English Pronouncing Dictionary

CAMBRIDGE
UNIVERSITY PRESS

PUBLISHED BY THE PRESS SYNDICATE OF THE UNIVERSITY OF CAMBRIDGE
The Pitt Building, Trumpington Street, Cambridge CB2 1RP, United Kingdom

CAMBRIDGE UNIVERSITY PRESS
The Edinburgh Buiding, Cambridge CB2 2RU, United Kingdom
40 West 20th Street, New York, NY 10011–4211, USA
477 Williamstown Road, Port Melbourne, VIC 3207, Australia
Ruiz de Alarcón 13, 28014 Madrid, Spain
Dock House, The Waterfront, Cape Town 8001, South Africa

Visit our website at http://www.cup.cam.ac.uk/elt/reference
Email comments about this book to epd@cup.cam.ac.uk

First published by J. M. Dent & Sons Ltd 1917

First published by Cambridge University Press 1991
This edition published 2003

Printed in Italy by G. Canale & C. S.p.A

Typeface Times Phonetic IPA 7/9 pt. *System* QuarkXPress® [UPH]

A catalogue record for this book is available from the British Library

Library of Congress Cataloguing in Publication data applied for

ISBN 0 521 81693 9 hardback
ISBN 0 521 01712 2 paperback
ISBN 0 521 01713 0 paperback & CD-ROM
ISBN 3 12 539683 2 Klett paperback & CD-ROM
ISBN 3 12 539684 0 Klett paperback

[redacted]

Contents

Editors' preface to the 16th Edition

The *English Pronouncing Dictionary* was first published in 1917, perhaps the greatest work of the greatest of British phoneticians, Daniel Jones (born in 1881). Jones was Professor of Phonetics at University College London from 1921 until his retirement in 1949. He was still an occasional visitor to the Department in 1967 when Peter Roach was there as a postgraduate student of phonetics, though he died in December of that year. The dictionary was preceded by a now forgotten work by Michaelis and Jones (1913) in which the phonemic transcription was presented first and the corresponding spelling followed it. The last edition in which Jones was directly involved was the 12th, and the 13th was substantially revised by his successor as Professor of Phonetics at University College, A. C. Gimson. From the 13th edition, Gimson was assisted by Dr. Susan Ramsaran, and in her preface to the 14th edition she notes that they had been making plans for a 15th edition at the time of Gimson's death. After this, the publishing rights were acquired from the original publishers, J. M. Dent & Sons, by Cambridge University Press.

With the publication of the 15th Edition in 1997, the *English Pronouncing Dictionary* entered the computer age. The type-set text of the 14th Edition was converted into a computer database, and the task of editing was carried out by a team of phonetics experts who worked by transferring the data of the developing new edition in electronic form between universities in Reading, Leeds, Kansas and Hong Kong, and the University Press in Cambridge. Despite the complexity of this operation, the process of updating and adding to the previous edition has been made more efficient, and has enabled this 16th Edition to be prepared much more rapidly. Versions of the database are available electronically, and are currently being used by language researchers in both academic and commercial institutions. For details of licensing the database, see the Cambridge Dictionaries website: www.dictionaries.cambridge.org

The *English Pronouncing Dictionary* has been in use for over 80 years, and during that time it has become established as a classic work of reference, both for native speakers of English wanting an authoritative guide to pronunciation and for users of English as a foreign or second language all over the world.

Above all, the aim of the Dictionary is to include information which is relevant to the needs of contemporary users and which is presented in the clearest possible way. This aim has informed both the choice of vocabulary covered and the range of pronunciations shown. The 15th edition saw a massive injection of 18,000 new words. Large numbers of terms connected with science and technology were added, as were hundreds of people and places which had acquired fame or notoriety in recent years. The more cosmopolitan nature of modern life was reflected in the increase of geographical names as well as a significant number of items of international cuisine. Personal names, both first names and family names, were based on census reports and statistical analysis, and many subject areas such as literature and law were revised and updated. For the first time, U.S. spellings and vocabulary items were included.

This 16th edition builds on that work, its wordlist fully updated with items which have become current since 1997. Another major feature is the addition of over 150 information panels explaining phonetics terminology and discussing the relationship between spelling and pronunciation.

Perhaps the most significant development of the 16th edition, and the one which truly takes it into the 21st century, is that it is now available with a CD-ROM which contains spoken pronunciations of every headword. The CD-ROM gives both linguists and learners of English a wealth of other features, from advanced search options on both alphabetic and phonetic characters, the ability to record the user's own voice and compare it with the spoken pronunciation on the CD-ROM, and a large number of interactive exercises.

In the Preface to the 15th Edition we thanked the many people who had contributed to our work, and our debt to them remains. Above all, we are very grateful to Liz Walter, our Commissioning Editor at Cambridge University Press who oversaw the production of the 15th Edition and has continued to advise and encourage us through the work on the 16th.

PETER ROACH, University of Reading
JAMES HARTMAN, University of Kansas
JANE SETTER, University of Reading

Introduction

It is strongly recommended that users of this dictionary read the introduction, since a full understanding of the information in it will ensure the most effective use of the dictionary.

(PART 1) **'What is the English Pronouncing Dictionary?'**: The intended use of the dictionary, the principles of its design and the accents of English represented in it.

(PART 2) **'Principles of Transcription'**: The main characteristics of the British and American accents.

(PART 3) **'Explanatory Notes'**: How to interpret the information provided with the individual words in the dictionary.

Part 1: Introduction to the English Pronouncing Dictionary

1.1 What is the English Pronouncing Dictionary?

This dictionary is designed to provide information on the current pronunciation of approximately 80,000 English words and phrases. For each entry, a British and an American pronunciation is shown (see Section 1.2 below). The pronunciation is given in modified phonemic transcription, and you need to understand the principles of phonemic transcription in order to be able to make proper use of this information (see Section 2.1 below).

The Pronouncing Dictionary provides much essential information that is not available in a general dictionary, such as the pronunciation of proper names, the pronunciation of all inflected forms of each word, and a larger amount of detail about variant pronunciations than is usual in a general dictionary.

1.2 Whose pronunciation is represented?

A pronouncing dictionary must base its recommendations on one or more *models*. A pronunciation model is a carefully chosen and defined accent of a language. In the first edition of this dictionary (1917), Daniel Jones described the type of pronunciation recorded as "that most usually heard in everyday speech in the families of Southern English persons whose menfolk have been educated at the great public boarding-schools". Accordingly, he felt able to refer to his model as "Public School Pronunciation" (PSP). In later editions, e.g. that of 1937, he added the remark that boys in boarding-schools tend to lose their markedly local peculiarities, whereas this is not the case for those in day-schools. He had by 1926, however, abandoned the term PSP in favour of "Received Pronunciation" (RP). The type of speech he had in mind had for centuries been regarded as a kind of standard, having its base in the educated pronunciation of London and the Home Counties (the counties surrounding London). Its use was not restricted to this region, however, being characteristic by the nineteenth century of upper-class speech throughout the country. The Editor of the 14th Edition of this dictionary, A. C. Gimson, commented in 1977 "Such a definition of RP is hardly tenable today", and went on "If I have retained the traditional, though imprecise, term 'received pronunciation', it is because the label has such wide currency in books on present-day English and because it is a convenient name for an accent which remains generally acceptable and intelligible within Britain".

For this edition a more broadly-based and accessible model accent for British English is represented, and pronunciations for one broadly-conceived accent of American English have been added. The time has come to abandon the archaic name *Received Pronunciation*. The model used for British English is what is referred to as *BBC English*; this is the pronunciation of professional speakers employed by the BBC as newsreaders and announcers on BBC1 and BBC2 television, the World Service and BBC Radio 3 and 4, as well as many commercial broadcasting organisations such as ITN. Of course, one finds differences between such speakers – individual broadcasters all have their own personal characteristics, and an increasing number of broadcasters with Scottish, Welsh and Irish accents are employed. However, the accent described here is typical of broadcasters with an English accent, and there is a useful degree of consistency in the broadcast speech of these speakers. Their speech does not carry for most people the connotations of high social class and privilege that PSP and RP have had in the past. An additional advantage in concentrating on the accent of broadcasters is that it is easy to gain access to examples, and the sound quality is usually of a very high standard.

For American English, the selection also follows what is frequently heard from professional voices on national network news and information programmes. It is similar to what has been termed "General American", which refers to a geographically (largely non-coastal) and socially based set of pronunciation features. It is important to note that no single dialect – regional or social – has been singled out as an American standard. Even national media (radio, television, movies, CD-ROM, etc.), with professionally trained voices have speakers with regionally mixed features. However, "Network English", in its most colourless form, can be described as a relatively homogeneous dialect that reflects the ongoing development of progressive American dialects (Canadian English has several notable differences). This "dialect" itself contains some variant forms. The variants included within this targeted accent involve vowels before /r/, possible differences in words like 'cot' and 'caught' and some vowels before /l/. It is fully rhotic. These differences largely pass unnoticed by the audiences for Network English, and are also reflective of age differences. What are thought to be the more progressive (used by educated, socially mobile, and younger speakers) variants are listed first in each entry. The intent is to list the variety of pronunciations with the least amount of regional or social marking, while still being sensitive to the traits of the individual word.

1.3 How are the pronunciations chosen?

It is important to remember that the pronunciation of English words is not governed by a strict set of rules; most words have more than one pronunciation, and the speaker's choice of which to use depends on a wide range of factors. These include the degree of formality, the amount of background noise, the speed of utterance, the speaker's perception of the listener and the frequency with which the speaker uses the word. For example, the two words 'virtuous' and 'virtuoso' are closely similar in spelling and share a common origin. However, the former is more common than the latter, and for British English /ˈvɜː.tʃu.əs/ is given as the first pronunciation of the former but /ˈvɜː.tju.əʊ.səʊ/ for the latter (which in general is typical of more careful speech). If such variation did not exist, most of the work of compiling a pronouncing dictionary could be done easily by means of one of the available computer programs that convert English spelling into a phonemic transcription. Ultimately, however, the decisions about which pronunciation to recommend, which pronunciations have dropped out of use, and so on, have been based on the editors' intuitions as professional phoneticians and observers of the pronunciation of English (particularly broadcast English) over many years. The opinion of many colleagues and acquaintances has also been a valuable source of advice.

In general, a pronunciation typical of a more casual, informal style of speaking is given for common words, and a more careful pronunciation for uncommon words. In real life, speakers tend to articulate most carefully when listeners are likely to have difficulty in recognising the words they hear. When more than one pronunciation of a word is given, the order of the alternatives is important. The first pronunciation given is believed to be the most usual one although the distance between the alternatives may vary, with some alternant forms rivalling the first-given in perceived frequency while others may be a more distant second.

1.4 Regional Accents

A pronouncing dictionary that systematically presented the pronunciations of a range of regional accents would be very valuable, but it would be very much bigger than the present volume and the job of ensuring an adequate coverage which treated all accents as equally important would have taken many years. In the case of some place-names, information about local pronunciations has been retained or added as well as "official" broadcasting ones, but the other words are given only in the standard accents chosen for British and American English.

1.5 Pronunciation of foreign words

Many of the words in an English dictionary are of foreign origin, and in previous editions of this dictionary many such words have been given both in an Anglicised pronunciation used by most English speakers, and in a broad phonetic transcription of the "authentic" pronunciation in the original language. This edition does not give detailed phonetic transcriptions of foreign words; the primary aim of this dictionary is to list pronunciations likely to be used by educated speakers of English, and an authentic pronunciation would in some circumstances be quite inappropriate (pronouncing 'Paris' as /pærˈiː/, for example). In some cases the information is unnecessary (very few English speakers would attempt, or even recognise, an authentic pronunciation of a word from a non-European language), while in other cases it is difficult to establish the authentic original (many African place-names, for example, have reached us after being adapted by British, French or Portuguese colonists; place-names in Spain may be pronounced in different ways according to their regional affiliation, so that the name of Barcelona might be given a Catalan or a Castilian Spanish pronunciation, while other Spanish names are different according to whether they originate in Spain or South America). Words and names of foreign origin are therefore given in what is felt to be the pronunciation likely to be used among educated speakers of English.

In some cases it is possible to identify an alternative pronunciation which represents an attempt to pronounce in a manner closer to the supposed original. This is marked by first indicating the language which the speaker would be aiming at, then giving the pronunciation, using where necessary additional phonetic symbols not required for the phonemic transcription of English. For example, the word 'bolognese' is widely used to refer to a sauce served with pasta. This is given as /ˌbɒl.əˈneɪz/ for British English and as /ˌboʊ.ləˈniːz/ for American; for speakers of both groups, a pronunciation aimed at being nearer to the Italian original would be /ˌbɒl.əˈnjeɪ.zeɪ/ (though this would still be different from the pronunciation that would be produced by an Italian speaker). To indicate that this last pronunciation is aimed at sounding Italian, it is marked in the entry as: *as if Italian:* ˌbɒl.əˈnjeɪ.zeɪ. In a few cases it has been necessary to mark separate British and American pronunciations within this field, as the degree of Anglicisation of any given word may vary between British and American English.

1.6 Usage notes

Usage notes are included with some words. In some cases these are needed so that users of the dictionary can understand how alternative pronunciations are to be used. In some cases the rules needed for correct pronunciation are quite complex, most noticeably in the case of the so-called "weak-form words" such as 'there', 'her'. Explanations with examples are given in such cases.

1.7 Syllable divisions

Earlier editions of this dictionary regularly marked the division between syllables. This practice was largely abandoned in the 14th Edition, but the present edition gives syllable divisions in all cases, since it is felt that foreign learners will find the information useful. Syllable division is marked with the symbol . recommended by the International Phonetic Association. The decision on where to place a syllable division is not always easy, and the rules used in this work are explained later in this Introduction (Section 2.6).

Part 2: Principles of transcription

2.1 The phoneme principle

The basic principle of the transcription used is, as in all previous editions, *phonemic*. This means that a small set of symbols is used to represent the sounds that can be shown to be distinctive in English, so that replacing one phoneme by another can change the identity of a word. We do not usually add phonetic detail such as the presence of glottal stops, aspiration or vowel devoicing. It is usual to put slant brackets before and after symbols representing phonemes (e.g. the word 'cat' would be represented phonemically as /kæt/). When non-phonemic symbols are used, the convention is to use square brackets (e.g. the glottal stop will be represented as [ʔ]). In entries in the dictionary itself, however, we do not use these brackets, in order to keep the information simple; only in explanatory notes do we use slant or square brackets. For an explanation of the principle of the phoneme and some of the problems associated with it, see Roach (2000), Chapters 5 and 13. The use of phonemic transcription in works on pronunciation (including this one) has remained in the "realist" tradition established by Jones, while approaches to the phoneme by theoretical phonologists have changed radically during recent decades and become much more abstract. There are a few exceptions to our general use of the phoneme principle that should be mentioned here, however. One is the use, in American pronunciations, of the [̬] diacritic to indicate the voicing and "flapping" of /t/ in words such as 'getting' /ˈget̬.ɪŋ/, and 'better' /ˈbet̬.ɚ/. This is an important feature of American pronunciation, but speakers of British English find it difficult to apply the rule which determines when /t/ is voiced and/or flapped. Another is the use of the symbols [i] and [u] , the use of which is explained below (Section 2.9). Finally, it is necessary to use a number of special symbols which are not normally used for English phonemes. This set includes some nasalised vowels used particularly in some words taken from French, the [x] sound found in Scottish words such as 'loch', and some non-linguistic sounds used in certain exclamations and interjections (see Section 2.4).

2.2 Vowels and diphthongs

It is standard practice in phonetics to represent the quality of vowels and diphthongs by placing them on a four-sided figure usually known as the *Cardinal Vowel quadrilateral* (see Roach (2000), pp. 13–14). This device is used in the vowel descriptions in the following section.

(a) British English

British English (BBC accent) is generally described as having short vowels, long vowels and diphthongs. There are said to be seven short vowels, five long ones and eight diphthongs. At the end of this section some attention is also given to triphthongs.

- Short vowels:
  pit pet pat putt pot put another
  ɪ e æ ʌ ɒ ʊ ə ə
- Long vowels:
  bean barn born boon burn
  iː ɑː ɔː uː ɜː
- Diphthongs:
  bay buy boy no now peer pair poor
  eɪ aɪ ɔɪ əʊ aʊ ɪə eə ʊə

These vowels and diphthongs may be placed on the Cardinal Vowel quadrilateral as shown in Figs. 1 -3. It should be noted that though each vowel (or diphthong starting-point) is marked with a point (●), it is misleading to think of this as a precise target; the point represents the centre of an area within which the typical vowel pronunciation falls.

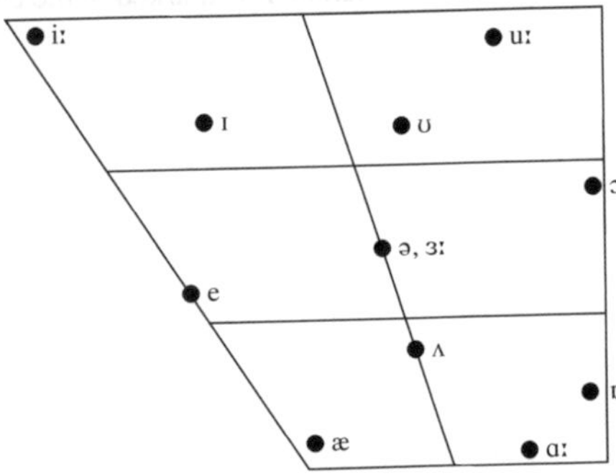

Fig. 1 BBC English pure vowels

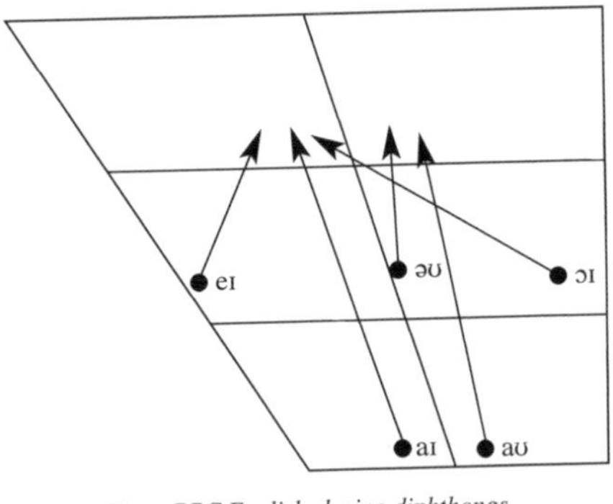

Fig. 2 BBC English closing diphthongs

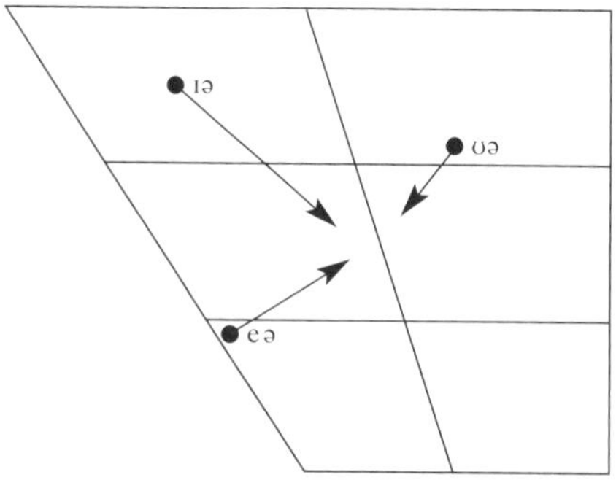

Fig. 3 BBC English centring diphthongs

A few comments on individual vowels and vowel symbols are needed. The pronunciation of any language is constantly changing, and a dictionary such as this one should reflect such changes. However, there is a general reluctance among users of phonemic transcription to change the symbols used too frequently, as this causes existing teaching materials and textbooks to become out of date. The following remarks apply chiefly to BBC pronunciation.

(a) The length of long vowels and diphthongs is very much reduced when they occur in syllables closed by the consonants / p, t, k, tʃ, f, θ, s, ʃ /. Thus /iː/ in 'beat' has only about half the length of /iː/ in 'bead' or 'bee'; similarly /eɪ/ in 'place' is much reduced in length compared with /eɪ/ in 'plays' or 'play'.

(b) The vowel /æ/, classified as a short vowel, is nevertheless generally lengthened before /b, d, g, dʒ, m, n/. Thus /æ/ in 'bag' is considerably longer than /æ/ in 'back'. The quality of this vowel is now more open than it used to be, and the symbol /a/ might one day be considered preferable. We have retained the /æ/ symbol partly because it is phonetically appropriate for the corresponding American vowel.

(c) The vowel /ʌ/ used to be a back vowel, and the symbol was chosen for this reason. This is no longer a back vowel, but a central one. Alternative symbols could be considered in the future.

(d) Among younger speakers, the /uː/ vowel has moved to a more front quality, with less lip-rounding, particularly when preceded by /j/ as in 'use'.

(e) Among the diphthongs, there seems to be a progressive decline in the use of /ʊə/, with /ɔː/ taking its place (e.g. the pronunciation of the word 'poor' as /pɔː/ is increasingly common).

(f) Triphthongs create some problems. These three-vowel sequences are generally held to be composed of one of the diphthongs /eɪ, aɪ, ɔɪ, əʊ, aʊ/ plus a schwa (e.g. 'layer' /leɪəʳ/; 'fire' /faɪəʳ/). In British English many of these triphthongs are pronounced with such slight movement in vowel quality that it is difficult for foreign learners to recognise them: for example, the name 'Ireland', which is generally transcribed /ˈaɪə.lənd/, frequently has an initial syllable which sounds virtually indistinguishable from /ɑː/. It seems reasonable in this case to treat these sounds as being monosyllabic (e.g. the word 'fire' is a single syllable), but in other words and names transcribed with the same symbols it seems necessary to insert a syllable division. This is usually done (i) when there is a morpheme boundary (e.g. 'buyer' /baɪ.əʳ/) and (ii) when the word is felt to be foreign (this includes many Biblical names originating from Hebrew, e.g. 'Messiah').

Another problem with triphthongs is that before an /r/ consonant at the beginning of a following syllable, the distinction between /aɪə/ and /aɪ/ seems to be neutralised – it seems to make no difference whether one represents 'Irish', 'irate' as /ˈaɪə.rɪʃ/, /aɪəˈreɪt/ or as /ˈaɪ.rɪʃ/ , /aɪˈreɪt/, since there is no regular distinction made in pronunciation. In general, the practice of this edition is to transcribe such cases as /aɪɚ- /.

(b) American English

American English is commonly described as having lax vowels, tense vowels, and wide diphthongs. Generally speaking, lax vowels are lower and made with less oral tension; they do not usually end syllables. Vowel length in American English is generally considered to be conditioned by phonological environment, so the long/short distinction described for BBC English is not usually present, though we have retained the length mark on the tense vowels /iː, ɑː, ɔː, ɜː, uː/ in order to mark their relationship to the English long vowels. Since the diphthongal movement in /eɪ/ and /oʊ/ is small in American pronunciation, these are treated as tense vowels. Vowels preceding /r/ are notably influenced by rhotic colouring. Word spellings such as 'bird', 'word', 'curd', 'earth', 'jerk', which now rhyme with /ɝ/ in American English, at one time in history had differing vowels. The retroflexed vowels /ɝ/ and /ɚ/, stressed and unstressed, are among those features that noticeably distinguish

American English from BBC English. All vowels occurring before /r/ within a syllable are likely to become "r-coloured" to some extent.

- lax vowels: ɪ e æ ʌ ʊ ə
- tense vowels: iː ɑː ɔː ɜː uː eɪ oʊ
- wide diphthongs: aʊ aɪ ɔɪ
- retroflexed vowels ("r-coloured") ɚ ɝ

There is an issue in the symbolization of the diphthong in the word "home". This has for many years been represented as /əʊ/, but in earlier editions of this and others of Jones' works the symbolization /ou/ indicated a rounded initial vowel. This is still the preferred transcription for the American English diphthong. In order to preserve compatibility with other works, we have chosen to use /əʊ/ for BBC English and /oʊ/ for American, though it can be argued that the latter symbolization would be suitable for both.

The American /æ/ vowel is somewhat closer than BBC /æ/, and seems to be evolving into an even closer vowel in many speakers. It is used in the same words as BBC /æ/ and also in most of the words which in BBC have /ɑː/ when there is no letter r in the spelling, e.g. 'pass', 'ask'. The quality of American /ɑː/ is similar to the BBC /ɑː/ vowel; it is used in some of the words which have /ɑː/ in BBC when there is no letter r in the spelling (e.g. 'father', 'calm'). It also replaces the BBC short /ɒ/ vowel in many words (e.g. 'hot', 'top', 'bother'): 'bother' rhymes with 'father'. American /ɔː/ is more open in quality than BBC /ɔː/. It is used where BBC has /ɔː/ (e.g. 'cause', 'walk'), and also replaces BBC short /ɒ/ in many words, e.g. 'long', 'dog'. American /uː/ is similar to BBC /uː/, but is also used where BBC has /juː/ after alveolar consonants (e.g. 'new', 'duty').

2.3 Consonants

(a) British English (BBC)

- Plosives: p b t d k g
  pin **b**in **t**in **d**in **k**in **g**um
- Affricates: tʃ dʒ
  chain **J**ane
- Fricatives: f v θ ð s z
  fine **v**ine **th**ink **th**is **s**eal **z**eal

  ʃ ʒ h
  sheep mea**s**ure **h**ow
- Nasals: m n ŋ
  su**m** su**n** su**ng**
- Approximants: l r w j
  light **r**ight **w**et **y**et

These consonants can be arranged in table form as shown below. The layout of the symbols follows the principle that, where there are two consonants which differ only in voicing, they are placed side by side with the voiceless one to the left.

(a) Certain types of consonant have a distinction such as that between /t/ and /d/; this is commonly classed as a distinction between voiceless and voiced consonants, but the distinction is in fact much more complex. Consonants usually classed as voiceless are /p, t, k, f, θ, s, ʃ, h, tʃ/, with voiced partners /b, d, g, v, ð, z, ʒ, dʒ/. Since the presence or absence of voicing is often less important than some other phonetic features, it has been suggested that instead the terms *fortis* (equivalent to voiceless) and *lenis* (equivalent to voiced) should be used. These terms imply that the main distinguishing factor is the amount of energy used in the articulation (fortis consonants being made with greater energy than lenis). These terms

Table of English Consonants

	Bilabial	*Labio-dental*	*Dental*	*Alveolar*	*Post-alveolar*	*Palatal*	*Velar*	*Glottal*
Plosive	p b			t d			k g	
Affricate					tʃ dʒ			
Fricative		f v	θ ð	s z	ʃ ʒ		(x)	h
Nasal	m			n			ŋ	
Lateral approximant				l				
Approximant	w				r	j		

are not used in this dictionary, since the usefulness of this terminology is uncertain. Some of the characteristics of the two types of consonant are set out below.

(b) /p,t,k/ are typically accompanied by aspiration (i.e. an interval of breath before the following vowel onset), especially when initial in a stressed syllable. Thus, 'pin' is distinguished from 'bin' very largely by the aspiration accompanying /p/. However, in the syllable-initial sequences /sp-, st-, sk- /, /p, t, k/ lack such aspiration. When /l/, /j/, /w/ or /r/ immediately follow /p,t,k/, they are devoiced and are pronounced as fricatives. Another characteristic of /p,t,k/ that is not marked in transcriptions is glottalization; when one of these consonants is followed by another consonant it is now usual to find that a glottal closure precedes the /p/, /t/ or /k/, particularly if the syllable in which they occur is stressed. Thus the pronunciation of 'captain', 'rightful', 'Yorkshire', which are phonemically /ˈkæp.tɪn/, /ˈraɪt.fᵊl/, /ˈjɔːk.ʃəʳ/, could be shown (using the symbol [ʔ] for glottal closure) as [ˈkæʔp.tɪn], [ˈraɪʔt.fl̩], [ˈjɔːʔk.ʃəʳ]. Similarly, in American English 'mountain' has one pronunciation that could be represented as [maʊ̃.ʔn̩].

(c) Voiceless consonants have a shortening effect on sounds preceding them within a syllable. Thus in the words 'right' and 'ride' (/raɪt/ and /raɪd/) the diphthong is noticeably shorter in the first word than in the second; in the words 'bent' and 'bend' (/bent/ and /bend/), both the vowel /e/ and the nasal consonant /n/ are shorter in the first word. This length difference is not always easy to observe in connected speech.

(d) The consonant /l/ has two different allophones in BBC English, the so-called "clear" and "dark" allophones. The "clear" one (which has an /iː/-like quality) occurs before vowels, the "dark" one (which has an /uː/-like quality) before consonants or before a pause.

(e) The consonants /ʃ/, /ʒ/, /tʃ/, dʒ/, /r/ are usually accompanied by lip-rounding.

(b) American English

The consonants of the American English model, at the phonemic level, may be represented by the same broad scheme used for British English above. Similarly, many of the distinguishing phonetic traits discussed for British English hold for American English as well: initial /p,t,k/ are normally aspirated except when immediately preceded by /s/. Glottalization preceding and, at times, replacing the plosives occurs often in rapid speech. There are, of course, numerous phonetic and phonological differences between British and American English, as there are within regional and social varieties within the two political entities. Two differences receive sufficient attention and have attained sufficient generality within the two varieties that they are represented here. One is phonetic: the "flapped" medial /t/ (as in 'butter') is transcribed as /t̬/ (see Section 2.1 above); the other is phonological: the presence (in American English) of postvocalic /r/ (as in 'farmer' /ˈfɑːr.mɚ/). It should also be noted that the difference between "clear" and "dark" /l/ is much less marked in American than in the BBC accent, so that even prevocalic /l/ in American pronunciation sounds dark to English ears.

2.4 Non-English sounds

In addition to the phonemes of English described above, most English speakers are aware of, and often attempt to pronounce, some sounds of languages other than English. The number of such sounds is small, since most foreign words and names are Anglicised so that they are pronounced with English phonemes. We find the voiceless velar fricative [x] in the Gaelic languages of Scotland and Ireland in words such as 'loch' and names such as 'Strachan'. The same sound is often used by English speakers for the German sound which is written 'ch' (e.g. 'Bach' [bɑːx]) and the Spanish sound spelt 'j' (e.g. 'Badajoz' [ˌbæd.əˈxɒθ]). The voiceless lateral fricative [ɬ] is found (always represented in spelling with 'll') in Welsh words and names such as 'Llanberis'; we give the pronunciation of this sound as *h*l to indicate that it may be pronounced as a voiceless [ɬ] (as many British English speakers do), but alternatively as a voiced one: thus /*h*lænˈber.ɪs/. The dictionary lists a few names with more than one of these sounds (e.g. Llanelli). Most non-Welsh speakers are unlikely to pronounce more than one [ɬ] sound in a word, so we give the pronunciation as /θl/ for 'll' sounds after the initial one.

The other case which needs special attention is the pronunciation of French nasalised vowels. Many English speakers attempt to produce something similar to the French vowels /ɛ̃/, /ɑ̃/, /ɔ̃/, /œ̃/ in words such as 'v**in** rouge', 'restaur**ant**', 'b**on** marché', 'Verd**un**'.

Although many speakers do not get close to the French vowels, the principle adopted here is to use symbols for English vowels, with added nasalisation. The equivalents are:

French	*English*
ɛ̃	æ̃
ɑ̃	ɑ̃ː
ɔ̃	ɔ̃ː
œ̃	ɜ̃ː

2.5 Stress

Stress patterns present one of the most difficult problems in a pronouncing dictionary. One reason for this is that many polysyllabic words have more than one possible stress pattern, and one must consider carefully which should be recommended. Secondly, the stress of many words changes in different contexts, and it is necessary to indicate how this happens. Thirdly, there is no straightforward way to decide on how many different levels of stress are recognisable.

(a) Where more than one stress pattern is possible, the preferred pronunciation is given first and then alternatives are listed. Many dictionaries use the convention of representing stress patterns using dashes to represent syllables: thus the two possible patterns for 'cigarette' (ˌciga'rette and 'cigarette) can be shown as ˌ--'- and '---. This convention, which is sometimes referred to (incorrectly) as "Morse Code", is used in this work for short words, since it is economical on space. However, in longer words users are likely to find it difficult to interpret. In the planning of this edition, an experiment was carried out to test this, and it was found that readers (both native speakers and non-native speakers of English) do indeed take less time to read word stress patterns when the whole word is given, rather than just a "dashes and dots" pattern (Stromberg and Roach, 1993). Consequently, words of more than three syllables are given in full when alternative stress patterns are being given.

(b) The most common case of variable stress placement caused by context is what is usually nowadays known as "stress-shift". As a general rule, when a word of several syllables has a stress near the end of the word, and is followed by another word with stress near its beginning, there is a tendency for the stress in the first word to move nearer the beginning if it contains a syllable that is capable of receiving stress. For example, the word 'academic' in isolation usually has the stress on the penultimate syllable /-dem-/. However, when the word 'year' follows, the stress is often found to move to the first syllable /æk-/. The whole phrase 'academic year' will have its primary stress on the word 'year', so the resulting stress pattern will be ˌacademic 'year (where ˌ represents secondary stress and ' represents primary stress). To make this process easier to understand, this dictionary now gives specific examples in each case where stress-shift is possible except where certain prefixes such as 'un-' produce hundreds of such cases. In general, this shift is not obligatory: it would not be a mispronunciation to say acaˌdemic 'year. However, it is undoubtedly widespread and in some cases is used almost without exception: for example, although the adjective 'compact' on its own is pronounced with the stress pattern -'- , in the phrase 'compact disc' it is virtually always pronounced with stress on the first syllable.

(c) It is necessary to decide how many levels of stress to mark. The minimum possible range is two: stressed and unstressed. This is inadequate for representing English words in a pronouncing dictionary: a word such as 'controversial' clearly has stress(es) on the first and third syllables, and equally clearly has stronger stress on the third syllable than on the first. It is therefore necessary to recognise an intermediate level of stress ("secondary"). The transcription of this word, therefore, is /ˌkɒn.trə'vɜː.ʃᵊl/. An argument can be made for recognising yet another level (tertiary stress): in a word such as 'indivisibility', for example, it can be claimed that the level of stress on the third syllable /vɪz/ is weaker than that on the first syllable /ɪn/, which has secondary stress (primary stress being placed on the penultimate syllable /bɪl/). However, introducing this extra level creates a degree of complexity that it is better to avoid. In EPD14 some long polysyllabic words were transcribed with two primary stress marks (e.g. 'cross-examination' was given as /'krɒsɪgˌzæmɪ'neɪʃn/): for the present edition only one primary stress may occur in a word or compound.

(d) Secondary stresses have only limited occurrence after a primary stress: such a secondary stress is only marked in closed or hyphenated compound words where the second element is polysyllabic (e.g. 'fishˌmonger).

(e) Stress assignment on prefixes:

(i) In words containing a prefix such as, for example, **con**-, **de**-, **im**-, **in**-, secondary stress is not applied to the prefix where the following (i.e., second) syllable is stressed. Examples include 'intoxicate' /ɪn'tɒk.sɪ.keɪt ⓊⓈ -'tɑːk-/.

(ii) Where the prefix is separable, however, as in **impossible**, a variant showing secondary stress on the prefix is listed, as follows: /ɪm'pɒs.ə.bl̩ ,ˌɪm -/.

(iii) In all other cases, primary or secondary stress is applied to the prefix where appropriate.

(f) In the case of words which do not have a prefix but have a stressed second syllable preceded by a syllable with a full vowel (e.g. 'shampoo', 'Chinese') the first syllable is usually treated as unstressed, though in some cases capable of receiving primary stress through stress-shift.

2.6 Syllable divisions

The 14th Edition of EPD marked syllable division (using hyphens) only when it was important to distinguish between the affricate /tʃ/ and the phonemes /t/ and /ʃ/ at a syllable juncture (e.g. 'satchel' /'sætʃəl/ and 'nutshell' /'nʌt-ʃel/). However, although native speakers may well find no difficulty in dividing words into syllables, it seems that learners of English have trouble in doing so, and the divisions are therefore marked. Descriptions of stress and rhythm are usually expressed in terms of syllables, and so it is helpful to have polysyllabic words clearly broken up into their constituent syllables. The syllabified transcription of a polysyllabic word is easier to read and interpret than an undivided one. In addition, the dictionary is likely to be of interest to the field of speech and language technology, where syllable divisions can be useful in developing automatic speech and language analysis systems.

A dot . is used to divide syllables, in accordance with the current recommendations of the International Phonetic Association. These may be read in the *IPA Handbook* (International Phonetic Association 1999). However, this is not used where a stress mark ˈ or ˌ occurs, as these are effectively also syllable division markers.

No completely satisfactory scheme of syllable division can be produced – all sets of rules will throw up some cases which cannot be dealt with properly. The principles used in this edition are set out below. This requires some discussion of *phonotactics*, the study of permissible phoneme sequences.

(a) As far as possible, syllables should not be divided in a way that violates what is known of English syllable structure. The 'Maximal Onsets Principle', which is widely recognised in contemporary phonology, is followed as far as possible. This means that, where possible, syllables should be divided in such a way that as many consonants as possible are assigned to the beginning of the syllable to the right (if one thinks in terms of how they are written in transcription), rather than to the end of the syllable to the left. However, when this would result in a syllable ending with a stressed /ɪ/, /e/, /æ/, /ʌ/, /ɒ/ or /ʊ/, it is considered that this would constitute a violation of English phonotactics, and the first (or only) intervocalic consonant is assigned to the preceding syllable; thus the word 'better' is divided /'bet.əʳ/, whereas 'beater' is divided /'biː.təʳ/. In the case of unstressed short vowels, /e/, /æ/, /ʌ/ and /ɒ/ are also prevented from appearing in syllable-final position; however, unstressed /ɪ/ and /ʊ/ are allowed the same "privilege of occurrence" as /ə/ when a consonant begins a following syllable, and may therefore occur in final position in unstressed syllables except pre-pausally. Thus in a word such as 'develop', the syllable division is /dɪ'vel.əp/.

(b) Notwithstanding the above, words in compounds should not be re-divided syllabically in a way that does not agree with perceived word boundaries. For example, 'hardware' could in theory be divided /'hɑː.dweəʳ/, but most readers would find this counter-intuitive and would prefer /'hɑːd.weəʳ/. This principle applies to open, closed and hyphenated compounds.

2.7 Assimilation

Assimilation is a process found in all languages which causes speech sounds to be modified in a way which makes them more similar to their neighbours. A well-known example is that of English alveolar consonants such as /t , d , n/, which, when they are followed by a consonant which does not have alveolar place of articulation, tend to adopt the place of articulation of the following consonant. Thus the /t/ at the end of 'foot' /fʊt/ changes to /p/ when followed by /b/ in the word 'football', giving the pronunciation /'fʊp.bɔːl/. A similar case is the assimilation of /s/ to a following /ʃ/ or /j/, resulting in the pronunciation of 'this ship' as /ðɪʃ'ʃɪp/ and 'this year' as /ðɪʃ'jɪəʳ/. This assimilation can be considered to be optional.

The assimilation of /n/ is a rather special case: many English words begin with the prefixes 'in-'

and 'un-', and in a number of cases the /n/ of these prefixes is followed by a consonant which is not alveolar. In some cases it seems to be normal that the /n/ is regularly assimilated to the place of articulation of the following consonant (e.g. 'inquest' /ˈɪŋ.kwest/), while in others this assimilation is optional (e.g. 'incautious' may be /ɪnˈkɔː.ʃəs/ or /ɪŋˈkɔː.ʃəs/). Where it is clear that the prefix is attached to a word that exists independently, so that prefix and stem are easily separable, the assimilation is normally treated as optional. When it seems more like an integral part of the word, the assimilation is shown as obligatory. The occurrence of assimilation in British and American English may differ.

2.8 Treatment of /r/

The accent used for British English is classed as *non-rhotic* – the phoneme /r/ is not usually pronounced except when a vowel follows it. The American pronunciations, on the other hand, do show a rhotic accent, and in general in the accent described, /r/ is pronounced where the letter r is found in the spelling.

It is necessary to show, in British English entries, cases of *potential* pronunciation of /r/, mainly in word-final position; in other words, it is necessary to indicate, in a word such as 'car', that though the word when said in isolation does not have /r/ in the pronunciation (/kɑː/), there is a *potential* /r/ which is realised if a vowel follows (e.g. in 'car owner'). This is indicated by giving the transcription as /kɑːʳ/, where the superscript /ʳ/ indicates the potential for pronunciation. This is traditionally known as 'linking r'. A controversial question is that of so-called 'intrusive r', where the phoneme /r/ is pronounced when no 'r' is seen in the spelling. For example, the phrase 'china and glass' will often be pronounced with /r/ at the end of the word 'china'; although this type of pronunciation is widespread in the speech of native speakers of the accent described, it is still safer not to recommend it to foreign learners, and it is therefore avoided in this dictionary.

2.9 Use of /i/ and /u/

There are many places in present-day British and American English where the distinction between /ɪ/ and /iː/ is neutralised. For example, the final vowel of 'city' and 'seedy' seems to belong neither to the /ɪ/ phoneme nor to /iː/. The symbol /i/ is used in this case (though it is not, strictly speaking, a phoneme symbol; there is no obvious way to choose suitable brackets for this symbol, but phoneme brackets // will be used for simplicity). A parallel argument can be made for the distinction between /ʊ/ and /uː/ (with a corresponding 'neutralised' symbol /u/), though this is needed much less frequently. This issue, and the issues which follow, are discussed in detail in Roach (2000), pp. 84–86.

(a) In word-final position, /ɪ/ and /ʊ/ do not occur. Word-final, close vowels are transcribed with /i/ and /u/ if unstressed. Word-final /iː/ and /uː/ are possible both with stress ('grandee', 'bamboo') and without ('Hindi', 'argue'), although in the unstressed case it is often not possible to draw a clear line between /iː/ and /i/, or between /uː/ and /u/.

(b) In compounds such as 'busybody' and names such as 'Merryweather', /i/ is permitted to occur word-medially, e.g. 'busybody' is transcribed /ˈbɪz.iˌbɒd.i ⓤⓢ ˈbɪz.i.bɑː.di/ and 'Merryweather' as /ˈmer.iˌweð.əʳ ⓤⓢ ˈmer.iˌ weð.ɚ/. In all other cases word-medially, /ɪ/ is used when the vowel is unstressed, unless a vowel follows (see below).

(c) The vowel symbols /ɪ/ and /ʊ/ only occur in front of another vowel symbol if they form part of a composite (diphthong or triphthong) phoneme symbol (e.g. /ɪə, ʊə/). Otherwise /i/ or /u/ is used (e.g. 'scurrying' /ˈskʌr.i.ɪŋ/, 'influenza' /ˌɪn.fluˈen.zə/.

(d) A matter related to this decision concerns words ending in '-ier', '-eer', '-ia'. The usual transcription in the 14th Edition of the EPD was /ɪə/. However, 'reindeer' and 'windier' (comparative form of 'windy') do not have identical pronunciations in their final syllables in British English (BBC). In this edition, the alternative /-jə/ previously given for the latter type of word has been dropped; 'reindeer' is transcribed as /ˈreɪn.dɪəʳ/ and 'windier' as /ˈwɪn.di.əʳ/. The latter transcription, which indicates a different (closer) vowel quality in the second syllable of 'windier', and implies a pronunciation with three rather than two syllables, is felt to be accurate in terms of contemporary pronunciation.

The long vowels /iː/ and /uː/ may also occur before other vowels, but only when in a stressed syllable (e.g. 'skiing' /ˈskiː.ɪŋ/, 'canoeing' /kəˈnuː.ɪŋ/).

2.10 Syllabic consonants

Syllabic consonants are frequently found in English pronunciation: these are cases where instead of an expected vowel-plus-consonant sequence, the consonant alone (usually one of /m, n, ŋ, l, r/) is pronounced with the rhythmical value of a syllable. (See Roach, 2000, pp. 86–90.) In EPD14, syllabic consonants were only marked where there is ambiguity in the pronunciation of a word; for example, in a word such as 'bottle', the transcription /ˈbɒtl/ is said to imply unambiguously that the /l/ is syllabic, whereas in the derived form 'bottling' there may be two pronunciations, one with and one without a syllabic /l/. In this instance the EPD14 preferred pronunciation was /ˈbɒtl̩ɪŋ/, with /ˈbɒtlɪŋ/ given as an alternative.

(a) The main problem here is how to deal with optional and obligatory syllabicity and the permissibility of vowels. The most frequently found case is where an item may have (i) a schwa vowel followed by a non-syllabic consonant, (ii) a syllabic consonant not preceded by schwa or (iii) a non-syllabic consonant not preceded by schwa. For example, 'lightening' may be (i) /ˈlaɪ.tə.nɪŋ/, (ii) /ˈlaɪt.n̩.ɪŋ/ or (iii) /ˈlaɪt.nɪŋ/. Such items are transcribed as /ˈlaɪ.tᵊn̩.ɪŋ/ and /ˈlaɪt.nɪŋ/, the first representing cases (i) and (ii), in which there are three syllables, and the second representing only the disyllabic pronunciation, (iii). The use of superscript schwa in words such as /ˈlaɪ.tᵊn̩.ɪŋ/ should be interpreted as meaning that the schwa may be pronounced, or may be omitted while giving its syllabic character to the following consonant.

(b) The problem remaining is that of /l/ corresponding to the '-le' spelling form, preceded by any plosive or homorganic fricative, as in 'bottle', 'wrestle'. It is not felt to be acceptable in BBC pronunciation to pronounce this with a vowel in the second syllable, and therefore the superscript schwa convention is not used in such cases: rather, the /l/ is marked as syllabic, i.e. /l̩/. The entry for 'bottle' is /ˈbɒt.l̩/, and for 'cycle', /ˈsaɪ.kl̩/.

(c) Where a word such as the above carries a suffix with an initial vowel, as in 'bottling', 'cycling', speakers' intuitions about the number of syllables are very divergent, so no single recommendation will be adequate. The entry for 'bottle' gives the syllabic /l̩/ (three-syllable) version of 'bottling' as the first recommendation, and it is therefore necessary to add for the -ing form the two-syllable alternative /ˈbɒt.lɪŋ/.

(d) Syllabic nasals are not usual where they would result in a nasal-plosive-syllabic consonant sequence (e.g. 'London', 'abandon' must contain a schwa vowel in the final syllable).

2.11 Optional sounds

The convention used in EPD14 of printing phoneme symbols in italics to indicate that they may be omitted is retained, though used more sparingly. It is not necessary to give alternative pronunciations that simply follow general rules of simplification that apply in rapid speech. For example, pointing out the possibility of omitting the [d] sound in 'engine' seems unnecessary, whereas it does seem worth recording the fact that some speakers pronounce words such as 'lunch' and 'French' with a final /ntʃ/ while others have final /nʃ/. There is a difference between the two cases: the former is a straightforward example of elision, and needs no special explanation that refers to a specific word or class of word, while the latter is a particular case of an insertion or deletion that is restricted to a particular phonological environment; speakers are usually consistent in using one or other of the alternative pronunciations in the latter case.

2.12 Elision

As mentioned in the preceding section, there are many cases where sounds which are produced in words pronounced on their own, or in slow, careful speech, are not found in a different style of speech. This is known as *elision*, and this dictionary normally does not show elisions in order to avoid adding a large number of additional pronunciations that are typical of casual speech. It is usual to explain elision in terms of the Principle of Least Effort – we try to avoid doing more work than is necessary. We find elision most commonly in the simplification of consonant clusters. A common example is the loss of /t/ and /d/ in combination with other consonants. Examples are:

'act badly' /ˌæktˈbæd.li/ (careful speech) /ˌækˈbæd.li/ (rapid speech)

'strange person' /ˌstreɪndʒˈpɜː.sᵊn (US) -ˈpɝː.sᵊn/ (careful speech) /ˌstreɪnʒˈpɜː.sᵊn (US) -ˈpɝː.sᵊn/ (rapid speech)

The fricative /θ/ is also frequently lost in clusters in rapid speech. Examples are:

'sixth place' /ˌsɪksθˈpleɪs/ (careful speech) /ˌsɪksˈpleɪs/ (rapid speech)

Elision of vowels is also found, and again this seems to be characteristic of rapid or casual speech. Examples are:

'philosophy' /fɪˈlɒs.ə.fi (US) -ˈlɑː.sə-/ (careful speech) /fəˈlɒs.fi (US) -ˈlɑːs.fi/ (rapid speech)

'persuade' /pəˈsweɪd (US) pɚˈ-/ (careful speech) /psweɪd/ (rapid speech)

Part 3: Explanatory notes

In order to explain the way in which the information in the dictionary is laid out, several entries are presented below with explanatory notes.

• Throughout the dictionary we use the convention of the cutback bar, a vertical line | which marks the place at which a word is divided so that alternative endings can be shown without having to print the entire word again.

• The brackets used for phonemic and phonetic transcriptions are not used in the entries in the dictionary, for the sake of clarity.

affectation ˌæf.ek'teɪ.ʃᵊn,-ɪk'- **-s** -z

Spelling of word. — Main pronunciation. — Variant pronunciation.

afar ə'fɑːʳ (US) -'fɑːr

British pronunciation. — This sign indicates that an American pronunciation follows. If this sign is not shown, pronunciation is the same for British and American. — American pronunciation.

affected ə'fek.tɪd **-ly** -li **-ness** -nəs, -nɪs

Derived forms of the headword (affectedly & affectedness).

addl|e 'æd.l̩ **-es** -z **-ing** -ɪŋ, 'æd.lɪŋ **-ed** -d

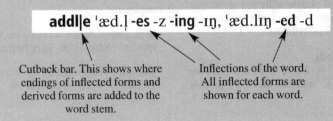

Cutback bar. This shows where endings of inflected forms and derived forms are added to the word stem. — Inflections of the word. All inflected forms are shown for each word.

Adam ˈæd.əm ˌ**Adam's** ˈ**apple** (US) ˈ**Adam's** ˌ**apple**

American stress pattern for compound word.

Stress pattern for compound word, British pronunciation.

Aden *in the Yemen:* ˈeɪ.dᵊn (US) ˈɑː-, ˈeɪ- *in Grampian region:* ˈæd.ᵊn

Glosses indicate where pronunciations differ according to meaning.

addict (*n.*) ˈæd.ɪkt **-s** -s
addict (*v.*) əˈdɪkt **-s** -s **-ing** -ɪŋ

Labels indicate where pronunciation differs according to part of speech.

Adriatic ˌeɪ.driˈæt.ɪk (US) -ˈæţ - *stress shift:* ˌAdriatic ˈSea

Example of stress shift when the word is used before a noun.

advent (A) ˈæd.vent, -vənt **-s** -s

This indicates that the word can be spelled with a capital letter in some contexts.

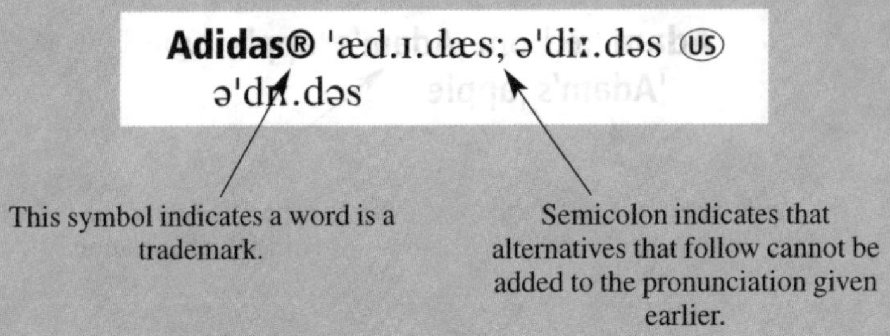

Adidas® 'æd.ɪ.dæs; ə'diː.dəs (US) ə'dɑː.dəs
This symbol indicates a word is a trademark.
Semicolon indicates that alternatives that follow cannot be added to the pronunciation given earlier.

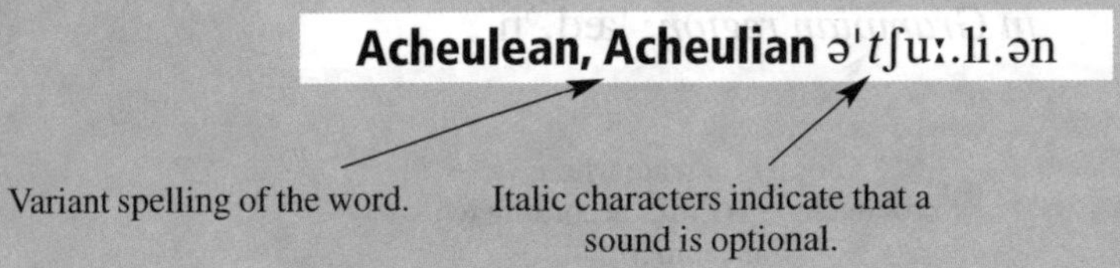

Variant spelling of the word.
Italic characters indicate that a sound is optional.

References in introduction

Roach, P. (2000) *English Phonetics and Phonology,* 3rd ed., Cambridge University Press.

Stromberg, K. and Roach, P. (1993) 'The representation of stress-patterns in pronunciation dictionaries: 'Morse-code' vs. orthographic marking', *Journal of the International Phonetic Association*, vol.23.3, pp. 55-58.

Michaelis, H., and Jones, D. (1913) *A Phonetic Dictionary of the English Language*, Carl Meyer (Gustav Prior), Hanover.

List of recommended reading

A. Works principally on British English

Brown, G. (1990) *Listening to Spoken English*, (2nd ed.), Longman.
An introductory book with many insights on connected speech.

Jones, D. (1960) *Outline of English Phonetics*, (9th ed.), Cambridge University Press.
The classic textbook written by the original author of the *English Pronouncing Dictionary*. First published in 1918, but still readable and informative.

Fudge, E. (1984) *English Word Stress*, Allen and Unwin.
A comprehensive and valuable treatment of stress.

Giegerich, H.J. (1992) *English Phonology*, Cambridge University Press.
A theoretical introduction to the phonology of English.

Gimson, A.C., revised by A.Cruttenden (2001) *The Pronunciation of English (6th Edition)*, Edward Arnold.
The best contemporary description of the phonetics of English, written by the person responsible for the 13th and 14th editions of the *English Pronouncing Dictionary*.

International Phonetic Association (1999) *Handbook of the International Phonetic Association*, Cambridge University Press.

Knowles, G.O., (1987) *Patterns of Spoken English*, Longman.
An introductory textbook on the phonetics of English.

Kreidler, C.W. (1989) *The Pronunciation of English*, Blackwell.
A modern treatment of the phonetics and phonology of English, with coverage of American as well as British English.

Roach, P. (2000) *English Phonetics and Phonology*, 3rd ed., Cambridge University Press.
An introductory textbook with practical exercises.

Roach. P. (2001) *Phonetics*, Oxford University Press.
A short introductory book.

Wells, J.C (1982) *Accents of English*, Cambridge University Press (3 vols).
A very detailed and comprehensive account of the different accents of English throughout the world.

Wells, J.C. (2000) *Longman Pronunciation Dictionary*, 2nd ed., Longman.
An alternative pronouncing dictionary to this one.

B. American English

Cassidy, F.G (ed.) (1985) *Dictionary of American Regional English*, Belknap Press, Harvard.
An ongoing publication, each entry listing pronunciations in designated regions.

Kenyon, J.S and Knott, T.A. (1953) *A Pronouncing Dictionary of American English*, G.&C. Merrian & Co.
One of the earlier pronouncing dictionaries for American English.

Lujan, B. (1999) *The American Accent*, Lingual Arts.

Wolfram, W. and Johnson, R. (1988) *Phonological Analysis: Focus on American English*, Prentice Hall.

Wolfram, W. and Schilling-Estes, N. (1998) 'American English: Dialects and Variation', *Language in Society*, vol. 25.

Van Riper, C. and Smith, D. (1992) *Introduction to General American Phonetics*, Waveland Press.
A practical workbook.

THE INTERNATIONAL PHONETIC ALPHABET (revised to 1993, updated 1996)

CONSONANTS (PULMONIC)

	Bilabial	Labiodental	Dental	Alveolar	Postalveolar	Retroflex	Palatal	Velar	Uvular	Pharyngeal	Glottal
Plosive	p b			t d		ʈ ɖ	c ɟ	k ɡ	q ɢ		ʔ
Nasal	m	ɱ		n		ɳ	ɲ	ŋ	ɴ		
Trill	ʙ			r					ʀ		
Tap or Flap				ɾ		ɽ					
Fricative	ɸ β	f v	θ ð	s z	ʃ ʒ	ʂ ʐ	ç ʝ	x ɣ	χ ʁ	ħ ʕ	h ɦ
Lateral fricative				ɬ ɮ							
Approximant		ʋ		ɹ		ɻ	j	ɰ			
Lateral approximant				l		ɭ	ʎ	ʟ			

Where symbols appear in pairs, the one to the right represents a voiced consonant. Shaded areas denote articulations judged impossible.

CONSONANTS (NON-PULMONIC)

Clicks		Voiced implosives		Ejectives	
ʘ	Bilabial	ɓ	Bilabial	ʼ	Examples:
ǀ	Dental	ɗ	Dental/alveolar	pʼ	Bilabial
ǃ	(Post)alveolar	ʄ	Palatal	tʼ	Dental/alveolar
ǂ	Palatoalveolar	ɠ	Velar	kʼ	Velar
ǁ	Alveolar lateral	ʛ	Uvular	sʼ	Alveolar fricative

VOWELS

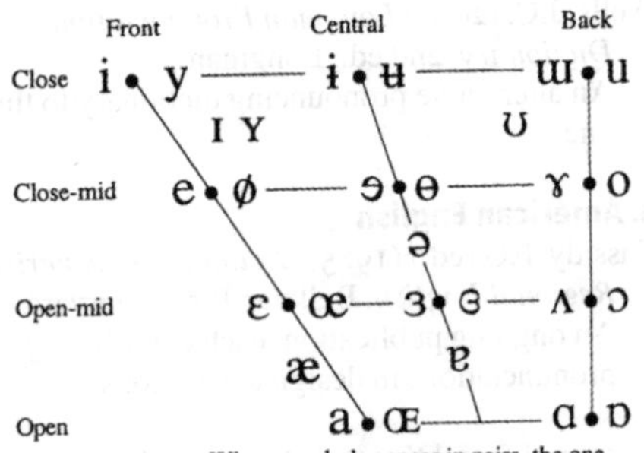

Where symbols appear in pairs, the one to the right represents a rounded vowel.

OTHER SYMBOLS

- ʍ Voiceless labial-velar fricative
- w Voiced labial-velar approximant
- ɥ Voiced labial-palatal approximant
- ʜ Voiceless epiglottal fricative
- ʢ Voiced epiglottal fricative
- ʡ Epiglottal plosive
- ɕ ʑ Alveolo-palatal fricatives
- ɺ Alveolar lateral flap
- ɧ Simultaneous ʃ and x

Affricates and double articulations can be represented by two symbols joined by a tie bar if necessary. k͡p t͜s

SUPRASEGMENTALS

ˈ	Primary stress	ˌfoʊnəˈtɪʃən
ˌ	Secondary stress	
ː	Long	eː
ˑ	Half-long	eˑ
˘	Extra-short	ĕ
|	Minor (foot) group	
‖	Major (intonation) group	
.	Syllable break	ɹi.ækt
‿	Linking (absence of a break)	

DIACRITICS Diacritics may be placed above a symbol with a descender, e.g. ŋ̊

̥ Voiceless	n̥ d̥	̤ Breathy voiced	b̤ a̤	̪ Dental	t̪ d̪
̬ Voiced	s̬ t̬	̰ Creaky voiced	b̰ a̰	̺ Apical	t̺ d̺
ʰ Aspirated	tʰ dʰ	̼ Linguolabial	t̼ d̼	̻ Laminal	t̻ d̻
̹ More rounded	ɔ̹	ʷ Labialized	tʷ dʷ	̃ Nasalized	ẽ
̜ Less rounded	ɔ̜	ʲ Palatalized	tʲ dʲ	ⁿ Nasal release	dⁿ
̟ Advanced	u̟	ˠ Velarized	tˠ dˠ	ˡ Lateral release	dˡ
̠ Retracted	e̠	ˤ Pharyngealized	tˤ dˤ	̚ No audible release	d̚
̈ Centralized	ë	̴ Velarized or pharyngealized	ɫ		
̽ Mid-centralized	e̽	̝ Raised	e̝ (ɹ̝ = voiced alveolar fricative)		
̩ Syllabic	n̩	̞ Lowered	e̞ (β̞ = voiced bilabial approximant)		
̯ Non-syllabic	e̯	̘ Advanced Tongue Root	e̘		
˞ Rhoticity	ɚ a˞	̙ Retracted Tongue Root	e̙		

TONES AND WORD ACCENTS

LEVEL		CONTOUR	
e̋ or ˥	Extra high	ě or ˩˥	Rising
é ˦	High	ê ˥˩	Falling
ē ˧	Mid	e᷄ ˦˥	High rising
è ˨	Low	e᷅ ˩˨	Low rising
ȅ ˩	Extra low	e᷈ ˧˦˧	Rising-falling
↓	Downstep	↗	Global rise
↑	Upstep	↘	Global fall

This chart is reproduced by courtesy of the International Phonetic Association

Index of Information Panels

Index of Information Panels

Pronouncing the letter A

See also AE, AEO, AI/AY, AU/AW

The vowel letter **a** has two main strong pronunciations linked to spelling: a 'short' pronunciation /æ/ and a 'long' pronunciation /eɪ/. In the 'short' pronunciation, the **a** is usually followed by a consonant which closes the syllable, or a double consonant before another vowel, e.g.:

tap	/tæp/
tapping	/ˈtæp.ɪŋ/

The 'long' pronunciation usually means the **a** is followed by a single consonant and then a vowel, e.g.:

tape	/teɪp/
taping	/ˈteɪ.pɪŋ/

When there is an **r** in the spelling, the strong pronunciation is one of three possibilities: /ɑː (US) ɑːr/, /eə (US) er/ or /æ (US) e, æ/, e.g.:

car	/kɑː^{r}/	(US) /kɑːr/
care	/keə^{r}/	(US) /ker/
carry	/kær.i/	(US) /ker.i, kær.i/

In addition

There are other vowel sounds associated with the letter **a**, e.g.:

/ɑː/	father	/ˈfɑː.ðə^{r}/	(US) /ˈfɑː.ðɚ/
/ɑː (US) æ/	bath	/bɑːθ/	(US) /bæθ/
/ɒ (US) ɑː/	swan	/swɒn/	(US) /swɑːn/
/ɔː (US) ɑː, ɔː/	walk	/wɔːk/	(US) /wɑːk/
	warm	/wɔːm/	(US) /wɔːrm/

And, in rare cases:

/e/	many	/ˈmen.i/

In weak syllables

The vowel letter **a** is realised with the vowels /ə/ and /ɪ/ in weak syllables, and may also not be pronounced at all in British English, due to compression, e.g.:

above	/əˈbʌv/	
village	/ˈvɪl.ɪdʒ/	
necessary	/ˈnes.ə.sri/	(US) /-ser.i/

a *indefinite article: strong form:* eɪ *weak form:* ə
Note: Weak form word. The strong form /eɪ/ is used mainly for contrast (e.g. 'This is *a* solution, but not the only one.'). The weak form only occurs before consonants, and is usually pronounced /ə/. In rapid speech, when /ə/ is preceded by a consonant, it may combine with a following /l/, /n/ or /r/ to produce a syllabic consonant (e.g. 'got a light' /ˌɡɒt.l̩ˈaɪt (US) ˌɡɑːt̬.əˈlaɪt/; 'get another' /ˌɡet.n̩ˈʌð.ə^{r} (US) -ɚ/).
a (A) *the letter:* eɪ **-'s** -z
A-1 ˌeɪˈwʌn *stress shift:* ˌA-1 conˈdition
A4 ˌeɪˈfɔː^{r} (US) -ˈfɔːr *stress shift:* ˌA4 ˈpaper
AA ˌeɪˈeɪ *stress shift:* ˌAA patˈrol
Aachen ˈɑː.kən
aah ɑː
Aalborg ˈɑːl.bɔːɡ (US) ˈɑːl.bɔːrɡ, ˈɔːl-
aardvark ˈɑːd.vɑːk (US) ˈɑːrd.vɑːrk **-s** -s
aardwol|f ˈɑːd.wʊl|f (US) ˈɑːrd- **-ves** -vz
Aarhus ˈɑː.hʊs (US) ˈɑːr-, ˈɔːr-
Aaron ˈeə.rən (US) ˈer.ən, ˈær-
ab- æb-, əb-
Note: Prefix. Examples include **abnegate** /ˈæb.nɪ.ɡeɪt/, in which it is stressed, and **abduct** /əbˈdʌkt/, where it is unstressed.
ab (A) æb
AB ˌeɪˈbiː
Abacha əˈbætʃ.ə (US) -bɑːtʃ-
aback əˈbæk
Abaco ˈæb.ə.kəʊ (US) -koʊ
abacus ˈæb.ə.kəs **-es** -ɪz
Abadan ˌæb.əˈdɑːn, -ˈdæn
Abaddon əˈbæd.^{ə}n
abaft əˈbɑːft (US) -ˈbæft
abalone æb.əˈləʊ.ni (US) -ˈloʊ-
abandon əˈbæn.dən **-s** -z **-ing** -ɪŋ **-ed** -d **-ment** -mənt
à bas æˈbɑː (US) æ-, ɑː-
abas|e əˈbeɪs **-es** -ɪz **-ing** -ɪŋ **-ed** -t **-ement** -mənt
abash əˈbæʃ **-es** -ɪz **-ing** -ɪŋ **-ed** -t
abatab|le əˈbeɪ.tə.b|l̩ (US) -t̬ə- **-ly** -li
a|bate ə|ˈbeɪt **-bates** -ˈbeɪts **-bating** -ˈbeɪ.tɪŋ (US) -ˈbeɪ.t̬ɪŋ **-bated** -ˈbeɪ.tɪd (US) -ˈbeɪ.t̬ɪd **-batement/s** -ˈbeɪt.mənt/s
abat(t)is ˈæb.ə.tɪs, -tiː (US) -ə.t̬ɪs, əˈbæt̬.ɪs **-es** ˈæb.ə.tɪ.sɪz (US) -t̬ɪ-, əˈbæt̬.ɪ.sɪz *alternative plur.:* ˈæb.ə.tiːz (US) -t̬iːz, əˈbæt̬.iːz
abattoir ˈæb.ə.twɑː^{r} (US) -twɑːr, -twɔːr **-s** -z
abaxial əˈbæk.si.əl, æbˈæk-
Abba ˈæb.ə
abbac|y ˈæb.ə.s|i **-ies** -iz
Abbado əˈbɑː.dəʊ (US) -oʊ
Abbas ˈæb.əs, əˈbæs
Abbassid, **Abbasid** əˈbæs.ɪd **-s** -z
abbé ˈæb.eɪ (US) ˈæb.eɪ, -ˈ- **-s** -z
abbess ˈæb.es, -ɪs (US) -əs **-es** -ɪz
Abbeville *in France:* ˈæb.viːl (US) ˌæbˈviːl *in US:* ˈæb.ɪ.vɪl
abbey (A) ˈæb.i **-s** -z
Abbie ˈæb.i
abbot (A) ˈæb.ət **-s** -s
Abbotsford ˈæb.əts.fəd (US) -fɚd
abbotship ˈæb.ət.ʃɪp **-s** -s
Abbott ˈæb.ət **-s** -s ˌ**Abbott and Cosˈtello**
abbrevi|ate əˈbriː.vi|.eɪt **-ates** -eɪts **-ating** -eɪ.tɪŋ (US) -eɪ.t̬ɪŋ **-ated** -eɪ.tɪd (US) -eɪ.t̬ɪd **-ator/s** -eɪ.tə^{r}/z (US) -eɪ.t̬ɚ/z
abbreviation əˌbriː.viˈeɪ.ʃ^{ə}n **-s** -z
abbreviatory əˈbriː.vi.ə.tri, əˌbriː.viˈeɪ.t^{ə}r.i (US) əˈbriː.vi.ə.tɔːr.i
Abbs æbz
Abby ˈæb.i
abc, **ABC** ˌeɪ.biːˈsiː **-'s** -z
Abdera æbˈdɪə.rə (US) -ˈdɪr.ə
abdicant ˈæb.dɪ.kənt **-s** -s
abdi|cate ˈæb.dɪ|.keɪt **-cates** -keɪts **-cating** -keɪ.tɪŋ (US) -keɪ.t̬ɪŋ **-cated** -keɪ.tɪd (US) -keɪ.t̬ɪd **-cator/s** -keɪ.tə^{r}/z (US) -keɪ.t̬ɚ/z
abdication ˌæb.dɪˈkeɪ.ʃ^{ə}n **-s** -z
Abdiel ˈæb.dɪəl (US) -di.əl
abdomen ˈæb.də.mən, -men; æbˈdəʊ.mən (US) ˈæb.də.mən, æbˈdoʊ- **-s** -z
abdominal æbˈdɒm.ɪ.n^{ə}l, əb-, -ˈdəʊ.mɪ- (US) -ˈdɑː.mə- **-ly** -i
abducent əbˈdjuː.s^{ə}nt, æb- (US) -ˈduː-, -ˈdjuː-
abduct əbˈdʌkt, æb- **-s** -s **-ing** -ɪŋ **-ed** -ɪd **-or/s** -ə^{r}/z (US) -ɚ/z
abduction əbˈdʌk.ʃ^{ə}n, æb- **-s** -z
Abdul ˈæb.dʊl
Abdulla(h) æbˈdʌl.ə, əb-, -ˈdʊl-

Abbreviations

The pronunciation of individual abbreviations is not predictable and must be treated on a word-by-word basis.

Examples

Some good examples of abbreviations which are spoken in full are to be found in titles used for people, e.g.:

Mr	/ˈmɪs.təʳ/	(US) /-tɚ/
Mrs	/ˈmɪs.ɪz/	
Dr	/ˈdɒk.təʳ/	(US) /ˈdɑːk.tɚ/
Esq	/ɪsˈkwaɪəʳ/	(US) /ˈes.kwaɪɚ/

However, in some cases, an abbreviation may be pronounced the way it is written, e.g.:

Bros. (*Brothers*)	/ˈbrʌð.əz/, /brɒs/ (US) /ˈbrʌð.ɚz/
des res (*desirable residence*)	/ˌdezˈrez/

Some words or phrases are abbreviated to initial letters. In this case, the item may be pronounced as the initial letters, or in full. This is not the same as an ACRONYM, in which the letters are pronounced as a word (see, for example, *NATO*), e.g.:

MS (*multiple sclerosis; manuscript*)	/ˌemˈes/
NBA (*National Basketball Association*)	/ˌen.biːˈeɪ/
UCLA (*University of California Los Angeles*)	/ˌjuː.siː.elˈeɪ/

Abbreviations derived from Latin words and phrases are common, but do not all follow the same pattern, some being pronounced in full, some as letters, and some as they are spelt, e.g.:

e.g. (*exempli gratia*)	/ˌiːˈdʒiː/	
et al (*et alia*)	/etˈæl/	(US) /-ˈɑːl/
etc. (*et cetera*)	/ɪtˈset.ər.ə/	(US) /-ˈset̬.ɚ-/
i.e. (*id est*)	/ˌaɪˈiː/	

Abe eɪb
abeam əˈbiːm
abecedarian ˌeɪ.biː.siːˈdeə.ri.ən (US) -ˈder.i-
à Becket əˈbek.ɪt
abed əˈbed
Abednego ˌæb.edˈniː.gəʊ, əˈbed.nɪ.gəʊ (US) -goʊ
Abel ˈeɪ.bᵊl
Abelard ˈæb.ə.lɑːd, ˈ-ɪ- (US) -lɑːrd
Abelmeholah ˌeɪ.bᵊl.miˈhəʊ.lə, -məˈ- (US) -ˈhoʊ-
Abenaki ˌæb.əˈnæk.i (US) ˌɑː.bəˈnɑː.ki, ˌæb.əˈ-, -ˈnæk.i **-s** -z
Aberavon ˌæb.əˈræv.ᵊn (US) -ɚˈæv-
Abercanaid ˌæb.əˈkæn.aɪd (US) ˌ-ɚ-
Abercarn ˌæb.əˈkɑːn (US) -ɚˈkɑːrn
Aberconway ˌæb.əˈkɒn.weɪ (US) -ɚˈkɑːn-
Aberconwy ˌæb.əˈkɒn.wi (US) -ɚˈkɑːn-
Abercorn ˈæb.ə.kɔːn (US) -ɚ.kɔːrn
Abercrombie, Abercromby ˈæb.ə.krɒm.bi, -krʌm-, ˌæb.əˈkrɒm.bi, -ˈkrʌm- (US) -ɚ.krɑːm-, -ɚˈkrɑːm-
Aberdare ˌæb.əˈdeəʳ (US) -ɚˈder
Aberdeen ˌæb.əˈdiːn (US) -ɚˈ- **-shire** -ʃəʳ, -ˌʃɪəʳ (US) -ʃɚ, -ˌʃɪr *stress shift:* ˌAberdeen ˈstation
Aberdonian ˌæb.əˈdəʊ.ni.ən (US) -ɚˈdoʊ- **-s** -z
Aberdour ˌæb.əˈdaʊəʳ (US) -ɚˈdaʊɚ
Aberdovey ˌæb.əˈdʌv.i (US) -ɚˈ-
Aberfan ˌæb.əˈvæn (US) -ɚˈ-
Abergavenny *place:* ˌæb.ə.gəˈven.i (US) -ɚˈ- *family name:* ˌæb.əˈgen.i (US) -ɚˈ-
Abergele ˌæb.əˈgel.i (US) -ɚˈ-
Aberkenfig ˌæb.əˈken.fɪg (US) -ɚˈ-
Abernathy ˌæb.əˈnæθ.i (US) ˈæb.ɚ.næθ-
Abernethy ˌæb.əˈneθ.i, -ˈniː.θi (US) ˈæb.ɚˈneθ.i
aberran|t æbˈer.ᵊn|t, əˈber-; ˈæb.ə.rᵊn|t **-ce** -*t*s **-cy** -*t*.si
aber|rate ˈæb.ə|.reɪt **-rates** -reɪts **-rating** -reɪ.tɪŋ (US) -reɪ.t̬ɪŋ **-rated** -reɪ.tɪd (US) -reɪ.t̬ɪd
aberration ˌæb.əˈreɪ.ʃᵊn **-s** -z
Abersychan ˌæb.əˈsɪk.ən (US) -ɚˈ-
Abert ˈeɪ.bɜːt, -bət (US) -bɝːt, -bɚt
Abertillery ˌæb.ə.tɪˈleə.ri, -təˈ- (US) -ɚ.təˈler.i
Abertridwr ˌæb.əˈtrɪd.ʊəʳ (US) -ʊr
Aberystwyth ˌæb.əˈrɪs.*t*wɪθ
a|bet ə|ˈbet **-bets** -ˈbets **-betting** -ˈbet.ɪŋ (US) -ˈbet̬.ɪŋ **-betted** -ˈbet.ɪd (US) -ˈbet̬.ɪd **-bettor/s** -ˈbet.əʳ/z (US) -ˈbet̬.ɚ/z **-betment** -ˈbet.mənt
abeyance əˈbeɪ.ən*t*s
abhor əbˈhɔːʳ, əˈbɔːʳ (US) æbˈhɔːr, əb- **-s** -z **-ring** -ɪŋ **-red** -d **-rer/s** -əʳ/z (US) -ɚ/z
abhorren|ce əbˈhɒr.ᵊn|*t*s, əˈbɒr- (US) æbˈhɔːr-, əb- **-t** -t
Abia *biblical name:* əˈbaɪ.ə *city:* ˈæb.i.ə
Abiathar əˈbaɪ.ə.θəʳ (US) -θɚ
abid|e əˈbaɪd **-es** -z **-ing** -ɪŋ **-ed** -ɪd
abode əˈbəʊd (US) -ˈboʊd
Abidjan ˌæb.iːˈdʒɑːn, -ɪˈ-
abigail (A) ˈæb.ɪ.geɪl **-s** -z
Abilene *in Syria:* ˌæb.ɪˈliː.ni, -əˈ- *in US:* ˈæb.ə.liːn
abilit|y əˈbɪl.ə.t|i, -ɪ.t|i (US) -ə.t̬|i **-ies** -iz
-ability -əˈbɪl.ə.ti, -ɪ.ti (US) -ə.t̬i
Note: Suffix. Words containing **-ability** always exhibit primary stress as shown above, e.g. **capability** /ˌkeɪ.pəˈbɪl.ə.ti (US) -ə.t̬i/.
Abimelech əˈbɪm.ə.lek
Abingdon ˈæb.ɪŋ.dən
Abinger ˈæb.ɪn.dʒəʳ (US) -dʒɚ
Abington ˈæb.ɪŋ.tən
ab initio ˌæb.ɪˈnɪʃ.i.əʊ, -əˈ-, -ˈnɪs- (US) -oʊ
abiogenesis ˌeɪ.baɪ.əʊˈdʒen.ə.sɪs, ˈ-ɪ- (US) -oʊˈ-
Abiola ˌæb.iˈəʊ.lə (US) -ˈoʊ-
abiotic ˌeɪ.baɪˈɒt.ɪk (US) -ˈɑː.t̬ɪk
abject ˈæb.dʒekt (US) ˈæb.dʒekt, -ˈ- **-ly** -li **-ness** -nəs, -nɪs
abjection æbˈdʒek.ʃᵊn
abjudi|cate æbˈdʒuː.dɪ|.keɪt, əb- (US) -də- **-cates** -keɪts **-cating** -keɪ.tɪŋ (US) -keɪ.t̬ɪŋ **-cated** -keɪ.tɪd (US) -keɪ.t̬ɪd
abjuration ˌæb.dʒʊˈreɪ.ʃᵊn, -dʒəˈ-, -dʒʊəˈ- (US) -dʒəˈ-, -dʒʊˈ- **-s** -z
abjur|e əbˈdʒʊəʳ, æb-, -ˈdʒɔːʳ (US) -ˈdʒʊr **-es** -z **-ing** -ɪŋ **-ed** -d **-er/s** -əʳ/z (US) -ɚ/z
ablat|e əˈbleɪt, æbˈleɪt, ˌæbˈleɪt **-es** -s **-ing** -ɪŋ (US) ˌæbˈleɪ.t̬ɪŋ **-ed** -ɪd (US) ˌæbˈleɪ.t̬ɪd
ablation əˈbleɪ.ʃᵊn, æbˈleɪ- (US) ˌæb-
ablatival ˈæb.ləˈtaɪ.vᵊl
ablative ˈæb.lə.tɪv (US) -t̬ɪv **-s** -z
ablaut ˈæb.laʊt **-s** -s
ablaze əˈbleɪz
ab|le ˈeɪ.b|l̩ **-ler** -l̩.əʳ, -ləʳ (US) -l̩.ɚ, -lɚ **-lest** -l̩.əst, -ləst, -l̩.ɪst, -lɪst **-ly** -l̩.i, -li
-able -ə.bl̩
Note: Suffix. Does not normally affect stress patterning, e.g. **knowledge** /ˈnɒl.ɪdʒ (US) ˈnɑː.lɪdʒ/, **knowledgeable** /ˈnɒl.ɪ.dʒə.bl̩ (US) ˈnɑː.lɪ-/; **rely** /rɪˈlaɪ/, **reliable** /rɪˈlaɪ.ə.bl̩/. In some cases, however,

the stress patterning may change, e.g. **admire** /əd'maɪəʳ ⓤⓢ -'maɪɚ/, **admirable** /'æd.mᵊr.ə.bl̩/.
able-bodied ˌeɪ.bl̩'bɒd.ɪd ⓤⓢ 'eɪ.bl̩ˌbɑː.dɪd, ˌeɪ.bl̩'bɑː- *stress shift, British only:* ˌable-bodied 'person
Ablett 'æb.lət, -lɪt
ablution ə'bluː.ʃᵊn **-s** -z
-ably -ə.bli
Note: Suffix. Behaves as **-able** above.
Abnaki æb'næk.i ⓤⓢ -'nɑː.ki **-s** -z
abneg|ate 'æb.nɪ.g|eɪt, -neg|.eɪt, -nə.g|eɪt **-ates** -eɪts **-ating** -eɪ.tɪŋ ⓤⓢ -eɪ.t̬ɪŋ **-ated** -eɪ.tɪd ⓤⓢ -eɪ.t̬ɪd
abnegation ˌæb.nɪ'geɪ.ʃᵊn, -neg'eɪ-, -nə'geɪ- **-s** -z
Abner 'æb.nəʳ ⓤⓢ -nɚ
abnormal æb'nɔː.mᵊl, əb- ⓤⓢ -'nɔːr- **-ly** -i
abnormalit|y ˌæb.nɔː'mæl.ə.t|i, -ɪ.t|i ⓤⓢ -nɔːr'mæl.ə.t̬|i **-ies** -iz
abnormit|y æb'nɔː.mə.t|i, əb-, -mɪ- ⓤⓢ -'nɔːr.mə.t̬|i **-ies** -iz
abo 'æb.əʊ ⓤⓢ -oʊ **-s** -z
ABO ˌeɪ.biː'əʊ ⓤⓢ -'oʊ
aboard ə'bɔːd ⓤⓢ -'bɔːrd
abode ə'bəʊd ⓤⓢ -'boʊd **-s** -z
abolish ə'bɒl.ɪʃ ⓤⓢ -'bɑː.lɪʃ **-es** -ɪz **-ing** -ɪŋ **-ed** -t **-er/s** -əʳ/z ⓤⓢ -ɚ/z
abolition ˌæb.ə'lɪʃ.ᵊn **-s** -z
abolition|ism ˌæb.ə'lɪʃ.ᵊn|.ɪ.zᵊm **-ist/s** -ɪst/s
abomas|um ˌæb.əʊ'meɪ.s|ᵊm ⓤⓢ -oʊ'- **-a** -ə
A-bomb 'eɪˌbɒm ⓤⓢ -ˌbɑːm **-s** -z
abominab|le ə'bɒm.ɪ.nə.b|l̩, -ᵊn.ə- ⓤⓢ -'bɑː.mɪ- **-ly** -li **-leness** -l̩.nəs, -nɪs
abomi|nate ə'bɒm.ɪ|.neɪt, '-ə- ⓤⓢ -'bɑː.mɪ- **-nates** -neɪts **-nating** -neɪ.tɪŋ ⓤⓢ -neɪ.t̬ɪŋ **-nated** -neɪ.tɪd ⓤⓢ -neɪ.t̬ɪd
abomination əˌbɒm.ɪ'neɪ.ʃᵊn, -ə'- ⓤⓢ -ˌbɑː.mɪ'- **-s** -z
à bon marché æˌbɔ̃ː.mɑː'ʃeɪ, -ˌbɒn- ⓤⓢ -ˌbõʊn.mɑːr'-
aboriginal (A) ˌæb.ə'rɪdʒ.ᵊn.ᵊl, -ɪ.nᵊl **-s** -z **-ly** -i
aborigine (A) ˌæb.ə'rɪdʒ.ᵊn.i, -ɪ.ni **-s** -z
a|bort ə|'bɔːt ⓤⓢ -'bɔrt **-borts** -'bɔːts ⓤⓢ -'bɔːrts **-borting** -'bɔː.tɪŋ ⓤⓢ -'bɔːr.t̬ɪŋ **-borted** -'bɔː.tɪd ⓤⓢ -'bɔːr.t̬ɪd
aborticide ə'bɔː.tɪ.saɪd ⓤⓢ -'bɔːr.t̬ə-
abortifacient əˌbɔː.tɪ'feɪ.ʃi.ənt, -ʃᵊnt ⓤⓢ -ˌbɔːr.t̬ə'-
abortion ə'bɔː.ʃᵊn ⓤⓢ -'bɔːr- **-s** -z **-ist/s** -ɪst/s
abortive ə'bɔː.tɪv ⓤⓢ -'bɔːr.t̬ɪv **-ly** -li **-ness** -nəs, -nɪs
Aboukir ˌæb.uː'kɪəʳ, -ʊ'- ⓤⓢ -'kɪr
abound ə'baʊnd **-s** -z **-ing** -ɪŋ **-ed** -ɪd
about ə'baʊt
about-fac|e əˌbaʊt'feɪs **-es** -ɪz **-ing** -ɪŋ **-ed** -d
about-turn əˌbaʊt'tɜːn ⓤⓢ -'tɝːn **-s** -z
above ə'bʌv
above-board əˌbʌv'bɔːd ⓤⓢ ə'bʌv.bɔːrd
aboveground əˌbʌv'graʊnd ⓤⓢ ə'bʌv.graʊnd
above-mentioned əˌbʌv'men.*t*ʃᵊnd ⓤⓢ -'men*t*.ʃᵊnd *stress shift:* aˌbove-mentioned 'person
ab ovo ˌæb'əʊ.vəʊ ⓤⓢ -'oʊ.voʊ
abracadabra ˌæb.rə.kə'dæb.rə **-s** -z
abrad|e ə'breɪd **-es** -z **-ing** -ɪŋ **-ed** -ɪd
Abraham 'eɪ.brə.hæm, -həm *as a biblical name in Britain often also:* 'ɑː-
Abrahams 'eɪ.brə.hæmz
Abram 'eɪ.brəm, -bræm *as a biblical name in Britain often also:* 'ɑː-
abranchi|al ˌeɪ'bræŋ.ki|.əl, ə'bræŋ-, æb'ræŋ- **-ate** -eɪt, -ət
abrasion ə'breɪ.ʒᵊn **-s** -z
abrasive ə'breɪ.sɪv, -zɪv **-ly** -li **-s** -z
abreact ˌæb.ri'ækt **-s** -s **-ing** -ɪŋ **-ed** -ɪd
abreaction ˌæb.ri'æk.ʃᵊn
abreast ə'brest
abridg|e ə'brɪdʒ **-es** -ɪz **-ing** -ɪŋ **-ed** -d
abridg(e)ment ə'brɪdʒ.mənt **-s** -s
abroad ə'brɔːd ⓤⓢ -'brɑːd, -'brɔːd
abro|gate 'æb.rəʊ|.geɪt ⓤⓢ -rə- **-gates** -geɪts **-gating** -geɪ.tɪŋ ⓤⓢ -geɪ.t̬ɪŋ **-gated** -geɪ.tɪd ⓤⓢ -geɪ.t̬ɪd
abrogation ˌæb.rəʊ'geɪ.ʃᵊn ⓤⓢ -rə'- **-s** -z
A'Brook ə'brʊk
abrupt ə'brʌpt **-er** -əʳ ⓤⓢ -ɚ **-est** -əst, -ɪst **-ly** -li **-ness** -nəs, -nɪs
abruption ə'brʌp.ʃᵊn
Abruzzi ə'brʊt.si, -bruːt-
Absalom 'æb.sᵊl.əm
abscess 'æb.ses, -sɪs **-es** -ɪz
abscis|e æb'saɪz, əb- **-es** -ɪz **-ing** -ɪŋ **-ed** -d
abscisin æb'sɪs.ɪn
absciss|a æb'sɪs|.ə, əb- **-ae** -i **-as** -əz
abscission æb'sɪʃ.ᵊn, -'sɪʒ- **-s** -z
abscond æb'skɒnd, əb- ⓤⓢ -'skɑːnd **-s** -z **-ing** -ɪŋ **-ed** -ɪd **-er/s** -əʳ/z ⓤⓢ -ɚ/z
Abse 'æb.si, -zi
abseil 'æb.seɪl, -saɪl **-s** -z **-ing** -ɪŋ **-ed** -d
absenc|e 'æb.sᵊnts **-es** -ɪz
absent *(adj.)* 'æb.sᵊnt **-ly** -li ˌ**absent without 'leave**
ab|sent *(v.)* æb|'sent, əb- **-sents** -'sents **-senting** -'sen.tɪŋ ⓤⓢ -'sen.t̬ɪŋ **-sented** -'sen.tɪd ⓤⓢ -'sen.t̬ɪd
absentee ˌæb.sᵊn'tiː, -sen'- **-s** -z **-ism** -ɪ.zᵊm *stress shift, see compounds:* ˌ**absentee 'ballot**; ˌ**absentee 'landlord**
absentia æb'sen.ti.ə, -ɑː, -'sen*t*.ʃi- ⓤⓢ -'sen*t*.ʃə, '-ʃi.ə
absent-minded ˌæb.sᵊnt'maɪn.dɪd **-ly** -li **-ness** -nəs, -nɪs *stress shift:* ˌabsent-minded 'person
absinth(e) 'æb.sæ̃θ, -sɪn*t*θ
absolut|e ˌæb.sə'luːt, -ljuːt, 'æb.sᵊl.uːt, -juːt ⓤⓢ ˌæb.sə'luːt, '--- **-es** -s **-est** -əst, -ɪst **-ness** -nəs, -nɪs
absolutely ˌæb.sə'luːt.li, -'ljuːt- ⓤⓢ ˌæb.sə'luːt-, 'æb.sə.luːt- *stress shift:* ˌabsolutely 'fabulous
absolution ˌæb.sə'luː.ʃᵊn, -'ljuː- ⓤⓢ -'luː- **-s** -z
absolut|ism 'æb.sᵊl.uː.t|ɪ.zᵊm, -juː- ⓤⓢ -sə.luː.t̬|ɪ- **-ist/s** -ɪst/s
absolutive ˌæb.sə'luː.tɪv, -'ljuː- ⓤⓢ -'luː.t̬ɪv
absolv|e əb'zɒlv, -'sɒlv ⓤⓢ -'zɑːlv, -'sɑːlv, -'zɔːlv, -'sɔːlv **-es** -z **-ing** -ɪŋ **-ed** -d **-er/s** -əʳ/z ⓤⓢ -ɚ/z
absorb əb'zɔːb, -'sɔːb ⓤⓢ -'sɔːrb, -'zɔːrb **-s** -z **-ed** -d **-edly** -ɪd.li, -əd.li **-able** -ə.bl̩
absorbency əb'zɔː.bənt.si, -'sɔː- ⓤⓢ -'sɔːr-, -'zɔːr-
absorbent əb'zɔː.bənt, -'sɔː- ⓤⓢ -'sɔːr-, -'zɔːr- **-ly** -li
absorbing əb'zɔː.bɪŋ, -'sɔː- ⓤⓢ -'sɔːr-, -'zɔːr- **-ly** -li
absorbing əb'zɔː.bɪŋ, -'sɔː- ⓤⓢ -'sɔːr-, -'zɔːr- **-ly** -li
absorption əb'zɔːp.ʃᵊn, -'sɔːp- ⓤⓢ -'sɔːrp-, -'zɔːrp-
absorptive əb'zɔːp.tɪv, -'sɔːp- ⓤⓢ -'sɔːrp-, -'zɔːrp-
abstain æb'steɪn, əb- **-s** -z **-ing** -ɪŋ **-ed** -d **-er/s** -əʳ/z ⓤⓢ -ɚ/z
abstemious æb'stiː.mi.əs, əb- **-ly** -li **-ness** -nəs, -nɪs
abstention æb'sten.*t*ʃᵊn, əb- ⓤⓢ -'sten*t*.ʃᵊn **-s** -z
abstergent æb'stɜː.dʒᵊnt, əb- ⓤⓢ -'stɝː- **-s** -s
abstinen|ce 'æb.stɪ.nən|*t*s, -stə- **-t** -t
abstract *(n. adj.)* 'æb.strækt **-s** -s
abstract *(v.)* æb'strækt, əb- **-s** -s **-ing** -ɪŋ **-ed/ly** -ɪd/li
abstraction æb'stræk.ʃᵊn, əb- **-s** -z
abstraction|ism æb'stræk.ʃᵊn|.ɪ.zᵊm, əb- **-ist/s** -ɪst/s
abstract|ly 'æb.stræk*t*|.li, əb'stræk*t*-, æb'- **-ness** -nəs, -nɪs
abstrict əb'strɪkt, æb- **-s** -s **-ing** -ɪŋ **-ed** -ɪd
abstriction əb'strɪk.ʃᵊn, æb-
abstruse æb'struːs, əb- **-ly** -li **-ness** -nəs, -nɪs
absurd əb'zɜːd, -'sɜːd ⓤⓢ -'sɝːd, -'zɝːd **-est** -ɪst, -əst **-ly** -li **-ness** -nəs, -nɪs
absurd|ism əb'zɜː.d|ɪ.zᵊm, -'sɜː- ⓤⓢ -'sɝː-, -'zɝː- **-ist** -ɪst

Accent

Accent may refer to prominence given to a syllable (see STRESS), or to a particular way of pronouncing. This panel concentrates on the latter definition.

Examples for English

Speakers may share the same grammar and vocabulary, but pronounce what they say with different accents.
In Britain, for example, there are accents such as Scots, Cockney (in London), and Scouse (in Liverpool), and in the United States the New York accent differs considerably from that commonly heard in Texas. There are also different world standard English accents, such as British, American, Australian, Indian or Singaporean.

Major differences between British and US English include the vowel in words such as *glass*, the use of a flapped /t/ in words like *butter*, and the fact that US English is RHOTIC while British English is non-rhotic, that is, an *r* in the spelling is always pronounced in US English, but only where a vowel follows in British English, e.g.:

glass	/ɡlɑːs/	US /ɡlæs/
butter	/ˈbʌt.əʳ/	US /ˈbʌt̬.ɚ/
car	/kɑːʳ/	US /kɑːr/

More information on the accents chosen to represent British and American English is given on pp xx.

absurdit|y əbˈzɜː.də.t|i, -ˈsɜː-, -dɪ- US -ˈsɝː.də.t̬|i, -ˈzɝː- **-ies** -iz
ABTA ˈæb.tə
Abu ˈɑː.buː, ˈæb.uː
Abu Dhabi ˌæb.uːˈdɑː.bi, ˌɑː.buː-, -ˈdæb.i US ˌɑː.buːˈdɑː.bi
Abuja əˈbuː.dʒə
abulia əˈbuː.li.ə, eɪ-, -ˈbjuː-
abundance əˈbʌn.dən*t*s
abundant əˈbʌn.dənt **-ly** -li
Abu Nidal ˌæb.uː.niːˈdɑːl, ˌɑː.buː-, -ˈdæl US ˌɑː.buː-
Abury ˈeɪ.bᵊr.i US -ber-, -bɚ-
abus|e (*n.*) əˈbjuːs **-es** -ɪz
abus|e (*v.*) əˈbjuːz **-es** -ɪz **-ing** -ɪŋ **-ed** -d **-er/s** -əʳ/z US -ɚ/z
Abu Simbel ˌæb.uːˈsɪm.bᵊl, -bel US ˌɑː.buːˈ-
abusive əˈbjuː.sɪv, -zɪv **-ly** -li **-ness** -nəs, -nɪs
a|but əˈbʌt **-buts** -ˈbʌts **-butting** -ˈbʌt.ɪŋ US -ˈbʌt̬.ɪŋ **-butted** -ˈbʌt.ɪd US -ˈbʌt̬.ɪd **-buttal** -ˈbʌt.ᵊl US -ˈbʌt̬.ᵊl
abutilon əˈbjuː.tɪ.lən, -lɒn US -t̬ə.lɑːn, -lən **-s** -z
abutment əˈbʌt.mənt **-s** -s
aabutter əˈbʌt.əʳ US -ˈbʌt̬.ɚ **-s** -z
abuzz əˈbʌz
Abydos əˈbaɪ.dɒs, -dəs; ˈæb.ɪ.dɒs US əˈbaɪ.dɑːs; ˈæb.ɪ-
abysm əˈbɪz.ᵊm **-s** -z
abysmal əˈbɪz.mᵊl **-ly** -i
abyss əˈbɪs **-es** -ɪz
abyssal əˈbɪs.ᵊl
Abyssini|a ˌæb.ɪˈsɪn.i|.ə, -əˈ- **-an/s** -ən/z
a/c *(abbrev. for* **account***)* əˈkaʊnt
AC *(US abbrev. for* **air conditioning***),* **a/c** ˌeɪˈsiː
-ac -æk, -ək
Note: Suffix. Does not normally affect stress patterning, e.g. **mania**, /ˈmeɪ.ni.ə/, **maniac** /ˈmeɪ.ni.æk/.
acacia əˈkeɪ.ʃə, -ˈsi.ə US -ˈ-ʃə **-s** -z
academe (A) ˈæk.ə.diːm
academia ˌæk.əˈdiː.mi.ə
academic ˌæk.əˈdem.ɪk **-s** -s *stress shift, see compound:* ˌ**academic** ˈ**year**
academic|al ˌæk.əˈdem.ɪ.k|ᵊl **-als** -ᵊlz **-ally** -ᵊl.i, -li
academician əˌkæd.əˈmɪʃ.ᵊn, ˌæk.ə.dəˈ-, -dɪˈ- US ˌæk.ə-, əˌkæd- **-s** -z
academicism ˌæk.əˈdem.ɪ.sɪ.zᵊm, ˈ-ə-
academism əˈkæd.ə.mɪ.zᵊm
academ|y əˈkæd.ə.m|i **-ies** -iz Aˌcademy Aˈward
Acadi|a əˈkeɪ.di|.ə **-an/s** -ən/z
acajou ˈæk.ə.ʒuː **-s** -z
acanth|oid əˈkæn*t*.θ|ɔɪd **-ous** -əs
acanth|us əˈkæn*t*.θ|əs **-i** -aɪ **-uses** -ə.sɪz **-ine** -aɪn
a cap(p)ella ˌæ.kəˈpel.ə, -kæpˈel- US ˌɑː.kəˈpel-
Acapulco ˌæk.əˈpʊl.kəʊ US ˌæk.əˈpuːl.koʊ, ˌɑː.kəˈ-, -ˈpʊl-
acarid ˈæk.ᵊr.ɪd **-s** -z
acarolog|y ˌæk.əˈrɒl.ə.dʒ|i US -ˈrɑː.lə- **-ist/s** -ɪst/s
acarpel(l)ous ˌeɪˈkɑː.pᵊl.əs US -ˈkɑːr-
acarpous ˌeɪˈkɑː.pəs US -ˈkɑːr-
ACAS, Acas ˈeɪˌkæs
acatalectic ˌeɪ.kæt.əˈlek.tɪk, əˌkæt- US -kæt̬.əˈ- **-s** -s *stress shift:* ˌacatalectic ˈverse, aˌcatalectic ˈverse
acatalepsy ˌeɪˈkæt.ə.lep.si, əˈkæt- US -ˈkæt̬.ə-
acataleptic ˌeɪ.kæt.əˈlep.tɪk, əˌkæt- US -kæt̬.əˈ-
Accad ˈæk.æd
Accadi|a əˈkeɪ.di|.ə, ækˈeɪ- **-an/s** -ən/z
acced|e əkˈsiːd, æk- **-es** -z **-ing** -ɪŋ **-ed** -ɪd **-er/s** -əʳ/z US -ɚ/z
accelerando ækˌsel.əˈræn.dəʊ, ək-, əˌtʃel- US -ˈrɑːn.doʊ
accelerant əkˈsel.ə.rᵊnt, æk- US -ɚ.ənt **-s** -s
accele|rate əkˈsel.ə|.reɪt, æk- **-rates** -reɪts **-rating** -reɪ.tɪŋ US -reɪ.t̬ɪŋ **-rated** -reɪ.tɪd US -reɪ.t̬ɪd
acceleration əkˌsel.əˈreɪ.ʃᵊn, æk- **-s** -z
accelerative əkˈsel.ə.rə.tɪv, æk- US -ɚ.ə.t̬ɪv
accelerator əkˈsel.ə.reɪ.təʳ, æk- US -t̬ɚ **-s** -z
accelerometer əkˌsel.əˈrɒm.ɪ.təʳ, æk-, ˈ-ə- US -ˈrɑː.mə.t̬ɚ **-s** -z
accent (*n.*) ˈæk.sᵊnt US -sent **-s** -s
ac|cent (*v.*) əkˈsent, æk- US æk-, ək- **-cents** -ˈsents **-centing** -ˈsen.tɪŋ US -ˈsen.t̬ɪŋ **-cented** -ˈsen.tɪd US -ˈsen.t̬ɪd
accentual əkˈsen.tʃu.əl, æk-, -tju- **-ly** -i
accentu|ate əkˈsen.tʃu.eɪt, æk-, -tju- **-ates** -eɪts **-ating** -eɪ.tɪŋ US -eɪ.t̬ɪŋ **-ated** -eɪ.tɪd US -eɪ.t̬ɪd
accentuation əkˌsen.tʃuˈeɪ.ʃᵊn, æk-, -tjuˈ- **-s** -z
accept əkˈsept, æk- **-s** -s **-ing** -ɪŋ **-ed** -ɪd **-er/s** -əʳ/z US -ɚ/z **-or/s** -əʳ/z US -ɚ/z
acceptability əkˌsep.təˈbɪl.ə.ti, æk-, -ɪ.ti US -ə.t̬i
acceptab|le əkˈsep.tə.b|l̩, æk- **-ly** -li **-leness** -l̩.nəs, -nɪs
acceptanc|e əkˈsep.tən*t*s, æk- **-es** -ɪz
acceptant əkˈsep.tᵊnt, æk- **-s** -s
acceptation ˌæk.sepˈteɪ.ʃᵊn **-s** -z
access (A®) ˈæk.ses **-es** -ɪz **-ing** -ɪŋ **-ed** -t
accessar|y əkˈses.ᵊr|.i, æk- **-ies** -iz
accessibility əkˌses.əˈbɪl.ə.ti, æk-, -ɪˈ-, -ɪ.ti US -ə.t̬i
accessible əkˈses.ə.bl̩, æk-, ˈ-ɪ-
accession əkˈseʃ.ᵊn, æk- **-s** -z
accessit ækˈses.ɪt, ək- **-s** -s

accessoriz|e, -is|e əkˈses.ᵊr.aɪz (US) -ə.raɪz **-es** -ɪz **-ing** -ɪŋ **-ed** -d

accessor|y əkˈses.ᵊr|.i, æk- **-ies** -iz

acciaccatur|a əˌtʃæk.əˈtʊə.r|ə (US) ɑːˌtʃɑː.kəˈtʊr|.ə **-as** -əz **-e** -eɪ, -iː

accidence ˈæk.sɪ.dᵊnts, -sə-

accident ˈæk.sɪ.dᵊnt, -sə- **-s** -s **ˈaccident-ˌprone**

accidental ˌæk.sɪˈden.tᵊl, -səˈ- (US) -t̬ᵊl **-ly** -i

accidia ækˈsɪd.i.ə

accidie ˈæk.sɪ.di, -sə-

accipiter ækˈsɪp.ɪ.təʳ, ək-, -ə.təʳ (US) -ə.t̬ɚ **-s** -z

acclaim əˈkleɪm **-s** -z **-ing** -ɪŋ **-ed** -d

acclamation ˌæk.ləˈmeɪ.ʃᵊn **-s** -z

acclamatory əˈklæm.ə.tᵊr.i (US) -ə.tɔːr.i

acclimatation əˌklaɪ.məˈteɪ.ʃᵊn

acclima|te ˈæk.lɪ.meɪ|t, -lə-; əˈklaɪ.mə|t (US) ˈæk.lə.meɪ|t; əˈklaɪ.mə|t **-tes** -ts **-ting** -tɪŋ (US) -t̬ɪŋ **-ted** -tɪd (US) -t̬ɪd

acclimation ˌæk.lɪˈmeɪ.ʃᵊn

acclimatization, -isa- əˌklaɪ.mə.taɪˈzeɪ.ʃᵊn, -tɪˈ- (US) -t̬əˈ-

acclimatiz|e, -is|e əˈklaɪ.mə.taɪz, -mɪ- **-es** -ɪz **-ing** -ɪŋ **-ed** -d

acclivit|y əˈklɪv.ə.t|i, ækˈlɪv-, -ɪt|i (US) -t̬|i **-ies** -iz

accolade ˈæk.ə.leɪd, ˌ--ˈ- **-s** -z

accommo|date əˈkɒm.ə|.deɪt (US) -ˈkɑː.mə- **-dates** -deɪts **-dated** -de.tɪd (US) -deɪ.t̬ɪd **-dator/s** -deɪ.təʳ/z (US) -deɪ.t̬ɚ/z **-dative/ly** -deɪ.tɪv/li (US) -deɪ.t̬ɪv/li

accommodating əˈkɒm.ə.deɪ.tɪŋ (US) əˈkɑː.mə.deɪ.t̬ɪŋ **-ly** -li

accommodation əˌkɒm.əˈdeɪ.ʃᵊn (US) əˌkɑː.məˈ- **-s** -z

accompaniment əˈkʌm.pᵊn.ɪ.mənt **-s** -s

accompanist əˈkʌm.pə.nɪst **-s** -s

accompan|y əˈkʌm.pə.n|i **-ies** -iz **-ying** -i.ɪŋ **-ied** -id **-yist/s** -i.ɪsts **-ier/s** -i.əʳ/z (US) -i.ɚ/z

accomplic|e əˈkʌm.plɪs, -ˈkɒm- (US) -ˈkɑːm-, -ˈkʌm- **-es** -ɪz

accomplish əˈkʌm.plɪʃ, -ˈkɒm- (US) -ˈkɑːm-, -ˈkʌm- **-es** -ɪz **-ing** -ɪŋ **-ed** -t

accomplishment əˈkʌm.plɪʃ.mənt, -ˈkɒm- (US) -ˈkɑːm-, -ˈkʌm- **-s** -s

accord əˈkɔːd (US) -ˈkɔːrd **-ed** -ɪd **-ing** -ɪŋ **-s** -z

accordan|ce əˈkɔː.dᵊn|*t*s (US) -ˈkɔːr- **-t** -t

according əˈkɔː.dɪŋ (US) -ˈkɔːr- **-ly** -li

accordion əˈkɔː.di.ən (US) -ˈkɔːr- **-s** -z

accost əˈkɒst (US) -ˈkɑːst **-s** -s **-ing** -ɪŋ **-ed** -ɪd

accouchement əˈkuːʃ.mɑ̃ː*ŋ* (US) -mɑːnt, ˌæk.uːʃˈmɑ̃ː

accoucheur ˌæk.uːˈʃɜːʳ, əˈkuː.ʃɜːʳ (US) ˌæk.uːˈʃɝː **-s** -z

accoucheus|e ˌæk.uːˈʃɜːz, əˈkuː.ʃɜːz (US) ˌæk.uːˈʃɜːz **-es** -ɪz

ac|count ə|ˈkaʊnt **-counts** -ˈkaʊnts **-counting** -ˈkaʊn.tɪŋ (US) -ˈkaʊn.t̬ɪŋ **-counted** -ˈkaʊn.tɪd (US) -ˈkaʊn.t̬ɪd **aˈccount ˌbook**

accountability əˌkaʊn.təˈbɪl.ə.ti, -ɪ.ti (US) -t̬əˈbɪl.ə.t̬i

accountab|le əˈkaʊn.tə.b|l̩ (US) -t̬ə- **-ly** -li **-leness** -l̩.nəs, -nɪs

accountancy əˈkaʊn.tən*t*.si (US) -t̬ən*t*-

accountant əˈkaʊn.tənt **-s** -s

accout|er əˈkuː.t|əʳ (US) -t̬|ɚ **-ers** -əz (US) -ɚz **-ering** -ᵊr.ɪŋ **-ered** -əd (US) -ɚd **-erment/s** -ə.mənt/s (US) -ɚ-

accout|re əˈkuː.t|əʳ (US) əˈkuː.t̬|ɚ **-res** -əz **-ring** -ᵊr.ɪŋ **-red** -əd (US) -ɚd **-rement/s** -rə.mənt/s, -ə.mənt/s (US) -ɚ.mənt/s

Accra əˈkrɑː, ækˈrɑː

accred|it əˈkred|.ɪt **-its** -ɪts **-iting** -ɪ.tɪŋ (US) -ɪ.t̬ɪŋ **-ited** -ɪ.tɪd (US) -ɪ.t̬ɪd

accreditation əˌkred.ɪˈteɪ.ʃᵊn (US) -əˈ-

accre|te əˈkriː|t, ækˈriː|t **-tes** -ts **-ting** -tɪŋ (US) -t̬ɪŋ **-ted** -tɪd (US) -t̬ɪd

accretion əˈkriː.ʃᵊn, ækˈriː- **-s** -z

accretive əˈkriː.tɪv, ækˈriː- (US) əˈkriː.t̬ɪv

Accrington ˈæk.rɪŋ.tən

accrual əˈkruː.əl, -ˈkrʊəl (US) -ˈkruː.əl

accru|e əˈkruː **-es** -z **-ing** -ɪŋ **-ed** -d

accruement əˈkruː.mənt

accultur|ate əˈkʌl.tʃᵊr|.eɪt, ækˈʌl- (US) -tʃə.r|eɪt **-ates** -eɪts **-ating** -eɪ.tɪŋ (US) -eɪ.t̬ɪŋ **-ated** -eɪ.tɪd (US) -eɪ.t̬ɪd

acculturation əˌkʌl.tʃᵊrˈeɪ.ʃᵊn, ækˌʌl- (US) -tʃəˈreɪ-

accumben|t əˈkʌm.bən|t **-cy** -*t*.si

accumu|late əˈkjuː.mjə|.leɪt, -mjʊ- **-lates** -leɪts **-lating** -leɪ.tɪŋ (US) -leɪ.t̬ɪŋ **-lated** -leɪ.tɪd (US) -leɪ.t̬ɪd **-lator/s** -leɪ.təʳ/z (US) -leɪ.t̬ɚ/z

accumulation əˌkjuː.mjəˈleɪ.ʃᵊn, -mjʊˈ- **-s** -z

accumulative əˈkjuː.mjə.lə.tɪv, -mjʊ- (US) -t̬ɪv

accuracy ˈæk.jə.rə.si, -jʊ- (US) -jɚ.ə-, -jʊ.rə-

accurate ˈæk.jə.rət, -jʊ-, -rɪt (US) -jɚ.ət, -jʊ.rət, -rɪt **-ly** -li **-ness** -nəs, -nɪs

accursed əˈkɜː.sɪd, -ˈkɜːst (US) əˈkɝːst, -ˈkɝː.səd, əˈkɜːst **-ly** -li

accusal əˈkjuː.zᵊl **-s** -z

accusation ˌæk.jʊˈzeɪ.ʃᵊn, -jəˈ- **-s** -z

accusatival əˌkjuː.zəˈtaɪ.vᵊl

accusative əˈkjuː.zə.tɪv (US) -t̬ɪv **-s** -z

accusativity əˌkjuː.zəˈtɪv.ə.ti, -ɪ.ti (US) -ə.t̬i

accusatory əˈkjuː.zə.tᵊr.i, ˌæk.jʊˈzeɪ-, -jəˈ-, -tri (US) əˈkjuː.zə.tɔːr.i

accus|e əˈkjuːz **-es** -ɪz **-ing/ly** -ɪŋ/li **-ed** -d **-er/s** -əʳ/z (US) -ɚ/z

accustom əˈkʌs.təm **-s** -z **-ing** -ɪŋ **-ed/ness** -d/nəs, -nɪs

AC/DC ˌeɪ.siːˈdiː.siː

ac|e eɪs **-es** -ɪz

acedia əˈsiː.di.ə

Aceldama əˈkel.də.mə, -ˈsel-; ˌæk.elˈdɑː- (US) əˈsel.də-

-aceous -ˈeɪ.ʃəs, -ˈeɪ.ʃi.əs

Note: Suffix. Words containing **-aceous** always exhibit primary stress as shown above, e.g. **herbaceous** /hɜːˈbeɪ.ʃəs (US) hɚ-/.

acephalous əˈsef.ᵊl.əs, ˌeɪ-, -ˈkef- (US) eɪˈsef-, ə-

acequia əˈseɪ.ki.ə, -ˈsiː- **-s** -z

acer|bate ˈæs.ə.|beɪt (US) ˈ-ɚ- **-bates** -beɪts **-bating** -beɪ.tɪŋ (US) -beɪ.t̬ɪŋ **-bated** -beɪ.tɪd (US) -beɪ.t̬ɪd

acerbic əˈsɜː.bɪk, æsˈɜː- (US) əˈsɝː- **-ally** -ᵊl.i, -li

acerbity əˈsɜː.bə.ti, -bɪ- (US) əˈsɝː.bə.t̬i

Acestes əˈses.tiːz, -ˈkes-

acetabul|um ˌæs.ɪˈtæb.jə.l|əm, -jʊ- **-ums** -əmz **-a** -ə **-ar** -əʳ (US) -ɚ

acetaldehyde ˌæs.ɪˈtæl.dɪ.haɪd, -də-

acetaminophen əˌsiː.təˈmɪn.ə.fən (US) ˌæs.ɪ.t̬əˈ-; əˌsiː.t̬əˈ-, -ˌset̬.əˈ-

acetate ˈæs.ɪ.teɪt, ˈ-ə- **-s** -s

acetic əˈsiː.tɪk, æsˈiː-, -ˈet.ɪk (US) əˈsiː.t̬ɪk **aˌcetic ˈacid**

acetif|y əˈsiː.tɪ.f|aɪ, æsˈiː-, -ˈset.ɪ- (US) -ˈset̬.ə- **-ies** -aɪz **-ying** -aɪ.ɪŋ **-ied** -aɪd

acetin ˈæs.ə.tɪn, ˈ-ɪ- (US) -t̬ɪn

acetone ˈæs.ɪ.təʊn, ˈ-ə- (US) -toʊn

acetose ˈæs.ɪ.təʊs, ˈ-ə-, -təʊz (US) -toʊs

acetous ˈæs.ɪ.təs, ˈ-ə- (US) ˈæs.ɪ.t̬əs; əˈsiː-

acetum əˈsiː.təm (US) -t̬əm

acetyl ˈæs.ɪ.taɪl, ˈ-ə-, -tɪl; əˈsiː-, -taɪl (US) ˈæs.ə.t̬ᵊl, -t̬iːl; əˈsiː.t̬ᵊl

acetyl|ate əˈset.ɪ.l|eɪt, -ᵊl|.eɪt (US) -ˈset̬.ə.l|eɪt, -ˈsiː.t̬ə- **-ates** -eɪts **-ating** -eɪ.tɪŋ (US) -eɪ.t̬ɪŋ **-ated** -eɪ.tɪd (US) -eɪ.t̬ɪd

acetylation əˌset.ɪˈleɪ.ʃᵊn, -ᵊlˈeɪ- (US) -ˌset̬.əˈleɪ-

acetylcholine ˌæs.ɪ.taɪlˈkəʊ.liːn, ˌ-ə- (US) əˌsiː.t̬ᵊlˈkoʊ-, -ˌset̬.ᵊlˈ-; ˌæs.ə.t̬ᵊlˈ-

acetylene əˈset.ɪ.liːn, -ᵊl.iːn (US) -ˈset̬.ə.liːn

Achae|a əˈkiː|.ə **-an/s** -ən/z

Achaia əˈkaɪ.ə

Achates əˈkeɪ.tiːz, -ˈkɑː- (US) -t̬iːz

ach|e eɪk **-es** -s **-ing/ly** -ɪŋ/li **-ed** -t **-er/s** -əʳ/z (US) -ɚ/z

Achebe əˈtʃeɪ.bi

Achernar ˈeɪ.kə.nɑːʳ (US) -kɚ.nɑːr

Acheron ˈæk.ə.rɒn, -rᵊn (US) -rɑːn

Acheson ˈætʃ.ɪ.sᵊn, ˈ-ə-

Acheulean, Acheulian əˈ*t*ʃuː.li.ən

à cheval ˌæ.ʃəˈvæl

achiev|e ə'tʃiːv **-es** -z **-ing** -ɪŋ **-ed** -d **-able** -ə.bl̩ **-er/s** -əʳ/z (US) -ɚ/z
achievement ə'tʃiːv.mənt **-s** -s
Achil(l) 'æk.ɪl
Achilles ə'kɪl.iːz **A,chilles 'heel** (US) **A'chilles ,heel**
Achille Serre æʃ.ɪl'seəʳ, -iːl'- (US) -'ser
Achin ə'tʃiːn
Achish 'eɪ.kɪʃ
achondro|plasia ə,kɒn.drəʊ|'pleɪ.zi.ə, -ʒə (US) -,kɑːn.drə|'pleɪ.ʒi.ə, ,eɪ- **-plastic** -'plæs.tɪk
Achray ə'kreɪ, ə'xreɪ
achromatic ,æk.rəʊ'mæt.ɪk, ,eɪ.krəʊ- (US) ,æk.rə'mæt̬- **-ally** -ᵊl.i *stress shift:* ,achromatic 'lens
achromatism ə'krəʊ.mə.tɪ.zᵊm, ,eɪ- (US) -'kroʊ-
achromatiz|e, -is|e ə'krəʊ.mə.taɪz, ,eɪ- (US) -'kroʊ- **-es** -ɪz **-ing** -ɪŋ **-ed** -d
achromatous ə'krəʊ.mə.təs, ,eɪ- (US) -'kroʊ.mə.t̬əs
achtung 'ɑːx.tʊŋ, 'æx- (US) 'ɑːx-, 'ɑːk-
achy 'eɪ.ki
acicul|a ə'sɪk.jʊ.l|ə, -jə- **-ae** -i **-ar** -ə
acid 'æs.ɪd **-s** -z **-ly** -li **-ness** -nəs, -nɪs **'acid ,drop; ,acid 'rain; ,acid 'test, 'acid ,test**
acidhead 'æs.ɪd.hed **-s** -z
acidic ə'sɪd.ɪk
acidif|y ə'sɪd.ɪ.f|aɪ, æs'ɪd- **-ies** -aɪz **-ying** -aɪ.ɪŋ **-ied** -aɪd
acidity ə'sɪd.ə.ti, æs'ɪd-, -ɪ.ti (US) -ə.t̬i
acidiz|e, -is|e 'æs.ɪ.daɪz **-es** -ɪz **-ing** -ɪŋ **-ed** -d
acidophilus ,æs.ɪ'dɒf.ɪ.ləs, -ᵊl.əs (US) -'dɑː.fᵊl-
acidosis ,æs.ɪ'dəʊ.sɪs (US) -'doʊ-
acidu|late ə'sɪd.jʊ|.leɪt, æs'ɪd-, -jə-, -'sɪdʒ.ʊ-, '-ə- **-lates** -leɪts **-lating** -leɪ.tɪŋ (US) -leɪ.t̬ɪŋ **-lated** -leɪ.tɪd (US) -leɪ.t̬ɪd
acidulous ə'sɪd.jʊ.ləs, æs'ɪd-, -jə-, -'sɪdʒ.ʊ-, '-ə-
acin|ose 'æs.ɪ.n|əʊs, -n|əʊz (US) -n|oʊs, -n|oʊz **-ous** -əs
acin|us 'æs.ɪ.n|əs **-i** -aɪ
Acis 'eɪ.sɪs
ack-ack ,æk'æk *stress shift:* ,ack-ack 'gun
ackee 'æk.i **-s** -z
Ackerley 'æk.ᵊl.i (US) -ɚ.li
Ackerman(n) 'æk.ə.mən, -mæn (US) '-ɚ-
Ackland 'æk.lənd
acknowledg|e ək'nɒl.ɪdʒ, æk- (US) -'nɑː.lɪdʒ **-es** -ɪz **-ing** -ɪŋ **-ed** -d **-eable** -ə.bl̩
acknowledg(e)ment ək'nɒl.ɪdʒ.mənt, æk- (US) -'nɑː.lɪdʒ- **-s** -s
Ackroyd 'æk.rɔɪd
Ackworth Moor Top ,æk.wəθ,mɔː'tɒp (US) -wɚθ,mʊr'tɑːp
Acland 'æk.lənd
ACLU ,eɪ.siː.el'juː
acme 'æk.mi **-s** -z
acne 'æk.ni
acnode 'æk.nəʊd (US) -noʊd **-s** -z
Acol *road in London, system of bridge playing:* 'æk.ᵊl *in Kent:* 'eɪ.kɒl (US) -kɑːl
acolyte 'æk.ᵊl.aɪt (US) -ə.laɪt **-s** -s
Acomb 'eɪ.kəm
Aconcagua ,æk.ɒn'kæg.wə, -ɒŋ'- (US) ,ɑː.kᵊn'-, -kᵊŋ'-, -kɑː.gwə
aconite 'æk.ə.naɪt **-s** -s
acorn 'eɪ.kɔːn (US) -kɔrn **-s** -z **'acorn ,squash**
acotyledon ə,kɒt.ɪ'liː.dᵊn, ,eɪ-, -ᵊl'iː- (US) -,kɑː.t̬ə'liː- **-s** -z
acouchi ə'kuː.ʃi (US) ɑː'kuː.ʃi, ə-
acoustic ə'kuː.stɪk **-s** -s **-ally** -ᵊl.i (US) -li
acoustician ,æ.kuː'stɪʃ.ᵊn **-s** -z
acoustooptic ə,kuː.stəʊ'ɒp.tɪk (US) -stoʊ'ɑːp- **-s** -s **-al** -ᵊl
ac|quaint ə|'kweɪnt **-quaints** -'kweɪnts **-quainting** -'kweɪn.tɪŋ (US) -'kweɪn.t̬ɪŋ **-quainted** -'kweɪn.tɪd (US) -'kweɪn.t̬ɪd
acquaintanc|e ə'kweɪn.tᵊnts **-es** -ɪz
acquaintanceship ə'kweɪn.tᵊnts.ʃɪp, -tᵊnt.ʃɪp **-s** -s
acquest ə'kwest **-s** -s
acquiesc|e ,æk.wi'es **-es** -ɪz **-ing** -ɪŋ **-ed** -t **-ence** -ᵊnts **-ent/ly** -ᵊnt/li
acquir|e ə'kwaɪəʳ (US) -'kwaɪɚ **-es** -z **-ing** -ɪŋ **-ed** -d **-ement/s** -mənt/s **-able** -ə.bl̩
acquisition ,æk.wɪ'zɪʃ.ᵊn, -wə-, -z
acquisitive ə'kwɪz.ɪ.tɪv, '-ə- (US) -ə.t̬ɪv **-ly** -li **-ness** -nəs, -nɪs
acquit ə'kwɪt **-s** -s **-ting** -ɪŋ (US) ə'kwɪt̬.ɪŋ **-ted** -ɪd (US) ə'kwɪt̬.ɪd
acquittal ə'kwɪt.ᵊl (US) -'kwɪt̬- **-s** -z
acquittance ə'kwɪt.ᵊnts
acre (A) 'eɪ.kəʳ (US) -kɚ **-s** -z
acreag|e 'eɪ.kᵊr.ɪdʒ, '-krɪdʒ **-es** -ɪz
acrid 'æk.rɪd **-ly** -li **-ness** -nəs, -nɪs
acridine 'æk.rɪ.diːn, -daɪn
acridity ə'krɪd.ə.ti, æk'rɪd-, -ɪ.ti (US) -ə.t̬i
Acrilan® 'æk.rɪ.læn, -rə-
acrimonious ,æk.rɪ'məʊ.ni.əs, -rə'- (US) -'moʊ- **-ly** -li **-ness** -nəs, -nɪs
acrimon|y 'æk.rɪ.mə.n|i, -rə- (US) -moʊ- **-ies** -iz
acritical ,eɪ'krɪt.ɪ.kᵊl, '-ə- (US) -'krɪt̬.ə-
acritude 'æk.rɪ.tjuːd, -rə-, -tʃuːd (US) -tuːd, -tjuːd
acro- æk.rəʊ-; ə'krɒ- (US) æk.rə-, -roʊ-; ə'krɑː-
Note: Prefix. Either takes primary or secondary stress on the first syllable, e.g. **acrosome** /'æk.rəʊ.səʊm (US) -rə.soʊm/, **acrosomal** /,æk.rəʊ'səʊ.mᵊl (US) -rə'soʊ-/, or primary stress only on the second syllable, e.g. **acropolis** /ə'krɒp.ə.lɪs (US) -'krɑː.pə-/.
acrobat 'æk.rə.bæt **-s** -s
acrobatic ,æk.rə'bæt.ɪk (US) -'bæt̬- **-s** -s **-ally** -ᵊl.i, -li *stress shift:* ,acrobatic 'leap
acrobatism 'æk.rə.bæt.ɪ.zᵊm, ,æk.rə'bæt- (US) 'æk.rə.bæt̬-, ,æk.rə'bæt̬-
acrogen 'æk.rəʊ.dʒən, -dʒen (US) -roʊ-, -rə- **-s** -z
acrolect 'æk.rəʊ.lekt (US) -roʊ-, -rə- **-s** -s **-al** -ᵊl
acrolith 'æk.rəʊ.lɪθ (US) -roʊ-, -rə- **-s** -s
acromegalic ,æk.rəʊ.mɪ'gæl.ɪk, -mə'- (US) -roʊ-
acromegaly ,æk.rəʊ'meg.ᵊl.i (US) -roʊ'-
acromion ə'krəʊ.mi.ən (US) -'kroʊ- **-s** -z
acronym 'æk.rəʊ.nɪm (US) -rə- **-s** -z
acropetal ə'krɒp.ɪ.tᵊl (US) -'krɑː.pə.t̬ᵊl **-ly** -i
acrophob|ia ,æk.rəʊ'fəʊ.b|i.ə (US) -rə'foʊ- **-ic** -ɪk
acropolis (A) ə'krɒp.ə.lɪs (US) -'krɑː.pə- **-es** -ɪz
acrosomal ,æk.rəʊ'səʊ.mᵊl (US) -rə'soʊ-
acrosome 'æk.rəʊ.səʊm (US) -rə.soʊm
across ə'krɒs (US) -'krɑːs
across-the-board ə,krɒs.ðə'bɔːd (US) -,krɑːs.ðə'bɔːrd
acrostic ə'krɒs.tɪk (US) -'krɑː.stɪk **-s** -s
Acrux 'eɪ.krʌks
acrylic ə'krɪl.ɪk, æk'rɪl- **-s** -s
act ækt **-s** -s **-ing** -ɪŋ **-ed** -ɪd **get ,in on the 'act; ,get one's 'act together**
ACT ,eɪ.siː'tiː
acta 'æk.tə
Actaeon 'æk.ti.ən (US) æk'tiː-
ACTH ,eɪ.siː.tiː'eɪtʃ, ækθ
actinic æk'tɪn.ɪk **-ly** -li
actinide 'æk.tɪn.aɪd **-s** -z
actinism 'æk.tɪn.ɪ.zᵊm
actinium æk'tɪn.i.əm
action 'æk.ʃᵊn **-s** -z **-ing** -ɪŋ **-ed** -d **'action ,man; 'action ,stations**
actionable 'æk.ʃᵊn.ə.bl̩
Actium 'æk.ti.əm
activable 'æk.tɪv.ə.bl̩
acti|vate 'æk.tɪ|.veɪt **-vates** -veɪts **-vating** -veɪ.tɪŋ (US) -veɪ.t̬ɪŋ **-vated** -veɪ.tɪd (US) -veɪ.t̬ɪd **-vator/s** -veɪ.təʳ/z (US) -veɪ.t̬ɚ/z
activation ,æk.tɪ'veɪ.ʃᵊn
active 'æk.tɪv **-ly** -li **-ness** -nəs, -nɪs
activ|ism 'æk.tɪ.v|ɪ.zᵊm **-ist/s** -ɪst/s
activit|y æk'tɪv.ə.t|i, -ɪ.t|i (US) -ə.t̬|i **-ies** -iz
activiz|e 'æk.tɪ.vaɪz **-es** -ɪz **-ing** -ɪŋ **-ed** -d
Acton 'æk.tən

Acronyms

Acronyms are words or phrases written in an abbreviated form, usually with their initial letters, and pronounced as if they were words, usually with the most obvious pronunciation. However, it is best to treat them on a word-by-word basis, since there are exceptions.

Examples

Many organisations, particularly those to do with government, charities and trade unions, use acronyms. Phrases can also be reduced to acronym form. Acronyms are usually written using capital letters, although there are exceptions. Where there is a letter *E* at the end of an acronym, it is usually pronounced /iː/, e.g.:

- NATFHE (*National Association of Teachers in Further and Higher Education*) /ˈnæt.fiː/
- NATO (*North Atlantic Treaty Organisation*) /ˈneɪ.təʊ/ (US) /-t̬oʊ/
- snafu (*situation normal, all fouled up*) /snæfˈuː/
- Tardis (*time and relative dimensions in space*) /ˈtɑː.dɪs/ (US) /ˈtɑːr-/

Some words or phrases are abbreviated to initial letters but do not become acronyms. See **ABBREVIATIONS**.

actor ˈæk.təʳ (US) -tɚ **-s** -z
actress ˈæk.trəs, -trɪs **-es** -ɪz
Acts ækts
actual ˈæk.tʃu.əl, -tju-, -tʃᵊl, -tʃʊl (US) -tʃu.əl, -tʃᵊl, -tʃʊl **-ly** -i
actualit|y ˌæk.tʃuˈæl.ə.t|i, -tju-, -ɪ.t|i (US) -tʃuˈæl.ə.t̬|i **-ies** -iz
actualiz|e, -is|e ˈæk.tʃu.ə.laɪz, -tju-, -ʃu- (US) -tʃu- **-es** -ɪz **-ing** -ɪŋ **-ed** -d
actuarial ˌæk.tʃuˈeə.ri.əl, -tju- (US) -tʃuˈer.i-
actuar|y ˈæk.tʃu.ə.r|i, -tju.er|i (US) -tʃu- **-ies** -iz
actu|ate ˈæk.tʃu|.eɪt, -tju- (US) -tʃu- **-ates** -eɪts **-ating** -eɪ.tɪŋ (US) -eɪ.t̬ɪŋ **-ated** -eɪ.tɪd (US) -eɪ.t̬ɪd
actuation ˌæk.tʃuˈeɪ.ʃᵊn, -tjuˈ- (US) -tʃuˈ- **-s** -z
Act-Up ˌæktˈʌp
acuity əˈkjuː.ə.ti, -ɪt.i (US) -ə.t̬i
acumen ˈæk.jʊ.mən, -jə-, -men (US) əˈkjuː.mən, ˈæk.jə-
acupressure ˈæk.jʊ.preʃ.əʳ, -jə- (US) -ɚ
acupunctur|e ˈæk.jʊ.pʌŋk.tʃəʳ, -jə- (US) -tʃɚ **-ist/s** -ɪst/s
a|cute ə|ˈkjuːt **-cuter** -ˈkjuː.təʳ (US) -ˈkjuː.t̬ɚ **-cutest** -ˈkjuː.tɪst, -təst (US) -ˈkjuː.t̬ɪst, -t̬əst **-cutely** -ˈkjuːt.li **-cuteness** -ˈkjuːt.nəs, -nɪs **aˌcute ˈangle**
acyl ˈæs.ɪl **-s** -z
ad- æd-, əd-
Note: Prefix. Examples include **adjective** /ˈædʒ.ɪk.tɪv/, in which it is stressed, and **admonish** /ədˈmɒn.ɪʃ (US) -ˈmɑː.nɪʃ/, where it is unstressed.
ad æd **-s** -z
AD *(abbrev. for* **Anno Domini***)* ˌeɪˈdiː, ˌæn.əʊˈdɒm.ɪ.naɪ (US) ˌeɪˈdiː, ˌæn.oʊˈdɑː.mə.niː, -ˈdoʊ-, -naɪ
ADA ˌeɪ.diːˈeɪ
Ada, **ADA** *woman's name, trademark, US town:* ˈeɪ.də
adactylous ˌeɪˈdæk.tɪ.ləs
adag|e ˈæd.ɪdʒ **-es** -ɪz
adagio əˈdɑː.dʒi.əʊ, ˈ-ʒi- (US) -ˈdɑː.dʒoʊ, -dʒi.oʊ **-s** -z
Adair əˈdeəʳ (US) -ˈder
Adalbert ˈæd.ᵊl.bɜːt (US) -bɝːt
Adam ˈæd.əm **ˌAdam's ˈapple** (US) **ˈAdam's ˌapple**
adamant ˈæd.ə.mənt **-ly** -li
adamantine ˌæd.əˈmæn.taɪn (US) -tiːn, -taɪn, -tᵊn
adamite (A) ˈæd.ə.maɪt **-s** -s
Adams ˈæd.əmz
adamsite ˈæd.əm.zaɪt
Adamson ˈæd.əm.sᵊn
Adamthwaite ˈæd.əm.θweɪt
Adana ˈɑː.də.nə; əˈdɑː-
Adapazari ˌɑː.dəˈpɑː.zᵊr.i (US) -ˌpɑː.zəˈriː
adapt əˈdæpt **-s** -s **-ing** -ɪŋ **-ed** -ɪd **-ive** -ɪv
adaptability əˌdæp.təˈbɪl.ə.ti, -ɪt.i (US) -ə.t̬i
adaptable əˈdæp.tə.bl̩ **-ness** -nəs, -nɪs
adaptation ˌæd.æpˈteɪ.ʃᵊn, -əpˈ- **-s** -z
adapter əˈdæp.təʳ (US) -tɚ **-s** -z
adaption əˈdæp.ʃən, ædˈæp- **-s** -z
adaptive əˈdæp.tɪv, ædˈæp- **-ly** -li
adaptor əˈdæp.təʳ (US) -tɚ **-s** -z
Adare əˈdeəʳ (US) -ˈder
Adar Sheni ɑːˌdɑːˈʃeɪ.ni (US) -ˌdɑːrˈ-
ADC ˌeɪ.diːˈsiː
Adcock ˈæd.kɒk (US) -kɑːk
add æd **-s** -z **-ing** -ɪŋ **-ed** -ɪd
Addams ˈæd.əmz
addax ˈæd.æks **-es** -ɪz
addend əˈdend, ædˈend (US) ˈæd.end; əˈdend **-s** -z
addend|um əˈden.d|əm, ædˈen- **-a** -ə
adder ˈæd.əʳ (US) -ɚ **-s** -z **ˈadder's ˌtongue**
adderwort ˈæd.ə.wɜːt (US) -ɚ.wɝːt, -wɔːrt
addict (*n.*) ˈæd.ɪkt **-s** -s
addict (*v.*) əˈdɪkt **-s** -s **-ing** -ɪŋ **-ed/ness** -ɪd/nəs, -nɪs
addiction əˈdɪk.ʃᵊn **-s** -z
addictive əˈdɪk.tɪv **-ly** -li **-ness** -nəs, -nɪs
Addington ˈæd.ɪŋ.tən
Addis ˈæd.ɪs
Addis Ababa ˌæd.ɪsˈæb.ə.bə, -ˈɑːb-
Addiscombe ˈæd.ɪ.skəm
Addison ˈæd.ɪ.sən
addition əˈdɪʃ.ᵊn **-s** -z
additional əˈdɪʃ.ᵊn.ᵊl **-ly** -i
additive ˈæd.ə.tɪv, ˈ-ɪ- (US) -ə.t̬ɪv **-s** -z
addl|e ˈæd.l̩ **-es** -z **-ing** -ɪŋ, ˈæd.lɪŋ **-ed** -d
addleheaded ˌæd.l̩ˈhed.ɪd (US) ˈæd.l̩ˌhed- *stress shift, British only:* ˌaddleheaded ˈperson
Addlestone ˈæd.l̩.stən
add-on ˈæd.ɒn (US) -ɑːn **-s** -z
address (*n.*) əˈdres (US) ˈæd.res, əˈdres **-es** -ɪz **aˈddress ˌbook** (US) **ˈaddress ˌbook**
address (*v.*) əˈdres **-es** -ɪz **-ing** -ɪŋ **-ed** -t
addressable əˈdres.ə.bl̩
addressee ˌæd.resˈiː **-s** -z
Addressograph® əˈdres.əʊ.grɑːf, -græf (US) -ə.græf **-s** -s
adduc|e əˈdjuːs, ædˈjuːs (US) əˈduːs, -ˈdjuːs **-es** -ɪz **-ing** -ɪŋ **-ed** -t **-er/s** -əʳ/z (US) -ɚ/z **-ible** -ə.bl̩, -ɪ.bl̩
adducent əˈdjuː.sᵊnt (US) -ˈduː-, -ˈdjuː-
adduct əˈdʌkt **-s** -s **-ing** -ɪŋ **-ed** -ɪd **-ive** -ɪv
adduction əˈdʌk.ʃᵊn
adductor əˈdʌk.təʳ (US) -tɚ **-s** -z
Ade eɪd
-ade -eɪd, -ɑːd
Note: Suffix. Generally carries primary stress, e.g. **lemonade**

/ˌlem.əˈneɪd/, but see individual entries. For instance, **escapade** is also /ˈes.kə.peɪd/. In words derived from French it is often pronounced /-ɑːd/, e.g. **roulade** is /ruːˈlɑːd/.

Adeane əˈdiːn
Adel ˈæd.ᵊl
Adela *English name:* ˈæd.ɪ.lə, ˈ-ə- *foreign name:* əˈdeɪ.lə
Adelaide ˈæd.ᵊl.eɪd, -ɪ.leɪd (US) -ə.leɪd
Adele əˈdel
Adelina ˌæd.ɪˈliː.nə, -ᵊlˈiː- (US) -əˈliː-
Adeline ˈæd.ɪ.liːn, -ᵊl.iːn, -aɪn (US) -ə.laɪn, -liːn
Adelphi əˈdel.fi
ademption əˈdemp.ʃᵊn **-s** -z
Aden *in the Yemen:* ˈeɪ.dᵊn (US) ˈɑː-, ˈeɪ- *in Grampian region:* ˈæd.ᵊn
Adenauer ˈæd.ᵊn.aʊ.əʳ, ˈɑː.dᵊn- (US) -ɚ
adenoid ˈæd.ᵊ.nɔɪd, -ɪn.ɔɪd (US) -ᵊn.ɔɪd; ˈæd.nɔɪd **-s** -z
adenoidal ˌæd.ᵊˈnɔɪ.dᵊl, -ɪnˈɔɪ- (US) -ᵊnˈɔɪ-; ædˈnɔɪ-
adenoidectom|y ˌæd.ᵊ.nɔɪˈdek.tə.m|i, -ɪn.ɔɪˈ- (US) -ᵊn.ɔɪˈ-; ˌæd.nɔɪˈ- **-ies** -iz
adenoma ˌæd.ɪˈnəʊ.mə, -əˈ- (US) -ˈnoʊ- **-s** -z **-tous** -təs (US) -t̬əs
adenosine ædˈen.əʊ.siːn, əˈden-; ˌæd.ɪˈnəʊ- (US) əˈden.ə.siːn, -sᵊn
adept (*n.*) ˈæd.ept, əˈdept, ædˈept **-s** -s
adept (*adj.*) əˈdept, ædˈept; ˈæd.ept (US) əˈdept **-ly** -li
adequacy ˈæd.ɪ.kwə.si, ˈ-ə-
adequate ˈæd.ɪ.kwət, ˈ-ə-, -kwɪt **-ly** -li **-ness** -nəs, -nɪs
adessive əˈdes.ɪv, ædˈes-
à deux æˈdɜː
adher|e ədˈhɪəʳ, æd-; əˈdɪəʳ (US) ədˈhɪr, æd- **-es** -z **-ing** -ɪŋ **-ed** -d **-er/s** -əʳ/z (US) -ɚ/z
adheren|ce ədˈhɪə.rᵊn|*t*s, æd-, -ˈher.ᵊn|*t*s; əˈdɪə.rᵊn|*t*s (US) ədˈhɪr.ᵊn|*t*s, æd- **-t/s** -t/s
adhesion ədˈhiː.ʒən, æd-; **-s** -z
adhesive ədˈhiː.sɪv, æd-, -zɪv; -zɪv **-ly** -li **-ness** -nɪs, -nəs
ad hoc ˌædˈhɒk, -ˈhəʊk (US) -ˈhɑːk, -ˈhoʊk
ad hominem ˌædˈhɒm.ɪ.nəm, ˈ-ə-, -nem (US) -ˈhɑː.mə.nəm, -nem
adiabatic ˌeɪ.daɪəˈbæt.ɪk, ˌæd.aɪə- (US) ˌæd.i.əˈbæt̬-; ˌeɪ.daɪəˈ- **-ally** -ᵊl.i, -li
Adidas® ˈæd.ɪ.dæs; əˈdiː.dəs (US) əˈdiː.dəs
Adie ˈeɪ.di
adieu əˈdjuː *as if French:* ædˈjɜː (US) əˈduː, -ˈdjuː
adieus, adieux əˈdjuː, -ˈdjuːz *as if French:* ædˈjɜː (US) əˈduːz, -ˈdjuːz
Adige ˈæd.ɪ.dʒeɪ (US) ˈɑː.di.dʒeɪ, -ə
ad infinitum ˌæd.ɪn.fɪˈnaɪ.təm (US) ˌæd.ɪn.fɪˈnaɪ.t̬əm, ˌɑːd-
adios ˈæd.i.ɒs, --ˈ- (US) ˌɑː.diˈoʊs, ˌæd.iˈ-
adipocere ˌæd.ɪ.pəʊˈsɪəʳ (US) ˈæd.ə.poʊ.sɪr, -pə-
adipose ˈæd.ɪ.pəʊs, -pəʊz (US) -ə.poʊs
adiposity ˌæd.ɪˈpɒs.ə.ti, -ɪ.ti (US) -əˈpɑː.sə.t̬i
Adirondack ˌæd.ɪˈrɒn.dæk, -əˈrɒn- (US) -rɑːn- **-s** -s
adit ˈæd.ɪt **-s** -s
adjacency əˈdʒeɪ.sᵊn*t*.si
adjacent əˈdʒeɪ.sᵊnt **-ly** -li
adjectival ˌædʒ.ɪkˈtaɪ.vᵊl, -ekˈ-, -əkˈ- **-ly** -i
adjective ˈædʒ.ɪk.tɪv, -ek-, -ək- **-s** -z
adjoin əˈdʒɔɪn **-s** -z **-ing** -ɪŋ **-ed** -d
adjourn əˈdʒɜːn (US) -ˈdʒɝːn **-s** -z **-ing** -ɪŋ **-ed** -d **-ment/s** -mənt/s
adjudg|e əˈdʒʌdʒ, ædʒˈʌdʒ (US) əˈdʒʌdʒ **-es** -ɪz **-ing** -ɪŋ **-ed** -d **-ment/s** -mənt/s
adjudi|cate əˈdʒuː.dɪ|.keɪt, -də- **-cates** -keɪts **-cating** -keɪ.tɪŋ (US) -keɪ.t̬ɪŋ **-cated** -keɪ.tɪd (US) -keɪ.t̬ɪd
adjudication əˌdʒuː.dɪˈkeɪ.ʃᵊn, -dəˈ- **-s** -z
adjudicator əˈdʒuː.dɪ.keɪ.təʳ, -də- (US) -t̬ɚ **-s** -z
adjunct ˈædʒ.ʌŋ*k*t **-s** -s **-ly** -li; əˈdʒʌŋ*k*t.li
adjunction əˈdʒʌŋ*k*.ʃᵊn, ædʒˈʌŋ*k*-
adjunctival ˌædʒ.ʌŋ*k*ˈtaɪ.vᵊl
adjuration ˌædʒ.əˈreɪ.ʃᵊn, -ʊəˈ-, -ɔːˈ- (US) -əˈ- **-s** -z
adjuratory əˈdʒʊə.rə.tᵊr.i, -ˈdʒɔː- (US) -ˈdʒʊr.ə.tɔːr-
adjur|e əˈdʒʊəʳ, -ɔːʳ (US) -dʒʊr **-es** -z **-ing** -ɪŋ **-ed** -d
adjust əˈdʒʌst **-s** -s **-ing** -ɪŋ **-ed** -ɪd **-able** -ə.bl̩ **-er/s** -əʳ/z (US) -ɚ/z
adjustment əˈdʒʌs*t*.mənt **-s** -s
adjutage ˈædʒ.ʊ.tɪdʒ; əˈdʒuː-
adjutan|cy ˈædʒ.ʊ.tᵊn|*t*.si, ˈ-ə- **-t/s** -t/s
Adkins ˈæd.kɪnz
Adkinson ˈæd.kɪn.sən
Adlai ˈæd.leɪ
Adler ˈæd.ləʳ, ˈɑːd.ləʳ (US) -lɚ
ad-lib ˌædˈlɪb **-s** -z **-bing** -ɪŋ **-bed** -d
Adlington ˈæd.lɪŋ.tən
ad|man ˈæd.mæn, -mən **-men** -men, -mən
admass ˈæd.mæs
admeasur|e ædˈmeʒ.əʳ, əd- (US) -ɚ, -ˈmeɪ.ʒɚ **-es** -z **-ing** -ɪŋ **-ed** -d **-ement/s** -mənt/s
Admetus ædˈmiː.təs (US) -t̬əs
admin ˈæd.mɪn
administer ədˈmɪn.ɪ.stəʳ, ˈ-ə- (US) -ɚ, æd- **-s** -z **-ing** -ɪŋ **-ed** -d
administr|able ədˈmɪn.ɪ.str|ə.bl̩, ˈ-ə- (US) əd-, æd- **-ant/s** -ᵊnt/s
admini|strate ədˈmɪn.ɪ|.streɪt, ˈ-ə- (US) əd-, æd- **-strates** -streɪts **-strating** -streɪ.tɪŋ (US) -streɪ.t̬ɪŋ **-strated** -streɪ.tɪd (US) -streɪ.t̬ɪd
administration ədˌmɪn.ɪˈstreɪ.ʃᵊn, -əˈ- (US) əd-, æd- **-s** -z
administrative ədˈmɪn.ɪ.strə.tɪv, ˈ-ə-, -streɪ- (US) əd-, æd- **-ly** -li
administrator ədˈmɪn.ɪ.streɪ.təʳ, ˈ-ə- (US) -t̬ɚ, æd- **-s** -z **-ship/s** -ʃɪp/s
administra|trix ədˈmɪn.ɪ.streɪ|.trɪks, ˈ-ə- (US) əd-, æd- **-trixes** -trɪk.sɪz **-trices** -trɪ.siːz
admirab|le ˈæd.mᵊr.ə.bl̩ **-ly** -li **-leness** -l̩.nəs, -nɪs
admiral ˈæd.mᵊr.əl, -mɪ.rəl **-s** -z
admiralt|y (A) ˈæd.mᵊr.əl.t|i, -mɪ.rəl- (US) -t̬|i **-ies** -iz
admiration ˌæd.məˈreɪ.ʃᵊn, -mɪˈ-
admir|e ədˈmaɪəʳ (US) -ˈmaɪɚ, æd- **-es** -z **-ing/ly** -ɪŋ/li **-ed** -d **-er/s** -əʳ/z (US) -ɚ/z
admissibility ədˌmɪs.əˈbɪl.ə.ti, æd-, -ɪˈ-, -ɪ.ti (US) -ə.t̬i
admissibl|e ədˈmɪs.ə.bl̩, æd-, -ɪ.bl̩ **-y** -i
admission ədˈmɪʃ.ᵊn, æd- **-s** -z
ad|mit əd|ˈmɪt **-mits** -ˈmɪts **-mitting** -ˈmɪt.ɪŋ (US) -ˈmɪt̬.ɪŋ **-mitted/ly** -ˈmɪt.ɪd/li (US) -ˈmɪt̬.ɪd/li
admittanc|e ədˈmɪt.ᵊn*t*s **-es** -ɪz
admix ædˈmɪks, əd- **-es** -ɪz **-ing** -ɪŋ **-ed** -t
admixture ədˈmɪks.tʃəʳ, æd- **-s** -z
admonish ədˈmɒn.ɪʃ, æd- (US) -ˈmɑː.nɪʃ **-es** -ɪz **-ing/ly** -ɪŋ **-ed** -t **-ment/s** -mənt/s
admonition ˌæd.məˈnɪʃ.ᵊn **-s** -z
admonitory ədˈmɒn.ɪ.tᵊr.i, æd- (US) -ˈmɑː.nə.tɔːr-
Adnams ˈæd.nəmz
ad nauseam ˌædˈnɔː.zi.æm, -si-, -əm (US) -ˈnɑː-, -ˈnɔː-
adnominal ˌædˈnɒm.ɪn.ᵊl (US) -ˈnɑːm- **-s** -z
ado əˈduː
adobe əˈdəʊ.bi, ædˈəʊ- (US) -ˈdoʊ- **-s** -z
adolescence ˌæd.ᵊlˈes.ᵊn*t*s, -əʊˈles- (US) -əˈles-
adolescent ˌæd.ᵊlˈes.ᵊnt, -əʊˈles- (US) -əˈles- **-s** -s
Adolf ˈæd.ɒlf (US) ˈeɪ.dɑːlf, ˈæd.ɑːlf
Adolphus əˈdɒl.fəs (US) -ˈdɑːl-
Adonai ˈæd.əʊ.naɪ (US) ˌɑː.dəˈnaɪ, -doʊˈ-, -ˈnɔɪ
Adonais ˌæd.əʊˈneɪ.ɪs (US) -əˈ-
Adonijah ˌæd.əʊˈnaɪ.dʒə (US) -əˈ-
Adonis əˈdəʊ.nɪs, -ˈdɒn.ɪs (US) -ˈdɑː.nɪs, -ˈdoʊ-
adopt əˈdɒpt (US) -ˈdɑːpt **-s** -s **-ing** -ɪŋ **-ed** -ɪd **-ive** -ɪv **-er/s**
adoption əˈdɒp.ʃᵊn (US) -ˈdɑːp- **-s** -z
adoptionism əˈdɒp.ʃᵊn.ɪ.zᵊm (US) -ˈdɑːp-
adorab|le əˈdɔː.rə.bl̩ (US) -ˈdɔːr.ə- **-ly** -li **-leness** -l̩.nəs, -nɪs

adoration ˌæd.əˈreɪ.ʃən, -ɔːˈ- ⓤⓢ -əˈreɪ- **-s** -z
ador|e əˈdɔːʳ ⓤⓢ -ˈdɔːr **-es** -z **-ing/ly** -ɪŋ/li **-ed** -d **-er/s** -əʳ/z ⓤⓢ -ɚ/z
adorn əˈdɔːn ⓤⓢ -ˈdɔːrn **-s** -z **-ing** -ɪŋ **-ed** -d **-ment/s** -mənt/s
Adorno əˈdɔː.nəʊ ⓤⓢ -ˈdɔːr.noʊ
ADP ˌeɪ.diːˈpiː
Adrastus əˈdræs.təs
adrenal əˈdriː.nəl **aˈdrenal ˌgland**
adrenalin(e) əˈdren.əl.ɪn ⓤⓢ -ə.lɪn
adrenocortical əˌdriː.nəʊˈkɔː.tɪ.kəl ⓤⓢ -noʊˈkɔːr.t̬ɪ-, -ˌdren.oʊˈ-, -əˈ-
adrenocorticotroph|ic əˌdriː.nəʊˌkɔː.tɪ.kəʊˈtrɒf|.ɪk ⓤⓢ -noʊˌkɔːr.t̬ɪ.koʊˈtroʊ.f|ɪk, -ˌdren.oʊˌ-, -əˌ-, -ˈtrɑː- **-in** -ɪn
Adria ˈeɪ.dri.ə
Adrian ˈeɪ.dri.ən
Adriana ˌeɪ.driˈɑː.nə, ˌæd.riˈ-
Adrianople ˌeɪ.dri.əˈnəʊ.pl̩, ˌæd.ri- ⓤⓢ -ˈnoʊ-
Adrianopolis ˌeɪ.dri.əˈnɒp.əl.ɪs, ˌæd.ri- ⓤⓢ -ˈnɑː.pəl-
Adriatic ˌeɪ.driˈæt.ɪk ⓤⓢ -ˈæt̬- *stress shift:* ˌAdriatic ˈSea
Adrienne ˌeɪ.driˈen, ˌæd.riˈ-; ˈeɪ.dri.ən, ˈæd.ri-
adrift əˈdrɪft
adroit əˈdrɔɪt **-est** -əst, -ɪst **-ly** -li **-ness** -nəs, -nɪs
adsorb ædˈzɔːb, əd-, -ˈsɔːb ⓤⓢ -ˈsɔːrb, -ˈzɔːrb **-s** -z **-ing** -ɪŋ **-ed** -d
adsorbent ædˈzɔː.bənt, ədˈ-, -ˈsɔː- ⓤⓢ -ˈsɔːr-, -ˈzɔːr-
adsorption ædˈzɔːp.ʃən, ədˈ-, -ˈsɔːp- ⓤⓢ -ˈsɔːrp-, -ˈzɔːrp-
adsorptive ædˈzɔːp.tɪv, ədˈ-, -ˈsɔːp- ⓤⓢ -ˈsɔːrp-, -ˈzɔːrp-
adsum ˈæd.sʌm, -sʊm, -səm
adularia ˌæd.jʊˈleə.ri.ə, -jəˈ-, ˌædʒ.ʊˈ- ⓤⓢ ˌædʒ.ʊˈler.i-, ˌæd.jəˈ-
adu|late ˈæd.jʊ|.leɪt, -jə-, ˈædʒ.ʊ-, ˈ-ə- ⓤⓢ ˈædʒ.ə-, ˈæd.jə-, ˈ-ə- **-lates** -leɪts **-lating** -leɪ.tɪŋ ⓤⓢ -leɪ.t̬ɪŋ **-lated** -leɪ.tɪd ⓤⓢ -leɪ.t̬ɪd
adulation ˌæd.jʊˈleɪ.ʃən, -jəˈ-, ˌædʒ.ʊˈ-, -əˈ- ⓤⓢ ˌædʒ.əˈ-, ˌæd.jəˈ-, -əˈ- **-s** -z
adulatory ˌæd.jʊˈleɪ.tər.i, -jəˈ-, ˌædʒ.ʊˈ-, -əˈ-; ˈæd.jʊ.leɪ-, -jə-, ˈædʒ.ʊ-, ˈ-ə-, -tər.i ⓤⓢ ˈædʒ.əl.ə.tɔːr-, ˈæd.jəl-, -əl-
Adullam əˈdʌl.əm **-ite/s** -aɪt/s
adult ˈæd.ʌlt, əˈdʌlt ⓤⓢ əˈdʌlt, ˈæd.ʌlt **-s** -s **ˌadult eduˈcation**
adulterant əˈdʌl.tər.ənt ⓤⓢ -t̬ər- **-s** -s
adulter|ate əˈdʌl.tər|.eɪt ⓤⓢ -t̬ə.r|eɪt **-ates** -eɪts **-ating** -eɪ.tɪŋ ⓤⓢ -eɪ.t̬ɪŋ **-ated** -eɪ.tɪd ⓤⓢ -eɪ.t̬ɪd **-ator/s** -eɪ.təʳ/z ⓤⓢ -eɪ.t̬ɚ/z
adulteration əˌdʌl.tərˈeɪ.ʃən ⓤⓢ -t̬əˈreɪ- **-s** -z
adulterer əˈdʌl.tər.əʳ ⓤⓢ -t̬ɚ.ɚ **-s** -z
adulteress əˈdʌl.tər.es, -ɪs, -əs ⓤⓢ -t̬ɚ-, ˈ-trɪs **-es** -ɪz
adulterous əˈdʌl.tər.əs, ˈ-trəs ⓤⓢ ˈ-t̬ɚ.əs, ˈ-trəs **-ly** -li
adulter|y əˈdʌl.tər|.i, ˈ-tr|i ⓤⓢ ˈ-t̬ɚ.i, ˈ-tri **-ies** -iz
adulthood ˈæd.ʌlt.hʊd, əˈdʌlt- ⓤⓢ əˈdʌlt-
adum|brate ˈæd.ʌm|.breɪt, -əm- **-brates** -breɪts **-brating** -breɪ.tɪŋ ⓤⓢ -breɪ.t̬ɪŋ **-brated** -breɪ.tɪd ⓤⓢ -breɪ.t̬ɪd
adumbration ˌæd.ʌmˈbreɪ.ʃən, -əm- **-s** -z
Adur ˈeɪ.dəʳ ⓤⓢ -dɚ
ad valorem ˌæd.vəˈlɔː.rem, -vælˈɔː-, -rəm ⓤⓢ -vəˈlɔːr.əm
advanc|e ədˈvɑːnts ⓤⓢ -ˈvænts, æd- **-es** -ɪz **-ing** -ɪŋ **-ed** -t **-ement/s** -mənt/s **adˌvance ˈnotice; adˌvance ˈpayment; Adˈvanced ˌLevel**
advantag|e ədˈvɑːn.tɪdʒ ⓤⓢ -ˈvæn.t̬ɪdʒ, æd- **-es** -ɪz
advantageous ˌæd.vənˈteɪ.dʒəs, -vɑːnˈ-, -vænˈ- ⓤⓢ -vænˈ-, -vənˈ- **-ly** -li **-ness** -nəs, -nɪs
adven|e ædˈviːn, əd- **-es** -z **-ing** -ɪŋ **-ed** -d
advent (A) ˈæd.vent, -vənt **-s** -s **ˈAdvent ˌcalendar**
Adventism ˈæd.ven.tɪ.zəm, -vən- ⓤⓢ -vən-
Adventist ˈæd.ven.tɪst, -vən- ⓤⓢ -vən-; ədˈven-
adventitious ˌæd.vənˈtɪʃ.əs, -ven- **-ly** -li
adventive ædˈven.tɪv ⓤⓢ -t̬ɪv **-ly** -li
advent|ure ədˈven.tʃ|əʳ ⓤⓢ -tʃ|ɚ, æd- **-ures** -əz, -ɚz **-uring** -ər.ɪŋ **-ured** -əd, -ɚd **-urer/s** -ər.əʳ/z ⓤⓢ -ɚ.ɚ/z **-uress/es** -ər.əs/ɪz, -ə.res/ɪz **adˌventure ˈplayground**
adventuresome ədˈven.tʃə.səm ⓤⓢ -tʃɚ-, æd-
adventurous ədˈven.tʃər.əs ⓤⓢ əd-, æd- **-ly** -li **-ness** -nəs, -nɪs
adverb ˈæd.vɜːb ⓤⓢ -vɝːb **-s** -z
adverbial ədˈvɜː.bi.əl, æd- ⓤⓢ -ˈvɝː- **-ly** -i
adversarial ˌæd.vəˈseə.ri.əl, -vɜːˈ- ⓤⓢ -vɚˈser.i- **-ly** -i
adversar|y ˈæd.və.sər|.i, ədˈvɜː- ⓤⓢ ˈæd.vɚ.ser- **-ies** -iz
adversative ədˈvɜː.sə.tɪv, æd- ⓤⓢ -ˈvɝː.sə.t̬ɪv
adverse ˈæd.vɜːs, -ˈ-, əd- ⓤⓢ ædˈvɝːs, ˈ-- **-ly** -li

Pronouncing the letters AE

The vowel digraph **ae** is a fairly low-frequency spelling. In some cases, the American spelling of words containing **ae** omits the **a**, e.g. in *aesthetic*, which is spelt in American English as *esthetic*.

The pronunciation of the digraph in strong syllables depends on whether or not it is followed by an **r** in the spelling. If so, the pronunciation is /eə ⓤⓢ er/, e.g:

aeroplane /ˈeə.rə.pleɪn/ ⓤⓢ /ˈer.ə-/

When not followed by **r**, the pronunciation is most usually one of /iː/, /ɪ/ or /e/, the latter being most common in American English pronunciation, e.g.:

Caesar /ˈsiː.zəʳ/ ⓤⓢ /-zɚ/
aesthetic /iːsˈθet.ɪk, ɪs-/ ⓤⓢ /esˈθet̬-/

In addition

Other vowel sounds associated with the digraph **ae** include /æ/, for Old English names, e.g.:

Aethelstan /ˈæθ.əl.stən/

In weak syllables

The vowel digraph is realised with the vowels /ə/ and /ɪ/ in weak syllables, e.g.:

gynaecology /ˌgaɪ.nəˈkɒl.ə.dʒi, -nɪˈ-/ ⓤⓢ /-ˈkɑː.lə-/

Pronouncing the letters AEO

The vowel letter combination **aeo** is low frequency, and is often spelt **eo** in American English. It has two pronunciations associated with it:

/iˈɒ US iˈɑː/	archaeology	/ˌɑː.kiˈɒl.ə.dʒi/ US /ˌɑːr.kiˈɑː.lə-/
/iəʊ US ioʊ, iə/	palaeotype	/ˈpæl.i.əʊ.taɪp/ US /ˈpeɪ.li.oʊ-, -ə-/

adversit|y ədˈvɜː.sə.t|i, -sɪ- US -ˈvɝː.sə.ţ|i, æd- **-ies** -iz
advert (*n.*) ˈæd.vɜːt US -vɝːt **-s** -s
ad|vert (*v.*) ədˈvɜːt, æd- US -ˈvɝːt **-verts** -ˈvɜːts US -ˈvɝːts **-verting** -ˈvɜː.tɪŋ US -ˈvɝː.ţɪŋ **-verted** -ˈvɜː.tɪd US -ˈvɝː.ţɪd
advertenc|e ədˈvɜː.tᵊnts US -ˈvɝː-, æd- **-y** -i
advertent ədˈvɜː.tᵊnt US -ˈvɝː-, æd- **-ly** -li
advertis|e, -iz|e ˈæd.və.taɪz US -vɚ- **-es** -ɪz **-ing** -ɪŋ **-ed** -d **-er/s** -əʳ/z US -ɚ/z
advertisement, -ize- ədˈvɜː.tɪs.mənt, -tɪz-, -təs-, -təz- US ˌæd.vɚˈtaɪz.mənt; ədˈvɝː.ţəs-, -ţəz- **-s** -s
advertorial ˌæd.vəˈtɔː.ri.əl US -vɚˈtɔːr.i-
advic|e ədˈvaɪs US əd-, æd- **-es** -ɪz
advisability ədˌvaɪ.zəˈbɪl.ə.ti, -ɪ- US -ə.ţi, æd-
advisab|le ədˈvaɪ.zə.b|l̩ US əd-, æd- **-ly** -li **-leness** -l̩.nəs, -nɪs
advis|e ədˈvaɪz US əd-, æd- **-es** -ɪz **-ing** -ɪŋ **-ed** -d **-edly** -ɪd.li **-edness** -ɪd.nəs, -nɪs
adviser, advisor ədˈvaɪ.zəʳ US -zɚ, æd- **-s** -z
advisor|y ədˈvaɪ.zᵊr|.i US əd-, æd- **-ies** -iz **adˈvisory ˌbody**
advocaat ˈæd.vəʊ.kɑː, -kɑːt US -voʊ-
advocacy ˈæd.və.kə.si
advocate (*n.*) ˈæd.və.kət, -keɪt, -kɪt **-s** -s
advo|cate (*v.*) ˈæd.və|.keɪt **-cates** -keɪts **-cating** -keɪ.tɪŋ US -keɪ.ţɪŋ **-cated** -keɪ.tɪd US -keɪ.ţɪd **-cator/s** -keɪ.təʳ/z US -keɪ.ţɚ/z
advocation ˌæd.vəˈkeɪ.ʃᵊn
advowson ədˈvaʊ.zᵊn **-s** -z
Adwa ˈɑː.dwə
Adwick le Street ˌæd.wɪk.lɪˈstriːt
Adye ˈeɪ.di
adynamia ˌeɪ.daɪˈneɪ.mi.ə, ˌæd.ɪˈ-
adynamic ˌeɪ.daɪˈnæm.ɪk, ˌæd.aɪˈ-, -ɪˈ-
adz|e, adz ædz **-es** -ɪz **-ing** -ɪŋ **-ed** -d
adzuki ædˈzuː.ki **adˈzuki ˌbean**
Aeacus ˈiː.ə.kəs
aedile ˈiː.daɪl **-s** -z **-ship/s** -ʃɪp/s
Aeetes iːˈiː.tiːz
Aegean iːˈdʒiː.ən, ɪˈ-
Aegeus ˈiː.dʒi.əs US ˈiː.dʒi.əs, ˈiː.dʒuːs
Aegina iːˈdʒaɪ.nə, ɪˈdʒaɪ-
aegis ˈiː.dʒɪs
Aegisthus iːˈdʒɪs.θəs, ɪˈdʒɪs-
aegrotat ˈaɪ.grəʊ.tæt, ˈiː- US -groʊ- **-s** -s
Aegyptus iːˈdʒɪp.təs
Aelfric ˈæl.frɪk
Aemilius iːˈmɪl.i.əs, ɪˈmɪl-
Aeneas iːˈniː.əs, ɪˈniː-, -æs
Aeneid ˈiː.ni.ɪd, iːˈniː.ɪd, ɪˈ- **-s** -z
Aeneus ˈiː.ni.əs, iːˈniː-, ɪ-
Aeoli|a iːˈəʊ.li|.ə US -ˈoʊ- **-an/s** -ən/z
Aeolic iːˈɒl.ɪk, -ˈəʊ.lɪk US -ˈɑː.lɪk
Aeolus ˈiː.əʊ.ləs US ˈ-ə-
aeon ˈiː.ən, -ɒn US -ɑːn **-s** -z
aera|te eəˈreɪ|t, ˈ-- US erˈeɪ|t **-tes** -ts **-ting** -tɪŋ US -ţɪŋ **-ted** -tɪd US -ţɪd **-tor/s** -təʳ/z US -ţɚ/z
aeration eəˈreɪ.ʃᵊn US erˈeɪ-
aerial ˈeə.ri.əl US ˈer.i- **-s** -z **-ly** -i
aerie ˈɪə.ri, ˈeə- US ˈer.i, ˈɪr-, ˈeɪ.ri **-s** -z
aerif|y ˈeə.rɪ.faɪ US ˈer.ə- **-ies** -z **-ying** -ɪŋ **-ied** -aɪd
Aer Lingus® ˌeəˈlɪŋ.gəs US ˌer-
aero- eə.rəʊ-; eəˈrɒ- US er.oʊ-, er.ə-; erˈɑː-
Note: Prefix. Either takes primary or secondary stress on the first syllable, e.g. **aeronaut** /ˈeə.rə.nɔːt US ˈer.ə.nɑːt/ **aeronautic** /ˌeə.rəˈnɔː.tɪk US ˌer.əˈnɑː.ţɪk/, or primary stress on the second syllable, e.g. **aerology** /eəˈrɒl.ə.dʒi US erˈɑː.lə-/.
aero ˈeə.rəʊ US ˈer.oʊ
aeroballistics ˌeə.rəʊ.bəˈlɪs.tɪks US ˌer.oʊ-
aerobatic ˌeə.rəʊˈbæt.ɪk US ˌer.oʊˈbæţ- **-s** -s **-ally** -ᵊl.i, -li
aerobe ˈeə.rəʊb US ˈer.oʊb **-s** -z
aerobic eəˈrəʊ.bɪk US erˈoʊ- **-s** -s
aerodrome ˈeə.rə.drəʊm US ˈer.ə.droʊm **-s** -z
aerodynamic ˌeə.rəʊ.daɪˈnæm.ɪk, -dɪˈ- US ˌer.oʊ- **-s** -s **-ally** -ᵊl.i, -li *stress shift:* ˌaerodynamic ˈfairing
aerodyne ˈeə.rəʊ.daɪn US ˈer.ə- **-s** -z
Aeroflot® ˈeə.rəʊ.flɒt US ˈer.ə.floʊt, -flɑːt
aerofoil ˈeə.rəʊ.fɔɪl US ˈer.oʊ- **-s** -z
aerogram, aerogramme ˈeə.rəʊ.græm US ˈer.ə- **-s** -z
aerolite ˈeə.rəʊ.laɪt US ˈer.ə- **-s** -s
aerolith ˈeə.rəʊ.lɪθ US ˈer.ə- **-s** -s
aerological ˌeə.rəʊˈlɒdʒ.ɪ.kᵊl US ˌer.oʊˈlɑː.dʒɪ-
aerologist eəˈrɒl.ə.dʒɪst US erˈɑː.lə- **-s** -s
aerolog|y eəˈrɒl.ə.dʒ|i US erˈɑː.lə- **-ist/s** -ɪst/s
aeronaut ˈeə.rə.nɔːt US ˈer.ə.nɑːt, -nɔːt **-s** -s
aeronautic ˌeə.rəˈnɔː.tɪk US ˌer.əˈnɑː.ţɪk, -ˈnɔː- **-s** -s **-al** -ᵊl
aerophone ˈeə.rə.fəʊn US ˈer.ə.foʊn **-s** -z
aeroplane ˈeə.rə.pleɪn US ˈer- **-s** -z
Aerosmith ˈeə.rəʊ.smɪθ US ˈe.roʊ-
aerosol ˈeə.rə.sɒl US ˈer.ə.sɑːl **-s** -z
aerospace ˈeə.rəʊ.speɪs US ˈer.oʊ-
aerostat ˈeə.rəʊ.stæt US ˈer.oʊ- **-s** -s
Aertex® ˈeə.teks US ˈer-
aer|y (*n.*) ˈɪə.r|i, ˈeə- US ˈer|.i, ˈɪr-, ˈeɪ|.ri **-ies** -iz
aery (*adj.*) ˈeə.ri US ˈer.i, ˈeɪ.ə.ri
Aeschines ˈiː.skɪ.niːz, -skə.niːz US ˈes.kə-, ˈiː.skə-
Aeschylus ˈiː.skɪ.ləs, -skə.ləs US ˈes.kə-, ˈiː.skə-
Aesculapi|us ˌiː.skjʊˈleɪ.pi|.əs US ˌes.kjəˈ-, -kəˈ- **-an** -ən
Aesop ˈiː.sɒp US -sɑːp, -səp
aesthete ˈiːs.θiːt US ˈes- **-s** -s
aesthetic iːsˈθet.ɪk, ɪs-, es- US esˈθeţ-, ɪs- **-s** -s **-al** -ᵊl **-ally** -ᵊl.i, -li
aestheticism iːsˈθet.ɪ.s|ɪ.zᵊm, ɪs-, es- US es-, ɪs- **-ist/s** -ɪst/s
aestival iːˈstaɪ.vᵊl US ˈes.tə-, esˈtaɪ-
Aethelstan ˈæθ.ᵊl.stən, -stæn
aether ˈiː.θəʳ US -θɚ
aetiolog|y ˌiː.tiˈɒl.ə.dʒ|i US -ţiˈɑː.lə- **-ist/s** -ɪst/s
Aetna ˈet.nə
afar əˈfɑːʳ US -ˈfɑːr
afeard əˈfɪəd US -ˈfɪrd
affability ˌæf.əˈbɪl.ə.ti, -ɪ.ti US -ə.ţi
affab|le ˈæf.ə.b|l̩ **-ly** -li **-leness** -l̩.nəs, -nɪs
affair əˈfeəʳ US -ˈfer **-s** -z
affect (*v.*) əˈfekt **-s** -s **-ing/ly** -ɪŋ/li **-ed** -ɪd
affect (*n.*) *in psychology:* ˈæf.ekt **-s** -s
affectation ˌæf.ekˈteɪ.ʃᵊn, -ɪkˈ- **-s** -z
affected əˈfek.tɪd **-ly** -li **-ness** -nəs, -nɪs

Affricate

A type of consonant consisting of a PLOSIVE followed by a FRICATIVE with the same place of ARTICULATION.

Examples for English

Examples are the /tʃ/ and /dʒ/ sounds (sometimes symbolised /č/ /ǰ/ by American writers) at the beginning and end of the words *church* and *judge*, where the first of these sounds is voiceless and the second voiced (see VOICING), e.g.:

church /tʃɜːtʃ/ (US) /tʃɝːtʃ/
judge /dʒʌdʒ/

It is often difficult to decide whether any particular combination of a plosive plus a fricative should be classed as a single affricate sound or as two separate sounds, and the question depends on whether these are to be regarded as separate PHONEMES or not. It is usual to regard /tʃ/ and /dʒ/ as affricate phonemes in English; /ts dz tr dr/ also occur in English but are not usually regarded as affricate phonemes, but are treated as clusters. The two phrases *why choose* and *white shoes* are said to show the difference between the /tʃ/ affricate (in the first example) and separate /t/ and /ʃ/ (in the second), e.g.:

why choose /*h*waɪ tʃuːz/
white shoes /*h*waɪt ʃuːz/

affection əˈfek.ʃᵊn **-s** -z
affectionate əˈfek.ʃᵊn.ət, -ɪt **-ly** -li **-ness** -nəs, -nɪs
affective əˈfek.tɪv, æfˈek-
affenpinscher ˈæf.ən,pɪn.*t*ʃəʳ (US) -,pɪn*t*.ʃɚ **-s** -z
afferent ˈæf.ᵊr.ənt
affettuoso ə,fet.juˈəʊ.səʊ, æf,et-, -zəʊ (US) ə,fet.juˈoʊ.soʊ, æf,et-, -,etʃ.uˈ-
affianc|e əˈfaɪən*t*s **-es** -ɪz **-ing** -ɪŋ **-ed** -t
affiant əˈfaɪənt **-s** -s
affich|e æfˈiːʃ, əˈfiːʃ **-es** -ɪz
affidavit ,æf.ɪˈdeɪ.vɪt, -əˈ- **-s** -s
affili|ate əˈfɪl.i|.eɪt **-ates** -eɪts **-ating** -eɪ.tɪŋ (US) -eɪ.t̬ɪŋ **-ated** -eɪ.tɪd (US) -eɪ.t̬ɪd
affiliation ə,fɪl.iˈeɪ.ʃᵊn **-s** -z
affinit|y əˈfɪn.ə.t|i, -ɪt|i (US) -ə.t̬|i **-ies** -iz
affirm əˈfɜːm (US) -ˈfɝːm **-s** -z **-ing** -ɪŋ **-ed** -d **-able** -ə.bl̩
affirmation ,æf.əˈmeɪ.ʃᵊn (US) -ɚˈ- **-s** -z
affirmative əˈfɜː.mə.tɪv (US) -ˈfɝː.mə.t̬ɪv **-ly** -li **af,firmative ˈaction**
affirmatory əˈfɜː.mə.tᵊr.i (US) -ˈfɝː.mə.tɔːr-
affix (*n.*) ˈæf.ɪks **-es** -ɪz
affix (*v.*) əˈfɪks, ˈæf.ɪks **-es** -ɪz **-ing** -ɪŋ **-ed** -d
affixation ,æf.ɪkˈseɪ.ʃᵊn
affixture æfˈɪks.tʃəʳ (US) -tʃɚ, æfˈɪks-
afflatus əˈfleɪ.təs (US) -t̬əs
Affleck ˈæf.lek
afflict əˈflɪkt **-s** -s **-ing** -ɪŋ **-ed** -ɪd **-ive** -ɪv
affliction əˈflɪk.ʃᵊn **-s** -z
affluence ˈæf.lu.ən*t*s
afflux ˈæf.lʌks **-es** -ɪz
afford əˈfɔːd (US) -ˈfɔːrd **-s** -z **-ing** -ɪŋ **-ed** -ɪd
affordab|le əˈfɔː.də.b|l̩ (US) -ˈfɔːr- **-ly** -li
afforest əˈfɒr.ɪst, æfˈɒr- (US) əˈfɔːr.əst **-s** -s **-ing** -ɪŋ **-ed** -ɪd
afforestation æf,ɒr.ɪˈsteɪ.ʃᵊn, ə,fɒr-, -əˈ- (US) ə,fɔːr.əˈ- **-s** -z
affranchis|e əˈfræn.*t*ʃaɪz, æfˈræn- (US) əˈfræn.tʃaɪz **-es** -ɪz **-ing** -ɪŋ **-ed** -d
affray əˈfreɪ **-s** -z
affricate ˈæf.rɪ.kət, -rə-, -kɪt, -keɪt (US) -kɪt **-s** -s
affricated ˈæf.rɪ.keɪ.tɪd, -rə- (US) -t̬ɪd
affrication ,æf.rɪˈkeɪ.ʃᵊn, -rəˈ-
affricative æfˈrɪk.ə.tɪv, əˈfrɪk- (US) -t̬ɪv **-s** -z
af|fright ə|ˈfraɪt **-frights** -ˈfraɪts **-frighting** -ˈfraɪ.tɪŋ (US) -ˈfraɪ.t̬ɪŋ **-frighted/ly** -ˈfraɪ.tɪd/li (US) -ˈfraɪ.t̬ɪd/li
af|front ə|ˈfrʌnt **-fronts** -ˈfrʌnts **-fronting** -ˈfrʌn.tɪŋ (US) -ˈfrʌn.t̬ɪŋ **-fronted** -ˈfrʌn.tɪd (US) -ˈfrʌn.t̬ɪd
Afghan ˈæf.gæn **-s** -z **,Afghan ˈhound**
afghani æfˈgæn.i, -ˈgɑː.ni **-s** -z
Afghanistan æfˈgæn.ɪ.stæn, ˈ-ə-, -stɑːn, æf,gæn.ɪˈstɑːn, -əˈ-, -ˈstæn (US) æfˈgæn.ə.stæn, -stɑːn
aficionado ə,fɪʃ.i.əˈnɑː.dəʊ, -,fɪs- *as if Spanish:* æf,ɪθ.jəˈnɑː.dəʊ (US) ə,fɪʃ.i.əˈnɑː.doʊ, -,fɪs-, -,fiː.si- **-s** -z
afield əˈfiːld
afire əˈfaɪəʳ (US) -ˈfaɪɚ
aflame əˈfleɪm
aflatoxin ,æf.ləˈtɒk.sɪn (US) -ˈtɑːk.sᵊn
AFL-CIO eɪ.ef,el.siː.aɪˈəʊ (US) -ˈoʊ
afloat əˈfləʊt (US) -ˈfloʊt
aflutter əˈflʌt.əʳ (US) -ˈflʌt̬.ɚ
afoot əˈfʊt
afore əˈfɔːʳ (US) -ˈfɔːr
aforementioned əˈfɔː.men.*t*ʃᵊnd, ə,fɔːˈmen- (US) əˈfɔːr.men*t*.ʃᵊnd
Note: In British English, the latter form is not used attributively.
aforesaid əˈfɔː.sed (US) -ˈfɔːr-
aforethought əˈfɔː.θɔːt (US) -ˈfɔːr.θɑːt, -θɔːt
aforetime əˈfɔː.taɪm (US) -ˈfɔːr-
a fortiori eɪ,fɔː.tiˈɔː.raɪ, ɑː,-, -ri (US) ,eɪ,fɔːr.t̬iˈɔːr.i, -ʃiˈ-, -aɪ
afraid əˈfreɪd
afreet ˈæf.riːt, əˈfriːt **-s** -s
afresh əˈfreʃ
Afric ˈæf.rɪk
Afric|a ˈæf.rɪ.k|ə **-an/s** -ən/z
African-American ,æf.rɪ.kən.əˈmer.ɪ.kən **-s** -z
Africander ,æf.rɪˈkæn.dəʳ (US) -dɚ **-s** -z
Africanist ˈæf.rɪ.kə.nɪst **-s** -s
Africanization, **-isa-** ,æf.rɪ.kə.naɪˈzeɪ.ʃᵊn, -rə-, -nɪˈ- (US) -nɪˈ-
Africaniz|e, **-is|e** ˈæf.rɪ.kə.naɪz **-es** -ɪz **-ing** -ɪŋ **-ed** -d
Africanus ,æf.rɪˈkɑː.nəs, -ˈkeɪ-
Afridi æfˈriː.di, əˈfriː- **-s** -z
Afrikaans ,æf.rɪˈkɑːn*t*s, -rəˈkɑːn*t*s, -rɪkˈɑːnz, -rəˈkɑːnz
Afrikaner ,æf.rɪˈkɑː.nəʳ (US) -nɚ **-s** -z
afrit ˈæf.riːt, əˈfriːt **-s** -s
Afro- ,æf.rəʊ- (US) ,æf.roʊ-
Note: Prefix. Normally carries secondary stress on the first syllable, e.g. **Afro-American** /,æf.rəʊ.əˈmer.ɪ.kən (US) -roʊ-/.
Afro ˈæf.rəʊ (US) -roʊ **-s** -z
Afro-American ,æf.rəʊ.əˈmer.ɪ.kən (US) -roʊ- **-s** -z
Afro-Asian ,æf.rəʊˈeɪ.ʃᵊn, -ʒᵊn (US) -roʊˈeɪ.ʒᵊn, -ʃᵊn **-s** -z
Afro-Asiatic ,æf.rəʊ.eɪ.ʃiˈæt.ɪk, -siˈ-, -ʒiˈ-, -ziˈ- (US) -roʊ.eɪ.ʒiˈ-, -ʃiˈ-
Afro-Caribbean ,æf.rəʊ.kær.ɪˈbiː.ən (US) -roʊ.ker-, -kær-; -kəˈrɪb.i- **-s** -z
aft ɑːft (US) æft
after- ˈɑːf.tə- (US) ˈæf.tɚ-

Note: Prefix. Words containing **after-** usually carry primary stress on the first syllable, e.g. **afterglow** /ˈɑːf.tə.gləʊ ⓤⓢ ˈæf.tɚ.gloʊ/, but there are exceptions, including **afternoon** /ˌɑːf.təˈnuːn ⓤⓢ ˌæf.tɚ-/.
after ˈɑːf.təʳ ⓤⓢ ˈæf.tɚ **ˌafter ˈall; ˌAfter ˈEights®**
afterbirth ˈɑːf.tə.bɜːθ ⓤⓢ ˈæf.tɚ.bɝːθ **-s** -s
after-burner ˈɑːf.təˌbɜː.nəʳ ⓤⓢ ˈæf.tɚˌbɝː.nɚ **-s** -z
aftercare ˈɑːf.tə.keəʳ ⓤⓢ ˈæf.tɚ.ker
after-crop ˈɑːf.tə.krɒp ⓤⓢ ˈæf.tɚ.krɑːp **-s** -s
aftereffect ˈɑːf.təʳ.ɪˌfekt, -əˌfekt ⓤⓢ ˈæf.tɚ- **-s** -s
afterglow ˈɑːf.tə.gləʊ ⓤⓢ ˈæf.tɚ.gloʊ **-s** -z
after-hours ˌɑːf.təʳˈaʊəz ⓤⓢ ˈæf.tɚˌaʊɚz, ˌ--ˈ-
afterli|fe ˈɑːf.tə.laɪ|f ⓤⓢ ˈæf.tɚ- **-ves** -vz
aftermath ˈɑːf.tə.mɑːθ, -mæθ ⓤⓢ ˈæf.tɚ.mæθ **-s** -s
afternoon ˌɑːf.təˈnuːn ⓤⓢ ˌæf.tɚˈ- **-s** -z *stress shift, see compounds:* **ˌafternoon ˈtea; good ˌafterˈnoon**
afterpiec|e ˈɑːf.tə.piːs ⓤⓢ ˈæf.tɚ- **-es** -ɪz
afters ˈɑːf.təz ⓤⓢ ˈæf.tɚz
after-sales ˌɑːf.təˈseɪlz ⓤⓢ ˌæf.tɚˈ- *stress shift:* ˌafter-sales ˈservice
aftershave ˈɑːf.tə.ʃeɪv ⓤⓢ ˈæf.tɚ- **-s** -z
aftershock ˈɑːf.tə.ʃɒk ⓤⓢ ˈæf.tɚ.ʃɑːk **-s** -s
aftertaste ˈɑːf.tə.teɪst ⓤⓢ ˈæf.tɚ- **-s** -s
afterthought ˈɑːf.tə.θɔːt ⓤⓢ ˈæf.tɚ.θɑːt, -θɔːt **-s** -s
afterward ˈɑːf.tə.wəd ⓤⓢ ˈæf.tɚ.wɚd **-s** -z
AFTRA ˈæf.trə
Aga® ˈɑː.gə
Agadir ˌæg.əˈdɪə ⓤⓢ ˌɑː.gəˈdɪr, ˌæg.əˈ-
Agag ˈeɪ.gæg
again əˈgen, -ˈgeɪn ⓤⓢ əˈgen
against əˈgentst, -ˈgeɪntst ⓤⓢ əˈgentst
Aga Khan ˌɑː.gəˈkɑːn
Agamemnon ˌæg.əˈmem.nən, -nɒn ⓤⓢ -nɑːn, -nən
agamete eɪˈgæm.iːt, əˈ- ⓤⓢ ˌæg.əˈmiːt **-s** -s
Agana ɑːˈgɑː.nə, -njə ⓤⓢ -njə
agape (*adj. adv.*) əˈgeɪp
agape (*n.*) ˈæg.ə.pi, -peɪ ⓤⓢ ɑːˈgɑː.peɪ, ˈɑː.gə- **-s** -z
Agar *family name:* ˈeɪ.gəʳ, -gɑːʳ ⓤⓢ -gɚ, -gɑːr
agar *jelly:* ˈeɪ.gɑːʳ, -əʳ ⓤⓢ -gɑːr, ˈɑː-, -gɚ
agar-agar ˌeɪ.gəʳˈeɪ.gəʳ, -gɑːʳˈ-, -gɑːʳ ⓤⓢ -gɚˈeɪ.gɚ, ˌɑː.gɚˈɑ-, -gɑːrˈ-, -gɑːr
agaric (*n.*) ˈæg.ə.rɪk; əˈgær.ɪk ⓤⓢ ˈæg.ɚ.ɪk, əˈger-; -ˈgær- **-s** -s
agaric (*adj.*) ægˈær.ɪk, əˈgær-
Agassi ˈæg.ə.si
Agassiz ˌæg.əˈsiː ⓤⓢ ˈæg.ə.si
Agassizhorn əˈgæs.ɪ.hɔːn ⓤⓢ -hɔːrn
agate *stone:* ˈæg.ət, -gɪt **-s** -s
Agate *surname:* ˈeɪ.gət, ˈæg.ət
Agatha ˈæg.ə.θə
Agathocles əˈgæθ.əʊ.kliːz ⓤⓢ ˈ-ə-
agave əˈgeɪ.vi, -ˈgɑː-, ˈæg.eɪ- ⓤⓢ əˈgɑː- **-s** -z
agaze əˈgeɪz
ag|e eɪdʒ **-es** -ɪz **-(e)ing** -ɪŋ **-ed** -d **ˌage of conˈsent; ˈgolden ˌage**
-age -ɪdʒ, -ɑːʒ
Note: Suffix. Normally pronounced /-ɪdʒ/, e.g. **advantage** /ədˈvɑːn.tɪdʒ ⓤⓢ -ˈvæn.t̬ɪdʒ/, which is unstressed, but in words of French origin it is often /-ɑːʒ/, which may be stress bearing; see for example, **corsage**, in which it has both stressed and unstressed variants.
aged (*adj.*) *old:* ˈeɪ.dʒɪd *of the age of:* eɪdʒd
agedness ˈeɪdʒ.ɪd.nəs, -nɪs
Agee ˈeɪ.dʒi
age|ism ˈeɪdʒ.|ɪ.zᵊm **-ist/s** -ɪst/s
ageless ˈeɪdʒ.ləs, -lɪs
agelong ˈeɪdʒ.lɒŋ ⓤⓢ -lɑːŋ, -lɔːŋ
agenc|y ˈeɪ.dʒᵊnt.s|i **-ies** -iz
agenda əˈdʒen.də **-s** -z
agendum əˈdʒen.dəm **-s** -z
agene ˈeɪ.dʒiːn
agenesis ˌeɪˈdʒen.ə.sɪs, ˈ-ɪ-
agent ˈeɪ.dʒᵊnt **-s** -s **ˌAgent ˈOrange**
agentival ˌeɪ.dʒᵊnˈtaɪ.vᵊl
agentive ˈeɪ.dʒᵊn.tɪv
agent(s) provocateur(s) ˌæʒ.ɑ̃ː.prəˌvɒk.əˈtɜːʳ, ˌæʒ.ɒŋ- ⓤⓢ ˌɑːʒ.ɑ̃ː.proʊˌvɑː.kəˈtɝː, -tʊr
age-old ˌeɪdʒˈəʊld ⓤⓢ ˈeɪdʒ.oʊld *stress shift, British only:* ˌage-old ˈcity
-ageous -ˈeɪ.dʒəs
Note: Suffix. Words containing **-ageous** are normally stressed on the penultimate syllable, e.g. **advantageous** /ˌæd.vənˈteɪ.dʒəs ⓤⓢ -vænˈ-/.
Ager ˈeɪ.dʒəʳ ⓤⓢ -dʒɚ
Agesilaus əˌdʒes.ɪˈleɪ.əs, ædʒˌes- ⓤⓢ -əˈ-
Agfa® ˈæg.fə
aggie (A) ˈæg.i **-s** -z
aggiornamento əˌdʒɔː.nəˈmen.təʊ ⓤⓢ -ˌdʒɔːr.nəˈmen.toʊ
agglomerate (*n. adj.*) əˈglɒm.ᵊr.ət, -ɪt ⓤⓢ -ˈglɑː.mɚ- **-s** -s
agglomer|ate (*v.*) əˈglɒm.ᵊr|.eɪt ⓤⓢ -ˈglɑː.mə.r|eɪt **-ates** -eɪts **-ating** -eɪ.tɪŋ ⓤⓢ -eɪ.t̬ɪŋ **-ated** -eɪ.tɪd ⓤⓢ -eɪ.t̬ɪd
agglomeration əˌglɒm.əˈreɪ.ʃᵊn ⓤⓢ -ˌglɑː.məˈ- **-s** -z
agglutinate (*adj.*) əˈgluː.tɪ.nət, -ɪt ⓤⓢ -tᵊn.ət
agglutin|ate (*v.*) əˈgluː.tɪ.n|eɪt ⓤⓢ -tᵊn|.eɪt **-ates** -eɪts **-ating** -eɪ.tɪŋ ⓤⓢ -eɪ.t̬ɪŋ **-ated** -eɪ.tɪd ⓤⓢ -eɪ.t̬ɪd
agglutination əˌgluː.tɪˈneɪ.ʃᵊn ⓤⓢ -tᵊnˈeɪ- **-s** -z
agglutinative əˈgluː.tɪ.nə.tɪv, -eɪ.tɪv ⓤⓢ -tᵊn.eɪ.t̬ɪv
agglutinin əˈgluː.tɪ.nɪn ⓤⓢ -tᵊn.ɪn
agglutinogen ˌæg.lʊˈtɪn.ə.dʒᵊn ⓤⓢ -luːˈ-
aggrandiz|e, -is|e əˈgræn.daɪz **-es** -ɪz **-ing** -ɪŋ **-ed** -d
aggrandizement, -ise- əˈgræn.dɪz.mənt ⓤⓢ -dɪz-, -daɪz-
aggra|vate ˈæg.rə|.veɪt **-vates** -veɪts **-vating/ly** -veɪ.tɪŋ/li ⓤⓢ -veɪ.t̬ɪŋ/li **-vated** -veɪ.tɪd ⓤⓢ -veɪ.t̬ɪd
aggravation ˌæg.rəˈveɪ.ʃᵊn **-s** -z
aggregate (*n. adj.*) ˈæg.rɪ.gət, -rə.gət, -gɪt **-s** -s
aggre|gate (*v.*) ˈæg.rɪ|.geɪt, -rə- **-gates** -geɪts **-gating** -geɪ.tɪŋ ⓤⓢ -geɪ.t̬ɪŋ **-gated** -geɪ.tɪd ⓤⓢ -geɪ.t̬ɪd
aggregation ˌæg.rɪˈgeɪ.ʃᵊn, -rəˈ- **-s** -z
aggregative ˈæg.rɪ.gə.tɪv, -rə-
aggress əˈgres, ægˈres **-es** -ɪz **-ing** -ɪŋ **-ed** -t
aggression əˈgreʃ.ᵊn, ægˈreʃ- **-s** -z
aggressive əˈgres.ɪv, ægˈres- **-ly** -li **-ness** -nəs, -nɪs
aggressor əˈgres.əʳ, ægˈres- ⓤⓢ -ɚ **-s** -z
aggriev|e əˈgriːv **-es** -z **-ing** -ɪŋ **-ed** -d
aggro ˈæg.rəʊ ⓤⓢ -roʊ
aghast əˈgɑːst ⓤⓢ -ˈgæst
agil|e ˈædʒ.aɪl ⓤⓢ -ᵊl **-ist** -əst, -ɪst **-ely** -li
agility əˈdʒɪl.ə.ti, -ɪ.ti ⓤⓢ -ə.t̬i
agin əˈgɪn
Agincourt ˈædʒ.ɪn.kɔːʳ, -kɔːt, -kʊəʳ ⓤⓢ -kɔːrt
agiotage ˈædʒ.ə.tɪdʒ, ˈædʒ.i.əʊ-, -tɑːʒ ⓤⓢ ˈædʒ.i.ə.tɪdʒ; ˌæʒ.əˈtɑːʒ
ag|ism ˈeɪ.dʒ|ɪ.zᵊm **-ist/s** -ɪst/s
agi|tate ˈædʒ.ɪ|.teɪt, ˈ-ə- **-tates** -teɪts **-tating** -teɪ.tɪŋ ⓤⓢ -teɪ.t̬ɪŋ **-tated** -teɪ.tɪd ⓤⓢ -teɪ.t̬ɪd **-tator/s** -teɪ.təʳ/z ⓤⓢ -teɪ.t̬ɚ/z
agitation ˌædʒ.ɪˈteɪ.ʃᵊn, -əˈ- **-s** -z
agitato ˌædʒ.ɪˈtɑː.təʊ ⓤⓢ -t̬oʊ
agitprop ˈædʒ.ɪt.prɒp ⓤⓢ -prɑːp
Aglaia əˈglaɪ.ə, -ˈgleɪ-
aglow əˈgləʊ ⓤⓢ -ˈgloʊ
AGM ˌeɪ.dʒiːˈem
agnail ˈæg.neɪl **-s** -z
agnate ˈæg.neɪt
agnation ægˈneɪ.ʃᵊn
Agnes ˈæg.nəs, -nɪs
Agnew ˈæg.njuː ⓤⓢ -nuː, -njuː
Agni ˈæg.ni

agnomen æɡˈnəʊ.men, -mən (US) -ˈnoʊ- **-s** -z
agnostic æɡˈnɒs.tɪk, əɡ- (US) -ˈnɑː.stɪk **-s** -s
agnosticism æɡˈnɒs.tɪ.sɪ.zᵊm, əɡ-, -tə- (US) -ˈnɑː.stɪ-, -stə-
Agnus Dei ˌæɡ.nəsˈdeɪ.i, -nʊs-, -ˈdiː.aɪ **-s** -z
ago əˈɡəʊ (US) -ˈɡoʊ
agog əˈɡɒɡ (US) -ˈɡɑːɡ, -ˈɡɔːɡ
-agogic -əˈɡɒdʒ.ɪk, -ˈɡɒɡ-, -ˈɡəʊ.dʒɪk (US) -əˈɡɑː.dʒɪk, -ˈɡoʊ-
Note: Suffix. Words containing **-agogic** are normally stressed on the penultimate syllable, e.g. **pedagogic** /ˌped.əˈɡɒdʒ.ɪk (US) -ˈɡɑː-/.
-agogue -ə.ɡɒɡ (US) -ə.ɡɑːɡ, -ə.ɡɔːɡ
Note: Suffix. Normally unstressed, e.g. **pedagogue** /ˈped.ə.ɡɒɡ (US) -ɡɑːɡ/.
-agogy -ə.ɡɒdʒ.i, -ɡɒɡ-, -ɡəʊ.dʒi (US) -ə.ɡɑː.dʒi, -ɡoʊ.ɡi
Note: Suffix. Normally unstressed, e.g. **pedagogy** /ˈped.ə.ɡɒdʒ.i (US) -ɡɑː.dʒi/.
agone əˈɡɒn (US) -ˈɡɑːn
agonist ˈæɡ.ə.nɪst **-s** -s
Agonistes ˌæɡ.əʊˈnɪs.tiːz (US) -əˈ-
agonistic ˌæɡ.əʊˈnɪs.tɪk (US) -əˈ- **-s** -s **-ally** -ᵊl.i
agoniz|e, -is|e ˈæɡ.ə.naɪz **-es** -ɪz **-ing/ly** -ɪŋ/li **-ed** -d
agon|y ˈæɡ.ə.n|i **-ies** -iz ˈ**agony** ˌ**aunt**; ˈ**agony** ˌ**column**
agor|a ˈæɡ.ə.r|ə, -ɒr.ə, ˌæɡ.əˈrɑː (US) ˈæɡ.ə.r|ə, -ɔːr.ə **-ae** -iː **-as** -əz
agoraphob|ia ˌæɡ.ᵊr.əˈfəʊ.b|i.ə, -ɔː.rə- (US) -ɚ.əˈfoʊ-; əˌɡɔːr.əˈ- **-ic/s** -ɪk
agouti əˈɡuː.ti (US) -t̬i **-s** -z
Agra ˈɑː.ɡrə, ˈæɡ.rə
agrarian əˈɡreə.ri.ən (US) -ˈɡrer.i- **-s** -z **-ism** -ɪ.zᵊm
agree əˈɡriː **-s** -z **-ing** -ɪŋ **-d** -d
agreeab|le əˈɡriː.ə.b|l̩ **-ly** -li **-leness** -l̩.nəs, -nɪs
agreement əˈɡriː.mənt **-s** -s
agribusiness ˈæɡ.riˌbɪz.nɪs, -nəs **-es** -ɪz
Agricola əˈɡrɪk.əʊ.lə (US) -ᵊl.ə
agricultural ˌæɡ.rɪˈkʌl.tʃᵊr.ᵊl, -rəˈ- **-ist/s** -ɪst/s
agriculture ˈæɡ.rɪ.kʌl.tʃəʳ, -rə- (US) -tʃɚ
agriculturist ˌæɡ.rɪˈkʌl.tʃᵊr.ɪst, -rəˈ- **-s** -s
Agrigento ˌæɡ.rɪˈdʒen.təʊ (US) -toʊ
agrimony ˈæɡ.rɪ.mə.ni, -rə- (US) -moʊ-
Agrippa əˈɡrɪp.ə
Agrippina ˌæɡ.rɪˈpiː.nə, -rəˈ-
agro- æɡ.rəʊ-; əˈɡrɒ- (US) æɡ.roʊ-, -rə-; əˈɡrɑː-
Note: Prefix. Either takes primary or secondary stress on the first syllable, e.g. **agronomics** /ˌæɡ.rəˈnɒm.ɪks (US) -ˈnɑː.mɪks/, or primary stress on the second syllable, e.g. **agronomy** /əˈɡrɒn.ə.mi (US) -ˈɡrɑː.nə-/.
agrobiologic ˌæɡ.rəʊ.baɪəˈlɒdʒ.ɪk (US) -roʊ.baɪəˈlɑː.dʒɪk **-al** -ᵊl **-ally** -ᵊl.i, -li
agrobiology ˌæɡ.rəʊ.baɪˈɒl.ə.dʒi (US) -roʊ.baɪˈɑː.lə-
agrochemical ˌæɡ.rəʊˈkem.ɪ.kᵊl (US) -roʊˈ- **-s** -z
agrolog|y əˈɡrɒl.ə.dʒ|i, æɡˈ- (US) əˈɡrɑː.lə- **-ist/s** -ɪst/s
agronomics ˌæɡ.rəˈnɒm.ɪks (US) -ˈnɑː.mɪks
agronom|y əˈɡrɒn.ə.m|i (US) -ˈɡrɑː.nə- **-ist/s** -ɪst/s
aground əˈɡraʊnd
Aguascalientes ˌæɡ.wɑːs.kæl.iˈen.tes (US) ˌɑː.ɡwɑːs.kælˈjen.tes, -iˈen-
ague ˈeɪɡ.juː **-s** -z
Aguecheek ˈeɪɡ.juː.tʃiːk
Agulhas əˈɡʌl.əs
Agutter ˈæɡ.ə.təʳ; əˈɡʌt.əʳ (US) əˈɡʌt̬.ɚ; ˈæɡ.ə.t̬ɚ
ah ɑː
aha ɑːˈhɑː, əˈhɑː
Ahab ˈeɪ.hæb
Ahasuerus eɪˌhæz.juˈɪə.rəs, əˌhæz- (US) -ˈɪr.əs
Ahaz ˈeɪ.hæz
Ahaziah ˌeɪ.həˈzaɪ.ə
ahead əˈhed
aheap əˈhiːp
ahem mˈʔm̩m, ˈʔm̩m, hm, əˈhem
Note: Interjection. The spelling attempts to represent a clearing of the throat to attract attention. The pronunciation /əˈhem/ represents the reading aloud of this word by someone who does not know what it stands for.
Ahenobarbus əˌhen.əʊˈbɑː.bəs (US) -oʊˈbɑːr-, -ˌhiː.noʊˈ-
A'Hern ˈeɪ.hɜːn (US) -hɝːn
Ahern(e) əˈhɜːn (US) -ˈhɝːn
Ahimsa ɑːˈhɪm.sɑː (US) ə-
ahistorical ˌeɪ.hɪˈstɒr.ɪ.kᵊl (US) -ˈstɔːr-
Ahithophel əˈhɪθ.əʊ.fel (US) ˈ-ə-
Ahmadabad ˈɑː.mə.də.bæd (US) -bɑːd
Ahmed ˈɑː.med
ahold əˈhəʊld (US) -hoʊld
ahoy əˈhɔɪ
ahungered əˈhʌŋ.ɡəd (US) -ɡɚd
AI ˌeɪˈaɪ
ai ˈɑː.i, aɪ
Aicken ˈeɪ.kᵊn
aid eɪd **-s** -z **-ing** -ɪŋ **-ed** -ɪd **-er/s** -əʳ/z (US) -ɚ/z ˌ**aid and a'bet**
Aïda, Aida aɪˈiː.də, ɑː-
Aidan ˈeɪ.dᵊn
aide eɪd **-s** -z
Aideed aɪˈdiːd
aide(s)-de-camp ˌeɪd.dəˈkɑ̃ː (US) -ˈkæmp
aide(s)-mémoire ˌeɪd.memˈwɑː (US) -ˈwɑːr
aid|-man ˈeid|.mən, -mæn **-men** -men, -mən
AIDS, Aids eɪdz
aigrette ˈeɪ.ɡret, eɪˈɡret **-s** -s
aiguille ˌeɪˈɡwiː, -ˈɡwiːl (US) ˌeɪˈɡwiːl, ˈ-- **-s** -z
Aiken ˈeɪ.kᵊn
aikido ˌaɪˈkiː.dəʊ, ˈaɪ.kɪ- (US) ˌaɪˈkiː.doʊ
Aikin ˈeɪ.kɪn, -kᵊn
Aikman ˈeɪk.mən
ail eɪl **-s** -z **-ing** -ɪŋ **-ed** -d
ailanthus ˌaɪˈlænt.θəs **-es** -ɪz
Aileen ˈeɪ.liːn (US) aɪˈliːn
aileron ˈeɪ.lᵊr.ɒn (US) -ə.rɑːn **-s** -z
Ailesbury ˈeɪlz.bᵊr.i (US) -ber-
ailment ˈeɪl.mənt **-s** -s
Ailred ˈeɪl.red, ˈaɪl-
Ailsa ˈeɪl.sə
ailuro- aɪˈljʊə.rəʊ-, eɪ-, ˈaɪ.ljʊə.rəʊ- (US) aɪˈlʊr.ə-
ailurophile aɪˈljʊə.rəʊ.faɪl, eɪ- (US) -ˈlʊr.ə- **-s** -z
ailurophobe aɪˈljʊə.rəʊ.fəʊb, eɪ- (US) -ˈlʊr.ə.foʊb **-s** -z
ailurophobia aɪˌljʊə.rəʊˈfəʊ.bi.ə, eɪ- (US) -ˌlʊr.əˈfoʊ-
aim eɪm **-s** -z **-ing** -ɪŋ **-ed** -d
aimless ˈeɪm.ləs, -lɪs **-ly** -li **-ness** -nəs, -nɪs
Ainger ˈeɪn.dʒəʳ (US) -dʒɚ
Ainsley, Ainslie ˈeɪnz.li
Ainsworth ˈeɪnz.wəθ, -wɜːθ (US) -wɚθ, -wɝːθ
ain't eɪnt
Aintree ˈeɪn.triː
Ainu ˈaɪ.nuː **-s** -z
aïoli, aioli aɪˈəʊ.li, eɪˈ- (US) -ˈoʊ-
air eəʳ (US) er **-s** -z **-ing/s** -ɪŋ/z **-ed** -d ˈ**air** ˌ**force**; ˈ**air ho**ˌ**stess**; ˈ**air** ˌ**letter**; ˈ**air** ˌ**pocket**; ˈ**air** ˌ**raid**; ˈ**air** ˌ**rifle**; ˈ**air** ˌ**route**; ˈ**air** ˌ**terminal**; ˌ**air traffic con'trol**; ˌ**air traffic con'troller**; ˌ**clear the 'air**
airbag ˈeə.bæɡ (US) ˈer- **-s** -z
airbase ˈeə.beɪs (US) ˈer- **-s** -ɪz
airbed ˈeə.bed (US) ˈer- **-s** -z
air-boat ˈeə.bəʊt (US) ˈer.boʊt **-s** -s
airborne ˈeə.bɔːn (US) ˈer.bɔːrn
airbrake ˈeə.breɪk (US) ˈer- **-s** -s
airbrick ˈeə.brɪk, ˈer-
airbridg|e ˈeə.brɪdʒ (US) ˈer- **-es** -ɪz
airbrush ˈeə.brʌʃ (US) ˈer- **-es** -ɪz **-ing** -ɪŋ **-ed** -d
air-burst ˈeə.bɜːst (US) ˈer.bɝːst **-s** -s
airbus (A®) ˈeə.bʌs (US) ˈer- **-es** -ɪz
air-check ˈeə.tʃek (US) ˈer- **-s** -s
air-condition ˈeə.kənˌdɪʃ.ᵊn, ˌeə.kənˈdɪʃ- (US) ˈer.kənˌdɪʃ- **-s** -z **-ing** -ɪŋ **-ed** -d **-er/s** -əʳ/z (US) -ɚ/z

Pronouncing the letters AI, AY

The vowel letter digraphs **ai** and **ay** are similar in that their most common pronunciation is /eɪ/, e.g.:

day /deɪ/
daily /ˈdeɪ.li/

However, in days of the week, **ay** is also frequently pronounced /i/, e.g.:

Monday /ˈmʌn.di/

When followed by an **r** in the spelling, **ai** and **ay** are pronounced as /eə, US er/, e.g.:

air /eəʳ/ US /er/
Ayr /eəʳ/ US /er/

In addition

There are other vowel sounds associated with the digraphs **ai** and ay, e.g.:

/e/ said, says /sed, sez/
/æ/ plait /plæt/
/aɪ/ aisle /aɪl/

And, in rare cases:

/eɪ.ɪ/ archaic /ɑːˈkeɪ.ɪk/ US /ɑːr-/

In weak syllables

The vowel digraphs **ai** and **ay** are realised with the vowels /ɪ/ and /i/ in weak syllables respectively, and **ai** may also result in a schwa vowel or a syllabic consonant, e.g.:

bargain /ˈbɑː.gɪn/ US /ˈbɑːr-/
Murray /ˈmʌr.i/ US /ˈmɝː-/
Britain /ˈbrɪt.ᵊn/

air-cool ˈeə.kuːl US ˈer- **-s** -z **-ing** -ɪŋ **-ed** -d
aircraft ˈeə.krɑːft US ˈer.kræft
aircraft|man ˈeə.krɑːft|.mən US ˈer.kræft- **-men** -mən
aircraft|woman ˈeə.krɑːft|ˌwʊm.ən US ˈer.kræft- **-women** -ˌwɪm.ɪn
aircrew ˈeə.kruː US ˈer- **-s** -z
Aird eəd US erd
airdate ˈeə.deɪt US ˈer- **-s** -s
Airdrie ˈeə.dri US ˈer-
Airdrieonian ˌeə.driˈəʊ.ni.ən US ˌer.driˈoʊ- **-s** -z
airdrome ˈeə.drəʊm US ˈer.droʊm **-s** -z
air-drop ˈeə.drɒp US ˈer.drɑːp **-s** -s **-ping** -ɪŋ **-ped** -t
air-dr|y ˈeə.dr|aɪ US ˈer- **-ies** -z **-ing** -ɪŋ **-ied** -d
Aire eəʳ US er
Airedale ˈeə.deɪl US ˈer- **-s** -z
air-engine ˈeəʳ.en.dʒɪn US ˈer- **-s** -z
airer ˈeə.rəʳ US ˈer.ɚ **-s** -z
Airey ˈeə.ri US ˈer.i
airfare ˈeə.feəʳ US ˈer.fer **-s** -z
airfield ˈeə.fiːld US ˈer- **-s** -z
airfleet ˈeə.fliːt US ˈer-
airflow ˈeə.fləʊ US ˈer.floʊ **-s** -z
air-foil ˈeə.fɔɪl US ˈer- **-s** -z
airgraph ˈeə.grɑːf, -græf US ˈer.græf **-s** -s
airgun ˈeəˌgʌn US ˈer- **-s** -z
airhead ˈeə.hed US ˈer- **-s** -z
airi|ly ˈeə.rɪ|.li, -rᵊl|.i US ˈer- **-ness** -nəs, -nɪs
airing ˈeə.rɪŋ US ˈer.ɪŋ **-s** -z ˈ**airing** ˌ**cupboard**
airless ˈeə.ləs, -lɪs US ˈer-
Airlie ˈeə.li US ˈer-
airlift ˈeə.lɪft US ˈer- **-s** -s **-ing** -ɪŋ **-ed** -ɪd
airlin|e ˈeə.laɪn US ˈer- **-es** -z **-er/s** -əʳ/z US -ɚ/z
airlock ˈeə.lɒk US ˈer.lɑːk **-s** -s
airmail ˈeə.meɪl US ˈer- **-s** -z
air|man ˈeə|.mən, -mæn US ˈer- **-men** -mən, -men
airmarshal ˈeəˌmɑː.ʃᵊl US ˈerˌmɑːr-
airmobile ˈeə.məʊ.biːl US ˈerˌmoʊ.bᵊl
airplane ˈeə.pleɪn US ˈer- **-s** -z
airplay ˈeə.pleɪ US ˈer-
airport ˈeə.pɔːt US ˈer.pɔːrt **-s** -s
air-sea ˌeəˈsiː US ˌer- *stress shift, see compound:* ˌ**air-sea** ˈ**rescue**
airship ˈeə.ʃɪp US ˈer- **-s** -s
airshow ˈeə.ʃəʊ US ˈer.ʃoʊ **-s** -z
airsick ˈeə.sɪk US ˈer- **-ness** -nəs, -nɪs
airspace ˈeə.speɪs US ˈer-
airspeed ˈeə.spiːd US ˈer- **-s** -z
airstream ˈeə.striːm US ˈer-
airstrike ˈeə.straɪk US ˈer- **-s** -s
airstrip ˈeə.strɪp US ˈer- **-s** -s
airtight ˈeə.taɪt US ˈer-
airtime ˈeə.taɪm US ˈer-
air-to-air ˌeə.tuˈeəʳ US ˌer.t̬əˈer, -tuˈ- *stress shift:* ˌair-to-air ˈmissile
air-to-surface ˌeə.təˈsɜː.fɪs US ˌer.t̬əˈsɝː.fəs *stress shift:* ˌair-to-surface ˈmissile
Airtours® ˈeə.tɔːz, -tʊəz US ˈer.tʊrz
air traffic ˈeəˌtræf.ɪk US ˈer-
airwave ˈeə.weɪv US ˈer- **-s** -z
airway ˈeə.weɪ US ˈer- **-s** -z
air|woman ˈeə|ˌwʊm.ən US ˈer- **-women** -ˌwɪm.ɪn
airworth|y ˈeəˌwɜː.ð|i US ˈerˌwɝː- **-iness** -ɪ.nəs, -ɪ.nɪs
air|y (A) ˈeə.r|i US ˈer|.i **-ier** -i.əʳ US -i.ɚ **-iest** -i.əst, -i.ɪst **-ily** -ɪ.li, -ə.li **-iness** -ɪ.nəs, -ɪ.nɪs
airy-fairy ˌeə.riˈfeə.ri US ˌer.iˈfer.i *stress shift:* ˌairy-fairy ˈconcept
Aisha aɪˈiː.ʃə
Aislaby ˈeɪz.lə.bi *locally:* ˈeɪ.zᵊl.bi
aisle aɪl **-s** -z **-d** -d
aitch eɪtʃ **-es** -ɪz
aitchbone ˈeɪtʃ.bəʊn US -boʊn **-s** -z
Aitchison ˈeɪ.tʃɪ.sᵊn
Aith eɪθ
Aitken ˈeɪt.kɪn, -kən
Aix eɪks, eks
Aix-en-Provence ˌeɪks.ɑ̃ːm.prəˈvɑ̃ːns, ˌeks- US -ɑːn.proʊˈvɑ̃ːs
Aix-la-Chapelle ˌeɪks.lɑː.ʃæpˈel, ˌeks-, -ʃəˈpel US -ʃɑːˈpel
Aix-les-Bains ˌeɪks.leɪˈbæ̃ː, ˌeks-, -ˈbæŋ
Ajaccio əˈjætʃ.i.əʊ, əˈdʒæs.i.əʊ US ɑːˈjɑː.tʃoʊ, -tʃi.oʊ
ajar əˈdʒɑːʳ US -dʒɑːr
Ajax *cleaning substance* ®ˈeɪ.dʒæks *football team:* ˈaɪ.æks
ajutage ˈædʒ.ʊ.tɪdʒ, əˈdʒuːt- US ˈædʒ.ə.t̬ɪdʒ, əˈdʒuː-
AKA, aka ˌeɪ.keɪˈeɪ, ˈæk.ə
Akaba ˈæk.ə.bə
Akabusi ˌæk.əˈbuː.si
Akahito ˌæk.əˈhiː.təʊ US ˌɑː.kəˈhiː.toʊ
Akbar ˈæk.bɑːʳ US -bɑːr
akela ɑːˈkeɪ.lə
Akenside ˈeɪ.kən.saɪd, -kɪn-
Akerman ˈæk.ə.mən US ˈ-ɚ-
Akers ˈeɪ.kəz US -kɚz

Akhmatova ək'mɑː.tə.və, ˌɑːk.mə'təʊ- (US) ʌk'mɑː.tə.və, ˌɑːk.mə'toʊ-
Akihito ˌæk.i'hiː.təʊ (US) ˌɑː.ki'hiː.toʊ
akimbo ə'kɪm.bəʊ (US) -boʊ
akin ə'kɪn
Akkad 'æk.æd (US) 'æk.æd, 'ɑː.kɑːd
Akkadian ə'keɪ.di.ən (US) -'keɪ-, -'kɑː- **-s** -z
Akond of Swat *former title of the Wali of Swat territory in Pakistan:* əˌkuːnd.əv'swɒt (US) -'swɑːt *name in poem by Edward Lear:* ˌæk.ənd.əv'swɒt (US) -'swɑːt
Akron 'æk.rɒn, -rən (US) -rən
Akrotiri 'æk.rəʊ'tɪə.ri (US) ˌɑːk.roʊ'tɪr.i
Akroyd 'æk.rɔɪd
al- əl-, æl-
Note: Prefix. Examples include **allocate** /'æl.ə.keɪt/, in which it is stressed, and **allure** /ə'ljʊər (US) -'lʊr/, where it is unstressed.
AL ˌeɪ'el
Al æl
-al -əl
Note: Suffix. When forming a noun, **-al** does not normally affect the stress pattern, e.g. **arouse** /ə'raʊz/, **arousal** /ə'raʊ.zəl/. In forming adjectives, however, the resulting item is usually either stressed one or two syllables before the suffix, e.g. **abdomen** becomes **abdominal** /æb'dɒm.ɪ.nəl (US) -'dɑː.mə-/, **adjective** becomes **adjectival** /ˌædʒ.ɪk'taɪ.vəl/.
Ala. *(abbrev. for* **Alabama***)* ˌæl.ə'bæm.ə, -'bɑː.mə (US) -'bæm.ə
à la 'æl.ɑː, 'ɑː.lɑː (US) 'ɑː.lɑː, 'ɑː.lə, 'æl.ə
Alabama ˌæl.ə'bæm.ə, -'bɑː.mə (US) -'bæm.ə
alabaster (A) ˌæl.ə'bæs.tər, -'bɑː.stər, 'æl.ə.bæs.tər, -bɑː.stər (US) 'æl.ə.bæs.tɚ
à la carte ˌæl.ə'kɑːt, ˌɑː.lɑː'- (US) ˌɑː.lə'kɑːrt, ˌæl.ə'-
alack ə'læk
alackaday ə'læk.ə.deɪ, əˌlæk.ə'deɪ
alacrity ə'læk.rə.ti, -rɪ.ti (US) -t̬i
Aladdin ə'læd.ɪn (US) -ən **Aˌladdin's 'cave**
Alagoas ˌæl.ə'gəʊ.əs (US) -'goʊ-
à la grecque ˌæl.ə'grek, ˌɑː.lɑː'- (US) ˌɑː.lə'-, ˌæl.ə'-
Alain *man's name:* æl'æ̃ (US) æl'ẽn *woman's name:* ə'leɪn
Alain-Fournier ælˌæ̃'fɔː.ni.eɪ *as if French:* -fʊə'njeɪ (US) -ˌẽn.fɔːr'njeɪ
Alameda æl.ə'miː.də, -'meɪ-
Alamein 'æl.ə.meɪn
Alamo 'æl.ə.məʊ (US) -moʊ
à la mode ˌæl.ə'məʊd, ˌɑː.lɑː-, -'mɒd (US) ˌɑː.lə'moʊd, ˌæl.ə'-
Alamogordo ˌæl.ə.mə'gɔː.dəʊ (US) -'gɔːr.doʊ
Alan 'æl.ən
Alana ə'lɑː.nə, -'læn.ə
Aland *islands:* 'ɑː.lənd, 'ɔː-
aland *(adv.)* ə'lænd
à l'anglaise ˌæl.ɑ̃ːŋ'gleɪz, ˌɑː.lɑ̃ːŋ'-, -'glez
alanine 'æl.ə.naɪn, -niːn
alar 'eɪ.lər, -lɑːr (US) -lɚ
Alaric 'æl.ə.rɪk
alarm ə'lɑːm (US) -'lɑːrm **-s** -z **-ing/ly** -ɪŋ/li **-ed** -d **a'larm ˌclock**
alarmist ə'lɑː.mɪst (US) -'lɑːr- **-s** -s
alarum ə'lær.əm, -'lɑː.rəm, -'leə- (US) -'ler.əm, -'lɑːr- **-s** -z
alas ə'læs, -'lɑːs (US) -'læs
Alasdair 'æl.ə.stər, -steər (US) -stɚ
Alask|a ə'læs.k|ə **-an/s** -ən/z
Alastair 'æl.ə.stər, -steər (US) -stɚ, -ster
Alastor ə'læs.tɔːr, æl'æs- (US) -tɔːr, -tɚ
alate 'eɪ.leɪt **-s** -s
alb ælb **-s** -z
Alba 'æl.bə
albacore 'æl.bə.kɔː (US) -kɔːr **-s** -z
Alba Longa ˌæl.bə'lɒŋ.gə (US) -'lɑːŋ.gə, -'lɔːŋ-
Alban 'ɔːl.bən, 'ɒl- (US) 'ɑːl-
Albani æl'bɑː.ni (US) ɑːl-, ɔːl-
Albani|a æl'beɪ.ni|.ə, ɔːl- **-an/s** -ən/z
Albany *in London:* 'ɔːl.bə.ni, 'ɒl-, 'æl- (US) 'ɑːl-, 'ɔːl- *in Australia:* 'æl.bə.ni (US) 'ɑːl.bə-, 'ɔːl- *in US:* 'ɔːl.bə.ni, 'ɒl- (US) 'ɑːl-
Albarn 'ɔːl.bɑːn, 'ɒl- (US) 'ɑːl.bɑːrn
albatross 'æl.bə.trɒs (US) -trɑːs, -trɔːs **-es** -ɪz
albedo æl'biː.dəʊ (US) -doʊ **-(e)s** -z
Albee 'ɔːl.biː, 'æl- (US) 'ɑːl-, 'ɔːl-, 'æl-
albeit ɔːl'biː.ɪt (US) ɔːl-, ɑːl-
Albemarle 'æl.bə.mɑːl, -bɪ- (US) -mɑːrl
Alberic 'æl.bə.rɪk
Alberich 'æl.bə.rɪk, -rɪx (US) -rɪk
Albers 'æl.bɜːz, 'ɔːl.bəz (US) 'æl.bɝːz, 'ɑːl.bɚz
albert (A) 'æl.bət (US) -bɚt **-s** -s **ˌAlbert 'Hall**
Alberta æl'bɜː.tə (US) -'bɝː.t̬ə
albertite 'æl.bə.taɪt (US) -bɚ-
Alberton 'æl.bə.tən (US) -bɚ-
albescen|ce æl'bes.ən|ts **-t** -t
Albi 'æl.bi
Albigenses ˌæl.bɪ'gent.siːz, -bɪ'dʒent-
albinism 'æl.bɪ.nɪ.zəm
albino æl'biː.nəʊ (US) -'baɪ.noʊ **-s** -z
Albinoni ˌæl.bɪ'nəʊ.ni (US) -'noʊ-
Albinus æl'biː.nəs
Albion 'æl.bi.ən
Albrecht 'æl.brekt, -brext (US) 'ɑːl.brekt
Albright 'ɔːl.braɪt, 'ɒl- (US) 'ɑːl-, 'ɔːl-
Albrighton 'ɔː.braɪ.tən, 'ɔːl-, 'ɒl- (US) 'ɑːl-
Albrow 'ɔːl.braʊ (US) 'ɑːl-
Albufeira ˌæl.bʊ'feə.rə (US) ˌɑːl.buː'feɪ.rə
Albula 'æl.bjʊ.lə (US) 'ɑːl.buː-, -bjuː-
album 'æl.bəm **-s** -z
albumen 'æl.bjʊ.mən, -men, -mɪn (US) æl'bjuː.mən
albumin 'æl.bjʊ.mɪn, -bjə.mɪn (US) æl'bjuː.mən
albuminoid æl'bjuː.mɪ.nɔɪd **-s** -z
albuminous æl'bjuː.mɪ.nəs
albuminuria ˌæl.bjuː.mɪ'njʊə.ri.ə (US) -'nʊr.i-, -'njʊr-
Albuquerque ˌæl.bə'kɜː.ki, 'æl.bəˌkɜː- (US) 'æl.bəˌkɝː- *esp. for person:* ˌ--'--
alburnum æl'bɜː.nəm (US) -'bɝː- **-s** -z
Albury 'ɔːl.bər.i, 'ɒl- (US) 'ɔːl-, 'ɑːl-
Alcaeus æl'siː.əs
alcaic (A) æl'keɪ.ɪk **-s** -s
alcalde æl'kæl.deɪ, -di (US) -'kɑːl.di, -deɪ **-s** -z
Alcan® 'æl.kæn
Alcatraz 'æl.kə.træz, ˌ--'-
Alcazar *Spanish palace:* ˌæl.kə'zɑː (US) 'æl.kə.zɑːr; æl'kæz.ɚ *music hall:* æl'kæz.ər (US) -ɚ
Alcester 'ɔːl.stər, 'ɒl- (US) 'ɔːl.stɚ, 'ɑːl-
Alcestis æl'ses.tɪs
alchemic æl'kem.ɪk **-al** -əl
alchemist 'æl.kə.mɪst, -kɪ- **-s** -s
alchemy 'æl.kə.mi, -kɪ-
Alcibiades ˌæl.sɪ'baɪ.ə.diːz
Alcinous ˌæl'sɪn.əʊ.əs (US) '-oʊ-
Alcmene ælk'miː.niː
Alcock 'æl.kɒk, 'ɔːl-, 'ɒl- (US) 'æl.kɑːk, 'ɑːl-, 'ɔːl-
alcohol 'æl.kə.hɒl (US) -hɑːl **-s** -z
alcoholic ˌæl.kə'hɒl.ɪk (US) -'hɑː.lɪk **-s** -s *stress shift:* ˌalcoholic 'drink
alcoholism 'æl.kə.hɒl.ɪ.zəm (US) -hɑː.lɪ-
Alconbury 'ɔːl.kən.bər.i, 'ɔː-, 'ɒl-, -kəm-, -bri (US) 'ɔːl.kən.ber.i, 'ɑːl-, -bɚ-
alcopop 'æl.kəʊ.pɒp (US) -koʊ.pɑːp **-s** -s
Alcott 'ɔːl.kət, 'ɒl-, -kɒt (US) 'ɑːl.kɑːt, 'æl-, -kət
alcove 'æl.kəʊv, 'ɒl- (US) 'æl.koʊv **-s** -z **-d** -d
Alcuin 'æl.kwɪn, 'ɒl- (US) 'æl-
Alcyone æl'saɪə.ni
Aldborough 'ɔːld.bər.ə, 'ɒl- *locally:* 'ɔː.brə (US) 'ɔːld.bɚ.oʊ, 'ɑːld-
Aldbury 'ɔːld.bər.i, 'ɒl- (US) 'ɔːld.ber-, 'ɑːld-, -bɚ-
Alde ɔːld (US) ɔːld, ɑːld
Aldebaran æl'deb.ə.rən, -ræn
Aldeburgh 'ɔːld.bər.ə, 'ɒl- (US) 'ɔːld.bɚ.oʊ, 'ɑːld-
aldehyde 'æl.dɪ.haɪd, -də- **-s** -z
Alden 'ɔːl.dən, 'ɒl- (US) 'ɔːl-, 'ɑːl-
Aldenham 'ɔːld.ən.əm, 'ɒl- (US) 'ɔːl-, 'ɑːl-

al dente æl'den.teɪ, ɑːl-
alder (A) 'ɔːl.dəʳ, 'ɒl- US 'ɔːl.dɚ, 'ɑːl- **-s** -z
Alderley Edge ˌɔːl.də.li'edʒ, ˌɒl- US ˌɔːl.dɚ-, ˌɑːl-
alder|man (A) 'ɔːl.də|.mən, 'ɒl- US 'ɔːl.dɚ-, 'ɑːl- **-men** -mən, -men
aldermanic ˌɔːl.də'mæn.ɪk, ˌɒl- US ˌɔːl.dɚ'-, ˌɑːl-
Aldermaston 'ɔːl.də.mɑː.stən US 'ɔːl.dɚ-, 'ɑːl-
aldern 'ɔːl.dən, 'ɒl-, -dɜːn US 'ɔːl.dɚn, 'ɑːl-
Alderney 'ɔːl.də.ni, 'ɒl- US 'ɔːl.dɚ-, 'ɑːl-
Aldersgate 'ɔːl.dəz.geɪt, 'ɒl-, -gɪt US 'ɔːl.dɚz-, 'ɑːl-
Aldershot 'ɔːl.də.ʃɒt, 'ɒl- US 'ɔːl.dɚ.ʃɑːt, 'ɑːl-
Alderson 'ɔːl.də.sᵊn, 'ɒl- US 'ɔːl.dɚ-, 'ɑːl-
Alderton 'ɔːl.də.tᵊn, 'ɒl- US 'ɔːl.dɚ-, 'ɑːl-
Aldgate 'ɔːl*d*.geɪt, 'ɒl-, -gɪt US 'ɔːl*d*-, 'ɑːl*d*-
Aldhelm 'ɔːld.helm, 'ɒl- US 'ɔːld-, 'ɑːld-
Aldi 'æl.di US 'ɑːl-
Aldine 'ɔːl.daɪn, ɒl-, -diːn US 'ɔːl-, 'ɑːl-
Aldington 'ɔːl.dɪŋ.tən, 'ɒl- US 'ɔːl-, 'ɑːl-
Aldis(s) 'ɔːl.dɪs, 'ɒl- US 'ɔːl-, 'ɑːl-
Aldous 'ɔːl.dəs, 'ɒl- US 'ɔːl.dəs, 'ɑːl-, 'æl-
Aldred 'ɔːl.drɪd, 'ɒl-, -dred US 'ɔːl-, 'ɑːl-
Aldrich 'ɔːl.drɪtʃ, 'ɒl-, -drɪdʒ US 'ɔːl-, 'ɑːl-
Aldridge 'ɔːl.drɪdʒ, 'ɒl- US 'ɔːl-, 'ɑːl-
Aldrin 'ɔːl.drɪn, 'ɒl- US 'ɔːl-, 'ɑːl-
Aldsworth 'ɔːldz.wəθ, 'ɒl-, -wɜːθ US 'ɔːldz.wɚθ, 'ɑːldz-, -wɝːθ
Aldus 'ɔːl.dəs, 'ɒl-, 'æl- US 'ɔːl-, 'ɑːl-
Aldwych 'ɔːld.wɪtʃ, 'ɒld- US 'ɔːld-, 'ɑːld-
ale (A) eɪl **-s** -z
aleatoric ˌæl.i.ə'tɒr.ɪk, ˌeɪ.li- US -'tɔːr-, -'tɑːr- **-ally** -ᵊl.i, -li
aleatory 'eɪ.li.ə.tᵊr.i, ˌæl.i'eɪ.tᵊr.i US 'eɪ.li.ə.tɔːr-
Alec(k) 'æl.ɪk, -lek
Alecto ə'lek.təʊ US -toʊ
Aled 'æl.ed, -ɪd
alehou|se 'eɪl.haʊ|s **-ses** -zɪz
Alemannic ˌæl.ɪ'mæn.ɪk, -ə'-
alembic ə'lem.bɪk **-s** -s
Alençon 'æl.ɑ̃ːn.sɔ̃ːŋ US ə'len.sən; ˌæl.ɑːn'soʊn
Aleppo ə'lep.əʊ, æl'ep- US -oʊ
a|lert ə|'lɜːt US -'lɝːt **-lerts** -'lɜːts US -'lɝːts **-lertly** -'lɜːt.li US -'lɝːt- **-lertness** -'lɜːt.nəs, -nɪs US -'lɝːt.nəs, -nɪs **-lerting** -'lɜː.tɪŋ US -'lɝː.t̬ɪŋ **-lerted** -'lɜː.tɪd US -'lɝː.t̬ɪd
Alessandria ˌæl.ɪ'sæn.dri.ə, -es'- US ˌɑː.lə'sɑːn-, ˌæl.ə'-, -'sæn-
Alessi ə'les.i
Alethea ˌæl.ə'θiː.ə; ə'liː.θi-; 'æl.ɪ.θi- US ˌæl.ɪ'θiː.ə; ə'liː.θi-
alethic æl'iː.θɪk, ə'liː-
Aletsch 'æl.ɪtʃ, 'ɑː.lɪtʃ, -letʃ US 'ɑː.letʃ
Aleut ə'ljuːt, -luːt; 'æl.juːt, -uːt US ə'luːt; 'æl.juːt, -i.uːt **-s** -s
Aleutian ə'ljuː.ʃən, -'luː- US -'luː-
A-level 'eɪ.lev.ᵊl **-s** -z
alewi|fe 'eɪl.waɪ|f **-ves** -vz
Alex 'æl.ɪks
Alexander ˌæl.ɪg'zɑːn.dəʳ, -eg'-, -əg'-, -'zæn-, -ɪk'sɑːn- US -'zæn.dɚ
Alex'ander tech,nique
Alexandra ˌæl.ɪg'zɑːn.drə, -eg'-, -əg'-, -'zæn-, -ɪk'sɑːn- US -'zæn-
Alexandria ˌæl.ɪg'zɑːn.dri.ə, -əg'-, -'zæn-, -ɪk'sɑːn-
alexandrian ˌæl.ɪg'zɑːn.dri.ən, -eg'-, -əg'-, -'zæn-, -ɪk'sɑːn- US -'zæn- **-s** -z
Alexandrina ˌæl.ɪg.zæn'driː.nə, -eg-, -əg'-, -zɑːn-, -ɪk.sɑːn'-
alexandrine ˌæl.ɪg'zæn.draɪn, -eg'-, -əg'-, -'zɑːn-, -ɪk'sɑːn- US -'zæn.drɪn, -'zæn.draɪn **-s** -z
alexia ˌeɪ'lek.si.ə, ə- US ə-
Alexis ə'lek.sɪs
Alf ælf
alfalfa ˌæl'fæl.fə
Alfa Romeo® ˌæl.fə.rəʊ'meɪ.əʊ US -roʊ'meɪ.oʊ
Alfie 'æl.fi
Alfonso æl'fɒn*t*.səʊ, -'fɒn.zəʊ US -'fɑːn*t*.soʊ, -'fɑːn.zoʊ
Alford 'ɔːl.fəd, 'ɒl- US 'ɔːl.fɚd, 'ɑːl-
Alfred 'æl.frɪd, -frəd
Alfreda æl'friː.də
Alfredian æl'friː.di.ən
alfresco, al fresco æl'fres.kəʊ US -koʊ
Alfreton 'ɔːl.frɪ.tᵊn, 'ɒl- US 'ɔːl.frɪ.tən, 'ɑːl-
Alfric 'æl.frɪk
Alfriston 'æl.frɪ.stən, 'ɔːl-
al|ga 'æl|.gə **-gae** -dʒiː, -dʒaɪ, -giː, -gaɪ
Algarve æl'gɑːv, 'æl.gɑːv US ɑːl'gɑːr.və
algebra 'æl.dʒɪ.brə, -dʒə- **-s** -z
algebraic ˌæl.dʒɪ'breɪ.ɪk, -dʒə'- **-al** -ᵊl **-ally** -ᵊl.i, -li *stress shift:* ˌalgebraic 'sum
algebraist ˌæl.dʒɪ'breɪ.ɪst, -dʒə'- **-s** -s
Algeciras ˌæl.dʒɪ'sɪə.rəs, -dʒə'-, -dʒes'ɪə-, -'sɪr.əs US -'sɪr-
Alger 'æl.dʒəʳ US -dʒɚ
Algeri|a æl'dʒɪə.ri|.ə US -'dʒɪr.i- **-an/s** -ən/z
Algerine ˌæl.dʒə'riːn
Algernon 'æl.dʒə.nən, -nɒn US -dʒɚ.nɑːn, -nən
Algiers æl'dʒɪəz US -'dʒɪrz
Algoa æl'gəʊ.ə US -'goʊ-
Algol, ALGOL 'æl.gɒl US -gɑːl
Algonquian æl'gɒŋ.kwi.ən, -ki.ən US -'gɑːŋ-, -'gɔːŋ-
Algonquin æl'gɒŋ.kwɪn, -kɪn US -'gɑːn-, -'gɔːŋ-
algorism 'æl.gᵊr.ɪ.zᵊm
algorithm 'æl.gᵊr.ɪ.ðᵊm **-s** -z
algorithmic ˌæl.gə'rɪð.mɪk *stress shift:* ˌalgorithmic de'sign
Algren 'ɔːl.grɪn, 'ɒl- US 'ɔːl-, 'ɑːl-
Algy 'æl.dʒi
Alhambra *in Spain:* æl'hæm.brə, əl-; ə'læm- *in California:* æl'hæm.brə
Ali *girl's name:* 'æl.i *boy's name and surname:* 'ɑː.li, ɑː'li
alias 'eɪ.li.əs, -æs **-es** -ɪz
Ali Baba ˌæl.i'bɑː.bə, ˌɑː.li-, -bɑː
alibi 'æl.ɪ.baɪ **-s** -z
Alicante ˌæl.ɪ'kæn.teɪ, -ti US -ti, -teɪ
Alice 'æl.ɪs ˌ**Alice 'Springs;** ˌ**Alice in 'Wonderland**
Alicia ə'lɪs.i.ə, -'lɪʃ.ə US -'lɪʃ.ə, -i.ə
Alick 'æl.ɪk
alien 'eɪ.li.ən **-s** -z **ing** -ɪŋ **-ed** -d **-age** -ɪdʒ
alienable 'eɪ.li.ə.nə.bl̩
alie|nate 'eɪ.li.ə|.neɪt **-nates** -neɪts **-nating** -neɪ.tɪŋ US -neɪ.t̬ɪŋ **-nated** -neɪ.tɪd US -neɪ.t̬ɪd **-nator/s** -neɪ.təʳ/z US -neɪ.t̬ɚ/z
alienation ˌeɪ.li.ə'neɪ.ʃᵊn **-s** -z
alien|ism 'eɪ.li.ə.nɪ|.zᵊm **-ist/s** -ɪst/s
a|light ə|'laɪt **-lights** -'laɪts **-lighting** -'laɪ.tɪŋ US -'laɪ.t̬ɪŋ **-lighted** -'laɪ.tɪd US -'laɪ.t̬ɪd
align ə'laɪn **-s** -z **-ing** -ɪŋ **-ed** -d
alignment ə'laɪn.mənt, -'laɪm- US -'laɪn- **-s** -s
alike ə'laɪk
aliment 'æl.ɪ.mənt **-s** -s
alimental ˌæl.ɪ'men.tᵊl US -t̬ᵊl
alimentary ˌæl.ɪ'men.tᵊr.i, '-tri US -t̬ᵊr.i, '-tri **ali,mentary ca'nal** US **ali'mentary ca,nal**
alimentation ˌæl.ɪ.men'teɪ.ʃᵊn
alimon|y 'æl.ɪ.mə.n|i US -moʊ- **-ies** -iz
A-line 'eɪ.laɪn
Aline *woman's name:* æl'iːn, ə'liːn; 'æl.iːn
alin|e ə'laɪn **-es** -z **-ing** -ɪŋ **-ed** -d
alineation əˌlɪn.i'eɪ.ʃᵊn **-s** -z
Alington 'æl.ɪŋ.tən
Ali Pasha ˌæl.i'pɑː.ʃə, ˌɑː.li-, -'pæʃ.ə US ˌɑː.li'pɑː.ʃɑː, ˌæl.i'-
aliqu|ant 'æl.ɪ.kw|ənt **-ot** -ɒt US -ɑːt
Alisha ə'lɪʃ.ə
Alison 'æl.ɪ.sᵊn
Alissa ə'lɪs.ə
Alistair, Alister 'æl.ɪ.stəʳ US -stɚ

alit ə'lɪt
Alitalia® ˌæl.ɪ'tæl.i.ə, ˌɑː.li'tɑː.li- (US) -jə
alive ə'laɪv
Alix 'æl.ɪks
alizarin ə'lɪz.ə.rɪn
alkahest 'æl.kə.hest
alkalescen|ce ˌæl.kᵊl'es.ᵊn|ts (US) -kə'les- **-cy** -*t*.si **-t** -t
alkali 'æl.kᵊl.aɪ (US) -kə.laɪ **-(e)s** -z
alkalic ˌæl'kæl.ɪk
alkalif|y æl'kæl.ɪ.f|aɪ **-ies** -aɪz **-ying** -aɪ.ɪŋ **-ied** -aɪd
alkaline 'æl.kᵊl.aɪn (US) -kə.laɪn
alkalinity ˌæl.kᵊl'ɪn.ə.ti, -ɪ.ti (US) -kə'lɪn.ə.t̬i
alkalization, **-isa-** ˌæl.kᵊl.aɪ'zeɪ.ʃᵊn, -ɪ'- (US) -ɪ'-
alkaliz|e, **-is|e** 'æl.kᵊl.aɪz (US) -kə.laɪz **-es** -ɪz **-ing** -ɪŋ **-ed** -d
alkaloid 'æl.kᵊl.ɔɪd (US) -kə.lɔɪd **-s** -z **-al** -ᵊl
alkane 'æl.keɪn **-s** -z
Alka Seltzer® ˌæl.kə'selt.səʳ (US) 'æl.kəˌselt.sɚ
alkene 'æl.kiːn **-s** -z
Alkoran ˌæl.kɒr'ɑːn, -kɔː'rɑːn, -kə'rɑːn (US) -kɔːr'ɑːn, -kə'rɑːn, -'ræn
alk|y 'æl.k|i **-ies** -iz
alkyl 'æl.kɪl (US) -kᵊl **-s** -z
alkyne 'æl.kaɪn **-s** -z
all ɔːl (US) ɔːl, ɑːl ˌ**all** '**fours**; ˌ**all** '**right**
alla breve ˌæl.ə'breɪ.veɪ, -vi (US) ˌɑː.lə'breɪ.vi, -veɪ
Allah 'æl.ə, -ɑː; ə'lɑː, æl'ɑː
Allahabad ˌæl.ə.hə'bɑːd, -'bæd
all-American ˌɔːl.ə'mer.ɪ.kᵊn (US) ˌɔːl-, ˌɑːl-
Allan 'æl.ən
Allan-a-Dale ˌæl.ən.ə'deɪl
Allandale 'æl.ən.deɪl
allantois ə'læn.təʊ.ɪs (US) -toʊ-
allantoides əˌlæn'təʊ.ɪ.diːz (US) ˌæl.ən'toʊ.ə-
Allard 'æl.ɑːd, -əd (US) -ɑːrd, -ɚd
Allardice, **Allardyce** 'æl.ə.daɪs (US) '-ɚ-
allargando ˌæl.ɑː'gæn.dəʊ (US) ˌɑː.lɑːr'gɑːn.doʊ
allative 'æl.ə.tɪv (US) -t̬ɪv
allay ə'leɪ **-s** -z **-ing** -ɪŋ **-ed** -d
All-Bran® 'ɔːl.bræn (US) 'ɔːl-, 'ɑːl-
Allbright 'ɔːl.braɪt, 'ɒl- (US) 'ɔːl-, 'ɑːl-
all-clear ˌɔːl'klɪəʳ (US) ˌɔːl'klɪr, ˌɑːl-
Allcock 'ɔːl.kɒk (US) 'ɔːl.kɑːk, 'ɑːl-
Allcroft 'ɔːl.krɒft, 'ɒl- (US) 'ɔːl.krɑːft, 'ɑːl-
allegation ˌæl.ɪ'geɪ.ʃᵊn, -ə'-, -eg'eɪ- **-s** -z
alleg|e ə'ledʒ **-es** -ɪz **-ing** -ɪŋ **-ed** -d
allegedly ə'ledʒ.ɪd.li, -əd-
Alleghany ˌæl.ɪ'geɪ.ni, -ə'- (US) -ə'-
Allegheny 'æl.ɪ.gen.i (US) ˌæl.ə'geɪ.ni
allegian|ce ə'liː.dʒᵊn|ts **-ces** -sɪz **-t** -t
allegoric ˌæl.ɪ'gɒr.ɪk, -ə'gɒr- (US) -'gɔːr- **-al** -ᵊl **-ally** -ᵊl.i, -li
allegorist 'æl.ɪ.gə.rɪst, '-ə- (US) -gɔːr.ɪst **-s** -s
allegoriz|e, **-is|e** 'æl.ɪ.gə.raɪz, '-ə- (US) -gɔː-, -gə- **-es** -ɪz **-ing** -ɪŋ **-ed** -d
allegor|y 'æl.ɪ.gə.r|i, '-ə- (US) -gɔːr|.i **-ies** -iz
allegretto ˌæl.ɪ'gret.əʊ, -ə'- (US) -'gret̬.oʊ **-s** -z
Allegri æl'eg.ri, -'eɪ.gri
allegro ə'leg.rəʊ, æl'eg-, -'eɪ.grəʊ (US) -'leg.roʊ, -'leɪ.groʊ **-s** -z
Allein(e) 'æl.ɪn
allele ə'liːl **-s** -z
allelic ə'liː.lɪk
allelism ə'liː.li.zᵊm
alleluia **(A)** ˌæl.ɪ'luː.jə, -ə'- **-s** -z
allemande 'æl.ə.mɑːnd, -mænd, -mɒnd (US) -mænd, -mɑːnd, -mæn, -mən **-s** -z
all-embracing ˌɔːl.ɪm'breɪ.sɪŋ, -em'- (US) ˌɔːl.em'-, ˌɑːl-, -ɪm'- *stress shift:* ˌall-embracing 'theory
Allen 'æl.ən, -ɪn '**Allen** ˌ**key**; '**Allen** ˌ**wrench**
Allenby 'æl.ən.bi
Allendale 'æl.ən.deɪl, -ɪn-
Allende aɪ'end.i, -eɪ (US) ɑː'jen.deɪ, ɑːl-
Allentown 'æl.ən.taʊn, -ɪn-
allergen 'æl.ə.dʒen, -dʒən (US) '-ɚ- **-s** -z
allergenic ˌæl.ə'dʒen.ɪk (US) -ɚ'-
allergic ə'lɜː.dʒɪk (US) -'lɝː-
allergist 'æl.ə.dʒɪst (US) '-ɚ- **-s** -s
allerg|y 'æl.ə.dʒ|i (US) '-ɚ- **-ies** -iz
Allerton 'æl.ə.tᵊn (US) '-ɚ.tən
allevi|ate ə'liː.vi|.eɪt **-ates** -eɪts **-ating** -eɪ.tɪŋ (US) -eɪ.t̬ɪŋ **-ated** -eɪ.tɪd (US) -eɪ.t̬ɪd **-ator/s** -eɪ.təʳ/z (US) -eɪ.t̬ɚ/z
alleviation əˌliː.vi'eɪ.ʃᵊn
alley 'æl.i **-s** -z '**alley** ˌ**cat**
Alleyn 'æl.ɪn
Alleyne æl'iːn, 'æl.ɪn, æl'eɪn
Alleynian ə'leɪ.ni.ən, æl'eɪ- **-s** -z
alleyway 'æl.i.weɪ **-s** -z
All Fools' Day ˌɔːl'fuːlz.deɪ (US) ˌɔːl-, ˌɑːl- **-s** -z
Allhallows ˌɔːl'hæl.əʊz (US) -oʊz, ˌɑːl-
allianc|e ə'laɪ.ən*t*s **-es** -ɪz
allicin 'æl.ə.sɪn, '-ɪ-
allied 'æl.aɪd
Allies 'æl.aɪz
alligator 'æl.ɪ.geɪ.təʳ (US) -t̬ɚ **-s** -z
all-important ˌɔːl.ɪm'pɔː.tᵊnt (US) ɔːl.ɪm'pɔːr-, ɑːl- *stress shift:* ˌall-important 'meeting
all-in ˌɔːl'ɪn (US) ˌɔːl-, ˌɑːl- *stress shift:* ˌall-in 'wrestling
all-inclusive ˌɔːl.ɪŋ'kluː.sɪv (US) -ɪn'-, ˌɑːl-, -ɪŋ'-
allineation əˌlɪn.i'eɪ.ʃᵊn, ælˌɪn- **-s** -z
Allingham 'æl.ɪŋ.əm
all-in-one ˌɔːl.ɪn'wʌn (US) ˌɔːl-, ˌɑːl- *stress shift:* ˌall-in-one sham'poo
Allison 'æl.ɪ.sᵊn
alliter|ate ə'lɪt.ᵊr|.eɪt, æl'ɪt- (US) ə'lɪt̬.ə.r|eɪt **-ates** -eɪts **-ating** -eɪ.tɪŋ (US) -eɪ.t̬ɪŋ **-ated** -eɪ.tɪd (US) -eɪ.t̬ɪd
alliteration əˌlɪt.ə'reɪ.ʃᵊn, ælˌɪt- (US) əˌlɪt̬- **-s** -z
alliterative ə'lɪt.ᵊr.ə.tɪv, æl'ɪt-, -eɪ- (US) ə'lɪt̬.ᵊr.ə.t̬ɪv, -ə.reɪ.t̬ɪv
Allman 'ɔːl.mən (US) 'ɔːl-, 'ɑːl-
all-nighter ˌɔːl'naɪ.təʳ (US) -t̬ɚ, ˌɑːl- **-s** -z
Alloa 'æl.əʊə (US) -oʊə
Allobroges ə'lɒb.rə.dʒiːz, æl'ɒb-, -rəʊ- (US) ə'lɑː.broʊ-
allo|cate 'æl.ə|.keɪt **-cates** -keɪts **-cating** -keɪ.tɪŋ (US) -keɪ.t̬ɪŋ **-cated** -keɪ.tɪd (US) -keɪ.t̬ɪd
allocation ˌæl.ə.keɪ.ʃᵊn **-s** -z
allocution ˌæl.ə'kjuː.ʃᵊn **-s** -z
allodi|al ə'ləʊ.di|.əl (US) -'loʊ- **-um** -əm
allogeneic ˌæl.əʊ.dʒə'niː.ɪk, -'neɪ- (US) ˌ-ə-, ˌ-oʊ- **-ally** -ᵊl.i
allokine 'æl.əʊ.kaɪn (US) '-ə- **-s** -z
allomorph 'æl.əʊ.mɔːf (US) -ə.mɔːrf, -oʊ- **-s** -s
Allon 'æl.ən
allopath 'æl.əʊ.pæθ (US) '-ə-, '-oʊ- **-s** -s
allopathic ˌæl.əʊ'pæθ.ɪk (US) -ə'-, -oʊ'-
allopath|y ə'lɒp.ə.θ|i, æl'ɒp- (US) ə'lɑː.pə- **-ist/s** -ɪst/s
allophone 'æl.əʊ.fəʊn (US) -ə.foʊn, -oʊ- **-s** -z
allophonic ˌæl.əʊ'fɒn.ɪk (US) -ə'fɑː.nɪk *stress shift:* ˌallophonic 'variant
all-or-nothing ˌɔːl.ɔː'nʌθ.ɪŋ, -ə'- (US) -ɔːr'-, ˌɑːl-, -ɚ'- *stress shift:* ˌall-or-nothing 'gamble
alloseme 'æl.əʊ.siːm (US) '-ə- **-s** -z
al|lot ə|'lɒt (US) -'lɑːt **-lots** -'lɒts (US) -'lɑːts **-lotting** -'lɒt.ɪŋ (US) -'lɑː.t̬ɪŋ **-lotted** -'lɒt.ɪd (US) -'lɑː.t̬ɪd
allotment ə'lɒt.mənt (US) -'lɑːt- **-s** -s
allotone 'æl.əʊ.təʊn (US) -ə.toʊn **-s** -z
allotrope 'æl.ə.trəʊp (US) -troʊp **-s** -s
allotropic ˌæl.ə'trɒp.ɪk (US) -'trɑː.pɪk
allotropy æl'ɒt.rə.pi, ə'lɒt- (US) ə'lɑː.trə-
all-out ˌɔːl'aʊt (US) ˌɔːl-, ˌɑːl- *stress shift:* ˌall-out 'effort
allow ə'laʊ **-s** -z **-ing** -ɪŋ **-ed** -d
allowab|le ə'laʊ.ə.b|l̩ **-ly** -li **-leness** -l̩.nəs, -nɪs
allowanc|e ə'laʊ.ən*t*s **-es** -ɪz **-ing** -ɪŋ **-ed** -t
Alloway 'æl.ə.weɪ
allowedly ə'laʊ.ɪd.li, -əd-
alloy (*n.*) 'æl.ɔɪ **-s** -z
alloy (*v.*) ə'lɔɪ **-s** -z **-ing** -ɪŋ **-ed** -d

Allophone

A variant of a phoneme.

Examples for English

Central to the concept of the PHONEME is the idea that it may be pronounced in many different ways. In English we take it for granted that the /r/ sound in *ray* and *tray* are "the same sound" (i.e. the same phoneme), but in reality the two sounds are very different – the /r/ in *ray* is voiced and non-fricative, while the /r/ sound in *tray* is voiceless and FRICATIVE. In phonemic transcription we use the same symbol /r/ for both (the slant brackets indicate that phonemic symbols are being used), but we know that the allophones of /r/ include the voiced non-fricative sound and the voiceless fricative one. Using the square brackets that indicate PHONETIC (allophonic) symbols, the former is [ɹ] and the latter [ɹ̥], e.g.:

ray	/reɪ/	[ɹeɪ]
tray	/treɪ/	[tɹ̥eɪ]

In theory a phoneme can have an infinite number of allophones, but in practice for descriptive purposes we tend to concentrate on the ones that occur most regularly and recognizably.

all-powerful ˌɔːlˈpaʊə.fəl, -fʊl ⓊⓈ -ˈpaʊɚ-, ˌɑːl- *stress shift:* ˌall-powerful ˈmonarch
all-purpose ˌɔːlˈpɜː.pəs ⓊⓈ ˌɔːlˈpɝː-, ˌɑːl- *stress shift:* ˌall-purpose ˈknife
all-round ˌɔːlˈraʊnd ⓊⓈ ˌɔːl-, ˌɑːl- *stress shift:* ˌall-round ˈathlete
all-rounder ˌɔːlˈraʊn.dəʳ ⓊⓈ -dɚ, ˌɑːl- **-s** -z
All Saints' Day ˌɔːlˈseɪntsˌdeɪ ⓊⓈ ˌɔːl-, ˌɑːl- **-s** -z
Allsop(p) ˈɔːl.sɒp ⓊⓈ ˈɔːl.sɑːp, ˈɑːl-
allsorts ˈɔːl.sɔːts ⓊⓈ -sɔːrts, ˈɑːl-
All Souls' Day ˌɔːlˈsəʊlzˌdeɪ ⓊⓈ ˌɔːlˈsoʊlz-, ˌɑːl- **-s** -z
allspice ˈɔːl.spaɪs ⓊⓈ ˈɔːl-, ˈɑːl-
all-star ˈɔːl.stɑːʳ ⓊⓈ ˈɔːl.stɑːr, ˈɑːl-
all-time ˌɔːlˈtaɪm ⓊⓈ ˈɔːl.taɪm, ˈɑːl- *stress shift, British only, see compound:* ˌ**all-time** ˈ**greats**
allud|e əˈluːd, -ˈljuːd ⓊⓈ -ˈluːd **-es** -z **-ing** -ɪŋ **-ed** -ɪd
Allum ˈæl.əm
allur|e əˈljʊəʳ, -ˈlʊəʳ, -ˈljɔːʳ ⓊⓈ -ˈlʊr **-es** -z **-ing/ly** -ɪŋ/li **-ed** -d **-ement/s** -mənt/s
allusion əˈluː.ʒən, əˈljuː- ⓊⓈ -ˈluː- **-s** -z
allusive əˈluː.sɪv, -ˈljuː- ⓊⓈ -ˈluː- **-ly** -li **-ness** -nəs, -nɪs
alluvi|al əˈluː.vi|.əl, -ˈljuː- ⓊⓈ -ˈluː- **-a** -ə
alluvion əˈluː.vi.ən, -ˈljuː- ⓊⓈ -ˈluː- **-s** -z
alluvi|um əˈluː.vi|.əm, -ˈljuː- ⓊⓈ -ˈluː- **-ums** -əmz **-a** -ə
Allworth ˈɔːl.wəθ, -wɜːθ ⓊⓈ -wɚθ, ˈɑːl-, -wɝːθ
Allworthy ˈɔːlˌwɜː.ði ⓊⓈ -ˌwɝː-, ɑːl-
all|y *(n.)* ˈæl.aɪ, əˈlaɪ **-ies** -z
all|y *(v.)* əˈl|aɪ, ælˈ|aɪ; ˈæl|.aɪ **-ies** -aɪz **-ying** -aɪ.ɪŋ **-ied** -aɪd
Note: **Allied** is usually pronounced /ˈæl.aɪd/ when attributive.
Ally ˈæl.i
-ally -əl.i, -li
Note: Suffix. Words containing **-ally** are stressed in the same manner as adjectives containing **-al**. Where the word ends **-ically**, two forms are possible, e.g. **musically** is either /ˈmjuː.zɪ.kəl.i/ or /ˈmjuː.zɪ.kli/.
Allyson ˈæl.ɪ.sən
Alma ˈæl.mə
Alma-Ata ˌæl.mɑː.əˈtɑː, ælˌmɑː-, ˌɑːl.məˈɑː.tə
Almack ˈɔːl.mæk, ˈɒl- ⓊⓈ ˈɔːl-, ˈɑːl-
almagest ˈæl.mə.dʒest **-s** -s
alma mater (A M) ˌæl.məˈmɑː.təʳ, -ˈmeɪ.təʳ ⓊⓈ -ˈmɑː.t̬ɚ, ˌɑːl- **-s** -z
almanac(k) ˈɔːl.mə.næk, ˈɒl-, ˈæl- ⓊⓈ ˈɔːl-, ˈɑːl-, ˈæl- **-s** -s
almandine ˈæl.mən.diːn, -dɪn **-s** -z
Almanzor ælˈmæn.zɔːʳ, -zəʳ ⓊⓈ -zɔːr, -zɚ
Alma-Tadema ˌæl.məˈtæd.ɪ.mə
Almeida ælˈmiː.də, -ˈmeɪ- ⓊⓈ -ˈmeɪ-
Almeria ˌæl.məˈri.ə
Almesbury ˈɑːmz.bər.i ⓊⓈ -ber-, -bɚ-
almight|y (A) ɔːlˈmaɪ.t|i ⓊⓈ -t̬|i, ɑːl- **-ily** -ɪ.li, -əl.i **-iness** -ɪ.nəs, -ɪ.nɪs
Almodovar ˌæl.məˈdəʊ.vɑːʳ, -ˈdɒ- ⓊⓈ -ˈdoʊ.vɑːr
Almon ˈæl.mən
almond (A) ˈɑː.mənd ⓊⓈ ˈɑː-, ˈɑːl-, ˈæl- **-s** -z
Almondbury ˈæl.mən*d*.bər.i, ˈɑː-, ˈɔː- ⓊⓈ ˈæl.mən*d*.ber.i, ˈɑː-, ˈɑːl-, -bɚ-
Almondsbury ˈɑː.mən*dz*.bər.i *locally also:* ˈeɪmz.bər.i ⓊⓈ ˈɑː.mən*dz*.ber.i, ˈɑːl-, -bɚ-
almoner ˈɑː.mə.nəʳ, ˈæl- ⓊⓈ ˈæl.mə.nɚ, ˈɑː-, ˈɑːl- **-s** -z
almonr|y ˈɑː.mən.r|i, ˈæl- ⓊⓈ ˈæl-, ˈɑː-, ˈɑːl- **-ies** -iz
almost ˈɔːl.məʊst, -məst ⓊⓈ ˈɔːl.moʊst, ˈɑːl-
alms ɑːmz
almsgiv|er ˈɑːmz.gɪ.v|əʳ ⓊⓈ -v|ɚ **-ers** -əz ⓊⓈ -ɚz **-ing** -ɪŋ
almshou|se ˈɑːmz.haʊ|s **-ses** -zɪz
Alne ɔːn
Alness ˈɔːl.nɪs, ˈæl-
Alnmouth ˈæln.maʊθ, ˈeɪl-
Alnwick ˈæn.ɪk
aloe ˈæl.əʊ ⓊⓈ -oʊ **-s** -z
aloe vera ˌæl.əʊˈvɪə.rə ⓊⓈ -oʊˈvɪr.ə
aloft əˈlɒft ⓊⓈ -ˈlɑːft
aloha əˈləʊ.hə, ælˈəʊ-, -hɑː, -ə ⓊⓈ əˈloʊ-
alone əˈləʊn ⓊⓈ -ˈloʊn **-ness** -nəs, -nɪs
along əˈlɒŋ ⓊⓈ -ˈlɑːŋ, -ˈlɔːŋ
alongside əˌlɒŋˈsaɪd ⓊⓈ əˈlɑːŋ.saɪd, -ˈlɔːŋ-, -ˌ-ˈ-
Alonso əˈlɒn*t*.səʊ, -ˈlɒn.zəʊ ⓊⓈ -ˈlɑːn*t*.soʊ, -ˈlɑːn.zoʊ
aloof əˈluːf **-ness** -nəs, -nɪs
alopecia ˌæl.əʊˈpiː.ʃə, ˈ-ʃi.ə ⓊⓈ -əˈ-, -oʊˈ-
aloud əˈlaʊd
Aloysius ˌæl.əʊˈɪʃ.əs, -ˈɪs.i.əs ⓊⓈ ˌæl.oʊˈɪʃ-, -ˈɪs.i.əs, -əˈwɪʃ.əs, -i.əs
alp (A) ælp **-s** -s
alpaca ælˈpæk.ə **-s** -z
Alpen® ˈæl.pən
alpenglow ˈæl.pən.gləʊ ⓊⓈ -gloʊ
alpenhorn ˈæl.pən.hɔːn, -pɪn- ⓊⓈ -hɔːrn **-s** -z
alpenstock ˈæl.pən.stɒk, -pɪn- ⓊⓈ -stɑːk **-s** -s
Alperton ˈæl.pə.tən ⓊⓈ -pɚ-
alpha ˈæl.fə **-s** -z ˈ**alpha** ˌ**particle**; ˈ**alpha** ˌ**ray**; ˈ**alpha** ˌ**rhythm**; ˈ**alpha** ˌ**wave**
alphabet ˈæl.fə.bet **-s** -s
alphabetic ˌæl.fəˈbet.ɪk ⓊⓈ -ˈbet̬- *stress shift:* ˌalphabetic ˈwriting
alphabetic|al ˌæl.fəˈbet.ɪ.k|əl ⓊⓈ -ˈbet̬- **-ally** -əl.i, -li ˌ**alphabetical** ˈ**order**, **alpha**ˌ**betical** ˈ**order**
alphabeticiz|e, -is|e ˌæl.fəˈbet.ɪ.saɪz ⓊⓈ -ˈbet̬.ə- **-es** -ɪz **-ing** -ɪŋ **-ed** -d
alphabetization, -isa- ˌæl.fə.bet.aɪˈzeɪ.ʃən ⓊⓈ -bet̬.ɪˈ-
alphabetiz|e, -is|e ˈæl.fə.bet.aɪz, -bə.taɪz, -bɪ- ⓊⓈ -bə.taɪz **-es** -ɪz **-ing** -ɪŋ **-ed** -d

Alveolar

Alveolar sounds are made with a place of articulation behind the upper front teeth, against the hard, bony ridge called the alveolar ridge; the skin covering it is corrugated with transverse wrinkles.

Examples for English

The tongue comes into contact with the alveolar ridge in some of the consonants of English and many other languages; sounds such as [t], [d], [s], [z], [n], [l] are consonants with alveolar place of articulation. Some examples for English follow, e.g.:

tip	/tɪp/	zip	/zɪp/
dip	/dɪp/	nip	/nɪp/
sip	/sɪp/	lip	/lɪp/

Although /r/ is described as alveolar or post-alveolar in British English, in US English it is in fact nearer to RETROFLEX, e.g.:

rip /rɪp/ [ɹɪʔp] (US) [ɻɪʔp]

Alpha Centauri ˌæl.fə.senˈtɔː.ri, -kenˈ-, -ˈtaʊ- (US) -senˈtɔːr.i

Alphaeus ælˈfiː.əs

alphanumeric ˌæl.fə.njuːˈmer.ɪk (US) -nuːˈ-, -njuːˈ- **-al** -ᵊl **-ally** -ᵊl.i, -li *stress shift:* ˌalphanumeric ˈcode

Alphonse ælˈfɒn*t*s, ˈ-- (US) ælˈfɑːn*t*s, -ˈfɔːn*t*s, ˈ--

Alphonso ælˈfɒn*t*.səʊ, -ˈfɒn.zəʊ (US) -ˈfɑːn*t*.soʊ, -ˈfɑːn.zoʊ

alpine (A) ˈæl.paɪn

alpin|ism ˈæl.pɪ.n|ɪ.zᵊm **-ist/s** -ɪst/s

Alps ælps

Al-Qaida, Al Qaeda ˌælˈkaɪ.də; ˌæl.kɑːˈiː.də (US) ˌælˈkeɪ.də, ˌɑːl-; ˌɑːlˈkaɪ.ə.də

already ɔːlˈred.i (US) ɔːl-, ɑːl- *stress shift:* ˌalready ˈhere

Alresford ˈɔːlz.fəd, ˈɔːls-, ˈɑːlz-, ˈɑːls- (US) -fɚd

alright ɔːlˈraɪt (US) ɔːl-, ɑːl-

Alsace ælˈsæs, -ˈzæs

Alsace-Lorraine ælˌsæs.lɒrˈeɪn, -ˈzæs (US) -loʊˈreɪn, -ˌseɪs-, -ləˈ-

Alsager ˈɔːl.sɪ.dʒəʳ, -sə.dʒəʳ, ɔːlˈseɪ.dʒəʳ (US) ˈɔːl.sə.dʒɚ, ˈɑːl-, ɔːlˈseɪ.dʒɚ, ɑːl-

Alsatia ælˈseɪ.ʃə, ˈ-ʃi.ə

alsatian (A) ælˈseɪ.ʃᵊn **-s** -z

also ˈɔːl.səʊ (US) ˈɔːl.soʊ, ˈɑːl-

Alsop(p) ˈɔːl.sɒp, ˈɒl-, -səp (US) ˈɔːl.sɑːp, ˈɑːl-

also-ran ˈɔːl.səʊˌræn (US) ˈɔːl.soʊ.ræn, ˈɑːl- **-s** -z

Alston ˈɔːl.stən, ˈɒl- (US) ˈɔːl-, ˈɑːl-

alt ælt, ɔːlt (US) ælt, ɑːlt

Altai ɑːlˈtaɪ

Altaic ælˈteɪ.ɪk

Altair ˈæl.teəʳ, -ˈ- (US) ælˈter, -ˈtær, -ˈtaɪr

altar ˈɔːl.təʳ, ˈɒl- (US) ˈɔːl.t̬ɚ, ˈɑːl- **-s** -z **ˈaltar ˌboy; ˈaltar ˌrail**

altarpiec|e ˈɔːl.tə.piːs, ˈɒl- (US) ˈɔːl.t̬ɚ-, ˈɑːl- **-es** -ɪz

AltaVista® ˌæl.təˈvɪs.tə, ˌɔːl- (US) ˌɑːl-, ˌæl-

altazimuth ælˈtæz.ɪ.məθ **-s** -s

Altdorf ˈælt.dɔːf (US) ˈɑːlt.dɔːrf, ˈælt-

alter ˈɔːl.təʳ, ˈɒl- (US) ˈɔːl.t̬ɚ, ˈɑːl- **-s** -z **-ing** -ɪŋ **-ed** -d **-able** -ə.bl̩ **-ant/s** -ᵊnt/s

alteration ˌɔːl.tᵊrˈeɪ.ʃᵊn, ˌɒl- (US) ˌɔːl.t̬əˈreɪ-, ˌɑːl- **-s** -z

alterative ˈɔːl.tᵊr.ə.tɪv, ˈɒl-, -tᵊr.eɪ- (US) ˈɔːl.t̬ə.reɪ.t̬ɪv, ˈɑːl-, -t̬ɚ.ə-

alter|cate ˈɔːl.tə|.keɪt, ˈɒl- (US) ˈɔːl.t̬ɚ-, ˈɑːl- **-cates** -keɪts **-cating** -keɪ.tɪŋ (US) -keɪ.t̬ɪŋ **-cated** -keɪ.tɪd (US) -keɪ.t̬ɪd

altercation ˌɔːl.təˈkeɪ.ʃᵊn, ˌɒl- (US) ˌɔːl.t̬ɚˈ-, ˌɑːl- **-s** -z

alter ego ˌɔːl.təʳˈiː.gəʊ, ˌɒl-, ˌæl-, -ˈeg.əʊ (US) ˌɔːl.t̬ɚˈiː.goʊ, ˌɑːl- **-s** -z

alternanc|e ɔːlˈtɜː.nən*t*s, ˈɒl- (US) ˈɔːl.tɝː-, ˈɑːl- **-es** -ɪz

alternant ɔːlˈtɜː.nənt, ɒl- (US) ˈɔːl.tɝː-, ˈɑːl- **-s** -s

alternate (*adj.*) ɔːlˈtɜː.nət, ɒl-, -nɪt (US) ɔːlˈtɝː-, ɑːl-; ˈɔːl.t̬ɚ-, ˈɑːl- **-ly** -li **-ness** -nəs, -nɪs

alter|nate (*v.*) ˈɔːl.tə|.neɪt, ˈɒl- (US) ˈɔːl.t̬ɚ-, ˈɑːl- **-nates** -neɪts **-nating** -neɪ.tɪŋ (US) -neɪ.t̬ɪŋ **-nated** -neɪ.tɪd (US) -neɪ.t̬ɪd

alternation ˌɔːl.təˈneɪ.ʃᵊn, ˌɒl- (US) ˌɔːl.t̬ɚˈ-, ˌɑːl- **-s** -z

alternative ɔːlˈtɜː.nə.tɪv, ɒl- (US) ɔːlˈtɝː.nə.t̬ɪv, ɑːl- **-s** -z **-ly** -li **alˌternative ˈmedicine**

alternator ˈɔːl.tə.neɪ.təʳ (US) ˈɔːl.tɚ.neɪ.t̬ɚ, ˈɑːl-, ˈæl- **-s** -z

Althea ˈæl.θi.ə (US) ælˈθiː-

Althorp ˈɔːl.θɔːp, ˈɒl-, -trəp (US) ˈɔːl.θɔːrp, ˈɑːl-

Note: Viscount Althorp pronounces /ˈɔːl.trəp/.

although ɔːlˈðəʊ (US) ɔːlˈðoʊ, ɑːl-

Althusser ˌæl.tʊˈseə (US) ˌɑːl.tuːˈser

altimeter ˈæl.tɪ.miː.təʳ, ˈɔːl-, ˈɒl-; ælˈtɪm.ɪ- (US) ælˈtɪm.ə.t̬ɚ, ˈæl.t̬ə.miː- **-s** -z

altimetry ælˈtɪm.ɪ.tri, ɔːl-, ɒl-, ˈ-ə- (US) ælˈtɪm.ə-

altissimo ælˈtɪs.ɪ.məʊ (US) -moʊ, ɑːl-

altitude ˈæl.tɪ.tjuːd, ˈɔːl-, ˈɒl-, -tʃuːd (US) ˈæl.tə.tuːd, -tjuːd **-s** -z

Altman ˈɔːlt.mən (US) ˈɔːlt-, ˈɑːlt-

alto ˈæl.təʊ, ˈɒl- (US) ˈæl.toʊ **-s** -z

altogether ˌɔːl.təˈgeð.əʳ (US) -ɚ, ˌɑːl- *stress shift:* ˌaltogether ˈmarvellous

Alton ˈɔːl.tᵊn, ˈɒl- (US) ˈɔːl-, ˈɑːl-

Altona ˈæl.təʊ.nə (US) ɑːlˈtoʊ-

Altoona ælˈtəʊ.nə (US) -ˈtuː-

alto-relievo, alto-rilievo ˌæl.təʊ.rɪˈliː.vəʊ (US) -toʊ.rəˈliː.voʊ, ˌɑːl-

Altrincham ˈɔːl.trɪŋ.əm, ˈɒl- (US) ˈɔːl-, ˈɑːl-

altru|ism ˈæl.tru|.ɪ.zᵊm **-ist/s** -ɪst/s

altruistic ˌæl.truˈɪs.tɪk **-ally** -ᵊl.i, -li *stress shift:* ˌaltruistic ˈaction

alum (A) ˈæl.əm **-s** -z

alumina əˈluː.mɪ.nə, ælˈuː-, -ˈljuː- (US) əˈluː-

aluminium ˌæl.jəˈmɪn.i.əm, -jʊˈ-, -ə-, ˈ-jəm *stress shift:* ˌaluminium ˈfoil

aluminiz|e, -is|e əˈljuː.mɪ.naɪz, əˈluː- (US) -ˈluː- **-es** -ɪz **-ing** -ɪŋ **-ed** -d

aluminous əˈluː.mɪ.nəs, -ˈljuː- (US) -ˈluː-

aluminum əˈluː.mɪ.nəm, -ˈljuː- (US) -ˈluː-

alumn|a əˈlʌm.n|ə **-ae** -iː

alumn|us əˈlʌm.n|əs **-i** -aɪ

Alun ˈæl.ɪn

Alva ˈæl.və

Alvar ˈæl.vɑːʳ, -vəʳ (US) -vɑːr, -vɚ

Alvarez ælˈvɑː.rez; ˈæl.və- (US) ˈæl.və.rez; ˈɑːl.vɑː.reθ

Alvary ˈæl.vᵊr.i

alveolar ˌæl.viˈəʊ.ləʳ; ælˈviː.ə-; ˈæl.vi- (US) ælˈviː.ə.lɚ **-s** -z

alveolate ælˈviː.ə.lət, -lɪt, -leɪt (US) -lɪt

alveole ˈæl.vi.əʊl (US) -oʊl **-s** -z

alveol|us ˌæl.viˈəʊ.l|əs; ælˈviː.ə-; ˈæl.vi.ə- (US) ælˈviː.ə- **-i** -aɪ, -iː

Alverstone ˈɔːl.və.stᵊn, ˈɒl- (US) ˈɔːl.vɚ-, ˈɑːl-

Alvescot ˈæl.vɪ.skɒt, -skət *locally:* ˈɔːl.skət (US) -skɑːt

Alveston ˈæl.vɪ.stən
Alvey ˈæl.vi
Alvin ˈæl.vɪn
alway ˈɔːl.weɪ, ˈɑːl-
always ˈɔːl.weɪz, -wəz, -wɪz US ˈɔːl-, ˈɑːl-
Alwyn ˈæl.wɪn, ˈɔːl-
Alyn ˈæl.ɪn, -ən
Alyson ˈæl.ɪ.sən
Alyssa ælˈɪs.ə
alyssum ˈæl.ɪ.səm
Alzheimer ˈælts.haɪ.məʳ US ˈɑːlts.haɪ.mɚ, ˈælts- **ˈAlzheimer's diˌsease**
a.m., AM ˌeɪˈem
am *strong form:* æm *weak forms:* əm, m
Note: Weak form word. The strong form /æm/ is used for emphasis (e.g. 'I **am** going to leave.'), for contrast (e.g. 'I know what I **am** and am **not** capable of.') and in final position (e.g. 'That's who I am.'). The weak form is usually /əm/ (e.g. 'How am I going to pay?' /ˌhaʊ.əm.aɪˌɡəʊ.ɪŋ.təˈpeɪ US -ɡoʊ.ɪŋ.t̬əˈ-/), but after 'I' /aɪ/ it is frequently shortened to /m/ (e.g. 'I am (I'm) here' /aɪmˈhɪəʳ US aɪmˈhɪr/).
AMA ˌeɪ.emˈeɪ
Amabel ˈæm.ə.bel
Amadeus ˌæm.əˈdeɪ.əs US ˌɑː.məˈdeɪ.ʊs, -əs
Amadis ˈæm.ə.dɪs
amadou ˈæm.ə.duː
amah ˈɑː.mə, ˈæm.ɑː US ˈɑː.mɑː **-s** -z
Amahl ˈæm.ɑːl US əˈmɑːl
amain əˈmeɪn
Amalekite əˈmæl.ə.kaɪt, ˈ-ɪ- US ˌæm.əˈlek.aɪt; əˈmæl.ə.kaɪt **-s** -s
Amalfi əˈmæl.fi, æmˈæl- US əˈmæl-, -ˈmɑːl
amalgam əˈmæl.ɡəm **-s** -z
amalga|mate əˈmæl.ɡə|.meɪt **-mates** -meɪts **-mating** -meɪ.tɪŋ US -meɪ.t̬ɪŋ **-mated** -meɪ.tɪd US -meɪ.t̬ɪd
amalgamation əˌmæl.ɡəˈmeɪ.ʃᵊn **-s** -z
amalgamative əˈmæl.ɡə.mə.tɪv US -t̬ɪv
Amalia əˈmɑː.li.ə, æmˈɑː- US əˈmeɪl.jə
Amalth(a)ea ˌæm.əlˈθiː.ə
Aman ˈæm.ən US ˈeɪ.mən
Amanda əˈmæn.də
amandine əˈmæn.daɪn; ˌɑː.mənˈdiːn US ˌɑː.mənˈdiːn, ˌæm.ənˈ-
Amantia əˈmæn.ʃi.ə
amanuens|is əˌmæn.juˈen*t*.s|ɪs **-es** -iːz
Amara əˈmɑː.rə
amaranth ˈæm.ᵊr.æn*t*θ US -ə.ræn*t*θ **-s** -s
amaranthine ˌæm.ᵊrˈæn*t*.θaɪn US -əˈræn*t*.θɪn, -θiːn, -θaɪn
amaretto (A) ˌæm.ᵊrˈet.əʊ US -əˈret̬.oʊ
Amarillo ˌæm.ᵊrˈɪl.əʊ US -əˈrɪl.oʊ
amaryllis (A) ˌæm.ᵊrˈɪl.ɪs US -əˈrɪl- **-es** -ɪz
Amasis əˈmeɪ.sɪs
amass əˈmæs **-es** -ɪz **-ing** -ɪŋ **-ed** -t
amateur ˈæm.ə.təʳ, -tɜːʳ, -tjʊəʳ, -tjəʳ, -tʃəʳ; ˌæm.əˈtɜːʳ US ˈæm.ə.tʃɚ, -tʃʊr, -t̬ɚ, -tɝː **-s** -z **ˌamateur draˈmatics**
Note: The final British form is not used attributively.
amateurish ˈæm.ə.tᵊr.ɪʃ, -tɜː.rɪʃ, -tjʊə-, -tjɔː-, -tjᵊr.ɪʃ, -tʃᵊr- US ˌæm.əˈtɝː.ɪʃ, -ˈtʃʊr-, -ˈtjʊr- **-ly** -li **-ness** -nəs, -nɪs
amateurism ˈæm.ə.tᵊr.ɪ.zᵊm, -tɜː.rɪ-, -tjʊə-, -tjɔː-, -tjᵊr.ɪ-, -tʃᵊr- US ˈæm.ə.tʃɚ.ɪ-, -tʃʊ.rɪ-, -t̬ɚ.ɪ-
Amati əˈmɑː.ti, æmˈɑː- US -t̬i **-s** -z
amatol ˈæm.ə.tɒl US -tɑːl
amatory ˈæm.ə.tᵊr.i US -tɔːr-
amaurosis ˌæm.ɔːˈrəʊ.sɪs US -ˈroʊ-
amaz|e əˈmeɪz **-es** -ɪz **-ed** -d **-edly** -ɪd.li **-edness** -ɪd.nəs, -nɪs **-ement/s** -mənt/s
amazing əˈmeɪ.zɪŋ **-ly** -li
amazon (A) ˈæm.ə.zᵊn US -zɑːn **-s** -z
Amazonia ˌæm.əˈzəʊ.ni.ə US -ˈzoʊ-
amazonian (A) ˌæm.əˈzəʊ.ni.ən US -ˈzoʊ-
amazonite ˈæm.ə.zə.naɪt **-s** -s
ambassador æmˈbæs.ə.dəʳ US -dɚ **-s** -z
ambassadorial æmˌbæs.əˈdɔː.ri.əl, ˌæm.bæs-
ambassadress æmˈbæs.ə.drəs, -drɪs, -dres US -drəs **-es** -ɪz
Ambato ɑːmˈbɑː.təʊ, æm- US -toʊ
amber (A) ˈæm.bəʳ US -bɚ
ambergris ˈæm.bə.ɡriːs, -bɚ.ɡrɪs
amberjack ˈæm.bə.dʒæk US -bɚ- **-s** -s
ambi- æm.bɪ-, æm.bi-; æmˈbɪ-
Note: Prefix. Normally either takes primary or secondary stress on the first syllable, e.g. **ambient** /ˈæm.bi.ənt/, **ambidextrous** /ˌæm.bɪˈdek.strəs/, or primary stress on the second syllable, e.g. **ambivalence** /æmˈbɪv.ᵊl.ən*t*s/.
ambianc|e ˈæm.bi.ən*t*s, -ɑ̃ːn*t*s US ˈæm.bi.ən*t*s, ˌɑːm.biˈɑːn*t*s **-es** -ɪz
ambidexter ˌæm.bɪˈdek.stəʳ US -stɚ **-s** -z
ambidexterity ˌæm.bɪ.dekˈster.ə.ti, -ɪ.ti US -ə.t̬i
ambidextrous ˌæm.bɪˈdek.strəs
ambienc|e ˈæm.bi.ən*t*s, -ɑ̃ːn*t*s US ˈæm.bi.ən*t*s, ˌɑːm.biˈɑːn*t*s **-es** -ɪz
ambient ˈæm.bi.ənt
ambiguit|y ˌæm.bɪˈɡjuː.ə.t|i, -ɪ.t|i US -bəˈɡjuː.ə.t̬|i **-ies** -iz
ambiguous æmˈbɪɡ.ju.əs **-ly** -li **-ness** -nəs, -nɪs
Ambiorix æmˈbaɪ.ə.rɪks US -ɚ.ɪks, -oʊ.rɪks
ambit ˈæm.bɪt **-s** -s
ambition æmˈbɪʃ.ᵊn **-s** -z
ambitious æmˈbɪʃ.əs **-ly** -li **-ness** -nəs, -nɪs
ambivalen|ce æmˈbɪv.ᵊl.ən|*t*s **-t/ly** -t/li
ambl|e (A) ˈæm.bl̩ **-es** -z **-ing** -ɪŋ, ˈæm.blɪŋ **-ed** -d **-er/s** -əʳ/z, ˈ-bləʳ/z US ˈ-bl̩.ɚ/z, ˈ-blɚ/z
Ambler ˈæm.bləʳ, ˈ-bl̩.əʳ US ˈ-blɚ, ˈ-bl̩.ɚ
Ambleside ˈæm.bl̩.saɪd
amboyna (A) æmˈbɔɪ.nə
Ambree ˈæm.bri
Ambridge ˈæm.brɪdʒ
Ambrose ˈæm.brəʊz, -brəʊs US -broʊz
ambrosi|a æmˈbrəʊ.zi|.ə, -ʒ|ə US -ˈbroʊ.ʒ|ə **-al** -əl **-ally** -ᵊl.i **-an** -ən
Ambrosius æmˈbrəʊ.zi.əs, -ʒəs US -ˈbroʊ.ʒəs
ambsace ˈeɪm.zeɪs, ˈæm-
ambulance ˈæm.bjə.lən*t*s, -bjʊ.lən*t*s, -bə- **-s** -ɪz **-man** -mæn **-men** -men **-woman** -ˌwʊm.ən **-women** -ˌwɪm.ɪn
ambulance-chaser ˈæm.bjə.lən*t*sˌtʃeɪ.səʳ, -bjʊ- US -sɚ **-s** -z
ambulant ˈæm.bjə.lənt, -bjʊ.lənt
ambu|late ˈæm.bjə|.leɪt, -bjʊ- **-lates** -leɪts **-lating** -leɪ.tɪŋ US -leɪ.t̬ɪŋ **-lated** -leɪ.tɪd US -leɪ.t̬ɪd
ambulation ˌæm.bjəˈleɪ.ʃᵊn, -bjʊˈ- **-s** -z
ambulator|y ˌæm.bjəˈleɪ.tᵊr|.i, -bjʊ-; ˈæm.bjə.lə-, -bjʊ- US ˈæm.bjə.lə.tɔːr-, -bjʊ- **-ies** -iz
ambuscad|e ˌæm.bəˈskeɪd **-es** -z **-ing** -ɪŋ **-ed** -ɪd
ambush ˈæm.bʊʃ **-es** -ɪz **-ing** -ɪŋ **-ed** -t
ameb|a əˈmiː.b|ə **-as** -əz **-ae** -iː **-ic** -ɪk
Amelia əˈmiː.li.ə US -ˈmiːl.jə, -ˈmiː.li.ə
amelior|ate əˈmiː.li.ᵊr|.eɪt US -ˈmiː.li.ə.r|eɪt, -ˈmiːl.jə- **-ates** -eɪts **-ating** -eɪ.tɪŋ US -eɪ.t̬ɪŋ **-ated** -eɪ.tɪd US -eɪ.t̬ɪd
amelioration əˌmiː.li.ᵊrˈeɪ.ʃᵊn US -ˌmiː.li.əˈreɪ-, -ˌmiːl.jəˈ- **-s** -z
ameliorative əˈmiː.li.ᵊr.ə.tɪv, -eɪ- US -ˈmiː.li.ə.reɪ.t̬ɪv, -ˈmiːl.jə-
amen ˌɑːˈmen, ˌeɪ- **-s** -z
amenability əˌmiː.nəˈbɪl.ə.ti, -ɪ.ti US -ə.t̬i
amenab|le əˈmiː.nə.b|l̩ US -ˈmiː.nə-, -ˈmen.ə- **-ly** -li **-leness** -l̩.nəs, -nɪs
Amen Corner ˌeɪ.menˈkɔː.nəʳ US -ˈkɔːr.nɚ
amend əˈmend **-s** -z **-ing** -ɪŋ **-ed** -ɪd
amendatory əˈmen.də.tᵊr.i US -tɔː.ri
amendment əˈmen*d*.mənt **-s** -s
amenit|y əˈmiː.nə.t|i, -ˈmen.ə-, -ɪ.t|i US əˈmen.ə.t̬|i **-ies** -iz

amenorrh(o)ea ˌeɪ.men.əˈriː.ə, ˌæm.en- (US) ˌeɪ.men-
Amerasian ˌæm.əˈreɪ.ʃən, -ʒən (US) -əˈreɪ.ʒən, -ʃən -s -z
amerc|e əˈmɜːs (US) -ˈmɝːs -es -ɪz -ing -ɪŋ -ed -t -ement/s -mənt/s
America əˈmer.ɪ.kə -s -z
American əˈmer.ɪ.kən -s -z -ist/s -ɪst/s **Aˌmerican Exˈpress®**
Americana əˌmer.ɪˈkɑː.nə (US) -ˈkæn.ə, -ˈkɑː.nə
Americanese əˌmer.ɪ.kəˈniːz (US) -ˈniːz, -ˈniːs
american|ism (A) əˈmer.ɪ.kə.n|ɪ.zəm -isms -ɪ.zəmz -ist/s -ɪst/s
americanization, -isa- (A) əˌmer.ɪ.kə.naɪˈzeɪ.ʃən, -nɪˈ- (US) -nɪˈ-
americaniz|e, -is|e (A) əˈmer.ɪ.kə.naɪz -es -ɪz -ing -ɪŋ -ed -d
americium ˌæm.əˈrɪs.i.əm, -ˈrɪʃ-
Amerindian ˌæm.əˈrɪn.di.ən -s -z
Amersham ˈæm.ə.ʃəm (US) -ɚ-
Amery ˈeɪ.mər.i
Ames eɪmz
Amesbury ˈeɪmz.bər.i (US) -ber.i
Ameslan ˈæm.ɪ.slæn
amethyst ˈæm.ə.θɪst, -ɪ.θɪst -s -s
amethystine ˌæm.əˈθɪs.taɪn, -ɪˈ- (US) -tən, -taɪn, -tɪn, -tiːn
Amex ˈæm.eks
AMF ˌeɪ.emˈef
Amharic æmˈhær.ɪk (US) -ˈhær-, -ˈhɑːr-
Amherst ˈæm.əst, -hɜːst (US) -ɚst, -hɝːst
amiability ˌeɪ.mi.əˈbɪl.ə.ti, -ɪ.ti (US) -ə.t̬i
amiab|le ˈeɪ.mi.ə.b|l̩ -ly -li -leness -l̩.nəs, -nɪs
amicability ˌæm.ɪ.kəˈbɪl.ə.ti, -ɪ.ti (US) -ə.t̬i
amicab|le ˈæm.ɪ.kə.b|l̩, əˈmɪk- -ly -li -leness -l̩.nəs, -nɪs
amic|e ˈæm.ɪs -es -ɪz
Amice ˈeɪ.mɪs
amid əˈmɪd
amide ˈæm.aɪd, ˈeɪ.maɪd (US) ˈæm.aɪd, -əd -s -z
amidships əˈmɪd.ʃɪps
amidst əˈmɪdst, -ˈmɪtst
Amiel ˈæm.i.əl, ˈeɪ.mi-
Amiens *French city:* ˈæm.jæ̃, -i.ɑ̃ː, -i.ɒŋ, -i.ənz *Shakespearean character:* ˈæm.i.ənz *street in Dublin:* ˈeɪ.mi.ənz
Amies ˈeɪ.miz
amiga (A®) əˈmiː.gə (US) əˈmiː.gə, ɑː- -s -z
amigo əˈmiː.gəʊ (US) -goʊ, ɑː- -s -z
Amin ɑːˈmiːn, æmˈiːn
amino əˈmiː.nəʊ, æmˈiː- (US) -noʊ **aˌmino ˈacid, aˈmino ˌacid**
amir əˈmɪəʳ (US) -ˈmɪr -s -z
Amis ˈeɪ.mɪs
Amish ˈɑː.mɪʃ, ˈæm.ɪʃ, ˈeɪ.mɪʃ (US) ˈɑːm-, ˈæm-
amiss əˈmɪs
amitosis ˌæm.ɪˈtəʊ.sɪs (US) -ˈtoʊ-
amitotic ˌæm.ɪˈtəʊ.tɪk (US) -ˈtoʊ-
amity ˈæm.ɪ.ti, -ə.ti (US) -ə.t̬i
Amlwch ˈæm.lʊk, -lʊx
Amman əˈmɑːn (US) ɑːˈmɑːn
Ammanford ˈæm.ən.fəd (US) -fɚd
ammeter ˈæm.iː.təʳ, -ɪ.təʳ (US) -t̬ɚ -s -z
ammo ˈæm.əʊ (US) -oʊ
Ammon ˈæm.ən, -ɒn (US) -ən
ammonia əˈməʊ.ni.ə (US) -ˈmoʊ.njə
ammoniac əˈməʊ.ni.æk (US) -ˈmoʊ-
ammoniacal ˌæm.əʊˈnaɪ.ə.kəl, -əˈ-
ammoniated əˈməʊ.ni.eɪ.tɪd (US) -ˈmoʊ.ni.eɪ.t̬ɪd
ammonification əˌməʊ.nɪ.fɪˈkeɪ.ʃən, -nə- (US) -mɑː-, -moʊ-
ammonif|y əˈməʊ.nɪ|.faɪ, -nə- (US) -ˈmɑː-, -ˈmoʊ- -ies -aɪz -ying -aɪ.ɪŋ -ied -aɪd -ier/s -aɪ.əʳ/z (US) -aɪ.ɚ/z
ammonite (A) ˈæm.ə.naɪt -s -s
ammonium əˈməʊ.ni.əm (US) -ˈmoʊ-
Ammons ˈæm.ənz
ammunition ˌæm.jəˈnɪʃ.ən, -jʊˈ- (US) -jəˈ-
amnesia æmˈniː.zi.ə, -ʒə (US) -ʒə
amnesiac æmˈniː.zi.æk (US) -ʒi- -s -s
amnesic æmˈniː.zɪk, -sɪk -s -s
amnest|y ˈæm.nə.st|i, -nɪ- -ies -iz **ˌAmnesty Interˈnational**
amniocentesis ˌæm.ni.əʊ.senˈtiː.sɪs, -sənˈ- (US) -oʊ-
amniotic ˌæm.niˈɒt.ɪk (US) -ˈɑː.t̬ɪk *stress shift:* ˌamniotic ˈmembrane
Amoco® ˈæm.ə.kəʊ; əˈməʊ- (US) ˈæm.ə-
amoeb|a əˈmiː.b|ə -ae -iː -as -əz -ic -ɪk
amoebiasis ˌæm.iːˈbaɪə.sɪs, -ɪˈ-
amok əˈmɒk, -ˈmʌk (US) -ˈmʌk, -ˈmɑːk
Amon ˈɑː.mən
among əˈmʌŋ
amongst əˈmʌŋst
Amon-Ra ˌɑː.mənˈrɑː
amontillado (A) əˌmɒn.tiˈjɑː.dəʊ, -tɪˈlɑː- (US) -ˌmɑːn.təˈlɑː.doʊ -s -z
amoral ˌeɪˈmɒr.əl, æmˈɒr- (US) ˌeɪˈmɔːr- -ly -li
Amoretti ˌæm.əˈret.i (US) -ˈret̬-, ˌɑː.məˈ-
amorett|o ˌæm.əˈret|.əʊ (US) -ˈret̬|.oʊ, ˌɑː.məˈ- -i -i
amorist ˈæm.ər.ɪst -s -s
Amorite ˈæm.ər.aɪt (US) -ə.raɪt -s -s
amorous ˈæm.ər.əs -ly -li -ness -nəs, -nɪs
amorph|ism əˈmɔː.f|ɪ.zəm (US) -ˈmɔːr- -ous -əs
amortizable, -isa- əˈmɔː.taɪ.zə.bl̩ (US) ˌæm.ɔːrˈtaɪ-
amortization, -isa- əˌmɔː.tɪˈzeɪ.ʃən, -təˈ- (US) æmˌɔːr.t̬əˈ- -s -z
amortiz|e, -is|e əˈmɔː.taɪz (US) æmˈɔːr- -es -ɪz -ing -ɪŋ -ed -d
amortizement, -ise- əˈmɔː.tɪz.mənt (US) ˈæm.ɚˈtaɪz.mənt, əˌmɔːr.t̬ɪz.mənt
Amory ˈeɪ.mər.i
Amos ˈeɪ.mɒs (US) -məs
a|mount ə|ˈmaʊnt -mounts -ˈmaʊnts -mounting -ˈmaʊn.tɪŋ (US) -ˈmaʊn.t̬ɪŋ -mounted -ˈmaʊn.tɪd (US) -ˈmaʊn.t̬ɪd
amour əˈmʊəʳ, æmˈʊəʳ, əˈmɔːʳ, æmˈɔːʳ (US) əˈmʊr, æmˈʊr -s -z
amour-propre ˌæm.ʊəˈprɒp.rə (US) ˌɑː.mʊrˈproʊ.prə, ˌæm.ʊrˈ-
Amoy əˈmɔɪ, æmˈɔɪ
amp æmp -s -s
ampelopsis ˌæm.pɪˈlɒp.sɪs (US) -ˈlɑːp-
amperage ˈæm.pər.ɪdʒ, -per-, -peə.rɪdʒ (US) ˈæm.prɪdʒ, -pɪ.rɪdʒ
ampère, ampere (A) ˈæm.peəʳ (US) -pɪr, -per -s -z
ampersand ˈæm.pə.sænd (US) -pɚ- -s -z
amphetamine æmˈfet.ə.miːn, -mɪn (US) -fet̬- -s -z
amphi- æmp.fɪ-; æmˈfɪ- (US) æmp.fɪ-, -fə-; æmˈfɪ-
Note: Prefix. Either takes primary or secondary stress on the first syllable, e.g. **amphora** /ˈæmp.fər.ə/, **amphibiotic** /ˌæmp.fɪ.baɪˈɒt.ɪk (US) -ˈɑː.t̬ɪk/, or primary stress on the second syllable, e.g. **amphibian** /æmˈfɪb.i.ən/.
amphibi|a æmˈfɪb.i|ə -ous -əs
amphibian æmˈfɪb.i.ən -s -z
amphibiotic ˌæmp.fɪ.baɪˈɒt.ɪk (US) -ˈɑː.t̬ɪk
amphibole ˈæmp.fɪ.bəʊl (US) -boʊl
amphibology ˌæmp.fɪˈbɒl.ə.dʒi (US) -ˈbɑː.lə-
amphiboll|y æmˈfɪb.ə.l|i -ies -iz
amphibrach ˈæmp.fɪ.bræk -s -s
Amphictyon æmˈfɪk.ti.ən -s -z
amphictyonic æmˌfɪk.tiˈɒn.ɪk (US) -ˈɑː.nɪk
amphimacer æmˈfɪm.ɪ.səʳ (US) -ə.sɚ
Amphion æmˈfaɪən
Amphipolis æmˈfɪp.ə.lɪs
amphitheatre, amphitheater ˈæmp.fɪˌθɪə.təʳ (US) -fəˌθiː.ə.t̬ɚ -s -z
Amphitrite ˌæmp.fɪˈtraɪ.ti (US) -t̬i
Amphitryon æmˈfɪt.ri.ən
amphor|a ˈæmp.fər|.ə -ae -iː -as -əz
amphoric æmˈfɒr.ɪk (US) -ˈfɔːr-
amphoteric ˌæmp.fəʊˈter.ɪk (US) -fəˈ-
ampicillin ˌæm.pɪˈsɪl.ɪn (US) -pəˈ-
amp|le ˈæm.p|l̩ -ler -ləʳ (US) -lɚ -lest -ləst, -lɪst -ly -li -leness -l̩.nəs, -nɪs
Ampleforth ˈæm.pl̩.fɔːθ, -fəθ
amplification ˌæm.plɪ.fɪˈkeɪ.ʃən, -plə- -s -z
amplificatory ˌæm.plɪ.fɪˈkeɪ.tər.i, -plə-, ˈ-tri (US) æmˈplɪf.ɪ.kə.tɔːr.i
amplifier ˈæm.plɪ.faɪ.əʳ (US) -ɚ -s -z

amplif|y ˈæm.plɪ.f|aɪ **-ies** -aɪz **-ying** -aɪ.ɪŋ **-ied** -aɪd

amplitude ˈæm.plɪ.tjuːd, -tʃuːd ⓤⓢ -tuːd, -tjuːd **-s** -z

ampoule ˈæm.puːl **-s** -z

Amps æmps

Ampthill ˈæmpt.hɪl

ampule ˈæm.pjuːl ⓤⓢ -pjuːl, -puːl **-s** -z

ampull|a æmˈpʊl|.ə **-ae** -iː

ampu|tate ˈæm.pjə|.teɪt, ˈæm.pjʊ- **-tates** -teɪts **-tating** -teɪ.tɪŋ ⓤⓢ -teɪ.t̬ɪŋ **-tated** -teɪ.tɪd ⓤⓢ -teɪ.t̬ɪd

amputation ˌæm.pjəˈteɪ.ʃᵊn, ˌæm.pjʊˈ- **-s** -z

amputee ˌæm.pjəˈtiː, -pjʊˈ- **-s** -z

Amram ˈæm.ræm

Amritsar æmˈrɪt.səʳ, -sɑːʳ ⓤⓢ -sɚ

Amsterdam ˌæmp.stəˈdæm, ˈ--ˌ- ⓤⓢ ˈæmp.stɚ.dæm

Note: In British English, the latter form is used when attributive.

Amstrad® ˈæm.stræd

Amtrak® ˈæm.træk

amuck əˈmʌk

amulet ˈæm.jʊ.lət, -jə-, -let, -lɪt **-s** -s

Amundsen ˈɑː.mənd.sᵊn, -mʊnd-

Amur əˈmʊəʳ, æmˈʊəʳ, ˈæm.ʊəʳ ⓤⓢ ɑːˈmʊr

amus|e əˈmjuːz **-es** -ɪz **-ing/ly** -ɪŋ/li **-ingness** -ɪŋ.nəs, -nɪs **-ed** -d

amusement əˈmjuːz.mənt **-s** -s **aˈmusement arˌcade; aˈmusement ˌpark**

Amway® ˈæm.weɪ

Amy ˈeɪ.mi

Amyas ˈeɪ.mi.əs

amygdalin əˈmɪg.də.lɪn, æmˈɪg-

amygdaloid əˈmɪg.də.lɔɪd

amyl ˈæm.ɪl, -əl **-s** -z

amylase ˈæm.ɪ.leɪz, ˈ-ə-, -leɪs

amylic æmˈɪl.ɪk, əˈmɪl-

amylopsin ˌæm.ɪˈlɒp.sɪn ⓤⓢ -ˈlɑːp-

amytal ˈæm.ɪ.tæl ⓤⓢ -tɑːl

an- æn-, ən-

Note: Prefix. When used as a negative prefix, **an-** is normally /æn-/, e.g. **anaerobic** /ˌæn.əˈrəʊ.bɪk ⓤⓢ -erˈoʊ-/, but in some items it may be reduced, e.g. **anomaly** /əˈnɒm.ə.li ⓤⓢ -ˈnɑː.mə-/. Otherwise, it contains /æ/ when stressed, e.g. **annular** /ˈænj.ə.ləʳ ⓤⓢ -lɚ/, and /ə/ when unstressed, e.g. **annul** /əˈnʌl/.

an *strong form:* æn *weak form:* ᵊn

Note: Weak form word. The strong form /æn/ is used mainly for contrast (e.g. 'This is **an** ideal, but it's not **the** ideal.'). The weak form is usually /ən/ (e.g., 'make an excuse' /ˌmeɪk.ən.ɪkˈskjuːs/); in rapid speech, and particularly after an alveolar or palatoalveolar consonant, it may be pronounced as a syllabic /n̩/ (e.g. 'find an example' /ˌfaɪnd.n̩.ɪgˈzɑːm.pl̩ ⓤⓢ -ˈzæm-/).

ana- æn.ə-, əˈnæ-

Note: Prefix. Either takes primary or secondary stress on the first syllable, e.g. **anagram** /ˈæn.ə.græm/, **anatomic** /ˌæn.əˈtɒm.ɪk/, or primary stress on the second syllable, e.g. **anachronism** /əˈnæk.rə.nɪ.zᵊm/.

ana (A) ˈɑː.nə

Anabapt|ism ˌæn.əˈbæp.t|ɪ.zᵊm **-ist/s** -ɪst/s

anabas|is əˈnæb.ə.s|ɪs **-es** -iːz

anabi|osis ˌæn.ə.baɪ|ˈəʊ.sɪs ⓤⓢ -ˈoʊ- **-otic** -ˈɒt.ɪk ⓤⓢ -ˈɑː.t̬ɪk

anabolic ˌæn.əˈbɒl.ɪk ⓤⓢ -ˈbɑː.lɪk *stress shift, see compound:* **ˌanabolic ˈsteroid**

anabolism əˈnæb.əʊ.lɪ.zᵊm ⓤⓢ -ᵊl.ɪ-

anachronism əˈnæk.rə.nɪ.zᵊm **-s** -z

anachronistic əˌnæk.rəˈnɪs.tɪk **-ally** -ᵊl.i, -li

anachronous əˈnæk.rə.nəs **-ly** -li

Anacin® ˈæn.ə.sɪn

anacoluth|on ˌæn.ə.kəʊˈluː.θ|ɒn, -ˈljuː-, -θ|ᵊn ⓤⓢ -kəˈluː.θ|ᵊn **-a** -ə

anaconda ˌæn.əˈkɒn.də ⓤⓢ -ˈkɑːn- **-s** -z

Anacreon əˈnæk.ri.ən ⓤⓢ -ɑːn, -ən

anacrus|is ˌæn.əˈkruː.s|ɪs **-es** -iːz

Anadin® ˈæn.ə.dɪn

anadiplosis ˌæn.ə.dɪˈpləʊ.sɪs ⓤⓢ -ˈploʊ-

anaemia əˈniː.mi.ə

anaemic əˈniː.mɪk

anaerobe ˈæn.ə.rəʊb, ˈæn.ɪ- ⓤⓢ -roʊb **-s** -z

anaerobic ˌæn.əˈrəʊ.bɪk, -eəˈ- ⓤⓢ -erˈoʊ-, -əˈroʊ-

anaesthesia ˌæn.əsˈθiː.zi.ə, -ɪsˈ-, -iːsˈ-, -ʒi-, ˈ-ʒə ⓤⓢ ˌæn.əsˈθiː.ʒə

anaesthesiology ˌæn.əsˌθiː.ziˈɒl.ə.dʒi, -ɪsˌ-, -iːsˌ-, -ʒiˈ- ⓤⓢ -ziˈɑː.lə-

anaesthetic ˌæn.əsˈθet.ɪk, -ɪsˈ-, -iːsˈ- ⓤⓢ -ˈθet̬- **-s** -s **-ally** -ᵊl.i, -li *stress shift:* ˌanaesthetic ˈmask

anaesthetist əˈniːs.θə.tɪst, ænˈiːs-, -θɪ- ⓤⓢ əˈnes.θə.t̬ɪst **-s** -s

anaesthetiz|e, -is|e əˈniːs.θə.taɪz, ænˈiːs-, -θɪ- ⓤⓢ əˈnes- **-es** -ɪz **-ing** -ɪŋ **-ed** -d

anaglyph ˈæn.ə.glɪf **-s** -s

anagram ˈæn.ə.græm **-s** -z

anagrammatic ˌæn.ə.grəˈmæt.ɪk ⓤⓢ -ˈmæt̬- **-al** -ᵊl **-ally** -ᵊl.i

Anaheim ˈæn.ə.haɪm

Anaïs ˌæn.aɪˈiːs

anal ˈeɪ.nᵊl **-ly** -i

analects ˈæn.ə.lekts

analeptic ˌæn.əˈlep.tɪk

analgesia ˌæn.əlˈdʒiː.zi.ə, -ælˈ-, -si- ⓤⓢ ˈ-ʒə

analgesic ˌæn.əlˈdʒiː.zɪk, -ælˈ-, -sɪk

analog ˈæn.ə.lɒg ⓤⓢ -lɑːg, -lɔːg **-s** -z

analogic ˌæn.əˈlɒdʒ.ɪk ⓤⓢ -ˈlɑː.dʒɪk **-al** -ᵊl **-ally** -ᵊl.i, -li

analogist əˈnæl.ə.dʒɪst **-s** -s

analogous əˈnæl.ə.gəs **-ly** -li **-ness** -nəs, -nɪs

analogue ˈæn.ə.lɒg ⓤⓢ -lɑːg, -lɔːg **-s** -z

analog|y əˈnæl.ə.dʒ|i **-ies** -iz

analphabetic ˌæn.æl.fəˈbet.ɪk ⓤⓢ -ˈbet̬- **-al** -ᵊl **-ally** -ᵊl.i, -li

anal-retentive ˌeɪ.nᵊl.rɪˈten.tɪv ⓤⓢ -t̬ɪv

analysable ˌæn.ᵊlˈaɪ.zə.bl̩ ⓤⓢ -əˈlaɪ-, ˈæn.ə.laɪ-

analysand əˈnæl.ɪ.sænd, ˈ-ə- **-s** -z

analys|e, -yz|e ˈæn.ᵊl.aɪz, -ə.laɪz **-es** -ɪz **-ing** -ɪŋ **-ed** -d

analys|is əˈnæl.ə.s|ɪs, -ɪ.sɪs **-es** -iːz

analyst ˈæn.ᵊl.ɪst ⓤⓢ -ə.lɪst **-s** -s

analytic ˌæn.ᵊlˈɪt.ɪk ⓤⓢ -əˈlɪt̬- **-s** -s **-al** -ᵊl **-ally** -ᵊl.i, -li *stress shift:* ˌanalytic ˈmind

analyzable ˌæn.ᵊlˈaɪ.zə.bl̩ ⓤⓢ -əˈlaɪ-, ˈæn.ə.laɪ-

analyz|e, -ys|e ˈæn.ᵊl.aɪz, -ə.laɪz **-es** -ɪz **-ing** -ɪŋ **-ed** -d

anamorphosis ˌæn.əˈmɔː.fə.sɪs; -mɔːˈfəʊ- ⓤⓢ -ˈmɔːr.fə-; -mɔːrˈfoʊ-

Anand ˈɑː.nənd

Ananias ˌæn.əˈnaɪ.əs

anap(a)est ˈæn.ə.pest, -piːst ⓤⓢ -pest **-s** -s

anap(a)estic ˌæn.əˈpes.tɪk, -ˈpiː.stɪk ⓤⓢ -ˈpes.tɪk

anaphor ˈæn.ə.fɔːʳ, -fəʳ ⓤⓢ -fɔːr **-s** -z

anaphora əˈnæf.ᵊr.ə **-s** -z

anaphoric ˌæn.əˈfɒr.ɪk ⓤⓢ -ˈfɔːr- *stress shift:* ˌanaphoric ˈreference

anaphrodisiac ˌæn.æf.rəʊˈdɪz.i.æk ⓤⓢ -roʊˈ- **-s** -s

anaptyctic ˌæn.əpˈtɪk.tɪk, -æpˈ-

anaptyxis ˌæn.əpˈtɪk.sɪs, -æpˈ-

Anapurna ˌæn.əˈpɜː.nə, -ˈpʊə- ⓤⓢ -ˈpɝː-, -ˈpʊr-

anarch ˈæn.ɑːk ⓤⓢ -ɑːrk **-s** -s

anarchic əˈnɑː.kɪk, ænˈɑː- ⓤⓢ ænˈɑːr-, əˈnɑːr- **-al** -ᵊl **-ally** -ᵊl.i, -li

anarchism ˈæn.ə.kɪ.zᵊm, -ɑː- ⓤⓢ -ɚ-, -ɑːr-

anarchist ˈæn.ə.kɪst, -ɑː- ⓤⓢ -ɚ-, -ɑːr- **-s** -s

anarchistic ˌæn.əˈkɪs.tɪk, -ɑːˈ- ⓤⓢ -ɚˈ-, -ɑːrˈ- *stress shift:* ˌanarchistic ˈviews

anarchy ˈæn.ə.ki, -ɑː- ⓤⓢ -ɚ-, -ɑːr-

Anastasia *English Christian name:* ˌæn.əˈsteɪ.zi.ə, ˈ-ʒə ⓤⓢ ˈ-ʒə *foreign name:* ˌæn.əˈstɑː.zi.ə ⓤⓢ ˈ-ʒə

Anastasius ˌæn.əˈstɑː.zi.əs, -ˈsteɪ- ⓤⓢ ˈ-ʒəs

anastigmat əˈnæs.tɪg.mæt, ænˈæs-; ˌæn.əˈstɪg- ⓤⓢ əˈnæs.tɪg-; ˌæn.əˈstɪg- **-s** -s
anastigmatic ˌæn.ə.stɪgˈmæt.ɪk; əˌnæs.tɪgˈ- ⓤⓢ əˌnæs.tɪgˈmæt̬-; ˌæn.ə.stɪgˈmæt̬-
anastomosis ˌæn.ə.stəˈməʊ.sɪs ⓤⓢ -ˈmoʊ-
anastrophe əˈnæs.trə.fi, ænˈæs- **-s** -z
anathema əˈnæθ.ə.mə, ænˈ-, ˈ-ɪ- **-s** -z
anathematization, -isa- əˌnæθ.ə.mə.taɪˈzeɪ.ʃən, ænˈ-, ˌ-ɪ-, -tɪˈ- **-s** -z
anathematiz|e, -is|e əˈnæθ.ə.mə.taɪz, ænˈ-, ˈ-ɪ- **-es** -ɪz **-ing** -ɪŋ **-ed** -d
Anatole ˈæn.ə.təʊl ⓤⓢ -toʊl
Anatoli|a ˌæn.əˈtəʊ.li|.ə ⓤⓢ -ˈtoʊ- **-an/s** -ən/z
anatomic ˌæn.əˈtɒm.ɪk ⓤⓢ -ˈtɑː.mɪk **-al** -əl **-ally** -əl.i, -li *stress shift:* ˌanatomic ˈdiagram
anatomist əˈnæt.ə.mɪst ⓤⓢ -ˈnæt̬- **-s** -s
anatomiz|e, -is|e əˈnæt.ə.maɪz ⓤⓢ -ˈnæt̬- **-es** -ɪz **-ing** -ɪŋ **-ed** -d
anatom|y əˈnæt.ə.m|i ⓤⓢ -ˈnæt̬- **-ies** -iz
Anaxagoras ˌæn.ækˈsæg.ə.rəs, -ræs ⓤⓢ -ɚ.əs
ANC ˌeɪ.enˈsiː
-ance -ənts
Note: Suffix. When attached to a free stem, **-ance** does not change the stress pattern of the word, e.g. **admit** /ədˈmɪt/, **admittance** /ədˈmɪt.ənts/. In other cases, the stress may be on the penultimate or antepenultimate syllable, e.g. **reluctance**/rɪˈlʌk.tənts/, **brilliance** /ˈbrɪl.i.ənts ⓤⓢ ˈ-jənts/. There are exceptions; see individual entries.
ancestor ˈæn.ses.təʳ, -sɪ.stəʳ, -sə- ⓤⓢ -ses.tɚ **-s** -z
ancestral ænˈses.trəl
ancestress ˈæn.ses.trəs; -sɪ.strəs, -ses.trɪs ⓤⓢ -ses.trɪs **-es** -ɪz
ancestr|y ˈæn.ses.tr|i, -sɪ.str|i, -sə- ⓤⓢ -ses.tr|i **-ies** -iz
Anchises ænˈkaɪ.siːz, æŋˈ-
anch|or ˈæŋ.k|əʳ ⓤⓢ -k|ɚ **-ors** -əz ⓤⓢ -ɚz **-oring** -ər.ɪŋ **-ored** -əd ⓤⓢ -ɚd
anchorag|e (A) ˈæŋ.kər.ɪdʒ **-es** -ɪz
anchoress ˈæŋ.kər.ɪs, -es, -əs **-es** -ɪz
anchoret ˈæŋ.kər.et, -ɪt **-s** -s
anchorhold ˈæŋ.kə.həʊld ⓤⓢ -kɚ.hoʊld **-s** -z
anchorite ˈæŋ.kər.aɪt ⓤⓢ -kə.raɪt **-s** -s
anchor|man ˈæŋ.kə|.mæn, -mən ⓤⓢ -kɚ- **-men** -men, -mən
anchorperson ˈæŋ.kəˌpɜː.sən ⓤⓢ -kɚˌpɝː-
anchor|woman ˈæŋ.kə|ˌwʊm.ən ⓤⓢ -kɚˌ- **-women** -ˌwɪm.ɪn
anchov|y ˈæn.tʃə.v|i, ænˈtʃəʊ- ⓤⓢ ˈæn.tʃoʊ-, -ˈ-- **-ies** -iz
ancien(s)-régime(s) ˌɑ̃ːnt.si.æ̃n.reɪˈʒiːm, ˌɑːnt-, ɒntˌsjæn- ⓤⓢ ˌɑːnt.si.æn-
ancient ˈeɪn.tʃənt ⓤⓢ ˈeɪnt.ʃənt **-est** -əst, -ɪst **-ly** -li **-s** -s ˌ**ancient** ˈ**Greek**; ˌ**ancient** ˈ**history**
ancillar|y ænˈsɪl.ər|.i ⓤⓢ ˈænt.sə.ler- **-ies** -iz
ancipit|al ænˈsɪp.ɪ.t|əl ⓤⓢ -t̬|əl **-ous** -əs
Ancona æŋˈkəʊ.nə ⓤⓢ ænˈ-, ɑːnˈ-, -ˈkoʊ-
Ancram ˈæŋ.krəm
Ancren Riwle ˌæŋ.krɪnˈri.ʊ.li, -krenˈ-, -krənˈ-, -lə
-ancy -ənt.si
Note: Suffix. Words containing **-ancy** are stressed in a similar way to those containing **-ance**; see above.
and *strong form:* ænd *weak forms:* ənd, ən, nd, n, m, ŋ
Note: Weak form word. The strong form /ænd/ is used for emphasis (e.g. 'The price included bed **and** breakfast.'), for contrast (e.g. 'It's not trick **and** treat, it's trick **or** treat.') or for citation (e.g. 'You should not begin a sentence with "and".').There are several weak pronunciations. In slow, careful speech the pronunciation may be /ənd/, but is more often /ən/ (e.g. 'Come and see.' /ˌkʌm.ənˈsiː/). In more rapid speech, when it occurs between consonants, the pronunciation may be a syllabic nasal consonant with a place of articulation assimilated to the neighbouring consonants (e.g. 'cut and dried' /ˌkʌt.n̩ˈdraɪd/; 'thick and creamy' /ˌθɪk.ŋ̍ˈkriː.mi/; 'up and back' /ˌʌp.m̩ˈbæk/).
Andalusi|a ˌæn.dəˈluː.si|.ə, -zi-, -lʊˈsiː|.ə ⓤⓢ -ˈluː.ʒ|ə, ˈ-ʒi|.ə, -ʃi- **-an** -ən
Andaman ˈæn.də.mæn, -mən
andante ænˈdæn.teɪ, -ti ⓤⓢ ɑːnˈdɑːn.teɪ, ænˈdæn.t̬i **-s** -z
andantino ˌæn.dænˈtiː.nəʊ ⓤⓢ ˌɑːn.dɑːnˈtiː.noʊ, ˌæn.dænˈ-
Andean ænˈdiː.ən, ˈæn.di.ən
Anderlecht ˈæn.də.lekt ⓤⓢ -dɚ-
Andersen, Anderson ˈæn.də.sən ⓤⓢ -dɚ-
Anderton ˈæn.də.tən ⓤⓢ -dɚ-
Andes ˈæn.diːz
Andhra Pradesh ˌæn.drə.prɑːˈdeʃ, -prəˈ-, ˌɑːn-, -ˈdeɪʃ
andiron ˈæn.daɪən ⓤⓢ -daɪɚn **-s** -z
Andizhan ˈæn.dɪ.ʒæn ⓤⓢ ˈɑːn.dɪ.ʒɑːn, ˈæn.dɪ.ʒæn
Andorra ænˈdɔː.rə, -ˈdɒr.ə ⓤⓢ -ˈdɔːr.ə
Andorra la Vella ænˌdɔː.rə.ləˈveɪ.jə ⓤⓢ -ˌdɔːr.ə.lɑːˈveɪl.jə
Andover ˈæn.dəʊ.vəʳ ⓤⓢ -doʊ.vɚ
Andow ˈæn.daʊ
Andrade ˈæn.dreɪd, -drɑːd
Andrassy ænˈdræs.i
Andre, André ˈɑ̃ːn.dreɪ, ˈɑːn-, ˈæn- ⓤⓢ ˈɑːn.dreɪ, ˈæn-, ˈɑ̃ː-
Andrea ˈæn.dri.ə; ænˈdreɪə ⓤⓢ ˈæn.dri.ə, ˈɑːn-; ænˈdreɪə, ɑːn-
Andrea del Sarto ænˌdreɪə.delˈsɑː.təʊ ⓤⓢ ɑːnˌdreɪə.delˈsɑːr.t̬oʊ, æn-
Andreas ˈæn.dri.əs, -dri.æs; ænˈdreɪəs ⓤⓢ ɑːnˈdreɪəs, æn-
Andrei ˈɒn.dreɪ, ˈæn- ⓤⓢ ˈɑːn.dreɪ, ˈæn-, ˈɑ-ˉ
Andrew ˈæn.druː
Andrewatha *Cornish family:* ænˈdruː.θə *Plymouth family:* ænˈdruː.ə.θə, ˌæn.druˈɒθ.ə ⓤⓢ -ˈɑː.θə
Andrews, Andrewes ˈæn.druːz
Andrex® ˈæn.dreks
Andria ˈæn.dri.ə ⓤⓢ ˈæn-, ˈɑːn-
andro- æn.drəʊ-; ænˈdrɒ- ⓤⓢ æn.drə-, -droʊ-; ænˈdrɑː-
Note: Prefix. Either takes primary or secondary stress on the first syllable, e.g. **androgen** /ˈæn.drəʊ.dʒən ⓤⓢ -drə-/ **androgenic** /ˌæn.drəʊˈdʒen.ɪk ⓤⓢ -drəˈ-/, or primary stress on the first syllable, e.g. **androgynous** /ænˈdrɒdʒ.ən.əs ⓤⓢ -drɑː.dʒən.əs/.
androcentric ˌæn.drəʊˈsen.trɪk ⓤⓢ -drəˈ-
Androcles ˈæn.drəʊ.kliːz ⓤⓢ -drə-
Androclus ænˈdrɒk.ləs ⓤⓢ -ˈdrɑː.kləs
androeci|um ænˈdriː.si|.əm ⓤⓢ -ʃi-, -si- **-ia** -ə
androgen ˈæn.drəʊ.dʒən, -dʒen, -dʒɪn ⓤⓢ -drə-, -droʊ- **-s** -z
androgenic ˌæn.drəʊˈdʒen.ɪk ⓤⓢ -drəˈ-, -droʊˈ-
androgenous ænˈdrɒdʒ.ən.əs, ˈ-ɪ.nəs ⓤⓢ -ˈdrɑː.dʒən.əs
androgynous ænˈdrɒdʒ.ɪ.nəs, -ən.əs ⓤⓢ -ˈdrɑː.dʒən-
androgyny ænˈdrɒdʒ.ɪ.ni, -ən.i ⓤⓢ -ˈdrɑː.dʒən-
android ˈæn.drɔɪd **-s** -z
Andromache ænˈdrɒm.ə.ki ⓤⓢ -ˈdrɑː.mə-
Andromeda ænˈdrɒm.ɪ.də, -ə.də ⓤⓢ -ˈdrɑː.mə-
Andronicus *Byzantine emperors and other figures in ancient history:* ˌæn.drəˈnaɪ.kəs, ænˈdrɒn.ɪ.kəs ⓤⓢ -ˈdrɑː.nə- *in Shakespeare's* **Titus Andronicus**: ænˈdrɒn.ɪ.kəs ⓤⓢ -ˈdrɑː.nɪ-

Andropov ˈæn.drə.pɒf, ænˈdrɒp.ɒf, -əf (US) ɑːnˈdrɔː.pəf, -ˈdroʊ-, -pɔːf
Andros ˈæn.drɒs (US) -ˈdrɑːs
Andvari ænˈdwɑː.ri (US) ɑːn-
Andy ˈæn.di
-ane -eɪn
Note: Suffix. Does not normally affect word stress, e.g. **alkane** /ˈæl.keɪn/.
anecdotage ˈæn.ɪk.dəʊ.tɪdʒ, -ək- (US) -doʊ.t̬ɪdʒ
anecdotal ˌæn.ɪkˈdəʊ.tᵊl, -ək- (US) -ˈdoʊ.t̬ᵊl
anecdote ˈæn.ɪk.dəʊt, -ək- (US) -doʊt **-s** -s
anecdotic ˌæn.ɪkˈdəʊ.tɪk, -ek-, -ək-, -ˈdɒt- (US) -ɪkˈdɑː.t̬ɪk **-al** -ᵊl **-ally** -ᵊl.i, -li
anechoic ˌæn.ɪˈkəʊ.ɪk, -ekˈəʊ-, -əˈkəʊ- (US) -əˈkoʊ-, -ɪˈ-, -ekˈoʊ- *stress shift:* ˌanechoic ˈchamber
anelectric ˌæn.ɪˈlek.trɪk, -əˈlek- **-s** -s
anelectrode ˌæn.ɪˈlek.trəʊd, -əˈlek- (US) -troʊd **-s** -z
anemia əˈniː.mi.ə
anemic əˈniː.mɪk
anemometer ˌæn.ɪˈmɒm.ɪ.təʳ, -ə.təʳ (US) -ˈmɑː.mə.t̬ɚ **-s** -z
anemometric ˌæn.ɪ.məʊˈmet.rɪk (US) -moʊˈ-
anemometry ˌæn.ɪˈmɒm.ɪ.tri, -ə.tri (US) -ˈmɑː.mə-
anemone əˈnem.ə.ni **-s** -z
anemoscope əˈnem.ə.skəʊp (US) -skoʊp **-s** -s
anent əˈnent
aneroid ˈæn.ə.rɔɪd, -ɪ.rɔɪd **-s** -z
anesthesia ˌæn.əsˈθiː.zi.ə, -ɪsˈ-, -iːsˈ-, -ʒi-, ˈ-ʒə (US) ˈ-ʒə
anesthesiolog|y ˌæn.əsˌθiː.ziˈɒl.ə.dʒ|i, -ɪsˌ-, -iːsˌ-, -ʒiˈ- (US) -ziˈɑː.lə- **-ist/s** -ɪst/s
anesthetic ˌæn.əsˈθet.ɪk, -ɪsˈ-, -iːsˈ- (US) -θet̬- **-s** -s **-ally** -ᵊl.i, -li *stress shift:* ˌanesthetic ˈmask
anesthetist əˈniːs.θə.tɪst, ænˈiːs-, -θɪ- (US) əˈnes.θə.t̬ɪst **-s** -s
anesthetiz|e, -is|e əˈniːs.θə.taɪz, ænˈiːs-, -θɪ- (US) əˈnes.θə- **-es** -ɪz **-ing** -ɪŋ **-ed** -d
aneurin əˈnjʊər.ɪn, -ˈnjʊə.rɪn (US) ˈæn.jɚ.ɪn, -jʊ.rɪn
Aneurin əˈnaɪə.rɪn (US) -ˈnaɪ-
aneurism ˈæn.jʊə.rɪ.zᵊm (US) ˈæn.jɚ.ɪ-, -jʊ.rɪ- **-s** -z
aneurismal ˌæn.jʊəˈrɪz.məl (US) -jəˈ-, -jʊˈ-
aneurysm ˈæn.jʊə.rɪ.zᵊm (US) -jɚ.ɪ-, -jʊ.rɪ- **-s** -z
aneurysmal ˌæn.jʊəˈrɪz.məl (US) -jəˈ-, -jʊˈ-
anew əˈnjuː (US) -ˈnuː, -ˈnjuː
Anfield ˈæn.fiːld
anfractuosity ˌæn.fræk.tjuˈɒs.ə.ti, -ɪ.ti (US) -tʃuˈɑː.sə.t̬i
angel (A) ˈeɪn.dʒᵊl **-s** -z ˈ**angel** ˌ**dust**
Angela ˈæn.dʒᵊl.ə, -dʒɪ.lə
Angeleno ˌæn.dʒᵊlˈiː.nəʊ (US) -dʒəˈliː.noʊ
Angeles ˈæn.dʒᵊl.iːz, -dʒɪ.liːz, -liz, -lis (US) -dʒᵊl.əs, -dʒə.liːz
angelfish ˈeɪn.dʒᵊl.fɪʃ **-es** -ɪz
angel-food cake ˌeɪn.dʒᵊlˈfuːdˌkeɪk (US) ˈeɪn.dʒᵊlˌfuːd-
angelic ænˈdʒel.ɪk **-al** -ᵊl **-ally** -ᵊl.i, -li
angelica (A) ænˈdʒel.ɪ.kə
Angelico ænˈdʒel.ɪ.kəʊ (US) -koʊ
Angelina ˌæn.dʒᵊlˈiː.nə, -dʒelˈ- (US) -dʒəˈliː-, -dʒelˈiː-
Angelo ˈæn.dʒᵊl.əʊ, -dʒɪ.ləʊ (US) -dʒə.loʊ
Angelou ˈæn.dʒᵊl.uː (US) -dʒə.luː, -loʊ
angelus (A) ˈæn.dʒᵊl.əs, -dʒɪ.ləs **-es** -ɪz
ang|er ˈæŋ.g|əʳ (US) -g|ɚ **-ers** -əz (US) -ɚz **-ering** -ᵊr.ɪŋ **-ered** -əd (US) -ɚd
Angers ɑ̃ːnˈʒeɪ
Angevin ˈæn.dʒɪ.vɪn, -dʒə-
Angharad æŋˈhær.əd, æn-; ˈæŋ.ᵊr- (US) æŋˈher-, æn- (US) -ˈhær-
Angie ˈæn.dʒi
Angier ˈæn.dʒɪəʳ
angina ænˈdʒaɪ.nə **-s** -z
angiogram ˈæn.dʒi.əʊ.græm (US) -ə-, -oʊ- **-s** -z
angiographic ˌæn.dʒi.əʊˈgræf.ɪk (US) -əˈ-, -oʊˈ-
angiography ˌæn.dʒiˈɒg.rə.fi (US) -ˈɑː.grə-
angioplasty ˈæn.dʒi.əʊ.plæs.ti (US) -ə-, -oʊ-
angiosperm ˈæn.dʒi.əʊ.spɜːm (US) -ə.spɝːm, -oʊ- **-s** -z
Angkor Thom ˌæŋ.kɔːˈtɔːm (US) -kɔːrˈtɑːm
angl|e (A) ˈæŋ.gl̩ **-es** -z **-ing** -ɪŋ, ˈ-glɪŋ **-ed** -d
Anglepoise® ˈæŋ.gl̩.pɔɪz ˌ**Anglepoise** ˈ**lamp** (US) ˈ**Anglepoise** ˌ**lamp**
angler ˈæŋ.gləʳ, -gl̩.əʳ (US) ˈ-glɚ, -gl̩.ɚ **-s** -z
Anglesea ˈæŋ.gl̩.si, -siː
Anglesey ˈæŋ.gl̩.si, -siː
Angli|a ˈæŋ.gli|.ə **-an/s** -ən/z
Anglican ˈæŋ.glɪ.kən **-s** -z **-ism** -ɪ.zᵊm
anglice ˈæŋ.glɪ.si, -glə-
anglicism ˈæŋ.glɪ.sɪ.zᵊm, -glə- **-s** -z
anglicist ˈæŋ.glɪ.sɪst, -glə- **-s** -s
anglicization, -isa- ˌæŋ.glɪ.saɪˈzeɪ.ʃᵊn, -glə-, -ɪˈ- (US) -ɪˈ-
angliciz|e, -is|e ˈæŋ.glɪ.saɪz, -glə- **-es** -ɪz **-ing** -ɪŋ **-ed** -d
angling ˈæŋ.glɪŋ, -gl̩.ɪŋ
Anglo- æŋ.gləʊ- (US) æŋ.gloʊ-
Note: Prefix. Words containing **anglo-** normally carry either primary or secondary stress on the first syllable, e.g. **anglophobe** /ˈæŋ.gləʊ.fəʊb (US) -gloʊ.foʊb/, **anglophobia** /ˌæŋ.gləʊˈfəʊ.bi.ə (US) -gloʊˈfoʊ-/. Where the prefix is used to mean "English and ...", it usually carries secondary stress, e.g. **Anglo-French** /ˌæŋ.gləʊˈfrentʃ (US) -gloʊˈ-/.
Anglo ˈæŋ.gləʊ (US) -gloʊ **-s** -z
Anglo-American ˌæŋ.gləʊ.əˈmer.ɪ.kən (US) -gloʊ- **-s** -z
Anglo-French ˌæŋ.gləʊˈfrentʃ (US) -gloʊˈ-
Anglo-Irish ˌæŋ.gləʊˈaɪə.rɪʃ (US) -gloʊˈaɪ-
anglomania ˌæŋ.gləʊˈmeɪ.ni.ə (US) -gloʊˈ-
Anglo-Norman ˌæŋ.gləʊˈnɔː.mən (US) -gloʊˈnɔːr-
anglophile (A) ˈæŋ.gləʊ.faɪl (US) -glə- **-s** -z
anglophilia ˌæŋ.gləʊˈfɪl.i.ə (US) -gləˈ-
anglophobe ˈæŋ.gləʊ.fəʊb (US) -glə.foʊb **-s** -z
anglophobia ˌæŋ.gləʊˈfəʊ.bi.ə (US) -gləˈfoʊ-
anglophone ˈæŋ.gləʊ.fəʊn (US) -glə.foʊn **-s** -z
Anglo-Saxon ˌæŋ.gləʊˈsæk.sᵊn (US) -gloʊˈ- **-s** -z
Anglo-Saxondom ˌæŋ.gləʊˈsæk.sᵊn.dəm (US) -gloʊˈ-
Anglo-Saxonism ˌæŋ.gləʊˈsæk.sᵊn.ɪ.zᵊm (US) -gloʊˈ- **-s** -z
Angmering ˈæŋ.mə.rɪŋ
Angol|a æŋˈgəʊ.l|ə (US) -ˈgoʊ-, æn- **-an/s** -ən/z
angora (A) *cat, rabbit, cloth:* æŋˈgɔː.rə (US) -ˈgɔːr.ə, æn- **-s** -z
Angora *old form of* ***Ankara*** *in Turkey:* ˈæŋ.gə.rə, æŋˈgɔː.rə (US) æŋˈgɔːr.ə, æn-
angostura (A) ˌæŋ.gəˈstjʊə.rə, -gɒsˈtjʊə-, -ˈstjɔː- (US) -gəˈstʊr.ə, -ˈstjʊr- ˌ**Angostura** ˈ**bitters®**
Angoulême ɑ̃ːŋ.guˈlem
angr|y ˈæŋ.gr|i **-ier** -i.əʳ (US) -i.ɚ **-iest** -i.əst, -i.ɪst **-ily** -ɪ.li, -ᵊl.i **-iness** -ɪ.nəs, -ɪ.nɪs ˌ**angry young** ˈ**man**
angst æŋkst (US) æŋkst, ɑːŋkst
angstrom ˈæŋk.strəm **-s** -z
Anguill|a æŋˈgwɪl|.ə **-an/s** -ən/z
anguine ˈæŋ.gwɪn
anguish ˈæŋ.gwɪʃ **-es** -ɪz **-ing** -ɪŋ **-ed** -t
angular ˈæŋ.gjʊ.ləʳ, -gjə- (US) -lɚ **-ly** -li **-ness** -nəs, -nɪs
angularit|y ˌæŋ.gjʊˈlær.ə.t|i, -gjə-, -ɪ.t|i (US) -ˈler.ə.t̬|i, -ˈlær- **-ies** -iz
angulate ˈæŋ.gjʊ.leɪt, -gjə-, -lɪt, -lət
angulated ˈæŋ.gjʊ.leɪ.tɪd, -gjə- (US) -t̬ɪd

Angus 'æŋ.gəs
Angustura ˌæŋ.gə'stjʊə.rə, -'stjɔː-, -'stʊr.ə US -'stʊr-, -'stjʊr-
anharmonic ˌæn.hɑː'mɒn.ɪk US -hɑːr'mɑː.nɪk *stress shift:* ˌanharmonic 'system
anhungered ən'hʌŋ.gəd, æn- US -gɚd
anhydride æn'haɪ.draɪd **-s** -z
anhydrite æn'haɪ.draɪt
anhydrous æn'haɪ.drəs
anil 'æn.ɪl
anile 'eɪ.naɪl, 'æn.aɪl
aniline 'æn.ɪ.liːn, -lɪn, -laɪn US -lɪn, -liːn, -laɪn
anility æn'ɪl.ə.ti, ə'nɪl-, -ɪ.ti US -ə.t̬i
anima 'æn.ɪ.mə
animadversion ˌæn.ɪ.mæd'vɜː.ʃᵊn, -məd'-, -ʒᵊn US -'vɝː.ʒᵊn, -ʃᵊn **-s** -z
animad|vert ˌæn.ɪ.mæd|'vɜːt, -məd'- US -'vɝːt **-verts** -'vɜːts US -'vɝːts **-verting** -'vɜː.tɪŋ US -'vɝː.t̬ɪŋ **-verted** -'vɜː.tɪd US -'vɝː.t̬ɪd
animal 'æn.ɪ.mᵊl, '-ə- **-s** -z
animalcule ˌæn.ɪ'mæl.kjuːl **-s** -z
animalism 'æn.ɪ.mᵊl.ɪ.zᵊm
animalistic ˌæn.ɪ.mᵊl'ɪs.tɪk US -mə'lɪs-, -məl'-
animate (*adj.*) 'æn.ɪ.mət, -mɪt, -meɪt
ani|mate (*v.*) 'æn.ɪ|.meɪt, '-ə- **-mates** -meɪts **-mating** -meɪ.tɪŋ US -meɪ.t̬ɪŋ **-mated/ly** -meɪ.tɪd/li US -meɪ.t̬ɪd/li
animation ˌæn.ɪ'meɪ.ʃᵊn, -ə'- **-s** -z
animator 'æn.ɪ.meɪ.təʳ, '-ə- US -t̬ɚ **-s** -z
animatronic ˌæn.ɪ.mə'trɒn.ɪk, ˌ-ə- US -'trɑː.nɪk **-s** -s
anim|ism 'æn.ɪ.m|ɪ.zᵊm, '-ə- **-ist/s** -ɪst/s
animosit|y ˌæn.ɪ'mɒs.ə.t|i, -ə'-, -ɪ.t|i US -'mɑː.sə.t̬|i **-ies** -iz
animus 'æn.ɪ.məs
anion 'æn.aɪən **-s** -z
anis 'æn.iːs, -i; æn'iːs US 'æn.iːs, 'ɑː.niːs, -i; æn'iːs, ɑː'niːs
anise 'æn.ɪs, æn'iːs
aniseed 'æn.ɪ.siːd, '-ə-
anisette ˌæn.ɪ'set, -ə'-, -'zet
anisometric ænˌaɪ.səʊ'met.rɪk US -soʊ'-
anisotropic ˌæn.aɪ.səʊ'trɒp.ɪk, -'trəʊ.pɪk US -soʊ'trɑː.pɪk, -'troʊ- **-ally** -ᵊl.i, -li
anisotropism ˌæn.aɪ'sɒt.rə.pɪ.zᵊm US -'sɑː.trə-
anisotropy ˌæn.aɪ'sɒt.rə.pi US -'sɑː.trə-
Aniston 'æn.ɪ.stən
Anita ə'niː.tə US -t̬ə
Anjou ɑ̃ːn'dʒuː, ɑːn'-
Ankara 'æŋ.kᵊr.ə US 'æŋ-, 'ɑːŋ-
ankerite 'æŋ.kᵊr.aɪt US -kə.raɪt
ankh ɑːŋk, æŋk **-s** -s
ankle 'æŋ.kl̩ **-s** -z **'ankle ˌsock**
anklet 'æŋ.klət, -klɪt **-s** -s
Ann æn
anna (A) 'æn.ə **-s** -z
Annaba æn'ɑː.bə
Annabel 'æn.ə.bel
Annabella ˌæn.ə'bel.ə
Annagh æn'ɑː, 'æn.ɑː
Annakin 'æn.ə.kɪn
annalist 'æn.ᵊl.ɪst **-s** -s
annals 'æn.ᵊlz
Annaly 'æn.ə.li
Annam æn'æm, 'æn.æm
Annamese ˌæn.ə'miːz
Annan 'æn.ən
Annandale 'æn.ən.deɪl
Annapolis ə'næp.ᵊl.ɪs, æn'æp-
Annapurna ˌæn.ə'pɜː.nə, -'pʊə- US -'pɝː-, -'pʊr-
Ann Arbor ˌæn'ɑː.bə US -'ɑːr.bɚ
Annas 'æn.æs, -əs
annatto ə'næt.əʊ, æn'æt- US ə'nɑː.toʊ, ə'næt.oʊ
Anne æn
anneal ə'niːl **-s** -z **-ing** -ɪŋ **-ed** -d
Anneka 'æn.ɪ.kə, -ə.kə
annelid 'æn.ə.lɪd **-s** -z
Annesley 'ænz.li
Annett 'æn.ɪt, -ət
Annette ə'net, æn'et US ə'net
annex (*n.*) 'æn.eks **-es** -ɪz
annex (*v.*) ə'neks, æn'eks **-es** -ɪz **-ing** -ɪŋ **-ed** -t **-ment/s** -mənt/s
annexation ˌæn.ek'seɪ.ʃᵊn, -ɪk'- **-s** -z
annex|e 'æn.eks **-es** -ɪz
Annfield Plain ˌæn.fiːld'pleɪn
Annie 'æn.i
Annigoni ˌæn.ɪ'gəʊ.ni US -'goʊ-
annihi|late ə'naɪ.ɪ|.leɪt, '-ə- US '-ə- **-lates** -leɪts **-lating** -leɪ.tɪŋ US -leɪ.t̬ɪŋ **-lated** -leɪ.tɪd US -leɪ.t̬ɪd **-lator/s** -leɪ.təʳ/z US -leɪ.t̬ɚ/z
annihilation əˌnaɪ.ɪ'leɪ.ʃᵊn, -ə'- US -ə'- **-s** -z
Anning 'æn.ɪŋ
Anniston 'æn.ɪ.stən
anniversar|y ˌæn.ɪ'vɜː.sᵊr|.i US -'vɝː- **-ies** -iz
anno Domini (A) ˌæn.əʊ'dɒm.ɪ.naɪ US -oʊ'dɑː.mə.niː, -'doʊ-, -naɪ
anno|tate 'æn.əʊ|.teɪt US '-ə-, '-oʊ- **-tates** -teɪts **-tating** -teɪ.tɪŋ US -teɪ.t̬ɪŋ **-tated** -teɪ.tɪd US -teɪ.t̬ɪd **-tator/s** -teɪ.təʳ/z US -teɪ.t̬ɚ/z **-tative** -teɪ.tɪv US -teɪ.t̬ɪv
annotation ˌæn.əʊ'teɪ.ʃᵊn US -ə'-, -oʊ'- **-s** -z
announc|e ə'naʊnts **-es** -ɪz **-ing** -ɪŋ **-ed** -t **-ement/s** -mənt/s
announcer ə'naʊnt.səʳ US -sɚ **-s** -z
annoy ə'nɔɪ **-s** -z **-ing/ly** -ɪŋ/li **-ed** -d
annoyanc|e ə'nɔɪ.ənts **-es** -ɪz
annual 'æn.ju.əl **-s** -z **-ly** -i
annualiz|e, -is|e 'æn.ju.ᵊl.aɪz US -ə.laɪz **annuali|ze** -jul'- **-es** -ɪz **-ing** -ɪŋ **-ed** -d
annuit|y ə'njuː.ə.t|i, -ɪ.t|i US -'nuː.ə.t̬|i, -'njuː- **-ies** -iz **-ant/s** -ᵊnt/s
annul ə'nʌl **-s** -z **-ling** -ɪŋ **-led** -d
annular 'æn.jə.ləʳ, '-jʊ- US -lɚ
annu|late 'æn.jə|.leɪt, '-jʊ- **-lated** -leɪ.tɪd US -leɪ.t̬ɪd
annulet 'æn.jʊ.lət, '-jə-, -lɪt **-s** -s
annulment ə'nʌl.mənt **-s** -s
annul|us æn.jə.l|əs, '-jʊ- **-uses** -əs.ɪz **-i** -aɪ, -iː
annum 'æn.əm
annunci|ate ə'nʌnt.si|.eɪt, -ʃi- **-ates** -eɪts **-ating** -eɪ.tɪŋ US -eɪ.t̬ɪŋ **-ated** -eɪ.tɪd US -eɪ.t̬ɪd
annunciation (A) əˌnʌnt.si'eɪ.ʃᵊn **-s** -z
annus mirabilis (A) ˌæn.əs.mɪ'rɑː.bᵊl.ɪs, -mə'- US ˌɑː.nəs-, ˌæn.əs-
anode 'æn.əʊd US -oʊd **-s** -z
anodiz|e, -ise 'æn.əʊ.daɪz US '-oʊ-, '-ə- **-es** -ɪz **-ing** -ɪŋ **-ed** -d
anodyne 'æn.əʊ.daɪn US '-oʊ-, '-ə- **-s** -z
a|noint ə|'nɔɪnt **-noints** -'nɔɪnts **-nointing** -'nɔɪn.tɪŋ US -'nɔɪn.t̬ɪŋ **-nointed** -'nɔɪn.tɪd US -'nɔɪn.t̬ɪd **-nointment/s** -'nɔɪnt.mənt/s
anomalous ə'nɒm.ə.ləs US -'nɑː.mə- **-ly** -li
anomal|y ə'nɒm.ə.l|i US -'nɑː.mə- **-ies** -iz
anon (A) ə'nɒn US -'nɑːn
anonym 'æn.ə.nɪm, -ɒn.ɪm US -ə.nɪm **-s** -z
anonymity ˌæn.ə'nɪm.ə.ti, -ɒn'ɪm-, -ɪ.ti US -ə'nɪm.ə.t̬i
anonymiz|e, -is|e ə'nɒn.ɪ.maɪz, '-ə- US -'nɑː.nə- **-es** -ɪz **-ing** -ɪŋ **-ed** -d
anonymous ə'nɒn.ɪ.məs, '-ə- US -'nɑː.nə- **-ly** -li
anopheles ə'nɒf.ɪ.liːz, '-ə- US -'nɑː.fə-
anorak 'æn.ᵊr.æk US -ə.ræk **-s** -s
anorectic ˌæn.ᵊr'ek.tɪk US -ə'rek- **-s** -s
anorexia ˌæn.ᵊr'ek.si.ə US -ə'rek- **anoˌrexia nerˈvosa**
anorexic ˌæn.ᵊr'ek.sɪk US -ə'rek- **-s** -s
anosmia æn'ɒz.mi.ə, -'ɒs- US æn'ɑːz-, -'ɑːs-
another ə'nʌð.əʳ US -ɚ
A N Other ˌeɪ,en'ʌð.əʳ US -ɚ
Anouilh 'æn.uː.iː, ˌæn.uː'iː US ɑː'nuː.jə, æn'uː-, -iː; ˌɑː.nuː'iː, ˌæn.uː'-
anoxia æn'ɒk.si.ə, eɪ'nɒk- US æn'ɑːk-
ansaphone, ansafone (A®) 'ɑːnt.sə.fəʊn US 'æn.sə.foʊn **-s** -z
anschauung (A) 'æn.ʃaʊ.ʊŋ US 'ɑːn.ʃaʊ.əŋ
anschluss (A) 'æn.ʃlʊs US 'ɑːn-, 'æn-
Ansell 'ænt.sᵊl
Anselm 'ænt.selm

anserine 'æn*t*.sə.raɪn, -riːn, -rɪn
Ansley 'ænz.li
Anson 'æn*t*.sən
Ansonia æn'səʊ.ni.ə ⓊⓈ -'soʊ-, '-njə
Ansted 'æn*t*.sted, -stɪd
Anster 'æn*t*.stəʳ ⓊⓈ -stɚ
Anstey 'æn*t*.sti
Anston 'æn*t*.stən
Anstruther 'æn*t*.strʌð.əʳ ⓊⓈ -ɚ
answ|er 'ɑːn*t*.s|əʳ ⓊⓈ 'æn*t*.s|ɚ **-ers** -əz ⓊⓈ -ɚz **-ering** -ᵊr.ɪŋ **-ered** -əd ⓊⓈ -ɚd **-erer/s** -ᵊr.əʳ/z ⓊⓈ -ɚ.ɚ/z **'answering ma,chine**
answerability ˌɑːn*t*.sᵊr.ə'bɪl.ə.ti, -ɪ.ti ⓊⓈ ˌæn*t*.sɚ.ə'bɪl.ə.t̬i
answerab|le 'ɑːn*t*.sᵊr.ə.b|l ⓊⓈ 'æn*t*- **-ly** -li
answerphone 'ɑːn*t*.sə.fəʊn ⓊⓈ 'æn*t*.sɚ.foʊn **-s** -z
ant- ænt-
Note: Prefix. Where **ant-** is attached to a free stem it often carries secondary stress, e.g. **antacid** /ˌæn'tæs.ɪd/. In other cases it may take primary, secondary or no stress at all, e.g. **antonym** /'æn.tə.nɪm ⓊⓈ -tᵊn.ɪm/, **antonymic** /ˌæn.tə'nɪm.ɪk/, **antonymous** /æn'tɒn.ɪ.məs ⓊⓈ -'tɑː.nə-/.
ant ænt **-s** -s **'ant ˌlion**
-ant -ənt
Note: Suffix. Words containing **-ant** are stressed in a similar way to those containing **-ance**; see above.
Antabuse® 'æn.tə.bjuːs, -bjuːz
antacid ˌæn'tæs.ɪd **-s** -z
Antaeus æn'tiː.əs, -'teɪ-
antagonism æn'tæg.ᵊn.ɪ.zᵊm **-s** -z
antagonist æn'tæg.ᵊn.ɪst **-s** -s
antagonistic ænˌtæg.ᵊn'ɪs.tɪk, ˌæn.tæg.ᵊn'- ⓊⓈ -ə'nɪs- **-ally** -ᵊl.i, -li
antagoniz|e, -is|e æn'tæg.ᵊn.aɪz ⓊⓈ -ə.naɪz **-es** -ɪz **-ing** -ɪŋ **-ed** -d
Antalya æn'tæl.jə ⓊⓈ ˌɑːn.tᵊl'jɑː, ˌæn-
Antananarivo ˌæn.təˌnæn.ə'riː.vəʊ ⓊⓈ -voʊ
Antarctic æn'tɑːk.tɪk ⓊⓈ -'tɑːrk-, -'tɑːr.t̬ɪk **Antˌarctic 'Circle; Antˌarctic 'Ocean**
Antarctica æn'tɑːk.tɪ.kə ⓊⓈ -'tɑːrk-, -'tɑːr.t̬ɪ-
Antares æn'teə.riːz ⓊⓈ -'ter.iːz
ant-bear 'ænt.beəʳ ⓊⓈ -ber **-s** -z
ante- æn.tɪ- ⓊⓈ -t̬i-, -t̬ə-
Note: Prefix. Words containing **ante-** carry either primary or secondary stress on the first syllable, e.g. **antechamber** /'æn.tɪˌtʃeɪm.bəʳ ⓊⓈ -t̬ɪˌtʃeɪm.bɚ/, **antenatal** /ˌæn.tɪ'neɪ.tᵊl ⓊⓈ -t̬ᵊl/.
ante 'æn.ti ⓊⓈ -t̬i **-s** -z **-ing** -ɪŋ **-d** -d
anteater 'ænt̬ˌiː.təʳ ⓊⓈ -t̬ɚ **-s** -z
antebellum ˌæn.tɪ'bel.əm ⓊⓈ -t̬ə'-
antecedence ˌæn.tɪ'siː.dᵊnts, 'æn.tɪ.siː- ⓊⓈ ˌæn.t̬ə'siː-
antecedent ˌæn.tɪ'siː.dᵊnt, -t̬ə'- **-s** -s **-ly** -li
antechamber 'æn.tɪˌtʃeɪm.bəʳ ⓊⓈ -t̬ɪˌtʃeɪm.bɚ **-s** -z
antechapel 'æn.tɪˌtʃæp.ᵊl ⓊⓈ -t̬ɪ- **-s** -z
ante|date ˌæn.tɪ|'deɪt ⓊⓈ 'æn.t̬ɪ|.deɪt **-dates** -'deɪts ⓊⓈ -deɪts **-dating** -'deɪ.tɪŋ ⓊⓈ -deɪ.t̬ɪŋ **-dated** -'deɪ.tɪd ⓊⓈ -deɪ.t̬ɪd
antediluvi|an ˌæn.tɪ.dɪ'luː.vi|.ən, -də'-, -daɪ'-, -'ljuː- ⓊⓈ -t̬ɪ.də'luː- **-ans** -ənz **-al** -ᵊl **-ally** -ᵊl.i
antelope 'æn.tɪ.ləʊp ⓊⓈ -t̬ᵊl.oʊp **-s** -s
antemeridian ˌæn.tɪ.mə'rɪd.i.ən ⓊⓈ -t̬ɪ-
ante meridiem ˌæn.tɪ.mə'rɪd.i.əm ⓊⓈ -t̬ɪ-
antenatal ˌæn.tɪ'neɪ.tᵊl ⓊⓈ -t̬ɪ'neɪ.t̬ᵊl
antenn|a æn'ten|.ə **-ae** -iː **-as** -əz **-al** -ᵊl **-ary** -ᵊr.i
Antenor æn'tiː.nɔːʳ ⓊⓈ -nɔːr
antenuptial ˌæn.tɪ'nʌp.ʃᵊl, -tʃᵊl ⓊⓈ -t̬ɪ'-
antepenult ˌæn.tɪ.pɪ'nʌlt, -pen'ʌlt, -pə'nʌlt ⓊⓈ ˌæn.t̬ɪ'piː.nʌlt; -pɪ'nʌlt **-s** -s
antepenultimate ˌæn.tɪ.pə'nʌl.tɪ.mət, -pɪ'nʌl-, -pen'ʌl-, -tə-, -mɪt ⓊⓈ -t̬ɪ.pɪ'nʌl.t̬ə.mət **-s** -s
anteprandial ˌæn.tɪ'præn.di.əl ⓊⓈ -t̬ɪ'-
anterior æn'tɪə.ri.əʳ ⓊⓈ -'tɪr.i.ɚ **-ly** -li
anteroom 'æn.tɪ.rʊm, -ruːm ⓊⓈ -t̬ɪ.ruːm, -rʊm **-s** -z
Anthea 'æn*t*.θi.ə ⓊⓈ æn'θiː-
ant-heap 'ænt.hiːp **-s** -s
antheli|on ænt'hiː.li|.ən, æn*t*'θiː- **-ons** -ənz **-a** -ə
anthelix ænt'hiː.lɪks, æn*t*'θiː- **-es** -ɪz
anthem 'æn*t*.θəm **-s** -z
anther 'æn*t*.θəʳ ⓊⓈ -θɚ **-s** -z
anthill 'ænt.hɪl **-s** -z
anthological ˌæn*t*.θə'lɒdʒ.ɪ.kᵊl ⓊⓈ -'lɑː.dʒɪ-
anthologist æn'θɒl.ə.dʒɪst ⓊⓈ -'θɑː.lə- **-s** -s
anthologiz|e, -is|e æn'θɒl.ə.dʒaɪz ⓊⓈ -'θɑː.lə- **-es** -ɪz **-ing** -ɪŋ **-ed** -d
antholog|y æn'θɒl.ə.dʒ|i ⓊⓈ -'θɑː.lə- **-ies** -iz
Anthon 'æn.tɒn ⓊⓈ 'æn*t*.θən, 'æn.tɑːn
Anthony 'æn.tə.ni, 'æn*t*.θə.ni ⓊⓈ 'æn.θə.ni, 'æn.tə.ni
anthracite 'æn*t*.θrə.saɪt
anthracitic ˌæn*t*.θrə'sɪt.ɪk ⓊⓈ -'sɪt̬-
anthrax 'æn*t*.θræks
anthropic æn'θrɒp.ɪk ⓊⓈ -'θrɑː.pɪk **-al** -ᵊl
anthropo- ˌæn*t*.θrəʊ.pəʊ-; ˌæn*t*.θrəʊ'pɒ- ⓊⓈ ˌæn*t*.θrə.pə-, -poʊ-; ˌæn*t*.θrə'pɑː-
Note: Prefix. Words containing **anthropo-** normally exhibit secondary stress on the first syllable, e.g. **anthropomorphic** /ˌæn*t*.θrə.pəʊ'mɔː.fɪk ⓊⓈ -pə'mɔːr-/, but may also have primary stress on the third syllable, e.g., **anthropology** /ˌæn*t*.θrə'pɒl.ə.dʒi ⓊⓈ -'pɑː.lə-/.
anthropocentric ˌæn*t*.θrəʊ.pəʊ'sen.trɪk ⓊⓈ -θrə.pə'-, -poʊ'-
anthropocentrism ˌæn.θrəʊ.pəʊ'sen.trɪ.zᵊm ⓊⓈ -θrə.pə'-, -poʊ'-
anthropoid 'æn*t*.θrəʊ.pɔɪd ⓊⓈ -θrə-, -θroʊ- **-s** -z
anthropoidal ˌæn*t*.θrəʊ'pɔɪd.ᵊl ⓊⓈ -θrə'-, -θroʊ'-
anthropological ˌæn*t*.θrə.pə'lɒdʒ.ɪ.kᵊl ⓊⓈ -'lɑː.dʒɪ- **-ly** -i
anthropologist ˌæn*t*.θrə'pɒl.ə.dʒɪst ⓊⓈ -'pɑː.lə- **-s** -s
anthropology ˌæn*t*.θrə'pɒl.ə.dʒi ⓊⓈ -'pɑː.lə-
anthropometric ˌæn*t*.θrəʊ.pəʊ'met.rɪk ⓊⓈ -θrə.pə'-
anthropometry ˌæn.θrə'pɒm.ɪ.tri, '-ə- ⓊⓈ -'pɑː.mə-
anthropomorph|ic ˌæn*t*.θrə.pəʊ'mɔː.f|ɪk ⓊⓈ -pə'mɔːr- **-ous** -əs
anthropomorph|ism ˌæn*t*.θrə.pəʊ'mɔː.f|ɪ.zᵊm ⓊⓈ -pə'mɔːr- **-ist/s** -ɪst/s
anthropomorphiz|e, -is|e ˌæn*t*.θrə.pəʊ'mɔː.faɪz ⓊⓈ -pə'mɔːr- **-es** -ɪz **-ing** -ɪŋ **-ed** -d
anthropomorphosis ˌæn*t*.θrə.pəʊ.mɔː'fəʊ.sɪs ⓊⓈ -pə.mɔːr'foʊ-
anthropopha|gus ˌæn*t*.θrəʊ'pɒf.ə|l.gəs ⓊⓈ -θrə'pɑː.fə- **-gi** -dʒaɪ, -gaɪ ⓊⓈ -dʒaɪ
anthropopha|gy ˌæn*t*.θrəʊ'pɒf.ə|l.dʒi ⓊⓈ -θrə'pɑː.fə- **-gous** -gəs
anthroposoph|y ˌæn*t*.θrəʊ'pɒs.ə.f|i ⓊⓈ -θrə'pɑː.sə- **-ist/s** -ɪst/s
anti- æn.tɪ-, -ti-; æn'tɪ- ⓊⓈ -t̬ɪ-, -t̬i-, -taɪ-; æn'tɪ-
Note: Prefix. Numerous compounds may be formed by prefixing **anti-** to other words. Most often, these compounds carry primary or secondary stress on the first syllable, e.g. **antihero** /'æn.tɪˌhɪə.rəʊ ⓊⓈ -t̬ɪˌhɪr.oʊ/, **anti-icer** /ˌæn.ti'aɪ.səʳ ⓊⓈ -t̬i'aɪ.sɚ/, but there are also cases in which the second syllable takes the primary stress, e.g. **antinomy** /æn'tɪn.ə.mi/.

anti ˈæn.ti US -t̬i, -taɪ **-s** -z

antiabortion ˌæn.ti.əˈbɔː.ʃᵊn US -t̬i.əˈbɔːr-, -taɪ- **-ist/s** -ɪst/s

anti-aircraft ˌæn.tiˈeə.krɑːft US -t̬iˈer.kræft, -taɪˈ-

antibacterial ˌæn.tɪ.bækˈtɪə.ri.əl US -t̬ɪ.bækˈtɪr.i-, -taɪ-

antiballistic ˌæn.tɪ.bəˈlɪs.tɪk US -t̬ɪ-, -taɪ-

Antibes ɑːnˈtiːb, æn-, ɒnˈ- US ɑːnˈ-

antibiosis ˌæn.tɪ.baɪˈəʊ.sɪs US -t̬ɪ.baɪˈoʊ-, -taɪ-

antibiotic ˌæn.tɪ.baɪˈɒt.ɪk US -t̬ɪ.baɪˈɑː.t̬ɪk, -taɪ- **-s** -s

antibod|y ˈæn.tɪˌbɒd|.i US -t̬ɪˌbɑː.d|i, -taɪˌ- **-ies** -iz

antic ˈæn.tɪk US -t̬ɪk **-s** -s

anticatholic ˌæn.tɪˈkæθ.ᵊl.ɪk US -t̬ɪˈ-, -taɪˈ- **-s** -s

anti-choice ˌæn.tɪˈtʃɔɪs US -t̬ɪˈ-, -taɪˈ-

antichrist (A) ˈæn.tɪ.kraɪst US -t̬ɪ-, -taɪ- **-s** -s

antichristian *opposing Christianity:* ˌæn.tɪˈkrɪs.tʃᵊn, -ˈkrɪʃ- US -t̬ɪˈ-, -taɪˈ- **-s** -z *pertaining to Antichrist:* ˈæn.tɪˌkrɪʃ.tʃᵊn US -t̬ɪˌ-, -taɪˌ- **-s** -z

anticipant ænˈtɪs.ɪ.pənt, ˈ-ə- **-s** -s

antici|pate ænˈtɪs.ɪ|.peɪt, ˈ-ə- US ˈ-ə- **-pates** -peɪts **-pating** -peɪ.tɪŋ US -peɪ.t̬ɪŋ **-pated** -peɪ.tɪd US -peɪ.t̬ɪd **-pative/ly** -peɪ.tɪv/li US -peɪ.t̬ɪv/li

anticipation ænˌtɪs.ɪˈpeɪ.ʃᵊn, -əˈ-; ˌæn.tɪ.sɪˈ-, -səˈ- US ænˌtɪs.əˈ- **-s** -z

anticipator|y ænˌtɪs.ɪˈpeɪ.tᵊr|.i, -əˈ-; ˌæn.tɪ.sɪˈ-, -səˈ- US ænˈtɪs.ə.pə.tɔːr- **-ily** -ᵊl.i, -ɪ.li

anticiz|e, -is|e ˈæn.tɪ.saɪz US -t̬ɪ-, -taɪ- **-es** -ɪz **-ing** -ɪŋ **-ed** -d

anticlerical ˌæn.tɪˈkler.ɪ.kᵊl US -t̬ɪˈ-, -taɪˈ- **-ism** -ɪ.zᵊm **-ist/s** -ɪst/s

anticlimactic ˌæn.tɪ.klaɪˈmæk.tɪk, -klɪˈ- US -t̬ɪ.klaɪˈ-, -taɪ- **-ally** -ᵊl.i, -li

anticlimatic ˌæn.tɪ.klaɪˈmæt.ɪk, -klɪˈ- US -t̬ɪ.klaɪˈmæt̬-, -taɪ- **-al** -ᵊl **-ally** -ᵊl.i, -li

anticlimax ˌæn.tɪˈklaɪ.mæks, ˈæn.tɪˌklaɪ- US ˌæn.t̬ɪˈklaɪ-, -taɪˌ- **-es** -ɪz

anticline ˈæn.tɪ.klaɪn US -t̬ɪ- **-s** -z

anticlockwise ˌæn.tɪˈklɒk.waɪz US -t̬ɪˈklɑːk-, -taɪˈ- *stress shift:* ˌanticlockwise ˈaction

anticoagulant ˌæn.tɪ.kəʊˈæg.jʊ.lənt, -jə- US -t̬ɪ.koʊˈæg.jə-, -taɪ- **-s** -s

anticonsumer|ism ˌæn.tɪ.kənˈsjuː.mᵊr|.ɪ.zᵊm, -ˈsuː- US -t̬ɪ.kənˈsuː- **-ist/s** -ɪst/s

anticonvulsant ˌæn.tɪ.kənˈvʌl.sᵊnt US -t̬ɪ-, -taɪ- **-s** -s

anticonvulsive ˌæn.tɪ.kənˈvʌl.sɪv US -t̬ɪ-, -taɪ- **-s** -z

anticyclone ˌæn.tɪˈsaɪ.kləʊn, ˈæn.tɪ.saɪ- US ˌæn.t̬ɪˈsaɪ.kloʊn, -taɪˈ- **-s** -z

anticyclonic ˌæn.tɪ.saɪˈklɒn.ɪk US -t̬ɪ.saɪˈklɑː.nɪk, -taɪ-

antidepressant ˌæn.tɪ.dɪˈpres.ᵊnt, -dəˈ- US -t̬ɪ-, -taɪ- **-s** -s

antidotal ˌæn.tɪˈdəʊ.tᵊl, ˈæn.tɪ.dəʊ- US ˈæn.t̬ɪ.doʊ-

antidote ˈæn.tɪ.dəʊt US -t̬ɪ.doʊt **-s** -s

Antietam ænˈtiː.təm US -t̬əm

antifebrile ˌæn.tɪˈfiː.braɪl, -ˈfeb.raɪl US -t̬ɪˈfiː.brɪl, -taɪˈ-, -ˈfeb.rɪl, -rəl

anti-federal ˌæn.tɪˈfed.ᵊr.ᵊl US -t̬ɪˈ-, -taɪˈ- **-ism** -ɪ.zᵊm **-ist/s** -ɪst/s

antifreeze ˈæn.tɪ.friːz US -t̬ɪ-

antigen ˈæn.tɪ.dʒən, -dʒen US -t̬ɪ- **-s** -z

Antigone ænˈtɪg.ə.ni

Antigonus ænˈtɪg.ə.nəs

Antigu|a ænˈtiː.g|ə US -gw|ə, -g|ə, -ˈtɪg.w|ə, ˈ-ə **-an/s** -ən/z

antihel|ix ˌæn.tɪˈhiː.l|ɪks US -t̬ɪˈ-, -taɪˈ- **-ixes** -ɪk.sɪz **-ices** -ɪ.siːz, -ˈhel.ɪs.iːz

antihero ˈæn.tɪˌhɪə.rəʊ US -t̬ɪˌher.oʊ, -t̬i-, -taɪ-, -hiː.roʊ **-es** -z

antiheroic ˌæn.tɪ.hɪˈrəʊ.ɪk, -həˈ-, -herˈəʊ- US -t̬ɪ.hɪˈroʊ-, -t̬i-, -taɪ-

antiheroine ˈæn.tɪˌher.əʊ.ɪn US -t̬ɪˌher.oʊ-, -taɪ- **-s** -z

antihistamine ˌæn.tɪˈhɪs.tə.miːn, -mɪn US -t̬ɪˈ- **-s** -z

anti-icer ˌæn.tiˈaɪ.səʳ US -t̬iˈaɪ.sɚ **-s** -z

anti-inflammatory ˌæn.ti.ɪnˈflæm.ə.tᵊr.i US -t̬i.ɪnˈflæm.ə.tɔːr-, -taɪ-

Anti-Jacobin ˌæn.tɪˈdʒæk.ə.bɪn, -ɒb.ɪn US -t̬ɪˈdʒæk.ə.bɪn, -taɪˈ-

antiknock ˌæn.tɪˈnɒk US ˈæn.t̬ɪˈnɑːk, -t̬iˈ-, -taɪˈ- **-ing** -ɪŋ

Antilles ænˈtɪl.iːz

antilock ˌæn.tɪˈlɒk US -t̬ɪˈlɑːk, -t̬iˈ-, -taɪˈ- *stress shift:* ˌantilock ˈbrakes

anti-locking ˌæn.tɪˈlɒk.ɪŋ US -t̬ɪˈlɑː.kɪŋ

antilog ˌæn.tɪˈlɒg US ˈæn.t̬ɪ.lɑːg, -taɪ-, -lɔːg **-s** -z

antilogarithm ˌæn.tɪˈlɒg.ə.rɪ.ðᵊm, -θᵊm US -t̬ɪˈlɑː.gɚ.ɪ.ðᵊm, -taɪˈ-, -ˈlɔː- **-s** -z

antilog|y ænˈtɪl.ə.dʒ|i **-ies** -iz

antimacassar ˌæn.tɪ.məˈkæs.əʳ US -t̬ɪ.məˈkæs.ɚ **-s** -z

Antimachus ænˈtɪm.ə.kəs

antimatter ˈæn.tɪˌmæt.əʳ US -t̬ɪˌmæt̬.ɚ, -t̬iˌ-, -taɪˌ-

anti-missile ˌæn.tɪˈmɪs.aɪl US -t̬ɪˈmɪs.ᵊl, -t̬iˈ-, -taɪˈ-

antimonarchical ˌæn.tɪ.mɒnˈɑː.kɪ.kᵊl, -məˈnɑː- US -t̬ɪ.məˈnɑːr-, -taɪ-

antimonarchist ˌæn.tɪˈmɒn.ə.kɪst US -t̬ɪˈmɑː.nɚ-, -taɪˈ-, -nɑːr- **-s** -s

antimonial ˌæn.tɪˈməʊ.ni.əl US -t̬ɪˈmoʊ- **-s** -z

antimonic ˌæn.tɪˈmɒn.ɪk US -t̬ɪˈmɑː.nɪk

antimony ˈæn.tɪ.mə.ni, ænˈtɪm.ə- US ˈæn.t̬ə.moʊ-

antinode ˈæn.tɪ.nəʊd US -t̬ɪ.noʊd

antinomian ˌæn.tɪˈnəʊ.mi.ən US -t̬ɪˈnoʊ-, -taɪˈ- **-s** -z

antinomic ˌæn.tɪˈnɒm.ɪk US -t̬ɪˈnɑː.mɪk **-al** -ᵊl **-ally** -ᵊl.i, -li

antinom|y ænˈtɪn.ə.m|i **-ies** -iz

Antinous ænˈtɪn.əʊ.əs US -oʊ-

antinovel ˈæn.tɪˌnɒv.ᵊl US -t̬ɪˌnɑː.vᵊl, -t̬iˌ-, -taɪˌ- **-s** -z

antinuclear ˌæn.tɪˈnjuː.kli.ə US -t̬ɪˈnuː-, -t̬iˈ-, -taɪˈ-, -ˈnjuː-

Antioch ˈæn.ti.ɒk US -t̬i.ɑːk

Antiochus ænˈtaɪ.ə.kəs

Antioquia ˌæn.ti.əʊˈkiː.ə US -t̬i.əˈ-; ɑːnˈtjoʊ.kjɑː

antioxidant ˌæn.tiˈɒk.sɪ.dᵊnt US -t̬iˈɑːk-, -taɪˈ- **-s** -s

Antipas ˈæn.tɪ.pæs US -t̬ɪ-

antipasti ˌæn.tɪˈpæs.ti US ˌæn.t̬ɪˈpɑː.sti, ˌɑːn.t̬ɪˈ-, -ˈpæs.ti

antipasto ˌæn.tiˈpæs.təʊ US ˌæn.t̬iˈpɑː.stoʊ, ˌɑːn-, -ˈpæs.toʊ **-s** -z

Antipater ænˈtɪp.ə.təʳ US -t̬ɚ

antipathetic ˌæn.tɪ.pəˈθet.ɪk, ænˌtɪp.əˈ- US ˌæn.t̬ɪ.pəˈθet̬.ɪk, ænˌtɪ.pəˈ- **-al** -ᵊl **-ally** -ᵊl.i, -li

antipath|y ænˈtɪp.ə.θ|i **-ies** -iz

anti-personnel ˌæn.tɪˌpɜː.sᵊnˈel US -t̬ɪˌpɝː-, -t̬iˌ-, -taɪˌ-

antiperspirant ˌæn.tɪˈpɜː.spᵊr.ənt, -spɪ.rənt US -t̬ɪˈpɝː.spɚ.ənt, -t̬iˈ-, -taɪˈ- **-s** -s

Antipholus ænˈtɪf.ə.ləs

antiphon ˈæn.tɪ.fən, -fɒn US -t̬ə.fɑːn, -fən **-s** -z

antiphonal ænˈtɪf.ə.nᵊl **-s** -z

antiphoner ænˈtɪf.ᵊn.əʳ US -ɚ **-s** -z

antiphonic ˌæn.tɪˈfɒn.ɪk US -t̬ɪˈfɑː.nɪk **-al** -ᵊl **-ally** -ᵊl.i, -li

antiphon|y ænˈtɪf.ə.n|i **-ies** -iz

antipodal ænˈtɪp.ə.dᵊl

antipodean (A) ænˌtɪp.əʊˈdiː.ən, ˌæn.tɪp- US -əˈ-

antipodes ænˈtɪp.ə.diːz

antipope ˈæn.tɪ.pəʊp US -t̬ɪ.poʊp **-s** -s

antipyretic ˌæn.tɪ.paɪəˈret.ɪk, -pɪˈret- US -t̬ɪ.paɪˈret̬-, -t̬i-, -taɪ- **-s** -s

antipyrin ˌæn.tɪˈpaɪə.rɪn, -riːn US -t̬ɪˈpaɪ-, -taɪˈ-

antiquarian ˌæn.tɪˈkweə.ri.ən US -t̬əˈkwer.i- **-s** -z **-ism** -ɪ.zᵊm

antiquar|y ˈæn.tɪ.kwᵊr|.i US -t̬ə.kwer- **-ies** -iz

anti|quate ˈæn.tɪ|.kweɪt US -t̬ə- **-quates** -kweɪts **-quating** -kweɪ.tɪŋ US -kweɪ.t̬ɪŋ **-quated** -kweɪ.tɪd US -kweɪ.t̬ɪd

antique æn'tiːk **-s** -s **-ly** -li **-ness** -nəs, -nɪs
antiquit|y æn'tɪk.wə.t|i, -wɪ- US -wə.t̬|i **-ies** -iz
anti-racial|ism ˌæn.tɪ'reɪ.ʃᵊl|.ɪ.zᵊm, -ʃi.ə.l|ɪ- US -t̬ɪ'reɪ.ʃᵊl|.ɪ-, -taɪ'- **-ist/s** -ɪst/s
anti-rac|ism ˌæn.tɪ'reɪ.s|ɪ.zᵊm US -t̬ɪ'-, -taɪ'- **-ist/s** -ɪst/s
antirrhinum ˌæn.tɪ'raɪ.nəm, -tə'- US -t̬ə'- **-s** -z
antiscorbutic ˌæn.tɪ.skɔː'bjuː.tɪk US -t̬ɪ.skɔːr'bjuː.t̬ɪk, -taɪ- **-s** -s
anti-Semite ˌæn.tɪ'siː.maɪt, -'sem.aɪt US -t̬ɪ'sem.aɪt, -t̬i'-, -taɪ'- **-s** -s
anti-Semitic ˌæn.tɪ.sɪ'mɪt.ɪk, -sə'- US -t̬ɪ.sə'mɪt̬-, -t̬i-, -taɪ- *stress shift:* ˌanti-Semitic 'views
anti-Semitism ˌæn.tɪ'sem.ɪ.tɪ.zᵊm, '-ə- US -t̬ɪ'sem.ə-, -t̬i'-, -taɪ'-
antisepsis ˌæn.tɪ'sep.sɪs US -t̬ə'-
antiseptic ˌæn.tɪ'sep.tɪk US -t̬ə'- **-s** -s **-ally** -ᵊl.i, -li *stress shift:* ˌantiseptic 'lozenge
antiser|um ˌæn.tɪ'sɪə.r|əm US -t̬ɪ'sɪr|.əm, -taɪ'- **-ums** -əmz **-a** -ə
antisocial ˌæn.tɪ'səʊ.ʃᵊl US -t̬ɪ'soʊ-, -t̬i'-, -taɪ'- **-ly** -i
antisocialist ˌæn.tɪ'səʊ.ʃᵊl.ɪst US -t̬ɪ'soʊ-, -t̬i'-, -taɪ'- **-s** -s
antistatic ˌæn.tɪ'stæt.ɪk US -t̬ɪ'stæt̬-, -taɪ'- *stress shift:* ˌantistatic 'cloth
Antisthenes æn'tɪs.θə.niːz, -θɪ-
antistrophe æn'tɪs.trə.fi **-s** -z
antistrophic ˌæn.tɪ'strɒf.ɪk US -t̬ə'strɑː.fɪk
anti-tank ˌæn.tɪ'tæŋk US -t̬ɪ'-, -t̬i'-, -taɪ'-
antithes|is æn'tɪθ.ə.s|ɪs, '-ɪ- **-es** -iːz
antithetic ˌæn.tɪ'θet.ɪk US -t̬ə'θet̬.ɪk **-al** -ᵊl **-ally** -ᵊl.i, -li
antitox|ic ˌæn.tɪ'tɒk.s|ɪk US -t̬ɪ'tɑːk-, -taɪ'- **-in/s** -sɪn/z
antitrust ˌæn.tɪ'trʌst US -t̬ɪ'-, -taɪ'-, -tiː-
antiviral ˌæn.tɪ'vaɪə.rᵊl US -t̬ɪ'vaɪ-, -t̬i'-, -taɪ'-
anti-vivisection ˌæn.tɪˌvɪv.ɪ'sek.ʃᵊn US -t̬i'vɪv.ɪ.sek-, -taɪ'- **-ist/s** -ɪst/s
antler 'ænt.ləʳ US -lɚ **-s** -z **-ed** -d
Antofagasta ˌæn.tə.fə'gæs.tə
Antoine ɑːn'twæn, ɒn'- US 'æn.twɑːn; 'ɑːn-
Antoinette ˌæn.twɑː'net, ˌɑːn-, -twə'- US ˌæn.twə'-, ˌɑːn-
Anton 'æn.tɒn US -tɑːn
Antonia æn'təʊ.ni.ə US -'toʊ-; ˌæn.toʊ'niː-
Antonine 'æn.tə.naɪn US -t̬ə- **-s** -z
Antoninus ˌæn.təʊ'naɪ.nəs US -t̬ə'-
Antonio æn'təʊ.ni.əʊ US -'toʊ.ni.oʊ
Antonius æn'təʊ.ni.əs US -'toʊ-
Antony 'æn.tə.ni US -tᵊn.i
antonym 'æn.tə.nɪm US -tᵊn.ɪm **-s** -z
antonymic ˌæn.tə'nɪm.ɪk US -tᵊn'ɪm-
antonymous æn'tɒn.ɪ.məs, '-ə- US -'tɑː.nə-
antonymy æn'tɒn.ɪ.mi, '-ə- US -'tɑː.nə-
Antrim 'æn.trɪm
Antrobus 'æn.trə.bəs
Antron 'æn.trɒn US -trɑːn
antr|um 'æn.tr|əm **-ums** -əmz **-a** -ə
antsy 'ænt.si
Antwerp 'æn.twɜːp US -twɝːp
ANU ˌeɪ.en'juː
Anubis ə'njuː.bɪs US -'nuː-, -'njuː-
anuresis ˌæn.jʊə'riː.sɪs, -jə- US -jʊ'-, -jə'-
anuria ˌæn'juː.ri.ə, -'jɔː- US -'jʊr.i-
anus 'eɪ.nəs **-es** -ɪz
anvil 'æn.vɪl US -vᵊl, -vɪl **-s** -z
Anwar 'æn.wɑːʳ US 'ɑːn.wɑːr, 'æn-
Anwick 'æn.ɪk US -wɪk
anxiet|y æŋ'zaɪ.ə.t|i, æŋg-, -ɪt|.i US -ə.t̬|i **-ies** -iz
anxious 'æŋ*k*.ʃəs **-ly** -li **-ness** -nəs, -nɪs
any *normal form:* 'en.i *occasional weak form:* ə.ni *occasional weak form after t or d:* ᵊn.i
Note: The usual pronunciation is /'en.i/, but when the word follows immediately after a strongly stressed word it may be weakened to /ə.ni/ (e.g. 'Have you got any change?' /hæv.ju,gɒt.ə.ni'tʃeɪndʒ US -ˌgɑːt-/). In more rapid speech, and when preceded by an alveolar consonant, the first syllable may be reduced to syllabic /n̩/ (e.g. 'Got any more?' /ˌgɒt.n̩.i'mɔːʳ US ˌgɑːt̬.n̩.i'mɔːr/).
anybody 'en.iˌbɒd.i, -bə.di US -ˌbɑː.di
anyhow 'en.i.haʊ
anymore ˌen.i'mɔːʳ US -'mɔːr
anyone 'en.i.wʌn, -wən
anyplace 'en.i.pleɪs
anyroad 'en.i.rəʊd US -roʊd
anything 'en.i.θɪŋ
anytime 'en.i.taɪm
anyway 'en.i.weɪ **-s** -z
anywhere 'en.i.*h*weəʳ US -*h*wer
anywise 'en.i.waɪz
Anzac 'æn.zæk **-s** -s **'Anzac ˌDay**
Anzio 'æn.zi.əʊ US -oʊ
AOB ˌeɪ.əʊ'biː US -oʊ'-
A-OK, A-Okay ˌeɪ.əʊ'keɪ US -oʊ'-
AOL® ˌeɪ.əʊ'el US -oʊ-
A-one ˌeɪ'wʌn *stress shift:* ˌA-one con'dition
Aoni|a eɪ'əʊ.ni|.ə US -'oʊ- **-an/s** -ən/z
aorist 'eɪ.ə.rɪst, 'eə.rɪst US 'eɪ.ə- **-s** -s
aort|a eɪ'ɔː.t|ə US -'ɔːr.t̬|ə **-as** -əz **-ae** -iː **-al** -ᵊl **-ic** -ɪk
Aosta ɑː'ɒs.tə US -'ɔː.stə, -'oʊ-
Aouita aʊ'iː.tə US -t̬ə
apace ə'peɪs
Apache ə'pætʃ.i **-s** -z
apart ə'pɑːt US -'pɑːrt **-ness** -nəs, -nɪs
apartheid ə'pɑː.taɪt, -teɪd, -teɪt, -'pɑːt.heɪt, -heɪd, -haɪt US -'pɑːr.teɪt, -taɪt
apartment ə'pɑːt.mənt US -'pɑːrt- **-s** -s **a'partment ˌblock; a'partment ˌhouse**
apathetic ˌæp.ə'θet.ɪk US -'θet̬- **-al** -ᵊl **-ally** -ᵊl.i, -li *stress shift:* ˌapathetic 'voters
apath|y 'æp.ə.θ|i **-ies** -iz
ap|e eɪp **-es** -s **-ing** -ɪŋ **-ed** -t
Apelles ə'pel.iːz
Apemantus æp.ɪ'mæn.təs US -t̬əs
Apennines 'æp.ə.naɪnz, -en.aɪnz
aperçu ˌæp.ɜː'sjuː, -ə'-, -'suː US -ɚ'suː, ˌɑː.pɚ'- **-s** -z
aperient ə'pɪə.ri.ənt US -'pɪr.i- **-s** -s
aperiodic ˌeɪ.pɪə.ri'ɒd.ɪk US -pɪr.i'ɑː.dɪk
aperiodicity ˌeɪ.pɪə.ri.ə'dɪs.ə.ti, -ɪ.ti US -pɪr.i.ə'dɪs.ə.t̬i
aperitif əˌper.ə'tiːf, æpˌer-, -ɪ'-, ə'per.ə.tɪf US ɑːˌper.ɪ'-, -ə'- **-s** -s
aperture 'æp.ə.tʃəʳ, -tjʊəʳ US -ɚ.tʃʊr, -tʃɚ **-s** -z
aper|y 'eɪ.pə.r|i **-ies** -iz
apeshit 'eɪp.ʃɪt
apex, APEX (A) 'eɪ.peks **-es** -ɪz
aphaeresis æf'ɪə.rə.sɪs, ə'fɪə-, -rɪ- US ə'fer.ə-
aphasia ə'feɪ.zi.ə, æf'eɪ-, eɪ'feɪ-, -ʒi.ə, -ʒə US ə'feɪ.ʒə, -ʒi.ə
aphasic ə'feɪ.zɪk, æf'eɪ-, eɪ'feɪ- US ə'feɪ-
apheli|on æf'iː.li.|ən **-a** -ə
apheresis æf'ɪə.rə.sɪs, ə'fɪə-, -rɪ- US ə'fer.ə-
aphes|is 'æf.ə.s|ɪs, '-ɪ- **-es** -iːz
aphid 'eɪ.fɪd US 'eɪ.fɪd, 'æf.ɪd, -əd **-s** -z
aphidian eɪ'fɪd.i.ən, æf'ɪd- **-s** -z
aph|is 'eɪ.f|ɪs, 'æf|.ɪs **-ides** -ɪ.diːz **-ises** -ɪ.sɪz
aphonia eɪ'fəʊ.ni.ə, æf'əʊ-, ə'fəʊ- US eɪ'foʊ-
aphonic eɪ'fɒn.ɪk, æf'ɒn-, ə'fɒn- US eɪ'fɑː.nɪk
aphony 'æf.ə.ni
aphorism 'æf.ᵊr.ɪ.zᵊm, -ɒr- US '-ɚ- **-s** -z
aphorist 'æf.ᵊr.ɪst, -ɒr- US '-ɚ- **-s** -s
aphoristic ˌæf.ᵊr'ɪs.tɪk, -ɒr'- US -ə'rɪs- **-ally** -ᵊl.i, -li
aphoriz|e, -is|e 'æf.ᵊr.aɪz, -ɒr- US -ə.raɪz **-es** -ɪz **-ing** -ɪŋ **-ed** -d **-er/s** -əʳ/z US -ɚ/z
Aphra 'æf.rə
aphrodisiac ˌæf.rəʊ'dɪz.i.æk US -rə'-, -roʊ'-, -'diː.zi- **-s** -s
aphrodisian ˌæf.rəʊ'dɪz.i.ən

US -rəˈdiː.zi-, -roʊˈ-, -ˈdɪz.i-, -ˈdʒ.ən **-s** -z
Aphrodite ˌæf.rəʊˈdaɪ.ti US -rəˈdaɪ.t̬i, -roʊˈ-
aphtha ˈæf.θə
Apia ɑːˈpiː.ə
apian ˈeɪ.pi.ən
apiarian ˌeɪ.piˈeə.ri.ən US -ˈer.i- **-s** -z
apiarist ˈeɪ.pi.ə.rɪst **-s** -s
apiar|y ˈeɪ.pi.ə.r|i US -er|.i **-ies** -iz
apical ˈæp.ɪ.kᵊl, ˈeɪ.pɪ- **-ly** -i
apices *(alternative plur. of* **apex)** ˈeɪ.pɪ.siːz, ˈæp.ɪ-
apiculture ˈeɪ.pɪ.kʌl.tʃəʳ US -tʃɚ
apiece əˈpiːs
apis ˈeɪ.pɪs
Apis ˈɑː.pɪs, ˈeɪ-
apish ˈeɪ.pɪʃ **-ly** -li **-ness** -nəs, -nɪs
aplenty əˈplen.ti US -t̬i
aplomb əˈplɒm, æpˈlɒm US əˈplɑːm, -ˈplʌm
apn(o)ea æpˈniː.ə, ˈæp.ni.ə
apn(o)eic æpˈniː.ɪk
apocalyps|e (A) əˈpɒk.ə.lɪps US -ˈpɑː.kə- **-es** -ɪz
apocalypt|ic əˌpɒk.əˈlɪp.t|ɪk US -ˌpɑː.kəˈ- **-ist/s** -ɪst/s **-ical** -ɪ.kᵊl
stress shift: aˌpocalyptic ˈvision
apocope əˈpɒk.əʊ.pi US -ˈpɑː.kə- **-s** -z
apocryph|a (A) əˈpɒk.rɪ.f|ə, -rə- US -ˈpɑː.krə- **-al** -ᵊl
apocryphal əˈpɒk.rɪ.fəl, -rə- US -ˈpɑː.krə-
apodeictic ˌæp.əʊˈdaɪk.tɪk US -əˈ-, -oʊˈ- **-al** -ᵊl **-ally** -ᵊl.i, -li
apodictic ˌæp.əʊˈdɪk.tɪk US -əˈ-, -oʊˈ- **-al** -ᵊl **-ally** -ᵊl.i, -li
apodos|is əˈpɒd.ə.s|ɪs US -ˈpɑː.də- **-es** -iːz
apogee ˈæp.əʊ.dʒiː US -ə- **-s** -z
apolitical ˌeɪ.pəˈlɪt.ɪ.kᵊl, ˈ-ə- US -ˈlɪt̬.ə-
Apollinaire əˌpɒl.ɪˈneəʳ US -ˌpɑː.lɪˈner
Apollinaris əˌpɒl.ɪˈnɑː.rɪs, -ˈeə- US -pɑː.lɪˈner.ɪs
Apollo əˈpɒl.əʊ US -ˈpɑː.loʊ
Apollodorus əˌpɒl.əˈdɔː.rəs US -ˌpɑː.ləˈdɔːr.əs
Apolloni|a ˌæp.əˈləʊ.ni.|ə, -ɒlˈəʊ- US -əˈloʊ- **-an** -ən **-us** -əs
Apollos əˈpɒl.əs US -ˈpɑː.ləs
Apollyon əˈpɒl.i.ən US -ˈpɑː.li-
apologetic əˌpɒl.əˈdʒet.ɪk US -ˌpɑː.ləˈdʒet̬.ɪk **-al** -ᵊl **-ally** -ᵊl.i, -li **-s** -s
apologia ˌæp.əˈləʊ.dʒə, -dʒi.ə US -ˈloʊ- **-s** -z
apologist əˈpɒl.ə.dʒɪst US -ˈpɑː.lə- **-s** -s
apologiz|e, -is|e əˈpɒl.ə.dʒaɪz US -ˈpɑː.lə- **-es** -ɪz **-ing** -ɪŋ **-ed** -d **-er/s** -əʳ/z, -ɚ/z
apologue ˈæp.əʊ.lɒg US -ə.lɑːg **-s** -z
apolog|y əˈpɒl.ə.dʒ|i US -ˈpɑː.lə- **-ies** -iz
apophthegm ˈæp.ə.θem **-s** -z
apoplectic ˌæp.əˈplek.tɪk **-al** -ᵊl **-ally** -ᵊl.i, -li
apoplex|y ˈæp.ə.plek.s|i **-ies** -iz
aposiopes|is ˌæp.ə.saɪ.əʊˈpiː.s|ɪs, əˌpɒs.i.əʊˈ- US ˌæp.oʊ.saɪ.oʊˈ-, -ə.saɪ.əˈ- **-es** -iːz
apostas|y əˈpɒs.tə.s|i US -ˈpɑː.stə- **-ies** -iz
apostate əˈpɒs.teɪt, -tɪt, -tət US -ˈpɑː.steɪt, -stɪt, -stət **-s** -s
apostatic ˌæp.əʊˈstæt.ɪk US -əˈstæt̬- **-al** -ᵊl
apostatiz|e, -is|e əˈpɒs.tə.taɪz US -ˈpɑː.stə- **-es** -ɪz **-ing** -ɪŋ **-ed** -d
a posteriori eɪ.pɒsˌter.iˈɔː.raɪ, ˌɑː-, -tɪə.ri- -riː- US eɪ.pɑːˌstɪr-
apostil əˈpɒs.tɪl US -ˈpɑː.stɪl **-s** -z
apostle əˈpɒs.l̩ US -ˈpɑː.sl̩ **-s** -z **-ship** -ʃɪp
apostolate əˈpɒs.tə.lət, -lɪt, -leɪt US -ˈpɑː.stə.lɪt, -leɪt **-s** -s
apostolic ˌæp.əˈstɒl.ɪk US -ˈstɑː.lɪk **-al** -ᵊl **-ally** -ᵊl.i
apostolicism ˌæp.əˈstɒl.ɪ.sɪ.zᵊm US -ˈstɑː.lɪ-
apostrophe əˈpɒs.trə.fi US -ˈpɑː.strə- **-s** -z
apostrophiz|e, -is|e əˈpɒs.trə.faɪz US -ˈpɑː.strə- **-es** -ɪz **-ing** -ɪŋ **-ed** -d
apothecar|y əˈpɒθ.ə.kᵊr.|i, ˈ-ɪ- US -ˈpɑː.θə- **-ies** -iz
apothegm ˈæp.ə.θem **-s** -z
apothegmatic ˌæp.ə.θegˈmæt.ɪk US -ˈmæt̬- **-al** -ᵊl
apotheos|is əˌpɒθ.iˈəʊ.s|ɪs, ˌæp.əʊ.θiˈ- US əˌpɑː.θiˈoʊ-, ˌæp.əˈθiː.ə- **-es** -iːz
apotheosiz|e, -is|e əˈpɒθ.i.əʊ.saɪz, ˌæp.əˈθiː.əʊ.saɪz US əˈpɑː.θi.oʊ-, ˌæp.əˈθiː.ə- **-es** -ɪz **-ing** -ɪŋ **-ed** -d
appal əˈpɔːl US -ˈpɔːl, -ˈpɑːl **-s** -z **-ling/ly** -ɪŋ/li **-led** -d
Appalachi|a ˌæp.əˈleɪ.ʃ|ə, -tʃ|ə, -ʃi|.ə US -ˈleɪ.tʃi-, -ˈlætʃ.i-, -ˈleɪ.tʃ|ə, -ˈlætʃ|.ə **-an/s** -ən/z
appall əˈpɔːl US -ˈpɔːl, -ˈpɑːl **-s** -z **-ing/ly** -ɪŋ/li **-ed** -d
Appaloosa ˌæp.əˈluː.sə
appanag|e ˈæp.ə.nɪdʒ **-es** -ɪz
apparat ˌæp.əˈrɑːt US ˌɑː.pəˈ-, ˈæp.ə.ræt **-s** -s
apparatchik ˌæp.əˈrætʃ.ɪk, -ˈræt.tʃɪk, -ˈrɑːt-, -ˈrɑː.tʃɪk US ˌɑː.pəˈrɑː.tʃɪk, -ˈrɑːt.tʃɪk **-s** -s **-i** -i
apparatus ˌæp.ᵊrˈeɪ.təs, -ˈæt.əs US -əˈræt̬- **-es** -ɪz
apparel əˈpær.ᵊl US -ˈper-, -ˈpær- **-s** -z **-ling** -ɪŋ **-led** -d
apparent əˈpær.ᵊnt, -ˈpeə.rᵊnt US -ˈper.ᵊnt, -ˈpær- **-ly** -li **-ness** -nəs, -nɪs
apparition ˌæp.ᵊrˈɪʃ.ᵊn US -əˈrɪʃ- **-s** -z
apparitor əˈpær.ɪ.təʳ US -ˈper.ɪ.t̬ɚ, -ˈpær- **-s** -z
appassionata əˌpæs.i.əˈnɑː.tə, -ˌpæs.jəˈ- US -ˌpɑː.si.əˈnɑː.t̬ə, -ˌpæs.i-
appeal əˈpiːl **-s** -z **-ing** -ɪŋ **-ed** -d **-er/s** -əʳ/z US -ɚ/z **Apˈpeal ˌCourt**
appealing əˈpiː.lɪŋ **-ly** -li **-ness** -nəs, -nɪs
appear əˈpɪəʳ US -ˈpɪr **-s** -z **-ing** -ɪŋ **-ed** -d **-er/s** -əʳ/z US -ɚ/z
appearanc|e əˈpɪə.rᵊnts US -ˈpɪr.ᵊnts **-es** -ɪz
appeas|e əˈpiːz **-es** -ɪz **-ing/ly** -ɪŋ/li **-ed** -d **-able** -ə.bl̩
appeasement əˈpiːz.mənt **-s** -s
appellant əˈpel.ənt **-s** -s
appellate əˈpel.ət, æpˈel-, -eɪt, -ɪt US -ɪt
appellation ˌæp.əˈleɪ.ʃᵊn, -ɪˈ-, -elˈeɪ- **-s** -z
appellation contrôlée *as if French:* æp.el.æsˌjɔ̃ːŋ.kɔ̃ːn.trəʊˈleɪ, æp.elˌæs.jɔ̃ːŋ-, -kɒnˈtrəʊ.leɪ US æp.elˌɑː.sjoʊn.kɑːn.troʊˈleɪ
appellative əˈpel.ə.tɪv, æpˈel- US -t̬ɪv **-ly** -li **-ness** -nəs, -nɪs
append əˈpend **-s** -z **-ing** -ɪŋ **-ed** -ɪd
appendag|e əˈpen.dɪdʒ **-es** -ɪz
appendant əˈpen.dənt **-s** -s
appendectom|y ˌæp.enˈdek.tə.m|i **-ies** -iz
appendicitis əˌpen.dɪˈsaɪ.tɪs, -dəˈ-
appendicular ˌæp.enˈdɪk.jʊ.ləʳ, -ənˈ-, -ɪnˈ-, -jə- US -ju.lɚ
append|ix əˈpen.d|ɪks **-ixes** -ɪk.sɪz **-ices** -ɪ.siːz
appercep|tion ˌæp.əˈsep.|ʃᵊn US -ɚˈ- **-tive** -tɪv
Apperley ˈæp.ə.li US -ɚ-
appertain ˌæp.əˈteɪn US -ɚˈ- **-s** -z **-ing** -ɪŋ **-ed** -d
appertinent əˈpɜː.tɪ.nənt, æpˈɜː- US əˈpɝː.tᵊn.ənt
appeten|ce ˈæp.ɪ.tᵊn|ts **-cy** -t.si **-t** -t
appetite ˈæp.ɪ.taɪt, ˈ-ə- US ˈ-ə- **-s** -s
appetizer, -iser ˈæp.ɪ.taɪ.zəʳ, ˈ-ə- US -ə.taɪ.zɚ **-s** -z
appetizing, -isi- ˈæp.ɪ.taɪ.zɪŋ, ˈ-ə- US ˈ-ə- **-ly** -li
Appi|an ˈæp.i|.ən **-us** -əs
applaud əˈplɔːd US -ˈplɑːd, -ˈplɔːd **-s** -z **-ing/ly** -ɪŋ/li **-ed** -ɪd **-er/s** -əʳ/z, -ɚ/z
applause əˈplɔːz US -ˈplɑːz, -ˈplɔːz
apple ˈæp.l̩ **-s** -z **ˈapple ˌblossom; ˈapple ˌbutter; ˌapple ˈsauce;** US **ˈapple ˌsauce; ˈapple ˌtree; the ˌapple of one's ˈeye**
Appleby ˈæp.l̩.bi
apple-cart ˈæp.l̩.kɑːt US -kɑːrt
Appledore ˈæp.l̩.dɔːʳ US -dɔːr

Approximant

A phonetic term of comparatively recent origin, used to denote a consonant which makes very little obstruction to the airflow.

Examples for English

Traditionally approximants have been divided into two groups. Sounds in the first group are known as 'semivowels' such as the /w/ and /j/, which are very similar to 'close vowels' such as [u] and [i] but are produced as a rapid glide, e.g.:

wet /wet/
yet /jet/

'Liquids' are sounds which have an identifiable constriction of the airflow but not one that is sufficiently obstructive to produce fricative noise, compression or the diversion of airflow through another part of the vocal tract as in nasals. This category includes laterals such as /l/ and non-fricative /r/ (phonetically [ɹ] in British English and [ɻ] in US English), e.g.:

lead /liːd/
read /riːd/

Approximants therefore are never fricative and never contain interruptions to the flow of air.

Appleford 'æp.l̩.fəd (US) -fɚd
Applegate 'æp.l̩.geɪt, -gɪt
applejack 'æp.l̩.dʒæk
apple-pie ˌæp.l̩'paɪ **-s** -z *stress shift, see compounds:* **in ˌapple-pie 'order**; *British only:* **ˌapple-pie 'bed**
Appleseed 'æp.l̩.siːd
applet 'æp.lət **-s** -s
Appleton 'æp.l̩.tən (US) -t̬ən
appliable ə'plaɪ.ə.bl̩ **-ness** -nəs, -nɪs
applianc|e ə'plaɪ.ənts **-es** -ɪz
applicability ˌæp.lɪ.kə'bɪl.ə.ti, əˌplɪk-, -ɪ.ti (US) -ə.t̬i
applicab|le ə'plɪk.ə.bl|̩, 'æp.lɪ- **-ly** -li **-leness** -l̩.nəs, -nɪs
applicant 'æp.lɪ.kənt, -lə- **-s** -s
applicate 'æp.lɪ.kət, -lə-, -kɪt, -keɪt
application ˌæp.lɪ'keɪ.ʃən, -lə'- **-s** -z
applicator 'æp.lɪ.keɪ.təʳ, -lə- (US) -t̬ɚ **-s** -z
appliqué æp'liː.keɪ, ə'pliː-; 'æp.lɪ.keɪ (US) 'æp.lə.keɪ, -lɪ- **-s** -z **-ing** -ɪŋ, **-d** -d
appl|y ə'pl|aɪ **-ies** -aɪz **-ying** -aɪ.ɪŋ **-ied** -aɪd
appoggiatura əˌpɒdʒ.ə'tʊə.rə, -i.ə'-, -'tjʊə- (US) əˌpɑː.dʒə'tʊr.ə **-s** -z
ap|point ə|'pɔɪnt **-points** -'pɔɪnts **-pointing** -'pɔɪn.tɪŋ (US) -'pɔɪn.t̬ɪŋ **-pointed** -'pɔɪn.tɪd (US) -'pɔɪn.t̬ɪd
appointee əˌpɔɪn'tiː, ˌæp.ɔɪn'- **-s** -z
appointive ə'pɔɪn.tɪv (US) -t̬ɪv
appointment ə'pɔɪnt.mənt **-s** -s
Appomattox ˌæp.ə'mæt.əks (US) -'mæt̬-
ap|port ə|'pɔːt (US) -'pɔːrt **-ports** -'pɔːts (US) -'pɔːrts **-porting** -'pɔː.tɪŋ (US) -'pɔːr.t̬ɪŋ **-ported** -'pɔː.tɪd (US) -'pɔːr.t̬ɪd
apportion ə'pɔː.ʃən (US) -'pɔːr- **-s** -z **-ing** -ɪŋ **-ed** -d **-ment/s** -mənt/s
appos|e ə'pəʊz, æp'əʊz (US) ə'poʊz **-es** -ɪz **-ing** -ɪŋ **-ed** -d
apposite 'æp.ə.zɪt, -zaɪt (US) -zɪt **-ly** -li **-ness** -nəs, -nɪs
apposition ˌæp.ə'zɪʃ.ən **-s** -z
appositional ˌæp.ə'zɪʃ.ən.əl
appraisal ə'preɪ.zəl **-s** -z
apprais|e ə'preɪz **-es** -ɪz **-ing** -ɪŋ **-ed** -d **-er/s** -əʳ/z (US) -ɚ/s **-able** -ə.bl̩
appraisee ˌæp.reɪ'ziː, -'-- (US) ˌæ.preɪ'ziː, ˌə- **-s** -z
appraisement ə'preɪz.mənt **-s** -s
appreciab|le ə'priː.ʃə.bl|̩, -ʃi.ə-, -si.ə- (US) '-ʃə-, '-ʃi.ə- **-ly** -li
appreci|ate ə'priː.ʃi|.eɪt, -si- (US) -ʃi- **-ates** -eɪts **-ating/ly** -eɪ.tɪŋ/li (US) -eɪ.t̬ɪŋ/li **-ated** -eɪ.tɪd (US) -eɪ.t̬ɪd **-ator/s** -eɪ.təʳ/z (US) -eɪ.t̬ɚ/z
appreciation əˌpriː.ʃi'eɪ.ʃən, -si'- (US) -ʃi'- **-s** -z
appreciative ə'priː.ʃə.tɪv, '-ʃi.ə.tɪv (US) -'priː.ʃə.t̬ɪv, '-ʃi.ə-, -eɪ- **-ly** -li **-ness** -nəs, -nɪs
appreciatory ə'priː.ʃi.ə.tər.i, -ʃi.eɪ-, -si.ə- (US) '-ʃə.tɔːr-, '-ʃi.ə-
apprehend ˌæp.rɪ'hend, -rə'- **-s** -z **-ing** -ɪŋ **-ed** -ɪd
apprehensibility ˌæp.rɪˌhent.sɪ'bɪl.ə.ti, -rə-, -sə'-, -ɪ.ti (US) -ə.t̬i
apprehensible ˌæp.rɪ'hent.sɪ.bl̩, -rə'-, -sə-
apprehension ˌæp.rɪ'hen.tʃən, -rə'- (US) -'hent.ʃən **-s** -z
apprehensive ˌæp.rɪ'hent.sɪv, -rə'- **-ly** -li **-ness** -nəs, -nɪs
apprentic|e ə'pren.tɪs (US) -t̬ɪs **-es** -ɪz **-ing** -ɪŋ **-ed** -t
apprenticeship ə'pren.tɪ.ʃɪp, -tɪs- (US) -t̬əs.ʃɪp, -t̬ə- **-s** -s
appris|e, -iz|e ə'praɪz **-es** -ɪz **-ing** -ɪŋ **-ed** -d **-er/s** -əʳ/z (US) -ɚ/z
appro 'æp.rəʊ (US) -roʊ
approach ə'prəʊtʃ (US) -'proʊtʃ **-es** -ɪz **-ing** -ɪŋ **-ed** -t
approachability əˌprəʊ.tʃə'bɪl.ə.ti, -ɪ.ti (US) -ˌproʊ.tʃə'bɪl.ə.t̬i
approachable ə'prəʊ.tʃə.bl̩ (US) -'proʊ-
appro|bate 'æp.rəʊ|.beɪt (US) -rə- **-bates** -beɪts **-bating** -beɪ.tɪŋ (US) -beɪ.t̬ɪŋ **-bated** -beɪ.tɪd (US) -beɪ.t̬ɪd **-bative** -beɪ.tɪv (US) -beɪ.t̬ɪv
approbation ˌæp.rəʊ'beɪ.ʃən (US) -rə'-, -roʊ'- **-s** -z
approbatory ˌæp.rəʊ'beɪ.tər.i (US) ə'proʊ.bə.tɔːr-
appropriate *(adj.)* ə'prəʊ.pri.ət, -ɪt (US) -'proʊ- **-ly** -li **-ness** -nəs, -nɪs
appropri|ate *(v.)* ə'prəʊ.pri|.eɪt (US) -'proʊ- **-ates** -eɪts **-ating** -eɪ.tɪŋ (US) -eɪ.t̬ɪŋ **-ated** -eɪ.tɪd (US) -eɪ.t̬ɪd **-ator/s** -eɪ.təʳ/z (US) -eɪ.t̬ɚ/z
appropriation əˌprəʊ.pri'eɪ.ʃən (US) -ˌproʊ- **-s** -z
approval ə'pruː.vəl **-s** -z
approv|e ə'pruːv **-es** -z **-ing/ly** -ɪŋ/li **-ed** -d **-er/s** -əʳ/z (US) -ɚ/z **-able** -ə.bl̩
approx *(abbrev. for* **approximate/ly***)* ə'prɒk.sɪ.mət/li, -sə-, -mɪt/li (US) -'prɑːk-
approximant ə'prɒk.sɪ.mənt, -sə- (US) -'prɑːk- **-s** -s
approximate *(adj.)* ə'prɒk.sɪ.mət, -sə-, -mɪt (US) -'prɑːk- **-ly** -li
approxi|mate *(v.)* ə'prɒk.sɪ|.meɪt, -sə- (US) -'prɑːk- **-mates** -meɪts **-mating** -meɪ.tɪŋ (US) -meɪ.t̬ɪŋ **-mated** -meɪ.tɪd (US) -meɪ.t̬ɪd
approximation əˌprɒk.sɪ'meɪ.ʃən, -sə'- (US) -ˌprɑːk- **-s** -z
approximative ə'prɒk.sɪ.mə.tɪv, -sə- (US) -'prɑːk.sə.mə.t̬ɪv
appui æp'wiː, ə'pwiː
appuls|e æp'ʌls, ə'pʌls, 'æp.ʌls **-es** -ɪz
appurtenan|ce ə'pɜː.tɪ.nən|ts, -tən.ən|ts (US) -'pɝː.tən- **-ces** -t.sɪz **-t** -t
APR ˌeɪ.pi'ɑːʳ (US) -'ɑːr
Apr. *(abbrev. for* **April***)* 'eɪ.prəl, -prɪl
après 'æp.reɪ (US) ˌɑː'preɪ, ˌæp'reɪ
après-ski ˌæp.reɪ'skiː (US) ˌɑː.preɪ'-, ˌæp.reɪ'- *stress shift:* ˌapräs-ski 'drinks

apricot ˈeɪ.prɪ.kɒt (US) -kɑːt, ˈæp.rɪ- **-s** -s
April ˈeɪ.prəl, -prɪl **-s** -z ˌ**April ˈFools' ˌDay**
a priori eɪ.praɪˈɔː.raɪ, ˌɑː.priːˈɔː.ri (US) ˌɑː.priːˈɔːr.aɪ, ˌeɪ-, -i
apriority ˌeɪ.praɪˈɒr.ə.ti, -ɪ.ti (US) -ˈɔːr.ə.t̬i
apron ˈeɪ.prən **-s** -z **-ed** -d ˈ**apron ˌstrings**
apropos ˌæp.rəˈpəʊ (US) -ˈpoʊ
aps|e æps **-es** -ɪz
apsidal ˈæp.sɪ.dəl
Apsley ˈæp.sli
apt æpt **-er** -əʳ (US) -ɚ **-est** -əst, -ɪst **-ly** -li **-ness** -nəs, -nɪs
apter|al ˈæp.tər|.əl **-ous** -əs
apteryx ˈæp.tər.ɪks **-es** -ɪz
aptitude ˈæp.tɪ.tjuːd, -tə-, -tʃuːd (US) -tuːd, -tjuːd **-s** -z
aptitudinal ˌæp.tɪˈtjuː.dɪ.nəl, -təˈ-, -ˈtʃuː- (US) -ˈtuː.dən.əl, -ˈtjuː- **-ly** -li
Apuli|a əˈpjuː.li|.ə **-an/s** -ən/z
apyretic ˌæp.aɪəˈret.ɪk, ˌeɪ.paɪəˈ-, -paɪ.ɪˈ- (US) -paɪˈret̬-
aqua ˈæk.wə (US) ˈɑːk-
aquacultural ˌæk.wəˈkʌl.tʃər.əl (US) ˌɑː.kwəˈ-, ˌæk.wəˈ-
aquaculture ˈæk.wəˌkʌl.tʃəʳ (US) ˈɑː.kwəˌkʌl.tʃɚ, ˈæk.wəˌ-
aqua fortis ˌæk.wəˈfɔː.tɪs (US) ˌɑː.kwəˈfɔːr.t̬ɪs, ˌæk.wəˈ-
aquamarine ˌæk.wə.məˈriːn, ˈæk.wə.mə.riːn (US) ˌɑː.kwə.məˈriːn, ˌæk.wə- **-s** -z
aquaplan|e ˈæk.wə.pleɪn (US) ˈɑː.kwə-, ˈæk.wə- **-es** -z **-ing** -ɪŋ **-ed** -d
aqua regia ˌæk.wəˈriː.dʒi.ə (US) ˌɑː.kwəˈ-, ˌæk.wəˈ-
aquarell|e ˌæk.wəˈrel (US) ˌɑː.kwəˈ-, ˌæk.wəˈ- **-es** -z **-ist/s** -ɪst/s
aquarist ˈæk.wə.rɪst (US) əˈkwer.ɪst **-s** -s
aquari|um əˈkweə.ri.|əm (US) -ˈkwer.i- **-ums** -əmz **-a** -ə
Aquari|us əˈkweə.ri.|əs (US) -ˈkwer.i- **-an/s** -ən/z
Aquascutum® ˌæk.wəˈskjuː.təm (US) ˌɑː.kwəˈskuː.t̬əm, ˌæk.wəˈ-
aquatic əˈkwæt.ɪk, -ˈkwɒt- (US) -ˈkwæt̬-, -ˈkwɑː.t̬ɪk **-s** -s **-ally** -əl.i, -li
aquatint ˈæk.wə.tɪnt (US) ˈɑː.kwə-, ˈæk.wə- **-s** -s
aquatube ˈæk.wə.tjuːb, -tʃuːb (US) ˈɑː.kwə.tuːb, ˈæk.wə-, -tjuːb **-s** -z
aquavit ˈæk.wə.vɪt, -viːt (US) ˈɑː.kwə.viːt
aqua vitae ˌæk.wəˈviː.taɪ, -ˈvaɪ.tiː (US) ˌɑː.kwəˈvaɪ.t̬iː, ˌæk.wəˈ-
aqueduct ˈæk.wɪ.dʌkt, -wə- **-s** -s
aqueous ˈeɪ.kwi.əs, ˈæk.wi- **-ly** -li
aquifer ˈæk.wɪ.fəʳ, -wə.fəʳ (US) ˈɑː.kwə.fɚ, ˈæk.wə- **-s** -z
Aquila ˈæk.wɪ.lə, -wə-; əˈkwɪl.ə
aquilegia ˌæk.wɪˈliː.dʒi.ə, -wə-, -ˈliː.dʒə **-s** -z
aquiline ˈæk.wɪ.laɪn, -wə- (US) -lən
Aquinas əˈkwaɪ.nəs, ækˈwaɪ-, -næs
Aquino əˈkiː.nəʊ (US) -noʊ
Aquitaine ˌæk.wɪˈteɪn, -wəˈteɪn, ˈ---
Aquitania ˌæk.wɪˈteɪ.ni.ə
aquiver əˈkwɪv.əʳ (US) -ɚ
ar- əˈr-; ˈær- (US) əˈr-; ˈer-, ˈær-
Note: Prefix. Examples include **arrogate** /ˈær.əʊ.geɪt (US) ˈer.ə-/, in which it is stressed, and **array** /əˈreɪ/, where it is unstressed.
-ar -əʳ, -ɑːʳ (US) -ɚ, -ɑːr
Note: Suffix. Normally pronounced /-əʳ (US) -ɚ/, e.g. **molecular** /məʊˈlek.jə.ləʳ (US) moʊˈlek.juː.lɚ/, but in some cases /-ɑːʳ (US) -ɑːr/, e.g. **sonar** /ˈsəʊ.nɑːʳ (US) ˈsoʊ.nɑːr/.
Arab ˈær.əb (US) ˈer-, ˈær- **-s** -z
Arabella ˌær.əˈbel.ə (US) ˌer-, ˌær-
arabesque ˌær.əˈbesk (US) ˌer-, ˌær- **-s** -s **-d** -t
Arabi|a əˈreɪ.bi|.ə **-an/s** -ən/z
Arabic *of Arabia:* ˈær.ə.bɪk (US) ˈer-, ˈær- *name of ship:* ˈær.ə.bɪk; əˈræb- (US) ˈer.ə-, ˈær-; əˈræb-
arabis ˈær.ə.bɪs (US) ˈer-, ˈær-
Arabist ˈær.ə.bɪst (US) ˈer-, ˈær- **-s** -s
arable ˈær.ə.bl̩ (US) ˈer-, ˈær-
Araby ˈær.ə.bi (US) ˈer-, ˈær-
Aracaju ˌær.ə.kæʒˈuː (US) ɑːˌrɑː.kəˈʒuː
Arachne əˈræk.ni
arachnid əˈræk.nɪd **-a** -ə **-s** -z
arachnoid əˈræk.nɔɪd **-s** -z
arachnologist ˌær.ækˈnɒl.ə.dʒɪst, -əkˈ- (US) ˌer.əkˈnɑː.lə-, ˌær- **-s** -s
arachnopho|bia əˌræk.nəʊˈfəʊ.|bi.ə (US) -nəˈfoʊ-, -noʊˈ- **-bic** -bɪk
Arafat ˈær.ə.fæt (US) ˈer-, ˈær-
Arafura ˌær.əˈfʊə.rə (US) ˌɑːr.əˈfʊr.ə
Aragon ˈær.ə.gən (US) ˈer.ə.gɑːn, ˈær-, -gən
aragonite əˈræg.ən.aɪt; ˈær.ə.gən- (US) əˈræg.ən-; ˈer.ə.gən-, ˈær-
Aral ˈɑː.rəl, ˈær.əl, -æl (US) ˈer.əl, ˈær-
Araldite® ˈær.əl.daɪt (US) ˈer-, ˈær-
Aram *biblical name:* ˈeə.ræm, -rəm (US) ˈer.æm, ˈær-, ˈeɪ.rəm, ˈɑːr.əm *surname:* ˈeə.rəm (US) ˈer.əm, ˈær-
Aramaean ˌær.əˈmiː.ən (US) ˌer-, ˌær-
Arama|ic ˌær.əˈmeɪ|.ɪk (US) ˌer-, ˌær- **-ism** -ɪ.zəm
Aramean ˌær.əˈmiː.ən (US) ˌer-, ˌær- **-s** -z
aramid ˈær.ə.mɪd (US) ˈer-, ˈær- **-s** -z
Aramite ˈær.ə.maɪt (US) ˈer-, ˈær- **-s** -s
Aran ˈær.ən (US) ˈer-, ˈær-
Arapaho əˈræp.ə.həʊ (US) -hoʊ
Ararat ˈær.ə.ræt (US) ˈer-, ˈær-
Araucani|a ˌær.ɔːˈkeɪ.ni|.ə (US) ˌer-, ˌær-, -ɑːˈ-; əˌraʊ.kɑːˈniː- **-an/s** -ən/z
araucaria ˌær.ɔːˈkeə.ri.ə (US) ˌer.ɔːˈker.i-, ˌær-, -ɑːˈ- **-s** -z
Arawak ˈær.ə.wæk, -wɑːk (US) ˈɑːr.ə.wɑːk; ˈær.ə.wæk, ˈer- **-s** -s
Arber ˈɑː.bəʳ (US) ˈɑːr.bɚ
Arberry ˈɑː.bər.i (US) ˈɑːr.ber-
Arbil ˈɑː.bɪl (US) ˈɑːr-
arbiter ˈɑː.bɪ.təʳ (US) ˈɑːr.bɪ.t̬ɚ **-s** -z
arbitrage *arbitration:* ˈɑː.bɪ.trɪdʒ (US) ˈɑːr- *of stocks, etc.:* ˌɑː.bɪˈtrɑːʒ, ˈɑː.bɪ.trɪdʒ (US) ˈɑːr.bɪ.trɑːʒ
arbitrageur ˌɑː.bɪ.trɑːˈʒɜːʳ (US) ˈɑːr.bɪ.trɑː.ʒɚ **-s** -z
arbitrament ɑːˈbɪt.rə.mənt (US) ɑːr- **-s** -s
arbitrarily ˌɑː.bɪˈtreə.rəl.i, ˈɑː.bɪ.trər.əl.i (US) ˌɑːr.bəˈtrer.əl-
arbitrar|y ˈɑː.bɪ.trər|.i (US) ˈɑːr.bə.trer- **-iness** -ɪ.nəs, -ɪ.nɪs
arbi|trate ˈɑː.bɪ|.treɪt (US) ˈɑːr.bə|.treɪt **-trates** -treɪts **-trating** -treɪ.tɪŋ (US) -treɪ.t̬ɪŋ **-trated** -treɪ.tɪd (US) -treɪ.t̬ɪd
arbitration ˌɑː.bɪˈtreɪ.ʃən (US) ˌɑːr.bəˈ- **-s** -z
arbitrator ˈɑː.bɪ.treɪ.təʳ (US) ˈɑːr.bə- **-s** -z
Arblay ˈɑː.bleɪ (US) ˈɑːr-
arbor *tree:* ˈɑː.bɔːʳ, -bəʳ (US) ˈɑːr.bɚ *axle, shaft:* ˈɑː.bəʳ (US) ˈɑːr.bɚ **-s** -z
Arbor ˈɑː.bəʳ (US) ˈɑːr.bɚ ˈ**Arbor ˌDay**
arboraceous ˌɑː.bərˈeɪ.ʃəs, -bɔːˈreɪ- (US) ˌɑːr.bəˈreɪ-, -bɔːˈ-
arbore|al ɑːˈbɔː.ri|.əl (US) ɑːrˈbɔːr.i- **-ous** -əs
arborescen|ce ˌɑː.bərˈes.ən|ts, -bɔːˈres- (US) ˌɑːr.bəˈres-, -bɔːˈ- **-t** -t
arbore|tum ˌɑː.bərˈiː.|təm, -bɔːˈriː- (US) ˌɑːr.bəˈriː-, -bɔːˈ- **-tums** -təmz (US) -t̬əmz **-ta** -tə (US) -t̬ə
arboriculture ˈɑː.bər.ɪˌkʌl.tʃəʳ, -bɔː-; ɑːˈbɒr.ɪ.- (US) ˈɑːr.bɚ.ɪˌkʌl.tʃɚ; ɑːrˈbɔːr-
arborization, -isa- ˌɑː.bər.aɪˈzeɪ.ʃən, -bɔː.raɪˈ-, -rɪˈ- (US) ˌɑːr.bɚ.ɪˈ-, -bɔːr-
arboriz|e, -is|e ˈɑː.bər.aɪz (US) ˈɑːr.bə.raɪz **-es** -ɪz **-ing** -ɪŋ **-ed** -d
arbor-vitae ˌɑː.bəˈviː.taɪ, -bɔː-, -ˈvaɪ-, -tiː (US) ˌɑːr.bɚˈvaɪ.tiː, -ˈviː- **-s** -z
arbour ˈɑː.bəʳ (US) ˈɑːr.bɚ **-s** -z
Arbroath ɑːˈbrəʊθ (US) ɑːrˈbroʊθ
Arbus ˈɑː.bəs (US) ˈɑːr-
Arbuthnot(t) ɑːˈbʌθ.nət, əˈbʌθ- (US) ɑːr-, -nɑːt
arbutus ɑːˈbjuː.təs (US) ɑːrˈbjuː.t̬əs **-es** -ɪz
arc (A) ɑːk (US) ɑːrk **-s** -s **-(k)ing** -ɪŋ **-(k)ed** -t ˈ**arc ˌlamp**; ˈ**arc ˌlight**
arcade ɑːˈkeɪd (US) ɑːr- **-s** -z

Arcadi|a ɑː'keɪ.di|.ə (US) ɑːr- **-an/s** -ən/z
Arcady 'ɑː.kə.di (US) 'ɑːr-
arcane ɑː'keɪn (US) ɑːr-
arcan|um ɑː'keɪ.n|əm (US) ɑːr- **-a** -ə
arch- ɑːtʃ-, ɑːk- (US) ɑːrtʃ-, ɑːrk-
Note: Prefix. Words containing **arch-** normally carry secondary stress on the first syllable, e.g. **archbishop** /ˌɑːtʃ'bɪʃ.əp (US) ˌɑːrtʃ-/, with the obvious exception of **archangel**.
arch *(adj.)* ɑːtʃ (US) ɑːrtʃ **-est** -əst, -ɪst **-ly** -li **-ness** -nəs, -nɪs
arch *(n. v.)* ɑːtʃ (US) ɑːrtʃ **-es** -ɪz **-ing** -ɪŋ **-ed** -t
-arch -ɑːk, -ək (US) -ɑːrk, -ɚk
Note: Suffix. Normally /-ɑːk (US) -ɑːrk/, e.g. **oligarch** /'ɒl.ɪ.gɑːk (US) 'ɑː.lɪ.gɑːrk/, but /-ək, -ɚk/ is preferred in some words, e.g. **monarch** /'mɒn.ək (US) 'mɑː.nɚk -nɑːrk/.
archaean (A) ɑː'kiː.ən (US) ɑːr-
archaeo- ˌɑː.ki.əʊ-; ˌɑː.ki'ɒ- (US) ˌɑːr.ki.oʊ-, -ə-; ˌɑːr.ki'ɑː-
Note: Prefix. Words containing **archaeo-** normally carry secondary stress on the first syllable, and in the items which follow have primary stress on the second syllable, e.g. **archaeology** /ˌɑː.ki'ɒl.ə.dʒi (US) ˌɑːr.ki'ɑː.lə-/, with the exception of **archaeological**.
archaeologic|al ˌɑː.ki.ə'lɒdʒ.ɪ.k|ᵊl (US) ˌɑːr.ki.ə'lɑː.dʒɪ- **-ally** -ᵊl.i, -i
archaeologist ˌɑː.ki'ɒl.ə.dʒɪst (US) ˌɑːr.ki'ɑː.lə- **-s** -s
archaeology ˌɑː.ki'ɒl.ə.dʒi (US) ˌɑːr.ki'ɑː.lə-
archaeopteryx ˌɑː.ki'ɒp.tᵊr.ɪks (US) ˌɑːr.ki'ɑːp- **-es** -ɪz
archaic ɑː'keɪ.ɪk (US) ɑːr- **-ally** -ᵊl.i, -li
archaism ɑː'keɪ.ɪ.zᵊm, 'ɑː.keɪ- (US) 'ɑːr.ki-, -keɪ- **-s** -z
archangel ɑː'keɪn.dʒᵊl, 'ɑː.keɪn- (US) 'ɑːr.keɪn- **-s** -z
Archangel 'ɑːˌkeɪn.dʒᵊl, ˌɑː'keɪn- (US) 'ɑːr.keɪn-
archbishop ˌɑːtʃ'bɪʃ.əp (US) ˌɑːrtʃ- **-s** -s *stress shift:* ˌArchbishop of 'Canterbury
archbishopric ˌɑːtʃ'bɪʃ.ə.prɪk (US) ˌɑːrtʃ- **-s** -s
Archbold 'ɑːtʃ.bəʊld (US) 'ɑːrtʃ.boʊld
Archdale 'ɑːtʃ.deɪl (US) 'ɑːrtʃ-
archdeacon ˌɑːtʃ'diː.kən (US) ˌɑːrtʃ- **-s** -z
archdeaconr|y ˌɑːtʃ'diː.kᵊn.r|i (US) ˌɑːrtʃ- **-ies** -iz
archdioces|e ˌɑːtʃ'daɪə.sɪs (US) ˌɑːrtʃ- **-es** -ɪz
archducal ˌɑːtʃ'djuː.kᵊl (US) ˌɑːrtʃ'duː-, -'djuː-
archduchess ˌɑːtʃ'dʌtʃ.ɪs, -əs (US) ˌɑːrtʃ- **-es** -ɪz
archduch|y ˌɑːtʃ'dʌtʃ.|i (US) ˌɑːrtʃ- **-ies** -iz
archduke ˌɑːtʃ'djuːk (US) ˌɑːrtʃ'duːk, -'djuːk **-s** -s *stress shift:* ˌArchduke 'Ferdinand
archdukedom ˌɑːtʃ'djuːk.dəm (US) ˌɑːrtʃ'duːk-, -'djuːk **-s** -z
Archelaus ˌɑː.kɪ'leɪ.əs, -kə'- (US) ˌɑːr-
archenem|y ˌɑːtʃ'en.ə.m|i, -ɪ.m|i (US) ˌɑːrtʃ- **-ies** -iz
archeo- ˌɑː.ki.əʊ-; ˌɑː.ki'ɒ- (US) ˌɑːr.ki.oʊ-, -ə-; ˌɑːr.ki'ɑː-
Note: Prefix. See **archaeo-**.
archeologic|al ˌɑː.ki.ə'lɒdʒ.ɪ.k|ᵊl (US) ˌɑr.ki.ə'lɑː.dʒɪ- **-ally** -ᵊl.i, -li
archeologist ˌɑː.ki'ɒl.ə.dʒɪst (US) ˌɑːr.ki'ɑː.lə- **-s** -s
archeology ˌɑː.ki'ɒl.ə.dʒi (US) ˌɑːr.ki'ɑː.lə-
archeopteryx ˌɑː.ki'ɒp.tə.rɪks (US) ˌɑːr.ki'ɑːp- **-es** -ɪz
archer (A) 'ɑː.tʃəʳ (US) 'ɑːr.tʃɚ **-s** -z
archeress 'ɑː.tʃᵊr.ɪs, -es (US) 'ɑːr.tʃɚ.əs **-es** -ɪz
archery 'ɑː.tʃᵊr.i (US) 'ɑːr-
archetypal ˌɑː.kɪ'taɪ.pᵊl, 'ɑː.kɪˌtaɪ- (US) ˌɑːr.kɪ'taɪ-
archetype 'ɑː.kɪ.taɪp (US) 'ɑːr- **-s** -s
archetypic|al ˌɑː.kɪ'tɪp.ɪ.k|ᵊl (US) ˌɑːr.kə'- **-ally** -ᵊl.i, -li *stress shift:* ˌarchetypical 'incident
archfiend ˌɑːtʃ'fiːnd (US) ˌɑːrtʃ- **-s** -z
arch-heretic ˌɑːtʃ'her.ə.tɪk, '-ɪ- (US) ˌɑːrtʃ'her.ə- **-s** -s
archi- ɑː.tʃi- (US) ɑːr.tʃi-
Archibald 'ɑː.tʃɪ.bɔːld, -bᵊld (US) 'ɑːr.tʃə.bɔːld, -bɑːld
-archic -ɑː.kɪk (US) -ɑːr.kɪk
Archie 'ɑː.tʃi (US) 'ɑːr-
Archilochus ɑː'kɪl.ə.kəs (US) ɑːr-
archimandrite ˌɑː.kɪ'mæn.draɪt (US) ˌɑːr.kə'- **-s** -s
archimedean ˌɑː.kɪ'miː.di.ən, -miː'diː.ən (US) ˌɑːr.kə- *stress shift:* ˌarchimedean 'screw
Archimedes ˌɑː.kɪ'miː.diːz (US) ˌɑːr.kə'-
archipelago ˌɑː.kɪ'pel.əg.əʊ (US) ˌɑːr.kə'pel.ə.goʊ **-(e)s** -z
archiphoneme ˌɑː.kɪ'fəʊ.niːm (US) 'ɑːr.kɪˌfoʊ-, ˌɑːr.kɪ'fo- **-s** -z
architect 'ɑː.kɪ.tekt (US) 'ɑːr.kə- **-s** -s
architectonic ˌɑː.kɪ.tek'tɒn.ɪk (US) ˌɑːr.kə.tek'tɑː.nɪk **-s** -s
architectural ˌɑː.kɪ'tek.tʃᵊr.ᵊl (US) ˌɑːr.kə'- **-ly** -i
architecture 'ɑː.kɪ.tek.tʃəʳ (US) 'ɑːr.kə.tek.tʃɚ
architrave 'ɑː.kɪ.treɪv (US) 'ɑːr.kə- **-s** -z **-d** -d
archival ˌɑː'kaɪ.vᵊl (US) ˌɑːr-
archive 'ɑː.kaɪv (US) 'ɑːr- **-s** -z
archivist 'ɑː.kɪ.vɪst (US) 'ɑːr.kaɪ-, -kə- **-s** -s
archon 'ɑː.kən, -kɒn (US) 'ɑːr.kɑːn **-s** -z
arch-prelate ˌɑːtʃ'prel.ət, -ɪt (US) ˌɑːrtʃ- **-s** -s
arch-priest ˌɑːtʃ'priːst (US) ˌɑːrtʃ- **-s** -s *stress shift:* ˌarch-priest's 'ceremony
arch-traitor ˌɑːtʃ'treɪ.təʳ (US) ˌɑːrtʃ'treɪ.t̬ɚ **-s** -z *stress shift:* ˌarch-traitor 'clique
archway (A) 'ɑːtʃ.weɪ (US) 'ɑːrtʃ- **-s** -z
archwise 'ɑːtʃ.waɪz (US) 'ɑːrtʃ-
Archytas ɑː'kaɪ.təs, -tæs (US) ɑːr'kaɪ.t̬əs
Arcite 'ɑː.saɪt (US) 'ɑːr-
Arcot 'ɑː.kɒt (US) 'ɑːr.kɑːt
arctic (A) 'ɑːk.tɪk (US) 'ɑːrk-; 'ɑːr.t̬ɪk ˌ**Arctic 'Circle**; ˌ**Arctic 'Ocean**
Arcturus ɑːk'tjʊə.rəs (US) ɑːrk'tʊr.əs
arcuate 'ɑː.kju.ət, -eɪt, -ɪt (US) 'ɑːr-
arcuated 'ɑː.kju.eɪ.tɪd (US) 'ɑːr.kju.eɪ.t̬ɪd
Arcy 'ɑː.si (US) 'ɑːr-
-ard -əd, -ɑːd (US) -ɚd, -ɑːrd
Note: Suffix. In frequently occurring words, normally /-əd (US) -ɚd/, e.g. **wizard** /'wɪz.əd (US) -ɚd/, but may also be /-ɑːd (US) -ɑːrd/, e.g. **dullard** /'dʌl.əd, -ɑːd (US) -ɚd/. See individual items.
Ardagh 'ɑː.də, -dɑː (US) 'ɑːr-
Ardèche ɑː'deʃ (US) ɑːr-
Ardee ɑː'diː (US) ɑːr-
Arden 'ɑː.dᵊn (US) 'ɑːr-
ardency 'ɑː.dᵊnt.si (US) 'ɑːr-
Ardennes ɑː'den, -denz (US) ɑːr-
ardent 'ɑː.dᵊnt (US) 'ɑːr- **-ly** -li
Arding 'ɑː.dɪŋ (US) 'ɑːr-
Ardingly 'ɑː.dɪŋ.laɪ, ˌ--'- (US) 'ɑːr.dɪŋ-, ˌ--'-
Ardleigh, Ardley 'ɑːd.li (US) 'ɑːrd-
Ardoch 'ɑː.dɒk, -dɒx (US) 'ɑːr.dɑːk
ardo(u)r 'ɑː.dəʳ (US) 'ɑːr.dɚ
Ardrishaig ɑː'drɪʃ.ɪg, -eɪg (US) ɑːr-
Ardrossan ɑː'drɒs.ᵊn (US) ɑːr'drɑː.sᵊn
Ards ɑːdz (US) ɑːrdz
Arduin 'ɑː.dwɪn (US) 'ɑːr-
arduous 'ɑː.dju.əs, -dʒu- (US) 'ɑːr.dʒu- **-ly** -li **-ness** -nəs, -nɪs
Ardwick 'ɑː.dwɪk (US) 'ɑːr-
are *(from* **be**) *strong form:* ɑːʳ (US) ɑːr *weak form:* əʳ (US) ɚ *occasional weak form before vowels:* r
Note: Weak form word. The strong form /ɑːʳ (US) ɑːr/ is used for emphasis (e.g. 'You **are** stupid.'), for contrast (e.g. 'You **are** rich, but you **aren't** handsome.') and in final position (e.g. 'Here you are.'). The weak form is usually /əʳ (US) ɚ/ (e.g. 'These are mine.' /ˌðiːz.ə'maɪn

(US) -ɚ'-/; 'These are old.' /ˌðiːz.əʳ'əʊld (US) -ɚ'oʊld/), but when the weak form precedes a vowel, as in the last example, it often happens that the word is pronounced as a syllabic /r̩/ (e.g. /ˌðiːz.r̩'əʊld (US) -'oʊld/).

are *surface measure:* ɑːʳ (US) ɑːr **-s** -z

area 'eə.ri.ə (US) 'er.i- **-s** -z **'area ˌcode**

areca ə'riː.kə; 'ær.ɪ- (US) ə'riː.kə; 'ær.ɪ-, 'er- **-s** -z

arena ə'riː.nə **-s** -z

Arendt 'ær.ənt, 'ɑː.rənt (US) 'ɑːr.ənt, 'er-

aren't ɑːnt (US) ɑːrnt

areol|a ə'riː.əl|.ə, ær'iː- **-as** -əz **-ae** -iː

areometer ˌær.i'ɒm.ɪ.təʳ, ˌeə.ri'-, '-ə- (US) ˌer.i'ɑː.mə.t̬ɚ, ˌær- **-s** -z

areometry ˌær.i'ɒm.ɪ.tri, ˌeə.ri'-, '-ə- (US) ˌer.i'ɑː.mə-, ˌær-

Areopagite ˌær.i'ɒp.ə.gaɪt, -dʒaɪt (US) ˌer.i'ɑː.pə-, ˌær- **-s** -s

Areopagitic ˌær.i.ɒp.ə'dʒɪt.ɪk (US) ˌer.iˌɑː.pə'-, ˌær- **-a** -ə

Areopagus ˌær.i'ɒp.ə.gəs (US) ˌer.i'ɑː.pə-, ˌær-

Arequipa ˌær.ɪ'kiː.pə, -ek'iː- (US) ˌɑː.rə'kiː-, ˌer.ə'-, ˌær-

Ares 'eə.riːz (US) 'er.iːz

arête ær'et, ə'ret

Aretha ə'riː.θə

Arethusa ˌær.ɪ'θjuː.zə, -eθ'juː- (US) ˌɑːr.ə'θuː-

Arezzo ær'et.səʊ, ə'ret- (US) ɑː'ret.soʊ

Arfon 'ɑː.vən, -vɒn (US) 'ɑːr-, -fən

Argand 'ɑː.gænd, -gənd (US) ˌɑːr'gɑːnd, -'gænd **-s** -z *stress shift, US only, see compound:* ˌ**Argand 'diagram**

argent (A) 'ɑː.dʒənt (US) 'ɑːr-

Argentina ˌɑː.dʒən'tiː.nə, -dʒen'- (US) ˌɑːr-

argentine (A) 'ɑː.dʒən.taɪn (US) 'ɑːr.dʒən.taɪn, -tiːn, -tɪn

Argentinian ˌɑː.dʒən'tɪn.i.ən (US) ˌɑːr- **-s** -z

argillaceous ˌɑː.dʒɪ'leɪ.ʃəs (US) ˌɑːr.dʒə'-

Argive 'ɑː.gaɪv (US) 'ɑːr- **-s** -z

Argo 'ɑː.gəʊ (US) 'ɑːr.goʊ

argol 'ɑː.gɒl, -gəl (US) 'ɑːr.gɑːl, -gəl

Argolis 'ɑː.gəl.ɪs (US) 'ɑːr-

argon 'ɑː.gɒn, -gən (US) 'ɑːr.gɑːn

Argonaut 'ɑː.gə.nɔːt (US) 'ɑːr.gə.nɑːt, -nɔːt **-s** -s

Argonautic ˌɑː.gə'nɔː.tɪk (US) ˌɑːr.gə'nɑː.t̬ɪk, -'nɔː-

Argos 'ɑː.gɒs (US) 'ɑːr.gɑːs, -gəs

argos|y 'ɑː.gə.s|i (US) 'ɑːr.gə.s|i **-ies** -iz

argot 'ɑː.gəʊ (US) 'ɑːr.goʊ, -gət **-s** -z

arguab|le 'ɑːg.ju.ə.b|l̩ (US) 'ɑːrg- **-ly** -li

argu|e 'ɑːg.juː (US) 'ɑːrg- **-es** -z **-ing** -ɪŋ **-ed** -d **-er/s** -əʳ/z (US) -ɚ/z

argument 'ɑːg.jə.mənt, -jʊ- (US) 'ɑːrg.jə-, -jʊ- **-s** -s

argumental ˌɑːg.jə'men.təl, -jʊ- (US) ˌɑːrg.jə'men.t̬əl, -jʊ'-

argumentation ˌɑːg.jə.men'teɪ.ʃən, -jʊ-, -mən- (US) ˌɑːrg.jə-, -jʊ- **-s** -z

argumentative ˌɑːg.jə'men.tə.tɪv, -jʊ- (US) ˌɑːrg.jə'men.t̬ə.t̬ɪv, -jʊ'- **-ly** -li **-ness** -nəs, -nɪs

argus (A) 'ɑː.gəs (US) 'ɑːr- **-es** -ɪz

argy-bargy ˌɑː.dʒi'bɑː.dʒi (US) ˌɑːr.dʒi'bɑːr-

Argyle ɑː'gaɪl (US) ɑːr-, '-- *stress shift:* ˌArgyle 'tartan

Argyllshire ɑː'gaɪl.ʃəʳ, -ˌʃɪəʳ (US) ɑːr'gaɪl.ʃɚ, -ˌʃɪr

aria 'ɑː.ri.ə (US) 'ɑːr.i- **-s** -z

Ariadne ˌær.i'æd.ni (US) ˌær-, ˌer-

Arian 'eə.ri.ən (US) 'er.i-, 'ær- **-s** -z **-ism** -ɪ.zəm

-arian -'eə.ri.ən (US) -'er.i-, -'ær-

Note: Suffix. Always carries primary stress, e.g. **grammarian** /grə'meə.ri.ən (US) -'mer.i-/.

arid 'ær.ɪd (US) 'er-, 'ær- **-ly** -li **-ness** -nəs, -nɪs

aridity ær'ɪd.ə.ti, ə'rɪd-, -ɪ.ti (US) er'ɪd.ə.t̬i, ær-

ariel (A) 'eə.ri.əl (US) 'er.i- **-s** -z

Aries 'eə.riːz, -ri.iːz (US) 'er.iːz

arietta ˌær.i'et.ə, ˌɑː.ri'- (US) ˌɑːr.i'et̬-, ˌær.i'-, ˌer- **-s** -z

aright ə'raɪt

-arily -ər.ə.li, -ɪ.li; -'er.əl.i, -ɪ.li (US) -er.ə.li, -ær-

Note: Suffix. The stress pattern of words containing **-arily** in British English is either unaffected by the affix or primary stress moves to the antepenultimate syllable, in which case it contains a full vowel, e.g. **momentarily** /'məʊ.mən.tər.əl.i, -ɪ.li ˌməʊ.mən'ter-/. In American English, **-arily** normally has a full vowel, but the antepenultimate syllable may or may not take primary stress, e.g. **momentarily** /'moʊ.mən.ter.əl.i, ˌmoʊ.mən'ter-/. See individual entries.

Arimathaea ˌær.ɪ.mə'θiː.ə (US) ˌer.ə-, ˌær-

Arion ə'raɪən, ær'aɪən (US) ə'raɪən

arioso ˌɑː.ri'əʊ.səʊ, ˌær.i'-, -zəʊ (US) ˌɑːr.i'oʊ.soʊ

Ariosto ˌær.i'ɒs.təʊ (US) ˌɑːr.i'ɑː.stoʊ, ˌer-, ˌær-, -'ɔː-, -'oʊ-

aris|e ə'raɪz **-es** -ɪz **-ing** -ɪŋ

arisen ə'rɪz.ən

Aristaeus ˌær.ɪ'stiː.əs, -ə'- (US) ˌer.ə'-, ˌær-

Aristarchus ˌær.ɪ'stɑː.kəs (US) ˌer.ə'stɑːr-, ˌær-

Aristide ˌær.ɪ'stiːd (US) ˌer-, ˌær-

Aristides ˌær.ɪ'staɪ.diːz (US) ˌer.ə'-, ˌær-

aristo ə'rɪs.təʊ (US) -toʊ **-s** -z

aristocrac|y ˌær.ɪ'stɒk.rə.s|i (US) ˌer.ə'stɑː.krə-, ˌær- **-ies** -iz

aristocrat 'ær.ɪ.stə.kræt; ə'rɪs.tə- (US) ə'rɪs-; 'er.ə.stə-, 'ær- **-s** -s

aristocratic ˌær.ɪ.stə'kræt.ɪk (US) əˌrɪs.tə'kræt̬.ɪk; ˌer.ə.stə'-, ˌær- **-al** -əl **-ally** -əl.i, -li *stress shift, British:* ˌaristocratic 'airs *stress shift, US:* aˌristocratic 'airs, ˌaristocratic 'airs

aristocratism ˌær.ɪ'stɒk.rə.tɪ.zəm (US) ˌer.ə'stɑː.krə-, ˌær-

Aristophanes ˌær.ɪ'stɒf.ə.niːz (US) ˌer.ə'stɑː.fə-, ˌær-

aristophanic ˌær.ɪ.stə'fæn.ɪk, -tɒf'æn- (US) ˌer.ə.stə'-, ˌær-

aristotelian (A) ˌær.ɪ.stɒt'iː.li.ən, -stə'tiː- (US) ˌer.ə.stə'tiː-, ˌær- **-s** -z

Aristotle 'ær.ɪ.stɒt.l̩ (US) 'er.ə.stɑː.t̬l̩, 'ær-

Aristoxenus ˌær.ɪ'stɒk.sɪ.nəs, -sə.nəs (US) ˌer.ə'stɑːk.sə-, ˌær-

arithmetic (*n.*) ə'rɪθ.mə.tɪk, -mɪ- **-s** -s

arithmetic (*adj.*) ˌær.ɪθ'met.ɪk (US) ˌer.ɪθ'met̬-, ˌær- **-al** -əl **-ally** -əl.i, -li *stress shift:* ˌarithmetic 'mean

arithmetician əˌrɪθ.mə'tɪʃ.ən, -mɪ'-; ˌær.ɪθ- (US) əˌrɪθ.mə'- **-s** -z

-arium -'eə.ri.əm (US) -'er.i-

Note: Suffix. Always carries primary stress, e.g. **solarium** /səʊ'ler.i.əm (US) soʊ-, sə-/.

Arius 'eə.ri.əs; ə'raɪ- (US) 'er.i-, 'ær-

Ariz. (*abbrev. for* **Arizona**) ˌær.ɪ'zəʊ.nə (US) ˌer.ɪ'zoʊ-, ˌær-, -ə'-

Arizona ˌær.ɪ'zəʊ.nə (US) ˌer.ɪ'zoʊ-, ˌær-, -ə'-

Arjuna ɑː'juː.nə (US) ɑːr-, ɜː-

ark (A) ɑːk (US) ɑːrk **-s** -s

Ark. (*abbrev. for* **Arkansas**) 'ɑː.kən.sɔː; ɑː'kæn.zəs (US) 'ɑːr.kən.sɑː, -sɔː; ɑːr'kæn.zəs

Arkan 'ɑː.kæn (US) 'ɑːr-

Arkansas *US state:* 'ɑː.kən.sɔː; (US) 'ɑːr.kən.sɑː, -sɔː; *river:* ɑː'kæn.zəs (US) ɑːr'kæn.zəs

Arkhangelsk ˌɑː.kæŋ'gelsk (US) ɑːr'kɑːn.gelsk

Arklow 'ɑː.kləʊ (US) 'ɑːr.kloʊ

Arkwright 'ɑː.kraɪt (US) 'ɑːr-

Arlen 'ɑː.lən (US) 'ɑːr-

Arlene 'ɑː.liːn (US) ɑːr'liːn

Arlington 'ɑː.lɪŋ.tən (US) 'ɑːr-

arm ɑːm (US) ɑːrm **-s** -z **-ing** -ɪŋ **-ed** -d **cost an ˌarm and a 'leg; ˌkeep someone at ˌarm's 'length; ˌarmed to the 'teeth**

armada (A) ɑː'mɑː.də (US) ɑːr'- **-s** -z

Armadale 'ɑː.mə.deɪl (US) 'ɑːr-
armadillo ˌɑː.mə'dɪl.əʊ (US) ˌɑːr.mə'dɪl.oʊ **-s** -z
Armado ɑː'mɑː.dəʊ (US) ɑːr'mɑː.doʊ
Armageddon ˌɑː.mə'ged.ᵊn (US) ˌɑːr-
Armagh ˌɑː'mɑː (US) ˌɑːr-
Armagnac 'ɑː.mə.njæk (US) 'ɑːr-, ˌ--'-
Armah 'ɑː.mə (US) 'ɑːr-
Armalite® 'ɑː.mᵊl.aɪt (US) 'ɑːr.mə.laɪt
armament 'ɑː.mə.mənt (US) 'ɑːr- **-s** -s
Armani ˌɑː'mɑː.ni (US) ˌɑːr-
Armatrading ˌɑː.mə'treɪ.dɪŋ, 'ɑː.mə.treɪ- (US) 'ɑːr.mə.treɪ-, ˌɑːr.mə'treɪ-
armature 'ɑː.mə.tʃəʳ, -tʃʊəʳ, -tjʊəʳ, -tjəʳ (US) 'ɑːr.mə.tʃɚ **-s** -z
armband 'ɑːm.bænd (US) 'ɑːrm- **-s** -z
armchair 'ɑːm.tʃeəʳ, -'- (US) 'ɑːrm.tʃer **-s** -z
Note: The latter British form is used when attributive.
armed ɑːmd (US) ɑːrmd ˌ**armed 'robbery**
Armeni|a ɑː'miː.ni|.ə (US) ɑːr- **-an/s** -ən/z
Armfield 'ɑːm.fiːld (US) 'ɑːrm-
armful 'ɑːm.fʊl (US) 'ɑːrm- **-s** -z
armhole 'ɑːm.həʊl (US) 'ɑːrm.hoʊl **-s** -z
armiger (A) 'ɑː.mɪ.dʒəʳ (US) 'ɑːr.mɪ.dʒɚ **-s** -z
Armin 'ɑː.mɪn (US) 'ɑːr-
arm-in-arm ˌɑːm.ɪn'ɑːm (US) ˌɑːrm.ɪn'ɑːrm
Arminian ɑː'mɪn.i.ən (US) ɑːr- **-s** -z
Armistead 'ɑː.mɪ.sted, -stɪd (US) 'ɑːr-
armistic|e 'ɑː.mɪ.stɪs (US) 'ɑːr.mə- **-es** -ɪz **'Armistice ˌDay**
Armitage 'ɑː.mɪ.tɪdʒ, -mə- (US) 'ɑːr.mə.t̬ɪdʒ
armless 'ɑːm.ləs, -lɪs (US) 'ɑːrm-
armlet 'ɑːm.lət, -lɪt (US) 'ɑːrm- **-s** -s
armload 'ɑːm.ləʊd (US) 'ɑːrm.loʊd **-s** -z
armlock 'ɑːm.lɒk (US) 'ɑːrm.lɑːk **-s** -s
arm|or 'ɑː.m|əʳ (US) 'ɑːr.m|ɚ **-ors** -əz (US) -ɚz **-oring** -ᵊr.ɪŋ **-ored** -əd (US) -ɚd ˌ**armored 'vehicle**
armorer 'ɑː.mᵊr.əʳ (US) 'ɑːr.mɚ.ɚ **-s** -z
armorial ɑː'mɔː.ri.əl (US) ɑːr'mɔːr.i-
Armoric ɑː'mɒr.ɪk (US) ɑːr'mɔːr-
Armoric|a ɑː'mɒr.ɪ.k|ə (US) ɑːr'mɔːr- **-an/s** -ən/z
armor-pla|te ˌɑː.mə'pleɪ|t, '--- (US) 'ɑːr.mɚ.pleɪ|t **-tes** -ts **-ting** -tɪŋ (US) -t̬ɪŋ **-ted** -tɪd (US) -t̬ɪd
armor|y 'ɑː.mᵊr|.i (US) 'ɑːr- **-ies** -iz
arm|our (A) 'ɑː.m|əʳ (US) 'ɑːr.m|ɚ **-ours** -əz (US) -ɚz **-ouring** -ᵊr.ɪŋ **-oured** -əd (US) -ɚd ˌ**armoured 'vehicle**
armourer 'ɑː.mᵊr.əʳ (US) 'ɑːr.mɚ.ɚ **-s** -z
armour-pla|te ˌɑː.mə'pleɪ|t, '--- (US) 'ɑːr.mɚ.pleɪ|t **-tes** -ts **-ting** -tɪŋ (US) -t̬ɪŋ **-ted** -tɪd (US) -t̬ɪd
Note: The latter British form is used attributively.
armour|y 'ɑː.mᵊr|.i (US) 'ɑːr- **-ies** -iz
armpit 'ɑːm.pɪt (US) 'ɑːrm- **-s** -s
armrest 'ɑːm.rest (US) 'ɑːrm- **-s** -s
arms ɑːmz (US) ɑːrmz **'arms conˌtrol; 'arms ˌrace; ˌup in 'arms**
Armstead 'ɑːm.sted, -stɪd (US) 'ɑːrm-
Armstrong 'ɑːm.strɒŋ (US) 'ɑːrm.strɑːŋ, -strɔːŋ
Armthorpe 'ɑːm.θɔːp (US) 'ɑːrm.θɔːrp
arm|y 'ɑː.m|i (US) 'ɑːr- **-ies** -iz
army-corps *sing.:* 'ɑː.mi.kɔːʳ (US) 'ɑːr.mi.kɔːr *plur.:* -kɔːz (US) -kɔːrz
Arnald 'ɑː.nəld (US) 'ɑːr-
Arndale 'ɑːn.deɪl (US) 'ɑːrn-
Arne ɑːn (US) ɑːrn
Arnfield 'ɑːn.fiːld (US) 'ɑːrn-
Arnhem 'ɑː.nəm, 'ɑːn.həm (US) 'ɑːr.nəm, 'ɑːrn.hem
arnica 'ɑː.nɪ.kə (US) 'ɑːr-
Arno 'ɑː.nəʊ (US) 'ɑːr.noʊ
Arnold 'ɑː.nᵊld (US) 'ɑːr- **-son** -sᵊn
Arnot(t) 'ɑː.nət, -nɒt (US) 'ɑːr.nət, -nɑːt
Arolla ə'rɒl.ə (US) -'rɑː.lə
aroma ə'rəʊ.mə (US) -'roʊ- **-s** -z
aromatherap|y əˌrəʊ.mə'θer.ə.p|i (US) -ˌroʊ- **-ist/s** -ɪst/s
aromatic ˌær.əʊ'mæt.ɪk (US) ˌer.ə'mæt̬-, ˌær- **-s** -s *stress shift:* ˌaromatic 'oils
arose *(from* **arise***)* ə'rəʊz (US) -'roʊz
around ə'raʊnd
arousal ə'raʊ.zᵊl **-s** -z
arous|e ə'raʊz **-es** -ɪz **-ing** -ɪŋ **-ed** -d
arpeggio ɑː'pedʒ.i.əʊ, -'pedʒ.əʊ (US) ɑːr'pedʒ.i.oʊ, -'peʒ-, -'pedʒ.oʊ **-s** -z
arquebus 'ɑː.kwɪ.bəs, -kwə.bəs, -bʌs (US) 'ɑːr- **-es** -ɪz
Arquette ɑː'ket (US) ɑːr-
arr *(abbrev. for* **arranged by***)* ə'reɪndʒdˌbaɪ *(abbrev. for* **arrives, arrival***)* ə'raɪ|vz; -vᵊl
arrack 'ær.ək (US) 'er-, 'ær-; ə'ræk
arraign ə'reɪn **-s** -z **-ing** -ɪŋ **-ed** -d **-er/s** -əʳ/z (US) -ɚ/z **-ment/s** -mənt/s
Arran 'ær.ᵊn (US) 'er-, 'ær-
arrang|e ə'reɪndʒ **-es** -ɪz **-ing** -ɪŋ **-ed** -d **-er/s** -əʳ/z (US) -ɚ/z
arrangement ə'reɪndʒ.mənt **-s** -s
arrant 'ær.ᵊnt (US) 'er-, 'ær- **-ly** -li
arras 'ær.əs (US) 'er-, 'ær- **-es** -ɪz
Arras *French town:* 'ær.əs, -æs (US) 'er-, 'ær-
Arrau ə'raʊ; 'ær.aʊ (US) ə'raʊ
array ə'reɪ **-s** -z **-ing** -ɪŋ **-ed** -d
arrear ə'rɪəʳ (US) -'rɪr **-s** -z **-age** -ɪdʒ
arrest ə'rest **-s** -s **-ing** -ɪŋ **-ed** -ɪd **-ment/s** -mənt/s
arrestable ə'res.tə.bl̩
arrestation ˌær.es'teɪ.ʃᵊn (US) ˌer-, ˌær-; əˌres'- **-s** -z
arrhythm|ia ə'rɪð.m|i.ə **-ic** -ɪk **-ical** -ɪ.kᵊl **-ically** -ɪ.kᵊl.i, -ɪ.kli
Arrian 'ær.i.ən (US) 'er-, 'ær-
arrière-ban ˌær.i.eə'bæn (US) -er'bɑːn, -'bæn **-s** -z
arrière pensée ˌær.i.eə'pɑ̃ː*nt*.seɪ, -pɑː*nt*'seɪ (US) -er.pɑː*n*'seɪ
arris 'ær.ɪs (US) 'er-, 'ær- **-es** -ɪz
arrival ə'raɪ.vᵊl **-s** -z
arriv|e ə'raɪv **-es** -z **-ing** -ɪŋ **-ed** -d
arrivederci ˌær.i.və'deə.tʃi (US) əˌriː.və'der-
arriviste ˌær.iː'viːst (US) ˌer-, ˌær- **-s** -s
arroganc|e 'ær.ə.gən*t*s (US) 'er-, 'ær- **-y** -i
arrogant 'ær.ə.gənt (US) 'er-, 'ær- **-ly** -li
arro|gate 'ær.əʊ|.geɪt (US) 'er.ə-, 'ær- **-gates** -geɪts **-gating** -geɪ.tɪŋ (US) -geɪ.t̬ɪŋ **-gated** -geɪ.tɪd (US) -geɪ.t̬ɪd
arrogation ˌær.əʊ'geɪ.ʃᵊn (US) ˌer.ə'-, ˌær- **-s** -z
arrogative ə'rɒg.ə.tɪv (US) -'rɑː.gə.t̬ɪv
arrondissement ˌær.ɒn'diː.sᵊm.ɑ̃ː (US) erˌɑːn.diːs'mɑːn, ær-; əˌrɑːn- **-s** -s
arrow 'ær.əʊ (US) 'er.oʊ, 'ær- **-s** -z **'arrow ˌhead**
arrowroot 'ær.əʊ.ruːt (US) 'er.oʊ-, 'ær-
Arrowsmith 'ær.əʊ.smɪθ (US) 'er.oʊ-, 'ær-
arrowwood 'ær.əʊ.wʊd (US) 'er.oʊ-, 'ær-
arroyo ə'rɔɪ.əʊ (US) -oʊ **-s** -z
ars ɑːz (US) ɑːrz
ars|e ɑːs (US) ɑːrs **-es** -ɪz
Note: In US dictionaries, **arse** is usually listed as a variant of **ass**, which is pronounced /æs/. **Arse** is a British term.
arsehole 'ɑːs.həʊl (US) 'ɑːrs.hoʊl **-s** -z
arsenal (A) 'ɑː.sᵊn.ᵊl (US) 'ɑːr- **-s** -z
arsenate 'ɑː.sᵊn.eɪt, -sɪ.neɪt, -nɪt, -nət (US) 'ɑːr- **-s** -s
arsenic *(n.)* 'ɑː.sᵊn.ɪk (US) 'ɑːr-
arsenic *(adj.)* ɑː'sen.ɪk (US) ɑːr- **-al** -ᵊl
arsenide 'ɑː.sᵊn.aɪd (US) 'ɑːr- **-s** -z
arsenite 'ɑː.sᵊn.aɪt, -sɪ.naɪt (US) 'ɑːr-
ars|is 'ɑː.s|ɪs (US) 'ɑːr- **-es** -iːz
arson 'ɑː.sᵊn (US) 'ɑːr-
arsonist 'ɑː.sᵊn.ɪst (US) 'ɑːr- **-s** -s
art *(n.)* ɑːt (US) ɑːrt **-s** -s **'art ˌgallery; ˌarts and 'crafts; 'art ˌschool**
art *(from* **be***) (v.) normal form:* ɑːt (US) ɑːrt *occasional weak form:* ət (US) ɚt
Artaxerxes ˌɑː.tə'zɜːk.siːz, -tək'sɜːk-, -təg'zɜːk-, 'ɑː.tə.zɜːk-, -tək.sɜːk-, -təg.zɜːk- (US) ˌɑːr.t̬ə'zɝːk-
Art Deco ˌɑːt'dek.əʊ (US) ˌɑːrt.deɪ'koʊ, ˌɑːr-, -'deɪ.koʊ
artefact 'ɑː.tɪ.fækt, -tə.fækt (US) 'ɑːr.t̬ə- **-s** -s
Artemis 'ɑː.tɪ.mɪs, -tə.mɪs (US) 'ɑːr.t̬ə-
Artemus 'ɑː.tɪ.məs, -tə.məs (US) 'ɑːr.t̬

Articulation

The movement of the vocal organs to produce speech sounds. The vocal organs are often referred to as 'articulators', and these include the tongue, the lips, the hard palate, the soft palate, the teeth, the pharynx and the larynx. In classifying CONSONANTS, phoneticians note the 'place of articulation' (the point in the vocal tract where the obstruction to the airflow is made) and the 'manner of articulation' (the type of obstruction made by the articulators). Thus the sound [s] is classified as ALVEOLAR (because the place of articulation is at the alveolar ridge, just behind the upper front teeth) and FRICATIVE (because the obstruction is one which allows air to escape with difficulty, creating a hissing noise).

arterial ɑːˈtɪə.ri.əl US ɑːrˈtɪr.i-

arteriolar ɑːˌtɪə.riˈəʊ.ləʳ US ɑːrˌtɪr.iˈoʊ.lɚ

arteriol|e ɑːˈtɪə.ri.əʊl US ɑːrˈtɪr.i.oʊl **-es** -z

arteriosclerosis ɑːˌtɪə.ri.əʊ.skləˈrəʊ.sɪs, -sklɪəˈ- US ɑːrˌtɪr.i.oʊ.skləˈroʊ.səs

arteritis ˌɑː.tᵊrˈaɪ.tɪs, -tɪˈraɪ-, -təs US ˌɑːr.t̬əˈraɪ.t̬ɪs

arter|y ˈɑː.tᵊr|.i US ˈɑːr.t̬ɚ- **-ies** -iz

artesian ɑːˈtiː.zi.ən, -ʒi.ən, -ʒᵊn US ɑːrˈtiː.ʒᵊn **arˌtesian ˈwell**

Artex® ˈɑː.teks US ˈɑːr-

artful ˈɑːt.fᵊl, -fʊl US ˈɑːrt- **-ly** -i **-ness** -nəs, -nɪs **ˌArtful ˈDodger**

arthouse ˈɑːtˌhaʊs US ˈɑːrt-

arthritic ɑːˈθrɪt.ɪk US ɑːrˈθrɪt̬.ɪk **-s** -s

arthritis ɑːˈθraɪ.tɪs, -təs US ɑːrˈθraɪ.t̬ɪs

arthropod ˈɑː.θrə.pɒd US ˈɑːr.θrə.pɑːd **-s** -z

arthroscope ˈɑː.θrə.skəʊp US ˈɑːr.θrə.skoʊp **-s** -s

arthroscopic ˌɑː.θrəˈskɒp.ɪk US ˌɑːr.θrəˈskɑː.pɪk

arthroscopy ɑːˈθrɒs.kə.pi US ɑːrˈθrɑː.skə-

Arthur ˈɑː.θəʳ US ˈɑːr.θɚ

Arthurian ɑːˈθjʊə.ri.ən, -ˈθʊə- US ɑːrˈθʊr.i-, -ˈθɝː-

artichoke ˈɑː.tɪ.tʃəʊk US ˈɑːr.t̬ə.tʃoʊk **-s** -s

articl|e ˈɑː.tɪ.kl̩ US ˈɑːr.t̬ɪ- **-es** -z **-ing** -ɪŋ, -klɪŋ **-ed** -d

articular ɑːˈtɪk.jə.ləʳ, -jʊ- US ɑːrˈtɪk.jə.lɚ

articulate (*adj.*) ɑːˈtɪk.jə.lət, -jʊ-, -lɪt US ɑːrˈtɪk.jə.lət **-ly** -li **-ness** -nəs, -nɪs

articu|late (*v.*) ɑːˈtɪk.jə|.leɪt, -jʊ- US ɑːrˈtɪk.jə- **-lates** -leɪts **-lating** -leɪ.tɪŋ US -leɪ.t̬ɪŋ **-lated** -leɪ.tɪd US -leɪ.t̬ɪd **-lator/s** -leɪ.təʳ/z US -leɪ.t̬ɚ/s **arˌticulated ˈlorry**

articulation ɑːˌtɪk.jəˈleɪ.ʃᵊn, -jʊˈ- US ɑːrˌtɪk.jəˈ- **-s** -z

articulatory ɑːˈtɪk.jə.lə.tᵊr.i, -jʊ-; ɑːˌtɪk.jəˈleɪ-, -jʊˈ- US ɑːrˈtɪk.jə.lə.tɔːr-

artifact ˈɑː.tɪ.fækt US ˈɑːr.t̬ə- **-s** -s

artific|e ˈɑː.tɪ.fɪs US ˈɑːr.t̬ə- **-es** -ɪz

artificer ɑːˈtɪf.ɪ.səʳ US ɑːrˈtɪf.ə.sɚ **-s** -z

artificial ˌɑː.tɪˈfɪʃ.ᵊl US ˌɑːr.t̬əˈ- **-ly** -i **-ness** -nəs, -nɪs *stress shift, see compounds:* **ˌartificial inseminˈnation**; **ˌartificial inˈtelligence**; **ˌartificial respiˈration**

artificialit|y ˌɑː.tɪˌfɪʃ.iˈæl.ə.t|i, -ɪ.t|i US ˌɑːr.t̬əˌfɪʃ.iˈæl.ə.t̬|i **-ies** -iz

artificializ|e, -is|e ˌɑː.tɪˈfɪʃ.ᵊl.aɪz US ˌɑːr.t̬ə- **-es** -ɪz **-ing** -ɪŋ **-ed** -d

artiller|y ɑːˈtɪl.ᵊr|.i US ɑːr- **-ies** -iz **-ist/s** -ɪst/s

artillery|-man ɑːˈtɪl.ᵊr.i|.mən, -mæn US ɑːrˈ- **-men** -mən, -men

artisan ˌɑː.tɪˈzæn, -təˈzæn, ˈ--- US ˈɑːr.t̬ə.zᵊn, -sᵊn **-s** -z

artist ˈɑː.tɪst US ˈɑːr.t̬əst, -t̬ɪst **-s** -s

artiste ɑːˈtiːst US ɑːr- **-s** -s

artistic ɑːˈtɪs.tɪk US ɑːr- **-al** -ᵊl **-ally** -ᵊl.i, -li

artistry ˈɑː.tɪ.stri US ˈɑːr.t̬ə-, -t̬ɪ-

artless ˈɑːt.ləs, -lɪs US ˈɑːrt- **-ly** -li **-ness** -nəs, -nɪs

Art Nouveau ˌɑːt.nuːˈvəʊ, ˌɑː-, ˌ-ˈ-- US ˌɑːrt.nuːˈvoʊ, ˌɑːr-

Artois ɑːˈtwɑː, ˈ-- US ɑːr-

arts|man ˈɑːts|.mæn US ˈɑːrts- **-men** -men

artsy ˈɑːt.si US ˈɑːrt-

artwork ˈɑːt.wɜːk US ˈɑːrt.wɝːk

arty ˈɑː.ti US ˈɑːr.t̬i

arty-farty ˌɑː.tiˈfɑː.ti US ˌɑːr.t̬iˈfɑːr.t̬i *stress shift:* ˌarty-farty ˈperson

Arub|a əˈruː.b|ə **-an/s** -ən/z

arugula əˈruː.gᵊl.ə, -gjʊ.lə, -gjᵊl.ə **-s** -z

arum ˈeə.rəm US ˈer- **-s** -z

Arun ˈær.ᵊn US ˈer-, ˈær-

Arundel ˈær.ᵊn.dᵊl; əˈrʌn- US ˈer.ᵊn-, ˈær-; əˈrʌn-

Arundell ˈær.ᵊn.del, -dᵊl US ˈer-, ˈær-

Arveragus ɑːˈver.ə.gəs US ɑːr-

-ary -ᵊr.i US -er.i, -ɚ.i

Note: Suffix. When added to a free stem, **-ary** does not normally affect the stress pattern, e.g. **imagine** /ɪˈmædʒ.ɪn/, **imaginary** /ɪˈmæʒd.ɪ.nᵊr.i US -ə.ner-/. Otherwise words containing **-ary** normally carry stress one or two syllables before the suffix, e.g. **centenary** /senˈtiː.nᵊr.i, -ˈten.ᵊr- US ˈsen.tᵊn.er-, senˈten.ᵊr-/, **culinary** /ˈkʌl.ɪ.nᵊr.i US -ə.ner-/. There are exceptions; see individual entries.

Aryan ˈeə.ri.ən, ˈɑː- US ˈer.i-, ˈær-, ˈɑːr- **-s** -z **-ism** -ɪ.zᵊm

arytenoid ˌær.ɪˈtiː.nɔɪd, -rəˈtiː-; ærˈɪt.ᵊn.ɔɪd US əˈrɪt.ᵊn-; ˌer.ɪˈtiː.nɔɪd, ˌær- **-s** -z

as (conj.) *strong form:* æz *weak form:* əz

Note: Weak form word. The strong form /æz/ is used in contrastive or coordinative constructions (e.g. 'as and when it's ready'), and in sentence-final position (e.g. 'That's what I bought it as.'). Quite frequently the strong form is found when the word occurs in initial position in a sentence if the following word is not stressed (e.g. 'As I was saying, ...'). The weak form is /əz/ (e.g. 'as good as gold' /əzˌgʊd.əzˈgəʊld US -ˈgoʊld/).

as (*n.*) *coin:* æs **-es** -ɪz

AS *(abbrev. for* **airspeed** *or* **Anglo-Saxon** *or* **antisubmarine***)* ˌeɪˈes

Asa *biblical name:* ˈeɪ.sə, ˈɑː.sə *as modern first name:* ˈeɪ.zə

asaf(o)etida ˌæs.əˈfet.ɪ.də, -ˈfiː.tɪ- US -ˈfet̬.ə-

a.s.a.p., ASAP ˌeɪ.es.eɪˈpiː, ˈeɪ.sæp

Asaph ˈæs.əf

ASAT ˈeɪ.sæt

asbest|ic æsˈbes.t|ɪk, əs-, æz-, əz- **-ous** -əs

asbestos æsˈbes.tɒs, æz-, əs-, əz-, -təs US -təs

asbestosis ˌæs.besˈtəʊ.sɪs, ˌæz-, -bɪs- US -ˈtoʊ-

Ascalon ˈæs.kə.lɒn, -lən US -lɑːn

Ascanius æsˈkeɪ.ni.əs

ascend əˈsend, æsˈend **-s** -z **-ing** -ɪŋ **-ed** -ɪd

ascendan|ce əˈsen.dən|*t*s, æsˈen- **-cy** -*t*.si **-t** -t

ascenden|ce ə'sen.dənt*s*, æs'en- **-cy** -*t*.si **-t** -t
ascender ə'sen.dəʳ (US) -dɚ **-s** -z
ascension (A) ə'sen.*t*ʃᵊn (US) -'sen*t*.ʃᵊn **-s** -z **A'scension ˌDay**
ascensional ə'sen.*t*ʃᵊn.ᵊl (US) -'sen*t*.ʃᵊn-
ascent ə'sent, æs'ent **-s** -s
ascertain ˌæs.ə'teɪn (US) -ɚ'- **-s** -z **-ing** -ɪŋ **-ed** -d **-ment** -mənt **-able** -ə.bl̩
ascetic ə'set.ɪk, æs'et- (US) ə'set̬.ɪk **-al** -ᵊl **-ally** -ᵊl.i, -li **-s** -s
asceticism ə'set.ɪ.sɪ.zᵊm, æs'et- (US) ə'set̬.ə-
Asch æʃ
Ascham 'æs.kəm
ASCII 'æs.kiː, -ki
Asclepius ə'skliː.pi.əs, æs'kliː-
ascorbate ə'skɔː.beɪt, æs'kɔː- (US) ə'skɔːr- **-s** -s
ascorbic ə'skɔː.bɪk, æs'kɔː- (US) ə'skɔːr- **aˌscorbic 'acid**
Ascot *place in Berkshire:* 'æs.kət (US) -kɑːt
ascot *item of clothing:* 'æs.kət (US) -kɑːt, -kət **-s** -s
ascrib|e ə'skraɪb **-es** -z **-ing** -ɪŋ **-ed** -d **-able** -ə.bl̩
ascription ə'skrɪp.ʃᵊn, æs'krɪp-
ascriptive ə'skrɪp.tɪv
Asda® 'æz.də
asdic 'æz.dɪk **-s** -s
-ase -eɪz, -eɪs
Note: Suffix. Does not normally affect stress pattern, e.g. **amylase** /'æm.ɪ.leɪz/.
asepsis ˌeɪ'sep.sɪs, ə-, æs'ep-
aseptic ˌeɪ'sep.tɪk, ə-, æ'sep- **-s** -s
asexual ˌeɪ'sek.ʃʊəl, -ʃu.əl, -sjʊəl, -ʃᵊl (US) -ʃu.əl **-ly** -i
asexuality ˌeɪ.sek.ʃu'æl.ə.ti, -sju'-, -ɪ.ti (US) -ʃu'æl.ə.t̬i
Asgard 'æs.gɑːd, 'æz- (US) -gɑːrd, 'ɑːs-, 'ɑːz-
Asgill 'æs.gɪl, 'æz-
ash (A) æʃ **-es** -ɪz **'ash ˌcan; ˌAsh 'Wednesday**
asham|ed ə'ʃeɪm|d **-edly** -ɪd.li **-edness** -ɪd.nəs, -nɪs
Ashanti ə'ʃæn.ti, æʃ'- (US) ə'ʃæn-, -'ʃɑːn- **-s** -z
Ashbee 'æʃ.bi
Ashbery 'æʃ.bᵊr.i (US) -ber-
Ashbourne 'æʃ.bɔːn (US) -bɔːrn
Ashburne 'æʃ.bɜːn (US) -bɝːn
Ashburnham æʃ'bɜː.nəm (US) -'bɝː-
Ashburton æʃ'bɜː.tᵊn (US) -'bɝː-
Ashbury 'æʃ.bᵊr.i (US) -ber-, -bɚ-
Ashby 'æʃ.bi
Ashby-de-la-Zouch ˌæʃ.bi.də.lɑː'zuːʃ, -de.lə'-
ashcan 'æʃ.kæn **-s** -z
Ashcombe 'æʃ.kəm
Ashcroft 'æʃ.krɒft (US) -krɑːft
Ashdod 'æʃ.dɒd (US) -dɑːd
Ashdown 'æʃ.daʊn
Ashe æʃ
ashen 'æʃ.ᵊn
Asher 'æʃ.əʳ (US) -ɚ
asher|y 'æʃ.ᵊr|.i **-ies** -iz
Ashfield 'æʃ.fiːld
Ashford 'æʃ.fəd (US) -fɚd
Ashington 'æʃ.ɪŋ.tən
Ashkenazy, Ashkenazi ˌæʃ.kə'nɑː.zi, -kɪ'nɑː- (US) ɑːʃ-
Ashkhabad ˌɑːʃ.kə'bɑːd (US) ˌɑːʃ.kɑː'bɑːd
Ashland 'æʃ.lənd
ashlar 'æʃ.ləʳ, -lɑːʳ (US) -lɚ
Ashley, Ashlee, Ashleigh 'æʃ.li
Ashman 'æʃ.mən
Ashmole 'æʃ.məʊl (US) -moʊl
Ashmolean æʃ'məʊ.li.ən, æʃ.məʊ'liː.ən (US) -'moʊ.li-
Ashmore 'æʃ.mɔːʳ (US) -mɔːr
ashore ə'ʃɔːʳ (US) -'ʃɔːr
Ashover 'æʃ.əʊ.vəʳ (US) -oʊ.vɚ
ashpan 'æʃ.pæn **-s** -z
ashram 'æʃ.rəm, -ræm **-s** -z
Ashtaroth 'æʃ.tə.rɒθ (US) -rɑːθ, -rɔːθ
Ashton 'æʃ.tᵊn
Ashton-in-Makerfield ˌæʃ.tᵊn.ɪn'meɪ.kə.fiːld (US) -kɚ-
Ashton-under-Lyne ˌæʃ.tᵊn.ʌn.də'laɪn, -'ʌn.dəˌlaɪn (US) -ʌn.dɚ'-, -'ʌn.dɚˌ-
Ashtoreth 'æʃ.tə.reθ, -tɒr.eθ (US) -tə.reθ
ashtray 'æʃ.treɪ **-s** -z
Ashurbanipal ˌæʃ.ɜː'bɑː.nɪ.pæl, -pᵊl (US) ˌɑː.ʃʊr'bɑː.nɪ.pɑːl
Ashwell 'æʃ.wel, -wᵊl
Ashworth 'æʃ.wəθ, -wɜːθ (US) -wɚθ, -wɝːθ
ash|y 'æʃ.|i **-ier** -i.əʳ (US) -i.ɚ **-iest** -i.əst, -i.ɪst **-iness** -ɪ.nəs, -ɪ.nɪs
Asia 'eɪ.ʒə, -ʃə (US) 'eɪ.ʒə **ˌAsia 'Minor**
Asian 'eɪ.ʒᵊn, -ʃᵊn (US) 'eɪ.ʒᵊn, -ʃᵊn **-s** -z **ˌAsian 'flu**
Asiatic ˌeɪ.zi'æt.ɪk, ˌeɪ.si-, ˌeɪ.ʒi-, ˌeɪ.ʃi- (US) ˌeɪ.ʒi'æt̬.ɪk, -ʃi'- **-s** -s *stress shift:* ˌAsiatic 'origin
aside ə'saɪd **-s** -z
Asimov 'æz.ɪ.mɒf, 'æs-, '-ə-, -mɒv (US) 'æz.ə.mɑːf, -mɑːv
asinine 'æs.ɪ.naɪn, -ə.naɪn
asininit|y ˌæs.ɪ'nɪn.ə.t|i, -ə'nɪn-, -ɪ.t|i (US) -ə'nɪn.ə.t̬|i **-ies** -iz
ask (*v.*) ɑːsk (US) æsk **-s** -s **-ing** -ɪŋ **-ed** -t
askance ə'skæn*t*s, -'skɑːn*t*s (US) ə'skæn*t*s
askant ə'skænt
Aske æsk
Askelon 'æs.kɪ.lən, -kə.lən, -lɒn (US) -kə.lɑːn
Askern 'æs.kɜːn, -kən (US) -kɝːn, -kɚn
askew ə'skjuː
Askew 'æs.kjuː
Askey 'æs.ki
Askrigg 'æs.krɪg
Askwith 'æs.kwɪθ
Aslam 'æz.ləm
aslant ə'slɑːnt (US) -'slænt
asleep ə'sliːp
ASLEF, Aslef 'æz.lef
Asmara æs'mɑː.rə, æz- (US) -'mɑːr.ə
Asmodeus æs'məʊ.di.əs (US) ˌæz.moʊ'diː-, ˌæs-, -mə'-
Note: For British English, the name must be pronounced /ˌæs.məʊ'diː.əs/ in Milton's 'Paradise Lost', iv, 168.
asocial ˌeɪ'səʊ.ʃᵊl (US) -'soʊ-
Asoka ə'ʃəʊ.kə, ə'səʊ- (US) -'soʊ-
asp æsp, ɑːsp (US) æsp **-s** -s
asparagus ə'spær.ə.gəs (US) -'sper-, -'spær-
aspartame ə'spɑː.teɪm; 'æs.pə- (US) 'æs.pɚ-; ə'spɑːr-
Aspasia æs'peɪ.zi.ə, ə'speɪ-, -ʒə (US) -ʒə
ASPCA ˌeɪ.es,piː.siː'eɪ
aspect 'æs.pekt **-s** -s
aspectable æs'pek.tə.bl̩
aspectual ə'spek.tʃu.əl, æs'pek-, -tju- (US) -tʃu-
Aspel(l) 'æs.pᵊl
aspen (A) 'æs.pən **-s** -z
asper 'æs.pəʳ (US) -pɚ
asperg|e ə'spɜːdʒ, æs'pɜːdʒ (US) ə'spɝːdʒ **-es** -ɪz **-ing** -ɪŋ **-ed** -d
asperges (A) *religious service:* æs'pɜː.dʒiːz, ə'spɜː- (US) ə'spɝː-
aspergill 'æs.pə.dʒɪl (US) -pɚ- **-s** -z
asperit|y æs'per.ə.t|i, ə'sper-, -ɪ.t|i (US) -ə.t̬|i **-ies** -iz
Aspern 'æs.pɜːn (US) -pɝːn
aspers|e ə'spɜːs, æs'pɜːs (US) ə'spɝːs **-es** -ɪz **-ing** -ɪŋ **-ed** -t
aspersion ə'spɜː.ʃᵊn, æs'pɜː- (US) ə'spɝː.ʒᵊn, -ʃᵊn **-s** -z
asphalt (*n.*) 'æs.fælt, -fɔːlt, -fəlt (US) -fɑːlt, -fɔːlt **-s** -s **ˌasphalt 'jungle**
asphal|t (*v.*) 'æs.fæl|t, æs'fæl|t (US) 'æs.fɑːl|t, -fɔːl|t **-ts** -ts **-ting** -tɪŋ (US) -t̬ɪŋ **-ted** -tɪd (US) -t̬ɪd
asphaltic æs'fæl.tɪk (US) -'fɑːl.t̬ɪk, -'fɔːl-
asphodel 'æs.fəʊ.del (US) -fə- **-s** -z
asphyxia əs'fɪks.i.ə, æs-
asphyxiant əs'fɪk.si.ənt, æs'- **-s** -s
asphyxi|ate əs'fɪk.si|.eɪt, æs- **-ates** -s **-ating** -eɪ.tɪŋ (US) -eɪ.t̬ɪŋ **-ated** -eɪ.tɪd (US) -eɪ.t̬ɪd **-ator/s** -eɪ.təʳ/z (US) -eɪ.t̬ɚ/z
asphyxiation əsˌfɪk.si'eɪ.ʃᵊn, æs- **-s** -z
asphyx|y æs'fɪk.s|i **-ies** -iz
aspic 'æs.pɪk

Aspiration

Noise made when the constriction of a plosive consonant is released and air is allowed to escape relatively freely.

Examples for English

English /p t k/ at the beginning of a syllable are aspirated in most accents. In words like *pea, tea, key,* there is a silent period during which the compressed air is prevented from escaping by the articulatory closure; this is followed by a sound similar to /h/ before the VOICING of the vowel begins, the result of the vocal folds being widely parted at the time of the articulatory release. Aspiration is an important factor in whether we perceive a sound to be /p t k/ or /b d g/ in syllable-initial position.

/p t k/ are aspirated at the beginning of a syllable containing a full vowel, e.g.:

pin	/pɪn/	[pʰɪ̃n]
tick	/tɪk/	[tʰɪʔk]
kin	/kɪn/	[kʰɪ̃n]
appease	/əˈpiːz/	[əˈpʰiːz̥]
attain	/əˈteɪn/	[əˈtʰeɪ̃n]
accord	/əˈkɔːd/	[əˈkʰɔːd̥] US /əˈkɔːrd/ [əˈkʰɔːɹ̥d̥]

When followed by /l r w/ or /j/ in initial consonant clusters, the release of the PLOSIVE gives the following sound a voiceless quality, e.g.:

play	/pleɪ/	[pl̥eɪ]
tree	/triː/	[tɹ̥iː]
queue	/kjuː/	[kj̊ʉː]
twice	/twaɪs/	[tw̥aɪs]

It is noticeable that when /p t k/ are preceded by /s/ at the beginning of a syllable they are not aspirated. This makes them very similar to /b d g/, and is an example of NEUTRALISATION – the distinctive difference between /p t k/ and /b d g/ is lost when there is a preceding /s/, e.g.:

spin	/spɪn/	[spɪ̃n]	(compare pɪn [pʰɪ̃n])
stick	/stɪk/	[stɪʔk]	(compare tɪk [tʰɪʔk])
skin	/skɪn/	[skɪ̃n]	(compare kɪn [kʰɪ̃n])

Word final /p t k/ may be aspirated or not, for stylistic reasons.

aspidistra ˌæs.pɪˈdɪs.trə US -pəˈ- **-s** -z

Aspinall ˈæs.pɪ.nɔːl, -nᵊl

Aspinwall ˈæs.pɪn.wɔːl US -wɔːl, -wɑːl

aspirant ˈæs.pɪ.rᵊnt; əˈspaɪə- US ˈæs.pɚ.ᵊnt, -pɪ.rᵊnt **-s** -s

aspirate (*n. adj.*) ˈæs.pᵊr.ət, -pɪ.rət-, -rɪt **-s** -s

aspir|ate (*v.*) ˈæs.pᵊr.|eɪt, -pɪ.r|eɪt US -pə.r|eɪt, -pɪ- **-ates** -eɪts **-ating** -eɪ.tɪŋ US -eɪ.t̬ɪŋ **-ated** -eɪ.tɪd US -eɪ.t̬ɪd **-ator/s** -eɪ.təʳ/z US -eɪ.t̬ɚ/z

aspiration ˌæs.pᵊrˈeɪ.ʃᵊn, -pɪˈreɪ- US -pəˈreɪ-, -pɪˈ- **-s** -z

aspirational ˌæs.pᵊrˈeɪ.ʃᵊn.ᵊl, -pɪˈreɪ- US -pəˈreɪ-, -pɪˈ- **-ly** -i

aspir|e əˈspaɪəʳ US -spaɪɚ **-es** -z **-ing/ly** -ɪŋ/li **-ed** -d **-er/s** -əʳ/z US -ɚ/z

aspirin ˈæs.pᵊr.ɪn, ˈ-prɪn **-s** -z

aspirine ˈæs.pᵊr.iːn, -pɪ.riːn US -pə.riːn, -pɪ- **-s** -z

asplenium æsˈpliː.ni.əm, əˈspliː- **-s** -z

Asquith ˈæs.kwɪθ

ass æs **-es** -ɪz

assaf(o)etida ˌæs.əˈfet.ɪ.də, -ˈfiː.tɪ- US -ˈfet̬.ə-

assagai ˈæs.ə.gaɪ **-s** -z

assai æsˈaɪ

assail əˈseɪl **-s** -z **-ing** -ɪŋ **-ed** -d **-able** -ə.bl̩ **-ant/s** -ənt/s

Assam æsˈæm, ˈæs.æm

Assamese ˌæs.əˈmiːz, -æmˈiːz US -əˈmiːz, -ˈmiːs

assassin əˈsæs.ɪn US -ən **-s** -z

assassi|nate əˈsæs.ɪ|.neɪt, ˈ-ə- **-nates** -neɪts **-nating** -neɪ.tɪŋ US -neɪ.t̬ɪŋ **-nated** -neɪ.tɪd US -neɪ.t̬ɪd **-nator/s** -neɪ.təʳ/z US -neɪ.t̬ɚ/z

assassination əˌsæs.ɪˈneɪ.ʃᵊn, -əˈ- **-s** -z

assault əˈsɔːlt, -ˈsɒlt US -ˈsɔːlt, -ˈsɑːlt **-s** -s **-ing** -ɪŋ US əˈsɔːl.t̬ɪŋ **-ed** -ɪd US əˈsɔːl.t̬ɪd **-er/s** -əʳ/z US əˈsɔːl.t̬ɚ/z **asˌsault and ˈbattery; asˈsault ˌcourse**

assay (*n.*) əˈseɪ; ˈæs.eɪ US ˈæs.eɪ; əˈseɪ **-s** -z

assay (*v.*) əˈseɪ, æsˈeɪ **-s** -z **-ing** -ɪŋ **-ed** -d **-er/s** -əʳ/z US -ɚ/z

Assaye æsˈeɪ

assegai ˈæs.ə.gaɪ, ˈ-ɪ- US ˈ-ə- **-s** -z

assemblag|e əˈsem.blɪdʒ **-es** -ɪz

assembl|e əˈsem.bl̩ **-es** -z **-ing** -ɪŋ, ˈ-blɪŋ **-ed** -d **-er/s** -əʳ/z, ˈ-bləʳ/z US ˈ-bl̩.ɚ/z, -blɚ/z

assembl|y əˈsem.bl|i **-ies** -iz **asˈsembly ˌline; asˈsembly ˌroom; asˈsembly ˌlanguage**

assembly|man əˈsem.bli|.mæn, -mən **-men** -men, -mən

assen|t əˈsen|t, æsˈen|t **-ts** -ts **-ting/ly** -tɪŋ/li US -t̬ɪŋ/li **-ted** -tɪd US -t̬ɪd

Asser ˈæs.əʳ US -ɚ

as|sert ə|ˈsɜːt US -ˈsɝːt **-serts** -ˈsɜːts US -ˈsɝːts **-serting** -ˈsɜː.tɪŋ US -ˈsɝː.t̬ɪŋ **-serted** -ˈsɜː.tɪd US -ˈsɝː.t̬ɪd **-serter/s** -ˈsɜː.təʳ/z US -ˈsɝː.t̬ɚ/s **-sertor/s** -ˈsɜː.təʳ/z US -ˈsɝː.t̬ɚ/z **-sertable** -ˈsɜː.tə.bl̩ US -ˈsɝː.t̬ə.bl̩

assertion əˈsɜː.ʃᵊn US -ˈsɝː- **-s** -z

assertive əˈsɜː.tɪv US -sɝː.t̬ɪv **-ly** -li **-ness** -nəs, -nɪs **asˈsertiveness ˌtraining**

assess əˈses **-es** -ɪz **-ing** -ɪŋ **-ed** -t **-or/s** -əʳ/z US -ɚ/z **-able** -ə.bl̩

assessment əˈses.mənt **-s** -s

asset ˈæs.et, -ɪt **-s** -s

asset-stripp|ing ˈæs.etˌstrɪp|.ɪŋ **-er/s** -əʳ/z US -ɚ/z

assev|er æsˈev|.əʳ, əˈsev- US -ɚ **-ers** -əz US -ɚs **-ering** -ᵊr.ɪŋ **-ered** -əd US -ɚd

assever|ate əˈsev.ᵊr|.eɪt, æsˈev- US -ə.r|eɪt **-ates** -eɪts **-ating** -eɪ.tɪŋ US -eɪ.t̬ɪŋ **-ated** -eɪ.tɪd US -eɪ.t̬ɪd

asseveration əˌsev.əˈreɪ.ʃᵊn, æsˌev- **-s** -z

asshole ˈɑːs.həʊl, ˈæs- US ˈæs.hoʊl **-s** -z

Note: Chiefly US; see note at **arse**.

assibi|late əˈsɪb.ɪ|.leɪt, æsˈɪb-, ˈ-ə- **-lates** -leɪts **-lating** -leɪ.tɪŋ US -leɪ.t̬ɪŋ **-lated** -leɪ.tɪd US -leɪ.t̬ɪd

assibilation əˌsɪb.ɪˈleɪ.ʃᵊn, æsˌɪb-, -əˈ- **-s** -z

assiduit|y ˌæs.ɪˈdjuː.ə.t|i, -ˈdʒuː-, -ɪ.t|i US -ˈduː.ə.t̬|i, -ˈdjuː- **-ies** -iz

assiduous əˈsɪd.ju.əs, -ˈsɪdʒ.u- US -ˈsɪdʒ.u- **-ly** -li **-ness** -nəs, -nɪs

assign əˈsaɪn **-s** -z **-ing** -ɪŋ **-ed** -d **-er/s** -əʳ/z US -ɚ/z **-able** -ə.bl̩

Assimilation

Assimilation is what happens to a sound when it is influenced by one of its neighbours; essentially it becomes more similar to a neighbour.

Examples for English

Assimilation is said to be 'progressive' when a sound influences a following sound, or 'regressive' when a sound influences one which precedes it. The most familiar case of regressive assimilation in English is that of ALVEOLAR consonants (e.g. /t d s z n/) which are followed by non-alveolar consonants: assimilation results in a change of place of articulation from alveolar to a different place. For example, the word *this* has the sound /s/ at the end if it is pronounced on its own, but when followed by post-alveolar /ʃ/ in a word such as *shop* it often changes in rapid speech (through assimilation) to /ʃ/, giving the pronunciation /ðɪʃʃɒp/. The following examples occur especially in British English:

batman	/ˈbæt.mæn/	→ [ˈbæp.mæn]
fruitcake	/ˈfruːt.keɪk/	→ [ˈfruːk.keɪk]
handbag	/ˈhænd.bæg/	→ [ˈhæmb .bæg]

Progressive assimilation is exemplified by the behaviour of the 's' plural ending in English, which is pronounced with a voiced /z/ after a voiced consonant but with a voiceless /s/ after a voiceless consonant, e.g.:

dog	/dɒg/	+ plural →	/dɒgz/
	(US) /dɑːg/		(US) /dɑːgz/
cat	/kæt/	+ plural →	/kæts/

assignat *as if French:* ˌæs.ɪnˈjɑː, æs.ɪgˈnæt **-s** -z, -s
assignation ˌæs.ɪgˈneɪ.ʃən **-s** -z
assignee ˌæs.aɪˈniː, -ɪˈniː (US) əˌsaɪˈniː, ˌæs.əˈ- **-s** -z
assignment əˈsaɪn.mənt, -ˈsaɪm- (US) -ˈsaɪn- **-s** -s
assimilable əˈsɪm.əl.ə.bl̩, -ɪ.lə-
assimil|ate əˈsɪm.ɪ.l|eɪt, -əl|.eɪt (US) -ə.l|eɪt **-ates** -eɪts **-ating** -eɪ.tɪŋ (US) -eɪ.t̬ɪŋ **-ated** -eɪ.tɪd (US) -eɪ.t̬ɪd
assimilation əˌsɪm.ɪˈleɪ.ʃən, -əlˈeɪ- (US) -əˈleɪ- **-s** -z
assimilative əˈsɪm.ɪ.lə.tɪv, -əl.ə-, -ə.leɪ- (US) -ə.leɪ.t̬ɪv, -lə-
assimilatory əˈsɪm.ɪ.lə.tər.i, -əl.ə-; əˌsɪm.ɪˈleɪ-, -əˈ- (US) əˈsɪm.əl.ə.tɔːr-
Assiniboine əˈsɪn.ɪ.bɔɪn, -ə.bɔɪn **-s** -z
Assisi əˈsiː.si, -zi, -ˈsɪs.i
assist əˈsɪst **-s** -s **-ing** -ɪŋ **-ed** -ɪd **-er/s** -ər/z (US) -ɚ/z
assistanc|e əˈsɪs.tənts **-es** -ɪz
assistant əˈsɪs.tənt **-s** -s
Assiut æsˈjuːt (US) ɑːˈsjuːt
assiz|e əˈsaɪz **-es** -ɪz **-er/s** -ər/z (US) -ɚ/z
assoc *(abbrev. for* **associated***)* əˈsəʊ.ʃi.eɪ.tɪd, -si- (US) -ˈsoʊ.ʃi.eɪ.t̬ɪd, -si-
associable əˈsəʊ.ʃi.ə.bl̩, -ʃə-, -si.ə- (US) -ˈsoʊ-
associate *(n.)* əˈsəʊ.ʃi.ət, -si.ət (US) -ˈsoʊ.ʃi.ɪt, -si-, -ət **-s** -s
associ|ate *(v.)* əˈsəʊ.ʃi|.eɪt, -si- (US) -ˈsoʊ- **-ates** -eɪts **-ating** -eɪ.tɪŋ (US) -eɪ.t̬ɪŋ **-ated** -eɪ.tɪd (US) -eɪ.t̬ɪd
association əˌsəʊ.ʃiˈeɪ.ʃən, -siˈ- (US) -ˌsoʊ **-s** -z
associative əˈsəʊ.ʃi.ə.tɪv, -si- (US) -ˈsoʊ-
assonanc|e ˈæs.ən.ənts **-es** -ɪz
assonant ˈæs.ən.ənt **-s** -s
asson|ate ˈæs.ən|.eɪt (US) -ə.n|eɪt **-ates** -eɪts **-ating** -eɪ.tɪŋ (US) -eɪ.t̬ɪŋ **-ated** -eɪ.tɪd (US) -eɪ.t̬ɪd
as|sort əˈsɔːt (US) -ˈsɔːrt **-sorts** -ˈsɔːts (US) -ˈsɔːrts **-sorting** -ˈsɔː.tɪŋ (US) -ˈsɔːr.t̬ɪŋ **-sorted** -ˈsɔː.tɪd (US) -ˈsɔːr.t̬ɪd
assortment əˈsɔːt.mənt (US) -ˈsɔːrt- **-s** -s
Assouan æsˈwæn, ɑːˈswæn, -ˈswɑːn (US) ˈæs.wɑːn, ˈɑː.swɑːn *stress shift, British only, see compound:* ˌ**Assouan** ˈ**Dam**
asst *(abbrev. for* **assistant***)* əˈsɪs.tənt
assuag|e əˈsweɪdʒ **-es** -ɪz **-ing** -ɪŋ **-ed** -d **-ement** -mənt
assum|e əˈsjuːm, -suːm (US) -suːm **-es** -z **-ing/ly** -ɪŋ/li **-ed** -d **-edly** -ɪd.li, -əd- **-able** -ə.bl̩ **-ably** -ə.bli
assumpsit əˈsʌmp.sɪt
assumption (A) əˈsʌmp.ʃən **-s** -z
assumptive əˈsʌmp.tɪv
assuranc|e əˈʃɔː.rənts, -ˈʃʊə- (US) -ˈʃʊr.ənts, -ˈʃɜː- **-es** -ɪz
assur|e əˈʃʊər, -ʃɔːr (US) -ˈʃʊr, -ˈʃɜː **-es** -z **-ing** -ɪŋ **-ed** -d **-edly** -ɪd.li, -əd- **-edness** -d.nəs, -nɪs **-er/s** -ər/z (US) -ɚ/z
Assyri|a əˈsɪr.i|.ə **-an/s** -ən/z
assyriologist (A) əˌsɪr.iˈɒl.ə.dʒɪst (US) -ˈɑː.lə- **-s** -s
assyriology (A) əˌsɪr.iˈɒl.ə.dʒi (US) -ˈɑː.lə-
Astaire əˈsteər (US) -ˈster
Astarte æsˈtɑː.ti (US) əˈstɑr.t̬i
astatine ˈæs.tə.tiːn, -tɪn
Astbury ˈæst.bər.i (US) -ber-
aster ˈæs.tər (US) -tɚ **-s** -z
asterisk ˈæs.tər.ɪsk **-s** -s **-ing** -ɪŋ **-ed** -t
asterism ˈæs.tər.ɪ.zəm **-s** -z
Asterix ˈæs.tər.ɪks
astern əˈstɜːn (US) -ˈstɝːn
asteroid ˈæs.tər.ɔɪd (US) -tə.rɔɪd **-s** -z
asthenia æsˈθiː.ni.ə
asthenic æsˈθen.ɪk **-al** -əl
asthma ˈæsθ.mə, ˈæs.mə (US) ˈæz.mə
asthmatic æsθˈmæt.ɪk, æsˈmæt.ɪk (US) æzˈmæt̬- **-al** -əl **-ally** -əl.i, -li **-s** -s
Asti ˈæs.ti, -tiː (US) ˈɑː.sti
astigmatic ˌæs.tɪgˈmæt.ɪk (US) -ˈmæt̬-
astigmatism əˈstɪg.mə.tɪ.zəm, æsˈtɪg-
astir əˈstɜːr (US) -ˈstɝː
Asti Spumante ˌæs.ti.spuˈmæn.ti, -teɪ (US) ˌɑː.sti.spuˈmɑːn-, ˌæs.ti-
Astle ˈæs.l̩, ˈæs.tl̩
Astley ˈæst.li
Aston ˈæs.tən ˌ**Aston** ˈ**Martin®**; ˌ**Aston** ˈ**Villa**
astonish əˈstɒn.ɪʃ (US) -ˈstɑː.nɪʃ **-es** -ɪz **-ed/ly** -t/li
astonishing əˈstɒn.ɪ.ʃɪŋ (US) -ˈstɑː.nɪ- **-ly** -li
astonishment əˈstɒn.ɪʃ.mənt (US) -ˈstɑː.nɪʃ-
Astor ˈæs.tər, -tɔːr (US) -tɚ
Astoria əˈstɔː.ri.ə, æsˈtɔː- (US) əˈstɔːr.i-, æsˈtɔːr-
astound əˈstaʊnd **-s** -z **-ing/ly** -ɪŋ **-ed** -ɪd
Astra® ˈæs.trə
Astraea æsˈtriː.ə
astragal ˈæs.trə.gəl **-s** -z
astrakhan (A) ˌæs.trəˈkæn, -kɑːn
astral ˈæs.trəl **-ly** -i
astray əˈstreɪ
Astrid ˈæs.trɪd
astride əˈstraɪd
astring|e əˈstrɪndʒ **-es** -ɪz **-ing** -ɪŋ **-ed** -d
astringency əˈstrɪn.dʒənt.si
astringent əˈstrɪn.dʒənt **-s** -s **-ly** -li
astro- æs.trəʊ-; əˈstrɒ- (US) æs.troʊ-; əˈstrɑː-

Note: Prefix. Either takes primary or secondary stress on the first syllable, e.g. **astrolabe** /ˈæs.trəʊ.leɪb ⓤⓢ -trə-/, **astronomic** /ˌæs.trəˈnɒm.ɪk ⓤⓢ -ˈnɑː.mɪk/, or primary stress on the second syllable, e.g. **astronomy** /əˈstrɒn.ə.mi ⓤⓢ əˈstrɑː.nə-/.

astrobiology ˌæs.trəʊ.baɪˈɒl.ə.dʒi ⓤⓢ -troʊ.baɪˈɑː.lə-, -trə-

astrodome ˈæs.trəʊ.dəʊm ⓤⓢ -trə.doʊm **-s** -z

astrolabe ˈæs.trəʊ.leɪb ⓤⓢ -trə- **-s** -z

astrologer əˈstrɒl.ə.dʒəʳ, æsˈ- ⓤⓢ əˈstrɑː.lə.dʒɚ **-s** -z

astrologic ˌæs.trəˈlɒdʒ.ɪk ⓤⓢ -ˈlɑː.dʒɪk **-al** -ᵊl **-ally** -ᵊl.i

astrologist əˈstrɒl.ə.dʒɪst, æsˈ- ⓤⓢ əˈstrɑː.lə- **-s** -s

astrology əˈstrɒl.ə.dʒi, æsˈ- ⓤⓢ əˈstrɑː.lə-

astromet|er əˈstrɒm.ɪ.t|əʳ, æsˈtrɒm-, -ə.təʳ ⓤⓢ əˈstrɑː.mə.t̬|ɚ **-ers** -əz ⓤⓢ -ɚz **-ry** -ri

astronaut ˈæs.trə.nɔːt ⓤⓢ -nɑːt, -nɔːt **-s** -s

astronautic|al ˌæs.trəʊˈnɔː.tɪ.k|ᵊl ⓤⓢ -trəˈnɑː.t̬ɪ-, -ˈnɔː- **-s** -s

astronomer əˈstrɒn.ə.məʳ, æsˈ- ⓤⓢ əˈstrɑː.nə.mɚ **-s** -z

astronomic ˌæs.trəˈnɒm.ɪk ⓤⓢ -ˈnɑː.mɪk **-al** -ᵊl **-ally** -ᵊl.i, -li *stress shift:* ˌastronomic ˈincrease

astronom|y əˈstrɒn.ə.m|i, æsˈ- ⓤⓢ əˈstrɑː.nə- **-ies** -iz

Astrophil ˈæs.trəʊ.fɪl ⓤⓢ -trə-

astrophysical ˌæs.trəʊˈfɪz.ɪ.kᵊl ⓤⓢ -troʊˈ-, -trəˈ-

astrophysicist ˌæs.trəʊˈfɪz.ɪ.sɪst ⓤⓢ -troʊˈ-, -trəˈ- **-s** -s

astrophysics ˌæs.trəʊˈfɪz.ɪks ⓤⓢ -troʊˈ-

Astros ˈæs.trəʊz ⓤⓢ -troʊz

astroturf (A®) ˈæs.trəʊ.tɜːf ⓤⓢ -troʊ.tɝːf

Asturias æsˈtʊə.ri.æs, əˈstʊə-, -stjʊə-, -əs ⓤⓢ əˈstʊr.i-

astu|te əˈstjuː|t, æsˈtjuː|t, -ˈtʃuː|t ⓤⓢ əˈstuː|t, -ˈstjuː|t **-ter** -təʳ ⓤⓢ -t̬ɚ **-test** -tɪst, -təst ⓤⓢ -t̬ɪst, -t̬əst **-tely** -t.li **-teness** -t.nəs, -t.nɪs

Astyanax əˈstaɪ.ə.næks, æsˈtaɪ-

astylar eɪˈstaɪ.ləʳ, -lɑːʳ ⓤⓢ -lɚ

Asunción əˌsʊnt.siˈəʊn, -ˈɒn ⓤⓢ ɑːˌsuːnt.siˈoʊn, ˌɑː.suːnt-

asunder əˈsʌn.dəʳ ⓤⓢ -dɚ

Aswan æsˈwæn, ɑːˈswæn, -swɑːn ⓤⓢ ˈæs.wɑːn, ˈɑː.swɑːn *stress shift, British only, see compound:* ˌ**Aswan ˈDam**

asyllabic ˌeɪ.sɪˈlæb.ɪk, -səˈ- ⓤⓢ -sɪˈ- *stress shift:* ˌasyllabic ˈvowel

asylum əˈsaɪ.ləm **-s** -z **aˈsylum ˌseeker**

asymmetric ˌeɪ.sɪˈmet.rɪk, ˌæs.ɪˈ-, -səˈ- **-al** -ᵊl **-ally** -ᵊl.i, -li *stress shift:* ˌasymmetric ˈbars

asymmetry eɪˈsɪm.ə.tri, æsˈɪm-, ˈ-ɪ-

asymptote ˈæs.ɪmp.təʊt ⓤⓢ -toʊt **-s** -s

asymptotic ˌæs.ɪmpˈtɒt.ɪk ⓤⓢ -ˈtɑː.t̬ɪk **-al** -ᵊl **-ally** -ᵊl.i, -li *stress shift:* ˌasymptotic ˈcurve

asyndet|on æsˈɪn.dɪ.t|ən, əˈsɪn- ⓤⓢ əˈsɪn.də.t|ɑːn, ˌeɪ- **-a** -ə

at- ət-, æt-

Note: Prefix. Examples include **attestation** /ˌæt.esˈteɪ.ʃᵊn ⓤⓢ æt̬-/, in which it is stressed, and **attest** /əˈtest/, where it is unstressed.

at *(prep.) strong form:* æt *weak form:* ət

Note: Weak form word. The strong form is /æt/, and is used mainly in sentence-final position (e.g. 'What are you playing at?'). It may also be used in sentence-initial position. The weak form is /ət/ (e.g. 'She's at home.' /ʃiz.ətˈhəʊm ⓤⓢ -ˈhoʊm/).

at *currency:* ɑːt, æt

Atalanta ˌæt.əˈlæn.tə ⓤⓢ ˌæt̬.əˈlæn.t̬ə

Atall ˈæt.ɔːl

Atari® əˈtɑː.ri ⓤⓢ -ˈtɑːr.i

AT&T® ˌeɪ.tiː.ᵊndˈtiː

Atatürk ˈæt.ə.tɜːk, ˌ--ˈ- ⓤⓢ ˈæt̬.ə.tɝːk

atavism ˈæt.ə.vɪ.zᵊm ⓤⓢ ˈæt̬-

atavistic ˌæt.əˈvɪs.tɪk ⓤⓢ ˌæt̬.əˈ- **-ally** -ᵊl.i, -li *stress shift:* ˌatavistic ˈfeelings

ataxia əˈtæk.si.ə, ætˈæk-, eɪˈ-

atax|y əˈtæk.s|i, eɪ- **-ies** -iz **-ic** -ɪk

Atbara ætˈbɑː.rə ⓤⓢ -ˈbɑːr.ə

ATC ˌeɪ.tiːˈsiː

Atchison ˈætʃ.ɪ.sᵊn, ˈeɪ.tʃɪ- ⓤⓢ ˈætʃ.ɪ-

Ate *(n.)* ˈɑː.ti, ˈeɪ- ⓤⓢ ˈɑː-

ate *(from* **eat***)* et, eɪt ⓤⓢ eɪt

-ate -eɪt, -ət, -ɪt

Note: Suffix. When forming a verb, **-ate** is always pronounced with a full vowel, and the verb itself is usually stressed two syllables before the suffix, e.g. **demonstrate** /ˈdem.ən.streɪt/, unless it is a word containing two syllables, in which case the suffix normally carries primary stress in British English, e.g. **rotate** /rəʊˈteɪt ⓤⓢ ˈroʊ.teɪt, -ˈ-/. In nouns, **-ate** is normally pronounced /-ət/ or /-ɪt/, e.g. **climate** /ˈklaɪ.mət, -mɪt/, but where the noun is a chemical term it generally has a full vowel, e.g. **nitrate** /ˈnaɪ.treɪt, -trɪt ⓤⓢ -treɪt/. There are numerous exceptions; see individual entries.

A-team ˈeɪˌtiːm

atelic əˈtel.ɪk, ætˈel.ɪk, -iː.lɪk ⓤⓢ ˌeɪˈtiː.lɪk, ˌætˈiː-, -ˈel.ɪk

atelier əˈtel.i.eɪ, ˈæt.el-, ˈæt.ə.li-, -jeɪ ⓤⓢ əˈtᵊl.jeɪ, ætˈel-; ˌæt.elˈjeɪ **-s** -z

Atfield ˈæt.fiːld

Athabasca ˌæθ.əˈbæs.kə

Athaliah ˌæθ.əˈlaɪ.ə

Athanasian ˌæθ.əˈneɪ.zi.ən, ˈ-ʒən, -si.ən, -ʒi- ⓤⓢ -ʒən

Athanasius ˌæθ.əˈneɪ.zi.əs, ˈ-ʒəs, -si.əs, -ʒi- ⓤⓢ -ʒəs

Athawes ˈæt.hɔːz, ˈæθ.ɔːz ⓤⓢ ˈæt̬.hɑːz, -hɔːz, ˈæθ.ɑːz, -ɔːz

atheism ˈeɪ.θi.ɪ.zᵊm

atheist ˈeɪ.θi.ɪst **-s** -s

atheistic ˌeɪ.θiˈɪs.tɪk **-al** -ᵊl **-ally** -ᵊl.i, -li *stress shift:* ˌatheistic ˈculture

atheling (A) ˈæθ.ə.lɪŋ **-s** -z

Athelney ˈæθ.ᵊl.ni

Athelstan ˈæθ.ᵊl.stən *as if Old English:* ˈæð.ᵊl.stɑːn

Athelston ˈæθ.ᵊl.stən

Athena əˈθiː.nə

Athenaeum ˌæθ.ɪˈniː.əm, -əˈ- **-s** -z

Athene əˈθiː.ni, -niː

Athenian əˈθiː.ni.ən **-s** -z

Athenry ˌæθ.ənˈraɪ, -ɪnˈ-

Athens ˈæθ.ᵊnz, -ɪnz

Atherley ˈæθ.ə.li ⓤⓢ ˈ-ɚ-

atherosclerosis ˌæθ.ə.rəʊ.skləˈrəʊ.sɪs, -sklerˈəʊ-, sklɪrˈ- ⓤⓢ -roʊ.skləˈroʊ.səs

atherosclerotic ˌæθ.ə.rəʊ.skləˈrɒt.ɪk, -sklerˈɒt-, -sklɪrˈ- ⓤⓢ -roʊ.skləˈrɑː.t̬ɪk

Atherston ˈæθ.ə.stᵊn ⓤⓢ ˈ-ɚ-

Atherstone ˈæθ.ə.stəʊn, -stᵊn ⓤⓢ -ɚ.stoʊn, -stᵊn

Atherton ˈæθ.ə.tᵊn ⓤⓢ ˈ-ɚ.t̬ən

athirst əˈθɜːst ⓤⓢ -ˈθɝːst

Athlestaneford ˈel.ʃən.fəd ⓤⓢ -fɚd

athlete ˈæθ.liːt **-s** -s ˌ**athlete's ˈfoot** ⓤⓢ ˈ**athlete's ˌfoot**

athletic æθˈlet.ɪk, əθ- ⓤⓢ -ˈlet̬.ɪk **-al** -ᵊl **-ally** -ᵊl.i, -li **-s** -s

athleticism æθˈlet.ɪ.sɪ.zᵊm, əθ-, ˈ-ə- ⓤⓢ -ˈlet̬.ə-

Athlone æθˈləʊn ⓤⓢ -ˈloʊn *stress shift:* ˌAthlone ˈPress

Athol ˈæθ.ᵊl, -ɒl ⓤⓢ -ɑːl, -ᵊl

Atholl, Athole ˈæθ.ᵊl

Athos ˈæθ.ɒs, ˈeɪ.θɒs ⓤⓢ ˈæθ.ɑːs, ˈeɪ.θɑːs; ˈæθ.oʊs

athwart əˈθwɔːt ⓤⓢ -ˈθwɔːrt

Athy əˈθaɪ

-ation -ˈeɪ.ʃᵊn

Note: Suffix. Always carries primary stress, e.g. **demonstration** /ˌdem.ənˈstreɪ.ʃᵊn/.

atishoo əˈtɪʃ.uː

-ative -ə.tɪv, -eɪ- ⓤⓢ -ə.t̬ɪv, -eɪ-

Note: Suffix. Words containing **-ative** are normally stressed one or two syllables before the suffix, e.g.

ablative /'æb.lə.tɪv (US) -t̬ɪv/, **operative** /'ɒp.ᵊr.ə.tɪv (US) 'ɑː.pɚ.ə.t̬ɪv/. See individual entries for exceptions.

Atkins 'æt.kɪnz

Atkinson 'æt.kɪn.sᵊn

Atlanta ət'læn.tə, æt- (US) -t̬ə

atlantean ˌæt.læn'tiː.ən, -lən'-; ət'læn.ti-, æt- (US) ˌæt.læn'tiː-, -lən'-

Atlantes *statues:* ət'læn.tiːz, æt- *in Ariosto's 'Orlando Furioso':* ət'læn.tes, æt-

Atlantic ət'læn.tɪk, æt- (US) -t̬ɪk **Atˌlantic 'City**

Atlantis ət'læn.tɪs, æt- (US) -t̬ɪs

atlas (A) 'æt.ləs **-es** -ɪz

ATM ˌeɪ.tiː'em **-s** -z

atman (A) 'ɑːt.mən

atmometer æt'mɒm.ɪ.təʳ, '-ə- (US) -'mɑː.mə.t̬ɚ **-s** -z

atmosphere 'æt.məs.fɪəʳ (US) -fɪr **-s** -z

atmospheric ˌæt.məs'fer.ɪk (US) -'fer-, -'fɪr- **-s** -s **-al** -ᵊl **-ally** -ᵊl.i, -li *stress shift:* ˌatmospheric 'pressure

atoll 'æt.ɒl; ə'tɒl (US) 'æt.ɑːl, 'eɪ.tɑːl, -tɔːl **-s** -z

atom 'æt.əm (US) 'æt̬- **-s** -z

atomic ə'tɒm.ɪk (US) -'tɑː.mɪk **-s** -s **-ally** -ᵊl.i, -li **aˌtomic 'energy**

atom|ism 'æt.ə.m|ɪ.zᵊm (US) 'æt̬- **-ist/s** -ɪst/s

atomistic ˌæt.ə'mɪs.tɪk (US) ˌæt̬-

atomization, -isa- ˌæt.ə.maɪ'zeɪ.ʃᵊn (US) ˌæt̬.ə.mɪ'-

atomiz|e, -is|e 'æt.ə.maɪz (US) 'æt̬- **-es** -ɪz **-ing** -ɪŋ **-ed** -d **-er/s** -əʳ/z (US) -ɚ/z

atonal eɪ'təʊ.nᵊl, ə-, æt'əʊ- (US) eɪ'toʊ-, æt'oʊ- **-ism** -ɪ.zᵊm **-ly** -i

atonality ˌeɪ.təʊ'næl.ə.ti, ə-, ˌæt.əʊ'-, -ɪ.ti (US) ˌeɪ.toʊ'næl.ə.t̬i, ˌæt.oʊ'-

aton|e ə'təʊn (US) -'toʊn **-es** -z **-ing/ly** -ɪŋ/li **-ed** -d **-er/s** -əʳ/z, -ɚ/z

atonement ə'təʊn.mənt, -'təʊm- (US) -'toʊn- **-s** -s

atonic eɪ'tɒn.ɪk, ə-, æt'ɒn- (US) eɪ'tɑː.nɪk, æt'ɑː- **-s** -s

atony 'æt.ᵊn.i (US) 'æt̬-

atop ə'tɒp (US) -'tɑːp

-ator -ə.təʳ, -eɪ.təʳ (US) -ə.t̬ɚ, -eɪ.t̬ɚ

Note: Suffix. Words containing **-ator** behave similarly to verbs containing **-ate**, e.g. **demonstrator** /'dem.ən.streɪ.təʳ (US) -t̬ɚ/.

-atory -ə.tᵊr.i, -eɪ- (US) -ə.tɔːr.i

Note: Suffix. The pronunciation differs between British and American English. In British English, the penultimate syllable is always reduced, but the antepenultimate syllable may be stressed, and in either case may be pronounced with a full vowel, e.g. **articulatory** /ɑː'tɪk.jə.lə.tᵊr.i, -jʊ-' ɑːˌtɪk.jə'leɪ-, -jʊ'-/. In American English, the penultimate syllable is pronounced with a full vowel (but does not carry primary stress), e.g. **articulatory** /ɑːr'tɪk.jə.lə.tɔːr.i/.

ATP ˌeɪ.tiː'piː

atrabilious ˌæt.rə'bɪl.i.əs (US) '-jəs

Atreus 'eɪ.tri.əs, -tri.uːs, -truːs

atri|um 'eɪ.tri.|əm, 'æt.ri- (US) 'eɪ.tri- **-a** -ə **-ums** -əmz

atrocious ə'trəʊ.ʃəs (US) -'troʊ- **-ly** -li **-ness** -nəs, -nɪs

atrocit|y ə'trɒs.ə.t|i, -ɪ.t|i, -'trɑː.sə.t̬|i **-ies** -iz

atrophic ə'trɒf.ɪk, æt'rɒf- (US) ə'trɑː.fɪk

atroph|y 'æt.rə.f|i **-ies** -iz **-ying** -i.ɪŋ **-ied** -id

atropine 'æt.rə.pɪn, -piːn

Atropos 'æt.rə.pɒs, -pəs (US) -pɑːs

attaboy 'æt.ə.bɔɪ (US) 'æt̬-

attach ə'tætʃ **-es** -ɪz **-ing** -ɪŋ **-ed** -t **-able** -ə.bl̩

attaché ə'tæʃ.eɪ, æt'æʃ- (US) ˌæt̬.ə'ʃeɪ, ə'tæʃ.eɪ **-s** -z **at'taché ˌcase** (US) **atta'ché ˌcase,** (US) **at'taché ˌcase**

attachment ə'tætʃ.mənt **-s** -s

attack ə'tæk **-s** -s **-ing** -ɪŋ **-ed** -t **-er/s** -əʳ/z, -ɚ/z

attain ə'teɪn **-s** -z **-ing** -ɪŋ **-ed** -d **-able** -ə.bl̩

attainability əˌteɪ.nə'bɪl.ə.ti, -ɪ.ti (US) -ə.t̬i

attainder ə'teɪn.dəʳ (US) -dɚ **-s** -z

attainment ə'teɪn.mənt, -'teɪm- (US) -'teɪn- **-s** -s

at|taint ə|'teɪnt **-taints** -'teɪnts **-tainting** -'teɪn.tɪŋ (US) -'teɪn.t̬ɪŋ **-tainted** -'teɪn.tɪd (US) -'teɪn.t̬ɪd

attar 'æt.əʳ (US) 'æt̬.ɚ, -ɑːr

attempt ə'tem*p*t **-s** -s **-ing** -ɪŋ **-ed** -ɪd **-er/s** -əʳ/z (US) -ɚ/z **-able** -ə.bl̩

Attenborough 'æt.ᵊn.bᵊr.ə, -ᵊm-, -ˌbʌr.ə (US) -ᵊnˌbɝː.oʊ

attend ə'tend **-s** -z **-ing** -ɪŋ **-ed** -ɪd **-er/s** -əʳ/z (US) -ɚ/z

attendanc|e ə'ten.dᵊn*t*s **-es** -ɪz

attendant ə'ten.dᵊnt **-s** -s

attendee ə.ten'diː, ˌæt.en- **-s** -z

attention ə'ten.*t*ʃᵊn **-s** -z

attentive ə'ten.tɪv (US) -t̬ɪv **-ly** -li **-ness** -nəs, -nɪs

attenuate *(adj.)* ə'ten.ju.ɪt, -ət, -eɪt

attenu|ate *(v.)* ə'ten.ju|.eɪt **-ates** -eɪts **-ating** -eɪ.tɪŋ (US) -eɪ.t̬ɪŋ **-ated** -eɪ.tɪd (US) -eɪ.t̬ɪd

attenuation əˌten.ju'eɪ.ʃᵊn **-s** -z

attenuator ə'ten.ju.eɪ.təʳ (US) -t̬ɚ **-s** -z

Atterbury 'æt.ə.bᵊr.i (US) 'æt̬.ɚ.ber.i, -bɚ-

Attercliffe 'æt.ə.klɪf (US) 'æt̬.ɚ-

attest ə'test **-s** -s **-ing** -ɪŋ **-ed** -ɪd **-or/s** -əʳ/z (US) -ɚ/z **-able** -ə.bl̩

attestation ˌæt.es'teɪ.ʃᵊn (US) ˌæt̬- **-s** -z

Attfield 'æt.fiːld

attic 'æt.ɪk (US) 'æt̬- **-s** -s

Attica 'æt.ɪ.kə (US) 'æt̬-

atticism 'æt.ɪ.sɪ.zᵊm (US) 'æt̬- **-s** -z

atticiz|e, -is|e 'æt.ɪ.saɪz (US) 'æt̬- **-es** -ɪz **-ing** -ɪŋ **-ed** -d

Attila ə'tɪl.ə; 'æt.ɪ.lə (US) ə'tɪl.ə; 'æt̬.ɪ.lə

attir|e ə'taɪəʳ (US) -'taɪɚ **-es** -z **-ing** -ɪŋ **-ed** -d **-ement** -mənt

Attis 'æt.ɪs (US) 'æt̬-

attitude 'æt.ɪ.tjuːd, -tʃuːd (US) 'æt̬.ə.tuːd, -tjuːd **-s** -z

attitudinal ˌæt.ɪ'tjuː.dɪ.nᵊl, -'tʃuː- (US) ˌæt̬.ə'tuː.dᵊn.ᵊl, -'tjuː-

attitudinarian ˌæt.ɪ.tjuː.dɪ'neə.ri.ən, -tʃuː- (US) ˌæt̬.əˌtuː.dɪ'ner.i-, -ˌtjuː- **-s** -z

attitudiniz|e, -is|e ˌæt.ɪ'tjuː.dɪ.naɪz, -'tʃuː- (US) ˌæt̬.ə'tuː.dᵊn.aɪz, -'tjuː- **-es** -ɪz **-ing** -ɪŋ **-ed** -d **-er/s** -əʳ/z, -ɚ/z

Attleborough 'æt.ᵊl.bᵊr.ə, -ˌbʌr.ə (US) -ˌbɝː.oʊ

Attlee 'æt.li

Attock ə'tɒk (US) -'tɑːk

attorn ə'tɜːn (US) -'tɝːn **-s** -z **-ing** -ɪŋ **-ed** -d

attorney ə'tɜː.ni (US) -'tɝː- **-s** -z **aˌttorney 'general**

attorney-at-law əˌtɜː.ni.ət'lɔː (US) -ˌtɝː.ni.ət'lɑː, -'lɔː **attorneys-at-law** əˌtɜː.niz.ət'lɔː (US) -ˌtɝː.niz.ət'lɑː, -'lɔː

attorneyship ə'tɜː.ni.ʃɪp (US) -'tɝː- **-s** -s

attract ə'trækt **-s** -s **-ing/ly** -ɪŋ/li **-ed** -ɪd **-or/s** -əʳ/z (US) -ɚ/z **-able** -ə.bl̩

attractability əˌtræk.tə'bɪl.ə.ti, -ɪ.ti (US) -ə.t̬i

attraction ə'træk.ʃᵊn **-s** -z

attractive ə'træk.tɪv **-ly** -li **-ness** -nəs, -nɪs

attributable ə'trɪb.jə.tə.bl̩, -jʊ- (US) -jə.t̬ə-

attribute *(n.)* 'æt.rɪ.bjuːt **-s** -s

attri|bute *(v.)* ə'trɪ|.bjuːt **-butes** -bjuːt **-buting** -bjʊ.tɪŋ (US) -bjə.t̬ɪŋ, -bjuː- **-buted** -bjʊ.tɪd (US) -bjə.t̬ɪd, -bjuː-

attribution ˌæt.rɪ'bjuː.ʃᵊn **-s** -z

attributive ə'trɪb.jə.tɪv, -jʊ- (US) -jə.t̬ɪv **-ly** -li

attrition ə'trɪʃ.ᵊn, æt'rɪʃ-

attun|e ə'tjuːn, æt'juːn (US) ə'tuːn, -'tjuːn **-es** -z **-ing** -ɪŋ **-ed** -d

Attwell 'æt.wel, -wəl

At(t)wood 'æt.wʊd

ATV ˌeɪ.tiː'viː **-s** -z

Atwater 'æt.wɔː.təʳ (US) -wɑː.t̬ɚ, -wɔː-

atypical ˌeɪ'tɪp.ɪ.kᵊl

aubade əʊ'bɑːd (US) oʊ- **-s** -z

Pronouncing the letters AU, AW

The vowel letter combinations **au** and **aw** are similar in that their most common pronunciation is /ɔː (US) ɑː/, e.g.:

sauce	/sɔːs/	(US) /sɑːs/
saw	/sɔː/	(US) /sɑː/

However, there is more variation in the case of **au**. When followed by **gh** in the spelling realised as /f/, it is pronounced as /ɑː, (US) æ/, e.g.:

laugh	/lɑːf/	(US) /læf/

The combination **au** may also be pronounced as /ɒ (US) ɑː/, e.g.:

Australia	/ɒsˈtreɪ.li.ə/	(US) /ɑːˈstreɪ-/
because	/bɪˈkɒz/	(US) /-ˈkɑːz/

In addition

Other sounds associated with the combinations **au** are:

/əʊ (US) oʊ/ chauffeur /ˈʃəʊ.fəʳ/ (US) /ʃoʊˈfɝː/

And, in rare cases:

/eɪ/ gauge /geɪdʒ/

In weak syllables

The vowel combinations **au** and **aw** are realised with the vowel /ə/ in weak syllables, and **au** may also result in a syllabic consonant or an elided vowel, e.g.:

awry	/əˈraɪ/
restaurant	/ˈres.tᵊr.ɔ̃ːŋ, ˈ-trɔ̃ːŋ/ (US) /-tə.rɑːnt, ˈ-trɑːnt/

auberg|e əʊˈbeəʒ, -ˈbɜːʒ (US) oʊˈberʒ **-es** -ɪz

aubergine ˈəʊ.bə.ʒiːn, -dʒiːn, ˌ--ˈ- (US) ˈoʊ.bɚ- **-s** -z

Auberon ˈɔː.bə.rən, ˈəʊ-, -rɒn, ˌ--ˈ- (US) ˈɑː.bə.rɑːn, ˈɔː-

aubretia ɔːˈbriː.ʃə, -ʃi.ə (US) ɑː-, ɔː-

Aubrey ˈɔː.bri (US) ˈɑː-, ˈɔː-

aubrietia ɔːˈbriː.ʃə, -ʃi.ə (US) ɑː-, ɔː- **-s** -z

auburn (A) ˈɔː.bən, -bɜːn (US) ˈɑː.bɚn, ˈɔː-

Auchindachie ˌɔː.kɪnˈdæk.i, -xɪnˈdæx- (US) ˌɑː.kɪnˈdæk-, ˌɔː-

Auchinleck ˌɔː.kɪnˈlek, -xɪnˈ-, ˈ--- (US) ˌɑː.kɪnˈlek, ˌɔː-, ˈ---

Auchmuty ɔːkˈmjuː.ti (US) ɑːk-, ɔːk-

Auchtermuchty ˌɔːk.təˈmʌk.ti, ˌɒk.tə-, ˌɔːx.təˈmʌx.ti, ˌɒx.tə- (US) ˌɑːk.tɚˈmʌk-, ˌɔːk-

Auckland ˈɔːk.lənd (US) ˈɑːk-, ˈɔːk-

au contraire ˌəʊ.kɒnˈtreəʳ (US) ˌoʊ.kɑːnˈtrer

au courant əʊˈkʊr.ɑ̃ːŋ (US) ˌoʊ.kuːˈrɑːn

auction ˈɔːk.ʃᵊn, ˈɒk- (US) ˈɑːk.ʃᵊn, ˈɔːk- **-s** -z **-ing** -ɪŋ **-ed** -d

auctionary ˈɔːk.ʃᵊn.ᵊr.i, ˈɒk- (US) ˈɑːk.ʃᵊn.er-, ˈɔːk-

auctioneer ˌɔːk.ʃᵊnˈɪəʳ, ˌɒk- (US) ˌɑːk.ʃəˈnɪr, ˌɔːk- **-s** -z **-ing** -ɪŋ **-ed** -d

audacious ɔːˈdeɪ.ʃəs (US) ɑː-, ɔː- **-ly** -li **-ness** -nəs, -nɪs

audacit|y ɔːˈdæs.ə.t|i, -ɪ.t|i (US) ɑːˈdæs.ə.ţ|i, ɔː- **-ies** -iz

Audelay ˈɔːd.leɪ (US) ˈɑːd-, ˈɔːd-

Auden ˈɔː.dᵊn (US) ˈɑː-, ˈɔː-

Audenshaw ˈɔː.dᵊn.ʃɔː (US) ˈɑː.dᵊn.ʃɑː, ˈɔː-, -ʃɔː

Audi® ˈaʊ.di (US) ˈaʊ-, ˈɑː-

audibility ˌɔː.dɪˈbɪl.ə.ti, -dəˈ-, -ɪ.ti (US) ˌɑː.dəˈbɪl.ə.ţi, ˌɔː-

audib|le ˈɔː.də.b|l̩, ˈ-dɪ- (US) ˈɑː.də-, ˈɔː- **-ly** -li **-leness** -l̩.nəs, -nɪs

audienc|e ˈɔː.di.ənts (US) ˈɑː-, ˈɔː- **-es** -ɪz

audio ˈɔː.di.əʊ (US) ˈɑː.di.oʊ, ˈɔː-

audiocassette ˌɔː.di.əʊ.kəˈset (US) ˌɑː.di.oʊ-, ˌɔː- **-s** -s

audiologist ˌɔː.diˈɒl.ə.dʒɪst (US) ˌɑː.diˈɑː.lə-, ˌɔː- **-s** -s

audiology ˌɔː.diˈɒl.ə.dʒi (US) ˌɑː.diˈɑː.lə-, ˌɔː-

audiometer ˌɔː.diˈɒm.ɪ.təʳ, -ə.təʳ (US) ˌɑː.diˈɑː.mə.ţɚ, ˌɔː- **-s** -z

audiometry ˌɔː.diˈɒm.ɪ.tri, ˈ-ə- (US) ˌɑː.diˈɑː.mə-, ˌɔː-

audiotape ˈɔː.di.əʊ.teɪp (US) ˈɑː.di.oʊ-, ˈɔː- **-s** -s

audio-typ|ing ˈɔː.di.əʊˌtaɪ.p|ɪŋ (US) ˈɑː.di.oʊ-, ˈɔː- **-ist/s** -ɪst/s

audio-visual ˌɔː.di.əʊˈvɪʒ.u.əl, -ˈvɪz.ju- (US) ˌɑː.di.oʊˈvɪʒ.ju-, ˌɔː-

audiphone ˈɔː.dɪ.fəʊn (US) ˈɑː.dɪ.foʊn, ˈɔː- **-s** -z

au|dit ˈɔː|.dɪt (US) ˈɑː-, ˈɔː- **-dits** -dɪts **-diting** -dɪ.tɪŋ (US) -də.ţɪŋ **-dited** -dɪ.tɪd (US) -də.ţɪd

audition ɔːˈdɪʃ.ᵊn (US) ɑː-, ɔː- **-s** -z **-ing** **-ed**

auditor ˈɔː.dɪt.əʳ (US) ˈɑː.də.ţɚ, ˈɔː- **-s** -z

auditori|um ˌɔː.dɪˈtɔː.ri|.əm (US) ˌɑː.dəˈtɔːr.i-, ˌɔː- **-ums** -əmz **-a** -ə

auditorship ˈɔː.dɪt.ə.ʃɪp (US) ˈɑː.də.ţɚ-, ˈɔː- **-s** -s

auditor|y ˈɔː.dɪ.tᵊr|.i (US) ˈɑː.də.tɔːr-, ˈɔː- **-ies** -iz

Audley ˈɔːd.li (US) ˈɑːd-, ˈɔːd-

Audrey ˈɔː.dri (US) ˈɑː-, ˈɔː-

Audubon ˈɔː.də.bɒn, -bən (US) ˈɑː.də.bɑːn, ˈɔː-, -bən

au fait ˌəʊˈfeɪ (US) ˌoʊ-

Aufidius ɔːˈfɪd.i.əs (US) ɑː-, ɔː-

Aufklärung ˈaʊf.kleə.rʊŋ (US) -kler.ʊŋ

Auf Wiedersehen ˌaʊfˈviː.də.zeɪ.ən, -zeɪn (US) -ˈviː.dɚ-

Aug. *(abbrev. for* **August***)* ˈɔː.gəst (US) ˈɑː-, ˈɔː-

Augean ɔːˈdʒiː.ən (US) ɑː-, ɔː-

Augeas ɔːˈdʒiː.æs (US) ɑː-, ɔː-

Augener ˈaʊ.gᵊn.əʳ (US) -ɚ

auger ˈɔː.gəʳ (US) ˈɑː.gɚ, ˈɔː- **-s** -z

Aughrim ˈɔː.grɪm (US) ˈɑː-, ˈɔː-

aught ɔːt (US) ɑːt, ɔːt

Aughton *Humberside, S. Yorks & Nr. Ormskirk, Lancashire:* ˈɔː.tᵊn (US) ˈɑː-, ˈɔː- *Nr. Lancaster, Lancashire:* ˈæf.tən

Augie ˈɔː.gi (US) ˈɑː-, ˈɔː-

augment *(n.)* ˈɔːg.mənt (US) ˈɑːg-, ˈɔːg- **-s** -s

aug|ment *(v.)* ɔːg|ˈment (US) ɑːg-, ɔːg- **-ments** -ˈments **-menting** -ˈmen.tɪŋ (US) -ˈmen.ţɪŋ **-mented** -ˈmen.tɪd (US) -ˈmen.ţɪd **-mentable** -ˈmen.tə.bl̩ (US) -ˈmen.ţə.bl̩

augmentation ˌɔːg.menˈteɪ.ʃᵊn, -mənˈ- (US) ˌɑːg-, ˌɔːg- **-s** -z

augmentative ɔːgˈmen.tə.tɪv (US) ɑːgˈmen.ţə.ţɪv, ɔːg-

au gratin ˌəʊˈgræt.æ̃ŋ (US) oʊˈgrɑː.tᵊn, -ˈgræt.ᵊn

Augsburg ˈaʊgz.bɜːg, ˈaʊks-, -bʊəg (US) ˈɑːgz.bɝːg, ˈɔːgz-, -bʊrg

aug|ur ˈɔː.g|əʳ (US) ˈɑː.g|ɚ, ˈɔː- **-urs** -əz (US) -ɚz **-uring** -ᵊr.ɪŋ **-ured** -əd (US) -ɚd

augural ˈɔːg.jʊ.rᵊl, -jᵊr.ᵊl (US) ˈɑːg.jɚ.ᵊl, ˈɔːg-

augur|y ˈɔːg.jʊ.r|i, -jᵊr.|i (US) ˈɑːg.jɚ|.i, ˈɔːg- **-ies** -iz

August *(n.)* ˈɔː.gəst (US) ˈɑː-, ˈɔː- **-s** -s
ˌ**August Bank** ˈ**Holiday**

august *(adj.)* ɔːˈgʌst (US) ɑː-, ɔː-, ˈ-- **-est** -ɪst **-ly** -li **-ness** -nəs, -nɪs

August|a ɔːˈɡʌs.t|ə, ə- (US) əˈ-, ɑːˈ-, ɔːˈ- **-an** -ən
Augustine ɔːˈɡʌs.tɪn, ə- (US) ɑː-, ɔː-; ˈɑː.ɡə.stɪn, ˈɔː-
Augustinian ˌɔː.ɡəˈstɪn.i.ən (US) ˌɑː-, ˌɔː-
Augustus ɔːˈɡʌs.təs, ə- (US) ə-, ɑː-, ɔː-
auk ɔːk (US) ɑːk, ɔːk **-s** -s
aul|a ˈɔː.l|ə, ˈaʊ- (US) ˈɑː-, ˈɔː- **-ae** -iː, -aɪ, -eɪ
auld (A) ɔːld (US) ɑːld, ɔːld
auld lang syne ˌɔːld.læŋˈsaɪn, -zaɪn (US) ˌɑːld-, ˌɔːld-
Aumerle ɔːˈmɜːl (US) ɑːˈmɝːl, ɔː-
au naturel ˌəʊ.næt.jʊˈrel (US) ˌoʊ.nætʃ.əˈrel; -nɑː.tʊˈ-
Aungier ˈeɪn.dʒəʳ (US) -dʒɚ
aunt ɑːnt (US) ænt, ɑːnt **-s** -s
Note: Although **aunt** is generally /ænt/ in American English, regional and social subgroups have persistent /ɑːnt/.
auntie, aunty ˈɑːn.ti (US) ˈæn.t̬i, ˈɑːn- **-s** -z
au pair ˌəʊˈpeəʳ (US) oʊˈper
aura ˈɔː.rə (US) ˈɔːr.ə **-s** -z
aural ˈɔː.rᵊl, ˈaʊ- (US) ˈɔːr.ᵊl **-ly** -i
aurate ˈɔː.reɪt, -rɪt (US) ˈɔːr.eɪt **-s** -s
aureate ˈɔː.ri.eɪt, -ət, -ɪt (US) ˈɔːr.i-
Aureli|a ɔːˈriː.li.|ə **-an** -ən **-us** -əs
aureola ɔːˈriː.ə.lə (US) ˌɔːr.iˈoʊ- **-s** -z
aureole ˈɔː.ri.əʊl (US) ˈɔːr.i.oʊl **-s** -z
aureomycin ˌɔː.ri.əʊˈmaɪ.sɪn (US) ˌɔːr.i-
au revoir ˌəʊ.rəvˈwɑːʳ, -rɪvˈ- (US) ˌoʊ.rəvˈwɑːr
auricle ˈɔː.rɪ.kl̩, ˈɒr.ɪ- (US) ˈɔːr.ɪ- **-s** -z
auricula ɔːˈrɪk.jʊ.lə, ɒrˈɪk-, -jə- (US) ɔːˈrɪk.jə- **-s** -z
auricular ɔːˈrɪk.jʊ.ləʳ, ɒrˈɪk-, -jə- (US) ɔːˈrɪk.jə.lɚ **-ly** -li
auricu|late ɔːˈrɪk.jʊ|.lət, -jə-, -lɪt, -leɪt (US) -jə- **-lated** -leɪ.tɪd (US) -leɪ.t̬ɪd
Auriel ˈɔː.ri.əl (US) ˈɔːr.i-
auriferous ɔːˈrɪf.ᵊr.əs
Auriga ɔːˈraɪ.ɡə
Aurignacian ˌɔː.rɪɡˈneɪ.ʃᵊn, -ʃi.ən (US) ˌɔːr.ɪɡ-
aurist ˈɔː.rɪst (US) ˈɔːr.ɪst **-s** -s
aurochs ˈɔː.rɒks, ˈaʊ- (US) ˈɔːr.ɑːks, ˈaʊ.rɑːks **-es** -ɪz
auror|a (A) ɔːˈrɔː.r|ə, ə- (US) -ˈrɔːr|.ə **-as** -əz **-al** -ᵊl
aurora australis ɔːˌrɔː.rə.ɒsˈtreɪ.lɪs, ə-, -ˈtrɑː- (US) -ˌrɔːr.ə.ɔːˈstreɪ-
aurora borealis ɔːˌrɔː.rə.bɔr.iˈeɪ.lɪs, ə-, -ˈɑː.lɪs (US) -ˌrɔːr.ə.bɔːr.iˈæl.ɪs, -ˈɑː.lɪs
Auschwitz ˈaʊʃ.wɪts *as if German:* -vɪts
auscul|tate ˈɔː.skᵊl|.teɪt, ˈɒs.kᵊl-, -kʌl- (US) ˈɑː.skᵊl-, ˈɔː- **-tates** -teɪts **-tating** -teɪ.tɪŋ (US) -teɪ.t̬ɪŋ **-tated** -teɪ.tɪd (US) -teɪ.t̬ɪd
auscultation ˌɔː.skᵊlˈteɪ.ʃᵊn, ˌɒs.kᵊlˈ-, -kʌlˈ- (US) ˌɑː.skᵊl-, ˌɔː- **-s** -z
auscultator ˈɔː.skᵊl.teɪ.təʳ, ˈɒs.kᵊl-, -kʌl- (US) ˈɑː.skᵊl.teɪ.t̬ɚ, ˈɔː- **-s** -z
auspic|e ˈɔː.spɪs, ˈɒs.pɪs (US) ˈɑː.spɪs, ˈɔː- **-es** -ɪz
auspicious ɔːˈspɪʃ.əs, ɒsˈpɪʃ- (US) ɑːˈspɪʃ-, ɔː- **-ly** -li **-ness** -nəs, -nɪs
Aussie ˈɒz.i (US) ˈɑː.zi, ˈɔː-, -si **-s** -z
Austell ˈɔː.stᵊl, ˈɒs.tᵊl *local Cornish pronunciation:* ˈɔː.sᵊl (US) ˈɑː.stᵊl, ˈɔː-
Austen ˈɒs.tɪn, ˈɔː.stɪn (US) ˈɑː.stɪn, ˈɔː-
Auster ˈɔː.stəʳ, ˈɒs.təʳ (US) ˈɑː.stɚ, ˈɔː-
auster|e ɒsˈtɪəʳ, ɔːˈstɪəʳ (US) ɑːˈstɪr, ɔː- **-er** -əʳ, -ɚ **-est** -ɪst, -əst **-ely** -li **-eness** -nəs, -nɪs
austerit|y ɒsˈter.ə.t|i, ɔːˈster-, -ɪ.t|i (US) ˈɑː.ster.ə.t̬|i, ˈɔː- **-ies** -iz
Austerlitz ˈɔː.stə.lɪts, ˈaʊ- (US) ˈɑː.stɚ-, ˈɔː-
Austin ˈɒs.tɪn, ˈɔː.stɪn (US) ˈɑː.stɪn, ˈɔː- **-s** -z
austral ˈɒs.trᵊl, ˈɔː.strᵊl (US) ˈɑː.strᵊl, ˈɔː-
Australasi|a ˌɒs.trəˈleɪ.ʒ|ə, ˌɔː.strə-, -zi|.ə, -ʃi|.ə, -ʃ|ə (US) ˌɑː.strəˈ-, ˌɔː- **-an/z** -ən/z
Australi|a ɒsˈtreɪ.li|.ə, ɔːˈstreɪ- (US) ɑːˈstreɪl.jə, ɔː- **-an/s** -ən/z
australopithecus ˌɒs.trə.ləʊˈpɪθ.ɪ.kəs, ˌɔː.strə-, -ə.kəs (US) ˌɑː.strə.loʊˈ-, ˌɔː-
Austri|a ˈɒs.tri|.ə, ˈɔː.stri- (US) ˈɑː.stri-, ˈɔː- **-an/s** -ən/z
Austro- ɒs.trəʊ-, ɔː.strəʊ- (US) ɑː.stroʊ-, ɔː-
Note: Prefix. Behaves as **Anglo-**.
Austro-German ˌɒs.trəʊˈdʒɜː.mən, ˌɔː.strəʊˈ- (US) ˌɑː.stroʊˈdʒɝː-, ˌɔː-
Austro-Hungarian ˌɒs.trəʊ.hʌŋˈɡeə.ri.ən, ˌɔː.strəʊ- (US) ˌɑː.stroʊ.hʌŋˈɡer.i-, ˌɔː-
Austronesi|a ˌɒs.trəʊˈniː.ʒ|ə, ˌɔː.strəʊˈ-, -zi|.ə, -si|.ə, -ʃ|ə (US) ˌɑː.stroʊˈ-, ˌɔː- **-an/s** -ən/z
autarchic ɔːˈtɑː.kɪk (US) ɑːˈtɑːr-, ɔː- **-al** -ᵊl
autarch|y ˈɔː.tɑː.k|i (US) ˈɑː.tɑːr-, ˈɔː- **-ies** -iz
autarkic ɔːˈtɑː.kɪk (US) ɑːˈtɑr-, ɔː- **-al** ᵊl
Auteuil əʊˈtɜːj (US) oʊˈtʊj, -ˈtɜːj
authentic ɔːˈθen.tɪk (US) ɑːˈθen.t̬ɪk, ɔː- **-al** -ᵊl **-ally** -ᵊl.i, -li
authenti|cate ɔːˈθen.tɪ|.keɪt (US) ɑːˈθen.t̬ɪ-, ɔː- **-cates** -keɪts **-cating** -keɪ.tɪŋ (US) -keɪ.t̬ɪŋ **-cated** -keɪ.tɪd (US) -keɪ.t̬ɪd **-cator/s** -keɪ.təʳ/z (US) -keɪ.t̬ɚ/z
authentication ɔːˌθen.tɪˈkeɪ.ʃᵊn (US) ɑːˌθen.t̬ɪˈ-, ɔː- **-s** -z
authenticit|y ˌɔː.θenˈtɪs.ə.t|i, -θᵊnˈ-, -ɪ.t|i (US) ˌɑː.θenˈtɪs.ə.t̬|i, ˌɔː- **-ies** -iz
author ˈɔː.θəʳ (US) ˈɑː.θɚ, ˈɔː- **-s** -z **-ing** **-ed**
authoress ˈɔː.θᵊr.es, -ɪs, -əs; ˌɔː.θᵊrˈes (US) ˈɑː.θɚ.ɪs, ˈɔː-, -əs **-es** -ɪz
authorial ɔːˈθɔː.ri.əl (US) ɑːˈθɔːr.i-, ɔː-
authoritarian ˌɔː.θɒr.ɪˈteə.ri.ən, ɔːˌθɒr-, -əˈ- (US) əˌθɔːr.əˈter.i-, ɑː-, ɔː- **-s** -z
authoritarianism ɔːˌθɒr.ɪˈteə.ri.ə.nɪ.zᵊm, -əˈ- (US) əˌθɔːr.əˈter.i-, ɑː-, ɔː-
authoritative ɔːˈθɒr.ɪ.tə.tɪv, ə-, ˈ-ə-, -teɪ- (US) əˈθɔːr.ə.teɪ.t̬ɪv, ɑː-, ɔː- **-ly** -li **-ness** -nəs, -nɪs
authorit|y ɔːˈθɒr.ə.t|i, ə-, -ɪ.t|i (US) əˈθɔːr.ə.t̬|i, ɑː-, ɔː- **-ies** -iz
authorization, -isa- ˌɔː.θᵊr.aɪˈzeɪ.ʃᵊn, -ɪˈ- (US) ˌɑː.θɚ.ɪˈ-, ˌɔː- **-s** -z
authoriz|e, -is|e ˈɔː.θᵊr.aɪz (US) ˈɑː-, ˈɔː- **-es** -ɪz **-ing** -ɪŋ **-ed** -d **-able** -ə.bl̩
authorship ˈɔː.θə.ʃɪp (US) ˈɑː.θɚ-, ˈɔː-
autism ˈɔː.tɪ.zᵊm (US) ˈɑː.tɪ-, ˈɔː-
autistic ɔːˈtɪs.tɪk (US) ɑː-, ɔː-
auto- ɔː.təʊ-; ɔːˈtɒ- (US) ɑː.t̬oʊ-, ɔː-; ɑːˈtɑː-, ɔː-
Note: Prefix. Either takes primary or secondary stress on the first syllable. e.g. **autocrat** /ˈɔː.tə.kræt (US) ˈɑː.t̬ə-, ɔː-/, **automatic** /ˌɔː.təˈmæt.ɪk (US) ˌɑː.t̬əˈmæt̬-, ɔː-/, or primary stress on the second syllable, e.g. **automaton** /ɔːˈtɒm.ə.tᵊn (US) ɑːˈtɑː.mə-, ɔː-, -tɑːn/.
auto ˈɔː.təʊ (US) ˈɑː.t̬oʊ, ˈɔː- **-s** -z
autobahn ˈɔː.təʊ.bɑːn, ˈaʊ- (US) ˈɑː.t̬oʊ-, ˈɔː-, -t̬ə- **-s** -z
autobiographer ˌɔː.tə.baɪˈɒɡ.rə.fəʳ (US) ˌɑː.t̬ə.baɪˈɑː.ɡrə.fɚ, ˌɔː-, -t̬oʊ- **-s** -z
autobiographic ˌɔː.təˌbaɪ.əʊˈɡræf.ɪk (US) ˌɑː.t̬əˌbaɪ.əˈ-, ˌɔː-, -t̬oʊˌ- **-al** -ᵊl **-ally** -ᵊl.i, -li *stress shift:* ˌautobiographic ˈnovel
autobiograph|y ˌɔː.tə.baɪˈɒɡ.rə.f|i (US) ˌɑː.t̬ə.baɪˈɑː.ɡrə-, ˌɔː-, -t̬oʊ- **-ies** -iz
autocade ˈɔː.təʊ.keɪd (US) ˈɑː.t̬oʊ-, ˈɔː-
auto-car ˈɔː.təʊ.kɑːʳ (US) ˈɑː.t̬oʊ.kɑːr, ˈɔː- **-s** -z
autochthon ɔːˈtɒk.θᵊn, -θɒn (US) ɑːˈtɑːk.θᵊn, ɔː- **-s** -z
autochthonous ɔːˈtɒk.θᵊn.əs (US) ɑːˈtɑːk-, ɔː-
autoclav|e ˈɔː.təʊ.kleɪv (US) ˈɑː.t̬oʊ-, ˈɔː- **-es** -z **-ing** -ɪŋ **-ed** -d
autocrac|y ɔːˈtɒk.rə.s|i (US) ɑːˈtɑː.krə-, ɔː- **-ies** -iz
autocrat ˈɔː.tə.kræt (US) ˈɑː.t̬ə-, ˈɔː- **-s**
autocratic ˌɔː.təˈkræt.ɪk (US) ˌɑː.t̬əˈkræt̬-, ˌɔː- **-al** -ᵊl **-ally** -ᵊl.i, *stress shift:* ˌautocratic ˈgovernment

autocross ˈɔː.təʊ.krɒs (US) ˈɑː.t̬oʊ.krɑːs, ˈɔː-
autocue (A®) ˈɔː.təʊ.kjuː (US) ˈɑː.t̬oʊ-, ˈɔː- **-s** -z
auto-da-fé ˌɔː.təʊ.dɑːˈfeɪ, ˌaʊ- (US) ˌɑː.t̬oʊ.dəˈ-, ˌɔː- **-s** -z
autodestruct ˌɔː.təʊ.dɪˈstrʌkt, -dəˈ- (US) ˌɑː.t̬oʊ-, ˌɔː- **-s** -s **-ing** -ɪŋ **-ed** -ɪd
autodidact ˌɔː.təʊˈdaɪ.dækt (US) ˌɑː.t̬oʊ-, ˌɔː- **-s** -s
autodidactic ˌɔː.təʊ.daɪˈdæk.tɪk, -dɪˈ- (US) ˌɑː.t̬oʊ-, ˌɔː-
autoerotic ˌɔː.təʊ.ɪˈrɒt.ɪk, -əˈrɒt- (US) ˌɑː.t̬oʊ.ɪˈrɑː.t̬ɪk, ˌɔː- *stress shift:* ˌautoerotic ˈfantasy
autoerot|ism ˌɔː.təʊ.ɪˈrɒt|.ɪ.zᵊm; -ˈer.ə.t|ɪ- (US) ˌɑː.t̬oʊ.ɪˈrɑː.t̬|ɪ-, ˌɔː- **-icism** -ɪ.sɪ.zᵊm (US) -ə.sɪ.zᵊm
autogam|ous ɔːˈtɒg.ə.m|əs (US) ɑːˈtɑː.gə-, ɔː- **-y** -i
autogenesis ˌɔː.təʊˈdʒen.ə.sɪs, ˈ-ɪ- (US) ˌɑː.t̬oʊˈdʒen.ə-, ˌɔː-
autogenetic ˌɔː.təʊ.dʒᵊnˈet.ɪk (US) ˌɑː.t̬oʊ.dʒəˈnet̬-, ˌɔː-
autogenic ˌɔː.təʊˈdʒen.ɪk (US) ˌɑː.t̬oʊˈ-, ˌɔː-
autogenous ɔːˈtɒdʒ.ə.nəs (US) ɑːˈt̬ɑː.dʒə-, ɔː- **-ly** -li
autogiro ˌɔː.təʊˈdʒaɪə.rəʊ (US) ˌɑː.t̬oʊˈdʒaɪ.roʊ, ˌɔː- **-s** -z
autograph ˈɔː.tə.grɑːf, -græf (US) ˈɑː.t̬ə.græf, ˈɔː- **-s** -s **-ing** -ɪŋ **-ed** -d
autographic ˌɔː.təʊˈgræf.ɪk (US) ˌɑː.t̬əˈ-, ˌɔː- **-al** -ᵊl **-ally** -ᵊl.i
autography ɔːˈtɒg.rə.fi (US) ɑːˈtɑː.grə-, ɔː-
autogyro ˌɔː.təʊˈdʒaɪə.rəʊ (US) ˌɑː.t̬oʊˈdʒaɪ.roʊ, ˌɔː- **-s** -z
Autoharp® ˈɔː.təʊ.hɑːp (US) ˈɑː.t̬oʊ.hɑːrp, ˈɔː-
auto-immun|e ˌɔː.təʊ.ɪˈmjuːn (US) ˌɑː.t̬oʊ-, ˌɔː- **-ity** -ə.ti, -ɪ.ti (US) -ə.t̬i
autolexic|al ˌɔː.təʊˈlek.sɪ.k|ᵊl (US) ˌɑː.t̬oʊˈlek.sə-, ˌɔː- **-ally** -ᵊl.i, -li
autolock ˈɔː.təʊ.lɒk (US) ˈɑː.t̬oʊ.lɑːk, ˈɔː-
Autolycus ɔːˈtɒl.ɪ.kəs (US) ɑːˈtɑː.lɪ-, ɔː-
automaker ˈɔː.təʊˌmeɪ.kəʳ (US) ˈɑː.t̬oʊˌmeɪ.kɚ, ˈɔː- **-s** -z
automat (A®) ˈɔː.tə.mæt (US) ˈɑː.t̬ə-, ˈɔː-
auto|mate ˈɔː.tə|.meɪt (US) ˈɑː.t̬ə-, ˈɔː- **-mates** -meɪts **-mating** -meɪ.tɪŋ (US) -meɪ.t̬ɪŋ **-mated** -meɪ.tɪd (US) -meɪ.t̬ɪd
automatic ˌɔː.təˈmæt.ɪk (US) ˌɑː.t̬əˈmæt̬-, ˌɔː- **-al** -ᵊl **-ally** -ᵊl.i, -li *stress shift, see compound:* **ˌautomatic ˈpilot**
automation ˌɔː.təˈmeɪ.ʃᵊn (US) ˌɑː.t̬əˈ-, ˌɔː-
automat|ism ɔːˈtɒm.ə.t|ɪ.zᵊm (US) ɑːˈtɑː.mə.t̬|ɪ-, ɔː- **-ist/s** -ɪst/s
automat|on ɔːˈtɒm.ə.t|ᵊn (US) ɑːˈtɑː.mə-, ɔː-, -t|ɑːn **-ons** -ᵊnz (US) -ᵊnz, -ɑːnz **-a** -ə
automobile ˈɔː.tə.məʊ.biːl, ˌɔː.tə.məʊˈbiːl (US) ˈɑː.t̬ə.moʊ.biːl, ˈɔː-, ˌɑː.t̬ə.moʊˈbiːl, ˌɔː-, ˌɑː.t̬əˈmoʊ-, ˈɔː- **-s** -z
automotive ˌɔː.təˈməʊ.tɪv (US) ˌɑː.t̬əˈmoʊ.t̬ɪv, ˌɔː-
autonomic ˌɔː.təˈnɒm.ɪk (US) ˌɑː.t̬əˈnɑː.mɪk, ˌɔː- *stress shift:* ˌautonomic ˈreflex
autonomous ɔːˈtɒn.ə.məs (US) ɑːˈtɑː.nə-, ɔː-
autonom|y ɔːˈtɒn.ə.m|i (US) ɑːˈtɑː.nə-, ɔː- **-ies** -iz
autonym ˈɔː.tə.nɪm (US) ˈɑː.t̬ə-, ˈɔː- **-s** -z
auto-pilot ˈɔː.təʊˌpaɪ.lət (US) ˈɑː.t̬oʊ-, ˈɔː- **-s** -s
autops|y ˈɔː.tɒp.s|i, -təp-, ɔːˈtɒp.s|i (US) ˈɑː.tɑːp-, ˈɔː-, -t̬əp- **-ies** -iz
autoroute ˈɔː.təʊ.ruːt (US) ˈɑː.t̬oʊ-, ˈɔː-, -raʊt **-s** -s
autosegment ˈɔː.təʊ.seg.mənt (US) ˈɑː.t̬oʊ-, ˈɔː- **-s** -s
autosegmental ˌɔː.təʊ.segˈmen.tᵊl (US) ˌɑː.t̬oʊ.segˈmen.t̬ᵊl, ˌɔː- **-ly** -i
autosug|gestion ˌɔː.təʊ.səˈdʒes.tʃᵊn, -ˈdʒeʃ- (US) ˌɑː.t̬oʊ.səgˈ-, ˌɔː- **-gestive** -ˈdʒes.tɪv
autotroph ˈɔː.təʊ.trɒf (US) ˈɑː.t̬oʊ.trɑːf, ˈɔː-, -troʊf
autotyp|e ˈɔː.təʊ.taɪp (US) ˈɑː.t̬oʊ-, ˈɔː- **-es** -s **-ing** -ɪŋ **-ed** -t
autotypography ˌɔː.təʊ.taɪˈpɒg.rə.fi (US) ˌɑː.t̬oʊ.taɪˈpɑː.grə-, ˌɔː-
autoworker ˈɔː.təʊˌwɜː.kəʳ (US) ˈɑː.t̬oʊˌwɝː.kɚ, ˈɔː- **-s** -z
autumn (A) ˈɔː.təm (US) ˈɑː.t̬əm, ˈɔː- **-s** -z
autumnal ɔːˈtʌm.nᵊl (US) ɑː-, ɔː- **-ly** -i
Auvergne əʊˈveən, -ˈvɜːn (US) oʊˈvern, -ˈvɝːn
auxiliar|y ɔːgˈzɪl.i.ᵊr|.i, ɔːkˈsɪl-, -jᵊr|.i (US) ɑːgˈzɪl.jᵊr-, ɔːg-, ˈ-i.er|.i **-ies** -iz
auxin ˈɔːk.sɪn (US) ˈɑːk-, ˈɔːk-
Ava ˈɑː.və, ˈeɪ.və (US) ˈeɪ-
avail əˈveɪl **-s** -z **-ing/ly** -ɪŋ/li **-ed** -d
availability əˌveɪ.ləˈbɪl.ə.ti, -ɪ.ti (US) -ə.t̬i
availab|le əˈveɪ.lə.b|l̩ **-ly** -li **-leness** -l̩.nəs, -nɪs
avalanch|e ˈæv.ᵊl.ɑːntʃ (US) -æntʃ **-es** -ɪz
Avalon ˈæv.ᵊl.ɒn (US) -ə.lɑːn
avant-courier ˌævɑ̃ːŋˈkʊr.i.eɪ (US) ˌɑː.vɑːnt-, ˌæv.ɑːnt-; əˌvɑːnt- **-s** -z
avant-garde ˌæv.ɑ̃ːŋˈgɑːd (US) ˌɑː.vɑːntˈgɑːrd, ˌæv.ɑːnt-; əˌvɑːnt-
avarice ˈæv.ᵊr.ɪs
avaricious ˌæv.ᵊrˈɪʃ.əs (US) -əˈrɪʃ- **-ly** -li **-ness** -nəs, -nɪs
avast əˈvɑːst (US) əˈvæst
avatar ˌæv.əˈtɑːʳ, ˈ--- (US) ˈæv.ə.tɑːr **-s** -z
avaunt əˈvɔːnt (US) -ˈvɑːnt, -ˈvɔːnt
AVC ˌeɪ.viːˈsiː
ave *prayer:* ˈɑː.veɪ, -viː **-s** -z
Ave. *(abbrev. for* **avenue***)* æv, ˈæv.ə.njuː, ˈ-ɪ- (US) ˈæv.ə.nuː, ˈ-ɪ-, -njuː
Avebury ˈeɪv.bᵊr.i (US) -ber-, -bɚ-
Aveley ˈeɪv.li
Aveline ˈæv.ə.laɪn, -liːn
Aveling ˈeɪv.lɪŋ
Ave Maria ˌɑː.veɪ.məˈriː.ə, -viː- **-s** -z
Ave Maria Lane ˌɑː.vi.mə.riː.əˈleɪn *formerly:* ˌeɪ.vi.məˌraɪəˈleɪn
aveng|e əˈvendʒ **-es** -ɪz **-ing** -ɪŋ **-ed** -d **-er/s** -əʳ/z (US) -ɚ/z **-eful** -fʊl
avenue ˈæv.ə.njuː, ˈ-ɪ- (US) -nuː, -njuː **-s** -z
aver əˈvɜːʳ (US) -ˈvɝː **-s** -z **-ring** -ɪŋ **-red** -d **-ment/s** -mənt/s
averag|e ˈæv.ᵊr.ɪdʒ, ˈ-rɪdʒ **-es** -ɪz **-ing** -ɪŋ **-ed** -d **-ely** -li
averse əˈvɜːs (US) -ˈvɝːs **-ly** -li **-ness** -nəs, -nɪs
aversion əˈvɜː.ʃᵊn, -ʒᵊn (US) -ˈvɝː.ʒᵊn, -ʃᵊn **-s** -z
a|vert ə|ˈvɜːt (US) -ˈvɝːt **-verts** -ˈvɜːts (US) -ˈvɝːts **-verting** -ˈvɜː.tɪŋ (US) -ˈvɝː.t̬ɪŋ **-verted** -ˈvɜː.tɪd (US) -ˈvɝː.t̬ɪd **-vertible** -ˈvɜː.tə.bl̩, -tɪ- (US) -ˈvɝː.t̬ə.bl̩
Avery ˈeɪ.vᵊr.i, ˈeɪv.ri
Aves ˈeɪ.viːz
Avesta əˈves.tə
avgolemono ˌæv.gəʊˈlem.ə.nəʊ (US) ˌɑːv.goʊˈlem.ə.noʊ
Avia® ˈeɪ.vi.ə (US) əˈviː-
avian ˈeɪ.vi.ən **-s** -z
aviarist ˈeɪ.vi.ᵊr.ɪst **-s** -s
aviar|y ˈeɪ.vi.ᵊr|.i (US) -er- **-ies** -iz
aviation ˌeɪ.viˈeɪ.ʃᵊn
aviator ˈeɪ.vi.eɪ.təʳ (US) -t̬ɚ **-s** -z
Avice ˈeɪ.vɪs
Avicenna ˌæv.ɪˈsen.ə
aviculture ˈeɪ.vɪˌkʌl.tʃəʳ, ˈæv.ɪ- (US) -tʃɚ
avid ˈæv.ɪd **-ly** -li
avidity əˈvɪd.ə.ti, ævˈɪd-, -ɪ.ti (US) -ə.t̬i
Aviemore ˈæv.ɪ.mɔːʳ, ˌ--ˈ- (US) ˌæv.ɪˈmɔːr
Avignon ˈæv.i.njɔ̃ːŋ (US) ˌæv.iːˈnjõʊn, -ˈnjɑːn
avionic ˌeɪ.viˈɒn.ɪk (US) -ˈɑː.nɪk **-s** -s *stress shift:* ˌavionic ˈsystem
Avis® ˈeɪ.vɪs
Avoca əˈvəʊ.kə (US) -ˈvoʊ-
avocado ˌæv.əˈkɑː.dəʊ (US) -doʊ, ɑː.vəˈ- **-s** -z
avocation ˌæv.əʊˈkeɪ.ʃᵊn (US) -əˈ-, -oʊˈ- **-s** -z

avocet 'æv.əʊ.set ⓤⓢ '-ə- **-s** -s
Avoch ɔːk, ɔːx
Avogadro ˌæv.əʊ'gæd.rəʊ, -'gɑː.drəʊ ⓤⓢ -ə'gɑː.droʊ, ˌɑː.və'-, -'gæd.roʊ
avoid ə'vɔɪd **-s** -z **-ing** -ɪŋ **-ed** -ɪd
avoidab|le ə'vɔɪ.də.b|l̩ **-ly** -li
avoidanc|e ə'vɔɪ.dənts **-es** -ɪz
avoirdupois ˌæv.ə.də'pɔɪz, ˌæv.wɑː.dju'pwɑː ⓤⓢ ˌæv.ɚ.də'pɔɪz, 'æv.ɚ.dəˌpɔɪz
Avon *in Avon:* 'eɪ.vən ⓤⓢ -vɑːn, -vən, 'æv.ən *in Devon:* 'æv.ən *in the Grampian region:* ɑːn *trademark:* 'eɪ.vɒn ⓤⓢ -vɑːn
Avondale 'eɪ.vən.deɪl ⓤⓢ 'eɪ.vən-, 'æv.ən-
Avonmouth 'eɪ.vən.maʊθ, -vəm- ⓤⓢ -vən-
Avory 'eɪ.vər.i ⓤⓢ 'eɪv.ri
avow ə'vaʊ **-s** -z **-ing** -ɪŋ **-ed** -d **-edly** -ɪd.li, -əd-
avowal ə'vaʊ.əl **-s** -z
Avril 'æv.rɪl, -rəl
avuncular ə'vʌŋ.kjə.lər, -kjʊ- ⓤⓢ -lɚ **-ly** -li
AWACS 'eɪ.wæks
a|wait ə|'weɪt **-waits** -'weɪts **-waiting** -'weɪ.tɪŋ ⓤⓢ -'weɪ.t̬ɪŋ **-waited** -'weɪ.tɪd ⓤⓢ -'weɪ.t̬ɪd
awak|e ə'weɪk **-es** -s **-ing** -ɪŋ **-ed** -t **awoke** ə'wəʊk ⓤⓢ -'woʊk
awaken ə'weɪ.kən **-s** -z **-ing/s** -ɪŋ/z **-ed** -d **-ment/s** -mənt/s
awakening *(n.)* ə'weɪ.kən.ɪŋ **-s** -z
award ə'wɔːd ⓤⓢ -'wɔːrd **-s** -z **-ing** -ɪŋ **-ed** -ɪd **-able** -ə.bl̩
aware ə'weər ⓤⓢ -'wer **-ness** -nəs, -nɪs
awash ə'wɒʃ ⓤⓢ -'wɑːʃ, -'wɔːʃ
away ə'weɪ
aw|e (A) ɔː ⓤⓢ ɑː, ɔː **-es** -z **-(e)ing** -ɪŋ **-ed** -d
awe-inspiring 'ɔː.ɪn.spaɪə.rɪŋ ⓤⓢ 'ɑː-, 'ɔː- **-ly** -li
aweless 'ɔː.ləs, -lɪs ⓤⓢ 'ɑː-, 'ɔː- **-ness** -nəs, -nɪs
awesome 'ɔː.səm ⓤⓢ 'ɑː-, 'ɔː- **-ly** -li **-ness** -nəs, -nɪs
awe-stricken 'ɔːˌstrɪk.ən ⓤⓢ 'ɑː-, 'ɔː-
awe-struck 'ɔː.strʌk ⓤⓢ 'ɑː-, 'ɔː-
awful *terrible:* 'ɔː.fəl, -fʊl ⓤⓢ 'ɑː-, 'ɔː- **-ness** -nəs, -nɪs *inspiring awe:* 'ɔː.fʊl ⓤⓢ 'ɑː-, 'ɔː- **-ness** -nəs, -nɪs
awfully 'ɔː.fəl.i, -fʊl- ⓤⓢ 'ɑː-, 'ɔː-
awhile ə'*h*waɪl
awkward 'ɔː.kwəd ⓤⓢ 'ɑː.kwɚd, 'ɔː- **-est** -əst, -ɪst **-ly** -li **-ness** -nəs, -nɪs **-ish** -ɪʃ
awl ɔːl ⓤⓢ ɔːl, ɑːl **-s** -z
awn ɔːn ⓤⓢ ɑːn, ɔːn **-s** -z **-ed** -d
awning 'ɔː.nɪŋ ⓤⓢ 'ɑː-, 'ɔː- **-s** -z
awoke *(from* **awake***)* ə'wəʊk ⓤⓢ -'woʊk
awoken ə'wəʊ.kən ⓤⓢ -'woʊ-
AWOL, Awol 'eɪ.wɒl ⓤⓢ -wɑːl
Awooner ə'wuː.nər ⓤⓢ -nɚ
awry ə'raɪ
Axa® 'æk.sə
ax|e, ax æks **-es** -ɪz **-ing** -ɪŋ **-ed** -t **have an 'axe to ˌgrind**
axel (A) 'æk.səl **-s** -z
axes *(plur. of* **axis***)* 'æk.siːz
axes *(plur. of* **axe***)* 'æk.sɪz
Axholm(e) 'æks.*h*əʊm, -əm ⓤⓢ -*h*oʊm
axial 'æk.si.əl **-ly** -i
axil 'æk.sɪl, -səl **-s** -z
axill|a æk'sɪl.|ə **-ae** -iː **-as** -əz **-ar** -ər ⓤⓢ -ɚ **-ary** -ər.i
axiom 'æk.si.əm **-s** -z
axiomatic ˌæk.si.ə'mæt.ɪk ⓤⓢ -'mæt̬- **-al** -əl **-ally** -əl.i, -li
ax|is 'æk.s|ɪs **-es** -iːz
axle 'æk.sl̩ **-s** -z **-d** -d
axle-tree 'æk.sl̩.triː **-s** -z
Axminster 'æks.mɪn.stər ⓤⓢ -stɚ **-s** -z
axolotl 'æk.sə.lɒt.l̩ ⓤⓢ 'æk.sə.lɑː.tl̩ **-s** -z
axon 'æk.sɒn ⓤⓢ -sɑːn **-s** -z
ay aɪ, eɪ **-es** -z
ayah 'aɪ.ə, 'ɑː.jə **-s** -z
ayatollah ˌaɪ.ə'tɒl.ə ⓤⓢ -'toʊ.lə; -toʊ'lɑː **-s** -z
Ayckbourn 'eɪk.bɔːn ⓤⓢ -bɔːrn
Aycliffe 'eɪ.klɪf
aye *ever:* eɪ *yes:* aɪ **-s** -z
aye-aye 'aɪ.aɪ **-s** -z
Ayenbite of Inwyt ˌeɪ.ən.baɪt.əv'ɪn.wɪt
Ayer eər ⓤⓢ er
Ayers eəz ⓤⓢ erz ˌ**Ayers 'Rock**
Ayesha aɪ'iː.ʃə
Aylesbury 'eɪlz.bər.i ⓤⓢ -ber-, -bɚ-
Aylesford 'eɪlz.fəd, 'eɪls- ⓤⓢ -fɚd
Ayling 'eɪ.lɪŋ
Aylmer 'eɪl.mər ⓤⓢ -mɚ
Aylsham 'eɪl.ʃəm
Aylward 'eɪl.wəd ⓤⓢ -wɚd
Aylwin 'eɪl.wɪn
Aymer 'eɪ.mər ⓤⓢ -mɚ
Ayot 'eɪ.ət
Ayr eər ⓤⓢ er **-shire** -ʃər, -ˌʃɪər ⓤⓢ -ʃɚ, -ˌʃɪr
Ayre eər ⓤⓢ er **-s** -z
Ayrton 'eə.tən ⓤⓢ 'er-
Ayscough 'æs.kə, 'æsk.juː, 'eɪ.skəf, 'eɪz.kɒf ⓤⓢ 'æs.kjuː
Ayscue 'eɪ.skjuː ⓤⓢ 'æs.kjuː
Ayton, Aytoun 'eɪ.tən
ayurved|a aɪ.ʊə'veɪ.d|ə, ɑː-, -'viː- ⓤⓢ ˌɑː.jʊr'veɪ- **-ic** -ɪk
A-Z ˌeɪ.tə'zed ⓤⓢ -t̬ə'ziː
azalea ə'zeɪ.li.ə ⓤⓢ -'zeɪl.jə **-s** -z
Azani|a ə'zeɪ.ni|.ə **-an/s** -ən/z
Azariah ˌæz.ə'raɪ.ə
Azerbaijan ˌæz.ə.baɪ'dʒɑːn, -'ʒɑːn ⓤⓢ ˌɑː.zɚ-, ˌæz.ɚ- **-i/s** -i/z
azimuth 'æz.ɪ.məθ, '-ə- **-s** -s
Aziz ə'ziːz, -'zɪz
Aznavour 'æz.nə.vɔːr, -vʊər ⓤⓢ ˌ--'vɔːr, -'vʊr
azodye 'eɪ.zəʊ.daɪ, 'æz.əʊ- ⓤⓢ -zoʊ- **-s** -z
azoic ə'zəʊ.ɪk, æz'əʊ-, eɪ'zəʊ- ⓤⓢ ə'zoʊ-, eɪ-
Azores ə'zɔːz ⓤⓢ 'eɪ.zɔːrz; ə'zɔːrz
Note: It is customary to pronounce /ə'zɔː.rɪz ⓤⓢ -'zɔːr.ɪz/ (or /-'zɔː.rez ⓤⓢ -'zɔːr.ez/) in reciting Tennyson's poem 'The Revenge'.
azote ə'zəʊt, æz'əʊt; 'æz.əʊt, 'eɪ.zəʊt ⓤⓢ 'æz.oʊt, 'eɪ.zoʊt; ə'zoʊt
azotic ə'zɒt.ɪk, æz'ɒt-, eɪ'zɒt- ⓤⓢ ə'zɑː.t̬ɪk
Azov 'ɑː.zɒv, 'eɪ-, 'æz.ɒv ⓤⓢ 'ɑː.zɑːf, 'eɪ-, 'æz.ɑːf, -ɔːf
AZT® ˌeɪ.zed'tiː ⓤⓢ -ziː'-
Aztec 'æz.tek **-s** -s
azure 'æz.jʊər, 'eɪ.zjʊər, 'æʒ.ər, 'eɪ.ʒər, ə'zjʊər, ə'zjʊər ⓤⓢ 'æʒ.ɚ, 'eɪ.ʒɚ
azygous ə'zaɪ.gəs, æz'aɪ-, ˌeɪ'zaɪ- ⓤⓢ 'æz.ɪ-; ˌeɪ'zaɪ-

Pronouncing the letter B

The consonant **b** is most often realised as /b/, e.g.:

boy /bɔɪ/
grab /græb/

In addition

b can be silent, or have a zero realisation. There are two combinations in which this can occur: **bt** and **mb**.

bt is either word medial or word final, e.g.:

doubt /daʊt/
subtle /ˈsʌt.l̩/ (US) /ˈsʌt̬.l̩/

Words containing **mb** in which **b** is silent have the **mb** in word final position, except where an inflection is added, e.g.:

bomb /bɒm/ (US) /bɑːm/
bombing /ˈbɒm.ɪŋ/ (US) /ˈbɑː.mɪŋ/

However, the appearance of **bt** and **mb** does not necessarily indicate a silent **b**. In the case of **mb**, the **b** is pronounced if it occurs inside a morpheme or unit of meaning. Compare:

number = arithmetical value /ˈnʌm.bə^{r}/ (US) /ˈnʌm.bɚ/
number = comparative of *numb* /ˈnʌm.ə^{r}/ (US) /ˈnʌm.ɚ/

For **bt**, the **b** is not silent if part of a prefix. Compare:

subtract /səbˈtrækt/
subtle /ˈsʌt.l̩/ (US) /ˈsʌt̬.l̩/

b (**B**) biː **-'s** -z
ba beɪ **-s** -z
BA ˌbiːˈeɪ
baa bɑː (US) bæ, bɑː **-s** -z **-ing** -ɪŋ **-ed** -d
Baader-Meinhof ˌbɑː.dəˈmaɪn.hɒf (US) -dɚˈmaɪn.hɑːf, -hoʊf
Baal ˈbeɪ.^{ə}l *Jewish pronunciation:* bɑːl
BAAL bɑːl
baa-lamb ˈbɑː.læm (US) ˈbɑː-, ˈbæ- **-s** -z
Baalim ˈbeɪ.^{ə}l.ɪm *Jewish pronunciation:* ˈbɑː.lɪm
baas *master:* bɑːs **-es** -ɪz
baas *(from* **baa***)* bɑːz (US) bæz, bɑːz
baaskaap ˈbɑːs.kæp (US) -kɑːp
Ba'ath bɑːθ (US) bɑːθ, bæθ **-ist/s** -ɪst/s
Bab bɑːb
baba ˈbɑː.bɑː, -bə **-s** -z
Babar ˈbɑː.bɑː^{r} (US) bəˈbɑːr; ˈbæb.ɑːr, ˈbɑː.bɑːr
Babbage ˈbæb.ɪdʒ
babbit (**B**) ˈbæb.ɪt **-s** -s
babbl|e ˈbæb.l̩ **-es** -z **-ing** -ɪŋ, ˈbæb.lɪŋ **-ed** -d **-er/s** -ə^{r}/z, ˈ-lə^{r}/z (US) ˈ-l̩.ɚ/z, ˈ-lɚ/z **-ement/s** -mənt/s
Babcock ˈbæb.kɒk (US) -kɑːk
babe beɪb **-s** -z
babel (**B**) ˈbeɪ.b^{ə}l (US) ˈbeɪ-, ˈbæb.^{ə}l **-s** -z
Babington ˈbæb.ɪŋ.tən
Bab|ism ˈbɑː.b|ɪ.z^{ə}m **-ist/s** -ɪst/s **-ite** -aɪt
Babi Yar ˌbɑː.biˈjɑː^{r} (US) -ˈjɑːr *stress shift:* ˌBabi Yar ˈmassacre
babka ˈbɑːb.kə **-s** -z
baboo (**B**) ˈbɑː.buː **-s** -z
baboon bəˈbuːn (US) bæbˈuːn, bəˈbuːn **-s** -z
babooner|y bəˈbuː.n^{ə}r|.i, bæbˈuː- **-ies** -iz
Babs bæbz
babu (**B**) ˈbɑː.buː **-s** -z
babushka bæbˈuːʃ.kə, bəˈbuːʃ-, -ˈbʊʃ- **-s** -z
bab|y (**B**) ˈbeɪ.b|i **-ies** -iz **-ying** -i.ɪŋ **-ied** -id **ˈbaby ˌboom; ˈbaby ˌboomer; ˌbaby ˈgrand; ˈbaby ˌtalk; ˈbaby ˌcarriage; throw the ˌbaby out with the ˈbath water**
Babycham® ˈbeɪ.bɪ.ʃæm
Babygro® ˈbeɪ.bɪ.grəʊ (US) -groʊ **-s** -z
babyhood ˈbeɪ.bi.hʊd
babyish ˈbeɪ.bi.ɪʃ **-ly** -li **-ness** -nəs, -nɪs
Babylon ˈbæb.ɪ.lɒn, -ə-, -lən (US) -lɑːn
Babyloni|a ˌbæb.ɪˈləʊ.ni|.ə, -əˈ- (US) -ˈloʊ- **-an/s** -ən/z
baby|sit ˈbeɪ.bɪ|.sɪt **-sitter/s** -ˌsɪt.ə^{r}/z (US) -ˌsɪt̬.ɚ/z **-sits** -sɪts **-sitting** -ˌsɪt.ɪŋ (US) -ˌsɪt̬.ɪŋ **-sat** -sæt
Bacall bəˈkɔːl (US) -ˈkɔːl, -ˈkɑːl
Bacardi® bəˈkɑː.di (US) -ˈkɑːr- **-s** -z
baccalaureate ˌbæk.əˈlɔː.ri.ət, -ɪt (US) -ˈlɔːr.i-, -ɪt **-s** -s
baccarat ˈbæk.ə.rɑː, ˌ--ˈ- (US) ˌbæk.əˈrɑː, ˌbɑː.kəˈ-, ˈ---
Bacchae ˈbæk.iː
bacchanal ˈbæk.ə.n^{ə}l; ˌbæk.əˈnæl (US) ˌbæk.əˈnæl **-s** -z
bacchanali|a ˌbæk.əˈneɪ.li|.ə (US) -jə **-an/s** -ən/z
bacchant ˈbæk.ənt **-s** -s
bacchante bəˈkæn.ti, bəˈkænt (US) -ˈkænt, -ˈkæn.ti, -ˈkɑːn- **-s** -z, -s
bacchic ˈbæk.ɪk
Bacchus ˈbæk.əs (US) ˈbæk.əs, ˈbɑː.kəs
Bacchylides bækˈɪl.ɪ.diːz, bəˈkɪl-
baccy ˈbæk.i
Bach *German composer:* bɑːk *as if German:* bɑːx (US) bɑːk *English surname:* beɪtʃ, bætʃ
bach *Welsh term of address:* bɑːk *as if Welsh:* bɑːx (US) bɑːk
Bacharach ˈbæk.ə.ræk
Bache beɪtʃ
bachelor (**B**) ˈbætʃ.^{ə}l.ə^{r}, -ɪ.lə^{r} (US) -^{ə}l.ɚ **-s** -z **-hood** -hʊd **-ship** -ʃɪp **ˌBachelor of ˈArts; ˌBachelor of ˈScience; ˈbachelor ˌgirl**
baciliform bəˈsɪl.ɪ.fɔːm, bæsˈɪl- (US) bəˈsɪl.ə.fɔːrm
bacillary bəˈsɪl.^{ə}r.i, bæsˈɪl- (US) bəˈsɪl-
bacill|us bəˈsɪl.|əs, bæsˈɪl- (US) bəˈsɪl- **-i** -aɪ, -iː
back (**B**) bæk **-s** -s **-ing** -ɪŋ **-ed** -t **ˈBack ˌBay; ˌback ˈdoor;** *stress shift:* ˌback door ˈdeal; **ˌback ˈgarden; ˌback of beˈyond; ˌback ˈseat; ˌback seat ˈdriver; ˈback ˌtalk; ˌback ˈyard** *stress shift:* ˌback yard ˈspecial; **have one's ˌback to the ˈwall; ˌput someone's ˈback up; ˌturn one's ˈback on someone/something**
backache ˈbæk.eɪk **-s** -s
backbeat ˈbæk.biːt
backbench ˌbækˈbentʃ **-es** -ɪz *stress shift:* ˌbackbench ˈspeaker
backbencher ˌbækˈben.tʃə^{r} (US) -tʃɚ **-s** -z *stress shift:* ˌbackbencher ˈvote
backbi|ting ˈbækˌbaɪ|.tɪŋ (US) -t̬ɪŋ **-ter/s** -tə^{r}/z (US) -t̬ɚ/z
backboard ˈbæk.bɔːd (US) -bɔːrd **-s** -z
backbone ˈbæk.bəʊn (US) -boʊn **-s** -z
backbreaker ˈbækˌbreɪ.kə^{r} (US) -kɚ **-s** -z
backbreaking ˈbækˌbreɪ.kɪŋ **-ly** -li
backchat ˈbæk.tʃæt
back|cloth ˈbæk|.klɒθ (US) -klɑːθ **-cloths** -klɒθs, -klɒðz (US) -klɑːθs, -klɑːðz
backcomb ˈbæk.kəʊm, ˌ-ˈ- (US) ˈbæk.koʊm **-s** -z **-ing** -ɪŋ **-ed** -d
back|date ˌbæk|ˈdeɪt (US) ˈbæk|.deɪt **-dates** -ˈdeɪts (US) -deɪts **-dating** -ˈdeɪ.tɪŋ (US) -deɪ.t̬ɪŋ **-dated** -ˈdeɪ.tɪd (US) -deɪ.t̬ɪd *stress shift:* ˌbackdated ˈcheque

backdrop 'bæk.drɒp US -drɑːp **-s** -s
backer 'bæk.əʳ US -ɚ **-s** -z
backfield 'bæk.fiːld
backfill 'bæk.fɪl **-s** -z **-ing** -ɪŋ **-ed** -d
backfir|e ˌbæk'faɪəʳ, '-- US ˌbæk'faɪɚ, '-- **-es** -z **-ing** -ɪŋ **-ed** -d
back-formation 'bæk.fɔːˌmeɪ.ʃᵊn US -fɔːrˌ- **-s** -z
backgammon 'bæk.gæm.ən, ˌ-'--
background 'bæk.graʊnd **-s** -z **'background ˌnoise, ˌbackground 'noise** US **'background ˌnoise**
backhand 'bæk.hænd **-s** -z
backhanded ˌbæk'hænd.ɪd **-ly** -li **-ness** -nəs, -nɪs *stress shift, see compound:* **ˌbackhanded 'compliment**
backhander ˌbæk'hænd.əʳ US -ɚ **-z** -z
backhoe 'bæk.həʊ US -hoʊ **-s** -z
Backhouse 'bæk.haʊs
backing 'bæk.ɪŋ **-s** -z
backlash 'bæk.læʃ
backless 'bæk.ləs, -lɪs
back|light 'bæk|.laɪt **-lights** -laɪts **-lighting** -ˌlaɪ.tɪŋ US -ˌlaɪ.t̬ɪŋ **-lighted** -ˌlaɪ.tɪd US -ˌlaɪ.t̬ɪd **backlit** 'bæk.lɪt
backlist 'bæk.lɪst **-s** -s **-ing** -ɪŋ **-ed** -ɪd
backlog 'bæk.lɒg US -lɑːg, -lɔːg **-s** -z
backpack 'bæk.pæk **-s** -s **-ing** -ɪŋ **-ed** -d **-er/s** -əʳ/z US -ɚ/z
back-pedal ˌbæk'ped.ᵊl, '-ˌ-- US 'bæk.ped- **-s** -z **-(l)ing** -ɪŋ **-(l)ed** -d
backrest 'bæk.rest **-s** -s
backroom ˌbæk'rʊm, -'ruːm, '-- US ˌbæk'ruːm, -'rʊm, '-- **'backroom ˌboy**
backscratcher 'bækˌskrætʃ.əʳ US -ɚ **-s** -z
backsheesh, backshish ˌbæk'ʃiːʃ, '--
backside ˌbæk'saɪd, '-- US '-- **-s** -z
backslap 'bæk.slæp **-s** -s **-ping** -ɪŋ **-ped** -t **-per/s** -əʳ/z US -ɚ/z
backslash 'bæk.slæʃ **-es** -ɪz
backslid|e 'bæk.slaɪd **-es** -z **-ing** -ɪŋ **-er/s** -əʳ/z US -ɚ/z **backslid** 'bæk.slɪd
backspac|e 'bæk.speɪs **-es** -ɪz **-ing** -ɪŋ **-ed** -t
backspin 'bæk.spɪn
backstage ˌbæk'steɪdʒ *stress shift:* ˌbackstage 'pass
backstairs ˌbæk'steəz US ˌbæk'sterz *stress shift:* ˌbackstairs 'gossip
backstay 'bæk.steɪ **-s** -z
backstitch 'bæk.stɪtʃ **-es** -ɪz **-ing** -ɪŋ **-ed** -t
backstop 'bæk.stɒp US -stɑːp **-s** -s **-ping** -ɪŋ **-ped** -t
backstrap 'bæk.stræp **-s** -s
backstreet 'bæk.striːt **-s** -s
backstroke 'bæk.strəʊk US -stroʊk
back-to-back ˌbæk.tə'bæk *stress shift:* ˌback-to-back 'house
backtrack 'bæk.træk **-s** -s **-ing** -ɪŋ **-ed** -t
backup 'bæk.ʌp **-s** -s
backward 'bæk.wəd US -wɚd **-ly** -li **-ness** -nəs, -nɪs **-s** -z **ˌbend over 'backwards**
backwash 'bæk.wɒʃ US -wɑːʃ, -wɔːʃ **-es** -ɪz
backwater 'bækˌwɔː.təʳ US -ˌwɑː.t̬ɚ, -ˌwɔː- **-s** -z
backwoods 'bæk.wʊdz
backwoods|man ˌbæk'wʊdz|.mən, '-ˌ-- **-men** -mən, -men
bacon (B) 'beɪ.kᵊn **ˌbring home the 'bacon**
Baconian beɪ'kəʊ.ni.ən, bə'kəʊ- US -'koʊ- **-s** -z
bacteria bæk'tɪə.ri.ə US bæk'tɪr.i.ə
bacterial bæk'tɪə.ri.əl US bæk'tɪr.i.əl
bacteriological bækˌtɪə.ri.ə'lɒdʒ.ɪ.kᵊl US -ˌtɪr.i.ə'lɑː.dʒɪ-
bacteriolog|y bækˌtɪə.ri'ɒl.ə.dʒ|i US -ˌtɪr.i'ɑː.lə- **-ist/s** -ɪst/s
bacteriophag|e bæk'tɪə.ri.əʊ.feɪdʒ US -'tɪr.i.ə- **-es** -ɪz
bacterium bæk'tɪə.ri.əm US bæk'tɪr.i.əm
Bactri|a 'bæk.tri|.ə **-an/s** -ən/z
Bacup 'beɪ.kəp
bad bæd **ˌbad 'blood; ˌbad 'language; ˌbad 'news; ˌbad 'temper; go from ˌbad to 'worse**
Bad bæd, bɑːd US bɑːd
Badajoz ˌbæd.ə'hɒs *as if Spanish:* ˌbæd.ə'xɒθ US ˌbɑː.dɑː'hoʊz, -ðɑː'hoʊθ
badass 'bæd.æs **-ed** -t
Badcock 'bæd.kɒk US -kɑːk
Baddeley 'bæd.ᵊl.i
baddie 'bæd.i **-s** -z
Baddiel bə'dɪəl, bæd'ɪəl
baddish 'bæd.ɪʃ
badd|y 'bæd|.i **-ies** -iz
bade *(from **bid**)* bæd, beɪd
Badedas® 'bæd.ɪ.dæs; bə'deɪ.dəs
Badel bə'del
Badely 'bæd.ᵊl.i
Baden 'bɑː.dᵊn
Baden-Powell ˌbeɪ.dᵊn'paʊəl, -'pəʊəl, -'pəʊ.ɪl, -'pəʊ.el US -'poʊ.əl, -'paʊəl
Baden-Württemberg ˌbɑː.dᵊn'vɜː.tᵊm.bɜːg US -'vɝː.tᵊm.bɜːrg
Bader 'bɑː.dəʳ, 'beɪ- US -dɚ
badg|e bædʒ **-es** -ɪz **-ing** -ɪŋ **-ed** -d
badg|er (B) 'bædʒ|.əʳ US -ɚ **-ers** -əz US -ɚz **-ering** -ᵊr.ɪŋ **-ered** -əd US -ɚd
badger-baiting 'bædʒ.əˌbeɪ.tɪŋ US -ɚˌbeɪ.t̬ɪŋ
badger-dog 'bædʒ.ə.dɒg US -ɚ.dɑːg, -dɔːg **-s** -z
Bad Godesburg ˌbɑːd'gəʊ.dəz.bɜːg, -'gəʊdz-, -beəg US -'goʊ.dəz.bɝːg
Badham 'bæd.əm
badinage 'bæd.ɪ.nɑːʒ, -nɑːdʒ, ˌ--'-
badlands 'bæd.lændz
badly 'bæd.li
badminton (B) 'bæd.mɪn.tən
bad-mouth 'bæd.maʊθ **-s** -z **-ing** -ɪŋ **-ed** -d
badness 'bæd.nəs, -nɪs
Badoit® 'bæd.wɑː, -'- US bɑː'dwɑː
bad-tempered ˌbæd'tem.pəd US 'bædˌtem.pɚd **-ly** -li **-ness** -nəs, -nɪs *stress shift, British only:* ˌbad-tempered 'person
Baeda 'biː.də
Baedeker 'beɪ.dek.əʳ, 'baɪ-, -dɪ.kəʳ US 'beɪ.də.kɚ, 'baɪ- **-s** -z
Baez 'baɪ.ez, -'-
Baffin 'bæf.ɪn **ˌBaffin 'Bay; ˌBaffin 'Island**
baffl|e 'bæf.l̩ **-es** -z **-ing/ly** -ɪŋ/li, '-lɪŋ **-ed** -d **-er/s** -əʳ/z, '-ləʳ/z US '-l̩.ɚ/z, '-lɚ/z **-ement** -mənt
BAFTA, Bafta 'bæf.tə
bag bæg **-s** -z **-ging** -ɪŋ **-ged** -d **'bag ˌlady; ˌbag of 'bones** **-ger/s** -gəʳ/z US -gɚ/z
bagatelle ˌbæg.ə'tel **-s** -z
Bagdad *in Iraq:* ˌbæg'dæd, '-- US 'bæg.dæd *in Tasmania, Florida:* 'bæg.dæd
Bagehot 'bædʒ.ət, 'bæg-
bagel 'beɪ.gᵊl **-s** -z
bagful 'bæg.fʊl **-s** -z
baggag|e 'bæg.ɪdʒ **-es** -ɪz
Baggie® 'bæg.i **-s** -z
bagg|y 'bæg|.i **-ier** -i.əʳ US -i.ɚ **-iest** -i.ɪst, -i.əst **-ily** -ɪ.li, -ᵊl.i **-iness** -ɪ.nəs, -ɪ.nɪs
Baghdad bæg'dæd, '-- US 'bæg.dæd
Bagheera bæg'ɪə.rə, bə'gɪə- US bə'gɪr.ə
Bagley 'bæg.li
Bagnall 'bæg.nəl, -nɔːl
Bagnell 'bæg.nəl
bagnio 'bæn.jəʊ, 'bɑː.njəʊ US 'bɑː.njoʊ, 'bæn.joʊ **-s** -z
Bagnold 'bæg.nəʊld US -noʊld
Bagot 'bæg.ət
bagpip|e 'bæg.paɪp **-es** -s **-er/s** -əʳ/z US -ɚ/z
bags bægz **-es** -ɪz **-ing** -ɪŋ **-ed** -d
Bagshaw(e) 'bæg.ʃɔː US -ʃɑː, -ʃɔː
Bagshot 'bæg.ʃɒt US -ʃɑːt
bags|y 'bæg.z|i **-ies** -iz **-ing** -ɪŋ **-ied** -id
baguette, baguet bæg'et, bə'get **-s** -s
Bagworthy 'bædʒ.ᵊr.i
bah bɑː US bɑː, bæ
bahadur bə'hɑː.dəʳ US -dɚ **-s** -z
Baha'i bə'haɪ, bɑː-, -'hɑː.i, -'haɪ.i **-s** -z
Baha|ism bə'haɪ|.ɪ.zᵊm, bɑː-, -'hɑː- **-ist/s** -ɪst/s
Bahama bə'hɑː.mə **-s** -z
Bahamian bə'heɪ.mi.ən, -'hɑː- **-s** -z

Bahasa bəˈhɑː.sə
Bahawalpur bɑːˈhɑː.wəl.pʊəʳ, bə- (US) -pʊr
Bahia bəˈhiː.ə
Bahrain, Bahrein bɑːˈreɪn **-i** -i
baht bɑːt **-s** -s
baignoire ˈbeɪn.wɑːʳ (US) benˈwɑːr, beɪn- **-s** -z
Baikal ˈbaɪ.kæl, -kɑːl, -ˈ-
bail beɪl **-s** -z **-ing** -ɪŋ **-ed** -d **-er/s** -əʳ/z (US) -ɚ/z
bailable ˈbeɪ.lə.bl̩
bail-bond ˈbeɪl.bɒnd, -ˈ- (US) ˈbeɪl.bɑːnd **-s** -z
bail-bonds|man ˈbeɪlˌbɒndz|.mən (US) -ˌbɑːndz- **-men** -mən
Baildon ˈbeɪl.dən
bailee ˌbeɪˈliː **-s** -z
bailey (B) ˈbeɪ.li
bailie (B) ˈbeɪ.li **-s** -z
bailiff ˈbeɪ.lɪf **-s** -s
bailiwick ˈbeɪ.lɪ.wɪk **-s** -s
Baille ˈbeɪ.li
Baillie ˈbeɪ.li
Baillieu ˈbeɪ.ljuː (US) ˈbeɪl.juː
Bailly ˈbeɪ.li
bailment ˈbeɪl.mənt **-s** -s
bailout ˈbeɪ.laʊt (US) ˈbeɪl.aʊt **-s** -s
Baily ˈbeɪ.li
Bain beɪn
Bainbridge ˈbeɪn.brɪdʒ, ˈbeɪm- (US) ˈbeɪn-
Baines beɪnz
bain-marie ˌbæn.məˈriː *as if French:* bæ̃m- (US) ˌbæn- **-s** -z
Baird beəd (US) berd
bairn beən (US) bern **-s** -z
Bairstow ˈbeə.stəʊ (US) ˈber.stoʊ
bait beɪt **-s** -s **-ing** -ɪŋ (US) ˈbeɪ.t̬ɪŋ **-ed** -ɪd (US) ˈbeɪ.t̬ɪd
bai|za ˈbaɪ|.zə (US) -zɑː **-zas** -zəz
baiz|e beɪz **-es** -ɪz
Baja California ˌbɑː.hɑː.kæl.ɪˈfɔː.njə (US) -əˈfɔːr-
bak|e beɪk **-es** -s **-ing** -ɪŋ **-ed** -t ˌ**baked Aˈlaska**; ˌ**baked ˈbeans**; ˈ**baking** ˌ**powder**; ˈ**baking** ˌ**soda**
bakehou|se ˈbeɪk.haʊ|s **-ses** -zɪz
Bakelite® ˈbeɪ.kᵊl.aɪt (US) ˈbeɪ.kə.laɪt, ˈbeɪk.laɪt
baker (B) ˈbeɪ.kəʳ (US) -kɚ **-s** -z
Bakerloo ˌbeɪ.kᵊlˈuː (US) -kɚˈluː
Bakersfield ˈbeɪ.kəz.fiːld (US) -kɚz-
baker|y ˈbeɪ.kᵊr|.i **-ies** -iz
Bakewell ˈbeɪk.wel, -wəl
Bakke ˈbɑː.ki
baklava ˈbæk.lə.vɑː, ˈbɑː.klə- *as if Greek:* ˌ--ˈ- **-s** -z
baksheesh ˌbækˈʃiːʃ, ˈ--
Baku bækˈuː (US) bɑːˈkuː
Bakunin bəˈkuː.nɪn, bɑː- (US) bɑːˈkuːn.jɪn, bə-
Bala ˈbæl.ə
balaam (B) ˈbeɪ.læm, -ləm **-s** -z
balaclava (B) ˌbæl.əˈklɑː.və, ˌbɑː.ləˈ- **-s** -z
Balakirev bəˈlæk.ɪ.rev, -ˈlɑː.kɪ- (US) ˌbɑː.lɑːˈkɪr.*jef*
balalaika ˌbæl.əˈlaɪ.kə **-s** -z
balanc|e ˈbæl.ən*t*s **-es** -ɪz **-ing** -ɪŋ **-ed** -t ˈ**balancing** ˌ**act**; ˌ**balance of ˈpayments**; ˈ**balance** ˌ**sheet**
Balanchine ˈbæl.ən.tʃiːn, ˌ--ˈ- (US) ˈbæl.ən*t*.ʃiːn
Balatka bəˈlæt.kə (US) -kɑː, -ˈlɑːt-
Balaton bælˈæt.ən *as if Hungarian:* bɒlˈɒt- (US) ˈbɑː.lɑː.tɑːn
Balboa bælˈbəʊ.ə (US) -ˈboʊ-
Balbriggan bælˈbrɪg.ən
Balbus ˈbæl.bəs
Balchin ˈbɔːl.tʃɪn, ˈbɒl- (US) ˈbɔːl-, ˈbɑːl-
balcon|y ˈbæl.kə.n|i **-ies** -iz
bald bɔːld (US) bɔːld, bɑːld **-er** -əʳ (US) -ɚ **-est** -ɪst, -əst **-ing** -ɪŋ **-ish** -ɪʃ **-ly** -li **-ness** -nəs, -nɪs ˌ**bald ˈeagle**
baldachin, baldaquin ˈbɔːl.də.kɪn (US) ˈbɔːl-, ˈbɑːl- **-s** -z
Balder ˈbɔːl.dəʳ, ˈbɒl- (US) ˈbɔːl.dɚ, ˈbɑːl-
balderdash ˈbɔːl.də.dæʃ, ˈbɒl- (US) ˈbɔːl.dɚ-, ˈbɑːl-
baldfaced ˌbɔːldˈfeɪst (US) ˈbɔːld.feɪst, ˈbɑːld- *stress shift, British only:* ˌbaldfaced ˈliar
bald-headed ˌbɔːldˈhed.ɪd (US) ˌbɔːld-, ˌbɑːld- *stress shift:* ˌbald-headed ˈman
Baldock ˈbɔːl.dɒk (US) ˈbɔːl.dɑːk, ˈbɑːl-
baldric (B) ˈbɔːl.drɪk, ˈbɒl- (US) ˈbɔːl-, ˈbɑːl- **-s** -s
Baldry ˈbɔːl.dri (US) ˈbɔːl-, ˈbɑːl-
Baldwin ˈbɔːld.wɪn (US) ˈbɔːld-, ˈbɑːld-
bald|y ˈbɔːl.d|i (US) ˈbɔːl-, ˈbɑːl- **-ies** -iz
bal|e (B) beɪl **-es** -z **-ing** -ɪŋ **-ed** -d
Bale, Bâle *in Switzerland:* bɑːl
Baleares ˌbæl.iˈɑː.rɪz (US) ˌbɑː.liˈ-, ˌbæl.iˈ-
Balearic ˌbæl.iˈær.ɪk (US) ˌbɑː.liˈ-, ˌbæl.iˈ-, -ˈer-
baleen bəˈliːn, bælˈiːn **-s** -z
baleful ˈbeɪl.fᵊl, -fʊl **-ly** -i **-ness** -nəs, -nɪs
baler ˈbeɪ.ləʳ (US) -lɚ **-s** -z
Balfour ˈbæl.fəʳ, -fɔːʳ (US) -fɚ, -fɔːr
Balguy ˈbɔːl.gi (US) ˈbɔːl-, ˈbɑːl-
Balham ˈbæl.əm
Bali ˈbɑː.li (US) ˈbɑː.li, ˈbæl.i
Balinese ˌbɑː.lɪˈniːz (US) ˌbɑː.ləˈ-, ˌbæl.əˈ-
Baliol ˈbeɪ.li.əl
balk bɔːlk, bɔːk (US) bɔːk, bɑːk **-s** -s **-ing** -ɪŋ **-ed** -t
Balkan ˈbɔːl.kən, bɒl- (US) ˈbɔːl-, ˈbɑːl- **-s** -z
Balkanization, -isa- ˌbɔːl.kə.naɪˈzeɪ.ʃᵊn, ˌbɒl-, -nɪˈ- (US) ˌbɔːl-, ˌbɑːl-
Balkaniz|e, -is|e ˈbɔːl.kə.naɪz, ˈbɒl- (US) ˈbɔːl-, ˈbɑːl- **-es** -ɪz **-ing** -ɪŋ **-ed** -d
Balkhash bælˈkæʃ (US) bɑːlˈkɑːʃ, bæl-, -ˈkæʃ
ball (B) bɔːl (US) bɔːl, bɑːl **-s** -z ˌ**ball and ˈchain**; ˌ**ball ˈbearing**; ˈ**ball** ˌ**boy**; ˈ**ball** ˌ**game**; ˈ**ball** ˌ**girl**; ˈ**ball** ˌ**park**; ˌ**on the ˈball**; ˌ**set the ball ˈrolling**, ˌ**set the ˈball** ˌ**rolling**
ballad ˈbæl.əd **-s** -z
ballade bælˈɑːd, bəˈlɑːd **-s** -z
balladeer ˌbæl.əˈdɪəʳ (US) -ˈdɪr **-s** -z
Ballantine, Ballantyne ˈbæl.ən.taɪn
Ballantrae ˌbæl.ənˈtreɪ
Ballarat ˌbæl.əˈræt, ˈ---
Ballard ˈbæl.əd, -ɑːd (US) -ɚd, -ɑːrd
ballast ˈbæl.əst **-s** -s
Ballater ˈbæl.ə.təʳ (US) -t̬ɚ
ballcarrier ˈbɔːlˌkær.i.əʳ (US) -ˌker.i.ɚ, ˈbɑːl-, -ˌkær- **-s** -z
ballcock ˈbɔːl.kɒk (US) ˈbɔːl.kɑːk, ˈbɑːl- **-s** -s
Balleine bælˈen
ballerina ˌbæl.ᵊrˈiː.nə (US) -əˈriː- **-s** -z
Ballesteros ˌbæl.ɪˈstɪə.rɒs, ˌbaɪ.ɪˈ-, -əˈ-, -ˈsteə- (US) ˌbaɪ.əˈster.oʊs, ˌbæl-
ballet ˈbæl.eɪ (US) bælˈeɪ, ˈ-- **-s** -z ˈ**ballet** ˌ**dancer**
balletic bælˈet.ɪk, bəˈlet- (US) bəˈlet̬.ɪk
balletomane ˈbæl.ɪ.təʊ.meɪn, -et.əʊ- (US) bəˈlet̬.ə- **-s** -z
ballgown ˈbɔːl.gaʊn (US) ˈbɔːl-, ˈbɑːl- **-s** -z
Ballingry bəˈlɪŋ.gri
Balliol ˈbeɪ.li.əl
ballistic bəˈlɪs.tɪk **-s** -s
balloon bəˈluːn **-s** -z **-ing** -ɪŋ **-ed** -d **-ist/s** -ɪst/s **go** ˌ**down/**ˌ**over like a** ˌ**lead baˈlloon**
ball|ot ˈbæl|.ət **-ots** -əts **-oting** -ə.tɪŋ (US) -ə.t̬ɪŋ **-oted** -ə.tɪd (US) -ə.t̬ɪd ˈ**ballot** ˌ**box**; ˈ**ballot** ˌ**paper**; ˈ**ballot** ˌ**rigging**
ballpark ˈbɔːl.pɑːk (US) -pɑːrk, ˈbɑːl- ˌ**ball-park ˈfigure**
ballplayer ˈbɔːlˌpleɪ.əʳ (US) -ɚ, ˈbɑːl- **-s** -z
ball|point ˈbɔːl|.pɔɪnt (US) ˈbɔːl-, ˈbɑːl- **-points** -pɔɪnts **-pointed** -ˌpɔɪn.tɪd (US) -ˌpɔɪn.t̬ɪd ˌ**ball-point ˈpen**
ballroom ˈbɔːl.rʊm, -ruːm (US) ˈbɔːl-, ˈbɑːl- **-s** -z ˌ**ballroom ˈdancing** (US) ˈ**ballroom** ˌ**dancing**
balls-up ˈbɔːlz.ʌp (US) ˈbɔːlz-, ˈbɑːlz-
balls|y ˈbɔːl.z|i (US) ˈbɔːl-, ˈbɑːl- **-ier** -i.əʳ (US) -i.ɚ **-iest** -i.əst, -i.ɪst
bally ˈbæl.i
Ballycastle ˌbæl.ɪˈkɑː.sl̩ (US) -ˈkæs.l̩
Ballyclare ˌbæl.ɪˈkleəʳ (US) -ˈkler
ballyhoo ˌbæl.ɪˈhuː (US) ˈ---

Ballymena ˌbæl.ɪˈmiː.nə
Ballymoney ˌbæl.ɪˈmʌn.i
balm bɑːm **-s** -z
Balmain ˈbæl.mæ̃n, -ˈ- ⓤⓢ ˈbæl.meɪn, -ˈ-
Balm(e) bɑːm
Balmer ˈbɑː.məʳ ⓤⓢ ˈbɑːl.mɚ, ˈbɑː-
Balmoral bælˈmɒr.ᵊl ⓤⓢ -ˈmɔːr-
balm|y ˈbɑː.m|i **-ier** -i.əʳ ⓤⓢ -i.ɚ **-iest** -i.ɪst, -i.əst **-ily** -ɪ.li, -ᵊl.i **-iness** -ɪ.nəs, -ɪ.nɪs
Balniel bælˈniː.ɪl
Balogh ˈbæl.ɒg ⓤⓢ -ɑːg
baloney bəˈləʊ.ni ⓤⓢ -ˈloʊ-
Baloo bəˈluː
balsa ˈbɔːl.sə, ˈbɒl- ⓤⓢ ˈbɔːl-, ˈbɑːl- ˈ**balsa** ˌ**wood**
balsam ˈbɔːl.səm, ˈbɒl- ⓤⓢ ˈbɔːl-, ˈbɑːl- **-s** -z
balsamic bɔːlˈsæm.ɪk, bɒl- ⓤⓢ bɔːl-, bɑːl- **bal**ˌ**samic** ˈ**vinegar**
Balta ˈbæl.tə ⓤⓢ ˈbæl-, ˈbɑːl-
Balthazar ˌbæl.θəˈzɑːʳ, ˈ---; bælˈθæz.əʳ ⓤⓢ ˌbæl.θəˈzɑːr, ˈ---; bælˈθeɪ.zɚ
Note: In Shakespeare, normally /ˌbæl.θəˈzɑːʳ, ˈ--- ⓤⓢ ˌbæl.θəˈzɑːr, ˈ---/.
balti (B) ˈbɔːl.ti, ˈbɒl- ⓤⓢ ˈbɔːl-, ˈbɑːl-, ˈbʌl-
Baltic ˈbɔːl.tɪk, ˈbɒl- ⓤⓢ ˈbɔːl-, ˈbɑːl- ˌ**Baltic** ˈ**Sea**; ˌ**Baltic** ˈ**States**
Baltimore ˈbɔːl.tɪ.mɔːʳ, ˈbɒl- ⓤⓢ ˈbɔːl.tə.mɔːr, ˈbɑːl-, -mɚ **-s** -z
Baluchistan bəˌluː.tʃɪˈstɑːn, bælˌuː-, -kɪˈ-, -ˈstæn ⓤⓢ -tʃəˈstæn, -ˈstɑːn
baluster ˈbæl.ə.stəʳ ⓤⓢ -stɚ **-s** -z **-ed** -d
balustrade ˌbæl.əˈstreɪd ⓤⓢ ˈ--- **-s** -z
Balzac ˈbæl.zæk ⓤⓢ ˈbɔːl-, ˈbɑːl-, ˈbæl-
Bamako ˌbæm.əˈkəʊ ⓤⓢ ˌbæm.əˈkoʊ, ˌbɑː.mə-
Bambi ˈbæm.bi
bambin|o bæmˈbiː.n|əʊ ⓤⓢ bæmˈbiː.n|oʊ, bɑːm- **-os** -əʊz ⓤⓢ -oʊz **-i** -i
bamboo bæmˈbuː **-s** -z
bamboozl|e bæmˈbuː.zl̩ **-es** -z **-ing** -ɪŋ, -ˈbuːz.lɪŋ **-ed** -d
Bamborough ˈbæm.bᵊr.ə ⓤⓢ -oʊ
Bamburgh ˈbæm.bᵊr.ə ⓤⓢ -bɚ.ə, -bɝːg
Bamfield ˈbæm.fiːld
Bamford ˈbæm.fəd ⓤⓢ -fɚd
ban *prohibit:* bæn **-s** -z **-ning** -ɪŋ **-ned** -d
ban *Romanian money:* bæn ⓤⓢ bɑːn **bani** ˈbɑː.ni
banal bəˈnɑːl, bænˈɑːl, -ˈnæl
banalit|y bəˈnæl.ə.t|i, bænˈæl-, -ɪ.t|i ⓤⓢ -ə.t̬|i **-ies** -iz
banana bəˈnɑː.nə ⓤⓢ -ˈnæn.ə **-s** -z **ba**ˌ**nana re**ˈ**public**; **ba**ˈ**nana** ˌ**skin**; **ba**ˌ**nana** ˈ**split**
Banaras bəˈnɑː.rəs ⓤⓢ -ˈnɑːr.əs
Banbridge ˈbæn.brɪdʒ, ˈbæm- ⓤⓢ ˈbæn-
Banbury ˈbæn.bᵊr.i, ˈbæm- ⓤⓢ ˈbæn.ber-, -bɚ-
Banchory ˈbæŋ.kᵊr.i
Bancroft ˈbæŋ.krɒft ⓤⓢ ˈbæn.krɑːft, ˈbæŋ-
band bænd **-s** -z **-ing** -ɪŋ **-ed** -ɪd ˈ**band** ˌ**shell**
Banda ˈbæn.də ⓤⓢ ˈbɑːn-, ˈbæn-
bandag|e ˈbæn.dɪdʒ **-es** -ɪz **-ing** -ɪŋ **-ed** -d
Band-Aid®, band-aid ˈbænd.eɪd **-s** -z
bandan(n)a bænˈdæn.ə **-s** -z
Bandaranaike ˌbæn.dᵊr.əˈnaɪ.ɪ.kə, -ˈnaɪ.kə ⓤⓢ ˌbɑːn-
Bandar Seri Begawan ˌbæn.də.ser.i.bəˈgɑː.wən, -beˈ-, -bɪˈ-, -ˈgaʊ.ən ⓤⓢ ˌbɑːn.dɚ-
B and B ˌbiː.ᵊn*d*ˈbiː, -ᵊmˈ- ⓤⓢ -ᵊn*d*ˈ- **-s** -z
bandbox ˈbæn*d*.bɒks ⓤⓢ -bɑːks **-es** -ɪz
bandeau ˈbæn.dəʊ *as if French:* bæ̃*n*ˈdəʊ ⓤⓢ bænˈdoʊ **bandeaux** ˈbæn.dəʊ, -dəʊz *as if French:* bæ̃*n*ˈdəʊ ⓤⓢ bænˈdoʊ, -doʊz
banderole ˈbæn.dᵊr.əʊl ⓤⓢ -də.roʊl **-s** -z
bandicoot ˈbæn.dɪ.kuːt **-s** -s
bandit ˈbæn.dɪt **-s** -s **-ry** -ri
bandleader ˈbændˌliː.dəʳ ⓤⓢ -dɚ **-s** -z
bandmaster ˈbæn*d*ˌmɑː.stəʳ ⓤⓢ -ˌmæs.tɚ **-s** -z
bandog ˈbæn.dɒg ⓤⓢ -dɑːg, -dɔːg **-s** -z
bandoleer, bandolier ˌbæn.dᵊlˈɪəʳ ⓤⓢ -dəˈlɪr **-s** -z
bandoline ˈbæn.dəʊ.liːn ⓤⓢ -də-, -doʊ-
bands|man ˈbæn*d*z|.mən **-men** -mən, -men
bandstand ˈbæn*d*.stænd **-s** -z
Bandung ˈbæn.dʊŋ, -ˈ- ⓤⓢ ˈbɑːn-, ˈbæn-
bandwagon ˈbæn*d*ˌwæg.ən **-s** -z
bandwidth ˈbæn.dwɪtθ, -dwɪdθ ⓤⓢ ˈbæn*d*.wɪtθ, -wɪdθ, -wɪθ **-s** -s
band|y ˈbæn.d|i **-ier** -i.əʳ ⓤⓢ -i.ɚ **-iest** -i.ɪst, -i.əst **-ies** -iz **-ying** -i.ɪŋ **-ied** -id
bandy-legged ˌbæn.diˈlegd, -ˈleg.ɪd, -ˈleg.əd *stress shift:* ˌbandy-legged ˈchild
bane beɪn **-s** -z
baneful ˈbeɪn.fᵊl, -fʊl **-ly** -i **-ness** -nəs, -nɪs
Banff bænf **-shire** -ʃəʳ, -ˌʃɪəʳ ⓤⓢ -ʃɚ, -ˌʃɪr
Banfield ˈbæn.fiːld
bang bæŋ **-s** -z **-ing** -ɪŋ **-ed** -d **go** ˌ**off with a** ˈ**bang**
Bangalore ˌbæŋ.gəˈlɔːʳ ⓤⓢ ˈbæŋ.gə.lɔːr, ˌ--ˈ-
banger ˈbæŋ.əʳ ⓤⓢ -ɚ **-s** -z
Banger ˈbeɪn.dʒəʳ ⓤⓢ -dʒɚ
Bangkok bæŋˈkɒk ⓤⓢ ˈbæŋ.kɑːk, -ˈ- *stress shift, British only:* ˌBangkok ˈtemple
Bangladesh ˌbæŋ.gləˈdeʃ, -ˈdeɪʃ ⓤⓢ ˌbæŋ.gləˈdeʃ, ˌbɑːŋ-
Bangladeshi ˌbæŋ.gləˈdeʃ.i, -ˈdeɪ.ʃi ⓤⓢ ˌbæŋ.gləˈdeʃ-, ˌbɑːŋ- **-s** -z
bangle ˈbæŋ.gl̩ **-s** -z **-d** -d
bang-on ˌbæŋˈɒn ⓤⓢ ˈbæŋ.ɑːn
Bangor *in Wales:* ˈbæŋ.gəʳ ⓤⓢ -gɚ *in US:* ˈbæŋ.gɔːʳ, -gəʳ ⓤⓢ -gɔːr, -gɚ
Bangui ˌbɑːŋˈgiː ⓤⓢ ˌbɑːŋ-
bang-up ˌbæŋˈʌp ⓤⓢ ˈ--
Banham ˈbæn.əm
bani *(plur. of* **ban***)* ˈbɑː.ni
banian ˈbæn.i.ən, ˈ-jæn **-s** -z
banish ˈbæn.ɪʃ **-es** -ɪz **-ing** -ɪŋ **-ed** -t **-ment/s** -mənt/s
banister (B) ˈbæn.ɪ.stəʳ ⓤⓢ -ə.stɚ **-s** -z
Banja Luka ˌbæn.jəˈluː.kə ⓤⓢ ˌbɑː.njəˈ-
banjo ˈbæn.dʒəʊ, -ˈ- ⓤⓢ ˈbæn.dʒoʊ **-(e)s** -z
Banjul bænˈdʒuːl ⓤⓢ ˈbɑːn.dʒuːl
bank bæŋk **-s** -s **-ing** -ɪŋ **-ed** -t ˈ**bank a**ˌ**ccount**; ˈ**bank** ˌ**card**; ˈ**bank** ˌ**clerk**; ˌ**bank** ˈ**holiday**; ˈ**bank** ˌ**manager**; ˈ**bank** ˌ**rate**; ˈ**bank** ˌ**statement**; ˌ**Bank of** ˈ**England**
bankability ˌbæŋ.kəˈbɪl.ə.ti, -ɪ.ti ⓤⓢ -ə.t̬i
bankable ˈbæŋ.kə.bl̩
banker ˈbæŋ.kəʳ ⓤⓢ -kɚ **-s** -z
Bankes bæŋks
Bankhead ˈbæŋk.hed
banknote ˈbæŋk.nəʊt ⓤⓢ -noʊt **-s** -s
bankroll ˈbæŋk.rəʊl ⓤⓢ -roʊl **-s** -z **-ing** -ɪŋ **-ed** -d
bankrupt ˈbæŋ.krʌpt, -krəpt **-s** -s **-ing** -ɪŋ **-ed** -ɪd
bankruptc|y ˈbæŋ.krəp*t*.s|i, -krʌp*t*- **-ies** -iz
Banks bæŋks
banksia ˈbæŋk.si.ə **-s** -z
Ban-Lon® ˈbæn.lɒn ⓤⓢ -lɑːn
Bann bæn
Bannatyne ˈbæn.ə.taɪn
banner (B) ˈbæn.əʳ ⓤⓢ -ɚ **-s** -z
Bannerman ˈbæn.ə.mən ⓤⓢ ˈ-ɚ-
Banning ˈbæn.ɪŋ
bannister (B) ˈbæn.ɪ.stəʳ ⓤⓢ -ə.stɚ **-s** -z
bannock ˈbæn.ək **-s** -s
Bannockburn ˈbæn.ək.bɜːn ⓤⓢ -bɝːn, -bɚn
Bannon ˈbæn.ən
banns bænz
banque|t ˈbæŋ.kwɪ|t ⓤⓢ -kwə|t, -kwɪ|t **-ts** -ts **-ting** -tɪŋ ⓤⓢ -t̬ɪŋ **-ted** -tɪd ⓤⓢ -t̬ɪd ˈ**banquet** ˌ**room**; ˈ**banqueting** ˌ**hall**
banquette bæŋˈket **-s** -s
Banquo ˈbæŋ.kwəʊ ⓤⓢ -kwoʊ
banshee ˈbæn.ʃiː, -ˈ- **-s** -z
Banstead ˈbæn*t*.stɪd, -sted
bant bænt **-s** -s **-ing** -ɪŋ ⓤⓢ ˈbæn.t̬ɪŋ **-ed** -ɪd ⓤⓢ ˈbæn.t̬ɪd
bantam (B) ˈbæn.təm ⓤⓢ -t̬əm **-s** -z

bantamweight 'bæn.təm.weɪt ⓤⓢ -t̬əm-

bant|er 'bæn.t|əʳ ⓤⓢ -t̬|ɚ **-ers** -əz ⓤⓢ -ɚz **-ering** -ᵊr.ɪŋ **-ered** -əd ⓤⓢ -ɚd

Banting 'bæn.tɪŋ ⓤⓢ -t̬ɪŋ

bantling 'bænt.lɪŋ **-s** -z

Bantry 'bæn.tri

Bantu ˌbæn'tuː, ˌbɑːn-, '-- ⓤⓢ 'bæn.tuː

bantustan (B) ˌbæn.tu'stɑːn, ˌbɑːn-, -'stæn

banyan 'bæn.jæn, -ni.ən, '-jən ⓤⓢ '-jən, '-jæn **-s** -z

Banyard 'bæn.jɑːd ⓤⓢ -jɑːrd

banzai bæn'zaɪ, bɑːn-, '-- ⓤⓢ bɑːn'zaɪ, '--

baobab 'beɪ.əʊ.bæb ⓤⓢ '-oʊ-, 'bɑː- **-s** -z

bap bæp **-s** -s

baptism 'bæp.tɪ.zᵊm **-s** -z ˌ**baptism of** '**fire**

baptismal bæp'tɪz.mᵊl **-ly** -i

baptist (B) 'bæp.tɪst **-s** -s ˌ**John the** '**Baptist**

baptister|y 'bæp.tɪ.stᵊr|.i **-ies** -iz

baptistr|y 'bæp.tɪ.str|i **-ies** -iz

baptiz|e, -is|e bæp'taɪz ⓤⓢ '-- **-es** -ɪz **-ing** -ɪŋ **-ed** -d

bar (B) bɑːʳ ⓤⓢ bɑːr **-s** -z **-ring** -ɪŋ **-red** -d '**bar** ˌ**code**; '**bar** ˌ**graph**; '**bar** ˌ**meal**; '**bar** ˌ**staff**

Barabbas bə'ræb.əs

barb bɑːb ⓤⓢ bɑːrb **-s** -z **-ing** -ɪŋ **-ed** -d

Barbadian bɑː'beɪ.di.ən, -dʒən ⓤⓢ bɑːr- **-s** -z

Barbados bɑː'beɪ.dɒs, -dəs ⓤⓢ bɑːr'beɪ.doʊs

Barbara 'bɑː.bᵊr.ə, '-brə ⓤⓢ 'bɑːr-

barbarian bɑː'beə.ri.ən ⓤⓢ bɑːr'ber.i- **-s** -z

barbaric bɑː'bær.ɪk ⓤⓢ bɑːr'ber-, -'bær- **-ally** -ᵊl.i, -li

barbarism 'bɑː.bᵊr.ɪ.zᵊm ⓤⓢ 'bɑːr- **-s** -z

barbarit|y bɑː'bær.ə.t|i, -ɪ.t|i ⓤⓢ bɑːr'ber.ə.t̬|i, -'bær- **-ies** -iz

barbariz|e, -ise 'bɑː.bᵊr.aɪz ⓤⓢ 'bɑːr- **-es** -ɪz **-ing** -ɪŋ **-ed** -d

Barbarossa ˌbɑː.bᵊr'ɒs.ə ⓤⓢ ˌbɑːr.bə'roʊ.sə, -'rɑː-

barbarous 'bɑː.bᵊr.əs ⓤⓢ 'bɑːr- **-ly** -li **-ness** -nəs, -nɪs

Barbary 'bɑː.bᵊr.i ⓤⓢ 'bɑːr- ˌ**Barbary** '**ape**; ˌ**Barbary** '**Coast**

barbate 'bɑː.beɪt, -bɪt, -bət ⓤⓢ 'bɑːr-

barbated 'bɑː.beɪ.tɪd, -bɪ-, -bə-; bɑː'beɪ- ⓤⓢ bɑːr'beɪ.t̬ɪd

Barbauld 'bɑː.bᵊld ⓤⓢ 'bɑːr-

barbecu|e 'bɑː.bɪ.kjuː, -bə- ⓤⓢ 'bɑːr- **-es** -z **-ing** -ɪŋ **-ed** -d

barbed bɑːbd ⓤⓢ bɑːrbd ˌ**barbed** '**wire**

barbell 'bɑː.bel ⓤⓢ 'bɑːr- **-s** -z

barber (B) 'bɑː.bəʳ ⓤⓢ 'bɑːr.bɚ **-s** -z

barberr|y 'bɑː.bᵊr|.i ⓤⓢ 'bɑːr.ber|.i **-ies** -iz

barbershop 'bɑː.bə.ʃɒp ⓤⓢ 'bɑːr.bɚ.ʃɑːp **-s** -s ˌ**barbershop quar'tet**

barbette bɑː'bet ⓤⓢ bɑːr- **-s** -s

barbican (B) 'bɑː.bɪ.kən ⓤⓢ 'bɑːr.bə- **-s** -z

barbie (B) 'bɑː.bi ⓤⓢ 'bɑːr- '**Barbie** ˌ**doll**®

Barbirolli ˌbɑː.bɪ'rɒl.i, -bə'- ⓤⓢ ˌbɑːr.bə'rɑː.li

barbitone 'bɑː.bɪ.təʊn ⓤⓢ 'bɑːr.bə.toʊn **-s** -z

barbiturate bɑː'bɪtʃ.ᵊr.ət, -'bɪt.jʊ.rət, -jᵊr.ət, -ɪt, -eɪt ⓤⓢ bɑːr'bɪtʃ.ᵊr.ət, -eɪt **-s** -s

barbituric ˌbɑː.bɪ'tʃʊə.rɪk; ˌbɑː'bɪt.jʊ-, -jᵊr.ɪk ⓤⓢ ˌbɑːr.bə'tʃʊr.ɪk, -'tʊr- **barbi**ˌ**turic** '**acid**

Barbour® 'bɑː.bəʳ ⓤⓢ 'bɑːr.bɚ **-s** -z

Barbuda bɑː'bjuː.də ⓤⓢ bɑːr'buː-, -'bjuː-

barbule 'bɑː.bjuːl ⓤⓢ 'bɑːr- **-s** -z

barbwire 'bɑːb.waɪəʳ ⓤⓢ 'bɑːrb.waɪɚ

Barca 'bɑː.kə ⓤⓢ 'bɑːr-

barcarol(l)e ˌbɑː.kə'rəʊl, -'rɒl, '--- ⓤⓢ 'bɑːr.kə.roʊl **-s** -z

Barcelona ˌbɑː.sᵊl'əʊ.nə, -sɪ'ləʊ- ⓤⓢ ˌbɑːr.sə'loʊ-

Barchester 'bɑː.tʃes.təʳ, -tʃɪ.stəʳ ⓤⓢ 'bɑːr.tʃə.stɚ, -tʃes.tɚ

Barclay 'bɑː.kli, -kleɪ ⓤⓢ 'bɑːr- **-'s** -z

Barclaycard® 'bɑː.kli.kɑːd, -kleɪ- ⓤⓢ 'bɑːr.kli.kɑːrd

bar code 'bɑː.kəʊd ⓤⓢ 'bɑːr.koʊd **-s** -z

Barcroft 'bɑː.krɒft ⓤⓢ 'bɑːr.krɑːft

bard (B) bɑːd ⓤⓢ bɑːrd **-s** -z **-ic** -ɪk

Bardell bɑː'del; 'bɑː.dᵊl, -del ⓤⓢ bɑːr'del; 'bɑːr.dᵊl, -del

Note: In Dickens' 'The Pickwick Papers' generally pronounced /bɑː'del ⓤⓢ bɑːr-/.

bardolatry bɑː'dɒl.ə.tri ⓤⓢ bɑːr'dɑː.lə-

Bardolph 'bɑː.dɒlf ⓤⓢ 'bɑːr.dɑːlf

Bardot bɑː'dəʊ ⓤⓢ bɑːr'doʊ

Bardsey 'bɑːd.si ⓤⓢ 'bɑːrd-

Bardsley 'bɑːdz.li ⓤⓢ 'bɑːrdz-

Bardswell 'bɑːdz.wəl, -wel ⓤⓢ 'bɑːrdz-

Bardwell 'bɑːd.wəl, -wel ⓤⓢ 'bɑːrd-

bar|e beəʳ ⓤⓢ ber **-er** -əʳ ⓤⓢ -ɚ **-est** -ɪst, -əst **-es** -z **-ing** -ɪŋ **-ed** -d

bareback 'beə.bæk ⓤⓢ 'ber- **-ed** -t

Barebones 'beə.bəʊnz ⓤⓢ 'ber.boʊnz

barefaced beə'feɪst ⓤⓢ 'ber.feɪst **-ly** -li, -ɪd.li **-ness** -nəs, -nɪs *stress shift, British only:* ˌbarefaced 'liar

barefoot beə'fʊt ⓤⓢ 'ber.fʊt *stress shift, British only:* ˌbarefoot 'child

barefooted ˌbeə'fʊt.ɪd ⓤⓢ 'ber.fʊt̬- *stress shift, British only:* ˌbarefooted 'child

barehanded ˌbeə'hæn.dɪd ⓤⓢ 'berˌhæn- *stress shift, British only:* ˌbarehanded 'warrior

bare-headed ˌbeə'hed.ɪd ⓤⓢ 'berˌhed- *stress shift, British only:* ˌbare-headed 'worshippers

Bareilly bə'reɪ.li

bare-legged ˌbeə'legd, -'leg.ɪd ⓤⓢ 'berˌleg.ɪd, -legd *stress shift, British only:* ˌbare-legged 'child

bare|ly 'beə|.li ⓤⓢ 'ber- **-ness** -nəs, -nɪs

Barenboim 'bær.ən.bɔɪm, 'bɑːr- ⓤⓢ 'ber-, 'bær-

Barents 'bær.ənts ⓤⓢ 'ber-, 'bær-

barf bɑːf ⓤⓢ bɑːrf **-s** -s **-ing** -ɪŋ **-ed** -t

Barfield 'bɑː.fiːld ⓤⓢ 'bɑːr-

bar|fly 'bɑː|.flaɪ ⓤⓢ 'bɑːr- **-flies** -flaɪz

Barfoot 'bɑː.fʊt ⓤⓢ 'bɑːr-

bargain 'bɑː.gɪn, -gən ⓤⓢ 'bɑːr- **-s** -z **-ing** -ɪŋ **-ed** -d **-er/s** -əʳ/z ⓤⓢ -ɚ/z ˌ**bargain** '**basement**; '**bargain** ˌ**hunter**

barg|e bɑːdʒ ⓤⓢ bɑːrdʒ **-es** -ɪz **-ing** -ɪŋ **-ed** -d

bargee bɑː'dʒiː, '-- ⓤⓢ bɑːr'dʒiː **-s** -z

barge|man 'bɑːdʒ|.mən, -mæn ⓤⓢ 'bɑːrdʒ- **-men** -mən, -men

bargepole 'bɑːdʒ.pəʊl ⓤⓢ 'bɑːrdʒ.poʊl **-s** -z

Barger 'bɑː.dʒəʳ ⓤⓢ 'bɑːr.dʒɚ

Bargh bɑːdʒ, bɑːf ⓤⓢ bɑːrdʒ, bɑːrf

Bargoed 'bɑː.gɔɪd ⓤⓢ 'bɑːr-

Bargrave 'bɑː.greɪv ⓤⓢ 'bɑːr-

Barham *surname:* 'bær.əm, 'bɑː.rəm ⓤⓢ 'ber-, 'bær-, 'bɑːr.əm *in Kent:* 'bær.əm ⓤⓢ 'ber-, 'bær-

Bari 'bɑː.ri ⓤⓢ 'bɑːr.i

Baring 'beə.rɪŋ, 'bær.ɪŋ ⓤⓢ 'ber.ɪŋ, 'bær-

Baring-Gould ˌbeə.rɪŋ'guːld ⓤⓢ ˌber.ɪŋ'-

baritone 'bær.ɪ.təʊn ⓤⓢ 'ber.ə.toʊn, 'bær- **-s** -z

barium 'beə.ri.əm ⓤⓢ 'ber.i-, 'bær- ˌ**barium** '**meal**

bark bɑːk ⓤⓢ bɑːrk **-s** -s **-ing** -ɪŋ **-ed** -t **-er/s** -əʳ/z ⓤⓢ -ɚ/z ˌ**bark up the wrong** '**tree**; **their** ˌ**bark is** ˌ**worse than their** '**bite**

barkeep 'bɑː.kiːp ⓤⓢ 'bɑːr- **-s** -s **-er/s** -əʳ/z ⓤⓢ -ɚ/z

Barker 'bɑː.kəʳ ⓤⓢ 'bɑːr.kɚ

Barking 'bɑː.kɪŋ ⓤⓢ 'bɑːr-

Barkston 'bɑːk.stən ⓤⓢ 'bɑːrk-

barley 'bɑː.li ⓤⓢ 'bɑːr- '**barley** ˌ**sugar**; '**barley** ˌ**water**; ˌ**barley** '**wine**

barleycorn (B) 'bɑː.li.kɔːn ⓤⓢ 'bɑːr.li.kɔːrn **-s** -z

Barlow(e) 'bɑː.ləʊ ⓤⓢ 'bɑːr.loʊ

barm bɑːm ⓤⓢ bɑːrm

barmaid 'bɑː.meɪd ⓤⓢ 'bɑːr- **-s** -z

bar|man 'bɑː|.mən, -mæn ⓤⓢ 'bɑːr- **-men** -mən, -men

Barmby 'bɑːm.bi ⓤⓢ 'bɑːrm-

Barmecide 'bɑː.mɪ.saɪd ⓤⓢ 'bɑːr.mə-
bar mi(t)zvah bɑː'mɪts.və ⓤⓢ bɑːr-
Barmouth 'bɑː.məθ ⓤⓢ 'bɑːr-
barm|y 'bɑː.m|i ⓤⓢ 'bɑːr- **-ier** -i.əʳ ⓤⓢ -i.ɚ **-iest** -i.ɪst, -i.əst **-iness** -ɪ.nəs, -ɪ.nɪs
barn bɑːn ⓤⓢ bɑːrn **-s** -z **'barn ˌdance; ˌbarn 'door**
Barnabas 'bɑː.nə.bəs, -bæs ⓤⓢ 'bɑːr-
Barnaby 'bɑː.nə.bi ⓤⓢ 'bɑːr-
barnacle 'bɑː.nə.kl̩ ⓤⓢ 'bɑːr- **-s** -z
Barnard 'bɑː.nəd, -nɑːd ⓤⓢ 'bɑːr.nɚd; bɑːr'nɑːrd
Barnardiston ˌbɑː.nə'dɪs.tən ⓤⓢ ˌbɑːr.nɚ'-
Barnardo bə'nɑː.dəʊ, bɑː- ⓤⓢ bɚ'nɑːr.doʊ
Barnby 'bɑːn.bi, 'bɑːm- ⓤⓢ 'bɑːrn-
Barnes bɑːnz ⓤⓢ bɑːrnz
Barnet(t) 'bɑː.nɪt ⓤⓢ bɑːr'net, '--
barney (B) 'bɑː.ni ⓤⓢ 'bɑːr- **-s** -z
Barnfield 'bɑːn.fiːld ⓤⓢ 'bɑːrn-
Barnham 'bɑː.nəm ⓤⓢ 'bɑːr-
Barnicott 'bɑː.nɪ.kət, -kɒt ⓤⓢ 'bɑːr.nə.kɑːt, -nɪ-, -kət
Barnoldswick bɑː'nəʊldz.wɪk *locally also:* 'bɑː.lɪk ⓤⓢ bɑːr'noʊldz.wɪk
Barnsley 'bɑːnz.li ⓤⓢ 'bɑːrnz-
Barnstaple 'bɑːn.stə.pl̩ *locally also:* -bl̩ ⓤⓢ 'bɑːrn.stə.pl̩
barnstorm 'bɑːn.stɔːm ⓤⓢ 'bɑːrn.stɔːrm **-s** -z **-ing** -ɪŋ **-ed** -d **-er/s** -əʳ/z ⓤⓢ -ɚ/z
Barnum 'bɑː.nəm ⓤⓢ 'bɑːr-
barnyard 'bɑːn.jɑːd ⓤⓢ 'bɑːrn.jɑːrd **-s** -z
Baroda bə'rəʊ.də ⓤⓢ -'roʊ-
barograph 'bær.əʊ.grɑːf, -græf ⓤⓢ 'ber.ə.græf, 'bær- **-s** -s
Barolo bə'rəʊ.ləʊ ⓤⓢ -'roʊ.loʊ
Barolong ˌbɑː.rəʊ'ləʊŋ, ˌbær.əʊ-, -'lɒŋ ⓤⓢ ˌbɑːr.ə'loʊŋ
barometer bə'rɒm.ɪ.təʳ, -ə.təʳ ⓤⓢ -'rɑː.mə.t̬ɚ **-s** -z
barometric ˌbær.əʊ'met.rɪk ⓤⓢ ˌber.ə'-, ˌbær- **-al** -əl **-ally** -əl.i, -li
barometry bə'rɒm.ɪ.tri, '-ə- ⓤⓢ -'rɑː.mə-
baron (B) 'bær.ən ⓤⓢ 'ber-, 'bær- **-s** -z
baronag|e 'bær.ən.ɪdʒ ⓤⓢ 'ber-, 'bær- **-es** -ɪz
baroness (B) 'bær.ən.es, -ɪs, -əs; ⓤⓢ 'ber.ən.əs, 'bær- **-es** -ɪz
baronet 'bær.ən.ət, -ɪt, ˌbær.ən'et ⓤⓢ 'ber.ən.ət, 'bær-, -ɪt **-s** -s
baronetag|e 'bær.ə.nə.tɪdʒ, ˌbær.ə'net.ɪdʒ ⓤⓢ 'ber.ə.nə.t̬ɪdʒ, 'bær- **-es** -ɪz
baronetc|y 'bær.ə.nət.s|i, -net- ⓤⓢ 'ber-, 'bær- **-ies** -iz
baronial bə'rəʊ.ni.əl ⓤⓢ -'roʊ-
baron|y 'bær.ən|.i ⓤⓢ 'ber-, 'bær- **-ies** -iz
baroque bə'rɒk, bær'ɒk ⓤⓢ bə'roʊk, bær'oʊk, -'ɑːk
baroscope 'bær.əʊ.skəʊp ⓤⓢ 'ber.ə.skoʊp, 'bær- **-s** -s
baroscopic ˌbær.əʊ'skɒp.ɪk ⓤⓢ ˌber.ə'skɑː.pɪk, ˌbær-
Barossa bə'rɒs.ə ⓤⓢ -'rɑː.sə **Baˌrossa 'Valley**
barouch|e bə'ruːʃ, bær'uːʃ ⓤⓢ bə'ruːʃ **-es** -ɪz
barperson 'bɑːˌpɜː.sən ⓤⓢ 'bɑːrˌpɝː- **-s** -z
barque bɑːk ⓤⓢ bɑːrk **-s** -s
Barquisimeto ˌbɑː.kɪ.sɪ'meɪ.təʊ ⓤⓢ bɑːrˌkə.sə'meɪ.toʊ
Barr bɑːʳ ⓤⓢ bɑːr
Barra 'bær.ə ⓤⓢ 'ber-, 'bær-
barrack 'bær.ək ⓤⓢ 'ber-, 'bær- **-s** -s **-ing** -ɪŋ **-ed** -t
Barraclough 'bær.ə.klʌf ⓤⓢ 'ber-, 'bær-
barracouta ˌbær.ə'kuː.tə ⓤⓢ ˌber.ə'kuː.t̬ə, ˌbær-, -də **-s** -z
barracuda ˌbær.ə'kjuː.də, -'kuː- ⓤⓢ ˌber.ə'kuː-, ˌbær-
barrag|e 'bær.ɑːdʒ ⓤⓢ bə'rɑːdʒ **-es** -ɪz
barramund|a ˌbær.ə'mʌn.d|ə ⓤⓢ ˌber-, ˌbær- **-as** -əz **-i** -i **-is** -ɪs
Barranquilla ˌbær.əŋ'kiː.ə ⓤⓢ ˌbɑːr.ɑːn'kiː.jɑː, ˌber-, ˌbær-
barratry 'bær.ə.tri ⓤⓢ 'ber-, 'bær-
Barrat(t) 'bær.ət ⓤⓢ 'ber-, 'bær-
barre bɑːʳ ⓤⓢ bɑːr **-s** -z
barrel 'bær.əl ⓤⓢ 'ber-, 'bær- **-s** -z **-(l)ing -(l)ed**
barrel-organ 'bær.əlˌɔː.gən ⓤⓢ 'ber.əlˌɔːr-, 'bær- **-s** -z
barren 'bær.ən ⓤⓢ 'ber-, 'bær- **-est** -ɪst, -əst **-ly** -li **-ness** -nəs, -nɪs
Barrett 'bær.ət, -et, -ɪt ⓤⓢ 'ber-, 'bær-
barrette bə'ret, bɑː- ⓤⓢ bə'ret **-s** -s
Barrhead 'bɑː.hed ⓤⓢ 'bɑːr-
barricad|e ˌbær.ɪ'keɪd, -ə'-, '--- ⓤⓢ 'ber.ə.keɪd, 'bær-, ˌ--'- **-es** -z **-ing** -ɪŋ **-ed** -ɪd
Barrie 'bær.i ⓤⓢ 'ber-, 'bær-
barrier (B) 'bær.i.əʳ ⓤⓢ 'ber.i.ɚ, 'bær- **-s** -z **ˌGreat ˌBarrier 'Reef**
barring 'bɑː.rɪŋ ⓤⓢ 'bɑːr.ɪŋ
Barrington 'bær.ɪŋ.tən ⓤⓢ 'ber-
barrio 'bær.i.əʊ ⓤⓢ 'bɑːr.i.oʊ, 'ber-, 'bær- **-s** -z
barrister 'bær.ɪ.stəʳ ⓤⓢ 'ber.ɪ.stɚ, 'bær- **-s** -z
barrister-at-law ˌbær.ɪ.stəʳ.ət'lɔː ⓤⓢ ˌber.ə.stɚ.ət'lɑː, ˌbær-, -'lɔː **barristers-at-law** ˌbær.ɪ.stəz.ət'lɔː ⓤⓢ ˌber.ə.stɚz.ət'lɑː, ˌbær-, -'lɔː
barristerial ˌbær.ɪ'stɪə.ri.əl ⓤⓢ ˌber.ə'stɪr.i-, ˌbær-
Barron 'bær.ən ⓤⓢ 'ber-, 'bær-
barroom 'bɑː.rʊm, -ruːm ⓤⓢ 'bɑːr.ruːm, -rʊm **-s** -z
barrow (B) 'bær.əʊ ⓤⓢ 'ber.oʊ, 'bær- **-s** -z
Barrow-in-Furness ˌbær.əʊ.ɪn'fɜː.nɪs, -nes, -nəs ⓤⓢ ˌber.oʊ.ɪn'fɝː-, ˌbær-
Barry 'bær.i ⓤⓢ 'ber-, 'bær-
Barrymore 'bær.ɪ.mɔːʳ ⓤⓢ 'ber.ɪ.mɔːr, 'bær-
Barset 'bɑː.sɪt, -set, -sət ⓤⓢ 'bɑːr- **-shire** -ʃəʳ, -ˌʃɪəʳ ⓤⓢ -ʃɚ, -ˌʃɪr
barstool 'bɑː.stuːl ⓤⓢ 'bɑːr- **-s** -z
Barstow 'bɑː.stəʊ ⓤⓢ 'bɑːr.stoʊ
bart (B) bɑːt ⓤⓢ bɑːrt **-s** -s
bartend 'bɑː.tend ⓤⓢ 'bɑːr- **-s** -z **-ing** -ɪŋ **-ed** -ɪd
bartender 'bɑːˌten.dəʳ ⓤⓢ 'bɑːrˌten.dɚ **-s** -z
bart|er (B) 'bɑː.t|əʳ ⓤⓢ 'bɑːr.t̬|ɚ **-ers** -əz ⓤⓢ -ɚz **-ering** -ər.ɪŋ **-ered** -əd ⓤⓢ -ɚd
Barth bɑːθ ⓤⓢ bɑːrθ
Barthelme 'bɑː.təl.meɪ ⓤⓢ 'bɑːr.t̬əl-
Barthes bɑːt ⓤⓢ bɑːrt
Bartholomew bɑː'θɒl.ə.mjuː, bə'- ⓤⓢ bɑːr'θɑː.lə-, bɚ-
Bartle 'bɑː.tl̩ ⓤⓢ 'bɑːr.t̬l̩
Bartleby 'bɑː.tl̩.bi ⓤⓢ 'bɑːr.t̬l̩-
Bartlett 'bɑːt.lət, -lɪt ⓤⓢ 'bɑːrt-
Bartók 'bɑː.tɒk ⓤⓢ 'bɑːr.tɑːk
Bartoli bɑː'təʊ.li ⓤⓢ bar'toʊ.li
Bartolommeo ˌbɑː.tɒl.ə'meɪ.əʊ ⓤⓢ bɑːrˌtɑː.lə'meɪ.oʊ
Bartolozzi ˌbɑː.tə'lɒt.si ⓤⓢ ˌbɑːr.t̬ə'lɑːt-
Barton 'bɑː.tən ⓤⓢ 'bɑːr-
Bartram 'bɑː.trəm ⓤⓢ 'bɑːr-
Bart's bɑːts ⓤⓢ bɑːrts
bartsia 'bɑːt.si.ə ⓤⓢ 'bɑːrt-
Baruch *biblical name:* 'bɑː.rʊk, 'beə-, -rək ⓤⓢ bə'ruːk; 'bɑːr.uːk, 'ber- *modern surname:* bə'ruːk
Barugh bɑːf ⓤⓢ bɑːrf
Barum 'beə.rəm ⓤⓢ 'ber.əm
Barwick *in the UK:* 'bær.ɪk ⓤⓢ 'ber.ɪk, 'bær- *in the US:* 'bɑː.wɪk; 'bær.ɪk ⓤⓢ 'bɑːr.wɪk
Baryshnikov bə'rɪʃ.nɪ.kɒf, bær'ɪʃ-, -kəf ⓤⓢ bə'rɪʃ.nɪ.kɔːf, bɑː'-, -kɑːf
barysphere 'bær.ɪ.sfɪəʳ ⓤⓢ 'ber.ɪ.sfɪr, 'bær- **-s** -z
barytone 'bar.ɪ.təʊn ⓤⓢ 'ber.ə.toʊn, 'bær- **-s** -z
basal 'beɪ.səl
basalt 'bæs.ɔːlt; -əlt; bə'sɔːlt, -'sɒlt ⓤⓢ bə'sɔːlt, -'sɑːlt; 'beɪ.sɔːlt, -sɑːlt
basaltic bə'sɔːl.tɪk, -'sɒl- ⓤⓢ bə'sɔːl.t̬ɪk, -'sɑːl-
Basan 'beɪ.sæn
bascule 'bæs.kjuːl **-s** -z
bas|e beɪs **-es** -ɪz **-er** -əʳ ⓤⓢ -ɚ **-est** -ɪst, -əst **-ely** -li **-eness** -nəs, -nɪs **-ing** -ɪŋ **-ed** -t **ˌbase 'metal; 'base ˌrate**
baseball 'beɪs.bɔːl ⓤⓢ -bɔːl, -bɑːl **'baseball ˌbat; 'baseball ˌcap**

baseboard 'beɪs.bɔːd (US) -bɔːrd **-s** -z

baseborn 'beɪs.bɔːn (US) -bɔːrn

Baseden 'beɪz.dən

Basel 'bɑː.zᵊl

baseless 'beɪs.ləs, -lɪs **-ly** -li **-ness** -nəs, -nɪs

baseline 'beɪs.laɪn **-s** -z

base|man 'beɪs|.mən, -mæn **-men** -mən, -men

basement 'beɪs.mənt **-s** -s

bases *(plur. of* **base***)* 'beɪ.sɪz *(plur. of* **basis***)* 'beɪ.siːz

Basford *in Nottinghamshire:* 'beɪs.fəd (US) -fɚd *in Staffordshire:* 'bæs.fəd (US) -fɚd

bash bæʃ **-es** -ɪz **-ing** -ɪŋ **-ed** -t

Basham 'bæʃ.əm

Bashan 'beɪ.ʃæn

Bashford 'bæʃ.fəd (US) -fɚd

bashful 'bæʃ.fᵊl, -fʊl **-lest** -ɪst, -əst **-ly** -i **-ness** -nəs, -nɪs

basho 'bæʃ.əʊ (US) bɑː'ʃoʊ **-s** (US) -z

basic (B) 'beɪ.sɪk **-s** -s **-ally** -ᵊl.i, -li

BASIC, Basic 'beɪ.sɪk

basicity bə'sɪs.ə.ti, -ɪ.ti (US) -ə.t̬i

Basie 'beɪ.si, -zi

basil (B) 'bæz.ᵊl, -ɪl (US) 'beɪ.zᵊl, -sᵊl; 'bæz.ᵊl

basilar 'bæz.ɪ.ləʳ, 'bæs-, -ᵊl.əʳ (US) -ɪ.lɚ, -ᵊl.ɚ **ˌbasilar 'membrane**

Basildon 'bæz.ᵊl.dən

basilect 'bæz.ɪ.lekt, '-ə- (US) 'bæz.ə-, 'beɪ.sə- **-s** -s **-al** -ᵊl

basilic|a bə'zɪl.ɪ.k|ə, -'sɪl- (US) -'sɪl- **-as** -əz **-an** -ən

basilisk 'bæz.ə.lɪsk, '-ɪ- (US) 'bæs-, 'bæz- **-s** -s

basin 'beɪ.sᵊn **-s** -z

basinet 'bæs.ɪ.net; '-ə-; -nɪt; ˌbæs.ɪ'net **-s** -s

Basinger 'beɪ.sɪŋ.gəʳ, 'bæs.ɪn.dʒəʳ (US) 'beɪ.sɪŋ.gɚ, 'bæs.ɪn.dʒɚ

Basingstoke 'beɪ.zɪŋ.stəʊk (US) -stoʊk

bas|is 'beɪ.s|ɪs **-es** -iːz

bask bɑːsk (US) bæsk **-s** -s **-ing** -ɪŋ **-ed** -t

Basker 'bɑː.skəʳ (US) 'bæs.kɚ

Baskervill(e) 'bæs.kə.vɪl (US) -kɚ-

basket 'bɑː.skɪt (US) 'bæs.kət **-s** -s **-ful/s** -fʊl/z **'basket ˌcase; put all one's ˌeggs in one 'basket**

basketball 'bɑː.skɪt.bɔːl (US) 'bæs.kət.bɔːl, -bɑːl

basketry 'bɑː.skɪ.tri (US) 'bæs.kə-

basketwork 'bɑː.skɪt.wɜːk (US) 'bæs.kət.wɝːk

Baskin-Robbins® ˌbæs.kɪn'rɒb.ɪnz (US) -'rɑː.bɪnz

Basle bɑːl

basmati bə'smɑː.ti, bæs'mɑː-, bəz-, bæz-

bas mi(t)zvah ˌbæs'mɪts.və (US) ˌbɑːs- **-ing** -ɪŋ **-ed** -d

Basnett 'bæz.nɪt, -nət, -net

Basotho bə'suː.tuː, -'səʊ.təʊ (US) -'soʊ.toʊ

basque (B) bæsk, bɑːsk (US) bæsk **-s** -s

Basra(h) 'bæz.rə, 'bʌz-, 'bæs- (US) 'bɑːz.rə, 'bæs-, 'bæz-, 'bɑːs-

bas-relief ˌbɑː.rɪ'liːf, ˌbæs-, ˌbɑːs-, -rə'liːf **-s** -s

bass (B) *fish, fibre, beer:* bæs

bass *in music:* beɪs **-es** -ɪz **ˌbass clari'net; ˌbass 'clef; ˌbass 'drum; ˌbass gui'tar**

Bassanio bə'sɑː.ni.əʊ, bæs'ɑː- (US) -oʊ

Bassenthwaite 'bæs.ᵊn.θweɪt

basset 'bæs.ɪt (US) -ət **-s** -s **'basset ˌhorn; 'basset ˌhound**

Basseterre bæs'teəʳ (US) -'ter

Basset(t) 'bæs.ɪt (US) -ət

Bassey 'bæs.i

bassinet(te) ˌbæs.ɪ'net, -ə'- **-s** -s

Bassingbourne 'bæs.ɪŋ.bɔːn (US) -bɔːrn

bassist 'beɪ.sɪst **-s** -s

bass|o 'bæs|.əʊ (US) -oʊ, 'bɑː.s|oʊ **-os** -z **-i** -iː

bassoon bə'suːn **-s** -z **-ist/s** -ɪst/s

basswood 'bæs.wʊd

bast (B) bæst

Bastable 'bæs.tə.bl̩

bastard 'bɑː.stəd, 'bæs.təd (US) 'bæs.tɚd **-s** -z **-y** -i

bastardiz|e, -is|e 'bɑː.stə.daɪz, 'bæs.tə- (US) 'bæs.tɚ- **-es** -ɪz **-ing** -ɪŋ **-ed** -d

bast|e beɪst **-es** -s **-ing** -ɪŋ **-ed** -ɪd

bastille (B) bæs'tiːl **-s** -z

bastinado ˌbæs.tɪ'nɑː.dəʊ, -'neɪ- (US) -doʊ **-es** -z **-ing** -ɪŋ **-ed** -d

bastion 'bæs.ti.ən (US) '-tʃən, '-ti.ən **-s** -z **-ed** -d

Basuto bə'suː.təʊ, -'zuː- (US) -toʊ **-s** -z

Basutoland bə'suː.təʊ.lænd, -'zuː- (US) -toʊ-

bat bæt **-s** -s **-ting** -ɪŋ (US) 'bæt̬.ɪŋ **-ted** -ɪd (US) 'bæt̬.ɪd

Ba'taan bə'tɑːn (US) -'tæn, -'tɑːn

Batavia bə'teɪ.vi.ə

batboy 'bæt.bɔɪ **-s** -z

batch bætʃ **-es** -ɪz

Batchelar, Batchelor 'bætʃ.ᵊl.əʳ, -ɪ.ləʳ (US) -ᵊl.ɚ

bat|e (B) beɪt **-es** -s **-ing** -ɪŋ (US) 'beɪ.t̬ɪŋ **-ed** -ɪd (US) 'beɪ.t̬ɪd

Bateman 'beɪt.mən **-s** -s

Bates beɪts

Bateson 'beɪt.sᵊn

Batey 'beɪ.ti (US) -t̬i

ba|th (B) *(n.)* bɑː|θ (US) bæ|θ **-ths** -ðz **ˌBath 'bun, 'Bath ˌbun; ˌbath 'chair; 'bath ˌcube; 'bath ˌmat; 'bath ˌsalts; 'Bath ˌstone; ˌBath 'Oliver**

bath *(v.)* bɑːθ (US) bæθ **-s** -s **-ing** -ɪŋ **-ed** -t

bath|e beɪð **-es** -z **-ing** -ɪŋ **-ed** -d **'bathing ˌcostume; 'bathing ˌbeauty; 'bathing ˌsuit**

bather 'beɪ.ðəʳ (US) -ðɚ **-s** -z

bathetic bə'θet.ɪk, bæθ'et- (US) bə'θet̬-

Bathgate 'bɑːθ.geɪt (US) 'bæθ-

bathhou|se 'bɑːθ.haʊ|s (US) 'bæθ- **-ses** -zɪz

bathmat 'bɑːθ.mæt (US) 'bæθ- **-s** -s

Batho 'bæθ.əʊ, 'beɪ.θəʊ (US) 'bæθ.oʊ, 'beɪ.θoʊ

batholite 'bæθ.əʊ.laɪt (US) '-ə- **-s** -s

batholith 'bæθ.əʊ.lɪθ (US) '-ə- **-s** -s

bathors|e 'bæt.hɔːs (US) -hɔːrs **-es** -ɪz

bathos 'beɪ.θɒs (US) -θɑːs

bathrobe 'bɑːθ.rəʊb (US) 'bæθ.roʊb **-s** -z

bathroom 'bɑːθ.rʊm, -ruːm (US) 'bæθ.ruːm, -rʊm **-s** -z

Bathsheba 'bæθ.ʃɪ.bə; bæθ'ʃiː-

bathtub 'bɑːθ.tʌb (US) 'bæθ- **-s** -z

Bathurst 'bæθ.ɜːst, -əst, -hɜːst, 'bɑː.θɜːst, -θəst, 'bɑːθ.hɜːst (US) 'bæθ.ɝːst, -hɝːst

bathyscaphe 'bæθ.ɪ.skæf **-s** -s

bathysphere 'bæθ.ɪ.sfɪəʳ (US) -sfɪr **-s** -z

batik bæt'iːk; 'bæt.ɪk (US) bə'tiːk; 'bæt̬.ɪk

batiste bæt'iːst, bə'tiːst

Batley 'bæt.li

bat|man *military:* 'bæt|.mən **-men** -mən

batman *oriental weight:* 'bæt.mən **-s** -z

Batman® 'bæt.mæn

baton 'bæt.ɒn; -ᵊn (US) bə'tɑːn **-s** -z

Baton Rouge ˌbæt.ᵊn'ruːʒ

bats bæts

bats|man 'bæts|.mən **-men** -mən

battalion bə'tæl.i.ən, '-jən (US) '-jən **-s** -z

Battambang 'bæt.əm.bæŋ (US) 'bæt̬-

battels 'bæt.ᵊlz (US) 'bæt̬-

batten (B) 'bæt.ᵊn **-s** -z **-ing** -ɪŋ **-ed** -d

Battenberg 'bæt.ᵊn.bɜːg, -ᵊm- (US) -ᵊn.bɝːg **'Battenberg ˌcake**

batt|er 'bæt|.əʳ (US) 'bæt̬|.ɚ **-ers** -əz (US) -ɚz **-ering** -ᵊr.ɪŋ **-ered** -əd (US) -ɚd **'battering ˌram**

Battersby 'bæt.əz.bi (US) 'bæt̬.ɚz-

Battersea 'bæt.ə.si (US) 'bæt̬.ɚ-

batter|y 'bæt.ᵊr|.i (US) 'bæt̬- **-ies** -iz **'battery ˌacid**

batting *(n.)* 'bæt.ɪŋ (US) 'bæt̬.ɪŋ **'batting ˌaverage; 'batting ˌorder**

Battishill 'bæt.ɪ.ʃɪl, -ʃᵊl (US) 'bæt̬-

battl|e (B) 'bæt.l̩ (US) 'bæt̬- **-es** -z **-ing** -ɪŋ, 'bæt.lɪŋ **-ed** -d **-er/s** -əʳ/z, '-ləʳ/z (US) '-l̩.ɚ/z, '-lɚ/z **'battle ˌcry; ˌBattle of 'Britain; ˌbattle 'royal; 'battle ˌstations**

battleax|e, battle-ax 'bæt.l̩.æks (US) 'bæt̬- **-es** -ɪz

battledore, battledoor 'bæt.l̩.dɔːʳ (US) 'bæt̬.l̩.dɔːr **-s** -z

battledress 'bæt.l̩.dres

battlefield 'bæt.l̩.fiːld (US) 'bæt̬- **-s** -z

battleground 'bæt.l̩.graʊnd **-s** -z
battlement 'bæt.l̩.mənt ⓤⓢ 'bæt̬- **-s** -s **-ed** -ɪd ⓤⓢ -mən.t̬ɪd
battleship 'bæt.l̩.ʃɪp ⓤⓢ 'bæt̬- **-s** -s
battue bæt'uː, -'juː **-s** -z
batt|y 'bæt.|i ⓤⓢ 'bæt̬- **-ier** -i.əʳ ⓤⓢ -i.ɚ **-iest** -i.ɪst, -i.əst
Battye 'bæt.i ⓤⓢ 'bæt̬-
Batumi bɑː'tuː.mi
batwing 'bæt.wɪŋ ˌ**batwing 'sleeve**
bauble 'bɔː.bl̩ ⓤⓢ 'bɑː-, 'bɔː- **-s** -z
Baucis 'bɔː.sɪs ⓤⓢ 'bɑː-, 'bɔː
Baudelaire 'bəʊ.də.leəʳ, ˌ--'- ⓤⓢ ˌboʊ.də'ler, ˌboʊd'ler
Baudouin 'bəʊ.dwæ̃n ⓤⓢ boʊ'dwɑːn
Bauer baʊəʳ ⓤⓢ baʊɚ
Baugh bɔː ⓤⓢ bɑː, bɔː
Baughan bɔːn ⓤⓢ bɑːn, bɔːn
Bauhaus 'baʊ.haʊs
baulk bɔːk, bɔːlk ⓤⓢ bɑːk, bɔːk **-s** -s **-ing** -ɪŋ **-ed** -t
Baum *US name:* bɔːm ⓤⓢ bɑːm, bɔːm *German name:* baʊm
bauxite 'bɔːk.saɪt ⓤⓢ 'bɑːk-, 'bɔːk-
Bavari|a bə'veə.ri|.ə ⓤⓢ -'ver.i- **-an/s** -ən/z
bawbee bɔː'biː, '-- ⓤⓢ 'bɑː.biː, 'bɔː-, -'- **-s** -z
bawd bɔːd ⓤⓢ bɑːd, bɔːd **-s** -z **-ry** -ri
Bawden 'bɔː.dᵊn ⓤⓢ 'bɑː-, 'bɔː-
bawd|y 'bɔː.d|i ⓤⓢ 'bɑː-, 'bɔː- **-ier** -i.əʳ ⓤⓢ -i.ɚ **-iest** -i.ɪst, -i.əst **-ily** -ɪ.li, -ᵊl.i **-iness** -ɪ.nəs, -ɪ.nɪs '**bawdy ˌhouse**
bawl bɔːl ⓤⓢ bɑːl, bɔːl **-s** -z **-ing** -ɪŋ **-ed** -d **-er/s** -əʳ/z ⓤⓢ -ɚ/z
Bax bæks
Baxandall 'bæk.sᵊn.dɔːl ⓤⓢ -dɔːl, -dɑːl
Baxter 'bæk.stəʳ ⓤⓢ -stɚ
bay **(B)** beɪ **-s** -z **-ing** -ɪŋ **-ed** -d '**bay ˌleaf**; ˌ**Bay of 'Pigs**; '**bay ˌtree**; ˌ**bay 'window**
bayard **(B)** *horse:* beɪəd ⓤⓢ beɪɚd **-s** -z
Bayard *surname:* 'beɪ.ɑːd ⓤⓢ -ɑːrd
Bayard *airship:* 'beɪ.ɑːd, -'-; beɪəd ⓤⓢ beɪɚd; 'beɪ.ɑːrd **-s** -z
bayberr|y 'beɪ.bᵊr|.i ⓤⓢ -ˌber- **-ies** -iz
Bayer® 'beɪ.əʳ ⓤⓢ -ɚ, ber
Bayeux baɪ'jɜː, beɪ- ⓤⓢ 'beɪ.juː, 'baɪ- *stress shift, British only: see compound:* ˌ**Bayeux 'Tapestry**
Bayley 'beɪ.li
Bayliss 'beɪ.lɪs
Bayly 'beɪ.li
Baynes beɪnz
Baynham 'beɪ.nəm
Baynton 'beɪn.tən ⓤⓢ -tᵊn
bayone|t 'beɪ.ə.nə|t, -nɪ|t, -ne|t; ˌbeɪ.ə'ne|t ⓤⓢ ˌbeɪ.ə'ne|t, '---- **-ts** -ts **-t(t)ing** -tɪŋ ⓤⓢ -t̬ɪŋ **-t(t)ed** -tɪd ⓤⓢ -t̬ɪd
Bayonne *in France:* baɪ'ɒn ⓤⓢ beɪ'oʊn, -'ɑːn, -'ɔːn *in New Jersey, U.S.A.:* beɪ'əʊn ⓤⓢ -'oʊn, -'joʊn
bayou 'baɪ.uː, -əʊ ⓤⓢ -*j*uː, -*j*oʊ **-s** -z
Bayreuth baɪ'rɔɪt, '--
bay-rum ˌbeɪ'rʌm
bay-salt ˌbeɪsɔːlt, -sɒlt ⓤⓢ
Bayston Hill ˌbeɪ.stᵊn'hɪl
Bayswater 'beɪzˌwɔː.təʳ ⓤⓢ -ˌwɑː.t̬ɚ, -ˌwɔː-
bazaar bə'zɑːʳ ⓤⓢ -'zɑːr **-s** -z
Bazalgette 'bæz.ᵊl.dʒɪt, -dʒet
bazooka bə'zuː.kə **-s** -z
BBC ˌbiː.biː'siː
BC biː'siː
BCG ˌbiː.siː'dʒiː
bdellium 'del.i.əm, bə'del-
be- bɪ-, bə-
Note: Prefix. Words containing **be-** are always stressed on the second syllable, e.g. **friend** /frend/, **befriend** /bɪ'frend/.
be *strong form:* biː *weak forms:* bi, bɪ **being** 'biː.ɪŋ **been** biːn, bɪn ⓤⓢ bɪn
Note: Weak form word. The strong form /biː/ is used contrastively, e.g. "the **be** all and **end** all" and in sentence-final position, e.g. "What'll it be?". The weak form is /bɪ/ before consonants, e.g. "We'll be going" /ˌwil.bɪ'gəʊ.ɪŋ ⓤⓢ -'goʊ-/; before vowels it is /bi/, e.g. "It'll be opening soon" /ˌɪt.l̩.bi'əʊ.pᵊn.ɪŋˌsuːn ⓤⓢ -'oʊ-/. See note at **been** for further weak form information.
Bea biː
beach **(B)** biːtʃ ⓤⓢ **-es** -ɪz **-ing** -ɪŋ **-ed** -t '**beach ˌball**; '**beach ˌbum**
beachchair 'biːtʃ.tʃeəʳ ⓤⓢ -tʃer **-s** -z
beachcomber **(B)** 'biːtʃˌkəʊ.məʳ ⓤⓢ -ˌkoʊ.mɚ **-s** -z
beachfront 'biːtʃ.frʌnt **-s** -s
beachhead 'biːtʃ.hed **-s** -z
beach-la-mar, Beach-la-Mar ˌbiːtʃ.lə'mɑːʳ ⓤⓢ -'mɑːr
beachwear 'biːtʃ.weəʳ ⓤⓢ -wer
beachy **(B)** 'biː.tʃi ˌ**Beachy 'Head**
beacon 'biː.kᵊn **-s** -z
Beaconsfield *place in Buckinghamshire:* 'bek.ᵊnz.fiːld *title of Benjamin Disraeli:* 'biː.kᵊnz.fiːld
bead biːd **-s** -z **-ing/s** -ɪŋ/z **-ed** -ɪd **-er/s** -əʳ/z ⓤⓢ -ɚ/z
beadle **(B)** 'biː.dl̩ **-s** -z
Beadon 'biː.dᵊn
beadwork 'biːd.wɜːk ⓤⓢ -wɝːk
bead|y 'biː.d|i **-ier** -i.əʳ ⓤⓢ -i.ɚ **-iest** -i.ɪst, -i.əst **-iness** -ɪ.nɪs, -ɪ.nəs
beagle 'biː.gl̩ **-s** -z
beak biːk **-s** -s **-ed** -t
beaker 'biː.kəʳ ⓤⓢ -kɚ **-s** -z
Beal(e) biːl
beam biːm **-s** -z **-ing** -ɪŋ **-ed** -d '**beam ˌengine**
beam-ends ˌbiːm'endz, '--
Beaminster 'bem.ɪn*t*.stəʳ *locally also:* 'bem.ɪ.stəʳ ⓤⓢ -stɚ
Note: /'biː.mɪn*t*-/ is sometimes heard from people unfamiliar with the place.
Beamish 'biː.mɪʃ
beam|y 'biː.m|i **-ily** -ɪ.li, -ᵊl.i **-iness** -ɪ.nɪs, -ɪ.nəs
bean biːn **-s** -z ˌ**full of 'beans**; ˌ**spill the 'beans**
beanbag 'biːn.bæg, 'biːm- ⓤⓢ 'biːn- **-s** -z
beanfeast 'biːn.fiːst **-s** -s **-er/s** -əʳ/z ⓤⓢ -ɚ/z
beanie 'biː.ni **-s** -z
beano **(B)** 'biː.nəʊ ⓤⓢ -noʊ **-s** -z
beanpole 'biːn.pəʊl, 'biːm- ⓤⓢ 'biːn.poʊl **-s** -z
beanshoot 'biːn.ʃuːt **-s** -s
beansprout 'biːn.spraʊt **-s** -s
beanstalk 'biːn.stɔːk ⓤⓢ -stɔːk, -stɑːk **-s** -s
bear beəʳ ⓤⓢ ber **-s** -z **-ing/s** -ɪŋ/z **bore** bɔːʳ ⓤⓢ bɔːr **borne** bɔːn ⓤⓢ bɔːrn '**bear ˌgarden**
bearab|le 'beə.rə.b|l̩ ⓤⓢ 'ber.ə- **-ly** -li **-leness** -l̩.nəs, -l̩.nɪs
bear-baiting 'beəˌbeɪ.tɪŋ ⓤⓢ 'berˌbeɪ.t̬ɪŋ
beard **(B)** bɪəd ⓤⓢ bɪrd **-s** -z **-ing** -ɪŋ **-ed** -ɪd
Bearder 'bɪə.dəʳ ⓤⓢ 'bɪr.dɚ
beardless 'bɪəd.ləs, -lɪs ⓤⓢ 'bɪrd-
Beardsley 'bɪədz.li ⓤⓢ 'bɪrdz-
Beare bɪəʳ ⓤⓢ bɪr
bearer 'beə.rəʳ ⓤⓢ 'ber.ɚ **-s** -z
bearhug 'beə.hʌg ⓤⓢ 'ber- **-s** -z
bearing *(n.)* 'beə.rɪŋ ⓤⓢ 'ber.ɪŋ **-s** -z
bearing rein 'beə.rɪŋ.reɪn ⓤⓢ 'ber.ɪŋ- **-s** -z
bearish 'beə.rɪʃ ⓤⓢ 'ber.ɪʃ **-ly** -li **-ness** -nəs, -nɪs
béarnaise **(B)** ˌbeɪə'neɪz, -'nez ⓤⓢ ˌber'neɪz, ˌbeɪ.ɑːr'-, ˌbeɪɚ'-
Bearsden beəz'den ⓤⓢ berz-
bearskin 'beə.skɪn ⓤⓢ 'ber- **-s** -z
Bearsted 'bɜː.sted, 'beə.sted ⓤⓢ 'bɝː-, 'ber-
Beasant 'beɪ.zᵊnt
Beasley 'biːz.li
beast biːst **-s** -s ˌ**beast of 'burden**
beastie 'biː.sti **-s** -z
beastings 'biː.stɪŋz
beastl|y 'biːs*t*.l|i **-ier** -i.əʳ ⓤⓢ -i.ɚ **-iest** -i.ɪst, -i.əst **-iness** -ɪ.nəs, -ɪ.nɪs
beat biːt **-s** -s **-ing/s** -ɪŋ/z ⓤⓢ 'biː.t̬ɪŋ/z **-en** -ᵊn ⓤⓢ 'biː.t̬ᵊn **-er/s** -əʳ/z ⓤⓢ 'biː.t̬ɚ/z ˌ**beat about the 'bush**; '**Beat Geneˌration**
beatific ˌbiː.ə'tɪf.ɪk **-al** -ᵊl **-ally** -ᵊl.i, -li
beatification biˌæt.ɪ.fɪ'keɪ.ʃᵊn, ˌ-ə- ⓤⓢ -ˌæt̬.ə- **-s** -z

beatif|y bi'æt.ɪ.f|aɪ, '-ə- (US) -'æt̬.ə- **-ies** -aɪz **-ying** -aɪ.ɪŋ **-ied** -aɪd
beatitude (B) bi'æt.ɪ.tjuːd, '-ə-, -tʃuːd (US) -'æt̬.ə.tuːd, -tjuːd **-s** -z
Beatles 'biː.tl̩z (US) -t̬l̩z
beatnik 'biːt.nɪk **-s** -s
Beaton 'biː.tən (US) -t̬ən
Beatrice 'bɪə.trɪs (US) 'biː.ə-
Beatrix 'bɪə.trɪks (US) 'biː.ə-
Beattie 'biː.ti (US) -t̬i, 'beɪ-
Beattock 'biː.tək (US) -t̬ək
Beatty 'biː.ti (US) 'beɪ.t̬i, 'biː-
beat-up ˌbiːt'ʌp
beau (B) bəʊ (US) boʊ **-s** -z ˌ**Beau** '**Brummell**
Beauchamp 'biː.tʃəm
Beauclerc(k) 'bəʊ.kleəʳ (US) 'boʊ.kler, -klɜːk
Beaufort *in South Carolina:* 'bjuː.fət, -fɔːt (US) 'bjuː.fɚt *other senses:* 'bəʊ.fət, -fɔːt (US) 'boʊ.fɚt
beau(x) geste(s) ˌbəʊ'ʒest (US) ˌboʊ-
Beauharnais ˌbəʊ.ɑː'neɪ (US) ˌboʊ.ɑːr'-
Beaujolais 'bəʊ.ʒəl.eɪ, -ʒɒl.eɪ (US) ˌboʊ.ʒə'leɪ
Beaujolais nouveau ˌbəʊ.ʒə.leɪ.nuː'vəʊ, -ʒɒl.eɪ- (US) ˌboʊ.ʒə.leɪ.nuː'voʊ
Beaulieu *in Hampshire:* 'bjuː.li *US family name:* 'bəʊ.juː (US) 'boʊ-, 'boʊl- *in France:* bəʊ'ljɜː (US) boʊ-
Beaumarchais 'bəʊ.mɑː.ʃeɪ, ˌ--'- (US) ˌboʊ.mɑːr'ʃeɪ
Beaumaris bəʊ'mær.ɪs, bjuː- (US) boʊ'mer-, -'mær-
beau(x) monde(s) bəʊ'mɒnd (US) ˌboʊ'mɑːnd
Beaumont 'bəʊ.mənt, -mɒnt (US) 'boʊ-, -mɑːnt
Beaune bəʊn (US) boʊn
Beauregard 'bəʊ.rɪ.gɑːd (US) 'boʊ.rə.gɑːrd
beaut bjuːt **-s** -s
beauteous 'bjuː.ti.əs (US) -t̬i- **-ly** -li **-ness** -nəs, -nɪs
beautician bjuː'tɪʃ.ən **-s** -z
beautification ˌbjuː.tɪ.fɪ'keɪ.ʃən, -tə- (US) -t̬ə-
beautiful 'bjuː.tɪ.fəl, -tə-, -fʊl (US) -t̬ə- **-ly** -i
beautif|y 'bjuː.tɪ.f|aɪ, -tə- (US) -t̬ə- **-ies** -aɪz **-ying** -aɪ.ɪŋ **-ied** -aɪd **-ier/s** -aɪ.əʳ/z (US) -aɪ.ɚ/z
beaut|y 'bjuː.t|i (US) -t̬|i **-ies** -iz '**beauty** ˌ**contest**; '**beauty** ˌ**mark**; '**beauty** ˌ**parlo(u)r**; '**beauty** ˌ**sleep**; '**beauty** ˌ**spot**
Beauvoir 'bəʊv.wɑː (US) boʊv'wɑːr
beaux-arts bəʊ'zɑːʳ (US) boʊ'zɑːr
Beaux' Stratagem ˌbəʊz'stræt.ə.dʒəm (US) ˌboʊz'stræt̬-
Beavan, Beaven 'bev.ən
beaver (B) 'biː.vəʳ (US) -vɚ **-s** -z
Beaverbrook 'biː.və.brʊk (US) -vɚ-
beaver|y 'biː.vər|.i **-ies** -iz
Beavis 'biː.vɪs
Beazley 'biːz.li
Bebb beb
Bebington 'beb.ɪŋ.tən
bebop 'biː.bɒp (US) -bɑːp **-per/s** -əʳ/z (US) -ɚ/z
becalm bɪ'kɑːm, bə- **-s** -z **-ing** -ɪŋ **-ed** -d
became *(from* **become***)* bɪ'keɪm, bə-
because bɪ'kɒz, bə-, -'kəz *colloquially also:* kɒz, kəz (US) bɪ'kɑːz, bə-, -'kʌz, -'kəz, kəz
Note: The form /bɪ'kəz/ or /bə-/ is unusual in having a stressed schwa vowel. This is found only in a few phrases, most commonly in "because of the/a ..." The pronunciation /kəz/ (also /kɒz/ in British English) is often spelt **'cos**.
Beccles 'bek.l̩z
bechamel, béchamel ˌbeɪ.ʃə'mel, ˌbeʃ.ə'- *stress shift:* ˌbechamel 'sauce
Becher 'biː.tʃəʳ (US) -tʃɚ
Bechstein 'bek.staɪn **-s** -z
Bechuana ˌbetʃ.u'ɑː.nə **-s** -z **-land** -lænd
beck (B) bek **-s** -s ˌ**beck and** '**call**
Becke bek
Beckenbauer 'bek.ən.baʊəʳ (US) -baʊɚ
Beckenham 'bek.ən.əm
Becker 'bek.əʳ (US) -ɚ
Becket(t) 'bek.ɪt
Beckford 'bek.fəd (US) -fɚd
Beckham 'bek.əm
Beckinsale 'bek.ɪn.seɪl
Beckles 'bek.l̩z
Beckley 'bek.li
beckon 'bek.ən **-s** -z **-ing** -ɪŋ **-ed** -d
Beckton 'bek.tən
Beckwith 'bek.wɪθ
Becky 'bek.i
becloud bɪ'klaʊd, bə- **-s** -z **-ing** -ɪŋ **-ed** -ɪd
becom|e bɪ'kʌm, bə- **-es** -z **-ing** -ɪŋ **became** bɪ'keɪm, bə-
becoming bɪ'kʌm.ɪŋ, bə'- **-ly** -li **-ness** -nəs, -nɪs
Becontree 'bek.ən.triː
becquerel (B) ˌbek.ə'rel; 'bek.ə.rel, -rəl **-s** -z
bed bed **-s** -z **-ding** -ɪŋ **-ded** -ɪd '**bed** ˌ**rest**; ˌ**bed and** '**breakfast**; ˌ**get out of** ˌ**bed on the** ˌ**wrong** '**side**
BEd biː'ed
bedad bɪ'dæd, bə-
Bedale 'biː.dəl, -deɪl
Bedales 'biː.deɪlz
bedaub bɪ'dɔːb, bə- (US) -'dɑːb, -'dɔːb **-s** -z **-ing** -ɪŋ **-ed** -d
bedazzl|e bɪ'dæz.l̩, bə- **-es** -z **-ing** -ɪŋ **-ed** -d
bedbug 'bed.bʌg **-s** -z
bedchamber 'bedˌtʃeɪm.bəʳ (US) -bɚ **-s** -z
bedclothes 'bed.kləʊðz, -kləʊz (US) -kloʊðz, -kloʊz
Beddau 'beð.aɪ
bedder 'bed.əʳ (US) -ɚ **-s** -z
Beddgelert beð'gel.ət, bed-, beɪð-, -ɜːt (US) -ɚt
bedding *(n.)* 'bed.ɪŋ
Beddoes 'bed.əʊz (US) -oʊz
beddy-bye 'bed.i.baɪ **-s** -z
Bede biːd
bedeck bɪ'dek, bə- **-s** -s **-ing** -ɪŋ **-ed** -t
Bedel 'biː.dəl; bɪ'del, bə-
bedel(l) bed'el, bɪ'del, bə- **-s** -z
Bedevere 'bed.ɪ.vɪəʳ, '-ə- (US) -ə.vɪr
bedevil bɪ'dev.əl, bə- **-s** -z **-(l)ing** -ɪŋ **-(l)ed** -d
bedevilment bɪ'dev.əl.mənt, bə-
bedew bɪ'djuː, bə- (US) -'duː, -'djuː **-s** -z **-ing** -ɪŋ **-ed** -d
bedfellow 'bedˌfel.əʊ (US) -oʊ **-s** -z
Bedford 'bed.fəd (US) -fɚd **-shire** -ʃəʳ, -ˌʃɪəʳ (US) -ʃɚ, -ˌʃɪr
bedim bɪ'dɪm, bə- **-s** -z **-ming** -ɪŋ **-med** -d
Bedivere 'bed.ɪ.vɪəʳ, '-ə- (US) -ə.vɪr
bedizen bɪ'daɪ.zən, bə-, -'dɪz.ən **-s** -z **-ing** -ɪŋ **-ed** -d
bedjacket 'bedˌdʒæk.ɪt **-s** -s
bedlam (B) 'bed.ləm
Bedlamite 'bed.lə.maɪt **-s** -s
bedlinen 'bedˌlɪn.ɪn, -ən (US) -ən
bedmaker 'bedˌmeɪ.kəʳ (US) -kɚ **-s** -z
Bedouin 'bed.u.ɪn **-s** -z
bedpan 'bed.pæn **-s** -z
bedpost 'bed.pəʊst (US) -poʊst **-s** -s
bedraggl|e bɪ'dræg.l̩, bə- **-es** -z **-ing** -ɪŋ **-ed** -d
bedridden 'bedˌrɪd.ən
bedrock 'bed.rɒk (US) -rɑːk **-s** -s
bedroll 'bed.rəʊl (US) -roʊl **-s** -z
bedroom 'bed.rʊm, -ruːm (US) -ruːm, -rʊm **-s** -z
Beds. *(abbrev. for* **Bedfordshire***)* bedz; 'bed.fəd.ʃəʳ, -ˌʃɪəʳ (US) bedz; 'bed.fɚd.ʃɚ, -ˌʃɪr
bedside 'bed.saɪd ˌ**bedside** '**manner**; ˌ**bedside** '**table**
bedsit 'bed.sɪt **-s** -s
bedsitter bed'sɪt.əʳ, '-ˌ-- (US) bed'sɪt.ɚ, '-ˌ-- **-s** -z
bedsore 'bed.sɔːʳ (US) -sɔːr **-s** -z
bedspread 'bed.spred **-s** -z
bedstead 'bed.sted **-s** -z
bedstraw 'bed.strɔː (US) -strɑː, -strɔː **-s** -z
bedtime 'bed.taɪm
Bedwas 'bed.wæs

Bedwell ˈbed.wel, -wəl
Bedworth ˈbed.wəθ (US) -wɚθ
bee (B) biː **-s** -z ˈ**bee ˌsting; have a ˈbee in one's ˌbonnet; the ˌbee's ˈknees**
Beeb biːb
Beeby ˈbiː.bi
beech (B) biːtʃ **-es** -ɪz **-en** -ᵊn
Beecham ˈbiː.tʃəm ˌ**Beecham's ˈPowders®**
Beecher ˈbiː.tʃəʳ (US) -tʃɚ
Beeching ˈbiː.tʃɪŋ
beechnut ˈbiːtʃ.nʌt **-s** -s
beechwood ˈbiːtʃ.wʊd
bee eater ˈbiːˌiː.təʳ (US) -t̬ɚ **-s** -z
beef *(n)* biːf **-s** -s **beeves** biːvz
beef *(v)* biːf **-s** -s **-ing** -ɪŋ **-ed** -t
beefalo ˈbiː.fᵊl.əʊ (US) -fə.loʊ **-(e)s** -z
beefburger ˈbiːfˌbɜː.gəʳ (US) -ˌbɝː.gɚ **-s** -z
beefcake ˈbiːf.keɪk **-s** -s
beefeater (B) ˈbiːfˌiː.təʳ (US) -t̬ɚ **-s** -z
beefsteak ˈbiːf.steɪk, -ˈ- **-s** -s
beef|y ˈbiː.f|i **-ier** -i.əʳ (US) -i.ɚ **-iest** -i.ɪst, -i.əst **-ily** -ɪ.li, -ᵊl.i **-iness** -ɪ.nəs, -ɪ.nɪs
beehive ˈbiː.haɪv **-s** -z
bee-keep|ing ˈbiːˌkiː.p|ɪŋ **-er/s** -əʳ/z (US) -ɚ/z
beeline ˈbiː.laɪn **-s** -z
Beelzebub biːˈel.zɪ.bʌb, -zə-
been *(from* **be***)* biːn, bɪn (US) bɪn
Note: Weak form word, British English. The pronunciation /bɪn/ may be used optionally as a weak form corresponding to /biːn/, e.g. "Jane's been invited" /ˈdʒeɪnz.bɪn.ɪnˌvaɪ.tɪd (US) -t̬ɪd/. In American English, /biːn/ does not usually occur.
beep biːp **-s** -s **-ing** -ɪŋ **-ed** -t
beeper ˈbiː.pəʳ (US) -pɚ **-s** -z
beer (B) bɪəʳ (US) bɪr **-s** -z ˈ**beer ˌgarden; ˈbeer ˌmat**
Beerbohm ˈbɪə.bəʊm (US) ˈbɪr.boʊm
Beersheba bɪəˈʃiː.bə, ˈbɪə.ʃɪ- (US) bɪrˈʃiː-, ber-
beer|y ˈbɪə.r|i (US) ˈbɪr|.i **-ier** -i.əʳ (US) -i.ɚ **-iest** -i.ɪst, -i.əst **-ily** -ɪ.li, -ᵊl.i **-iness** -ɪ.nəs, -ɪ.nɪs
Beesl(e)y ˈbiːz.li
beestings ˈbiː.stɪŋz
Beeston ˈbiː.stᵊn
beeswax ˈbiːz.wæks
beeswing ˈbiːz.wɪŋ
beet biːt **-s** -s
Beetham ˈbiː.θəm
Beethoven *composer:* ˈbeɪt.həʊ.vᵊn, ˈbeɪ.təʊ- (US) ˈbeɪ.toʊ- *London street:* ˈbiːt.həʊ.vᵊn, ˈbiː.təʊ- (US) ˈbiː.toʊ-
beetl|e ˈbiː.tl̩ (US) -t̬l̩ **-es** -z **-ing** -ɪŋ, ˈbiːt.lɪŋ **-ed** -d
Beeton ˈbiː.tᵊn
beetroot ˈbiːt.ruːt **-s** -s
beeves *(plur. of* **beef***)* biːvz
befall bɪˈfɔːl, bə- (US) -ˈfɔːl, -ˈfɑːl **-s** -z **-ing** -ɪŋ **-en** -ən
befell *(from* **befall***)* bɪˈfel, bə-
befit bɪˈfɪt, bə- **-s** -s **-ting/ly** -ɪŋ/li (US) -ˈfɪt̬.ɪŋ/li **-ted** -ɪd (US) -ˈfɪt̬.ɪd
before bɪˈfɔːʳ, bə- (US) -ˈfɔːr
beforehand bɪˈfɔː.hænd, bə- (US) -ˈfɔːr-
before-mentioned bɪˈfɔːˌmen.*t*ʃᵊnd, -ˌ-ˈ-- (US) bəˈfɔːrˌmen-
beforetime bɪˈfɔː.taɪm, bə- (US) -ˈfɔːr-
befoul bɪˈfaʊl, bə- **-s** -z **-ing** -ɪŋ **-ed** -d
befriend bɪˈfrend, bə- **-s** -z **-ing** -ɪŋ **-ed** -ɪd
befuddl|e bɪˈfʌd.l̩, bə- **-es** -z **-ing** -ɪŋ, -ˈfʌd.lɪŋ **-ed** -d
befuddlement bɪˈfʌd.l̩.mᵊnt, bə-
beg beg **-s** -z **-ging** -ɪŋ **-ged** -d
begad bɪˈgæd, bə-
began *(from* **begin***)* bɪˈgæn, bə-
begat *(from* **beget***)* bɪˈgæt, bə-
beget bɪˈget, bə- **-s** -s **-ting** -ɪŋ (US) -ˈget̬.ɪŋ **begat** bɪˈgæt, bə- **begot** bɪˈgɒt, bə- (US) -ˈgɑːt **begotten** bɪˈgɒt.ᵊn, bə- (US) -ˈgɑː.tᵊn
Begg beg
beggar ˈbeg.əʳ (US) -ɚ **-s** -z **-ing** -ɪŋ **-ed** -d
beggarl|y ˈbeg.ᵊl|.i (US) -ɚ.l|i **-iness** -ɪ.nəs, -ɪ.nɪs
beggar-my-neighbour ˌbeg.ə.mɪˈneɪ.bəʳ, -maɪˈ- (US) -ɚ.maɪˈneɪ.bɚ
beggarweed ˈbeg.ə.wiːd (US) ˈ-ɚ- **-s** -z
beggary ˈbeg.ᵊr.i
Beggs begz
begin bɪˈgɪn, bə- **-s** -z **-ning/s** -ɪŋ/z
Begin ˈbeɪ.gɪn
beginner bɪˈgɪn.əʳ, bə- (US) -ɚ **-s** -z
Begley ˈbeg.li
begone bɪˈgɒn, bə- (US) -ˈgɑːn
begonia bɪˈgəʊ.ni.ə, bə- (US) -ˈgoʊ.njə **-s** -z
begorra bɪˈgɒr.ə, bə- (US) -ˈgɔːr.ə
begot *(from* **beget***)* bɪˈgɒt, bə- (US) -ˈgɑːt **-ten** -ᵊn (US) -ˈgɑː.t̬ᵊn
begrim|e bɪˈgraɪm, bə- **-es** -z **-ing** -ɪŋ **-ed** -d
begrudg|e bɪˈgrʌdʒ, bə- **-es** -ɪz **-ing** -ɪŋ **-ed** -d
beguil|e bɪˈgaɪl, bə- **-es** -z **-ing/ly** -ɪŋ/li **-ed** -d
beguine bɪˈgiːn
begum (B) ˈbeɪ.gəm **-s** -z
begun *(from* **begin***)* bɪˈgʌn, bə-
behalf bɪˈhɑːf, bə- (US) -ˈhæf
Behan ˈbiː.ən
behav|e bɪˈheɪv, bə- **-es** -z **-ing** -ɪŋ **-ed** -d
behavio(u)r bɪˈheɪ.vjəʳ, bə- (US) -vjɚ **-s** -z
behavio(u)ral bɪˈheɪ.vjər.əl- (US) -vjɚ.əl
behavio(u)r|ism bɪˈheɪ.vjᵊr|.ɪ.zᵊm, bə- **-ist/s** -ɪst/s
behead bɪˈhed, bə- **-s** -z **-ing** -ɪŋ **-ed** -ɪd
beheld *(from* **behold***)* bɪˈheld, bə-
behemoth (B) bɪˈhiː.mɒθ, bə-, -məθ (US) -mɑːθ, -məθ; ˈbiː.ə.məθ **-s** -s
behest bɪˈhest, bə- **-s** -s
behind bɪˈhaɪnd, bə-
behindhand bɪˈhaɪnd.hænd, bə-
behind-the-scenes bɪˌhaɪn*d*.ðəˈsiːnz (US) bə- *stress shift:* ˌbehind-the-scenes ˈtour
Behn ben
behold bɪˈhəʊld, bə- (US) -ˈhoʊld **-s** -z **-ing** -ɪŋ **beheld** bɪˈheld, bə- **beholder/s** bɪˈhəʊl.dəʳ/z, bə- (US) -ˈhoʊl.dɚ/z
beholden bɪˈhəʊl.dᵊn, bə- (US) -ˈhoʊl-
behoof bɪˈhuːf, bə-
behoov|e bɪˈhuːv, bə- **-es** -z **-ing** -ɪŋ **-ed** -d
behov|e bɪˈhəʊv, bə- (US) -ˈhoʊv **-es** -z **-ing** -ɪŋ **-ed** -d
Behrens ˈbeə.rənz (US) ˈber.ənz
Behrman ˈbeə.mən (US) ˈber-
Beiderbecke ˈbaɪ.də.bek (US) -dɚ-
beige beɪʒ
Beighton ˈbeɪ.tᵊn, ˈbaɪ-
beignet ˈbeɪ.njeɪ, -ˈ- (US) ˌbeɪˈnjeɪ **-s** -z
Beijing beɪˈ*d*ʒɪŋ
being ˈbiː.ɪŋ **-s** -z
Beira ˈbaɪ.rə (US) ˈbeɪ-
Beirut beɪˈruːt
Beit baɪt
Beith *surname:* biːθ *place in Scotland:* biːð
Bejam® ˈbiː.dʒæm
bejan ˈbiː.dʒᵊn **-s** -z
bejesus, bejezus bɪˈdʒiː.zəz, bə-, -zəs
bejewel bɪˈdʒuː.əl **-s** -z **-(l)ing** -ɪŋ **-(l)ed** -d
bel bel **-s** -z
belabo(u)r bɪˈleɪ.bəʳ, bə- (US) -bɚ **-s** -z **-ing** -ɪŋ **-ed** -d
Belarius bɪˈleə.ri.əs, bə-, -ˈlɑː- (US) -ˈler.i-
Belarus ˌbel.əˈruːs, ˌbjel- **-rusian** -ruːs.jən, -rus.i.ən, -ru.ʃən
Belasco bɪˈlæs.kəʊ, bə- (US) -koʊ
belated bɪˈleɪ.tɪd, bə- (US) -t̬ɪd **-ly** -li **-ness** -nəs, -nɪs
belay bɪˈleɪ, bə- **-s** -z **-ing** -ɪŋ **-ed** -d
bel canto ˌbelˈkæn.təʊ (US) -toʊ
belch (B) beltʃ **-es** -ɪz **-ing** -ɪŋ **-ed** -t **-er/s** -əʳ/z (US) -ɚ/z
Belcher ˈbel.*t*ʃəʳ (US) -*t*ʃɚ
beldam(e) ˈbel.dəm **-s** -z
beleagu|er bɪˈliː.g|əʳ, bə- (US) -g|ɚ **-ers** -əz (US) -ɚz **-ering** -ᵊr.ɪŋ **-ered** -əd (US) -ɚd **-erer/s** -əʳ/z (US) -ɚ/z
Belém bəˈlem, belˈem
belemnite ˈbel.əm.naɪt **-s** -s

Belfast bel'fɑːst, '-- ⓤⓢ 'bel.fæst, ,-'-
belfr|y 'bel.fr|i **-ies** -iz
Belgian 'bel.dʒən **-s** -z
Belgic 'bel.dʒɪk
Belgium 'bel.dʒəm
Belgrade bel'greɪd ⓤⓢ '-- *stress shift, British only:* ,Belgrade 'streets
Belgrano bel'grɑː.nəʊ ⓤⓢ -noʊ
Belgrave bel'greɪv ⓤⓢ '-- *stress shift, British only:* ,Belgrave 'Square
Belgravia bel'greɪ.vi.ə
Belial 'biː.li.əl
bel|ie bɪ'l|aɪ, bə- **-ies** -aɪz **-ying** -aɪ.ɪŋ **-ied** -aɪd
belief bɪ'liːf, bə- **-s** -s
believab|le bɪ'liː.və.b|l̩, bə- **-ly** -li
believ|e bɪ'liːv, bə- **-es** -z **-ing/ly** -ɪŋ/li **-ed** -d
believer bɪ'liː.vəʳ, bə- ⓤⓢ -vɚ **-s** -z
belike bɪ'laɪk, bə-
Belinda bə'lɪn.də, bɪ-
Belisha bə'liː.ʃə, bɪ- **Be,lisha 'beacon**
belittl|e bɪ'lɪt.l̩, bə- ⓤⓢ -'lɪt̬- **-es** -z **-ing** -ɪŋ, -'lɪt.lɪŋ **-ed** -d
Belize bə'liːz, bel'iːz
bell (B) bel **-s** -z **-ing** -ɪŋ **-ed** -d **'bell ,jar; 'bell ,pepper; 'bell ,tent; 'bell ,tower**
Bella 'bel.ə
belladonna ,bel.ə'dɒn.ə ⓤⓢ -'dɑː.nə
Bellamy 'bel.ə.mi
Bellatrix 'bel.ə.trɪks, bə'leɪ- ⓤⓢ 'bel.ə-
bell-bottom 'bel,bɒt.əm ⓤⓢ -,bɑː.t̬əm **-s** -z **-ed** -d
bellboy 'bel.bɔɪ **-s** -z
belle (B) bel **-s** -z **,Southern 'belle; ,belle of the 'ball**
belle époque ,bel.eɪ'pɒk ⓤⓢ -'pɑːk
Belle Isle ,bel'aɪl
Bellerophon bə'ler.ə.fən, bɪ- ⓤⓢ -fən, -fɑːn
belles lettres ,bel'let.rə
Bellevue bel'vjuː, '-- ⓤⓢ 'bel.vjuː
Bellew 'bel.juː
bellhop 'bel.hɒp ⓤⓢ -hɑːp **-s** -s
bellicose 'bel.ɪ.kəʊs, '-ə-, -kəʊz ⓤⓢ -koʊs **-ly** -li
bellicosity ,bel.ɪ'kɒs.ə.ti, -ɪ.ti ⓤⓢ -ə'kɑː.sə.t̬i
belligeren|ce bə'lɪdʒ.ᵊr.ənt|s, bɪ'- **-cy** -si
belligerent bə'lɪdʒ.ᵊr.ənt, bɪ- **-s** -s **-ly** -li
Bellingham *in Northumberland:* 'bel.ɪn.dʒəm *surname:* 'bel.ɪn.dʒəm, -ɪŋ.əm, -hæm *in London:* 'bel.ɪŋ.əm *in the US:* 'bel.ɪŋ.hæm
Bellini bel'iː.ni, bə'liː-
bell|man 'bel|.mən, -mæn **-men** -mən, -men
Belloc 'bel.ɒk ⓤⓢ -ɑːk
Bellot 'bel.əʊ ⓤⓢ bel'oʊ
bellow (B) 'bel.əʊ ⓤⓢ -oʊ **-s** -z **-ing** -ɪŋ **-ed** -d
bellringer 'bel,rɪŋ.əʳ ⓤⓢ -ɚ **-s** -z
Bellshill belz'hɪl
bellwether 'bel,weð.əʳ ⓤⓢ -ɚ **-s** -z
bell|y 'bel|.i **-ies** -iz **-ying** -i.ɪŋ **-ied** -id **'belly ,button; 'belly ,dance; 'belly ,flop; 'belly ,laugh**
bellyach|e 'bel.i.eɪk **-es** -s **-ing** -ɪŋ **-ed** -t
bellyful 'bel.ɪ.fʊl **-s** -z
belly-up ,bel.i'ʌp
Belmont 'bel.mɒnt, -mənt ⓤⓢ -mɑːnt
Belmopan ,bel.məʊ'pæn ⓤⓢ -moʊ'-
Belo Horizonte ,beɪ.ləʊ.hɒr.ɪ'zɒn.ti ⓤⓢ -loʊ.hɔːr.ə'zɑːn-, ,bel.oʊ-
belong bɪ'lɒŋ, bə- ⓤⓢ -'lɑːŋ, -'lɔːŋ **-s** -z **-ing** -ɪŋ **-ed** -d
Belorussi|a ,bel.əʊ'rʌʃ.ə, ,bjel-, -'ruː.si- ⓤⓢ -oʊ'-, -ə'- **-an/s** -ən/z
beloved *used predicatively:* bɪ'lʌvd, bə- *used attributively or as a noun:* bɪ'lʌv.ɪd, bə-, -'lʌvd
below bɪ'ləʊ, bə- ⓤⓢ -'loʊ
Bel Paese ,bel.pɑː'eɪ.zeɪ, -zi ⓤⓢ -zi
Belper 'bel.pəʳ ⓤⓢ -pɚ
Belsen 'bel.sᵊn
Belsham 'bel.ʃəm
Belshaw 'bel.ʃɔː ⓤⓢ -ʃɑː, -ʃɔː
Belshazzar bel'ʃæz.əʳ ⓤⓢ -ɚ
Belsize 'bel.saɪz
Belstead 'bel.stɪd, -sted
belt (B) belt **-s** -s **-ing/s** -ɪŋ/z ⓤⓢ 'bel.t̬ɪŋ **-ed** -ɪd ⓤⓢ 'bel.t̬ɪd **be,low the 'belt**
Beltingham 'bel.tɪn.dʒəm
Belton 'bel.tən
beltway 'belt.weɪ **-s** -z
Beluchistan bə'luː.tʃɪ.stɑːn, bɪ-, -stæn, bə,luː.tʃɪ'stɑːn, bə-, -kɪ'-, -'stæn
beluga bə'luː.gə, bɪ'-, bel'uː- **-s** -z
belvedere (B) 'bel.və.dɪəʳ, -vɪ-, ,--'- ⓤⓢ 'bel.və.dɪr, ,--'- **-s** -z
Belvoir 'biː.vəʳ ⓤⓢ -vɚ
bema 'biː.mə **-s** -z **-ta** -tə ⓤⓢ -t̬ə
Bembridge 'bem.brɪdʒ
bemoan bɪ'məʊn, bə- ⓤⓢ -'moʊn **-s** -z **-ing** -ɪŋ **-ed** -d
bemus|e bɪ'mjuːz, bə- **-es** -ɪz **-ing** -ɪŋ **-ed** -d **-ement** -mənt
Ben ben
Benares bɪ'nɑː.rɪz, bə-, ben'ɑː- ⓤⓢ bə'nɑːr.iːz
Benbecula ben'bek.jʊ.lə, bem-, -jə- ⓤⓢ ben-
Benbow 'ben.bəʊ, 'bem- ⓤⓢ 'ben.boʊ
bench bentʃ **-es** -ɪz
bencher 'ben.tʃəʳ ⓤⓢ -tʃɚ **-s** -z
Benchley 'bentʃ.li
benchmark 'bentʃ.mɑːk ⓤⓢ -mɑːrk **-s** -s **-ing** -ɪŋ
bend bend **-s** -z **-ing** -ɪŋ **-ed** -ɪd **bent** bent **bendable** 'ben.də.bl̩ **,round the 'bend**
Bendall 'ben.dᵊl, -dɔːl ⓤⓢ -dᵊl, -dɔːl, -dɑːl
bender (B) 'ben.dəʳ ⓤⓢ -dɚ **-s** -z
Bendix® 'ben.dɪks
bend|y 'ben.d|i **-ier** -i.əʳ ⓤⓢ -i.ɚ **-iest** -i.ɪst, -i.əst **-iness** -ɪ.nəs, -ɪ.nɪs
beneath bɪ'niːθ, bə-
Benedicite ,ben.ɪ'daɪ.sɪ.ti, -'diː.tʃɪ-, -tʃə-, -teɪ ⓤⓢ -ə'dɪs.ə.t̬i, ,beɪ.neɪ'diː.tʃiː.teɪ **-s** -z
Benedick 'ben.ɪ.dɪk, '-ə- **-s** -s
Benedict 'ben.ɪ.dɪkt, '-ə-
benedictine *liqueur:* ,ben.ɪ'dɪk.tiːn, -ə'- **-s** -z
Benedictine *monk:* ,ben.ɪ'dɪk.tɪn, -ə'-, -taɪn ⓤⓢ -tɪn, -tiːn **-s** -z
Note: Members of the Order pronounce /-tɪn/.
benediction ,ben.ɪ'dɪk.ʃᵊn, -ə'- **-s** -z
Benedictus ,ben.ɪ'dɪk.təs, -ə'-, -tʊs **-es** -ɪz
benefaction ,ben.ɪ'fæk.ʃᵊn, -ə'- ⓤⓢ ,ben.ə'fæk-, 'ben.ə.fæk- **-s** -z
benefactive 'ben.ɪ.fæk.tɪv, -ə-, ,ben.ɪ'fæk-, -ə'- ⓤⓢ 'ben.ə.fæk-, ,ben.ə'fæk-
benefactor 'ben.ɪ.fæk.təʳ, '-ə- ⓤⓢ -tɚ **-s** -z
benefactress 'ben.ɪ.fæk.trəs, '-ə-, -trɪs, ,ben.ɪ'fæk-, -ə'- ⓤⓢ 'ben.ə.fæk- **-es** -ɪz
benefic bɪ'nef.ɪk
benefic|e 'ben.ɪ.fɪs, '-ə- **-es** -ɪz **-ed** -t
beneficen|ce bɪ'nef.ɪ.sᵊn|ts, bə- **-t/ly** -t/li
beneficial ,ben.ɪ'fɪʃ.ᵊl, -ə'- **-ly** -li **-ness** -nəs, -nɪs
beneficiar|y ,ben.ɪ'fɪʃ.ᵊr|.i, -ə'- **-ies** -iz
bene|fit 'ben.ɪ|.fɪt, '-ə- **-fits** -fɪts **-fit(t)ing** -fɪ.tɪŋ ⓤⓢ -fɪ.t̬ɪŋ **-fit(t)ed** -fɪ.tɪd ⓤⓢ -fɪ.t̬ɪd
Benelux 'ben.ɪ.lʌks
Benenden 'ben.ən.dən
Bene't 'ben.ɪt
Benet 'ben.ɪt
Benét *US surname:* ben'eɪ ⓤⓢ bə'neɪ, ben'eɪ
Benetton® 'ben.ɪ.tᵊn, '-ə-, -tɒn ⓤⓢ -ə.t̬ən, -tɑːn
benevolence bɪ'nev.ᵊl.ənts, bə-
benevolent bɪ'nev.ᵊl.ənt, bɪ- **-ly** -li
Benfleet 'ben.fliːt
BEng ,biː'endʒ
Bengal ,beŋ'gɔːl, ,ben- ⓤⓢ -'gɔːl; 'beŋ.gᵊl, 'ben- *stress shift, British only:* ,Bengal 'tiger
Bengalese ,beŋ.gᵊl'iːz, ,ben-, -gɔː'- ⓤⓢ -gə'liːz, -'liːs
Bengali beŋ'gɔː.li, ben- **-s** -z
Bengasi beŋ'gɑː.zi, ben-
Benge bendʒ
Benghazi beŋ'gɑː.zi, ben-

Ben-Gurion ben'gʊə.ri.ən, beŋ-, -'gʊr.i- ⓤⓢ -'gʊr.i-, ˌben.gʊr'jɑːn
Benham 'ben.əm
Ben-Hur ben'hɜːʳ ⓤⓢ -'hɝː
Benidorm 'ben.ɪ.dɔːm, '-ə- ⓤⓢ -dɔːrm
benighted bɪ'naɪ.tɪd, bə- ⓤⓢ -t̬ɪd
benign bɪ'naɪn, bə- **-est** -ɪst, -əst **-ly** -li
benignancy bɪ'nɪg.nən*t*.si, bə-
benignant bɪ'nɪg.nənt, bə- **-ly** -li
Benigni bə'niː.ni
benignity bɪ'nɪg.nə.ti, bə-, -nɪ- ⓤⓢ -nə.t̬i
Benin ben'iːn, bɪ'niːn, bə-
Bening 'ben.ɪŋ
benison 'ben.ɪ.sᵊn, '-ə-, -zᵊn **-s** -z
Benis(s)on 'ben.ɪ.sᵊn, '-ə-
Benito ben'iː.təʊ, bə'niː- ⓤⓢ bə'niː.t̬oʊ
Benjamin 'ben.dʒə.mɪn, -ən
Benjamite 'ben.dʒə.maɪt **-s** -s
Benn ben
Bennet(t) 'ben.ɪt
Bennette ben'et, bə'net
Ben Nevis ˌben'nev.ɪs
Bennington 'ben.ɪŋ.tən
Benny 'ben.i
Bensham 'ben*t*.ʃəm
Bensley 'benz.li
Benson 'ben*t*.sᵊn
Benstead 'ben*t*.stɪd, -sted
bent (B) *(from* **bend***)* bent **-s** -s
Bentham 'ben.təm, 'ben*t*.θəm ⓤⓢ 'ben*t*.θəm **-ism** -ɪ.zᵊm **-ite/s** -aɪt/s
benthic 'ben*t*.θɪk
Bentinck 'ben.tɪŋk
Bentine ben'tiːn, '--
Bentley 'bent.li **-s** -z
Benton 'ben.tən
bentwood 'bent.wʊd
benumb bɪ'nʌm, bə- **-s** -z **-ing** -ɪŋ **-ed** -d
Benvolio ben'vəʊ.li.əʊ ⓤⓢ -'voʊ.li.oʊ
Benz benz, bents
Benzedrine® 'ben.zɪ.driːn, -zə-, -drɪn
benzene, benzine 'ben.ziːn, -'-
benzoate 'ben.zəʊ.eɪt ⓤⓢ -zoʊ-
benzoic ben'zəʊ.ɪk ⓤⓢ -'zoʊ-
benzoin 'ben.zəʊ.ɪn, -'-- ⓤⓢ 'ben.zoʊ-, ben'zoʊ-
benzol 'ben.zɒl ⓤⓢ -zɑːl
benzoline 'ben.z*əʊ*.liːn ⓤⓢ -zə-
benzyl 'ben.zɪl ⓤⓢ -ziː.əl, -zᵊl
Beowulf 'beɪ.*əʊ*.wʊlf, 'biː- ⓤⓢ 'beɪə.wʊlf
beque|ath bɪ'kwiː|ð, bə-, -'kwiː|θ **-ths** -ðz, -θs **-thing** -ðɪŋ **-thed** -ðd, -θt
bequest bɪ'kwest, bə- **-s** -s
be|rate bɪ|'reɪt, bə-, bɪ- **-rates** -'reɪts **-rating** -'reɪ.tɪŋ ⓤⓢ -'reɪ.t̬ɪŋ **-rated** -'reɪ.tɪd ⓤⓢ -'reɪ.t̬ɪd
Berber 'bɜː.bəʳ ⓤⓢ 'bɝː.bɚ **-s** -z
berceuse beə'sɜːz ⓤⓢ ber'sʊz, -'sɜːz
Bere bɪəʳ ⓤⓢ bɪr
Berea bə'riː.ə, bɪ- ⓤⓢ bə-
bereav|e bɪ'riːv, bə- ⓤⓢ bɪ- **-es** -z **-ing** -ɪŋ **-ed** -d
bereavement bɪ'riːv.mənt, bə- **-s** -s
bereft bɪ'reft, bə-
Berengaria ˌber.ᵊŋ'geə.ri.ə, -ɪŋ'-, -eŋ'- ⓤⓢ -'ger.i-
Berenice *in ancient Egypt, etc.:* ˌber.ɪ'naɪ.si, -ki, -'niː.tʃeɪ *opera by Handel:* ˌber.ɪ'niː.tʃi *modern name:* ˌber.ə'niːs, -ɪ'-
Berenson 'ber.ᵊn*t*.sən
Beresford 'ber.ɪs.fəd, -ɪz- ⓤⓢ -fɚd
beret 'ber.eɪ, -i ⓤⓢ bə'reɪ **-s** -z
berg (B) bɜːg, beəg ⓤⓢ bɝːg **-s** -z
bergamot 'bɜː.gə.mɒt, -mət ⓤⓢ 'bɝː.gə.mɑːt **-s** -s
Bergen 'bɜː.gən, 'beə- ⓤⓢ 'bɝː-
Berger *English surname:* 'bɜː.dʒəʳ ⓤⓢ 'bɝː.dʒɚ *US surname:* 'bɜː.gəʳ ⓤⓢ 'bɝː.gɚ
Bergerac 'bɜː.ʒə.ræk ⓤⓢ ˌbɝː.ʒə'ræk, -'rɑːk
Bergkamp 'bɜːg.kæmp ⓤⓢ 'bɝːg-, -kɑːmp
Bergman 'bɜːg.mən ⓤⓢ 'bɝːg-
Bergson 'bɜːg.sən ⓤⓢ 'berg-, 'bɝːg-
Bergsonian bɜːg'səʊ.ni.ən ⓤⓢ berg'soʊ-, bɝːg-
beribboned bɪ'rɪb.ᵊnd, bə-
beriberi ˌber.ɪ'ber.i
Bering 'beə.rɪŋ, 'ber- ⓤⓢ 'ber.ɪŋ **ˌBering 'Strait**
Berio 'ber.i.əʊ ⓤⓢ -oʊ
Berisford 'ber.ɪs.fəd ⓤⓢ -fɚd
berk bɜːk ⓤⓢ bɝːk **-s** -z
Berkeleian bɑːk'liː.ən ⓤⓢ 'bɝː.kli.ən
Berkeley *in England:* 'bɑː.kli ⓤⓢ 'bɑːr-, 'bɝː- *in US:* 'bɜː.kli ⓤⓢ 'bɝː-
berkelium bɜː'kiː.li.əm ⓤⓢ 'bɝː.kli.əm, bɝː'kliː.əm
Berkhamsted, Berkhampstead 'bɜː.kəm*p*.stɪd, -sted ⓤⓢ 'bɝː-

Note: The usual British pronunciation is /'bɜː-/, but the form /'bɑː-/ is used by some residents.

Berkley 'bɜː.kli ⓤⓢ 'bɝː-
Berkoff 'bɜː.kɒf ⓤⓢ 'bɝː.kɑːf
Berks. *(abbrev. for* **Berkshire***)* bɑːks, 'bɑːk.ʃəʳ, -ˌʃɪəʳ ⓤⓢ bɝːks; 'bɝːk.ʃɚ, -ˌʃɪr
Berkshire 'bɑːk.ʃəʳ, -ˌʃɪəʳ ⓤⓢ 'bɝːk.ʃɚ, -ˌʃɪr
Berlin *in Germany:* bɜː'lɪn ⓤⓢ bɝː- *stress shift, British only, see compound:* **ˌBerlin 'Wall**
Berlin *surname:* 'bɜː.lɪn, -'- ⓤⓢ 'bɝː-, -'- *town in US:* 'bɜː.lɪn ⓤⓢ 'bɝː-
Berliner bɜː'lɪn.əʳ ⓤⓢ bɚ'lɪn.ɚ **-s** -z
Berlioz 'beə.li.əʊz, 'bɜː- ⓤⓢ 'ber.li.oʊz
Berlitz bɜː'lɪts, '-- ⓤⓢ 'bɝː.lɪts, ˌ-'-
Berlusconi ˌbɜː.lʊ'skəʊ.ni, ˌbeə- ⓤⓢ ˌbɝː.lʊ'skoʊ-, ˌber-
Bermondsey 'bɜː.mən*d*.zi ⓤⓢ 'bɝː-
Bermuda bə'mjuː.də ⓤⓢ bɚ- **-s** -z **Berˌmuda 'shorts; Berˌmuda 'triangle**
Bern bɜːn, beən ⓤⓢ bɝːn
Bernadette ˌbɜː.nə'det ⓤⓢ ˌbɝː-
Bernard *first name:* 'bɜː.nəd ⓤⓢ 'bɝː.nɚd *surname:* bɜː'nɑːd, bə'-; 'bɜː.nəd ⓤⓢ bɚ'nɑːrd; 'bɝː.nɚd
Berne bɜːn, beən ⓤⓢ bɝːn
Berners 'bɜː.nəz ⓤⓢ 'bɝː.nɚz
Bernese bɜː'niːz ⓤⓢ bɝː-, -'niːs *stress shift:* ˌBernese 'Oberland
Bernhardt 'bɜːn.hɑːt ⓤⓢ 'bɝːn.hɑːrt
Bernice *biblical name:* bɜː'naɪ.si ⓤⓢ bɚ- *modern name:* 'bɜː.nɪs, bɜː'niːs ⓤⓢ 'bɝː-; bɚ'niːs
Bernini bɜː'niː.ni, bə- ⓤⓢ bɚ-, ber-
Bernoulli bɜː'nuː.ji, bə'-, -li ⓤⓢ bɚ'nuː.li
Bernstein 'bɜːn.staɪn, -stiːn ⓤⓢ 'bɝːn-
Berol® 'biː.rɒl, -rəʊl ⓤⓢ -rɑːl, -roʊl
Berowne bə'rəʊn ⓤⓢ -'roʊn
Berra 'ber.ə
Berridge 'ber.ɪdʒ
berr|y (B) 'ber|.i **-ies** -iz
Berryman 'ber.ɪ.mæn, -mən
berserk bə'zɜːk, -'sɜːk ⓤⓢ bɚ'sɝːk, -'zɝːk **-s** -s
Bert bɜːt ⓤⓢ bɝːt
Bertelsmann® 'bɜː.tᵊlz.mæn, -mən ⓤⓢ 'bɝː.t̬ᵊlz-
berth *(n.)* bɜːθ ⓤⓢ bɝːθ **-s** -s, bɜːðz ⓤⓢ bɝːðz
berth *(v.)* bɜːθ ⓤⓢ bɝːθ **-s** -s **-ing** -ɪŋ **-ed** -t
Bertha 'bɜː.θə ⓤⓢ 'bɝː-
Bertie *first name:* 'bɜː.ti ⓤⓢ 'bɝː.t̬i *surname:* 'bɑː.ti, 'bɜː- ⓤⓢ 'bɑːr.t̬i, 'bɝː-
Bertolucci ˌbɜː.təʊ'luː.tʃi, -tə'-, -'lʊtʃ ⓤⓢ ˌbɝː.t̬ə'luː.tʃi, ˌber-
Bertram 'bɜː.trəm ⓤⓢ 'bɝː-
Bertrand 'bɜː.trənd ⓤⓢ 'bɝː-
Berwick 'ber.ɪk **-shire** -ʃəʳ, -ˌʃɪəʳ ⓤⓢ -ʃɚ, -ˌʃɪr
Berwick-on-Tweed ˌber.ɪk.ɒn'twiːd ⓤⓢ -ɑːn'-
beryl (B) 'ber.ᵊl, -ɪl ⓤⓢ -ᵊl **-s** -z
beryllium bə'rɪl.i.əm, ber'ɪl- ⓤⓢ bə'rɪl
Besançon bə'zɑ̃ː*n*.sɔ̃ːŋ ⓤⓢ -'zɑ̃ːn.sõʊ
Besant 'bes.ᵊnt, 'bez-; bə-
beseech bɪ'siːtʃ, bə- **-es** -ɪz **-ing/ly** -ɪŋ/ **-ed** -t **besought** bɪ'sɔːt, bə- ⓤⓢ -'sɑː -'sɔːt
beseem bɪ'siːm, bə- **-s** -z **-ing** -ɪŋ **-ed** -
beset bɪ'set, bə- **-s** -s **-ting** -ɪŋ ⓤⓢ -'set̬.ɪŋ
beshrew bɪ'ʃruː, bə-
beside bɪ'saɪd, bə- **-s** -z
besieg|e bɪ'siːdʒ, bə- **-es** -ɪz **-ing** -ɪŋ **-ed** -d **-er/s** -əʳ/z ⓤⓢ -ɚ/z

Besley ˈbez.li
besmear bɪˈsmɪəʳ, bə- (US) -ˈsmɪr **-s** -z **-ing** -ɪŋ **-ed** -d
besmirch bɪˈsmɜːtʃ, bə- (US) -ˈsmɝːtʃ **-es** -ɪz **-ing** -ɪŋ **-ed** -t
besom ˈbiː.zᵊm **-s** -z
besotted bɪˈsɒt.ɪd, bə- (US) -ˈsɑː.t̬ɪd **-ly** -li **-ness** -nəs, -nɪs
besought *(from* **beseech***)* bɪˈsɔːt, bə- (US) -ˈsɑːt, -ˈsɔːt
bespangl|e bɪˈspæŋ.gl̩, bəˈspæŋ- **-es** -z **-ing** -ɪŋ, ˈ-glɪŋ **-ed** -d
bespatt|er bɪˈspæt|.əʳ, bə- (US) -ˈspæt̬|.ɚ **-ers** -əz (US) -ɚz **-ering** -ᵊr.ɪŋ **-ered** -əd (US) -ɚd
bespeak bɪˈspiːk, bə- **-s** -s **-ing** -ɪŋ
bespoke bɪˈspəʊk, bə- (US) -ˈspoʊk
bespoken bɪˈspəʊ.kᵊn, bə- (US) -ˈspoʊ-
bespectacled bɪˈspek.tə.kl̩d, -tɪ.kl̩d
besprinkl|e bɪˈsprɪŋ.kl̩, bə- **-es** -z **-ing** -ɪŋ, ˈ-klɪŋ **-ed** -d
Bess bes
Bessacarr ˈbes.ə.kəʳ (US) -kɚ
Bessarabia ˌbes.əˈreɪ.bi.ə
Bessborough ˈbez.bᵊr.ə (US) -oʊ
Bessemer ˈbes.ɪ.məʳ, ˈ-ə- (US) -mɚ
Besses o' th' Barn ˌbes.ɪz.əðˈbɑːn (US) -ˈbɑːrn
Bessette bəˈset
Bessie ˈbes.i
best (B) best **-s** -s **-ing** -ɪŋ **-ed** -ɪd **ˌbest ˈman; ˌmake the ˈbest of ˌsomething; the ˌbest of ˈboth ˌworlds** (US) **the ˌbest of ˌboth ˈworlds**
bestial ˈbes.ti.əl, ˈbiː.sti- (US) ˈbes.tʃᵊl, ˈbiːs-, -ti.əl **-ly** -i **-ism** -ɪ.zᵊm
bestialit|y ˌbes.tiˈæl.ə.t|i, ˌbiː.stiˈ-, -ɪ.t|i (US) ˌbes.tʃiˈæl.ə.t̬|i, ˌbiːs- **-ies** -iz
bestiar|y ˈbes.ti.ᵊr|.i, ˈbiː.sti- (US) -tʃi.er|.i **-ies** -iz
bestir bɪˈstɜːʳ, bə- (US) -ˈstɝː **-s** -z **-ring** -ɪŋ **-red** -d
bestow bɪˈstəʊ, bə- (US) -ˈstoʊ **-s** -z **-ing** -ɪŋ **-ed** -d
bestowal bɪˈstəʊ.əl, bə- (US) -ˈstoʊ- **-s** -z
bestrew bɪˈstruː, bə- **-s** -z **-ing** -ɪŋ **-ed** -d
bestrewn bɪˈstruːn, bə-
bestrid|e bɪˈstraɪd, bə- **-es** -z **-ing** -ɪŋ
bestrode bɪˈstrəʊd, bə- (US) -ˈstroʊd
bestridden bɪˈstrɪ.dᵊn, bə-
bestseller ˌbestˈsel.əʳ (US) -ɚ **-s** -z *stress shift:* ˌbestseller ˈlistings
best-selling ˌbestˈsel.ɪŋ *stress shift:* ˌbest-selling ˈbook
Beswick ˈbez.ɪk
bet (B) bet **-s** -s **-ting** -ɪŋ (US) ˈbet̬.ɪŋ **-ted** -ɪd (US) ˈbet̬.ɪd **ˌhedge one's ˈbets**
beta ˈbiː.tə (US) ˈbeɪ.t̬ə **-s** -z
beta-blocker ˈbiː.təˌblɒk.əʳ (US) ˈbeɪ.t̬əˌblɑː.kɚ **-s** -z
betak|e bɪˈteɪk, bə- **-es** -s **-ing** -ɪŋ
betook bɪˈtʊk, bə- **betaken** bɪˈteɪ.kᵊn, bə-
betel ˈbiː.tᵊl (US) -t̬ᵊl **-nut/s** -nʌt/s
Betelgeuse, Betelgeux ˈbiː.tᵊl.dʒɜːz, ˈbet.ᵊl-, -dʒuːz (US) ˈbiː.t̬ᵊl.dʒuːz, ˈbet̬.ᵊl-, -dʒuːs, -dʒɜːz
bête noire ˌbetˈnwɑːʳ (US) -ˈnwɑːr, ˌbeɪt- **bêtes noires** ˌbetˈnwɑːʳ, -ˈnwɑːz (US) -nwɑːr, beɪt-, -nwɑːrz
Beth beθ
Bethany ˈbeθ.ᵊn.i
Bethel ˈbeθ.ᵊl
Bethell ˈbeθ.ᵊl, bəˈθel
Bethesda beθˈez.də, bɪˈθez-, bə- (US) bəˈθez-, bɪ-
bethink bɪˈθɪŋk, bə- **-s** -s **-ing** -ɪŋ
bethought bɪˈθɔːt, bə- (US) -ˈθɑːt, -ˈθɔːt
Bethlehem ˈbeθ.lɪ.hem, -lə- (US) -lə.hem, -həm
Bethnal ˈbeθ.nᵊl
bethought *(from* **bethink***)* bɪˈθɔːt, bə- (US) -ˈθɑːt, -ˈθɔːt
Bethsaida beθˈseɪ.də, -ˈsaɪ-
Bethune *surname:* ˈbiː.tᵊn (US) bəˈθuːn *in names of streets, etc.:* beθˈjuːn, bɪˈθjuːn, bə- (US) bəˈθuːn, -ˈθjuːn
betid|e bɪˈtaɪd, bə-
betimes bɪˈtaɪmz, bə-
Betjeman ˈbetʃ.ə.mən
betoken bɪˈtəʊ.kᵊn, bə- (US) -ˈtoʊ- **-s** -z **-ing** -ɪŋ **-ed** -ᵊnd
betony ˈbet.ə.ni
betook *(from* **betake***)* bɪˈtʊk, bəˈtʊk
betray bɪˈtreɪ, bə- **-s** -z **-ing** -ɪŋ **-ed** -d **-er/s** -əʳ/z (US) -ɚ/z
betrayal bɪˈtreɪ.əl, bə- **-s** -z
betro|th bɪˈtrəʊ|ð, bə-, -ˈtrəʊ|θ (US) -ˈtroʊ|ð, -ˈtrɑː|θ **-ths** -ðz, -θs **-thing** -ðɪŋ, -θɪŋ **-thed** -ðd, -θt
Note: In British English, the voiceless version is unlikely before **-ing**.
betrothal bɪˈtrəʊ.ðᵊl, bə- (US) -ˈtroʊ-, -θᵊl **-s** -z
Betsy ˈbet.si
Bette bet; ˈbet.i (US) bet; ˈbet̬.i
Betteley ˈbet.ᵊl.i (US) ˈbet̬-
bett|er ˈbet|.əʳ (US) ˈbet̬|.ɚ **-ers** -əz (US) -ɚz **-ering** -ᵊr.ɪŋ **-ered** -əd (US) -ɚd **for ˌbetter or (for) ˈworse**
betterment ˈbet.ə.mənt (US) ˈbet̬.ɚ-
betting ˈbet.ɪŋ (US) ˈbet̬- **-s** -z **ˈbetting ˌshop**
bettor ˈbet.əʳ (US) ˈbet̬.ɚ **-s** -z
Bettws ˈbet.əs (US) ˈbet̬-
Bettws-y-Coed ˌbet.ə.siˈkɔɪd, -ʊ.siˈ-, -kəʊ.ɪd, -əd (US) ˌbet̬.ə.siˈkɔɪd
Betty ˈbet.i (US) ˈbet̬-
between bɪˈtwiːn, bə-
betweentimes bɪˈtwiːn.taɪmz, bə-
betwixt bɪˈtwɪkst, bə-
Beulah ˈbjuː.lə
Bevan ˈbev.ᵊn
bevel ˈbev.ᵊl **-s** -z **-(l)ing** -ɪŋ **-(l)ed** -d
Beven ˈbev.ᵊn
beverag|e ˈbev.ᵊr.ɪdʒ, ˈ-rɪdʒ **-es** -ɪz
Beveridge ˈbev.ᵊr.ɪdʒ, ˈ-rɪdʒ
Beverley ˈbev.ᵊl.i (US) -ɚ.li
Beverly ˈbev.ᵊl.i (US) -ɚ.li **ˌBeverly ˈHills**
Beves ˈbiː.vɪs
Bevin ˈbev.ɪn
Bevis ˈbiː.vɪs, ˈbev.ɪs
bevv|y ˈbev|.i **-ies** -iz **-ied** -id
bev|y ˈbev|.i **-ies** -iz
bewail bɪˈweɪl, bə- **-s** -z **-ing** -ɪŋ **-ed** -d
beware bɪˈweəʳ, bə- (US) -ˈwer
Bewdley ˈbjuːd.li
bewhiskered bɪˈ*h*wɪs.kəd, bə- (US) -kɚd
Bewick(e) ˈbjuː.ɪk
bewigged bɪˈwɪgd, bə-
bewild|er bɪˈwɪl.d|əʳ, bə- (US) -d|ɚ **-ers** -əz (US) -ɚ/z **-ering/ly** -ᵊr.ɪŋ/li **-ered** -əd (US) -ɚd **-erment/s** -ə.mənt/s (US) -ɚ.mənt/s
bewitch bɪˈwɪtʃ, bə- **-es** -ɪz **-ing/ly** -ɪŋ/li **-ed** -t **-ment/s** -mənt/s
Bewley ˈbjuː.li
Bexhill beksˈhɪl *stress shift:* ˌBexhill ˈstation
Bexley ˈbek.sli
Bexleyheath ˌbek.slɪˈhiːθ
Bey beɪ **-s** -z
Beynon ˈbaɪ.nən, ˈbeɪ-
beyond biˈɒnd (US) -ˈ*j*ɑːnd
Beyrout(h) beɪˈruːt
bezant ˈbez.ᵊnt **-s** -s
bezel ˈbez.ᵊl **-s** -z
Béziers ˈbez.i.eɪ
bezique bɪˈziːk, bə-
BFPO ˌbiː.ef.piːˈəʊ (US) -ˈoʊ
Bhagavad-Gita ˌbæg.ə.vədˈgiː.tə, ˌbʌg-, -vædˈ- (US) ˌbɑː.gə.vɑːdˈ-
bhagwan (B) ˈbæg.wɑːn
bhaji ˈbɑː.dʒi **-s** -z
bhang bæŋ
bhangra ˈbæŋ.grə, ˈbɑːŋ-
bhindi ˈbɪn.di
Bhopal bəʊˈpɑːl (US) boʊ-
Bhutan buːˈtɑːn, -ˈtæn
Bhutanese ˌbuː.təˈniːz
Bhutto ˈbuː.təʊ, ˈbʊt.əʊ (US) ˈbuː.t̬oʊ
bi- baɪ-
Note: Prefix. Words containing **bi-** normally take secondary stress, but sometimes primary stress, on the first syllable, e.g. **bimetallic** /ˌbaɪ.metˈæl.ɪk/, British English **bicarb** /ˈbaɪ.kɑːb/, or primary stress on the second syllable, e.g. **biathlete** /baɪˈæθ.liːt/.
Biafr|a biˈæf.r|ə, baɪˈ- **-an/s** -ən/z
Bialystok biˈæl.ɪ.stɒk; ˈ-ə-; ˌbiː.əˈlɪs.tɒk (US) biˈɑː.lə.stɑːk, -ˈæl.ə-

Bianca bi'æŋ.kə (US) -'æŋ-, -'ɑːŋ-
biannual baɪ'æn.ju.əl **-s** -z **-ly** -li
Biarritz ˌbɪə'rɪts, '-- (US) ˌbiː.ə'rɪts, '---
bias 'baɪəs **-(s)es** -ɪz **-(s)ing** -ɪŋ **-(s)ed** -t
biathlete baɪ'æθ.liːt **-s** -s
biathlon baɪ'æθ.lən, -lɒn (US) -lɑːn **-s** -z
biaxal baɪ'æk.səl
biaxial baɪ'æk.si.əl
bib bɪb **-s** -z
Bibby 'bɪb.i
bibelot 'bɪb.ləʊ, -əl.əʊ (US) -ə.loʊ, 'biː.bloʊ **-s** -z
Bible 'baɪ.bl̩ **-s** -z **'Bible ˌBelt**
biblic|al 'bɪb.lɪ.k|əl **-ally** -əl.i, -li
biblio- bɪb.li.əʊ-; ˌbɪb.li'ɒ- (US) bɪb.li.oʊ-, -ə-; ˌbɪb.li'ɑː-
Note: Prefix. Normally takes either primary or secondary stress on the first syllable, e.g. **bibliophile** /'bɪb.li.əʊ.faɪl (US) -ə-/, **bibliomania** /ˌbɪb.li.əʊ'meɪ.ni.ə (US) -ə'-/, or secondary stress on the first syllable, with primary stress occurring on the third syllable, e.g. **bibliography** /ˌbɪb.li'ɒg.rə.fi (US) -'ɑː.grə-/.
bibliograph|y ˌbɪb.li'ɒg.rə.f|i (US) -'ɑː.grə- **-ies** -iz **-er/s** -əʳ/z (US) -ɚ/z
bibliolat|ry ˌbɪb.li'ɒl.ə.t|ri (US) -'ɑː.lə- **-er/z** -əʳ/z (US) -ɚ/z
bibliomania ˌbɪb.li.əʊ'meɪ.ni.ə (US) -ə'-, -oʊ'-
bibliomaniac ˌbɪb.li.əʊ'meɪ.ni.æk (US) -ə'-, -oʊ'- **-s** -s
bibliophile 'bɪb.li.əʊ.faɪl (US) -ə-, -oʊ- **-s** -z
bibulous 'bɪb.jə.ləs, -jʊ- (US) -jə- **-ly** -li
Bic® bɪk
bicameral ˌbaɪ'kæm.ər.əl **-ism** -ɪ.zəm
bicarb 'baɪ.kɑːb (US) baɪ'kɑːrb
bicarbonate ˌbaɪ'kɑː.bən.ət, -eɪt, -ɪt (US) -'kɑːr- **-s** -s **biˌcarbonate of 'soda**
bice baɪs
Bice 'biː.tʃi; baɪs
bicentenar|y ˌbaɪ.sen'tiː.nər|.i, -sən'-, -'ten.ər- (US) baɪ'sen.tən.er|.i; ˌbaɪ.sen'ten.ər- **-ies** -iz
bicentennial ˌbaɪ.sen'ten.i.əl, -sən'- **-s** -z
biceps 'baɪ.seps
Bicester 'bɪs.təʳ (US) -tɚ
bichloride ˌbaɪ'klɔː.raɪd (US) -'klɔːr.aɪd
bichromate ˌbaɪ'krəʊ.meɪt, -met, -mɪt (US) -'kroʊ-
bick|er 'bɪk|.əʳ (US) -ɚ **-ers** -əz (US) -ɚz **-ering/s** -ər.ɪŋ/z **-ered** -əd (US) -ɚd **-erer/s** -ər.əʳ/z (US) -ɚ.ɚ/z
Bickerstaff(e) 'bɪk.ə.stɑːf (US) -ɚ.stæf
Bickersteth 'bɪk.ə.steθ, -stɪθ (US) '-ɚ-
Bickerton 'bɪk.ə.tən (US) '-ɚ-
Bickford 'bɪk.fəd (US) -fɚd
Bickleigh, Bickley 'bɪk.li
Bicknell 'bɪk.nəl
bicoastal baɪ'kəʊ.stəl (US) -'koʊ-
bicuspid baɪ'kʌs.pɪd **-s** -z
bicyc|le 'baɪ.sɪ.k|l̩, -sə- **-les** -l̩z **-ling** -lɪŋ **-led** -l̩d
bicyclist 'baɪ.sɪ.klɪst, -sə- **-s** -s
bid bɪd **-s** -z **-ding** -ɪŋ **-der/s** -əʳ/z (US) -ɚ/z **bade** bæd, beɪd **bidden** 'bɪd.ən
biddable 'bid.ə.bl̩
bidder (B) 'bɪd.əʳ (US) -ɚ **-s** -z
Biddle 'bɪd.l̩
Biddulph 'bɪd.ʌlf, -əlf
bidd|y (B) 'bɪd|.i **-ies** -iz
bid|e (B) baɪd **-es** -z **-ing** -ɪŋ **-ed** -ɪd
Bideford 'bɪd.ɪ.fəd (US) -fɚd
Biden 'baɪ.dən
bidet 'biː.deɪ (US) bɪ'deɪ, biː- **-s** -z
bidialectal ˌbaɪ.daɪə'lek.təl
bidialectalism ˌbaɪ.daɪə'lek.təl.ɪ.zəm
Bidwell 'bɪd.wel
Bielefeld 'biː.lə.felt, -feld
biennial baɪ'en.i.əl **-ly** -i
bier bɪəʳ (US) bɪr **-s** -z
Bierce bɪəs (US) bɪrs
biff bɪf **-s** -s **-ing** -ɪŋ **-ed** -t
Biffen 'bɪf.ɪn, -ən
bifocal baɪ'fəʊ.kəl (US) 'baɪˌfoʊ-, ˌ-'-- **-s** -z
bifur|cate 'baɪ.fə.keɪt, -fɜː- (US) -fɚ- **-cates** -keɪts **-cating** -keɪ.tɪŋ (US) -keɪ.t̬ɪŋ **-cated** -keɪ.tɪd (US) -keɪ.t̬ɪd
bifurcation ˌbaɪ.fə'keɪ.ʃən, -fɜː'- (US) -fɚ'- **-s** -z
big bɪg **-ger** -əʳ (US) -ɚ **-gest** -ɪst, -əst **-ness** -nəs, -nɪs **ˌBig 'Apple; ˌBig 'Bang; ˌBig 'Ben; ˌbig 'business; ˌBig 'Dipper; ˌbig 'game; ˌbig 'screen; ˌbig 'wheel; ˌhit the 'big ˌtime**
bigamist 'bɪg.ə.mɪst **-s** -s
bigamous 'bɪg.ə.məs **-ly** -li
bigam|y 'bɪg.ə.m|i **-ies** -iz
Bigelow 'bɪg.əl.əʊ, -ɪ.ləʊ (US) -ə.loʊ
Bigfoot 'bɪg.fʊt
Bigge bɪg
biggie 'bɪg.i
Biggin 'bɪg.ɪn
biggish 'bɪg.ɪʃ
Biggles 'bɪg.l̩z
Biggleswade 'bɪg.l̩z.weɪd
Biggs bɪgz
biggl|y 'bɪg|.i **-ies** -iz
Bigham 'bɪg.em
bighead 'bɪg.hed **-s** -z
bigheaded ˌbɪg'hed.ɪd, -əd (US) '-ˌ-- **-ly** -li **-ness** -nəs, -nɪs *stress shift:* ˌbigheaded 'bully
bighorn 'bɪg.hɔːn (US) -hɔːrn **-s** -z
bight baɪt **-s** -s **-ing** -ɪŋ (US) 'baɪ.t̬ɪŋ **-ed** -ɪd (US) 'baɪ.t̬ɪd
big-league 'bɪg.liːg
Biglow 'bɪg.ləʊ (US) -loʊ
Bignell 'bɪg.nəl
big|ot 'bɪg|.ət **-ots** -əts **-oted** -ə.tɪd (US) -ə.t̬ɪd
bigotr|y 'bɪg.ə.tr|i **-ies** -iz
bigraph 'baɪ.grɑːf, -græf (US) -græf **-s** -s
Big Sur ˌbɪg'sɜːʳ (US) -'sɝː
big-ticket 'bɪgˌtɪk.ɪt
big-time 'bɪg.taɪm **-er/s** -əʳ/z (US) -ɚ/z
bigwig 'bɪg.wɪg **-s** -z
Bihar bɪ'hɑːʳ, biː- (US) -hɑːr
bijou 'biː.ʒuː, -'-
bik|e baɪk **-es** -s **-ing** -ɪŋ **-ed** -t
biker (B) 'baɪ.kəʳ (US) -kɚ **-s** -z
bikini (B) bɪ'kiː.ni, bə- **-s** -z
Biko 'biː.keʊ (US) -koʊ
bilabial (*n. adj.*) baɪ'leɪ.bi.əl **-s** -z **-ly** -i

Bilabial

Bilabial articulations involve both of the lips.

Examples for English

In English, /p b/ and /m/ are examples of bilabial sounds. These are all made with a complete closure of the lips, e.g.:

pan	/pæn/
ban	/bæn/
man	/mæn/

(/w/ is also sometimes referred to as bilabial, but, as it has tongue movement towards the velum in addition to lip rounding, it is more accurately described as 'labial-velar')

The plosives /p/ and /b/ are one of the pairs which are said to be distinguished by being FORTIS and LENIS respectively, rather than voiceless and voiced.

bilateral baɪˈlæt.ᵊr.ᵊl, ˈ-rᵊl (US) -ˈlæt̬.ɚ.ᵊl **-y** -i **-ness** -nəs, -nɪs

Bilbao bɪlˈbaʊ, -ˈbɑː.əʊ (US) -ˈbɑː.oʊ, -ˈbaʊ

bilberr|y ˈbɪl.bᵊr|.i (US) -ber- **-ies** -iz

Bilborough ˈbɪl.bᵊr.ə (US) -oʊ

Bilbrough ˈbɪl.brə (US) -broʊ

bilb|y ˈbɪl.bi **-ies** -iz

Bildungsroman ˈbɪl.dʊŋz.rəʊ.mɑːn (US) -roʊ- **-s** -z **-e** -ə

bile baɪl

bilg|e bɪldʒ **-es** -ɪz **-ing** -ɪŋ **-ed** -d ˈ**bilge** ˌ**pump**; ˈ**bilge** ˌ**water**

bilgy ˈbɪl.dʒi

bilharzia bɪlˈhɑː.zi.ə, -ˈhɑːt.si- (US) -ˈhɑːr.zi-

biliary ˈbɪl.i.ᵊr.i

bilingual baɪˈlɪŋ.gwᵊl **-s** -z **-ly** -i **-ism** -ɪ.zᵊm *stress shift, see first compound:* ˌ**bilingual** ˈ**secretary** **bi**ˌ**lingual** ˈ**secretary**

bilious ˈbɪl.i.əs (US) ˈ-jəs, ˈ-i.əs **-ly** -li **-ness** -nəs, -nɪs

bilirubin ˌbɪl.ɪˈruː.bɪn

biliteral baɪˈlɪt.ᵊr.ᵊl, ˈ-rᵊl (US) -ˈlɪt̬.ɚ.ᵊl **-ly** -i

bilk bɪlk **-s** -s **-ing** -ɪŋ **-ed** -t

bill (B) bɪl **-s** -z **-ing** -ɪŋ **-ed** -d ˌ**bill of** ˈ**fare**; ˌ**fit the** ˈ**bill**

billable ˈbɪl.ə.bl̩

billabong ˈbɪl.ə.bɒŋ (US) -bɑːŋ, -bɔːŋ **-s** -z

billboard ˈbɪl.bɔːd (US) -bɔːrd **-s** -z

Billericay ˌbɪl.əˈrɪk.i

bille|t ˈbɪl|.ɪt, -ət (US) -ət **-ts** -ts **-ting** -tɪŋ (US) -t̬ɪŋ **-ted** -tɪd (US) -t̬ɪd

billet-doux ˌbɪl.eɪˈduː **billets-doux** ˌbɪl.eɪˈduː, -duːz

billfold ˈbɪl.fəʊld (US) -foʊld **-s** -z

billhook ˈbɪl.hʊk **-s** -s

billiard ˈbɪl.i.əd, ˈ-jəd (US) ˈ-jɚd **-s** -z ˈ**billiard** ˌ**ball**; ˈ**billiard** ˌ**cue**; ˈ**billiard** ˌ**room**; ˈ**billiard** ˌ**table**

Billie ˈbɪl.i

Billie-Jean ˌbɪl.iˈdʒiːn

Billing ˈbɪl.ɪŋ **-s** -z

Billinge ˈbɪl.ɪndʒ

Billingham ˈbɪl.ɪŋ.*h*əm

Billinghurst ˈbɪl.ɪŋ.hɜːst (US) -hɝːst

Billingsgate ˈbɪl.ɪŋz.geɪt

Billington ˈbɪl.ɪŋ.tən

billion ˈbɪl.i.ən, -jən (US) -jən **-s** -z

billionaire ˌbɪl.i.əˈneəʳ, ˌ-jəˈ- (US) -jəˈner **-s** -z

billionth ˈbɪl.i.ənθ, ˈ-jənθ (US) ˈ-jənθ **-s** -s

billow ˈbɪl.əʊ (US) -oʊ **-s** -z **-ing** -ɪŋ **-ed** -d **-y** -i

billposter ˈbɪlˌpəʊ.stəʳ (US) -ˌpoʊ.stɚ **-s** -z

billsticker ˈbɪlˌstɪk.əʳ (US) -kɚ **-s** -z

bill|y (B) ˈbɪl|.i **-ies** -iz ˈ**billy** ˌ**can**; ˈ**billy** ˌ**club**; ˈ**billy** ˌ**goat**

billycock ˈbɪl.i.kɒk (US) -kɑːk **-s** -s

billy-o ˈbɪl.i.əʊ (US) -oʊ

Biloxi bɪˈlʌk.si, bə-, -ˈlɒk- (US) -ˈlɑːk-, -ˈlʌk-

Bilston(e) ˈbɪl.stən

Bilton ˈbɪl.tᵊn

biltong ˈbɪl.tɒŋ (US) -tɑːŋ, -tɔːŋ

bimbo ˈbɪm.bəʊ (US) -boʊ **-(e)s** -z

bimestrial baɪˈmes.tri.əl

bimetallic ˌbaɪ.metˈæl.ɪk, -mɪˈtæl-, -mə-

bimetall|ism baɪˈmet.ᵊl|.ɪ.zᵊm (US) -ˈmet̬- **-ist/s** -ɪst/s

bimolecular ˌbaɪ.məˈlek.jə.ləʳ, -jʊ- (US) -lɚ

bimonthl|y baɪˈmʌn*t*θ.l|i **-ies** -iz

bin bɪn **-s** -z **-ning** -ɪŋ **-ned** -d

binar|y ˈbaɪ.nᵊr|.i **-ies** -iz ˌ**binary** ˈ**number**

binaural baɪˈnɔː.rᵊl, bɪ- (US) -ˈnɔːr.ᵊl

Binchy ˈbɪn.*t*ʃi (US) ˈbɪn*t*.ʃi

bind baɪnd **-s** -z **-ing** -ɪŋ **bound** baʊnd

binder ˈbaɪn.dəʳ (US) -dɚ **-s** -z

binder|y ˈbaɪn.dᵊr|.i **-ies** -iz

bindweed ˈbaɪnd.wiːd

Binet ˈbiː.neɪ (US) bɪˈneɪ

Binet-Simon ˌbiː.neɪˈsaɪ.mən (US) bɪˌneɪ.siˈmoʊn

Bing bɪŋ

bing|e bɪndʒ **-es** -ɪz **-(e)ing** -ɪŋ **-ed** -d

Bingen ˈbɪŋ.ən

Bingham ˈbɪŋ.əm

Bingley ˈbɪŋ*g*.li

bingo ˈbɪŋ.gəʊ (US) -goʊ

Bink(e)s bɪŋks

bin Laden ˌbɪnˈlɑː.dᵊn

bin|man ˈbɪn|.mæn, ˈbɪm-, -mən (US) ˈbɪn- **-men** -men, -mən

binnacle ˈbɪn.ə.kl̩ **-s** -z

Binney, Binnie ˈbɪn.i

Binns bɪnz

Binoche bɪˈnɒʃ, biː- (US) -noʊʃ

binocular (*adj.*) baɪˈnɒk.jə.ləʳ, bɪ-, bə-, -jʊ- (US) -ˈnɑː.kjə.lɚ, -kjʊ-

binoculars (*n.*) bɪˈnɒk.jə.ləz, baɪ-, bə-, -jʊ- (US) -ˈnɑː.kjə.lɚz, -kjʊ-

binomial baɪˈnəʊ.mi.əl (US) -ˈnoʊ- **-s** -z **-ly** -i

Binste(a)d ˈbɪn.stɪd, -sted

bint bɪnt **-s** -s

Binyon ˈbɪn.jən

bio- baɪ.əʊ-; baɪˈɒ- (US) baɪ.oʊ-, -ə-; baɪˈɑː-

Note: Prefix. Normally carries primary or secondary stress on the first syllable, e.g. **biograph** /ˈbaɪ.əʊ.grɑːf (US) -ə.græf/, **biographic** /ˌbaɪ.əʊˈgræf.ɪk (US) -əˈ-/, or primary stress on the second syllable, e.g. **biographer** /baɪˈɒg.rə.fəʳ (US) -ˈɑː.grə.fɚ/. There are exceptions; see individual entries.

biochemic|al ˌbaɪ.əʊˈkem.ɪ.k|ᵊl (US) -oʊˈ- **-als** -ᵊlz **-ally** -ᵊl.i, -li

biochemist ˌbaɪ.əʊˈkem.ɪst (US) -oʊˈ- **-s** -s **-ry** -ri

biocoenosis ˌbaɪ.əʊ.sɪˈnəʊ.sɪs, -siːˈ- (US) -oʊ.sɪˈnoʊ-

biodegradability ˌbaɪ.əʊ.dɪ.greɪ.dəˈbɪl.ɪ.ti, -də.greɪ-, -ə.ti (US) -oʊ.dɪ.greɪ.dəˈbɪl.ə.t̬i, -də-

biodegradab|le ˌbaɪ.əʊ.dɪˈgreɪ.də.b|l̩, -dəˈ- (US) -oʊ- **-ly** -li

biodegradation ˌbaɪ.əʊ.deg.rəˈdeɪ.ʃᵊn (US) ˌ-oʊ-

biodegrad|e ˌbaɪ.əʊ.dɪˈgreɪd, -dəˈ- (US) -oʊ- **-es** -z **-ing** -ɪŋ **-ed** -ɪd

biodiversity ˌbaɪ.əʊ.daɪˈvɜː.sə.ti, -dɪˈ-, -sɪ- (US) -oʊ.dɪˈvɝː.sə.t̬i, -daɪˈ-

bioengineer ˌbaɪ.əʊ.en.dʒɪˈnɪəʳ, -dʒəˈ- (US) -oʊ.en.dʒɪˈnɪr, -dʒəˈ- **-s** -z

bioengineering ˌbaɪ.əʊ.en.dʒɪˈnɪə.rɪŋ, -dʒəˈ- (US) -oʊ.en.dʒɪˈnɪr.ɪŋ, -dʒəˈ-

biofeedback ˌbaɪ.əʊˈfiːd.bæk (US) -oʊˈ-

biogenesis ˌbaɪ.əʊˈdʒen.ə.sɪs, ˈ-ɪ- (US) -oʊˈ-

biogenetic ˌbaɪ.əʊ.dʒəˈnet.ɪk, -dʒɪˈ- (US) -oʊ.dʒəˈnet̬- **-ally** -ᵊl.i, -li

biogenic ˌbaɪ.əʊˈdʒen.ɪk (US) -oʊˈ-

biograph ˈbaɪ.əʊ.grɑːf, -græf (US) -ə.græf **-s** -s

biographer baɪˈɒg.rə.fəʳ (US) -ˈɑː.grə.fɚ **-s** -z

biographic ˌbaɪ.əʊˈgræf.ɪk (US) -əˈ- **-al** -ᵊl **-ally** -ᵊl.i, -li

biograph|y baɪˈɒg.rə.f|i (US) -ˈɑː.grə- **-ies** -iz

biolinguistics ˌbaɪ.əʊ.lɪŋˈgwɪs.tɪks (US) ˌ-oʊ-

biologic ˌbaɪ.əˈlɒdʒ.ɪk (US) -ˈlɑː.dʒɪk

biologic|al ˌbaɪ.əˈlɒdʒ.ɪ.k|ᵊl (US) -ˈlɑː.dʒɪ- **-ally** -ᵊl.i, -li **bio**ˌ**logical** ˈ**clock**; **bio**ˌ**logical** ˈ**warfare**

biologist baɪˈɒl.ə.dʒɪst (US) -ˈɑː.lə- **-s** -s

biology baɪˈɒl.ə.dʒi (US) -ˈɑː.lə-

biome ˈbaɪ.əʊm (US) -oʊm

biomedical ˌbaɪ.əʊˈmed.ɪ.kᵊl (US) -oʊˈ-

biometric ˌbaɪ.əʊˈmet.rɪk (US) -oʊˈ- **-s** -s **-al** -ᵊl

biometry baɪˈɒm.ə.tri, ˈ-ɪ- (US) -ˈɑː.mə-

bionic baɪˈɒn.ɪk (US) -ˈɑː.nɪk **-s** -s

biophysicist ˌbaɪ.əʊˈfɪz.ɪ.sɪst, -oʊˈ- **-s** -s

biophysic|s ˌbaɪ.əʊˈfɪz.ɪk|s (US) -oʊˈ- **-al** -ᵊl

biopic ˈbaɪ.əʊ.pɪk (US) -oʊ- **-s** -s

biops|y ˈbaɪ.ɒp.s|i (US) -ɑːp- **-ies** -iz

biorhythm ˈbaɪ.əʊˌrɪð.ᵊm (US) -oʊˌ- **-s** -z

bioscope ˈbaɪ.əʊ.skəʊp (US) -skoʊp **-s** -s

biosphere ˈbaɪ.əʊ.sfɪəʳ (US) -ə.sfɪr **-s** -z

biotech ˈbaɪ.əʊ.tek (US) -oʊ-

biotechnology ˌbaɪ.əʊ.tekˈnɒl.ə.dʒi (US) -oʊ.tekˈnɑː.lə-

biotope ˈbaɪ.əʊ.təʊp (US) -toʊp **-s** -s

biparous ˈbɪp.ᵊr.əs
bipartisan baɪˈpɑː.tɪ.zæn; ˌbaɪ.pɑː.tɪˈzæn, -zən (US) baɪˈpɑːr.t̬ə.zən
bipartite baɪˈpɑː.taɪt (US) baɪˈpɑːr- *stress shift:* ˌbipartite ˈtreaty
biped ˈbaɪ.ped **-s** -z
bipedal baɪˈpiː.dᵊl, -ˈped.ᵊl (US) -ˈped.ᵊl **-ism** -ɪ.zᵊm
biplane ˈbaɪ.pleɪn **-s** -z
bipod ˈbaɪ.pɒd (US) -pɑːd **-s** -z
bipolar baɪˈpəʊ.ləʳ (US) -ˈpoʊ.lɚ
bipolarity ˌbaɪ.pəʊˈlær.ɪ.ti, -ə.ti (US) -poʊˈler.ə.t̬i, -ˈlær-
biquadratic ˌbaɪ.kwɒdˈræt.ɪk, -kwəˈdræt- (US) -kwɑːˈdræt̬.ɪk **-s** -s
birch (B) bɜːtʃ (US) bɝːtʃ **-es** -ɪz **-ing** -ɪŋ **-ed** -t
Birchall ˈbɜː.tʃɔːl, -tʃᵊl (US) ˈbɝː.tʃɔːl, -tʃɑːl, -tʃᵊl
Birchenough ˈbɜː.tʃɪ.nʌf (US) ˈbɝː-
Bircher ˈbɜː.tʃəʳ (US) ˈbɝː.tʃɚ
Birchwood ˈbɜːtʃ.wʊd (US) ˈbɝːtʃ-
Bircotes ˈbɜː.kəʊts (US) ˈbɝː.koʊts
bird (B) bɜːd (US) bɝːd **-s** -z **ˈbird ˌcage; ˈbird ˌdog; ˈbird ˌfancier; ˌbird of ˈparadise; ˌbird of ˈprey; ˌkill two ˌbirds with ˌone ˈstone**
bird-brain ˈbɜːd.breɪn (US) ˈbɝːd-
bird-brained ˈbɜːd.breɪnd (US) ˈbɝːd-
birdhou|se ˈbɜːd.haʊ|s (US) ˈbɝːd- **-ses** -zɪz
birdie ˈbɜː.di (US) ˈbɝː- **-s** -z **-d** -d
birdlike ˈbɜːd.laɪk (US) ˈbɝːd-
birdlime ˈbɜːd.laɪm (US) ˈbɝːd-
birdseed ˈbɜːd.siːd (US) ˈbɝːd-
bird's-eye *(n. adj.)* ˈbɜːdz.aɪ (US) ˈbɝːdz- **-s** -z **ˌbird's-eye ˈview**
Birds Eye® ˈbɜːdz.aɪ (US) ˈbɝːdz-
bird's-nest ˈbɜːdz.nest (US) ˈbɝːdz- **-s** -s **-ing** -ɪŋ **-ed** -ɪd **ˌbird's nest ˈsoup**
birdwatch|ing ˈbɜːdˌwɒtʃ|.ɪŋ (US) ˈbɝːdˌwɑː.tʃ|ɪŋ, -ˌwɔː- **-er/s** -əʳ/z (US) -ɚ/z
bireme ˈbaɪ.riːm, -ˈ- (US) baɪˈriːm **-s** -z
biretta bɪˈret.ə (US) -ˈret̬- **-s** -z
Birgit ˈbɜː.gɪt, ˈbɪə- (US) ˈbɝː-, -giːt
biriani ˌbɪr.iˈɑː.ni **-s** -z
Birkbeck *surname:* ˈbɜː.bek, ˈbɜːk- (US) ˈbɝː-, ˈbɝːk- *college in London:* ˈbɜːk.bek (US) ˈbɝːk-
Birkenau ˈbɜː.kᵊn.aʊ (US) ˈbɝː-
Birkenhead ˌbɜː.kᵊnˈhed, ˈ--- (US) ˌbɝː.kᵊnˈhed, ˈ---
Birkenstocks® ˈbɜː.kᵊn.stɒks (US) ˈbɝː.kᵊn.stɑːks
Birkett ˈbɜː.kɪt (US) ˈbɝː-
Birkin ˈbɜː.kɪn (US) ˈbɝː-
Birley ˈbɜː.li (US) ˈbɝː-
Birling ˈbɜː.lɪŋ (US) ˈbɝː-
Birmingham *place in UK:* ˈbɜː.mɪŋ.əm (US) ˈbɝː- *places in US:* ˈbɜː.mɪŋ.hæm (US) ˈbɝː-
Birnam ˈbɜː.nəm (US) ˈbɝː-
Birney ˈbɜː.ni (US) ˈbɝː-
Biro® ˈbaɪə.rəʊ (US) ˈbaɪ.roʊ **-s** -z
Biron ˈbaɪ.rən
Note: /bɪˈruːn/ in 'Love's Labour's Lost'.
birr bɜːʳ (US) bɝː **birrotch** ˈbɜː.rɒtʃ (US) ˈbɝː.ɑːtʃ
Birrell ˈbɪr.ᵊl
birrotch *(plur. of* **birr***)* ˈbɜː.rɒtʃ (US) ˈbɝː.ɑːtʃ
Birstall ˈbɜː.stɔːl (US) ˈbɝː.stɔːl, -stɑːl
Birt bɜːt (US) bɝːt
birth bɜːθ (US) bɝːθ **-s** -s **ˈbirth cerˌtificate; ˈbirth conˌtrol; ˈbirthing ˌcenter**
birthday ˈbɜːθ.deɪ, -di (US) ˈbɝːθ.deɪ **-s** -z **ˈbirthday ˌcake; ˈbirthday ˌcard; ˈbirthday ˌparty; ˈbirthday ˌpresent; in one's ˈbirthday ˌsuit**
birthmark ˈbɜːθ.mɑːk (US) ˈbɝːθ.mɑːrk **-s** -s
birthplac|e ˈbɜːθ.pleɪs (US) ˈbɝːθ- **-es** -ɪz
birthrate ˈbɜːθ.reɪt (US) ˈbɝːθ- **-s** -s
birthright ˈbɜːθ.raɪt (US) ˈbɝːθ- **-s** -s
Birtwistle ˈbɜː.twɪ.sl̩ (US) ˈbɝː-
biryani ˌbɪr.iˈɑː.ni **-s** -z
bis bɪs
Biscay ˈbɪs.keɪ, -ki **ˌBay of ˈBiscay**
biscuit ˈbɪs.kɪt **-s** -s **ˈbiscuit ˌbarrel**
bisect baɪˈsekt (US) ˈbaɪ.sekt, -ˈ- **-s** -s **-ing** -ɪŋ **-ed** -ɪd
bisection baɪˈsek.ʃᵊn **-s** -z
bisector baɪˈsek.təʳ (US) -tɚ **-s** -z
bisexual baɪˈsek.ʃʊəl, -ʃu.əl, -sjʊəl, -sjʊ.əl (US) -ʃu.əl
bisexuality baɪˌsek.ʃuˈæl.ɪ.ti, -sjuˈæl-, -ə.ti (US) -ʃuˈæl.ə.t̬i
bishop (B) ˈbɪʃ.əp **-s** -s
bishopric ˈbɪʃ.ə.prɪk **-s** -s
Bishopsgate ˈbɪʃ.əps.geɪt, -gɪt
Bishop's Stortford ˌbɪʃ.əpsˈstɔːt.fəd, -ˈstɔː- (US) -ˈstɔːrt.fɚd, -ˈstɔːr-
Bishopstoke ˈbɪʃ.əp.stəʊk (US) -stoʊk
Bishopston ˈbɪʃ.əp.stən
Bishopton ˈbɪʃ.əp.tən
Bisley ˈbɪz.li **-s** -z
Bismarck ˈbɪz.mɑːk (US) -mɑːrk
bismuth ˈbɪz.məθ
bison ˈbaɪ.sᵊn **-s** -z
Bispham *surname:* ˈbɪs.fəm, ˈbɪs.pəm *place:* ˈbɪs.pəm
bisque biːsk, bɪsk (US) bɪsk **-s** -s
Bissau ˈbɪs.aʊ, -ˈ- (US) bɪˈsaʊ
Bissell ˈbɪs.ᵊl
Bissett ˈbɪs.ɪt, ˈbɪz-
bissextile bɪˈsek.staɪl (US) -stᵊl, -staɪl **-s** -z
bister ˈbɪs.təʳ (US) -tɚ
Bisto® ˈbɪs.təʊ (US) -toʊ
bistour|y ˈbɪs.tᵊr|.i **-ies** -iz
bistre ˈbɪs.təʳ (US) -tɚ
bistro, bistrot ˈbiː.strəʊ, ˈbɪs- (US) -stroʊ **-s** -z
bisulph|ate baɪˈsʌl.f|eɪt, -f|ɪt, -f|ət (US) -f|eɪt **-ite** -aɪt
bit bɪt **-s** -s **ˌbits and ˈpieces; take the ˌbit between one's ˈteeth**
bitch bɪtʃ **-es** -ɪz **-ed** -d
bitch|y ˈbɪtʃ|.i **-iness** -ɪ.nəs, -ɪ.nɪs **-iest** -i.ɪst, -i.əst **-ier** -i.əʳ (US) -i.ɚ
bit|e baɪt **-es** -s **-ing** -ɪŋ (US) ˈbaɪ.t̬ɪŋ **bit** bɪt **bitten** ˈbɪt.ᵊn **biter/s** ˈbaɪ.təʳ/z (US) -t̬ɚ/z **ˌbite off ˌmore than one can ˈchew; ˌbite one's ˈtongue; ˌbite someone's ˈhead off; ˌbite the ˈbullet; ˌbite the ˈdust; ˌbite the ˌhand that ˈfeeds one**
Bithell ˈbɪθ.ᵊl, bɪˈθel
Bithynia bɪˈθɪn.i.ə, baɪ-
Bitola ˈbiː.təʊ.lə (US) -toʊ-, -t̬ᵊl.ə
Bitolj ˈbiː.təʊ.ljə (US) -toʊ-, -t̬ᵊl.jə
bitten *(from* **bite***)* ˈbɪt.ᵊn **once ˌbitten twice ˈshy**
bitt|er ˈbɪt|.əʳ (US) ˈbɪt̬|.ɚ **-erer** -ᵊr.əʳ (US) -ɚ.ɚ **-erest** -ᵊr.ɪst, -əst **-erly** -ə.li (US) -ɚ.li **-erness** -ə.nəs, -nɪs (US) -ɚ.nəs, -nɪs **to the ˌbitter ˈend**
bittern ˈbɪt.ən, -ɜːn (US) ˈbɪt̬.ɚn **-s** -z
bitters ˈbɪt.əz (US) ˈbɪt̬.ɚz
bittersweet ˈbɪt.ə.swiːt, ˌ--ˈ- (US) ˈbɪt̬.ɚ.swiːt
bitt|y ˈbɪt|.i (US) ˈbɪt̬- **-ier** -i.əʳ (US) -i.ɚ **-iest** -i.ɪst, -i.əst **-iness** -ɪ.nəs, -ɪ.nɪs
bitumen ˈbɪtʃ.ə.mən, ˈ-ʊ-, -mɪn (US) bɪˈtuː.mən, baɪ-, -ˈtjuː- **-s** -z
bituminous bɪˈtʃuː.mɪ.nəs, bə-, -ˈtjuː-, -mə- (US) -ˈtuː-, -ˈtjuː-
bivalen|ce ˌbaɪˈveɪ.lən|*t*s, bɪ-; (US) ˌbaɪˈveɪ.lən|*t*s, ˈbaɪ.veɪ- **-cy** -*t*.si **-t** -t
bivalve ˈbaɪ.vælv **-s** -z
bivouac ˈbɪv.u.æk (US) -u.æk, ˈ-wæk **-s** -s **-king** -ɪŋ **-ked** -t
bi-weekl|y baɪˈwiː.kl|i **-ies** -iz *stress shift:* ˌbi-weekly ˈjournal
bizarre bɪˈzɑːʳ, bə- (US) -ˈzɑːr **-ly** -li **-ness** -nəs, -nɪs
Bizerte, Bizerta bɪˈzɜː.tə (US) -ˈzɝː-
Bizet ˈbiː.zeɪ (US) -ˈ-
Bjork, Björk bjɔːk, bjɜːk, biˈɔːk (US) bjɔːrk
Bjorn, Björn bjɔːn, bjɜːn; biˈɔːn, -ˈɜːn (US) bjɔːrn, bjɝːn
BL ˌbiːˈel
blab blæb **-s** -z **-bing** -ɪŋ **-bed** -d **-ber/s** -əʳ/z (US) -ɚ/z
blabb|er ˈblæb|.əʳ (US) -ɚ **-ers** -əz (US) -ɚz **-ering** -ᵊr.ɪŋ **-ered** -əd (US) -ɚd
blabber|mouth ˈblæb.ə|.maʊθ (US) ˈ-ɚ- **-mouths** -maʊðz, -maʊθs
Blaby ˈbleɪ.bi

Blachford ˈblæʃ.fəd (US) -fɚd
black (B) blæk **-s** -s **-er** -əʳ (US) -ɚ **-est** -ɪst, -əst **-ish** -ɪʃ **-ly** -li **-ness** -nəs, -nɪs **-ing** -ɪŋ **-ed** -t ˌ**black ˈbelt**; ˌ**black ˈbox**; ˌ**black ˈeye**; ˌ**Black ˈForest**; ˌ**Black Forest ˈgateau**; ˌ**black ˈhole**; ˌ**black ˌhole of Calˈcutta**; ˌ**black ˈice**; ˌ**black ˈmagic**; ˌ**black ˈmarket**; ˌ**black ˈpepper**; ˌ**black ˈpudding**; ˌ**Black ˈRod**; ˌ**black ˈtreacle**; ˌ**black and ˈblue**; ˌ**black and ˈtan**; ˌ**black and ˈwhite**; ˌ**black ˌsheep of the ˈfamily**
Blackadder ˈblækˌæd.əʳ, ˌ-ˈ-- (US) ˈblækˌæd.ɚ
blackamoor ˈblæk.ə.mɔːʳ (US) -mʊr **-s** -z
blackball (*v.*) ˈblæk.bɔːl (US) -bɔːl, -bɑːl **-s** -z **-ing** -ɪŋ **-ed** -d
blackbeetle ˌblækˈbiː.tl̩ (US) ˈblækˌbiː.t̬l̩ **-s** -z
blackberr|y ˈblæk.bᵊr|.i, -ˌber- (US) -ˌber- **-ies** -iz
blackberrying ˈblæk.bᵊr.i.ɪŋ, -ˌber- (US) -ˌber-
blackbird ˈblæk.bɜːd (US) -bɝːd **-s** -z
blackboard ˈblæk.bɔːd (US) -bɔːrd **-s** -z
black box ˌblækˈbɒks (US) -ˈbɑːks **-es** -ɪz
blackboy ˈblæk.bɔɪ **-s** -z
Blackburn(e) ˈblæk.bɜːn (US) -bɝːn
blackcap ˈblæk.kæp **-s** -s
blackcock ˈblæk.kɒk (US) -kɑːk **-s** -s
blackcurrant ˌblækˈkʌr.ᵊnt (US) ˈblækˌkɝː- **-s** -s *stress shift, British only:* ˌblackcurrant ˈpie
Blackdown ˈblæk.daʊn
blacken ˈblæk.ᵊn **-s** -z **-ing** -ɪŋ **-ed** -d
Blackett ˈblæk.ɪt
black-eyed ˌblækˈaɪd *stress shift:* ˌblack-eyed ˈpeas
black|fly ˈblæk|.flaɪ **-flies** -flaɪz
Black|foot ˈblæk|.fʊt **-feet** -fiːt
Blackford ˈblæk.fəd (US) -fɚd
Blackfriars ˌblækˈfraɪəz (US) -ˈfraɪɚz *stress shift:* ˌBlackfriars ˈBobby
blackgame ˈblæk.geɪm **-s** -z
blackguard ˈblæg.ɑːd, ˈ-əd (US) -ɑːrd, -ɚd **-s** -z **-ly** -li
blackhead ˈblæk.hed **-s** -z
Blackheath ˌblækˈhiːθ *stress shift:* ˌBlackheath ˈHarriers
Blackie ˈblæk.i, ˈbleɪ.ki (US) ˈblæk.i
blacking (*n.*) ˈblæk.ɪŋ **-s** -z
blackjack ˈblæk.dʒæk **-s** -s
blacklead (*n.*) ˈblæk.led
blacklead (*v.*) ˌblækˈled, ˈ-- **-s** -z **-ing** -ɪŋ **-ed** -ɪd
blackleg ˈblæk.leg **-s** -z
Blackley *Manchester:* ˈbleɪ.kli *surname:* ˈblæk.li
blacklist ˈblæk.lɪst **-s** -s **-ing** -ɪŋ **-ed** -ɪd
blackmail ˈblæk.meɪl **-s** -z **-ing** -ɪŋ **-ed** -d **-er/s** -əʳ/z (US) -ɚ/z
Blackman ˈblæk.mən
Black Maria ˌblæk.məˈraɪə
Blackmoor, Blackmore ˈblæk.mɔːʳ (US) -mɔːr
blackout ˈblæk.aʊt **-s** -s
Blackpool ˈblæk.puːl
Blackpudlian ˌblækˈpʌd.li.ən **-s** -z
Blackrock ˈblæk.rɒk (US) -rɑːk
Blackshirt ˈblæk.ʃɜːt (US) -ʃɝːt **-s** -s
blacksmith ˈblæk.smɪθ **-s** -s
Blackston ˈblæk.stᵊn
Blackstone ˈblæk.stəʊn, -stᵊn (US) -stoʊn, -stᵊn
blackthorn (B) ˈblæk.θɔːn (US) -θɔːrn **-s** -z
blacktop ˈblæk.tɒp (US) -tɑːp **-s** -s **-ping** -ɪŋ **-ped** -t
Blackwall ˈblæk.wɔːl (US) -wɔːl, -wɑːl
blackwater (B) ˈblækˌwɔː.təʳ (US) -ˌwɑː.t̬ɚ, -ˌwɔː-
Blackwell ˈblæk.wel, -wᵊl
Blackwood *surname:* ˈblæk.wʊd *place in Gwent:* ˌblækˈwʊd
bladder ˈblæd.əʳ (US) -ɚ **-s** -z
bladderwort ˈblæd.ə.wɜːt (US) -ɚ.wɝːt, -wɔːrt **-s** -s
bladderwrack ˈblæd.ᵊr.æk
blade bleɪd **-s** -z
Bladon ˈbleɪ.dᵊn
blaeberr|y ˈbleɪ.bᵊr|.i (US) -ber- **-ies** -iz
Blaenau Ffestiniog ˌblaɪ.naɪ.fesˈtɪn.i.ɒg, ˌbleɪ.ni- (US) -ɑːg
Blaenau Gwent ˌblaɪ.naɪˈgwent, ˌbleɪ.ni-
Blaenavon blaɪˈnæv.ᵊn
blah-blah ˈblɑː.blɑː, ˌ-ˈ-
Blaikie ˈbleɪ.ki
Blaikley ˈbleɪ.kli
blain bleɪn **-s** -z
Blair bleəʳ (US) bler **-ite/s** -aɪt/s **-ism** -ɪ.zᵊm
Blair Atholl ˌbleəʳˈæθ.ᵊl (US) ˌbler-
Blairgowrie ˌbleəˈgaʊə.ri (US) ˌbler-
Blaise bleɪz
Blake bleɪk
Blakelock ˈbleɪ.klɒk (US) -klɑːk
Blakely ˈbleɪ.kli
Blakeney ˈbleɪk.ni
Blakey ˈbleɪ.ki
Blakiston ˈblæk.ɪ.stᵊn, ˈbleɪ.kɪ-
blamab|le ˈbleɪ.mə.b|l̩ **-ly** -li **-leness** -l̩.nəs, -nɪs
blam|e bleɪm **-es** -z **-ing** -ɪŋ **-ed** -d
blameless ˈbleɪm.ləs, -lɪs **-ly** -li **-ness** -nəs, -nɪs
blameworth|y ˈbleɪmˌwɜː.ð|i (US) -ˌwɝː- **-iness** -ɪ.nəs, -ɪ.nɪs
Blamires bləˈmaɪəz (US) -ˈmaɪɚz
Blanc *Mont:* blɑ̃ːŋ (US) blɑ̃ːŋ, blɑːŋk
blanch blɑːntʃ (US) blæntʃ **-es** -ɪz **-ing** -ɪŋ **-ed** -t
Blanchard ˈblæn.tʃəd, -tʃɑːd (US) ˈblænt.ʃɚd, -ʃɑːrd
Blanche blɑːntʃ (US) blæntʃ
Blanchett ˈblɑːn.tʃɪt (US) ˈblæn-
Blanchflower ˈblɑːntʃ.flaʊəʳ (US) ˈblæntʃ.flaʊɚ
blancmang|e bləˈmɒndʒ, -ˈmɒ̃nʒ (US) -ˈmɑːndʒ **-es** -ɪz
blanco ˈblæŋ.kəʊ (US) -koʊ
bland (B) blænd **-er** -əʳ (US) -ɚ **-est** -ɪst, -əst **-ly** -li **-ness** -nəs, -nɪs
Blandford ˈblænd.fəd (US) -fɚd
blandish ˈblæn.dɪʃ **-es** -ɪz **-ing** -ɪŋ **-ed** -t
blandishment ˈblæn.dɪʃ.mᵊnt
Blandy ˈblæn.di
Blaney ˈbleɪ.ni
blank (*n. adj. v.*) blæŋk **-s** -s **-er** -əʳ (US) -ɚ **-est** -ɪst, -əst **-ly** -li **-ness** -nəs, -nɪs **-ing** -ɪŋ **-ed** -t ˌ**blank ˈcheque/check**; ˌ**blank ˈverse**
blan|ket ˈblæŋ|.kɪt **-kets** -kɪts **-keting** -kɪ.tɪŋ (US) -kɪ.t̬ɪŋ **-keted** -kɪ.tɪd (US) -kɪ.t̬ɪd
Blankley ˈblæŋ.kli
blanquette ˌblɒŋˈket, ˌblæŋ-, ˌblɑ̃ːŋ- (US) ˌblɑːŋ- **-s** -s
Blantyre blænˈtaɪəʳ, ˈ-- (US) blænˈtaɪɚ
Note: In Malawi the preferred stress pattern is /ˈ--/.
blar|e bleəʳ (US) bler **-es** -z **-ing** -ɪŋ **-ed** -d
blarney (B) ˈblɑː.ni (US) ˈblɑːr-
blasé ˈblɑː.zeɪ, blɑːˈzeɪ (US) -ˈ-
blasphem|e ˌblæsˈfiːm, ˌblɑːs- (US) ˈblæs.fiːm **-es** -z **-ing/ly** -ɪŋ/li **-ed** -d **-er/s** -əʳ/z (US) -ɚ/z
blasphemous ˈblæs.fə.məs, ˈblɑːs-, -fɪ- (US) ˈblæs- **-ly** -li
blasphem|y ˈblæs.fə.m|i, ˈblɑːs-, -fɪ- (US) ˈblæs- **-ies** -iz
blast blɑːst (US) blæst **-s** -s **-ing** -ɪŋ **-ed** -ɪd ˈ**blast ˌfurnace**
blastoderm ˈblæs.təʊ.dɜːm (US) -tə.dɝːm **-s** -z
blast-off ˈblɑːst.ɒf (US) ˈblæst.ɑːf **-s** -s
blatancy ˈbleɪ.tᵊnt.si
blatant ˈbleɪ.tᵊnt **-ly** -li
Blatchford ˈblætʃ.fəd (US) -fɚd
blath|er ˈblæð|.əʳ (US) -ɚ **-ers** -əz (US) -ɚz **-ering** -ᵊr.ɪŋ **-ered** -əd (US) -ɚd
Blawith *in Cumbria:* ˈblɑːð *road in Harrow:* ˈbleɪ.wɪθ
blaxploitation ˌblæk.splɔɪˈteɪ.ʃᵊn
Blaydes bleɪdz
Blaydon ˈbleɪ.dᵊn
blaz|e bleɪz **-es** -ɪz **-ing** -ɪŋ **-ed** -d
blazer ˈbleɪ.zəʳ (US) -zɚ **-s** -z
Blazes ˈbleɪ.zɪz
Blazey ˈbleɪ.zi
blazon ˈbleɪ.zᵊn *in original heraldic sense also:* ˈblæz.ᵊn **-s** -z **-ing** -ɪŋ **-ed** -d
bleach bliːtʃ **-es** -ɪz **-ing** -ɪŋ **-ed** -t ˈ**bleaching ˌpowder**
bleachers ˈbliː.tʃəz (US) -tʃɚz

bleak bliːk **-er** -əʳ (US) -ɚ **-est** -ɪst, -əst **-ly** -li **-ness** -nəs, -nɪs
Bleakley ˈbliː.kli
blear blɪəʳ (US) blɪr
blear|y ˈblɪə.r|i (US) ˈblɪr|.i **-ier** -i.əʳ (US) -i.ɚ **-iest** -i.ɪst (US) -i.əst **-ily** -ᵊl.i, -ɪ.li **-iness** -ɪ.nəs, -ɪ.nɪs
bleary-eyed ˌblɪə.riˈaɪd (US) ˈblɪr.i.aɪd- *stress shift, British only:* ˌbleary-eyed ˈchild
Bleasdale ˈbliːz.deɪl
Bleasedale ˈbliːz.deɪl
bleat bliːt **-s** -s **-ing** -ɪŋ (US) ˈbliː.t̬ɪŋ **-ed** -ɪd (US) ˈbliː.t̬ɪd
bleb bleb **-s** -z
bled *(from* **bleed***)* bled
Bledisloe ˈbled.ɪ.sləʊ (US) -sloʊ
bleed bliːd **-s** -z **-ing** -ɪŋ **-er/s** -əʳ/z (US) -ɚ/z **bled** bled
bleep bliːp **-s** -s **-ing** -ɪŋ **-ed** -t
bleeper ˈbliː.pəʳ (US) -pɚ **-s** -z
blemish ˈblem.ɪʃ **-es** -ɪz **-ing** -ɪŋ **-ed** -t
blench (B) blen*t*ʃ **-es** -ɪz **-ing** -ɪŋ **-ed** -t
Blencowe ˈbleŋ.kəʊ (US) -koʊ
blend blend **-s** -z **-ing** -ɪŋ **-ed** -ɪd
blende blend
blender ˈblen.dəʳ (US) -dɚ **-s** -z
Blenheim ˈblen.ɪm, -əm
Blenkinsop ˈbleŋ.kɪn.sɒp (US) -sɑːp
Blennerhassett ˌblen.əˈhæs.ɪt (US) ˈblen.ɚ.hæs-
Blériot ˈbler.i.əʊ (US) ˌbler.iˈoʊ, ˈ--- **-s** -z
bless bles **-es** -ɪz **-ing** -ɪŋ **-ed** -t **blest** blest
blessed *(adj.)* ˈbles.ɪd, -əd **-ly** -li **-ness** -nəs, -nɪs
blessing ˈbles.ɪŋ **-s** -z **a ˌblessing in disˈguise**
Blessington ˈbles.ɪŋ.tən
blest *(from* **bless***)* blest
Bletchley ˈbletʃ.li
bleth|er ˈbleð|.əʳ (US) -ɚ **-ers** -əz (US) -ɚz **-ering** -ᵊr.ɪŋ **-ered** -əd (US) -ɚd
blew *(from* **blow***)* bluː
Blewett, Blewitt bluː.ɪt
Blickling ˈblɪk.lɪŋ
Bligh blaɪ
blight blaɪt **-s** -s **-ing** -ɪŋ (US) ˈblaɪ.t̬ɪŋ **-ed** -ɪd (US) ˈblaɪ.t̬ɪd
blighter ˈblaɪ.təʳ (US) -t̬ɚ **-s** -z
Blighty ˈblaɪ.ti (US) -t̬i
blimey ˈblaɪ.mi
blimp blɪmp **-s** -s **-ish** -ɪʃ
blind blaɪnd **-er** -əʳ (US) -ɚ **-est** -ɪst, -est **-ly** -li **-ness** -nəs, -nɪs **-s** -z **-ing** -ɪŋ **-ed** -ɪd **ˌblind ˈdate; ˈblind ˌside; ˈblind ˌspot; as ˌblind as a ˈbat; (a ˌcase of) the ˌblind ˌleading the ˈblind; ˌturn a ˌblind ˈeye (to)**
blinder ˈblaɪn.dəʳ (US) -dɚ **-s** -z
blindfold ˈblaɪn*d*.fəʊld (US) -foʊld **-s** -z **-ing** -ɪŋ **-ed** -ɪd
blinding ˈblaɪn.dɪŋ **-ly** -li
blindman's-buff ˌblaɪn*d*.mænzˈbʌf
blindsid|e ˈblaɪn*d*.saɪd **-s** -z **-ing** -ɪŋ **-ed** -ɪd
blindworm ˈblaɪnd.wɜːm (US) -wɝːm **-s** -z
blini ˈblɪn.i, ˈbliː.ni **-s** -z
blink blɪŋk **-s** -s **-ing** -ɪŋ **-ed** -t
blinker ˈblɪŋ.kəʳ (US) -kɚ **-s** -z **-ed** -d
blip blɪp **-s** -s **-ping** -ɪŋ **-ped** -t
bliss (B) blɪs
Blissett ˈblɪs.ɪt
blissful ˈblɪs.fᵊl, -fʊl **-ly** -i **-ness** -nəs, -nɪs
blist|er ˈblɪs.t|əʳ (US) -t|ɚ **-ers** -əz (US) -ɚz **-ering** -ᵊr.ɪŋ **-ered** -əd (US) -ɚd
blith|e blaɪð **-er** -əʳ (US) -ɚ **-est** -ɪst, -əst **-ely** -li **-eness** -nəs, -nɪs
Blithedale ˈblaɪð.deɪl
blithering ˈblɪð.ᵊr.ɪŋ
blithesome ˈblaɪð.səm **-ly** -li **-ness** -nəs, -nɪs
BLit(t) ˌbiːˈlɪt
blitz blɪts **-es** -ɪz **-ing** -ɪŋ **-ed** -t
blitzkrieg ˈblɪts.kriːg **-s** -z
Blixen ˈblɪk.sᵊn
blizzard ˈblɪz.əd (US) -ɚd **-s** -z
bloat bləʊt (US) bloʊt **-s** -s **-ing** -ɪŋ (US) ˈbloʊ.t̬ɪŋ **-ed/ness** -ɪd/nəs, -nɪs (US) ˈbloʊ.t̬ɪd/nəs, -nɪs
bloater ˈbləʊ.təʳ (US) ˈbloʊ.t̬ɚ **-s** -z
blob blɒb (US) blɑːb **-s** -z
blobb|y ˈblɒb|.i (US) ˈblɑː.b|i **-ier** -i.əʳ (US) -i.ɚ **-iest** -i.ɪst, -ɪ.əst
bloc blɒk (US) blɑːk **-s** -s
Bloch blɒk *as if German:* blox (US) blɑːk
block (B) blɒk (US) blɑːk **-s** -s **-ing** -ɪŋ **-ed** -t **-er/s** -əʳ/z (US) -ɚ/z **ˌblock ˈcapitals; ˌblock ˈbooking**
blockad|e blɒkˈeɪd, bləˈkeɪd (US) blɑːˈkeɪd **-es** -z **-ing** -ɪŋ **-ed** -ɪd **-er/s** -əʳ/z (US) -ɚ/z
blockag|e ˈblɒk.ɪdʒ (US) ˈblɑː.kɪdʒ **-es** -ɪz
blockbust|er ˈblɒkˌbʌs.t|əʳ (US) ˈblɑːkˌbʌs.t|ɚ **-ers** -əz (US) -ɚz **-ering** -ᵊr.ɪŋ
blockhead ˈblɒk.hed (US) ˈblɑːk- **-s** -z
blockhou|se ˈblɒk.haʊ|s (US) ˈblɑːk- **-ses** -zɪz
Blodwen ˈblɒd.wɪn, -wen (US) ˈblɑːd-
Bloemfontein ˈbluːm.fən.teɪn, -fɒn- (US) -fɑːn-
Blofeld ˈbləʊ.felt, -feld (US) ˈbloʊ-
Blois *town in France:* blwɑː *surname:* blɔɪs
bloke bləʊk (US) bloʊk **-s** -s **-ish/ly** -ɪʃ/li
Blom blɒm (US) blɑːm
Blomefield ˈbluːm.fiːld
Blomfield ˈblɒm.fiːld, ˈblʊm-, ˈblʌm-, ˈbluːm- (US) ˈblɑːm-, ˈblʊm-, ˈblʌm-, ˈbluːm-
blond(e) blɒnd (US) blɑːnd **-s** -z
Blondel(l) ˈblʌn.dᵊl, ˈblɒn-; blɒnˈdel (US) blɑːnˈdel; ˈblɑːn.dᵊl, ˈblʌn-
Blondin ˈblɒn.dɪn *as if French:* blɔ̃ː*n*ˈdæ̃*ŋ* (US) blɑːnˈdæn
blood blʌd **-s** -z **-ing** -ɪŋ **-ed** -ɪd **ˈblood ˌcell; ˈblood ˌdonor; ˈblood ˌgroup; ˈblood ˌmoney; ˈblood ˌpoisoning; ˈblood ˌpressure; ˌblood reˈlation; ˈblood ˌsport; ˈblood ˌtest; ˈblood transˌfusion; ˈblood ˌvessel; ˌblood is thicker than ˈwater; get ˌblood out of a ˈstone; in ˌcold ˈblood**
bloodba|th ˈblʌd.bɑː|θ (US) -bæ|θ **-ths** -ðz
bloodcurdling ˈblʌdˌkɜː.dl̩.ɪŋ, -ˌkɜːd.lɪŋ (US) -ˌkɝː.dl̩.ɪŋ, -ˌkɝːd.lɪŋ **-ly** -li
bloodhound ˈblʌd.haʊnd **-s** -z
bloodied ˈblʌd.id
bloodless ˈblʌd.ləs, -lɪs **-ly** -li **-ness** -nəs, -nɪs
bloodletting ˈblʌdˌlet.ɪŋ (US) -ˌlet̬.ɪŋ
bloodline ˈblʌd.laɪn
blood-red ˌblʌdˈred *stress shift:* ˌblood-red ˈlips
bloodshed ˈblʌd.ʃed
bloodshot ˈblʌd.ʃɒt (US) -ʃɑːt
bloodstain ˈblʌd.steɪn **-s** -z **-ed** -d
bloodstock ˈblʌd.stɒk (US) -stɑːk
bloodstone ˈblʌd.stəʊn (US) -stoʊn **-s** -z
bloodstream ˈblʌd.striːm **-s** -z
bloodsucker ˈblʌdˌsʌk.əʳ (US) -ɚ **-s** -z
bloodthirst|y ˈblʌdˌθɜː.st|i (US) -ˌθɝː- **-ier** -i.əʳ (US) -i.ɚ **-iest** -i.ɪst, -i.əst **-ily** -ɪ.li, -ᵊl.i **-iness** -ɪ.nəs, -ɪ.nɪs
blood|y ˈblʌd|.i **-ier** -i.əʳ (US) -i.ɚ **-iest** -i.ɪst, -i.əst **-ily** -ɪ.li, -ᵊl.i **-iness** -ɪ.nəs, -ɪ.nɪs **ˌBloody ˈMary**
bloody-minded ˌblʌd.iˈmaɪn.dɪd *stress shift:* ˌbloody-minded ˈperson
bloom (B) bluːm **-s** -z **-ing** -ɪŋ **-ed** -d
bloomer (B) ˈbluː.məʳ (US) -mɚ **-s** -z
Bloomfield ˈbluːm.fiːld
Bloomingdale ˈbluː.mɪŋ.deɪl **-'s** -z
Bloomington ˈbluː.mɪŋ.tən
Bloomsbury ˈbluːmz.bᵊr.i (US) -ber-, -bɚ-
bloop bluːp **-s** -s **-ing** -ɪŋ **-ed** -t
blooper ˈbluː.pəʳ (US) -pɚ **-s** -z
Blore blɔːʳ (US) blɔːr
blossom (B) ˈblɒs.ᵊm (US) ˈblɑː.sᵊm **-s** -z **-ing** -ɪŋ **-ed** -d
blot blɒt (US) blɑːt **-s** -s **-ting** -ɪŋ (US) ˈblɑː.t̬ɪŋ **-ted** -ɪd (US) ˈblɑː.t̬ɪd
blotch blɒtʃ (US) blɑːtʃ **-es** -ɪz **-ing** -ɪŋ **-ed** -t
blotch|y ˈblɒtʃ|.i (US) ˈblɑː.tʃ|i **-ier** -i.əʳ (US) -i.ɚ **-iest** -i.ɪst, -i.əst **-ily** -ɪ.li, -ᵊl.i **-iness** -ɪ.nəs, -ɪ.nɪs
blotter ˈblɒt.əʳ (US) ˈblɑː.t̬ɚ **-s** -z
blotting ˈblɒt.ɪŋ (US) ˈblɑːt̬.ɪŋ **ˈblotting ˌpaper**

blotto ˈblɒt.əʊ (US) ˈblɑː.t̬oʊ
Blount blʌnt, blaʊnt
blous|e blaʊz (US) blaʊs **-es** -ɪz
blouson ˈbluː.zɒn (US) -sɑːn, ˈblaʊ-, -zɑːn **-s** -z
blow (B) bləʊ (US) bloʊ **-s** -z **-ing** -ɪŋ **blew** bluː **blown** bləʊn (US) bloʊn **blowed** bləʊd (US) bloʊd **blower/s** ˈbləʊ.əʳ/z (US) ˈbloʊ.ɚ/s
blow-by-blow ˌbləʊ.baɪˈbləʊ (US) ˌbloʊ.baɪˈbloʊ *stress shift:* ˌblow-by-blow acˈcount
blow|dry ˈbləʊ|.draɪ (US) ˈbloʊ- **-dries** -draɪz **-drying** -ˌdraɪ.ɪŋ **-dried** -draɪd **-drier/s** -ˌdraɪ.əʳ/z (US) -ˌdraɪ.ɚ/z
blowfl|y ˈbləʊ.fl|aɪ (US) ˈbloʊ- **-ies** -aɪz
blowgun ˈbləʊ.gʌn (US) ˈbloʊ- **-s** -z
blowhard ˈbləʊ.hɑːd (US) ˈbloʊ.hɑːrd **-s** -z
blowhole ˈbləʊ.həʊl (US) ˈbloʊ.hoʊl **-s** -z
blowlamp ˈbləʊ.læmp (US) ˈbloʊ- **-s** -s
blown *(from* **blow**) bləʊn (US) bloʊn
blowout ˈbləʊ.aʊt (US) ˈbloʊ- **-s** -s
blowpipe ˈbləʊ.paɪp (US) ˈbloʊ- **-s** -s
blows|y ˈblaʊ.z|i **-ier** -i.əʳ (US) -i.ɚ **-iest** -i.ɪst, -i.əst **-ily** -ɪ.li, -əl.i **-iness** -ɪ.nəs, -ɪ.nɪs
blowtorch ˈbləʊ.tɔːtʃ (US) ˈbloʊ.tɔːrtʃ **-es** -ɪz
blow|y ˈbləʊ|.i (US) ˈbloʊ- **-ier** -i.əʳ (US) -i.ɚ **-iest** -i.ɪst, -i.əst **-ily** -ɪ.li, -əl.i **-iness** -ɪ.nəs, -ɪ.nɪs
blowz|y ˈblaʊ.z|i **-ier** -i.əʳ (US) -i.ɚ **-iest** -i.ɪst, -i.əst **-ily** -ɪ.li, -əl.i **-iness** -ɪ.nəs, -ɪ.nɪs
Blox(h)am ˈblɒk.səm (US) ˈblɑːk-
BLT ˌbiː.elˈtiː
blub blʌb **-s** -z **-bing** -ɪŋ **-bed** -d
blubb|er ˈblʌb|.əʳ (US) -ɚ **-ers** -əz (US) -ɚz **-ering** -ər.ɪŋ **-ered** -əd (US) -ɚd **-erer/s** -ər.əʳ/z
bludgeon ˈblʌdʒ.ən **-s** -z **-ing** -ɪŋ **-ed** -d
blu|e bluː **-es** -z **-er** -əʳ (US) -ɚ **-est** -ɪst, -əst **-(e)ing** -ɪŋ **-ed** -d ˌ**blue** ˈ**cheese**; ˈ**blue** ˌ**law**; ˌ**blue** ˈ**movie**; ˈ**blue** ˌ**jay**; ˈ**blue** ˌ**tit**; ˌ**out of the** ˈ**blue**
Bluebeard ˈbluː.bɪəd (US) -bɪrd
bluebell ˈbluː.bel **-s** -z
blueberr|y ˈbluː.bər|.i, -ˌber- (US) -ˌber- **-ies** -iz
bluebird ˈbluː.bɜːd (US) -bɝːd **-s** -z
blue-blooded ˌbluːˈblʌd.ɪd (US) ˈ-ˌ-- *stress shift, British only:* ˌblue-blooded ˈmonarch
bluebottle ˈbluːˌbɒt.l̩ (US) -ˌbɑː.t̬l̩ **-s** -z
blue-chip ˈbluː.tʃɪp
bluecoat ˈbluː.kəʊt (US) -koʊt **-s** -s
blue-collar ˌbluːˈkɒl.əʳ (US) ˈbluːˌkɑː.lɚ *stress shift, British only:* ˌblue-collar ˈworker
blue-eyed ˌbluːˈaɪd, ˈ-- *stress shift, British only: see compound:* ˌ**blue-eyed** ˈ**boy**
bluegrass ˈbluː.grɑːs (US) -græs
bluejacket ˈbluːˌdʒæk.ɪt **-s** -s
bluejay ˈbluː.dʒeɪ **-s** -z
bluejeans, blue jeans ˌbluːˈdʒiːnz (US) ˈ--
blueness ˈbluː.nəs, -nɪs
blue-pencil ˌbluːˈpent*.*səl, -sɪl (US) ˈ-ˌ-- **-s** -z **-(l)ing** -ɪŋ **-(l)ed** -d
blueprint ˈbluː.prɪnt **-s** -s
bluestocking ˈbluːˌstɒk.ɪŋ (US) -ˌstɑː.kɪŋ **-s** -z
bluesy ˈbluː.zi
Bluett ˈbluː.ɪt
bluey ˈbluː.i
bluff blʌf **-s** -s **-er** -əʳ (US) -ɚ **-est** -ɪst, -əst **-ly** -li **-ness** -nəs, -nɪs **-ing** -ɪŋ **-ed** -t
bluish ˈbluː.ɪʃ
Blum bluːm
Blume bluːm
Blundell ˈblʌn.dəl; blʌnˈdel
Blunden ˈblʌn.dən
blund|er ˈblʌn.d|əʳ (US) -d|ɚ **-ers** -əz (US) -ɚz **-ering** -ər.ɪŋ **-ered** -əd (US) -ɚd **-erer/s** -ər.əʳ/z (US) -ɚ.ɚ/z
blunderbuss ˈblʌn.də.bʌs (US) -dɚ- **-es** -ɪz
Blunkett ˈblʌŋ.kɪt
Blunn blʌn
blunt (B) blʌnt **-er** -əʳ (US) ˈblʌn.t̬ɚ **-est** -ɪst, -əst (US) ˈblʌn.t̬ɪst, -t̬əst **-ly** -li **-ness** -nəs, -nɪs **-s** -s **-ing** -ɪŋ (US) ˈblʌn.t̬ɪŋ **-ed** -ɪd (US) ˈblʌn.t̬ɪd ˌ**blunt** ˈ**instrument**
blur (B) blɜːʳ (US) blɝː **-s** -z **-ring** -ɪŋ **-red** -d
blurb blɜːb (US) blɝːb **-s** -z
blurt blɜːt (US) blɝːt **-s** -s **-ing** -ɪŋ (US) ˈblɝː.t̬ɪŋ **-ed** -ɪd (US) ˈblɝː.t̬ɪd
blush blʌʃ **-es** -ɪz **-ing/ly** -ɪŋ/li **-ed** -t
blusher ˈblʌʃ.əʳ (US) -ɚ **-s** -z
blust|er ˈblʌs.t|əʳ (US) -t|ɚ **-ers** -əz (US) -ɚz **-ering/ly** -ər.ɪŋ/li **-ered** -əd (US) -ɚd **-erer/s** -ər.əʳ/z (US) -ɚ.ɚ/z
bluster|y ˈblʌs.tər|.i **-iness** -ɪ.nəs, -ɪ.nɪs
Blu-Tack® ˈbluː.tæk
Bly blaɪ
Blyth blaɪð, blaɪθ, blaɪ
Blythborough ˈblaɪ.bər.ə (US) -oʊ
Blythe blaɪð
Blyton ˈblaɪ.tən
B-movie ˈbiːˌmuː.vi **-s** -z
BMus ˌbiːˈmʌz
BMW® ˌbiː.emˈdʌb.l̩.juː
BMX ˌbiː.emˈeks *stress shift, see compound:* ˌ**BMX** ˈ**bike**
bn *(abbrev. for* **billion**) ˈbɪl.i.ən, ˈ-jən (US) ˈ-jən
Bo bəʊ (US) boʊ
BO ˌbiːˈəʊ (US) -ˈoʊ
boa bəʊə (US) boʊə **-s** -z
Boadicea ˌbəʊ.dɪˈsiː.ə, -dəˈ- (US) ˌboʊ.ə-
Boag bəʊg; ˈbəʊ.æg, -əg (US) boʊg
Boal bəʊl (US) boʊl
Boanas ˈbəʊ.nəs (US) ˈboʊ-
Boanerges ˌbəʊəˈnɜː.dʒiːz (US) ˌboʊəˈnɝː-
boar bɔːʳ (US) bɔːr **-s** -z
board bɔːd (US) bɔːrd **-s** -z **-ing** -ɪŋ **-ed** -ɪd ˈ**board** ˌ**game**; ˈ**boarding** ˌ**house**; ˈ**boarding** ˌ**pass**; ˈ**boarding** ˌ**school**; ˌ**go by the** ˈ**board**
boarder ˈbɔː.dəʳ (US) ˈbɔːr.dɚ **-s** -z
boardroom ˈbɔːd.rʊm, -ruːm (US) ˈbɔːrd.ruːm, -rʊm **-s** -z
boardwalk ˈbɔːd.wɔːk (US) ˈbɔːrd.wɔːk, -wɑːk **-s** -s
boarish ˈbɔː.rɪʃ (US) ˈbɔːr.ɪʃ
Boas ˈbəʊ.æz, -əz, -æs, -əs (US) ˈboʊ-
Boase bəʊz (US) boʊz
boast bəʊst (US) boʊst **-s** -s **-ing/ly** -ɪŋ/li **-ed** -ɪd **-er/s** -əʳ/z (US) -ɚ/z
boastful ˈbəʊst.fəl, -fʊl (US) ˈboʊst- **-ly** -li **-ness** -nəs, -nɪs
boat bəʊt (US) boʊt **-s** -s **-er/s** -əʳ/z (US) ˈboʊ.t̬ɚ/z ˈ**boat** ˌ**race**; ˈ**boat** ˌ**train**; ˌ**burn one's** ˈ**boats**
Boateng ˈbwɑː.teŋ, ˈbəʊ- (US) ˈbwɑː-, ˈboʊ-
boathook ˈbəʊt.hʊk (US) ˈboʊt- **-s** -s
boathou|se ˈbəʊt.haʊ|s (US) ˈboʊt- **-ses** -zɪz
boating ˈbəʊ.tɪŋ (US) ˈboʊ.t̬ɪŋ
boatload ˈbəʊt.ləʊd (US) ˈboʊt.loʊd **-s** -z
boat|man ˈbəʊt|.mən (US) ˈboʊt- **-men** -mən, -men
boatswain ˈbəʊ.sən, ˈbəʊt.sweɪn (US) ˈboʊ.sən **-s** -z
boatyard ˈbəʊt.jɑːd (US) ˈboʊt.jɑːrd **-s** -z
Boaz ˈbəʊ.æz (US) ˈboʊ-
bob (B) bɒb (US) bɑːb **-s** -z **-bing** -ɪŋ **-bed** -d
Bobbie ˈbɒb.i (US) ˈbɑː.bi
bobbin ˈbɒb.ɪn (US) ˈbɑː.bɪn **-s** -z
bobbish ˈbɒb.ɪʃ (US) ˈbɑː.bɪʃ **-ly** -li **-ness** -nəs, -nɪs
bobbl|e ˈbɒb.l̩ (US) ˈbɑː.bl̩ **-es** -z **-ing** -ɪŋ **-ed** -d
bobb|y (B) ˈbɒb|.i (US) ˈbɑː.b|i **-ies** -iz ˈ**bobby** ˌ**pin**
bobbysox ˈbɒb.i.sɒks (US) ˈbɑː.bi.sɑːks **-er/s** -əʳ/z (US) -ɚ/z
bobcat ˈbɒb.kæt (US) ˈbɑːb- **-s** -s
Bobo Dioulasso ˌbəʊ.bəʊ.djuˈlæs.əʊ (US) ˌboʊ.boʊ.djuˈlæs.oʊ
bobolink ˈbɒb.ə.lɪŋk (US) ˈbɑː.bə- **-s** -s
bobsled ˈbɒb.sled (US) ˈbɑːb- **-s** -z **-ding** -ɪŋ **-ded** -ɪd
bobsleigh ˈbɒb.sleɪ (US) ˈbɑːb- **-s** -z
bobstay ˈbɒb.steɪ (US) ˈbɑːb- **-s** -z
bobtail ˈbɒb.teɪl (US) ˈbɑːb- **-s** -z
bobwig ˈbɒb.wɪg (US) ˈbɑːb- **-s** -z

Boca Raton ˌbəʊ.kə.rəˈtəʊn (US) ˌboʊ.kə.rəˈtoʊn
Boccaccio bɒkˈɑː.tʃi.əʊ, bəˈkɑː- (US) boʊˈkɑː-
Boccherini ˌbɒk.^{ə}rˈiː.ni (US) ˌbɑː.kəˈriː-, ˌboʊ-
Boche(s) bɒʃ (US) bɑːʃ, bɔːʃ
Bochum ˈbəʊ.k^{ə}m (US) ˈboʊ-
bod bɒd (US) bɑːd **-s** -z
bodacious bəʊˈdeɪ.ʃəs (US) boʊ- **-ly** -li
Boddington ˈbɒd.ɪŋ.tən (US) ˈbɑː.dɪŋ-
Boddy ˈbɒd.i (US) ˈbɑː.di
bod|e (B) bəʊd (US) boʊd **-es** -z **-ing** -ɪŋ **-ed** -ɪd
bodega (B) bəˈdeɪ.gə, bɒdˈeɪ- (US) boʊˈdeɪ- **-s** -z
Boden ˈbəʊ.d^{ə}n (US) ˈboʊ-
Bodey ˈbəʊ.di (US) ˈboʊ-
bodg|e bɒdʒ (US) bɑːdʒ **-es** -ɪz **-ing** -ɪŋ **-ed** -d
bodger ˈbɒdʒ.ə^r (US) ˈbɑː.dʒɚ **-s** -z
Bodiam ˈbəʊ.di.əm (US) ˈboʊ-
bodic|e ˈbɒd.ɪs (US) ˈbɑː.dɪs **-es** -ɪz
Bodie ˈbəʊ.di (US) ˈboʊ-
-bodied -ˈbɒd.id (US) -ˈbɑː.did
Note: Suffix. Always carries primary stress unless used attributively, e.g. **full-bodied** /ˌfʊlˈbɒd.id (US) -ˈbɑː.did/, **ˈfull-bodied ˌwine**.
bodily ˈbɒd.ɪ.li, -^{ə}l.i (US) ˈbɑː.d^{ə}l.i **ˌbodily ˈfunction**
bodkin (B) ˈbɒd.kɪn (US) ˈbɑːd- **-s** -z
Bodleian ˈbɒd.li.ən, bɒdˈliː- (US) ˈbɑːd.li.ən, bɑːdˈliː-
Bodley ˈbɒd.li (US) ˈbɑːd-
Bodmin ˈbɒd.mɪn (US) ˈbɑːd-
Bodnant ˈbɒd.nænt (US) ˈbɑːd-
bod|y ˈbɒd|.i (US) ˈbɑː.d|i **-ies** -iz **ˈbody ˌbag; ˈbody ˌbuilder; ˈbody ˌbuilding; ˈbody ˌlanguage; ˈbody ˌsnatcher; keep ˌbody and ˌsoul toˈgether; over ˌmy ˌdead ˈbody**
bodyguard ˈbɒd.i.gɑːd (US) ˈbɑː.di.gɑːrd **-s** -z
bodysuit ˈbɒd.i.suːt, -sjuːt (US) ˈbɑː.di.suːt **-s** -s
bodysurf ˈbɒd.i.sɜːf (US) ˈbɑː.di.sɝːf **-s** -s **-ing** -ɪŋ **-ed** -t **-er/s** -ə^r/z (US) -ɚ/z
bodywarmer ˈbɒd.iˌwɔː.mə^r (US) ˈbɑː.diˌwɔːr.mɚ **-s** -z
bodywork ˈbɒd.i.wɜːk (US) ˈbɑː.di.wɝːk
Boeing® ˈbəʊ.ɪŋ (US) ˈboʊ-
Boeoti|a biˈəʊ.ʃ|ə, -ʃi|.ə (US) -ˈoʊ.ʃ|ə **-an/s** -ən/z
Boer bəʊə^r, bɔː^r, bʊə^r (US) bɔːr, boʊɚ, bʊr **-s** -z
Boethius bəʊˈiː.θi.əs (US) boʊ-
boeuf bourguignon ˌbɜːfˌbʊə.giːˈnjɔ̃ːŋ, -ˌbɔː-, -gɪˈ- (US) ˌbɜːfˌbʊr.giːˈnjõʊn
boff bɒf (US) bɑːf **-s** -s **-ing** -ɪŋ **-ed** -t

boffin (B) ˈbɒf.ɪn (US) ˈbɑː.fɪn **-s** -z
Bofors ˈbəʊ.fəz (US) ˈboʊ.fɔːrz, -fɔːrs
bog bɒg (US) bɑːg, bɔːg **-s** -z **-ging** -ɪŋ **-ged** -d
Bogan ˈbəʊ.g^{ə}n (US) ˈboʊ-
Bogarde ˈbəʊ.gɑːd (US) ˈboʊ.gɑːrd
Bogart ˈbəʊ.gɑːt (US) ˈboʊ.gɑːrt
Bogdan ˈbɒg.dæn (US) ˈbɑːg-, ˈbɔːg-
Bogdanovich bɒgˈdæn.ə.vɪtʃ (US) bɑːgˈdɑːn-, bɔːg-
bogey ˈbəʊ.gi (US) ˈboʊ- **-s** -z
bogey|man ˈbəʊ.gi|.mæn (US) ˈboʊ- **-men** -men
boggl|e ˈbɒg.l̩ (US) ˈbɑː.gl̩ **-es** -z **-ing** -ɪŋ, ˈ-lɪŋ (US) ˈ-glɪŋ **-ed** -d **-er/s** -ə^r/z, ˈ-lə^r/z (US) ˈbɑː.gl̩.ɚ/z, ˈbɑːg.lɚ/z
bogg|y ˈbɒg|.i (US) ˈbɑː.g|i **-ier** -i.ə^r (US) -i.ɚ **-iest** -i.ɪst, -i.əst **-iness** -ɪ.nəs, -ɪ.nɪs
bogie ˈbəʊ.gi (US) ˈboʊ- **-s** -z **ˈbogie ˌengine; ˈbogie ˌwheel**
Bognor ˈbɒg.nə^r (US) ˈbɑːg.nɚ, ˈbɔːg- **ˌBognor ˈRegis**
bog-oak ˌbɒgˈəʊk (US) ˈbɑːg.oʊk, ˈbɔːg-
Bogota *in Columbia:* ˌbɒg.əʊˈtɑː, ˌbəʊ.gə- (US) ˌboʊ.gəˈtɑː, ˈ--- *in New Jersey:* bəˈgəʊ.tə (US) -ˈgoʊ.t̬ə
bogstandard ˌbɒgˈstæn.dəd (US) ˈbɑːgˌstæn.dɚd, ˈbɔːg-
bogus ˈbəʊ.gəs (US) ˈboʊ-
bog|y ˈbəʊ.g|i (US) ˈboʊ- **-ies** -iz
bohea bəʊˈhiː (US) boʊ-
Bohème bəʊˈem, -ˈeɪm (US) boʊ-
Bohemia bəʊˈhiː.mi.ə (US) boʊ-
bohemian (B) bəʊˈhiː.mi.ən (US) boʊ- **-s** -z
Böhm bɜːm
Bohn bəʊn (US) boʊn
Bohr bɔː^r (US) bɔːr
Bohun ˈbəʊ.ən, buːn (US) ˈboʊ-, buːn
Note: /buːn/ in Shaw's 'You never can tell'.
boil bɔɪl **-s** -z **-ing** -ɪŋ **-ed** -d **ˈboiling ˌpoint**
boiler ˈbɔɪ.lə^r (US) -lɚ **-s** -z **ˈboiler ˌsuit**
boilermaker ˈbɔɪ.ləˌmeɪ.kə^r (US) -lɚˌmeɪ.kɚ **-s** -z
boilerplate ˈbɔɪ.lə.pleɪt (US) -lɚ- **-s** -s
boil-in-the-bag ˌbɔɪl.ɪn.ðəˈbæg *stress shift:* ˌboil-in-the-bag ˈmeal
boing bɔɪŋ
Boipatong ˌbɔɪ.pəˈtɒŋ, -pætˈɒŋ (US) ˈbɔɪ.pə.tɑːŋ, -tɔːŋ
Bois bɔɪs, bwɑː
Boise ˈbɔɪ.zi, ˈbɔɪ.si
boisterous ˈbɔɪ.st^{ə}r.əs **-ly** -li **-ness** -nəs, -nɪs
Boker ˈbəʊ.kə^r (US) ˈboʊ.kɚ
Bokhara bəʊˈkɑː.rə (US) boʊˈkɑːr.ə
Bolan ˈbəʊ.lən (US) ˈboʊ-
bolas ˈbəʊ.ləs, -læs (US) ˈboʊ- **-es** -ɪz

bold bəʊld (US) boʊld **-er** -ə^r (US) -ɚ **-est** -ɪst, -əst **-ly** -li **-ness** -nəs, -nɪs
bold-face ˌbəʊldˈfeɪs (US) ˈboʊld.feɪs, ˈboʊl- **-d** -t *stress shift, British only:* ˌbold-face ˈtype
Boldon ˈbəʊl.d^{ə}n (US) ˈboʊl-
Boldre ˈbəʊl.də^r (US) ˈboʊl.dɚ
bole bəʊl (US) boʊl **-s** -z
bolero *dance:* bəˈleə.rəʊ, bɒlˈeə-, -ˈlɪə- (US) bəˈler.oʊ, boʊ- **-s** -z *garment:* ˈbɒl.ə.rəʊ (US) bəˈler.oʊ **-s** -z
bolet|us bəʊˈliː.t|əs (US) boʊˈliː.t̬|əs **-uses** -ə.sɪz **-i** -aɪ
Boleyn bəˈlɪn; bʊ-; bəʊ-; -ˈliːn; (US) ˈbʊ.lɪn, bʊˈlɪn
Bolingbroke ˈbɒl.ɪŋ.brʊk (US) ˈbɑː.lɪŋ-, ˈboʊ-
Bolinger ˈbɒl.ɪn.dʒə^r, ˈbəʊ.lɪn- (US) ˈbɑː.lən.dʒɚ
Bolitho bəˈlaɪ.θəʊ, bɒlˈaɪ- (US) bəˈlaɪ.θoʊ
Bolivar *S. American general:* ˈbɒl.ɪ.vɑː^r; bɒlˈiː- (US) ˈbɑː.lə.vɚ *places in US:* ˈbɒl.ɪ.və^r, ˈ-ə-, -vɑː^r (US) ˈbɑː.lə.vɚ
bolivar *money:* bɒlˈiː.vɑː^r; ˈbɒl.ɪ.və^r (US) boʊˈliː.vɑːr; ˈbɑː.lə.vɚ **-s** -z
bolivares *(alternative plur. of* **bolivar***)* ˌbɒl.ɪˈvɑː.reɪz (US) boʊˌliː.vɑːˈreɪs; ˌboʊ.lɪˈvɑːr.es
Bolivi|a bəˈlɪv.i|.ə, bɒlˈɪv- (US) bəˈlɪv-, boʊ- **-an/s** -ən/z
bolivia|no bəʊˌlɪv.iˈɑː|.nəʊ, bɒlˌɪv-; ˌbəʊ.lɪ.viˈ-, ˌbɒl.ɪv- (US) bəˌlɪv.iˈɑː.noʊ, boʊ- **-nos** -nɒs (US) -noʊs
boll bəʊl, bɒl (US) boʊl **-s** -z **-ed** -d **ˌboll ˈweevil** (US) **ˈboll ˌweevil**
Böll bɜːl (US) bɜːl, boʊl
bollard ˈbɒl.ɑːd, -əd (US) ˈbɑː.lɚd **-s** -z
Bolling ˈbəʊ.lɪŋ (US) ˈboʊ-
Bollinger ˈbɒl.ɪn.dʒə^r (US) ˈbɑː.lən.dʒɚ
Bollington ˈbɒl.ɪŋ.tən (US) ˈbɑː.lɪŋ-
bollix ˈbɒl.ɪks (US) ˈbɑː.lɪks **-es** -ɪz **-ing** -ɪŋ **-ed** -t
bollocking ˈbɒl.ə.kɪŋ (US) ˈbɑː.lə-
bollocks ˈbɒl.əks (US) ˈbɑː.ləks
Bollywood ˈbɒl.i.wʊd (US) ˈbɑː.li-
bolo ˈbəʊ.ləʊ (US) ˈboʊ.loʊ **-s** -z
Bologna bəˈlɒn.jə, bɒlˈɒn-, -ˈləʊ.njə, -ni.ə (US) bəˈloʊ.njə, -ˈlɑː-
bologna *sausage:* bəˈləʊ.ni (US) -ˈloʊ-
bolognaise ˌbɒl.əˈneɪz, -ˈnjeɪz (US) ˌboʊ.ləˈnjeɪz
Bolognese ˌbɒl.əˈneɪz *as if Italian:* -ˈnjeɪ.zeɪ (US) ˌboʊ.ləˈniːz, -ˈnjiːz
bolometer bəʊˈlɒm.ɪ.tə^r, ˈ-ə- (US) boʊˈlɑː.mə.t̬ɚ **-s** -z
boloney bəˈləʊ.ni (US) -ˈloʊ-
Bolshevik ˈbɒl.ʃə.vɪk, -ʃɪ- (US) ˈboʊl-, ˈbɑːl- **-s** -s

Bolshev|ist 'bɒl.ʃə.v|ɪst, -ʃɪ- (US) 'boʊl-, 'bɑːl- -ism -ɪ.zᵊm

bolshie 'bɒl.ʃi (US) 'boʊl-, 'bɑːl- -s -z

Bolshoi, Bolshoy bɒl'ʃɔɪ, '-- (US) 'boʊl.ʃɔɪ, 'bɑːl-; boʊl'ʃɔɪ

bolsh|y 'bɒl.ʃ|i (US) 'boʊl-, 'bɑːl- -ies -z -ier -i.əʳ (US) -i.ɚ -iest -i.ɪst, -i.əst

Bolsover *surname, street in London:* 'bɒl.səʊ.vəʳ (US) 'boʊl.soʊ.vɚ *in Derbyshire:* 'bəʊl.zəʊ.vəʳ; 'bəʊl.səʊ- (US) 'boʊl.zoʊ.vɚ

bolst|er 'bəʊl.st|əʳ (US) 'boʊl.st|ɚ -ers -əz (US) -ɚz -ering -ᵊr.ɪŋ -ered -əd (US) -ɚd

bolt (B) bəʊlt (US) boʊlt -s -s -ing -ɪŋ (US) 'boʊl.t̬ɪŋ -ed -ɪd (US) 'boʊl.t̬ɪd ˌbolt 'upright

bolter (B) 'bəʊl.təʳ (US) 'boʊl.t̬ɚ -s -z

Bolton 'bəʊl.tᵊn (US) 'boʊl-

Bolton-le-Sands ˌbəʊl.tən.lə'sændz, -lɪ'- (US) ˌboʊl.tᵊn-

bolus 'bəʊ.ləs (US) 'boʊ- -es -ɪz

Bolzano bɒlt'zɑː.nəʊ (US) boʊlt'sɑː.noʊ, boʊl'zɑː-

bomb bɒm (US) bɑːm -s -z -ing/s -ɪŋ/z -ed -d ˌbomb dis'posal ˌunit, 'bomb diˌsposal ˌunit

bombard (*n.*) 'bɒm.bɑːd (US) 'bɑːm.bɑːrd -s -z

bombard (*v.*) bɒm'bɑːd (US) bɑːm'bɑːrd -s -z -ing -ɪŋ -ed -ɪd -ment/s -mənt/s

bombardier ˌbɒm.bə'dɪəʳ (US) ˌbɑːm.bə'dɪr -s -z

bombardon 'bɒm.bə.dᵊn; bɒm'bɑː- (US) 'bɑːm.bɚ-; bɑːm'bɑːr- -s -z

bombasine 'bɒm.bə.ziːn, -siːn, ˌ--'- (US) ˌbɑːm.bə'ziːn

bombast 'bɒm.bæst (US) 'bɑːm-

bombastic bɒm'bæs.tɪk (US) bɑːm- -ally -ᵊl.i, -li

Bombay ˌbɒm'beɪ (US) ˌbɑːm- *stress shift, see compound:* ˌBombay 'duck

bombe bɒm, bɒmb (US) bɑːm -s -z

bomber 'bɒm.əʳ (US) 'bɑː.mɚ -s -z

bombshell 'bɒm.ʃel (US) 'bɑːm- -s -z

bombsite 'bɒm.saɪt (US) 'bɑːm- -s -s

Bompas 'bʌm.pəs

bon bɔ̃ːŋ (US) bɔ̃ːn

bona fid|e ˌbəʊ.nə'faɪ.d|i, -d|eɪ (US) ˌboʊ.nə'- -es -iːz, -eɪz

bonanza bə'næn.zə -s -z

Bonapart|e 'bəʊ.nə.pɑːt (US) 'boʊ.nə.pɑːrt -ist/s -ɪst/s

Bonar 'bɒn.əʳ, 'bəʊ.nəʳ (US) 'bɑː.nɚ, 'boʊ-

bonbon 'bɒn.bɒn, 'bɒm- (US) 'bɑːn.bɑːn -s -z

Bonchurch 'bɒn.tʃɜːtʃ (US) 'bɑːn.tʃɝːtʃ

bond (B) bɒnd (US) bɑːnd -s -z -ing -ɪŋ -ed -ɪd 'bond ˌholder

bondage 'bɒn.dɪdʒ (US) 'bɑːn-

Bondi *in Australia:* 'bɒn.daɪ (US) 'bɑːn- ˌBondi 'Beach

Bondi *mathematician:* 'bɒn.di (US) 'bɑːn-

bondmaid 'bɒnd.meɪd (US) 'bɑːnd- -s -z

bond|man 'bɒnd|.mən (US) 'bɑːnd- -men -mən, -men

bonds|man 'bɒndz|.mən (US) 'bɑːndz- -men -mən, -men

bonds|woman 'bɒndz|ˌwʊm.ən (US) 'bɑːndz- -women -ˌwɪm.ɪn

bond|woman 'bɒnd|ˌwʊm.ən (US) 'bɑːnd- -women -ˌwɪm.ɪn

bon|e (B) bəʊn (US) boʊn -es -z -ing -ɪŋ -ed -d -er/s -əʳ/z (US) -ɚ/z -eless -ləs, -lɪs 'bone ˌmeal; 'bone ˌmarrow; ˌchilled to the 'bone; have a 'bone to pick with ˌsomeone; ˌmake no 'bones about something

bone-dry ˌbəʊn'draɪ (US) ˌboʊ- *stress shift:* ˌbone-dry 'desert

bonehead 'bəʊn.hed (US) 'boʊn- -s -z

bonesetter 'bəʊnˌset.əʳ (US) 'boʊnˌset̬.ɚ -s -z

bone-shaker 'bəʊnˌʃeɪ.kəʳ (US) 'boʊnˌʃeɪ.kɚ -s -z

Bo'ness bəʊ'nes (US) boʊ-

bonfire 'bɒn.faɪəʳ (US) 'bɑːn.faɪɚ -s -z 'Bonfire ˌNight

bong bɒŋ (US) bɑːŋ, bɔːŋ -s -z

bongo 'bɒŋ.gəʊ (US) 'bɑːŋ.goʊ -(e)s -z 'bongo ˌdrum

Bonham 'bɒn.əm (US) 'bɑː.nəm

Bonham-Carter ˌbɒn.əm'kɑː.təʳ (US) ˌbɑː.nəm'kɑːr.t̬ɚ

bonhomie 'bɒn.ɒm.i, -ə.mi, -miː, ˌ--'- (US) ˌbɑː.nə'miː, '---

Boniface 'bɒn.ɪ.feɪs, -fæs (US) 'bɑː.nɪ-

Bonifacio ˌbɒn.ɪ'fæʃ.i.əʊ, -'fæs- (US) ˌboʊ.ni'fɑː.ʃoʊ, '-ʃi.oʊ

Bonington 'bɒn.ɪŋ.tən (US) 'bɑː.nɪŋ.t̬ən

bonk bɒŋk (US) bɑːŋk, bɔːŋk -s -s -ing -ɪŋ -ed -t

bonkers 'bɒŋ.kəz (US) 'bɑːŋ.kɚz, 'bɔːŋ-

bon(s) mot(s) ˌbɔ̃ːm'məʊ (US) ˌbɔ̃ːn'moʊ

Bonn bɒn (US) bɑːn

Bonnard bɒn'ɑːʳ (US) bɑː'nɑːr, bɔː-

Bonner 'bɒn.əʳ (US) 'bɑː.nɚ

bonn|et 'bɒn|.ɪt (US) 'bɑː.n|ɪt -ets -ɪts -eting -ɪ.tɪŋ (US) -ɪ.t̬ɪŋ -eted -ɪ.tɪd (US) -ɪ.t̬ɪd

Bonnett 'bɒn.ɪt (US) 'bɑː.nɪt

Bonnie 'bɒn.i (US) 'bɑː.ni

bonn|y 'bɒn|.i (US) 'bɑː.n|i -ier -i.əʳ (US) -i.ɚ -iest -i.ɪst, -i.əst -ily -ɪ.li, -ᵊl.i -iness -ɪ.nəs, -ɪ.nɪs

Bono 'bəʊ.nəʊ, 'bɒn.əʊ (US) 'boʊ.noʊ, 'bɑː-

bonsai 'bɒn.saɪ (US) ˌbɑːn'saɪ, ˌboʊn- -s -z

Bonsor 'bɒnt.səʳ, -zəʳ (US) 'bɑːnt.sɚ, -zɚ

bonus 'bəʊ.nəs (US) 'boʊ- -es -ɪz

bon(s) vivant(s) ˌbɔ̃ːŋ.vi.'vɑ̃ːŋ (US) ˌbɑːn.viː'vɑːnt, ˌbɔ̃ː-

bon(s) viveur(s) ˌbɔ̃ːŋ.vi'vɜːʳ (US) ˌbɑːn.viː'vɝː

bon voyage ˌbɔ̃ːŋ.vɔɪ'ɑːʒ, -vwaɪ'- (US) ˌbɑːn.vwaɪ'-, -vɔɪ'-

bon|y 'bəʊ.n|i (US) 'boʊ- -ier -i.əʳ (US) -i.ɚ -iest -i.ɪst, -i.əst -iness -ɪ.nəs, -ɪ.nɪs

bonz|e bɒnz (US) bɑːnz -es -ɪz

bonzer 'bɒn.zəʳ (US) 'bɑːn.zɚ

boo buː -s -z -ing -ɪŋ -ed -d -er/s -əʳ/z (US) -ɚ/z ˌcouldn't say ˌboo to a 'goose

boob buːb -s -z -ing -ɪŋ -ed -d

boo-boo 'buː.buː -s -z

boob|y 'buː.b|i -ies -iz -yish -i.ɪʃ 'booby ˌprize; 'booby ˌtrap

boodle (B) 'buː.dl̩

booger 'buː.gəʳ, 'bʊg.əʳ (US) 'bʊg.ɚ, 'buː.gɚ -s -z

boogey|man 'bʊg.i|.mæn, 'buː.gi- -men -men

boog|ie 'buː.g|i (US) 'bʊg-, 'buː- -ies -iz -ieing -i.ɪŋ -ied -id

boogie-woogie ˌbuː.gi'wuː.gi, 'buː.giˌwuː-, ˌbʊg.i'wʊg.i

boohoo ˌbuː'huː -s -z -ing -ɪŋ -ed -d

book bʊk -s -s -ing -ɪŋ -ed -t -er/s -əʳ/z (US) -ɚ/z 'book ˌclub; 'book ˌtoken; ˌbring someone to 'book; in someone's 'good/bad ˌbooks, in someone's ˌgood/ˌbad 'books

bookable 'bʊk.ə.bl̩

bookbind|er 'bʊkˌbaɪn.d|əʳ (US) -d|ɚ -ers -əz (US) -ɚz -ing -ɪŋ

bookcas|e 'bʊk.keɪs -es -ɪz

bookend 'bʊk.end -s -z

Booker 'bʊk.əʳ (US) -ɚ

Bookham 'bʊk.əm

bookie 'bʊk.i -s -z

booking 'bʊk.ɪŋ -s -z 'booking ˌoffice

bookish 'bʊk.ɪʃ -ly -li -ness -nəs, -nɪs

bookkeep|er 'bʊkˌkiː.p|əʳ (US) -p|ɚ -ers -əz (US) -ɚz -ing -ɪŋ

bookland 'bʊk.lænd

book-learning 'bʊkˌlɜː.nɪŋ (US) -ˌlɝː-

booklet 'bʊk.lət, -lɪt -s -s

bookmak|er 'bʊkˌmeɪ.k|əʳ (US) -k|ɚ -ers -əz (US) -ɚz -ing -ɪŋ

book|man 'bʊk|.mən, -mæn -men -mən, -men

bookmark 'bʊk.mɑːk (US) -mɑːrk -s -s -ing -ɪŋ -ed -t -er/s -əʳ/z (US) -ɚ/z

bookmobile 'bʊk.məʊˌbiːl (US) -mə-, -moʊ- -s -z

bookplate 'bʊk.pleɪt -s -s

booksell|er 'bʊkˌsel|.əʳ (US) -ɚ -ers -əz (US) -ɚz -ing -ɪŋ

bookshel|f 'bʊk.ʃel|f -ves -vz

bookshop 'bʊk.ʃɒp (US) -ʃɑːp -s -s

bookstall 'bʊk.stɔːl (US) -stɔːl, -stɑːl -s -z

bookstand ˈbʊk.stænd **-s** -z
bookstore ˈbʊk.stɔːʳ (US) -stɔːr **-s** -z
bookwork ˈbʊk.wɜːk (US) -wɝːk
bookworm ˈbʊk.wɜːm (US) -wɝːm **-s** -z
Boolean ˈbuː.li.ən **-s** -z
boom buːm **-s** -z **-ing** -ɪŋ **-ed** -d ˈ**boom** ˌ**box**
boomerang ˈbuː.mᵊr.æŋ (US) -mə.ræŋ **-s** -z **-ing** -ɪŋ **-ed** -d
boomlet ˈbuːm.lət, -lɪt **-s** -s
boon buːn **-s** -z
boondock ˈbuːn.dɒk (US) -dɑːk **-s** -s
boondoggl|e ˈbuːnˌdɒg.l̩ (US) -ˌdɑː.gl̩, -ˌdɔː- **-es** -z **-ing** -ɪŋ, ˌ-lɪŋ (US) -ˌdɑː.gl̩.ɪŋ, -ˌdɔː-, ˌ-glɪŋ **-ed** -d **-er/s** -əʳ/z, ˌ-ləʳ/z (US) -ˌdɑː.gl̩.ɚ/z, -ˌdɔː-, ˌ-glɚ/z
Boon(e) buːn
boonies ˈbuː.niz
boor bɔːʳ, bʊə (US) bʊr **-s** -z
Boord bɔːd (US) bɔːrd
boorish ˈbɔː.rɪʃ, ˈbʊə- (US) ˈbʊr.ɪʃ **-ly** -li **-ness** -nəs, -nɪs
Boosey ˈbuː.zi
boost buːst **-s** -s **-ing** -ɪŋ **-ed** -ɪd
booster ˈbuː.stəʳ (US) -stɚ **-s** -z
boot (B) buːt **-s** -s **-ing** -ɪŋ (US) ˈbuː.t̬ɪŋ **-ed** -ɪd (US) ˈbuː.t̬ɪd ˈ**boot** ˌ**sale; ˌput the ˈboot in; too ˌbig for one's ˈboots**
bootblack ˈbuːt.blæk **-s** -s
bootee ˌbuːˈtiː; ˈbuː.ti (US) ˈbuː.t̬i **-s** -z
Boötes bəʊˈəʊ.tiːz (US) boʊˈoʊ-
booth (B) buːð, buːθ **-s** -z, -s
Boothby ˈbuːð.bi
Boothe buːð
Boothroyd ˈbuːθ.rɔɪd, ˈbuːð-
bootie ˈbuː.ti (US) -t̬i **-s** -z
bootjack ˈbuːt.dʒæk **-s** -s
bootlac|e ˈbuːt.leɪs **-es** -ɪz
Bootle ˈbuː.tl̩ (US) ˈbuː.t̬l̩
bootleg ˈbuːt.leg **-s** -z **-ging** -ɪŋ **-ged** -d
bootlegger ˈbuːtˌleg.əʳ (US) -ɚ **-s** -z
bootless ˈbuːt.ləs, -lɪs **-ly** -li **-ness** -nəs, -nɪs
boots (*sing.*) *hotel servant:* buːts (*plur.*) buːts, ˈbuːt.sɪz
Boots® buːts
bootstrap ˈbuːt.stræp **-s** -s **-ping** -ɪŋ **-ped** -t
booty ˈbuː.ti (US) -t̬i
booz|e buːz **-es** -ɪz **-ing** -ɪŋ **-ed** -d **-er/s** -əʳ/z (US) -ɚ/z
booze-up ˈbuːz.ʌp **-s** -s
booz|y ˈbuː.z|i **-ier** -i.əʳ (US) -i.ɚ **-iest** -i.ɪst, -i.əst **-ily** -ɪ.li, -ᵊl.i
bop bɒp (US) bɑːp **-s** -s **-ping** -ɪŋ **-ped** -t **-py** -i
Bo-peep ˌbəʊˈpiːp (US) ˌboʊ-
Bophuthatswana ˌbɒp.uː.tætˈswɑː.nə, ˌboʊ.puː-, -tətˈ- (US) ˌboʊ.puː.tɑːtˈswɑː-, -t̬ətˈ-
boracic bəˈræs.ɪk, bɒrˈæs- (US) bəˈræs-, bɔː-
borage ˈbɒr.ɪdʒ, ˈbʌr- (US) ˈbɔːr-
borate ˈbɔː.reɪt, -rɪt, -rət (US) ˈbɔːr.eɪt, -ɪt, -ət **-s** -s
borax ˈbɔː.ræks (US) ˈbɔːr.æks
borborygmus ˌbɔː.bəˈrɪg.məs (US) ˌbɔːr-
Bord bɔːd (US) bɔːrd
Bordeaux bɔːˈdəʊ (US) bɔːrˈdoʊ
bordello bɔːˈdel.əʊ (US) bɔːrˈdel.oʊ **-s** -z
bord|er ˈbɔː.d|əʳ (US) ˈbɔːr.d|ɚ **-ers** -əz (US) -ɚz **-ering** -ᵊr.ɪŋ **-ered** -əd (US) -ɚd **-erer/s** -ᵊr.əʳ/z (US) -ɚ.ɚ/z
borderland ˈbɔː.dᵊl.ænd (US) ˈbɔːr.dɚ.lænd **-s** -z
borderline ˈbɔː.dᵊl.aɪn (US) ˈbɔːr.dɚ.laɪn **-s** -z
Borders ˈbɔː.dəz (US) ˈbɔːr.dɚz
Bordon ˈbɔː.dᵊn (US) ˈbɔːr-
bordure ˈbɔː.djʊəʳ (US) ˈbɔːr.djɚ, -dʒɚ **-s** -z
bor|e bɔːʳ (US) bɔːr **-es** -z **-ing** -ɪŋ **-ed** -d
bore *(from* **bear***)* bɔːʳ (US) bɔːr
borealis ˌbɒr.iˈɑː.lɪs, ˌbɔː.riˈ-, -ˈeɪ- (US) ˌbɔːr.iˈæl.ɪs, -ˈeɪ.lɪs
Boreas ˈbɒr.i.æs, ˈbɔː.ri-, -əs (US) ˈbɔːr.i-
boredom ˈbɔː.dəm (US) ˈbɔːr-
Boreham ˈbɔː.rəm (US) ˈbɔːr.əm
Borehamwood ˌbɔː.rəmˈwʊd (US) ˌbɔːr.əm-
borehole ˈbɔː.həʊl (US) ˈbɔːr.hoʊl **-s** -z
borer ˈbɔː.rəʳ (US) ˈbɔːr.ɚ **-s** -z
Borg bɔːg (US) bɔːrg
Borges ˈbɔː.ges, -xes (US) ˈbɔːr.hes
Borgia ˈbɔː.*dʒ*i.ə, -*dʒ*ə (US) ˈbɔːr.*dʒ*ə
boric ˈbɔː.rɪk, ˈbɒr.ɪk (US) ˈbɔːr.ɪk ˌ**boric** ˈ**acid**
Boris ˈbɒr.ɪs (US) ˈbɔːr-
Borland ˈbɔː.lənd (US) ˈbɔːr-
borlotti (B) bɔːˈlɒt.i (US) bɔːrˈlɑː.t̬i
born bɔːn (US) bɔːrn
born-again ˌbɔːn.əˈgen, -ˈgeɪn (US) ˌbɔːrn.əˈgen *stress shift, see compound:* ˌ**born-again** ˈ**Christian**
borne *(from* **bear***)* bɔːn (US) bɔːrn
Borneo ˈbɔː.ni.əʊ (US) ˈbɔːr.ni.oʊ
Borodin ˈbɒr.ə.dɪn (US) ˈbɔːr-
boron ˈbɔː.rɒn (US) ˈbɔːr.ɑːn
borough ˈbʌr.ə (US) ˈbɝː.oʊ, -ə **-s** -z
borrow (B) ˈbɒr.əʊ (US) ˈbɑːr.oʊ **-s** -z **-ing/s** -ɪŋ/z **-ed** -d **-er/s** -əʳ/z (US) -ɚ/z
Borrowash ˈbɒr.əʊ.wɒʃ (US) ˈbɑːr.oʊ.wɑːʃ, -wɔːʃ
Borrowdale ˈbɒr.ə.deɪl (US) ˈbɑːr-
Bors bɔːs (US) bɔːrs
borsch bɔːʃ (US) bɔːrʃ
borscht bɔːʃt (US) bɔːrʃt
borstal (B) ˈbɔː.stᵊl (US) ˈbɔːr- **-s** -z
borstch bɔːʃ, bɔːstʃ, bɔːʃtʃ (US) bɔːrʃt
Borthwick ˈbɔːθ.wɪk (US) ˈbɔːrθ-
Borwick ˈbɒr.ɪk (US) ˈbɔːr.wɪk
borzoi ˈbɔː.zɔɪ, -ˈ- (US) ˈbɔːr- **-s** -z
Bosanquet ˈbəʊ.zᵊn.ket, -kɪt (US) ˈboʊ-
boscag|e ˈbɒs.kɪdʒ (US) ˈbɑːs- **-es** -ɪz
Boscastle ˈbɒs.kɑː.sl̩, -kæs.l̩ (US) ˈbɑː.skæs-
Boscawen bɒsˈkəʊ.ən; -ɪn; -ˈkɔː-; ˈbɒs.kwɪn (US) bɑːˈskoʊ.ən; ˈbɑː.skwɪn
Bosch bɒʃ (US) bɑːʃ
bosh bɒʃ (US) bɑːʃ
Bosham ˈbɒz.əm, ˈbɒs- (US) ˈbɑː.zəm, -səm
Note: A new pronunciation /ˈbɒʃ.əm/ is also heard.
Bosher ˈbəʊ.ʃəʳ (US) ˈboʊ.ʃɚ
bosky ˈbɒs.ki (US) ˈbɑː.ski
bos'n, bo's'n ˈbəʊ.sᵊn (US) ˈboʊ- **-s** -z
Bosni|a ˈbɒz.ni|.ə (US) ˈbɑːz- **-an/s** -ən/z
Bosnia-Herzegovina ˌbɒz.ni.əˌhɜːt.səˈgɒv.ɪ.nə; -gəʊˈviː- (US) ˌbɑːz.ni.əˌhert.səˈgoʊˈviː.nə, -gəˈ-
bosom ˈbʊz.ᵊm **-s** -z **-y** -i
Bosphorus ˈbɒs.fᵊr.əs, -pᵊr- (US) ˈbɑːs.fɚ-, ˈbɑː.spɚ-
Bosporus ˈbɒs.pᵊr.əs (US) ˈbɑː.spɚ-
boss (B) bɒs (US) bɑːs **-es** -ɪz **-ing** -ɪŋ **-ed** -t
bossa nova ˌbɒs.əˈnəʊ.və (US) ˌbɑː.səˈnoʊ-
boss-eyed ˌbɒsˈaɪd (US) ˈbɑːs.aɪd *stress shift:* ˌboss-eyed ˈcat
Bossuet ˈbɒs.u.eɪ (US) ˈbɑː.sweɪ
boss|y ˈbɒs|.i (US) ˈbɑː.s|i **-ier** -i.əʳ (US) -i.ɚ **-iest** -i.ɪst, -i.əst **-ily** -ɪ.li, -ᵊl.i **-iness** -ɪ.nəs, -ɪ.nɪs
Bostik® ˈbɒs.tɪk (US) ˈbɑː.stɪk
Bostock ˈbɒs.tɒk (US) ˈbɑː.stɑːk
Boston ˈbɒs.tᵊn (US) ˈbɑː.stᵊn, ˈbɔː-
Bostonian bɒsˈtəʊ.ni.ən (US) bɑːˈstoʊ-, bɔː- **-s** -z
Bostridge ˈbɒs.trɪdʒ (US) ˈbɑː.strɪdʒ
bosun ˈbəʊ.sᵊn (US) ˈboʊ- **-s** -z
Boswell ˈbɒz.wəl, -wel (US) ˈbɑːz-
Bosworth ˈbɒz.wəθ, -wɜːθ (US) ˈbɑːz.wɚθ, -wɝːθ
botanic bəˈtæn.ɪk, bɒtˈæn- (US) bəˈtæn- **-al** -ᵊl **-ally** -ᵊl.i, -li **boˌtanic ˈgarden**
botanist ˈbɒt.ᵊn.ɪst (US) ˈbɑː.tᵊn- **-s** -s
botaniz|e, -is|e ˈbɒt.ᵊn.aɪz (US) ˈbɑː.tᵊn- **-es** -ɪz **-ing** -ɪŋ **-ed** -d
botany ˈbɒt.ᵊn.i (US) ˈbɑː.tᵊn- ˌ**Botany** ˈ**Bay**
botch bɒtʃ (US) bɑːtʃ **-es** -ɪz **-ing** -ɪŋ **-ed** -t **-er/s** -əʳ/z (US) -ɚ/z
botch-up ˈbɒtʃ.ʌp (US) ˈbɑːtʃ- **-s** -s
both bəʊθ (US) boʊθ
Botha ˈbəʊ.tə (US) ˈboʊ.t̬ə
Botham ˈbəʊ.θəm, ˈbɒð.əm (US) ˈboʊ.θəm, ˈbɑː.ðəm
both|er ˈbɒð|.əʳ (US) ˈbɑː.ð|ɚ **-ers** -əz (US) -ɚz **-ering** -ᵊr.ɪŋ **-ered** -əd (US) -ɚd
botheration ˌbɒð.ᵊrˈeɪ.ʃᵊn (US) ˌbɑː.ðəˈreɪ-

bothersome 'bɒð.ə.səm (US) 'bɑː.ðɚ-
Bothnia 'bɒθ.ni.ə (US) 'bɑːθ-
Bothwell 'bɒθ.wəl, 'bɒð-, -wel (US) 'bɑːθ-, 'bɑːð-
both|y 'bɒθ|.i, bɒð- (US) 'bɑː.θ|i, -ð|i **-ies** -iz
Botolph 'bɒt.ɒlf, -əlf (US) 'bɑː.tɑːlf
Botox® 'bəʊ.tɒks (US) 'boʊ.tɑːks
botrytis bɒt'raɪ.tɪs (US) boʊ'traɪ.t̬əs
Botswana bɒt'swɑː.nə (US) bɑːt-
Botticelli ˌbɒt.ɪ'tʃel.i (US) ˌbɑː.t̬ə'- **-s** -z
bottl|e 'bɒt.l̩ (US) 'bɑː.t̬l̩ **-es** -z **-ing** -ɪŋ, '-lɪŋ (US) 'bɑː.t̬l̩.ɪŋ, 'bɑːt.lɪŋ **-ed** -d **-er/s** -ər/z, '-lər/z (US) 'bɑː.t̬l̩.ɚ/z, 'bɑːt.lɚ/z '**bottle** ˌ**bank**
bottle-green ˌbɒt.l̩'griːn (US) ˌbɑː.t̬l̩'- *stress shift:* ˌbottle-green 'jacket
bottleneck 'bɒt.l̩.nek (US) 'bɑː.t̬l̩- **-s** -s
bottle-nos|e 'bɒt.l̩.nəʊz (US) 'bɑː.t̬l̩.noʊz **-es** -ɪz **-ed** -d
bottle-wash|er 'bɒt.l̩ˌwɒʃ.ər (US) 'bɑː.t̬l̩ˌwɑː.ʃɚ **-ers** -əz (US) -ɚs **-ing** -ɪŋ
bottom (B) 'bɒt.əm (US) 'bɑː.t̬əm **-s** -z **-ing** -ɪŋ **-ed** -d
Bottome bə'təʊm (US) -'toʊm
bottomless 'bɒt.əm.ləs, -lɪs, -les (US) 'bɑː.t̬əm-
Bottomley 'bɒt.əm.li (US) 'bɑː.t̬əm-
bottomry 'bɒt.əm.ri (US) 'bɑː.t̬əm-
botulism 'bɒtʃ.ə.lɪ.zəm, -ʊ-; 'bɒt.jʊ-, '-jə- (US) 'bɑː.tʃə-
Bouaké 'bwɑː.keɪ
Boucicault 'buː.si.kəʊ *as if French:* ˌ--'- (US) 'buː.si.koʊ, -kɑːlt
bouclé 'buː.kleɪ (US) -'-
Boudicca 'buː.dɪ.kə, 'bəʊ- (US) buː'dɪk.ə
boudoir 'buːd.wɑːr (US) 'buːd.wɑːr, 'bʊd- **-s** -z
bouffant 'buː.fɑ̃ːŋ, -fɒnt (US) buː'fɑːnt, '--
bougainvillaea ˌbuː.gən'vɪl.i.ə (US) -i.ə, '-jə **-s** -z
Bougainville 'buː.gən.vɪl, -viːl
bougainvillea ˌbuː.gən'vɪl.i.ə (US) -i.ə, '-jə **-s** -z
bough baʊ **-s** -z
Bough bɒf (US) bɑːf
Boughey 'bəʊ.i (US) 'boʊ-
bought *(from* **buy***)* bɔːt (US) bɑːt, bɔːt
Boughton 'bɔː.tən, 'baʊ- (US) 'bɑː.tən, 'bɔː-, 'baʊ-
bougie 'buː.dʒiː, -'- **-s** -z
bouillabaisse ˌbuː.jə'bes, ˌbwiː-, -jɑː'-, -'beɪs, '---
bouillon 'buː.jɔ̃ːŋ, 'bwiː-, -jɒn (US) 'bʊl.jɑːn, 'buː-, -jən
boulanger ˌbuː.lɑ̃ːn'ʒeɪ, '---
Boulby 'bəʊl.bi (US) 'boʊl-
boulder 'bəʊl.dər (US) 'boʊl.dɚ **-s** -z
Bouler 'buː.lər (US) -lɚ
boules buːl
boulevard 'buː.lə.vɑːd, -lɪ-, 'buːl.vɑːr (US) 'bʊl.ə.vɑːrd **-s** -z
Boulez 'buː.lez, -leɪ (US) buː'lez
Boulogne bʊ'lɔɪn, bə- (US) -'loʊn, -'lɔɪn
Boult bəʊlt (US) boʊlt
Boulter 'bəʊl.tər (US) 'boʊl.tɚ
Boulton 'bəʊl.tən (US) 'boʊl-
bounc|e baʊnts **-es** -ɪz **-ing** -ɪŋ **-ed** -t
bouncer (B) 'baʊnt.sər (US) -sɚ **-s** -z
bounc|y 'baʊnt.s|i **-ier** -i.ər (US) -i.ɚ **-iest** -i.ɪst, -i.əst
bound baʊnd **-s** -z **-ing** -ɪŋ **-ed** -ɪd
boundar|y 'baʊn.dər|.i **-ies** -iz
bounden 'baʊn.dən ˌ**bounden** '**duty**
bounder 'baʊn.dər (US) -dɚ **-s** -z
Bounderby 'baʊn.də.bi (US) -dɚ-
boundless 'baʊnd.ləs, -lɪs **-ly** -li **-ness** -nəs, -nɪs
bounteous 'baʊn.ti.əs, -tʃəs (US) -t̬i.əs **-ly** -li **-ness** -nəs, -nɪs
bountiful 'baʊn.tɪ.fəl, -tə-, -fʊl (US) -t̬ə-, -t̬ɪ- **-ly** -i **-ness** -nəs, -nɪs
bount|y 'baʊn.t|i (US) -t̬|i **-ies** -iz '**bounty** ˌ**hunter**
bouquet bʊ'keɪ; bəʊ-; 'buː.keɪ (US) boʊ'keɪ, buː- **-s** -z
bouquet(s) garni(s) bʊˌkeɪ.gɑː'niː, ˌbuː.keɪ- (US) ˌboʊ.keɪ.gɑːr'-
Bourbon *French royal house:* 'bʊə.bən, 'bɔː-, -bɒn (US) 'bʊr.bən, -bɔːn **-s** -z
bourbon *drink:* 'bɜː.bən, 'bʊə- (US) 'bɝː- *biscuit:* 'bɔː.bən, 'bʊə-, -bɒn (US) 'bɝː-
Bourchier 'baʊ.tʃər (US) -tʃɚ
Bourdillon bə'dɪl.i.ən, bɔː-, -'dɪl.ən (US) bɔːr'dɪl.jən, bɚ-
bourdon 'bɔː.dən, 'bʊə- (US) 'bʊr-, 'bɔːr- **-s** -z
bourgeois *middle class:* 'bɔː.ʒwɑː, 'bʊəʒ- (US) 'bʊrʒ- *printing type:* bɜː'dʒɔɪs (US) bɝː-
bourgeoisie ˌbɔː.ʒwɑː'ziː, ˌbʊəʒ-, -wə'- (US) ˌbʊrʒ-
Bourke bɜːk (US) bɝːk
bourn(e) bɔːn, bʊən (US) bɔːrn, bʊrn **-s** -z
Bourne bɔːn, bʊən *as surname also:* bɜːn (US) bɔːrn, bʊrn, bɝːn
Bournemouth 'bɔːn.məθ (US) 'bɔːrn-
Bournville 'bɔːn.vɪl (US) 'bɔːrn-
bourrée 'bʊr.eɪ, 'bʊə.reɪ (US) bʊ'reɪ **-s** -z
bours|e (B) bʊəs, bɔːs (US) bʊrs, bɔːrs **-es** -ɪz
boustrophedon ˌbuː.strə'fiː.dən, ˌbaʊ-, -dɒn (US) -ɑːn
bout baʊt **-s** -s
boutique buː'tiːk **-s** -s
Boutros-Ghali ˌbuː.trɒs'gɑː.li (US) -troʊs'-
Bouverie 'buː.vər.i
bouzouki bʊ'zuː.ki, bə-, buː- **-s** -z
Bovary 'bəʊ.vər.i (US) 'boʊ-
Bovey *place:* 'bʌv.i *surname:* 'buː.vi, 'bəʊ-, 'bʌv.i (US) 'buː.vi, 'boʊ-, 'bʌv.i
Bovey Tracey ˌbʌv.i'treɪ.si
Bovill 'bəʊ.vɪl (US) 'boʊ-
bovine 'bəʊ.vaɪn (US) 'boʊ-, -viːn
Bovingdon 'bʌv.ɪŋ.dən, 'bɒv- (US) 'bʌv-, 'bɑː.vɪŋ-
Note: Locally /'bʌv-/.
Bovington 'bɒv.ɪŋ.tən (US) 'bɑː.vɪŋ-
Bovis 'bəʊ.vɪs (US) 'boʊ-
Bovril® 'bɒv.rɪl, -rəl (US) 'bɑːv-
bovver 'bɒv.ər, 'bɑː.vɚ '**bovver** ˌ**boot**; '**bovver** ˌ**boy**
bow *(n.) bending, fore end of ship:* baʊ **-s** -z
bow (B) *(n.) for shooting, etc., knot:* bəʊ (US) boʊ **-s** -z ˌ**bow** '**tie**; ˌ**bow** '**window**
bow *(v.) in playing the violin, etc.:* bəʊ (US) boʊ **-s** -z **-ing/s** -ɪŋ/z **-ed** -d
bow *(v.) bend body:* baʊ **-s** -z **-ing** -ɪŋ **-ed** -d
Bowater 'bəʊˌwɔː.tər (US) 'boʊˌwɑː.t̬ɚ, -ˌwɔː-
Bowden 'bəʊ.dən, 'baʊ- (US) 'boʊ-, 'baʊ-
Bowdler 'baʊd.lər (US) 'boʊd.lɚ, 'baʊd-
bowdlerism 'baʊd.lər.ɪ.zəm (US) 'boʊd-, 'baʊd- **-s** -z
bowdlerization, -isa- ˌbaʊd.lər.aɪ'zeɪ.ʃən, -ɪ'- (US) ˌboʊd.lɚ.ɪ'-, ˌbaʊd-
bowdleriz|e, -is|e 'baʊd.lər.aɪz (US) 'boʊd.lə.raɪz, 'baʊd- **-es** -ɪz **-ing** -ɪŋ **-ed** -d
Bowdoin, Bowdon 'bəʊ.dən (US) 'boʊ-
bowel baʊəl **-s** -z
Bowen 'bəʊ.ɪn (US) 'boʊ-
bower (B) baʊər (US) baʊɚ **-s** -z
Bowering 'baʊə.rɪŋ (US) 'baʊɚ.ɪŋ
bowery (B) 'baʊə.ri (US) 'baʊɚ.i, 'baʊ.ri
Bowes bəʊz (US) boʊz
Bowie 'baʊ.i, 'bəʊ- (US) 'boʊ-, 'buː-
bowie-kni|fe 'bəʊ.i.naɪ|f, 'buː- (US) 'boʊ-, 'buː- **-ves** -vz
Bowker 'baʊ.kər (US) -kɚ
bowl bəʊl (US) boʊl **-s** -z **-ing** -ɪŋ **-ed** -d '**bowling** ˌ**alley**; '**bowling** ˌ**green**
Bowland 'bəʊ.lənd (US) 'boʊ-
bow-legged bəʊ'legd, -'leg.ɪd, -əd (US) boʊ- *stress shift:* ˌbow-legged 'child
bowler (B) 'bəʊ.lər (US) 'boʊ.lɚ **-s** -z
Bowles bəʊlz (US) boʊlz
bowline 'bəʊ.lɪn (US) 'boʊ- **-s** -z
Bowling 'bəʊ.lɪŋ (US) 'boʊ-
Bowlker 'bəʊ.kər (US) 'boʊ.kɚ
bow|man (B) 'bəʊ|.mən (US) 'boʊ- **-men** -mən, -men
Bowmer 'bəʊ.mər (US) 'boʊ.mɚ
Bown baʊn
Bowness bəʊ'nes (US) boʊ-
Bowra 'baʊ.rə
Bowring 'baʊ.rɪŋ

bowshot 'bəʊ.ʃɒt (US) 'boʊ.ʃɑːt **-s** -s
bowsprit 'bəʊ.sprɪt, 'baʊ- (US) 'baʊ-, 'boʊ- **-s** -s
bowstring 'bəʊ.strɪŋ (US) 'boʊ- **-s** -z
Bowtell bəʊ'tel (US) boʊ-
bow-wow *(interj.) sound made by a dog:* ˌbaʊ'waʊ **-s** -z *(n.) dog:* 'baʊ.waʊ **-s** -z
bowyer (B) 'bəʊ.jəʳ (US) 'boʊ.jɚ
box (B) bɒks (US) bɑːks **-es** -ɪz **-ing** -ɪŋ **-ed** -t ˌ**box 'bed**; '**box ˌcloth**; ˌ**box 'junction**; '**box ˌnumber**; '**box ˌoffice**; '**box ˌseat**; ˌ**boxed 'set**; '**box ˌscore**
boxcar 'bɒks.kɑːʳ (US) 'bɑːks.kɑːr **-s** -z
boxer (B) 'bɒk.səʳ (US) 'bɑːk.sɚ **-s** -z '**boxer ˌshorts**
boxing 'bɒk.sɪŋ (US) 'bɑːk- '**Boxing ˌDay**; '**boxing ˌglove**; '**boxing ˌmatch**
Boxmoor 'bɒks.mɔːʳ *also locally:* -'- (US) 'bɑːks.mʊr, -mɔːr
boxroom 'bɒks.rʊm, -ruːm (US) 'bɑːks.ruːm, -rʊm **-s** -z
boxwood 'bɒks.wʊd (US) 'bɑːks-
box|y 'bɒk.s|i (US) 'bɑːk- **-iness** -ɪ.nəs, -ɪ.nɪs
boy bɔɪ **-s** -z ˌ**boy 'scout** (US) '**boy ˌscout**
boyar 'bɔɪ.əʳ, -ɑːʳ; 'bəʊ.jɑːʳ, -'- (US) boʊ'jɑːr; 'bɔɪ.ɚ **-s** -z
Boyce bɔɪs
boyco|tt (B) 'bɔɪ.kɒ|t, -kə|t (US) -kɑː|t **-tts** -ts **-tting** -tɪŋ (US) -t̬ɪŋ **-tted** -tɪd (US) -t̬ɪd **-tter/s** -təʳ/z (US) -t̬ɚ/z
Boyd bɔɪd
Boyer 'bwaɪ.eɪ; 'bɔɪ.əʳ (US) bɔɪ'eɪ; 'bɔɪ.ɚ
Boyet 'bɔɪ.et, -'- (US) bwɑː'jeɪ
boyfriend 'bɔɪ.frend **-s** -z
boyhood 'bɔɪ.hʊd **-s** -z
boyish 'bɔɪ.ɪʃ **-ly** -li **-ness** -nəs, -nɪs
Boyle bɔɪl
Boyne bɔɪn
boyo 'bɔɪ.əʊ (US) -oʊ **-s** -z
boysenberr|y 'bɔɪ.zᵊn.bᵊr|.i, -ˌber- (US) -ˌber- **-ies** -iz
Boyson 'bɔɪ.sᵊn
Boyton 'bɔɪ.tᵊn
Boyzone 'bɔɪ.zəʊn (US) -zoʊn
Boz bɒz (US) bɑːz
Note: This pen-name of Charles Dickens was originally pronounced /bəʊz (US) boʊz/, but this pronunciation is not often heard now.
bozo 'bəʊ.zəʊ (US) 'boʊ.zoʊ **-s** -z
BP ˌbiː'piː
BPhil ˌbiː'fɪl
BR ˌbiː'ɑːʳ (US) -'ɑːr
bra brɑː **-s** -z
braai braɪ **-s** -z **-ing** -ɪŋ **-ed** -d
Brabant brə'bænt; 'bræb.ənt
Brabantio brə'bæn.ti.əʊ, bræb'æn-, -tʃi- (US) brə'bæn.t̬i.oʊ, -'bænt.ʃi-
Brabazon 'bræb.ə.zᵊn (US) -zɑːn
Brabham 'bræb.əm
Brabourne *place:* 'breɪ.bɔːn (US) -bɔːrn *family name:* 'breɪ.bən, 'breɪ.bɔːn (US) -bɚn, -bɔːrn
brac|e (B) breɪs **-es** -ɪz **-ing** -ɪŋ **-ed** -t
Bracebridge 'breɪs.brɪdʒ
bracelet 'breɪs.lət, -lɪt **-s** -s
brach brætʃ (US) brætʃ, bræk **-es** -ɪz
brachial 'breɪ.ki.əl (US) 'breɪ-, 'bræk.i-
brachy- 'bræk.i-
brachycephalic ˌbræk.i.sə'fæl.ɪk, -sɪ'-
brack bræk **-s** -s
bracken 'bræk.ᵊn
Brackenbury 'bræk.ᵊn.bᵊr.i (US) -ber-
Brackenridge 'bræk.ᵊn.rɪdʒ
brack|et 'bræk|.ɪt **-ets** -ɪts **-eting** -ɪ.tɪŋ (US) -ɪ.t̬ɪŋ **-eted** -ɪ.tɪd (US) -ɪ.t̬ɪd
brackish 'bræk.ɪʃ **-ness** -nəs, -nɪs
Brackley 'bræk.li
Bracknell 'bræk.nəl
brad (B) bræd **-s** -z
bradawl 'bræd.ɔːl (US) -ɑːl, -ɔːl **-s** -z
Bradbury 'bræd.bᵊr.i, 'bræb- (US) -ber-
Braddon 'bræd.ᵊn
Braden 'breɪ.dᵊn
Bradfield 'bræd.fiːld
Bradford 'bræd.fəd (US) -fɚd
Bradgate 'bræd.geɪt, -gɪt
Bradlaugh, Bradlaw 'bræd.lɔː (US) -lɑː, -lɔː
Bradley 'bræd.li
Bradman 'bræd.mən
Bradshaw 'bræd.ʃɔː (US) -ʃɑː, -ʃɔː
Bradstreet 'bræd.striːt
Bradwardine 'bræd.wə.diːn (US) -wɚ-
Brady 'breɪ.di
bradycardia ˌbræd.ɪ'kɑː.di.ə (US) -'kɑːr-
brae breɪ **-s** -z
Braemar breɪ'mɑːʳ (US) -'mɑːr *stress shift:* ˌBraemar 'games
brag bræg **-s** -z **-ging/ly** -ɪŋ/li **-ged** -d
Bragg bræg
braggadocio ˌbræg.ə'dəʊ.tʃi.əʊ (US) -'doʊ- **-s** -z
braggart 'bræg.ət, -ɑːt (US) -ɚt **-s** -s
Braham 'breɪ.əm
Brahe 'brɑː.hə, -ə, -hi
brahma (B) *god:* 'brɑː.mə *breed of fowl or cattle:* 'breɪ.mə (US) 'brɑː-, 'breɪ-, 'bræm.ə **-s** -z
Brahman 'brɑː.mən **-s** -z **-ism** -ɪ.zᵊm
Brahmaputra ˌbrɑː.mə'puː.trə
brahmin (B) 'brɑː.mɪn **-s** -z **-ism** -ɪ.zᵊm
brahminical ˌbrɑː'mɪn.ɪ.kᵊl
Brahms brɑːmz
braid (B) breɪd **-s** -z **-ing** -ɪŋ **-ed** -ɪd
brail breɪl **-s** -z
Braille breɪl
Brailsford 'breɪls.fəd (US) -fɚd
brain (B) breɪn **-s** -z **-ing** -ɪŋ **-ed** -d '**brain ˌdamage**; '**brain ˌdeath**; '**brain ˌdrain**
brain|child 'breɪn|.tʃaɪld **-children** -ˌtʃɪl.drən
Braine breɪn
brainless 'breɪn.ləs, -lɪs **-ness** -nəs, -nɪs
brainsick 'breɪn.sɪk
brainstorm 'breɪn.stɔːm (US) -stɔːrm **-s** -z **-ing** -ɪŋ **-ed** -d
brainstorming 'breɪnˌstɔː.mɪŋ (US) -ˌstɔːr-
brainteaser 'breɪnˌtiː.zəʳ (US) -zɚ **-s** -z
Braintree 'breɪn.triː, -tri
brainwash 'breɪn.wɒʃ (US) -wɑːʃ, -wɔːʃ **-es** -ɪz **-ing** -ɪŋ **-ed** -t
brainwave 'breɪn.weɪv **-s** -z
brain|y 'breɪ.n|i **-ier** -i.əʳ (US) -i.ɚ **-iest** -i.ɪst, -i.əst
brais|e breɪz **-es** -ɪz **-ing** -ɪŋ **-ed** -d
Braithwaite 'breɪ.θweɪt
brak|e breɪk **-es** -s **-ing** -ɪŋ **-ed** -t '**brake ˌfluid**; '**brake ˌlight**
Brakenridge 'bræk.ᵊn.rɪdʒ
Bram bræm
Bramah 'brɑː.mə, 'bræm.ə
Bramall 'bræm.ɔːl (US) -ɔːl, -ɑːl
bramble 'bræm.bl̩ **-s** -z '**bramble ˌbush**
Brambler 'bræm.bləʳ (US) -blɚ
brambly 'bræm.bli
Bramhall 'bræm.hɔːl (US) -hɔːl, -hɑːl
Bramley 'bræm.li **-s** -z
Brampton 'bræm*p*.tən
Bramwell 'bræm.wel, -wəl
bran (B) bræn ˌ**bran 'mash**; ˌ**bran 'pie**
Branagh 'bræn.ə
branch (B) brɑːn*t*ʃ (US) bræn*t*ʃ **-es** -ɪz **-ing** -ɪŋ **-ed** -t
branchi|a 'bræŋ.ki|.ə **-ae** -iː
branchial 'bræŋ.ki.əl
branchiate 'bræŋ.ki.eɪt, -ət
Brancusi bræŋ'kuː.zi (US) bræn-, brɑːŋ
brand (B) brænd **-s** -z **-ing** -ɪŋ **-ed** -ɪd '**brand ˌname**; ˌ**brand 'new**; '**brandi ˌiron**
Brandeis 'bræn.daɪs
Brandenburg 'bræn.dən.bɜːg (US) -bɝ ˌ**Brandenburg 'Gate**
Brandi 'bræn.di
brandish 'bræn.dɪʃ **-es** -ɪz **-ing** -ɪŋ **-ed**
Brando 'bræn.dəʊ (US) -doʊ
Brandon 'bræn.dən
Brandram 'bræn.drəm
Brandreth 'bræn.drɪθ, -drəθ, -dreθ
Brandt brænt
brand|y (B) 'bræn.d|i **-ies** -iz **-ied** -id **-ying** -i.ɪŋ ˌ**brandy 'butter** (US) '**bran ˌbutter**; '**brandy ˌsnap**
brank bræŋk **-s** -s
Branksome 'bræŋk.səm
Branson 'bræn*t*.sᵊn
Branston 'bræn*t*.stən
brant brænt **-s** -s
Brant brɑːnt (US) brænt
brant|-goose brænt|'guːs **-geese** -'g

Braque brɑːk, bræk
Brasenose ˈbreɪz.nəʊz (US) -noʊz
brash bræʃ **-er** -əʳ (US) -ɚ **-est** -ɪst, -əst **-es** -ɪz **-ly** -li **-ness** -nəs, -nɪs
Brasher ˈbreɪ.ʃəʳ (US) -ʃɚ
brasier ˈbreɪ.zi.əʳ, ˈ-ʒəʳ (US) ˈ-ʒɚ **-s** -z
Brasilia brəˈzɪl.i.ə (US) -i.ə, ˈ-jə
Brasov ˈbræʃ.ɒv (US) ˈbrɑː.ʃɔv
brass brɑːs (US) bræs **-es** -ɪz ˌ**brass ˈband**; ˌ**brass ˈknuckles**; ˌ**brass ˈmonkey**; ˌ**brassed ˈoff**
brassard ˈbræs.ɑːd, -ˈ- (US) ˈbræs.ɑːrd; brəˈsɑːrd **-s** -z
brasserie ˈbræs.ᵊr.i (US) ˌbræs.əˈriː **-s** -z
Brassey ˈbræs.i
brassica ˈbræs.ɪ.kə **-s** -z
brassière ˈbræs.i.əʳ, ˈbræz- (US) brəˈzɪr **-s** -z
Brasso® ˈbrɑː.səʊ (US) ˈbræs.oʊ
brass|y, brass|ie *golf club:* ˈbrɑː.s|i (US) ˈbræs|.i **-ies** -iz
brass|y *(adj.)* ˈbrɑː.s|i (US) ˈbræs|.i **-ier** -i.əʳ (US) -i.ɚ **-iest** -i.ɪst, -i.əst
Brasted ˈbreɪ.stɪd, ˈbræs.tɪd
brat bræt **-s** -s ˈ**brat** ˌ**pack**
Bratislava ˌbræt.ɪˈslɑː.və (US) ˌbrɑː.t̬ɪˈ-
Bratsk brætsk, brɑːtsk (US) brɑːtsk
Brattleboro ˈbræt.l̩.bᵊr.ə (US) -oʊ
Braughing ˈbræf.ɪŋ
Braun brɔːn, braʊn (US) brɑːn, brɔːn, braʊn
Note: The trademark is pronounced /brɔːn/ in British English, /brɑːn, brɔːn/ in American English.
Braunton ˈbrɔːn.tən (US) ˈbrɑːn-, ˈbrɔːn-
Brautigan ˈbraʊ.tɪ.gən, ˈbrɔː-, ˈbræt.ɪ- (US) ˈbrɑː.t̬ɪ-, ˈbrɔː-
bravado brəˈvɑː.dəʊ (US) -doʊ **-(e)s** -z
brav|e breɪv **-er** -əʳ (US) -ɚ **-est** -ɪst, -əst **-ely** -li **-es** -z **-ing** -ɪŋ **-ed** -d
Braveheart ˈbreɪv.hɑːt (US) -hɑːrt
braver|y ˈbreɪ.vᵊr|.i **-ies** -iz
Bravington ˈbræv.ɪŋ.tən
bravo brɑːˈvəʊ, ˈ-- (US) ˈbrɑː.voʊ, -ˈ- **-(e)s** -z
Note: Always /ˈ--/ in the ICAO alphabet.
bravura brəˈvjʊə.rə, -ˈvjɔː-, -ˈvʊə- (US) -ˈvjʊr.ə, -ˈvʊr-
brawl brɔːl (US) brɑːl, brɔːl **-s** -z **-ing** -ɪŋ **-ed** -d **-er/s** -əʳ/z (US) -ɚ/z
brawn brɔːn (US) brɑːn, brɔːn
Brawne brɔːn (US) brɑːn, brɔːn
brawn|y ˈbrɔː.n|i (US) ˈbrɑː-, ˈbrɔː- **-ier** -i.əʳ (US) -i.ɚ **-iest** -i.ɪst, -i.əst **-iness** -ɪ.nəs, -ɪ.nɪs
Braxton ˈbræk.stᵊn
bray **(B)** breɪ **-s** -z **-ing** -ɪŋ **-ed** -d
Braybrooke ˈbreɪ.brʊk
Brayley ˈbreɪ.li
braz|e breɪz **-es** -ɪz **-ing** -ɪŋ **-ed** -d
brazen ˈbreɪ.zᵊn **-ly** -li **-ness** -nəs, -nɪs
brazen-faced ˌbreɪ.zᵊnˈfeɪst *stress shift:* ˌbrazen-faced ˈchild
brazier ˈbreɪ.zi.əʳ, ˈ-ʒəʳ (US) ˈ-ʒɚ **-s** -z
Brazier ˈbreɪ.ʒəʳ (US) -ʒɚ
Brazil *country:* brəˈzɪl *English surname:* ˈbræz.ɪl, -ᵊl; brəˈzɪl **Braˈzil** ˌ**nut**
Brazilian brəˈzɪl.i.ən (US) -jən **-s** -z
Brazzaville ˈbræz.ə.vɪl, ˈbrɑː.zə-
breach briːtʃ **-es** -ɪz **-ing** -ɪŋ **-ed** -t ˌ**breach of the ˈpeace**
bread bred **-s** -z **-ed** -ɪd ˈ**bread** ˌ**basket**; ˌ**bread and ˈbutter**
Breadalbane *Earl:* brəˈdɔːl.bɪn, brɪ-, -bᵊn (US) -ˈdɔːl-, -ˈdɑːl- *place:* brəˈdæl.bɪn, -ˈdɔːl-, -bən (US) -ˈdæl-, -ˈdɔːl-, -ˈdɑːl-
breadboard ˈbred.bɔːd (US) -bɔːrd **-s** -z
breadbox ˈbred.bɒks (US) -bɑːks **-es** -ɪz
breadcrumb ˈbred.krʌm **-s** -z
breadfruit ˈbred.fruːt **-s** -s
breadline ˈbred.laɪn
breadth bretθ, bredθ **-s** -s
breadth|ways ˈbretθ|.weɪz, ˈbredθ- **-wise** -waɪz
breadwinner ˈbredˌwɪn.əʳ (US) -ɚ **-s** -z
break breɪk **-s** -s **-ing** -ɪŋ **broke** brəʊk (US) broʊk **broken** ˈbrəʊ.kᵊn (US) ˈbroʊ- ˌ**breaking and ˈentering**
breakable ˈbreɪ.kə.bl̩ **-s** -z
breakag|e ˈbreɪ.kɪdʒ **-es** -ɪz
breakaway ˈbreɪ.kə.weɪ **-s** -z
breakdown ˈbreɪk.daʊn **-s** -z
breaker ˈbreɪ.kəʳ (US) -kɚ **-s** -z
break-even ˌbreɪkˈiː.vᵊn
breakfast ˈbrek.fəst **-s** -s **-ing** -ɪŋ **-ed** -ɪd
break-in ˈbreɪk.ɪn **-s** -z
breakneck ˈbreɪk.nek
breakout ˈbreɪk.aʊt **-s** -s
Breakspear ˈbreɪk.spɪəʳ (US) -spɪr
breakthrough ˈbreɪk.θruː **-s** -z
breakup ˈbreɪk.ʌp **-s** -s
breakwater ˈbreɪkˌwɔː.təʳ (US) -ˌwɑː.t̬ɚ, -ˌwɔː- **-s** -z
bream **(B)** briːm (US) briːm, brɪm **-s** -z
Breamore ˈbrem.əʳ (US) -ɚ
breast brest **-s** -s **-ing** -ɪŋ **-ed** -ɪd ˌ**make a** ˌ**clean ˈbreast of something**
breastbone ˈbrest.bəʊn (US) -boʊn **-s** -z
breast-feed ˈbres*t*.fiːd **-s** -z **-ing** -ɪŋ **breast-fed** ˈbres*t*.fed
Breaston ˈbriː.stᵊn
breastplate ˈbres*t*.pleɪt **-s** -s
breaststroke ˈbres*t*.strəʊk (US) -stroʊk
breastwork ˈbrest.wɜːk (US) -wɝːk **-s** -s
breath breθ **-s** -s ˈ**breath** ˌ**test**; ˌ**take someone's ˈbreath away**; ˌ**waste one's ˈbreath**
breathalyz|e, -ys|e ˈbreθ.ᵊl.aɪz (US) -ə.laɪz **-es** -ɪz **-ed** -d **-ing** -ɪŋ **-er/s** -əʳ/z (US) -ɚ/z
breath|e briːð **-es** -z **-ing** -ɪŋ **-ed** -d ˈ**breathing** ˌ**room**; ˈ**breathing** ˌ**space**; ˌ**breathe** ˌ**down someone's ˈneck**
breathed *phonetic term:* breθt, briːðd
breather ˈbriː.ðəʳ (US) -ðɚ **-s** -z
breathiness ˈbreθ.ɪ.nəs, -nɪs
breathless ˈbreθ.ləs, -lɪs **-ly** -li **-ness** -nəs, -nɪs
breathtaking ˈbreθˌteɪ.kɪŋ **-ly** -li
breath|y ˈbreθ|.i **-ier** -i.əʳ (US) -i.ɚ **-iest** -i.ɪst, -i.əst **-iness** -ɪ.nəs, -ɪ.nɪs
Brebner ˈbreb.nəʳ (US) -nɚ
Brechin ˈbriː.kɪn, -xɪn (US) -kɪn
Brecht brekt *as if German:* brext **-ian** -i.ən
Breckenridge, -kin- ˈbrek.ᵊn.rɪdʒ, -ɪn-
Brecknock ˈbrek.nɒk, -nək (US) -nɑːk **-shire** -ʃəʳ, -ˌʃɪəʳ (US) -ʃɚ, -ˌʃɪr
Brecon ˈbrek.ᵊn ˌ**Brecon ˈBeacons**
bred *(from* **breed***)* bred
Bredbury ˈbred.bᵊr.i, ˈbreb- (US) ˈbred.ber-, -bɚ-
Bredon ˈbriː.dᵊn
bree briː
breech *(n.)* briːtʃ **-es** -ɪz **-ed** -t ˈ**breech** ˌ**birth**, ˌ**breech ˈbirth** (US) ˈ**breech** ˌ**birth**
breeches *trousers:* ˈbrɪtʃ.ɪz, ˈbriː.tʃɪz
breeching ˈbrɪtʃ.ɪŋ, ˈbriː.tʃɪŋ **-s** -z
breech-loader ˈbriːtʃˌləʊ.dəʳ (US) -ˌloʊ.dɚ **-s** -z
breed briːd **-s** -z **-ing** -ɪŋ **bred** bred ˈ**breeding** ˌ**ground**
breeder ˈbriː.dəʳ (US) -dɚ **-s** -z ˈ**breeder reˌactor**
breeks briːks
breez|e briːz **-es** -ɪz **-ing** -ɪŋ **-ed** -d
breez|y ˈbriː.z|i **-ier** -i.əʳ (US) -i.ɚ **-iest** -i.ɪst, -i.əst **-ily** -ɪ.li, -ᵊl.i **-iness** -ɪ.nəs, -ɪ.nɪs
Bremen *in Germany:* ˈbreɪ.mən (US) ˈbrem.ən, ˈbreɪ.mən *in US:* ˈbriː.mᵊn, ˈbrem.ən
Bremerhaven ˈbreɪ.məˌhɑː.vᵊn (US) ˈbrem.ɚ-, ˈbreɪ.mɚ-
Bremner ˈbrem.nəʳ (US) -nɚ
Bren bren
Brenda ˈbren.də
Brendan ˈbren.dən
Brendel ˈbren.dᵊl
Brendon ˈbren.dən
Brennan ˈbren.ən
Brenner ˈbren.əʳ (US) -ɚ
Brent brent
Brentford ˈbrent.fəd (US) -fɚd
brent|-goose ˌbrent|ˈguːs **-geese** -giːs
Brenton ˈbren.tən
Brentwood ˈbrent.wʊd
bre'r, br'er **(B)** brɜːʳ, breəʳ (US) brɝː, brer
Brereton ˈbrɪə.tᵊn (US) ˈbrɪr-
Brescia ˈbreʃ.ə, ˈbreɪ.ʃə (US) ˈbreʃ.ɑː, ˈbreɪ.ʃɑː
Breslau ˈbrez.laʊ, ˈbres-

Brest *in France:* brest
brethren ˈbreð.rən, -rɪn
Breton ˈbret.ɒn *as if French:* bretˈɔ̃ːŋ (US) ˈbret.ᵊn **-s** -z
Bret(t) bret
Bretwalda bretˈwɔːl.də, -ˈwɒl-, ˈ--- (US) -ˈwɑːl-, -ˈwɔːl-
Breughel ˈbrɔɪ.gᵊl, ˈbrɜː-, ˈbruː- *as if Dutch:* -xəl (US) ˈbruː.gᵊl, ˈbrɔɪ-, ˈbrɔː-
breve briːv (US) briːv, brev **-s** -z
brev|et ˈbrev|.ɪt **-ets** -ɪts **-eting** -ɪ.tɪŋ (US) -ɪ.t̬ɪŋ **-eted** -ɪ.tɪd (US) -ɪ.t̬ɪd
breviar|y ˈbrev.i.ᵊr|.i, ˈbriː.vi- (US) -er|.i, -ɚ|.i **-ies** -iz
breviate ˈbriː.vi.ət, -ɪt **-s** -s
brevier brəˈvɪəʳ, brɪ- (US) -ˈvɪr
brevity ˈbrev.ə.ti, -ɪ.ti (US) -ə.t̬i
brew (B) bruː **-s** -z **-ing** -ɪŋ **-ed** -d
brewer (B) ˈbruː.əʳ (US) -ɚ **-s** -z ˌ**brewer's** ˈ**yeast**
brewer|y ˈbruː.ᵊr|.i (US) ˈbruː.ɚ|.i, ˈ-ri **-ies** -iz
brewpub ˈbruː.pʌb **-s** -z
Brewster ˈbruː.stəʳ (US) -stɚ
Brezhnev ˈbreʒ.nef, -njef (US) -nef, -nev
Brian braɪən
Note: /ˈbriː.ən/ for the novelist Brian Moore.
Bria(n)na briˈæn.ə
Brianne briˈæn
briar braɪəʳ (US) braɪɚ **-s** -z
Briareus ˌbraɪˈeə.ri.əs (US) -ˈer.i-
brib|e braɪb **-es** -z **-ing** -ɪŋ **-ed** -d **-er/s** -əʳ/z (US) -ɚ/z
briber|y ˈbraɪ.bᵊr|.i **-ies** -iz
bric-à-brac ˈbrɪk.əˌbræk
Brice braɪs
brick brɪk **-s** -s ˈ**brick** ˌ**dust**; ˈ**brick** ˌ**field**
brickbat ˈbrɪk.bæt **-s** -s
brickie ˈbrɪk.i **-s** -z
brick-kiln ˈbrɪk.kɪln, -kɪl **-s** -z
Note: The pronunciation /-kɪl/ is used chiefly by those concerned with the working of kilns.
bricklay|er ˈbrɪkˌleɪ|.əʳ (US) -ɚ **-ers** -əz (US) -ɚz **-ing** -ɪŋ
brickmak|er ˈbrɪkˌmeɪ|.kəʳ (US) -kɚ **-ers** -əz (US) -ɚz **-ing** -ɪŋ
brickwork ˈbrɪk.wɜːk (US) -wɝːk
bricolage ˌbrɪk.əʊˈlɑːʒ, ˈ--- (US) ˌbriː.koʊˈlɑːʒ, ˌbrɪk.oʊˈ-
bridal ˈbraɪ.dᵊl
bride braɪd **-s** -z
bridegroom ˈbraɪd.grʊm, -gruːm (US) -gruːm, -grʊm **-s** -z
Brideshead ˈbraɪdz.hed
bridesmaid ˈbraɪdz.meɪd **-s** -z
brides|man ˈbraɪdz|.mən **-men** -mən, -men
bride-to-be ˌbraɪd.təˈbiː (US) -tuːˈ- **brides-to-be** ˌbraɪdz.təˈbiː (US) -tuːˈ-
Bridewell ˈbraɪd.wel, -wəl
bridg|e (B) brɪdʒ **-es** -ɪz **-ing** -ɪŋ **-ed** -d ˌ**burn one's** ˈ**bridges**
bridgeable ˈbrɪdʒ.ə.bl̩
bridgehead ˈbrɪdʒ.hed **-s** -z
Bridgeman ˈbrɪdʒ.mən
Bridgend ˌbrɪdʒˈend, ˈ--
Bridgenorth ˈbrɪdʒ.nɔːθ, -ˈ- (US) ˈbrɪdʒ.nɔːrθ, -ˈ-
Bridgeport ˈbrɪdʒ.pɔːt (US) -pɔːrt
Bridger ˈbrɪdʒ.əʳ (US) -ɚ
Bridges ˈbrɪdʒ.ɪz
Bridget ˈbrɪdʒ.ɪt
Bridgetown ˈbrɪdʒ.taʊn
Bridgewater ˈbrɪdʒˌwɔː.təʳ (US) -ˌwɑː.t̬ɚ, -ˌwɔː-
bridgework ˈbrɪdʒ.wɜːk (US) -wɝːk
Bridgnorth ˈbrɪdʒ.nɔːθ, ˌ-ˈ- (US) ˈbrɪdʒ.nɔːrθ, ˌ-ˈ-
Bridgwater ˈbrɪdʒˌwɔː.təʳ (US) -ˌwɑː.t̬ɚ, -ˌwɔː-
bridie (B) ˈbraɪ.di **-s** -z
bridl|e ˈbraɪ.dl̩ **-es** -z **-ing** -ɪŋ, ˈbraɪd.lɪŋ **-ed** -d ˈ**bridle** ˌ**path**
bridleway ˈbraɪ.dl̩.weɪ **-s** -z
Bridlington ˈbrɪd.lɪŋ.tən
bridoon brɪˈduːn **-s** -z
Bridport ˈbrɪd.pɔːt (US) -pɔːrt
brie (B) briː
brief briːf **-s** -s **-er** -əʳ (US) -ɚ **-est** -ɪst, -əst **-ly** -li **-ness** -nəs, -nɪs **-ing/s** -ɪŋ/z **-ed** -t
briefcas|e ˈbriːf.keɪs **-es** -ɪz, -əz
briefless ˈbriː.fləs, -flɪs
brier braɪəʳ (US) braɪɚ **-s** -z
Brierfield ˈbraɪə.fiːld (US) ˈbraɪɚ-
Brierley ˈbraɪə.li, ˈbrɪə- (US) ˈbraɪɚ-, ˈbrɪr-
Briers braɪəz (US) braɪɚz
brig brɪg **-s** -z
brigade brɪˈgeɪd, brə- **-s** -z
brigadier ˌbrɪg.əˈdɪəʳ (US) -ˈdɪr **-s** -z *stress shift, see compound:* ˌ**brigadier** ˈ**general**
Brigadoon ˌbrɪg.əˈduːn
brigand ˈbrɪg.ᵊnd **-s** -z **-age** -ɪdʒ
brigantine ˈbrɪg.ᵊn.tiːn, -taɪn **-s** -z
Briges ˈbrɪdʒ.ɪz
Brigg brɪg **-s** -z
Brigham ˈbrɪg.əm
Brighouse ˈbrɪg.haʊs
bright (B) braɪt **-er** -əʳ (US) ˈbraɪ.t̬ɚ **-est** -ɪst, -əst (US) ˈbraɪ.t̬ɪst, -t̬əst **-ly** -li **-ness** -nəs, -nɪs
brighten ˈbraɪ.tᵊn **-s** -z **-ing** -ɪŋ **-ed** -d
Brightlingsea ˈbraɪt.lɪŋ.siː
Brighton ˈbraɪ.tᵊn
brights braɪts
Brigid ˈbrɪdʒ.ɪd
Brigit ˈbrɪdʒ.ɪt
Brignell ˈbrɪg.nəl
Brigstock(e) ˈbrɪg.stɒk (US) -stɑːk
brill (B) brɪl **-s** -z
brillian|ce ˈbrɪl.i.ənt|s (US) ˈ-jənt|s **-cy** -si
brilliant ˈbrɪl.i.ənt (US) ˈ-jənt **-s** -s **-ly** -li **-ness** -nəs, -nɪs
brilliantine ˈbrɪl.i.ən.tiːn (US) ˈ-jən- **-d** -d
Brillo® ˈbrɪl.əʊ (US) -oʊ
Brillo pad® ˈbrɪl.əʊˌpæd (US) -oʊˌ-
brim brɪm **-s** -z **-ming** -ɪŋ **-med** -d
brimful brɪmˈfʊl, ˈ--
brimstone ˈbrɪm.stəʊn (US) -stoʊn
Brind brɪnd
Brindisi ˈbrɪn.dɪ.si, -də-, -zi
brindle (B) ˈbrɪn.dl̩ **-s** -z **-d** -d
brine braɪn
bring brɪŋ **-s** -z **-ing** -ɪŋ **brought** brɔːt (US) brɑːt, brɔːt **bringer/s** ˈbrɪŋ.əʳ/z (US) -ɚ/z
brinjal ˈbrɪn.dʒᵊl
brink (B) brɪŋk **-s** -s
brinkmanship ˈbrɪŋk.mən.ʃɪp
brinksmanship ˈbrɪŋks.mən.ʃɪp
Brinks-Mat® ˌbrɪŋksˈmæt
Brinsley ˈbrɪnz.li
brin|y ˈbraɪ.n|i **-ier** -i.əʳ (US) -i.ɚ **-iest** -i.ɪst, -i.əst **-iness** -ɪ.nəs, -ɪ.nɪs
Bri-Nylon® ˌbraɪˈnaɪ.lɒn (US) -lɑːn
brio ˈbriː.əʊ (US) -oʊ
brioch|e briˈɒʃ, -ˈəʊʃ (US) -ˈoʊʃ, -ˈɑːʃ **-es** -ɪz
Briony ˈbraɪə.ni
briquet(te) brɪˈket **-s** -s
Brisbane ˈbrɪz.bən (US) -bən, -beɪn
Note: /ˈbrɪz.bən/ is the pronunciation in Australia.
Briscoe ˈbrɪs.kəʊ (US) -koʊ
brisk brɪsk **-er** -əʳ (US) -ɚ **-est** -ɪst, -əst **-ly** -li **-ness** -nəs, -nɪs
brisket ˈbrɪs.kɪt **-s** -s
bristl|e ˈbrɪs.l̩ **-es** -z **-ing** -ɪŋ, ˈbrɪs.lɪŋ **-ed** -d
bristl|y ˈbrɪs|.l̩.i, ˈbrɪs|.li **-liness** -l̩.ɪ.nəs, ˈbrɪs|.li-, -nɪs
Bristol ˈbrɪs.tᵊl
Bristow(e) ˈbrɪs.təʊ (US) -toʊ
Brit brɪt **-s** -s
Brit. *(abbrev. for* **Britain***)* brɪt; ˈbrɪt.ᵊn
Brit. *(abbrev. for* **British***)* brɪt; ˈbrɪt.ɪʃ (US) brɪt; ˈbrɪt̬.ɪʃ
Britain ˈbrɪt.ᵊn
Britannia brɪˈtæn.i.ə, ˈ-jə (US) ˈ-jə
Britannic brɪˈtæn.ɪk **-a** -ə
britches ˈbrɪtʃ.ɪz, -əz
Briticism ˈbrɪt.ɪ.sɪ.zᵊm (US) ˈbrɪt̬- **-s** -z
British ˈbrɪt.ɪʃ (US) ˈbrɪt̬- **-er/s** -əʳ/z (US) -ɚ/z ˌ**British** ˈ**English**; ˌ**British** ˈ**Isles**; ˌ**British** ˈ**Summer** ˌ**Time**
Britishism ˈbrɪt.ɪ.ʃɪ.zᵊm (US) ˈbrɪt̬- **-s** -z
British Leyland® ˌbrɪt.ɪʃˈleɪ.lənd (US) ˌbrɪt̬-
Britling ˈbrɪt.lɪŋ
Britney ˈbrɪt.ni
Britomart ˈbrɪt.əʊ.mɑːt (US) -oʊ.mɑːrt

Briton ˈbrɪt.ᵊn **-s** -z
Britpop ˈbrɪt.pɒp (US) -pɑːp
Britt brɪt
Brittain ˈbrɪt.ᵊn; brɪˈteɪn (US) ˈbrɪt.ᵊn; brɪˈteɪn
Brittan ˈbrɪt.ᵊn
Brittany ˈbrɪt.ᵊn.i
Britten ˈbrɪt.ᵊn
brittl|e ˈbrɪt.l̩ (US) ˈbrɪt̬- **-er** -əʳ (US) -ɚ **-est** -ɪst, -əst **-eness** -nəs, -nɪs
Brittney ˈbrɪt.ni
Britton ˈbrɪt.ᵊn
Britvic® ˈbrɪt.vɪk
Brixham ˈbrɪk.sᵊm
Brixton ˈbrɪk.stᵊn
Brize Norton ˌbraɪzˈnɔː.tᵊn (US) -ˈnɔːr-
Brno ˈbɜː.nəʊ *as if Czech:* ˈbɚ- (US) ˈbɜː.noʊ
bro brəʊ (US) broʊ **-s** -z
broach brəʊtʃ (US) broʊtʃ **-es** -ɪz **-ing** -ɪŋ **-ed** -t
broad brɔːd (US) brɑːd, brɔːd **-er** -əʳ (US) -ɚ **-est** -ɪst, -əst **-ly** -li **-ness** -nəs, -nɪs ˌ**broad** ˈ**bean**
Broad brɔːd (US) brɑːd, brɔːd **-s** -z
broadband ˈbrɔːd.bænd (US) ˈbrɑːd-, ˈbrɔːd-
Broadbent ˈbrɔːd.bent (US) ˈbrɑːd-, ˈbrɔːd-
broadbrimmed ˌbrɔːdˈbrɪmd (US) ˌbrɑːd-, ˌbrɔːd- *stress shift:* ˌbroadbrimmed ˈhat
broadcast ˈbrɔːd.kɑːst (US) ˈbrɑːd.kæst, ˈbrɔːd- **-s** -s **-ing** -ɪŋ **-er/s** -əʳ/z (US) -ɚ/z
broadcloth ˈbrɔːd.klɒθ (US) ˈbrɑːd.klɑːθ, ˈbrɔːd-
broaden ˈbrɔː.dᵊn (US) ˈbrɑː-, ˈbrɔː- **-s** -z **-ing** -ɪŋ **-ed** -d
broad-gauge ˈbrɔːd.geɪdʒ (US) ˈbrɑːd-, ˈbrɔːd-
Broadhurst ˈbrɔːd.hɜːst (US) ˈbrɑːd.hɝːst, ˈbrɔːd-
Broadlands ˈbrɔːd.ləndz (US) ˈbrɑːd-, ˈbrɔːd-
broadloom ˈbrɔːd.luːm (US) ˈbrɑːd-, ˈbrɔːd-
broad-minded ˌbrɔːdˈmaɪn.dɪd (US) ˌbrɑːd-, ˌbrɔːd-, ˈ-ˌ-- **-ness** -nəs, -nɪs *stress shift, British only:* ˌbroad-minded ˈperson
Broadmoor ˈbrɔːd.mɔːʳ (US) ˈbrɑːd.mʊr, ˈbrɔːd-, -mɔːr
broadsheet ˈbrɔːd.ʃiːt (US) ˈbrɑːd-, ˈbrɔːd- **-s** -s
broadside ˈbrɔːd.saɪd (US) ˈbrɑːd-, ˈbrɔːd- **-s** -z
Broadstairs ˈbrɔːd.steəz (US) ˈbrɑːd.sterz, ˈbrɔːd-
broadsword ˈbrɔːd.sɔːd (US) ˈbrɑːd.sɔːrd, ˈbrɔːd- **-s** -z
Broadwater ˈbrɔːdˌwɔː.təʳ (US) ˈbrɑːdˌwɑː.t̬ɚ, -ˌwɔː-
Broadway ˈbrɔːd.weɪ (US) ˈbrɑːd-, ˈbrɔːd-
Broadwood ˈbrɔːd.wʊd (US) ˈbrɑːd-, ˈbrɔːd- **-s** -z
Brobdingnag ˈbrɒb.dɪŋ.næg (US) ˈbrɑːb-
Brobdingnagian ˌbrɒb.dɪŋˈnæg.i.ən (US) ˌbrɑːb- **-s** -z
brocade brəʊˈkeɪd (US) broʊ- **-s** -z **-d** -ɪd
brocard ˈbrəʊ.kəd, -kɑːd (US) ˈbroʊ.kɚd, ˈbrɑː-, -kɑːrd **-s** -z
broc(c)oli ˈbrɒk.ᵊl.i, -aɪ (US) ˈbrɑː.kᵊl-
Broch brɒk *as if German:* brox (US) broʊk
brochette brɒʃˈet (US) broʊˈʃet **-s** -s
brochure ˈbrəʊ.ʃəʳ, -ʃʊəʳ, brɒʃˈʊəʳ, brəˈʃʊəʳ (US) broʊˈʃʊr **-s** -z
brock (B) brɒk (US) brɑːk **-s** -s
Brocken ˈbrɒk.ᵊn (US) ˈbrɑː.kᵊn
Brockenhurst ˈbrɒk.ᵊn.hɜːst (US) ˈbrɑː.kᵊn.hɝːst
Brocket ˈbrɒk.ɪt (US) ˈbrɑː.kɪt
Brocklehurst ˈbrɒk.l̩.hɜːst (US) ˈbrɑː.kl̩.hɝːst
Brockley ˈbrɒk.li (US) ˈbrɑː.kli
Brockman ˈbrɒk.mən (US) ˈbrɑːk-
Brockovich ˈbrɒk.ə.vɪtʃ (US) ˈbrɑː.kə-
Brockwell ˈbrɒk.wəl, -wel (US) ˈbrɑː.kwəl, -kwel
Broderick ˈbrɒd.ᵊr.ɪk (US) ˈbrɑː.dᵊr-
broderie anglaise ˌbrəʊ.dᵊr.iˈɑ̃ː*ŋ*.gleɪz, ˌbrɒd.ᵊr-, -ˈglez, -ɑ̃ː*ŋ*ˈgleɪz, -ˈglez (US) ˌbroʊ.də.riː.ɑːŋˈgleɪz
Brodie ˈbrəʊ.di (US) ˈbroʊ-
Brodrick ˈbrɒd.rɪk (US) ˈbrɑː.drɪk
Brogan ˈbrəʊ.gᵊn (US) ˈbroʊ-
brogue brəʊg (US) broʊg **-s** -z
broil brɔɪl **-s** -z **-ing** -ɪŋ **-ed** -d
broiler ˈbrɔɪ.ləʳ (US) -lɚ **-s** -z
brok|e (*v.*) brəʊk (US) broʊk **-es** -s **-ing** -ɪŋ **-ed** -t
broke (*from* **break**) brəʊk (US) broʊk
Broke brʊk
broken ˈbrəʊ.kᵊn (US) ˈbroʊ- **-ly** -li
broken-down ˌbrəʊ.kᵊnˈdaʊn (US) ˌbroʊ- *stress shift:* ˌbroken-down ˈcar
broken-hearted ˌbrəʊ.kᵊnˈhɑː.tɪd (US) ˌbroʊ.kᵊnˈhɑːr.t̬ɪd *stress shift:* ˌbroken-hearted ˈsuitor
broker ˈbrəʊ.kəʳ (US) ˈbroʊ.kɚ **-s** -z **-ing** -ɪŋ **-ed** -d
brokerag|e ˈbrəʊ.kᵊr.ɪdʒ (US) ˈbroʊ- **-es** -ɪz
broll|y ˈbrɒl|.i (US) ˈbrɑː.l|i **-ies** -iz
bromate ˈbrəʊ.meɪt (US) ˈbroʊ- **-s** -s
brome brəʊm, bruːm (US) broʊm **-s** -z
Brome brəʊm, bruːm (US) broʊm, bruːm
bromeliad brəʊˈmiː.li.æd (US) broʊ-
Bromfield ˈbrɒm.fiːld (US) ˈbrɑːm-
Bromham ˈbrɒm.əm (US) ˈbrɑː.məm
bromic ˈbrəʊ.mɪk (US) ˈbroʊ-
bromide ˈbrəʊ.maɪd (US) ˈbroʊ- **-s** -z
bromine ˈbrəʊ.miːn, -mɪn (US) ˈbroʊ-
Bromley ˈbrɒm.li, ˈbrʌm- (US) ˈbrɑːm-
Brompton ˈbrɒm*p*.tən, ˈbrʌm*p*- (US) ˈbrɑːm*p*-
Bromsgrove ˈbrɒmz.grəʊv (US) ˈbrɑːmz.groʊv
Bromwich *in place names:* ˈbrɒm.ɪtʃ, ˈbrʌm-, -ɪdʒ (US) ˈbrɑːm.wɪtʃ *surname:* ˈbrʌm.ɪdʒ (US) -wɪtʃ
Bromyard ˈbrɒm.jɑːd, -jəd (US) ˈbrɑːm.jɑːrd, -jɚd
bronchi|a ˈbrɒŋ.ki|.ə, ˈbrɒn- (US) ˈbrɑːŋ-, ˈbrɑːn- **-ae** -iː
bronchial ˈbrɒŋ.ki.əl, ˈbrɒn- (US) ˈbrɑːŋ-, ˈbrɑːn-
bronchiole ˈbrɒŋ.ki.əʊl, ˈbrɒn- (US) ˈbrɑːŋ.ki.oʊl, ˈbrɑːn- **-s** -z
bronchitic brɒŋˈkɪt.ɪk, brɒn- (US) brɑːŋˈkɪt̬-, brɑːn-
bronchitis brɒŋˈkaɪ.tɪs, brɒn- (US) brɑːŋˈkaɪ.t̬ɪs, brɑːn-
broncho-pneumonia ˌbrɒŋ.kəʊ.njuːˈməʊ.ni.ə, ˌbrɒn-, -njʊˈ- (US) ˌbrɑːŋ.koʊ.nuːˈmoʊ.njə, ˌbrɑːn-, -njuːˈ-
bronch|us ˈbrɒŋ.k|əs, ˈbrɒn- (US) ˈbrɑːŋ-, ˈbrɑːn- **-i** -iː, -aɪ
bronco ˈbrɒŋ.kəʊ (US) ˈbrɑːŋ.koʊ **-s** -z
Bronson ˈbrɒn*t*.sən (US) ˈbrɑːn*t*-
Bronstein ˈbrɒn.stiːn (US) ˈbrɑːn-
Bronte, Brontë ˈbrɒn.teɪ, -ti (US) ˈbrɑːn.teɪ, -t̬i
brontosaur ˈbrɒn.tə.sɔːʳ (US) ˈbrɑːn.t̬ə.sɔːr **-s** -z
brontosaur|us ˌbrɒn.təˈsɔː.r|əs (US) ˌbrɑːn.t̬əˈsɔːr|.əs **-uses** -ə.sɪz **-i** -aɪ
Bronwen ˈbrɒn.wen, -wɪn (US) ˈbrɑːn-
Bronx brɒŋks (US) brɑːŋks ˌ**Bronx** ˈ**cheer**
bronz|e brɒnz (US) brɑːnz **-es** -ɪz **-ing** -ɪŋ **-ed** -d **-y** -i ˈ**Bronze** ˌ**Age**
bronzer ˈbrɒn.zəʳ (US) ˈbrɑːn.zɚ **-s** -z
brooch brəʊtʃ (US) broʊtʃ, bruːtʃ **-es** -ɪz
brood bruːd **-s** -z **-ing** -ɪŋ **-ed** -ɪd
brood|y ˈbruː.d|i **-ily** -ɪ.li, -ᵊl.i **-iness** -ɪ.nəs, -ɪ.nɪs
brook brʊk **-s** -s **-ing** -ɪŋ **-ed** -t
Brook(e) brʊk **-s** -s
Brooker ˈbrʊk.əʳ (US) -ɚ
Brookfield ˈbrʊk.fiːld
Brookland ˈbrʊk.lənd **-s** -z
brooklet ˈbrʊk.lət, -lɪt **-s** -s
Brookline ˈbrʊk.laɪn
Brooklyn ˈbrʊk.lɪn (US) -lɪn, -lən ˌ**Brooklyn** ˈ**Bridge**
Brookner ˈbrʊk.nəʳ (US) -nɚ
Brooks brʊks
Brookside ˈbrʊk.saɪd
Brooksmith ˈbrʊk.smɪθ
Brookwood ˈbrʊk.wʊd
broom bruːm, brʊm **-s** -z

Broom(e) bruːm
Broomfield ˈbruːm.fiːld, ˈbrʊm-
broomstick ˈbruːm.stɪk, ˈbrʊm- **-s** -s
Brophy ˈbrəʊ.fi (US) ˈbroʊ-
Bros. ˈbrʌð.əz *sometimes humorously:* brɒs, brɒz (US) ˈbrʌð.ɚz
Broseley ˈbrəʊz.li (US) ˈbroʊz-
Brosnahan ˈbrɒz.nə.hən, ˈbrɒs- (US) ˈbrɑːz-, ˈbrɑːs-
Brosnan ˈbrɒz.nən (US) ˈbrɑːz-
broth brɒθ (US) brɑːθ **-s** -s
brothel ˈbrɒθ.ᵊl (US) ˈbrɑː.θᵊl **-s** -z
brother ˈbrʌð.əʳ (US) -ɚ **-s** -z
brotherhood ˈbrʌð.ə.hʊd (US) ˈ-ɚ- **-s** -z
broth|er-in-law ˈbrʌð|.əʳ.ɪn.lɔː (US) -ɚ.ɪn.lɑː, -lɔː **-ers-in-law** -əz.ɪn.lɔː (US) -ɚz.ɪn.lɑː, -lɔː
brotherl|y ˈbrʌð.ᵊl|.i (US) -ɚ.l|i **-iness** -ɪ.nəs, -ɪ.nɪs
Brotton ˈbrɒt.ᵊn (US) ˈbrɑː.tᵊn
Brough brʌf
brougham ˈbruː.əm, bruːm (US) broʊm, ˈbruː.əm, bruːm **-s** -z
Brougham brʊm, bruːm, ˈbruː.əm, ˈbrəʊ- (US) brʊm, bruːm, ˈbruː.əm, ˈbroʊ-
Brougham and Vaux ˌbrʊm.ənd̚ˈvɔːks (US) -ˈvɑːks, -ˈvɔːks
brought *(from* **bring***)* brɔːt (US) brɑːt, brɔːt
Broughton *in Northamptonshire:* ˈbraʊ.tᵊn *all others in England:* ˈbrɔː.tᵊn (US) ˈbrɑː-, ˈbrɔː-
brouhaha ˈbruː.hɑː.hɑː **-s** -z
brow braʊ **-s** -z
brow|beat ˈbraʊ|.biːt **-beats** -biːts **-beating** -biː.tɪŋ (US) -biː.t̬ɪŋ **-beaten** -biː.tᵊn (US) -biː.t̬ᵊn
brown (B) braʊn **-s** -z **-er** -əʳ (US) -ɚ **-est** -ɪst, -əst **-ness** -nəs, -nɪs **-ing** -ɪŋ **-ed** -d ˌ**brown ˈale**; ˌ**brown ˈBetty**; ˌ**brown ˈbread**; ˌ**brown ˈowl**; ˌ**brown ˈsauce**; ˌ**brown ˈsugar**
brown-bag ˌbraʊnˈbæg **-s** -z **-ging** -ɪŋ **-ged** -d
Browne braʊn
brownfield ˈbraʊn.fiːld
Brownhills ˈbraʊn.hɪlz
Brownian ˈbraʊ.ni.ən ˌ**Brownian ˈmotion** (US) ˈ**Brownian** ˌ**motion**; ˌ**Brownian ˈmovement** (US) ˈ**Brownian** ˌ**movement**
brownie (B) ˈbraʊ.ni **-s** -z ˈ**Brownie** ˌ**Guide**; ˈ**brownie** ˌ**point**
browning (B) ˈbraʊ.nɪŋ
brownish ˈbraʊ.nɪʃ
Brownjohn ˈbraʊn.dʒɒn (US) -dʒɑːn
Brownlee, Brownlie ˈbraʊn.li
Brownlow ˈbraʊn.ləʊ (US) -loʊ
brown-nos|e ˌbraʊnˈnəʊz (US) -ˈnoʊz **-es** -ɪz **-ing** -ɪŋ **-ed** -d
brownout ˈbraʊn.aʊt **-s** -s
Brownrigg ˈbraʊn.rɪg
brownshirt (B) ˈbraʊn.ʃɜːt (US) -ʃɝːt **-s** -s
Brownsmith ˈbraʊn.smɪθ
Brownson ˈbraʊn.sᵊn
brownstone ˈbraʊn.stəʊn (US) -stoʊn **-s** -z
brows|e (B) braʊz **-es** -ɪz **-ing** -ɪŋ **-ed** -d
browser ˈbraʊ.zəʳ (US) -zɚ **-s** -z
Broxbourne ˈbrɒks.bɔːn (US) ˈbrɑːks.bɔːrn
Broxburn ˈbrɒks.bɜːn (US) ˈbrɑːks.bɝːn
Brubeck ˈbruː.bek
Bruce bruːs
brucellosis ˌbruː.sɪˈləʊ.sɪs, -səˈ- (US) -ˈloʊ-
Brucesmith ˈbruːs.smɪθ
Bruch brʊk *as if German:* brʊx
Bruckner ˈbrʊk.nəʳ (US) -nɚ
Brueg(h)el ˈbrɔɪ.gᵊl, ˈbrɜː-, ˈbruː- *as if Dutch:* -xəl (US) ˈbruː.gᵊl, ˈbrɔɪ-, ˈbrɔː-
Bruges bruːʒ
bruin (B) ˈbruː.ɪn, brʊɪn (US) ˈbruː.ɪn **-s** -z
bruis|e bruːz **-es** -ɪz **-ing** -ɪŋ **-ed** -d
bruiser ˈbruː.zəʳ (US) -zɚ **-s** -z
bruit bruːt **-s** -s **-ing** -ɪŋ (US) ˈbruː.t̬ɪŋ **-ed** -ɪd (US) ˈbruː.t̬ɪd
Brum brʌm
Brumaire bruˈmeəʳ (US) -ˈmer
brumb|y ˈbrʌm.b|i **-ies** -iz
brume bruːm
brummagem (B) ˈbrʌm.ə.dʒəm
Brummel ˈbrʌm.ᵊl
brunch brʌntʃ **-es** -ɪz
Brunei bruːˈnaɪ, ˈ-- (US) bruːˈnaɪ
Brunel bruːˈnel
brunette, brunet bruːˈnet **-s** -s
Brünnhilde brʊnˈhɪl.də, ˈ-ˌ--
Brunning ˈbrʌn.ɪŋ
Bruno ˈbruː.nəʊ (US) -noʊ
Brunswick ˈbrʌnz.wɪk
brunt brʌnt
Brunton ˈbrʌn.tən
bruschetta brʊˈsket.ə (US) -ˈsket̬-, bruːˈʃet̬.ə
brush brʌʃ **-es** -ɪz **-ing** -ɪŋ **-ed** -t
brush-off ˈbrʌʃ.ɒf (US) -ɑːf **-s** -s ˌ**give someone the ˈbrush-off**
brushstroke ˈbrʌʃ.strəʊk (US) -stroʊk **-s** -s
brushwood ˈbrʌʃ.wʊd
brushwork ˈbrʌʃ.wɜːk (US) -wɝːk
brusque bruːsk, brʊsk, brʌsk (US) brʌsk **-ly** -li **-ness** -nəs, -nɪs
Brussels ˈbrʌs.ᵊlz ˌ**brussels ˈsprout(s)** (US) ˈ**brussels** ˌ**sprout(s)**
brut (B®) bruːt
brutal ˈbruː.tᵊl (US) -t̬ᵊl **-ly** -i
brutalit|y bruːˈtæl.ə.t|i, -ɪ.t|i (US) -ə.t̬|i **-ies** -iz
brutaliz|e, -is|e ˈbruː.tᵊl.aɪz (US) -t̬ᵊl- **-es** -ɪz **-ing** -ɪŋ **-ed** -d
brute bruːt **-s** -s
brutish ˈbruː.tɪʃ (US) -t̬ɪʃ **-ly** -li **-ness** -nəs, -nɪs
Brutnell ˈbruːt.nel, -nᵊl
Bruton ˈbruː.tᵊn (US) -tᵊn
Brutus ˈbruː.təs (US) -t̬əs
Bryan braɪən **-s** -z
Bryant braɪənt
Bryce braɪs
Brydon ˈbraɪ.dᵊn
Bryers braɪəz (US) braɪɚz
Brylcreem® ˈbrɪl.kriːm **-ed** -d
Brymbo ˈbrɪm.bəʊ, ˈbrʌm- (US) ˈbrɪm.boʊ
Bryn brɪn
Brynamman brɪˈnæm.ən
Bryncoch brɪnˈkəʊx (US) -ˈkoʊx
Brynhild ˈbrɪn.hɪld
Brynmawr *in Wales:* brɪnˈmaʊəʳ, brɪm- (US) -ˈmaʊɚ
Bryn Mawr *in US:* brɪnˈmɔːʳ (US) -ˈmɑːr
Brynmor ˈbrɪn.mɔːʳ, ˈbrɪm- (US) ˈbrɪn.mɔːr
bryony (B) ˈbraɪə.ni
Bryson ˈbraɪ.sᵊn
BS ˌbiːˈes
BSc ˌbiː.esˈsiː
BSE ˌbiː.esˈiː
BSkyB ˌbiː.skaɪˈbiː
BST ˌbiː.esˈtiː
BT ˌbiːˈtiː
bub bʌb **-s** -z
bubbl|e ˈbʌb.l̩ **-es** -z **-ing** -ɪŋ, ˈbʌb.lɪŋ **-ed** -d ˌ**bubble-and-ˈsqueak**; ˈ**bubble** ˌ**bath**; ˈ**bubble** ˌ**gum**; ˈ**bubble** ˌ**wrap**
Bubblejet® ˈbʌb.l̩.dʒet
bubbly ˈbʌb.l̩.i, -li
Buber ˈbuː.bəʳ (US) -bɚ
bubo ˈbjuː.bəʊ, ˈbuː- (US) -boʊ **-es** -z
bubonic bjuːˈbɒn.ɪk, buː- (US) -ˈbɑː.nɪk buˌ**bonic ˈplague**
Bucaramanga bʊˌkær.əˈmæŋ.gə (US) ˌbuː.kə.rɑːˈmɑːŋ.gɑː, -kɑːr.ɑːˈ-
buccal ˈbʌk.ᵊl
buccaneer ˌbʌk.əˈnɪəʳ (US) -ˈnɪr **-s** -z
Buccleuch bəˈkluː
Bucephalus bjuːˈsef.ᵊl.əs
Buchan ˈbʌk.ᵊn, ˈbʌx-
Buchanan bjuːˈkæn.ən, bə-
Bucharest ˌbuː.kəˈrest, ˌbjuː-, ˌbʊk.əˈ-, ˈ--- (US) ˈbuː.kə.rest, ˈbjuː-
Buchel ˈbjuː.ʃᵊl
Buchenwald ˈbuː.kᵊn.væld *as if German:* ˈbʊx.ən.vælt (US) ˈbuː.kᵊn.wɑːld, -wɔːld
Büchner ˈbuːk.nəʳ *as if German:* ˈbuːx- (US) ˈbʊk.nɚ, ˈbuːk-
buck (B) bʌk **-s** -s **-ing** -ɪŋ **-ed** -t ˌ**buck's ˈfizz**; ˌ**buck ˈteeth**; ˌ**pass the ˈbuck**
buckboard ˈbʌk.bɔːd (US) -bɔːrd **-s** -z
buck|et ˈbʌk|.ɪt **-ets** -ɪts **-eting** -ɪ.tɪŋ (US) -ɪ.t̬ɪŋ **-eted** -ɪ.tɪd (US) -ɪ.t̬ɪd ˌ**kick the ˈbucket**

bucketful 'bʌk.ɪt.fʊl **-s** -z
Buckhaven 'bʌkˌheɪ.vᵊn
buckhorn 'bʌk.hɔːn (US) -hɔːrn
Buckhurst 'bʌk.*h*ɜːst (US) -*h*ɝːst
Buckie 'bʌk.i
Buckingham 'bʌk.ɪŋ.əm **-shire** -ʃəʳ, -ˌʃɪəʳ (US) -ʃɚ, -ˌʃɪr ˌ**Buckingham 'Palace**
Buckland 'bʌk.lənd
buckl|e (B) 'bʌk.l̩ **-es** -z **-ing** -ɪŋ, 'bʌk.lɪŋ **-ed** -d
buckler 'bʌk.ləʳ (US) -lɚ **-s** -z
Buckley 'bʌk.li
Buckmaster 'bʌkˌmɑː.stəʳ (US) -ˌmæs.tɚ
Bucknall 'bʌk.nəl
Bucknell 'bʌk.nᵊl; bʌk'nel
Bucknill 'bʌk.nɪl, -nᵊl
buck-passing 'bʌkˌpɑː.sɪŋ (US) -ˌpæs.ɪŋ
buckram 'bʌk.rəm **-s** -z
Bucks. *(abbrev. for* **Buckinghamshire***)* bʌks; 'bʌk.ɪŋ.əm.ʃəʳ, -ˌʃɪəʳ (US) bʌks; 'bʌk.ɪŋ.əm.ʃɚ, -ˌʃɪr
buckshee ˌbʌk'ʃiː, '--
buckshot 'bʌk.ʃɒt (US) -ʃɑːt
buckskin 'bʌk.skɪn **-s** -z
Buckston 'bʌk.stən
buckwheat 'bʌk.*h*wiːt
bucolic bjuː'kɒl.ɪk (US) -'kɑː.lɪk **-al** -ᵊl **-ally** -ᵊl.i, -li
Buczacki bʊ'tʃæt.ski, bjuː-
bud (B) bʌd **-s** -z **-ding** -ɪŋ **-ded** -ɪd ˌ**nip something in the 'bud**
Budapest ˌbjuː.də'pest, ˌbuː- (US) 'buː.də.pest; ˌbuː.də'peʃt
Budd bʌd
Buddha 'bʊd.ə (US) 'buː.də, 'bʊd.ə
Buddh|ism 'bʊd|.ɪ.zᵊm (US) 'buː.d|ɪ-, 'bʊd|.ɪ- **-ist/s** -ɪst/s
Buddhistic bʊ'dɪs.tɪk (US) buː-, bʊ-
budding 'bʌd.ɪŋ
Buddle 'bʌd.l̩, 'bʊd-
buddleia 'bʌd.li.ə (US) bʌd'liː-; 'bʌd.li- **-s** -z
budd|y 'bʌd|.i **-ies** -iz
Bude bjuːd
budg|e (B) bʌdʒ **-es** -ɪz **-ing** -ɪŋ **-ed** -d
Budgens® 'bʌdʒ.ənz
budgerigar 'bʌdʒ.ᵊr.ɪ.gɑːʳ (US) -gɑːr **-s** -z
budg|et 'bʌdʒ|.ɪt **-ets** -ɪts **-eting** -ɪ.tɪŋ (US) -ɪ.t̬ɪŋ **-eted** -ɪ.tɪd (US) -ɪ.t̬ɪd
budgetary 'bʌdʒ.ɪ.tᵊr.i, '-ə- (US) -ter.i
budgie 'bʌdʒ.i **-s** -z
Budleigh 'bʌd.li
Budweiser® 'bʌd.waɪ.zəʳ (US) -zɚ
Buenos Aires ˌbweɪ.nɒs'aɪə.rez, -nəs-, -riːz, -rɪs (US) ˌbweɪ.nəs'er.iːz, -noʊs'-, ˌboʊ.nəs'-, -aɪ.riːz
buff bʌf **-s** -s **-ing** -ɪŋ **-ed** -d
buffalo (B) 'bʌf.ᵊl.əʊ (US) -ə.loʊ **-es** -z ˌ**Buffalo 'Bill**

buffer 'bʌf.əʳ (US) -ɚ **-s** -z **-ing** -ɪŋ **-ed** -d **'buffer ˌzone**
buffet *(n.) blow:* 'bʌf.ɪt **-s** -s
buffet *(n.) refreshment, sideboard:* 'bʊf.eɪ, 'bʌf-, -i (US) bə'feɪ, buː- **-s** -z
buff|et *(v.) hit against:* 'bʌf|.ɪt **-ets** -ɪts **-eting** -ɪ.tɪŋ, -ə.tɪŋ (US) -ɪ.t̬ɪŋ, -ə.t̬ɪŋ **-eted** -ɪ.tɪd, -ə.tɪd (US) -ɪ.t̬ɪd, -ə.t̬ɪd
buffo 'bʊf.əʊ (US) 'buː.foʊ **-s** -z
buffoon bə'fuːn, bʌf'uːn (US) bə'fuːn **-s** -z
buffooner|y bə'fuː.nᵊr|.i, bʌf'uː- (US) bə'fuː- **-ies** -iz
Buffs bʌfs
Buffy 'bʌf.i
bug bʌg **-s** -z **-ging** -ɪŋ **-ged** -d
Bug *river:* buːg
bugaboo 'bʌg.ə.buː **-s** -z
Buganda buː'gæn.də
Bugatti bjʊ'gæt.i, bʊ- (US) -'gɑː.t̬i
bugbear 'bʌg.beəʳ (US) -ber **-s** -z
bug-eyed ˌbʌg'aɪd (US) '-- *stress shift, British only:* ˌbug-eyed 'monster
bugg|er 'bʌg|.əʳ (US) -ɚ **-ers** -əz (US) -ɚz **-ering** -ᵊr.ɪŋ **-ered** -əd (US) -ɚd
buggery 'bʌg.ᵊr.i
Buggins 'bʌg.ɪnz
Buggs bjuːgz, bʌgz
bugg|y 'bʌg|.i **-ies** -iz
bugl|e (B) 'bjuː.gl̩ **-es** -z **-ing** -ɪŋ, 'bjuː.glɪŋ **-ed** -d
bugler 'bjuː.gləʳ (US) -glɚ **-s** -z
bugloss 'bjuː.glɒs (US) -glɑːs
Bugner 'bʌg.nəʳ (US) -nɚ
Bugs Bunny ˌbʌgz'bʌn.i
Buick® 'bjuː.ɪk **-s** -s
build bɪld **-s** -z **-ing** -ɪŋ **built** bɪlt **'building soˌciety**
builder 'bɪl.dəʳ (US) -dɚ **-s** -z
build-up 'bɪld.ʌp **-s** -s
built *(from* **build***)* bɪlt
Builth bɪlθ
built-in ˌbɪlt'ɪn (US) 'bɪlt.ɪn *stress shift, British only:* ˌbuilt-in 'microphone
Buist bjuːst, 'bjuː.ɪst
Buitoni® bjuː'təʊ.ni, bwiː- (US) -'toʊ-
Bujumbura ˌbuː.dʒəm'bʊə.rə, -dʒʊm'- (US) -'bʊr.ə
Bukowski bjʊ'kɒf.ski, bjuː-, -'kaʊ- (US) bjuː'kaʊ-
Bulawayo ˌbʊl.ə'weɪ.əʊ, ˌbuː.lə- (US) -oʊ
bulb bʌlb **-s** -z
bulbaceous bʌl'beɪ.ʃəs
bulbous 'bʌl.bəs
bulbul 'bʊl.bʊl **-s** -z
Bulford 'bʊl.fəd (US) -fɚd
Bulgakov bʊl'gɑː.kɒf (US) -kɔːf, -kɔːv
bulgar 'bʌl.gəʳ, 'bʊl- (US) -gɚ **'bulgar ˌwheat**
Bulgar 'bʌl.gɑːʳ, 'bʊl-, -gəʳ (US) -gɑːr, -gɚ **-s** -z

Bulgari|a bʌl'geə.ri|.ə (US) -'ger.i- **-an/s** -ən/z
bulg|e bʌldʒ **-es** -ɪz **-ing** -ɪŋ **-ed** -d
Bulger 'bʊl.dʒəʳ, 'bʌl- (US) -dʒɚ
bulgur 'bʊl.gəʳ (US) -gɚ
bulg|y 'bʌl.dʒ|i **-iness** -ɪ.nəs, -ɪ.nɪs
bulim|ia bʊ'lɪm|.i.ə, buː-, bjuː-, -'liː.m|i- (US) bjuː'liː.m|i-, buː- **-ic/s** -ɪk/s **buˌlimia ner'vosa**
Bulins 'bjuː.lɪnz
bulk bʌlk **-s** -s **-ing** -ɪŋ **-ed** -t
bulkhead 'bʌlk.hed **-s** -z
Bulkington 'bʌl.kɪŋ.tən
bulk|y 'bʌl.k|i **-ier** -i.əʳ (US) -i.ɚ **-iest** -i.ɪst, -i.əst **-ily** -ɪ.li, -ᵊl.i **-iness** -ɪ.nəs, -ɪ.nɪs
bull (B) bʊl **-s** -z **-ing** -ɪŋ **-ed** -d ˌ**bull 'terrier; 'bull's ˌeye; like a ˌbull in a 'china shop; take the ˌbull by the 'horns**
bullac|e 'bʊl.ɪs **-es** -ɪz
Bullard 'bʊl.ɑːd, -əd (US) -ɑːrd, -ɚd
bull-baiting 'bʊlˌbeɪ.tɪŋ (US) -t̬ɪŋ
bull-cal|f 'bʊlˌkɑː|f, ˌ-'- (US) 'bʊl.kæ|f **-ves** -vz
bulldog 'bʊl.dɒg (US) -dɑːg, -dɔːg **-s** -z
bulldoz|e 'bʊl.dəʊz (US) -doʊz **-es** -ɪz **-ing** -ɪŋ **-ed** -d
bulldozer 'bʊlˌdəʊ.zəʳ (US) -ˌdoʊ.zɚ **-s** -z
Bulleid 'bʊl.iːd
Bullen 'bʊl.ən, -ɪn
Buller 'bʌl.əʳ (US) -ɚ
bullet 'bʊl.ɪt, -ət **-s** -s
bulletin 'bʊl.ə.tɪn, '-ɪ- (US) -ə.t̬ɪn **-s** -z **'bulletin ˌboard**
bullet-proof 'bʊl.ɪt.pruːf ˌ**bullet-proof 'vest**
bullfight 'bʊl.faɪt **-s** -s
bullfight|er 'bʊlˌfaɪ.t|əʳ (US) -t̬|ɚ **-ers** -əz (US) -ɚz **-ing** -ɪŋ
bullfinch 'bʊl.fɪntʃ **-es** -ɪz
bullfrog 'bʊl.frɒg (US) -frɑːg, -frɔːg **-s** -z
bullheaded ˌbʊl'hed.ɪd (US) '-ˌ-- **-ly** -li **-ness** -nəs, -nɪs *stress shift, British only:* ˌbullheaded 'person
bullhorn 'bʊl.hɔːn (US) -hɔːrn **-s** -z
bullion 'bʊl.i.ən, '-jən (US) '-jən
bullish 'bʊl.ɪʃ **-ly** -li **-ness** -nəs, -nɪs
Bullman 'bʊl.mən
bullock (B) 'bʊl.ək **-s** -s
Bullokar 'bʊl.ə.kɑːʳ, -kəʳ (US) -kɑːr
Bullough 'bʊl.əʊ (US) -oʊ
bullpen 'bʊl.pen **-s** -z
bullring 'bʊl.rɪŋ **-s** -z
bullrush 'bʊl.rʌʃ **-es** -ɪz
bull|shit 'bʊl|.ʃɪt **-shits** -ʃɪts **-shitting** -ˌʃɪt.ɪŋ (US) -ˌʃɪt̬.ɪŋ **-shitted** -ˌʃɪt.ɪd (US) -ˌʃɪt̬.ɪd
bullshitter 'bʊlˌʃɪt.əʳ (US) -ˌʃɪt̬.ɚ **-s** -z
bull|y 'bʊl|.i **-ies** -iz **-ying** -i.ɪŋ **-ied** -id
Bulmer 'bʊl.məʳ (US) -mɚ

bulrush 'bʊl.rʌʃ **-es** -ɪz
Bulstrode 'bʊl.strəʊd, 'bʌl.strəʊd ⓤⓢ -stroʊd
Bultitude 'bʊl.tɪ.tjuːd, '-tə- ⓤⓢ -tuːd, -tjuːd
bulwark 'bʊl.wək, 'bʌl-, -wɜːk ⓤⓢ -wɚk, -wɝːk **-s** -s
Bulwer 'bʊl.wəʳ ⓤⓢ -wɚ
Bulwer-Lytton ˌbʊl.wə'lɪt.ən ⓤⓢ -wɚ'lɪt̬-
bum bʌm **-s** -z **-ming** -ɪŋ **-med** -d
bumbag 'bʌm.bæg **-s** -z
bumbl|e 'bʌm.bl̩ **-es** -z **-ing** -ɪŋ, 'bʌm.blɪŋ **-ed** -d **-er/s** -əʳ/z, '-bləʳ/z ⓤⓢ '-bl̩.ɚ/z, '-blɚ/z
bumblebee 'bʌm.bl̩.biː **-s** -z
bumboat 'bʌm.bəʊt ⓤⓢ -boʊt **-s** -s
bumf bʌmpf
Bumford 'bʌm.fəd ⓤⓢ -fɚd
bumkin 'bʌmp.kɪn **-s** -z
bummaree ˌbʌm.ə'riː, '--- ⓤⓢ 'bʌm.ə.riː **-s** -z
bummer 'bʌm.əʳ ⓤⓢ -ɚ **-s** -z
bump bʌmp **-s** -s **-ing** -ɪŋ **-ed** -t
bumper 'bʌm.pəʳ ⓤⓢ -pɚ **-s** -z **'bumper ˌcar; 'bumper ˌsticker; ˌbumper to 'bumper**
bumph bʌmpf
bumpkin 'bʌmp.kɪn **-s** -z
bumptious 'bʌmp.ʃəs **-ly** -li **-ness** -nəs, -nɪs
Bumpus 'bʌm.pəs
bump|y 'bʌm.p|i **-ier** -i.əʳ ⓤⓢ -i.ɚ **-iest** -i.ɪst, -i.əst **-ily** -ɪ.li, -əl.i **-iness** -ɪ.nəs, -ɪ.nɪs
bun bʌn **-s** -z **have a 'bun in the ˌoven**
Bunce bʌnts
bunch (B) bʌntʃ **-es** -ɪz **-ing** -ɪŋ **-ed** -t
buncombe (B) 'bʌŋ.kəm
Bundesbank 'bʊn.dəz.bæŋk
Bundesrat 'bʊn.dəz.rɑːt
Bundestag 'bʊn.dəz.tɑːg *as if German:* -də.ztɑːk ⓤⓢ -dəz.tɑːg
bundl|e 'bʌn.dl̩ **-es** -z **-ing** -ɪŋ, 'bʌnd.lɪŋ **-ed** -d
bung bʌŋ **-s** -z **-ing** -ɪŋ **-ed** -d
bungalow 'bʌŋ.gəl.əʊ ⓤⓢ -oʊ **-s** -z
Bungay 'bʌŋ.gi
Bunge 'bʌŋ.i
bungee 'bʌn.dʒi **'bungee ˌjumping**
bungl|e 'bʌŋ.gl̩ **-es** -z **-ing** -ɪŋ, 'bʌŋ.glɪŋ **-ed** -d **-er/s** -əʳ/z, '-gləʳ/z ⓤⓢ '-gl̩.ɚ/z, '-glɚ/z
bunion 'bʌn.jən **-s** -z
bunk bʌŋk **-s** -s **-ing** -ɪŋ **-ed** -t
bunk|er (B) 'bʌŋ.k|əʳ ⓤⓢ -k|ɚ **-ers** -əz ⓤⓢ -ɚz **-ering** -ər.ɪŋ **-ered** -əd ⓤⓢ -ɚd
bunkhou|se 'bʌŋk.haʊ|s **-ses** -zɪz
bunkum 'bʌŋ.kəm
Bunnett 'bʌn.ɪt
bunn|y 'bʌn|.i **-ies** -iz
Bunsen 'bʌnt.sən ⓤⓢ -sɪn ˌ**Bunsen 'burner** ⓤⓢ **'Bunsen ˌburner**
bunt bʌnt **-s** -s
Bunter 'bʌn.təʳ ⓤⓢ -t̬ɚ
bunting (B) 'bʌn.tɪŋ ⓤⓢ -t̬ɪŋ **-s** -z
Bunty 'bʌn.ti ⓤⓢ -t̬i
Buñuel ˌbuː.nju'el, '---; ˌbuːn'wel, ˌbʊn- ⓤⓢ ˌbuːn'wel, ˌbʊn-
Bunyan 'bʌn.jən
buoy bɔɪ ⓤⓢ bɔɪ, 'buː.i **-s** -z **-ing** -ɪŋ **-ed** -d
buoyancy 'bɔɪ.ənt.si ⓤⓢ 'bɔɪ-, 'buː.jənt-
buoyant 'bɔɪ.ənt ⓤⓢ 'bɔɪ-, 'buː.jənt **-ly** -li
BUPA 'buː.pə, 'bjuː-
bur bɜːʳ ⓤⓢ bɝː **-s** -z
Burbage 'bɜː.bɪdʒ ⓤⓢ 'bɝː-
Burberr|y® 'bɜː.bər|.i ⓤⓢ 'bɝː.ber-, -bɚ- **-y's** -iz **-ies** -iz
burbl|e 'bɜː.bl̩ ⓤⓢ 'bɝː- **-es** -z **-ing** -ɪŋ, '-blɪŋ **-ed** -d
Burbridge 'bɜː.brɪdʒ ⓤⓢ 'bɝː-
Burbury 'bɜː.bər.i ⓤⓢ 'bɝː.ber-, -bɚ-
Burch bɜːtʃ ⓤⓢ bɝːtʃ
Burchell, Burchall 'bɜː.tʃəl ⓤⓢ 'bɝː-
Burchill 'bɜː.tʃəl, -tʃɪl ⓤⓢ 'bɝː-
Burco 'bɜː.kəʊ ⓤⓢ 'bɝː.koʊ
burden (B) 'bɜː.dən ⓤⓢ 'bɝː- **-s** -z **-ing** -ɪŋ **-ed** -d
burdensome 'bɜː.dən.səm ⓤⓢ 'bɝː-
Burdett 'bɜː.det, -'- ⓤⓢ bɝː'det, '--
Burdett-Coutts ˌbɜː.det'kuːts, -ˌ-'- ⓤⓢ bɝːˌdet'-
burdock 'bɜː.dɒk ⓤⓢ 'bɝː.dɑːk **-s** -s
Burdon 'bɜː.dən ⓤⓢ 'bɝː-
Bure bjʊəʳ ⓤⓢ bjʊr
bureau 'bjʊə.rəʊ, 'bjɔː-, bjʊə'rəʊ ⓤⓢ 'bjʊr.oʊ **-s** -z
bureaucrac|y bjʊə'rɒk.rə.s|i, bjə'-, bjɔː'- ⓤⓢ bjʊ'rɑː.krə- **-ies** -iz
bureaucrat 'bjʊə.rəʊ.kræt, 'bjɔː- ⓤⓢ 'bjʊr.ə- **-s** -s
bureaucratic ˌbjʊə.rəʊ'kræt.ɪk, ˌbjɔː- ⓤⓢ ˌbjʊr.ə'kræt̬- **-ally** -əl.i, -li
bureaux *(alternative plur. of* **bureau***)* 'bjʊə.rəʊ, 'bjɔː-, -rəʊz; ˌbjʊə'rəʊ, -'rəʊz ⓤⓢ 'bjʊr.oʊ, -oʊz
burette, buret bjʊə'ret ⓤⓢ bjʊr'et **-s** -s
Burford 'bɜː.fəd ⓤⓢ 'bɝː.fɚd
burg bɜːg ⓤⓢ bɝːg **-s** -z
Burgar 'bɜː.gəʳ ⓤⓢ 'bɝː.gɚ
Burg|e bɜːdʒ ⓤⓢ bɝːdʒ **-es** -ɪz
burgee 'bɜː.dʒiː, -'- ⓤⓢ 'bɝː.dʒi **-s** -z
burgeon 'bɜː.dʒən ⓤⓢ 'bɝː- **-s** -z **-ing** -ɪŋ **-ed** -d
burger 'bɜː.gəʳ ⓤⓢ 'bɝː.gɚ **-s** -z
burgess (B) 'bɜː.dʒəs, -dʒɪs, -dʒes ⓤⓢ 'bɝː- **-es** -ɪz
burgh 'bʌr.ə ⓤⓢ bɝːg, 'bɜː.rə, 'bɝː.oʊ **-s** -z
Burgh bɜːg ⓤⓢ bɝːg *in Suffolk:* bɜːg; 'bʌr.ə ⓤⓢ bɝːg; 'bɝː.oʊ *Baron, Heath in Surrey, place in Lincolnshire:* 'bʌr.ə ⓤⓢ 'bɝː.oʊ *Burgh-by-Sands:* brʌf
Burghclere 'bɜː.kleəʳ ⓤⓢ 'bɝː.kler
burgher 'bɜː.gəʳ ⓤⓢ 'bɝː.gɚ **-s** -z
Burghersh 'bɜː.gəʃ ⓤⓢ 'bɝː.gɚʃ
Burghley 'bɜː.li ⓤⓢ 'bɝː-
burglar 'bɜː.gləʳ ⓤⓢ 'bɝː.glɚ **-s** -z
burglariz|e 'bɜː.glər.aɪz ⓤⓢ 'bɝː.glə.raɪz **-es** -ɪz **-ing** -ɪŋ **-ed** -d
burglar|y 'bɜː.glər|.i ⓤⓢ 'bɝː- **-ies** -iz
burgl|e 'bɜː.gl̩ ⓤⓢ 'bɝː- **-es** -z **-ing** -ɪŋ, '-glɪŋ **-ed** -d
burgomaster 'bɜː.gəʊˌmɑː.stəʳ ⓤⓢ 'bɝː.gəˌmæs.tɚ **-s** -z
Burgos 'bʊə.gɒs ⓤⓢ 'bʊr.gɑːs
Burgoyne 'bɜː.gɔɪn, -'- ⓤⓢ bɝː'gɔɪn, '--
burgund|y (B) 'bɜː.gən.d|i ⓤⓢ 'bɝː- **-ies** -iz
burial 'ber.i.əl **-s** -z **'burial ˌground; 'burial ˌplace**
burin 'bjʊə.rɪn ⓤⓢ 'bʊr.ɪn, 'bɝː- **-s** -z
burk bɜːk ⓤⓢ bɝːk **-s** -s
burk|e (B) bɜːk ⓤⓢ bɝːk **-es** -s **-ing** -ɪŋ **-ed** -t
Burkina Faso bɜːˌkiː.nə'fæs.əʊ ⓤⓢ bʊrˌkiː.nə'fɑː.soʊ
burlap 'bɜː.læp ⓤⓢ 'bɝː-
Burleigh 'bɜː.li ⓤⓢ 'bɝː-
burlesqu|e bɜː'lesk ⓤⓢ bɝː- **-es** -s **-ing** -ɪŋ **-ed** -t
Burley 'bɜː.li ⓤⓢ 'bɝː-
Burling 'bɜː.lɪŋ ⓤⓢ 'bɝː-
Burlington 'bɜː.lɪŋ.tən ⓤⓢ 'bɝː-
burl|y (B) 'bɜː.l|i ⓤⓢ 'bɝː- **-ier** -i.əʳ ⓤⓢ -i.ɚ **-iest** -i.ɪst, -i.əst **-iness** -ɪ.nəs, -ɪ.nɪs
Burma 'bɜː.mə ⓤⓢ 'bɝː-
Burmah 'bɜː.mə ⓤⓢ 'bɝː-
Burman 'bɜː.mən ⓤⓢ 'bɝː- **-s** -z
Burmese bɜː'miːz ⓤⓢ bɝː-, -'miːs
burn bɜːn ⓤⓢ bɝːn **-s** -z **-ing** -ɪŋ **-ed** -d **burnt** bɜːnt ⓤⓢ bɝːnt
Burnaby 'bɜː.nə.bi ⓤⓢ 'bɝː-
Burnand bɜː'nænd, bə- ⓤⓢ bɚ-
Burne bɜːn ⓤⓢ bɝːn
burner 'bɜː.nəʳ ⓤⓢ 'bɝː.nɚ **-s** -z ˌ**put something on a/the ˌback 'burner**
burnet (B) 'bɜː.nɪt ⓤⓢ 'bɝː- **-s** -s
Burnett bɜː'net, bə-; 'bɜː.nɪt ⓤⓢ bɚ'net; 'bɝː.nɪt
Burney 'bɜː.ni ⓤⓢ 'bɝː-
Burnham 'bɜː.nəm ⓤⓢ 'bɝː-
Burnham-on-Crouch ˌbɜː.nəm.ɒn'kraʊtʃ ⓤⓢ ˌbɝː.nəm.ɑːn'-
Burnham-on-Sea ˌbɜː.nəm.ɒn'siː ⓤⓢ ˌbɝː.nəm.ɑːn'-
burnish 'bɜː.nɪʃ ⓤⓢ 'bɝː- **-es** -ɪz **-ing** -ɪŋ **-ed** -t **-er/s** -əʳ/z ⓤⓢ -ɚ/z

Burnley 'bɜːn.li ⓤⓢ 'bɝːn-
burnous, burnous|e bɜː'nuːs ⓤⓢ bɚ- **-es** -ɪz
burnout 'bɜːn.aʊt ⓤⓢ 'bɝːn-
Burns bɜːnz ⓤⓢ bɝːnz
Burnside 'bɜːn.saɪd ⓤⓢ 'bɝːn-
burnt *(from* **burn***)* bɜːnt ⓤⓢ bɝːnt **ˌburnt ˈoffering**
Burntisland ˌbɜːnt'aɪ.lənd ⓤⓢ ˌbɝːnt-
Burntwood 'bɜːnt.wʊd ⓤⓢ 'bɝːnt-
burp bɜːp ⓤⓢ bɝːp **-s** -s **-ing** -ɪŋ **-ed** -t
burqa 'bɜː.kə ⓤⓢ 'bɝː- **-s** -z
burr (B) bɜːʳ ⓤⓢ bɝː **-s** -z
Burrell 'bʌr.ᵊl, 'bɜːr-
Burridge 'bʌr.ɪdʒ ⓤⓢ 'bɝː-
burrito bə'riː.təʊ, bʊr'iː- ⓤⓢ bə'riː.t̬oʊ **-s** -z
Burrough(e)s 'bʌr.əʊz ⓤⓢ 'bɝː.oʊz
burrow 'bʌr.əʊ ⓤⓢ 'bɝː.oʊ **-s** -z **-ing** -ɪŋ **-ed** -d
Burrows 'bʌr.əʊz ⓤⓢ 'bɝː.oʊz
Burry Port ˌbʌr.i'pɔːt ⓤⓢ ˌbɝː.i'pɔːrt
Bursa 'bɜː.sə ⓤⓢ bʊr'sɑː, bɝː-
bursar 'bɜː.səʳ ⓤⓢ 'bɝː.sɚ, -sɑːr **-s** -z
bursarship 'bɜː.sə.ʃɪp ⓤⓢ 'bɝː.sɚ-, -sɑːr- **-s** -s
bursar|y 'bɜː.sᵊr|.i ⓤⓢ 'bɝː- **-ies** -iz
Burscough Bridge ˌbɜː.skəʊ'brɪdʒ ⓤⓢ ˌbɝː.skoʊ'-
Bursledon 'bɜː.zᵊl.dᵊn ⓤⓢ 'bɝː-
Burslem 'bɜːz.ləm ⓤⓢ 'bɝːz-
burst bɜːst ⓤⓢ bɝːst **-s** -s **-ing** -ɪŋ
Burt bɜːt ⓤⓢ bɝːt
burthen 'bɜː.ðᵊn ⓤⓢ 'bɝː- **-s** -z
Burton (B) 'bɜː.tᵊn ⓤⓢ 'bɝː-
Burundi bʊ'rʊn.di, bə- **-an/s** -ən/z
Burwash 'bɜː.wɒʃ *locally also:* 'bʌr.əʃ ⓤⓢ 'bɝː.wɑːʃ, -wɔːʃ
bur|y *(v.)* 'ber|.i **-ies** -iz **-ying** -i.ɪŋ **-ied** -id
Bury *place:* 'ber.i *surname:* 'bjʊə.ri, 'ber.i ⓤⓢ 'bʊr.i, 'ber-
bus bʌs **-(s)es** -ɪz **-(s)ing** -ɪŋ **-(s)ed** -t **ˈbus conˌductor; ˈbus ˌstop**
busbar 'bʌs.bɑːʳ ⓤⓢ -bɑːr **-s** -z
busboy 'bʌs.bɔɪ **-s** -z
busb|y 'bʌz.b|i **-ies** -iz
bush (B) bʊʃ **-es** -ɪz **-ing** -ɪŋ **-ed** -t **ˈbush ˌbaby; ˌbeat about the ˈbush**
bushel 'bʊʃ.ᵊl **-s** -z
Bushell 'bʊʃ.ᵊl ⓤⓢ 'bʊʃ.ᵊl, bʊ'ʃel
Bushey 'bʊʃ.i
Bushire bjuː'ʃaɪəʳ, buː-, -'ʃɪəʳ ⓤⓢ buː'ʃɪr
bush-league 'bʊʃ.liːg **-s** -z
bush|man (B) 'bʊʃ|.mən **-men** -mən, -men
Bushmills 'bʊʃ.mɪlz
Bushnell 'bʊʃ.nᵊl ⓤⓢ -nᵊl, -nel
bushranger 'bʊʃˌreɪn.dʒəʳ ⓤⓢ -dʒɚ **-s** -z
bushwhack 'bʊʃ.*h*wæk **-s** -s **-ing** -ɪŋ **-ed** -t
bushwhacker 'bʊʃˌ*h*wæk.əʳ ⓤⓢ -ɚ **-s** -z
bush|y (B) 'bʊʃ|.i **-ier** -i.əʳ ⓤⓢ -i.ɚ **-iest** -i.ɪst, -i.əst **-ily** -ɪ.li, -ᵊl.i **-iness** -ɪ.nəs, -ɪ.nɪs
business 'bɪz.nɪs, -nəs **-es** -ɪz **ˌmind one's ˌown ˈbusiness**
businesslike 'bɪz.nɪs.laɪk, -nəs-
business|man 'bɪz.nɪs|.mæn, -nəs-, -mən **-men** -men, -mən
business|person 'bɪz.nɪs|ˌpɜː.sᵊn, -nəsˌ- **-people** -ˌpiː.pl̩
business|woman 'bɪz.nɪs|ˌwʊm.ən, -nəsˌ- **-women** -ˌwɪm.ɪn
busk (B) bʌsk **-s** -s **-ing** -ɪŋ **-ed** -t **-er/s** -əʳ/z ⓤⓢ -ɚ/z
buskin 'bʌs.kɪn **-s** -z **-ed** -d
bus|man 'bʌs|.mən, -mæn **-men** -mən, -men **ˌbusman's ˈholiday**
Busoni buː'zəʊ.ni, bjuː-, -'səʊ- ⓤⓢ bʊ'zoʊ.ni, bjuː-
buss (B) bʌs **-es** -ɪz **-ing** -ɪŋ **-ed** -t
bust bʌst **-s** -s **-ing** -ɪŋ **-ed** -ɪd
bustard 'bʌs.təd ⓤⓢ -tɚd **-s** -z
buster (B) 'bʌs.təʳ ⓤⓢ -tɚ **-s** -z
bustier 'bʌs.ti.əʳ, 'bʊs-, 'buː.sti- ⓤⓢ 'buː.sti.eɪ, 'bʊs.tjeɪ **-s** -z
bustl|e 'bʌs.l̩ **-es** -z **-ing** -ɪŋ, 'bʌs.lɪŋ **-ed** -d
bust|y 'bʌs.t|i **-ier** -i.əʳ ⓤⓢ -i.ɚ **-iest** -i.ɪst, -i.əst **-iness** -ɪ.nəs, -ɪ.nɪs
bus|y 'bɪz|.i **-ies** -ɪz **-ying** -i.ɪŋ **-ied** -ɪd **-ier** -i.əʳ ⓤⓢ -i.ɚ **-iest** -i.ɪst, -i.əst **-ily** -ɪ.li, -ᵊl.i **ˈbusy ˌsignal**
busybod|y 'bɪz.iˌbɒd|.i ⓤⓢ -ˌbɑː.d|i **-ies** -iz
busyness 'bɪz.i.nəs, -nɪs
but *strong form:* bʌt *weak form:* bət
Note: Weak form word. The strong form /bʌt/ is used contrastively (e.g. **ifs** and **buts**) and in sentence-final position (e.g. "It's anything but"). The weak form is /bət/ (e.g. "It's good but expensive" /ɪtsˌgʊd.bət.ɪk'spen*t*.sɪv/)
butane 'bjuː.teɪn ⓤⓢ 'bjuː.teɪn, -'-
butch (B) bʊtʃ
butch|er (B) 'bʊtʃ|.əʳ ⓤⓢ -ɚ **-ers** -əz ⓤⓢ -ɚz **-ering** -ᵊr.ɪŋ **-ered** -əd ⓤⓢ -ɚd
butcher|y 'bʊtʃ.ᵊr|.i **-ies** -iz
Bute bjuːt **-shire** -ʃəʳ, -ˌʃɪəʳ ⓤⓢ -ʃɚ, -ˌʃɪr
Buthelezi ˌbuː.tə'leɪ.zi
butler (B) 'bʌt.ləʳ ⓤⓢ -lɚ **-s** -z
butler|age 'bʌt.lᵊr|.ɪdʒ **-y** -i **-ies** -iz
Butlin 'bʌt.lɪn **-s** -z
butt (B) bʌt **-s** -s **-ing** -ɪŋ ⓤⓢ 'bʌt̬.ɪŋ **-ed** -ɪd ⓤⓢ 'bʌt̬.ɪd
butt-end 'bʌt.end **-s** -z
butt|er 'bʌt|.əʳ ⓤⓢ 'bʌt̬|.ɚ **-ers** -əz ⓤⓢ -ɚz **-ering** -ᵊr.ɪŋ **-ered** -əd ⓤⓢ -ɚd **ˈbutter ˌbean; ˈbutter ˌdish; ˈbutter ˌknife; ˌbutter wouldn't ˌmelt in his/her ˈmouth**
butterball 'bʌt.ə.bɔːl ⓤⓢ 'bʌt̬.ɚ.bɔːl, -bɑːl **-s** -z
buttercup 'bʌt.ə.kʌp ⓤⓢ 'bʌt̬.ɚ- **-s** -s
butterfat 'bʌt.ə.fæt ⓤⓢ 'bʌt̬.ɚ-
Butterfield 'bʌt.ə.fiːld ⓤⓢ 'bʌt̬.ɚ-
butterfinger|s 'bʌt.əˌfɪŋ.gə|z ⓤⓢ 'bʌt̬.ɚˌfɪŋ.gɚ|z **-ed** -d
butterfl|y 'bʌt.ə.fl|aɪ ⓤⓢ 'bʌt̬.ɚ- **-ies** -aɪz
Butterick 'bʌt.ᵊr.ɪk ⓤⓢ 'bʌt̬-
Butterleigh, Butterley 'bʌt.ᵊl.i ⓤⓢ 'bʌt̬.ɚ.li
Buttermere 'bʌt.ə.mɪəʳ ⓤⓢ 'bʌt̬.ɚ.mɪr
buttermilk 'bʌt.ə.mɪlk ⓤⓢ 'bʌt̬.ɚ-
butternut 'bʌt.ə.nʌt ⓤⓢ 'bʌt̬.ɚ- **-s** -s
butterscotch 'bʌt.ə.skɒtʃ ⓤⓢ 'bʌt̬.ɚ.skɑːtʃ
Butterwick 'bʌt.ᵊr.ɪk, -ə.wɪk ⓤⓢ 'bʌt̬.ɚ.ɪk, -wɪk
Butterworth 'bʌt.ə.wəθ, -wɜːθ ⓤⓢ 'bʌt̬.ɚ.wɚθ, -wɝːθ
butter|y 'bʌt.ᵊr|.i ⓤⓢ 'bʌt̬- **-ies** -iz
buttock 'bʌt.ək ⓤⓢ 'bʌt̬- **-s** -s
button (B) 'bʌt.ᵊn **-s** -z **-ing** -ɪŋ **-ed** -d
button-down ˌbʌt.ᵊn'daʊn *stress shift:* ˌbutton-down 'collar
buttonhol|e 'bʌt.ᵊn.həʊl ⓤⓢ -hoʊl **-es** -z **-ing** -ɪŋ **-ed** -d
buttonhook 'bʌt.ᵊn.hʊk **-s** -s
buttress (B) 'bʌt.rəs, -rɪs **-es** -ɪz **-ing** -ɪŋ **-ed** -d
butt|y 'bʌt|.i ⓤⓢ 'bʌt̬- **-ies** -iz
butut buː'tuːt
butyric bjʊ'tɪr.ɪk ⓤⓢ bjuː-
buxom 'bʌk.səm **-ness** -nəs, -nɪs
Buxtehude ˌbʊk.stə'huː.də
Buxton 'bʌk.stən
buy baɪ **-s** -z **-ing** -ɪŋ **bought** bɔːt ⓤⓢ bɑːt, bɔːt
buyable 'baɪ.ə.bl̩
buyback 'baɪ.bæk **-s** -s
buyer 'baɪ.əʳ ⓤⓢ -ɚ **-s** -z
buyout 'baɪ.aʊt **-s** -s
Buzfuz 'bʌz.fʌz
buzz bʌz **-es** -ɪz, -əz **-ing** -ɪŋ **-ed** -d
buzzard 'bʌz.əd ⓤⓢ -ɚd **-s** -z
buzzer 'bʌz.əʳ ⓤⓢ -ɚ **-s** -z
buzzword 'bʌz.wɜːd ⓤⓢ -wɝːd **-s** -z
bwana 'bwɑː.nə
by *normal form:* baɪ *occasional weak forms:* bɪ, bə
Note: Weak form word. The strong form is /baɪ/. The weak forms /bɪ, bə/ are rarely used, but can be found occasionally, particularly in measurements (e.g. "two by three" /ˌtuː.bə'θriː/).
by-and-by ˌbaɪ.ᵊn*d*'baɪ, -ᵊm- ⓤⓢ -ᵊn*d*'-
Byard baɪəd ⓤⓢ baɪɚd
Byars baɪəz ⓤⓢ baɪɚz
Byas(s) baɪəs
Byatt baɪət

Bydgoszcz 'bɪd.gɒʃt *as if Polish:* -gɒtʃtʃ ⓤⓢ -gɔːʃtʃ
bye (B) baɪ **-s** -z
bye-bye *goodbye:* ˌbaɪ'baɪ, bə-, bʌb'aɪ; 'baɪ.baɪ, 'bʌb.aɪ
bye-bye *sleep:* 'baɪ.baɪ **-s** -z
byelaw 'baɪ.lɔː ⓤⓢ -lɑː, -lɔː **-s** -z
by-election 'baɪ.ɪˌlek.ʃᵊn, -əˌ- **-s** -z
Byelorussi|a ˌbjel.əʊ'rʌʃ|.ə, ˌbel-, -'ruː.si- ⓤⓢ -oʊ'-, -ə'- **-an/s** -ᵊn/z
Byers baɪəz ⓤⓢ baɪɚz
Byfleet 'baɪ.fliːt
Byford 'baɪ.fəd ⓤⓢ -fɚd
bygone 'baɪ.gɒn ⓤⓢ -gɑːn **-s** -z
Bygraves 'baɪ.greɪvz
bylaw 'baɪ.lɔː ⓤⓢ -lɑː, -lɔː **-s** -z
Byles baɪlz
byline 'baɪ.laɪn **-s** -z
Byng bɪŋ
Bynoe 'baɪ.nəʊ ⓤⓢ -noʊ
BYO ˌbiː.waɪ'əʊ ⓤⓢ -'oʊ
bypass 'baɪ.pɑːs ⓤⓢ -pæs **-es** -ɪz **-ing** -ɪŋ **-ed** -d
bypa|th 'baɪ.pɑː|θ ⓤⓢ -pæ|θ **-ths** -ðz
byplay 'baɪ.pleɪ
by-product 'baɪˌprɒd.ʌkt, -əkt ⓤⓢ -ˌprɑː.dəkt **-s** -s
Byrd bɜːd ⓤⓢ bɝːd
byre baɪəʳ ⓤⓢ baɪɚ **-s** -z
Byrne bɜːn ⓤⓢ bɝːn
byroad 'baɪ.rəʊd ⓤⓢ -roʊd **-s** -z
Byrom 'baɪ.rəm
Byron 'baɪ.rən
Byronic baɪ'rɒn.ɪk ⓤⓢ -'rɑː.nɪk **-ally** -ᵊl.i, -li
Bysshe bɪʃ
bystander 'baɪˌstæn.dəʳ ⓤⓢ -dɚ **-s** -z
bystreet 'baɪ.striːt **-s** -s
byte baɪt **-s** -s
Bythesea 'baɪθ.siː
byway 'baɪ.weɪ **-s** -z
byword 'baɪ.wɜːd ⓤⓢ -wɝːd **-s** -z
Byzantian baɪ'zæn.ti.ən, bɪ-, bə-, '-*t*ʃᵊn ⓤⓢ bɪ'zæn.ti.ən, bə-, baɪ-, -'zæn*t*.ʃᵊn
Byzantine bɪ'zæn.taɪn, baɪ-, bə-, -tiːn; 'bɪz.ᵊn- ⓤⓢ 'bɪz.ᵊn.tiːn, -taɪn
Byzantium bɪ'zæn.ti.əm, baɪ-, bə-, '-*t*ʃᵊm ⓤⓢ bɪ'zæn.ti.əm, bə-, baɪ-, -'zæn*t*.ʃᵊm

Pronouncing the letter C

See also CC, CCH, CH, CK, CQU

The consonant letter **c** has four pronunciations: /s, k, ʃ/ and /tʃ/.

Before the vowel letters **i, e** or **y** (when functioning as a vowel letter), it is pronounced as /s/, e.g.:

specific /spəˈsɪf.ɪk/
cell /sel/
cycle /ˈsaɪ.kl̩/

In suffixes *-cial, -cious, -ciate, -cient* and their derivatives, **c** is realised as /ʃ/, e.g.:

social /ˈsəʊ.ʃᵊl/ Ⓤⓢ /ˈsoʊ-/
vicious /ˈvɪʃ.əs/

In most other situations, **c** is pronounced as /k/, e.g.:

cat /kæt/
critic /ˈkrɪt.ɪk/ Ⓤⓢ /ˈkrɪt̬-/

In addition

C can be silent. There are two occasions when this can occur: the combination **ct** in some words, and in British place names such as *Leicester*, e.g.:

Leicester /ˈles.təʳ/ Ⓤⓢ /-tɚ/
indict /ɪnˈdaɪt/

An exceptional pronunciation for **c** is /tʃ/ in some words borrowed from Italian, e.g.:

cello /ˈtʃel.əʊ/ Ⓤⓢ /-oʊ/
Cinquecento /ˌtʃɪŋ.kweɪˈtʃen.təʊ/ Ⓤⓢ /-toʊ/

A final exception:

Caesar /ˈsiː.zəʳ/ Ⓤⓢ /-zɚ/

c (C) siː -'s -z
ca *(abbrev. for* **circa**) ˈsɜː.kə Ⓤⓢ ˈsɝː-
CAA ˌsiː.eɪˈeɪ
cab kæb **-s** -z
CAB ˌsiː.eɪˈbiː
cabal kəˈbæl, kæbˈæl Ⓤⓢ kəˈbɑːl, -ˈbæl **-s** -z
cabala (C) kəˈbɑː.lə, kæbˈɑː-
cabalism ˈkæb.ə.lɪ.zᵊm
cabalistic ˌkæb.əˈlɪs.tɪk **-al** -ᵊl **-ally** -ᵊl.i, -li
caballero ˌkæb.əˈleə.rəʊ, -ˈljeə- Ⓤⓢ -ˈler.oʊ, -əlˈjer- **-s** -z
cabana kəˈbɑː.nə Ⓤⓢ -ˈbæn.ə, -ˈbɑː.nə, -njə **-s** -z
abaret ˈkæb.ə.reɪ, ˌ--ˈ- Ⓤⓢ ˌkæb.əˈreɪ, ˈ--- **-s** -z
abbag|e ˈkæb.ɪdʒ **-es** -ɪz **ˈcabbage ˌrose**
abbala (C) kəˈbɑː.lə, kæbˈɑː- **-s** -z
abbal|ism ˈkæb.ə.l|ɪ.zᵊm **-ist/s** -ɪst/s
abbalistic ˌkæb.əˈlɪs.tɪk **-al** -ᵊl **-ally** -ᵊl.i, -li
abb|ie, **cabb|y** ˈkæb|.i **-ies** -iz
abdriver ˈkæbˌdraɪ.vəʳ Ⓤⓢ -vɚ **-s** -z
abell ˈkæb.ᵊl
aber ˈkeɪ.bəʳ Ⓤⓢ -bɚ **-s** -z
abernet Sauvignon ˌkæb.ə.neɪ.səʊ.viːˈnjɔ̃ːŋ, -jɒn Ⓤⓢ -ɚ.neɪˌsoʊ.viːˈnjoʊn
abin ˈkæb.ɪn **-s** -z **ˈcabin ˌboy; ˈcabin ˌcruiser; ˈcabin ˌfever**
abinet (C) ˈkæb.ɪ.nət, -ə-, -nɪt **-s** -s **ˈCabinet ˌMinister, ˌCabinet ˈMinister**
abinetmak|er ˈkæb.ɪ.nətˌmeɪ.k|əʳ, -nɪt- Ⓤⓢ -kɚ **-ers** -əz Ⓤⓢ -ɚz **-ing** -ɪŋ
abl|e (C) ˈkeɪ.bl̩ **-es** -z **-ing** -ɪŋ, ˈ-blɪŋ **-ed** -d **ˈcable ˌcar; ˌcable ˈtelevision, ˌcable teleˈvision**
cablecast ˈkeɪ.bl̩.kɑːst Ⓤⓢ -kæst **-s** -s **-ing** -ɪŋ **-er/s** -əʳ/z Ⓤⓢ -ɚ/z
cablegram ˈkeɪ.bl̩.græm **-s** -z
cab|man ˈkæb|.mən **-men** -mən, -men
caboodle kəˈbuː.dl̩
caboos|e kəˈbuːs **-es** -ɪz
Caborn ˈkeɪ.bɔːn Ⓤⓢ -bɔːrn
Cabot ˈkæb.ət
cabotage ˈkæb.ə.tɑːʒ, -tɪdʒ
Cabrini kəˈbriː.ni
cabriole ˈkæb.ri.əʊl Ⓤⓢ -oʊl **-s** -z
cabriolet ˈkæb.ri.əʊ.leɪ, ˌkæb.ri.əʊˈleɪ Ⓤⓢ ˌkæb.ri.əˈleɪ **-s** -z
cabstand ˈkæb.stænd **-s** -z
ca-ca ˈkɑː.kɑː
cacao kæˈkaʊ, kækˈaʊ; kəˈkɑː.əʊ, kækˈɑː-, -ˈeɪ- Ⓤⓢ -oʊ **-s** -z
cachalot ˈkæʃ.ə.lɒt Ⓤⓢ -lɑːt, -loʊ **-s** -s, -z
cach|e kæʃ **-es** -ɪz
cachepot ˈkæʃ.pəʊ, ˌkæʃˈpɒt Ⓤⓢ ˈkæʃ.pɑːt, -poʊ **-s** -s, -z
cachet ˈkæʃ.eɪ Ⓤⓢ -ˈ- **-s** -z
cachinnat|e ˈkæk.ɪ.neɪt, ˈ-ə- **-es** -s **-ing** -ɪŋ **-ed** -ɪd
cachinnation ˌkæk.ɪˈneɪ.ʃᵊn
cachou kæʃˈuː, kəˈʃuː; ˈkæʃ.uː **-s** -z
cachucha kəˈtʃuː.tʃə **-s** -z
cacique kæsˈiːk, kəˈsiːk **-s** -s
cack-handed ˌkækˈhæn.dɪd, ˈ--- **-ly** -li **-ness** -nəs, -nɪs
cackl|e ˈkæk.l̩ **-es** -z **-ing** -ɪŋ, ˈ-lɪŋ **-ed** -d **-er/s** -əʳ/z, ˈ-ləʳ/z Ⓤⓢ ˈ-l̩.ɚ/z, ˈ-lɚ/z
cacodyl ˈkæk.əʊ.daɪl, -dɪl Ⓤⓢ ˈkæk.oʊ.dɪl, ˈ-ə-
cacoepy kækˈəʊ.ɪ.pi, -ep.i Ⓤⓢ -ˈoʊ.ə-
cacographic ˌkæk.əʊˈgræf.ɪk Ⓤⓢ -oʊˈ-, -əˈ- **-al** -ᵊl
cacography kækˈɒg.rə.fi, kəˈkɒg- Ⓤⓢ kəˈkɑː.grə-
cacology kækˈɒl.ə.dʒi, kəˈkɒl- Ⓤⓢ kəˈkɑː.lə-
cacophonic ˌkæk.əʊˈfɒn.ɪk Ⓤⓢ -oʊˈfɑː.nɪk, -əˈ- **-al** -ᵊl **-ally** -ᵊl.i, -li
cacophonous kəˈkɒf.ə.nəs, kækˈɒf- Ⓤⓢ kəˈkɑː.fə-
cacophon|y kəˈkɒf.ə.n|i, kækˈɒf- Ⓤⓢ kəˈkɑː.fə- **-ies** -iz
cactus ˈkæk.təs **-es** -ɪz **cacti** ˈkæk.taɪ
cacuminal kækˈjuː.mɪ.nᵊl, kəˈkjuː- Ⓤⓢ kəˈkjuː.mə- **-s** -z
cad kæd **-s** -z
CAD kæd
cadaster kəˈdæs.təʳ Ⓤⓢ -tɚ
cadastral kəˈdæs.trəl
cadastre kəˈdæs.təʳ Ⓤⓢ -tɚ
cadaver kəˈdɑː.vəʳ, -ˈdeɪ-, -ˈdæv.əʳ Ⓤⓢ -ˈdæv.ɚ **-s** -z
cadaveric kəˈdæv.ə.rɪk Ⓤⓢ -ɚ.ɪk
cadaverous kəˈdæv.ᵊr.əs **-ness** -nəs, -nɪs
Cadbury ˈkæd.bᵊr.i Ⓤⓢ ˈkæd.ber.i, -bɚ-
Cadby ˈkæd.bi, ˈkæb-
CAD/CAM ˈkæd.kæm
Caddell kəˈdel
Caddick ˈkæd.ɪk
caddie ˈkæd.i **-s** -z
caddis ˈkæd.ɪs **ˈcaddis ˌfly**
caddish ˈkæd.ɪʃ **-ly** -li **-ness** -nəs, -nɪs
cadd|y ˈkæd|.i **-ies** -iz **-ying** -i.ɪŋ **-ied** -ɪd
cade (C) keɪd **-s** -z
Cadell ˈkæd.ᵊl, kəˈdel

cadenc|e 'keɪ.dᵊnts **-es** -ɪz
cadency 'keɪ.dᵊnt.si
Cadenus kə'diː.nəs
cadenza kə'den.zə **-s** -z
Cader Idris ˌkæd.əʳ'ɪd.rɪs (US) -ɚ'-
cadet kə'det **-s** -s **ca'det ˌcorps**
cadetship kə'det.ʃɪp **-s** -s
cadg|e kædʒ **-es** -ɪz **-ing** -ɪŋ **-ed** -d **-er/s** -əʳ/z (US) -ɚ/z
cadi 'kɑː.di, 'keɪ- **-s** -z
Cadillac® 'kæd.ɪ.læk, -ᵊl.æk (US) -ə.læk, -ᵊl.æk **-s** -s
Cadiz *in Spain:* kə'dɪz *as if Spanish:* 'kæd.ɪθ (US) kə'dɪz; 'keɪ.dɪz *in Phillipines:* 'kɑː.diːs (US) kə'dɪz; 'keɪ.dɪz *in the US:* kæd'ɪz; 'keɪ.dɪz (US) kə'dɪz; 'keɪ.dɪz
Cadman 'kæd.mən
Cadmean 'kæd.mi.ən, kæd'miː- (US) kæd'miː-
cadmic 'kæd.mɪk
cadmium 'kæd.mi.əm, 'kæb- (US) 'kæd-
Cadmus 'kæd.məs
Cadogan kə'dʌg.ən
cadre 'kɑː.dəʳ, 'keɪ-, -drə (US) 'kæd.riː, 'kɑː.dri, -dreɪ **-s** -z
caduce|us kə'djuː.si|.əs, -'dʒuː- (US) -'duː-, -'djuː-, -ʃ|əs **-i** -aɪ
Cadwallader kæd'wɒl.ə.dəʳ (US) -'wɑː.lə.dɚ
CAE ˌsiː.eɪ'iː
caec|um 'siː.k|əm **-a** -ə
Caedmon 'kæd.mən
Caen kɑ̃ː (US) kɑːn
Caerleon kɑː'liː.ən, kə-, -'lɪən (US) kɑːr-
Caernarvon, Caernarfon kə'nɑː.vᵊn (US) kɑːr'nɑːr- **-shire** -ʃəʳ, -ˌʃɪəʳ (US) -ʃɚ, -ˌʃɪr
Caerphilly keə'fɪl.i, kɑː-, kə'fɪl- (US) kɑːr-
Caesar 'siː.zəʳ (US) -zɚ **-s** -z
Caesarea ˌsiː.zə'riː.ə
caesarean, caesarian *way of having a baby:* sɪ'zeə.ri.ən, sə- (US) sɪ'zer.i- **caeˌsarean 'section**
Caesarean *of Caesarea:* ˌsiː.zə'riː.ən *of Caesar:* siː'zeə.ri.ən, sɪ- (US) sɪ'zer.i-
caesium 'siː.zi.əm
caesura sɪ'zjʊə.rə, siː-, -'zjɔː-, -'ʒʊə- (US) sə'zʊr.ə, -'ʒʊr- **-s** -z
café, cafe 'kæf.eɪ (US) kæf'eɪ, kə'feɪ **-s** -z
cafeteria ˌkæf.ə'tɪə.ri.ə, -ɪ'- (US) -'tɪr.i- **-s** -z
cafetière, cafetiere ˌkæf.ə'tjeəʳ (US) -'tjer **-s** -z
caff kæf **-s** -s
caffein 'kæf.iːn, -eɪn (US) kæf'iːn
caffeinated 'kæf.ɪ.neɪ.tɪd, '-ə- (US) -ə.neɪ.t̬ɪd
caffeine 'kæf.iːn, -eɪn (US) kæf'iːn
caftan 'kæf.tæn (US) -tæn, -tən **-s** -z
cag|e (C) keɪdʒ **-es** -ɪz **-ing** -ɪŋ **-ed** -d
cageling 'keɪdʒ.lɪŋ **-s** -z
cager 'keɪ.dʒəʳ (US) -dʒɚ **-s** -z
cag|ey 'keɪ.dʒ|i **-ier** -i.əʳ (US) -i.ɚ **-iest** -i.ɪst, -i.əst **-ily** -ɪ.li, -ᵊl.i **-iness** -ɪ.nəs, -ɪ.nɪs
Cagliari ˌkæl.ji'ɑː.ri, 'kæl.jə.ri (US) 'kɑːl.jɑːr.i, -jɚ-
Cagliostro kæl.ji'ɒs.trəʊ (US) kɑːl'jɔː.stroʊ
Cagney 'kæg.ni
cagoule kə'guːl, kæg'uːl **-s** -z
cag|y 'keɪ.dʒ|i **-ier** -i.əʳ (US) -i.ɚ **-iest** -i.ɪst, -i.əst **-ily** -ɪ.li, -ᵊl.i **-iness** -ɪ.nəs, -ɪ.nɪs
Cahal kə'hæl, 'kæ.hᵊl
Cahan kɑːn
Cahill 'kɑː.hɪl, 'keɪ.hɪl
Cahoon kə'huːn, kæ-
cahoots kə'huːts
CAI ˌsiː.eɪ'aɪ
Caiaphas 'kaɪ.ə.fæs, -fəs
Caicos 'keɪ.kɒs, -kəs (US) -kəs
Caillard 'kaɪ.ɑːʳ (US) -ɑːr
caiman 'keɪ.mən, 'kaɪ-, -mæn (US) 'keɪ- **-s** -z
Cain(e) keɪn
caique, caïque kaɪ'iːk, kɑː- (US) kɑː'iːk **-s** -s
Caird keəd (US) kerd
Cairene 'kaɪə.riːn (US) 'kaɪ-, -'-
cairn keən (US) kern **-s** -z
cairngorm (C) ˌkeən'gɔːm, ˌkeəŋ-, '-- (US) 'kern.gɔːrm **-s** -z
Cairns keənz (US) kernz
Cairo *in Egypt:* 'kaɪə.rəʊ (US) 'kaɪ.roʊ *in the US:* 'keə.rəʊ (US) 'ker.oʊ
caisson 'keɪ.sɒn, -sᵊn *sometimes in engineering:* kə'suːn (US) 'keɪ.sᵊn, -sɑːn **-s** -z
Caister 'keɪ.stəʳ (US) -stɚ
Caister-on-Sea ˌkeɪ.stəʳ.ɒn'siː (US) -stɚ.ɑːn'-
Caistor 'keɪ.stəʳ (US) -stɚ
Caithness 'keɪθ.nes, -nəs;
caitiff 'keɪ.tɪf (US) -t̬ɪf **-s** -s
Caitlin, Caitlín 'keɪt.lɪn, 'kæt.lɪn
Caius *Roman name, character in Shakespeare's Merry Wives:* 'kaɪ.əs, 'keɪ.əs *as if Latin:* 'gaɪ- *Cambridge college:* kiːz
cajol|e kə'dʒəʊl (US) -'dʒoʊl **-es** -z **-ing** -ɪŋ **-ed** -d **-er/s** -əʳ/z (US) -ɚ/z
cajoler|y kə'dʒəʊ.lᵊr|.i (US) -'dʒoʊ- **-ies** -iz
Cajun 'keɪ.dʒən **-s** -z
cak|e keɪk **-es** -s **-ing** -ɪŋ **-ed** -t **(sell/go) like ˌhot 'cakes** (US) **(sell/go) like 'hot ˌcakes; ˌhave one's ˌcake and 'eat it** (US) **ˌhave one's ˌcake and ˌeat it 'too**
cakewalk 'keɪk.wɔːk (US) -wɑːk, -wɔːk **-s** -s
Cakovec tʃɑː'kəʊ.vets (US) -'koʊ-
CAL kæl, ˌsiː.eɪ'el
Calabar ˌkæl.ə'bɑːʳ, '--- (US) 'kæl.ə.bɑːr, ˌ--'-
calabash 'kæl.ə.bæʃ **-es** -ɪz, -əz
calaboos|e 'kæl.ə.buːs, --'- **-es** -ɪz
calabrese 'kæl.ə.briːs, -briːz
Calabri|a kə'læb.ri|.ə, kæl'æb-, -'ɑː.bri- (US) kə'leɪ.bri-, -'lɑː- **-an/s** -ən/z
Calais 'kæl.eɪ (US) kæl'eɪ
calamari ˌkæl.ə'mɑː.ri (US) -'mɑːr.i
calamine 'kæl.ə.maɪn
calamitous kə'læm.ɪ.təs, -ə.təs (US) -ə.t̬əs **-ly** -li **-ness** -nəs, -nɪs
calamit|y kə'læm.ə.t|i, -ɪ.t|i (US) -ə.t̬|i **-ies** -iz **Caˌlamity 'Jane**
calamus 'kæl.ə.məs
calash kə'læʃ **-es** -ɪz
calcareous kæl'keə.ri.əs (US) -'ker.i-, -'kær- **-ness** -nəs, -nɪs
calceolaria ˌkæl.si.ə'leə.ri.ə (US) -'ler.i-, -'lær- **-s** -z
calces 'kæl.siːz
Calchas 'kæl.kæs
calciferol kæl'sɪf.ə.rɒl (US) -roʊl, -rɑːl
calciferous kæl'sɪf.ᵊr.əs
calcification ˌkæl.sɪ.fɪ'keɪ.ʃᵊn, -sə-
calcifug|e 'kæl.sɪ.fjuːdʒ **-es** -ɪz
calcifugous kæl'sɪf.jə.gəs
calcif|y 'kæl.sɪ.f|aɪ, -sə- **-ies** -aɪz **-ying** -aɪ.ɪŋ **-ied** -aɪd
calcination ˌkæl.sɪ'neɪ.ʃᵊn, -sə'-
calcin|e 'kæl.saɪn, -sɪn **-es** -z **-ing** -ɪŋ **-ed** -d
calcite 'kæl.saɪt **-s** -s
calcium 'kæl.si.əm
Calcot(t) 'kɔːl.kət, 'kɒl-, 'kæl- (US) 'kɔːl.kɑːt, 'kɑːl-, 'kæl-
Note: In Calcot Row, Berkshire, the pronunciation is /'kæl.kət/.
calculab|le 'kæl.kjə.lə.b|l̩, -kjʊ- (US) -kjə- **-ly** -li
calcu|late 'kæl.kjə|.leɪt, -kjʊ- (US) -kjə [illegible] **-lates** -leɪts **-lating** -leɪ.tɪŋ (US) -leɪ.t̬ɪŋ **-lated** -leɪ.tɪd (US) -leɪ.t̬[illegible]
calculation ˌkæl.kjə'leɪ.ʃᵊn, -kjʊ'- (US) -kjə'- **-s** -z
calculative 'kæl.kjə.lə.tɪv, -kjʊ- (US) -kjə.lə.t̬ɪv
calculator 'kæl.kjə.leɪ.təʳ, -kjʊ- (US) -kjə.leɪ.t̬ɚ **-s** -z
calcul|us 'kæl.kjə.l|əs, -kjʊ- (US) -kjə- **-uses** -ə.sɪz **-i** -aɪ
Calcutt 'kæl.kʌt
Calcutta kæl'kʌt.ə (US) -'kʌt̬-
Caldecote 'kɔːl.dɪ.kət, 'kɒl-, -də- (US) 'kɑːl.də.koʊt, 'kɔːl-, -kət
Caldecott 'kɔːl.də.kət, 'kɒl-, -dɪ-, -k[illegible] (US) 'kɑːl.də.kɑːt, 'kɔːl-, -kət
Calder 'kɔːl.dəʳ, 'kɒl- (US) 'kɔːl.dɚ, 'k[illegible]
caldera kæl'deə.rə, 'kɔːl.də.rə (US) kæl'der.ə

Calderon *English name:* 'kɔːl.də.rən, 'kɒl-, 'kæl- US 'kɔːl.də.rɑːn, 'kɑːl- *Spanish name:* ˌkæl.də'rɒn US ˌkɑːl.ðə'rɔːn

Caldicot(t) 'kɔːl.dɪ.kɒt, 'kɒl-, -də-, -kət US 'kɑːl.də.kɑːt, 'kɔːl-, -kət

caldron 'kɔːl.drən, 'kɒl- US 'kɑːl-, 'kɔːl- -s -z

Caldwell 'kɔːld.wəl, 'kɒld-, -wel US 'kɔːld-, 'kɑːld-

Caleb 'keɪ.leb, -lɪb, -ləb

Caledon 'kæl.ɪ.dᵊn, '-ə-

Caledoni|a ˌkæl.ɪ'dəʊ.ni|.ə, -ə'- US -'doʊ- **-an/s** -ən/z

calefaction ˌkæl.ɪ'fæk.ʃᵊn, -ə'-

calefactor|y ˌkæl.ɪ'fæk.tᵊr|.i, -ə'-, -tr|i **-ies** -iz

calendar 'kæl.ən.dəʳ, -ɪn- US -dɚ **-s** -z

calend|er 'kæl.ən.d|əʳ, -ɪn- US -d|ɚ **-ers** -əz US -ɚz **-ering** -ᵊr.ɪŋ **-ered** -əd US -ɚd

calends 'kæl.ɪndz, -endz, -əndz US 'kæl.ɪndz, 'keɪ.lɪndz, -lendz, -ləndz

calendula kə'len.djə.lə, kæl'en-, -djʊ- US -dʒə- **-s** -z

calenture 'kæl.ən.tʃʊəʳ, -ɪn-, -tjʊəʳ, -tʃəʳ US -tʃɚ, -tʃʊr **-s** -z

cal|f kɑː|f US kæ|f **-ves** -vz ˌ**calf's-foot 'jelly**

calfskin 'kɑːf.skɪn US 'kæf-

Calgary 'kæl.gᵊr.i

Calhoun kæl'huːn, -'haʊn, kə'huːn US kæl'huːn, -'hoʊn, kə'huːn

Cali 'kɑː.li

Caliban 'kæl.ɪ.bæn, '-ə-, -bən

caliber 'kæl.ɪ.bəʳ, '-ə- US 'kæl.ə.bɚ **-s** -z

Calibra® kə'liː.brə

cali|brate 'kæl.ɪ|.breɪt, '-ə- **-brates** -breɪts **-brating** -breɪ.tɪŋ US -breɪ.t̬ɪŋ **-brated** -breɪ.tɪd US -breɪ.t̬ɪd

calibration ˌkæl.ɪ'breɪ.ʃᵊn, -ə'-

calibrator 'kæl.ɪ.breɪ.təʳ, '-ə- US -t̬ɚ **-s** -z

calibre 'kæl.ɪ.bəʳ, '-ə- US 'kæl.ə.bɚ **-s** -z

calicle 'kæl.ɪ.kl̩ **-s** -z

calico 'kæl.ɪ.kəʊ, '-ə- US -koʊ **-(e)s** -z

Calicut 'kæl.ɪ.kət, '-ə-, -kʌt

calif 'keɪ.lɪf, 'kæl.ɪf **-s** -s

Calif. *(abbrev. for* **California***)* ˌkæl.ɪ'fɔː.ni.ə, -ə'-, '-njə US -ə'fɔːr.njə, -ni.ə

Californi|a ˌkæl.ɪ'fɔː.ni|.ə, -ə'-, '-nj|ə US -ə'fɔːr.nj|ə, -ni|.ə **-an/s** -ən/z

californium ˌkæl.ɪ'fɔː.ni.əm, -ə'- US -ə'fɔːr-

Caligula kə'lɪg.jʊ.lə, -jə-

calipash 'kæl.ɪ.pæʃ

calipee 'kæl.ɪ.piː, ˌ--'-

caliper 'kæl.ɪ.pəʳ US -ə.pɚ **-s** -z

caliph 'keɪ.lɪf, 'kæl.ɪf **-s** -s

caliphate 'kæl.ɪ.feɪt, 'keɪ.lɪ-, -fɪt, -fət US 'keɪ.lɪ.fət, 'kæl.ɪ.feɪt **-s** -s

calisthenic ˌkæl.ɪs'θen.ɪk, -əs'- US -əs'- **-s** -s

Calisto kə'lɪs.təʊ US -toʊ

cal|ix 'keɪ.l|ɪks, 'kæl|.ɪks **-ices** -ɪs.iːz

calk kɔːk US kɔːk, kɑːk **-s** -s **-ing** -ɪŋ **-ed** -t

calkin 'kæl.kɪn, 'kɔː- US 'kɔː-, 'kɑː- **-s** -z

call kɔːl US kɔːl, kɑːl **-s** -z **-ing** -ɪŋ **-ed** -d **'call ˌgirl**

Callaghan 'kæl.ə.hən, -hæn, -gən US -hæn

Callahan 'kæl.ə.hæn, -hən US -hæn

Callan 'kæl.ən

Callander 'kæl.ən.dəʳ US -dɚ

callanetics® ˌkæl.ə'net.ɪks US -'net̬-

Callao kə'jaʊ US kə'jɑː.oʊ

Callas 'kæl.əs, -æs

callback 'kɔːl.bæk US 'kɔːl-, 'kɑːl-

callboy 'kɔːl.bɔɪ US 'kɔːl-, 'kɑːl- **-s** -z

Callcott 'kɔːl.kət, 'kɒl- US 'kɔːl.kɑːt, 'kɑːl-

Callender 'kæl.ɪn.dəʳ, -ən- US -dɚ

caller 'kɔː.ləʳ US 'kɔː.lɚ, 'kɑː- **-s** -z

Caller 'kæl.əʳ US -ɚ

Callie *surname:* 'kɔː.li US 'kɔː-, 'kɑː-

Callie *girl's name:* 'kæl.i

calligraphic ˌkæl.ɪ'græf.ɪk, -ə'- **-al** -ᵊl **-ally** -ᵊl.i, -li

calligraph|y kə'lɪg.rə.f|i, kæl'ɪg- **-ist/s** -ɪst/s **-er/s** -əʳ/z US -ɚ/z

calling 'kɔː.lɪŋ US 'kɔː-, 'kɑː- **-s** -z **'calling ˌcard**

Calliope kə'laɪə.pi, kæl'aɪə-

calliper 'kæl.ɪ.pəʳ US -ə.pɚ **-s** -z

callipygian ˌkæl.ɪ'pɪdʒ.i.ən, -ə'- US -ə'-

callipygous ˌkæl.ɪ'paɪ.gəs, -ə'- US -ə'-

Callirrhoe kæl'ɪr.əʊ.iː, kə'lɪr- US kə'lɪr.oʊ-

Callisthenes kæl'ɪs.θə.niːz, kə'lɪs- US kə'lɪs-

callisthenic ˌkæl.ɪs'θen.ɪk **-s** -s

Callistratus kæl'ɪs.trə.təs, kə'lɪs- US kə'lɪs-

callosit|y kæl'ɒs.ə.t|i, kə'lɒs-, -ɪt|.i US kə'lɑː.sə.t̬|i **-ies** -iz

callous 'kæl.əs **-ly** -li **-ness** -nəs, -nɪs **-ed** -t

callow (C) 'kæl.əʊ US -oʊ **-er** -əʳ US -ɚ **-est** -ɪst, -əst

Calloway 'kæl.ə.weɪ

call-up 'kɔːl.ʌp US 'kɔːl-, 'kɑːl-

callus 'kæl.əs **-es** -ɪz **-ed**

calm kɑːm US kɑː/m **-s** -z **-er** -əʳ US -ɚ **-est** -ɪst, -əst **-ly** -li **-ness** -nəs, -nɪs **-ing** -ɪŋ **-ed** -d

calmative 'kæl.mə.tɪv, 'kɑː.mə- US 'kɑː.mə.t̬ɪv, 'kæl- **-s** -z

calmodulin kəl'mɒd.jə.lɪn, -jʊ- US -'mɑː.dʒə-, -dʒʊ-

Calne kɑːn

calomel 'kæl.əʊ.mel US -ə.mel, -məl

calor 'kæl.əʳ US -ɚ **'Calor ˌgas**

caloric kə'lɒr.ɪk; 'kæl.ᵊr- US kə'lɔːr-

calorie 'kæl.ᵊr.i **-s** -z

calorific ˌkæl.ə'rɪf.ɪk, -ɔː'- US -ə'-

calorification kəˌlɒr.ɪ.fɪ'keɪ.ʃᵊn; ˌkæl.ə.rɪ-, ˌkæl.ɔː-, ˌkæl.ɒr.ɪ- US kəˌlɔːr-, kælˌɔːr-

calorimeter ˌkæl.ə'rɪm.ɪ.təʳ, -ɔː'-, -ɒr'ɪm-, '-ə- US -ə'rɪm.ə.t̬ɚ **-s** -z

calorimetry ˌkæl.ə'rɪm.ɪ.tri, -ɔː'-, -ɒr'ɪm-, '-ə- US -ə'rɪm.ə-

calotte kə'lɒt US -lɑːt **-s** -s

caloyer 'kæl.ɔɪ.əʳ US 'kæl.ə.jɚ; kə'lɔɪ- **-s** -z

Calpurnia ˌkæl'pɜː.ni.ə US -'pɝː-

calque kælk **-s** -s

Calshot 'kæl.ʃɒt US -ʃɑːt

Calthorpe *district in Birmingham:* 'kæl.θɔːp US -θɔːrp *surname:* 'kɔːl.θɔːp, 'kɒl-, 'kæl.θɔːp US 'kɔːl.θɔːrp, 'kɑːl-, 'kæl-

Calton *in Edinburgh:* 'kɔːl.tᵊn US 'kɔːl-, 'kɑːl- *in Glasgow:* 'kɑːl.tᵊn

caltrop 'kæl.trəp, -trɒp **-s** -s

calumet 'kæl.jʊ.met US 'kæl.jə.met, -mɪt; ˌkæl.jə'met **-s** -s

calumni|ate kə'lʌm.ni|.eɪt **-ates** -eɪts **-ating** -eɪ.tɪŋ US -eɪ.t̬ɪŋ **-ated** -eɪ.tɪd US -eɪ.t̬ɪd **-ator/s** -eɪ.təʳ/z US -eɪ.t̬ɚ/z

calumniation kəˌlʌm.ni'eɪ.ʃᵊn **-s** -z

calumn|y 'kæl.əm.n|i **-ies** -iz

calvados (C) 'kæl.və.dɒs US ˌkæl.və'doʊs, ˌkɑːl-

calvar|y (C) 'kæl.vᵊr|.i **-ies** -iz

calv|e kɑːv US kæv **-es** -z **-ing** -ɪŋ **-ed** -d

Calverley *surname:* 'kæl.vᵊl.i US -vɚ.li *place in West Yorkshire:* 'kɑː.və.li, 'kɔːv.li US 'kɑː.vɚ-, 'kɔːv-

Calvert 'kæl.vɜːt, -vət, 'kɔːl.vət US 'kæl.vɝːt, -vɚt

Calverton 'kæl.və.tᵊn, 'kɔːl- US 'kæl.vɚ.t̬ən

calves'-foot 'kɑːvz.fʊt US 'kævz-

Calvin 'kæl.vɪn

Calvin|ism 'kæl.vɪ.n|ɪ.zᵊm, -və- **-ist/s** -ɪst/s

Calvinistic ˌkæl.vɪ'nɪs.tɪk, -və'- **-al** -ᵊl **-ally** -ᵊl.i, -li

cal|x kæl|ks **-ces** -siːz **-xes** -k.sɪz

Calydon 'kæl.ɪ.dᵊn, '-ə-

calypso (C) kə'lɪp.səʊ US -soʊ **-(e)s** -z

ca|lyx 'keɪ|.lɪks, 'kæ|l.ɪks **-lyces** -lɪ.siːz **-lyxes** -lɪk.sɪz

calzone kælt'soʊ.ni, kæl'zəʊ-, -neɪ US kæl'zoʊ.ni, -'zoʊn **-s** -z

cam (C) kæm **-s** -z

CAm *(abbrev. for* **Central America***)* ˌsen.trᵊl.ə'mer.ɪ.kə

CAM kæm

Camalodunum ˌkæm.ə.ləʊˈdjuː.nəm ⓤⓢ -loʊˈduː-, -ˈdjuː-
camaraderie ˌkæm.əˈrɑː.dᵊr.i, -ˈræd.ᵊr-, -iː ⓤⓢ ˌkæm.əˈrɑː.dɚ.i, ˌkɑː.məˈ-, -ˈræd.ɚ-
Camargue kæmˈɑːg, kəˈmɑːg ⓤⓢ kəˈmɑːrg
camarilla ˌkæm.əˈrɪl.ə **-s** -z
Camay® ˈkæm.eɪ ⓤⓢ ˌkæmˈeɪ
camber (C) ˈkæm.bəʳ ⓤⓢ -bɚ **-s** -z
Camberley ˈkæm.bᵊl.i ⓤⓢ -bɚ.li
Camberwell ˈkæm.bə.wel, -wəl ⓤⓢ -bɚ-
cambial ˈkæm.bi.əl
cambium ˈkæm.bi.əm
Cambodi|a ˌkæmˈbəʊ.di|.ə ⓤⓢ -ˈboʊ- **-an/s** -ən
Camborne ˈkæm.bɔːn, -bən ⓤⓢ -bɔːrn
Cambray ˈkɑ̃ːm.breɪ, ˈkɒm- ⓤⓢ kɑːmˈbreɪ
Cambri|a ˈkæm.bri|.ə **-an/s** -ən/z
cambric ˈkæm.brɪk, ˈkeɪm-
Cambridge ˈkeɪm.brɪdʒ **-shire** -ʃəʳ, -ˌʃɪəʳ ⓤⓢ -ʃɚ, -ˌʃɪr
Cambs. *(abbrev. for* **Cambridgeshire***)* kæm*bz*; ˈkeɪm.brɪdʒ.ʃəʳ, -ˌʃɪəʳ ⓤⓢ kæm*bz*; ˈkeɪm.brɪdʒ.ʃɚ, -ˌʃɪr
Cambyses kæmˈbaɪ.siːz
camcorder ˈkæmˌkɔː.dəʳ ⓤⓢ -ˌkɔːr.dɚ **-s** -z
Camden ˈkæm.dən
came *(from* **come***)* keɪm
camel ˈkæm.ᵊl **-s** -z
Camelford ˈkæm.ᵊl.fəd ⓤⓢ -fɚd
camelhair ˈkæm.ᵊl.heəʳ ⓤⓢ -her
camel(l)ia (C) kəˈmiː.li.ə, -ˈmel.i- ⓤⓢ -ˈmiːl.jə, -ˈmiː.li.ə **-s** -z
Camelot ˈkæm.ə.lɒt, ˈ-ɪ- ⓤⓢ -lɑːt
Camembert ˈkæm.əm.beəʳ ⓤⓢ -ber
cameo ˈkæm.i.əʊ ⓤⓢ -oʊ **-s** -z **ˈcameo ˌrole**
camera ˈkæm.ᵊr.ə, ˈkæm.rə **-s** -z
cameral ˈkæm.ᵊr.ᵊl
camera|man ˈkæm.ᵊr.ə|.mæn, ˈkæm.rə-, -mən **-men** -men
camera obscura ˌkæm.ᵊr.ə.əbˈskjʊə.rə, ˌkæm.rə-, -ɒbˈ- ⓤⓢ -əbˈskjʊr.ə
camera|woman ˈkæm.ᵊr.ə|ˌwʊm.ən, -rəˌ- **-women** -ˌwɪm.ɪn
Camero kəˈmeə.rəʊ ⓤⓢ -ˈmer.oʊ
Cameron ˈkæm.ᵊr.ən, ˈkæm.rən
Cameronian ˌkæm.ᵊrˈəʊ.ni.ən ⓤⓢ -ˈroʊ- **-s** -z
Cameroon ˌkæm.əˈruːn, ˈ--- **-s** -z
camiknickers ˈkæm.iˌnɪk.əz, ˌkæm.iˈnɪk- ⓤⓢ ˈkæm.iˌnɪk.ɚz
Camilla kəˈmɪl.ə
Camille kəˈmiːl, -ˈmɪl
camis|e kəˈmiːz **-es** -ɪz
camisole ˈkæm.ɪ.səʊl ⓤⓢ -soʊl **-s** -z
Camlachie kæmˈlæk.i, -ˈlæx-
Cammell Laird ˌkæm.ᵊlˈleəd ⓤⓢ -ˈlerd
camomile ˈkæm.əʊ.maɪl ⓤⓢ -ə.miːl
Camorra kəˈmɒr.ə ⓤⓢ -ˈmɔːr-
camouflag|e ˈkæm.ə.flɑːʒ, ˈ-ʊ- ⓤⓢ -flɑː*d*ʒ **-es** -ɪz **-ing** -ɪŋ **-ed** -d
Camoys kəˈmɔɪz
camp (C) kæmp **-s** -s **-ing** -ɪŋ **-ed** -t **-y** -i **ˈcamp ˌstool ˌcamp ˈbed ˈcamp ˌbed; ˌCamp ˈDavid; ˈcamp ˌfollower**
Campagna kæmˈpɑː.njə ⓤⓢ -njɑː
campaign kæmˈpeɪn **-s** -z **-ing** -ɪŋ **-ed** -d **-er/s** -əʳ/z ⓤⓢ -ɚ/z
campanile ˌkæm.pəˈniː.leɪ ⓤⓢ -leɪ, -li **-s** -z
campanolog|y ˌkæm.pəˈnɒl.ə.dʒ|i ⓤⓢ -ˈnɑː.lə- **-ist/s** -ɪst/s
campanula kəmˈpæn.jʊ.lə, kæm-, -jə- **-s** -z
Campari® kæmˈpɑː.ri ⓤⓢ -ˈpɑːr.i
Campbell ˈkæm.bᵊl **-s** -z
Campbellite ˈkæm.bᵊl.aɪt ⓤⓢ -bə.laɪt **-s** -s
Campbeltown ˈkæm.bᵊl.taʊn
Campden ˈkæm*p*.dən
Campeche kæmˈpiː.tʃi
camper ˈkæm.pəʳ ⓤⓢ -pɚ **-s** -z **ˈcamper ˌvan**
Camperdown ˈkæm.pə.daʊn ⓤⓢ -pɚ-
campfire ˈkæmp.faɪəʳ ⓤⓢ -faɪɚ **-s** -z
campground ˈkæmp.graʊnd **-s** -z
camphire ˈkæm*p*.faɪəʳ ⓤⓢ -faɪɚ
camphor ˈkæm*p*.fəʳ ⓤⓢ -fɚ **-s** -z
camphor|ate ˈkæm*p*.fə.r|eɪt **-ates** -eɪts **-ating** -eɪ.tɪŋ ⓤⓢ -eɪ.t̬ɪŋ **-ated** -eɪ.tɪd ⓤⓢ -eɪ.t̬ɪd ˌ**camphorated ˈoil**
camphoric kæmˈfɒr.ɪk ⓤⓢ -ˈfɔːr-
camping ˈkæm.pɪŋ
campion (C) ˈkæm.pi.ən **-s** -z
Camps kæmps
campsite ˈkæmp.saɪt **-s** -s
campus ˈkæm.pəs **-es** -ɪz
CAMRA ˈkæm.rə
camshaft ˈkæm.ʃɑːft ⓤⓢ -ʃæft **-s** -s
Camus kæmˈuː ⓤⓢ kæmˈuː, kɑːˈmuː, kə-
camwood ˈkæm.wʊd
can *(n.)* kæn **-s** -z **ˈcan ˌopener; (ˌopen a) ˌcan of ˈworms; ˌcarry theˈcan**
can *(v.) put in cans:* kæn **-s** -z **-ning** -ɪŋ **-ned** -d
can *(auxil. v.) strong form:* kæn *weak forms:* kən, kn̩, kŋ
Note: Weak form word. The strong form /kæn/ is used for emphasis (e.g. "You **can** do it", and for contrast (e.g. "I don't know if he can or he can't"). It is also used finally in a sentence (e.g. "I don't know if I can"). The form /kŋ/ occurs only before words beginning with /k/ or /g/.
Cana ˈkeɪ.nə
Canaan ˈkeɪ.nən, -ni.ən *Jewish pronunciation:* kəˈneɪ.ən
Canaanite ˈkeɪ.nə.naɪt, -ni.ə- *Jewish pronunciation:* kəˈneɪ.ə.naɪt **-s** -s
Canada ˈkæn.ə.də
Canadian kəˈneɪ.di.ən **-s** -z
canaille kəˈneɪəl, -naɪ ⓤⓢ kəˈneɪl
canal kəˈnæl **-s** -z
Canaletto ˌkæn.ᵊlˈet.əʊ ⓤⓢ -əˈlet̬.oʊ
canalization, -isa- ˌkæn.ᵊl.aɪˈzeɪ.ʃᵊn, -ɪˈ- ⓤⓢ -ɪˈ-
canaliz|e, -is|e ˈkæn.ᵊl.aɪz ⓤⓢ -ə.laɪz **-es** -ɪz **-ing** -ɪŋ **-ed** -d
Cananite ˈkæn.ə.naɪt, ˈkeɪ.nə- **-s** -s
canapé ˈkæn.ə.peɪ **-s** -z
canard ˈkæn.ɑːd, kəˈnɑːd, kænˈɑːd ⓤⓢ kəˈnɑːrd **-s** -z
canar|y (C) kəˈneə.r|i ⓤⓢ -ˈner|.i **-ies** -iz **Caˈnary ˌIslands**
canasta kəˈnæs.tə
canaster kəˈnæs.təʳ ⓤⓢ -tɚ **-s** -z
Canaveral kəˈnæv.ᵊr.ᵊl
Canberra ˈkæn.bᵊr.ə, ˈkæm- ⓤⓢ ˈkæn.ber-, -bɚ-
cancan ˈkæn.kæn, ˈkæŋ- **-s** -z
cancel ˈkæn*t*.sᵊl **-s** -z **-(l)ing** -ɪŋ **-(l)ed** -d
cancell|ate ˈkæn*t*.sᵊl|.eɪt, -sɪ.l|eɪt ⓤⓢ -sə.l|eɪt **-ates** -eɪts **-ating** -eɪ.tɪŋ ⓤⓢ -eɪ.t̬ɪŋ **-ated** -eɪ.tɪd ⓤⓢ -eɪ.t̬ɪd
cancellation ˌkæn*t*.sᵊlˈeɪ.ʃᵊn, -sɪˈleɪ- ⓤⓢ -səˈleɪ- **-s** -z
cancellous ˈkæn*t*.sᵊl.əs
cancer (C) ˈkæn*t*.səʳ ⓤⓢ -sɚ **-s** -z
Cancerean, Cancerian kæn*t*ˈsɪə.ri.ən, -ˈseə- ⓤⓢ -ˈser.i-, -ˈsɪr- **-s** -z
cancerous ˈkæn*t*.sᵊr.əs
cancroid ˈkæŋ.krɔɪd
Candace kænˈdeɪ.si, ˈkæn.dɪs, -dəs
candela kænˈdel.ə, -ˈdeɪ.lə, -ˈdiː- **-s** -z
candelabr|a ˌkæn.dᵊlˈɑː.br|ə, -dɪˈlɑː-, -ˈlæb.r|ə ⓤⓢ -dəˈlɑː.br|ə, -ˈlæb.r|ə **-as** -əz **-um** -əm
Canderel® ˌkæn.dᵊrˈel, ˈ---
candescen|ce kænˈdes.ᵊn|*t*s **-t** -t
Candia ˈkæn.di.ə
Candice ˈkæn.dɪs, -diːs
candid ˈkæn.dɪd **-ly** -li **-ness** -nəs, -nɪs
Candida ˈkæn.dɪ.də
candida|cy ˈkæn.dɪ.də|.si **-cies** -siz
candidate ˈkæn.dɪ.dət, -deɪt, -dɪt **-s** -s
candidature ˈkæn.dɪ.də.tʃəʳ, ˈ-də-, -deɪ-, -dɪtʃ.əʳ ⓤⓢ ˈkæn.də.də.tʃʊr, -tʃɚ **-s** -z
Candide kɑ̃ː*n*ˈdiːd ⓤⓢ kɑːn-, kæn-
candidias|is ˌkæn.dɪˈdaɪə.s|ɪs, -dəˈ- **-es** -iːz
candle ˈkæn.dl̩ **-s** -z ˌ**burn the ˌcandle ˌboth ˈends**
candlelight ˈkæn.dl̩.laɪt
candle-lit ˈkæn.dl̩.lɪt ˌ**candle-lit ˈdinner**
Candlemas ˈkæn.dl̩.məs, -mæs

candlepower 'kæn.dl̩.paʊəʳ ⓤⓢ -paʊɚ **-s** -z
candlestick 'kæn.dl̩.stɪk **-s** -s
candlewick 'kæn.dl̩.wɪk
cando(u)r 'kæn.dəʳ ⓤⓢ -dɚ
cand|y **(C)** 'kæn.d|i **-ies** -iz **-ying** -i.ɪŋ **-ied** -id
candyfloss 'kæn.di.flɒs ⓤⓢ -flɑːs
candytuft 'kæn.di.tʌft
can|e **(C)** keɪn **-es** -z **-ing** -ɪŋ **-ed** -d ˌ**cane 'sugar**, **'cane ˌsugar**
Canford 'kæn.fəd ⓤⓢ -fɚd
Canham 'kæn.əm
canicular kə'nɪk.jʊ.ləʳ, kæn'ɪk-, -jə- ⓤⓢ -jə.lɚ
canine 'keɪ.naɪn, 'kæn.aɪn ⓤⓢ 'keɪ.naɪn **-s** -z
Canis 'keɪ.nɪs, 'kæn.ɪs
canister 'kæn.ɪ.stəʳ ⓤⓢ -ə.stɚ **-s** -z
cank|er 'kæŋ.k|əʳ ⓤⓢ -k|ɚ **-ers** -əz ⓤⓢ -ɚz **-ering** -ᵊr.ɪŋ **-ered** -əd ⓤⓢ -ɚd
ankerous 'kæŋ.kᵊr.əs
anna 'kæn.ə **-s** -z
annabis 'kæn.ə.bɪs
annan 'kæn.ən
annelloni ˌkæn.ᵊl'əʊ.ni, -ɪ'ləʊ- ⓤⓢ -ə'loʊ-
anner|y 'kæn.ᵊr|.i **-ies** -iz
annes kæn, kænz ⓤⓢ kæn, kænz, kɑːn ˌ**Cannes 'Film ˌFestival**
annibal 'kæn.ɪ.bᵊl, '-ə- **-s** -z
annibalism 'kæn.ɪ.bᵊl.ɪ.zᵊm, '-ə-
annibalistic ˌkæn.ɪ.bᵊl'ɪs.tɪk, ˌ-ə- ⓤⓢ -bə'lɪs-
annibaliz|e, **-is|e** 'kæn.ɪ.bᵊl.aɪz, '-ə- ⓤⓢ -bə.laɪz **-es** -ɪz **-ing** -ɪŋ **-ed** -d
annikin 'kæn.ɪ.kɪn ⓤⓢ '-ə- **-s** -z
anning 'kæn.ɪŋ
annizzaro ˌkæn.ɪ'zɑː.rəʊ, -ə'- ⓤⓢ -roʊ
annock 'kæn.ək
nnon **(C)** 'kæn.ən **-s** -z **-ing** -ɪŋ **-ed** -d **'cannon ˌfodder**
nnonad|e ˌkæn.ə'neɪd **-es** -z **-ing** -ɪŋ **-ed** -ɪd
nnonball 'kæn.ən.bɔːl ⓤⓢ -bɔːl, -bɑːl **-s** -z **-ing** -ɪŋ **-ed** -d
nnoneer ˌkæn.ə'nɪəʳ ⓤⓢ -'nɪr **-s** -z
nnonry 'kæn.ən.ri
nnonshot 'kæn.ən.ʃɒt ⓤⓢ -ʃɑːt **-s** -s
nnot 'kæn.ɒt, -ət ⓤⓢ 'kæn.ɑːt, kə'nɑːt
te: This word is usually contracted to /kɑːnt ⓤⓢ kænt/. See **can't**.
nnul|a 'kæn.jə.l|ə, -jʊ- ⓤⓢ -jə- **-ae** -iː, -aɪ **-as** -əz
nn|y 'kæn|.i **-ier** -i.əʳ ⓤⓢ -i.ɚ **-iest** -i.ɪst, -i.əst **-ily** -ɪ.li, -ᵊl.i **-iness** -ɪ.nəs, -ɪ.nɪs
noe kə'nuː **-s** -z **-ing** -ɪŋ **-d** -d
noeist kə'nuː.ɪst **-s** -s
non 'kæn.ən **-s** -z ˌ**canon 'law**

Canonbury 'kæn.ən.bᵊr.i, -əm- ⓤⓢ -ən.ber-, -bɚ-
canoness ˌkæn.ə'nes, 'kæn.ə.nɪs, -nes ⓤⓢ 'kæn.ə.nəs **-es** -ɪz
Canongate 'kæn.ən.geɪt, -əŋ-
canonic kə'nɒn.ɪk, kæn'ɒn- ⓤⓢ kə'nɑː.nɪk **-al/s** -ᵊl/z **-ally** -ᵊl.i, -li
canonization, **-isa-** ˌkæn.ə.naɪ'zeɪ.ʃᵊn, -nɪ'- ⓤⓢ -nɪ'- **-s** -z
canoniz|e, **-is|e** 'kæn.ə.naɪz **-es** -ɪz **-ing** -ɪŋ **-ed** -d
canonr|y 'kæn.ən.r|i **-ies** -iz
canoodl|e kə'nuː.dl̩ **-es** -z **-ing** -ɪŋ, -'nuːd.lɪŋ **-ed** -d
Canopus kə'nəʊ.pəs ⓤⓢ -'noʊ-
canop|y 'kæn.ə.p|i **-ies** -iz
Canossa kə'nɒs.ə, kæn'ɒs- ⓤⓢ kə'nɑː.sə
canst *(from* **can***) strong form:* kænst *weak form:* kənst
cant **(C)** kænt **-s** -s **-ing** -ɪŋ **-ed** -ɪd **-er/s** -əʳ/z ⓤⓢ -ɚ/z
can't kɑːnt ⓤⓢ kænt
Cantab. 'kæn.tæb
cantabile kæn'tɑː.bɪ.leɪ, -bə-
Cantabria kæn'tæb.ri.ə ⓤⓢ -'teɪ.bri-
Cantabrian kæn'tæb.ri.ən ⓤⓢ -'teɪ.bri-
Cantabrigian ˌkæn.tə'brɪdʒ.i.ən **-s** -z
cantaloup(e) 'kæn.tə.luːp ⓤⓢ -t̬ə.loʊp **-s** -s
cantankerous ˌkæn'tæŋ.kᵊr.əs, kən- **-ly** -li **-ness** -nəs, -nɪs
cantata kæn'tɑː.tə, kən- ⓤⓢ kən'tɑː.t̬ə **-s** -z
cantatrice 'kæn.tə.triːs *as if French:* ˌkɑ̃ːn.tæt'riːs *as if Italian:* ˌkɑːn.tə'triː.tʃeɪ ⓤⓢ ˌkɑːn.tə'triːs **-s** -ɪz
canteen kæn'tiːn **-s** -z *stress shift:* ˌcanteen 'food
cant|er **(C)** 'kæn.t|əʳ ⓤⓢ -t̬|ɚ **-ers** -əz ⓤⓢ -ɚz **-ering** -ᵊr.ɪŋ **-ered** -əd ⓤⓢ -ɚd
Canterbury 'kæn.tə.bᵊr.i, -ber- ⓤⓢ -t̬ɚ.ber-, -bɚ- ˌ**Canterbury 'Tales**
cantharides kæn*t*'θær.ɪ.diːz, kən*t*- ⓤⓢ -'θer-, -'θær-
canticle 'kæn.tɪ.kl̩ ⓤⓢ -t̬ə- **-s** -z
Canticles *(Song of Solomon)* 'kæn.tɪ.kl̩z ⓤⓢ -t̬ə-
cantilena ˌkæn.tɪ'leɪn.ə ⓤⓢ -t̬ə'-
cantilever 'kæn.tɪ.liː.vəʳ, -tə- ⓤⓢ -t̬ə.liː.vɚ, -lev.ɚ **-s** -z
Cantire kæn'taɪəʳ ⓤⓢ -'taɪɚ
Cantling 'kænt.lɪŋ
canto 'kæn.təʊ ⓤⓢ -toʊ **-s** -z
canton *Swiss state:* 'kæn.tɒn, ˌ-'- ⓤⓢ 'kæn.tɑːn, -tᵊn **-s** -z *in heraldry:* 'kæn.tən
Canton *in China:* ˌkæn'tɒn ⓤⓢ -'tɑːn *in Wales, surname, place in US:* 'kæn.tən ⓤⓢ -tᵊn

canton *(v.) divide into portions or districts:* kæn'tɒn ⓤⓢ -'tɑːn **-s** -z **-ing** -ɪŋ **-ed** -d
canton *(v.) provide accommodation:* kæn'tuːn, kən- ⓤⓢ kæn'toʊn, -'tɑːn **-s** -z **-ing** -ɪŋ **-ed** -d **-ment/s** -mənt/s
Cantona 'kæn.tə.nɑː
cantonal 'kæn.tə.nᵊl, kæn'təʊ.nᵊl ⓤⓢ 'kæn.tə.nᵊl, kæn'tɑː.nəl
Cantonese ˌkæn.tə'niːz, -tɒn'iːz ⓤⓢ -tᵊn'iːz, -'iːs
cantor 'kæn.tɔːʳ ⓤⓢ -tɚ, -tɔːr **-s** -z
cantoris kæn'tɔː.rɪs ⓤⓢ -'tɔːr.ɪs
cantus 'kæn.təs ⓤⓢ -t̬əs
Cantwell 'kænt.wel
Canty 'kæn.ti ⓤⓢ -t̬i
Canuck kə'nʌk **-s** -s
Canute kə'njuːt ⓤⓢ -'nuːt, -'njuːt
canvas 'kæn.vəs **-es** -ɪz
canvasback 'kæn.vəs.bæk **-s** -s
canvass 'kæn.vəs **-es** -ɪz **-ing** -ɪŋ **-ed** -t **-er/s** -əʳ/z ⓤⓢ -ɚ/z
Canvey 'kæn.vi
canyon 'kæn.jən **-s** -z **-ing** -ɪŋ **-ed** -d
Canyonlands 'kæn.jən.lændz
canzone kænt'səʊ.neɪ, kæn'zəʊ- ⓤⓢ kæn'zoʊ.ni, kɑːnt'soʊ.neɪ **-s** -z
canzonet kænt'səʊ.net, kæn'zəʊ- ⓤⓢ ˌkæn.zə'net **-s** -s
caoutchouc 'kaʊ.tʃʊk, -tʃuːk, -tʃuː, -'-
cap kæp **-s** -s **-ping** -ɪŋ **-ped** -t
CAP ˌsiː.ei'piː
capabilit|y ˌkeɪ.pə'bɪl.ə.t|i, -ɪ.t|i ⓤⓢ -ə.t̬|i **-ies** -iz
capab|le 'keɪ.pə.b|l̩ **-ly** -li **-leness** -l̩.nəs, -nɪs
capacious kə'peɪ.ʃəs **-ly** -li **-ness** -nəs, -nɪs
capacitance kə'pæs.ɪ.tᵊn*t*s ⓤⓢ '-ə-
capaci|tate kə'pæs.ɪ|.teɪt ⓤⓢ '-ə- **-tates** -teɪts **-tating** -teɪ.tɪŋ ⓤⓢ -teɪ.t̬ɪŋ **-tated** -teɪ.tɪd ⓤⓢ -teɪ.t̬ɪd
capacitor kə'pæs.ɪ.təʳ, '-ə- ⓤⓢ -ə.t̬ɚ **-s** -z
capacit|y kə'pæs.ə.t|i, -ɪ.t|i ⓤⓢ -ə.t̬|i **-ies** -iz
cap-à-pie ˌkæp.ə'piː
caparison kə'pær.ɪ.sᵊn ⓤⓢ -'per.ə-, -'pær- **-s** -z **-ing** -ɪŋ **-ed** -d
cape **(C)** keɪp **-s** -s **-d** -t ˌ**Cape Ca'naveral**; ˌ**Cape 'Cod**; ˌ**Cape 'Horn**; ˌ**Cape of Good 'Hope**; **'Cape ˌProvince**; ˌ**caped cru'sader**
Capel *surname, places in Kent and Surrey:* 'keɪ.pᵊl *in Wales:* 'kæp.ᵊl
Capel Curig ˌkæp.ᵊl'kɪr.ɪg
Capell 'keɪ.pᵊl
capel(l)et 'kæp.ə.let, -lɪt **-s** -s
cap|er 'keɪ.p|əʳ ⓤⓢ -p|ɚ **-ers** -əz ⓤⓢ -ɚz **-ering** -ᵊr.ɪŋ **-ered** -əd ⓤⓢ -ɚd **-erer/s** -ᵊr.əʳ/z ⓤⓢ -ɚ.ɚ/z
caper *bird:* 'kæp.əʳ ⓤⓢ -ɚ **-s** -z

capercailzie, capercaillie ˌkæp.əˈkeɪ.li, -ˈkeɪ.lji, -ˈkeɪl.zi (US) -ɚˈkeɪ.li, -ˈkeɪl.ji, -zi -s -z

Capernaum kəˈpɜː.ni.əm (US) -ˈpɝː-

Cape Town, Capetown ˈkeɪp.taʊn

Cape Verde ˌkeɪpˈvɜːd, -ˈveəd (US) -ˈvɝːd

Capgrave ˈkæp.greɪv

capias ˈkeɪ.pi.æs, -pjæs, -pjəs (US) ˈkeɪ.pi.əs -es -ɪz

capillarity ˌkæp.ɪˈlær.ə.ti, -əˈ-, -ɪ.ti (US) -ˈler.ə.t̬i, -ˈlær-

capillary kəˈpɪl.ᵊr.i (US) ˈkæp.ə.ler-

capital ˈkæp.ɪ.tᵊl (US) -ə.t̬ᵊl -s -z -ly -i ˌcapital ˈletter; ˌcapital ˈpunishment

capitalism ˈkæp.ɪ.tᵊl.ɪ.zᵊm, kəˈpɪt.ᵊl-, kæpˈɪt- (US) ˈkæp.ə.t̬ᵊl-

capitalist ˈkæp.ɪ.tᵊl.ɪst, kəˈpɪt.ᵊl-, kæpˈɪt- (US) ˈkæp.ə.t̬ᵊl- -s -s

capitalistic ˌkæp.ɪ.tᵊlˈɪs.tɪk (US) -ə.t̬əˈlɪs- -ally -ᵊl.i, -li

capitalization, -isa- ˌkæp.ɪ.tᵊl.aɪˈzeɪ.ʃᵊn, kæpˌɪt.ᵊl-, kəˌpɪt- (US) ˌkæp.ə.t̬ᵊl.ɪˈ- -s -z

capitaliz|e, -is|e ˈkæp.ɪ.tᵊl.aɪz, kæpˈɪt.ᵊl-, kəˈpɪt- (US) ˈkæp.ə.t̬ə.laɪz -es -ɪz -ing -ɪŋ -ed -d

capitation ˌkæp.ɪˈteɪ.ʃᵊn (US) -əˈ- -s -z

capitol (C) ˈkæp.ɪ.tᵊl (US) -ə.t̬ᵊl -s -z ˌCapitol ˈHill

capitolian ˌkæp.ɪˈtəʊ.li.ən (US) -əˈtoʊ-

capitoline (C) kəˈpɪt.əʊ.laɪn (US) ˈkæp.ə.t̬ə.laɪn, -liːn

capitular kəˈpɪt.jʊ.ləʳ, -jə-, -ˈpɪtʃ.ʊ-, ˈ-ə- (US) -ˈpɪtʃ.ᵊl.ɚ -s -z

capitular|y kəˈpɪt.jʊ.lə.r|i, -jə-, -ˈpɪtʃ.ʊ-, ˈ-ə- (US) -ˈpɪtʃ.ə.ler|.i -ies -iz

capitu|late kəˈpɪt.jʊ|.leɪt, -jə-, -ˈpɪtj.ʊ-, ˈ-ə- (US) -ˈpɪtʃ.ə|.leɪt, ˈ-ʊ- -lates -leɪts -lating -leɪ.tɪŋ (US) -leɪ.t̬ɪŋ -lated -leɪ.tɪd (US) -leɪ.t̬ɪd

capitulation kəˌpɪt.jʊˈleɪ.ʃᵊn, -jəˈ-, -ˌpɪtʃ.ʊˈ-, -əˈ- (US) -ˌpɪtʃ.əˈ-, -jʊˈ- -s -z

capitul|um kəˈpɪt.jʊ.l|əm, -jə-, -ˈpɪtʃ.ʊ-, ˈ-ə- (US) -ˈpɪtʃ.ə- -a -ə

capo *for guitar:* ˈkæp.əʊ, ˈkeɪ.pəʊ (US) ˈkeɪ.poʊ -s -z *criminal chieftain:* ˈkɑː.pəʊ, ˈkæp.əʊ (US) ˈkɑː.poʊ, ˈkæp.oʊ

capon ˈkeɪ.pən, -pɒn (US) -pɑːn, -pᵊn -s -z

Capone kəˈpəʊn, keɪ- (US) kəˈpoʊn

capot kəˈpɒt (US) -ˈpɑːt -s -s -ting -ɪŋ (US) -ˈpɑː.t̬ɪŋ -ted -ɪd (US) -ˈpɑː.t̬ɪd

capote kəˈpəʊt (US) -ˈpoʊt -s -s

Capote kəˈpəʊ.ti (US) -ˈpoʊ.t̬i

Cappadoci|a ˌkæp.əˈdəʊ.si|.ə, -ʃi|.ə, -ʃ|ə (US) -ˈdoʊ.ʃ|ə -an/s -ən/z

Capper ˈkæp.əʳ (US) -ɚ

cappuccino ˌkæp.ʊˈtʃiː.nəʊ, -əˈ- (US) ˌkæp.əˈtʃiː.noʊ, ˌkɑː.pəˈ- -s -z

Capra ˈkæp.rə

Capri kæpˈriː, kəˈpriː

Capriati ˌkæp.riˈɑː.ti (US) -ˈɑː.t̬i, ˌkɑːp-

capric ˈkæp.rɪk

capriccio kəˈprɪtʃ.i.əʊ, -ˈpriː.tʃi- (US) -ˈpriː.tʃoʊ -s -z

capriccioso kəˌprɪtʃ.iˈəʊ.zəʊ, -ˌpriː.tʃiˈ-, -səʊ (US) ˌkɑː.priːˈtʃoʊ.soʊ, -tʃiˈoʊ-; kəˌpriː-

capric|e kəˈpriːs -es -ɪz

capricious kəˈprɪʃ.əs -ly -li -ness -nəs, -nɪs

Capricorn ˈkæp.rɪ.kɔːn (US) -rə.kɔːrn

Capricornus ˌkæp.rɪˈkɔː.nəs (US) -rəˈkɔːr-

capriol|e ˈkæp.ri.əʊl (US) -oʊl -es -z -ing -ɪŋ -ed -d

capsicum ˈkæp.sɪ.kəm

capsiz|e kæpˈsaɪz (US) ˈ--, -ˈ- -es -ɪz -ing -ɪŋ -ed -d

capstan ˈkæp.stən -s -z

capsular ˈkæp.sjʊ.ləʳ, -sjə- (US) -sə.lɚ, -sjʊ-

capsule ˈkæp.sjuːl (US) -sᵊl, -sjʊl -s -z

captain ˈkæp.tɪn (US) -tᵊn -s -z -ing -ɪŋ -ed -d

captainc|y ˈkæp.tɪn.s|i, -tən- -ies -iz

caption ˈkæp.ʃᵊn -s -z -ing -ɪŋ -ed -d

captious ˈkæp.ʃəs -ly -li -ness -nəs, -nɪs

capti|vate ˈkæp.tɪ|.veɪt (US) -tə- -vates -veɪts -vating -veɪ.tɪŋ (US) -veɪ.t̬ɪŋ -vated -veɪ.tɪd (US) -veɪ.t̬ɪd

captivation ˌkæp.tɪˈveɪ.ʃᵊn (US) -təˈ-

captive ˈkæp.tɪv -s -z

captivit|y kæpˈtɪv.ə.t|i, -ɪ.t|i (US) -ə.t̬|i -ies -iz

captor ˈkæp.təʳ, -tɔːʳ (US) -tɚ, -tɔːr -s -z

capt|ure ˈkæp.tʃ|əʳ (US) -tʃ|ɚ -ures -əz (US) -ɚz -uring -ᵊr.ɪŋ -ured -əd (US) -ɚd

Capua ˈkæp.ju.ə

capuch|e kəˈpuːʃ, -ˈpuːtʃ -es -ɪz

capuchin (C) ˈkæp.jʊ.tʃɪn, -ʃɪn; (US) ˈkæp.jʊ.tʃɪn, -jə-, -ʃɪn; kəˈpjuː- -s -z

Capulet ˈkæp.jʊ.let, -jə-, -lət, -lɪt

capybara ˌkæp.ɪˈbɑː.rə (US) -ˈbɑːr.ə -s -z

car kɑːʳ (US) kɑːr -s -z ˈcar aˌlarm; ˈcar ˌferry; ˈcar ˌpark; ˈcar ˌpool; ˈcar ˌport; ˈcar ˌwash

Cara ˈkɑː.rə (US) ˈker.ə, ˈkær-, ˈkɑːr-

carabineer ˌkær.ə.bɪˈnɪəʳ (US) ˌker.ə.bɪˈnɪr, ˌkær- -s -z

carabiner ˌkær.əˈbiː.nəʳ (US) ˌker.əˈbiː.nɚ, ˌkær- -s -z

carabinieri ˌkær.ə.bɪ.niˈeə.ri (US) ˌker.ə.bənˈjer.i, ˌkær-

caracal ˈkær.ə.kæl (US) ˈker-, ˈkær- -s -z

Caracas kəˈræk.əs, -ˈrɑː.kəs (US) -ˈrɑː-

caracole ˈkær.ə.kəʊl (US) ˈker.ə.koʊl, ˈkær- -s -z

Caractacus kəˈræk.tə.kəs

Caradoc kəˈræd.ək; ˈkær.ə.dɒk (US) ˈker.ə.dɑːk, ˈkær-; kəˈræd.ək

carafe kəˈræf, -ˈrɑːf -s -s

carambola ˌkær.əmˈbəʊ.lə (US) ˌker.əmˈboʊ-, ˌkær- -s -z

caramel ˈkær.ə.mᵊl, -mel (US) ˈkɑːr.mᵊl; ˈker.ə-, ˈkær- -s -z

carameliz|e, -is|e ˈkær.ə.mᵊl.aɪz, -mel- (US) ˈkɑːr.mə.laɪz, ˈker.ə-, ˈkær- -es -ɪz -ing -ɪŋ -ed -d

Caran d'Ache® ˌkær.ᵊnˈdæʃ (US) ˌkɑːr.ɑːnˈdɑːʃ

carapac|e ˈkær.ə.peɪs (US) ˈker-, ˈkær- -es -ɪz

carat ˈkær.ət (US) ˈker-, ˈkær- -s -s

Caratacus kəˈræt.ə.kəs (US) -ˈræt̬-

Caravaggio ˌkær.əˈvædʒ.i.əʊ, ˌkɑː.rəˈ-, -ˈvɑː.dʒi- (US) ˌker.əˈvɑː.dʒi.oʊ, ˌkær-

caravan ˈkær.ə.væn, ˌ--ˈ- (US) ˈker.ə.væn, ˈkær- -s -z -ning -ɪŋ

caravansar|y ˌkær.əˈvæn.sᵊr|.i (US) ˌker-, ˌkær- -ies -iz

caravanserai ˌkær.əˈvæn.sᵊr.aɪ, -eɪ, -i (US) ˌker-, ˌkær- -s -z

caravel ˈkær.ə.vel, ˌ--ˈ- (US) ˈker.ə.vel, ˈkær- -s -z

caraway ˈkær.ə.weɪ (US) ˈker-, ˈkær- -s -z ˈcaraway ˌseed

Carbery ˈkɑː.bᵊr.i (US) ˈkɑːr.ber-, -bɚ-

carbide ˈkɑː.baɪd (US) ˈkɑːr- -s -z

carbine ˈkɑː.baɪn (US) ˈkɑːr.biːn, -baɪn -s -z

carbineer ˌkɑː.bɪˈnɪəʳ, -bəˈ- (US) ˌkɑːr.bəˈnɪr -s -z

carbohydrate ˌkɑː.bəʊˈhaɪ.dreɪt, -dr (US) ˌkɑːr.boʊˈhaɪ.dreɪt, -bəˈ- -s -s

carbolic kɑːˈbɒl.ɪk (US) kɑːrˈbɑː.lɪk carˌbolic ˈacid

carbon ˈkɑː.bᵊn (US) ˈkɑːr- -s -z ˌcarbon ˈcopy (US) ˈcarbon ˌcopy; ˌcarbon diˈoxide

carbonaceous ˌkɑː.bəʊˈneɪ.ʃəs (US) ˌkɑːr.bəˈ-

carbonade ˌkɑː.bəˈneɪd, ˈ--- (US) ˌkɑːr.bəˈneɪd -s -z

carbonara ˌkɑː.bəˈnɑː.rə (US) ˌkɑːr.bəˈnɑːr.ə

carbonate *(n.)* ˈkɑː.bᵊn.eɪt, -ɪt, -ət (US) ˈkɑːr- -s -s

carbon|ate *(v.)* ˈkɑː.bᵊn|.eɪt (US) ˈkɑːr- -ates -eɪts -ating -eɪ.tɪŋ (US) -eɪ.t̬ɪŋ -ated -eɪ.tɪd (US) -eɪ.t̬ɪd

carbon|-date ˌkɑː.bᵊn|ˈdeɪt (US) ˌkɑːr- -dates -ˈdeɪts -dating -ˈdeɪ.tɪŋ (US) -ˈdeɪ.t̬ɪŋ -dated -ˈdeɪ.tɪd (US) -ˈdeɪ.t̬ɪd

carbonic kɑːˈbɒn.ɪk (US) kɑːrˈbɑː.nɪk

carboniferous ˌkɑː.bəˈnɪf.ᵊr.əs (US) ˌkɑːr-

carbonization, -isa- ˌkɑː.bᵊn.aɪˈzeɪ. -ɪˈ- (US) ˌkɑːr.bᵊn.ɪˈ-

Cardinal Vowel

One of the vowels of the standard classification system used in phonetics.

Description

Phoneticians have always needed some way of classifying vowels which is independent of the vowel system of a particular language. With most consonants it is quite easy to observe how their articulation is organised, and to specify the place and manner of the constriction formed; vowels, however, are much less easy to observe.

Early in the 20th century, the English phonetician Daniel Jones worked out a set of "Cardinal Vowels" that students learning phonetics could be taught to make and which would serve as reference points that other vowels could be related to.

The vowels are located on the four-sided figure shown below:

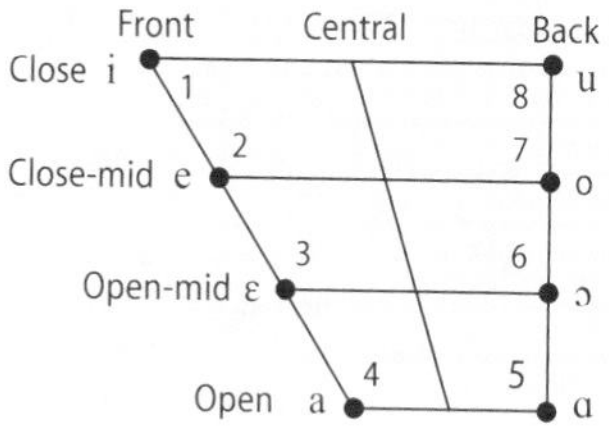

The primary cardinal vowels

The cardinal vowel figure is used to specify the qualities of the English vowels and diphthongs on pp xx and xx in the Introduction to this dictionary.

The Cardinal Vowel diagram is used both for rounded and unrounded vowels, and Jones proposed that there should be a **primary** set of Cardinal Vowels and a **secondary** set. The primary includes the unrounded front vowels [i e ɛ a], the back unrounded vowel [ɑ] and the back rounded vowels [ɔ o u], while the secondary set comprises the front rounded vowels [y ø œ ɶ], the back rounded vowel [ɒ] and the back unrounded vowels [ʌ ɤ ɯ].

Phonetic "ear-training" makes much use of the Cardinal Vowel system, and students can learn to identify and discriminate a very large number of different vowels in relation to the Cardinal vowels.

carboniz|e, **-is|e** 'kɑː.b^{ə}n.aɪz (US) 'kɑːr- **-es** -ɪz **-ing** -ɪŋ **-ed** -d

carbonnade ˌkɑː.b^{ə}n'eɪd, -'ɑːd, '--- (US) ˌkɑːr.b^{ə}n'eɪd **-s** -z

carbonyl 'kɑː.bə.nɪl, -naɪl (US) 'kɑːr-, -niːl **-s** -z

Carborundum® ˌkɑː.b^{ə}r'ʌn.dəm (US) ˌkɑːr.bɚ-

carboxyl kɑː'bɒk.sɪl, -saɪl (US) kɑːr'bɑːk.s^{ə}l

carboy 'kɑː.bɔɪ (US) 'kɑːr- **-s** -z

carbuncle 'kɑː.bʌŋ.kl̩ (US) 'kɑːr- **-s** -z

carburation ˌkɑː.bjə'reɪ.ʃ^{ə}n, -bjʊ'- (US) ˌkɑːr.bə-, -bjə-

carburetter, **carbure(t)tor** ˌkɑː.bjə'ret.ə^{r}, -bjʊ'-, 'kɑː.bjə.ret.ə (US) 'kɑːr.bə.reɪ.t̬ɚ, -bjə- **-s** -z

carburization, **-isa-** ˌkɑː.bjə.raɪ'zeɪ.ʃ^{ə}n, -bjʊ-, -rɪ'- (US) ˌkɑːr.bɚ.ɪ'-, -bjɚ-

carburiz|e, **-is|e** 'kɑː.bjə.raɪz, -bjʊ- (US) 'kɑːr.bə-, -bjə- **-es** -ɪz **-ing** -ɪŋ **-ed** -d

carcanet 'kɑː.kə.net, -nɪt (US) 'kɑːr- **-s** -s

carcas|e 'kɑː.kəs (US) 'kɑːr- **-es** -ɪz

carcass 'kɑː.kəs (US) 'kɑːr- **-es** -ɪz

Carcassonne ˌkɑː.kə'sɒn (US) ˌkɑːr.kə'soʊn, -'sɔːn

Carchemish 'kɑː.kə.mɪʃ, -kɪ-; kɑː'kiː- (US) 'kɑːr.kə-; kɑːr'kiː-

carcinogen kɑː'sɪn.ə.dʒ^{ə}n, -dʒen; 'kɑː.sɪ.nə-, -s^{ə}n.ə- (US) kɑːr'sɪn.ə-; 'kɑːr.s^{ə}n.ə- **-s** -z

carcinogenic ˌkɑː.sɪ.nəʊ'dʒen.ɪk, -s^{ə}n.əʊ'- (US) ˌkɑːr.s^{ə}n.oʊ'-; kɑːrˌsɪn-

carcinom|a ˌkɑː.sɪ'nəʊ.m|ə (US) ˌkɑːr.s^{ə}n'oʊ- **-as** -əz **-ata** -ə.tə (US) -ə.t̬ə

Carcroft 'kɑː.krɒft (US) 'kɑːr.krɑːft

card kɑːd (US) kɑːrd **-s** -z **-ing** -ɪŋ **-ed** -ɪd **'card ˌindex; 'card ˌkey; put one's ˌcards on the 'table**

cardamom, **cardamum** 'kɑː.də.məm (US) 'kɑːr-, -mɑːm **-s** -z

cardboard 'kɑːd.bɔːd (US) 'kɑːrd.bɔːrd

card-carrying 'kɑːdˌkær.i.ɪŋ (US) 'kɑːrdˌker-, -ˌkær-

Cardenden ˌkɑː.dən'dən (US) ˌkɑːr-

Cardew 'kɑː.djuː (US) 'kɑːr.duː

cardholder 'kɑːdˌhəʊl.də^{r} (US) 'kɑːrdˌhoʊl.dɚ **-s** -z

cardiac 'kɑː.di.æk (US) 'kɑːr- **ˌcardiac a'rrest**

cardiacal kɑː'daɪə.k^{ə}l (US) kɑːr-

Cardiff 'kɑː.dɪf (US) 'kɑːr-

cardigan 'kɑː.dɪ.gən (US) 'kɑːr- **-s** -z

Cardigan 'kɑː.dɪ.gən (US) 'kɑːr- **-shire** -ʃə^{r}, -ˌʃɪə^{r} (US) -ʃɚ, -ʃɪr

Cardin 'kɑː.dæ̃n, -dæn (US) kɑːr'dæn

cardinal 'kɑː.dɪ.n^{ə}l, -d^{ə}n.^{ə}l (US) 'kɑːr- **-s** -z **ˌcardinal 'number; ˌcardinal 'point; ˌcardinal 'rule; ˌcardinal 'vowel**

cardio- 'kɑː.di.əʊ-, ˌkɑː.di'ɒ- (US) 'kɑːr.di.oʊ-, ˌkɑːr.di'ɑː-

Note: Prefix. Normally takes either primary or secondary stress on the first syllable, e.g. **cardiogram** /'kɑː.di.əʊ.græm (US) 'kɑːr.di.oʊ-/, **cardiological** /ˌkɑː.di.əʊ'lɒdʒ.ɪ.k^{ə}l (US) ˌkɑːr.di.ə'lɑː.dʒɪ-/, or primary stress on the third syllable, e.g. **cardiology** /ˌkɑː.di'ɒl.ə.dʒi (US) ˌkɑːr.di'ɑː.lə-/.

cardiogram 'kɑː.di.əʊ.græm (US) 'kɑːr.di.oʊ- **-s** -z

cardiograph 'kɑː.di.əʊ.grɑːf, -græf (US) 'kɑːr.di.oʊ.græf **-s** -s

cardiography ˌkɑː.di'ɒg.rə.fi (US) ˌkɑːr.di'ɑː.grə-

cardioid 'kɑː.di.ɔɪd (US) 'kɑːr- **-s** -z

cardiological ˌkɑː.di.əʊ'lɒdʒ.ɪ.k^{ə}l (US) ˌkɑːr.di.ə'lɑː.dʒɪ-

cardiolog|y ˌkɑː.di'ɒl.ə.dʒ|i (US) ˌkɑːr.di'ɑː.lə- **-ist/s** -ɪst/s

cardiometer ˌkɑː.diˈɒm.ɪ.təʳ, -mə- US ˌkɑːr.diˈɑː.mə.t̬ɚ -s -z
cardiopulmonary ˌkɑː.di.əʊˈpʌl.mən.ᵊr.i, -ˈpʊl- US ˌkɑːr.di.oʊˈpʊl.mə.ner-, -ˈpʌl-
cardiovascular ˌkɑː.di.əʊˈvæs.kjʊ.ləʳ, -kjə- US ˌkɑːr.di.oʊˈvæs.kjə.lɚ
cardoon kɑːˈduːn US kɑːr- -s -z
cardphone ˈkɑːd.fəʊn US ˈkɑːrd.foʊn -s -z
cardpunch ˈkɑːd.pʌntʃ US ˈkɑːrd- -es -ɪz
cardsharp ˈkɑːd.ʃɑːp US ˈkɑːrd.ʃɑːrp -s -z **-er/s** -əʳ/z US -ɚ/z
Cardwell ˈkɑːd.wəl, -wel US ˈkɑːrd-
Cardy ˈkɑː.di US ˈkɑːr-
card|y, card|ie ˈkɑː.d|i US ˈkɑːr- **-ies** -iz
car|e keəʳ US ker **-es** -z **-ing** -ɪŋ **-ed** -d **-er/s** -əʳ/z US -ɚ/z
careen kəˈriːn **-s** -z **-ing** -ɪŋ **-ed** -d
career kəˈrɪəʳ US -ˈrɪr **-s** -z **-ing** -ɪŋ **-ed** -d **caˈreers adˌvisor; caˈreers ˌoffice**
careerist kəˈrɪə.rɪst US -ˈrɪr.ɪst **-s** -s
carefree ˈkeə.friː US ˈker-
careful ˈkeə.fᵊl, -fʊl US ˈker- **-lest** -ɪst **-ly** -i **-ness** -nəs, -nɪs
caregiver ˈkeəˌɡɪv.əʳ US ˈkerˌɡɪv.ɚ -s -z
careless ˈkeə.ləs, -lɪs US ˈker- **-ly** -li **-ness** -nəs, -nɪs
caress kəˈres **-es** -ɪz **-ing/ly** -ɪŋ/li **-ed** -t
caret ˈkær.ət, -ɪt, -et US ˈker-, ˈkær- **-s** -s
caretaker ˈkeəˌteɪ.kəʳ US ˈkerˌteɪ.kɚ **-s** -z **ˌcaretaker ˈgovernment** US **ˈcaretaker ˌgovernment**
Carew kəˈruː; ˈkeə.ri US kəˈruː; ˈker.u, -i
careworn ˈkeə.wɔːn US ˈker.wɔːrn
Carey ˈkeə.ri US ˈker.i, ˈkær-
carfare ˈkɑː.feəʳ US ˈkɑːr.fer **-s** -z
Carfax ˈkɑː.fæks US ˈkɑːr-
Cargill ˈkɑː.gɪl, -ˈ- US ˈkɑːr.gɪl, -ˈ-
cargo ˈkɑː.gəʊ US ˈkɑːr.goʊ **-(e)s** -z
carhop ˈkɑː.hɒp US ˈkɑːr.hɑːp **-s** -s
Caria ˈkeə.ri.ə US ˈker.i-
Carib ˈkær.ɪb US ˈker-, ˈkær- **-s** -z
Caribbean ˌkær.ɪˈbiː.ən, -ə-; kəˈrɪb.i.ən US ˌker.ɪˈbiː-, ˌkær-; kəˈrɪb.i-
Caribbees ˈkær.ɪ.biːz US ˈker-, ˈkær-
caribou (C) ˈkær.ɪ.buː US ˈker-, ˈkær- **-s** -z
caricatur|e ˈkær.ɪ.kə.tʃʊəʳ, -tʃɔːʳ, -tjʊəʳ, ˌkær.ɪ.kəˈtʃʊəʳ, -ˈtʃɔːʳ, -ˈtjʊəʳ US ˈker.ə.kə.tʃʊr, ˈkær-, -tʊr, -tʃɚ **-es** -z **-ing** -ɪŋ **-ed** -d
caricaturist ˈkær.ɪ.kə.tʃʊə.rɪst, -tʃɔː-, -tjʊə-, ˌkær.ɪ.kəˈtʃʊə.rɪst, -ˈtʃɔː-, -ˈtjʊə- US ˈker.ə.kə.tʃʊr.ɪst, ˈkær-, -tʊr-, -tʃɚ- **-s** -s
caries ˈkeə.riːz, -ri.iːz US ˈker.iːz, -i.ːz
carillon kærˈɪl.jən, kəˈrɪl-, -ɒn; ˈkær.ɪ.ljən, -ᵊl.jən, -ɒn US ˈker.ə.lɑːn, ˈkær- **-s** -z
Carinthia kəˈrɪnt.θi.ə, kærˈɪnt- US kəˈrɪnt-
carious ˈkeə.ri.əs US ˈker.i-
Carisbrooke ˈkær.ɪs.brʊk, -ɪz- US ˈker-, ˈkær-
carjack ˈkɑː.dʒæk US ˈkɑːr- **-s** -z **-ing/s** -ɪŋ/z **-ed** -t **-er/s** -əz US -ɚz
Carl kɑːl US kɑːrl
Carla ˈkɑː.lə US ˈkɑːr-
Carle kɑːl US kɑːrl **-s** -z
Carless ˈkɑː.ləs US ˈkɑːr-
Carleton ˈkɑːl.tᵊn US ˈkɑːrl-
Carlile kɑːˈlaɪl US kɑːr-
Carlin ˈkɑː.lɪn US ˈkɑːr-
Carling ˈkɑː.lɪŋ US ˈkɑːr-
Carlingford ˈkɑː.lɪŋ.fəd US ˈkɑːr.lɪŋ.fɚd
Carlisle kɑːˈlaɪl *locally:* ˈ-- US kɑːrˈlaɪl, kɚˈ-; ˈkɑːr.laɪl
Carlist ˈkɑː.lɪst US ˈkɑːr- **-s** -s
Carlos ˈkɑː.lɒs US ˈkɑːr.ləs, -loʊs
Carlovingian ˌkɑː.ləʊˈvɪn.dʒi.ən, -dʒᵊn US ˌkɑːr.lə-
Carlow ˈkɑː.ləʊ US ˈkɑːr.loʊ
Carlsbad ˈkɑːlz.bæd US ˈkɑːrlz-
Carlsberg® ˈkɑːlz.bɜːɡ US ˈkɑːrlz.bɝːɡ **-s** -z
Carlson ˈkɑːl.sᵊn US ˈkɑːrl-
Carlsruhe ˈkɑːlzˌruː.ə US ˈkɑːrlz-
Carlton ˈkɑːl.tᵊn US ˈkɑːrl-
Carluccio kɑːˈluː.tʃi.əʊ US kɑːrˈluː.tʃi.oʊ
Carluke kɑːˈluːk US kɑːr-
Carly ˈkɑː.li US ˈkɑːr-
Carlyle kɑːˈlaɪl, ˈ-- US kɑːrˈlaɪl, ˈ--
carmaker ˈkɑːˌmeɪ.kəʳ US ˈkɑːrˌmeɪ.kɚ **-s** -z
car|man ˈkɑː|.mən US ˈkɑːr- **-men** -mən, -men
Carmarthen kəˈmɑː.ðᵊn US kɑːrˈmɑːr- **-shire** -ʃəʳ, -ˌʃɪəʳ US -ʃɚ, -ʃɪr
Carmel ˈkɑː.mel, -mᵊl, kɑːˈmel US ˈkɑːr.mel, -mᵊl; kɑːrˈmel
Note: The form /kɑːˈmel US kɑːr-/ is preferred for the city in California.
Carmelite ˈkɑː.mᵊl.aɪt, -mɪ.laɪt, -mel.aɪt US ˈkɑːr.mə.laɪt, -mɪ-, -mel.aɪt **-s** -s
Carmen ˈkɑː.men US ˈkɑːr-
Carmichael kɑːˈmaɪ.kᵊl, ˈ--- US ˈkɑːr.maɪ-
Carmina Burana ˌkɑː.mɪ.nə.bəˈrɑː.nə, kɑːˌmiː-, -bjʊˈ-, -bʊˈ- US kɑːrˌmiː.nə.bəˈ-
carminative ˈkɑː.mɪ.nə.tɪv, -mə- US ˈkɑːr.mə.nə.t̬ɪv **-s** -z
carmine ˈkɑː.maɪn, -mɪn US ˈkɑːr-
Carnaby ˈkɑː.nə.bi US ˈkɑːr- **ˈCarnaby ˌStreet**
Carnac ˈkɑː.næk US kɑːrˈnæk
carnage ˈkɑː.nɪdʒ US ˈkɑːr-
Carnaghan ˈkɑː.nə.gən, -hən US ˈkɑːr.nə.hæn
carnal ˈkɑː.nᵊl US ˈkɑːr- **-ly** -i
carnality kɑːˈnæl.ə.ti, -ɪ.ti US kɑːrˈnæl.ə.t̬i
Carnarvon kəˈnɑː.vᵊn US kɑːrˈnɑːr-
Carnatic kɑːˈnæt.ɪk US kɑːrˈnæt̬-
carnation (C) kɑːˈneɪ.ʃᵊn US kɑːr- **-s** -z
Carné kɑːˈneɪ US kɑːr-
Carnegie kɑːˈneg.i, -ˈneɪ.gi, -ˈniː-; ˈkɑː.nə.gi US ˈkɑːr.nə.gi; kɑːrˈneɪ-, -ˈneg.i, -ˈniː.gi **Carˌnegie ˈHall**
carnelian kɑːˈniː.li.ən, kə- US kɑːr-, -ˈniːl.jən **-s** -z
carnet ˈkɑː.neɪ US kɑːrˈneɪ **-s** -z
Carnforth ˈkɑːn.fɔːθ, -fəθ US ˈkɑːrn.fɔːrθ, -fɚθ
carnival ˈkɑː.nɪ.vᵊl US ˈkɑːr.nə- **-s** -z
carnivore ˈkɑː.nɪ.vɔːʳ, -nə- US ˈkɑːr.nə.vɔːr **-s** -z
carnivorous kɑːˈnɪv.ᵊr.əs US kɑːr-
Carnochan ˈkɑː.nə.kən, -nɒk.ən, -nɒx- US ˈkɑːr.nə.kən, -nɑː.kən
Carnoustie kɑːˈnuː.sti US kɑːr-
carob ˈkær.əb US ˈker-, ˈkær- **-s** -z
carol (C) ˈkær.ᵊl US ˈker-, ˈkær- **-s** -z **-(l)ing** -ɪŋ **-(l)ed** -d **ˈcarol ˌsinger**
Carole ˈkær.ᵊl US ˈker-, ˈkær-
Carolina ˌkær.ᵊlˈaɪ.nə US ˌker.əˈlaɪ-, ˌkær-
Caroline ˈkær.ᵊl.aɪn, -ɪn US ˈker.ə.laɪn, ˈkær-, -ᵊl.ɪn
carolus (C) ˈkær.ᵊl.əs US ˈker-, ˈkær- **-es** -ɪz
Carolyn ˈkær.ᵊl.ɪn US ˈker-, ˈkær-
carotene ˈkær.ə.tiːn US ˈker-, ˈkær-
carotid kəˈrɒt.ɪd US -ˈrɑː.t̬ɪd **-s** -z
carotin ˈkær.ə.tɪn US ˈker-, ˈkær-
carousal kəˈraʊ.zᵊl **-s** -z
carous|e kəˈraʊz **-es** -ɪz **-ing** -ɪŋ **-ed** -d **-er/s** -əʳ/z US -ɚ/z
carousel ˌkær.əˈsel, -ʊˈ- US ˈker.ə.sel, ˈkær-, ˌ--ˈ- **-s** -z
carp kɑːp US kɑːrp **-s** -s **-ing** -ɪŋ **-ed** -t **-er/s** -əʳ/z US -ɚ/z
carpaccio kɑːˈpætʃ.i.əʊ, -ˈpætʃ.əʊ US kɑːrˈpɑːtʃ.oʊ
carpal ˈkɑː.pᵊl US ˈkɑːr- **-s** -z
Carpathian kɑːˈpeɪ.θi.ən US kɑːr- **-s** -z
carpe diem ˌkɑː.peɪˈdiː.em, -piˈ- US ˌkɑːr.pəˈ-, -peɪˈ-
carpel ˈkɑː.pel, -pᵊl US ˈkɑːr- **-s** -z
Carpentaria ˌkɑː.pᵊnˈteə.ri.ə, -penˈ-, -pᵊmˈ- US ˌkɑːr.pᵊnˈter.i-
carpent|er (C) ˈkɑː.pᵊn.t|əʳ, -pɪn- US ˈkɑːr.pᵊn.t̬|ɚ **-ers** -əz US -ɚz **-ering** -ᵊr.ɪŋ **-ered** -əd US -ɚd
carpentry ˈkɑː.pᵊn.tri, -pɪn- US ˈkɑːr.pᵊn-
carp|et ˈkɑː.p|ɪt US ˈkɑːr.p|ət **-ets** -ɪts

(US) -əts **-eting** -ɪ.tɪŋ (US) -ə.t̬ɪŋ **-eted** -ɪ.tɪd (US) -ə.t̬ɪd **ˈcarpet ˌbroom; ˈcarpet ˌslipper; ˈcarpet ˌsweeper**

carpetbag ˈkɑː.pɪt.bæg (US) ˈkɑːr.pət- **-s** -z **-ging** -ɪŋ

carpetbagger ˈkɑː.pɪtˌbæg.əʳ (US) ˈkɑːr.pətˌbæg.ɚ **-s** -z

carpet-bomb ˈkɑː.pɪt.bɒm (US) ˈkɑːr.pət.bɑːm **-s** -z **-ing** -ɪŋ **-ed** -d

carport ˈkɑː.pɔːt (US) ˈkɑːr.pɔːrt **-s** -s

carp|us ˈkɑː.p|əs (US) ˈkɑːr- **-i** -aɪ, -iː

Carr kɑːʳ (US) kɑːr

carrag(h)een ˈkær.ə.giːn, --ˈ- (US) ˈker.ə.giːn, ˈkær-

Carrara kəˈrɑː.rə (US) kəˈrɑːr.ə

Carrauntoohill ˌkær.ənˈtuː.hᵊl (US) ˌker-, ˌkær-

carraway ˈkær.ə.weɪ (US) ˈker-, ˈkær- **-s** -z

Carrhae ˈkær.iː (US) ˈker-, ˈkær-

carriag|e ˈkær.ɪdʒ (US) ˈker-, ˈkær- **-es** -ɪz **ˈcarriage ˌclock**

carriageway ˈkær.ɪdʒ.weɪ (US) ˈker-, ˈkær- **-s** -z

carrick (C) ˈkær.ɪk (US) ˈker-, ˈkær-

Carrickfergus ˌkær.ɪkˈfɜː.gəs (US) ˌker.ɪkˈfɝː-, ˌkær-

Carrie ˈkær.i (US) ˈker-, ˈkær-

carrier ˈkær.i.əʳ (US) ˈker.i.ɚ, ˈkær- **-s** -z **ˈcarrier ˌbag; ˈcarrier ˌpigeon**

Carrington ˈkær.ɪŋ.tən (US) ˈker-, ˈkær-

carrion ˈkær.i.ən (US) ˈker-, ˈkær- **ˌcarrion ˈcrow** (US) **ˈcarrion ˌcrow**

Carrodus ˈkær.ə.dəs (US) ˈker-, ˈkær-

Carroll ˈkær.ᵊl (US) ˈker-, ˈkær-

Carron ˈkær.ᵊn (US) ˈker-, ˈkær-

carrot ˈkær.ət (US) ˈker-, ˈkær- **-s** -s

carroty ˈkær.ə.ti (US) ˈker.ə.t̬i, ˈkær-

carrousel ˌkær.əˈsel, -ʊˈ- (US) ˌker.əˈsel, ˌkær-, ˈ--- **-s** -z

Carruthers kəˈrʌð.əz (US) -ɚz

carr|y ˈkær|.i (US) ˈker-, ˈkær- **-ies** -iz **-ying** -i.ɪŋ **-ied** -id **-ier/s** -i.əʳ/z (US) -i.ɚ/z

carryall ˈkær.i.ɔːl (US) ˈker.i.ɔːl, ˈkær-, -ɑːl **-s** -z

carrycot ˈkær.i.kɒt (US) ˈker.i.kɑːt, ˈkær- **-s** -s

carryings-on ˌkær.i.ɪŋzˈɒn (US) ˌker.i.ɪŋzˈɑːn, ˌkær-

carry-on ˈkær.i.ɒn (US) ˈker.i.ɑːn, ˈkær- **-s** -z

carryout ˈkær.i.aʊt (US) ˈker-, ˈkær- **-s** -z

Carse kɑːs (US) kɑːrs

Carshalton kɑːˈʃɔːl.tᵊn, kəˈ- *old-fashioned local pronunciation:* keɪsˈhɔː.tᵊn (US) kɑːrˈʃɔːl-, kɚ-, -ˈʃɑːl-

carsick ˈkɑː.sɪk (US) ˈkɑːr- **-ness** -nəs, -nɪs

Carson ˈkɑː.sᵊn (US) ˈkɑːr-

Carstairs ˈkɑː.steəz, ˌ-ˈ- (US) ˈkɑːr.sterz

cart (C) kɑːt (US) kɑːrt **-s** -s **-ing** -ɪŋ (US) ˈkɑːr.t̬ɪŋ **-ed** -ɪd (US) ˈkɑːr.t̬ɪd **-er/s** -əʳ/z (US) ˈkɑːr.t̬ɚ/z **put the ˌcart before the ˈhorse**

Carta ˈkɑː.tə (US) ˈkɑːr.t̬ə

cartage ˈkɑː.tɪdʒ (US) ˈkɑːr.t̬ɪdʒ

Cartagena ˌkɑː.təˈgeɪ.nə (US) ˌkɑːr.t̬əˈdʒiː.nə, -ˈheɪ-, -ˈgeɪ-

carte (C) kɑːt (US) kɑːrt

carte blanche ˌkɑːtˈblɑ̃ːntʃ (US) ˌkɑːrtˈblɑːnʃ, -ˈblæntʃ

cartel kɑːˈtel (US) kɑːr- **-s** -z

Carter ˈkɑː.təʳ (US) ˈkɑːr.t̬ɚ

Carteret *surname:* ˈkɑː.tə.ret, -rɪt (US) ˈkɑːr.t̬ɚ.ɪt *US place name:* ˌkɑː.təˈret (US) ˌkɑːr.t̬əˈ-

Cartesian kɑːˈtiː.zi.ən, -ʒᵊn (US) kɑːrˈtiː.ʒᵊn **-ism** -ɪ.zᵊm

Carteton ˈkɑː.tə.tᵊn (US) ˈkɑːr.t̬ə.tən

Carthage ˈkɑː.θɪdʒ (US) ˈkɑːr-

Carthaginian ˌkɑː.θəˈdʒɪn.i.ən (US) ˌkɑːr- **-s** -z

cart-hors|e ˈkɑːt.hɔːs (US) ˈkɑːrt.hɔːrs **-es** -ɪz

Carthusian kɑːˈθjuː.zi.ən, -ˈθuː- (US) kɑːrˈθuː.ʒᵊn, -ˈθjuː- **-s** -z

Cartier ˈkɑː.ti.eɪ (US) ˌkɑːr.tiˈeɪ; kɑːrˈtjeɪ

Cartier-Bresson ˌkɑː.ti.eɪˈbres.ɔ̃ːn (US) ˌkɑːr.tjeɪ.breɪˈsõʊn, -bresˈõʊn

cartilag|e ˈkɑː.tɪ.lɪdʒ, -tᵊl.ɪdʒ (US) ˈkɑːr.t̬ᵊl.ɪdʒ **-es** -ɪz

cartilaginous ˌkɑː.tɪˈlædʒ.ɪ.nəs, -tᵊlˈædʒ-, -ᵊn.əs (US) ˌkɑːr.təˈlædʒ.ᵊn.əs

carting ˈkɑː.tɪŋ (US) ˈkɑːr.t̬ɪŋ

Cartland ˈkɑːt.lənd (US) ˈkɑːrt-

cartload ˈkɑːt.ləʊd (US) ˈkɑːrt.loʊd **-s** -z

Cartmel(e) ˈkɑːt.mel, -mᵊl (US) ˈkɑːrt-

cartographic ˌkɑː.təʊˈgræf.ɪk, ˌkɑːr.t̬əˈ- **-ally** -ᵊl.i, -li

cartograph|y kɑːˈtɒg.rə.f|i (US) kɑːrˈtɑː.grə- **-er/s** -əʳ/z (US) -ɚ/z

cartomancy ˈkɑː.təʊ.mænt.si (US) ˈkɑːr.t̬ə-

carton ˈkɑː.tᵊn (US) ˈkɑːr- **-s** -z

cartoon kɑːˈtuːn (US) kɑːr- **-s** -z **-ist/s** -ɪst/s

cartouch|e, cartouch kɑːˈtuːʃ (US) kɑːr- **-es** -ɪz

cartridg|e ˈkɑː.trɪdʒ (US) ˈkɑːr- **-es** -ɪz **ˈcartridge ˌpaper**

cartwheel ˈkɑːt.hwiːl (US) ˈkɑːrt- **-s** -z **-ing** -ɪŋ **-ed** -d

cartwright (C) ˈkɑːt.raɪt (US) ˈkɑːrt- **-s** -s

caruncle ˈkær.əŋ.kl̩; kəˈrʌŋ- (US) kəˈrʌŋ-, kerˈʌŋ-, kær- **-s** -z

Carus ˈkeə.rəs (US) ˈker.əs, ˈkɑːr-

Caruso kəˈruː.zəʊ, -səʊ (US) -soʊ, -zoʊ

Caruthers kəˈrʌð.əz (US) -ɚz

carv|e kɑːv (US) kɑːrv **-es** -z **-ing/s** -ɪŋ/z **-ed** -d **ˈcarving ˌknife**

carver (C) ˈkɑː.vəʳ (US) ˈkɑːr.vɚ **-s** -z

carver|y ˈkɑː.vᵊr|.i (US) ˈkɑːr- **-ies** -iz

Carville ˈkɑː.vɪl (US) ˈkɑːr-

Carwardine ˈkɑː.wə.diːn (US) ˈkɑːr.wɚ-

carwash ˈkɑː.wɒʃ (US) ˈkɑːr.wɑːʃ, -wɔːʃ **-es** -ɪz

Cary *surname:* ˈkeə.ri (US) ˈker.i *first name:* ˈkær.i (US) ˈker.i, ˈkær-

caryatid ˌkær.iˈæt.ɪd, ˈkær.i.ə.tɪd (US) ˌker.iˈæt̬.ɪd, ˌkær-; kəˈraɪ.ə.t̬ɪd **-s** -z **-es** -iːz

Caryll ˈkær.ɪl, -ᵊl (US) ˈker-, ˈkær-

Carysfort ˈkær.ɪs.fɔːt, -əs- (US) ˈker.ɪs.fɔːrt, ˈkær-

Casablanca ˌkæs.əˈblæŋ.kə (US) ˌkæs.əˈblæŋ.kə, ˌkɑː.səˈblɑːŋ.kə

Casals kəˈsæls (US) -ˈsɑːlz, -ˈsælz

Casamassima ˌkæs.əˈmæs.ɪ.mə

Casanova ˌkæs.əˈnəʊ.və, ˌkæz- (US) ˌkæs.əˈnoʊ-, ˌkæz-

Casaubon kəˈsɔː.bᵊn; ˈkæz.ə.bɒn, -ɔː- (US) kəˈsɑː.bᵊn, -ˈsɔː-; ˈkæz.ə.bɑːn

casbah (C) ˈkæz.bɑː (US) ˈkæz.bɑː, ˈkɑːz- **-s** -z

cascad|e kæsˈkeɪd **-es** -z **-ing** -ɪŋ **-ed** -ɪd

cascara kæsˈkɑː.rə, kəˈskɑː- (US) kæsˈker.ə, -ˈkær- **-s** -z

cascarilla ˌkæs.kəˈrɪl.ə

cas|e (C) keɪs **-es** -ɪz **-ing** -ɪŋ **-ed** -t **ˈcase ˌending; ˌcase ˈhistory; ˈcase ˌknife; ˈcase ˌlaw; ˈcase ˌshot; ˈcase ˌstudy**

casebook ˈkeɪs.bʊk **-s** -s

casein ˈkeɪ.siːn, -siː.ɪn (US) -siː.ɪn, -siːn

caseload ˈkeɪs.ləʊd (US) -loʊd **-s** -z

casemate ˈkeɪs.meɪt **-s** -s

casement ˈkeɪs.mənt **-s** -s

Casement ˈkeɪs.mənt

casern kəˈzɜːn (US) -ˈzɝːn **-s** -z

casework ˈkeɪs.wɜːk (US) -wɝːk **-er/s** -əʳ/z (US) -ɚ/z

Casey ˈkeɪ.si

cash (C) kæʃ **-es** -ɪz **-ing** -ɪŋ **-ed** -t **-less** -ləs, -lɪs **ˈcash ˌcrop; ˈcash ˌdesk; ˈcash disˌpenser; ˈcash ˌflow; ˈcash maˌchine; ˈcash ˌregister**

cash-and-carry ˌkæʃ.ᵊndˈkær.i, -ᵊŋˈ- (US) -ᵊndˈker-, -ˈkær-

cashback ˈkæʃ.bæk

cashbook ˈkæʃ.bʊk **-s** -s

cashbox ˈkæʃ.bɒks (US) -bɑːks **-es** -ɪz

cashew ˈkæʃ.uː; -ˈ-, kəˈʃuː (US) ˈkæʃ.uː; kəˈʃuː **-s** -z **ˈcashew ˌnut, caˈshew ˌnut** (US) **caˈshew ˌnut**

cashier *(n.)* kæʃˈɪəʳ, kəˈʃɪəʳ (US) kæʃˈɪr **-s** -z

cashier *(v.)* kəˈʃɪəʳ, kæʃˈɪəʳ (US) kəˈʃɪr, kæʃˈɪr **-s** -z **-ing** -ɪŋ **-ed** -d

cash-in-hand ˌkæʃ.ɪnˈhænd *stress shift:* ˌcash-in-hand ˈpayment

cashless ˈkæʃ.ləs, -lɪs

Cashmere *place:* ˈkæʃ.mɪəʳ, ˌ-ˈ- (US) ˈkæʃ.mɪr **-s** -z

cashmere *fabric:* 'kæʃ.mɪəʳ, ,-'- ⓤⓢ 'kæʒ.mɪr, 'kæʃ-
Cashmore 'kæʃ.mɔːʳ ⓤⓢ -mɔːr
cashpoint 'kæʃ.pɔɪnt **-s** -s
Casimir 'kæs.ɪ.mɪəʳ ⓤⓢ -ə.mɪr
casing 'keɪ.sɪŋ **-s** -z
casino kə'siː.nəʊ ⓤⓢ -noʊ **-s** -z
Casio® 'kæs.i.əʊ ⓤⓢ -oʊ
cask kɑːsk ⓤⓢ kæsk **-s** -s **-ing** -ɪŋ **-ed** -t
casket 'kɑː.skɪt ⓤⓢ 'kæs.kɪt **-s** -s
Caslon 'kæz.lᵊn, -lɒn ⓤⓢ -lᵊn, -lɑːn
Caspar 'kæs.pəʳ, -pɑːʳ ⓤⓢ -pɚ
Caspian 'kæs.pi.ən
casque kæsk, kɑːsk ⓤⓢ kæsk **-s** -s
Cass kæs
Cassandra kə'sæn.drə, -'sɑːn-
Cassani kə'sɑː.ni
cassareep 'kæs.ə.riːp
cassata kə'sɑː.tə, kæs'ɑː- ⓤⓢ kə'sɑː.t̬ə
cassation kæs'eɪ.ʃᵊn, kə'seɪ- ⓤⓢ kə'seɪ- **-s** -z
Cassatt kə'sæt
cassava kə'sɑː.və
Cassavetes ,kæs.ə'viː.tiːz ⓤⓢ -t̬iːz
Cassel(l) 'kæs.ᵊl
casserol|e 'kæs.ᵊr.əʊl ⓤⓢ -ə.roʊl **-es** -z **-ing** -ɪŋ **-ed** -d
cassette kə'set, kæs'et ⓤⓢ kə'set **-s** -s **ca'ssette re,corder**
cassia 'kæs.i.ə
Cassidy 'kæs.ə.di, -ɪ.di ⓤⓢ -ə.di
Cassie 'kæs.i
Cassil(l)is 'kæs.ᵊlz, 'kɑː.sᵊlz
Cassio 'kæs.i.əʊ ⓤⓢ -oʊ
Cassiopeia ,kæs.i.əʊ'piː.ə *as name of constellation also:* ,kæs.i'əʊ.pi- ⓤⓢ ,kæs.i.ə'piː-
cassis kæs'iːs, '-- ⓤⓢ kæs'iːs
Cassius 'kæs.i.əs ⓤⓢ 'kæʃ.əs, 'kæs.i-
Cassivelaunus ,kæs.ɪ.vɪ'lɔː.nəs, ,-ə-, -və'- ⓤⓢ -ɪ.və'lɑː-, -'lɔː-
cassock 'kæs.ək **-s** -s **-ed** -t
cassoulet ,kæs.ʊ'leɪ, '--- ⓤⓢ ,kæs.ʊ'leɪ **-s** -z
cassowar|y 'kæs.ə.weə.r|i, -wə- ⓤⓢ -wer|.i **-ies** -iz
Cass Timberlane ,kæs'tɪm.bə.leɪn ⓤⓢ -bɚ-
cast kɑːst ⓤⓢ kæst **-s** -s **-ing** -ɪŋ **,cast-'iron**
Castali|a kæs'teɪ.li|.ə ⓤⓢ -li|.ə, -'teɪl.j|ə **-an/s** -ən/z
castanet ,kæs.tə'net **-s** -s
castaway 'kɑː.stə.weɪ ⓤⓢ 'kæs.tə- **-s** -z
caste kɑːst ⓤⓢ kæst **-s** -s
Castel Gandolfo ,kæs.tel.gæn'dɒl.fəʊ ⓤⓢ -'dɑːl.foʊ, -'dɔːl-
castellated 'kæs.tə.leɪ.tɪd, -tɪ-, -tel.eɪ- ⓤⓢ -tə.leɪ.t̬ɪd
Castelnau 'kɑː.sᵊl.nɔː, -nəʊ ⓤⓢ 'kæs.ᵊl.nɔː, -noʊ
caster 'kɑː.stəʳ ⓤⓢ 'kæs.tɚ **-s** -z **'caster ,sugar**
Casterbridge 'kɑː.stə.brɪdʒ ⓤⓢ 'kæs.tɚ-
casti|gate 'kæs.tɪ|.geɪt, -tə|.geɪt ⓤⓢ -tə- **-gates** -geɪts **-gating** -geɪ.tɪŋ ⓤⓢ -geɪ.t̬ɪŋ **-gated** -geɪ.tɪd ⓤⓢ -geɪ.t̬ɪd **-gator/s** -geɪ.təʳ/z ⓤⓢ -geɪ.t̬ɚ/z
castigation ,kæs.tɪ'geɪ.ʃᵊn, -tə'- ⓤⓢ -ə'- **-s** -z
Castile kæs'tiːl
Castilian kæs'tɪl.i.ən, kə'stɪl- ⓤⓢ -i.ən, -jən **-s** -z
casting 'kɑː.stɪŋ ⓤⓢ 'kæs.tɪŋ **-s** -z **'casting ,couch; 'casting ,net; ,casting 'vote**
castl|e (C) 'kɑː.sl̩ ⓤⓢ 'kæs.l̩ **-es** -z **-ing** -ɪŋ **-ed** -d
Castlebar ,kɑː.sl̩'bɑːʳ ⓤⓢ ,kæs.l̩'bɑːr
Castleford 'kɑː.sl̩.fəd ⓤⓢ 'kæs.l̩.fɚd
Castlemaine 'kɑː.sl̩.meɪn ⓤⓢ 'kæs.l̩-
Castlenau 'kɑː.sl̩.nɔː ⓤⓢ 'kæs.l̩.nɑː, -nɔː
Castlerea(gh) 'kɑː.sl̩.reɪ, ,--'- ⓤⓢ 'kæs.l̩-
Castleton 'kɑː.sl̩.tən ⓤⓢ 'kæs.l̩.t̬ən
Castlewellan ,kɑː.sl̩'wel.ən ⓤⓢ ,kæs.l̩'-
cast-off 'kɑːst.ɒf, ,-'- ⓤⓢ 'kæst.ɑːf **-s** -s
castor (C) 'kɑː.stəʳ ⓤⓢ 'kæs.tɚ **-s** -z **,castor 'oil; 'castor ,sugar**
cas|trate kæs|'treɪt ⓤⓢ '-- **-trates** -'treɪts ⓤⓢ -treɪts **-trating** -'treɪ.tɪŋ ⓤⓢ -treɪ.t̬ɪŋ **-trated** -'treɪ.tɪd ⓤⓢ -treɪ.t̬ɪd
castration kæs'treɪ.ʃᵊn **-s** -z
castrat|o kæs'trɑː.t|əʊ ⓤⓢ -t|oʊ **-i** -iː
Castries kæs'triːz, -'triːs
Castro 'kæs.trəʊ ⓤⓢ -troʊ
Castrol® 'kæs.trɒl ⓤⓢ -trɑːl, -troʊl
casual 'kæʒ.ju.əl, -zju- ⓤⓢ '-uː- **-ly** -i **,casual 'sex**
casualt|y 'kæʒ.ju.əl.t|i, 'kæz- ⓤⓢ 'kæʒ.uː- **-ies** -iz
casuarina ,kæz.jʊə'riː.nə, ,kæʒ-, 'kæʒ.jʊə.riː- ⓤⓢ ,kæʒ.uː.ə'riː- **-s** -z
casuist 'kæz.ju.ɪst, 'kæʒ- ⓤⓢ 'kæʒ.u- **-s** -s
casuistic ,kæz.ju'ɪs.tɪk, ,kæʒ- ⓤⓢ ,kæʒ.u'- **-al** -ᵊl
casuistry 'kæz.ju.ɪ.stri, 'kæʒ- ⓤⓢ 'kæʒ.u-
casus belli ,kɑː.sʊs'bel.iː, ,keɪ.səs'bel.aɪ ⓤⓢ ,keɪ.səs'bel.i, ,kɑː-
Caswell 'kæz.wəl, -wel ⓤⓢ 'kæz-, 'kæs-
cat kæt **-s** -s **'cat ,burglar; ,cat's 'whiskers; let the ,cat out of the 'bag; play ,cat and 'mouse with; set the ,cat among the 'pigeons**
CAT kæt **'CAT ,scan**
cata- 'kæt.ə- ⓤⓢ 'kæt̬.ə-, kə'tæ-
Note: Prefix. This usually takes primary or secondary stress on the first syllable, e.g. **catalogue** /'kæt.ə.lɒg ⓤⓢ 'kæt̬.ə.lɑːg/, or on the second syllable, e.g. **catastrophe** /kə'tæs.trə.fi/.
catabolic ,kæt.ə'bɒl.ɪk ⓤⓢ ,kæt̬.ə'bɑː.lɪk **-ally** -ᵊl.i, -li
catabolism kə'tæb.ᵊl.ɪ.zᵊm
catachresis ,kæt.ə'kriː.sɪs ⓤⓢ ,kæt̬.ə'-
cataclysm 'kæt.ə.klɪ.zᵊm ⓤⓢ 'kæt̬- **-s** -z
cataclysmal ,kæt.ə'klɪz.məl ⓤⓢ ,kæt̬.ə'- **-ly** -li
cataclysmic ,kæt.ə'klɪz.mɪk ⓤⓢ ,kæt̬.ə'- **-ally** -ᵊl.i, -li
catacomb 'kæt.ə.kuːm, -kəʊm ⓤⓢ 'kæt̬.ə.koʊm **-s** -z
catafalque 'kæt.ə.fælk ⓤⓢ 'kæt̬.ə.fælk, -fɔːlk, -fɑːlk **-s** -s
Catalan ,kæt.ə'læn, '---, -lən ⓤⓢ 'kæt̬.ə.læn, -ᵊl.ən **-s** -z
catalectic ,kæt.ə'lek.tɪk ⓤⓢ ,kæt̬.ə'let̬.ɪk
catalepsy|y 'kæt.ə.lep.s|i ⓤⓢ 'kæt̬.ə- **-ies** -iz
cataleptic ,kæt.ə'lep.tɪk ⓤⓢ ,kæt̬.ə'-
catalexis 'kæt.ə.lek.sɪs ⓤⓢ 'kæt̬.ə-
catalog 'kæt.ᵊl.ɒg ⓤⓢ 'kæt̬.ə.lɑːg, -lɔːg **-s** -z **-ing** -ɪŋ **-ed** -d **-er/s** -əʳ/z ⓤⓢ -ɚ/z **-ist/s** -ɪst/s
catalogu|e 'kæt.ᵊl.ɒg ⓤⓢ 'kæt̬.ə.lɑːg, -lɔːg **-es** -z **-ing** -ɪŋ **-ed** -d **-er/s** -əʳ/z ⓤⓢ -ɚ/z **-ist/s** -ɪst/s
Cataloni|a ,kæt.ə'ləʊ.ni|.ə, -nj|ə ⓤⓢ -'loʊ-, -nj|ə **-an/s** -ən/z
catalpa kə'tæl.pə **-s** -z
catalysis kə'tæl.ə.sɪs, '-ɪ-
catalyst 'kæt.ᵊl.ɪst ⓤⓢ 'kæt̬- **-s** -s
catalytic ,kæt.ə'lɪt.ɪk ⓤⓢ ,kæt̬'ə- *stress shift, see compound:* **,catalytic con'verter**
catamaran ,kæt.ə.mə'ræn, 'kæt.ə.mə.ræn ⓤⓢ ,kæt̬.ə.mə'ræn **-s** -z
Catania kə'teɪ.ni.ə, -'tɑː-, -njə ⓤⓢ -njə, -ni.ə
cataphora kə'tæf.ᵊr.ə
cataphoric ,kæt.ə'fɒr.ɪk ⓤⓢ ,kæt̬.ə'fɔːr-
cataplasm 'kæt.ə.plæz.ᵊm ⓤⓢ 'kæt̬- **-s** -z
cata|pult 'kæt.ə|.pʌlt ⓤⓢ 'kæt̬- **-pults** -pʌlts **-pulting** -pʌl.tɪŋ ⓤⓢ -pʌl.t̬ɪŋ **-pulted** -pʌl.tɪd ⓤⓢ -pʌl.t̬ɪd
cataract 'kæt.ᵊr.ækt ⓤⓢ 'kæt̬.ər.ækt **-s** -s
catarrh kə'tɑːʳ, kæt'ɑːʳ ⓤⓢ kə'tɑːr **-s** -z **-al** -ᵊl
catastas|is kə'tæs.tə.s|ɪs **-es** -iːz
catastrophe kə'tæs.trə.fi **-s** -z
catastrophic ,kæt.ə'strɒf.ɪk ⓤⓢ ,kæt̬.ə'strɑː.fɪk **-ally** -ᵊl.i, -li

catatonia ˌkæt.əˈtəʊ.ni.ə (US) ˌkæt̬.əˈtoʊ-

catatonic ˌkæt.əˈtɒn.ɪk (US) ˌkæt̬.əˈtɑː.nɪk

catawba (C) kəˈtɔː.bə (US) -ˈtɔː-, -ˈtɑː-

catbird ˈkæt.bɜːd (US) -bɝːd **-s** -z

catboat ˈkæt.bəʊt (US) -boʊt **-s** -s

catcall ˈkæt.kɔːl (US) -kɔːl, -kɑːl **-s** -z **-ing** -ɪŋ **-ed** -d

catch kætʃ **-es** -ɪz **-ing** -ɪŋ **caught** kɔːt (US) kɑːt, kɔːt

catch-22 (C) ˌkætʃˌtwen.tiˈtuː (US) -t̬iˈ-

catchall ˈkætʃ.ɔːl (US) -ɔːl, -ɑːl **-s** -z

catcher ˈkætʃ.əʳ (US) -ɚ **-s** -z

catching ˈkætʃ.ɪŋ

catchment ˈkætʃ.mənt **-s** -s ˈ**catchment** ˌ**area**

catchpenn|y ˈkætʃ.pen|.i **-ies** -iz

catchphras|e ˈkætʃ.freɪz **-es** -ɪz

catchpole (C) ˈkætʃ.pəʊl (US) -poʊl **-s** -z

catchpoll ˈkætʃ.pəʊl (US) -poʊl **-s** -z

catchword ˈkætʃ.wɜːd (US) -wɝːd **-s** -z

catch|y ˈkætʃ|.i **-ier** -i.əʳ (US) -i.ɚ **-iest** -i.ɪst, -i.əst **-iness** -ɪ.nəs, -ɪ.nɪs

catechism ˈkæt.ə.kɪ.zᵊm, ˈ-ɪ- (US) ˈkæt̬.ə- **-s** -z

catechist ˈkæt.ə.kɪst, ˈ-ɪ- (US) ˈkæt̬.ə- **-s** -s

catechiz|e, -is|e ˈkæt.ə.kaɪz, ˈ-ɪ- (US) ˈkæt̬.ə- **-es** -ɪz **-ing** -ɪŋ **-ed** -d **-er/s** -əʳ/z (US) -ɚ/z

catechu ˈkæt.ə.tʃuː, ˈ-ɪ- (US) ˈkæt̬.ə.tʃuː, -kjuː

catechumen ˌkæt.ɪˈkjuː.men, -əˈ-, -mɪn (US) ˌkæt̬.əˈkjuː.mən **-s** -z

categoric|al ˌkæt.əˈgɒr.ɪ.k|ᵊl, -ɪˈ- (US) ˌkæt̬.əˈgɔːr- **-ally** -ᵊl.i, -li

categorization, -isa- ˌkæt.ə.gᵊr.aɪˈzeɪ.ʃᵊn, ˌ-ɪ-, -ɪˈ- (US) ˌkæt̬.ə.gɚ.ɪˈ- **-s** -z

categoriz|e, -is|e ˈkæt.ə.gᵊr.aɪz, ˈ-ɪ- (US) ˈkæt̬.ə.gə.raɪz **-es** -ɪz **-ing** -ɪŋ **-ed** -d

categor|y ˈkæt.ə.gᵊr|.i, ˈ-ɪ- (US) ˈkæt̬.ə.gɔːr- **-ies** -iz

catenar|y kəˈtiː.nᵊr|.i **-ies** -iz

caten|ate ˈkæt.ɪ.n|eɪt, ˈ-ə- (US) ˈkæt.ᵊn|.eɪt **-ates** -eɪts **-ating** -eɪ.tɪŋ (US) -eɪ.t̬ɪŋ **-ated** -eɪ.tɪd (US) -eɪ.t̬ɪd

catenation ˌkæt.ɪˈneɪ.ʃᵊn, -əˈ- (US) ˌkæt̬.ənˈeɪ- **-s** -z

catenative kəˈtiː.nə.tɪv

cateniz|e, -is|e ˈkæt.ɪ.naɪz, ˈ-ə- (US) ˈkæt.ᵊn.aɪz **-es** -ɪz **-ing** -ɪŋ **-ed** -d

cat|er (C) ˈkeɪ.t|əʳ (US) -t̬|ɚ **-ers** -əz (US) -ɚz **-ering** -ᵊr.ɪŋ **-ered** -əd (US) -ɚd **-erer/s** -ᵊr.əʳ/z (US) -ɚ.ɚ/z

Caterham ˈkeɪ.tᵊr.əm (US) -t̬ɚ-

Caterina ˌkæt.ᵊrˈiː.nə (US) ˌkæt̬-

caterpillar ˈkæt.ə.pɪl.əʳ (US) ˈkæt̬.ɚ.pɪl.ɚ, ˈ-ə- **-s** -z

caterwaul ˈkæt.ə.wɔːl (US) ˈkæt̬.ɚ-, -wɑːl **-s** -z **-ing** -ɪŋ **-ed** -d

Catesby ˈkeɪts.bi

catfish ˈkæt.fɪʃ **-es** -ɪz

Catford ˈkæt.fəd (US) -fɚd

catgut ˈkæt.gʌt

Cathar ˈkæθ.əʳ, -ɑːʳ (US) -ɑːr **-ism** -ɪ.zᵊm **-ist/s** -ɪst/s

Catharine ˈkæθ.ᵊr.ɪn, ˈkæθ.rɪn

cathars|is kəˈθɑː.s|ɪs, kæθˈɑː- (US) kəˈθɑːr- **-es** -iːz

cathartic kəˈθɑː.tɪk, kæθˈɑː- (US) kəˈθɑːr.t̬ɪk **-s** -s

Cathay kæθˈeɪ, kəˈθeɪ

Cathcart ˈkæθ.kət, -kɑːt; kæθˈkɑːt, kəθ- (US) ˈkæθ.kɑːrt, -kɚt; kæθˈkɑːrt, kəθ-

cathead ˈkæt.hed **-s** -z

cathedra kəˈθiː.drə, -ˈθed.rə (US) kəˈθiː.drə, ˈkæθ.ə- **-s** -z

cathedra *(in phrase* **ex cathedra***)* kəˈθiː.drə, kæθˈed.rɑː, kəˈθed-

cathedral kəˈθiː.drᵊl **-s** -z

Cather ˈkæð.əʳ (US) -ɚ

Catherine ˈkæθ.ᵊr.ɪn, ˈkæθ.rɪn ˈ**catherine** ˌ**wheel**

catheter ˈkæθ.ɪ.təʳ, ˈ-ə- (US) -ət̬.ɚ **-s** -z

catheterization, -isa- ˌkæθ.ɪ.tᵊr.aɪˈzeɪ.ʃᵊn, ˌ-ə-, -ɪˈ- (US) -ə.t̬ɚ.ɪˈ-

catheteriz|e, -is|e ˈkæθ.ɪ.tᵊr.aɪz, ˈ-ə- (US) ˈ-ə.t̬ɚ- **-es** -ɪz **-ing** -ɪŋ **-ed** -d

cathetometer ˌkæθ.ɪˈtɒm.ɪ.təʳ, -əˈ-, ˈ-ə- (US) -əˈtɑː.mə.t̬ɚ **-s** -z

cathex|is kəˈθek.s|ɪs, kæθˈek- **-es** -iːz

Cathleen ˈkæθ.liːn, -ˈ- (US) -ˈ-, ˈ--

cathode ˈkæθ.əʊd (US) -oʊd **-s** -z ˌ**cathode** ˈ**ray**; ˌ**cathode-**ˈ**ray** ˌ**tube**

catholic (C) ˈkæθ.ᵊl.ɪk **-s** -s

catholicism (C) kəˈθɒl.ɪ.sɪ.zᵊm, ˈ-ə- (US) -ˈθɑː.lə-

catholicity (C) ˌkæθ.əʊˈlɪs.ə.ti, -ɪ.ti (US) ˌkæθ.əˈlɪs.ə.t̬i

catholiciz|e, -is|e kəˈθɒl.ɪ.saɪz, ˈ-ə- (US) -ˈθɑː.lə- **-es** -ɪz **-ing** -ɪŋ **-ed** -d

Cathy ˈkæθ.i

Catiline ˈkæt.ɪ.laɪn, -ᵊl.aɪn (US) -ɪ.laɪn, ˈ-ə-

cation ˈkæt.aɪən **-s** -z

catkin ˈkæt.kɪn **-s** -z

catlike ˈkæt.laɪk

catmint ˈkæt.mɪnt

catnap ˈkæt.næp **-s** -s **-ping** -ɪŋ **-ped** -t

catnip ˈkæt.nɪp

Cato ˈkeɪ.təʊ (US) -t̬oʊ

cat-o'-nine-tails ˌkæt.əˈnaɪn.teɪlz (US) ˌkæt̬-

Cator ˈkeɪ.təʳ (US) -t̬ɚ

Catriona kəˈtriː.ə.nə, kæˈtriː-, -triː.nə, ˌkæt.riˈəʊ.nə (US) -ˈoʊ-

cat's-cradle ˌkætsˈkreɪ.dl̩ (US) ˌ-ˈ--, ˈ-ˌ--

cat's-eye ˈkæts.aɪ **-s** -z

Catshill kætsˈhɪl *stress shift:* ˌCatshill ˈstores

Catskill ˈkæt.skɪl

catsuit ˈkæt.suːt, -sjuːt (US) -suːt **-s** -s

catsup ˈkæt.səp, ˈkætʃ.əp, ˈketʃ.əp **-s** -s

Cattegat ˈkæt.ɪ.gæt (US) ˈkæt̬-

Cattell kætˈel, kəˈtel

Catterick ˈkæt.ᵊr.ɪk (US) ˈkæt̬-

Cattermole ˈkæt.ə.məʊl (US) ˈkæt̬.ɚ.moʊl

catter|y ˈkæt.ᵊr|.i (US) ˈkæt̬- **-ies** -iz

cattish ˈkæt.ɪʃ (US) ˈkæt̬-

cattle ˈkæt.l̩ (US) ˈkæt̬- ˈ**cattle** ˌ**grid**; ˈ**cattle** ˌ**market**; ˈ**cattle** ˌ**pen**; ˈ**cattle** ˌ**truck**

cattle-show ˈkæt.l̩.ʃəʊ (US) ˈkæt̬.l̩.ʃoʊ **-s** -z

catt|y ˈkæt|.i (US) ˈkæt̬- **-ier** -i.əʳ (US) -i.ɚ **-iest** -i.ɪst, -i.əst **-ily** -ɪ.li, -ᵊl.i **-iness** -ɪ.nəs, -ɪ.nɪs

Catullus kəˈtʌl.əs

catwalk ˈkæt.wɔːk (US) -wɑːk, -wɔːk **-s** -s

Caucasi|a kɔːˈkeɪ.ʒ|ə, -ʒi|.ə, -zi- (US) kɑːˈkeɪ.ʒ|ə, kɔː-, -ʃ|ə **-an/s** -ən/z

Caucasus ˈkɔː.kə.səs, -zəs (US) ˈkɑː-, ˈkɔː-

caucus ˈkɔː.kəs (US) ˈkɑː-, ˈkɔː- **-es** -ɪz

caudal ˈkɔː.dᵊl (US) ˈkɑː-, ˈkɔː-

caudate ˈkɔː.deɪt (US) ˈkɑː-, ˈkɔː-

caudillo kaʊˈdiː.əʊ, kɔːˈdɪl-, -jəʊ (US) kaʊˈdiː.joʊ, -ˈdɪl- **-s** -z

Caudine ˈkɔː.daɪn (US) ˈkɑː-, ˈkɔː-

caudle (C) ˈkɔː.dl̩ (US) ˈkɑː-, ˈkɔː-

caught *(from* **catch***)* kɔːt (US) kɑːt, kɔːt

caul kɔːl (US) kɑːl, kɔːl **-s** -z

cauldron ˈkɔːl.drᵊn, ˈkɒl- (US) ˈkɑːl-, ˈkɔːl- **-s** -z

Caulfield ˈkɔː.fiːld, ˈkɔːl- (US) ˈkɑː-, ˈkɔː-, ˈkɑːl-, ˈkɔːl-

cauliflower ˈkɒl.ɪˌflaʊəʳ (US) ˈkɑː.lɪˌflaʊɚ, ˈkɔː- **-s** -z ˌ**cauliflower** ˈ**ear**

caulk kɔːk (US) kɑːk, kɔːk **-s** -s **-ing** -ɪŋ **-ed** -t

caulker ˈkɔː.kəʳ (US) ˈkɑː.kɚ, ˈkɔː- **-s** -z

causa ˈkaʊ.sɑː, -zɑː

causal ˈkɔː.zᵊl (US) ˈkɑː-, ˈkɔː- **-ly** -i

causality kɔːˈzæl.ə.ti, -ɪ.ti (US) kɑːˈzæl.ə.t̬i, kɔː-

causa mortis ˌkaʊ.sɑːˈmɔː.tɪs, -zɑːˈ- (US) -mɔːr.t̬ɪs

causation kɔːˈzeɪ.ʃᵊn (US) kɑː-, kɔː-

causative ˈkɔː.zə.tɪv (US) ˈkɑː.zə.t̬ɪv, ˈkɔː- **-ly** -li

caus|e kɔːz (US) kɑːz, kɔːz **-es** -ɪz **-ing** -ɪŋ **-ed** -d

cause(s) célèbre(s) ˌkɔːz.selˈeb.rə, ˌkəʊz-, -səˈleb-, -ˈleɪ.brə (US) ˌkɑːz.səˈleb.rə, ˌkɔːz-, ˌkoʊz-

causeless ˈkɔːz.ləs, -lɪs (US) ˈkɑːz-, ˈkɔːz- **-ly** -li

Pronouncing the letters CC

The consonant digraph **cc** has two pronuncations: /ks/ and /k/.

Before the vowel letters **i** or **e**, it is pronounced as /ks/, e.g.:

accident /ˈæk.sɪ.dᵊnt/

In most other situations, **cc** is pronounced as /k/, e.g.:

acclaim /əkˈleɪm/

In addition

The word *flaccid* has two possible pronunciations.

/ˈflæk.sɪd, ˈflæs.ɪd/

Words borrowed from Italian may have /tʃ/, e.g.:

cappuccino /ˌkæp.ʊˈtʃiː.nəʊ/ ⓊⓈ /-əˈtʃiː.noʊ/

causerie ˈkəʊ.zᵊr.i, -iː ⓊⓈ ˌkoʊ.zəˈriː **-s** -z

causeway ˈkɔːz.weɪ ⓊⓈ ˈkɑːz-, ˈkɔːz- **-s** -z

caustic ˈkɔː.stɪk, ˈkɒs.tɪk ⓊⓈ ˈkɑː.stɪk, ˈkɔː- **-al** -ᵊl **-ally** -ᵊl.i, -li ˌ**caustic** ˈ**soda**

causticity kɔːˈstɪs.ə.ti, kɒsˈtɪs-, -ɪ.ti ⓊⓈ kɑːˈstɪs.ə.t̬i, kɔː-

cauterization, -isa- ˌkɔː.tᵊr.aɪˈzeɪ.ʃᵊn, -ɪˈ- ⓊⓈ ˌkɑː.t̬ɚ.ɪˈ-, ˌkɔː- **-s** -z

cauteriz|e, -is|e ˈkɔː.tᵊr.aɪz ⓊⓈ ˈkɑː.t̬ə.raɪz, ˈkɔː- **-es** -ɪz **-ing** -ɪŋ **-ed** -d

cauter|y ˈkɔː.tᵊr|.i ⓊⓈ ˈkɑː.t̬ɚ-, ˈkɔː- **-ies** -iz

Cauthen ˈkɔː.θᵊn ⓊⓈ ˈkɑː-, ˈkɔː-

caution ˈkɔː.ʃᵊn ⓊⓈ ˈkɑː-, ˈkɔː- **-s** -z **-ing** -ɪŋ **-ed** -d **-er/s** -əʳ/z ⓊⓈ -ɚ/z ˈ**caution** ˌ**money; throw** ˌ**caution to the** ˈ**wind**

cautionary ˈkɔː.ʃᵊn.ᵊr.i, -ʃᵊn.ri ⓊⓈ ˈkɑː.ʃᵊn.er-, ˈkɔː- ˌ**cautionary** ˈ**tale**

cautious ˈkɔː.ʃəs ⓊⓈ ˈkɑː-, ˈkɔː- **-ly** -li **-ness** -nəs, -nɪs

cavalcade ˌkæv.ᵊlˈkeɪd, ˈ--- **-s** -z

cavalier ˌkæv.ᵊlˈɪəʳ ⓊⓈ -əˈlɪr **-s** -z

Cavalleria Rusticana kə.væl.əˌriː.ə.rʊs.tɪˈkɑː.nə, ˌkæv.ᵊl-, -ˌrɪə-

cavalr|y ˈkæv.ᵊl.r|i **-ies** -iz

cavalry|man ˈkæv.ᵊl.ri|.mən, -mæn **-men** -mən, -men

Cavan ˈkæv.ᵊn

Cavanagh ˈkæv.ə.nə

Cavanaugh ˈkæv.ə.nɔː ⓊⓈ -nɑː, -nɔː

cavatina ˌkæv.əˈtiː.nə **-s** -z

cav|e (C) *(n. v.)* keɪv **-es** -z **-ing** -ɪŋ **-ed** -d **-er/s** -əʳ/z ⓊⓈ -ɚ/z ˈ**cave** ˌ**dweller**

cave *beware:* ˈkeɪ.vi

caveat ˈkæv.i.æt, ˈkeɪ.vi- ⓊⓈ ˈkæv.i.-, ˈkeɪ.vi-, ˈkɑː- **-s** -s

caveat emptor ˌkæv.i.ætˈemp.tɔːʳ, ˌkeɪ.vi-, -təʳ ⓊⓈ -tɔːr, ˌkɑː-, -ɑːtˈ-, -tɚ

Cavell ˈkæv.ᵊl, kəˈvel

Note: The family of Nurse Edith Cavell pronounces /ˈkæv.ᵊl/.

Pronouncing the letters CCH

The consonant letter combination **cch** only has one possible realisation: /k/, e.g.:

saccharine /ˈsæk.ᵊr.ɪn/

cave|man ˈkeɪv|.mæn **-men** -men

Cavendish ˈkæv.ᵊn.dɪʃ

cavern ˈkæv.ᵊn, -ɜːn ⓊⓈ -ɚn **-s** -z

cavernous ˈkæv.ᵊn.əs ⓊⓈ -ɚn- **-ly** -li

Caversham ˈkæv.ə.ʃəm ⓊⓈ ˈ-ɚ-

cave|woman ˈkeɪv|ˌwʊm.ən **-women** -ˌwɪm.ɪn

caviar(e) ˈkæv.i.ɑːʳ, ˌ--ˈ- ⓊⓈ ˈkæv.i.ɑːr

cavil ˈkæv.ᵊl, -ɪl **-s** -z **-(l)ing** -ɪŋ **-(l)ed** -d **-(l)er/s** -əʳ/z ⓊⓈ -ɚ/z

cavit|y ˈkæv.ə.t|i, -ɪ.t|i ⓊⓈ -ə.t̬|i **-ies** -iz

ca|vort kəˈvɔːt ⓊⓈ -ˈvɔːrt **-vorts** -ˈvɔːts ⓊⓈ -ˈvɔːrts **-vorting** -ˈvɔː.tɪŋ ⓊⓈ -ˈvɔːr.t̬ɪŋ **-vorted** -ˈvɔː.tɪd ⓊⓈ -ˈvɔːr.t̬ɪd

cav|y ˈkeɪ.v|i **-ies** -iz

caw kɔː ⓊⓈ kɑː, kɔː **-s** -z **-ing** -ɪŋ **-ed** -d

Cawdor ˈkɔː.dəʳ, -dɔːʳ ⓊⓈ ˈkɑː.dɚ, ˈkɔː-, -dɔːr

Cawdrey ˈkɔː.dri ⓊⓈ ˈkɑː-, ˈkɔː-

Cawley ˈkɔː.li ⓊⓈ ˈkɑː-, ˈkɔː-

Cawse kɔːz ⓊⓈ kɑːz, kɔːz

Caxton ˈkæk.stᵊn

cay kiː, keɪ **-s** -z

cayenne (C) keɪˈen ⓊⓈ kaɪ-, keɪ- *stress shift:* ˌ**cayenne** ˈ**pepper**

Cayley ˈkeɪ.li

cayman (C) ˈkeɪ.mən **-s** -z ˈ**Cayman** ˌ**Islands**

Cazenove ˈkæz.ᵊn.əʊv ⓊⓈ -oʊv

CB ˌsiːˈbiː

CBC ˌsiː.biːˈsiː

CBE ˌsiː.biːˈiː

CBI ˌsiː.biːˈaɪ

CBS ˌsiː.biːˈes *stress shift:* ˌ**CBS** ˈ**records**

cc ˌsiːˈsiː

CD ˌsiːˈdiː **-s** -z ˌ**C**ˈ**D** ˌ**player**

CDI ˌsiː.diːˈaɪ

Cdr. *(abbrev. for* **commander***)* kəˈmɑːn.dəʳ ⓊⓈ -ˈmæn.dɚ

CD-ROM ˌsiː.diːˈrɒm ⓊⓈ -ˈrɑːm **-s** -z

CDT ˌsiː.diːˈtiː

ceas|e siːs **-es** -ɪz **-ing** -ɪŋ **-ed** -t

cease-fire ˈsiːs.faɪəʳ ⓊⓈ -faɪɚ

ceaseless ˈsiː.sləs, -slɪs **-ly** -li **-ness** -nəs, -nɪs

Ceausescu ˌtʃaʊˈʃes.kuː

Cebu siˈbuː

Cecil ˈses.ᵊl, -ɪl, ˈsɪs.ᵊl, -ɪl ⓊⓈ ˈsiː.sᵊl, ˈses.ᵊl

Note: The family name of the Marquess of Exeter and that of the Marquess of Salisbury is /ˈsɪs.ᵊl, -ɪl/.

Cecile sesˈiːl, ˈ--, ˈses.ɪl, -ᵊl; ⓊⓈ sɪˈsiːl

Cecilia sɪˈsiː.li.ə, sə-, -ˈsɪl.i- ⓊⓈ -ˈsiːl.jə, -ˈsɪl-

Cecily ˈses.ɪ.li, ˈsɪs-, -ᵊl.i ⓊⓈ ˈses-

cec|um ˈsiː.k|əm **-a** -ə

cedar ˈsiː.dəʳ ⓊⓈ -dɚ **-s** -z

ced|e siːd **-es** -z **-ing** -ɪŋ **-ed** -ɪd

cedi ˈsiː.di **-s** -z

cedilla səˈdɪl.ə, sɪ- **-s** -z

Cedric ˈsed.rɪk, ˈsiː.drɪk

Ceefax® ˈsiː.fæks

Cefn-Mawr ˌkev.ᵊnˈmaʊəʳ ⓊⓈ -ˈmaʊɚ

CEGB ˌsiː.iː.dʒiːˈbiː

ceilidh ˈkeɪ.li **-s** -z

ceiling ˈsiː.lɪŋ **-s** -z

celadon ˈsel.ə.dɒn, -dən ⓊⓈ -dɑːn

celandine ˈsel.ən.daɪn, -diːn **-s** -z

Celanese® ˌsel.əˈniːz ⓊⓈ -ˈniːz, -ˈniːs

celeb səˈleb, sɪ- **-s** -z

Celebes selˈiː.biz, səˈliː-, sɪ- ⓊⓈ ˈsel.ə.biːz, səˈliː.biz

celebrant ˈsel.ə.brᵊnt, ˈ-ɪ- **-s** -s

cele|brate ˈsel.ə|.breɪt, ˈ-ɪ- **-brates** -breɪts **-brating** -breɪ.tɪŋ

US -breɪ.t̬ɪŋ **-brated** -breɪ.tɪd US -breɪ.t̬ɪd **-brator/s** -breɪ.təʳ/z US -breɪ.t̬ɚ/z
celebration ˌsel.əˈbreɪ.ʃᵊn, -ɪˈ- **-s** -z
celebratory ˌsel.əˈbreɪ.tᵊr.i, -ɪˈ-; -tri; ˈsel.ɪ.brə-, ˈ-ə- US ˈsel.ə.brə.tɔːr.i; səˈleb.rə-
celebrit|y səˈleb.rə.t|i, sɪ-, -rɪ- US səˈleb.rə.t̬|i **-ies** -iz
celeriac səˈler.i.æk, sɪ-;
celerity səˈler.ə.ti, sɪ-, -ɪ.ti US -ə.t̬i
Celeron® ˈsel.ᵊr.ɒn US -ɑːn
celery ˈsel.ᵊr.i
celeste **(C)** səˈlest, sɪ- **-s** -s
celestial **(C)** səˈles.ti.əl, sɪ- US ˈ-tʃᵊl **-ly** -i
celestine ˈsel.ə.staɪn, ˈ-ɪ-, -stɪn
Celestine ˈsel.ə.staɪn, ˈ-ɪ-; sɪˈles.taɪn, sə-, -tɪn, -tiːn **-s** -z
Celia ˈsiː.li.ə
celiac ˈsiː.li.æk
celibacy ˈsel.ə.bə.si, ˈ-ɪ-
celibatarian ˌsel.ə.bəˈteə.ri.ən, ˌ-ɪ- US -ˈter.i- **-s** -z
celibate ˈsel.ə.bət, ˈ-ɪ-, -bɪt **-s** -s
Céline selˈiːn, seɪˈliːn
cell sel **-s** -z
cellar ˈsel.əʳ US -ɚ **-s** -z
cellarage ˈsel.ᵊr.ɪdʒ
cellarer ˈsel.ᵊr.əʳ US -ɚ **-s** -z
cellaret ˌsel.ᵊrˈet, ˈsel.ᵊr.et US ˌsel.ɚˈet **-s** -s
cellarist ˈsel.ᵊr.ɪst **-s** -s
cellar|man ˈsel.ə|.mən, -mæn US -ɚ- **-men** -mən, -men
Cellini tʃelˈiː.ni, tʃɪˈliː-, tʃə-
cellist ˈtʃel.ɪst **-s** -s
cellmate ˈsel.meɪt **-s** -s
Cellnet® ˈsel.net
cello ˈtʃel.əʊ US -oʊ **-s** -z
Cellophane® ˈsel.ə.feɪn
cellphone ˈsel.fəʊn US -foʊn **-s** -z
cellular ˈsel.jə.ləʳ, -jʊ- US -lɚ ˌ**cellular ˈphone**; ˌ**cellular ˈradio**
cellule ˈsel.juːl **-s** -z
cellulite ˈsel.jə.laɪt, -jʊ-
celluloid **(C)** ˈsel.jə.lɔɪd, -jʊ-
cellulose ˈsel.jə.ləʊs, -jʊ- US -loʊs
Celsius ˈsel.si.əs US ˈsel.si.əs, -ʃəs
celt *axe:* selt **-s** -s
Celt *people, tribe:* kelt, selt **-s** -s *member of football or baseball team:* selt **-s** -s
Celtic *(of the people or tribe)* ˈkel.tɪk, ˈsel.tɪk
Note: In names of football and baseball teams /ˈsel.tɪk/; for **Sea** /ˈkel.tɪk/.
cembal|o ˈtʃem.bə.l|əʊ, ˈsem- US -loʊ **-os** -əʊz US -oʊz **-i** -iː
cement sɪˈment, sə- **-s** -s **-ing** -ɪŋ **-ed** -ɪd **ceˈment-ˌmixer**
cementation ˌsiː.menˈteɪ.ʃᵊn **-s** -z
cementium sɪˈmen.ʃi.əm, sə-, ˈ-ti- US -t̬i-
cemeter|y ˈsem.ə.tr|i, ˈ-ɪ- US -ə.ter|.i **-ies** -iz
Cenci ˈtʃen.*t*ʃi
CENELEC ˈsen.ɪ.lek, ˈ-ə-
cenematics ˌsen.ɪˈmæt.ɪks, -əˈ- US -ˈmæt̬-
cenetics səˈnet.ɪks, sɪ- US -ˈnet̬-
CEng *(abbrev. for* **Chartered Engineer***)* ˌsiːˈendʒ, ˌtʃɑː.təd.en.dʒɪˈnɪəʳ, -dʒəˈ- US ˌsiːˈendʒ, ˌtʃɑːr.t̬ɚd.en.dʒɪˈnɪr, -dʒəˈ-
Cenis səˈniː, senˈiː
cenobite ˈsiː.nə.baɪt, ˈsen.ə- US ˈsen.ə- **-s** -s
cenotaph ˈsen.əʊ.tæf, -tɑːf US -ə.tæf **-s** -s
cens|e sen*t*s **-es** -ɪz **-ing** -ɪŋ **-ed** -t
censer ˈsen*t*.səʳ US -sɚ **-s** -z
cens|or ˈsen*t*.s|əʳ US -s|ɚ **-ors** -əz US -ɚz **-oring** -ᵊr.ɪŋ **-ored** -əd US -ɚd
censorial sen*t*ˈsɔː.ri.əl US -ˈsɔːr.i- **-ly** -i
censorian sen*t*ˈsɔː.ri.ən US -ˈsɔːr.i-
censorious sen*t*ˈsɔː.ri.əs US -ˈsɔːr.i- **-ly** -li **-ness** -nəs, -nɪs
censorship ˈsen*t*.sə.ʃɪp US -sɚ- **-s** -s
censurable ˈsen*t*.sjᵊr.ə.bl̩, -ʃᵊr- US -ʃɚ-
cens|ure ˈsen*t*.ʃ|əʳ, -sj|əʳ US ˈsen*t*.ʃ|ɚ **-ures** -əz US -ɚz **-uring** -ᵊr.ɪŋ **-ured** -əd US -ɚd
census ˈsen*t*.səs **-es** -ɪz ˈ**census ˌpaper**
cent sent **-s** -s
centage ˈsen.tɪdʒ
cental ˈsen.tᵊl **-s** -z
centaur ˈsen.tɔːʳ US -tɔːr **-s** -z
Centaur|us senˈtɔː.r|əs US -ˈtɔːr|.əs **-i** -aɪ, -iː
centaur|y ˈsen.tɔː.r|i US -tɔːr|.i **-ies** -iz
centavo senˈtɑː.vəʊ US -voʊ **-s** -z
centenarian ˌsen.tɪˈneə.ri.ən, -təˈ- US -tᵊnˈer.i- **-s** -z
centenar|y senˈtiː.nᵊr|.i, sᵊn-, -ˈten.ᵊr- US ˈsen.tᵊn.er-; senˈten.ᵊr- **-ies** -iz
centennial senˈten.i.əl, sᵊn- **-s** -z **-ly** -i
cent|er ˈsen.t|əʳ US -t̬|ɚ **-ers** -əz US -ɚz **-ering** -ᵊr.ɪŋ **-ered** -əd US -ɚd ˌ**center of ˈgravity**; ˌ**center ˈstage**
centerboard ˈsen.tə.bɔːd US -t̬ɚ.bɔːrd **-s** -z
center-field ˌsen.təˈfiːld US -t̬ɚˈ- **-s** -z **-er/s** -əʳ/z US -ɚ/z
centerfold ˈsen.tə.fəʊld US -t̬ɚ.foʊld **-s** -z
center-forward ˌsen.təˈfɔː.wəd US -t̬ɚˈfɔːr.wɚd **-s** -z
center-|half ˌsen.tə|ˈhɑːf US -t̬ɚ|ˈhæf **-halves** -ˈhɑːvz US -ˈhævz
centerpiec|e ˈsen.tə.piːs US -t̬ɚ- **-es** -ɪz
centesimal senˈtes.ɪ.mᵊl, ˈ-ə- **-ly** -i
centesim|o senˈtes.ɪ.m|əʊ, ˈ-ə- US -m|oʊ **-i** -aɪ, -iː **-os** -əʊz US -oʊz
centigrade ˈsen.tɪ.greɪd US -t̬ə-
centigram, **centigramme** ˈsen.tɪ.græm US -t̬ə- **-s** -z
centigram(me) ˈsen.tɪ.græm US -t̬ə- **-s** -z
centilitre, **centiliter** ˈsen.tɪˌliː.təʳ US -t̬əˌliː.t̬ɚ **-s** -z
centime ˈsɑ̃ːn.tiːm, ˈsɔ̃ːn-, ˈsɑːn-; -ˈ- US ˈsɑːn-, ˈsen- **-s** -z
centimetre, **centimeter** ˈsen.tɪˌmiː.təʳ US -t̬əˌmiː.t̬ɚ **-s** -z
centimo ˈsen.tɪ.məʊ US -moʊ **-s** -z
centipede ˈsen.tɪ.piːd US -t̬ə- **-s** -z
centipois|e ˈsen.tɪ.pɔɪz US -t̬ə- **-es** -ɪz
centner ˈsent.nəʳ US -nɚ **-s** -z
cento ˈsen.təʊ US -toʊ **-s** -z
CENTO ˈsen.təʊ US -toʊ
central **(C)** ˈsen.trᵊl **-ly** -i ˌ**Central ˌAfrican ReˈpubIic**; ˌ**Central AˈmerIca**; ˌ**Central ˈDaylight ˌTime**; ˌ**central ˈheating**; ˌ**central reserˈvation**; ˌ**Central ˈStandard ˌTime**
centralism ˈsen.trᵊl.ɪ.zᵊm
centralist ˈsen.trᵊl.ɪst **-s** -s
centrality senˈtræl.ə.ti, -ɪ.ti US -ə.t̬i
centralization, **-isa-** ˌsen.trᵊl.aɪˈzeɪ.ʃᵊn, -lɪˈ- US -lɪˈ-
centraliz|e, **-is|e** ˈsen.trᵊl.aɪz **-es** -ɪz **-ing** -ɪŋ **-ed** -d
cent|re ˈsen.t|əʳ US -t̬|ɚ **-res** -əz US -ɚz **-ring** -ᵊr.ɪŋ **-red** -əd US -ɚd ˌ**centre of ˈgravity**; ˌ**centre ˈstage**
centreboard ˈsen.tə.bɔːd US -t̬ɚ.bɔːrd **-s** -z
centre-field ˌsen.təˈfiːld US -t̬ɚ- **-s** -z **-er/s** -əʳ/z US -ɚ/z
centrefold ˈsen.tə.fəʊld US -t̬ɚ.foʊld **-s** -z
centre-forward ˌsen.təˈfɔː.wəd US -t̬ɚˈfɔːr.wɚd **-s** -z
centre-|half ˌsen.tə|ˈhɑːf US -t̬ɚ|ˈhæf **-halves** -ˈhɑːvz US -ˈhævz
centrepiec|e ˈsen.tə.piːs US -t̬ɚ- **-es** -ɪz
Centrepoint ˈsen.tə.pɔɪnt US -t̬ɚ-
centric ˈsen.trɪk **-al** -ᵊl **-ally** -ᵊl.i, -li
centrifugal ˌsen.trɪˈfjuː.gᵊl, -trəˈ-, senˈtrɪf.jʊ-, -jə- US senˈtrɪf.jə.gᵊl, ˈ-ə-, -juː-
centrifug|e ˈsen.trɪ.fjuːdʒ, -trə- US -trə- **-es** -ɪz **-ing** -ɪŋ **-ed** -d
centriole ˈsen.tri.əʊl US -oʊl **-s** -z
centripetal ˌsen.trɪˈp.iː.tᵊl, ˈ-ə-, senˈtrɪ.pɪ- US senˈtrɪ.pə.t̬ᵊl
centr|ism ˈsen.tr|ɪ.zᵊm **-ist/s** -ɪst/s
centro- ˈsen.trəʊ- US ˈsen.trə-
centr|um ˈsen.tr|əm **-a** -ə
centumvirate senˈtʌm.vɪ.rət, -və-, -rɪt US senˈtʌm.vɚ.ət, ken-, -vɪ.rət **-s** -s
Centumviri ˌsen.tʌmˈvɪ.riː US ˈsen.təm.vɪ-, ˈken.tʊm-, -raɪ
centuple ˈsen.tjʊ.pl̩; senˈtjuː- US ˈsen.t̬ə-; senˈtuː-, -ˈtjuː-

centurion sen'tjʊə.ri.ən, -'tʃʊə-, -'tjɔː-, -'tʃɔː- (US) -'tʊr.i-, -'tjʊr- **-s** -z
centur|y 'sen.tʃᵊr|.i **-ies** -iz
CEO ˌsiː.iː'əʊ (US) -'oʊ
cep sep **-s** -s
cèpe sep **-s** -s
cephalic sef'æl.ɪk, sɪf-, sə'fæl-, kef'æl-, kɪf- (US) sə'fæl.ɪk
Cephalonia ˌsef.ə'ləʊ.ni.ə (US) -'loʊ-
cephalopod 'sef.ᵊl.əʊ.pɒd (US) -ə.pɑːd **-s** -z
cephalopoda ˌsef.ə'lɒp.ə.də (US) -'lɑː.pə-
cephalous 'sef.ᵊl.əs
Cephas 'siː.fæs
Cepheid 'siː.fi.ɪd, 'sef.i- **-s** -z
Cepheus 'siː.fi.əs, -fjəs
ceramic sə'ræm.ɪk, sɪ-, kɪ-, kə- (US) sə'ræm- **-s** -s
Note: In the UK, experts tend to use the forms with /kɪ-, kə-/.
ceramicist sə'ræm.ɪ.sɪst, sɪ-, '-ə- (US) sə'ræm.ə- **-s** -s
ceramist 'ser.ə.mɪst, sə'ræm.ɪst **-s** -s
cerastes sə'ræs.tiːz, sɪ- (US) sə-
cerate 'sɪə.reɪt, -rɪt, -rət (US) 'sɪr.eɪt, -ɪt **-s** -s
Cerberus 'sɜː.bᵊr.əs (US) 'sɝː-
cercari|a sɜː'keə.ri|.ə (US) sɚ'ker.i- **-ae** -iː
cer|e sɪəʳ (US) sɪr **-es** -z **-ing** -ɪŋ **-ed** -d
cereal 'sɪə.ri.əl (US) 'sɪr.i- **-s** -z
cerebell|um ˌser.ɪ'bel|.əm, -ə'- (US) -ə'- **-ums** -əmz **-a** -ə
Cerebos® 'ser.ə.bɒs, '-ɪ- (US) -bɑːs
cerebral 'ser.ə.brᵊl, '-ɪ-; sə'riː-, sɪ- (US) 'ser.ə-; sə'riː- **-s** -z ˌ**cerebral 'palsy**
cere|brate 'ser.ə|.breɪt, '-ɪ- (US) '-ə- **-brates** -breɪts **-brating** -breɪ.tɪŋ (US) -breɪ.t̬ɪŋ **-brated** -breɪ.tɪd (US) -breɪ.t̬ɪd
cerebration ˌser.ɪ'breɪ.ʃᵊn, -ə'- (US) -ə'- **-s** -z
cerebr|um sə'riː.br|əm, sɪ-; ser.ɪ-, '-ə- (US) 'ser.ə-; sə'riː- **-a** -ə **-ums** -əmz
Ceredigion ˌker.ə'dɪg.i.ɒn, -ɪ'- (US) -ɑːn
cerement 'sɪə.mənt, 'ser.ə.mənt (US) 'sɪr.mənt **-s** -s
ceremonial ˌser.ɪ'məʊ.ni.əl, -ə'- (US) -ə'moʊ- **-s** -z **-ly** -i **-ism** -ɪ.zᵊm
ceremonious ˌser.ɪ'məʊ.ni.əs, -ə'- (US) -ə'moʊ- **-ly** -li **-ness** -nəs, -nɪs
ceremon|y 'ser.ɪ.mə.n|i, '-ə- (US) '-ə.moʊ.n|i **-ies** -iz
Ceres 'sɪə.riːz (US) 'sɪr.iːz
cerif 'ser.ɪf **-s** -s
cerise sə'riːz, sɪ-, -'riːs (US) sə-
cerium 'sɪə.ri.əm (US) 'sɪr.i-
ceroplastic ˌsɪə.rəʊ'plæs.tɪk, -'plɑː.stɪk (US) 'sɪr.oʊ.plæs-, 'ser-
cert sɜːt (US) sɝːt **-s** -s
certain 'sɜː.tᵊn, -tɪn (US) 'sɝː- **-ly** -li
certaint|y 'sɜː.tᵊn.t|i, -tɪn- (US) 'sɝː- **-ies** -iz
certes 'sɜː.tiːz, -tɪz, sɜːts (US) 'sɝː.tiːz
certifiab|le ˌsɜː.tɪ'faɪ.ə.b|l̩, -tə'-, 'sɜː.tɪ.faɪ-, -tə- (US) 'sɝː.t̬ə.faɪ- **-ly** -li
certificate *(n.)* sə'tɪf.ɪ.kət, sɜː-, '-ə-, -kɪt (US) sɚ- **-s** -s
certifi|cate *(v.)* sə'tɪf.ɪ|.keɪt, sɜː-, '-ə- (US) sɚ- **-cates** -keɪts **-cating** -keɪ.tɪŋ (US) -keɪ.t̬ɪŋ **-cated** -keɪ.tɪd, -kə.tɪd, -kɪ- (US) -keɪ.t̬ɪd
certification *act of certifying:* ˌsɜː.tɪ.fɪ'keɪ.ʃᵊn, -fə'- (US) ˌsɝː.t̬ə- **-s** -z *providing with a certificate:* ˌsɜː.tɪ.fɪ'keɪ.ʃᵊn, səˌtɪ- (US) ˌsɝː.t̬ə- **-s** -z
certificatory sə'tɪf.ɪ.kə.tᵊr.i, sɜː-, -keɪ-, -tri (US) sɚ'tɪf.ɪ.kə.tɔːr.i
certif|y 'sɜː.tɪ.f|aɪ, -tə- (US) -t̬ə- **-ies** -aɪz **-ying** -aɪ.ɪŋ **-ied** -aɪd **-ier/s** -aɪ.əʳ/z (US) -aɪ.ɚ/z ˌ**certified 'mail**
certiorari ˌsɜː.ʃi.ɔː'reə.raɪ, -ti.ə'-, -'rɑː.ri (US) ˌsɝː.ʃi.ə'rer.i, -'rɑːr- **-s** -z
certitude 'sɜː.tɪ.tjuːd (US) 'sɝː.t̬ə.tuːd, -tjuːd
cerulean sə'ruː.li.ən, sɪ- (US) sə'ruː-
cerumen sə'ruː.men, sɪ-, -mən (US) sə'ruː-
Cervantes sɜː'væn.tiːz, -tɪz (US) sɚ-
cervical sə'vaɪ.kᵊl, sɜː-; 'sɜː.vɪ- (US) 'sɝː.vɪ- **cer**ˌ**vical 'smear,** ˌ**cervical 'smear** (US) ˌ**cervical 'smear**
cervine 'sɜː.vaɪn (US) 'sɝː-
cer|vix 'sɜː|.vɪks (US) 'sɝː- **-vices** -vɪ.siːz **-vixes** -vɪk.sɪz
Cerynean sə'rɪn.i.ən (US) ˌser.ə'niː.ən
César 'seɪ.zɑːʳ, -zəʳ (US) seɪ'zɑːr
cesarean, cesarian sɪ'zeə.ri.ən, sə- (US) sə'zer.i- **-s** -z **ce**ˌ**sarean 'section**
Cesarewitch *Russian prince:* sɪ'zɑː.rə.vɪtʃ, sə- (US) -'zɑːr.ə- *race:* sɪ'zær.ə.wɪtʃ, -'zɑː.rə-, -rɪ- (US) -'zɑːr.ə-
Cesario siː'zɑː.ri.əʊ, -'zær.i- (US) -'zɑːr.i.oʊ
cesium 'siː.zi.əm
cess ses **-es** -ɪz
cessation ses'eɪ.ʃᵊn, sɪ'seɪ-, sə- **-s** -z
cession 'seʃ.ᵊn **-s** -z
cessionar|y 'seʃ.ᵊn.ᵊr|.i, -ᵊn.r|i (US) -er- **-ies** -iz
Cessna® 'ses.nə
cesspit 'ses.pɪt **-s** -s
cesspool 'ses.puːl **-s** -z
c'est la vie ˌseɪ.læ'viː, -lɑː'-, -lə'-
cestui que trust ˌset.ɪ.kɪ'trʌst (US) ˌset̬-, ˌses.twɪ- **-s** -s
cestui que vie ˌset.ɪ.kɪ'viː (US) ˌset̬-, ˌses.twɪ- **-s** -z
cestuis que trust ˌset.ɪz.kɪ'trʌst (US) ˌset̬-, ˌses.twɪz-
cestuis que vie ˌset.ɪz.kɪ'viː (US) ˌset̬-, ˌses.twɪz-
cestus 'ses.təs **-es** -ɪz
cesura sɪ'zjʊə.rə, siː-, -'zjɔː-, -'ʒʊə- (US) sə'zʊr.ə, -'ʒʊr- **-s** -z
Cetacea sɪ'teɪ.ʃə, sə-, -ʃi.ə, -si.ə (US) -ʃə
cetacean sɪ'teɪ.ʃᵊn, sə-, -ʃi.ən, -si.ən (US) -ʃᵊn **-s** -z
cetaceous sɪ'teɪ.ʃəs, sə-, -ʃi.əs, -si.əs (US) -ʃəs
cetane 'siː.teɪn
Cetewayo ketʃ'waɪ.əʊ, ˌket.i'waɪ-, -wɑː.jəʊ (US) -'waɪ.oʊ
Ceuta 'sjuː.tə (US) 'seɪ.uː.t̬ə
Cévennes sev'en, sə'ven, sɪ-, -venz (US) seɪ'ven
ceviche sə'viː.tʃeɪ, -tʃiː
Ceylon sɪ'lɒn, sə- (US) sɪ'lɑːn, seɪ-
Ceylonese ˌsel.ə'niːz, ˌsiː.lə- (US) ˌsiː.lə'niːz, ˌseɪ-, -'niːs
Cézanne seɪ'zæn, sɪ-, sez'æn (US) seɪ'zɑːn
cf. *(abbrev. for* **compare***)* kəm'peəʳ, kən'fɜːʳ; ˌsiː'ef (US) kəm'per, kən'fɜ… ˌsiː'ef
CFC ˌsiː.ef'siː **-s** -z
cg *(abbrev. for* **centigramme, centigram***)* 'sen.tɪ.græm (US) -t̬ə-
Chablis 'ʃæb.liː, -bli, -'- (US) ʃæb'li, ʃɑː'b…
Chabrier 'ʃæb.ri.eɪ, 'ʃɑː.bri-, --'- (US) ˌʃɑː.bri'eɪ
cha-cha 'tʃɑː.tʃɑː **-s** -z **-ing** -ɪŋ **-ed** -d
cha-cha-cha ˌtʃɑː.tʃɑː'tʃɑː **-s** -z
chaconne ʃæk'ɒn, ʃə'kɒn (US) ʃɑː'kɑːn, ʃæk'ɑːn, -'ɔːn **-s** -z
chacun à son goût ˌʃæk.ɜːn.ɑː.sɔ̃ːŋ'guː, -æ.sɒŋ'- (US) ʃɑːˌkuːn.ɑː.sɑːn'-, ʃækˌuːn-, -sɔːn'-
chad (C) tʃæd **-s** -z **-ian/s** -i.ən/z
Chadband 'tʃæd.bænd
Chadderton 'tʃæd.ə.tᵊn (US) -ɚ.t̬ən
Chadwick 'tʃæd.wɪk
chaf|e tʃeɪf **-es** -s **-ing** -ɪŋ **-ed** -t
chafer 'tʃeɪ.fəʳ (US) -fɚ **-s** -z
chaff tʃæf, tʃɑːf (US) tʃæf **-s** -s **-ing/ly** -ɪŋ/li **-ed** -t
chaff|er 'tʃæf|.əʳ (US) -ɚ **-ers** -əz (US) -ɚz **-ering** -ᵊr.ɪŋ **-ered** -əd (US) -ɚd
Chaffey 'tʃeɪ.fi
chaffinch 'tʃæf.ɪntʃ **-es** -ɪz
chaff|y 'tʃæf|.i, 'tʃɑː.f|i (US) 'tʃæf|.i **-iness** -ɪ.nəs, -ɪ.nɪs
chafing-dish 'tʃeɪ.fɪŋ.dɪʃ **-es** -ɪz
Chagall ʃæg'æl, ʃə'gæl, -gɑːl (US) ʃə'g…
chagrin *(n.)* 'ʃæg.rɪn, -rᵊn (US) ʃə'grɪn
chagrin *(v.)* 'ʃæg.rɪn, ʃə'griːn (US) ʃə'grɪn **-s** -z **-ing** -ɪŋ **-ed** -d
Chaim haɪm, xaɪm
chain tʃeɪn **-s** -z **-ing** -ɪŋ **-ed** -d **'chain** ˌ**gang;** ˌ**chain 'letter; 'chain** ˌ**mail;** ˌ**chain re'action; 'chain** ˌ**store**

Pronouncing the letters CH

The consonant digraph **ch** has three main pronunciations: /tʃ, k/ and /ʃ/. Before the letter **r**, **ch** is always realised as /k/, e.g.:

Christmas	/ˈkrɪs*t*.məs/
anachronism	/əˈnæk.rə.nɪ.zᵊm/

However, there is no reliable way of predicting whether **ch** will be pronounced as /tʃ k/ or /ʃ/ in most other situations by looking at the spelling alone, e.g.:

chap	/tʃæp/
stomach	/ˈstʌm.ək/
champagne	/ʃæmˈpeɪn/

In general, /k/ words are those originating from Greek (e.g. *chaos, chorus*). Words containing /ʃ/ are usually late borrowings from French (e.g. *champagne, chauffeur*).

The remainder, pronounced /tʃ/, are more long-established, often being common everyday words (e.g. *lunch, chew*).

In addition

Occasionally, **ch** is pronounced /dʒ/, as in the British place name *Greenwich*.

/ˈgren.ɪdʒ/

Words from Scots ending **ch** may be pronounced /x/, but can also have the realisation /k/, e.g.:

loch	/lɒk, lɒx/	(US) /lɑːk, lɑːx/

In the case of *yacht* **ch** is silent:

yacht	/jɒt/	(US) /jɑːt/

chainless ˈtʃeɪn.ləs, -lɪs

chain-link ˈtʃeɪn.lɪŋk **ˌchain-link ˈfence**

chainsaw ˈtʃeɪn.sɔː (US) -sɑː, -sɔː **-s** -z **-ing** -ɪŋ **-ed** -d

chain-smok|e ˈtʃeɪn.sməʊk (US) -smoʊk **-es** -s **-ing** -ɪŋ **-ed** -t **-er/s** -əʳ/z (US) -ɚ/z

chainstitch ˈtʃeɪn.stɪtʃ

chainwork ˈtʃeɪn.wɜːk (US) -wɝːk

chair tʃeəʳ (US) tʃer **-s** -z **-ing** -ɪŋ **-ed** -d

chairlift ˈtʃeə.lɪft (US) ˈtʃer- **-s** -s

chair|man ˈtʃeə|.mən (US) ˈtʃer- **-men** -mən

chairmanship ˈtʃeə.mən.ʃɪp (US) ˈtʃer- **-s** -s

chairperson ˈtʃeəˌpɜː.sᵊn (US) ˈtʃerˌpɝː- **-s** -z

chair|woman ˈtʃeə|ˌwʊm.ən (US) ˈtʃer- **-women** -ˌwɪm.ɪn

chais|e ʃeɪz (US) ʃeɪz, tʃeɪs **-es** -ɪz

chaise(s) longue(s) ˌʃeɪzˈlɒŋ, ˌʃez-, -ˈlɒŋg, -ˈlɔ̃ːŋg (US) ˌʃeɪzˈlɔːŋ, ˌtʃeɪs-, -ˈlɑːŋ

Chalcedon ˈkæl.sɪ.dᵊn, -dɒn (US) -sə.dɑːn

chalcedony kælˈsed.ᵊn.i (US) kælˈsed.ᵊn.i, ˈkæl.sə.doʊ.ni

chalcedonyx ˌkæl.sɪˈdɒn.ɪks (US) -ˈdɑː.nɪks; kælˈsed.ᵊn.ɪks; **-es** -ɪz

Chalcis ˈkæl.sɪs

chalcography kælˈkɒg.rə.fi (US) -ˈkɑː.grə-

Chalde|a kælˈdiː|.ə, kɔːl- (US) kæl- **-an/s** -ən/z

Chaldee kælˈdiː, kɔːl- (US) kæl- **-s** -z

chaldron ˈtʃɔːl.drᵊn (US) ˈtʃɔːl-, ˈtʃɑːl- **-s** -z

chalet ˈʃæl.eɪ, ˈʃæl.i (US) ʃælˈeɪ **-s** -z

Chalfont *in Buckinghamshire:* ˈtʃæl.fənt, -fɒnt *old-fashioned:* ˈtʃɑː- (US) -fɑːnt

chalic|e ˈtʃæl.ɪs **-es** -ɪz **-ed** -t

chalk (C) tʃɔːk (US) tʃɔːk, tʃɑːk **-s** -s **-ing** -ɪŋ **-ed** -t **ˈchalk ˌpit; as ˌdifferent as ˌchalk and ˈcheese**

chalkboard ˈtʃɔːk.bɔːd (US) -bɔːrd, ˈtʃɑːk- **-s** -z

Chalker ˈtʃɔː.kəʳ (US) ˈtʃɔː.kɚ, ˈtʃɑː-

chalkface ˈtʃɔːk.feɪs (US) ˈtʃɔːk-, ˈtʃɑːk-

Chalkley ˈtʃɔːk.li (US) ˈtʃɔːk-, ˈtʃɑːk-

chalkstone ˈtʃɔːk.stəʊn (US) ˈtʃɔːk.stoʊn, ˈtʃɑːk- **-s** -z

chalk|y ˈtʃɔː.k|i (US) ˈtʃɔː-, ˈtʃɑː- **-ier** -i.əʳ (US) -i.ɚ **-iest** -i.ɪst, -i.əst **-ily** -ɪ.li, -ᵊl.i **-iness** -ɪ.nəs, -ɪ.nɪs

challeng|e ˈtʃæl.ɪndʒ, -əndʒ **-es** -ɪz **-ing** -ɪŋ **-ed** -d **-er/s** -əʳ/z (US) -ɚ/z

Challenor ˈtʃæl.ə.nəʳ, ˈ-ɪ- (US) -ə.nɚ

challis (C) ˈʃæl.ɪs, ˈʃæl.i

Challoner ˈtʃæl.ə.nəʳ (US) -nɚ

Chalmers ˈtʃɑː.məz, ˈtʃæl- (US) -mɚz

Chaloner ˈtʃæl.ə.nəʳ (US) -nɚ

chalybeate kəˈlɪb.i.ət, -ɪt, -eɪt

chamber ˈtʃeɪm.bəʳ (US) -bɚ **-s** -z **-ed** -d **ˈchamber ˌmusic; ˈchamber ˌpot**

chamberlain ˈtʃeɪm.bᵊl.ɪn, -ən (US) -bɚ- **-s** -z

Chamberlain ˈtʃeɪm.bᵊl.ɪn, -ən, -eɪn (US) -bɚ-

chamberlainship ˈtʃeɪm.bᵊl.ɪn.ʃɪp, -ən- (US) -bɚ- **-s** -s

chambermaid ˈtʃeɪm.bə.meɪd (US) -bɚ- **-s** -z

Chambers ˈtʃeɪm.bəz (US) -bɚz

Chambourcy® ʃæmˈbʊə.si, -ˈbɔː- (US) ˌʃɑːm.bʊrˈsiː

chambray ˈʃæm.breɪ

chambré ˈʃɑ̃ː*m*.breɪ (US) ʃɑːmˈbreɪ

chameleon kəˈmiː.li.ən (US) -li.ən, -ˈmiːl.jən **-s** -s

chamfer ˈʃæm*p*.fəʳ, ˈtʃæm*p*- (US) -fɚ **-s** -z

chamois (*sing.*) *goat-antelope:* ˈʃæm.wɑː (US) ˈʃæm.i, ʃæmˈwɑː (*plur.*)ˈʃæm.wɑːz (US) ˈʃæm.iz, ʃæmˈwɑːz

chamois *leather:* ˈʃæm.i **ˈchamois ˌleather ˌchamois ˈleather**

chamomile ˈkæm.ə.maɪl (US) -miːl, -maɪl

Chamonix ˈʃæm.ə.niː, -ɒn.iː (US) ˌʃæm.əˈniː

champ tʃæmp **-s** -s **-ing** -ɪŋ **-ed** -t

champagne (C) ʃæmˈpeɪn **-s** -z *stress shift:* ˌchampagne ˈsocialist

champaign ˈtʃæm.peɪn **-s** -z

champers ˈʃæm.pəz (US) -pɚz

champerty ˈtʃæm.pɜː.ti, -pə- (US) -pɝː.t̬i

champignon ˈʃæm.piː.njɔ̃ː, ˈʃɑ̃ː*m*-, ˌ--ˈ-; ʃæmˈpɪn.jɒn, ˈ--- (US) ʃæmˈpɪn.jən, tʃæm- **-s** -z

champion (C) ˈtʃæm.pi.ən (US) -pi.ən, -pjən **-s** -z **-ing** -ɪŋ **-ed** -d

championship ˈtʃæm.pi.ən.ʃɪp (US) ˈtʃæm.pi.ən.ʃɪp, -pjən- **-s** -s

Champlain *French explorer:* ʃæmˈpleɪn; ʃɔ̃ː*ŋ*ˈplɑ̃ː*ŋ* (US) ʃæmˈpleɪn; ʃɑ̃ːˈplɑ̃ː*ŋ* *lake in US:* ʃæmˈpleɪn

Champneys ˈtʃæmp.niz

Champs Elysées ˌʃɑ̃ː*nz*.elˈiː.zeɪ, ˌʃɔ̃ː*nz*- (US) ˌʃɑːnz.eɪ.liːˈzeɪ

chanc|e tʃɑːn*t*s (US) tʃæn*t*s **-es** -ɪz **-ing** -ɪŋ **-ed** -t **-er/s** -əʳ/z (US) -ɚ/z

chancel ˈtʃɑːn*t*.sᵊl (US) ˈtʃæn*t*- **-s** -z

chanceller|y ˈtʃɑːn*t*.sᵊl.ᵊr|.i (US) ˈtʃæn*t*- **-ies** -iz

chancellor (C) ˈtʃɑːn*t*.sᵊl.əʳ, -sɪ.ləʳ (US) ˈtʃæn*t*- **-s** -z **-ship/s** -ʃɪp/s **ˌchancellor of the exˈchequer**

Chancellorsville ˈtʃɑːn*t*.sᵊl.əz.vɪl (US) ˈtʃæn*t*.sᵊl.ɚz-

chancer|y (C) ˈtʃɑːn*t*.sᵊr|.i (US) ˈtʃæn*t*- **-ies** -iz

chancre 'ʃæŋ.kəʳ ⓤⓢ -kɚ
chancroid 'ʃæŋ.krɔɪd **-s** -z
chanc|y 'tʃɑːnt.s|i ⓤⓢ 'tʃænt- **-ier** -i.əʳ ⓤⓢ -i.ɚ **-iest** -i.ɪst, -i.əst
chandelier ˌʃæn.də'lɪəʳ, -dɪ'- ⓤⓢ -'lɪr **-s** -z
Chandigarh ˌtʃæn.dɪ'gɜːʳ, ˌtʃʌn-, -'gɑːʳ, '--- ⓤⓢ -'gɝː, -'gɑːr
chandler (C) 'tʃɑːnd.ləʳ ⓤⓢ 'tʃænd.lɚ **-s** -z
Chandos 'ʃæn.dɒs, 'tʃæn.dɒs ⓤⓢ -dɑːs
Note: Lord Chandos pronounces /'ʃæn-/. **Chandos Street** in London is generally pronounced with /'tʃæn-/.
Chanel ʃə'nel, ʃæn'el
Chaney 'tʃeɪ.ni
Chang tʃæŋ
chang|e tʃeɪndʒ **-es** -ɪz **-ing** -ɪŋ **-ed** -d **-er/s** -əʳ/z ⓤⓢ -ɚ/z
changeability ˌtʃeɪn.dʒə'bɪl.ə.ti, -ɪ.ti ⓤⓢ -ə.t̬i
changeab|le 'tʃeɪn.dʒə.bl̩ **-ly** -li **-leness** -l̩.nəs, -l̩.nɪs
changeful 'tʃeɪndʒ.fᵊl, -fʊl **-ly** -i **-ness** -nəs, -nɪs
changeless 'tʃeɪndʒ.ləs, -lɪs
changeling 'tʃeɪndʒ.lɪŋ **-s** -z
changeover 'tʃeɪndʒˌəʊ.vəʳ ⓤⓢ -ˌoʊ.vɚ **-s** -z
Chang Jiang ˌtʃæŋ.dʒi'æŋ ⓤⓢ ˌtʃɑːŋ.dʒi'ɑːŋ, ˌtʃæŋ-, -'æŋ
channel 'tʃæn.ᵊl **-s** -z **-(l)ing** -ɪŋ **-(l)ed** -d 'Channel ˌIslands; ˌChannel 'Tunnel
channelization, -isa- ˌtʃæn.ᵊl.aɪ'zeɪ.ʃᵊn, -ɪ'- ⓤⓢ -ɪ'-
channeliz|e, -is|e 'tʃæn.ᵊl.aɪz ⓤⓢ -ə.laɪz **-es** -ɪz **-ing** -ɪŋ **-ed** -d
Channell 'tʃæn.ᵊl
Channing 'tʃæn.ɪŋ
Channon 'tʃæn.ən, 'ʃæn.ən
chanson 'ʃɑ̃ːn.sɔ̃ːŋ, -sɒn, -'- ⓤⓢ ʃɑ̃ːn'soʊn, -'sɑːn, -'sɔːn **-s** -z
chant (C) tʃɑːnt ⓤⓢ tʃænt **-s** -s **-ing** -ɪŋ ⓤⓢ 'tʃæn.t̬ɪŋ **-ed** -ɪd ⓤⓢ 'tʃæn.t̬ɪd **-er/s** -əʳ/z ⓤⓢ 'tʃæn.t̬ɚ/z
Chantal ʃɑ̃ːn'tɑːl, ʃæn-, -tæl ⓤⓢ ʃɑːn'tɑːl
Chantelle ʃɑ̃ːn'tel, ʃæn- ⓤⓢ ʃɑːn'tel, ʃæn-
Chanter 'tʃɑːn.təʳ ⓤⓢ 'tʃæn.t̬ɚ
chanterelle ˌʃɑ̃ːn.tə'rel, ˌʃæn-, ˌtʃæn- ⓤⓢ ˌʃæn.t̬ə'-, ˌʃɑːn- **-s** -z
chanteus|e ʃɑ̃ːn'tɜːz, ʃɑːn- ⓤⓢ ʃɑ̃ːn'tuːz, ʃæn-, -'tuːs **-es** -ɪz
chantey 'ʃæn.ti, 'tʃæn-, 'tʃɑːn- ⓤⓢ 'ʃæn.t̬i **-s** -z
chanticleer (C) 'tʃɑːn.tɪ.klɪəʳ, 'tʃænt-, 'ʃɑːn-, -tə-, ˌ--'- ⓤⓢ 'tʃæn.t̬ə.klɪr, 'ʃæn- **-s** -z
Chantilly *in France:* ʃæn'tɪl.i, ʃɑ̃ːn- ⓤⓢ ʃæn'tɪl.i; ˌʃɑːn.ti'ji
Note: In the song "Chantilly Lace", it is pronounced /ʃæn'tɪl.i/.
Chantilly *in US:* ʃæn'tɪli
Chantrey 'tʃɑːn.tri ⓤⓢ 'tʃæn-
chantr|y 'tʃɑːn.tr|i ⓤⓢ 'tʃæn- **-ies** -iz
chant|y 'tʃɑːn.t|i ⓤⓢ 'tʃæn.t̬|i **-ies** -iz
Chanukah 'hʌn.ʊ.kə, 'xʌn- ⓤⓢ 'hɑː.nə.kə, 'xɑː-, -nʊ.kɑː
chaos 'keɪ.ɒs ⓤⓢ -ɑːs
chaotic keɪ'ɒt.ɪk ⓤⓢ -'ɑː.t̬ɪk **-ally** -ᵊl.i, -li
chap tʃæp **-s** -s **-ping** -ɪŋ **-ped** -t
chapat(t)i tʃə'pɑː.ti, -'pæt.i **-(e)s** -z
chapbook 'tʃæp.bʊk **-s** -s
chape tʃeɪp **-s** -s
chapeau 'ʃæp.əʊ, -'- ⓤⓢ ʃæp'oʊ **-s** -z
chapeaux *(alternative plur. of* **chapeau***)* 'ʃæp.əʊ, -əʊz ⓤⓢ ʃæp'oʊ, -'oʊz
chapel 'tʃæp.ᵊl **-s** -z
Chapel-en-le-Frith ˌtʃæp.ᵊl.ən.lə'frɪθ, -en.lə'-
chapelr|y 'tʃæp.ᵊl.r|i **-ies** -iz
Chapeltown 'tʃæp.ᵊl.taʊn
chaperon|e, chaperon 'ʃæp.ᵊr.əʊn ⓤⓢ -ə.roʊn **-es** -z **-ing** -ɪŋ **-ed** -d **-age** -ɪdʒ
chapfallen 'tʃæpˌfɔː.lən ⓤⓢ -ˌfɔː-, -ˌfɑː-
chaplain 'tʃæp.lɪn **-s** -z
chaplainc|y 'tʃæp.lɪnt.s|i, -lənt- **-ies** -iz
chaplet 'tʃæp.lət, -lɪt, -let **-s** -s
Chaplin 'tʃæp.lɪn
Chapman 'tʃæp.mᵊn
Chapone ʃə'pəʊn ⓤⓢ -poʊn
Chappaquiddick ˌtʃæp.ə'kwɪd.ɪk
Chappell 'tʃæp.ᵊl
chappie, chappy 'tʃæp.i **-s** -z
Chapple 'tʃæp.l̩
chapstick 'tʃæp.stɪk **-s** -s
chapter 'tʃæp.təʳ ⓤⓢ -tɚ **-s** -z 'chapter ˌhouse; ˌchapter and 'verse
Chapultepec tʃə'puːl.təˌpek, -'pʊl-
char tʃɑːʳ ⓤⓢ tʃɑːr **-s** -z **-ring** -ɪŋ **-red** -d
charabanc 'ʃær.ə.bæŋ, -bɑ̃ːŋ ⓤⓢ -bæŋ **-s** -s
character 'kær.ək.təʳ, -ɪk- ⓤⓢ 'ker.ək.tɚ, 'kær- **-s** -z
characteristic ˌkær.ək.tə'rɪs.tɪk, -ɪk- ⓤⓢ ˌker.ək-, ˌkær- **-s** -s **-al** -ᵊl **-ally** -ᵊl.i, -li
characterization, -isa- ˌkær.ək.tᵊr.aɪ'zeɪ.ʃᵊn, -ɪk-, -ɪ'- ⓤⓢ ˌker.ək.tɚ.ɪ'-, ˌkær- **-s** -z
characteriz|e, -is|e 'kær.ək.tᵊr.aɪz, -ɪk- ⓤⓢ 'ker.ək.tə.raɪz, 'kær- **-es** -ɪz **-ing** -ɪŋ **-ed** -d
characterless 'kær.ək.tə.ləs, -ɪk-, -lɪs ⓤⓢ 'ker.ək.tɚ-, 'kær- **-ness** -nəs, -nɪs
charade ʃə'rɑːd ⓤⓢ -'reɪd **-s** -z
charbroil 'tʃɑː.brɔɪl ⓤⓢ 'tʃɑːr- **-s** -z **-ing** -ɪŋ **-ed** -d
charcoal 'tʃɑː.kəʊl ⓤⓢ 'tʃɑːr.koʊl
chard (C) tʃɑːd ⓤⓢ tʃɑːrd
Chardin 'ʃɑː.dæ̃ŋ, -'- ⓤⓢ ʃɑːr'dæ̃n
chardonnay (C) 'ʃɑː.dᵊn.eɪ ⓤⓢ 'ʃɑːr-, ˌ--'- **-s** -z
char|e tʃeəʳ ⓤⓢ tʃer **-es** -z **-ing** -ɪŋ **-ed** -d
charg|e tʃɑːdʒ ⓤⓢ tʃɑːrdʒ **-es** -ɪz **-ing** -ɪŋ **-ed** -d 'charge ˌcard
chargeab|le 'tʃɑː.dʒə.bl̩ ⓤⓢ 'tʃɑːr- **-ly** -li **-leness** -l̩.nəs, -nɪs
chargé(s) d'affaires *sing:* ˌʃɑː.ʒeɪ.dæf'eəʳ, -də'feəʳ ⓤⓢ ˌʃɑːr.ʒeɪ.də'fer, -dæf'er *plur:* -z
charger 'tʃɑː.dʒəʳ ⓤⓢ 'tʃɑːr.dʒɚ **-s** -z
Charing Cross ˌtʃær.ɪŋ'krɒs, ˌtʃeər- ⓤⓢ ˌtʃer.ɪŋ'krɑːs, ˌtʃær-
chariot 'tʃær.i.ət ⓤⓢ 'tʃer-, 'tʃær- **-s** -s
charioteer ˌtʃær.i.ə'tɪəʳ ⓤⓢ ˌtʃer.i.ə'tɪr, ˌtʃær- **-s** -z
charisma kə'rɪz.mə
charismatic ˌkær.ɪz'mæt.ɪk ⓤⓢ ˌker.ɪz'mæt̬-, ˌkær-
charitab|le 'tʃær.ɪ.tə.bl̩, '-ə- ⓤⓢ 'tʃer-, 'tʃær- **-ly** -li **-leness** -l̩.nəs, -nɪs
charit|y (C) 'tʃær.ɪ.t|i, -ə.t|i ⓤⓢ 'tʃer.ə.t̬|i, 'tʃær- **-ies** -iz
charivari ˌʃɑː.rɪ'vɑː.ri ⓤⓢ ʃəˌrɪv.ə'riː; ˌʃɑː.rɪ'vɑː.ri, ˌʃɪv.ə'riː **-s** -z
charivaria ˌʃɑː.rɪv'ɑː.ri.ə ⓤⓢ ˌʃɑːr.ɪ'vɑːr.i-
charlad|y 'tʃɑː.leɪ.d|i ⓤⓢ 'tʃɑːr- **-ies** -iz
charlatan 'ʃɑː.lə.tᵊn, -tæn ⓤⓢ 'ʃɑːr.lə.tᵊn **-s** -z
charlatanism 'ʃɑː.lə.tᵊn.ɪ.zᵊm ⓤⓢ 'ʃɑːr.lə.tᵊn-, -t̬ə.nɪ- **-s** -z
charlatanry 'ʃɑː.lə.tᵊn.ri ⓤⓢ 'ʃɑːr.lə.tᵊn-, -t̬ən-
Charlbury 'tʃɑːl.bᵊr.i ⓤⓢ 'tʃɑːrl.ber.i, -bɚ-
Charlecote 'tʃɑːl.kəʊt ⓤⓢ 'tʃɑːrl.koʊt
Charlemagne 'ʃɑː.lə.meɪn, -maɪn, ˌ--'- ⓤⓢ 'ʃɑːr.lə.meɪn
Charlemont 'tʃɑː.lɪ.mənt, 'tʃɑːl.mənt ⓤⓢ 'tʃɑːr.lɪ.mənt, 'tʃɑːrl.mənt
Charlene 'tʃɑː.liːn, 'ʃɑː-, ʃɑː'liːn ⓤⓢ ʃɑːr'liːn, '--
Charleroi 'ʃɑː.lə.rɔɪ *as if French:* ˌʃɑː.lə'rwɑː ⓤⓢ 'ʃɑːr-
Charles tʃɑːlz ⓤⓢ tʃɑːrlz
Charleston 'tʃɑːl.stən ⓤⓢ 'tʃɑːrl-
Charlestown 'tʃɑːlz.taʊn ⓤⓢ 'tʃɑːrlz-
Charlesworth 'tʃɑːlz.wəθ, -wɜːθ ⓤⓢ 'tʃɑːrlz.wɚθ, -wɝːθ
Charleville 'ʃɑː.lə.vɪl ⓤⓢ 'ʃɑːr-
Charley 'tʃɑː.li ⓤⓢ 'tʃɑːr- 'charley ˌhorse
charlie (C) 'tʃɑː.li ⓤⓢ 'tʃɑːr- **-s** -z
charlock 'tʃɑː.lɒk ⓤⓢ 'tʃɑːr.lɑːk
charlotte (C) 'ʃɑː.lət ⓤⓢ 'ʃɑːr- **-s** -s
Charlottenburg ʃɑː'lɒt.ᵊn.bɜːg ⓤⓢ ʃɑːr'lɑː.tᵊn.bɝːg

Charlottesville ˈtʃɑː.ləts.vɪl ⓤⓢ ˈtʃɑːr-
Charlton ˈtʃɑːl.tᵊn ⓤⓢ ˈtʃɑːrl-
charm tʃɑːm ⓤⓢ tʃɑːrm **-s** -z **-ed** -d **-ing** -ɪŋ **-er/s** -əʳ/z ⓤⓢ -ɚ/z **-less/ly** -ləs/li, -lɪs/li
Charmaine ʃɑːˈmeɪn ⓤⓢ ʃɑːr-
Charmian ˈtʃɑː.mi.ən, ˈʃɑː-, ˈkɑː- ⓤⓢ ˈtʃɑːr-, ˈʃɑːr-, ˈkɑːr-
Charmin® ˈtʃɑː.mɪn ⓤⓢ ˈʃɑːr-
charming ˈtʃɑː.mɪŋ ⓤⓢ ˈtʃɑːr- **-ly** -li
charnel ˈtʃɑː.nᵊl ⓤⓢ ˈtʃɑːr- **ˈcharnel ˌhouse**
Charnock ˈtʃɑː.nɒk, -nək ⓤⓢ ˈtʃɑːr.nɑːk
Charnwood ˈtʃɑːn.wʊd, -wəd ⓤⓢ ˈtʃɑːrn-
Charolais *sing:* ˈʃær.ə.leɪ ⓤⓢ ˌʃɑːr.əˈleɪ *plur:* ˈʃær.ə.leɪ, -leɪz ⓤⓢ ˌʃɑːr.əˈleɪ, -ˈleɪz
Charon ˈkeə.rᵊn, -rɒn ⓤⓢ ˈker.ᵊn
Charpentier ʃɑː.ˈpɑ̃ːn.ti.eɪ ⓤⓢ ˌʃɑːr.pɑ̃ːn.tiˈeɪ, -ˈtjeɪ
Charrington ˈtʃær.ɪŋ.tən ⓤⓢ ˈtʃer-, ˈtʃær-
chart tʃɑːt ⓤⓢ tʃɑːrt **-s** -s **-ing** -ɪŋ ⓤⓢ ˈtʃɑːr.t̬ɪŋ **-ed** -ɪd ⓤⓢ ˈtʃɑːr.t̬ɪd
chart|er (C) ˈtʃɑː.t|əʳ ⓤⓢ ˈtʃɑːr.t̬|ɚ **-ers** -əz ⓤⓢ -ɚz **-ering** -ᵊr.ɪŋ **-ered** -əd ⓤⓢ -ɚd **-erer/s** -ᵊr.əʳ/z ⓤⓢ -ɚ.ɚ/z **ˈcharter ˌflight; ˌchartered aˈccountant**
Charterhouse ˈtʃɑː.tə.haʊs ⓤⓢ ˈtʃɑːr.t̬ɚ-
Charteris ˈtʃɑː.təz, -tᵊr.ɪs ⓤⓢ ˈtʃɑːr.t̬ɚ.ɪs
charterpart|y ˈtʃɑː.təˌpɑː.t|i ⓤⓢ ˈtʃɑːr.t̬ɚˌpɑːr.t̬|i **-ies** -iz
chart|ism (C) ˈtʃɑː.t|ɪ.zᵊm ⓤⓢ ˈtʃɑːr.t̬|ɪ- **-ist/s** -ɪst/s
Chartres ˈʃɑː.trə; ʃɑːt ⓤⓢ ˈʃɑːr.trə; ʃɑːrt
Chartreuse® ʃɑːˈtrɜːz ⓤⓢ ʃɑːrˈtruːz
Chartwell ˈtʃɑːt.wel, -wəl ⓤⓢ ˈtʃɑːrt-
char|woman ˈtʃɑː|ˌwʊm.ən ⓤⓢ ˈtʃɑːr- **-women** -ˌwɪm.ɪn
char|y ˈtʃeə.r|i ⓤⓢ ˈtʃer|.i **-ier** -i.əʳ ⓤⓢ -i.ɚ **-iest** -i.ɪst, -i.əst **-ily** -ɪ.li, -ᵊl.i **-iness** -ɪ.nəs, -ɪ.nɪs
Charybdis kəˈrɪb.dɪs
Chas tʃæz, tʃɑːlz ⓤⓢ tʃæz, tʃɑːrlz
chas|e (C) tʃeɪs **-es** -ɪz **-ing** -ɪŋ **-ed** -t **-er/s** -əʳ/z ⓤⓢ -ɚ/z
chasm ˈkæz.ᵊm **-s** -z
chassé ˈʃæs.eɪ ⓤⓢ -ˈ- **-s** -z
chasseur ʃæsˈɜːʳ ⓤⓢ -ˈɝː **-s** -z
chassis *sing:* ˈʃæs.i, -iː ⓤⓢ ˈtʃæs-, ˈʃæs- *plur:* ˈʃæs.iz, -iːz ⓤⓢ ˈtʃæs-, ˈʃæs-
chaste tʃeɪst **-ly** -li **-ness** -nəs, -nɪs
chasten ˈtʃeɪ.sᵊn **-s** -z **-ing** -ɪŋ **-ed** -d
chastis|e tʃæsˈtaɪz ⓤⓢ ˈ-- **-es** -ɪz **-ing** -ɪŋ **-ed** -d
chastisement tʃæsˈtaɪz.mənt, ˈtʃæs.tɪz- ⓤⓢ ˈtʃæs.taɪz-, -ˈ-- **-s** -s
chastiser tʃæsˈtaɪ.zəʳ ⓤⓢ -zɚ **-s** -z
chastity (C) ˈtʃæs.tə.ti, -tɪ- ⓤⓢ -tə.t̬i **ˈchastity ˌbelt**
chasuble ˈtʃæz.jʊ.bl̩, -jə- ⓤⓢ -jə-, ˈ-ə- **-s** -z
chat tʃæt **-s** -s **-ting** -ɪŋ ⓤⓢ ˈtʃæt̬.ɪŋ **-ted** -ɪd ⓤⓢ ˈtʃæt̬.ɪd **ˈchat ˌshow**
Chataway ˈtʃæt.ə.weɪ ⓤⓢ ˈtʃæt̬-
château ˈʃæt.əʊ, -ˈ- ⓤⓢ ʃætˈoʊ **-s** -z
chateaubriand (C) ˌʃæt.əʊ.briˈɑ̃ː*nd*, ˌʃæt.əʊˈbriː-, ʃætˈəʊ- ⓤⓢ ˌʃæt.oʊ.briˈɑ̃ː*nd*, ˌʃɑː.toʊ- **-s** -z
Châteauneuf-du-Pape ˌʃæt.əʊ.nɜːf.djuˈpæp ⓤⓢ -oʊˌnɜːf.du-, -dju-, -ˈpɑːp
châteaux *(alternative plur. of* **chateau***)* ˈʃæt.əʊ, -əʊz, -ˈ- ⓤⓢ ʃætˈoʊ, -ˈoʊz
chatelain ˈʃæt.ᵊl.eɪn, -æ̃ŋ ⓤⓢ ˈʃæt̬.ə.leɪn **-s** -z
chatelaine ˈʃæt.ᵊl.eɪn ⓤⓢ ˈʃæt̬.ə.leɪn **-s** -z
Chater ˈtʃeɪ.təʳ ⓤⓢ -tɚ
Chatham ˈtʃæt.əm ⓤⓢ ˈtʃæt̬-
chatline ˈtʃæt.laɪn **-s** -z
chatroom ˈtʃæt.ruːm, -rʊm **-s** -z
Chatsworth ˈtʃæts.wəθ, -wɜːθ ⓤⓢ -wɚθ, -wɝːθ
Chattanooga ˌtʃæt.ᵊnˈuː.gə ⓤⓢ ˌtʃæt̬.əˈnuː-, ˌtʃæt.ᵊnˈuː-
chattel ˈtʃæt.ᵊl ⓤⓢ ˈtʃæt̬- **-s** -z
chatt|er ˈtʃæt|.əʳ ⓤⓢ ˈtʃæt̬|.ɚ **-ers** -əz ⓤⓢ -ɚz **-ering** -ᵊr.ɪŋ **-ered** -əd ⓤⓢ -ɚd **-erer/s** -ᵊr.əʳ/z ⓤⓢ -ɚ.ɚ/z **ˈchattering ˌclasses**
chatterbox ˈtʃæt.ə.bɒks ⓤⓢ ˈtʃæt̬.ɚ.bɑːks **-es** -ɪz
Chatteris ˈtʃæt.ᵊr.ɪs
Chatterley ˈtʃæt.ᵊl.i ⓤⓢ ˈtʃæt̬.ɚ.li
Chatterton ˈtʃæt.ə.tᵊn ⓤⓢ ˈtʃæt̬.ɚ-
Chatto ˈtʃæt.əʊ ⓤⓢ -oʊ, ˈtʃæt̬-
chatt|y ˈtʃæt|.i ⓤⓢ ˈtʃæt̬|.i **-ier** -i.əʳ ⓤⓢ -i.ɚ **-iest** -i.ɪst, -i.əst **-ily** -ɪ.li, -ᵊl.i **-iness** -ɪ.nəs, -ɪ.nɪs
Chatwin ˈtʃæt.wɪn
Chaucer ˈtʃɔː.səʳ ⓤⓢ ˈtʃɑː.sɚ, ˈtʃɔː-
Chaucerian tʃɔːˈsɪə.ri.ən ⓤⓢ tʃɑːˈsɪr.i-, tʃɔː-, -ˈser-
chaudfroid ˈʃəʊ.fwɑː, -frwɑː ⓤⓢ ˈʃoʊ-
Chaudhuri ˈtʃaʊ.dᵊr.i
chauffer ˈtʃɔː.fəʳ ⓤⓢ ˈtʃɑː.fɚ, ˈtʃɔː- **-s** -z
chauffeur ˈʃəʊ.fəʳ, ʃəʊˈfɜːʳ ⓤⓢ ʃoʊˈfɝː **-s** -z **-ing** -ɪŋ **-ed** -d
Chauncey ˈtʃɔːn*t*.si ⓤⓢ ˈtʃɑːn*t*-, ˈtʃɔːn*t*-
chauvin|ism ˈʃəʊ.vɪ.n|ɪ.zᵊm, -və- ⓤⓢ ˈʃoʊ- **-ist/s** -ɪst/s
chauvinistic ˌʃəʊ.vɪˈnɪs.tɪk, -vəˈ- ⓤⓢ ˌʃoʊ- **-ally** -ᵊl.i, -li
Chavez ˈtʃæv.es ⓤⓢ ˈʃɑː.vez, ˈtʃɑː-, -ves
Chaworth ˈtʃɑː.wəθ, -wɜːθ ⓤⓢ -wɚθ, -wɝːθ
Chayefsky tʃaɪˈef.ski
Che tʃeɪ
Cheadle ˈtʃiː.dl̩
Cheam tʃiːm
cheap tʃiːp **-er** -əʳ ⓤⓢ -ɚ **-est** -ɪst, -əst **-ly** -li **-ness** -nəs, -nɪs **ˌcheap ˈshot**
cheapen ˈtʃiː.pᵊn **-s** -z **-ing** -ɪŋ **-ed** -d
cheapie ˈtʃiː.pi **-s** -z
cheap-jack ˈtʃiːp.dʒæk **-s** -s
cheapo ˈtʃiː.pəʊ ⓤⓢ -poʊ **-s** -z
Cheapside ˈtʃiːp.saɪd, tʃiːpˈsaɪd
cheapskate ˈtʃiːp.skeɪt **-s** -s
cheat tʃiːt **-s** -s **-ing** -ɪŋ ⓤⓢ ˈtʃiː.t̬ɪŋ **-ed** -ɪd ⓤⓢ ˈtʃiː.t̬ɪd
Cheatham ˈtʃiː.təm ⓤⓢ -t̬əm
Chechen ˌtʃetʃˈen **-s** -z *stress shift:* ˌChechen ˈfighters
Chechenia ˈtʃetʃ.ni.ɑː, -ni.ə; tʃetʃ.ɪˈnjɑː ⓤⓢ -ni.ə
Chechnya ˈtʃetʃ.ni.ə, -ni.ɑː; tʃetʃ.ɪˈnjɑː ⓤⓢ -ni.ə
check tʃek **-s** -s **-ing** -ɪŋ **-ed** -t **ˈchecking acˌcount**
checkbook ˈtʃek.bʊk **-s** -s
check|er (C) ˈtʃek|.əʳ ⓤⓢ -ɚ **-ers** -əz ⓤⓢ -ɚz **-ering** -ᵊr.ɪŋ **-ered** -əd ⓤⓢ -ɚd
checkerboard ˈtʃek.ə.bɔːd ⓤⓢ -ɚ.bɔːrd **-s** -z
checkers ˈtʃek.əz ⓤⓢ -ɚz
check-in ˈtʃek.ɪn **-s** -z **ˈcheck-in ˌdesk**
Checkland ˈtʃek.lənd
checklist ˈtʃek.lɪst **-s** -s
checkma|te ˈtʃek.meɪ|t, ˌ-ˈ- **-tes** -ts **-ting** -tɪŋ ⓤⓢ -t̬ɪŋ **-ted** -tɪd ⓤⓢ -t̬ɪd
checkout ˈtʃek.aʊt **-s** -s
checkpoint ˈtʃek.pɔɪnt **-s** -s **ˌCheckpoint ˈCharlie**
checkrein ˈtʃek.reɪn **-s** -z
checkroom ˈtʃek.rʊm, -ruːm ⓤⓢ -ruːm **-s** -z
checkup ˈtʃek.ʌp **-s** -s
cheddar (C) ˈtʃed.əʳ ⓤⓢ -ɚ **-s** -z **-ing** -ɪŋ **-ed** -d
cheek tʃiːk **-s** -s **-ing** -ɪŋ **-ed** -t **ˌturn the other ˈcheek**
cheekbone ˈtʃiːk.bəʊn ⓤⓢ -boʊn **-s** -z
Cheeke tʃiːk
cheek|y ˈtʃiː.k|i **-ier** -i.əʳ ⓤⓢ -i.ɚ **-iest** -i.ɪst, -i.əst **-ily** -ɪ.li, -ᵊl.i **-iness** -ɪ.nəs, -ɪ.nɪs
cheep tʃiːp **-s** -s **-ing** -ɪŋ **-ed** -t
cheer tʃɪəʳ ⓤⓢ tʃɪr **-s** -z **-ing** -ɪŋ **-ed** -d
cheerful ˈtʃɪə.fᵊl, -fʊl ⓤⓢ ˈtʃɪr- **-ly** -i **-ness** -nəs, -nɪs
cheerio ˌtʃɪə.riˈəʊ ⓤⓢ ˌtʃɪr.iˈoʊ **-s** -z
Cheerios® ˈtʃɪə.ri.əʊz, ˈtʃɪr.i.oʊz
cheerleader ˈtʃɪəˌliː.dəʳ ⓤⓢ ˈtʃɪrˌliː.dɚ **-s** -z
cheerless ˈtʃɪə.ləs, -lɪs ⓤⓢ ˈtʃɪr- **-ly** -li **-ness** -nəs, -nɪs
cheer|y ˈtʃɪə.r|i ⓤⓢ ˈtʃɪr|.i **-ier** -i.əʳ ⓤⓢ -i.ɚ **-iest** -i.ɪst, -i.əst **-ily** -ɪ.li, -ᵊl.i **-iness** -ɪ.nəs, -ɪ.nɪs

chees|e tʃiːz **-es** -ɪz **-ed** -d ˌ**cheesed 'off**
cheeseboard 'tʃiːz.bɔːd US -bɔːrd **-s** -z
cheeseburger 'tʃiːzˌbɜː.gəʳ US -ˌbɝː.gɚ **-s** -z
cheesecake 'tʃiːz.keɪk **-s** -s
cheesecloth 'tʃiːz.klɒθ US -klɑːθ
Cheeseman 'tʃiːz.mən
cheesemonger 'tʃiːzˌmʌŋ.gəʳ US -gɚ, -ˌmɑːŋ- **-s** -z
cheeseparing 'tʃiːzˌpeə.rɪŋ US -ˌper.ɪŋ
Cheesewright 'tʃiːz.raɪt, 'tʃez-
chees|y 'tʃiː.z|i **-ier** -i.əʳ US -i.ɚ **-iest** -i.ɪst, -i.əst **-iness** -ɪ.nəs, -ɪ.nɪs
cheetah 'tʃiː.tə US -t̬ə **-s** -z
Cheetham 'tʃiː.təm US -t̬əm
Cheever 'tʃiː.vəʳ US -vɚ
chef ʃef **-s** -s
chef d'équipe ˌʃef.dek'iːp
chef(s) d'oeuvre, chef(s)-d'oeuvre ˌʃeɪ'dɜːv.rə, -əʳ US ˌʃeɪ'dɜːv.rə, -'dɝːv
Cheke tʃiːk
Chekhov 'tʃek.ɒf, -ɒv US -ɑːf, -ɔːf, -ɑːv
chela 'tʃeɪ.lə, 'tʃiː.lə **-s** -z
chela|te kiː'leɪ|t, kə-, tʃiː-, kɪ-; 'kiː.leɪ|t, 'tʃiː- US 'kiː.leɪ|t **-tes** -ts **-ting** -tɪŋ US -t̬ɪŋ **-ted** -tɪd US -t̬ɪd
chelation kiː'leɪ.ʃᵊn, kə-, tʃiː-, kɪ-
Chelmer 'tʃel.məʳ US -mɚ
Chelmsford 'tʃelmz.fəd, 'tʃelmps- *old-fashioned local pronunciations:* 'tʃemz-, 'tʃɒmz- US -fɚd
Chelsea 'tʃel.si ˌ**Chelsea 'bun, 'Chelsea ˌbun;** ˌ**Chelsea 'pensioner**
Chelsey 'tʃel.si
Cheltenham 'tʃel.tᵊn.əm
Chelyabinsk tʃel'jɑː.bɪnsk
chemic 'kem.ɪk
chemical 'kem.ɪ.kᵊl **-ly** -i **-s** -z ˌ**chemical engi'neering;** ˌ**chemical 'warfare**
chemis|e ʃə'miːz **-es** -ɪz
chemist 'kem.ɪst **-s** -s
chemistry 'kem.ɪ.stri, -ə-
Chemnitz 'kem.nɪts
chemo- 'kiː.məʊ-, 'kem.əʊ- US 'kiː.moʊ-, 'kem.oʊ-
chemotherapy ˌkiː.məʊ'θer.ə.pi, ˌkem.əʊ- US ˌkiː.moʊ'-, ˌkem.oʊ'-
Chenevix 'tʃen.ə.vɪks, 'ʃen.ə.vɪks
Cheney 'tʃiː.ni, 'tʃeɪ- US 'tʃeɪ-
Chengdu ˌtʃʌŋ'duː
Chenies *in Buckinghamshire:* 'tʃeɪ.niz *street in London:* 'tʃiː.niz
chenille ʃə'niːl
cheongsam ˌtʃɒŋ'sæm, tʃiˌɒŋ- US ˌtʃɔːŋ-, ˌtʃɑːŋ- **-s** -z
Cheops 'kiː.ɒps US -ɑːps
Chepstow 'tʃep.stəʊ US -stoʊ
cheque tʃek **-s** -s **'cheque ˌcard**
chequebook 'tʃek.bʊk **-s** -s
chequecard 'tʃek.kɑːd US -kɑːrd **-s** -z
chequ|er 'tʃek|.əʳ US -ɚ **-ers** -əz US -ɚz **-ering** -ᵊr.ɪŋ **-ered** -əd US -ɚd
Chequers 'tʃek.əz US -ɚz
Cher ʃeəʳ US ʃer
Cherbourg 'ʃeə.bʊəg, ʃɜː-, -bɔːg, -bɜːg US 'ʃer.bʊrg, -bʊr, -'-
Cherie ʃə'riː, 'ʃer.i
cherish 'tʃer.ɪʃ **-es** -ɪz **-ing** -ɪŋ **-ed** -t
Cheriton 'tʃer.ɪ.tᵊn
Chernobyl tʃɜː'nəʊ.bᵊl, tʃə-, -'nɒb.ᵊl, -ɪl US tʃɚ'noʊ.bᵊl
Chernomyrdin ˌtʃɜː.nə'mɪə.dɪn, ˌtʃeə-, -'mɜː-, -dᵊn US ˌtʃɝː.nə'mɪr-, -noʊ'-, ˌtʃer-, -'mɝː-
Cherokee 'tʃer.ə.kiː, ˌ--'- **-s** -z
cheroot ʃə'ruːt **-s** -s
cherr|y (C) 'tʃer|.i **-ies** -iz ˌ**cherry 'brandy;** ˌ**cherry 'pie;** ˌ**cherry to'mato**
cherrystone 'tʃer.i.stəʊn US -stoʊn **-s** -z
chersonese 'kɜː.sə.niːs, -niːz, ˌ--'- US ˌkɝː.sə.niːz, -niːs
Chertsey 'tʃɜːt.si US 'tʃɝːt-
cherub 'tʃer.əb **-s** -z
cherubic tʃə'ruː.bɪk, tʃer'uː- US tʃə'ruː- **-ally** -ᵊl.i, -li
cherubim 'tʃer.ə.bɪm, '-ʊ-
Cherubini ˌker.ʊ'biː.niː, -ə'-, -ni
chervil 'tʃɜː.vɪl, -vᵊl US 'tʃɝː-
Cherwell 'tʃɑː.wəl, -wel US 'tʃɑːr-
Cheryl 'tʃer.ᵊl, 'ʃer-, -ɪl US 'ʃer.ᵊl
Chesapeake 'tʃes.ə.piːk
Chesebro, Chesebrough 'tʃiːz.brə
Chesham 'tʃeʃ.ᵊm *old-fashioned local pronunciation:* 'tʃes-
Cheshire 'tʃeʃ.əʳ, -ɪəʳ US -ɚ, -ɪr ˌ**Cheshire 'cat;** ˌ**Cheshire 'cheese**
Cheshunt 'tʃes.ᵊnt, 'tʃeʃ-
Chesil 'tʃez.ᵊl ˌ**Chesil 'Bank;** ˌ**Chesil 'Beach**
Chesney 'tʃes.ni, 'tʃez.ni
Chesnutt 'tʃes.nʌt
chess tʃes
chessboard 'tʃes.bɔːd US -bɔːrd **-s** -z
chess|man 'tʃes|.mæn, -mən **-men** -men, -mən
chest tʃest **-s** -s **-ed** -ɪd ˌ**chest of 'drawers**
Chester 'tʃes.təʳ US -tɚ
chesterfield (C) 'tʃes.tə.fiːld US -tɚ- **-s** -z
Chester-le-Street ˌtʃes.tə.lɪ'striːt, '---ˌ- US -tɚ-
Chesterton 'tʃes.tə.tᵊn US -tɚ.t̬ən
chestnut 'tʃes.nʌt, 'tʃest- **-s** -s
Chestre 'tʃes.təʳ US -tɚ
chest|y 'tʃes.t|i **-ier** -i.əʳ US -i.ɚ **-iest** -i.ɪst, -i.əst **-ily** -ɪ.li, -ᵊl.i **-iness** -ɪ.nəs, -ɪ.nɪs
Chetham 'tʃet.əm
chetrum 'tʃet.rʊm, -rəm
Chettle 'tʃet.l̩ US 'tʃet̬-
Chetwode 'tʃet.wʊd
Chetwynd 'tʃet.wɪnd
cheval-glass ʃə'væl.glɑːs US -glæs **-es** -ɪz
chevalier ˌʃev.ə'lɪəʳ US -'lɪr **-s** -z
Chevalier *surname:* ʃə'væl.i.eɪ, ʃɪ- US -i.eɪ, -jeɪ
Chevening 'tʃiːv.nɪŋ
Cheves tʃiːvz
Chevette® ʃə'vet, ʃev'et **-s** -s
Cheviot *hills, sheep:* 'tʃiː.vi.ət, 'tʃev.i-, 'tʃɪv.i- US 'ʃev.i- *cloth:* 'tʃev.i.ət US 'ʃev-
Chevis 'tʃev.ɪs
Chevrolet® 'ʃev.rə.leɪ, ˌ--'- US ˌʃev.rə'leɪ **-s** -z
chevron 'ʃev.rᵊn, -rɒn US -rᵊn **-s** -z
chev|y (C) 'tʃev|.i **-ies** -iz **-ying** -i.ɪŋ **-ied** -id
Chevy 'ʃev.i
chew tʃuː **-s** -z **-ing** -ɪŋ **-ed** -d **'chewing ˌgum**
chew|y 'tʃuː|.i **-ier** -i.əʳ US -i.ɚ **-iest** -i.ɪst, -i.əst **-iness** -ɪ.nəs, -ɪ.nɪs
Cheyenne ˌʃaɪ'æn, -'en US -'en, -'æn
Cheyne 'tʃeɪ.ni, tʃeɪn
Cheyney 'tʃeɪ.ni
chez ʃeɪ
Chiang Kai-Shek ˌtʃæŋ.kaɪ'ʃek US ˌtʃæŋ-, ˌdʒæŋ-
Chiang Mai tʃiˌæŋ'maɪ US ˌdʒɑːŋ'maɪ, tʃiˌɑːŋ-
chianti (C) ki'æn.ti US -'ɑːn.t̬i, -'æn-
Chiantishire ki'æn.ti.ʃəʳ, -ˌʃɪəʳ US -'ɑːn.t̬i.ʃɚ, -'æn-, -ˌʃɪr
Chiapas tʃi'æp.əs US -'ɑː.pəs
chiaroscuro kiˌɑː.rə'skʊə.rəʊ, -rɒs'kʊə-, -'kjʊə- US -ˌɑːr.ə'skjʊr.oʊ
chias|ma kaɪ'æz|.mə **-mata** -mə.tə US -mə.t̬ə **-mas** -məz
chiasmus kaɪ'æz.məs
chic ʃiːk, ʃɪk
Chicago ʃɪ'kɑː.gəʊ, ʃə- US -goʊ, -'kɔː-
chican|e ʃɪ'keɪn, ʃə- **-es** -z **-ing** -ɪŋ **-ed** -d **-er/s** -əʳ/z US -ɚ/z
chicaner|y ʃɪ'keɪ.nᵊr|.i, ʃə- **-ies** -iz
chicano tʃɪ'kɑː.nəʊ US -noʊ **-s** -z
Chichele 'tʃɪtʃ.ᵊl.i, -ɪ.li
Chichén Itzá tʃiˌtʃen.ɪt'sɑː US -iːt'-
Chichester 'tʃɪtʃ.ɪ.stəʳ, '-ə- US -stɚ
chi-chi 'ʃiː.ʃiː
chick (C) tʃɪk **-s** -s
chickabidd|y 'tʃɪk.əˌbɪd|.i **-ies** -iz
chickadee 'tʃɪk.əˌdiː, ˌ--'- **-s** -z
Chickasaw 'tʃɪk.ə.sɔː US -sɔː, -sɑː **-s** -z
chicken 'tʃɪk.ɪn, -ᵊn **-s** -z **-ing** -ɪŋ **-ed** -d **'chicken ˌfeed;** ˌ**chicken 'Kiev; 'chicken ˌpox;** ˌ**don't count your ˌchickens before they 'hatch**
chickenhearted ˌtʃɪk.ɪn'hɑː.tɪd, -ᵊn'-, -təd, 'tʃɪk.ɪnˌhɑː-, -ᵊnˌ- US ˌtʃɪk.ɪn'hɑːr.t̬ɪd, -ᵊn'-, -t̬əd

chickenshit 'tʃɪk.ɪn.ʃɪt, -ᵊn- -s -s
Chicklets® 'tʃɪk.ləts, -lɪts
chickpea 'tʃɪk.piː -s -z
chickweed 'tʃɪk.wiːd
Chiclayo tʃi'klaɪ.jəʊ ⓤⓢ -joʊ
chicory 'tʃɪk.ᵊr.i
Chiddingly ˌtʃɪd.ɪŋ'laɪ, '---
chid|e tʃaɪd **-es** -z **-ing** -ɪŋ **-ed** -ɪd **chid** tʃɪd **chidden** 'tʃɪd.ᵊn
chief tʃiːf **-s** -s **-ly** -li ˌ**chief in'spector;** ˌ**chief of 'staff**
chieftain 'tʃiːf.tᵊn, -tɪn **-s** -z
chieftanc|y 'tʃiːf.tᵊnt.s|i, -tɪnt- **-ies** -iz
chiff-chaff 'tʃɪf.tʃæf **-s** -s
chiffon 'ʃɪf.ɒn, ʃɪ'fɒn ⓤⓢ ʃɪ'fɑːn **-s** -z
chiffon(n)ier ˌʃɪf.ə'nɪəʳ, -ni.eɪ *as if French:* ʃiː.fɔ̃ː'nje ⓤⓢ -'nɪr **-s** -z
chifforobe 'ʃɪf.ə.rəʊb ⓤⓢ 'ʃɪf.roʊb **-s** -z
chignon 'ʃiː.njɒn, -njɒŋ, -njɔ̃ː *old-fashioned:* ʃɪ'nɒn ⓤⓢ 'ʃiː.njɑːn **-s** -z
Chigwell 'tʃɪg.wel, -wəl
chihuahua (C) tʃɪ'wɑː.wə, tʃə-, ʃɪ-, ʃə-, -wɑː **-s** -z
chilblain 'tʃɪl.bleɪn **-s** -z
child (C) tʃaɪld **children** 'tʃɪl.drᵊn '**child a**ˌ**buse;** ˌ**child 'benefit;** '**child's** ˌ**play;** ˌ**child 'prodigy;** ˌ**child sup'port**
childbearing 'tʃaɪldˌbeə.rɪŋ ⓤⓢ -ˌber.ɪŋ
childbed 'tʃaɪld.bed
childbirth 'tʃaɪld.bɜːθ ⓤⓢ -bɝːθ
childcare 'tʃaɪld.keəʳ ⓤⓢ -ker
Childe tʃaɪld
Childermas 'tʃɪl.də.mæs, -məs ⓤⓢ -dɚ.mæs
Childers 'tʃɪl.dəz ⓤⓢ -dɚz
childhood 'tʃaɪld.hʊd ˌ**childhood 'sweetheart**
childish 'tʃaɪl.dɪʃ **-ly** -li **-ness** -nəs, -nɪs
childless 'tʃaɪld.ləs, -lɪs **-ness** -nəs, -nɪs
childlike 'tʃaɪld.laɪk
childmind|er 'tʃaɪldˌmaɪn.d|əʳ ⓤⓢ -d|ɚ **-ers** -əz ⓤⓢ -ɚz **-ing** -ɪŋ
childproof 'tʃaɪld.pruːf
children *(from* **child***)* 'tʃɪl.drᵊn '**children's** ˌ**home**
Childs tʃaɪldz
Chile 'tʃɪl.i, 'tʃiː.leɪ
Chilean 'tʃɪl.i.ən, tʃɪ'liː.ən ⓤⓢ tʃɪ'liː-, 'tʃɪl.i- **-s** -z
chili 'tʃɪl.i **-s** -z
chiliad 'kɪl.i.æd, 'kaɪ.li-, -əd **-s** -z
chili|asm 'kɪl.i|.æz.ᵊm **-ast/s** -æst/s
chilidog 'tʃɪl.i.dɒg ⓤⓢ -dɑːg, -dɔːg **-s** -z
chill tʃɪl **-s** -z **-ing/ly** -ɪŋ/li **-ed** -d **-ness** -nəs, -nɪs **-er** -əʳ ⓤⓢ -ɚ
chiller 'tʃɪl.əʳ ⓤⓢ -ɚ **-s** -z
chilli 'tʃɪl.i **-es** -z '**chilli** ˌ**pepper;** '**chilli** ˌ**powder**
chilli con carne ˌtʃɪl.i.kɒn'kɑː.ni, -kɒŋ'-, -kən'-, -kəŋ'-, -neɪ ⓤⓢ -kɑːn'kɑːr.ni, -kən'-
Chillingham 'tʃɪl.ɪŋ.əm
Chillingly 'tʃɪl.ɪŋ.li
Chillingworth 'tʃɪl.ɪŋ.wəθ, -wɜːθ ⓤⓢ -wɚθ, -wɝːθ
Chillon ʃɪ'lɒn, ʃə-; 'ʃɪl.ən, -ɒn ⓤⓢ ʃə'lɑːn, ʃɪ-; 'ʃɪl.ən; ʃi'joʊn
Note: In Byron's 'Castle of Chillon' it is usual to pronounce /'ʃɪl.ən/ or /'ʃɪl.ɒn ⓤⓢ -ɑːn/.
chill|y 'tʃɪl|.i **-ier** -i.əʳ ⓤⓢ -i.ɚ **-iest** -i.ɪst, -i.əst **-iness** -ɪ.nəs, -ɪ.nɪs
Chiltern 'tʃɪl.tᵊn ⓤⓢ -tɚn ˌ**Chiltern 'Hills;** ˌ**Chiltern 'Hundreds**
Chilton 'tʃɪl.tᵊn
chimaera kaɪ'mɪə.rə, kɪ-, kə-, ʃɪ-, ʃə-, -'meə-; ⓤⓢ kaɪ'mɪr.ə, kɪ- **-s** -z
Chimborazo ˌtʃɪm.bə'rɑː.zəʊ, ˌʃɪm-, -bɒr'ɑː- ⓤⓢ -bə'rɑː.zoʊ
chim|e tʃaɪm **-es** -z **-ing** -ɪŋ **-ed** -d **-er/s** -əʳ/z ⓤⓢ -ɚ/z
chimera kaɪ'mɪə.rə, kɪ-, kə-, ʃɪ-, ʃə-, -'meə-; 'kɪm.ᵊr.ə ⓤⓢ kaɪ'mɪr.ə, kɪ- **-s** -z
chimere tʃɪ'mɪəʳ, ʃɪ-, kɪ-, kaɪ- ⓤⓢ -'mɪr **-s** -z
chimeric kaɪ'mer.ɪk, kɪ-, kə- **-al** -ᵊl **-ally** -ᵊl.i, -li
Chimkent tʃɪm'kent
chimney 'tʃɪm.ni **-s** -z '**chimney** ˌ**breast;** '**chimney** ˌ**pot;** '**chimney** ˌ**stack;** '**chimney** ˌ**sweep;** '**chimney** ˌ**sweeper**
chimneypiec|e 'tʃɪm.ni.piːs **-es** -ɪz
chimp tʃɪmp **-s** -s
chimpanzee ˌtʃɪm.pᵊn'ziː, -pæn'- ⓤⓢ tʃɪm'pæn.ziː, ˌtʃɪm.pᵊn'zi **-s** -z
chin tʃɪn **-s** -z ˌ**chin-'deep**
china (C) 'tʃaɪ.nə '**china** ˌ**clay** ˌ**china 'clay; like a** ˌ**bull in a 'china shop**
China|man 'tʃaɪ.nə|.mən **-men** -mən
Chinatown 'tʃaɪ.nə.taʊn
chinchilla tʃɪn'tʃɪl.ə **-s** -z
Chindit 'tʃɪn.dɪt **-s** -s
chin|e tʃaɪn **-es** -z **-ing** -ɪŋ **-ed** -d
Chinese tʃaɪ'niːz ⓤⓢ -'niːz, -'niːs *stress shift, see compounds:* ˌ**Chinese 'gooseberry;** ˌ**Chinese 'lantern;** ˌ**Chinese 'restaurant**
Chingford 'tʃɪŋ.fəd ⓤⓢ -fɚd
chink (C) tʃɪŋk **-s** -s **-ing -ed**
Chinkie, Chinky 'tʃɪŋ.ki
chinless 'tʃɪn.ləs, -lɪs ˌ**chinless 'wonder**
Chinnock 'tʃɪn.ək
Chinnor 'tʃɪn.əʳ ⓤⓢ -ɚ
chino 'tʃiː.nəʊ ⓤⓢ -noʊ **-s** -z
Chinook tʃɪ'nʊk, -'nuːk ⓤⓢ ʃə'nʊk, tʃə-
chinstrap 'tʃɪn.stræp **-s** -s
chintz tʃɪnts **-es** -ɪz **-y** -i
chinwag 'tʃɪn.wæg **-s** -s **-ging** -ɪŋ
Chios 'kaɪ.ɒs, 'kiː- ⓤⓢ -ɑːs
chip tʃɪp **-s** -s **-ping** -ɪŋ **-ped** -t '**chip** ˌ**shop; have a 'chip on one's** ˌ**shoulder**
chipboard 'tʃɪp.bɔːd ⓤⓢ -bɔːrd
chipmunk 'tʃɪp.mʌŋk **-s** -s
chipolata ˌtʃɪp.ᵊl'ɑː.tə ⓤⓢ -ə'lɑː.t̬ə **-s** -z
Chipp tʃɪp
Chippendale 'tʃɪp.ᵊn.deɪl **-s** -z
Chippenham 'tʃɪp.ᵊn.əm
chipper 'tʃɪp.əʳ ⓤⓢ -ɚ
Chipperfield 'tʃɪp.ə.fiːld ⓤⓢ -ɚ-
Chippewa 'tʃɪp.ɪ.wɑː, -wə **-s** -z
chippie 'tʃɪp.i **-s** -z
Chipping 'tʃɪp.ɪŋ
Chipping Sodbury ˌtʃɪp.ɪŋ'sɒd.bᵊr.i ⓤⓢ -'sɑːd.ber-, -bɚ-
chipp|y 'tʃɪp|.i **-ier** -i.əʳ ⓤⓢ -i.ɚ **-iest** -i.ɪst, -i.əst **-iness** -ɪ.nəs, -ɪ.nɪs
Chips tʃɪps
Chirac 'ʃɪə.ræk, ʃi'ræk ⓤⓢ ʃə'rɑːk, ʃɪ'ræk
Chirk tʃɜːk ⓤⓢ tʃɝːk
chirograph 'kaɪə.rəʊ.grɑːf, -græf ⓤⓢ 'kaɪ.rə.græf **-s** -s
chirographer kaɪə'rɒg.rə.fəʳ ⓤⓢ kaɪ'rɑː.grə.fɚ **-s** -z
chirographic ˌkaɪə.rəʊ'græf.ɪk ⓤⓢ ˌkaɪ.roʊ'-
chirographist kaɪə'rɒg.rə.fɪst ⓤⓢ kaɪ'rɑː.grə- **-s** -s
chirography kaɪə'rɒg.rə.fi ⓤⓢ kaɪ'rɑː.grə-
Chirol 'tʃɪr.ᵊl
chiromancer 'kaɪə.rəʊ.mænt.səʳ ⓤⓢ 'kaɪ.roʊ.mænt.sɚ **-s** -z
chiromancy 'kaɪə.rəʊ.mænt.si ⓤⓢ 'kaɪ.roʊ-
Chiron 'kaɪə.rən ⓤⓢ 'kaɪ-
chiropodist kɪ'rɒp.ə.dɪst, ʃɪ-, tʃɪ- ⓤⓢ kɪ'rɑː.pə-, kaɪ-, ʃɪ- **-s** -s
chiropody kɪ'rɒp.ə.di, ʃɪ-, tʃɪ- ⓤⓢ kɪ'rɑː.pə-, kaɪ-, ʃɪ-
chiropractic ˌkaɪə.rəʊ'præk.tɪk ⓤⓢ ˌkaɪ.roʊ'-, 'kaɪ.roʊ.præk-
chiropractor 'kaɪə.rəʊ.præk.təʳ ⓤⓢ 'kaɪ.roʊ.præk.tɚ **-s** -z
chirp tʃɜːp ⓤⓢ tʃɝːp **-s** -s **-ing** -ɪŋ **-ed** -t
chirp|y 'tʃɜː.p|i ⓤⓢ 'tʃɝː- **-ier** -i.əʳ ⓤⓢ -i.ɚ **-iest** -i.ɪst, -i.əst **-ily** -ɪ.li, -ᵊl.i **-iness** -ɪ.nəs, -ɪ.nɪs
chirr tʃɜːʳ ⓤⓢ tʃɝː **-s** -z **-ing** -ɪŋ **-ed** -d
chirrup 'tʃɪr.əp ⓤⓢ 'tʃɪr-, 'tʃɝː- **-s** -s **-ing** -ɪŋ **-ed** -t
chisel 'tʃɪz.ᵊl **-s** -z **-(l)ing** -ɪŋ **-(l)ed** -d **-(l)er/s** -əʳ/z ⓤⓢ -ɚ/z
Chisholm 'tʃɪz.ᵊm
Chislehurst 'tʃɪz.l̩.hɜːst ⓤⓢ -hɝːst
Chiswick 'tʃɪz.ɪk
chit tʃɪt **-s** -s
chit-chat, chitchat 'tʃɪt.tʃæt
chitin 'kaɪ.tɪn, -tᵊn ⓤⓢ -tᵊn
Chittagong 'tʃɪt.ə.gɒŋ ⓤⓢ 'tʃɪt̬.ə.gɑːŋ, -gɔːŋ
Chittenden 'tʃɪt.ᵊn.dən
chitterling 'tʃɪt.ᵊl.ɪŋ ⓤⓢ 'tʃɪt̬.ɚ.lɪŋ **-s** -z

Chitty 'tʃɪt.i ⓤⓢ 'tʃɪţ-
chivalric 'ʃɪv.əl.rɪk ⓤⓢ ʃɪ'væl-; 'ʃɪv.əl-
chivalrous 'ʃɪv.əl.rəs **-ly** -li **-ness** -nəs, -nɪs
chivalry 'ʃɪv.əl.ri
chive tʃaɪv **-s** -z
Chivers 'tʃɪv.əz ⓤⓢ -ɚz
chivv|y 'tʃɪv|.i **-ies** -iz **-ying** -i.ɪŋ **-ied** -id
chiv|y 'tʃɪv|.i **-ies** -iz **-ying** -i.ɪŋ **-ied** -id
chlamid|ia, chlamyd|ia klə'mɪd|.i.ə **-iae** -i.i **-ial** -i.əl
chlamy|s 'klæm.ɪ|s, 'kleɪ.mɪ|s **-des** -diːz
Chloe, Chloë 'kləʊ.i ⓤⓢ 'kloʊ-
chloral 'klɔː.rəl ⓤⓢ 'klɔːr.əl
chloramine 'klɔː.rə.miːn; -mɪn ⓤⓢ 'klɔːr.ə.miːn, ,--'-; klɔː'ræm.iːn, -ɪn
chlorate 'klɔː.reɪt, -rɪt ⓤⓢ 'klɔːr.eɪt, -ɪt **-s** -s
chloric 'klɔː.rɪk, 'klɒr.ɪk ⓤⓢ 'klɔːr.ɪk
chloride 'klɔː.raɪd ⓤⓢ 'klɔːr.aɪd **-s** -z
chlori|nate 'klɔː.rɪ|.neɪt, 'klɒr.ɪ- ⓤⓢ 'klɔːr.ɪ- **-nates** -neɪts **-nating** -neɪ.tɪŋ ⓤⓢ -neɪ.ţɪŋ **-nated** -neɪ.tɪd ⓤⓢ -neɪ.ţɪd
chlorine 'klɔː.riːn ⓤⓢ 'klɔːr.iːn, -ɪn
Chloris 'klɔː.rɪs, 'klɒr.ɪs ⓤⓢ 'klɔːr.ɪs
chlorite 'klɔː.raɪt ⓤⓢ 'klɔːr.aɪt **-s** -s
chloro- 'klɔː.rəʊ-, 'klɒr.əʊ- ⓤⓢ 'klɔːr.ə-, '-oʊ-
chlorodyne 'klɔː.rə.daɪn, 'klɒr.ə- ⓤⓢ 'klɔːr.ə-
chlorofluorocarbon ,klɔː.rəʊ,flɔː.rəʊ'kɑː.bən, ,klɒr.əʊ-, -,flʊə- ⓤⓢ ,klɔːr.oʊ,flɔːr.oʊ'kɑːr-, -,flʊr- **-s** -z
chloroform 'klɔː.rə.fɔːm, 'klɒr.ə- ⓤⓢ 'klɔːr.ə.fɔːrm **-s** -z **-ing** -ɪŋ **-ed** -d
Chloromycetin® ,klɔː.rəʊ.maɪ'siː.tɪn, ,klɒr.əʊ- ⓤⓢ ,klɔːr.oʊ.maɪ'siː.tən
chlorophyl(l) 'klɔː.rə.fɪl, 'klɒr.ə- ⓤⓢ 'klɔːr.ə-
chlorophyllose ,klɔː.rə'fɪl.əʊs, ,klɒr.ə'- ⓤⓢ ,klɔːr.ə'fɪl.oʊs
chloroplast 'klɒr.ə.plɑːst, -plæst ⓤⓢ 'klɔːr.ə.plæst
chlorous 'klɔː.rəs ⓤⓢ 'klɔːr.əs
Choate tʃəʊt ⓤⓢ tʃoʊt
choc tʃɒk ⓤⓢ tʃɑːk **-s** -s
choc-ic|e 'tʃɒk.aɪs ⓤⓢ 'tʃɑːk- **-es** -ɪz
chock tʃɒk ⓤⓢ tʃɑːk **-s** -s ,**chock-'full**
chock-a-block ,tʃɒk.ə'blɒk, '--- ⓤⓢ 'tʃɑːk.ə.blɑːk
chocker, chocka 'tʃɒk.əʳ ⓤⓢ 'tʃɑː.kɚ
chocoholic, chocaholic ,tʃɒk.ə'hɒl.ɪk ⓤⓢ ,tʃɑː.kə'hɑː.lɪk **-s** -s
chocolate 'tʃɒk.əl.ət, -ɪt, '-lət, -lɪt ⓤⓢ 'tʃɑːk.lət, 'tʃɔːk-, 'tʃɑː.kəl.ət, 'tʃɔː-, -ɪt **-s** -s ,**chocolate 'cake,** '**chocolate ,cake;** ,**chocolate chip 'cookie;** '**drinking ,chocolate**
Choctaw 'tʃɒk.tɔː ⓤⓢ 'tʃɑːk.tɔː, -tɑː
choic|e tʃɔɪs **-es** -ɪz **-er** -əʳ ⓤⓢ -ɚ **-est** -ɪst, -əst **-ely** -li **-eness** -nəs, -nɪs
choir kwaɪəʳ ⓤⓢ kwaɪɚ **-s** -z '**choir ,screen**
choirboy 'kwaɪə.bɔɪ ⓤⓢ 'kwaɪɚ- **-s** -z
choirmaster 'kwaɪə,mɑː.stəʳ ⓤⓢ 'kwaɪɚ,mæs.tɚ **-s** -z
chok|e tʃəʊk ⓤⓢ tʃoʊk **-es** -s **-ing** -ɪŋ **-ed** -t
choker 'tʃəʊ.kəʳ ⓤⓢ 'tʃoʊ.kɚ **-s** -z
chok|y 'tʃəʊ.k|i ⓤⓢ 'tʃoʊ- **-ier** -i.əʳ ⓤⓢ -i.ɚ **-iest** -i.ɪst, -i.əst **-iness** -ɪ.nəs, -ɪ.nɪs
Cholderton 'tʃəʊl.də.tən ⓤⓢ 'tʃoʊl.dɚ.ţən
choler 'kɒl.əʳ ⓤⓢ 'kɑː.lɚ
cholera 'kɒl.ər.ə ⓤⓢ 'kɑː.lɚ-
choleraic ,kɒl.ə'reɪ.ɪk ⓤⓢ ,kɑː.lə'-
choleric 'kɒl.ər.ɪk; kɒl'er- ⓤⓢ 'kɑː.lɚ-; kə'ler-
cholesterol kə'les.tər.ɒl, kɒl'es-, -əl ⓤⓢ kə'les.tə.rɑːl, -rɔːl, -roʊl
choliamb 'kəʊ.li.æmb ⓤⓢ 'koʊ- **-s** -z
choliambic ,kəʊ.li'æm.bɪk ⓤⓢ ,koʊ-
choline 'kəʊ.liːn ⓤⓢ 'koʊ-, -lɪn
Cholmeley 'tʃʌm.li
Cholmondeley 'tʃʌm.li
Cholsey 'tʃəʊl.zi, 'tʃɒl.si ⓤⓢ 'tʃoʊl-
Chomley 'tʃʌm.li
chomp tʃɒmp ⓤⓢ tʃɑːmp **-s** -s **-ing** -ɪŋ **-ed** -t
Chomsky 'tʃɒmp.ski ⓤⓢ 'tʃɑːmp- **-an** -ən
chon tʃəʊn ⓤⓢ tʃoʊn
Chongquing ,tʃʊŋ'tʃɪŋ
choo-choo 'tʃuː.tʃuː **-s** -z
chook tʃʊk **-s** -s
choos|e tʃuːz **-es** -ɪz **-ing** -ɪŋ **chose** tʃəʊz ⓤⓢ tʃoʊz **chosen** 'tʃəʊ.zən ⓤⓢ 'tʃoʊ- **chooser/s** 'tʃuː.zəʳ/z ⓤⓢ -zɚ/z
choos|y, choos|ey 'tʃuː.z|i **-ier** -i.əʳ ⓤⓢ -i.ɚ **-iest** -i.ɪst, -i.əst **-iness** -ɪ.nəs, -ɪ.nɪs
chop tʃɒp ⓤⓢ tʃɑːp **-s** -s **-ping** -ɪŋ **-ped** -t '**chopping ,board;** ,**chop 'suey**
chop-chop ,tʃɒp'tʃɒp ⓤⓢ ,tʃɑːp'tʃɑːp
chophou|se 'tʃɒp.haʊ|s ⓤⓢ 'tʃɑːp- **-ses** -zɪz
Chopin 'ʃɒp.æ̃ŋ, 'ʃəʊ.pæ̃ŋ, -pæŋ ⓤⓢ 'ʃoʊ.pæn; ʃoʊ'pæ̃n
chopper 'tʃɒp.əʳ ⓤⓢ 'tʃɑː.pɚ **-s** -z
chopp|y 'tʃɒp|.i ⓤⓢ 'tʃɑː.p|i **-ier** -i.əʳ ⓤⓢ -i.ɚ **-iest** -i.ɪst, -i.əst **-ily** -ɪ.li, -əl.i **-iness** -ɪ.nəs, -ɪ.nɪs
chopstick 'tʃɒp.stɪk ⓤⓢ 'tʃɑːp- **-s** -s
chop-suey ,tʃɒp'suː.i ⓤⓢ ,tʃɑːp-
choral 'kɔː.rəl ⓤⓢ 'kɔːr.əl **-ly** -i
chorale kɒr'ɑːl, kə'rɑːl, kɔː- ⓤⓢ kə'ræl, -'rɑːl **-s** -z
chord kɔːd ⓤⓢ kɔːrd **-s** -z
chordate 'kɔː.deɪt, -dɪt, -dət ⓤⓢ 'kɔːr-
chore tʃɔːʳ ⓤⓢ tʃɔːr **-s** -z
chorea kɒr'ɪə, kɔː'rɪə, kə- ⓤⓢ kə'riː.ə, kɔːr'iː-
choreograph 'kɒr.i.ə.grɑːf, 'kɔː.ri-, -græf ⓤⓢ 'kɔːr.i.ə.græf **-s** -s **-ing** -ɪŋ **-ed** -t
choreographer ,kɒr.i'ɒg.rə.fəʳ, ,kɔː.ri- ⓤⓢ ,kɔːr.i'ɑː.grə.fɚ **-s** -z
choreographic ,kɒr.i.əʊ'græf.ɪk, ,kɔː.ri- ⓤⓢ ,kɔːr.i.ə'-
choreography ,kɒr.i'ɒg.rə.fi, ,kɔː.ri- ⓤⓢ ,kɔːr.i'ɑː.grə-
choriamb 'kɒr.i.æmb, 'kɔː.ri- ⓤⓢ 'kɔːr.i- **-s** -z
choriambic ,kɒr.i'æm.bɪk, ,kɔː.ri- ⓤⓢ ,kɔːr.i'-
choric 'kɒr.ɪk ⓤⓢ 'kɔːr-
chorion 'kɔː.ri.ən, -ɒn ⓤⓢ 'kɔːr.i.ɑːn **-s** -z
chorionic ,kɔː.ri'ɒn.ɪk ⓤⓢ ,kɔːr.i'ɑː.nɪk
chorister 'kɒr.ɪ.stəʳ ⓤⓢ 'kɔːr.ɪ.stɚ **-s** -z
chorizo tʃə'riː.zəʊ, tʃɒr'iː- ⓤⓢ tʃə'riː.zoʊ, tʃoʊ-, -soʊ **-s** -z
Chorley 'tʃɔː.li ⓤⓢ 'tʃɔːr-
Chorleywood ,tʃɔː.li'wʊd ⓤⓢ ,tʃɔːr-
choroid 'kɔː.rɔɪd ⓤⓢ 'kɔːr.ɔɪd
chortl|e 'tʃɔː.tl̩ ⓤⓢ 'tʃɔːr.ţl̩ **-es** -z **-ing** -ɪŋ, 'tʃɔːt.lɪŋ ⓤⓢ 'tʃɔːr.ţl̩.ɪŋ, 'tʃɔːrt.lɪŋ **-ed** -d
chorus 'kɔː.rəs ⓤⓢ 'kɔːr.əs **-es** -ɪz **-ing** -ɪŋ **-ed** -t
chose *legal term:* ʃəʊz ⓤⓢ ʃoʊz
chose *(from* **choose***)* tʃəʊz ⓤⓢ tʃoʊz
Chosen *Japanese name for Korea:* ,tʃəʊ'sen ⓤⓢ ,tʃoʊ-
chosen *(from* **choose***)* 'tʃəʊ.zən ⓤⓢ 'tʃoʊ-
Chou En-lai ,tʃəʊ.en'laɪ, ,dʒəʊ- ⓤⓢ ,dʒoʊ-
chough tʃʌf **-s** -s
choux ʃuː ,**choux 'pastry**
chow tʃaʊ **-s** -z
chow-chow ,tʃaʊ'tʃaʊ, '-- **-s** -z
chowder 'tʃaʊ.dəʳ ⓤⓢ -dɚ **-s** -z
Chowles tʃəʊlz ⓤⓢ tʃoʊlz
chow mein ,tʃaʊ'meɪn
chrestomath|y kres'tɒm.ə.θ|i ⓤⓢ -'tɑː.mə- **-ies** -iz
Chrétien de Troyes kreɪ,tjæ̃n.də'trwɑː
Chris krɪs **-'s** -ɪz
chrism 'krɪz.əm
chrisom 'krɪz.əm **-s** -z
Chrissie 'krɪs.i
Christ kraɪst **-s** -s
Christa 'krɪs.tə
Christabel 'krɪs.tə.bel, -bəl
Christadelphian ,krɪs.tə'del.fi.ən **-s** -z
Christchurch 'kraɪst.tʃɜːtʃ ⓤⓢ -tʃɝːtʃ
Christdom 'kraɪst.dəm
christen 'krɪs.ən **-s** -z **-ing** -ɪŋ **-ed** -d
Christendom 'krɪs.ən.dəm

christening ˈkrɪs.ᵊn.ɪŋ **-s** -z
Christensen ˈkrɪs.tᵊn.sᵊn
Christi *(in* **Corpus Christi***)* ˈkrɪs.ti
Christian ˈkrɪs.tʃən, ˈkrɪʃ-; ˈkrɪs.ti.ən US ˈkrɪs.tʃən, -ti.ən **-s** -z ˈ**Christian** ˌ**name**; ˌ**Christian** ˈ**Science**; ˌ**Christian** ˈ**Scientist**
Christiana ˌkrɪs.tiˈɑː.nə US -tiˈæn.ə, -tʃiˈ-, -ˈɑː.nə
Christiania ˌkrɪs.tiˈɑː.ni.ə US -tiˈæn.i-, -tʃiˈ-, -ˈɑː.ni-
Christianism ˈkrɪs.tʃᵊn.ɪ.zᵊm, ˈkrɪʃ-; ˈkrɪs.ti.ə.nɪ- US ˈkrɪs.tʃᵊn.ɪ-, -ti.ə.nɪ-
Christianity ˌkrɪs.tiˈæn.ə.ti, -ˈtʃæn-, -ɪ.ti US -tʃiˈæn.ə.t̬i, -tiˈ-
christianiz|e, -is|e (C) ˈkrɪs.tʃə.naɪz, ˈkrɪʃ-; ˈkrɪs.ti.ə- US ˈkrɪs.tʃə- **-es** -ɪz **-ing** -ɪŋ **-ed** -d
christianly (C) ˈkrɪs.tʃən.li, ˈkrɪʃ-; ˈkrɪs.ti.ən- US ˈkrɪs.tʃən-
Christie ˈkrɪs.ti **-'s** -z
Christina krɪˈstiː.nə
Christine ˈkrɪs.tiːn, krɪˈstiːn
Christlike ˈkraɪst.laɪk **-ness** -nəs, -nɪs
Christmas ˈkrɪst.məs US ˈkrɪs- **-es** -ɪz ˈ**Christmas** ˌ**box**; ˈ**Christmas** ˌ**cake**; ˈ**Christmas** ˌ**card**; ˌ**Christmas** ˈ**Day**; ˌ**Christmas** ˈ**Eve**; ˈ**Christmas** ˌ**present**; ˌ**Christmas** ˈ**pudding**; ˈ**Christmas** ˌ**tree**
Christmassy ˈkrɪst.mə.si US ˈkrɪs-
Christmastide ˈkrɪst.məs.taɪd US ˈkrɪs-
Christminster ˈkraɪstˌmɪnt.stəʳ, ˈkrɪst- US -stɚ
Christobel ˈkrɪs.tə.bel
Christophe krɪˈstɒf; ˈkrɪs.tɒf US kriːˈstɑːf, krɪ-, -ˈstɔːf
christophene ˈkrɪs.tə.fiːn **-s** -z
Christopher ˈkrɪs.tə.fəʳ US -fɚ
Christopherson krɪˈstɒf.ə.sᵊn US -ˈstɑː.fɚ-
Christy ˈkrɪs.ti
chroma ˈkrəʊ.mə US ˈkroʊ-
chromate ˈkrəʊ.meɪt, -mɪt US ˈkroʊ- **-s** -s
chromatic krəʊˈmæt.ɪk US kroʊˈmæt̬-, krə- **-ally** -ᵊl.i, -li
chromaticity ˌkrəʊ.məˈtɪs.ə.ti, -ɪ.ti US ˌkroʊ.məˈtɪs.ə.t̬i
chromatin ˈkrəʊ.mə.tɪn US ˈkroʊ-
chromatogram ˈkrəʊ.mə.tə.græm, krəʊˈmæt.ə- US kroʊˈmæt̬- **-s** -z
chromatographic ˌkrəʊ.mə.təˈgræf.ɪk, krəʊˌmæt.əˈ- US kroʊˌmæt̬-
chromatography ˌkrəʊ.məˈtɒg.rə.fi US ˌkroʊ.məˈtɑː.grə-
chrome krəʊm US kroʊm
chrom|ic ˈkrəʊ.m|ɪk US ˈkroʊ- **-ous** -əs
chromite ˈkrəʊ.maɪt US ˈkroʊ- **-s** -s
chromium ˈkrəʊ.mi.əm US ˈkroʊ-
chromolithograph ˌkrəʊ.məʊˈlɪθ.əʊ.grɑːf, -græf US ˌkroʊ.moʊˈlɪθ.ə.græf **-s** -s
chromolithography ˌkrəʊ.məʊ.lɪˈθɒg.rə.fi US ˌkroʊ.moʊ.lɪˈθɑː.grə-
chromosomal ˌkrəʊ.məˈsəʊ.mᵊl US ˌkroʊ.məˈsoʊ-
chromosome ˈkrəʊ.mə.səʊm US ˈkroʊ.mə.soʊm **-s** -z
chromosphere ˈkrəʊ.mə.sfɪəʳ US ˈkroʊ.mə.sfɪr **-s** -z
chromotype ˈkrəʊ.məʊ.taɪp US ˈkroʊ.moʊ-
chronic ˈkrɒn.ɪk US ˈkrɑː.nɪk **-al** -ᵊl **-ally** -ᵊl.i, -li
chronicl|e ˈkrɒn.ɪ.kl̩ US ˈkrɑː.nɪ- **-es** -z **-ing** -ɪŋ, -klɪŋ **-ed** -d **-er/s** -kləʳ/z US -klɚ/z
Chronicles ˈkrɒn.ɪ.kl̩z US ˈkrɑː.nɪ-
chrono- ˈkrɒn.əʊ-, ˈkrəʊ.nəʊ-, krəˈnɒ- US ˈkrɑː.noʊ-, ˈkroʊ.noʊ-, ˈ-nə-, krəˈnɑː-

Note: Prefix. This may take primary or secondary stress on the first syllable (e.g. **chronograph** /ˈkrɒn.əʊ.grɑːf US ˈkrɑː.nə.græf/) or primary stress on the second syllable (e.g. **chronometer** /krəˈnɒm.ɪ.təʳ US krəˈnɑː.mə.t̬ɚ/).

chronogram ˈkrɒn.ə.græm, ˈkrəʊ.nə- US ˈkrɑː.nə-, ˈkroʊ- **-s** -z
chronograph ˈkrɒn.ə.grɑːf, ˈkrəʊ.nə-, -græf US ˈkrɑː.nə.græf, ˈkroʊ- **-s** -s
chronologic ˌkrɒn.əˈlɒdʒ.ɪk US ˌkrɑː.nəˈlɑː.dʒɪk **-al** -ᵊl **-ally** -ᵊl.i, -li
chronolog|y krɒnˈɒl.ə.dʒ|i, krəˈnɒl- US krəˈnɑː.lə-, krɑː- **-ies** -iz **-ist/s** -ɪst/s
chronometer krɒnˈɒm.ɪ.təʳ, krəˈnɒm-, -ə.təʳ US krəˈnɑː.mə.t̬ɚ, krɑː- **-s** -z
chronometric ˌkrɒn.əˈmet.rɪk US ˌkrɑː.nəˈ- **-al** -ᵊl **-ally** -ᵊl.i
chronometry krɒnˈɒm.ɪ.tri, krəˈnɒm-, -ə.tri US krəˈnɑː.mə-, krɑː-
chrysalid ˈkrɪs.ᵊl.ɪd **-s** -z
chrysalides krɪˈsæl.ɪ.diːz, krə-, ˈ-ə-
chrysalis ˈkrɪs.ᵊl.ɪs **-es** -ɪz
chrysanth krɪˈsæntθ, krə-, -ˈzæntθ **-s** -s
chrysanthemum krɪˈsæntθ.ə.məm, krə-, -ˈzæntθ-, ˈ-ɪ- **-s** -z
chryselephantine ˌkrɪs.el.ɪˈfæn.taɪn, -əˈ- US -taɪn, -tiːn, -tɪn
Chrysler® ˈkraɪz.ləʳ US ˈkraɪs.lɚ **-s** -z
chrysolite ˈkrɪs.əʊ.laɪt US ˈ-ə- **-s** -s
chrysopras|e ˈkrɪs.əʊ.preɪz US ˈ-ə- **-es** -ɪz
Chrysostom ˈkrɪs.ə.stəm US ˈkrɪs.ə.stəm, krɪˈsɑː-
Chryston ˈkraɪ.stən
chthonian ˈθəʊ.ni.ən, ˈkθəʊ- US ˈθoʊ-
chthonic ˈθɒn.ɪk, ˈkθɒn- US ˈθɑː.nɪk
chub tʃʌb **-s** -z
Chubb tʃʌb
chubb|y ˈtʃʌb|.i **-ier** -i.əʳ US -i.ɚ **-iest** -i.ɪst, -i.əst **-ily** -ɪ.li, -ᵊl.i **-iness** -ɪ.nəs, -ɪ.nɪs
Chuchulain(n) kuːˈkʌl.ɪn
chuck (C) tʃʌk **-s** -s **-ing** -ɪŋ **-ed** -t ˈ**chuck** ˌ**wagon**
chuckl|e ˈtʃʌk.l̩ **-es** -z **-ing** -ɪŋ, ˈ-lɪŋ **-ed** -d
Chudleigh ˈtʃʌd.li
chuff tʃʌf **-s** -s **-ing** -ɪŋ **-ed** -t
Chuffey ˈtʃʌf.i
chug tʃʌg **-s** -z **-ging** -ɪŋ **-ged** -d
chugalug ˈtʃʌg.ə.lʌg **-s** -z **-ging** -ɪŋ **-ged** -d
chukka ˈtʃʌk.ə **-s** -z
chukker ˈtʃʌk.əʳ US -ɚ **-s** -z
chum tʃʌm **-s** -z **-ming** -ɪŋ **-med** -d
Chumbi ˈtʃʊm.bi
chumm|y ˈtʃʌm|.i **-ier** -i.əʳ US -i.ɚ **-iest** -i.ɪst, -i.əst **-ily** -ɪ.li, -ᵊl.i **-iness** -ɪ.nəs, -ɪ.nɪs
chump tʃʌmp **-s** -s
chund|er ˈtʃʌn.d|əʳ US -d|ɚ **-ers** -əz US -ɚz **-ering** -ᵊr.ɪŋ **-ered** -əd US -ɚd
Chungking ˌtʃʊŋˈkɪŋ, ˌtʃʌŋ- US ˌtʃʊŋˈkɪŋ, ˌtʃʌŋ-, ˌdʒʊŋ-, ˌdʒʌŋ-, -ˈgɪŋ *stress shift:* ˌChungking ˈMansions
chunk tʃʌŋk **-s** -s
chunk|y ˈtʃʌŋ.k|i **-ier** -i.əʳ US -i.ɚ **-iest** -i.ɪst, -i.əst **-ily** -ɪ.li, -ᵊl.i **-iness** -ɪ.nəs, -ɪ.nɪs
Chunnel ˈtʃʌn.ᵊl
chunt|er ˈtʃʌn.t|əʳ US -t̬|ɚ **-ers** -əz US -ɚz **-ering** -ᵊr.ɪŋ **-ered** -əd US -ɚd
church (C) tʃɜːtʃ US tʃɝːtʃ **-es** -ɪz ˌ**Church of** ˈ**England**
Churchdown ˈtʃɜːtʃ.daʊn US ˈtʃɝːtʃ-

Note: There was until recently a local pronunciation /ˈtʃəʊ.zᵊn/, which is preserved as the name of a hill near by, which is now written **Chosen**.

churchgo|er ˈtʃɜːtʃˌgəʊ|.əʳ US ˈtʃɝːtʃˌgoʊ|.ɚ **-ers** -əz US -ɚz **-ing** -ɪŋ
Churchill ˈtʃɜː.tʃɪl US ˈtʃɝː-
Churchillian tʃɜːˈtʃɪl.i.ən US tʃɝː-
church|man (C) ˈtʃɜːtʃ|.mən US ˈtʃɝːtʃ- **-men** -mən
churchwarden ˌtʃɜːtʃˈwɔː.dᵊn US ˌtʃɝːtʃˈwɔːr- **-s** -z *stress shift:* ˌchurchwarden ˈpipe
church|woman ˈtʃɜːtʃ|ˌwʊm.ən US ˈtʃɝːtʃ- **-women** -ˌwɪm.ɪn
church|y ˈtʃɜː.tʃ|i US ˈtʃɝː- **-ier** -i.əʳ US -i.ɚ **-iest** -i.ɪst, -i.əst **-ily** -ɪ.li, -ᵊl.i **-iness** -ɪ.nəs, -ɪ.nɪs
churchyard *outside church:* ˈtʃɜːtʃ.jɑːd US ˈtʃɝːtʃ.jɑːrd **-s** -z

Churchyard *surname:* 'tʃɜː.tʃəd (US) 'tʃɝː.tʃɚd

churl tʃɜːl (US) tʃɝːl **-s** -z

churlish 'tʃɜː.lɪʃ (US) 'tʃɝː- **-ly** -li **-ness** -nəs, -nɪs

churn tʃɜːn (US) tʃɝːn **-s** -z **-ing** -ɪŋ **-ed** -d

chute ʃuːt **-s** -s

Chute tʃuːt

Chuter 'tʃuː.tə^r (US) -t̬ɚ

chutney 'tʃʌt.ni **-s** -z

chutzpa(h) 'hʊt.spɑː, 'xʊt-, -spə

Chuzzlewit 'tʃʌz.l̩.wɪt

chyle kaɪl

chyme kaɪm

CIA ˌsiː.aɪ'eɪ

ciabatta tʃə'bæt.ə, -'bɑː.tə

Cian 'kiː.ən

ciao tʃaʊ

Ciara 'kɪə.rə (US) 'kɪr.ə

Ciaran 'kɪə.r^{ə}n (US) 'kɪr.^{ə}n

Ciba-Geigy® ˌsiː.bə'gaɪ.gi

Cibber 'sɪb.ə^r (US) -ɚ

cibori|um sɪ'bɔː.ri|.əm, sə- (US) -'bɔːr.i- **-ums** -əmz **-a** -ə

cicada sɪ'kɑː.də, -'keɪ- (US) -'keɪ-, -'kɑː- **-s** -z

cicala sɪ'kɑː.lə **-s** -z

cicatric|e 'sɪk.ə.trɪs **-es** -ɪz

cicatrix 'sɪk.ə.trɪks; sə'keɪ-, sɪ- **cicatrices** ˌsɪk.ə'traɪ.siːz; sə'keɪ.trɪ-, sɪ-

cicatriz|e, -is|e 'sɪk.ə.traɪz **-es** -ɪz **-ing** -ɪŋ **-ed** -d

cicel|y (C) 'sɪs.^{ə}l|.i, -ɪ.l|i **-ies** -iz

Cicero 'sɪs.^{ə}r.əʊ (US) -ə.roʊ

cicerone ˌtʃɪtʃ.ə'rəʊ.ni, ˌsɪs.ə'-, ˌtʃiː.tʃə'- (US) ˌsɪs.ə'roʊ- **-s** -z

Ciceronian ˌsɪs.^{ə}r'əʊ.ni.ən (US) -ə'roʊ- **-s** -z

cicisbe|o ˌtʃɪtʃ.ɪz'beɪ|.əʊ (US) sɪ'sɪs.biː|.oʊ **-i** -iː

Cid sɪd

CID ˌsiː.aɪ'diː

-cidal -'saɪ.d^{ə}l

-cide -saɪd

cider 'saɪ.də^r (US) -dɚ **-s** -z **'cider-ˌcup**

cig sɪg **-s** -z

cigar sɪ'gɑː^r, sə- (US) -gɑːr **-s** -z ci'gar-ˌshaped

cigarette ˌsɪg.^{ə}r'et, '--- (US) ˌsɪg.ə'ret **-s** -s **ciga'rette ˌholder** (US) **'cigarette ˌholder; ciga'rette ˌlighter** (US) **'cigarette ˌlighter**

cigarillo ˌsɪg.ə'rɪl.əʊ (US) -oʊ **-s** -z

cigg|y, cigg|ie 'sɪg|.i **-ies** -iz

cilantro sɪ'læn.trəʊ, sə- (US) -'lɑːn.troʊ, -'læn-

cilia 'sɪl.i.ə

ciliary 'sɪl.i.^{ə}r.i (US) -er-

cilic|e 'sɪl.ɪs **-es** -ɪz

Cilicia saɪ'lɪʃ.i.ə, sɪ-, -'lɪs- (US) sə'lɪʃ.ə

cilium 'sɪl.i.əm

Cilla 'sɪl.ə

Ciller 'sɪl.ə^r (US) -ɚ

Cimabue ˌtʃɪm.ə'buː.eɪ, ˌtʃiː.mə'-, -i

Cimmeri|an sɪ'mɪə.ri|.ən (US) -'mɪr.i- **-i** -aɪ

C-in-C ˌsiː.ɪn'siː **-s** -z

cinch sɪntʃ **-es** -ɪz **-ing** -ɪŋ **-ed** -d

cinchona sɪŋ'kəʊ.nə (US) -'koʊ-, sɪn- **-s** -z

cinchonic sɪŋ'kɒn.ɪk (US) -'kɑː.nɪk, sɪn-

Cincinnati ˌsɪn*t*.sɪ'næt.i, -sə'- (US) -'næt̬-

Cincinnatus ˌsɪn*t*.sɪ'nɑː.təs, -'neɪ- (US) -'næt̬.əs-, -'nɑː.t̬əs, -'neɪ-

cincture 'sɪŋ*k*.tʃə^r (US) -tʃɚ **-s** -z

cinder 'sɪn.də^r (US) -dɚ **-s** -z **'cinder ˌblock; 'cinder ˌpath; 'cinder ˌtrack**

Cinderella ˌsɪn.d^{ə}r'el.ə

Cinderford 'sɪn.də.fəd (US) -dɚ.fɚd

Cindy 'sɪn.di

cine- 'sɪn.i-

cinecamera 'sɪn.iˌkæm.^{ə}r.ə, -ˌkæm.rə, ˌsɪn.i'kæm- **-s** -z

cinefilm 'sɪn.i.fɪlm **-s** -z

cinema 'sɪn.ə.mə, '-ɪ-, -mɑː (US) -mə **-s** -z

cinemago|er 'sɪn.ə.məˌgəʊ|.ə^r, '-ɪ- (US) -goʊ|.ɚ **-ers** -əz (US) -ɚz **-ing** -ɪŋ

CinemaScope® 'sɪn.ə.mə.skəʊp, '-ɪ- (US) -skoʊp **-s** -s

cinematic ˌsɪn.ɪ'mæt.ɪk, -ə'- (US) -ə'mæt̬- **-ally** -^{ə}l.i, -li

cinematograph ˌsɪn.ɪ'mæt.ə.grɑːf, -ə'-, -græf (US) -ə'mæt̬.ə.græf **-s** -s

cinematographic ˌsɪn.ɪ.mæt.ə'græf.ɪk, ˌ-ə-; sɪ.nɪˌmæt- (US) ˌsɪn.əˌmæt̬- **-al** -^{ə}l **-ally** -^{ə}l.i, -li

cinematograph|y ˌsɪn.ɪ.mə'tɒg.rə.f|i, ˌ-ə- (US) -ə.mə'tɑː.grə- **-er/s** -ə^r/z (US) -ɚ/z

cinema verité ˌsɪn.ɪ.mɑː'ver.ɪ.teɪ, ˌ-ə-, -ə.mə'- (US) ˌsɪn.ɪ.mɑː.ver.ə'teɪ, -mə'ver.ə.teɪ

cine-projector 'sɪn.i.prəˌdʒek.tə^r (US) -tɚ **-s** -z

Cinerama® ˌsɪn.ə'rɑː.mə, -ɪ'- (US) -ə'rɑː-, -'ræm.ə

cineraria ˌsɪn.ə'reə.ri.ə (US) -'rer.i- **-s** -z

cinerari|um ˌsɪn.ə'reə.ri|.əm (US) -'rer.i- **-a** -ə

cinerary 'sɪn.ə.r^{ə}r.i (US) -rer-

cineration ˌsɪn.ə'reɪ.ʃ^{ə}n

cinnabar 'sɪn.ə.bɑː^r (US) -bɑːr

cinnamon 'sɪn.ə.mən

cinque (C) sɪŋk **'Cinque ˌPorts**

Cinquecento® ˌtʃɪŋ.kweɪ'tʃen.təʊ, -kwɪ'- (US) -toʊ

cinquefoil 'sɪŋk.fɔɪl

Cinzano® tʃɪn'zɑː.nəʊ, sɪn-, tʃɪnt'sɑː-, sɪnt'sɑː- (US) -noʊ

ciph|er 'saɪ.f|ə^r (US) -f|ɚ **-ers** -əz (US) -ɚz **-ering** -^{ə}r.ɪŋ **-ered** -əd (US) -ɚd **'cipher ˌkey**

Cipriani ˌsɪp.ri'ɑː.ni

circa 'sɜː.kə (US) 'sɝː-

circadian sɜː'keɪ.di.ən, sə- (US) sɚ-; ˌsɝː.kə'diː.ən

Circassi|a sɜː'kæs.i|.ə, sə-, -'kæʃ|.ə, -i|.ə (US) sɚ- **-an/s** -ən/z

Circe 'sɜː.si (US) 'sɝː-

circl|e 'sɜː.kl̩ (US) 'sɝː- **-es** -z **-ing** -ɪŋ, '-klɪŋ (US) '-kl̩.ɪŋ, '-klɪŋ **-ed** -d

circlet 'sɜː.klət, -klɪt (US) 'sɝː- **-s** -s

circuit 'sɜː.kɪt (US) 'sɝː- **-s** -s **-ry** -ri **'circuit ˌbreaker; 'circuit ˌtraining**

circuitous sə'kjuː.ɪ.təs, sɜː-, '-ə- (US) sɚ'kjuː.ə.t̬əs **-ly** -li **-ness** -nəs, -nɪs

circular 'sɜː.kjə.lə^r, -kjʊ- (US) 'sɝː.kjə.lɚ **-s** -z **'circular ˌsaw, ˌcircular 'saw**

circularity ˌsɜː.kjə'lær.ə.ti, -kjʊ'-, -ɪ.ti (US) -kjə'ler.ə.t̬i, -'lær-

circulariz|e, -is|e 'sɜː.kjə.l^{ə}r.aɪz, -kjʊ- (US) 'sɝː.kjə.lə.raɪz **-es** -ɪz **-ing** -ɪŋ **-ed** -d

circu|late 'sɜː.kjə|.leɪt, -kjʊ- (US) 'sɝː.kjə- **-lates** -leɪts **-lating** -leɪ.tɪŋ (US) -leɪ.t̬ɪŋ **-lated** -leɪ.tɪd (US) -leɪ.t̬ɪd **-lator/s** -leɪ.tə^r/z (US) -leɪ.t̬ɚ/z

circulation ˌsɜː.kjə'leɪ.ʃ^{ə}n, -kjʊ'- (US) ˌsɝː- **-s** -z

circulatory ˌsɜː.kjə'leɪ.t^{ə}r.i, -kjʊ'-, -tri; 'sɜː.kjə.lə-, -kjʊ- (US) 'sɝː.kjə.lə.tɔːr.i

circum- 'sɜː.kəm-, sə'kʌm- (US) 'sɝː.kəm-, sɚ'kʌm-

Note: Prefix. This may have primary or secondary stress on the first syllable, e.g. **circumstance** /'sɜː.kəm.stɑːn*t*s (US) 'sɜːr.kəm.stæns/ or on the second syllable, e.g. **circumference** /sə'kʌm*p*.f^{ə}r.^{ə}n*t*s (US) sɚ- /.

circumambient ˌsɜː.kəm'æm.bi.ənt (US) ˌsɝː-

circumambu|late ˌsɜː.kəm'æm.bjə|.leɪt, -bjʊ- (US) ˌsɝː.kəm'æm.bjə- **-lates** -leɪts **-lating** -leɪ.tɪŋ (US) -leɪ.t̬ɪŋ **-lated** -leɪ.tɪd (US) -leɪ.t̬ɪd

circumcis|e 'sɜː.kəm.saɪz (US) 'sɝː- **-es** -ɪz **-ing** -ɪŋ **-ed** -d

circumcision ˌsɜː.kəm'sɪʒ.^{ə}n (US) ˌsɝː- **-s** -z

circumferenc|e sə'kʌm*p*.f^{ə}r.^{ə}n*t*s (US) sɚ- **-es** -ɪz

circumferential səˌkʌm*p*.f^ə'ren.*t*ʃ^{ə}l (US) sɚˌkʌm*p*.fɚ'ren*t*.ʃ^{ə}l

circumflex 'sɜː.kəm.fleks (US) 'sɝː- **-es** -ɪz

circumlocution ˌsɜː.kəm.lə'kjuː.ʃ^{ə}n (US) ˌsɝː- **-s** -z

circumlocutory ˌsɜː.kəm.lə'kjuː.t^{ə}r.i,

-tri; -ˈlɒk.jʊ- (US) ˌsɝː.kəmˈlɑː.kjuː.tɔːr.i

circumnavi|gate ˌsɜː.kəmˈnæv.ɪ|.geɪt (US) ˌsɝː- **-gates** -geɪts **-gating** -geɪ.tɪŋ (US) -geɪ.t̬ɪŋ **-gated** -geɪ.tɪd (US) -geɪ.t̬ɪd **-gator/s** -geɪ.təʳ/z (US) -geɪ.t̬ɚ/z

circumnavigation ˌsɜː.kəmˌnæv.ɪˈgeɪ.ʃᵊn (US) ˌsɝː- **-s** -z

circumpolar ˌsɜː.kəmˈpəʊ.ləʳ (US) ˌsɝː.kəmˈpoʊ.lɚ

circumscrib|e ˈsɜː.kəm.skraɪb, ˌ--ˈ- (US) ˈsɝː-, ˌ--ˈ- **-es** -z **-ing** -ɪŋ **-ed** -d

circumscription ˌsɜː.kəmˈskrɪp.ʃᵊn (US) ˌsɝː- **-s** -z

circumspect ˈsɜː.kəm.spekt (US) ˈsɝː- **-ly** -li **-ness** -nəs, -nɪs

circumspection ˌsɜː.kəmˈspek.ʃᵊn (US) ˌsɝː-

circumstanc|e ˈsɜː.kəm.stæn*t*s, -stən*t*s, -stɑːn*t*s (US) ˈsɝː.kəm.stæn*t*s, -stən*t*s **-es** -ɪz **-ed** -t

circumstantial ˌsɜː.kəmˈstæn.*t*ʃᵊl (US) ˌsɝː.kəmˈstæn*t*.ʃᵊl **-ly** -i ˌcircumstantial ˈevidence

circumstantiality ˌsɜː.kəmˌstæn.*t*ʃiˈæl.ə.ti, -ɪ.ti (US) ˌsɝː.kəmˌstæn*t*.ʃiˈæl.ə.t̬i

circumstanti|ate ˌsɜː.kəmˈstæn.*t*ʃi|.eɪt (US) ˌsɝː.kəmˈstæn*t*.ʃi- **-ates** -eɪts **-ating** -eɪ.tɪŋ (US) -eɪ.t̬ɪŋ **-ated** -eɪ.tɪd (US) -eɪ.t̬ɪd

circumvallation ˌsɜː.kəm.vəˈleɪ.ʃᵊn, -vælˈeɪ- (US) ˌsɝː- **-s** -z

circum|vent ˌsɜː.kəm|ˈvent, ˈ--|- (US) ˌsɝː- **-vents** -ˈvents **-venting** -ˈven.tɪŋ (US) -ˈven.t̬ɪŋ **-vented** -ˈven.tɪd (US) -ˈven.t̬ɪd

circumvention ˌsɜː.kəmˈven.*t*ʃᵊn (US) ˌsɝː.kəmˈven*t*.ʃᵊn **-s** -z

circus (C) ˈsɜː.kəs (US) ˈsɝː- **-es** -ɪz

Cirencester ˈsaɪə.rᵊn.ses.təʳ, ˈsɪs.ɪ.təʳ, -stəʳ (US) ˈsaɪ.rᵊn.ses.tɚ

Note: The pronunciation most usually heard in the town is /ˈsaɪə.rᵊn.ses.təʳ/ (or /-tər/ with the dialectal retroflex /r/).

cirque sɜːk, sɪək (US) sɝːk **-s** -s

cirrhosis sɪˈrəʊ.sɪs, sə- (US) səˈroʊ-

cirrocumulus ˌsɪr.əʊˈkjuː.mjə.ləs, -mjʊ- (US) -oʊˈkjuː.mjə-

cirrostratus ˌsɪr.əʊˈstrɑː.təs, -ˈstreɪ- (US) -oʊˈstreɪ.t̬əs, -ˈstræt̬.əs

cirrus ˈsɪr.əs

CIS ˌsiː.aɪˈes

Cisalpine sɪˈsæl.paɪn

Cisco® ˈsɪs.kəʊ (US) -koʊ

Ciskei sɪˈskaɪ, ˈsɪs.kaɪ (US) ˈsɪs.kaɪ

Cissie ˈsɪs.i

cissoid ˈsɪs.ɔɪd **-s** -z

cissy (C) ˈsɪs.i

cist sɪst **-s** -s

Cistercian sɪˈstɜː.ʃᵊn, sə- (US) -ˈstɝː- **-s** -z

cistern ˈsɪs.tən (US) -tɚn **-s** -z

cistus ˈsɪs.təs **-es** -ɪz

citadel ˈsɪt.ə.del, -dᵊl (US) ˈsɪt̬- **-s** -z

citation saɪˈteɪ.ʃᵊn **-s** -z

citatory ˈsaɪ.tə.tᵊr.i, ˈsɪ-, -tri; saɪˈteɪ- (US) ˈsaɪ.t̬ə.tɔːr.i

cit|e saɪt **-es** -s **-ing** -ɪŋ (US) ˈsaɪ.t̬ɪŋ **-ed** -ɪd (US) ˈsaɪ.t̬ɪd

cithar|a ˈsɪθ.ᵊr|.ə **-ae** -iː

cither ˈsɪθ.əʳ (US) -ɚ, ˈsɪð- **-s** -z

Citibank® ˈsɪt.i.bæŋk (US) ˈsɪt̬-

citizen ˈsɪt.ɪ.zᵊn, ˈ-ə- (US) ˈsɪt̬- **-s** -z ˌcitizen's arˈrest

citizenry ˈsɪt.ɪ.zᵊn.ri, ˈ-ə- (US) ˈsɪt̬-

citizenship ˈsɪt.ɪ.zᵊn.ʃɪp, ˈ-ə- (US) ˈsɪt̬-

citole ˈsɪt.əʊl, sɪˈtəʊl (US) ˈsɪt.oʊl, sɪˈtoʊl **-s** -z

citrate ˈsɪt.reɪt, ˈsaɪ.treɪt, -trɪt **-s** -s

citric ˈsɪt.rɪk ˌcitric ˈacid

citrine sɪˈtriːn, sə-

Citroën® ˈsɪt.rəʊən, ˈsɪt.rᵊn (US) ˌsɪt.roʊˈen, ˌsiː.troʊˈ- **-s** -z

citron ˈsɪt.rᵊn **-s** -z

citronella ˌsɪt.rᵊnˈel.ə (US) -rəˈnel-

citrous ˈsɪt.rəs

citrus ˈsɪt.rəs **-es** -ɪz ˈcitrus ˌfruit

cittern ˈsɪt.ɜːn, -ən (US) ˈsɪt̬.ɚn **-s** -z

cit|y (C) ˈsɪt|.i (US) ˈsɪt̬|.i **-ies** -iz ˌcity ˈfather; ˌcity ˈgent; ˌcity ˈhall; ˌcity ˈslicker (US) ˈcity ˌslicker

city-dweller ˈsɪt.iˌdwel.əʳ (US) ˈsɪt̬.iˌdwel.ɚ **-s** -z

citywide ˌsɪt.iˈwaɪd (US) ˈsɪt̬- *stress shift, British only:* ˌcitywide ˈmeetings

Ciudad Bolívar θjʊˌdɑːd.bɒlˈiː.vɑːʳ, θiː.ʊˌdɑːd- (US) sjuːˌdɑːd.boʊˈliː.vɑːr, ˌsiː.uː-

Ciudad Guayana θjʊˌdɑːd.gwaɪˈjɑː.nə, θiː.ʊˌdɑːd- (US) sjuːˌdɑːd.gəˈ-, ˌsiː.uː-, -gwəˈ-, -gwɑːˈ-

Ciudad Juárez θjʊˌdɑːdˈhwɑː.rez, θiː.ʊ-, -ˈwɑː- (US) sjuːˌdɑːdˈhwɑːr.es, ˌsiː.uː-, -ˈwɑːr.eʒ

civet ˈsɪv.ɪt **-s** -s

civic ˈsɪv.ɪk **-s** -s ˌcivic ˈcentre (US) ˈcivic ˌcenter

civil ˈsɪv.ᵊl, -ɪl **-ly** -i ˌcivil deˈfence; ˌcivil disoˈbedience; ˌcivil engiˈneer; ˌcivil engiˈneering; ˌcivil ˈliberty; ˌcivil ˈrights ˌmovement; ˌcivil ˈservant; ˌcivil ˈservice; ˌcivil ˈwar

civilian sɪˈvɪl.i.ən, sə- (US) ˈ-jən **-s** -z

civilit|y sɪˈvɪl.ə.t|i, sə-, -ɪ.t|i (US) -ə.t̬|i **-ies** -iz

civilizable, -isa- ˈsɪv.ɪ.laɪ.zə.bl̩, ˈ-ə-

civilization, -isa- ˌsɪv.ᵊl.aɪˈzeɪ.ʃᵊn, -ɪ.laɪˈ-, -lɪˈ- (US) -ᵊl.ɪˈ- **-s** -z

civiliz|e, -is|e ˈsɪv.ᵊl.aɪz, -ɪ.laɪz (US) -ə.laɪz, ˈ-ɪ- **-es** -ɪz **-ing** -ɪŋ **-ed** -d

civitas ˈsɪv.ɪ.tæs, ˈkɪv-

civv|y ˈsɪv|.i **-ies** -iz ˈcivvy ˌstreet

CJD ˌsiː.dʒeɪˈdiː

cl *(abbrev. for* **centilitre/s***) singular:* ˈsen.tɪˌliː.təʳ (US) -t̬əˌliː.t̬ɚ *plural:* -z

clack klæk **-s** -s **-ing** -ɪŋ **-ed** -t

Clackmannan klækˈmæn.ən **-shire** -ʃəʳ, -ˌʃɪəʳ (US) -ʃɚ, -ˌʃɪr

Clacton ˈklæk.tən

clad klæd

cladding ˈklæd.ɪŋ

cladistics kləˈdɪs.tɪks, klædˈɪs-

Claggart ˈklæg.ət (US) -ɚt

Claiborne ˈkleɪ.bɔːn (US) -bɔːrn

claim kleɪm **-s** -z **-ing** -ɪŋ **-ed** -d

claimant ˈkleɪ.mənt **-s** -s

claimer ˈkleɪ.məʳ (US) -mɚ **-s** -z

clairaudien|ce ˌkleəˈrɔː.di.ən|*t*s (US) ˌklerˈɑː-, -ˈɔː- **-t** -t

Claire kleəʳ (US) kler

Clairol® ˈkleə.rɒl (US) ˈkler.ɑːl

clairvoyan|ce ˌkleəˈvɔɪ.ən*t*|s (US) ˌkler- **-cy** -si

clairvoyant ˌkleəˈvɔɪ.ənt (US) ˌkler- **-s** -s

clam klæm **-s** -z **-ming** -ɪŋ **-med** -d

clamant ˈkleɪ.mənt, ˈklæm.ənt **-ly** -li

clambake ˈklæm.beɪk **-s** -s

clamb|er ˈklæm.b|əʳ (US) -b|ɚ **-ers** -əz (US) -ɚz **-ering** -ᵊr.ɪŋ **-ered** -əd (US) -ɚd

clamm|y ˈklæm|.i **-ier** -i.əʳ (US) -i.ɚ **-iest** -i.ɪst, -i.əst **-ily** -ɪ.li, -ᵊl.i **-iness** -ɪ.nəs, -ɪ.nɪs

clam|or ˈklæm|.əʳ (US) -ɚ **-ors** -əz (US) -ɚz **-oring** -ᵊr.ɪŋ **-ored** -əd (US) -ɚd **-orer/s** -ᵊr.əʳ/z (US) -ɚ.ɚ/z

clamorous ˈklæm.ᵊr.əs **-ly** -li **-ness** -nəs, -nɪs

clam|our ˈklæm|.əʳ (US) -ɚ **-ours** -əz (US) -ɚz **-ouring** -ᵊr.ɪŋ **-oured** -əd (US) -ɚd **-ourer/s** -ᵊr.əʳ/z (US) -ɚ.ɚ/z

clamp klæmp **-s** -s **-ing** -ɪŋ **-ed** -t

clampdown ˈklæmp.daʊn **-s** -z

Pronouncing the letters CK

The consonant digraph **ck** only has one possible realisation in English words: /k/, e.g.:

sock /sɒk/ (US) /sɑːk/

clan klæn -s -z

clandestine klæn'des.tɪn, -taɪn, 'klæn.dɪs- US klæn'des.tɪn -ly -li

clang klæŋ -s -z -ing -ɪŋ -ed -d

clanger 'klæŋ.ə^r US -ɚ -s -z

clangor 'klæŋ.gə^r, -ə^r US -ɚ, -gɚ

clangorous 'klæŋ.g^{ə}r.əs, -^{ə}r- US '-ɚ-, -gɚ- -ly -li

clangour 'klæŋ.gə^r, -ə^r US -ɚ, -gɚ

clank klæŋk -s -s -ing -ɪŋ -ed -t

Clanmaurice klæn'mɒr.ɪs, klæm- US -'mɔːr-, -'mɑːr-

Clanmorris klæn'mɒr.ɪs, klæm- US klæn'mɔːr-

clannish 'klæn.ɪʃ -ly -li -ness -nəs, -nɪs

Clanricarde klæn'rɪk.əd US -ɚd

clanship 'klæn.ʃɪp

clans|man 'klænz|.mən -men -mən

clap klæp -s -s -ping -ɪŋ -ped -t ˌclapped 'out *stress shift:* ˌclapped-out 'car

clapboard 'klæp.bɔːd US -bɔːrd; 'klæb.ɚd -s -z

Clapham 'klæp.^{ə}m ˌClapham 'omnibus

clapometer klæp'ɒm.ɪ.tə^r US -'ɑː.mə.t̬ɚ -s -z

clapper 'klæp.ə^r US -ɚ -s -z

clapperboard 'klæp.ə.bɔːd US -ɚ.bɔːrd -s -z

Clapton 'klæp.tən

claptrap 'klæp.træp

claque klæk -s -s

Clara 'klɑː.rə, 'kleə- US 'kler.ə, 'klær-

clarabella (C) ˌklær.ə'bel.ə US ˌkler-, ˌklær- -s -z

Clare kleə^r US kler

Clarel 'kleə.r^{ə}l US 'kler.^{ə}l, 'klær.^{ə}l; klə'rel

Claremont 'kleə.mɒnt, -mənt US 'kler.mɑːnt

Clarence 'klær.^{ə}n*t*s US 'kler-, 'klær-

Clarenc(i)eux 'klær.^{ə}n.suː, -sjuː US 'kler-, 'klær-

clarendon (C) 'klær.^{ə}n.dən US 'kler-, 'klær-

claret 'klær.ət, -ɪt US 'kler-, 'klær- -s -s

Clarges 'klɑː.dʒɪz, -dʒəz US 'klɑːr-

Clarice 'klær.ɪs US 'kler-, 'klær-; kler'iːs, klær-

Claridge 'klær.ɪdʒ US 'kler-, 'klær- -'s -ɪz

clarification ˌklær.ɪ.fɪ'keɪ.ʃ^{ə}n, ˌ-ə- US ˌkler-, ˌklær- -s -z

clari|fy 'klær.ɪ|.faɪ, '-ə- US 'kler-, 'klær- -fies -faɪz -fying -faɪ.ɪŋ -fied -faɪd -fier/s -faɪ.ə^r/z US -faɪ.ɚ/z

Clarina klə'raɪ.nə

clarinet ˌklær.ɪ'net, -ə'- US ˌkler-, ˌklær- -s -s

clarinet(t)ist ˌklær.ɪ'net.ɪst, -ə'- US ˌkler.ə'net̬-, ˌklær- -s -s

clarion 'klær.i.ən US 'kler-, 'klær- -s -z 'clarion ˌcall

Clarissa klə'rɪs.ə, klær'ɪs- US klə'rɪs-

clarity 'klær.ə.ti, -ɪ.ti US 'kler.ə.t̬i, 'klær-

Clark(e) klɑːk US klɑːrk

clarkia 'klɑː.ki.ə US 'klɑːr- -s -z

Clarkson 'klɑːk.s^{ə}n US 'klɑːrk-

Clarrie 'klær.i US 'kler-, 'klær-

Clary 'kleə.ri US 'kler.i, 'klær-

clash klæʃ -es -ɪz -ing -ɪŋ -ed -t

clasp klɑːsp US klæsp -s -s -ing -ɪŋ -ed -t 'clasp ˌknife

class klɑːs US klæs -es -ɪz -ing -ɪŋ -ed -t 'class ˌsystem; 'class ˌwar; ˌclass 'war

class-conscious 'klɑːsˌkɒn.*t*ʃəs, ˌ-'-- US 'klæsˌkɑːn*t*.ʃəs -ness -nəs, -nɪs

classic 'klæs.ɪk -s -s

classic|al 'klæs.ɪ.k|^{ə}l, '-ə- -ally -^{ə}l.i, -li -alness -^{ə}l.nəs, -nɪs ˌclassical 'music

classicism 'klæs.ɪ.sɪ.z^{ə}m, '-ə- -s -z

classicist 'klæs.ɪ.sɪst, '-ə- -s -s

classifiable 'klæs.ɪ.faɪ.ə.bl̩, ˌklæs.ɪ'faɪ- US 'klæs.ə.faɪ-

classification ˌklæs.ɪ.fɪ'keɪ.ʃ^{ə}n, ˌ-ə- US ˌ-ə- -s -z

classificatory ˌklæs.ɪ.fɪ'keɪ.t^{ə}r.i, ˌ-ə-, -tri; 'klæs.ɪ.fɪ.kə-, '-ə- US 'klæs.ə.fɪ.kə.tɔːr.i; klə'sɪf.ə-

classi|fy 'klæs.ɪ|.faɪ, '-ə- -fies -faɪz -fying -faɪ.ɪŋ -fied -faɪd -fier/s -faɪ.ə^r/z US -faɪ.ɚ/z ˌclassified 'ad US 'classified ˌad; ˌclassified infor'mation

class|ism 'klɑː.s|ɪ.z^{ə}m US 'klæs|.ɪ- -ist/s -ɪst/s

classless 'klɑːs.ləs, -lɪs US 'klæs- -ness -nəs, -nɪs

class|man 'klɑːs|.mæn, -mən US 'klæs- -men -men, -mən

classmate 'klɑːs.meɪt US 'klæs- -s -s

classroom 'klɑːs.rʊm, -ruːm US 'klæs.ruːm, -rʊm -s -z

classwork 'klɑːs.wɜːk US 'klæs.wɝːk

class|y 'klɑː.s|i US 'klæs|.i -ier -i.ə^r US -i.ɚ -iest -i.ɪst, -i.əst -ily -ɪ.li, -^{ə}l.i -iness -ɪ.nəs, -ɪ.nɪs

clatt|er 'klæt|.ə^r US 'klæt̬|.ɚ -ers -əz US -ɚz -ering -^{ə}r.ɪŋ -ered -əd US -ɚd

Claud(e) klɔːd US klɑːd, klɔːd

Claudette klɔː'det US klɑː-, klɔː-

Claudi|a 'klɔː.di|.ə, 'klaʊ- US 'klɑː-, 'klɔː-, 'klaʊ- -an -ən

Claudine klɔː'diːn US klɑː-, klɔː-

Claudio 'klaʊ.di.əʊ, 'klɔː- US 'klɑː.di.oʊ, 'klɔː-, 'klaʊ-

Claudius 'klɔː.di.əs US 'klɑː-, 'klɔː-

claus|e klɔːz US klɑːz, klɔːz -es -ɪz -al -^{ə}l

Clausewitz 'klaʊ.sə.vɪts, -zə-

claustral 'klɔː.str^{ə}l US 'klɑː-, 'klɔː-

claustrophob|ia ˌklɔː.strə'fəʊ.b|i.ə, ˌklɒs.trə- US ˌklɑː.strə'foʊ-, ˌklɔː- -ic -ɪk

clave *(archaic past of* **cleave***)* kleɪv

clavecin 'klæv.sɪn, -ə.sɪn, '-ɪ- -s -z

Claverhouse 'kleɪ.və.haʊs US -vɚ-

Clavering 'kleɪ.v^{ə}r.ɪŋ, 'klæv.^{ə}r-

clavichord 'klæv.ɪ.kɔːd US -kɔːrd -s -z

clavicle 'klæv.ɪ.kl̩ -s -z

clavicular klə'vɪk.jʊ.lə^r, klæv'ɪk-, -jə- US -jə.lɚ

clavier *keyboard:* 'klæv.i.ə^r; klæv'ɪə^r, klə'vɪə^r US 'klæv.i.ɚ; klə'vɪr -s -z *instrument:* klə'vɪə^r, klæv'ɪə^r US 'klæv.i.ɚ; klə'vɪr -s -z

claw klɔː US klɑː, klɔː -s -z -ing -ɪŋ -ed -d

clawback 'klɔː.bæk US 'klɑː-, 'klɔː- -s -s

Claxton 'klæk.st^{ə}n

clay (C) kleɪ -s -z ˌclay 'pigeon

Clayden, Claydon 'kleɪ.d^{ə}n

clayey 'kleɪ.i

Clayhanger 'kleɪ.hæŋ.ə^r US -ɚ

claymore 'kleɪ.mɔː^r US -mɔːr -s -z

Clayton 'kleɪ.t^{ə}n

Clayton-le-Moors ˌkleɪ.t^{ə}n.li'mɔː^r US -'mɔːr

clean kliːn -s -z -ing -ɪŋ -ed -d -est -ɪst, -əst -ly -li -ness -nəs, -nɪs

clean-cut ˌkliːn'kʌt, ˌkliːŋ- US ˌkliːn- *stress shift:* ˌclean-cut 'image

cleaner 'kliː.nə^r US -nɚ -s -z

cleanliness 'klen.lɪ.nəs, -nɪs

cleanl|y 'kliːn.l|i -ier -i.ə^r US -i.ɚ -iest -i.ɪst, -i.əst

cleans|e klenz -es -ɪz -ing -ɪŋ -ed -d -er/s -ə^r/z US -ɚ/z -able -ə.bl̩

cleanshaven ˌkliːn'ʃeɪ.v^{ə}n *stress shift:* ˌcleanshaven 'chin

clean-up 'kliːn.ʌp -s -s

clear klɪə^r US klɪr -er -ə^r US -ɚ -est -ɪst, -əst -ly -li -ness -nəs, -nɪs -s -z -ing -ɪŋ -ed -d ˌclear-'headed US 'clear-ˌheaded *stress shift, British only:* ˌclear-headed 'thinking ˌclear-'sighted US 'clear-ˌsighted *stress shift, British only:* ˌclear-sighted 'planning

clearage 'klɪə.rɪdʒ US 'klɪr.ɪdʒ

clearanc|e 'klɪə.r^{ə}n*t*s US 'klɪr.^{ə}n*t*s -es -ɪz 'clearance ˌsale

clear-cut ˌklɪə'kʌt US ˌklɪr- *stress shift:* ˌclear-cut 'difference

clearing-hou|se 'klɪə.rɪŋ.haʊ|s US 'klɪr.ɪŋ- -ses -zɪz

clearout 'klɪə.raʊt US 'klɪr- -s -s

clearway 'klɪə.weɪ US 'klɪr- -s -z

Cleary 'klɪə.ri US 'klɪr.i

cleat kliːt -s -s

Cleator Moor ˌkliː.tə'mɔː^r US -tɚ'mɔːr

cleavag|e 'kliː.vɪdʒ -es -ɪz

cleav|e kliːv -es -z -ing -ɪŋ -ed -d clove kləʊv US kloʊv cleft kleft cloven 'kləʊ.v^{ə}n US 'kloʊ- clave kleɪv

Clear l

A type of LATERAL sound in which the air escapes past the sides of the tongue, found normally only before vowels. Usually contrasted with DARK L.

Examples for English

In the case of an alveolar lateral (e.g. English /l/) the blade of the tongue (the part further back than the tip) is in contact with the alveolar ridge, but the rest of the tongue is free to take up different shapes. One possibility is for the front of the tongue (the part behind the blade) to be raised in the same shape as that for a close front vowel [i]. This gives the /l/ an [i]-like sound, and the result is a "clear l". It is found in BBC English only before vowels, but in some other accents, notably Irish and Welsh ones, it is found is all positions. However, the variant most often found in all positions is "DARK L", e.g.:

pill /pɪl/ [pʰɪɫ]

cleaver (C) ˈkliː.vəʳ US -vɚ -s -z
Cleckheaton klekˈhiː.tᵊn US -t̬ᵊn
Clee kliː
cleek kliːk -s -s -ing -ɪŋ -ed -t
Cleese kliːz
Cleethorpes ˈkliː.θɔːps US -θɔːrps
clef klef -s -s
cleft kleft -s -s ˌcleft ˈpalate
cleg kleg -s -z
Clegg kleg
Cleland ˈklel.ənd, ˈkliː.lənd
Clem klem
clematis ˈklem.ə.tɪs; klɪˈmeɪ.tɪs, klə-, klemˈeɪ- US ˈklem.ə.t̬əs; kləˈmæt̬.əs, -ˈmɑː.t̬əs
Clemence ˈklem.ənts
Clemenceau ˈklem.ən.səʊ, -ɑ̃ːn- US -soʊ
clemency ˈklem.ənt.si
Clemens ˈklem.ənz
clement (C) ˈklem.ənt -ly -li
Clementi klɪˈmen.ti, klə-, klemˈen- US -t̬i
Clementina ˌklem.ənˈtiː.nə
clementine (C) ˈklem.ən.tiːn, -taɪn US -taɪn, -tiːn -s -z
Clements ˈklem.ᵊnts
Clemo ˈklem.əʊ US -oʊ
clench klentʃ -es -ɪz -ing -ɪŋ -ed -t
Cleo ˈkliː.əʊ US -oʊ
Cleobury *places in Shropshire:* ˈklɪb.ᵊr.i, ˈkleb-, ˈklɪə.bᵊr- US -er-, ˈ-ɚ-
Cleobury *surname:* ˈkləʊ.bᵊr.i, ˈkliː- US ˈkloʊ.ber-, ˈkliː-, -bɚ-
Cleopatra ˌkli.əˈpæt.rə, -ˈpɑː.trə US ˌkli.oʊˈpæt.rə, -əˈ-, -ˈpeɪ.trə, -ˈpɑː-
clepsydr|a ˈklep.sɪ.dr|ə, klepˈsɪd.r|ə US ˈklep.sɪ.dr|ə -ae -iː
clerestor|y ˈklɪə.stɔː.r|i, -stə- US ˈklɪr.stɔːr|.i -ies -iz
clergy ˈklɜː.dʒi US ˈklɝː-
clergy|man ˈklɜː.dʒɪ|.mən US ˈklɝː- -men -mən
clergy|woman ˈklɜː.dʒɪ|ˌwʊm.ən US ˈklɝː- -women -ˌwɪm.ɪn
cleric ˈkler.ɪk -s -s
clerical ˈkler.ɪ.kᵊl -s -z -ly -i
Clerides klerˈiː.diːz, kləˈriː- US klerˈiː.ðiːz, -diːz
clerihew (C) ˈkler.ɪ.hjuː, ˈ-ə- US ˈ-ə- -s -z
clerisy ˈkler.ɪ.si, ˈ-ə- US ˈ-ə-
clerk (C) klɑːk US klɝːk -s -s
Clerke klɑːk US klɝːk, klɑːrk
Clerkenwell ˈklɑː.kᵊn.wel, -wəl US ˈklɝː-, ˈklɑːr-
clerkship ˈklɑːk.ʃɪp US ˈklɝːk- -s -s
Clermont *towns in Ireland, village in Norfolk:* ˈkleə.mɒnt, -mənt US ˈkler.mɑːnt *in US:* ˈkleə.mɒnt, ˈklɜː- US ˈkler.mɑːnt, ˈklɝː-
Clermont-Ferrand ˌkleə.mɔ̃ːn.ferˈɑ̃ːŋ US ˌkler.mɑːn.ferˈɑ̃ːn
Clery ˈklɪə.ri US ˈklɪr.i
Clevedon ˈkliːv.dən
Cleveland ˈkliːv.lənd
Cleveleys ˈkliːv.liz
clev|er ˈklev|.əʳ US -ɚ -erer -ᵊr.əʳ US -ɚ.ɚ -erest -ᵊr.ɪst, -əst -erly -ᵊl.i US -ɚ.li -erness -ə.nəs, -nɪs US -ɚ.nəs, -nɪs -erish -ᵊr.ɪʃ ˈclever ˌclogs; too ˌclever by ˈhalf
clever-dick ˈklev.ə.dɪk US ˈ-ɚ- -s -s
Cleverdon ˈklev.ə.dᵊn US ˈ-ɚ-
Cleves kliːvz
clew kluː -s -z -ing -ɪŋ -ed -d
Clews kluːz
Cley klaɪ, kleɪ
cliché ˈkliː.ʃeɪ, -ˈ- US -ˈ- -s -z -d -d
click klɪk -s -s -ing -ɪŋ -ed -t
client klaɪənt -s -s
clientage ˈklaɪən.tɪdʒ
clientele ˌkliː.ɑ̃ːnˈtel, -ɑːnˈ-, -ənˈ- US ˌklaɪ.ənˈtel, ˌkliː-, -ɑːnˈ- -s -z
cliff klɪf -s -s
Cliff(e) klɪf
cliffhanger ˈklɪfˌhæŋ.əʳ US -ɚ -s -z
Clifford ˈklɪf.əd US -ɚd
clifftop ˈklɪf.tɒp US -tɑːp -s -s
clift (C) klɪft -s -s
Clifton ˈklɪf.tᵊn
climacteric klaɪˈmæk.tᵊr.ɪk; ˌklaɪ.mækˈter- US klaɪˈmæk.tɚ.ɪk; ˌklaɪ.mækˈter-, -ˈtɪr- -s -s
climacterical ˌklaɪ.mækˈter.ɪ.kᵊl
climactic klaɪˈmæk.tɪk -al -ᵊl -ally -ᵊl.i, -li
climate ˈklaɪ.mət, -mɪt -s -s
climatic klaɪˈmæt.ɪk US -ˈmæt̬- -al -ᵊl -ally -ᵊl.i, -li
climatolog|y ˌklaɪ.məˈtɒl.ə.dʒ|i US -ˈtɑː.lə- -ist/s -ɪst/s
climax ˈklaɪ.mæks -es -ɪz -ing -ɪŋ -ed -t
climb klaɪm -s -z -ing -ɪŋ -ed -d -able -ə.bl̩ ˈclimbing ˌframe
climb-down ˈklaɪm.daʊn -s -z
climber ˈklaɪ.məʳ US -mɚ -s -z
clime klaɪm -s -z
clinch (C) klɪntʃ -es -ɪz -ing -ɪŋ -ed -t -er/s -əʳ/z US -ɚ/z
cline (C) klaɪn -s -z
cling klɪŋ -s -z -ing -ɪŋ clung klʌŋ
clingfilm (C®) ˈklɪŋ.fɪlm
clingstone ˈklɪŋ.stəʊn US -stoʊn -s -z
cling|y ˈklɪŋ|.i -ier -i.əʳ US -i.ɚ -iest -i.ɪst, -i.əst -iness -ɪ.nəs, -ɪ.nɪs
clinic ˈklɪn.ɪk -s -s -al -ᵊl -ally -ᵊl.i, -li
clinician klɪˈnɪʃ.ᵊn US klɪ-, klə- -s -z
Clinique® klɪˈniːk
clink klɪŋk -s -s -ing -ɪŋ -ed -t
clinker (C) ˈklɪŋ.kəʳ US -kɚ -s -z
clinometer klaɪˈnɒm.ɪ.təʳ, klɪ-, ˈ-ə- US -ˈnɑː.mə.t̬ɚ -s -s
clinometric ˌklaɪ.nəʊˈmet.rɪk, ˌklɪn.əʊˈ- US -noʊˈ-
clinometry klaɪˈnɒm.ɪ.tri, klɪ-, ˈ-ə- US klaɪˈnɑː.mə-
Clint klɪnt
Clinton ˈklɪn.tən US ˈklɪn.tən, -tᵊn
Clio ˈkliː.əʊ, ˈklaɪ- US -oʊ
Note: The pronunciation /ˈkliː.əʊ US -oʊ/ is suitable for the motor car.
clip klɪp -s -s -ping -ɪŋ -ped -t ˈclip ˌjoint
clipboard ˈklɪp.bɔːd US -bɔːrd -s -z
clip-clop ˈklɪp.klɒp US -klɑːp -s -s -ping -ɪŋ -ped -t
clipper ˈklɪp.əʳ US -ɚ -s -z
clippie ˈklɪp.i -s -z
clipping ˈklɪp.ɪŋ -s -z

clique kliːk ⓤⓢ kliːk, klɪk **-s** -s **-y** -i

cliquish 'kliː.kɪʃ ⓤⓢ 'kliː.kɪʃ, 'klɪk.ɪʃ **-ly** -li **-ness** -nəs, -nɪs

cliqu|y 'kliː.k|i ⓤⓢ 'kliː.k|i, 'klɪk|.i **-ier** -i.əʳ ⓤⓢ -i.ɚ **-iest** -i.ɪst, -i.əst **-iness** -ɪ.nəs, -ɪ.nɪs

Clissold 'klɪs.ᵊld, -əʊld ⓤⓢ -oʊld

Clitheroe 'klɪð.ə.rəʊ ⓤⓢ -roʊ

clitic 'klɪt.ɪk ⓤⓢ 'klɪt̬- **-s** -s

clitoral 'klɪt.ᵊr.ᵊl ⓤⓢ 'klɪt̬.ɚ-, 'klaɪ.t̬ɚ-

clitoridectom|y ˌklɪt.ᵊr.ɪ'dek.tə.m|i ⓤⓢ ˌklɪt- **-ies** -iz

clitor|is 'klɪt.ᵊr|.ɪs ⓤⓢ 'klɪt̬.ɚ|.əs, 'klaɪ.t̬ɚ-; klɪ'tɔːr- **-ic** -ɪk

Clive klaɪv

Cliveden 'klɪv.dᵊn, 'kliːv-

cloa|ca kləʊ'eɪ|.kə ⓤⓢ kloʊ- **-cae** -kiː, -siː ⓤⓢ -siː, -kiː **-cal** -kᵊl

cloak (C) kləʊk ⓤⓢ kloʊk **-s** -s **-ing** -ɪŋ **-ed** -t

cloak-and-dagger ˌkləʊk.ᵊn'dæg.əʳ ⓤⓢ ˌkloʊk.ᵊn'dæg.ɚ

cloakroom 'kləʊk.rʊm, -ruːm ⓤⓢ 'kloʊk.ruːm, -rʊm **-s** -z

clobb|er 'klɒb|.əʳ ⓤⓢ 'klɑː.b|ɚ **-ers** -əz ⓤⓢ -ɚz **-ering** -ᵊr.ɪŋ **-ered** -əd ⓤⓢ -ɚd

cloch|e klɒʃ, kləʊʃ ⓤⓢ kloʊʃ **-es** -ɪz

clock klɒk ⓤⓢ klɑːk **-s** -s **-ing** -ɪŋ **-ed** -t **'clock ˌface; put the 'clock ˌback**

clockwise 'klɒk.waɪz ⓤⓢ 'klɑːk-

clockwork 'klɒk.wɜːk ⓤⓢ 'klɑːk.wɝːk

clod klɒd ⓤⓢ klɑːd **-s** -z **-dy** -i

clodhopp|ing 'klɒdˌhɒp|.ɪŋ ⓤⓢ 'klɑːdˌhɑː.p|ɪŋ **-er/s** -əʳ/z ⓤⓢ -ɚ/z

Cloete kləʊ'iː.ti; 'kluː.ti ⓤⓢ 'kluː.t̬i; kloʊ'iː.t̬i

clog klɒg ⓤⓢ klɑːg, klɔːg **-s** -z **-ging** -ɪŋ **-ged** -d

clogg|y 'klɒg|.i ⓤⓢ 'klɑː.g|i **-ier** -i.əʳ ⓤⓢ -i.ɚ **-iest** -i.ɪst, -i.əst **-ily** -ɪ.li, -ᵊl.i **-iness** -ɪ.nəs, -ɪ.nɪs

Clogher 'klɒ.həʳ, 'klɒx.əʳ, 'klɔː-, klɔːʳ ⓤⓢ 'klɑː.hɚ, -xɚ

cloisonné klwɑː'zɒn.eɪ, klwʌz'ɒn-; ⓤⓢ ˌklɔɪ.zə'neɪ

cloist|er 'klɔɪ.st|əʳ ⓤⓢ -st|ɚ **-ers** -əz ⓤⓢ -ɚz **-ering** -ᵊr.ɪŋ **-ered** -əd ⓤⓢ -ɚd

cloistral 'klɔɪ.strᵊl

clonal 'kləʊ.nᵊl ⓤⓢ 'kloʊ- **-ly** -i

clon|e kləʊn ⓤⓢ kloʊn **-es** -z **-ing** -ɪŋ **-ed** -d

Clonmel 'klɒn.mel, -'- ⓤⓢ 'klɑːn.mel, -'-

clos|e (*v.*) kləʊz ⓤⓢ kloʊz **-es** -ɪz **-ing** -ɪŋ **-ed** -d **-er/s** -əʳ/z ⓤⓢ -ɚ/z **ˌclosed 'book; ˌclosed 'circuit** *stress shift:* ˌclosed circuit 'television; **ˌclosed 'shop**

clos|e (*n.*) *end:* kləʊz ⓤⓢ kloʊz **-es** -ɪz

clos|e (*adj.*) *near:* kləʊs ⓤⓢ kloʊs **-er** -əʳ ⓤⓢ -ɚ **-est** -ɪst, -əst **-ely** -li **-eness** -nəs, -nɪs **ˌclose 'quarters; ˌclose 'season**

close-cut ˌkləʊs'kʌt ⓤⓢ ˌkloʊs-

closefisted ˌkləʊs'fɪs.tɪd ⓤⓢ ˌkloʊs- *stress shift:* ˌclosefisted 'miser

close-grained ˌkləʊs'greɪnd ⓤⓢ ˌkloʊs- *stress shift:* ˌclose-grained 'wood

close-hauled ˌkləʊs'hɔːld ⓤⓢ ˌkloʊs'hɔːld, -'hɑːld *stress shift:* ˌclose-hauled 'sailing

close-knit ˌkləʊs'nɪt ⓤⓢ ˌkloʊs- *stress shift:* ˌclose-knit 'family

closely 'kləʊ.sli ⓤⓢ 'kloʊ-

closely-guarded ˌkləʊ.sli'gɑː.dɪd ⓤⓢ ˌkloʊ.sli'gɑːr- *stress shift:* ˌclosely-guarded 'secret

clos|et 'klɒz|.ɪt ⓤⓢ 'klɑː.z|ɪt **-ets** -ɪts **-eting** -ɪ.tɪŋ ⓤⓢ -ɪ.t̬ɪŋ, '-ə- **-eted** -ɪ.tɪd ⓤⓢ -ɪ.t̬ɪd, '-ə- **come ˌout of the 'closet**

close-up 'kləʊs.ʌp ⓤⓢ 'kloʊs- **-s** -s

closure 'kləʊ.ʒəʳ ⓤⓢ 'kloʊ.ʒɚ **-s** -z

clot klɒt ⓤⓢ klɑːt **-s** -s **-ting** -ɪŋ ⓤⓢ 'klɑː.t̬ɪŋ **-ted** -ɪd ⓤⓢ 'klɑː.t̬ɪd **ˌclotted 'cream**

cloth klɒθ ⓤⓢ klɑːθ **-s** klɒθs, klɒðz ⓤⓢ klɑːθs, klɑːðz **'cloth ˌyard; cut one's ˌcoat according to one's 'cloth**

cloth|e kləʊð ⓤⓢ kloʊð **-es** -z **-ing** -ɪŋ **-ed** -d **clad** klæd

cloth-eared ˌklɒθ'ɪəd ⓤⓢ ˌklɑːθ'ɪrd *stress shift:* ˌcloth-eared 'listener

clothes kləʊðz ⓤⓢ kloʊðz **'clothes ˌbrush; 'clothes ˌhanger**

clotheshors|e 'kləʊðz.hɔːs ⓤⓢ 'kloʊðz.hɔːrs **-es** -ɪz

clothesline 'kləʊðz.laɪn ⓤⓢ 'kloʊðz- **-s** -z

clothespeg 'kləʊðz.peg ⓤⓢ 'kloʊðz- **-s** -z

clothespin 'kləʊðz.pɪn ⓤⓢ 'kloʊðz- **-s** -z

clothier 'kləʊ.ði.əʳ ⓤⓢ 'kloʊ.ði.ɚ **-s** -z

Clothilde 'klɒt.ɪld, -'- ⓤⓢ kloʊ'tɪl.də

clothing 'kləʊ.ðɪŋ ⓤⓢ 'kloʊ-

Clotho 'kləʊ.θəʊ ⓤⓢ 'kloʊ.θoʊ

cloud klaʊd **-s** -z **-ing** -ɪŋ **-ed** -ɪd **'cloud-ˌcapped**

cloudberr|y 'klaʊd.bᵊr|.i, 'klaʊb-, -ber- ⓤⓢ 'klaʊd.ber- **-ies** -iz

cloudburst 'klaʊd.bɜːst ⓤⓢ -bɝːst **-s** -s

cloud-cuckoo-land ˌklaʊd'kʊk.uː.lænd ⓤⓢ -'kuː.kuː-, -'kʊk.ʊ-

Cloudesley 'klaʊdz.li

cloudless 'klaʊd.ləs, -lɪs **-ly** -li **-ness** -nəs, -nɪs

cloud|y 'klaʊ.d|i **-ier** -i.əʳ ⓤⓢ -i.ɚ **-iest** -i.ɪst, -i.əst **-ily** -ɪ.li, -ᵊl.i **-iness** -ɪ.nəs, -ɪ.nɪs

clough klʌf **-s** -s

Clough *surname:* klʌf, kluː *in Ireland:* klɒx ⓤⓢ klʌf

Clouseau kluː'səʊ, '-- ⓤⓢ kluː'zoʊ, '--

clout klaʊt **-s** -s **-ing** -ɪŋ ⓤⓢ 'klaʊ.t̬ɪŋ **-ed** -ɪd ⓤⓢ 'klaʊ.t̬ɪd

clove (*n.*) kləʊv ⓤⓢ kloʊv **-s** -z

clov|e (*from* **cleave**) kləʊv ⓤⓢ kloʊv **-en** -ᵊn

Clovelly klə'vel.i

cloven 'kləʊ.vᵊn ⓤⓢ 'kloʊ- **ˌcloven-'footed** *stress shift:* ˌcloven-footed 'beast

clover (C) 'kləʊ.vəʳ ⓤⓢ 'kloʊ.vɚ **-s** -z

clover|leaf 'kləʊ.və|.liːf ⓤⓢ 'kloʊ.vɚ- **-leafs** -liːfs **-leaves** -liːvz

Clovis 'kləʊ.vɪs ⓤⓢ 'kloʊ-

Clow kləʊ ⓤⓢ kloʊ, klaʊ

Clowes *in Norfolk:* kluːz *surname:* klaʊz, kluːz

clown klaʊn **-s** -z **-ing** -ɪŋ **-ed** -d

Clowne klaʊn

clownish 'klaʊ.nɪʃ **-ly** -li **-ness** -nəs, -nɪs

cloy klɔɪ **-s** -z **-ing/ly** -ɪŋ/li **-ed** -d

cloze kləʊz ⓤⓢ kloʊz

club klʌb **-s** -z **-bing** -ɪŋ **-bed** -d **ˌclub 'sandwich; ˌclub 'soda; ˌclub 'moss** ⓤⓢ **'club ˌmoss**

clubbable 'klʌb.ə.bl̩

clubber 'klʌb.əʳ ⓤⓢ -ɚ **-s** -z

club|foot ˌklʌb|'fʊt, '-- ⓤⓢ '-- **-feet** -'fiːt ⓤⓢ -fiːt

clubfooted ˌklʌb'fʊt.ɪd, '--- ⓤⓢ 'klʌbˌfʊt̬.ɪd

clubhou|se 'klʌb.haʊ|s **-ses** -zɪz

clubland 'klʌb.lænd, -lənd

club|man 'klʌb|.mən, -mæn **-men** -mən, -men

Club Med ˌklʌb'med

Club Méditerranée® ˌklʌbˌmed.ɪˌter.ə'neɪ

club-room 'klʌb.rʊm, -ruːm ⓤⓢ -ruːm, -rʊm **-s** -z

cluck klʌk **-s** -s **-ing** -ɪŋ **-ed** -t

clu|e kluː **-es** -z **-(e)ing** -ɪŋ **-ed** -d **ˌclued 'up**

clueless 'kluː.ləs, -lɪs **-ness** -nəs, -nɪs

Cluj kluːʒ

clumber (C) 'klʌm.bəʳ ⓤⓢ -bɚ **-s** -z

clump klʌmp **-s** -s **-ing** -ɪŋ **-ed** -t

clumpy 'klʌm.pi

clums|y 'klʌm.z|i **-ier** -i.əʳ ⓤⓢ -i.ɚ **-iest** -i.ɪst, -i.əst **-ily** -ɪ.li, -ᵊl.i **-iness** -ɪ.nəs, -ɪ.nɪs

Clun klʌn

clunch klʌntʃ

clung (*from* **cling**) klʌŋ

clunk klʌŋk **-s** -s **-ing** -ɪŋ **-ed** -t

clunk|y 'klʌŋ.k|i **-ier** -i.əʳ ⓤⓢ -i.ɚ **-iest** -i.ɪst, -i.əst

clust|er 'klʌs.t|əʳ ⓤⓢ -tɚ **-ers** -əz ⓤⓢ -ɚz **-ering** -ᵊr.ɪŋ **-ered** -əd ⓤⓢ -ɚd

clutch klʌtʃ **-es** -ɪz **-ing** -ɪŋ **-ed** -t **'clutch ˌbag**

clutt|er 'klʌt|.əʳ ⓤⓢ 'klʌt̬|.ɚ **-ers** -əz ⓤⓢ -ɚz **-ering** -ᵊr.ɪŋ **-ered** -əd ⓤⓢ -ɚd

Clutterbuck 'klʌt.ə.bʌk ⓤⓢ 'klʌt̬.ɚ-

Clutton 'klʌt.ᵊn ⓤⓢ 'klʌt̬-

Cluster

Two or more CONSONANT PHONEMES in sequence, with no vowel sound between them.

Examples for English

English can allow up to three consonants in a cluster syllable initially in the ONSET, and four syllable finally in the CODA. For example, the word *stray* /streɪ/ begins with three consonants, and *sixths* /sɪksθs/ ends with four.

Some types of grammatical information are shown by adding certain consonants at the ends of words in English, giving rise to consonant clusters, e.g.:

likes	/laɪks/	
lives	/lɪvz/	
liked	/laɪkt/	
lived	/lɪvd/	
Mark's	/mɑːks/	(US) /mɑːrks/
John's	/dʒɒnz/	(US) /dʒɑːnz/
cats	/kæts/	
dogs	/dɒgz/	(US) /dɑːgz/

Coalescence

A kind of ASSIMILATION in which a fusion of neighbouring sounds takes place during rapid or CONNECTED SPEECH.

Examples for English

The most frequently observed situation in which coalescence occurs in English is when ALVEOLAR consonants /t d s z/ are followed by /j/, e.g.:

won't you	/wəʊnt ju/ (US) /woʊnt-/	→	/ˈwəʊntʃu/ (US) /woʊnt-/
would you	/wʊd ju/	→	/ˈwʊdʒu/
miss you	/mɪs ju/	→	/ˈmɪʃu/
lose you	/luːz ju/	→	/ˈluːʒu/

In the case of coalescence with /s z/, there will usually be extra length to the resulting fricative sounds, e.g.:

miss you	/mɪs ju/	→	/ˈmɪʃʃu/
lose you	/luːz ju/	→	/ˈluːʒʒu/

A common very much reduced example of coalescence is *do you* being pronounced as /dʒə/.

Clwyd ˈkluː.ɪd
Clwydian kluˈɪd.i.ən
Clydach ˈklɪd.ək, ˈklʌd-, -əx (US) -ək
Clyde klaɪd
Clydebank ˈklaɪd.bæŋk, -ˈ-
Clydesdale ˈklaɪdz.deɪl **-s** -z
Clydeside ˈklaɪd.saɪd
Clym klɪm
lyster ˈklɪs.tə^{r} (US) -tɚ **-s** -z
lytemnestra ˌklaɪ.təmˈnes.trə, ˌklɪt.əmˈ-, -ɪmˈ-, -emˈ-, -ˈniː.strə (US) ˌklaɪ.t̬əmˈnes.trə
lytie *in Greek mythology:* ˈklɪt.i.iː, ˈklaɪ.tiː (US) ˈklaɪ.t̬i.iː, ˈklɪt̬.i.iː *modern first name, chignon:* ˈklaɪ.ti, -tiː (US) ˈklaɪ.t̬i, klɪˈʃiː.ə
m *(abbrev. for* **centimetre/s***)* *singular:* ˈsen.tɪˌmiː.tə^{r} (US) -t̬əˌmiː.t̬ɚ *plural:* -z
ND ˌsiː.enˈdiː
nidus ˈnaɪ.dəs, ˈknaɪ-
NN ˌsiː.enˈen
nut kəˈnjuːt, knuːt
o *(abbrev. for* **care of***)* ˈkeə^{r}.ɒv (US) ˈker.ɑːv, -əv
o *(abbrev. for* **carried over***)* ˌkær.idˈəʊ.və^{r} (US) ˌker.idˈoʊ.vɚ, ˌkær-
co- kəʊ- (US) koʊ-
Co. *(abbrev. for* **company***)* kəʊ, ˈkʌm.p^{ə}n.i (US) koʊ, ˈkʌm.p^{ə}n.i
CO ˌsiːˈəʊ (US) -ˈoʊ
coach kəʊtʃ (US) koʊtʃ **-es** -ɪz **-ing** -ɪŋ **-ed** -t **ˈcoach ˌhorse; ˈcoach ˌhouse; ˈcoach ˌparty; ˈcoach ˌstation**
coach|man ˈkəʊtʃ|.mən (US) ˈkoʊtʃ- **-men** -mən
coac|tion kəʊˈæk|.ʃ^{ə}n (US) koʊ- **-tive** -tɪv
coadjacent ˌkəʊ.əˈdʒeɪ.s^{ə}nt (US) ˌkoʊ-
coadjutant kəʊˈædʒ.ʊ.t^{ə}nt, ˈ-ə- (US) koʊˈædʒ.ə.t̬^{ə}nt **-s** -s
coadjutor kəʊˈædʒ.ʊ.tə^{r}, ˈ-ə- (US) koʊˈædʒ.ə.t̬ɚ **-s** -z
co-administrator ˌkəʊ.ədˈmɪn.ɪ.streɪ.tə^{r} (US) ˌkoʊ.ædˈmɪn.ɪ.streɪ.t̬ɚ, -ədˈ- **-s** -z
coagulant kəʊˈæg.jʊ.lənt, -jə- (US) koʊˈæg.jə- **-s** -s
coagu|late kəʊˈæg.jə|.leɪt, -jʊ- (US) koʊˈæg.jə- **-lates** -leɪts **-lating** -leɪ.tɪŋ (US) -leɪ.t̬ɪŋ **-lated** -leɪ.tɪd (US) -leɪ.t̬ɪd
coagulation kəʊˌæg.jəˈleɪ.ʃ^{ə}n, -jʊˈ- (US) koʊˌæg.jəˈ-
coal kəʊl (US) koʊl **-s** -z **-ing** -ɪŋ **-ed** -d **ˈcoal ˌbed; ˈcoal ˌblack; ˈcoal ˌbunker; ˈcoal ˌscuttle; ˈcoal ˌtar; ˌhaul someone over the ˈcoals**
coalesc|e kəʊəˈles (US) koʊə- **-es** -ɪz **-ing** -ɪŋ **-ed** -t
coalescen|ce kəʊəˈles.^{ə}n|*t*s (US) koʊə- **-t** -t
coalfac|e ˈkəʊl.feɪs (US) ˈkoʊl- **-es** -ɪz
coalfield ˈkəʊl.fiːld (US) ˈkoʊl- **-s** -z
coalhole ˈkəʊl.həʊl (US) ˈkoʊl.hoʊl **-s** -z
coalhou|se ˈkəʊl.haʊ|s (US) ˈkoʊl- **-ses** -zɪz
Coalite® ˈkəʊ.laɪt (US) ˈkoʊ-
coalition kəʊəˈlɪʃ.^{ə}n (US) koʊə- **-s** -z
coal|man ˈkəʊl|.mən, -mæn (US) ˈkoʊl- **-men** -men, -mən
coalmine ˈkəʊl.maɪn (US) ˈkoʊl- **-s** -z
coalminer ˈkəʊlˌmaɪ.nə^{r} (US) ˈkoʊlˌmaɪ.nɚ **-s** -z
coalpit ˈkəʊl.pɪt (US) ˈkoʊl- **-s** -s
Coalville ˈkəʊl.vɪl (US) ˈkoʊl-
coanchor ˈkəʊˌæŋ.kə^{r} (US) ˈkoʊˌæŋ.kɚ **-s** -z
coars|e kɔːs (US) kɔːrs **-er** -ə^{r} (US) -ɚ **-est** -ɪst, -əst **-ely** -li **-eness** -nəs, -nɪs **ˈcoarse ˌfishing, ˌcoarse ˈfishing**
coarse-grained ˌkɔːsˈgreɪnd (US) ˈkɔːrs.greɪnd *stress shift:* ˌcoarse-grained ˈpicture

Coarticulation

The influence of phonetic context on the articulation of speech sounds.

Examples for English

Phonetics studies coarticulation as a way of finding out how the brain controls the production of speech. When we speak, many muscles are active at the same time and sometimes the brain tries to make them do things that they are not capable of. For example, in the word *mum* the vowel phoneme is one that is normally pronounced with the soft palate raised to prevent the escape of air through the nose, while the two /m/ phonemes must have the soft palate lowered. The soft palate cannot be raised very quickly, so the vowel is likely to be pronounced with the soft palate still lowered, giving a nasalized quality to the vowel, e.g.:

mum /mʌm/ [mʌ̃m]

Another example is the lip-rounding of a consonant in the environment of rounded vowels: in the phrase 'you too', the /t/ occurs between two rounded vowels, and there is not enough time in normal speech for the lips to move from rounded to unrounded and back again in a few hundredths of a second; consequently the /t/ is pronounced with lip-rounding, e.g.:

you too /juː tuː/ [juːtʷuː]

Coarticulation is a phenomenon closely related to ASSIMILATION. The major difference is that assimilation is used as a name for the process whereby one sound becomes like another neighbouring sound, while coarticulation, though it refers to a similar process, is concerned with articulatory explanations for why the assimilation occurs, and considers cases where the changes may occur over a number of segments.

coarsen ˈkɔː.sᵊn US ˈkɔːr- **-s** -z **-ing** -ɪŋ **-ed** -d
coarticulation ˌkəʊ.ɑː.tɪ.kjəˈleɪ.ʃᵊn, -jʊˈ- US ˌkoʊ.ɑːr.tɪ.kjəˈ-
coast kəʊst US koʊst **-s** -s **-ing** -ɪŋ **-ed** -ɪd
coastal ˈkəʊs.tᵊl US ˈkoʊ-
coaster ˈkəʊ.stəʳ US ˈkoʊ.stɚ **-s** -z
coastguard ˈkəʊst.gɑːd US ˈkoʊst.gɑːrd **-s** -z
coastline ˈkəʊst.laɪn US ˈkoʊst- **-s** -z
coastwise ˈkəʊst.waɪz US ˈkoʊst-
coat kəʊt US koʊt **-s** -s **-ing** -ɪŋ **-ed** -ɪd **ˈcoat ˌcheck; ˈcoat ˌhanger; ˌcoat of ˈarms; ˈcoat ˌroom; ˈcoat ˌtail(s); ˌcut one's ˌcoat according to one's ˈcloth**
Coatbridge ˈkəʊt.brɪdʒ US ˈkoʊt-
Coat(e)s kəʊts US koʊts
coati kəʊˈɑː.ti US koʊˈɑː.t̬i **-s** -z
coating ˈkəʊ.tɪŋ US ˈkoʊ.t̬ɪŋ **-s** -z
coauthor kəʊˈɔː.θəʳ, ˈ-,-- US koʊˈɑː.θɚ, -ˈɔː- **-s** -z **-ing** -ɪŋ **-ed** -d
coax kəʊks US koʊks **-es** -ɪz **-ing/ly** -ɪŋ/li **-ed** -t **-er/s** -əʳ/z US -ɚ/z
co-axial ˌkəʊˈæk.si.əl US ˌkoʊ- **-ly** -i
cob kɒb US kɑːb **-s** -z
Cobain kəʊˈbeɪn US ˈkoʊ-, ˌkoʊˈbeɪn
cobalt ˈkəʊ.bɔːlt, -bɒlt US ˈkoʊ.bɔːlt, -bɑːlt
Cobb(e) kɒb US kɑːb
cobber ˈkɒb.əʳ US ˈkɑː.bɚ **-s** -z
Cobbett ˈkɒb.ɪt US ˈkɑː.bɪt
cobbl|e ˈkɒb.l̩ US ˈkɑː.bl̩ **-es** -z **-ing** -ɪŋ, ˈ-lɪŋ US ˈkɑː.bl̩.ɪŋ, ˈ-blɪŋ **-ed** -d
Cobbleigh ˈkɒb.li US ˈkɑː.bli
cobbler ˈkɒb.ləʳ, ˈkɒb.l̩.əʳ US ˈkɑː.blɚ **-s** -z
cobblestone ˈkɒb.l̩.stəʊn US ˈkɑː.bl̩.stoʊn **-s** -z
Cobbold ˈkɒb.əʊld, -ᵊld US ˈkɑː.boʊld
Cobden ˈkɒb.dᵊn US ˈkɑːb-
Cobh kəʊv US koʊv
Cobham ˈkɒb.ᵊm US ˈkɑː.bᵊm
Coblenz kəʊˈblents, ˈkəʊ.blents US ˈkoʊ-
cobnut ˈkɒb.nʌt US ˈkɑːb- **-s** -s
COBOL, Cobol ˈkəʊ.bɒl US ˈkoʊ.bɔːl, -bɑːl
cobra ˈkəʊ.brə, ˈkɒb.rə US ˈkoʊ.brə **-s** -z
Coburg ˈkəʊ.bɜːg US ˈkoʊ.bɝːg **-s** -z
cobweb ˈkɒb.web US ˈkɑːb- **-s** -z
coca ˈkəʊ.kə US ˈkoʊ.kə **-s** -z
Coca-Cola® ˌkəʊ.kəˈkəʊ.lə US ˌkoʊ.kəˈkoʊ-
cocaine kəʊˈkeɪn US koʊ-, ˈ--
coccal ˈkɒk.ᵊl US ˈkɑː.kᵊl
coccid ˈkɒk.sɪd US ˈkɑːk-
cocciferous kɒkˈsɪf.ᵊr.əs US kɑːk-
coccoid ˈkɒk.ɔɪd US ˈkɑː.kɔɪd
coccus ˈkɒk.əs US ˈkɑː.kəs **cocci** ˈkɒk.aɪ, ˈkɒk.saɪ US ˈkɑːk.saɪ
coccyx ˈkɒk.sɪks US ˈkɑːk- **-es** -ɪz **coccyges** -saɪ.dʒiːz
Cochabamba ˌkəʊ.tʃəˈbæm.bə US ˌkoʊ.tʃəˈbɑːm-
Cochin ˈkəʊ.tʃɪn, ˈkɒtʃ.ɪn US ˈkoʊ.tʃɪn
Cochin-China ˌkɒtʃ.ɪnˈtʃaɪ.nə US ˌkoʊ.tʃɪnˈ-, ˌkɑː-
cochineal ˌkɒtʃ.ɪˈniːl, -əˈ-, ˈ--- US ˈkɑː.tʃə.niːl, ˌ--ˈ-
Cochise kəʊˈtʃiːs US koʊ-, -ˈtʃiːz
cochle|a ˈkɒk.li|.ə US ˈkɑːk-, ˈkoʊk- **-as** -əz **-ae** -iː **-ar** -əʳ US -ɚ
Cochran(e) ˈkɒk.rən, ˈkɒx- US ˈkɑːk-
cock kɒk US kɑːk **-s** -s **-ing** -ɪŋ **-ed** -t
cockade kɒkˈeɪd US kɑːˈkeɪd **-s** -z
cock-a-doodle-doo ˌkɒk.ə.duː.dl̩ˈduː US ˌkɑːk-
cock-a-hoop ˌkɒk.əˈhuːp US ˌkɑːk-
Cockaigne kɒkˈeɪn, kəˈkeɪn US kɑːˈkeɪn
cock-a-leekie ˌkɒk.əˈliː.ki US ˌkɑːk-
cockalorum ˌkɒk.əˈlɔː.rᵊm US ˌkɑː.kəˈlɔːr.ᵊm **-s** -z
cockamamie ˌkɒk.əˈmeɪ.mi US ˈkɑː.kə.meɪ-
cock-and-bull ˌkɒk.ᵊndˈbʊl, -ᵊmˈ- US ˌkɑːk.ᵊnd- *stress shift, British only, see compound:* **ˌcock-and-bull ˈstory** US **ˌcock-and-ˈbull ˌstory**
cockateel, cockatiel ˌkɒk.əˈtiːl US ˌkɑː.kəˈ- **-s** -z
cockatoo ˌkɒk.əˈtuː US ˈkɑː.kə.tuː **-s** -z
cockatric|e ˈkɒk.ə.traɪs, -trɪs, -trəs US ˈkɑː.kə- **-es** -ɪz
Cockaygne kɒkˈeɪn, kəˈkeɪn US kɑːˈkeɪn
Cockburn ˈkəʊ.bɜːn, -bən US ˈkoʊ.bɝːn
cockchafer ˈkɒkˌtʃeɪ.fəʳ US ˈkɑːkˌtʃeɪ.fɚ **-s** -z
Cockcroft ˈkəʊk.krɒft, ˈkɒk.krɒft US ˈkɑːk.krɑːft, ˈkoʊ.krɑːft
cockcrow ˈkɒk.krəʊ US ˈkɑːk.kroʊ
Cocke *place:* kɒk US kɑːk *surname:* kəʊk, kɒk US koʊk, kɑːk
Cockell ˈkɒk.ᵊl US ˈkɑː.kᵊl
cocker (C) ˈkɒk.əʳ US ˈkɑː.kɚ **-s** -z **ˌcocker ˈspaniel**
cockerel ˈkɒk.ᵊr.ᵊl US ˈkɑː.kɚ- **-s** -z
Cockerell ˈkɒk.ᵊr.ᵊl US ˈkɑː.kɚ-
Cockermouth ˈkɒk.ə.məθ, -maʊθ *locally:* -məθ US ˈkɑː.kɚ-
cockeye ˈkɒk.aɪ US ˈkɑːk.aɪ **-d** kɒkˈaɪd US ˈkɑːk.aɪd *stress shift, British only:* ˌcockeyed ˈoptimist

Coda

The end of a syllable, which is said to be made up of an ONSET, a peak and a coda. The peak and the coda constitute the RHYME (or RIME) of the syllable.

Examples for English

English allows up to four consonants to occur in the coda, so the total number of possible codas in English is very large – several hundred in fact, e.g.

sick	/sɪk/	sixth	/sɪksθ/
six	/sɪks/	sixths	/sɪksθs/

The central part of a syllable is almost always a vowel, and if the syllable contains nothing after the vowel it is said to have no coda ('zero coda'), e.g.:

bough	baʊ
buy	baɪ

In other languages

Some languages (e.g. Japanese) have no codas in any syllables.

cock|fight 'kɒk|.faɪt ⓤⓢ 'kɑːk- **-fights** -faɪts **-fighting** -ˌfaɪ.tɪŋ ⓤⓢ -ˌfaɪ.t̬ɪŋ

Cockfosters ˌkɒk'fɒs.təz, '-ˌ-- ⓤⓢ 'kɑːkˌfɑː.stɚz, ˌ-'--

cockhors|e ˌkɒk'hɔːs ⓤⓢ 'kɑːk.hɔːrs **-es** -ɪz

cockl|e (C) 'kɒk.l̩ ⓤⓢ 'kɑː.kl̩ **-es** -z **-ing** -ɪŋ, '-lɪŋ ⓤⓢ 'kɑː.kl̩.ɪŋ, '-klɪŋ **-ed** -d

cockleshell 'kɒk.l̩.ʃel ⓤⓢ 'kɑː.kl̩- **-s** -z

cockney (C) 'kɒk.ni ⓤⓢ 'kɑːk- **-s** -z

cockneyism 'kɒk.ni.ɪ.zᵊm ⓤⓢ 'kɑːk- **-s** -z

cockpit 'kɒk.pɪt ⓤⓢ 'kɑːk- **-s** -s

cockroach 'kɒk.rəʊtʃ ⓤⓢ 'kɑːk.roʊtʃ **-es** -ɪz

Cockroft 'kɒk.rɒft, 'kəʊ.krɒft ⓤⓢ 'kɑː.krɑːft, 'koʊ-

cockscomb 'kɒk.skəʊm ⓤⓢ 'kɑːk.skoʊm **-s** -z

Cocksedge 'kɒk.sɪdʒ, 'kɒs.ɪdʒ, -edʒ, 'kəʊ.sɪdʒ ⓤⓢ 'kɑːk.sɪdʒ, 'kɑː-, 'koʊ-, -sedʒ

Cockshott 'kɒk.ʃɒt ⓤⓢ 'kɑːk.ʃɑːt

cocksh|y 'kɒk.ʃ|aɪ ⓤⓢ 'kɑːk- **-ies** -aɪz

cockspur (C) 'kɒk.spɜːʳ, -spəʳ ⓤⓢ 'kɑːk.spɝː **-s** -z

cocksure ˌkɒk'ʃʊəʳ, -'ʃɔːʳ ⓤⓢ ˌkɑːk'ʃʊr, -'ʃɝː

cocktail 'kɒk.teɪl ⓤⓢ 'kɑːk- **-s** -z
'cocktail ˌdress; 'cocktail ˌlounge; 'cocktail ˌparty; 'cocktail ˌstick

cock-up 'kɒk.ʌp ⓤⓢ 'kɑːk- **-s** -s

Cockwood 'kɒk.wʊd ⓤⓢ 'kɑːk-
Note: There exists also a local pronunciation /'kɒk.ʊd ⓤⓢ 'kɑː.kʊd/.

cock|y 'kɒk|.i ⓤⓢ 'kɑː.k|i **-ier** -i.əʳ ⓤⓢ -i.ɚ **-iest** -i.ɪst, -i.əst **-ily** -ɪ.li, -ᵊl.i **-iness** -ɪ.nəs, -ɪ.nɪs

cocky-leeky ˌkɒk.i'liː.ki ⓤⓢ ˌkɑː.ki-

coco 'kəʊ.kəʊ ⓤⓢ 'koʊ.koʊ **-s** -z

cocoa 'kəʊ.kəʊ ⓤⓢ 'koʊ.koʊ **-s** -z
'cocoa ˌbutter

cocoanut 'kəʊ.kə.nʌt ⓤⓢ 'koʊ- **-s** -s

co-conspirator ˌkəʊ.kən'spɪr.ə.təʳ, '-ɪ- ⓤⓢ ˌkoʊ.kən'spɪr.ə.t̬ɚ **-s** -z

coconut 'kəʊ.kə.nʌt ⓤⓢ 'koʊ- **-s** -s
ˌcoconut 'ice; 'coconut ˌshy

cocoon kə'kuːn **-s** -z **-ing** -ɪŋ **-ed** -d

Cocos 'kəʊ.kəs, -kɒs ⓤⓢ 'koʊ.koʊs, -kəs

cocotte kə'kɒt, kəʊ-, kɒk'ɒt ⓤⓢ koʊ'kɑːt **-s** -s

Cocteau 'kɒk.təʊ ⓤⓢ kɑːk'toʊ

Cocytus kəʊ'saɪ.təs ⓤⓢ koʊ'saɪ.t̬əs

cod (C) kɒd ⓤⓢ kɑːd **-s** -z **-ding** -ɪŋ **-ded** -ɪd **ˌcod-liver 'oil**

COD ˌsiː.əʊ'diː ⓤⓢ -oʊ'-

coda 'kəʊ.də ⓤⓢ 'koʊ- **-s** -z

Coddington 'kɒd.ɪŋ.tən ⓤⓢ 'kɑː.dɪŋ-

coddl|e 'kɒd.l̩ ⓤⓢ 'kɑː.dl̩ **-es** -z **-ing** -ɪŋ, '-lɪŋ ⓤⓢ 'kɑː.dl̩.ɪŋ, 'kɑːd.lɪŋ **-ed** -d

cod|e kəʊd ⓤⓢ koʊd **-es** -z **-ing** -ɪŋ **-ed** -ɪd **-er/s** -əʳ/z ⓤⓢ -ɚ/s

co-defendant ˌkəʊ.dɪ'fen.dənt, -də'- ⓤⓢ ˌkoʊ-

codeine 'kəʊ.diːn ⓤⓢ 'koʊ-

co-determination ˌkəʊ.dɪ.tɜː.mɪ'neɪ.ʃᵊn, -də- ⓤⓢ ˌkoʊ.dɪ.tɝː-, -də-

cod|ex 'kəʊ.d|eks ⓤⓢ 'koʊ- **-exes** -ek.sɪz, -səz **-ices** -ɪ.siːz, 'kɒd.ɪ.siːz ⓤⓢ 'koʊ.də.siːz, 'kɑː-

codger 'kɒdʒ.əʳ ⓤⓢ 'kɑː.dʒɚ **-s** -z

codicil 'kəʊ.dɪ.sɪl, 'kɒd.ɪ-, '-ə- ⓤⓢ 'kɑː.də.sᵊl, -sɪl **-s** -z

codicillary ˌkəʊ.dɪ'sɪl.ᵊr.i, ˌkɒd.ɪ'- ⓤⓢ ˌkɑː.də'-

Codicote 'kəʊ.dɪ.kəʊt, 'kɒd.ɪ.kət ⓤⓢ 'koʊ.dɪ.koʊt, 'kɑː.dɪ.kət

codification ˌkəʊ.dɪ.fɪ'keɪ.ʃᵊn, -də- ⓤⓢ ˌkɑː-, ˌkoʊ- **-s** -z

codi|fy 'kəʊ.dɪ|.faɪ, -də- ⓤⓢ 'kɑː-, 'koʊ- **-fies** -faɪz **-fying** -faɪ.ɪŋ **-fied** -faɪd

codling 'kɒd.lɪŋ ⓤⓢ 'kɑːd- **-s** -z

codpiec|e 'kɒd.piːs ⓤⓢ 'kɑːd- **-es** -ɪz

Codrington 'kɒd.rɪŋ.tən ⓤⓢ 'kɑːd-

Codsall 'kɒd.sᵊl ⓤⓢ 'kɑːd-

codswallop 'kɒdzˌwɒl.əp ⓤⓢ 'kɑːdzˌwɑː.ləp, -ˌwɔː-

Cody 'kəʊ.di ⓤⓢ 'koʊ-

Coe kəʊ ⓤⓢ koʊ

coed ˌkəʊ'ed ⓤⓢ 'koʊ.ed **-s** -z *stress shift, British only:* ˌcoed 'school

Coed kɔɪd

coeducation ˌkəʊ.edʒ.ʊ'keɪ.ʃᵊn, -ed.jʊ'- ⓤⓢ ˌkoʊ.edʒ.ʊ'-, -ə'-

coeducational ˌkəʊ.edʒ.ʊ'keɪ.ʃᵊn.ᵊl, -ed.jʊ'-, -'keɪʃ.nᵊl ⓤⓢ ˌkoʊ.edʒ.ə'- **-ly** -i

coefficient ˌkəʊ.ɪ'fɪʃ.ᵊnt, -ə'fɪʃ- ⓤⓢ ˌkoʊ- **-s** -s

coelacanth 'siː.lə.kæn*t*θ **-s** -s

coeliac 'siː.li.æk

coenobite 'siː.nəʊ.baɪt ⓤⓢ 'sen.ə- **-s** -s

coequal ˌkəʊ'iː.kwᵊl ⓤⓢ ˌkoʊ- **-ly** -i

coequality ˌkəʊ.ɪ'kwɒl.ə.ti, -ɪ.ti ⓤⓢ ˌkoʊ.iː'kwɑː.lə.t̬i

coerc|e kəʊ'ɜːs ⓤⓢ koʊ'ɝːs **-es** -ɪz **-ing** -ɪŋ **-ed** -t

coercib|le kəʊ'ɜː.sɪ.b|l̩, -sə- ⓤⓢ koʊ'ɝː- **-ly** -li

coercion kəʊ'ɜː.ʃᵊn ⓤⓢ koʊ'ɝː.ʒᵊn, -ʃᵊn

coercionist kəʊ'ɜː.ʃᵊn.ɪst ⓤⓢ koʊ'ɝː.ʒᵊn-, -ʃᵊn- **-s** -s

coercive kəʊ'ɜː.sɪv ⓤⓢ koʊ'ɝː- **-ly** -li

co-eternal ˌkəʊ.ɪ'tɜː.nᵊl ⓤⓢ ˌkoʊ.ɪ'tɝː-

Coetzee kuːt'sɪə, -siː

Coeur de Lion ˌkɜː.də'liː.ɔ̃ːŋ, -dᵊl'iː-, -ɒn ⓤⓢ ˌkɝː.də'liː.ən, -'laɪən

coeval kəʊ'iː.vᵊl ⓤⓢ koʊ- **-s** -z

co-executor ˌkəʊ.ɪg'zek.jʊ.təʳ, -eg'-, -jə-; -ɪk'sek-, -ek'- ⓤⓢ ˌkoʊ.ɪg'zek.juː.t̬ɚ, -eg'- **-s** -z

co-exist ˌkəʊ.ɪg'zɪst, -eg'-, -əg'-; -ɪk'sɪst, -ek'-, -ək'- ⓤⓢ ˌkoʊ.ɪg'zɪst, -eg'- **-s** -s **-ing** -ɪŋ **-ed** -ɪd

co-existen|ce ˌkəʊ.ɪg'zɪs.tᵊn|*t*s, -eg'-, -əg'-; -ɪk'sɪs-, -ek'-, -ək'- ⓤⓢ ˌkoʊ.ɪg'-, -eg'- **-t** -t

co-extend ˌkəʊ.ɪk'stend, -ek'-, -ək'- ⓤⓢ ˌkoʊ.ɪk'-, -ek'- **-s** -z **-ing** -ɪŋ **-ed** -ɪd

co-extension ˌkəʊ.ɪk'sten.*t*ʃᵊn, -ek'-, -ək'- ⓤⓢ ˌkoʊ.ɪk'-, -ek'- **-s** -z

co-extensive ˌkəʊ.ɪk'sten*t*.sɪv, -ek'-, -ək'- ⓤⓢ ˌkoʊ.ɪk'-, -ek'-

Coey ˈkəʊ.i ⓤⓢ ˈkoʊ-

C of E *(abbrev. for* **Church of England***)* ˌsiː.əvˈiː

coffee ˈkɒf.i ⓤⓢ ˈkɑː.fi, ˈkɔː- **-s** -z
ˈcoffee ˌbar; ˈcoffee ˌbean; ˈcoffee ˌbreak; ˈcoffee ˌcup; ˈcoffee ˌmill; ˈcoffee ˌtable

coffeehou|se ˈkɒf.i.haʊ|s ⓤⓢ ˈkɑː.fi-, ˈkɔː- **-ses** -zɪz

coffee klatch, coffee klatsch ˈkɒf.iˌklætʃ ⓤⓢ ˈkɑː.fi-, ˈkɔː-

coffeemaker ˈkɒf.iˌmeɪ.kəʳ ⓤⓢ ˈkɑː.fiˌmeɪ.kɚ, ˈkɔː- **-s** -z

coffeepot ˈkɒf.i.pɒt ⓤⓢ ˈkɑː.fi.pɑːt, ˈkɔː- **-s** -s

coffer ˈkɒf.əʳ ⓤⓢ ˈkɑː.fɚ, ˈkɔː- **-s** -z

cofferdam ˈkɒf.ə.dæm ⓤⓢ ˈkɑː.fɚ-, -dᵊm **-s** -z

Coffey ˈkɒf.i ⓤⓢ ˈkɑː.fi, ˈkɔː-

coffin (C) ˈkɒf.ɪn ⓤⓢ ˈkɔː.fɪn, ˈkɑː- **-s** -z **-ing** -ɪŋ **-ed** -d

cog kɒg ⓤⓢ kɑːg, kɔːg **-s** -z **-ging** -ɪŋ **-ged** -d

cogen|ce ˈkəʊ.dʒᵊnt|s ⓤⓢ ˈkoʊ- **-cy** -si

Cogenhoe ˈkʊk.nəʊ ⓤⓢ -noʊ

cogent ˈkəʊ.dʒᵊnt ⓤⓢ ˈkoʊ- **-ly** -li

Coggeshall *in Essex:* ˈkɒg.ɪ.ʃᵊl; ˈkɒk.sᵊl ⓤⓢ ˈkɑː.gɪ.ʃᵊl, ˈkɔː-; ˈkɑːk.sᵊl *surname:* ˈkɒg.zɔːl ⓤⓢ ˈkɑːg.zɔːl, ˈkɔːg-, -zɑːl

Coggin ˈkɒg.ɪn ⓤⓢ ˈkɑː.gɪn, ˈkɔː-

Coghill ˈkɒg.ɪl, -hɪl ⓤⓢ ˈkɑː.gɪl, ˈkɔː-, ˈkɑːg.hɪl, ˈkɔːg-

cogi|tate ˈkɒdʒ.ɪ|.teɪt, ˈ-ə- ⓤⓢ ˈkɑː.dʒə- **-tates** -teɪts **-tating** -teɪ.tɪŋ ⓤⓢ -teɪ.t̬ɪŋ **-tated** -teɪ.tɪd ⓤⓢ -teɪ.t̬ɪd **-tator/s** -teɪ.təʳ/z ⓤⓢ -teɪ.t̬ɚ/z

cogitation ˌkɒdʒ.ɪˈteɪ.ʃᵊn, -əˈ- ⓤⓢ ˌkɑː.dʒəˈ- **-s** -z

cogitative ˈkɒdʒ.ɪ.tə.tɪv, ˈ-ə-, -teɪ- ⓤⓢ ˈkɑː.dʒə.teɪ.t̬ɪv

cogito ergo sum ˌkɒg.ɪ.təʊˌɜː.gəʊˈsʊm ⓤⓢ ˌkɑː.giː.toʊˌer.goʊˈsʌm, ˌkoʊ.gə-, -dʒiː-, -ˌɝː-, -ˈsʊm

cognac ˈkɒn.jæk ⓤⓢ ˈkoʊ.njæk **-s** -s

cognate ˈkɒg.neɪt, -ˈ- ⓤⓢ ˈkɑːg.neɪt, ˈkɔːg- **-s** -s

cognation kɒgˈneɪ.ʃᵊn ⓤⓢ kɑːg-, kɔːg-

cognition kɒgˈnɪʃ.ᵊn ⓤⓢ kɑːg-, kɔːg- **-s** -z

cognitive ˈkɒg.nə.tɪv, -nɪ- ⓤⓢ ˈkɑːg.nə.t̬ɪv, ˈkɔːg-

cognizable, -isa- ˈkɒg.nɪ.zə.bl̩, ˈkɒn.ɪ-; kɒgˈnaɪ- ⓤⓢ ˈkɑːg.nɪ-, ˈkɔːg-, ˈkɑː-, kɑːgˈnaɪ-, kɔːg-

cognizanc|e, -isa- ˈkɒg.nɪ.zᵊnts, ˈkɒn.ɪ-; kɒgˈnaɪ- ⓤⓢ ˈkɑːg.nə-, ˈkɔːg-, ˈkɑː- **-es** -ɪz

cognizant, -isa- ˈkɒg.nɪ.zᵊnt, ˈkɒn.ɪ-; kɒgˈnaɪ- ⓤⓢ ˈkɑːg.nə-, ˈkɔːg-, ˈkɑː-

cognomen kɒgˈnəʊ.men, -mən ⓤⓢ kɑːgˈnoʊ-, kɔːg- **-s** -z

cognominal kɒgˈnəʊ.mɪ.nᵊl, -ˈnɒm.ɪ- ⓤⓢ kɑːgˈnɑː.mə-, kɔːg-

cognoscent|e ˌkɒn.jəʊˈʃen.t|i, ˌkɒg.nəʊˈ-, -ˈsen- ⓤⓢ ˌkɑːg.nəˈʃen.t̬|i, ˌkɔːg-, ˌkɑː.njəˈ- **-i** -iː, -i

cognovit kɒgˈnəʊ.vɪt ⓤⓢ kɑːgˈnoʊ-, kɔːg- **-s** -s

cogwheel ˈkɒg.wiːl, -hwiːl ⓤⓢ ˈkɑːg-, ˈkɔːg- **-s** -z

cohab|it kəʊˈhæb|.ɪt ⓤⓢ koʊ- **-its** -ɪts **-iting** -ɪ.tɪŋ ⓤⓢ -ɪ.t̬ɪŋ **-ited** -ɪ.tɪd ⓤⓢ -ɪ.t̬ɪd

cohabitant kəʊˈhæb.ɪ.tᵊnt ⓤⓢ koʊˈhæb.ɪ.t̬ᵊnt **-s** -s

cohabitation kəʊˌhæb.ɪˈteɪ.ʃᵊn, ˌkəʊ.hæb- ⓤⓢ koʊˌhæb-

cohabitee ˌkəʊ.hæb.ɪˈtiː, kəʊˌhæb.ɪˈtiː ⓤⓢ ˌkoʊ- **-s** -z

co-heir ˌkəʊˈeəʳ, ˈ-- ⓤⓢ ˈkoʊ.er, -ˈ- **-s** -z

co-heiress ˌkəʊˈeə.res, -rɪs, -rəs, ˌ--ˈ- ⓤⓢ ˈkoʊ.er.əs, ˌ-ˈ-- **-es** -ɪz

Cohen ˈkəʊ.ɪn, -ən ⓤⓢ ˈkoʊ.ən

coher|e kəʊˈhɪəʳ ⓤⓢ koʊˈhɪr **-es** -z **-ing** -ɪŋ **-ed** -d

coheren|ce kəʊˈhɪə.rᵊnt|s ⓤⓢ koʊˈhɪr.ᵊnt|s **-cy** -si

coherent kəʊˈhɪə.rᵊnt ⓤⓢ koʊˈhɪr.ᵊnt **-ly** -li

cohesion kəʊˈhiː.ʒᵊn ⓤⓢ koʊ-

cohesive kəʊˈhiː.sɪv, -zɪv ⓤⓢ koʊ- **-ly** -li **-ness** -nəs, -nɪs

Cohn kəʊn ⓤⓢ koʊn

Cohn-Bendit ˌkəʊnˈben.dɪt, ˌkəʊm- ⓤⓢ ˌkoʊn-

cohort ˈkəʊ.hɔːt ⓤⓢ ˈkoʊ.hɔːrt **-s** -s

COHSE ˈkəʊ.zi ⓤⓢ ˈkoʊ-

coif *(n.)* kɔɪf **-s** -s

coif *(v.)* kwɑːf **-s** -s **-fing** -ɪŋ **-fed** -t

coiffé ˈkwɑː.feɪ, ˈkwɒf.eɪ, ˈkwæf-, -ˈ- ⓤⓢ kwɑːˈfeɪ **-s** -z **-ing** -ɪŋ **-d** -d

coiffeur kwɑːˈfɜːʳ, kwɒfˈɜːʳ, kwæf- ⓤⓢ kwɑːˈfɝː **-s** -z

coiffeus|e kwɑːˈfɜːz, kwɒfˈɜːz, kwæf- ⓤⓢ kwɑːˈfɜːz **-es** -ɪz

coiffure kwɒˈfjʊəʳ, kwɒfˈjʊəʳ, kwæf- ⓤⓢ kwɑːˈfjʊr **-s** -z

coign kɔɪn **-s** -z

coil kɔɪl **-s** -z **-ing** -ɪŋ **-ed** -d

Coimbra ˈkwɪm.brə, ˈkwiːm-

coin kɔɪn **-s** -z **-ing** -ɪŋ **-ed** -d **-er/s** -əʳ/z ⓤⓢ -ɚ/z

coinag|e ˈkɔɪ.nɪdʒ **-es** -ɪz

coin-box ˈkɔɪn.bɒks, ˈkɔɪm- ⓤⓢ ˈkɔɪn.bɑːks **-es** -ɪz

coincid|e ˌkəʊ.ɪnˈsaɪd, -ənˈ- ⓤⓢ ˌkoʊ- **-es** -z **-ing** -ɪŋ **-ed** -ɪd

coincidenc|e kəʊˈɪnt.sɪ.dᵊnts ⓤⓢ koʊ- **-es** -ɪz

coincidental kəʊˌɪnt.sɪˈden.tᵊl, ˌkəʊ.ɪn- ⓤⓢ koʊˌɪnt.sɪˈden.t̬ᵊl **-ly** -i

co-inheritor ˌkəʊ.ɪnˈher.ɪ.təʳ, ˈ-ə- ⓤⓢ ˌkoʊ.ɪnˈher.ə.t̬ɚ **-s** -z

coinsurance ˌkəʊ.ɪnˈʃʊə.rᵊnts, -ˈʃɔː- ⓤⓢ ˌkoʊ.ɪnˈʃʊr.ᵊnts, -ˈʃɝː-

coinsur|e ˌkəʊ.ɪnˈʃʊəʳ, -ˈʃɔːʳ ⓤⓢ ˌkoʊ.ɪnˈʃʊr, -ˈʃɝː **-es** -z **-ing** -ɪŋ **-ed** -d **-er/s** -əʳ/z ⓤⓢ -ɚ/z

Cointreau® ˈkwɒn.trəʊ, ˈkwɑːn-, ˈkwæn- ⓤⓢ ˈkwɑːn.troʊ

coir kɔɪəʳ ⓤⓢ kɔɪr

coition kəʊˈɪʃ.ᵊn ⓤⓢ koʊ-

coit|us ˈkəʊ.ɪ.t|əs, ˈkɔɪ.t|əs ⓤⓢ ˈkoʊ.ə.t̬|əs **-al** -ᵊl **-ally** -ᵊl.i

coitus interruptus ˌkəʊ.ɪ.təs.ɪn.təˈrʌp.təs, ˌkɔɪ- ⓤⓢ ˌkoʊ.ə.t̬əs.ɪn.t̬əˈ-

coke kəʊk ⓤⓢ koʊk

Coke *surname:* kəʊk, kʊk ⓤⓢ koʊk
Note: Members of the Essex family pronounce /kʊk/. So also the family name of the Earl of Leicester.

Coke® kəʊk ⓤⓢ koʊk

Coker ˈkəʊ.kəʳ ⓤⓢ ˈkoʊ.kɚ

col kɒl ⓤⓢ kɑːl **-s** -z

Col. *(abbrev. for* **Colonel***)* ˈkɜː.nᵊl ⓤⓢ ˈkɝː-

cola ˈkəʊ.lə ⓤⓢ ˈkoʊ-

colander ˈkʌl.ən.dəʳ, ˈkɒl- ⓤⓢ ˈkʌl.ən.dɚ, ˈkɑː.lən- **-s** -z

Colbert kɒlˈbeəʳ ⓤⓢ kɔːlˈber, koʊl-

Colby ˈkəʊl.bi, ˈkɒl- ⓤⓢ ˈkoʊl-

colcannon kəlˈkæn.ən, ˈkɒl.kæn- ⓤⓢ kəlˈkæn.ən, ˈkɑːl.kæn-

Colchester ˈkəʊl.tʃɪ.stəʳ, -tʃə- ⓤⓢ ˈkoʊl.tʃes.tɚ

colchicum ˈkɒl.tʃɪ.kəm, -kɪ- ⓤⓢ ˈkɑːl-

Colchis ˈkɒl.kɪs ⓤⓢ ˈkɑːl-

Colclough ˈkɒl.klʌf, ˈkəʊl-, ˈkəʊ.kli ⓤⓢ ˈkɑːl.klʌf, ˈkoʊl-, ˈkoʊ.kli

cold kəʊld ⓤⓢ koʊld **-s** -z **-er** -əʳ ⓤⓢ -ɚ **-est** -ɪst, -əst **-ly** -li **-ness** -nəs, -nɪs
ˌcold ˈcomfort; ˈcold ˌcream; ˌcold ˈfeet; ˈcold ˌframe; ˈcold ˌsore; ˌcold ˈstorage; ˌcold ˈturkey; ˌcold ˈwar; ˌcold ˈwater; blow ˌhot and ˈcold

cold-blooded ˌkəʊldˈblʌd.ɪd ⓤⓢ ˌkoʊld- **-ly** -li **-ness** -nəs, -nɪs
stress shift: ˌcold-blooded ˈkiller

cold-call *(v.)* ˈkəʊld.kɔːl ⓤⓢ ˈkoʊld-, -kɑːl **-s** -z **-ing** -ɪŋ **-ed** -d

cold-hearted ˌkəʊldˈhɑː.tɪd ⓤⓢ ˌkoʊldˈhɑːr.t̬ɪd **-ness** -nəs, -nɪs

coldish (C) ˈkəʊl.dɪʃ ⓤⓢ ˈkoʊl-

Colditz ˈkəʊl.dɪts ⓤⓢ ˈkoʊl-, ˈkɑːl-

cold-should|er ˌkəʊldˈʃəʊl.d|əʳ ⓤⓢ ˌkoʊldˈʃoʊl.d|ɚ **-ers** -əz ⓤⓢ -ɚz **-ering** -ᵊr.ɪŋ **-ered** -əd ⓤⓢ -ɚd

Coldstream ˈkəʊld.striːm ⓤⓢ ˈkoʊld-

cole (C) kəʊl ⓤⓢ koʊl **-s** -z

Colebrook(e) ˈkəʊl.brʊk ⓤⓢ ˈkoʊl-

Coleby 'kəʊl.bi US 'koʊl-
Coleclough 'kəʊl.klaʊ, -klʌf US 'koʊl-
Coleen kɒl'iːn, '-- US kɑː'liːn, koʊ'liːn
Coleford 'kəʊl.fəd US 'koʊl.fɚd
Coleman 'kəʊl.mən US 'koʊl-
Colenso kə'len.zəʊ US -zoʊ
coleopter|a ˌkɒl.i'ɒp.tᵊr|.ə US ˌkɑː.li'ɑːp- **-al** -ᵊl
Coleraine kəʊl'reɪn US koʊl-
Coleridge 'kəʊ.lᵊr.ɪdʒ US 'koʊ-
Coles kəʊlz US koʊlz
Coleshill 'kəʊlz.hɪl US 'koʊlz-
coleslaw 'kəʊl.slɔː US 'koʊl.slɑː, -slɔː
Colet 'kɒl.ɪt US 'kɑː.lɪt
cole-tit 'kəʊl.tɪt US 'koʊl- **-s** -s
Colette kɒl'et, kə'let US koʊ'let, kɑː-
coley (C) 'kəʊ.li US 'koʊ- **-s** -z
Colgan 'kɒl.gən US 'kɑːl-
Colgate® 'kəʊl.geɪt, 'kɒl-, -gət, -gɪt US 'koʊl.geɪt
colic 'kɒl.ɪk US 'kɑː.lɪk **-ky** -i
Colin 'kɒl.ɪn US 'kɑː.lɪn
Colindale 'kɒl.ɪn.deɪl, -ən- US 'kɑː.lɪn-, -lən-
Coling 'kəʊ.lɪŋ US 'koʊ-
coliseum (C) ˌkɒl.ɪ'siː.əm, -ə'- US ˌkɑː.lə'-
colitis kɒl'aɪ.tɪs, kəʊ'laɪ- US koʊ'laɪ.t̬ɪs, kə-
collabor|ate kə'læb.ᵊr|.eɪt, kɒl'æb- US kə'læb.ə.r|eɪt **-ates** -eɪts **-ating** -eɪ.tɪŋ US -eɪ.t̬ɪŋ **-ated** -eɪ.tɪd US -eɪ.t̬ɪd
collaboration kəˌlæb.ᵊ'reɪ.ʃᵊn, kɒlˌæb- US kəˌlæb- **-s** -z
collaborative kə'læb.ᵊr.ə.tɪv, kɒl'æb- US kə'læb.ɚ.ə.t̬ɪv, -rə.t̬ɪv **-ly** -li
collaborator kə'læb.ᵊr.eɪ.təʳ, kɒl'æb- US kə'læb.ə.reɪ.t̬ɚ **-s** -z
collag|e kɒl'ɑːʒ, kə'lɑːʒ; 'kɒl.ɑːʒ US kə'lɑːʒ, kɑː-, koʊ- **-es** -ɪz
collagen 'kɒl.ə.dʒən, -dʒɪn US 'kɑː.lə-
collagenic ˌkɒl.ə'dʒen.ɪk US ˌkɑː.lə'-
collagenous kə'lædʒ.ɪ.nəs, '-ə-
collaps|e kə'læps **-es** -ɪz **-ing** -ɪŋ **-ed** -t
collapsible kə'læp.sə.bl̩, -sɪ-
coll|ar 'kɒl|.əʳ US 'kɑː.l|ɚ **-ars** -əz US -ɚz **-aring** -ər.ɪŋ **-ared** -əd US -ɚd ˌ**hot under the 'collar**
collarbone 'kɒl.ə.bəʊn US 'kɑː.lɚ.boʊn **-s** -z
collard 'kɒl.əd US 'kɑː.lɚd
coll|ate kə'l|eɪt, kɒl'|eɪt US kə'l|eɪt, koʊ-, kɑː- **-ates** -eɪts **-ating** -eɪ.tɪŋ US -eɪ.t̬ɪŋ **-ated** -eɪ.tɪd US -eɪ.t̬ɪd **-ator/s** -eɪ.təʳ/z US -eɪ.t̬ɚ/z
collateral kə'læt.ᵊr.ᵊl, kɒl'æt- US kə'læt̬- **-s** -z **-ly** -i
collation kə'leɪ.ʃᵊn, kɒl'eɪ- US kɑː'leɪ-, kə-, koʊ- **-s** -z
colleague 'kɒl.iːg US 'kɑː.liːg **-s** -z
collect (*n.*) 'kɒl.ekt, -ɪkt US 'kɑːl.ekt, -ɪkt **-s** -s
collect (*v.*) kə'lekt **-s** -s **-ing** -ɪŋ **-ed** -ɪd
collectable kə'lek.tə.bl̩ **-s** -z
collectanea ˌkɒl.ek'teɪ.ni.ə, -'tɑː- US ˌkɑː.lek'-
collected kə'lek.tɪd, -təd **-ly** -li **-ness** -nəs, -nɪs
collectible kə'lek.tə.bl̩, -tɪ- **-s** -z
collection kə'lek.ʃᵊn **-s** -z
collective kə'lek.tɪv **-ly** -li **coˌllective 'bargaining**
collectiv|ism kə'lek.tɪ.v|ɪ.zᵊm US -tə- **-ist/s** -ɪst/s
collectivity ˌkɒl.ek'tɪv.ɪ.ti, kəˌlek-, -ə.ti US ˌkɑː.lek'tɪv.ə.t̬i, kəˌlek'-
collectivization, -isa- kəˌlek.tɪ.vaɪ'zeɪ.ʃᵊn, -tə-, -vɪ'- US -tɪ.vɪ'zeɪ-
collectiviz|e, -is|e kə'lek.tɪ.vaɪz, -tə- **-es** -ɪz **-ing** -ɪŋ **-ed** -d
collector kə'lek.təʳ US -tɚ **-s** -z **co'llector's ˌitem, coˌllector's 'item**
colleen (C) 'kɒl.iːn *in Ireland:* -'- US kɑː'liːn, '-- **-s** -z
colleg|e (C) 'kɒl.ɪdʒ US 'kɑː.lɪdʒ **-es** -ɪz **'College ˌBoard; ˌcollege 'try**
collegian kə'liː.dʒi.ən, kɒl'iː-, '-dʒᵊn US kə'liː.dʒən, '-dʒi.ən **-s** -z
collegiate kə'liː.dʒi.ət, kɒl'iː-, -dʒət US kə'liː.dʒɪt, -dʒi.ɪt
Colles 'kɒl.ɪs, -əs US 'kɑː.lɪs
collet (C) 'kɒl.ɪt, -ət US 'kɑː.lɪt **-s** -s
Collett 'kɒl.ɪt, -et, -ət US 'kɑː.lɪt
Colley 'kɒl.i US 'kɑː.li
collid|e kə'laɪd **-es** -z **-ing** -ɪŋ **-ed** -ɪd
collie (C) 'kɒl.i US 'kɑː.li **-s** -z
collier (C) 'kɒl.i.əʳ, '-jəʳ US 'kɑːl.jɚ **-s** -z
collier|y 'kɒl.jə.r|i, -i.ᵊr|.i US 'kɑːl.jɚ|.i **-ies** -iz
colli|gate 'kɒl.ɪ|.geɪt, '-ə- US 'kɑː.lə- **-gates** -geɪts **-gating** -geɪ.tɪŋ US -geɪ.t̬ɪŋ **-gated** -geɪ.tɪd US -geɪ.t̬ɪd
colligation ˌkɒl.ɪ'geɪ.ʃᵊn, -ə'- US ˌkɑː.lə'-
colli|mate 'kɒl.ɪ|.meɪt, '-ə- US 'kɑː.lə- **-mates** -meɪts **-mating** -meɪ.tɪŋ US -meɪ.t̬ɪŋ **-mated** -meɪ.tɪd US -meɪ.t̬ɪd
collimation ˌkɒl.ɪ'meɪ.ʃᵊn, -ə'- US ˌkɑː.lə'-
collimator 'kɒl.ɪ.meɪ.təʳ, '-ə- US 'kɑː.lə.meɪ.t̬ɚ **-s** -z
collinear kɒl'ɪn.i.əʳ, kəʊ'lɪn- US kə'lɪn.i.ɚ, kɑː-
Collingham 'kɒl.ɪŋ.əm US 'kɑː.lɪŋ-
Collings 'kɒl.ɪŋz US 'kɑː.lɪŋz
Collingwood 'kɒl.ɪŋ.wʊd US 'kɑː.lɪŋ-
Collins 'kɒl.ɪnz US 'kɑː.lɪnz
Collinson 'kɒl.ɪn.sᵊn, -ən- US 'kɑː.lɪn-
Collis 'kɒl.ɪs US 'kɑː.lɪs
collision kə'lɪʒ.ᵊn **-s** -z **co'llision ˌcourse**
collo|cate 'kɒl.əʊ|.keɪt US 'kɑː.lə- **-cates** -keɪts **-cating** -keɪ.tɪŋ US -keɪ.t̬ɪŋ **-cated** -keɪ.tɪd US -keɪ.t̬ɪd
collocation ˌkɒl.əʊ'keɪ.ʃᵊn US ˌkɑː.lə'- **-s** -z
collodi|on kə'ləʊ.di|.ən US -'loʊ- **-um** -əm
colloid 'kɒl.ɔɪd US 'kɑː.lɔɪd **-s** -z
colloidal kə'lɔɪ.dᵊl, kɒl'ɔɪ- US kə'lɔɪ-
collop 'kɒl.əp US 'kɑː.ləp **-s** -s
colloquial kə'ləʊ.kwi.əl US -'loʊ- **-ly** -i **-ism/s** -ɪ.zᵊm/z
colloquium kə'ləʊ.kwi.əm US -'loʊ-
colloqu|y 'kɒl.ə.kw|i US 'kɑː.lə- **-ies** -iz
collotype 'kɒl.əʊ.taɪp US 'kɑː.lə- **-s** -s
Colls kɒlz US kɑːlz
collud|e kə'luːd, -ljuːd US -'luːd **-es** -z **-ing** -ɪŋ **-ed** -ɪd **-er/s** -əʳ/z US -ɚ/z
collusion kə'luː.ʒᵊn, -'ljuː- US -'luː- **-s** -z
collusive kə'luː.sɪv, -'ljuː- US -'luː- **-ly** -li
Collyns 'kɒl.ɪnz US 'kɑː.lɪnz
collywobbles 'kɒl.iˌwɒb.l̩z US 'kɑː.liˌwɑː-
Colman 'kəʊl.mən, 'kɒl- US 'koʊl-, 'kɑːl-
Colnaghi kɒl'nɑː.gi US kɑːl-
Colnbrook 'kəʊln.brʊk, 'kəʊn- US 'koʊln-, 'koʊn-
Colne kəʊn, kəʊln US koʊn, koʊln
Colney 'kəʊ.ni US 'koʊ-
Colo. (*abbrev. for* **Colorado**) ˌkɒl.ᵊr'ɑː.dəʊ US ˌkɑː.lə'ræd.oʊ, -'rɑː.doʊ
cologne (C) kə'ləʊn US -'loʊn **-s** -z
Colombi|a kə'lɒm.bi|.ə, -'lʌm- US -'lʌm- **-an/s** -ən/z
Colombo kə'lʌm.bəʊ, -'lɒm- US -'lʌm.boʊ
colon *punctuation, part of intestine:* 'kəʊ.lɒn, -lən US 'koʊ.lən **-s** -z **cola** 'kəʊ.lə US 'koʊ-
colon, colón *currency:* kɒl'ɒn, kə'lɒn US kə'loʊn **-s** -z **-es** -es, -əs
colonel (C) 'kɜː.nᵊl US 'kɝː- **-s** -z ˌ**Colonel 'Blimp**
colonelc|y 'kɜː.nᵊl.s|i US 'kɝː- **-ies** -iz
colonelship 'kɜː.nᵊl.ʃɪp US 'kɝː- **-s** -s
colonial kə'ləʊ.ni.əl US -'loʊ- **-s** -z
colonial|ism kə'ləʊ.ni.ə.l|ɪ.zᵊm US -'loʊ- **-ist/s** -ɪst/s
colonist 'kɒl.ə.nɪst US 'kɑː.lə- **-s** -s
colonization, -isa- ˌkɒl.ə.naɪ'zeɪ.ʃᵊn, -nɪ'- US ˌkɑː.lə.nɪ'-
coloniz|e, -is|e 'kɒl.ə.naɪz US 'kɑː.lə- **-es** -ɪz **-ing** -ɪŋ **-ed** -d **-er/s** -əʳ/z US -ɚ/z
colonnade ˌkɒl.ə'neɪd US ˌkɑː.lə'- **-s** -z

Colonus kəˈləʊ.nəs ⓤⓢ -ˈloʊ-
colon|y ˈkɒl.ə.n|i ⓤⓢ ˈkɑː.lə- **-ies** -iz
colophon ˈkɒl.ə.fən, -fɒn ⓤⓢ ˈkɑː.lə.fən, -fɑːn **-s** -z
col|or ˈkʌl|.əʳ ⓤⓢ -ɚ **-ors** -əz ⓤⓢ -ɚz **-oring** -ər.ɪŋ **-ored/s** -əd/z ⓤⓢ -ɚd/s **-orer/s** -ər.əʳ/z ⓤⓢ -ɚ.ɚ/z **-orist/s** -ər.ɪst/s
colorab|le ˈkʌl.ər.ə.b|l̩ **-ly** -li
Colorado ˌkɒl.ərˈɑː.dəʊ ⓤⓢ ˌkɑː.ləˈræd.oʊ, -ˈrɑː.doʊ *stress shift, see compounds:* ˌ**Colorado** ˈ**beetle**; ˌ**Colorado** ˈ**Springs**
colorant ˈkʌl.ər.ənt **-s** -s
coloration ˌkʌl.əˈreɪ.ʃən
coloratura ˌkɒl.ər.əˈtjʊə.rə, -ˈtʊə- ⓤⓢ ˌkʌl.ɚ.əˈtʊr.ə, ˌkɑː.lɚ-, -ˈtjʊr-
color|-blind ˈkʌl.ə|.blaɪnd ⓤⓢ ˈ-ɚ- **-blindness** -ˌblaɪnd.nəs, -nɪs
colorcast ˈkʌl.ə.kɑːst ⓤⓢ -ɚ.kæst **-s** -s **-ing** -ɪŋ **-ed** -ɪd
color-coded ˈkʌl.əˌkəʊ.dɪd ⓤⓢ -ɚ.koʊ-
colorfast ˈkʌl.ə.fɑːst ⓤⓢ -ɚ.fæst **-ness** -nəs, -nɪs
colorful ˈkʌl.ə.fəl, -fʊl ⓤⓢ ˈ-ɚ- **-ly** -i
colorific ˌkɒl.əˈrɪf.ɪk, ˌkʌl- ⓤⓢ ˌkʌl-
coloring ˈkʌl.ər.ɪŋ **-s** -z
Colorization® ˌkɒl.ə.raɪˈzeɪ.ʃən, ˌkʌl-, -rɪˈ- ⓤⓢ ˌkʌl.ɚ.ɪˈ-
colorless ˈkʌl.ə.ləs, -lɪs ⓤⓢ ˈ-ɚ- **-ly** -li **-ness** -nəs, -nɪs
colossal kəˈlɒs.əl ⓤⓢ -ˈlɑː.səl **-ly** -i
colosseum (C) ˌkɒl.əˈsiː.əm ⓤⓢ ˌkɑː.ləˈ-
Colossian kəˈlɒs.i.ən, -ˈlɒʃ.i.ən, -ˈlɒʃ.ən ⓤⓢ -ˈlɑː.ʃən **-s** -z
coloss|us kəˈlɒs|.əs ⓤⓢ -ˈlɑː.s|əs **-i** -aɪ **-uses** -ə.sɪz
colostom|y kəˈlɒs.tə.m|i, kɒlˈɒs- ⓤⓢ kəˈlɑː.stə- **-ies** -iz
colostrum kəˈlɒs.trəm, kɒlˈɒs- ⓤⓢ kəˈlɑː.strəm
col|our ˈkʌl|.əʳ ⓤⓢ -ɚ **-ours** -əz ⓤⓢ -ɚz **-ouring** -ər.ɪŋ **-oured/s** -əd/z ⓤⓢ -ɚd/s **-ourer/s** -ər.əʳ/z ⓤⓢ -ɚ.ɚ/z **-ourist/s** -ər.ɪst/s
colourab|le ˈkʌl.ər.ə.b|l̩ **-ly** -li
colourant ˈkʌl.ər.ənt **-s** -s
colouration ˌkʌl.əˈreɪ.ʃən
colour|-blind ˈkʌl.ə|.blaɪnd ⓤⓢ ˈ-ɚ- **-blindness** -ˌblaɪnd.nəs, -nɪs
colourcast ˈkʌl.ə.kɑːst ⓤⓢ -ɚ.kæst **-s** -s
colour-coded ˈkʌl.əˌkəʊ.dɪd ⓤⓢ -ɚˌkoʊ-
colourfast ˈkʌl.ə.fɑːst ⓤⓢ -ɚ.fæst **-ness** -nəs, -nɪs
colourful ˈkʌl.ə.fəl, -fʊl ⓤⓢ ˈ-ɚ- **-ly** -i
colouring ˈkʌl.ər.ɪŋ **-s** -z
colourless ˈkʌl.ə.ləs, -lɪs ⓤⓢ ˈ-ɚ- **-ly** -li **-ness** -nəs, -nɪs
colourway ˈkʌl.ə.weɪ ⓤⓢ -ɚ- **-s** -z
colpo- ˈkɒl.pəʊ-; kɒlˈpɒ- ⓤⓢ ˈkɑːl.pə-, ˈkɑːl.poʊ-; kɑːlˈpɑː-
Note: Prefix. This may carry primary or secondary stress on the first syllable, e.g. **colposcope** /ˈkɒl.pə.skəʊp ⓤⓢ ˈkɑːl.pə.skoʊp/, or on the second syllable, e.g. **colposcopy** /kɒlˈpɒs.kə.pi ⓤⓢ kɑːlˈpɑː-/.
colporteur ˈkɒl.pɔː.təʳ, ˌkɒl.pɔːˈtɜːʳ ⓤⓢ ˈkɑːl.pɔːr.t̬ɚ, ˌkɑːl.pɔːrˈtɝː **-s** -z
colposcope ˈkɒl.pə.skəʊp ⓤⓢ ˈkɑːl.pə.skoʊp **-s** -s
colposcopic ˌkɒl.pəˈskɒp.ɪk ⓤⓢ ˌkɑːl.pəˈskɑː.pɪk
colposcopy kɒlˈpɒs.kə.pi ⓤⓢ kɑːlˈpɑː.skə-
Colquhoun kəˈhuːn
Cols. *(abbrev. for* **Colonels***)* ˈkɜː.nəlz ⓤⓢ ˈkɝː-
Colson ˈkəʊl.sən ⓤⓢ ˈkoʊl-
Colston ˈkəʊl.stən ⓤⓢ ˈkoʊl-
colt kəʊlt ⓤⓢ koʊlt **-s** -s
coltish ˈkəʊl.tɪʃ ⓤⓢ ˈkoʊl.t̬ɪʃ **-ly** -li **-ness** -nəs, -nɪs
Coltrane kɒlˈtreɪn, kəʊl- ⓤⓢ ˈkoʊl.treɪn
coltsfoot ˈkəʊlts.fʊt ⓤⓢ ˈkoʊlts- **-s** -s
colubrine ˈkɒl.jʊ.braɪn, -brɪn ⓤⓢ ˈkɑː.lə-, ˈkɑːl.jə-
Columba kəˈlʌm.bə
columbari|um ˌkɒl.əmˈbeə.ri|.əm ⓤⓢ ˌkɑː.ləmˈber.i- **-ums** -əmz **-a** -ə
Columbi|a kəˈlʌm.bi|.ə **-an/s** -ən/z
Columbiad kəˈlʌm.bi.æd
columbine (C) ˈkɒl.əm.baɪn ⓤⓢ ˈkɑː.ləm- **-s** -z
Columbo kəˈlʌm.bəʊ ⓤⓢ -boʊ
Columbus kəˈlʌm.bəs
column ˈkɒl.əm ⓤⓢ ˈkɑː.ləm **-s** -z **-ed** -d
column|al kəˈlʌm.n|əl **-ar** -əʳ ⓤⓢ -ɚ
columnist ˈkɒl.əm.nɪst, -ə.mɪst ⓤⓢ ˈkɑː.ləm.nɪst, -lə.mɪst **-s** -s
colure kəˈljʊəʳ, -ˈlʊəʳ; ˈkəʊ.ljʊəʳ, -lʊəʳ ⓤⓢ koʊˈlʊr, kə-; ˈkoʊ.lʊr **-s** -z
Colwyn ˈkɒl.wɪn ⓤⓢ ˈkɑːl- ˌ**Colwyn** ˈ**Bay**
Colyton ˈkɒl.ɪ.tən ⓤⓢ ˈkɑː.lɪ.t̬ən
colza ˈkɒl.zə ⓤⓢ ˈkɑːl-
com- kɒm-, kəm- ⓤⓢ kɑːm-, kəm-
Note: Prefix. This may carry primary or secondary stress, e.g. **combat** /ˈkɒm.bæt ⓤⓢ ˈkɑːm.bæt/ or be unstressed, e.g. **complete** /kəmˈpliːt/.
coma *deep sleep:* ˈkəʊ.mə ⓤⓢ ˈkoʊ- **-s** -z
com|a *tuft:* ˈkəʊ.m|ə ⓤⓢ ˈkoʊ- **-as** -əz **-ae** -iː
Coma Berenices ˌkəʊ.məˌber.ɪˈnaɪ.siːz ⓤⓢ ˌkoʊ.məˌber.əˈ-
Comanche kəˈmæn.tʃi, kəʊ- ⓤⓢ kə- **-s** -z
Comaneci ˌkɒm.əˈnetʃ.i, -ˈnetʃ ⓤⓢ ˌkoʊ.mə.ˈniː.tʃi, -ˈnetʃ.i
comatose ˈkəʊ.mə.təʊs, -təʊz ⓤⓢ ˈkoʊ.mə.toʊs, ˈkɑː-
comb kəʊm ⓤⓢ koʊm **-s** -z **-ing/s** -ɪŋ/z **-ed** -d
combat (*n.*) ˈkɒm.bæt, ˈkʌm-, -bət ⓤⓢ ˈkɑːm.bæt **-s** -s
comba|t (*v.*) ˈkɒm.bæ|t, ˈkʌm-, -bə|t; kəmˈbæ|t ⓤⓢ kəmˈbæ|t, kɑːm-; ˈkɑːm.bæ|t **-ts** -ts **-(t)ting** -tɪŋ ⓤⓢ -t̬ɪŋ **-(t)ted** -tɪd ⓤⓢ -t̬ɪd
combatant ˈkɒm.bə.tənt, ˈkʌm-; kəmˈbæt.ənt ⓤⓢ kəmˈbæt.ənt; ˈkɑːm.bə.tənt **-s** -s
combative ˈkɒm.bə.tɪv, ˈkʌm-; kəmˈbæt.ɪv ⓤⓢ kəmˈbæt̬.ɪv; ˈkɑːm.bə.t̬ɪv **-ly** -li **-ness** -nəs, -nɪs
combe (C) kuːm, kəʊm ⓤⓢ kuːm, koʊm **-s** -z
comber *combing machine:* ˈkəʊ.məʳ ⓤⓢ ˈkoʊ.mɚ **-s** -z
comber (C) *fish:* ˈkɒm.bəʳ ⓤⓢ ˈkɑːm.bɚ **-s** -z
combination ˌkɒm.bɪˈneɪ.ʃən, -bəˈ- ⓤⓢ ˌkɑːm.bəˈ-, -bɪˈ- **-s** -z ˌ**combiˈnation** ˌ**lock**; ˌ**combiˈnation** ˌ**room**
combinative ˈkɒm.bɪ.nə.tɪv, -bə-, -neɪ- ⓤⓢ ˈkɑːm.bə.neɪ.t̬ɪv, -nə-; -bɪ-; kəmˈbaɪ.nə.t̬ɪv
combinatorial ˌkɒm.bɪ.nəˈtɔː.ri.əl, -bən.əˈ- ⓤⓢ ˌkɑːm.bə.nəˈtɔːr.i-; -bɪn.əˈ-; kəmˌbaɪ-
combinatory ˈkɒm.bɪ.nə.tər.i, -tri; ˌkɒm.bɪˈneɪ- ⓤⓢ ˈkɑːm.bə.nə.tɔːr.i; -bɪ-; kəmˈbaɪ-
combine (*n.*) ˈkɒm.baɪn; kəmˈbaɪn ⓤⓢ ˈkɑːm.baɪn **-s** -z
combin|e (*v.*) *join:* kəmˈbaɪn **-es** -z **-ing** -ɪŋ **-ed** -d *harvest:* ˈkɒm.baɪn ⓤⓢ ˈkɑːm- **-es** -z **-ing** -ɪŋ **-ed** -d ˌ**combine** ˈ**harvester**
combo ˈkɒm.bəʊ ⓤⓢ ˈkɑːm.boʊ **-s** -z
Combs kəʊmz, kuːmz ⓤⓢ koʊmz
combust kəmˈbʌst **-s** -s **-ing** -ɪŋ **-ed** -ɪd **-er/s** -əʳ/z ⓤⓢ -ɚ/z
combustibility kəmˌbʌs.təˈbɪl.ə.ti, -tɪˈ-, -ɪ.ti ⓤⓢ -ə.t̬i
combustible kəmˈbʌs.tə.bl̩, -tɪ- **-ness** -nəs, -nɪs
combustion kəmˈbʌs.tʃən **-s** -z comˈ**bustion** ˌ**engine**
com|e kʌm **-es** -z **-ing/s** -ɪŋ/z **came** keɪm
come-at-able ˌkʌmˈæt.ə.bl̩ ⓤⓢ -ˈæt̬-
comeback ˈkʌm.bæk **-s** -s
Comecon ˈkɒm.ɪ.kɒn ⓤⓢ ˈkɑː.mɪ.kɑːn
comedian kəˈmiː.di.ən **-s** -z
comedic kəˈmiː.dɪk **-ally** -əl.i, -li
comedienne kəˌmiː.diˈen, ˌkɒm.iː- ⓤⓢ kəˌmiː- **-s** -z
comedown ˈkʌm.daʊn, ˌ-ˈ- ⓤⓢ ˈ-- **-s** -z
comed|y ˈkɒm.ə.d|i, ˈ-ɪ- ⓤⓢ ˈkɑː.mə- **-ies** -iz

come-hither ˌkʌmˈhɪð.əʳ ⓊⓈ ˌkʌmˈhɪð.ɚ *stress shift:* ˌcome-hither ˈlook
comel|y ˈkʌm.l|i **-ier** -i.əʳ ⓊⓈ -i.ɚ **-iest** -i.ɪst, -i.əst **-iness** -ɪ.nəs, -ɪ.nɪs
Comenius kəˈmeɪ.ni.əs, kɒmˈeɪ-, -ˈiː- ⓊⓈ kəˈmiː-
come-on ˈkʌm.ɒn ⓊⓈ -ɑːn **-s** -z
-comer -ˌkʌm.əʳ ⓊⓈ -ɚ
comer ˈkʌm.əʳ ⓊⓈ -ɚ **-s** -z
comestible kəˈmes.tɪ.bl̩, -tə- **-s** -z
comet ˈkɒm.ɪt ⓊⓈ ˈkɑː.mɪt **-s** -s **-ary** -ᵊr.i ⓊⓈ -er.i
come-uppanc|e kʌmˈʌp.ənts **-es** -ɪz
comfit ˈkʌm.fɪt, ˈkɒm- ⓊⓈ ˈkʌm-, ˈkɑːm- **-s** -s
com|fort ˈkʌmp|.fət ⓊⓈ -fɚt **-forts** -fəts ⓊⓈ -fɚts **-forting/ly** -fə.tɪŋ/li ⓊⓈ -fɚ.t̬ɪŋ/li **-forted** -fə.tɪd ⓊⓈ -fɚ.t̬ɪd **-forter/s** -fə.təʳ/z ⓊⓈ -fɚ.t̬ɚ/z ˈ**comfort** ˌ**station**
comfortab|le ˈkʌmpf.tə.b|l̩, ˈkʌmp.fə.tə- ⓊⓈ ˈkʌmp.fɚ.t̬ə-, ˈkʌmpf.tə- **-ly** -li
comforter ˈkʌmp.fə.təʳ ⓊⓈ -fɚ.t̬ɚ **-s** -z
comfortless ˈkʌmp.fət.ləs, -lɪs ⓊⓈ -fɚt-
comfrey ˈkʌmp.fri
comf|y ˈkʌmp.f|i **-ier** -i.əʳ ⓊⓈ -i.ɚ **-iest** -i.ɪst, -i.əst **-ily** -ɪ.li, -ᵊl.i **-iness** -ɪ.nəs, -ɪ.nɪs
comic ˈkɒm.ɪk ⓊⓈ ˈkɑː.mɪk **-s** -s ˈ**comic** ˌ**book**; ˈ**comic** ˌ**strip**, ˌ**comic** ˈ**strip**
comic|al ˈkɒm.ɪ.k|ᵊl ⓊⓈ ˈkɑː.mɪ- **-ally** -ᵊl.i, -li **-alness** -ᵊl.nəs, -nɪs
Cominform ˈkɒm.ɪn.fɔːm, -ən-, ˌ--ˈ- ⓊⓈ ˈkɑː.mən.fɔːrm
Comintern ˈkɒm.ɪn.tɜːn, -ən-, ˌ--ˈ- ⓊⓈ ˈkɑː.mən.tɝːn
comity ˈkɒm.ɪ.ti, -ə.ti ⓊⓈ ˈkɑː.mə.t̬i, ˈkoʊ-
comma ˈkɒm.ə ⓊⓈ ˈkɑː.mə **-s** -z
command kəˈmɑːnd ⓊⓈ -ˈmænd **-s** -z **-ing** -ɪŋ **-ed** -ɪd
commandant ˈkɒm.ən.dænt, -dɑːnt, ˌ--ˈ- ⓊⓈ ˈkɑː.mən.dænt, -dɑːnt **-s** -s
commandantship ˌkɒm.ənˈdænt.ʃɪp, -ˈdɑːnt-, ˈkɒm.ən.dænt.ʃɪp, -dɑːnt- ⓊⓈ ˈkɑː.mən.dænt-, -dɑːnt- **-s** -s
commandeer ˌkɒm.ənˈdɪəʳ ⓊⓈ ˌkɑː.mənˈdɪr **-s** -z **-ing** -ɪŋ **-ed** -d
commander kəˈmɑːn.dəʳ ⓊⓈ -ˈmæn.dɚ **-s** -z
commander-in-chief kəˌmɑːn.də.rɪnˈtʃiːf ⓊⓈ -ˌmæn.dɚ- **commanders-in-chief** kəˌmɑːn.dəz.ɪnˈtʃiːf ⓊⓈ -ˌmænd.ɚz-
commandership kəˈmɑːn.də.ʃɪp ⓊⓈ -ˈmæn.dɚ- **-s** -s
commanding kəˈmɑːn.dɪŋ ⓊⓈ -ˈmæn- **-ly** -li
commandment kəˈmɑːnd.mənt, -ˈmɑːm- ⓊⓈ -ˈmænd- **-s** -s
commando kəˈmɑːn.dəʊ ⓊⓈ -ˈmæn.doʊ **-(e)s** -z
Comme des Garçons ˌkɒm.deɪ.gɑːˈsɔ̃ːŋ, ˌkɒm.deɪˈgɑː.sɔŋ ⓊⓈ ˌkɑːm.deɪ.gɑːrˈsoʊ̃n
commedia dell'arte kɒmˌeɪ.di.ə.delˈɑː.teɪ, kəˌmeɪ-, -ˌmed.i- ⓊⓈ kəˌmeɪ.di.ə.delˈɑːr.t̬i
comme il faut ˌkɒm.iːlˈfəʊ ⓊⓈ ˌkʌm.iːlˈfoʊ, ˌkɑːm-
commemo|rate kəˈmem.ə|.reɪt **-rates** -reɪts **-rating** -reɪ.tɪŋ ⓊⓈ -reɪ.t̬ɪŋ **-rated** -reɪ.tɪd ⓊⓈ -reɪ.t̬ɪd **-rator/s** -reɪ.təʳ/z ⓊⓈ -reɪ.t̬ɚ/z
commemoration kəˌmem.əˈreɪ.ʃᵊn **-s** -z
commemorative kəˈmem.ᵊr.ə.tɪv, -eɪ- ⓊⓈ -ə.t̬ɪv, -eɪ- **-ly** -li
commenc|e kəˈments **-es** -ɪz **-ing** -ɪŋ **-ed** -t
commencement kəˈments.mənt **-s** -s
commend kəˈmend **-s** -z **-ing** -ɪŋ **-ed** -ɪd
commendab|le kəˈmen.də.b|l̩ **-ly** -li **-leness** -l̩.nəs, -nɪs
commendation ˌkɒm.enˈdeɪ.ʃᵊn, -ənˈ- ⓊⓈ ˌkɑː.mənˈ- **-s** -z
commendatory kəˈmen.də.tᵊr.i, -tri; ˌkɒm.enˈdeɪ-, -ənˈ- ⓊⓈ kəˈmen.də.tɔːr.i
commensal kəˈment.sᵊl
commensalism kəˈment.sᵊl.ɪ.zᵊm
commensurability kəˌment.ʃᵊr.əˈbɪl.ə.ti, -ʃʊ.rə-, -sjᵊr.ə-, -ɪ.ti ⓊⓈ -sɚ.əˈbɪl.ə.t̬i, -ʃɚ-
commensurab|le kəˈment.ʃᵊr.ə.b|l̩, -ʃʊ.rə-, -sjᵊr.ə- ⓊⓈ -sɚ.ə-, -ʃɚ- **-ly** -li **-leness** -l̩.nəs, -nɪs
commensurate kəˈment.ʃᵊr.ət, -ʃʊ.rət, -sjᵊr.ət, -ɪt ⓊⓈ -sɚ.ət, -ʃɚ- **-ly** -li **-ness** -nəs, -nɪs
comment *(n.)* ˈkɒm.ent ⓊⓈ ˈkɑː.ment **-s** -s
commen|t *(v.)* ˈkɒm.en|t, -ən|t; kɒmˈent, kəˈmen|t; ⓊⓈ ˈkɑː.men|t **-ts** -ts **-ting** -tɪŋ ⓊⓈ -t̬ɪŋ **-ted** -tɪd ⓊⓈ -t̬ɪd
commentar|y ˈkɒm.ən.tᵊr|.i, -tr|i ⓊⓈ ˈkɑː.mən.ter|.i **-ies** -iz
commen|tate ˈkɒm.ən|.teɪt, -en- ⓊⓈ ˈkɑː.mən- **-tates** -teɪts **-tating** -teɪ.tɪŋ ⓊⓈ -teɪ.t̬ɪŋ **-tated** -teɪ.tɪd ⓊⓈ -teɪ.t̬ɪd
commentator ˈkɒm.ən.teɪ.təʳ, -en- ⓊⓈ ˈkɑː.mən.teɪ.t̬ɚ **-s** -z
commerce ˈkɒm.ɜːs ⓊⓈ ˈkɑː.mɝːs
commercial kəˈmɜː.ʃᵊl ⓊⓈ -ˈmɝː- **-s** -z **-ly** -i
commercialese kəˌmɜː.ʃᵊlˈiːz ⓊⓈ -ˌmɝː.ʃəˈliːz
commercial|ism kəˈmɜː.ʃᵊl|.ɪ.zᵊm ⓊⓈ -ˈmɝː- **-ist/s** -ɪst/s
commerciality kəˌmɜː.ʃiˈæl.ə.ti, -ɪ.ti ⓊⓈ -ˌmɝː.ʃiˈæl.ə.t̬i
commercialization, -isa- kəˌmɜː.ʃᵊ.laɪˈzeɪ.ʃᵊn, -lɪˈ- ⓊⓈ -mɝː.ʃə.lɪˈ-
commercializ|e, -is|e kəˈmɜː.ʃᵊl.aɪz ⓊⓈ -ˈmɝː.ʃə.laɪz **-es** -ɪz **-ing** -ɪŋ **-ed** -d
commie ˈkɒm.i ⓊⓈ ˈkɑː.mi **-s** -z
commi|nate ˈkɒm.ɪ|.neɪt ⓊⓈ ˈkɑː.mə- **-nates** -neɪts **-nating** -neɪ.tɪŋ ⓊⓈ -neɪ.t̬ɪŋ **-nated** -neɪ.tɪd ⓊⓈ -neɪ.t̬ɪd
commination ˌkɒm.ɪˈneɪ.ʃᵊn ⓊⓈ ˌkɑː.məˈ- **-s** -z
comminatory ˈkɒm.ɪ.nə.tᵊr.i, -neɪ-, -tri ⓊⓈ ˈkɑː.mɪ.nə.tɔːr.i; kəˈmɪn.ə-
commingl|e kɒmˈɪŋ.gl̩, kəˈmɪŋ- ⓊⓈ kəˈmɪŋ-, kɑː- **-es** -z **-ing** -ɪŋ, ˈ-glɪŋ **-ed** -d
commi|nute ˈkɒm.ɪ.njuːt ⓊⓈ ˈkɑː.mə.nuːt, -njuːt **-nutes** -njuːts ⓊⓈ -nuːts, -njuːts **-nuting** -njuː.tɪŋ ⓊⓈ -nuː.t̬ɪŋ, -njuː- **-nuted** -njuː.tɪd ⓊⓈ -nuː.t̬ɪd, -njuː-
comminution ˌkɒm.ɪˈnjuː.ʃᵊn ⓊⓈ ˌkɑː.məˈnuː-, -ˈnjuː-
commis ˈkɒm.i, -ɪs ⓊⓈ ˌkɑːˈmi *stress shift, American only, see compound:* ˈ**commis** ˌ**chef**, ˌ**commis** ˈ**chef**
commiser|ate kəˈmɪz.ᵊr|.eɪt, kɒmˈɪz- ⓊⓈ kəˈmɪz- **-ates** -eɪts **-ating** -eɪ.tɪŋ ⓊⓈ -eɪ.t̬ɪŋ **-ated** -eɪ.tɪd ⓊⓈ -eɪ.t̬ɪd
commiseration kəˌmɪz.ᵊrˈeɪ.ʃᵊn, kɒmˌɪz- ⓊⓈ kəˌmɪz-
commissar ˌkɒm.ɪˈsɑːʳ, -əˈ-, ˈ--- ⓊⓈ ˈkɑː.mə.sɑːr **-s** -z
commissarial ˌkɒm.ɪˈseə.ri.əl, -əˈ-, -ˈsɑː-, -ˈsær.i- ⓊⓈ ˌkɑː.məˈser-
commissariat ˌkɒm.ɪˈseə.ri.ət, -əˈ-, -ˈsɑː-, -ˈsær.i-, -æt ⓊⓈ ˌkɑː.məˈser-
commissar|y ˈkɒm.ɪ.sᵊr|.i, kəˈmɪs.ᵊr- ⓊⓈ ˈkɑː.mə.ser- **-ies** -iz
commission kəˈmɪʃ.ᵊn **-s** -z **-ing** -ɪŋ **-ed** -d **-er/s** -əʳ/z, ˈ-nəʳ/z ⓊⓈ ˈ-ᵊn.ɚ/z, ˈ-nɚ/z **com**ˈ**mission** ˌ**agent**; **com**ˌ**missioned** ˈ**officer**
commissionaire kəˌmɪʃ.ᵊnˈeəʳ ⓊⓈ -ˈer **-s** -z
commissive kəˈmɪs.ɪv, ˈkɒm.ɪ.sɪv ⓊⓈ kəˈmɪs-
commissure ˈkɒm.ɪ.sjʊəʳ, ˈ-ə-, -ʃʊəʳ ⓊⓈ ˈkɑː.mə.ʃʊr **-s** -z
com|mit kə|ˈmɪt **-mits** -s **-mitting** -ˈmɪt.ɪŋ ⓊⓈ -ˈmɪt̬.ɪŋ **-mitted** -ˈmɪt.ɪd ⓊⓈ -ˈmɪt̬.ɪd **-mitter/s** -ˈmɪt.əʳ/z ⓊⓈ -ˈmɪt̬.ɚ/z
commitment kəˈmɪt.mənt **-s** -s
committal kəˈmɪt.ᵊl ⓊⓈ -ˈmɪt̬- **-s** -z
committee *council:* kəˈmɪt.i ⓊⓈ -ˈmɪt̬- **-s** -z **com**ˈ**mittee** ˌ**meeting**
committee *one committed:* ˌkɒm.ɪˈtiː ⓊⓈ ˌkɑː.mɪˈtiː **-s** -z

committor ˌkɒm.ɪˈtɔːʳ, kəˈmɪt.əʳ (US) ˌkɑː.mɪˈt̬ɔːr; kəˈmɪt̬.ɚ **-s** -z

commixture kəˈmɪks.tʃəʳ (US) -tʃɚ **-s** -z

commode kəˈməʊd (US) -ˈmoʊd **-s** -z

commodious kəˈməʊ.di.əs (US) -ˈmoʊ- **-ly** -li **-ness** -nəs, -nɪs

commodit|y kəˈmɒd.ə.t|i, -ɪ.t|i (US) -ˈmɑː.də.t̬|i **-ies** -iz

commodore ˈkɒm.ə.dɔːʳ (US) ˈkɑː.mə.dɔːr **-s** -z

Commodus ˈkɒm.ə.dəs (US) ˈkɑː.mə-

common ˈkɒm.ən (US) ˈkɑː.mən **-s** -z **-er** -əʳ (US) -ɚ **-est** -ɪst, -əst **-ly** -li **-ness** -nəs, -nɪs ˌ**common deˈnominator; ˌCommon ˈMarket; ˈcommon ˌroom; ˌcommon ˈsense; ˈcommon ˌtouch**

commonage ˈkɒm.ə.nɪdʒ (US) ˈkɑː.mə-

commonality ˌkɒm.əˈnæl.ə.ti, -ɪ.ti (US) ˌkɑː.məˈnæl.ə.t̬i

commonalt|y ˈkɒm.ə.nᵊl.t|i (US) ˈkɑː.mə- **-ies** -iz

Commondale ˈkɒm.ən.deɪl (US) ˈkɑː.mən-

commoner ˈkɒm.ə.nəʳ (US) ˈkɑː.mə.nɚ **-s** -z

common-law ˌkɒm.ənˈlɔː (US) ˈkɑː.mən.lɑː, -lɔː *stress shift, British only:* ˌcommon-law ˈwife

common-or-garden ˌkɒm.ən.ɔːˈgɑː.dᵊn, -əˈgɑː- (US) ˌkɑː.mən.ɔːrˈgɑːr-

commonplac|e ˈkɒm.ən.pleɪs, -əm- (US) ˈkɑː.mən- **-es** -ɪz

commons (C) ˈkɒm.ənz (US) ˈkɑː.mənz

commonsense ˌkɒm.ənˈsen*t*s (US) ˌkɑː.mənˈ-

commonsensical ˌkɒm.ənˈsen*t*.sɪ.kᵊl (US) ˌkɑː.mənˈ-

commonwealth (C) ˈkɒm.ən.welθ (US) ˈkɑː.mən- **-s** -s

commotion kəˈməʊ.ʃᵊn (US) -ˈmoʊ- **-s** -z

communal ˈkɒm.jʊ.nᵊl, -jə-; kəˈmjuː- (US) kəˈmjuː-; ˈkɑː.mjə- **-ly** -i

communard (C) ˈkɒm.jʊ.nɑːd, ˌkɒm.jʊˈnɑː (US) ˈkɑː.mjʊ.nɑːrd, -nɑːr **-s** -z

commune (*n.*) ˈkɒm.juːn (US) ˈkɑː.mjuːn **-s** -z

commun|e (*v.*) kəˈmjuːn **-es** -z **-ing** -ɪŋ **-ed** -d

communicab|le kəˈmjuː.nɪ.kə.b|l̩ **-ly** -li **-leness** -l̩.nəs, -nɪs

communicant kəˈmjuː.nɪ.kənt **-s** -s

communi|cate kəˈmjuː.nɪ|.keɪt, -nə- **-cates** -keɪts **-cating** -keɪ.tɪŋ (US) -keɪ.t̬ɪŋ **-cated** -keɪ.tɪd (US) -keɪ.t̬ɪd **-cator/s** -keɪ.təʳ/z (US) -keɪ.t̬ɚ/z

communication kəˌmjuː.nɪˈkeɪ.ʃᵊn, -nəˈ- **-s** -z

communicative kəˈmjuː.nɪ.kə.tɪv, -nə-, -keɪ- (US) -nə.keɪ.t̬ɪv, -kə- **-ly** -li **-ness** -nəs, -nɪs

communion kəˈmjuː.ni.ən (US) -njən **-s** -z

communiqué kəˈmjuː.nɪ.keɪ, kɒmˈjuː-, -nə- (US) kəˌmjuː.nɪˈkeɪ, kəˈmjuː.nɪ.keɪ **-s** -z

commun|ism ˈkɒm.jə.n|ɪ.zᵊm, -jʊ- (US) ˈkɑː.mjə- **-ist/s** -ɪst/s

communit|y kəˈmjuː.nə.t|i, -nɪ- (US) -nə.t̬|i **-ies** -iz **comˈmunity ˌcentre; comˈmunity ˌchest** (US) **community ˈchest; comˈmunity ˌcollege**

commutability kəˌmjuː.təˈbɪl.ə.ti, -ɪ.ti (US) -t̬əˈbɪl.ə.t̬i

commutable kəˈmjuː.tə.bl̩ (US) -t̬ə-

commu|tate ˈkɒm.jʊ|.teɪt (US) ˈkɑː.mjə- **-tates** -teɪts **-tating** -teɪ.tɪŋ (US) -teɪ.t̬ɪŋ **-tated** -teɪ.tɪd (US) -teɪ.t̬ɪd **-tator/s** -teɪ.təʳ/z (US) -teɪ.t̬ɚ/z

commutation ˌkɒm.jʊˈteɪ.ʃᵊn (US) ˌkɑː.mjəˈ- **-s** -z

commutative kəˈmjuː.tə.tɪv, ˈkɒm.jʊ.teɪ- (US) ˈkɑː.mjə.teɪ.t̬ɪv, kəˈmjuː.t̬ə- **-ly** -li

com|mute kə|ˈmjuːt **-mutes** -ˈmjuːts **-muting** -ˈmjuː.tɪŋ (US) -ˈmjuː.t̬ɪŋ **-muted** -ˈmjuː.tɪd (US) -ˈmjuː.t̬ɪd

commuter kəˈmjuː.təʳ (US) -t̬ɚ **-s** -z

Como ˈkəʊ.məʊ (US) ˈkoʊ.moʊ

Comorin ˈkɒm.ə.rɪn (US) ˈkɑː.mɚ.ɪn

Comoros ˈkɒm.ə.rəʊz (US) ˈkɑː.mə.roʊz

comose ˈkəʊ.məʊs, -məʊz, -ˈ- (US) ˈkoʊ.moʊs

compact (*n.*) ˈkɒm.pækt (US) ˈkɑːm- **-s** -s

compact (*adj. v.*) kəmˈpækt (US) kəm-, kɑːm- **-er** -əʳ (US) -ɚ **-est** -ɪst, -əst **-ly** -li **-ness** -nəs, -nɪs **-s** -s **-ing** -ɪŋ **-ed** -ɪd *stress shift, see compound:* ˌ**compact ˈdisc/ˌcompact ˈdisk**

compactor kəmˈpæk.təʳ; ˈkɒm.pæk- (US) kəmˈpæk.tɚ; ˈkɑːm.pæk- **-s** -z

companion kəmˈpæn.jən **-s** -z **-ship** -ʃɪp

companionab|le kəmˈpæn.jə.nə.b|l̩ **-ly** -li **-leness** -l̩.nəs, -nɪs

companionate kəmˈpæn.jə.nət, -nɪt

companionway kəmˈpæn.jən.weɪ **-s** -z

compan|y ˈkʌm.pə.n|i **-ies** -iz

Compaq® ˈkɒm.pæk (US) ˈkɑːm-

comparability ˌkɒm.pᵊr.əˈbɪl.ə.ti; kəmˌpær-, -ɪ.ti (US) ˌkɑːm.pɚ.əˈbɪl.ə.t̬i

comparab|le ˈkɒm.pᵊr.ə.b|l̩ (US) ˈkɑːm-; kəmˈper.ə-, -ˈpær- **-ly** -li **-leness** -l̩.nəs, -nɪs

comparative kəmˈpær.ə.tɪv (US) -ˈper.ə.t̬ɪv, -ˈpær- **-s** -z **-ly** -li

compar|e kəmˈpeəʳ (US) -per **-es** -z **-ing** -ɪŋ **-ed** -d

comparison kəmˈpær.ɪ.sᵊn (US) -ˈper-, -ˈpær- **-s** -z

compartment kəmˈpɑːt.mənt (US) -ˈpɑːrt- **-s** -s

compartmentalization, -isa- ˌkɒm.pɑːt.men.tᵊl.aɪˈzeɪ.ʃᵊn, kɒm.pɑːtˌmen-, -ɪˈ- (US) kəm.pɑːrtˌmen.t̬ᵊl.ɪˈ-, ˌkɑːm-

compartmentaliz|e, -is|e ˌkɒm.pɑːtˈmen.tᵊl.aɪz (US) kəm.pɑːrtˈmen.t̬ə.laɪz, ˌkɑːm- **-es** -ɪz **-ing** -ɪŋ **-ed** -d

compass ˈkʌm.pəs (US) ˈkʌm-, ˈkɑːm- **-es** -ɪz **-ing** -ɪŋ **-ed** -t

compassion kəmˈpæʃ.ᵊn

compassionate kəmˈpæʃ.ᵊn.ət, -ɪt **-ly** -li **-ness** -nəs, -nɪs

compatibility kəmˌpæt.əˈbɪl.ə.ti, -ɪˈ-, -ɪ.ti (US) -ˌpæt̬.əˈbɪl.ə.t̬i

compatib|le kəmˈpæt.ɪ.b|l̩, ˈ-ə- (US) -ˈpæt̬- **-ly** -li **-leness** -l̩.nəs, -nɪs

compatriot kəmˈpæt.ri.ət, kɒm- (US) kəmˈpeɪ.tri-, kɑːm- **-s** -s

compeer ˈkɒm.pɪəʳ, -ˈ- (US) ˈkɑːm.pɪr; -ˈ-, kəm- **-s** -z

compel kəmˈpel **-s** -z **-ling/ly** -ɪŋ/li **-led** -d **-lable** -ə.bl̩

compendious kəmˈpen.di.əs **-ly** -li **-ness** -nəs, -nɪs

compendi|um kəmˈpen.di|.əm **-ums** -əmz **-a** -ə

compen|sate ˈkɒm.pən|.seɪt, -pen- (US) ˈkɑːm- **-sates** -seɪts **-sating** -seɪ.tɪŋ (US) -seɪ.t̬ɪŋ **-sated** -seɪ.tɪd (US) -seɪ.t̬ɪd

compensation ˌkɒm.pənˈseɪ.ʃᵊn, -pen- (US) ˌkɑːm- **-s** -z

compensative kəmˈpen*t*.sə.tɪv, ˌkɒm.pənˈseɪ- (US) kəmˈpen*t*.sə.t̬ɪv, ˈkɑːm.pən.seɪ-

compensatory ˌkɒm.pənˈseɪ.tᵊr.i, -tri; kəmˈpen*t*.sə-; ˈkɒm.pen.seɪ-, -pən- (US) kəmˈpen*t*.sə.tɔːr.i

comper|e, compèr|e ˈkɒm.peəʳ (US) ˈkɑːm.per **-es** -z **-ing** -ɪŋ **-ed** -d

com|pete kəmˈpiːt **-petes** -ˈpiːts **-peting** -ˈpiː.tɪŋ (US) -ˈpiː.t̬ɪŋ **-peted** -ˈpiː.tɪd (US) -ˈpiː.t̬ɪd

competen|ce ˈkɒm.pɪ.tᵊn*t*|s, -pə- (US) ˈkɑːm- **-cies** -siz **-cy** -si

competent ˈkɒm.pɪ.tᵊnt, -pə- (US) ˈkɑːm.pɪ.t̬ᵊnt, -pə- **-ly** -li

competition ˌkɒm.pəˈtɪʃ.ᵊn, -pɪˈ- (US) ˌkɑːm- **-s** -z

competitive kəmˈpet.ɪ.tɪv, ˈ-ə- (US) -ˈpet̬.ə.t̬ɪv **-ly** -li **-ness** -nəs, -nɪs

competitor kəmˈpet.ɪ.təʳ, ˈ-ə- (US) -ˈpet̬.ə.t̬ɚ **-s** -z

compilation ˌkɒm.pɪˈleɪ.ʃᵊn, -pəˈ-, -paɪˈ- (US) ˌkɑːm.pəˈ- **-s** -z

compil|e kəmˈpaɪl **-es** -z **-ing** -ɪŋ **-ed** -d **-er/s** -əʳ/z (US) -ɚ/z

complacen|ce kəmˈpleɪ.sᵊn*t*|s **-cy** -si

complacent kəmˈpleɪ.sᵊnt **-ly** -li

Compounds

This panel looks at word stress in compounds. Compounds are words made up of two other words which can exist independently in English. They are written in a variety of ways: closed, e.g. *armchair, sunflower*; hyphenated, e.g., *front-runner, she-devil*; open, e.g. *side salad, bank manager*. Sometimes it is possible for the same compounds to be written in different ways, e.g. *shoulder blade* or *shoulderblade*.

There are some rules for compound word stress in English but they are not completely reliable. In addition, British and US English differ. The rules which follow are therefore guidelines, but exceptions exist.

Examples

Words that combine two nouns usually have primary stress on the first element, e.g.:

coffee pot	/ˈkɒf.i.pɒt/	(US) /ˈkɑː.fi.pɑːt/
suitcase	/ˈsuːt.keɪs/	

In US English, it is more frequently the case that compound nouns have first element stress, and this tendency is appearing among some British English speakers. For example, *ice cream* can have first or second-element stress in British English, but tends to be stressed on the first element in US English.

Other types of compound are usually stressed on the second element. These include words ending in *-ed* which are used as adjectives, words with a number as a first element, and words functioning as adverbs or verbs, e.g.:

kind-hearted	/ˌkaɪndˈhɑː.tɪd/	(US) /-ˈhɑːr.t̬ɪd/
three-piece	/ˌθriːˈpiːs/	
southeast	/ˌsaʊθˈiːst/	

These words are subject to stress-shift when a stressed syllable follows closely (e.g., *a ˌkindhearted ˈman*).

complain kəmˈpleɪn **-s** -z **-ing** -ɪŋ **-ed** -d **-er/s** -əʳ/z (US) -ɚ/z
complainant kəmˈpleɪ.nənt **-s** -s
complaint kəmˈpleɪnt **-s** -s
complaisance kəmˈpleɪ.zᵊnts (US) -sᵊnts
complaisant kəmˈpleɪ.zᵊnt (US) -sᵊnt **-ly** -li
compleat kəmˈpliːt
complement (*n.*) ˈkɒm.plɪ.mənt, -plə- (US) ˈkɑːm- **-s** -s
comple|ment (*v.*) ˈkɒm.plɪ|.ment, ˌkɒm.plɪ|ˈment (US) ˈkɑːm.plɪ- **-ments** -ments, -ˈments (US) -ments **-menting** -men.tɪŋ, -ˈmen.tɪŋ (US) -men.t̬ɪŋ **-mented** -men.tɪd, -ˈmen.tɪd (US) -men.t̬ɪd
omplemental ˌkɒm.plɪˈmen.tᵊl (US) ˌkɑːm.plɪˈmen.t̬ᵊl
omplementary ˌkɒm.plɪˈmen.tᵊr.i, -pləˈ-, ˈ-tri (US) ˌkɑːm.pləˈmen.t̬ɚ.i, ˈ-tri
omplementation ˌkɒm.plɪ.menˈteɪ.ʃᵊn, -plə-, -mənˈ- (US) ˌkɑːm-
omplementiser, -izer ˈkɒm.plɪ.men.taɪ.zəʳ, -plə-, -mən- (US) ˈkɑːm.plə.mən.taɪ.zɚ, -men- **-s** -z
om|plete kəm|ˈpliːt **-pletest** -ˈpliː.tɪst, -təst (US) -ˈpliː.t̬ɪst, -t̬əst **-pletely** -ˈpliːt.li **-pleteness** -ˈpliːt.nəs, -nɪs **-pletes** -ˈpliːts **-pleting** -ˈpliː.tɪŋ (US) -ˈpliː.t̬ɪŋ **-pleted** -ˈpliː.tɪd (US) -ˈpliː.t̬ɪd
ompletion kəmˈpliː.ʃᵊn
mplex (*adj.*) ˈkɒm.pleks, kəmˈpleks (US) kɑːmˈpleks, kəm-; ˈkɑːm.pleks
complex (*n.*) ˈkɒm.pleks (US) ˈkɑːm- **-es** -ɪz
complexion kəmˈplek.ʃᵊn **-s** -z **-ed** -d
complexit|y kəmˈplek.sə.t|i, -sɪ- (US) -sə.t̬|i **-ies** -iz
complianc|e kəmˈplaɪ.ənts **-es** -ɪz
compliant kəmˈplaɪ.ənt **-ly** -li
compli|cate ˈkɒm.plɪ|.keɪt (US) ˈkɑːm.plə- **-cates** -keɪts **-cating** -keɪ.tɪŋ (US) -keɪ.t̬ɪŋ **-cated** -keɪ.tɪd (US) -keɪ.t̬ɪd
complication ˌkɒm.plɪˈkeɪ.ʃᵊn (US) ˌkɑːm.pləˈ- **-s** -z
complicit kəmˈplɪs.ɪt
complicity kəmˈplɪs.ə.ti, -ɪ.ti (US) -ə.t̬i
compliment (*n.*) ˈkɒm.plɪ.mənt, -plə- (US) ˈkɑːm.plə- **-s** -s
compli|ment (*v.*) ˈkɒm.plɪ|.ment, -plə-, ˌkɒm.plɪ|ˈment (US) ˈkɑːm.plə- **-ments** -ments, -ˈments (US) -ments **-menting** -men.tɪŋ, -ˈmen.tɪŋ (US) -men.t̬ɪŋ **-mented** -men.tɪd, -ˈmen.tɪd (US) -men.t̬ɪd
complimentarily ˌkɒm.plɪˈmen.tᵊr.ᵊl.i, -plə- (US) ˌkɑːm.plə.menˈter-; -ˈmen.t̬ɚ-
complimentar|y ˌkɒm.plɪˈmen.tᵊr|.i, -pləˈ-, ˈ-tr|i (US) ˌkɑːm.pləˈmen.t̬ɚ|.i, ˈ-tr|i **-ies** -iz
complin ˈkɒm.plɪn (US) ˈkɑːm- **-s** -z
compline ˈkɒm.plɪn, -plaɪn (US) ˈkɑːm- **-s** -z
compl|y kəmˈpl|aɪ **-ies** -aɪz **-ying** -aɪ.ɪŋ **-ied** -aɪd **-ier/s** -aɪ.əʳ/z (US) -aɪ.ɚ/z
compo ˈkɒm.pəʊ (US) ˈkɑːm.poʊ
component kəmˈpəʊ.nənt (US) -ˈpoʊ- **-s** -s
componential ˌkɒm.pəʊˈnen.tʃᵊl (US) ˌkɑːm.pəˈ- ˌcompoˌnential aˈnalysis
com|port kəm|ˈpɔːt (US) -ˈpɔːrt **-ports** -ˈpɔːts (US) -ˈpɔːrts **-porting** -ˈpɔː.tɪŋ (US) -ˈpɔːr.t̬ɪŋ **-ported** -ˈpɔː.tɪd (US) -ˈpɔːr.t̬ɪd
comportment kəmˈpɔːt.mənt (US) -ˈpɔːrt-
compos|e kəmˈpəʊz (US) -ˈpoʊz **-es** -ɪz **-ing** -ɪŋ **-ed** -d
compos|ed kəmˈpəʊz|d (US) -ˈpoʊz|d **-edly** -ɪd.li, -əd.li **-edness** -ɪd.nəs, -d.nəs, -nɪs
composer kəmˈpəʊ.zəʳ (US) -ˈpoʊ.zɚ **-s** -z
composite ˈkɒm.pə.zɪt, -sɪt, -zaɪt, -saɪt (US) kəmˈpɑː.zɪt **-ly** -li **-ness** -nəs, -nɪs
composition ˌkɒm.pəˈzɪʃ.ᵊn (US) ˌkɑːm- **-s** -z
compositor kəmˈpɒz.ɪ.təʳ (US) -ˈpɑː.zɪ.t̬ɚ **-s** -z
compos mentis ˌkɒm.pəsˈmen.tɪs, -pɒs- (US) ˌkɑːm.pəsˈmen.t̬əs
compost ˈkɒm.pɒst (US) ˈkɑːm.poʊst **-s** -s **-ing** -ɪŋ **-ed** -ɪd ˈ**compost** ˌ**heap**
composure kəmˈpəʊ.ʒəʳ (US) -ˈpoʊ.ʒɚ
compote ˈkɒm.pɒt, -pəʊt (US) ˈkɑːm.poʊt **-s** -s
compound (*n. adj.*) ˈkɒm.paʊnd (US) ˈkɑːm- **-s** -z ˌ**compound** ˈ**fracture**
compound (*v.*) kəmˈpaʊnd, kɒm-; ˈkɒm.paʊnd (US) kɑːmˈpaʊnd, kəm-; ˈkɑːm.paʊnd **-s** -z **-ing** -ɪŋ **-ed** -ɪd **-able** -ə.bl̩
comprehend ˌkɒm.prɪˈhend, -prəˈ- (US) ˌkɑːm- **-s** -z **-ing** -ɪŋ **-ed** -ɪd

comprehensibility ˌkɒm.prɪ.hent.səˈbɪl.ə.ti, -prə-, -sɪˈ-, -ɪ.ti (US) ˌkɑːm.prə.hent.səˈbɪl.ə.t̬i, -prɪ-
comprehensib|le ˌkɒm.prɪˈhent.sə.b|l̩, -prəˈ-, -sɪ- (US) ˌkɑːm- **-ly** -li **-leness** -l̩.nəs, -nɪs
comprehension ˌkɒm.prɪˈhen.tʃᵊn, -prəˈ- (US) ˌkɑːm.prɪˈhent.ʃᵊn-, -prəˈ-
comprehensive ˌkɒm.prɪˈhent.sɪv, -prəˈ- (US) ˌkɑːm.prə-, -prɪ- **-s** -z **-ly** -li **-ness** -nəs, -nɪs **compreˈhensive ˌschool**
compress (*n.*) ˈkɒm.pres (US) ˈkɑːm- **-es** -ɪz
compress (*v.*) kəmˈpres **-es** -ɪz **-ing** -ɪŋ **-ed** -t **-or/s** -əʳ/z (US) -ɚ/z
compressibility kəmˌpres.əˈbɪl.ə.ti, -ɪˈ-, -ɪ.ti (US) -ə.t̬i
compressible kəmˈpres.ə.bl̩, ˈ-ɪ- **-ness** -nəs, -nɪs
compression kəmˈpreʃ.ᵊn **-s** -z **-al** -ᵊl
compressive kəmˈpres.ɪv
compris|e kəmˈpraɪz **-es** -ɪz **-ing** -ɪŋ **-ed** -d **-able** -ə.bl̩
compromis|e ˈkɒm.prə.maɪz (US) ˈkɑːm- **-es** -ɪz **-ing/ly** -ɪŋ/li **-ed** -d **-er/s** -əʳ/z (US) -ɚ/z
Comptometer® ˌkɒmpˈtɒm.ɪ.təʳ, ˈ-ə- (US) ˌkɑːmpˈtɑː.mə.t̬ɚ **-s** -z
Compton ˈkɒmp.tən, ˈkʌmp- (US) ˈkɑːmp-
Note: For British English, as surname more often /ˈkʌmp-/, as place name more often /ˈkɒmp-/. The London street is generally /ˈkɒmp-/.
Compton-Burnett ˌkɒmp.tən.bɜːˈnet, -ˈbɜː.nɪt (US) ˌkɑːmp.tən.bɝːˈnet
comptroller kənˈtrəʊ.ləʳ, kəmp-, kɒmp- (US) kənˈtroʊ.lɚ, kəmp-, kɑːmp-; ˈkɑːmp.troʊ- **-s** -z
compulsion kəmˈpʌl.ʃᵊn
compulsive kəmˈpʌl.sɪv **-ly** -li
compulsor|y kəmˈpʌl.sᵊr|.i **-ily** -ᵊl.i, -ɪ.li
compunction kəmˈpʌŋk.ʃᵊn
compunctious kəmˈpʌŋk.ʃəs
compurgation ˌkɒm.pɜːˈgeɪ.ʃᵊn (US) ˌkɑːm.pɚˈ-
computability kəmˌpjuː.təˈbɪl.ə.ti, ˌkɒm.pjʊ-, -ɪ.ti (US) kəmˌpjuː.t̬əˈbɪl.ə.t̬i
computable kəmˈpjuː.tə.bl̩; ˈkɒm.pjʊ- (US) kəmˈpjuː.t̬ə-
computation ˌkɒm.pjəˈteɪ.ʃᵊn, -pjʊˈ- (US) ˌkɑːm.pjəˈ- **-s** -z
computational ˌkɒm.pjəˈteɪ.ʃᵊn.ᵊl, -pjʊˈ-, -ˈteɪʃ.nᵊl (US) ˌkɑːm- **-ly** -i **compuˌtational linˈguistics**
computator ˈkɒm.pjə.teɪ.təʳ, -pjʊ- (US) ˈkɑːm.pjə.teɪ.t̬ɚ **-s** -z
com|pute kəm|ˈpjuːt **-putes** -ˈpjuːts **-puting** -ˈpjuː.tɪŋ (US) -ˈpjuː.t̬ɪŋ **-puted** -ˈpjuː.tɪd (US) -ˈpjuː.t̬ɪd
computer kəmˈpjuː.təʳ (US) -t̬ɚ **-s** -z **comˈputer ˌgame; comˌputer ˈprogrammer; comˌputer aided deˈsign**
computerate kəmˈpjuː.tᵊr.ət (US) -t̬ɚ-
computerization, -isa- kəmˌpjuː.tᵊr.aɪˈzeɪ.ʃᵊn, -ɪˈ- (US) -t̬ɚ.ɪˈ-
computeriz|e, -is|e kəmˈpjuː.tᵊr.aɪz (US) -t̬ə.raɪz **-es** -ɪz **-ing** -ɪŋ **-ed** -d
computist kəmˈpjuː.tɪst (US) -t̬ɪst **-s** -s
comrade ˈkɒm.reɪd, ˈkʌm-, -rɪd (US) ˈkɑːm.ræd, -rəd **-s** -z **-ship** -ʃɪp
Comsat® ˈkɒm.sæt (US) ˈkɑːm- **-s** -s
Comte kɔ̃ːnt, kɔːnt, kɒnt (US) kɔ̃ːnt, koʊnt
Comus ˈkəʊ.məs (US) ˈkoʊ-
Comyn ˈkʌm.ɪn
con- kɒn-, kən- (US) kɑːn-, kən-
Note: Prefix. This may carry primary or secondary stress, e.g. **concept** /ˈkɒn.sept (US) ˈkɑːn-/, or may be unstressed, e.g. **consume** /kənˈsjuːm (US) kənˈsuːm/.
con kɒn (US) kɑːn **-s** -z **-ning** -ɪŋ **-ned** -d **ˈcon ˌman; ˈcon ˌtrick**
Conakry ˌkɒn.əˈkriː, ˈkɒn.ə.kri (US) ˈkɑː.nə.kri
Conall ˈkɒn.ᵊl (US) ˈkɑː.nᵊl
Conan *personal name:* ˈkəʊ.nən, ˈkɒn.ən (US) ˈkoʊ.nən, ˈkɑː- *place in Scotland:* ˈkɒn.ən, ˈkəʊ.nən (US) ˈkɑː-, ˈkoʊ-
Conant ˈkɒn.ənt (US) ˈkoʊ.nənt
conation kəʊˈneɪ.ʃᵊn (US) koʊ-
conative ˈkəʊ.nə.tɪv (US) ˈkoʊ.nə.t̬ɪv
Concannon kɒnˈkæn.ən, kɒŋ- (US) kɑːn-
concaten|ate kənˈkæt.ᵊn|.eɪt, kəŋ-, kɒn-, kɒŋ-, ˈ-ɪ- (US) kənˈkæt̬-, kɑːn- **-ates** -eɪts **-ating** -eɪ.tɪŋ (US) -eɪ.t̬ɪŋ **-ated** -eɪ.tɪd (US) -eɪ.t̬ɪd
concatenation kənˌkæt.əˈneɪ.ʃᵊn, kəŋ-, kɒn-, kɒŋ-, -ɪˈ-; ˈkɒn.kæt-, ˈkɒŋ- (US) kənˌkæt̬.əˈ-; ˌkɑːn.kæt̬- **-s** -z
concave kɒŋˈkeɪv, kəŋ-, kɒn-, kən-; ˈkɒŋ.keɪv (US) kɑːnˈkeɪv, ˈkɑːn- *stress shift:* ˌconcave ˈlens
concavit|y kɒnˈkæv.ə.t|i, kən-, kɒŋ-, kəŋ-, -ɪ.t|i (US) kɑːnˈkæv.ə.t̬|i **-ies** -iz
conceal kənˈsiːl **-s** -z **-ing** -ɪŋ **-ed** -d **-able** -ə.bl̩ **-er/s** -əʳ/z (US) -ɚ/z
concealment kənˈsiːl.mənt **-s** -s
conced|e kənˈsiːd **-es** -z **-ing** -ɪŋ **-ed** -ɪd
conceit kənˈsiːt **-s** -s
conceited kənˈsiː.tɪd (US) -t̬ɪd **-ly** -li **-ness** -nəs, -nɪs
conceivab|le kənˈsiː.və.b|l̩ **-ly** -li **-leness** -l̩.nəs, -nɪs
conceiv|e kənˈsiːv **-es** -z **-ing** -ɪŋ **-ed** -d
concele|brate kɒnˈsel.əl|.breɪt, kən-, ˈ-ɪ- (US) kən-, kɑːn- **-brates** -breɪts **-brating** -breɪ.tɪŋ (US) -breɪ.t̬ɪŋ **-brated** -breɪ.tɪd (US) -breɪ.t̬ɪd
concelebration ˌkɒn.sel.əˈbreɪ.ʃᵊn, -ɪˈ-; kənˌsel- (US) kənˌsel-; ˌkɑːn.sel- **-s** -z
concent kənˈsent, ˌkɒn- (US) kən-
concent|er kɒnˈsen.t|əʳ (US) kənˈsen.t̬|ɚ, kɑːn- **-ers** -əz (US) -ɚz **-ering** -ᵊr.ɪŋ **-ered** -əd (US) -ɚd
concen|trate ˈkɒnt.sᵊn|.treɪt, -sɪn-, -sen- (US) ˈkɑːnt.sᵊn- **-trates** -treɪts **-trating** -treɪ.tɪŋ (US) -treɪ.t̬ɪŋ **-trated** -treɪ.tɪd (US) -treɪ.t̬ɪd
concentration ˌkɒnt.sᵊnˈtreɪ.ʃᵊn, -sɪnˈ-, -senˈ- (US) ˌkɑːnt.sᵊnˈ- **-s** -z **concenˈtration ˌcamp**
concentrative ˈkɒnt.sᵊn.treɪ.tɪv, -sɪn-, -sen- (US) ˈkɑːnt.sən.treɪ.t̬ɪv; kənˈsen.trə-
concent|re kɒnˈsen.t|əʳ (US) kənˈsen.t̬|ɚ, kɑːn- **-res** -əz (US) -ɚz **-ring** -rɪŋ **-ering** -ᵊr.ɪŋ **-red** -əd (US) -ɚd
concentric kənˈsen.trɪk, kɒn- (US) kən- **-ally** -ᵊl.i, -li
Concepción kənˌsep.siˈəʊn, ˌkɒn.sep- (US) kən-, kɑːn-, -ˈoʊn
concept ˈkɒn.sept (US) ˈkɑːn- **-s** -s
conception kənˈsep.ʃᵊn **-s** -z
conceptual kənˈsep.tʃu.əl, -ʃu-, -tju- (US) -tʃu- **-ly** -i
conceptualization, -isa- kənˌsep.tʃu.ə.laɪˈzeɪ.ʃᵊn, -ʃu-, -tju-, -ɪˈ- (US) -tʃu.ᵊl.ɪˈ-
conceptualiz|e, -is|e kənˈsep.tʃu.ə.laɪz, -ʃu-, -tju-, -tʃʊ.laɪz, -tʃə- (US) -tʃu.ə- **-es** -ɪz **-ing** -ɪŋ **-ed** -d
conceptually kənˈsep.tʃu.ə.li, -ʃu-, -tju- (US) -tʃu-
conceptus kənˈsep.təs **-es** -ɪz
concern kənˈsɜːn (US) -ˈsɝːn **-s** -z **-ing** -ɪŋ **-ed** -d **-ment/s** -mənt/s
concern|ed kənˈsɜːn|d (US) -ˈsɝːn|d **-edly** -ɪd.li **-edness** -ɪd.nəs, -d.nəs, -nɪs
concert (*n.*) *musical entertainment:* ˈkɒn.sət (US) ˈkɑːn.sɚt **-s** -s
concert (C) (*n.*) *union:* ˈkɒn.sɜːt, -sət (US) ˈkɑːn.sɚt **-s** -s
con|cert (*v.*) kən|ˈsɜːt (US) -ˈsɝːt **-certs** -ˈsɜːts (US) -ˈsɝːts **-certing** -ˈsɜː.tɪŋ (US) -ˈsɝː.t̬ɪŋ **-certed** -ˈsɜː.tɪd (US) -ˈsɝː.t̬ɪd
concerti (*plur. of* **concerto**) kənˈtʃeə.ti, -ˈtʃɜː- (US) -ˈtʃer.t̬i
concertina ˌkɒnt.səˈtiː.nə (US) ˌkɑːnt.sɚˈ- **-s** -z **-ing** -ɪŋ **-ed** -d
concertino ˌkɒn.tʃəˈtiː.nəʊ (US) ˌkɑːn.tʃɚˈtiː.noʊ **-s** -z
concerto kənˈtʃeə.təʊ, -ˈtʃɜː-

US -ˈtʃer.t̬oʊ **-s** -z **concerti** kənˈtʃeə.ti, -ˈtʃɜː- US -ˈtʃer.t̬i
concerto grosso kənˌtʃeə.təʊˈɡrɒs.əʊ, kɒn-, -ˌtʃɜː- US kənˌtʃer.t̬oʊˈɡroʊ.soʊ, kɑːn- **concerti grossi** kənˌtʃeə.tiˈɡrɒs.i US -ˌtʃer.t̬iˈɡroʊ.si
concession kənˈseʃ.ᵊn **-s** -z
concessionaire kənˌseʃ.ᵊnˈeəʳ US -ˈer **-s** -z
concessional kənˈseʃ.ᵊn.ᵊl, ˈ-nᵊl US -ən.ᵊl **-ly** -i
concessionary kənˈseʃ.ᵊn.ᵊr.i, -ᵊn.ri US -ʃᵊn.er.i
concessive kənˈses.ɪv **-ly** -li
conch kɒntʃ, kɒŋk US kɑːŋk, kɑːntʃ **conches** ˈkɒn.tʃɪz US ˈkɑːn.tʃɪz **conchs** kɒŋks US kɑːŋks
concha ˈkɒŋ.kə US ˈkɑːŋ-, ˈkɔːŋ- **-s** -z
conchie ˈkɒn.tʃi US ˈkɑːn- **-s** -z
Conchobar ˈkɒŋ.kəʊ.əʳ, ˈkɒn.u.əʳ US ˈkɑː.nu.ɚ, ˈkɑːŋ.koʊ.ɚ, ˈkɔːŋ-
conchoid ˈkɒŋ.kɔɪd US ˈkɑːn- **-s** -z
conchologist kɒŋˈkɒl.ə.dʒɪst US kɑːŋˈkɑː.lə-, kɔːŋ- **-s** -s
conchology kɒŋˈkɒl.ə.dʒi US kɑːŋˈkɑː.lə-, kɔːŋ-
concierge ˌkɒn.siˈeəʒ, ˌkɔːn-, ˌkɔ̃ːn-, ˈ--- US koʊnˈsjerʒ, kɑːn-, -siˈerʒ **-s** -ɪz
concili|ate kənˈsɪl.i|.eɪt **-ates** -eɪts **-ating** -eɪ.tɪŋ US -eɪ.t̬ɪŋ **-ated** -eɪ.tɪd US -eɪ.t̬ɪd
conciliation kənˌsɪl.iˈeɪ.ʃᵊn
conciliative kənˈsɪl.i.ə.tɪv, -eɪ- US -eɪ.t̬ɪv
conciliator kənˈsɪl.i.eɪ.təʳ US -t̬ɚ **-s** -z
conciliatory kənˈsɪl.i.ə.tᵊr.i, -eɪ-, -tri; kənˌsɪl.iˈeɪ- US kənˈsɪl.i.ə.tɔːr.i
concis|e kənˈsaɪs **-er** -əʳ US -ɚ **-est** -ɪst, -əst **-ely** -li **-eness** -nəs, -nɪs
concision kənˈsɪʒ.ᵊn **-s** -z
conclave ˈkɒŋ.kleɪv, ˈkɒn- US ˈkɑːn- **-s** -z
conclud|e kənˈkluːd, kəŋ- US kən- **-es** -z **-ing** -ɪŋ **-ed** -ɪd
conclusion kənˈkluː.ʒᵊn, kəŋ- US kən- **-s** -z
conclusive kənˈkluː.sɪv, kəŋ- US kən- **-ly** -li **-ness** -nəs, -nɪs
concoct kənˈkɒkt, kəŋ- US kənˈkɑːkt **-s** -s **-ing** -ɪŋ **-ed** -ɪd **-er/s** -əʳ/z US -ɚ/z
concoction kənˈkɒk.ʃᵊn, kəŋ- US kənˈkɑːk- **-s** -z
concomitan|ce kənˈkɒm.ɪ.tᵊnt|s, kəŋ-, ˈ-ə- US kənˈkɑː.mə.t̬ᵊnt|s **-cy** -si
concomitant kənˈkɒm.ɪ.tᵊnt, kəŋ-, ˈ-ə- US kənˈkɑː.mə.t̬ᵊnt **-ly** -li
concord (*n.*) ˈkɒŋ.kɔːd, ˈkɒn- US ˈkɑːn.kɔːrd, ˈkɑːŋ-, ˈkɔːŋ- **-s** -z
concord (*v.*) kənˈkɔːd, kəŋ- US kənˈkɔːrd **-s** -z **-ing** -ɪŋ **-ed** -ɪd
Concord *place in the US, type of grape:* ˈkɒŋ.kəd US ˈkɑːŋ.kɚd
concordanc|e kənˈkɔː.dᵊnts, kəŋ- US kənˈkɔːr- **-es** -ɪz **-ing** -ɪŋ **-ed** -d
concordant kənˈkɔː.dᵊnt, kəŋ- US kənˈkɔːr- **-ly** -li
concordat kɒnˈkɔː.dæt, kɒŋ-, kən-, kəŋ- US kənˈkɔːr- **-s** -s
Concorde ˈkɒŋ.kɔːd, ˈkɒn- US ˈkɑːn.kɔːrd, ˈkɑːŋ- **-s** -z
concours|e ˈkɒŋ.kɔːs, ˈkɒn-, -kʊəs US ˈkɑːn.kɔːrs **-es** -ɪz
concrete (*n. adj.*) ˈkɒŋ.kriːt, ˈkɒn- US ˈkɑːn- ˌ**concrete** ˈ**jungle**
con|crete (*v.*) *cover with concrete:* ˈkɒŋ|.kriːt, ˈkɒn- US ˈkɑːn- **-cretes** -kriːts **-creting** -kriː.tɪŋ US -t̬ɪŋ **-creted** -kriː.tɪd US -kriː.t̬ɪd
con|crete (*v.*) *solidify:* kən|ˈkriːt, kəŋ- US kən- **-cretes** -ˈkriːts **-creting** -ˈkriː.tɪŋ US -ˈkriː.t̬ɪŋ **-creted** -ˈkriː.tɪd US -ˈkriː.t̬ɪd
concrete|ly kɒŋˈkriːt|.li, kɒn- US kɑːn- **-ness** -nəs, -nɪs
concretion kənˈkriː.ʃᵊn, kəŋ-, kɒn- US kən-, kɑːn- **-s** -z
concretiz|e, -is|e ˈkɒŋ.kriː.taɪz, ˈkɒn-, -krɪ- US ˈkɑːn.kriː-, kɑːnˈkriː.taɪz, kɑːŋ- **-es** -ɪz **-ing** -ɪŋ **-ed** -d
concubinage kɒnˈkjuː.bɪ.nɪdʒ, kɒŋ-, kən-, kəŋ- US kənˈkjuː.bə-, kɑːn-
concubine ˈkɒŋ.kjʊ.baɪn, ˈkɒn-, -kjə- US ˈkɑːŋ-, ˈkɑːn- **-s** -z
concupiscen|ce kənˈkjuː.pɪ.sᵊn|ts, kəŋ-, ˌkɒn-, ˌkɒŋ- US kɑːn-, kənˈkjuː.pə- **-t** -t
concur kənˈkɜːʳ, kəŋ- US -ˈkɝː **-s** -z **-ring** -ɪŋ **-red** -d
concurren|ce kənˈkʌr.ᵊnt|s, kəŋ- US kən- **-cy** -si
concurrent kənˈkʌr.ᵊnt, kəŋ- US kən- **-ly** -li
concuss kənˈkʌs, kəŋ- US kən- **-es** -ɪz **-ing** -ɪŋ **-ed** -t
concussion kənˈkʌʃ.ᵊn, kəŋ- US kən- **-s** -z
condemn kənˈdem **-s** -z **-ing** -ɪŋ **-ed** -d **-able** -nə.bl̩
condemnation ˌkɒn.demˈneɪ.ʃᵊn, -dəmˈ- US ˌkɑːn- **-s** -z
condemnatory kənˈdem.nə.tᵊr.i, -tri; ˌkɒn.demˈneɪ-, -dəmˈ- US kənˈdem.nə.tɔːr.i
condensation ˌkɒn.denˈseɪ.ʃᵊn, -dənˈ- US ˌkɑːn- **-s** -z
condens|e kənˈdents **-es** -ɪz **-ing** -ɪŋ **-ed** -t **-able** -ə.bl̩ **con**ˌ**densed** ˈ**milk**
condenser kənˈden.səʳ US -sɚ **-s** -z
condescend ˌkɒn.dɪˈsend, -dəˈ- US ˌkɑːn- **-s** -z **-ing** -ɪŋ **-ed** -ɪd
condescending ˌkɒn.dɪˈsen.dɪŋ, -dəˈ- US ˌkɑːn- **-ly** -li
condescension ˌkɒn.dɪˈsen.ʃᵊn, -dəˈ- US ˌkɑːn-
condign kənˈdaɪn, kɒn- US kənˈdaɪn, ˈkɑːn.daɪn **-ly** -li **-ness** -nəs, -nɪs
condiment ˈkɒn.dɪ.mənt US ˈkɑːn.də- **-s** -s
condition kənˈdɪʃ.ᵊn **-s** -z **-ing** -ɪŋ **-ed** -d
conditional kənˈdɪʃ.ᵊn.ᵊl, ˈ-nᵊl **-ly** -i
conditioner kənˈdɪʃ.ᵊn.əʳ, ˈ-nəʳ US ˈ-ᵊn.ɚ, ˈ-nɚ **-s** -z
condo ˈkɒn.dəʊ US ˈkɑːn.doʊ **-s** -z
condol|e kənˈdəʊl US -ˈdoʊl **-es** -z **-ing** -ɪŋ **-ed** -d **-ement/s** -mənt/s
condolenc|e kənˈdəʊ.lənts US -ˈdoʊ- **-es** -ɪz
condolent kənˈdəʊ.lənt US -ˈdoʊ-
condom ˈkɒn.dɒm, -dəm US ˈkɑːn.dəm, ˈkʌn- **-s** -z
condominium ˌkɒn.dəˈmɪn.i.əm US ˌkɑːn.dəˈ- **-s** -z
Condon ˈkɒn.dən US ˈkɑːn-
condonation ˌkɒn.dəʊˈneɪ.ʃᵊn US ˌkɑːn.doʊˈ- **-s** -z
condon|e kənˈdəʊn US -ˈdoʊn **-es** -z **-ing** -ɪŋ **-ed** -d
condor (C) ˈkɒn.dɔːʳ, -dəʳ US ˈkɑːn.dɚ, -dɔːr **-s** -z
conduc|e kənˈdjuːs US -ˈduːs, -ˈdjuːs **-es** -ɪz **-ing** -ɪŋ **-ed** -t **-ement/s** -mənt/s
conducive kənˈdjuː.sɪv US -ˈduː-, -ˈdjuː- **-ly** -li **-ness** -nəs, -nɪs
conduct (*n.*) ˈkɒn.dʌkt, -dəkt US ˈkɑːn- **-s** -s
conduct (*v.*) kənˈdʌkt **-s** -s **-ing** -ɪŋ **-ed** -ɪd
conductance kənˈdʌk.tᵊnts
conductibility kənˌdʌk.təˈbɪl.ə.ti, -tɪˈ-, -ɪ.ti US -ə.t̬i
conductible kənˈdʌk.tə.bl̩, -tɪ-
conduction kənˈdʌk.ʃᵊn
conductive kənˈdʌk.tɪv
conductivity ˌkɒn.dʌkˈtɪv.ə.ti, -dəkˈ-, -ɪ.ti US ˌkɑːn.dʌkˈtɪv.ə.t̬i
conductor kənˈdʌk.təʳ US -tɚ **-s** -z
conductress kənˈdʌk.trəs, -trɪs **-es** -ɪz
conduit ˈkɒn.dju.ɪt, ˈkʌn-, -du-, -dʒu-, -dɪt US ˈkɑːn.du.ɪt, -dɪt **-s** -s
Conduit *street:* ˈkɒn.dɪt, ˈkʌn- US ˈkɑːn-
Condy ˈkɒn.di US ˈkɑːn-
condyle ˈkɒn.dɪl, -daɪl US ˈkɑːn- **-s** -z
cone kəʊn US koʊn **-s** -z
Conestoga ˌkɒn.əˈstəʊ.ɡə US ˌkɑː.nəˈstoʊ- **Cones**ˈ**toga** ˌ**wagon**
coney (C) ˈkəʊ.ni US ˈkoʊ- **-s** -z ˌ**Coney** ˈ**Island** *stress shift:* ˌConey Island ˈresident
confab ˈkɒn.fæb; kɒnˈfæb, kən- US ˈkɑːn.fæb **-s** -z
confabu|late kənˈfæb.jʊ|.leɪt, kɒn- US kənˈfæb.jə- **-lates** -leɪts **-lating** -leɪ.tɪŋ US -leɪ.t̬ɪŋ **-lated** -leɪ.tɪd US -leɪ.t̬ɪd

confabulation kənˌfæb.jʊˈleɪ.ʃᵊn, kɒn- (US) kənˌfæb.jəˈ- **-s** -z
confect (*n.*) ˈkɒn.fekt (US) ˈkɑːn- **-s** -s
confect (*v.*) kənˈfekt **-s** -s **-ing** -ɪŋ **-ed** -ɪd
confection kənˈfek.ʃᵊn **-s** -z **-ing** -ɪŋ **-ed** -d **-er/s** -əʳ/z (US) -ɚ/z
confectionery kənˈfek.ʃᵊn.ᵊr.i, -ʃᵊn.ri (US) -er-
confederac|y (C) kənˈfed.ᵊr.ə.s|i **-ies** -iz
confederate (C) (*n. adj.*) kənˈfed.ᵊr.ət, -ɪt **-s** -s
confede|rate (*v.*) kənˈfed.ər|.reɪt **-rates** -reɪts **-rating** -reɪ.tɪŋ (US) -reɪ.t̬ɪŋ **-rated** -reɪ.tɪd (US) -reɪ.t̬ɪd
confederation kənˌfed.əˈreɪ.ʃᵊn **-s** -z
confer kənˈfɜːʳ (US) -ˈfɝː **-s** -z **-ring** -ɪŋ **-red** -d **-rable** -ə.bl̩ **-ment** -mənt
conferenc|e ˈkɒn.fᵊr.ᵊn*t*s (US) ˈkɑːn.fɚ- **-es** -ɪz **-ing** -ɪŋ
conferral kənˈfɜː.rᵊl (US) -ˈfɝː.ᵊl **-s** -z
confess kənˈfes **-es** -ɪz **-ing** -ɪŋ **-ed** -t **-edly** -ɪd.li
Confessio Amantis kɒnˌfes.i.əʊ.əˈmæn.tɪs, kən- (US) kɑːnˌfes.i.oʊ.əˈmɑːn-
confession kənˈfeʃ.ᵊn **-s** -z
confessional kənˈfeʃ.ᵊn.ᵊl, ˈ-nᵊl **-s** -z
confessor kənˈfes.əʳ, kɒn- (US) kənˈfes.ɚ **-s** -z
Note: In British English, may also be pronounced /kɒnˈfes.ɔːʳ/ in the sense of "Father Confessor".
confetti kənˈfet.i, kɒn- (US) kənˈfet̬-
confidant(e) ˈkɒn.fɪ.dænt, -fə-, -dᵊnt; ˌkɒn.fɪˈdænt, -ˈdɑːnt (US) ˈkɑːn.fə.dænt, -dɑːnt, ˌ--ˈ- **-s** -s
confid|e kənˈfaɪd **-es** -z **-ing/ly** -ɪŋ/li **-ed** -ɪd **-er/s** -əʳ/z (US) -ɚ/z
confidenc|e ˈkɒn.fɪ.dᵊn*t*s, -fə- (US) ˈkɑːn.fə- **-es** -ɪz
confident ˈkɒn.fɪ.dᵊnt, -fə- (US) ˈkɑːn.fə- **-ly** -li
confidential ˌkɒn.fɪˈden.*t*ʃᵊl (US) ˌkɑːn.fəˈden*t*.ʃᵊl **-ly** -i
confidentiality ˌkɒn.fɪ.den.*t*ʃiˈæl.ə.ti, -fə-, -ɪ.ti (US) ˌkɑːn.fə.den*t*.ʃiˈæl.ə.t̬i
configuration kənˌfɪg.əˈreɪ.ʃᵊn, ˌkɒn.fɪg-, -jəˈ- (US) kənˌfɪg.jəˈ- **-s** -z
config|ure kənˈfɪg|.əʳ, -j|əʳ (US) -j|ɚ **-ures** -əz (US) -ɚz **-uring** -ᵊr.ɪŋ **-ured** -əd (US) -ɚd
confine (*n.*) ˈkɒn.faɪn (US) ˈkɑːn- **-s** -z
confin|e (*v.*) kənˈfaɪn **-es** -z **-ing** -ɪŋ **-ed** -d
confinement kənˈfaɪn.mənt **-s** -s
confirm kənˈfɜːm (US) -ˈfɝːm **-s** -z **-ing** -ɪŋ **-ed** -d **-er/s** -əʳ/z (US) -ɚ/z
confirmation ˌkɒn.fəˈmeɪ.ʃᵊn (US) ˌkɑːn.fɚˈ- **-s** -z
confirma|tive kənˈfɜː.mə|.tɪv (US) -ˈfɝː.mə|.t̬ɪv **-tory** -tᵊr.i, -tri (US) -tɔːr.i
confi|scate ˈkɒn.fɪ|.skeɪt, -fə- (US) ˈkɑːn.fə-, -fɪ- **-scates** -skeɪts **-scating** -skeɪ.tɪŋ (US) -skeɪ.t̬ɪŋ **-scated** -skeɪ.tɪd (US) -skeɪ.t̬ɪd **-scator/s** -skeɪ.təʳ/z (US) -skeɪ.t̬ɚ/z
confiscation ˌkɒn.fɪˈskeɪ.ʃᵊn, -fəˈ- (US) ˌkɑːn.fəˈ-, -fɪ- **-s** -z
confiscatory kənˈfɪs.kə.tᵊr.i, kɒn-, -tri; ˌkɒn.fɪˈskeɪ-, -fəˈ-, ˈkɒn.fɪ.skeɪ-, -fə- (US) kənˈfɪs.kə.tɔːr.i
confit kɒnˈfiː (US) koʊn-, kɔ̃ː*n*- **-s** -z
confiteor (C) kɒnˈfɪt.i.ɔːʳ, kən-, ˈ-eɪ- (US) kənˈfɪt̬.i.ɔːr, -ˈfiː.t̬i- **-s** -z
confiture ˈkɒn.fɪ.tjʊəʳ, -tjɔːʳ (US) ˈkɑːn.fə.tʃʊr **-s** -z
conflagration ˌkɒn.fləˈgreɪ.ʃᵊn (US) ˌkɑːn- **-s** -z
con|flate kən|ˈfleɪt, kɒn- (US) kən- **-flates** -ˈfleɪts **-flating** -ˈfleɪ.tɪŋ (US) -ˈfleɪ.t̬ɪŋ **-flated** -ˈfleɪ.tɪd (US) -ˈfleɪ.t̬ɪd
conflation kənˈfleɪ.ʃᵊn, kɒn- (US) kən-
conflict (*n.*) ˈkɒn.flɪkt (US) ˈkɑːn- **-s** -s
conflict (*v.*) kənˈflɪkt **-s** -s **-ing** -ɪŋ **-ed** -ɪd
confluenc|e ˈkɒn.flu.ən*t*s (US) ˈkɑːn- **-es** -ɪz
confluent ˈkɒn.flu.ənt (US) ˈkɑːn- **-s** -s **-ly** -li
conform kənˈfɔːm (US) -ˈfɔːrm **-s** -z **-ing** -ɪŋ **-ed** -d **-er/s** -əʳ/z (US) -ɚ/z
conformability kənˌfɔː.məˈbɪl.ə.ti, -ɪ.ti (US) -ˌfɔːr.məˈbɪl.ə.t̬i
conformab|le kənˈfɔː.mə.bl|̩ (US) -ˈfɔːr- **-ly** -li
conformation ˌkɒn.fɔːˈmeɪ.ʃᵊn, -fəˈ- (US) ˌkɑːn.fɚˈ-, -fɔːrˈ- **-s** -z
conformist kənˈfɔː.mɪst (US) -ˈfɔːr- **-s** -s
conformit|y kənˈfɔː.mə.t|i, -ɪ.t|i (US) -ˈfɔːr.mə.t̬|i **-ies** -iz
confound kənˈfaʊnd, ˌkɒn- (US) kən-, ˌkɑːn- **-s** -z **-ing** -ɪŋ **-ed/ly** -ɪd/li
confraternit|y ˌkɒn.frəˈtɜː.nə.t|i, -nɪ- (US) ˌkɑːn.frəˈtɝː.nə.t̬|i **-ies** -iz
confrère ˈkɒn.freəʳ (US) kɑːnˈfrer **-s** -z
con|front kən|ˈfrʌnt **-fronts** -ˈfrʌnts **-fronting** -ˈfrʌn.tɪŋ (US) -ˈfrʌn.t̬ɪŋ **-fronted** -ˈfrʌn.tɪd (US) -ˈfrʌn.t̬ɪd
confrontation ˌkɒn.frʌnˈteɪ.ʃᵊn, -frənˈ- (US) ˌkɑːn.frənˈ- **-s** -z
confrontational ˌkɒn.frʌnˈteɪ.ʃᵊn.ᵊl, -frənˈ-, -ˈteɪʃ.nᵊl (US) ˌkɑːn.frənˈ- **-ly** -i
Confucian kənˈfjuː.ʃᵊn **-s** -z
Confucian|ism kənˈfjuː.ʃᵊn|.ɪ.zᵊm **-ist/s** -ɪst/s
confus|e kənˈfjuːz **-es** -ɪz **-ing/ly** -ɪŋ/li **-ed** -d **-edly** -ɪd.li, -d.li **-edness** -ɪd.nəs, -d.nəs, -nɪs
confusing kənˈfjuː.zɪŋ **-ly** -li
confusion kənˈfjuː.ʒᵊn **-s** -z
confutable kənˈfjuː.tə.bl̩ (US) -t̬ə-
confutation ˌkɒn.fjʊˈteɪ.ʃᵊn (US) ˌkɑːn.fjuːˈ- **-s** -z
con|fute kən|ˈfjuːt **-futes** -ˈfjuːts **-futing** -ˈfjuː.tɪŋ (US) -ˈfjuː.t̬ɪŋ **-futed** -ˈfjuː.tɪd (US) -ˈfjuː.t̬ɪd
conga ˈkɒŋ.gə (US) ˈkɑːŋ-, ˈkɔːŋ- **-s** -z
congé ˈkɔ̃ː*n*.ʒeɪ, ˈkɔːn-, ˈkɒn- (US) koʊnˈʒeɪ, kɑːn-, ˈ-- **-s** -z
congeal kənˈdʒiːl **-s** -z **-ing** -ɪŋ **-ed** -d **-able** -ə.bl̩
congee ˈkɒn.dʒiː (US) ˈkɑːn- **-s** -z
congelation ˌkɒn.dʒɪˈleɪ.ʃᵊn, -dʒəˈ- (US) ˌkɑːn.dʒəˈ-
congener kənˈdʒiː.nəʳ; ˈkɒn.dʒɪ-, -dʒə- (US) ˈkɑːn.dʒᵊn.ɚ; kənˈdʒiː.nɚ **-s** -z
congenial kənˈdʒiː.ni.əl (US) ˈ-njəl, ˈ-ni.əl **-ly** -i
congeniality kənˌdʒiː.niˈæl.ə.ti, -ɪ.ti (US) -ə.t̬i
congenital kənˈdʒen.ɪ.tᵊl (US) -ə.t̬ᵊl **-ly** -i
conger ˈkɒŋ.gəʳ (US) ˈkɑːŋ.gɚ, ˈkɔːŋ- **-s** -z ˌ**conger** ˈ**eel**, ˈ**conger** ˌ**eel**
congeries ˈkɒn.dʒᵊr.iːz, -ɪz; kənˈdʒɪə.riːz, -rɪz (US) ˈkɑːn.dʒə.riːz
congest kənˈdʒest **-s** -s **-ing** -ɪŋ **-ed** -ɪd **-ive** -ɪv
congestion kənˈdʒes.tʃᵊn, -ˈdʒeʃ- **-s** -z
Congleton ˈkɒŋ.gl̩.tən (US) ˈkɑːŋ-, ˈkɔːŋ-
conglo|bate ˈkɒŋ.gləʊ|.beɪt, ˈkɒn- (US) kənˈgloʊ|.beɪt; ˈkɑːŋ.gloʊ-, ˈkɔːŋ- **-bates** -beɪts **-bating** -beɪ.tɪŋ (US) -beɪ.t̬ɪŋ **-bated** -beɪ.tɪd (US) -beɪ.t̬ɪd
conglobation ˌkɒn.gləʊˈbeɪ.ʃᵊn, ˌkɒŋ- (US) ˌkɑːn.gloʊˈ-, kɑːŋ-, ˌkɔːŋ-
conglomerate (*n. adj.*) kənˈglɒm.ᵊr.ət, kəŋ-, kɒn-, -eɪt, -ɪt (US) kənˈglɑː.mɚ- **-s** -s
conglomer|ate (*v.*) kənˈglɒm.ᵊr|.eɪt, kəŋ-, kɒn- (US) kənˈglɑː.mə.r|eɪt **-ates** -eɪts **-ating** -eɪ.tɪŋ (US) -eɪ.t̬ɪŋ **-ated** -eɪ.tɪd (US) -eɪ.t̬ɪd
conglomeration kənˌglɒm.əˈreɪ.ʃᵊn, kəŋ-, kɒn-, ˌkɒn.glɒm-, ˌkɒŋ.glɒm- (US) kənˌglɑː.məˈ- **-s** -z
Congo ˈkɒŋ.gəʊ (US) ˈkɑːŋ.goʊ, ˈkɔːŋ-
Congolese ˌkɒŋ.gəʊˈliːz (US) ˌkɑːŋ.gəˈ-, ˌkɔːŋ-, -ˈliːs
congratu|late kənˈgrætʃ.ʊ|.leɪt, kəŋ-, -ˈgræt.jʊ-, -jə- (US) -ˈgrætʃ.ə-, -ˈgrædʒ-, ˈ-ʊ- **-lates** -leɪts **-lating** -leɪ.tɪŋ (US) -leɪ.t̬ɪŋ **-lated** -leɪ.tɪd (US) -leɪ.t̬ɪd **-lator/s** -leɪ.təʳ/z (US) -leɪ.t̬ɚ/z
congratulation kənˌgrætʃ.ʊˈleɪ.ʃᵊn, kəŋ-, -ˌgræt.jʊˈ-, -jəˈ- (US) -ˌgrætʃ.əˈ-, -ˌgrædʒ-, -ʊˈ- **-s** -z
congratulatory kənˌgrætʃ.ʊˈleɪ.tᵊr.i, kəŋ-, -ˌgræt.jʊˈ-, -jəˈ-, -tri; kənˈgrætʃ.ᵊl.ə- (US) kənˈgrætʃ.ᵊl.ə.tɔːr.i, -ˈgrædʒ-

Connected speech phenomena

The processes which result in words being pronounced differently from their dictionary form when they occur in close contact with other words.

Examples for English

In natural speech we rarely leave gaps between words, and we can observe many processes that result in differences between isolated words and the same words occurring in connected speech: examples are ASSIMILATION and ELISION, e.g.:

(assimilation) one boy /wʌn bɔɪ/ → /wʌm bɔɪ/

(elision) last time /lɑːst taɪm/ → /lɑːs taɪm/
US /læst taɪm/ US /læs taɪm/

The study of connected speech also involves looking at the process of VOWEL REDUCTION in weak syllables (see also WEAK FORM), at RHYTHM and at prosodic phenomena such as INTONATION and STRESS.

congre|gate ˈkɒŋ.grɪ|.geɪt, -grə- US ˈkɑːŋ-, ˈkɔːŋ- **-gates** -geɪts **-gating** -geɪ.tɪŋ US -geɪ.t̬ɪŋ **-gated** -geɪ.tɪd US -geɪ.t̬ɪd
congregation ˌkɒŋ.grɪˈgeɪ.ʃən, -grəˈ- US ˌkɑːŋ-, ˌkɔːŋ- **-s** -z
congregational (C) ˌkɒŋ.grɪˈgeɪ.ʃən.əl, -grəˈ-, -ˈgeɪʃ.nəl US ˌkɑːŋ-, ˌkɔːŋ- **-ism** -ɪ.zəm **-ist/s** -ɪst/s
Congresbury ˈkɒŋz.bri, ˈkuːmz.bər.i US ˈkɑːŋz.ber-, ˈkɔːŋz-, ˈkuːmz-, -bɚ-
congress (C) ˈkɒŋ.gres US ˈkɑːŋ-, ˈkɔːŋ-, -grəs **-es** -ɪz
congressional (C) kənˈgreʃ.ən.əl, kəŋ-, kɒŋ-, ˈ-nəl US kəŋ-
congress|man ˈkɒŋ.gres|.mən US ˈkɑːŋ-, ˈkɔːŋ-, -grəs- **-men** -mən, -men
congress|woman ˈkɒŋ.gres|ˌwʊm.ən US ˈkɑːŋ-, ˈkɔːŋ-, -grəs- **-women** -ˌwɪm.ɪn
Congreve ˈkɒŋ.griːv US ˈkɑːn-, ˈkɑːŋ-
congruenc|e ˈkɒŋ.gru.ənts US ˈkɑːŋ-, ˈkɔːŋ-, kənˈgruː- **-es** -ɪz **-y** -i **-ies** -iz
congruent ˈkɒŋ.gru.ənt US ˈkɑːŋ-; kənˈgruː- **-ly** -li
congruit|y kɒŋˈgruː.ə.t|i, kən-, kəŋ-, -ɪ.t|i US kɑːnˈgruː.ə.t̬|i, kən- **-ies** -iz
congruous ˈkɒŋ.gru.əs US ˈkɑːŋ-, ˈkɔːŋ- **-ly** -li **-ness** -nəs, -nɪs
conic ˈkɒn.ɪk US ˈkɑː.nɪk **-s** -s
conical ˈkɒn.ɪ.kəl US ˈkɑː.nɪ- **-ly** -i **-ness** -nəs, -nɪs
conifer ˈkɒn.ɪ.fər, ˈkəʊ.nɪ-, -nə- US ˈkɑː.nə.fɚ, ˈkoʊ- **-s** -z
coniferous kəʊˈnɪf.ər.əs, kɒnˈɪf- US koʊˈnɪf-, kə-
coniform ˈkəʊ.nɪ.fɔːm US ˈkoʊ.nɪ.fɔːrm
Coningham ˈkʌn.ɪŋ.əm US -hæm
Coningsby ˈkɒn.ɪŋz.bi, ˈkʌn- US ˈkʌn-
Conisbrough ˈkɒn.ɪs.brə, ˈkʌn- US ˈkɑː.nɪs.bɚ.oʊ
Coniston ˈkɒn.ɪ.stən US ˈkɑː.nɪ-
conjecturable kənˈdʒek.tʃər.ə.bl̩
conjectural kənˈdʒek.tʃər.əl **-ly** -i
conject|ure kənˈdʒek.tʃ|əʳ US -tʃ|ɚ **-ures** -əz US -ɚz **-uring** -ər.ɪŋ **-ured** -əd US -ɚd
conjoin kənˈdʒɔɪn, kɒn- US kən- **-s** -z **-ing** -ɪŋ **-ed** -d
conjoint kənˈdʒɔɪnt, kɒn- US kən- **-ly** -li
conjugal ˈkɒn.dʒʊ.gəl, -dʒə- US ˈkɑːn.dʒə- **-ly** -i ˌ**conjugal** ˈ**rights**
conjugality ˌkɒn.dʒʊˈgæl.ə.ti, -ɪ.ti US ˌkɑːn.dʒəˈgæl.ə.t̬i
conjugate (*n. adj*) ˈkɒn.dʒʊ.gət, -dʒə-, -gɪt, -geɪt US ˈkɑːn.dʒə- **-s** -s
conju|gate (*v.*) ˈkɒn.dʒʊ|.geɪt, -dʒə- US ˈkɑːn.dʒə- **-gates** -geɪts **-gating** -geɪ.tɪŋ US -geɪ.t̬ɪŋ **-gated** -geɪ.tɪd US -geɪ.t̬ɪd
conjugation ˌkɒn.dʒʊˈgeɪ.ʃən, -dʒəˈ- US ˌkɑːn.dʒəˈ- **-s** -z
conjunct (*n.*) ˈkɒn.dʒʌŋ*k*t US ˈkɑːn- **-s** -s
conjunct (*adj.*) kənˈdʒʌŋ*k*t, kɒn- US kən-; ˈkɑːn.dʒʌŋ*k*t **-ly** -li
conjunction kənˈdʒʌŋk.ʃən **-s** -z
conjunctiva ˌkɒn.dʒʌŋ*k*ˈtaɪ.və US ˌkɑːn.dʒəŋˈ-
conjunctive kənˈdʒʌŋ*k*.tɪv **-ly** -li
conjunctivitis kənˌdʒʌŋ*k*.tɪˈvaɪ.tɪs, -təˈ- US -təˈvaɪ.t̬ɪs
conjuncture kənˈdʒʌŋ*k*.tʃəʳ US -tʃɚ **-s** -z
conjuration ˌkɒn.dʒʊəˈreɪ.ʃən US ˌkɑːn.dʒʊˈreɪ- **-s** -z
conjur|e *charge solemnly:* kənˈdʒʊəʳ US -ˈdʒʊr **-es** -z **-ing** -ɪŋ **-ed** -d
conj|ure *summon by magic:* ˈkʌn.dʒ|əʳ US -dʒ|ɚ **-ures** -əz US -ɚz **-uring** -ər.ɪŋ **-ured** -əd US -ɚd **-urer/s** -ər.əʳ/z US -ɚ.ɚ/z **-uror/s** -ər.əʳ/z US -ɚ.ɚ/z ˈ**conjuring** ˌ**trick**
conk kɒŋk US kɑːŋk, kɔːŋk **-s** -s **-ing** -ɪŋ **-ed** -t
conker ˈkɒŋ.kəʳ US ˈkɑːŋ.kɚ, ˈkɔːŋ- **-s** -z
Conleth ˈkɒn.ləθ US ˈkɑːn-
Conley ˈkɒn.li US ˈkɑːn-
Conlon ˈkɒn.lən US ˈkɑːn-
con|man ˈkɒn|.mæn US ˈkɑːn- **-men** -men
Conn. (*abbrev. for* **Connaught**) ˈkɒn.ɔːt US ˈkɑː.nɑːt, -nɔːt
Conn. (*abbrev. for* **Connecticut**) kəˈnet.ɪ.kət US -ˈnet̬-, -kɪt
Connah's Quay ˌkɒn.əzˈkiː US ˌkɑː.nəzˈkiː, -ˈkeɪ, -ˈkweɪ
Connally ˈkɒn.əl.i US ˈkɑː.nəl-
connate ˈkɒn.eɪt, -ˈ- US ˈkɑː.neɪt, -ˈ-
Connaught ˈkɒn.ɔːt US ˈkɑː.nɑːt, -nɔːt
connect kəˈnekt **-s** -s **-ing** -ɪŋ **-ed/ly** -ɪd/li **-able** -ə.bl̩ **-or/s** -əʳ/z US -ɚ/z
connectible kəˈnek.tə.bəl, -tɪ-
Connecticut kəˈnet.ɪ.kət US -ˈnet̬-, -kɪt
connection kəˈnek.ʃən **-s** -z
connective kəˈnek.tɪv **-s** -z **-ly** -li
connectivity ˌkɒn.ekˈtɪv.ɪ.ti; kəˌnekˈ-, ˈ-ə- US ˌkɑː.nekˈtɪv.ə.t̬i
Connelly ˈkɒn.əl.i US ˈkɑː.nəl-
Connemara ˌkɒn.ɪˈmɑː.rə, -əˈ- US ˌkɑː.nəˈ-
Conner ˈkɒn.əʳ US ˈkɑː.nɚ
Connery ˈkɒn.ər.i US ˈkɑː.nɚ-
Connex® ˈkɒn.eks US ˈkɑː.neks
connexion kəˈnek.ʃən **-s** -z
Connie ˈkɒn.i US ˈkɑː.ni
conning tower ˈkɒn.ɪŋˌtaʊəʳ US ˈkɑː.nɪŋˌtaʊɚ **-s** -z
conniption kəˈnɪp.ʃən
connivance kəˈnaɪ.vənts
conniv|e kəˈnaɪv **-es** -z **-ing** -ɪŋ **-ed** -d **-er/s** -əʳ/z US -ɚ/z
connoisseur ˌkɒn.əˈsɜːʳ, -ɪˈ- US ˌkɑː.nəˈsɝː **-s** -z
Connolly ˈkɒn.əl.i US ˈkɑː.nəl-
Connor ˈkɒn.əʳ US ˈkɑː.nɚ
conno|tate ˈkɒn.əʊ|.teɪt US ˈkɑː.nə- **-tates** -teɪts **-tating** -teɪ.tɪŋ US -teɪ.t̬ɪŋ **-tated** -teɪ.tɪd US -teɪ.t̬ɪd
connotation ˌkɒn.əʊˈteɪ.ʃən US ˌkɑː.nəˈ- **-s** -z

connotative 'kɒn.əʊ.teɪ.tɪv; kə'nəʊ.tə- ⓊⓈ kə'noʊ.t̬ə.t̬ɪv, 'kɑː.nə.teɪ-
connot|e kə'nəʊt, kɒn'əʊt ⓊⓈ kə'noʊt **-es** -s **-ing** -ɪŋ ⓊⓈ kə'noʊ.t̬ɪŋ **-ed** -ɪd ⓊⓈ kə'noʊ.t̬ɪd
connubial kə'njuː.bi.əl, kɒn'juː- ⓊⓈ kə'nuː-, -'njuː- **-ly** -i
connubiality kə,njuː.bi'æl.ə.ti, kɒn,juː-, -ɪ.ti ⓊⓈ kə,nuː.bi'æl.ə.t̬i, -,njuː-
conoid 'kəʊ.nɔɪd ⓊⓈ 'koʊ- **-s** -z
conoidal kəʊ'nɔɪ.dəl ⓊⓈ koʊ-
Conolly 'kɒn.əl.i ⓊⓈ 'kɑː.nəl-
Conor 'kɒn.ər ⓊⓈ 'kɑː.nɚ
conqu|er 'kɒŋ.k|ər ⓊⓈ 'kɑːŋ.k|ɚ, 'kɔːŋ- **-ers** -əz ⓊⓈ -ɚz **-ering** -ər.ɪŋ **-ered** -əd ⓊⓈ -ɚd **-erable** -ər.ə.bl̩
conqueror 'kɒŋ.kər.ər ⓊⓈ 'kɑːŋ.kɚ.ɚ, 'kɔːŋ- **-s** -z
conquest (C) 'kɒŋ.kwest ⓊⓈ 'kɑːn-, 'kɑːŋ- **-s** -s
conquistador kɒn'kɪs.tə.dɔːr, kɒŋ-, -'kwɪs-; ,kɒn.kɪ.stə'dɔːr, kɒŋ-, -kwɪ- ⓊⓈ kɑːŋ'kiː.stə.dɔːr, kɔːŋ-, kɑːn-, -'kwɪs.tə- **-s** -z
Conrad 'kɒn.ræd ⓊⓈ 'kɑːn-
Conran 'kɒn.rən, -ræn ⓊⓈ 'kɑːn-
Conroy 'kɒn.rɔɪ ⓊⓈ 'kɑːn-
consanguine kɒn'sæŋ.gwɪn ⓊⓈ kɑːn-
consanguineous ,kɒn.sæŋ'gwɪn.i.əs ⓊⓈ ,kɑːn.sæŋ'-
consanguinity ,kɒn.sæŋ'gwɪn.ə.ti, -ɪ.ti ⓊⓈ ,kɑːn.sæŋ'gwɪn.ə.t̬i
conscienc|e 'kɒn.tʃənts ⓊⓈ 'kɑːn- **-es** -ɪz **'conscience-,stricken**
conscientious ,kɒn.tʃi'en.tʃəs ⓊⓈ ,kɑːn.tʃi'ent.ʃəs **-ly** -li **-ness** -nəs, -nɪs **consci,entious ob'jector**
conscionab|le 'kɒn.tʃən.ə.b|l̩ ⓊⓈ 'kɑːn- **-ly** -li **-leness** -l̩.nəs, -nɪs
conscious 'kɒn.tʃəs ⓊⓈ 'kɑːnt.ʃəs **-ly** -li **-ness** -nəs, -nɪs **'consciousness ,raising**
conscrib|e kən'skraɪb **-es** -z **-ing** -ɪŋ **-ed** -d
conscript (*n.*) 'kɒn.skrɪpt ⓊⓈ 'kɑːn- **-s** -s
conscript (*v.*) kən'skrɪpt **-s** -s **-ing** -ɪŋ **-ed** -ɪd
conscription kən'skrɪp.ʃən **-s** -z
conse|crate 'kɒnt.sɪ|.kreɪt, -sə- ⓊⓈ 'kɑːnt.sə- **-crates** -kreɪts **-crating** -kreɪ.tɪŋ ⓊⓈ -kreɪ.t̬ɪŋ **-crated** -kreɪ.tɪd ⓊⓈ -kreɪ.t̬ɪd **-crator/s** -kreɪ.tər/z ⓊⓈ -kreɪ.t̬ɚ/z
consecration ,kɒnt.sɪ'kreɪ.ʃən, -sə'- ⓊⓈ ,kɑːnt.sə'- **-s** -z
consecutive kən'sek.jʊ.tɪv, -jə- ⓊⓈ -jə.t̬ɪv **-ly** -li **-ness** -nəs, -nɪs
consensual kən'sent.sju.əl, kɒn-, -'sen.tʃu- ⓊⓈ kən'sent.ʃu-, '-ʃəl **-ly** -li
consensus kən'sent.səs, kɒn- ⓊⓈ kən-
con|sent kən|'sent **-sents** -'sents **-senting** -'sen.tɪŋ ⓊⓈ -'sen.t̬ɪŋ **-sented** -'sen.tɪd ⓊⓈ -'sen.t̬ɪd
consequenc|e 'kɒnt.sɪ.kwənts, -sə- ⓊⓈ 'kɑːnt- **-es** -ɪz
consequent 'kɒnt.sɪ.kwənt, -sə- ⓊⓈ 'kɑːnt- **-ly** -li
consequential ,kɒnt.sɪ'kwen.tʃəl, -sə'- ⓊⓈ ,kɑːnt- **-ly** -i
conservable kən'sɜː.və.bl̩ ⓊⓈ -'sɝː-
conservanc|y kən'sɜː.vənt.s|i ⓊⓈ -'sɝː- **-ies** -iz
conservation ,kɒnt.sə'veɪ.ʃən ⓊⓈ ,kɑːnt.sɚ'-
conservationist ,kɒnt.sə'veɪ.ʃən.ɪst ⓊⓈ ,kɑːnt.sɚ'- **-s** -s
conservatism kən'sɜː.və.tɪ.zəm ⓊⓈ -'sɝː-
conservative (C) kən'sɜː.və.tɪv ⓊⓈ -'sɝː.və.t̬ɪv **-s** -z **-ly** -li **-ness** -nəs, -nɪs
conservatoire kən'sɜː.və.twɑːr, kɒn- ⓊⓈ kən'sɝː.və.twɑːr, -,sɝː.və'twɑːr **-s** -z
conservator *preserver:* 'kɒnt.sə.veɪ.tər ⓊⓈ 'kɑːnt.sɚ.veɪ.t̬ɚ **-s** -z
conservator *official guardian:* kən'sɜː.və.tər ⓊⓈ -'sɝː.və.t̬ɚ **-s** -z
conservator|y kən'sɜː.və.tr|i ⓊⓈ -'sɝː.və.tɔːr|.i **-ies** -iz
conserve (*n.*) kən'sɜːv; 'kɒn.sɜːv ⓊⓈ 'kɑːn.sɝːv **-s** -z
conserv|e (*v.*) kən'sɜːv ⓊⓈ -'sɝːv **-es** -z **-ing** -ɪŋ **-ed** -d
Consett 'kɒn.sɪt, -set, -sət ⓊⓈ 'kɑːn-
consid|er kən'sɪd|.ər ⓊⓈ -ɚ **-ers** -əz ⓊⓈ -ɚz **-ering** -ər.ɪŋ **-ered** -əd ⓊⓈ -ɚd
considerab|le kən'sɪd.ər.ə.b|l̩ **-ly** -li **-leness** -l̩.nəs, -nɪs
considerate kən'sɪd.ər.ət, -ɪt **-ly** -li **-ness** -nəs, -nɪs
consideration kən,sɪd.ər'eɪ.ʃən **-s** -z
consign kən'saɪn **-s** -z **-ing** -ɪŋ **-ed** -d **-er/s** -ər/z ⓊⓈ -ɚ/z **-able** -ə.bl̩
consignation ,kɒn.saɪ'neɪ.ʃən ⓊⓈ ,kɑːn.sɪg'-, -sɪ'-
consignee ,kɒn.saɪ'niː, -sɪ'- ⓊⓈ ,kɑːn- **-s** -z
Consignia® kən'sɪg.ni.ə
consignment kən'saɪn.mənt, -'saɪm- ⓊⓈ -'saɪn- **-s** -s
consist kən'sɪst **-s** -s **-ing** -ɪŋ **-ed** -ɪd
consisten|ce kən'sɪs.tənt|s **-cy** -si **-cies** -siz
consistent kən'sɪs.tənt **-ly** -li
consistorial ,kɒn.sɪ'stɔː.ri.əl ⓊⓈ ,kɑːn.sɪ'stɔːr.i-
consistor|y kən'sɪs.tər|.i, -tr|i ⓊⓈ -tɚ|.i **-ies** -iz
consolable kən'səʊ.lə.bl̩ ⓊⓈ -'soʊ-
consolation ,kɒn.sə'leɪ.ʃən ⓊⓈ ,kɑːn- **-s** -z **,conso'lation ,prize**
consolatory kən'sɒl.ə.tər.i, -'səʊ.lə-, -tri ⓊⓈ -'sɑː.lə.tɔːr.i, -'soʊ-
console (*n.*) 'kɒn.səʊl ⓊⓈ 'kɑːn.soʊl **-s** -z
consol|e (*v.*) kən'səʊl ⓊⓈ -'soʊl **-es** -z **-ing** -ɪŋ **-ed** -d **-er/s** -ər/z ⓊⓈ -ɚ/z
consoli|date kən'sɒl.ɪ|.deɪt, '-ə- ⓊⓈ -'sɑː.lə- **-dates** -deɪts **-dating** -deɪ.tɪŋ ⓊⓈ -deɪ.t̬ɪŋ **-dated** -deɪ.tɪd ⓊⓈ -deɪ.t̬ɪd **-dator/s** -deɪ.tər/z ⓊⓈ -deɪ.t̬ɚ/z **-dative** -deɪ.tɪv ⓊⓈ -deɪ.t̬ɪv
consolidation kən,sɒl.ɪ'deɪ.ʃən, -ə'- ⓊⓈ -,sɑː.lə'- **-s** -z
consols kən'sɒlz; 'kɒnt.səlz ⓊⓈ 'kɑːn.sɑːlz; kən'sɑːlz
consommé kən'sɒm.eɪ, kɒn-; 'kɒnt.sə.meɪ ⓊⓈ ,kɑːnt.sə'meɪ, '---
consonanc|e 'kɒnt.sən.ənts ⓊⓈ 'kɑːnt- **-es** -ɪz
consonant 'kɒnt.sən.ənt ⓊⓈ 'kɑːnt- **-s** -s **-ly** -li
consonantal ,kɒnt.sən'æn.təl ⓊⓈ ,kɑːnt.sə'næn.t̬əl **-ly** -i
consort (*n.*) 'kɒn.sɔːt ⓊⓈ 'kɑːn.sɔːrt **-s** -s
con|sort (*v.*) kən|'sɔːt, kɒn- ⓊⓈ kən|'sɔːrt **-sorts** -'sɔːts ⓊⓈ -'sɔːrts **-sorting** -'sɔː.tɪŋ ⓊⓈ -'sɔːr.t̬ɪŋ **-sorted** -'sɔː.tɪd ⓊⓈ -'sɔːr.t̬ɪd
consorti|um kən'sɔː.ti|.əm, -ʃi-, '-ʃ|əm ⓊⓈ -'sɔːr.t̬i|.əm, -ʃi-, '-ʃ|əm **-ums** -əmz **-a** -ə
conspectus kən'spek.təs **-es** -ɪz
conspicuous kən'spɪk.ju.əs **-ly** -li **-ness** -nəs, -nɪs
conspirac|y kən'spɪr.ə.s|i **-ies** -iz **con'spiracy ,theory**
conspirator kən'spɪr.ə.tər, -ɪ.tər ⓊⓈ -ə.t̬ɚ **-s** -z
conspiratorial kən,spɪr.ə'tɔː.ri.əl, kɒn- ⓊⓈ kən,spɪr.ə'tɔːr.i-
conspir|e kən'spaɪər ⓊⓈ -'spaɪɚ **-es** -z **-ing** -ɪŋ **-ed** -d **-er/s** -ər/z ⓊⓈ -ɚ/z
constable (C) 'kʌnt.stə.bl̩, 'kɒnt- ⓊⓈ 'kɑːnt-, 'kʌnt- **-s** -z
constabular|y kən'stæb.jʊ.lər|.i, -jə- ⓊⓈ -jə.ler|.i **-ies** -iz
Constance 'kɒnt.stənts ⓊⓈ 'kɑːnt-
constancy 'kɒnt.stənt.si ⓊⓈ 'kɑːnt-
constant 'kɒnt.stənt ⓊⓈ 'kɑːnt- **-s** -s **-ly** -li **-ness** -nəs, -nɪs
Constanta kən'stæn.tə ⓊⓈ -t̬ə
Constantine *Kings and Emperors:* 'kɒnt.stən.taɪn, -tiːn ⓊⓈ 'kɑːnt.stən.tiːn, -taɪn *city:* 'kɒnt.stən.taɪn, -tiːn ⓊⓈ 'kɑːnt-
Constantinople ,kɒn.stæn.tɪ'nəʊ.pl̩ ⓊⓈ ,kɑːn.stæn.tən'oʊ-
constative kən'stæt.ɪv ⓊⓈ -'stæt̬-

Consonant

A speech sound which obstructs the flow of air though the vocal tract or a letter of the alphabet representing such a vowel.

Examples for English

There are many types of consonant, but what all have in common is that they obstruct the flow of air through the vocal tract. Some do this a lot, some not very much: those which make the maximum obstruction (i.e. PLOSIVES, which form a complete stoppage of the airstream) are the most consonantal, e.g.:

bat	/bæt/
keep	/kiːp/

NASAL consonants result in complete stoppage of the oral cavity but are less obstructive than plosives since air is allowed to escape through the nose, e.g.:

man	/mæn/
name	/neɪm/

FRICATIVES make a considerable obstruction to the flow of air, but not a total closure, e.g.:

sheaf	/ʃiːf/
south	/saʊθ/

The class of sounds called APPROXIMANTS comprises sounds which make very little obstruction of the flow of air.

The post-alveolar approximant that is the usual pronunciation of /r/ in BBC English involves no contact between the tongue and the palate, e.g.:

red	/red/	[ɹed]
arrive	/ə'raɪv/	[ə'ɹaɪv]

LATERAL approximants obstruct the flow of air only in the centre of the mouth, not at the sides, so obstruction is slight, e.g.:

lull	/lʌl/

Other sounds classed as approximants make so little obstruction to the flow of air that they could almost be thought to be vowels if they were in a different context. These are sometimes referred to as 'semi-vowels', e.g.:

you	/juː/
woo	/wuː/

Finally, AFFRICATES begin as plosives and are released as fricatives, with no intervening gap, e.g.:

church	/tʃɜːtʃ/	(US) /tʃɝːtʃ/
judge	/dʒʌdʒ/	

The above explanation is based on phonetic criteria. An alternative approach is to look at the *phonological* characteristics of consonants: for example, consonants are typically found at the beginning and end of syllables while vowels are typically found in the middle.

constellation ˌkɒn*t*.stə'leɪ.ʃᵊn, -stɪ'- (US) ˌkɑːn*t*- **-s** -z

conster|nate 'kɒn*t*.stə|.neɪt (US) 'kɑːn*t*.stɚ- **-nates** -neɪts **-nating** -neɪ.tɪŋ (US) -neɪ.t̬ɪŋ **-nated** -neɪ.tɪd (US) -neɪ.t̬ɪd

consternation ˌkɒn*t*.stə'neɪ.ʃᵊn (US) ˌkɑːn*t*.stɚ'-

consti|pate 'kɒn*t*.stɪ|.peɪt, -stə- (US) 'kɑːn*t*.stə- **-pates** -peɪts **-pating** -peɪ.tɪŋ (US) -peɪ.t̬ɪŋ **-pated** -peɪ.tɪd (US) -peɪ.t̬ɪd

constipation ˌkɒn*t*.stɪ'peɪ.ʃᵊn, -stə'- (US) ˌkɑːn*t*.stə'-

constituen|cy kən'stɪt.ju.ən*t*|.si, kɒn-, -'stɪtʃ.u- (US) kən'stɪtʃ.u- **-cies** -siz

constituent kən'stɪt.ju.ənt, kɒn-, -'stɪtʃ.u- (US) kən'stɪtʃ.u- **-s** -s

consti|tute 'kɒn*t*.stɪ|.tjuːt, -stə-, -tʃuːt (US) 'kɑːn*t*.stə|.tuːt, -tjuːt **-tutes** -tjuːts, -tʃuːts (US) -tuːts, -tjuːts **-tuting** -tjuː.tɪŋ, -tʃuː.tɪŋ (US) -tuː.t̬ɪŋ, -tjuː- **-tuted** -tjuː.tɪd, -tʃuː.tɪd (US) -tuː.t̬ɪd, -tjuː-

constitution ˌkɒn*t*.stɪ'tjuː.ʃᵊn, -stə'-, -'tʃuː- (US) ˌkɑːn*t*.stə'tuː-, -'tjuː- **-s** -z

constitutional ˌkɒn*t*.stɪ'tjuː.ʃᵊn.ᵊl, -stə'-, -'tʃuː-, -'tjuːʃ.nᵊl, -'tʃuːʃ- (US) ˌkɑːn*t*.stə'tuː-, -'tjuː-, -'tuːʃ.nᵊl, -'tjuːʃ- **-ly** -i

constitutional|ism ˌkɒn*t*.stɪ'tjuː.ʃᵊn.ᵊl|.ɪ.zᵊm, -stə'-, -'tʃuː- (US) ˌkɑːn*t*.stə'tuː-, -'tjuː- **-ist/s** -ɪst/s

constitutionaliz|e, **-is|e** ˌkɒn*t*.stɪ'tjuː.ʃᵊn.ᵊl.aɪz, -stə'-, -'tʃuː- (US) ˌkɑːn*t*.stə'tuː.ʃᵊn.ə.laɪz, -'tjuː- **-es** -ɪz **-ing** -ɪŋ **-ed** -d

constitutive kən'stɪt.jʊ.tɪv, kɒn-, -'stɪtʃ.ə-; 'kɒn*t*.stɪ.tjuː-, -stə-, -tʃuː- (US) 'kɑːn*t*.stə.tuː.t̬ɪv, -tjuː-; kən'stɪtʃ.ə-

constrain kən'streɪn **-s** -z **-ing** -ɪŋ **-ed** -d **-edly** -ɪd.li, -d.li **-able** -ə.bl̩

constraint kən'streɪnt **-s** -s

constrict kən'strɪkt **-s** -s **-ing** -ɪŋ **-ed** -ɪd **-or/s** -əʳ/z (US) -ɚ/z **-ive** -ɪv

constriction kən'strɪk.ʃᵊn **-s** -z

construct (*n.*) 'kɒn.strʌkt (US) 'kɑːn- **-s** -s

construct (*v.*) kən'strʌkt **-s** -s **-ing** -ɪŋ **-ed** -ɪd

construction kən'strʌk.ʃᵊn **-s** -z

constructional kən'strʌk.ʃᵊn.ᵊl **-ly** -i

constructionist kən'strʌk.ʃᵊn.ɪst **-s** -s

constructive kən'strʌk.tɪv **-ly** -li **-ness** -nəs, -nɪs

constructor kən'strʌk.təʳ (US) -tɚ **-s** -z

constru|e kən'struː, kɒn- (US) kən- **-es** -z **-ing** -ɪŋ **-ed** -d

consubstantial ˌkɒn.səb'stæn.*t*ʃᵊl, -'stɑːn- (US) ˌkɑːn.səb'stæn*t*.ʃᵊl **-ly** -i

consubstanti|ate ˌkɒn.səb'stæn.*t*ʃi|.eɪt, -'stɑːn-, -'stæn*t*.si-, -'stɑːn*t*.si- (US) ˌkɑːn.səb'stæn*t*.ʃi- **-ates** -eɪts **-ating** -eɪ.tɪŋ (US) -eɪ.t̬ɪŋ **-ated** -eɪ.tɪd (US) -eɪ.t̬ɪd

consubstantiation ˌkɒn.səbˌstæn.*t*ʃi'eɪ.ʃᵊn, -ˌstɑːn-, -ˌstæn*t*.si'-, -ˌstɑːn*t*.si'- (US) ˌkɑːn.səbˌstæn*t*.ʃi'-

consuetude 'kɒn*t*.swɪ.tjuːd, -tʃuːd (US) 'kɑːn*t*.swɪ.tuːd, -tjuːd

consuetudinary ˌkɒn*t*.swɪ'tjuː.dɪ.nᵊr.i (US) ˌkɑːn*t*.swɪ'tuː.dɪ.ner-, -'tjuː-

consul 'kɒn*t*.sᵊl (US) 'kɑːn*t*- **-s** -z **-ship/s** -ʃɪp/s

consular 'kɒn*t*.sjʊ.ləʳ, -sjə- (US) 'kɑːn*t*-

consulate 'kɒn*t*.sjʊ.lət, -sjə-, -lɪt (US) 'kɑːn*t*- **-s** -s

con|sult kən|'sʌlt **-sults** -'sʌlts **-sulting** -'sʌl.tɪŋ (US) -'sʌl.t̬ɪŋ **-sulted** -'sʌl.tɪd (US) -'sʌl.t̬ɪd

consultanc|y kən'sʌl.tᵊn*t*.s|i **-ies** -iz

consultant kən'sʌl.tᵊnt **-s** -s
consultation ˌkɒn.sᵊl'teɪ.ʃᵊn, -sʌl'- (US) ˌkɑːn- **-s** -z
consultative kən'sʌl.tə.tɪv (US) -t̬ə.t̬ɪv; 'kɑːnt.səl.teɪ-
consultatory kən'sʌl.tə.tᵊr.i, -tri; ˌkɒnt.sᵊl'teɪ- (US) kən'sʌl.t̬ə.tɔːr.i
consumable kən'sjuː.mə.bl̩, -'suː- (US) -'suː- **-s** -z
consum|e kən'sjuːm, -'suːm (US) -'suːm **-es** -z **-ing** -ɪŋ **-ed** -d
consumer kən'sjuː.məʳ, -'suː- (US) -'suː.mɚ **-s** -z **con'sumer ˌgoods; con'sumer soˌciety**
consumer|ism kən'sjuː.mə.r|ɪ.zᵊm, -'suː- (US) -'suː.mɚ.ɪ- **-ist** -ɪst
consummate *(adj.)* kən'sʌm.ət, -ɪt; 'kɒnt.sə.mət, -sjʊ-, -mɪt (US) 'kɑːnt.sə.mɪt; kən'sʌm.ɪt **-ly** -li
consum|mate *(v.)* 'kɒnt.sə|.meɪt, -sjʊ- (US) 'kɑːnt.sə- **-mates** -meɪts **-mating** -meɪ.tɪŋ (US) -meɪ.t̬ɪŋ **-mated** -meɪ.tɪd (US) -meɪ.t̬ɪd **-mator/s** -meɪ.təʳ/z (US) -meɪ.t̬ɚ/z
consummation ˌkɒnt.sə'meɪ.ʃᵊn, -sjʊ'- (US) ˌkɑːnt.sə'- **-s** -z
consummative 'kɒnt.sə.meɪ.tɪv, -sʌm.eɪ-, -sjʊ.meɪ-; kən'sʌm.ə- (US) 'kɑːnt.sə.meɪ.t̬ɪv; kən'sʌm.ə-
consumption kən'sʌmp.ʃᵊn
consumptive kən'sʌmp.tɪv **-s** -z **-ly** -li **-ness** -nəs, -nɪs
contact *(n. adj.)* 'kɒn.tækt (US) 'kɑːn- **-s** -s **'contact ˌlens**
contact *(v.)* 'kɒn.tækt; -'-, kən- (US) 'kɑːn.tækt **-s** -s **-ing** -ɪŋ **-ed** -ɪd
contagion kən'teɪ.dʒᵊn **-s** -z
contagious kən'teɪ.dʒəs **-ly** -li **-ness** -nəs, -nɪs
contain kən'teɪn **-s** -z **-ing** -ɪŋ **-ed** -d **-able** -ə.bl̩
container kən'teɪ.nəʳ (US) -nɚ **-s** -z **con'tainer ˌship**
containerization, -isa- kənˌteɪ.nᵊr.aɪ'zeɪ.ʃᵊn, -ɪ'- (US) -ɪ'-
containeriz|e, is|e kən'teɪ.nᵊr.aɪz (US) -nə.raɪz **-es** -ɪz **-ing** -ɪŋ **-ed** -d
containment kən'teɪn.mənt, -'teɪm- (US) -'teɪn-
contaminant kən'tæm.ɪ.nənt, '-ə- **-s** -s
contami|nate kən'tæm.ɪ|.neɪt, '-ə- **-nates** -neɪts **-nating** -neɪ.tɪŋ (US) -neɪ.t̬ɪŋ **-nated** -neɪ.tɪd (US) -neɪ.t̬ɪd **-nater/s** -neɪ.təʳ/z (US) -neɪ.t̬ɚ/z
contamination kənˌtæm.ɪ'neɪ.ʃᵊn, -ə'- **-s** -z
contaminative kən'tæm.ɪ.nə.tɪv, '-ə-, -neɪ- (US) -t̬ɪv
contango kən'tæŋ.gəʊ, kɒn- (US) kən'tæŋ.goʊ **-s** -z

contd *(abbrev. for* **continued***)* kən'tɪn.juːd, -jud
contemn kən'tem **-s** -z **-ing** -ɪŋ **-ed** -d **-er/s** -əʳ/z, -nəʳ/z (US) -ɚ/z, -nɚ/z
contem|plate 'kɒn.təm|.pleɪt, -tem- (US) 'kɑːn.t̬əm-, -tem- **-plates** -pleɪts **-plating** -pleɪ.tɪŋ (US) -pleɪ.t̬ɪŋ **-plated** -pleɪ.tɪd (US) -pleɪ.t̬ɪd **-plator/s** -pleɪ.təʳ/z (US) -pleɪ.t̬ɚ/z
contemplation ˌkɒn.təm'pleɪ.ʃᵊn, -tem'- (US) ˌkɑːn.t̬əm'-, -tem'- **-s** -z
contemplative *pensive:* kən'tem.plə.tɪv, 'kɒn.tem.pleɪ.tɪv, -təm- (US) kən'tem.plə.t̬ɪv; 'kɑːn.t̬əm.pleɪ- **-ly** -li **-ness** -nəs, -nɪs
contemplative *of religious orders:* kən'tem.plə.tɪv (US) -t̬ɪv
contemporaneity kənˌtem.pᵊr.ə'niː.ə.ti, kɒn-, -'neɪ-, -ɪ.ti; ˌkɒn.tem- (US) kənˌtem.pɚ.ə'niː.ə.t̬i, -'neɪ-
contemporaneous kənˌtem.pᵊr'eɪ.ni.əs, kɒn-; ˌkɒn.tem- (US) kən- **-ly** -li **-ness** -nəs, -nɪs
contemporar|y kən'tem.pᵊr.ᵊr|.i (US) -pə.rer- **-ies** -iz **-ily** -ᵊl.i, -ɪ.li
contempt kən'tempt
contemptibility kənˌtemp.tə'bɪl.ə.ti, -tɪ'-, -ɪ.ti (US) -tə'bɪl.ə.t̬i
contemptib|le kən'temp.tə.b|l̩, -tɪ- **-ly** -li **-leness** -l̩.nəs, -nɪs
contemptuous kən'temp.tʃu.əs, -tju- (US) -tʃu- **-ly** -li **-ness** -nəs, -nɪs
contend kən'tend **-s** -z **-ing** -ɪŋ **-ed** -ɪd **-er/s** -əʳ/z (US) -ɚ/z
content *(n.) what is contained:* 'kɒn.tent (US) 'kɑːn- *contentment:* kən'tent
con|tent *(adj. v.)* kən|'tent **-tents** -'tents **-tenting** -'ten.tɪŋ (US) -'ten.t̬ɪŋ **-tented/ly** -'ten.tɪd/li (US) -'ten.t̬ɪd/li **-tentedness** -'ten.tɪd.nəs, -nɪs (US) -'ten.t̬ɪd-
contention kən'ten.tʃᵊn **-s** -z
contentious kən'ten.tʃəs **-ly** -li **-ness** -nəs, -nɪs
contentment kən'tent.mənt
contents *(n.) what is contained:* 'kɒn.tents, kən'tents (US) 'kɑːn.tents
contermin|al kɒn'tɜː.mɪ.n|ᵊl, kən-, -mə- (US) kən'tɝː- **-ous** -əs
contest *(n.)* 'kɒn.test (US) 'kɑːn- **-s** -s
contest *(v.)* kən'test **-s** -s **-ing** -ɪŋ **-ed** -ɪd **-able** -ə.bl̩
contestant kən'tes.tᵊnt **-s** -s
contestation ˌkɒn.tes'teɪ.ʃᵊn (US) ˌkɑːn- **-s** -z
context 'kɒn.tekst (US) 'kɑːn- **-s** -s
contextual kən'tek.stju.əl, kɒn-, -'teks.tʃu- (US) kən'teks.tʃu-, kɑːn-, -tʃᵊl **-ly** -i

contextualization, -isa- kənˌtek.stju.ə.laɪ'zeɪ.ʃᵊn, -ˌteks.tʃu-, -lɪ'- (US) kənˌteks.tʃu.ə.lɪ'-, kɑːn-, -tʃᵊl.ɪ'-
contextualiz|e, is|e kən'tek.stju.ə.laɪz, -'teks.tʃu- (US) kən'teks.tʃu-, -tʃə.laɪz **-es** -ɪz **-ing** -ɪŋ **-ed** -d
Conti 'kɒn.ti (US) 'kɑːn.t̬i
contiguity ˌkɒn.tɪ'gjuː.ə.ti, -tə'-, -ɪ.ti (US) ˌkɑːn.t̬ə'gjuː.ə.t̬i
contiguous kən'tɪg.ju.əs **-ly** -li **-ness** -nəs, -nɪs
continen|ce 'kɒn.tɪ.nənt|s (US) 'kɑːn.tᵊn.ənt|s **-cy** -si
continent (C) 'kɒn.tɪ.nənt (US) 'kɑːn.tᵊn.ənt **-s** -s **-ly** -li
continental ˌkɒn.tɪ'nen.tᵊl, -tə'- (US) ˌkɑːn.t̬ᵊn'en.t̬ᵊl **ˌcontinental 'breakfast; ˌcontinental 'quilt**
contingen|ce kən'tɪn.dʒᵊnt|s **-cy** -si **-cies** -siz
contingent kən'tɪn.dʒᵊnt **-s** -s **-ly** -li
continual kən'tɪn.ju.əl **-ly** -i
continuan|ce kən'tɪn.ju.ənt|s **-t/s** -t/s
continuation kənˌtɪn.ju'eɪ.ʃᵊn **-s** -z
continuative kən'tɪn.ju.ə.tɪv, -eɪ.tɪv (US) kən'tɪn.ju.eɪ.t̬ɪv, -ə-
continuator kən'tɪn.ju.eɪ.təʳ (US) -t̬ɚ **-s** -z
contin|ue kən'tɪn|.juː, -ju **-ues** -juːz, -juz **-uing** -ju.ɪŋ **-ued** -juːd, -jud **-uer/s** -ju.əʳ/z (US) -ju.ɚ/z
continuity ˌkɒn.tɪ'njuː.ə.ti, -tə'-, -ɪ.ti (US) ˌkɑːn.tᵊn'uː.ə.t̬i, -'juː-
continuo kən'tɪn.ju.əʊ, kɒn-, -u.əʊ (US) kən'tɪn.ju.oʊ
continuous kən'tɪn.ju.əs **-ly** -li **-ness** -nəs, -nɪs **conˌtinuous as'sessment**
continu|um kən'tɪn.ju|.əm **-ums** -əmz **-a** -ə
contoid 'kɒn.tɔɪd (US) 'kɑːn- **-s** -z
con|tort kən|'tɔːt (US) -'tɔːrt **-torts** -'tɔːts (US) -'tɔːrts **-torting** -'tɔː.tɪŋ (US) -'tɔːr.t̬ɪŋ **-torted** -'tɔː.tɪd (US) -'tɔːr.t̬ɪd
contortion kən'tɔː.ʃᵊn (US) -'tɔːr- **-s** -z
contortionist kən'tɔː.ʃᵊn.ɪst, kɒn- (US) kən'tɔːr- **-s** -s
contour 'kɒn.tʊəʳ, -tɔːʳ (US) 'kɑːn.tʊr **-s** -z **-ing** -ɪŋ **-ed** -d
contra- 'kɒn.trə- (US) 'kɑːn.trə-
Note: Prefix. In the sense of "against" this always carries primary or secondary stress on the first syllable.
contra (C) 'kɒn.trə, -trɑː (US) 'kɑːn.trə **-s** -z
contraband 'kɒn.trə.bænd (US) 'kɑːn- **-ist/s** -ɪst/s
contrabass ˌkɒn.trə'beɪs, '--- (US) 'kɑːn.trə.beɪs **-es** -ɪz

contra bonos mores ˌkɒn.trɑːˌbəʊ.nəʊsˈmɔː.reɪs, -ˌbɒn.əʊs- (US) ˌkɑːn.trɑːˌboʊ.noʊsˈmɔːr.iːz
contraception ˌkɒn.trəˈsep.ʃᵊn (US) ˌkɑːn-
contraceptive ˌkɒn.trəˈsep.tɪv (US) ˌkɑːn- -s -z
contract (*n.*) ˈkɒn.trækt (US) ˈkɑːn- -s -s
contract (*v.*) kənˈtrækt -s -s -ing -ɪŋ -ed -ɪd -ive -ɪv
contractibility kənˌtræk.təˈbɪl.ə.ti, -tɪˈ-, -ɪ.ti (US) kənˌtræk.təˈbɪl.ə.t̬i; ˌkɑːn.træk-
contractib|le kənˈtræk.tə.b|l̩, -tɪ- -ly -li -leness -l̩.nəs, -nɪs
contractile kənˈtræk.taɪl (US) -tᵊl, -taɪl
contraction kənˈtræk.ʃᵊn -s -z
contractionary kənˈtræk.ʃᵊn.ᵊr.i, -ʃᵊn.ri (US) -ʃᵊn.er.i
contractor *builder:* kənˈtræk.təʳ; ˈkɒn.træk- (US) ˈkɑːn.træk.tɚ -s -z *other senses:* kənˈtræk.təʳ (US) -tɚ -s -z
contractual kənˈtræk.tʃu.ᵊl, -tju- (US) kənˈtræk.tʃu-, kɑːn-, -tʃᵊl -ly -i
contracture kənˈtræk.tʃəʳ, -tjʊəʳ, -ʃəʳ (US) -tʃɚ -s -z
contradict ˌkɒn.trəˈdɪkt (US) ˌkɑːn- -s -s -ing -ɪŋ -ed -ɪd
contradiction ˌkɒn.trəˈdɪk.ʃᵊn (US) ˌkɑːn- -s -z
contradictor|y ˌkɒn.trəˈdɪk.tᵊr|.i, -tr|i (US) ˌkɑːn- -ily -ᵊl.i, -ɪ.li -iness -ɪ.nəs, -ɪ.nɪs
contradistinc|tion ˌkɒn.trə.dɪˈstɪŋk|.ʃᵊn, -dəˈ- (US) ˌkɑːn.trə.dɪˈ-, -dəˈ- -tive -tɪv
contradistinguish ˌkɒn.trə.dɪˈstɪŋ.gwɪʃ, -dəˈ- (US) ˌkɑːn.trə.dɪˈ-, -dəˈ- -es -ɪz -ing -ɪŋ -ed -t
contrafactive ˌkɒn.trəˈfæk.tɪv (US) ˌkɑːn-
contraflow ˈkɒn.trə.fləʊ (US) ˈkɑːn.trə.floʊ -s -z
contraindi|cate ˌkɒn.trəˈɪn.dɪ|.keɪt (US) ˌkɑːn.trə- -cates -keɪts -cating -keɪ.tɪŋ (US) -keɪ.t̬ɪŋ -cated -keɪ.tɪd (US) -keɪ.t̬ɪd
contraindication ˌkɒn.trə.ɪn.dɪˈkeɪ.ʃᵊn (US) ˌkɑːn.trə- -s -z
contraindicative ˌkɒn.trə.ɪnˈdɪk.ə.tɪv (US) ˌkɑːn.trə.ɪnˈdɪk.ə.t̬ɪv
contralti (*plur. of* **contralto**) kənˈtræl.ti, -ˈtrɑːl- (US) -ˈtræl.t̬i
contralto kənˈtræl.təʊ, -ˈtrɑːl- (US) -ˈtræl.t̬oʊ -s -z
contra pacem ˌkɒn.trɑːˈpɑː.kem, -ˈpɑː.tʃem (US) ˌkɑːn.trɑːˈpɑː.kem, -ˈpeɪ.sem
contraposition ˌkɒn.trə.pəˈzɪʃ.ᵊn (US) ˌkɑːn-
contraption kənˈtræp.ʃᵊn -s -z
contrapuntal ˌkɒn.trəˈpʌn.tᵊl (US) ˌkɑːn.trəˈpʌn.t̬ᵊl -ly -i
contrapuntist ˌkɒn.trəˈpʌn.tɪst (US) ˌkɑːn.trəˈpʌn.t̬ɪst -s -s
contrariety ˌkɒn.trəˈraɪ.ə.ti, -ɪ.ti (US) ˌkɑːn.trəˈraɪ.ə.t̬i
contrariwise kənˈtreə.ri.waɪz; ˈkɒn.trə- (US) kənˈtrer.i-; ˈkɑːn.trɚ-
contrar|y *opposed:* ˈkɒn.trᵊr|.i (US) ˈkɑːn.trɚ|.i -ies -iz -ily -ᵊl.i, -ɪ.li
contrar|y *perverse, obstinate:* kənˈtreə.r|i (US) -ˈtrer|.i -ies -iz -ily -ɪ.li, -ᵊl.i -iness -ɪ.nəs, -ɪ.nɪs
contrast (*n.*) ˈkɒn.trɑːst (US) ˈkɑːn.træst -s -s
contrast (*v.*) kənˈtrɑːst (US) -ˈtræst -s -s -ing/ly -ɪŋ/li -ed -ɪd
contrastive kənˈtrɑː.stɪv (US) -ˈtræs.tɪv
contraven|e ˌkɒn.trəˈviːn (US) ˌkɑːn- -es -z -ing -ɪŋ -ed -d
contravention ˌkɒn.trəˈven.*t*ʃᵊn (US) ˌkɑːn- -s -z
contretemps (*sing.*) ˈkɒn.trə.tɑ̃ːŋ, ˈkɔːn-, ˈkɔ̃ːn- (US) ˈkɑːn.trə.tɑ̃ː (*plur.*) ˈkɒn.trə.tɑ̃ː, -z (US) ˈkɑːn.trə.tɑ̃ː, -z
contrib|ute kənˈtrɪb|.juːt, ˈkɒn.trɪ.b|juːt, -jət (US) kənˈtrɪb|.juːt, -jət -utes -juːts (US) -juːts, -jəts -uting -jʊ.tɪŋ (US) -juː.t̬ɪŋ, -jə- -uted -jʊ.tɪd (US) -juː.t̬ɪd, -jə-
contribution ˌkɒn.trɪˈbjuː.ʃᵊn (US) ˌkɑːn- -s -z
contributive kənˈtrɪb.jʊ.tɪv, -jə- (US) -jə.t̬ɪv
contributor kənˈtrɪb.jə.təʳ, -jʊ-; ˈkɒn.trɪ.bjuː- (US) kənˈtrɪb.jə.t̬ɚ, -juː.t̬ɚ -s -z
contributory kənˈtrɪb.jʊ.tᵊr.i, -jə-, -tri; ˌkɒn.trɪˈbjuː- (US) kənˈtrɪb.jə.tɔːr.i
contrite kənˈtraɪt, kɒn- (US) kən-, kɑːn- -ly -li -ness -nəs, -nɪs
contrition kənˈtrɪʃ.ᵊn
contrivanc|e kənˈtraɪ.vᵊn*t*s -es -ɪz
contriv|e kənˈtraɪv -es -z -ing -ɪŋ -ed -d -er/s -əʳ/z (US) -ɚ/z
control (*n.*) kənˈtrəʊl *in machinery also:* ˈkɒn.trəʊl (US) kənˈtroʊl -s -z
control (*v.*) kənˈtrəʊl (US) -ˈtroʊl -s -z -ling -ɪŋ -led -d -lable -ə.bl̩
controller kənˈtrəʊ.ləʳ (US) -ˈtroʊ.lɚ -s -z
controversial ˌkɒn.trəˈvɜː.ʃᵊl, ˈ-si.əl (US) ˌkɑːn.trəˈvɝː.ʃᵊl -ly -i
controversialist ˌkɒn.trəˈvɜː.ʃᵊl.ɪst, ˈ-si.ᵊl- (US) ˌkɑːn.trəˈvɝː.ʃᵊl- -s -s
controvers|y ˈkɒn.trə.vɜː.s|i, -və.s|i; kənˈtrɒv.ə.s|i (US) ˈkɑːn.trə.vɝː- -ies -iz
controver|t ˌkɒn.trəˈvɜː|t, ˈ--- (US) ˈkɑːn.trə.vɝː|t, ˌ--ˈ- -ts -ts -ting -tɪŋ (US) -t̬ɪŋ -ted -tɪd (US) -t̬ɪd
controvertib|le ˌkɒn.trəˈvɜː.tə.b|l̩, -tɪ- (US) ˌkɑːn.trəˈvɝː.t̬ə- -ly -li
contumacious ˌkɒn.tjʊˈmeɪ.ʃəs (US) ˌkɑːn.tʊˈ-, -tjuːˈ-, -t̬əˈ-, -tjəˈ- -ly -li -ness -nəs, -nəs
contumacy ˈkɒn.tjʊ.mə.si (US) ˈkɑːn.tuː-; -tjʊ-; kənˈtuː-
contumelious ˌkɒn.tjʊˈmiː.li.əs (US) ˌkɑːn.tʊˈ-, -tjuːˈ-, -təˈ-, -tjəˈ- -ly -li -ness -nəs, -nɪs
contumel|y ˈkɒn.tjuː.mᵊl|.i, -tjʊ-, -mɪ.l|i; kənˈtjʊm.ɪ.l|i, -ᵊl|.i, -ˈtjuː.mɪ.l|i, -mᵊl|.i (US) ˈkɑːn.tuː.mᵊl|.i, -tjuː-, ˈ-t̬əm.l|i; kənˈtuː.mə.l|i, -ˈtjuː-, -ˈtʊm.ə- -ies -iz
contus|e kənˈtjuːz (US) -ˈtuːz, -ˈtjuːz -es -ɪz -ing -ɪŋ -ed -d
contusion kənˈtjuː.ʒᵊn (US) -ˈtuː-, -ˈtjuː- -s -z
conundrum kəˈnʌn.drəm -s -z
conurbation ˌkɒn.ɜːˈbeɪ.ʃᵊn, -əˈ- (US) ˌkɑː.nɝːˈ-, -nɚˈ- -s -z
convalesc|e ˌkɒn.vəˈles (US) ˌkɑːn- -es -ɪz -ing -ɪŋ -ed -t
convalescence ˌkɒn.vəˈles.ᵊn*t*s (US) ˌkɑːn-
convalescent ˌkɒn.vəˈles.ᵊnt (US) ˌkɑːn- -s -s
convection kənˈvek.ʃᵊn
convector kənˈvek.təʳ (US) -tɚ -s -z
convenanc|e ˈkɔ̃ːn.və.nɑ̃ːns, ˈkɒn-, -nɑːn*t*s (US) ˈkɑːn.və.nən*t*s, -næn*t*s -es -ɪz
conven|e kənˈviːn -es -z -ing -ɪŋ -ed -d -er/s -əʳ/z (US) -ɚ/z -or/s -əʳ/z (US) -ɚ/z
convenienc|e kənˈviː.ni.ən*t*s (US) -ˈviːn.jən*t*s -es -ɪz **conˈvenience ˌfood; conˈvenience ˌstore**
convenient kənˈviː.ni.ənt (US) -ˈviːn.jənt -ly -li
convent ˈkɒn.vənt, -vent (US) ˈkɑːn- -s -s
conventicle kənˈven.tɪ.kᵊl (US) -t̬ə- -s -z
convention kənˈven.*t*ʃᵊn (US) -ˈven*t*.ʃᵊn -s -z
conventional kənˈven.*t*ʃᵊn.ᵊl (US) -ˈven*t*.ʃᵊn- -ly -i
conventional|ism kənˈven.*t*ʃᵊn.ᵊl|.ɪ.zᵊm (US) -ˈven*t*.ʃᵊn- -ist/s -ɪst/s
conventionalit|y kənˌven.*t*ʃəˈnæl.ə.t|i, -ɪ.t|i (US) -ˌven*t*.ʃəˈnæl.ə.t̬|i -ies -iz
conventionaliz|e, -is|e kənˈven.*t*ʃᵊn.ᵊl.aɪz (US) -ˈven*t*.ʃᵊn.ə.laɪz -es -ɪz -ing -ɪŋ -ed -d
conventual kənˈven.tju.əl, -tʃu-, -tʃᵊl (US) -tʃu.əl -s -z

converg|e kən'vɜːdʒ, kɒn- US kən'vɝːdʒ **-es** -ɪz **-ing** -ɪŋ **-ed** -d
convergen|ce kən'vɜː.dʒ^{ə}n*t*|s, kɒn- US kən'vɝː- **-ces** -sɪz **-cy** -si
convergent kən'vɜː.dʒ^{ə}nt, kɒn- US kən'vɝː- **-ly** -li
conversable kən'vɜː.sə.bl̩ US -'vɝː-
conversan|ce kən'vɜː.s^{ə}n*t*|s; 'kɒn.və- US kən'vɝː-; 'kɑːn.vɚ- **-cy** -si
conversant kən'vɜː.s^{ə}nt; 'kɒn.və- US kən'vɝː-; 'kɑːn.vɚ- **-ly** -li
conversation ˌkɒn.və'seɪ.ʃ^{ə}n US ˌkɑːn.vɚ'- **-s** -z **conver'sation ˌpiece**
conversational ˌkɒn.və'seɪ.ʃ^{ə}n.^{ə}l, -'seɪʃ.n^{ə}l US ˌkɑːn.vɚ'- **-ly** -i
conversationalist ˌkɒn.və'seɪ.ʃ^{ə}n.^{ə}l.ɪst, -'seɪʃ.n^{ə}l- US ˌkɑːn.vɚ'- **-s** -s
conversazione ˌkɒn.və.sæt.si'əʊ.neɪ, -ni US ˌkɑːn.vɚ.sɑːt.si'oʊ.ni, ˌkoʊn- **-s** -z
convers|e (*n. adj.*) 'kɒn.vɜːs; kən'vɜːs US 'kɑːn.vɝːs; kən'vɝːs **-es** -ɪz **-ely** -li
convers|e (*v.*) kən'vɜːs US -'vɝːs **-es** -ɪz **-ing** -ɪŋ **-ed** -t
conversion kən'vɜː.ʃ^{ə}n, -ʒ^{ə}n US -'vɝː.ʒ^{ə}n, -ʃ^{ə}n **-s** -z **con'version ˌcourse**
convert (*n.*) 'kɒn.vɜːt US 'kɑːn.vɝːt **-s** -s
con|vert (*v.*) kən|'vɜːt US -'vɝːt **-verts** -'vɜːts US -'vɝːts **-verting** -'vɜː.tɪŋ US -'vɝː.t̬ɪŋ **-verted** -'vɜː.tɪd US -'vɝː.t̬ɪd **-verter/s** -'vɜː.tə^{r}/z US -'vɝː.t̬ɚ/z **-vertor/s** -'vɜː.tə^{r}/z US -'vɝː.t̬ɚ/z
convertibility kənˌvɜː.tə'bɪl.ə.ti, -tɪ'-, -ɪ.ti US -ˌvɝː.t̬ə'bɪl.ə.t̬i
convertib|le kən'vɜː.tə.bl̩, -tɪ- US -'vɝː.t̬ə- **-les** -l̩z **-ly** -li
convex kɒn'veks, '-- US 'kɑːn.veks; kən'veks **-ly** -li
convexit|y kɒn'vek.sə.t|i, kən-, -ɪt|.i US kən'vek.sə.t̬|i **-ies** -iz
convey kən'veɪ **-s** -z **-ing** -ɪŋ **-ed** -d **-er/s** -ə^{r}/z US -ɚ/z **-or/s** -ə^{r}/z US -ɚ/z **-able** -ə.bl̩ **con'veyor ˌbelt**
conveyanc|e kən'veɪ.ən*t*s **-es** -ɪz
conveyanc|er kən'veɪ.ən*t*.s|ə^{r} US -s|ɚ **-ers** -əz US -ɚz **-ing** -ɪŋ
convict (*n.*) 'kɒn.vɪkt US 'kɑːn- **-s** -s
convict (*v.*) kən'vɪkt **-s** -s **-ing** -ɪŋ **-ed** -ɪd
conviction kən'vɪk.ʃ^{ə}n **-s** -z
convinc|e kən'vɪn*t*s **-es** -ɪz **-ing** -ɪŋ **-ed** -t
convincible kən'vɪn*t*.sə.bl̩
convincing kən'vɪn*t*.sɪŋ **-ly** -li
convivial kən'vɪv.i.əl **-ly** -i
conviviality kənˌvɪv.i'æl.ə.ti, -ɪ.ti US -ə.t̬i
convocation ˌkɒn.vəʊ'keɪ.ʃ^{ə}n US ˌkɑːn.və'- **-s** -z
convok|e kən'vəʊk US -'voʊk **-es** -s **-ing** -ɪŋ **-ed** -t
convolu|te 'kɒn.və.luː|t, -ljuː|t, ˌ--'- US 'kɑːn.və.luː|t **-ted/ly** -tɪd/li US -t̬ɪd/li
convolution ˌkɒn.və'luː.ʃ^{ə}n, -'ljuː- US ˌkɑːn.və'luː- **-s** -z
convolv|e kən'vɒlv US -'vɑːlv, -'vɔːlv **-es** -z **-ing** -ɪŋ **-ed** -d
convolvul|us kən'vɒl.vjʊ.l|əs, -vjə- US -'vɑːl.vjuː-, -vjə- **-i** -aɪ **-uses** -ə.sɪz
convoy 'kɒn.vɔɪ US 'kɑːn- **-s** -z **-ing** -ɪŋ **-ed** -d
convulsant kən'vʌl.s^{ə}nt **-s** -s
convuls|e kən'vʌls **-es** -ɪz **-ing** -ɪŋ **-ed** -t
convulsion kən'vʌl.ʃ^{ə}n **-s** -z
convulsive kən'vʌl.sɪv **-ly** -li **-ness** -nəs, -nɪs
Conway 'kɒn.weɪ US 'kɑːn-
Conwy 'kɒn.wi US 'kɑːn-
con|y 'kəʊ.n|i US 'koʊ- **-ies** -iz
Conybeare 'kɒn.ɪ.bɪə^{r}, 'kʌn- US 'kɑː.nɪ.bɪr, 'kʌn.ɪ-
coo kuː **-(e)s** -z **-ing** -ɪŋ **-ed** -d
Coober Pedy ˌkuː.bə'piː.di US -bɚ'-
Cooch kuːtʃ
cooee 'kuː.i, -iː, ˌ-'- **-s** -z **-ing** -ɪŋ **-d** -d
cook kʊk **-s** -s **-ing** -ɪŋ **-ed** -t
cookbook 'kʊk.bʊk **-s** -s
cook-chill ˌkʊk'tʃɪl **-s** -z **-ing** -ɪŋ **-ed** -d
Cook(e) kʊk
cooker 'kʊk.ə^{r} US -ɚ **-s** -z
cookery 'kʊk.^{ə}r.i **'cookery ˌbook**
Cookham 'kʊk.əm US -əm, -hæm
cookhou|se 'kʊk.haʊ|s **-ses** -zɪz
cookie 'kʊk.i **-s** -z
cookout 'kʊk.aʊt **-s** -s
Cookson 'kʊk.s^{ə}n
Cookstown 'kʊks.taʊn
cookware 'kʊk.weə^{r} US -wer
cook|y 'kʊk|.i **-ies** -iz
cool kuːl **-er** -ə^{r} US -ɚ **-est** -ɪst, -əst **-ly** -li, -i **-ness** -nəs, -nɪs **-s** -z **-ing** -ɪŋ **-ed** -d
coolant 'kuː.lənt **-s** -s
coolbox 'kuːl.bɒks US -bɑːks **-es** -ɪz
cooler 'kuː.lə^{r} US -lɚ **-s** -z
coolheaded ˌkuːl'hed.ɪd **-ness** -nəs, -nɪs *stress shift:* ˌcoolheaded 'thinking
coolibah 'kuː.lɪ.bɑː, -lə- **-s** -z
Coolidge 'kuː.lɪdʒ
coolie 'kuː.li **-s** -z
Cooling 'kuː.lɪŋ
cooling-off period ˌkuː.lɪŋ'ɒfˌpɪə.ri.əd US -'ɑːfˌpɪr.i- **-s** -z
coom kuːm **-s** -z
coomb kuːm **-s** -z
Coomb(e) kuːm
Coomber 'kuːm.bə^{r} US -bɚ
Coombes kuːmz
coon kuːn **-s** -z
coop kuːp **-s** -s **-ing** -ɪŋ **-ed** -t
co-op 'kəʊ.ɒp, -'- US 'koʊ.ɑːp **-s** -s
coop|er (C) 'kuː.p|ə^{r} US -p|ɚ **-ers** -əz US -ɚz **-ering** -^{ə}r.ɪŋ **-ered** -əd US -ɚd
cooperag|e 'kuː.p^{ə}r.ɪdʒ **-es** -ɪz
cooper|ate kəʊ'ɒp.^{ə}r|.eɪt US koʊ'ɑː.pə.r|eɪt **-ates** -eɪts **-ating** -eɪ.tɪŋ US -eɪ.t̬ɪŋ **-ated** -eɪ.tɪd US -eɪ.t̬ɪd **-ator/s** -eɪ.tə^{r}/z US -eɪ.t̬ɚ/z
cooperation kəʊˌɒp.ə'reɪ.ʃ^{ə}n, ˌkəʊ.ɒp- US koʊˌɑː.pə'- **-s** -z
cooperative kəʊ'ɒp.^{ə}r.ə.tɪv US koʊ'ɑː.pɚ.ə.t̬ɪv **-s** -z **-ly** -li
Cooperstown 'kuː.pəz.taʊn US -pɚz-
coopery 'kuː.p^{ə}r.i
Coopman 'kuːp.mən
co-opt kəʊ'ɒpt US koʊ'ɑːpt, '-- **-s** -s **-ing** -ɪŋ **-ed** -ɪd
co-optation ˌkəʊ.ɒp'teɪ.ʃ^{ə}n US ˌkoʊ.ɑːp'-
co-option kəʊ'ɒp.ʃ^{ə}n US koʊ'ɑːp- **-s** -z
coordinate (*n. adj.*) kəʊ'ɔː.dɪ.nət, -d^{ə}n.ət US koʊ'ɔːr.d^{ə}n-, -eɪt **-s** -s **-ly** -li **-ness** -nəs, -nɪs
coordin|ate (*v.*) kəʊ'ɔː.dɪ.n|eɪt, -d^{ə}n|.eɪt US koʊ'ɔːr.d^{ə}n- **-ates** -eɪts **-ating** -eɪ.tɪŋ US -eɪ.t̬ɪŋ **-ated** -eɪ.tɪd US -eɪ.t̬ɪd **-ator/s** -eɪ.tə^{r}/z US -eɪ.t̬ɚ/z
coordination kəʊˌɔː.dɪ'neɪ.ʃ^{ə}n, -d^{ə}n'eɪ- US koʊˌɔːr.d^{ə}n'eɪ-
coordinative kəʊ'ɔː.dɪ.nə.tɪv, -d^{ə}n.ə-, -eɪ- US koʊ'ɔːr.d^{ə}n.ə.t̬ɪv
Coors® kɔːz, kʊəz US kʊrz
coot kuːt **-s** -s
Coote kuːt
co-ownership ˌkəʊ'əʊ.nə.ʃɪp US ˌkoʊ'oʊ.nɚ-
cop kɒp US kɑːp **-s** -s **-ping** -ɪŋ **-ped** -t
Copacabana ˌkəʊ.pə.kə'bæn.ə US ˌkoʊ-, -'bɑː.nə
copaiba kəʊ'paɪ.bə, kɒp'aɪ- US koʊ'paɪ-
copal 'kəʊ.p^{ə}l; kəʊ'pæl US 'koʊ.p^{ə}l, -pæl
coparcener ˌkəʊ'pɑː.s^{ə}n.ə^{r}, -sɪ.nə^{r} US ˌkoʊ'pɑːr.s^{ə}n.ɚ **-s** -z
copartner ˌkəʊ'pɑːt.nə^{r} US 'koʊˌpɑːrt.nɚ, ˌ-'-- **-s** -z **-ship/s** -ʃɪp/s
cop|e (C) kəʊp US koʊp **-es** -s **-ing** -ɪŋ **-ed** -t
copeck 'kəʊ.pek, 'kɒp.ek US 'koʊ.pe **-s** -s
Copeland 'kəʊp.lənd US 'koʊp-
Copenhagen ˌkəʊ.p^{ə}n'heɪ.g^{ə}n, -'hɑː- 'kəʊ.p^{ə}nˌheɪ-, -ˌhɑː-

(US) 'koʊ.pᵊn,heɪ.gᵊn, -,hɑː-, ,koʊpᵊn'heɪ-, -'hɑː-

coper 'kəʊ.pəʳ (US) 'koʊ.pɚ **-s** -z

Copernican kəʊ'pɜː.nɪ.kᵊn (US) koʊ'pɝː-, kə-

Copernicus kəʊ'pɜː.nɪ.kəs (US) koʊ'pɝː-, kə-

copestone 'kəʊp.stəʊn (US) 'koʊp.stoʊn **-s** -z

Cophetua kəʊ'fet.ju.ə (US) koʊ-

copier 'kɒp.i.əʳ (US) 'kɑː.pi.ɚ **-s** -z

co-pilot 'kəʊ,paɪ.lət, ,-'-- (US) 'koʊ,paɪ- **-s** -s

coping 'kəʊ.pɪŋ (US) 'koʊ- **-s** -z

copingstone 'kəʊ.pɪŋ.stəʊn (US) 'koʊ.pɪŋ.stoʊn **-s** -z

copious 'kəʊ.pi.əs (US) 'koʊ- **-ly** -li **-ness** -nəs, -nɪs

Copland 'kɒp.lənd, 'kəʊp- (US) 'kɑːp-, 'koʊp-

Note: The name of the composer Aaron Copland is pronounced /'kəʊp.lənd (US) 'koʊp-/.

Copleston 'kɒp.l̩.stən (US) 'kɑː.pl̩-

Copley 'kɒp.li (US) 'kɑː.pli

cop-out 'kɒp.aʊt (US) 'kɑːp- **-s** -s

Copp kɒp (US) kɑːp

copp|er 'kɒp|.əʳ (US) 'kɑː.p|ɚ **-ers** -əz (US) -ɚz **-ering** -ᵊr.ɪŋ **-ered** -əd (US) -ɚd **,copper 'beech; ,copper 'sulphate**

copperas 'kɒp.ᵊr.əs (US) 'kɑː.pɚ-

copper-bottomed ,kɒp.ə'bɒt.əmd (US) ,kɑː.pɚ'bɑː.t̬əmd *stress shift:* ,copper-bottomed 'prospect

Copperfield 'kɒp.ə.fiːld (US) 'kɑː.pɚ-

copperhead 'kɒp.ə.hed (US) 'kɑː.pɚ- **-s** -z

copperplate 'kɒp.ə.pleɪt, ,--'- (US) 'kɑː.pɚ-

coppersmith **(C)** 'kɒp.ə.smɪθ (US) 'kɑː.pɚ- **-s** -s

coppery 'kɒp.ᵊr.i (US) 'kɑː.pɚ-

coppic|e 'kɒp.ɪs (US) 'kɑː.pɪs **-es** -ɪz **-ing** -ɪŋ **-ed** -t

copping 'kɒp.ɪŋ (US) 'kɑː.pɪŋ

Coppola 'kɒp.ᵊl.ə, 'kɑː.pᵊl.ə (US) 'kɑː.pᵊl.ə, 'koʊ.pᵊl.ə

Coppull 'kɒp.ᵊl (US) 'kɑː.pᵊl

copra 'kɒp.rə (US) 'kɑː.prə

copro- 'kɒp.rəʊ- (US) 'kɑː.proʊ-, -prə-

coproduc|e ,kəʊ.prə'djuːs, -'dʒuːs (US) ,koʊ.prə'duːs, -'djuːs **-es** -ɪz **-ing** -ɪŋ **-ed** -t **-er/s** -əʳ/z (US) -ɚ/z

coproduction ,kəʊ.prə'dʌk.ʃᵊn (US) ,koʊ- **-s** -z

cops|e kɒps (US) kɑːps **-es** -ɪz

Copt kɒpt (US) kɑːpt **-s** -s

copter 'kɒp.təʳ (US) 'kɑːp- **-s** -z

Copthall 'kɒp.tɔːl, 'kɒpt.hɔːl (US) 'kɑːp.tɔːl, -tɑːl, 'kɑːpt.hɔːl, -hɑːl

Coptic 'kɒp.tɪk (US) 'kɑːp-

copul|a 'kɒp.jə.l|ə, -jʊ- (US) 'kɑː.pjə- **-ae** -iː **-as** -əz

copu|late 'kɒp.jə|.leɪt, -jʊ- (US) 'kɑː.pjə- **-lates** -leɪts **-lating** -leɪ.tɪŋ (US) -leɪ.t̬ɪŋ **-lated** -leɪ.tɪd (US) -leɪ.t̬ɪd

copulation ,kɒp.jə'leɪ.ʃᵊn, -jʊ'- (US) ,kɑː.pjə'- **-s** -z

copula|tive 'kɒp.jə.lə|.tɪv, -jʊ-, -leɪ- (US) 'kɑː.pjə.lə|.t̬ɪv **-tory** -tᵊr.i, -tri (US) -tɔːr.i

cop|y 'kɒp|.i (US) 'kɑː.p|i **-ies** -iz **-ying** -i.ɪŋ **-ied** -id

copybook 'kɒp.i.bʊk (US) 'kɑː.pi- **-s** -s **,blot one's 'copybook**

copycat 'kɒp.i.kæt (US) 'kɑː.pi- **-s** -s

Copydex® 'kɒp.i.deks (US) 'kɑː.pi-

copy-ed|it 'kɒp.i,ed|.ɪt (US) 'kɑː.pi- **-its** -ɪts **-iting** -ɪ.tɪŋ (US) -ɪ.t̬ɪŋ **-ited** -ɪ.tɪd (US) -ɪ.t̬ɪd **-itor/s** -ɪ.təʳ/z (US) -ɪ.t̬ɚ/z

copyhold 'kɒp.i.həʊld (US) 'kɑː.pi.hoʊld **-s** -z **-er/s** -əʳ/z (US) -ɚ/z

copyist 'kɒp.i.ɪst (US) 'kɑː.pi- **-s** -s

copy|right 'kɒp.i|.raɪt (US) 'kɑː.pi- **-rights** -raɪts **-righting** -,raɪ.tɪŋ (US) -,raɪ.t̬ɪŋ **-righted** -,raɪ.tɪd (US) -,raɪ.t̬ɪd

copywrit|er 'kɒp.i,raɪ.t|əʳ (US) 'kɑː.pi,raɪ.t̬|ɚ **-ers** -əz (US) -ɚz **-ing** -ɪŋ

coq au vin ,kɒk.əʊ'væn, -'væ̃ŋ (US) ,koʊk.oʊ'-, ,kɑːk-

Coquelles kɒk'el, kəʊ'kel (US) koʊ'kel

coqu|et kɒk|'et, kəʊ'k|et (US) koʊ'k|et **-ets** -ets **-etting** -et.ɪŋ (US) -et̬.ɪŋ **-etted** -et.ɪd (US) -et̬.ɪd

Coquet 'kəʊ.kɪt (US) 'koʊ-

coquetr|y 'kɒk.ɪ.tr|i, 'kəʊ.kɪ-, -kə- (US) 'koʊ.kə.tr|i, koʊ'ket.r|i **-ies** -iz

coquette kɒk'et, kəʊ'ket (US) koʊ'ket **-s** -s

coquettish kɒk'et.ɪʃ, kəʊ'ket- (US) koʊ'ket̬- **-ly** -li **-ness** -nəs, -nɪs

cor kɔːʳ (US) kɔːr **-s** -z

Cora 'kɔː.rə (US) 'kɔːr.ə

coracle 'kɒr.ə.kl̩ (US) 'kɔːr- **-s** -z

coral 'kɒr.əl (US) 'kɔːr- **-s** -z **,coral 'reef**

corallaceous ,kɒr.ə'leɪ.ʃəs (US) ,kɔːr-

corall|ine 'kɒr.ᵊl|.aɪn (US) 'kɔːr.ə.l|aɪn **-ite** -aɪt

Coram 'kɔː.rəm (US) 'kɔːr.əm

coram nobis ,kɔː.rəm'nəʊ.bɪs, -ræm- (US) ,kɔːr.æm'noʊ.bɪs

cor(s) anglais ,kɔː'rɒŋ.gleɪ, -'rɑːŋ- (US) ,kɔːr.ɑːŋ'gleɪ

corban 'kɔː.bæn, -bᵊn (US) 'kɔːr-

corbel 'kɔː.bᵊl (US) 'kɔːr- **-s** -z

Corbett 'kɔː.bɪt, -bet, -bət (US) 'kɔːr-

Corbishley 'kɔː.bɪʃ.li (US) 'kɔːr-

Corbridge 'kɔː.brɪdʒ (US) 'kɔːr-

Corbusier kɔː'bjuː.zi.eɪ, -'buː- (US) ,kɔːr.buː'zjeɪ

Corby 'kɔː.bi (US) 'kɔːr-

Corbyn 'kɔː.bɪn (US) 'kɔːr-

Corcoran 'kɔː.kᵊr.ᵊn (US) 'kɔːr-

Corcyra ,kɔː'saɪə.rə (US) ,kɔːr'saɪ-

cord kɔːd (US) kɔːrd **-s** -z **-ing** -ɪŋ **-ed** -ɪd **-age** -ɪdʒ

Cordelia kɔː'diː.li.ə (US) kɔːr'diːl.jə

cordelier **(C)** ,kɔː.dɪ'lɪəʳ (US) ,kɔːr.dɪ'lɪr **-s** -z

Cordero kɔː'deə.rəʊ (US) kɔːr'der.oʊ

cordial 'kɔː.di.əl (US) 'kɔːr.dʒəl, -djəl **-s** -z **-ly** -i

cordialit|y ,kɔː.di'æl.ə.t|i, -ɪ.t|i (US) ,kɔːr.dʒi'æl.ə.t̬|i, -'djæl.ə- **-ies** -iz

cordillera **(C)** ,kɔː.dɪ'ljeə.rə, -dᵊl'jeə-, -'eə- (US) ,kɔːr.dᵊl'jer.ə; kɔːr'dɪl.ɚ-

cordite 'kɔː.daɪt (US) 'kɔːr-

cordless 'kɔːd.ləs, -lɪs (US) 'kɔːrd-

Cordoba, **Córdoba** 'kɔː.də.bə (US) 'kɔːr-

cordon 'kɔː.dᵊn (US) 'kɔːr- **-s** -z **-ing** -ɪŋ **-ed** -d

cordon bleu ,kɔː.dɔ̃ːm'blɜː, -dɒn'- (US) ,kɔːr.dɔ̃ː'bluː

cordon(s) sanitaire(s) ,kɔː.dɔ̃ːn.sæn.ɪ'teəʳ, -dɒn-, -ə'- (US) kɔːr,dɔ̃ː.sɑː.ni'ter

Cordov|a 'kɔː.də.v|ə (US) 'kɔːr- **-an/s** -ən/z

corduroy 'kɔː.djə.rɔɪ, -djʊ-, -dʒə-, -dʒʊ-, ,--'- (US) 'kɔːr.də- **-s** -z

cordwainer 'kɔːd,weɪ.nəʳ (US) 'kɔːrd,weɪ.nɚ **-s** -z

cor|e kɔːʳ (US) kɔːr **-es** -z **-ing** -ɪŋ **-ed** -d **-er/s** -əʳ/z (US) -ɚ/z

CORE kɔːʳ (US) kɔːr

co-referential ,kəʊ.ref.ə'ren.tʃᵊl (US) ,koʊ.ref.ə'rent.ʃᵊl

co-regent ,kəʊ'riː.dʒᵊnt (US) ,koʊ- **-s** -s

coreligionist ,kəʊ.rɪ'lɪdʒ.ᵊn.ɪst, -rə'- (US) ,koʊ.rə'-, -rɪ'- **-s** -s

Corelli kə'rel.i, kɒr'el- (US) koʊ'rel-, kə'-

co-representational ,kəʊ.rep.rɪ.zen'teɪ.ʃᵊn.ᵊl, -rə-, -'teɪʃ.nᵊl (US) koʊ-

co-respondent ,kəʊ.rɪ'spɒn.dənt, -rə'- (US) ,koʊ.rɪ'spɑːn-, -rə'- **-s** -s

Corey 'kɔː.ri (US) 'kɔːr.i

corf kɔːf (US) kɔːrf **-s** -s

Corfe kɔːf (US) kɔːrf

Corfu kɔː'fuː, -'fjuː (US) 'kɔːr.fuː, -fjuː, -'-

corgi **(C)** 'kɔː.gi (US) 'kɔːr- **-s** -z

coriander ,kɒr.i'æn.dəʳ, 'kɒr.i.æn- (US) 'kɔːr.i.æn.dɚ, ,kɔːr.i'æn-

Corin 'kɒr.ɪn, -ᵊn (US) 'kɔːr-

Corinne kə'rɪn

Corinth 'kɒr.ɪntθ (US) 'kɔːr-

Corinthian kə'rɪnt.θi.ən **-s** -z

Coriolanus ,kɒr.i.əʊ'leɪ.nəs, -'lɑː- (US) ,kɔːr.i.ə'-

Corioles kəˈraɪə.liːz, kɒrˈaɪə- (US) kəˈraɪə-
Coriolis kəˈraɪə.lɪs, kɒrˈaɪə- (US) kəˈraɪə-
cork (C) kɔːk (US) kɔːrk **-s** -s **-ing** -ɪŋ **-ed** -t
corkage ˈkɔː.kɪdʒ (US) ˈkɔːr-
corker (C) ˈkɔː.kəʳ (US) ˈkɔːr.kɚ **-s** -z
Corkery ˈkɔː.kᵊr.i (US) ˈkɔːr-
corkscrew ˈkɔːk.skruː (US) ˈkɔːrk- **-s** -z **-ing** -ɪŋ **-ed** -d
corky ˈkɔː.ki (US) ˈkɔːr-
Corleone ˌkɔː.liˈəʊ.ni (US) ˌkɔːr.liˈoʊ-
corm kɔːm (US) kɔːrm **-s** -z
Cormac ˈkɜː.mæk, ˈkɔː- (US) ˈkɔːr-
Cormack ˈkɔː.mæk (US) ˈkɔːr-
cormorant ˈkɔː.mᵊr.ənt (US) ˈkɔːr- **-s** -s
corn kɔːn (US) kɔːrn **-s** -z **-ing** -ɪŋ **-ed** -d **ˈCorn ˌBelt; ˈcorn ˌdolly; ˌcorned ˈbeef; ˈcorn ˌexchange**
cornball ˈkɔːn.bɔːl, ˈkɔːm- (US) ˈkɔːrn-, -bɑːl **-s** -z
cornbread ˈkɔːn.bred, ˈkɔːm- (US) ˈkɔːrn-
Cornbury ˈkɔːn.bᵊr.i, ˈkɔːm- (US) ˈkɔːrn.ber-, -bɚ-
corncob ˈkɔːn.kɒb (US) ˈkɔːrn.kɑːb **-s** -z
corncrake ˈkɔːn.kreɪk, ˈkɔːŋ- (US) ˈkɔːrn- **-s** -s
corndog ˈkɔːn.dɒg (US) ˈkɔːrn.dɑːg, -dɔːg **-s** -z
corne|a ˈkɔː.ni|.ə; kɔːˈniː- (US) ˈkɔːr.ni- **-as** -əz **-al** -ᵊl
Corneille kɔːˈneɪ, -ˈneɪl (US) kɔːrˈneɪ
Cornelia kɔːˈniː.li.ə (US) kɔːrˈniːl.jə
cornelian kɔːˈniː.li.ən (US) kɔːrˈniːl.jən **-s** -z
Cornelius kɔːˈniː.li.əs (US) kɔːrˈniːl.jəs
Cornell kɔːˈnel (US) kɔːr-
corn|er ˈkɔː.n|əʳ (US) ˈkɔːr.n|ɚ **-ers** -əz (US) -ɚz **-ering** -ᵊr.ɪŋ **-ered** -əd (US) -ɚd **ˌcorner ˈshop**
cornerback ˈkɔː.nə.bæk (US) ˈkɔːr.nɚ- **-s** -s
-cornered -ˈkɔː.nəd (US) -ˈkɔr.nɚd
cornerstone ˈkɔː.nə.stəʊn (US) ˈkɔːr.nɚ.stoʊn **-s** -z
cornet ˈkɔː.nɪt (US) kɔːrˈnet **-s** -s
Cornetto® kɔːˈnet.əʊ (US) kɔːrˈneţ.oʊ
cornfield ˈkɔːn.fiːld (US) ˈkɔːrn- **-s** -z
cornflakes ˈkɔːn.fleɪks (US) ˈkɔːrn-
cornflour ˈkɔːn.flaʊəʳ (US) ˈkɔːrn.flaʊɚ
cornflower ˈkɔːn.flaʊəʳ (US) ˈkɔːrn.flaʊɚ **-s** -z
Cornhill ˌkɔːnˈhɪl (US) ˈkɔːrn.hɪl, ˌ-ˈ-
cornic|e ˈkɔː.nɪs (US) ˈkɔːr- **-es** -ɪz
corrnich|e (C) kɔːˈniːʃ; ˈ--, -nɪʃ (US) kɔːrˈniːʃ **-es** -ɪz
Cornish ˈkɔː.nɪʃ (US) ˈkɔːr- **-man** -mən **-men** -mən, -men **-woman** -ˌwʊm.ən **-women** -ˌwɪm.ɪn **ˌCornish ˈpasty**
cornmeal ˈkɔːn.miːl, ˈkɔːm- (US) ˈkɔːrn-
cornrow ˈkɔːn.rəʊ (US) ˈkɔːrn.roʊ **-s** -z **-ing** -ɪŋ **-ed** -d
cornstarch ˈkɔːn.stɑːtʃ (US) ˈkɔːrn.stɑːrtʃ
cornsyrup ˈkɔːnˌsɪr.əp (US) ˈkɔːrnˌsɪr-, -ˌsɝː-
cornucopi|a ˌkɔː.njuˈkəʊ.pi|.ə (US) ˌkɔːr.nəˈkoʊ-, -njəˈ- **-as** -əz **-an** -ən
Cornwall ˈkɔːn.wɔːl, -wəl (US) ˈkɔːrn.wɔːl, -wɑːl
Cornwallis kɔːnˈwɒl.ɪs (US) kɔːrnˈwɑː.lɪs
Cornwell ˈkɔːn.wel, -wəl (US) ˈkɔːrn-
corn|y ˈkɔː.n|i (US) ˈkɔːr- **-ier** -i.əʳ (US) -i.ɚ **-iest** -i.ɪst, -i.əst
corolla (C) kəˈrɒl.ə, -ˈrəʊ.lə (US) -ˈroʊ-, -ˈrɑː- **-s** -z
Note: The suitable pronunciation for the car in Amercian English is /kəˈroʊ-/.
corollar|y kəˈrɒl.ᵊr|.i (US) ˈkɔːr.ə.ler- **-ies** -iz
Coromandel ˌkɒr.əʊˈmæn.dᵊl (US) ˌkɔːr.oʊˈ-
coron|a kəˈrəʊ.n|ə (US) -ˈroʊ- **-ae** -iː **-as** -əz
Corona *female name:* ˈkɒr.ə.nə (US) ˈkɔːr-
coronach (C) ˈkɒr.ə.nək, -nəx, -næk (US) ˈkɔːr.ə.nək **-s** -s
coronal (*n.*) ˈkɒr.ə.nᵊl (US) ˈkɔːr- **-s** -z
coronal (*adj.*) *pertaining to the sun's corona:* kəˈrəʊ.nᵊl (US) -ˈroʊ- *medical, botanical and phonetic senses:* ˈkɒr.ə.nᵊl; kəˈrəʊ- (US) ˈkɔːr.ə-; kəˈroʊ-
coronar|y ˈkɒr.ə.nᵊr|.i (US) ˈkɔːr.ə.ner- **-ies** -iz
coronation ˌkɒr.əˈneɪ.ʃᵊn (US) ˌkɔːr- **-s** -z
Coronel ˈkɒr.ə.nel (US) ˈkɔːr-
coroner ˈkɒr.ə.nəʳ (US) ˈkɔːr.ᵊn.ɚ **-s** -z
coronet ˈkɒr.ə.nɪt, -net, -nət; ˌkɒr.əˈnet (US) ˌkɔːr.əˈnet **-s** -s
corpora (*plur. of* **corpus**) ˈkɔː.pᵊr.ə, -pə.rɑː (US) ˈkɔːr.pɚ.ə
corporal ˈkɔː.pᵊr.ᵊl, ˈ-prᵊl (US) ˈkɔːr- **-s** -z **-ly** -i **ˌcorporal ˈpunishment**
corporality ˌkɔː.pəˈræl.ə.ti, -ɪ.ti (US) ˌkɔːr.pəˈræl.ə.ţi
corporate ˈkɔː.pᵊr.ət, -ɪt, ˈ-prət, ˈ-prɪt (US) ˈkɔːr- **-ly** -li **-ness** -nəs, -nɪs
corporation ˌkɔː.pᵊrˈeɪ.ʃᵊn (US) ˌkɔːr.pəˈreɪ- **-s** -z
corporative ˈkɔː.pᵊr.ə.tɪv (US) ˈkɔːr.pɚ.ə.ţɪv
corporator ˈkɔː.pᵊr.eɪ.təʳ (US) ˈkɔːr.pə.reɪ.ţɚ **-s** -z
corporeal kɔːˈpɔː.ri.əl (US) kɔːrˈpɔːr- **-ly** -i
corps (*sing.*) kɔːʳ (US) kɔːr (*plur.*) kɔːz (US) kɔːrz
corps de ballet ˌkɔː.dəˈbæl.eɪ, -li (US) ˌkɔːr.də.bælˈeɪ
corps|e kɔːps (US) kɔːrps **-es** -ɪz **-ing** -ɪŋ **-ed** -t
corpulen|ce ˈkɔː.pjʊ.lənt|s, -pjə- (US) ˈkɔːr.pjə- **-cy** -si
corpulent ˈkɔː.pjʊ.lənt, -pjə- (US) ˈkɔːr.pjə-
corp|us ˈkɔː.p|əs (US) ˈkɔːr- **-ora** -ə.rə (US) -ɚ.ə **-uses** -ə.sɪz
Corpus Christi ˌkɔː.pəsˈkrɪs.ti (US) ˌkɔːr-
corpuscle ˈkɔː.pʌs.l̩, -pə.sl̩; kɔːˈpʌs- (US) ˈkɔːr.pʌs.l̩, -pə.sl̩ **-s** -z
corpuscular kɔːˈpʌs.kjə.ləʳ, -kjʊ- (US) kɔːrˈpʌs.kjə.lɚ
corpuscule kɔːˈpʌs.kjuːl, -kjʊl (US) kɔːrˈpʌs.kjuːl **-s** -z
corpus delicti ˌkɔː.pʌs.dɪˈlɪk.taɪ, -pəs- (US) ˌkɔːr-
corpus juris ˌkɔː.pʌsˈdʒʊə.rɪs, -pəs- (US) ˌkɔːr.pʌsˈdʒʊr.ɪs
Corr kɔːʳ (US) kɔːr **-s** -z
corral kəˈrɑːl, kɒrˈɑːl (US) kəˈræl **-s** -z **-ling** -ɪŋ **-led** -d
correct kəˈrekt **-ly** -li **-ness** -nəs, -nɪs **-s** -s **-ing** -ɪŋ **-ed** -ɪd **-or/s** -əʳ/z (US) -ɚ/z
correction kəˈrek.ʃᵊn **-s** -z
correctional kəˈrek.ʃᵊn.ᵊl
correctitude kəˈrek.tɪ.tjuːd, -tʃuːd (US) -tə.tuːd, -tjuːd
corrective kəˈrek.tɪv **-s** -z
Correggio kəˈredʒ.i.əʊ (US) ˈ-oʊ
correlate (*n.*) ˈkɒr.ᵊl.ət, -ɪ.lət, -leɪt (US) ˈkɔːr.ə.leɪt **-s** -s
corre|late (*v.*) ˈkɒr.ə|.leɪt, ˈ-ɪ- (US) ˈkɔːr.ə- **-lates** -leɪts **-lating** -leɪ.tɪŋ (US) -leɪ.ţɪŋ **-lated** -leɪ.tɪd (US) -leɪ.ţɪd **-latable** -leɪ.tə.bl̩ (US) -leɪ.ţə.bl̩
correlation ˌkɒr.əˈleɪ.ʃᵊn, -ɪˈ- (US) ˌkɔːr.əˈ- **-s** -z
correlative kɒrˈel.ə.tɪv, kəˈrel- (US) kəˈrel.ə.ţɪv **-ly** -li **-ness** -nəs, -nɪ
correspond ˌkɒr.ɪˈspɒnd, -əˈ- (US) ˌkɔːr.əˈ- **-s** -z **-ing** -ɪŋ **-ed** -ɪd
correspondenc|e ˌkɒr.ɪˈspɒn.dənts, -əˈ- (US) ˌkɔːr.əˈspɑːn- **-es** -ɪz **correˈspondence ˌcourse**
correspondent ˌkɒr.ɪˈspɒn.dᵊnt, -əˈ- (US) ˌkɔːr.əˈspɑːn- **-s** -s
corresponding ˌkɒr.ɪˈspɒn.dɪŋ, -əˈ- (US) ˌkɔːr.əˈspɑːn- **-ly** -li
corridor ˈkɒr.ɪ.dɔːʳ, ˈ-ə-, -dəʳ (US) ˈkɔːr.ə.dɚ, ˈ-ɪ-, -dɔːr **-s** -z
corrie (C) ˈkɒr.i (US) ˈkɔːr-
Corrientes ˌkɒr.iˈen.tes (US) ˌkɔːr-
Corrigan ˈkɒr.ɪ.gᵊn, ˈ-ə- (US) ˈkɔːr.ə-,
corrigend|um ˌkɒr.ɪˈdʒen.d|əm, -əˈ-, -ˈgen- (US) ˌkɔːr- **-a** -ə
corrigible ˈkɒr.ɪ.dʒə.bl̩, -dʒɪ- (US) ˈkɔː
Corringham ˈkɒr.ɪŋ.əm (US) ˈkɔːr-, -hæm
corroborant kəˈrɒb.ᵊr.ᵊnt (US) -ˈrɑː.b **-s** -s

corrobor|ate kəˈrɒb.ᵊr|.eɪt (US) -ˈrɑː.bə.r|eɪt **-ates** -eɪts **-ating** -eɪ.tɪŋ (US) -eɪ.t̬ɪŋ **-ated** -eɪ.tɪd (US) -eɪ.t̬ɪd **-ator/s** -eɪ.təʳ/z (US) -eɪ.t̬ɚ/z

corroboration kəˌrɒb.əˈreɪ.ʃᵊn (US) -ˌrɑː.bəˈ- **-s** -z

corroborative kəˈrɒb.ᵊr.ə.tɪv, -eɪ- (US) -ˈrɑː.bɚ.ə.t̬ɪv

corroboratory kəˈrɒb.ᵊr.ə.tᵊr.i, -tri; kəˌrɒb.əˈreɪ- (US) -ˈrɑː.bɚ.ə.tɔːr.i

corroboree kəˈrɒb.ᵊr.i, kəˌrɒb.əˈriː (US) -ˌrɑː.bəˈriː **-s** -z

corrod|e kəˈrəʊd (US) -ˈroʊd **-es** -z **-ing** -ɪŋ **-ed** -ɪd

corrodible kəˈrəʊ.də.bl̩, -dɪ- (US) -ˈroʊ.də-

corrosion kəˈrəʊ.ʒᵊn (US) -ˈroʊ- **-s** -z

corrosive kəˈrəʊ.sɪv, -zɪv (US) -ˈroʊ- **-s** -z **-ly** -li **-ness** -nəs, -nɪs

corru|gate ˈkɒr.ə|.geɪt, ˈ-ʊ- (US) ˈkɔːr.ə- **-gates** -geɪts **-gating** -geɪ.tɪŋ (US) -geɪ.t̬ɪŋ **-gated** -geɪ.tɪd (US) -geɪ.t̬ɪd ˌ**corrugated** ˈ**iron**

corrugation ˌkɒr.əˈgeɪ.ʃᵊn, -ʊˈ- (US) ˌkɔːr.əˈ- **-s** -z

corrupt kəˈrʌpt **-est** -ɪst, -əst **-ly** -li **-ness** -nəs, -nɪs **-s** -s **-ing** -ɪŋ **-ed** -ɪd **-er/s** -əʳ/z (US) -ɚ/z

corruptibility kəˌrʌp.təˈbɪl.ə.ti, -tɪˈ-, -ɪ.ti (US) -təˈbɪl.ə.t̬i

corruptib|le kəˈrʌp.tə.b|l̩, -tɪ- (US) -tə- **-ly** -li **-leness** -l̩.nəs, -nɪs

corruption kəˈrʌp.ʃᵊn **-s** -z

corruptive kəˈrʌp.tɪv

Corry ˈkɒr.i (US) ˈkɔːr-

Corsa® ˈkɔː.sə (US) ˈkɔːr-

corsag|e kɔːˈsɑːʒ, ˈ-- (US) kɔːrˈsɑːʒ, -sɑːdʒ **-es** -ɪz

corsair ˈkɔː.seəʳ, -ˈ- (US) ˈkɔːr.ser, -ˈ- **-s** -z

cors|e kɔːs (US) kɔːrs **-es** -ɪz

corselet ˈkɔː.slət, -slɪt (US) ˈkɔːr- **-s** -s

corset ˈkɔː.sɪt, -sət (US) ˈkɔːr- **-s** -s

corsetry ˈkɔː.sɪ.tri, -sə- (US) ˈkɔːr-

Corsham ˈkɔː.ʃəm (US) ˈkɔːr-

Corsic|a ˈkɔː.sɪ.k|ə (US) ˈkɔːr- **-an/s** -ən/z

corslet ˈkɔː.slət, -slɪt (US) ˈkɔːr- **-s** -s

cortèg|e kɔːˈteɪʒ, -ˈteʒ, ˈ-- (US) kɔːrˈteʒ **-es** -ɪz

Cortes, Cortés ˈkɔː.tes, -tez, -ˈ- (US) kɔːrˈtez

cort|ex ˈkɔː.t|eks (US) ˈkɔːr- **-exes** -ek.sɪz **-ices** -ɪ.siːz

Corti ˈkɔː.ti (US) ˈkɔːr.ti

cortical ˈkɔː.tɪ.kᵊl (US) ˈkɔːr.t̬ɪ-

corticosteroid ˌkɔː.tɪ.kəʊˈstɪə.rɔɪd, -ˈster.ɔɪd (US) ˌkɔːr.t̬ɪ.koʊˈster.ɔɪd, -ˈstɪr- **-s** -z

Cortina® kɔːˈtiː.nə (US) kɔːr- **-s** -z

cortisone ˈkɔː.tɪ.zəʊn, -tə-, -səʊn (US) ˈkɔːr.t̬ə.zoʊn, -soʊn

Cortney ˈkɔːt.ni (US) ˈkɔːrt-

corundum kəˈrʌn.dəm

Corunna kɒrˈʌn.ə, kəˈrʌn- (US) kəˈrʌn-

Corus® ˈkɔː.rəs (US) ˈkɔːr.əs

corus|cate ˈkɒr.ə.s|keɪt, -ʌs|.keɪt (US) ˈkɔːr.ə.s|keɪt **-cates** -keɪts **-cating** -keɪ.tɪŋ (US) -keɪ.t̬ɪŋ **-cated** -keɪ.tɪd (US) -keɪ.t̬ɪd

coruscation ˌkɒr.əˈskeɪ.ʃᵊn, -ʌsˈkeɪ- (US) ˌkɔːr.əˈskeɪ- **-s** -z

corvée ˈkɔː.veɪ (US) kɔːrˈveɪ **-s** -z

corvette kɔːˈvet (US) kɔːr- **-s** -s

Corwen ˈkɔː.wen, -wɪn (US) ˈkɔːr-

Cory ˈkɔː.ri (US) ˈkɔːr.i

Corybant ˈkɒr.ɪ.bænt (US) ˈkɔːr- **-s** -s **Corybantes** ˌkɒr.ɪˈbæn.tiːz (US) ˌkɔːr-

Corydon ˈkɒr.ɪ.dᵊn, ˈ-ə-, -dɒn (US) ˈkɔːr.ə.dᵊn, -dɑːn

corymb ˈkɒr.ɪmb, -ɪm (US) ˈkɔːr-

coryphae|us ˌkɒr.ɪˈfiː|.əs (US) ˌkɔːr.əˈ- **-i** -aɪ

coryphée ˌkɒr.ɪˈfeɪ (US) ˌkɔːr-

Coryton *in Devon:* ˈkɒr.ɪ.tᵊn, ˈ-ə- (US) ˈkɔːr- *in Essex:* ˈkɔː.rɪ.tən, ˈ-rə- (US) ˈkɔːr-

cos *because:* kəz, kəs, kɒz, kɒs (US) kəz, kəs, kɑːz, kɑːs

Note: Weak form word.

cos (C) *lettuce:* kɒs, kɒz (US) kɑːs, koʊs

Cosa Nostra ˌkəʊ.zəˈnɒs.trə (US) ˌkoʊ.səˈnoʊ.strə, -zəˈ-

Cosby ˈkɒz.bi (US) ˈkɑːz-

cosec ˈkəʊ.sek (US) ˈkoʊ-

cosecant ˌkəʊˈsiː.kᵊnt (US) ˌkoʊ- **-s** -s

co-set ˈkəʊ.set (US) ˈkoʊ- **-s** -s

Cosgrave ˈkɒz.greɪv (US) ˈkɑːz-

cosh kɒʃ (US) kɑːʃ **-es** -ɪz **-ing** -ɪŋ **-ed** -t

Cosham ˈkɒs.əm (US) ˈkɑː.səm

cosh|er *feast, pamper:* ˈkɒʃ|.əʳ (US) ˈkɑː.ʃ|ɚ **-ers** -əz (US) -ɚz **-ering** -ᵊr.ɪŋ **-ered** -əd (US) -ɚd

cosher *according to Jewish law:* ˈkəʊ.ʃəʳ, ˈkɒʃ.əʳ (US) ˈkoʊ.ʃɚ

Cosi Fan Tutte ˌkəʊ.si.fænˈtʊt.eɪ, -zi-, kəʊˌsiː-, -i (US) koʊˌsiː.fɑːnˈtuː.teɪ

cosignator|y ˌkəʊˈsɪg.nə.tᵊr|.i, -tr|i (US) ˌkoʊˈsɪg.nə.tɔːr|.i **-ies** -iz

Cosima ˈkəʊ.sɪ.mə (US) ˈkoʊ.zi-, -mɑː

cosine ˈkəʊ.saɪn (US) ˈkoʊ- **-s** -z

CoSIRA kəʊˈsaɪə.rə (US) koʊˈsaɪə-

cosmetic kɒzˈmet.ɪk (US) kɑːzˈmet̬- **-s** -s **-al** -ᵊl **-ally** -ᵊl.i, -li

cosmic ˈkɒz.mɪk (US) ˈkɑːz- **-al** -ᵊl **-ally** -ᵊl.i, -li

cosm|ism ˈkɒz.m|ɪ.zᵊm (US) ˈkɑːz- **-ist/s** -ɪst/s

cosmo- ˈkɒz.məʊ-, kɒzˈmɒ- (US) ˈkɑːz.moʊ-, -mə-, kɑːzˈmɑː-

Note: Prefix. This may be stressed on the initial syllable (as in **cosmonaut** /ˈkɒz.mə.nɔːt (US) ˈkɑːz.mə.nɑːt/) or on the second syllable (e.g. **cosmology** /kɒzˈmɒl.ə.dʒi (US) kɑːzˈmɑː.lə.dʒi/).

Cosmo ˈkɒz.məʊ (US) ˈkɑːz.moʊ

cosmogonic ˌkɒz.məʊˈgɒn.ɪk (US) ˌkɑːz.məˈgɑː.nɪk **-al** -ᵊl **-ally** -ᵊl.i, -li

cosmogon|y kɒzˈmɒg.ᵊn|.i (US) kɑːzˈmɑː.gᵊn- **-ist/s** -ɪst/s

cosmographic ˌkɒz.məʊˈgræf.ɪk (US) ˌkɑːz.məˈ- **-al** -ᵊl **-ally** -ᵊl.i, -li

cosmograph|y kɒzˈmɒg.rə.f|i (US) kɑːzˈmɑː.grə- **-er/s** -əʳ/z (US) -ɚ/z

cosmological ˌkɒz.məˈlɒdʒ.ɪ.kᵊl (US) ˌkɑːz.məˈlɑː.dʒɪ-

cosmolog|y kɒzˈmɒl.ə.dʒ|i (US) kɑːzˈmɑː.lə- **-ist/s** -ɪst/s

cosmonaut ˈkɒz.mə.nɔːt (US) ˈkɑːz.mə.nɑːt, -nɔːt **-s** -s

cosmopolitan (C®) ˌkɒz.məˈpɒl.ɪ.tᵊn, ˈ-ə- (US) ˌkɑːz.məˈpɑː.lɪ- **-s** -z

cosmopolitanism ˌkɒz.məˈpɒl.ɪ.tᵊn.ɪ.zᵊm, ˈ-ə-, -tɪ.nɪ- (US) ˌkɑːz.məˈpɑː.lɪ.tᵊn.ɪ-

cosmos (C®) ˈkɒz.mɒs (US) ˈkɑːz.moʊs, -məs, -mɑːs

Cossack ˈkɒs.æk (US) ˈkɑː.sæk **-s** -s

coss|et ˈkɒs|.ɪt (US) ˈkɑː.s|ɪt **-ets** -ɪts **-e(t)ting** -ɪ.tɪŋ (US) -ɪ.t̬ɪŋ **-e(t)ted** -ɪ.tɪd (US) -ɪ.t̬ɪd

cost kɒst (US) kɑːst **-s** -s **-ing** -ɪŋ **-ed** -ɪd ˌ**cost-efˈfective**; ˌ**cost of** ˈ**living**

Costa ˈkɒs.tə (US) ˈkɑː.stə

Costa Blanca ˌkɒs.təˈblæŋ.kə (US) ˌkɑː.stəˈblɑːŋ-, ˌkoʊ-

Costa Brava ˌkɒs.təˈbrɑː.və (US) ˌkɑː.stə-, ˌkoʊ-

Costa del Sol ˌkɒs.tə.delˈsɒl (US) ˌkɑː.stə.delˈsoʊl, ˌkoʊ-

Costain kɒsˈteɪn, ˈ-- (US) ˈkɑː.steɪn, -ˈ-

costal ˈkɒs.tᵊl (US) ˈkɑː.stᵊl

co-star (*n.*) ˈkəʊ.stɑːʳ (US) ˈkoʊ.stɑːr **-s** -z

co-star (*v.*) kəʊˈstɑːʳ (US) ˈkoʊ.stɑːr **-s** -z **-ring** -ɪŋ **-red** -d

costard ˈkʌs.təd, ˈkɒs- (US) ˈkɑː.stɚd **-s** -z

Costard ˈkɒs.təd, -tɑːd (US) ˈkɑː.stɚd, -stɑːrd

Costa Ric|a ˌkɒs.təˈriː.k|ə (US) ˌkoʊ.stəˈ-, ˌkɑː- **-an/s** -ən/z

cost-effective ˌkɒst.ɪˈfek.tɪv, -əˈ-, ˈkɒst.ɪ.fek-, ˈ-ə- (US) ˈkɑːst.ɪˌfek-, -əˌ-, ˌkɑːst.ɪˈfekt-, -əˈ- **-ly** -li **-ness** -nəs, -nɪs

Costello kɒsˈtel.əʊ, kəˈstel-, ˈkɒs.tᵊl.əʊ (US) kɑːˈstel.oʊ, kə-; ˈkɑː.stə.loʊ

coster ˈkɒs.təʳ (US) ˈkɑː.stɚ **-s** -z

costermonger ˈkɒs.təˌmʌŋ.gəʳ (US) ˈkɑː.stɚˌmʌŋ.gɚ, -ˌmɑːŋ- **-s** -z

costive ˈkɒs.tɪv (US) ˈkɑː.stɪv **-ly** -li **-ness** -nəs, -nɪs

costl|y 'kɒst.l|i US 'kɑːst- **-ier** -i.əʳ US -i.ɚ **-iest** -i.ɪst, -i.əst **-iness** -ɪ.nəs, -ɪ.nɪs

costmary 'kɒst.meə.ri US 'kɑːst.mer.i

Costner 'kɒs*t*.nəʳ US 'kɑːs*t*.nɚ

cost-plus ˌkɒs*t*'plʌs US ˌkɑːs*t*-

costum|e 'kɒs.tjuːm US 'kɑː.stuːm, -stjuːm **-es** -z **-ing** -ɪŋ **-ed** -d ˌ**costume 'jewellery**

costumier kɒs'tjuː.mi.əʳ, -eɪ US kɑː'stuː.mi.eɪ, -'stjuː-, -ɚ **-s** -z

Cosway 'kɒz.weɪ US 'kɑːz- **-s** -z

cos|y 'kəʊ.z|i US 'koʊ- **-ies** -iz **-ier** -i.əʳ US -i.ɚ **-iest** -i.ɪst, -i.əst **-ily** -ɪ.li, -ᵊl.i **-iness** -ɪ.nəs, -ɪ.nɪs

cot kɒt US kɑːt **-s** -s **'cot ˌdeath**

cotangent ˌkəʊ'tæn.dʒənt, '-ˌ-- US ˌkoʊ'tæn-, '-ˌ-- **-s** -s

cot|e kəʊt US koʊt **-es** -s **-ing** -ɪŋ US 'koʊ.t̬ɪŋ **-ed** -ɪd US 'koʊ.t̬ɪd

Côte d'Azur ˌkəʊt.dæ'zjʊəʳ, -də'- US ˌkoʊt.də'zʊr, -dɑː'-

Côte d'Ivoire ˌkəʊt.diː'vwɑːʳ US ˌkoʊt.diː'vwɑːr

Côte d'Or ˌkəʊt'dɔːʳ US ˌkoʊt'dɔːr

cotenancy ˌkəʊ'ten.ən*t*.si US ˌkoʊ-

coterie 'kəʊ.tᵊr.i US 'koʊ.t̬ɚ- **-s** -z

coterminous ˌkəʊ'tɜː.mɪ.nəs US ˌkoʊ'tɝː- **-ly** -li

Cotgrave 'kɒt.greɪv US 'kɑːt-

cotill(i)on kə'tɪl.i.ən, kəʊ-, kɒt'ɪl- US koʊ'tɪl.jən, kə- **-s** -z

Coton 'kəʊ.tᵊn US 'koʊ-

cotoneaster kəˌtəʊ.ni'æs.təʳ US -ˌtoʊ.ni'æs.tɚ **-s** -z

Cotonou ˌkəʊ.tə'nuː, ˌkɒt.ɒn'uː US ˌkoʊ.toʊ'nuː, -tᵊn'uː

Cotopaxi ˌkɒt.əʊ'pæk.si, ˌkəʊ.təʊ'- US ˌkoʊ.t̬ə'-

Cotswold 'kɒt.swəʊld, -swəld US 'kɑːt.swoʊld **-s** -z

Cotsworth 'kɒt.swəθ, -wɜːθ US 'kɑːt.swɝːθ, -swɚθ

cottag|e 'kɒt.ɪdʒ US 'kɑː.t̬ɪdʒ **-es** -ɪz **-ing** -ɪŋ **-ey** -i ˌ**cottage 'cheese**; ˌ**cottage 'industry**; ˌ**cottage 'pie**

cottager 'kɒt.ɪ.dʒəʳ US 'kɑː.t̬ɪ.dʒɚ **-s** -z

Cottam 'kɒt.əm US 'kɑː.t̬əm

Cottbus 'kɒt.bəs, -bʊs US 'kɑːt.bəs, -bʊs

Cottenham 'kɒt.ᵊn.əm US 'kɑː.tᵊn-, -hæm

cotter (C) 'kɒt.əʳ US 'kɑː.t̬ɚ **-s** -z

Cotterell 'kɒt.ᵊr.ᵊl US 'kɑː.t̬ɚ-

Cotterill 'kɒt.ᵊr.ᵊl, -ɪl US 'kɑː.t̬ɚ-

Cottesloe 'kɒt.sləʊ, -əz.ləʊ US 'kɑːt.sloʊ, -əz.loʊ

Cottian 'kɒt.i.ən US 'kɑː.t̬i-

Cottingham 'kɒt.ɪŋ.əm US 'kɑː.t̬ɪŋ-, -hæm

cotton (C) 'kɒt.ᵊn US 'kɑː.tᵊn **-s** -z **-ing** -ɪŋ **-ed** -d **'Cotton ˌBelt**; ˌ**cotton 'candy**; ˌ**cotton 'wool**

cotton grass 'kɒt.ᵊn.grɑːs US 'kɑː.tᵊn.græs

cottonseed 'kɒt.ᵊn.siːd US 'kɑː.tᵊn-

cottontail 'kɒt.ᵊn.teɪl US 'kɑː.tᵊn- **-s** -z

cottonwood 'kɒt.n̩.wʊd US 'kɑː.tn̩- **-s** -z

cottony 'kɒt.ᵊn.i US 'kɑː.tᵊn-

Cottrell 'kɒt.rᵊl; kə'trel US 'kɑː.trᵊl; kə'trel

cotyledon ˌkɒt.ɪ'liː.dᵊn, -ᵊl'iː- US ˌkɑː.t̬ə'liː- **-s** -z

cotyledonous ˌkɒt.ɪ'liː.dᵊn.əs, -ᵊl'iː- US ˌkɑː.t̬ə'liː-

couch *all verb senses, item of furniture:* kaʊtʃ **-es** -ɪz **-ing** -ɪŋ **-ed** -t **'couch poˌtato**, ˌ**couch po'tato**

couch *grass:* kuːtʃ, kaʊtʃ

Couch kuːtʃ

couchant 'kaʊ.tʃᵊnt, 'kuː-

couchée 'kuː.ʃeɪ, -'- US kuː'ʃeɪ **-s** -z

couchette kuː'ʃet **-s** -s

Coué 'kuː.eɪ **-ism** -ɪ.zᵊm

cougar 'kuː.gəʳ US -gɚ **-s** -z

cough kɒf US kɑːf, kɔːf **-s** -s **-ing** -ɪŋ **-ed** -t **-er/s** -əʳ/z US -ɚ/z **'cough ˌdrop**; **'cough ˌmixture**; **'cough ˌsyrup**

Coughlan 'kɒg.lən, 'kɒf-, 'kɒk-, 'kɒx-, 'kəʊ- US 'kɑː.glən, 'koʊ.lən

Coughlin 'kɒg.lɪn, 'kɒf-, 'kɒk-, 'kɒx- US 'kɑː.glɪn, 'kɑːf-

could *(from* **can**) *strong form:* kʊd *weak form:* kəd

Note: Weak form word. The strong form is used for emphasis, e.g. "You **could** be right", for contrast, e.g. "whether she could or not", and in sentence-final position, e.g. "as well as he could.".

couldn't 'kʊd.ᵊnt

couldst kʊdst

coulee 'kuː.li **-s** -z

coulisse kuː'liːs, kʊ- **-s** -ɪz

couloir 'kuːl.wɑːʳ, -wɔːʳ US kuːl'wɑːr **-s** -z

coulomb (C) 'kuː.lɒm US -lɑːm, -loʊm **-s** -z

Coulsdon 'kəʊlz.dᵊn, 'kuːlz- US 'koʊlz-, 'kuːlz-

Note: /'kəʊlz- US 'koʊlz-/ is the traditional local pronunciation. People unfamiliar with the place generally pronounce /'kuːlz-/, as also do new residents in the district.

Coulson 'kəʊl.sᵊn, 'kuːl- US 'koʊl-, 'kuːl-

coulter 'kəʊl.təʳ, 'kuː- US 'koʊl.t̬ɚ **-s** -z

Coulthard 'kuːl.tɑːd, 'kəʊl- US -tɑːrd

Coulton 'kəʊl.tᵊn US 'koʊl-

council 'kaʊn*t*.sᵊl, -sɪl **-s** -z **'council ˌhouse**; **'council ˌtax**

counci(l)lor 'kaʊn*t*.sᵊl.əʳ, -sɪ.ləʳ US -sᵊl.ɚ **-s** -z

council|man 'kaʊn*t*.sᵊl|.mən, -sɪl-, -mæn **-men** -mən, -men **-woman** -ˌwʊm.ən **-women** -ˌwɪm.ɪn

counsel 'kaʊn*t*.sᵊl **-s** -z **-(l)ing** -ɪŋ **-(l)ed** -d

counsel(l)or 'kaʊn*t*.sᵊl.əʳ US -ɚ **-s** -z

count (C) kaʊnt **-s** -s **-ing** -ɪŋ US 'kaʊn.t̬ɪŋ **-ed** -ɪd US 'kaʊn.t̬ɪd

countab|le 'kaʊn.tə.b|l̩ US -t̬ə- **-ly** -li

countdown 'kaʊnt.daʊn

countenanc|e 'kaʊn.tᵊn.ən*t*s, -tɪ.nən*t*s US -tᵊn.ən*t*s **-es** -ɪz **-ing** -ɪŋ **-ed** -t

counter- 'kaʊn.təʳ- US 'kaʊn.t̬ɚ-

count|er 'kaʊn.t|əʳ US 'kaʊn.t̬|ɚ **-ers** -əz US -ɚz **-ering** -ᵊr.ɪŋ **-ered** -əd US -ɚd ˌ**Counter-Refor'mation**

counteract ˌkaʊn.tᵊr'ækt, '--- US ˌkaʊn.t̬ɚ'ækt **-s** -s **-ing** -ɪŋ **-ed** -ɪd

counteraction *counteracting:* ˌkaʊn.tᵊr'æk.ʃᵊn US -t̬ɚ'- **-s** -z

counter-action *action by way of reply:* 'kaʊn.tᵊrˌæk.ʃᵊn US -t̬ɚˌ- **-s** -z

counteractive ˌkaʊn.tᵊr'æk.tɪv US -t̬ɚ'- **-ly** -li

counterargument 'kaʊn.tᵊrˌɑːg.jə.mənt, -jʊ- US -t̬ɚˌɑːrg.jə- **-s** -s

counterattack 'kaʊn.tᵊr.əˌtæk, ˌkaʊn.tᵊr.ə'tæk US 'kaʊn.t̬ɚ.əˌtæk, ˌkaʊn.t̬ɚ.ə'tæk **-s** -s **-ing** -ɪŋ **-ed** -t

counterattraction ˌkaʊn.tᵊr.ə'træk.ʃᵊn, 'kaʊn.tᵊr.əˌtræk- US ˌkaʊn.t̬ɚ.ə'træk-, 'kaʊn.t̬ɚ.əˌtræk- **-s** -z

counterbalanc|e (*n.*) 'kaʊn.təˌbæl.ən*t*s US -t̬ɚ- **-es** -ɪz

counterbalanc|e (*v.*) ˌkaʊn.tə'bæl.ən*t*s US -t̬ɚ'- **-es** -ɪz **-ing** -ɪŋ **-ed** -t

counterbid 'kaʊn.tə.bɪd US -t̬ɚ- **-s** -z **-ding** -ɪŋ

counterblast 'kaʊn.tə.blɑːst US -t̬ɚ.blæst **-s** -s

counterblow 'kaʊn.tə.bləʊ US -t̬ɚ.bloʊ **-s** -z

countercharg|e 'kaʊn.tə.tʃɑːdʒ US -t̬ɚ.tʃɑːrdʒ **-es** -ɪz **-ing** -ɪŋ **-ed** -d

counterclaim 'kaʊn.tə.kleɪm US -t̬ɚ- **-s** -z **-ing** -ɪŋ **-ed** -d

counterclockwise ˌkaʊn.tə'klɒk.waɪz US -t̬ɚ'klɑː.kwaɪz

counterespionage ˌkaʊn.tᵊr'es.pi.ə.nɑːʒ, -nɑːdʒ US -t̬ɚ'-

counter|feit 'kaʊn.tə|.fɪt, -fiːt US -t̬ɚ|.fɪt **-feits** -fɪts, -fiːts US -fɪts **-feiting** -fɪ.tɪŋ, -fiː- US -fɪ.t̬ɪŋ **-feited** -fɪ.tɪd, -fiː- US -fɪ.t̬ɪd **-feiter/s** -fɪ.təʳ/z, -fiː- US -fɪ.t̬ɚ/z

counterfoil 'kaʊn.tə.fɔɪl US -t̬ɚ- **-s** -z

counterinsurgen|cy ˌkaʊn.təʳ.ɪnˈsɜː.dʒᵊn|t.si (US) -t̬ɚ.ɪnˈsɝː- **-t** -t

counterintelligence ˌkaʊn.təʳ.ɪnˈtel.ɪ.dʒənts, ˈkaʊn.təʳ.ɪn.tel- (US) ˌkaʊn.t̬ɚ.ɪnˈtel-, ˈkaʊn.t̬ɚ.ɪnˌtel-

counterintuitive ˌkaʊn.təʳ.ɪnˈtjuː.ə.tɪv, -ɪ.tɪv (US) -t̬ɚ.ɪnˈtuː.ə.t̬ɪv, -ˈtjuː- **-ly** -li

countermand ˌkaʊn.təˈmɑːnd, ˈ--- (US) ˌkaʊn.tɚˈmænd, ˈ--- **-s** -z **-ing** -ɪŋ **-ed** -ɪd

countermeasure ˈkaʊn.təˌmeʒ.əʳ (US) -t̬ɚˌmeʒ.ɚ **-s** -z

countermove ˈkaʊn.tə.muːv (US) -t̬ɚ- **-s** -z

counteroffensive ˌkaʊn.təʳ.əˈfent.sɪv, ˈkaʊn.təʳ.əˌfent- (US) ˈkaʊn.t̬ɚ.əˌfent- **-s** -z

counterpane ˈkaʊn.tə.peɪn, -pɪn (US) -t̬ɚ- **-s** -z

counterpart ˈkaʊn.tə.pɑːt (US) -tɚ.pɑːrt **-s** -s

counterplot ˈkaʊn.tə.plɒt (US) -tɚ.plɑːt **-s** -s

counterpoint ˈkaʊn.tə.pɔɪnt (US) -tɚ-

counterpois|e ˈkaʊn.tə.pɔɪz (US) -tɚ- **-es** -ɪz **-ing** -ɪŋ **-ed** -d

counterproductive ˌkaʊn.tə.prəˈdʌk.tɪv (US) -tɚ- **-ly** -li **-ness** -nəs, -nɪs

counterrevolution ˌkaʊn.tə.rev.əˈluː.ʃᵊn, -ˈljuː-, ˈkaʊn.tə.rev.əˌluː-, -ˌljuː- (US) ˌkaʊn.t̬ɚ.rev.əˈluː-, ˈkaʊn.t̬ɚ.rev.əˌluː- **-s** -z

counterrevolutionar|y ˌkaʊn.tə.rev.əˈluː.ʃᵊn.ᵊr|.i, -ˈljuː-, ˈkaʊn.tə.rev.əˌluː-, -ˌljuː- (US) ˌkaʊn.t̬ɚ.rev.əˈluː.ʃᵊn.er-, ˈkaʊn.t̬ɚ.rev.əˌluː- **-ies** -iz

counterscarp ˈkaʊn.tə.skɑːp (US) -t̬ɚ.skɑːrp **-s** -s

countersign (*n.*) ˈkaʊn.tə.saɪn (US) -t̬ɚ- **-s** -z **-ed** -d

countersign (*v.*) ˈkaʊn.tə.saɪn, ˌ--ˈ- (US) -tɚ- **-s** -z **-ing** -ɪŋ **-ed** -d

counter|sink ˈkaʊn.tə|.sɪŋk (US) -tɚ- **-sinks** -sɪŋks **-sinking** -sɪŋ.kɪŋ **-sunk** -sʌŋk

countertenor ˌkaʊn.təˈten.əʳ, ˈkaʊn.təˌten- (US) ˈkaʊn.t̬ɚˌten.ɚ **-s** -z

counterterror|ism ˌkaʊn.təˈter.ə.r|ɪ.zᵊm (US) -t̬ɚˈter.ɚ|.ɪ- **-ist/s** -ɪst/s

countervail ˌkaʊn.təˈveɪl, ˈ--- (US) ˈkaʊn.tɚ.veɪl, ˌ--ˈ- **-s** -z **-ing** -ɪŋ **-ed** -d

counterweight ˈkaʊn.tə.weɪt (US) -tɚ- **-s** -s

countess (C) ˈkaʊn.tɪs, -tes, -təs; ˌkaʊnˈtes (US) ˈkaʊn.t̬ɪs, -təs **-es** -ɪz

Countesthorpe ˈkaʊn.tɪs.θɔːp (US) -θɔːrp

countinghou|se ˈkaʊn.tɪŋ.haʊ|s **-ses** -zɪz

countless ˈkaʊnt.ləs, -lɪs

countrified ˈkʌn.trɪ.faɪd

countr|y ˈkʌn.tr|i **-ies** -iz ˌ**country and ˈwestern**; ˌ**country ˈbumpkin**; ˌ**country ˈdancing** (US) ˈ**country ˌdancing**; ˌ**country ˈhouse**; ˌ**country ˈseat**

country-danc|e ˌkʌn.triˈdɑːnts (US) -ˈdænts **-es** -ɪz **-ing** -ɪŋ

country|man ˈkʌn.trɪ|.mən **-men** -mən

countryside ˈkʌn.trɪ.saɪd

countrywide ˌkʌn.triˈwaɪd (US) ˈ--- *stress shift, British only:* ˌcountrywide ˈvoting

country|woman ˈkʌn.trɪ|ˌwʊm.ən **-women** -ˌwɪm.ɪn

count|y ˈkaʊn.t|i (US) -t̬|i **-ies** -iz ˌ**county ˈcourt**; ˌ**county ˈfair**; ˌ**county ˈhall**; ˌ**county ˈtown**

coup kuː **-s** -z

coup(s) de foudre ˌkuː.dəˈfuː.drə

coup(s) de grâce ˌkuː.dəˈgrɑːs

coup(s) de main ˌkuː.dəˈmæ̃ŋ, -ˈmæn

coup(s) d'état ˌkuː.deɪˈtɑː, -detˈɑː

coup(s) de théâtre ˌkuː.də.teɪˈɑː.trə

coupé, coupe ˈkuː.peɪ, -ˈ- (US) kuːˈpeɪ, koʊp **-s** -z

Couper ˈkuː.pəʳ (US) -pɚ

Couperin ˈkuː.pə.ræ̃ŋ, -ræn

Coupland ˈkuːp.lənd, ˈkəʊp- (US) ˈkuːp-, ˈkoʊp-

coupl|e ˈkʌp.l̩ **-es** -z **-ing** -ɪŋ, ˈ-lɪŋ **-ed** -d

coupler ˈkʌp.ləʳ (US) -lɚ **-s** -z

couplet ˈkʌp.lət, -lɪt **-s** -s

coupling ˈkʌp.lɪŋ **-s** -z

coupon ˈkuː.pɒn (US) ˈkuː.pɑːn, ˈkjuː- **-s** -z

courage (C) ˈkʌr.ɪdʒ

courageous kəˈreɪ.dʒəs **-ly** -li **-ness** -nəs, -nɪs

courante kʊˈrɑ̃ːnt, -ˈrɑːnt, -ˈrænt (US) -ˈrɑːnt **-s** -s

courgette kɔːˈʒet, kʊə- (US) kʊr- **-s** -s

courier (C) ˈkʊr.i.əʳ, ˈkʌr- (US) ˈkʊr.i.ɚ, ˈkɝː- **-s** -z

Courland ˈkʊə.lənd, -lænd (US) ˈkʊr-

cours|e (C) kɔːs (US) kɔːrs **-es** -ɪz **-ing** -ɪŋ **-ed** -t

coursebook ˈkɔːs.bʊk (US) ˈkɔːrs- **-s** -s

courser ˈkɔː.səʳ (US) ˈkɔːr.sɚ **-s** -s

coursework ˈkɔːs.wɜːk (US) ˈkɔːrs.wɝːk

court (C) kɔːt (US) kɔːrt **-s** -s **-ing** -ɪŋ (US) ˈkɔːr.t̬ɪŋ **-ed** -ɪd (US) ˈkɔːr.t̬ɪd ˈ**court ˌcard**; ˌ**court of apˈpeal**; ˈ**court ˌorder**, ˌ**court ˈorder**; ˈ**court ˌshoe**

Courtauld ˈkɔː.təʊld, ˈkɔː.təʊ (US) ˈkɔːr.toʊld, -toʊ **-s** -z

court-bouillon ˌkɔːtˈbuː.jɒn, ˈkʊət-, ˈkʊə-, ˌ--ˈ- (US) ˌkɔːr.buːˈjɑːn

Courtelle® kɔːˈtel, kʊə- (US) kɔːr-

Courtenay ˈkɔːt.ni (US) ˈkɔːrt-

courteous ˈkɜː.ti.əs (US) ˈkɝː.t̬i- **-ly** -li **-ness** -nəs, -nɪs

courtesan ˈkɔː.tɪ.zæn, ˈkʊə-, -tə-, --ˈ- (US) ˈkɔːr.t̬ə.zᵊn, -zæn **-s** -z

courtes|y ˈkɜː.tə.s|i, -tɪ- (US) ˈkɝː.t̬ə- **-ies** -iz

Courthope ˈkɔː.təp, ˈkɔːt.həʊp (US) ˈkɔːr.təp, ˈkɔːrt.hoʊp

courthou|se ˈkɔːt.haʊ|s (US) ˈkɔːrt- **-ses** -zɪz

courtier ˈkɔː.ti.əʳ (US) ˈkɔːr.t̬i.ɚ **-s** -z

courtl|y ˈkɔːt.l|i (US) ˈkɔːrt- **-ier** -i.əʳ (US) -i.ɚ **-iest** -i.ɪst, -i.əst **-iness** -ɪ.nəs, -ɪ.nɪs

court-martial ˌkɔːtˈmɑː.ʃᵊl (US) ˈkɔːrtˌmɑːr- **-s** -z **-(l)ing** -ɪŋ **-(l)ed** -d **courts-martial** ˌkɔːts- (US) ˈkɔːrts-

Courtneidge ˈkɔːt.nɪdʒ (US) ˈkɔːrt-

Courtney ˈkɔːt.ni (US) ˈkɔːrt-

courtroom ˈkɔːt.rʊm, -ruːm (US) ˈkɔːrt.ruːm, -rʊm **-s** -z

courtship ˈkɔːt.ʃɪp (US) ˈkɔːrt- **-s** -s

courtyard ˈkɔːt.jɑːd (US) ˈkɔːrt.jɑːrd **-s** -z

Courvoisier® kʊəˈvwæz.i.eɪ, kɔːˈ-, -ˈvwɑː.zi- (US) ˌkɔːr.vwɑː.ziˈeɪ

couscous ˈkuːs.kuːs

cousin ˈkʌz.ᵊn **-s** -z

Cousins ˈkʌz.ᵊnz

Cousteau kuːˈstəʊ, ˈ-- (US) kuːˈstoʊ

couth kuːθ **-ly** -li **-ness** -nəs, -nɪs

Coutts kuːts

couture kuːˈtjʊəʳ, -ˈtʊəʳ (US) kuːˈtʊr

couturier kuːˈtjʊə.ri.eɪ, -ˈtʊə-, -əʳ (US) -ˈtʊr.i.eɪ, -ɚ **-s** -z

Couzens ˈkʌz.ᵊnz

covalenc|y ˌkəʊˈveɪ.lənt.s|i, ˈkəʊ.veɪ- (US) ˌkoʊˈveɪ.lənt- **-ies** -iz

covalent ˌkəʊˈveɪ.lənt, ˈ--- (US) ˌkoʊˈveɪ-

covariance ˌkəʊˈveə.ri.ənts, ˈkəʊ.veə- (US) ˌkoʊˈver.i-, -ˈvær-

cove (C) kəʊv (US) koʊv **-s** -z

coven ˈkʌv.ᵊn **-s** -z

coven|ant ˈkʌv.ᵊn|.ənt (US) -ænt **-ants** -ənts (US) -ænts **-anting** -ən.tɪŋ (US) -ən.t̬ɪŋ, -æn- **-anted** -ən.tɪd (US) -ən.t̬ɪd, -æn- **-anter/s** -ən.təʳ/z (US) -ən.t̬ɚ/z, -æn-

covenantee ˌkʌv.ᵊn.ənˈtiː (US) -ænˈtiː, -ənˈ- **-s** -z

covenantor ˈkʌv.ᵊn.ən.təʳ (US) ˈkʌv.ən.æn.t̬ɚ; ˌkʌv.ən.ænˈtɔːr **-s** -z

Covent ˈkɒv.ᵊnt, ˈkʌv- (US) ˈkʌv-, ˈkɑː.vᵊnt ˌ**Covent ˈGarden**

Coventry ˈkɒv.ᵊn.tri, ˈkʌv- (US) ˈkʌv-, ˈkɑː.vᵊn-

Pronouncing the letters CQU

The letter combination **cqu** has two possible pronunciations: /kw/ and /k/. Generally speaking, /kw/ is used where the combination begins a stressed syllable, e.g.:

acquire /əˈkwaɪəʳ/ (US) /-ˈkwaɪɚ/
acquiesce /ˌæk.wiˈes/

The realisation /k/ tends to appear before unstressed syllables, e.g.:

racquet /ˈræk.ɪt/

cov|er ˈkʌv|.əʳ (US) -ɚ **-ers** -əz (US) -ɚz **-ering/s** -ᵊr.ɪŋ/z **-ered** -əd (US) -ɚd ˈ**cover** ˌ**charge**; ˈ**cover** ˌ**girl**; ˌ**covered** ˈ**wagon**
Coverack ˈkɒv.ᵊr.æk, ˈkʌv-, -ək (US) ˈkʌv.ə.ræk, ˈkɑː.və-
coverage ˈkʌv.ᵊr.ɪdʒ
coverall ˈkʌv.ᵊr.ɔːl (US) -ɔːl, -ɑːl **-s** -z
Coverdale ˈkʌv.ə.deɪl (US) ˈ-ɚ-
coverlet ˈkʌv.ə.lət, -lɪt (US) ˈ-ɚ- **-s** -s
Coverley ˈkʌv.ə.li (US) ˈ-ɚ-
cover-point ˌkʌv.əˈpɔɪnt (US) -ɚˈ- **-s** -s
covert (*n.*) *shelter, cloth:* ˈkʌv.ət, -ə (US) ˈkʌv.ɚt, ˈkoʊ.vɚt **-s** -z
covert (*adj.*) ˈkəʊ.vɜːt, ˈkʌv.ət, kəʊˈvɜːt (US) ˈkoʊ.vɝːt, ˈkʌv.ɚt; koʊˈvɝːt **-ly** -li
coverture ˈkʌv.ə.tʃəʳ, -tʃʊəʳ, -tjʊəʳ (US) -ɚ.tʃɚ
cover-up ˈkʌv.əʳ.ʌp (US) ˈ-ɚ- **-s** -s
cov|et ˈkʌv|.ɪt, -ət **-ets** -ɪts, -əts **-eting/ly** -ɪ.tɪŋ/li, -ə.tɪŋ/li (US) -ə.t̬ɪŋ/li **-eted** -ɪ.tɪd, -ə.tɪd (US) -ə.t̬ɪd **-etable** -ɪ.tə.bl̩, -ə.tə.bl̩ (US) -ə.t̬ə.bl̩
covetous ˈkʌv.ɪ.təs, -ə.təs (US) -ə.t̬əs **-ly** -li **-ness** -nəs, -nɪs
covey ˈkʌv.i **-s** -z
Covington ˈkʌv.ɪŋ.tən
cow kaʊ **-s** -z **-ing** -ɪŋ **-ed** -d ˈ**cow** ˌ**parsley**, ˌ**cow** ˈ**parsley**; **till the** ˈ**cows come** ˌ**home**
Cowan kaʊən
coward (C) kaʊəd (US) kaʊɚd **-s** -z
cowardice ˈkaʊə.dɪs (US) ˈkaʊɚ-
cowardl|y ˈkaʊəd.l|i (US) ˈkaʊɚd- **-iness** -ɪ.nəs, -ɪ.nɪs
cowbane ˈkaʊ.beɪn
cowbell ˈkaʊ.bel **-s** -z
cowboy ˈkaʊ.bɔɪ **-s** -z ˈ**cowboy** ˌ**boots**; ˈ**cowboy** ˌ**hat**
cowcatcher ˈkaʊˌkætʃ.əʳ (US) -ɚ **-s** -z
Cowden ˈkaʊ.den, -dᵊn; kaʊˈden
Cowdenbeath ˌkaʊ.dᵊnˈbiːθ
Cowdray ˈkaʊ.dreɪ, -dri
Cowdrey ˈkaʊ.dri
Cowell kaʊəl, kaʊl, kəʊəl (US) kaʊəl, kaʊl, koʊəl
Cowen kaʊən, kaʊɪn, kəʊən, kəʊɪn (US) kaʊən, kaʊɪn, koʊən, koʊɪn
cower kaʊəʳ (US) kaʊɚ **-s** -z **-ing** -ɪŋ **-ed** -d
Cowes kaʊz
cowgirl ˈkaʊ.gɜːl (US) -gɝːl **-s** -z
cowhand ˈkaʊ.hænd **-s** -z
cowherd ˈkaʊ.hɜːd (US) -hɝːd **-s** -z
cowhide ˈkaʊ.haɪd
Cowie ˈkaʊ.i
cowl kaʊl **-s** -z **-ing** -ɪŋ **-ed** -d
Cowley ˈkaʊ.li
cowlick ˈkaʊ.lɪk **-s** -s
cowlike ˈkaʊ.laɪk
Cowling ˈkaʊ.lɪŋ
cow|-man ˈkaʊ|.mæn **-men** -mən
co-worker ˈkəʊˌwɜː.kəʳ (US) ˈkoʊˌwɝː.kɚ, ˌ-ˈ-- **-s** -z
cowpat ˈkaʊ.pæt **-s** -s
Cowper ˈkaʊ.pəʳ, ˈkuː- (US) ˈkaʊ.pɚ, ˈkuː-
Note: The poet called himself /ˈkuː.pəʳ (US) -pɚ/. /ˈkuː.pəʳ (US) -pɚ/ is also the pronunciation in **Cowper Powys** /ˌkuː.pəˈpəʊ.ɪs (US) -pɚˈpoʊ-/ and **Cowper-Black** /ˌkuː.pəˈblæk (US) -pɚˈ-/.
cowpoke ˈkaʊ.pəʊk (US) -poʊk **-s** -s
cowpox ˈkaʊ.pɒks (US) -pɑːks
cowpuncher ˈkaʊˌpʌn.tʃəʳ (US) -ˌpʌnt.ʃɚ **-s** -z
cowr|ie, cowr|y ˈkaʊ.r|i **-ies** -iz
co-writer ˈkəʊˌraɪ.təʳ (US) ˈkoʊˌraɪ.t̬ɚ, ˌ-ˈ-- **-s** -z
cowshed ˈkaʊ.ʃed **-s** -z
cowslip ˈkaʊ.slɪp **-s** -s
cox (C) kɒks (US) kɑːks **-es** -ɪz **-ing** -ɪŋ **-ed** -t **-less** -ləs, -lɪs
Coxall ˈkɒk.sᵊl, -sɑːl (US) ˈkɑːk-
coxcomb ˈkɒk.skəʊm (US) ˈkɑːk.skoʊm **-s** -z
coxswain ˈkɒk.sᵊn, -sweɪn (US) ˈkɑːk- **-s** -z
coy kɔɪ **-er** -əʳ (US) -ɚ **-est** -ɪst, -əst **-ly** -li **-ness** -nəs, -nɪs
coyish ˈkɔɪ.ɪʃ **-ly** -li **-ness** -nəs, -nɪs
Coyle kɔɪl
coyote kɔɪˈəʊ.ti, kaɪ-; ˈkɔɪ.əʊt, ˈkaɪ- (US) kaɪˈoʊ.t̬i; ˈkaɪ.oʊt **-s** -z
coypu ˈkɔɪ.puː, -pjuː, -ˈ- **-s** -z
coz kʌz
cozen ˈkʌz.ᵊn **-s** -z **-ing** -ɪŋ **-ed** -d **-er/s** -əʳ/z (US) -ɚ/z
Cozens, Cozzens ˈkʌz.ᵊnz
coz|y ˈkəʊ.z|i (US) koʊ- **-ier** -i.əʳ (US) -i.ɚ **-iest** -i.ɪst, -i.əst
CPU ˌsiː.piːˈjuː
crab kræb **-s** -z **-bing** -ɪŋ **-bed** -d ˈ**crab** ˌ**apple**
Crabbe kræb
crabbed kræbd, ˈkræb.ɪd **-ly** -li **-ness** -nəs, -nɪs
crabb|y ˈkræb|.i **-ier** -i.əʳ (US) -i.ɚ **-iest** -i.ɪst, -i.əst **-ily** -ɪ.li, -ᵊl.i **-iness** -ɪ.nəs, -ɪ.nɪs
crabtree (C) ˈkræb.triː **-s** -z
crabwise ˈkræb.waɪz
Crace kreɪs
crack kræk **-s** -s **-ing** -ɪŋ **-ed** -t ˌ**crack of** ˈ**dawn**
crackdown ˈkræk.daʊn **-s** -z
Crackenthorpe ˈkræk.ᵊn.θɔːp (US) -θɔːrp
cracker ˈkræk.əʳ (US) -ɚ **-s** -z
cracker-barrel ˈkræk.əˌbær.ᵊl (US) -ɚˌber.ᵊl, -ˌbær-
crackerjack (*adj.*) ˈkræk.ə.dʒæk (US) ˈ-ɚ-
Cracker Jack® ˈkræk.ə.dʒæk (US) ˈ-ɚ-
crackhead ˈkræk.hed **-s** -z
crackhou|se ˈkræk.haʊ|s **-ses** -zɪz
crackl|e ˈkræk.l̩ **-es** -z **-ing** -ɪŋ, ˈ-lɪŋ **-ed** -d
crackling ˈkræk.lɪŋ
crackly ˈkræk.l̩.i, ˈkræk.li
cracknel ˈkræk.nᵊl **-s** -z
Cracknell ˈkræk.nᵊl
crackpot ˈkræk.pɒt (US) -pɑːt **-s** -s
cracks|man ˈkræks|.mən **-men** -mən
Cracow ˈkræk.ɒf, -ɒv, -aʊ, -əʊ (US) ˈkrɑː.kaʊ, ˈkræk.aʊ; ˈkrɑː.kʊf
-cracy -krə.si
Craddock ˈkræd.ək
cradl|e ˈkreɪ.dl̩ **-es** -z **-ing** -ɪŋ, ˈkreɪd.lɪŋ **-ed** -d
cradlesnatch ˈkreɪ.dl̩.snætʃ **-ing** -ɪŋ **-er/s** -əʳ/z (US) -ɚ/z
Cradley ˈkreɪd.li, ˈkræd-
craft krɑːft (US) kræft **-s** -s **-ing** **-ed**
-craft -krɑːft (US) -kræft
crafts|man ˈkrɑːfts|.mən (US) ˈkræfts- **-men** -mən **-manship** -mən.ʃɪp
crafts|woman ˈkrɑːfts|ˌwʊm.ən (US) ˈkræfts- **-women** -ˌwɪm.ɪn

craft|y 'krɑːf.t|i ⓤⓢ 'kræf- -ier -i.əʳ ⓤⓢ -i.ɚ -iest -i.ɪst, -i.əst -ily -ɪ.li, -əl.i -iness -ɪ.nəs, -ɪ.nɪs
crag kræg -s -z
Cragg kræg
cragg|y 'kræg|.i -ier -i.əʳ ⓤⓢ -i.ɚ -iest -i.ɪst, -i.əst -ily -ɪ.li, -əl.i -iness -ɪ.nəs, -ɪ.nɪs
crags|man 'krægz|.mən -men -mən, -men
craic kræk
Craig kreɪg
Craigavon ˌkreɪ'gæv.ən
Craigie 'kreɪ.gi
Craik kreɪk
Craiova krə'jəʊ.və, krɑː- ⓤⓢ krɑː'joʊ-
crak|e kreɪk -es -s -ing -ɪŋ -ed -t
cram (C) kræm -s -z -ming -ɪŋ -med -d
crambo 'kræm.bəʊ ⓤⓢ -boʊ
Cramer 'krɑː.məʳ, 'kreɪ- ⓤⓢ 'kreɪ.mɚ
cram-full ˌkræm'fʊl
Cramlington 'kræm.lɪŋ.tən
crammer 'kræm.əʳ ⓤⓢ -ɚ -s -z
cramp (C) kræmp -s -s -ing -ɪŋ -ed -t
cramp-iron 'kræmp.aɪən ⓤⓢ -aɪɚn -s -z
crampon 'kræm.pɒn, -pən ⓤⓢ -pɑːn -s -z
Crampton 'kræm*p*.tən
cran kræn -s -z
cranage 'kreɪ.nɪdʒ
Cranage 'kræn.ɪdʒ
cranberr|y 'kræn.bər|.i, 'kræm- ⓤⓢ -ˌber- -ies -iz
Cranborne 'kræn.bɔːn, 'kræm- ⓤⓢ 'kræn.bɔːrn
Cranbourn(e) 'kræn.bɔːn, 'kræm- ⓤⓢ 'kræn.bɔːrn
ranbrook 'kræn.brʊk, 'kræm- ⓤⓢ 'kræn-
ran|e (C) kreɪn -es -z -ing -ɪŋ -ed -d 'crane ˌfly
ranesbill 'kreɪnz.bɪl -s -z
ranfield 'kræn.fiːld
ranford 'kræn.fəd ⓤⓢ -fɚd
ranial 'kreɪ.ni.əl
ranio- 'kreɪ.ni.əʊ- ⓤⓢ 'kreɪ.ni.oʊ-, -ə-
raniolog|y ˌkreɪ.ni'ɒl.ə.dʒ|i ⓤⓢ -'ɑː.lə- -ist/s -ɪst/s
rani|um 'kreɪ.ni|.əm -ums -əmz -a -ə
ank kræŋk -s -s -ing -ɪŋ -ed -t
ankshaft 'kræŋk.ʃɑːft ⓤⓢ -ʃæft -s -s
ankshaw 'kræŋk.ʃɔː ⓤⓢ -ʃɑː, -ʃɔː
ank|y 'kræŋ.k|i -ier -i.əʳ ⓤⓢ -i.ɚ -iest -i.ɪst, -i.əst -ily -ɪ.li, -əl.i -iness -ɪ.nəs, -ɪ.nɪs
anleigh, Cranley 'kræn.li
anmer 'kræn.məʳ, 'kræm- ⓤⓢ 'kræn.mɚ
ann|y 'kræn|.i -ies -iz -ied -id
anston 'kræn.stən
anwell 'kræn.wəl, -wel
anworth 'kræn.wəθ, -wɜːθ ⓤⓢ -wɚθ, -wɝːθ

crap kræp -s -s -ping -ɪŋ -ped -t
crape kreɪp -s -s
crapper 'kræp.əʳ ⓤⓢ -ɚ -s -z
crapp|y 'kræp|.i -ier -i.əʳ ⓤⓢ -i.ɚ -iest -i.ɪst, -i.əst
craps kræps
crapshooter 'kræpˌʃuː.təʳ ⓤⓢ -t̬ɚ -s -z
crapulen|ce 'kræp.jə.lən|*t*s, -jʊ- -t/ly -t/li
crapulous 'kræp.jə.ləs, -jʊ- -ly -li
crash kræʃ -es -ɪz -ing -ɪŋ -ed -t 'crash ˌbarrier; 'crash ˌhelmet, ˌcrash 'helmet
Crashaw 'kræʃ.ɔː ⓤⓢ -ɑː, -ɔː
crash-div|e 'kræʃ.daɪv, ˌ-'- -es -z -ing -ɪŋ -ed -d crash-dove 'kræʃ.dəʊv ⓤⓢ -doʊv
crash-land ˌkræʃ'lænd ⓤⓢ 'kræʃ.lænd, ˌ-'- -s -z -ing/s -ɪŋ/z -ed -ɪd *stress shift, British only:* ˌcrash-land 'heavily
cra|sis 'kreɪ|.sɪs -ses -siːz
crass kræs -er -əʳ ⓤⓢ -ɚ -est -ɪst, -əst -ly -li -ness -nəs, -nɪs
-crat -kræt
cratch krætʃ -es -ɪz
Cratchit 'krætʃ.ɪt
crat|e kreɪt -es -s -ing -ɪŋ -ed -ɪd
crater 'kreɪ.təʳ ⓤⓢ -t̬ɚ -s -z
Crathie 'kræθ.i
-cratic -'kræt.ɪk ⓤⓢ -'kræt̬.ɪk
cra|vat krə|'væt -vats -væts -vatted -væt.ɪd ⓤⓢ -væt̬.ɪd
crav|e kreɪv -es -z -ing -ɪŋ -ed -d -er/s -əʳ/z ⓤⓢ -ɚ/z
craven (C) 'kreɪ.vən -s -z -ly -li
craving 'kreɪ.vɪŋ -s -z
craw krɔː ⓤⓢ krɑː, krɔː -s -z
crawfish 'krɔː.fɪʃ ⓤⓢ 'krɑː-, 'krɔː- -es -ɪz
Crawford 'krɔː.fəd ⓤⓢ 'krɑː.fɚd, 'krɔː-
crawl krɔːl ⓤⓢ krɑːl, krɔːl -s -z -ing -ɪŋ -ed -d -er/s -əʳ/z ⓤⓢ -ɚ/z
Crawley 'krɔː.li ⓤⓢ 'krɑː-, 'krɔː-
crawl|y 'krɔː.l|i ⓤⓢ 'krɑː-, 'krɔː- -ier -i.əʳ ⓤⓢ -i.ɚ -iest -i.ɪst, -i.əst -iness -ɪ.nəs, -ɪ.nɪs
Craxi 'kræk.si
Cray kreɪ
crayfish 'kreɪ.fɪʃ -es -ɪz
Crayford 'kreɪ.fəd ⓤⓢ -fɚd
Crayola® kreɪ'əʊ.lə ⓤⓢ -'oʊ-
crayon 'kreɪ.ɒn, -ən ⓤⓢ -ɑːn, -ən -s -z -ing -ɪŋ -ed -d
craz|e kreɪz -es -ɪz -ed -d
craz|y 'kreɪ.z|i -ier -i.əʳ ⓤⓢ -i.ɚ -iest -i.ɪst, -i.əst -ily -ɪ.li, -əl.i -iness -ɪ.nəs, -ɪ.nɪs 'Crazy ˌHorse; ˌcrazy 'paving
CRE ˌsiː.ɑːʳ'iː ⓤⓢ -ɑːr'-
Creagh kreɪ
creak kriːk -s -s -ing -ɪŋ -ed -t

creak|y 'kriː.k|i -ier -i.əʳ ⓤⓢ -i.ɚ -iest -i.ɪst, -i.əst -ily -ɪ.li, -əl.i -iness -ɪ.nəs, -ɪ.nɪs
cream kriːm -s -z -ing -ɪŋ -ed -d -er/s -əʳ/z ⓤⓢ -ɚ/z ˌcream 'cheese; ˌcream 'cracker; ˌcream 'soda; ˌcream 'tea
creamer|y 'kriː.mər|.i -ies -iz
cream|y 'kriː.m|i -ier -i.əʳ ⓤⓢ -i.ɚ -iest -i.ɪst, -i.əst -ily -ɪ.li, -əl.i -iness -ɪ.nəs, -ɪ.nɪs
creas|e kriːs -es -ɪz -ing -ɪŋ -ed -t
Creas(e)y 'kriː.si
creasy 'kriː.si
cre|ate kri|'eɪt -ates -eɪts -ating -eɪ.tɪŋ ⓤⓢ -eɪ.t̬ɪŋ -ated -eɪ.tɪd ⓤⓢ -eɪ.t̬ɪd
creation (C) kri'eɪ.ʃən -s -z
creation|ism kri'eɪ.ʃən|.ɪ.zəm -ist/s -ɪst/s
creative kri'eɪ.tɪv ⓤⓢ -t̬ɪv -ly -li -ness -nəs, -nɪs
creativity ˌkriː.eɪ'tɪv.ə.ti, -ɪ.ti ⓤⓢ -ə.t̬i
creator (C) kri'eɪ.təʳ ⓤⓢ -t̬ɚ -s -z
creature 'kriː.tʃəʳ ⓤⓢ -tʃɚ -s -z ˌcreature 'comfort ⓤⓢ 'creature ˌcomfort
crèch|e kreʃ, kreɪʃ -es -ɪz
Crécy 'kres.i ⓤⓢ kreɪ'siː
cred kred
Creda® 'kriː.də
credence 'kriː.dən*t*s
credential krɪ'den.*t*ʃəl, krə- ⓤⓢ -'den*t*.ʃəl -s -z
credibility ˌkred.ə'bɪl.ə.ti, -ɪ'-, -ɪ.ti ⓤⓢ -ə'bɪl.ə.t̬i
credib|le 'kred.ə.b|l̩, '-ɪ- -ly -li -leness -l̩.nəs, -nɪs
cred|it 'kred|.ɪt -its -ɪts -iting -ɪ.tɪŋ ⓤⓢ -ɪ.t̬ɪŋ -ited -ɪ.tɪd ⓤⓢ -ɪ.t̬ɪd 'credit ˌcard
creditab|le 'kred.ɪ.tə.b|l̩ ⓤⓢ -t̬ə- -ly -li -leness -l̩.nəs, -nɪs
Crediton 'kred.ɪ.tən
creditor 'kred.ɪ.təʳ ⓤⓢ -t̬ɚ -s -z
creditworth|y 'kred.ɪtˌwɜː.ð|i ⓤⓢ -ˌwɝː- -iness -ɪ.nəs, -ɪ.nɪs
credo 'kreɪ.dəʊ, 'kriː- ⓤⓢ 'kriː.doʊ, 'kreɪ- -s -z
credulity krə'djuː.lə.ti, krɪ-, kred'juː-, -lɪ- ⓤⓢ krə'duː.lə-, -'djuː-
credulous 'kred.jʊ.ləs, -jə- ⓤⓢ 'kredʒ.ə-, 'kred.jə- -ly -li -ness -nəs, -nɪs
Cree kriː
creed (C) kriːd -s -z
creek (C) kriːk -s -s
creel kriːl -s -z
creep kriːp -s -s -ing -ɪŋ crept krept
creeper 'kriː.pəʳ ⓤⓢ -pɚ -s -z
creep|y 'kriː.p|i -ier -i.əʳ ⓤⓢ -i.ɚ -iest -i.ɪst, -i.əst -ily -ɪ.li, -əl.i -iness -ɪ.nəs, -ɪ.nɪs

creepy-crawl|y ˌkriː.pi'krɔː.l|i, 'kriː.pi.krɔː- ⓤⓢ ˌkriː.pi'krɑː-, -'krɔː-, 'kriː.pi.krɑː-, -ˌkrɔː- **-ies** -iz
Crees kriːs, kriːz
Creevey 'kriː.vi
Creighton 'kraɪ.tᵊn, 'kreɪ- ⓤⓢ 'kreɪ-, 'kraɪ-
crema|te krɪ'meɪ|t, krə- ⓤⓢ 'kriː.meɪ|t; krɪ'meɪ|t **-tes** -ts **-ting** -tɪŋ ⓤⓢ -t̬ɪŋ **-ted** -tɪd ⓤⓢ -t̬ɪd **-tor/s** -təʳ/z ⓤⓢ -t̬ɚ/z
cremation krɪ'meɪ.ʃᵊn, krə- ⓤⓢ krɪ-, kriː- **-s** -z
crematori|um ˌkrem.ə'tɔː.ri|.əm ⓤⓢ ˌkriː.mə'tɔːr.i-, ˌkrem.ə'- **-ums** -əmz **-a** -ə
cremator|y 'krem.ə.tᵊr|.i, -tr|i ⓤⓢ 'kriː.mə.tɔːr|.i, 'krem.ə- **-ies** -iz
creme krem, kriːm
crème brulée ˌkrem.bruː'leɪ, ˌkreɪm-, ˌ-'--
crème caramel ˌkrem.kær.ə'mel, ˌkreɪm-, -'kær.ə.mel ⓤⓢ -ker.ə'mel, -kær-, -'ker.ə.mel, -'kær-
crème de la crème ˌkrem.də.lɑː'krem, ˌkreɪm-, -'kreɪm
crème de menthe ˌkrem.də'mɑ̃ːnθ, ˌkreɪm-, -'mɑːntθ, -'mɒntθ, -'mɒnt ⓤⓢ -'mɑːnt, -'mentθ
crème fraîche ˌkrem'freɪʃ, ˌkreɪm- ⓤⓢ -'freɪʃ, -'freʃ
Cremona krɪ'məʊ.nə, krə- ⓤⓢ -'moʊ-
Cremora® krɪ'mɔː.rə, krə-
crenate 'kriː.neɪt
crenel(l)|ate 'kren.ᵊl|.eɪt, -ɪ.l|eɪt ⓤⓢ -ə.l|eɪt **-ates** -eɪts **-ating** -eɪ.tɪŋ ⓤⓢ -eɪ.t̬ɪŋ **-ated** -eɪ.tɪd ⓤⓢ -eɪ.t̬ɪd
crenel(l)ation ˌkren.ᵊl'eɪ.ʃᵊn, -ɪ'leɪ- ⓤⓢ -ə'leɪ- **-s** -z
creole (C) 'kriː.əʊl, 'kreɪ-, -'- ⓤⓢ 'kriː.oʊl, -'- **-s** -z
Creolian kriː'əʊ.li.ən, kreɪ- ⓤⓢ -'oʊ-
Creon 'kriː.ən, -ɒn ⓤⓢ -ɑːn
creo|sote 'kriː.ə|.səʊt ⓤⓢ -soʊt **-sotes** -səʊts ⓤⓢ -soʊts **-soting** -səʊ.tɪŋ ⓤⓢ -soʊ.t̬ɪŋ **-soted** -səʊ.tɪd ⓤⓢ -soʊ.t̬ɪd
crepe kreɪp **-s** -s ˌ**crepe 'paper** ⓤⓢ '**crepe ˌpaper**
crêpe de chine ˌkreɪp.də'ʃiːn, ˌkrep-
crêpe(s) suzette ˌkrep.suː'zet, ˌkreɪp-
crepi|tate 'krep.ɪ|.teɪt **-tates** -teɪts **-tating** -teɪ.tɪŋ ⓤⓢ -teɪ.t̬ɪŋ **-tated** -teɪ.tɪd ⓤⓢ -teɪ.t̬ɪd
crepitation ˌkrep.ɪ'teɪ.ʃᵊn **-s** -z
crépon 'krep.ɔ̃ːŋ, 'kreɪ.pɔ̃ːŋ, -pɒn ⓤⓢ 'kreɪ.pɑːn
crept *(from* **creep)** krept
crepuscular krɪ'pʌs.kjə.ləʳ, krə-, krep'ʌs-, -kjʊ- ⓤⓢ -kjə.lɚ
crepuscule 'krep.ə.skjuːl ⓤⓢ krɪ'pʌs.kjuːl
crescendo krɪ'ʃen.dəʊ, krə- ⓤⓢ -doʊ **-s** -z
crescent *moon, shape:* 'kres.ᵊnt, 'krez- ⓤⓢ 'kres- **-s** -s
crescent *growing, when applied to objects other than the moon:* 'kres.ᵊnt
Crespigny *surname:* 'krep.ɪ.ni, 'krep.ni, 'kres.pɪ.ni *in London streets:* kres'pɪn.i
cress kres **-es** -ɪz
Cressida 'kres.ɪ.də
Cresson 'kres.ɔ̃ːŋ, -ɒn ⓤⓢ -ɑːn, -oʊn, -ɔ̃
Cresswell 'krez.wəl, -wel, 'kres- ⓤⓢ 'kres.wel, 'krez-, -wəl
Cressy 'kres.i
crest krest **-s** -s **-ing** -ɪŋ **-ed** -ɪd
Cresta 'kres.tə ˌ**Cresta 'Run**
crestfallen 'krestˌfɔː.lᵊn ⓤⓢ -ˌfɔː-, -ˌfɑː- **-ness** -nəs, -nɪs
Creswell 'kres.wəl, -wel, 'krez-
Creswick 'krez.ɪk ⓤⓢ 'kres.wɪk; 'krez.ɪk
cretaceous (C) krɪ'teɪ.ʃəs, krə-, kret'eɪ-, -ʃi.əs
Cretan 'kriː.tᵊn **-s** -z
Crete kriːt
Cretic 'kriː.tɪk ⓤⓢ -t̬ɪk **-s** -s
cretin 'kret.ɪn ⓤⓢ 'kriː.tᵊn **-s** -z
cretinism 'kret.ɪ.nɪ.zᵊm, -ᵊn.ɪ- ⓤⓢ 'kriː.tᵊn-
cretinous 'kret.ɪ.nəs, -ᵊn.əs ⓤⓢ 'kriː.tᵊn- **-ly** -li
cretonne kret'ɒn, krɪ'tɒn, krə-; 'kret.ɒn ⓤⓢ 'kriː.tɑːn, krɪ'tɑːn **-s** -z
Creusa kri'uː.zə ⓤⓢ -sə
Creuse krɜːz ⓤⓢ krɝːz
Creutzfeldt-Jacob ˌkrɔɪts.felt'jæk.ɒb ⓤⓢ -'jɑː.koʊb, -kɑːb ˌ**Creutzfeldt-'Jacob diˌsease**
crevass|e krɪ'væs, krə- ⓤⓢ krə- **-es** -ɪz **-ed** -t
Crèvecoeur krev'kɜːʳ ⓤⓢ -'kʊr
crevic|e 'krev.ɪs **-es** -ɪz
crew kruː **-s** -z **-ing** -ɪŋ **-ed** -d '**crew ˌcut**; ˌ**crew 'neck**, '**crew ˌneck**
Crewe kruː
crewel 'kruː.əl, -ɪl **-s** -z
Crewkerne 'kruː.kɜːn, 'krʊk.ən, kruː'kɜːn ⓤⓢ 'kruː.kɜːn
Crianlarich ˌkriː.ən'lær.ɪk, -ɪx ⓤⓢ -'ler.ɪk, -'lær-
crib krɪb **-s** -z **-bing** -ɪŋ **-bed** -d **-ber/s** -əʳ/z ⓤⓢ -ɚ/z '**crib ˌdeath**
cribbage 'krɪb.ɪdʒ
Cribbins 'krɪb.ɪnz
Criccieth 'krɪk.i.eθ, -əθ
Crich kraɪtʃ
Crichel 'krɪtʃ.ᵊl
Crichton 'kraɪ.tᵊn
crick (C) krɪk **-s** -s **-ing** -ɪŋ **-ed** -t
crick|et 'krɪk|.ɪt **-ets** -ɪts **-eter/s** -ɪ.təʳ/z ⓤⓢ -ɪ.t̬ɚ/z **-eting** -ɪ.tɪŋ ⓤⓢ -ɪ.t̬ɪŋ
Crickhowell krɪk'haʊəl, -'haʊl
cricoid 'kraɪ.kɔɪd
cri(s) de coeur ˌkriː.də'kɜːʳ ⓤⓢ -'kɝː
cried *(from* **cry)** kraɪd
Crieff kriːf
crier 'kraɪ.əʳ ⓤⓢ -ɚ **-s** -z
cries *(from* **cry)** kraɪz
crikey 'kraɪ.ki
crime kraɪm **-s** -z ˌ**crime of 'passion**
Crime|a kraɪ'miː|.ə **-an** -ən
crimen falsi ˌkrɪm.en'fæl.si
crime(s) passionel(s) ˌkriːm.pæs.i.ə'nel, -pæʃ.ə'-
Crimewatch 'kraɪm.wɒtʃ ⓤⓢ -wɑːtʃ, -wɔːtʃ
criminal 'krɪm.ɪ.nᵊl, '-ə- **-s** -z **-ly** -li ˌ**criminal 'damage**; ˌ**criminal 'law**, ⓤⓢ '**criminal ˌlaw**
criminality ˌkrɪm.ɪ'næl.ə.ti, -ə'-, -ɪ.ti ⓤⓢ -ə'næl.ə.t̬i
criminalization, -isa- ˌkrɪm.ɪ.nᵊl.aɪ'zeɪ.ʃᵊn, -ɪ'- ⓤⓢ -ɪ'-
criminaliz|e, -is|e 'krɪm.ɪ.nᵊl.aɪz ⓤⓢ -nə.laɪz **-es** -ɪz **-ing** -ɪŋ **-ed** -d
crimi|nate 'krɪm.ɪ|.neɪt, '-ə- **-nates** -neɪts **-nating** -neɪ.tɪŋ ⓤⓢ -neɪ.t̬ɪŋ **-nated** -neɪ.tɪd ⓤⓢ -neɪ.t̬ɪd
crimination ˌkrɪm.ɪ'neɪ.ʃᵊn, -ə'- **-s** -z
criminolog|y ˌkrɪm.ɪ'nɒl.ə.dʒ|i, -ə'- ⓤⓢ -'nɑː.lə- **-ist/s** -ɪst/s
crimp krɪmp **-s** -s **-ing** -ɪŋ **-ed** -t
Crimplene® 'krɪm.pliːn
crimson 'krɪm.zᵊn **-s** -z **-ing** -ɪŋ **-ed** -d
cring|e krɪndʒ **-es** -ɪz **-ing** -ɪŋ **-ed** -d **-er/s** -əʳ/z ⓤⓢ -ɚ/z
crinkl|e 'krɪŋ.kl̩ **-es** -z **-ing** -ɪŋ, '-klɪŋ **-ed** -d
crinkly 'krɪŋ.kli
crinoid 'kraɪ.nɔɪd, 'krɪn.ɔɪd **-s** -z
crinoline 'krɪn.ᵊl.ɪn **-s** -z
cripes kraɪps
Crippen 'krɪp.ɪn, -ᵊn
crippl|e 'krɪp.l̩ **-es** -z **-ing** -ɪŋ, '-lɪŋ **-ed**
Cripplegate 'krɪp.l̩.geɪt
Cripps krɪps
Crisco® 'krɪs.kəʊ ⓤⓢ -koʊ
Criseyde krɪ'seɪ.də
cris|is 'kraɪ.s|ɪs **-es** -iːz '**crisis ˌmanagement**
crisp (C) krɪsp **-er** -əʳ ⓤⓢ -ɚ **-est** -ɪst, **-s** -s **-ly** -li **-ness** -nəs, -nɪs
crispbread 'krɪsp.bred **-s** -z
Crispian 'krɪs.pi.ən
Crispin 'krɪs.pɪn
crisp|y 'krɪs.p|i **-ier** -i.əʳ ⓤⓢ -i.ɚ **-iest** -i.ɪst, -i.əst **-ily** -ɪ.li, -ᵊl.i **-iness** -ɪ.nəs, -ɪ.nɪs
crisscross 'krɪs.krɒs ⓤⓢ -krɑːs **-es** -ɪz **-ing** -ɪŋ **-ed** -t
Cristina krɪ'stiː.nə
crit krɪt **-s** -s
Critchley 'krɪtʃ.li

criteri|on (C) kraɪˈtɪə.ri|.ən (US) -ˈtɪr.i- -ons -ənz -a -ə

critic ˈkrɪt.ɪk (US) ˈkrɪt̬- -s -s

critic|al ˈkrɪt.ɪ.k|əl (US) ˈkrɪt̬- -ally -əl.i, -li -alness -əl.nəs, -nɪs

criticism ˈkrɪt.ɪ.sɪ.zəm, ˈ-ə- (US) ˈkrɪt̬- -s -z

criticizable, -isa- ˈkrɪt.ɪ.saɪ.zə.bl̩, ˈ-ə-, ˌkrɪt.ɪˈsaɪ-, -əˈ- (US) ˈkrɪt̬.ɪ.saɪ-

criticiz|e, -is|e ˈkrɪt.ɪ.saɪz, ˈ-ə- (US) ˈkrɪt̬- -es -ɪz -ing -ɪŋ -ed -d

critique krɪˈtiːk, krə- -s -s

Crittenden ˈkrɪt.ən.dən

critter ˈkrɪt.əʳ (US) ˈkrɪt̬.ɚ -s -z

crittur ˈkrɪt.əʳ (US) ˈkrɪt̬.ɚ -s -z

croak krəʊk (US) kroʊk -s -s -ing/s -ɪŋ/z -ed -t -er/s -əʳ/z (US) -ɚ/z

croak|y ˈkrəʊ.k|i (US) ˈkroʊ- -ier -i.əʳ (US) -i.ɚ -iest -i.ɪst, -i.əst -ily -ɪ.li, -əl.i -iness -ɪ.nəs, -ɪ.nɪs

Croat ˈkrəʊ.æt, -ət (US) ˈkroʊ- -s -s

Croatia krəʊˈeɪ.ʃə (US) kroʊ-

Croatian krəʊˈeɪ.ʃən (US) kroʊ- -s -z

croc krɒk (US) krɑːk -s -s

crochet ˈkrəʊ.ʃeɪ, -ʃi (US) kroʊˈʃeɪ -s -z -ing -ɪŋ -ed -d ˈcrochet ˌhook (US) croˈchet ˌhook

crock krɒk (US) krɑːk -s -s

Crocker ˈkrɒk.əʳ (US) ˈkrɑː.kɚ

crockery ˈkrɒk.ər.i (US) ˈkrɑː.kɚ-

crocket ˈkrɒk.ɪt (US) ˈkrɑː.kɪt -s -s

Crockett ˈkrɒk.ɪt (US) ˈkrɑː.kɪt

Crockford ˈkrɒk.fəd (US) ˈkrɑːk.fɚd

Crockpot® ˈkrɒk.pɒt (US) ˈkrɑːk.pɑːt

crocodile ˈkrɒk.ə.daɪl (US) ˈkrɑː.kə- -s -z ˌcrocodile ˈtears (US) ˈcrocodile ˌtears

crocodilian ˌkrɒk.əˈdɪl.i.ən (US) ˌkrɑː.kəˈdɪl.jən -s -z

crocus ˈkrəʊ.kəs (US) ˈkroʊ- -es -ɪz

Croesus ˈkriː.səs

croft (C) krɒft (US) krɑːft -s -s

crofter ˈkrɒf.təʳ (US) ˈkrɑːf.tɚ -s -z

Crofton ˈkrɒf.tən (US) ˈkrɑːf-

Crohn krəʊn (US) kroʊn ˈCrohn's diˌsease

croissant ˈkwæs.ɑ̃ːŋ, ˈkrwæs-, -ɒnt (US) kwɑːˈsɑ̃ː, krə-, krwɑː-, -ˈsɑːnt -s -z

Croker ˈkrəʊ.kəʳ (US) ˈkroʊ.kɚ

Cro-Magnon ˌkrəʊˈmæn.jɔ̃ːŋ, -jən, -ˈmæg.nən, -nɒn (US) kroʊˈmæg.nən, -nɑːn, -ˈmæn.jən, -jɑːn

Cromarty ˈkrɒm.ə.ti (US) ˈkrɑː.mɚ.t̬i

Crombie ˈkrɒm.bi, ˈkrʌm- (US) ˈkrɑːm-, ˈkrʌm-

Crome krəʊm (US) kroʊm

Cromer ˈkrəʊ.məʳ (US) ˈkroʊ.mɚ

cromlech ˈkrɒm.lek (US) ˈkrɑːm- -s -s

Crommelin ˈkrʌm.lɪn, ˈkrɒm- (US) ˈkrɑːm-, ˈkrʌm-

Crompton ˈkrʌmp.tən, ˈkrɒmp- (US) ˈkrɑːmp-

Cromwell ˈkrɒm.wəl, ˈkrʌm-, -wel (US) ˈkrɑːm-

Cromwellian krɒmˈwel.i.ən, krʌm- (US) krɑːm-

crone krəʊn (US) kroʊn -s -z

Cronin ˈkrəʊ.nɪn (US) ˈkroʊ-

Cronkite ˈkrɒŋ.kaɪt (US) ˈkrɑːn.kaɪt, ˈkrɑːŋ-

Cronos ˈkrəʊ.nɒs (US) ˈkroʊ.nɑːs

cron|y ˈkrəʊ.n|i (US) ˈkroʊ- -ies -iz

cronyism ˈkrəʊ.ni.ɪ.zəm (US) ˈkroʊ-

crook (C) krʊk -s -s -ing -ɪŋ -ed -t by ˌhook or by ˈcrook

Crookback ˈkrʊk.bæk

crookbacked ˈkrʊk.bækt

Crooke krʊk -s -s

crooked *not straight:* ˈkrʊk.ɪd -er -əʳ (US) -ɚ -est -ɪst, -əst -ly -li -ness -nəs, -nɪs

crooked *having a crook:* krʊkt

Croome kruːm

croon kruːn -s -z -ing -ɪŋ -ed -d -er/s -əʳ/z (US) -ɚ/z

crop krɒp (US) krɑːp -s -s -ping -ɪŋ -ped -t

cropper ˈkrɒp.əʳ (US) ˈkrɑː.pɚ -s -z

croquet ˈkrəʊ.keɪ, -ki (US) kroʊˈkeɪ -s -z -ing -ɪŋ -ed -d

croquette krɒkˈet, krəʊˈket (US) kroʊˈket -s -s

crore krɔːʳ (US) krɔːr -s -z

Crosby ˈkrɒz.bi, ˈkrɒs- (US) ˈkrɑːz-

Crosfield ˈkrɒs.fiːld (US) ˈkrɑːs-

Croshaw ˈkrəʊ.ʃɔː (US) ˈkroʊ.ʃɑː, -ʃɔː

crosier (C) ˈkrəʊ.zi.əʳ, -ʒəʳ (US) ˈkroʊ.ʒɚ -s -z

cross- krɒs- (US) krɑːs-

cross (C) krɒs (US) krɑːs -es -ɪz -er -əʳ (US) -ɚ -est -ɪst, -əst -ly -li -ness -nəs, -nɪs -ing -ɪŋ -ed -t ˈcross ˌaction; ˈcross ˌbench

crossbar ˈkrɒs.bɑːʳ (US) ˈkrɑːs.bɑːr -s -z

crossbeam ˈkrɒs.biːm (US) ˈkrɑːs- -s -z

crossbencher ˈkrɒsˌben.tʃəʳ, ˌ-ˈ-- (US) ˈkrɑːsˌben.tʃɚ -s -z

crossbill ˈkrɒs.bɪl (US) ˈkrɑːs- -s -z

crossbones ˈkrɒs.bəʊnz (US) ˈkrɑːs.boʊnz

cross-border ˌkrɒsˈbɔː.dəʳ (US) ˌkrɑːsˈbɔːr.dɚ *stress shift:* ˌcross-boarder ˈtalks

crossbow ˈkrɒs.bəʊ (US) ˈkrɑːs.boʊ -s -z

crossbred ˈkrɒs.bred (US) ˈkrɑːs-

crossbreed ˈkrɒs.briːd (US) ˈkrɑːs- -s -z -ing -ɪŋ

cross-Channel ˌkrɒsˈtʃæn.əl (US) ˌkrɑːs- *stress shift:* ˌcross-Channel ˈferry

crosscheck (*n.*) ˈkrɒs.tʃek (US) ˈkrɑːs-

crosscheck (*v.*) ˌkrɒsˈtʃek, ˈ-- (US) ˈkrɑːs.tʃek -s -s -ing -ɪŋ -ed -t

cross-claim ˈkrɒs.kleɪm (US) ˈkrɑːs- -s -z

cross-country ˌkrɒsˈkʌn.tri (US) ˌkrɑːs- *stress shift:* ˌcross-country ˈrunner

crosscourt ˈkrɒs.kɔːt (US) ˈkrɑːs.kɔːrt

cross-cultural ˌkrɒsˈkʌl.tʃə.rəl (US) ˌkrɑːsˈkʌl.tʃɚ.əl -ly -li

crosscut ˈkrɒs.kʌt, ˌ-ˈ- (US) ˈkrɑːs.kʌt -s -s

cross-dress|ing ˌkrɒsˈdres|.ɪŋ (US) ˌkrɑːs- -er/s -əʳ/z (US) -ɚ/z

Crosse krɒs (US) krɑːs

cross-examination ˌkrɒs.ɪgˌzæm.ɪˈneɪ.ʃən, -egˌ-, -ɪkˌsæm-, -ekˌ-, -əˈ- (US) ˌkrɑːs.ɪgˌzæm-, -egˌ- -s -z

cross-examin|e ˌkrɒs.ɪgˈzæm.ɪn, -egˈ-, -ɪkˈsæm-, -ekˈ- (US) ˌkrɑːs.ɪgˈzæm-, -egˈ- -es -z -ing -ɪŋ -ed -d -er/s -əʳ/z (US) -ɚ/z

cross-eyed ˌkrɒsˈaɪd, ˈ-- (US) ˈkrɑːsˌaɪd *stress shift, British only:* ˌcross-eyed ˈstare

cross-fertilization, -isa- ˌkrɒsˌfɜː.tɪ.laɪˈzeɪ.ʃən, -tə-, -lɪˈ-, -ləˈ- (US) ˌkrɑːsˌfɝː.t̬əl.ɪˈ-

cross-fertiliz|e, -is|e ˌkrɒsˈfɜː.tɪ.laɪz, -tə- (US) ˌkrɑːsˈfɝː.t̬ə- -es -ɪz -ing -ɪŋ -ed -d

cross-fire ˈkrɒs.faɪəʳ (US) ˈkrɑːs.faɪɚ

cross-grained ˌkrɒsˈgreɪnd (US) ˌkrɑːs-, ˈ-ˌ- *stress shift:* ˌcross-grained ˈcutting

crosshatch ˈkrɒs.hætʃ (US) ˈkrɑːs- -es -ɪz -ing -ɪŋ -ed -t

crossing ˈkrɒs.ɪŋ (US) ˈkrɑː.sɪŋ -s -z

cross-legged ˌkrɒsˈlegd, ˈ--; -əd (US) ˌkrɑːsˈleg.əd, -ˈlegd

Crossley ˈkrɒs.li (US) ˈkrɑː.sli

Crossman ˈkrɒs.mən (US) ˈkrɑːs-

crossover ˈkrɒsˌəʊ.vəʳ (US) ˈkrɑːsˌoʊ.vɚ -s -z

cross-party ˌkrɒsˈpɑː.ti (US) ˌkrɑːsˈpɑːr.t̬i *stress shift:* ˌcross-party ˈquestions

crosspatch ˈkrɒs.pætʃ (US) ˈkrɑːs- -es -ɪz

cross-purpos|e ˌkrɒsˈpɜː.pəs (US) ˌkrɑːsˈpɝː-, ˈ-ˌ-- -es -ɪz

cross-question ˌkrɒsˈkwes.tʃən, -ˈkweʃ- (US) ˌkrɑːs-, ˈ-ˌ-- -s -z -ing -ɪŋ -ed -d

cross-refer ˌkrɒs.rɪˈfɜːʳ, -rəˈ- (US) ˌkrɑːs.rəˈfɝː -s -z -ring -ɪŋ -red -d

cross-referenc|e ˌkrɒsˈref.ər.ənts, ˈ-rənts (US) ˌkrɑːs-, ˈkrɑːsˌref.ɚ.ənts, ˌ-rənts -es -ɪz

crossroad ˈkrɒs.rəʊd (US) ˈkrɑːs.roʊd -s -z

cross-section ˈkrɒs.sek.ʃən, ˌ-ˈ-- (US) ˈkrɑːs.sek- -s -z

cross-stitch ˈkrɒs.stɪtʃ (US) ˈkrɑːs-

crosswalk ˈkrɒs.wɔːk (US) ˈkrɑːs.wɑːk, -wɔːk -s -s

crossway ˈkrɒs.weɪ (US) ˈkrɑːs- -s -z

crosswind ˈkrɒs.wɪnd (US) ˈkrɑːs- -s -z

crosswise ˈkrɒs.waɪz (US) ˈkrɑːs-

crossword 'krɒs.wɜːd (US) 'krɑːs.wɝːd **-s** -z **'crossword ˌpuzzle**
Crosthwaite 'krɒs.θweɪt (US) 'krɑːs-
crotch (C) krɒtʃ (US) krɑːtʃ **-es** -ɪz
crotch|et (C) 'krɒtʃ|.ɪt, -ət (US) 'krɑː.tʃ|ət **-ets** -ɪts, -əts (US) -əts
crotchet|y 'krɒtʃ.ɪ.t|i, -ə.t|i (US) 'krɑː.tʃə.ţ|i **-iness** -ɪ.nəs, -ɪ.nɪs
Crothers 'krʌð.əz (US) -ɚz
croton (C) 'krəʊ.t^{ə}n (US) 'kroʊ-
crouch (C) (*v.*) kraʊtʃ **-es** -ɪz **-ing** -ɪŋ **-ed** -t
Crouch *village in Kent:* kruːtʃ
Crouchback 'kraʊtʃ.bæk
croup kruːp **-s** -s
croupier 'kruː.pi.ə^{r}, -eɪ (US) -eɪ, -ɚ **-s** -z
croustade kruː'stɑːd **-s** -z
crouton 'kruː.tɒn, -tɔ̃ːŋ (US) 'kruː.tɑːn, -'- **-s** -z
crow (C) krəʊ (US) kroʊ **-s** -z **-ing** -ɪŋ **-ed** -d **crew** kruː **'crow's ˌnest, ˌcrow's 'nest; as the ˌcrow 'flies**
crowbar 'krəʊ.bɑː^{r} (US) 'kroʊ.bɑːr **-s** -z
Crowborough 'krəʊ.b^{ə}r.ə (US) 'kroʊ.bɚ.oʊ
crowd kraʊd **-s** -z **-ing** -ɪŋ **-ed** -ɪd
Crowe krəʊ (US) kroʊ
crow|foot 'krəʊ|.fʊt (US) 'kroʊ- **-foots** -fʊts **-feet** -fiːt
Crowhurst 'krəʊ.hɜːst (US) 'kroʊ.hɝːst
Crowland 'krəʊ.lənd (US) 'kroʊ-
Crowley 'krəʊ.li, 'kraʊ- (US) 'kroʊ-, 'kraʊ-
crown kraʊn **-s** -z **-ing** -ɪŋ **-ed** -d **ˌCrown 'Court; ˌcrown 'glass; ˌcrown 'jewels; ˌcrown 'land; ˌcrown 'prince**
Crowndale 'kraʊn.deɪl
crow's|-foot 'krəʊz|.fʊt (US) 'kroʊz- **-feet** -fiːt
Crowther 'kraʊ.ðə^{r} (US) -ðɚ
Crowthorne 'krəʊ.θɔːn (US) 'kroʊ.θɔːrn
Croxteth 'krɒk.stəθ (US) 'krɑːk-
Croyden, Croydon 'krɔɪ.d^{ə}n
crozier (C) 'krəʊ.zi.ə^{r}, -ʒə^{r} (US) 'kroʊ.ʒɚ **-s** -z
CRT ˌsiː.ɑː'tiː (US) -ɑːr'-
cru kruː
crucial 'kruː.ʃ^{ə}l **-ly** -i
crucible 'kruː.sɪ.bl̩, -sə- **-s** -z
crucifer 'kruː.sɪ.fə^{r}, -sə- (US) -fɚ **-s** -z
cruciferous kruː'sɪ.f^{ə}r.əs
crucifix 'kruː.sɪ.fɪks, -sə- **-es** -ɪz
crucifixion (C) ˌkruː.sə'fɪk.ʃ^{ə}n, -sɪ'- **-s** -z
cruciform 'kruː.sɪ.fɔːm, -sə- (US) -fɔːrm
cruci|fy 'kruː.sɪ|.faɪ, -sə- **-fies** -faɪz **-fying** -faɪ.ɪŋ **-fied** -faɪd **-fier/s** -faɪ.ə^{r}/z (US) -faɪ.ɚ/z
crud krʌd **-s** -z **-ding** -ɪŋ **-ded** -ɪd
crudd|y 'krʌd|.i **-ier** -i.ə^{r} (US) -i.ɚ **-iest** -i.ɪst, -i.əst
crud|e kruːd **-er** -ə^{r} (US) -ɚ **-est** -ɪst, -əst **-ely** -li **-eness** -nəs, -nɪs

Cruden 'kruː.d^{ə}n
crudité(s) 'kruː.dɪ.teɪ, -də- (US) ˌkruː.dɪ'teɪ
crudit|y 'kruː.də.t|i, -dɪ.t|i (US) -də.ţ|i **-ies** -iz
cruel 'kruː.əl, krʊəl (US) 'kruː.əl **-(l)er** -ə^{r} (US) -ɚ **-(l)est** -ɪst, -əst **-(l)y** -li **-ness** -nəs, -nɪs
cruelt|y 'kruː.əl.t|i, 'krʊəl- (US) 'kruː.əl.ţ|i **-ies** -iz
cruet 'kruː.ɪt **-s** -s
Cruft krʌft **-s** -s
Crui(c)kshank 'krʊk.ʃæŋk
cruis|e (C) kruːz **-es** -ɪz **-ing** -ɪŋ **-ed** -d **-er/s** -ə^{r}/z (US) -ɚ/z **'cruise conˌtrol; ˌcruise 'missile** (US) **'cruise ˌmissile**
cruiserweight 'kruː.zə.weɪt (US) -zɚ- **-s** -s
cruller 'krʌl.ə^{r} (US) -ɚ **-s** -z
crumb krʌm **-s** -z **-ing** -ɪŋ **-ed** -d
crumbl|e 'krʌm.bl̩ **-es** -z **-ing** -ɪŋ, '-blɪŋ **-ed** -d
crumbl|y 'krʌm.bl|i, -bl̩|.i **-ier** -i.ə^{r} (US) -i.ɚ **-iest** -i.ɪst, -i.əst
crumby 'krʌm.i
crumhorn 'krʌm.hɔːn (US) -hɔːrn **-s** -z
Crumlin 'krʌm.lɪn
Crummock 'krʌm.ək
crumm|y 'krʌm|.i **-ier** -i.ə^{r} (US) -i.ɚ **-iest** -i.ɪst
crump (C) krʌmp **-s** -s **-ing** -ɪŋ **-ed** -t
crumpet 'krʌm.pɪt **-s** -s
crumpl|e 'krʌm.pl̩ **-es** -z **-ing** -ɪŋ, '-plɪŋ **-ed** -d
crunch krʌntʃ **-es** -ɪz **-ing** -ɪŋ **-ed** -t
Crunchie® 'krʌn.tʃi
crunch|y 'krʌn.tʃ|i **-ier** -i.ə^{r} (US) -i.ɚ **-iest** -i.ɪst, -i.əst **-iness** -ɪ.nəs, -ɪ.nɪs
Crundale 'krʌn.d^{ə}l (US) -deɪl
crupper 'krʌp.ə^{r} (US) -ɚ **-s** -z
crusad|e (C) kruː'seɪd **-es** -z **-ing** -ɪŋ **-ed** -ɪd
crusader kruː'seɪ.də^{r} (US) -dɚ **-s** -z
crus|e kruːz **-es** -ɪz
crush krʌʃ **-es** -ɪz **-ing** -ɪŋ **-ed** -t **-er/s** -ə^{r}/z (US) -ɚ/z **-able** -ə.bl̩
Crusoe 'kruː.səʊ (US) -soʊ
crust krʌst **-s** -s
crustace|an krʌs'teɪ.ʃ|^{ə}n, -ʃi|.ən **-a** -ə **-ans** -ənz
crustaceous krʌs'teɪ.ʃəs, -ʃi.əs
crustate 'krʌs.teɪt
crustated krʌs'teɪ.tɪd (US) -ţɪd
crustation krʌs'teɪ.ʃ^{ə}n **-s** -z
crusted 'krʌs.tɪd
crust|y 'krʌs.t|i **-ier** -i.ə^{r} (US) -i.ɚ **-iest** -i.ɪst, -i.əst **-ily** -ɪ.li, -^{ə}l.i **-iness** -ɪ.nəs, -ɪ.nɪs
crutch krʌtʃ **-es** -ɪz **-ed** -t
Crutched Friars ˌkrʌtʃt'fraɪəz, ˌkrʌtʃ.ɪd'- (US) -'fraɪɚz
Cruttwell 'krʌt.wəl, -wel

crux krʌks **-es** -ɪz
Cruyff kraɪf, krɔɪf (US) krɔɪf
Cruz kruːz
cruzado kruː'zɑː.dəʊ (US) -doʊ, -'zeɪ- **-(e)s** -z
cruzeiro kruː'zeə.rəʊ (US) -'zer.oʊ **-s** -z
cr|y kr|aɪ **-ies** -aɪz **-ying** -aɪ.ɪŋ **-ied** -aɪd
cry-bab|y 'kraɪˌbeɪ.b|i **-ies** -iz
cryo- ˌkraɪ.əʊ- (US) ˌkraɪ.oʊ-, -ə-
cryogenic ˌkraɪ.əʊ'dʒen.ɪk (US) -ə'- **-s** -s
cryonic kraɪ'ɒn.ɪk (US) -'ɑː.nɪk **-s** -s
crypt- krɪpt-
crypt krɪpt **-s** -s
cryptic 'krɪp.tɪk **-al** -^{ə}l **-ally** -^{ə}l.i, -li
crypto 'krɪp.təʊ (US) -toʊ **-s** -z
cryptogam 'krɪp.təʊ.gæm (US) -tə- **-s** -z
cryptogram 'krɪp.təʊ.græm (US) -tə- **-s** -z **-ic** -ɪk
cryptograph 'krɪp.təʊ.grɑːf, -græf (US) -tə.græf **-s** -s
cryptographer krɪp'tɒg.rə.fə^{r} (US) -'tɑː.grə.fɚ **-s** -z
cryptography krɪp'tɒg.rə.fi (US) -'tɑː.grə-
cryptolog|y krɪp'tɒl.ə.dʒ|i (US) -'tɑː.lə- **-ist/s** -ɪst/s
crystal (C) 'krɪs.t^{ə}l **-s** -z **ˌcrystal 'ball; 'crystal ˌgazing**
crystalizable, -isa- 'krɪs.t^{ə}l.aɪ.zə.bl̩ (US) -tə.laɪ-
crystalline 'krɪs.t^{ə}l.aɪn (US) -tə.laɪn
crystallization, -isa- ˌkrɪs.t^{ə}l.aɪ'zeɪ.ʃ^{ə}n, -ɪ'- (US) -ɪ'- **-s** -z
crystalliz|e, -is|e 'krɪs.t^{ə}l.aɪz (US) -tə.laɪz **-es** -ɪz **-ing** -ɪŋ **-ed** -d
crystallographer ˌkrɪs.t^{ə}l'ɒg.rə.fə^{r} (US) -tə'lɑː.grə.fɚ **-s** -z
crystallography krɪs.t^{ə}l'ɒg.rə.fi (US) -tə'lɑː.grə-
crystalloid 'krɪs.t^{ə}l.ɔɪd (US) -tə.lɔɪd **-s** -
CSE ˌsiː.es'iː
C-section 'siːˌsek.ʃ^{ə}n **-s** -z
ct (*abbrev. for* **carat**) 'kær.ət (US) 'ker-, 'kær-
cub kʌb **-s** -z **-bing** -ɪŋ **-bed** -d
Cub|a 'kjuː.b|ə **-an/s** -ən/z **ˌCuban 'he**
cubage 'kjuː.bɪdʒ
cubb|y 'kʌb|.i **-ies** -iz
cubbyhole 'kʌb.i.həʊl (US) -hoʊl **-s** -z
cub|e kjuːb **-es** -z **-ing** -ɪŋ **-ed** -d
cubic 'kjuː.bɪk **-al** -^{ə}l **-ally** -^{ə}l.i, -li
cubicle 'kjuː.bɪ.kl̩ **-s** -z
cub|ism 'kjuː.b|ɪ.z^{ə}m **-ist/s** -ɪst/s
cubistic kjuː'bɪs.tɪk
cu|bit 'kjuː|.bɪt **-bits** -bɪts **-bital** -bɪ.t^{ə}l (US) -bɪ.ţ^{ə}l
Cubitt 'kjuː.bɪt
cuboid 'kjuː.bɔɪd **-s** -z
cuchul(l)inn, cuchulain (C) kuː'kʊl.ɪn, -'xʊl- (US) -'kʊl-
Cuckfield 'kʊk.fiːld
Cuckmere 'kʊk.mɪə^{r} (US) -mɪr

cuckold ˈkʌk.əʊld, -ᵊld ⓤⓢ -oʊld, -ᵊld **-s** -z **-ing** -ɪŋ **-ed** -ɪd **-er/s** -əʳ/z ⓤⓢ -ɚ/z **-ry** -ri
cuckoo ˈkʊk.uː ⓤⓢ ˈkuː.kuː, ˈkʊk.uː **-s** -z **-ing** -ɪŋ **-ed** -d ˈ**cuckoo** ˌ**clock**; ˈ**cuckoo** ˌ**spit**
cuckooflower ˈkʊk.uː.flaʊəʳ ⓤⓢ ˈkuː.kuː.flaʊɚ, ˈkʊk.uːˌ- **-s** -z
cuckoopint ˈkʊk.uː.paɪnt ⓤⓢ ˈkuː.kuː-, ˈkʊk.uː **-s** -s
cucumber ˈkjuː.kʌm.bəʳ ⓤⓢ -bɚ **-s** -z
cud kʌd **-s** -z
cuddl|e ˈkʌd.l̩ **-es** -z **-ing** -ɪŋ, ˈ-lɪŋ **-ed** -d **-y** -i
cudd|y ˈkʌd|.i **-ies** -iz
cudgel ˈkʌdʒ.ᵊl **-s** -z **-(l)ing** -ɪŋ **-(l)ed** -d
Cudworth ˈkʌd.wəθ, -wɜːθ ⓤⓢ -wɚθ, -wɝːθ
cu|e kjuː **-es** -z **-ing** -ɪŋ **-ed** -d
Cuenca ˈkweŋ.kɑː, -kə
Cuernavaca ˌkweə.nəˈvæk.ə ⓤⓢ ˌkwer.nəˈvɑː.kə, -nɑːˈvɑː.kɑː
cuff kʌf **-s** -s **-ing** -ɪŋ **-ed** -t
Cuffley ˈkʌf.li
cufflink ˈkʌf.lɪŋk **-s** -s
cui bono ˌkuː.iˈbəʊn.əʊ, ˌkwiː-, -ˈbɒn.əʊ ⓤⓢ ˌkwiːˈboʊ.noʊ
cuirass kwɪˈræs, kjuᵊ- ⓤⓢ kwɪˈræs **-es** -ɪz
cuirassier ˌkwɪ.rəˈsi.əʳ, ˌkjuᵊ.rəˈ- ⓤⓢ ˌkwiː.rəˈsɪr, ˈkwɪr.ə.sɪr **-s** -z
cuisenaire ˌkwiː.zᵊnˈeəʳ ⓤⓢ -er
Cuisinart® ˈkwiː.zᵊn.ɑːt ⓤⓢ -ɑːrt
cuisine kwɪzˈiːn, kwəˈziːn
cuisine minceur kwɪˌziːn.mæ̃nˈsɜːʳ, kwə- ⓤⓢ -ˈsɝː
cuiss|e kwɪs **-es** -ɪz
cuke kjuːk **-s** -s
Culcheth ˈkʌl.tʃəθ, -tʃɪθ
cul-de-sac ˈkʌl.də.sæk, ˈkʊl-, ˌ--ˈ- **-s** -s
Culham ˈkʌl.əm
culinary ˈkʌl.ɪ.nᵊr.i, ˈ-ə-, ˈkjuː.lɪ- ⓤⓢ ˈkʌl.ə.ner-
Culkin ˈkʌl.kɪn
cull kʌl **-s** -z **-ing** -ɪŋ **-ed** -d
Cullen ˈkʌl.ən, -ɪn
cullender ˈkʌl.ən.dəʳ, -ɪn- ⓤⓢ -dɚ **-s** -z
Culley ˈkʌl.i
Cullinan ˈkʌl.ɪ.nən, ˈ-ə-, -næn
Culloden kəˈlɒd.ᵊn, kʌlˈɒd-; kəˈləʊ.dᵊn ⓤⓢ kəˈloʊ.dᵊn, -ˈlɑː-
Cullompton kəˈlʌmp.tᵊn, ˈkʌl.əmp-
Cullum ˈkʌl.əm
culm (C) kʌlm **-s** -z
Culme kʌlm
culmi|nate ˈkʌl.mɪ|.neɪt **-nates** -neɪts **-nating** -neɪ.tɪŋ ⓤⓢ -neɪ.t̬ɪŋ **-nated** -neɪ.tɪd ⓤⓢ -neɪ.t̬ɪd
culmination ˌkʌl.mɪˈneɪ.ʃᵊn, -məˈ- **-s** -z
culottes kjuːˈlɒts, kuː- ⓤⓢ ˈkuː.lɑːts, ˈkjuː-, -ˈ-
culpability ˌkʌl.pəˈbɪl.ə.ti, -ɪ.ti ⓤⓢ -ə.t̬i
culpab|le ˈkʌl.pə.b|l̩ **-ly** -li **-leness** -l̩.nəs, -nɪs
culprit ˈkʌl.prɪt **-s** -s
Culross *Scottish surname & place:* ˈkuː.rɒs, -rəs ⓤⓢ -rɑːs
Culross *English surname and London street:* ˈkʌl.rɒs, -ˈ- ⓤⓢ ˈkʌl.rɑːs, -ˈ-
cult kʌlt **-s** -s
Culter ˈkuː.təʳ ⓤⓢ -t̬ɚ
cultivable ˈkʌl.tɪ.və.bl̩, -tə- ⓤⓢ -t̬ə-
culti|vate ˈkʌl.tɪ|.veɪt, -tə- ⓤⓢ -t̬ə- **-vates** -veɪts **-vating** -veɪ.tɪŋ ⓤⓢ -veɪ.t̬ɪŋ **-vated** -veɪ.tɪd ⓤⓢ -veɪ.t̬ɪd **-vatable** -veɪ.tə.bl̩ ⓤⓢ -veɪ.t̬ə-
cultivation ˌkʌl.tɪˈveɪ.ʃᵊn, -təˈ- ⓤⓢ -t̬əˈ-
cultivator ˈkʌl.tɪ.veɪ.təʳ, -tə- ⓤⓢ -t̬ə.veɪ.t̬ɚ **-s** -z
Cults kʌlts
cultural ˈkʌl.tʃᵊr.ᵊl **-ly** -i
culturality ˌkʌl.tʃᵊrˈæl.ɪ.ti, -ə.ti ⓤⓢ -tʃəˈræl.ə.t̬i
culture ˈkʌl.tʃəʳ ⓤⓢ -tʃɚ **-s** -z **-d** -d ˈ**culture** ˌ**shock**
culver (C) ˈkʌl.vəʳ ⓤⓢ -vɚ **-s** -z
culverin ˈkʌl.vᵊr.ɪn **-s** -z
culvert ˈkʌl.vət ⓤⓢ -vɚt **-s** -s **-age** -ɪdʒ ⓤⓢ ˈkʌl.vɚ.t̬ɪdʒ
Culzean kəˈleɪn
cum kʌm, kʊm
Cumaean kjuːˈmiː.ən
cumbent ˈkʌm.bᵊnt
cumb|er ˈkʌm.b|əʳ ⓤⓢ -b|ɚ **-ers** -əz ⓤⓢ -ɚz **-ering** -ᵊr.ɪŋ **-ered** -əd ⓤⓢ -ɚd **-erer/s** -ᵊr.əʳ/z ⓤⓢ -ɚ.ɚ/z
Cumberland ˈkʌm.bᵊl.ənd ⓤⓢ -bɚ.lənd
Cumbernauld ˌkʌm.bəˈnɔːld, ˈ--- ⓤⓢ ˌkʌm.bɚˈnɑːld, -ˈnɔːld
cumbersome ˈkʌm.bə.səm ⓤⓢ -bɚ- **-ly** -li **-ness** -nəs, -nɪs
Cumbri|a ˈkʌm.bri|.ə **-an/s** -ən/z
cumbrous ˈkʌmb.rəs **-ly** -li **-ness** -nəs, -nɪs
cumin ˈkjuː.mɪn, ˈkʌm.ɪn ⓤⓢ ˈkuː-, ˈkjuː-
cum laude ˌkʌmˈlaʊ.deɪ, ˌkʊm-, -ˈlɔː.di ⓤⓢ ˌkʊmˈlaʊ.deɪ, -ˈlɑː-, -ˈlɔː-, -di, -də
cummerbund ˈkʌm.ə.bʌnd ⓤⓢ ˈ-ɚ- **-s** -z
cummin ˈkʌm.ɪn
Cumming ˈkʌm.ɪŋ **-s** -z
cummings (C) ˈkʌm.ɪŋz
Cumnock ˈkʌm.nək
Cumnor ˈkʌm.nəʳ ⓤⓢ -nɚ
cumquat ˈkʌm.kwɒt ⓤⓢ -kwɑːt **-s** -s
cumulate *(adj.)* ˈkjuː.mjə.lət, -mjʊ-, -lɪt, -leɪt ⓤⓢ -mjə-
cumu|late *(v.)* ˈkjuː.mjə|.leɪt, -mjʊ- ⓤⓢ -mjə- **-lates** -leɪts **-lating** -leɪ.tɪŋ ⓤⓢ -leɪ.t̬ɪŋ **-lated** -leɪ.tɪd ⓤⓢ -leɪ.t̬ɪd
cumulation ˌkjuː.mjəˈleɪ.ʃᵊn, -mjʊˈ- ⓤⓢ -mjəˈ- **-s** -z
cumulative ˈkjuː.mjə.lə.tɪv, -mjʊ-, -leɪ- ⓤⓢ -mjə.lə.t̬ɪv **-ly** -li **-ness** -nəs, -nɪs
cumulonimbus ˌkjuː.mjə.ləʊˈnɪm.bəs, -mjʊ- ⓤⓢ -mjə.loʊˈ- **-es** -ɪz
cumul|us ˈkjuː.mjə.l|əs, -mjʊ- ⓤⓢ -mjə- **-i** -aɪ, -iː ⓤⓢ -aɪ
Cunard ˌkjuːˈnɑːd ⓤⓢ ˌkuːˈnɑːrd, ˌkjuː- **-er/s** -əʳ/z ⓤⓢ -ɚ/z
cunctation kʌŋkˈteɪ.ʃᵊn **-s** -z
cunctator kʌŋkˈteɪ.təʳ ⓤⓢ -t̬ɚ **-s** -z
cuneiform ˈkjuː.nɪ.fɔːm, -ni.ɪ-, -ə.fɔːm ⓤⓢ ˈkjuː.nə.fɔːrm, -ni.ə-
Cunliffe ˈkʌn.lɪf
cunnilingus ˌkʌn.ɪˈlɪŋ.gəs ⓤⓢ -əˈ-
cunning ˈkʌn.ɪŋ **-est** -ɪst **-ly** -li **-ness** -nəs, -nɪs
Cunningham ˈkʌn.ɪŋ.əm ⓤⓢ -hæm
cunt kʌnt **-s** -s
cup kʌp **-s** -s **-ping** -ɪŋ **-ped** -t ˈ**Cup** ˌ**Final**, ˌ**Cup** ˈ**Final**
Cupar ˈkuː.pəʳ ⓤⓢ -pɚ
cupbearer ˈkʌpˌbeə.rəʳ ⓤⓢ -ˌber.ɚ **-s** -z
cupboard ˈkʌb.əd ⓤⓢ -ɚd **-s** -z ˈ**cupboard** ˌ**love**
cupcake ˈkʌp.keɪk **-s** -s
cupful ˈkʌp.fʊl **-s** -z
cupid (C) ˈkjuː.pɪd **-s** -z
cupidity kjuˈpɪd.ə.ti, -ɪ.ti ⓤⓢ -ə.t̬i
cupola ˈkjuː.pᵊl.ə **-s** -z
cuppa ˈkʌp.ə **-s** -z
cupreous ˈkjuː.pri.əs
cupric ˈkjuː.prɪk
Cuprinol® ˈkjuː.prɪ.nɒl, -prə- ⓤⓢ -nɑːl
cuprous kjuː.prəs
cur kɜːʳ ⓤⓢ kɝː **-s** -z
curability ˌkjʊə.rəˈbɪl.ə.ti, ˌkjɔː-, -ɪ.ti ⓤⓢ ˌkjʊr.əˈbɪl.ə.t̬i
curable ˈkjʊə.rə.bl̩, ˈkjɔː- ⓤⓢ ˈkjʊr-
curaç|ao (C) ˈkjʊə.rə.s|aʊ, ˈkjɔː-, -s|əʊ, ˌ--ˈ- ⓤⓢ ˈkjʊr.ə.s|oʊ, ˈkʊr-, -s|aʊ, ˌ--ˈ- **-oa** -əʊə ⓤⓢ -oʊə
curac|y ˈkjʊə.rə.s|i, ˈkjɔː- ⓤⓢ ˈkjʊr.ə- **-ies** -iz
Curan ˈkʌr.ən
curare kjʊəˈrɑː.ri ⓤⓢ kjʊˈrɑːr.i
curate *(n.)* ˈkjʊə.rət, ˈkjɔː-, -rɪt ⓤⓢ ˈkjʊr.ət, -eɪt **-s** -s ˌ**curate's** ˈ**egg**
cura|te *(v.)* ˈkjʊə.r|eɪt, ˈkjɔː-; -ˈ-, kjə- ⓤⓢ ˈkjʊr.|eit; -ˈ-, kjɚ- **-tes** -ts **-ting** -tɪŋ ⓤⓢ -t̬ɪŋ **-ted** -tɪd ⓤⓢ -t̬ɪd
curative ˈkjʊə.rə.tɪv, ˈkjɔː- ⓤⓢ ˈkjʊr.ə.t̬ɪv **-ly** -li
curator kjʊəˈreɪ.təʳ, kjɔː- ⓤⓢ ˈkjʊr.eɪ.t̬ɚ, ˈkjɝː- **-s** -z **-ship/s** -ʃɪp/s
curb kɜːb ⓤⓢ kɝːb **-s** -z **-ing** -ɪŋ **-ed** -d
curbstone ˈkɜːb.stəʊn ⓤⓢ ˈkɝːb.stoʊn **-s** -z
curd kɜːd ⓤⓢ kɝːd **-s** -z
curdl|e ˈkɜː.dl̩ ⓤⓢ ˈkɝː- **-es** -z **-ing** -ɪŋ, ˈkɜːd.lɪŋ ⓤⓢ ˈkɝː.dl̩.ɪŋ, ˈkɝːd.lɪŋ **-ed** -d

curd|y 'kɜː.d|i US 'kɝː- **-ier** -i.əʳ US -i.ɚ **-iest** -i.ɪst, -i.əst **-iness** -ɪ.nəs, -ɪ.nɪs

cur|e kjʊəʳ, kjɔːʳ US kjʊr **-es** -z **-ing** -ɪŋ **-ed** -d **-er/s** -əʳ/z US -ɚ/z

cure-all 'kjʊəʳ.ɔːl, 'kjɔːʳ- US 'kjʊr.ɑːl, 'kjɝː-, -ɔːl **-s** -z

cu|ret kjʊə|'ret US kjʊ|'ret **-rets** -'rets **-retting** -'ret.ɪŋ US -'ret̬.ɪŋ **-retted** -'ret.ɪd US -'ret̬.ɪd

curettage ˌkjʊə.rɪ'tɑːʒ, kjʊə'ret.ɪdʒ US kjʊ'ret̬.ɪdʒ, ˌkjʊr.ə'tɑːʒ

cu|rette kjʊə|'ret US kjʊ- **-rettes** -'rets **-retting** -'ret.ɪŋ US -'ret̬.ɪŋ **-retted** -'ret.ɪd US -'ret̬.ɪd

curettment kjʊə'ret.mənt US kjʊ-

curfew 'kɜː.fjuː US 'kɝː- **-s** -z

cur|ia 'kjʊə.r|i.ə, 'kjɔː-, 'kʊə- US 'kjʊr|.i- **-iae** -i.iː, -i.aɪ

curie (C) 'kjʊə.ri, -iː US 'kjʊr.i, -iː **-s** -z

curio 'kjʊə.ri.əʊ, 'kjɔː- US 'kjʊr.i.oʊ **-s** -z

curiosit|y ˌkjʊə.ri'ɒs.ə.t|i, ˌkjɔː-, -ɪ.t|i US ˌkjʊr.i'ɑː.sə.t̬|i **-ies** -iz

curious 'kjʊə.ri.əs, 'kjɔː- US 'kjʊr.i- **-ly** -li **-ness** -nəs, -nɪs

curium 'kjʊə.ri.əm, 'kjɔː- US 'kjʊr.i-

curl kɜːl US kɝːl **-s** -z **-ing** -ɪŋ **-ed** -d **'curling ˌtongs**

curler 'kɜː.ləʳ US 'kɝː.lɚ **-s** -z

curlew 'kɜː.ljuː US 'kɝː.luː, 'kɝːl.juː **-s** -z

curlicue 'kɜː.lɪ.kjuː US 'kɝː- **-s** -z

curling 'kɜː.lɪŋ US 'kɝː-

curl|y 'kɜː.l|i US 'kɝː- **-ier** -i.əʳ US -i.ɚ **-iest** -i.ɪst, -i.əst **-iness** -ɪ.nəs, -ɪ.nɪs

curmudgeon kɜː'mʌdʒ.ᵊn, kə- US kɚ- **-s** -z **-ly** -li

curragh, currach (C) 'kʌr.ə US 'kɝː- **-s** -z

Curran 'kʌr.ᵊn US 'kɝː-

currant 'kʌr.ᵊnt US 'kɝː- **-s** -s

currawong 'kʌr.ə.wɒŋ US -wɑːŋ, -wɔːŋ **-s** -z

currenc|y 'kʌr.ᵊnt.s|i US 'kɝː- **-ies** -iz

current 'kʌr.ᵊnt US 'kɝː- **-s** -s **-ly** -li **-ness** -nəs, -nɪs **ˌcurrent ac'count; ˌcurrent af'fairs**

Currer 'kʌr.əʳ US 'kɝː.ɚ

curricle 'kʌr.ɪ.kl̩ US 'kɝː- **-s** -z

curricul|um kə'rɪk.jə.l|əm, -jʊ- US -jə- **-a** -ə **-ums** -əmz **-ar** -əʳ US -ɚ

curriculum vitae kəˌrɪk.jə.ləm'viː.taɪ, -jʊ-, -teɪ US -jə.ləm'viː.taɪ, -tiː, -'vaɪ.t̬i **-s** -s **curricula vitae** kəˌrɪk.jə.lə'viː.taɪ, -jʊ-, -teɪ US -jə.lə'viː.taɪ, -tiː, -'vaɪ.t̬i

Currie 'kʌr.i US 'kɝː.i

Currier 'kʌr.i.əʳ US 'kɝː.i.ɚ

currish 'kɜː.rɪʃ US 'kɝː.ɪʃ **-ly** -li **-ness** -nəs, -nɪs

curr|y (C) 'kʌr|.i US 'kɝː- **-ies** -iz **-ying** -i.ɪŋ **-ied** -id **-ier/s** -i.əʳ/z US -i.ɚ/z **'curry ˌpowder**

curs|e kɜːs US kɝːs **-es** -ɪz **-ing** -ɪŋ **-ed** -t

cursed *(adj.)* 'kɜː.sɪd US 'kɝː- **-ly** -li **-ness** -nəs, -nɪs

cursive 'kɜː.sɪv US 'kɝː- **-ly** -li **-ness** -nəs, -nɪs

cursor 'kɜː.səʳ US 'kɝː.sɚ **-s** -z

Cursor Mundi ˌkɜː.sɔː'mʊn.diː, -'mʌn.daɪ US ˌkɝː.sɔːr'mʊn.di, -sɚ'-

cursor|y 'kɜː.sᵊr|.i US 'kɝː- **-ily** -ᵊl.i, -ɪ.li **-iness** -ɪ.nəs, -ɪ.nɪs

curst kɜːst US kɝːst

cursus 'kɜː.səs US 'kɝː-

curt kɜːt US kɝːt **-er** -əʳ US 'kɝː.t̬ɚ **-est** -ɪst, -əst US 'kɝː.t̬ɪst, -t̬əst **-ly** -li **-ness** -nəs, -nɪs

curtail kɜː'teɪl US kɚ- **-s** -z **-ing** -ɪŋ **-ed** -d **-ment/s** -mənt/s

curtain 'kɜː.tᵊn, -tɪn US 'kɝː.tᵊn **-s** -z **-ed** -d **'curtain ˌcall; 'curtain ˌraiser**

curtes|y 'kɜː.tə.s|i, -tɪ.s|i US 'kɝː.t̬ə- **-ies** -ɪz

Curtice 'kɜː.tɪs US 'kɝː.t̬ɪs

curtilage 'kɜː.tᵊl.ɪdʒ, -tɪ.lɪdʒ US 'kɝː.t̬ᵊl-

Curtis(s) 'kɜː.tɪs US 'kɝː.t̬ɪs

curtsey 'kɜːt.si US 'kɝːt- **-s** -z **-ing** -ɪŋ **-ed** -d

curts|y 'kɜːt.s|i US 'kɝːt- **-ies** -iz **-ying** -i.ɪŋ **-ied** -id

curvaceous kɜː'veɪ.ʃəs US kɝː- **-ly** -li **-ness** -nəs, -nɪs

curvation kɜː'veɪ.ʃᵊn US kɝː- **-s** -z

curvature 'kɜː.və.tʃəʳ, -tjʊəʳ US 'kɝː.və.tʃɚ **-s** -z

curv|e kɜːv US kɝːv **-es** -z **-ing** -ɪŋ **-ed** -d **'curve ˌball**

curveball 'kɜːv.bɔːl US 'kɝːv-, -bɑːl **-s** -z

cur|vet kɜː|'vet US kɝː- **-vets** -'vets **-vet(t)ing** -'vet.ɪŋ US -'vet̬.ɪŋ **-vet(t)ed** -'vet.ɪd US -'vet̬.ɪd

curviline|al ˌkɜː.vɪ'lɪn.i|.əl, -və'- US ˌkɝː.və'- **-ar** -əʳ US -ɚ

curv|y 'kɜː.v|i US 'kɝː- **-ier** -i.əʳ US -i.ɚ **-iest** -i.ɪst, -i.əst

Curwen 'kɜː.wɪn, -wən US 'kɝː-

Curzon 'kɜː.zᵊn US 'kɝː-

Cusack 'kjuː.sæk, -zæk, -zək US 'kuː-, 'kjuː-

Cush kʊʃ, kʌʃ **-ite/s** -aɪt/s

Cushing 'kʊʃ.ɪŋ

cushion 'kʊʃ.ᵊn **-s** -z **-ing** -ɪŋ **-ed** -d

cush|y 'kʊʃ|.i **-ier** -i.əʳ US -i.ɚ **-iest** -i.əst, -i.ɪst **-ily** -ɪ.li, -ᵊl.i **-iness** -ɪ.nəs, -ɪ.nɪs

cusp kʌsp **-s** -s

cuspid 'kʌs.pɪd

cuspidor 'kʌs.pɪ.dɔːʳ US -ə.dɔːr **-s** -z

cuss kʌs **-es** -ɪz **-ing** -ɪŋ **-ed** -t

cussed *(adj.)* 'kʌs.ɪd, -əd **-ly** -li **-ness** -nəs, -nɪs

custard 'kʌs.təd US -tɚd **-s** -z **'custard ˌapple; ˌcustard 'pie**

Custer 'kʌs.təʳ US -tɚ kʌs'təʊ.diːz US -'toʊ-

custodial kʌs'təʊ.di.əl US -'toʊ-

custodian kʌs'təʊ.di.ən US -'toʊ- **-s** -z

custody 'kʌs.tə.di

custom 'kʌs.təm **-s** -z

customarily 'kʌs.tə.mᵊr.ᵊl.i, -ɪ.li; ˌkʌs.tə'mer- US ˌkʌs.tə'mer-

customar|y 'kʌs.tə.mᵊr|.i US -mer- **-iness** -ɪ.nəs, -ɪ.nɪs

customer 'kʌs.tə.məʳ US -mɚ **-s** -z

customhou|se 'kʌs.təm.haʊ|s **-ses** -zɪz

customiz|e, -is|e 'kʌs.tə.maɪz **-es** -ɪz **-ing** -ɪŋ **-ed** -d **-er/s** -əʳ/z US -ɚ/z

custom-made ˌkʌs.təm'meɪd *stress shift, British only:* ˌcustom-made 'suit

custos *(sing.)* 'kʌs.tɒs, -təʊs US -tɑːs; 'kʊs.toʊs *(plur.)* **custodes** kʌs'təʊ.diːz US -'toʊ-

cut kʌt **-s** -s **-ting** -ɪŋ US 'kʌt̬.ɪŋ **-ter/s** -əʳ/z US 'kʌt̬.ɚ/z

cut-and-|dried ˌkʌt.ᵊn|'draɪd **-dry** -'dra

cut-and-paste ˌkʌt.ᵊnd'peɪst, -ᵊm'- US -ᵊnd'-

cutaneous kjuː'teɪ.ni.əs **-ly** -li

cutaway 'kʌt.ə.weɪ US 'kʌt̬-

cutback 'kʌt.bæk **-s** -s

Cutch kʌtʃ

cut|e kjuːt **-er** -əʳ US 'kjuː.t̬ɚ **-est** -ɪst, -əst US 'kjuː.t̬ɪst, -t̬əst **-ely** -li **-enes** -nəs, -nɪs

cutesy 'kjuːt.si

cutey 'kjuː.ti US -t̬i **-s** -z

Cutforth 'kʌt.fɔːθ US -fɔːrθ

Cuthbert 'kʌθ.bət US -bɚt

Cuthbertson 'kʌθ.bət.sᵊn US -bɚt-

cuticle 'kjuː.tɪ.kl̩ US -t̬ə- **-s** -z

cuticular kjuː'tɪk.jə.ləʳ, -jʊ- US -lɚ

Cuticura® ˌkjuː.tɪ'kjʊə.rə, -'kjɔː- US -t̬ə'kjʊr.ə

cutie 'kjuː.ti US -t̬i **-s** -z

cutie-pie 'kjuː.ti.paɪ US -t̬i-

cutis 'kjuː.tɪs US -t̬ɪs

cutlass 'kʌt.ləs **-es** -ɪz

cutler (C) 'kʌt.ləʳ US -lɚ **-s** -z

cutlery 'kʌt.lᵊr.i

cutlet 'kʌt.lət, -lɪt **-s** -s

cutoff 'kʌt.ɒf US 'kʌt̬.ɑːf, -ɔːf **-s** -s

cutout 'kʌt.aʊt US 'kʌt̬- **-s** -s

cut-price ˌkʌt'praɪs *stress shift:* ˌcut-price 'goods

Cuttell kə'tel

cutter 'kʌt.əʳ US 'kʌt̬.ɚ **-s** -z

cutthroat 'kʌt.θrəʊt US -θroʊt **-s** -s

cutting 'kʌt.ɪŋ US 'kʌt̬- **-s** -z **ˌcutting 'edge**

cuttle (C) 'kʌt.l̩ US 'kʌt̬- **-s** -z **-bone** -bəʊn US -boʊn

cuttlefish 'kʌt.l̩.fɪʃ US 'kʌt̬- **-es** -ɪz

cutt|y 'kʌt|.i US 'kʌt̬- **-ies** -iz **ˌCutty 'Sark**

cutwater ˈkʌtˌwɔː.təʳ (US) -ˌwɑː.t̬ɚ, -ˌwɔː- **-s** -z
cutworm ˈkʌt.wɜːm (US) -wɝːm **-s** -z
cuvette kjuːˈvet (US) kjuː-, kuː- **-s** -s
Cuvier ˈkjuː.vi.eɪ, ˈkuː- (US) ˈkjuː.vi.eɪ; ˌkuːˈvjeɪ
Cuxhaven ˈkʊksˌhɑː.vᵊn
Cuyahoga ˌkaɪ.əˈhəʊ.gə (US) -ˈhoʊ-, -ˈhɑː-, -ˈhɔː-
Cuyp kaɪp, kɔɪp (US) kɔɪp **-s** -s
Cuzco ˈkʊs.kəʊ, ˈkuː.skəʊ (US) ˈkuː.skoʊ
CV ˌsiːˈviː **-s** -z
cwm kʊm, kuːm **-s** -z
Cwm Avon kʊmˈæv.ᵊn, kuːm-
Cwmbach kʊmˈbɑːx, kuːm- (US) -ˈbɑːk
Cwmbran kʊmˈbrɑːn, kuːm-
cwt *(abbrev. for* **hundredweight***)* ˈhʌn.drəd.weɪt, -drɪd- **-s** -s
cyan ˈsaɪ.æn, -ən
cyanate ˈsaɪə.neɪt
cyanic saɪˈæn.ɪk
cyanide ˈsaɪə.naɪd **-s** -z
cyanogen saɪˈæn.ə.dʒᵊn, -dʒɪn, -dʒen
cyanosis ˌsaɪəˈnəʊ.sɪs (US) -ˈnoʊ-
cybercafe ˈsaɪ.bəˌkæf.eɪ (US) ˌsaɪ.bɚ-.kæfˈeɪ, -kəˈfeɪ **-s** -z
cybernetic ˌsaɪ.bəˈnet.ɪk (US) -bɚˈnet̬- **-s** -s
cyberpet ˈsaɪ.bə.pet (US) -bɚ- **-s** -s
cyberpunk ˈsaɪ.bə.pʌŋk (US) -bɚ- **-s** -s
cyberspace ˈsaɪ.bə.speɪs (US) -bɚ-
cybrarian saɪˈbreə.ri.ən (US) -ˈbrer.i- **-s** -z
cybrar|y ˈsaɪ.brᵊr|.i, -br|i (US) -brer|.i, -bræːr.i **-ies** -iz
cycad ˈsaɪ.kæd, -kəd **-s** -z
Cyclades ˈsaɪ.klə.diːz, ˈsɪk.lə-
cyclamate ˈsaɪ.klə.meɪt, ˈsɪk.lə- (US) ˈsaɪ.klə- **-s** -s
cyclamen ˈsɪk.lə.mən, ˈsaɪ.klə-, -men (US) ˈsaɪ.klə- **-s** -z
cycl|e ˈsaɪ.kl̩ **-es** -z **-ing** -ɪŋ, ˈ-klɪŋ **-ed** -d
cyclic ˈsaɪ.klɪk, ˈsɪk.lɪk **-al** -ᵊl **-ally** -ᵊl.i, -li
cyclist ˈsaɪ.klɪst **-s** -s
cyclo- ˈsaɪ.kləʊ-, saɪˈklɒ-, ˈsɪk.ləʊ- (US) ˈsaɪ.kloʊ-, saɪˈklɑː-
Note: Prefix. This may be stressed on the initial syllable, e.g. **cyclostyle** /ˈsaɪ.kləʊ.staɪl (US) ˈsaɪ.kloʊ-/ or on the second syllable, e.g. **cyclometer** /saɪˈklɒm.ɪ.tə (US) saɪˈklɑː.mə.tɚ/.
cyclograph ˈsaɪ.kləʊ.grɑːf, -græf (US) -klə.græf **-s** -s
cycloid ˈsaɪ.klɔɪd **-s** -z
cycloidal saɪˈklɔɪ.dᵊl
cyclometer saɪˈklɒm.ɪ.təʳ, ˈ-ə- (US) -ˈklɑː.mə.t̬ɚ **-s** -z
cyclone ˈsaɪ.kləʊn (US) -kloʊn **-s** -z
cyclonic saɪˈklɒn.ɪk (US) -ˈklɑː.nɪk
cyclopaed|ia ˌsaɪ.kləʊˈpiː.d|i.ə (US) -kloʊˈ-, -kləˈ- **-ias** -i.əz **-ic** -ɪk
cyclopean ˌsaɪ.kləʊˈpiː.ən; saɪˈkləʊ.pi- (US) ˌsaɪ.kloʊˈpiː-, -kləˈ-; saɪˈkloʊ.pi-
cycloped|ia ˌsaɪ.kləʊˈpiː.d|i.ə (US) -kloʊˈ-, -kləˈ- **-ias** -i.əz **-ic** -ɪk saɪˈkləʊ.piːz (US) -ˈkloʊ-
cyclops *(sing.)* ˈsaɪ.klɒps (US) -klɑːps *(plur.)* **cyclopes** saɪˈkləʊ.piːz (US) -ˈkloʊ-
cyclorama ˌsaɪ.kləˈrɑː.mə (US) -kloʊˈræm.ə, -kləˈ-, -ˈrɑː.mə **-s** -z
cyclostyl|e ˈsaɪ.kləʊ.staɪl (US) -klə- **-es** -z **-ing** -ɪŋ **-ed** -d
cyclothymia ˌsaɪ.kləʊˈθaɪ.mi.ə, ˌsɪk.ləʊˈ- (US) ˌsaɪ.kloʊˈ-, -kləˈ-
cyclotron ˈsaɪ.kləʊ.trɒn (US) -klə.trɑːn **-s** -z
cyder ˈsaɪ.dəʳ (US) -dɚ **-s** -z
cygnet ˈsɪg.nət, -nɪt **-s** -s
Cygnus ˈsɪg.nəs
cylinder ˈsɪl.ɪn.dəʳ, -ən- (US) -dɚ **-s** -z
cylindric səˈlɪn.drɪk, sɪ- **-al** -ᵊl **-ally** -ᵊl.i, -li
cylindriform səˈlɪn.drɪ.fɔːm, sɪ- (US) -drɪ.fɔːrm, -drə-
cylindroid ˈsɪl.ɪn.drɔɪd, səˈlɪn-, sɪ- **-s** -z
cyli|x ˈsaɪ.lɪ|ks, ˈsɪl.ɪ|ks **-ces** -siːz
cy|ma ˈsaɪ|.mə **-mae** -miː
cymbal ˈsɪm.bᵊl **-s** -z
cymbal|o ˈsɪm.bə.l|əʊ (US) -l|oʊ **-o(e)s** -əʊz (US) -oʊz
Cymbeline ˈsɪm.bə.liːn, -bɪ-
cyme saɪm **-s** -z
Cymric ˈkɪm.rɪk, ˈkʌm- (US) ˈkɪm-
Cymru ˈkɪm.ri, ˈkʌm- (US) ˈkʌm-
Cymry ˈkɪm.ri, ˈkʌm- (US) ˈkɪm-
Cynewulf ˈkɪn.ɪ.wʊlf, ˈ-ə-
cynic ˈsɪn.ɪk **-s** -s
cynical ˈsɪn.ɪ.kᵊl **-ly** -i
cynicism ˈsɪn.ɪ.sɪ.zᵊm, ˈ-ə- **-s** -z
cynocephalic ˌsaɪ.nəʊ.sefˈæl.ɪk, -kefˈ- (US) -noʊ-
cynocephalous ˌsaɪ.nəʊˈsef.ə.ləs, -ˈkef- (US) -noʊˈ-
Cynon ˈkɪn.ən, ˈkʌn-
cynosure ˈsaɪ.nə.sjʊəʳ, ˈsɪn.ə-, -ˌʃʊəʳ (US) -ʃʊr **-s** -z
Cynthi|a ˈsɪnt.θi|.ə **-us** -əs
cyph|er ˈsaɪ.f|əʳ (US) -f|ɚ **-ers** -əz (US) -ɚz **-ering** -ᵊr.ɪŋ **-ered** -əd (US) -ɚd
cy près ˌsiːˈpreɪ, ˌsaɪ-
cypress ˈsaɪ.prəs, -prɪs **-es** -ɪz
Cyprian ˈsɪp.ri.ən **-s** -z
Cypriot ˈsɪp.ri.ət **-s** -s
Cypriote ˈsɪp.ri.əʊt (US) -oʊt **-s** -s
Cyprus ˈsaɪ.prəs
Cyrano ˈsɪr.ə.nəʊ; sɪˈrɑː-, sə- (US) ˈsɪr.ə.noʊ **ˌCyrano de ˈBergerac**
Cyrenaica ˌsɪr.əˈneɪ.ɪ.kə, ˌsaɪə.rəˈ-, -ɪˈ-, -ˈnaɪ- (US) ˌsaɪ.rəˈ-
Cyrene saɪəˈriː.ni (US) saɪ-
Cyrenian saɪəˈriː.ni.ən (US) saɪ-
Cyrenius saɪəˈriː.ni.əs (US) saɪ-
Cyril ˈsɪr.ᵊl, -ɪl
Cyrillic səˈrɪl.ɪk, sɪ- (US) sə-
Cyrus ˈsaɪə.rəs (US) ˈsaɪ-
cyst sɪst **-s** -s
cystic ˈsɪs.tɪk **ˌcystic fibˈrosis**
cystitis sɪˈstaɪ.tɪs (US) -t̬ɪs
cystoid ˈsɪs.tɔɪd
Cythera sɪˈθɪə.rə, sə- (US) -ˈθɪr.ə
cyto- ˈsaɪ.təʊ-, saɪˈtɒ- (US) ˈsaɪ.t̬oʊ-, -t̬ə-, saɪˈtɑː-
Note: Prefix. This may carry primary or secondary stress on the initial syllable, e.g. **cytoplasm** /ˈsaɪ.tə.plæz.ᵊm (US) ˈsaɪ.t̬ə-/ or on the second syllable, e.g. **cytology** /saɪˈtɒl.ədʒi (US) saɪˈtɑːl-/.
cytogenetics ˌsaɪ.təʊ.dʒəˈnet.ɪks, -dʒenˈet-, -dʒɪˈnet- (US) ˌsaɪ.t̬oʊ.dʒəˈnet̬-
cytology saɪˈtɒl.ə.dʒi (US) -ˈtɑː.lə-
cytoplasm ˈsaɪ.təʊ.plæz.ᵊm (US) -t̬ə- **-s** -z
cytoplasmic ˌsaɪ.təʊˈplæz.mɪk (US) -t̬əˈ-
czar **(C)** zɑːʳ, tsɑːʳ (US) zɑːr, tsɑːr **-s** -z
czardas ˈtʃɑː.dæʃ, ˈzɑː.dæs, -dəs (US) ˈtʃɑːr.dɑːʃ, -dæʃ **-es** -ɪz
czarevitch **(C)** ˈzɑː.rə.vɪtʃ, -rɪ- (US) ˈzɑːr.ə-, ˈtsɑːr- **-es** -ɪz
czarevna **(C)** zɑːˈrev.nə, tsɑː- **-s** -z
czarina zɑːˈriː.nə, tsɑː- **-s** -z
czarist ˈzɑː.rɪst, ˈtsɑː- (US) ˈzɑːr.ɪst, ˈtsɑːr- **-s** -s
Czech tʃek **-s** -s
Czechoslovak ˌtʃek.əʊˈsləʊ.væk (US) -oʊˈsloʊ.vɑːk, -væk **-s** -s
Czechoslovaki|a ˌtʃek.əʊ.sləʊˈvæk.i|.ə, -ˈvɑː.ki- (US) -oʊ.sloʊˈvɑː.ki-, -ˈvæk.i- **-an** -ən
Czerny ˈtʃɜː.ni, ˈzɜː-, tʃeə- (US) ˈtʃer-

Pronouncing the letter D

When not used in the grammatical inflection *-ed*, the consonant letter **d** is most often realised as /d/, e.g.:

duck /dʌk/

However, in consonant clusters /d/ may be elided, e.g.:

grandson /ˈgræn*d*.sʌn/
Wednesday /ˈwenz.deɪ/

In addition

d is sometimes realised as /dʒ/, e.g.:

procedure /prəʊˈsiː.dʒə^r/ (US) /prəˈsiː.dʒɚ/
soldier /ˈsəʊl.dʒə^r/ (US) /ˈsoʊl.dʒɚ/

Due to COALESCENCE between /d/ and /j/ in British English and omission of /j/ in American English, syllables beginning with **du** may have different pronunciations, e.g.:

due /dʒuː/ (US) /duː/

The grammatical inflection -ed

There are three possible ways of pronouncing the grammatical inflection *-ed*.

Following /t/ and /d/ the inflection is realised as /ɪd/, e.g.:

started /ˈstɑː.tɪd/ (US) /ˈstɑːr.t̬ɪd/

Following all other voiceless consonant sounds the inflection is realised as /t/, e.g.:

shaped /ʃeɪpt/

Following all other voiced consonant sounds and after vowel sounds, the inflection is realised as /d/, e.g.:

played /pleɪd/

d (D) diː **-'s** -z
d' *(from* **do***)* də, d
Note: See also **d'you**.
'd *(from* **had, would***)* d
DA ˌdiːˈeɪ **-s** -z
dab dæb **-s** -z **-bing** -ɪŋ **-bed** -d **-ber/s** -ə^r/z (US) -ɚ/z ˌ**dab 'hand**
dabbl|e ˈdæb.l̩ **-es** -z **-ing** -ɪŋ, ˈdæb.lɪŋ **-ed** -d **-er/s** -ə^r/z, ˈdæb.lə^r/z (US) -ɚ/z
dabchick ˈdæb.tʃɪk **-s** -s
da capo dɑːˈkɑː.pəʊ, də- (US) -poʊ
Dacca ˈdæk.ə (US) ˈdæk.ə, ˈdɑː.kə
dace deɪs
dacha ˈdætʃ.ə (US) ˈdɑː.tʃə **-s** -z
Dachau *as if German:* ˈdæx.aʊ, ˈdæk- (US) ˈdɑː.kaʊ
dachshund ˈdæk.s^{ə}nd, ˈdæʃ.^{ə}nd, -hʊnd, -hʊnt (US) ˈdɑːks.hʊnd, ˈdɑːk.sənd **-s** -z
Daci|a ˈdeɪ.si|.ə, -ʃi|-, ˈ-ʃ|ə (US) ˈ-ʃ|ə **-an/s** -ən/z
dacoit dəˈkɔɪt **-s** -s
Dacre ˈdeɪ.kə^r (US) -kɚ **-s** -z
Dacron® ˈdæk.rɒn, ˈdeɪ.krɒn (US) ˈdeɪ.krɑːn, ˈdæk.rɑːn
dactyl ˈdæk.tɪl, -t^{ə}l **-s** -z
dactylic dækˈtɪl.ɪk
dactylogram dækˈtɪl.əʊ.græm; ˈdæk.tɪ.ləʊ-, -t^{ə}l.əʊ- (US) dækˈtɪl.ə- **-s** -z
dactylography ˌdæk.tɪˈlɒg.rə.fi (US) -təˈlɑː.grə-
dad (D) dæd **-s** -z
Dada ˈdɑː.dɑː, -də **-ism** -ɪ.z^{ə}m **-ist/s** -ɪst/s
dadaistic (D) ˌdɑː.dɑːˈɪs.tɪk
Daddies® ˈdæd.iz
dadd|y ˈdæd|.i **-ies** -iz
daddy longlegs ˌdæd.iˈlɒŋ.legz (US) -ˈlɑːŋ-, -ˈlɔːŋ-
dado ˈdeɪ.dəʊ (US) -doʊ **-s** -z
Daedalus ˈdiː.d^{ə}l.əs (US) ˈded.^{ə}l-
daemon ˈdiː.mən, ˈdaɪ-, ˈdeɪ- **-s** -z
daemonic diːˈmɒn.ɪk, dɪ-, də- (US) -ˈmɑː.nɪk
D'Aeth deɪθ, deθ, diːθ
Daewoo® ˈdeɪ.uː (US) ˌdeɪˈwuː
DAF® dæf
daffodil ˈdæf.ə.dɪl **-s** -z
daff|y ˈdæf|.i **-ier** -i.ə^r (US) -i.ɚ **-iest** -i.ɪst, -i.əst **-iness** -ɪ.nəs, -ɪ.nɪs
Daffyd ap Gwilym ˌdæv.ɪð.ɑːpˈgwɪl.ɪm, -ɪd- (US) ˌdɑː.vɪð-
daft dɑːft (US) dæft **-er** -ə^r (US) -ɚ **-est** -ɪst, -əst **-ly** -li **-ness** -nəs, -nɪs
Dafydd ˈdæv.ɪð, ˈdæf-
dag dæg **-s** -z **-ging** -ɪŋ **-ged** -d
da Gama dəˈgɑː.mə (US) -ˈgɑː-, -ˈgæm.ə
Dagenham ˈdæg.^{ə}n.əm
Dagestan ˌdɑː.gɪˈstɑːn, -gəˈ-
dagga ˈdæx.ə, ˈdʌx-, ˈdɑː.xə (US) ˈdæg.ə, ˈdɑː.gə
dagger ˈdæg.ə^r (US) -ɚ **-s** -z **at ˌdaggers 'drawn; look 'daggers at someone**
Daggett ˈdæg.ɪt
dagg|y ˈdæg|.i **-ier** -i.ə^r (US) -i.ɚ **-iest** -i.ɪst, -i.əst
Dagmar ˈdæg.mɑː^r (US) -mɑːr
dago ˈdeɪ.gəʊ (US) -goʊ **-(e)s** -z
Dagobert ˈdæg.əʊ.bɜːt (US) -ə.bɝːt
Dagon ˈdeɪ.gɒn, -gən (US) -gɑːn
Dagonet ˈdæg.ə.nət, -nɪt
daguerreotype dəˈger.əʊ.taɪp (US) ˈ-ə- **-s** -s
Dagwood ˈdæg.wʊd
dahl (D) dɑːl
dahlia (D) ˈdeɪ.li.ə, ˈ-ljə (US) ˈdæl.jə, ˈdɑːl-, ˈdeɪl- **-s** -z
Dahomey dəˈhəʊ.mi (US) -ˈhoʊ-
Dahrendorf ˈdɑː.r^{ə}n.dɔːf, ˈdær.^{ə}n- (US) -dɔːrf
Dai daɪ
Daiches ˈdeɪ.*t*ʃɪz, -*t*ʃəz, -*t*ʃɪs, -*t*ʃəs
Daihatsu® ˌdaɪˈhæt.suː (US) -ˈhɑːt-
daikon ˈdaɪ.kɒn, -kən (US) -kən, -kɑːn **-s** -z
Dail, Dáil dɔɪl
Dáil Eireann ˌdɔɪlˈeə.rən (US) -ˈer.ən, -ˈeɪ.rən
daill|y ˈdeɪ.l|i **-ies** -iz
Daimler® ˈdeɪm.lə^r (US) -lɚ, ˈdaɪm- **-s** -z
Daintree ˈdeɪn.triː, -tri
daint|y ˈdeɪn.t|i (US) -t̬|i **-ies** -iz **-ier** -i.ə^r (US) -i.ɚ **-iest** -i.ɪst, -i.əst **-ily** -ɪ.li, -^{ə}l.i **-iness** -ɪ.nəs, -ɪ.nɪs
daiquiri (D) ˈdaɪ.kɪ.ri, ˈdæk.ɪ-, -^{ə}r.i; daɪˈkɪə.ri, də- (US) ˈdæk.ɚ.i, ˈdaɪ.kɚ-
dair|y ˈdeə.r|i (US) ˈder|.i **-ies** -iz **-ying** -i.ɪŋ **ˈdairy ˌfarm; ˈdairy ˌproducts**
Dairylea® ˌdeə.riˈliː, ˈ--- (US) ˌder.iˈliː, ˈ---
dairymaid ˈdeə.ri.meɪd (US) ˈder.i- **-s** -z
dairy|man ˈdeə.ri|.mən, -mæn (US) ˈder.i- **-men** -mən, -men
dais ˈdeɪ.ɪs, deɪs (US) ˈdeɪ.ɪs, ˈdaɪ- **-es** -ɪz
dais|y (D) ˈdeɪ.z|i **-ies** -iz ˈ**daisy ˌchain**; ˈ**daisy ˌwheel**
daisywheel ˈdeɪ.zi.*h*wiːl **-s** -z

Dakar 'dæk.ɑːʳ, -əʳ (US) də'kɑːr; 'dæk.ɑːr
Dakota də'kəʊ.tə (US) -'koʊ.t̬ə -s -z
dal *food:* dɑːl
dal *in Italian phrases:* dæl, dɑːl (US) dɑːl
Dalai Lama ˌdæl.aɪ'lɑː.mə, ˌdɑː.laɪ'- (US) ˌdɑː.laɪ'- -s -z
dalasi də'lɑː.si -s -z
Dalbeattie dæl'biː.ti, dəl- (US) -t̬i
Dalby 'dɔːl.bi, 'dɒl-, 'dæl- (US) 'dɑːl-, 'dɔːl-, 'dæl-
Daldy 'dæl.di (US) 'dɑːl.di
dale (D) deɪl -s -z
Dalek 'dɑː.lek, -lɪk -s -s
dales|man 'deɪlz|.mən, -mæn **-men** -mən, -men **-woman** -ˌwʊm.ən **-women** -ˌwɪm.ɪn
Daley 'deɪ.li
Dalgety dæl'get.i, dəl- (US) -'get̬ - *stress shift, see compound:* ˌDalgety 'Bay
Dalgleish, Dalglish dæl'gliːʃ, dəl-
Dalhousie dæl'haʊ.zi, -'huː-
Dali 'dɑː.li
Dalkeith dæl'kiːθ
Dalkey 'dɔː.ki, 'dɔːl-
Dallas 'dæl.əs
dallianc|e 'dæl.i.ənts -es -ɪz
Dalloway 'dæl.ə.weɪ
dall|y 'dæl|.i -ies -iz -ying -i.ɪŋ -ied -id -ier/s -i.əʳ/z (US) -i.ɚ/z
Dalmatia dæl'meɪ.ʃə, -ʃi.ə
dalmatian (D) dæl'meɪ.ʃᵊn, -ʃi.ən -s -z
Dalmeny dæl'men.i, dəl-
Dalny 'dæl.ni
Dalry dæl'raɪ, dəl-
Dalrymple dæl'rɪm.pl̩, dəl-; 'dæl.rɪm- (US) 'dæl.rɪm-

Note: The family name of the Earl of Stair is /dæl'rɪm-, dəl-/.

dal segno dæl'sen.jəʊ, dɑːl- (US) dɑːl'seɪ.njoʊ, -'sen.joʊ
Dalston 'dɔːl.stᵊn, 'dɒl- (US) 'dɔːl-, 'dɑːl-
Dalton 'dɔːl.tᵊn, 'dɒl- (US) 'dɔːl-, 'dɑːl-
Dalton-in-Furness ˌdɔːl.tᵊn.ɪn'fɜː.nɪs, ˌdɒl- (US) ˌdɔːl.tᵊn.ɪn'fɝː-, ˌdɑːl-
Daltonism 'dɔːl.tᵊn.ɪ.zᵊm, 'dɒl- (US) 'dɔːl-, 'dɑːl-
Daltr(e)y 'dɔːl.tri, 'dɒl- (US) 'dɔːl-, 'dɑːl-
Dalwhinnie dæl'hwɪn.i, dəl-
Daly 'deɪ.li
Dalyell diː'el
Dalzell diː'el; 'dæl.zel
Dalziel diː'el; 'dæl.ziːl, -zi.əl

Note: The form /diː'el/ is chiefly used in Scotland.

dam dæm (US) -s -z (US) -ming -ɪŋ (US) -med -d (US)
damag|e 'dæm.ɪdʒ -es -ɪz -ing/ly -ɪŋ/li -ed -d
damaging 'dæm.ɪ.dʒɪŋ -ly -li
Damaraland də'mɑː.rə.lænd; 'dæm.ə.rə- (US) də'mɑːr.ə-
Damart® 'dæm.ɑːt, 'deɪ.mɑːt (US) 'dæm.ɑːrt, 'deɪ.mɑːrt
damascene 'dæm.ə.siːn -s -z
Damascus də'mæs.kəs, -'mɑː.skəs (US) -'mæs.kəs
damask 'dæm.əsk -s -s
dame (D) deɪm -s -z
Damian, Damien 'deɪ.mi.ən
Damman 'dæm.æn (US) dæm'æn
dammit 'dæm.ɪt
damn dæm -s -z -ing -ɪŋ -ed -d
damnab|le 'dæm.nə.b|l̩ -ly -li -leness -l̩.nəs, -l̩.nɪs
damnation dæm'neɪ.ʃᵊn -s -z
damnatory 'dæm.nə.tᵊr.i, -tri (US) -tɔːr.i
damnedest 'dæm.dɪst, -dəst
damni|fy 'dæm.nɪ|.faɪ -fies -faɪz -fying -faɪ.ɪŋ -fied -faɪd
damnum sine injuria ˌdæm.nəmˌsiː.neɪ.ɪn'dʒʊə.ri.ə (US) -'dʒʊr.i.ə
Damoclean ˌdæm.ə'kliː.ən
Damocles 'dæm.ə.kliːz
Damon 'deɪ.mən
damosel, damozel ˌdæm.əʊ'zel (US) -ə'-, -oʊ'- -s -z
damp dæmp -er -əʳ (US) -ɚ -est -ɪst, -əst -ly -li -ness -nəs, -nɪs -ish -ɪʃ -s -s -ing -ɪŋ -ed -t 'damp ˌcourse; ˌdamp 'squib
dampen 'dæm.pən -s -z -ing -ɪŋ, 'dæmp.nɪŋ -ed -d
damper 'dæm.pəʳ (US) -pɚ -s -z
Dampier 'dæm.pi.əʳ, -pɪəʳ (US) -pi.ɚ
damp-proof 'dæmp.pruːf -s -s -ing -ɪŋ -ed -d
damsel 'dæm.zᵊl -s -z
damson 'dæm.zᵊn -s -z
dan (D) dæn -s -z
Dana *first name in UK:* 'dɑː.nə *in US:* 'deɪ.nə *in Canada:* 'dæn.ə
Danaan 'dæn.i.ən -s -z
Danaë 'dæn.eɪ.iː, '-i-
Danaides, Danäides də'neɪ.ɪ.diːz, dæn'eɪ-, '-ə-
Dan-Air® ˌdæn'eəʳ (US) -'er
Danakil ˌdæn.ə'kiːl, -'kɪl (US) 'dæn.ə.kɪl; də'nɑː.kiːl
Da Nang ˌdɑː'næŋ (US) də'næŋ, dɑː'nɑːŋ
Danbury 'dæn.bᵊr.i, 'dæm- (US) 'dæn.ber-, -bɚ-
Danby 'dæn.bi, 'dæm- (US) 'dæn-
danc|e dɑːnts (US) dænts -es -ɪz -ing -ɪŋ -ed -t -er/s -əʳ/z (US) -ɚ/z
Dance dɑːnts, dænts (US) dænts
Dancer 'dɑːnt.səʳ (US) 'dænt.sɚ
dandelion 'dæn.dɪ.laɪən (US) -də-, -dɪ- -s -z
dandi|fy 'dæn.dɪ|.faɪ (US) -də- -fies -faɪz -fying -faɪ.ɪŋ -fied -faɪd
dandl|e 'dæn.dl̩ -es -z -ing -ɪŋ, 'dænd.lɪŋ -ed -d
Dando 'dæn.dəʊ (US) -doʊ
dandruff 'dæn.drʌf (US) -drəf
dand|y 'dæn.d|i -ies -iz -yish -i.ɪʃ -yism -i.ɪ.zᵊm
Dane deɪn -s -z
Danebury 'deɪn.bᵊr.i, 'deɪm- (US) 'deɪn.ber-, -bɚ-
danegeld 'deɪn.geld, 'deɪŋ- (US) 'deɪn-
Danelaw 'deɪn.lɔː (US) -lɑː, -lɔː
danger 'deɪn.dʒəʳ (US) -dʒɚ -s -z
Dangerfield 'deɪn.dʒə.fiːld (US) -dʒɚ-
dangerous 'deɪn.dʒᵊr.əs -ly -li -ness -nəs, -nɪs
dangerously 'deɪn.dʒᵊr.ə.sli
dangl|e (D) 'dæŋ.gl̩ -es -z -ing -ɪŋ, 'dæŋ.glɪŋ -ed -d -er/s -əʳ/z, '-gləʳ/z (US) '-gl̩.ɚ/z, '-glɚ/z
dangly 'dæŋ.gl̩.i, '-gli
Daniel 'dæn.jəl -s -z
Danielle ˌdæn.i'el, dæn'jel
Danish 'deɪ.nɪʃ ˌDanish 'blue; ˌDanish 'pastry
dank dæŋk -er -əʳ (US) -ɚ -est -ɪst, -əst -ly -li -ness -nəs, -nɪs
Danks dæŋks
Dankworth 'dæŋk.wəθ, -wɜːθ (US) -wɚθ, -wɝːθ
Dann dæn
d'Annunzio dæn'ʊnt.si.əʊ (US) dɑː'nʊnt.si.oʊ
Danny 'dæn.i
Danone dæn'əʊn, dæn'ɒn (US) -oʊn, -ɑːn
danse(s) macabre(s) ˌdɑ̃ːns.mə'kɑː.brə, -mæk'ɑː- (US) ˌdɑːnts.mə'kɑː.brə
danseuse(s) ˌdɑ̃ːn'sɜːz (US) ˌdɑːnt'suːz, -'sʊz
Dansville 'dænz.vɪl
Dante 'dæn.ti, 'dɑːn-, -teɪ (US) 'dɑːn.teɪ
Dantesque dæn'tesk (US) dɑːn-
Danton 'dæn.tɒn, -tən; *as if French:* dɑ̃ːn'tɔ̃ːŋ (US) dɑːn'tɑːn, -toʊn; '--, -tən
Danube 'dæn.juːb
Danubian dæn'juː.bi.ən, də'njuː-
Danuta də'nuː.tə, dæn'uː- (US) də'nuː.t̬ə
Danvers 'dæn.vəz (US) -vɚz
Danville 'dæn.vɪl
Danzig 'dænt.sɪg, -sɪk
daphne (D) 'dæf.ni
Daphnis 'dæf.nɪs
dapp|er (D) 'dæp|.əʳ (US) -ɚ -erest -ᵊr.ɪst, -ᵊr.əst
dappl|e 'dæp.l̩ -es -z -ing -ɪŋ, '-lɪŋ -ed -d
dapple-grey ˌdæp.l̩'greɪ
DAR ˌdiː.eɪ'ɑːʳ (US) -'ɑːr
Darbishire 'dɑː.bi.ʃəʳ, -ˌʃɪəʳ (US) 'dɑːr.bi.ʃɚ, -ˌʃɪr
Darby 'dɑː.bi (US) 'dɑːr- ˌDarby and 'Joan
d'Arc dɑːk (US) dɑːrk

Dark l

A type of LATERAL sound, recognizably different from CLEAR L.

Examples for English

If, when pronouncing the sound /l/, the back of the tongue is raised as for an [u] vowel, the quality is [u]-like and 'dark'; this effect is even more noticeable if the lips are rounded at the same time. This sound is typically found when /l/ occurs before a consonant or before a pause, e.g.:

help	/help/	[heɫp]
hill	/hɪl/	[hɪɫ]

In several accents of English, particularly those close to London, the dark l has given way to a [w] sound, so that *help* and *hill* might be transcribed /hewp/ and /hɪw/; this process is known as 'l vocalisation'.

In other languages

The process of l vocalisation took place in Polish some time ago, and the sound represented in Polish writing with the letter ł is almost always pronounced as [w], though foreigners usually try to pronounce it as [l].

D'Arcy, Darcy 'dɑː.si (US) 'dɑːr-
Dardanelles ˌdɑː.d^{ə}n'elz (US) ˌdɑːr-
Dardanus 'dɑː.d^{ə}n.əs (US) 'dɑːr-
dar|e (D) deə^{r} (US) der **-es** -z **-ing** -ɪŋ **-ed** -d **durst** dɜːst (US) dɝːst
daredevil 'deəˌdev.^{ə}l (US) 'der- **-s** -z
daren't deənt (US) dernt
Darent 'dær.^{ə}nt (US) 'der-, 'dær-
Darenth 'dær.ənθ (US) 'der-, 'dær-
Dares 'deə.riːz (US) 'der.iːz
daresay, dare say ˌdeə'seɪ (US) ˌder-
Daresbury 'dɑːz.b^{ə}r.i (US) 'dɑːrz.ber-, -bɚ-
Dar es Salaam ˌdɑː.res.sə'lɑːm, -rɪs-, -rez-, -rɪz- (US) ˌdɑːr.es-
Darfield 'dɑː.fiːld (US) 'dɑːr-
Darien 'deə.ri.ən, 'dær.i.ən (US) 'der.i-, 'dær-; ˌder.i'en, ˌdær-
Darin 'dær.ɪn (US) 'der-, 'dær-
daring 'deə.rɪŋ (US) 'der.ɪŋ **-ly** -li
Dario 'dær.i.əʊ (US) dɑː'riː.oʊ
dariole 'dær.i.əʊl (US) 'der.i.oʊl, 'dær- **-s** -z
Darius də'raɪ.əs, 'deə.ri-, 'dær.i-, 'dɑː.ri- (US) də'raɪ-; 'der.i-, 'dær-
Darjeeling dɑː'dʒiː.lɪŋ (US) dɑːr-
dark dɑːk (US) dɑːrk **-er** -ə^{r} (US) -ɚ **-est** -ɪst, -əst **-ly** -li **-ness** -nəs, -nɪs **'Dark ˌAges; ˌdark 'glasses; ˌdark 'horse**
darken 'dɑː.k^{ə}n (US) 'dɑːr- **-s** -z **-ing** -ɪŋ, 'dɑːk.nɪŋ (US) 'dɑːr.k^{ə}n.ɪŋ, 'dɑːrk.nɪŋ **-ed** -d
dark|ie 'dɑː.k|i (US) 'dɑːr- **-ies** -iz
darkish 'dɑː.kɪʃ (US) 'dɑːr-
darkling 'dɑː.klɪŋ (US) 'dɑːr-
darkroom 'dɑːk.rʊm, -ruːm (US) 'dɑːrk.ruːm, -rʊm **-s** -z
darksome 'dɑːk.səm (US) 'dɑːrk-
dark|y 'dɑː.k|i (US) 'dɑːr- **-ies** -iz
Darlaston 'dɑː.lə.stən (US) 'dɑːr-
Darleen, Darlene 'dɑː.liːn (US) dɑːr'liːn
Darley 'dɑː.li (US) 'dɑːr-
darling (D) 'dɑː.lɪŋ (US) 'dɑːr- **-s** -z
Darlington 'dɑː.lɪŋ.tən (US) 'dɑːr-
Darlow 'dɑː.ləʊ (US) 'dɑːr.loʊ
Darmstadt 'dɑːm.stæt *as if German:* -ʃtæt (US) 'dɑːrm-
darn dɑːn (US) dɑːrn **-s** -z **-ing** -ɪŋ **-ed** -d **-er/s** -ə^{r}/z (US) -ɚ/z **'darning ˌneedle**
darnation dɑː'neɪ.ʃ^{ə}n (US) dɑːr-
darnel 'dɑː.n^{ə}l (US) 'dɑːr-
Darnell dɑː'nel (US) dɑːr-, '--
Darney 'dɑː.ni (US) 'dɑːr-
Darnley 'dɑːn.li (US) 'dɑːrn-
Darracq 'dær.ək, dær'æk (US) 'der-, 'dær-
Darragh 'dær.ə, -əx (US) 'der.ə, 'dær-
Darrell 'dær.^{ə}l (US) 'der-, 'dær-
Darren, Darron 'dær.^{ə}n (US) 'der-, 'dær-
Darrow 'dær.əʊ (US) 'der.oʊ, 'dær-
Darryl 'dær.^{ə}l, -ɪl (US) 'der-, 'dær-
dart (D) dɑːt (US) dɑːrt **-s** -s **-ing** -ɪŋ (US) 'dɑːr.t̬ɪŋ **-ed** -ɪd (US) 'dɑːr.t̬ɪd
D'Artagnan dɑː'tæn.jən, -jɑ̃ːŋ (US) dɑːr'tæn.jən; ˌdɑːr.t^{ə}n'jɑːn
dartboard 'dɑːt.bɔːd (US) 'dɑːrt.bɔːrd **-s** -z
darter 'dɑː.tə^{r} (US) 'dɑːr.t̬ɚ **-s** -z
Dartford 'dɑːt.fəd (US) 'dɑːrt.fɚd
Darth Vader ˌdɑːθ'veɪ.də^{r} (US) ˌdɑːrθ'veɪ.dɚ
Dartie 'dɑː.ti (US) 'dɑːr.t̬i
Dartington 'dɑː.tɪŋ.tən (US) 'dɑːr.t̬ɪŋ-
Dartle 'dɑː.tl̩ (US) 'dɑːr.t̬l̩
Dartmoor 'dɑːt.mɔː^{r}, -mʊə^{r} (US) 'dɑːrt.mʊr, -mɔːr
Dartmouth 'dɑːt.məθ (US) 'dɑːrt-
Darton 'dɑː.t^{ə}n (US) 'dɑːr-
darts dɑːts (US) dɑːrts
Darwen 'dɑː.wɪn (US) 'dɑːr-
Darwin 'dɑː.wɪn (US) 'dɑːr- **-ism** -ɪ.z^{ə}m
Darwinian dɑː'wɪn.i.ən (US) dɑːr-
Daryl(l) 'dær.^{ə}l, -ɪl (US) 'der-, 'dær-
Daschle 'dæʃ.l̩
Dasent 'deɪ.s^{ə}nt
dash (D) dæʃ **-es** -ɪz **-ing** -ɪŋ **-ed** -t **-er/s** -ə^{r}/z (US) -ɚ/z
dashboard 'dæʃ.bɔːd (US) -bɔːrd **-s** -z
dashing 'dæʃ.ɪŋ **-ly** -li
Dashwood 'dæʃ.wʊd
dastard 'dæs.təd, 'dɑː.stəd (US) 'dæs.tɚd **-s** -z **-ly** -li **-liness** -lɪ.nəs, -nɪs
DAT dæt; ˌdiː.eɪ'tiː
data 'deɪ.tə, 'dɑː- (US) 'deɪ.t̬ə, 'dæt̬.ə, 'dɑː.t̬ə
databank 'deɪ.tə.bæŋk, 'dɑː- (US) 'deɪ.t̬ə-, 'dæt̬.ə-, 'dɑː.t̬ə- **-s** -s
databas|e 'deɪ.tə.beɪs, 'dɑː- (US) 'deɪ.t̬ə-, 'dæt̬.ə-, 'dɑː.t̬ə- **-es** -ɪz
databus 'deɪ.tə.bʌs, 'dɑː- (US) 'deɪ.t̬ə-, 'dæt̬.ə-, 'dɑː.t̬ə- **-es** -ɪz
datafile 'deɪ.tə.faɪl, 'dɑː- (US) 'deɪ.t̬ə-, 'dæt̬.ə-, 'dɑː.t̬ə- **-s** -z
dataflow 'deɪ.tə.fləʊ, 'dɑː- (US) 'deɪ.t̬ə.floʊ, 'dæt̬.ə-, 'dɑː.t̬ə-
dataglove 'deɪ.tə.glʌv, 'dɑː- (US) 'deɪ.t̬ə-, 'dæt̬.ə- (US) 'dɑː.t̬ə- **-s** -z
Datapost® 'deɪ.tə.pəʊst, 'dɑː- (US) -t̬ə.poʊst
Datchery 'dætʃ.^{ə}r.i
Datchet 'dætʃ.ɪt
dat|e deɪt **-es** -s **-ing** -ɪŋ (US) 'deɪ.t̬ɪŋ **-ed** -ɪd (US) 'deɪ.t̬ɪd **'dating ˌagency**
dated 'deɪ.tɪd (US) -t̬ɪd
Datel® 'deɪ.tel
Dateline® 'deɪt.laɪn **-s** -z
date-stamp 'deɪt.stæmp **-s** -s **-ing** -ɪŋ **-ed** -t
datival də'taɪ.v^{ə}l, deɪ-
dative 'deɪ.tɪv (US) -t̬ɪv **-s** -z
Datsun® 'dæt.s^{ə}n (US) 'dɑːt-, 'dæt-
dat|um 'deɪ.t|əm, 'dɑː- (US) 'deɪ.t̬|əm, 'dæt̬|.əm, 'dɑː.t̬|əm **-a** -ə
daub dɔːb (US) dɑːb, dɔːb **-s** -z **-ing** -ɪŋ **-ed** -d **-er/s** -ə^{r}/z (US) -ɚ/z
daube dəʊb (US) doʊb **-s** -z
Daubeney 'dɔː.b^{ə}n.i (US) 'dɑː-, 'dɔː-
Daudet 'dəʊ.deɪ (US) doʊ'deɪ
Daugavpils 'daʊ.gæf.pɪls (US) 'doʊ.gʌv-, 'daʊ-, -gʌf-, -gɑːf-, -pɪlz, -piːlz
daughter 'dɔː.tə^{r} (US) 'dɑː.t̬ɚ, 'dɔː- **-s**
daughter-in-law 'dɔː.tə^{r}.ɪn.lɔː (US) 'dɑː.t̬ɚ.ɪn.lɑː, 'dɔː-, -lɔː

daughters-in-law ˈdɔː.təz.ɪn.lɔː (US) ˈdɑː.t̬ɚz.ɪn.lɑː, ˈdɔː-, -lɔː
daughterl|y ˈdɔː.tə.l|i (US) ˈdɑː.t̬ɚ-, ˈdɔː- **-iness** -ɪ.nəs, -ɪ.nɪs
Daun dɔːn (US) dɑːn, dɔːn
daunt **(D)** dɔːnt (US) dɑːnt, dɔːnt **-s** -s **-ing** -ɪŋ (US) ˈdɑːn.t̬ɪŋ, ˈdɔːn- **-ed** -ɪd (US) ˈdɑːn.t̬ɪd, ˈdɔːn-
dauntless ˈdɔːnt.ləs, -lɪs (US) ˈdɑːnt-, ˈdɔːnt **-ly** -li **-ness** -nəs, -nɪs
dauphin **(D)** ˈdɔː.fɪn, ˈdəʊ-, -fæ̃ŋ (US) ˈdɑː.fɪn, ˈdɔː-; doʊˈfæn **-s** -z
Dauphiné ˈdɔː.fɪ.neɪ, ˈdəʊ-, --ˈ- (US) ˌdoʊ.fiːˈneɪ
dauphine **(D)** ˈdɔː.fiːn, ˈdəʊ-, -fɪn (US) dɑːˈfiːn, dɔː-, doʊ- **-s** -z
Davao dævˈɑː.əʊ, dəˈvɑː- (US) dɑːˈvaʊ
Dave deɪv
Davenant, **D'Avenant** ˈdæv.ən.ənt, -ɪ.nənt
davenport **(D)** ˈdæv.ən.pɔːt, -əm- (US) -ən.pɔːrt **-s** -s
Daventry ˈdæv.ən.tri *old-fashioned local pronunciation:* ˈdeɪn.tri
Davey ˈdeɪ.vi
David ˈdeɪ.vɪd **-s** -z
Davidge ˈdæv.ɪdʒ
Davidson ˈdeɪ.vɪd.sən
Davie ˈdeɪ.vi
Davies ˈdeɪ.vɪs (US) -viːz
Davina dəˈviː.nə
da Vinci dəˈvɪn.tʃi
Davis ˈdeɪ.vɪs
Davison ˈdeɪ.vɪ.sən
davit ˈdæv.ɪt, ˈdeɪ.vɪt **-s** -s
Davos dævˈəʊs, dɑːˈvəʊs, -ˈvɒs; ˈdɑː.vɒs, -vəʊs (US) dɑːˈvoʊs
dav|y **(D)** ˈdeɪ.v|i **-ies** -iz **ˈdavy ˌlamp; ˌDavy ˌJones's ˈlocker**
daw **(D)** dɔː (US) dɑː, dɔː **-s** -z
dawdl|e ˈdɔː.dl̩ (US) ˈdɑː-, ˈdɔː- **-es** -z **-ing** -ɪŋ, ˈdɔːd.lɪŋ (US) ˈdɑːd-, ˈdɔːd- **-ed** -d **-er/s** -əʳ/z, ˈdɔːd.ləʳ/z (US) ˈdɑː.dl̩.ɚ/z, ˈdɔː- (US) ˈdɑːd.lɚ/z, ˈdɔːd-
Dawe dɔː (US) dɑː, dɔː **-s** -z
Dawkes dɔːks (US) dɑːks, dɔːks
Dawkins ˈdɔː.kɪnz (US) ˈdɑː-, ˈdɔː-
Dawley ˈdɔː.li (US) ˈdɑː-, ˈdɔː-
Dawlish ˈdɔː.lɪʃ (US) ˈdɑː-, ˈdɔː-
dawn **(D)** dɔːn (US) dɑːn, dɔːn **-s** -z **-ing** -ɪŋ **-ed** -d
Dawson ˈdɔː.sən (US) ˈdɑː-, ˈdɔː-
day **(D)** deɪ **-s** -z **ˈday ˌboy; ˈday ˌcamp; ˈday ˌgirl; ˈday ˌjob; ˈday ˌlily; ˈday ˌnursery; ˌday ˈout; ˈday ˌroom; ˈday ˌschool; at the ˌend of the ˈday; ˌcall it a ˈday**
daybreak ˈdeɪ.breɪk **-s** -s
daycare ˈdeɪ.keəʳ (US) -ker
day|dream ˈdeɪ|.driːm **-dreams** -driːmz **-dreaming** -ˌdriː.mɪŋ **-dreamed** -drempt, -driːmd **-dreamt** -drempt **-dreamer/s** -ˌdriː.məʳ/z (US) -ˌdriː.mɚ/z
Day-Glo®, **dayglo** ˈdeɪ.gləʊ (US) -gloʊ
Daylesford ˈdeɪlz.fəd, ˈdeɪls- (US) -fɚd
Day-Lewis ˌdeɪˈluː.ɪs
daylight ˈdeɪ.laɪt **-s** -s **ˌdaylight ˈrobbery; ˌdaylight ˈsaving; ˈdaylight ˌtime; ˌbeat the living ˈdaylights out of sb**
dayspring ˈdeɪ.sprɪŋ
daystar ˈdeɪ.stɑːʳ (US) -stɑːr **-s** -z
daytime ˈdeɪ.taɪm
day-to-day ˌdeɪ.təˈdeɪ (US) -t̬əˈ-
Dayton ˈdeɪ.tən
Daytona deɪˈtəʊ.nə (US) -ˈtoʊ- **DayˌtonaˈBeach**
daywork ˈdeɪ.wɜːk (US) -wɝːk
Daz® dæz
daz|e deɪz **-es** -ɪz **-ing** -ɪŋ **-ed** -d **-edly** -əd.li, -ɪd.li
dazzl|e ˈdæz.l̩ **-es** -z **-ing/ly** -ɪŋ/li, ˈdæz.lɪŋ/li **-ed** -d **-er/s** -əʳ/z, ˈ-ləʳ/z (US) ˈ-l̩.ɚ/z, ˈ-lɚ/z
DBMS ˌdiː.biː.emˈes
DC ˌdiːˈsiː
D-Day ˈdiː.deɪ
DDT ˌdiː.diːˈtiː
de- diː-, dɪ-, də-
Note: Prefix. In verbs containing **de-** where the stem is free, usually a noun, it is normally pronounced /ˌdiː-/, e.g. **debag** /ˌdiːˈbæg/, **declutch** /ˌdiːˈklʌtʃ/. Attached to bound stems the pronunciation is normally /dɪ-/ or /də-/, e.g. **debilitate** /dɪˈbɪl.ɪ.teɪt/, **demand** /dɪˈmɑːnd (US) -mænd/. There are exceptions; see individual entries.
de *in French names:* də, dɪ, di
deacon **(D)** ˈdiː.kən **-s** -z
deaconess ˌdiː.kəˈnes; ˈ---, -nɪs (US) ˈdiː.kən.əs **-es** -ɪz
deacon|hood ˈdiː.kən|.hʊd **-ship/s** -ʃɪp/s
deaconr|y ˈdiː.kən.r|i **-ies** -iz
deacti|vate ˌdiˈæk.tɪ|.veɪt, -tə- **-vates** -veɪts **-vating** -veɪ.tɪŋ (US) -veɪ.t̬ɪŋ **-vated** -veɪ.tɪd (US) -veɪ.t̬ɪd
deactivation diˌæk.tɪˈveɪ.ʃən, ˌdiː.æk-, -təˈ- (US) diˌæk-
dead ded **-ness** -nəs, -nɪs **ˌdead ˈend; ˌdead ˈheat; ˌdead ˈletter; ˌdead or ˈalive; ˌdead ˈreckoning; ˌdead ˈringer; ˌDead ˈSea; ˌdead ˈset; as ˌdead as a ˈdoor-nail**
dead-and-alive ˌded.ənd.əˈlaɪv
deadbeat *(n.)* ˈded.biːt, ˈdeb- (US) ˈded- **-s** -s
dead beat *(adj.)* ˌdedˈbiːt, ˌdeb- (US) ˌded- *stress shift:* ˌdead beat ˈworker
deadbolt ˈded.bəʊlt, ˈdeb- (US) ˈded.boʊlt **-s** -s
deaden ˈded.ən **-s** -z **-ing** -ɪŋ **-ed** -d
dead-end ˌdedˈend *stress shift:* ˌdead-end ˈstreet
deadeye **(D)** ˈded.aɪ **-s** -z
deadhead ˈded.hed, -ˈ- **-s** -z
deadline ˈded.laɪn **-s** -z
deadlock ˈded.lɒk (US) -lɑːk **-s** -s **-ed** -t
deadl|y ˈded.l|i **-ier** -i.əʳ (US) -i.ɚ **-iest** -i.ɪst, -i.əst **-iness** -ɪ.nəs, -ɪ.nɪs **ˌdeadly ˈnightshade**
deadnettle ˈded.net.l̩, ˌ-ˈ-- (US) ˌdedˈnet̬-, ˈ-ˌ-- **-s** -z
deadpan ˈded.pæn, ˈdeb-, ˌ-ˈ- (US) ˈded.pæn
deadweight ˌdedˈweɪt, ˈ-- **-s** -s
deadwood ˈded.wʊd, ˌ-ˈ-
deaf def **-er** -əʳ (US) -ɚ **-est** -ɪst, -əst **-ly** -li **-ness** -nəs, -nɪs **ˌfall on ˌdeaf ˈears**
deaf-aid ˈdef.eɪd **-s** -z
deaf-and-dumb ˌdef.əndˈdʌm
deafen ˈdef.ən **-s** -z **-ing/ly** -ɪŋ/li, ˈ-nɪŋ/li **-ed** -d
deaf-mute ˌdefˈmjuːt, ˈ-- **-s** -s
Deakin ˈdiː.kɪn
deal **(D)** diːl **-s** -z **-ing** -ɪŋ **dealt** delt
dealer ˈdiː.ləʳ (US) -lɚ **-s** -z
dealership ˈdiː.lə.ʃɪp (US) -lɚ- **-s** -s
dealing ˈdiː.lɪŋ **-s** -z
dealt *(from* **deal***)* delt
Dealtry *surname:* ˈdɔːl.tri, ˈdɪəl- (US) ˈdɑːl-, ˈdɔːl-, ˈdiːl- *road in London:* ˈdel.tri
deami|nate diˈæm.ɪ.neɪt, ˌdiː-, ˈ-ə- (US) ˈ-ə- **-nates** -neɪts **-nating** -neɪ.tɪŋ (US) -neɪ.t̬ɪŋ **-nated** -neɪ.tɪd (US) -neɪ.t̬ɪd
deamination diˌæm.ɪˈneɪ.ʃən, ˌdiː-, -əˈ- (US) -əˈ-
dean diːn **-s** -z **-ship/s** -ʃɪp/s
Dean(e) diːn
deaner|y ˈdiː.nər|.i **-ies** -iz
Deanna diˈæn.ə; ˈdiː.nə (US) diˈæn.ə
Deans diːnz
dear **(D)** dɪəʳ (US) dɪr **-s** -z **-er** -əʳ (US) -ɚ **-est** -ɪst, -əst **-ly** -li **-ness** -nəs, -nɪs
dear|ie ˈdɪə.r|i (US) ˈdɪr|.i **-ies** -iz
Dearing ˈdɪə.rɪŋ (US) ˈdɪr.ɪŋ
Dearne dɜːn (US) dɝːn
dearth **(D)** dɜːθ (US) dɝːθ **-s** -s
dear|y ˈdɪə.r|i (US) ˈdɪr|.i **-ies** -iz
death deθ **-s** -s **ˈdeath ˌduty; ˈdeath ˌmask; ˈdeath ˌpenalty; ˈdeath ˌrate; ˈdeath ˌrattle; ˌdeath ˈrow; ˈdeath ˌtoll; ˈdeath ˌtrap; ˈdeath ˌwarrant; ˌDeath ˈValley; ˈdeath ˌwish; like ˌdeath warmed ˈup; like ˌgrim ˈdeath**
Death *surname:* deɪθ, deθ, diːθ; diːˈæθ, deɪ-, -ˈɑːθ
deathbed ˈdeθ.bed **-s** -z
deathblow ˈdeθ.bləʊ (US) -bloʊ **-s** -z
deathless ˈdeθ.ləs, -lɪs
deathlike ˈdeθ.laɪk

deathl|y ˈdeθ.l|i **-ier** -i.əʳ (US) -i.ɚ **-iest** -i.ɪst, -i.əst **-iness** -ɪ.nəs, -ɪ.nɪs
death's-head ˈdeθs.hed **-s** -z
deathwatch ˈdeθ.wɒtʃ (US) -wɑːtʃ, -wɔːtʃ ˌ**deathwatch** ˈ**beetle**
Deauville ˈdəʊ.vɪl, -viːl (US) ˈdoʊ-
Deayton ˈdiː.tᵊn
deb deb **-s** -z
débâcle deɪˈbɑː.kḷ, də-, debˈɑː-, dɪˈbɑː-; ˈdeɪ.bɑː- (US) dɪˈbɑː-, də-, deɪ-, -ˈbæk.ḷ **-s** -z
debag ˌdiːˈbæg **-s** -z **-ging** -ɪŋ **-ged** -d
debar ˌdiːˈbɑːʳ, dɪ- (US) -ˈbɑːr **-s** -z **-ring** -ɪŋ **-red** -d
debark ˌdiːˈbɑːk, dɪ- (US) -ˈbɑːrk **-s** -s **-ing** -ɪŋ **-ed** -t
debarkation ˌdiː.bɑːˈkeɪ.ʃᵊn (US) -bɑːrˈ- **-s** -z
debas|e dɪˈbeɪs **-es** -ɪz **-ing/ly** -ɪŋ/li **-ed** -t **-ement** -mənt
debatab|le dɪˈbeɪ.tə.b|ḷ, də- (US) dɪˈbeɪ.t̬ə- **-ly** -li
de|bate dɪ|ˈbeɪt, də- (US) dɪ- **-bates** -ˈbeɪts **-bating** -ˈbeɪ.tɪŋ (US) -ˈbeɪ.t̬ɪŋ **-bated** -ˈbeɪ.tɪd (US) -ˈbeɪ.t̬ɪd **-bater/s** -ˈbeɪ.təʳ/z (US) -ˈbeɪ.t̬ɚ/z
debauch dɪˈbɔːtʃ (US) -ˈbɑːtʃ, -ˈbɔːtʃ **-es** -ɪz **-ing** -ɪŋ **-ed** -t **-er/s** -əʳ/z (US) -ɚ/z
debauchee ˌdeb.ɔːˈtʃiː, -ˈʃiː, ˌdɪb-; dɪˌbɔː-, də- (US) ˌdeb.ɑːˈʃiː, -ɔːˈ-; dɪˌbɑːˈtʃiː, -ˌbɔːˈ- **-s** -z
debaucher|y dɪˈbɔː.tʃᵊr|.i, dəˈ- (US) dɪˈbɑː-, -ˈbɔː- **-ies** -iz
Debbie ˈdeb.i
de Beauvoir dəˈbəʊ.vwɑːʳ (US) -ˌboʊˈvwɑːr
Deben ˈdiː.bᵊn
de bene esse ˌdeɪˌben.iˈes.i, dəˌbiː.niːˈes.iː
Debenham ˈdeb.ᵊn.əm (US) -hæm **-'s** -z
debenture dɪˈben.*t*ʃəʳ, də- (US) dɪˈben*t*.ʃɚ **-s** -z
debili|tate dɪˈbɪl.ɪ|.teɪt, də-, ˈ-ə- (US) dɪ- **-tates** -teɪts **-tating** -teɪ.tɪŋ (US) -teɪ.t̬ɪŋ **-tated** -teɪ.tɪd (US) -teɪ.t̬ɪd
debilitation dɪˌbɪl.ɪˈteɪ.ʃᵊn, də-, -əˈ- (US) dɪ-
debility dɪˈbɪl.ə.ti, də-, -ɪ.ti (US) dɪˈbɪl.ə.t̬i
deb|it ˈdeb|.ɪt **-its** -ɪts **-iting** -ɪ.tɪŋ (US) -ɪ.t̬ɪŋ **-ited** -ɪ.tɪd (US) -ɪ.t̬ɪd
Debnam ˈdeb.nəm
debonair ˌdeb.əˈneəʳ (US) -ˈner **-ly** -li **-ness** -nəs, -nɪs
de Bono dəˈbəʊ.nəʊ (US) -ˈboʊ.noʊ
Deborah ˈdeb.ᵊr.ə, ˈ-rə
debouch dɪˈbaʊtʃ, ˌdiː-, -buːʃ **-es** -ɪz **-ing** -ɪŋ **-ed** -t **-ment** -mənt
Debra ˈdeb.rə
Debrecen ˈdeb.rət.sᵊn (US) ˌdeb.rətˈsen, ˈ---
Debrett dəˈbret, dɪ- **-'s** -s

debridement, débridement dɪˈbriːd.mənt, ˌdiː-, deɪ-; *as if French:* -ˌbriːdˈmɑ̃ːŋ (US) dɪˈbriːd.mənt, deɪ-, -ˈbriːd.mɑ̃ːŋ
debrief ˌdiːˈbriːf **-s** -s **-ing** -ɪŋ **-ed** -t
debris ˈdeɪ.briː, ˈdeb.riː (US) dəˈbriː; ˈdeɪ.briː
debt det **-s** -s
debtor ˈdet.əʳ (US) ˈdet̬.ɚ **-s** -z
debug ˌdiːˈbʌg **-s** -z **-ging** -ɪŋ **-ged** -d
debunk ˌdiːˈbʌŋk **-s** -s **-ing** -ɪŋ **-ed** -t
De Burgh dəˈbɜːg (US) -ˈbɝːg
Debussy dəˈbuː.siː, -ˈbjuː-; (US) ˈdeɪ.bjuː.si; ˌdeɪ.bjuːˈsiː; dəˈbjuː.si
Note: US street names are always /də-/.
début ˈdeɪ.bjuː, -buː; ˈdeb.juː (US) deɪˈbjuː, ˈ-- **-s** -z **-ing** -ɪŋ **-ed** -d
débutant ˈdeb.jʊ.tɑ̃ːŋ, ˈdeɪ.bjʊ- (US) ˈdeb.juː.tɑːnt, ˌ--ˈ- **-s** -z
débutante ˈdeb.juː.tɑ̃ːŋt, ˈdeɪ.bjuː- (US) ˈdeb.juː.tɑːnt, ˌ--ˈ- **-s** -s
Dec. *(abbrev. for* **December***)* dɪˈsem.bəʳ, də- (US) dɪˈsem.bɚ
deca- dek.ə-
Note: Prefix. Normally carries primary or secondary stress on the first syllable, e.g. **decagon** /ˈdek.ə.gən (US) -gɑːn/, **decahedron** /ˌdek.əˈhiː.drən/.
decachord ˈdek.ə.kɔːd (US) -kɔːrd **-s** -z
decade *ten years:* ˈdek.eɪd; dekˈeɪd, dɪˈkeɪd **-s** -z *division of the rosary:* ˈdek.əd
decaden|ce ˈdek.ə.dᵊn*t*|s (US) ˈdek.ə-; dɪˈkeɪ- **-cy** -si
decadent ˈdek.ə.dᵊnt (US) ˈdek.ə-; dɪˈkeɪ- **-ly** -li
decaf, decaff ˈdiː.kæf
decaffei|nate dɪˈkæf.ɪ|.neɪt, ˌdiː-, ˈ-ə- **-nates** -neɪts **-nating** -neɪ.tɪŋ (US) -neɪ.t̬ɪŋ **-nated** -neɪ.tɪd (US) -neɪ.t̬ɪd
decagon ˈdek.ə.gən (US) -gɑːn **-s** -z
decagram, decagramme ˈdek.ə.græm **-s** -z
decahedr|on ˌdek.əˈhiː.dr|ən, -ˈhed.r|ən (US) -ˈhiː.dr|ən **-ons** -ənz **-a** -ə **-al** -ᵊl
decal ˈdiː.kæl; dɪˈkæl; **-s** -z
decalcification ˌdiːˌkæl.sɪ.fɪˈkeɪ.ʃᵊn, -sə-
decalci|fy ˌdiːˈkæl.sɪ|.faɪ, -sə- **-fies** -faɪz **-fying** -faɪ.ɪŋ **-fied** -faɪd
decalitre, decaliter ˈdek.əˌliː.təʳ (US) -t̬ɚ **-s** -z
Decalogue ˈdek.ə.lɒg (US) -lɑːg, -lɔːg **-s** -z
Decameron dɪˈkæm.ᵊr.ᵊn, dekˈæm-, dəˈkæm-
decametre, decameter ˈdek.əˌmiː.təʳ (US) -t̬ɚ **-s** -z

decamp ˌdiːˈkæmp, dɪ- **-s** -s **-ing** -ɪŋ **-ed** -t
decanal dɪˈkeɪ.nᵊl, dekˈeɪ-, dəˈkeɪ-; ˈdek.ᵊn.ᵊl
decani dɪˈkeɪ.naɪ, dekˈeɪ-
de|cant dɪ|ˈkænt, ˌdiː- **-cants** -ˈkænts **-canting** -ˈkæn.tɪŋ (US) -ˈkæn.t̬ɪŋ **-canted** -ˈkæn.tɪd (US) -ˈkæn.t̬ɪd
decantation ˌdiː.kænˈteɪ.ʃᵊn **-s** -z
decanter dɪˈkæn.təʳ, də- (US) dɪˈkæn.t̬ɚ **-s** -z
decapi|tate dɪˈkæp.ɪ|.teɪt, ˌdiː-, ˈ-ə- **-tates** -teɪts **-tating** -teɪ.tɪŋ (US) -teɪ.t̬ɪŋ **-tated** -teɪ.tɪd (US) -teɪ.t̬ɪd
decapitation dɪˌkæp.ɪˈteɪ.ʃᵊn, ˌdiː-, -əˈ- **-s** -z
decapod ˈdek.ə.pɒd (US) -pɑːd **-s** -z
Decapolis dekˈæp.ə.lɪs, dɪˈkæp-
decarbo|nate ˌdiːˈkɑː.bəl.neɪt (US) -ˈkɑːr- **-nates** -neɪts **-nating** -neɪ.tɪŋ (US) -neɪ.t̬ɪŋ **-nated** -neɪ.tɪd (US) -neɪ.t̬ɪd
decarbonization, -isa- diːˌkɑː.bᵊn.aɪˈzeɪ.ʃᵊn, ˌdɪ.kɑː-, -ɪˈ- (US) ˌdiː.kɑːr.bə.nɪˈ-
decarboniz|e, -is|e ˌdiːˈkɑː.bə.naɪz (US) -ˈkɑːr- **-es** -ɪz **-ing** -ɪŋ **-ed** -d
decarburiz|e, -is|e ˌdiːˈkɑː.bjʊ.raɪz, -bjᵊr.aɪz (US) -ˈkɑːr.bə.raɪz, -bjə-, -bjʊ- **-es** -ɪz **-ing** -ɪŋ **-ed** -d
decasyllabic ˌdek.ə.sɪˈlæb.ɪk, -səˈ-
decasyllable ˈdek.əˌsɪl.ə.bḷ, ˌdek.əˈsɪl.ə- **-s** -z
decathlete dɪˈkæθ.liːt, dekˈæθ-, dəˈkæθ- **-s** -s
decathlon dɪˈkæθ.lɒn, dekˈæθ-, dəˈkæθ-, -lən (US) dɪˈkæθ.lɑːn, -lən, də- **-s** -z
decay dɪˈkeɪ, də- **-s** -z **-ing** -ɪŋ **-ed** -d
Decca ˈdek.ə
Deccan ˈdek.ən, -æn
deceas|e dɪˈsiːs, də- (US) dɪ- **-es** -ɪz **-ing** -ɪŋ **-ed** -t
decedent dɪˈsiː.dᵊnt, də- (US) dɪ- **-s** -s
deceit dɪˈsiːt, də- (US) dɪ- **-s** -s
deceitful dɪˈsiːt.fᵊl, də-, -fʊl (US) dɪ- **-ly** -li **-ness** -nəs, -nɪs
deceivable dɪˈsiː.və.bḷ, də- (US) dɪ-
deceiv|e dɪˈsiːv, də- (US) dɪ- **-es** -z **-ing** -ɪŋ **-ed** -d **-er/s** -əʳ/z (US) -ɚ/z
deceler|ate dɪˈsel.ᵊr|.eɪt, ˌdiː- (US) -ə.r|eɪt **-ates** -eɪts **-ating** -eɪ.tɪŋ (US) -eɪ.t̬ɪŋ **-ated** -eɪ.tɪd (US) -eɪ.t̬ɪd
deceleration ˌdɪˌsel.əˈreɪ.ʃᵊn, ˌdiː.sel- **-s** -z
December dɪˈsem.bəʳ, də- (US) dɪˈsem.bɚ **-s** -z
decemvir dɪˈsem.vəʳ, də-, -vɜːʳ (US) diːˈsem.vɪr **-s** -z
decemvirate dɪˈsem.vɪ.rət, də-, -vᵊr.ət, -ɪt, -eɪt (US) diːˈsem.vɚ.ɪt, -və.reɪt **-s** -s

decenc|y 'diː.sᵊnt.s|i **-ies** -iz

decennial dɪ'sen.i.əl, des'en-, də'sen-, diː- ⓤⓢ dɪ'sen-, diː-

decent 'diː.sᵊnt **-ly** -li

decentralization, -isa- diːˌsen.trᵊl.aɪ'zeɪ.ʃᵊn, ˌdɪ.sen-, -ɪ'- ⓤⓢ -ɪ'-

decentraliz|e, -is|e diː'sen.trə.laɪz, ˌdɪ- **-es** -ɪz **-ing** -ɪŋ **-ed** -d

deception dɪ'sep.ʃᵊn, də- ⓤⓢ dɪ- **-s** -z

deceptive dɪ'sep.tɪv, də- ⓤⓢ dɪ- **-ly** -li **-ness** -nəs, -nɪs

de Chastelain də'tʃæs.tə.leɪn ⓤⓢ -t̬ə.lən

deci- des.i-

Note: Prefix. Normally carries primary or secondary stress on the first syllable, e.g. **decimal** /'des.ɪ.mᵊl/, **decimalization** /ˌdes.ɪ.mᵊl.aɪ'zeɪ.ʃᵊn ⓤⓢ -ɪ'-/. There are exceptions; see individual entries.

decibel 'des.ɪ.bel, -bəl, -bᵊl **-s** -z

decid|e dɪ'saɪd, də- ⓤⓢ dɪ- **-es** -z **-ing** -ɪŋ **-ed/ly** -ɪd/li **-er/s** -əʳ/z ⓤⓢ -ɚ/z

deciduous dɪ'sɪd.ju.əs, də- ⓤⓢ dɪ'sɪdʒ.u- **-ly** -li **-ness** -nəs, -nɪs

decigram, decigramme 'des.ɪ.græm **-s** -z

decilitre, deciliter 'des.ɪˌliː.təʳ ⓤⓢ -t̬ɚ **-s** -z

decillion dɪ'sɪl.i.ən, '-jən ⓤⓢ '-jən **-s** -z

decimal 'des.ɪ.mᵊl, '-ə- **-s** -z **-ly** -i ˌ**decimal** '**point** ⓤⓢ '**decimal** ˌ**point**

decimalization, -isa- ˌdes.ɪ.mᵊl.aɪ'zeɪ.ʃᵊn, ˌ-ə-, -ɪ'- ⓤⓢ -ɪ'-

decimaliz|e, -is|e 'des.ɪ.mᵊl.aɪz, -ə- ⓤⓢ -mə.laɪz **-es** -ɪz **-ing** -ɪŋ **-ed** -d

deci|mate 'des.ɪ|.meɪt, '-ə- **-mates** -meɪts **-mating** -meɪ.tɪŋ ⓤⓢ -meɪ.t̬ɪŋ **-mated** -meɪ.tɪd ⓤⓢ -meɪ.t̬ɪd **-mator/s** -meɪ.təʳ/z ⓤⓢ -meɪ.t̬ɚ/z

decimation ˌdes.ɪ'meɪ.ʃᵊn, -ə'-

decimetre, decimeter 'des.ɪˌmiː.təʳ ⓤⓢ -t̬ɚ **-s** -z

deciph|er dɪ'saɪ.f|əʳ, ˌdiː- ⓤⓢ -f|ɚ **-ers** -əz ⓤⓢ -ɚz **-ering** -ᵊr.ɪŋ **-ered** -əd ⓤⓢ -ɚd

decipherable dɪ'saɪ.fᵊr.ə.bl̩, ˌdiː-

decision dɪ'sɪʒ.ᵊn, də- ⓤⓢ dɪ- **-s** -z

decision-mak|er dɪ'sɪʒ.ᵊnˌmeɪ.k|əʳ, də-, -ᵊm- ⓤⓢ dɪ'sɪʒ.ᵊnˌmeɪ.k|ɚ **-ers** -əz ⓤⓢ -ɚz **-ing** -ɪŋ

decisive dɪ'saɪ.sɪv, də-, -zɪv ⓤⓢ dɪ'saɪ.sɪv **-ly** -li **-ness** -nəs, -nɪs

Decius 'diː.ʃi.əs, '-ʃəs, '-si.əs; 'dek.i.əs, 'des- ⓤⓢ 'diː.ʃi.əs, '-ʃəs, '-si.əs; 'des.i.əs

deck dek **-s** -s **-ing** -ɪŋ **-ed** -t **-er/s** -əʳ/z ⓤⓢ -ɚ/z ˌ**clear the** '**decks**; ˌ**hit the** '**deck**

deckchair 'dek.tʃeəʳ ⓤⓢ -tʃer **-s** -z

Decker 'dek.əʳ ⓤⓢ -ɚ

deckhand 'dek.hænd **-s** -z

deckhou|se 'dek.haʊ|s **-ses** -zɪz

deckle 'dek.l̩ **-s** -z ˌ**deckle** '**edged**

declaim dɪ'kleɪm, də- ⓤⓢ dɪ- **-s** -z **-ing** -ɪŋ **-ed** -d **-er/s** -əʳ/z ⓤⓢ -ɚ/z **-ant/s** -ənt/s

declamation ˌdek.lə'meɪ.ʃᵊn **-s** -z

declamatory dɪ'klæm.ə.tᵊr.i, də-, -tri ⓤⓢ dɪ'klæm.ə.tɔːr.i

Declan 'dek.lən

declarable dɪ'kleə.rə.bl̩, də- ⓤⓢ dɪ'kler.ə-, -'klær-

declaration ˌdek.lə'reɪ.ʃᵊn **-s** -z

declarative dɪ'klær.ə.tɪv, də-, -kleə.rə- ⓤⓢ dɪ'kler.ə.t̬ɪv, -'klær- **-ly** -li

declaratory dɪ'klær.ə.tᵊr.i, də-, -'kleə.rə-, -tri ⓤⓢ dɪ'kler.ə.tɔːr.i, -'klær-

declar|e dɪ'kleəʳ, də- ⓤⓢ dɪ'kler **-es** -z **-ing** -ɪŋ **-ed** -d **-er/s** -əʳ/z ⓤⓢ -ɚ/z

declaredly dɪ'kleə.rɪd.li, də-, -rəd- ⓤⓢ dɪ'kler-

declass ˌdiː'klɑːs ⓤⓢ -'klæs **-es** -ɪz **-ing** -ɪŋ **-ed** -t

declassification ˌdiːˌklæs.ɪ.fɪ'keɪ.ʃᵊn, ˌ-ə-

declassi|fy ˌdiː'klæs.ɪ|.faɪ, '-ə- **-fies** -faɪz **-fying** -faɪ.ɪŋ **-fied** -faɪd

declension dɪ'klen.*t*ʃᵊn, də- ⓤⓢ dɪ'klen*t*.ʃᵊn **-s** -z

declination ˌdek.lɪ'neɪ.ʃᵊn, -lə'- **-s** -z

declin|e dɪ'klaɪn, də- ⓤⓢ dɪ- **-es** -z **-ing** -ɪŋ **-ed** -d **-able** -ə.bl̩

declivit|y dɪ'klɪv.ə.t|i, də-, -ɪ.t|i ⓤⓢ dɪ'klɪv.ə.t̬|i **-ies** -iz

declutch ˌdiː'klʌtʃ **-es** -ɪz **-ing** -ɪŋ **-ed** -t

decoct dɪ'kɒkt, ˌdiː- ⓤⓢ -'kɑːkt **-s** -s **-ing** -ɪŋ **-ed** -ɪd

decod|e ˌdiː'kəʊd ⓤⓢ -'koʊd **-es** -z **-ing** -ɪŋ **-ed** -ɪd

decoder ˌdiː'kəʊ.dəʳ, dɪ- ⓤⓢ -'koʊ.dɚ **-s** -z

decok|e ˌdiː'kəʊk ⓤⓢ -'koʊk **-es** -s **-ing** -ɪŋ **-ed** -t

décolletage ˌdeɪ.kɒl'tɑːʒ; -kɒl.ɪ'-, -ə'- ⓤⓢ -kɑː.lə'-, -kɑːl'-

décolleté(e) ˌdeɪ.kɒl'teɪ; -kɒl.ɪ'-, -ə'- ⓤⓢ -kɑː.lə'-, -kɑːl'-

decolonization ˌdiːˌkɒl.ə.naɪ'zeɪ.ʃᵊn, -nɪ'- ⓤⓢ -ˌkɑː.lə.nɪ'-

decoloniz|e, -is|e ˌdiː'kɒl.ə.naɪz ⓤⓢ -'kɑː.lə- **-es** -ɪz **-ing** -ɪŋ **-ed** -d

decolo(u)rization, -isa- ˌdiː.kʌl.ə.raɪ'zeɪ.ʃᵊn, dɪˌkʌl-, -ᵊr.ɪ'- ⓤⓢ dɪˌkʌl.ɚ.ɪ'-

decolo(u)riz|e, -is|e ˌdiː'kʌl.ᵊr.aɪz ⓤⓢ -ə.raɪz **-es** -ɪz **-ing** -ɪŋ **-ed** -d

decommission ˌdiː.kə'mɪʃ.ᵊn **-s** -z **-ing** -ɪŋ **-ed** -d

decompos|e ˌdiː.kəm'pəʊz ⓤⓢ -'poʊz **-es** -ɪz **-ing** -ɪŋ **-ed** -d **-able** -ə.bl̩

decomposition ˌdiː.kɒm.pə'zɪʃ.ᵊn, dɪˌkɒm- ⓤⓢ ˌdiː.kɑːm- **-s** -z

decompound ˌdiː.kəm'paʊnd **-s** -z **-ing** -ɪŋ **-ed** -ɪd

decompress ˌdiː.kəm'pres **-es** -ɪz **-ing** -ɪŋ **-ed** -t **-er/s** -əʳ/z ⓤⓢ -ɚ/z

decompression ˌdiː.kəm'preʃ.ᵊn

decongestant ˌdiː.kən'dʒest.ᵊnt **-s** -s

deconsecrat|e ˌdiː'kɒn*t*.sɪ.kreɪt, -sə- ⓤⓢ -'kɑːn*t*- **-es** -s **-ing** -ɪŋ **-ed** -ɪd

deconsecration ˌdiː.kɒn*t*.sɪ'kreɪ.ʃᵊn, dɪˌkɒn*t*-, -sə'- ⓤⓢ ˌdiː.kɑːn*t*- **-s** -z

deconstruct ˌdiː.kən'strʌkt **-s** -s **-ing** -ɪŋ **-ed** -ɪd **-ive** -ɪv

deconstruction ˌdiː.kən'strʌk.ʃᵊn **-ism** -ɪ.zᵊm **-ist/s** -ɪst/s

decontami|nate ˌdiː.kən'tæm.ɪ|.neɪt, '-ə- **-nates** -neɪts **-nating** -neɪ.tɪŋ ⓤⓢ -neɪ.t̬ɪŋ **-nated** -neɪ.tɪd ⓤⓢ -neɪ.t̬ɪd

decontamination ˌdiː.kənˌtæm.ɪ'neɪ.ʃᵊn, -ə'-

decontrol ˌdiː.kən'trəʊl ⓤⓢ -'troʊl **-s** -z **-ling** -ɪŋ **-led** -d

decor, décor 'deɪ.kɔːʳ, 'dek.ɔːʳ, 'dɪk- ⓤⓢ deɪ'kɔːr, '-- **-s** -z

decor|ate 'dek.ᵊr|.eɪt ⓤⓢ -ə.r|eɪt **-ates** -eɪts **-ating** -eɪ.tɪŋ ⓤⓢ -eɪ.t̬ɪŋ **-ated** -eɪ.tɪd ⓤⓢ -eɪ.t̬ɪd

decoration ˌdek.ᵊ'reɪ.ʃᵊn ⓤⓢ -ə'reɪ- **-s** -z

decorative 'dek.ᵊr.ə.tɪv ⓤⓢ -t̬ɪv **-ly** -li **-ness** -nəs, -nɪs

decorator 'dek.ᵊr.eɪ.təʳ ⓤⓢ -ə.reɪ.t̬ɚ **-s** -z

decorous 'dek.ᵊ.rəs; dɪ'kɔː- ⓤⓢ 'dek.ɚ.əs **-ly** -li **-ness** -nəs, -nɪs

decorum dɪ'kɔː.rəm, də- ⓤⓢ dɪ'kɔːr-

De Courcy də'kʊə.si, -'kɔː-, -'kɜː- ⓤⓢ -'kʊr-, -'kɔːr-, -'kɝː-

decoy (*n.*) 'diː.kɔɪ; dɪ'kɔɪ, də- ⓤⓢ 'diː.kɔɪ; dɪ'kɔɪ **-s** -z

decoy (*v.*) dɪ'kɔɪ, də- ⓤⓢ dɪ- **-s** -z **-ing** -ɪŋ **-ed** -d

decreas|e (*n.*) 'diː.kriːs; dɪ'-, diː-, də- ⓤⓢ 'diː.kriːs **-es** -ɪz

decreas|e (*v.*) dɪ'kriːs, diː-, də-; 'diː.kriːs ⓤⓢ dɪ'kriːs; 'diː.kriːs **-es** -ɪz **-ing/ly** -ɪŋ/li **-ed** -t

decree dɪ'kriː, də- ⓤⓢ dɪ- **-s** -z **-ing** -ɪŋ **-d** -d

decree nisi dɪˌkriː'naɪ.saɪ, -si

decrement 'dek.rɪ.mənt, -rə- **-s** -s

decrepit dɪ'krep.ɪt, də- ⓤⓢ dɪ- **-est** -ɪst, -əst

decrepitation dɪˌkrep.ɪ'teɪ.ʃᵊn, də-, -ə'- ⓤⓢ dɪ- **-s** -z

decrepitude dɪ'krep.ɪ.tjuːd, də-, '-ə-, -tʃuːd ⓤⓢ dɪ'krep.ɪ.tuːd, '-ə-, -tjuːd

decrescendo ˌdiː.krɪ'ʃen.dəʊ, ˌdeɪ-, -krə'- ⓤⓢ -doʊ **-s** -z

De Crespigny də'krep.ɪ.ni, -'kres.pɪ-

decrial dɪˈkraɪ.əl **-s** -z

decriminalization, -isa- diːˌkrɪm.ɪ.nᵊl.aɪˈzeɪ.ʃᵊn, ˌdɪ.krɪ.mɪ-, -mᵊn.ᵊl-, -ɪˈ- US ˌdiː.krɪ.mɪ.nᵊl.ɪˈ-

decriminaliz|e, -is|e ˌdiːˈkrɪm.ɪ.nᵊl.aɪz, dɪ-, -ᵊn.ᵊl- US -ɪ.nᵊl- **-es** -ɪz **-ing** -ɪŋ **-ed** -d

decr|y dɪˈkr|aɪ, də- US dɪ- **-ies** -aɪz **-ying** -aɪ.ɪŋ **-ied** -aɪd **-ier/s** -aɪ.əʳ/z US -aɪ.ɚ/z

decumben|ce dɪˈkʌm.bənt|s, ˌdiː- **-cy** -si

decumbent dɪˈkʌm.bənt, ˌdiː- **-ly** -li

decuple ˈdek.jʊ.pḷ US -jʊ-, -jə- **-es** -z **-ing** -ɪŋ, ˈdek.jʊ.plɪŋ, -juː- **-ed** -d

Dedalus ˈdiː.dᵊl.əs US ˈded.ᵊl.əs, ˈdiː.dᵊl-

Deddington ˈded.ɪŋ.tᵊn

Dedham ˈded.əm

dedi|cate ˈded.ɪ|.keɪt **-cates** -keɪts **-cating** -keɪ.tɪŋ US -keɪ.t̬ɪŋ **-cated/ly** -keɪ.tɪd/li US -keɪ.t̬ɪd/li **-cator/s** -keɪ.təʳ/z US -keɪ.t̬ɚ/z

dedicatee ˌded.ɪ.kəˈtiː **-s** -z

dedication ˌded.ɪˈkeɪ.ʃᵊn **-s** -z

dedicatory ˈded.ɪ.kə.tᵊr.i, -keɪ-, -tri; ˌded.ɪˈkeɪ- US ˈded.ɪ.kə.tɔːr-

de Dion dəˈdiː.ən, -ɒn *as if French:* -ɔ̃ːŋ US dəˈdiː.ɑːn *as if French:* -ɔ̃ːŋ **-s** -z

Dedlock ˈded.lɒk US -lɑːk

Dedman ˈded.mən, ˈdeb-, -mæn US ˈded-

deduc|e dɪˈdjuːs, də- US dɪˈduːs, -ˈdjuːs **-es** -ɪz **-ing** -ɪŋ **-ed** -t

deducibility dɪˌdjuː.səˈbɪl.ə.ti, də-, -sɪˈ-, -ɪ.ti US dɪˌduː.səˈbɪl.ə.t̬i, -ˌdjuː-

deducible dɪˈdjuː.sə.bḷ, də-, -sɪ- US dɪˈduː-, -ˈdjuː-

deduct dɪˈdʌkt, də- US dɪ- **-s** -s **-ing** -ɪŋ **-ed** -ɪd **-ible** -ə.bḷ

deduction dɪˈdʌk.ʃᵊn, də- US dɪ- **-s** -z

deductive dɪˈdʌk.tɪv, də- US dɪ- **-ly** -li

Dee diː

deed diːd **-s** -z ˈ**deed** ˌ**poll**

Deedes diːdz

deejay ˈdiː.dʒeɪ **-s** -z

Deek(e)s diːks

Deeley ˈdiː.li

deem diːm **-s** -z **-ing** -ɪŋ **-ed** -d

Deems diːmz

deemster ˈdiːm.stəʳ US -stɚ **-s** -z

deep diːp **-s** -s **-er** -əʳ US -ɚ **-est** -ɪst, -əst **-ly** -li **-ness** -nəs, -nɪs ˌ**deep** ˈ**freeze** US ˈ**deep** ˌ**freeze**; ˌ**Deep** ˈ**South**; **go off the** ˈ**deep** ˌ**end**; ˌ**throw (someone) in at the** ˈ**deep** ˌ**end**

deepen ˈdiː.pᵊn **-s** -z **-ing** -ɪŋ **-ed** -d

deep-fr|y ˌdiːpˈfr|aɪ, ˈ-- **-ies** -aɪz **-ying** -aɪ.ɪŋ **-ied** -aɪd *stress shift:* ˌdeep-fried ˈchicken

deep-laid ˌdiːpˈleɪd *stress shift:* ˌdeep-laid ˈplans

deep-rooted ˌdiːpˈruː.tɪd US -t̬ɪd *stress shift:* ˌdeep-rooted ˈfears

deep-sea ˌdiːpˈsiː *stress shift:* ˌdeep-sea ˈdiving

deep-seated ˌdiːpˈsiː.tɪd US -t̬ɪd *stress shift:* ˌdeep-seated ˈsorrow

deep-six ˌdiːpˈsɪks **-es** -ɪz **-ing** -ɪŋ **-ed** -t

deer dɪəʳ US dɪr ˈ**deer** ˌ**forest**; ˈ**deer** ˌ**park**; ˈ**Deer** ˌ**Park**

Deerfield ˈdɪə.fiːld US ˈdɪr-

deerhound ˈdɪə.haʊnd US ˈdɪr- **-s** -z

deerskin ˈdɪə.skɪn US ˈdɪr-

Deerslayer ˈdɪəˌsleɪ.əʳ US ˈdɪrˌsleɪ.ɚ

deerstalk|ing ˈdɪəˌstɔː.k|ɪŋ US ˈdɪr-, -ˌstɑː-, -ˌstɔː- **-er/s** -əʳ/z US -ɚ/z

Deery ˈdɪə.ri US ˈdɪr.i

de-escal|ate ˌdiːˈes.kᵊl|.eɪt US -kə.l|eɪt **-ates** -eɪts **-ating** -eɪ.tɪŋ US -eɪ.t̬ɪŋ **-ated** -eɪ.tɪd US -eɪ.t̬ɪd

de-escalation ˌdiː.es.kəˈleɪ.ʃᵊn, diːˌes- US diːˌes-

Deeside ˈdiː.saɪd

defac|e dɪˈfeɪs **-es** -ɪz **-ing** -ɪŋ **-ed** -t **-er/s** -əʳ/z US -ɚ/z **-ement/s** -mənt/s

de facto ˌdeɪˈfæk.təʊ, ˌdiː- US -toʊ

defae|cate ˈdef.ə|.keɪt, ˈdiː.fə-, -fɪ- US ˈdef.ə-, ˈ-ɪ- **-cates** -keɪts **-cating** -keɪ.tɪŋ US -keɪ.t̬ɪŋ **-cated** -keɪ.tɪd US -keɪ.t̬ɪd

defaecation ˌdef.əˈkeɪ.ʃᵊn, ˌdiː.fəˈ-, -fɪˈ- US ˌdef.əˈ-, -ɪˈ-

defal|cate ˈdiː.fæl|.keɪt, diːˈfæl-; ˈdiː.fɔːl- US diːˈfæl-, -ˈfɔːl- **-cates** -keɪts **-cating** -keɪ.tɪŋ US -keɪ.t̬ɪŋ **-cated** -keɪ.tɪd US -keɪ.t̬ɪd

defalcation ˌdiː.fælˈkeɪ.ʃᵊn, -fɔːlˈ- **-s** -z

defamation ˌdef.əˈmeɪ.ʃᵊn, ˌdiː.fəˈ- US ˌdef.əˈ- **-s** -z

defamatory dɪˈfæm.ə.tᵊr.i, də-, -tri US dɪˈfæm.ə.tɔːr.i

defam|e dɪˈfeɪm, də- US dɪ- **-es** -z **-ing** -ɪŋ **-ed** -d **-er/s** -əʳ/z US -ɚ/z

Defarge dəˈfɑːʒ US -ˈfɑːrʒ

default (*n.*) dɪˈfɔːlt, də-, -ˈfɒlt; ˈdiː.fɔːlt, -fɒlt US dɪˈfɑːlt, -ˈfɔːlt

defaul|t (*v.*) dɪˈfɔːl|t, də-, -ˈfɒl|t US dɪˈfɑːl|t, -ˈfɔːl|t **-ts** -ts **-ting** -tɪŋ US -t̬ɪŋ **-ted** -tɪd US -t̬ɪd **-ter/s** -təʳ/z US -t̬ɚ/z

defeasance dɪˈfiː.zᵊnts, də- US dɪ-

defeasib|le dɪˈfiː.zə.bl|l, də-, -zɪ- US dɪ- **-ly** -li **-leness** -l̩.nəs, -nɪs

de|feat dɪ|ˈfiːt, də- US dɪ- **-feats** -ˈfiːts **-feating** -ˈfiː.tɪŋ US -ˈfiː.t̬ɪŋ **-feated** -ˈfiː.tɪd US -ˈfiː.t̬ɪd

defeat|ism dɪˈfiː.t|ɪ.zᵊm, də- US dɪˈfiː.t̬|ɪ- **-ist/s** -ɪst/s

defe|cate ˈdef.ə|.keɪt, ˈdiː.fə-, -fɪ- US ˈdef.ə-, ˈ-ɪ- **-cates** -keɪts **-cating** -keɪ.tɪŋ US -keɪ.t̬ɪŋ **-cated** -keɪ.tɪd US -keɪ.t̬ɪd

defecation ˌdef.əˈkeɪ.ʃᵊn, ˌdiː.fəˈ-, -fɪˈ- US ˌdef.əˈ-, -ɪˈ- **-s** -z

defect (*n.*) ˈdiː.fekt; dɪˈfekt, də- US ˈdiː.fekt; dɪˈfekt **-s** -s

defect (*v.*) dɪˈfekt, də- US dɪ- **-s** -s **-ing** -ɪŋ **-ed** -ɪd

defection dɪˈfek.ʃᵊn, də- US dɪ- **-s** -z

defective dɪˈfek.tɪv, də- US dɪ- **-ly** -li **-ness** -nəs, -nɪs

defector dɪˈfek.təʳ, də- US dɪˈfek.tɚ **-s** -z

defenc|e dɪˈfents, də- US dɪ- **-es** -ɪz

defenceless dɪˈfent.sləs, də-, -slɪs US dɪ- **-ly** -li **-ness** -nəs, -nɪs

defend dɪˈfend, də- US dɪ- **-s** -z **-ing** -ɪŋ **-ed** -ɪd **-able** -ə.bḷ

defendant dɪˈfen.dənt, də- US dɪ- **-s** -s

defender dɪˈfen.dəʳ, də- US dɪˈfen.dɚ **-s** -z

defens|e dɪˈfents, də- US dɪ-; *esp. in sports:* ˈdiː.fents **-es** -ɪz

defenseless dɪˈfent.sləs, də-, -slɪs US dɪ- **-ly** -li **-ness** -nəs, -nɪs

defense|man dɪˈfents|.mən, də- US dɪ-, -mæn **-men** -mən

defensibility dɪˌfent.səˈbɪl.ə.ti, də-, -sɪˈ-, -ɪ.ti US dɪˌfent.səˈbɪl.ə.t̬i

defensib|le dɪˈfent.sə.bl|l, də-, -sɪ- US dɪ- **-ly** -li

defensive dɪˈfent.sɪv, də- US dɪ- **-ly** -li **-ness** -nəs, -nɪs

defer dɪˈfɜːʳ, də- US dɪˈfɝː **-s** -z **-ring** -ɪŋ **-red** -d **-rer/s** -əʳ/z US -ɚ/z

deferen|ce ˈdef.ᵊr.ᵊn|ts **-t** -t

deferential ˌdef.ᵊˈren.tʃᵊl US -ˈrent.ʃᵊl **-ly** -i

deferment dɪˈfɜː.mənt, də- US dɪˈfɝː- **-s** -s

deferral dɪˈfɜː.rᵊl, də- US dɪˈfɝː.ᵊl **-s** -z

defiance dɪˈfaɪ.ənts, də- US dɪ-

defiant dɪˈfaɪ.ənt, də- US dɪ- **-ly** -li **-ness** -nəs, -nɪs

defibrill|ate ˌdiːˈfɪb.rɪ.l|eɪt, -ˈfaɪ.brɪ-, -brᵊl|.eɪt US -rɪ.l|eɪt, -rə- **-ates** -eɪts **-ating** -eɪ.tɪŋ US -eɪ.t̬ɪŋ **-ated** -eɪ.tɪd US -eɪ.t̬ɪd

defibrillation diːˌfɪb.rɪˈleɪ.ʃᵊn, -ˌfaɪ.brɪˈ-, -brəˈ-; ˌdiː.fɪ.brɪˈ-

defibrillator ˌdiːˈfɪb.rɪ.leɪ.təʳ, -ˈfaɪ.brɪ-, -brə- US -t̬ɚ **-s** -z

deficienc|y dɪˈfɪʃ.ᵊnt.s|i, də- US dɪ- **-ies** -iz

deficient dɪˈfɪʃ.ᵊnt, də- US dɪ- **-ly** -li

deficit ˈdef.ɪ.sɪt, ˈ-ə-; dəˈfɪs-, dɪ- US ˈdef.ɪ.sɪt, ˈ-ə- **-s** -s

defilad|e ˌdef.ɪˈleɪd, -əˈ-, ˈ--- **-es** -z **-ing** -ɪŋ **-ed** -ɪd

defile (*n.*) dɪˈfaɪl, ˌdiː-; ˈdiː.faɪl **-s** -z

defil|e (*v.*) dɪˈfaɪl, də- US dɪ- **-es** -z **-ing**

-ɪŋ -ed -d -er/s -ə^r/z (US) -ɚ/z -ement -mənt

definable dɪˈfaɪ.nə.bl̩, də- (US) dɪ-

defin|e dɪˈfaɪn, də- (US) dɪ- -es -z -ing -ɪŋ -ed -d -er/s -ə^r/z (US) -ɚ/z

definite ˈdef.ɪ.nət, -^{ə}n.ət, -ɪt -ly -li -ness -nəs, -nɪs

definition ˌdef.ɪˈnɪʃ.^{ə}n, -əˈ- -s -z

definitive dɪˈfɪn.ə.tɪv, də-, ˈ-ɪ- (US) dɪˈfɪn.ə.t̬ɪv -ly -li -ness -nəs, -nɪs

defla|grate ˈdiː.flə|.greɪt, ˈdef.lə- (US) ˈdef.lə- -grates -greɪts -grating -greɪ.tɪŋ (US) -greɪ.t̬ɪŋ -grated -greɪ.tɪd (US) -greɪ.t̬ɪd -grator/s -greɪ.tə^r/z (US) -greɪ.t̬ɚ/z

deflagration ˌdiː.fləˈgreɪ.ʃ^{ə}n, ˌdef.ləˈ- (US) ˌdef.ləˈ- -s -z

de|flate dɪ|ˈfleɪt, ˌdiː- -flates -ˈfleɪts -flating -ˈfleɪ.tɪŋ (US) -ˈfleɪ.t̬ɪŋ -flated -ˈfleɪ.tɪd (US) -ˈfleɪ.t̬ɪd

deflation dɪˈfleɪ.ʃ^{ə}n, ˌdiː- -ary -^{ə}r.i (US) -er.i

deflect dɪˈflekt, də- (US) dɪ- -s -s -ing -ɪŋ -ed -ɪd -or/s -ə^r/z (US) -ɚ/z

deflection, deflexion dɪˈflek.ʃ^{ə}n, də- (US) dɪ- -s -z

defloration ˌdiː.flɔːˈreɪ.ʃ^{ə}n, ˌdef.lɔːˈ- (US) ˌdef.ləˈ-, ˌdiː.fləˈ-, -flɔːˈ- -s -z

deflower dɪˈflaʊə^r, ˌdiː- (US) -ˈflaʊɚ -s -z -ing -ɪŋ -ed -d

Defoe dɪˈfəʊ, də- (US) -ˈfoʊ

defog ˌdiːˈfɒg (US) -ˈfɑːg, -ˈfɔːg -s -z -ging -ɪŋ -ged -d -ger/s -ə^r/z (US) -ɚ/z

defoliant ˌdiːˈfəʊ.li.ənt, dɪ- (US) -ˈfoʊ- -s -s

defoli|ate ˌdiːˈfəʊ.li|.eɪt, dɪ- (US) -ˈfoʊ- -ates -eɪts -ating -eɪ.tɪŋ (US) -eɪ.t̬ɪŋ -ated -eɪ.tɪd (US) -eɪ.t̬ɪd

defoliation ˌdiː.fəʊ.liˈeɪ.ʃ^{ə}n; diːˌfəʊ-, dɪ- (US) diːˌfoʊ-, dɪ-

deforest ˌdiːˈfɒr.ɪst, dɪ-, -əst (US) -ˈfɔːr- -s -s -ing -ɪŋ -ed -ɪd

deforestation diːˌfɒr.ɪˈsteɪ.ʃ^{ə}n, dɪ-; ˌdiː.fɔːr-, -əˈ- (US) diːˌfɔːr-, dɪ-

deform dɪˈfɔːm, də-, ˌdiː- (US) dɪˈfɔːrm, ˌdiː- -s -z -ing -ɪŋ -ed -d -er/s -ə^r/z (US) -ɚ/z

deformation ˌdiː.fɔːˈmeɪ.ʃ^{ə}n, ˌdef.əˈ- (US) ˌdiː.fɔːrˈ-, ˌdef.ɚˈ- -s -z

deformit|y dɪˈfɔː.mə.t|i, də-, -mɪ- (US) dɪˈfɔːr.mə.t̬|i -ies -iz

defraud dɪˈfrɔːd, ˌdiː-, də- (US) dɪˈfrɑːd, ˌdiː-, -ˈfrɔːd -s -z -ing -ɪŋ -ed -ɪd -er/s -ə^r/z (US) -ɚ/z

defray dɪˈfreɪ, də- (US) dɪ- -s -z -ing -ɪŋ -ed -d -er/s -ə^r/z (US) -ɚ/z -ment -mənt

defrayal dɪˈfreɪ.əl, də- (US) dɪ- -s -z

De Freitas dəˈfreɪ.təs (US) -t̬əs

defrock ˌdiːˈfrɒk (US) -ˈfrɑːk -s -s -ing -ɪŋ -ed -t

defrost ˌdiːˈfrɒst, dɪ- (US) -ˈfrɑːst -s -s -ing -ɪŋ -ed -ɪd -er/s -ə^r/z (US) -ɚ/z

deft deft -er -ə^r (US) -ɚ -est -ɪst, -əst -ly -li -ness -nəs, -nɪs

defunct dɪˈfʌŋkt, də-; ˈdiː.fʌŋkt (US) dɪˈfʌŋkt, ˌdiː- -s -s

defus|e ˌdiːˈfjuːz, dɪ-, də- (US) ˌdiː-, dɪ- -es -ɪz -ing -ɪŋ -ed -d

def|y dɪˈf|aɪ, də- (US) dɪ- -ies -aɪz -ying -aɪ.ɪŋ -ied -aɪd -ier/s -aɪ.ə^r/z (US) -aɪ.ɚ/z

Deganwy dɪˈgæn.wi, də-

Degas dəˈgɑː, ˈdeɪ.gɑː

De Gaulle dəˈgəʊl, dɪ-, -ˈgɔːl (US) -ˈgoʊl, -ˈgɔːl, -ˈgɑːl

degauss ˌdiːˈgaʊs, -ˈgɔːs (US) -ˈgaʊs -es -ɪz -ing -ɪŋ -ed -t

degeneracy dɪˈdʒen.^{ə}r.ə.si, də- (US) dɪ-

degenerate *(adj.)* dɪˈdʒen.^{ə}r.ət, də-, -ɪt (US) dɪ- -ly -li -ness -nəs, -nɪs

degener|ate *(v.)* dɪˈdʒen.^{ə}r|.eɪt, də- (US) dɪˈdʒen.ə.r|eɪt -ates -eɪts -ating -eɪ.tɪŋ (US) -eɪ.t̬ɪŋ -ated -eɪ.tɪd (US) -eɪ.t̬ɪd

degeneration dɪˌdʒen.əˈreɪ.ʃ^{ə}n, də- (US) dɪ-

degenerative dɪˈdʒen.^{ə}r.ə.tɪv, də-, -ə.reɪ- (US) dɪˈdʒen.ɚ.ə.t̬ɪv, -ə.reɪ-

deglutin|ate ˌdiːˈgluː.tɪ.n|eɪt, dɪ- (US) -t^{ə}n|.eɪt -ates -eɪts -ating -eɪ.tɪŋ (US) -eɪ.t̬ɪŋ -ated -eɪ.tɪd (US) -eɪ.t̬ɪd

deglutition ˌdiː.gluːˈtɪʃ.^{ə}n

degradation ˌdeg.rəˈdeɪ.ʃ^{ə}n -s -z

degrad|e dɪˈgreɪd, də- (US) dɪ- -es -z -ed -ɪd -able -ə.bl̩

degrading dɪˈgreɪ.dɪŋ, də- (US) dɪ- -ly -li

degree dɪˈgriː, də- (US) dɪ- -s -z

dehisc|e dɪˈhɪs, ˌdiː- (US) ˌdiː-, dɪ- -es -ɪz -ing -ɪŋ -ed -t

dehiscen|ce dɪˈhɪs.^{ə}n|ts, ˌdiː- (US) ˌdiː-, dɪ- -t -t

Dehra Dun ˌdeə.rəˈduːn, ˌdeɪ^ə- (US) ˌder.əˈ-

dehumaniz|e, -is|e ˌdiːˈhjuː.mə.naɪz -es -ɪz -ing -ɪŋ -ed -d

dehumidifier ˌdiː.hjuːˈmɪd.ɪ.faɪ.ə^r (US) -ə.faɪ.ɚ -s -z

dehy|drate ˌdiː.haɪ|ˈdreɪt, ˈ--- -drates -ˈdreɪts -drating -ˈdre.tɪŋ (US) -ˈdreɪ.t̬ɪŋ -drated -ˈdreɪ.tɪd (US) -ˈdreɪ.t̬ɪd

dehydration ˌdiː.haɪˈdreɪ.ʃ^{ə}n

dehypnotiz|e, -is|e ˌdiːˈhɪp.nə.taɪz -es -ɪz -ing -ɪŋ -ed -d

de-ic|e ˌdiːˈaɪs -es -ɪz -ing -ɪŋ -ed -t -er/s -ə^r/z (US) -ɚ/z

deicide ˈdeɪ.ɪ.saɪd, ˈdiː-, ˈ-ə- (US) ˈdiː.ə- -s -z

dei|ctic ˈdaɪ|k.tɪk, ˈdeɪ- -xis -k.sɪs

deification ˌdeɪ.ɪ.fɪˈkeɪ.ʃ^{ə}n, ˌdiː-, ˌ-ə- (US) ˌdiː.ə- -s -z

dei|fy ˈdeɪ.ɪ|.faɪ, ˈdiː-, ˈ-ə- (US) ˈdiː- -fies -faɪz -fying -faɪ.ɪŋ -fied -faɪd

Deighton *surname:* ˈdeɪ.t^{ə}n, ˈdaɪ- *place in North Yorkshire:* ˈdiː.t^{ə}n

deign deɪn -s -z -ing -ɪŋ -ed -d

deindustrialization, -isa- ˌdiː.ɪnˌdʌs.tri.^{ə}l.aɪˈzeɪ.ʃ^{ə}n, -ɪˈ- (US) -ɪˈ-

Deirdre ˈdɪə.dri, -dreɪ (US) ˈdɪr.drə, -dri

de|ism ˈdeɪ|.ɪ.z^{ə}m, ˈdiː- (US) ˈdiː- -ist/s -ɪst/s

deistic deɪˈɪs.tɪk, diː- (US) diː- -al -^{ə}l

deit|y (D) ˈdeɪ.ɪ.t|i, ˈdiː-, ˈ-ə- (US) ˈdiː.ə.t̬|i -ies -iz

déjà vu ˌdeʒ.ɑːˈvuː, -ˈvjuː (US) ˌdeɪ.ʒɑːˈvuː, -vjuː

deject dɪˈdʒekt, də- (US) dɪ- -s -s -ing -ɪŋ -ed/ly -ɪd/li -edness -ɪd.nəs, -nɪs

dejection dɪˈdʒek.ʃ^{ə}n, də- (US) dɪ-

déjeuner ˈdeɪ.ʒə.neɪ, -ʒɜː- (US) -ʒə- -s -z

de jure ˌdeɪˈdʒʊə.reɪ, di-, ˌdiː-, -ri (US) diːˈdʒʊr.i, deɪ-

Dekker ˈdek.ə^r (US) -ɚ

dekko ˈdek.əʊ (US) -oʊ -s -z

de Klerk dəˈklɜːk, dəˈkleək (US) -ˈklerk, -ˈklɝːk

de Kooning dəˈkəʊ.nɪŋ, -ˈkuː- (US) -ˈkuː-

Del. *(abbrev. for* **Delaware***)* ˈdel.ə.weə^r (US) -wer

de la Bère də.ləˈbɪə^r (US) də.ləˈbɪr

Delacroix ˈdel.ə.krwɑː, ˌ--ˈ-

Delafield ˈdel.ə.fiːld

Delagoa ˌdel.əˈgəʊə (US) -ˈgoʊə

Delamain ˈdel.ə.meɪn

de la Mare də.lɑːˈmeə^r, ˌdel.əˈ- (US) də.ləˈmer, ˌdel.əˈ-

Delamere ˈdel.ə.mɪə^r (US) -mɪr

De Lancey dəˈlɑːnt.si (US) -ˈlænt-

Delane dəˈleɪn, dɪ-

Delaney dəˈleɪ.ni, dɪ-

Delany dəˈleɪ.ni, dɪ-

De la Pole ˌdel.əˈpəʊl, də.lɑːˈ- (US) də.ləˈpoʊl

de la Roche ˌdel.əˈrɒʃ, -ˈrəʊʃ; də.ləˈ- (US) də.lɑːˈroʊʃ, -lə-, -ˈrɑːʃ

De la Rue ˌdel.əˈruː; də.lɑːˈ-; ˈdel.ə.ruː

de la Torre ˌdel.əˈtɔː^r, də.lɑːˈ- (US) -ˈtɔːr

Delaunay dəˈlɔː.neɪ (US) -lɔːˈneɪ

Delaware ˈdel.ə.weə^r (US) -wer

De La Warr ˌdel.əˈweə^r, də.lɑːˈ- (US) -ˈwer

delay dɪˈleɪ, də- (US) dɪ- -s -z -ing -ɪŋ -ed -d -er/s -ə^r/z (US) -ɚ/z

Delbert ˈdel.bət (US) -bɚt

del credere ˌdelˈkred.ər.eɪ, -ˈkreɪ.dər-, -i (US) -ˈkreɪ.dɚ-

dele ˈdiː.liː, -li

delectab|le dɪˈlek.tə.b|l̩, də- (US) dɪ- -ly -li -leness -l̩.nəs, -nɪs

delectation ˌdiː.lekˈteɪ.ʃ^{ə}n

delegac|y ˈdel.ɪ.gə.s|i, ˈ-ə- -ies -iz

delegate *(n.)* ˈdel.ɪ.gət, ˈ-ə-, -geɪt, -gɪt (US) -gət, -gɪt, -geɪt -s -s

dele|gate (*v.*) 'del.ɪ|.geɪt, '-ə- **-gates** -geɪts **-gating** -geɪ.tɪŋ (US) -geɪ.t̬ɪŋ **-gated** -geɪ.tɪd (US) -geɪ.t̬ɪd

delegation ˌdel.ɪ'geɪ.ʃᵊn, -ə'- **-s** -z

delend|um dɪ'len.d|əm, diː- **-a** -ə

de|lete dɪ|'liːt, də- (US) dɪ- **-letes** -'liːts **-leting** -'liː.tɪŋ (US) -'liː.t̬ɪŋ **-leted** -'liː.tɪd (US) -'liː.t̬ɪd

deleterious ˌdel.ɪ'tɪə.ri.əs, ˌdɪl-, ˌdiː.lɪ'-, -lə'tɪə- (US) ˌdel.ə'tɪr.i- **-ly** -li **-ness** -nəs, -nɪs

deletion dɪ'liː.ʃᵊn, də- (US) dɪ- **-s** -z

delf delf

Delft delft **-ware** -weəʳ (US) -wer

Delham 'del.əm

Delhi 'del.i

deli 'del.i **-s** -z

Deli|a 'diː.li|.ə (US) 'diːl.j|ə, -li|.ə, -li **-an/s** -ən/z

deliberate (*adj.*) dɪ'lɪb.ᵊr.ət, də-, -ɪt (US) dɪ- **-ly** -li **-ness** -nəs, -nɪs

deliber|ate (*v.*) dɪ'lɪb.ᵊr|.eɪt, də- (US) dɪ'lɪb.ə.r|eɪt **-ates** -eɪts **-ating** -eɪ.tɪŋ (US) -eɪ.t̬ɪŋ **-ated** -eɪ.tɪd (US) -eɪ.t̬ɪd **-ator/s** -eɪ.təʳ/z (US) -eɪ.t̬ɚ/z

deliberation dɪˌlɪb.ə'reɪ.ʃᵊn, də- (US) dɪ- **-s** -z

deliberative dɪ'lɪb.ᵊr.ə.tɪv, də- (US) dɪ'lɪb.ɚ.ə.t̬ɪv, -rə.t̬ɪv **-ly** -li

Delibes də'liːb, dɪ-

delicac|y 'del.ɪ.kə.s|i, '-ə- **-ies** -iz

delicate 'del.ɪ.kət, '-ə-, -kɪt **-ly** -li **-ness** -nəs, -nɪs

delicatessen ˌdel.ɪ.kə'tes.ᵊn, ˌ-ə- **-s** -z

delicious dɪ'lɪʃ.əs, də- (US) dɪ- **-ly** -li **-ness** -nəs, -nɪs

delict dɪ'lɪkt; 'diː.lɪkt (US) dɪ'lɪkt **-s** -s

de|light dɪ|'laɪt, də- (US) dɪ- **-lights** -'laɪts **-lighting** -'laɪ.tɪŋ (US) -'laɪ.t̬ɪŋ **-lighted/ly** -'laɪ.tɪd/li (US) -'laɪ.t̬ɪd/li

delightful dɪ'laɪt.fᵊl, də-, -fʊl (US) dɪ- **-ly** -i **-ness** -nəs, -nɪs

delightsome dɪ'laɪt.səm, də- (US) dɪ-

Delilah dɪ'laɪ.lə, də- (US) dɪ-

delim|it dɪ'lɪm|.ɪt, ˌdiː-, də- (US) dɪ- **-its** -ɪts **-iting** -ɪ.tɪŋ (US) -ɪ.t̬ɪŋ **-ited** -ɪ.tɪd (US) -ɪ.t̬ɪd

delimitation dɪˌlɪm.ɪ'teɪ.ʃᵊn, ˌdiː-, də- (US) dɪ- **-s** -z

deline|ate dɪ'lɪn.i|.eɪt, də- (US) dɪ- **-ates** -eɪts **-ating** -eɪ.tɪŋ (US) -eɪ.t̬ɪŋ **-ated** -eɪ.tɪd (US) -eɪ.t̬ɪd **-ator/s** -eɪ.təʳ/z (US) -eɪ.t̬ɚ/z

delineation dɪˌlɪn.i'eɪ.ʃᵊn, də- (US) dɪ- **-s** -z

delinquenc|y dɪ'lɪŋ.kwənt.s|i, də- (US) dɪ- **-ies** -iz

delinquent dɪ'lɪŋ.kwənt, də- (US) dɪ- **-s** -s

deliquesc|e ˌdel.ɪ'kwes, -ə'- **-es** -ɪz **-ing** -ɪŋ **-ed** -t

deliquescen|ce ˌdel.ɪ'kwes.ᵊn|*t*s **-t** -t

delirious dɪ'lɪr.i.əs, də-, -'lɪə.ri- (US) dɪ'lɪr.i- **-ly** -li **-ness** -nəs, -nɪs

delirium dɪ'lɪr.i.əm, də-, -'lɪə.ri- (US) dɪ'lɪr.i-

delirium tremens dɪˌlɪr.i.əm'triː.menz, -'trem.enz, -ənz

De l'Isle *English name:* də'laɪl

Delisle *French name:* də'liːl

Delius 'diː.li.əs

deliv|er dɪ'lɪv|.əʳ, də- (US) dɪ'lɪv|.ɚ **-ers** -əz (US) -ɚz **-ering** -ᵊr.ɪŋ **-ered** -əd (US) -ɚd **-erer/s** -ᵊr.əʳ/z (US) -ɚ.ɚ/z

deliverable dɪ'lɪv.ᵊr.ə.bl̩, də- (US) dɪ- **-s** -z

deliveranc|e dɪ'lɪv.ᵊr.ᵊn*t*s, də- (US) dɪ- **-es** -ɪz

deliver|y dɪ'lɪv.ᵊr|.i, də- (US) dɪ- **-ies** -iz

delivery|man dɪ'lɪv.ᵊr.ɪ|.mən, də-, -mæn (US) də'lɪv.ri.mæn **-men** -mən, -men

dell (D) del **-s** -z

Della 'del.ə

Dellar 'del.əʳ (US) -ɚ

della Robbia ˌdel.ə'rɒb.i.ə (US) ˌdel.ə'roʊ.biə, -ɑː'-, -'rɑː-, -bjə

Delma 'del.mə

Delmar del'mɑːʳ, '-- (US) 'del.mɑːr, -'-

Delmarva del'mɑː.və (US) -'mɑːr- **Del'marva Peˌninsula**

Del Monte® del'mɒn.teɪ, -ti (US) -'mɑːn.t̬i

Deloitte də'lɔɪt, dɪ-

Delores də'lɔː.rɪz, dɪ- (US) dɪ'lɔːr.ɪs, də-

Deloria də'lɔː.ri.ə (US) -'lɔːr.i-

Delors də'lɔːʳ (US) -'lɔːr

Delos 'diː.lɒs (US) -lɑːs, 'del.oʊs

delous|e ˌdiː'laʊs (US) -'laʊs, -'laʊz **-es** -ɪz **-ing** -ɪŋ **-ed** -t (US) -t, -d

Delph delf

Delphi *in Greece:* 'del.faɪ, -fi *city in US:* 'del.faɪ

Delph|ian 'del.f|i.ən **-ic** -ɪk ˌ**Delphic 'oracle**

Delphine del'fiːn

delphinium del'fɪn.i.əm **-s** -z

Delroy 'del.rɔɪ

delta 'del.tə (US) -t̬ə **-s** -z

deltoid 'del.tɔɪd

delud|e dɪ'luːd, də-, -'ljuːd (US) dɪ'luːd **-es** -z **-ing** -ɪŋ **-ed** -ɪd **-er/s** -əʳ/z (US) -ɚ/z

delug|e 'del.juːdʒ **-es** -ɪz **-ing** -ɪŋ **-ed** -d

delusion dɪ'luː.ʒᵊn, də-, -'ljuː- (US) dɪ'luː- **-s** -z

delusive dɪ'luː.sɪv, də-, -'ljuː- (US) dɪ'luː- **-ly** -li **-ness** -nəs, -nɪs

delusory dɪ'luː.sᵊr.i, də-, -'ljuː-, -zᵊr- (US) dɪ'luː-

de luxe, deluxe dɪ'lʌks, də-, -'luːks, -'lʊks (US) dɪ'lʌks, də-, -'lʊks

delv|e delv **-es** -z **-ing** -ɪŋ **-ed** -d **-er/s** -əʳ/z (US) -ɚ/z

Delyn 'del.ɪn

Dem *(abbrev. for* **Democrat***)* 'dem.ə.kræt ˌdem.ə'kræt.ɪk

demagnetization, -isa- diːˌmæg.nə.taɪ'zeɪ.ʃᵊn, ˌdiː.mæg-, -nɪ-, -ɪ'- (US) diːˌmæg.nə.t̬ɪ'- **-s** -z

demagnetiz|e, -is|e ˌdiː'mæg.nə.taɪz, -nɪ- **-es** -ɪz **-ing** -ɪŋ **-ed** -d

demagog 'dem.ə.gɒg (US) -gɑːg, -gɔːg **-s** -z

demagogic ˌdem.ə'gɒg.ɪk, -'gɒdʒ- (US) -'gɑː.dʒɪk, -gɪk; -goʊ.dʒɪk **-al** -ᵊl **-ally** -ᵊl.i, -li

demagogue 'dem.ə.gɒg (US) -gɑːg, -gɔːg **-s** -z

demagoguery 'dem.ə.gɒg.ᵊr.i (US) -gɑː.gɚ-

demagogy 'dem.ə.gɒg.i, -gɒdʒ- (US) -gɑː.dʒi, -gi; -goʊ.dʒi

demand dɪ'mɑːnd, də- (US) dɪ'mænd **-s** -z **-ing/ly** -ɪŋ/li **-ed** -ɪd

demanding dɪ'mɑːn.dɪŋ, də- (US) dɪ'mæn- **-ly** -li

demar|cate 'diː.mɑː|.keɪt (US) diː'mɑːr|.keɪt, 'diː.mɑːr- **-cates** -keɪts **-cating** -keɪ.tɪŋ (US) -keɪ.t̬ɪŋ **-cated** -keɪ.tɪd (US) -keɪ.t̬ɪd

demarcation ˌdiː.mɑː'keɪ.ʃᵊn (US) -mɑːr'-

demarcative ˌdiː'mɑː.kə.tɪv (US) -'mɑːr.kə.t̬ɪv

démarch|e 'deɪ.mɑːʃ, -'- (US) deɪ'mɑːrʃ, dɪ- **-es** -ɪz

demark dɪ'mɑːk, ˌdiː- (US) -'mɑːrk **-s** -s **-ing** -ɪŋ **-ed** -t

demarkation ˌdiː.mɑː'keɪ.ʃᵊn (US) -mɑːr'-

Demas 'diː.mæs

dematerializ|e, -is|e ˌdiː.mə'tɪə.ri.ə.laɪz (US) -'tɪr.i- **-es** -ɪz **-ing** -ɪŋ **-ed** -d

demean dɪ'miːn, də- (US) dɪ- **-s** -z **-ing** -ɪŋ **-ed** -d

demeano(u)r dɪ'miː.nəʳ, də- (US) dɪ'miː.nɚ **-s** -z

Demelza dɪ'mel.zə, də-, dem'el-

de|ment dɪ|'ment, də- (US) dɪ- **-ments** -'ments **-menting** -'men.tɪŋ (US) -'men.t̬ɪŋ **-mented/ly** -'men.tɪd/li (US) -'men.t̬ɪd/li

dementia dɪ'men.*t*ʃə, də-, -*t*ʃi.ə (US) dɪ'men*t*.ʃə

dementia praecox dɪˌmen.*t*ʃə'priː.kɒks, -'praɪ- (US) -men*t*.ʃə'priː.kɑːks

demerara *sugar:* ˌdem.ᵊ'reə.rə, -'rɑː- (US) -'rɑːr.ə

Demerara *district in Guyana:* ˌdem.ə'rɑː.rə (US) -'rɑːr.ə

demerg|e ˌdiːˈmɜːdʒ (US) -ˈmɝːrdʒ, də- **-es** -ɪz **-ing** -ɪŋ **-ed** -d
demerger ˌdiːˈmɜː.dʒəʳ (US) -ˈmɝː.dʒɚ **-s** -z
demerit ˌdiːˈmer.ɪt, ˈdiː.mer- (US) dɪˈmer-, diː- **-s** -s
Demerol® ˈdem.ə.rɒl (US) -rɑːl
demesne dɪˈmeɪn, də-, -ˈmiːn (US) dɪ- **-s** -z
Demeter dɪˈmiː.təʳ, də- (US) -t̬ɚ
Demetrius dɪˈmiː.tri.əs, də-
demi- dem.i-
Note: Prefix. Normally carries primary or secondary stress on the first syllable, e.g. **demigod** /ˈdem.i.gɒd (US) -gɑːd/, **demisemiquaver** /ˌdem.iˈsem.iˌkweɪ.vəʳ (US) -vɚ/.
demigod ˈdem.i.gɒd (US) -gɑːd **-s** -z
demigoddess ˈdem.iˌgɒd.es (US) -ˌgɑː.des **-es** -ɪz
demijohn ˈdem.i.dʒɒn (US) -dʒɑːn **-s** -z
demilitarization, -isa- diːˌmɪl.ɪ.tᵊr.aɪˈzeɪ.ʃᵊn, ˌdiː.mɪ.lɪ-, -lə-, -ɪˈ- (US) diːˌmɪl.ɪ.t̬ɚ.ɪˈ-
demilitariz|e, -is|e ˌdiːˈmɪl.ɪ.tᵊr.aɪz, ˈ-ə- (US) -t̬ə.raɪz **-es** -ɪz **-ing** -ɪŋ **-ed** -d
De Mille dəˈmɪl, dɪ-
demimondaine ˌdem.i.mɒnˈdeɪn (US) -mɑːnˈ- **-s** -z
demimonde ˌdem.iˈmɔ̃ːnd, -ˈmɔːnd, -ˈmɒnd, ˈ--- (US) ˈdem.i.mɑːnd
de minimis ˌdeɪˈmɪn.ɪ.miːs, ˈ-ə-
demis|e dɪˈmaɪz, də- (US) dɪ- **-es** -ɪz **-ing** -ɪŋ **-ed** -d
demisemiquaver ˈdem.i.sem.iˌkweɪ.vəʳ, ˌdem.iˈsem.i- (US) ˌdem.iˈsem.iˌkweɪ.vɚ **-s** -z
demission dɪˈmɪʃ.ᵊn **-s** -z
demist ˌdiːˈmɪst **-s** -s **-ing** -ɪŋ **-ed** -ɪd **-er/s** -əʳ/z (US) -ɚ/z
demitass|e ˈdem.i.tæs, -tɑːs **-es** -ɪz
demiurg|e ˈdem.i.ɜːdʒ, ˈdiː.mi- (US) -ɝːdʒ **-es** -ɪz
demo ˈdem.əʊ (US) -oʊ **-s** -z
demob ˌdiːˈmɒb (US) -ˈmɑːb **-s** -z **-bing** -ɪŋ **-bed** -d
demobilization, -isa- diːˌməʊ.bᵊl.aɪˈzeɪ.ʃᵊn, dɪ-, -bɪ.laɪˈ-, -lɪˈ- (US) -ˌmoʊ.bᵊl.ɪˈ-, -bɪ.lɪˈ- **-s** -z
demobiliz|e, -is|e ˌdiːˈməʊ.bᵊl.aɪz, dɪ-, -bɪ.laɪz (US) -ˈmoʊ.bə.laɪz, -bɪ- **-es** -ɪz **-ing** -ɪŋ **-ed** -d
democrac|y dɪˈmɒk.rə.s|i, də- (US) dɪˈmɑː- **-ies** -iz
democrat (D) ˈdem.ə.kræt **-s** -s
democratic (D) ˌdem.əˈkræt.ɪk (US) -ˈkræt̬- **-al** -ᵊl **-ally** -ᵊl.i, -li
democratization, -isa- dɪˌmɒk.rə.taɪˈzeɪ.ʃᵊn, də-, -tɪˈ- (US) dɪˌmɑː.krə.t̬ɪˈ-
democratiz|e, -is|e dɪˈmɒk.rə.taɪz, də- (US) dɪˈmɑː.krə- **-es** -ɪz **-ing** -ɪŋ **-ed** -d
Democritus dɪˈmɒk.rɪ.təs, də-, -rə- (US) dɪˈmɑːk.krə.t̬əs
démodé ˌdeɪˈməʊ.deɪ (US) -moʊˈdeɪ
demodu|late ˌdiːˈmɒd.jə|.leɪt, dɪ-, -jʊ-; -ˈmɒdʒ.ə-, ˈ-ʊ- (US) -ˈmɑː.dʒə-, -dʒʊ- **-lates** -leɪts **-lating** -leɪ.tɪŋ (US) -leɪ.t̬ɪŋ **-lated** -leɪ.tɪd (US) -leɪ.t̬ɪd
demodulation ˌdiːˌmɒd.jəˈleɪ.ʃᵊn, dɪ-, -jʊˈ-; -mɒdʒ.əˈ-, -ʊˈ- (US) -ˌmɑː.dʒəˈ-, -dʒʊ-
demodulator ˌdiːˈmɒd.jə.leɪ.təʳ, dɪ-, -jʊ-; -ˈmɒdʒ.ə-, ˈ-ʊ- (US) -ˈmɑː.dʒə.leɪ.t̬ɚ, -dʒʊ- **-s** -z
demographer dɪˈmɒg.rə.fəʳ, də-, ˌdiː- (US) dɪˈmɑː.grə.fɚ, ˌdiː- **-s** -z
demographic ˌdem.əʊˈgræf.ɪk, ˌdiː.məʊˈ- (US) ˌdem.əˈ-, ˌdiː.məˈ- **-s** -s
demography dɪˈmɒg.rə.fi, də-, ˌdiː- (US) dɪˈmɑː.grə-, ˌdiː-
demoiselle ˌdem.wɑːˈzel, -wəˈ- **-s** -z
De Moivre dəˈmɔɪ.vəʳ, dɪ- (US) -vɚ
demolish dɪˈmɒl.ɪʃ, də- (US) dɪˈmɑː.lɪʃ **-es** -ɪz **-ing** -ɪŋ **-ed** -t **-er/s** -əʳ/z (US) -ɚ/z
demolition ˌdem.əˈlɪʃ.ᵊn, ˌdiː.məˈ- **-s** -z
demon ˈdiː.mən **-s** -z
demoniz|e, -is|e ˈdiː.mᵊn.aɪz **-es** -ɪz **-ing** -ɪŋ **-ed** -d
demonetization, -isa- ˌdiːˌmʌn.ɪ.taɪˈzeɪ.ʃᵊn, -ˌmɒn-, -ə-, -tɪˈ- (US) -ˌmɑː.nə.tɪˈ-
demonetiz|e, -is|e ˌdiːˈmʌn.ɪ.taɪz, -ˈmɒn-, ˈ-ə- (US) -ˈmɑː.nə- **-es** -ɪz **-ing** -ɪŋ **-ed** -d
demoniac dɪˈməʊ.ni.æk, də-, diː- (US) dɪˈmoʊ-, diː- **-s** -s
demoniac|al ˌdiː.məʊˈnaɪə.k|ᵊl (US) -məˈ- **-ally** -ᵊl.i, -li
demonic dɪˈmɒn.ɪk, də-, diː- (US) dɪˈmɑː.nɪk, diː- **-al** -ᵊl **-ally** -ᵊl.i, -li
demon|ism ˈdiː.mə.n|ɪ.zᵊm **-ist/s** -ɪst/s
demoniz|e, -is|e ˈdiː.mᵊn.aɪz **-es** -ɪz **-ing** -ɪŋ **-ed** -d
demonology ˌdiː.məˈnɒl.ə.dʒi (US) -ˈnɑː.lə-
demonstrability dɪˌmɒnt.strəˈbɪl.ə.ti, də-, -ɪ.ti; ˌdem.ən- (US) dɪˌmɑːnt.strəˈbɪl.ə.t̬i; ˌdem.ən-
demonstrab|le dɪˈmɒnt.strə.b|l̩, də-; ˈdem.ən- (US) dɪˈmɑːnt-, də-; ˈdem.ən- **-ly** -li
demon|strate ˈdem.ən|.streɪt **-strates** -streɪts **-strating** -streɪ.tɪŋ (US) -streɪ.t̬ɪŋ **-strated** -streɪ.tɪd (US) -streɪ.t̬ɪd
demonstration ˌdem.ənˈstreɪ.ʃᵊn **-s** -z
demonstrative dɪˈmɒnt.strə.tɪv, də- (US) dɪˈmɑːnt.strə.t̬ɪv **-s** -z **-ly** -li **-ness** -nəs, -nɪs
demonstrator ˈdem.ən.streɪ.təʳ (US) -t̬ɚ **-s** -z
de Montfort dəˈmɒnt.fət, -fɔːt (US) -ˈmɑːnt.fɚt, -fɔːrt
demoralization, -isa- dɪˌmɒr.ᵊl.aɪˈzeɪ.ʃᵊn, ˌdiː.mɒr-, -ɪˈ- (US) dɪˌmɔːr.ᵊl.ɪˈ-
demoraliz|e, -is|e dɪˈmɒr.ə.laɪz, ˌdiː- (US) -ˈmɔːr- **-es** -ɪz **-ing** -ɪŋ **-ed** -d
De Morgan dəˈmɔː.gən (US) -ˈmɔːr-
Demos ˈdiː.mɒs (US) -mɑːs
Demosthenes dɪˈmɒs.θə.niːz, də-, -θɪ- (US) -ˈmɑːs-
de|mote dɪ|ˈməʊt, ˌdiː- (US) -ˈmoʊt **-motes** -ˈməʊts (US) -ˈmoʊts **-moting** -ˈməʊ.tɪŋ (US) -ˈmoʊ.t̬ɪŋ **-moted** -ˈməʊ.tɪd (US) -ˈmoʊ.t̬ɪd
demotic dɪˈmɒt.ɪk, də-, diː- (US) dɪˈmɑː.t̬ɪk, diː-
demotion dɪˈməʊ.ʃᵊn, ˌdiː- (US) -ˈmoʊ-
demoti|vate ˌdiːˈməʊ.tɪ|.veɪt, -tə- (US) -ˈmoʊ.t̬ə- **-vates** -veɪts **-vating** -veɪ.tɪŋ (US) -veɪ.t̬ɪŋ **-vated** -veɪ.tɪd (US) -veɪ.t̬ɪd
Dempsey ˈdem*p*.si
Dempster ˈdem*p*.stəʳ (US) -stɚ
demulcent dɪˈmʌl.sᵊnt, də-, ˌdiː- (US) dɪ-, ˌdiː- **-s** -s
demur dɪˈmɜːʳ, də- (US) dɪˈmɝː **-s** -z **-ring** -ɪŋ **-red** -d
demur|e dɪˈmjʊəʳ, də-, -mjɔːʳ (US) dɪˈmjʊr **-er** -əʳ (US) -ɚ **-est** -ɪst, -əst **-ely** -li **-eness** -nəs, -nɪs
demurrage dɪˈmʌr.ɪdʒ, də- (US) dɪˈmɝː-
demurrer *person who demurs:* dɪˈmɜː.rəʳ, də- (US) -ˈmɝː.ɚ **-s** -z
demurrer *objection on grounds of irrelevance:* dɪˈmʌr.əʳ, də- (US) dɪˈmɝː.ɚ **-s** -z
demutualization, -isa- ˌdiː.mjuː.tʃu.ə.laɪˈzeɪ.ʃᵊn, dɪˌmjuː-, -tju-, -ɪˈ- (US) -tʃu.ə.lɪˈ-, -tʃə.laɪ-
demutualiz|e, -is|e ˌdiːˈmjuː.tʃu.ə.laɪz, dɪˈmjuː-, -tju- (US) -tʃu-, -tʃə.laɪz **-es** -ɪz **-ing** -ɪŋ **-ed** -d
dem|y dɪˈm|aɪ, də- (US) dɪ- **-ies** -aɪz
demystification ˌdiː.mɪ.stɪ.fɪˈkeɪ.ʃᵊn, -stə-; diːˌmɪs.tɪ-, -tə- (US) diːˌmɪs-
demysti|fy ˌdiːˈmɪs.tɪ|.faɪ, -tə- **-fies** -faɪz **-fying** -faɪ.ɪŋ **-fied** -faɪd
demythologiz|e, -is|e ˌdiː.mɪˈθɒl.ə.dʒaɪz, -maɪˈ-, -məˈ- (US) -mɪˈθɑː.lə- **-es** -ɪz **-ing** -ɪŋ **-ed** -d
den den **-s** -z
Denali dəˈnɑː.li
denari|us dɪˈneə.ri|.əs, də-, denˈeə-, -ˈɑː- (US) dɪˈner.i-, -ˈnær- **-i** -aɪ, -iː
denary ˈdiː.nᵊr.i, ˈden.ᵊr-
denationalization, -isa- diːˌnæʃ.ᵊn.ᵊl.aɪˈzeɪ.ʃᵊn, ˌdiː.næʃ-, -nᵊl.aɪ-, -ɪˈ- (US) diːˌnæʃ.ᵊn.ᵊl.ɪˈ-, -nᵊl.ɪ-

Dental

A sound in which there is contact between the tongue and the front teeth.

Examples for English

In English, the dentals usually referred to are the FRICATIVES /θ/ and /ð/, of which /θ/ is voiceless and /ð/ is voiced. In a careful production of these sounds, the tongue tip may be protruded between the upper and lower teeth; the sounds are sometimes referred to as 'interdental' for this reason, e.g.:

thigh	/θaɪ/	
ether	/'iː.θər/	US /-θɚ/
breath	/breθ/	
thy	/ðaɪ/	
either	/'aɪ.ðər/	US /'iː.ðɚ/
breathe	/briːð/	

denationaliz|e, -is|e ˌdiː'næʃ.ᵊn.ᵊl.aɪz, '-nᵊl- **-es** -ɪz **-ing** -ɪŋ **-ed** -d
denaturalization, -isa- diːˌnætʃ.ᵊr.ᵊl.aɪ'zeɪ.ʃᵊn, ˌdiː.nætʃ-, -ɪ'- US diːˌnætʃ.ɚ.ᵊl.ɪ'-
denaturaliz|e, -is|e ˌdiː'nætʃ.ᵊr.ᵊl.aɪz **-es** -ɪz **-ing** -ɪŋ **-ed** -d
denatur|e ˌdiː'neɪ.tʃəʳ US -tʃɚ **-es** -z **-ing** -ɪŋ **-ed** -d
Denbigh 'den.bi, 'dem- US 'den- **-shire** -ʃəʳ, -ˌʃɪəʳ US -ʃɚ, -ˌʃɪr
Denby 'den.bi, 'dem- US 'den-
Dench dentʃ
dendrite 'den.draɪt **-s** -s
dendritic den'drɪt.ɪk US -'drɪţ- **-al** -ᵊl
dendroid 'den.drɔɪd
dendrology den'drɒl.ə.dʒi US -'drɑː.lə-
dendron 'den.drən US -drən, -drɑːn **-s** -z
dene (D) diːn **-s** -z
Deneb 'den.eb
Denebola dɪ'neb.ə.lə, den'eb-, də'neb-
Deneuve də'nɜːv
dengue 'deŋ.gi, -geɪ
Deng Xiaoping ˌdeŋ.ʃaʊ'pɪŋ US ˌdʌŋ-, ˌdeŋ-
Denham 'den.əm
Denholm *place in West Yorkshire:* 'den.hɒlm US -hoʊlm
Denholm(e) *name:* 'den.əm
Denia 'diː.ni.ə **-s** -z
deniable dɪ'naɪ.ə.bl̩, də- US dɪ-
denial dɪ'naɪ.əl, də- US dɪ- **-s** -z
denier *coin:* 'den.i.əʳ, -eɪ; də'nɪəʳ US də'nɪr **-s** -z
denier *thickness of yarn:* 'den.i.əʳ, -eɪ US 'den.jɚ
denier *person who denies:* dɪ'naɪ.əʳ, də- US dɪ'naɪ.ɚ **-s** -z
deni|grate 'den.ɪ|.greɪt, '-ə- **-grates** -greɪts **-grating** -greɪ.tɪŋ US -greɪ.ţɪŋ **-grated** -greɪ.tɪd US -greɪ.ţɪd
denigration ˌden.ɪ'greɪ.ʃᵊn, -ə'-
denim 'den.ɪm, -əm **-s** -z
De Niro də'nɪə.rəʊ US -'nɪr.oʊ
Denis 'den.ɪs
Denise də'niːz, den'iːz, dɪ'niːz, -'niːs US də'niːs, den'iːs, dɪ'niːs, -'niːz
Denison 'den.ɪ.sᵊn
denizen 'den.ɪ.zᵊn, '-ə- **-s** -z
Denktash 'deŋk.tæʃ US -tɑːʃ
Denman 'den.mən, 'dem- US 'den-
Denmark 'den.mɑːk, 'dem- US 'den.mɑːrk
Denning 'den.ɪŋ
Dennis 'den.ɪs
Dennison 'den.ɪ.sᵊn
Denny 'den.i **-s** -z
denomi|nate dɪ'nɒm.ɪ|.neɪt, də'-, '-ə- US dɪ'nɑː.mə- **-nates** -neɪts **-nating** -neɪ.tɪŋ US -neɪ.ţɪŋ **-nated** -neɪ.tɪd US -neɪ.ţɪd
denomination dɪˌnɒm.ɪ'neɪ.ʃᵊn, də-, -ə'- US dɪˌnɑː.mə'- **-s** -z
denominational dɪˌnɒm.ɪ'neɪ.ʃᵊn.ᵊl, də-, -ə'- US dɪˌnɑː.mə'-
denominationalism dɪˌnɒm.ɪ'neɪ.ʃᵊn.ᵊl.ɪ.zᵊm, də-, -ə'- US dɪˌnɑː.mə'-
denominative dɪ'nɒm.ɪ.nə.tɪv, də-, '-ə- US dɪ'nɑː.mə.nə.ţɪv
denominator dɪ'nɒm.ɪ.neɪ.təʳ, də-, '-ə- US dɪ'nɑː.mə.neɪ.ţɚ **-s** -z
denotation ˌdiː.nəʊ'teɪ.ʃᵊn US -noʊ'-, -nə'- **-s** -z
denotative dɪ'nəʊ.tə.tɪv, də-; 'diː.nəʊ.teɪ- US 'diː.noʊ.teɪ.ţɪv; dɪ'noʊ.ţə-
de|note dɪ|'nəʊt, də- US dɪ|'noʊt **-notes** -'nəʊts US -'noʊts **-noting** -'nəʊ.tɪŋ US -'noʊ.ţɪŋ **-noted** -'nəʊ.tɪd US -'noʊ.ţɪd
dénouement deɪ'nuː.mɑ̃ːŋ, dɪ-, də- US ˌdeɪ.nuː'mɑ̃ːŋ
dénouements deɪ'nuː.mɑ̃ːŋ, dɪ-, də-, -mɑ̃ːŋz US ˌdeɪ.nuː'mɑ̃ːŋ, -'mɑ̃ːŋz
denounc|e dɪ'naʊnts, də- US dɪ- **-es** -ɪz **-ing** -ɪŋ **-ed** -t **-er/s** -əʳ/z US -ɚ/z **-ement/s** -mənt/s
de novo deɪ'nəʊ.vəʊ, diː-, də- US -'noʊ.voʊ
dens|e dents **-er** -əʳ US -ɚ **-est** -ɪst, -əst **-ely** -li **-eness** -nəs, -nɪs
densit|y 'dent.sɪ.t|i, -sə- US -sə.ţ|i **-ies** -iz
dent (D) dent **-s** -s **-ing** -ɪŋ **-ed** -ɪd
dental 'den.tᵊl **-s** -z **'dental ˌfloss; 'dental ˌsurgeon**
dentaliz|e, -is|e 'den.tᵊl.aɪz US -ţə.laɪ- **-es** -ɪz **-ing** -ɪŋ **-ed** -d
dentate 'den.teɪt
dentated den'teɪ.tɪd, 'den.teɪ- US -ţɪ-
denticle 'den.tɪ.kl̩ US -ţɪ- **-s** -z
dentific|e 'den.tɪ.friːs, -tə-, -frɪs US -ţə.frɪs **-es** -ɪz
dentil 'den.tɪl, -tᵊl US -tᵊl **-s** -z
dentilingual ˌden.ti'lɪŋ.gwəl US -ţi'- **-s** -z
dentine 'den.tiːn
dentist 'den.tɪst US -ţɪst **-s** -s
dentistry 'den.tɪ.stri, -tə- US -ţɪ-
dentition den'tɪʃ.ᵊn
Denton 'den.tən US -tᵊn
denture 'den.tʃəʳ US 'dent.ʃɚ **-s** -z
denudation ˌdiː.njuː'deɪ.ʃᵊn, ˌden.ju- US ˌdiː.nuː'-, -njuː'-; ˌden.juː'- **-s** -z
denud|e dɪ'njuːd, də-, ˌdiː- US dɪ'nuːd, ˌdiː-, -'njuːd **-es** -z **-ing** -ɪŋ **-ed** -ɪd
denunci|ate dɪ'nʌnt.si|.eɪt, də-, -ʃi- US dɪ'nʌnt.si- **-ates** -eɪts **-ating** -eɪ.tɪŋ US -eɪ.ţɪŋ **-ated** -eɪ.tɪd US -eɪ.ţɪd **-ator/s** -eɪ.təʳ/z US -eɪ.ţɚ/z
denunciation dɪˌnʌnt.si'eɪ.ʃᵊn, də-, -ʃi'- US dɪˌnʌnt.si'- **-s** -z
denunciatory dɪ'nʌnt.si.ə.tᵊr.i, də-, -ʃi-, -tri US dɪ'nʌnt.si.ə.tɔːr.i
Denver 'den.vəʳ US -vɚ
den|y dɪ'n|aɪ, də- US dɪ- **-ies** -aɪz **-ying** -aɪ.ɪŋ **-ied** -aɪd **-ier/s** -aɪ.əʳ/z US -aɪ.ɚ/z
Denys 'den.ɪs
Denzel 'den.zᵊl, -zel, -zɪl, ˌden'zel
Denzil 'den.zɪl, -zᵊl US -zᵊl
deodand 'diː.əʊ.dænd US '-ə- **-s** -z
deodar 'diː.əʊ.dɑːʳ US -ə.dɑːr **-s** -z
deodorant di'əʊ.dᵊr.ᵊnt US -'oʊ- **-s**
deodorization, -isa- diˌəʊ.dᵊr.aɪ'zeɪ.ʃᵊn, -ɪ'- US -oʊ.dɚ.ɪ'- **-s** -z

deodoriz|e, **-is|e** di'əʊ.dᵊr.aɪz (US) -'oʊ.də.raɪz **-es** -ɪz **-ing** -ɪŋ **-ed** -d **-er/s** -əʳ/z (US) -ɚ/z
deontic di'ɒn.tɪk, diː-, deɪ- (US) -'ɑːn.t̬ɪk
deoxidization, **-isa-** di,ɒk.sɪ.daɪ'zeɪ.ʃᵊn, ,diː-, -sə-, -dɪ'- (US) -,ɑːk.sə.dɪ'- **-s** -z
deoxidiz|e, **-is|e** di'ɒk.sɪ.daɪz, ,diː-, -sə- (US) -'ɑːk.sə- **-es** -ɪz **-ing** -ɪŋ **-ed** -d **-er/s** -əʳ/z (US) -ɚ/z
Depardieu ,dep.ɑː'djɜː, də.pɑː'-; 'dep.ɑː.djɜː (US) ,dep.ɑːr'djɜː, '---
de|part dɪ|'pɑːt, də- (US) dɪ|'pɑːrt **-parts** -'pɑːts (US) -'pɑːrts **-parting** -'pɑː.tɪŋ (US) -'pɑːr.t̬ɪŋ **-parted** -'pɑː.tɪd (US) -'pɑːr.t̬ɪd
department dɪ'pɑːt.mənt, də- (US) dɪ'pɑːrt- **-s** -s **de'partment ,store**
departmental ,diː.pɑːt'men.tᵊl (US) -pɑːrt'men.t̬ᵊl **-ism** -ɪ.zᵊm
departure dɪ'pɑː.tʃəʳ, də- (US) dɪ'pɑːr.tʃɚ **-s** -z **de'parture ,lounge**
depast|ure ,diː'pɑːs.tʃ|əʳ (US) -'pæs.tʃ|ɚ **-ures** -əz (US) -ɚz **-uring** -ᵊr.ɪŋ **-ured** -əd (US) -ɚd
depend dɪ'pend, də- (US) dɪ- **-s** -z **-ing** -ɪŋ **-ed** -ɪd
dependability dɪ,pen.də'bɪl.ə.ti, də-, -ɪ.ti (US) dɪ,pen.də'bɪl.ə.t̬i
dependab|le dɪ'pen.də.b|l̩, də-, dɪ- **-ly** -li **-leness** -l̩.nəs, -nɪs
dependant dɪ'pen.dənt, də- (US) dɪ- **-s** -s
dependenc|e dɪ'pen.dənts, də- (US) dɪ- **-y** -i **-ies** -iz
dependent dɪ'pen.dənt, də- (US) dɪ- **-s** -s **-ly** -li
De Pere dɪ'pɪəʳ, də- (US) -'pɪr
depersonaliz|e, **is|e** ,diː'pɜː.sᵊn.ᵊl.aɪz (US) -'pɝː- **-es** -ɪz **-ing** -ɪŋ **-ed** -d
Depew dɪ'pjuː, də-
depict dɪ'pɪkt, də- (US) dɪ- **-s** -s **-ing** -ɪŋ **-ed** -ɪd
depiction dɪ'pɪk.ʃᵊn, də- (US) dɪ- **-s** -z
depi|late 'dep.ɪ|.leɪt, '-ə- **-lates** -leɪts **-lating** -leɪ.tɪŋ (US) -leɪ.t̬ɪŋ **-lated** -leɪ.tɪd (US) -leɪ.t̬ɪd
depilation ,dep.ɪ'leɪ.ʃᵊn, -ə'-
depilator 'dep.ɪ.leɪ.təʳ, '-ə- (US) -t̬ɚ **-s** -z
depilator|y dɪ'pɪl.ə.tᵊr|.i, də-, -tr|i (US) dɪ'pɪl.ə.tɔːr|.i **-ies** -iz
deplan|e ,diː'pleɪn **-es** -z **-ing** -ɪŋ **-ed** -d
de|plete dɪ|'pliːt, də- (US) dɪ- **-pletes** -'pliːts **-pleting** -'pliː.tɪŋ (US) -'pliː.t̬ɪŋ **-pleted** -'pliː.tɪd (US) -'pliː.t̬ɪd
depletion dɪ'pliː.ʃᵊn, də- (US) dɪ- **-s** -z
deplet|ive dɪ'pliː.t|ɪv, də- (US) dɪ'pliː.t̬|ɪv **-ory** -ᵊr.i
deplorab|le dɪ'plɔː.rə.b|l̩, də- (US) dɪ'plɔːr.ə- **-ly** -li **-leness** -l̩.nəs, -nɪs
deplor|e dɪ'plɔːʳ, də- (US) dɪ'plɔːr **-es** -z **-ing** -ɪŋ **-ed** -d
deploy dɪ'plɔɪ, də- (US) dɪ- **-s** -z **-ing** -ɪŋ **-ed** -d
deployment dɪ'plɔɪ.mənt, də-, dɪ- **-s** -s
depolarization, **-isa-** diː,pəʊ.lᵊr.aɪ'zeɪ.ʃᵊn, ,diː.pəʊ-, -ɪ'- (US) diː,poʊ.lɚ.ɪ'-
depolariz|e, **-is|e** ,diː'pəʊ.lᵊr.aɪz (US) -'poʊ.lə.raɪz **-es** -ɪz **-ing** -ɪŋ **-ed** -d
depoliticization ,diː.pə,lɪt.ɪ.saɪ'zeɪ.ʃᵊn, ,-ə-, -sɪ'- (US) ,-lɪt̬.ɪ.sɪ'-, ,-ə-
depoliticiz|e, **-is|e** ,diː.pə'lɪt.ɪ.saɪz, '-ə- (US) -'lɪt̬- **-es** -ɪz **-ing** -ɪŋ **-ed** -d
de Pompadour də'pɒm.pə.dɔːʳ, -dʊəʳ (US) -'pɑːm.pə.dɔːr
deponent dɪ'pəʊ.nənt, də- (US) dɪ'poʊ- **-s** -s
Depo-Provera® ,dep.əʊ.prəʊ'vɪə.rə (US) -oʊ.proʊ'ver.ə
depopu|late ,diː'pɒp.jə|.leɪt, -jʊ- (US) -'pɑː.pjə- **-lates** -leɪts **-lating** -leɪ.tɪŋ (US) -leɪ.t̬ɪŋ **-lated** -leɪ.tɪd (US) -leɪ.t̬ɪd **-lator/s** -leɪ.təʳ/z (US) -leɪ.t̬ɚ/z
depopulation diː,pɒp.jə'leɪ.ʃᵊn, ,diː.pɒp-, -jʊ'- (US) diː,pɑː.pjə'-
de|port dɪ|'pɔːt, də- (US) dɪ|'pɔːrt **-ports** -'pɔːts (US) -'pɔːrts **-porting** -'pɔː.tɪŋ (US) -'pɔːr.t̬ɪŋ **-ported** -'pɔː.tɪd (US) -'pɔːr.t̬ɪd
deportation ,diː.pɔː'teɪ.ʃᵊn (US) -pɔːr'- **-s** -z
deportee ,diː.pɔː'tiː (US) -pɔːr'- **-s** -z
deportment dɪ'pɔːt.mənt, də- (US) dɪ'pɔːrt-
deposal dɪ'pəʊ.zᵊl, də- (US) dɪ'poʊ- **-s** -z
depos|e dɪ'pəʊz, də- (US) dɪ'poʊz **-es** -ɪz **-ing** -ɪŋ **-ed** -d
depos|it dɪ'pɒz|.ɪt, də- (US) dɪ'pɑː.z|ɪt **-its** -ɪts **-iting** -ɪ.tɪŋ (US) -ɪ.t̬ɪŋ **-ited** -ɪ.tɪd (US) -ɪ.t̬ɪd **de'posit ac,count**
depositar|y dɪ'pɒz.ɪ.tᵊr|.i, də-, '-ə- (US) dɪ'pɑː.zə.ter- **-ies** -iz
deposition ,dep.ə'zɪʃ.ᵊn, ,diː.pə'- **-s** -z
depositor dɪ'pɒz.ɪ.təʳ, də-, '-ə- (US) dɪ'pɑː.zə.t̬ɚ **-s** -z
depositor|y dɪ'pɒz.ɪ.tᵊr|.i, də-, '-ə-, -tr|i (US) dɪ'pɑː.zə.tɔːr|.i **-ies** -iz
depot 'dep.əʊ (US) 'diː.poʊ, 'dep.oʊ **-s** -z
Depp dep
depravation ,dep.rə'veɪ.ʃᵊn
deprav|e dɪ'preɪv, də- (US) dɪ- **-es** -z **-ing** -ɪŋ **-ed** -d **-edly** -d.li, -ɪd.li **-edness** -d.nəs, -ɪd.nəs, -nɪs
depravity dɪ'præv.ə.ti, də-, -ɪ.ti (US) dɪ'præv.ə.t̬i
depre|cate 'dep.rə|.keɪt, -rɪ- **-cates** -keɪts **-cating/ly** -keɪ.tɪŋ/li (US) -keɪ.t̬ɪŋ/li **-cated** -keɪ.tɪd (US) -keɪ.t̬ɪd **-cator/s** -keɪ.təʳ/z (US) -keɪ.t̬ɚ/z
deprecation ,dep.rə'keɪ.ʃᵊn, -prɪ'- **-s** -z
deprecatory 'dep.rə.kə.tᵊr.i, -rɪ-, -tri; ,dep.rə'keɪ- (US) 'dep.rə.kə.tɔːr.i
depreciable dɪ'priː.ʃi.ə.bl̩, də-, -si- (US) dɪ'priː.ʃi.ə.bl̩, '-ʃə.bl̩
depreci|ate dɪ'priː.ʃi|.eɪt, də-, -si- (US) dɪ'priː.ʃi- **-ates** -eɪts **-ating/ly** -eɪ.tɪŋ/li (US) -eɪ.t̬ɪŋ/li **-ated** -eɪ.tɪd (US) -eɪ.t̬ɪd **-ator/s** -eɪ.təʳ/z (US) -eɪ.t̬ɚ/z
depreciation dɪ,priː.ʃi'eɪ.ʃᵊn, də-, -si'- (US) dɪ,priː.ʃi'-
depreciatory dɪ'priː.ʃi.ə.tᵊr.i, də-, -si-, '-ʃə.tᵊr-, -tri (US) dɪ'priː.ʃi.ə.tɔːr.i, '-ʃə.tɔːr-
depre|date 'dep.rə|.deɪt, -rɪ- **-dates** -deɪts **-dating** -deɪ.tɪŋ (US) -deɪ.t̬ɪŋ **-dated** -deɪ.tɪd (US) -deɪ.t̬ɪd **-dator/s** -deɪ.təʳ/z (US) -deɪ.t̬ɚ/z
depredation ,dep.rə'deɪ.ʃᵊn, -rɪ'- **-s** -z
depredatory dɪ'pred.ə.tᵊr.i, də-, -tri; ,dep.rə'deɪ- (US) 'dep.rə.də.tɔːr.i, -deɪ.t̬ɚ-; dɪ'pred.ə.tɔːr-
depress dɪ'pres, də- (US) dɪ- **-es** -ɪz **-ing** -ɪŋ **-ed** -t **-or/s** -əʳ/z (US) -ɚ/z **-ant/s** -ᵊnt/s
depressing dɪ'pres.ɪŋ, də- (US) dɪ- **-ly** -li
depression dɪ'preʃ.ᵊn, də- (US) dɪ- **-s** -z
depressive dɪ'pres.ɪv, də- (US) dɪ- **-s** -z
depressor dɪ'pres.əʳ, də- (US) dɪ'pres.ɚ **-s** -z
depressurization, **-isation** diː,preʃ.ᵊr.aɪ'zeɪ.ʃᵊn, ,diː.preʃ-, -ɪ'- (US) diː,preʃ.ɚ.ɪ'-
depressuriz|e, **-is|e** ,diː'preʃ.ᵊr.aɪz (US) -ə.raɪz **-es** -ɪz **-ing** -ɪŋ **-ed** -d
deprivation ,dep.rɪ'veɪ.ʃᵊn, -rə'-; ,diː.praɪ'- **-s** -z
depriv|e dɪ'praɪv, də- (US) dɪ- **-es** -z **-ing** -ɪŋ **-ed** -d
de profundis ,deɪ.prɒf'ʊn.diːs, -prə'fʊn- (US) -proʊ'fʊn.dɪs
deprogram ,diː'prəʊ.græm (US) -'proʊ- **-s** -z **-(m)ing** -ɪŋ **-(m)ed** -d
deprogramm|e ,diː'prəʊ.græm (US) -'proʊ- **-s** -z **-ing** -ɪŋ **-er** -d
dept *(abbrev. for* **department***)* dɪ'pɑːt.mənt, də- (US) dɪ'pɑːrt-
Deptford 'det.fəd, 'dep.fəd (US) -fɚd
depth depθ **-s** -s **'depth ,charge**
deputation ,dep.jə'teɪ.ʃᵊn, -jʊ'- (US) -jə'- **-s** -z
de|pute dɪ|'pjuːt, də- (US) dɪ- **-putes** -'pjuːts **-puting** -'pjuː.tɪŋ (US) -'pjuː.t̬ɪŋ **-puted** -'pjuː.tɪd (US) -'pjuː.t̬ɪd
deputiz|e, **-is|e** 'dep.jə.taɪz, -jʊ- **-es** -ɪz **-ing** -ɪŋ **-ed** -d
deput|y 'dep.jə.t|i, -jʊ- (US) -t̬|i **-ies** -iz
De Quincey də'kwɪnt.si, dɪ-
deraci|nate dɪ'ræs.ɪ|.neɪt, ,diː-, '-ə- **-nates** -neɪts **-nating** -neɪ.tɪŋ (US) -neɪ.t̬ɪŋ **-nated** -neɪ.tɪd, -neɪ.t̬ɪd

deracination diː,ræs.ɪ'neɪ.ʃᵊn, ,diː.ræs-, -ə'- ⓤⓢ diː,ræs-

derail dɪ'reɪl, ,diː- **-s** -z **-ing** -ɪŋ **-ed** -d

derailleur dɪ'reɪ.ljəʳ, də-, -ləʳ ⓤⓢ dɪ'reɪ.lɚ

derailment dɪ'reɪl.mənt, ,diː- **-s** -s

derang|e dɪ'reɪndʒ, də- ⓤⓢ dɪ- **-es** -ɪz **-ing** -ɪŋ **-ed** -d **-ement/s** -mənt/s

de|rate ,diː|'reɪt **-rates** -'reɪts **-rating** -'reɪ.tɪŋ ⓤⓢ -'reɪ.t̬ɪŋ **-rated** -'reɪ.tɪd ⓤⓢ -'reɪ.t̬ɪd

deration ,diː'ræʃ.ᵊn **-s** -z **-ing** -ɪŋ **-ed** -d

derb|y 'dɑː.b|i ⓤⓢ 'dɝː- **-ies** -iz

Der|by 'dɑː|.bi ⓤⓢ 'dɑːr-, 'dɝː- **-byshire** -bɪ.ʃəʳ, -,ʃɪəʳ ⓤⓢ -ʃɚ, -,ʃɪr

Note: American pronunciation uses /'dɑːr-/ for British references.

Derbys. *(abbrev. for* **Derbyshire***)* 'dɑː.bɪ.ʃəʳ, -,ʃɪəʳ ⓤⓢ 'dɑːr.bɪ.ʃɚ, 'dɝː-, -,ʃɪr

Note: American pronunciation uses /'dɑːr-/ for British references.

deregu|late ,diː'reg.jə|.leɪt, -jʊ- ⓤⓢ -jə- **-lates** -leɪts **-lating** -leɪ.tɪŋ ⓤⓢ -leɪ.t̬ɪŋ **-lated** -leɪ.tɪd ⓤⓢ -leɪ.t̬ɪd

deregulation ,diː.reg.jə'leɪ.ʃᵊn, -jʊ'- ⓤⓢ -jə'-

Dereham 'dɪə.rəm ⓤⓢ 'dɪr.əm

Derek 'der.ɪk

derelict 'der.ə.lɪkt, '-ɪ- **-s** -s

dereliction ,der.ə'lɪk.ʃᵊn, -ɪ'-

derequisition diː,rek.wɪ'zɪʃ.ᵊn, ,diː.rek-, -wə'- ⓤⓢ diː,rek- **-s** -z **-ing** -ɪŋ **-ed** -d

De Reszke də'res.ki

Derg(h) dɜːg ⓤⓢ dɝːg

Derham 'der.əm

derid|e dɪ'raɪd, də- ⓤⓢ dɪ- **-es** -z **-ing/ly** -ɪŋ/li **-ed** -ɪd **-er/s** -əʳ/z ⓤⓢ -ɚ/z

de rigueur də.rɪ'gɜːʳ, ,deɪ-, ,diː-, -riː'- ⓤⓢ -'gɝː

Dering 'dɪə.rɪŋ ⓤⓢ 'dɪr.ɪŋ

derision dɪ'rɪʒ.ᵊn, də- ⓤⓢ dɪ-

derisive dɪ'raɪ.sɪv, də'raɪ-, -zɪv, -'rɪz.ɪv ⓤⓢ dɪ'raɪ.sɪv, -zɪv **-ly** -li **-ness** -nəs, -nɪs

derisory dɪ'raɪ.sᵊr.i, də-, -zᵊr- ⓤⓢ dɪ'raɪ-

derivation ,der.ɪ'veɪ.ʃᵊn, -ə'- **-s** -z **-al** -ᵊl

derivative dɪ'rɪv.ə.tɪv, də- ⓤⓢ dɪ'rɪv.ə.t̬ɪv **-s** -z **-ly** -li

deriv|e dɪ'raɪv, də- ⓤⓢ dɪ- **-es** -z **-ing** -ɪŋ **-ed** -d **-able** -ə.bl̩

d'Erlanger ,deə.lɑ̃ː*n*'ʒeɪ ⓤⓢ ,der.lɑːn'-

derm dɜːm ⓤⓢ dɝːm **-al** -ᵊl

-derm -dɜːm ⓤⓢ -dɝːm

Note: Suffix. Does not normally carry stress, e.g. **pachyderm** /'pæk.ɪ.dɜːm ⓤⓢ -ə.dɝːm/.

dermabrasion ,dɜː.mə'breɪ.ʒᵊn ⓤⓢ ,dɝː-

-dermal -dɜː.mᵊl ⓤⓢ -dɝː-

Note: Suffix. May or may not carry stress, e.g. **epidermal** /,ep.ɪ'dɜː.mᵊl ⓤⓢ -'dɝːr-/; see individual entries.

dermatitis ,dɜː.mə'taɪ.tɪs ⓤⓢ ,dɝː.mə'taɪ.t̬ɪs

dermatolog|y ,dɜː.mə'tɒl.ə.dʒ|i ⓤⓢ ,dɝː.mə'tɑː.lə- **-ist/s** -ɪst/s

dermatos|is ,dɜː.mə'təʊ.s|ɪs ⓤⓢ ,dɝː.mə'toʊ- **-es** -iːz

dermis 'dɜː.mɪs ⓤⓢ 'dɝː-

Dermot(t) 'dɜː.mət ⓤⓢ 'dɝː-

dernier cri ,dɜː.ni.eɪ'kriː, ,deə- ⓤⓢ ,der.njeɪ'-, ,dɝː-

dero|gate 'der.əʊ|.geɪt, 'diː.rəʊ- ⓤⓢ 'der.ə- **-gates** -geɪts **-gating** -geɪ.tɪŋ ⓤⓢ -geɪ.t̬ɪŋ **-gated** -geɪ.tɪd ⓤⓢ -geɪ.t̬ɪd

derogation ,der.əʊ'geɪ.ʃᵊn, ,diː.rəʊ'- ⓤⓢ ,der.ə'-

derogator|y dɪ'rɒg.ə.tᵊr|.i, də-, -tr|i ⓤⓢ dɪ'rɑː.gə.tɔːr|.i **-ily** -ᵊl.i, -ɪ.li **-iness** -ɪ.nəs, -ɪ.nɪs

Deronda də'rɒn.də, dɪ- ⓤⓢ də'rɑːn-

derrick (D) 'der.ɪk **-s** -s

Derrida də'riː.də, der'iː-; 'der.ɪ- ⓤⓢ 'der.iː.dɑː

derrière 'der.i.eəʳ, ,--'- ⓤⓢ ,der.i'er, '--- **-s** -z

derring-do ,der.ɪŋ'duː, ,deə.rɪŋ'- ⓤⓢ ,der.ɪŋ'-

derringer (D) 'der.ɪn.dʒəʳ, -ᵊn- ⓤⓢ -dʒɚ **-s** -z

Derry 'der.i

derv dɜːv ⓤⓢ dɝːv

dervish (D) 'dɜː.vɪʃ ⓤⓢ 'dɝː- **-es** -ɪz

Dervla 'dɜːv.lə ⓤⓢ 'dɝːv-

Derwent 'dɜː.wənt, 'dɑː-, -went, -wɪnt ⓤⓢ 'dɝː-, 'dɑːr- **'Derwent ,Water**

Note: /'dɑː- ⓤⓢ 'dɑːr-/ is the normal pronunciation for the Baron.

Des dez ⓤⓢ des

DES ,diː.iː'es

Desai des'aɪ; 'deɪ.saɪ

desali|nate ,diː'sæl.ɪ|.neɪt, '-ə- **-nates** -neɪts **-nating** -neɪ.tɪŋ ⓤⓢ -neɪ.t̬ɪŋ **-nated** -neɪ.tɪd ⓤⓢ -neɪ.t̬ɪd

desalination diː,sæl.ɪ'neɪ.ʃᵊn, ,diː.sæl-, -ə'- ⓤⓢ diː,sæl- **-s** -z

desalinization, -isa- diː,sæl.ɪ.naɪ'zeɪ.ʃᵊn, ,diː.sæl-, ,-ə-, -nɪ'- ⓤⓢ diː,sæl.ə.nɪ'-

desaliniz|e, -is|e ,diː'sæl.ɪ.naɪz, '-ə- **-es** -ɪz **-ing** -ɪŋ **-ed** -d

Desart 'dez.ət ⓤⓢ -ɚt

Desborough 'dez.brə ⓤⓢ -bɚ.oʊ, '-brə

descal|e ,diː'skeɪl **-es** -z **-ing** -ɪŋ **-ed** -d

descant *(n.)* 'des.kænt **-s** -s

descan|t *(v.)* dɪ'skæn|t, des'kæn|t ⓤⓢ 'des.kæn|t, -'- **-ts** -ts **-ting** -tɪŋ ⓤⓢ -t̬ɪŋ **-ted** -tɪd ⓤⓢ -t̬ɪd

Descartes 'deɪ.kɑːt, deɪ'kɑːt ⓤⓢ deɪ'kɑːrt

descend dɪ'send, də- ⓤⓢ dɪ- **-s** -z **-ing** -ɪŋ **-ed** -ɪd

descendant, descendent dɪ'sen.dənt, də- ⓤⓢ dɪ- **-s** -s

descender dɪ'sen.dəʳ, də- ⓤⓢ dɪ'sen.dɚ **-s** -z

descent dɪ'sent, də- ⓤⓢ dɪ- **-s** -s

describ|e dɪ'skraɪb, də- ⓤⓢ dɪ- **-es** -z **-ing** -ɪŋ **-ed** -d **-er/s** -əʳ/z ⓤⓢ -ɚ/z **-able** -ə.bl̩

description dɪ'skrɪp.ʃᵊn, də- ⓤⓢ dɪ- **-s** -z

descriptive dɪ'skrɪp.tɪv, də- ⓤⓢ dɪ- **-ly** -li **-ness** -nəs, -nɪs

descriptiv|ism dɪ'skrɪp.tɪ.v|ɪ.zᵊm, də- ⓤⓢ dɪ- **-ist** -ɪst

descr|y dɪ'skr|aɪ, də- ⓤⓢ dɪ- **-ies** -aɪz **-ying** -aɪ.ɪŋ **-ied** -aɪd

Desdemona ,dez.dɪ'məʊ.nə, -də'- ⓤⓢ -də'moʊ-

dese|crate 'des.ɪ|.kreɪt, '-ə- **-crates** -kreɪts **-crating** -kreɪ.tɪŋ ⓤⓢ -kreɪ.t̬ɪŋ **-crated** -kreɪ.tɪd ⓤⓢ -kreɪ.t̬ɪd **-crator/s** -kreɪ.təʳ/z ⓤⓢ -kreɪ.t̬ɚ/z

desecration ,des.ɪ'kreɪ.ʃᵊn, -ə'- **-s** -z

deseed ,diː'siːd **-s** -z **-ing** -ɪŋ **-ed** -d

desegre|gate ,diː'seg.rɪ|.geɪt, -rə- **-gates** -geɪts **-gating** -geɪ.tɪŋ ⓤⓢ -geɪ.t̬ɪŋ **-gated** -geɪ.tɪd ⓤⓢ -geɪ.t̬ɪd

desegregation diː,seg.rɪ'geɪ.ʃᵊn, ,diː.seg-, -rə'- ⓤⓢ diː,seg-

deselect ,diː.sə'lekt, -sɪ'- **-s** -s **-ing** -ɪŋ **-ed** -ɪd

deselection ,diː.sə'lek.ʃᵊn, -sɪ'-

de Selincourt də'sel.ɪŋ.kɔːt, -ɪn- ⓤⓢ -kɔːrt

desensitization diː,sen*t*.sɪ.taɪ'zeɪ.ʃᵊn, ,diː.sen*t*-, -sə-, -tɪ'- ⓤⓢ diː,sen*t*.sɪ.tɪ'-, ,-sə-

desensitiz|e, -is|e ,diː'sen*t*.sɪ.taɪz, -sə- **-es** -ɪz **-ing** -ɪŋ **-ed** -d

desert *(n. adj.) dry place:* 'dez.ət ⓤⓢ -ɚt **-s** -s ,**desert 'island**; ,**desert 'rat**

desert *(n.) what is deserved:* dɪ'zɜːt, də- ⓤⓢ dɪ'zɝːt **-s** -s **get one's ,just de'serts**

de|sert *(v.)* dɪ|'zɜːt, də- ⓤⓢ dɪ|'zɝːt **-serts** -'zɜːts ⓤⓢ -'zɝːts **-serting** -'zɜː.tɪŋ ⓤⓢ -'zɝː.t̬ɪŋ **-serted** -'zɜː.tɪd ⓤⓢ -'zɝː.t̬ɪd **-serter/s** -'zɜː.təʳ/z ⓤⓢ -'zɝː.t̬ɚ/z

desertification dɪ,zɜː.tɪ.fɪ'keɪ.ʃᵊn, də-, -tə- ⓤⓢ dɪ,zɝː.t̬ə-

desertion dɪ'zɜː.ʃᵊn, də- ⓤⓢ dɪ'zɝː- **-s** -z

deserv|e dɪ'zɜːv, də- ⓤⓢ dɪ'zɝːv **-es** -z **-ing/ly** -ɪŋ/li **-ed** -d **-edly** -ɪd.li

desex ,diː'seks **-es** -ɪz **-ing** -ɪŋ **-ed** -t

desexualiz|e, -is|e diːˈsek.ʃʊə.laɪz, -ʃu.^{ə}l.aɪz, -sjʊə.laɪz, -sjʊ.^{ə}l.aɪz US -ʃu.ə.laɪz **-es** -ɪz **-ing** -ɪŋ **-ed** -d

deshabille ˌdez.æbˈiːl, ˌdeɪ.zæbˈ-, ˌdes.æbˈ-, -əˈbiːl, ˈ--- US ˌdes.æbˈ-, ˌdez-; ˈdɪs.ə.biːl

déshabillé ˌdeɪ.zæbˈiː.eɪ, ˌdez.æb-, ˌdes-, -əˈbiː-, -ˈbiːl

desiccant ˈdes.ɪ.k^{ə}nt, ˈ-ə- **-s** -s

desic|cate ˈdes.ɪ|.keɪt, ˈ-ə- **-cates** -keɪts **-cating** -keɪ.tɪŋ US -keɪ.t̬ɪŋ **-cated** -keɪ.tɪd US -keɪ.t̬ɪd

desiccation ˌdes.ɪˈkeɪ.ʃ^{ə}n, -əˈ-

desiccative ˈdes.ɪ.kə.tɪv; desˈɪk.ə-, dɪˈsɪk- US ˈdes.ɪ.keɪ.t̬ɪv; dəˈsɪk.ə-

desiccator ˈdes.ɪ.keɪ.tə^r, ˈ-ə- US -t̬ɚ **-s** -z

desider|ate dɪˈzɪd.^{ə}r|.eɪt, də-, -ˈsɪd- US dɪˈsɪd.ə.r|eɪt, -ˈzɪd- **-ates** -eɪts **-ating** -eɪ.tɪŋ US -eɪ.t̬ɪŋ **-ated** -eɪ.tɪd US -eɪ.t̬ɪd

desideration dɪˌzɪd.^{ə}ˈreɪ.ʃ^{ə}n, də-, -ˌsɪd- US dɪˌsɪd-, -ˌzɪd- **-s** -z

desiderative dɪˈzɪd.^{ə}r.ə.tɪv, də-, -ˈsɪd- US dɪˈsɪd.ɚ.ə.t̬ɪv, -ˈzɪd-

desiderat|um dɪˌzɪd.^{ə}ˈrɑː.t|əm, də-, -ˌsɪd-, -ˈreɪ- US dɪˌsɪd.əˈrɑː.t̬|əm, -ˌzɪd-, -ˈreɪ- **-a** -ə

design dɪˈzaɪn, də- US dɪ- **-s** -z **-ing** -ɪŋ **-ed** -d **-edly** -ɪd.li **-able** -ə.bl̩

designate (*adj.*) ˈdez.ɪg.neɪt, -nɪt, -nət

desig|nate (*v.*) ˈdez.ɪg|.neɪt **-nates** -neɪts **-nating** -neɪ.tɪŋ US -neɪ.t̬ɪŋ **-nated** -neɪ.tɪd US -neɪ.t̬ɪd **-nator/s** -neɪ.tə^r/z US -neɪ.t̬ɚ/z

designation ˌdez.ɪgˈneɪ.ʃ^{ə}n **-s** -z

designer dɪˈzaɪ.nə^r, də- US dɪˈzaɪ.nɚ **-s** -z

desinenc|e ˈdes.ɪ.nənts, ˈdez-, -^{ə}n.ənts **-es** -ɪz

desirability dɪˌzaɪə.rəˈbɪl.ə.ti, də-, -ɪ.ti US dɪˌzaɪ.rəˈbɪl.ə.t̬i

desirab|le dɪˈzaɪə.rə.b|l̩, də- US dɪˈzaɪ- **-ly** -li **-leness** -l̩.nəs, -nɪs

desir|e dɪˈzaɪə^r, də US dɪˈzaɪɚ **-es** -z **-ing** -ɪŋ **-ed** -d **-er/s** -ə^r/z US -ɚ/z

désirée deɪˈzɪə.reɪ, dezˈɪə- US ˌdez.əˈreɪ

desirous dɪˈzaɪə.rəs, də- US dɪˈzaɪ.rəs **-ly** -li

desist dɪˈsɪst, də-, dɪˈzɪst **-s** -s **-ing** -ɪŋ **-ed** -ɪd

desistance dɪˈsɪs.t^{ə}nts, dəˈ-, dɪˈzɪs-

desk desk **-s** -s ˈ**desk** ˌ**job**

desk-skill ˌdiːˈskɪl **-s** -z **-ing** -ɪŋ **-ed** -d

desktop ˈdesk.tɒp US -tɑːp ˌ**desktop** ˈ**publishing**

Des Moines dəˈmɔɪn, dɪ-, -ˈmɔɪnz US -ˈmɔɪn

Desmond ˈdez.mənd

desolate (*adj.*) ˈdes.^{ə}l.ət, ˈdez-, -ɪt **-ly** -li **-ness** -nəs, -nɪs

desol|ate (*v.*) ˈdes.^{ə}l|.eɪt, ˈdez.ə.l|eɪt **-ates** -eɪts **-ating** -eɪ.tɪŋ US -eɪ.t̬ɪŋ **-ated** -eɪ.tɪd US -eɪ.t̬ɪd **-ator/s** -eɪ.tə^r/z US -eɪ.t̬ɚ/z

desolation ˌdes.^{ə}lˈeɪ.ʃ^{ə}n, ˌdez- **-s** -z

de Soto dəˈsəʊ.təʊ US -ˈsoʊ.toʊ

despair dɪˈspeə^r, də- US dɪˈsper **-s** -z **-ing/ly** -ɪŋ/li **-ed** -d

Despard ˈdes.pəd, -pɑːd US -pɚd, -pɑːrd

despatch dɪˈspætʃ, də- US dɪ- **-es** -ɪz **-ing** -ɪŋ **-ed** -t **-er/s** -ə^r/z US -ɚ/z **des**ˈ**patch** ˌ**box; des**ˈ**patch** ˌ**rider**

desperado ˌdes.pəˈrɑː.dəʊ, -ˈreɪ- US -doʊ **-(e)s** -z

desperate ˈdes.p^{ə}r.ət, -ɪt **-ly** -li **-ness** -nəs, -nɪs

desperation ˌdes.p^{ə}ˈreɪ.ʃ^{ə}n

despicability dɪˌspɪk.əˈbɪl.ə.ti, də-, -ɪ.ti; ˌdes.pɪ.kəˈ- US dɪˌspɪk.əˈbɪl.ə.t̬i; ˌdes.pɪ.kəˈ-

despicab|le dɪˈspɪk.ə.b|l̩, də-; ˈdes.pɪ.kə- US dɪˈspɪk.ə-; ˈdes.pɪ.kə- **-ly** -li **-leness** -l̩.nəs, -nɪs

despis|e dɪˈspaɪz, də- US dɪ- **-es** -ɪz **-ing** -ɪŋ **-ed** -d **-er/s** -ə^r/z US -ɚ/z

despite dɪˈspaɪt, də- US dɪ-

despiteful dɪˈspaɪt.f^{ə}l, də-, -fʊl US dɪ- **-ly** -li

despoil dɪˈspɔɪl, də- US dɪ- **-s** -z **-ing** -ɪŋ **-ed** -d **-er/s** -ə^r/z US -ɚ/z

despoliation dɪˌspəʊ.liˈeɪ.ʃ^{ə}n, də-, -ˌspɒl.iˈ- US dɪˌspoʊ.liˈ-

despond (D) dɪˈspɒnd, də- US dɪˈspɑːnd **-s** -z **-ing/ly** -ɪŋ/li **-ed** -ɪd

desponden|ce dɪˈspɒn.dən*t*|s, də- US dɪˈspɑːn- **-cy** -si

despondent dɪˈspɒn.dənt, də- US dɪˈspɑːn- **-ly** -li

despot ˈdes.pɒt, -pət US -pət **-s** -s

despotic dɪˈspɒt.ɪk, desˈpɒt-, dəˈspɒt- US desˈpɑː.t̬ɪk **-al** -^{ə}l **-ally** -^{ə}l.i, -li **-alness** -^{ə}l.nəs, -nɪs

despotism ˈdes.pə.tɪ.z^{ə}m **-s** -z

desqua|mate ˈdes.kwə|.meɪt **-mates** -meɪts **-mating** -meɪ.tɪŋ US -meɪ.t̬ɪŋ **-mated** -meɪ.tɪd US -meɪ.t̬ɪd

des res ˌdezˈrez

dessert dɪˈzɜːt, də- US dɪˈzɝːt **-s** -s **des**ˈ**sert** ˌ**wine, des**ˌ**sert** ˈ**wine**

dessertspoon dɪˈzɜːt.spuːn, də- US dɪˈzɝːt- **-s** -z

dessert|spoonful dɪˈzɜːt|ˌspuːn.fʊl, də- US dɪˈzɝːt- **-spoonsful** -ˌspuːnz.fʊl **-spoonfuls** -ˌspuːn.fʊlz

destabilization, -isa- ˌdiːˌsteɪ.b^{ə}l.aɪˈzeɪ.ʃ^{ə}n, dɪ-, -bɪ.laɪˈ- US -b^{ə}l.ɪˈ-, -bɪ.lɪˈ-

destabiliz|e, -is|e ˌdiːˈsteɪ.b^{ə}l.aɪz, dɪ-, -bɪ.laɪz **-es** -ɪz **-ing** -ɪŋ **-ed** -d

destination ˌdes.tɪˈneɪ.ʃ^{ə}n, -təˈ- **-s** -z

destin|e ˈdes.tɪn, -t^{ə}n **-es** -z **-ing** -ɪŋ **-ed** -d

destin|y ˈdes.tɪ.n|i, -t^{ə}n|.i **-ies** -iz

destitute ˈdes.tɪ.tjuːt, -tə- US -tuːt, -tjuːt **-ly** -li **-ness** -nəs, -nɪs

destitution ˌdes.tɪˈtjuː.ʃ^{ə}n, -təˈ- US -ˈtuː-, -ˈtjuː-

destroy dɪˈstrɔɪ, də- US dɪ- **-s** -z **-ing** -ɪŋ **-ed** -d

destroyer dɪˈstrɔɪ.ə^r, də- US dɪˈstrɔɪ.ɚ **-s** -z

destruct dɪˈstrʌkt, də- US dɪ- **-s** -s **-ing** -ɪŋ **-ed** -ɪd

destructibility dɪˌstrʌk.təˈbɪl.ə.ti, də-, -tɪˈ-, -ɪ.ti US dɪˌstrʌk.təˈbɪl.ə.t̬i, -tɪˈ-

destructible dɪˈstrʌk.tə.bl̩, də-, -tɪ- US dɪ-

destruction dɪˈstrʌk.ʃ^{ə}n, də- US dɪ- **-s** -z

destructive dɪˈstrʌk.tɪv, də- US dɪ- **-ly** -li **-ness** -nəs, -nɪs

destructor dɪˈstrʌk.tə^r, də- US dɪˈstrʌk.tɚ **-s** -z

desuetude dɪˈsjuː.ɪ.tjuːd, -tʃuːd; ˈdes.wɪ-, ˈdiː.swɪ- US ˈdes.wɪ.tuːd, -tjuːd; dɪˈsuː.ə-

desultor|y ˈdes.^{ə}l.t^{ə}r|.i, ˈdez-, -tr|i US -tɔːr|.i **-ily** -^{ə}l.i, -ɪ.li **-iness** -ɪ.nəs, -ɪ.nɪs

Des Voeux deɪˈvɜː

detach dɪˈtætʃ, də- US dɪ- **-es** -ɪz **-ing** -ɪŋ **-ed** -t **-edly** -t.li, -ɪd.li **-able** -ə.bl̩

detachment dɪˈtætʃ.mənt, də- US dɪ- **-s** -s

detail ˈdiː.teɪl; dɪˈteɪl, də- US dɪˈteɪl; ˈdiː.teɪl **-s** -z **-ing** -ɪŋ **-ed** -d

detain dɪˈteɪn, də- US dɪ- **-s** -z **-ing** -ɪŋ **-ed** -d **-er/s** -ə^r/z US -ɚ/z

detainee ˌdiː.teɪˈniː; dɪˌteɪˈ-, də- US ˌdiː.teɪˈ- **-s** -z

detect dɪˈtekt, də- US dɪ- **-s** -s **-ing** -ɪŋ **-ed** -ɪd

detectab|le dɪˈtek.tə.b|l̩, də- US dɪ- **-ly** -li

detection dɪˈtek.ʃ^{ə}n, də- US dɪ- **-s** -z

detective dɪˈtek.tɪv, də- US dɪ- **-s** -z

detector dɪˈtek.tə^r, də- US dɪˈtek.tɚ **-s** -z

detent dɪˈtent, də- US dɪ- **-s** -s

détente ˈdeɪ.tɑ̃ː*n*t US deɪˈtɑːnt, ˈ--

detention dɪˈten.*t*ʃ^{ə}n, də- US dɪ- **-s** -z **de**ˈ**tention** ˌ**centre**

deter dɪˈtɜː^r, də- US dɪˈtɝː **-s** -z **-ring** -ɪŋ **-red** -d

Deterding ˈdet.ə.dɪŋ US ˈdet̬.ɚ-

detergent dɪˈtɜː.dʒ^{ə}nt, də- US dɪˈtɝː- **-s** -s

deterior|ate dɪˈtɪə.ri.^{ə}r|.eɪt, də- US dɪˈtɪr.i.ə.r|eɪt **-ates** -eɪts **-ating** -eɪ.tɪŋ US -eɪ.t̬ɪŋ **-ated** -eɪ.tɪd US -eɪ.t̬ɪd

deterioration dɪˌtɪə.ri.əˈreɪ.ʃ^{ə}n, də- US dɪˌtɪr.i-

determinable dɪˈtɜː.mɪ.nə.bl̩, də-, -m^{ə}n.ə- US dɪˈtɝː-

determinant dɪˈtɜː.mɪ.nənt, də- US dɪˈtɝː- **-s** -s
determinate dɪˈtɜː.mɪ.nət, də-, -nɪt US dɪˈtɝː- **-ly** -li **-ness** -nəs, -nɪs
determination dɪˌtɜː.mɪˈneɪ.ʃᵊn, də-, -məˈ- US dɪˌtɝː- **-s** -z
determinative dɪˈtɜː.mɪ.nə.tɪv, də-, -mᵊn.ə- US dɪˈtɝː.mɪ.neɪ.t̬ɪv, -nə-
determin|e dɪˈtɜː.mɪn, də-, -mən US dɪˈtɝː- **-es** -z **-ing** -ɪŋ **-ed/ly** -d/li
determined dɪˈtɜː.mɪnd, də- US dɪˈtɝː- **-ly** -li
determiner dɪˈtɜː.mɪ.nəʳ, də-, -mə- US dɪˈtɝː.mɪ.nɚ **-s** -z
determin|ism dɪˈtɜː.mɪ.n|ɪ.zᵊm, də-, -mə- US dɪˈtɝː- **-ist/s** -ɪst/s
deterrence dɪˈter.ᵊnts, də- US dɪ-
deterrent dɪˈter.ᵊnt, də- US dɪ- **-s** -s
detest dɪˈtest, də- US dɪ- **-s** -s **-ing** -ɪŋ **-ed** -ɪd
detestab|le dɪˈtes.tə.b|l̩, də- US dɪ- **-ly** -li **-leness** -l̩.nəs, -nɪs
detestation ˌdiː.tesˈteɪ.ʃᵊn, dɪˌtes- US ˌdiː.tes-
dethron|e diːˈθrəʊn, ˌdɪ-, də- US dɪˈθroʊn, ˌdiː- **-es** -z **-ing** -ɪŋ **-ed** -d **-ement** -mənt
detinue ˈdet.ɪ.njuː US -ᵊn.juː, -uː
Detlev ˈdet.lef US -ləf, -lef
Detmold ˈdet.məʊld US -moʊld
de Tocqueville dəˈtəʊk.vɪl, -ˈtɒk-, -viːl US -ˈtoʊk.vɪl, -ˈtɑːk-
deton|ate ˈdet.ᵊn|.eɪt **-ates** -eɪts **-ating** -eɪ.tɪŋ US -eɪ.t̬ɪŋ **-ated** -eɪ.tɪd US -eɪ.t̬ɪd
detonation ˌdet.ᵊnˈeɪ.ʃᵊn **-s** -z
detonator ˈdet.ᵊn.eɪ.təʳ US -t̬ɚ **-s** -z
detour ˈdiː.tʊəʳ, ˈdeɪ-, -tɔːʳ US ˈdiː.tʊr; -ˈ-, dɪ- **-s** -z
detox ˈdiː.tɒks, ˌdiːˈtɒks US diːˈtɑːks, ˈ-- **-es** -ɪz **-ing** -ɪŋ **-ed** -t
detoxi|cate ˌdiːˈtɒk.sɪ|.keɪt, dɪ-, -sə- US -ˈtɑːk- **-cates** -keɪts **-cating** -keɪ.tɪŋ US -keɪ.t̬ɪŋ **-cated** -keɪ.tɪd US -keɪ.t̬ɪd
detoxification diːˌtɒk.sɪ.fɪˈkeɪ.ʃᵊn, dɪ-, -sə-; ˌdiː.tɒk- US diːˌtɑːk-
detoxi|fy ˌdiːˈtɒk.sɪ|.faɪ, dɪ-, -sə- US ˌdiːˈtɑːk- **-fies** -faɪz **-fying** -faɪ.ɪŋ **-fied** -faɪd
detract dɪˈtrækt, də- US dɪ- **-s** -s **-ing/ly** -ɪŋ/li **-ed** -ɪd
detraction dɪˈtræk.ʃᵊn, də- US dɪ- **-s** -z
detract|ive dɪˈtræk.t|ɪv, də- US dɪ- **-ory** -ᵊr.i
detractor dɪˈtræk.təʳ, də- US dɪˈtræk.tɚ **-s** -z
detrain ˌdiːˈtreɪn **-s** -z **-ing** -ɪŋ **-ed** -d
detriment ˈdet.rɪ.mənt, -rə- **-s** -s
detrimental ˌdet.rɪˈmen.tᵊl, -rəˈ- US -t̬ᵊl
detrition dɪˈtrɪʃ.ᵊn, də- US dɪ-
detritus dɪˈtraɪ.təs, də- US dɪˈtraɪ.t̬əs
Detroit dəˈtrɔɪt, dɪ-
de trop dəˈtrəʊ US -troʊ
detrun|cate ˌdiːˈtrʌŋ|.keɪt, ˈ--- US ˌdiːˈtrʌŋ- **-cates** -keɪts **-cating** -keɪ.tɪŋ US -keɪ.t̬ɪŋ **-cated** -keɪ.tɪd US -keɪ.t̬ɪd
detruncation ˌdiː.trʌŋˈkeɪ.ʃᵊn **-s** -z
Dettol® ˈdet.ɒl, -ᵊl US -tɑːl, -t̬ᵊl
Dettori detˈɔː.ri US -ɔːr.i
detumescen|ce ˌdiː.tjuːˈmes.ᵊn|ts, -tjʊˈ- US -tuːˈ-, -tjuːˈ- **-t** -t
Deucalion djuːˈkeɪ.li.ən US duː-, djuː-
deuc|e djuːs, dʒuːs US duːs, djuːs **-es** -ɪz
deuc|ed djuːs|t, dʒuːs|t; ˈdjuː.s|ɪd, ˈdʒuː- US ˈduː.s|ɪd, ˈdjuː-; duːs|t, djuːs|t **-edly** -ɪd.li
deus ex machina ˌdeɪ.əs.eksˈmɑː.k.ɪ.nə, -ˈmæk-, ˌdiː-, -ʊs-;
deuterium djuːˈtɪə.ri.əm US duːˈtɪr.i-, djuː-
deuteronomic ˌdjuː.tᵊr.əˈnɒm.ɪk US ˌduː.t̬ɚ.əˈnɑː.mɪk, ˌdjuː-
Deuteronomy ˌdjuː.təˈrɒn.ə.mi US ˌduː.t̬əˈrɑː.nə-, ˌdjuː-
Deutsche Mark ˌdɔɪ.tʃəˈmɑːk US -ˈmɑːrk **-s** -s
deutschmark (D) ˈdɔɪtʃ.mɑːk US -mɑːrk **-s** -s
deutzia ˈdjuːt.si.ə, ˈdɔɪt- US ˈduːt-, ˈdjuːt- **-s** -z
deux chevaux ˌdɜː.ʃəˈvəʊ, -ʃɪˈ- US -ˈvoʊ
deva ˈdeɪ.və, ˈdiː.və **-s** -z
de Valera də.vəˈleə.rə, -ˈlɪə-; ˌdev.əˈ- US -ler.ə, -ˈlɪr-
de Valois dəˈvæl.wɑː
devaluation ˌdiː.væl.juˈeɪ.ʃᵊn; dɪˌvæl- US ˌdiː.væl- **-s** -z
devalu|e ˌdiːˈvæl.juː, dɪ- **-es** -z **-ing** -ɪŋ **-ed** -d
Devanagari ˌdeɪ.vəˈnɑː.gᵊr.i, ˌdev.əˈ-
Devant dəˈvænt, dɪ-
deva|state ˈdev.ə|.steɪt **-states** -steɪts **-stating/ly** -steɪ.tɪŋ/li US -steɪ.t̬ɪŋ/li **-stated** -steɪ.tɪd US -steɪ.t̬ɪd
devastation ˌdev.əˈsteɪ.ʃᵊn **-s** -z
develop dɪˈvel.əp, də- US dɪ- **-s** -s **-ing** -ɪŋ **-ed** -t **deˌveloping ˈcountry**
developer dɪˈvel.ə.pəʳ, də- US -pɚ **-s** -z
development dɪˈvel.əp.mənt, də- **-s** -s
developmental dɪˌvel.əpˈmen.tᵊl, də- US -t̬ᵊl **-ly** -li
Devenish ˈdev.ᵊn.ɪʃ
Deventer ˈdev.ᵊn.təʳ US -tɚ
De Vere dəˈvɪəʳ, dɪ- US -ˈvɪr
Devereux ˈdev.ə.ruː, -ruːks, -rɜː, -rəʊ, -reks, ˈ-ᵊr.ə US -ə.ruː, -rɜː, -rə, -uːks
Deveron ˈdev.ə.rᵊn US -ɚ.ᵊn
Devers ˈdiː.vəz, ˈdev.əz US ˈdiː.vɚz, ˈdev.ɚz
Devi ˈdeɪ.vi
devian|ce ˈdiː.vi.ənt|s **-cy** -si
deviant ˈdiː.vi.ənt **-s** -s
devi|ate ˈdiː.vi|.eɪt **-ates** -eɪts **-ating** -eɪ.tɪŋ US -eɪ.t̬ɪŋ **-ated** -eɪ.tɪd US -eɪ.t̬ɪd **-ator/s** -eɪ.təʳ/z US -eɪ.t̬ɚ/z
deviation ˌdiː.viˈeɪ.ʃᵊn **-s** -z
deviation|ism ˌdiː.viˈeɪ.ʃᵊn|.ɪ.zᵊm **-ist/s** -ɪst/s
devic|e dɪˈvaɪs, də- US dɪ- **-es** -ɪz **ˌleave someone to their ˌown deˈvices**
devil ˈdev.ᵊl **-s** -z **-(l)ing** -ɪŋ **-(l)ed** -d **ˌdevil's ˈadvocate; ˌdevil's ˈfood ˌcake, ˈdevil's food ˌcake** US **ˈdevil's food ˌcake; between the ˌdevil and the ˌdeep blue ˈsea; give the ˌdevil his ˈdue; ˌtalk of the ˈdevil**
devilfish ˈdev.ᵊl.fɪʃ **-es** -ɪz
devilish ˈdev.ᵊl.ɪʃ **-ly** -li **-ness** -nəs, -nɪ…
devil-may-care ˌdev.ᵊl.meɪˈkeəʳ US -ˈker *stress shift:* ˌdevil-may-care ˈattitude
devilment ˈdev.ᵊl.mənt **-s** -s
devilr|y ˈdev.ᵊl.r|i **-ies** -iz
Devine dəˈvaɪn, dɪ-
devious ˈdiː.vi.əs **-ly** -li **-ness** -nəs, -nɪ…
devis|e dɪˈvaɪz, də- US dɪ- **-es** -ɪz **-ing** -ɪŋ **-ed** -d **-er/s** -əʳ/z US -ɚ/z **-able** -ə…
devisee dɪˌvaɪˈziː, də-; ˌdev.ɪˈ- US dɪˌvaɪˈ-; ˌdev.əˈ- **-s** -z
devisor dɪˈvaɪ.zəʳ, də-; dəˌvaɪˈzɔːʳ, d… ˌdev.aɪˈ- US dɪˈvaɪ.zɚ; ˌdev.əˈzɔːr **-s** -z
devitalization, -isa- diːˌvaɪ.tᵊl.aɪˈzeɪ.ʃᵊn, ˌdiː.vaɪ-, -ɪˈ- US diːˌvaɪ.t̬ᵊl.ɪˈ-
devitaliz|e, -is|e ˌdiːˈvaɪ.tᵊl.aɪz US -t̬… **-es** -ɪz **-ing** -ɪŋ **-ed** -d
Devizes dɪˈvaɪ.zɪz, də-, -zəz
Devlin ˈdev.lɪn, -lən
devocalization, -isa- diːˌvəʊ.kᵊl.aɪˈzeɪ.ʃᵊn, ˌdiː.vəʊ-, -… US diːˌvoʊ- **-s** -z
devocaliz|e, -is|e ˌdiːˈvəʊ.kᵊl.aɪz US -ˈvoʊ- **-es** -ɪz **-ing** -ɪŋ **-ed** -d
devoic|e ˌdiːˈvɔɪs **-es** -ɪz **-ing** -ɪŋ **-ed** …
devoid dɪˈvɔɪd, də- US dɪ-
devolution ˌdiː.vəˈluː.ʃᵊn, ˌdev.əˈ-, -ˈljuː- US ˌdev.əˈluː-, ˌdiː.vəˈ- **-s** -…
devolv|e dɪˈvɒlv, də- US dɪˈvɑːlv **-es** … **-ing** -ɪŋ **-ed** -d
Devon ˈdev.ᵊn **-shire** -ʃəʳ, -ˌʃɪəʳ US -… -ˌʃɪr
Devonian devˈəʊ.ni.ən, dɪˈvəʊ-, də… US dɪˈvoʊ- **-s** -z
Devonport ˈdev.ᵊn.pɔːt, -ᵊm- US -ᵊn.pɔːrt
de|vote dɪ|ˈvəʊt, də- US dɪ|ˈvoʊt **-v…** -vəʊts US -voʊts **-voting** -vəʊ.tɪ… US -voʊ.t̬ɪŋ **-voted** -vəʊ.tɪd US -voʊ.t̬ɪd

Devoicing

A process affecting a sound which we would normally expect to be voiced but which is pronounced without VOICING in a particular context.

Examples for English

In English, the /l/ in *blade* /bleɪd/ [bleɪd̥] is usually voiced, but in *played* /pleɪd/ [pl̥eɪd̥] the /l/ is usually voiceless because of the preceding voiceless plosive. Note also that the /d/ at the end of the word in each case is devoiced if it is followed by a voiceless consonant or a pause.

The notion of devoicing leads to a rather confusing use of phonetic symbols in cases where there are separate symbols for voiced and voiceless pairs of sounds: a devoiced /d/ can be symbolised by adding a diacritic that indicates lack of voice – [d̥], but one is then left in doubt as to what the difference is between this sound and [t]. The usual reason for doing this is to leave the symbol looking like the phoneme it represents.

devoted dɪˈvəʊ.tɪd, də- (US) dɪˈvoʊ.t̬ɪd **-ly** -li **-ness** -nəs, -nɪs

devotee ˌdev.əʊˈtiː (US) -əˈtiː, -ˈteɪ, -oʊ- **-s** -z

devotion dɪˈvəʊ.ʃᵊn, də- (US) dɪˈvoʊ- **-s** -z

devotional dɪˈvəʊ.ʃᵊn.ᵊl, də- (US) dɪˈvoʊ- **-ly** -i

devour dɪˈvaʊəʳ, də- (US) dɪˈvaʊɚ **-s** -z **-ing** -ɪŋ **-ed** -d **-er/s** -əʳ/z (US) -ɚ/z

de|vout dɪ|ˈvaʊt, də- (US) dɪ- **-vouter** -ˈvaʊ.təʳ (US) -ˈvaʊ.t̬ɚ **-voutest** -ˈvaʊ.tɪst, -təst (US) -ˈvaʊ.t̬ɪst, -t̬əst **-voutly** -ˈvaʊt.li **-voutness** -ˈvaʊt.nəs, -nɪs

ew djuː, dʒuː (US) duː, djuː **-s** -z ˈ**dew** ˌ**pond**; ˈ**dew** ˌ**point**

ewali dɪˈwɑː.li (US) də-, dɪ-

ewar ˈdjuː.əʳ, ˈdʒuː-; djʊəʳ, dʒʊəʳ (US) ˈduː.ɚ, ˈdjuː-

ewberr|y ˈdjuː.bᵊr|.i, ˈdʒuː-, -ber- (US) ˈduː.ber-, ˈdjuː- **-ies** -iz

ewclaw ˈdjuː.klɔː, ˈdʒuː- (US) ˈduː.klɑː, ˈdjuː-, -klɔː **-s** -z

ewdrop ˈdjuː.drɒp, ˈdʒuː- (US) ˈduː.drɑːp, ˈdjuː- **-s** -s

'Ewes djuːz, dʒuːz (US) duːz, djuːz

e Wet dəˈvet, -ˈwet

ewey ˈdjuː.i, ˈdʒuː- (US) ˈduː-, ˈdjuː-

ewhurst ˈdjuː.hɜːst, ˈdʒuː- (US) ˈduː.hɝːst, ˈdjuː-

ewi ˈde.wi

ote: This is a Welsh place name. The anglicized pronunciation /ˈdjuː.i/ should be considered incorrect.

ewlap ˈdjuː.læp, ˈdʒuː- (US) ˈduː-, ˈdjuː- **-s** -s

ewsbury ˈdjuːz.bᵊr.i, ˈdʒuːz- (US) ˈduːz.ber-, ˈdjuːz-, -bɚ-

w|y ˈdjuː|.i, ˈdʒuː- (US) ˈduː-, ˈdjuː- **-iness** -ɪ.nəs, -ɪ.nɪs

xedrine® ˈdek.sɪ.driːn, -sə-

xter **(D)** ˈdek.stəʳ (US) -stɚ

xterity dekˈster.ə.ti, -ɪ.ti (US) -ə.t̬i

xterous ˈdek.stᵊr.əs **-ly** -li **-ness** -nəs, -nɪs

dextrose ˈdek.strəʊs, -strəʊz (US) -stroʊs

dextrous ˈdek.strəs **-ly** -li **-ness** -nəs, -nɪs

De Zoete dəˈzuːt

de Zoete Wedd dəˌzuːtˈwed

dg *(abbrev. for* **decigram***)* ˈdes.ɪ.græm

Dhaka ˈdæk.ə (US) ˈdæk.ə, ˈdɑː.kɑː

dhal dɑːl

dharma ˈdɑː.mə (US) ˈdɑːr-

dhobi ˈdəʊ.bi (US) ˈdoʊ- **-es** -z

dhoti ˈdəʊ.ti (US) ˈdoʊ.t̬i **-es** -z

dhow daʊ **-s** -z

DHSS ˌdiː.eɪtʃ.esˈes

dhurrie ˈdʌr.i (US) ˈdɝː- **-s** -z

di- daɪ-, dɪ-

Note: Prefix. Where the meaning is **two**, it may carry either primary or secondary stress and is pronounced /daɪ-/, e.g. **digraph** /ˈdaɪ.grɑːf (US) -græf/, **diglossia** /ˌdaɪˈglɒs.i.ə (US) -ˈglɑː.si-/. In other instances, it may be pronounced /daɪ-/, /dɪ-/ or occasionally /də-/, and is not normally stressed in verbs and adjectives, e.g. **digest** /daɪˈdʒest/, **diverse** /daɪˈvɜːs (US) dɪˈvɜːrs/. In nouns, however, it may carry stress, e.g. **digest** /ˈdaɪ.dʒest/. There are exceptions; see individual entries.

Di daɪ

dia- daɪə-; daɪˈæ-

Note: Prefix. Normally carries primary or secondary stress on the first syllable, e.g. **diadem** /ˈdaɪə.dem/, **diabolic** /ˌdaɪəˈbɒl.ɪk (US) -ˈbɑː.lɪk/, or primary stress on the second syllable, e.g. **diagonal** /daɪˈæg.ᵊn.ᵊl/.

diabetes ˌdaɪəˈbiː.tiːz, -tɪz, -tɪs (US) -t̬əs, -t̬iːz

diabetic ˌdaɪəˈbet.ɪk (US) -ˈbet̬- **-s** -s

diabolic ˌdaɪəˈbɒl.ɪk (US) -ˈbɑː.lɪk **-al** -ᵊl **-ally** -ᵊl.i, -li

diabolism daɪˈæb.ᵊl.ɪ.zᵊm

diaboliz|e, **-is|e** daɪˈæb.ᵊl.aɪz (US) -ə.laɪz **-es** -ɪz **-ing** -ɪŋ **-ed** -d

diabolo diˈæb.ᵊl.əʊ, daɪ-, -ɑː.bᵊl- (US) daɪˈæb.ə.loʊ

diachronic ˌdaɪ.əˈkrɒn.ɪk (US) -ˈkrɑː.nɪk **-ally** -ᵊl.i, -li

diacid daɪˈæs.ɪd **-s** -z

diaconal daɪˈæk.ə.nᵊl, di-

diaconate daɪˈæk.ə.neɪt, di-, -nɪt, -nət **-s** -s

diacritic ˌdaɪəˈkrɪt.ɪk (US) -ˈkrɪt̬- **-s** -s **-al** -ᵊl

diadem ˈdaɪə.dem, -dəm **-s** -z

diaeres|is daɪˈer.ə.s|ɪs, -ˈɪr.ə-, -ˈɪə.rə-, -rɪ- (US) -ˈer.ə-, -ˈɪr- **-es** -iːz

Diaghilev diˈæg.ɪ.lef, ˈ-ə- (US) -ˈɑː.gə.lef, -gɪ-

diagnos|e ˈdaɪəg.nəʊz, ˌ--ˈ- (US) ˌdaɪəgˈnoʊs, -ˈnoʊz, ˈ--- **-es** -ɪz **-ing** -ɪŋ **-ed** -d

diagnos|is ˌdaɪəgˈnəʊ.s|ɪs (US) -ˈnoʊ- **-es** -iːz

diagnostic ˌdaɪəgˈnɒs.tɪk (US) -ˈnɑː.stɪk **-s** -s

diagnostician ˌdaɪəg.nɒsˈtɪʃ.ᵊn (US) -nɑːˈstɪʃ- **-s** -z

diagonal daɪˈæg.ᵊn.ᵊl **-s** -z **-ly** -i

diagram ˈdaɪə.græm **-s** -z

diagrammatic ˌdaɪə.grəˈmæt.ɪk (US) -ˈmæt̬- **-al** -ᵊl **-ally** -ᵊl.i, -li

dial daɪəl (US) daɪəl **-s** -z **-(l)ing** -ɪŋ **-(l)ed** -d ˈ**dialling** ˌ**code**; ˈ**dialling** ˌ**tone**; ˈ**dial** ˌ**tone**

dialect ˈdaɪə.lekt **-s** -s

dialectal ˌdaɪəˈlek.tᵊl

dialectic ˌdaɪəˈlek.tɪk **-s** -s **-al** -ᵊl **-ally** -ᵊl.i, -li

dialectician ˌdaɪə.lekˈtɪʃ.ᵊn **-s** -z

dialectolog|y ˌdaɪə.lekˈtɒl.ə.dʒ|i (US) -ˈtɑː.lə- **-ist/s** -ɪst/s

diallage *figure of speech:* daɪˈæl.ə.gi, -dʒi

diallage *mineral:* ˈdaɪə.lɪdʒ

dialog|ism daɪˈæl.ə.dʒ|ɪ.zᵊm **-ist/s** -ɪst/s

dialogue, dialog 'daɪə.lɒg (US) -lɑːg -s -z
dial-up 'daɪəl.ʌp
dialys|is daɪ'æl.ə.s|ɪs, '-ɪ- -es -iːz
diamagnetic ˌdaɪə.mæg'net.ɪk, -məg'- (US) -mæg'neţ- -s -s -ally -ᵊl.i, -li
diamagnetism ˌdaɪə'mæg.nə.tɪ.zᵊm, -nɪ-
diamanté ˌdiː.ə'mɑ̃ŋ.teɪ, ˌdaɪə'-, -'mæn-, -ti (US) ˌdiː.ə.mɑːn'teɪ, -'mɑːn.teɪ
diameter daɪ'æm.ɪ.təʳ, '-ə- (US) -ə.ţɚ -s -z
diametral daɪ'æm.ɪ.trəl, '-ə- -ly -i
diametric ˌdaɪə'met.rɪk -al -ᵊl -ally -ᵊl.i, -li
diamond (D) 'daɪə.mənd (US) 'daɪə-, 'daɪ- -s -z
diamondback 'daɪə.mənd.bæk (US) 'daɪə-, 'daɪ- -s -s
diamorphine ˌdaɪ.ə'mɔː.fiːn (US) -'mɔːr-
Diana daɪ'æn.ə
Diane daɪ'æn, di-
dianthus daɪ'ænt.θəs -es -ɪz
diapason ˌdaɪə'peɪ.zᵊn, -sᵊn -s -z
diap|er 'daɪə.p|əʳ (US) -p|ɚ -ers -əz (US) -ɚz -ering -ᵊr.ɪŋ -ered -əd (US) -ɚd
diaphanous daɪ'æf.ᵊn.əs
diaphone 'daɪə.fəʊn (US) -foʊn -s -z
diaphragm 'daɪə.fræm, -frəm (US) -fræm -s -z
diaphragmatic ˌdaɪə.fræg'mæt.ɪk, -frəg'- (US) -'mæţ-
diapositive ˌdaɪə'pɒz.ɪ.tɪv, '-ə- (US) -'pɑː.zə.ţɪv -s -z
diarch|y 'daɪ.ɑː.k|i (US) -ɑːr- -ies -iz
diarist 'daɪə.rɪst -s -s
diarrh(o)ea ˌdaɪə'rɪə (US) -'riː.ə
diar|y 'daɪə.r|i -ies -iz
diaspora (D) daɪ'æs.pᵊr.ə
diastase 'daɪə.steɪs, -steɪz
diastas|is daɪ'æs.tə.s|ɪs, ˌdaɪə'steɪ.s|ɪs -es -iːz
diastole daɪ'æs.tᵊl.i -s -z
diastolic ˌdaɪə'stɒl.ɪk (US) -'stɑː.lɪk
diasystem 'daɪəˌsɪs.təm
diatherm|ic ˌdaɪə'θɜː.m|ɪk (US) -'θɝː- -ous -əs
diatom 'daɪə.təm, -tɒm (US) -tɑːm -s -z
diatomaceous ˌdaɪə.tə'meɪ.ʃəs
diatomic ˌdaɪə'tɒm.ɪk (US) -'tɑː.mɪk
diatomite daɪ'æt.ə.maɪt (US) -'æţ-
diatonic ˌdaɪə'tɒn.ɪk (US) -'tɑː.nɪk -ally -ᵊl.i, -li
diatribe 'daɪə.traɪb -s -z
diatype 'daɪə.taɪp
Diaz 'diː.əs, -æs, -æθ (US) -ɑːs, -ɑːz, -əs, -æz
diazepam daɪ'æz.ə.pæm, -'eɪ.zə-, -zɪ- (US) -'æz.ə-
dib dɪb -s -z -bing -ɪŋ -bed -d -ber/s -əʳ/z (US) -ɚ/z
dibasic daɪ'beɪ.sɪk
dibasicity ˌdaɪ.beɪ'sɪs.ə.ti, -ɪ.ti (US) -ə.ţi
Dibb dɪb
dibbl|e 'dɪb.l̩ -es -z -ing -ɪŋ, 'dɪb.lɪŋ -ed -d -er/s -əʳ/z, '-ləʳ/z (US) '-l̩.ɚ/z, '-lɚ/z
Dibdin 'dɪb.dɪn
dibs dɪbz
DiCaprio dɪ'kæp.ri.əʊ, diː'- (US) -oʊ
dicast 'dɪk.æst (US) 'dɪk.æst, 'daɪ.kæst -s -s
dice *(plur. of* **die***)* daɪs
dic|e *(v.)* daɪs -es -ɪz -ing -ɪŋ -ed -t
dicey (D) 'daɪ.si
dichloride ˌdaɪ'klɔː.raɪd (US) -'klɔːr.aɪd -s -z
dichotomous daɪ'kɒt.ə.məs, dɪ- (US) -'kɑː.ţə-
dichotom|y daɪ'kɒt.ə.m|i, dɪ- (US) -'kɑː.ţə- -ies -iz
dichromate ˌdaɪ'krəʊ.meɪt (US) -'kroʊ- -s -s
dick (D) dɪk
dickens (D) 'dɪk.ɪnz
Dickensian dɪ'ken.zi.ən, də-, -si-
dick|er (D) 'dɪk|.əʳ (US) -ɚ -ers -əz (US) -ɚz -ering -ᵊr.ɪŋ -ered -əd (US) -ɚd
Dickerson 'dɪk.ə.sᵊn (US) '-ɚ-
dickey (D) 'dɪk.i -s -z 'dickey ˌbow
dickhead 'dɪk.hed -s -z
Dickie 'dɪk.i
Dickins 'dɪk.ɪnz
Dickinson 'dɪk.ɪn.sᵊn
Dickson 'dɪk.sᵊn
dick|y (D) 'dɪk|.i -ies -iz
dickybird 'dɪk.i.bɜːd (US) -bɝːd -s -z
dicotyledon ˌdaɪ.kɒt.ɪ'liː.dᵊn, -ᵊl'iː- (US) -kɑː.ţᵊl'- -s -z
Dictaphone® 'dɪk.tə.fəʊn (US) -foʊn -s -z
dictate *(n.)* 'dɪk.teɪt -s -s
dic|tate *(v.)* dɪk|'teɪt (US) 'dɪk|.teɪt, -|'- -tates -'teɪts (US) -teɪts, -'teɪts -tating -'teɪ.tɪŋ (US) -teɪ.ţɪŋ, -'teɪ- -tated -'teɪ.tɪd (US) -teɪ.ţɪd, -'teɪ-
dictation dɪk'teɪ.ʃᵊn -s -z
dictator dɪk'teɪ.təʳ (US) 'dɪk.teɪ.ţɚ, -'-- -s -z
dictatorial ˌdɪk.tə'tɔː.ri.əl (US) -'tɔːr.i- -ly -i
dictatorship dɪk'teɪ.tə.ʃɪp (US) -ţɚ- -s -s
diction 'dɪk.ʃᵊn
dictionar|y 'dɪk.ʃᵊn.ᵊr|.i, -ʃᵊn.r|i (US) -er|.i -ies -iz
dict|um 'dɪk.t|əm -a -ə -ums -əmz
did *(from* **do***)* dɪd
Didache 'dɪd.ə.ki
didact 'daɪ.dækt -s -s
didactic dɪ'dæk.tɪk, daɪ-, də- (US) daɪ-, dɪ- -al -ᵊl -ally -ᵊl.i, -li
didacticism dɪ'dæk.tɪ.sɪ.zᵊm, daɪ-, də- (US) daɪ-, dɪ-, -tə-
Didcot 'dɪd.kət, -kɒt (US) -kɑːt
diddl|e 'dɪd.l̩ -es -z -ing -ɪŋ, '-lɪŋ -ed -d -er/s -əʳ/z, '-ləʳ/z (US) '-l̩.ɚ/z, '-lɚ/z
diddly 'dɪd.l̩.i, '-li
diddlysquat ˌdɪd.l̩.i'skwɒt, -li'- (US) -'skwɑːt
diddums 'dɪd.əmz
Diderot 'diː.də.rəʊ (US) ˌdiː.də'roʊ
didgeridoo ˌdɪdʒ.ᵊr.i'duː -s -z
Didier 'dɪd.i.eɪ, 'diː.di-
didn't 'dɪd.ᵊnt
Dido 'daɪ.dəʊ (US) -doʊ
didst dɪdst
Didymus 'dɪd.ɪ.məs, '-ə-
die *(n.) stamp:* daɪ -s -z
die *(n.) cube:* daɪ **dice** daɪs
die *(v.)* daɪ -s -z **dying** 'daɪ.ɪŋ **died** daɪd
die-casting 'daɪˌkɑː.stɪŋ (US) -ˌkæs.tɪŋ
Diego di'eɪ.gəʊ (US) -goʊ
diehard 'daɪ.hɑːd (US) -hɑːrd -s -z
dielectric ˌdaɪ.ɪ'lek.trɪk, -ə'- -s -s
Dieppe diː'ep, di-
dieres|is daɪ'er.ə.s|ɪs, -'ɪr-, -'ɪə.rə-, -rɪ- (US) -'er.ə- -es -iːz
dieretic ˌdaɪə'ret.ɪk (US) -'reţ-
diesel 'diː.zᵊl (US) -sᵊl, -zᵊl -s -z 'diesel ˌengine
diesink 'daɪ.sɪŋk -er/s -əʳ/z (US) -ɚ/z -ing -ɪŋ
dies irae ˌdiː.eɪz'ɪə.raɪ, -ez'-, -es'-, -re- (US) -eɪz'ɪr.eɪ, -es'-
dies|is 'daɪ.ə.s|ɪs, '-ɪ- -es -iːz
dies non ˌdaɪ.iːz'nɒn, ˌdiː.eɪz- (US) 'diː.eɪs.nɑːn, -es-; ˌdiː.eɪz'nɑːn, ˌdaɪ.iːz'- -s -z
diet daɪət -s -s -ing -ɪŋ (US) 'daɪə.ţɪŋ -ed -ɪd (US) 'daɪə.ţɪd -er/s -əʳ/z (US) -ɚ/z
dietar|y 'daɪə.tᵊr|.i, 'daɪ.ɪ-, -tr|i (US) 'daɪə.ter- -ies -iz ˌdietary 'fibre
dietetic ˌdaɪə'tet.ɪk, ˌdaɪ.ɪ'- (US) -'teţ- -s -al -ᵊl -ally -ᵊl.i, -li
dietician, dietitian ˌdaɪə'tɪʃ.ᵊn, ˌdaɪ.ɪ- (US) ˌdaɪə'- -s -z
Dietrich 'diː.trɪk, -trɪx, -trɪʃ
Dieu et mon droit ˌdjɜː.eɪ.mɔ̃ːn'drwɑː
diff|er 'dɪf|.əʳ (US) -ɚ -ers -əz (US) -ɚz -ering -ᵊr.ɪŋ -ered -əd (US) -ɚd
differenc|e 'dɪf.ᵊr.ᵊnts, '-rᵊnts -es -ɪz
different 'dɪf.ᵊr.ᵊnt, '-rᵊnt -ly -li
differenti|a ˌdɪf.ᵊ'ren.tʃi|.ə, '-tʃ|ə (US) -'rent.ʃi|.ə, '-ʃə -ae -iː
differentiable ˌdɪf.ᵊ'ren.tʃi.ə.bl̩, '-tʃə- (US) -'rent.ʃi.ə-, '-ʃə-
differential ˌdɪf.ᵊ'ren.tʃᵊl (US) -'rent.ʃᵊl -s -z -ly -i
differenti|ate ˌdɪf.ᵊ'ren.tʃi|.eɪt (US) -'rent.ʃi- -ates -eɪts -ating -eɪ.tɪŋ (US) -eɪ.ţɪŋ -ated -eɪ.tɪd (US) -eɪ.ţɪd
differentiation ˌdɪf.ᵊr.en.tʃi'eɪ.ʃᵊn, -ent.si'- (US) -ə.rent.ʃi'-, -si'- -s -z
difficult 'dɪf.ɪ.kᵊlt, '-ə-
difficult|y 'dɪf.ɪ.kᵊl.t|i, '-ə- (US) -ţ|i -ies -iz
diffidence 'dɪf.ɪ.dᵊnts
diffident 'dɪf.ɪ.dᵊnt -ly -li

diffract dɪˈfrækt **-s** -s **-ing** -ɪŋ **-ed** -ɪd
diffraction dɪˈfræk.ʃᵊn
diffuse *(adj.)* dɪˈfjuːs **-ly** -li **-ness** -nəs, -nɪs
diffus|e *(v.)* dɪˈfjuːz **-es** -ɪz **-ing** -ɪŋ **-ed** -d **-edly** -ɪd.li, -d.li **-edness** -ɪd.nəs, -d.nəs, -nɪs **-er/s** -əʳ/z US -ɚ/z
diffusibility dɪˌfjuː.zəˈbɪl.ə.ti, -zɪˈ-, -ɪ.ti US -zəˈbɪl.ə.t̬i
diffusible dɪˈfjuː.zə.bl̩, -zɪ-
diffusion dɪˈfjuː.ʒᵊn
diffusive dɪˈfjuː.sɪv **-ly** -li **-ness** -nəs, -nɪs
dig *(n. v.)* dɪɡ **-s** -z **-ging** -ɪŋ **-ged** -d **dug** dʌɡ
dig. *(in phrase* **infra dig.**) dɪɡ
digamma daɪˈɡæm.ə, ˈ--- **-s** -z
Digby ˈdɪɡ.bi
digest *(n.)* ˈdaɪ.dʒest **-s** -s
digest *(v.)* daɪˈdʒest, dɪ-, də- **-s** -s **-ing** -ɪŋ **-ed** -ɪd
digestibility daɪˌdʒes.təˈbɪl.ə.ti, dɪ-, də-, -tɪˈ-, -ɪ.ti US -ə.t̬i
digestible daɪˈdʒes.tə.bl̩, dɪ-, də-, -tɪ-
digestif ˌdiː.ʒesˈtɪf **-s** -s
digestion daɪˈdʒes.tʃᵊn, dɪ-, də-, -ˈdʒeʃ- **-s** -z
digestive daɪˈdʒes.tɪv, dɪ-, də- **-s** -z **-ly** -li **-ness** -nəs, -nɪs **diˌgestive ˈbiscuit, diˈgestive ˌbiscuit**
digger ˈdɪɡ.əʳ US -ɚ **-s** -z
Digges dɪɡz
diggings ˈdɪɡ.ɪŋz
Diggle ˈdɪɡ.l̩ **-s** -z
Diggory ˈdɪɡ.ᵊr.i
dight daɪt
Dighton ˈdaɪ.tᵊn
digit ˈdɪdʒ.ɪt **-s** -s
digital ˈdɪdʒ.ɪ.tᵊl, ˈ-ə- US -t̬ᵊl **-s** -z **-ly** -li
digitalin ˌdɪdʒ.ɪˈteɪ.lɪn, -əˈ-, -ˈtɑː- US -ˈtæl.ɪn, -ˈteɪ.lɪn
digitalis ˌdɪdʒ.ɪˈteɪ.lɪs, -əˈ-, -ˈtɑː- US -ˈtæl.ɪs, -ˈteɪ.lɪs
digitalization, -isa- ˌdɪdʒ.ɪ.tᵊl.aɪˈzeɪ.ʃᵊn, ˌ-ə-, -ɪˈ- US -t̬ᵊl.ɪˈ-
digitaliz|e, -is|e ˈdɪdʒ.ɪ.tᵊl.aɪz, ˈ-ə- US -t̬ə.laɪz **-es** -ɪz **-ing** -ɪŋ **-ed** -d
digitization, -isa- ˌdɪdʒ.ɪ.taɪˈzeɪ.ʃᵊn, ˌ-ə-, -tɪˈ- US -t̬ɪˈ-
digitiz|e, -is|e ˈdɪdʒ.ɪ.taɪz, ˈ-ə- **-es** -ɪz **-ing** -ɪŋ **-ed** -d
digloss|ia ˌdaɪˈɡlɒs|.i.ə US -ˈɡlɑː.s|i- **-ic** -ɪk
digni|fy ˈdɪɡ.nɪ|.faɪ, -nə- **-fies** -faɪz **-fying** -faɪ.ɪŋ **-fied** -faɪd
dignitar|y ˈdɪɡ.nɪ.tᵊr|.i, -nə- US -nə.ter- **-ies** -iz
dignit|y ˈdɪɡ.nə.t|i, -nɪ- US -t̬|i **-ies** -iz
digraph ˈdaɪ.ɡrɑːf US -ɡræf **-s** -s
digress daɪˈɡres, dɪ- **-es** -ɪz **-ing** -ɪŋ **-ed** -t
digression daɪˈɡreʃ.ᵊn, dɪ- **-s** -z
digressive daɪˈɡres.ɪv, dɪ- **-ly** -li **-ness** -nəs, -nɪs
digs dɪɡz
Dijon ˈdiː.ʒɔ̃ːŋ US diːˈʒoʊn, -ˈʒɔːn
dik|e daɪk **-es** -s **-ing** -ɪŋ **-ed** -t
diktat ˈdɪk.tæt, -tɑːt US dɪkˈtɑːt, ˈ-- **-s** -s
dilapi|date dɪˈlæp.ɪ|.deɪt, də-, ˈ-ə- **-dates** -deɪts **-dating** -deɪ.tɪŋ US -deɪ.t̬ɪŋ **-dated** -deɪ.tɪd US -deɪ.t̬ɪd
dilapidation dɪˌlæp.ɪˈdeɪ.ʃᵊn, də-, -əˈ- **-s** -z
dilatability daɪˌleɪ.təˈbɪl.ə.ti, dɪ-, də-, -ɪ.ti US -t̬əˈbɪl.ə.t̬i
dilatation ˌdɪl.əˈteɪ.ʃᵊn, ˌdaɪ-, -leɪˈ- US ˌdɪl.əˈteɪ.ʃᵊn; ˈdaɪ.lə.teɪ- **-s** -z
dila|te daɪˈleɪ|t, dɪ-, də- US ˈdaɪ.leɪ|t; -ˈ-, də- **-tes** -ts **-ting** -tɪŋ US -t̬ɪŋ **-ted** -tɪd US -t̬ɪd **-ter/s** -təʳ/z US -t̬ɚ/z **-table** -tə.bl̩ US -t̬ə.bl̩
dilation daɪˈleɪ.ʃᵊn, dɪ-, də- **-s** -z
dilator daɪˈleɪ.təʳ, dɪ-, də- US -t̬ɚ **-s** -z
dilator|y ˈdɪl.ə.tᵊr|.i, -tr|i US -tɔːr|.i **-ily** -ᵊl.i, -ɪ.li **-iness** -i.nəs, -i.nɪs
Dilbert ˈdɪl.bət US -bɚt
dildo ˈdɪl.dəʊ US -doʊ **-(e)s** -z
dilemma dɪˈlem.ə, daɪ-, də- **-s** -z
dilettante ˌdɪl.ɪˈtæn.ti, -əˈ-, -teɪ US ˌdɪl.əˈtɑːnt, -ˈtænt, ˈ---; ˌdɪl.əˈtæn.ti, -ˈtɑːn- **-s** -z
dilettanti *(alternative plur. of* **dilettante***)* ˌdɪl.ɪˈtæn.ti, -əˈ-, -teɪ US ˌdɪl.əˈtɑːn.taɪ, -ˈtæn-, -ti
dilettantism ˌdɪl.ɪˈtæn.tɪ.zᵊm, -əˈ- US -ˈtɑːn-, -ˈtæn-
Dili ˈdɪl.i
diligenc|e ˈdɪl.ɪ.dʒᵊnts, ˈ-ə-
diligent ˈdɪl.ɪ.dʒᵊnt, ˈ-ə- **-ly** -li
Dilke dɪlk **-s** -s
dill (D) dɪl **-s** -z
Diller ˈdɪl.əʳ US -ɚ
Dilley ˈdɪl.i
Dillinger ˈdɪl.ɪn.dʒəʳ US -dʒɚ
Dillon ˈdɪl.ən
Dillwyn ˈdɪl.ɪn, ˈdɪl.wɪn
dill|y ˈdɪl|.i **-ies** -iz
dillydall|y ˈdɪl.iˌdæl|.i, ˌ--ˈ-- **-ies** -iz **-ying** -i.ɪŋ **-ied** -id
diluent ˈdɪl.ju.ənt **-s** -s
dilu|te daɪˈluː|t, dɪ-, -ˈljuː|t US -ˈluː|t **-tes** -ts **-ting** -tɪŋ US -t̬ɪŋ **-ted** -tɪd US -t̬ɪd **-teness** -t.nəs, -t.nɪs
dilution daɪˈluː.ʃᵊn, dɪ-, -ˈljuː- US -ˈluː- **-s** -z
diluvi|al daɪˈluː.vi|.əl, dɪ-, -ˈljuː- US dɪˈluː-, daɪ- **-an** -ən
diluvi|um daɪˈluː.vi|.əm, dɪ-, -ˈljuː- US dɪˈluː-, daɪ- **-a** -ə
Dilwyn, Dilwen ˈdɪl.wɪn
Dilys ˈdɪl.ɪs
dim dɪm **-mer/s** -əʳ/z US -ɚ/z **-mest** -ɪst, -əst **-ly** -li **-ness** -nəs, -nɪs **-s** -z **-ming** -ɪŋ **-med** -d
Di Maggio dɪˈmædʒ.i.əʊ US -oʊ, dəˈmɑː.ʒ.i.oʊ
Dimbleby ˈdɪm.bl̩.bi
dime daɪm **-s** -z
dimension ˌdaɪˈmen.tʃᵊn, dɪ-, də- US dɪˈment.ʃᵊn, də-, ˌdaɪ- **-s** -z
dimensional ˌdaɪˈmen.tʃᵊ.nᵊl, dɪ-, də- US dɪˈment.ʃᵊn-, də-, ˌdaɪ-
dimeter ˈdɪm.ɪ.təʳ, ˈ-ə- US -ə.t̬ɚ **-s** -z
diminish dɪˈmɪn.ɪʃ, də- **-es** -ɪz **-ing** -ɪŋ **-ed** -t **-able** -ə.bl̩
diminuendo dɪˌmɪn.juˈen.dəʊ, də- US -doʊ **-s** -z
diminution ˌdɪm.ɪˈnjuː.ʃᵊn US -əˈnuː-, -ˈnjuː- **-s** -z
diminutive dɪˈmɪn.jə.tɪv, də-, -jʊ- US -jə.t̬ɪv **-ly** -li **-ness** -nəs, -nɪs
dimity ˈdɪm.ɪ.ti, -ə.ti US -ə.t̬i, -ɪ.t̬i
dimmer ˈdɪm.əʳ US -ɚ **-s** -z
Dimmesdale ˈdɪmz.deɪl
dimmish ˈdɪm.ɪʃ
Dimmock ˈdɪm.ək
dimorphism daɪˈmɔː.fɪ.zᵊm US -ˈmɔːr-
dimorphous daɪˈmɔː.fəs US -ˈmɔːr-
dimout ˈdɪm.aʊt **-s** -s
dimpl|e ˈdɪm.pl̩ **-es** -z **-ing** -ɪŋ, ˈdɪm.plɪŋ **-ed** -d
Dimplex® ˈdɪm.pleks
dimply ˈdɪm.pli
dim sum ˌdɪmˈsʊm, -ˈsʌm
dimwit ˈdɪm.wɪt **-s** -s
dim-witted ˌdɪmˈwɪt.ɪd US ˈdɪmˌwɪt̬-, ˌ-ˈ-- **-ly** -li **-ness** -nəs, -nɪs *stress shift, British only:* ˌdimwitted ˈidiot
din dɪn **-s** -z **-ning** -ɪŋ **-ned** -d
Dina ˈdiː.nə, ˈdaɪ.nə
Dinah ˈdaɪ.nə
dinar ˈdiː.nɑːʳ, -ˈ- US diːˈnɑːr, ˈ-- **-s** -z
Dinaric dɪˈnær.ɪk, də-, daɪ- US -ˈner-, -ˈnær-
Dinas Powis ˌdiː.næsˈpaʊ.ɪs
din|e (D) daɪn **-es** -z **-ing** -ɪŋ **-ed** -d **ˈdining ˌcar; ˈdining ˌroom; ˈdining ˌtable**
Dinefwr dɪˈnev.ʊəʳ US -ʊr
diner ˈdaɪ.nəʳ US -nɚ **-s** -z
Dinesen ˈdɪn.ɪ.sᵊn, ˈ-ə- US ˈdiː.nə-, ˈdɪn.ə-, ˈ-ɪ-, -sɪn
dinette daɪˈnet, dɪ- US daɪ- **-s** -s
ding dɪŋ **-s** -z **-ing** -ɪŋ **-ed** -d
ding-a-ling ˈdɪŋ.ə.lɪŋ **-s** -z
dingbat ˈdɪŋ.bæt **-s** -s
ding-dong ˈdɪŋ.dɒŋ US -dɑːŋ, -dɔːŋ
dingh|y ˈdɪŋ.ɡ|i, -i US ˈdɪŋ|.i, -ɡ|i **-ies** -iz
dingle (D) ˈdɪŋ.ɡl̩ **-s** -z
Dingley ˈdɪŋ.li
dingo ˈdɪŋ.ɡəʊ US -ɡoʊ **-es** -z
Dingwall ˈdɪŋ.wɔːl, -wəl US -wɑːl, -wɔːl, -wəl

Diphthong

A sound in which there is a glide from one vowel quality to another.

Examples for English

BBC English and US English contain a large number of diphthongs: in both accents, there are three ending in [ɪ] (/eɪ aɪ ɔɪ/), sometimes referred to as 'front closing', and two ending in [ʊ] (/aʊ əʊ/), sometimes referred to as 'back closing'. In US English, the preferred transcription of the BBC vowel /əʊ/ is /oʊ/, which indicates a rounded initial vowel.

BBC English also has three diphthongs ending in [ə] (/ɪə eə ʊə/), which are sometimes known as 'centring'. The /ʊə/ diphthong is now less commonly used than /ɔː/. These diphthongs usually appear in US English with an /r/ final (/ɪr er ʊr/), as words containing them generally end with an *r* in the spelling, e.g.:

bay	/beɪ/	
buy	/baɪ/	
boy	/bɔɪ/	
go	/gəʊ/	(US) /goʊ/
cow	/kaʊ/	
pier	/pɪə/	(US) /pɪr/
pear	/peə/	(US) /per/
poor	/pʊə/ (more often) /pɔː/	(US) /pʊr/

Opinions differ as to whether diphthongs should be treated as phonemes in their own right, or as combinations of two phonemes.

ding|y 'dɪn.dʒ|i **-ier** -i.əʳ (US) -i.ɚ **-iest** -i.ɪst, -i.əst **-ily** -ɪ.li, -ᵊl.i **-iness** -ɪ.nəs, -ɪ.nɪs
dink dɪŋk **-s** -s
Dinkins 'dɪŋ.kɪnz (US) 'dɪŋ-, 'dɪn-
dinkum 'dɪŋ.kəm
dink|y 'dɪŋ.k|i **-ier** -i.əʳ (US) -i.ɚ **-iest** -i.ɪst, -i.əst **-iness** -ɪ.nəs, -ɪ.nɪs
Dinmont 'dɪn.mɒnt, 'dɪm-, -mənt (US) 'dɪn.mɑːnt, -mənt
Dinneford 'dɪn.ɪ.fəd (US) -fɚd
dinner 'dɪn.əʳ (US) -ɚ **-s** -z **'dinner ˌhour; 'dinner ˌjacket; 'dinner ˌlady; 'dinner ˌparty; 'dinner ˌplate; 'dinner ˌservice; 'dinner ˌset; 'dinner ˌtable; 'dinner ˌtime**
Dinnington 'dɪn.ɪŋ.tᵊn
Dinocrates daɪ'nɒk.rə.tiːz, dɪ- (US) -'nɑː.krə-
Dinorah dɪ'nɔː.rə (US) -'nɔːr.ə
dinosaur 'daɪ.nə.sɔːʳ (US) -sɔːr **-s** -z
dinosaur|us ˌdaɪ.nə'sɔː.r|əs (US) -'sɔːr|.əs **-i** -aɪ
dinotheri|um ˌdaɪ.nəʊ'θɪə.ri|.əm (US) -oʊ'-, -ə'- (US) -'θɪr.i- **-a** -ə
dint dɪnt
Dinwiddie dɪn'wɪd.i, '---
diocesan daɪ'ɒs.ɪ.sᵊn, '-ə-, -zᵊn (US) -'ɑː.sə-
dioces|e 'daɪə.sɪs, -siːs, -siːz **-es** -ɪz
Diocles 'daɪə.kliːz
Diocletian ˌdaɪə'kliː.ʃᵊn, -ʃi.ən
diode 'daɪ.əʊd (US) -oʊd **-s** -z
Diodorus ˌdaɪə'dɔː.rəs (US) -'dɔːr.əs
Diogenes daɪ'ɒdʒ.ɪ.niːz, '-ə- (US) -'ɑː.dʒə-
Diomede 'daɪə.miːd
Diomedes ˌdaɪə'miː.diːz; daɪ'ɒm.ɪ- (US) ˌdaɪə'miː-
Dion *Greek:* 'daɪ.ən (US) -ɑːn *French:* 'diː.ən, -ɔ̃ːŋ, -ɒŋ, -ɒn (US) di'oʊn
Dionne diː'ɒn, di-; 'diː.ɒn (US) -'ɑːn
Dionysi|a ˌdaɪə'nɪs.i|.ə, -'nɪz- (US) -'nɪʃ.i|.ə, -'nɪs-, -'nɪz-, -'nɪʃ|.ə **-an** -ən
Dionysiac ˌdaɪə'nɪs.i.æk, -'nɪz-
Dionysius ˌdaɪə'nɪs.i.əs, -'nɪz- (US) -'nɪʃ.əs, '-i.əs, -'nɪs.i-, -'naɪ.si-
Dionysus ˌdaɪə'naɪ.səs (US) -'naɪ.səs, -'niː-
dioptre, diopter daɪ'ɒp.təʳ (US) -'ɑːp.tɚ **-s** -z
dioptric daɪ'ɒp.trɪk (US) -'ɑːp-
Dior 'diː.ɔːʳ, di'ɔːʳ (US) di'ɔːr
diorama ˌdaɪə'rɑː.mə (US) -'ræm.ə, -'rɑː.mə **-s** -z
dioramic ˌdaɪə'ræm.ɪk
Dioscuri ˌdaɪə'skjʊə.ri; ˌdaɪ.ɒs'kjʊə-; daɪ'ɒs.kjʊ.ri, -raɪ (US) ˌdaɪ.ɑː'skjʊr.aɪ
Diosy di'əʊ.si (US) -'oʊ-
dioxide daɪ'ɒk.saɪd (US) -'ɑːk- **-s** -z
dioxin daɪ'ɒk.sɪn (US) -'ɑːk- **-s** -z
dip dɪp **-s** -s **-ping** -ɪŋ **-ped** -t **-per/s** -əʳ/z (US) -ɚ/z
diphenyl daɪ'fiː.naɪl, -'fen.aɪl, -ᵊl, -ɪl, -'fen.ɪl (US) -'fen.ᵊl, -'fiː.nᵊl
diphtheria dɪf'θɪə.ri.ə, dɪp- (US) -'θɪr.i-
diphthong 'dɪf.θɒŋ, 'dɪp- (US) -θɑːŋ, -θɔːŋ **-s** -z
diphthongal 'dɪf.θɒŋ.ᵊl, 'dɪp-, -gᵊl, -'-- (US) dɪf'θɑːŋ.ᵊl, dɪp-, -'θɔːŋ-, -gᵊl **-ly** -i
diphthongization, -isa- ˌdɪf.θɒŋ.aɪ'zeɪ.ʃᵊn, ˌdɪp-, -gaɪ'-, -gɪ'- (US) -θɑːŋ.ɪ'-, -θɔːŋ-, -gɪ'- **-s** -z
diphthongiz|e, -is|e 'dɪf.θɒŋ.aɪz, 'dɪp-, -gaɪz (US) -θɑːŋ.aɪz, -θɔːŋ-, -gaɪz **-es** -ɪz **-ing** -ɪŋ **-ed** -d
Diplock 'dɪp.lɒk (US) -lɑːk
diplodoc|us dɪ'plɒd.ə.k|əs, ˌdɪp.ləʊ'dəʊ- (US) dɪ'plɑː.də-, -'ploʊ- **-uses** -ə.sɪz **-i** -aɪ
diploid 'dɪp.lɔɪd **-s** -z
diploma dɪ'pləʊ.mə (US) -'ploʊ-, də- **-s** -z
diplomacy dɪ'pləʊ.mə.si (US) -'ploʊ-, də-
diplomat 'dɪp.lə.mæt **-s** -s
diplomatic ˌdɪp.lə'mæt.ɪk (US) -'mæt̬- **-s** -s **-al** -ᵊl **-ally** -ᵊl.i, -li
diplomatist dɪ'pləʊ.mə.tɪst (US) -'ploʊ-, də- **-s** -s
diplomatiz|e, -is|e dɪ'pləʊ.mə.taɪz (US) -'ploʊ-, də- **-es** -ɪz **-ing** -ɪŋ **-ed** -d
diplosis dɪ'pləʊ.sɪs (US) -'ploʊ-
dipole 'daɪ.pəʊl (US) -poʊl **-s** -z
dipper 'dɪp.əʳ (US) -ɚ **-s** -z
dipp|y 'dɪp|.i **-ier** -i.əʳ (US) -i.ɚ **-iest** -i.ɪst, -i.əst
dipsomania ˌdɪp.səʊ'meɪ.ni.ə (US) -sə'-, -soʊ'-
dipsomaniac ˌdɪp.səʊ'meɪ.ni.æk (US) -sə'-, -soʊ'- **-s** -s
dipstick 'dɪp.stɪk **-s** -s
dipswitch 'dɪp.swɪtʃ **-es** -ɪz
dipteran 'dɪp.tə.rən (US) -tɚ.ən **-s** -z
dipter|on 'dɪp.tə.r|ən (US) -r|ɑːn **-ons** -ənz (US) -ɑːnz **-a** -ə **-ous** -əs
diptych 'dɪp.tɪk **-s** -s
dir|e daɪəʳ (US) daɪɚ **-er** -əʳ (US) -ɚ **-est** -ɪst, -əst **-ely** -li **-eness** -nəs, -nɪs
direct dɪ'rekt, daɪ-, də- (US) dɪ'rekt, daɪ- **-s** -s **-ing** -ɪŋ **-ed** -ɪd **-est** -ɪst, -əst **-ness** -nəs, -nɪs **ˌdirect 'mail; ˌdirect 'object**
direction dɪ'rek.ʃᵊn, daɪ-, də- (US) dɪ'rek-, daɪ- **-s** -z **-less** -ləs, -lɪs
directional dɪ'rek.ʃᵊn.ᵊl, daɪ-, də- (US) dɪ'rek-, daɪ-
directive dɪ'rek.tɪv, daɪ-, də- (US) dɪ'rek-, daɪ- **-s** -z

directly dɪˈrekt.li, daɪ-, də- (US) dɪ-, daɪ-
director dɪˈrek.təʳ, daɪ-, də- (US) dɪˈrek.tɚ, daɪ- **-s** -z
directorate dɪˈrek.tᵊr.ət, daɪ-, də-, -ɪt (US) dɪˈrek-, daɪ- **-s** -s
directorial dɪˌrekˈtɔː.ri.əl, daɪ-, də- (US) dɪˌrekˈtɔːr.i-, daɪ-
directorship dɪˈrek.tə.ʃɪp, daɪ-, də- (US) dɪˈrek.tɚ-, daɪ- **-s** -s
director|y dɪˈrek.tᵊr|.i, daɪ-, də- (US) dɪˈrek-, daɪ- **-ies** -iz
direful ˈdaɪə.fᵊl, -fʊl (US) ˈdaɪɚ- **-ly** -i **-ness** -nəs, -nɪs
dirg|e dɜːdʒ (US) dɝːdʒ **-es** -ɪz
dirham ˈdɪ.ræm, ˈdɪər.æm, -əm (US) dɪrˈhæm; dəˈræm **-s** -z
dirigible ˈdɪr.ɪ.dʒə.bl̩, -dʒɪ-; dɪˈrɪdʒ-, də- (US) ˈdɪr.ə.dʒə-; dɪˈrɪdʒ.ə-, də- **-s** -z
dirigisme ˌdɪr.ɪˈʒiː.zᵊm; ˈdɪr.ɪ.ʒɪ- (US) ˌdɪr.ɪˈʒiː-
dirigiste ˌdɪr.ɪˈʒiːst; ˈdɪr.ɪ.ʒɪst (US) ˈdɪr.ɪ.ʒɪst; ˌdɪr.ɪˈʒiːst **-s** -s
dirk (D) dɜːk (US) dɝːk **-s** -s
dirndl ˈdɜːn.dl̩ (US) ˈdɝːn- **-s** -z
dirt dɜːt (US) dɝːt **ˌdirt ˈcheap; ˌdirt ˈpoor; ˈdirt ˌtrack**
dirt|y ˈdɜː.t|i (US) ˈdɝː.t̬|i **-ies** -iz **-ying** -i.ɪŋ **-ied** -id **-ier** -i.əʳ (US) -i.ɚ **-iest** -i.ɪst, -i.əst **-ily** -ɪ.li, -ᵊl.i **-iness** -ɪ.nəs, -ɪ.nɪs **ˌdirty ˈtrick; do someone's ˈdirty ˌwork**
dis- dɪs-, dɪz-

Note: Prefix. In words containing **dis-**, the prefix will normally either not be stressed, e.g. **disable** /dɪˈseɪ.bl̩/, or will take secondary stress if the stem is stressed on its second syllable, e.g. **ability** /əˈbɪl.ə.ti (US) -t̬i/, **disability** /ˌdɪs.əˈbɪl.ə.ti (US) -t̬i/. There is sometimes a difference in stress between nouns and verbs, e.g. **discharge**, noun /ˈdɪs.tʃɑːdʒ (US) -tʃɑːrdʒ/, verb /dɪsˈtʃɑːdʒ (US) -ˈtʃɑːrdʒ/. There are exceptions; see individual entries.

is dɪs
isabilit|y ˌdɪs.əˈbɪl.ə.t|i, -ɪ.t|i (US) -ə.t̬|i **-ies** -iz
isabl|e dɪˈseɪ.bl̩ **-es** -z **-ing** -ɪŋ, -ˈeɪ.blɪŋ **-ed** -d **-ement** -mənt
isabus|e ˌdɪs.əˈbjuːz **-es** -ɪz **-ing** -ɪŋ **-ed** -d
isaccharide daɪˈsæk.ᵊr.aɪd, -ɪd (US) -ə.raɪd **-s** -z
isaccustom ˌdɪs.əˈkʌs.təm **-s** -z **-ing** -ɪŋ **-ed** -d
isadvantag|e ˌdɪs.ədˈvɑːn.tɪdʒ (US) -ˈvæn.t̬ɪdʒ **-es** -ɪz **-ing** **-ed** -d
isadvantageous ˌdɪsˌæd.vənˈteɪ.dʒəs, -əd-, -vɑːnˈ-, -vænˈ-; dɪˌsæd- (US) ˌdɪsˌæd.vænˈ-, -vənˈ- **-ly** -li **-ness** -nəs, -nɪs
disaffect ˌdɪs.əˈfekt **-s** -s **-ing** -ɪŋ **-ed/ly** -ɪd/li **-edness** -ɪd.nəs, -nɪs
disaffection ˌdɪs.əˈfek.ʃᵊn
disafforest ˌdɪs.əˈfɒr.ɪst, -əst (US) -ˈfɔːr- **-s** -s **-ing** -ɪŋ **-ed** -ɪd
disafforestation ˌdɪs.əˌfɒr.ɪˈsteɪ.ʃᵊn, -əˈ- (US) -ˌfɔːr-
disagree ˌdɪs.əˈgriː **-s** -z **-ing** -ɪŋ **-d** -d
disagreeab|le ˌdɪs.əˈgriː.ə.b|l̩ **-ly** -li **-leness** -l̩.nəs, -nɪs
disagreement ˌdɪs.əˈgriː.mᵊnt **-s** -s
disallow ˌdɪs.əˈlaʊ **-s** -z **-ing** -ɪŋ **-ed** -d
disallowable ˌdɪs.əˈlaʊ.ə.bl̩ *stress shift:* ˌdisallowable ˈgoals
disallowance ˌdɪs.əˈlaʊ.ənts
disambigu|ate ˌdɪs.æmˈbɪg.ju|.eɪt **-ates** -eɪts **-ating** -eɪ.tɪŋ (US) -eɪ.t̬ɪŋ **-ated** -eɪ.tɪd (US) -eɪ.t̬ɪd
disambiguation ˌdɪs.æmˌbɪg.juˈeɪ.ʃᵊn
disappear ˌdɪs.əˈpɪəʳ (US) -ˈpɪr **-s** -z **-ing** -ɪŋ **-ed** -d
disappearanc|e ˌdɪs.əˈpɪə.rᵊnts (US) -ˈpɪr.ᵊnts **-es** -ɪz
disap|point ˌdɪs.ə|ˈpɔɪnt **-points** -ˈpɔɪnts **-pointing/ly** -ˈpɔɪn.tɪŋ/li (US) -ˈpɔɪn.t̬ɪŋ/li **-pointed** -ˈpɔɪn.tɪd (US) -ˈpɔɪn.t̬ɪd
disappointment ˌdɪs.əˈpɔɪnt.mənt **-s** -s
disapprobation ˌdɪs.æp.rəʊˈbeɪ.ʃᵊn, -rʊˈ-; dɪˌsæp- (US) ˌdɪsˌæp.rəˈ-, -roʊˈ-
disapproval ˌdɪs.əˈpruː.vᵊl
disapprov|e ˌdɪs.əˈpruːv **-es** -z **-ing/ly** -ɪŋ/li **-ed** -d
disarm dɪˈsɑːm, -ˈzɑːm (US) -ˈsɑːrm **-s** -z **-ing/ly** -ɪŋ/li **-ed** -d **-er/s** -əʳ/z (US) -ɚ/z
disarmament dɪˈsɑː.mə.mənt, -ˈzɑː- (US) -ˈsɑːr-
disarrang|e ˌdɪs.ᵊˈreɪndʒ **-es** -ɪz **-ing** -ɪŋ **-ed** -d
disarrangement ˌdɪs.ᵊˈreɪndʒ.mənt **-s** -s
disarray ˌdɪs.ᵊrˈeɪ **-s** -z **-ing** -ɪŋ **-ed** -d
disarticu|late ˌdɪs.ɑːˈtɪk.jə|.leɪt, -jʊ- (US) -ɑːrˈ- **-lates** -leɪts **-lating** -leɪ.tɪŋ (US) -leɪ.t̬ɪŋ **-lated** -leɪ.tɪd (US) -leɪ.t̬ɪd
disarticulation ˌdɪs.ɑːˌtɪk.jəˈleɪ.ʃᵊn, -jʊˈ- (US) -ɑːr-
disassoci|ate ˌdɪs.əˈsəʊ.si|.eɪt, -ʃi- (US) -ˈsoʊ.ʃi-, -si- **-ates** -eɪts **-ating** -eɪ.tɪŋ (US) -eɪ.t̬ɪŋ **-ated** -eɪ.tɪd (US) -eɪ.t̬ɪd
disassociation ˌdɪs.ə.səʊ.siˈeɪ.ʃᵊn, -ʃiˈ- (US) -soʊ.ʃiˈ-, -siˈ-
disaster dɪˈzɑː.stəʳ, də- (US) dɪˈzæs.tɚ **-s** -z
disastrous dɪˈzɑː.strəs, də- (US) dɪˈzæs.trəs **-ly** -li **-ness** -nəs, -nɪs
disavow ˌdɪs.əˈvaʊ **-s** -z **-ing** -ɪŋ **-ed** -d **-al** -ᵊl
disband dɪsˈbænd **-s** -z **-ing** -ɪŋ **-ed** -ɪd **-ment** -mənt
disbar dɪsˈbɑːʳ (US) -ˈbɑːr **-s** -z **-ring** -ɪŋ **-red** -d
disbark dɪsˈbɑːk (US) -ˈbɑːrk **-s** -s **-ing** -ɪŋ **-ed** -t
disbelief ˌdɪs.bɪˈliːf, -bəˈ-
disbeliev|e ˌdɪs.bɪˈliːv, -bəˈ- **-es** -z **-ing** -ɪŋ **-ed** -d **-er/s** -əʳ/z (US) -ɚ/z
disburden dɪsˈbɜː.dᵊn (US) -ˈbɝː- **-s** -z **-ing** -ɪŋ **-ed** -d
disburdenment dɪsˈbɜː.dᵊn.mənt (US) -ˈbɝː-
disburs|e dɪsˈbɜːs (US) -ˈbɝːs **-es** -ɪz **-ing** -ɪŋ **-ed** -t
disbursement dɪsˈbɜːs.mənt (US) -ˈbɝːs- **-s** -s
disc dɪsk **-s** -s **ˈdisc ˌjockey**
discard (*n.*) ˈdɪs.kɑːd (US) -kɑːrd **-s** -z
discard (*v.*) dɪˈskɑːd (US) -ˈskɑːrd **-s** -z **-ing** -ɪŋ **-ed** -ɪd
discern dɪˈsɜːn, də- (US) dɪˈsɝːn, -ˈzɝːn **-s** -z **-ing** -ɪŋ **-ed** -d **-er/s** -əʳ/z (US) -ɚ/z
discernib|le dɪˈsɜː.nə.b|l̩, də-, -nɪ- (US) dɪˈsɝː-, -ˈzɝː- **-ly** -li **-leness** -l̩.nəs, -nɪs
discerning dɪˈsɜː.nɪŋ, də- (US) dɪˈsɝː-, -ˈzɝː- **-ly** -li
discernment dɪˈsɜːn.mənt, də- (US) dɪˈsɝːn-, -ˈzɝːn-
discharg|e (*n.*) ˈdɪs.tʃɑːdʒ, -ˈ- (US) ˈdɪs.tʃɑːrdʒ, -ˈ- **-es** -ɪz
discharg|e (*v.*) dɪsˈtʃɑːdʒ (US) -ˈtʃɑːrdʒ **-es** -ɪz **-ing** -ɪŋ **-ed** -d **-er/s** -əʳ/z (US) -ɚ/z
disciple dɪˈsaɪ.pl̩, də- (US) dɪ- **-s** -z **-ship** -ʃɪp
disciplinarian ˌdɪs.ə.plɪˈneə.ri.ən, ˌ-ɪ-, -pləˈ- (US) -ˈner.i- **-s** -z
disciplinary ˌdɪs.əˈplɪ.nᵊr.i, -ɪˈ-, ˈdɪs.ə.plɪ-, ˈ-ɪ- (US) ˈdɪs.ə.plɪ.ner- **ˌdisciplinary ˈaction, disciˌplinary ˈaction** (US) **ˈdisciplinary ˌaction**
disciplin|e ˈdɪs.ə.plɪn, ˈ-ɪ- **-es** -z **-ing** -ɪŋ **-ed** -d
disclaim dɪsˈkleɪm **-s** -z **-ing** -ɪŋ **-ed** -d
disclaimer dɪsˈkleɪ.məʳ (US) -mɚ **-s** -z
disclos|e dɪsˈkləʊz (US) -ˈkloʊz **-es** -ɪz **-ing** -ɪŋ **-ed** -d
disclosure dɪsˈkləʊ.ʒəʳ (US) -ˈkloʊ.ʒɚ **-s** -z
disco ˈdɪs.kəʊ (US) -koʊ **-s** -z **-ing** -ɪŋ
discobol|us dɪˈskɒb.ᵊl|.əs (US) -ˈskɑː.bᵊl- **-i** -aɪ
discol|o(u)r dɪˈskʌl|.əʳ (US) -ˈskʌl|.ɚ **-o(u)rs** -əz (US) -ɚz **-o(u)ring** -ᵊr.ɪŋ **-o(u)red** -əd (US) -ɚd
discolo(u)ration dɪˌskʌl.əˈreɪ.ʃᵊn; ˌdɪs.kʌl- (US) dɪˌskʌl- **-s** -z
discombobu|late ˌdɪs.kəmˈbɒb.jə|.leɪt, -jʊ- (US) -ˈbɑː.bjə-, -bjʊ- **-lates** -leɪts **-lating** -leɪ.tɪŋ (US) -leɪ.t̬ɪŋ **-lated** -leɪ.tɪd (US) -leɪ.t̬ɪd

discom|fit dɪ'skʌmp|.fɪt **-fits** -fɪts **-fiting** -fɪ.tɪŋ (US) -fɪ.t̬ɪŋ **-fited** -fɪ.tɪd (US) -fɪ.t̬ɪd
discomfiture dɪ'skʌmp.fɪ.tʃəʳ, -fə- (US) -tʃɚ
discom|fort dɪ'skʌmp|.fət (US) -fɚt **-forts** -fəts (US) -fɚts **-forting** -fə.tɪŋ (US) -fɚ.t̬ɪŋ **-forted** -fə.tɪd (US) -fɚ.t̬ɪd
discommod|e ˌdɪs.kə'məʊd (US) -'moʊd **-es** -z **-ing** -ɪŋ **-ed** -ɪd
discompos|e ˌdɪs.kəm'pəʊz (US) -'poʊz **-es** -ɪz **-ing** -ɪŋ **-ed** -d
discomposure ˌdɪs.kəm'pəʊ.ʒəʳ (US) -'poʊ.ʒɚ
discon|cert ˌdɪs.kən|'sɜːt (US) -'sɝːt **-certs** -'sɜːts (US) -'sɝːts **-certing/ly** -'sɜː.tɪŋ/li (US) -'sɝː.t̬ɪŋ/li **-certed** -'sɜː.tɪd (US) -'sɝː.t̬ɪd
disconnect ˌdɪs.kə'nekt **-s** -s **-ing** -ɪŋ **-ed** -ɪd
disconnection ˌdɪs.kə'nek.ʃᵊn
disconsolate dɪ'skɒnt.sᵊl.ət, -ɪt (US) -'skɑːnt- **-ly** -li **-ness** -nəs, -nɪs
discon|tent ˌdɪs.kən|'tent **-tented** -'ten.tɪd (US) -'ten.t̬ɪd **-tentedly** -'ten.tɪd.li (US) -'ten.t̬ɪd.li **-tentedness** -'ten.tɪd.nəs, -nɪs (US) -'ten.t̬ɪd.nəs, -nɪs **-tentment** -'tent.mənt
discontinuance ˌdɪs.kən'tɪn.ju.ənts
discontinuation ˌdɪs.kənˌtɪn.ju'eɪ.ʃᵊn
discontinu|e ˌdɪs.kən'tɪn.juː **-es** -z **-ing** -ɪŋ **-ed** -d
discontinuit|y ˌdɪsˌkɒn.tɪ'njuː.ə.t|i, -kɒn-, -ɪ.t|i; dɪˌskɒn- (US) ˌdɪs.kɑːn.tᵊn'uː.ə.t̬|i, -'juː- **-ies** -iz
discontinuous ˌdɪs.kən'tɪn.ju.əs **-ly** -li
discord (*n.*) 'dɪs.kɔːd (US) -kɔːrd **-s** -z
discord (*v.*) dɪ'skɔːd (US) -'skɔːrd **-s** -z **-ing** -ɪŋ **-ed** -ɪd
discordan|ce dɪ'skɔː.dᵊnt|s (US) -'skɔːr- **-cy** -si
discordant dɪ'skɔː.dᵊnt (US) -'skɔːr- **-ly** -li
discotheque, discothèque 'dɪs.kə.tek **-s** -s
discount (*n.*) 'dɪs.kaʊnt **-s** -s
dis|count (*v.*) dɪ's|kaʊnt **-counts** -kaʊnts **-counting** -kaʊn.tɪŋ (US) -kaʊn.t̬ɪŋ **-counted** -kaʊn.tɪd (US) -kaʊn.t̬ɪd **-counter/s** -kaʊn.təʳ/z (US) -kaʊn.t̬ɚ/z
discountenanc|e dɪ'skaʊn.tɪ.nənts, -tə- (US) -tᵊn.ənts **-es** -ɪz **-ing** -ɪŋ **-ed** -t
discourag|e dɪ'skʌr.ɪdʒ (US) -'skɝː- **-es** -ɪz **-ing/ly** -ɪŋ/li **-ed** -d
discouragement dɪ'skʌr.ɪdʒ.mənt (US) -'skɝː- **-s** -s
discours|e (*n.*) 'dɪs.kɔːs (US) -kɔːrs **-es** -ɪz
discours|e (*v.*) dɪ'skɔːs (US) -'skɔːrs **-es** -ɪz **-ing** -ɪŋ **-ed** -t **-er/s** -əʳ/z (US) -ɚ/z
discourteous dɪ'skɜː.ti.əs (US) -'skɝː.t̬i- **-ly** -li **-ness** -nəs, -nɪs
discourtesy dɪ'skɜː.tə.si, -tɪ- (US) -'skɝː.t̬ə-
discov|er dɪ'skʌv|.əʳ (US) -ɚ **-ers** -əz (US) -ɚz **-ering** -ᵊr.ɪŋ **-ered** -əd (US) -ɚd **-erer/s** -ᵊr.əʳ/z (US) -ɚ.ɚ/z
discoverable dɪ'skʌv.ᵊr.ə.bl̩
discovert dɪ'skʌv.ət (US) -ɚt
discover|y dɪ'skʌv.ᵊr|.i **-ies** -iz
discred|it dɪ'skred|.ɪt **-its** -ɪts **-iting** -ɪ.tɪŋ (US) -ɪ.t̬ɪŋ **-ited** -ɪ.tɪd (US) -ɪ.t̬ɪd
discreditab|le dɪ'skred.ɪ.tə.bl|̩ (US) -t̬ə- **-ly** -li **-leness** -l̩.nəs, -nɪs
dis|creet dɪ's|kriːt **-creetest** -'kriː.tɪst, -təst (US) -'kriː.t̬ɪst, -t̬əst **-creetly** -'kriːt.li **-creetness** -'kriːt.nəs, -nɪs
discrepan|cy dɪ'skrep.ᵊn|t.si **-cies** -t.siz **-t** -t
discrete dɪ'skriːt **-ly** -li **-ness** -nəs, -nɪs
discretion dɪ'skreʃ.ᵊn **-s** -z
discretional dɪ'skreʃ.ᵊn.ᵊl **-ly** -i
discretionar|y dɪ'skreʃ.ᵊn.ᵊr|.i, -r|i (US) -er|.i **-ily** -ᵊl.i, -ɪ.li
discriminate (*adj.*) dɪ'skrɪm.ɪ.nət, '-ə-, -nɪt **-ly** -li
discrimi|nate (*v.*) dɪ'skrɪm.ɪ|.neɪt, '-ə- **-nates** -neɪts **-nating/ly** -neɪ.tɪŋ/li (US) -neɪ.t̬ɪŋ/li **-nated** -neɪ.tɪd (US) -neɪ.t̬ɪd
discrimination dɪˌskrɪm.ɪ'neɪ.ʃᵊn, -ə'- **-s** -z
discriminative dɪ'skrɪm.ɪ.nə.tɪv, '-ə-, -neɪ- (US) -neɪ.t̬ɪv, -nə- **-ly** -li
discriminatory dɪ'skrɪm.ɪ.nə.tᵊr.i, '-ə-, -tri; dɪˌskrɪm.ɪ'neɪ-, -ə'- (US) dɪ'skrɪm.ɪ.nə.tɔːr.i
discursion dɪ'skɜː.ʃᵊn, -ʒᵊn (US) -'skɝː.ʒᵊn, -ʃᵊn **-s** -z
discursive dɪ'skɜː.sɪv (US) -skɝː- **-ly** -li **-ness** -nəs, -nɪs
discursory dɪ'skɜː.sᵊr.i (US) -'skɝː-
disc|us 'dɪs.k|əs **-i** -aɪ **-uses** -ə.sɪz
discuss dɪ'skʌs **-es** -ɪz **-ing** -ɪŋ **-ed** -t **-able** -ə.bl̩
discussant dɪ'skʌs.ᵊnt **-s** -s
discussion dɪ'skʌʃ.ᵊn **-s** -z
disdain dɪs'deɪn, dɪz- **-s** -z **-ing** -ɪŋ **-ed** -d
disdainful dɪs'deɪn.fᵊl, dɪz-, -fʊl **-ly** -i **-ness** -nəs, -nɪs
diseas|e dɪ'ziːz, də- (US) dɪ- **-es** -ɪz **-ed** -d
disembark ˌdɪs.ɪm'bɑːk, -em'- (US) -'bɑːrk, '--- **-s** -s **-ing** -ɪŋ **-ed** -t
disembarkation ˌdɪs.ɪm.bɑː'keɪ.ʃᵊn, -em- (US) -bɑːr'- **-s** -z
disembarkment ˌdɪs.ɪm'bɑːk.mənt, -em'- (US) -'bɑːrk- **-s** -s
disembarrass ˌdɪs.ɪm'bær.əs, -em'- (US) -'ber-, -'bær- **-es** -ɪz **-ing** -ɪŋ **-ed** -t
disembarrassment ˌdɪs.ɪm'bær.əs.mənt, -em'- (US) -'ber-, -'bær- **-s** -s
disembod|y ˌdɪs.ɪm'bɒd|.i, -em'- (US) -'bɑː.d|i **-ies** -iz **-ying** -i.ɪŋ **-ied** -id
disembowel ˌdɪs.ɪm'baʊəl, -em'- **-s** -z **-(l)ing** -ɪŋ **-(l)ed** -d
disen|chant ˌdɪs.ɪn|'tʃɑːnt, -en'-, -ᵊn'- (US) -'tʃænt **-chants** -'tʃɑːnts (US) -'tʃænts **-chanting** -'tʃɑːn.tɪŋ (US) -'tʃæn.t̬ɪŋ **-chanted** -'tʃɑːn.tɪd (US) -'tʃæn.t̬ɪd
disenchantment ˌdɪs.ɪn'tʃɑːnt.mənt, -en'-, -ᵊn'- (US) -'tʃænt- **-s** -s
disencumb|er ˌdɪs.ɪn'kʌm.b|əʳ, -ɪŋ'-, -en'-, -eŋ'- (US) -b|ɚ **-ers** -əz (US) -ɚz **-ering** -ᵊr.ɪŋ **-ered** -əd (US) -ɚd
disendow ˌdɪs.ɪn'daʊ, -en'- **-s** -z **-ing** -ɪŋ **-ed** -d
disendowment ˌdɪs.ɪn'daʊ.mənt, -en'-
disenfranchis|e ˌdɪs.ɪn'fræn.tʃaɪz, -en'- **-es** -ɪz **-ing** -ɪŋ **-ed** -d
disenfranchisement ˌdɪs.ɪn'fræn.tʃɪz.mənt, -en'-, -tʃaɪz- (US) -tʃaɪz-, -tʃɪz-
disengag|e ˌdɪs.ɪn'geɪdʒ, -ɪŋ'-, -en'-, -eŋ'- (US) -ɪn'-, -en'- **-es** -ɪz **-ing** -ɪŋ **-ed** -d
disengagement ˌdɪs.ɪn'geɪdʒ.mənt, -ɪŋ'-, -en'-, -eŋ'- (US) -ɪn'-, -en'-
disentail ˌdɪs.ɪn'teɪl, -en'-, -ᵊn'- **-s** -z **-ing** -ɪŋ **-ed** -d
disentangl|e ˌdɪs.ɪn'tæŋ.gl̩, -en'- **-es** -z **-ing** -ɪŋ, -'tæŋ.glɪŋ **-ed** -d
disentanglement ˌdɪs.ɪn'tæŋ.gl̩.mənt, -en'-
disequilibrium ˌdɪs.ek.wɪ'lɪb.ri.əm, -iː.kwɪ'-, -kwə'- (US) ˌdɪs.iː.kwɪ'-; dɪˌsek.wɪ'-
disestablish ˌdɪs.ɪ'stæb.lɪʃ, -es'tæb-, -ə'stæb- (US) -ɪ'stæb-, -es'tæb-, 'dɪs.ɪ.stæb-, -es.tæb- **-es** -ɪz **-ing** -ɪŋ **-ed** -t
disestablishment ˌdɪs.ɪ'stæb.lɪʃ.mənt, -es'tæb-, -ə'stæb- (US) -ɪ'stæb-, -es'tæb-
disestablishmentarian ˌdɪs.ɪˌstæb.lɪʃ.mən'teə.ri.ən, -esˌtæb-, -əˌstæb- (US) -ɪˌstæb.lɪʃ.mən'ter.i-, -esˌtæb-
disfavo(u)r dɪs'feɪ.vəʳ (US) -vɚ
disfiguration dɪsˌfɪg.ə'reɪ.ʃᵊn, ˌdɪs.fɪg-, -jʊ'- (US) dɪsˌfɪg.jə'- **-s** -z
disfig|ure dɪs'fɪg|.əʳ (US) -j|ɚ **-ures** -əz (US) -ɚz **-uring** -ᵊr.ɪŋ **-ured** -əd (US) -ɚd **-urement/s** -ə.mənt/s (US) -ɚ.mənt/s
disforest dɪs'fɒr.ɪst, -əst (US) -'fɔːr- **-s** -s **-ing** -ɪŋ **-ed** -ɪd
disfranchis|e dɪs'fræn.tʃaɪz **-es** -ɪz **-ing** -ɪŋ **-ed** -d
disfranchisement dɪs'fræn.tʃɪz.mənt, -tʃəz-, -tʃaɪz- (US) -tʃaɪz-, -tʃɪz-
disgorg|e dɪs'gɔːdʒ (US) -'gɔːrdʒ **-es** -ɪz **-ing** -ɪŋ **-ed** -d

disgrac|e dɪsˈɡreɪs, dɪz- (US) dɪs- **-es** -ɪz **-ing** -ɪŋ **-ed** -t
disgraceful dɪsˈɡreɪs.fᵊl, dɪz-, -fʊl (US) dɪs- **-ly** -i **-ness** -nəs, -nɪs
disgruntled dɪsˈɡrʌn.tl̩d (US) -t̬l̩d
disgruntlement dɪsˈɡrʌn.tl̩.mənt (US) -t̬l̩-
disguis|e dɪsˈɡaɪz, dɪz- (US) dɪs- **-es** -ɪz **-ing** -ɪŋ **-ed** -d **-er/s** -əʳ/z (US) -ɚ/z
disgust dɪsˈɡʌst, dɪz- (US) dɪs- **-s** -s **-ing** -ɪŋ **-ed/ly** -ɪd/li
disgusting dɪsˈɡʌs.tɪŋ, dɪz- (US) dɪs- **-ly** -li
dish dɪʃ **-es** -ɪz **-ing** -ɪŋ **-ed** -t
dishabille ˌdɪs.æbˈiːl, -əˈbiːl (US) -əˈ-
disharmony dɪsˈhɑː.mᵊn.i (US) -ˈhɑːr-
dish|cloth ˈdɪʃ|.klɒθ (US) -klɑːθ **-cloths** -klɒθs, -klɒðz (US) -klɑːθs, -klɑːðz
dishearten dɪsˈhɑː.tᵊn (US) -ˈhɑːr- **-s** -z **-ing/ly** -ɪŋ/li **-ed** -d
dishevel dɪˈʃev.ᵊl **-s** -z **-(l)ing** -ɪŋ **-(l)ed** -d
dishful ˈdɪʃ.fʊl **-s** -z
dishonest dɪˈsɒn.ɪst, -ˈzɒn-, -əst (US) -ˈsɑː.nɪst, -nəst **-ly** -li
dishonest|y dɪˈsɒn.ɪ.st|i, -ˈzɒn-, ˈ-ə- (US) -ˈsɑː.nə- **-ies** -iz
dishono(u)r dɪˈsɒn.əʳ, -ˈzɒn- (US) -ˈsɑː.nɚ **-s** -z **-ing** -ɪŋ **-ed** -d **-er/s** -əʳ/z (US) -ɚ/z
dishono(u)rab|le dɪˈsɒn.ᵊr.ə.b|l̩, -ˈzɒn- (US) -ˈsɑː.nɚ- **-ly** -li **-leness** -l̩.nəs, -nɪs
dishrag ˈdɪʃ.ræɡ **-s** -z
dishtowel ˈdɪʃ.taʊəl **-s** -z
dishwash|er ˈdɪʃˌwɒʃ|.əʳ (US) -ˌwɑː.ʃ|ɚ, -ˌwɔː- **-ers** -əz (US) -ɚz **-ing** -ɪŋ
dishwater ˈdɪʃˌwɔː.təʳ (US) -ˌwɑː.t̬ɚ, -ˌwɔː-
dish|y ˈdɪʃ|.i **-ier** -i.əʳ (US) -i.ɚ **-iest** -i.ɪst, -i.əst
disillusion ˌdɪs.ɪˈluː.ʒᵊn, -əˈ-, -ˈljuː- (US) -ˈluː- **-s** -z **-ing** -ɪŋ **-ed** -d **-ment/s** -mənt/s
disincentive ˌdɪs.ɪnˈsen.tɪv (US) -t̬ɪv **-s** -z
disinclination ˌdɪs.ɪn.klɪˈneɪ.ʃᵊn, -ɪŋ-, -kləˈ- (US) -ɪn-
disinclin|e ˌdɪs.ɪnˈklaɪn, -ɪŋˈ- (US) -ɪn- **-es** -z **-ing** -ɪŋ **-ed** -d
disinfect ˌdɪs.ɪnˈfekt **-s** -s **-ing** -ɪŋ **-ed** -ɪd
disinfectant ˌdɪs.ɪnˈfek.tᵊnt **-s** -s
disinfection ˌdɪs.ɪnˈfek.ʃᵊn **-s** -z
disinfestation ˌdɪs.ɪn.fesˈteɪ.ʃᵊn
disinflation ˌdɪs.ɪnˈfleɪ.ʃᵊn
disinformation ˌdɪs.ɪn.fəˈmeɪ.ʃᵊn, -fɔːˈ- (US) -fɚˈ-
disingenuous ˌdɪs.ɪnˈdʒen.ju.əs **-ly** -li **-ness** -nəs, -nɪs
disinher|it ˌdɪs.ɪnˈher|.ɪt **-its** -ɪts **-iting** -ɪ.tɪŋ (US) -ɪ.t̬ɪŋ **-ited** -ɪ.tɪd (US) -ɪ.t̬ɪd
disinheritance ˌdɪs.ɪnˈher.ɪ.tᵊnts (US) -t̬ᵊnts
disintegrable dɪˈsɪn.tɪ.ɡrə.bl̩, -tə- (US) -t̬ə-
disinte|grate dɪˈsɪn.tɪ|.ɡreɪt, -tə- (US) -t̬ə- **-grates** -ɡreɪts **-grating** -ɡreɪ.tɪŋ (US) -ɡreɪ.t̬ɪŋ **-grated** -ɡreɪ.tɪd (US) -ɡreɪ.t̬ɪd **-grator/s** -ɡreɪ.təʳ/z (US) -ɡreɪ.t̬ɚ/z
disintegration dɪˌsɪn.tɪˈɡreɪ.ʃᵊn, -təˈ-; ˌdɪs.ɪn- (US) ˌdɪs.ɪn.t̬əˈ- **-s** -z
disinter ˌdɪs.ɪnˈtɜːʳ (US) -ˈtɝː **-s** -z **-ring** -ɪŋ **-red** -d
disinterest dɪˈsɪn.trəst, -trest, -trɪst; ˈ-tᵊr.əst, -est, -ɪst (US) -ˈsɪn.trɪst, -trəst, -trest; ˈ-t̬ɚ.ɪst, -əst, -est
disinterested dɪˈsɪn.trə.stɪd, -tres.tɪd, -trɪ.stɪd; ˈ-tᵊr.ə.stɪd, -es.tɪd, -ɪ.stɪd (US) -ˈsɪn.trɪ.stɪd, -trə-, -tres.tɪd; ˈ-t̬ɚ.ɪ.stɪd, -ə-, -es.tɪd **-ly** -li **-ness** -nəs, -nɪs
disinterment ˌdɪs.ɪnˈtɜː.mənt (US) -ˈtɝː- **-s** -s
disinvest ˌdɪs.ɪnˈvest **-s** -s **-ing** -ɪŋ **-ed** -ɪd **-ment** -mənt
disjoin dɪsˈdʒɔɪn, dɪz- (US) dɪs- **-s** -z **-ing** -ɪŋ **-ed** -d
disjoint dɪsˈdʒɔɪnt, dɪz- (US) dɪs- **-s** -s **-ing** -ɪŋ **-ed** -ɪd
disjointed dɪsˈdʒɔɪn.tɪd, dɪz- (US) dɪsˈdʒɔɪn.t̬ɪd **-ly** -li **-ness** -nəs, -nɪs
disjunct dɪsˈdʒʌŋkt, ˈ--
disjunction dɪsˈdʒʌŋk.ʃᵊn **-s** -z
disjunctive dɪsˈdʒʌŋk.tɪv **-ly** -li
disk dɪsk **-s** -s ˈ**disk** ˌ**drive**
diskette dɪˈsket **-s** -s
dislik|e dɪˈslaɪk, dɪzˈlaɪk (US) dɪˈslaɪk **-es** -s **-ing** -ɪŋ **-ed** -t **-able** -ə.bl̩
Note: The stress /ˈ--/ is, however, used in the expression **likes and dislikes**.
dislo|cate ˈdɪs.ləʊ|.keɪt (US) dɪˈsloʊ-; ˈdɪs.loʊ- **-cates** -keɪts **-cating** -keɪ.tɪŋ (US) -keɪ.t̬ɪŋ **-cated** -keɪ.tɪd (US) -keɪ.t̬ɪd
dislocation ˌdɪs.ləʊˈkeɪ.ʃᵊn (US) -loʊˈ- **-s** -z
dislodg|e dɪˈslɒdʒ (US) -ˈslɑːdʒ **-es** -ɪz **-ing** -ɪŋ **-ed** -d **-(e)ment** -mənt
disloyal dɪˈslɔɪəl; ˌdɪsˈlɔɪəl **-ly** -i
disloyalt|y dɪˈslɔɪəl.t|i; ˌdɪsˈlɔɪəl- (US) -t̬|i **-ies** -iz
dismal ˈdɪz.məl **-ly** -i **-ness** -nəs, -nɪs
dismantl|e dɪˈsmæn.tl̩, dɪzˈmæn- (US) dɪˈsmæn.t̬l̩ **-es** -z **-ing** -ɪŋ, dɪˈsmænt.lɪŋ, dɪzˈmænt- (US) dɪˈsmæn.t̬l̩.ɪŋ, -ˈsmænt.lɪŋ **-ed** -d
dismast ˌdɪsˈmɑːst (US) -ˈmæst **-s** -s **-ing** -ɪŋ **-ed** -ɪd
dismay dɪˈsmeɪ, dɪzˈmeɪ **-s** -z **-ing** -ɪŋ **-ed** -d
dismemb|er dɪˈsmem.b|əʳ (US) -b|ɚ **-ers** -əz (US) -ɚz **-ering** -ᵊr.ɪŋ **-ered** -əd (US) -ɚd **-erment** -ə.mənt (US) -ɚ.mənt
dismiss dɪˈsmɪs **-es** -ɪz **-ing** -ɪŋ **-ed** -t
dismissal dɪˈsmɪs.ᵊl **-s** -z
dismissive dɪˈsmɪs.ɪv **-ly** -li **-ness** -nəs, -nɪs
dis|mount dɪˈs|maʊnt **-mounts** -maʊnts **-mounting** -maʊn.tɪŋ (US) -maʊn.t̬ɪŋ **-mounted** -maʊn.tɪd (US) -maʊn.t̬ɪd
Disney ˈdɪz.ni ˈ**Disney** ˌ**World®**
Disneyland® ˈdɪz.ni.lænd
disobedience ˌdɪs.əʊˈbiː.di.ənts (US) -əˈ-, -oʊˈ-
disobedient ˌdɪs.əʊˈbiː.di.ənt (US) -əˈ-, -oʊˈ- **-ly** -li
disobey ˌdɪs.əʊˈbeɪ (US) -əˈ-, -oʊˈ- **-s** -z **-ing** -ɪŋ **-ed** -d
disoblig|e ˌdɪs.əˈblaɪdʒ **-es** -ɪz **-ing/ly** -ɪŋ/li **-ingness** -ɪŋ.nəs, -nɪs **-ed** -d
disord|er dɪˈsɔː.d|əʳ, -ˈzɔː- (US) -ˈsɔːr.d|ɚ, -ˈzɔːr- **-ers** -əz (US) -ɚz **-ering** -ᵊr.ɪŋ **-ered** -əd (US) -ɚd
disorderl|y dɪˈsɔː.dᵊl|.i, -ˈzɔː- (US) -ˈsɔːr.dɚ.l|i, -ˈzɔːr- **-iness** -ɪ.nəs, -ɪ.nɪs
disorganization, -isa- dɪˌsɔː.ɡə.naɪˈzeɪ.ʃᵊn, -ˌzɔː-, -nɪˈ-; ˌdɪs.ɔː-, ˌdɪz- (US) dɪˌsɔːr.ɡə.nɪˈ-, -ˌzɔːr-
disorganiz|e, -is|e dɪˈsɔː.ɡə.naɪz, -ˈzɔː-; ˌdɪsˈɔː-, ˌdɪzˈɔː- (US) dɪˈsɔːr-, -ˈzɔːr- **-es** -ɪz **-ing** -ɪŋ **-ed** -d
disorien|t dɪˈsɔː.ri.ən|t, -en|t (US) -ˈsɔːr.i.en|t **-ts** -ts **-ting** -tɪŋ (US) -t̬ɪŋ **-ted** -tɪd (US) -t̬ɪd
disorien|tate dɪˈsɔː.ri.ən|.teɪt, -en-; ˌdɪsˈɔːr- (US) dɪˈsɔːr.i- **-tates** -teɪts **-tating** -teɪ.tɪŋ (US) -teɪ.t̬ɪŋ **-tated** -teɪ.tɪd (US) -teɪ.t̬ɪd
disorientation dɪˌsɔː.ri.ənˈteɪ.ʃᵊn, -enˈ-; ˌdɪsˌɔː- (US) dɪˌsɔːr.i-
disown dɪˈsəʊn; ˌdɪsˈəʊn (US) dɪˈsoʊn **-s** -z **-ing** -ɪŋ **-ed** -d
disparag|e dɪˈspær.ɪdʒ (US) -ˈsper-, -ˈspær- **-es** -ɪz **-ing/ly** -ɪŋ/li **-ed** -d **-er/s** -əʳ/z (US) -ɚ/z **-ement** -mənt
disparate ˈdɪs.pᵊr.ət, -ɪt, -eɪt (US) -ət, -ɪt; dɪˈsper-, -ˈspær- **-s** -s
disparit|y dɪˈspær.ə.t|i, -ɪ.t|i (US) -ˈper.ə.t̬|i, -ˈpær- **-ies** -iz
dispassionate dɪˈspæʃ.ᵊn.ət, -ɪt **-ly** -li **-ness** -nəs, -nɪs
dispatch (*n.*) dɪˈspætʃ, də-; ˈdɪs.pætʃ (US) dɪˈspætʃ; ˈdɪs.pætʃ **-es** -ɪz **disˈpatch** ˌ**box**; **disˈpatch** ˌ**rider**
dispatch (*v.*) dɪˈspætʃ, də- (US) dɪ- **-es** -ɪz **-ing** -ɪŋ **-ed** -t **-er/s** -əʳ/z (US) -ɚ/z
dispel dɪˈspel **-s** -z **-(l)ing** -ɪŋ **-(l)ed** -d
dispensable dɪˈspent.sə.bl̩
dispensar|y dɪˈspent.sᵊr|.i **-ies** -iz
dispensation ˌdɪs.penˈseɪ.ʃᵊn, -pənˈ- **-s** -z
dispensator|y dɪˈspen.sə.tᵊr|.i, -tr|i (US) -tɔːr|.i **-ies** -iz

dispens|e dɪ'spen*t*s **-es** -ɪz **-ing** -ɪŋ **-ed** -t **-er/s** -əʳ/z ⓤⓢ -ɚ/z
dispersal dɪ'spɜː.sᵊl ⓤⓢ -'spɝː- **-s** -z
dispers|e dɪ'spɜːs ⓤⓢ -spɝːs **-es** -ɪz **-ing** -ɪŋ **-ed** -t **-er/s** -əʳ/z ⓤⓢ -ɚ/z **-ant/s** -ᵊnt/s
dispersion (D) dɪ'spɜː.ʃᵊn ⓤⓢ -'spɝː.ʒᵊn, -ʃᵊn **-s** -z
dispersive dɪ'spɜː.sɪv ⓤⓢ -'spɝː.zɪv, -sɪv
dispir|it dɪ'spɪr|.ɪt **-its** -ɪts **-iting** -ɪ.tɪŋ ⓤⓢ -ɪ.t̬ɪŋ **-ited/ly** -ɪ.tɪd/li ⓤⓢ -ɪ.t̬ɪd/li **-itedness** -ɪ.tɪd.nəs, -nɪs ⓤⓢ -ɪ.t̬ɪd.nəs, -nɪs
displac|e dɪ'spleɪs **-es** -ɪz **-ing** -ɪŋ **-ed** -t
displacement dɪ'spleɪs.mənt
display dɪ'spleɪ **-s** -z **-ing** -ɪŋ **-ed** -d **-er/s** -əʳ/z ⓤⓢ -ɚ/z
displeas|e dɪ'spliːz **-es** -ɪz **-ing/ly** -ɪŋ/li **-ed** -d
displeasure dɪ'spleʒ.əʳ ⓤⓢ -ɚ
di|sport dɪ|'spɔːt ⓤⓢ -|'spɔːrt **-sports** -'spɔːts ⓤⓢ -'spɔːrts **-sporting** -'spɔː.tɪŋ ⓤⓢ -'spɔːr.t̬ɪŋ **-sported** -'spɔː.tɪd ⓤⓢ -'spɔːr.t̬ɪd
disposable dɪ'spəʊ.zə.bl̩, də- ⓤⓢ dɪ'spoʊ-
disposal dɪ'spəʊ.zᵊl, də- ⓤⓢ dɪ'spoʊ- **-s** -z
Disposall® dɪ'spəʊ.zɔːl, də- ⓤⓢ dɪ'spoʊ.zɑːl, -zɔːl
dispos|e dɪ'spəʊz, də- ⓤⓢ -'spoʊz **-es** -ɪz **-ing** -ɪŋ **-ed** -d **-er/s** -əʳ/z ⓤⓢ -ɚ/z
disposition ˌdɪs.pə'zɪʃ.ᵊn **-s** -z
dispossess ˌdɪs.pə'zes **-es** -ɪz **-ing** -ɪŋ **-ed** -t
dispossession ˌdɪs.pə'zeʃ.ᵊn
Disprin® 'dɪs.prɪn **-s** -z
disproof dɪ'spruːf
disproportion ˌdɪs.prə'pɔː.ʃᵊn ⓤⓢ -'pɔːr- **-ed** -d
disproportional ˌdɪs.prə'pɔː.ʃᵊn.ᵊl, -'pɔːʃ.nᵊl ⓤⓢ -'pɔːr.ʃᵊn.ᵊl, -'pɔːrʃ.nᵊl **-ly** -i
disproportionate ˌdɪs.prə'pɔː.ʃᵊn.ət, -ɪt ⓤⓢ -'pɔːr- **-ly** -li **-ness** -nəs, -nɪs
disproval dɪ'spruː.vᵊl; ˌdɪs'pruː-
disprov|e dɪ'spruːv; ˌdɪs'pruːv **-es** -z **-ing** -ɪŋ **-ed** -d
disputable dɪ'spjuː.tə.bl̩, də-; 'dɪs.pjʊ- ⓤⓢ dɪ'spjuː.t̬ə-; 'dɪs.pjʊ-, -pjə-
disputableness dɪ'spjuː.tə.bl̩.nəs, də-, -nɪs ⓤⓢ dɪ'spjuː.t̬ə-
disputant dɪ'spjuː.tᵊnt; 'dɪs.pjʊ- ⓤⓢ 'dɪs.pjʊ.tᵊnt, -pjə-; dɪ'spjuː- **-s** -s
disputation ˌdɪs.pjʊ'teɪ.ʃᵊn ⓤⓢ -pjuː'- **-s** -z
disputatious ˌdɪs.pjʊ'teɪ.ʃəs ⓤⓢ -pjuː'- **-ly** -li **-ness** -nəs, -nɪs
disputative dɪ'spjuː.tə.tɪv ⓤⓢ -t̬ə.t̬ɪv
dispute (*n.*) dɪ'spjuːt; 'dɪs.pjuːt ⓤⓢ dɪ'spjuːt **-s** -s
di|spute (*v.*) dɪ|'spjuːt **-sputes** -'spjuːts **-sputing** -'spjuː.tɪŋ ⓤⓢ -'spjuː.t̬ɪŋ **-sputed** -'spjuː.tɪd ⓤⓢ -'spjuː.t̬ɪd **-sputer/s** -'spjuː.təʳ/z ⓤⓢ -'spjuː.t̬ɚ/z
disqualification dɪˌskwɒl.ɪ.fɪ'keɪ.ʃᵊn, ˌ-ə-; ˌdɪsˌkwɒl- ⓤⓢ dɪˌskwɑː.lə- **-s** -z
disquali|fy dɪ'skwɒl.ɪ|.faɪ, '-ə-; ˌdɪs'kwɒl- ⓤⓢ dɪ'skwɑː.lə- **-fies** -faɪz **-fying** -faɪ.ɪŋ **-fied** -faɪd
di|squiet (*n. v.*) dɪ|'skwaɪət **-squiets** -'skwaɪəts **-squieting** -'skwaɪə.tɪŋ ⓤⓢ -'skwaɪə.t̬ɪŋ **-squieted** -'skwaɪə.tɪd ⓤⓢ -'skwaɪə.t̬ɪd
disquietude dɪ'skwaɪə.tjuːd, -'skwaɪ.ɪ- ⓤⓢ -'skwaɪə.tuːd, -tjuːd
disquisition ˌdɪs.kwɪ'zɪʃ.ᵊn, -kwə'- **-s** -z
disquisitional ˌdɪs.kwɪ'zɪʃ.ᵊn.ᵊl, -kwə'-, '-nᵊl
disquisitive dɪ'skwɪz.ə.tɪv, -ɪ.tɪv ⓤⓢ -ə.t̬ɪv
Disraeli dɪz'reɪ.li, dɪs-
d'Israeli dɪz'reɪ.li, dɪs-
disregard ˌdɪs.rɪ'gɑːd, -rə'- ⓤⓢ -rɪ'gɑːrd **-s** -z **-ing** -ɪŋ **-ed** -ɪd
disregardful ˌdɪs.rɪ'gɑːd.fᵊl, -rə'-, -fʊl ⓤⓢ -rɪ'gɑːrd- **-ly** -i
disrepair ˌdɪs.rɪ'peəʳ, -rə'- ⓤⓢ -rɪ'per
disreputability dɪsˌrep.jə.tə'bɪl.ə.ti, -jʊ-, -ɪ.ti ⓤⓢ -jə.t̬ə'-
disreputab|le dɪs'rep.jə.tə.b|l̩, -jʊ- ⓤⓢ -jə.t̬ə- **-ly** -li **-leness** -l̩.nəs, -nɪs
disrepute ˌdɪs.rɪ'pjuːt, -rə'- ⓤⓢ -rɪ'-
disrespect ˌdɪs.rɪ'spekt, -rə'- ⓤⓢ -rɪ'-
disrespectful ˌdɪs.rɪ'spekt.fᵊl, -rə'-, -fʊl ⓤⓢ -rɪ'- **-ly** -i **-ness** -nəs, -nɪs
disrob|e dɪs'rəʊb ⓤⓢ -'roʊb **-es** -z **-ing** -ɪŋ **-ed** -d
disrupt dɪs'rʌpt **-s** -s **-ing** -ɪŋ **-ed** -ɪd
disruption dɪs'rʌp.ʃᵊn **-s** -z
disruptive dɪs'rʌp.tɪv **-ly** -li **-ness** -nəs, -nɪs
Diss dɪs
dis(s) dɪs **-es** -ɪz **-ing** -ɪŋ **-ed** -t
dissatisfaction dɪsˌsæt.ɪs'fæk.ʃᵊn, ˌdɪs.sæt-, -əs'- ⓤⓢ ˌdɪs.sæt̬.əs'-
dissatisfactor|y dɪsˌsæt.ɪs'fæk.tᵊr|.i, ˌdɪs.sæt-, -əs'- ⓤⓢ ˌdɪs.sæt̬.əs'- **-ily** -ᵊl.i, -ɪ.li **-iness** -i.nəs, -i.nɪs
dissatis|fy dɪs'sæt.ɪs|.faɪ, ˌdɪs-, -əs- ⓤⓢ -'sæt̬.əs- **-fies** -faɪz **-fying** -faɪ.ɪŋ **-fied** -faɪd
dissect dɪ'sekt, də-, daɪ- ⓤⓢ dɪ'sekt, daɪ-; 'daɪ.sekt **-s** -s **-ing** -ɪŋ **-ed** -ɪd **-or/s** -əʳ/z ⓤⓢ -ɚ/z **-ible** -ə.bl̩, -ɪ.bl̩
dissection dɪ'sek.ʃᵊn, də-, daɪ- ⓤⓢ dɪ'sek-, daɪ-; 'daɪ.sek- **-s** -z
dissemblanc|e dɪ'sem.blən*t*s **-es** -ɪz
dissembl|e dɪ'sem.bl̩ **-es** -z **-ing** -ɪŋ, '-blɪŋ **-ed** -d **-er/s** -əʳ/z, '-bləʳ/z ⓤⓢ -ə/z
dissemi|nate dɪ'sem.ɪ|.neɪt, '-ə- **-nates** -neɪts **-nating** -neɪ.tɪŋ ⓤⓢ -neɪ.t̬ɪŋ **-nated** -neɪ.tɪd ⓤⓢ -neɪ.t̬ɪd **-nator/s** -neɪ.təʳ/z ⓤⓢ -neɪ.t̬ɚ/z
dissemination dɪˌsem.ɪ'neɪ.ʃᵊn, -ə'-
dissension, dissention dɪ'sen.*t*ʃᵊn **-s** -z
dis|sent dɪ|'sent **-sents** -'sents **-senting** -'sen.tɪŋ ⓤⓢ -'sen.t̬ɪŋ **-sented** -'sen.tɪd ⓤⓢ -'sen.t̬ɪd **-senter/s** -'sen.təʳ/z ⓤⓢ -'sen.t̬ɚ/z
dissentient dɪ'sen.*t*ʃi.ənt, -*t*ʃᵊnt ⓤⓢ -'sen*t*.ʃᵊnt **-s** -s
dissertation ˌdɪs.ə'teɪ.ʃᵊn, -ɜː'- ⓤⓢ -ɚ'- **-s** -z
dissservic|e ˌdɪs'sɜː.vɪs, dɪ- ⓤⓢ -'sɝː- **-es** -ɪz
dissev|er dɪs'sev|.əʳ ⓤⓢ -ɚ **-ers** -əz ⓤⓢ -ɚz **-ering** -ᵊr.ɪŋ **-ered** -əd ⓤⓢ -ɚd **-erment** -ə.mənt ⓤⓢ -ɚ.mənt **-erance** -ᵊr.ᵊn*t*s
dissidence 'dɪs.ɪ.dᵊn*t*s, '-ə-
dissident 'dɪs.ɪ.dᵊnt, '-ə- **-s** -s
dissimilar ˌdɪs'sɪm.ɪ.ləʳ, dɪ-, '-ə- ⓤⓢ -lɚ **-ly** -li
dissimilarit|y ˌdɪsˌsɪm.ɪ'lær.ə.t|i, dɪ-, -ə'-, -ɪ.t|i ⓤⓢ -'ler.ə.t̬|i, -'lær- **-ies** -iz
dissimi|late dɪ'sɪm.ɪ|.leɪt, ˌdɪs-, '-ə- **-lates** -leɪts **-lating** -leɪ.tɪŋ ⓤⓢ -leɪ.t̬ɪŋ **-lated** -leɪ.tɪd ⓤⓢ -leɪ.t̬ɪd
dissimilation ˌdɪsˌsɪm.ɪ'leɪ.ʃᵊn, dɪ-, -ə'- **-s** -z
dissimilitude ˌdɪs.sɪ'mɪl.ɪ.tjuːd, -ɪ'-, '-ə- ⓤⓢ -tuːd, -tjuːd
dissimu|late dɪ'sɪm.jə|.leɪt, ˌdɪs-, -jʊ- **-lates** -leɪts **-lating** -leɪ.tɪŋ ⓤⓢ -leɪ.t̬ɪŋ **-lated** -leɪ.tɪd ⓤⓢ -leɪ.t̬ɪd **-lator/s** -leɪ.təʳ/z ⓤⓢ -leɪ.t̬ɚ/z
dissimulation ˌdɪsˌsɪm.jə'leɪ.ʃᵊn, dɪ-, -jʊ'- **-s** -z
dissi|pate 'dɪs.ɪ|.peɪt, '-ə- **-pates** -peɪts **-pating** -peɪ.tɪŋ ⓤⓢ -peɪ.t̬ɪŋ **-pated** -peɪ.tɪd ⓤⓢ -peɪ.t̬ɪd **-pative** -peɪ.tɪv ⓤⓢ -peɪ.t̬ɪv
dissipation ˌdɪs.ɪ'peɪ.ʃᵊn, -ə'- **-s** -z
dissociable *separable:* dɪ'səʊ.ʃi.ə.bl̩, ˌdɪs- ⓤⓢ -'soʊ-, -ʃə.bl̩ *unsociable:* ˌdɪs'səʊ.ʃə.bl̩, dɪ- ⓤⓢ -'soʊ-
dissoci|ate dɪ'səʊ.ʃi|.eɪt, -si- ⓤⓢ -'soʊ- **-ates** -eɪts **-ating** -eɪ.tɪŋ ⓤⓢ -eɪ.t̬ɪŋ **-ated** -eɪ.tɪd ⓤⓢ -eɪ.t̬ɪd
dissociation dɪˌsəʊ.ʃi'eɪ.ʃᵊn, ˌdɪs-, -s- ⓤⓢ -ˌsoʊ-
dissolubility dɪˌsɒl.jə'bɪl.ə.ti, -jʊ'-, -ɪ.ti ⓤⓢ -ˌsɑːl.jə'bɪl.ə.t̬i, -jʊ'-
dissolub|le dɪ'sɒl.jə.b|l̩, -jʊ- ⓤⓢ -'sɑːl- **-ly** -li **-leness** -l̩.nəs, -nɪs
dissolute 'dɪs.ə.luːt, -ljuːt ⓤⓢ -luːt **-ly** -li **-ness** -nəs, -nɪs
dissolution ˌdɪs.ə'luː.ʃᵊn, -'ljuː- ⓤⓢ -'luː- **-s** -z
dissolvability dɪˌzɒl.və'bɪl.ə.ti,

dəˌzɒl-, -ˌsɒl-, -ɪ.ti
(US) dɪˌzɑːl.vəˈbɪl.ə.t̬i, -ˌzɔːl-
dissolv|e dɪˈzɒlv, -ˈsɒlv (US) -ˈzɑːlv, -ˈzɔːlv **-es** -z **-ing** -ɪŋ **-ed** -d **-able** -ə.bl̩
dissolvent dɪˈzɒl.vənt, -ˈsɒl- (US) -ˈzɑːl-, -ˈzɔːl- **-s** -s
dissonanc|e ˈdɪs.ən.ənts **-es** -ɪz
dissonant ˈdɪs.ən.ənt **-ly** -li
dissuad|e dɪˈsweɪd **-es** -z **-ing** -ɪŋ **-ed** -ɪd
dissuasion dɪˈsweɪ.ʒən
dissuasive dɪˈsweɪ.sɪv, -zɪv (US) -sɪv **-ly** -li **-ness** -nəs, -nɪs
dissymmetric ˌdɪs.ɪˈmet.rɪk, -sɪmˈ-
dissymmetry dɪˈsɪm.ɪ.tri, ˌdɪs-, ˈ-ə-
distaff ˈdɪs.tɑːf (US) -tæf **-s** -s
distanc|e ˈdɪs.tənts **-es** -ɪz **-ing** -ɪŋ **-ed** -t
distant ˈdɪs.tənt **-ly** -li
distaste dɪˈsteɪst **-s** -s
distasteful dɪˈsteɪst.fəl, -fʊl **-ly** -i **-ness** -nəs, -nɪs
distemp|er dɪˈstem.p|əʳ (US) -p|ɚ **-ers** -əz (US) -ɚz **-ering** -ər.ɪŋ **-ered** -əd (US) -ɚd
distend dɪˈstend **-s** -z **-ing** -ɪŋ **-ed** -ɪd
distensible dɪˈstent.sə.bl̩, -sɪ-
distension dɪˈsten.tʃən (US) -ˈstent.ʃən
distich ˈdɪs.tɪk **-s** -s **-ous** -əs
distil(l) dɪˈstɪl, də- (US) dɪ- **-s** -z **-ing** -ɪŋ **-ed** -d
distillate ˈdɪs.tɪ.lət, -təl.ət, -eɪt, -ɪt (US) -tə.leɪt, -təl.ɪt; dɪˈstɪl.ɪt **-s** -s
distillation ˌdɪs.tɪˈleɪ.ʃən, -təˈ- **-s** -z
distillatory dɪˈstɪl.ə.tər.i, də-, -tri (US) dɪˈstɪl.ə.tɔːr.i
distiller dɪˈstɪl.əʳ, də- (US) dɪˈstɪl.ɚ **-s** -z
distiller|y dɪˈstɪl.ər|.i, də- (US) dɪ- **-ies** -iz
distinct dɪˈstɪŋkt, də- (US) dɪ- **-est** -ɪst, -əst **-ly** -li **-ness** -nəs, -nɪs
distinction dɪˈstɪŋk.ʃən, də- (US) dɪ- **-s** -z
distinctive dɪˈstɪŋk.tɪv, də- (US) dɪ- **-ly** -li **-ness** -nəs, -nɪs
distinguish dɪˈstɪŋ.gwɪʃ, də- (US) dɪ- **-es** -ɪz **-ing** -ɪŋ **-ed** -t
distinguishab|le dɪˈstɪŋ.gwɪ.ʃə.b|l̩, də- (US) dɪ- **-ly** -li
di|stort dɪ|ˈstɔːt (US) -ˈstɔːrt **-storts** -ˈstɔːts (US) -ˈstɔːrts **-storting** -ˈstɔː.tɪŋ (US) -ˈstɔːr.t̬ɪŋ **-storted** -ˈstɔː.tɪd (US) -ˈstɔːr.t̬ɪd
distortion dɪˈstɔː.ʃən (US) -ˈstɔːr- **-s** -z
distract dɪˈstrækt, dəˈstrækt (US) dɪ- **-s** -s **-ing** -ɪŋ **-ed/ly** -ɪd/li **-edness** -ɪd.nəs, -nɪs
distraction dɪˈstræk.ʃən, də- **-s** -z
distrain dɪˈstreɪn, də- (US) dɪ- **-s** -z **-ing** -ɪŋ **-ed** -d **-er/s** -əʳ/z (US) -ɚ/z **-able** -ə.bl̩
distrainee ˌdɪs.treɪˈniː **-s** -z
distrainor ˌdɪs.treɪˈnɔːʳ (US) -ˈnɔːr, dɪˈstreɪ.nɚ **-s** -z
distraint dɪˈstreɪnt **-s** -s
distrait dɪˈstreɪ; ˈdɪs.treɪ (US) dɪˈstreɪ
distraught dɪˈstrɔːt (US) -ˈstrɑːt, -ˈstrɔːt
distress dɪˈstres **-es** -ɪz **-ing/ly** -ɪŋ/li **-ed** -t
distressful dɪˈstres.fəl, -fʊl **-ly** -i
distributable dɪˈstrɪb.jə.tə.bl̩, -jʊ- (US) -t̬ə-
distribu|te dɪˈstrɪb.juː|t; ˈdɪs.trɪ.bjuː|t, -trə- (US) dɪˈstrɪb.juː|t, -jʊ|t, -jə|t **-tes** -ts **-ting** -tɪŋ (US) -t̬ɪŋ **-ted** -tɪd (US) -t̬ɪd
distribution ˌdɪs.trɪˈbjuː.ʃən, -trəˈ- **-s** -z
distributive dɪˈstrɪb.jə.tɪv, -jʊ- (US) -jə.t̬ɪv **-ly** -li
distributor dɪˈstrɪb.jə.təʳ, -jʊ- (US) -t̬ɚ **-s** -z
district ˈdɪs.trɪkt **-s** -s ˌ**district atˈtorney; ˌDistrict of Coˈlumbia**
distrust dɪˈstrʌst; ˌdɪsˈtrʌst **-s** -s **-ing** -ɪŋ **-ed** -ɪd
distrustful dɪˈstrʌst.fəl, -fʊl; ˌdɪsˈtrʌst- **-ly** -i **-ness** -nəs, -nɪs
disturb dɪˈstɜːb (US) -ˈstɝːb **-s** -z **-ing/ly** -ɪŋ/li **-ed** -d **-er/s** -əʳ/z (US) -ɚ/z
disturbanc|e dɪˈstɜː.bənts (US) -ˈstɝː- **-es** -ɪz
distyle ˈdɪs.taɪl; ˈdaɪ.staɪl **-s** -z
disulphate daɪˈsʌl.feɪt, -fɪt **-s** -s
disulphide daɪˈsʌl.faɪd **-s** -z
disunion dɪˈsjuː.njən, -ni.ən (US) ˈ-njən **-s** -z
disu|nite ˌdɪs.juː|ˈnaɪt **-nites** -ˈnaɪts **-niting** -ˈnaɪ.tɪŋ (US) -ˈnaɪ.t̬ɪŋ **-nited** -ˈnaɪ.tɪd (US) -ˈnaɪ.t̬ɪd
disunity dɪˈsjuː.nɪ.ti, -nə- (US) -t̬i
disuse (*n.*) dɪˈsjuːs
disus|e (*v.*) dɪˈsjuːz **-es** -ɪz **-ing** -ɪŋ **-ed** -d
disyllabic ˌdaɪ.sɪˈlæb.ɪk, ˌdɪs.ɪˈ-, -əˈ-
disyllable daɪˈsɪl.ə.bl̩, dɪ- **-s** -z
ditch dɪtʃ **-es** -ɪz **-ing** -ɪŋ **-ed** -t **-er/s** -əʳ/z (US) -ɚ/z
Ditchling ˈdɪtʃ.lɪŋ
ditchwater ˈdɪtʃˌwɔː.təʳ (US) -ˌwɑː.t̬ɚ, -ˌwɔː- **as ˌdull as ˈditch-water**
dith|er ˈdɪð|.əʳ (US) -ɚ **-ers** -əz (US) -ɚz **-ering** -ər.ɪŋ **-ered** -əd (US) -ɚd **-erer/s** -ər.əʳ/z (US) -ɚ.ɚ/z **-ery** -ər.i
dithyramb ˈdɪθ.ɪ.ræmb, ˈ-ə- **-s** -z
Note: The /b/ is rarely pronounced.
dithyramb|us ˌdɪθ.ɪˈræm.b|əs, -əˈ- **-i** -aɪ **-ic/s** -ɪk/s
ditransitive ˌdaɪˈtræn.sɪ.tɪv, -ˈtrɑːn-, -sə- (US) -ˈtræn.sə.t̬ɪv **-s** -z **-ly** -li
dits|y ˈdɪt.s|i **-ier** -i.əʳ (US) -i.ɚ **-iest** -i.ɪst, -i.əst
ditto ˈdɪt.əʊ (US) ˈdɪt̬.oʊ **-s** -z
Ditton ˈdɪt.ən
ditt|y ˈdɪt|.i (US) ˈdɪt̬- **-ies** -iz
diures|is ˌdaɪ.jʊəˈriː.s|ɪs, -jəˈ- (US) -jəˈ-, -əˈ-, -jʊrˈ- **-es** -iːz
diuretic ˌdaɪ.jʊəˈret.ɪk, -jəˈ- (US) -jəˈret̬-, -əˈ- **-s** -s
diurnal ˌdaɪˈɜː.nəl (US) -ˈɝː- **-s** -z **-ly** -i
diva ˈdiː.və **-s** -z
diva|gate ˈdaɪ.və|.geɪt; -veɪ-; ˈdɪv.ə- (US) ˈdaɪ.və-, ˈdɪv.ə- **-gates** -geɪts **-gating** -geɪ.tɪŋ (US) -geɪ.t̬ɪŋ **-gated** -geɪ.tɪd (US) -geɪ.t̬ɪd
divagation ˌdaɪ.vəˈgeɪ.ʃən, -veɪˈ- (US) ˌdaɪ.vəˈ-, ˌdɪv.əˈ- **-s** -z
divalent ˌdaɪˈveɪ.lənt, ˈdaɪ.veɪ-
Divali dɪˈvɑː.li
divan dɪˈvæn, də-, daɪ-; ˈdaɪ.væn (US) dɪˈvæn, daɪ-; ˈdaɪ.væn **-s** -z
div|e daɪv **-es** -z **-ing** -ɪŋ **-ed** -d **dove** dəʊv (US) doʊv ˈ**diving ˌbell**; ˈ**diving ˌboard**; ˈ**diving ˌsuit**
dive-bomb ˈdaɪv.bɒm (US) -bɑːm **-s** -z **-ing** -ɪŋ **-ed** -d **-er/s** -əʳ/z (US) -ɚ/z
diver **(D)** ˈdaɪ.vəʳ (US) -vɚ **-s** -z
diverg|e daɪˈvɜːdʒ, dɪ- (US) dɪˈvɝːdʒ, daɪ- **-es** -ɪz **-ing** -ɪŋ **-ed** -d
divergenc|e daɪˈvɜː.dʒənts, dɪ- (US) dɪˈvɝː-, daɪ- **-es** -ɪz **-y** -i **-ies** -iz
divergent daɪˈvɜː.dʒənt, dɪ- (US) dɪˈvɝː-, daɪ- **-ly** -li
divers ˈdaɪ.vəz, -vɜːz, -vɜːs; daɪˈvɜːs (US) ˈdaɪ.vɚz
diverse daɪˈvɜːs, ˈ-- (US) dɪˈvɝːs, daɪ-; ˈdaɪ.vɝːs **-ly** -li
diversification daɪˌvɜː.sɪ.fɪˈkeɪ.ʃən, dɪ-, də-, -sə- (US) dɪˌvɝː-, daɪ- **-s** -z
diversi|fy daɪˈvɜː.sɪ|.faɪ, dɪ- (US) dɪˈvɝː-, daɪ- **-fies** -faɪz **-fying** -faɪ.ɪŋ **-fied** -faɪd
diversion daɪˈvɜː.ʃən, dɪ-, -ʒən (US) dɪˈvɝː-, daɪ- **-s** -z
diversionary daɪˈvɜː.ʃən.ər.i, dɪ-, -ʒən- (US) dɪˈvɝː.ʒən.er.i, daɪ-, -ʃən-
diversionist daɪˈvɜː.ʃən.ɪst, dɪ-, -ʒən- (US) dɪˈvɝː-, daɪ- **-s** -s
diversit|y daɪˈvɜː.sə.t|i, dɪ-, -ɪ.t|i (US) dɪˈvɝː.sə.t̬|i, daɪ- **-ies** -iz
di|vert daɪ|ˈvɜːt, dɪ- (US) dɪ|ˈvɝːt, daɪ- **-verts** -ˈvɜːts (US) -ˈvɝːts **-verting/ly** -ˈvɜː.tɪŋ/li (US) -ˈvɝː.t̬ɪŋ/li **-verted** -ˈvɜː.tɪd (US) -ˈvɝː.t̬ɪd
diverticulitis ˌdaɪ.vəˌtɪk.jʊˈlaɪ.tɪs, -vɜːˌ-, -jəˈ- (US) -vɚˌtɪk.jəˈlaɪ.t̬ɪs, -jʊˈ-
diverticulosis ˌdaɪ.vəˌtɪk.jʊˈləʊ.sɪs, -vɜːˌ-, -jəˈ- (US) -vɚˌtɪk.jəˈloʊ-, -jʊˈ-
diverticulum ˌdaɪ.vəˈtɪk.jʊ.ləm, -vɜːˈ-, -jə- (US) -vɚˈtɪk.jə-, -jʊ-
divertimento dɪˌvɜː.tɪˈmen.təʊ, -ˌveə-, -təˈ- (US) -ˌvɝː.t̬əˈmen.toʊ
divertissement ˌdiː.veəˈtiːs.mɑ̃ːŋ, -vəˈ-, -vɜːˈ-, dɪˈvɜː.tɪs.mənt (US) ˌdɪv.erˈtiːs.mɑ̃
Dives *in Bible:* ˈdaɪ.viːz *surname:* daɪvz
divest daɪˈvest, dɪ- (US) dɪ-, daɪ- **-s** -s **-ing** -ɪŋ **-ed** -ɪd
divestiture daɪˈves.tɪ.tʃəʳ, dɪ- (US) dɪˈves.tɪ.tʃɚ, daɪ-

divestment daɪ'vest.mənt, dɪ- ⓤⓢ dɪ-, daɪ- **-s** -s
divid|e dɪ'vaɪd, də- **-es** -z **-ing** -ɪŋ **-ed/ly** -ɪd/li **-able** -ə.bl̩
dividend 'dɪv.ɪ.dend, '-ə-, -dənd **-s** -z
divider dɪ'vaɪ.dəʳ, də- ⓤⓢ -dɚ **-s** -z
divination ˌdɪv.ɪ'neɪ.ʃən, -ə'- **-s** -z
divin|e (*n. adj.*) dɪ'vaɪn, də- **-es** -z **-er** -əʳ ⓤⓢ -ɚ **-est** -ɪst, -əst **-ely** -li **-eness** -nəs, -nɪs **diˌvine 'right**
divin|e (*v.*) dɪ'vaɪn, də- **-es** -z **-ing** -ɪŋ **-ed** -d **-er/s** -əʳ/z ⓤⓢ -ɚ/z **di'vining ˌrod**
divinit|y dɪ'vɪn.ə.t|i, də-, -ɪ.t|i ⓤⓢ -ə.t̬|i **-ies** -iz
divisibility dɪˌvɪz.ɪ'bɪl.ə.ti, də-, -ə'-, -ɪ.ti ⓤⓢ -ə'bɪl.ə.t̬i
divisib|le dɪ'vɪz.ə.b|l̩, də-, '-ɪ- **-ly** -li
division dɪ'vɪʒ.ən, də- **-s** -z
divisional dɪ'vɪʒ.ən.əl, də-, '-nəl
divisive dɪ'vaɪ.sɪv, də- **-ly** -li **-ness** -nəs, -nɪs
divisor dɪ'vaɪ.zəʳ, də- ⓤⓢ -zɚ **-s** -z
divorc|e dɪ'vɔːs, də- ⓤⓢ -'vɔːrs **-es** -ɪz **-ing** -ɪŋ **-ed** -t **-er/s** -əʳ/z ⓤⓢ -ɚ/z
divorcé(e), divorcee dɪˌvɔː'siː, də-, -'seɪ; ˌdɪv.ɔː'- ⓤⓢ dɪˌvɔːr'seɪ, də-, -'siː; -'vɔːr.seɪ, -siː **-s** -z
divot 'dɪv.ət **-s** -s
divulg|e daɪ'vʌldʒ, dɪ- ⓤⓢ dɪ-, daɪ- **-es** -ɪz **-ing** -ɪŋ **-ed** -d
divulsion daɪ'vʌl.ʃən, dɪ- ⓤⓢ dɪ-, daɪ- **-s** -z
divv|y 'dɪv|.i **-ies** -iz **-ying** -i.ɪŋ **-ied** -id
divvy-up ˌdɪv.i'ʌp
Diwali dɪ'wɑː.li
Dix dɪks
Dixey, Dixie 'dɪk.si
dixieland (D) 'dɪk.si.lænd
Dixon 'dɪk.sən
Dixwell 'dɪk.swəl, -swel
DIY ˌdiː.aɪ'waɪ
dizz|y 'dɪz|.i **-ier** -i.əʳ ⓤⓢ -i.ɚ **-iest** -i.ɪst, -i.əst **-ily** -ɪ.li, -əl.i **-iness** -ɪ.nəs, -ɪ.nɪs **-ies** -iz **-ying/ly** -i.ɪŋ **-ied** -id
DJ ˌdiː'dʒeɪ ⓤⓢ '-- **-s** -z *stress shift, British only:* ˌDJ 'culture
Djakarta dʒə'kɑː.tə ⓤⓢ -'kɑːr.t̬ə
Django 'dʒæŋ.gəʊ ⓤⓢ -goʊ
djellaba(h) dʒə'lɑː.bə **-s** -z
Djibouti dʒɪ'buː.ti, dʒə- ⓤⓢ -t̬i
djinn dʒɪn **-s** -z
djinni dʒɪ'ni, 'dʒɪn.i
Djukanovic dʒʊ'kæn.ə.vɪtʃ ⓤⓢ -'kɑːn-, dʒuː-, -oʊ-
dl (*abbrev. for* **decilitres/s, deciliter/s**) *singular:* 'des.ɪˌliː.təʳ ⓤⓢ -t̬ɚ *plural:* -z
DLit(t) ˌdiː'lɪt
dm (*abbrev. for* **decimetre/s, decimeter/s**) *singular:* 'des.ɪˌmiː.təʳ ⓤⓢ -t̬ɚ *plural:* -z
D-mark 'dɔɪtʃ.mɑːk ⓤⓢ -mɑːrk **-s** -s

DNA ˌdiː.en'eɪ
Dnepropetrovsk ˌ*d*njep.rɒp.jet'rɒfsk ⓤⓢ ˌnep.roʊ.pə'trɔːfsk, ˌdjnep-, -pjə'-
Dnieper '*d*niː.pəʳ ⓤⓢ -pɚ
D-notic|e 'diːˌnəʊ.tɪs ⓤⓢ -ˌnoʊ.t̬ɪs **-es** -ɪz
do (*v.*) *strong form:* duː *weak forms:* də, du *strong form:* **dost** dʌst *weak form:* dəst *strong form:* **doth** dʌθ *weak form:* dəθ **doeth** 'duː.ɪθ *strong form:* **does** dʌz *weak form:* dəz **doing** 'duː.ɪŋ **did** dɪd **done** dʌn **doer/s** 'duː.əʳ/z ⓤⓢ -ɚ/z

Note: Weak form word. The strong form /duː/ is normally used in final position (e.g. "Yes, I do"), when it is used as a full verb rather than as an auxilliary (e.g. "Do it yourself"), for emphasis (e.g. "Why **do** you like him?") or for contrast (e.g. "I do and I don't"). There are two weak forms: /də/ before consonants (e.g. "How do they do it" /ˌhaʊ.də.ðeɪ'duː.ɪt/) and /du/ before vowels (e.g. "Why do all the books disappear?" /ˌwaɪ.duˌɔːl.ðə'bʊks.dɪs.ə.pɪəʳ ⓤⓢ -pɪɚ/).

do (*n.*) *entertainment:* duː **-s** -z
do (*n.*) *musical note:* dəʊ ⓤⓢ doʊ **-s** -z
do. (*abbrev. for* **ditto**) 'dɪt.əʊ ⓤⓢ 'dɪt̬.oʊ
DOA ˌdiː.əʊ'eɪ ⓤⓢ -oʊ'-
doable 'duː.ə.bl̩
Doane dəʊn ⓤⓢ doʊn
dob dɒb ⓤⓢ dɑːb **-s** -z **-bing** -ɪŋ **-bed** -d **-ber/s** -əʳ/z ⓤⓢ -ɚ/z
Dobb dɒb ⓤⓢ dɑːb **-s** -z
dobbin (D) 'dɒb.ɪn ⓤⓢ 'dɑː.bɪn **-s** -z
Dobell dəʊ'bel, 'dəʊ.bəl ⓤⓢ 'doʊ.bəl, -bel
doberman (D) 'dəʊ.bə.mən ⓤⓢ 'doʊ.bɚ- **-s** -z
Doberman pinscher ˌdəʊ.bə.mən'pɪn.*t*ʃəʳ ⓤⓢ ˌdoʊ.bɚ.mən'pɪn*t*.ʃɚ
Dobie 'dəʊ.bi ⓤⓢ 'doʊ-
dobra 'dəʊ.brə ⓤⓢ 'doʊ- **-s** -z
Dobrée 'dəʊ.breɪ ⓤⓢ 'doʊ-
Dobson 'dɒb.sən ⓤⓢ 'dɑːb-
doc dɒk ⓤⓢ dɑːk **-s** -s
docent 'dəʊ.sənt, dəʊ'sent ⓤⓢ 'doʊ.sənt, -sent; doʊ'sent **-s** -s
Docet|ism dəʊ'siː.t|ɪ.zəm; 'dəʊ.sɪ- ⓤⓢ doʊ'siː.t|ɪ-; 'doʊ.sə.t̬|ɪ- **-ist/s** -ɪst/s
Docherty 'dɒk.ə.ti, 'dɒx- ⓤⓢ 'dɑː.kɚ.t̬i
docile 'dəʊ.saɪl, 'dɒs.aɪl ⓤⓢ 'dɑː.səl, -saɪl **-ly** -li
docility dəʊ'sɪl.ə.ti, -ɪ.ti ⓤⓢ dɑː'sɪl.ə.t̬i, doʊ-
dock dɒk ⓤⓢ dɑːk **-s** -s **-ing** -ɪŋ **-ed** -t
dockage 'dɒk.ɪdʒ ⓤⓢ 'dɑː.kɪdʒ

docker (D) 'dɒk.əʳ ⓤⓢ 'dɑː.kɚ **-s** -z
Dockerill 'dɒk.ər.əl ⓤⓢ 'dɑː.kɚ-
dock|et 'dɒk|.ɪt ⓤⓢ 'dɑː.k|ɪt **-ets** -ɪts **-eting** -ɪ.tɪŋ ⓤⓢ -ɪ.t̬ɪŋ **-eted** -ɪ.tɪd ⓤⓢ -ɪ.t̬ɪd
dockland (D) 'dɒk.lænd, -lənd ⓤⓢ 'dɑːk- **-s** -z
dockside 'dɒk.saɪd ⓤⓢ 'dɑːk-
dockworker 'dɒkˌwɜː.kəʳ ⓤⓢ 'dɑːkˌwɝː.kɚ **-s** -z
dockyard 'dɒk.jɑːd ⓤⓢ 'dɑːk.jɑːrd **-s** -z
Doc Martens® ˌdɒk'mɑː.tɪnz ⓤⓢ ˌdɑːk'mɑːr.tənz
doct|or 'dɒk.t|əʳ ⓤⓢ 'dɑːk.t|ɚ **-ors** -əz ⓤⓢ -ɚz **-oring** -ər.ɪŋ **-ored** -əd ⓤⓢ -ɚd
doctoral 'dɒk.tər.əl ⓤⓢ 'dɑːk-
doctorate 'dɒk.tər.ət, -ɪt ⓤⓢ 'dɑːk- **-s** -s
Doctorow 'dɒk.tər.əʊ ⓤⓢ 'dɑːk.tə.roʊ
doctrinaire ˌdɒk.trɪ'neəʳ, -trə'- ⓤⓢ ˌdɑːk.trə'ner **-s** -z
doctrinal dɒk'traɪ.nəl; 'dɒk.trɪ- ⓤⓢ 'dɑːk.trɪ- **-ly** -i
doctrinarian ˌdɒk.trɪ'neə.ri.ən, -trə'- ⓤⓢ ˌdɑːk.trɪ'ner.i- **-s** -z
doctrine 'dɒk.trɪn ⓤⓢ 'dɑːk- **-s** -z
docudrama 'dɒk.juˌdrɑː.mə ⓤⓢ 'dɑː.kjʊˌdrɑː.mə, -ˌdræm.ə **-s** -z
document (*n.*) 'dɒk.jə.mənt, -jʊ- ⓤⓢ 'dɑː.kjə-, -jʊ- **-s** -s
docu|ment (*v.*) 'dɒk.jə|.ment, -jʊ- ⓤⓢ 'dɑː.kjə-, -jʊ- **-ments** -ments **-menting** -men.tɪŋ ⓤⓢ -men.t̬ɪŋ **-mented** -men.tɪd ⓤⓢ -men.t̬ɪd
documental ˌdɒk.jə'men.təl, -jʊ'- ⓤⓢ ˌdɑː.kjə'men'tᵊl, -jʊ-
documentar|y (*n. adj.*) ˌdɒk.jə'men.tər|.i, -jʊ'-, '-tr|i ⓤⓢ ˌdɑː.kjə'men.t̬ɚ|.i, -kjʊ'- **-ies** -iz
documentation ˌdɒk.jə.men'teɪ.ʃən, -jʊ-, -mən'- ⓤⓢ ˌdɑː.kjə-, -jʊ-
docusoap 'dɒk.ju.səʊp, -jʊ- ⓤⓢ 'dɑː.kjə.soʊp, -kjʊ- **-s** -s
Docwra 'dɒk.rə ⓤⓢ 'dɑːk-
Dod(d) dɒd ⓤⓢ dɑːd **-s** -z
dodd|er 'dɒd|.əʳ ⓤⓢ 'dɑː.d|ɚ **-ers** -əz ⓤⓢ -ɚz **-ering** -ər.ɪŋ **-ered** -əd ⓤⓢ -ɚd **-erer/s** -ər.əʳ/z ⓤⓢ -ɚ.ɚ/z
doddery 'dɒd.ər.i ⓤⓢ 'dɑː.dɚ-
Doddington 'dɒd.ɪŋ.tən ⓤⓢ 'dɑː.dɪŋ-
doddle 'dɒd.l̩ ⓤⓢ 'dɑː.dl̩ **-s** -z
Doddridge 'dɒd.rɪdʒ ⓤⓢ 'dɑː.drɪdʒ
dodecagon ˌdəʊ'dek.ə.gən ⓤⓢ ˌdoʊ- **-s** -z
dodecahedr|on ˌdəʊ.dek.ə'hiː.dr|ən, -dɪk-, -'hed.r|ən ⓤⓢ ˌdoʊ.dek.ə'hiː.dr|ən **-ons** -ənz **-a** -ə **-al** -əl
Dodecanese ˌdəʊ.dɪ.kə'niːz, -dek.ə'- ⓤⓢ ˌdoʊ.dek-, -'niːs
dodg|e (D) dɒdʒ ⓤⓢ dɑːdʒ **-es** -ɪz **-ing** -ɪŋ **-ed** -d **-er/s** -əʳ/z ⓤⓢ -ɚ/z ˌ**Dodge 'City**

dodgem ˈdɒdʒ.əm (US) ˈdɑː.dʒəm **-s** -z

Dodgson ˈdɒdʒ.sᵊn (US) ˈdɑːdʒ-

dodg|y ˈdɒdʒ|.i (US) ˈdɑː.dʒ|i **-ier** -i.əʳ (US) -i.ɚ **-iest** -i.ɪst, -i.əst **-ily** -ɪ.li, -ᵊl.i **-iness** -ɪ.nəs, -ɪ.nɪs

Dodington ˈdɒd.ɪŋ.tən (US) ˈdɑː.dɪŋ-

dodo (D) ˈdəʊ.dəʊ (US) ˈdoʊ.doʊ **-(e)s** -z

Dodoma ˈdəʊ.də.mə, -mɑː (US) ˈdoʊ.də.mɑː, -doʊ-, doʊˈ-

Dodona dəʊˈdəʊ.nə (US) dəˈdoʊ-

Dodsley ˈdɒdz.li (US) ˈdɑːdz-

Dodson ˈdɒd.sᵊn (US) ˈdɑːd-

Dodsworth ˈdɒdz.wəθ, -wɜːθ (US) ˈdɑːdz.wɚθ, -wɝːθ

Dodwell ˈdɒd.wəl, -wel (US) ˈdɑːd-

doe (D) dəʊ (US) doʊ **-s** -z

doer ˈduː.əʳ (US) -ɚ **-s** -z

-doer -ˌduː.əʳ (US) -ɚ

Note: Suffix. Normally carries secondary stress, e.g. **wrongdoer** /ˈrɒŋˌduː.əʳ (US) ˈrɑːŋˌduː.ɚ/.

does *(from* **do***) strong form:* dʌz *weak form:* dəz

Note: Weak form word. The strong form is used when **does** is used as a full verb (e.g. "That's what he does for a living"), for emphasis (e.g. "That **does** look nice") and for contrast (e.g. "It **does** cost a lot, but it **doesn't** need repairing"). The strong form also occurs in final position (e.g. "I don't like it as much as she does"). When **does** occurs in other positions as an auxiliary, the weak form is normally used (e.g. "Why does it stop?" /ˌwaɪ.dəz.ɪtˈstɒp (US) -stɑːp/).

doeskin ˈdəʊ.skɪn (US) ˈdoʊ- **-s** -z

doesn't ˈdʌz.ᵊnt

doeth *(from* **do***)* ˈduː.ɪθ

Note: Archaic.

doff (D) dɒf (US) dɑːf, dɔːf **-s** -s **-ing** -ɪŋ **-ed** -t **-er/s** -əʳ/z (US) -ɚ/z

dog dɒg (US) dɑːg, dɔːg **-s** -z **-ging** -ɪŋ **-ged** -d **ˈdog ˌbiscuit; ˈdog ˌcollar; ˈdog ˌdays; ˈdog ˌpaddle; ˈdog ˌrose; ˌdog's ˈbreakfast; ˈDog ˌStar; dressed up like a ˌdog's ˈdinner; it's a ˈdog's ˌlife; let ˌsleeping dogs ˈlie; ˌgo to the ˈdogs**

dogbane ˈdɒg.beɪn (US) ˈdɑːg-, ˈdɔːg-

Dogberry ˈdɒg.ber.i, -bᵊr- (US) ˈdɑːg.ber-, ˈdɔːg-

dogcart ˈdɒg.kɑːt (US) ˈdɑːg.kɑːrt, ˈdɔːg- **-s** -s

dogcatcher ˈdɒgˌkætʃ.əʳ (US) ˈdɑːgˌkætʃ.ɚ, ˈdɔːg- **-s** -z

dog|e dəʊdʒ, dəʊʒ (US) doʊdʒ **-es** -ɪz

dog-ear ˈdɒg.ɪəʳ (US) ˈdɑːg.ɪr, ˈdɔːg- **-s** -z **-ing** -ɪŋ **-ed** -d

dog-eat-dog ˌdɒg.iːtˈdɒg (US) ˌdɑːg.iːtˈdɑːg; ˌdɔːg.iːtˈdɔːg

dog-end ˈdɒg.end (US) ˈdɑːg-, ˈdɔːg- **-s** -z

dogfight ˈdɒg.faɪt (US) ˈdɑːg-, ˈdɔːg- **-s** -s

dogfish ˈdɒg.fɪʃ (US) ˈdɑːg-, ˈdɔːg- **-es** -ɪz

Doggart ˈdɒg.ət (US) ˈdɑː.gɚt, ˈdɔː-

dogged ˈdɒg.ɪd (US) ˈdɑː.gɪd, ˈdɔː- **-ly** -li **-ness** -nəs, -nɪs

dogger (D) ˈdɒg.əʳ (US) ˈdɑː.gɚ, ˈdɔː- **-s** -z **ˌDogger ˈBank** (US) **ˈDogger ˌBank**

doggerel ˈdɒg.ᵊr.ᵊl, -ɪl (US) ˈdɑː.gɚ.ᵊl, ˈdɔː-, ˈ-grᵊl

Doggert ˈdɒg.ət (US) ˈdɑː.gɚt, ˈdɔː-

Doggett ˈdɒg.ɪt (US) ˈdɑː.gɪt, ˈdɔː-

doggo ˈdɒg.əʊ (US) ˈdɑː.goʊ, ˈdɔː-

doggone ˈdɒg.ɒn (US) ˈdɑː.gɑːn; ˈdɔː.gɔːn **-d** -d

dogg|y, dogg|ie ˈdɒg|.i (US) ˈdɑː.g|i, ˈdɔː- **-ies** -iz **ˈdoggie ˌbag**

doghou|se ˈdɒg.haʊ|s (US) ˈdɑːg-, ˈdɔːg- **-ses** -zɪz

dogie ˈdəʊ.gi (US) ˈdoʊ- **-s** -z

dogleg ˈdɒg.leg (US) ˈdɑːg-, ˈdɔːg- **-s** -z **-ging** -ɪŋ **-ged** -ɪd, -legd

dogma ˈdɒg.mə (US) ˈdɑːg-, ˈdɔːg- **-s** -z

dogmatic dɒgˈmæt.ɪk (US) dɑːgˈmæt̬-, dɔːg- **-s** -s **-al** -ᵊl **-ally** -ᵊl.i, -li

dogmat|ism ˈdɒg.mə.t|ɪ.zᵊm (US) ˈdɑːg.mə.t|ɪ-, ˈdɔːg- **-ist/s** -ɪst/s

dogmatiz|e, -is|e ˈdɒg.mə.taɪz (US) ˈdɑːg-, ˈdɔːg- **-es** -ɪz **-ing** -ɪŋ **-ed** -d **-er/s** -əʳ/z (US) -ɚ/z

do-good|er ˌduːˈgʊd|.əʳ (US) ˈduːˌgʊd|.ɚ **-ers** -əz (US) -ɚz **-ing** -ɪŋ

dogsbod|y ˈdɒgz.bɒd|.i (US) ˈdɑːgz.bɑː.d|i, ˈdɔːgz- **-ies** -iz

dogsled ˈdɒg.sled (US) ˈdɑːg-, ˈdɔːg- **-s** -z

dog-tired ˌdɒgˈtaɪəd (US) ˌdɑːgˈtaɪɚd, ˌdɔːg- *stress shift:* ˌdog-tired ˈworker

dog|tooth ˈdɒg|.tuːθ (US) ˈdɑːg-, ˈdɔːg- **-teeth** -tiːθ

dogwatch ˈdɒg.wɒtʃ (US) ˈdɑːg.wɑːtʃ, ˈdɔːg- **-es** -ɪz

dogwood ˈdɒg.wʊd (US) ˈdɑːg-, ˈdɔːg-

doh dəʊ (US) doʊ **-s** -z

Doha ˈdəʊ.hɑː, -ə (US) ˈdoʊ-

Doherty ˈdəʊ.ə.ti; ˈdɒ.hə-; ˈdɒx.ə-; dəʊˈhɜː- (US) ˈdɔːr.ə.t̬i; ˈdoʊ.ɚ-

Dohnanyi dɒkˈnɑːn.jiː, dɒx-, -ji (US) ˈdoʊ.ɑː.nji; dɑːkˈnɑːn.ji, dɑːx-

Doig dɔɪg, ˈdəʊ.ɪg (US) dɔɪg, ˈdoʊ.ɪg

doil|y ˈdɔɪ.l|i **-ies** -iz

doing *(from* **do***)* ˈduː.ɪŋ **-s** -z

Doister ˈdɔɪ.stəʳ (US) -stɚ

doit dɔɪt **-s** -s

do-it-yourself ˌduː.ɪ.tʃəˈself, -ɪt.jɔːˈ-, -jəˈ- (US) ˌduː.ɪt.jɚˈself, -ɪ.tʃɚˈ-

Dokic ˈdɒk.ɪtʃ (US) ˈdɑː.kɪtʃ

Dolan ˈdəʊ.lən (US) ˈdoʊl-

Dolby ˈdɒl.bi (US) ˈdɑːl-, ˈdoʊl-

dolce ˈdɒl.tʃi, ˈdəʊl-, -tʃeɪ (US) ˈdoʊl.tʃeɪ

dolce vita ˌdɒl.tʃiˈviː.tə, ˌdəʊ-, -tʃeɪˈ- (US) ˌdoʊl.tʃeɪˈviː.tə

Dolcis® ˈdɒl.sɪs, -tʃɪs (US) ˈdɑːl-

doldrum ˈdɒl.drəm (US) ˈdoʊl-, ˈdɑːl- **-s** -z

dol|e (D) dəʊl (US) doʊl **-es** -z **-ing** -ɪŋ **-ed** -d

doleful ˈdəʊl.fᵊl, -fʊl (US) ˈdoʊl- **-ly** -i **-ness** -nəs, -nɪs

dolerite ˈdɒl.ə.raɪt (US) ˈdɑː.lə-

Dolgellau, Dolgelley dɒlˈgeθ.laɪ, -li (US) dɑːl-

dolichocephalic ˌdɒl.ɪ.kəʊ.sefˈæl.ɪk, -sɪˈfæl-, -səˈ-, -kefˈæl-, -kɪˈfæl- (US) ˌdɑː.lɪ.koʊ-

Dolittle ˈduː.lɪ.tl̩ (US) -t̬l̩

doll dɒl (US) dɑːl **-s** -z **ˈdoll's ˌhouse**

dollar (D) ˈdɒl.əʳ (US) ˈdɑː.lɚ **-s** -z **ˌbet one's ˌbottom ˈdollar**

Dollond ˈdɒl.ənd (US) ˈdɑː.lənd

dollop ˈdɒl.əp (US) ˈdɑː.ləp **-s** -s

doll|y (D) ˈdɒl|.i (US) ˈdɑː.l|i **-ies** -iz **ˈdolly ˌmixture**

dolman ˈdɒl.mən (US) ˈdoʊl- **-s** -z

dolmen ˈdɒl.men (US) ˈdoʊl- **-s** -z

dolomite (D) ˈdɒl.ə.maɪt (US) ˈdoʊ.lə-, ˈdɑː- **-s** -s

dolor ˈdɒl.əʳ, ˈdəʊ.ləʳ (US) ˈdoʊ.lɚ, ˈdɑː-

Dolores dəˈlɔː.res, dɒlˈɔː-, -rɪs, -rəs, -rez, -rɪz, -rəz (US) dəˈlɔːr.əs, -ɪs

dolorous ˈdɒl.ᵊr.əs (US) ˈdoʊ.lɚ-, ˈdɑː- **-ly** -li **-ness** -nəs, -nɪs

dolour ˈdɒl.əʳ, ˈdəʊ.ləʳ (US) ˈdoʊ.lɚ, ˈdɑː-

dolphin ˈdɒl.fɪn (US) ˈdɑːl- **-s** -z

dolt dəʊlt (US) doʊlt **-s** -s

doltish ˈdəʊl.tɪʃ (US) ˈdoʊl- **-ly** -li **-ness** -nəs, -nɪs

-dom -dəm

Note: Suffix. Normally unstressed, e.g. **kingdom** /ˈkɪŋ.dəm/.

domain dəʊˈmeɪn (US) doʊ-, də- **-s** -z

Dombey ˈdɒm.bi (US) ˈdɑːm-

dome dəʊm (US) doʊm **-s** -z **-d** -d

Domecq dəʊˈmek, dɒmˈek (US) doʊ-

Domesday ˈduːmz.deɪ **ˈDomesday ˌbook**

domestic dəˈmes.tɪk **-s** -s **-ally** -ᵊl.i, -li **doˌmestic ˈanimal; doˌmestic ˈviolence**

domesti|cate dəˈmes.tɪ|.keɪt **-cates** -keɪts **-cating** -keɪ.tɪŋ (US) -keɪ.t̬ɪŋ **-cated** -keɪ.tɪd (US) -keɪ.t̬ɪd

domestication dəˌmes.tɪˈkeɪ.ʃᵊn

domesticity ˌdɒm.esˈtɪs.ə.ti, ˌdəʊ.mes-, -ɪ.ti (US) ˌdoʊ.mesˈ-, dəˌmesˈ-

Domestos® dəˈmes.tɒs, dəʊ- (US) dəˈmes.toʊs

domett dəʊˈmet (US) də-, doʊ-; ˈdɑː.mət

Domett ˈdɒm.ɪt (US) ˈdɑː.mɪt

domicil|e ˈdɒm.ɪ.saɪl, ˈdəʊ.mɪ-, -sɪl (US) ˈdɑː.mə-, ˈdoʊ.mə- **-es** -z **-ing** -ɪŋ **-ed** -d

domiciliary ˌdɒm.ɪˈsɪl.i.ər.i, -əˈ- ⓤⓢ ˌdɑː.məˈsɪl.i.er-, ˌdoʊ-
dominance ˈdɒm.ɪ.nənts, ˈ-ə- ⓤⓢ ˈdɑː.mə-
dominant ˈdɒm.ɪ.nənt, ˈ-ə- ⓤⓢ ˈdɑː.mə- **-s** -s **-ly** -li
domi|nate ˈdɒm.ɪ|.neɪt, ˈ-ə- ⓤⓢ ˈdɑː.mə- **-nates** -neɪts **-nating** -neɪ.tɪŋ ⓤⓢ -neɪ.t̬ɪŋ **-nated** -neɪ.tɪd ⓤⓢ -neɪ.t̬ɪd **-nator/s** -neɪ.tər/z ⓤⓢ -neɪ.t̬ɚ/z
domination ˌdɒm.ɪˈneɪ.ʃən, -əˈ- ⓤⓢ ˌdɑː.məˈ- **-s** -z
dominatr|ix ˌdɒm.ɪˈneɪ.tr|ɪks, -əˈ- ⓤⓢ ˌdɑː.məˈ- **-ixes** -ɪk.sɪz **-ices** -ɪ.siːz
domineer ˌdɒm.ɪˈnɪər, -əˈ- ⓤⓢ ˌdɑː.məˈnɪr **-s** -z **-ing/ly** -ɪŋ/li **-ed** -d
Domingo dəˈmɪŋ.gəʊ, dɒmˈɪŋ- ⓤⓢ dəˈmɪŋ.goʊ
Dominic ˈdɒm.ɪ.nɪk, ˈ-ə- ⓤⓢ ˈdɑː.mə-
Dominica dəˈmɪn.ɪ.kə; dɒm.ɪnˈiː- ⓤⓢ ˌdɑː.mɪˈniː-, dəˈmɪn.ɪ-
dominical dəˈmɪn.ɪ.kəl, dɒmˈɪn-, dəʊˈmɪn- ⓤⓢ doʊˈmɪn-, də-
Dominican *republic, religious order:* dəˈmɪn.ɪ.kən, dɒmˈɪn- ⓤⓢ doʊˈmɪn-, də- **-s** -z *of Dominica:* ˌdɒm.ɪˈniː.kən ⓤⓢ ˌdɑː.mɪˈniː- **-s** -z
dominie ˈdɒm.ɪ.ni, ˈ-ə- ⓤⓢ ˈdɑː.mɪ- **-s** -z
dominion (D) dəˈmɪn.jən, -i.ən ⓤⓢ ˈ-jən **-s** -z
Dominique ˌdɒm.ɪˈniːk, -əˈ-, ˈ--- ⓤⓢ ˌdɑː.məˈ-, ˈ---
domino (D) ˈdɒm.ɪ.nəʊ, ˈ-ə- ⓤⓢ ˈdɑː.mə.noʊ **-(e)s** -z **ˈdomino efˌfect**
Domitian dəʊˈmɪʃ.i.ən, dɒmˈɪʃ-, -ˈɪʃ.ən ⓤⓢ dəˈmɪʃ.ən, -i.ən
don (D) dɒn ⓤⓢ dɑːn **-s** -z **-ning** -ɪŋ **-ned** -d
doña, dona ˈdɒn.jə ⓤⓢ ˈdoʊ.njə, -nə
dona(h) ˈdəʊ.nə ⓤⓢ ˈdoʊ- **-s** -z
Donal ˈdəʊ.nəl ⓤⓢ ˈdoʊ-
Donalbain ˈdɒn.əl.beɪn ⓤⓢ ˈdɑː.nəl-
Donald ˈdɒn.əld ⓤⓢ ˈdɑː.nəld
Donaldson ˈdɒn.əld.sən ⓤⓢ ˈdɑː.nəld-
Donat ˈdəʊ.næt ⓤⓢ ˈdoʊ-
do|nate dəʊ|ˈneɪt ⓤⓢ ˈdoʊ|.neɪt, -|ˈ- **-nates** -ˈneɪts ⓤⓢ -neɪts, -ˈneɪts **-nating** -ˈneɪ.tɪŋ ⓤⓢ -neɪ.t̬ɪŋ, -ˈneɪ- **-nated** -ˈneɪ.tɪd ⓤⓢ -neɪ.t̬ɪd, -ˈneɪ-
Donatello ˌdɒn.əˈtel.əʊ ⓤⓢ ˌdɑː.nəˈtel.oʊ
donatio dəʊˈnɑː.ti.əʊ ⓤⓢ doʊˈnɑː.ti.oʊ, -ˈneɪ-, -ʃi-
donation dəʊˈneɪ.ʃən ⓤⓢ doʊˈneɪ- **-s** -z
Donatist ˈdəʊ.nə.tɪst, ˈdɒn.ə- ⓤⓢ ˈdoʊ.nə-, ˈdɑː- **-s** -s
donative ˈdəʊ.nə.tɪv, ˈdɒn.ə- ⓤⓢ ˈdoʊ.nə.t̬ɪv, ˈdɑː- **-s** -z
donator dəʊˈneɪ.tər ⓤⓢ ˈdoʊ.neɪ.t̬ɚ, ˌdoʊˈneɪ- **-s** -z
donatory ˈdəʊ.nə.tər.i, ˈdɒn.ə-; -tri, dəʊˈneɪ- ⓤⓢ ˈdoʊ.nə.tɔːr.i
Donatus dəʊˈneɪ.təs, -ˈnɑː- ⓤⓢ doʊˈneɪ.t̬əs, -ˈnɑː-
Don Carlos ˌdɒnˈkɑː.lɒs, ˌdɒŋ- ⓤⓢ ˌdɑːnˈkɑːr.loʊs
Doncaster ˈdɒŋ.kə.stər, -ˌkɑː-, -ˌkæs.tər ⓤⓢ ˈdɑːŋˌkæs.tɚ, -kə.stɚ, ˈdɑːn-
done *(from* **do***)* dʌn
Done dəʊn ⓤⓢ doʊn
donee dəʊˈniː ⓤⓢ doʊ- **-s** -z
Donegal ˌdɒn.ɪˈgɔːl, ˌdʌn-, ˈ--- ⓤⓢ ˌdɑː.nɪˈgɔːl, -ˈgɑːl, ˈ---
Note: /ˌdʌn.ɪˈgɔːl/ appears to be the most usual pronunciation in Ireland.
Donegall ˈdɒn.ɪ.gɔːl ⓤⓢ ˈdɑː.nɪ.gɔːl, -gɑːl
Donelson ˈdɒn.əl.sən ⓤⓢ ˈdɑː.nəl-
doner ˈdɒn.ər ⓤⓢ ˈdoʊ.nɚ **ˌdoner keˈbab**
Donetsk dɒnˈjetsk ⓤⓢ dəˈnjetsk, doʊ-
Donetz dɒnˈjets ⓤⓢ dəˈnets, dɑːˈnjets
dong (*v.*) dɒŋ ⓤⓢ dɑːŋ, dɔːŋ **-s** -z **-ing** -ɪŋ **-ed** -d
dông *Vietnam currency:* dɒŋ ⓤⓢ dɑːŋ, dɔːŋ
donga ˈdɒŋ.gə ⓤⓢ ˈdɑːŋ.gə, ˈdɔːŋ- **-s** -z
Dönges ˈdɜːn.jes
Don Giovanni ˌdɒn.dʒəʊˈvɑː.ni, -dʒi.əʊˈ-, -ˈvæn.i ⓤⓢ ˌdɑːn.dʒi.əˈvɑː.ni, -dʒoʊˈ-
Dongola ˈdɒŋ.gə.lə ⓤⓢ ˈdɑːŋ-
Donington ˈdɒn.ɪŋ.tən, ˈdʌn- ⓤⓢ ˈdɑː.nɪŋ-
Donizetti ˌdɒn.ɪˈzet.i, -ɪdˈze-, -ɪtˈset- ⓤⓢ ˌdɑː.nəˈzet̬.i, -nətˈset̬-
donjon ˈdɒn.dʒən, ˈdʌn- ⓤⓢ ˈdɑːn- **-s** -z
Don Juan ˌdɒnˈdʒuː.ən, -ˈhwɑːn ⓤⓢ ˌdɑːn-
donkey ˈdɒŋ.ki ⓤⓢ ˈdɑːŋ-, ˈdɔːŋ-, ˈdʌŋ- **-s** -z **ˈdonkey ˌengine; ˈdonkey ˌjacket; ˈdonkey's ˌyears**
donkeywork ˈdɒŋ.ki.wɜːk ⓤⓢ ˈdɑːŋ.ki.wɝːk, ˈdɔːŋ-, ˈdʌŋ-
Donleavy, Donlevy dɒnˈliː.vi, -ˈlev.i ⓤⓢ ˈdɑːn.liː.vi, ˈdʌn-, -lev.i, -ˈ--
Donmar ˈdɒn.mɑːr ⓤⓢ ˈdɑːn-
donna (D) ˈdɒn.ə ⓤⓢ ˈdɑː.nə
Donnan ˈdɒn.ən ⓤⓢ ˈdɑː.nən
Donne dʌn, dɒn ⓤⓢ dʌn, dɑːn
Donnell ˈdɒn.əl ⓤⓢ ˈdɑː.nəl
Donnelly ˈdɒn.əl.i ⓤⓢ ˈdɑː.nəl-
Donnington ˈdɒn.ɪŋ.tən ⓤⓢ ˈdɑː.nɪŋ-
donnish ˈdɒn.ɪʃ ⓤⓢ ˈdɑː.nɪʃ **-ly** -li **-ness** -nəs, -nɪs
Donny ˈdɒn.i ⓤⓢ ˈdɑː.ni
Donnybrook ˈdɒn.i.brʊk ⓤⓢ ˈdɑː.ni-
Donoghue ˈdʌn.ə.hjuː, ˈdɒn-, -hjuː ⓤⓢ ˈdɑː.nə.huː, ˈdʌn.ə-, -huː
Donohoe ˈdʌn.ə.həʊ, ˈdɒn-, -huː ⓤⓢ ˈdɑː.nə.hoʊ, ˈdʌn.ə-, -huː
Donohue ˈdʌn.ə.hjuː, ˈdɒn-, -huː ⓤⓢ ˈdɑː.nə.hjuː, ˈdʌn.ə-, -huː
donor ˈdəʊ.nər, -nɔːr ⓤⓢ ˈdoʊ.nɚ **-s** -z
Donovan ˈdɒn.ə.vən ⓤⓢ ˈdɑː.nə-, ˈdʌn.ə-
Don Pasquale ˌdɒn.pæsˈkwɑː.leɪ, ˈdɒm-, -li ⓤⓢ ˌdɑːn.pəˈ-
Don Quixote ˌdɒnˈkwɪk.sət, ˌdɒŋ-, -səʊt, -sɒt; *as if Spanish:* ˌdɒn.kiˈhəʊ.teɪ, ˌdɒŋ-, -ti ⓤⓢ ˌdɑːn.kiːˈhoʊ.teɪ, -t̬i; -ˈkwɪk.sət
donship ˈdɒn.ʃɪp ⓤⓢ ˈdɑːn- **-s** -s
don't dəʊnt ⓤⓢ doʊnt
Note: Weak forms /dən, dn̩/ may sometimes be heard in the expression "I don't know", and a weak form /dəm/ in the expression "I don't mind".
do|nut ˈdəʊ|.nʌt ⓤⓢ ˈdoʊ- **-nuts** -nʌts **-nutting** -nʌt.ɪŋ ⓤⓢ -nʌt̬.ɪŋ
Doo duː
Doobie ˈduː.bi
doodad ˈduː.dæd **-s** -z
doodah ˈduː.dɑː **-s** -z
doodl|e ˈduː.dl̩ **-es** -z **-ing** -ɪŋ, ˈduːd.lɪŋ **-ed** -d **-er/s** -ər/z, ˈduːd.lər/z ⓤⓢ ˈduː.dl̩.ɚ/z, ˈduːd.lɚ/z
doodlebug ˈduː.dl̩.bʌg **-s** -z
doohickey ˈduːˌhɪk.i **-s** -z
Doolittle ˈduː.lɪ.tl̩ ⓤⓢ -t̬l̩
doom duːm **-s** -z **-ing** -ɪŋ **-ed** -d
doomsayer ˈduːmˌseɪ.ər ⓤⓢ -ɚ **-s** -z
doomsday (D) ˈduːmz.deɪ
Doona® ˈduː.nə **-s** -z
Doon(e) duːn
door dɔːr ⓤⓢ dɔːr **-s** -z **ˌshut the ˌdoor in someone's ˈface; ˌshow someone the ˈdoor**
doorbell ˈdɔː.bel ⓤⓢ ˈdɔːr- **-s** -z
doorframe ˈdɔː.freɪm ⓤⓢ ˈdɔːr- **-s** -z
doorjamb ˈdɔː.dʒæm ⓤⓢ ˈdɔːr- **-s** -z
doorkeeper ˈdɔːˌkiː.pər ⓤⓢ ˈdɔːrˌkiː.pɚ **-s** -z
doorknob ˈdɔː.nɒb ⓤⓢ ˈdɔːr.nɑːb **-s** -z
doorknocker ˈdɔːˌnɒk.ər ⓤⓢ ˈdɔːrˌnɑː.kɚ **-s** -z
door|man ˈdɔː|.mən, -mæn ⓤⓢ ˈdɔːr- **-men** -mən, -men
doormat ˈdɔː.mæt ⓤⓢ ˈdɔːr- **-s** -s
doornail ˈdɔː.neɪl ⓤⓢ ˈdɔːr- **-s** -z **as ˌdead as a ˈdoornail**
doorplate ˈdɔː.pleɪt ⓤⓢ ˈdɔːr- **-s** -s
doorpost ˈdɔː.pəʊst ⓤⓢ ˈdɔːr.poʊst **-s** -s
doorstep ˈdɔː.step ⓤⓢ ˈdɔːr- **-s** -s **-ping** -ɪŋ **-ped** -t **-per/s** -ər/z ⓤⓢ -ɚ/z
doorstop ˈdɔː.stɒp ⓤⓢ ˈdɔːr.stɑːp **-s** -s
door-to-door ˌdɔː.təˈdɔːr ⓤⓢ ˌdɔːr.t̬əˈdɔːr
doorway ˈdɔː.weɪ ⓤⓢ ˈdɔːr- **-s** -z
doo-wop ˈduː.wɒp ⓤⓢ -wɑːp
dopa ˈdəʊ.pə ⓤⓢ ˈdoʊ-, -pɑː
dopamine ˈdəʊ.pə.miːn, -mɪn ⓤⓢ ˈdoʊ-

dop|e dəʊp ⓤⓢ doʊp **-es** -s **-ing** -ɪŋ **-ed** -t **-er/s** -əʳ/z ⓤⓢ -ɚ/z
dop|ey ˈdəʊ.p|i ⓤⓢ ˈdoʊ- **-ier** -i.əʳ ⓤⓢ -i.ɚ **-iest** -i.ɪst, -i.əst **-ily** -ɪ.li, -əl.i **-iness** -ɪ.nəs, -ɪ.nɪs
doppelganger ˈdɒp.əlˌgæŋ.əʳ ⓤⓢ ˈdɑː.pəlˌgæŋ.ɚ **-s** -z
doppelgänger ˈdɒp.əlˌgeŋ.əʳ ⓤⓢ ˈdɑː.pəlˌgeŋ.ɚ **-s** -z
Doppler ˈdɒp.ləʳ ⓤⓢ ˈdɑː.plɚ **ˈDoppler efˌfect**
dop|y ˈdəʊ.p|i ⓤⓢ ˈdoʊ- **-ier** -i.əʳ ⓤⓢ -i.ɚ **-iest** -i.ɪst, -i.əst **-ily** -ɪ.li, -əl.i **-iness** -ɪ.nəs, -ɪ.nɪs
Dora ˈdɔː.rə ⓤⓢ ˈdɔːr.ə
dorado **(D)** dəˈrɑː.dəʊ, dɒrˈɑː- ⓤⓢ doʊˈrɑː.doʊ, də'- **-s** -z
Doran ˈdɔː.rən ⓤⓢ ˈdɔːr.ən
Dorando dəˈræn.dəʊ, dɒrˈæn- ⓤⓢ dɔːrˈæn.doʊ
Dorcas ˈdɔː.kəs, -kæs ⓤⓢ ˈdɔːr-
Dorchester ˈdɔː.tʃɪ.stəʳ ⓤⓢ ˈdɔːr.tʃes.tɚ
Dordogne dɔːˈdɔɪn ⓤⓢ dɔːrˈdoʊn
Dordon ˈdɔː.dən ⓤⓢ ˈdɔːr-
Dordrecht ˈdɔː.drext, -drekt ⓤⓢ ˈdɔːr.drekt, -drext
Dore dɔːʳ ⓤⓢ dɔːr
Doreen ˈdɔː.riːn; -ˈ-, də-, dɒrˈiːn ⓤⓢ dɔːˈriːn
Dorian ˈdɔː.ri.ən ⓤⓢ ˈdɔːr.i- **-s** -z
Doric ˈdɒr.ɪk ⓤⓢ ˈdɔːr-
Doricism ˈdɒr.ɪ.sɪ.zəm, ˈ-ə- ⓤⓢ ˈdɔːr- **-s** -z
Dorigen ˈdɒr.ɪ.gən ⓤⓢ ˈdɔːr-
Doris *modern first name:* ˈdɒr.ɪs ⓤⓢ ˈdɔːr-, ˈdɑːr- *district and female name in Greek history:* ˈdɔː.rɪs, ˈdɒr.ɪs ⓤⓢ ˈdɔːr.ɪs, ˈdɑːr-
dork dɔːk ⓤⓢ dɔːrk **-s** -s
Dorking ˈdɔː.kɪŋ ⓤⓢ ˈdɔːr-
Dorling ˈdɔː.lɪŋ ⓤⓢ ˈdɔːr-
dorm dɔːm ⓤⓢ dɔːrm **-s** -z
dormancy ˈdɔː.mənt.si ⓤⓢ ˈdɔːr-
dormant ˈdɔː.mənt ⓤⓢ ˈdɔːr-
dormer **(D)** ˈdɔː.məʳ ⓤⓢ ˈdɔːr.mɚ **-s** -z **ˌdormer ˈwindow**
dormie ˈdɔː.mi ⓤⓢ ˈdɔːr-
dormitor|y ˈdɔː.mɪ.tər|.i, -mə-, -tr|i ⓤⓢ ˈdɔːr.mə.tɔːr|.i **-ies** -iz
Dormobile® ˈdɔː.mə.biːl ⓤⓢ ˈdɔːr- **-s** -z
dor|mouse ˈdɔː|.maʊs ⓤⓢ ˈdɔːr- **-mice** -maɪs
dormy ˈdɔː.mi ⓤⓢ ˈdɔːr-
Dornoch ˈdɔː.nɒk, -nək, -nɒx, -nəx ⓤⓢ ˈdɔːr.nɑːk, -nək
Dornton ˈdɔːn.tən ⓤⓢ ˈdɔːrn-
Dorothea ˌdɒr.əˈθiː.ə ⓤⓢ ˌdɔːr-, ˌdɑːr-
Dorothy ˈdɒr.ə.θi ⓤⓢ ˈdɔːr-, ˈdɑːr-
Dorr dɔːʳ ⓤⓢ dɔːr
Dorriforth ˈdɒr.ɪ.fɔːθ ⓤⓢ ˈdɔːr.ɪ.fɔːrθ, ˈdɑːr-
Dorrit ˈdɒr.ɪt ⓤⓢ ˈdɔːr-
Dors dɔːz ⓤⓢ dɔːrz
dorsal ˈdɔː.səl ⓤⓢ ˈdɔːr- **-ly** -i
Dorset ˈdɔː.sɪt, -sət ⓤⓢ ˈdɔːr- **-shire** -ʃəʳ, -ˌʃɪəʳ ⓤⓢ -ʃɚ, -ˌʃɪr
Dorsey ˈdɔː.si ⓤⓢ ˈdɔːr-
dorsum ˈdɔː.səm ⓤⓢ ˈdɔːr-
Dortmund ˈdɔːt.mənd, -mʊnd ⓤⓢ ˈdɔːrt-
dor|y **(D)** ˈdɔː.r|i ⓤⓢ ˈdɔːr|.i **-ies** -iz
DOS dɒs ⓤⓢ dɑːs
dosag|e ˈdəʊ.sɪdʒ ⓤⓢ ˈdoʊ- **-es** -ɪz
dos|e dəʊs ⓤⓢ doʊs **-es** -ɪz **-ing** -ɪŋ **-ed** -t **like a ˌdose of ˈsalts**
dosh dɒʃ ⓤⓢ dɑːʃ
do-si-do ˌdəʊ.siˈdəʊ, -saɪˈ- ⓤⓢ ˌdoʊ.siˈdoʊ **-s** -z
Dos Passos ˌdɒsˈpæs.ɒs ⓤⓢ ˌdoʊsˈpæs.oʊs, dəs-, ˌdɑːs-
doss dɒs ⓤⓢ dɑːs **-es** -ɪz **-ing** -ɪŋ **-ed** -t **-er/s** -əʳ/z ⓤⓢ -ɚ/z
dossal ˈdɒs.əl ⓤⓢ ˈdɑː.səl **-s** -z
dosshou|se ˈdɒs.haʊ|s ⓤⓢ ˈdɑːs- **-ses** -zɪz
dossier ˈdɒs.i.eɪ, -əʳ ⓤⓢ ˈdɑː.si.eɪ, -ɚ **-s** -z
dost (*from* **do**) *strong form:* dʌst *weak form:* dəst
Dostoievski, **Dostoevsky** ˌdɒs.tɔɪˈef.ski ⓤⓢ ˌdɔː.stəˈjef-, ˌdɑː-, ˈdʌs.təˈ-, -tɔɪˈ-
dot **(D)** dɒt ⓤⓢ dɑːt **-s** -s **-ting** -ɪŋ ⓤⓢ ˈdɑː.t̬ɪŋ **-ted** -ɪd ⓤⓢ ˈdɑː.t̬ɪd **ˌdotted ˈline**
dotage ˈdəʊ.tɪdʒ ⓤⓢ ˈdoʊ.t̬ɪdʒ
dotard ˈdəʊ.təd, -ɑːd ⓤⓢ ˈdoʊ.t̬ɚd **-s** -z
dot.com ˌdɒtˈkɒm ⓤⓢ ˈdɑːt.kɑːm, ˌ-ˈ- **-s** -z *stress shift:* ˌdot.com ˈcompany
dot|e dəʊt ⓤⓢ doʊt **-es** -s **-ing/ly** -ɪŋ/li ⓤⓢ ˈdoʊ.t̬ɪŋ/li **-ed** -ɪd ⓤⓢ ˈdoʊ.t̬ɪd **-er/s** -əʳ/z ⓤⓢ ˈdoʊ.t̬ɚ/z
doth (*from* **do**) *strong form:* dʌθ *weak form:* dəθ
Dotheboys Hall ˌduː.ðə.bɔɪzˈhɔːl ⓤⓢ -ˈhɔːl, -ˈhɑːl
dot-matrix ˌdɒtˈmeɪ.trɪks, ˈ-ˌ-- ⓤⓢ ˌdɑːtˈmeɪ- **ˌdot-matrix ˈprinter, dot-ˌmatrix ˈprinter** ⓤⓢ **ˌdot-ˈmatrix printer**
dotterel ˈdɒt.rəl ⓤⓢ ˈdɑː.trəl **-s** -z
dottle ˈdɒt.l̩ ⓤⓢ ˈdɑː.t̬l̩ **-s** -z
dott|y ˈdɒt|.i ⓤⓢ ˈdɑː.t̬|i **-ier** -i.əʳ ⓤⓢ -i.ɚ **-iest** -i.ɪst, -i.əst **-ily** -ɪ.li, -əl.i **-iness** -ɪ.nəs, -ɪ.nɪs
Douai *French town:* ˈduː.eɪ ⓤⓢ -ˈ- *school near Reading:* ˈdaʊ.eɪ, ˈduː-, -i ⓤⓢ duːˈeɪ *version of Bible:* ˈdaʊ.eɪ, ˈduː-, -i ⓤⓢ duːˈeɪ, ˈ--
Douala duˈɑː.lə
doubl|e ˈdʌb.l̩ **-y** -i, ˈ-li **-eness** -nəs, -nɪs **-es** -z **-ing** -ɪŋ, ˈ-lɪŋ **-ed** -d **ˌdouble ˈagent; ˌdouble ˈbass; ˌdouble ˈchin; ˌdouble ˈdutch; ˌdouble ˈentry; ˌdouble ˈfirst; ˌDouble ˈGloucester; ˌdouble inˈdemnity; ˌdouble ˈjeopardy; ˌdouble ˈtake;** ⓤⓢ **ˈdouble ˌtake;**
double-barrel(l)ed ˌdʌb.l̩ˈbær.l̩d ⓤⓢ -ˈber-, -ˈbær- *stress shift:* ˌdouble-barrel(l)ed ˈname
double-breasted ˌdʌb.l̩ˈbres.tɪd *stress shift:* ˌdouble-breasted ˈjacket
double-check ˌdʌb.l̩ˈtʃek ⓤⓢ ˈdʌb.l̩ˌtʃek, ˌ--ˈ- **-s** -s **-ing** -ɪŋ **-ed** -t
double-cross ˌdʌb.l̩ˈkrɒs ⓤⓢ -ˈkrɑːs **-es** -ɪz **-ing** -ɪŋ **-ed** -t
Doubleday ˈdʌb.l̩.deɪ
double-deal|er ˌdʌb.l̩ˈdiː.l|əʳ ⓤⓢ -l|ɚ **-ers** -əʳ/z ⓤⓢ -ɚ/z **-ing** -ɪŋ
double-decker ˌdʌb.l̩ˈdek.əʳ ⓤⓢ ˈdʌb.l̩ˌdek.ɚ, ˌdʌb.l̩ˈdek- **-s** -z *stress shift, British only:* ˌdouble-decker ˈbus
double-dip ˌdʌb.l̩ˈdɪp **-s** -s **-ping** -ɪŋ **-ped** -t
double-edged ˌdʌb.l̩ˈedʒd *stress shift:* ˌdouble-edged ˈsword
double entendre ˌduː.bl̩.ɑ̃ːnˈtɑ̃ːn.drə, -ɑːnˈtɑːn- ⓤⓢ ˌdʌb.l̩.ɑːnˈtɑːn.drə, ˌduː.blɑːnˈtrɑːn
double-glaz|e ˌdʌb.l̩ˈgleɪz **-es** -ɪz **-ing** -ɪŋ **-ed** -d *stress shift:* ˌdouble-glazed ˈwindows
double-glazing ˌdʌb.l̩ˈgleɪ.zɪŋ
double-header ˌdʌb.l̩ˈhed.əʳ ⓤⓢ -ɚ **-s** -z
double-jointed ˌdʌb.l̩ˈdʒɔɪn.tɪd ⓤⓢ -t̬ɪd *stress shift:* ˌdouble-jointed ˈgymnast
double-park ˌdʌb.l̩ˈpɑːk ⓤⓢ -ˈpɑːrk **-s** -s **-ing** -ɪŋ **-ed** -t
double-quick ˌdʌb.l̩ˈkwɪk *stress shift:* ˌdouble-quick ˈtime
doublespeak ˈdʌb.l̩.spiːk
double-stop ˌdʌb.l̩ˈstɒp ⓤⓢ -ˈstɑːp **-s** -s **-ping** -ɪŋ **-ped** -t
doublet ˈdʌb.lɪt, -lət **-s** -s
doubletalk ˈdʌb.l̩.tɔːk ⓤⓢ -tɔːk, -tɑːk
doublethink ˈdʌb.l̩.θɪŋk
double-tongued ˌdʌb.l̩ˈtʌŋd
doubloon dʌbˈluːn **-s** -z
doubt daʊt **-s** -s **-ing/ly** -ɪŋ/li ⓤⓢ ˈdaʊ.t̬ɪŋ/li **-ed** -ɪd ⓤⓢ ˈdaʊ.t̬ɪd **-er/s** -əʳ/z ⓤⓢ ˈdaʊ.t̬ɚ/z **ˌdoubting ˈThomas**
doubtful ˈdaʊt.fəl, -fʊl **-lest** -ɪst, -əst **-ly** -i **-ness** -nəs, -nɪs
doubtless ˈdaʊt.ləs, -lɪs **-ly** -li
douch|e duːʃ **-es** -ɪz **-ing** -ɪŋ **-ed** -t
Doug dʌg
Dougal(l) ˈduː.gəl
Dougan ˈduː.gən
dough dəʊ ⓤⓢ doʊ
Dougherty ˈdɒx.ə.ti, ˈdəʊ-, ˈdaʊ- ⓤⓢ ˈdɔːr.ə.t̬i, ˈdɔːr.t̬i, ˈdoʊ.ɚ-, ˈdaʊ-, ˈdɑː.kɚ-

doughfaced ˈdəʊ.feɪst ⓤⓢ ˈdoʊ-
dough|nut ˈdəʊ|.nʌt ⓤⓢ ˈdoʊ- **-nuts** -nʌts **-nutting** -nʌt.ɪŋ ⓤⓢ -nʌt̬.ɪŋ
dought|y (D) ˈdaʊ.t|i ⓤⓢ -t̬|i **-ier** -i.əʳ ⓤⓢ -i.ɚ **-iest** -i.ɪst, -i.əst **-ily** -ɪ.li, -əl.i **-iness** -ɪ.nəs, -ɪ.nɪs
dough|y ˈdəʊ|.i ⓤⓢ ˈdoʊ- **-ily** -ɪ.li, -əl.i **-iness** -ɪ.nəs, -ɪ.nɪs
Douglas-Home ˌdʌg.ləsˈhjuːm
Douglas(s) ˈdʌg.ləs
douloureux ˌduː.ləˈrɜː, -luːˈ-, -lʊˈ-
Doulton ˈdəʊl.tən ⓤⓢ ˈdoʊl-
Dounreay ˈduːn.reɪ, -ˈ-
dour dʊəʳ, daʊəʳ ⓤⓢ dʊr, daʊɚ **-ly** -li **-ness** -nəs, -nɪs
Douro ˈdʊə.rəʊ ⓤⓢ ˈdɔːr.oʊ
dous|e daʊs **-es** -ɪz **-ing** -ɪŋ **-ed** -t
dove (D) dʌv **-s** -z
dove *(from* **dive***)* dəʊv ⓤⓢ doʊv
dovecot(e) ˈdʌv.kɒt ⓤⓢ -kɑːt **-s** -s
Dovedale ˈdʌv.deɪl
Dover ˈdəʊ.vəʳ ⓤⓢ ˈdoʊ.vɚ ˌ**Dover** ˈ**sole**
dovetail ˈdʌv.teɪl **-s** -z **-ing** -ɪŋ **-ed** -d
Dovey ˈdʌv.i
Dow daʊ ˌ**Dow** ˈ**Jones**; ˌ**Dow Jones** ˈ**index**
dowager ˈdaʊə.dʒəʳ, ˈdaʊɪ- ⓤⓢ -dʒɚ **-s** -z
Dowden ˈdaʊ.dən
Dowds daʊdz
dowd|y ˈdaʊ.d|i **-ies** -iz **-ier** -i.əʳ ⓤⓢ -i.ɚ **-iest** -i.ɪst, -i.əst **-ily** -ɪ.li, -əl.i **-iness** -ɪ.nəs, -ɪ.nɪs
dowel daʊəl **-s** -z **-(l)ing** -ɪŋ **-(l)ed** -d
Dowell daʊəl; ˈdaʊ.ɪl, -el
dower daʊəʳ ⓤⓢ daʊɚ **-s** -z **-less** -ləs, -lɪs
Dowgate ˈdaʊ.gɪt, -geɪt
Dowie ˈdaʊ.i
Dowland ˈdaʊ.lənd
dowlas (D) ˈdaʊ.ləs
Dowler ˈdaʊ.ləʳ ⓤⓢ -lɚ
Dowling ˈdaʊ.lɪŋ
down (D) daʊn **-s** -z **-ing** -ɪŋ **-ed** -d ˌ**down** ˈ**payment**; ˈ**Down's** ˌ**syndrome**; ˌ**down** ˈ**under**
Down *county:* daʊn **-shire** -ʃəʳ, -ˌʃɪəʳ ⓤⓢ -ʃɚ, -ˌʃɪr
down-and-out ˌdaʊn.əndˈaʊt **-s** -s *stress shift:* ˌdown-and-out ˈperson
down-at-heel ˌdaʊn.ətˈhiːl *stress shift:* ˌdown-at-heel ˈperson
downbeat ˈdaʊn.biːt, ˈdaʊm- ⓤⓢ ˈdaʊn- **-s** -s
downcast ˈdaʊn.kɑːst, ˈdaʊŋ-, ˌ-ˈ- ⓤⓢ ˈdaʊn.kæst
downdraught ˈdaʊn.drɑːft ⓤⓢ -dræft **-s** -s
downdrift ˈdaʊn.drɪft
Downe daʊn **-s** -z
downer ˈdaʊ.nəʳ ⓤⓢ -nɚ **-s** -z
Downey ˈdaʊ.ni
downfall ˈdaʊn.fɔːl ⓤⓢ -fɔːl, -fɑːl **-s** -z
downgrad|e ˌdaʊnˈgreɪd, ˌdaʊŋ- ⓤⓢ ˈdaʊn.greɪd **-es** -z **-ing** -ɪŋ **-ed** -ɪd *stress shift, British only:* ˌdowngraded ˈworker
Downham ˈdaʊ.nəm
downhearted ˌdaʊnˈhɑː.tɪd ⓤⓢ -ˈhɑːr.t̬ɪd **-ly** -li **-ness** -nəs, -nɪs *stress shift:* ˌdownhearted ˈperson
downhill ˌdaʊnˈhɪl *stress shift:* ˌdownhill ˈslide
down-home ˌdaʊnˈhəʊm ⓤⓢ -ˈhoʊm
Downie ˈdaʊ.ni
Downing ˈdaʊ.nɪŋ ˈ**Downing** ˌ**Street**
downland (D) ˈdaʊn.lænd, -lənd
download ˌdaʊnˈləʊd, ˈ-- ⓤⓢ ˈdaʊn.loʊd **-s** -z **-ing** -ɪŋ **-ed** -ɪd **-able**
downmarket ˌdaʊnˈmɑː.kɪt, ˌdaʊm- ⓤⓢ ˈdaʊnˌmɑːr- *stress shift, British only:* ˌdownmarket ˈarea
Downpatrick ˌdaʊnˈpæt.rɪk, ˌdaʊm- ⓤⓢ ˌdaʊn-
downpipe ˈdaʊn.paɪp, ˈdaʊm- ⓤⓢ ˈdaʊn- **-s** -s
downplay ˌdaʊnˈpleɪ, ˌdaʊm- ⓤⓢ ˈdaʊn.pleɪ **-s** -z **-ing** -ɪŋ **-ed** -d *stress shift, British only:* ˌdownplayed ˈincident
downpour ˈdaʊn.pɔːʳ, ˈdaʊm- ⓤⓢ ˈdaʊn.pɔːr **-s** -z
downright ˈdaʊn.raɪt **-ness** -nəs, -nɪs
downriver ˌdaʊnˈrɪv.əʳ, -ɚ *stress shift:* ˌdownriver ˈsettlement
downrush ˈdaʊn.rʌʃ **-es** -ɪz
Downs daʊnz
downside (D) ˈdaʊn.saɪd
downsiz|e ˌdaʊnˈsaɪz ⓤⓢ ˈ-- **-es** -ɪz **-ing** -ɪŋ **-ed** -d *stress shift, British only:* ˌdownsized ˈpayments
downspout ˈdaʊn.spaʊt **-s** -s
downstage ˌdaʊnˈsteɪdʒ ⓤⓢ ˈ-- *stress shift, British only:* ˌdownstage ˈaction
downstairs ˌdaʊnˈsteəz ⓤⓢ -ˈsterz *stress shift:* ˌdownstairs ˈbathroom
downstream ˌdaʊnˈstriːm *stress shift:* ˌdownstream ˈsettlement
downswing ˈdaʊn.swɪŋ **-s** -z
downtime ˈdaʊn.taɪm
down-to-earth ˌdaʊn.tuˈɜːθ ⓤⓢ -ˈɝːθ *stress shift:* ˌdown-to-earth ˈperson
Downton ˈdaʊn.tən ⓤⓢ -tən
downtown ˌdaʊnˈtaʊn ⓤⓢ ˌdaʊnˈtaʊn, ˈ-- *stress shift, British only:* ˌdowntown ˈarea
downtrodden ˈdaʊnˌtrɒd.ən, ˌ-ˈ-- ⓤⓢ ˈdaʊnˌtrɑː.dən
downturn ˈdaʊn.tɜːn ⓤⓢ -tɝːn **-s** -z
downward ˈdaʊn.wəd ⓤⓢ -wɚd **-s** -z
downwind ˌdaʊnˈwɪnd ⓤⓢ ˌdaʊnˈwɪnd, ˈ--
down|y ˈdaʊ.n|i **-ier** -i.əʳ ⓤⓢ -i.ɚ **-iest** -i.ɪst, -i.əst
dowr|y ˈdaʊ.r|i **-ies** -iz
dows|e daʊz, daʊs **-es** -ɪz **-ing** -ɪŋ **-ed** -d **-er/s** -əʳ/z ⓤⓢ -ɚ/z ˈ**dowsing** ˌ**rod**
Dowse daʊs
Dowson ˈdaʊ.sən
Dowton ˈdaʊ.tən
doxolog|y dɒkˈsɒl.ə.dʒ|i ⓤⓢ dɑːkˈsɑː.lə- **-ies** -iz
dox|y ˈdɒk.s|i ⓤⓢ ˈdɑːk- **-ies** -iz
doyen ˈdɔɪ.en, -ən; ˈdwaɪ.æ̃ŋ; dɔɪˈen ⓤⓢ ˈdɔɪ.ən, -ən, dwɑːˈjen **-s** -z
doyenne dɔɪˈen; dwaɪˈæ̃ŋ ⓤⓢ dɔɪˈen, -ˈjen, dwɑːˈjen **-s** -z
Doyle dɔɪl
doyl|(e)y ˈdɔɪ.li **-l(e)ys** -z **-lies** -z
D'Oyl(e)y ˈdɔɪ.li
d'Oyly Carte ˌdɔɪ.liˈkɑːt ⓤⓢ -ˈkɑːrt
doz|e dəʊz ⓤⓢ doʊz **-es** -ɪz **-ing** -ɪŋ **-ed** -d **-er/s** -əʳ/z ⓤⓢ -ɚ/z
dozen ˈdʌz.ən **-s** -z **-th** -θ
doz|y ˈdəʊ.z|i ⓤⓢ ˈdoʊ- **-ier** -i.əʳ ⓤⓢ -i.ɚ **-iest** -i.ɪst, -i.əst **-ily** -ɪ.li, -əl.i **-iness** -ɪ.nəs, -ɪ.nɪs
DPhil ˌdiːˈfɪl
dr *(abbrev. for* **dram***)* dræm
Dr. *(abbrev. for* **Doctor***)* ˈdɒk.təʳ ⓤⓢ ˈdɑːk.tɚ
drab dræb **-s** -z **-ber** -əʳ ⓤⓢ -ɚ **-best** -ɪst, -əst **-ness** -nəs, -nɪs
drabbl|e (D) ˈdræb.l̩ **-es** -z **-ing** -ɪŋ, ˈ-lɪŋ **-ed** -d
dracaena drəˈsiː.nə **-s** -z
drachm dræm **-s** -z
drachm|a ˈdræk.m|ə **-as** -əz **-ae** -iː, -eɪ
Draco *Greek legislator:* ˈdreɪ.kəʊ ⓤⓢ -koʊ *English surname:* ˈdrɑː.kəʊ ⓤⓢ -koʊ
draconian (D) drəˈkəʊ.ni.ən, drækˈəʊ- ⓤⓢ drəˈkoʊ-, dreɪ-
Dracula ˈdræk.jə.lə, -jʊ-
draff dræf, drɑːf ⓤⓢ dræf
draft drɑːft ⓤⓢ dræft **-s** -s **-ing** -ɪŋ **-ed** -ɪd **-er/s** -əʳ/z ⓤⓢ -ɚ/z ˈ**draft** ˌ**dodger**
draftee ˌdrɑːfˈtiː ⓤⓢ ˌdræf- **-s** -z
drafts|man ˈdrɑːfts|.mən ⓤⓢ ˈdræfts- **-men** -mən, -men **-manship** -mən.ʃɪp
drafts|woman ˈdrɑːfts|ˌwʊm.ən ⓤⓢ ˈdræfts- **-women** -ˌwɪm.ɪn
draft|y ˈdrɑːf.t|i ⓤⓢ ˈdræf- **-ier** -i.əʳ ⓤⓢ -i.ɚ **-iest** -i.ɪst, -i.əst **-iness** -ɪ.nəs, -ɪ.nɪs
drag dræg **-s** -z **-ging** -ɪŋ **-ged** -d ˈ**drag** ˌ**race**; ˈ**drag** ˌ**queen**
Drage dreɪdʒ
dragee, dragée dræʒˈeɪ ⓤⓢ dræʒˈeɪ, drɑːˈʒeɪ **-s** -z
draggl|e ˈdræg.l̩ **-es** -z **-ing** -ɪŋ, ˈ-lɪŋ **-ed** -d
draggl|y ˈdræg|.i **-ier** -i.əʳ ⓤⓢ -i.ɚ **-iest** -i.ɪst, -i.əst
dragnet ˈdræg.net **-s** -s
drago|man ˈdræg.əʊ|.mən, -mæn

(US) -ə-, -oʊ- **-mans** -mənz, -mænz **-men** -mən, -men

dragon ˈdræg.ᵊn **-s** -z ˈ**dragon's** ˌ**blood**, ˌ**dragon's** ˈ**blood**

dragonet ˈdræg.ə.nɪt, -net **-s** -s

dragonfl|y ˈdræg.ᵊn.fl|aɪ **-ies** -aɪz

dragonnade ˌdræg.əˈneɪd **-s** -z

dragoon drəˈguːn **-s** -z

dragster ˈdræg.stəʳ (US) -stɚ **-s** -z

drain dreɪn **-s** -z **-ing** -ɪŋ **-ed** -d **-er/s** -əʳ/z (US) -ɚ/z ˈ**draining** ˌ**board**

drainage ˈdreɪ.nɪdʒ

drainpipe ˈdreɪn.paɪp, ˈdreɪm- (US) ˈdreɪn- **-s** -s

drake (**D**) dreɪk **-s** -s

Drakensberg ˈdræk.ənz.bɜːg (US) ˈdrɑː.kənz.bɝːg

Dralon® ˈdreɪ.lɒn (US) -lɑːn

dram dræm **-s** -z **-ming** -ɪŋ **-med** -d

drama ˈdrɑː.mə (US) ˈdrɑːm.ə, ˈdræm.ə **-s** -z

Dramamine® ˈdræm.ə.miːn

dramatic drəˈmæt.ɪk (US) -ˈmæt̬- **-al** -ᵊl **-ally** -ᵊl.i, -li **-s** -s

dramatis personae ˌdrɑː.mə.tɪs.pɜːˈsəʊ.naɪ, ˌdræm.ə-, -pəˈ- (US) ˌdrɑː.mə.t̬ɪs.pɚˈsoʊ-, ˌdræm.ə-, -ni

dramatist ˈdræm.ə.tɪst, ˈdrɑː.mə- (US) ˈdrɑː.mə.t̬ɪst, ˈdræm.ə- **-s** -s

dramatization, -isa- ˌdræm.ə.taɪˈzeɪ.ʃᵊn, ˌdrɑː.mə-, -tɪˈ- (US) ˌdrɑː.mə.t̬ɪˈ-, ˌdræm.ə- **-s** -z

dramatiz|e, -is|e ˈdræm.ə.taɪz, ˈdrɑː.mə- (US) ˈdrɑː.mə-, ˈdræm.ə- **-es** -ɪz **-ing** -ɪŋ **-ed** -d **-able** -ə.bl̩

dramaturg|e ˈdræm.ə.tɜːdʒ, ˈdrɑː.mə- (US) ˈdrɑː.mə-, ˈdræm.ə.tɝːdʒ **-es** -ɪz

dramaturgic ˌdræm.əˈtɜː.dʒɪk, ˌdrɑː.mə- (US) ˈdrɑː.mə.tɝː-; ˌdræm.əˈtɝː- **-al** -ᵊl **-ally** -ᵊl.i, -li

dramaturgy ˈdræm.ə.tɜː.dʒi, ˈdrɑː.mə- (US) ˈdrɑː.mə.tɝː-, ˈdræm.ə-

Drambuie® dræmˈbjuː.i, -ˈbuː-

Drane dreɪn

drank (*from* **drink**) dræŋk

drap|e dreɪp **-es** -s **-ing** -ɪŋ **-ed** -t

draper (**D**) ˈdreɪ.pəʳ (US) -pɚ **-s** -z

draper|y ˈdreɪ.pᵊr|.i **-ies** -iz

Drapier ˈdreɪ.pi.əʳ (US) -ɚ

Draskovic ˈdræs.kə.vɪtʃ (US) drɑːs-

drastic ˈdræs.tɪk, ˈdrɑː.stɪk (US) ˈdræs.tɪk **-ally** -ᵊl.i, -li

drat dræt

draught drɑːft (US) dræft **-s** -s

draughtboard ˈdrɑːft.bɔːd (US) ˈdræft.bɔːrd **-s** -z

draught-proof ˈdrɑːft.pruːf (US) ˈdræft- **-s** -s **-ing** -ɪŋ **-d** -t

draughts|man ˈdrɑːfts|.mən (US) ˈdræfts- **-men** -mən

draughts|woman ˈdrɑːfts|ˌwʊm.ən (US) ˈdræfts- **-women** -ˌwɪm.ɪn

draught|y ˈdrɑːf.t|i (US) ˈdræf- **-ier** -i.əʳ (US) -i.ɚ **-iest** -i.ɪst, -i.əst **-ily** -ɪ.li, -ᵊl.i **-iness** -ɪ.nəs, -ɪ.nɪs

Drava ˈdrɑː.və

Dravidian drəˈvɪd.i.ən **-s** -z

draw drɔː (US) drɑː, drɔː **-s** -z **-ing** -ɪŋ **drew** druː **drawn** drɔːn (US) drɑːn, drɔːn **drawable** ˈdrɔː.ə.bl̩ (US) ˈdrɑː-, ˈdrɔː- ˈ**drawing** ˌ**board**; ˈ**drawing** ˌ**pin**; ˈ**drawing** ˌ**room**; ˈ**drawing** ˌ**table**; **go** ˌ**back to the** ˈ**drawing** ˌ**board**

drawback ˈdrɔː.bæk (US) ˈdrɑː-, ˈdrɔː- **-s** -s

drawbridg|e ˈdrɔː.brɪdʒ (US) ˈdrɑː-, ˈdrɔː- **-es** -ɪz

drawdown ˈdrɔː.daʊn (US) ˈdrɑː-, ˈdrɔː-

drawee ˌdrɔːˈiː (US) ˌdrɑː-, ˌdrɔː- **-s** -z

drawer *sliding box:* drɔːʳ (US) drɔːr **-s** -z

drawer *person who draws:* ˈdrɔː.əʳ (US) ˈdrɑː.ɚ, ˈdrɔː- **-s** -z

drawers *garment:* drɔːz (US) drɔːrz

drawl drɔːl (US) drɑːl, drɔːl **-s** -z **-ing** -ɪŋ **-ed** -d **-er/s** -əʳ/z (US) -ɚ/z

drawn (*from* **draw**) drɔːn (US) drɑːn, drɔːn

drawstring ˈdrɔː.strɪŋ (US) ˈdrɑː-, ˈdrɔː- **-s** -z

Drax dræks

dray dreɪ **-s** -z

dray|man ˈdreɪ|.mən, -mæn **-men** -mən, -men

Drayton ˈdreɪ.tᵊn

dread dred **-s** -z **-ing** -ɪŋ **-ed** -ɪd

dreadful ˈdred.fᵊl, -fʊl **-ly** -i **-ness** -nəs, -nɪs

dreadlocks ˈdred.lɒks (US) -lɑːks

dreadnought, dreadnaught (**D**) ˈdred.nɔːt (US) -nɑːt, -nɔːt **-s** -s

dream driːm **-s** -z **-ing/ly** -ɪŋ/li **-ed** drempt, driːmd (US) driːmd, drempt **-t** drempt **-er/s** ˈdriː.məʳ/z (US) -mɚ/z **-like** -laɪk ˈ**dream** ˌ**world**

dreamboat ˈdriːm.bəʊt (US) -boʊt **-s** -s

Dreamcast® ˈdriːm.kɑːst (US) -kæst

dreamland ˈdriːm.lænd

dreamless ˈdriːm.ləs, -lɪs **-ly** -li

dreamtime ˈdriːm.taɪm

dream|y ˈdriː.m|i **-ier** -i.əʳ (US) -i.ɚ **-iest** -i.ɪst, -i.əst **-ily** -ɪ.li, -ᵊl.i **-iness** -ɪ.nəs, -ɪ.nɪs

drear drɪəʳ (US) drɪr

drear|y ˈdrɪə.r|i (US) ˈdrɪr|.i **-ier** -i.əʳ (US) -i.ɚ **-iest** -i.ɪst, -i.əst **-ily** -ɪ.li, -ᵊl.i **-iness** -ɪ.nəs, -ɪ.nɪs

dredg|e dredʒ **-es** -ɪz **-ing** -ɪŋ **-ed** -d

dredger ˈdredʒ.əʳ (US) -ɚ **-s** -z

Dre-fach Felindre drevˌɑːx.velˈɪn.drə

dregg|y ˈdreg|.i **-ily** -ɪ.li, -ᵊl.i **-iness** -ɪ.nəs, -ɪ.nɪs

dregs dregz

Dreiser ˈdraɪ.zəʳ, -səʳ (US) -zɚ, -sɚ

drench drentʃ **-es** -ɪz **-ing** -ɪŋ **-ed** -t **-er/s** -əʳ/z (US) -ɚ/z

Dresden ˈdrez.dᵊn

dress dres **-es** -ɪz **-ing** -ɪŋ **-ed** -t ˌ**dress** ˈ**circle** (US) ˈ**dress** ˌ**circle**; ˌ**dress** ˈ**coat** (US) ˈ**dress** ˌ**coat**; ˈ**dress** ˌ**code**; ˌ**dress** **re**ˈ**hearsal** (US) ˈ**dress re**ˌ**hearsal**; ˈ**dress** ˌ**sense**; ˌ**dress** ˈ**suit**; (US) ˈ**dress** ˌ**suit**

dressage ˈdres.ɑːʒ; -ɑːdʒ; -ɪdʒ; drəˈsɑːʒ (US) drəˈsɑːʒ, dresˈɑːʒ

dresser ˈdres.əʳ (US) -ɚ **-s** -z

dressing ˈdres.ɪŋ **-s** -z ˈ**dressing** ˌ**gown**; ˈ**dressing** ˌ**room**; ˈ**dressing** ˌ**table**;

dressing-down ˌdres.ɪŋˈdaʊn **-s** -z

dressmak|er ˈdresˌmeɪ.k|əʳ (US) -k|ɚ **-ers** -əz (US) -ɚz **-ing** -ɪŋ

dress|y ˈdres|.i **-ier** -i.əʳ (US) -i.ɚ **-iest** -i.ɪst, -i.əst **-ily** -ɪ.li, -ᵊl.i **-iness** -ɪ.nəs, -ɪ.nɪs

drew (*from* **draw**) druː

Drew druː **-s** -z

Dreyfus(s) ˈdreɪ.fəs, ˈdraɪ-, -fʊs

dribbl|e ˈdrɪb.l̩ **-es** -z **-ing** -ɪŋ **-ed** -d, ˈ-lɪŋ **-er/s** -əʳ/z, ˈ-ləʳ/z (US) ˈ-l̩.ɚ/z, ˈ-lɚ/z

driblet ˈdrɪb.lət, -lɪt **-s** -s

dribs and drabs ˌdrɪbz.ənˈdræbz

dried (*from* **dry**) draɪd

drier ˈdraɪ.əʳ (US) -ɚ **-s** -z

dries (*from* **dry**) draɪz

driest ˈdraɪ.ɪst, -əst

Driffield ˈdrɪf.iːld

drift drɪft **-s** -s **-ing** -ɪŋ **-ed** -ɪd

drifter ˈdrɪf.təʳ (US) -tɚ **-s** -z

driftless ˈdrɪft.ləs, -lɪs

driftnet ˈdrɪft.net **-s** -s

driftwood ˈdrɪft.wʊd

drifty ˈdrɪf.ti

drill drɪl **-s** -z **-ing** -ɪŋ **-ed** -d ˈ**drill** ˌ**sergeant**

drily ˈdraɪ.li

drink drɪŋk **-s** -s **-ing** -ɪŋ **drank** dræŋk **drunk** drʌŋk **drinker/s** ˈdrɪŋ.kəʳ/z (US) -kɚ/z ˈ**drinking** ˌ**fountain**; ˈ**drinking** ˌ**horn**; ˈ**drinking** ˌ**water**

drinkable ˈdrɪŋ.kə.bl̩

drink-driv|ing ˌdrɪŋkˈdraɪ.v|ɪŋ **-er/s** -əʳ/z (US) -ɚ/z

Drinkwater ˈdrɪŋkˌwɔː.təʳ (US) -ˌwɑː.t̬ɚ, -ˌwɔː-

drip drɪp **-s** -s **-ping** -ɪŋ **-ped** -t

drip|-dry ˈdrɪp|.draɪ, ˌ-ˈ- **-dries** -draɪz **-drying** -ˌdraɪ.ɪŋ **-dried** -draɪd

drip|-feed ˈdrɪp|.fiːd **-feeds** -fiːdz **-feeding** -ˌfiː.dɪŋ **-fed** -fed

dripping ˈdrɪp.ɪŋ **-s** -z

dripp|y ˈdrɪp|.i **-ier** -i.əʳ (US) -i.ɚ **-iest** -i.ɪst, -i.əst

dripstone ˈdrɪp.stəʊn (US) -stoʊn **-s** -z

Driscoll ˈdrɪs.kᵊl

driv|e draɪv **-es** -z **-ing** -ɪŋ **drove** drəʊv ⓤⓢ droʊv **driven** 'drɪv.ᵊn **'driving ˌiron; 'driving ˌlicence/license; 'driving ˌseat; 'driving ˌtest**

driveaway 'draɪv.əˌweɪ

drive-by 'draɪv.baɪ

drive-in 'draɪv.ɪn **-s** -z

drivel 'drɪv.ᵊl **-s** -z **-(l)ing** -ɪŋ **-(l)ed** -d **-(l)er/s** -əʳ/z ⓤⓢ -ɚ/z

driven *(from* **drive***)* 'drɪv.ᵊn

driver (D) 'draɪ.vəʳ ⓤⓢ -vɚ **-s** -z **'driver's ˌlicense; in the 'driver's ˌseat**

driveway 'draɪv.weɪ **-s** -z

Driza-bone® 'draɪ.zə.bəʊn ⓤⓢ -boʊn

drizzl|e 'drɪz.l̩ **-es** -z **-ing** -ɪŋ, '-lɪŋ **-ed** -d

drizzly 'drɪz.l̩.i, '-li

Drogheda *place:* 'drɔɪ.ɪ.də, 'drɔː-, '-ə-, 'drɒ.hə- ⓤⓢ 'drɔː.ɪ-, 'drɑː-, '-ə- *Earl:* 'drɔɪ.ɪ.də

droid drɔɪd **-s** -z

droit drɔɪt, drwɑː **-s** -s

droit de seigneur ˌdrwɑː.də.seɪ'njɜːʳ, -sen'jɜːʳ, -siː'njɜːʳ ⓤⓢ -seɪ'njʊr, -sen'jʊr, -'jɝː

Droitwich 'drɔɪ.twɪtʃ

droll drəʊl ⓤⓢ droʊl **-ness** -nəs, -nɪs **-er** -əʳ ⓤⓢ -ɚ **-est** -ɪst, -əst **-y** -li, 'drəʊ.li ⓤⓢ 'droʊ.li

droller|y 'drəʊ.lᵊr|.i ⓤⓢ 'droʊ- **-ies** -iz

-drome -drəʊm ⓤⓢ -droʊm

Note: Suffix. Normally unstressed, e.g. **aerodrome** /'eə.rə.drəʊm ⓤⓢ 'er.ə.droʊm/.

dromedar|y 'drɒm.ə.dᵊr|.i, 'drʌm-, '-ɪ- ⓤⓢ 'drɑː.mə.der-, 'drʌm.ə- **-ies** -iz

Dromio 'drəʊ.mi.əʊ ⓤⓢ 'droʊ.mi.oʊ

Dromore 'drəʊ.mɔːʳ; drə'mɔːʳ ⓤⓢ 'droʊ.mɔːr; drə'mɔːr

dron|e drəʊn ⓤⓢ droʊn **-es** -z **-ing** -ɪŋ **-ed** -d

Dronfield 'drɒn.fiːld ⓤⓢ 'drɑːn-

drongo 'drɒŋ.gəʊ ⓤⓢ 'drɑːŋ.goʊ **-(e)s** -z

Drood druːd

drool druːl **-s** -z **-ing** -ɪŋ **-ed** -d

droop druːp **-s** -s **-ing/ly** -ɪŋ/li **-ed** -t

droop|y 'druː.p|i **-ier** -i.əʳ ⓤⓢ -i.ɚ **-iest** -i.ɪst, -i.əst **-ily** -ɪ.li, -ᵊl.i **-iness** -ɪ.nəs, -ɪ.nɪs

drop drɒp ⓤⓢ drɑːp **-s** -s **-ping** -ɪŋ **-ped** -t **'drop ˌscone; 'drop ˌshot; a ˌdrop in the 'ocean; at the ˌdrop of a 'hat**

drop-in 'drɒp.ɪn ⓤⓢ 'drɑːp-

dropkick 'drɒp.kɪk ⓤⓢ 'drɑːp- **-s** -s

droplet 'drɒp.lət, -lɪt ⓤⓢ 'drɑːp- **-s** -s

dropout 'drɒp.aʊt ⓤⓢ 'drɑːp- **-s** -s

dropper 'drɒp.əʳ ⓤⓢ 'drɑː.pɚ **-s** -z

dropping 'drɒp.ɪŋ ⓤⓢ 'drɑː.pɪŋ **-s** -z

dropsic|al 'drɒp.sɪ.k|ᵊl ⓤⓢ 'drɑːp- **-ally** -ᵊl.i, -li **-alness** -ᵊl.nəs, -nɪs

dropsy 'drɒp.si ⓤⓢ 'drɑːp-

droshk|y 'drɒʃ.k|i ⓤⓢ 'drɑːʃ- **-ies** -iz

drosophila drə'sɒf.ɪ.lə, drɒs'ɒf-, -ᵊl.ə ⓤⓢ droʊ'sɑː.fᵊl.ə, drə- **-s** -z

dross drɒs ⓤⓢ drɑːs **-y** -i

drought draʊt **-s** -s **-y** -i

drove drəʊv ⓤⓢ droʊv **-s** -z

drover 'drəʊ.vəʳ ⓤⓢ 'droʊ.vɚ **-s** -z

Drower draʊəʳ ⓤⓢ draʊɚ

drown draʊn **-s** -z **-ing** -ɪŋ **-ed** -d

drows|e draʊz **-es** -ɪz **-ing** -ɪŋ **-ed** -d

drows|y 'draʊ.z|i **-ier** -i.əʳ ⓤⓢ -i.ɚ **-iest** -i.ɪst, -i.əst **-ily** -ɪ.li, -ᵊl.i **-iness** -ɪ.nəs, -ɪ.nɪs

Droylsden 'drɔɪlz.dᵊn

Drs. *(abbrev. for* **Doctors***)* 'dɒk.təz ⓤⓢ 'dɑːk.tɚz

drub drʌb **-s** -z **-bing** -ɪŋ **-bed** -d

Druce druːs

Drucker 'drʊk.əʳ ⓤⓢ 'drʌk.ɚ, 'drʊk-

drudg|e drʌdʒ **-es** -ɪz **-ing/ly** -ɪŋ/li **-ed** -d

drudgery 'drʌdʒ.ᵊr.i

drug drʌg **-s** -z **-ging** -ɪŋ **-ged** -d

drugget 'drʌg.ɪt **-s** -s

druggie 'drʌg.i **-s** -z

druggist 'drʌg.ɪst **-s** -s

druggl|y 'drʌg|.i **-ies** -iz

drugstore 'drʌg.stɔːʳ ⓤⓢ -stɔːr **-s** -z

druid 'druː.ɪd **-s** -z **-ess/es** -ɪs/ɪz, -es/ɪz **-ism** -ɪ.zᵊm

druidic druː'ɪd.ɪk **-al** -ᵊl

drum drʌm **-s** -z **-ming** -ɪŋ **-med** -d **ˌdrum 'major** ⓤⓢ **'drum ˌmajor; ˌdrum major'ette**

drumbeat 'drʌm.biːt **-s** -s

Drumcree drʌm'kriː *stress shift:* ˌDrumcree 'residents

drumfire 'drʌm.faɪəʳ ⓤⓢ -faɪɚ

drumhead 'drʌm.hed **-s** -z

drummer 'drʌm.əʳ ⓤⓢ -ɚ **-s** -z

Drummond 'drʌm.ənd

drumroll 'drʌm.rəʊl ⓤⓢ -roʊl **-s** -z

drumstick 'drʌm.stɪk **-s** -s

drunk *(n. adj.) (also from* **drink***)* drʌŋk **-s** -s **-er** -əʳ ⓤⓢ -ɚ

drunkard 'drʌŋ.kəd ⓤⓢ -kɚd **-s** -z

drunk-driv|ing ˌdrʌŋk'draɪ.v|ɪŋ **-er/s** -əʳ/z ⓤⓢ -ɚ/z

drunken 'drʌŋ.kən **-ly** -li **-ness** -nəs, -nɪs

drupe druːp **-s** -s

Drury 'drʊə.ri ⓤⓢ 'drʊr.i

drus|e *geological term:* druːz **-es** -ɪz

Druse *surname:* druːz, druːs

Drus|e, Druz|e *member of sect in Syria and Lebanon:* druːz **-es** -ɪz

Drusilla druː'sɪl.ə, drʊ-

druthers 'drʌð.əz ⓤⓢ -ɚz

dr|y dr|aɪ **-ier** -aɪ.əʳ ⓤⓢ -aɪ.ɚ **-iest** -aɪ.ɪst, -əst **-yly** -aɪ.li **-yness** -aɪ.nəs, -nɪs **-ies** -aɪz **-ying** -aɪ.ɪŋ **-ied** -aɪd **ˌdry 'goods** ⓤⓢ **'dry ˌgoods; ˌdry 'ice; ˌdry 'land; ˌdry 'rot**

dryad 'draɪ.æd, -əd **-s** -z

Dryburgh 'draɪ.bᵊr.ə ⓤⓢ -bɝːg, -bɚ.ə

dry-clean ˌdraɪ'kliːn ⓤⓢ '-- **-s** -z **-ing** -ɪŋ **-ed** -d **-er/s** -əʳ/z ⓤⓢ -ɚ/z

Dryden 'draɪ.dᵊn

dry-dock ˌdraɪ'dɒk, '-- ⓤⓢ 'draɪ.dɑːk **-s** -s **-ing** -ɪŋ **-ed** -t

dryer 'draɪ.əʳ ⓤⓢ -ɚ **-s** -z

Dryfesdale 'draɪfs.deɪl

Dryhurst 'draɪ.hɜːst ⓤⓢ -hɝːst

drying *(from* **dry***)* 'draɪ.ɪŋ

dryly 'draɪ.li

dryness 'draɪ.nəs, -nɪs

dry-nurs|e 'draɪ.nɜːs ⓤⓢ -nɝːs **-es** -ɪz **-ing** -ɪŋ **-ed** -t

drypoint 'draɪ.pɔɪnt

Drysdale 'draɪz.deɪl

dryshod 'draɪ.ʃɒd ⓤⓢ ʃɑːd

drywall 'draɪ.wɔːl ⓤⓢ -wɔːl, -wɑːl **-s** -z **-ing** -ɪŋ **-ed** -d

DTI ˌdiː.tiː'aɪ

DTP ˌdiː.tiː'piː

DTs ˌdiː'tiːz

dual 'djuː.əl, 'dʒuː-; djʊəl, dʒʊəl ⓤⓢ 'duː.ᵊl, 'djuː- **ˌdual 'carriageway**

dual|ism 'djuː.ə.l|ɪ.zᵊm, 'dʒuː-; 'djʊə.l|ɪ-, 'dʒʊə- ⓤⓢ 'duː.ᵊl|.ɪ-, 'djuː- **-ist/s** -ɪst/s

dualistic ˌdjuː.ə'lɪs.tɪk, ˌdʒuː-; ˌdjʊə'lɪs-, ˌdʒʊə- ⓤⓢ ˌduː.ᵊl'ɪs-, ˌdjuː-

dualit|y dju'æl.ə.t|i, dʒu-, -ɪ.t|i ⓤⓢ du'æl.ə.t̬|i, dju- **-ies** -iz

dual-purpose ˌdjuː.əl'pɜː.pəs, ˌdʒuː-; ˌdjʊəl-, ˌdʒʊəl- ⓤⓢ ˌduː.ᵊl'pɝː-, ˌdjuː- *stress shift:* ˌdual-purpose 'implement

Duane dweɪn; du'eɪn

dub dʌb **-s** -z **-bing** -ɪŋ **-bed** -d

Dubai duː'baɪ, dʊ-, djʊ- ⓤⓢ duː-, də-

Du Barry djuː'bær.i, duː- ⓤⓢ duː'ber-, djuː-, -'bær-

dubbin 'dʌb.ɪn

Dubcek 'dʊb.tʃek ⓤⓢ 'duːb-

dubiety djuː'baɪ.ə.ti, djʊ-, dʒuː-, dʒʊ-, -ɪ.ti ⓤⓢ duː'baɪ.ə.t̬i, djuː-

dubious 'djuː.bi.əs, 'dʒuː- ⓤⓢ 'duː-, 'djuː- **-ly** -li **-ness** -nəs, -nɪs

dubi|tate 'djuː.bɪ|.teɪt, 'dʒuː- ⓤⓢ 'duː.bə-, 'djuː- **-tates** -teɪts **-tating** -teɪ.tɪŋ ⓤⓢ -teɪ.t̬ɪŋ **-tated** -teɪ.tɪd ⓤⓢ -teɪ.t̬ɪd

dubitation ˌdjuː.bɪ'teɪ.ʃᵊn, ˌdʒuː- ⓤⓢ ˌduː.bə'-, ˌdjuː- **-s** -z

dubitative 'djuː.bɪ.tə.tɪv, 'dʒuː-, -teɪ- ⓤⓢ 'duː.bə-, 'djuː- **-ly** -li

Dublin 'dʌb.lɪn

Dubliner 'dʌb.lɪ.nəʳ ⓤⓢ -nɚ **-s** -z

DuBois, Du Bois duː'bwɑː, djuː-

Dubonnet® djuː'bɒn.eɪ, duː-, '--- ⓤⓢ ˌduː.bə'neɪ, ˌdjuː-

Dubrovnik djʊ'brɒv.nɪk, dʊ- ⓤⓢ duː'brɑːv-

Dubya 'dʌb.jə

ducal ˈdjuː.k^{ə}l, ˈdʒuː- (US) ˈduː-, ˈdjuː- **-ly** -i
Du Cane djuːˈkeɪn, duː- (US) du-, djuː-
ducat ˈdʌk.ət **-s** -s
duce **(D)** ˈduː.tʃeɪ, -tʃi (US) ˈduː.tʃeɪ
duces tecum ˌduː.kesˈteɪ.kʊm (US) -siːzˈ-
Duchamp ˈdjuː.ʃɑ̃ŋ, ˈduː-, ˌ-ˈ- (US) ˌ-ˈ-, ˌduˈʃɑːmp
Duchesne djuːˈʃeɪn, duː-
duchess **(D)** ˈdʌtʃ.ɪs, -es; dʌtʃˈes (US) ˈdʌtʃ.ɪs **-es** -ɪz
duchesse duːˈʃes; ˈdʌtʃ.ɪs, -es (US) ˈdʌtʃ.ɪs
Duchovny dʊˈkɒv.ni, duː- (US) -ˈkɑːv-
duch|y ˈdʌtʃ|.i **-ies** -iz
Ducie ˈdjuː.si, ˈdʒuː- (US) ˈduː-, ˈdjuː-
duck dʌk **-s** -s **-ing** -ɪŋ **-ed** -t **ˈduck ˌpond; ˌducks and ˈdrakes; ˌtake to something like a ˌduck to ˈwater**
duckbill ˈdʌk.bɪl **-s** -z **-ed** -d **ˌduckbilled ˈplatypus**
duckboard ˈdʌk.bɔːd (US) -bɔːrd **-s** -z
duck-egg ˈdʌk.eg **-s** -z
duckling ˈdʌk.lɪŋ **-s** -z
duckweed ˈdʌk.wiːd
Duckworth ˈdʌk.wəθ, -wɜːθ (US) -wɚθ, -wɝːθ
duck|y ˈdʌk|.i **-ies** -iz
duct dʌkt **-s** -s
ductile ˈdʌk.taɪl (US) -tɪl, -taɪl
ductility dʌkˈtɪl.ə.ti, -ɪ.ti (US) -ə.t̬i
ductless ˈdʌkt.ləs, -lɪs **ˌductless ˈgland**
dud dʌd **-s** -z
Duddeston ˈdʌd.ɪ.st^{ə}n
Duddington ˈdʌd.ɪŋ.t^{ə}n
Duddon ˈdʌd.^{ə}n
dude duːd, djuːd **-s** -z **ˈdude ˌranch**
Dudeney ˈduːd.ni, ˈdjuːd-
dudgeon ˈdʌdʒ.^{ə}n **-s** -z
Dudley ˈdʌd.li
due djuː, dʒuː (US) duː, djuː **-s** -z
duel ˈdjuː.əl, ˈdʒuː- (US) ˈduː.əl, ˈdjuː- **-s** -z **-(l)ing** -ɪŋ **-(l)ed** -d **-(l)er/s** -ə^{r}/z (US) -ɚ/z
duel(l)ist ˈdjuː.^{ə}l.ɪst, ˈdʒuː- (US) ˈduː-, ˈdjuː- **-s** -s
duenna djuˈen.ə, du- (US) du-, dju- **-s** -z
duer ˈdjuː.ə^{r}, ˈdʒuː- (US) ˈduː.ɚ, ˈdjuː-
Duessa djuˈes.ə, dʒu- (US) du-, dju-
duet djuˈet, dʒu- (US) du-, dju- **-s** -s
duettino ˌdjuː.etˈiː.nəʊ, ˌdʒuː- (US) ˌduː.etˈiː.noʊ, ˌdjuː- **-s** -z
duettist djuˈet.ɪst, dʒu- (US) duˈet̬-, dju- **-s** -s
duetto djuˈet.əʊ, dʒu- (US) duˈet̬.oʊ, dju- **-s** -z
duff **(D)** dʌf **-s** -s **-ing** -ɪŋ **-ed** -t
duffel ˈdʌf.^{ə}l **ˈduffel ˌbag; ˈduffel ˌcoat**
duffer ˈdʌf.ə^{r} (US) -ɚ **-s** -z
Dufferin ˈdʌf.^{ə}r.ɪn
Duffield ˈdʌf.iːld
Duffin ˈdʌf.ɪn
Duffy ˈdʌf.i
Dufy ˈduː.fi (US) duːˈfiː
dug *(n.) (also from* **dig***)* dʌg **-s** -z
Dugald ˈduː.g^{ə}ld
Dugan ˈduː.g^{ə}n
Dugdale ˈdʌg.deɪl
Duggan ˈdʌg.^{ə}n
Dugmore ˈdʌg.mɔː^{r} (US) -mɔːr
dugong ˈdjuː.gɒŋ, ˈduː- (US) ˈduː.gɑːŋ, -gɔːŋ **-s** -z
dugout ˈdʌg.aʊt **-s** -s
Duguid ˈdjuː.gɪd, ˈduː.gɪd (US) ˈduː-, ˈdjuː-
DUI ˌdiː.juːˈaɪ
duiker ˈdaɪ.kə^{r} (US) -kɚ **-s** -z
Duisburg ˈdjuːz.bɜːg, ˈdjuːs- (US) ˈduːs.bɝːg, ˈduːz-
Duisenberg ˈdaɪ.z^{ə}n.bɜːg, ˈdɔɪ-, -z^{ə}m- (US) ˈduː.z^{ə}n.bɝg, daɪ-
Dukakis dʊˈkɑː.kɪs, djʊ-, dʒʊ-, də- (US) dʊˈkɑː.kəs, də-
Dukas ˈdjuː.kɑː, ˈduː-, -ˈ- (US) duːˈkɑː, djuː-
duke **(D)** djuːk, dʒuːk (US) duːk, djuːk **-s** -s
dukedom ˈdjuːk.dəm, ˈdʒuːk- (US) ˈduːk-, ˈdjuːk- **-s** -z
duker|y ˈdjuː.k^{ə}r|.i, ˈdʒuː- (US) ˈduː-, ˈdjuː- **-ies** -iz
Dukinfield ˈdʌk.ɪn.fiːld
Dulce ˈdʌl.si
dulcet ˈdʌl.sɪt, -sət
Dulcie ˈdʌl.si
dulci|fy ˈdʌl.sɪ|.faɪ, -sə- **-fies** -faɪz **-fying** -faɪ.ɪŋ **-fied** -faɪd
dulcimer ˈdʌl.sɪ.mə^{r}, -sə- (US) -mɚ **-s** -z
Dulcinea ˌdʌl.sɪˈniː.ə, -ˈneɪ-; dʌlˈsɪn.i- (US) ˌdʌl.səˈniː-; dʌlˈsɪn.i-
dulia djʊˈlaɪə, dʊ- (US) duːˈlaɪə, djuː-; ˈduː.li.ə
dull dʌl **-er** -ə^{r} (US) -ɚ **-est** -ɪst, -əst **-y** -li, -i **-ness** -nəs, -nɪs **-s** -z **-ing** -ɪŋ **-ed** -d **as ˌdull as ˈditch-water**
dullard ˈdʌl.əd, -ɑːd (US) -ɚd **-s** -z
Dulles ˈdʌl.ɪs, -əs
dullish ˈdʌl.ɪʃ
dullsville ˈdʌlz.vɪl
dulness ˈdʌl.nəs, -nɪs
Duluth dəˈluːθ, djʊ-, dʊ-, də- (US) də-
Dulux® ˈdjuː.lʌks
Dulwich ˈdʌl.ɪdʒ, -ɪtʃ
duly ˈdjuː.li, ˈdʒuː- (US) ˈduː-, ˈdjuː-
Duma ˈduː.mə, ˈdjuː- (US) ˈduː-
Dumain djʊˈmeɪn, dʒʊ- (US) duː-, djuː-
Dumas ˈdjuː.mɑː, ˈduː-; dʊˈmɑː (US) duːˈmɑː, djuː-
Du Maurier djuːˈmɔː.ri.eɪ, duː-, -ˈmɒr.i- (US) duːˈmɔːr.i-, djuː-
dumb dʌm **-er -est -ly** -li **-ness** -nəs, -nɪs **-s** -z **-ing** -ɪŋ **-ed** -d **ˈdumb ˌshow; ˌdumb ˈwaiter** (US) **ˈdumb ˌwaiter**
Dumbarton dʌmˈbɑː.t^{ə}n, dəm- (US) -ˈbɑːr-
Note: In **Dumbarton Oaks** (Washington DC), however, the pronunciation is /ˌdʌm.bɑːr.t^{ə}nˈəʊks (US) -bɑːr.t^{ə}nˈoʊks/.
dumbbell ˈdʌm.bel **-s** -z
dumbfound ˌdʌmˈfaʊnd, ˈ-- (US) ˈdʌm.faʊnd, ˌ-ˈ- **-s** -z **-ing** -ɪŋ **-ed** -ɪd
dumbo **(D)** ˈdʌm.bəʊ (US) -boʊ
dumbstricken ˈdʌmˌstrɪk.^{ə}n
dumbstruck ˈdʌm.strʌk
dum-dum ˈdʌm.dʌm **-s** -z
dumfound ˌdʌmˈfaʊnd, ˈ-- (US) ˈdʌm.faʊnd, ˌ-ˈ- **-s** -z **-ing** -ɪŋ **-ed** -ɪd
Dumfries dʌmˈfriːs, dəm- **-shire** -ʃə^{r}, -ˌʃɪə^{r}, dʌmˈfriːʃ.ʃə^{r} (US) dʌmˈfriːs.ʃɚ, -ˌʃɪr
dumm|y ˈdʌm|.i **-ies** -iz
dump dʌmp **-s** -s **-ing** -ɪŋ **-ed** -t **ˈdump ˌtruck**
dumper ˈdʌm.pə^{r} (US) -pɚ **-s** -z
Dumphreys ˈdʌmp.frɪz, -friz
dumpish ˈdʌm.pɪʃ **-ly** -li **-ness** -nəs, -nɪs
dumpling ˈdʌm.plɪŋ **-s** -z
dumps dʌmps
Dumpster® ˈdʌmp.stə^{r} (US) -stɚ
dump|y ˈdʌm.p|i **-ier** -i.ə^{r} (US) -i.ɚ **-iest** -i.ɪst, -i.əst **-iness** -ɪ.nəs, -ɪ.nɪs
dun dʌn **-s** -z **-ning** -ɪŋ **-ned** -d
Dunalley dʌnˈæl.i
Dunaway ˈdʌn.ə.weɪ
Dunbar dʌnˈbɑː^{r}, dʌm-, ˈ-- (US) ˈdʌn.bɑːr, -ˈ-
Note: In Scotland always -ˈ-.
Dunbarton dʌnˈbɑː.t^{ə}n, dʌm- (US) dʌnˈbɑːr- **-shire** -ʃə^{r}, -ˌʃɪə^{r} (US) -ʃɚ, -ˌʃɪr
Dunblane dʌnˈbleɪn, dʌm- (US) dʌn-
Duncan ˈdʌŋ.kən, ˈdʌn-
Duncannon dʌnˈkæn.ən, dʌŋ- (US) dʌn-
Duncansby ˈdʌŋ.kənz.bi, ˈdʌn-
dunc|e dʌnts **-es** -ɪz
Dunciad ˈdʌnt.si.æd
Duncombe ˈdʌn.kəm, ˈdʌŋ-
Dundalk dʌnˈdɔːk, -ˈdɔːlk (US) -ˈdɔːk, -ˈdɑːk
Dundas dʌnˈdæs, ˈdʌn.dæs, ˈdʌn.dəs (US) dʌnˈdæs, ˈdʌn.dəs
Dundee dʌnˈdiː, ˌdʌn- *stress shift:* ˌDundee ˈstation
dunderhead ˈdʌn.də.hed (US) -dɚ- **-s** -z
Dundonald dʌnˈdɒn.^{ə}ld (US) -ˈdɑː.n^{ə}ld
dundrear|y **(D)** dʌnˈdrɪə.r|i (US) -ˈdrɪr|.i **-ies** -iz
Dundrum dʌnˈdrʌm, ˈdʌn.drəm
dune djuːn, dʒuːn (US) duːn, djuːn **-s** -z
Dunedin dʌnˈiː.dɪn, -d^{ə}n

Dunell djʊ'nel, ˌdjuː-, dʒʊ-, ˌdʒuː- (US) duː-, djuː-
Dunfermline dʌn'fɜːm.lɪn, -lən (US) -'fɝːm-
dung dʌŋ
Dungannon dʌn'gæn.ən, dʌŋ-
dungaree ˌdʌŋ.gə'riː, '--- **-s** -z
Dungarvan dʌn'gɑː.vən, dʌŋ- (US) dʌn'gɑːr-
Dungeness ˌdʌn.*dʒ*ə'nes, -*dʒ*ɪ'-
dungeon 'dʌn.dʒᵊn **-s** -z
dunghill 'dʌŋ.hɪl **-s** -z
Dunglison 'dʌŋ.glɪ.sᵊn
dungy 'dʌŋ.i
Dunham 'dʌn.ᵊm
Dunhill 'dʌn.hɪl
Dunholme 'dʌn.əm
dunk (D) dʌŋk **-s** -s **-ing** -ɪŋ **-ed** -t
Dunkeld dʌn'keld, dʌŋ- (US) dʌn-
Dunker 'dʌŋ.kəʳ (US) -kɚ **-s** -z
Dunkirk dʌn'kɜːk, ˌdʌn-, dʌŋ-, ˌdʌŋ- (US) 'dʌn.kɝːk, dʌn'kɝːk, ˌdʌn-
Dunkley 'dʌŋ.kli
Dun Laoghaire dʌn'lɪə.ri, duːn-, 'leə-, -rə (US) -'ler.ə, -i
Dunlap 'dʌn.ləp, -læp (US) -læp, -ləp
dunlin 'dʌn.lɪn, -lən **-s** -z
Dunlop *surname:* 'dʌn.lɒp, -'- (US) 'dʌn.lɑːp, -'-
Dunlop® 'dʌn.lɒp (US) -lɑːp **-s** -s
Dunmail dʌn'meɪl, dʌm- (US) dʌn-
Dunmore dʌn'mɔːʳ, dʌm- (US) dʌn'mɔːr
Dunmow 'dʌn.məʊ, 'dʌm- (US) 'dʌn.moʊ
dunnage 'dʌn.ɪdʒ
Dunn(e) dʌn
Dunnet(t) 'dʌn.ɪt
Dunning 'dʌn.ɪŋ
dunno də'nəʊ (US) -'noʊ
dunnock 'dʌn.ək **-s** -s
Dunnottar dʌn'ɒt.əʳ, də'nɒt- (US) dʌn'ɑː.t̬ɚ, də'nɑː-
dunn|y 'dʌn|.i **-ies** -ɪz
Dunoon dʌn'uːn, də'nuːn
Dunraven dʌn'reɪ.vᵊn
Dunrobin dʌn'rɒb.ɪn (US) -'rɑː.bɪn
Dunsany dʌn'seɪ.ni, -'sæn.i
Dunse dʌn*t*s
Dunsinane dʌn'sɪn.ən
Note: This name has to be pronounced /ˌdʌn*t*.sɪ'neɪn/ in Shakespeare's 'Macbeth'.
Duns Scotus ˌdʌnz'skɒt.əs, -'skəʊ.təs (US) -'skoʊ.t̬əs
Dunstable 'dʌn*t*.stə.bl̩
Dunstaffnage dʌn'stæf.nɪdʒ, -'stɑːf- (US) -'stæf-
Dunstan 'dʌn*t*.stᵊn
Dunster 'dʌn*t*.stəʳ (US) -stɚ
Dunston 'dʌn*t*.stᵊn
Dunton 'dʌn.tən (US) -tᵊn
Dunwich 'dʌn.ɪtʃ
Dunwoody dʌn'wʊd.i
duo- djuː.əʊ-, dʒuː.əʊ-; dju'ɒ-, dʒu'ɒ- (US) duː.oʊ-, djuː-, -ə-; du'ɑː-, dju'ɑː-
Note: Prefix. Either carries primary or secondary stress on the first syllable, e.g. **duologue** /'djuː.ə.lɒg (US) 'duː.ə.lɑːg/, **duodecimal** /ˌdjuː.əʊ'des.ɪ.mᵊl (US) ˌduː.oʊ'-/, or primary stress on the second syllable, e.g. **duopoly** /dju'ɒp.ᵊl.i (US) du'ɑː.pᵊl-/.
duo 'djuː.əʊ, 'dʒuː- (US) 'duː.oʊ, 'djuː- **-s** -z
duodecennial ˌdjuː.əʊ.dɪ'sen.i.əl, ˌdʒuː-, -də'- (US) ˌduː.oʊ.də'-, ˌdjuː-
duodecimal ˌdjuː.əʊ'des.ɪ.mᵊl, ˌdʒuː-, '-ə- (US) ˌduː.oʊ'-, ˌdjuː- **-s** -z
duodecimo ˌdjuː.əʊ'des.ɪ.məʊ, ˌdʒuː- (US) ˌduː.oʊ'des.ə.moʊ, ˌdjuː- **-s** -z
duodenal ˌdjuː.əʊ'diː.nᵊl, ˌdʒuː- (US) ˌduː.ə'-, ˌdjuː-; duː'ɑː.dᵊn.ᵊl, djuː-
duodenary ˌdjuː.əʊ'diː.nᵊr.i, ˌdʒuː- (US) ˌduː.ə'-, ˌdjuː-, -'dən.ɚ.i
duoden|um ˌdjuː.əʊ'diː.n|əm, ˌdʒuː- (US) ˌduː.ə'-, ˌdjuː-; duː'ɑː.dᵊn|.əm, djuː- **-ums** -əmz **-a** -ə
duologue 'djuː.ə.lɒg, 'dʒuː- (US) 'duː.ə.lɑːg, 'djuː- **-s** -z
duopol|y dju'ɒp.ᵊl|.i, dʒu- (US) du'ɑː.pᵊl-, dju- **-ies** -iz
dup|e djuːp, dʒuːp (US) duːp, djuːp **-es** -s **-ing** -ɪŋ **-ed** -t
dupery 'djuː.pᵊr.i, 'dʒuː- (US) 'duː-, 'djuː-
duple 'djuː.pl̩, 'dʒuː- (US) 'duː-, 'djuː-
Dupleix *governor in India:* djuː'pleɪks (US) duː'pleɪks, djuː- *historian:* djuː'pleɪ (US) duː'pleɪ, djuː-
duplex 'djuː.pleks, 'dʒuː- (US) 'duː-, 'djuː- **-es** -ɪz
duplicate (*n. adj.*) 'djuː.plɪ.kət, 'dʒuː-, -plə-, -kɪt (US) 'duː-, 'djuː- **-s** -s
dupli|cate (*v.*) 'djuː.plɪ|.keɪt, 'dʒuː-, -plə- (US) 'duː-, 'djuː- **-cates** -keɪts **-cating** -keɪ.tɪŋ (US) -keɪ.t̬ɪŋ **-cated** -keɪ.tɪd (US) -keɪ.t̬ɪd **-cator/s** -keɪ.təʳ/z (US) -keɪ.t̬ɚ/z
duplication ˌdjuː.plɪ'keɪ.ʃᵊn, ˌdʒuː-, -plə'- (US) ˌduː-, ˌdjuː- **-s** -z
duplicature 'djuː.plɪ.keɪ.tʃəʳ, 'dʒuː-, -kə- (US) 'duː.plə.kə.tʃʊr, 'djuː-, -keɪ-, -tʃɚ **-s** -z
duplicitous djʊ'plɪs.ɪ.təs, dʒʊ-, '-ə- (US) duː'plɪs.ə.t̬əs, djuː- **-ly** -li **-ness** -nəs, -nɪs
duplicity djʊ'plɪs.ə.ti, dʒʊ-, -ɪ.ti (US) duː'plɪs.ə.t̬i, djuː-
dupl|y djʊ'pl|aɪ, dʒʊ- (US) duː-, djuː- **-ies** -aɪz
Dupont djʊ'pɒnt; 'djuː.pɒnt (US) duː'pɑːnt, djuː-, '--
du Pré dʊ'preɪ, djʊ- (US) duː-, djuː-
Dupré(e) dʊ'preɪ, djʊ-, -'priː (US) duː-, djuː-
Dupuytren dʊ'pwiː.trᵊn, djʊ-; 'djuː.pɪ.træ̃ŋ, ˌ--'- (US) 'duː.pwiː.træn, 'djuː-
Duquesne *French naval commander:* djʊ'keɪn, dʊ- (US) duː-, djuː- *place in US:* djuː'keɪn, duː- (US) duː-, dju-
durability ˌdjʊə.rə'bɪl.ə.ti, ˌdjɔː-, ˌdʒʊə-, ˌdʒɔː-, -ɪ.ti (US) ˌdʊr.ə'bɪl.ə.t̬i, ˌdjʊr-, ˌdɝː-
durab|le 'djʊə.rə.b|l̩, 'djɔː-, 'dʒʊə-, 'dʒɔː- (US) 'dʊr.ə-, 'djʊr-, 'dɝː- **-ly** -li **-leness** -l̩.nəs, -nɪs
Duracell® 'djʊə.rə.sel, 'dʒʊə-, 'djɔː-, 'dʒɔː- (US) 'dʊr.ə-, 'djʊr-, 'dɝː-
Duraglit® 'djʊə.rə.glɪt, 'dʒʊə- (US) 'dʊr.ə-, 'djʊr-
dural 'djʊə.rᵊl, 'djɔː-, 'dʒʊə-, 'dʒɔː- (US) 'dʊr.ᵊl, 'djʊr-
Duralumin® djʊə'ræl.jʊ.mɪn, djɔː-, dʒʊə-, dʒɔː-, -jə- (US) duː'ræl.jə-, djuː-
duramen djʊə'reɪ.men, dʒʊə- (US) dʊ-, djʊ-, -mən
Duran djʊə'ræn, dʊə-, dʒʊə- (US) dʊ'ræn, də- **Duˌran Du'ran**
durance 'djʊə.rᵊn*t*s, 'dʒʊə- (US) 'dʊr.ᵊn*t*s, 'djʊr-
Durand djʊə'rænd, dʒʊə- (US) dʊ'rænd, də-
Durango də'ræŋ.gəʊ, dʊ- (US) -goʊ
Durant djʊ'rɑːnt, dʒʊ-, -'rænt (US) 'duː.rænt; də'rænt
Durante djʊ'ræn.ti, dʒʊ-, -teɪ (US) də'ræn.t̬i, dʊ-
duration djʊə'reɪ.ʃᵊn, djɔː-, dʒʊə-, dʒɔː- (US) dʊ-, djʊ-, də- **-s** -z
durative 'djʊə.rə.tɪv, 'djɔː-, 'dʒʊə-, 'dʒɔː- (US) 'dʊr.ə.t̬ɪv, 'djʊr-
Durban 'dɜː.bən (US) 'dɝː-
durbar 'dɜː.bɑːʳ, ˌ-'- (US) 'dɝː.bɑːr **-s** -z
d'Urberville 'dɜː.bə.vɪl (US) 'dɝː.bɚ- **-s** -z
Durbin 'dɜː.bɪn (US) 'dɝː-
Durden 'dɜː.dᵊn (US) 'dɝː-
durdle 'dɜː.dl̩ (US) 'dɝː- **-s** -z
Durell djʊə'rel, dʒʊə- (US) duː-, djuː-
Dürer 'djʊə.rəʳ (US) 'djuː.rɚ **-s** -z
duress djʊ'res, dʒʊ- (US) dʊ-, djʊ-
durex® (D) 'djʊə.reks, 'djɔː-, 'dʒʊə-, 'dʒɔː- (US) 'dʊr.eks, 'djʊr- **-es** -ɪz
Durham 'dʌr.ᵊm (US) 'dɝː-
durian, durion 'djʊə.ri.ən, 'dʊr.i-, -a (US) 'dʊr.i- **-s** -z
during 'djʊə.rɪŋ, 'djɔː-, 'dʒʊə-, 'dʒɔ (US) 'dʊr.ɪŋ, 'djʊr-, 'dɝː-
Durnford 'dɜːn.fəd (US) 'dɝːn.fɚd
Durocher də'rəʊ.ʃəʳ, -tʃəʳ (US) -'roʊ.ʃ -tʃɚ

Durran dʌr'æn, də'ræn ⓤⓢ də'ræn
Durrant 'dʌr.ᵊnt ⓤⓢ 'dɝː-; də'rænt
Durrell 'dʌr.ᵊl ⓤⓢ 'dɝː-
Dürrenmat 'djʊə.rᵊn.mæt, 'dʊə- ⓤⓢ 'dʊr.ən.mɑːt
durrie 'dʌr.i ⓤⓢ 'dɝː- **-s** -z
Durrington 'dʌr.ɪŋ.tᵊn ⓤⓢ 'dɝː-
Dursley 'dɜːz.li ⓤⓢ 'dɝːz-
durst *(from* **dare***)* dɜːst ⓤⓢ dɝːst **-n't** 'dɜː.sᵊnt ⓤⓢ 'dɝː-
durum 'djʊə.rəm, 'dʒʊə-, 'djɔː-, 'dʒɔː- ⓤⓢ 'dʊr.əm, 'dɝː-
Durward 'dɜː.wəd ⓤⓢ 'dɝː.wɚd
Dury 'djʊə.ri, 'dʒʊə- ⓤⓢ 'dʊr.i, 'djʊr-
Duse 'duː.zi
Dushanbe duː'ʃæn.bə, -'ʃæm-, -'ʃɑːn-, -'ʃɑːm-, -bi ⓤⓢ duː'ʃɑːn.bi
dusk dʌsk **-s** -s **-ing** -ɪŋ **-ed** -t
dusk|y 'dʌs.k|i **-ier** -i.əʳ ⓤⓢ -i.ɚ **-iest** -i.ɪst, -i.əst **-ily** -ɪ.li, -ᵊl.i **-iness** -ɪ.nəs, -ɪ.nɪs
Düsseldorf 'dʊs.ᵊl.dɔːf ⓤⓢ 'duː.sᵊl.dɔːrf, 'dʊs.ᵊl-
dust dʌst **-s** -s **-ing** -ɪŋ **-ed** -ɪd **'Dust ˌBowl; 'dust ˌcover; 'dust ˌjacket; ˌbite the 'dust**
dustbin 'dʌst.bɪn **-s** -z
dustcart 'dʌst.kɑːt ⓤⓢ -kɑːrt **-s** -s
dustcoat 'dʌst.kəʊt ⓤⓢ -koʊt **-s** -s
duster 'dʌs.təʳ ⓤⓢ -tɚ **-s** -z
dustin 'dʌs.tɪn
dust|man 'dʌst|.mən **-men** -mən
dustpan 'dʌst.pæn **-s** -z
dustproof 'dʌst.pruːf
dustsheet 'dʌst.ʃiːt **-s** -s
dust-up 'dʌst.ʌp **-s** -s
dust|y (D) 'dʌs.t|i **-ier** -i.əʳ ⓤⓢ -i.ɚ **-iest** -i.ɪst, -i.əst **-ily** -ɪ.li, -ᵊl.i **-iness** -ɪ.nəs, -ɪ.nɪs
Dutch dʌtʃ **-man** -mən **-men** -mən **ˌDutch 'cap; ˌDutch 'courage; ˌDutch 'elm diˌsease; ˌDutch 'oven; ˌDutch 'treat**
Dutch|woman 'dʌtʃ|ˌwʊm.ən **-women** -ˌwɪm.ɪn
duteous 'djuː.ti.əs, 'dʒuː- ⓤⓢ 'duː.ţi-, 'djuː- **-ly** -li **-ness** -nəs, -nɪs
Duthie 'dʌθ.i
dutiable 'djuː.ti.ə.bl̩, 'dʒuː- ⓤⓢ 'duː.ţi-, 'djuː-
dutiful 'djuː.tɪ.fᵊl, 'dʒuː-, -fʊl ⓤⓢ 'duː.ţɪ-, 'djuː- **-ly** -i **-ness** -nəs, -nɪs
Dutton 'dʌt.ᵊn
dut|y 'djuː.t|i, 'dʒuː- ⓤⓢ 'duː.ţ|i, 'djuː- **-ies** -iz
duty-free ˌdjuː.ti'friː, ˌdʒuː- ⓤⓢ ˌduː.ţi-, ˌdjuː- **ˌduty-'free shop**
duumvir dju'ʌm.vəʳ, du-, -'ʊm-; 'djuː.əm.vəʳ, 'duː- ⓤⓢ du'ʌm.vɚ, dju- **-s** -z **-i** -aɪ, -iː
duumvirate dju'ʌm.vɪ.rət, du-, -vᵊr.ət, -ɪt, -eɪt ⓤⓢ du'ʌm.vɪ.rət, dju-, -vɚ.ət, -ɪt **-s** -s
Duvalier djʊ'væl.i.eɪ, dʊ- ⓤⓢ duː'vɑːl.jeɪ, djuː-
Duveen djʊ'viːn ⓤⓢ duː-, djuː-, də-
duvet 'djuː.veɪ, 'duː- ⓤⓢ duː'veɪ, djuː- **-s** -z
dux dʌks **-es** -ɪz
Duxbury 'dʌks.bᵊr.i ⓤⓢ -ber-, -bɚ-
Duxford 'dʌks.fəd ⓤⓢ -fɚd
DV ˌdiː'viː
DVD ˌdiː.viː'diː **-s** -z
Dvorák *Czech composer:* 'dvɔː.ʒɑːk, 'vɔː-, -ʒæk ⓤⓢ 'dvɔːr.ʒɑːk
Dvorak *US family name:* 'dvɔː.ræk ⓤⓢ 'dvɔːr.æk
dwale dweɪl
dwar|f *(n.)* dwɔː|f ⓤⓢ dwɔːr|f **-s** -s **-ves** -vz
dwarf *(v.)* dwɔːf ⓤⓢ dwɔːrf **-s** -s **-ing** -ɪŋ **-ed** -t
dwarfish 'dwɔː.fɪʃ ⓤⓢ 'dwɔːr- **-ly** -li **-ness** -nəs, -nɪs
Dwayne dweɪn
dweeb dwiːb **-s** -z
dwell dwel **-s** -z **-ing** -ɪŋ **-ed** -t, -d **dwelt** dwelt **dweller/s** 'dwel.əʳ/z ⓤⓢ -ɚ/z
dwelling 'dwel.ɪŋ **-s** -z
dwelt *(from* **dwell***)* dwelt
DWI ˌdiː.dʌb.l̩.juː'aɪ ⓤⓢ -juː'-, -jə'-
Dwight dwaɪt
dwindl|e 'dwɪn.dl̩ **-es** -z **-ing** -ɪŋ **-ed** -d
Dworkin 'dwɔː.kɪn ⓤⓢ 'dwɔːr-
Dwyer dwaɪəʳ ⓤⓢ dwaɪɚ
dyad 'daɪ.æd, -əd **-s** -z
Dyak 'daɪ.æk, -ək **-s** -s
dyarch|y 'daɪ.ɑː.k|i ⓤⓢ -ɑːr- **-ies** -iz
Dyce daɪs
dy|e (D) daɪ **-es** -z **-eing** -ɪŋ **-ed** -d **-er/s** -əʳ/z ⓤⓢ -ɚ/z
dyed-in-the-wool ˌdaɪd.ɪn.ðə'wʊl
Dyer daɪəʳ ⓤⓢ daɪɚ
dyestuff 'daɪ.stʌf **-s** -s
dyewood 'daɪ.wʊd
dyeworks 'daɪ.wɜːks ⓤⓢ -wɝːks
Dyfed 'dʌv.ɪd, -ed, -əd
Dyffryn 'dʌf.rɪn, -rᵊn
dying *(from* **die***)* 'daɪ.ɪŋ
dyk|e (D) daɪk **-es** -s **-ing** -ɪŋ **-ed** -t
Dylan 'dɪl.ən, 'dʌl- ⓤⓢ 'dɪl-
Dymchurch 'dɪm.tʃɜːtʃ ⓤⓢ -tʃɝːtʃ
Dymock, Dymoke 'dɪm.ək
Dymond 'daɪ.mənd
Dymphna 'dɪmp.nə
dynameter daɪ'næm.ɪ.təʳ, dɪ-, '-ə- ⓤⓢ -ə.ţɚ **-s** -z
dynamic daɪ'næm.ɪk, dɪ- **-al** -ᵊl **-ally** -ᵊl.i, -li **-s** -s
dynamism 'daɪ.nə.mɪ.zᵊm
dyna|mite 'daɪ.nə|.maɪt **-mites** -maɪts **-miting** -maɪ.tɪŋ ⓤⓢ -maɪ.ţɪŋ **-mited** -maɪ.tɪd ⓤⓢ -maɪ.ţɪd **-miter/s** -maɪ.təʳ/z ⓤⓢ -maɪ.ţɚ/z
dynamo 'daɪ.nə.məʊ ⓤⓢ -moʊ **-s** -z
dynamometer ˌdaɪ.nə'mɒm.ɪ.təʳ, '-ə- ⓤⓢ -'mɑː.mə.ţɚ **-s** -z
dynamometric ˌdaɪ.nə.məʊ'met.rɪk ⓤⓢ -moʊ'- **-al** -ᵊl
dynast 'dɪn.əst, 'daɪ.nəst, -næst ⓤⓢ 'daɪ.næst, -nəst **-s** -s
dynastic dɪ'næs.tɪk, daɪ-, də- ⓤⓢ daɪ-
dynast|y 'dɪn.ə.st|i, 'daɪ.nə- ⓤⓢ 'daɪ.nə- **-ies** -iz
dynatron 'daɪ.nə.trɒn ⓤⓢ -trɑːn **-s** -z
dyne daɪn **-s** -s
Dynevor 'dɪn.ɪ.vəʳ, '-ə- ⓤⓢ -vɚ
d'you *strong forms:* dʒuː, djuː *weak forms:* dʒə, djə, dʒu, dju
Note: Abbreviated form of "do you": the spelling represents a pronunciation that is usually unstressed, and the pronunciation therefore parallels that of unstressed **you**, which has weak forms /jə/ before a consonant and /ju/ before vowels. When used contrastively, the strong form /djuː/ or /dʒuː/ may be used (e.g. "I don't like it. **D'you** like it?").
Dysart 'daɪ.sət, -zət, -sɑːt, -zɑːt ⓤⓢ -sɑːrt, -zɑːrt, -sɚt
dysarthria dɪ'sɑː.θri.ə ⓤⓢ -'sɑːr-
dysenteric ˌdɪs.ᵊn'ter.ɪk, -en'- ⓤⓢ -en'-
dysentery 'dɪs.ᵊn.tᵊr.i, -tri ⓤⓢ -ter.i
dysfunction dɪs'fʌŋk.ʃᵊn **-s** -z **-ing** -ɪŋ **-ed** -d **-al** -ᵊl
dysfunctional dɪs'fʌŋk.ʃᵊn.ᵊl
dysgraphia dɪs'græf.i.ə
dysgraphic dɪs'græf.ɪk
dyslalia dɪ'sleɪ.li.ə, -'slæl.i-
dyslexia dɪ'slek.si.ə
dyslexic dɪ'slek.sɪk
dysmenorrh(o)ea ˌdɪs.men.ə'rɪə ⓤⓢ -'riː.ə
Dyson 'daɪ.sᵊn
dyspepsia dɪ'spep.si.ə
dyspeptic dɪ'spep.tɪk **-s** -s
dysphagia dɪs'feɪ.dʒi.ə ⓤⓢ -dʒə, -dʒi.ə
dysphasia dɪs'feɪ.zi.ə, -ʒi-, '-ʒə ⓤⓢ '-ʒə, '-ʒi.ə
dysphasic dɪs'feɪ.zɪk **-s** -s
dysphonia dɪs'fəʊ.ni.ə ⓤⓢ -'foʊ-
dysphonic dɪs'fɒn.ɪk ⓤⓢ -'fɑː.nɪk
dyspn(o)ea dɪsp'niː.ə
dysprosium dɪ'sprəʊ.zi.əm, -si- ⓤⓢ -'sproʊ-
dystrophic dɪ'strɒf.ɪk ⓤⓢ -'strɑː.fɪk, -'stroʊ-
dystrophy 'dɪs.trə.fi
dysuria dɪ'sjʊə.ri.ə ⓤⓢ -'sjʊr.i-
dziggetai 'dzɪg.ɪ.taɪ, '-ə-, --'- ⓤⓢ 'dʒɪg.ɪ.taɪ, **-s** -z

Pronouncing the letter E

See also EA, EE, EI, EO, EOU, EU/EW, EY

The vowel letter **e** has two main strong pronunciations linked to spelling: a 'short' pronunciation /e/ and a 'long' pronunciation /iː/. However, the situation is not clear cut and other pronunciations are available.

The 'short' pronunciation always occurs when the **e** is followed by a consonant which closes the syllable, or a double consonant before another vowel, e.g.:

bed	/bed/	
bedding	/ˈbed.ɪŋ/	

The 'long' pronunciation is usually found when the **e** is followed by a single consonant and then a vowel, e.g.:

Eve	/iːv/	
credence	/ˈkriː.dənts/	

However, the 'short' pronunciation occurs in many cases where the **e** is followed by a single consonant and then a vowel, e.g.:

ever	/ˈev.əʳ/	(US) /-ɚ/
prejudice	/ˈpredʒ.ə.dɪs/	

The 'long' pronunciation may also occur where the **e** is followed by two consonants, e.g.:

negro	/ˈniː.grəʊ/	(US) /-roʊ/
secret	/ˈsiː.krət/	

When there is an **r** in the spelling, the strong pronunciation is one of four possibilities: /ɪə (US) ɪr/, /eə (US) er/, /ɜː (US) ɝː/ or /e/, e.g.:

here	/hɪəʳ/	(US) /hɪr/
there	/ðeəʳ/	(US) /ðer/
were	/wɜːʳ/	(US) /wɝː/
very	/ˈver.i/	

It frequently happens that the letter **e** has no pronunciation at all, but is used as a spelling convention to show that a preceding vowel is realised with its 'long' pronunciation, e.g.:

brave	/breɪv/	
mice	/maɪs/	
hope	/həʊp/	(US) /hoʊp/
use (v.)	/juːz/	

In addition

There are other vowel sounds associated with the letter **e**, e.g.:

eɪ	ballet	/ˈbæl.eɪ/	(US) /bælˈeɪ/

And, in rare cases:

/ɑː/ (US) /ɝː/	clerk	/klɑːk/	(US) /klɝːk/
/ɪ/	women	/ˈwɪm.ɪn/	

In weak syllables

The vowel letter **e** is realised with the vowels /ɪ/, /i/ and /ə/ in weak syllables, or may also not be pronounced at all due to syllabic consonant formation or compression, e.g.:

begin	/bɪˈgɪn/	
react	/riˈækt/	
arithmetic	/əˈrɪθ.mə.tɪk/	
castle	/ˈkɑː.sl̩/	(US) /ˈkæs.l̩/

e (E) iː -**'s** -z ˈ**E** ˌ**number**
E *(abbrev. for **east**)* iːst
E111 ˌiːˌwʌn.ɪˈlev.ən, -əˈ-
each iːtʃ ˌ**each** ˈ**other**
EACSO iːˈæk.səʊ, -ˈɑːk- (US) -soʊ
Eadie, Eady ˈiː.di
eager ˈiː.gəʳ (US) -gɚ -**ly** -li -**ness** -nəs, -nɪs ˌ**eager** ˈ**beaver**
eagle (E) ˈiː.gl̩ -**s** -z ˈ**eagle** ˌ**owl**; ˌ**Eagle** ˈ**Scout** (US) ˈ**Eagle** ˌ**Scout**
eagle-eyed ˌiː.gl̩ˈaɪd, ˈiː.gl̩.aɪd
Eaglefield ˈiː.gl̩.fiːld
Eaglehawk ˈiː.gl̩.hɔːk (US) -hɑːk, -hɔːk
Eaglescliffe ˈiː.gl̩z.klɪf
eaglet ˈiː.glɪt, -lət -**s** -s
eagre ˈeɪ.gəʳ, ˈiː- (US) ˈiː.gɚ, ˈeɪ- -**s** -z
Eakin ˈeɪ.kɪn, ˈiː- -**s** -z
Ealing ˈiː.lɪŋ
Eames iːmz, eɪmz
Eamon(n) ˈeɪ.mən

-ean -iː.ən, -i.ən
Note: Suffix. **-ean** may take primary stress or alternatively words containing it may be stressed on the syllable before the prefix. An example where both possibilities occur is **Caribbean**, which is either /ˌkær.ɪˈbiː.ən (US) ˌker-/, or /kəˈrɪb.i.ən/.
ear ɪəʳ (US) ɪr -**s** -z ˈ**ear** ˌ**trumpet**; ˌ**turn a** ˌ**deaf** ˈ**ear to**; ˌ**keep one's** ˌ**ear to the** ˈ**ground**; ˌ**prick up one's** ˈ**ears**; ˌ**give someone a** ˌ**thick** ˈ**ear**
earache ˈɪə.reɪk (US) ˈɪr-
Eardley ˈɜːd.li (US) ˈɝːd-
eardrop ˈɪə.drɒp (US) ˈɪr.drɑːp -**s** -s
eardrum ˈɪə.drʌm (US) ˈɪr- -**s** -z
eared ɪəd (US) ɪrd
earful ˈɪə.fʊl (US) ˈɪr-
Earhart ˈeə.hɑːt (US) ˈer.hɑːrt

earl (E) ɜːl (US) ɝːl -**s** -z -**dom/s** -dəm
ˌ**Earl's** ˈ**Court**; ˌ**Earl** ˈ**Grey**; ˌ**earl** ˈ**marshal**
Earl(e) ɜːl (US) ɝːl
earlobe ˈɪə.ləʊb (US) ˈɪr.loʊb -**s** -z
earl|y ˈɜː.l|i (US) ˈɝː- -**ier** -i.əʳ (US) -i.ɚ -i.ɪst, -i.əst -**iness** -ɪ.nəs, -ɪ.nɪs ˈ ˌ**bird**; ˌ**early** ˈ**warning** ˌ**system**
earmark ˈɪə.mɑːk (US) ˈɪr.mɑːrk -**s** - -**ing** -ɪŋ -**ed** -t
earmuffs ˈɪə.mʌfs (US) ˈɪr-
earn (E) ɜːn (US) ɝːn -**s** -z -**ing** -ɪŋ -**ed** ɜːnt (US) ɝːnt -**er/s** -əʳ/z (US) -ɚ/z
earnest ˈɜː.nɪst, -nəst (US) ˈɝː- -**s** -s -**ness** -nəs, -nɪs
earnings ˈɜː.nɪŋz (US) ˈɝː-
Earnshaw ˈɜːn.ʃɔː (US) ˈɝːn.ʃɑː, -ʃɔ
Earp ɜːp (US) ɝːp
earphone ˈɪə.fəʊn (US) ˈɪr.foʊn -**s** -
earpiec|e ˈɪə.piːs (US) ˈɪr- -**es** -ɪz

Pronouncing the letters EA

The vowel digraph **ea** has two main strong pronunciations linked to spelling: a 'short' pronunciation /e/ and a 'long' pronunciation /iː/. However, it is not normally predictable which one will occur, e.g.:

bread	/bred/
bead	/biːd/
cleanse	/klenz/
clean	/kliːn/

When the digraph is followed by an **r** in the spelling, the strong pronunciation is one of four possibilities: /ɪə (US) ɪr/, /eə (US) er/, /ɜː (US) ɝː/ or /ɑː (US) ɑːr/, e.g:

fear (n.)	/fɪəʳ/	(US) /fɪr/
tear (v.)	/teəʳ/	(US) /ter/
pearl	/pɜːl/	(US) /pɝːl/
heart	/hɑːt/	(US) /hɑːrt/

In addition

There are other vowel sounds associated with the digraph **ea**, e.g.:

/ɪə/	idea	/aɪˈdɪə/	
/i.ə/	area	/ˈeə.ri.ə/	(US) /ˈer.i-/
/eɪ/	great	/greɪt/	
/i.æ/	theatrical	/θiˈæt.rɪ.kᵊl/	
/i.eɪ/	create	/kriˈeɪt/	

In addition, there are instances when the two letters **e** and **a** come together in closed compounds, e.g.:

whereas	/*h*weəˈræz/	(US) /*h*werˈæz/
hereafter	/hɪərˈɑːf.təʳ/	(US) /hɪrˈæf.tɚ/

In weak syllables

The vowel digraph **ea** is realised with the vowels /i/ and /ə/ in weak syllables and may result in a syllabic consonant, e.g.:

guinea	/ˈgɪn.i/	
ocean	/ˈəʊ.ʃᵊn/	(US) /ˈoʊ-/

arplug ˈɪə.plʌg (US) ˈɪr- **-s** -z
arring ˈɪə.rɪŋ (US) ˈɪr.ɪŋ, -rɪŋ **-s** -z
arshot ˈɪə.ʃɒt (US) ˈɪr.ʃɑːt
arsplitting ˈɪəˌsplɪt.ɪŋ (US) ˈɪrˌsplɪt̬.ɪŋ **-ly** -li
rth **(E)** (*n.*) ɜːθ (US) ɝːθ **-s** -s, ɜːðz (US) ɝːðz ˈ**earth** ˌ**mother**
rth (*v.*) ɜːθ (US) ɝːθ **-s** -s **-ing** -ɪŋ **-ed** -t
rthborn ˈɜːθ.bɔːn (US) ˈɝːθ.bɔːrn
rthbound ˈɜːθ.baʊnd (US) ˈɝːθ-
rthen ˈɜː.θᵊn, -ðᵊn (US) ˈɝː-
rthenware ˈɜː.θᵊn.weəʳ, -ðᵊn- (US) ˈɝː.θᵊn.wer, -ðᵊn-
rthiness ˈɜː.θɪ.nəs, -nɪs (US) ˈɝː-
rthling ˈɜːθ.lɪŋ (US) ˈɝːθ- **-s** -z
rthl|y ˈɜːθ.l|i (US) ˈɝːθ- **-ier** -i.əʳ (US) -i.ɚ **-iest** -i.ɪst, -i.əst **-iness** -ɪ.nəs, -ɪ.nɪs
rthmover ˈɜːθˌmuː.vəʳ (US) ˈɝːθˌmuː.vɚ **-s** -z
rthquake ˈɜːθ.kweɪk (US) ˈɝːθ- **-s** -s
rthsea ˈɜːθ.siː (US) ˈɝːθ-
rthshaking ˈɜːθˌʃeɪ.kɪŋ (US) ˈɝːθ-
rth-shattering ˈɜːθˌʃæt.ᵊr.ɪŋ (US) ˈɝːθˌʃæt̬- **-ly** -li
thward ˈɜːθ.wəd (US) ˈɝːθ.wɚd **-s** -z
thwork ˈɜːθ.wɜːk (US) ˈɝːθ.wɜːrk **-s** -s
thworm ˈɜːθ.wɜːm (US) ˈɝːθ.wɜːrm **-s** -z
th|y ˈɜː.θ|i (US) ˈɝː- **-ier** -i.əʳ (US) -i.ɚ **iest** -i.əst, -i.ɪst **-ily** -ɪ.li, -ᵊl.i **-iness** ɪ.nəs, -ɪ.nɪs
wax ˈɪə.wæks (US) ˈɪr-
wig ˈɪə.wɪg (US) ˈɪr- **-s** -z **-ging** -ɪŋ **ged** -d

Easdale ˈiːz.deɪl
Easdaq iˈæz.dæk
eas|e iːz **-es** -ɪz **-ing** -ɪŋ **-ed** -d
Easebourne ˈiːz.bɔːn (US) -bɔːrn
easeful ˈiːz.fᵊl, -fʊl **-ly** -li **-ness** -nəs, -nɪs
easel ˈiː.zᵊl **-s** -z
easement ˈiːz.mənt **-s** -s
Easey ˈiː.zi
easiness (*from* **easy**) ˈiː.zɪ.nəs, -nɪs
Easington ˈiː.zɪŋ.tən
east **(E)** iːst ˌ**East** ˈ**Anglia**; ˌ**East** ˈ**End** *stress shift:* ˌEast End ˈpub; ˌEast ˈCoast *stress shift:* ˌEast Coast ˈaccent
East Bergholt ˌiːstˈbɜːg.həʊlt (US) -ˈbɝːg.hoʊlt
eastbound ˈiːst.baʊnd
Eastbourne ˈiːst.bɔːn (US) -bɔːrn
Eastcheap ˈiːst.tʃiːp
Eastender ˌiːstˈen.dəʳ (US) -dɚ **-s** -z
Easter ˈiː.stəʳ (US) -stɚ **-s** -z ˌ**Easter** ˈ**bonnet** (US) ˈ**Easter** ˌ**bonnet**; ˌ**Easter** ˈ**Bunny** (US) ˈ**Easter** ˌ**Bunny**; ˌ**Easter** ˈ**Day**; ˈ**Easter** ˌ**egg**; ˈ**Easter** ˌ**Island**; ˌ**Easter** ˈ**Sunday**
Easterby ˈiː.stə.bi (US) -stɚ-
easterl|y ˈiː.stᵊl|.i (US) -stɚ.l|i **-ies** -iz
eastern **(E)** ˈiː.stᵊn (US) -stɚn **-most** -məʊst, -məst (US) -moʊst, -məst ˌ**Eastern** ˈ**Shore**; ˌ**Eastern** ˈ**Standard** ˌ**Time**
easterner **(E)** ˈiː.stᵊn.əʳ (US) -tɚ.nɚ **-s** -z
Eastertide ˈiː.stə.taɪd (US) -stɚ-
Eastfield ˈiːst.fiːld
Eastham ˈiːst.*h*əm

Easthampton ˌiːstˈhæm*p*.tən
easting ˈiː.stɪŋ **-s** -z
East Kilbride ˌiːst.kɪlˈbraɪd
Eastlake ˈiːst.leɪk
Eastleigh ˈiːst.liː, ˌiːstˈliː
Eastman ˈiːs*t*.mən
east-northeast ˌiːst.nɔːθˈiːst (US) -nɔːrθˈ- *in nautical usage also:* -nɔːˈriːst (US) -nɔːrˈiːst
Easton ˈiː.stən
Easton-in-Gordano ˌiː.stᵊn.ɪn.gɔːˈdɑː.nəʊ, -ɪŋ- (US) -gɔːrˈdɑː.noʊ
Eastport ˈiːs*t*.pɔːt (US) -pɔːrt
east-southeast ˌiːst.saʊθˈiːst *in nautical usage also:* -saʊˈ-
eastward ˈiːst.wəd (US) -wɚd **-ly** -li **-s** -z
East-West ˌiːstˈwest *stress shift, see compound:* ˌ**East-West** **re**ˈ**lations**
Eastwood ˈiːst.wʊd
eas|y **(E)** ˈiː.z|i **-ier** -i.əʳ (US) -i.ɚ **-iest** -i.ɪst, -i.əst **-ily** -ɪ.li, -ᵊl.i **-iness** -ɪ.nəs, -ɪ.nɪs ˈ**easy** ˌ**chair**; **as** ˌ**easy as** ˈ**pie**; ˌ**take it** ˈ**easy**; **on** ˈ**easy** ˌ**street**
easygoing ˌiː.ziˈgəʊ.ɪŋ (US) -ˈgoʊ- *stress shift:* ˌeasygoing ˈperson
EasyJet® ˈiː.zi.dʒet
eat iːt **-s** -s **-ing** -ɪŋ (US) ˈiː.t̬ɪŋ **ate** et, eɪt (US) eɪt **eaten** ˈiː.tᵊn (US) -t̬ən **eater/s** ˈiː.təʳ/z (US) -t̬ɚ/z ˈ**eating di**ˌ**sorder**; ˌ**eat one's** ˈ**heart out**; ˌ**eat one's** ˈ**words**; ˌ**eat someone out of** ˌ**house and** ˈ**home**
eatable ˈiː.tə.bl̩ (US) -t̬ə- **-s** -z
eaterie ˈiː.tᵊr.i (US) -t̬ɚ- **-s** -z

eater|y ˈiː.tᵊr|.i US -t̬ɚ- **-ies** -iz

Eaton ˈiː.tᵊn

Eaton Socon ˌiː.tᵊnˈsəʊ.kᵊn US -ˈsoʊ-

eau de cologne ˌəʊ.də.kəˈləʊn, -dɪ- US ˌoʊ.də.kəˈloʊn *stress shift:* ˌeau de cologne ˈspray

eau de nil ˌəʊ.dəˈniːl US ˌoʊ- *stress shift:* ˌeau de nil ˈpaint

eau de parfum ˌəʊ.də.pɑːˈfʌm US ˌoʊ.də.pɑːrˈ-

eau de toilette ˌəʊ.də.twɑːˈlet, -twəˈ- US ˌoʊ-

eau-de-vie ˌəʊ.dəˈviː US ˌoʊ-

eave (E) iːv **-s** -z

eavesdrop ˈiːvz.drɒp US -drɑːp **-s** -s **-ping** -ɪŋ **-ped** -t **-per/s** -əʳ/z US -ɚ/z

ebb eb **-s** -z **-ing** -ɪŋ **-ed** -d **ˌebb ˈtide**

Ebbsfleet ˈebz.fliːt

Ebbw ˈeb.uː, -ə

Ebel ebˈel, ˈiː.bᵊl

Ebenezer ˌeb.əˈniː.zəʳ, -ɪˈ- US -zɚ *stress shift:* ˌEbenezer ˈScrooge

Eberhart ˈeɪ.bə.hɑːt US ˈeb.ɚ.hɑːrt, ˈeɪ.bɚ-

Ebionite ˈiː.bjə.naɪt, -bɪə- **-s** -s

Eblis ˈeb.lɪs

ebola (E) ɪˈbəʊ.lə, ˈeb.əʊ.lə US -ˈboʊ-

ebon ˈeb.ən

ebonite ˈeb.ə.naɪt

eboniz|e, -is|e ˈeb.ə.naɪz **-es** -ɪz **-ing** -ɪŋ **-ed** -d

ebony (E) ˈeb.ᵊn.i

Eboracum iːˈbɒr.ə.kəm, ɪ- US ɪˈbɔːr-

Ebrington ˈeb.rɪŋ.tən

Ebro ˈiː.brəʊ, ˈeb.rəʊ US ˈeɪ.broʊ, ˈiː-, ˈeb.roʊ

ebullien|ce ɪˈbʌl.i.ən|*t*s, -ˈbʊl- US -ˈbʊl.jən|*t*s, -ˈbʌl- **-cy** -*t*si

ebullient ɪˈbʌl.i.ənt, -ˈbʊl- US -ˈbʊl.jənt, -ˈbʌl- **-ly** -li

ebullition ˌeb.əˈlɪʃ.ᵊn, -ʊˈ- US -əˈ-, -juːˈ- **-s** -z

Ebury ˈiː.bᵊr.i US -ˌber-, -bɚ-

e-business ˈiːˌbɪz.nɪs, -nəs **-es** -ɪz

EC ˌiːˈsiː

écarté eɪˈkɑː.teɪ US ˌeɪ.kɑːrˈteɪ

Ecbatana ekˈbæt.ᵊn.ə, ˌek.bəˈtɑː.nə US ekˈbæt.ᵊn.ə

ecce homo ˌek.eɪˈhəʊ.məʊ, ˌetʃ-, -ˈhɒm.əʊ US -ˈhoʊ.moʊ

eccentric ɪkˈsen.trɪk, ek- **-s** -s **-al** -ᵊl **-ally** -ᵊl.i, -li

eccentricit|y ˌek.senˈtrɪs.ə.t|i, -sᵊnˈ-, -ɪ.t|i US -ə.t̬|i **-ies** -iz

Ecclefechan ˌek.l̩ˈfek.ᵊn, -ˈfex-

Eccles ˈek.l̩z **ˈEccles ˌcake**

Ecclesfield ˈek.l̩z.fiːld

ecclesi|a ɪˈkliː.zi|.ə US ɪˈkliː-, ekˈliː-, -ˈleɪ- **-ast/s** -æst/s

Ecclesiastes ɪˌkliː.ziˈæs.tiːz US ɪˌkliː-, ekˌliː-

ecclesiastic ɪˌkliː.ziˈæs.tɪk US ɪˌkliː-, ekˌliː- **-s** -s **-al** -ᵊl **-ally** -ᵊl.i, -li

ecclesiasticism ɪˌkliː.ziˈæs.tɪ.sɪ.zᵊm US ɪˌkliː-, ekˌliː-

Ecclesiasticus ɪˌkliː.ziˈæs.tɪ.kəs US ɪˌkliː-, ekˌliː-

Eccleston ˈek.l̩.stən

Ecclestone ˈek.l̩.stən

eccrine ˈek.rɪn, -riːn, -rən, -raɪn

ECG ˌiː.siːˈdʒiː

echelon ˈeʃ.ə.lɒn, ˈeɪ.ʃə- US ˈeʃ.ə.lɑːn **-s** -z **-ned** -d

echidn|a ekˈɪd.n|ə, ɪˈkɪd- US iːˈkɪd- **-ae** -iː **-as** -əz

echinacea ˌek.ɪˈneɪ.ʃə, -əˈ-, -si.ə

echin|us ekˈaɪ.n|əs; ɪˈkaɪ-; ə-; ˈek.ɪn|.əs US ɪˈkaɪ.n|əs **-i** -aɪ

echo ˈek.əʊ US -oʊ **-es** -z **-ing** -ɪŋ **-ed** -d

echocardio|gram ˌek.əʊˈkɑː.di.əʊ|.græm US -oʊˈkɑːr.di.ə-, -oʊ- **-s** -z **-graph/s** -grɑːf/s, -græf/s US -græf/s

echoic ekˈəʊ.ɪk, ɪˈkəʊ-, ə- US ekˈoʊ-

echolalia ˌek.əʊˈleɪ.li.ə US -oʊˈ-

echolo|cate ˌek.əʊ.ləʊ|ˈkeɪt US -oʊ.loʊˈ- **-cates** -ˈkeɪts **-cating** -ˈkeɪ.tɪŋ US -ˈkeɪ.t̬ɪŋ **-cated** -ˈkeɪ.tɪd US -ˈkeɪ.t̬ɪd

echolocation ˌek.əʊ.ləʊˈkeɪ.ʃᵊn US -oʊ.loʊˈ-

echt ext, ekt

Eckersl(e)y ˈek.əz.li US -ɚz-

Eckert ˈek.ət US -ɚt

Eckertford ˈek.ət.fəd US -ɚt.fɚd

Eckington ˈek.ɪŋ.tən

éclair eɪˈkleəʳ, ɪ-; ˈeɪ.kleəʳ US eɪˈkler, ɪ- **-s** -z

eclampsia ɪˈklæm*p*.si.ə, ekˈlæm*p*-, əˈklæm*p*-

éclat eɪˈklɑː, ˈ-- **-s** -z

eclectic ekˈlek.tɪk, ɪˈklek-, iː- US ekˈlek- **-s** -s **-al** -ᵊl **-ally** -ᵊl.i, -li

eclecticism ekˈlek.tɪ.sɪ.zᵊm, ɪˈklek-, iː-, -tə- US ekˈlek.tə-

eclips|e ɪˈklɪps, ə-, iː- **-es** -ɪz **-ing** -ɪŋ **-ed** -t

ecliptic ɪˈklɪp.tɪk, ə-, iː- **-s** -s

eclogue ˈek.lɒg US -lɑːg, -lɔːg **-s** -z

eco- iː.kəʊ-, ek.əʊ-; ɪ.kɒ- US ek.oʊ-, -ə-, iː.koʊ-, -kə-; ɪ.kɑː-

Note: Prefix. Either takes primary or secondary stress on the first syllable, e.g. **ecosphere** /ˈiː.kəʊ.sfɪəʳ US ˈek.oʊ.sfɪr/, **economic** /ˌiː.kəˈnɒm.ɪk US ˌiː.kəˈnɑː.mɪk/, or primary or secondary stress on the second syllable, e.g. **ecology** /iːˈkɒl.ə.dʒi US -ˈkɑː.lə-/, **econometric** /ɪˌkɒn.əˈmet.rɪk US -kɑː.nəˈ-/.

eco-friendly ˈiː.kəʊˌfrend.li US ˈek.oʊˌ-, ˈiː.koʊˌ-

E coli ˌiːˈkəʊ.laɪ US -ˈkoʊ-

ecologic|al ˌiː.kəˈlɒdʒ.ɪ.k|ᵊl, ˌek.əˈ- US -ˈlɑː.dʒɪ- **-ally** -ᵊl.i, -li **ˌecoˌlogically ˈsound**

ecolog|y iːˈkɒl.ə.dʒ|i, ɪ-, ekˈɒl- US iːˈkɑː.lə-, ɪˈkɑː-, ekˈɑː- **-ist/s** -ɪs

e-commerce ˈiːˌkɒm.ɜːs US -ˌkɑː.mɝ

econometric ɪˌkɒn.əˈmet.rɪk, iː- US -ˌkɑː.nəˈ- **-s** -s

econometrician ɪˌkɒn.ə.metˈrɪʃ.ᵊn, -məˈtrɪʃ- US -ˌkɑː.nə.məˈ- **-s** -z

econometrics ɪˌkɒn.əˈmet.rɪks, iː- US -ˌkɑː.nəˈ-

economic ˌiː.kəˈnɒm.ɪk, ˌek.əˈ- US -ˈnɑː.mɪk **-s** -s **-al** -ᵊl **-ally** -ᵊl.i, - **ˌeconomic ˈgrowth**

economist ɪˈkɒn.ə.mɪst, iː- US -ˈkɑː.nə- **-s** -s

economiz|e, -is|e ɪˈkɒn.ə.maɪz, əˈkɒ US ɪˈkɑː.nə-, iː- **-es** -ɪz **-ing** -ɪŋ **-ed** **-er/s** -əʳ/z US -ɚ/z

econom|y ɪˈkɒn.ə.m|i, əˈkɒn- US ɪˈkɑː.nə-, iː- **-ies** -iz **eˈconomy ˌclass**

ecosphere ˈiː.kəʊ.sfɪəʳ, ˈek.əʊ- US ˈek.oʊ.sfɪr, ˈiː.koʊ-

ecosystem ˈiː.kəʊˌsɪs.təm, ˈek.əʊ-, -tɪm US ˈek.oʊˌsɪs.təm, ˈiː.koʊ- **-s**

eco-tour|ism ˈiː.kəʊˌtʊə.r|ɪ.zᵊm, ˈek.əʊ-, -ˌtɔː- US ˈiː.koʊˌtʊr-, ˈek **-ist/s** -ɪst/s

ecru ˈeɪ.kruː, ˈek.ruː

ecstas|y ˈek.stə.s|i **-ies** -iz

ecstatic ɪkˈstæt.ɪk, ek-, ək- US ekˈstæt̬-, ɪk- **-al** -ᵊl **-ally** -ᵊl.i, -

ECT ˌiː.siːˈtiː

ecto- ek.təʊ- US ek.toʊ-, -tə-

Note: Prefix. Normally takes prima or secondary stress on the first syllable, e.g. **ectomorph** /ˈek.təʊ.mɔːf US ˈek.toʊ.mɔːrf/, **ectomorphic** /ˌek.təʊˈmɔː.fɪk US ˌek.toʊˈmɔːr-/.

ectoderm ˈek.təʊ.dɜːm US -toʊ.dɜ -tə-

ectoderm|al ˌek.təʊˈdɜː.m|ᵊl US -toʊˈdɝː-, -təˈ- **-ic** -ɪk

ectomorph ˈek.təʊ.mɔːf US -toʊ.mɔːrf, -tə- **-s** -s

ectomorph|ic ˌek.təʊˈmɔː.f|ɪk US -toʊˈmɔːr-, -təˈ- **-ism** -ɪ.zᵊm -

-ectomy -ˈek.tə.mi

Note: Suffix. Always carries prima stress, e.g. **appendix** /əˈpen.dɪk **appendectomy** /ˌæp.enˈdek.tə

ectopic ekˈtɒp.ɪk, ˌek-, ɪk- US ekˈtɑː.pɪk **ecˌtopic ˈpregnan**

ectoplasm ˈek.təʊ.plæz.ᵊm US -tc -tə-

ecu *(abbrev. for* **European Curre Unit***)*, **ECU** ˈek.juː, ˈeɪ.kjuː, ˈiː-, ˌiː.siːˈjuː US ˈeɪ.kuː, ˌiː.siːˈjuː **-s**

Ecuador ˈek.wə.dɔːʳ (US) -dɔːr

ecumenic ˌiː.kjʊˈmen.ɪk, ˌek.jʊˈ-, -jəˈ- (US) ˌek.jʊˈ-, -jəˈ- **-al** -ᵊl

ecumenicism ˌiː.kjʊˈmen.ɪ.sɪ.zᵊm, ˌek.jʊˈ-, -jəˈ- (US) ˌek.jʊˈ-, -jəˈ-

ecumen|ism iːˈkjuː.mə.n|ɪ.zᵊm; ɪ-; ˈek.jʊ-, -jə- (US) ˈek.juː-, -jə-; ekˈjuː-, ɪˈkjuː- **-ist/s** -ɪst/s

eczema ˈek.sɪ.mə, -sᵊm.ə (US) ˈek.sə.mə; ˈeg.zə-; ɪgˈziː.mə

eczematous ekˈsem.ə.təs, ɪk-; ɪgˈzem- (US) ɪgˈzem.ə.t̬əs, eg-; ɪkˈsem-

Ed ed

-ed -t, -d, -ɪd

Note: Suffix. Unstressed. When preceded by /t/ or /d/, the pronunciation is /-ɪd/, e.g. **batted** /ˈbæt.ɪd (US) ˈbæt̬.ɪd/. When preceded by a voiceless consonant other than /t/, the pronunciation is /t/, e.g. **picked** /pɪkt/. When preceded by a voiced sound, including vowels and consonants, the pronunciation is /d/, e.g. **rigged** /rɪgd/. There are, however, exceptions, particularly in adjectival forms, including **dogged** /ˈdɒg.ɪd (US) ˈdɑː.gɪd/, and **learned** /ˈlɜː.nɪd (US) ˈlɜːr-/; see individual entries.

edacious ɪˈdeɪ.ʃəs, iː-, edˈeɪ- (US) ɪˈdeɪ-, iː-

Edam ˈiː.dæm (US) ˈiː.dəm, -dæm

edaphic ɪˈdæf.ɪk, iː-

Edda ˈed.ə **-s** -z

Eddery ˈed.ᵊr.i

Eddie ˈed.i

Eddington ˈed.ɪŋ.tən

edd|y (E) ˈed|.i **-ies** -iz **-ying** -i.ɪŋ **-ied** -id

Eddystone ˈed.ɪ.stᵊn, -stəʊn (US) -stoʊn, -stən

Ede iːd

edelweiss ˈeɪ.dᵊl.vaɪs

edem|a ɪˈdiː.m|ə, iː- **-as** -əz **-ata** -ə.tə (US) -ə.t̬ə

edematous ɪˈdiː.mə.təs, iː- (US) -t̬əs

Eden ˈiː.dᵊn ˌ**Garden of ˈEden**

Edenbridge ˈiː.dᵊn.brɪdʒ

Edenfield ˈiː.dᵊn.fiːld

edentate iːˈden.teɪt, ɪ- **-s** -s

Edessa ɪˈdes.ə, iː-

Edgar ˈed.gəʳ (US) -gɚ

Edgbaston ˈedʒ.bə.stᵊn, -bæs.tᵊn

edg|e (E) edʒ **-es** -ɪz **-ing** -ɪŋ **-ed** -d

Edgecomb(e) ˈedʒ.kəm

Edgecote ˈedʒ.kəʊt, -kət (US) -koʊt

Edgecumbe ˈedʒ.kəm, -kuːm

Edgehill *name of a hill:* ˌedʒˈhɪl *surname:* ˈedʒ.hɪl

edgeless ˈedʒ.ləs, -lɪs

Edgerton ˈedʒ.ə.tᵊn (US) -ɚ.t̬ən

edge|ways ˈedʒ|.weɪz **-wise** -waɪz

edgewise ˈedʒ.waɪz

Edgeworth ˈedʒ.wəθ, -wɜːθ (US) -wɚθ, -wɝːθ

edging ˈedʒ.ɪŋ **-s** -z

Edgington ˈedʒ.ɪŋ.tən

Edgley ˈedʒ.li

Edgware ˈedʒ.weəʳ (US) -wer

edg|y ˈedʒ|.i **-ier** -i.əʳ (US) -i.ɚ **-iest** -i.ɪst, -i.əst **-ily** ɪ.li, ᵊl.i

edibility ˌed.ɪˈbɪl.ə.ti, -əˈ-, -ɪ.ti (US) -ə.t̬i

edible ˈed.ɪ.bl̩, ˈ-ə- **-s** -z **-ness** -nəs, -nɪs

edict ˈiː.dɪkt **-s** -s

Edie ˈiː.di

edification ˌed.ɪ.fɪˈkeɪ.ʃᵊn, ˌ-ə-

edific|e ˈed.ɪ.fɪs, ˈ-ə- **-es** -ɪz

edi|fy ˈed.ɪ|.faɪ, ˈ-ə- **-fies** -faɪz **-fying** -faɪ.ɪŋ **-fied** -faɪd

Edina ɪˈdaɪ.nə, iː-, edˈaɪ-, -ˈiː-

Edinburgh ˈed.ɪn.bᵊr.ə, -ɪm-, -ᵊn-, -bʌr- (US) -bʌr.ə, -oʊ

Edington ˈed.ɪŋ.tən

Edison ˈed.ɪ.sᵊn, ˈ-ə-

ed|it ˈed|.ɪt **-its** -ɪts **-iting** -ɪ.tɪŋ (US) -ɪ.t̬ɪŋ **-ited** -ɪ.tɪd (US) -ɪ.t̬ɪd

Edith ˈiː.dɪθ

edition ɪˈdɪʃ.ᵊn, ə- (US) ɪ- **-s** -z

editor ˈed.ɪ.təʳ (US) -t̬ɚ **-s** -z

editorial ˌed.ɪˈtɔː.ri.əl, -əˈ- (US) -əˈtɔːr.i- **-s** -z **-ly** -i

editorializ|e, -is|e ˌed.ɪˈtɔː.ri.ᵊl.aɪz, -əˈ- (US) -əˈtɔːr.i.ə.laɪz **-es** -ɪz **-ing** -ɪŋ **-ed** -d

editor-in-chief ˌed.ɪ.təʳ.ɪnˈtʃiːf (US) -t̬ɚ-

editorship ˈed.ɪ.tə.ʃɪp (US) -t̬ɚ- **-s** -s

Edmond ˈed.mənd **-s** -z

Edmonton ˈed.mən.tən

Edmund ˈed.mənd **-s** -z

Edna ˈed.nə

Edom ˈiː.dəm **-ite/s** -aɪt/s

Edridge ˈed.rɪdʒ

Edsall ˈed.sᵊl

educability ˌedʒ.ʊ.kəˈbɪl.ə.ti, ˌed.jʊ-, -ɪt.i (US) ˌedʒ.ʊ.kəˈbɪl.ə.t̬i, ˌ-ə-

educable ˈedʒ.ʊ.kə.bl̩, ˈed.jʊ- (US) ˈedʒ.ʊ-, ˈ-ə-

edu|cate ˈedʒ.ʊ|.keɪt, ˈed.jʊ- (US) ˈedʒ.ʊ|.keɪt, ˈ-ə- **-cates** -keɪts **-cating** -keɪ.tɪŋ (US) -keɪ.t̬ɪŋ **-cated** -keɪ.tɪd (US) -keɪ.t̬ɪd **-cator/s** -keɪ.təʳ/z (US) -keɪ.t̬ɚ/z

education ˌedʒ.ʊˈkeɪ.ʃᵊn, ˌed.jʊˈ- (US) ˌedʒ.ʊˈkeɪ.ʃᵊn, -əˈ-

educational ˌedʒ.ʊˈkeɪ.ʃᵊn.ᵊl, ˌed.jʊˈ- (US) ˌedʒ.ʊˈkeɪ.ʃᵊn.ᵊl, -əˈ- **-ly** -i

educationalist ˌedʒ.ʊˈkeɪ.ʃᵊn.ᵊl.ɪst, ˌed.jʊˈ- (US) ˌedʒ.ʊˈkeɪ.ʃᵊn.ᵊl.ɪst, -əˈ- **-s** -s

educationist ˌedʒ.ʊˈkeɪ.ʃᵊn.ɪst, ˌed.jʊˈ- (US) ˌedʒ.ʊˈkeɪ.ʃᵊn.ɪst, -əˈ- **-s** -s

educative ˈedʒ.ʊ.kə.tɪv, ˈed.jʊ-, -keɪ- (US) ˈedʒ.ʊ.keɪ.t̬ɪv, ˈ-ə-

educ|e ɪˈdjuːs, iː-, -ˈdʒuːs (US) -ˈduːs, -ˈdjuːs **-es** -ɪz **-ing** -ɪŋ **-ed** -t

eduction ɪˈdʌk.ʃᵊn, iː- **-s** -z

Edward ˈed.wəd (US) -wɚd **-(e)s** -z

Edwardian edˈwɔː.di.ən (US) -ˈwɔːr-, -ˈwɑːr- **-s** -z

Edwin ˈed.wɪn

Edwina edˈwiː.nə

Edwinstowe ˈed.wɪn.stəʊ (US) -stoʊ

-ee -iː, -i

Note: Suffix. May be stressed or unstressed, e.g. **employee** /ˌem.plɔɪˈiː, ɪmˈplɔɪ.iː/, **committee** /kəˈmɪt.i (US) -ˈmɪt̬-/.

-ée, -ee -eɪ

Note: Suffix. May be stressed or unstressed in British English, e.g. **soirée** /ˈswɑː.reɪ, -ˈ-/, but normally stressed in American English, e.g. /swɑːˈreɪ/.

EEC ˌiː.iːˈsiː

EEG ˌiː.iːˈdʒiː

eejit ˈiː.dʒɪt **-s** -s

eel iːl **-s** -z

eelgrass ˈiːl.grɑːs (US) -græs

eelworm ˈiːl.wɜːm (US) -wɝːm **-s** -z

e'en iːn

eeny, meeny, miney, mo ˌiː.niˌmiː.niˌmaɪ.niˈməʊ (US) -ˈmoʊ

e'er eəʳ (US) er

-eer -ˈɪəʳ (US) -ˈɪr

Note: Suffix. Normally carries stress, e.g., **musket** /ˈmʌs.kɪt/, **musketeer** /ˌmʌs.kɪˈtɪəʳ (US) -kəˈtɪr/.

eer|ie ˈɪə.r|i (US) ˈɪr|.i **-y** -i **-ily** -ɪ.li, -ᵊl.i **-iness** -ɪ.nəs, -ɪ.nɪs

Eeyore ˈiː.ɔːʳ (US) -ɔːr

eff ef **-ing** -ɪŋ ˌ**eff** ˈ**off**; ˌ**effing and** ˈ**blinding**

effac|e ɪˈfeɪs, efˈeɪs (US) ɪˈfeɪs, ə- **-es** -ɪz **-ing** -ɪŋ **-ed** -t **-ement** -mənt **-eable** -ə.bl̩

effect ɪˈfekt (US) ɪˈfekt, ə-, iː- **-s** -s **-ing** -ɪŋ **-ed** -ɪd

effective ɪˈfek.tɪv (US) ɪˈfek-, ə-, iː- **-s** -z **-ly** -li **-ness** -nəs, -nɪs

effectual ɪˈfek.tʃu.əl, -tju-, -tʃʊl, -tjʊl (US) ɪˈfek.tʃuː.əl, ə-, iː- **-ly** -i

effectuality ɪˌfek.tʃuˈæl.ə.ti, -tjuˈ-, -ɪ.ti (US) ɪˌfek.tʃuːˈæl.ə.t̬i, ə-, iː-

effectu|ate ɪˈfek.tʃu|.eɪt, -tju- (US) ɪˈfek.tʃuː-, ə-, iː- **-ates** -eɪts **-ating** -eɪ.tɪŋ (US) -eɪ.t̬ɪŋ **-ated** -eɪ.tɪd (US) -eɪ.t̬ɪd

effeminacy ɪˈfem.ɪ.nə.si, efˈem-, əˈfem-, ˈ-ə-

effeminate (*adj.*) ɪˈfem.ɪ.nət, efˈem-, əˈfem-, ˈ-ə-, -nɪt **-ly** -li **-ness** -nəs, -nɪs

effemi|nate (*v.*) ɪˈfem.ɪ|.neɪt, efˈem-, ˈ-ə- **-nates** -neɪts **-nating** -neɪ.tɪŋ (US) -neɪ.t̬ɪŋ **-nated** -neɪ.tɪd (US) -neɪ.t̬ɪd

Pronouncing the letters EE

The most common pronunciation for the vowel digraph **ee** is /iː/, e.g.:

bee /biː/

When followed by an **r** in the spelling, **ee** is pronounced as either /ɪə US ɪr/ or /iː.ə US iː.ɚ/, e.g.:

steer /stɪəʳ/ US /stɪr/
freer (comparative adj.) /ˈfriː.əʳ/ US /-ɚ/

In addition

There are other vowel sounds associated with the digraph **ee**, e.g.:

eɪ fiancée /fiˈɑ̃ː*n*.seɪ/ US /fiˈɑːn.seɪ/
iː.ɪst freest (superlative adj.) /ˈfriː.ɪst/

In weak syllables

The vowel digraph **ee** is realised with the vowel sound /i/ in weak syllables, e.g.:

coffee /ˈkɒf.i/ US /ˈkɑː.fi/

effendi efˈen.di, ɪˈfen-
efferent ˈef.ᵊr.ᵊnt, ˈiː.fᵊr- US ˈef.ᵊr-
effervesc|e ˌef.əˈves US -ɚˈ- **-es** -ɪz **-ing** -ɪŋ **-ed** -t
effervescen|t ˌef.əˈves.ən|t US -ɚˈ- **-ce** -*t*s *stress shift:* ˌeffervescent ˈpowder
effete ɪˈfiːt, efˈiːt
efficacious ˌef.ɪˈkeɪ.ʃəs, -əˈ- **-ly** -li **-ness** -nəs, -nɪs
efficacity ˌef.ɪˈkæs.ə.ti, -əˈ-, -ɪ.ti US -ə.t̬i
efficacy ˈef.ɪ.kə.si, ˈ-ə-
efficienc|y ɪˈfɪʃ.ᵊn*t*.s|i, ə- US ɪˈfɪʃ-, ə-, iː- **-ies** -iz
efficient ɪˈfɪʃ.ᵊnt, ə- US ɪˈfɪʃ-, ə-, iː- **-ly** -li
Effie ˈef.i
effig|y ˈef.ɪ.dʒ|i, ˈ-ə- **-ies** -iz
Effingham *in the UK:* ˈef.ɪŋ.əm US ˈef.ɪŋ.əm, -hæm *in the US:* ˈef.ɪŋ.hæm
effloresc|e ˌef.lɔːˈres, -lɒrˈes, -ləˈres US -ləˈres, -lɔːrˈ- **-es** -ɪz **-ing** -ɪŋ **-ed** -t
efflorescen|t ˌef.lɔːˈres.ᵊn|t US -ləˈ-, -lɔːrˈ- **-ce** -*t*s
effluence ˈef.lu.ən*t*s
effluent ˈef.lu.ənt **-s** -s
effluvi|um ɪˈfluː.vi|.əm, efˈluː- **-a** -ə **-al** -əl
efflux ˈef.lʌks **-es** -ɪz
effluxion efˈluk.ʃᵊn, ɪˈflʌk- **-s** -z
effort ˈef.ət US -ɚt **-s** -s
effortless ˈef.ət.ləs, -lɪs US -ɚt- **-ly** -li **-ness** -nəs, -nɪs
effronter|y ɪˈfrʌn.tᵊr|.i, efˈrʌn- US efˈrʌn-, ɪˈfrʌn- **-ies** -iz
effulg|e ɪˈfʌldʒ, efˈʌldʒ **-es** -ɪz **-ing** -ɪŋ **-ed** -d
effulgen|ce ɪˈfʌl.dʒᵊn|*t*s, efˈʌl- **-t/ly** -t/li
effuse (*adj.*) ɪˈfjuːs, efˈjuːs
effus|e (*v.*) ɪˈfjuːz, efˈjuːz **-es** -ɪz **-ing** -ɪŋ **-ed** -d
effusion ɪˈfjuː.ʒᵊn, efˈjuː- **-s** -z
effusive ɪˈfjuː.sɪv, efˈjuː- **-ly** -li **-ness** -nəs, -nɪs
Efik ˈef.ɪk
EFL ˌiː.efˈel
eft eft **-s** -s
EFTA ˈef.tə
e.g. ˌiːˈdʒiː; fᵊr.ɪgˈzɑːm.pl̩ US ˌiːˈdʒiː; fɚ.ɪgˈzæm.pl̩
egad iːˈgæd, ɪ-
egalitarian ɪˌgæl.ɪˈteə.ri.ən, iː-, -əˈ-; ˌiː.gæl- US -ˈter.i- **-ism** -ɪ.zᵊm
Egan ˈiː.gᵊn
Egbert ˈeg.bət, -bɜːt US -bɚt, -bɝːt
Egdon ˈeg.dən
Egeria ɪˈdʒɪə.ri.ə, iː- US -ˈdʒɪr.i-
Egerton ˈedʒ.ə.tᵊn US ˈ-ɚ-
Egeus *in Greek mythology:* ˈiː.dʒuːs; ɪˈdʒiː.əs, iː- US iːˈdʒiː.əs *Shakespearean character:* iːˈdʒiː.əs, ɪ-
egg eg **-s** -z **-ing** -ɪŋ **-ed** -d **ˈegg ˌtimer; have ˈegg on one's ˌface; put ˌall one's ˌeggs in one ˈbasket**
eggcup ˈeg.kʌp **-s** -s
egghead ˈeg.hed **-s** -z
Eggleston ˈeg.l̩z.tᵊn US -l̩.stᵊn
Eggleton ˈeg.l̩.tᵊn
eggnog ˌegˈnɒg, ˈ-- US ˈeg.nɑːg **-s** -z
eggplant ˈeg.plɑːnt US -plænt **-s** -s
egg-shaped ˈeg.ʃeɪpt
eggshell ˈeg.ʃel **-s** -z
Egham ˈeg.əm
Eglamore, Eglamour ˈeg.lə.mɔːʳ US -mɔːr
eglantine (E) ˈeg.lən.taɪn, -tiːn
Eglingham ˈeg.lɪn.dʒəm
Eglinton ˈeg.lɪn.tən
Eglon ˈeg.lɒn US -lɑːn
Egmont ˈeg.mɒnt, -mənt US -mɑːnt
ego ˈiː.gəʊ, ˈeg.əʊ US ˈiː.goʊ, ˈeg.oʊ **-s** -z **ˈego ˌtrip**
egocentric ˌiː.gəʊˈsen.trɪk, ˌeg.əʊˈ- US ˌiː.goʊˈ-, ˌeg.oʊˈ- **-ally** -ᵊl.i, -li
egocentricity ˌiː.gəʊ.senˈtrɪs.ɪ.ti, ˌeg.əʊ-, -ə.ti US ˌiː.goʊ.senˈtrɪs.ə.t̬i, ˌeg.oʊ-
egocentrism ˌiː.gəʊˈsen.trɪ.zᵊm, ˌeg.əʊˈ- US ˌiː.goʊˈ-, ˌeg.oʊˈ-
ego|ism ˈiː.gəʊ|.ɪ.zᵊm, ˈeg.əʊ- US ˈiː.goʊ-, ˈeg.oʊ- **-ist/s** -ɪst/s
egoistic ˌiː.gəʊˈɪs.tɪk, ˌeg.əʊˈ- US ˌiː.goʊˈ-, ˌeg.oʊˈ- **-al** -ᵊl **-ally** -ᵊl.i, -li
egomania ˌiː.gəʊˈmeɪ.ni.ə, ˌeg.əʊˈ- US ˌiː.goʊˈ-, ˌeg.oʊˈ-
egomaniac ˌiː.gəʊˈmeɪ.ni.æk, ˌeg.əʊˈ- US ˌiː.goʊˈ-, ˌeg.oʊˈ- **-s** -s
Egon ˈeg.ən, ˈiː.gən, -gɒn US ˈeɪ.gɑːn -gən
Note: The restaurant critic Egon Ronay is popularly pronounced as /ˈiː.gɒn/ in the UK.
egot|ism ˈiː.gəʊ.t|ɪ.zᵊm, ˈeg.əʊ- US ˈiː.goʊ-, ˈeg.oʊ- **-ist/s** -ɪst/s
egotistic ˌiː.gəʊˈtɪs.tɪk, ˌeg.əʊˈ- US ˌiː.goʊˈ-, ˌeg.oʊˈ- **-al** -ᵊl **-ally** -ᵊl.i, -li
egregious ɪˈgriː.dʒəs, əˈgriː-, -dʒi.əs US iː-, ɪ- **-ly** -li **-ness** -nəs, -nɪs
Egremont ˈeg.rə.mənt, -rɪ-, -mɒnt US -mɑːnt
egress ˈiː.gres **-es** -ɪz
egression ɪˈgreʃ.ᵊn, iː- **-s** -z
egressive ɪˈgres.ɪv, iː-
egret ˈiː.grət, -grɪt, -gret US ˈiː.gret, ˈeg.ret, -rɪt **-s** -s
Egton ˈeg.tən
Egypt ˈiː.dʒɪpt
Egyptian ɪˈdʒɪp.ʃᵊn, ə-, iː- **-s** -z
Egyptolog|y ˌiː.dʒɪpˈtɒl.ə.dʒ|i US -ˈtɑː.lə- **-ist/s** -ɪst/s
eh eɪ
Ehrlich *European family name:* ˈeə.lɪk, -lɪx US ˈer- *US family name:* ˈɜː.lɪk US ˈɝː-, ˈer-

Pronouncing the letters EI

There are several pronunciation possibilities for the vowel digraph **ei**. One is /iː/ when following a **c**; this is immortalised in the spelling rhyme "**I** before **E** except after **C**, but only if the sound is /iː/", e.g.:

receive /rɪˈsiːv/

When followed by a silent **gh** in the spelling, it is usually pronounced as /eɪ/ but may be pronounced /aɪ/, e.g.:

eight /eɪt/
height /haɪt/

The pronunciation /aɪ/ also occurs in two words which do not include **gh**, but only in British English, e.g.:

either /ˈaɪ.ðəʳ/ US /ˈiː.ðɚ/
neither /ˈnaɪ.ðəʳ/ US /ˈniː.ðɚ/

When followed by an **r** in the spelling, **ei** is pronounced as /eə US er/ and /ɪə US ɪr/, e.g.:

their /ðeəʳ/ US /ðer/
weir /wɪəʳ/ US /wɪr/

In addition

Other vowel sounds are associated with the digraph **ei**, e.g.:

e Leicester /ˈles.təʳ/ US /-tɚ/
eɪ rein /reɪn/

In weak syllables

The vowel digraph **ei** is realised with the vowel /ɪ/ in weak syllables, e.g.:

foreign /ˈfɒr.ɪn/ US /ˈfɔːr-/

eider ˈaɪ.dəʳ US -dɚ **-s** -z ˈ**eider** ˌ**duck**
eiderdown ˈaɪ.də.daʊn US -dɚ- **-s** -z
Eidos® ˈaɪ.dɒs, ˈeɪ- US -dɑːs, -doʊs
Eifel ˈaɪ.fᵊl
Eiffel Tower ˌaɪ.fᵊlˈtaʊəʳ US -ˈtaʊɚ **-s** -z
Eiger ˈaɪ.gəʳ US -gɚ
Eigg eg
eight eɪt **-s** -s
eighteen ˌeɪˈtiːn **-s** -z **-th/s** -θ/s *stress shift:* ˌeighteen ˈmonths
eightfold ˈeɪt.fəʊld US -foʊld
eighth eɪtθ **-s** -s
eightieth ˈeɪ.ti.əθ, -ti.ɪθ US -t̬i.əθ **-s** -s
eightsome ˈeɪt.sᵊm
eight|y ˈeɪ.t|i US -t̬|i **-ies** -iz
eightyfold ˈeɪ.ti.fəʊld US -t̬i.foʊld
eighty-six ˌeɪ.tiˈsɪks US -t̬iˈ- **-es** -ɪz **-ing** -ɪŋ **-ed** -t
ilat eɪˈlɑːt, -ˈlæt US -ˈlɑːt
ilean ˈel.ən, ˈiː.lən
ileen ˈaɪ.liːn US aɪˈliːn
iloart ˈaɪ.ləʊ.ɑːt US -loʊ.ɑːrt
indhoven ˈaɪnd.həʊ.vᵊn US -hoʊ-
instein ˈaɪn.staɪn
insteinium ˌaɪnˈstaɪ.ni.əm
ire ˈeə.rə US ˈer.ə, -iː; ˈaɪ.rə, -riː
irenicon aɪəˈriː.nɪ.kɒn, -ˈren.ɪ- US aɪˈriː.nɪ.kɑːn **-s** -z
isenhower ˈaɪ.zᵊn.haʊəʳ US -haʊɚ
isteddfod **(E)** aɪˈsteð.vɒd, ɪ-, -ˈsted.fəd US -ˈsteð.vɑːd, eɪ- **-s** -z
ither ˈaɪ.ðəʳ, ˈiː- US ˈiː.ðɚ, ˈaɪ-
acu|late *(v.)* ɪˈdʒæk.jə|.leɪt, iː-, -jʊ- **-lates** -leɪts **-lating** -leɪ.tɪŋ US -leɪ.t̬ɪŋ **-lated** -leɪ.tɪd US -leɪ.t̬ɪd
aculate *(n.)* ɪˈdʒæk.jə.lət, iː-, -jʊ-, -lɪt, -leɪt US -lət, -lɪt
aculation ɪˌdʒæk.jəˈleɪ.ʃᵊn, iː-, -jʊˈ- **-s** -z
ejaculative ɪˈdʒæk.jə.lə.tɪv, -jʊ-, -leɪ.tɪv US -jə.lə.t̬ɪv
ejaculatory ɪˈdʒæk.jə.lə.tᵊr.i, iː-, -jʊ-, -leɪ-, -tri; ɪˌdʒæk.jəˈleɪ-, iː-, -jʊˈ- US ɪˈdʒæk.jə.lə.tɔːr.i, iː-, -jʊ-
eject ɪˈdʒekt, iː- **-s** -s **-ing** -ɪŋ **-ed** -ɪd
ejection ɪˈdʒek.ʃᵊn, iː- **-s** -z
ejective ɪˈdʒek.tɪv, iː- **-s** -z
ejectment ɪˈdʒekt.mənt, iː- **-s** -s
ejector ɪˈdʒek.təʳ, iː- US -tɚ **-s** -z
ejusdem generis eɪˌʊs.demˈgen.ᵊr.ɪs US edʒˌuːs.demˈgen.ɚ.əs; iː.dʒəs.demˈdʒen-
Ekaterinburg ɪˌkæt.ᵊrˈiːn.bɜːg US -bɝːg
ek|e iːk **-es** -s **-ing** -ɪŋ **-ed** -t
EKG ˌiː.keɪˈdʒiː
Ekron ˈek.rɒn US -rɑːn
Ektachrome® ˈek.tə.krəʊm US -kroʊm
el el
elaborate *(adj.)* ɪˈlæb.ᵊr.ət, -ɪt **-ly** -li **-ness** -nəs, -nɪs
elabor|ate *(v.)* ɪˈlæb.ᵊr|eɪt **-ates** -eɪts **-ating** -eɪ.tɪŋ US -eɪ.t̬ɪŋ **-ated** -eɪ.tɪd US -eɪ.t̬ɪd **-ator/s** -eɪ.təʳ/z US -eɪ.t̬ɚ/z
elaboration ɪˌlæb.əˈreɪ.ʃᵊn **-s** -z
elaborative ɪˈlæb.ᵊr.ə.tɪv, -eɪ- US -ə.t̬ɪv
Elaine ɪˈleɪn, ə-, elˈeɪn
El Al® ˌelˈæl
El Alamein ˌelˈæl.ə.meɪn; elˌæl.əˈmeɪn US ˌelˈæl.ə.mein, -ˈɑː.lə-; elˌæl.əˈmeɪn, -ˌɑː.ləˈ-
Elam ˈiː.ləm **-ite/s** -aɪt/s
élan eɪˈlɑ̃ːn, ɪ-, -ˈlæn US -ˈlɑːn, -ˈlɑ̃ːŋ, -ˈlæn *stress shift, see compound:* ˌ**élan viˈtal**
eland **(E)** ˈiː.lənd **-s** -z
elaps|e ɪˈlæps **-es** -ɪz **-ing** -ɪŋ **-ed** -t
elastic ɪˈlæs.tɪk, -ˈlɑː.stɪk US -ˈlæs.tɪk **-s** -s **-ally** -ᵊl.i, -li eˌ**lastic** ˈ**band**
elasti|cate ɪˈlæs.tɪ|.keɪt, -ˈlɑː.stɪ-, -stə- US -ˈlæs.tɪ- **-cates** -keɪts **-cating** -keɪ.tɪŋ US -keɪ.t̬ɪŋ **-cated** -keɪ.tɪd US -keɪ.t̬ɪd
elasticity ˌɪl.æsˈtɪs.ə.ti, ˌel-, ˌiː.læs-, -ləˈstɪs-, -lɑːˈ-, -ɪ.ti; ɪˌlæsˈtɪs-, -ˌlɑːˈstɪs- US ɪˌlæsˈtɪs.ə.t̬i; ˌiː.læsˈ-
elasticiz|e, -ise ɪˈlæs.tɪ.saɪz, -ˈlɑː.stɪ-, -stə-, -ˈlæs.tɪ- **-es** -ɪz **-ing** -ɪŋ **-ed** -d
elastin ɪˈlæs.tɪn, ə-, -ˈlɑː.stɪn US ɪˈlæs.tɪn
Elastoplast® ɪˈlæs.təʊ.plɑːst, el-, iːˈlæs-, -plæst; -ˈlɑː.stəʊ.plɑːst US ɪˈlæs.toʊ.plæst, iː-, -tə-
e|late ɪˈleɪt, iː- **-lates** -leɪts **-lating** -leɪ.tɪŋ US -leɪ.t̬ɪŋ **-lated/ly** -leɪ.tɪd/li US -leɪ.t̬ɪd/li
elation ɪˈleɪ.ʃᵊn, iː-
Elba ˈel.bə
Elbe ˈel.bə, elb
elbow ˈel.bəʊ US -boʊ **-s** -z **-ing** -ɪŋ **-ed** -d ˈ**elbow** ˌ**grease**; ˈ**elbow** ˌ**room**
El Cid ˌelˈsɪd
elder **(E)** ˈel.dəʳ US -dɚ **-s** -z ˌ**elder** ˈ**statesman**
elderberr|y ˈel.dəˌber|.i, -bᵊr- US -dɚˌber- **-ies** -iz
elderflower ˈel.dəˌflaʊəʳ US -dɚˌflaʊɚ **-s** -z
elderl|y ˈel.dᵊl|.i US -dɚ.l|i **-iness** -ɪ.nəs, -ɪ.nɪs
eldest ˈel.dɪst, -dəst
Eldon ˈel.dᵊn
El Dorado, **Eldorado** ˌel.dəˈrɑː.dəʊ, -dɒrˈɑː- US -dəˈrɑː.doʊ, -ˈreɪ-
Eldred ˈel.drɪd, -dred, -drəd

Eldridge 'el.drɪdʒ
Eleanor 'el.ɪ.nəʳ, '-ə- (US) -nɚ, -nɔːr
Eleanora ˌel.i.ə'nɔː.rə (US) -'nɔːr.ə-
Eleazar ˌel.i'eɪ.zəʳ (US) -zɚ
elecampane ˌel.ɪ.kæm'peɪn, ˌ-ə- **-s** -z
elect ɪ'lekt **-s** -s **-ing** -ɪŋ **-ed** -ɪd **-able** -ə.bl̩
election ɪ'lek.ʃᵊn **-s** -z
electioneer ɪˌlek.ʃə'nɪəʳ (US) -'nɪr **-s** -z **-ing** -ɪŋ **-ed** -d **-er/s** -əʳ/z (US) -ɚ/z
elective ɪ'lek.tɪv **-ly** -li
elector ɪ'lek.təʳ (US) -tɚ **-s** -z
electoral ɪ'lek.tᵊr.ᵊl, '-trᵊl
electorate ɪ'lek.tᵊr.ət, -ɪt, '-trət, '-trɪt **-s** -s
Electra ɪ'lek.trə **E'lectra ˌcomplex**
electric ɪ'lek.trɪk **-al** -ᵊl **-ally** -ᵊl.i, -li **-s** -s **eˌlectric 'blanket; eˌlectric 'chair; eˌlectric gui'tar; eˌlectric 'shock; eˌlectric 'shock ˌtherapy**
electrician ˌel.ɪk'trɪʃ.ᵊn, ˌiː.lek'-; ɪˌlek'- (US) ɪˌlek'-; ˌiː.lek'- **-s** -z
electricity ˌel.ɪk'trɪs.ə.ti, ˌiː.lek-, -ɪ.ti; ɪˌlek'- (US) ɪˌlek'-; ˌiː.lek'-
electrification ɪˌlek.trɪ.fɪ'keɪ.ʃᵊn, -trə- **-s** -z
electri|fy ɪ'lek.trɪ|.faɪ, -trə- **-fies** -faɪz **-fying** -faɪ.ɪŋ **-fied** -faɪd **-fiable** -faɪ.ə.bl̩
electro- ɪ.lek.trəʊ-; ˌel.ɪk'trɒ-, ˌiː.lek'-; ɪˌlek'- (US) ɪ.lek.troʊ-; ɪˌlek'trɑː-; ˌiː.lek'-
Note: Prefix. Either takes primary or secondary stress on the second syllable, e.g. **electrocute** /ɪ'lek.trə.kjuːt/, **electrocution** /ɪˌlek.trə'kjuː.ʃᵊn/, or primary stress on the third syllable, with secondary stress on either the first or second syllable,e.g. **electrolysis** /ˌel.ɪk'trɒl.ɪ.sɪs, ɪˌlek'- (US) ɪˌlek'trɑː.lə-, ˌiː.lek'-/.
electrobiology ɪˌlek.trəʊ.baɪ'ɒl.ə.dʒi (US) -troʊ.baɪ'ɑː.lə-
electrocardiogram ɪˌlek.trəʊ'kɑː.di.əʊ.græm (US) -troʊ'kɑːr.di.ə- **-s** -z
electrocardiograph ɪˌlek.trəʊ'kɑː.di.əʊ.grɑːf, -græf (US) -troʊ'kɑːr.di.ə.græf **-s** -s
electrochemistry ɪˌlek.trəʊ'kem.ɪ.stri, -ə.stri (US) -troʊ'kem.ə-
electroconvulsive ɪˌlek.trəʊ.kən'vʌl.sɪv (US) -troʊ- **eˌlectroconˌvulsive 'therapy**
electro|cute ɪ'lek.trə|.kjuːt **-cutes** -kjuːts **-cuting** -kjuː.tɪŋ (US) -kjuː.t̬ɪŋ **-cuted** -kjuː.tɪd (US) -kjuː.t̬ɪd
electrocution ɪˌlek.trə'kjuː.ʃᵊn **-s** -z
electrode ɪ'lek.trəʊd (US) -troʊd **-s** -z
electrodynamic ɪˌlek.trəʊ.daɪ'næm.ɪk, -dɪ'- (US) -troʊ.daɪ'- **-s** -s
electroencephalo|gram ɪˌlek.trəʊ.en'sef.ᵊl.əʊ|.græm, -ɪn'-, -'kef-, -eŋ'kef-, -ɪŋ'kef- (US) -troʊ.en'sef.ə.loʊ-, -lə- **-s** -z **-graph/s** -grɑːf/s, -græf/s (US) -græf/s
electrokinetic ɪˌlek.trəʊ.kɪ'net.ɪk, -kaɪ'- (US) -troʊ.kɪ'net̬-, -trə- **-s** -s
electrolier ɪˌlek.trəʊ'lɪəʳ (US) -trə'lɪr **-s** -z
Electrolux® ɪ'lek.trəʊ.lʌks (US) -trə-
electrolys|is ˌel.ɪk'trɒl.ə.s|ɪs, ˌiː.lek-, -ɪ.s|ɪs; ɪˌlek'-, ə- (US) ɪˌlek'trɑː.lə-; ˌiː.lek- **-es** -iːz
electrolyte ɪ'lek.trə.laɪt **-s** -s
electrolytic ɪˌlek.trə'lɪt.ɪk (US) -'lɪt̬-
electrolyz|e, -ys|e ɪ'lek.trᵊl.aɪz (US) -trə.laɪz **-es** -ɪz **-ing** -ɪŋ **-ed** -d
electromagnet ɪˌlek.trəʊ'mæg.nɪt, -nət (US) -troʊ'-, -trə'- **-s** -s **-ism** -ɪ.zᵊm
electromagnetic ɪˌlek.trəʊ.mæg'net.ɪk, -məg'- (US) -troʊ.mæg'net̬-, -trə-
electrometer ˌel.ɪk'trɒm.ɪ.təʳ, ˌiː.lek-, -mə.təʳ; ɪˌlek'- (US) ɪ.lek'trɑː.mə.t̬ɚ; ˌiː.lek'- **-s** -z
electromotive ɪˌlek.trəʊ'məʊ.tɪv (US) -troʊ'moʊ.t̬ɪv, -trə'-
electromotor ɪˌlek.trəʊ'məʊ.təʳ (US) -troʊ'moʊ.t̬ɚ, -trə'- **-s** -z
electron ɪ'lek.trɒn (US) -trɑːn **-s** -z
electronic ˌel.ek'trɒn.ɪk, -ɪk'-, ˌiː.lek'-; ɪˌlek'- (US) ɪˌlek'trɑː.nɪk; ˌiː.lek'- **-s** -s **-ally** -ᵊl.i, -li *stress shift, see compound:* **ˌelectronic 'mail**
electropalatogram ɪˌlek.trəʊ'pæl.ə.təʊ.græm (US) -troʊ'pæl.ə.t̬ə- **-s** -z
electropalatography ɪˌlek.trəʊˌpæl.ə'tɒg.rə.fi (US) -troʊˌpæl.ə'tɑː.grə-
electrophone ɪ'lek.trə.fəʊn (US) -foʊn **-s** -z
electrophorus ˌel.ɪk'trɒf.ᵊr.əs, ˌiː.lek'- (US) ɪˌlek'trɑː.fɚ-; ˌiː.lek'- **-es** -ɪz
electropla|te ɪ'lek.trəʊ.pleɪ|t, ɪˌlek.trəʊ'pleɪ|t (US) ɪ'lek.troʊ.pleɪ|t, iː-, -trə- **-tes** -ts **-ting** -tɪŋ (US) -t̬ɪŋ **-ted** -tɪd (US) -t̬ɪd **-ter/s** -təʳ/z (US) -t̬ɚ/z
electropolar ɪˌlek.trəʊ'pəʊ.ləʳ (US) -troʊ'poʊ.lɚ
electropositive ɪˌlek.trəʊ'pɒz.ə.tɪv, -ɪ.tɪv (US) -troʊ'pɑː.zə.t̬ɪv
electroscope ɪ'lek.trəʊ.skəʊp (US) -troʊ.skoʊp, -trə- **-s** -s
electrostatic ɪˌlek.trəʊ'stæt.ɪk (US) -troʊ'stæt̬- **-s** -s
electrotherapeutic ɪˌlek.trəʊˌθer.ə'pjuː.tɪk (US) -troʊˌθer.ə'pjuː.t̬ɪk **-s** -s
electrotherapy ɪˌlek.trəʊ'θer.ə.pi (US) -troʊ'-
electrothermal ɪˌlek.trəʊ'θɜː.mᵊl (US) -troʊ'θɝː-
electrotype ɪ'lek.trəʊ.taɪp (US) -troʊ- **-s** -s
electrovalency ɪˌlek.trəʊ'veɪ.lənt.si (US) -troʊ'-
electrum ɪ'lek.trəm
electuar|y ɪ'lek.tjʊə.r|i (US) -tʃuː.er|.i **-ies** -iz
eleemosynary ˌel.i.iː'mɒs.ɪ.nᵊr.i, ˌel.iː'-, ˌel.ɪ'-, -'mɒz-, -'məʊ.zɪ-, -zᵊn.ᵊr- (US) ˌel.ɪ'mɑː.sə.ner.i, -iː.ə'-
elegance 'el.ɪ.gᵊnts (US) '-ə-
elegant 'el.ɪ.gᵊnt (US) '-ə- **-ly** -li
elegiac ˌel.ɪ'dʒaɪ.ək, -ə'-, -æk (US) ˌel.ɪ'dʒaɪ.ək, -ə'-, -æk; ɪ'liː.dʒiː.æk **-s** -s **-al** -ᵊl
elegist 'el.ɪ.dʒɪst, '-ə- **-s** -s
elegit ɪ'liː.dʒɪt, el'iː-
elegiz|e, -is|e 'el.ɪ.dʒaɪz, '-ə- **-es** -ɪz **-ing** -ɪŋ **-ed** -d
eleg|y 'el.ɪ.dʒ|i, '-ə- **-ies** -iz
Elektra ɪ'lek.trə
element 'el.ɪ.mənt, '-ə- (US) '-ə- **-s** -s
elemental ˌel.ɪ'men.tᵊl, -ə'- (US) -ə'men.t̬ᵊl **-s** -z **-ly** -i
elementar|y ˌel.ɪ'men.tᵊr|.i, -ə'-, '-tr|i (US) -ə'men.t̬ɚ|.i, '-tr|i **-ily** -ɪ.li, -ᵊl.i **-iness** -ɪ.nəs, -ɪ.nɪs **ele'mentary ˌschool**
elemi 'el.ɪ.mi
elenchus ɪ'leŋ.kəs, ə-
Eleonora ˌel.i.ə'nɔː.rə (US) -'nɔːr.ə
Eleonore 'el.i.ə.nɔːʳ (US) -nɔːr
elephant 'el.ɪ.fənt, '-ə- **-s** -s
elephantiasis ˌel.ɪ.fən'taɪə.sɪs, ˌ-ə-, -fæn'-
elephantine ˌel.ɪ'fæn.taɪn, -ə'- (US) -taɪn, -tiːn, 'el.ə.fən-
Eleusinian ˌel.juː'sɪn.i.ən, -uː'-
Eleusis el'juː.sɪs, ɪ'ljuː-, ə-, -'luː- (US) ɪ'luː.sɪs
Eleuthera ɪ'luː.θᵊr.ə, el'uː-, -'juː- (US) ɪ'luː-
ele|vate 'el.ɪ|.veɪt, '-ə- **-vates** -veɪts **-vating** -veɪ.tɪŋ (US) -veɪ.t̬ɪŋ **-vated** -veɪ.tɪd (US) -veɪ.t̬ɪd
elevation ˌel.ɪ'veɪ.ʃᵊn, -ə'- **-s** -z
elevator 'el.ɪ.veɪ.təʳ, '-ə- (US) -t̬ɚ **-s** -z
elevatory ˌel.ɪ'veɪ.tᵊr.i, -ə'-, '-tri (US) -t̬ɚ.i
eleven ɪ'lev.ᵊn, ə- **-s** -z **-th/s** -θ/s
eleven-plus ɪˌlev.ᵊn'plʌs, ə-, -əm'- (US) -ən'- **-es** -ɪz
elevenses ɪ'lev.ᵊn.zɪz, ə-
el|f el|f **-ves** -vz
elfin 'el.fɪn **-s** -z
elfish 'el.fɪʃ **-ly** -li
Elfrida el'friː.də
Elgar *composer:* 'el.gɑːʳ (US) -gɑːr *surname:* 'el.gɑːʳ, -gəʳ (US) -gɑːr, -gɚ

Elision

The omission of sounds which are normally present if words are pronounced slowly and clearly but appear not to be pronounced when the same words are produced in a rapid, colloquial style, or when the words occur in a different context. These missing sounds are said to have been 'elided'. See also CONNECTED SPEECH PHENOMENA.

Examples for English

It is easy to find examples of elision, but very difficult to state rules that govern which sounds may be elided and which may not. Elision of vowels in English usually happens when a short, unstressed vowel occurs between voiceless consonants, e.g. in the first syllable of *perhaps*, *potato*, the second syllable of *bicycle*, or the third syllable of *philosophy*.

Elision also occurs when a weak vowel occurs between a PLOSIVE or FRICATIVE consonant and a consonant such as a NASAL or a LATERAL: this process leads to SYLLABIC CONSONANTS, e.g.:

sudden	/ˈsʌd.ən/	→	/ˈsʌd.n̩/
awful	/ˈɔː.fʊl/	→	/ˈɔː.fl̩/
	(US) /ˈɑː-/		(US) /ˈɑː-/

Elision of consonants in English happens most commonly when a speaker 'simplifies' a complex consonant cluster, e.g.

acts	/ækts/	→	/æks/
twelfth night	/ˌtwelfθˈnaɪt/	→	/ˌtwelθˈnaɪt or ˌtwelfˈnaɪt/

In *twelfth night* above, it seems much less likely that any of the other consonants could be left out: the /l/ and the /n/ seem to be unelidable.

It is very important to note that sounds do not simply 'disappear' like a light being switched off. A transcription such as /æks/ for *acts* implies that the /t/ phoneme has dropped out altogether, but detailed examination of speech shows that such effects are more gradual: in slow speech the /t/ may be fully pronounced, with an audible transition from the preceding /k/ and to the following /s/, while in a more rapid style it may be articulated but not given any audible realisation, and in very rapid speech it may be observable, if at all, only as a rather early movement of the tongue blade towards the /s/ position. Much more research in this area is needed (not only on English) for us to understand what processes are involved when speech is 'reduced' in rapid articulation.

Elgin ˈel.gɪn (US) -gɪn, -dʒɪn ˌ**Elgin ˈMarbles**
El Greco ˌelˈgrek.əʊ (US) -oʊ
Elham ˈiː.ləm
Eli ˈiː.laɪ
Elia ˈiː.li.ə
Elias ɪˈlaɪəs, elˈaɪ-, əˈlaɪ-, -ˈlaɪ.æs
Elibank ˈel.ɪ.bæŋk
elic|it ɪˈlɪs|.ɪt, ə-, iː- **-its** -ɪts **-iting** -ɪ.tɪŋ (US) -ɪ.t̬ɪŋ **-ited** -ɪ.tɪd (US) -ɪ.t̬ɪd
elicitation ɪˌlɪs.ɪˈteɪ.ʃən, ə-, iː-, -əˈ-
elid|e ɪˈlaɪd, iː- **-es** -z **-ing** -ɪŋ **-ed** -ɪd **-able** -ə.bl̩
Elie ˈiː.li
eligibility ˌel.ɪ.dʒəˈbɪl.ə.ti, ˌ-ə-, -dʒɪˈ-, -ɪ.ti (US) -dʒəˈbɪl.ə.t̬i
eligib|le ˈel.ɪ.dʒə.b|l̩, ˈ-ə-, -dʒɪ- (US) -dʒə- **-ly** -li **-leness** -l̩.nəs, -nɪs
Elihu ɪˈlaɪ.hjuː, elˈaɪ- (US) ˈel.ɪ-; iːˈlaɪ-, ɪ-
Elijah ɪˈlaɪ.dʒə
Eliman ˈel.ɪ.mən
elimi|nate ɪˈlɪm.ɪ|.neɪt, ə-, ˈ-ə- **-nates** -neɪts **-nating** -neɪ.tɪŋ (US) -neɪ.t̬ɪŋ **-nated** -neɪ.tɪd (US) -neɪ.t̬ɪd **-nator/s** -neɪ.təʳ/z (US) -neɪ.t̬ɚ/z
elimination ɪˌlɪm.ɪˈneɪ.ʃən, ə-, -əˈ- **-s** -z
Elinor ˈel.ɪ.nəʳ, ˈ-ə- (US) -nɚ, -nɔːr
Eliot ˈel.i.ət
Eliotson ˈel.i.ət.sən
Eliott ˈel.i.ət
Eliphaz ˈel.ɪ.fæz
Elis ˈiː.lɪs
Elisabeth ɪˈlɪz.ə.bəθ, ə-
Elise ɪˈliːz (US) ɪˈliːz, -ˈliːs
Elisha *prophet:* ɪˈlaɪ.ʃə *place in Northumberland:* elˈɪʃ.ə
elision ɪˈlɪʒ.ən **-s** -z
elite, élite ɪˈliːt, eɪ- **-s** -s
elitism, élitism ɪˈliː.tɪ.zəm, eɪˈliː-
elitist, élitist ɪˈliː.tɪst, eɪˈliː- **-s** -s
elixir ɪˈlɪk.səʳ, elˈɪk-, əˈlɪk-, iː-, -sɪəʳ (US) -sɚ **-s** -z
Eliza ɪˈlaɪ.zə
Elizabeth ɪˈlɪz.ə.bəθ, ə-
Elizabethan ɪˌlɪz.əˈbiː.θən, ə- **-s** -z *stress shift:* Eˌlizabethan ˈpoet
Elizabethian ɪˌlɪz.əˈbiː.θi.ən, ə- **-s** -z *stress shift:* Eˌlizabethian ˈpoet
elk elk **-s** -s
Elkhart ˈelk.hɑːt (US) -hɑːrt
Elkin ˈel.kɪn
Elkington ˈel.kɪŋ.tən
Elkins ˈel.kɪnz
ell el **-s** -z
Ella ˈel.ə
Elland ˈel.ənd
Ellangowan ˌel.ənˈgaʊən, -əŋˈ-
Elle el
Ellen ˈel.ən, -ɪn
Ellenborough ˈel.ən.bəʳr.ə, -ɪn- (US) -oʊ
Ellery ˈel.əʳr.i
Ellesmere ˈelz.mɪəʳ (US) -mɪr
Ellice ˈel.ɪs
Ellicott ˈel.ɪ.kət, -kɒt (US) -kət, -kɑːt
Elliman ˈel.ɪ.mən
Ellingham *in Northumberland:* ˈel.ɪn.dʒəm *surname:* ˈel.ɪŋ.əm
Ellington ˈel.ɪŋ.tən
Elliot ˈel.i.ət
Elliotson ˈel.i.ət.sən
Elliott ˈel.i.ət
ellipse ɪˈlɪps **-s** -ɪz
ellips|is ɪˈlɪp.s|ɪs **-es** -iːz
ellipsoid ɪˈlɪp.sɔɪd **-s** -z
ellipsoidal ˌel.ɪpˈsɔɪ.dəl; ɪˌlɪpˈ-; elˌɪp- (US) ɪˌlɪpˈ-; ˌel.ɪpˈ-
elliptic ɪˈlɪp.tɪk **-al** -əl **-ally** -əl.i, -li
ellipticity ˌel.ɪpˈtɪs.ə.ti, ˌɪl-, -ɪ.ti (US) ɪˌlɪpˈtɪs.ə.t̬i; ˌel.ɪpˈ-
Ellis ˈel.ɪs
Ellison ˈel.ɪ.sən
Elliston ˈel.ɪ.stən
Ellon ˈel.ən
Ellsworth ˈelz.wəθ, -wɜːθ (US) -wɚθ, -wɝːθ
Ellwood ˈel.wʊd
elm (E) elm **-s** -z
Elmer ˈel.məʳ (US) -mɚ
Elmer Gantry ˌel.məˈgæn.tri (US) -mɚˈ-
Elmes elmz
Elmhurst ˈelm.hɜːst (US) -hɝːst
Elmina elˈmiː.nə
Elmo ˈel.məʊ (US) -moʊ
Elmore ˈel.mɔːʳ (US) -mɔːr
Elmsley ˈelmz.li
Elmwood ˈelm.wʊd

elocution ˌel.əˈkjuː.ʃᵊn
elocutionary ˌel.əˈkjuː.ʃᵊn.ᵊr.i, -ri US -er.i
elocutionist ˌel.əˈkjuː.ʃᵊn.ɪst **-s** -s
Elohim elˈəʊ.hɪm, ɪˈləʊ-, ə-, -hiːm; ˌel.əʊˈhiːm US elˈoʊ.hɪm, ɪˈloʊ-, ə-, -hiːm, ˌel.oʊˈhɪm, -ˈoʊ-
Eloi ɪˈləʊ.aɪ; ˈiː.ləʊ.aɪ, -lɔɪ US ˈiː.lɔɪ, ˈeɪ-
Eloisa ˌel.əʊˈiː.zə, -sə US -oʊˈ-
Éloise, Eloise ˌel.əʊˈiːz US -oʊˈ-
elon|gate ˈiː.lɒŋ|.geɪt US ɪˈlɑːŋ-, -ˈlɔːŋ- **-gates** -geɪts **-gating** -geɪ.tɪŋ US -geɪ.t̬ɪŋ **-gated** -geɪ.tɪd US -geɪ.t̬ɪd
elongation ˌiː.lɒŋˈgeɪ.ʃᵊn US ˌiː.lɑːŋˈ-, -lɔːŋˈ-; ɪˌlɑːŋˈ-, -ˌlɔːŋˈ- **-s** -z
elop|e ɪˈləʊp US -ˈloʊp **-es** -s **-ing** -ɪŋ **-ed** -t **-ement/s** -mənt/s
eloquence ˈel.ə.kwənts
eloquent ˈel.ə.kwənt **-ly** -li
El Paso ˌelˈpæs.əʊ US -oʊ
Elphick ˈel.fɪk
Elphin ˈel.fɪn
Elphinstone ˈel.fɪn.stən
Els els
Elsa *English name:* ˈel.sə *German name:* ˈel.zə
El Salvador ˌelˈsæl.və.dɔːʳ US -dɔːr
Elsan® ˈel.sæn
else els **-'s** -ɪz
elsewhere ˌelsˈ*h*weəʳ, ˈ-- US ˈels.*h*wer
Elsie ˈel.si
Elsinore ˈel.sɪ.nɔːʳ, ˌ--ˈ- US ˈel.sə.nɔːr, ˌ--ˈ-
Note: The stressing /ˌ--ˈ-/ has to be used in Shakespeare's 'Hamlet'.
Elsmere ˈelz.mɪəʳ US -mɪr
Elson ˈel.sᵊn
Elspeth ˈel.spəθ, -speθ
Elstree ˈel.striː, ˈelz.triː, -tri
Elswick ˈel.sɪk, ˈel.zɪk, ˈelz.wɪk
Note: **Elswick** in Tyne and Wear is locally /ˈel.sɪk/ or /ˈel.zɪk/.
Elsworthy ˈelz.wɜː.ði US -wɝː-
ELT ˌiː.elˈtiː
Eltham ˈel.təm
Elton ˈel.tᵊn
eluci|date ɪˈluː.sɪ|.deɪt, əˈluː-, -ˈljuː-, -sə- US ɪˈluː.sɪ-, -sə- **-dates** -deɪts **-dating** -deɪ.tɪŋ US -deɪ.t̬ɪŋ **-dated** -deɪ.tɪd US -deɪ.t̬ɪd **-dator/s** -deɪ.təʳ/z US -deɪ.t̬ɚ/z
elucidation ɪˌluː.sɪˈdeɪ.ʃᵊn, əˌluː-, -ˌljuː-, -səˈ- US ɪˌluː.sɪˈdeɪ-, -səˈ- **-s** -z
elucidative ɪˈluː.sɪ.deɪ.tɪv, əˈluː-, -ˈljuː-, -sə-, -də- US ɪˈluː.sɪ.deɪ.t̬ɪv, -sə-
elucidatory ɪˈluː.sɪ.deɪ.tᵊr.i, əˈluː-, -ˈljuː-, -sə-, -tri; ɪˌluː.sɪˈdeɪ-, ə-, -ˌljuː-, -səˈ- US ɪˈluː.sɪ.deɪ.tɔːr.i, -sə-; ɪˌluː.sɪˈdeɪ.t̬ɚ-, -səˈ-
elud|e ɪˈluːd, əˈluːd, -ˈljuːd US ɪˈluːd **-es** -z **-ing** -ɪŋ **-ed** -ɪd
elusion ɪˈluː.ʒᵊn, əˈluː, -ˈljuː- US ɪˈluː- **-s** -z
elusive ɪˈluː.sɪv, əˈluː-, -ˈljuː- US ɪˈluː- **-ly** -li **-ness** -nəs, -nɪs
elusory ɪˈluː.sᵊr.i, əˈluː-, -ˈljuː- US ɪˈluː-
elvan ˈel.vən
Elvedon ˈelv.dən, ˈel.dən
elver ˈel.vəʳ US -vɚ **-s** -z
elves *(plur. of* **elf***)* elvz
Elvey ˈel.vi
Elvin ˈel.vɪn
Elvira elˈvɪə.rə, -ˈvaɪə- US -ˈvaɪ.rə, -ˈvɪr.ə
Elvis ˈel.vɪs
Elwell ˈel.wel, -wəl
Elwes ˈel.wɪz, -wɪs, -wez
Ely *cities:* ˈiː.li *first name in US:* ˈiː.laɪ
Elyot ˈel.i.ət
Elyse elˈiːz US ɪˈliːs
Elysée eɪˈliː.zeɪ, ɪ-, ə- US ˌeɪ.liːˈzeɪ
Elysi|an ɪˈlɪz.i|.ən, iː- US ɪˈlɪʒ|.ən **-um** -əm **EˌlysianˈFields**
elzevir (E) ˈel.zɪ.vɪəʳ, -sɪ-, -zə-, -sə- US -vɪr
em- em-, ɪm-
Note: Prefix. Either takes primary or secondary stress and is pronounced /em-/, e.g. **emblem** /ˈem.bləm/, **emblematic** /ˌem.bləˈmæt.ɪk US -ˈmæt̬-/, or is unstressed and may be pronounced either /ɪm-/ or /em-/, e.g. **embed** /ɪmˈbed, em- US em-, ɪm-/.
em em **-s** -z
'em *(weak form of* **them***)* əm, m
emaci|ate ɪˈmeɪ.ʃi|.eɪt, iː-, -si- **-ates** -eɪts **-ating** -eɪ.tɪŋ US -eɪ.t̬ɪŋ **-ated** -eɪ.tɪd US -eɪ.t̬ɪd
emaciation ɪˌmeɪ.ʃiˈeɪ.ʃᵊn, iː-, -siˈ-
e-mail, E-mail ˈiː.meɪl **-s** -z **-ing** -ɪŋ **-ed** -d
emalangeni *(plur. of* **lilangeni***)* ˈem.ə.lɑːŋˌgen.i US ˌem.ə.lənˈgen-
ema|nate ˈem.ə|.neɪt **-nates** -neɪts **-nating** -neɪ.tɪŋ US -neɪ.t̬ɪŋ **-nated** -neɪ.tɪd US -neɪ.t̬ɪd **-native** -neɪ.tɪv US -neɪ.t̬ɪv
emanation ˌem.əˈneɪ.ʃᵊn **-s** -z
emanci|pate ɪˈmænt.sɪ|.peɪt, -sə- **-pates** -peɪts **-pating** -peɪ.tɪŋ US -peɪ.t̬ɪŋ **-pated** -peɪ.tɪd US -peɪ.t̬ɪd **-pator/s** -peɪ.təʳ/z US -peɪ.t̬ɚ/z
emancipation ɪˌmænt.sɪˈpeɪ.ʃᵊn, -səˈ- **-s** -z
Emanuel ɪˈmæn.ju.əl, -el
emasculate *(adj.)* ɪˈmæs.kjʊ.lɪt, iː-, -kjə-, -lət
emascu|late *(v.)* ɪˈmæs.kjʊ|.leɪt, iː-, -kjə- **-lates** -leɪts **-lating** -leɪ.tɪŋ US -leɪ.t̬ɪŋ **-lated** -leɪ.tɪd US -leɪ.t̬ɪd **-lator/s** -leɪ.təʳ/z US -leɪ.t̬ɚ/z
emasculation ɪˌmæs.kjʊˈleɪ.ʃᵊn, iː-, -kjəˈ- **-s** -z
embalm ɪmˈbɑːm, em- US em-, ɪm- **-s** -z **-ing** -ɪŋ **-ed** -d **-er/s** -əʳ/z US -ɚ/z **-ment/s** -mənt/s
embank ɪmˈbæŋk, em- US em-, ɪm- **-s** -s **-ing** -ɪŋ **-ed** -t
embankment (E) ɪmˈbæŋk.mənt, em- US em-, ɪm- **-s** -s
embarcation ˌem.bɑːˈkeɪ.ʃᵊn US -bɑːrˈ- **-s** -z
embargo ɪmˈbɑː.gəʊ, em- US emˈbɑːr.goʊ, ɪm- **-es** -z **-ing** -ɪŋ **-ed** -d
embark ɪmˈbɑːk, em- US emˈbɑːrk, ɪm- **-s** -s **-ing** -ɪŋ **-ed** -t
embarkation ˌem.bɑːˈkeɪ.ʃᵊn US -bɑːrˈ- **-s** -z
embarras de richesses ˌɑːm.bærˌɑː.də.riːˈʃes, ɑ̃ːm- US ˌɑːm.bɑː.rɑː-
embarrass ɪmˈbær.əs, em- US emˈber-, ɪm-, -ˈbær- **-es** -ɪz **-ing/ly** -ɪŋ/li **-ed** -t
embarrassment ɪmˈbær.əs.mənt, em- US emˈber-, ɪm-, -ˈbær- **-s** -s
embass|y ˈem.bə.s|i **-ies** -iz
embattl|e ɪmˈbæt.l̩, em- US emˈbæt̬-, ɪm- **-es** -z **-ing** -ɪŋ, -ˈbæt.lɪŋ **-ed** -d
embay ɪmˈbeɪ, em- US em-, ɪm- **-s** -z **-ing** -ɪŋ **-ed** -d
embed ɪmˈbed, em- US em-, ɪm- **-s** -z **-ding** -ɪŋ **-ded** -ɪd **-ment** -mənt
embellish ɪmˈbel.ɪʃ, em- US em-, ɪm- **-es** -ɪz **-ing** -ɪŋ **-ed** -t **-er/s** -əʳ/z US -ɚ/z
embellishment ɪmˈbel.ɪʃ.mənt, em- US em-, ɪm- **-s** -s
ember (E) ˈem.bəʳ US -bɚ **-s** -z **ˈEmber ˌday**
embezzl|e ɪmˈbez.l̩, em- US em-, ɪm- **-es** -z **-ing** -ɪŋ, -ˈ-lɪŋ **-ed** -d **-er/s** -əʳ/z, ˈ-ləʳ/z US -ɚ/z, ˈ-lɚ/z
embezzlement ɪmˈbez.l̩.mənt, em- US em-, ɪm-
embitt|er ɪmˈbɪt|.əʳ, em- US emˈbɪt̬|.ɚ, ɪm- **-ers** -əz US -ɚz **-ering** -ᵊr.ɪŋ **-ered** -əd US -ɚd **-erment** -ə.mənt US -ɚ.mənt
emblazon ɪmˈbleɪ.zᵊn, em- US em-, ɪm- **-s** -z **-ing** -ɪŋ **-ed** -d **-ment/s** -mənt/s **-ry** -ri
emblem ˈem.bləm, -blem, -blɪm US -bləm **-s** -z
emblematic ˌem.bləˈmæt.ɪk, -blɪˈ- US -bləˈmæt̬- **-al** -ᵊl **-ally** -ᵊl.i, -li
emblematiz|e, -is|e emˈblem.ə.taɪz, ˈ-ɪ-; ˈem.blem.ə- US emˈblem.ə- **-es** -ɪz **-ing** -ɪŋ **-ed** -d
emblements ˈem.blə.mənts, -bl̩- US -blə-

embodiment ɪmˈbɒd.ɪ.mənt, em- (US) emˈbɑː.di-, ɪm- **-s** -s
embod|y ɪmˈbɒd|.i, em- (US) emˈbɑː.d|i, ɪm- **-ies** -iz **-ying** -i.ɪŋ **-ied** -id
embolden ɪmˈbəʊl.dᵊn, em- (US) emˈboʊl-, ɪm- **-s** -z **-ing** -ɪŋ **-ed** -d
embolism ˈem.bə.lɪ.zᵊm **-s** -z
embonpoint ˌɑ̃ː*m*.bɔ̃ː*m*ˈpwɑ̃ː*ŋ* (US) ˌɑ̃ːm.bõʊnˈpwæ̃n, -ˈpwɑ̃ːn
embosom ɪmˈbʊz.ᵊm, em- (US) em-, ɪm- **-s** -z **-ing** -ɪŋ **-ed** -d
emboss ɪmˈbɒs, em- (US) emˈbɑːs, ɪm- **-es** -ɪz **-ing** -ɪŋ **-ed** -t **-er/s** -əʳ/z (US) -ɚ/z **-ment/s** -mənt/s
embouchure ˌɑ̃ːm.buːˈʃʊəʳ, ˈ--- (US) ˌɑːm.buːˈʃʊr, ˈ--- **-s** -z
embowel ɪmˈbaʊəl, em- (US) emˈbaʊᵊl, ɪm- **-s** -z **-(l)ing** -ɪŋ **-(l)ed** -d
embower ɪmˈbaʊəʳ, em- (US) emˈbaʊɚ, ɪm- **-s** -z **-ing** -ɪŋ **-ed** -d
embrac|e ɪmˈbreɪs, em- (US) em-, ɪm- **-es** -ɪz **-ing** -ɪŋ **-ed** -t
embracery ɪmˈbreɪ.sᵊr.i, em- (US) em-, ɪm-
embranchment ɪmˈbrɑːn*t*ʃ.mənt, em- (US) emˈbræn*t*ʃ-, ɪm- **-s** -s
embrasure ɪmˈbreɪ.ʒəʳ, em-, -ʒʊəʳ (US) emˈbreɪ.ʒɚ, ɪm- **-s** -z
embro|cate ˈem.brəʊ|.keɪt (US) -broʊ-, -brə- **-cates** -keɪts **-cating** -keɪ.tɪŋ (US) -keɪ.t̬ɪŋ **-cated** -keɪ.tɪd (US) -keɪ.t̬ɪd
embrocation ˌem.brəʊˈkeɪ.ʃᵊn (US) -broʊˈ-, -brəˈ- **-s** -z
embroglio ɪmˈbrəʊ.li.əʊ, em- (US) emˈbroʊ.ljoʊ, ɪm- **-s** -z
embroid|er ɪmˈbrɔɪ.d|əʳ, em- (US) emˈbrɔɪ.d|ɚ, ɪm- **-ers** -əz (US) -ɚz **-ering** -ᵊr.ɪŋ **-ered** -əd (US) -ɚd **-erer/s** -ᵊr.əʳ/z (US) -ɚ.ɚ/z
embroider|y ɪmˈbrɔɪ.dᵊr|.i, em- (US) em-, ɪm- **-ies** -iz
embroil ɪmˈbrɔɪl, em- (US) em-, ɪm- **-s** -z **-ing** -ɪŋ **-ed** -d **-ment/s** -mənt/s
embryo ˈem.bri.əʊ (US) -oʊ **-s** -z
embryolog|y ˌem.briˈɒl.ə.dʒ|i (US) -ˈɑː.lə- **-ist/s** -ɪst/s
embryonic ˌem.briˈɒn.ɪk (US) -ˈɑː.nɪk
Embury, Emburey ˈem.bᵊr.i, -bjʊ.ri, -bjə.ri (US) -bɚ.i
emcee ˌemˈsiː **-s** -z **-ing** -ɪŋ **-d** -d
-eme -iːm
Note: Suffix. Unstressed, e.g. **lexeme** /ˈlek.siːm/.
Emeline ˈem.ɪ.liːn, ˈ-ə- (US) -ə.laɪn, -liːn
emend ɪˈmend, iː- **-s** -z **-ing** -ɪŋ **-ed** -ɪd **-able** -ə.bl̩
emen|date ˈiː.men|.deɪt, ˈem.en- (US) ˈiː.men-, -mən-; ɪˈmen- **-dates** -deɪts **-dating** -deɪ.tɪŋ (US) -deɪ.t̬ɪŋ **-dated** -deɪ.tɪd (US) -deɪ.t̬ɪd **-dator/s** -deɪ.təʳ/z (US) -deɪ.t̬ɚ/z
emendation ˌiː.menˈdeɪ.ʃᵊn, ˌem.enˈ-, -ənˈ- **-s** -z
emendatory ɪˈmen.də.tᵊr.i, iː-, -tri (US) -tɔːr.i
emerald ˈem.ᵊr.ᵊld, ˈ-rᵊld **-s** -z ˈ**Emerald** ˌ**Isle**
emerg|e ɪˈmɜːdʒ, iː- (US) -ˈmɝːdʒ **-es** -ɪz **-ing** -ɪŋ **-ed** -d
emergen|ce ɪˈmɜː.dʒᵊn|*t*s, iː- (US) -ˈmɝː- **-t** -t
emergenc|y ɪˈmɜː.dʒᵊn*t*.s|i, iː- (US) -ˈmɝː- **-ies** -iz **e**ˈ**mergency** ˌ**room**
emeritus ɪˈmer.ɪ.təs, iː-, -ə.təs (US) -ə.t̬əs
emersion ɪˈmɜː.ʃᵊn, iː-, -ʒᵊn (US) -ˈmɝː.ʒᵊn, -ʃᵊn **-s** -z
Emerson ˈem.ə.sᵊn (US) ˈ-ɚ-
emery (E) ˈem.ᵊr.i ˈ**emery** ˌ**board**; ˈ**emery** ˌ**paper**
emetic ɪˈmet.ɪk, iː- (US) -ˈmet̬- **-s** -s **-al** -ᵊl **-ally** -ᵊl.i, -li
émeute eɪˈmɜːt **-s** -s
EMF ˌiː.emˈef
EMI® ˌiː.emˈaɪ
emigrant ˈem.ɪ.grənt (US) ˈ-ɪ-, ˈ-ə- **-s** -s
emi|grate ˈem.ɪ|.greɪt (US) ˈ-ɪ-, ˈ-ə- **-grates** -greɪts **-grating** -greɪ.tɪŋ (US) -greɪ.t̬ɪŋ **-grated** -greɪ.tɪd (US) -greɪ.t̬ɪd **-grator/s** -greɪ.təʳ/z (US) -greɪ.t̬ɚ/z
emigration ˌem.ɪˈgreɪ.ʃᵊn (US) -ɪˈ-, -əˈ- **-s** -z
emigratory ˈem.ɪ.grə.tᵊr.i, -greɪ-, -tri; ˌem.ɪˈgreɪ- (US) ˈem.ɪ.grə.tɔːr.i, ˈ-ə-
émigré ˈem.ɪ.greɪ **-s** -z
Emil emˈiːl, eɪˈmiːl (US) ˈiː.məl, ˈeɪ-
Emile, Émile emˈiːl, eɪˈmiːl (US) ˈiː.məl; eɪˈmiːl
Emilia ɪˈmɪl.i.ə, -ˈjə, emˈiː.li.ə (US) ɪˈmɪl.jə, emˈiː.ljə
Emily ˈem.ɪ.li, ˈ-ə-
Emin ˈem.ɪn
Eminem ˌem.ɪˈnem
eminen|ce ˈem.ɪ.nən*t*|s, ˈ-ə- **-ces** -sɪz **-cy** -si
éminence grise ˌem.ɪ.nən*t*sˈgriːz *as if French:* ˌeɪ.mɪˌnɑ̃ː*n*tsˈgriːz (US) ˌeɪ.miː.nɑːn*t*sˈ-
eminent ˈem.ɪ.nənt, ˈ-ə- **-ly** -li
emir (E) emˈɪəʳ, ɪˈmɪr, ə-, eɪ-; ˈem.ɪəʳ (US) emˈɪr, əˈmɪr; ˌeɪˈmɪr **-s** -z
emirate ˈem.ɪ.rət, -ᵊr.ət, -ɪt, -eɪt; emˈɪə.rət, ɪˈmɪə-, ə-, eɪ-, -rɪt, -reɪt (US) emˈɪr.eɪt, əˈmɪr-, -ət **-s** -s
emissar|y ˈem.ɪ.sᵊr|.i (US) -ser- **-ies** -iz
emission ɪˈmɪʃ.ᵊn, iː- **-s** -z
emissive ɪˈmɪs.ɪv, iː-
e|mit ɪ|ˈmɪt, iː- **-mits** -ˈmɪts **-mitting** -ˈmɪt.ɪŋ (US) -ˈmɪt̬- **-mitted** -ˈmɪt.ɪd (US) -ˈmɪt̬- **-mitter/s** -ˈmɪt.əʳ/z (US) -ˈmɪt̬.ɚ/z
Emley ˈem.li
Emlyn ˈem.lɪn
Emma ˈem.ə
Emmanuel ɪˈmæn.ju.əl, -el
Emmanuelle ɪˌmæn.juˈel, emˌæn-
Emmaus emˈeɪ.əs, ɪˈmeɪ-
Emmeline ˈem.ɪ.liːn, ˈ-ə- (US) -ə.laɪn, -liːn
Emmental, Emmenthal ˈem.ən.tɑːl
Emmerdale ˈem.ə.deɪl (US) ˈ-ɚ-
emmet (E) ˈem.ɪt **-s** -s
Emmie ˈem.i
Emmy ˈem.i **-s** -z ˈ**Emmy A**ˌ**ward**
emollient ɪˈmɒl.i.ənt, iː- (US) -ˈmɑːl.jənt **-s** -s
emolument ɪˈmɒl.jʊ.mənt, -jə- (US) -ˈmɑːl- **-s** -s
Emory ˈem.ᵊr.i
e|mote ɪ|ˈməʊt, iː- (US) -ˈmoʊt **-motes** -ˈməʊts (US) -ˈmoʊts **-moting** -ˈməʊ.tɪŋ (US) -ˈmoʊ.t̬ɪŋ **-moted** -ˈməʊ.tɪd (US) -ˈmoʊ.t̬ɪd
emoticon ɪˈməʊ.tɪ.kɒn (US) -ˈmoʊ.t̬ɪ.kɑːn **-s** -z
emotion ɪˈməʊ.ʃᵊn (US) -ˈmoʊ- **-s** -z **-less** -ləs, -lɪs
emotional ɪˈməʊ.ʃᵊn.ᵊl (US) -ˈmoʊ- **-ly** -i
emotionalism ɪˈməʊ.ʃᵊn.ᵊl.ɪ.zᵊm (US) -ˈmoʊ-
emotionaliz|e, -is|e ɪˈməʊ.ʃᵊn.ᵊl.aɪz (US) -ˈmoʊ.ʃᵊn.ə.laɪz **-es** -ɪz **-ing** -ɪŋ **-ed** -d
emotive ɪˈməʊ.tɪv (US) -ˈmoʊ.t̬ɪv **-ly** -li
empanel ɪmˈpæn.ᵊl, em- (US) em-, ɪm- **-s** -z **-(l)ing** -ɪŋ **-(l)ed** -d **-ment/s** -mənt/s
empathetic ˌem.pəˈθet.ɪk (US) -ˈθet̬-
empathic emˈpæθ.ɪk, ɪm-
empathiz|e, -is|e ˈem.pə.θaɪz **-es** -ɪz **-ing** -ɪŋ **-ed** -d
empathy ˈem.pə.θi
Empedocles emˈped.ə.kliːz, ɪm-
emperor (E) ˈem.pᵊr.əʳ (US) -ɚ.ɚ **-s** -z
emphas|is ˈem*p*.fə.s|ɪs **-es** -iːz
emphasiz|e, -is|e ˈem*p*.fə.saɪz **-es** -ɪz **-ing** -ɪŋ **-ed** -d
emphatic ɪmˈfæt.ɪk, em- (US) emˈfæt̬-, ɪm- **-al** -ᵊl **-ally** -ᵊl.i, -li
emphysema ˌem*p*.fɪˈsiː.mə (US) -fəˈsiː-, -ˈziː- **-s** -z
empire (E) ˈem.paɪəʳ (US) -paɪɚ **-s** -z ˌ**Empire** ˈ**State** ˌ**Building**
empiric ɪmˈpɪr.ɪk, em- (US) em-, ɪm- **-s** -s **-al** -ᵊl **-ally** -ᵊl.i, -li
empiric|ism ɪmˈpɪr.ɪ.s|ɪ.zᵊm, em-, ˈ-ə- (US) em-, ɪm- **-ist/s** -ɪst/s
emplacement ɪmˈpleɪs.mənt, em- (US) em-, ɪm- **-s** -s
employ ɪmˈplɔɪ, em- (US) em-, ɪm- **-s** -z **-ing** -ɪŋ **-ed** -d **-able** -ə.bl̩
employé ɑ̃ː*m*ˈplɔɪ.eɪ, ɔ̃ː*m*- **-s** -z
employee ɪmˈplɔɪ.iː, em-, əm-; ˌem.plɔɪˈiː (US) emˈplɔɪ.iː, ɪm-; ˌem.plɔɪˈiː **-s** -z

employer ɪmˈplɔɪ.əʳ, em- (US) emˈplɔɪ.ɚ, ɪm- **-s** -z

employment ɪmˈplɔɪ.mənt, em- (US) em-, ɪm- **-s** -s **emˈployment ˌagency**

empori|um emˈpɔː.ri|.əm, ɪm- (US) -ˈpɔːr.i- **-ums** -əmz **-a** -ə

empower ɪmˈpaʊəʳ, em- (US) emˈpaʊɚ, ɪm- **-s** -z **-ing** -ɪŋ **-ed** -d

empowerment ɪmˈpaʊə.mənt, em- (US) emˈpaʊɚ-, ɪm-

empress (E) ˈem.prəs, -prɪs, -pres **-es** -ɪz

Empson ˈemp.sᵊn

emption ˈemp.ʃᵊn

empt|y ˈemp.t|i **-ier** -i.əʳ (US) -i.ɚ **-iest** -i.ɪst, -i.əst **-ily** -ɪ.li, -ᵊl.i **-iness** -ɪ.nəs, -ɪ.nɪs **-ies** -iz **-ying** -i.ɪŋ **-ied** -id

empty-handed ˌemp.tiˈhæn.dɪd *stress shift:* ˌempty-handed ˈbeggar

empty-headed ˌemp.tiˈhed.ɪd **-ness** -nəs, -nɪs *stress shift:* ˌempty-headed ˈnonsense

empyema ˌem.paɪˈiː.mə (US) -paɪˈ-, -piˈ-

empyre|al ˌem.paɪəˈriː|.əl, -pɪˈ- (US) emˈpɪr.i-, -ˈpaɪ.ri-; ˌem.paɪˈriː-, -pəˈ- **-an** -ən

EMS ˌiː.emˈes

Emsworth ˈemz.wəθ, -wɜːθ (US) -wɚθ, -wɝːθ

emu ˈiː.mjuː (US) -mjuː, -muː **-s** -z

EMU ˌiː.emˈjuː, ˈiː.mjuː

emu|late ˈem.jə|.leɪt, -jʊ- **-lates** -leɪts **-lating** -leɪ.tɪŋ (US) -leɪ.t̬ɪŋ **-lated** -leɪ.tɪd (US) -leɪ.t̬ɪd **-lator/s** -leɪ.təʳ/z (US) -leɪ.t̬ɚ/z

emulation ˌem.jəˈleɪ.ʃᵊn, -jʊˈ-

emulative ˈem.jə.lə.tɪv, -jʊ-, -leɪ- (US) -leɪ.t̬ɪv

emulous ˈem.jə.ləs, -jʊ- **-ly** -li

emulsifier ɪˈmʌl.sɪ.faɪ.əʳ, -sə- (US) -ɚ **-s** -z

emulsi|fy ɪˈmʌl.sɪ|.faɪ, -sə- **-fies** -faɪz **-fying** -faɪ.ɪŋ **-fied** -faɪd

emulsion ɪˈmʌl.ʃᵊn **-s** -z

emunctor|y ɪˈmʌŋ*k*.tᵊr|.i **-ies** -iz

en *in French phrases:* ɑ̃ːŋ, ɒn, ɑːn

en- ɪn-, en-, ən-

Note: Prefix. Either takes primary or secondary stress and is pronounced /en-/, e.g. **energy** /ˈen.ə.dʒi (US) ˈ-ɚ-/, **energetic** /ˌen.əˈdʒet.ɪk (US) -ɚˈdʒet̬.ɪk/, or is unstressed and may be pronounced either /ɪn-/ or /en-/, e.g. **endear** /ɪnˈdɪəʳ, en- (US) -ˈdɪr/. NB When followed by a /k/ or /g/, assimilation may take place, e.g. **encage** may also be /ɪŋˈkeɪdʒ, eŋ-/.

enabl|e ɪˈneɪ.bl̩, enˈeɪ- **-es** -z **-ing** -ɪŋ, ˈ-blɪŋ **-ed** -d

enabler ɪˈneɪ.bləʳ, enˈeɪ-, -bl̩.əʳ (US) ˈ-blɚ, ˈ-bl̩.ɚ **-s** -z

enact ɪˈnækt, enˈækt **-s** -s **-ing** -ɪŋ **-ed** -ɪd **-or/s** -əʳ/z (US) -ɚ/z **-ment/s** -mənt/s **-ive** -ɪv

enaction ɪˈnæk.ʃᵊn, enˈæk- **-s** -z

enamel ɪˈnæm.ᵊl **-s** -z **-(l)ing** -ɪŋ **-(l)ed** -d **-(l)er/s** -əʳ/z (US) -ɚ/z **-(l)ist/s** -ɪst/s

enamelware ɪˈnæm.ᵊl.weəʳ (US) -wer

enamo(u)r ɪˈnæm.əʳ, enˈæm- (US) -ɚ **-s** -z **-ing** -ɪŋ **-ed** -d

en banc ɑ̃ː*m*ˈbɑ̃ːŋk (US) ɑ̃ːnˈbɑ̃ːŋ

en bloc ˌɑ̃ː*m*ˈblɒk (US) ɑ̃ːnˈblɑːk, en-

Encaenia enˈsiː.ni.ə

encag|e ɪnˈkeɪdʒ, ɪŋ-, en-, eŋ- (US) en-, ɪn- **-es** -ɪz **-ing** -ɪŋ **-ed** -d

encamp ɪnˈkæmp, ɪŋ-, en-, eŋ- (US) en-, ɪn- **-s** -s **-ing** -ɪŋ **-ed** -t, -kæmt **-ment/s** -mənt/s

encapsu|late ɪnˈkæp.sjə|.leɪt, ɪŋ-, en-, eŋ-, -sjʊ- (US) en-, ɪn- **-lates** -leɪts **-lating** -leɪ.tɪŋ (US) -leɪ.t̬ɪŋ **-lated** -leɪ.tɪd (US) -leɪ.t̬ɪd

encapsulation ɪnˌkæp.sjəˈleɪ.ʃᵊn, ɪŋ-, en-, eŋ-, -sjʊˈ- (US) en-, ɪn-

Encarta® enˈkɑː.tə, eŋ-, ɪn-, ɪŋ- (US) -ˈkɑːr.t̬ə

encas|e ɪnˈkeɪs, ɪŋ-, en-, eŋ- (US) en-, ɪn- **-es** -ɪz **-ing** -ɪŋ **-ed** -t **-ement/s** -mənt/s

encaustic ɪnˈkɔː.stɪk, ɪŋ-, en-, eŋ-, enˈkɒs.tɪk (US) enˈkɑː.stɪk, -ˈkɔː-, ɪn- **-s** -s **-ally** -ᵊl.i, -li

-ence -ᵊn*t*s

Note: Suffix. Normally, **-ence** does not affect the stress pattern of the word it is attached to, e.g. **depend** /dɪˈpend/, **dependence** /dɪˈpen.dən*t*s/. In other cases, the stress may be on the penultimate or antepenultimate syllable, e.g. **excellence**/ˈek.sᵊl.ᵊn*t*s/. See individual entries.

enceinte ˌɑ̃ː*n*ˈsæ̃nt (US) ˌɑ̃ː*n*-; enˈseɪnt **-s** -s

Enceladus enˈsel.ə.dəs

encephalic ˌen.kəˈfæl.ɪk, ˌeŋ-, ˌɪn-, ˌɪŋ-, -kɪˈ-; ˌen.səˈ-, ˌɪn-, -sefˈæl-, -sɪˈfæl- (US) ˌen.səˈfæl.ɪk, -sɪˈ-

encephalitis ˌen.kef.əˈlaɪ.tɪs, ˌeŋ-, ˌɪn-, ˌɪŋ-, -kɪ.fəˈ-; ˌen.sə-, ˌɪn-, -sef.əˈ-; enˌkef-, eŋ-, ɪn-, ɪŋ-; enˌsef-, ɪn- (US) enˌsef.əˈlaɪ.t̬ɪs

encephalogram enˈkef.ə.lə.græm, eŋ-, ɪn-, ɪŋ-; enˈsef-, ɪn- (US) enˈsef.ə.loʊ- **-s** -z

encephalograph enˈkef.ə.lə.grɑːf, eŋ-, ɪn-, ɪŋ; enˈsef-, ɪn-, -græf (US) enˈsef.ə.loʊ.græf **-s** -s

encephalomyelitis enˌkef.ə.ləʊ.maɪəˈlaɪ.tɪs, eŋ-, ɪn-, ɪŋ-; enˌsef-, ɪnˌsef-; ˌen.kef-, ˌeŋ-, ˌɪn-, ˌɪŋ-; ˌen.sef-, ˌɪn.sef- (US) enˌsef.ə.loʊ.maɪəˈlaɪ.t̬ɪs

encephalopathic enˌkef.ə.ləʊˈpæθ.ɪk, eŋ-, ɪn-, ɪŋ-, enˌsef-, ɪnˌsef- (US) enˌsef.ə.loʊˈ-

encephalopathy enˌkef.əˈlɒp.ə.θi, eŋ-, ɪn-, ɪŋ-; enˌsef-, ɪnˌsef-; ˌen.kef-, ˌeŋ-, ˌɪn-, ˌɪŋ-; ˌen.sef-, ˌɪn.sef- (US) enˌsef.əˈlɑː.pə-

enchain ɪnˈtʃeɪn, en- (US) en-, ɪn- **-s** -z **-ing** -ɪŋ **-ed** -d **-ment** -mənt

enchan|t ɪnˈtʃɑːn|t, en- (US) enˈtʃæn|t, ɪn- **-ts** -ts **-ting/ly** -tɪŋ/li (US) -t̬ɪŋ/li **-ted** -tɪd (US) -t̬ɪd **-ter/s** -təʳ/z (US) -t̬ɚ/z **-tress/es** -trɪs/ɪz **-tment/s** -t.mənt/s

enchilada ˌen.tʃɪˈlɑː.də **-s** -z

enchiridion ˌen.kaɪˈrɪd.i.ən, ˌeŋ-, -kɪˈ-, -ɒn (US) ˌen.kaɪˈrɪd.i.ən, -kɪˈ- **-s** -z

enciph|er ɪnˈsaɪ.f|əʳ, en- (US) enˈsaɪ.f|ɚ, ɪn- **-ers** -əz (US) -ɚz **-ering** -ᵊr.ɪŋ **-ered** -əd (US) -ɚd

encircl|e ɪnˈsɜː.kl̩, en- (US) enˈsɝː-, ɪn- **-es** -z **-ing** -ɪŋ, ˈ-klɪŋ **-ed** -d **-ement/s** -mənt/s

Encke ˈeŋ.kə

enclasp ɪnˈklɑːsp, ɪŋ-, en-, eŋ- (US) enˈklæsp, ɪn- **-s** -s **-ing** -ɪŋ **-ed** -t

enclave ˈen.kleɪv, ˈeŋ- (US) ˈen-, ˈɑːn- **-s** -z

enclitic ɪnˈklɪt.ɪk, ɪŋ-, en-, eŋ- (US) enˈklɪt̬-, ɪn- **-s** -s **-ally** -ᵊl.i, -li

enclos|e ɪnˈkləʊz, ɪŋ-, en-, eŋ- (US) enˈkloʊz, ɪn- **-es** -ɪz **-ing** -ɪŋ **-ed** -

enclosure ɪnˈkləʊ.ʒəʳ, ɪŋ-, en-, eŋ- (US) enˈkloʊ.ʒɚ, ɪn- **-s** -z

encod|e ɪnˈkəʊd, en-, eŋ-, ɪŋ- (US) enˈkoʊd, ɪn- **-es** -z **-ing** -ɪŋ **-ed** -ɪ **-er/s** -əʳ/z (US) -ɚ/z

encomi|ast ɪnˈkəʊ.mi|.æst, ɪŋ-, en-, e (US) enˈkoʊ-, ɪn- **-asts** -æsts **-um/s** -əm/z **-a** -ə

encompass ɪnˈkʌm.pəs, ɪŋ-, en-, eŋ- (US) en-, ɪn- **-es** -ɪz **-ing** -ɪŋ **-ed** -t

encore ˈɒŋ.kɔːʳ, ˈɑ̃ː*ŋ*-, -ˈ- (US) ˈɑːn.kɔːr -ˈ- **-es** -z **-ing** -ɪŋ **-ed** -d

encoun|ter ɪnˈkaʊn|.təʳ, ɪŋ-, en-, eŋ- (US) enˈkaʊn|.t̬ɚ, ɪn- **-ters** -təz (US) -t̬ɚz **-tering** -tᵊr.ɪŋ (US) -t̬ɚ.ɪŋ **-tered** -təd (US) -t̬ɚd

encourag|e ɪnˈkʌr.ɪdʒ, ɪŋ-, en-, eŋ- (US) en.kɝː-, ɪn- **-es** -ɪz **-ing/ly** -ɪŋ/li **-ed** -d

encouragement ɪnˈkʌr.ɪdʒ.mənt, ɪŋ en-, eŋ- (US) en.kɝː-, ɪn- **-s** -s

encroach ɪnˈkrəʊtʃ, ɪŋ-, en-, eŋ- (US) enˈkroʊtʃ, ɪn- **-es** -ɪz **-ing** -ɪŋ **-e** -t **-ment/s** -mənt/s

en croûte ˌɑ̃ː*ŋ*ˈkruːt (US) ˌɑːnˈkruːt

encrust ɪnˈkrʌst, ɪŋ-, en-, eŋ- (US) en-, ɪn- **-s** -s **-ing** -ɪŋ **-ed** -ɪd

encrustation ˌen.krʌsˈteɪ.ʃᵊn, ˌeŋ- (US) ˌen- **-s** -z

encrypt ɪnˈkrɪpt, ɪŋ-, en-, eŋ- (US) en-, ɪn- **-s** -s **-ing** -ɪŋ **-ed** -ɪd

encryption ɪnˈkrɪp.ʃᵊn, ɪŋ-, en-, eŋ- (US) en-, ɪn-

encumb|er ɪnˈkʌm.b|əʳ, ɪŋ-, en-, eŋ- (US) enˈkʌm.b|ɚ, ɪn- **-ers** -əz (US) -ɚz **-ering** -ᵊr.ɪŋ **-ered** -əd (US) -ɚd

encumbranc|e ɪnˈkʌm.brənts, ɪŋ-, en-, eŋ- (US) en-, ɪn- **-es** -ɪz

-ency -ᵊnt.si

Note: Suffix. Words containing **-ency** are stressed in a similar way to those containing **-ence**; see above.

encyclic ɪnˈsɪk.lɪk, en-, -ˈsaɪ.klɪk (US) en-, ɪn- **-s** -s **-al/s** -ᵊl/z

encyclop(a)edia ɪnˌsaɪ.kləˈpiː.di.ə, enˌsaɪ-, ˌɪn.saɪ-, ˌen- (US) enˌsaɪ-, ɪn-, ˌen.saɪ-, ˌɪn- **-s** -z

encyclop(a)edic ɪnˌsaɪ.kləˈpiː.dɪk, enˌsaɪ-, ˌɪn.saɪ-, ˌen- (US) enˌsaɪ-, ɪn-, ˌen.saɪ-, ˌɪn- **-ally** -ᵊl.i, -li

encyclop(a)ed|ism ɪnˌsaɪ.kləˈpiː.d|ɪ.zᵊm, enˌsaɪ-, ˌɪn.saɪ-, ˌen- (US) enˌsaɪ-, ɪn-, ˌen.saɪ-, ˌɪn- **-ist/s** -ɪst/s

end end **-s** -z **-ing** -ɪŋ **-ed** -ɪd **ˌend ˈproduct; ˈend ˌuser; be at a ˌloose ˈend; be at ˌloose ˈends; ˌmake ends ˈmeet** (US) **ˌmake ˈends ˌmeet; go off the ˈdeep ˌend; ˌthrown in at the ˈdeep ˌend; at the ˌend of the ˈday**

endang|er ɪnˈdeɪn.dʒ|əʳ, en- (US) enˈdeɪn.dʒ|ɚ, ɪn- **-ers** -əz (US) -ɚz **-ering** -ᵊr.ɪŋ **-ered** -əd (US) -ɚd **-erment** -ə.mənt (US) -ɚ.mənt

endear ɪnˈdɪəʳ, en- (US) enˈdɪr, ɪn- **-s** -z **-ing/ly** -ɪŋ/li **-ed** -d **-ment** -mənt

endeav|o(u)r ɪnˈdev|.əʳ, en- (US) enˈdev|.ɚ, ɪn- **-o(u)rs** -əz (US) -ɚz **-o(u)ring** -ᵊr.ɪŋ **-o(u)red** -əd (US) -ɚd

Endell ˈen.dᵊl

endemic enˈdem.ɪk **-s** -s **-al** -ᵊl **-ally** -ᵊl.i, -li

Enderby ˈen.də.bi (US) -dɚ-

endermic enˈdɜː.mɪk (US) -ˈdɝː- **-al** -ᵊl **-ally** -ᵊl.i, -li

endgame ˈen*d*.geɪm, ˈeŋ- (US) ˈen*d*- **-s** -z

Endicott ˈen.dɪ.kət, -də-, -kɒt (US) -kɑːt, -kət

ending ˈen.dɪŋ **-s** -z

endive ˈen.daɪv, -dɪv (US) ˈen.daɪv, ˈɑːn.diːv **-s** -z

endless ˈend.ləs, -lɪs **-ly** -li **-ness** -nəs, -nɪs

endlong ˈend.lɒŋ (US) -lɑːŋ, -lɔːŋ

endmost ˈen*d*.məʊst (US) -moʊst

endnote ˈend.nəʊt (US) -noʊt **-s** -s

endo- en.dəʊ-; enˈdɒ-, ɪn- (US) en.doʊ-, -də-; enˈdɑː-, ɪn-

Note: Prefix. Either carries primary or secondary stress on the first syllable, e.g. **endomorph** /ˈen.dəʊ.mɔːf (US) -doʊ.mɔːrf/, **endomorphic** /ˌen.dəʊˈmɔː.fɪk (US) -doʊˈmɔːr-/, or primary stress on the second syllable, e.g. **endogenous** /ɪnˈdɒdʒ.ɪ.nəs (US) enˈdɑː.dʒə-/.

endocentric ˌen.dəʊˈsen.trɪk (US) -doʊˈ-

endocrine ˈen.dəʊ.kraɪn, -krɪn, -kriːn (US) -də.krɪn, -kriːn, -kraɪn **ˈendocrine ˌgland**

endocrinolog|y ˌen.dəʊ.kraɪˈnɒl.ə.dʒ|i, -krɪˈ- (US) -doʊ.krɪˈnɑː.lə- **-ist/s** -ɪst/s

endoderm ˈen.dəʊ.dɜːm (US) -doʊ.dɝːm

endoderm|al ˌen.dəʊˈdɜː.m|ᵊl (US) -doʊˈdɝː- **-ic** -ɪk

endogamy ɪnˈdɒg.ə.mi, en- (US) enˈdɑː.gə-, ɪn-

endogenous ɪnˈdɒdʒ.ə.nəs, en-, ˈ-ɪ- (US) enˈdɑː.dʒə-, ɪn-

endometrial ˌen.dəʊˈmiː.tri.əl (US) -doʊˈ-

endometriosis ˌen.dəʊˌmiː.triˈəʊ.sɪs (US) -doʊˌmiː.triˈoʊ-

endometri|um ˌen.dəʊˈmiː.tri|.əm (US) -doʊˈ- **-a** -ə

endomorph ˈen.dəʊ.mɔːf (US) -doʊ.mɔːrf **-s** -s **-y** -i

endomorph|ic ˌen.dəʊˈmɔː.f|ɪk (US) -doʊˈmɔːr- **-ism** -ɪ.zᵊm

endophoric ˌen.dəʊˈfɒr.ɪk (US) -doʊˈfɔːr-

endoplasm ˈen.dəʊ.plæz.ᵊm (US) -doʊ-

endoplasmic ˌen.dəʊˈplæz.mɪk (US) -doʊˈ-

Endor ˈen.dɔːʳ (US) -dɔːr

endorphin enˈdɔː.fɪn (US) -ˈdɔːr-, ɪn- **-s** -z

endors|e ɪnˈdɔːs, en- (US) enˈdɔːrs, ɪn- **-es** -ɪz **-ing** -ɪŋ **-ed** -t **-er/s** -əʳ/z (US) -ɚ/z **-ement/s** -mənt/s **-able** -ə.bl̩

endorsee ˌen.dɔːˈsiː (US) -dɔːrˈ- **-s** -z

endoscope ˈen.dəʊ.skəʊp (US) -doʊ.skoʊp, -də- **-s** -s

endoscop|y enˈdɒs.kə.p|i (US) -ˈdɑː.skə- **-ies** -iz

endoskeleton ˌen.dəʊˈskel.ɪ.tᵊn, ˈ-ə- (US) -doʊˈ- **-s** -z

endosperm ˈen.dəʊ.spɜːm (US) -doʊ.spɝːm **-s** -z

endow ɪnˈdaʊ, en- (US) en-, ɪn- **-s** -z **-ing** -ɪŋ **-ed** -d **-ment/s** -mənt/s

endpaper ˈendˌpeɪ.pəʳ (US) -pɚ **-s** -z

endpoint ˈend.pɔɪnt **-s** -s

end-stopped ˈend.stɒpt (US) -stɑːpt

endu|e ɪnˈdjuː, en- (US) enˈduː, ɪn-, -ˈdjuː **-es** -z **-ing** -ɪŋ **-ed** -d

endurab|le ɪnˈdjʊə.rə.b|l̩, en-, -ˈdjɔː- (US) enˈdʊr.ə-, ɪn-, -ˈdjʊr- **-ly** -li

endurance ɪnˈdjʊə.rᵊnts, en-, -ˈdjɔː- (US) enˈdʊr.ᵊnts, ɪn-, -ˈdjʊr-

endur|e ɪnˈdjʊəʳ, en-, -ˈdjɔːʳ (US) enˈdʊr, ɪn, -ˈdjʊr **-es** -z **-ing/ly** -ɪŋ/li **-ed** -d

end|ways ˈend|.weɪz **-wise** -waɪz

Endymion enˈdɪm.i.ən, ɪn-

-ene -iːn

Note: Suffix. **-ene** is not stressed, e.g. **ethylene** /ˈeθ.ɪ.liːn/.

ENE ˌiːst.nɔːθˈiːst (US) -nɔːrθ- *in nautical usage also:* -nɔːˈriːst (US) -nɔːrˈiːst

Eneas iːˈniː.əs, ɪ-, -æs

Eneid ˈiː.ni.ɪd, ɪˈniː-

enema ˈen.ə.mə, ˈ-ɪ- (US) ˈ-ə- **-s** -z

enem|y ˈen.ə.m|i, ˈ-ɪ- **-ies** -iz

energetic ˌen.əˈdʒet.ɪk (US) -ɚˈdʒet̬- **-s** -s **-ally** -ᵊl.i, -li

energiz|e, -is|e ˈen.ə.dʒaɪz (US) ˈ-ɚ- **-es** -ɪz **-ing** -ɪŋ **-ed** -d **-er/s** -əʳ/z (US) -ɚ/z

energumen ˌen.əˈgjuː.men (US) -ɚˈ- **-s** -z

energ|y ˈen.ə.dʒ|i (US) ˈ-ɚ- **-ies** -iz

ener|vate ˈen.ə|.veɪt, -ɜː- (US) ˈ-ɚ- **-vates** -veɪts **-vating** -veɪ.tɪŋ (US) -veɪ.t̬ɪŋ **-vated** -veɪ.tɪd (US) -veɪ.t̬ɪd

enervation ˌen.əˈveɪ.ʃᵊn, -ɜːˈ- (US) -ɚˈ-

en famille ˌɑ̃ːn.fæmˈiː (US) ˌɑ̃ːn.fɑːˈmiː.jə

enfant(s) terrible(s) ˌɑ̃ːn.fɑ̃ːn.terˈiː.blə, ˌɒn.fɒn-, -təˈriː- (US) ˌɑːn.fɑːn.terˈiː-, ˌɑ̃n.fɑ̃n-

enfeebl|e ɪnˈfiː.bl̩, en- (US) en-, ɪn- **-es** -z **-ing** -ɪŋ, ˈ-blɪŋ **-ed** -d **-ement** -mənt

enfeoff ɪnˈfiːf, en-, -ˈfef (US) en-, ɪn- **-s** -s **-ing** -ɪŋ **-ed** -t **-ment/s** -mənt/s

Enfield ˈen.fiːld

enfilad|e ˌen.fɪˈleɪd, ˈ--- (US) ˈen.fə.leɪd **-es** -z **-ing** -ɪŋ **-ed** -ɪd

enfold ɪnˈfəʊld, en- (US) enˈfoʊld, ɪn- **-s** -z **-ing** -ɪŋ **-ed** -ɪd **-ment** -mənt

enforc|e ɪnˈfɔːs, en- (US) enˈfɔːrs, ɪn- **-es** -ɪz **-ing** -ɪŋ **-ed** -t **-edly** -ɪd.li **-eable** -ə.bl̩

enforcement ɪnˈfɔːs.mənt, en- (US) enˈfɔːrs-, ɪn-

enforcer ɪnˈfɔː.səʳ (US) -ˈfɔːr.sɚ **-s** -z

enfranchis|e ɪnˈfræn.tʃaɪz, en- (US) en-, ɪn- **-es** -ɪz **-ing** -ɪŋ **-ed** -d

enfranchisement ɪnˈfræn.tʃɪz.mənt, en-, -tʃəz- (US) enˈfræn.tʃaɪz-, ɪn-, -tʃəz- **-s** -s

Engadine ˈeŋ.gə.diːn, ˌ--ˈ-

engag|e ɪnˈgeɪdʒ, ɪŋ-, en-, eŋ- (US) en-, ɪn- **-es** -ɪz **-ing/ly** -ɪŋ/li **-ed** -d

engagement ɪnˈgeɪdʒ.mənt, ɪŋ-, en-, eŋ- (US) en-, ɪn- **-s** -s **enˈgagement ˌring**

en garde ɑ̃ːŋˈgɑːd (US) ˌɑːnˈgɑːrd, ˌɑ̃ːn-

Engels ˈeŋ.gᵊlz

engend|er ɪnˈdʒen.d|əʳ, en- (US) enˈdʒen.d|ɚ, ɪn- **-ers** -əz (US) -ɚz **-ering** -ᵊr.ɪŋ **-ered** -əd (US) -ɚd

engine ˈen.dʒɪn **-s** -z **ˈengine ˌdriver**

engineer ˌen.dʒɪˈnɪəʳ, -dʒəˈ- (US) -ˈnɪr **-s** -z **-ing** -ɪŋ **-ed** -d
engird ɪnˈgɜːd, ɪŋ-, en-, eŋ- (US) enˈgɝːd, ɪn- **-s** -z **-ing** -ɪŋ **-ed** -ɪd
England ˈɪŋ.glənd **-er/s** -əʳ/z (US) -ɚ/z
Englefield ˈeŋ.gl̩.fiːld
Englewood ˈeŋ.gl̩.wʊd
English ˈɪŋ.glɪʃ ˌ**English** ˈ**Channel**; ˌ**English** ˈ**horn** (US) ˈ**English** ˌ**horn**
English|man ˈɪŋ.glɪʃ|.mən **-men** -mən, -men
English|woman ˈɪŋ.glɪʃ|ˌwʊm.ən **-women** -ˌwɪm.ɪn
engorg|e ɪnˈgɔːdʒ, ɪŋ-, en-, eŋ- (US) -ˈgɔːrdʒ **-es** -iz **-ing** -ɪŋ **-ed** -d
engraft ɪnˈgrɑːft, ɪŋ-, en-, eŋ- (US) enˈgræft, ɪn- **-s** -s **-ing** -ɪŋ **-ed** -ɪd **-ment** -mənt
engrailed ɪnˈgreɪld, ɪŋ-, en-, eŋ- (US) en-, ɪn-
engrain ɪnˈgreɪn, ɪŋ-, en-, eŋ- (US) en-, ɪn- **-s** -z **-ing** -ɪŋ **-ed** -d
engrav|e ɪnˈgreɪv, ɪŋ-, en-, eŋ- (US) en-, ɪn- **-es** -z **-ing/s** -ɪŋ/z **-ed** -d **-er/s** -əʳ/z (US) -ɚ/z **-ery** -ᵊr.i
en gros ˌɑ̃ːŋˈgrəʊ, ˌɑːnˈgroʊ
engross ɪnˈgrəʊs, ɪŋ-, en-, eŋ- (US) enˈgroʊs, ɪn- **-es** -ɪz **-ing** -ɪŋ **-ed** -t **-ment** -mənt
engulf ɪnˈgʌlf, ɪŋ-, en-, eŋ- (US) en-, ɪn- **-s** -s **-ing** -ɪŋ **-ed** -t **-ment** -mənt
enhanc|e ɪnˈhɑːnts, en- (US) -ˈhænts **-es** -ɪz **-ing** -ɪŋ **-ed** -t **-ement/s** -mənt/s **-er/s** -əʳ/z (US) -ɚ/z
enharmonic ˌen.hɑːˈmɒn.ɪk (US) -hɑːrˈmɑː.nɪk **-al** -ᵊl **-ally** -ᵊl.i, -li
Enid ˈiː.nɪd
enigma ɪˈnɪg.mə, enˈɪg-, əˈnɪg- (US) ɪˈnɪg.mə, ə-, enˈɪg- **-s** -z
enigmatic ˌen.ɪgˈmæt.ɪk (US) -ˈmæţ- **-al** -ᵊl **-ally** -ᵊl.i, -li *stress shift:* ˌenigmatic ˈsmile
enigmatist ɪˈnɪg.mə.tɪst, enˈɪg-, əˈnɪg- (US) ɪˈnɪg-, ə-, enˈɪg- **-s** -s
enigmatiz|e, -is|e ɪˈnɪg.mə.taɪz, enˈɪg-, əˈnɪg- (US) ɪˈnɪg-, ə-, enˈɪg- **-es** -ɪz **-ing** -ɪŋ **-ed** -d
enjamb(e)ment ɪnˈdʒæm*b*.mənt, en- (US) en-, ɪn- **-s** -s
enjoin ɪnˈdʒɔɪn, en- (US) en-, ɪn- **-s** -z **-ing** -ɪŋ **-ed** -d
enjoy ɪnˈdʒɔɪ, en- (US) en-, ɪn- **-s** -z **-ing** -ɪŋ **-ed** -d
enjoyab|le ɪnˈdʒɔɪ.ə.b|l̩, en- (US) en-, ɪn- **-ly** -li **-leness** -l̩.nəs, -nɪs
enjoyment ɪnˈdʒɔɪ.mənt, en- (US) en-, ɪn- **-s** -s
enkindl|e ɪnˈkɪn.dl̩, en-, ɪŋ-, eŋ- (US) en-, ɪn- **-es** -z **-ing** -ɪŋ, ˈ-lɪŋ **-ed** -d
enlac|e ɪnˈleɪs, en- (US) en-, ɪn- **-es** -ɪz **-ing** -ɪŋ **-ed** -t **-ement/s** -mənt/s
Enlai ˌenˈlaɪ
enlarg|e ɪnˈlɑːdʒ, en- (US) enˈlɑːrdʒ, ɪn- **-es** -ɪz **-ing** -ɪŋ **-ed** -d **-er/s** -əʳ/z (US) -ɚ/z **-ement/s** -mənt/s
enlighten ɪnˈlaɪ.tᵊn, en- (US) en-, ɪn- **-s** -z **-ing** -ɪŋ **-ed** -d
enlightenment (E) ɪnˈlaɪ.tᵊn.mənt, en- (US) en-, ɪn-
enlist ɪnˈlɪst, en- (US) en-, ɪn- **-s** -s **-ing** -ɪŋ **-ed** -ɪd **-ment/s** -mənt/s
enliven ɪnˈlaɪ.vᵊn, en- (US) en-, ɪn- **-s** -z **-ing** -ɪŋ **-ed** -d
en masse ɑ̃ːˈ*m*ˈmæs, ɒn- (US) ɑːn-, ɑ̃ːn-
enmesh ɪnˈmeʃ, en- (US) en-, ɪn- **-es** -ɪz **-ing** -ɪŋ **-ed** -t
enmit|y ˈen.mə.t|i, -mɪ- **-ies** -iz
Ennis ˈen.ɪs
Enniscorthy ˌen.ɪˈskɔː.θi (US) -ˈskɔːr-
Enniskillen ˌen.ɪˈskɪl.ən, -əˈ-, -ɪn
Ennius ˈen.i.əs
ennobl|e ɪˈnəʊ.bl̩, enˈəʊ- (US) enˈoʊ-, ɪˈnoʊ- **-es** -z **-ing** -ɪŋ, ˈ-blɪŋ **-ed** -d **-ement** -mənt
ennui ˈɑ̃ː.n.wiː, ˈɒn-, -ˈ- (US) ˌɑːnˈwiː, ˈ--
Eno® ˈiː.nəʊ (US) -noʊ **-'s** -z
Enoch ˈiː.nɒk (US) -nɑːk, -nək
enormit|y ɪˈnɔː.mə.t|i, ə-, -mɪ- (US) -ˈnɔːr.mə.ţ|i **-ies** -iz
enormous ɪˈnɔː.məs, ə- (US) -ˈnɔːr- **-ly** -li **-ness** -nəs, -nɪs
Enos ˈiː.nɒs (US) -nɑːs, -nəs
enough ɪˈnʌf, ə-
enounc|e ɪˈnaʊnts **-es** -ɪz **-ing** -ɪŋ **-ed** -t
enow ɪˈnaʊ
en passant ˌɑ̃ːˈ*m*ˈpæs.ɑ̃ːŋ, ˌ--ˈ- (US) ˌɑ̃ːn.pɑːˈsɑ̃ːn, -pəˈ-
enquir|e ɪnˈkwaɪəʳ, ɪŋ-, en-, eŋ- (US) enˈkwaɪɚ, ɪn- **-es** -z **-ing/ly** -ɪŋ/li **-ed** -d **-er/s** -əʳ/z (US) -ɚ/z
enquir|y ɪnˈkwaɪə.r|i, ɪŋ-, en-, eŋ- (US) enˈkwaɪ-, ɪn-; ˈɪn.kwɚ.i **-ies** -iz
enrag|e ɪnˈreɪdʒ, en- (US) en-, ɪn- **-es** -ɪz **-ing** -ɪŋ **-ed** -d
enrapt ɪnˈræpt, en- (US) en-, ɪn-
enrapt|ure ɪnˈræp.tʃ|əʳ, en- (US) enˈræp.tʃ|ɚ, ɪn- **-ures** -əz (US) -ɚz **-uring** -ᵊr.ɪŋ **-ured** -əd (US) -ɚd
enregist|er ɪnˈredʒ.ɪ.st|əʳ, en-, ˈ-ə- (US) enˈredʒ.ɪ.st|ɚ, ɪn-, ˈ-ə- **-ers** -əz (US) -ɚz **-ering** -ᵊr.ɪŋ **-ered** -əd (US) -ɚd
enrich ɪnˈrɪtʃ, en- (US) en-, ɪn- **-es** -ɪz **-ing** -ɪŋ **-ed** -t **-ment** -mənt
Enright ˈen.raɪt
enrob|e ɪnˈrəʊb, en- (US) enˈroʊb, ɪn- **-es** -z **-ing** -ɪŋ **-ed** -d
enrol ɪnˈrəʊl, en- (US) enˈroʊl, ɪn- **-s** -z **-ling** -ɪŋ **-led** -d
enroll ɪnˈrəʊl, en- (US) enˈroʊl, ɪn- **-s** -z **-ing** -ɪŋ **-ed** -d
enrol(l)ment ɪnˈrəʊl.mənt, en- (US) enˈroʊl-, ɪn- **-s** -s
Enron® ˈen.rɒn (US) -rɑːn
en route ˌɑ̃ːˈ*n*ˈruːt, ˌɒn- (US) ˌɑːn-
en|s en|z **-tia** -ʃi.ə, -ʃə, -ti.ə
ENSA ˈen*t*.sə
ensample enˈsɑːm.pl̩, ɪn- (US) -ˈsæm- **-s** -z
ensanguined ɪnˈsæŋ.gwɪnd, en- (US) en-, ɪn-
ensconc|e ɪnˈskɒnts, en- (US) enˈskɑːnts, ɪn- **-es** -ɪz **-ing** -ɪŋ **-ed** -t
ensemble ɑ̃ːˈ*n*ˈsɑ̃ːm.bᵊl, ɒnˈsɒm- (US) ˌɑːnˈsɑːm- **-s** -z
enshrin|e ɪnˈʃraɪn, en- (US) en-, ɪn- **-es** -z **-ing** -ɪŋ **-ed** -d **-ement** -mənt
enshroud ɪnˈʃraʊd, en- (US) en-, ɪn- **-s** -z **-ing** -ɪŋ **-ed** -ɪd
ensign *flag:* ˈen.saɪn *in the navy:* ˈen*t*.sᵊn **-s** -z
ensign *officer:* ˈen.saɪn (US) ˈen.sɪn **-s** -z
ensign (*v.*) enˈsaɪn, ɪn- **-s** -z **-ing** -ɪŋ **-ed** -d
ensilag|e ˈen*t*.sɪ.lɪdʒ, -sə; ɪnˈsaɪ-, en- (US) ˈen*t*.sə- **-es** -ɪz
ensil|e enˈsaɪl, ˈen*t*.saɪl **-es** -z **-ing** -ɪŋ **-ed** -d
enslav|e ɪnˈsleɪv, en- (US) en-, ɪn- **-es** -z **-ing** -ɪŋ **-ed** -d **-er/s** -əʳ/z (US) -ɚ/z **-ement** -mənt
ensnar|e ɪnˈsneəʳ, en- (US) enˈsner, ɪn- **-es** -z **-ing** -ɪŋ **-ed** -d **-er/s** -əʳ/z (US) -ɚ
ensoul ɪnˈsəʊl, en- (US) enˈsoʊl, ɪn- **-s** - **-ing** -ɪŋ **-ed** -d
ensu|e ɪnˈsjuː, en-, -ˈsuː (US) enˈsuː, ɪn -ˈsjuː **-es** -z **-ing** -ɪŋ **-ed** -d
en suite ˌɑ̃ːˈ*n*ˈswiːt, ˌɒn- (US) ˌɑːn- *stres shift:* ˌen suite ˈbathroom
ensur|e ɪnˈʃɔːʳ, en-, -ˈʃʊəʳ, -ˈsjʊəʳ (US) enˈʃʊr, ɪn- **-es** -z **-ing** -ɪŋ **-ed** -d
-ent -ᵊnt
Note: Suffix. Words containing **-ent** stressed in a similar way to those containing **-ence**; see above.
entablature enˈtæb.lə.tʃəʳ, ɪn-, -lɪ-, -tʃʊəʳ, -tjʊəʳ (US) -lə.tʃɚ **-s** -z
entail ɪnˈteɪl, en- (US) en-, ɪn- **-s** -z **-ing** -ɪŋ **-ed** -d **-er/s** -əʳ/z (US) -ɚ/z **-ment** -mənt
entangl|e ɪnˈtæŋ.gl̩, en- (US) en-, ɪn- -z **-ing** -ɪŋ, ˈ-glɪŋ **-ed** -d **-ement/s** -mənt/s
Entebbe enˈteb.i, ɪn- (US) -ə
entendre ɑ̃ːˈ*n*ˈtɑ̃ː*n*.drə (US) ɑːnˈtɑːn.
entente ɑ̃ːˈ*n*ˈtɑ̃ː*nt* (US) ɑːnˈtɑːnt **-s** -s
entente cordiale ˌɑ̃ː*n*.tɑ̃ː*nt*.kɔː.diˈ (US) ˌɑːn.tɑːnt.kɔːr-
ent|er ˈen.t|əʳ (US) -ţ|ɚ **-ers** -əz (US) -ɚ **-ering** -ᵊr.ɪŋ **-ered** -əd (US) -ɚd
enteric enˈter.ɪk
enteritis ˌen.təˈraɪ.tɪs (US) -ţɪs
enterokinas|e ˌen.tᵊr.əʊˈkaɪ.neɪz (US) -ţə.roʊˈkaɪ.neɪs, -ˈkɪn.eɪs, -e **-es** -ɪz
enterology ˌen.təˈrɒl.ə.dʒi (US) -ţəˈrɑː.lə-

enterotomy ˌen.təˈrɒt.ə.mi ⓤⓢ -t̬əˈrɑː.t̬ə-
enterovirus ˌen.tᵊr.əʊˈvaɪə.rəs ⓤⓢ -t̬ə.roʊˈvaɪ.rəs **-es** -ɪz
enterpris|e ˈen.tə.praɪz ⓤⓢ -t̬ɚ- **-es** -ɪz **-ing/ly** -ɪŋ/li
entertain ˌen.təˈteɪn ⓤⓢ -t̬ɚˈ- **-s** -z **-ing/ly** -ɪŋ/li **-ed** -d **-er/s** -əʳ/z ⓤⓢ -ɚ/z
entertainment ˌen.təˈteɪn.mənt ⓤⓢ -t̬ɚˈ- **-s** -s
enthral ɪnˈθrɔːl, en- ⓤⓢ enˈθrɔːl, ɪn-, -ˈθrɑːl **-s** -z **-ling** -ɪŋ **-led** -d **-ment** -mənt
enthrall ɪnˈθrɔːl, en- ⓤⓢ enˈθrɔːl, ɪn-, -ˈθrɑːl **-s** -z **-ing** -ɪŋ **-ed** -d **-ment** -mənt
enthron|e ɪnˈθrəʊn, en- ⓤⓢ enˈθroʊn, ɪn- **-es** -z **-ing** -ɪŋ **-ed** -d **-ement/s** -mənt/s
enthus|e ɪnˈθjuːz, en- ⓤⓢ enˈθuːz, ɪn-, -ˈθjuːz **-es** -ɪz **-ing** -ɪŋ **-ed** -d
enthusi|asm ɪnˈθjuː.zi|.æz.ᵊm, en-, -ˈθuː- ⓤⓢ enˈθuː-, ɪn-, -ˈθjuː- **-asms** -æzmz **-ast/s** -æst/s
enthusiastic ɪnˌθjuː.ziˈæs.tɪk, en-, -ˌθuː- ⓤⓢ enˌθuː-, ɪn-, -ˌθjuː- **-ally** -ᵊl.i, -li
entia *(plur. of* **ens***)* ˈen.ʃi.ə, -ʃə, -ti.ə
entic|e ɪnˈtaɪs, en- ⓤⓢ en-, ɪn- **-es** -ɪz **-ing/ly** -ɪŋ/li **-ed** -t **-ement/s** -mənt/s
entire ɪnˈtaɪəʳ, en- ⓤⓢ enˈtaɪɚ, ɪn- **-ly** -li **-ness** -nəs, -nɪs
entiret|y ɪnˈtaɪə.rə.t|i, en- ⓤⓢ enˈtaɪ.rə.t̬|i, -ˈtaɪr.t̬|i, ɪn- **-ies** -iz
entitl|e ɪnˈtaɪ.tl̩, en- ⓤⓢ enˈtaɪ.t̬l̩, ɪn- **-es** -z **-ing** -ɪŋ, -ˈtaɪt.lɪŋ **-ed** -d
entitlement ɪnˈtaɪ.tl̩.mənt, en- ⓤⓢ enˈtaɪ.t̬l̩-, ɪn- **-s** -s
entit|y ˈen.tɪ.t|i, -tə- ⓤⓢ -t̬ə.t̬|i **-ies** -iz
entomb ɪnˈtuːm, en- ⓤⓢ en-, ɪn- **-s** -z **-ing** -ɪŋ **-ed** -d **-ment/s** -mənt/s
entomological ˌen.tə.məˈlɒdʒ.ɪ.kl̩ ⓤⓢ -t̬ə.məˈlɑː.dʒɪ- **-ly** -i
entomologiz|e, -is|e ˌen.təˈmɒl.ə.dʒaɪz ⓤⓢ -t̬əˈmɑː.lə- **-es** -ɪz **-ing** -ɪŋ **-ed** -d
entomolog|y ˌen.təˈmɒl.ə.dʒ|i ⓤⓢ -t̬əˈmɑː.lə- **-ist/s** -ɪst/s
entourag|e ˈɒn.tʊ.rɑːʒ, ˈɑ̃ːn-, -tʊə-, ˌ--ˈ- ⓤⓢ ˌɑːn.tʊˈrɑːʒ **-es** -ɪz
entr'acte ˈɒn.trækt, ˈɑ̃ːn-, ˌ-ˈ- ⓤⓢ ˈɑːnˌtrækt, ɑ̃ːn-, ˌ-ˈ- **-s** -s
entrails ˈen.treɪlz
entrain ɪnˈtreɪn, en- ⓤⓢ en-, ɪn- **-s** -z **-ing** -ɪŋ **-ed** -d
entrammel ɪnˈtræm.ᵊl, en- ⓤⓢ en-, ɪn- **-s** -z **-(l)ing** -ɪŋ **-(l)ed** -d
entranc|e *(n.) entry, place of entry, etc.:* ˈen.trənts **-es** -ɪz
entranc|e *(v.) put in state of trance, delight:* ɪnˈtrɑːnts, en- ⓤⓢ enˈtrænts, ɪn- **-es** -ɪz **-ing** -ɪŋ **-ed** -t **-ement/s** -mənt/s
entrant ˈen.trənt **-s** -s
entrap ɪnˈtræp, en- ⓤⓢ en-, ɪn- **-s** -s **-ping** -ɪŋ **-ped** -t **-ment** -mənt
en|treat ɪn|ˈtriːt, en- ⓤⓢ en-, ɪn- **-treats** -ˈtriːts **-treating/ly** -ˈtriː.tɪŋ/li ⓤⓢ -ˈtriː.t̬ɪŋ/li **-treated** -ˈtriː.tɪd ⓤⓢ -ˈtriː.t̬ɪd **-treatment** -ˈtriːt.mənt
entreat|y ɪnˈtriː.t|i, en- ⓤⓢ enˈtriː.t̬|i, ɪn- **-ies** -iz
entrechat ˈɑ̃ːn.trə.ʃɑː, ˈɒn- ⓤⓢ ˌɑːn.trəˈʃɑː, ˈ--- **-s** -z
entrecôte ˈɑ̃ːn.trə.kəʊt, ˈɒn- ⓤⓢ ˈɑːn.trə.koʊt, ˈɑ̃ːn-, ˌ--ˈ- **-s** -s
entrée ˈɑ̃ːn.treɪ, ˈɒn- ⓤⓢ ˈɑːn-, ˌ-ˈ- **-s** -z
entremets *(sing.)* ˈɑ̃ːn.trə.meɪ, ˈɒnt- ⓤⓢ ˈɑːn.trə-, ˌ--ˈ- *(plur.)* -z
entrench ɪnˈtrentʃ, en- ⓤⓢ en-, ɪn- **-es** -ɪz **-ing** -ɪŋ **-ed** -t **-ment/s** -mənt/s
entre nous ˌɑ̃ːn.trəˈnuː, ˌɒn- ⓤⓢ ˌɑːn-
entrepôt ˈɑ̃ːn.trə.pəʊ, ˈɒn- ⓤⓢ ˈɑːn.trə.poʊ; ˌ--ˈ- **-s** -z
entrepreneur ˌɒn.trə.prəˈnɜːʳ, ˌɑ̃ːn-, -prenˈɜːʳ ⓤⓢ ˌɑːn.trə.prəˈnɝː, -ˈnʊr, -ˈnjʊr **-s** -z **-ship** -ʃɪp
entrepreneurial ˌɒn.trə.prəˈnɜː.ri.əl, ˌɑ̃ːn- ⓤⓢ ˌɑːn.trə.prəˈnɝː.i-, -ˈnʊr-, -ˈnjʊr-
entresol ˈɑ̃ːn.trə.sɒl, ˈɒn- ⓤⓢ ˈɑːn.trə.sɑːl, ˌ--ˈ- **-s** -z
entropy ˈen.trə.pi
entrust ɪnˈtrʌst, en- ⓤⓢ en-, ɪn- **-s** -s **-ing** -ɪŋ **-ed** -ɪd
entr|y ˈen.tr|i **-ies** -iz
entry|ism ˈen.tri|.ɪ.zᵊm **-ist/s** -ɪst/s
entryphone ˈen.tri.fəʊn ⓤⓢ -foʊn **-s** -z
entryway ˈen.tri.weɪ **-s** -z
entwin|e ɪnˈtwaɪn, en- ⓤⓢ en-, ɪn- **-es** -z **-ing** -ɪŋ **-ed** -d
entwist ɪnˈtwɪst, en- ⓤⓢ en-, ɪn- **-s** -s **-ing** -ɪŋ **-ed** -ɪd
enumerable ɪˈnjuː.mᵊr.ə.bl̩ ⓤⓢ -ˈnuː-, -ˈnjuː-
enumer|ate ɪˈnjuː.mᵊr|.eɪt ⓤⓢ -ˈnuː.mə.r|eɪt, -ˈnjuː- **-ates** -eɪts **-ating** -eɪ.tɪŋ ⓤⓢ -eɪ.t̬ɪŋ **-ated** -eɪ.tɪd ⓤⓢ -eɪ.t̬ɪd **-ator/s** -eɪ.təʳ/z ⓤⓢ -eɪ.t̬ɚ/z
enumeration ɪˌnjuː.mᵊrˈeɪ.ʃᵊn ⓤⓢ -ˌnuː.məˈreɪ-, -ˌnjuː- **-s** -z
enumerative ɪˈnjuː.mᵊr.ə.tɪv, -eɪ.tɪv ⓤⓢ -ˈnuː.mɚ.ə.t̬ɪv, -ˈnjuː-
enunciable ɪˈnʌnt.si.ə.bl̩, -ʃi.ə-
enunci|ate ɪˈnʌnt.si|.eɪt, -ʃi- **-ates** -eɪts **-ating** -eɪ.tɪŋ ⓤⓢ -eɪ.t̬ɪŋ **-ated** -eɪ.tɪd ⓤⓢ -eɪ.t̬ɪd **-ator/s** -eɪ.təʳ/z ⓤⓢ -eɪ.t̬ɚ/z
enunciation ɪˌnʌnt.siˈeɪ.ʃᵊn **-s** -z
enunciative ɪˈnʌnt.si.ə.tɪv, -ʃi.ə-, -eɪ.tɪv ⓤⓢ -ə.t̬ɪv
enur|e ɪˈnjʊəʳ ⓤⓢ -ˈnjʊr **-es** -z **-ing** -ɪŋ **-ed** -d
enuresis ˌen.jʊəˈriː.sɪs ⓤⓢ -juːˈ-
envelop ɪnˈvel.əp, en- ⓤⓢ en-, ɪn- **-s** -s **-ing** -ɪŋ **-ed** -t **-ment/s** -mənt/s
envelope ˈen.və.ləʊp, ˈɒn- ⓤⓢ ˈen.və.loʊp, ˈɑːn- **-s** -s
envenom ɪnˈven.əm, en- ⓤⓢ en-, ɪn- **-s** -z **-ing** -ɪŋ **-ed** -d
enviab|le ˈen.vi.ə.b|l̩ **-ly** -li **-leness** -l̩.nəs, -nɪs
envious ˈen.vi.əs **-ly** -li **-ness** -nəs, -nɪs
environ *(v.)* ɪnˈvaɪə.rᵊn, en- ⓤⓢ enˈvaɪ-, ɪn-, -ɚn **-s** -z **-ing** -ɪŋ **-ed** -d
environment ɪnˈvaɪə.rᵊn.mənt, en- ⓤⓢ enˈvaɪ-, ɪn-, -ɚn- **-s** -s
environmental ɪnˌvaɪə.rᵊnˈmen.tᵊl, en-, -rᵊmˈ- ⓤⓢ enˌvaɪ.rənˈmen.t̬ᵊl, ɪn-, -ɚnˈ- **-ly** -i
environmental|ism ɪnˌvaɪə.rᵊnˈmen.tᵊl|.ɪ.zᵊm, en-, -rᵊmˈ- ⓤⓢ enˌvaɪ.rᵊnˈmen.t̬ᵊl-, ɪn-, -ɚnˈ- **-ist/s** -ɪst/s
environmentally-friendly ɪnˌvaɪᵊ.rᵊnˌmen.tᵊl.iˈfrend.li, en-, -rᵊmˌ- ⓤⓢ enˌvaɪ.rᵊn.men.t̬ᵊl-, ɪn-, ˌ-ɚn-
environs *(n.)* ɪnˈvaɪə.rᵊnz, en-; ˈen.vɪ-, -vᵊr.ᵊnz ⓤⓢ enˈvaɪ.rᵊnz, ɪn-, -ɚnz
envisag|e ɪnˈvɪz.ɪdʒ, en- ⓤⓢ en-, ɪn- **-es** -ɪz **-ing** -ɪŋ **-ed** -d
envision ɪnˈvɪʒ.ᵊn, en- ⓤⓢ en-, ɪn- **-s** -z **-ing** -ɪŋ **-ed** -d
envoy ˈen.vɔɪ ⓤⓢ ˈɑːn-, ˈen- **-s** -z
env|y ˈen.v|i **-ies** -iz **-ying** -i.ɪŋ **-ied** -id
enwrap ɪnˈræp, en- ⓤⓢ en-, ɪn- **-s** -s **-ping** -ɪŋ **-ped** -t
enwreath|e ɪnˈriːð, en- ⓤⓢ en-, ɪn- **-es** -z **-ing** -ɪŋ **-ed** -d
enzyme ˈen.zaɪm **-s** -z
enzymolog|y ˌen.zaɪˈmɒl.ə.dʒ|i ⓤⓢ -zɪˈ-, -ˈmɑː.lə- **-ist/s** -ɪst/s
Eocene ˈiː.əʊ.siːn ⓤⓢ -oʊ-, -ə-
eolian (E) iˈəʊ.li.ən ⓤⓢ -ˈoʊ-
eolith ˈiː.əʊ.lɪθ ⓤⓢ -oʊ-, -ə- **-s** -s
eolithic ˌiː.əʊˈlɪθ.ɪk ⓤⓢ -oʊˈ-, -əˈ-
eon ˈiː.ɒn ⓤⓢ -ɑːn **-s** -z
-eous -i.əs, -əs
Note: Suffix. Words containing **-eous** are normally stressed on the syllable preceding the suffix, e.g. **advantage** /ədˈvɑːn.tɪdʒ ⓤⓢ -ˈvæn.t̬ɪdʒ/, **advantageous** /ˌæd.vənˈteɪ.dʒəs ⓤⓢ -vænˈ-/.
EP ˌiːˈpiː
EPA ˌiː.piːˈeɪ
epact ˈiː.pækt, ˈep.ækt **-s** -s
Epaminondas epˌæm.ɪˈnɒn.dæs, ɪˌpæm-, -əˈ- ⓤⓢ ɪˌpæm.əˈnɑːn-
eparch ˈep.ɑːk ⓤⓢ -ɑːrk **-s** -s **-y** -i **-ies** -iz
epaulette, epaulet ˌep.əˈlet, -ɔːˈ-, ˈ--- ⓤⓢ ˌep.əˈlet, ˈ--- **-s** -s
Epcot® ˈep.kɒt ⓤⓢ -kɑːt ˈ**Epcot** ˌ**Center**
epee, épée ˈep.eɪ, ˈeɪ.peɪ, -ˈ- ⓤⓢ eɪˈpeɪ; ˈep.eɪ **-s** -z **-ist/s** -ɪst/s

Pronouncing the letters EO

There are several pronunciation possibilities for the vowel digraph **eo**, e.g.:

iː	people	/ˈpiː.pl̩/	
e	leopard	/ˈlep.əd/	(US) /-ɚd/
i.ə	chameleon	/kəˈmiː.li.ən/	

When followed by an **r** in the spelling, **eo** is pronounced as /ɔː (US) ɔːr/ and /ɪə (US) ɪr/, e.g.:

George	/dʒɔːdʒ/	(US) /dʒɔːrdʒ/
theory	/ˈθɪə.ri/	(US) /ˈθɪr.i/

Where *geo-* is a prefix, there are several possible realisations, e.g.:

/i.ɒ (US) i.ɑː/	geography	/dʒiˈɒg.rə.fi/	(US) /-ˈɑː.grə-/
/iː.əʊ (US) iː.oʊ/	geothermal	/ˌdʒiː.əʊˈθɜː.məl/	(US) /-oʊˈθɝː-/

(In *geography*, the prefix may also be pronounced as /ˈdʒɒg-/ in British English.)

In addition

There are instances when the two letters **e** and **o** come together in closed compounds, e.g.:

thereof	/ðeəˈrɒv/	(US) /ðerˈɑːv/
whereon	/*h*weəˈrɒn/	(US) /*h*werˈɑːn/

In weak syllables

The vowel digraph **eo** is realised with the vowel /ə/ in weak syllables, e.g.:

pigeon	/ˈpɪdʒ.ən/
luncheon	/ˈlʌntʃ.ən/

Pronouncing the letters EOU

The vowel letter combination **eou** has two possible pronunciations. After **c** or **g** the pronunciation is /ə/, e.g.:

cretaceous	/krɪˈteɪ.ʃəs/	
gorgeous	/ˈgɔː.dʒəs/	(US) /ˈgɔːr-/

After other letters, the pronunciation is /i.ə/, e.g.:

spontaneous	/spɒnˈteɪ.ni.əs/	(US) /spɑːn-/

epenthes|is epˈent.θə.s|ɪs, ɪˈpent-, -θɪ- (US) ɪˈpent.θə- **-es** -iːz
epenthetic ˌep.enˈθet.ɪk, -ənˈ- (US) -enˈθeţ-
epergne ɪˈpɜːn, epˈɜːn, -ˈeən (US) iːˈpɝːn, eɪ- **-s** -z
epexegesis epˌek.sɪˈdʒiː.sɪs, ɪˌpek-, -səˈ- (US) -səˈ-
epexegetic epˌek.sɪˈdʒet.ɪk, ɪˌpek-, -səˈ- (US) -səˈdʒeţ- **-al** -əl **-ally** -əl.i, -li
ephah ˈiː.fə **-s** -z
ephedrine ˈef.ə.drɪn, ˈ-ɪ-, -driːn, ɪˈfed.rɪn, -riːn (US) ɪˈfed.rin; ˈef.ə.driːn, -drɪn
ephemer|a ɪˈfem.ər|.ə, efˈem-, əˈfem-, -ˈfiː.mər- (US) ɪˈfem.ɚ-, efˈem-, ˈ-r|ə **-as** -əz **-al** -əl
ephemeralit|y ɪˌfem.əˈræl.ə.t|i, efˌem-, əˌfem-, -ˌfiː.məˈ-, -ɪ.t|i (US) ɪˌfem.əˈræl.ə.ţ|i, efˌem- **-ies** -iz
ephemeris ɪˈfem.ər.ɪs, efˈem-, əˈfem-, -ˈfiː.mər- (US) ɪˈfem-, efˈem-
ephemerides ˌef.ɪˈmer.ɪ.diːz (US) -əˈmer.ə-
ephemeron ɪˈfem.ər.ɒn, efˈem-, əˈfem-, -ˈfiː.mər-, -ən (US) ɪˈfem.ə.rɑːn, efˈem-, -rən **-s** -z
ephemerous ɪˈfem.ər.əs, efˈem-, əˈfem-, -ˈfiː.mər- (US) ɪˈfem.ɚ-, efˈem-
Ephesian ɪˈfiː.ʒən, efˈiː-, -ʒi.ən, -zi- **-s** -z
Ephesus ˈef.ə.səs, ˈ-ɪ-
ephod ˈiː.fɒd, ˈef.ɒd (US) -ɑːd **-s** -z
Ephraim ˈiː.freɪ.ɪm, -fri-, -əm, -frəm (US) ˈiː.fri.əm, -frəm
Ephron ˈef.rɒn, ˈiː.frɒn (US) -frɑːn
epi- ep.i-, ep.ə-; epˈɪ-
Note: Prefix. Normally takes either primary or secondary stress on the first syllable, e.g. **epicycle** /ˈep.ɪ.saɪ.kl̩/, **epicyclic** /ˌep.ɪˈsɪk.lɪk/, but may also be stressed on the second syllable, e.g. **epigraphy** /eˈpɪg.rə.fi/.
epiblast ˈep.ɪ.blæst **-s** -s
epic ˈep.ɪk **-s** -s
epicanth|ic ˌep.ɪˈkænt.θ|ɪk **-us/es** -əs/ɪz **-i** -aɪ
epicene ˈep.ɪ.siːn **-s** -z
epicenter ˈep.ɪ.sen.tər (US) -ţɚ **-s** -z
epicentral ˌep.ɪˈsen.trəl
epicentre ˈep.ɪ.sen.tər (US) -ţɚ **-s** -z
epicentr|um ˌep.ɪˈsen.tr|əm **-ums** -əmz **-a** -ə
Epicharmus ˌep.ɪˈkɑː.məs (US) -ˈkɑːr-
epic|ism ˈep.ɪ.s|ɪ.zəm **-ist/s** -ɪst/s
Epicoene ˈep.ɪ.siː.ni (US) ˈep.ɪ.siːn
epicotyl ˈep.ɪ.kɒt.ɪl (US) -kɑː.ţəl **-s** -z
Epictetus ˌep.ɪkˈtiː.təs (US) -ţəs
epicure ˈep.ɪ.kjʊər, -kjɔːr (US) -kjʊr -
epicurean (E) ˌep.ɪ.kjʊəˈriː.ən, -kjɔ (US) -kjʊrˈiː- **-s** -z
epicurism ˈep.ɪ.kjʊə.rɪ.zəm, -kjɔː- (US) -kjʊr.ɪ-
Epicurus ˌep.ɪˈkjʊə.rəs, -ˈkjɔː- (US) -əˈkjʊr.əs
epicycle ˈep.ɪ.saɪ.kl̩ (US) ˈ-ə- **-s** -z
epicyclic ˌep.ɪˈsaɪ.klɪk, -ˈsɪk.lɪk (US)
epicycloid ˌep.ɪˈsaɪ.klɔɪd (US) -əˈ- **-s**
Epidaurus ˌep.ɪˈdɔː.rəs (US) -əˈdɔːr.ə
epideictic ˌep.ɪˈdaɪk.tɪk (US) -əˈ-
epidemic ˌep.ɪˈdem.ɪk (US) -əˈ- **-s** -s -əl **-ally** -əl.i, -li
epidemiological ˌep.ɪˌdiː.mi.əˈlɒdʒ.ɪ.kəl (US) -əˌdiː.mi.əˈlɑː.dʒɪ-, -ˌdem.i-
epidemiolog|y ˌep.ɪˌdiː.miˈɒl.ə.dʒ (US) -əˌdiː.miˈɑː.lə-, -ˌdem.iˈ- **-ist/s** -ɪst/s
epiderm|al ˌep.ɪˈdɜː.m|əl (US) -əˈdɝ -ɪk **-oid** -ɔɪd

epidermis ˌep.ɪˈdɜː.mɪs (US) -əˈdɝː-

epidiascope ˌep.ɪˈdaɪə.skəʊp (US) -əˈdaɪə.skoʊp **-s** -s

epididymis ˌep.ɪˈdɪd.ə.mɪs, ˈ-ɪ- (US) -əˈ- **epididymides** ˌep.ɪ.dɪˈdɪm.ɪ.diːz (US) -ə-

epidural ˌep.ɪˈdjʊə.rᵊl, -ˈdjɔː- (US) -əˈdʊr.ᵊl, -ˈdjʊr- **-s** -z

epige|al ˌep.ɪˈdʒiː|.əl (US) -əˈ- **-an** -ən

epigene ˈep.ɪ.dʒiːn (US) ˈ-ə-

epigenesis ˌep.ɪˈdʒen.ə.sɪs, ˈ-ɪ- (US) -əˈ-

epiglott|al ˌep.ɪˈglɒt|.ᵊl, ˈep.ɪ.glɒt- (US) ˌep.əˈglɑː.t̬|ᵊl **-ic** -ɪk

epiglottis ˌep.ɪˈglɒt.ɪs, ˈep.ɪ.glɒt- (US) -əˈglɑː.t̬ɪs **-es** -ɪz

epigone ˈep.ɪ.gəʊn (US) -ə.goʊn **-s** -z

Epigoni epˈɪ.gə.naɪ, ɪˈpɪg-, -niː

epigram ˈep.ɪ.græm (US) ˈ-ə- **-s** -z

epigrammatic ˌep.ɪ.grəˈmæt.ɪk (US) -ə.grəˈmæt̬- **-al** -ᵊl **-ally** -ᵊl.i, -li

epigrammatist ˌep.ɪˈgræm.ə.tɪst (US) -əˈgræm.ə.t̬ɪst **-s** -s

epigrammatiz|e, -is|e ˌep.ɪˈgræm.ə.taɪz (US) -əˈ- **-es** -ɪz **-ing** -ɪŋ **-ed** -d

epigraph ˈep.ɪ.grɑːf, -græf (US) -ə.græf **-s** -s

epigrapher epˈɪg.rə.fəʳ, ɪˈpɪg- (US) -fɚ **-s** -z

epigraphic ˌep.ɪˈgræf.ɪk (US) -əˈ-

epigraph|y epˈɪg.rə.f|i, ɪˈpɪg- **-ist/s** -ɪst/s

epilepsy ˈep.ɪ.lep.si, ˈ-ə-

epileptic ˌep.ɪˈlep.tɪk, -əˈ- **-s** -s **-al** -ᵊl

epilog ˈep.ɪ.lɒg (US) -ə.lɑːg, -lɔːg **-s** -z

epilogic ˌep.ɪˈlɒdʒ.ɪk, -əˈ- (US) -əˈlɑː.dʒɪk

epilogiz|e, -is|e epˈɪl.ə.dʒaɪz, ɪˈpɪl- **-es** -ɪz **-ing** -ɪŋ **-ed** -d

epilogue ˈep.ɪ.lɒg (US) -ə.lɑːg, -lɔːg **-s** -z

Epimenides ˌep.ɪˈmen.ɪ.diːz, -ə.diːz (US) -əˈ-

Epinal ˈep.ɪ.nᵊl (US) ˌeɪ.piːˈnɑːl

Epiphan|y (E) ɪˈpɪf.ᵊn|.i, epˈɪf-, əˈpɪf- (US) ɪˈpɪf.ə.n|i **-ies** -iz

epiphyte ˈep.ɪ.faɪt (US) ˈ-ə- **-s** -s

Epirus epˈaɪə.rəs, ɪˈpaɪə- (US) ɪˈpaɪ-

episcopac|y ɪˈpɪs.kə.pə.s|i, epˈɪs- **-ies** -iz

episcopal ɪˈpɪs.kə.pᵊl, epˈɪs- **-ly** -i

Episcopalian (E) ɪˌpɪs.kəˈpeɪ.li.ən, epˌɪs- (US) -ˈpeɪ.li.ən, -ˈpeɪl.jən **-s** -z **-ism** -ɪ.zᵊm

episcopate ɪˈpɪs.kə.pət, epˈɪs-, -pɪt, -peɪt **-s** -s

episcope ˈep.ɪ.skəʊp (US) -ə.skoʊp **-s** -s

episcopiz|e, -is|e ɪˈpɪs.kə.paɪz, epˈɪs- **-es** -ɪz **-ing** -ɪŋ **-ed** -d

episiotom|y ɪˌpɪz.iˈɒt.ə.m|i, epˌɪz-, -ˌiː.ziˈ-; ˌep.ɪ.ziˈ- (US) ɪˌpiː.ziːˈɑː.t̬ə-; ˌep.ɪ.saɪˈ- **-ies** -iz

episode ˈep.ɪ.səʊd (US) -ə.soʊd **-s** -z

episodic ˌep.ɪˈsɒd.ɪk (US) -əˈsɑː.dɪk **-al** -ᵊl **-ally** -ᵊl.i, -li

epistemic ˌep.ɪˈstiː.mɪk, -ˈstem.ɪk

epistemological ɪˌpɪs.tɪ.məˈlɒdʒ.ɪ.kᵊl, epˌɪs-, -tə-, -tiː- (US) -ˈlɑː.dʒɪ- **-ly** -li

epistemology ɪˌpɪs.təˈmɒl.ə.dʒi, epˌɪs-, -tɪˈ- (US) -təˈmɑː.lə-

epistle (E) ɪˈpɪs.l̩, epˈɪs- (US) ɪˈpɪs- **-s** -z

epistler ɪˈpɪst.ləʳ, epˈɪs- (US) ɪˈpɪst.lɚ **-s** -z

epistolary ɪˈpɪs.tᵊl.ᵊr.i, epˈɪs- (US) ɪˈpɪs.tᵊl.er-

epistoler ɪˈpɪs.tᵊl.əʳ, epˈɪs- (US) ɪˈpɪs.tᵊl.ɚ **-s** -z

epistoliz|e, -is|e ɪˈpɪs.tᵊl.aɪz, epˈɪs- (US) ɪˈpɪs.tə.laɪz **-es** -ɪz **-ing** -ɪŋ **-ed** -d

epistyle ˈep.ɪ.staɪl **-s** -z

epitaph ˈep.ɪ.tɑːf, -tæf (US) -ə.tæf **-s** -s

Epithalamion ˌep.ɪ.θəˈleɪ.mi.ən

epithalami|um ˌep.ɪ.θəˈleɪ.mi|.əm **-a** -ə **-ums** -əmz

epitheli|um ˌep.ɪˈθiː.li|.əm **-ums** -əmz **-a** -ə

epithet ˈep.ɪ.θet (US) -θet, -θət **-s** -s

epithetic ˌep.ɪˈθet.ɪk (US) -əˈθet̬-

epitome ɪˈpɪt.ə.mi, epˈɪt-, əˈpɪt- (US) ɪˈpɪt̬- **-s** -z

epitomic ˌep.ɪˈtɒm.ɪk (US) -ˈtɑː.mɪk **-al** -ᵊl

epitomist ɪˈpɪt.ə.mɪst, epˈɪt- (US) ɪˈpɪt̬- **-s** -s

epitomiz|e, -is|e ɪˈpɪt.ə.maɪz, epˈɪt- (US) ɪˈpɪt̬- **-es** -ɪz **-ing** -ɪŋ **-ed** -d

epoch ˈiː.pɒk, ˈep.ək (US) ˈep.ək, -ɑːk, ˌiːˈpɑːk **-s** -s

epochal ˈiː.pɒk.ᵊl, ˈep.ɒk-, -ə.kᵊl; iːˈpɒk.ᵊl (US) ˈep.ə.kᵊl; -ɑː.kᵊl

epoch-making ˈiː.pɒkˌmeɪ.kɪŋ (US) ˈep.əkˌ-, -ɑːkˌ-

epode ˈep.əʊd (US) -oʊd **-s** -z

eponym ˈep.ə.nɪm **-s** -z

eponymous ɪˈpɒn.ɪ.məs, epˈɒn-, ˈ-ə- (US) ɪˈpɑː.nə-

eponymy ɪˈpɒn.ɪ.mi, epˈɒn-, ˈ-ə- (US) ɪˈpɑː.nə-

epos ˈep.ɒs, ˈiː.pɒs (US) ˈep.ɑːs **-es** -ɪz

Epos, EPOS ˈiː.pɒs (US) -pɑːs

epox|y ɪˈpɒk.si, epˈɒk- (US) ɪˈpɑːk- **-ies** -ɪz **-ing** -ɪŋ **ied** -ɪd **eˌpoxy ˈresin**

Epping ˈep.ɪŋ

Epps eps

EPROM ˈiː.prɒm (US) -prɑːm **-s** -z

epsilon epˈsaɪ.lən, -lɒn; ˈep.sɪ.lən, -sə-, -lɒn (US) ˈep.sə.lɑːn, -lən **-s** -z

Epsom ˈep.səm **ˈEpsom ˌsalts, ˌEpsom ˈsalts**

Epstein ˈep.staɪn

Epstein-Barr ˌep.staɪnˈbɑːʳ, -staɪmˈ- (US) -staɪn.ˈbɑːr

Epworth ˈep.wəθ, -wɜːθ (US) -wɚθ, -wɝːθ

epylli|on epˈɪl.i|.ɒn, ɪˈpɪl-, -ən (US) -ɑːn, -ən **-a** -ə

equability ˌek.wəˈbɪl.ə.ti, ˌiː.kwəˈ-, -ɪ.ti (US) -ə.t̬i

equab|le ˈek.wə.b|l̩, ˈiː.kwə- **-ly** -li **-leness** -l̩.nəs, -nɪs

equal ˈiː.kwəl **-ly** -i **-ness** -nəs, -nɪs **-s** -z **-(l)ing** -ɪŋ **-(l)ed** -d **ˌEqual Opporˈtunities Comˌmission; ˌEqual ˈRights Aˌmendment; ˌequal ˈrights; ˈequals ˌsign**

equalit|y ɪˈkwɒl.ə.t|i, iː-, -ɪ.t|i (US) -ˈkwɑː.lə.t̬|i, -ˈkwɔː- **-ies** -iz

equalization, -isa- ˌiː.kwᵊl.aɪˈzeɪ.ʃᵊn, -ɪˈ- (US) -ɪˈ- **-s** -z

equaliz|e, -is|e ˈiː.kwᵊl.aɪz (US) -kwə.laɪz **-es** -ɪz **-ing** -ɪŋ **-ed** -d

equalizer, -iser ˈiː.kwə.laɪ.zəʳ (US) -zɚ **-s** -z

equanimity ˌek.wəˈnɪm.ə.ti, ˌiː.kwəˈ-, -ɪ.ti (US) -ə.t̬i

equanimous ɪˈkwæn.ɪ.məs, iː-, ekˈwæn-, -ˈwɒn-, -ə.məs (US) ɪˈkwæn-, iː-, ekˈwæn- **-ly** -li **-ness** -nəs, -nɪs

e|quate ɪˈkweɪt, iː- **-quates** -kweɪts **-quating** -kweɪ.tɪŋ (US) -kweɪ.t̬ɪŋ **-quated** -kweɪ.tɪd (US) -kweɪ.t̬ɪd **-quatable** -kweɪ.tə.bl̩ (US) -kweɪ.t̬ə.bl̩

equation ɪˈkweɪ.ʒᵊn (US) ɪˈ-, iːˈ- **-s** -z

equational ɪˈkweɪ.ʒᵊn.ᵊl, iː-

equative ɪˈkweɪ.tɪv (US) -t̬ɪv

equator ɪˈkweɪ.təʳ (US) -t̬ɚ **-s** -z

equatorial ˌek.wəˈtɔː.ri.əl, ˌiː.kwəˈ- (US) -ˈtɔːr.i- **-ly** -i

equerr|y ˈek.wə.r|i; ɪˈkwer|.i (US) ˈek.wɚ|.i; ɪˈkwer- **-ies** -iz

Note: The pronunciation at court is /ɪˈkwer.i/.

equestrian ɪˈkwes.tri.ən, ekˈwes- (US) ɪˈkwes- **-s** -z **-ism** -ɪ.zᵊm

equestrienne ɪˌkwes.triˈen, ekˌwes- (US) ɪˌkwes- **-s** -z

equi- iː.kwɪ-, ek.wɪ-, -wi-, -wə-; ɪˈkwɪ-

Note: Prefix. Either takes primary or secondary stress on the first syllable, e.g. **equinox** /ˈiː.kwɪ.nɒks (US) -nɑːks/, **equinoctial** /ˌiː.kwɪnˈɒk.ʃᵊl (US) -ˈnɑːk-/, or primary or secondary stress on the second syllable, e.g. **equivocate** /ɪˈkwɪv.ə.keɪt/, **equivocation** /ɪˌkwɪv.əˈkeɪ.ʃᵊn/.

equiangular ˌiː.kwiˈæŋ.gjʊ.ləʳ, -gjə- (US) -lɚ

equidistant ˌiː.kwɪˈdɪs.tᵊnt, ˌek.wɪˈ-, -wəˈ- **-ly** -li

equilateral ˌiː.kwɪˈlæt.ᵊr.ᵊl, -kwəˈ- (US) -ˈlæt̬-, ˌek.wəˈ-

equilib|rate ˌiː.kwɪˈlaɪ.b|reɪt, ˌek.wɪˈ-, -wəˈ-, -ˈlɪb|.reɪt; iːˈkwɪl.ɪ.b|reɪt, ɪ- (US) ɪˈkwɪl-, iː- **-rates** -reɪts **-rating**

-reɪ.tɪŋ (US) -reɪ.t̬ɪŋ **-rated** -reɪ.tɪd (US) -reɪ.t̬ɪd

equilibration ˌiː.kwɪ.laɪˈbreɪ.ʃᵊn, ˌek.wɪ-, -wə-, -lɪˈbreɪ-; iːˌkwɪl.ɪˈ-, ɪ- (US) ɪˌkwɪl.ɪˈ-, iːˌ-

equilibrist iːˈkwɪl.ɪ.brɪst, ɪ-; ˌiː.kwɪˈlɪb.rɪst, ˌek.wɪˈ-, -wəˈ- (US) ɪˈkwɪl.ə.brɪst, iː-; ˌiː.kwəˈlɪb.rɪst **-s** -s

equilibrium ˌiː.kwɪˈlɪb.ri.əm, ˌek.wɪˈ-, -wəˈ-

equimultiple ˌiː.kwɪˈmʌl.tɪ.pl̩, ˌek.wɪˈ-, -wəˈ-, -tə- (US) -t̬ə- **-s** -z

equine ˈek.waɪn, ˈiː.kwaɪn (US) ˈiː.kwaɪn, ˈek.waɪn

equinoctial ˌiː.kwɪˈnɒk.ʃᵊl, ˌek.wɪˈ-, -wəˈ- (US) -ˈnɑːk- **-s** -z

equinox ˈiː.kwɪ.nɒks, ˈek.wɪ-, -wə- (US) -nɑːks **-es** -ɪz

equip ɪˈkwɪp **-s** -s **-ping** -ɪŋ **-ped** -t

equipag|e ˈek.wɪ.pɪdʒ, -wə- **-es** -ɪz

equipment ɪˈkwɪp.mənt

equipois|e ˈek.wɪ.pɔɪz, ˈiː.kwɪ-, -kwə- **-es** -ɪz **-ing** -ɪŋ **-ed** -d

equipollent ˌiː.kwɪˈpɒl.ənt, ˌek.wɪˈ-, -wəˈ- (US) -ˈpɑː.lənt

equitab|le ˈek.wɪ.tə.bl|, -wə- (US) -t̬ə- **-ly** -li **-leness** -l̩.nəs, -nɪs

equitation ˌek.wɪˈteɪ.ʃᵊn, -wəˈ-

equit|y (E) ˈek.wɪ.t|i, -wə- (US) -t̬|i **-ies** -iz

equivalen|ce ɪˈkwɪv.ᵊl.ən*t*|s **-cy** -si

equivalent ɪˈkwɪv.ᵊl.ənt **-s** -s **-ly** -li

equivocal ɪˈkwɪv.ə.kᵊl, ˈ-ɪ- **-ly** -i **-ness** -nəs, -nɪs

equivo|cate ɪˈkwɪv.ə|l.keɪt **-cates** -keɪts **-cating** -keɪ.tɪŋ (US) -keɪ.t̬ɪŋ **-cated** -keɪ.tɪd (US) -keɪ.t̬ɪd **-cator/s** -keɪ.təʳ/z (US) -keɪ.t̬ɚ/z

equivocation ɪˌkwɪv.əˈkeɪ.ʃᵊn **-s** -z

equivoque, equivoke ˈek.wɪ.vəʊk, -wə- (US) -voʊk **-s** -s

Equuleus ekˈwʊl.i.əs

er ɜːʳ (US) ɝː

-er -əʳ (US) -ɚ

Note: Suffix. Normally unstressed, e.g. **paint** /peɪnt/, **painter** /ˈpeɪn.təʳ (US) -t̬ɚ/, **soon** /suːn/, **sooner** /ˈsuː.nəʳ (US) -nɚ/.

ER ˌiːˈɑːʳ (US) -ˈɑːr

era ˈɪə.rə (US) ˈɪr.ə, ˈer- **-s** -z

ERA ˌiː.ɑːʳˈeɪ (US) -ɑːrˈ-

eradi|ate ɪˈreɪ.di|.eɪt, iː- **-ates** -eɪts **-ating** -eɪ.tɪŋ (US) -eɪ.t̬ɪŋ **-ated** -eɪ.tɪd (US) -eɪ.t̬ɪd

eradiation ɪˌreɪ.diˈeɪ.ʃᵊn, iː-

eradicable ɪˈræd.ɪ.kə.bl̩

eradi|cate ɪˈræd.ɪ|.keɪt **-cates** -keɪts **-cating** -keɪ.tɪŋ (US) -keɪ.t̬ɪŋ **-cated** -keɪ.tɪd (US) -keɪ.t̬ɪd

eradication ɪˌræd.ɪˈkeɪ.ʃᵊn

eradicative ɪˈræd.ɪ.kə.tɪv, -keɪ- (US) -kə.t̬ɪv

Érard ˈer.ɑːd (US) eɪˈrɑːrd, ˈer.ɑːrd **-s** -z

eras|e ɪˈreɪz (US) -ˈreɪs **-es** -ɪz **-ing** -ɪŋ **-ed** -d **-er/s** -əʳ/z (US) -ɚ/z **-able** -ə.bl̩

erasion ɪˈreɪ.ʒᵊn **-s** -z

Erasmian ɪˈræz.mi.ən, erˈæz- **-s** -z **-ism** -ɪ.zᵊm

Erasmus ɪˈræz.məs, erˈæz-

Erastian ɪˈræs.ti.ən, erˈæs- **-s** -z **-ism** -ɪ.zᵊm

Erastus ɪˈræs.təs, erˈæs-

erasure ɪˈreɪ.ʒəʳ (US) -ʃɚ **-s** -z

erbium ˈɜː.bi.əm (US) ˈɝː-

Erdington ˈɜː.dɪŋ.tən (US) ˈɝː-

ere eəʳ (US) er

Erebus ˈer.ɪ.bəs, ˈ-ə-

Erec ˈɪə.rek (US) ˈiː.rek, ˈer.ek

Erechtheum ˌer.ekˈθiː.əm, -ɪkˈ-, -əkˈ-

Erechtheus ɪˈrek.θjuːs, erˈek-, -θi.əs

erect ɪˈrekt **-ly** -li **-ness** -nəs, -nɪs **-s** -s **-ing** -ɪŋ **-ed** -ɪd

erectile ɪˈrek.taɪl (US) -təl, -taɪl

erection ɪˈrek.ʃᵊn **-s** -z

erector ɪˈrek.təʳ (US) -tɚ **-s** -z

eremite ˈer.ɪ.maɪt, ˈ-ə- **-s** -s

eremitic ˌer.ɪˈmɪt.ɪk, -əˈ- (US) -əˈmɪt̬- **-al** -ᵊl

erepsin ɪˈrep.sɪn

Eretri|a ɪˈret.ri|.ə, erˈet- **-an/s** -ən/z

erewhile eəˈ*h*waɪl (US) erˈ-

Erewhon ˈer.ɪ.*h*wɒn (US) -*h*wɑːn, -*h*wʌn

Erfurt ˈeə.fɜːt *as if German:* -fʊət (US) ˈer.fʊrt, -fɝːt

erg ɜːg (US) ɝːg **-s** -z

ergative ˈɜː.gə.tɪv (US) ˈɝː.gə.t̬ɪv

ergativity ˌɜː.gəˈtɪv.ə.ti, -ɪ.ti (US) ˌɝː.gəˈtɪv.ə.t̬i

ergo ˈɜː.gəʊ, ˈeə- (US) ˈer.goʊ, ˈɝː-

ergon ˈɜː.gɒn (US) ˈɝː.gɑːn **-s** -z

ergonic ɜːˈgɒn.ɪk (US) ɝːˈgɑː.nɪk **-s** -s **-ally** -ᵊl.i, -li

ergonomic ˌɜː.gəˈnɒm.ɪk (US) ˌɝː.gəˈnɑː.mɪk **-s** -s

ergonomical ˌɜː.gəˈnɒm.ɪ.kᵊl (US) ˌɝː.gəˈnɑː.mɪ- **-ly** -i

ergonomist ɜːˈgɒn.ə.mɪst (US) ɝːˈgɑː.nə- **-s** -s

ergosterol ɜːˈgɒs.tə.rɒl, -tɪᵊ- (US) ɝːˈgɑː.stə.rɑːl, -rɔːl, -roʊl

ergot ˈɜː.gət, -gɒt (US) ˈɝː.gət, -gɑːt **-ism** -ɪ.zᵊm

Eric ˈer.ɪk

Erica, erica ˈer.ɪ.kə

ericaceous ˌer.ɪˈkeɪ.ʃəs

Ericht ˈer.ɪxt

Eric(k)son ˈer.ɪk.sᵊn

Ericsson® ˈer.ɪ.ksᵊn

Erie ˈɪə.ri (US) ˈɪr.i

Erik ˈer.ɪk

Erika ˈer.ɪ.kə

Erin ˈɪə.rɪn, ˈer.ɪn, ˈeə.rɪn (US) ˈer.ɪn, ˈɪr-

Eris ˈer.ɪs (US) ˈɪr-, ˈer-

eristic erˈɪs.tɪk (US) ɪˈrɪs-, erˈɪs- **-s** -s

Erith ˈɪə.rɪθ (US) ˈɪr.ɪθ

Eritre|a ˌer.ɪˈtreɪ|.ə, -əˈtreɪ-, -ˈtriː- (US) -ˈtriː- **-an/s** -ən/z

Erle ɜːl (US) ɝːl

erl-king ˈɜːl.kɪŋ, ˌ-ˈ- (US) ˈɝːl.kɪŋ, ˈerl- **-s** -z

ERM ˌiː.ɑːʳˈem (US) -ɑːrˈ-

ermine ˈɜː.mɪn (US) ˈɝː- **-s** -z **-d** -d

erne (E) ɜːn (US) ɝːn **-s** -z

Ernest ˈɜː.nɪst, -nəst (US) ˈɝː-

Ernie ˈɜː.ni (US) ˈɝː-

Ernle ˈɜːn.li (US) ˈɝːn-

Ernst ɜːn*t*st *as if German:* eən*t*st (US) ɝːn*t*st *as if German:* ernst

erod|e ɪˈrəʊd (US) -ˈroʊd **-es** -z **-ing** -ɪŋ **-ed** -ɪd

erogenous ɪˈrɒdʒ.ɪ.nəs, erˈɒdʒ-, əˈrɒdʒ-, ˈ-ə- (US) ɪˈrɑː.dʒɪ-, -dʒə-

Eroica erˈəʊ.ɪ.kə, ɪˈrəʊ-, əˈrəʊ- (US) ɪˈroʊ-, erˈoʊ-

Eros ˈɪə.rɒs, ˈer.ɒs (US) ˈer.ɑːs, ˈɪr-, ˈer.oʊs

erosion ɪˈrəʊ.ʒᵊn (US) -ˈroʊ- **-s** -z

erosive ɪˈrəʊ.sɪv, -zɪv (US) -ˈroʊ-

erotic ɪˈrɒt.ɪk (US) -ˈrɑː.t̬ɪk **-s** -s **-a** -ə **-ally** -ᵊl.i, -li

eroticism ɪˈrɒt.ɪ.sɪ.zᵊm, ˈ-ə- (US) -ˈrɑː.t̬ə-

eroticization, -isa- ɪˌrɒt.ɪ.saɪˈzeɪ.ʃᵊn, ˌ-ə-, -sɪˈ- (US) -ˌrɑː.t̬ə.sɪˈ-

eroticiz|e, -is|e ɪˈrɒt.ɪ.saɪz, ˈ-ə- (US) -ˈrɑː.t̬ə- **-es** -ɪs **-ing** -ɪŋ **-ed** -d

erotogenic ɪˌrɒt.əˈdʒen.ɪk, -ˌrəʊ.təˈ- (US) ɪˌrɑː.t̬əˈdʒen-, -ˌroʊ- **-ally** -ᵊl.i,

erotomani|a ɪˌrɒt.əʊˈmeɪ.ni|.ə, -ˌrəʊ.təʊˈ- (US) ɪˌrɑː.t̬əˈmeɪ.ni|.ə, -ˌroʊ- **-ac/s** -æk/s

err ɜːʳ (US) ɝː, er **-s** -z **-ing** -ɪŋ **-ed** -d

errand ˈer.ənd **-s** -z

errant ˈer.ənt **-ly** -li **-ry** -ri

errata *(plur. of* **erratum***)* erˈɑː.tə, ɪˈrɑː-, -ˈreɪ- (US) -t̬ə

erratic ɪˈræt.ɪk, erˈæt- (US) ɪˈræt̬- **-ally** -ᵊl.i, -li

errat|um erˈɑː.t|əm, ɪˈrɑː-, -ˈreɪ- (US) -t̬|əm **-a** -ə

Errol(l) ˈer.əl

erroneous ɪˈrəʊ.ni.əs, erˈəʊ- (US) əˈro[…] erˈoʊ-, ɪˈroʊ- **-ly** -li **-ness** -nəs, -nɪs

error ˈer.əʳ (US) -ɚ **-s** -z

ersatz ˈeə.sæts *as if German:* ˈeə.zɑ[…] (US) ˈer.zɑːts, -ˈ-

Erse ɜːs (US) ɝːs

Erskine ˈɜː.skɪn (US) ˈɝː-

erst ɜːst (US) ɝːst

erstwhile ˈɜːst.*h*waɪl (US) ˈɝːst-

erubescen|ce ˌer.ʊˈbes.ᵊn|*t*s, -uːˈ- […] -*t*si **-t** -t

eruct ɪˈrʌkt, iː- **-s** -s **-ing** -ɪŋ **-ed** -ɪd

eruc|tate ɪˈrʌk|.teɪt, iː- **-tates** -teɪts **-tating** -teɪ.tɪŋ (US) -teɪ.t̬ɪŋ **-tated** -teɪ.tɪd (US) -teɪ.t̬ɪd

eructation ˌiː.rʌkˈteɪ.ʃᵊn, ˌer.ʌk-, -əkˈ-; ɪˌrʌkˈ- (US) ˌiː.rʌkˈ-, ɪˌrʌkˈ- -s -z
erudite ˈer.ʊ.daɪt, -jʊ- (US) -jə-, -ə-, -juː-, -uː- -ly -li -ness -nəs, -nɪs
erudition ˌer.ʊˈdɪʃ.ᵊn, -jʊˈ- (US) -juːˈ-, -uːˈ-, -jəˈ-, -əˈ-
erupt ɪˈrʌpt -s -s -ing -ɪŋ -ed -ɪd
eruption ɪˈrʌp.ʃᵊn -s -z
eruptive ɪˈrʌp.tɪv -ly -li -ness -nəs, -nɪs
Ervine ˈɜː.vɪn (US) ˈɝː-
Erving ˈɜː.vɪŋ (US) ˈɝː-
erysipelas ˌer.ɪˈsɪp.ᵊl.əs, -əˈ-, -ɪ.ləs, -lɪs
erythema ˌer.ɪˈθiː.mə, -əˈ-
erythrocyte ɪˈrɪθ.rəʊ.saɪt (US) erˈɪθ.roʊ- -s -s
erythrocytic ɪˌrɪθ.rəʊˈsɪt.ɪk (US) erˌɪθ.roʊˈsɪţ-
erythromycin ɪˌrɪθ.rəʊˈmaɪ.sɪn, əˌrɪθ- (US) ɪ.rɪθ.roʊˈ-, -rəˈ-
Erzerum ˈeə.zə.ruːm (US) ˈer-
Esau ˈiː.sɔː (US) -sɑː, -sɔː
Esbjerg ˈes.bjɜːg (US) -bjerg
escalad|e ˌes.kəˈleɪd, ˈ--- -es -z -ing -ɪŋ -ed -ɪd
esca|late ˈes.kə|.leɪt -lates -leɪts -lating -leɪ.tɪŋ (US) -leɪ.ţɪŋ -lated -leɪ.tɪd (US) -leɪ.ţɪd
escalation ˌes.kəˈleɪ.ʃᵊn
escalator ˈes.kə.leɪ.təʳ (US) -ţɚ -s -z
scal(l)op ɪˈskɒl.əp, esˈkɒl-, -ˈkæl-, -ɒp; ˈes.kə.lɒp (US) esˈkɑː.ləp, ɪˈskɑː-, -ˈskæl- -ed -t
escalope ˈes.kə.lɒp, ˈɪs-, -ləp; esˈkæl.əp, -ɒp (US) ˌes.kəˈloʊp -s -s
escapade ˌes.kəˈpeɪd, ˈ--- -s -z
escap|e ɪˈskeɪp, esˈkeɪp, əˈskeɪp -es -s -ing -ɪŋ -ed -t -ement/s -mənt/s
escapee ɪˌskeɪˈpiː, ˌes.keɪˈ- -s -z
escap|ism ɪˈskeɪ.p|ɪ.zᵊm, esˈkeɪ- -ist/s -ɪst/s
escapolog|y ˌes.kəˈpɒl.ə.dʒ|i, -keɪˈ- (US) -keɪˈpɑː.lə- -ist/s -ɪst/s
escargot ɪˈskɑː.gəʊ, esˈkɑː- *as if French:* ˌes.kɑːˈgəʊ (US) ˌes.kɑːrˈgoʊ -s -z
escarole ˈes.kə.rəʊl (US) -kə.roʊl
escarp ɪˈskɑːp, esˈkɑːp (US) esˈkɑːrp -s -s -ing -ɪŋ -ed -t
escarpment ɪˈskɑːp.mənt, esˈkɑːp- (US) esˈkɑːrp- -s -s
-esce -ˈes
Note: Suffix. Always carries primary stress, e.g. **convalesce** /ˌkɒn.vəˈles (US) ˌkɑːn-/.
-escen|ce -ˈes.ᵊn|*t*s -t -t
Note: Suffix. Always carries primary stress, e.g. **convalescence** /ˌkɒn.vəˈles.ᵊn*t*s (US) ˌkɑːn-/.
eschar ˈes.kɑːʳ (US) -kɑːr, -kɚ -s -z
eschatological ˌes.kə.təˈlɒdʒ.ɪ.kᵊl, esˌkæt.əˈ- (US) -kə.ţəˈlɑː.dʒɪ-; esˌkæţ.ᵊlˈɑː-
eschatolog|y ˌes.kəˈtɒl.ə.dʒ|i (US) -ˈtɑː.lə- -ist/s -ɪst/s
es|cheat ɪs|ˈtʃiːt, es- -cheats -ˈtʃiːts -cheating -ˈtʃiː.tɪŋ (US) -ˈtʃiː.ţɪŋ -cheated -ˈtʃiː.tɪd (US) -ˈtʃiː.ţɪd
Escher ˈeʃ.əʳ (US) -ɚ
eschew ɪsˈtʃuː, es- (US) es-, ɪs- -s -z -ing -ɪŋ -ed -d
eschscholtzia ɪˈskɒl.ʃə, esˈkɒl-, -tʃə; ɪʃˈɒlt.si.ə, eʃ-, əˈʃɒlt-, -ˈskɒlt- (US) eʃˈoʊlt.si.ə -s -z
Escoffier ɪˈskɒf.i.eɪ, esˈkɒf- (US) ˌes.kɑːˈfjeɪ
Escom ˈes.kɒm, -kɑːm (US) -kɑːm
Escombe ˈes.kəm
Escondido ˌes.kənˈdiː.dəʊ (US) -doʊ
Escorial ˌes.kɒr.iˈɑːl, -ˈæl; esˈkɔː.ri.æl, -ɑːl (US) esˈkɔːr.i.əl; esˌkɔːr.iˈæl
escort® **(E)** *(n.)* ˈes.kɔːt (US) -kɔːrt -s -s
escor|t *(v.)* ɪˈskɔː|t, esˈkɔː|t; ˈes.kɔː|t (US) esˈkɔːr|t, ɪˈskɔːr|t; ˈes.kɔːr|t -ts -ts -ting -tɪŋ (US) -ţɪŋ -ted -tɪd (US) -ţɪd
Escott ˈes.kɒt (US) -kɑːt
Escow ˈes.kəʊ (US) -koʊ
escritoire ˌes.kriːˈtwɑːʳ, ˈ--- (US) ˌes.kriːˈtwɑːr -s -z
escrow ˈes.krəʊ, -ˈ- (US) ˈes.kroʊ, -ˈ-
escudo esˈkuː.dəʊ, ɪˈskuː-, -ˈskjuː-; ɪʃˈkuː-, eʃ- (US) esˈkuː.doʊ, ɪˈskuː- -s -z
esculent ˈes.kjə.lənt, -kjʊ- -s -s
Escurial esˈkjʊə.ri.əl (US) -ˈkjʊr.i-
escutcheon ɪˈskʌtʃ.ᵊn, esˈkʌtʃ- -s -z
Esda ˈes.də, ˈez- ˈ**Esda** ˌ**test**
Esdaile ˈez.deɪl
Esdras ˈez.dræs, -drəs
-ese -ˈiːz (US) -ˈiːz, -ˈiːs
Note: Suffix. Always carries primary stress, e.g. **Japan** /dʒəˈpæn/, **Japanese** /ˌdʒæp.əˈniːz/.
ESE ˌiːst.saʊθˈiːst *in nautical usage also:* -saʊˈ-
Esfahan ˈeʃ.fə.hɑːn, ˈes- (US) ˌes.fəˈhɑːn
Esher ˈiː.ʃəʳ (US) -ʃɚ
Esias ɪˈzaɪ.əs, ezˈaɪ-, -æs
Esk esk
Eskimo ˈes.kɪ.məʊ (US) -kə.moʊ -s -z
ESL ˌiː.esˈel
Esmé ˈez.mi, -meɪ
Esmeralda ˌez.məˈræl.də, -mɪˈ-
Esmond(e) ˈez.mənd
ESN ˌiː.esˈen
ESOL ˈiː.sɒl (US) -sɑːl
ESOP ˈiː.sɒp (US) -sɑːp
esophageal ɪˌsɒf.əˈdʒiː.əl, iː-, ə-; ˌiː.sɒf- (US) ɪˌsɑː.fəˈ-; ˌiː.sɑː-
esopha|gus iːˈsɒf.ə|.gəs, ɪ-, ə- (US) ɪˈsɑː.fə-, iː- -gi -gaɪ, -dʒaɪ -guses -gə.sɪz
esoteric ˌes.əʊˈter.ɪk, ˌiː.səʊˈ- (US) ˌes.əˈ- -al -ᵊl -ally -ᵊl.i, -li
ESP ˌiː.esˈpiː
Espace® esˈpæs
espadrille ˌes.pəˈdrɪl, ˈ--- (US) ˈes.pə.drɪl -s -z
espalier ɪˈspæl.i.eɪ, esˈpæl-, -i.əʳ (US) -ˈspæl.jɚ, -jeɪ -s -z -ing -ɪŋ -ed -d
esparto esˈpɑː.təʊ, ɪˈspɑː- (US) esˈpɑːr.ţoʊ -s -z
especial ɪˈspeʃ.ᵊl, esˈpeʃ-, əˈspeʃ- -ly -i
Esperant|o ˌes.pᵊrˈæn.t|əʊ (US) -pəˈræn.t|oʊ, -ˈrɑːn- -ist/s -ɪst/s
espial ɪˈspaɪ.əl, esˈpaɪ-
espionage ˈes.pi.ə.nɑːʒ, -nɑːdʒ, -nɪdʒ; ˌes.pi.əˈnɑːʒ, -ˈnɑːdʒ
esplanade ˌes.pləˈneɪd, -ˈnɑːd, ˈ--- (US) ˈes.plə.nɑːd, -neɪd -s -z
Esplanade *in Western Australia:* ˈes.plə.nɑːd
ESPN ˌiː.esˌpiːˈen
Espoo ˈes.pəʊ (US) -poʊ
espous|e ɪˈspaʊz, esˈpaʊz -es -ɪz -ing -ɪŋ -ed -d -er/s -əʳ/z (US) -ɚ/z -al/s -ᵊl/z
espressivo ˌes.presˈiː.vəʊ (US) -voʊ
espresso esˈpres.əʊ, ɪˈspres- (US) -oʊ -s -z
esprit esˈpriː, ɪˈspriː, əˈspriː; ˈes.priː (US) esˈpriː, ɪˈspriː
esprit de corps esˌpriː.dəˈkɔːʳ, ɪˌspriː-, əˌspriː-; ˌes.priː- (US) esˌpriː.dəˈkɔːr, ɪˌspriː-
esp|y ɪˈsp|aɪ, esˈp|aɪ -ies -aɪz -ying -aɪ.ɪŋ -ied -aɪd
Espy ˈes.pi
Esq. *(abbrev. for* **Esquire***)* ɪˈskwaɪəʳ, esˈkwaɪəʳ (US) ˈes.kwaɪɚ; ɪˈskwaɪɚ, esˈkwaɪɚ
-esque -ˈesk
Note: Suffix. Always carries primary stress, e.g. **picturesque** /ˌpɪk.tʃᵊrˈesk/.
Esquiline ˈes.kwɪ.laɪn, -kwᵊl.aɪn (US) -kwə.laɪn
Esquimalt esˈkwaɪ.mɔːlt, ɪˈskwaɪ-, -mɒlt (US) -mɑːlt, -mɔːlt
esquire ɪˈskwaɪəʳ, esˈkwaɪəʳ (US) ˈes.kwaɪɚ; ɪˈskwaɪɚ, esˈkwaɪɚ -s -z
ess es -es -ɪz
essay *(n.) piece of writing:* ˈes.eɪ -s -z -ist/s -ɪst/s
essay *(n. v.) attempt:* esˈeɪ, ˈ-- -s -z -ing -ɪŋ -ed -d -er/s -əʳ/z (US) -ɚ/z
esse ˈes.i
Essen ˈes.ᵊn
essenc|e ˈes.ᵊn*t*s -es -ɪz
Essene ˈes.iːn, -ˈ- -s -z
essential ɪˈsen.*t*ʃᵊl (US) ɪˈsen*t*.ʃᵊl, esˈen*t*- -s -z -ly -i -ness -nəs, -nɪs esˌsential ˈoil
essentiality ɪˌsen.*t*ʃiˈæl.ə.ti, esˌen-, -ɪ.ti (US) -ə.ţi
Essex ˈes.ɪks
essive ˈes.ɪv -s -z

Esso® 'es.əʊ (US) -oʊ
-est -ɪst, -əst
Note: Suffix. Does not affect the stress pattern of the word, e.g. **happy** /'hæp.i/, **happiest** /'hæp.i.ɪst/.
EST ˌiː.es'tiː
establish ɪ'stæb.lɪʃ, es'tæb- **-es** -ɪz **-ing** -ɪŋ **-ed** -t **-er/s** -əʳ/z (US) -ɚ/z **-ment/s** -mənt/s
estate ɪ'steɪt, es'teɪt **-s** -s **es'tate ˌagent; es'tate ˌcar**
Estcourt 'est.kɔːt (US) -kɔːrt
Este 'es.ti (US) -teɪ
Estée 'es.teɪ, -tiː (US) -teɪ
esteem ɪ'stiːm, es'tiːm **-s** -z **-ing** -ɪŋ **-ed** -d
Estelle ɪ'stel, es'tel
ester 'es.təʳ (US) -tɚ **-s** -z
Esterhazy 'es.tə.hɑː.zi (US) -tɚ.hɑː.zi
Esther 'es.təʳ, -θəʳ (US) -tɚ
esthete 'iːs.θiːt (US) 'es- **-s** -s
esthetic es'θet.ɪk, ɪs- (US) es'θeţ- **-al** -əl **-ally** -əl.i, -li **-s** -s
esthetic|ism es'θet.ɪ.s|ɪ.zəm, ɪs- (US) es'θeţ- **-ist/s** -ɪst/s
estimab|le 'es.tɪ.mə.b|l̩, -tə- **-ly** -li **-leness** -l̩.nəs, -nɪs
estimate (*n.*) 'es.tɪ.mət, -tə-, -mɪt, -meɪt (US) -mɪt, -mət **-s** -s
esti|mate (*v.*) 'es.tɪ|.meɪt, -tə-, -mət (US) -meɪt **-mates** -meɪts, -məts (US) -meɪts **-mating** -meɪ.tɪŋ, -mə- (US) -meɪ.ţɪŋ **-mated** -meɪ.tɪd, -mə- (US) -meɪ.ţɪd **-mator/s** -meɪ.təʳ/z, -mə- (US) -meɪ.ţɚ/z
estimation ˌes.tɪ'meɪ.ʃən, -tə'-
estival iː'staɪ.vəl, es'taɪ- (US) 'es.tə-, es'taɪ-
Eston 'es.tən
Estoni|a es'təʊ.ni|.ə, ɪ'stəʊ- (US) es'toʊ- **-an/s** -ən/z
estop ɪ'stɒp, es'tɒp (US) es'tɑːp **-s** -s **-ping** -ɪŋ **-ped** -t **-page** -ɪdʒ **-pel/s** -əl/z
Estoril ˌes.tər'ɪl (US) ˌiː.stə'rɪl
estovers ɪ'stəʊ.vəz, es'təʊ- (US) es'toʊ.vɚz
estrade es'trɑːd, ɪ'strɑːd (US) es'trɑːd **-s** -z
Estragon 'es.trə.gɒn (US) -gɑːn
estrang|e ɪ'streɪndʒ, es'treɪndʒ **-es** -ɪz **-ing** -ɪŋ **-ed** -d
estrangement ɪ'streɪndʒ.mənt, es'treɪndʒ- **-s** -s
estrea|t ɪ'striː|t, es'triː|t (US) es'triː|t **-ts** -ts **-ting** -tɪŋ (US) -ţɪŋ **-ted** -tɪd (US) -ţɪd
Estremadura ˌes.trə.mə'dʊə.rə, -'dɔː- (US) -'dʊr.ə
estrogen 'iː.strə.dʒən, 'es.trə- (US) 'es.trə.dʒən, -dʒen
estr(o)us 'iː.strəs, 'es.trəs (US) 'es.trəs **-es** -ɪz
estuarine 'es.tju.ə.raɪn, -riːn, -rɪn (US) 'es.tʃuː.ə.raɪn, -ɚ.ɪn
estuar|y 'es.tjʊə.r|i, -tju.ə-, -tʃʊə-, -tʃu.ə-, -tjʊr|.i, -tʃʊr|.i (US) 'es.tʃuː.er|.i **-ies** -iz
esurien|ce ɪ'sjʊə.ri.ən|ts (US) iː'sʊr.i-, -'sjʊr- **-cy** -*t*.si **-t** -t
eta *Greek alphabet:* 'iː.tə (US) 'eɪ.ţə, 'iː-
ETA *estimated time of arrival:* ˌiː.tiː'eɪ
ETA *Basque separatist group:* 'et.ə (US) 'eţ-
étagère, etagere ˌeɪ.tə'ʒeəʳ, ˌet.ə-, -tæʒ'eəʳ, -tɑː'ʒeəʳ (US) -tɑː'ʒer **-s** -z
Etah 'iː.tə (US) -ţə
e-tail 'iː.teɪl **-er/s** -əʳ/z (US) -ɚz
Etain 'et.eɪn
et al et'æl (US) et'ɑːl, -'æl, -'ɔːl
Etam® 'iː.tæm
etc. ɪt'set.ər.ə, et-, ət- (US) -'seţ.ɚ-
etcetera ɪt'set.ər.ə, et-, ət- (US) -'seţ.ɚ- **-s** -z
etch etʃ **-es** -ɪz **-ing/s** -ɪŋ/z **-ed** -t **-er/s** -əʳ/z (US) -ɚ/z
eternal ɪ'tɜː.nəl (US) -'tɝː- **-ly** -i
eternaliz|e, -is|e ɪ'tɜː.nəl.aɪz (US) -'tɝː.nə.laɪz **-es** -ɪz **-ing** -ɪŋ **-ed** -d
eternit|y ɪ'tɜː.nə.t|i, -nɪ.t|i (US) -'tɝː.nə.ţ|i **-ies** -iz
eterniz|e, -is|e ɪ'tɜː.naɪz (US) -'tɝː- **-es** -ɪz **-ing** -ɪŋ **-ed** -d
Etesian ɪ'tiː.ʒi.ən, -zi-, -ʒən
Ethan 'iː.θən
ethane 'iː.θeɪn, 'eθ.eɪn (US) 'eθ.eɪn
ethanoic ˌeθ.ə'nəʊ.ɪk, 'iː.θə'- (US) ˌeθ.ə'noʊ-
ethanol 'eθ.ə.nɒl, 'iː.θə- (US) 'eθ.ə.nɑːl, -noʊl
Ethel 'eθ.əl
Ethelbald 'eθ.əl.bɔːld (US) -bɔːld, -bɑːld
Ethelbert 'eθ.əl.bɜːt, -bət (US) -bɝːt, -bɚt
Ethelberta ˌeθ.əl'bɜː.tə, 'eθ.əlˌbɜː- (US) ˌeθ.əl'bɝː.ţə
Ethelburga ˌeθ.əl'bɜː.gə, 'eθ.əlˌbɜː- (US) ˌeθ.əl'bɝː-
Ethelred 'eθ.əl.red
Ethelwulf 'eθ.əl.wʊlf
ethene 'eθ.iːn
ether 'iː.θəʳ (US) -θɚ **-s** -z
ethereal ɪ'θɪə.ri.əl, iː-, ə- (US) -'θɪr.i- **-ly** -i
etherealiz|e, -is|e ɪ'θɪə.ri.əl.aɪz, iː-, ə- (US) -'θɪr.i.ə.laɪz **-es** -ɪz **-ing** -ɪŋ **-ed** -d
Etherege 'eθ.ər.ɪdʒ
etheric iː'θer.ɪk, ɪ- **-s** -s **-ally** -əl.i, -li
Etherington 'eð.ər.ɪŋ.tən
etheriz|e, -is|e 'iː.θər.aɪz (US) -θə.raɪz **-es** -ɪz **-ing** -ɪŋ **-ed** -d
ethic 'eθ.ɪk **-s** -s **-al** -əl **-ally** -əl.i, -li
Ethiop 'iː.θi.ɒp (US) -ɑːp **-s** -s
Ethiopi|a ˌiː.θi'əʊ.pi|.ə (US) -'oʊ- **-an/s** -ən/z
Ethiopic ˌiː.θi'ɒp.ɪk, -'əʊ.pɪk (US) -'ɑː-, -'oʊ-
ethnic 'eθ.nɪk **-al** -əl **-ally** -əl.i, -li
ethnicity eθ'nɪs.ə.ti, -ɪ.ti (US) -ə.ţi
ethno- eθ.nəʊ-; eθ'nɒ- (US) eθ.noʊ-; eθ'nɑː-
Note: Prefix. Either takes primary or secondary stress on the first syllable, e.g. **ethnographic** /ˌeθ.nəʊ'græf.ɪk (US) -noʊ'-/, or primary stress on the second syllable, e.g. **ethnographer** /eθ'nɒg.rə.fəʳ (US) -'nɑː.grə.fɚ/.
ethnocentr|ic ˌeθ.nəʊ'sen.tr|ɪk (US) -noʊ'-, -nə'- **-ism** -ɪ.zəm **-ically** -ɪ.kəl.i, -ɪ.kli
ethnocentricity ˌeθ.nəʊ.sen'trɪs.ə.t[i], -ɪ.ti (US) -noʊ.sen'trɪs.ə.ţi
ethnographer eθ'nɒg.rə.fəʳ (US) -'nɑː.grə.fɚ **-s** -z
ethnographic ˌeθ.nəʊ'græf.ɪk (US) -noʊ'-, -nə'- **-al** -əl
ethnography eθ'nɒg.rə.fi (US) -'nɑː.grə-
ethnologic ˌeθ.nəʊ'lɒdʒ.ɪk (US) -noʊ'lɑː.dʒɪk, -nə'- **-al** -əl **-ally** -əl.i, -li
ethnolog|y eθ'nɒl.ə.dʒ|i (US) -'nɑː.lə- **-ist/s** -ɪst/s
ethologic ˌiː.θə'lɒdʒ.ɪk (US) -'lɑː.dʒɪk **-al** -əl
etholog|y iː'θɒl.ə.dʒ|i, ɪ- (US) iː'θɑː.lə-, ɪ'- **-ist/s** -ɪst/s
ethos 'iː.θɒs (US) -θɑːs, 'eθ.ɑːs, -oʊs
ethyl *commercial and general pronunciation:* 'eθ.ɪl, -əl (US) -əl *chemists' pronunciation:* 'iː.θaɪl
ethylene 'eθ.ɪ.liːn, -əl.iːn (US) -ə.liːn
etio|late 'iː.ti.əʊ|.leɪt (US) -ə- **-lates** -leɪts **-lating** -leɪ.tɪŋ (US) -leɪ.ţɪŋ **-lated** -leɪ.tɪd (US) -leɪ.ţɪd
etiolog|y ˌiː.ti'ɒl.ə.dʒ|i (US) -'ɑː.lə- **-ist/s** -ɪst/s
etiquette 'et.ɪ.ket, -kət; (US) 'eţ.ɪ.k[ɪt], -ket
Etna 'et.nə
Eton 'iː.tən
Etonian iː'təʊ.ni.ən, ɪ- (US) -'toʊ- **-s**
Etruri|a ɪ'trʊə.ri|.ə (US) -'trʊr.i- **-an/s** -ən/z
Etruscan ɪ'trʌs.kən **-s** -z
-ette -et
Note: Suffix. Normally takes prim[ary] stress, e.g. **majorette** /ˌmeɪ.dʒ[ə'ret]/; there are exceptions, however, e[.g.] **etiquette** /'et.ɪ.ket (US) 'eţ.ɪ.kɪt/; see individual entries.
Ettrick 'et.rɪk
Etty 'et.i (US) 'eţ-
étude 'eɪ.tjuːd, -'- (US) 'eɪ.tuːd, -tj[uːd] **-s** -z
etui et'wiː (US) eɪ'twiː **-s** -z

etymologic ˌet.ɪ.məˈlɒdʒ.ɪk, ˌ-ə- (US) ˌet̬.ɪ.məˈlɑː.dʒɪk **-al** -ᵊl **-ally** -ᵊl.i, -li

etymologist ˌet.ɪˈmɒl.ə.dʒɪst, -əˈ- (US) ˌet̬.ɪˈmɑː.lə- **-s** -s

etymologiz|e, -is|e ˌet.ɪˈmɒl.ə.dʒaɪz, -əˈ- (US) ˌet̬.ɪˈmɑː.lə- **-es** -ɪz **-ing** -ɪŋ **-ed** -d

etymolog|y ˌet.ɪˈmɒl.ə.dʒ|i, -əˈ- (US) ˌet̬.ɪˈmɑː.lə- **-ies** -iz

etymon ˈet.ɪ.mɒn, ˈ-ə- (US) ˈet̬.ə.mɑːn **-s** -z

EU ˌiːˈjuː

Euan ˈjuː.ən

Eubank ˈjuː.bæŋk

Euboea juːˈbiː.ə

eucalyptus ˌjuː.kᵊlˈɪp.təs **-es** -ɪz

Eucharist ˈjuː.kᵊr.ɪst **-s** -s

eucharistic ˌjuː.kᵊrˈɪs.tɪk **-al** -ᵊl **-ally** -ᵊl.i, -li

euchre ˈjuː.kəʳ (US) -kɚ **-s** -z **-ing** -ɪŋ **-d** -d

Euclid ˈjuː.klɪd **-s** -z

Euclidean juːˈklɪd.i.ən

eud(a)emon|ism juːˈdiː.mə.n|ɪ.zᵊm **-ist/s** -ɪst/s

eudiometer ˌjuː.diˈɒm.ɪ.təʳ, ˈ-ə- (US) -ˈɑː.mə.t̬ɚ **-s** -z

Eudocia juːˈdəʊ.ʃi.ə, -ʃə, -si.ə (US) -ˈdoʊ-

Eudora juːˈdɔː.rə (US) -ˈdɔːr.ə

Eudoxia juːˈdɒk.si.ə (US) -ˈdɑːk-

Eudoxus juːˈdɒk.səs (US) -ˈdɑːk-

Eugen *English name:* ˈjuː.dʒen, -dʒɪn, -dʒən *German name:* ˈɔɪ.gən

Eugene juːˈdʒiːn, -ˈdʒeɪn; ˈjuː.dʒiːn (US) juːˈdʒiːn, ˈ--

Eugene Onegin ˌjuː.dʒiːn.ɒnˈjeɪ.gɪn (US) -ɑːnˈ-, -oʊnˈ-

Eugénia juːˈdʒiː.ni.ə, -ˈʒiː-, -ˈdʒeɪ-, -ˈʒeɪ-

eugenic juːˈdʒen.ɪk **-s** -s

eugenicist juːˈdʒen.ɪ.sɪst, ˈ-ə- **-s** -s

Eugénie juːˈʒeɪ.ni, -ˈʒiː-, -ˈdʒiː-

Eugenius juːˈdʒiː.ni.əs, -ˈʒiː-, -ˈdʒeɪ- (US) -ˈʒeɪ-

Eulalia juːˈleɪ.li.ə

Eulenspiegel ˈɔɪ.lᵊnˌʃpiː.gᵊl

Euler *English name:* ˈjuː.ləʳ (US) -lɚ *German name:* ˈɔɪ.ləʳ (US) -lɚ

eulogist ˈjuː.lə.dʒɪst **-s** -s

eulogistic ˌjuː.ləˈdʒɪs.tɪk **-al** -ᵊl **-ally** -ᵊl.i, -li

eulogi|um juːˈləʊ.dʒi|.əm (US) -ˈloʊ- **-ums** -z **-a** -ə

eulogiz|e, -is|e ˈjuː.lə.dʒaɪz **-es** -ɪz **-ing** -ɪŋ **-ed** -d

eulog|y ˈjuː.lə.dʒ|i **-ies** -iz

Eumenides juːˈmen.ɪ.diːz, ˈ-ə-

Eunice *modern Christian name:* ˈjuː.nɪs *biblical name:* juːˈnaɪ.si

eunuch ˈjuː.nək **-s** -s **-ism** -ɪ.zᵊm

euonymus juːˈɒn.ɪ.məs, ˈ-ə- (US) -ˈɑː.nə- **-es** -ɪz

eupepsia juːˈpep.si.ə

eupeptic juːˈpep.tɪk

Euphemia juːˈfiː.mi.ə

euphemism ˈjuː.fə.mɪ.zᵊm, -fɪ- **-s** -z

euphemistic ˌjuː.fəˈmɪs.tɪk, -fɪˈ- **-al** -ᵊl **-ally** -ᵊl.i, -li

euphemiz|e, -is|e ˈjuː.fə.maɪz, -fɪ- **-es** -ɪz **-ing** -ɪŋ **-ed** -d

euphonic juːˈfɒn.ɪk (US) -ˈfɑː.nɪk **-al** -ᵊl **-ally** -ᵊl.i, -li

euphonious juːˈfəʊ.ni.əs (US) -ˈfoʊ- **-ly** -li

euphonium juːˈfəʊ.ni.əm (US) -ˈfoʊ- **-s** -z

euphoniz|e, -is|e ˈjuː.fə.naɪz **-es** -ɪz **-ing** -ɪŋ **-ed** -d

euphony ˈjuː.fᵊn.i

euphorbia juːˈfɔː.bi.ə (US) -ˈfɔːr-

euphoria juːˈfɔː.ri.ə (US) -ˈfɔːr.i-

euphoric juːˈfɒr.ɪk (US) -ˈfɔːr.ɪk **-ally** -ᵊl.i, -li

euphrasy ˈjuː.frə.si

Euphrates juːˈfreɪ.tiːz (US) -t̬iːz

Euphronius juːˈfrəʊ.ni.əs (US) -ˈfroʊ-

Euphrosyne juːˈfrɒz.ɪ.niː, ˈ-ə- (US) -ˈfrɑː.zə-

Euphues ˈjuː.fju.iːz

euphu|ism ˈjuː.fju.|ɪ.zᵊm **-isms** -ɪ.zᵊmz **-ist/s** -ɪst/s

euphuistic ˌjuː.fjuˈɪs.tɪk

eupnoea ˈjuːp.niː.ə (US) -ˈ--

Eurasi|a jʊəˈreɪ.ʒ|ə, jɔːˈ-, ˈ-ʒi|.ə, ˈ-ʃ|ə (US) jʊˈreɪ.ʒ|ə **-a** -ə **-an** -ᵊn

Euratom jʊəˈræt.əm, jɔːˈ- (US) jʊˈræt̬-

eureka (E) jʊəˈriː.kə, jɔːˈ- (US) jʊ-

eurhythm|ic jʊəˈrɪð.m|ɪk, jɔːˈ-, -ˈrɪθ- (US) jʊˈrɪð- **-ics** -ɪks **-y** -i

Euripides jʊəˈrɪp.ɪ.diːz, jɔːˈ-, ˈ-ə- (US) jʊ-

Euripus jʊəˈraɪ.pəs, jɔːˈ- (US) jʊ-

Euro- ˈjʊə.rəʊ-, jɔː-; jʊəˈrɒ- (US) ˈjʊr.oʊ-, -ə-; jʊˈrɑː-

Note: Prefix. Usually takes primary stress on the first syllable, e.g. **Eurocrat** /ˈjʊə.rəʊ.kræt (US) ˈjʊr.ə-/.

euro ˈjʊə.rəʊ, ˈjɔː- (US) ˈjʊr.oʊ **-s** -z

Pronouncing the letters **EU, EW**

The vowel digraphs **eu** and **ew** are similar in that their most common pronunciation is one of /juː/ or /uː/, e.g.:

feud	/fjuːd/
flew	/fluː/

Many words in British English which have /juː/ are pronounced without the /j/ in American English, e.g.:

news	/njuːz/	(US) /nuːz/

When the digraph **eu** is followed by an **r** in the spelling, the strong pronunciation is usually /jʊə (US) jʊr/, although words borrowed from French may have /ɜː (US) ɝː/ in stressed syllables, and /əʳ (US) ɚ/ in unstressed syllables, e.g.:

European	/ˌjʊə.rəˈpiː.ən/	(US) /ˌjʊr.ə-/
connoisseur	/ˌkɒn.əˈsɜːʳ/	(US) /ˌkɑː.nəˈsɝː/
amateur	/ˈæm.ə.təʳ/	(US) /-tʃɚ/

In addition

Other sounds associated with the digraphs **eu** and **ew** are as follows:

/əʊ (US) oʊ/	sew	/səʊ/ (US) /soʊ/
/i.ə/	museum	/mjuːˈziː.əm/
/ɔɪ/	schadenfreude	/ˈʃɑː.dᵊnˌfrɔɪ.də/
/ɜː (US) ɝː, uː/	masseuse	/mæsˈɜːz/ (US) /məˈsɝːz, -suːz/

In words borrowed from German, **eu** is pronounced /ɔɪ/, e.g.:

/ɔɪ/	schadenfreude	/ˈʃɑː.dᵊnˌfrɔɪ.də/

Eurobond 'jʊə.rəʊ.bɒnd, 'jɔː- ⓤⓢ 'jʊr.oʊ.bɑːnd **-s** -z
eurocentric ˌjʊə.rəʊ'sen.trɪk, ˌjɔː- ⓤⓢ ˌjʊr.oʊ'-
Eurocheque® 'jʊə.rəʊ.tʃek, 'jɔː- ⓤⓢ 'jʊr.oʊ- **-s** -s
Eurocommun|ism ˌjʊə.rəʊ'kɒm.jə.n|ɪ.zᵊm, ˌjɔː-, -jʊ-, 'jʊə.rəʊˌkɒm-, 'jɔː- ⓤⓢ ˌjʊr.oʊ'kɑːm.jə-, -ə'- **-ist/s** -ɪst/s
Eurocrat 'jʊə.rəʊ.kræt, 'jɔː- ⓤⓢ 'jʊr.ə- **-s** -s
Eurodisney® 'jʊə.rəʊˌdɪz.ni, 'jɔː- ⓤⓢ 'jʊr.oʊ-
Eurodollar® 'jʊə.rəʊˌdɒl.əʳ, 'jɔː- ⓤⓢ 'jʊr.oʊˌdɑː.lɚ **-s** -z
Europa jʊə'rəʊ.pə, jɔː'- ⓤⓢ jʊ'roʊ-
Europe 'jʊə.rəp, 'jɔː- ⓤⓢ 'jʊr.əp
European ˌjʊə.rə'piː.ən, ˌjɔː- ⓤⓢ ˌjʊr.ə'- **-s** -z *stress shift:* ˌEuropean Com'munity; ˌEuropean Eco'nomic Com'munity; ˌEuropean 'Monetary System
europeaniz|e, -is|e ˌjʊə.rə'piː.ə.naɪz, ˌjɔː- ⓤⓢ ˌjʊr.ə'- **-es** -ɪz **-ing** -ɪŋ **-ed** -d
europium jʊə'rəʊ.pi.əm, jɔː'- ⓤⓢ jʊ'roʊ-
Eurosceptic 'jʊə.rəʊˌskep.tɪk, 'jɔː- ⓤⓢ 'jʊr.oʊ-, '-ə- **-s** -s
Eurostar® 'jʊə.rəʊ.stɑːʳ, 'jɔː- ⓤⓢ 'jʊr.oʊ.stɑːr, -ə-
Eurotunnel® 'jʊə.rəʊˌtʌn.ᵊl, 'jɔː- ⓤⓢ 'jʊr.oʊ-, '-ə-
Eurovision® 'jʊə.rəʊ.vɪ.ʒᵊn, 'jɔː- ⓤⓢ 'jʊr.ə-, -oʊ- ˌ**Eurovision 'Song ˌContest**
eurozone 'jʊə.rəʊ.zəʊn, 'jɔː- ⓤⓢ 'jʊr.oʊ.zoʊn, -ə- **-s** -z
Eurus 'jʊə.rəs, 'jɔː- ⓤⓢ 'jʊr.əs
Eurydice jʊə'rɪd.ɪ.si, jɔː'-, '-ə- ⓤⓢ jʊ-
eurythm|ic jʊə'rɪð.m|ɪk, jɔː'-, -'rɪθ- ⓤⓢ jʊ'rɪð- **-ics** -ɪks **-y** -i
Eusden 'juːz.dən
Eusebius juː'siː.bi.əs
Eustace 'juː.stəs, -stɪs
eustachian juː'steɪ.ʃᵊn, -ʃi.ən, -ki.ən euˌ**stachian 'tube** ⓤⓢ **eu'stachian ˌtube**
Eustachius juː'steɪ.ki.əs
Eustacia juː'steɪ.si.ə, -ʃə
Euston 'juː.stᵊn
Euterpe juː'tɜː.pi ⓤⓢ -'tɝː-
euthanasia ˌjuː.θə'neɪ.zi.ə, '-ʒə ⓤⓢ '-ʒə, '-zi.ə
Eutropius juː'trəʊ.pi.əs ⓤⓢ -'troʊ-
Euxine 'juːk.saɪn
Euxton 'ek.stən
Eva 'iː.və ⓤⓢ 'iː.və, 'eɪ-
evacu|ate ɪ'væk.ju|.eɪt **-ates** -eɪts **-ating** -eɪ.tɪŋ ⓤⓢ -eɪ.t̬ɪŋ **-ated** -eɪ.tɪd ⓤⓢ -eɪ.t̬ɪd **-ator/s** -eɪ.təʳ/z ⓤⓢ -eɪ.t̬ɚ/z
evacuation ɪˌvæk.ju'eɪ.ʃᵊn **-s** -z
evacuee ɪˌvæk.ju'iː **-s** -z
evad|e ɪ'veɪd **-es** -z **-ing** -ɪŋ **-ed** -ɪd **-er/s** -əʳ/z ⓤⓢ -ɚ/z
Evadne ɪ'væd.ni
evalu|ate ɪ'væl.ju|.eɪt **-ates** -eɪts **-ating** -eɪ.tɪŋ ⓤⓢ -eɪ.t̬ɪŋ **-ated** -eɪ.tɪd ⓤⓢ -eɪ.t̬ɪd
evaluation ɪˌvæl.ju'eɪ.ʃᵊn **-s** -z
evaluative ɪ'væl.ju.ə.tɪv ⓤⓢ -eɪ.t̬ɪv **-ly** -li
Evan 'ev.ᵊn
Evander ɪ'væn.dəʳ ⓤⓢ -dɚ
evanesc|e ˌiː.və'nes, ˌev.ə'- ⓤⓢ ˌev.ə'- **-es** -ɪz **-ing** -ɪŋ **-ed** -t
evanescen|ce ˌiː.və'nes.ᵊn|*t*s, ˌev.ə'- ⓤⓢ ˌev.ə'- **-t/ly** -t/li
evangel ɪ'væn.dʒəl, -dʒel **-s** -z
evangelic ˌiː.væn'dʒel.ɪk, ˌev.æn'-, -ən'- **-s** -s
evangelic|al ˌiː.væn'dʒel.ɪ.k|ᵊl, ˌev.æn'-, -ən'- **-als** -ᵊlz **-ally** -li **-alism** -ᵊl.ɪ.zᵊm
Evangeline ɪ'væn.dʒɪ.liːn, -dʒᵊl.iːn, -aɪn ⓤⓢ -dʒə.lɪn, -dʒɪ-, -liːn, -laɪn
evangel|ism ɪ'væn.dʒə.l|ɪ.zᵊm, -dʒɪ- **-ist/s** -ɪst/s
evangelistic ɪˌvæn.dʒə'lɪs.tɪk, -dʒɪ'-
evangelization, -isa- ɪˌvæn.dʒᵊl.aɪ'zeɪ.ʃᵊn, -dʒɪ.laɪ'-, -lɪ'- ⓤⓢ -dʒᵊl.ɪ'-
evangeliz|e, -is|e ɪ'væn.dʒᵊl.aɪz, -dʒɪ- ⓤⓢ -dʒə.laɪz, -dʒɪ- **-es** -ɪz **-ing** -ɪŋ **-ed** -d
Evans 'ev.ᵊnz
Evanson 'ev.ᵊn.sᵊn
Evanston 'ev.ᵊn.stən
Evansville 'ev.ᵊnz.vɪl
evaporable ɪ'væp.ᵊr.ə.bl̩
evapor|ate ɪ'væp.ᵊr|.eɪt ⓤⓢ -ə.r|eɪt **-ates** -eɪts **-ating** -eɪ.tɪŋ ⓤⓢ -eɪ.t̬ɪŋ **-ated** -eɪ.tɪd ⓤⓢ -eɪ.t̬ɪd **-ator/s** -eɪ.təʳ/z ⓤⓢ -eɪ.t̬ɚ/z **eˌvaporated 'milk**
evaporation ɪˌvæp.ə'reɪ.ʃᵊn **-s** -z
evasion ɪ'veɪ.ʒᵊn **-s** -z
evasive ɪ'veɪ.sɪv **-ly** -li **-ness** -nəs, -nɪs
eve (E) iːv **-s** -z
Evele(i)gh 'iːv.li
Evelina ˌev.ɪ'liː.nə, -ə'-
Eveline 'iːv.lɪn, 'ev.lɪn, 'ev.ɪ.liːn
Evelyn 'iːv.lɪn, 'ev.lɪn, 'ev.ə- ⓤⓢ 'ev.ə-, 'ev.lɪn, 'iːv-

Note: The pronunciation /'iːv.lɪn/ is used in the US only for British people of that name.

even 'iː.vᵊn **-ly** -li **-ness** -nəs, -nɪs **-s** -z **-ing** -ɪŋ **-ed** -d
Evenden 'ev.ᵊn.dən
evenhanded ˌiː.vᵊn'hæn.dɪd **-ly** -li **-ness** -nəs, -nɪs *stress shift:* ˌevenhanded ad'ministrator
evening *(n.)* 'iːv.nɪŋ **-s** -z **'evening ˌdress, ˌevening 'dress; 'evening ˌgown; ˌevening 'primrose; ˌevening 'primrose ˌoil**
Evens 'ev.ᵊnz
evensong 'iː.vᵊn.sɒŋ ⓤⓢ -sɑːŋ, -sɔːŋ **-s** -z
even-steven ˌiː.vᵊn'stiː.vᵊn **-s** -z
e|vent ɪ|'vent **-vents** -'vents **-venting** -'ven.tɪŋ ⓤⓢ -'ven.t̬ɪŋ **-vented** -'ven.tɪd ⓤⓢ -'ven.t̬ɪd **-venter/s** -'ven.təʳ/z ⓤⓢ -'ven.t̬ɚ/z
eventful ɪ'vent.fᵊl, -fʊl **-ly** -i
eventide 'iː.vᵊn.taɪd **-s** -z
eventive ɪ'ven.tɪv ⓤⓢ -t̬ɪv
eventual ɪ'ven.tʃu.əl, -tju-, -tʃʊl, -tjʊl ⓤⓢ -tʃu.əl **-ly** -i
eventualit|y ɪˌven.tʃu'æl.ə.t|i, -tju'-, -ɪ.t|i ⓤⓢ -tʃu'æl.ə.t̬|i **-ies** -iz
eventu|ate ɪ'ven.tʃu|.eɪt, -tju- ⓤⓢ -tʃu- **-ates** -eɪts **-ating** -eɪ.tɪŋ ⓤⓢ -eɪ.t̬ɪŋ **-ated** -eɪ.tɪd ⓤⓢ -eɪ.t̬ɪd
ever 'ev.əʳ ⓤⓢ -ɚ
Everard 'ev.ᵊr.ɑːd ⓤⓢ -ə.rɑːrd
Everest 'ev.ᵊr.est ⓤⓢ -ə.rest, -ɚ.ɪst, '-rɪst
Everett 'ev.ᵊr.et ⓤⓢ -ə.ret, 'ev.rɪt
Everglades 'ev.ə.gleɪdz ⓤⓢ '-ɚ-
evergreen 'ev.ə.griːn ⓤⓢ '-ɚ- **-s** -z
Everitt 'ev.ᵊr.ɪt
everlasting ˌev.ə'lɑː.stɪŋ ⓤⓢ -ɚ'læs.tɪŋ **-ly** -li **-ness** -nəs, -nɪs
Everl(e)y 'ev.ə.li ⓤⓢ '-ɚ-
evermore ˌev.ə'mɔːʳ ⓤⓢ -ɚ'mɔːr
EverReady® 'ev.əˌred.i ⓤⓢ -ɚˌ-
Evers 'ev.əz ⓤⓢ -ɚz
Evershed 'ev.ə.ʃed ⓤⓢ '-ɚ-
eversion ɪ'vɜː.ʃᵊn, iː- ⓤⓢ -'vɝː.ʒᵊn, -ʃᵊn
Eversley 'ev.əz.li ⓤⓢ -ɚz-
e|vert ɪ|'vɜːt, iː- ⓤⓢ -'vɝːt **-verts** -'vɜːts ⓤⓢ -'vɝːts **-verting** -'vɜː.tɪŋ ⓤⓢ -'vɝː.t̬ɪŋ **-verted** -'vɜː.tɪd ⓤⓢ -'vɝː.t̬ɪd
Evert 'ev.ət ⓤⓢ -ɚt
Everton 'ev.ə.tᵊn ⓤⓢ '-ɚ-
every 'ev.ri ˌ**every ˌwhich 'way** ⓤⓢ ˌ**every 'which ˌway** ⓤⓢ **'every ˌwhich ˌway**

Note: The meaning is slightly different in American English depending on the stress pattern. ˌ**Every which way** means "akimbo". '**Every which ˌway** means "in all possible ways.".

everybody 'ev.riˌbɒd.i ⓤⓢ -ˌbɑː.di
everyday 'ev.ri.deɪ, ˌ--'-
Everyman 'ev.ri.mæn
everyone 'ev.ri.wʌn
everyplace 'ev.ri.pleɪs
everything 'ev.ri.θɪŋ

everywhere ˈev.ri.*h*weəʳ (US) -*h*wer
Evesham ˈiːv.ʃᵊm *locally also:* ˈiː.vɪ-
Evett ˈev.ɪt
Evian® ˈev.i.ɒ̃ŋ (US) ˌev.iˈɑːn, ˈev.i.ən
evict ɪˈvɪkt **-s** -s **-ing** -ɪŋ **-ed** -ɪd
eviction ɪˈvɪk.ʃᵊn **-s** -z
evidenc|e ˈev.ɪ.dᵊn*t*s, ˈ-ə- **-es** -ɪz **-ing** -ɪŋ **-ed** -t
evident ˈev.ɪ.dᵊnt, ˈ-ə- **-ly** -li
evidential ˌev.ɪˈden.*t*ʃᵊl, -əˈ- (US) -ʃᵊl **-ly** -i
evidentiary ˌev.ɪˈden.*t*ʃᵊr.i, -əˈ- (US) -ˈden*t*.ʃɚ.i
evil ˈiː.vᵊl, -vɪl (US) -vᵊl **-s** -z **-ly** -i ˌ**evil** ˈ**eye** (US) ˈ**evil** ˌ**eye**
evildoer ˈiː.vᵊlˌduː.əʳ, -vɪlˌ-, ˌiː.vᵊlˈduː-, -vɪlˈ- (US) ˈiː.vᵊlˌduː.ɚ, ˌiː.vᵊlˈduː- **-s** -z
evil-minded ˌiː.vᵊlˈmaɪn.dɪd, -vɪlˈ-, ˈiː.vᵊlˌmaɪn-, -vɪlˌ- (US) ˌiː.vᵊlˈmaɪn-, ˈiː.vᵊlˌmaɪn- **-ness** -nəs, -nɪs
evinc|e ɪˈvɪn*t*s **-es** -ɪz **-ing** -ɪŋ **-ed** -t **-ive** -ɪv
evincib|le ɪˈvɪn*t*.sə.bl̩, -sɪ- **-ly** -li
evi|rate ˈiː.vɪ|.reɪt, ˈev.ɪ- **-rates** -reɪts **-rating** -reɪ.tɪŋ (US) -reɪ.t̬ɪŋ **-rated** -reɪ.tɪd (US) -reɪ.t̬ɪd
evisce|rate ɪˈvɪs.ə|.reɪt, iː- **-rates** -reɪts **-rating** -reɪ.tɪŋ (US) -reɪ.t̬ɪŋ **-rated** -reɪ.tɪd (US) -reɪ.t̬ɪd
evisceration ɪˌvɪs.əˈreɪ.ʃᵊn, iːˌvɪs-
Evita evˈiː.tə, ɪˈviː- (US) -tə, -t̬ə
evo|cate ˈev.əʊ|.keɪt, ˈiː.vəʊ- (US) ˈev.ə-, ˈiː.voʊ- **-cates** -keɪts **-cating** -keɪ.tɪŋ (US) -keɪ.t̬ɪŋ **-cated** -keɪ.tɪd (US) -keɪ.t̬ɪd
evocation ˌev.əʊˈkeɪ.ʃᵊn, ˌiː.vəʊˈ- (US) ˌev.əˈ-, ˌiː.voʊˈ- **-s** -z
evocative ɪˈvɒk.ə.tɪv (US) -ˈvɑː.kə.t̬ɪv **-ly** -li
evok|e ɪˈvəʊk (US) -ˈvoʊk **-es** -s **-ing** -ɪŋ **-ed** -t
evolute ˌiː.vəˈluːt, ˌev.əˈ-, -ˈljuːt (US) ˌev.əˈluːt, ˌiː.vəˈ- **-s** -s
evolution ˌiː.vəˈluː.ʃᵊn, ˌev.əˈ-, -ˈljuː- (US) ˌev.əˈluː.ʃᵊn, ˌiː.vəˈ- **-s** -z
evolutional ˌiː.vəˈluː.ʃᵊn.ᵊl, ˌev.əˈ-, -ˈljuː- (US) ˌev.əˈluː-, ˌiː.vəˈ-
evolutionary ˌiː.vəˈluː.ʃᵊn.ᵊr.i, ˌev.əˈ-, -ˈljuː-, -ri (US) ˌev.əˈluː.ʃᵊn.er-, ˌiː.vəˈ-
evolution|ism ˌiː.vəˈluː.ʃᵊn|.ɪ.zᵊm, ˌev.əˈ-, -ˈljuː- (US) ˌev.əˈluː-, ˌiː.vəˈ- **-ist/s** -ɪst/s
evolutive ɪˈvɒl.jə.tɪv, iː-, -jʊ- (US) ˌev.əˈluː.t̬ɪv, ˌiː.vəˈ-; iːˈvɑːl.jə-
evolv|e ɪˈvɒlv (US) -ˈvɑːlv **-es** -z **-ing** -ɪŋ **-ed** -d **-able** -ə.bl̩
Évora ˈev.ə.rə (US) evˈʊr.ə
Evo-stik® ˈiː.vəʊ.stɪk (US) -voʊ-
evulsion ɪˈvʌl.ʃᵊn, iː- **-s** -z
Ewan ˈjuː.ən
Ewart ˈjuː.ət, jʊət (US) ˈjuː.ɚt
Ewbank ˈjuː.bæŋk
ewe juː **-s** -z
Ewell ˈjuː.əl, jʊəl (US) ˈjuː.əl
Ewen ˈjuː.ən, -ɪn; jʊən (US) ˈjuː.ən
ewer ˈjuː.əʳ, jʊəʳ (US) ˈjuː.ɚ **-s** -z
Ewing ˈjuː.ɪŋ
ex- eks-, ɪks-, egz-, ɪgz-
Note: Prefix. Takes either primary or secondary stress, e.g. **excellent** /ˈek.sᵊl.ᵊnt/, **excitation** /ˌek.sɪˈteɪ.ʃᵊn (US) -saɪˈ-/ or may be unstressed, e.g. **excel** /ɪkˈsel/.
ex eks
exacer|bate ɪgˈzæs.ə|.beɪt, eg-; ɪkˈsæs-, ek- (US) ɪgˈzæs.ɚ-, egˈ- **-bates** -beɪts **-bating** -beɪ.tɪŋ (US) -beɪ.t̬ɪŋ **-bated** -beɪ.tɪd (US) -beɪ.t̬ɪd
exacerbation ɪgˌzæs.əˈbeɪ.ʃᵊn, egˌ-; ɪkˌsæs-, ekˌ- (US) ɪgˌzæs.ɚˈ-, egˈ- **-s** -z
exact ɪgˈzækt, egˈ-; ɪkˈsækt, ekˈ- (US) ɪgˈzækt, egˈ- **-ly** -li, -ˈzæk.li, -ˈsæk- (US) -ˈzæk- **-ness** -nəs, -nɪs **-s** -s **-ing/ly** -ɪŋ/li **-ed** -ɪd **-er/s** -əʳ/z (US) -ɚ/z **-or/s** -əʳ/z (US) -ɚ/z
exaction ɪgˈzæk.ʃᵊn, egˈ-; ɪkˈsæk-, ekˈ- (US) ɪgˈzæk-, egˈ- **-s** -z
exactitude ɪgˈzæk.tɪ.tjuːd, egˈ-, -tə-; ɪkˈsæk-, ekˈ- (US) ɪgˈzæk.tə.tuːd, egˈ-, -tjuːd
exactly ɪgˈzækt.li, egˈ-; ɪkˈsækt-, ekˈ- (US) ɪgˈzækt-, egˈ-
exagger|ate ɪgˈzædʒ.ᵊr|.eɪt, egˈ-; ɪkˈsædʒ-, ekˈ- (US) ɪgˈzædʒ.ə.r|eɪt, egˈ- **-ates** -eɪts **-ating** -eɪ.tɪŋ (US) -eɪ.t̬ɪŋ **-ated/ly** -eɪ.tɪd/li (US) -eɪ.t̬ɪd/li **-ator/s** -eɪ.təʳ/z (US) -eɪ.t̬ɚ/z
exaggeration ɪgˌzædʒ.ᵊrˈeɪ.ʃᵊn, egˌ-; ɪkˌsædʒ-, ekˌ- (US) ɪgˌzædʒ-, egˌ- **-s** (US) -z
exaggerative ɪgˈzædʒ.ᵊr.ə.tɪv, egˈ-; ɪkˈsædʒ-, ekˈ- (US) ɪgˈzædʒ.ɚ.ə.t̬ɪv, egˈ-
exal|t ɪgˈzɔːl|t, egˈ-, -ˈzɒl|t; ɪkˈsɔːl|t, ekˈ-, -ˈsɒl|t (US) ɪgˈzɔːl|t, eg-, -ˈzɑːl|t **-ts** -ts **-ting** -tɪŋ (US) -t̬ɪŋ **-ted/ly** -tɪd/li (US) -t̬ɪd/li **-tedness** -tɪd.nəs (US) -t̬ɪd.nəs, -nɪs
exaltation ˌeg.zɔːlˈteɪ.ʃᵊn, ˌek.sɔːlˈ-, -sɒlˈ- (US) ˌeg.zɔːlˈ-, -zɑːlˈ-; ˌek.sɔːlˈ-, -sɑːlˈ- **-s** -z
exam ɪgˈzæm, egˈ-; ɪkˈsæm, ekˈ- (US) ɪgˈzæm, egˈ- **-s** -z
examen egˈzeɪ.men, ɪgˈ- **-s** -z
examination ɪgˌzæm.ɪˈneɪ.ʃᵊn, egˌ-; ɪkˌsæm-, ekˌ-, -əˈ- (US) ɪgˌzæm-, egˌ- **-s** -z **exˌamiˈnation** ˌ**paper**
examin|e ɪgˈzæm.ɪn, egˈ-; ɪkˈsæm-, ekˈ- (US) ɪgˈzæm-, egˈ- **-es** -z **-ing** -ɪŋ **-ed** -d **-er/s** -əʳ/z (US) -ɚ/z
examinee ɪgˌzæm.ɪˈniː, egˌ-; ɪkˌsæm-, ekˌ-, -əˈ- (US) ɪgˌzæm-, egˌ- **-s** -z
exampl|e ɪgˈzɑːm.pl̩, egˈ-; ɪkˈsɑːm-, ekˈ- (US) ɪgˈzæm-, egˈ- **-es** -z **-ing** -ɪŋ, ˈ-plɪŋ **-ed** -d
exarch ˈek.sɑːk (US) -sɑːrk **-s** -s **-ate/s** -eɪt/s
exasper|ate ɪgˈzæs.pᵊr|.eɪt, egˈ-; ɪkˈsæs-, ekˈ-, -ˈzɑː.spᵊr- (US) ɪgˈzæs.pə.r|eɪt, egˈ- **-ates** -eɪts **-ating/ly** -eɪ.tɪŋ/li (US) -eɪ.t̬ɪŋ/li **-ated/ly** -eɪ.tɪd/li (US) -eɪ.t̬ɪd/li
exasperation ɪgˌzæs.pəˈreɪ.ʃᵊn, egˌ-; ɪkˌsæs-, ekˌ-, -ˌzɑː.spəˈ- (US) ɪgˈzæs.pəˈ-, eg-
Excalibur ekˈskæl.ɪ.bəʳ, ɪkˈ-, ˈ-ə- (US) -bɚ
ex cathedra ˌeks.kəˈθiː.drə, -ˈθed.rə, -rɑː (US) -kəˈθiː.drə; -ˈkæθ.ɪ-
exca|vate ˈek.skə|.veɪt **-vates** -veɪts **-vating** -veɪ.tɪŋ (US) -veɪ.t̬ɪŋ **-vated** -veɪ.tɪd (US) -veɪ.t̬ɪd **-vator/s** -veɪ.təʳ/z (US) -veɪ.t̬ɚ/z
excavation ˌeks.kəˈveɪ.ʃᵊn **-s** -z
exceed ɪkˈsiːd, ek- **-s** -z **-ing/ly** -ɪŋ/li **-ed** -ɪd
exceeding ɪkˈsiː.dɪŋ, ek- **-ly** -li
excel ɪkˈsel, ek- **-s** -z **-ling** -ɪŋ **-led** -d
excellenc|e ˈek.sᵊl.ᵊn*t*s **-es** -ɪz
excellenc|y (E) ˈek.sᵊl.ᵊn*t*.s|i **-ies** -iz
excellent ˈek.sᵊl.ᵊnt **-ly** -li
excelsior ekˈsel.si.ɔːʳ, ɪk-, -əʳ (US) -ɔːr, -ɚ
except ɪkˈsept, ek- **-s** -s **-ing** -ɪŋ **-ed** -ɪd
exception ɪkˈsep.ʃᵊn, ek- **-s** -z
exceptionab|le ɪkˈsep.ʃᵊn.ə.b|l̩, ek- **-ly** -li **-leness** -l̩.nəs, -nɪs
exceptional ɪkˈsep.ʃᵊn.ᵊl, ek- **-ly** -i
excerpt (*n.*) ˈek.sɜːpt, ˈeg.zɜːpt (US) ˈek.sɝːpt, ˈeg.zɝːpt **-s** -s
excerpt (*v.*) ekˈsɜːpt, ɪkˈ- (US) ekˈsɝːpt, egˈzɝːpt **-s** -s **-ing** -ɪŋ **-ed** -ɪd
excerption ekˈsɜːp.ʃᵊn, ɪk- (US) ekˈsɝːp-, egˈzɝːp- **-s** -z
excess ɪkˈses, ekˈ- **-es** -ɪz **-ing** -ɪŋ **-ed** -t *stress shift:* ˌexcess ˈbaggage
excessive ɪkˈses.ɪv, ekˈ- **-ly** -li **-ness** -nəs, -nɪs
exchang|e ɪksˈtʃeɪndʒ, eksˈ- **-es** -ɪz **-ing** -ɪŋ **-ed** -d **-er/s** -əʳ/z (US) -ɚ/z **-eable** -ə.bl̩ **exˈchange** ˌ**rate**; **Exˈchange** ˌ**Rate** ˌ**Mechanism**
exchangeability ɪksˌtʃeɪn.dʒəˈbɪl.ə.ti, eksˌ-, -ɪ.ti (US) -ə.t̬i
exchangee ˌeks.tʃeɪnˈdʒiː; ɪksˌtʃeɪnˈ- **-s** -z
exchequer (E) ɪksˈtʃek.əʳ, eksˈ- (US) -ɚ **-s** -z ˌ**Chancellor of the Exˈchequer**
excisable ekˈsaɪ.zə.bl̩, ɪkˈ- (US) ekˈsaɪ-, ˈek.saɪ-

excise (*n.*) *tax:* ˈek.saɪz; ekˈsaɪz, ɪkˈ- US ˈek.saɪz, -saɪs **-man** -mæn **-men** -men
excis|e (*v.*) *cut out:* ekˈsaɪz, ɪk- **-es** -ɪz **-ing** -ɪŋ **-ed** -d
excision ekˈsɪʒ.ᵊn, ɪkˈ- **-s** -z
excitability ɪkˌsaɪ.təˈbɪl.ə.ti, ekˌ-, -ɪ.ti US -ə.t̬i
excitab|le ɪkˈsaɪ.tə.bl̩, ekˈ- US -t̬ə- **-ly** -li **-leness** -l̩.nəs, -nɪs
excitant ˈek.sɪ.tᵊnt; ɪkˈsaɪ-, ekˈ- US ɪkˈsaɪ.tᵊnt **-s** -s
excitation ˌek.sɪˈteɪ.ʃᵊn, -səˈ-, -saɪˈ- US ˌek.saɪˈ- **-s** -z
excita|tive ekˈsaɪ.tə|.tɪv, ɪkˈ- US -t̬ə|.t̬ɪv **-tory** -tᵊr.i, -tri US -tɔːr.i
ex|cite ɪk|ˈsaɪt, ek|ˈ- **-cites** -ˈsaɪts **-citing/ly** -ˈsaɪ.tɪŋ/li US -ˈsaɪ.t̬ɪŋ/li **-cited** -ˈsaɪ.tɪd US -ˈsaɪ.t̬ɪd **-citer/s** -ˈsaɪ.təʳ/z US -ˈsaɪ.t̬ɚ/z
excitement ɪkˈsaɪt.mənt, ekˈ- **-s** -s
exclaim ɪksˈkleɪm, eksˈ- **-s** -z **-ing** -ɪŋ **-ed** -d
exclamation ˌeks.kləˈmeɪ.ʃᵊn **-s** -z **excla'mation ˌmark; excla'mation ˌpoint**
exclamatory eksˈklæm.ə.tᵊr.i, ɪksˈ-, -tri US -tɔːr.i
exclave ˈeks.kleɪv **-s** -z
exclud|e ɪksˈkluːd, eksˈ- **-es** -z **-ing** -ɪŋ **-ed** -ɪd
exclusion ɪksˈkluː.ʒᵊn, eksˈ- **-s** -z
exclusionary ɪksˈkluː.ʒᵊn.ᵊr.i, eksˈ- US -er-
exclusionist ɪksˈkluː.ʒᵊn.ɪst, eksˈ- **-s** -s
exclusive ɪksˈkluː.sɪv, eksˈ- **-ly** -li **-ness** -nəs, -nɪs
exclusiv|ism ɪksˈkluː.sɪ.v|ɪ.zᵊm, eksˈ-, -sə- **-ist/s** -ɪst/s
exclusivistic ɪksˌkluː.sɪˈvɪs.tɪk, eksˈ-, -səˈ-
exclusivity ˌeks.kluːˈsɪv.ə.ti, -ɪ.ti US -ə.t̬i
excogi|tate ekˈskɒdʒ.ɪ|.teɪt, ɪkˈ- US -ˈskɑː.dʒɪ- **-tates** -teɪts **-tating** -teɪ.tɪŋ US -teɪ.t̬ɪŋ **-tated** -teɪ.tɪd US -teɪ.t̬ɪd
excogitation ˌek.skɒdʒ.ɪˈteɪ.ʃᵊn; ɪkˌskɒdʒ.ɪˈ-, ekˌ- US ɪkˌskɑː.dʒɪˈ-, ekˌ- **-s** -z
excommuni|cate ˌek.skəˈmjuː.nɪ|.keɪt, -nə- **-cates** -keɪts **-cating** -keɪ.tɪŋ US -keɪ.t̬ɪŋ **-cated** -keɪ.tɪd US -keɪ.t̬ɪd
excommunication ˌek.skəˌmjuː.nɪˈkeɪ.ʃᵊn, -nəˈ- **-s** -z
excori|ate ekˈskɔː.ri|.eɪt, ɪkˈ-, -ˈskɒr.i- US -ˈskɔːr.i- **-ates** -eɪts **-ating** -eɪ.tɪŋ US -eɪ.t̬ɪŋ **-ated** -eɪ.tɪd US -eɪ.t̬ɪd
excoriation ekˌskɔː.riˈeɪ.ʃᵊn, ɪkˌ-, -ˌskɒr.iˈ- US -ˌskɔːr.iˈ- **-s** -z
excrement ˈek.skrə.mənt, -skrɪ- **-s** -s
excremental ˌek.skrəˈmen.tᵊl, -skrɪˈ- US -t̬ᵊl
excrescen|ce ɪkˈskres.ᵊn|*t*s, ekˈ- **-ces** -*t*.sɪz **-t** -t
excreta ɪkˈskriː.tə, ekˈ- US -t̬ə
ex|crete ɪkˈs|kriːt, ekˈ- **-cretes** -kriːts **-creting** -kriː.tɪŋ US -kriː.t̬ɪŋ **-creted** -kriː.tɪd US -kriː.t̬ɪd **-cretive** -kriː.tɪv US -kriː.t̬ɪv **-cretory** -kriː.tᵊr.i US -kriː.t̬ɚ.i
excretion ɪkˈskriː.ʃᵊn, ekˈ- **-s** -z
excret|um ɪkˈskriː.t|əm, ekˈ- US -t̬|əm **-a** -ə
excruci|ate ɪkˈskruː.ʃi|.eɪt, ekˈ-, -si- US -ʃi- **-ates** -eɪts **-ating/ly** -eɪ.tɪŋ/li US -eɪ.t̬ɪŋ/li **-ated** -eɪ.tɪd US -eɪ.t̬ɪd
excruciation ɪkˌskruː.ʃiˈeɪ.ʃᵊn, ekˌ-, -siˈ- US -ʃiˈ-
excul|pate ˈek.skʌl|.peɪt; ɪkˈskʌl-, ekˈ- **-pates** -peɪts **-pating** -peɪ.tɪŋ US -peɪ.t̬ɪŋ **-pated** -peɪ.tɪd US -peɪ.t̬ɪd
exculpation ˌek.skʌlˈpeɪ.ʃᵊn
exculpatory ekˈskʌl.pə.tᵊr.i, -tri US -tɔːr.i
excurs|e ɪkˈskɜːs, ekˈ- US -ˈskɝːs **-es** -ɪz **-ing** -ɪŋ **-ed** -t
excursion ɪkˈskɜː.ʃᵊn, ekˈ-, -ʒᵊn US -ˈskɝː.ʒᵊn **-s** -z
excursionist ɪkˈskɜː.ʃᵊn.ɪst, ekˈ-, -ʒᵊn- US -ˈskɝː.ʒᵊn- **-s** -s
excursioniz|e, -is|e ɪkˈskɜː.ʃᵊn.aɪz, ekˈ-, -ʒᵊn- US -ˈskɝː.ʒᵊn- **-es** -ɪz **-ing** -ɪŋ **-ed** -d
excursive ɪkˈskɜː.sɪv, ekˈ- US -ˈskɝː- **-ly** -li **-ness** -nəs, -nɪs
excursus ekˈskɜː.səs, ɪkˈ- US -ˈskɝː- **-es** -ɪz
excusab|le ɪkˈskjuː.zə.bl̩, ekˈ- **-ly** -li **-leness** -l̩.nəs, -nɪs
excusatory ɪkˈskjuː.zə.tᵊr.i, ekˈ-, -tri US -tɔːr.i
excus|e (*n.*) ɪkˈskjuːs, ekˈ- **-es** -ɪz
excus|e (*v.*) ɪkˈskjuːz, ekˈ- **-es** -ɪz **-ing** -ɪŋ **-ed** -d
ex delicto ˌeks.delˈɪk.təʊ US -diːˈlɪk.toʊ, -dɪˈ-
ex-directory ˌeks.dəˈrek.tᵊr.i, -dɪˈ-, -daɪˈ-, ˈ-tri
Exe eks
exeat ˈek.si.æt, -seɪ- **-s** -s
exec ɪgˈzek, eg-, ɪkˈsek, ek- US ɪgˈzek, əg- **-s** -s
execrab|le ˈek.sɪ.krə.bl̩, -sə- **-ly** -li **-leness** -l̩.nəs, -nɪs
exe|crate ˈek.sɪ|.kreɪt, -sə- **-crates** -kreɪts **-crating** -kreɪ.tɪŋ US -kreɪ.t̬ɪŋ **-crated** -kreɪ.tɪd US -kreɪ.t̬ɪd
execration ˌek.sɪˈkreɪ.ʃᵊn, -səˈ- **-s** -z
execra|tive ˈek.sɪ.kreɪ|.tɪv, -sə- US -t̬ɪv **-tively** -tɪv.li US -t̬ɪv.li **-tory** -tᵊr.i, -tri US -tɔːr.i
executant ɪgˈzek.jə.tənt, eg-, -jʊ-; ɪkˈsek-, ek- US ɪgˈzek.jə-, eg- **-s** -s
exe|cute ˈek.sɪ|.kjuːt, -sə- **-cutes** -kjuːts **-cuting** -kjuː.tɪŋ US -kjuː.t̬ɪŋ **-cuted** -kjuː.tɪd US -kjuː.t̬ɪd **-cuter/s** -kjuː.təʳ/z US -kjuː.t̬ɚ/z **-cutable** -kjuː.tə.bl̩ US -kjuː.t̬ə.bl̩
execution ˌek.sɪˈkjuː.ʃᵊn, -səˈ- **-s** -z
executioner ˌek.sɪˈkjuː.ʃᵊn.əʳ, -səˈ- US -ɚ **-s** -z
executive ɪgˈzek.jə.tɪv, eg-, -jʊ-; ɪkˈsek-, ek- US ɪgˈzek.jə.t̬ɪv, eg- **-s** US -z **-ly** US -li **exˌecutive 'privilege**
executor ɪgˈzek.jə.təʳ, eg-, -jʊ-; ɪkˈsek-, ek- US ɪgˈzek.jə.t̬ɚ, eg- **-s** -z **-ship/s** -ʃɪp/s
executory ɪgˈzek.jə.tᵊr.i, eg-, -jʊ-, -tri, ɪkˈsek-, ek- US ɪgˈzek.jə.tɔːr.i, eg-
executr|ix ɪgˈzek.jə.tr|ɪks, eg-, -jʊ-; ɪkˈsek-, ek- US ɪgˈzek.jə-, eg- **-ixes** -ɪk.sɪz **executrices** ɪgˌzek.jəˈtraɪ.siːz, eg-, -jʊ-; ɪkˌsek-, ek- US ɪgˌzek.jəˈ-, eg-
exeges|is ˌek.sɪˈdʒiː.s|ɪs, -səˈ- **-es** -iːz
exegetic ˌek.sɪˈdʒet.ɪk, -səˈ-, ˈdʒiː.tɪk US -ˈdʒet̬- **-al** -ᵊl **-ally** -ᵊl.i, -li **-s** -s
exemplar ɪgˈzem.pləʳ, eg-; ɪkˈsem-, ek-, -plɑːʳ US ɪgˈzem.plɚ, eg-, -plɑːr **-s** -z
exemplarity ˌeg.zemˈplær.ə.ti, -ɪ.ti US -ˈpler-, -ˈplær-, -ə.t̬i
exemplar|y ɪgˈzem.plᵊr|.i, eg-; ɪkˈsem-, ek- US ɪgˈzem-, eg- **-ily** -ᵊl.i, -ɪ.li **-iness** -ɪ.nəs, -ɪ.nɪs
exemplification ɪgˌzem.plɪ.fɪˈkeɪ.ʃᵊn, eg-, -plə-; ɪkˌsem-, ek- US ɪgˌzem.plə-, eg- **-s** -z
exempli|fy ɪgˈzem.plɪ|.faɪ, eg-, -plə-; ɪkˈsem-, ek- US ɪgˈzem-, eg- **-fies** -faɪz **-fying** -faɪ.ɪŋ **-fied** -faɪd
exemplum ɪgˈzem.pləm, egˈ-; ɪkˈsem-, ekˈ-
exempt ɪgˈzempt, egˈ-; ɪkˈsempt, ekˈ- US ɪgˈzempt, egˈ- **-s** -s **-ing** -ɪŋ **-ed** -ɪd
exemption ɪgˈzemp.ʃᵊn, egˈ-; ɪkˈsemp-, ekˈ- US ɪgˈzemp-, egˈ **-s** -z
exequatur ˌek.sɪˈkweɪ.təʳ, -səˈ- US -t̬ɚ **-s** -z
exequies ˈek.sɪ.kwɪz, -sə- US -kwiːz
exercis|e ˈek.sə.saɪz US -sɚ- **-es** -ɪz **-ing** -ɪŋ **-ed** -d **-er/s** -əʳ/z US -ɚ/z **'exercise ˌbook**
exercitation egˌzɜː.sɪˈteɪ.ʃᵊn, ɪgˌ- US -ˌzɝː-
exergue ekˈsɜːg, ˈ-- US ˈek.sɝːg, ˈeg.zɝːg **-s** -z
exer|t ɪgˈzɜː|t, eg-; ɪkˈsɜː|t, ek- US ɪgˈzɝː|t, eg- **-ts** -ts **-ting** -tɪŋ

(US) -ţɪŋ **-ted** -tɪd (US) -ţɪd **-tive** -tɪv (US) -ţɪv

exertion ɪɡˈzɜː.ʃᵊn, eɡ-; ɪkˈsɜː-, ek- (US) ɪɡˈzɝː-, eɡ- **-s** -z

Exeter ˈek.sɪ.təʳ, -sə- (US) -ţɚ

exeunt ˈek.si.ʌnt, -seɪ-, -ʊnt, -si.ənt (US) -si.ʌnt, -ənt

exfoli|ate eksˈfəʊ.li|.eɪt (US) -ˈfoʊ- **-ates** -eɪts **-ating** -eɪ.tɪŋ (US) -eɪ.ţɪŋ **-ated** -eɪ.tɪd (US) -eɪ.ţɪd **-ator** -eɪ.təʳ (US) -eɪ.ţɚ/z

exfoliation eksˌfəʊ.liˈeɪ.ʃᵊn, ˌeks.fəʊ- (US) eksˌfoʊ- **-s** -z

ex gratia eksˈɡreɪ.ʃə, -ʃi.ə

exhalant, exhalent eksˈheɪ.lənt, ɪks-; eɡˈzeɪ- (US) eksˈheɪ-

exhalation ˌeks.*h*əˈleɪ.ʃᵊn **-s** -z

exhal|e eksˈheɪl, ɪks-; eɡˈzeɪl (US) eksˈheɪl, ˈ-- **-es** -z **-ing** -ɪŋ **-ed** -d

exhaust ɪɡˈzɔːst, eɡˈ-; ɪkˈsɔːst, ekˈ- (US) ɪɡˈzɑːst, eɡˈ-, -ˈzɔːst **-s** -s **-ing** -ɪŋ **-ed** -ɪd **-er/s** -əʳ/z (US) -ɚ/z **-ible** -ə.bl̩, -ɪ.bl̩ **-less** -ləs, -lɪs **exˈhaust ˌpipe**

exhaustion ɪɡˈzɔːs.tʃᵊn, eɡ-; ɪkˈsɔː-, ek- (US) ɪɡˈzɑː-, eɡ-, -ˈzɔː-

exhaustive ɪɡˈzɔː.stɪv, eɡ-; ɪkˈsɔː-, ek- (US) ɪɡˈzɑː-, eɡ-, -ˈzɔː- **-ly** -li **-ness** -nəs, -nɪs

exhibit (*n.*) ɪɡˈzɪb.ɪt, eɡ-; ɪkˈsɪb-, ek-; ˈeɡ.zɪb-, ˈek.sɪb- (US) ɪɡˈzɪb-, eɡ- **-s** -s

exhib|it (*v.*) ɪɡˈzɪb|.ɪt, eɡ-; ɪkˈsɪb-, ek- (US) ɪɡˈzɪb-, eɡ- **-its** -ɪts **-iting** -ɪ.tɪŋ (US) -ɪ.ţɪŋ **-ited** -ɪ.tɪd (US) -ɪ.ţɪd **-itor/s** -ɪ.təʳ/z (US) -ɪ.ţɚ/z **-itive** -ɪ.tɪv (US) -ɪ.ţɪv **-itory** -ɪ.tᵊr.i, -ɪ.tri (US) -ɪ.tɔːr.i

exhibition ˌek.sɪˈbɪʃ.ᵊn, -səˈ- **-s** -z

exhibitioner ˌek.sɪˈbɪʃ.ᵊn.əʳ, -səˈ- (US) -ɚ **-s** -z

exhibitionism ˌek.sɪˈbɪʃ.ᵊn.ɪ.zᵊm, -səˈ-

exhibitionist ˌek.sɪˈbɪʃ.ᵊn.ɪst, -səˈ- **-s** -s

exhibitionistic ˌek.sɪ.bɪ.ʃᵊnˈɪs.tɪk, -sə- **-ally** -ᵊl.i, -li

exhilarant ɪɡˈzɪl.ᵊr.ᵊnt, eɡ-; ɪkˈsɪl-, ek- (US) ɪɡˈzɪl-, eɡ- **-s** -s

exhilar|ate ɪɡˈzɪl.ᵊr|.eɪt, eɡ-; ɪkˈsɪl-, ek- (US) ɪɡˈzɪl-, eɡ- **-ates** -eɪts **-ating** -eɪ.tɪŋ (US) -eɪ.ţɪŋ **-ated** -eɪ.tɪd (US) -eɪ.ţɪd

exhilaration ɪɡˌzɪl.ᵊrˈeɪ.ʃᵊn, eɡ-; ɪkˌsɪl-, ek- (US) ɪɡˌzɪl-, eɡ-

exhilarative ɪɡˈzɪl.ᵊr.ə.tɪv, eɡ-, -eɪ-; ɪkˈsɪl-, ek- (US) ɪɡˈzɪl.ə.reɪ.ţɪv, eɡ-

exhor|t ɪɡˈzɔː|t, eɡ-; ɪkˈsɔː|t, ek- (US) ɪɡˈzɔːr|t, eɡ- **-ts** -ts **-ting** -tɪŋ (US) -ţɪŋ **-ted** -tɪd (US) -ţɪd

exhortation ˌeɡ.zɔːˈteɪ.ʃᵊn, ˌek.sɔːˈ- (US) ˌeɡ.zɔːrˈ-, -zɚˈ-; ˌek.sɔːrˈ-, -sɚˈ- **-s** -z

exhorta|tive ɪɡˈzɔː.tə|.tɪv, eɡ-; ɪkˈsɔː-, ek- (US) ɪɡˈzɔːr.ţə|.ţɪv, eɡ- **-tory** -tᵊr.i, -tri (US) -tɔːr.i

exhumation ˌeks.*h*juːˈmeɪ.ʃᵊn (US) ˌeks.*h*juːˈ-, ˌeɡ.zjuːˈ- **-s** -z

exhum|e eksˈ*h*juːm, ɪksˈ-; ɪɡˈzjuːm, eɡˈ- (US) eɡˈzuːm, ɪɡˈ-, -ˈzjuːm **-es** -z **-ing** -ɪŋ **-ed** -d **-er/s** -əʳ/z (US) -ɚ/z

exigen|ce ˈek.sɪ.dʒən*t*|s, -sə-; ˈeɡ.zɪ-, -zə- **-ces** -sɪz

exigenc|y ˈek.sɪ.dʒən*t*.s|i, -sə-; ˈeɡ.zɪ-, -zə-; ɪɡˈzɪdʒ.ən*t*-, eɡ-; ɪkˈsɪdʒ-, ek- **-ies** -iz

exigent ˈek.sɪ.dʒənt, -sə-; ˈeɡ.zɪ-, -zə- **-ly** -li

exiguity ˌek.sɪˈɡjuː.ə.ti, -ɪ.ti (US) ˌek.sɪˈɡjuː.ə.ţi, ˌeɡ.zɪˈ-

exiguous eɡˈzɪɡ.ju.əs, ɪɡ-; ekˈsɪɡ-, ɪk- (US) eɡˈzɪɡ-, ɪɡ- **-ness** -nəs, -nɪs

exil|e ˈek.saɪl, ˈeɡ.zaɪl **-es** -z **-ing** -ɪŋ **-ed** -d

exility eɡˈzɪl.ə.ti, ekˈsɪl-, -ɪ.ti (US) -ə.ţi

exist ɪɡˈzɪst, eɡ-; ɪkˈsɪst, ek- (US) ɪɡˈzɪst, eɡ- **-s** -s **-ing** -ɪŋ **-ed** -ɪd

existen|ce ɪɡˈzɪs.tᵊn|*t*s, eɡ-; ɪkˈsɪs-, ek- (US) ɪɡˈzɪs-, eɡ- **-ces** -*t*.sɪz

existent ɪɡˈzɪs.tᵊnt, eɡ-; ɪkˈsɪs-, ek- (US) ɪɡˈzɪs-, eɡ-

existential ˌeɡ.zɪˈsten.*t*ʃᵊl, -zəˈ-; ˌek.sɪˈ-, -səˈ-

existential|ism ˌeɡ.zɪˈsten.*t*ʃᵊl|.ɪ.zᵊm, -zəˈ-; ˌek.sɪˈ-, -səˈ- **-ist/s** -ɪst/s

exit ˈek.sɪt, ˈeɡ.zɪt **-s** -s **ˈexit ˌpoll** **-ing** -ɪŋ **-ed** -ɪd

ex libris ˌeksˈlɪb.riːs, -rɪs, -ˈlaɪ.brɪs (US) -ˈliː.brɪs

Exmoor ˈek.smɔːʳ, -smʊəʳ (US) -smʊr

Exmouth *in Devon:* ˈek.smaʊθ, -sməθ *in Australia:* ˈek.smaʊθ

exo- ek.səʊ-; ɪkˈsɒ-, ek- (US) ek.soʊ-; ɪkˈsɑː-, ek-

Note: Prefix. Either carries primary or secondary stress on the first syllable, e.g. **exocrine** /ˈek.səʊ.kraɪn (US) -sə.krən/, **exocentric** /ˌek.səʊˈsen.trɪk (US) -soʊˈ-/, or primary stress on the second syllable, e.g. **exogamy** /ekˈsɒɡ.ə.mi (US) -ˈsɑː.ɡə-/.

exocentric ˌek.səʊˈsen.trɪk (US) -soʊˈ- **-ally** -ᵊ.li, -li

Exocet® ˈek.səʊ.set (US) -soʊ- **-s** -s

exocrine ˈek.səʊ.kraɪn, -krɪn (US) ˈek.sə.krən, -soʊ-, -kraɪn, -kriːn

exode ˈek.səʊd (US) -soʊd **-s** -z

exodus (E) ˈek.sə.dəs **-es** -ɪz

ex officio ˌeks.əˈfɪʃ.i.əʊ, -ɒfˈɪʃ-, -ˈɪs- (US) -əˈfɪʃ.i.oʊ, -ˈfɪs-

exogam|y ekˈsɒɡ.ə.m|i (US) -ˈsɑː.ɡə- **-ous** -əs

exogenous ɪkˈsɒdʒ.ə.nəs, ek-, -ɪ.nəs (US) -ˈsɑː.dʒə-

exon ˈek.sɒn (US) -sɑːn **-s** -z

exoner|ate ɪɡˈzɒn.ᵊr|.eɪt, eɡ-; ɪkˈsɒn-, ek- (US) ɪɡˈzɑː.nə.r|eɪt, eɡ- **-ates** -eɪts **-ating** -eɪ.tɪŋ (US) -eɪ.ţɪŋ **-ated** -eɪ.tɪd (US) -eɪ.ţɪd

exoneration ɪɡˌzɒn.əˈreɪ.ʃᵊn, eɡ-; ɪkˌsɒn-, ek- (US) ɪɡˌzɑː.nəˈ-, eɡ-

exonerative ɪɡˈzɒn.ᵊr.ə.tɪv, eɡ-, -eɪ-; ɪkˈsɒn-, ek-, -eɪ.tɪv (US) ɪɡˈzɑː.nə.reɪ.ţɪv, eɡ-

exophora ekˈsɒf.ᵊr.ə (US) -ˈsɑː.fɚ-

exophoric ˌek.səʊˈfɒr.ɪk (US) -səˈfɔːr-

exorbitan|ce ɪɡˈzɔː.bɪ.tᵊn*t*|s, eɡ-, -bə-; ɪkˈsɔː-, ek- (US) ɪɡˈzɔːr.bə.ţᵊn*t*|s, eɡ- **-cy** -si

exorbitant ɪɡˈzɔː.bɪ.tᵊnt, eɡ-, -bə-; ɪkˈsɔː-, ek- (US) ɪɡˈzɔːr.bə.ţᵊnt, eɡ- **-ly** -li

exorc|ism ˈek.sɔː.s|ɪ.zᵊm, -sə-; ˈeɡ.zɔː-, -zə- (US) ˈek.sɔːr-, -sɚ- **-ist/s** -ɪst/s

exorciz|e, -is|e ˈek.sɔː.saɪz, -sə-; ˈeɡ.zɔː-, -zə- (US) ˈek.sɔːr-, -sɚ- **-es** -ɪz **-ing** -ɪŋ **-ed** -d

exordi|um ekˈsɔː.di|.əm; eɡˈzɔː- (US) eɡˈzɔːr.di-, ɪɡ-; ekˈsɔːr-, ɪk- **-ums** -əmz **-a** -ə

exoskelet|on ˌek.səʊˈskel.ɪ.t|ᵊn, ˈ-ə-, ˈek.səʊˌskel- (US) ˌek.soʊˈskel.ə- **-ons** -ənz **-al** -ᵊl

exoteric ˌek.səʊˈter.ɪk (US) -səˈ-, -soʊˈ- **-s** -s **-al** -ᵊl **-ally** -ᵊl.i, -li

exotic ɪɡˈzɒt.ɪk, eɡ-; ɪkˈsɒt-, ek- (US) ɪɡˈzɑː.ţɪk, eɡ- **-s** -s **-a** -ə **-ally** -ᵊl.i, -li

exoticism ɪɡˈzɒt.ɪ.sɪ.zᵊm, eɡ-, ˈ-ə-; ɪkˈsɒt-, ek-, ək- (US) ɪɡˈzɑː.ţə-, eɡ-

expand ɪkˈspænd, ek- **-s** -z **-ing** -ɪŋ **-ed** -ɪd **-er/s** -əʳ/z (US) -ɚ/z **-able** -ə.bl̩

expans|e ɪkˈspæn*t*s, ek- **-es** -ɪz

expansibility ɪkˌspæn*t*.səˈbɪl.ə.ti, ek-, -sɪˈ-, -ɪ.ti (US) -ə.ţi

expansib|le ɪkˈspæn*t*.sə.b|l̩, ek-, -sɪ- **-ly** -li **-leness** -l̩.nəs, -nɪs

expansile ɪkˈspæn*t*.saɪl, ek- (US) -sɪl

expansion ɪkˈspæn.*t*ʃᵊn, ek- **-s** -z

expansion|ism ɪkˈspæn.*t*ʃᵊn|.ɪ.zᵊm, ek-, ək- **-ist/s** -ɪst/s

expansive ɪkˈspæn*t*.sɪv, ek- **-ly** -li **-ness** -nəs, -nɪs

ex parte ˌeksˈpɑː.teɪ, -ti (US) -ˈpɑːr.ţi

expat ˌekˈspæt **-s** -s *stress shift:* ˌexpat comˈmunity

expati|ate ekˈspeɪ.ʃi|.eɪt, ɪk- **-ates** -eɪts **-ating** -eɪ.tɪŋ (US) -eɪ.ţɪŋ **-ated** -eɪ.tɪd (US) -eɪ.ţɪd

expatiation ekˌspeɪ.ʃiˈeɪ.ʃᵊn, ɪk- **-s** -z

expatia|tive ekˈspeɪ.ʃi.ə|.tɪv, ɪk-, -tɪv (US) -eɪ|.ţɪv **-tory** -tᵊr.i, -tri (US) -tɔːr.i

expatriate (*n. adj.*) ɪk'spæt.ri.ət, ek'-, -'speɪ.tri-, -ɪt, -eɪt ⓤⓢ ek'speɪ-, ɪk'- **-s** -s
expatri|ate (*v.*) ɪk'spæt.ri|.eɪt, ek'-, -'speɪ.tri- ⓤⓢ ek'speɪ-, ɪk'- **-ates** -eɪts **-ating** -eɪ.tɪŋ ⓤⓢ -eɪ.t̬ɪŋ **-ated** -eɪ.tɪd ⓤⓢ -eɪ.t̬ɪd
expatriation ek,spæt.ri'eɪ.ʃᵊn, ɪk-, -,speɪ.tri'-, ,ek.speɪ-, ,ek.spæt.ri'- ⓤⓢ ek,speɪ.tri'eɪ-, ɪk-
expect ɪk'spekt, ek- **-s** -s **-ing** -ɪŋ **-ed** -ɪd
expectan|cy ɪk'spek.tᵊnt|si, ek- **-ce** -s **-cies** -siz
expectant ɪk'spek.tᵊnt, ek- **-ly** -li
expectation ,ek.spek'teɪ.ʃᵊn **-s** -z
expectorant ɪk'spek.tᵊr.ᵊnt, ek- **-s** -s
expector|ate ɪk'spek.tᵊr|.eɪt, ek- **-ates** -eɪts **-ating** -eɪ.tɪŋ ⓤⓢ -eɪ.t̬ɪŋ **-ated** -eɪ.tɪd ⓤⓢ -eɪ.t̬ɪd
expectoration ɪk,spek.tᵊr'eɪ.ʃᵊn, ek-
Expedia ɪk'spiː.di.ə, ek-
expedien|cy ɪk'spiː.di.ənt|si, ek- **-ce** -s
expedient ɪk'spiː.di.ənt, ek- **-s** -s **-ly** -li
expe|dite 'ek.spɪ|.daɪt, -spə- **-dites** -daɪts **-diting** -daɪ.tɪŋ ⓤⓢ -daɪ.t̬ɪŋ **-dited** -daɪ.tɪd ⓤⓢ -daɪ.t̬ɪd
expediter 'ek.spɪ.daɪ.təʳ, -spə- ⓤⓢ -t̬ɚ **-s** -z
expedition ,ek.spɪ'dɪʃ.ᵊn, -spə'- **-s** -z
expeditionary ,ek.spɪ'dɪʃ.ᵊn.ᵊr.i, -spɪ'-, -ri ⓤⓢ -er-
expeditious ,ek.spɪ'dɪʃ.əs, -spə'- **-ly** -li **-ness** -nəs, -nɪs
expeditor 'ek.spɪ.daɪ.təʳ, -spə- ⓤⓢ -t̬ɚ **-s** -z
expel ɪk'spel, ek- **-s** -z **-ling** -ɪŋ **-led** -d **-lable** -ə.bl̩
expend ɪk'spend, ek- **-s** -z **-ing** -ɪŋ **-ed** -ɪd
expendable ɪk'spen.də.bl̩, ek- **-s** -z
expenditure ɪk'spen.dɪ.tʃəʳ, ek-, -də- ⓤⓢ -tʃɚ **-s** -z
expens|e ɪk'spents, ek- **-es** -ɪz **ex'pense ac,count**
expensive ɪk'spent.sɪv, ek- **-ly** -li **-ness** -nəs, -nɪs
experienc|e ɪk'spɪə.ri.ənts, ek- ⓤⓢ -'spɪr.i- **-es** -ɪz **-ing** -ɪŋ **-ed** -t
experiential ɪk,spɪə.ri'en.tʃᵊl, ek- ⓤⓢ -,spɪr.i'- **-ly** -li
experiment (*n.*) ɪk'sper.ɪ.mənt, ek-, '-ə- **-s** -s
experiment (*v.*) ɪk'sper.ɪ.ment, ek-, '-ə- **-s** -s **-ing** -ɪŋ **-ed** -ɪd **-er/s** -əʳ/z ⓤⓢ -ɚ/z
experimental ɪk,sper.ɪ'men.tᵊl, ek-, -ə'-; ,ek.sper- ⓤⓢ ek,sper-, ɪk- **-ly** -i
experimental|ism ɪk,sper.ɪ'ment.ᵊl|.ɪ.zᵊm, ek-, -ə'-; ,ek.sper-, -ə'men- ⓤⓢ ek,sper-, ɪk- **-ist/s** -ɪst/s
experimentaliz|e, -is|e ɪk,sper.ɪ'men.tᵊl.aɪz, ek-, -ə'-; ,ek.sper- ⓤⓢ ek,sper.ɪ'men.t̬ᵊ.laɪz, ɪk- **-es** -ɪz **-ing** -ɪŋ **-ed** -d
experimentation ɪk,sper.ɪ.men'teɪ.ʃᵊn, ek-, ,-ə- **-s** -z
expert 'ek.spɜːt ⓤⓢ -spɝːt **-s** -s **-ly** -li **-ness** -nəs, -nɪs
expertise ,ek.spɜː'tiːz, -spə'tiːz ⓤⓢ -spɝː'-, -spɚ'-
expiable 'ek.spi.ə.bl̩
expi|ate 'ek.spi|.eɪt **-ates** -eɪts **-ating** -eɪ.tɪŋ ⓤⓢ -eɪ.t̬ɪŋ **-ated** -eɪ.tɪd ⓤⓢ -eɪ.t̬ɪd **-ator/s** -eɪ.təʳ/z ⓤⓢ -eɪ.t̬ɚ/z
expiation ,ek.spi'eɪ.ʃᵊn **-s** -z
expiatory 'ek.spi.ə.tᵊr.i, -eɪ-, -tri; ,ek.spi'eɪ- ⓤⓢ 'ek.spi.ə.tɔːr.i
expiration ,ek.spɪ'reɪ.ʃᵊn, -spə'-, -spaɪə'- ⓤⓢ -spə'- **-s** -z
expiratory ɪk'spɪr.ə.tᵊr.i, ek-, -'spaɪə.rə-, -tri ⓤⓢ -'spaɪ.rə.tɔːr.i
expir|e ɪk'spaɪəʳ, ek'- ⓤⓢ -'spaɪɚ **-es** -z **-ing** -ɪŋ **-ed** -d
expiry ɪk'spaɪə.ri, ek- ⓤⓢ -'spaɪ-; 'ek.spɚ.i **ex'piry ,date**
explain ɪk'spleɪn, ek'- **-s** -z **-ing** -ɪŋ **-ed** -d **-er/s** -əʳ/z ⓤⓢ -ɚ/z **-able** -ə.bl̩
explanation ,ek.splə'neɪ.ʃᵊn **-s** -z
explanator|y ɪk'splæn.ə.tᵊr|.i, ek'-, '-ɪ-, -tr|i ⓤⓢ -ə.tɔːr|.i **-ily** -ᵊl.i, -ɪ.li **-iness** -ɪ.nəs, -ɪ.nɪs
expletive ɪk'spliː.tɪv, ek'- ⓤⓢ 'ek.splə.t̬ɪv **-s** -z
expletory ɪk'spliː.tᵊr.i, ek'-, '-tri ⓤⓢ -t̬ɚ.i
explicab|le ɪk'splɪk.ə.b|l̩, ek-; 'ek.splɪ.kə- **-ly** -li
expli|cate 'ek.splɪ|.keɪt **-cates** -keɪts **-cating** -keɪ.tɪŋ ⓤⓢ -keɪ.t̬ɪŋ **-cated** -keɪ.tɪd ⓤⓢ -keɪ.t̬ɪd
explication ,ek.splɪ'keɪ.ʃᵊn **-s** -z
explicative ek'splɪk.ə.tɪv, ɪk-; 'ek.splɪ.keɪ.tɪv ⓤⓢ -t̬ɪv
explicatory ek'splɪk.ə.tᵊr.i, ɪk-, -tri; 'ek.splɪ.keɪ-, ,ek.splɪ'keɪ- ⓤⓢ 'ek.splɪ.kə.tɔːr.i; ɪk'splɪk.ə-, ek-
explicit ɪk'splɪs.ɪt, ek- **-ly** -li **-ness** -nəs, -nɪs
explod|e ɪk'spləʊd, ek- ⓤⓢ -'sploʊd **-es** -z **-ing** -ɪŋ **-ed** -ɪd **-er/s** -əʳ/z ⓤⓢ -ɚ/z
exploit (*n.*) 'ek.splɔɪt **-s** -s
exploi|t (*v.*) ɪk'splɔɪ|t, ek- **-ts** -ts **-ting** -tɪŋ ⓤⓢ -t̬ɪŋ **-ted** -tɪd ⓤⓢ -t̬ɪd **-ter/s** -təʳ/z ⓤⓢ -t̬ɚ/z
exploitation ,ek.splɔɪ'teɪ.ʃᵊn
exploitative ɪk'splɔɪ.tə.tɪv, ek- ⓤⓢ -t̬ə.t̬ɪv **-ly** -li
exploitive ɪk'splɔɪ.tɪv, ek- ⓤⓢ -t̬ɪv **-ly** -li
exploration ,ek.splə'reɪ.ʃᵊn, -splɔː'- ⓤⓢ -splɔːr- **-s** -z
explorative ɪk'splɒr.ə.tɪv, ek-, -'splɔː.rə- ⓤⓢ -'splɔːr.ə.t̬ɪv
exploratory ɪk'splɒr.ə.tᵊr.i, ek-, -'splɔː.rə-, -tri ⓤⓢ -'splɔːr.ə.tɔːr.i
explor|e ɪk'splɔːʳ, ek- ⓤⓢ -'splɔːr **-es** -z **-ing** -ɪŋ **-ed** -d **-er/s** -əʳ/z ⓤⓢ -ɚ/z
explosion ɪk'spləʊ.ʒᵊn, ek- ⓤⓢ -'sploʊ- **-s** -z
explosive ɪk'spləʊ.sɪv, ek-, -zɪv ⓤⓢ -'sploʊ.sɪv **-s** -z **-ly** -li **-ness** -nəs, -nɪs
expo 'ek.spəʊ ⓤⓢ -spoʊ **-s** -z
exponent ɪk'spəʊ.nənt, ek- ⓤⓢ -'spoʊ- **-s** -s
exponential ,ek.spəʊ'nen.tʃᵊl ⓤⓢ -spoʊ'nent.ʃᵊl **-ly** -li
export (*n.*) 'ek.spɔːt ⓤⓢ -spɔːrt **-s** -s
expor|t (*v.*) ɪk'spɔː|t, ek-; 'ek.spɔː|t ⓤⓢ ɪk'spɔːr|t, ek-; 'ek.spɔːr|t **-ts** -ts **-ting** -tɪŋ ⓤⓢ -t̬ɪŋ **-ted** -tɪd ⓤⓢ -t̬ɪd **-ter/s** -təʳ/z ⓤⓢ -t̬ɚ/z
exportable ɪk'spɔː.tə.bᵊl, ek- ⓤⓢ -'spɔːr.t̬ə-
exportation ,ek.spɔː'teɪ.ʃᵊn ⓤⓢ -spɔːr'-
expos|e ɪk'spəʊz, ek- ⓤⓢ -'spoʊz **-es** -ɪz **-ing** -ɪŋ **-ed** -d **-edness** -d.nəs, -nɪs **-er/s** -əʳ/z ⓤⓢ -ɚ/z
exposé ek'spəʊ.zeɪ, ɪk- ⓤⓢ ,ek.spoʊ'zeɪ, '--- **-s** -z
exposition ,ek.spəʊ'zɪʃ.ᵊn ⓤⓢ -pə'- **-s**
expositive ɪk'spɒz.ɪ.tɪv, ek-, -ə.tɪv ⓤⓢ -'spɑː.zə.t̬ɪv
exposi|tor ɪk'spɒz.ɪ|.təʳ, ek-, -ə|.təʳ ⓤⓢ -'spɑː.zə|.t̬ɚ **-tors** -təz ⓤⓢ -t̬ɚz **-tory** -tᵊr.i, -tri ⓤⓢ -tɔːr.i
ex post facto ,eks.pəʊst'fæk.təʊ ⓤⓢ -poʊst'fæk.toʊ
expostu|late ɪk'spɒs.tʃə|.leɪt, ek-, -tʃʊ-, -tjə-, -tjʊ- ⓤⓢ -'spɑːs.tʃə- **-lates** -leɪts **-lating** -leɪ.tɪŋ ⓤⓢ -leɪ.t̬ɪŋ **-lated** -leɪ.tɪd ⓤⓢ -leɪ.t̬ɪd **-lator/s** -leɪ.təʳ/z ⓤⓢ -leɪ.t̬ɚ/z
expostulation ɪk,spɒs.tʃə'leɪ.ʃᵊn, ek-, -tʃʊ'-, -tjə'-, -tjʊ'- ⓤⓢ -,pɑːs.tʃə'- **-s** -z
expostulative ɪk'spɒs.tʃə.lə.tɪv, ek-, -tʃʊ-, -tjə-, -tjʊ-, -leɪ- ⓤⓢ -'pɑːs.tʃə.leɪ.t̬ɪv
expostulatory ɪk'spɒs.tʃə.lə.tᵊr.i, ek-, -tʃʊ-, -tjə-, -tjʊ-, -leɪ-, -tri ⓤⓢ -'spɑːs.tʃə.lə.tɔːr.i
exposure ɪk'spəʊ.ʒəʳ, ek- ⓤⓢ -'spoʊ.ʒ- **-s** -z
expound ɪk'spaʊnd, ek- **-s** -z **-ing** -ɪŋ **-ed** -ɪd **-er/s** -əʳ/z ⓤⓢ -ɚ/z
express ɪk'spres, ek- **-es** -ɪz **-ly** -li **-ness** -nəs, -nɪs **-ing** -ɪŋ **-ed** -t **,express de'livery, ex,press de'livery** ⓤⓢ **,express de'livery**
expressible ɪk'spres.ə.bl̩, ek-, -sɪ-
expression ɪk'spreʃ.ᵊn, ek- **-s** -z
expressional ɪk'spreʃ.ᵊn.ᵊl, ek-

expression|ism ɪkˈspreʃ.ən|.ɪ.zəm, ek- **-ist/s** -ɪst/s
expressionistic ɪkˌspreʃ.əˈnɪs.tɪk, ek- **-ally** -əl.i, -li
expressionless ɪkˈspreʃ.ən.ləs, ek-, -lɪs **-ly** -li **-ness** -nəs, -nɪs
expressive ɪkˈspres.ɪv, ek- **-ly** -li **-ness** -nəs, -nɪs
expresso ɪkˈspres.əʊ, ek- (US) -oʊ **-s** -z
expressway ɪkˈspres.weɪ, ek- **-s** -z
expropri|ate ɪkˈsprəʊ.pri|.eɪt, ek- (US) -ˈsproʊ- **-ates** -eɪts **-ating** -eɪ.tɪŋ (US) -eɪ.t̬ɪŋ **-ated** -eɪ.tɪd (US) -eɪ.t̬ɪd **-ator/s** -eɪ.təʳ/z (US) -eɪ.t̬ɚ/z
expropriation ɪkˌsprəʊ.priˈeɪ.ʃən, ek-; ˌek.sprəʊ- (US) ɪkˌsproʊ-, ek- **-s** -z
expulsion ɪkˈspʌl.ʃən, ek- **-s** -z
expulsive ɪkˈspʌl.sɪv, ek-
expung|e ɪkˈspʌndʒ, ek- **-es** -ɪz **-ing** -ɪŋ **-ed** -d
expur|gate ˈek.spə|.geɪt, -spɜː- (US) -spɚ- **-gates** -geɪts **-gating** -geɪ.tɪŋ (US) -geɪ.t̬ɪŋ **-gated** -geɪ.tɪd (US) -geɪ.t̬ɪd **-gator/s** -geɪ.təʳ/z (US) -geɪ.t̬ɚ/z
expurgation ˌek.spəˈgeɪ.ʃən, -spɜːˈ- (US) -spɚˈ- **-s** -z
expurgatory ekˈspɜː.gə.tər.i, ɪkˈ-, -tri (US) -ˈspɝː.gə.tɔːr.i
exquisite ɪkˈskwɪz.ɪt, ek-; ˈek.skwɪ.zɪt, -zət **-s** -s **-ly** -li **-ness** -nəs, -nɪs
exscind ekˈsɪnd, ɪk- **-s** -z **-ing** -ɪŋ **-ed** -ɪd
exsect ekˈsekt, ɪk- **-s** -s **-ing** -ɪŋ **-ed** -ɪd
exsection ekˈsek.ʃən, ɪk- **-s** -z
ex-service ˌeksˈsɜː.vɪs (US) ˌeksˈsɝː-
exsic|cate ˈek.sɪ|.keɪt, ˈeks- **-cates** -keɪts **-cating** -keɪ.tɪŋ (US) -keɪ.t̬ɪŋ **-cated** -keɪ.tɪd (US) -keɪ.t̬ɪd **-cator/s** -keɪ.təʳ/z (US) -keɪ.t̬ɚ/z
extant ekˈstænt, ɪk-; ˈek.stənt (US) ˈek.stənt; ˌekˈstænt
extemporaneous ɪkˌstem.pəˈreɪ.ni.əs, ek-; ˌek.stem- (US) ɪkˌstem.pəˈ-, ek- **-ly** -li **-ness** -nəs, -nɪs
extemporary ɪkˈstem.pər.ə.ri, ek- (US) -er.i
extempore ɪkˈstem.pər.i, ek-
extemporization, -isa- ɪkˌstem.pər.aɪˈzeɪ.ʃən, ek-, -ɪˈ- (US) -ɪˈ- **-s** -z
extemporiz|e, -is|e ɪkˈstem.pər.aɪz, ek- (US) -pə.raɪz **-es** -ɪz **-ing** -ɪŋ **-ed** -d **-er/s** -əʳ/z (US) -ɚ/z
extend ɪkˈstend, ek- **-s** -z **-ing** -ɪŋ **-ed** -ɪd **-able** -ə.bl̩ **exˌtended ˈfamily**
extensibility ɪkˌstent.səˈbɪl.ə.ti, ek-, -sɪˈ-, -ɪ.ti (US) -ə.t̬i
extensible ɪkˈstent.sə.bl̩, ek-, -sɪ-
extensile ɪkˈstent.saɪl, ek- (US) -sɪl
extension ɪkˈsten.tʃən, ek- **-s** -z **exˈtension ˌlead**
extensive ɪkˈstent.sɪv, ek- **-ly** -li **-ness** -nəs, -nɪs
extensor ɪkˈstent.səʳ, ek- (US) -sɚ **-s** -z
extent ɪkˈstent, ek- **-s** -s
extenu|ate ɪkˈsten.ju|.eɪt, ek- **-ates** -eɪts **-ating/ly** -eɪ.tɪŋ/li (US) -eɪ.t̬ɪŋ/li **-ated** -eɪ.tɪd (US) -eɪ.t̬ɪd **exˌtenuating ˈcircumstances**
extenuation ɪkˌsten.juˈeɪ.ʃən, ek- **-s** -z
extenuative ɪkˈsten.ju.ə.tɪv, ek-, -eɪ- (US) -eɪ.t̬ɪv
extenuatory ɪkˈsten.ju.ə.tər.i, ek-, -eɪ-, -tri (US) -ə.tɔːr.i
exterior ɪkˈstɪə.ri.əʳ, ek- (US) -ˈstɪr.i.ɚ **-s** -z **-ly** -li
exteriority ɪkˌstɪə.riˈɒr.ə.ti, ek-, -ɪ.ti; ˌek.stɪə- (US) ɪkˌstɪr.iˈɔːr.ə.t̬i, ek-
exterioriz|e, -is|e ɪkˈstɪə.ri.ər.aɪz, ek- (US) -ˈstɪr.i.ə.raɪz **-es** -ɪz **-ing** -ɪŋ **-ed** -d
exterminable ɪkˈstɜː.mɪ.nə.bl̩, ek-, -mə- (US) -ˈstɝː-
extermi|nate ɪkˈstɜː.mɪ|.neɪt, ek-, -mə- (US) -ˈstɝː- **-nates** -neɪts **-nating** -neɪ.tɪŋ (US) -neɪ.t̬ɪŋ **-nated** -neɪ.tɪd (US) -neɪ.t̬ɪd **-nator/s** -neɪ.təʳ/z (US) -neɪ.t̬ɚ/z
extermination ɪkˌstɜː.mɪˈneɪ.ʃən, ek-, -məˈ- (US) -ˌstɝː- **-s** -z
exterminative ɪkˈstɜː.mɪ.nə.tɪv, ek-, -mə-, -neɪ- (US) -ˈstɝː.mə.neɪ.t̬ɪv, -nə-
exterminatory ɪkˈstɜː.mɪ.nə.tər.i, ek-, -mə-, -neɪ-, -tri (US) -ˈstɝː.mə.nə.tɔːr.i
extern ˈek.stɜːn; ɪkˈstɜːn, ek- (US) ˈek.stɝːn **-s** -z
external ɪkˈstɜː.nəl, ek-; ˈek.stɜː- (US) ɪkˈstɝː-, ek-; ˈek.stɝː- **-s** -z **-ly** -i
external|ism ɪkˈstɜː.nəl|.ɪ.zəm, ek- (US) -ˈstɝː- **-ist/s** -ɪst/s
externality ˌek.stɜːˈnæl.ə.ti, -ɪ.ti (US) -stɝːˈnæl.ə.t̬i
externalization, -isa- ɪkˌstɜː.nəl.aɪˈzeɪ.ʃən, ek-, -ɪˈ- (US) -ˌstɝː.nəl.ɪˈ-
externaliz|e, -is|e ɪkˈstɜː.nəl.aɪz, ek- (US) -ˈstɝː.nə.laɪz **-es** -ɪz **-ing** -ɪŋ **-ed** -d
exterritorial ˌek.ster.ɪˈtɔː.ri.əl (US) -ˈtɔːr.i-
extinct ɪkˈstɪŋkt, ek-
extinction ɪkˈstɪŋk.ʃən, ek- **-s** -z
extinctive ɪkˈstɪŋk.tɪv, ek-
extinguish ɪkˈstɪŋ.gwɪʃ, ek- **-es** -ɪz **-ing** -ɪŋ **-ed** -t **-er/s** -əʳ/z (US) -ɚ/z **-ment** -mənt **-able** -ə.bl̩
extir|pate ˈek.stɜː|.peɪt, -stə- (US) -stɚ-; ɪkˈstɝː-, ek- **-pates** -peɪts **-pating** -peɪ.tɪŋ (US) -peɪ.t̬ɪŋ **-pated** -peɪ.tɪd (US) -peɪ.t̬ɪd **-pator/s** -peɪ.təʳ/z (US) -peɪ.t̬ɚ/z
extirpation ˌek.stɜːˈpeɪ.ʃən, -stəˈ- (US) -stɚˈ- **-s** -z
extol ɪkˈstəʊl, ek-, -ˈstɒl (US) -ˈstoʊl, -ˈstɑːl **-s** -z **-ling** -ɪŋ **-led** -d
extoll ɪkˈstəʊl, ek-, -stɒl (US) -ˈstoʊl, -ˈstɑːl **-s** -z **-ing** -ɪŋ **-ed** -d
Exton ˈek.stən
extor|t ɪkˈstɔː|t, ek- (US) -ˈstɔːr|t **-ts** -ts **-ting** -tɪŋ (US) -t̬ɪŋ **-ted** -tɪd (US) -t̬ɪd **-ter/s** -təʳ/z (US) -t̬ɚ/z
extortion ɪkˈstɔː.ʃən, ek- (US) -ˈstɔːr- **-s** -z
extortionate ɪkˈstɔː.ʃən.ət, ek-, -ɪt (US) -ˈstɔːr- **-ly** -li
extortioner ɪkˈstɔː.ʃən.əʳ, ek- (US) -ˈstɔːr.ʃən.ɚ **-s** -z
extortionist ɪkˈstɔː.ʃən.ɪst, ek- (US) -ˈstɔːr- **-s** -s
extra- ˈek.strə-; ɪkˈstræ-, ek-
Note: Prefix. Normally takes either primary or secondary stress on the first syllable, e.g. **extradite** /ˈek.strə.daɪt/, **extramural** /ˌeks.trəˈmjʊə.rəl (US) -ˈmjʊr.əl/, but may also take primary stress on the second syllable, e.g. **extrapolate** /ɪkˈstræp.ə.leɪt/. In some cases, the second syllable seems to disappear altogether, e.g. **extraordinary** /ekˈstrɔː.dən.ər.i (US) -ˈstrɔːr.dən.er-/.
extra ˈek.strə **-s** -z **ˌextra ˈtime**
extract *(n.)* ˈek.strækt **-s** -s
extract *(v.)* ɪkˈstrækt, ek- **-s** -s **-ing** -ɪŋ **-ed** -ɪd **-able** -ə.bl̩ **exˈtractor ˌfan**
extraction ɪkˈstræk.ʃən, ek- **-s** -z
extractive ɪkˈstræk.tɪv, ek- **-ly** -li
extractor ɪkˈstræk.təʳ, ek- (US) -tɚ **-s** -z **exˈtractor ˌfan**
extracurricular ˌek.strə.kəˈrɪk.jə.ləʳ, -jʊ- (US) -kəˈrɪk.jə.lɚ **ˌextracurˌricular acˈtivities**
extra|dite ˈek.strə|.daɪt **-dites** -daɪts **-diting** -daɪ.tɪŋ (US) -daɪ.t̬ɪŋ **-dited** -daɪ.tɪd (US) -daɪ.t̬ɪd **-ditable** -daɪ.tə.bl̩ (US) -daɪ.t̬ə.bl̩
extradition ˌek.strəˈdɪʃ.ən **-s** -z
extrados ekˈstreɪ.dɒs (US) -dɑːs, -doʊs **-es** -ɪz
extragalactic ˌek.strə.gəˈlæk.tɪk
extrajudicial ˌek.strə.dʒuːˈdɪʃ.əl **-ly** -i
extramarital ˌek.strəˈmær.ɪ.təl (US) -ˈmer.ə.t̬əl, -ˈmær- **ˌextramarital ˈsex**
extramural ˌek.strəˈmjʊə.rəl, -ˈmjɔː- (US) -ˈmjʊr.əl
extraneous ɪkˈstreɪ.ni.əs, ek- **-ly** -li
extranet ˈek.strə.net **-s** -s
extraordinaire ɪkˌstrɔː.dɪˈneəʳ, ek-, -dənˈeəʳ (US) -ˌstrɔːr.dəˈner

extraordinar|y ɪk'strɔː.dᵊn.ᵊr|.i, ek-, -dɪ.nᵊr-; ˌek.strə'ɔː- Ⓤⓢ ɪk'strɔːr.dᵊn.er-, ek-; ˌek.strə'ɔːr- **-ily** -ᵊl.i, -ɪ.li **-iness** -ɪ.nəs, -ɪ.nɪs

extrapo|late ɪk'stræp.ə|.leɪt, ek- **-lates** -leɪts **-lating** -leɪ.tɪŋ Ⓤⓢ -leɪ.t̬ɪŋ **-lated** -leɪ.tɪd Ⓤⓢ -leɪ.t̬ɪd

extrapolation ɪkˌstræp.ə'leɪ.ʃᵊn, ek- **-s** -z

extrasensory ˌek.strə'sent.sᵊr.i **ˌextraˌsensory per'ception**

extraterrestrial ˌeks.trə.tə'res.tri.əl, -ter'es-, -tɪ'res- Ⓤⓢ -tə'- **-s** -z

extraterritorial ˌeks.trəˌter.ɪ'tɔː.ri.əl, -ə'- Ⓤⓢ -'tɔːr.i-

extravagan|ce ɪk'stræv.ə.gənt|s, ek-, '-ɪ- **-ces** -sɪz

extravagant ɪk'stræv.ə.gənt, '-ɪ- **-ly** -li

extravaganza ɪkˌstræv.ə'gæn.zə, ek-; ˌek.stræv- Ⓤⓢ ɪkˌstræv-, ek- **-s** -z

extrava|sate ek'stræv.ə|.seɪt, ɪk- **-sates** -seɪts **-sating** -seɪ.tɪŋ Ⓤⓢ -seɪ.t̬ɪŋ **-sated** -seɪ.tɪd Ⓤⓢ -seɪ.t̬ɪd

extravasation ekˌstræv.ə'seɪ.ʃᵊn, ɪk-; -'zeɪ-, ˌek.stræv- Ⓤⓢ ɪkˌstræv-, ek- **-s** -z

extra|vert 'ek.strə|.vɜːt Ⓤⓢ -vɝːt **-verts** -vɜːts Ⓤⓢ -vɝːts **-verted** -vɜː.tɪd Ⓤⓢ -vɝː.t̬ɪd

Extremadura ˌek.strə.mə'djʊə.rə Ⓤⓢ -'dʊr.ə, -'djʊr.ə

extrem|e ɪk'striːm, ek- **-es** -z **-est** -ɪst, -əst **-ly** -li **-eness** -nəs, -nɪs

extrem|ism ɪk'striː.m|ɪ.zᵊm, ek- **-ist/s** -ɪst/s

extremit|y ɪk'strem.ə.t|i, ek-, -ɪ.t|i Ⓤⓢ -ə.t̬|i **-ies** -iz

extricable ɪk'strɪk.ə.bl̩, ek-; 'ek.strɪ.kə-

extri|cate 'ek.strɪ|.keɪt **-cates** -keɪts **-cating** -keɪ.tɪŋ Ⓤⓢ -keɪ.t̬ɪŋ **-cated** -keɪ.tɪd Ⓤⓢ -keɪ.t̬ɪd

extrication ˌek.strɪ'keɪ.ʃᵊn

extrinsic ek'strɪnt.sɪk, ɪk-, -'strɪn.zɪk **-al** -ᵊl **-ally** -ᵊl.i, -li

extroversion ˌek.strə'vɜː.ʃᵊn, -ʒᵊn Ⓤⓢ 'ek.strə.vɝ.ʒən, -stroʊ-

extro|vert 'ek.strə|.vɜːt Ⓤⓢ -strə|.vɝːt, -stroʊ- **-verts** -vɜːts Ⓤⓢ -vɝːts **-verted** -vɜː.tɪd Ⓤⓢ -vɝː.t̬ɪd

extrud|e ɪk'struːd, ek- **-es** -z **-ing** -ɪŋ **-ed** -ɪd

extrusion ɪk'struː.ʒᵊn, ek- **-s** -z

extrus|ive ɪk'struː.s|ɪv, ek- **-ory** -ᵊr.i Ⓤⓢ -ɔːr.i

exuberan|ce ɪg'zjuː.bᵊr.ᵊnt|s, eg-, -'zuː-; ɪk'sjuː-, ek-, -'suː- Ⓤⓢ ɪg'zuː-, eg- **-cy** -si

exuberant ɪg'zjuː.bᵊr.ᵊnt, eg-, -'zuː-; ɪk'sjuː-, ek-, -'suː- Ⓤⓢ ɪg'zuː-, eg- **-ly** -li

exuber|ate ɪg'zjuː.bᵊr|.eɪt, eg-, -'zuː-; ɪk'sjuː-, ek-, -'suː- Ⓤⓢ ɪg'zuː.bə.r|eɪt, eg- **-ates** -eɪts **-ating** -eɪ.tɪŋ Ⓤⓢ -eɪ.t̬ɪŋ **-ated** -eɪ.tɪd Ⓤⓢ -eɪ.t̬ɪd

exudation ˌek.sjuː'deɪ.ʃᵊn, ˌeg.zjuː'- Ⓤⓢ ˌek.sjuː'-, -suː'-, -sə'-, ˌeg.zjuː'-, -zuː'- **-s** -z

exud|e ɪg'zjuːd, eg-, -'zuːd; ɪk'sjuːd, ek-, -'suːd Ⓤⓢ ɪg'zuːd, ɪk'suːd, ek- **-es** -z **-ing** -ɪŋ **-ed** -ɪd

exul|t ɪg'zʌl|t, eg-; ɪk'sʌl|t, ek- Ⓤⓢ ɪg'zʌl|t, eg- **-ts** -ts **-ting/ly** -tɪŋ/li Ⓤⓢ -t̬ɪŋ/li **-ted** -tɪd Ⓤⓢ -t̬ɪd

exultan|ce ɪg'zʌl.tᵊnt|s, eg-; ɪk'sʌl-, ek- Ⓤⓢ ɪg'zʌl-, eg- **-cy** -si

exultant ɪg'zʌl.tᵊnt, eg-; ɪk'sʌl-, ek- Ⓤⓢ ɪg'zʌl-, eg- **-ly** -li

exultation ˌeg.zʌl'teɪ.ʃᵊn, -zᵊl'-; ˌek.sʌl'-, -sᵊl'- Ⓤⓢ ˌek.sʌl'-, -sᵊl'-; ˌeg.zʌl'-, -zᵊl'- **-s** -z

exurb 'ek.sɜːb; 'eg.zɜːb Ⓤⓢ 'ek.sɝːb; 'eg.zɝːb

exur|ban ek'sɜː|.bᵊn; eg'zɜː- Ⓤⓢ ek'sɝː-; eg'zɝː- **-banite** -bᵊn.aɪt **-bia** -bi.ə

exuviae ɪg'zjuː.vi.iː, eg-; -'zuː-; ɪk'sjuː-, ek-, -'suː-, -aɪ Ⓤⓢ ɪg'zuː.vi.iː, ek'suː-, eg'zuː-, -aɪ

exuvial ɪg'zjuː.vi.əl, eg-, -'zuː-; ɪk'sjuː-, ek-, -'suː- Ⓤⓢ ɪg'zuː-, ek'suː-, eg'zuː-

exuvi|ate ɪg'zjuː.vi|.eɪt, eg-, -'zuː-; ɪk'sjuː-, ek-, -'suː- Ⓤⓢ ɪg'zuː-, ek'suː-, eg'zuː- **-ates** -eɪts **-ating** -eɪ.tɪŋ Ⓤⓢ -eɪ.t̬ɪŋ **-ated** -eɪ.tɪd Ⓤⓢ -eɪ.t̬ɪd

exuviation ɪgˌzjuː.vi'eɪ.ʃᵊn, eg-, -ˌzuː-; ɪkˌsjuː-, ek-, -ˌsuː- Ⓤⓢ ɪg'zuː-, ek'suː-, eg'zuː-

ex voto ˌeks'vəʊ.təʊ Ⓤⓢ -'voʊ.t̬oʊ

Exxon® 'ek.sɒn Ⓤⓢ -sɑːn

Eyam 'iː.əm, iːm

eyas aɪəs **-es** -ɪz

Eyck aɪk

eye (*n. v.*) aɪ **-s** -z **-ing** -ɪŋ **-d** -d **have ˌeyes in the ˌback of one's 'head; in a ˌpig's 'eye; ˌone in the 'eye; ˌup to one's 'eyes; ˌgive one's ˌeye 'teeth; see ˌeye to 'eye**

Eye *place:* aɪ

eyeball 'aɪ.bɔːl Ⓤⓢ -bɔːl, -bɑːl **-s** -z **-ing** -ɪŋ **-ed** -d

eyebath 'aɪ.bɑːθ Ⓤⓢ -bæθ **-s** -s

eyebright 'aɪ.braɪt

eyebrow 'aɪ.braʊ **-s** -z **'eyebrow ˌpencil**

eye-catching 'aɪˌkætʃ.ɪŋ **-ly** -li

eyeful 'aɪ.fʊl **-s** -z

eyeglass 'aɪ.glɑːs Ⓤⓢ -glæs **-es** -ɪz

eyelash 'aɪ.læʃ **-es** -ɪz

eyelet 'aɪ.lət, -lɪt **-s** -s

eyelid 'aɪ.lɪd **-s** -z

eyeliner 'aɪˌlaɪ.nəʳ Ⓤⓢ -nɚ **-s** -z

Eyemouth 'aɪ.maʊθ

eye-open|er 'aɪˌəʊ.pᵊn|.əʳ, -ˌəʊp.n|əʳ Ⓤⓢ -ˌoʊ.pᵊn|.ɚ **-ers** -əz, -ɚz **-ing** -ɪŋ

eyepatch 'aɪ.pætʃ **-es** -ɪz

eyepiec|e 'aɪ.piːs **-es** -ɪz

eyeshade 'aɪ.ʃeɪd **-s** -z

eyeshot 'aɪ.ʃɒt Ⓤⓢ -ʃɑːt

eyesight 'aɪ.saɪt

eyesore 'aɪ.sɔːʳ Ⓤⓢ -sɔːr **-s** -z

eyestrain 'aɪ.streɪn

Eyetie 'aɪ.taɪ **-s** -z

eye|tooth 'aɪ|.tuːθ **-teeth** -tiːθ

eyewash 'aɪ.wɒʃ Ⓤⓢ -wɑːʃ, -wɔːʃ

Pronouncing the letters EY

The most common position for the vowel digraph **ey** is in word final position in an unstressed syllable.

In weak syllables the vowel digraph **ey** is realised with the vowel /i/, e.g.:

donkey	/'dɒŋ.ki/	Ⓤⓢ /'dɑːŋ-/
Surrey	/'sʌr.i/	Ⓤⓢ /'sɝː-/

However, there are several pronunciation possibilities for the digraph in stressed syllables, e.g.:

/eɪ/	they	/ðeɪ/	
/iː/	key	/kiː/	
/aɪ/	geyser	/'giː.zəʳ, 'gaɪ-/	Ⓤⓢ /-zɚ/

eyewitness ˈaɪ.wɪt.nɪs, -nəs, -ˈ-- **-es** -ɪz
Eynon ˈaɪ.nən ⓤⓢ -nɑːn
Eynsford ˈeɪnz.fəd, ˈeɪnts- ⓤⓢ -fɚd
Eynsham *in Oxfordshire:* ˈeɪn.ʃᵊm *locally:* ˈen.ʃᵊm
eyot eɪt, eɪət, aɪt **-s** -s
Note: The local pronunciation in the Thames valley is /eɪt/.
Eyre, eyre eəʳ ⓤⓢ er
eyr|ie, eyr|y ˈaɪə.r|i, ˈɪə-, ˈeə- ⓤⓢ ˈer.i, ˈɪr- **-ies** -iz
Eysenck ˈaɪ.zeŋk
Eyton *in Shropshire:* ˈaɪ.tᵊn *in Hereford and Worcester:* ˈeɪ.tᵊn *surname:* ˈaɪ.tᵊn, ˈiː-
Ezekiel ɪˈziː.ki.əl, ezˈiː-
Ezra ˈez.rə

Pronouncing the letter F

The consonant letter **f** is most often realised as /f/, and is given as a double consonant **ff** at the ends of many words, e.g.:

fit /fɪt/
cuff /kʌf/

However, in one of the most common words containing **f** it is pronounced /v/:

of /ɒv, əv/ (US) /ɑːv, əv/

f (F) ef **-'s** -s
fa fɑː *stress shift:* ˌFA 'cup;
FA ˌef'eɪ ˌ**sweet** ˌ**F'A**
fab fæb
Faber *English name:* 'feɪ.bəʳ (US) -bɚ *German name:* 'fɑː.bəʳ (US) -bɚ
Fabergé 'fæb.ə.ʒeɪ, -dʒeɪ (US) ˌfæb.ɚ'ʒeɪ
Fabian 'feɪ.bi.ən **-s** -z **-ism** -ɪ.zᵊm **'Fabian Soˌciety**
Fabius 'feɪ.bi.əs
fable 'feɪ.bl̩ **-s** -z **-d** -d
fabliau 'fæb.li.əʊ (US) -oʊ **-x** -z
Fablon® 'fæb.lɒn (US) -lɑːn
fabric 'fæb.rɪk **-s** -s **'fabric ˌsoftener**
fabri|cate 'fæb.rɪ|.keɪt **-cates** -keɪts **-cating** -keɪ.tɪŋ (US) -keɪ.t̬ɪŋ **-cated** -keɪ.tɪd (US) -keɪ.t̬ɪd **-cator/s** -keɪ.təʳ/z (US) -keɪ.t̬ɚ/z
fabrication ˌfæb.rɪ'keɪ.ʃᵊn, -rə'- **-s** -z
Fabricius fə'brɪʃ.i.əs, -ʃəs
fabulist 'fæb.jə.lɪst, -jʊ- (US) -jə- **-s** -s
fabulous 'fæb.jə.ləs, -jʊ- (US) -jə- **-ly** -li **-ness** -nəs, -nɪs
Fabyan 'feɪ.bi.ən
facade, façade fə'sɑːd, fæs'ɑːd (US) fə'sɑːd **-s** -z
fac|e (*n. v.*) feɪs **-es** -ɪz **-ing** -ɪŋ **-ed** -t **'face ˌpack; ˌface 'value; ˌcut off one's ˌnose to ˌspite one's 'face; put a ˌbrave 'face on; ˌfly in the 'face of; ˌlaugh on the other ˌside of one's 'face**
face|cloth 'feɪs|.klɒθ (US) -klɑːθ **-cloths** -klɒθs, -klɒðz (US) -klɑːθs, -klɑːðz
faceless 'feɪs.ləs, -lɪs **-ness** -nəs, -nɪs
face-lift 'feɪs.lɪft **-s** -s
facemask 'feɪs.mɑːsk (US) -mæsk **-s** -s
face-off 'feɪs.ɒf (US) -ɑːf **-s** -s
faceplate 'feɪs.pleɪt **-s** -s
facer 'feɪ.səʳ (US) -sɚ **-s** -z
face-sav|er 'feɪsˌseɪ|.vəʳ (US) -vɚ **-ers** -z **-ing** -ɪŋ
fac|et 'fæs|.ɪt, -ət, -et (US) -ɪt **-ets** -ɪts **-et(t)ed** -ɪ.tɪd (US) -ɪ.t̬ɪd
facetiae fə'siː.ʃi.iː, -ʃiː (US) -ʃi.iː
facetious fə'siː.ʃəs **-ly** -li **-ness** -nəs, -nɪs
face-to-face ˌfeɪs.tə'feɪs (US) -t̬ə- *stress shift:* ˌface-to-face 'talk
facia 'feɪ.ʃə (US) -ʃi.ə, -ʃə **-s** -z
facial 'feɪ.ʃᵊl **-ly** -i **-s** -z
facies 'feɪ.ʃi.iːz, -ʃiːz
facile 'fæs.aɪl (US) -ɪl, -əl **-ly** -li **-ness** -nəs, -nɪs
facili|tate fə'sɪl.ɪ|.teɪt, '-ə- **-tates** -teɪts **-tating** -teɪ.tɪŋ (US) -teɪ.t̬ɪŋ **-tated** -teɪ.tɪd (US) -teɪ.t̬ɪd **-tator/s** -teɪ.təʳ/z (US) -teɪ.t̬ɚ/z
facilitation fəˌsɪl.ɪ'teɪ.ʃᵊn, -ə'-
facilit|y fə'sɪl.ə.t|i, -ɪ.t|i (US) -ə.t̬|i **-ies** -iz
facing 'feɪ.sɪŋ **-s** -z
facsimile fæk'sɪm.ᵊl.i, -ɪ.li **-s** -z
fact fækt **-s** -s ˌ**fact of 'life**
fact-find|ing 'fæktˌfaɪn.d|ɪŋ **-er/s** -əʳ/z (US) -ɚ/z
faction 'fæk.ʃᵊn **-s** -z
factional 'fæk.ʃᵊn.ᵊl
factional|ism 'fæk.ʃᵊn.ᵊl|.ɪ.zᵊm **-ist/s** -ɪst/s
factionalization, -isa- ˌfæk.ʃᵊn.ᵊl.aɪ'zeɪ.ʃᵊn, -ɪ'- (US) -ɪ'-
factionaliz|e, -is|e 'fæk.ʃᵊn.ᵊl.aɪz (US) -ə.laɪz **-es** -ɪz **-ing** -ɪŋ **-ed** -d
factious 'fæk.ʃəs **-ly** -li **-ness** -nəs, -nɪs
factitious fæk'tɪʃ.əs **-ly** -li **-ness** -nəs, -nɪs
factitive 'fæk.tɪ.tɪv, -tə.tɪv (US) -tə.t̬ɪv
factive 'fæk.tɪv
factivity fæk'tɪv.ə.ti, -ɪ.ti (US) -ə.t̬i
fact|or 'fæk.t|əʳ (US) -t|ɚ **-ors** -əz (US) -ɚz **-oring** -ᵊr.ɪŋ **-ored** -ᵊrd **-orage** -ᵊr.ɪdʒ ˌ**Factor '5**
factorial fæk'tɔː.ri.əl (US) -'tɔːr.i-
factorization, -isa- ˌfæk.tᵊr.aɪ'zeɪ.ʃᵊn, -ɪ'- (US) -ɪ'-
factoriz|e, -is|e 'fæk.tᵊr.aɪz (US) -tə.raɪz **-es** -ɪz **-ing** -ɪŋ **-ed** -d
factor|y 'fæk.tᵊr|.i, '-tr|i **-ies** -iz **'factory ˌfarming, ˌfactory 'farming; ˌfactory 'floor**
factotum fæk'təʊ.təm (US) -'toʊ.t̬əm **-s** -z
factsheet 'fækt.ʃiːt **-s** -s
factual 'fæk.tʃʊəl, -tjʊəl (US) -tʃuː.əl **-ly** -li **-ness** -nəs, -nɪs
factum 'fæk.təm
factum probandum ˌfæk.təm.prəʊ'bæn.dəm (US) -proʊ'bɑːn-
facul|a 'fæk.jə.l|ə, -jʊ- (US) -jə-, -juː- **-ae** -iː
facultative 'fæk.ᵊl.tə.tɪv, -teɪ- (US) -teɪ.t̬ɪv **-ly** -li
facult|y 'fæk.ᵊl.t|i (US) -t̬|i **-ies** -iz
fad fæd **-s** -z
faddish 'fæd.ɪʃ **-ly** -li **-ness** -nəs, -nɪs
fadd|ism 'fæd|.ɪ.zᵊm **-ist/s** -ɪst/s
fadd|y 'fæd|.i **-ier** -i.əʳ (US) -i.ɚ **-iest** -i.ɪst, -i.əst **-ily** -ɪ.li, -ᵊl.i **-iness** -ɪ.nəs, -ɪ.nɪs
fad|e feɪd **-es** -z **-ing** -ɪŋ **-ed** -ɪd
fadeout 'feɪd.aʊt **-s** -s
fado 'fɑː.du (US) 'fɑː.ðuː, -ðoʊ, -doʊ **-s**
faecal 'fiː.kᵊl
faeces 'fiː.siːz
Faed feɪd
faerie, faery (F) 'feə.ri, 'feɪ.ᵊr.i (US) 'fe…
Faeroe 'feə.rəʊ (US) 'fer.oʊ **-s** -z
Faeroese ˌfeə.rəʊ'iːz (US) ˌfer.oʊ'-
faff fæf **-s** -s **-ing** -ɪŋ **-ed** -t
Fafner 'fɑːf.nəʳ, 'fæf- (US) -nɚ
Fafnir 'fæf.nɪəʳ, 'fæv- (US) -nɪr
fag fæg **-s** -z **-ging** -ɪŋ **-ged** -d **'fag ˌen…** ˌ**fag 'end; 'fag ˌhag**
Fagan 'feɪ.gən
Fagg(e) fæg
faggot 'fæg.ət **-s** -s
Fagin 'feɪ.gɪn
fagot 'fæg.ət **-s** -s
fah fɑː
Fahd fɑːd
Fahey, Fahie 'feɪ.i; feɪ
Fahrenheit 'fær.ᵊn.haɪt, 'fɑː.rᵊn- (US) 'fer.ᵊn-, 'fær-
Fahy 'fɑː.i, -hi; feɪ (US) 'feɪ.i; feɪ
faience, faïence faɪ'ɑ̃ːns, feɪ-, -ɑːnt… (US) faɪ'ɑːnts, feɪ'-; 'faɪ.ənts
fail feɪl **-s** -z **-ing/s** -ɪŋ/z **-ed** -d
faille feɪəl (US) faɪl, feɪl
failsafe 'feɪl.seɪf, -'- (US) '--
Failsworth 'feɪlz.wəθ, -wɜːθ (US) -w… -wɝːθ
failure 'feɪ.ljəʳ (US) 'feɪl.jɚ **-s** -z
fain feɪn
Fainall 'feɪ.nɔːl (US) -nɔːl, -nɑːl
faint feɪnt **-er** -əʳ (US) 'feɪn.t̬ɚ **-est** -… -əst (US) 'feɪn.t̬ɪst, 'feɪn.t̬əst **-ly** … **-ness** -nəs, -nɪs **-s** -s **-ing** -ɪŋ (US) 'feɪn.t̬ɪŋ **-ed** -ɪd (US) 'feɪn.t̬ɪd
fainthearted ˌfeɪnt'hɑː.tɪd (US) -'hɑːr.t̬ɪd **-ly** -li **-ness** -nəs, -n… *stress shift:* ˌfainthearted 'hero

ainwell 'feɪn.wel, -wəl
air (F) feəʳ (US) fer **-s** -z **-er** -əʳ (US) -ɚ **-est** -ɪst, -əst **-ness** -nəs, -nɪs ˌ**fair 'do's**; ˌ**fair 'dinkum**; ˌ**fair 'game**; '**Fair ˌIsle**; ˌ**fair 'play**; ˌ**fair's 'fair**; ˌ**fair and 'square**
airbairn 'feə.beən (US) 'fer.bern **-s** -z
airbank 'feə.bæŋk (US) 'fer- **-s** -s
airbeard 'feə.bɪəd (US) 'fer.bɪrd
airbrother 'feəˌbrʌð.əʳ (US) 'ferˌbrʌð.ɚ
airburn 'feə.bɜːn (US) 'fer.bɝːn
airbury 'feə.bᵊr.i (US) 'ferˌber-, -bɚ-
airchild 'feə.tʃaɪld (US) 'fer-
airclough 'feə.klʌf, -kləʊ (US) 'fer.klʌf
airfaced ˌfeə'feɪst (US) ˌfer- *stress shift:* ˌfairfaced 'child
airfax 'feə.fæks (US) 'fer-
airfield 'feə.fiːld (US) 'fer-
airford 'feə.fəd (US) 'fer.fɚd
airgrieve 'feə.griːv (US) 'fer-
airground 'feə.graʊnd (US) 'fer- **-s** -z
air-haired ˌfeə'heəd (US) ˌfer'herd *stress shift:* ˌfair-haired 'child
airhaven 'feəˌheɪ.vᵊn (US) 'fer-
airholme 'feə.həʊm (US) 'fer.hoʊm, -hoʊlm
airholt 'feə.həʊlt (US) 'fer.hoʊlt
airish 'feə.rɪʃ (US) 'fer.ɪʃ
airleigh 'feə.li, -liː (US) 'fer-
airlight 'feə.laɪt (US) 'fer-
airly 'feə.li (US) 'fer-
airman 'feə.mən (US) 'fer-
air-minded ˌfeə'maɪn.dɪd (US) ˌfer- **-ly** -li **-ness** -nəs, -nɪs *stress shift:* ˌfair-minded 'judge
airmont 'feə.mɒnt, -mənt (US) 'fer.mɑːnt
airmount 'feə.maʊnt (US) 'fer-
airport 'feə.pɔːt (US) 'fer.pɔːrt
airscribe 'feə.skraɪb (US) 'fer-
airview 'feə.vjuː (US) 'fer-
airway 'feə.weɪ (US) 'fer- **-s** -z
airweather 'feəˌweð.əʳ (US) 'ferˌweð.ɚ
air-weather 'feəˌweð.əʳ (US) 'ferˌweð.ɚ
air|y 'feə.r|i (US) 'fer|.i **-ies** -iz ˌ**fairy 'godmother**; '**fairy ˌlight**; ˌ**fairy 'ring** (US) '**fairy ˌring**; '**fairy ˌstory**; '**fairy ˌtale**
airyland 'feə.ri.lænd (US) 'fer.i-
airylike 'feə.ri.laɪk (US) 'fer.i-
aisal 'faɪ.sᵊl
aisalabad 'faɪ.sᵊl.ə.bæd, -zᵊl- (US) ˌfaɪ.sɑː.lə'bɑːd, -sæl.ə'bæd
ait accompli ˌfeɪt.ə'kɒm.pliː, ˌfet-, -'kʌm- *as if French:* -kɔ̃ːm'pliː (US) ˌfeɪt.ə.kɑːm'pliː, ˌfet- **faits accomplis** ˌfeɪz-, ˌfeɪts-, ˌfeɪt-, ˌfez-, -pliːz (US) ˌfeɪt.ə.kɑːm'pliː, ˌfet-, -'pliːz
aith (F) feɪθ **-s** -s '**faith ˌhealer**
aithful (F) 'feɪθ.fᵊl, -fʊl **-ly** -i **-ness** -nəs, -nɪs

Faithfull 'feɪθ.fᵊl, -fʊl
faithless 'feɪθ.ləs, -lɪs **-ly** -li **-ness** -nəs, -nɪs
Faithorne 'feɪ.θɔːn (US) -θɔːrn
fajita fæ'hiː.tə (US) fæ-, fə-, -t̬ə
fak|e feɪk **-es** -s **-ing** -ɪŋ **-ed** -t **-er/s** -əʳ/z (US) -ɚ/z
Fakenham 'feɪ.kᵊn.əm
fakir 'feɪ.kɪəʳ, 'fɑː-, 'fæk.ɪəʳ, fə'kɪəʳ, fæk'ɪəʳ (US) fɑː'kɪr, fæk'ɪr; 'feɪ.kɚ **-s** -z **-ism** -ɪ.zᵊm
Fal fæl
falafel fə'lɑː.fᵊl, -'læf.ᵊl (US) -'lɑː.fᵊl
Falange fə'lændʒ; 'fæl.ændʒ (US) fə'lændʒ, -'lɑːndʒ
Falangist fə'læn.dʒɪst **-s** -s
Falasha fə'læʃ.ə (US) -'lɑː.ʃə, fɑː'- **-s** -z
fal|cate 'fæl|.keɪt **-cated** -keɪ.tɪd (US) -keɪ.t̬ɪd
falchion 'fɔːl.*t*ʃᵊn (US) 'fɔːl-, 'fɑːl- **-s** -z
falcon (F) 'fɔːl.kᵊn, 'fɔː-, 'fɒl-, 'fæl- (US) 'fæl-, 'fɔːl-, 'fɑːl-, 'fɔː- **-s** -z **-er/s** -əʳ/z (US) -ɚ/z
Note: /'fɔː-/ is the usual British pronunciation among people who practise the sport of falconry, with /'fɔː-/ and /'fɔːl-/ most usual among them in the US.
Falconbridge 'fɔːl.kᵊn.brɪdʒ, 'fɔː-, 'fɒl-, 'fæl-, -kᵊm- (US) 'fɔː.kᵊn-, 'fɔːl-, 'fæl-, 'fɑːl-
Falconer 'fɔːl.kᵊn.əʳ, 'fɔː-, 'fɒl-, 'fæl- (US) 'fɔː.kᵊn.ɚ, 'fɔːl-, 'fæl-, 'fɑːl-
falconry 'fɔːl.kᵊn.ri, 'fɔː-, 'fɒl-, 'fæl- (US) 'fæl-, 'fɔːl-, 'fɑːl-, 'fɔː-
Note: See note at **falcon**.
Falder 'fɔːl.dəʳ, 'fɒl- (US) 'fɑːl.dɚ, 'fɔːl-
falderal 'fæl.də.ræl, -dɪ-, ˌ--'- (US) 'fɑːl.də.rɑːl, 'fæl.də.ræl **-s** -z
Faldo 'fæl.dəʊ (US) -doʊ
faldstool 'fɔːl*d*.stuːl **-s** -z
Falerii fə'lɪə.ri.aɪ, fæl'ɪə-, -iː (US) fə'lɪr.i-
Falernian fə'lɜː.ni.ən (US) -'lɝː-
Falk fɔːk, fɔːlk (US) fɔːk, fɔːlk, fɑːlk
Falkenbridge 'fɔː.kᵊn.brɪdʒ, 'fɔːl-, 'fɒl-, 'fæl-, -kᵊm- (US) 'fɔː.kᵊn-, 'fɔːl-, 'fæl-, 'fɑːl-
Falkender 'fɔːl.kən.dəʳ (US) -dɚ
Falkirk 'fɔːl.kɜːk, 'fɒl-, -kək (US) 'fɔːl.kɝːk, -kɚk
Falkland *Viscount:* 'fɔː.klənd, 'fɒl- (US) 'fɔː- *place in Scotland:* 'fɔːl.klənd, 'fɒl- (US) 'fɔːl-
Falkland Islands 'fɔː.kləndˌaɪ.ləndz, 'fɔːl-, 'fɒl- (US) 'fɔː-, 'fɔːl-
Falkner 'fɔːk.nəʳ, 'fɔːlk-, 'fɒlk-, 'fælk- (US) 'fɔːk.nɚ, 'fɔːlk-, 'fɑːlk-, 'fælk-
fall fɔːl (US) fɔːl, fɑːl **-s** -z **-ing** -ɪŋ **fell** fel **fallen** 'fɔː.lən (US) 'fɔː-, 'fɑː- '**fall ˌguy**; ˌ**falling 'star**
Falla 'faɪ.jə; 'fɑː.ljə, 'fæl.jə, -ə (US) 'faɪ.jə; 'fɑː.jɑː

fallacious fə'leɪ.ʃəs **-ly** -li **-ness** -nəs, -nɪs
fallac|y 'fæl.ə.s|i **-ies** -iz
fallal fæl'æl, -'læl (US) fæl'æl, fɑː'lɑːl **-s** -z
fallback 'fɔːl.bæk (US) 'fɔːl-, 'fɑːl- **-s** -s
Faller 'fæl.əʳ (US) -ɚ
fallibility ˌfæl.ə'bɪl.ə.ti, -ɪ'-, -ɪ.ti (US) -ə.t̬i
fallib|le 'fæl.ə.b|l, '-ɪ- **-ly** -li **-leness** -l̩.nəs, -nɪs
falling-out ˌfɔː.lɪŋ'aʊt (US) ˌfɔː-, ˌfɑː- **fallings-out** ˌfɔː.lɪŋz'aʊt (US) ˌfɔː-, ˌfɑː- **falling-outs** ˌfɔː.lɪŋ'aʊts (US) ˌfɔː-, ˌfɑː-
fall-off 'fɔːl.ɒf (US) -ɑːf, 'fɑːl- **-s** -s
Fallon 'fæl.ən
fallopian (F) fə'ləʊ.pi.ən, fæl'əʊ- (US) fə'loʊ- **faˌllopian 'tube**
fallout 'fɔːl.aʊt (US) 'fɔːl-, 'fɑːl-
fallow (F) 'fæl.əʊ (US) -oʊ **-s** -z **-ness** -nəs, -nɪs **-ing** -ɪŋ **-ed** -d '**fallow ˌdeer**, ˌ**fallow 'deer**
Fallowfield 'fæl.əʊ.fiːld (US) -oʊ-
Fallows 'fæl.əʊz (US) -oʊz
Falls fɔːlz (US) fɔːlz, fɑːlz ˌ**Falls 'Road**
Falmer 'fæl.məʳ, 'fɔːl- (US) 'fɑːl.mɚ, 'fɔːl-
Falmouth 'fæl.məθ
fals|e fɔːls, fɒls (US) fɔːls, fɑːls **-er** -əʳ (US) -ɚ **-est** -ɪst, -əst **-eness** -nəs, -nɪs ˌ**false a'larm**; ˌ**false pre'tences**; ˌ**false 'start**; ˌ**false 'teeth**
falsehood 'fɔːls.*h*ʊd, 'fɒls- (US) 'fɔːls.hʊd, 'fɑːls- **-s** -z
falsely 'fɔːl.sli, 'fɒl- (US) 'fɔːl-, 'fɑːl-
falsetto fɒl'set.əʊ, fɔːl- (US) fɔːl'set̬.oʊ, fɑːl- **-s** -z
Falshaw 'fɔːl.ʃɔː, 'fɒl- (US) 'fɔːl.ʃɑː, 'fɑːl-, -ʃɔː
falsification ˌfɔːl.sɪ.fɪ'keɪ.ʃᵊn, ˌfɒl-, -sə- (US) ˌfɔːl-, ˌfɑːl- **-s** -z
falsi|fy 'fɔːl.sɪ|.faɪ, 'fɒl-, -sə- (US) 'fɔːl-, 'fɑːl- **-fies** -faɪz **-fying** -faɪ.ɪŋ **-fied** -faɪd **-fier/s** -faɪ.əʳ/z (US) -faɪ.ɚ/z
falsit|y 'fɔːl.sə.t|i, 'fɒl-, -ɪ.t|i (US) 'fɔːl.sə.t̬|i, 'fɑːl- **-ies** -iz
Falstaff 'fɔːl.stɑːf, 'fɒl- (US) 'fɔːl.stæf, 'fɑːl-
Falstaffian fɔːl'stɑː.fi.ən, fɒl- (US) fɔːl'stæf.i-, fɑːl-
falt|er 'fɔːl.t|əʳ, 'fɒl- (US) 'fɔːl.t̬|ɚ, 'fɑːl- **-ers** -əz (US) -ɚz **-ering/ly** -ᵊr.ɪŋ/li **-ered** -əd (US) -ɚd **-erer/s** -ᵊr.əʳ/z (US) -ɚ.ɚ/z
Faludi fə'luː.di, fæl'uː.di
Famagusta ˌfæm.ə'gʊs.tə, ˌfɑː.mə'- (US) ˌfɑː.mə'guː.stə
fame feɪm **-d** -d
familial fə'mɪl.i.əl
familiar fə'mɪl.i.əʳ (US) '-jɚ, -i.ɚ **-s** -z **-ly** -li
familiarit|y fəˌmɪl.i'ær.ə.t|i, -ɪ.t|i (US) -'er.ə.t̬|i, -'ær- **-ies** -iz

familiariz|e, -is|e fə'mɪl.i.ᵊr.aɪz (US) '-jə.raɪz, '-i.ə- **-es** -ɪz **-ing** -ɪŋ **-ed** -d
famil|y 'fæm.ᵊl|.i, -ɪ.l|i **-ies** -iz **ˌfamily alˈlowance; ˌfamily ˈcredit; ˈfamily ˌman; ˌfamily ˈplanning; ˈfamily ˌroom; ˈfamily ˌstyle; ˌfamily ˈtree**
famine 'fæm.ɪn **-s** -z
famish 'fæm.ɪʃ **-es** -ɪz **-ing** -ɪŋ **-ed** -t
famosus libellus fæmˌəʊ.səs.lɪ'bel.əs (US) -ˌoʊ-
famous 'feɪ.məs **-ly** -li **-ness** -nəs, -nɪs
fan fæn **-s** -z **-ning** -ɪŋ **-ned** -d
Fan *Welsh mountains:* væn
fan-assisted ˌfæn.ə'sɪs.tɪd *stress shift:* ˌfan-assisted 'oven
fanatic fə'næt.ɪk (US) -'næt̬- **-s** -s **-al** -ᵊl **-ally** -ᵊl.i, -li
fanaticism fə'næt.ɪ.sɪ.zᵊm, '-ə- (US) -'næt̬-
fanaticiz|e, -is|e fə'næt.ɪ.saɪz (US) -'næt̬- **-es** -ɪz **-ing** -ɪŋ **-ed** -d
fanbelt 'fæn.belt **-s** -s
fanciful 'fænt.sɪ.fᵊl, -fʊl **-ly** -i **-ness** -nəs, -nɪs
Fancourt 'fæn.kɔːt, 'fæŋ- (US) -kɔːrt
fanc|y 'fænt.s|i **-ies** -iz **-ying** -i.ɪŋ **-ied** -id **-ier/s** -i.əʳ/z (US) -i.ɚ/z **ˌfancy ˈdress**
fancy-free ˌfænt.si'friː **ˌfootloose and ˌfancy-ˈfree** (US) **ˈfootloose and ˌfancy ˌfree**
fancywork 'fænt.si.wɜːk (US) -wɝːk
fandango fæn'dæŋ.gəʊ (US) -goʊ **-s** -z
fane (F) feɪn **-s** -z
Faneuil 'fæn.ᵊl, -jəl, -jʊəl (US) -jə.wəl
fanfare 'fæn.feəʳ (US) -fer **-s** -z
fanfaronade ˌfæn.fær.ə'nɑːd, -fᵊr-, -'neɪd (US) -fər.ə'neɪd, -'nɑːd **-s** -z
fang (F) fæŋ **-s** -z **-ed** -d
fanjet 'fæn.dʒet **-s** -s
fanlight 'fæn.laɪt **-s** -s
fanner 'fæn.əʳ (US) -ɚ **-s** -z
Fanning 'fæn.ɪŋ
fann|y (F) 'fæn|.i **-ies** -iz **ˈfanny ˌpack**
Fanshawe 'fæn.ʃɔː (US) -ʃɑː, -ʃɔː
Fanta® 'fæn.tə (US) -t̬ə
fantabulous fæn'tæb.jə.ləs, -jʊ-
fantail 'fæn.teɪl **-s** -z
fantasia fæn'teɪ.zi.ə, -'tɑː-, '-ʒə; ˌfæn.tə'ziː.ə, -'siː- (US) fæn'teɪ.ʒə, -ʒi.ə; ˌfæn.t̬ə'ziː.ə **-s** -z
fantasist 'fæn.tə.sɪst (US) -t̬ə- **-s** -s
fantasiz|e, -is|e 'fæn.tə.saɪz (US) -t̬ə- **-es** -ɪz **-ing** -ɪŋ **-ed** -d
fantasm 'fæn.tæz.ᵊm **-s** -z
fantastic fæn'tæs.tɪk, fən- (US) fæn- **-al** -ᵊl **-ally** -ᵊl.i, -li **-alness** -ᵊl.nəs, -nɪs
fantas|y 'fæn.tə.s|i, -z|i (US) -t̬ə- **-ies** -iz
Fanti, Fante 'fæn.ti (US) 'fæn.ti, 'fɑːn- **-s** -z
fanzine 'fæn.ziːn **-s** -z
far fɑːʳ (US) fɑːr **ˌFar ˈEast**
farad 'fær.əd, -æd (US) 'fer-, 'fær- **-s** -z
faraday (F) 'fær.ə.deɪ (US) 'fer-, 'fær- **-s** -z
faradic fə'ræd.ɪk
faraway ˌfɑː.rə'weɪ (US) ˌfɑːr.ə'- *stress shift:* ˌfaraway 'look
farc|e fɑːs (US) fɑːrs **-es** -ɪz
farceur ˌfɑː'sɜːʳ (US) ˌfɑːr'sɝː **-s** -z
farcical 'fɑː.sɪ.kᵊl, -sə- (US) 'fɑːr- **-ly** -i
farci(e) ˌfɑː'siː (US) ˌfɑːr-
farcy 'fɑː.si (US) 'fɑːr-
far|e (*n. v.*) feəʳ (US) fer **-es** -z **-ing** -ɪŋ **-ed** -d
Far East ˌfɑːʳ'iːst (US) ˌfɑːr-
Farebrother 'feəˌbrʌð.əʳ (US) 'ferˌbrʌð.ɚ
Fareham 'feə.rəm (US) 'fer.əm
farewell ˌfeə'wel (US) ˌfer- **-s** -z *stress shift:* ˌfarewell 'kiss
Farewell 'feə.wel, -wᵊl (US) 'fer-
farfalle fɑː'fæl.eɪ (US) fɑːr-
far-fetched ˌfɑː'fetʃt (US) ˌfɑːr- *stress shift:* ˌfar-fetched 'tale
far-flung ˌfɑː'flʌŋ (US) ˌfɑːr- *stress shift:* ˌfar-flung 'places
Fargo 'fɑː.gəʊ (US) 'fɑːr.goʊ
Farhi 'fɑː.hi (US) 'fɑːr-
Faribault 'fær.ɪ.bəʊ (US) 'fer.ɪ.boʊ, 'fær-
farina fə'riː.nə, -'raɪ- (US) -'riː-
Farina fə'riː.nə
farinaceous ˌfær.ɪ'neɪ.ʃəs, -ə'- (US) ˌfer-, ˌfær-
Faringdon 'fær.ɪŋ.dən (US) 'fer-, 'fær-
Faringford 'fær.ɪŋ.fəd (US) 'fer.ɪŋ.fɚd, 'fær-
Farington 'fær.ɪŋ.tən (US) 'fer-, 'fær-
farinose 'fær.ɪ.nəʊs, -nəʊz (US) 'fer.ə.noʊs, 'fær-
Farjeon 'fɑː.dʒᵊn (US) 'fɑːr-
Farleigh, Farley 'fɑː.li (US) 'fɑːr-
farm fɑːm (US) fɑːrm **-s** -z **-ing** -ɪŋ **-ed** -d
Farman 'fɑː.mən (US) 'fɑːr-
Farmaner 'fɑː.mə.nəʳ (US) 'fɑːr.mə.nɚ
farmer (F) 'fɑː.məʳ (US) 'fɑːr.mɚ **-s** -z
farmhand 'fɑːm.hænd (US) 'fɑːrm- **-s** -z
farmhou|se 'fɑːm.haʊ|s (US) 'fɑːrm- **-ses** -zɪz
Farmington 'fɑː.mɪŋ.tən (US) 'fɑːr-
farmland 'fɑːm.lænd, -lənd (US) 'fɑːrm.lænd
farmstead 'fɑːm.sted (US) 'fɑːrm- **-s** -z
farmyard 'fɑːm.jɑːd (US) 'fɑːrm.jɑːrd **-s** -z
Farnaby 'fɑː.nə.bi (US) 'fɑːr-
Farnborough 'fɑːn.bᵊr.ə, 'fɑːm- (US) 'fɑːrn-, -oʊ
Farn(e) fɑːn (US) fɑːrn
Farnham 'fɑː.nəm (US) 'fɑːr-
Farnhamworth 'fɑː.nəm.wəθ, -wɜːθ (US) 'fɑːr.nəm.wɚθ, -wɝːθ
faro *gambling game:* 'feə.rəʊ (US) 'fer.oʊ, 'fær-
Faro *in Portugal:* 'fɑː.rəʊ, 'feə- (US) 'fɑːr.oʊ, 'fer-
Faroe 'feə.rəʊ (US) 'fer.oʊ
Faroese ˌfeə.rəʊ'iːz (US) ˌfer.oʊ'-
far-off ˌfɑːʳ'ɒf (US) ˌfɑːr'ɑːf *stress shift:* ˌfar-off 'town
farouche fə'ruːʃ, fɑː-
Farouk fə'ruːk, fær'uːk (US) fə'ruːk
far-out ˌfɑːʳ'aʊt (US) ˌfɑːr- *stress shift:* ˌfar-out 'music
Farquhar 'fɑː.kwəʳ, -kəʳ (US) 'fɑːr.kwɚ, -kwɑːr, -kɚ
Farquharson 'fɑː.kwə.sᵊn, -kə- (US) 'fɑːr.kwɚ-, -kɚ-
Farr fɑːʳ (US) fɑːr
farraginous fə'reɪ.dʒɪ.nəs, -'rædʒ.ɪ-, -ᵊn.əs (US) fə'rædʒ.ɪ.nəs, '-ə-
farrago fə'rɑː.gəʊ, -'reɪ- (US) fə'rɑː.goʊ, -'reɪ- **-(e)s** -z
Farragut 'fær.ə.gət (US) 'fer-, 'fær-
Farrah 'fær.ə (US) 'fer-, 'fær-
Farrakhan 'fær.ə.kæn (US) 'fer-, 'fær-, -kɑːn, 'fer.kɑːn
Farrant 'fær.ᵊnt (US) 'fer-, 'fær-
far-reaching ˌfɑː'riː.tʃɪŋ (US) ˌfɑːr- *stress shift:* ˌfar-reaching 'consequences
Farrell 'fær.ᵊl (US) 'fer-, 'fær-
Farren 'fær.ᵊn (US) 'fer-, 'fær-
Farrener 'fær.ə.nəʳ (US) 'fer.ə.nɚ, 'fær-
farrier 'fær.i.əʳ (US) 'fer.i.ɚ, 'fær- **-s** -z **-y** -i **-ies** -iz
Farringdon 'fær.ɪŋ.dən (US) 'fer-, 'fær-
Farringford 'fær.ɪŋ.fəd (US) 'fer.ɪŋ.fɚd, 'fær-
Farrington 'fær.ɪŋ.tən (US) 'fer-, 'fær-
farrow (F) 'fær.əʊ (US) 'fer.oʊ, 'fær- **-s** -z **-ing** -ɪŋ **-ed** -d
farseeing ˌfɑː'siː.ɪŋ (US) ˌfɑːr- *stress shift:* ˌfarseeing 'leader
Farsi 'fɑː.siː, ˌ-'- (US) 'fɑːr- **-s** -z
farsighted fɑː'saɪ.tɪd (US) fɑːr'saɪ.t̬ɪd **-ly** -li **-ness** -nəs, -nɪs
Farsley 'fɑːz.li (US) 'fɑːrz-
fart fɑːt (US) fɑːrt **-s** -s **-ing** -ɪŋ (US) 'fɑːr.t̬ɪŋ **-ed** -ɪd (US) 'fɑːr.t̬ɪd
farth|er 'fɑː.ð|əʳ (US) 'fɑːr.ð|ɚ **-est** -ɪst, -əst
farthing 'fɑː.ðɪŋ (US) 'fɑːr- **-s** -z
farthingale 'fɑː.ðɪŋ.geɪl (US) 'fɑːr- **-s** -z
fartlek 'fɑːt.lek (US) 'fɑːrt- **-s** -s
Faruk fə'ruːk, fær'uːk (US) fə'ruːk
Farwell 'fɑː.wel, -wəl (US) 'fɑːr-
fasces 'fæs.iːz
fasci|a *medical term:* 'fæʃ.i|.ə, -ʃ|ə (US) -ʃi|.ə **-as** -əs **-ae** -iː *other senses:* 'feɪ.ʃ|ə, -ʃi|.ə (US) 'fæʃ.i|.ə, 'fæʃ|.ə *also when referring to classical architecture:* 'feɪ.si|.ə (US) -ʃi- **-as** -əz **-ae** -iː
fasciated 'fæʃ.i.eɪ.tɪd (US) -t̬ɪd

fascicle ˈfæs.ɪ.kḷ, ˈ-ə- **-s** -z

fascicule ˈfæs.ɪ.kjuːl, ˈ-ə- **-s** -z

fascin|ate ˈfæs.ɪ.n|eɪt, -ən|.eɪt (US) -ən|.eɪt **-ates** -eɪts **-ated** -eɪ.tɪd (US) -eɪ.t̬ɪd **-ator/s** -eɪ.təʳ/z (US) -eɪ.t̬ɚ/z

fascinating ˈfæs.ɪ.neɪ.tɪŋ, -ən.eɪ- (US) -ən.eɪ.t̬ɪŋ **-ly** -li

fascination ˌfæs.ɪˈneɪ.ʃən, -ənˈeɪ- (US) -ənˈeɪ- **-s** -z

fascine fæsˈiːn, fəˈsiːn **-s** -z

fascism (F) ˈfæʃ.ɪ.zəm

fascist (F) ˈfæʃ.ɪst **-s** -s

fascisti fæʃˈɪs.tiː, fəˈʃɪs-

fascistic (F) fæʃˈɪs.tɪk, fəˈʃɪs- **-ally** -əl.i, -li

fash fæʃ **-es** -ɪz **-ing** -ɪŋ **-ed** -t

fashion ˈfæʃ.ən **-s** -z **-ing** -ɪŋ **-ed** -d **-er/s** -əʳ/z (US) -ɚ/z ˈ**fashion** ˌ**plate**

fashionab|le ˈfæʃ.ən.ə.b|ḷ, ˈfæʃ.nə- **-ly** -li **-leness** -ḷ.nəs, -nɪs

Faslane fæzˈleɪn, fəˈsleɪn

Fassbinder ˈfæs.bɪn.dəʳ (US) ˈfɑːs.bɪn.dɚ

fast (F) fɑːst (US) fæst **-s** -s **-est** -ɪst, -əst **-ness** -nəs, -nɪs **-ing** -ɪŋ **-ed** -ɪd **-er/s** -əʳ/z (US) -ɚ/z ˌ**fast and** ˈ**loose**; ˈ**fast** ˌ**day**; ˌ**fast** ˈ**food**; ˈ**fast** ˌ**lane**; ˌ**fast reˈactor**; ˈ**fast** ˌ**track**; ˌ**life in the** ˈ**fast** ˌ**lane** ˌ**pull a** ˈ**fast** ˌ**one**

fastball ˈfɑːst.bɔːl (US) ˈfæst-, -bɑːl **-s** -z

fasten ˈfɑː.sən (US) ˈfæs.ən **-s** -z **-ing** -ɪŋ, ˈfɑːs.nɪŋ (US) ˈfæs- **-ed** -d

fastener ˈfɑː.sən.əʳ (US) ˈfæs.ən.ɚ **-s** -z

fastening ˈfɑː.sən.ɪŋ; ˈfɑːs.nɪŋ (US) ˈfæs.ən.ɪŋ; ˈfæs.nɪŋ **-s** -z

fast-forward ˌfɑːstˈfɔː.wəd (US) ˌfæstˈfɔːr.wɚd **-s** -z **-ing** -ɪŋ **-ed** -ɪd

fasti (F) ˈfæs.tiː, -taɪ

fastidious fæsˈtɪd.i.əs, fəˈstɪd- **-ly** -li **-ness** -nəs, -nɪs

fastness ˈfɑːst.nəs, -nɪs (US) ˈfæst- **-es** -ɪz

fastnet ˈfɑːst.net, -nɪt (US) ˈfæst-

fast-talk ˌfɑːstˈtɔːk (US) ˌfæst-, -ˈtɑːk **-s** -s **-ing** -ɪŋ **-ed** -t **-er/s** -əʳ/z (US) -ɚ/z

fast-track ˈfɑːst.træk (US) ˈfæst- **-s** -s **-ing** -ɪŋ **-ed** -t

fat fæt **-ter** -əʳ (US) ˈfæt̬.ɚ **-test** -ɪst, -əst (US) ˈfæt̬.ɪst, -əst **-ness** -nəs, -nɪs ˈ**fat cat**; ˌ**fat** ˈ**city**

fatal ˈfeɪ.təl (US) -t̬əl **-ly** -i

fatal|ism ˈfeɪ.təl|.ɪ.zəm (US) -t̬əl- **-ist/s** -ɪst/s

fatalistic ˌfeɪ.təlˈɪs.tɪk (US) -t̬əlˈ- **-ally** -əl.i, -li

fatalit|y fəˈtæl.ə.t|i, feɪ-, -ɪ.t|i (US) -ə.t̬|i **-ies** -iz

fate (F) feɪt **-es** -s **-ed** -ɪd (US) ˈfeɪ.t̬ɪd

fateful ˈfeɪt.fəl, -fʊl **-ly** -i

fathead ˈfæt.hed **-s** -z

fath|er (F) ˈfɑː.ð|əʳ (US) -ð|ɚ **-ers** -əz (US) -ɚz **-ering** -ər.ɪŋ **-ered** -əd (US) -ɚd ˌ**Father** ˈ**Christmas**; ˈ**father** ˌ**figure**

fatherhood ˈfɑː.ðə.hʊd (US) -ðɚ-

father-in-law ˈfɑː.ðər.ɪn.lɔː (US) -ðɚ.ɪn.lɑː, -lɔː **fathers-in-law** ˈfɑː.ðəz- (US) -ðɚz-

fatherland ˈfɑː.ðə.lænd (US) -ðɚ- **-s** -z

fatherless ˈfɑː.ðə.ləs, -lɪs (US) -ðɚ-

fatherl|y ˈfɑː.ðəl|.i (US) -ðɚ.l|i **-iness** -ɪ.nəs, -ɪ.nɪs

fathom ˈfæð.əm **-s** -z **-ing** -ɪŋ **-ed** -d **-able** -ə.bḷ **-less** -ləs, -lɪs

fatigu|e fəˈtiːg **-es** -z **-ing/ly** -ɪŋ/li **-ed** -d ˌ**chronic faˈtigue** ˌ**syndrome**

Fatima ˈfæt.ɪ.mə (US) ˈfæt̬-, ˈfɑː.t̬ɪ-; fəˈtiː-

fatling ˈfæt.lɪŋ **-s** -z

fatsia ˈfæt.si.ə **-s** -z

fatso ˈfæt.səʊ (US) -soʊ **-es** -z

fatted ˈfæt.ɪd (US) ˈfæt̬- ˌ**fatted** ˈ**calf**

fatten ˈfæt.ən **-s** -z **-ing** -ɪŋ **-ed** -d **-er/s** -əʳ/z (US) -ɚ/z

fattish ˈfæt.ɪʃ (US) ˈfæt̬-

fatt|y ˈfæt|.i (US) ˈfæt̬- **-ies** -iz **-ier** -i.əʳ (US) -i.ɚ **-iest** -i.ɪst, -i.əst **-iness** -ɪ.nəs, -ɪ.nɪs ˌ**fatty** ˈ**acid**

fatuity fəˈtjuː.ə.ti, fætˈjuː-, -ɪ.ti (US) fəˈtuː.ə.t̬i, -ˈtjuː-

fatuous ˈfæt.ju.əs (US) ˈfætʃ.u- **-ly** -li **-ness** -nəs, -nɪs

fatwa ˈfæt.wɑː, -wə (US) ˈfæt.wɑː, ˈfʌt- **-s** -z

fatwood ˈfæt.wʊd

faubourg ˈfəʊ.bʊəg, -bɜːg (US) ˈfoʊ.bʊr, -bɔrg **-s** -z

faucal ˈfɔː.kəl (US) ˈfɑː-, ˈfɔː-

fauces ˈfɔː.siːz (US) ˈfɑː-, ˈfɔː-

faucet ˈfɔː.sɪt, -sət (US) ˈfɑː-, ˈfɔː- **-s** -s

Faucett, Faucit ˈfɔː.sɪt, -ət (US) ˈfɑː-, ˈfɔː-

Faulconbridge ˈfɔː.kən.brɪdʒ, ˈfɔːl-, -kəm- (US) ˈfɑː.kən-, ˈfɑːl-, ˈfɔː-, ˈfɔːl-

Fauldhouse ˈfɔːld.haʊs (US) ˈfɑːld-, ˈfɔːld-

Faulds fəʊldz, fɔːldz (US) foʊldz, fɑːldz, fɔːldz

Faulhorn ˈfaʊl.hɔːn (US) -hɔːrn

Faulk fɔːk (US) fɑːk, fɔːk, fɑːlk

Faulkes fɔːks, fɔːlks (US) fɑːks, fɑːlks, fɔːks, fɔːlks

Faulkland ˈfɔː.klənd, ˈfɔːl- (US) ˈfɑː-, ˈfɑːl-, ˈfɔː-, ˈfɔːl-

Faulkner ˈfɔːk.nəʳ (US) ˈfɑːk.nɚ, ˈfɔːk-, ˈfɑːlk-

Faulks fəʊks (US) foʊks

faul|t fɔːl|t, fɒl|t (US) fɔːl|t, fɑːl|t **-ts** -ts **-ting** -tɪŋ (US) -t̬ɪŋ **-ted** -tɪd (US) -t̬ɪd

faultfind|er ˈfɔːltˌfaɪn.d|əʳ, ˈfɒlt- (US) ˈfɔːltˌfaɪn.d|ɚ, ˈfɑːlt- **-ers** -əz (US) -ɚz **-ing** -ɪŋ

faultless ˈfɔːlt.ləs, ˈfɒlt-, -lɪs (US) ˈfɔːlt-, ˈfɑːlt- **-ly** -li **-ness** -nəs, -nɪs

fault|y ˈfɔːl.t|i, ˈfɒl- (US) ˈfɔːl.t̬|i, ˈfɑːl- **-ier** -i.əʳ (US) -i.ɚ **-iest** -i.ɪst, -i.əst **-ily** -ɪ.li, -əl.i **-iness** -ɪ.nəs, -ɪ.nɪs

faun fɔːn (US) fɑːn, fɔːn **-s** -z

fauna ˈfɔː.nə (US) ˈfɑː-, ˈfɔː-

Faunch fɔːntʃ (US) fɑːntʃ, fɔːntʃ

Fauntleroy ˈfɔːnt.lə.rɔɪ, ˈfɒnt- (US) ˈfɑːnt-, ˈfɔːnt-

Fauré ˈfɔː.reɪ, ˈfɒr.eɪ (US) foʊˈreɪ, fɔː-

Faust faʊst

Faustian ˈfaʊ.sti.ən

Faustina fɔːˈstiː.nə, faʊ- (US) faʊ-, fɔː-

Faustus ˈfɔː.stəs, ˈfaʊ- (US) ˈfaʊ-, ˈfɔː-

fauteuil ˈfəʊ.tɜː.i, fəʊˈtɜː.i, -ˈtɜːl (US) ˈfoʊ.tɪl; foʊˈtɜː.jə **-s** -z

fauve fəʊv (US) foʊv

fauv|ism (F) ˈfəʊ.v|ɪ.zəm (US) ˈfoʊ- **-ist/s** -ɪst/s

Faux fəʊ, fɔːks (US) foʊ

faux ami ˌfəʊz.æmˈi (US) ˌfoʊz- **-s** -z

faux-naïf ˌfəʊ.naɪˈiːf (US) ˌfoʊ.nɑːˈ- **-s** -s

faux pas *singular:* ˌfəʊˈpɑː (US) ˌfoʊ-

faux pas *plural:* ˌfəʊˈpɑː, -ˈpɑːz (US) ˌfoʊ-

fave feɪv **-s** -z

Favel ˈfeɪ.vəl

Faversham ˈfæv.ə.ʃəm (US) ˈ-ɚ-

Favoni|an fəˈvəʊ.ni|.ən, feɪ- (US) -ˈvoʊ- **-us** -əs

Favorit® ˈfæv.ər.ɪt

fav|o(u)r ˈfeɪ.v|əʳ (US) -v|ɚ **-o(u)rs** -əz (US) -ɚz **-o(u)ring** -ər.ɪŋ **-o(u)red** -əd (US) -ɚd **-o(u)rer/s** -ər.əʳ/z (US) -ɚ.ɚ/z

favo(u)rab|le ˈfeɪ.vər.ə.b|ḷ **-ly** -li **-leness** -ḷ.nəs, -nɪs

favo(u)rit|e ˈfeɪ.vər.ɪt, -ət, ˈfeɪv.rɪt **-es** -s **-ism** -ɪ.zəm ˌ**favo(u)rite** ˈ**son**

favo(u)rless ˈfeɪ.və.ləs, -lɪs (US) -vɚ-

Fawcett ˈfɔː.sɪt, -sət, ˈfɒs.ɪt, -ət (US) ˈfɑː.sɪt, ˈfɔː-, -sət

Fawkes fɔːks (US) fɑːks, fɔːks

Fawkner ˈfɔːk.nəʳ (US) ˈfɑːk.nɚ, ˈfɔːk-

Fawley ˈfɔː.li (US) ˈfɑː-, ˈfɔː-

Fawlty ˈfɔːl.ti (US) ˈfɑːl-, ˈfɔːl-

fawn fɔːn (US) fɑːn, fɔːn **-s** -z **-ing/ly** -ɪŋ/li **-ed** -d **-er/s** -əʳ/z (US) -ɚ/z

Fawssett ˈfɔː.sɪt, -sət (US) ˈfɑː.sɪt, ˈfɔː-, -sət

fax fæks **-es** -ɪz **-ing** -ɪŋ **-ed** -t ˈ**fax maˌchine**

fay (F) feɪ **-s** -z

Faye feɪ

Fayette feɪˈet *stress shift, see compound:* ˌ**Fayette** ˈ**City**

Fayetteville ˈfeɪ.et.vɪl, -ɪt-, -ət- *locally also:* (US) ˈfeɪt.vəl

Faygate ˈfeɪ.geɪt

Faza(c)kerley fəˈzæk.əl.i (US) -ɚ.li

faz|e feɪz **-es** -ɪz **-ing** -ɪŋ **-ed** -d

FBI ˌef.biːˈaɪ

FC ˌefˈsiː

FCO ˌef.siːˈəʊ (US) -ˈoʊ

FDA ˌef.diːˈeɪ
fe *name of note in Tonic Sol-fa:* fiː
fe *syllable used in Tonic Sol-fa for counting a short note off the beat:* fi
FE *(abbrev. for* **Further Education***)* ˌefˈiː
fealty ˈfiːl.ti
fear fɪəʳ (US) fɪr **-s** -z **-ing** -ɪŋ **-ed** -d
fearful ˈfɪə.fᵊl, -fʊl (US) ˈfɪr- **-ly** -i **-ness** -nəs, -nɪs
Fearghal ˈfɜː.gᵊl (US) ˈfɝː-
Feargus ˈfɜː.gəs (US) ˈfɝː-
Fearing ˈfɪə.rɪŋ (US) ˈfɪr.ɪŋ
fearless ˈfɪə.ləs, -lɪs (US) ˈfɪr- **-ly** -li **-ness** -nəs, -nɪs
Fearn(e) fɜːn (US) fɝːn
Fearnside ˈfɜːn.saɪd (US) ˈfɝːn-
Fearon ˈfɪə.rᵊn (US) ˈfɪr.ᵊn
fearsome ˈfɪə.səm (US) ˈfɪr- **-ly** -li **-ness** -nəs, -nɪs
feasibility ˌfiː.zəˈbɪl.ə.ti, -zɪˈ-, -ɪ.ti (US) -ə.t̬i
feasib|le ˈfiː.zə.b|l̩, -zɪ- **-ly** -li **-leness** -l̩.nəs, -nɪs
feast (F) fiːst **-s** -s **-ing** -ɪŋ **-ed** -ɪd **-er/s** -əʳ/z (US) -ɚ/z
feat fiːt **-s** -s
feath|er ˈfeð|.əʳ (US) -ɚ **-ers** -əz (US) -ɚz **-ering** -ᵊr.ɪŋ **-ered** -əd (US) -ɚd ˌ**feather** ˈ**bed**
featherbed ˈfeð.ə.bed, ˌ--ˈ- (US) -ɚ- **-s** -z **-ding** -ɪŋ **-ded** -ɪd
featherbrain ˈfeð.ə.breɪn (US) ˈ-ɚ- **-s** -z **-ed** -d
featheredg|e ˈfeð.əʳ.edʒ, ˌ--ˈ- (US) -ɚ- **-es** -ɪz
featherhead ˈfeð.ə.hed (US) ˈ-ɚ- **-s** -z **-ed** -ɪd
featherstitch ˈfeð.ə.stɪtʃ (US) ˈ-ɚ- **-es** -ɪz **-ing** -ɪŋ **-ed** -t
Featherston ˈfeð.ə.stən (US) ˈ-ɚ-
Featherstone ˈfeð.ə.stən, -stəʊn (US) -ɚ.stən, -stoʊn
Featherstonehaugh ˈfeð.ə.stᵊn.hɔː; ˈfæn.ʃɔː; ˈfes.tᵊn.hɔː, ˈfɪə.stᵊn-; ˈfiː.sᵊn.heɪ (US) ˈfeð.ɚ.stᵊn.θɑː, -hɔː; ˈfæn.ʃɑː, -ʃɔː; ˈfes.tᵊn.hɑː, ˈfɪr.stᵊn-, -hɔː; ˈfiː.sᵊn.heɪ
featherweight ˈfeð.ə.weɪt (US) ˈ-ɚ- **-s** -s
feather|y ˈfeð.ᵊr|.i **-iness** -ɪ.nəs, -ɪ.nɪs
Featley ˈfiːt.li
featly ˈfiːt.li
feat|ure ˈfiː.tʃ|əʳ (US) -tʃ|ɚ **-ures** -əz (US) -ɚz **-uring** -ᵊr.ɪŋ **-ured** -əd (US) -ɚd **-ureless** -ə.ləs, -lɪs (US) -ɚ.ləs, -lɪs
Feaver ˈfiː.vəʳ (US) -vɚ
Feb. *(abbrev. for* **February***)* feb, ˈfeb.ru.ᵊr.i, ˈ-jʊ.ᵊr.i, ˈ-jʊ.ri, ˈ-jᵊr.i (US) ˈfeb.ruː.er.i, ˈ-juː-, ˈ-jə.wer-
febrifug|e ˈfeb.rɪ.fjuːdʒ, -rə- **-es** -ɪz
febrile ˈfiː.braɪl (US) -brɪl, ˈfeb.rɪl
February ˈfeb.ru.ᵊr.i, ˈ-ju.ᵊr.i, ˈ-jʊ.ri, ˈ-jᵊr.i (US) ˈfeb.ruː.er.i, ˈ-juː-, ˈ-jə.wer-
fecal ˈfiː.kᵊl
feces ˈfiː.siːz
fecit ˈfiː.sɪt, ˈfeɪ.kɪt
Feckenham ˈfek.ᵊn.əm
feckless ˈfek.ləs, -lɪs **-ly** -li **-ness** -nəs, -nɪs
feculen|t ˈfek.jə.lən|t, -jʊ- (US) -jə-, -juː- **-ce** -*ts*
fecund ˈfek.ənd, ˈfiː.kənd, -kʌnd
fecun|date ˈfek.ᵊn|.deɪt, ˈfiː.kᵊn-, -kʌn- **-dates** -deɪts **-dating** -deɪ.tɪŋ (US) -deɪ.t̬ɪŋ **-dated** -deɪ.tɪd (US) -deɪ.t̬ɪd
fecundation ˌfek.ᵊnˈdeɪ.ʃᵊn, ˌfiː.kᵊnˈ-, -kʌnˈ-
fecundity fɪˈkʌn.də.ti, fiːˈkʌn-, fekˈʌn-, -dɪ.ti (US) -də.t̬i
fed *(from* **feed***)* fed ˌ**fed** ˈ**up**
Fed fed
federal (F) ˈfed.ᵊr.ᵊl, ˈ-rəl **-ly** -i ˌ**Federal** **Re**ˈ**serve**
federal|ism ˈfed.ᵊr.ᵊl|.ɪ.zᵊm, ˈ-rᵊl- **-ist/s** -ɪst/s
federalization, -isa- ˌfed.ᵊr.ᵊl.aɪˈzeɪ.ʃᵊn, ˌ-rᵊl-, -ɪˈ- (US) -ɪˈ-
federaliz|e, -is|e ˈfed.ᵊr.ᵊl.aɪz, ˈ-rᵊl- (US) ˈ-ɚ.ə.laɪz, ˈ-rə- **-es** -ɪz **-ing** -ɪŋ **-ed** -d
federate *(n. adj.)* ˈfed.ᵊr.ət, -ɪt, -eɪt **-s** -s
feder|ate *(v.)* ˈfed.ᵊr|.eɪt **-ates** -eɪts **-ating** -eɪ.tɪŋ (US) -eɪ.t̬ɪŋ **-ated** -eɪ.tɪd (US) -eɪ.t̬ɪd
federation ˌfed.ᵊrˈeɪ.ʃᵊn (US) -əˈreɪ- **-s** -z
federative ˈfed.ᵊr.ə.tɪv, -eɪ- (US) -ɚ.ə.t̬ɪv, -ə.reɪ- **-ly** -li
fedora (F) fɪˈdɔː.rə, fə-, fedˈɔː- (US) fəˈdɔːr.ə **-s** -z
fed up ˌfedˈʌp
fee fiː **-s** -z **-ing** -ɪŋ **-d** -d ˌ**fee** ˈ**simple**; ˌ**fee** ˈ**tail**
feeb|le ˈfiː.b|l̩ **-ler** -ləʳ (US) -lɚ **-lest** -l̩.ɪst, -əst, -lɪst, -ləst **-ly** -li **-leness** -l̩.nəs, -nɪs
feebleminded ˌfiː.bl̩ˈmaɪn.dɪd (US) ˌfiː.bl̩ˈmaɪn.dɪd, ˈfiː.bl̩ˌmaɪn.dɪd **-ness** -nəs, -nɪs *stress shift, British only:* ˌfeebleminded ˈsimpleton
feed fiːd **-s** -z **-ing** -ɪŋ **fed** fed **feeder/s** ˈfiː.dəʳ/z (US) -dɚ/z ˈ**feeding** ˌ**bottle**; ˈ**feed** ˌ**pipe**; ˈ**feed** ˌ**tank**
feedback ˈfiːd.bæk
feedbag ˈfiːd.bæg **-s** -z
feel fiːl **-s** -z **-ing** -ɪŋ **felt** felt
feeler ˈfiː.ləʳ (US) -lɚ **-s** -z
feelgood ˈfiːl.gʊd ˈ**feelgood** ˌ**factor**
feeling ˈfiː.lɪŋ **-s** -z **-ly** -li
Feeney ˈfiː.ni
feet *(plur. of* **foot***)* fiːt ˌ**drag one's** ˈ**feet**; ˌ**fall on one's** ˈ**feet**; ˌ**find one's** ˈ**feet**; **have/keep** ˌ**both feet on the** ˈ**groun**; **be** ˌ**rushed off one's** ˈ**feet**; ˌ**sweep someone off their** ˈ**feet**
Fegan ˈfiː.gən
Feiffer ˈfaɪ.fəʳ (US) -fɚ
feign feɪn **-s** -z **-ing** -ɪŋ **-ed** -d **-edly** -ɪ **-edness** -ɪd.nəs, -nɪs
Feilden ˈfiːl.dən
Feilding ˈfiːl.dɪŋ
Feinstein ˈfaɪn.staɪn
feint feɪnt **-s** -s **-ing** -ɪŋ (US) ˈfeɪn.t̬ɪŋ **-ed** -ɪd (US) ˈfeɪn.t̬ɪd
Feisal ˈfaɪ.sᵊl, ˈfeɪ-
Feist fiːst
feist|y ˈfaɪ.st|i **-ier** -i.əʳ (US) -i.ɚ **-iest** -i.ɪst, -i.əst **-ily** -ɪ.li, -ᵊl.i
felafel fəˈlɑː.fᵊl, -ˈlæf.ᵊl (US) -ˈlɑː.fᵊl **-s** -z
Feldman ˈfeld.mən
feldspar ˈfeld.spɑːʳ, ˈfel- (US) ˈfeld.sp
Felicia fəˈlɪs.i.ə, felˈɪs-, fɪˈlɪs-, -ˈlɪʃ- (US) fəˈlɪʃ.ə, -i.ə, -ˈliː.ʃə, -ˈlɪs.i.ə
felicitat|e fɪˈlɪs.ɪ|.teɪt, fə-, felˈɪs-, ˈ- (US) fəˈlɪs- **-es** -teɪts **-ing** -teɪ.tɪŋ (US) -teɪ.t̬ɪŋ **-ed** -teɪ.tɪd (US) -teɪ.t̬ɪ
felicitation fɪˌlɪs.ɪˈteɪ.ʃᵊn, fə-, felˌɪ -əˈ- (US) fəˌlɪs- **-s** -z
felicitous fɪˈlɪs.ɪ.təs, fə-, felˈɪs-, ˈ-ə (US) fəˈlɪs.ɪ.t̬əs, ˈ-ə- **-ly** -li **-ness** -n -nɪs
felicity (F) fɪˈlɪs.ə.ti, fə-, felˈɪs-, -ɪ.t (US) fəˈlɪs.ə.t̬i
feline ˈfiː.laɪn **-s** -z
felinity fɪˈlɪn.ə.ti, fiː-, fə-, -ɪ.ti (US) - -ɪ.t̬i
Felix ˈfiː.lɪks
Felixstowe ˈfiː.lɪk.stəʊ (US) -stoʊ
Felkin ˈfel.kɪn
fell (F) fel **-s** -z **-ing** -ɪŋ **-ed** -d
fella ˈfel.ə **-s** -z
fellah ˈfel.ə (US) ˈfel.ə; fəˈlɑː **-in** -hiː ˌfel.əˈhiːn (US) -hiːn **-een** -hiːn, ˌfel.əˈhiːn (US) -hiːn
fella|te felˈeɪ|t, fəˈleɪ|t, fɪ- (US) ˈfel. -ˈ- **-tes** -ts **-ting** -tɪŋ (US) -t̬ɪŋ **-ted** (US) -t̬ɪd **-tor/s** -təʳ/z (US) -t̬ɚ/z **-tri** -trɪks/ɪz **-trice/s** -trɪs/ɪz
fellatio fəˈleɪ.ʃi.əʊ, felˈeɪ-, fɪˈleɪ- (US) fəˈleɪ.ʃi.oʊ, -ʃoʊ; -ˈlɑː.ti.oʊ
fellation fəˈleɪ.ʃᵊn, felˈeɪ-, fɪˈleɪ-
feller ˈfel.əʳ (US) -ɚ **-z** -z
Felling ˈfel.ɪŋ
Fellini felˈiː.ni, fəˈliː-, fɪ- (US) fə-
felloe ˈfel.əʊ (US) -oʊ **-s** -z
fellow ˈfel.əʊ (US) -oʊ **-s** -z ˌ**fellow** ˈ**citizen**; ˌ**fellow** ˈ**feeling**; ˌ**fellow** ˈ**traveller**
Fellow(e)s ˈfel.əʊz (US) -oʊz
fellowship ˈfel.əʊ.ʃɪp (US) -oʊ- **-s**
Felltham ˈfel.θəm
felo-de-se ˌfiː.ləʊ.diːˈsiː, ˌfel.əʊ-ˈseɪ (US) ˌfiː.loʊ.dɪˈsiː, ˌfel.oʊ-

felos-de-se ˌfiː.ləʊz-, ˌfel.əʊz- ⓤⓢ ˌfiː.loʊz-, ˌfel.oʊz- **felones-de-se** ˌfiː.ləʊ.niːz-, ˌfel.əʊ.niːz- ⓤⓢ ˌfel.oʊ.niː.dɪˈsiː, ˌfiː.loʊ-

elon ˈfel.ən **-s** -z

elonious fəˈləʊ.ni.əs, felˈəʊ-, fɪˈləʊ- ⓤⓢ fəˈloʊ- **-ly** -li **-ness** -nəs, -nɪs

elon|y ˈfel.ə.n|i **-ies** -iz

elpham ˈfel.pəm

elspar ˈfel.spɑːʳ ⓤⓢ -spɑːr

elste(a)d ˈfel.stɪd, -sted

elt felt **-s** -s

eltham *place:* ˈfel.təm *personal name:* ˈfel.θəm

elting ˈfel.tɪŋ **-s** -z

elton ˈfel.tᵊn

elt-tip ˌfeltˈtɪp **-s** -s *stress shift, see compound:* **ˌfelt-tip ˈpen**

elucca felˈʌk.ə, fəˈlʌk-, fɪ- ⓤⓢ fəˈlʌk-, -ˈluː.kə **-s** -z

emale ˈfiː.meɪl **-s** -z **-ness** -nəs, -nɪs

eme fiːm, fem ⓤⓢ fem **-s** -z

emidom® ˈfem.ɪ.dɒm ⓤⓢ -dɑːm

eminine ˈfem.ɪ.nɪn, ˈ-ə- **-ly** -li **-ness** -nəs, -nɪs

emininit|y ˌfem.ɪˈnɪn.ə.t|i, -əˈ-, -ɪ.t|i ⓤⓢ -ə.t̬|i **-ies** -iz

emin|ism ˈfem.ɪ.n|ɪ.zᵊm, ˈ-ə- **-ist/s** -ɪst/s

eminiz|e, -is|e ˈfem.ɪ.naɪz, ˈ-ə- **-es** -ɪz **-ing** -ɪŋ **-ed** -d

emme(s) fatale(s) ˌfæm.fəˈtɑːl ⓤⓢ ˌfem.fəˈtæl

emora *(alternative plur. of* **femur***)* ˈfem.ᵊr.ə, ˈfiː.mᵊr- ⓤⓢ ˈfem.ᵊr-

emoral ˈfem.ᵊr.ᵊl, ˈfiː.mᵊr- ⓤⓢ ˈfem.ᵊr-

emur ˈfiː.məʳ ⓤⓢ -mɚ **-s** -z **femora** ˈfem.ᵊr.ə, ˈfiː.mᵊr- ⓤⓢ ˈfem.ᵊr-

n (F) fen **-s** -z

nc|e fents **-es** -ɪz **-ing** -ɪŋ **-ed** -t **-er/s** -əʳ/z ⓤⓢ -ɚ/z **-eless** -ləs, -lɪs **ˌsit on the ˈfence**

ncesitt|er ˈfents,sɪt|.əʳ ⓤⓢ -ˌsɪt̬- **-ers** -əʳ/z ⓤⓢ -ɚ/z **-ing** -ɪŋ

nchurch ˈfen.tʃɜːtʃ ⓤⓢ -tʃɝːtʃ

nd fend **-s** -z **-ing** -ɪŋ **-ed** -ɪd

nder ˈfen.dəʳ ⓤⓢ -dɚ **-s** -z

nder-bender ˈfen.dəˌben.dəʳ ⓤⓢ -dɚˌben.dɚ **-s** -z

ndi ˈfen.di

nella fɪˈnel.ə, fə-

nestr|a fɪˈnes.tr|ə, fə- **-ae** -iː **-al** -ᵊl

nes|trate fɪˈnes|.treɪt, fəˈnes-; ˈfen.ɪ.s|treɪt, ˈ-ə- ⓤⓢ ˈfen.ɪ.s|treɪt; əˈnes|.treɪt **-trates** -treɪts **-trating** -treɪ.tɪŋ ⓤⓢ -treɪ.t̬ɪŋ **-trated** -treɪ.tɪd ⓤⓢ -treɪ.t̬ɪd

nestration ˌfen.ɪˈstreɪ.ʃᵊn, -əˈ- **-s** -z

ng shui ˌfeŋˈʃuː.i ⓤⓢ ˌfʌŋˈʃweɪ

nham ˈfen.əm

nian ˈfiː.ni.ən **-s** -z **-ism** -ɪ.zᵊm

nimore ˈfen.ɪ.mɔːʳ ⓤⓢ -mɔːr

fenland (F) ˈfen.lənd, -lænd

Fenn fen

fennec ˈfen.ek, -ɪk **-s** -s

fennel ˈfen.ᵊl

Fennell ˈfen.ᵊl

Fennessy ˈfen.ɪ.si, ˈ-ə-

Fennimore ˈfen.ɪ.mɔːʳ ⓤⓢ -mɔːr

fenny (F) ˈfen.i

Fenrir ˈfen.rɪəʳ ⓤⓢ -rɪr

Fenton ˈfen.tən ⓤⓢ -tᵊn

fenugreek ˈfen.jʊ.griːk, -ʊ- ⓤⓢ -juː-, -jə-

Fenwick *English surname:* ˈfen.ɪk, -wɪk *American surname:* ˈfen.wɪk *places in UK:* ˈfen.ɪk

Feodor ˈfiː.əʊ.dɔːʳ ⓤⓢ -ə.dɔːr

Feodora ˌfiː.əʊˈdɔː.rə ⓤⓢ -əˈdɔːr.ə

feoff fiːf, fef **-s** -s **-ing** -ɪŋ **-ed** -t **-er/s** -əʳ/z ⓤⓢ -ɚ/z **-ment/s** -mənt/s

feoffee fiːˈfiː, fefˈiː **-s** -z

feoffor fiːˈfɔːʳ, fefˈɔːʳ ⓤⓢ fiːˈfɔːr, fefˈɔːr **-s** -z

ferae naturae ˌfer.aɪˌnɑːˈtjʊə.raɪ, -ˈtjɔː- ⓤⓢ ˌfiː.riː.nəˈtuː.riː, -ˈtʊr.iː

feral ˈfer.ᵊl, ˈfɪə.rᵊl ⓤⓢ ˈfer.ᵊl, ˈfɪr-

Ferdinand ˈfɜː.dɪ.nænd, -də-, -dᵊn.ænd, -ənd ⓤⓢ ˈfɝː.dᵊn.ænd

feretor|y ˈfer.ɪ.tᵊr|.i, -tr|i ⓤⓢ -tɔːr|.i **-ies** -iz

Fergal ˈfɜː.gᵊl ⓤⓢ ˈfɝː-

Fergie ˈfɜː.gi ⓤⓢ ˈfɝː-

Fergus ˈfɜː.gəs ⓤⓢ ˈfɝː-

Fergus(s)on ˈfɜː.gə.sᵊn ⓤⓢ ˈfɝː-

feri|a ˈfer.i.ə, ˈfɪə.ri- ⓤⓢ ˈfɪr-, ˈfer- **-al** -əl

Feringhee fəˈrɪŋ.gi **-s** -z

Fermanagh fəˈmæn.ə, fɜː- ⓤⓢ fɚ-, fɝː-

ferment *(n.)* ˈfɜː.ment ⓤⓢ ˈfɝː- **-s** -s

fer|ment *(v.)* fə|ˈment, fɜː- ⓤⓢ fɚ- **-ments** -ˈments **-menting** -ˈmen.tɪŋ ⓤⓢ -ˈmen.t̬ɪŋ **-mented** -ˈmen.tɪd ⓤⓢ -ˈmen.t̬ɪd **-mentable** -ˈmen.tə.bl̩ ⓤⓢ -ˈmen.t̬ə.bl̩

fermentation ˌfɜː.menˈteɪ.ʃᵊn, -mənˈ- ⓤⓢ ˌfɝː- **-s** -z

fermentative fəˈmen.tə.tɪv ⓤⓢ -t̬ə.t̬ɪv **-ly** -li **-ness** -nəs, -nɪs

Fermi ˈfeə.mi ⓤⓢ ˈfer-

fermium ˈfɜː.mi.əm ⓤⓢ ˈfɝː-

Fermor ˈfɜː.mɔːʳ ⓤⓢ ˈfɝː.mɔːr

Fermoy *near Cork:* fəˈmɔɪ, fɜː- ⓤⓢ fɚ-, fɝː- *street in London:* ˈfɜː.mɔɪ ⓤⓢ ˈfɝː-

fern (F) fɜːn ⓤⓢ fɝːn **-s** -z

Fernandez fɜːˈnæn.dez, fə- ⓤⓢ fɚ-

Fernando fəˈnæn.dəʊ ⓤⓢ fɚˈnæn.doʊ

Ferndale ˈfɜːn.deɪl ⓤⓢ ˈfɝːn-

Ferndown ˈfɜːn.daʊn ⓤⓢ ˈfɝːn-

ferner|y ˈfɜː.nᵊr|.i ⓤⓢ ˈfɝː- **-ies** -iz

Fernhough ˈfɜːn.həʊ ⓤⓢ ˈfɝːn.hoʊ

Fernihough, Fernyhough ˈfɜː.ni.hʌf, -həʊ ⓤⓢ ˈfɝː.ni.hʌf, -hoʊ

ferny ˈfɜː.ni ⓤⓢ ˈfɝː-

ferocious fəˈrəʊ.ʃəs, fɪ- ⓤⓢ fəˈroʊ- **-ly** -li **-ness** -nəs, -nɪs

ferocity fəˈrɒs.ə.ti, fɪ-, -ɪ.ti ⓤⓢ fəˈrɑː.sə.t̬i

-ferous -fᵊr.əs

Note: Suffix. Words containing **-ferous** are normally stressed on the preceding syllable, e.g. **conifer** /ˈkɒn.ɪ.fəʳ ⓤⓢ ˈkɑː.nə.fɚ/, **coniferous** /kəʊˈnɪf.ᵊr.əs ⓤⓢ koʊˈnɪf-/.

Ferrand ˈfer.ᵊnd

Ferranti fəˈræn.ti, fɪ-, ferˈæn- ⓤⓢ fəˈrɑːn.t̬i

Ferrar ˈfer.əʳ; fəˈrɑːʳ ⓤⓢ ˈfer.ɚ; fəˈrɑːr

Ferrara fəˈrɑː.rə, fɪˈ-, ferˈɑː- ⓤⓢ -ˈrɑːr.ə

Ferrari® fəˈrɑː.ri, fɪˈ-, ferˈɑː- ⓤⓢ fəˈrɑːr.i

Ferraro fəˈrɑː.rəʊ, fɪˈ-, ferˈɑː- ⓤⓢ fəˈrɑːr.oʊ

Ferraud fəˈrəʊ, ferˈəʊ ⓤⓢ fəˈroʊ

ferrel (F) ˈfer.ᵊl **-s** -z

ferreous ˈfer.i.əs

Ferrer ˈfer.əʳ; fəˈreəʳ ⓤⓢ ˈfer.ɚ; fəˈrer **-s** -z

ferre|t (F) ˈfer.ɪ|t, -ə|t **-ts** -ts **-ting** -tɪŋ ⓤⓢ -t̬ɪŋ **-ted** -tɪd ⓤⓢ -t̬ɪd

ferri- ˈfer.i-

ferric ˈfer.ɪk

Ferrier ˈfer.i.əʳ ⓤⓢ -ɚ

ferris (F) ˈfer.ɪs **ˈferris ˌwheel**

Ferrisburg ˈfer.ɪs.bɜːg ⓤⓢ -bɝːg

ferrite ˈfer.aɪt

ferritic ferˈɪt.ɪk, fəˈrɪt- ⓤⓢ fəˈrɪt̬-, ferˈɪt̬-

ferro- fer.əʊ- ⓤⓢ fer.oʊ-

Note: Prefix. Normally carries either primary or secondary stress on the first syllable, e.g. **ferrotype** /ˈfer.əʊ.taɪp ⓤⓢ -oʊ-/, **ferromagnetic** /ˌfer.əʊ.mægˈnet.ɪk ⓤⓢ -oʊ.mægˈnet̬-/.

ferroconcrete ˌfer.əʊˈkɒŋ.kriːt ⓤⓢ -oʊˈkɑːn.kriːt

ferromagnetic ˌfer.əʊ.mægˈnet.ɪk ⓤⓢ -oʊ.mægˈnet̬-

ferromagnetism ˌfer.əʊˈmæg.nə.tɪ.zᵊm ⓤⓢ -oʊˈ-

ferrotype ˈfer.əʊ.taɪp ⓤⓢ -oʊ- **-s** -s

ferrous ˈfer.əs

ferruginous ferˈuː.dʒɪ.nəs, fəˈruː-, fɪ-, -dʒᵊn- ⓤⓢ fəˈruː.dʒɪ.nəs, ferˈuː-

ferrule ˈfer.uːl, -ᵊl, -juːl ⓤⓢ -ᵊl, -uːl **-s** -z

Note: /ˈfer.ᵊl/ is the pronunciation used by those connected with the umbrella trade.

ferr|y (F) ˈfer|.i **-ies** -iz **-ying** -i.ɪŋ **-ied** -id

ferryboat ˈfer.i.bəʊt ⓤⓢ -boʊt **-s** -s

Ferryhill ˈfer.i.hɪl

ferry|man ˈfer.i|.mən, -mæn **-men** -mən, -men

fertile 'fɜː.taɪl ⓤⓢ 'fɝː.ţəl **-ly** -li
fertility fə'tɪl.ə.ti, fɜː-, -ɪ.ti ⓤⓢ fɚ'tɪl.ə.ţi
fertilization, -isa- ˌfɜː.tɪ.laɪ'zeɪ.ʃən, -təl.aɪ'-, -ɪ'- ⓤⓢ ˌfɝː.ţəl.ɪ'-
fertiliz|e, -is|e 'fɜː.tɪ.laɪz, -təl.aɪz ⓤⓢ 'fɝː.ţə.laɪz **-es** -ɪz **-ing** -ɪŋ **-ed** -d
fertilizer, -ise- 'fɜː.tɪ.laɪ.zər, -təl.aɪ- ⓤⓢ 'fɝː.ţəl- **-s** -z
ferule 'fer.uːl, -əl, -juːl ⓤⓢ -əl, -uːl **-s** -z
fervency 'fɜː.vənt.si ⓤⓢ 'fɝː-
fervent 'fɜː.vənt ⓤⓢ 'fɝː- **-ly** -li **-ness** -nəs, -nɪs
fervid 'fɜː.vɪd ⓤⓢ 'fɝː- **-ly** -li **-ness** -nəs, -nɪs
fervo(u)r 'fɜː.vər ⓤⓢ 'fɝː.vɚ
fescue 'fes.kjuː **-s** -z
fess fes **-es** -ɪs **-ing** -ɪŋ **-ed** -t
fess|e fes **-es** -ɪz
Fessenden 'fes.ən.dən
fest fest **-s** -s
festal 'fes.təl **-ly** -i
Feste 'fes.ti ⓤⓢ -teɪ
fest|er 'fes.t|ər ⓤⓢ -t|ɚ **-ers** -əz ⓤⓢ -ɚz **-ering** -ər.ɪŋ **-ered** -əd ⓤⓢ -ɚd
Festiniog fes'tɪn.i.ɒg ⓤⓢ -ɑːg, -ɔːg
festival 'fes.tɪ.vəl, -tə- **-s** -z
festive 'fes.tɪv **-ly** -li **-ness** -nəs, -nɪs
festivit|y fes'tɪv.ə.t|i, -ɪ.t|i ⓤⓢ -ə.ţ|i **-ies** -iz
festoon fes'tuːn ⓤⓢ fes'tuːn, fə'stuːn **-s** -z **-ing** -ɪŋ **-ed** -d
festschrift 'fest.ʃrɪft, 'feʃ- **-en** -ən **-s** -s
Festus 'fes.təs
feta 'fet.ə ⓤⓢ 'feţ- ˌ**feta** '**cheese**
fetal 'fiː.təl ⓤⓢ -ţəl '**fetal po**ˌ**sition**
fetch fetʃ **-es** -ɪz **-ing** -ɪŋ **-ed** -t **-er/s** -ər/z ⓤⓢ -ɚ/z
fetching 'fetʃ.ɪŋ **-ly** -li
fet|e, fêt|e feɪt ⓤⓢ feɪt, fet **-es** -s **-ing** -ɪŋ ⓤⓢ 'feɪ.ţɪŋ, 'feţ.ɪŋ **-ed** -ɪd ⓤⓢ 'feɪ.ţɪd, 'feţ.ɪd ˌ**garden** '**fete** ⓤⓢ '**garden** ˌ**fete**
fête(s) champêtre(s) ˌfet.ʃɑ̃ːm'pet.rə ⓤⓢ -ʃɑːm'-
fetich 'fet.ɪʃ ⓤⓢ 'feţ- **-es** -ɪz
fetich|ism 'fet.ɪ.ʃ|ɪ.zəm ⓤⓢ 'feţ- **-ist/s** -ɪst/s
fetichistic ˌfet.ɪ'ʃɪs.tɪk ⓤⓢ ˌfeţ- **-ally** -əl.i, -li
fetid 'fet.ɪd, 'fiː.tɪd ⓤⓢ 'feţ.ɪd, 'fiː.ţɪd **-ly** -li **-ness** -nəs, -nɪs
fetish 'fet.ɪʃ ⓤⓢ 'feţ- **-es** -ɪz
fetish|ism 'fet.ɪ.ʃ|ɪ.zəm ⓤⓢ 'feţ- **-ist/s** -ɪst/s
fetishistic ˌfet.ɪ'ʃɪs.tɪk ⓤⓢ ˌfeţ- **-ally** -əl.i, -li
fetlock 'fet.lɒk ⓤⓢ -lɑːk **-s** -s **-ed** -t
fetolog|y fiː'tɒl.ə.dʒ|i ⓤⓢ -'tɑː.lə- **-ist/s** -ɪst/s
fetta 'fet.ə ⓤⓢ 'feţ- ˌ**fetta** '**cheese**

fett|er (F) 'fet|.ər ⓤⓢ 'feţ|.ɚ **-ers** -əz ⓤⓢ -ɚz **-ering** -ər.ɪŋ **-ered** -əd ⓤⓢ -ɚd
Fettes *place:* 'fet.ɪs ⓤⓢ 'feţ- *surname:* 'fet.ɪs, -ɪz ⓤⓢ 'feţ-
Fettesian fet'iː.zi.ən, -ʒən **-s** -z
fettl|e 'fet.l̩ ⓤⓢ 'feţ- **-es** -z **-ing** -ɪŋ, '-lɪŋ ⓤⓢ 'feţ.l̩.ɪŋ, 'fet.lɪŋ **-ed** -d
fettuccine ˌfet.ʊ'tʃiː.ni ⓤⓢ ˌfeţ.ə'-
fetus 'fiː.təs ⓤⓢ -ţəs **-es** -ɪz
feu fjuː **-s** -z **-ing** -ɪŋ **-ed** -d
feud fjuːd **-s** -z **-ing** -ɪŋ
feudal 'fjuː.dəl **-ly** -i
feudal|ism 'fjuː.dəl|.ɪ.zəm **-ist/s** -ɪst/s
feudality fjuː'dæl.ə.ti, -ɪ.ti ⓤⓢ -ə.ţi
feudalization, -isa- ˌfjuː.dəl.aɪ'zeɪ.ʃən, -ɪ'- ⓤⓢ -ɪ'-
feudaliz|e, -is|e 'fjuː.dəl.aɪz ⓤⓢ -də.laɪz **-es** -ɪz **-ing** -ɪŋ **-ed** -d
feudatory 'fjuː.də.tər.i, -tri ⓤⓢ -tɔːr.i
feuilleton 'fɜː.ɪ.tɔ̃ːŋ, 'fɜːl.tɔ̃ːŋ ⓤⓢ 'fɜː.jə.tɑːn, 'fɝː-, -tɔ̃ːn **-s** -z
fever 'fiː.vər ⓤⓢ -vɚ **-s** -z **-ed** -d '**fever** ˌ**blister**; '**fever** ˌ**pitch**
feverfew 'fiː.və.fjuː ⓤⓢ -vɚ-
feverish 'fiː.vər.ɪʃ **-ly** -li **-ness** -nəs, -nɪs
Feversham 'fev.ə.ʃəm ⓤⓢ '-ɚ-
few (F) fjuː **-er** -ər ⓤⓢ -ɚ **-est** -ɪst, -əst **-ness** -nəs, -nɪs
fey feɪ **-ness** -nəs, -nɪs
Feydeau 'feɪ.dəʊ ⓤⓢ feɪ'doʊ
Feynman 'faɪn.mən
fez (F) fez **-(z)es** -ɪz
Fezzan fez'ɑːn, -'æn ⓤⓢ -'æn
Ffestiniog fes'tɪn.i.ɒg ⓤⓢ -ɑːg, -ɔːg
Ffion 'fiː.ɒn ⓤⓢ -ɑːn
Ffitch fɪtʃ
Ffoulkes fəʊks, fəʊlks, faʊks, fuːks ⓤⓢ foʊks, foʊlks, faʊks, fuːks
Ffrangcon 'fræŋ.kən
-fiable -faɪ.ə.bl̩
Note: Suffix. Normally unstressed, e.g. **rectifiable** /'rek.tɪ.faɪ.ə.bl̩ ⓤⓢ -tə-/, although some words containing -**fiable** may also be stressed on the antepenultimate syllable, especially in British English (e.g. **justifiable** /ˌdʒʌs.tɪ'faɪ.ə.bl̩/); see alsoentry for **-fy**.
fiacre fi'ɑː.krə ⓤⓢ -kɚ **-s** -z
fiancé(e) fi'ɑ̃ːn.seɪ, -'ɒnt- ⓤⓢ ˌfiː.ɑːn'seɪ, -'--- **-s** -z
Fianna Fail, Fianna Fáil ˌfiː.ə.nə'fɔɪl, ˌfiː.nə'-, -'fɔːl ⓤⓢ -'fɔɪl, -'fiːl
fiasco fi'æs.kəʊ ⓤⓢ -koʊ **-(e)s** -z
fiat *decree:* 'faɪ.æt ⓤⓢ 'fiː.ət, -æt, -ɑːt **-s** -s
Fiat® fɪət, 'fiː.æt ⓤⓢ 'fiː.ɑːt **-s** -s
fiat justicia ˌfiː.æt.jʊs'tɪs.i.ə ⓤⓢ ˌfiː.ɑːt'jʊs.tɪ.ʃə
fib fɪb **-s** -z **-bing** -ɪŋ **-bed** -d **-ber/s** -ər/z ⓤⓢ -ɚ/z
fiber 'faɪ.bər ⓤⓢ -bɚ **-s** -z

fiberglass 'faɪ.bə.glɑːs ⓤⓢ -bɚ.glæs
fiberlike 'faɪ.bə.laɪk ⓤⓢ -bɚ-
Fibonacci ˌfɪb.ə'nɑː.tʃi, ˌfiː.bə'-
fibre 'faɪ.bər ⓤⓢ -bɚ **-s** -z **-d** -d **-less** -lə -lɪs
fibreglass 'faɪ.bə.glɑːs ⓤⓢ -bɚ.glæs
fibreoptic ˌfaɪ.bər'ɒp.tɪk ⓤⓢ -bɚ'ɑːp- **-s** -s
fibre optics ˌfaɪ.bər'ɒp.tɪks ⓤⓢ -bɚ'ɑː
fibriform 'faɪ.brɪ.fɔːm, 'fɪb.rɪ- ⓤⓢ -fɔːrm
fibril 'faɪ.brɪl, -brəl ⓤⓢ 'faɪ.brɪl, 'fɪb.r **-s** -s **-lar** -ər ⓤⓢ -ɚ **-lose** -əʊs ⓤⓢ -oʊs
fibril|late 'faɪ.brɪ|.leɪt, 'fɪb.rɪ-, -rə- ⓤⓢ 'fɪb.rɪ-, 'faɪ.brɪ- **-lates** -leɪts **-lating** -leɪ.tɪŋ ⓤⓢ -leɪ.ţɪŋ **-lated** -leɪ.tɪd ⓤⓢ -leɪ.ţɪd
fibrillation ˌfaɪ.brɪ'leɪ.ʃən, ˌfɪb.rɪ'-, -rə'- ⓤⓢ ˌfɪb.rɪ'-, ˌfaɪ.brɪ'- **-s** -z
fibrilliform faɪ'brɪl.ɪ.fɔːm, fɪ- ⓤⓢ fɪ'-, faɪ'-, -fɔːrm
fibrin 'fɪb.rɪn, 'faɪ.brɪn ⓤⓢ 'faɪ- **-ous**
fibrinogen fɪ'brɪn.əʊ.dʒən, faɪ-, -dʒe ⓤⓢ faɪ'brɪn.ə-
fibro- faɪ.brəʊ-; faɪ'brəʊ- ⓤⓢ faɪ.bro -brə-; faɪ'broʊ-
Note: Prefix. Normally carries primary or secondary stress on th first syllable, e.g. **fibrositis** /ˌfaɪ.brəʊ'saɪ.tɪs ⓤⓢ -broʊ'saɪ.ţɪs or primary stress on the second syllable, e.g. **fibrosis** /faɪ'brəʊ.sɪ ⓤⓢ -'broʊ-/.
fibroid 'faɪ.brɔɪd **-s** -z
fibroma faɪ'brəʊ.mə ⓤⓢ -'broʊ- **-s** -z **-ta** -tə ⓤⓢ -ţə
fibrosis faɪ'brəʊ.sɪs ⓤⓢ -'broʊ-
fibrositis ˌfaɪ.brəʊ'saɪ.tɪs ⓤⓢ -broʊ'saɪ.ţɪs
fibrous 'faɪ.brəs **-ly** -li **-ness** -nəs, -n
fibul|a 'fɪb.jə.l|ə, -jʊ- ⓤⓢ -jə- **-as** -əz **-ae** -iː
FICA 'fiː.kə ⓤⓢ 'faɪ-, 'fiː-
fich|e fiːʃ **-es** -ɪz
fichu 'fiː.ʃuː, 'fɪʃ.uː ⓤⓢ 'fɪʃ.uː; fiː'ʃ **-s** -z
fickl|e 'fɪk.l̩ **-er** -ər, '-lər ⓤⓢ '-lɚ, -l̩.ɚ -ɪst, -əst **-eness** -nəs, -nɪs
fiction 'fɪk.ʃən **-s** z
fictional 'fɪk.ʃən.əl **-ly** -i
fictionalization ˌfɪk.ʃən.əl.aɪ'zeɪ. -ɪ'- ⓤⓢ -ɪ'-
fictionaliz|e, -is|e 'fɪk.ʃən.əl.aɪz ⓤⓢ -ə.laɪz **-es** -ɪz **-ing** -ɪŋ **-ed** -d
fictionist 'fɪk.ʃən.ɪst **-s** -s
fictitious fɪk'tɪʃ.əs **-ly** -li **-ness** -nə -nɪs
fictive 'fɪk.tɪv
fid fɪd **-s** -z
fiddl|e 'fɪd.l̩ **-es** -z **-ing** -ɪŋ, '-lɪŋ **-e** **-er/s** -ər/z, '-lər/z, '-l̩.ɚ/z ⓤⓢ '-lɚ ˌ**fit as a** '**fiddle**

fiddlededee ˌfɪd.l̩.dɪˈdiː ⓊⓈ -diːˈdiː
fiddle-faddl|e ˈfɪd.l̩ˌfæd.l̩ **-es** -z **-ing** -ɪŋ, ˌ-lɪŋ **-ed** -d
fiddlesticks ˈfɪd.l̩.stɪks
fiddl|y ˈfɪd.l̩|.i, ˈfɪd.l|i **-ier** -i.əʳ ⓊⓈ -i.ɚ **-iest** -i.ɪst, -i.əst **-iness** -ɪ.nəs, -ɪ.nɪs
Fidel fɪˈdel, fiː-, ˈfɪd.el
Fidelia fɪˈdiː.li.ə, fə-, -ˈdeɪ- ⓊⓈ -ˈdiː.li.ə, -ˈdiːl.jə
Fidelio fɪˈdeɪ.li.əʊ ⓊⓈ -oʊ
fidelity fɪˈdel.ə.ti, fə-, -ɪ.ti ⓊⓈ -ə.t̬i
fidg|et ˈfɪdʒ|.ɪt **-ets** -ɪts **-eting** -ɪ.tɪŋ ⓊⓈ -ɪ.t̬ɪŋ **-eted** -ɪ.tɪd ⓊⓈ -ɪ.t̬ɪd
fidget|y ˈfɪdʒ.ɪ.t|i, ˈ-ə- **-ier** -i.əʳ ⓊⓈ -i.ɚ **-iest** -i.ɪst, -i.əst **-iness** -ɪ.nəs, -ɪ.nɪs
Fido ˈfaɪ.dəʊ ⓊⓈ -doʊ
fiducial fɪˈdjuː.ʃi.əl, fə-, faɪ-, -si- ⓊⓈ -ˈduː.ʃᵊl, -ˈdjuː- **-ly** -i
fiduciar|y fɪˈdjuː.ʃi.ə.r|i, fə-, faɪ-, -si-, -ʃᵊr|.i ⓊⓈ fɪˈduː.ʃi.er-, -ʃᵊr-, -ˈdjuː- **-ies** -iz
fie faɪ
fiedler ˈfiːd.ləʳ ⓊⓈ -lɚ
fief fiːf **-s** -s
fiefdom ˈfiːf.dəm **-s** -z
field (F) ˈfiːld **-s** -z **-ing** -ɪŋ **-ed** -ɪd **-er/s** -əʳ/z ⓊⓈ -ɚ/z ˈ**field** ˌ**glass**; ˈ**field** ˌ**goal**; ˈ**field** ˌ**gun**; ˌ**field** ˈ**hospital** ⓊⓈ ˈ**field** ˌ**hospital**; ˌ**field** ˈ**marshal** ⓊⓈ ˈ**field** ˌ**marshal**; ˈ**field** ˌ**mouse**; ˈ**field** ˌ**officer**; ˌ**field of** ˈ**vision**; ˈ**field** ˌ**trip**; **have a** ˈ**field** ˌ**day**
fielden ˈfiːl.dᵊn
fieldener ˈfiːl.dᵊn.əʳ ⓊⓈ -ɚ
fielder (F) ˈfiːl.dəʳ ⓊⓈ -dɚ **-s** -z
fieldfare ˈfiːld.feəʳ ⓊⓈ -fer **-s** -z
fielding ˈfiːl.dɪŋ
fields fiːldz
fields|man ˈfiːldz|.mən **-men** -mən, -men
field-test ˈfiːld.test **-s** -s **-ing** -ɪŋ **-ed** -ɪd
fieldwork ˈfiːld.wɜːk ⓊⓈ -wɝːk **-s** -s **-er/s** -əʳ/z ⓊⓈ -ɚ/z
fiend (F) fiːnd **-s** -z
fiendish ˈfiːn.dɪʃ **-ly** -li **-ness** -nəs, -nɪs
Fiennes faɪnz
fierc|e fɪəs ⓊⓈ fɪrs **-er** -əʳ ⓊⓈ -ɚ **-est** -ɪst, -əst **-ely** -li **-eness** -nəs, -nɪs
fier|y ˈfaɪə.r|i ⓊⓈ ˈfaɪ-, ˈfaɪɚ|.i **-ier** -i.əʳ ⓊⓈ -i.ɚ **-iest** -i.ɪst, -i.əst **-ily** -ɪ.li, -ᵊl.i **-iness** -ɪ.nəs, -ɪ.nɪs
fiesta® (F) fiˈes.tə **-s** -z
FIFA, Fifa ˈfiː.fə
fife (F) faɪf **-es** -s **-ing** -ɪŋ **-ed** -t **-er/s** -əʳ/z ⓊⓈ -ɚ/z
Fife faɪf **-shire** -ʃəʳ, -ˌʃɪəʳ ⓊⓈ -ʃɚ, -ʃɪr
fifi ˈfiː.fiː
Fifield ˈfaɪ.fiːld
fifteen ˌfɪfˈtiːn **-s** -z **-th/s** -θ/s *stress shift:* ˌfifteen ˈyears
fifth fɪfθ **-s** -s **-ly** -li ˌ**Fifth A**ˈ**mendment**; **Fifth** ˈ**Avenue**
fifth-column ˌfɪfθˈkɒl.əm ⓊⓈ -ˈkɑː.ləm **-ist/s** -ɪst/s, -nɪst/s **-ism** -ɪ.zᵊm, -nɪ.zᵊm
fiftieth ˈfɪf.ti.əθ **-s** -s
fift|y ˈfɪf.t|i **-ies** -iz
fifty-fifty ˌfɪf.tiˈfɪf.ti
fiftyfold ˈfɪf.ti.fəʊld ⓊⓈ -foʊld
fig fɪg **-s** -z ˈ**fig** ˌ**leaf**; ˈ**fig** ˌ**tree**
Figaro ˈfɪg.ə.rəʊ ⓊⓈ -roʊ
Figes ˈfɪg.ɪs
Figg fɪg
Figgis ˈfɪg.ɪs
fight faɪt **-s** -s **-ing** -ɪŋ ⓊⓈ ˈfaɪ.t̬ɪŋ **fought** fɔːt ⓊⓈ fɑːt, fɔːt ˈ**fighting** ˌ**cock**
fightback ˈfaɪt.bæk **-s** -s
fighter ˈfaɪ.təʳ ⓊⓈ -t̬ɚ **-s** -z
figment ˈfɪg.mənt **-s** -s
Figo ˈfiː.gəʊ ⓊⓈ -goʊ
Figueroa ˌfɪg.əˈrəʊ.ə ⓊⓈ -ˈroʊ-
figurability ˌfɪg.jᵊr.əˈbɪl.ə.ti, -ᵊr-, -jʊ.rəˈ-, -ɪ.ti ⓊⓈ -jɚ.əˈbɪl.ə.t̬i, -jʊ.rəˈ-
figurable ˈfɪg.jᵊr.ə.bl̩, -ᵊr-, -jʊ.rə- ⓊⓈ -jɚ.ə-, -jʊ.rə-
figurative ˈfɪg.jᵊr.ə.tɪv, -ᵊr-, -jʊ.rə- ⓊⓈ -jɚ.ə.t̬ɪv, -jʊ.rə- **-ly** -li **-ness** -nəs, -nɪs
figur|e ˈfɪg.əʳ ⓊⓈ -jɚ, -jʊr **-es** -z **-ing** -ɪŋ **-ed** -d ˌ**figure** ˈ**eight**; ˌ**figure of** ˈ**eight**; ˌ**figure of** ˈ**speech**; ˈ**figure** ˌ**skating**
figurehead ˈfɪg.ə.hed ⓊⓈ -jɚ- **-s** -z
figurine ˈfɪg.jə.riːn, ˈ-ə-, -jʊ-, ˌ--ˈ- ⓊⓈ ˌfɪg.juːˈriːn, -jəˈ- **-s** -z
Fiji ˈfiː.dʒiː, -ˈ- ⓊⓈ ˈ--
Fijian fɪˈdʒiː.ən, fiː- ⓊⓈ ˈfiː.dʒiː-, -ˈ-- **-s** -z
filament ˈfɪl.ə.mənt **-s** -s
filamentous ˌfɪl.əˈmen.təs
filari|a fɪˈleə.ri|.ə ⓊⓈ -ˈler.i- **-ae** -iː **-al** -əl
filarias|is ˌfɪl.əˈraɪə.s|ɪs; fɪˌleə.riˈeɪ-, fə- ⓊⓈ ˌfɪl.əˈraɪ.ə.s|ɪs **-es** -iːz
filature ˈfɪl.ə.tʃəʳ, -tjəʳ ⓊⓈ -tʃɚ **-s** -z
filbert ˈfɪl.bət ⓊⓈ -bɚt **-s** -s
filch fɪltʃ **-es** -ɪz **-ing** -ɪŋ **-ed** -t
Fildes faɪldz
fil|e faɪl **-es** -z **-ing/s** -ɪŋ/z **-ed** -d ˈ**filing** ˌ**clerk**
filemot ˈfɪl.ɪ.mɒt ⓊⓈ -mɑːt
filet ˈfɪl.eɪ, ˈfiː.leɪ ⓊⓈ fɪˈleɪ, ˈfɪl.eɪ **-s** -z **-(t)ing** -ɪŋ **-(t)ed** -d
filet(s) mignon(s) ˌfɪl.eɪˈmiː.njɔ̃ːŋ, ˌfiː.leɪ-, -ˈmɪn.jɒn ⓊⓈ ˌfɪl.eɪ.miːˈnjɑːn, -ˈnjoʊn; fɪˌleɪ-
Filey ˈfaɪ.li
filial ˈfɪl.i.əl **-ly** -i **-ness** -nəs, -nɪs
filiation ˌfɪl.iˈeɪ.ʃᵊn
filibeg ˈfɪl.ɪ.beg, ˈ-ə- **-s** -z
filibust|er ˈfɪl.ɪ.bʌs.t|əʳ, ˈ-ə- ⓊⓈ -t|ɚ **-ers** -əz ⓊⓈ -ɚz **-ering** -ᵊr.ɪŋ **-ered** -əd ⓊⓈ -ɚd
filigree ˈfɪl.ɪ.griː, ˈ-ə- **-s** -z **-ing** -ɪŋ **-d** -d
filing ˈfaɪ.lɪŋ **-s** -z ˈ**filing** ˌ**cabinet**
Filioque ˌfiː.liˈəʊ.kwi, ˌfaɪ-, ˌfɪl.iˈ- ⓊⓈ -ˈoʊ-
Filipino ˌfɪl.ɪˈpiː.nəʊ, -əˈ- ⓊⓈ -noʊ **-s** -z
Filkin ˈfɪl.kɪn **-s** -z
fill fɪl **-s** -z **-ing/s** -ɪŋ/z **-ed** -d ˈ**filling** ˌ**station**; ˌ**fill the** ˈ**bill**
filler *thing or person that fills:* ˈfɪl.əʳ ⓊⓈ -ɚ **-s** -z
filler, fillér *Hungarian currency:* ˈfiː.leəʳ ⓊⓈ ˈfɪl.er, ˈfiː.ler **-s** -z
fill|et ˈfɪl|.ɪt **-ets** -ɪts **-eting** -ɪ.tɪŋ ⓊⓈ -ɪ.t̬ɪŋ **-eted** -ɪ.tɪd ⓊⓈ -ɪ.t̬ɪd
fillibeg ˈfɪl.ɪ.beg, ˈ-ə- **-s** -z
fillip ˈfɪl.ɪp **-s** -s **-ing** -ɪŋ **-ed** -t
Fillmore ˈfɪl.mɔːʳ ⓊⓈ -mɔːr
fill|y ˈfɪl|.i **-ies** -iz
film fɪlm **-s** -z **-ing** -ɪŋ **-ed** -d ˈ**film** ˌ**star**
filmgoer ˈfɪlmˌgəʊ.əʳ ⓊⓈ -ˌgoʊ.ɚ **-s** -z
filmgoing ˈfɪlmˌgəʊ.ɪŋ ⓊⓈ -ˌgoʊ-
filmic ˈfɪl.mɪk
filmmaker ˈfɪlmˌmeɪ.kəʳ ⓊⓈ -kɚ **-s** -z
film(s) noir(s) ˌfɪlmˈnwɑː, -ˈnwɑːr
film|set ˈfɪlm|.set **-sets** -sets **-setting** -ˌset.ɪŋ ⓊⓈ -ˌset̬.ɪŋ
filmstrip ˈfɪlm.strɪp **-s** -s
film|y ˈfɪl.m|i **-ier** -i.əʳ ⓊⓈ -i.ɚ **-iest** -i.ɪst, -i.əst **-ily** -ɪ.li, -ᵊl.i **-iness** -ɪ.nəs, -ɪ.nɪs
filo ˈfaɪ.ləʊ, ˈfiː-, ˈfɪl.əʊ ⓊⓈ ˈfiː.loʊ, ˈfaɪ- ˌ**filo** ˈ**pastry** ⓊⓈ ˈ**filo** ˌ**pastry**
Filofax® ˈfaɪ.ləʊ.fæks ⓊⓈ -loʊ-, -lə- **-es** -ɪz
Filon ˈfaɪ.lən, -lɒn ⓊⓈ ˌfiːˈlɑːn
fils *son:* fiːs
fils *monetary unit:* fɪls
filt|er (*n. v.*) ˈfɪl.t|əʳ ⓊⓈ -t̬|ɚ **-ers** -əz ⓊⓈ -ɚz **-ering** -ᵊr.ɪŋ **-ered** -əd ⓊⓈ -ɚd ˈ**filter** ˌ**coffee**; ˈ**filter** ˌ**paper**; ˈ**filter** ˌ**tip**
filth fɪlθ
filth|y ˈfɪl.θ|i **-ier** -i.əʳ ⓊⓈ -i.ɚ **-iest** -i.ɪst, -i.əst **-ily** -ɪ.li, -ᵊl.i **-iness** -ɪ.nəs, -ɪ.nəs
filtrate (*n.*) ˈfɪl.treɪt **-s** -s
fil|trate (*v.*) fɪl|ˈtreɪt ⓊⓈ ˈ-- **-trates** -ˈtreɪts ⓊⓈ -treɪts **-trating** -ˈtreɪ.tɪŋ ⓊⓈ -treɪ.t̬ɪŋ **-trated** -ˈtreɪ.tɪd ⓊⓈ -treɪ.t̬ɪd
filtration fɪlˈtreɪ.ʃᵊn **-s** -z
FIMBRA ˈfɪm.brə
fin fɪn **-s** -z
Fina® ˈfiː.nə, ˈfaɪ-
finable ˈfaɪ.nə.bl̩
finagl|e fɪˈneɪ.gl̩ **-es** -z **-ing** -ɪŋ, ˈ-glɪŋ **-ed** -d **-er/s** -əʳ/z, ˈ-gləʳ/z ⓊⓈ ˈ-ɚ/z, ˈ-glɚ/z
final ˈfaɪ.nᵊl **-s** -z **-ly** -i
finale fɪˈnɑː.li, fə-, -leɪ ⓊⓈ -ˈnæl.i, -ˈnɑː.leɪ, -li **-s** -z
finalist ˈfaɪ.nᵊl.ɪst **-s** -s
finality faɪˈnæl.ə.ti, -ɪ.ti ⓊⓈ faɪˈnæl.ə.t̬i, fə-

finaliz|e, -is|e 'faɪ.n^{ə}l.aɪz US -nə.laɪz **-es** -ɪz **-ing** -ɪŋ **-ed** -d
financ|e 'faɪ.nænts; faɪ'nænts, fɪ-, fə- **-es** -ɪz **-ing** -ɪŋ **-ed** -t
financial faɪ'næn.tʃ^{ə}l, fɪ-, fə- US -'nænt.ʃ^{ə}l **-ly** -i **Fi,nancial 'Times**
financier faɪ'nænt.si.ə^{r}, fɪ-, fə- US fɪ'nænt.si.ɚ, fə-; ˌfɪn.ən'sɪr, ˌfaɪ.næn'-, -nən'- **-s** -z
Finbar 'fɪn.bɑː^{r}, 'fɪm- US 'fɪn.bɑːr
finch (F) fɪntʃ **-es** -ɪz
Finchale 'fɪŋ.k^{ə}l
Fincham 'fɪn.tʃəm
Finchampsted 'fɪn.tʃəm.sted, -tʃəmp-, -stɪd
Finchley 'fɪntʃ.li
find faɪnd **-s** -z **-ing/s** -ɪŋ/z **found** faʊnd **finder/s** 'faɪn.də^{r}/z US -dɚ/z
fin de siècle ˌfæ̃n.də'sjek.l̩, ˌfæn-, -si'ek-, -lə US ˌfæ̃n.də.si'ek.lə, -'sjek-, -l̩
Findlater 'fɪnd.lə.tə^{r}, -leɪ.tə^{r} US -t̬ɚ
Findlay 'fɪnd.leɪ, -li
Findley 'fɪnd.li
Findus 'fɪn.dəs
fin|e faɪn **-es** -z **-er** -ə^{r} US -ɚ **-est** -ɪst, -əst **-eness** -nəs, -nɪs **-ing** -ɪŋ **-ed** -d **ˌfine 'art; 'fine ˌprint, ˌfine 'print**
finely 'faɪn.li
finery 'faɪ.n^{ə}r.i
fines herbes ˌfiːn'eəb, -'ɜːb US ˌfiːn'zerb
finespun ˌfaɪn'spʌn US '-- *stress shift, British only:* ˌfinespun 'yarn
finess|e (*n. v.*) fɪ'nes, fə- **-es** -ɪz **-ing** -ɪŋ **-ed** -t
fine-tooth ˌfaɪn'tuːθ **-ed** -t **ˌfine-toothed 'comb**
fine-tun|e ˌfaɪn'tjuːn, -'tʃuːn US -'tuːn, -'tjuːn **-es** -z **-ing** -ɪŋ **-ed** -d *stress shift:* ˌfine-tuned 'instrument
Fingal 'fɪŋ.g^{ə}l **ˌFingal's 'Cave**
Fingall 'fɪŋ.gɔːl US -gɔːl, -gɑːl
fing|er 'fɪŋ.g|ə^{r} US -g|ɚ **-ers** -əz US -ɚz **-ering/s** -^{ə}r.ɪŋ/z **-ered** -əd US -ɚd **'finger ˌbowl; 'Finger ˌLakes; ˌburn one's 'fingers; ˌall ˌfingers and 'thumbs; have a ˌfinger in every 'pie; keep one's 'fingers ˌcrossed; ˌtwist someone round one's ˌlittle 'finger; ˌwork one's ˌfingers to the 'bone**
fingerboard 'fɪŋ.gə.bɔːd US -gɚ.bɔːrd **-s** -z
fingermark 'fɪŋ.gə.mɑːk US -gɚ.mɑːrk **-s** -s
fingernail 'fɪŋ.gə.neɪl US -gɚ- **-s** -z
fingerplate 'fɪŋ.gə.pleɪt US -gɚ- **-s** -s
fingerpost 'fɪŋ.gə.pəʊst US -gɚ.poʊst **-s** -s
fingerprint 'fɪŋ.gə.prɪnt US -gɚ- **-s** -s **-ing** -ɪŋ
fingerstall 'fɪŋ.gə.stɔːl US -gɚ.stɔːl, -stɑːl **-s** -z
fingertip 'fɪŋ.gə.tɪp US -gɚ- **-s** -s
Fingest 'fɪn.dʒɪst
finial 'fɪn.i.əl, 'faɪ.ni- US 'fɪn.i- **-s** -z
finical 'fɪn.ɪ.k^{ə}l **-ly** -i **-ness** -nəs, -nɪs
finicking 'fɪn.ɪ.kɪŋ
finick|y 'fɪn.ɪ.k|i **-ier** -i.ə^{r} US -i.ɚ **-iest** -i.ɪst, -i.əst **-ily** -ɪ.li, -^{ə}l.i **-iness** -ɪ.nəs, -ɪ.nɪs
finis 'fɪn.ɪs, 'fiː.nɪs US 'fɪn.ɪs; fiː'niː; 'faɪ.nɪs
finish 'fɪn.ɪʃ **-es** -ɪz **-ing** -ɪŋ **-ed** -t **-er/s** -ə^{r}/z US -ɚ/z **'finishing ˌschool**
Finisterre ˌfɪn.ɪ'steə^{r}, -ə'-, '--- US ˌfɪn.ɪ'ster
finite 'faɪ.naɪt **-ly** -li **-ness** -nəs, -nɪs
finito fɪ'niː.təʊ, fə- US -toʊ
finitude 'faɪ.nɪ.tjuːd, 'fɪn.ɪ-, -tʃuːd US 'fɪn.ɪ.tuːd, -tjuːd
fink fɪŋk **-s** -s **-ing** -ɪŋ **-ed** -t
Finlaison 'fɪn.lɪ.s^{ə}n
Finland 'fɪn.lənd **-er/s** -ə^{r}/z US -ɚ/z
Finlandization, -isa- ˌfɪn.lən.daɪ'zeɪ.ʃ^{ə}n, -dɪ'- US -dɪ'-
Finlandiz|e, -is|e 'fɪn.lən.daɪz **-es** -ɪz **-ing** -ɪŋ **-ed** -d
Finlay 'fɪn.leɪ, -li
Finlayson 'fɪn.lɪ.s^{ə}n
Finley 'fɪn.li
Finn fɪn **-s** -z
Finnan 'fɪn.ən
Finnegan 'fɪn.ɪ.gən, '-ə-
Finney 'fɪn.i
Finnic 'fɪn.ɪk
Finnie 'fɪn.i
Finnish 'fɪn.ɪʃ
Finnon 'fɪn.ən
Finno-Ugrian ˌfɪn.əʊ'juː.gri.ən US -oʊ'uː-, -'juː-
Finno-Ugric ˌfɪn.əʊ'juː.grɪk US -oʊ'uː-, -'juː-
fino 'fiː.nəʊ US -noʊ **-s** -z
Finsberg 'fɪnz.bɜːg US -bɝːg
Finsbury 'fɪnz.b^{ə}r.i US -ˌber-, -bɚ- **ˌFinsbury 'Park**
Finucane fɪ'nuː.k^{ə}n, fə-, fɪn.ə'keɪn
Finzi 'fɪn.zi
Fiona fi'əʊ.nə US -'oʊ-
fiord fjɔːd; fi'ɔːd; 'fiː.ɔːd US fjɔːrd; fi'ɔːrd **-s** -z
fiorin 'faɪə.rɪn US 'faɪɚ.ɪn
Fiorino® ˌfiː.ɔː'riː.nəʊ US -noʊ
fioritur|a ˌfjɔː.ri'tjʊə.r|ə, ˌfiː.ə.ri'- US ˌfjɔː.riː'tuː.r|ɑː **-e** -eɪ
fir fɜː^{r} US fɝː **-s** -z **'fir ˌtree**
Firbank 'fɜː.bæŋk US 'fɝː-
fir|e faɪə^{r} US faɪɚ **-es** -z **-ing** -ɪŋ **-ed** -d **-er/s** -ə^{r}/z US -ɚ/z **'fire aˌlarm; 'fire briˌgade; 'fire conˌtrol; 'fire deˌpartment; 'fire ˌdrill; 'fire ˌengine; 'fire esˌcape; 'fire exˌtinguisher; 'fire ˌfighter; 'fire ˌhydrant; 'fire ˌiron; 'fir[e] ˌscreen; ˌout of the ˌfrying pan ˌinto the 'fire**
firearm 'faɪə^{r}.ɑːm US 'faɪɚ.ɑːrm **-s** -z
fireball 'faɪə.bɔːl US 'faɪɚ.bɔːl, -bɑːl **-s** -z
firebomb 'faɪə.bɒm US 'faɪɚ.bɑːm **-s** -z **-ing** -ɪŋ **-ed** -d
firebox 'faɪə.bɒks US 'faɪɚ.bɑːks **-es** -ɪz
firebrand 'faɪə.brænd US 'faɪɚ- **-s** -z
firebreak 'faɪə.breɪk US 'faɪɚ- **-s** -s
firebrick 'faɪə.brɪk US 'faɪɚ- **-s** -s
firebug 'faɪə.bʌg US 'faɪɚ- **-s** -z
fireclay 'faɪə.kleɪ US 'faɪɚ-
firecracker 'faɪəˌkræk.ə^{r} US 'faɪɚˌkræk.ɚ **-s** -z
firecrest 'faɪə.krest US 'faɪɚ- **-s** -s
firedamp 'faɪə.dæmp US 'faɪɚ-
firedog 'faɪə.dɒg US 'faɪɚ.dɑːg, -dɔː[g] **-s** -z
fire-eat|er 'faɪə^{r}ˌiː.t|ə^{r} US 'faɪɚˌiː.t̬|ɚ **-ers** -əz US -ɚz **-ing** -ɪŋ
firefighter 'faɪəˌfaɪ.tə^{r} US 'faɪɚˌfaɪ.[t̬ɚ] **-s** -z
firefl|y 'faɪə.fl|aɪ US 'faɪɚ- **-ies** -aɪz
fireguard 'faɪə.gɑːd US 'faɪɚ.gɑːrd **-s** -z
firehou|se 'faɪə.haʊ|s US 'faɪɚ- **-ses** -zɪz
fire|light 'faɪə|.laɪt US 'faɪɚ- **-lighte[r/s]** -ˌlaɪ.tə^{r}/z US -ˌlaɪ.t̬ɚ/z
firelock 'faɪə.lɒk US 'faɪɚ.lɑːk **-s** -s
fire|man 'faɪə|.mən US 'faɪɚ- **-men** -mən, -men
fireplac|e 'faɪə.pleɪs US 'faɪɚ- **-es** -ɪ[z]
fireplug 'faɪə.plʌg US 'faɪɚ- **-s** -z
firepower 'faɪəˌpaʊə^{r} US 'faɪɚˌpaʊ[ɚ]
fireproof 'faɪə.pruːf US 'faɪɚ-
fireship 'faɪə.ʃɪp US 'faɪɚ- **-s** -s
fireside 'faɪə.saɪd US 'faɪɚ- **-s** -z
firestone 'faɪə.stəʊn US 'faɪɚ.stoʊ[n]
firestorm 'faɪə.stɔːm US 'faɪɚ.stɔː[rm] **-s** -z
firetrail 'faɪə.treɪl US 'faɪɚ- **-s** -z
firetrap 'faɪə.træp US 'faɪɚ- **-s** -s
firewall 'faɪə.wɔːl US 'faɪɚ-, -wɑːl [-s -z]
firewarden 'faɪəˌwɔː.d^{ə}n US 'faɪɚˌwɔːr- **-s** -z
firewater 'faɪəˌwɔː.tə^{r} US 'faɪɚˌwɑː.t̬ɚ, -ˌwɔː-
firewood 'faɪə.wʊd US 'faɪɚ-
firework 'faɪə.wɜːk US 'faɪɚ.wɝːk **-s** -s
firing 'faɪə.rɪŋ US 'faɪɚ.ɪŋ **'firing ˌli[ne];** **'firing ˌparty; 'firing ˌsquad**
firkin 'fɜː.kɪn US 'fɝː- **-s** -z
firm fɜːm US fɝːm **-s** -z **-er** -ə^{r} US -ɚ **-est** -ɪst, -əst **-ing** -ɪŋ **-ed** -d **-ly** -li **-ne[ss]** -nəs, -nɪs
firmament 'fɜː.mə.mənt US 'fɝː-
firmware 'fɜːm.weə^{r} US 'fɝːm.we[r]

Firsby ˈfɜːz.bi ⓊⓈ ˈfɝːz-
first ˈfɜːst ⓊⓈ ˈfɝːst **-s** -s **-ly** -li ˌ**first** ˈ**aid**; ˌ**first** ˈ**base**; ˌ**first** ˈ**class**; ˌ**first** ˈ**floor**; ˌ**first** ˈ**lady**; ˌ**First** ˌ**World** ˈ**War**
first base ˌfɜːs*t*ˈbeɪs ⓊⓈ ˌfɝːs*t*-
firstborn ˈfɜːs*t*.bɔːn ⓊⓈ ˈfɝːs*t*.bɔːrn
first-degree ˌfɜːs*t*.dɪˈgriː, -dəˈ- ⓊⓈ ˌfɝːs*t*.dɪˈ- *stress shift, see compound:* ˌ**first-degree** ˈ**murder**
firstfruits ˈfɜːs*t*.fruːts ⓊⓈ ˈfɝːs*t*-
firsthand ˌfɜːstˈhænd ⓊⓈ ˌfɝːst- *stress shift:* ˌfirsthand acˈcount
firstling ˈfɜːs*t*.lɪŋ ⓊⓈ ˈfɝːs*t*- **-s** -z
firstly ˈfɜːs*t*.li ⓊⓈ ˈfɝːs*t*-
first-past-the-post ˌfɜːs*t*ˌpɑːs*t*.ðəˈpəʊst ⓊⓈ ˌfɝːs*t*ˌpæs*t*.ðəˈpoʊst *stress shift:* ˌfirst-past-the-post ˈsystem
first-rate ˌfɜːs*t*ˈreɪt ⓊⓈ ˌfɝːst- *stress shift:* ˌfirst-rate ˈgame
first-time ˌfɜːs*t*ˈtaɪm ⓊⓈ ˌfɝːst- *stress shift, see compound:* ˌ**first-time** ˈ**buyer**
firth (F) fɜːθ ⓊⓈ fɝːθ **-s** -s
fisc fɪsk
fiscal ˈfɪs.kəl **-s** -z
Fischer ˈfɪʃ.əʳ ⓊⓈ -ɚ
Fischler ˈfɪʃ.ləʳ ⓊⓈ -lɚ
fish (F) fɪʃ **-es** -ɪz **-ing** -ɪŋ **-ed** -t ˌ**fish and** ˈ**chips**; ˌ**fish** ˈ**finger**; ˈ**fishing** ˌ**rod**; ˈ**fishing** ˌ**tackle**; ˈ**fish** ˌ**knife**; ˈ**fish** ˌ**slice**; ˈ**fish** ˌ**stick**; **have** ˌ**other** ˈ**fish to** ˌ**fry**; **like a** ˌ**fish out of** ˈ**water**; **a** ˈ**pretty** ˌ**kettle of** ˌ**fish**
fishbone ˈfɪʃ.bəʊn ⓊⓈ -boʊn **-s** -z
fishbowl ˈfɪʃ.bəʊl ⓊⓈ -boʊl **-s** -z
fishcake ˈfɪʃ.keɪk **-s** -s
fisher (F) ˈfɪʃ.əʳ ⓊⓈ -ɚ **-s** -z
fisher|man ˈfɪʃ.ə|.mən ⓊⓈ ˈ-ɚ- **-men** -mən, -men
fisher|y ˈfɪʃ.ər|.i **-ies** -iz
fisheye ˈfɪʃ.aɪ ˌ**fisheye** ˈ**lens**
Fishguard ˈfɪʃ.gɑːd ⓊⓈ -gɑːrd
fishhook ˈfɪʃ.*h*ʊk ⓊⓈ -hʊk **-s** -s
Fishkill ˈfɪʃ.kɪl
fishmonger ˈfɪʃˌmʌŋ.gəʳ ⓊⓈ -ˌmʌŋ.gɚ, -ˌmɑːŋ- **-s** -z
fish 'n' chips ˌfɪʃ.ənˈtʃɪps
fishnet ˈfɪʃ.net **-s** -s ˌ**fishnet** ˈ**stockings**
fishplate ˈfɪʃ.pleɪt **-s** -s
fishpond ˈfɪʃ.pɒnd ⓊⓈ -pɑːnd **-s** -z
fishtail ˈfɪʃ.teɪl **-s** -z **-ing** -ɪŋ **-ed** -d
fishtank ˈfɪʃ.tæŋk **-s** -s
Fishwick ˈfɪʃ.wɪk
fish|wife ˈfɪʃ|.waɪf **-wives** -waɪvz
fish|y ˈfɪʃ|.i **-ier** -i.əʳ ⓊⓈ -i.ɚ **-iest** -i.ɪst, -i.əst **-ily** -ɪ.li, -əl.i **-iness** -ɪ.nəs, -ɪ.nɪs
Fisk(e) fɪsk
Fison ˈfaɪ.sən
fissile ˈfɪs.aɪl ⓊⓈ -ɪl
fission ˈfɪʃ.ən ⓊⓈ ˈfɪʃ-, ˈfɪʒ- **-s** -z **-al** -əl
fissionable ˈfɪʃ.ən.ə.bl̩ ⓊⓈ ˈfɪʃ-, ˈfɪʒ-
fissiparous fɪˈsɪp.ər.əs, fə-
fiss|ure ˈfɪʃ|.əʳ, -ʊəʳ ⓊⓈ -ɚ **-ures** -əz ⓊⓈ -ɚz **-uring** -ər.ɪŋ **-ured** -əd ⓊⓈ -ɚd
fist fɪst **-s** -s **-ing** -ɪŋ **-ed** -ɪd **-ic** -ɪk
fistfight ˈfɪst.faɪt **-s** -s
fistful ˈfɪst.fʊl **-s** -z
fisticuffs ˈfɪs.tɪ.kʌfs
fistul|a ˈfɪs.tjə.l|ə, -tjʊ-, -tʃə-, -tʃʊ- ⓊⓈ -tjə-, -tʃuː- **-as** -əz **-ae** -iː **-ous** -əs
fit fɪt **-s** -s **-ting/ly** -ɪŋ/li ⓊⓈ ˈfɪt̬.ɪŋ/li **-ted** -ɪd ⓊⓈ ˈfɪt̬.ɪd **-ter/s** -əʳ/z ⓊⓈ ˈfɪt̬.ɚ/z **-test** -ɪst ⓊⓈ ˈfɪt̬.ɪst, -əst **-ly** -li ˌ**fitted** ˈ**kitchen**; ˈ**fitting** ˌ**room**; **as** ˌ**fit as a** ˈ**fiddle**
fitch (F) fɪtʃ **-es** -ɪz
Fitchburg ˈfɪtʃ.bɜːg ⓊⓈ -bɝːg
fitchew ˈfɪtʃ.uː **-s** -z
fitful ˈfɪt.fəl, -fʊl **-ly** -i **-ness** -nəs, -nɪs
fitment ˈfɪt.mənt **-s** -s
fitness ˈfɪt.nəs, -nɪs
fitt fɪt **-s** -s
Fitzalan fɪtsˈæl.ən
Fitzcharles fɪtsˈtʃɑːlz ⓊⓈ -ˈtʃɑːrlz
Fitzclarence fɪtsˈklær.ən*t*s ⓊⓈ -ˈkler-, -ˈklær-
Fitzgeorge fɪtsˈdʒɔːdʒ ⓊⓈ -ˈdʒɔːrdʒ
Fitzgerald, FitzGerald fɪtsˈdʒer.əld
Fitzgibbon fɪtsˈgɪb.ən
Fitzhardinge fɪtsˈhɑː.dɪŋ ⓊⓈ -ˈhɑːr-
Fitzharris fɪtsˈhær.ɪs ⓊⓈ -ˈher-, -ˈhær-
Fitzherbert fɪtsˈhɜː.bət ⓊⓈ -ˈhɝː.bɚt
Fitzhugh fɪtsˈhjuː
Fitzjames fɪtsˈdʒeɪmz
Note: In **James Fitzjames** often /ˈfɪts.dʒeɪmz/.
Fitzjohn fɪtsˈdʒɒn ⓊⓈ -ˈdʒɑːn
Fitzmaurice fɪtsˈmɒr.ɪs ⓊⓈ -ˈmɑːr-, -ˈmɔːr-
Fitzpatrick fɪtsˈpæt.rɪk
Fitzroy *surname:* fɪtsˈrɔɪ, ˈ-- *square and street in London:* ˈfɪts.rɔɪ
Fitzsimmons fɪtsˈsɪm.ənz
Fitzstephen fɪtsˈstiː.vən
Fitzwalter fɪtsˈwɔːl.təʳ, -ˈwɒl- ⓊⓈ -ˈwɔːl.t̬ɚ, -ˈwɑːl-
Fitzwilliam fɪtsˈwɪl.jəm, ˈ-i.əm ⓊⓈ ˈ-jəm
five faɪv **-s** -z **-fold** -fəʊld ⓊⓈ -foʊld
five-and-dime ˌfaɪv.ənˈdaɪm **-s** -z
fivepen|ce ˈfaɪf.pən*t*|s, ˈfaɪv- **-ces** -sɪz
fivepenny ˈfaɪv.pən.i
fiver ˈfaɪ.vəʳ ⓊⓈ -vɚ **-s** -z
fix fɪks **-es** -ɪz **-ing** -ɪŋ **-ed** -t **-edness** -ɪd.nəs, -nɪs **-er/s** -əʳ/z ⓊⓈ -ɚ/z
fixable ˈfɪk.sə.bl̩
fixa|te fɪkˈseɪ|t ⓊⓈ ˈ-- **-tes** -ts **-ting** -tɪŋ ⓊⓈ -t̬ɪŋ **-ted** -tɪd ⓊⓈ -t̬ɪd
fixation fɪkˈseɪ.ʃən **-s** -z
fixative ˈfɪk.sə.tɪv ⓊⓈ -t̬ɪv **-s** -z
fixedly ˈfɪk.sɪd.li, -səd-
fixit|y ˈfɪk.sə.t|i, -ɪ.t|i ⓊⓈ -ə.t̬|i **-ies** -iz
fixture ˈfɪks.tʃəʳ ⓊⓈ -tʃɚ **-s** -z
fizz fɪz **-es** -ɪz **-ing** -ɪŋ **-ed** -d **-er/s** -əʳ/z ⓊⓈ -ɚ/z
fizzl|e ˈfɪz.l̩ **-es** -z **-ing** -ɪŋ, ˈ-lɪŋ **-ed** -d
fizz|y ˈfɪz|.i **-ier** -i.əʳ ⓊⓈ -i.ɚ **-iest** -i.ɪst, -i.əst **-iness** -ɪ.nəs, -ɪ.nɪs
fjord fjɔːd; fiˈɔːd; ˈfiː.ɔːd ⓊⓈ fjɔːrd **-s** -z
Fla. *(abbrev. for* **Florida***)* ˈflɒr.ɪ.də ⓊⓈ ˈflɔːr-, ˈflɑːr-
flab flæb
flabbergast ˈflæb.ə.gɑːst ⓊⓈ -ɚ.gæst **-s** -s **-ing** -ɪŋ **-ed** -ɪd
flabb|y ˈflæb|.i **-ier** -i.əʳ ⓊⓈ -i.ɚ **-iest** -i.ɪst, -i.əst **-ily** -ɪ.li, -əl.i **-iness** -ɪ.nəs, -ɪ.nɪs
flaccid ˈflæk.sɪd, ˈflæs.ɪd **-ly** -li **-ness** -nəs, -nɪs
flaccidity flækˈsɪd.ə.ti, flæsˈɪd-, -ɪ.ti ⓊⓈ -ə.t̬i
flack (F) flæk **-s** -s
Flackwell ˈflæk.wel, -wəl
flag flæg **-s** -z **-ging** -ɪŋ **-ged** -d ˈ**flag** ˌ**day**; ˈ**flag** ˌ**officer**
flagellant ˈflædʒ.əl.ənt, -ɪ.lənt; fləˈdʒel.ənt, flædʒˈel- ⓊⓈ ˈflædʒ.əl.ənt, -ɪ.lənt; fləˈdʒel.ənt **-s** -s
flagellate *(n, adj.)* ˈflædʒ.əl.ət, -ɪ.lət, -ɪt, -eɪt ⓊⓈ ˈflædʒ.əl.eɪt, -ɪt; fləˈdʒel.ɪt **-s** -s
flagell|ate *(v.)* ˈflædʒ.əl|.eɪt, ˈ-ɪ- ⓊⓈ -ə.l|eɪt **-ates** -eɪts **-ating** -eɪ.tɪŋ ⓊⓈ -eɪ.t̬ɪŋ **-ated** -eɪ.tɪd ⓊⓈ -eɪ.t̬ɪd **-ator/s** -eɪ.təʳ/z ⓊⓈ -eɪ.t̬ɚ/z
flagellation ˌflædʒ.əˈleɪ.ʃən, -ɪˈ- **-s** -z
flagell|um fləˈdʒel|.əm, flædʒˈel- ⓊⓈ fləˈdʒel- **-ums** -əmz **-a** -ə
flageolet ˌflæd.ʒəʊˈlet, -ˈleɪ, ˈ--- ⓊⓈ ˌflædʒ.əˈlet, -ˈleɪ **-s** -s
Flagg flæg
flag|man ˈflæg|.mən, -mæn **-men** -mən, -men
flagon ˈflæg.ən **-s** -z
flagpole ˈflæg.pəʊl ⓊⓈ -poʊl **-s** -z
flagrancy ˈfleɪ.grən*t*.si
flagrant ˈfleɪ.grənt **-ly** -li
flagrante delicto fləˌgræn.teɪ.dɪˈlɪk.təʊ, flægˌræn-, -ti-, -dəˈ-, -deɪˈ- ⓊⓈ fləˌgræn.ti.diːˈlɪk.toʊ
flagship ˈflæg.ʃɪp **-s** -s
flagstaff ˈflæg.stɑːf ⓊⓈ -stæf **-s** -s
flagstone ˈflæg.stəʊn ⓊⓈ -stoʊn **-s** -z
flag-waving ˈflægˌweɪ.vɪŋ
Flaherty ˈfleə.ti, ˈflɑː.*h*ə.ti, ˈflæ.hə.ti ⓊⓈ ˈflæ.ɚ.t̬i, ˈflɑː-; ˈfler.ə-
flail fleɪl **-s** -z **-ing** -ɪŋ **-ed** -d
flair fleəʳ ⓊⓈ fler **-s** -z
flak flæk
flak|e fleɪk **-es** -s **-ing** -ɪŋ **-ed** -t ˌ**flake** ˈ**white**

Flap

A type of consonant sound that is closely similar to the TAP. It is usually voiced, and is produced by slightly curling back the tip of the tongue, then throwing it forward and allowing it to strike the alveolar ridge as it descends. The phonetic symbol for the sound is [ɽ]

Examples in English

This sound, although occurring in some accents of English, is not a PHONEME, and is uncommon in British English. It appears, however, in US English, where it is sometimes heard in words like *party* and *birdie*, where the /r/ consonant causes retroflexion of the tongue and the stress pattern favours a flap-like articulation, e.g.:

party	/'pɑː.ti/	US /'pɑːr.t̬i/ ['pʰɑːɻ.ɽti]
birdie	/'bɜː.di/	US /'bɝː.di/ ['bɝ̥ː.ɽi]

In other languages

A flap is most commonly heard in languages which have other RETROFLEX consonants, such as languages of the Indian sub-continent; it is also heard in the English of native speakers of such languages, often as a realisation of /r/.

flak|y 'fleɪ.k|i **-ily** -ɪ.li, -^{ə}l.i **-iness** -ɪ.nəs, -ɪ.nɪs ˌ**flaky** '**pastry**
flam flæm **-s** -z
Flambard 'flæm.bɑːd, -bəd US -bɑːrd, -bɚd
flambé, flambe 'flɑ̃ː*m*.beɪ US flɑːm'beɪ **-s** -z **-ing** -ɪŋ **-ed** -d
flambeau (F) 'flæm.bəʊ US -boʊ **-s** -z
flambée, flambee 'flɑ̃ː*m*.beɪ US flɑːm'beɪ **-d** -d
Flamborough 'flæm.b^{ə}r.ə US -oʊ
flamboyance flæm'bɔɪ.ən*t*s
flamboyant flæm'bɔɪ.ənt **-ly** -li
flam|e fleɪm **-es** -z **-ing** -ɪŋ **-ed** -d
flamen 'fleɪ.men **-s** -z
flamenco flə'meŋ.kəʊ US -koʊ **-s** -z
flameproof 'fleɪm.pruːf **-s** -s **-ing** -ɪŋ **-ed** -t
flamethrower 'fleɪmˌθrəʊ.ə^{r} US -ˌθroʊ.ɚ **-s** -z
flamingo flə'mɪŋ.gəʊ, flæm'ɪŋ- US flə'mɪŋ.goʊ **-(e)s** -z
Flaminius flə'mɪn.i.əs, flæm'ɪn- US flə'mɪn-
flammability ˌflæm.ə'bɪl.ə.ti, -ɪ.ti US -ə.t̬i
flammable 'flæm.ə.bl̩
Flamstead 'flæm.stiːd, -stɪd
Flamsteed 'flæm.stiːd
flan flæn **-s** -z
Flanagan 'flæn.ə.g^{ə}n
Flanders 'flɑːn.dəz US 'flæn.dɚz
flang|e flændʒ **-es** -ɪz **-ing** -ɪŋ **-ed** -d
flank flæŋk **-s** -s **-ing** -ɪŋ **-ed** -t **-er/s** -ə^{r}/z US -ɚ/z
Flann flæn
flannel 'flæn.^{ə}l **-s** -z **-(l)ing** -ɪŋ **-(l)ed** -d
flannelette, flannelet ˌflæn.^{ə}l'et US ˌflæn.^{ə}l'et, -ə'let
flannelly 'flæn.^{ə}l.i
flap flæp **-s** -s **-ping** -ɪŋ **-ped** -t
flapdoodle 'flæpˌduː.dl̩
flapjack 'flæp.dʒæk **-s** -s
flapper 'flæp.ə^{r} US -ɚ **-s** -z
flar|e fleə^{r} US fler **-es** -z **-ing/ly** -ɪŋ/li **-ed** -d
flarepa|th 'fleə.pɑː|θ US 'fler.pæ|θ **-ths** -ðz
flare-up 'fleə^{r}.ʌp US 'fler- **-s** -s
flash (F) flæʃ **-es** -ɪz **-ing** -ɪŋ **-ed** -t '**flash** ˌ**card**; '**flash** ˌ**point**; ˌ**flash in the** '**pan**; ˌ**quick as a** '**flash**
flashback 'flæʃ.bæk **-s** -s
flashbulb 'flæʃ.bʌlb **-s** -z
flasher 'flæʃ.ə^{r} US -ɚ **-s** -z
flashgun 'flæʃ.gʌn **-s** -z
flashlight 'flæʃ.laɪt **-s** -s
Flashman 'flæʃ.mən
flash|y 'flæʃ|.i **-ier** -i.ə^{r} US -i.ɚ **-iest** -i.ɪst, -i.əst **-ily** -ɪ.li, -^{ə}l.i **-iness** -ɪ.nəs, -ɪ.nɪs
flask flɑːsk US flæsk **-s** -s
flat flæt **-s** -s **-ter** -ə^{r} US 'flæt̬.ɚ **-test** -ɪst, -əst US 'flæt̬.ɪst, -əst **-ly** -li **-ness** -nəs, -nɪs
Flatbush 'flæt.bʊʃ
flat-chested ˌflæt'tʃes.tɪd **-ness** -nəs, -nɪs *stress shift:* ˌflat-chested 'waif
flatfish 'flæt.fɪʃ **-es** -ɪz
flatfoot 'flæt.fʊt
flat-footed ˌflæt'fʊt.ɪd US -'fʊt̬-, '--- **-ly** -li **-ness** -nəs, -nɪs *stress shift, British only:* ˌflat-footed 'person
flathead (F) 'flæt.hed **-s** -z
flatiron 'flætˌaɪən US 'flætˌaɪɚn **-s** -z
Flatland 'flæt.lænd
flatlet 'flæt.lət, -lɪt **-s** -s
flatmate 'flæt.meɪt **-s** -s
flat-out ˌflæt'aʊt *stress shift:* ˌflat-out 'dash
flatten 'flæt.^{ə}n **-s** -z **-ing** -ɪŋ **-ed** -d
flatt|er 'flæt|.ə^{r} US 'flæt̬|.ɚ **-ers** -əz, -ɚz **-ering/ly** -^{ə}r.ɪŋ/li **-ered** -əd, -ɚd **-erer/s** -^{ə}r.ə^{r}/z US -ɚ.ɚ/z
flatter|y 'flæt.^{ə}r|.i US 'flæt̬- **-ies** -iz
flatties 'flæt.iz US 'flæt̬-
flattish 'flæt.ɪʃ US 'flæt̬-
flattop 'flæt.tɒp US -tɑːp **-s** -s
flatulen|ce 'flæt.jə.lən*t*|s, -jʊ-, 'flætʃ.ə- US 'flætʃ.ə- **-cy** -si
flatulent 'flæt.jə.lənt, -jʊ-, 'flætʃ.ə-, '-ʊ- US 'flætʃ.ə- **-ly** -li
flatus 'fleɪ.təs US -t̬əs **-es** -ɪz
flatware 'flæt.weə^{r} US -wer
flat|ways 'flæt|.weɪz **-wise** -waɪz
flatworm 'flæt.wɜːm US -wɝːm **-s** -z
Flaubert 'fləʊ.beə^{r} US 'floʊ.ber, -'-
flaun|t flɔːn|t US flɑːn|t, flɔːn|t **-ts** -ts **-ting/ly** -tɪŋ/li US -t̬ɪŋ/li **-ted** -tɪd US -t̬ɪd
flautist 'flɔː.tɪst US 'flɑː.t̬ɪst, 'flɔː-, 'flaʊ- **-s** -s
Flavel 'flæv.^{ə}l, 'fleɪ.v^{ə}l
Flavell flə'vel, 'fleɪ.v^{ə}l
Flavi|a 'fleɪ.vi|.ə **-an** -ən
flavin 'fleɪ.vɪn, 'flæv.ɪn US 'fleɪ.vɪn **-s** -z
flavin(e) 'fleɪ.viːn, 'flæv.iːn, -ɪn US 'fleɪ.viːn
Flavius 'fleɪ.vi.əs
flav|or 'fleɪ.v|ə^{r} US -v|ɚ **-ors** -əz US -ɚz **-oring/s** -^{ə}r.ɪŋ/z **-ored** -əd US -ɚd ˌ**flavor of the** '**month**
flavorful 'fleɪ.və.f^{ə}l, -fʊl US -vɚ-
flavoring 'fleɪ.v^{ə}r.ɪŋ
flavorless 'fleɪ.və.ləs, -lɪs US -vɚ- **-ness** -nəs, -nɪs
flavorous 'fleɪ.v^{ə}r.əs
flavorsome 'fleɪ.və.səm US -vɚ-
flav|our (*n. v.*) 'fleɪ.v|ə^{r} US -v|ɚ **-ours** -əz US -ɚz **-ouring/s** -^{ə}r.ɪŋ/z **-oured** -əd US -ɚd ˌ**flavour of the** '**month**
flavourful 'fleɪ.və.f^{ə}l, -fʊl US -vɚ-
flavouring 'fleɪ.v^{ə}r.ɪŋ **-s** -z
flavourless 'fleɪ.və.ləs, -lɪs US -vɚ- **-ness** -nəs, -nɪs
flavoursome 'fleɪ.və.səm US -vɚ-
flaw flɔː US flɑː, flɔː **-s** -z **-ing** -ɪŋ **-ed** -d
flawless 'flɔː.ləs, -lɪs US 'flɑː-, 'flɔː- **-ly** -li **-ness** -nəs, -nɪs
flax flæks **-en** -^{ə}n
Flaxman 'flæks.mən

flay fleɪ -s -z -ing -ɪŋ -ed -d -er/s -əʳ/z (US) -ɚ/z
flea fliː -s -z 'flea ˌmarket
fleabag 'fliː.bæg -s -z
fleabane 'fliː.beɪn
flea|bite 'fliː|.baɪt -bites -baɪts -bitten -bɪt.ᵊn (US) -bɪt̬-
fleadh flɑː
fleam fliːm -s -z
fleapit 'fliː.pɪt -s -s
flèch|e, flech|e fleɪʃ, fleʃ -es -ɪz
fleck flek -s -s -ing -ɪŋ -ed -t
Flecker 'flek.əʳ (US) -ɚ
Flecknoe 'flek.nəʊ (US) -noʊ
flection 'flek.ʃᵊn -s -z
flectional 'flek.ʃᵊn.ᵊl
fled (*from* **flee**) fled
fledg|e fledʒ -es -ɪz -ing -ɪŋ -ed -d
fledg(e)ling 'fledʒ.lɪŋ -s -z
flee fliː -s -z -ing -ɪŋ **fled** fled
fleec|e fliːs -es -ɪz -ing -ɪŋ -ed -t
fleec|y 'fliː.s|i -ier -i.əʳ (US) -i.ɚ -iest -i.ɪst, -i.əst -iness -ɪ.nəs, -ɪ.nɪs
fleer flɪəʳ (US) flɪr -s -z -ing -ɪŋ -ed -d
fleet (F) fliːt -s -s -er -əʳ (US) 'fliː.t̬ɚ -est -ɪst, -əst (US) 'fliː.t̬ɪst, -t̬əst -ly -li -ness -nəs, -nɪs -ing -ɪŋ (US) 'fliː.t̬ɪŋ -ed -ɪd (US) 'fliː.t̬ɪd 'Fleet ˌStreet
fleeting 'fliː.tɪŋ (US) -t̬ɪŋ -ly -li
Fleetwood 'fliːt.wʊd
Fleming 'flem.ɪŋ -s -z
Flemings 'flem.ɪŋz
Flemington 'flem.ɪŋ.tən
Flemish 'flem.ɪʃ
Flemming 'flem.ɪŋ
flens|e flenz, flen*t*s (US) flen*t*s -es -ɪz -ing -ɪŋ -ed -d
flesh fleʃ -es -ɪz -ing/s -ɪŋ/z -ed -t ˌflesh and 'blood; 'flesh ˌwound; ˌmake someone's 'flesh ˌcreep
fleshless 'fleʃ.ləs, -lɪs
fleshl|y 'fleʃ.l|i -iness -ɪ.nəs, -ɪ.nɪs
fleshpot 'fleʃ.pɒt (US) -pɑːt -s -s
flesh|y 'fleʃ|.i -iness -ɪ.nəs, -ɪ.nɪs
fletcher (F) 'fletʃ.əʳ (US) -ɚ -s -z
Flete fliːt
fletton (F) 'flet.ᵊn (US) 'flet̬-
Fleur flɜːʳ (US) flɝː
fleur-de-lis ˌflɜː.də'liː, -liːs (US) ˌflɝː-, ˌflʊr-
fleuron 'flʊə.rɒn, 'flɜː-, -rən (US) 'flɝː.ɑːn, 'flʊr- -s -z
flew (*from* **fly**) fluː
flex fleks -es -ɪz -ing -ɪŋ -ed -t
flexibility ˌflek.sɪ'bɪl.ə.ti, -sə'-, -ɪ.ti (US) -ə.t̬i
flexib|le 'flek.sɪ.b|l̩, -sə- -ly -li -leness -l̩.nəs, -nɪs
flexion 'flek.ʃᵊn -s -z
flexitime 'flek.si.taɪm
flexor 'flek.səʳ (US) -sɚ, -sɔːr -s -z
flextime 'fleks.taɪm
flexure 'flek.ʃəʳ (US) -ʃɚ -s -z
flibbertigibbet ˌflɪb.ə.ti'dʒɪb.ɪt, -ət (US) 'flɪb.ɚ.t̬iˌdʒɪb- -s -s
flick flɪk -s -s -ing -ɪŋ -ed -t
flick|er 'flɪk|.əʳ (US) -ɚ -ers -əz (US) -ɚz -ering -ᵊr.ɪŋ -ered -əd (US) -ɚd
flick-kni|fe 'flɪk.naɪ|f -ves -vz
flier 'flaɪ.əʳ (US) -ɚ -s -z
flight (F) flaɪt -s -s -less -ləs, -lɪs 'flight atˌtendant; 'flight ˌdeck; 'flight ˌpath
flight|y 'flaɪ.t|i (US) -t̬|i -ier -i.əʳ (US) -i.ɚ -iest -i.ɪst, -i.əst -ily -ɪ.li, -ᵊl.i -iness -ɪ.nəs, -ɪ.nɪs
flimflam 'flɪm.flæm -s -z -ming -ɪŋ -med -d
flims|y 'flɪm.z|i -ier -i.əʳ (US) -i.ɚ -iest -i.ɪst, -i.əst -ily -ɪ.li, -ᵊl.i -iness -ɪ.nəs, -ɪ.nɪs
flinch flɪn*t*ʃ -es -ɪz -ing/ly -ɪŋ/li -ed -t -er/s -əʳ/z (US) -ɚ/z
flinders (F) 'flɪn.dəz (US) -dɚz
fling flɪŋ -s -z -ing -ɪŋ **flung** flʌŋ
flint flɪnt -s -s 'flint ˌglass
Flint flɪnt -shire -ʃəʳ, -ˌʃɪəʳ (US) -ʃɚ, -ˌʃɪr
flintlock 'flɪnt.lɒk (US) -lɑːk -s -s
Flintoff 'flɪn.tɒf (US) -tɑːf
Flintshire 'flɪnt.ʃəʳ, -ˌʃɪəʳ (US) -ʃɚ, -ˌʃɪr
flintstone (F) 'flɪnt.stəʊn (US) -stoʊn -s -z
flint|y 'flɪn.t|i (US) -t̬|i -ier -i.əʳ (US) -i.ɚ -iest -i.ɪst, -i.əst -ily -ɪ.li, -ᵊl.i -iness -ɪ.nəs, -ɪ.nɪs
flip flɪp -s -s -ping -ɪŋ -ped -t 'flip ˌside
flip-flap 'flɪp.flæp -s -s -ping -ɪŋ -ped -t
flip-flop 'flɪp.flɒp (US) -flɑːp -s -s -ping -ɪŋ -ped -t
flippancy 'flɪp.ᵊn*t*.si
flippant 'flɪp.ᵊnt -ly -li -ness -nəs, -nɪs
flipper 'flɪp.əʳ (US) -ɚ -s -z
flipside 'flɪp.saɪd -s -z
flirt flɜːt (US) flɝːt -s -s -ing/ly -ɪŋ/li (US) 'flɝː.t̬ɪŋ/li -ed -ɪd (US) 'flɝː.t̬ɪd
flirtation flɜː'teɪ.ʃᵊn (US) flɝː- -s -z
flirtatious flɜː'teɪ.ʃəs (US) flɝː- -ly -li -ness -nəs, -nɪs
flirty 'flɜː.ti (US) 'flɝː.t̬i
flit flɪt -s -s -ting -ɪŋ (US) 'flɪt̬.ɪŋ -ted -ɪd (US) 'flɪt̬.ɪd
flitch (F) flɪtʃ -es -ɪz
flitt|er 'flɪt|.əʳ (US) 'flɪt̬|.ɚ -ers -əz (US) -ɚz -ering -ᵊr.ɪŋ -ered -əd (US) -ɚd
Flitwick 'flɪt.ɪk (US) 'flɪt̬-
flivver 'flɪv.əʳ (US) -ɚ -s -z
Flixton 'flɪk.stᵊn
float fləʊt (US) floʊt -s -s -ing -ɪŋ (US) 'floʊ.t̬ɪŋ -ed -ɪd (US) 'floʊ.t̬ɪd -er/s -əʳ/z (US) 'floʊ.t̬ɚ/z -age -ɪdʒ (US) 'floʊ.t̬ɪdʒ ˌfloating 'bridge; ˌfloating 'dock
floatation fləʊ'teɪ.ʃᵊn (US) floʊ-
floatplane 'fləʊt.pleɪn (US) 'floʊt- -s -z
floccu|late 'flɒk.jə|.leɪt, -jʊ- (US) 'flɑː.kjuː-, -kjə- -lates -leɪts -lating -leɪ.tɪŋ (US) -leɪ.t̬ɪŋ -lated -leɪ.tɪd (US) -leɪ.t̬ɪd
flocculent 'flɒk.jə.lənt, -jʊ- (US) 'flɑː.kjuː-, -kjə-
flock flɒk (US) flɑːk -s -s -ing -ɪŋ -ed -t
Flockhart 'flɒk.hɑːt (US) 'flɑːk.hɑːrt
Flockton 'flɒk.tən (US) 'flɑːk-
Flodden 'flɒd.ᵊn (US) 'flɑː.dᵊn
floe fləʊ (US) floʊ -s -z
Floella fləʊ'el.ə (US) floʊ-
flog flɒg (US) flɑːg, flɔːg -s -z -ging/s -ɪŋ/z -ged -d
Flo-Jo 'fləʊ.dʒəʊ (US) 'floʊ.dʒoʊ
flood (F) flʌd -s -z -ing -ɪŋ -ed -ɪd ˌflood 'tide
floodgate 'flʌd.geɪt -s -s
flood|light 'flʌd|.laɪt -lights -laɪts -lighting -laɪ.tɪŋ (US) -laɪ.t̬ɪŋ -lit -lɪt
floodwater 'flʌdˌwɔː.təʳ (US) -ˌwɑː.t̬ɚ, -ˌwɔː- -s -z
Flook flʊk, fluːk
floor flɔːʳ (US) flɔːr -s -z -ing -ɪŋ -ed -d -er/s -əʳ/z (US) -ɚ/z 'floor ˌcloth; 'floor ˌplan; 'floor ˌshow
floorboard 'flɔː.bɔːd (US) 'flɔːr.bɔːrd -s -z
floorwalker 'flɔːˌwɔː.kəʳ (US) 'flɔːrˌwɔː.kɚ, -ˌwɑː- -s -z
floosie 'fluː.zi -s -z
flooz|y, flooz|ie 'fluː.z|i -ys -iz -ies -iz
flop flɒp (US) flɑːp -s -s -ping -ɪŋ -ped -t
flophou|se 'flɒp.haʊ|s (US) 'flɑːp- -ses -zɪz
flopp|y 'flɒp|.i (US) 'flɑː.p|i -ier -i.əʳ (US) -i.ɚ -iest -i.ɪst, -i.əst -ily -ɪ.li, -ᵊl.i -iness -ɪ.nəs, -ɪ.nɪs ˌfloppy 'disk
Flopsy 'flɒp.si (US) 'flɑːp-
floptical 'flɒp.tɪ.kᵊl (US) 'flɑːp- ˌfloptical 'disk
flor|a (F) 'flɔː.r|ə (US) 'flɔːr|.ə, 'floʊ.r|ə -as -əz -ae -iː
floral 'flɔː.rᵊl, 'flɒr.ᵊl (US) 'flɔːr-, 'floʊ.rᵊl
Florence 'flɒr.ᵊn*t*s (US) 'flɔːr-
florentine (F) 'flɒr.ᵊn.taɪn, -tiːn (US) 'flɔːr- -s -z
Flores 'flɔː.rɪz (US) 'flɔːr.es, -ɪz
florescen|ce flɔː'res.ᵊn|*t*s, flɒr'es-, flə'res- (US) flɔː'res-, flə-, floʊ- -t -t
floret 'flɒr.ɪt, 'flɔː.rɪt, -ret (US) 'flɔːr.ɪt-, 'floʊ.rɪt -s -s
Florian 'flɔː.ri.ən (US) 'flɔːr.i-
flori|ate 'flɔː.ri|.eɪt (US) 'flɔːr.i-, 'floʊ.ri- -ates -eɪts -ating -eɪ.tɪŋ (US) -eɪ.t̬ɪŋ -ated -eɪ.tɪd (US) -eɪ.t̬ɪd
floribunda ˌflɒr.ɪ'bʌn.də, ˌflɔː.rɪ'- (US) ˌflɔːr.ɪ'-, ˌfloʊ.rɪ'-
floricultur|al ˌflɔː.rɪ'kʌl.tʃᵊr|.ᵊl, ˌflɒr.ɪ'-, -tʃʊ.r|ᵊl (US) ˌflɔːr.ɪ'kʌl.tʃɚ|.ᵊl, ˌfloʊ.rɪ'- -ist/s -ɪst/s

floriculture 'flɔː.rɪ.kʌl.tʃəʳ, 'flɒr.ɪ- Ⓤⓢ 'flɔːr.ɪ.kʌl.tʃɚ, 'floʊ.rɪ-
florid 'flɒr.ɪd Ⓤⓢ 'flɔːr- **-est** -ɪst, -əst **-ly** -li **-ness** -nəs, -nɪs
Florida 'flɒr.ɪ.də Ⓤⓢ 'flɔːr-, 'flɑːr- ˌ**Florida** ˈ**Keys**
Floridian flɒr'ɪd.i.ən, flə'rɪd- Ⓤⓢ flɔː'rɪd-, flɑː'- **-s** -z
floridity flɒr'ɪd.ə.ti, flə'rɪd-, flɔː-, -ɪ.ti Ⓤⓢ flɔː'rɪd.ə.t̬i
floriferous flɔː'rɪf.ər.əs, flɒr'ɪf-, flə'rɪf- Ⓤⓢ flɔː'rɪf-, floʊ'-
florin 'flɒr.ɪn Ⓤⓢ 'flɔːr- **-s** -z
Florinda flɔː'rɪn.də, flɒr'ɪn-, flə'rɪn- Ⓤⓢ flɔː'rɪn-, floʊ-
Florio 'flɔː.ri.əʊ Ⓤⓢ 'flɔːr.i.oʊ
florist 'flɒr.ɪst, 'flɔː.rɪst Ⓤⓢ 'flɔːr.ɪst, 'floʊ.rɪst **-s** -s
floristry 'flɒr.ɪ.stri, 'flɔː.rɪ- Ⓤⓢ 'flɔːr.ɪ-, 'floʊ.rɪ-
Florrie 'flɒr.i Ⓤⓢ 'flɔːr-
floruit 'flɔː.ru.ɪt, 'flɒr.u- Ⓤⓢ 'flɔːr.ju-, 'floʊr-
floss (F) flɒs Ⓤⓢ flɑːs **-y** -i **-es** -ɪz **-ing** -ɪŋ **-ed** -t
Flossie 'flɒs.i Ⓤⓢ 'flɑː.si
flotage 'fləʊ.tɪdʒ Ⓤⓢ 'floʊ.t̬ɪdʒ
flotation fləʊ'teɪ.ʃən Ⓤⓢ floʊ- **-s** -z
flotilla fləʊ'tɪl.ə Ⓤⓢ floʊ- **-s** -z
flotsam 'flɒt.səm Ⓤⓢ 'flɑːt- ˌ**flotsam and** ˈ**jetsam**
Flotta 'flɒt.ə Ⓤⓢ 'flɑː.t̬ə
flounc|e flaʊnts **-es** -ɪz **-ing** -ɪŋ **-ed** -t
flouncy 'flaʊnt.si
flound|er 'flaʊn.d|əʳ Ⓤⓢ -d|ɚ **-ers** -əz Ⓤⓢ -ɚz **-ering** -ər.ɪŋ **-ered** -əd Ⓤⓢ -ɚd
flour flaʊəʳ Ⓤⓢ flaʊɚ **-s** -z **-ing** -ɪŋ **-ed** -d
flourish 'flʌr.ɪʃ Ⓤⓢ 'flɝː.ɪʃ **-es** -ɪz **-ing/ly** -ɪŋ/li **-ed** -t
floury 'flaʊə.ri Ⓤⓢ 'flaʊə.ri
flout flaʊt **-s** -s **-ing** -ɪŋ Ⓤⓢ 'flaʊ.t̬ɪŋ **-ed** -ɪd Ⓤⓢ 'flaʊ.t̬ɪd
flow fləʊ Ⓤⓢ floʊ **-s** -z **-ing/ly** -ɪŋ/li **-ingness** -ɪŋ.nəs, -nɪs **-ed** -d ˈ**flow** ˌ**chart**; ˈ**flow** ˌ**diagram**
flower (F) flaʊəʳ Ⓤⓢ flaʊɚ **-s** -z **-ing** -ɪŋ **-ed** -d **-er/s** -əʳ/z Ⓤⓢ -ɚ/z ˈ**flower** ˌ**child**; ˈ**flower** ˌ**garden**; ˈ**flower** ˌ**girl**; ˈ**flower** ˌ**power**
flowerbed 'flaʊə.bed Ⓤⓢ 'flaʊɚ- **-s** -z
floweret 'flaʊə.rɪt, -ret Ⓤⓢ 'flaʊɚ.ɪt, -et **-s** -s
flowerless 'flaʊə.ləs, -lɪs Ⓤⓢ 'flaʊɚ-
flowerpot 'flaʊə.pɒt Ⓤⓢ 'flaʊɚ.pɑːt **-s** -s
flowery 'flaʊə.ri
flown *(from* **fly***)* fləʊn Ⓤⓢ floʊn
Floyd flɔɪd
Floyder 'flɔɪ.dəʳ Ⓤⓢ -dɚ
fl oz *(abbrev. for* **fluid ounce***) singular:* ˌfluː.ɪd'aʊnts *plural:* -'aʊnt.sɪz
flu, ˈ**flu** fluː
flub flʌb **-s** -z **-bing** -ɪŋ **-bed** -d
fluctuant 'flʌk.tʃu.ənt, -tju- Ⓤⓢ -tʃu-, -tʃə.wənt
fluctu|ate 'flʌk.tʃu|.eɪt, -tju- Ⓤⓢ -tʃu-, -tʃə.w|eɪt **-ates** -eɪts **-ating** -eɪ.tɪŋ Ⓤⓢ -eɪ.t̬ɪŋ **-ated** -eɪ.tɪd Ⓤⓢ -eɪ.t̬ɪd
fluctuation ˌflʌk.tʃu'eɪ.ʃən, -tju'- Ⓤⓢ -tʃu-, -tʃə'weɪ- **-s** -z
Flud(d) flʌd
Fludyer 'flʌd.jəʳ, -i.əʳ Ⓤⓢ 'flʌd.jɚ
flue fluː **-s** -z ˈ**flue** ˌ**pipe**
Fluellen flu'el.ɪn, -ən
fluency 'fluː.ənt.si
fluent 'fluː.ənt **-ly** -li **-ness** -nəs, -nɪs
fluff flʌf **-s** -s **-ing** -ɪŋ **-ed** -t
fluff|y 'flʌf|.i **-ier** -i.əʳ Ⓤⓢ -i.ɚ **-iest** -i.ɪst, -i.əst **-iness** -ɪ.nəs, -ɪ.nɪs
flugelhorn, flügelhorn 'fluː.gəl.hɔːn Ⓤⓢ -hɔːrn **-s** -z
fluid 'fluː.ɪd **-s** -z ˌ**fluid** ˈ**ounce**
fluidity flu'ɪd.ə.ti, -ɪ.ti Ⓤⓢ -ə.t̬i
fluidization, -isa- ˌfluː.ɪ.daɪ'zeɪ.ʃən, -dɪ'- Ⓤⓢ -dɪ'-
fluidiz|e, -is|e 'fluː.ɪ.daɪz **-es** -ɪz **-ing** -ɪŋ **-ed** -d **-er/s** -əʳ/z Ⓤⓢ -ɚ/z
fluk|e fluːk **-es** -s **-ing** -ɪŋ **-ed** -t **-er/s** -əʳ/z Ⓤⓢ -ɚ/z **-ish** -ɪʃ
fluk|y, fluk|ey 'fluː.k|i **-ier** -i.əʳ Ⓤⓢ -i.ɚ **-iest** -i.ɪst, -i.əst **-iness** -ɪ.nəs, -ɪ.nɪs
flume fluːm **-s** -z
flummery 'flʌm.ər.i
flummox 'flʌm.əks **-es** -ɪz **-ing** -ɪŋ **-ed** -t
flung *(from* **fling***)* flʌŋ
flunk flʌŋk **-s** -s **-ing** -ɪŋ **-ed** -t
flunkey 'flʌŋ.ki **-s** -z **-ism** -ɪ.zəm
flunk|y 'flʌŋ.k|i **-ys** -iz **-ies** -iz **-yism** -i.ɪ.zəm
fluor 'fluː.ɔːʳ, -əʳ Ⓤⓢ -ɔːr, -ɚ
fluorescence flɔː'res.ənts, flʊə-, flə-; Ⓤⓢ flɔː-, flʊ-, fluː-, floʊ-
fluorescent flɔː'res.ənt, flʊə-, flə- Ⓤⓢ flɔː-, flʊ-, fluː-, floʊ-
fluoric flu'ɒr.ɪk Ⓤⓢ -'ɔːr-
fluori|date 'flɔː.rɪ|.deɪt, 'flʊə-, -rə- Ⓤⓢ 'flɔːr.ə-, 'flʊr- **-dates** -deɪts **-dating** -deɪ.tɪŋ Ⓤⓢ -deɪ.t̬ɪŋ **-dated** -deɪ.tɪd Ⓤⓢ -deɪ.t̬ɪd
fluoridation ˌflɔː.rɪ'deɪ.ʃən, ˌflʊə-, -raɪ'-, -rə'- Ⓤⓢ ˌflɔːr.ə'-, ˌflʊr.ə'-
fluoride 'flɔː.raɪd, 'flʊə- Ⓤⓢ 'flɔːr.aɪd, 'flʊr- **-s** -z
fluoridization, -isa- ˌflɔː.rɪ.daɪ'zeɪ.ʃən, ˌflʊə-, -raɪ-, -dɪ'- Ⓤⓢ ˌflɔːr.ə.dɪ'-, ˌflʊr-
fluoridiz|e, -is|e- 'flɔː.rɪ.daɪz, 'flʊə- Ⓤⓢ 'flɔːr.ə-, 'flʊr- **-es** -ɪz **-ing** -ɪŋ **-ed** -d
fluori|nate 'flɔː.rɪ|.neɪt, 'flʊə-, 'flɒr.ɪ-, '-ə- Ⓤⓢ 'flɔːr.ə-, 'flʊr- **-nates** -neɪts **-nating** -neɪ.tɪŋ Ⓤⓢ -neɪ.t̬ɪŋ **-nated** -neɪ.tɪd Ⓤⓢ -neɪ.t̬ɪd
fluorination ˌflɔː.rɪ'neɪ.ʃən, ˌflʊə-, ˌflɒr.ɪ'-, -ə'- Ⓤⓢ ˌflɔːr.ə'-, ˌflʊr-
fluorine 'flɔː.riːn, 'flʊə- Ⓤⓢ 'flɔːr.iːn, 'flʊr-, -ɪn
fluorisis flɔː'raɪ.sɪs, flʊə-, flə- Ⓤⓢ flɔː-, flʊ-
fluorite 'flɔː.raɪt, 'flʊə- Ⓤⓢ 'flɔːr.aɪt, 'flʊr-
fluoro- flɔː.rəʊ-, flʊə-; flɔː'rɒ-, flʊə-, flə-, -'rəʊ- Ⓤⓢ flɔːr.ə-, flʊr-, '-oʊ-; flɔː'rɑː-, flʊ-, -'roʊ-
Note: Prefix. Either takes primary or secondary stress on the first syllable, e.g. **fluoroscope** /'flɔː.rəʊ.skəʊp Ⓤⓢ 'flɔːr.ə.skoʊp/, **fluoroscopic** /ˌflɔː.rəʊ'skɒp.ɪk Ⓤⓢ ˌflɔːr.ə'skɑː.pɪk/, or primary stress on the second syllable, e.g. **fluoroscopy** /flɔː'rɒs.kə.pi Ⓤⓢ -'rɑː.skə-/.
fluorocarbon ˌflɔː.rəʊ'kɑː.bən, ˌflʊə- Ⓤⓢ ˌflɔːr.ə'kɑːr-, ˌflʊr-, -oʊ'- **-s** -z *stress shift:* ˌfluorocarbon 'dating techˌnique
fluoroscop|e 'flɔː.rəʊ.skəʊp, 'flʊə- Ⓤⓢ 'flɔːr.ə-, 'flʊr-, -oʊ- **-es** -s **-ing** -ɪŋ **-ed** -t
fluoroscopic ˌflɔː.rəʊ'skɒp.ɪk, ˌflʊə- Ⓤⓢ ˌflɔːr.ə'-, ˌflʊr-, -oʊ'- **-ally** -əl.i, -li
fluoroscop|y flɔː'rɒs.kə.p|i, flʊə-, flə- Ⓤⓢ flɔː'rɑː.skə-, flʊ- **-ies** -iz **-ist/s** -ɪst/s
fluorosis flɔː'rəʊ.sɪs, flʊə-, flə- Ⓤⓢ flɔː'roʊ-, flʊ-
fluorspar 'flɔː.spɑːʳ, 'flʊə- Ⓤⓢ 'flɔːr.spɑːr, 'fluː.ɔːr-
flurr|y 'flʌr|.i Ⓤⓢ 'flɝː- **-ies** -iz **-ying** -i.ɪŋ **-ied** -id
flush flʌʃ **-es** -ɪz **-ing** -ɪŋ **-ed** -t
flushing (F) 'flʌʃ.ɪŋ **-s** -z
flust|er 'flʌs.t|əʳ Ⓤⓢ -t|ɚ **-ers** -əz Ⓤⓢ -ɚz **-ering** -ər.ɪŋ **-ered** -əd Ⓤⓢ -ɚd
flut|e (F) fluːt **-es** -s **-ing** -ɪŋ Ⓤⓢ 'fluː.t̬ɪŋ **-ed** -ɪd Ⓤⓢ 'fluː.t̬ɪd **-y** -i Ⓤⓢ 'fluː.t̬i **-ier** -i.əʳ Ⓤⓢ 'fluː.t̬i.ɚ **-iest** -i.ɪst, -i.əst Ⓤⓢ 'fluː.t̬i.ɪst, -əst **-iness** -ɪ.nəs, -ɪ.nɪs Ⓤⓢ 'fluː.t̬ɪ.nəs, -nɪs
flutist 'fluː.tɪst Ⓤⓢ -t̬ɪst **-s** -s
flutt|er (F) 'flʌt|.əʳ Ⓤⓢ 'flʌt̬|.ɚ **-ers** -əz Ⓤⓢ -ɚz **-ering** -ər.ɪŋ **-ered** -əd Ⓤⓢ -ɚd **-erer/s** -ər.əʳ/z Ⓤⓢ -ɚ.ɚ/z
fluvial 'fluː.vi.əl
flux flʌks **-es** -ɪz
fluxion 'flʌk.ʃən **-s** -z
fluxional 'flʌk.ʃən.əl
fl|y (F) fl|aɪ **-ies** -aɪz **-ying** -aɪ.ɪŋ **flew** fluː **flown** fləʊn Ⓤⓢ floʊn **flier/s** 'flaɪ.əʳ/z Ⓤⓢ -ɚ/z ˈ**fly** ˌ**ball**; ˌ**flying** ˈ**buttress**; ˈ**flying** ˌ**fish**; ˈ**flying** ˌ**officer** ˌ**flying** ˈ**saucer**; ˈ**flying** ˌ**squad**; ˌ**flying** ˈ**start**; ˈ**fly** ˌ**sheet**; **he/she** ˌ**wouldn't** ˌ**harm a** ˈ**fly**

flyable ˈflaɪ.ə.bl̩

flyaway ˈflaɪ.ə.weɪ

flyb|y ˈflaɪ.b|aɪ **-ies** -aɪz

fly-by-night ˈflaɪ.baɪ.naɪt **-s** -s **-er/s** -əʳ/z (US) -ɚ/z

fly-by-wire ˈflaɪ.baɪ.waɪəʳ, ˌ--ˈ- (US) -waɪɚ

flycatcher ˈflaɪˌkætʃ.əʳ (US) -ɚ **-s** -z

fly-drive ˈflaɪ.draɪv, ˌ-ˈ- **-s** -z

flyer ˈflaɪ.əʳ (US) -ɚ **-s** -z

fly-fishing ˈflaɪˌfɪʃ.ɪŋ

flyingsaucer ˌflaɪ.ɪŋˈsɔː.səʳ (US) -ˈsɑː.sɚ, -ˈsɔː- **-s** -z

flying squad ˈflaɪ.ɪŋ.skwɒd (US) -skwɑːd **-s** -z

flylea|f ˈflaɪ.liː|f **-ves** -vz

Flymo® ˈflaɪ.məʊ (US) -moʊ

Flyn(n) flɪn

Flynt flɪnt

flyover ˈflaɪˌəʊ.vəʳ (US) -ˌoʊ.vɚ **-s** -z

flypaper ˈflaɪˌpeɪ.pəʳ (US) -pɚ **-s** -z

flypast ˈflaɪ.pɑːst (US) -pæst **-s** -s

flyposter ˈflaɪˌpəʊ.stəʳ (US) -ˌpoʊ.stɚ **-s** -z

flyswatter ˈflaɪˌswɒt.əʳ (US) -ˌswɑː.t̬ɚ **-s** -z

Flyte flaɪt

flyway ˈflaɪ.weɪ **-s** -z

flyweight ˈflaɪ.weɪt **-s** -s

flywheel ˈflaɪ.*h*wiːl **-s** -z

FM ˌefˈem

Fo fəʊ (US) foʊ

foal fəʊl (US) foʊl **-s** -z **-ing** -ɪŋ **-ed** -d

foam fəʊm (US) foʊm **-s** -z **-ing** -ɪŋ **-ed** -d **-y** -i **-iness** -ɪ.nəs, -ɪ.nɪs

Foard fɔːd (US) fɔːrd

fob fɒb (US) fɑːb **-s** -z **-bing** -ɪŋ **-bed** -d

focal ˈfəʊ.kəl (US) ˈfoʊ- **ˈfocal ˌpoint, ˌfocal ˈpoint**

Foch fɒʃ (US) fɑːʃ, fɔːʃ

Fochabers ˈfɒk.ə.bəz, ˈfɒx- (US) ˈfɑːk.ə.bɚz

Focke fɒk (US) fɑːk

fo'c'sle ˈfəʊk.səl (US) ˈfoʊk- **-s** -z

fo|cus (*n.*) ˈfəʊ|.kəs (US) ˈfoʊ- **-cuses** -kə.sɪz **-ci** -saɪ, -kiː

focus (*v.*) ˈfəʊ.kəs (US) ˈfoʊ- **-(s)es** -ɪz **-(s)ing** -ɪŋ **-(s)ed** -t

fodder ˈfɒd.əʳ (US) ˈfɑː.dɚ

foe fəʊ (US) foʊ **-s** -z

FoE (*abbrev. for* **Friends of the Earth**) ˌef.əʊˈiː (US) -oʊˈ-

Foehn fɜːn (US) feɪn, fɜːn

foe|man ˈfəʊ|.mən, -mæn (US) ˈfoʊ- **-men** -mən, -men

foetal ˈfiː.təl (US) -t̬əl **ˈfoetal poˌsition**

foetid ˈfiː.tɪd, ˈfet.ɪd (US) ˈfet̬.ɪd, ˈfiː.t̬ɪd **-ly** -li **-ness** -nəs, -nɪs

foetus ˈfiː.təs (US) -t̬əs **-es** -ɪz

fog fɒg (US) fɑːg, fɔːg **-s** -z **-ging** -ɪŋ **-ged** -d **ˈfog ˌlamp**

fogbound ˈfɒg.baʊnd (US) ˈfɑːg-, ˈfɔːg-

Fogerty ˈfəʊ.gə.ti, ˈfɒg.ə.ti (US) ˈfoʊ.gɚ.t̬i

fogey ˈfəʊ.gi (US) ˈfoʊ- **-s** -z **-ish** -ɪʃ **-ism** -ɪ.zəm

Fogg fɒg (US) fɑːg, fɔːg

fogg|y ˈfɒg|.i (US) ˈfɑː.g|i, ˈfɔː- **-ier** -i.əʳ (US) -i.ɚ **-iest** -i.ɪst, -i.əst **-ily** -ɪ.li, -əl.i **-iness** -ɪ.nəs, -ɪ.nɪs **ˌFoggy ˈBottom**

foghorn ˈfɒg.hɔːn (US) ˈfɑːg.hɔːrn, ˈfɔːg- **-s** -z

fog|y ˈfəʊ.g|i (US) ˈfoʊ- **-ies** -iz **-yish** -i.ɪʃ **-yism** -i.ɪ.zəm

fohn, föhn fɜːn (US) feɪn, fɜːn

foible ˈfɔɪ.bl̩ **-s** -z

foie gras ˌfwɑːˈgrɑː

foil fɔɪl **-s** -z **-ing** -ɪŋ **-ed** -d

foist fɔɪst **-s** -s **-ing** -ɪŋ **-ed** -ɪd

Fokker® ˈfɒk.əʳ (US) ˈfɑː.kɚ

fold fəʊld (US) foʊld **-s** -z **-ing** -ɪŋ **-ed** -ɪd

foldaway ˈfəʊld.ə.weɪ (US) ˈfoʊld-

folder ˈfəʊl.dəʳ (US) ˈfoʊl.dɚ **-s** -z

folderol ˈfɒl.dɪ.rɒl, -də- (US) ˈfɑːl.də.rɑːl **-s** -z

foldout ˈfəʊld.aʊt (US) ˈfoʊld- **-s** -s

Foley ˈfəʊ.li (US) ˈfoʊ-

Folgate ˈfɒl.gɪt, -geɪt (US) ˈfɑːl.geɪt

Folger ˈfəʊl.dʒəʳ, ˈfɒl- (US) ˈfoʊl.dʒɚ

foliage ˈfəʊ.li.ɪdʒ (US) ˈfoʊ- **-d** -d

foliar ˈfəʊ.li.ə (US) ˈfoʊ.li.ɚ

foliate (*adj.*) ˈfəʊ.li.ət, -ɪt, -eɪt (US) ˈfoʊ-

foli|ate (*v.*) ˈfəʊ.li|.eɪt (US) ˈfoʊ- **-ates** -eɪts **-ating** -eɪ.tɪŋ (US) -eɪ.t̬ɪŋ **-ated** -eɪ.tɪd (US) -eɪ.t̬ɪd

foliation ˌfəʊ.liˈeɪ.ʃən (US) ˌfoʊ- **-s** -z

folic ˈfɒl.ɪk, ˈfəʊ.lɪk (US) ˈfoʊ- **ˌfolic ˈacid**

Folies Bergère ˌfɒl.i.bɜːˈʒeəʳ, -bəˈ-, -beəˈ- (US) ˌfoʊ.li.berˈʒer

folio ˈfəʊ.li.əʊ (US) ˈfoʊ.li.oʊ **-s** -z

Foliot ˈfɒl.i.ət (US) ˈfɑː.li-

folk fəʊk (US) foʊk **-s** -s **ˈfolk ˌdance; ˈfolk ˌsong**

Folkes fəʊlks, fuːks (US) foʊlks

Folkestone ˈfəʊk.stən (US) ˈfoʊk-

folklore ˈfəʊk.lɔːʳ (US) ˈfoʊk.lɔːr

folklorist ˈfəʊkˌlɔː.rɪst (US) ˈfoʊkˌlɔːr.ɪst **-s** -s

folksinger ˈfəʊkˌsɪŋ.əʳ (US) ˈfoʊkˌsɪŋ.ɚ **-s** -z

folks|y ˈfəʊk.s|i (US) ˈfoʊk- **-ier** -i.əʳ (US) -i.ɚ **-iest** -i.ɪst, -i.əst **-ily** -ɪ.li, -əl.i **-iness** -ɪ.nəs, -ɪ.nɪs

folktale ˈfəʊk.teɪl (US) ˈfoʊk- **-s** -z

Follen ˈfɒl.ɪn, -ən (US) ˈfɑː.lɪn, -lən

Follett ˈfɒl.ɪt, -ət (US) ˈfɑː.lɪt, -lət

Follick ˈfɒl.ɪk (US) ˈfɑː.lɪk

follicle ˈfɒl.ɪ.kl̩ (US) ˈfɑː.lɪ- **-s** -z

follow ˈfɒl.əʊ (US) ˈfɑː.loʊ **-s** -z **-ing/s** -ɪŋ/z **-ed** -d **-er/s** -əʳ/z (US) -ɚ/z

follow-my-leader ˌfɒl.əʊ.məˈliː.dəʳ, -mɪˈ-, -maɪˈ- (US) ˌfɑː.loʊ.maɪˈliː.dɚ

follow-on ˈfɒl.əʊ.ɒn (US) ˈfɑː.loʊ.ɑːn **-s** -z

follow-the-leader ˌfɒl.əʊ.ðəˈliː.dəʳ (US) ˌfɑː.loʊ.ðəˈliː.dɚ

follow-through ˌfɒl.əʊˈθruː (US) ˈ---, ˈfɑː.loʊ.θruː **-s** -z

follow-up ˈfɒl.əʊ.ʌp (US) ˈfɑː.loʊ- **-s** -s

foll|y (F) ˈfɒl|.i (US) ˈfɑː.l|i **-ies** -iz

Fomalhaut ˈfəʊ.mə.ləʊt, ˈfɒm-, -əl.hɔːt (US) ˈfoʊ.məl.hɑːt, -hɔːt, -mə.loʊ

fo|ment fəʊ|ˈment (US) foʊ- **-ments** -ˈments **-menting** -ˈmen.tɪŋ (US) -ˈmen.t̬ɪŋ **-mented** -ˈmen.tɪd (US) -ˈmen.t̬ɪd **-menter/s** -ˈmen.təʳ/z (US) -ˈmen.t̬ɚ/z

fomentation ˌfəʊ.menˈteɪ.ʃən, -mənˈ- (US) ˌfoʊ- **-s** -z

fond fɒnd (US) fɑːnd **-er** -əʳ (US) -ɚ **-est** -ɪst, -əst **-ly** -li **-ness** -nəs, -nɪs

Fonda ˈfɒn.də (US) ˈfɑːn-

fondant ˈfɒn.dənt (US) ˈfɑːn- **-s** -s

fondl|e ˈfɒn.dl̩ (US) ˈfɑːn- **-es** -z **-ing** -ɪŋ, ˈfɒnd.lɪŋ (US) ˈfɑːnd- **-ed** -d

fondly ˈfɒnd.li (US) ˈfɑːnd-

fondu(e) ˈfɒn.djuː, -duː, -ˈ- (US) fɑːnˈduː, -ˈdjuː, ˈ-- **-s** -z

font fɒnt (US) fɑːnt **-s** -s **-al** -əl (US) ˈfɑːn.t̬əl

Fontainebleau ˈfɒn.tɪn.bləʊ, -tɪm-, -təm- (US) ˈfɑːn.tən.bloʊ

Fontane ˈfɒn.teɪn *as if German:* fɒnˈtɑː.nə (US) ˈfɑːn-

fontanelle, fontanel ˌfɒn.təˈnel (US) ˌfɑːn.tənˈel **-s** -z

Fontenoy ˈfɒn.tə.nɔɪ, -tɪ.nɔɪ (US) ˈfɑːn.tən.ɔɪ

Fonteyn fɒnˈteɪn, ˈ-- (US) fɑːnˈteɪn, ˈ--

Fonthill ˈfɒnt.hɪl (US) ˈfɑːnt-

Foochow ˌfuːˈtʃaʊ

food fuːd **-s** -z **-less** -ləs, -lɪs **ˈfood ˌpoisoning; ˈfood ˌprocessor**

foodie ˈfuː.di **-s** -z

foodstuff ˈfuːd.stʌf **-s** -s

fool fuːl **-s** -z **-ing** -ɪŋ **-ed** -d **ˌfool's ˈgold, ˈfool's ˌgold; ˌmake a ˈfool of oneˌself**

fooler|y ˈfuː.lər|.i **-ies** -iz

foolhard|y ˈfuːlˌhɑː.d|i (US) -ˌhɑːr- **-iest** -i.ɪst, -i.əst **-ily** -ɪ.li, -əl.i **-iness** -ɪ.nəs, -ɪ.nɪs

foolish ˈfuː.lɪʃ **-ly** -li **-ness** -nəs, -nɪs

foolproof ˈfuːl.pruːf

foolscap, fool's cap *hat:* ˈfuːlz.kæp **-s** -s

foolscap *paper size:* ˈfuːl.skæp, ˈfuːlz.kæp

foot (F) (*n.*) fʊt **feet** fiːt **ˈfoot ˌfault; ˈfoot ˌpassenger; ˈfoot ˌsoldier; ˌone foot in the ˈgrave; put one's ˌbest foot ˈforward; ˌput one's ˈfoot down; ˌput one's ˈfoot in it**

foot (*v.*) fʊt **-s** -s **-ing** -ɪŋ (US) ˈfʊt̬.ɪŋ **-ed** -ɪd (US) ˈfʊt̬.ɪd

footage ˈfʊt.ɪdʒ (US) ˈfʊt̬-

foot-and-mouth ˌfʊt.ᵊndˈmaʊθ, -ᵊmˈ- (US) -ᵊndˈ- ˌ**foot-and-ˈmouth diˌsease**
football ˈfʊt.bɔːl (US) -bɔːl, -bɑːl **-s** -z **-ing** -ɪŋ **-er/s** -əʳ/z (US) -ɚ/z ˈ**football ˌmatch**; ˈ**football ˌpools**
footba|th ˈfʊt.bɑː|θ (US) -bæ|θ **-ths** -ðz
footboard ˈfʊt.bɔːd (US) -bɔːrd **-s** -z
footbridg|e ˈfʊt.brɪdʒ **-es** -ɪz
Foote fʊt
footer ˈfʊt.əʳ (US) ˈfʊt̬.ɚ
footfall ˈfʊt.fɔːl (US) -fɔːl, -fɑːl **-s** -z
foothill ˈfʊt.hɪl **-s** -z
foothold ˈfʊt.həʊld (US) -hoʊld **-s** -z
footie ˈfʊt.i (US) ˈfʊt̬-
footing ˈfʊt.ɪŋ (US) ˈfʊt̬- **-s** -z
footl|e ˈfuː.tl̩ (US) -t̬l̩ **-es** -z **-ing** -ɪŋ, ˈfuːt.lɪŋ **-ed** -d
footlight ˈfʊt.laɪt **-s** -s
footlocker ˈfʊtˌlɒk.əʳ (US) -ˌlɑː.kɚ **-s** -z
footloose ˈfʊt.luːs ˌ**footloose and ˌfancy-ˈfree**
foot|man ˈfʊt|.mən **-men** -mən
footmark ˈfʊt.mɑːk (US) -mɑːrk **-s** -s
footnote ˈfʊt.nəʊt (US) -noʊt **-s** -s
footpad ˈfʊt.pæd **-s** -z
footpa|th ˈfʊt.pɑː|θ (US) -pæ|θ **-ths** -ðz
footplate ˈfʊt.pleɪt **-s** -s
foot-pound ˈfʊt.paʊnd **-s** -z
footprint ˈfʊt.prɪnt **-s** -s
footrac|e ˈfʊt.reɪs **-es** -ɪz
footrest ˈfʊt.rest **-s** -s
footrule ˈfʊt.ruːl **-s** -z
footsie (F) ˈfʊt.si
footslog ˈfʊt.slɒg (US) -slɑːg, -slɔːg **-s** -z **-ging** -ɪŋ **-ged** -d
footsore ˈfʊt.sɔːʳ (US) -sɔːr
footstep ˈfʊt.step **-s** -s
footstool ˈfʊt.stuːl **-s** -z
footsure ˈfʊt.ʃʊəʳ, -ʃɔːʳ (US) -ʃʊr, -ʃɝː **-ness** -nəs, -nɪs
footwear ˈfʊt.weəʳ (US) -wer
footwork ˈfʊt.wɜːk (US) -wɝːk
footy ˈfʊt.i (US) ˈfʊt̬-
foozl|e (F) ˈfuː.zl̩ **-es** -z **-ing** -ɪŋ, ˈfuːz.lɪŋ **-ed** -d **-er/s** -əʳ/z, ˈfuːz.ləʳ/z (US) ˈfuː.zl̩.ɚ/z, ˈfuːz.lɚ/z
fop fɒp (US) fɑːp **-s** -s
fopper|y ˈfɒp.ᵊr|.i (US) ˈfɑː.pɚ- **-ies** -iz
foppish ˈfɒp.ɪʃ (US) ˈfɑː.pɪʃ **-ly** -li **-ness** -nəs, -nɪs
for (*prep. conj.*) *strong form:* fɔːʳ (US) fɔːr *weak form:* fəʳ (US) fɚ *alternative weak form before vowels:* frʊ
Note: Weak form word. The strong form /fɔːʳ (US) fɔːr/ is used contrastively (e.g. "**for** and **against**") and in sentence-final position (e.g. "That's what it's for"). The weak form is /fə (US) fɚ/ before consonants (e.g. "Thanks for coming" /ˌθæŋks.fəˈkʌm.ɪŋ (US) -fɚˈ-/); before vowels it is /fər (US) fɚ/ (e.g. "One for all" /ˌwʌn.fərˈɔːl (US) -fɚˈɑːl/) or, in rapid speech, /frʊ/ (e.g. "Time for another" /ˌtaɪm.frʊ.əˈnʌð.əʳ (US) -ɚ/).
forag|e ˈfɒr.ɪdʒ (US) ˈfɔːr- **-es** -ɪz **-ing** -ɪŋ **-ed** -d **-er/s** -əʳ/z (US) -ɚ/z
foramen fəˈreɪ.men, fɒrˈeɪ-, -mən (US) fəˈreɪ.mən, fɔː-, foʊ- **foramina** fəˈræm.ɪ.nə, fɒrˈeɪ- (US) fəˈræm.ə-, fɔː-, foʊ-
forasmuch fᵊr.əzˈmʌtʃ, ˌfɔː.rəz-, ˌfɒr.əz- (US) ˌfɔːr.æzˈ-, ˌfɚ-, -əzˈ-
foray ˈfɒr.eɪ (US) ˈfɔːr- **-s** -z **-ing** -ɪŋ **-ed** -d
forbad *(from* **forbid***)* fəˈbæd, fɔː- (US) fɚ-, fɔːr-
forbade *(from* **forbid***)* fəˈbæd, fɔː-, -beɪd (US) fɚˈbæd, fɔːr-
forbear (*n.*) ˈfɔː.beəʳ (US) ˈfɔːr.ber **-s** -z
for|bear (*v.*) fɔː|ˈbeəʳ, fə- (US) fɔːr|ˈber **-bears** -ˈbeəz (US) -ˈberz **-bearing/ly** -ˈbeə.rɪŋ/li (US) -ˈber.ɪŋ/li **-bore** -ˈbɔːʳ (US) -ˈbɔːr **-borne** -ˈbɔːn (US) -ˈbɔːrn
forbearance fɔːˈbeə.rᵊnts, fə- (US) fɔːrˈber.ᵊnts
Forbes fɔːbz, ˈfɔː.bɪs (US) fɔːrbz
for|bid fə|ˈbɪd, fɔː- (US) fɚ-, fɔːr- **-bids** -ˈbɪdz **-bidding/ly** -ˈbɪd.ɪŋ/li **-bad** -ˈbæd **-bade** -ˈbæd, -ˈbeɪd (US) -ˈbæd **-bidden** -ˈbɪd.ᵊn
forbore *(from* **forbear***)* fɔːˈbɔːʳ (US) fɔːrˈbɔːr
forc|e (F) fɔːs (US) fɔːrs **-es** -ɪz **-ing** -ɪŋ **-ed** -t **-edly** -ɪd.li **-edness** -ɪd.nəs, -nɪs ˈ**force ˌpump**; ˌ**forced ˈmarch**
forcefeed ˌfɔːsˈfiːd, ˈ-- (US) ˈfɔːrs.fiːd, ˌ-ˈ- **-s** -z **-ing** -ɪŋ **forcefed** ˌfɔːsˈfed, ˈ-- (US) ˈfɔːrs.fed, ˌ-ˈ-
forceful ˈfɔːs.fᵊl, -fʊl (US) ˈfɔːrs- **-ly** -i **-ness** -nəs, -nɪs
force majeure ˌfɔːs.mæʒˈɜːʳ, -mædʒˈʊəʳ (US) ˌfɔːrs.mɑːˈʒɝː
forcemeat ˈfɔːs.miːt (US) ˈfɔːrs-
forceps ˈfɔː.seps, -sɪps, -səps (US) ˈfɔːr-
forcer ˈfɔː.səʳ (US) ˈfɔːr.sɚ **-s** -z
forcib|le ˈfɔː.sə.bl̩, -sɪ- (US) ˈfɔːr- **-ly** -li **-leness** -l̩.nəs, -nɪs
ford (F) fɔːd (US) fɔːrd **-s** -z **-ing** -ɪŋ **-ed** -ɪd **-able** -ə.bl̩
Fordcombe ˈfɔːd.kəm (US) ˈfɔːrd-
Forde fɔːd (US) fɔːrd
Forder ˈfɔː.dəʳ (US) ˈfɔːr.dɚ
Fordham ˈfɔː.dəm (US) ˈfɔːr-
Fordingbridge ˈfɔː.dɪŋ.brɪdʒ (US) ˈfɔːr-
Fordoun ˈfɔː.dᵊn (US) ˈfɔːr-
Fordyce ˈfɔː.daɪs (US) ˈfɔːr-
fore fɔːʳ (US) fɔːr
forearm (*n.*) ˈfɔːʳ.ɑːm (US) ˈfɔːr.ɑːrm **-s** -z
forearm (*v.*) fɔːʳˈɑːm (US) fɔːrˈɑːrm **-s** -z **-ing** -ɪŋ **-ed** -d
forebear ˈfɔː.beəʳ (US) ˈfɔːr.ber **-s** -s
forebod|e fɔːˈbəʊd, fə- (US) fɔːrˈboʊd, fɚ- **-es** -z **-ing/ly** -ɪŋ/li **-ed** -ɪd **-er/s** -əʳ/z (US) -ɚ/z
foreboding fɔːˈbəʊ.dɪŋ, fə- (US) fɔːrˈboʊ-, fɚ- **-s** -z
forecast (*n.*) ˈfɔː.kɑːst (US) ˈfɔːr.kæst **-s** -s
forecast (*v.*) ˈfɔː.kɑːst (US) ˈfɔːr.kæst **-s** -s **-ing** -ɪŋ **-ed** -ɪd **-er/s** -əʳ/z (US) -ɚ/z
forecastle ˈfəʊk.sᵊl (US) ˈfoʊk- **-s** -z
foreclos|e fɔːˈkləʊz (US) fɔːrˈkloʊz **-es** -ɪz **-ing** -ɪŋ **-ed** -d
foreclosure fɔːˈkləʊ.ʒəʳ (US) fɔːrˈkloʊ.ʒɚ **-s** -z
forecourt ˈfɔː.kɔːt (US) ˈfɔːr.kɔːrt **-s** -s
forefather ˈfɔːˌfɑː.ðəʳ (US) ˈfɔːrˌfɑː.ðɚ **-s** -z
forefinger ˈfɔːˌfɪŋ.gəʳ (US) ˈfɔːrˌfɪŋ.gɚ **-s** -z
fore|foot ˈfɔː|.fʊt (US) ˈfɔːr- **-feet** -fiːt
forefront ˈfɔː.frʌnt (US) ˈfɔːr-
fore|go fɔː|ˈgəʊ (US) fɔːr|ˈgoʊ **-goes** -ˈgəʊz (US) -ˈgoʊz **-going** -ˈgəʊ.ɪŋ (US) -ˈgoʊ.ɪŋ **-went** -ˈwent **-gone** -ˈgɒn (US) -ˈgɑːn **-goer/s** -ˈgəʊ.əʳ/z (US) -ˈgoʊ.ɚ/z
foregone *(from* **forego***)* fɔːˈgɒn (US) fɔːrˈgɑːn
foregone (*adj.*) ˈfɔː.gɒn (US) ˈfɔːr.gɑːn ˌ**foregone conˈclusion**
foreground ˈfɔː.graʊnd (US) ˈfɔːr- **-s** -z
foregrounding ˈfɔːˌgraʊn.dɪŋ (US) ˈfɔːr-
forehand ˈfɔː.hænd (US) ˈfɔːr- **-s** -z
forehanded fɔːˈhæn.dɪd (US) ˈfɔːrˌ-, ˌ-ˈ-- **-ly** -li **-ness** -nəs, -nɪs *stress shift, British only:* ˌforehanded ˈvolley
forehead ˈfɔː.hed, ˈfɒr.ɪd, -ed; (US) ˈfɔːr.ed, -hed **-s** -z
foreign ˈfɒr.ɪn, -ən (US) ˈfɔːr- ˌ**foreign afˈfairs**; ˌ**foreign correˈspondent**; ˌ**foreign exˈchange**; ˌ**foreign ˈlegion**; ˈ**Foreign ˌOffice**; ˌ**foreign ˈpolicy**; ˌ**foreign ˈsecretary**; ˌ**Foreign ˈService**
foreigner ˈfɒr.ɪ.nəʳ, ˈ-ə- (US) ˈfɔːr- **-s** -z
forejudg|e fɔːˈdʒʌdʒ (US) fɔːr- **-es** -ɪz **-ing** -ɪŋ **-ed** -d
fore|know fɔː|ˈnəʊ (US) fɔːr|ˈnoʊ **-knows** -ˈnəʊz (US) -ˈnoʊz **-knowing** -ˈnəʊ.ɪŋ (US) -ˈnoʊ.ɪŋ **-knew** -ˈnjuː (US) -ˈnuː, -ˈnjuː **-known** -ˈnəʊn (US) -ˈnoʊn
foreknowledge fɔːˈnɒl.ɪdʒ (US) fɔːrˈnɑː.lɪdʒ
foreland (F) ˈfɔː.lənd (US) ˈfɔːr- **-s** -z
foreleg ˈfɔː.leg (US) ˈfɔːr- **-s** -z
forelock ˈfɔː.lɒk (US) ˈfɔːr.lɑːk **-s** -s
fore|man (F) ˈfɔː|.mən (US) ˈfɔːr- **-men** -mən
foremast ˈfɔː.mɑːst (US) ˈfɔːr.mæst *nautical pronunciation:* -məst **-s** -s
foremost ˈfɔː.məʊst, -məst (US) ˈfɔːr.moʊst

forename ˈfɔː.neɪm (US) ˈfɔːr- **-s** -z

forenoon ˈfɔː.nuːn (US) ˈfɔːr-, ˌ-ˈ- **-s** -z

forensic fəˈrent.sɪk, fɒrˈent-, -ˈen.zɪk (US) fəˈrent.sɪk, -ˈren.zɪk **-s** -s

foreordain ˌfɔːr.ɔːˈdeɪn (US) ˌfɔːr.ɔːrˈ- **-s** -z **-ing** -ɪŋ **-ed** -d

forepart ˈfɔː.pɑːt (US) ˈfɔːr.pɑːrt **-s** -s

foreplay ˈfɔː.pleɪ (US) ˈfɔːr-

fore|run fɔːˈ|rʌn (US) fɔːr- **-runs** -ˈrʌnz **-running** -ˈrʌn.ɪŋ **-ran** -ˈræn

forerunner ˈfɔːˌrʌn.əʳ, ˌ-ˈ-- (US) ˈfɔːrˌrʌn.ɚ, ˌ-ˈ-- **-s** -z

foresail ˈfɔː.seɪl (US) ˈfɔːr- *nautical pronunciation:* -sᵊl **-s** -z

fore|see fɔːˈ|siː, fə- (US) fɔːr-, fɚ- **-sees** -ˈsiːz **-seeing** -ˈsiː.ɪŋ **-saw** -ˈsɔː (US) -ˈsɑː, -ˈsɔː **-seen** -ˈsiːn **-seeable** -ˈsiː.ə.bl̩

foreseeability fɔːˌsiː.əˈbɪl.ə.ti, ˌfɔː.siː-; fəˌsiː- (US) fɔːrˌsiː.əˈbɪl.ə.t̬i, fɚ-

foreshadow fɔːˈʃæd.əʊ (US) fɔːrˈʃæd.oʊ **-s** -z **-ing** -ɪŋ **-ed** -d **-er/s** -əʳ/z (US) -ɚ/z

foreshore ˈfɔː.ʃɔːʳ (US) ˈfɔːr.ʃɔːr **-s** -z

foreshorten fɔːˈʃɔː.tᵊn (US) fɔːrˈʃɔːr- **-s** -z **-ing** -ɪŋ **-ed** -d

foreshow fɔːˈʃəʊ (US) fɔːrˈʃoʊ **-s** -z **-ing** -ɪŋ **-ed** -d **-n** -n

foresight ˈfɔː.saɪt (US) ˈfɔːr- **-s** -s

foreskin ˈfɔː.skɪn (US) ˈfɔːr- **-s** -z

forest (F) ˈfɒr.ɪst (US) ˈfɔːr- **-s** -s ˌ**Forest ˈHills; ˌforest ˈranger** (US) **ˈforest ˌranger; not see the ˌforest for the ˈtrees**

forestall fɔːˈstɔːl (US) fɔːrˈstɔːl, -ˈstɑːl **-s** -z **-ing** -ɪŋ **-ed** -d **-er/s** -əʳ/z (US) -ɚ/z

forester (F) ˈfɒr.ɪ.stəʳ, ˈ-ə- (US) ˈfɔːr- **-s** -z

forestry ˈfɒr.ɪ.stri, ˈ-ə- (US) ˈfɔːr-

foretaste (*n.*) ˈfɔː.teɪst (US) ˈfɔːr- **-s** -s

foretast|e (*v.*) fɔːˈteɪst (US) fɔːr- **-es** -s **-ing** -ɪŋ **-ed** -ɪd

fore|tell fɔːˈ|tel (US) fɔːr- **-tells** -ˈtelz **-telling** -ˈtel.ɪŋ **-told** -ˈtəʊld (US) -ˈtoʊld **-teller/s** -ˈtel.əʳ/z (US) -ˈtel.ɚ/z

forethought ˈfɔː.θɔːt (US) ˈfɔːr.θɑːt, -θɔːt

foretop, fore-top ˈfɔː.tɒp (US) ˈfɔːr.tɑːp *nautical pronunciation:* -təp **-s** -s

fore-topmast fɔːˈtɒp.mɑːst (US) fɔːrˈtɑːp.mæst *nautical pronunciation:* -məst **-s** -s

fore-topsail fɔːˈtɒp.seɪl (US) fɔːrˈtɑːp- *nautical pronunciation:* -sᵊl **-s** -z

forever fəˈre.vəʳ (US) fɔːrˈev.ɚ, fɚ-

forewarn fɔːˈwɔːn (US) fɔːrˈwɔːrn **-s** -z **-ing** -ɪŋ **-ed** -d

forewent (*from* **forego**) fɔːˈwent (US) fɔːr-

fore|woman ˈfɔː|ˌwʊm.ən (US) ˈfɔːr- **-women** -ˌwɪm.ɪn

foreword ˈfɔː.wɜːd (US) ˈfɔːr.wɝːd **-s** -z

Forfar ˈfɔː.fəʳ, -fɑːʳ (US) ˈfɔːr.fɚ, -fɑːr

forfei|t ˈfɔː.fɪ|t (US) ˈfɔːr-, -fə|t **-ts** -ts **-ting** -tɪŋ (US) -t̬ɪŋ **-ted** -tɪd (US) -t̬ɪd **-ter/s** -təʳ/z (US) -t̬ɚ/z **-table** -tə.bl̩ (US) -t̬ə.bl̩

forfeiture ˈfɔː.fɪ.tʃəʳ (US) ˈfɔːr.fə- **-s** -z

forfend fɔːˈfend (US) fɔːr- **-s** -z **-ing** -ɪŋ **-ed** -ɪd

forgath|er fɔːˈgæð|.əʳ (US) fɔːrˈgæð|.ɚ **-ers** -əz (US) -ɚz **-ering** -ᵊr.ɪŋ **-ered** -əd (US) -ɚd

forgave (*from* **forgive**) fəˈgeɪv (US) fɚ-, fɔːr-

forg|e fɔːdʒ (US) fɔːrdʒ **-es** -ɪz **-ing** -ɪŋ **-ed** -d **-er/s** -əʳ/z (US) -ɚ/z

forger|y ˈfɔː.dʒᵊr|.i (US) ˈfɔːr- **-ies** -iz

for|get fə|ˈget (US) fɚ-, fɔːr- **-gets** -ˈgets **-getting** -ˈget.ɪŋ (US) -ˈget̬.ɪŋ **-got** -ˈgɒt (US) -ˈgɑːt **-gotten** -ˈgɒt.ᵊn (US) -ˈgɑː.tᵊn

forgetful fəˈget.fᵊl, -fʊl (US) fɚ-, fɔːr- **-ly** -i **-ness** -nəs, -nɪs

forget-me-not fəˈget.mi.nɒt (US) fɚˈget.mi.nɑːt, fɔːr- **-s** -s

forgettab|le fəˈget.ə.b|l̩ (US) fɚˈget̬-, fɔːr- **-ly** -li

for|give fə|ˈgɪv (US) fɚ-, fɔːr- **-gives** -ˈgɪvz **-giving** -ˈgɪv.ɪŋ **-gave** -ˈgeɪv **-given** -ˈgɪv.ᵊn **-givable** -ˈgɪv.ə.bl̩ **-giveness** -ˈgɪv.nəs, -nɪs

for|go fɔː|ˈgəʊ (US) fɔːr|ˈgoʊ **-goes** -ˈgəʊz (US) -ˈgoʊz **-going** -ˈgəʊ.ɪŋ (US) -ˈgoʊ.ɪŋ **-went** -ˈwent **-gone** -ˈgɒn (US) -ˈgɑːn

forgot (*from* **forget**) fəˈgɒt (US) fɚˈgɑːt, fɔːr-

forgotten (*from* **forget**) fəˈgɒt.ᵊn (US) fɚˈgɑː.tᵊn, fɔːr-

Forington ˈfɒr.ɪŋ.tən (US) ˈfɔːr-

forint ˈfɒr.ɪnt (US) ˈfɔːr- **-s** -s

fork fɔːk (US) fɔːrk **-s** -s **-ing** -ɪŋ **-ed** -t **-ful/s**

forklift ˈfɔːk.lɪft, ˌ-ˈ- (US) ˈfɔːrk.lɪft **-s** -s **-ing** -ɪŋ **-ed** -ɪd ˌ**forklift ˈtruck**

forlorn fəˈlɔːn, fɔː- (US) fɔːrˈlɔːrn, fɚ- **-ly** -li **-ness** -nəs, -nɪs

form fɔːm (US) fɔːrm **-s** -z **-ing** -ɪŋ **-ed** -d

formal ˈfɔː.mᵊl (US) ˈfɔːr- **-ly** -i

formaldehyde fɔːˈmæl.dɪ.haɪd, -də- (US) fɔːr-, fɚ-

formalin ˈfɔː.mᵊl.ɪn (US) ˈfɔːr.mə.lɪn

formal|ism ˈfɔː.mᵊl|.ɪ.zᵊm (US) ˈfɔːr- **-ist/s** -ɪst/s

formalit|y fɔːˈmæl.ə.t|i, -ɪ.t|i (US) -ə.t̬|i **-ies** -iz

formalization, -isa- ˌfɔː.mᵊl.aɪˈzeɪ.ʃᵊn, -ɪˈ- (US) ˌfɔːr.mᵊl.ɪˈ- **-s** -z

formaliz|e, -is|e ˈfɔː.mᵊl.aɪz (US) ˈfɔːr.mə.laɪz **-es** -ɪz **-ing** -ɪŋ **-ed** -d

Forman ˈfɔː.mən (US) ˈfɔːr-

formant ˈfɔː.mənt (US) ˈfɔːr- **-s** -s

for|mat ˈfɔː|.mæt (US) ˈfɔːr- **-mats** -mæts **-matting** -mæt.ɪŋ (US) -mæt̬.ɪŋ **-matted** -mæt.ɪd (US) -mæt̬.ɪd **-matter/s** -mæt.əʳ/z (US) -mæt̬.ɚ/z

formation fɔːˈmeɪ.ʃᵊn (US) fɔːr- **-s** -z

formative ˈfɔː.mə.tɪv (US) ˈfɔːr.mə.t̬ɪv **-ly** -li **-ness** -nəs, -nɪs

Formby ˈfɔːm.bi (US) ˈfɔːrm-

forme fɔːm (US) fɔːrm **-s** -z

former ˈfɔː.məʳ (US) ˈfɔːr.mɚ **-ly** -li

formic ˈfɔː.mɪk (US) ˈfɔːr- ˌ**formic ˈacid**

Formica® fɔːˈmaɪ.kə, fəˈmaɪ- (US) fɔːr-, fɚ-

formidab|le ˈfɔː.mɪ.də.b|l̩; fɔːˈmɪd.ə-, fə- (US) ˈfɔːr.mə.də.b|l̩; fɔːrˈmɪd.ə-, fɚ- **-ly** -li **-leness** -l̩.nəs, -nɪs

Formidable *name of ship:* fɔːˈmɪd.ə.bl̩; ˈfɔː.mɪ.də- (US) ˈfɔːr.mə.də-; fɔːrˈmɪd.ə-

formless ˈfɔːm.ləs (US) ˈfɔːrm-, -lɪs **-ness** -nəs, -nɪs

Formos|a fɔːˈməʊ.s|ə, -z|ə (US) fɔːrˈmoʊ- **-an/s** -ən/z

formul|a ˈfɔː.mjə.l|ə, -mjʊ- (US) ˈfɔːr.mjʊ-, -mjə- **-ae** -iː **-as** -əz

formulaic ˌfɔː.mjəˈleɪ.ɪk, -mjʊˈ- (US) ˌfɔːr.mjʊˈ-, -mjəˈ-

formular|y ˈfɔː.mjə.lə.r|i, -mjʊ- (US) ˈfɔːr.mjʊ.ler|.i, -mjə- **-ies** -iz

formu|late ˈfɔː.mjə|.leɪt, -mjʊ- (US) ˈfɔːr.mjʊ-, -mjə- **-lates** -leɪts **-lating** -leɪ.tɪŋ (US) -leɪ.t̬ɪŋ **-lated** -leɪ.tɪd (US) -leɪ.t̬ɪd

formulation ˌfɔː.mjəˈleɪ.ʃᵊn, -mjʊˈ- (US) ˌfɔːr.mjʊˈ-, -mjəˈ- **-s** -z

Fornax ˈfɔː.næks (US) ˈfɔːr-

Forney ˈfɔː.ni (US) ˈfɔːr-

forni|cate ˈfɔː.nɪ|.keɪt, -nə- (US) ˈfɔːr- **-cates** -keɪts **-cating** -keɪ.tɪŋ (US) -keɪ.t̬ɪŋ **-cated** -keɪ.tɪd (US) -keɪ.t̬ɪd **-cator/s** -keɪ.təʳ/z (US) -keɪ.t̬ɚ/z

fornication ˌfɔː.nɪˈkeɪ.ʃᵊn, -nəˈ- (US) ˌfɔːr-

Forres ˈfɒr.ɪs (US) ˈfɔːr-

Forrest ˈfɒr.ɪst (US) ˈfɔːr-

Forrester ˈfɒr.ɪ.stəʳ (US) ˈfɔːr.ɪ.stɚ

for|sake fə|ˈseɪk, fɔː- (US) fɔːr-, fɚ- **-sakes** -ˈseɪks **-saking** -ˈseɪ.kɪŋ **-sook** -ˈsʊk **-saken** -ˈseɪ.kᵊn

Forshaw ˈfɔː.ʃɔː (US) ˈfɔːr.ʃɑː, -ʃɔː

forsooth fəˈsuːθ, fɔː- (US) fɔːr-, fɚ-

Forster ˈfɔː.stəʳ (US) ˈfɔːr.stɚ

for|swear fɔː|ˈsweəʳ (US) fɔːr|ˈswer **-swears** -ˈsweəz (US) -ˈswerz **-swearing** -ˈsweə.rɪŋ (US) -ˈswer.ɪŋ **-swore** -ˈswɔːʳ (US) -ˈswɔːr **-sworn** -ˈswɔːn (US) -ˈswɔːrn

Forsyte ˈfɔː.saɪt (US) ˈfɔːr-

Forsyth ˈfɔː.saɪθ, -ˈ- (US) ˈfɔːr-, -ˈ-

forsythia fɔːˈsaɪ.θi.ə, fə-, -ˈsɪθ.i- (US) fɔːrˈsɪθ-, -ˈsaɪ.θi- **-s** -z

fort fɔːt (US) fɔːrt **-s** -s ˌ**Fort ˈKnox; ˌFort**

Fortis

Fortis sounds are said to be made with a relatively high degree of effort.

Examples for English

It is claimed that in some languages (including English) there are pairs of consonants whose members can be distinguished from each other in terms of whether they are 'strong' (fortis) or 'weak' (LENIS). These terms refer to the amount of energy used in their production, and are similar to the terms TENSE and LAX more usually used in relation to vowels. It is argued that English /b d g v ð z ʒ/ often have little or no voicing in normal speech, and it is therefore a misnomer to call them voiced. Since they seem to be more weakly articulated than /p t k f θ s ʃ/ it would be appropriate to use the term lenis instead, e.g.:

pin	/pɪn/	[pʰɪ̃n]
bin	/bɪn/	[b̥ɪ̃n]
fine	/faɪn/	[faɪ̃n]
vine	/vaɪn/	[v̥aɪ̃n]

ˌLauderdale; ˌFort ˈWorth; ˌhold the ˈfort

Fortaleza ˌfɔː.təˈleɪ.zə ⓊⓈ ˌfɔːr.t̬əˈ-

forte *strong point:* ˈfɔː.teɪ, -ti ⓊⓈ fɔːrt, ˈfɔːr.teɪ **-s** -z ⓊⓈ fɔːrts; ˈfɔːr.teɪz

forte *in music:* ˈfɔː.teɪ, -ti ⓊⓈ ˈfɔːr- **-s** -z

Fortescue ˈfɔː.tɪ.skjuː, -tə- ⓊⓈ ˈfɔːr.t̬ə-

Forteviot fɔːˈtiː.vi.ət ⓊⓈ fɔːr-

forth (F) fɔːθ ⓊⓈ fɔːrθ

forthcoming ˌfɔːθˈkʌm.ɪŋ ⓊⓈ ˌfɔːrθˈ-, ˈ-ˌ-- *stress shift, British only:* ˌforthcoming ˈbook

forthright ˈfɔːθ.raɪt, ˌ-ˈ- ⓊⓈ ˈfɔːrθ-, ˌ-ˈ- **-ness** -nəs, -nɪs

forthwith ˌfɔːθˈwɪθ, -ˈwɪð ⓊⓈ ˌfɔːrθˈ-

Forties *area in the North Sea:* ˈfɔː.tiz, -tɪz ⓊⓈ ˈfɔːr.t̬iz

fortieth ˈfɔː.ti.əθ, -ɪθ ⓊⓈ ˈfɔːr.t̬i- **-s** -s

fortification ˌfɔː.tɪ.fɪˈkeɪ.ʃən, -tə- ⓊⓈ ˌfɔːr.t̬ə- **-s** -z

forti|fy ˈfɔː.tɪ|.faɪ, -tə- ⓊⓈ ˈfɔːr.t̬ə- **-fies** -faɪz **-fying** -faɪ.ɪŋ **-fied** -faɪd **-fier/s** -faɪ.əʳ/z ⓊⓈ -faɪ.ɚ/z **-fiable** -faɪ.ə.bl̩

Fortinbras ˈfɔː.tɪn.bræs, -tɪm- ⓊⓈ ˈfɔːr.tən-, -t̬ɪn-

fort|is ˈfɔː.t|ɪs ⓊⓈ ˈfɔːr.t̬|ɪs **-es** -iːz, -eɪz

fortissimo fɔːˈtɪs.ɪ.məʊ, -ə- ⓊⓈ fɔːrˈtɪs.ə.moʊ **-s** -z

fortition fɔːˈtɪʃ.ən ⓊⓈ fɔːr-

fortitude ˈfɔː.tɪ.tjuːd, -tʃuːd ⓊⓈ ˈfɔːr.t̬ə.tuːd, -tjuːd

fortnight ˈfɔːt.naɪt ⓊⓈ ˈfɔːrt- **-s** -s

fortnightl|y (F) ˈfɔːt.naɪt.l|i ⓊⓈ ˈfɔːrt- **-ies** -iz

Fortnum ˈfɔːt.nəm ⓊⓈ ˈfɔːrt-

Fortran, FORTRAN ˈfɔː.træn ⓊⓈ ˈfɔːr-

fortress ˈfɔː.trəs, -trɪs ⓊⓈ ˈfɔːr- **-es** -ɪz

fortuitous fɔːˈtjuː.ɪ.təs, -ˈtʃuː-, ˈ-ə- ⓊⓈ fɔːrˈtuː.ə.t̬əs, -ˈtjuː- **-ly** -li **-ness** -nəs, -nɪs

fortuit|y fɔːˈtjuː.ɪ.t|i, -ˈtʃuː-, ˈ-ə- ⓊⓈ fɔːrˈtuː.ə.t̬|i, -ˈtjuː- **-ies** -iz

Fortuna fɔːˈtjuː.nə ⓊⓈ fɔːrˈtuː-, -ˈtjuː-

fortunate ˈfɔː.tʃən.ət, -ɪt ⓊⓈ ˈfɔːr- **-ly** -li **-ness** -nəs, -nɪs

Fortunatus ˌfɔː.tjuːˈneɪ.təs, -ˈnɑː- ⓊⓈ ˌfɔːr.tuːˈnɑː.t̬əs, -ˈneɪ-

fortune (F) ˈfɔː.tʃuːn, -tjuːn, -tʃən ⓊⓈ ˈfɔːr.tʃən **-s** -z **-less** -ləs, -lɪs **ˈfortune ˌcookie**

fortune-teller ˈfɔː.tʃuːnˌtel.əʳ, -tjuːnˌ-, -tʃənˌ- ⓊⓈ ˈfɔːr.tʃənˌtel.ɚ **-s** -z

fort|y ˈfɔː.t|i ⓊⓈ ˈfɔːr.t̬|i **-ies** -iz **ˌforty ˈwinks**

forty-five ˌfɔː.tiˈfaɪv ⓊⓈ ˌfɔːr.t̬iˈ- **-s** -z

fortyfold ˈfɔː.ti.fəʊld ⓊⓈ ˈfɔːr.t̬i-

forty-niner ˌfɔː.tiˈnaɪ.nəʳ ⓊⓈ ˌfɔːr.t̬iˈnaɪ.nɚ **-s** -z

forum ˈfɔː.rəm ⓊⓈ ˈfɔːr.əm **-s** -z

forward ˈfɔː.wəd ⓊⓈ ˈfɔːr.wɚd *nautical pronunciation:* ˈfɒr.əd ⓊⓈ ˈfɔːr- **-ly** -li **-ness** -nəs, -nɪs **-er** -əʳ ⓊⓈ -ɚ **-est** -ɪst, -əst **-s** -z **-ing** -ɪŋ **-ed** -ɪd **ˌbackwards and ˈforwards**

forwards ˈfɔː.wədz ⓊⓈ ˈfɔːr.wɚdz

forwent *(from* **forgo***)* fɔːˈwent ⓊⓈ fɔːr-

Fosbery ˈfɒz.bər.i ⓊⓈ ˈfɑːzˌber-, -bɚ-

Fosbroke ˈfɒz.brʊk ⓊⓈ ˈfɑːz-

Fosbury ˈfɒz.bər.i ⓊⓈ ˈfɑːzˌber-, -bɚ-

Fosco ˈfɒs.kəʊ ⓊⓈ ˈfɑː.skoʊ

Foss fɒs ⓊⓈ fɑːs

foss|e fɒs ⓊⓈ fɑːs **-es** -ɪz

fossick ˈfɒs.ɪk ⓊⓈ ˈfɑː.sɪk **-s** -s **-ing** -ɪŋ **-ed** -t

fossil ˈfɒs.əl, -ɪl ⓊⓈ ˈfɑː.səl **-s** -z

fossilization, -isa- ˌfɒs.əl.aɪˈzeɪ.ʃən, -ɪ.laɪˈ-, -lɪˈ- ⓊⓈ ˌfɑː.səl.ɪˈ-

fossiliz|e, -is|e ˈfɒs.əl.aɪz, -ɪ.laɪz ⓊⓈ ˈfɑː.sə.laɪz **-es** -ɪz **-ing** -ɪŋ **-ed** -d

fost|er (F) ˈfɒs.t|əʳ ⓊⓈ ˈfɑː.st|ɚ **-ers** -əz ⓊⓈ -ɚz **-ering** -ər.ɪŋ **-ered** -əd ⓊⓈ -ɚd **-erer/s** -ər.əʳ/z ⓊⓈ -ɚ.ɚ/z **-erage** -ər.ɪdʒ **ˈfoster ˌbrother; ˈfoster ˌchild; ˈfoster ˌchildren; ˈfoster ˌfather; ˈfoster ˌhome; ˈfoster ˌmother; ˈfoster ˌparent; ˈfoster ˌsister**

Fothergill ˈfɒð.ə.gɪl ⓊⓈ ˈfɑː.ðɚ-

Fotheringay ˈfɒð.ər.ɪŋ.heɪ, -geɪ ⓊⓈ ˈfɑː.ðɚ-

Fotheringham ˈfɒð.ər.ɪŋ.əm ⓊⓈ ˈfɑː.ðɚ-

Foucault ˈfuː.kəʊ, -ˈ- ⓊⓈ ˌfuːˈkoʊ

fouetté ˈfuː.ə.teɪ ⓊⓈ fwetˈeɪ **-s** -z

fought *(from* **fight***)* fɔːt ⓊⓈ fɑːt, fɔːt

foul faʊl **-er** -əʳ ⓊⓈ -ɚ **-est** -ɪst, -əst **-ly** -li, ˈfaʊ.li **-ness** -nəs, -nɪs **-s** -z **-ing** -ɪŋ **-ed** -d **ˌfoul ˈplay**

foulard ˈfuː.lɑːʳ, -lɑːd, -ˈ- ⓊⓈ fuːˈlɑːrd

Foulden ˈfəʊl.dən ⓊⓈ ˈfoʊl-

Foulds fəʊldz ⓊⓈ foʊldz

Foulerton ˈfʊl.ə.tən ⓊⓈ ˈ-ɚ-

Foulger ˈfuːl.dʒəʳ, -gəʳ ⓊⓈ ˈfuːl.dʒɚ, ˈfoʊl-, -gɚ

Foulis faʊlz

Foulkes fəʊks, faʊks ⓊⓈ foʊks, faʊks

foulmouthed ˌfaʊlˈmaʊðd, -ˈmaʊθt ⓊⓈ ˌ-ˈ-, ˈ-ˌ- *stress shift, British only:* ˌfoulmouthed ˈlanguage

foulness ˈfaʊl.nəs

Foulness ˌfaʊlˈnes, -nɪs *stress shift:* ˌFoulness ˈbeach

Foulsham ˈfəʊl.ʃəm ⓊⓈ ˈfoʊl-

foul-up ˈfaʊl.ʌp **-s** -s

found faʊnd **-s** -z **-ing** -ɪŋ **-ed** -ɪd

found *(from* **find***)* faʊnd

foundation faʊnˈdeɪ.ʃən **-s** -z **founˈdation ˌcourse; founˈdation ˌstone**

foundationer faʊnˈdeɪ.ʃən.əʳ ⓊⓈ -ɚ **-s** -z

found|er ˈfaʊn.d|əʳ ⓊⓈ -d|ɚ **-ers** -əz ⓊⓈ -ɚz **-ering** -ər.ɪŋ **-ered** -əd ⓊⓈ -ɚd **ˌfounder ˈmember**

foundling (F) ˈfaʊnd.lɪŋ **-s** -z

foundr|y ˈfaʊn.dr|i **-ies** -iz

fount *fountain, source:* faʊnt **-s** -s

fount *in printing:* faʊnt, fɒnt ⓊⓈ faʊnt fɑːnt **-s** -s

Note: Those connected with the printing trade generally pronounce /fɒnt, ⓊⓈ fɑːnt/.

fountain (F) ˈfaʊn.tɪn, -tən ⓤⓢ -tᵊn **-s** -z ˈ**fountain** ˌ**pen**

fountainhead ˈfaʊn.tɪn.hed, -tən-, ˌ--ˈ- ⓤⓢ ˈfaʊn.tᵊn.hed **-s** -z

four fɔːʳ ⓤⓢ fɔːr **-s** -z **-th/s** -θ/s **-thly** -θ.li ˌ**Four** ˈ**Corners**

four-cornered ˌfɔːˈkɔː.nəd ⓤⓢ ˌfɔːrˈkɔːr.nɚd *stress shift:* ˌfour-cornered ˈhat

four-dimensional ˌfɔː.dɪˈmen.*t*ʃᵊn.ᵊl, -daɪˈ- ⓤⓢ ˌfɔːr.dəˈmen*t*.ʃᵊn- *stress shift:* ˌfour-dimensional ˈmodel

fourfold ˈfɔː.fəʊld ⓤⓢ ˈfɔːr.foʊld

four-footed ˌfɔːˈfʊt.ɪd ⓤⓢ ˌfɔːrˈfʊt̬- *stress shift:* ˌfour-footed ˈbeast

Fourier ˈfʊə.ri.əʳ, ˈfʊr.i-, -eɪ ⓤⓢ ˈfʊr.i.eɪ

four-in-hand ˌfɔːʳ.ɪnˈhænd ⓤⓢ ˈfɔːr.ɪnˌhænd **-s** -z

four-legged ˌfɔːˈlegd, -ˈleg.ɪd ⓤⓢ ˌfɔːr-, ˈfɔːrˌ- *stress shift:* ˌfour-legged ˈfriend

four-letter ˌfɔːˈlet.əʳ ⓤⓢ ˌfɔːrˈlet̬.ɚ *stress shift, see compound:* ˌ**four-letter** ˈ**word**

fourpence ˈfɔː.pᵊn*t*s ⓤⓢ ˈfɔːr-

fourpenny ˈfɔː.pᵊn.i ⓤⓢ ˈfɔːr-

four-ply ˈfɔː.plaɪ, ˌ-ˈ- ⓤⓢ ˈfɔːr.plaɪ, ˌ-ˈ-

four-poster ˌfɔːˈpəʊ.stəʳ ⓤⓢ ˌfɔːrˈpoʊ.stɚ **-s** -z *stress shift, see compound:* ˌ**four-poster** ˈ**bed**

fourscore ˌfɔːˈskɔːʳ ⓤⓢ ˌfɔːrˈskɔːr *stress shift:* ˌfourscore ˈyears

foursome ˈfɔː.səm ⓤⓢ ˈfɔːr- **-s** -z

foursquare ˌfɔːˈskweəʳ, ˈ-- ⓤⓢ ˌfɔːrˈskwer, ˈ--

fourteen ˌfɔːˈtiːn ⓤⓢ ˌfɔːr- **-s** -z **-th/s** -θ/s *stress shift:* ˌfourteen ˈyears

fourteener fɔːˈtiː.nəʳ ⓤⓢ fɔːrˈtiː.nɚ **-s** -z

fourth fɔːθ ⓤⓢ fɔːrθ **-s** -s **-ly** -li ˌ**Fourth of Ju**ˈ**ly**

four-wheel drive ˌfɔː.*h*wiːlˈdraɪv ⓤⓢ ˌfɔːr- *stress shift, British only:* ˌfour-wheel drive ˈcar

four-wheeler ˌfɔːˈ*h*wiː.ləʳ ⓤⓢ ˌfɔːrˈ*h*wiː.lɚ **-s** -z

fov|ea ˈfɒv|.i.ə, ˈfəʊ.v|i- ⓤⓢ ˈfoʊ- **-eae** -i.iː

Fowey fɔɪ, ˈfəʊ.i ⓤⓢ fɔɪ, ˈfoʊ.i

Fowke faʊk, fəʊk ⓤⓢ faʊk, foʊk

Fowkes fəʊks, faʊks ⓤⓢ foʊks, faʊks

fowl faʊl **-s** -z **-ing** -ɪŋ **-ed** -d **-er/s** -əʳ/z ⓤⓢ -ɚ/z ˈ**fowling** ˌ**piece**

Fowler ˈfaʊ.ləʳ ⓤⓢ -lɚ

Fowles faʊlz

fox (F) fɒks ⓤⓢ fɑːks **-es** -ɪz **-ing** -ɪŋ **-ed** -t ˌ**fox** ˈ**terrier**

Foxboro' ˈfɒks.bᵊr.ə ⓤⓢ ˈfɑːks.bɚ.oʊ

Foxcroft ˈfɒks.krɒft ⓤⓢ ˈfɑːks.krɑːft

Foxe fɒks ⓤⓢ fɑːks

Foxfield ˈfɒks.fiːld ⓤⓢ ˈfɑːks-

foxglove ˈfɒks.glʌv ⓤⓢ ˈfɑːks- **-s** -z

foxhole ˈfɒks.həʊl ⓤⓢ ˈfɑːks.hoʊl **-s** -z

foxhound ˈfɒks.haʊnd ⓤⓢ ˈfɑːks- **-s** -z

fox|hunt ˈfɒks|.hʌnt ⓤⓢ ˈfɑːks- **-hunts** -hʌnts **-hunting** -ˌhʌn.tɪŋ ⓤⓢ -ˌhʌn.t̬ɪŋ

foxtrot ˈfɒks.trɒt ⓤⓢ ˈfɑːks.trɑːt **-s** -s

Foxwell ˈfɒks.wəl, -wel ⓤⓢ ˈfɑːks-

fox|y ˈfɒk.s|i ⓤⓢ ˈfɑːk- **-ier** -i.əʳ ⓤⓢ -i.ɚ **-iest** -i.ɪst, -i.əst **-ily** -ɪ.li, -ə.li **-iness** -ɪ.nəs, -ɪ.nɪs

Foy fɔɪ

foyer ˈfɔɪ.eɪ, -əʳ; ˈfwaɪ.eɪ ⓤⓢ ˈfɔɪ.ɚ, -eɪ; fɔɪˈeɪ, fwɑːˈ- **-s** -z

Foyers ˈfɔɪ.əz ⓤⓢ -ɚz

Foyle fɔɪl

Fr. *(abbrev. for* **Father***)* ˈfɑː.ðəʳ ⓤⓢ -ðɚ

frabjous ˈfræb.dʒəs

fracas *singular:* ˈfræk.ɑː ⓤⓢ ˈfreɪ.kəs, ˈfræk.əs *American usage only:* **-es** ⓤⓢ -ɪz *plural:* ˈfræk.ɑːz ⓤⓢ ˈfreɪ.kəs, ˈfræk.əs

fractal ˈfræk.tᵊl **-s** -z

fraction ˈfræk.ʃᵊn **-s** -z

fractional ˈfræk.ʃᵊn.ᵊl **-ly** -i

fraction|ate ˈfræk.ʃᵊn|.eɪt **-ates** -eɪts **-ating** -eɪ.tɪŋ ⓤⓢ -eɪ.t̬ɪŋ **-ated** -eɪ.tɪd ⓤⓢ -eɪ.t̬ɪd

fractious ˈfræk.ʃəs **-ly** -li **-ness** -nəs, -nɪs

fract|ure ˈfræk.*t*ʃ|əʳ ⓤⓢ -*t*ʃ|ɚ **-ures** -əz ⓤⓢ -ɚz **-uring** -ᵊr.ɪŋ **-ured** -əd ⓤⓢ -ɚd

fragile ˈfrædʒ.aɪl ⓤⓢ ˈfrædʒ.ᵊl **-ly** -li

fragility frəˈdʒɪl.ə.ti, frædʒˈɪl-, -ɪ.ti ⓤⓢ frəˈdʒɪl.ə.t̬i

fragment *(n.)* ˈfræg.mənt **-s** -s

fragmen|t *(v.)* frægˈmen|t ⓤⓢ ˈfræg.men|t, -ˈ- **-ts** -ts **-ting** -tɪŋ ⓤⓢ -t̬ɪŋ **-ted** -tɪd ⓤⓢ -t̬ɪd

fragmental frægˈmen.tᵊl ⓤⓢ -t̬ᵊl

fragmentar|y ˈfræg.mən.tᵊr|.i, -tr|i; frægˈmen- ⓤⓢ ˈfræg.mən.ter|.i **-ily** -ᵊl.i, -ɪ.li **-iness** -ɪ.nəs, -ɪ.nɪs

fragmentation ˌfræg.mənˈteɪ.ʃᵊn, -menˈ-

Fragonard ˈfræg.ɒn.ɑːʳ, -ən- ⓤⓢ ˌfræg.əˈnɑːr, ˌfrɑː.goʊˈ-

fragranc|e ˈfreɪ.grən*t*s **-es** -ɪz **-ed** -t

fragrant ˈfreɪ.grənt **-ly** -li **-ness** -nəs, -nɪs

frail freɪl **-er** -əʳ ⓤⓢ -ɚ **-est** -ɪst, -əst **-ly** -li **-ness** -nəs, -nɪs

frailt|y ˈfreɪl.t|i ⓤⓢ -t̬|i **-ies** -iz

frambesia, framboesia fræmˈbiː.zi.ə, -ʒə, ʒi.ə ⓤⓢ -ʒə, -ʒi.ə

fram|e (F) freɪm **-es** -z **-ing** -ɪŋ **-ed** -d **-er/s** -əʳ/z ⓤⓢ -ɚ/z

frame-up ˈfreɪm.ʌp **-s** -s

framework ˈfreɪm.wɜːk ⓤⓢ -wɝːk **-s** -s

Framingham *in UK:* ˈfreɪ.mɪŋ.əm *in US:* ˈfræm.ɪŋ.hæm

Framley ˈfræm.li

Framlingham ˈfræm.lɪŋ.əm

Framlington ˈfræm.lɪŋ.tən

Frampton ˈfræm*p*.tən

Fran fræn

franc fræŋk **-s** -s

France frɑːn*t*s ⓤⓢ fræn*t*s

Frances ˈfrɑːn*t*.sɪs ⓤⓢ ˈfræn*t*-

Francesca frænˈ*t*ʃes.kə ⓤⓢ fræn-, frɑːn-

Franche-Comté ˌfrɑ̃ːn*ʃ*.kɔ̃ːnˈteɪ ⓤⓢ -koʊ̃nˈ-

franchis|e ˈfræn.*t*ʃaɪz **-es** -ɪz **-ing** -ɪŋ **-ed** -d **-er/s** -əʳ/z ⓤⓢ -ɚ/z

franchisee ˌfræn.*t*ʃaɪˈziː **-s** -z

Francie ˈfrɑːn*t*.si ⓤⓢ ˈfræn*t*-

Francine fræn*t*ˈsiːn, ˈ--

Francis ˈfrɑːn*t*.sɪs ⓤⓢ ˈfræn*t*-

Franciscan frænˈsɪs.kən **-s** -z

Francisco frænˈsɪs.kəʊ ⓤⓢ -koʊ *in* ***San Francisco:*** frənˈsɪs.kəʊ, fræn- ⓤⓢ -koʊ

francium ˈfræn*t*.si.əm

Franck frɑ̃ːŋk, frɑːŋk, fræŋk ⓤⓢ frɑ̃ːŋk

Franco-, franco- fræŋ.kəʊ- ⓤⓢ fræŋ.koʊ-, -kə-

Note: Prefix. Normally either takes primary or secondary stress on the first syllable, e.g. **francophile** /ˈfræŋ.kəʊ.faɪl ⓤⓢ -koʊ-/, **Franco-German** /ˌfræŋ.kəʊˈdʒɜː.mən ⓤⓢ -koʊˈdʒɝːr-/.

Franco ˈfræŋ.kəʊ ⓤⓢ -koʊ

Franco-German ˌfræŋ.kəʊˈdʒɜː.mən ⓤⓢ -koʊˈdʒɝː-

Francois, François ˈfrɑ̃ː*n*.swɑː, -ˈ- ⓤⓢ frɑ̃ːn*t*ˈswɑː, fræn*t*ˈ-, ˈ-ˌ-

Francoise, Françoise ˈfrɑːn*t*.swɑːz, ˈfrɒn*t*-, ˈfræn*t*-, ˌ-ˈ- ⓤⓢ ˌfrɑːn*t*ˈswɑːz

francolin ˈfræŋ.kəʊ.lɪn ⓤⓢ -koʊ- **-s** -z

Franconi|a fræŋˈkəʊ.ni|.ə ⓤⓢ fræŋˈkoʊ-, fræn- **-an** -ən

francophile ˈfræŋ.kəʊ.faɪl ⓤⓢ -koʊ-, -kə- **-s** -z

francophobe ˈfræŋ.kəʊ.fəʊb ⓤⓢ -koʊ.foʊb, -kə- **-s** -z

francophone (F) ˈfræŋ.kəʊ.fəʊn ⓤⓢ -koʊ.foʊn, -kə- **-s** -z

francophonic (F) ˌfræŋ.kəʊˈfɒn.ɪk ⓤⓢ -koʊˈfɑː.nɪk, -kəˈ-

frangibility ˌfræn.dʒɪˈbɪl.ə.ti, -dʒəˈ-, -ɪ.ti ⓤⓢ -ə.t̬i

frangible ˈfræn.dʒɪ.bl̩, -dʒə- **-ness** -nəs, -nɪs

frangipani ˌfræn.dʒɪˈpɑː.ni, -ˈpæn.i **-s** -z

franglais ˈfrɑ̃ː*ŋ*.gleɪ, ˈfrɒŋ- ⓤⓢ frɑ̃ːnˈgleɪ

frank (F) fræŋk **-er** -əʳ ⓤⓢ -ɚ **-est** -ɪst, -əst **-ly** -li **-ness** -nəs, -nɪs **-s** -s **-ing** -ɪŋ **-ed** -t

Frankau ˈfræŋ.kəʊ, -kaʊ ⓤⓢ -kaʊ

Frankenstein ˈfræŋ.kᵊn.staɪn, -kɪn-

Frankfort *places in US:* ˈfræŋk.fət ⓤⓢ -fɚt

Frankfurt *in Germany:* 'fræŋk.fɜːt, -fət US -fɝːt, -fɚt
frankfurter (F) 'fræŋk.fɜː.təʳ US -fɝː.t̬ɚ **-s** -z
Frankie 'fræŋ.ki
frankincense 'fræŋ.kɪn.sen*t*s, -kᵊn-
Frankish 'fræŋ.kɪʃ
Frankland 'fræŋk.lənd
franklin (F) 'fræŋk.lɪn **-s** -z
Franklyn 'fræŋk.lɪn
Franks fræŋks
frantic 'fræn.tɪk US -t̬ɪk **-ally** -ᵊl.i, -li **-ness** -nəs, -nɪs
Franz *German name:* fræn*t*s, frɑːn*t*s *US name:* frænz
frap fræp **-s** -s **-ping** -ɪŋ **-ped** -t
frappé 'fræp.eɪ US -'-
Frascati fræs'kɑː.ti
Fraser 'freɪ.zəʳ US -zɚ
Fraserburgh 'freɪ.zə.bᵊr.ə, -bʌr- US -zɚ.bɚ-
Frasier 'freɪ.ʒəʳ, 'freɪ.zi.ə US -ʒɚ
frat fræt **-s** -s
fraternal frə'tɜː.nᵊl US -'tɝː- **-ly** -i
fraternit|y frə'tɜː.nə.t|i, -ɪ.t|i US -'tɝː.nə.t̬|i **-ies** -iz
fraternization, -isa- ˌfræt.ᵊn.aɪ'zeɪ.ʃᵊn, -ɪ'- US -ɚ.nɪ'-
fraterniz|e, -is|e 'fræt.ə.naɪz US '-ɚ- **-es** -ɪz **-ing** -ɪŋ **-ed** -d **-er/s** -əʳ/z US -ɚ/z
fratricidal ˌfræt.rɪ'saɪ.dᵊl, ˌfreɪ.trɪ'-, -trə'- US ˌfræt.rə'saɪ-
fratricide 'fræt.rɪ.saɪd, 'freɪ.trɪ-, -trə- US 'fræt.rə- **-s** -z
Fratton 'fræt.ᵊn
Frau fraʊ
fraud frɔːd US frɑːd, frɔːd **-s** -z
fraudster 'frɔːd.stəʳ US 'frɑːd.stɚ, 'frɔːd- **-s** -z
fraudulence 'frɔː.djə.lən*t*s, -djʊ-, -dʒə-, -dʒʊ- US 'frɑː.dʒə-, 'frɔː-, -djuː-, -djə-
fraudulent 'frɔː.djə.lənt, -djʊ-, -dʒə-, -dʒʊ- US 'frɑː.dʒə-, 'frɔː-, -djuː-, -djə- **-ly** -li
fraught frɔːt US frɑːt, frɔːt
fraülein 'frɔɪ.laɪn, 'fraʊ- **-s** -z
fray freɪ **-s** -z **-ing** -ɪŋ **-ed** -d
Fray Bentos® ˌfreɪ'ben.tɒs US -toʊs
Frayn freɪn
Frazer 'freɪ.zəʳ US -zɚ
Frazier 'freɪ.zi.əʳ US -ʒɚ, -ʒi.ɚ
frazil 'freɪ.zɪl, 'fræz.ɪl, -ᵊl US 'freɪ.zɪl; 'fræz.ᵊl; frə'zɪl, -'ziːl
frazzl|e 'fræz.l̩ **-es** -z **-ing** -ɪŋ, '-lɪŋ **-ed** -d
freak friːk **-s** -s **-ing** -ɪŋ **-ed** -t
Freake friːk
freakish 'friː.kɪʃ **-ly** -li **-ness** -nəs, -nɪs
freak|y 'friː.k|i **-ier** -i.əʳ US -i.ɚ **-iest** -i.ɪst, -i.əst **-ily** -ɪ.li, -ᵊl.i **-iness** -ɪ.nəs, -ɪ.nɪs
Frean friːn
Frears frɪəz, freəz US frɪrz, frerz
freckl|e 'frek.l̩ **-es** -z **-ing** -ɪŋ, '-lɪŋ **-ed** -d
Freckleton 'frek.l̩.tən
freckly 'frek.l̩.i, 'frek.li
Fred fred
Freda 'friː.də
Freddie, Freddy 'fred.i
Frederica ˌfred.ᵊr'iː.kə US -ə'riː-
Frederic(k) 'fred.ᵊr.ɪk
Fredericksburg 'fred.ᵊr.ɪks.bɜːg US -bɝːg
free (F) friː **-r** -əʳ US -ɚ **-st** -ɪst, -əst **-ly** -li **-s** -z **-ing** -ɪŋ **-d** -d **-r/s** -əʳ/z US -ɚ/z **ˌfree 'enterprise; 'free ˌhouse; ˌfree 'kick; ˌfree 'market; ˌfree 'ride; ˌfree 'trade; ˌfree 'will; give someone a ˌfree 'hand**
freebas|e 'friː.beɪs **-es** -ɪz **-ing** -ɪŋ **-ed** -t
freebie, freebee 'friː.bi **-s** -z
freeboard 'friː.bɔːd US -bɔːrd
freebooter 'friːˌbuː.təʳ US -t̬ɚ **-s** -z
freeborn ˌfriː'bɔːn US -'bɔːrn *stress shift:* ˌfreeborn 'citizen
Freeborn 'friː.bɔːn US -bɔːrn
Freeburn 'friː.bɜːn US -bɝːn
freed|man 'friːd|.mæn, -mən **-men** -men, -mən
freedom 'friː.dəm **-s** -z **'freedom ˌfighter**
free-fall (*v.*) 'friː.fɔːl, ˌ-'- US 'friː.fɔːl, -fɑːl **-ing** -ɪŋ **-er/s** -əʳ/z US -ɚ/z
Freefone® 'friː.fəʊn US -foʊn
free-for-all 'friː.fəʳˌɔːl, ˌ--'- US 'friː.fɚ.ɔːl, -ɑːl
freehand 'friː.hænd
freehearted ˌfriː'hɑː.tɪd US -'hɑːr.t̬ɪd, '-ˌ-- **-ly** -li **-ness** -nəs, -nɪs *stress shift, British only:* ˌfreehearted 'friend
freehold 'friː.həʊld US -hoʊld **-s** -z **-er/s** -əʳ/z US -ɚ/z
freelanc|e 'friː.lɑːn*t*s, ˌ-'- US 'friː.læn*t*s **-es** -ɪz **-ing** -ɪŋ **-ed** -t **-er/s** -əʳ/z US -ɚ/z
Freeling 'friː.lɪŋ
freeload 'friː.ləʊd US -loʊd **-s** -z **-ing** -ɪŋ **-ed** -ɪd **-er/s** -əʳ/z US -ɚ/z
free|man 'friː|.mən, -mæn **-men** -mən, -men
Freeman *surname:* 'friː.mən
free-market (*adj.*) 'friːˌmɑː.kɪt US -ˌmɑːr-
free market (*n.*) ˌfriː'mɑː.kɪt US -'mɑːr-
freemason 'friːˌmeɪ.sᵊn **-s** -z
freemasonry 'friːˌmeɪ.sᵊn.ri, ˌfriː'meɪ-
freephone 'friː.fəʊn US -foʊn
Freeport 'friː.pɔːt US -pɔːrt
Freepost® 'friː.pəʊst US -poʊst
free-range ˌfriː'reɪndʒ *stress shift, see compounds:* **ˌfree-range 'eggs; ˌfree-range 'chickens**
Freeserve® 'friː.sɜːv US -sɝːv
freesheet 'friː.ʃiːt **-s** -s
freesia 'friː.zi.ə, -ʒə, -ʒi.ə US -ʒi.ə, -ʒə **-s** -z
free-spoken ˌfriː'spəʊ.kᵊn US ˌfriː'spoʊ-, '-ˌ-- *stress shift, British only:* ˌfree-spoken 'person
free-standing ˌfriː'stæn.dɪŋ US ˌfriː'stæn.dɪŋ, '-ˌ-- *stress shift, British only:* ˌfree-standing 'column
freestone (F) 'friː.stəʊn US -stoʊn
freestyle 'friː.staɪl
Freeth friːθ
freethinker ˌfriː'θɪŋ.kəʳ US -kɚ, '-ˌ-- **-s** -z
Freetown 'friː.taʊn
freeway 'friː.weɪ **-s** -z
freewheel ˌfriː'*h*wiːl US 'friː.*h*wiːl **-s** -z **-ing** -ɪŋ **-ed** -d *stress shift, British only:* ˌfreewheel 'mechanism
freewill ˌfriː'wɪl, '--
freez|e friːz **-es** -ɪz **-ing** -ɪŋ **froze** frəʊz US froʊz **frozen** 'frəʊ.zᵊn US 'froʊ- **freezer/s** 'friː.zəʳ/z US -zɚ/z **'freeze ˌframe ˌfreeze 'frame**
freeze|-dry 'friːz|.draɪ **-dries** -draɪz **-drying** -ˌdraɪ.ɪŋ **-dried** -draɪd
Freiburg 'fraɪ.bɜːg US -bɝːg
freight freɪt **-s** -s **-ing** -ɪŋ US 'freɪ.t̬ɪŋ **-ed** -ɪd US 'freɪ.t̬ɪd **-age** -ɪdʒ US 'freɪ.t̬ɪdʒ **'freight ˌcar**
freighter 'freɪ.təʳ US -t̬ɚ **-s** -z
freightliner 'freɪtˌlaɪ.nəʳ US -nɚ **-s** -z
Fremantle 'friː.mæn.tl̩ US -t̬l̩
fremitus 'frem.ɪ.təs US -t̬əs
Fremont 'friː.mɒnt, frɪ'mɒnt US 'friː.mɑːnt
French, french fren*t*ʃ **ˌFrench 'bean; ˌFrench 'bread; ˌFrench 'dressing; ˌfrench 'fry;** US **'french ˌfry; ˌFrench 'loaf; ˌFrench Revo'lution; ˌFrench 'stick; ˌFrench 'windows**
frenchi|fy 'fren.*t*ʃɪ|.faɪ US 'fren*t*.ʃɪ- **-fies** -faɪz **-fying** -faɪ.ɪŋ **-fied** -faɪd
French|man 'fren*t*ʃ|.mən **-men** -mən
french-polish ˌfren*t*ʃ'pɒl.ɪʃ US -'pɑː.lɪʃ **-es** -ɪz **-ing** -ɪŋ **-ed** -t **-er/s** -əʳ/z US -ɚ/z
French|woman 'fren*t*ʃ|ˌwʊm.ən **-women** -ˌwɪm.ɪn
frenetic frə'net.ɪk, frɪ-, fren'et- US frə'net̬- **-ally** -ᵊl.i, -li
frenz|y 'fren.z|i **-ies** -iz **-ied/ly** -ɪd/li
frequen|ce 'friː.kwən*t*|s **-cy** -si **-cies** -siz
frequent (*adj.*) 'friː.kwənt **-ly** -li **-ness** -nəs, -nɪs
frequen|t (*v.*) frɪ'kwen|t, friː-, frə- US friː-; 'friː.kwen|t, -kwən|t **-ts** -ts **-ting** -tɪŋ US -t̬ɪŋ **-ted** -tɪd US -t̬ɪd **-ter/s** -təʳ/z US -t̬ɚ/z
frequentative frɪ'kwen.tə.tɪv, friː-, frə- US friː'kwen.t̬ə.t̬ɪv **-s** -z

French words and phrases

French has provided a substantial proportion of English vocabulary since the Norman Conquest in 1066, with new words being incorporated all the time. The longest-established and the most commonly-used words are usually the most completely anglicised, and the most noticeable changes from the French original are found where English phonology does not easily accommodate them. Often there are many possible anglicised pronunciations: see for example the many listed for *restaurant*.

Examples

Word-final /r/: this is not usually pronounced in British English unless followed by a vowel in a following word. However, it is pronounced in US English, e.g.:

savoir faire /ˌsæv.wɑːˈfeəʳ/ (US) /-wɑːrˈfer, -wɑːˈ-/

Nasalized vowels: although some English speakers who have a good command of French may attempt to produce the French nasalized vowels /ɛ̃ ɑ̃ ɔ̃/ and even occasionally /œ̃/, these are pronounced by many people with a following /ŋ/. *Croissant* is given the pronunciation /ˈkwæs.ɑ̃ːŋ/ for British English, indicating that the vowel in the last syllable will be pronounced with a nasalised vowel but possibly also a velar nasal consonant. In US English, however, a velar nasal is not usually produced following a nasalised vowel, and *croissant* is pronounced /kwɑːˈsɑ̃ː/. (It should be noted that in both cases other pronunciations exist.) This example also shows the simplification of the initial consonant cluster /krw/, which occurs in French but not in English.

Word-final stress: many French words and names with final stress are modified by British English speakers to have the stress at the beginning of the word. In US English, this occurs in some words, but not in others, e.g.:

ballet /ˈbæl.eɪ/ (US) /bælˈeɪ, ˈ--/
Paris /ˈpær.ɪs/ (US) /ˈper-, ˈpær-/
restaurant /ˈres.tᵊr.ɔ̃ːŋ/ (US) /-tə.rɑːnt/

The phoneme /ʒ/: while this phoneme occurs frequently in the middle of words, it is rare at the beginning and end. Many such cases are in words of French origin. English speakers sometimes substitute /dʒ/ for this sound, e.g.:

gigolo /ˈdʒɪg.ə.ləʊ, ˈʒɪg-/ (US) /-loʊ/
garage /ˈgær.ɑːʒ, -ɪdʒ, -ɑːdʒ/ (US) /gəˈrɑːʒ, -ˈrɑːdʒ/

Frere frɪəʳ (US) frer
fresco ˈfres.kəʊ (US) -koʊ **-(e)s** -z
fresh freʃ **-er** -əʳ (US) -ɚ **-est** -ɪst, -əst **-ly** -li **-ness** -nəs, -nɪs
freshen ˈfreʃ.ᵊn **-s** -z **-ing** -ɪŋ **-ed** -d
fresher ˈfreʃ.əʳ (US) -ɚ **-s** -z
freshet ˈfreʃ.ɪt, -ət **-s** -s
fresh|man ˈfreʃ|.mən **-men** -mən
freshwater (F) ˈfreʃˌwɔː.təʳ, ˌ-ˈ-- (US) ˈfreʃˌwɑː.t̬ɚ, -ˌwɔː-
Fresno ˈfrez.nəʊ (US) -noʊ
fret fret **-s** -s **-ting** -ɪŋ (US) ˈfret̬.ɪŋ **-ted** -ɪd (US) ˈfret̬.ɪd
fretboard ˈfret.bɔːd, ˈfrep- (US) ˈfret.bɔːrd **-s** -z
fretful ˈfret.fᵊl, -fʊl **-ly** -i **-ness** -nəs, -nɪs
fretsaw ˈfret.sɔː (US) -sɑː, -sɔː **-s** -z
Fretwell ˈfret.wel, -wəl
fretwork ˈfret.wɜːk (US) -wɝːk
Freud frɔɪd **-ian** -i.ən ˌ**Freudian** ˈ**slip**
Frew fruː
Frey freɪ
Freya freɪə
Freyberg ˈfraɪ.bɜːg (US) -bɝːg
Freyer frɪəʳ; ˈfraɪ.əʳ (US) ˈfraɪ.ɚ, -ɚ; frɪr
Freyja freɪə
Fri. *(abbrev. for* **Friday***)* ˈfraɪ.deɪ, -di
friability ˌfraɪ.əˈbɪl.ə.ti, -ɪ.ti (US) -ə.t̬i
friable ˈfraɪ.ə.bl̩ **-ness** -nəs, -nɪs
friar fraɪəʳ (US) fraɪɚ **-s** -z
friar|y ˈfraɪə.r|i **-ies** -iz
fribbl|e ˈfrɪb.l̩ **-es** -z **-ing** -ɪŋ, ˈ-lɪŋ **-ed** -d
fricandeau ˈfrɪk.ən.dəʊ, -ɑ̃ːn- (US) ˌfrɪk.ənˈdoʊ, ˈ--- **-s** -z
fricandeaux *(alternative plur. of* **fricandeau***)* ˈfrɪk.ən.dəʊ, -ɑ̃ːn-, -dəʊz (US) ˌfrɪk.ənˈdoʊ, -ˈdoʊz, ˈ---
fricassee ˌfrɪk.əˈsiː, -ˈseɪ, ˈ--- (US) ˌfrɪk.əˈsiː, ˈ--- **-s** -z **-ing** -ɪŋ **-d** -d
fricative ˈfrɪk.ə.tɪv (US) -t̬ɪv **-s** -z
friction ˈfrɪk.ʃᵊn **-s** -z **-less** -ləs, -les, -lɪs
frictional ˈfrɪk.ʃᵊn.ᵊl
Friday ˈfraɪ.deɪ, -di **-s** -z
fridg|e frɪdʒ **-es** -ɪz ˌ**fridge-**ˈ**freezer**
fried *(from* **fry***)* fraɪd
Frieda ˈfriː.də
Friedan friːˈdæn, frɪ-
Friedland ˈfriːd.lənd, -lænd
Friedman ˈfriːd.mən
Friel friːl
friend (F) frend **-s** -z
friendless ˈfrend.ləs, -lɪs **-ness** -nəs, -nɪs
friendl|y (F) ˈfrend.l|i **-ies** -iz **-ier** -i.əʳ (US) -i.ɚ **-iest** -i.ɪst, -i.əst **-iness** -ɪ.nəs, -ɪ.nɪs
Friendl|y ˈfrend.l|i **-ies** -iz
friendship ˈfrend.ʃɪp **-s** -s
Friern ˈfraɪ.ən, ˈfriː- (US) -ɚn
fries *(from* **fry***)* fraɪz
Fries friːs, friːz
Friesian ˈfriː.ʒən, ˈ-zi.ən (US) ˈfriː.ʒᵊn
Friesland ˈfriːz.lənd, -lænd **-er/s** -əʳ/z (US) -ɚ/z
friez|e (F) friːz **-es** -ɪz
frig frɪg **-s** -z **-ging** -ɪŋ **-ged** -d
frigate ˈfrɪg.ət, -ɪt **-s** -s
fright fraɪt **-s** -s **-ing** -ɪŋ (US) ˈfraɪ.t̬ɪŋ **-ed** -ɪd (US) ˈfraɪ.t̬ɪd
frighten ˈfraɪ.tᵊn **-s** -z **-ing/ly** -ɪŋ/li **-ed** -d **-er/s** -əʳ/z (US) -ɚ/z
frightful ˈfraɪt.fᵊl, -fʊl **-ly** -i **-ness** -nəs, -nɪs
frigid ˈfrɪdʒ.ɪd **-ly** -li **-ness** -nəs, -nɪs
Frigidaire® ˌfrɪdʒ.ɪˈdeəʳ, -əˈ- (US) -ˈder, ˈ--ˌ-
frigidity frɪˈdʒɪd.ə.ti, -ɪ.ti (US) -ə.t̬i
Friis friːs
frijole frɪˈhəʊ.li, -eɪ (US) friːˈhoʊ.liː, -ˈhoʊ, -ˈhoʊl **-s** -z
frill frɪl **-s** -z **-ing** -ɪŋ **-ed** -d
frill|y ˈfrɪl|.i **-ier** -i.əʳ (US) -i.ɚ **-iest** -i.ɪst, -i.əst **-iness** -ɪ.nəs, -ɪ.nɪs
Frimley ˈfrɪm.li
fring|e frɪndʒ **-es** -ɪz **-ing** -ɪŋ **-ed** -d **-eless** -ləs, -lɪs ˈ**fringe** ˌ**benefit**, ˌ**fringe** ˈ**benefit**; ˌ**fringe** ˈ**theatre**/ˈ**theater**
Frink frɪŋk
Frinton ˈfrɪn.tən
fripper|y ˈfrɪp.ᵊr|.i **-ies** -iz
Frisbee® ˈfrɪz.bi **-s** -z

Fricative

A type of consonant made by forcing air through a narrow gap so that a hissing noise is generated. This may be accompanied by VOICING, in which case the sound is a voiced fricative, such as [z], or it may be voiceless, such as [s].

Examples for English

British and US English have nine fricative phonemes: /f θ s ʃ h/ (voiceless) and /v ð z ʒ/ (voiced).

All except /h/are permitted to occur in all positions in English, but /ʒ/ as in 'measure' /ˈmeʒə/ is of rather low frequency compared to the other eight sounds. /h/may not end a syllable.

The quality and intensity of fricative sounds varies greatly, but all are acoustically composed of energy at relatively high frequency – an indication of this is that much of the fricative sound is too high to be transmitted over a phone (which usually cuts out the highest and lowest frequencies in order to reduce the cost), giving rise to the confusions that often arise over sets of words like English *fin, thin, sin* and *shin*. In order for the sound quality to be produced accurately, the size and direction of the jet of air has to be very precisely controlled.

A distinction is sometimes made between 'sibilant' or 'strident' fricatives (such as [s] and [ʃ]) which are strong and clearly audible and others which are weak and less audible (such as [θ] and [f]).

frisé(e) ˈfriː.zeɪ (US) friːˈzeɪ, frɪ- **-s** -z
frisette frɪˈzet, friː- **-s** -s
Frisian ˈfrɪz.i.ən, ˈfriː.zi-, -ʒi-, -ʒᵊn (US) ˈfrɪʒ.ᵊn, ˈfriː.ʒᵊn **-s** -z
frisk frɪsk **-s** -s **-ing** -ɪŋ **-ed** -t **-er/s** -əʳ/z (US) -ɚ/z
frisket ˈfrɪs.kɪt **-s** -s
frisk|y ˈfrɪs.k|i **-ier** -i.əʳ (US) -i.ɚ **-iest** -i.ɪst, -i.əst **-ily** -ɪ.li, -ᵊl.i **-iness** -ɪ.nəs, -ɪ.nɪs
frisson ˈfriː.sɔ̃ːŋ, -ˈ- (US) friːˈsõʊn **-s** -z
Friston ˈfrɪs.tᵊn
Friswell ˈfrɪz.wəl, -wel
frit frɪt **-s** -s **-ting** -ɪŋ (US) ˈfrɪt̬.ɪŋ **-ted** -ɪd (US) ˈfrɪt̬.ɪd
frith (F) frɪθ **-s** -s
Frithsden ˈfriːz.dən, ˈfrɪz-, ˈfrɪθs.dən
fritillar|y frɪˈtɪl.ᵊr|.i, frə- (US) ˈfrɪt̬.ᵊl.er|.i **-ies** -iz
Fritos® ˈfriː.təʊz (US) -t̬oʊz, -toʊz
fritt|er ˈfrɪt|.əʳ (US) ˈfrɪt̬|.ɚ **-ers** -əz (US) -ɚz **-ering** -ᵊr.ɪŋ **-ered** -əd (US) -ɚd
fritz (F) frɪts
Friuli friˈuː.li
frivol ˈfrɪv.ᵊl **-s** -z **-(l)ing** -ɪŋ **-(l)ed** -d
frivolit|y frɪˈvɒl.ə.t|i, frə-, -ɪ.t|i (US) -ˈvɑː.lə.t̬|i **-ies** -iz
frivolous ˈfrɪv.ᵊl.əs **-ly** -li **-ness** -nəs, -nɪs
Frizelle frɪˈzel
friz(z) frɪz **-es** -ɪz **-ing** -ɪŋ **-ed** -d
frizzl|e ˈfrɪz.l̩ **-es** -z **-ing** -ɪŋ, ˈ-lɪŋ **-ed** -d
frizzl|y ˈfrɪz.l̩|.i, ˈfrɪz.l|i **-iness** -ɪ.nəs, -ɪ.nɪs
frizz|y ˈfrɪz|.i **-ier** -i.əʳ (US) -i.ɚ **-iest** -i.ɪst, -i.əst **-iness** -ɪ.nəs, -ɪ.nɪs
fro frəʊ (US) froʊ
Frobisher ˈfrəʊ.bɪ.ʃəʳ (US) ˈfroʊ.bɪ.ʃɚ
frock frɒk (US) frɑːk **-s** -s ˌ**frock** ˈ**coat**
Frodo ˈfrəʊ.dəʊ (US) ˈfroʊ.doʊ
Frodsham ˈfrɒd.ʃᵊm (US) ˈfrɑːd-
Froebel ˈfrəʊ.bᵊl, ˈfrɜː- (US) ˈfrɜː-, ˈfroʊ-
frog frɒg (US) frɑːg, frɔːg **-s** -z **have a** ˈ**frog in one's** ˌ**throat**
Froggatt ˈfrɒg.ɪt, -ət (US) ˈfrɑː.gɪt, -gət
frogg|y ˈfrɒg|.i (US) ˈfrɑː.g|i **-ies** -iz
frog|man ˈfrɒg|.mən (US) ˈfrɑːg-, ˈfrɔːg- **-men** -mən
frogmarch ˈfrɒg.mɑːtʃ (US) ˈfrɑːg.mɑːrtʃ, ˈfrɔːg- **-es** -ɪz **-ing** -ɪŋ **-ed** -t
Frogmore ˈfrɒg.mɔːʳ (US) ˈfrɑːg.mɔːr, ˈfrɔːg-
frogspawn ˈfrɒg.spɔːn (US) ˈfrɑːg.spɑːn, ˈfrɔːg-, -spɔːn
Froissart ˈfrɔɪ.sɑːt, ˈfrwæs.ɑː (US) -sɑːrt; *as if French:* ˌfrwɑːˈsɑːr
frolic ˈfrɒl.ɪk (US) ˈfrɑː.lɪk **-s** -s **-king** -ɪŋ **-ked** -t
frolicsome ˈfrɒl.ɪk.səm (US) ˈfrɑː.lɪk- **-ness** -nəs, -nɪs
from *strong form:* frɒm (US) frɑːm *weak forms:* frəm, frm
Note: Weak form word. The strong from /frɒm (US) frɑːm/ is used contrastively (e.g. "Travelling **to** and **from** London") and in sentence-final position (e.g. "Where is it from?"). The weak form is /frəm/ (e.g. "back from abroad" /ˌbæk.frəm.əˈbrɔːd (US) -ˈbrɑːd/). In rapid speech this may be further weakened to /frm/ (e.g. "one from each" /ˌwʌn.frmˈiːtʃ/).
fromage frais ˌfrɒm.ɑːʒˈfreɪ (US) frəˌmɑːʒˈ-; ˌfrɑː.mɑːʒˈ-
Frome *in Somerset:* fruːm *lake in Australia:* frəʊm (US) froʊm
Note: /frəʊm (US) froʊm/ is suitable in the Edith Wharton novel "Ethan Frome".
Fromm frɒm (US) frɑːm
frond frɒnd (US) frɑːnd **-s** -z
front frʌnt **-s** -s **-ing** -ɪŋ (US) ˈfrʌn.t̬ɪŋ **-ed** -ɪd (US) ˈfrʌn.t̬ɪd ˌ**front** ˈ**line**; ˈ**front** ˌ**matter**; ˈ**front** ˌ**money**
frontag|e ˈfrʌn.tɪdʒ (US) -t̬ɪdʒ **-es** -ɪz
frontal ˈfrʌn.tᵊl (US) -t̬ᵊl **-s** -z
frontbench ˌfrʌntˈbentʃ **-er/s** -əʳ/z (US) -ɚ/z *stress shift:* ˌfrontbench ˈspokesman
Frontera® frʌnˈteə.rə, frɒn- (US) frʌnˈter.ə, frɑːn-
frontier frʌnˈtɪəʳ; ˈ--, ˈfrɒn- (US) frʌnˈtɪr, frɑːn- **-s** -z
frontispiec|e ˈfrʌn.tɪs.piːs, -təs- (US) -t̬ɪs- **-es** -ɪz
frontless ˈfrʌnt.ləs, -lɪs, -les
frontlet ˈfrʌnt.lɪt, -lət **-s** -s
front-load ˌfrʌntˈləʊd (US) -ˈloʊd, ˈ-- **-s** -z **-ing** -ɪŋ **-ed** -ɪd **-er/s** -əʳ/z (US) -ɚ/z *stress shift, British only:* ˌfront-loading ˈdrier
front|man ˈfrʌnt|.mæn **-men** -men
front-page ˌfrʌntˈpeɪdʒ *stress shift, see compound:* ˌ**front-page** ˈ**news**
front-runner ˈfrʌntˌrʌn.əʳ, ˌ-ˈ-- (US) ˈfrʌntˌrʌn.ɚ **-s** -z
frosh frɒʃ (US) frɑːʃ **-es** -ɪz
frost (F) frɒst (US) frɑːst **-s** -s **-ing/s** -ɪŋ/z **-ed** -ɪd
frost|bite ˈfrɒst|.baɪt (US) ˈfrɑːst- **-bitten** -ˌbɪt.ᵊn (US) -ˌbɪt̬-
Frosties® ˈfrɒs.tiz (US) ˈfrɑː.stiz
frostwork ˈfrɒst.wɜːk (US) ˈfrɑːst.wɝːk
frost|y ˈfrɒs.t|i (US) ˈfrɑː.st|i **-ier** -i.əʳ (US) -i.ɚ **-iest** -i.ɪst, -i.əst **-ily** -ɪ.li, -ᵊl.i **-iness** -ɪ.nəs, -ɪ.nɪs
froth (*n.*) frɒθ (US) frɑːθ **-s** -s
fro|th (*v.*) frɒ|θ (US) frɑː|θ, frɑː|ð **-ths** -θs (US) -θs, -ðz **-thing** -θɪŋ (US) -θɪŋ, -ðɪŋ **-thed** -θt (US) -θt, -ðd
Frothingham ˈfrɒð.ɪŋ.əm (US) ˈfrɑː.ðɪŋ-

froth|y ˈfrɒθ|.i (US) ˈfrɑː.θ|i, -ð|i **-ier** -i.əʳ (US) -i.ɚ **-iest** -i.ɪst, -i.əst **-ily** -ɪ.li, -əl.i **-iness** -ɪ.nəs, -ɪ.nɪs
frottage ˈfrɒt.ɑːʒ, -ɪdʒ; frɒtˈɑːʒ (US) frəˈtɑːʒ, frɑː-
Froud fraʊd, fruːd
Froude fruːd
froufrou ˈfruː.fruː
froward ˈfrəʊ.əd (US) ˈfroʊ.ɚd **-ly** -li **-ness** -nəs, -nɪs
frown fraʊn **-s** -z **-ing/ly** -ɪŋ/li **-ed** -d
frowst fraʊst **-s** -s **-ing** -ɪŋ **-ed** -ɪd
frowst|y ˈfraʊ.st|i **-iness** -ɪ.nəs, -ɪ.nɪs
frows|y, frowz|y ˈfraʊ.z|i **-ier** -i.əʳ (US) -i.ɚ **-iest** -i.ɪst, -i.əst **-iness** -ɪ.nəs, -ɪ.nɪs
froz|e *(from* **freeze***)* frəʊz (US) froʊz **-en** -ən
fructiferous frʌkˈtɪf.ər.əs (US) frʌk-, frʊk-
fructification ˌfrʌk.tɪ.fɪˈkeɪ.ʃən (US) ˌfrʌk.tə-, ˌfrʊk-
fructi|fy ˈfrʌk.tɪ|.faɪ (US) ˈfrʌk.tə-, ˈfrʊk- **-fies** -faɪz **-fying** -faɪ.ɪŋ **-fied** -faɪd
fructose ˈfrʌk.təʊs, ˈfrʊk-, -təʊz (US) -toʊs
frugal ˈfruː.gəl **-ly** -i
frugality fruːˈgæl.ə.ti, -ɪ.ti (US) -ə.t̬i
fruit fruːt **-s** -s **-ing** -ɪŋ (US) ˈfruː.t̬ɪŋ **-ed** -ɪd (US) ˈfruː.t̬ɪd **ˈfruit maˌchine**
fruitarian fruːˈteə.ri.ən (US) -ˈter.i- **-s** -z
fruitcake ˈfruːt.keɪk **-s** -s
fruiterer ˈfruː.tər.əʳ (US) -t̬ɚ.ɚ **-s** -z
fruitful ˈfruːt.fəl, -fʊl **-ly** -i **-ness** -nəs, -nɪs
fruition fruˈɪʃ.ən
fruitless ˈfruːt.ləs, -lɪs **-ly** -li **-ness** -nəs, -nɪs
fruit|y ˈfruː.t|i (US) -t̬|i **-ier** -i.əʳ (US) -i.ɚ **-iest** -i.ɪst, -i.əst **-iness** -ɪ.nəs, -ɪ.nɪs
frumenty ˈfruː.mən.ti (US) -t̬i
frump frʌmp **-s** -s **-ish** -ɪʃ
frump|y ˈfrʌm.p|i **-ier** -i.əʳ (US) -i.ɚ **-iest** -i.ɪst, -i.əst **-ily** -ɪ.li, -əl.i **-iness** -ɪ.nəs, -ɪ.nɪs
frustra|te frʌsˈtreɪ|t, ˈ-- (US) ˈfrʌs.treɪ|t **-tes** -ts **-ting/ly** -tɪŋ/li (US) -t̬ɪŋ/li **-ted** -tɪd (US) -t̬ɪd
frustration frʌsˈtreɪ.ʃən **-s** -z
frust|um ˈfrʌs.t|əm **-a** -ə **-ums** -əmz
fr|y (F) fr|aɪ **-ies** -aɪz **-ying** -aɪ.ɪŋ **-ied** -aɪd **-yer** -aɪ.əʳ (US) -aɪ.ɚ **ˈfrying ˌpan; ˌout of the ˌfrying pan ˌinto the ˈfire**
Frye fraɪ
ft *(abbrev. for* **foot** *or* **feet***) singular:* fʊt *plural:* fiːt
FT ˌefˈtiː
FTSE, FT-SE ˈfʊt.si **ˈFT-SE ˌIndex**
FT-SE 100 ˌfʊt.si.wʌnˈhʌn.drəd, -drɪd
Fuad fuːˈɑːd, -ˈæd (US) ˈfuː.ɑːd
fuchsia ˈfjuː.ʃə **-s** -z
fuchsine ˈfuːk.siːn, -sɪn (US) ˈfuːk.sɪn, ˈfjuːk-, ˈfʊk-, -siːn
fuck fʌk **-s** -s **-ing** -ɪŋ **-ed** -t **-er/s** -əʳ/z (US) -ɚ/z
fu|cus ˈfjuː|.kəs **-ci** -saɪ **-cuses** -kə.sɪz
fuddl|e ˈfʌd.l̩ **-es** -z **-ing** -ɪŋ, ˈ-lɪŋ **-ed** -d
fuddy-dudd|y ˈfʌd.iˌdʌd|.i **-ies** -iz
fudg|e fʌdʒ **-es** -ɪz **-ing** -ɪŋ **-ed** -d
Fudge fʌdʒ, fjuːdʒ
fuehrer ˈfjʊə.rə, ˈfjɔː- (US) ˈfjʊr.ɚ
fuel ˈfjuː.əl, fjʊəl (US) ˈfjuː.əl, fjuːl **-s** -z **-(l)ing** -ɪŋ **-(l)ed** -d **add ˌfuel to the ˈfire**
Fuentes ˈfwen.tes, -teɪz
fug fʌg **-s** -z
fugacious fjuːˈgeɪ.ʃəs **-ly** -li **-ness** -nəs, -nɪs
fugacity fjuːˈgæs.ə.ti, -ɪ.ti (US) -ə.t̬i
fugal ˈfjuː.gəl
Fugard ˈfuː.gɑːd, ˈfjuː- (US) -gɑːrd
fuggles ˈfʌg.l̩z
fugg|y ˈfʌg|.i **-ier** -i.əʳ (US) -i.ɚ **-iest** -i.ɪst, -i.əst **-iness** -ɪ.nəs, -ɪ.nɪs
fugitive ˈfjuː.dʒə.tɪv, -dʒɪ- (US) -t̬ɪv **-s** -z **-ly** -li **-ness** -nəs, -nɪs
fugle|man ˈfjuː.gl̩|.mæn, -mən **-men** -men, -mən
fugue fjuːg **-s** -z
führer (F) ˈfjʊə.rəʳ, ˈfjɔː- (US) ˈfjʊr.ɚ **-s** -z
Fujairah fuːˈdʒaɪə.rə (US) -ˈdʒaɪ-
Fuji ˈfuː.dʒi
Fujian fuːˈdʒɑːn
Fujimori ˌfuː.dʒiˈmɔːr.i
Fuji-san ˈfuː.dʒi.sæn (US) -sɑːn
Fujitsu fʊˈdʒɪt.suː, fuː- (US) fuː-ˈ, fʊ-
Fujiyama ˌfuː.dʒiˈjɑː.mə
Fukuoka ˌfʊk.uːˈəʊ.kə, ˌfuː.kuːˈ- (US) ˌfuː.kuːˈoʊ-, ˌfʊk.uːˈ-
-ful -fəl, -fʊl
Note: Two suffixes are covered by this entry, both of which are not stressed. The first forms an adjective, e.g. **beauty** /ˈbjuː.ti (US) -t̬i/, **beautiful** /ˈbjuː.tɪ.fəl (US) -t̬ɪ-/; in this the pronunciation /-fəl/ is preferred. The second forms a measuring noun, e.g. **bucket** /ˈbʌk.ɪt/, **bucketful** /ˈbʌk.ɪt.fʊl/, and is normally /-fʊl/.
Fulani fuːˈlɑː.ni, ˈ--- **-s** -z
Fulbright ˈfʊl.braɪt **-s** -s
Fulcher ˈfʊl.tʃəʳ (US) -tʃɚ
fulcr|um ˈfʊl.kr|əm, ˈfʌl- **-a** -ə **-ums** -əmz
fuler|um fʊlkr|əm, fʌl- **-a** -ə **-ums** -əmz
fulfil fʊlˈfɪl **-s** -z **-ling** -ɪŋ **-led** -d **-ment** -mənt
fulfill fʊlˈfɪl **-s** -z **-ing** -ɪŋ **-ed** -d **-ment** -mənt
Fulford ˈfʊl.fəd (US) -fɚd
fulgent ˈfʌl.dʒənt **-ly** -li
Fulham ˈfʊl.əm
fuliginous fjuːˈlɪdʒ.ɪ.nəs **-ly** -li
Fulke fʊlk
full fʊl **-er** -əʳ (US) -ɚ **-est** -ɪst, -əst **-ness** -nəs, -nɪs **ˌfull ˈboard; ˌfull ˈface; ˌfull ˈmoon; ˌfull ˈstop**
fullback ˈfʊl.bæk, ˌ-ˈ- (US) ˈ-- **-s** -s
full-blooded ˌfʊlˈblʌd.ɪd *stress shift:* ˌfull-blooded ˈmale
full-blown ˌfʊlˈbləʊn (US) -ˈbloʊn *stress shift:* ˌfull-blown ˈargument
full-bodied ˌfʊlˈbɒd.ɪd (US) -ˈbɑː.did *stress shift:* ˌfull-bodied ˈwine
fuller (F) ˈfʊl.əʳ (US) -ɚ **-s** -z
Fullerton ˈfʊl.ə.tən (US) -ɚ-
full-face ˌfʊlˈfeɪs *stress shift:* ˌfull-face ˈphotograph
full-fledged ˌfʊlˈfledʒd *stress shift:* ˌfull-fledged ˈbird
full-grown ˌfʊlˈgrəʊn (US) -ˈgroʊn *stress shift:* ˌfull-grown ˈman
full-length ˌfʊlˈleŋkθ *stress shift:* ˌfull-length ˈcoat
full-scale ˌfʊlˈskeɪl *stress shift:* ˌfull-scale ˈwar
full-time ˌfʊlˈtaɪm *stress shift:* ˌfull-time ˈmother
fully ˈfʊl.i
-fully -fəl.i, -fʊl.i
Note: Suffix. Words containing **-fully** are stressed in a similar way to adjectives containing **-ful**; see above.
fully-fledged ˌfʊl.iˈfledʒd *stress shift:* ˌfully-fledged ˈbird
fulmar ˈfʊl.məʳ, -mɑːʳ (US) -mɚ, -mɑːr **-s** -z
Fulmer ˈfʊl.məʳ (US) -mɚ
fulmi|nate ˈfʊl.mɪ|.neɪt, ˈfʌl-, -mə- **-nates** -neɪts **-nating** -neɪ.tɪŋ (US) -neɪ.t̬ɪŋ **-nated** -neɪ.tɪd (US) -neɪ.t̬ɪd
fulmination ˌfʊl.mɪˈneɪ.ʃən, ˌfʌl-, -məˈ- **-s** -z
fulness ˈfʊl.nəs, -nɪs
fulsome ˈfʊl.səm **-ly** -li **-ness** -nəs, -nɪs
Fulton ˈfʊl.tən
Fulvia ˈfʊl.vi.ə, ˈfʌl-
fulvous ˈfʌl.vəs, ˈfʊl-
Fulwood ˈfʊl.wʊd
Fu Manchu ˌfuː.mænˈtʃuː
fumbl|e ˈfʌm.bl̩ **-es** -z **-ing** -ɪŋ, ˈ-blɪŋ **-ed** -d **-er/s** -əʳ/z, ˈ-bləʳ/z (US) ˈ-bl̩.ɚ/z, ˈ-blɚ/z
fum|e fjuːm **-es** -z **-ing** -ɪŋ **-ed** -d
fumi|gate ˈfjuː.mɪ|.geɪt, -mə- **-gates** -geɪts **-gating** -geɪ.tɪŋ (US) -geɪ.t̬ɪŋ **-gated** -geɪ.tɪd (US) -geɪ.t̬ɪd **-gator/s** -geɪ.təʳ/z (US) -geɪ.t̬ɚ/z
fumigation ˌfjuː.mɪˈgeɪ.ʃən, -məˈ- **-s** -z
fun fʌn
Funafuti ˌfuː.nəˈfuː.ti

funambulist fjuːˈnæm.bjə.lɪst, fjʊ-, -bjʊ- ⓤⓢ fjuːˈnæm.bjə-, -bjuː- **-s** -s
Funchal fʊnˈʃɑːl, -ˈtʃɑːl
function ˈfʌŋ*k*.ʃᵊn **-s** -z **-ing** -ɪŋ **-ed** -d
functional ˈfʌŋ*k*.ʃᵊn.ᵊl **-ly** -i
functional|ism ˈfʌŋ*k*.ʃᵊn.ᵊl|.ɪ.zᵊm **-ist/s** -ɪst/s
functionality ˌfʌŋ*k*.ʃᵊnˈæl.ɪ.ti, -ə.ti ⓤⓢ -ə.t̬i
functionar|y ˈfʌŋ*k*.ʃᵊn.ᵊr.|i, -r|i ⓤⓢ -er|.i **-ies** -iz
functor ˈfʌŋ*k*.təʳ, -tɔːʳ ⓤⓢ -tɚ, -tɔːr **-s** -z
fund fʌnd **-s** -z **-ing** -ɪŋ **-ed** -ɪd
fundament ˈfʌn.də.mənt **-s** -s
fundamental ˌfʌn.dəˈmen.tᵊl ⓤⓢ -t̬ᵊl **-s** -z **-ly** -i
fundamental|ism (F) ˌfʌn.dəˈmen.tᵊl|.ɪ.zᵊm ⓤⓢ -t̬ᵊl- **-ist/s** -ɪst/s
fundamentality ˌfʌn.də.menˈtæl.ə.ti, -ɪ.ti ⓤⓢ -ə.t̬i
fundless ˈfʌnd.ləs, -lɪs, -les
fundrais|er ˈfʌndˌreɪ.z|əʳ ⓤⓢ -z|ɚ **-er/s** -əz ⓤⓢ -ɚz **-ing** -ɪŋ
Fundy ˈfʌn.di
funeral ˈfjuː.nᵊr.əl **-s** -z ˈ**funeral** ˌ**home**; ˈ**funeral** ˌ**parlo(u)r**
funerary ˈfjuː.nᵊr.ə.ri ⓤⓢ -er.i
funereal fjuːˈnɪə.ri.əl ⓤⓢ -ˈnɪr.i- **-ly** -i
funfair ˈfʌn.feəʳ ⓤⓢ -fer **-s** -z
fungal ˈfʌŋ.gᵊl
fungible ˈfʌn.dʒɪ.bl̩, -dʒə- **-s** -z
fungicidal ˌfʌŋ.gɪˈsaɪ.dᵊl, ˌfʌn.dʒɪˈ- ⓤⓢ ˌfʌn.dʒɪˈ-, ˌfʌŋ.gəˈ- **-li** -i
fungicide ˈfʌŋ.gɪ.saɪd, ˈfʌn.dʒɪ- ⓤⓢ ˈfʌn.dʒɪ-, ˈfʌŋ.gə- **-s** -z
fungo ˈfʌŋ.gəʊ ⓤⓢ -goʊ **-es** -z
fun|gus ˈfʌŋ.|gəs **-gi** -gaɪ, -giː, ˈfʌn.dʒiː, -dʒaɪ **-guses** -gə.sɪz **-goid** -gɔɪd **-gous** -gəs
funicle ˈfjuː.nɪ.kl̩ **-s** -z
funicular fjuːˈnɪk.jə.ləʳ, fə-, -jʊ- ⓤⓢ -juː.lɚ **-s** -z
funicul|us fjuːˈnɪk.jə.l|əs, fə-, -jʊ- ⓤⓢ -juː- **-i** -aɪ
funk (F) fʌŋk **-s** -s **-ing** -ɪŋ **-ed** -t
funk|y ˈfʌŋ.k|i **-ier** -i.əʳ ⓤⓢ -i.ɚ **-iest** -i.ɪst, -i.əst **-ily** -ɪ.li, -ᵊl.i **-iness** -ɪ.nəs, -ɪ.nɪs
funnel ˈfʌn.ᵊl **-s** -z **-(l)ing** -ɪŋ **-(l)ed** -d
funnies ˈfʌn.iz
funn|y ˈfʌn|.i **-ier** -i.əʳ ⓤⓢ -i.ɚ **-iest** -i.ɪst, -i.əst **-ily** -ɪ.li, -ᵊl.i **-iness** -ɪ.nəs, -ɪ.nɪs ˈ**funny** ˌ**bone**; ˈ**funny** ˌ**business**
funny|man ˈfʌn.i|.mæn **-men** -men
fur fɜːʳ ⓤⓢ fɝː **-s** -z **-ring** -ɪŋ **-red** -d
fur *(abbrev. for* **furlong***)* ˈfɜː.lɒŋ ⓤⓢ ˈfɝː.lɑːŋ, -lɔːŋ
Furbear ˈfɜː.beəʳ ⓤⓢ ˈfɝː.ber
furbelow ˈfɜː.bɪ.ləʊ, -bə- ⓤⓢ ˈfɝː.bɪ.loʊ, -bə- **-s** -z
furbish ˈfɜː.bɪʃ ⓤⓢ ˈfɝː- **-es** -ɪz **-ing** -ɪŋ **-ed** -t
furcate *(adj.)* ˈfɜː.keɪt, -kɪt, -kət ⓤⓢ ˈfɝː-
fur|cate *(v.)* ˈfɜː|.keɪt, -|ˈ- ⓤⓢ ˈfɝː|.keɪt **-cates** -keɪts, -ˈkeɪts ⓤⓢ -keɪts **-cating** -keɪ.tɪŋ, -ˈkeɪ- ⓤⓢ -keɪ.t̬ɪŋ **-cated** -keɪ.tɪd, -ˈkeɪ- ⓤⓢ -keɪ.t̬ɪd
furcation fɜːˈkeɪ.ʃᵊn ⓤⓢ fɝː- **-s** -z
furibund ˈfjʊə.rɪ.bʌnd, ˈfjɔː-, -bənd ⓤⓢ ˈfjʊr.ɪ-
furioso ˌfjʊə.riˈəʊ.zəʊ, ˌfjɔː-, -səʊ ⓤⓢ ˌfjʊr.iˈoʊ.soʊ, ˌfjɝː-, -zoʊ
furious ˈfjʊə.ri.əs, ˈfjɔː- ⓤⓢ ˈfjʊr.i-, ˈfjɝː- **-ly** -li
furl fɜːl ⓤⓢ fɝːl **-s** -z **-ing** -ɪŋ **-ed** -d
furlong ˈfɜː.lɒŋ ⓤⓢ ˈfɝː.lɑːŋ, -lɔːŋ **-s** -z
furlough ˈfɜː.ləʊ ⓤⓢ ˈfɝː.loʊ **-s** -z
furnac|e ˈfɜː.nɪs, -nəs ⓤⓢ ˈfɝː- **-es** -ɪz
Furneaux ˈfɜː.nəʊ ⓤⓢ fɝːˈnoʊ
Furness ˈfɜː.nɪs, fɜːˈnes ⓤⓢ ˈfɝː.nɪs, fɝːˈnes
Furneux ˈfɜː.nɪks, -nəʊ ⓤⓢ ˈfɝː.nɪks, -nuː, -noʊ
Note: /ˈfɜː.nɪks/ is the more usual local pronunciation.
furnish ˈfɜː.nɪʃ ⓤⓢ ˈfɝː- **-es** -ɪz **-ing/s** -ɪŋ/z **-ed** -t **-er/s** -əʳ/z ⓤⓢ -ɚ/z
furniture ˈfɜː.nɪ.tʃəʳ ⓤⓢ ˈfɝː.nɪ.tʃɚ
Furnival(l) ˈfɜː.nɪ.vᵊl ⓤⓢ ˈfɝː-
furor ˈfjʊr.ɔː ⓤⓢ ˈfjʊr.ɔːr, -ɚ
furore fjʊəˈrɔː.ri, -reɪ; ˈfjʊə.rɔːʳ, ˈfjɔː- ⓤⓢ ˈfjʊr.ɔːr, -ɚ **-s** -z
furph|y (F) ˈfɜː.f|i ⓤⓢ ˈfɝː- **-ies** -iz
furrier ˈfʌr.i.əʳ ⓤⓢ ˈfɝː.i.ɚ **-s** -z
furrier|y ˈfʌr.i.ᵊr|.i ⓤⓢ ˈfɝː- **-ies** -iz
furrow ˈfʌr.əʊ ⓤⓢ ˈfɝː.oʊ **-s** -z **-ing** -ɪŋ **-ed** -d
furr|y ˈfɜː.r|i ⓤⓢ ˈfɝː|.i **-ier** -i.əʳ ⓤⓢ -i.ɚ **-iest** -i.ɪst, -i.əst **-iness** -ɪ.nəs, -ɪ.nɪs
furth|er ˈfɜː.ð|əʳ ⓤⓢ ˈfɝː.ð|ɚ **-ers** -əz ⓤⓢ -ɚz **-ering** -ᵊr.ɪŋ **-ered** -əd ⓤⓢ -ɚd **-erer/s** -ᵊr.əʳ/z ⓤⓢ -ɚ.ɚ/z ˌ**further** **eduˈcation**
furtherance ˈfɜː.ðᵊr.ᵊn*t*s ⓤⓢ ˈfɝː-
furthermore ˌfɜː.ðəˈmɔːʳ, ˈ--- ⓤⓢ ˈfɝː.ðɚ.mɔːr
furthermost ˈfɜː.ðə.məʊst ⓤⓢ ˈfɝː.ðɚ.moʊst
furthest ˈfɜː.ðɪst, -ðəst ⓤⓢ ˈfɝː-
furtive ˈfɜː.tɪv ⓤⓢ ˈfɝː.t̬ɪv **-ly** -li **-ness** -nəs, -nɪs
furuncle ˈfjʊə.rʌŋ.kᵊl, ˈfjɔː- ⓤⓢ ˈfjʊr.ʌŋ- **-s** -z
fur|y (F) ˈfjʊə.r|i, ˈfjɔː- ⓤⓢ ˈfjʊr|.i **-ies** -iz
furze fɜːz ⓤⓢ fɝːz
fus|e fjuːz **-es** -ɪz **-ing** -ɪŋ **-ed** -d ˈ**fuse** ˌ**box**
fusee fjuːˈziː ⓤⓢ fjuːˈziː, ˈ-- **-s** -z
fusel ˈfjuː.zᵊl ⓤⓢ ˈfjuː.zᵊl, -sᵊl ˈ**fusel** ˌ**oil**, ˌ**fusel** ˈ**oil**
fuselag|e ˈfjuː.zᵊl.ɑːʒ, -zɪ.lɑːʒ ⓤⓢ -sə.lɑːʒ, -zə-, -lɑːdʒ **-es** -ɪz
fusibility ˌfjuː.zɪˈbɪl.ə.ti, -zəˈ-, -ɪ.ti ⓤⓢ -ə.t̬i
fusible ˈfjuː.zɪ.bl̩, -zə-
fusil ˈfjuː.zɪl ⓤⓢ -zɪl, -sɪl **-s** -z
fusile ˈfjuː.saɪl, -zaɪl ⓤⓢ -zᵊl, -zaɪl, -sɪl
fusilier ˌfjuː.zᵊlˈɪəʳ, -zɪˈlɪəʳ ⓤⓢ -zɪˈlɪr **-s** -z
fusillade ˌfjuː.zəˈleɪd, -zɪˈ- ⓤⓢ ˌfjuː.səˈlɑːd, -zəˈ-, -ˈleɪd, ˈ--- **-s** -z
fusilli fʊˈsiː.li, fjʊˈzɪl.i ⓤⓢ ˈfjuː.siː.li, -zə-
fusion ˈfjuː.ʒᵊn **-s** -z
fuss fʌs **-es** -ɪz **-ing** -ɪŋ **-ed** -t **-er/s** -əʳ/z ⓤⓢ -ɚ/z
fussbudget ˈfʌsˌbʌdʒ.ɪt **-s** -s
fusspot ˈfʌs.pɒt ⓤⓢ -pɑːt **-s** -s
fuss|y ˈfʌs|.i **-ier** -i.əʳ ⓤⓢ -i.ɚ **-iest** -i.ɪst, -i.əst **-ily** -ɪ.li, -ᵊl.i **-iness** -ɪ.nəs, -ɪ.nɪs
fustian ˈfʌs.ti.ən ⓤⓢ -tʃᵊn
fustic ˈfʌs.tɪk
fusti|gate ˈfʌs.tɪ|.geɪt, -tə- **-gates** -geɪts **-gating** -geɪ.tɪŋ ⓤⓢ -geɪ.t̬ɪŋ **-gated** -geɪ.tɪd ⓤⓢ -geɪ.t̬ɪd
fustigation ˌfʌs.tɪˈgeɪ.ʃᵊn, -təˈ- **-s** -z
fust|y ˈfʌs.t|i **-ier** -i.əʳ ⓤⓢ -i.ɚ **-iest** -i.ɪst, -i.əst **-ily** -ɪ.li, -ᵊl.i **-iness** -ɪ.nəs, -ɪ.nɪs
futhark ˈfuː.θɑːk ⓤⓢ -θɑːrk
futile ˈfjuː.taɪl ⓤⓢ -t̬əl, -taɪl **-ly** -li **-ness** -nəs, -nɪs
futilit|y fjuːˈtɪl.ə.t|i, -ɪ.t|i ⓤⓢ -ə.t̬|i **-ies** -iz
futon ˈfuː.tɒn, ˈfjuː-, ˈfʊt.ɒn, -ᵊn; ˌfuːˈtɒn ⓤⓢ ˈfuː.tɑːn **-s** -z
futtock ˈfʌt.ək ⓤⓢ ˈfʌt̬- **-s** -s
future ˈfjuː.tʃəʳ ⓤⓢ -tʃɚ **-s** -z
futur|ism ˈfjuː.tʃᵊr|.ɪ.zᵊm **-ist/s** -ɪst/s
futuristic ˌfjuː.tʃəˈrɪs.tɪk **-ally** -ᵊl.i, -li
futurit|y fjuːˈtjʊə.rə.t|i, -ˈtjɔː-, -ˈtʃʊə-, -ˈtʃɔː-, -ɪ.t|i ⓤⓢ fjuːˈtʊr.ə.t̬|i, -ˈtjʊr-, -ˈtʃʊr-, -ˈtʃɝː- **-ies** -iz
futurolog|ist ˌfjuː.tʃəˈrɒl.ə.dʒ|ɪst ⓤⓢ -ˈrɑː.lə- **-ists** -ɪsts **-y** -i
fuz|e fjuːz **-es** -ɪz **-ing** -ɪŋ **-ed** -d
fuzee fjuːˈziː ⓤⓢ fjuːˈziː, ˈ-- **-s** -z
Fuzhou ˈfuː.dʒəʊ ⓤⓢ -dʒoʊ
fuzz fʌz **-es** -ɪz **-ing** -ɪŋ **-ed** -d
fuzz|y ˈfʌz|.i **-ier** -i.əʳ ⓤⓢ -i.ɚ **-iest** -i.ɪst, -i.əst **-ily** -ɪ.li, -ᵊl.i **-iness** -ɪ.nəs, -ɪ.nɪs
fuzzy-wuzz|y ˈfʌz.iˌwʌz|.i, ˌ--ˈ-- **-ies** -iz
f-word ˈefˌwɜːd ⓤⓢ -ˌwɝːd
Fyf(f)e faɪf
Fyfield ˈfaɪ.fiːld
Fylingdales ˈfaɪ.lɪŋ.deɪlz
Fyne faɪn

Pronouncing the letter G

See also GG, GH, GU, NG

There are two main pronunciations for the consonant letter **g**: /dʒ/ and /g/, e.g.:

gem	/dʒem/
age	/eɪdʒ/
geese	/giːs/
gig	/gɪg/

A following vowel letter **e**, **i** or **y** may lead to the pronunciation /dʒ/. However, as can be seen in the above examples, this is not reliable as an indicator of which pronunciation to use. More reliably, before vowel letters **a**, **o** or **u** the pronunciation is highly likely to be /g/, although there are exceptions, e.g.:

gaol	/dʒeɪl/

In addition

g is often silent before a consonant letter **m** or **n** at the beginning and end of words, e.g.:

gnat	/næt/
paradigm	/ˈpær.ə.daɪm/

g (G) dʒiː **-'s** -z
g *(abbrev. for* **gram/s***) singular:* græm *plural:* -z
Ga. *(abbrev. for* **Georgia***)* ˈdʒɔː.dʒə US ˈdʒɔːr-
gab gæb **-s** -z **-bing** -ɪŋ **-bed** -d
gabardine ˌgæb.əˈdiːn, ˈ--- US ˈgæb.ɚ.diːn, ˌ--ˈ- **-s** -z
Gabbatha ˈgæb.ə.θə
gabbl|e ˈgæb.l̩ **-es** -z **-ing** -ɪŋ, ˈ-lɪŋ **-ed** -d **-er/s** -əʳ/z, ˈ-ləʳ/z US ˈ-l̩.ɚ/z, ˈ-lɚ/z
gabbro ˈgæb.rəʊ US -roʊ **-s** -z
gabb|y ˈgæb|.i **-ier** -i.əʳ US -i.ɚ **-iest** -i.ɪst, -i.əst
gaberdine ˌgæb.əˈdiːn, ˈ--- US ˈgæb.ɚ.diːn, ˌ--ˈ- **-s** -z
gaberlunzie ˌgæb.əˈlʌn.zi, -ˈluː.nji, ˈgæb.ə.lʌn.zi, -luː.nji US ˌgæb.ɚˈlʌn.zi **-s** -z
gabfest ˈgæbˌfest **-s** -s
Gabii ˈgæb.i.iː, -bi.aɪ US ˈgæb.i.aɪ, ˈgeɪ.bi-
gabion ˈgeɪ.bi.ən **-s** -z
gable (G) ˈgeɪ.bl̩ **-s** -z **-d** -d
gablet ˈgeɪ.blɪt, -blət US -blət **-s** -s
Gabon gæbˈɒn, gəˈbɒn; ˈgæb.ɒn *as if French:* gæbˈɔ̃ːŋ US gæbˈoʊn, gəˈboʊn
Gabonese ˌgæb.ɒnˈiːz, -əˈniːz US -əˈniːz
Gaboon gəˈbuːn
Gabor gəˈbɔːʳ; ˈgɑː.bɔːʳ US gəˈbɔːr; ˈgɑː.bɔːr
Gaborone ˌgæb.əˈrəʊ.ni US ˌgɑː.bəˈroʊ.neɪ, -ni
Gabriel ˈgeɪ.bri.əl
Gabriella ˌgæb.riˈel.ə, ˌgeɪ.briˈ-
Gabrielle ˌgæb.riˈel, ˌgeɪ.briˈ-
gab|y ˈgeɪ.b|i **-ies** -iz
Gaby ˈgæb.i, ˈgɑː.bi
gad (G) gæd **-s** -z **-ding** -ɪŋ **-ded** -ɪd
gadabout ˈgæd.ə.baʊt **-s** -s
Gadafy, Gadaffi gəˈdæf.i, -ˈdɑː.fi US -ˈdɑː-
Gadara ˈgæd.ᵊr.ə
Gadarene ˌgæd.əˈriːn, ˈ--- US ˈ--- **-s** -z
Gaddafi gəˈdæf.i, -ˈdɑː.fi US -ˈdɑː-
Gaddesden ˈgædz.dᵊn
Gaddis ˈgæd.ɪs
Gade *English river:* geɪd *Danish composer:* ˈgɑː.də
Gades ˈgeɪ.diːz
gadfl|y ˈgæd.fl|aɪ **-ies** -aɪz
gadget ˈgædʒ.ɪt, -ət **-s** -s
gadgetry ˈgædʒ.ɪ.tri, ˈ-ə-
Gadhafi gəˈdæf.i, -ˈdɑː.fi US -ˈdɑː-
Gadhel ˈgæd.el US -əl **-s** -z
Gadhelic gædˈel.ɪk, gəˈdel-
gadolinium ˌgæd.əʊˈlɪn.i.əm, -ᵊlˈɪn- US -oʊˈlɪn-, gædˈlɪn-
gadroon gəˈdruːn **-s** -z
Gadsby ˈgædz.bi
Gadsden ˈgædz.dᵊn
Gadshill ˈgædz.hɪl
gadwall ˈgæd.wɔːl US -wɔːl **-s** -z
gadzooks ˌgædˈzuːks, gæd- US -ˈzuːks, -ˈzʊks
Gael geɪl **-s** -z
Gaelic ˈgeɪ.lɪk, ˈgæl.ɪk
Gaeltacht ˈgeɪl.tæxt, -təxt
Gaetulia *in Ireland:* giːˈtjuː.li.ə, gaɪ-, dʒi-, -ˈtuː- US dʒiˈtuː-, giː- *in Libya:* dʒɪˈtjuː.li.ə US -ˈtuː-, -ˈtjuː-
gaff gæf **-s** -s **-ing** -ɪŋ **-ed** -t
gaffe gæf **-s** -s
gaffer ˈgæf.əʳ US -ɚ **-s** -z
gag gæg **-s** -z **-ging** -ɪŋ **-ged** -d
gaga ˈgɑː.gɑː, ˈgæg.ɑː US ˈgɑː.gɑː **-s** -z
Gagarin gəˈgɑː.rɪn, gægˈɑː- US gəˈgɑːr.ɪn
gag|e (G) geɪdʒ **-es** -ɪz **-ing** -ɪŋ **-ed** -d
gaggle ˈgæg.l̩ **-s** -z
Gaia ˈgaɪ.ə, ˈgeɪ-
gaiet|y (G) ˈgeɪ.ə.t|i, -ɪ.t|i US -ə.t̬|i **-ies** -iz
Gail ˈgeɪl
gaily *(from* **gay***)* ˈgeɪ.li
gain geɪn **-s** -z **-ing/s** -ɪŋ/z **-ed** -d **-er/s** -əʳ/z US -ɚ/z
Gaines geɪnz
Gainesville ˈgeɪnz.vɪl US -vɪl, -vəl
gainful ˈgeɪn.fᵊl, -fʊl **-ly** -i **-ness** -nəs, -nɪs
gain|say ˌgeɪn|ˈseɪ **-says** -ˈseɪz, -ˈsez **-saying** -ˈseɪ.ɪŋ **-sayed** -ˈseɪd **-said** -ˈsed, -ˈseɪd **-sayer/s** -ˈseɪ.əʳ/z US -ˈseɪ.ɚ/z
Gainsborough ˈgeɪnz.bᵊr.ə US -oʊ, -ə **-s** -z
Gairdner ˈgeəd.nəʳ, ˈgɑːd- US ˈgerd.nɚ, ˈgɑːrd-
Gairloch ˈgeə.lɒx, -lɒk US ˈger.lɑːk
Gaisford ˈgeɪs.fəd US -fɚd
gait geɪt **-s** -s
gaiter ˈgeɪ.təʳ US -t̬ɚ **-s** -z
Gaitskell ˈgeɪt.skᵊl, -skɪl
Gaius ˈgaɪ.əs US ˈgeɪ-, ˈgaɪ-
gal *girl:* gæl **-s** -z
gal *(abbrev. for* **gallon***)* ˈgæl.ən
gala *special occasion:* ˈgɑː.lə, ˈgeɪ- US ˈgeɪ-, ˈgæl.ə, ˈgɑː.lə **-s** -z
Gala *river:* ˈgɑː.lə US ˈgɑː.lə, ˈgæl.ə
galactic gəˈlæk.tɪk **-ally** -ᵊl.i, -li
galacto- gəˈlæk.təʊ- US ˈ-tə-, ˈ-toʊ-
galactose gəˈlæk.təʊs, -təʊz US -toʊs
galah gəˈlɑː **-s** -z
Galahad ˈgæl.ə.hæd
galantine ˈgæl.ən.tiːn, ˌ--ˈ- **-s** -z
Galapagos gəˈlæp.ə.gəs, -gɒs US gəˈlɑː.pə.goʊs, -gəz
Galashiels ˌgæl.əˈʃiːlz *stress shift:* ˌGalashiels ˈstreets
Galata ˈgæl.ə.tə US -t̬ə
Galatasaray ˌgæl.əˈtæs.ə.raɪ
Galatea ˌgæl.əˈtiː.ə
Galatia gəˈleɪ.ʃə, -ʃi.ə, ˌgæl.əˈti.ə
Galatian gəˈleɪ.ʃᵊn, -ʃi.ən, ˌgæl.əˈti.ən **-s** -z
galax|y ˈgæl.ək.s|i **-ies** -iz
Galba ˈgæl.bə
galbanum ˈgæl.bə.nəm

Galbraith gælˈbreɪθ US ˈ--
gale (G) geɪl **-s** -z
Galen ˈgeɪ.lən, -lɪn
galena (G) gəˈliː.nə
Galenic gəˈlen.ɪk, geɪ-, -ˈliː.nɪk **-al** -əl
Galerius gəˈlɪə.ri.əs US -ˈlɪr.i-
Galesburg ˈgeɪlz.bɜːg US -bɝːg
Galic|ia gəˈlɪs|.i.ə, gælˈɪs-, -ˈɪʃ|.ə, -ˈɪʃ|.i.ə US gəˈlɪʃ|.ə **-ian/s** -i.ən/z US -ən/z, -i.ən/z
Galilean ˌgæl.ɪˈliː.ən, -əˈ- US -əˈ- **-s** -z
Galilee ˈgæl.ɪ.liː, ˈ-ə- US ˈ-ə-
Galileo ˌgæl.ɪˈleɪ.əʊ, -əˈ-, -ˈliː.əʊ US -əˈliː-, -ˈleɪ-
galingale ˈgæl.ɪŋ.geɪl
Galion ˈgæl.i.ən US ˈgæl.jən
galipot ˈgæl.ɪ.pɒt US -pɑːt
gall gɔːl US gɔːl, gɑːl **-s** -z **-ing** -ɪŋ **-ed** -d ˈ**gall** ˌ**bladder**
Gallacher ˈgæl.ə.həʳ, -xəʳ US -hɚ
Gallagher ˈgæl.ə.həʳ, -xəʳ US -gɚ, -hɚ
Gallaher ˈgæl.ə.həʳ, -xəʳ US -hɚ
gallant (*n.*) ˈgæl.ənt **-s** -s
gallant (*adj.*) *brave:* ˈgæl.ənt **-ly** -li **-ness** -nəs, -nɪs
gallant (*adj.*) *attentive to women:* ˈgæl.ənt; gəˈlænt US ˈgæl.ənt; gəˈlænt, -ˈlɑːnt **-ly** -li **-ness** -nəs, -nɪs
Gallant gəˈlɔ̃ːŋ
gallantr|y ˈgæl.ən.tr|i **-ies** -iz
Gallatin ˈgæl.ə.tɪn
Gallaudet gæl.əˈdet *stress shift:* ˌGallaudet ˈCollege
Galle *port in Sri Lanka:* gɑːl US gɑːl, gæl
Galle *German astronomer:* ˈgæl.ə
galleon ˈgæl.i.ən US -i.ən, ˈ-jən **-s** -z
galler|y ˈgæl.ᵊr|.i **-ies** -iz **-ied** -id
galley ˈgæl.i **-s** -z ˈ**galley** ˌ**proof**; ˈ**galley** ˌ**slave**
gallfl|y ˈgɔːl.fl|aɪ US ˈgɔːl-, ˈgɑːl- **-ies** -aɪz
Gallia ˈgæl.i.ə
galliambic ˌgæl.iˈæm.bɪk **-s** -s
galliard ˈgæl.i.ɑːd, -əd US ˈ-jɚd **-s** -z
gallic (G) ˈgæl.ɪk
Gallican ˈgæl.ɪ.kən **-s** -z
gallice ˈgæl.ɪ.siː, -si
gallicism ˈgæl.ɪ.sɪ.zᵊm, ˈ-ə- US ˈ-ə- **-s** -z
gallicizle, -is|e ˈgæl.ɪ.saɪz, ˈ-ə- US ˈ-ə- **-es** -ɪz **-ing** -ɪŋ **-ed** -d
gallimaufr|y ˌgæl.ɪˈmɔː.fr|i, -əˈ- US -əˈmɑː-, -ˈmɔː- **-ies** -iz
gallinaceous ˌgæl.ɪˈneɪ.ʃəs, -əˈ- US -əˈ-
Gallio ˈgæl.i.əʊ US -oʊ
galliot ˈgæl.i.ət **-s** -s
Gallipoli gəˈlɪp.ᵊl.i, gæˈlɪp-
Gallipolis *in US:* ˌgæl.ɪ.pəˈliːs US ˌ-ə-, -ˈlɪs
gallipot ˈgæl.ɪ.pɒt US -ə.pɑːt **-s** -s
gallium ˈgæl.i.əm
gallivant ˈgæl.ɪ.vænt, ˈ-ə-, ˌ--ˈ- US ˈgæl.ə.vænt, ˌ--ˈ- **-s** -s **-ing** -ɪŋ **-ed** -ɪd
gallnut ˈgɔːl.nʌt US ˈgɔːl-, ˈgɑːl- **-s** -s
gallon ˈgæl.ən **-s** -z
galloon gəˈluːn
gallop ˈgæl.əp **-s** -s **-ing** -ɪŋ **-ed** -t **-er/s** -əʳ/z US -ɚ/s
gallopade ˌgæl.əˈpeɪd, -ˈpɑːd US -ˈpeɪd **-s** -z
Gallovidian ˌgæl.əʊˈvɪd.i.ən US -əˈ- **-s** -z
galloway (G) ˈgæl.ə.weɪ **-s** -z
gallows ˈgæl.əʊz US -oʊz
gallstone ˈgɔːl.stəʊn US -stoʊn, ˈgɑːl- **-s** -z
Gallup ˈgæl.əp ˈ**Gallup** ˌ**poll**
Gallus ˈgæl.əs
galoot gəˈluːt **-s** -s
galop ˈgæl.əp; gælˈɒp US ˈgæl.əp **-s** -s
galore gəˈlɔːʳ US -ˈlɔːr
galosh gəˈlɒʃ US -ˈlɑːʃ **-es** -ɪz
Galpin ˈgæl.pɪn
Galsham ˈgɔːl.səm, ˈgɒl- US ˈgɔːl-, ˈgɑːl-
Galston ˈgɔːl.stᵊn, ˈgɒl- US ˈgɔːl-, ˈgɑːl-
Galsworthy ˈgɔːlz.wɜː.ði, ˈgɒlz-, ˈgælz- US ˈgɔːlz.wɝː-, ˈgɑːlz-, ˈgælz-
Note: John Galsworthy, the author, is commonly called /ˈgɔːlz.wɜː.ði US -wɜːr-/.
Galt gɔːlt, gɒlt US gɑːlt, gɔːlt
Galton ˈgɔːl.tᵊn, ˈgɒl- US ˈgɔːl-, ˈgɑːl-
Galvani gælˈvɑː.ni
galvanic gælˈvæn.ɪk
galvanism ˈgæl.və.nɪ.zᵊm
galvaniz|e, -is|e ˈgæl.və.naɪz **-es** -ɪz **-ing** -ɪŋ **-ed** -d **-er/s** -əʳ/z US -ɚ/z
galvanometer ˌgæl.vəˈnɒm.ɪ.təʳ, -ə.təʳ US -ˈnɑː.mə.t̬ɚ **-s** -z
Galveston, Galvestone ˈgæl.vɪ.stᵊn, -və-
Galway ˈgɔːl.weɪ US ˈgɔːl-, ˈgɑːl-
gam gæm **-s** -z
Gama ˈgɑː.mə
Gamage ˈgæm.ɪdʒ **-'s** -ɪz
Gamaliel gəˈmeɪ.li.əl *in Jewish usage also:* -ˈmɑː-; ˌgæm.əˈliː.əl
Gamay ˈgæm.eɪ, -ˈ- US gæmˈeɪ
gamba ˈgæm.bə US ˈgɑːm-, ˈgæm- **-s** -z
gambado *jump:* gæmˈbeɪ.dəʊ, -ˈbɑː- US -ˈbeɪ.doʊ **-(e)s** -z
gambadoes *leggings:* gæmˈbeɪ.dəʊz US -doʊz
Gambetta gæmˈbet.ə US -ˈbet̬-
Gambia ˈgæm.bi.ə **-n/s** -n/z
gambier *substance used in dyeing:* ˈgæm.bɪəʳ US ˈgæm.bɪr
Gambier *surname:* ˈgæm.bi.əʳ, -bɪəʳ, -bi.eɪ US ˈgæm.bɪr
gambit ˈgæm.bɪt **-s** -s
gambl|e (G) ˈgæm.bl̩ **-es** -z **-ing** -ɪŋ, ˈ-blɪŋ **-ed** -d **-er/s** -əʳ/z, ˈ-bləʳ/z US ˈ-bl̩.ɚ/z, ˈ-blɚ/z
gamboge gæmˈbəʊʒ, -ˈbəʊdʒ, -ˈbuːʒ US -ˈboʊdʒ
gambol ˈgæm.bᵊl **-s** -z **-(l)ing** -ɪŋ **-(l)ed** -d
Gambon ˈgæm.bən
gambrel ˈgæm.brəl **-s** -z
gam|e geɪm **-es** -z **-er** -əʳ US -ɚ **-est** -ɪst, -əst **-ely** -li **-eness** -nəs, -nɪs **-ing** -ɪŋ **-ed** -d ˈ**game** ˌ**show**
gamebag ˈgeɪm.bæg **-s** -z
gamecock ˈgeɪm.kɒk US -kɑːk **-s** -s
gamekeeper ˈgeɪmˌkiː.pəʳ US -pɚ **-s** -z
gamelan ˈgæm.ə.læn, ˈ-ɪ- **-s** -z
gameplay ˈgeɪm.pleɪ
gamesmanship ˈgeɪmz.mən.ʃɪp
games|-master ˈgeɪmz|ˌmɑː.stəʳ US -ˌmæs.tɚ **-masters** -ˌmɑː.stəz US -ˌmæs.tɚz **-mistress/es** -ˌmɪs.trəs/ɪz, -trɪs/ɪz
gamester ˈgeɪm.stəʳ US -stɚ **-s** -z
gamete ˈgæm.iːt, gəˈmiːt **-s** -s
gametic gəˈmet.ɪk, gæmˈet- US gəˈmet̬-
gamin ˈgæm.ɪn, gæˈmæ̃ŋ **-s** -z
gamine ˈgæm.iːn, -ˈ- **-s** -z
gamma ˈgæm.ə **-s** -z ˈ**gamma** ˌ**ray**
Gammell ˈgæm.ᵊl
gammer ˈgæm.əʳ US -ɚ **-s** -z
gammon ˈgæm.ən **-s** -z **-ing** -ɪŋ **-ed** -d
gamm|y ˈgæm|.i **-ier** -i.əʳ US -i.ɚ **-iest** -i.ɪst, -i.əst
-gamous -gə.məs
Note: Suffix. Usually unstressed, e.g. **monogamous** /məˈnɒg.ə.məs US -ˈnɑː.gə-/.
gamp (G) gæmp **-s** -s
gamut ˈgæm.ət, -ʌt **-s** -s
gam|y ˈgeɪ.m|i **-ier** -i.əʳ US -i.ɚ **-iest** -i.ɪst, -i.əst **-iness** -ɪ.nəs, -ɪ.nɪs
-gamy -gə.mi
Note: Suffix. Normally unstressed, e.g. **monogamy** /məˈnɒg.ə.mi US -ˈnɑː.gə-/.
Gandalf ˈgæn.dælf US -dælf, -dɑːlf
gander (G) ˈgæn.dəʳ US -dɚ **-s** -z
Gandh|i ˈgæn.d|i, ˈgɑːn- US ˈgɑːn-, ˈgæn- **-ian** -i.ən
Ganes(h)a gænˈiː.sə, -ˈeɪ.sə US -ʃə
gang gæŋ **-s** -z **-ing** -ɪŋ **-ed** -d
gang-bang ˈgæŋˌbæŋ **-s** -z **-ing** -ɪŋ **-ed** -d
Ganges ˈgæn.dʒiːz
gangland ˈgæŋ.lænd, -lənd
gangling ˈgæŋ.glɪŋ
gangli|on ˈgæŋ.gli|.ən, -ɒn US -ən **-a** -ə **-ons** -ənz, -ɒnz US -ənz
gangl|y ˈgæŋ.gl|i **-ier** -i.əʳ US -i.ɚ **-iest** -i.ɪst, -i.əst
gangplank ˈgæŋ.plæŋk **-s** -s
gangren|e ˈgæŋ.griːn US ˈ--, ˌ-ˈ- **-es** -z **-ing** -ɪŋ **-ed** -d

gangrenous 'gæŋ.grɪ.nəs (US) -grə-
gangsta 'gæŋk.stə
gangster 'gæŋk.stəʳ (US) -stɚ **-s** -z **-ism** -ɪ.zᵊm
gangway 'gæŋ.weɪ **-s** -z
ganister 'gæn.ɪ.stəʳ (US) -stɚ
ganja 'gæn.dʒə, 'gɑːn- (US) 'gɑːn-
gannet 'gæn.ɪt, -ət **-s** -s
Gannett 'gæn.ɪt, -ət
gannister 'gæn.ɪ.stəʳ (US) -stɚ
Gannon 'gæn.ən
gantr|y (G) 'gæn.tr|i **-ies** -iz
Ganymede 'gæn.ɪ.miːd (US) '-ə-
gaol dʒeɪl **-s** -z **-ing** -ɪŋ **-ed** -d
gaolbird 'dʒeɪl.bɜːd (US) -bɝːd **-s** -z
gaolbreak 'dʒeɪl.breɪk **-s** -s
gaoler 'dʒeɪ.ləʳ (US) -lɚ **-s** -z
gap gæp **-s** -s
gap|e geɪp **-es** -s **-ing** -ɪŋ **-ed** -t
garag|e 'gær.ɑːʒ, -ɪdʒ, -ɑːdʒ *occasionally:* gə'rɑːdʒ, -rɑːʒ (US) gə'rɑːʒ, -'rɑːdʒ **-es** -ɪz **-ing** -ɪŋ **-ed** -d **'garage ˌsale** (US) **ga'rage ˌsale**
garam masala ˌgɑː.rəm.mə'sɑː.lə, -mɑː'sɑː-
Garamond 'gær.ə.mɒnd (US) 'ger-, 'gær-, -mɑːnd
garb gɑːb (US) gɑːrb **-s** -z **-ed** -d
garbage 'gɑː.bɪdʒ (US) 'gɑːr- **'garbage ˌcan**; **'garbage disˌposal**; **'garbage ˌman**
garbanzo gɑː'bæn.zəʊ (US) gɑːr'bɑːn.zoʊ **-s** -z
garbl|e 'gɑː.bḷ (US) 'gɑːr- **-es** -z **-ing** -ɪŋ, '-blɪŋ **-ed** -d
Garbo 'gɑː.bəʊ (US) 'gɑːr.boʊ
Garcia *English surname:* 'gɑː.si.ə, 'gɑː.ʃi.ə (US) gɑːr'siː.ə, 'gɑːr.si-
Garcia, Garcia *Spanish surname:* gɑː'siː.ə (US) gɑːr-
Garcia Lorca gɑːˌsiː.ə'lɔː.kə (US) gɑːrˌsiː.ə'lɔːr.kə
Garcia Márquez gɑːˌsiː.ə'mɑː.kez, -kes (US) gɑːrˌsiː.ə.mɑːr'kez, -'kes, -'keθ
garçon, garcon 'gɑː.sɒŋ, -sɒn; gɑː'sɔ̃ŋ (US) gɑːr'soʊn, -'sɔ̃ː **-s** -z
garda *Irish police:* 'gɑː.də (US) 'gɑːr- **gardai** gɑː'diː (US) gɑːr-
Garda *Italian lake:* 'gɑː.də (US) 'gɑːr-
garden (G) 'gɑː.dᵊn (US) 'gɑːr- **-s** -z **-ing** -ɪŋ **-ed** -d **'garden ˌcentre**; **ˌgarden 'city**; **'garden ˌparty**
gardener 'gɑː.dᵊn.əʳ; 'gɑːd.nəʳ (US) 'gɑːr.dᵊn.ɚ; 'gɑːrd.nɚ **-s** -z
gardenia gɑː'diː.ni.ə (US) gɑːr-, '-njə **-s** -z
Gardiner 'gɑː.dᵊn.əʳ; 'gɑːd.nəʳ (US) 'gɑːr.dᵊn.ɚ; 'gɑːrd.nɚ
Gardner 'gɑːd.nəʳ (US) 'gɑːrd.nɚ
Gare du Nord ˌgɑː.djuː'nɔːʳ (US) ˌgɑːr.duː'nɔːr, -djuː'-
garefowl 'geə.faʊl (US) 'ger- **-s** -z
Gareth 'gær.əθ, -eθ, -ɪθ (US) 'ger-, 'gær-
Garfield 'gɑː.fiːld (US) 'gɑːr-
garfish 'gɑː.fɪʃ (US) 'gɑːr-
Garforth 'gɑː.fəθ, -fɔːθ (US) 'gɑːr.fɚθ, -fɔːrθ
Garfunkel ˌgɑː'fʌŋ.kᵊl, '--- (US) 'gɑːr.fʌŋ-
garganey 'gɑː.gᵊn.i (US) 'gɑːr- **-s** -z
Gargantua gɑː'gæn.tju.ə, -tʃu- (US) gɑːr'gæn.tʃu-, -tju-
gargantuan gɑː'gæn.tju.ən, -tʃu- (US) gɑːr'gæn.tʃu-, -tʃu-
Gargery 'gɑː.dʒᵊr.i (US) 'gɑːr-
gargl|e 'gɑː.gḷ (US) 'gɑːr- **-es** -z **-ing/s** -ɪŋ/z, '-glɪŋ **-ed** -d
gargoyle 'gɑː.gɔɪl (US) 'gɑːr- **-s** -z
garibaldi (G) ˌgær.ɪ'bɔːl.di, -ə'-, -'bæl-, -'bɒl- (US) ˌger-, ˌgær-, -'bɑːl- **-s** -z
Garioch 'gær.i.ɒk, -ɒx (US) 'ger.i.ɑːk, 'gær-
garish 'geə.rɪʃ, 'gɑː- (US) 'ger.ɪʃ, 'gær- **-ly** -li **-ness** -nəs, -nɪs
garland (G) 'gɑː.lənd (US) 'gɑːr- **-s** -z **-ing** -ɪŋ **-ed** -ɪd
garlic 'gɑː.lɪk (US) 'gɑːr- **-ky** -i
Garlick 'gɑː.lɪk (US) 'gɑːr-
Garman 'gɑː.mən (US) 'gɑːr-
gar|ment 'gɑː|.mənt (US) 'gɑːr- **-ments** -mənts **-mented** -mən.tɪd (US) -mən.t̬ɪd
garner (G) 'gɑː.nəʳ (US) 'gɑːr.nɚ **-s** -z **-ing** -ɪŋ **-ed** -d
garnet 'gɑː.nɪt, -nət (US) 'gɑːr- **-s** -s
Garnet(t) 'gɑː.nɪt, -nət (US) 'gɑːr-
Garnham 'gɑː.nəm (US) 'gɑːr-
garnish 'gɑː.nɪʃ (US) 'gɑːr- **-es** -ɪz **-ing** -ɪŋ **-ed** -t
garnishee ˌgɑː.nɪ'ʃiː (US) ˌgɑːr- **-s** -z **-ing** -ɪŋ **-d** -d
garnishment 'gɑː.nɪʃ.mənt (US) 'gɑːr- **-s** -s
garniture 'gɑː.nɪ.tʃəʳ (US) 'gɑːr.nɪ.tʃɚ
Garonne gær'ɒn (US) -'ɔːn, -'ɑːn
Garrard 'gær.əd, -ɑːd (US) 'ger.ɚd, 'gær-; gə'rɑːrd
Garratt 'gær.ət (US) 'ger-, 'gær-
Garraway 'gær.ə.weɪ (US) 'ger-, 'gær-
garret 'gær.ət, -ɪt (US) 'ger-, 'gær- **-s** -s
Garret(t) 'gær.ət, -ɪt (US) 'ger-, 'gær-
Garrick 'gær.ɪk (US) 'ger-, 'gær-
Garrioch *district in Scotland:* 'gɪə.ri (US) 'ger.i *surname:* 'gær.i.ək, -əx (US) 'ger-, 'gær-
garrison (G) 'gær.ɪ.sᵊn, '-ə- (US) 'ger.ə-, 'gær- **-s** -z **-ing** -ɪŋ **-ed** -d
Garrod 'gær.əd (US) 'ger-, 'gær-
Garrold 'gær.ᵊld (US) 'ger-, 'gær-
garrot 'gær.ət (US) 'ger-, 'gær- **-s** -s
garro|t(t)e gə'rɒ|t (US) -'rɑː|t, -'roʊ|t; 'ger.ə|t **-t(t)es** -ts **-t(t)ing** -tɪŋ (US) -t̬ɪŋ **-t(t)ed** -tɪd (US) -t̬ɪd **-t(t)er/s** -təʳ/z (US) -t̬ɚ/z
garrulity gær'uː.lə.ti, gə'ruː-, -'rjuː-, -lɪ- (US) ger'uː.lə.t̬i, gær-
garrulous 'gær.ᵊl.əs, -ʊl-, -jʊl- (US) 'ger.ᵊl-, -jᵊl- **-ly** -li **-ness** -nəs, -nɪs
Garston 'gɑː.stᵊn (US) 'gɑːr-
gart|er 'gɑː.t|əʳ (US) 'gɑːr.t̬|ɚ **-ers** -əz (US) -ɚz **-ering** -ᵊr.ɪŋ **-ered** -əd (US) -ɚd
garth (G) gɑːθ (US) gɑːrθ **-s** -s
Gartmore 'gɑːt.mɔːʳ (US) 'gɑːrt.mɔːr
Gartward 'gɑːt.wəd, -wɔːd (US) 'gɑːrt.wɚd
Garuda gær'uː.də (US) ger-, gær-
Garvagh 'gɑː.və (US) 'gɑːr-
Garvaghy ˌgɑː'væ.hi (US) 'gɑːr-
Garwood 'gɑː.wʊd (US) 'gɑːr-
Gary 'gær.i (US) 'ger-, 'gær-
Garza 'gɑː.zə (US) 'gɑːr-
gas (*n.*) gæs **-(s)es** -ɪz **'gas ˌchamber**; **'gas ˌmask**; **'gas ˌstation**
gas (*v.*) gæs **-ses** -ɪz **-sing** -ɪŋ **-sed** -t
gasbag 'gæs.bæg **-s** -z
Gascoigne 'gæs.kɔɪn (US) gæs'kɔɪn, '--
Gascon 'gæs.kən **-s** -z
gasconad|e ˌgæs.kə'neɪd **-es** -z **-ing** -ɪŋ **-ed** -ɪd
Gascony 'gæs.kə.ni
Gascoyne 'gæs.kɔɪn (US) gæs'kɔɪn, '--
gaselier ˌgæs.ə'lɪəʳ (US) -'lɪr **-s** -z
gaseous 'gæs.i.əs, 'geɪ.si-, '-ʃəs; 'gæʃ.əs (US) 'gæs.i.əs, 'gæʃ-; 'gæʃ.əs **-ness** -nəs, -nɪs
gas-guzzler 'gæsˌgʌz.ləʳ, -ˌgʌz.ḷ.əʳ (US) ˌ-ḷ.ɚ, ˌ-lɚ **-s** -z
gash gæʃ **-es** -ɪz **-ing** -ɪŋ **-ed** -t
gasholder 'gæsˌhəʊl.dəʳ (US) -ˌhoʊl.dɚ **-s** -z
gasi|fy 'gæs.ɪ|.faɪ, '-ə- (US) '-ə- **-fies** -faɪz **-fying** -faɪ.ɪŋ **-fied** -faɪd
Gaskell 'gæs.kᵊl, -kel
gasket 'gæs.kɪt **-s** -s
gaskin (G) 'gæs.kɪn **-s** -z
gaslight 'gæs.laɪt **-s** -s
gas|man 'gæs|.mæn **-men** -men
gasohol 'gæs.ə.hɒl (US) -hɔːl, -hɑːl
gasoline, gasolene 'gæs.ᵊl.iːn, ˌ--'-
gasometer gæs'ɒm.ɪ.təʳ, gə'sɒm-, -ə.təʳ (US) gæs'ɑː.mə.t̬ɚ **-s** -z
gasp gɑːsp (US) gæsp **-s** -s **-ing** -ɪŋ **-ed** -t
Gaspé gæs'peɪ
gasper 'gɑː.spəʳ (US) 'gæs.pɚ **-s** -z
gass|y 'gæs|.i **-ier** -i.əʳ (US) -i.ɚ **-iest** -i.ɪst, -i.əst **-iness** -ɪ.nəs, -ɪ.nɪs
gasteropod 'gæs.tᵊr.əʊ.pɒd (US) -ə.pɑːd **-s** -z
Gaston 'gæs.tɒn, gæs'tɔ̃ːŋ (US) -tən, gæs'tɑːn, -ɔ̃ːn
gastric 'gæs.trɪk
gastrin 'gæs.trɪn
gastritis gæs'traɪ.tɪs (US) -t̬ɪs
gastro- gæs.trəʊ-; gæs'trɒ- (US) gæs.troʊ-, -trə-; gæs'trɑː-

Note: Prefix. Normally takes either primary or secondary stress on the first syllable, e.g. **gastronome** /ˈgæs.trə.nəʊm ⓊⓈ -noʊm/, **gastronomic** /ˌgæs.trəˈnɒm.ɪk ⓊⓈ -ˈnɑː.mɪk/, or primary stress on the second syllable, e.g. **gastronomy** /gæsˈtrɒn.ə.mi ⓊⓈ -ˈtrɑː.nə-/.

gastroenteritis ˌgæs.trəʊˌen.təˈraɪ.tɪs ⓊⓈ -troʊˌen.t̬əˈraɪ.t̬ɪs

gastroenterolog|ist ˌgæs.trəʊˌen.təˈrɒl.ə.dʒ|ɪst ⓊⓈ -troʊˌen.t̬əˈrɑː.lə.dʒ|ɪst **-ists** -ɪsts **-y** -i

gastrointestinal ˌgæs.trəʊˌɪn.tesˈtaɪ.nəl, -ɪnˈtes.tɪ.nəl, -tən.əl ⓊⓈ -troʊ.ɪnˈtes.tən.əl

gastronome ˈgæs.trə.nəʊm ⓊⓈ -noʊm **-s** -z

gastronomic ˌgæs.trəˈnɒm.ɪk ⓊⓈ -ˈnɑː.mɪk **-al** -əl

gastronom|y gæsˈtrɒn.ə.m|i ⓊⓈ -ˈtrɑː.nə- **-ist/s** -ɪst/s

gastropod ˈgæs.trəʊ.pɒd ⓊⓈ -trə.pɑːd **-s** -z

gastropub ˈgæs.trəʊ.pʌb ⓊⓈ -troʊ- **-s** -z

gasworks ˈgæs.wɜːks ⓊⓈ -wɝːks

gat|e geɪt **-es** -s **-ing** -ɪŋ ⓊⓈ ˈgeɪ.t̬ɪŋ **-ed** -ɪd ⓊⓈ ˈgeɪ.t̬əd

gâteau, gateau ˈgæt.əʊ ⓊⓈ gætˈoʊ **-s** -z

gâteaux, gateaux ⓊⓈ gætˈoʊ, -z

gatecrash ˈgeɪt.kræʃ **-es** -ɪz **-ing** -ɪŋ **-ed** -t **-er/s** -əʳ/z ⓊⓈ -ɚ/z

gatehou|se ˈgeɪt.haʊ|s **-ses** -zɪz

gatekeeper ˈgeɪtˌkiː.pəʳ ⓊⓈ -pɚ **-s** -z

gateleg ˈgeɪt.leg **-s** -z

gate-legged ˈgeɪtˌlegd

gateless ˈgeɪt.ləs, -lɪs

gatepost ˈgeɪt.pəʊst ⓊⓈ -poʊst **-s** -s

Gates geɪts

Gateshead ˈgeɪts.hed, ˌgeɪtsˈhed

gateway (G) ˈgeɪt.weɪ **-s** -z

Gath gæθ

gath|er ˈgæð|.əʳ ⓊⓈ -ɚ **-ers** -əz ⓊⓈ -ɚz **-ering/s** -ər.ɪŋ/z **-ered** -əd ⓊⓈ -ɚd **-erer/s** -ər.əʳ/z ⓊⓈ -ɚ.ɚ/z

Gatley ˈgæt.li

Gatling ˈgæt.lɪŋ

gator ˈgeɪ.tə ⓊⓈ -t̬ɚ **-s** -z

Gatorade® ˌgeɪ.tərˈeɪd ⓊⓈ ˈgeɪ.t̬əˌreɪd

Gatsby ˈgæts.bi

Gatt, GATT gæt

Gatting ˈgæt.ɪŋ ⓊⓈ ˈgæt̬-

Gatty ˈgæt.i ⓊⓈ ˈgæt̬-

Gatwick ˈgæt.wɪk ˌ**Gatwick ˈAirport**

gauche gəʊʃ ⓊⓈ goʊʃ **-ly** -li **-ness** -nəs, -nɪs

gaucherie ˈgəʊ.ʃər.i; ˌgəʊ.ʃərˈiː ⓊⓈ ˌgoʊ.ʃəˈriː **-s** -z

gaucho ˈgaʊ.tʃəʊ ⓊⓈ -tʃoʊ **-s** -z

gaud gɔːd ⓊⓈ gɑːd, gɔːd **-s** -z

Gauden ˈgɔː.dən ⓊⓈ ˈgɑː-, ˈgɔː-

Gaudí ˈgaʊ.di, -ˈ-

gaud|y ˈgɔː.d|i ⓊⓈ ˈgɑː-, ˈgɔː- **-ier** -i.əʳ ⓊⓈ -i.ɚ **-iest** -i.ɪst, -i.əst **-ily** -ɪ.li, -əl.i **-iness** -ɪ.nəs, -ɪ.nɪs

gaug|e geɪdʒ **-es** -ɪz **-ing** -ɪŋ **-ed** -d **-eable** -ə.bl̩

gauger ˈgeɪ.dʒəʳ ⓊⓈ -dʒɚ **-s** -z

Gauguin ˈgəʊ.gæ̃n, -gæn ⓊⓈ goʊˈgæ̃, -ˈgæn

Gaul gɔːl **-s** -z **-ish** -ɪʃ

gauleiter ˈgaʊ.laɪ.təʳ ⓊⓈ -t̬ɚ **-s** -z

Gaull|ism ˈgəʊ.l|ɪ.zəm ⓊⓈ ˈgɑː-, ˈgoʊ- **-ist/s** -ɪst/s

Gauloise(s)® ˈgəʊl.wɑːz, ˌ-ˈ- ⓊⓈ goʊlˈwɑːz, gɑːl-

Gault gɔːlt, gɒlt ⓊⓈ gɔːlt, gɑːlt

Gaultier ˈgɔːl.ti.eɪ ⓊⓈ ˈgɔːl-, ˈgɑːl-

Gaumont® ˈgəʊ.mɒnt, -mənt ⓊⓈ ˈgoʊ.mɑːnt

gaun|t (G) gɔːn|t ⓊⓈ gɑːn|t, gɔːn|t **-ter** -təʳ ⓊⓈ -t̬ɚ **-test** -tɪst, -təst ⓊⓈ -t̬ɪst, -t̬əst **-tly** -t.li **-tness** -t.nəs, -nɪs

gauntle|t (G) ˈgɔːnt.lə|t, -lɪ|t ⓊⓈ ˈgɑːnt-, ˈgɔːnt- **-ts** -ts **-ted** -tɪd ⓊⓈ -t̬ɪd

Gauntlett ˈgɔːnt.lət, -lɪt ⓊⓈ ˈgɑːnt-, ˈgɔːnt

gauss (G) gaʊs **-es** -ɪz

gauz|e gɔːz ⓊⓈ gɑːz, gɔːz **-es** -ɪz **-y** -i **-iness** -ɪ.nəs, -ɪ.nɪs

gave *(from* **give)** geɪv

gavel ˈgæv.əl **-s** -z

gavelkind ˈgæv.əl.kaɪnd, -kɪnd

gavel-to-gavel ˌgæv.əl.təˈgæv.əl

Gaveston ˈgæv.ɪ.stən, ˈ-ə-

Gavey ˈgeɪ.vi

Gavin ˈgæv.ɪn

gavotte gəˈvɒt, gæ- ⓊⓈ -ˈvɑːt **-s** -s

Gawain ˈgɑː.weɪn, ˈgæw.eɪn, -ɪn;

gawd gɔːd ⓊⓈ gɔːd, gɑːd

Gawith ˈgeɪ.wɪθ, ˈgaʊ.ɪθ

gawk gɔːk ⓊⓈ gɑːk, gɔːk **-s** -s **-ing** -ɪŋ **-ed** -t

gawk|y ˈgɔː.k|i ⓊⓈ ˈgɑː-, ˈgɔː- **-ier** -i.əʳ ⓊⓈ -i.ɚ **-iest** -i.ɪst, -i.əst **-iness** -ɪ.nəs, -ɪ.nɪs

gawp gɔːp ⓊⓈ gɑːp, gɔːp **-s** -s **-ing** -ɪŋ **-ed** -t

Gawthrop ˈgɔː.θrɒp, -θrəp ⓊⓈ ˈgɑː.θrɑːp, ˈgɔː-, -θrəp

gay (G) geɪ **-er** -əʳ ⓊⓈ -ɚ **-est** -ɪst, -əst **-s** -z **gaily** ˈgeɪ.li **gayness** ˈgeɪ.nəs, -nɪs

Gaye geɪ

Gayle geɪl

Gaylord ˈgeɪ.lɔːd ⓊⓈ -lɔːrd

Gay-Lussac ˌgeɪˈluː.sæk ⓊⓈ -ləˈsæk

Gaynham ˈgeɪ.nəm

Gaynor ˈgeɪ.nəʳ ⓊⓈ -nɚ

Gaza *in the Middle East:* ˈgɑː.zə *in biblical use also:* ˈgeɪ.zə ⓊⓈ ˈgɑː.zə, ˈgæz.ə, ˈgeɪ.zə ˌ**Gaza ˈStrip**

Gaza *Greek scholar:* ˈgɑː.zə

gaz|e geɪz **-es** -ɪz **-ing** -ɪŋ **-ed** -d **-er/s** -əʳ/z ⓊⓈ -ɚ/z

gazebo gəˈziː.bəʊ ⓊⓈ -ˈziː.boʊ, -ˈzeɪ- **-s** -z

gazelle gəˈzel **-s** -z

ga|zette gə|ˈzet **-zettes** -ˈzets **-zetting** -ˈzet.ɪŋ ⓊⓈ -ˈzet̬.ɪŋ **-zetted** -ˈzet.ɪd ⓊⓈ -ˈzet̬.əd

gazetteer ˌgæz.əˈtɪəʳ, -ɪˈ- ⓊⓈ -ˈtɪr **-s** -z

Gaziantep ˌgɑː.zi.ɑːnˈtep

gazogene ˈgæz.əʊ.dʒiːn ⓊⓈ ˈ-ə-

gazpacho gæsˈpætʃ.əʊ ⓊⓈ gəˈspɑː.tʃoʊ, gəzˈpɑː-

gazump gəˈzʌmp **-s** -s **-ing** -ɪŋ **-ed** -t, -ˈzʌmt

gazunder gəˈzʌn.dəʳ ⓊⓈ -dɚ **-s** -s **-ing** -ɪŋ **-ed** -d

Gazza ˈgæz.ə

GB ˌdʒiːˈbiː

GBH ˌdʒiː.biːˈeɪtʃ

GCE ˌdʒiː.siːˈiː **-s** -z

GCHQ ˌdʒiː.siː.eɪtʃˈkjuː

GCSE ˌdʒiː.siː.esˈiː **-s** -z

Gdansk gəˈdæntsk, -ˈdaɪntsk ⓊⓈ -ˈdɑːntsk, -ˈdæntsk

g'day gəˈdeɪ

GDP ˌdʒiː.diːˈpiː

GDR ˌdʒiː.diːˈɑːʳ ⓊⓈ -ˈɑːr

GE® ˌdʒiːˈiː

gear gɪəʳ ⓊⓈ gɪr **-s** -z **-ing** -ɪŋ **-ed** -d ˈ**gear** ˌ**lever**

gearbox ˈgɪə.bɒks ⓊⓈ ˈgɪr.bɑːks **-es** -ɪz

Geare gɪəʳ ⓊⓈ gɪr

gearshift ˈgɪə.ʃɪft ⓊⓈ ˈgɪr- **-s** -s

Geary ˈgɪə.ri ⓊⓈ ˈgɪr.i

Geat giːt **-s** -s

gecko ˈgek.əʊ ⓊⓈ -oʊ **-(e)s** -z

Ged ged, dʒed

GED ˌdʒiː.iːˈdiː

Geddes ˈged.ɪs ⓊⓈ -iːz

geddit ˈged.ɪt ⓊⓈ -ət

gee (G) dʒiː **-s** -z **-ing** -ɪŋ **-d** -d ˌ**gee ˈwhiz**

geegaw ˈgiː.gɔː ⓊⓈ -gɑː, -gɔː **-s** -z

geegee ˈdʒiː.dʒiː **-s** -z

geek giːk **-s** -s

geek|y ˈgiː.k|i **-ier** -i.əʳ ⓊⓈ -i.ɚ **-iest** -i.ɪst, -i.əst

Geelong dʒɪˈlɒŋ, dʒə- ⓊⓈ -ˈlɑːŋ, -ˈlɔːŋ

Geering ˈgɪə.rɪŋ ⓊⓈ ˈgɪr.ɪŋ

geese *(plur. of* **goose)** giːs

Geeson ˈdʒiː.sən, ˈgiː-

gee-up ˌdʒiːˈʌp, ˈdʒiː.ʌp

geezer ˈgiː.zəʳ ⓊⓈ -zɚ **-s** -z

Geffen ˈgef.ən

gefilte gəˈfɪl.tə, gɪ- **geˈfilte** ˌ**fish, geˌfilte ˈfish**

Gehazi gɪˈheɪ.zaɪ, ge-, gə-, -ˈhɑː-, -zi

Gehenna gɪˈhen.ə, gə-

Gehrig ˈger.ɪg

Gehry ˈgeə.ri ⓊⓈ ˈger.i

Geierstein ˈgaɪə.staɪn ⓊⓈ ˈgaɪɚ-

Geiger 'gaɪ.gəʳ ⓤⓢ -gɚ 'Geiger ˌcounter
Geikie 'giː.ki
geisha 'geɪ.ʃə ⓤⓢ 'geɪ-, 'giː- -s -z
gel *girl:* gel -s -z
gel *jelly:* dʒel -s -s -ling -ɪŋ -led -d
gelatin 'dʒel.ə.tɪn
gelatine 'dʒel.ə.tiːn, -tɪn, ˌ--'-
gelatiniz|e, -is|e dʒə'læt.ɪ.naɪz, dʒel'æt-, dʒɪ'læt-, -ᵊn.aɪz ⓤⓢ dʒə'læt.ᵊn.aɪz -es -ɪz -ing -ɪŋ -ed -d
gelatinous dʒə'læt.ɪ.nəs, dʒel'æt-, dʒɪ'læt-, -ᵊn.əs ⓤⓢ dʒə'læt.ᵊn.əs -ly -li
geld geld -s -z -ing -ɪŋ -ed -ɪd
Gelderland 'gel.də.lænd ⓤⓢ -dɚ-
gelding 'gel.dɪŋ -s -z
Geldof 'gel.dɒf ⓤⓢ -dɑːf
gelid 'dʒel.ɪd -ly -li -ness -nəs, -nɪs
gelignite 'dʒel.ɪg.naɪt, -əg-
Gell gel, dʒel
Gellan 'gel.ən
Gellatl(e)y 'gel.ət.li, gel'æt-, gə'læt- ⓤⓢ gel'æt-, gə'læt-
Geller 'gel.əʳ ⓤⓢ -ɚ
Gelligaer ˌgeθ.li'geəʳ, -'gaɪ.əʳ ⓤⓢ -'ger, -'gaɪɚ
gem (G) dʒem -s -z
Gemara gə'mɑː.rə, gem'ɑː-, gɪ'mɑː-
gemfish 'dʒem.fɪʃ -es -ɪz
gemi|nate (*v.*) 'dʒem.ɪ|.neɪt, '-ə- -nates -neɪts -nating -neɪ.tɪŋ ⓤⓢ -neɪ.t̬ɪŋ -nated -neɪ.tɪd ⓤⓢ -neɪ.t̬əd
geminate (*adj.*) 'dʒem.ɪ.nət
gemination ˌdʒem.ɪ'neɪ.ʃᵊn, -ə'-
Gemini *constellation:* 'dʒem.ɪ.naɪ, '-ə-, -niː *aircraft:* 'dʒem.ɪ.ni, '-ə-
Geminian ˌdʒem.ɪ'naɪ.ən, -ə'-, -'niː- -s -z
gem|ma (G) 'dʒem|.ə -mae -iː
gemmiferous dʒə'mɪf.ᵊr.əs, dʒem'ɪf-
gemmology dʒem'ɒl.ə.dʒi ⓤⓢ -'ɑː.lə-
gemmule 'dʒem.juːl -s -z
gemology dʒem'ɒl.ə.dʒi ⓤⓢ -'ɑː.lə-
Gemsbok 'gemz.bɒk, -bʌk ⓤⓢ -bɑːk -s -s
gemshorn 'gemz.hɔːn ⓤⓢ -hɔːrn -s -z
gemstone 'dʒem.stəʊn ⓤⓢ -stoʊn -s -z
gen dʒen -s -z -ning -ɪŋ -ed -d
gendarme 'ʒɑ̃ːn.dɑːm, 'ʒɔ̃ːn-, 'ʒɑːn- ⓤⓢ 'ʒɑːn.dɑːrm -s -z
gender 'dʒen.dəʳ ⓤⓢ -dɚ -s -z -ing -ɪŋ -ed -d
gender-bender 'dʒen.dəˌben.dəʳ ⓤⓢ -dɚˌben.dɚ -s -z
gene (G) dʒiːn -s -z
genealogical ˌdʒiː.ni.ə'lɒdʒ.ɪ.kᵊl ⓤⓢ ˌdʒiː.ni.ə'lɑː.dʒɪ-, ˌdʒen.i- -ly -i
genealogist ˌdʒiː.ni'æl.ə.dʒɪst ⓤⓢ ˌdʒiː.ni'-, ˌdʒen.i'- -s -s
genealog|y ˌdʒiː.ni'æl.ə.dʒ|i ⓤⓢ ˌdʒiː.ni'-, ˌdʒen.i'- -ies -iz
genera (*plur. of* **genus**) 'dʒen.ᵊr.ə

general 'dʒen.ᵊr.ᵊl -s -z -ly -i ˌgeneral as'sembly; ˌgeneral e'lection; ˌgeneral prac'titioner; ˌgeneral 'store; ˌGeneral 'Motors®
generalissimo ˌdʒen.ᵊr.ə'lɪs.ɪ.məʊ, '-ə- ⓤⓢ -ə.moʊ -s -z
generalist 'dʒen.ᵊr.ᵊl.ɪst, 'dʒen.rᵊl- -s -s
generalit|y ˌdʒen.ᵊ'ræl.ə.t|i, -ɪ.t|i ⓤⓢ -ə.t̬|i -ies -iz
generalization, -isa- ˌdʒen.ᵊr.ᵊl.aɪ'zeɪ.ʃᵊn, -ɪ'- ⓤⓢ -ɪ'- -s -z
generaliz|e, -is|e 'dʒen.ᵊr.ᵊl.aɪz ⓤⓢ -ə.laɪz -es -ɪz -ing -ɪŋ -ed -d -able -ə.bl̩
generalship 'dʒen.ᵊr.ᵊl.ʃɪp -s -s
gener|ate 'dʒen.ᵊr|.eɪt ⓤⓢ -ə.r|eɪt -ates -eɪts -ating -eɪ.tɪŋ ⓤⓢ -eɪ.t̬ɪŋ -ated -eɪ.tɪd ⓤⓢ -eɪ.t̬ɪd
generation ˌdʒen.ə'reɪ.ʃᵊn -al -s -z geneˈration ˌgap
generative 'dʒen.ᵊr.ə.tɪv ⓤⓢ -ə.t̬ɪv, '-ə.reɪ.t̬ɪv
generator 'dʒen.ᵊ.reɪ.təʳ ⓤⓢ -t̬ɚ -s -z
generatri|x 'dʒen.ᵊ.reɪ.trɪ|ks ⓤⓢ ˌdʒen.ə'reɪ- -ces -siːz
generic dʒə'ner.ɪk, dʒɪ-, dʒen'er- -ally -ᵊl.i, -li
generosity ˌdʒen.ᵊ'rɒs.ə.ti, -ɪ.ti ⓤⓢ -'rɑː.sə.t̬i
generous 'dʒen.ᵊr.əs -ly -li -ness -nəs, -nɪs
gene|sis (G) 'dʒen.ə|.sɪs, '-ɪ- -ses -siːz
Genesius dʒə'niː.si.əs, dʒen'iː-, dʒɪ'niː- ⓤⓢ -si-, -ʃi-, -zi-
Genesta dʒə'nes.tə, dʒen'es-, dʒɪ'nes-
genet *(D) animal:* 'dʒen.ɪt ⓤⓢ 'dʒen.ɪt, dʒə'net -s -s
Genet *French writer:* ʒə'neɪ
genetic dʒə'net.ɪk, dʒɪ- ⓤⓢ -'net̬.ɪk -s -s -ally -ᵊl.i, -li geˌnetic engi'neering; geˌnetic 'fingerprint
geneticist dʒə'net.ɪ.sɪst, dʒɪ-, '-ə- ⓤⓢ -'net̬.ə- -s -s
Geneva dʒə'niː.və, dʒɪ- Geˌneva Con'vention
Geneviève *French name:* ˌʒen.ə'vjev ⓤⓢ ˌʒen.ə'vjev, 'dʒen.ə.viːv
Genevieve *English name:* 'dʒen.ə.viːv, '-ɪ-, ˌ--'-
Genghis Khan ˌgeŋ.gɪs'kɑːn, ˌdʒeŋ-, -gɪz'-
genial *amiable:* 'dʒiː.ni.əl -ly -i -ness -nəs, -nɪs
genial *of the chin:* dʒɪ'niː.əl, dʒə-, -'naɪ-
geniality ˌdʒiː.ni'æl.ə.ti, -ɪ.ti ⓤⓢ -ə.t̬i
-genic -'dʒen.ɪk, -'dʒiː.nɪk
Note: Suffix. Words ending **-genic** normally carry primary stress on the penultimate syllable, e.g. **photogenic** /ˌfəʊ.təʊ'dʒen.ɪk ⓤⓢ ˌfoʊ.t̬oʊ'-/.

genie (G) 'dʒiː.ni -s -z
genii *(from* **genius***)* 'dʒiː.ni.aɪ
genista dʒə'nɪs.tə, dʒɪ-, dʒen'ɪs- -s -z
genital 'dʒen.ɪ.tᵊl, '-ə- ⓤⓢ -ət̬.ᵊl -s -z -ly -li
genitalia ˌdʒen.ɪ'teɪ.li.ə, -ə'- ⓤⓢ -'teɪ.li.ə, -'teɪl.jə
genitival ˌdʒen.ɪ'taɪ.vᵊl, -ə'-
genitive 'dʒen.ɪ.tɪv, '-ə- ⓤⓢ -ə.t̬ɪv -s -z
genito-urinary ˌdʒen.ɪ.təʊ'jʊə.rɪ.nᵊr.i, ˌ-ə-, -'jɔː-, -rᵊn.ᵊr- ⓤⓢ -ə.t̬oʊ'jʊr.ə.ner.i
geni|us 'dʒiː.ni|.əs -i -aɪ -uses -ə.sɪz
genius loci ˌdʒiː.ni.əs'ləʊ.saɪ ⓤⓢ -'loʊ- **genii loci** ˌdʒiː.ni.aɪ'-
Gennadi dʒə'nɑː.di, ge-
Gennesare|t gə'nez.ᵊr.ɪ|t, gɪ-, gen'ez-, -e|t, -ə|t ⓤⓢ gə'nes-, dʒə- -th -θ
Genoa 'dʒen.əʊ.ə, dʒə'nəʊ-, dʒɪ-, dʒen'əʊ- ⓤⓢ 'dʒen.ə.wə, dʒə'noʊ.ə
genocidal ˌdʒen.ə'saɪ.dᵊl *stress shift:* ˌgenocidal 'policies
genocide 'dʒen.ə.saɪd
Genoese ˌdʒen.əʊ'iːz ⓤⓢ -oʊ'iːz *stress shift:* ˌGenoese 'sailor
genome 'dʒiː.nəʊm ⓤⓢ -noʊm -s -z
genotype 'dʒen.əʊ.taɪp ⓤⓢ '-oʊ-
-genous -dʒə.nəs, -dʒɪ.nəs
Note: Suffix. Words containing **-genous** are normally stressed on the antepenultimate syllable, e.g. **androgenous** /æn'drɒdʒ.ᵊn.əs ⓤⓢ -'drɑː.dʒᵊn-/. Exceptions exist: see individual entries.
genre 'ʒɑ̃ː*n*.rə ⓤⓢ 'ʒɑːn.rə -s -z
gen|s dʒen|z -tes -tiːz
Genseric 'gen.sᵊr.ɪk, 'dʒen-
Gensing 'gen.zɪŋ, 'gen*t*.sɪŋ
gent *gentleman:* dʒent -s -s
Gent *surname:* gent
Gent *place in Belgium:* gent, xent
genteel dʒen'tiːl, dʒən- -ly -li -ness -nəs, -nɪs
gentes *(plur. of* **gens***)* 'dʒen.tiːz
gentian 'dʒen.*t*ʃᵊn, -*t*ʃi.ən -s -z
gentile (G) 'dʒen.taɪl -s -z
gentility ˌdʒen'tɪl.ə.ti ⓤⓢ -t̬i
gent|le (G) 'dʒen.t|l̩ -ler -l̩.əʳ, 'dʒent.ləʳ ⓤⓢ 'dʒen.t̬l̩.ɚ, 'dʒent.lɚ -lest -l̩.əst, -ɪst, 'dʒent.lɪst, -ləst -ly -li -leness -l̩.nəs, -nɪs 'gentle ˌsex
gentlefolk 'dʒen.tl̩.fəʊk ⓤⓢ 'dʒen.t̬l̩-foʊk -s -s
gentle|man 'dʒen.tl̩|.mən ⓤⓢ 'dʒen.t̬l̩- -men -mən, -men ˌgentleman's 'gentleman
gentle|man-at-arms ˌdʒen.tl̩|.mən.ət'ɑːmz ⓤⓢ -t̬l̩|.mən.ət'ɑːrmz -men-at-arms -mən.ət'ɑːmz, -men- ⓤⓢ -'ɑːrmz
gentlemanlike 'dʒen.tl̩.mən.laɪk ⓤⓢ 'dʒen.t̬l̩.-

gentlemanl|y 'dʒen.tl̩.mən.l|i (US) 'dʒen.t̬l̩- **-iness** -ɪ.nəs, -ɪ.nɪs
gentle|woman 'dʒen.tl̩|ˌwʊm.ən (US) 'dʒen.t̬l̩- **-women** -ˌwɪm.ɪn
gentrification ˌdʒen.trɪ.fɪ'keɪ.ʃᵊn, -trə- **-s** -z
gentrifier 'dʒen.trɪ.faɪ.əʳ, -trə- (US) -ɚ **-s** -z
gentrif|y 'dʒen.trɪ.f|aɪ, -trə- **-ies** -aɪz **-ying** -aɪ.ɪŋ **-ied** -aɪd
gentry (G) 'dʒen.tri
genuflect 'dʒen.jʊ.flekt, -jə- **-s** -s **-ing** -ɪŋ **-ed** -ɪd
genuflection, genuflexion ˌdʒen.jʊ'flek.ʃᵊn, -jə- **-s** -z
genuine 'dʒen.ju.ɪn **-ly** -li **-ness** -nəs, -nɪs
genus 'dʒiː.nəs, 'dʒen.əs **genera** 'dʒen.ᵊr.ə
-geny -dʒə.ni, -dʒɪ.ni
Note: Suffix. Words containing **-geny** are stressed in a similar way to those containing **-genous**; see above.
geo- dʒiː.əʊ-; dʒi'ɒ-, 'dʒɒ- (US) dʒiː.oʊ-, -ə-; dʒi'ɑː-
Note: Prefix. Normally takes either primary or secondary stress on the first syllable, e.g. **geomancy** /'dʒiː.əʊ.mænt.si (US) '-ə-/, **geocentric** /ˌdʒiː.əʊ'sen.trɪk (US) -oʊ'-/, or primary stress on the second syllable, e.g. **geography** /dʒi'ɒg.rə.fi (US) -'ɑː.grə-/.
geocentric ˌdʒiː.əʊ'sen.trɪk (US) -oʊ'- **-al** -ᵊl **-ally** -ᵊl.i, -li
geochemical ˌdʒiː.əʊ'kem.ɪ.kᵊl (US) -oʊ'-
geochemist ˌdʒiː.əʊ'kem.ɪst, 'dʒiː.əʊˌkem- (US) ˌdʒiː.oʊ'kem- **-s** -s
geochemistry ˌdʒiː.əʊ'kem.ɪ.stri (US) -oʊ'-
geode 'dʒiː.əʊd (US) -oʊd **-s** -z
geodesic ˌdʒiː.əʊ'des.ɪk, -'diː.sɪk (US) -ə'- **-al** -ᵊl
geodesy dʒi'ɒd.ɪ.si, '-ə- (US) -'ɑː.də-
geodic dʒi'ɒd.ɪk (US) -'ɑː.dɪk
Geoff dʒef
Geoffr(e)y 'dʒef.ri
Geoghegan 'geɪ.gᵊn, 'gəʊ.gᵊn, gɪ'heɪ.gᵊn (US) 'goʊ.gᵊn
geographer dʒi'ɒg.rə.fəʳ (US) -'ɑː.grə.fɚ **-s** -z
geographic ˌdʒiː.əʊ'græf.ɪk (US) -ə'- **-al** -ᵊl **-ally** -ᵊl.i, -li
geograph|y dʒi'ɒg.rə.f|i; 'dʒɒg- (US) dʒi'ɑː.grə- **-ies** -iz
geologic ˌdʒi.əʊ'lɒdʒ.ɪk (US) -ə'lɑː.dʒɪk **-al** -ᵊl **-ally** -ᵊl.i, -li
geologist dʒi'ɒl.ə.dʒɪst (US) -'ɑː.lə- **-s** -s
geologiz|e, -is|e dʒi'ɒl.ə.dʒaɪz (US) -'ɑː.lə- **-es** -ɪz **-ing** -ɪŋ **-ed** -d
geology dʒi'ɒl.ə.dʒi (US) -'ɑː.lə-
geomagnetic ˌdʒiː.əʊ.mæg'net.ɪk, -məg'- (US) -oʊ.mæg'net̬.ɪk
geomagnetism ˌdʒiː.əʊ'mæg.nɪ.tɪ.zᵊm, -nə- (US) -oʊ'mæg.nə-
geomancy 'dʒiː.əʊ.mænt.si (US) '-ə-
geometer dʒi'ɒm.ɪ.təʳ, '-ə- (US) -'ɑː.mə.t̬ɚ **-s** -z
geometric ˌdʒiː.əʊ'met.rɪk (US) -ə'- **-al** -ᵊl **-ally** -ᵊl.i, -li
geometrician ˌdʒiː.əʊ.mə'trɪʃ.ᵊn, dʒiˌɒm.ə'-, -ɪ'- (US) ˌdʒiː.ə.mə'-; dʒiˌɑː- **-s** -z
geometr|y dʒi'ɒm.ɪ.tr|i, '-ə-; 'dʒɒm- (US) dʒi'ɑː.mə- **-ies** -iz
geomorphologic ˌdʒiː.əʊˌmɔː.fə'lɒdʒ.ɪk (US) -oʊˌmɔːr.fə'lɑː.dʒɪk **-al** -ᵊl **-ally** -ᵊl.i, -li
geomorpholog|y ˌdʒiː.əʊ.mɔː'fɒl.ə.dʒ|i (US) -oʊ.mɔːr'fɑː.lə- **-ist/s** -ɪst/s
geophysical ˌdʒiː.əʊ'fɪz.ɪ.kᵊl (US) -oʊ'-
geophysicist ˌdʒi.əʊ'fɪz.ɪ.sɪst (US) -oʊ'- **-s** -s
geophysics ˌdʒiː.əʊ'fɪz.ɪks (US) -oʊ'-
geopolitical ˌdʒiː.əʊ.pə'lɪt.ɪ.kᵊl (US) -oʊ.pə'lɪt̬- **-ly** -i
geopolitics ˌdʒiː.əʊ'pɒl.ə.tɪks, '-ɪ- (US) -oʊ'pɑː.lə-
Geordie 'dʒɔː.di (US) 'dʒɔːr- **-s** -z
George dʒɔːdʒ (US) dʒɔːrdʒ
Georgetown 'dʒɔːdʒ.taʊn (US) 'dʒɔːrdʒ-
georgette dʒɔː'dʒet (US) dʒɔːr-
Georgi|a 'dʒɔː.dʒ|ə, -dʒi|.ə (US) 'dʒɔːr- **-an/s** -ən/z
Georgiana ˌdʒɔː.dʒi'ɑː.nə (US) ˌdʒɔːr'dʒæn.ə, -dʒi'æn-
georgic (G) 'dʒɔː.dʒɪk (US) 'dʒɔːr- **-s** -s
Georgina dʒɔː'dʒiː.nə (US) dʒɔːr'-
geoscience ˌdʒiː.əʊ'saɪ.ənts (US) -oʊ'-
geostationary ˌdʒiː.əʊ'steɪ.ʃᵊn.ᵊr.i, -ri (US) -oʊ'steɪ.ʃᵊn.er-
geothermal ˌdʒiː.əʊ'θɜː.mᵊl (US) -oʊ'θɝː-
geotropic ˌdʒiː.əʊ'trɒp.ɪk (US) -ə'trɑː.pɪk
geotropism dʒi'ɒt.rə.pɪ.zᵊm (US) -'ɑː.trə- **-s** -z
Geraint 'ger.aɪnt, -'- (US) dʒə'reɪnt
Gerald 'dʒer.ᵊld
Geraldine 'dʒer.ᵊl.diːn, -daɪn
Note: /'dʒer.ᵊl.daɪn/ in Coleridge's 'Christabel'.
Geraldton 'dʒer.ᵊld.tᵊn
geranium dʒə'reɪ.ni.əm, dʒɪ- **-s** -z
Gerard 'dʒer.ɑːd, 'dʒer.əd, dʒer'ɑːd, dʒə'rɑːd (US) dʒə'rɑːrd
Gerbeau dʒeə'bəʊ, dʒɜː-, '-- (US) dʒer'boʊ, '--
gerbil 'dʒɜː.bᵊl, -bɪl (US) 'dʒɝː.bᵊl **-s** -z
gerfalcon 'dʒɜːˌfɔːl.kᵊn, -ˌfɔː.kᵊn (US) 'dʒɝːˌfɑːl-, -ˌfæl-, -ˌfɔː- **-s** -z
Note: In British English, those who practise the sport of falconry pronounce /-ˌfɔː-/.
Gergesene 'gɜː.gɪ.siːn, -gə-, -ges.iːn, ˌ-'-- (US) 'gɝː.gə- **-s** -z
Gerhardt 'geə.hɑːt (US) 'ger.hɑːrd, -hɑːrt
geriatric ˌdʒer.i'æt.rɪk **-s** -s
geriatrician ˌdʒer.i.ə'trɪʃ.ᵊn **-s** -z
geriatry 'dʒer.i.ə.tri, -æt.ri
Geritol® 'dʒer.ɪ.tɒl (US) -tɑːl
Gerizim ger'aɪ.zɪm, gə'raɪ-, -'riː-; 'ger.ɪ.zɪm
germ dʒɜːm (US) dʒɝːm **-s** -z ˌ**germ 'warfare**
Germain 'dʒɜː.mən, -meɪn (US) 'dʒɝː-
Germaine dʒə'meɪn, dʒɜː- (US) dʒɚ-
German 'dʒɜː.mən (US) 'dʒɝː- **-s** -z ˌ**German 'measles**
germander dʒə'mæn.dəʳ, dʒɜː- (US) dʒɚ'mæn.dɚ
germane (G) dʒə'meɪn, dʒɜː-; 'dʒɜː.meɪn (US) dʒɚ'meɪn **-ly** -li **-nes** -nəs, -nɪs
Germanic dʒə'mæn.ɪk, dʒɜː- (US) dʒɚ-
German|ism 'dʒɜː.mə.n|ɪ.zᵊm (US) 'dʒɝː- **-isms** -ɪ.zᵊmz **-ist/s** -ɪst/s
germanium dʒə'meɪ.ni.əm, dʒɜː- (US) dʒɚ-
germanization, -isa- ˌdʒɜː.mə.naɪ'zeɪ.ʃᵊn, -ɪ'- (US) ˌdʒɝː.mə.nɪ'-
germaniz|e, -is|e 'dʒɜː.mə.naɪz (US) 'dʒɝː- **-es** -ɪz **-ing** -ɪŋ **-ed** -d
German|y 'dʒɜː.mə.n|i (US) 'dʒɝː- **-ies** -iz
germicidal ˌdʒɜː.mɪ'saɪ.dᵊl, -mə'-, 'dʒɜː.mɪ.saɪ-, -mə- (US) ˌdʒɝː.mə'sa
germicide 'dʒɜː.mɪ.saɪd, -mə- (US) 'dʒɝː.mə- **-s** -z
germinal 'dʒɜː.mɪ.nᵊl, -mə- (US) 'dʒɝː.mə-
germi|nate 'dʒɜː.mɪ|.neɪt, -mə- (US) 'dʒɝː.mə- **-nates** -neɪts **-nating** -neɪ.tɪŋ (US) -neɪ.t̬ɪŋ **-nated** -neɪ.tɪ (US) -neɪ.t̬ɪd
germination ˌdʒɜː.mɪ'neɪ.ʃᵊn, -mə'- (US) ˌdʒɝː.mə'- **-s** -z
Germiston 'dʒɜː.mɪ.stᵊn (US) 'dʒɝː.m -mə-
Germolene® 'dʒɜː.mə.liːn (US) 'dʒɝː
Geronimo dʒə'rɒn.ɪ.məʊ, dʒɪ-, dʒer'ɒn-, '-ə- (US) -'rɑː.nə.moʊ
Gerontius gə'rɒn.ti.əs, gɪ-, dʒə-, dʒ ger'ɒn-, -ʃi.əs, -ʃəs (US) dʒə'rɑːn-
gerontocrac|y ˌdʒer.ɒn'tɒk.rə.s|i, -ən'- (US) -ᵊn'tɑː.krə- **-cies** -iz
gerontocratic dʒəˌrɒn.tə'kræt.ɪk, ˌdʒer.ɒn-, -ən.tə'- (US) dʒəˌrɑːn.t̬ə'kræt̬.ɪk

Pronouncing the letters GG

The main pronunciation for the consonant digraph **gg** is /g/, e.g.:

rugged /ˈrʌg.ɪd/

In addition

gg may be pronounced as /dʒ/, e.g.:

exaggerate /ɪgˈzædʒ.ᵊr.eɪt/ (US) /-ə.reɪt/

And in rare cases for American English as /gdʒ/:

suggest /səˈdʒest/ (US) /səgˈdʒest/

Pronouncing the letters GH

The consonant digraph **gh** can be pronounced as /g/, /f/ or may be silent.

In syllable-initial position, **gh** is always pronounced as /g/, e.g.:

ghost /gəʊst/ (US) /goʊst/
aghast /əˈgɑːst/ (US) /-ˈgæst/

Following a vowel letter, the pronunciation may be silent. This is always the case after **i** and **ei**, e.g.:

high /haɪ/
height /haɪt/
plough /plaʊ/
caught /kɔːt/ (US) /kɑːt/

Alternatively, the pronunciation may be /f/, e.g.:

rough /rʌf/
laugh /lɑːf/ (US) /læf/

In addition

A unique pronunciation of the consonant digraph **gh** is /p/, e.g.:

hiccough /ˈhɪk.ʌp/

gerontolog|y ˌdʒer.ɒnˈtɒl.ə.dʒ|i, ˌger-, -ənˈ- (US) ˌdʒer.ᵊnˈtɑː.lə- **-ist/s** -ɪst/s
Gerrard ˈdʒer.əd, -ɑːd; dʒerˈɑːd, dʒəˈrɑːd (US) ˈdʒer.ɚd ˌ**Gerrard's ˈCross**
Gerry ˈdʒer.i
gerrymand|er ˈdʒer.i.mæn.d|əʳ, ˌdʒer.iˈmæn- (US) -d|ɚ **-ers** -əz (US) -ɚz **-ering** -ᵊr.ɪŋ **-ered** -əd (US) -ɚd
Gershwin ˈgɜːʃ.wɪn (US) ˈgɝːʃ-, -wən
Gertie ˈgɜː.ti (US) ˈgɝː.t̬i
Gertrude ˈgɜː.truːd (US) ˈgɝː-
Gerty ˈgɜː.ti (US) ˈgɝː.t̬i
gerund ˈdʒer.ᵊnd, -ʌnd **-s** -z
gerundival ˌdʒer.ᵊnˈdaɪ.vᵊl
gerundive dʒəˈrʌn.dɪv, dʒɪ-, dʒerˈʌn- **-s** -z
Gerva(i)se ˈdʒɜː.veɪz, -vɪz; dʒɜːˈveɪz, -ˈveɪs (US) ˈdʒɝː-
Geryon ˈger.i.ən (US) ˈdʒɪr-, ˈger-
gesso ˈdʒes.əʊ (US) -oʊ **-es** -z
gest dʒest **-s** -s
gestalt gəˈʃtælt, -ʃtɑːlt; ˈgeʃ.tælt (US) gəˈʃtɑːlt
Gestapo gesˈtɑː.pəʊ, geʃ- (US) gəˈstɑː.poʊ, gəʃˈtɑː-
Gesta Romanorum ˌdʒes.tə.rəʊ.məˈnɔː.rəm, -mɑː-, ˌges- (US) -roʊ.mə.nɔːr.əm, -mɑ-
ges|tate dʒes|ˈteɪt, ˈ-- (US) ˈdʒes|.teɪt **-tates** -ˈteɪts (US) -teɪts **-tating** -ˈteɪ.tɪŋ (US) -teɪ.t̬ɪŋ **-tated** -ˈteɪ.tɪd (US) -teɪ.t̬ɪd
gestation dʒesˈteɪ.ʃᵊn **-s** -z
gestatorial ˌdʒes.təˈtɔː.ri.əl
gestatory dʒesˈteɪ.tᵊr.i; ˈdʒes.tə- (US) ˈdʒes.tə.tɔːr-
Gestetner® gesˈtet.nəʳ, gɪˈstet-, gə- (US) -nɚ
gesticu|late dʒesˈtɪk.jə|.leɪt, -jʊ- (US) -jə- **-lates** -leɪts **-lating** -leɪ.tɪŋ (US) -leɪ.t̬ɪŋ **-lated** -leɪ.tɪd (US) -leɪ.t̬ɪd **-lator/s** -leɪ.təʳ/z (US) -leɪ.t̬ɚ/z
gesticulation dʒesˌtɪk.jəˈleɪ.ʃᵊn, -jʊˈ- (US) -jəˈ- **-s** -z
gesticulatory dʒesˈtɪk.jʊ.leɪ.tᵊr.i, -lə-, -je- (US) -jə.lə.tɔːr-
gestur|e ˈdʒes.tʃəʳ (US) -tʃɚ **-es** -z **-ing** -ɪŋ **-ed** -d
Gesundheit gəˈzʊnd.haɪt
get get **-s** -s **-ting** -ɪŋ (US) ˈget̬.ɪŋ **got** gɒt (US) gɑːt **gotten** ˈgɒt.ᵊn (US) ˈgɑː.tᵊn ˌ**give as** ˌ**good as one** ˈ**gets**
Getae ˈgeɪ.taɪ, ˈdʒiː.tiː
getatable getˈæt.ə.bl̩ (US) get̬ˈæt̬-
getaway ˈget.ə.weɪ (US) ˈget̬- **-s** -z
Gethin ˈgeθ.ɪn
Gethsemane geθˈsem.ə.ni
get-rich-quick ˌget.rɪtʃˈkwɪk
get-together ˈget.tə.geð.ə (US) -geð.ɚ **-s** -z
Getty ˈget.i (US) ˈget̬.i
Gettysburg ˈget.iz.bɜːg (US) ˈget̬.iz.bɝːg ˌ**Gettysburg Adˈdress**
getup ˈget.ʌp (US) ˈget̬- **-s** -s
get-up-and-go ˌget.ʌp.ᵊnˈgəʊ, -ᵊŋˈ- (US) ˌget̬.ʌp.ᵊnˈgoʊ
geum ˈdʒiː.əm **-s** -z
gewgaw ˈgjuː.gɔː (US) ˈguː.gɑː, ˈgjuː-, -gɔː **-s** -z
Gewürztraminer gəˈvʊət.strəˌmiː.nə, -ˈvɜːt- (US) -ˈvɝːt.strəˌmiː.nɚ
geyser *hot spring:* ˈgiː.zəʳ, ˈgaɪ- (US) ˈgaɪ.zɚ **-s** -z
Note: In New Zealand the pronunciation is /ˈgaɪ.zəʳ/.
apparatus for heating water: ˈgiː.zəʳ (US) -zɚ **-s** -z
Ghana ˈgɑː.nə
Ghanaian gɑːˈneɪ.ən (US) -ˈniː-, -ˈneɪ- **-s** -z
ghastl|y ˈgɑːst.l|i (US) ˈgæst.l|i **-ier** -i.əʳ (US) -i.ɚ **-iest** -i.ɪst, -i.əst **-iness** -ɪ.nəs, -ɪ.nɪs
Ghat gɑːt, gɔːt **-s** -s
ghee giː
Ghent gent

gherkin 'gɜː.kɪn ⓤⓢ 'gɝː- **-s** -z
ghetto 'get.əʊ ⓤⓢ 'get̬.oʊ **-(e)s** -z **'ghetto ˌblaster**
ghettoiz|e, -i|se 'get.əʊ.aɪz ⓤⓢ 'get̬.oʊ- **-es** -ɪz **-ing** -ɪŋ **-ed** -d
Ghia 'giː.ə
Ghibelline 'gɪb.ɪ.laɪn, '-ə-, -liːn **-s** -z
ghillie 'gɪl.i **-s** -z
ghost gəʊst ⓤⓢ goʊst **-s** -s **-ing** -ɪŋ **-ed** -ɪd **-like** -laɪk **'ghost ˌtown; ˌgive up the 'ghost**
ghostl|y 'gəʊst.l|i ⓤⓢ 'goʊst- **-iness** -ɪ.nəs, -ɪ.nɪs
ghost|write 'gəʊst|.raɪt ⓤⓢ 'goʊst- **-writes** -raɪts **-writing** -ˌraɪ.tɪŋ ⓤⓢ -ˌraɪ.t̬ɪŋ **-wrote** -rəʊt ⓤⓢ -roʊt
ghostwriter 'gəʊstˌraɪ.təʳ ⓤⓢ 'goʊstˌraɪ.t̬ɚ **-s** -z
ghoul guːl **-s** -z **-ish/ly** -ɪʃ/li
ghyll gɪl **-s** -z
GI ˌdʒiː'aɪ *stress shift:* ˌGI 'bride
giant dʒaɪənt **-s** -s **-like** -laɪk **ˌGiant's 'Causeway**
giantess 'dʒaɪən.tes, -tɪs, -təs; ⓤⓢ 'dʒaɪən.t̬əs **-es** -ɪz
Giaour 'dʒaʊəʳ ⓤⓢ -ɚ
Gibb gɪb
gibb|er 'dʒɪb|.əʳ ⓤⓢ -ɚ **-ers** -əz ⓤⓢ -ɚz **-ering** -ᵊr.ɪŋ **-ered** -əd ⓤⓢ -ɚd
gibberish 'dʒɪb.ᵊr.ɪʃ
gibbet 'dʒɪb.ɪt, -ət **-s** -s **-ing** -ɪŋ ⓤⓢ 'dʒɪb.ɪ.t̬ɪŋ **-ed** -ɪd ⓤⓢ 'dʒɪb.ɪ.t̬ɪd
Gibbie 'dʒɪb.i
Gibbins 'gɪb.ɪnz
gibbon (G) 'gɪb.ᵊn **-s** -z
gibbosity gɪ'bɒs.ə.ti, dʒɪ-, -ɪ.ti ⓤⓢ gɪ'bɑː.sə.t̬i
gibbous 'gɪb.əs, 'dʒɪb- ⓤⓢ 'gɪb- **-ly** -li **-ness** -nəs, -nɪs
Gibbs gɪbz
gib|e dʒaɪb **-es** -z **-ing/ly** -ɪŋ/li **-ed** -d **-er/s** -əʳ/z ⓤⓢ -ɚ/z
Gibeon 'gɪb.i.ən
giblet 'dʒɪb.lət, -lɪt **-s** -s
Gibraltar dʒɪ'brɔːl.təʳ, dʒə-, -'brɒl- ⓤⓢ -'brɑːl.tɚ, -'brɔːl-
Gibraltarian ˌdʒɪb.rɔːl'teə.ri.ən, -rɒl'-; dʒɪˌbrɔːl'-, dʒə-, -ˌbrɒl'- ⓤⓢ ˌdʒɪb.rɑːlˌter.i-, -rɔːl'- **-s** -z
Gibson 'gɪb.sᵊn
Gidding 'gɪd.ɪŋ **-s** -z
Giddis 'gɪd.ɪs
gidd|y (G) 'gɪd|.i **-ier** -i.əʳ ⓤⓢ -i.ɚ **-iest** -i.ɪst, -i.əst **-ily** -ɪ.li, -ᵊl.i **-iness** -ɪ.nəs, -ɪ.nɪs
Gide ʒiːd
Gidea 'gɪd.i.ə
Gideon 'gɪd.i.ən
Gielgud 'giːl.gʊd
GIF gɪf, dʒɪf
Giffard 'dʒɪf.əd, 'gɪf- ⓤⓢ -ɚd
Giffen 'gɪf.ɪn, 'dʒɪf.ɪn, -ən
Giffnock 'gɪf.nək
Gifford *place near Haddington:* 'gɪf.əd ⓤⓢ -ɚd *surname:* 'gɪf.əd, 'dʒɪf.əd ⓤⓢ -ɚd
gift gɪft **-s** -s **-ed** -ɪd **'gift cerˌtificate; 'gift ˌtoken; ˌgift of the 'gab; ˌlook a ˌgift horse in the 'mouth**
gift-wrap 'gɪft.ræp **-s** -s **-ping** -ɪŋ **-ped** -t
gig gɪg **-s** -z
giga- 'gɪg.ə-, 'gaɪ.gə-, 'dʒɪg.ə-
gigabyte 'gɪg.ə.baɪt, 'gaɪ.gə-, 'dʒɪg.ə- **-s** -s
gigahertz 'gɪg.ə.hɜːts, 'gaɪ.gə-, 'dʒɪg.ə- ⓤⓢ -hɝːts
gigantesque ˌdʒaɪ.gæn'tesk, -gən-
gigantic dʒaɪ'gæn.tɪk, ˌdʒaɪ- ⓤⓢ -t̬ɪk **-ally** -ᵊl.i, -li
gigantism dʒaɪ'gæn.tɪ.zᵊm, 'dʒaɪ.gæn- ⓤⓢ -t̬ɪ-
giggl|e (*n. v.*) 'gɪg.l̩ **-es** -z **-ing** -ɪŋ, '-lɪŋ **-ed** -d **-er/s** -əʳ/z, '-ləʳ/z ⓤⓢ '-l̩.ɚ/z, '-lɚ/z
giggleswick (G) 'gɪg.l̩z.wɪk
giggly 'gɪg.l̩.i, 'gɪg.li
Giggs gɪgz
Gight gɪkt, gɪxt
Gigi 'ʒiː.ʒiː
Gigli 'dʒiː.li, -lji ⓤⓢ 'dʒiː.li, 'dʒiːl.ji
Giglio 'dʒiː.li.əʊ, '-ljəʊ ⓤⓢ '-li.oʊ
GIGO 'gaɪ.gəʊ, 'dʒaɪ- ⓤⓢ 'gɪg.oʊ, 'gaɪ.goʊ, 'giː-
gigolo 'dʒɪg.ə.ləʊ, 'ʒɪg- ⓤⓢ -loʊ **-s** -z
gigot 'dʒɪg.ət, 'zɪg-, -əʊ, 'dʒiː.gəʊ ⓤⓢ ziː'goʊ **-s** -s
gigue ʒiːg, ʒɪg **-s** -z
Gihon 'gaɪ.hɒn *in Jewish usage sometimes:* 'giː.həʊn
gila (G) 'hiː.lə, 'giː- ⓤⓢ 'hiː- **-s** -z
Gilbert 'gɪl.bət ⓤⓢ -bɚt
Gilbertian gɪl'bɜː.ti.ən, -ʃᵊn ⓤⓢ -'bɝː.t̬i.ən
Gilbey 'gɪl.bi
Gilboa gɪl'bəʊ.ə ⓤⓢ -'boʊ-
Gilchrist 'gɪl.krɪst
gild gɪld **-s** -z **-ing** -ɪŋ **-ed** -ɪd **gilt** gɪlt
Gildas 'gɪl.dæs
gilder (G) 'gɪl.dəʳ ⓤⓢ -dɚ **-s** -z
Gildersleeve 'gɪl.də.sliːv ⓤⓢ -dɚ-
Gildersome 'gɪl.də.səm ⓤⓢ -dɚ-
Gilding 'gɪl.dɪŋ
Gildredge 'gɪl.drɪdʒ, -dredʒ
Gilead 'gɪl.i.æd ⓤⓢ -əd
Giles dʒaɪlz
Gilfil 'gɪl.fɪl
Gilfillan gɪl'fɪl.ən
Gilford 'gɪl.fəd ⓤⓢ -fɚd
Gilgal 'gɪl.gæl, -gɔːl
Gilgamesh 'gɪl.gə.meʃ
Gilham 'gɪl.əm
Gilkes dʒɪlks
gill *respiratory organ, ravine:* gɪl **-s** -z *measure:* dʒɪl **-s** -z
Gill gɪl, dʒɪl
Gillam 'gɪl.əm
Gillard 'gɪl.ɑːd, -əd; gɪ'lɑːd ⓤⓢ 'gɪl.ɚd
Gillen 'gɪl.ən
Gilleney 'gɪl.ən.i
Gillespie gɪ'les.pi, gə-
Gillett 'gɪl.ɪt, 'gɪl.et, gɪ'let, dʒɪ'let, dʒə'let
Gillette® dʒɪ'let ⓤⓢ dʒə'let, dʒɪ- **-s** -s
Gilley 'gɪl.i
Gilliam 'gɪl.i.əm
Gillian 'dʒɪl.i.ən, 'gɪl-
Gilliat 'gɪl.i.ət, -æt
Gillick 'gɪl.ɪk
gillie (G) 'gɪl.i **-s** -z
Gillies 'gɪl.ɪs
Gilliland 'gɪl.ɪ.lænd
Gilling 'gɪl.ɪŋ **-s** -z
Gillingham *in Kent:* 'dʒɪl.ɪŋ.əm *in Dorset & Norfolk:* 'gɪl- *surname:* 'gɪl-, 'dʒɪl-
Gillison 'gɪl.ɪ.sᵊn
Gillmore 'gɪl.mɔːʳ ⓤⓢ -mɔːr
Gillon 'gɪl.ən
Gillott 'dʒɪl.ət, 'gɪl.ət
Gillow 'gɪl.əʊ ⓤⓢ -oʊ
Gillray 'gɪl.reɪ
Gills gɪlz
Gillson 'dʒɪl.sᵊn
gilly 'gɪl.i **-s** -z
gillyflower 'dʒɪl.ɪˌflaʊəʳ ⓤⓢ -ˌflaʊɚ **-s** -z
Gilman 'gɪl.mən
Gilmer 'gɪl.məʳ ⓤⓢ -mɚ
Gilmore 'gɪl.mɔːʳ, -məʳ ⓤⓢ -mɔːr
Gilmour 'gɪl.mɔːʳ, -məʳ ⓤⓢ -mɔːr
Gilpatrick gɪl'pæt.rɪk
Gilpin 'gɪl.pɪn
Gilroy 'gɪl.rɔɪ
Gilson 'dʒɪl.sᵊn, 'gɪl.sᵊn
gilt gɪlt **-s** -s
gilt-edged ˌgɪlt'edʒd *stress shift:* ˌgilt-edged 'stocks
gimbal 'gɪm.bəl, 'dʒɪm- **-s** -z
gimbl|e 'gɪm.bl̩ **-es** -z **-ing** -ɪŋ, '-blɪŋ **-ed** -d
Gimblett 'gɪm.*b*lɪt, -ət
gimcrack 'dʒɪm.kræk **-s** -s
gimlet 'gɪm.lət, -lɪt **-s** -s
gimme 'gɪm.i
gimmick 'gɪm.ɪk **-s** -s **-ry** -ri **-y** -i
gimp gɪmp
Gimson 'gɪm*p*.sᵊn, 'dʒɪm*p*.sᵊn
gin dʒɪn **-s** -z **'gin ˌmill; ˌgin 'rummy; ˌgin 'sling**
Gina 'dʒiː.nə
Gingell 'gɪn.dʒᵊl
ginger 'dʒɪn.dʒəʳ ⓤⓢ -dʒɚ **-s** -z **ˌginger 'ale; ˌginger 'beer**
gingerbread (G) 'dʒɪn.dʒə.bred ⓤⓢ -dʒɚ- **-s** -z **'gingerbread ˌman**
gingerly 'dʒɪn.dʒᵊl.i ⓤⓢ -dʒɚ.li

ginger|y 'dʒɪn.dʒᵊr|.i **-iness** -ɪ.nəs, -ɪ.nɪs
gingham 'gɪŋ.əm **-s** -z
gingival dʒɪn'dʒaɪ.vᵊl, 'dʒɪn.dʒɪ.vᵊl
gingivitis ˌdʒɪn.dʒɪ'vaɪ.tɪs, -dʒə'- (US) -dʒə'vaɪ.t̬ɪs
gingko 'gɪŋ.kəʊ (US) -koʊ **-s** -z
ingold 'gɪŋ.gəʊld (US) -goʊld
ingrich 'gɪŋ.grɪtʃ
inkel(l) 'gɪŋ.kᵊl
inkgo 'gɪŋ.kəʊ, 'gɪŋk.gəʊ (US) 'gɪŋ.koʊ, 'gɪŋk.goʊ **-es** -z
inn gɪn
innel 'gɪn.ᵊl, 'dʒɪn- **-s** -z
inny 'dʒɪn.i
inola 'dʒɪ.nəʊ.lə, 'ʒɪn- (US) -nə-, -ˌnoʊ-
inormous dʒaɪ'nɔː.məs (US) -'nɔːr-
insberg 'gɪnz.bɜːg (US) -bɝːg
inseng 'dʒɪn.seŋ
ioconda ˌdʒɪə'kɒn.də (US) -'kɑːn-
iotto 'dʒɒt.əʊ, dʒɪ'ɒt- (US) 'dʒɑː.t̬oʊ
iovanni ˌdʒiː.əʊ'vɑː.ni, dʒəʊ'-, -'væn.i (US) dʒoʊ'vɑː-, dʒə-
ip gɪp **-s** -s **-ping** -ɪŋ **-ped** -t
ipp gɪp
ppsland 'gɪps.lænd
ppy 'dʒɪp.i
ps|y 'dʒɪp.s|i **-ies** -iz
raffe dʒɪ'rɑːf, dʒə-, -'ræf (US) dʒə'ræf **-s** -s
ralda dʒɪ'ræl.də, hɪ-
randole 'dʒɪr.ən.dəʊl (US) -doʊl **-s** -z
rd gɜːd (US) gɝːd **-s** -z **-ing** -ɪŋ **-ed** -ɪd **girt** gɜːt (US) gɝːt
rder 'gɜː.dəʳ (US) 'gɝː.dɚ **-s** -z
rdl|e 'gɜː.dl̩ (US) 'gɝː- **-es** -z **-ing** -ɪŋ, 'gɜːd.lɪŋ (US) 'gɝː.dl̩.ɪŋ, 'gɝːd.lɪŋ **-ed** -d
rdlestone 'gɜː.dl̩.stᵊn (US) 'gɝː-
l gɜːl (US) gɝːl **-s** -z **-hood** -hʊd
lfriend 'gɜːl.frend (US) 'gɝːl- **-s** -z
lie 'gɜː.li (US) 'gɝː-
lish 'gɜː.lɪʃ (US) 'gɝː- **-ly** -li **-ness** -nəs, -nɪs
y 'gɜː.li (US) 'gɝː-
o **(G)** 'dʒaɪə.rəʊ (US) 'dʒaɪ.roʊ **-s** -z
obank® 'dʒaɪə.rəʊ.bæŋk (US) 'dʒaɪ.roʊ-
onde dʒɪ'rɒnd, ʒɪ-; (US) dʒə'rɑːnd
ondist dʒɪ'rɒn.dɪst, ʒɪ- (US) dʒə'rɑːn- **-s** -s
t *(n.)* gɜːt (US) gɝːt **-s** -s
t *(from* **gird***)* gɜːt (US) gɝːt
h gɜːθ (US) gɝːθ **-s** -s
tin 'gɜː.tɪn (US) 'gɝː.tɪn, -tᵊn
ton 'gɜː.tᵊn (US) 'gɝː-
onian gɜː'təʊ.ni.ən (US) gɝː'toʊ- **-s** -z
van 'gɜː.vən (US) 'gɝː.vᵊn
ourne 'gɪz.bɔːn, -bən (US) -bɔːrn
ard d'Estaing *ʒɪs.kɑː.des.'tæŋ, ʒiː-, -'tæ̃ŋ* (US) *ʒiːsˌkɑːr.des'tæ̃ŋ*

Giselle ʒɪ'zel, dʒɪ-
Gish gɪʃ
gismo 'gɪz.məʊ (US) -moʊ **-s** -z
Gissing 'gɪs.ɪŋ
gist dʒɪst **-s** -s
git gɪt **-s** -s
Gita 'giː.tə (US) -t̬ə
Gitane® ʒɪ'tɑːn (US) -'tɑːn, -'tæn **-s** -z
gîte, **gite** ʒiːt **-s** -s
gittern 'gɪt.ɜːn (US) -ɚn **-s** -z
Gitty 'gɪt.i (US) 'gɪt̬.i
Giuliani ˌdʒuː.li'ɑː.ni
Giuseppe dʒu'sep.i
giv|e gɪv **-es** -z **-ing** -ɪŋ **gave** geɪv **giv|en** 'gɪv|.ᵊn **-er/s** -əʳ/z (US) -ɚ/z **'given ˌname; ˌgive as ˌgood as one 'gets**
give-and-take ˌgɪv.ᵊnd'teɪk
giveaway 'gɪv.ə.weɪ **-s** -z
giveback 'gɪv.bæk **-s** -s
Givenchy® ʒiː'vɑ̃ːn.ʃi, gɪ- (US) ʒiː'vɑ̃ːn-, -'ʃiː
Giza, **Gîza** 'giː.zə
Gizeh 'giː.zeɪ, -zə
gizmo 'gɪz.məʊ (US) -moʊ **-s** -z
gizzard 'gɪz.əd (US) -ɚd **-s** -z
glabrous 'gleɪ.brəs
glacé, **glace** 'glæs.eɪ (US) glæs'eɪ **-ed** -d
glacial 'gleɪ.si.əl, -ʃᵊl; 'glæs.i.əl (US) 'gleɪ.ʃəl **-ly** -i
glaciation ˌgleɪ.si'eɪ.ʃᵊn, ˌglæs- (US) ˌgleɪ.ʃi'-
glacier 'glæs.i.əʳ, 'gleɪ.si- (US) 'gleɪ.ʃɚ **-s** -z
glacis 'glæs.ɪs, -i (US) 'gleɪ.sɪs, 'glæs.ɪs, glæs'iː 'glæs.ɪz (US) 'gleɪ.siːz, 'glæs.iːz, -'-
glacises *(alternative plur. of* **glacis***)* 'glæs.ɪ.sɪz (US) 'gleɪ.sɪ.ziːz, 'glæs.ɪ-
glad glæd **-der** -əʳ (US) -ɚ **-dest** -ɪst, -əst **-ness** -nəs, -nɪs **'glad ˌrags**
gladden 'glæd.ᵊn **-s** -z **-ing** -ɪŋ **-ed** -d
glade gleɪd **-s** -z
glad-hand 'glædˌhænd, ˌ-'- **-s** -z **-ing** -ɪŋ **-ed** -ɪd **-er/s** -əʳ/z
gladiator 'glæd.i.eɪ.təʳ (US) -t̬ɚ **-s** -z
gladiatorial ˌglæd.i.ə'tɔː.ri.əl (US) -tɔːr.i.əl
gladiole 'glæd.i.əʊl (US) -oʊl **-s** -z
gladiol|us ˌglæd.i'əʊ.l|əs (US) -'oʊ- **-i** -aɪ **-uses** -əs.ɪz
gladly 'glæd.li
gladsome 'glæd.səm **-ly** -li **-ness** -nəs, -nɪs
Gladstone 'glæd.stᵊn (US) -stoʊn, -stᵊn
Gladstonian glæd'stəʊ.ni.ən (US) -'stoʊ-
Gladwin 'glæd.wɪn
Gladys 'glæd.ɪs
glagolitic **(G)** ˌglæg.əʊ'lɪt.ɪk (US) -ə'lɪt̬-
glair gleəʳ (US) gler
Glaisdale 'gleɪz.deɪl *locally:* -dᵊl
Glaisher 'gleɪ.ʃəʳ (US) -ʃɚ
glam glæm

Glam. *(abbrev. for* **Glamorgan***)* glə'mɔː.gən (US) -'mɔːr-
Glamis glɑːmz
Note: In Shakespeare /'glæm.ɪs/.
Glamorgan glə'mɔː.gən (US) -'mɔːr- **-shire** -ʃə, -ˌʃɪəʳ (US) -ʃɚ, -ˌʃɪr
glamoriz|e, **-is|e** 'glæm.ᵊr.aɪz (US) -ə.raɪz **-es** -ɪz **-ing** -ɪŋ **-ed** -d
glamorous 'glæm.ᵊr.əs **-ly** -li **-ness** -nəs, -nɪs
glamour 'glæm.əʳ (US) -ɚ
glamourous 'glæm.ᵊr.əs **-ly** -li **-ness** -nəs, -nɪs
glamourpuss 'glæm.ə.pʊs (US) -ɚ- **-es** -ɪz
glanc|e glɑːnts (US) glænts **-es** -ɪz **-ing/ly** -ɪŋ/li **-ed** -t
gland glænd **-s** -z
glander|s 'glæn.də|z, 'glɑːn- (US) 'glæn.dɚ|z **-ed** -d
glandes *(plur. of* **glans***)* 'glæn.diːz
glandular 'glæn.djʊ.ləʳ, -dʒə.ləʳ (US) -dʒə.lɚ **ˌglandular 'fever**
glandule 'glæn.djuːl (US) -dʒuːl **-s** -z
glans glænz **glandes** 'glæn.diːz
Glanvill(e) 'glæn.vɪl
Glapthorne 'glæp.θɔːn (US) -θɔːrn
glar|e gleəʳ (US) gler **-es** -z **-ing/ly** -ɪŋ/li **-ingness** -ɪŋ.nəs, -nɪs **-ed** -d
Glarus *place in US:* 'glær.əs (US) 'gler-, 'glær- *other senses:* 'glɑː.rəs
Glasgow 'glɑːz.gəʊ, 'glɑːs-, 'glɑːs.kəʊ, 'glæz.gəʊ, 'glæs-, 'glæs.kəʊ (US) 'glæs.koʊ, 'glæz.goʊ
glasier **(G)** 'gleɪ.zi.əʳ, -ʒəʳ (US) -ʒɚ **-s** -z
glasnost 'glæs.nɒst, 'glæz- (US) 'glæs.nɑːst, -noʊst
glass **(G)** glɑːs (US) glæs **-es** -ɪz **ˌglass 'ceiling; 'glass ˌcutter**
glassblow|er 'glɑːsˌbləʊ|.əʳ (US) 'glæsˌbloʊ|.ɚ **-ers** -əz (US) -ɚz **-ing** -ɪŋ
Glasscock 'glɑːs.kɒk, -kəʊ (US) 'glæs.kɑːk, -koʊ
glassful 'glɑːs.fʊl, -fᵊl (US) 'glæs- **-s** -z
glasshou|se 'glɑːs.haʊ|s (US) 'glæs- **-ses** -zɪz
glasspaper, **glass-paper** 'glɑːsˌpeɪ.pəʳ (US) 'glæsˌpeɪ.pɚ
glassware 'glɑːs.weəʳ (US) 'glæs.wer
glasswork 'glɑːs.wɜːk (US) 'glæs.wɝːk **-s** -s
glasswort 'glɑːs.wɜːt (US) 'glæs.wɝːt, -wɔːrt
glass|y 'glɑː.s|i (US) 'glæs|.i **-ier** -i.əʳ (US) -i.ɚ **-iest** -i.ɪst, -i.əst **-ily** -ɪ.li, -ᵊl.i **-iness** -ɪ.nəs, -ɪ.nɪs
Glastonbury 'glæs.tᵊn.bᵊr.i, 'glɑː.stᵊn- (US) 'glæs.tᵊnˌber.i, -bᵊr.i
Glaswegian glæz'wiː.dʒᵊn, glɑːz-, glæs-, glɑːs-, -dʒi.ən (US) glæs-, glæz- **-s** -z

glaucoma glɔːˈkəʊ.mə, glaʊ- US glɑːˈkoʊ-, glɔː- **-tous** -təs
glaucous ˈglɔː.kəs US ˈglɑː-, ˈglɔː-
Glaxo® ˈglæk.səʊ US -soʊ
glaz|e gleɪz **-es** -ɪz **-ing** -ɪŋ **-ed** -d **-er/s** -əʳ/z US -ɚ/z
Glazebrook ˈgleɪz.brʊk
glazier ˈgleɪ.zi.əʳ, ˈ-ʒəʳ US ˈ-ʒɚ **-s** -z
Glazunov ˈglæz.u.nɒf US ˈglæz.ə.nɑːf, ˈglɑː.zə-, -noʊf
gleam gliːm **-s** -z **-ing** -ɪŋ **-ed** -d **-y** -i
glean gliːn **-s** -z **-ing/s** -ɪŋ/z **-ed** -d **-er/s** -əʳ/z **-er/z** US -ɚ/z
Gleason ˈgliː.sᵊn
glebe gliːb **-s** -z
glee gliː **ˈglee ˌclub**
gleeful ˈgliː.fᵊl, -fʊl **-ly** -i **-ness** -nəs, -nɪs
glee|man ˈgliː|.mən, -mæn **-men** -mən, -men
Glegg gleg
Gleichen ˈglaɪ.kən
Glemsford ˈglems.fəd, ˈglemz- US -fɚd
glen (G) glen **-s** -z
Glenallan glenˈæl.ən
Glenalmond glenˈɑː.mənd
Glenavon glenˈæv.ᵊn
Glenavy glenˈeɪ.vi
Glencairn glenˈkeən, gleŋ- US glenˈkern
Glencoe glenˈkəʊ, gleŋ- US glenˈkoʊ
Glenda ˈglen.də
Glendale glenˈdeɪl, ˈglen.deɪl US ˈglen-
Glendenning glenˈden.ɪŋ
Glendin(n)ing glenˈdɪn.ɪŋ
Glendower glenˈdaʊ.əʳ US -ɚ
Gleneagles glenˈiː.gl̩z
Glenelg glenˈelg
Glenfiddich glenˈfɪd.ɪk, -ɪx
Glenfinnan glenˈfɪn.ən
glengarr|y (G) glenˈgær|.i, gleŋ- US glenˈger-, -ˈgær-, ˈ--- **-ies** -iz
Glenlivet glenˈlɪv.ɪt, -ət
Glenmorangie ˌglen.məˈræn.dʒi, ˌglem-, glenˈmɒr.ən.dʒi US ˌglen-
Glenmore glenˈmɔːʳ, glem- US ˈglen.mɔːr, -ˈ-
Glenn glen
Glenrothes glenˈrɒθ.ɪs US -ˈrɑː.θəs
Glen Trool ˌglenˈtruːl
Glenwood ˈglen.wʊd
Glenys ˈglen.ɪs
glib glɪb **-ber** -əʳ US -ɚ **-best** -ɪst, -əst **-ly** -li **-ness** -nəs, -nɪs
glid|e glaɪd **-es** -z **-ing/ly** -ɪŋ/li **-ed** -ɪd
glider ˈglaɪ.dəʳ US -dɚ **-s** -z
glimmer ˈglɪm.əʳ US -ɚ **-s** -z **-ing/s** -ɪŋ/z **-ingly** -ɪŋ.li **-ed** -d
glimps|e glɪmps **-es** -ɪz **-ing** -ɪŋ **-ed** -t
glinch glɪntʃ **-es** -ɪz
Glinka ˈglɪŋ.kə
glint glɪnt **-s** -s **-ing** -ɪŋ **-ed** -ɪd
gliom|a glaɪˈəʊ.m|ə US -ˈoʊ-, gli- **-as** -əz **-ata** -ə.tə US -ə.t̬ə
glissad|e (*n. v.*) glɪˈsɑːd, -ˈseɪd **-es** -z **-ing** -ɪŋ **-ed** -ɪd
glissand|o glɪˈsæn.d|əʊ US -ˈsɑːn.d|oʊ **-i** -iː **-os** -əʊz US -oʊz
Glisson ˈglɪs.ᵊn
glisten ˈglɪs.ᵊn **-s** -z **-ing** -ɪŋ **-ed** -d
glist|er ˈglɪs.t|əʳ US -t|ɚ **-ers** -əz US -ɚz **-ering** -ᵊr.ɪŋ **-ered** -əd US -ɚd
glitch glɪtʃ **-es** -ɪz
glitt|er ˈglɪt|.əʳ US ˈglɪt̬|.ɚ **-ers** -əz US -ɚz **-ering/ly** -ᵊr.ɪŋ/li **-ered** -əd US -ɚd **-ery** -ᵊr.i
glitterati ˌglɪt.əˈrɑː.tiː, -ti US ˌglɪt̬.əˈrɑː.t̬i
glitz glɪts
glitz|y ˈglɪt.s|i **-ier** -i.əʳ US -i.ɚ **-iest** -i.ɪst, -i.əst **-iness** -ɪ.nəs, -ɪ.nɪs
Gloag gləʊg US gloʊg
gloaming ˈgləʊ.mɪŋ US ˈgloʊ-
gloat gləʊt US gloʊt **-s** -s **-ing/ly** -ɪŋ US ˈgloʊ.t̬ɪŋ **-ed** -ɪd US ˈgloʊ.t̬əd
glob glɒb US glɑːb **-s** -z
global ˈgləʊ.bᵊl US ˈgloʊ- **-ly** -i **-ism** -ɪ.zᵊm **ˌglobal ˈvillage**; **ˌglobal ˈwarming**
globalization, -isa- ˌgləʊ.bᵊl.aɪˈzeɪ.ʃᵊn, -ɪˈ- US ˌgloʊ.bᵊl.ɪˈ-
globaliz|e, -is|e ˈgləʊ.bᵊl.aɪz US ˈgloʊ.bə.laɪz **-es** -ɪz **-ing** -ɪŋ **-ed** -d
globe gləʊb US gloʊb **-s** -z
globe-trott|er ˈgləʊbˌtrɒt|.əʳ US ˈgloʊbˌtrɑː.t̬|ɚ **-ers** -əz US -ɚz **-ing** -ɪŋ
globose ˈgləʊ.bəʊs, gləʊˈbəʊs US ˈgloʊ.boʊs, -ˈ-
globosity gləʊˈbɒs.ə.ti, -ɪ.ti US gloʊˈbɑː.sə.t̬i
globous ˈgləʊ.bəs US ˈgloʊ-
globular ˈglɒb.jʊ.ləʳ, -jə- US ˈglɑː.bjə.lɚ **-ly** -li
globule ˈglɒb.juːl US ˈglɑː.bjuːl **-s** -z
globulin ˈglɒb.jʊ.lɪn, -jə- US ˈglɑː.bjə- **-s** -z
glockenspiel ˈglɒk.ᵊn.ʃpiːl, -spiːl US ˈglɑː.kᵊn.spiːl, -ʃpiːl **-s** -z
glom glɒm US glɑːm **-s** -z **-ming** -ɪŋ **-med** -d
gloom gluːm **-s** -z **-ing** -ɪŋ **-ed** -d
gloom|y ˈgluː.m|i **-ier** -i.əʳ US -i.ɚ **-iest** -i.ɪst, -i.əst **-ily** -ɪ.li, -ᵊl.i **-iness** -ɪ.nəs, -ɪ.nɪs
glop glɒp US glɑːp **-py** -i
Gloria ˈglɔː.ri.ə US ˈglɔːr.i- **-s** -z
Gloriana ˌglɔː.riˈɑː.nə US ˌglɔːr.iˈæn.ə, -ˈeɪ.nə
glorification ˌglɔː.rɪ.fɪˈkeɪ.ʃᵊn, -rə- US ˌglɔːr.ə.fəˈ-
glori|fy ˈglɔː.rɪ|.faɪ, -rə- US ˈglɔːr.ə- **-fies** -faɪz **-fying** -faɪ.ɪŋ **-fied** -faɪd **-fier/s** -faɪ.əʳ/z US -faɪ.ɚ/z
glorious ˈglɔː.ri.əs US ˈglɔːr.i- **-ly** -li **-ness** -nəs, -nɪs
glor|y ˈglɔː.r|i US ˈglɔːr|.i **-ies** -iz **-ying** -i.ɪŋ **-ied** -id **ˈglory ˌhole**
Glos. (*abbrev. for* **Gloucestershire**) ˈglɒs.tə.ʃəʳ, -ˌʃɪəʳ US ˈglɑː.stɚ.ʃɚ, -ˌʃɪr
gloss glɒs US glɑːs **-es** -ɪz **-ing** -ɪŋ **-ed** **-er/s** -əʳ/z US -ɚ/z
glossal ˈglɒs.ᵊl US ˈglɑː.sᵊl
glossarial glɒsˈeə.ri.əl US glɑːˈser.i-
glossar|y ˈglɒs.ᵊr|.i US ˈglɑː.sᵊr- **-ies**
glossectomy glɒsˈek.tə.mi US glɑːˈsek-
glossematics ˌglɒs.ɪˈmæt.ɪks, -əˈ- US ˌglɑː.səˈmæt̬.ɪks
glosseme ˈglɒs.iːm US ˈglɑː.siːm **-s**
glossitis glɒsˈaɪ.tɪs US glɑːˈsaɪ.t̬ɪs
glossolalia ˌglɒs.əʊˈleɪ.li.ə US ˌglɑː.səˈ-
Glossop ˈglɒs.əp US ˈglɑː.səp
glossopharyngeal ˌglɒs.əʊˌfær.ɪnˈdʒiː.əl, -fəˈrɪn.dʒi.əl US ˌglɑː.soʊˌfer.ᵊnˈdʒiː.əl, -ˌfær-
gloss|y ˈglɒs|.i US ˈglɑː.s|i **-ies** -iz **-ier** -i.əʳ US -i.ɚ **-iest** -i.ɪst, -i.əst **-ily** -ᵊl.i **-iness** -ɪ.nəs, -ɪ.nɪs
Gloster ˈglɒs.təʳ US ˈglɑː.stɚ
glottal ˈglɒt.ᵊl US ˈglɑː.t̬əl **ˌglottal ˈstop**
glottalic glɒtˈæl.ɪk, gləˈtæl- US glɑːˈtæl-
glott|is ˈglɒt|.ɪs US ˈglɑː.t̬|əs **-ises** -ɪ.sɪz, -ə.sɪz **-ides** -ɪ.diːz
glottochronology ˌglɒt.əʊ.krəˈnɒl.ə.dʒi US ˌglɑː.t̬oʊ.krəˈnɑː.lə-
glottology glɒtˈɒl.ə.dʒi US glɑːˈtɑː
Gloucester *in the UK:* ˈglɒs.təʳ US ˈglɑː.stɚ **-shire** -ʃəʳ, -ˌʃɪəʳ US -ʃɚ, -ˌʃɪr *in the US:* ˈglaʊ.stəʳ US -stɚ
glove glʌv **-s** -z **-d** -d **ˈglove comˌpartment**; **ˈglove ˌpuppet**
glover (G) ˈglʌv.əʳ US -ɚ **-s** -z
glow gləʊ US gloʊ **-s** -z **-ing/ly** -ɪŋ/li **-ed** -d
glower glaʊəʳ US glaʊɚ **-s** -z **-ing** **-ed** -d
glowworm ˈgləʊ.wɜːm US ˈgloʊ.w **-s** -z
gloxinia glɒkˈsɪn.i.ə US glɑːkˈ- **-s**
gloz|e gləʊz US gloʊz **-es** -ɪz **-ing** **-ed** -d
Gluck glʊk, gluːk, glʌk
glucose ˈgluː.kəʊs, -kəʊz US -koʊ -koʊz
glu|e gluː **-es** -z **-(e)ing** -ɪŋ **-ed** -d **-e** -əʳ/z US -ɚ/z
gluesniff|ing ˈgluːˌsnɪf|.ɪŋ **-er/s** -ə US -ɚz
gluey ˈgluː.i **-ness** -nəs, -nɪs

Glottal stop

A consonant made by closure of the vocal folds. The phonetic symbol for a glottal stop is [ʔ].

Examples for English

In some British accents, a glottal stop can actually replace the voiceless alveolar plosive [t] as the realisation of the /t/ phoneme when it follows a stressed vowel, e.g.:

getting better /ˌget.ɪŋˈbet.əʳ/ → [ˌgeʔ.ɪ̃ŋˈbeʔ.ə]

This type of pronunciation is found in many urban accents, notably London (Cockney), Leeds, Glasgow, Edinburgh and others, and is increasingly accepted among educated young people.

Sometimes a glottal stop is pronounced in front of a /p t/ or /k/ if there is not a vowel immediately following (see GLOTTALISATION).

In a true glottal stop there is complete obstruction to the passage of air, and the result is a period of silence. In casual speech it often happens that a speaker aims to produce a complete glottal stop but instead makes a low-pitched creak-like sound.

Glottalisation

The addition of a glottal stop before a consonant.

Examples for English

Adding a glottal stop before certain consonants has the effect of making the preceding vowel somewhat shorter. In English this usually happens before a voiceless PLOSIVE or AFFRICATE consonant if there is not a vowel immediately following (e.g. in *captive, catkin, arctic*; a similar case is that of /tʃ/ when following a stressed vowel or when syllable-final, as in *butcher*). This addition of a glottal stop is sometimes called 'glottal reinforcement', e.g.:

back	/bæk/	[b̥a̟ʔk]	(US)	/bæk/	[b̥æʔk]
captive	/ˈkæp.tɪv/	[ˈkʰa̟ʔp̚.tɪv]	(US)	/ˈkæp.tɪv/	[ˈkʰæʔp̚.tɪv]
catkin	/ˈkæt.kɪn/	[ˈkʰa̟ʔk̚.kɪ̃n]	(US)	/ˈkæt.kɪn/	[ˈkʰæʔk̚.kɪ̃n]
arctic	/ˈɑːk.tɪk/	[ˈɑˑʔk̚.tɪk]	(US)	/ˈɑːrk.tɪk/	[ˈɑˑɻʔk̚.tɪk]
butcher	/ˈbʊtʃ.əʳ/	[ˈbʊʔ.t͡ʃə]	(US)	/ˈbʊtʃ.ɚ/	[ˈbʊʔ.t͡ʃɚ]

This feature of English is an important one for perception. As the difference in voicing between /p t k tʃ/ and /b d g dʒ/ in syllable-final position is negligible, it is the length of the vowel rather than the voicing of the final consonant which contributes strongly to a native speaker's decision of whether a speaker has produced e.g. *back* or *bag*.

lühwein ˈgluː.vaɪn
lum glʌm **-mer** -əʳ (US) -ɚ **-mest** -ɪst, -əst **-ly** -li **-ness** -nəs, -nɪs
lusburn ˈglʌz.bɜːn (US) -bɝːn
lut glʌt **-s** -s **-ting** -ɪŋ (US) ˈglʌt̬.ɪŋ **-ted** -ɪd (US) ˈglʌt̬.əd
lutamate ˈgluː.tə.meɪt (US) -t̬ə- **-s** -s
luteal ˈgluː.ti.əl (US) -t̬i-
luten ˈgluː.tᵊn, -tɪn
lute|us ˈgluː.ti|.əs (US) -t̬i- **-i** -aɪ
luteus maximus ˌgluː.ti.əsˈmæk.sɪm.əs (US) -t̬i-
lutinous ˈgluː.tɪ.nəs, -tᵊn.əs (US) -tᵊn- **-ly** -li **-ness** -nəs, -nɪs
lutton ˈglʌt.ᵊn **-s** -z
luttoniz|e, **-is|e** ˈglʌt.ᵊn.aɪz **-es** -ɪz **-ing** -ɪŋ **-ed** -d
luttonous ˈglʌt.ᵊn.əs **-ly** -li
luttony ˈglʌt.ᵊn.i
lyceride ˈglɪs.ᵊ.raɪd **-s** -z
lycerin ˈglɪs.ᵊr.ɪn, -iːn; ˌglɪs.əˈriːn
lycerine ˈglɪs.ᵊr.iːn, -ɪn; ˌglɪs.əˈriːn
lycerol ˈglɪs.ᵊ.rɒl (US) -rɑːl, -roʊl
lycogen ˈglaɪ.kəʊ.dʒən, ˈglɪk.əʊ-, -dʒen (US) ˈglaɪ.koʊ-, -kə-
glycol ˈglaɪ.kɒl, ˈglɪk.ɒl (US) ˈglaɪ.kɑːl, -koʊl
Glyde glaɪd
Glyn glɪn
Glynde glaɪnd
Glyndebourne ˈglaɪn*d*.bɔːn, ˈglaɪm- (US) ˈglaɪn*d*.bɔːrn
Glyndwr glɪnˈdaʊəʳ, glen- (US) -ˈdaʊɚ
Glynis ˈglɪn.ɪs
Glynne glɪn
Glyn-Neath ˌglɪnˈniːθ
glyph glɪf **-s** -s
glyptic ˈglɪp.tɪk
gm *(abbrev. for* **gram/s***) singular:* græm *plural:* -z
GM ˌdʒiːˈem *stress shift:* ˌGM ˈfood
G|-man ˈdʒiː|ˌmæn **-men** -ˌmen
GMT ˌdʒiː.emˈtiː
gnarl nɑːl (US) nɑːrl **-s** -z **-ed** -d
gnash næʃ **-es** -ɪz **-ing** -ɪŋ **-ed** -t
gnat næt **-s** -s
gnathic ˈnæθ.ɪk
gnaw nɔː (US) nɑː, nɔː **-s** -z **-ing** -ɪŋ **-ed** -d
gneiss naɪs, gəˈnaɪs
gnocchi ˈnjɒk.i (US) ˈnjɑː.ki
gnome *goblin:* nəʊm (US) noʊm **-s** -z
gnome *maxim:* ˈnəʊ.miː (US) noʊm **-s** -z
gnomic ˈnəʊ.mɪk (US) ˈnoʊ-
gnomish ˈnəʊ.mɪʃ (US) ˈnoʊ-
gnomon ˈnəʊ.mɒn, -mən (US) ˈnoʊ.mɑːn, -mən **-s** -z
gnomonic nəʊˈmɒn.ɪk (US) noʊˈmɑː.nɪk **-al** -ᵊl **-ally** -ᵊl.i, -li
Gnosall ˈnəʊ.səl (US) ˈnoʊ-
gnostic **(G)** ˈnɒs.tɪk (US) ˈnɑː.stɪk **-s** -s
gnosticism **(G)** ˈnɒs.tɪ.sɪ.zᵊm (US) ˈnɑː.stə-
gnu nuː, -njuː **-s** -z
go gəʊ (US) goʊ **-es** -z **-ing** -ɪŋ **went** went **gone** gɒn (US) gɑːn, gɔːn **goer/s** ˈgəʊ.əʳ/z (US) ˈgoʊ.ɚ/z
Goa gəʊə (US) goʊə
goad gəʊd (US) goʊd **-s** -z **-ing** -ɪŋ **-ed** -ɪd
go-ahead *(adj.)* ˈgəʊ.ə.hed, ˌ--ˈ- (US) ˈgoʊ-
go-ahead *(n.)* ˈgəʊ.ə.hed (US) ˈgoʊ-
goal gəʊl (US) goʊl **-s** -z
goalie ˈgəʊ.li (US) ˈgoʊ.li **-s** -z
goalkeeper ˈgəʊlˌkiː.pəʳ (US) ˈgoʊlˌkiː.pɚ **-s** -z

goalless ˈɡəʊl.ləs, -lɪs ⓊⓈ ˈɡoʊl-
goalmouth ˈɡəʊl.maʊθ ⓊⓈ ˈɡoʊl-
goalpost ˈɡəʊl.pəʊst ⓊⓈ ˈɡoʊl.poʊst **-s** -s
goalscorer ˈɡəʊlˌskɔː.rəʳ ⓊⓈ ˈɡoʊlˌskɔːr.ɚ **-s** -z
goaltender ˈɡəʊlˌten.dəʳ ⓊⓈ ˈɡoʊlˌten.dɚ **-s** -z
Goan ɡəʊ.ən ⓊⓈ ɡoʊ.ən
Goanese ˌɡəʊ.əˈniːz ⓊⓈ ˌɡoʊ.ə-
goanna ɡəʊˈæn.ə ⓊⓈ ɡoʊ- **-s** -z
goat ɡəʊt ⓊⓈ ɡoʊt **-s** -s ˌ**get someone's** ˈ**goat**
goatee ɡəʊˈtiː ⓊⓈ ɡoʊ- **-s** -z *stress shift, British only, see compounds:* ˌ**goatee** ˈ**beard** ⓊⓈ **goaˈtee** ˌ**beard**
goatherd ˈɡəʊt.hɜːd ⓊⓈ ˈɡoʊt.hɝːd **-s** -z
Goathland ˈɡəʊθ.lənd ⓊⓈ ˈɡoʊθ-
goatish ˈɡəʊ.tɪʃ ⓊⓈ ˈɡoʊ-
goatskin ˈɡəʊt.skɪn ⓊⓈ ˈɡoʊt- **-s** -z
goatsucker ˈɡəʊtˌsʌk.əʳ ⓊⓈ ˈɡoʊtˌsʌk.ɚ **-s** -z
gob ɡɒb ⓊⓈ ɡɑːb **-s** -z **-bing** -ɪŋ **-bed** -d
gobbet ˈɡɒb.ɪt ⓊⓈ ˈɡɑː.bɪt **-s** -s
Gobbi ˈɡɒb.i ⓊⓈ ˈɡɑː.bi
gobbl|e ˈɡɒb.l̩ ⓊⓈ ˈɡɑː.bl̩ **-es** -z **-ing** -ɪŋ, ˈɡɒb.lɪŋ ⓊⓈ ˈɡɑː.bl̩.ɪŋ, ˈ-blɪŋ **-ed** -d **-er/s** -əʳ/z, ˈɡɒb.ləʳ/z ⓊⓈ ˈɡɑː.bl̩.ɚ/z, ˈ-blɚ/z
gobbledygook, gobbledegook ˈɡɒb.l̩.diˌɡuːk, -ˌɡʊk ⓊⓈ ˈɡɑː.bl̩-
Gobbo ˈɡɒb.əʊ ⓊⓈ ˈɡɑː.boʊ
Gobelin ˈɡəʊ.bəl.ɪn, ˈɡɒb.əl- ⓊⓈ ˈɡoʊ.bəl-
go-between ˈɡəʊ.bɪˌtwiːn, -bə- ⓊⓈ ˈɡoʊ.bə- **-s** -z
Gobi ˈɡəʊ.bi ⓊⓈ ˈɡoʊ-
goblet ˈɡɒb.lət, -lɪt ⓊⓈ ˈɡɑː.blət **-s** -s
goblin ˈɡɒb.lɪn ⓊⓈ ˈɡɑː.blɪn **-s** -z
gobsmack ˈɡɒb.smæk ⓊⓈ ˈɡɑːb- **-s** -s **-ing** -ɪŋ **-ed** -t
gobstopper ˈɡɒbˌstɒp.əʳ ⓊⓈ ˈɡɑːbˌstɑː.pɚ **-s** -z
gob|y ˈɡəʊ.b|i ⓊⓈ ˈɡoʊ- **-ies** -iz
go-by ˈɡəʊˌbaɪ ⓊⓈ ˈɡoʊ-
go-cart ˈɡəʊ.kɑːt ⓊⓈ ˈɡoʊ.kɑːrt **-s** -s
god (G) ɡɒd ⓊⓈ ɡɑːd **-s** -z
Godalming ˈɡɒd.əl.mɪŋ ⓊⓈ ˈɡɑː.dəl-
Godard ˈɡɒd.ɑː ⓊⓈ ɡoʊˈdɑːr
god-awful ˌɡɒdˈɔː.fəl ⓊⓈ ˌɡɑːdˈɑː-, -ˈɔː- *stress shift:* ˌgod-awful ˈnoise
god|child ˈɡɒd|.tʃaɪld ⓊⓈ ˈɡɑːd- **-children** -ˌtʃɪl.drən
goddam(n) ˈɡɒd.æm, ˈɡɒd.dæm ⓊⓈ ˌɡɑːdˈdæm, ˈɡɑːd-
goddamned ˈɡɒd.æmd, ˈɡɒd.dæmd ⓊⓈ ˈɡɑːd.æmd
Goddard ˈɡɒd.ɑːd, -əd ⓊⓈ ˈɡɑː.dɚd, -dɑːrd
goddaughter ˈɡɒdˌdɔː.təʳ ⓊⓈ ˈɡɑːdˌdɑː.t̬ɚ, -ˌdɔː- **-s** -z
Godden ˈɡɒd.ən ⓊⓈ ˈɡɑː.dən
goddess ˈɡɒd.es, -ɪs, -əs ⓊⓈ ˈɡɑː.dɪs, -dəs **-es** -ɪz
Goderich ˈɡəʊ.drɪtʃ ⓊⓈ ˈɡoʊ-
godetia ɡəʊˈdiː.ʃə, -ʃi.ə ⓊⓈ ɡə- **-s** -z
godfather (G) ˈɡɒd.fɑː.ðəʳ ⓊⓈ ˈɡɑːdˌfɑː.ðɚ **-s** -z
god-fearing (G) ˈɡɒdˌfɪə.rɪŋ ⓊⓈ ˈɡɑːd.fɪr.ɪŋ
godforsaken ˈɡɒd.fəˌseɪ.kən ⓊⓈ ˈɡɑːd.fɚ-
Godfrey ˈɡɒd.fri ⓊⓈ ˈɡɑːd-
god-given ˈɡɒdˌɡɪv.ən ⓊⓈ ˈɡɑːd-
godhead (G) ˈɡɒd.hed ⓊⓈ ˈɡɑːd- **-s** -z
Godiva ɡəˈdaɪ.və
Godkin ˈɡɒd.kɪn ⓊⓈ ˈɡɑːd-
godless ˈɡɒd.ləs, -lɪs ⓊⓈ ˈɡɑːd- **-ly** -li **-ness** -nəs, -nɪs
godlike ˈɡɒd.laɪk ⓊⓈ ˈɡɑːd-
godl|y ˈɡɒd.l|i ⓊⓈ ˈɡɑːd- **-ier** -i.əʳ ⓊⓈ -i.ɚ **-iest** -i.ɪst, -i.əst **-iness** -ɪ.nəs, -ɪ.nɪs
Godman ˈɡɒd.mən ⓊⓈ ˈɡɑːd-
Godmanchester ˈɡɒd.mənˌtʃes.təʳ ⓊⓈ ˈɡɑːd.mənˌtʃes.tɚ
godmother ˈɡɒdˌmʌð.əʳ ⓊⓈ ˈɡɑːdˌmʌð.ɚ **-s** -z
Godolphin ɡəˈdɒl.fɪn ⓊⓈ -ˈdɑːl-
Godot ˈɡɒd.əʊ ⓊⓈ ɡəˈdoʊ, ɡɑː-
godown ˈɡəʊ.daʊn ⓊⓈ ˈɡoʊ- **-s** -z
godparent ˈɡɒdˌpeə.rənt ⓊⓈ ˈɡɑːdˌper.ənt, -ˌpær- **-s** -s
godsend ˈɡɒd.send ⓊⓈ ˈɡɑːd- **-s** -z
God-slot ˈɡɒdˌslɒt ⓊⓈ ˈɡɑːdˌslɑːt **-s** -s
godson ˈɡɒd.sʌn ⓊⓈ ˈɡɑːd- **-s** -z
Godspeed ˌɡɒdˈspiːd ⓊⓈ ˌɡɑːd-
Godunov ˈɡɒd.ə.nɒf, ˈɡʊd-, -u- ⓊⓈ ˈɡʊd.ə.nɑːf
Godward ˈɡɒd.wəd ⓊⓈ ˈɡɑːd.wɚd
Godwin ˈɡɒd.wɪn ⓊⓈ ˈɡɑːd-
godwit ˈɡɒd.wɪt ⓊⓈ ˈɡɑːd- **-s** -s
Godzilla ɡɒdˈzɪl.ə ⓊⓈ ɡɑːd-
Goebbels ˈɡɜː.bəlz, -bəls
Goering ˈɡɜː.rɪŋ ⓊⓈ ˈɡɝː-
Goethe ˈɡɜː.tə
gofer ˈɡəʊ.fəʳ ⓊⓈ ˈɡoʊ.fɚ **-s** -z
Goff(e) ɡɒf ⓊⓈ ɡɑːf
goff|er ˈɡəʊ.f|əʳ, ˈɡɒf|.əʳ ⓊⓈ ˈɡɑː.f|ɚ **-ers** -əz ⓊⓈ -ɚz **-ering** -ər.ɪŋ **-ered** -əd ⓊⓈ -ɚd
Gog ɡɒɡ ⓊⓈ ɡɑːɡ, ɡɔːɡ
Gogarty ˈɡəʊ.ɡə.ti ⓊⓈ ˈɡoʊ.ɡɚ.t̬i
go-getter ˈɡəʊˌɡet.əʳ, ˌ-ˈ-- ⓊⓈ ˈɡoʊˌɡet̬.ɚ **-s** -z
goggl|e ˈɡɒɡ.l̩ ⓊⓈ ˈɡɑː.ɡl̩ **-es** -z **-ing** -ɪŋ, ˈ-lɪŋ ⓊⓈ ˈ-ɡl̩.ɪŋ, ˈ-ɡlɪŋ **-ed** -d
goggle-box ˈɡɒɡ.l̩.bɒks ⓊⓈ ˈɡɑː.ɡl̩.bɑːks **-es** -ɪz
goggle-eyed ˌɡɒɡ.l̩ˈaɪd ⓊⓈ ˈɡɑː.ɡl̩ˌaɪd *stress shift, British only:* ˌgoggle-eyed ˈcrowd
Gogmagog ˈɡɒɡ.mə.ɡɒɡ ⓊⓈ ˈɡɑːɡ.mə.ɡɑːɡ, ˈɡɔːɡ-, -ɡɔːɡ
a go-go, à go-go əˈɡəʊ.ɡəʊ ⓊⓈ -ˈɡoʊ.ɡoʊ
go-go ˈɡəʊ.ɡəʊ ⓊⓈ ˈɡoʊ.ɡoʊ ˈ**go-go** ˌ**dancer**
Gogo ˈɡəʊ.ɡəʊ ⓊⓈ ˈɡoʊ.ɡoʊ
Gogol ˈɡəʊ.ɡɒl ⓊⓈ ˈɡoʊ.ɡɑːl, -ɡəl
Goiânia ɡɔɪˈɑː.ni.ə
Goidelic ɡɔɪˈdel.ɪk
goings ˈɡəʊ.ɪŋz ⓊⓈ ˈɡoʊ- ˌ**comings and** ˈ**goings**; ˌ**goings-**ˈ**on**
goiter ˈɡɔɪ.təʳ ⓊⓈ -t̬ɚ **-s** -z **-ed** -d
goitre ˈɡɔɪ.təʳ ⓊⓈ -t̬ɚ **-s** -z **-d** -d
goitrous ˈɡɔɪ.trəs
go-kart ˈɡəʊ.kɑːt ⓊⓈ ˈɡoʊ.kɑːrt **-s** -s
Golan ˈɡəʊ.læn, -lɑːn; ⓊⓈ ˈɡoʊ.lɑːn ˌ**Golan** ˈ**Heights**
Golborne ˈɡəʊl.bɔːn ⓊⓈ ˈɡoʊl.bɔːrn
Golby ˈɡəʊl.bi ⓊⓈ ˈɡoʊl-
Golconda ɡɒlˈkɒn.də ⓊⓈ ɡɑːlˈkɑːn.də
gold (G) ɡəʊld ⓊⓈ ɡoʊld **-s** -z ˈ**Gold** ˌ**Coast**; ˈ**gold** ˌ**dust**; ˌ**gold** ˈ**leaf**; ˌ**gold** ˈ**medal**; ˈ**gold** ˌ**mine**; ˈ**gold** ˌ**rush**; **as** ˌ**good as** ˈ**gold**
Golda ˈɡəʊl.də ⓊⓈ ˈɡoʊl-
Goldberg ˈɡəʊl*d*.bɜːɡ ⓊⓈ ˈɡoʊl*d*.bɝːɡ
goldbrick ˈɡəʊl*d*.brɪk ⓊⓈ ˈɡoʊl*d*- **-s** -s **-ing** -ɪŋ **-ed** -d **-er/s** -əʳ/z ⓊⓈ -ɚ/z
goldcrest ˈɡəʊl*d*.krest ⓊⓈ ˈɡoʊl*d*- **-s** -s
gold-digger ˈɡəʊl*d*ˌdɪɡ.əʳ ⓊⓈ ˈɡoʊl*d*ˌdɪɡ.ɚ **-s** -z
golden (G) ˈɡəʊl.dən ⓊⓈ ˈɡoʊl- ˌ**golden** ˈ**age** ⓊⓈ ˈ**golden** ˌ**age**; ˌ**golden** ˈ**handshake**; ˌ**golden** ˈ**rule**; ˌ**golden** ˈ**syrup**
goldeneye ˈɡəʊl.dən.aɪ ⓊⓈ ˈɡoʊl- **-s** -z
goldfield ˈɡəʊl*d*.fiːld ⓊⓈ ˈɡoʊl*d*- **-s** -z
goldfinch ˈɡəʊl*d*.fɪntʃ ⓊⓈ ˈɡoʊl*d*- **-es** -ɪz
goldfish ˈɡəʊl*d*.fɪʃ ⓊⓈ ˈɡoʊl*d*- **-es** -ɪz ˈ**goldfish** ˌ**bowl**
Goldilocks ˈɡəʊl.dɪ.lɒks ⓊⓈ ˈɡoʊl.di.lɑːks
Golding ˈɡəʊl.dɪŋ ⓊⓈ ˈɡoʊl-
Goldman ˈɡəʊl*d*.mən ⓊⓈ ˈɡoʊl*d*-
Goldsborough ˈɡəʊldz.bər.ə ⓊⓈ ˈɡoʊldz.bɚ.oʊ
Goldschmidt ˈɡəʊld.ʃmɪt ⓊⓈ ˈɡoʊld-
goldsmith (G) ˈɡəʊld.smɪθ ⓊⓈ ˈɡoʊld- **-s** -s
Goldstein ˈɡəʊld.staɪn, -stiːn ⓊⓈ ˈɡoʊld-
Goldwyn ˈɡəʊl.dwɪn ⓊⓈ ˈɡoʊl-
golem ˈɡəʊ.lem ⓊⓈ ˈɡoʊ- **-s** -z
golf (*n. v.*) ɡɒlf *old-fashioned, sometimes used by players:* ɡɒf ⓊⓈ ɡɑːlf **-s** -s **-ing** -ɪŋ **-ed** -t ˈ**golf** ˌ**club**; ˈ**golf** ˌ**course**; ˈ**golf** ˌ**links**
golfer ˈɡɒl.fəʳ, ˈɡɒf.əʳ ⓊⓈ ˈɡɑːl.fɚ **-s**
Golgotha ˈɡɒl.ɡə.θə ⓊⓈ ˈɡɑːl-
Goliath ɡəʊˈlaɪ.əθ ⓊⓈ ɡə-
Golightly ɡəʊˈlaɪt.li ⓊⓈ ɡoʊ-
Gollancz ɡəˈlænts, -ˈlæŋ*k*s, ɡɒlˈænts,

-'æŋks, 'gɒl.ənts, -æŋks (US) gə'lænts, 'gɑː.lənts, -lænts
golliwog 'gɒl.ɪ.wɒg (US) 'gɑː.li.wɔːg, -wɑːg -s -z
jolly 'gɒl.i (US) 'gɑː.li
gollywog 'gɒl.ɪ.wɒg (US) 'gɑː.lɪ.wɔːg, -wɑːg -s -z
golosh gə'lɒʃ (US) gə'lɑːʃ -es -ɪz
Gomar 'gəʊ.məʳ (US) 'goʊ.mɚ
Gomer 'gəʊ.məʳ (US) 'goʊ.mɚ
Gomersal 'gɒm.ə.səl (US) 'gɑː.mɚ.səl
Gomes 'gəʊ.mez (US) 'goʊ-
Gomez, **Gómez** 'gəʊ.mez (US) 'goʊ-
gomme gɒm (US) gɑːm
Gomorrah gə'mɒr.ə (US) -'mɔːr.ə, -'mɑːr-
Gompers 'gɒm.pəz (US) 'gɑːm.pɚz
Gomshall 'gʌm.ʃəl, 'gɒm- (US) 'gɑːm-
gonad 'gəʊ.næd (US) 'goʊ- -s -z
Goncourt ˌgɒn'kʊəʳ, ˌgɒŋ-, ˌgɔ̃ːŋ- (US) ˌgoʊn'kʊr
gondola 'gɒn.dəl.ə (US) 'gɑːn- -s -z
gondolier ˌgɒn.də'lɪəʳ, -dəl'ɪəʳ (US) ˌgɑːn.də'lɪr -s -z
Gondwana gɒnd'wɑː.nə (US) gɑːnd- **-land** -lænd
gone (*from* **go**) gɒn (US) gɑːn
goner 'gɒn.əʳ (US) 'gɑː.nɚ -s -z
Goneril 'gɒn.ər.ɪl, -əl (US) 'gɑː.nər.əl
gonfalon 'gɒn.fəl.ən (US) 'gɑːn- -s -z
gong gɒŋ (US) gɑːŋ, gɔːŋ -s -z
goniometer ˌgəʊ.ni'ɒm.ɪ.təʳ, '-ə- (US) ˌgoʊ.ni'ɑː.mə.t̬ɚ -s -z
goniometric ˌgəʊ.ni.ə'met.rɪk (US) ˌgoʊ-
gonk gɒŋk (US) gɑːŋk, gɔːŋk -s -s
gonna gən.ə, 'gɒn.ə (US) 'gɑː.nə, 'gɔː-
gonorrh(o)e|a ˌgɒn.ə'riː|.ə (US) ˌgɑː.nə'- **-al** -əl
Gonville 'gɒn.vɪl (US) 'gɑːn-
Gonzales gɒn'zɑː.lɪs, gən-, -lez (US) gən'zɑː.ləs, gɑːn-, -'sɑː-, -leɪs
Gonzalez gɒn'zɑː.lɪs, gən-, -lez (US) gən'zɑːl.əs, gɑːn-, -'sɑː-, -leɪs
Gonzo 'gɒn.zəʊ (US) 'gɑːn.zoʊ
goo guː
goober 'guː.bəʳ (US) -bɚ -s -z
gooch guːtʃ
good (**G**) (*n. adj. interj.*) gʊd -s -z **-ness** -nəs, -nɪs ˌ**good** '**day**; ˌ**Good** '**Friday**; ˌ**good** '**grief!**; ˌ**Good** '**Heavens!**; '**goods** ˌ**train**; **as** ˌ**good as** '**gold**
Goodale 'gʊd.eɪl
Goodall 'gʊd.ɔːl (US) -ɔːl, -ɑːl
Goodbody 'gʊd.bɒd.i (US) -bɑː.di
goodbye (*n.*) gʊd'baɪ -s -z
goodbye (*interj.*) gʊd'baɪ
godchild 'gʊd.tʃaɪld
Goode gʊd
Goodell gʊ'del
goodenough 'gʊd.ɪ.nʌf, '-ə-, -ən.ʌf
goodfellow 'gʊdˌfel.əʊ (US) -oʊ
good-for-nothing 'gʊd.fəˌnʌθ.ɪŋ, ˌgʊd.fə'nʌθ- (US) 'gʊd.fɚˌnʌθ-, ˌgʊd.fɚ'nʌθ- -s -z
Goodge guːdʒ, gʊdʒ
Goodhart 'gʊd.hɑːt (US) -hɑːrt
good-hearted ˌgʊd'hɑː.tɪd (US) -'hɑːr.t̬əd **-ness** -nəs, -nɪs *stress shift:* ˌgood-hearted 'person
good-humo(u)red ˌgʊd'hjuː.məd (US) -'hjuː.mɚd, -'juː- **-ly** -li **-ness** -nəs, -nɪs *stress shift:* ˌgood-humo(u)red 'friend
goodie 'gʊd.i -s -z
goodish 'gʊd.ɪʃ
Goodison 'gʊd.ɪ.sən, -ə-
Goodliffe 'gʊd.lɪf
good-looking ˌgʊd'lʊk.ɪŋ *stress shift:* ˌgood-looking 'guy
goodl|y 'gʊd.l|i **-ier** -i.əʳ (US) -i.ɚ **-iest** -i.ɪst, -i.əst **-iness** -ɪ.nəs, -ɪ.nɪs
good|man 'gʊd|.mæn **-men** -men
Goodman 'gʊd.mən
good morning gʊd'mɔː.nɪŋ (US) -'mɔːr-
good-natured ˌgʊd'neɪ.tʃəd (US) -tʃɚd **-ly** -li **-ness** -nəs, -nɪs *stress shift:* ˌgood-natured 'smile
goodness 'gʊd.nəs, -nɪs
good night ˌgʊd'naɪt
Goodrich 'gʊd.rɪtʃ
Goodson 'gʊd.sən
goods-train 'gʊdz.treɪn -s -z
good-tempered ˌgʊd'tem.pəd (US) -pɚd **-ly** -li **-ness** -nəs, -nɪs *stress shift:* ˌgood-tempered 'horse
goodwill gʊd'wɪl -s -z
Goodwin 'gʊd.wɪn
Goodwood 'gʊd.wʊd
good|y (**G**) 'gʊd|.i **-ies** -iz ˌ**goody-**'**two-shoes**
Goodyear® 'gʊd.jɪəʳ, -jəʳ, -jɜːʳ (US) -jɪr, -jɚ, 'gʊdʒ.ɪr
Goodyer 'gʊd.jəʳ
goody-good|y 'gʊd.iˌgʊd|.i **-ies** -iz
goo|ey 'guː|.i **-ier** -i.əʳ (US) -i.ɚ **-iest** -i.ɪst, -i.əst **-iness** -ɪ.nəs, -ɪ.nɪs
goof guːf -s -s **-ing** -ɪŋ **-ed** -t
goofball 'guːf.bɔːl (US) -bɔːl, -bɑːl -s -z
goof|y (**G**) 'guː.f|i **-ier** -i.əʳ (US) -i.ɚ **-iest** -i.ɪst, -i.əst **-ily** -ɪ.li, -əl.i **-iness** -ɪ.nəs, -ɪ.nɪs
Googe guːdʒ, gʊdʒ
Googie 'guː.gi
Google 'guː.gl̩
googl|y 'guː.gl|i **-ies** -iz
googol 'guː.gɒl, -gəl (US) -gɑːl, -gəl -s -z
googolplex 'guː.gɒl.pleks, -gəl- (US) -gɑːl-, -gəl-
Goole guːl
gooll|ie, **gooll|y** 'guː.l|i **-ies** -iz
goon guːn -s -z
Goonhilly ˌguːn'hɪl.i, ˌgʊn- *stress shift:* ˌGoonhilly 'Down
goop guːp
goop|y 'guː.p|i **-ier** -i.əʳ (US) -i.ɚ **-iest** -i.ɪst, -i.əst **-ily** -ɪ.li, -əl.i **-iness** -ɪ.nəs, -ɪ.nɪs
goosander guː'sæn.dəʳ (US) -dɚ -s -z
goose *bird:* guːs **geese** giːs '**goose** ˌ**bumps**; '**goose** ˌ**grass**; '**goose** ˌ**pimples**; ˌ**cook someone's** '**goose**; **(kill) the** ˌ**goose that** ˌ**lays the** ˌ**golden** '**eggs**; ˌ**couldn't say** ˌ**boo to a** '**goose**
goos|e (*v.*) guːs **-es** -ɪz **-ing** -ɪŋ **-ed** -t
goos|e *tailor's iron:* guːs **-es** -ɪz
gooseberr|y 'gʊz.bər|.i, 'guːz-, '-br|i (US) 'guːsˌber|.i, 'guːz-, -bɚ- **-ies** -iz ˌ**gooseberry** '**fool**
gooseflesh 'guːs.fleʃ
goose-step 'guːsˌstep -s -s **-ping** -ɪŋ **-ped** -t
goosey 'guː.si -s -z
GOP ˌdʒiː.əʊ'piː (US) -oʊ'-
gopher 'gəʊ.fəʳ (US) 'goʊ.fɚ -s -z
Gorazde gɔː'ræʒ.deɪ, gə'-
Gorbachev 'gɔː.bə.tʃɒf, ˌ--'- (US) 'gɔːr.bə.tʃɑːf, ˌ--'-
Gorbals 'gɔː.bəlz (US) 'gɔːr-
gorblimey ˌgɔː'blaɪ.mi (US) ˌgɔːr-
Gorboduc 'gɔː.bə.dʌk (US) 'gɔːr-
Gordale 'gɔː.deɪl (US) 'gɔːr-
Gordano gɔː'dɑː.nəʊ, -'deɪ- (US) gɔːr'dɑːn.oʊ
Gordian knot ˌgɔː.di.ən'nɒt (US) ˌgɔːr.di.ən'nɑːt
Gordimer 'gɔː.dɪ.məʳ (US) 'gɔːr-
Gordon 'gɔː.dən (US) 'gɔːr-
Gordonstoun 'gɔː.dən.stən (US) 'gɔːr-
gor|e (**G**) gɔːʳ (US) gɔːr **-es** -z **-ing** -ɪŋ **-ed** -d
Gorebridge 'gɔː.brɪdʒ (US) 'gɔːr-
Gorell 'gɒr.əl (US) ˌgɔː'rel, 'gɑː.rəl
Gore-Tex® 'gɔː.teks (US) 'gɔːr-
gorg|e gɔːdʒ (US) gɔːrdʒ **-es** -ɪz **-ing** -ɪŋ **-ed** -d
gorgeous 'gɔː.dʒəs (US) 'gɔːr- **-ly** -li **-ness** -nəs, -nɪs
Gorges 'gɔː.dʒɪz (US) 'gɔːr-
gorget 'gɔː.dʒɪt, -dʒət (US) 'gɔːr.dʒət -s -s
Gorgie 'gɔː.gi (US) 'gɔːr-
gorgon (**G**) 'gɔː.gən (US) 'gɔːr- -s -z
Gorgonzola ˌgɔː.gən'zəʊ.lə (US) ˌgɔːr.gən'zoʊ-
Gorham 'gɔː.rəm (US) 'gɔːr.əm
gorilla gə'rɪl.ə -s -z
Goring 'gɔː.rɪŋ (US) 'gɔːr.ɪŋ 'gɜː.rɪŋ (US) 'gɝː.ɪŋ, 'gɔːr-
Gorki, **Gorky** 'gɔː.ki (US) 'gɔːr-
Gorleston 'gɔːl.stən (US) 'gɔːrl-
Gorman 'gɔː.mən (US) 'gɔːr-
gormandiz|e, **-is|e** 'gɔː.mən.daɪz (US) 'gɔːr- **-es** -ɪz **-ing** -ɪŋ **-ed** -d **-er/s** -əʳ/z (US) -ɚ/z

Gormenghast ˈgɔː.mən.gɑːst, -məŋ- US ˈgɔːr.mən.gæst, -məŋ-
gormless ˈgɔːm.ləs, -lɪs US ˈgɔːrm- **-ly** -li **-ness** -nəs, -nɪs
Gormley ˈgɔːm.li US ˈgɔːrm-
Goronwy gəˈrɒn.wi US -ˈrɑːn-
gorp gɔːp US gɔːrp
Gorringe ˈgɒr.ɪndʒ, -əndʒ US ˈgɑː.rɪndʒ, ˈgɔː-
gorse gɔːs US gɔːrs
Gorseinon gɔːˈsaɪ.nən US gɔːr-
Gorst gɔːst US gɔːrst
Gorton ˈgɔː.tᵊn US ˈgɔːr-
gor|y ˈgɔː.r|i US ˈgɔːr|.i **-ier** -i.əʳ US -i.ɚ **-iest** -i.ɪst, -i.əst **-ily** -ᵊl.i, -ɪ.li **-iness** -ɪ.nəs, -ɪ.nɪs
Goschen ˈgəʊ.ʃᵊn, ˈgɒʃ.ᵊn US ˈgoʊ-
gosh gɒʃ US gɑːʃ
goshawk ˈgɒs.hɔːk US ˈgɑːs.hɑːk, -hɔːk **-s** -s
Goshen ˈgəʊ.ʃᵊn, ˈgɒʃ.ᵊn US ˈgoʊ-
gosling (G) ˈgɒz.lɪŋ US ˈgɑːz- **-s** -z
go-slow ˌgəʊˈsləʊ, ˈ-- US ˈgoʊ.sloʊ **-s** -z
gospel (G) ˈgɒs.pᵊl, -pel US ˈgɑːs- **-s** -z ˈ**gospel** ˌ**music**
gospel(l)er ˈgɒs.pᵊl.əʳ US ˈgɑː.spᵊl.ɚ **-s** -z
Gosport ˈgɒs.pɔːt US ˈgɑːs.pɔːrt
gossamer ˈgɒs.ə.məʳ US ˈgɑː.sə.mɚ
Goss(e) gɒs US gɑːs
gossip (*n. v.*) ˈgɒs.ɪp US ˈgɑː.səp **-s** -s **-ing** -ɪŋ **-ed** -t **-y** -i
got *(from* **get***)* gɒt US gɑːt
Göteborg ˈjɜː.tə.bɔː US -bɔːr
goth (G) gɒθ US gɑːθ **-s** -s
Gotha *in Germany:* ˈgəʊ.θə, ˈgəʊ.tə US ˈgoʊ.t̬ə *old-fashioned English spelling of* **Göta** *in Sweden:* ˈgəʊ.tə US ˈgoʊ.t̬ə
Gotham *in Nottinghamshire:* ˈgəʊ.təm US ˈgoʊ.t̬əm *New York:* ˈgɒθ.əm US ˈgɑː.θəm
Gothenburg ˈgɒθ.ᵊn.bɜːg, ˈgɒt-, -ᵊm- US ˈgɑː.θᵊn.bɝːg, -tᵊn-
gothic (G) ˈgɒθ.ɪk US ˈgɑː.θɪk
Gothicism ˈgɒθ.ɪ.sɪ.zᵊm, ˈ-ə- US ˈgɑː.θə-
gothiciz|e, -is|e ˈgɒθ.ɪ.saɪz, ˈ-ə- US ˈgɑː.θə- **-es** -ɪz **-ing** -ɪŋ **-ed** -d
Gothland ˈgɒθ.lənd US ˈgɑːt-
Gotland ˈgɒt.lənd US ˈgɑːt-
gotta ˈgɒt.ə US ˈgɑː.t̬ə
gotten *(from* **get***)* ˈgɒt.ᵊn US ˈgɑː.tᵊn
götterdämmerung (G) ˌgɜː.təˈdem.ə.rʊŋ, -ˈdeɪ.mə- US ˌgɜː.t̬ɚˈdem-
Gotthard ˈgɒt.ɑːd US ˈgɑː.tɑːrd
Gotti ˈgɒt.i US ˈgɑː.t̬i
Göttingen ˈgɜː.tɪŋ.ən US ˈgɝː-
gouache guˈɑːʃ, -ˈæʃ, gwɑːʃ, gwæʃ
Gouda ˈgaʊ.də US ˈguː-
Goudie ˈgaʊ.di
goug|e gaʊdʒ, guːdʒ US gaʊdʒ **-es** -ɪz **-ing** -ɪŋ **-ed** -d
Gough gɒf US gɑːf
goujon ˈguː.dʒɒn, -ʒɒn, -ʒɔ̃ːŋ US guːˈʒoʊn **-s** -z
goulash ˈguː.læʃ US -lɑːʃ, -læʃ **-es** -ɪz
Goulburn *place-name:* ˈgəʊl.bɜːn US ˈgoʊl.bɝːn *surname:* ˈguːl.bɜːn, ˈgəʊl.bən US ˈguːl.bɝːn, ˈgoʊl.bɚn
Gould guːld
Goulden ˈguːl.dən
Goulding ˈguːl.dɪŋ
Gouler ˈguː.ləʳ US -lɚ
Gounod ˈguː.nəʊ US -noʊ
gourd gʊəd, gɔːd US gɔːrd, gʊrd **-s** -z
gourde gʊəd, gɔːd US gɔːrd, gʊrd **-s** -z
Gourl|ay ˈgʊə.l|eɪ, -l|i US ˈgʊr.l|i **-ey** -i
gourmand ˈgʊə.mənd, ˈgɔː-, -mɑ̃ŋ US ˈgʊr.mɑːnd, -mənd; **-s** -z
gourmet ˈgʊə.meɪ, ˈgɔː- US ˈgʊr.meɪ, -ˈ- **-s** -z
Gourock ˈgʊə.rək US ˈgʊr.ək
gout gaʊt **-y** -i US ˈgaʊ.t̬i **-ily** -ɪ.li, -ᵊl.i US ˈgaʊ.t̬ɪ.li, -t̬ᵊl.i **-iness** -ɪ.nəs, -ɪ.nɪs US ˈgaʊ.t̬ɪ.nəs, -t̬ɪ-
Govan ˈgʌv.ᵊn
Gover ˈgəʊ.vəʳ US ˈgoʊ.vɚ
govern ˈgʌv.ᵊn US -ɚn **-s** -z **-ing** -ɪŋ **-ed** -d **-able** -ə.bl̩
governance ˈgʌv.ᵊn.ənts US -ɚ.nᵊnts
governess ˈgʌv.ᵊn.əs, -ɪs, -es US -ɚ.nəs **-es** -ɪz
government ˈgʌv.ᵊn.mənt, -ᵊm.mənt, -və.mənt US -ɚn- **-s** -s
governmental ˌgʌv.ᵊnˈmen.tᵊl, -ᵊmˈmen-, -əˈmen- US -ɚnˈmen.t̬ᵊl
governor ˈgʌv.ᵊn.əʳ US -ɚ.nɚ **-s** -z
governor-general ˌgʌv.ᵊn.əˈdʒen.ᵊr.ᵊl US -ɚ.nɚˈ- **-s** -z
governorship ˈgʌv.ᵊn.ə.ʃɪp US -ɚ.nɚ- **-s** -s
Govey ˈgəʊ.vi US ˈgoʊ-
Govier ˈgəʊ.vi.əʳ US ˈgoʊ.vi.ɚ
Gow gaʊ
Gowan gaʊən
Gowdy ˈgaʊ.di
Gowen gaʊən, gaʊɪn
Gower gaʊəʳ, gɔːʳ US gaʊɚ
Note: /gaʊəʳ/ is used in **Gower Street** and for the place in Wales. /gɔːʳ/ is the family name of the Duke of Sutherland; this pronunciation is also used in **Leveson-Gower** .
Gowing ˈgaʊ.ɪŋ
gowk gaʊk **-s** -s
Gowlett ˈgaʊ.lət, -lɪt
gown gaʊn **-s** -z **-ed** -d
gowns|man ˈgaʊnz|.mən **-men** -mən, -men
Gowrie ˈgaʊ.ri
Gowther ˈgaʊ.ðəʳ US -ðɚ
Gowy ˈgaʊ.i
goy gɔɪ **-s** -z **-im** -ɪm **-ish** -ɪʃ
Goya ˈgɔɪ.ə
Gozo ˈgəʊ.zəʊ US ˈgoʊ.zoʊ
GP ˌdʒiːˈpiː **-s** -z
GPA ˌdʒiː.piːˈeɪ
GPO ˌdʒiː.piːˈəʊ US -ˈoʊ
GPS ˌdʒiː.piːˈes
grab græb **-s** -z **-bing** -ɪŋ **-bed** -d **-be**[...] -əʳ/z US -ɚ/z ˈ**grab** ˌ**bag**; ˌ**up for** ˈ**grabs**
grabbl|e ˈgræb.l̩ **-es** -z **-ing** -ɪŋ, ˈ-lɪŋ **-ed** -d
grabb|y ˈgræb|.i **-ier** -i.əʳ US -i.ɚ **-ie**[...] -i.ɪst, -i.əst
Grabham ˈgræb.əm
Gracch|us ˈgræk|.əs **-i** -iː, -aɪ
grac|e (G) greɪs **-es** -ɪz **-ing** -ɪŋ **-ed** [...] ˈ**grace** ˌ**note**; ˌ**fall from** ˈ**grace**
Gracechurch ˈgreɪs.tʃɜːtʃ US -tʃɝː[...]
graceful ˈgreɪs.fᵊl, -fʊl **-ly** -i **-ness** [...] -nɪs
Graceland ˈgreɪs.lænd, -lənd
graceless ˈgreɪ.sləs, -slɪs **-ly** -li **-ne**[...] -nəs, -nɪs
Gracie ˈgreɪ.si
gracious ˈgreɪ.ʃəs **-ly** -li **-ness** -nəs[...]
grackle ˈgræk.l̩ **-s** -z
grad græd **-s** -z ˈ**grad** ˌ**school**
gradability ˌgreɪ.dəˈbɪl.ə.ti, -ɪ.ti US -ə.t̬i
gradable ˈgreɪ.də.bl̩
gra|date grə|ˈdeɪt US ˈgreɪ|.deɪt [...] -ˈdeɪts US -deɪts **-dating** -ˈdeɪ.t[...] US -deɪ.t̬ɪŋ **-dated** -ˈdeɪ.tɪd US -deɪ.t̬əd
gradation grəˈdeɪ.ʃᵊn US greɪ- **-s**
gradational grəˈdeɪ.ʃᵊn.ᵊl US gre[...]
grad|e greɪd **-es** -z **-ing** -ɪŋ **-ed** -ɪd ˌ**grade point** ˈ**average** US ˈ**grad**[...] ˌ**average**; ˈ**grade** ˌ**school**; ˌ**make** ˈ**grade**
gradeable ˈgreɪ.də.bl̩
gradely ˈgreɪd.li
Gradgrind ˈgræd.graɪnd
gradient ˈgreɪ.di.ənt **-s** -s
gradin ˈgreɪ.dɪn **-s** -z
graditative ˈgreɪ.dɪ.tə.tɪv, -də-[...]
gradual ˈgrædʒ.u.əl, ˈgræd.ju.ə[...] US ˈgrædʒ.u.əl **-s** -z **-ly** -i
graduate (*n.*) ˈgrædʒ.u.ət, ˈgræd[...] -ɪt US ˈgrædʒ.u.ət, -ɪt **-s** -s
gradu|ate (*v.*) ˈgræd.ju|.eɪt, ˈgræ[...] US ˈgrædʒ.u- **-ates** -eɪts **-ating** -eɪ.tɪŋ US -eɪ.t̬ɪŋ **-ated** -eɪ.tɪd US -eɪ.t̬ɪd
graduation ˌgrædʒ.uˈeɪ.ʃᵊn, ˌgr[...] US ˌgrædʒ.uˈ- **-s** -z
graduator ˈgrædʒ.u.eɪ.təʳ, ˈgræ[...] US ˈgrædʒ.u.eɪ.t̬ɚ **-s** -z
gradus ˈgræd.əs, ˈgreɪ.dəs **-es** -[...]
Grady ˈgreɪ.di
Graecism ˈgriː.sɪ.zᵊm

raeco- 'griː.kəʊ-, 'grek.əʊ- (US) 'grek.oʊ-, 'griː.koʊ-
raeme greɪəm, greɪm
raf grɑːf, græf (US) græf
raf(f)ham 'græf.əm
raffiti grə'fiː.ti, græf'iː- (US) grə'fiː.t̬i
raft grɑːft (US) græft -s -s -ing -ɪŋ -ed -ɪd -er/s -əʳ/z (US) -ɚ/z
rafton 'grɑːf.tᵊn (US) 'græf-
raham cracker 'greɪəm,kræk.əʳ (US) -ɚ, 'græm- -s -z
raham(e) 'greɪəm
raham flour 'greɪəm,flaʊəʳ (US) -,flaʊɚ
rahamston 'greɪəm.stᵊn
rahamstown 'greɪəmz.taʊn
rail (G) greɪl -s -z
rain greɪn -s -z -ing -ɪŋ -ed -d -er/s -əʳ/z (US) -ɚ/z ,go a,gainst the 'grain
rainger 'greɪn.dʒəʳ (US) -dʒɚ
rain|y 'greɪ.n|i -ier -i.əʳ (US) -i.ɚ -iest -i.ɪst, -i.əst
am græm -s -z
amercy grə'mɜː.si (US) -'mɝː-
aminaceous ,græm.ɪ'neɪ.ʃəs, ,greɪ.mɪ'-, -mə'- (US) ,græm.ə'-
amineous grə'mɪn.i.əs, græm'ɪn-
aminivorous ,græm.ɪ'nɪv.ᵊr.əs, ,greɪ-
ammalogue 'græm.ə.lɒg (US) -lɑːg, -lɔːg -s -z
ammar 'græm.əʳ (US) -ɚ -s -z 'grammar ,school
ammarian grə'meə.ri.ən (US) -'mer.i- -s -z
ammatical grə'mæt.ɪ.kᵊl (US) -mæt̬.ɪ- -ly -i
ammaticality grə,mæt.ɪ'kæl.ə.ti, -ɪ.ti (US) -,mæt̬.ə'kæl.ə.t̬i
ammaticiz|e, -is|e grə'mæt.ɪ.saɪz, -ə- (US) -'mæt̬.ə- -es -ɪz -ing -ɪŋ -ed -d
amme græm -s -z
ammer 'græm.əʳ (US) -ɚ
amm|y 'græm|.i -ys -iz -ies -iz
mophone 'græm.ə.fəʊn (US) -foʊn -s -z
mpian 'græm.pi.ən -s -z
mps græmps
mpus 'græm.pəs -es -ɪz
n græn -s -z
nada grə'nɑː.də
nar|y 'græn.ᵊr|.i -ies -iz 'granary bread
nbury 'græn.bᵊr.i, 'græm- (US) 'græn,ber-, -bɚ-
nby 'græn.bi, 'græm- (US) 'græn-
n Canaria ,græn.kə'neə.ri.ə, ,græŋ- (US) ,grɑːn.kə'nɑː-, -'ner-
n Chaco ,græn'tʃɑː.kəʊ, -'tʃæk.əʊ (US) ,grɑːn'tʃɑː.koʊ
nd grænd -er -əʳ (US) -ɚ -est -ɪst, -əst -ly -li -ness -nəs, -nɪs, 'græn.nəs, -nɪs ,Grand Ca'nary; ,Grand 'Canyon; ,grand 'duchess; ,grand 'duke; ,Grand 'Forks; ,grand 'jury; ,Grand 'National; ,grand pi'ano

grandad (G) 'græn.dæd -s -z
grandadd|y 'græn.dæd|.i -ies -iz
grandam 'græn.dæm, -dəm -s -z
grandaunt 'grænd,ɑːnt (US) -,ænt, -,ɑːnt -s -s
grand|child 'grænd|.tʃaɪld -children -,tʃɪl.drᵊn
granddad (G) 'grænd.dæd -s -z
granddadd|y 'grænd.dæd|.i -ies -iz
granddaughter 'grænd,dɔː.təʳ (US) -,dɑː.t̬ɚ, -,dɔː- -s -z
grande dame ,grɑːnd'dɑːm, ,grɑ̃ːn-, -'dæm -s -z
grandee græn'diː -s -z
grandeur 'græn.djəʳ, -dʒəʳ, -djʊəʳ (US) -dʒɚ, -dʒʊr
grandfather 'grænd,fɑː.ðəʳ (US) -ðɚ -s -z 'grandfather ,clause; ,grandfather 'clock (US) 'grandfather ,clock
Grand Guignol ,grɑ̃ːŋ.giː'njɒl (US) ,grɑ̃ː.giː'njoʊl, ,grɑːn-, -'njɑːl
grandiloquen|ce græn'dɪl.ə.kwən|ts -t/ly -t/li
grandiose 'græn.di.əʊs, -əʊz (US) -oʊs, -oʊz, ,--'- -ly -li
grandiosity ,græn.di'ɒs.ə.ti, -ɪ.ti (US) -'ɑː.sə.t̬i
Grandison 'græn.dɪ.sᵊn
Grandissimes 'grænd.ɪ.siːmz
grandma 'grænd.mɑː, 'græm- -s -z ,Grandma 'Moses
grand mal ,grɑ̃ːnd'mæl (US) ,grɑːnd'mɑːl, ,grænd-, -'mæl
grandmamma 'grænd.mə,mɑː, 'græm- -s -z
Grand Marnier® ,grɑ̃ːnd'mɑː.ni.eɪ (US) ,grɑːn.mɑːr'njeɪ -s -z
grandmaster 'grænd,mɑː.stəʳ, 'græm- (US) 'grænd,mæs.tɚ -s -z
grandmother 'grænd,mʌð.əʳ, 'græm- (US) 'grænd,mʌð.ɚ -s -z
grandnephew 'grænd,nev.juː, -,nef-, ,-'-- (US) 'grænd,nef.juː -s -z
grandniec|e 'grænd.niːs, ,-'- -es -ɪz
grandpa 'grænd.pɑː, 'græm- -s -z
grandpapa 'grænd.pə,pɑː, 'græm- -s -z
grandparent 'grænd,peə.rᵊnt, 'græm- (US) 'grænd,per.ᵊnt, -,pær- -s -s
grand prix ,grɑ̃ːn'priː, ,grɒn-, ,grɒm- (US) ,grɑːn- grands prix ,grɑ̃ː'priː, ,grɒn-, ,grɒm- (US) ,grɑːn-
grandsire 'grænd.saɪəʳ (US) -saɪɚ -s -z
grandson 'grænd.sʌn -s -z
grands prix ,grɑ̃ː'priː, ,grɒn-, ,grɒm- (US) ,grɑːn
grandstand 'grænd.stænd -s -z -ing -ɪŋ -ed -ɪd
granduncle 'grænd,ʌŋ.kl̩ -s -z
grang|e (G) 'greɪndʒ -es -ɪz
Grangemouth 'greɪndʒ.məθ, -maʊθ
Granger 'greɪn.dʒəʳ (US) -dʒɚ
grangeriz|e, -is|e 'greɪn.dʒᵊr.aɪz (US) -dʒə.raɪz -es -ɪz -ing -ɪŋ -ed -d
Grangetown 'greɪndʒ.taʊn
Grangeville 'greɪndʒ.vɪl
granite (G) 'græn.ɪt, -ət -s -s
granitic græn'ɪt.ɪk, grə'nɪt- (US) grə'nɪt̬-
grann|y 'græn|.i -ies -iz 'granny ,flat; 'granny ,knot; ,Granny 'Smith
granola grə'nəʊ.lə, græn'əʊ- (US) grə'noʊ-
granolithic ,græn.əʊ'lɪθ.ɪk (US) -ə'-
grant (G) grɑːnt (US) grænt -s -s -ing -ɪŋ (US) 'græn.t̬ɪŋ -ed -ɪd (US) 'græn.t̬ɪd
Granta 'græn.tə, 'grɑːn- (US) 'græn-
Grantchester 'grɑːn.tʃɪ.stəʳ, 'græn-, -tʃə, -tʃes.təʳ (US) 'græn,tʃes-
grantee ,grɑːn'tiː (US) ,græn- -s -z
Granth grʌnt
Grantham 'grænt.θəm
Granton 'grɑːn.tən, 'græn- (US) 'græn-
grantor ,grɑːn'tɔːʳ; 'grɑːn.təʳ (US) 'græn.t̬ɚ; ,græn'tɔːr -s -z
Grantown 'græn.taʊn
granular 'græn.jə.ləʳ, -jʊ- (US) -jə.lɚ -ly -li
granularity ,græn.jə'lær.ə.ti, -jʊ'-, -ɪ.ti (US) -jə'ler.ə.t̬i, -'lær-
granu|late 'græn.jə|.leɪt, -jʊ- (US) -jə- -lates -leɪts -lating -leɪ.tɪŋ (US) -leɪ.t̬ɪŋ -lated -leɪ.tɪd (US) -leɪ.t̬ɪd
granulation ,græn.jə'leɪ.ʃᵊn, -jʊ'- (US) -jə'- -s -z
granule 'græn.juːl -s -z
granulite 'græn.jə.laɪt, -jʊ- (US) -jə-
granulitic ,græn.jə'lɪt.ɪk, -jʊ'- (US) -jə'lɪt̬-
Granville 'græn.vɪl
Granville-Barker ,græn.vɪl'bɑː.kəʳ (US) -'bɑːr.kɚ
grape (G) greɪp -s -s 'grape ,sugar
grapefruit 'greɪp.fruːt -s -s
grapeshot 'greɪp.ʃɒt (US) -ʃɑːt
grapevine 'greɪp.vaɪn -s -z
graph grɑːf, græf (US) græf -s -s 'graph ,paper
grapheme 'græf.iːm -s -z
graphemic græf'iː.mɪk, grə'fiː- -ally -ᵊl.i, -li
-grapher -grə.fəʳ (US) -grə.fɚ
Note: Suffix. Words containing -**grapher** are normally stressed on the antepenultimate syllable, e.g. **photographer** /fə'tɒg.rə.fəʳ (US) -'tɑː.grə.fɚ/.
graphic (G) 'græf.ɪk -s -s -al -ᵊl -ally -ᵊl.i, -li ,graphic de'sign
-graphic -'græf.ɪk
Note: Suffix. Normally carries primary stress, e.g. **photographic** /,fəʊ.tə'græf.ɪk (US) ,foʊ.t̬ə'-/.

graphite ˈgræf.aɪt
graphitic græfˈɪt.ɪk, grəˈfɪt- US grəˈfɪt̬-
graphological ˌgræf.əˈlɒdʒ.ɪ.kᵊl US -ˈlɑː.dʒɪ- **-ly** -i
grapholog|y græfˈɒl.ə.dʒ|i, grəˈfɒl- US grəˈfɑː.lə- **-ist/s** -ɪst/s
graphometer græfˈɒm.ɪ.təʳ, grəˈfɒm-, ˈ-ə- US grəˈfɑː.mə.t̬ɚ **-s** -z
-graphy -grə.fi
Note: Suffix. Words containing **-graphy** are normally stressed on the antepenultimate syllable, e.g. **photography** /fəˈtɒg.rə.fi US -ˈtɑː.grə-/.
grapnel ˈgræp.nᵊl **-s** -z
grappa ˈgræp.ə US ˈgrɑː.pə **-s** -z
Grappelli græpˈel.i, grəpˈ-
grappl|e ˈgræp.l̩ **-es** -z **-ing** -ɪŋ, ˈ-lɪŋ **-ed** -d **-er/s** -əʳ/z, ˈ-ləʳ/z US ˈ-l̩.ɚ/z, ˈ-lɚ/z ˈ**grappling** ˌ**iron**
grapy ˈgreɪ.pi
Grasmere ˈgrɑːs.mɪəʳ US ˈgræs.mɪr
grasp grɑːsp US græsp **-s** -s **-ing** -ɪŋ **-ed** -t **-er/s** -əʳ/z US -ɚ/z **-able** -ə.bl̩
grass (G) grɑːs US græs **-es** -ɪz **-ing** -ɪŋ **-ed** -t ˌ**grass** ˈ**widow; let the** ˌ**grass** ˌ**grow under one's** ˈ**feet**
grasshopper ˈgrɑːsˌhɒp.əʳ US ˈgræsˌhɑː.pɚ **-s** -z
grassland ˈgrɑːs.lænd, -lənd US ˈgræs-
grass-roots *(adj.)* ˌgrɑːsˈruːts US ˌgræs- *stress shift:* ˌgrass-roots ˈfeeling
grass roots *(n.)* ˌgrɑːsˈruːts US ˌgræs-
grasstree ˈgrɑːs.triː US ˈgræs.triː **-s** -z
grass|y ˈgrɑː.s|i US ˈgræs|.i **-ier** -i.əʳ US -i.ɚ **-iest** -i.ɪst, -i.əst
grat|e *(n. v.)* greɪt **-es** -s **-ing/ly** -ɪŋ/li US ˈgreɪ.t̬ɪŋ/li **-ed** -ɪd US ˈgreɪ.t̬ɪd **-er/s** -əʳ/z US ˈgreɪ.t̬ɚ/z
grateful ˈgreɪt.fᵊl, -fʊl **-ly** -i **-ness** -nəs, -nɪs
Gratian ˈgreɪ.ʃᵊn, -ʃi.ən
graticule ˈgræt.ɪ.kjuːl, ˈ-ə- US ˈ-ə- **-s** -z
gratification ˌgræt.ɪ.fɪˈkeɪ.ʃᵊn, ˌ-ə- US ˌgræt̬.ə- **-s** -z
grati|fy ˈgræt.ɪ|.faɪ, ˈ-ə- US ˈgræt̬.ə- **-fies** -faɪz **-fying/ly** -faɪ.ɪŋ/li **-fied** -faɪd
gratin ˈgræ.tæ̃ŋ, -tæn US ˈgrɑː.tᵊn
grating *(n.)* ˈgreɪ.tɪŋ US -t̬ɪŋ **-s** -z
Gratiot ˈgræʃ.i.ət, ˈgræʃ.ət, ˈgreɪ.ʃi.ət, -ʃət US ˈgræʃ.ət
gratis ˈgrɑː.tɪs, ˈgreɪ-, ˈgræt.ɪs, -əs US ˈgræt̬.əs, ˈgrɑː.t̬əs, ˈgreɪ-
gratitude ˈgræt.ɪ.tjuːd, -tʃuːd, ˈ-ə- US ˈgræt̬.ə.tuːd, -tjuːd
Grattan ˈgræt.ᵊn
gratuitous grəˈtjuː.ɪ.təs, -ˈtʃuː- US -ˈtuː.ə.t̬əs, -ˈtjuː- **-ly** -li **-ness** -nəs, -nɪs
gratuit|y grəˈtjuː.ə.t|i, -ˈtʃuː-, -ɪ.t|i US -ˈtuː.ə.t̬|i, -ˈtjuː- **-ies** -iz
graupel ˈgraʊ.pᵊl
gravadlax ˈgræv.əd.læks US ˈgrɑː.vəd.lɑːks
gravamen grəˈveɪ.men, -ˈvɑː-, -mən US -mən **-s** -z **gravamina** grəˈveɪ.mɪ.nə, -ˈvɑː- US -ˈvæm.ɪn-
grave *accent above a letter:* grɑːv US grɑːv, greɪv
grav|e *other senses:* greɪv **-es** -z **-er** -əʳ US -ɚ **-est** -ɪst, -əst **-ely** -li **-eness** -nəs, -nɪs **-ing** -ɪŋ **-ed** -d **-er/s** -əʳ/z US -ɚ/z ˌ**turn in one's** ˈ**grave**
graveclothes ˈgreɪv.kləʊðz US -kloʊðz
gravedigger ˈgreɪvˌdɪg.əʳ US -ɚ **-s** -z
gravel ˈgræv.ᵊl **-s** -z **-(l)ing** -ɪŋ **-(l)ed** -d **-ly** -i
graven ˈgreɪ.vᵊn ˌ**graven** ˈ**image**
Graves *surname:* greɪvz *wine:* grɑːv
Gravesend ˌgreɪvzˈend
graveside ˈgreɪv.saɪd
gravestone ˈgreɪv.stəʊn US -stoʊn **-s** -z
graveyard ˈgreɪv.jɑːd US -jɑːrd **-s** -z ˈ**graveyard** ˌ**shift,** ˌ**graveyard** ˈ**shift**
gravid ˈgræv.ɪd **-ly** -li **-ness** -nəs, -nɪs
gravid|a ˈgræv.ɪ.d|ə **-as** -əz **-ae** -iː
gravidity grævˈɪd.ɪ.ti, grəˈvɪd- US grəˈvɪd.ə.t̬i
gravitas ˈgræv.ɪ.tæs, ˈ-ə-, -tɑːs
gravi|tate ˈgræv.ɪ|.teɪt, ˈ-ə- **-tates** -teɪts **-tating** -teɪ.tɪŋ US -teɪ.t̬ɪŋ **-tated** -teɪ.tɪd US -teɪ.t̬ɪd
gravitation ˌgræv.ɪˈteɪ.ʃᵊn, -əˈ- **-al** -ᵊl **-ally** -ᵊl.i
gravitative ˈgræv.ɪ.teɪ.tɪv, ˈ-ə-, -tə.tɪv US -teɪ.t̬ɪv
gravity ˈgræv.ə.ti, -ɪ.ti US -ə.t̬i
gravlax ˈgræv.læks US ˈgrɑːv.lɑːks
gravure grəˈvjʊəʳ, -ˈvjɔːʳ US -ˈvjʊr
grav|y ˈgreɪ.v|i **-ies** -iz ˈ**gravy** ˌ**train**
gray (G) greɪ **-s** -z **-er** -əʳ US -ɚ **-est** -ɪst, -əst **-ness** -nəs, -nɪs **-ing** -ɪŋ
grayish ˈgreɪ.ɪʃ
grayling ˈgreɪ.lɪŋ **-s** -z
Grayson ˈgreɪ.sᵊn
graystone (G) ˈgreɪ.stəʊn US -stoʊn
Graz grɑːts
graz|e greɪz **-es** -ɪz **-ing** -ɪŋ **-ed** -d
grazier ˈgreɪ.zi.əʳ, -ʒəʳ US -ʒɚ **-s** -z
GRE ˌdʒiː.ɑːrˈiː **-s** -z
Greasby ˈgriːz.bi
greas|e griːs **-es** -ɪz **-ing** -ɪŋ **-ed** -t
greasepaint ˈgriːs.peɪnt
greaseproof ˈgriːs.pruːf ˌ**greaseproof** ˈ**paper**
greaser ˈgriː.səʳ US -sɚ, -zɚ **-s** -z
Greasley ˈgriːz.li
greas|y ˈgriː.s|i **-ier** -i.əʳ US -i.ɚ **-iest** -i.ɪst, -i.əst **-ily** -ɪ.li, -ᵊl.i **-iness** -ɪ.nəs, -ɪ.nɪs
great greɪt **-er** -əʳ US ˈgreɪ.t̬ɚ **-est** -ɪst, -əst US ˈgreɪ.t̬ɪst, -t̬əst **-s** -s **-ness** -nəs, -nɪs ˌ**Great** ˌ**Barrier** ˈ**Reef;** ˌ**Great** ˈ**Britain;** ˌ**Great** ˈ**Falls;** ˌ**Great** ˈ**Lakes** ˌ**Great** ˈ**Plains**
great-aunt ˌgreɪtˈɑːnt US ˌgreɪtˈænt, -ˈɑːnt **-s** -s *stress shift:* ˌgreat-aunt ˈMaud
Note: p
greatcoat ˈgreɪt.kəʊt US -koʊt **-s** -s
great-grand|child ˌgreɪtˈgrænd|.tʃa[ɪld] **-children** -ˌtʃɪl.drᵊn
great-granddaughter ˌgreɪtˈgrændˌdɔː.təʳ US -ˌdɑː.t̬ɚ, -ˌdɔː- **-s** -z
great-grandfather ˌgreɪtˈgrændˌfɑː.ðəʳ US -ðɚ **-s** -z
great-grandmother ˌgreɪtˈgrændˌmʌð.əʳ, -ˈgræm- US -ˈgrændˌmʌð.ɚ **-s** -z
great-grandparent ˌgreɪtˈgrændˌpeə.rᵊnt US -ˌper.ᵊn[t], -ˌpær- **-s** -s
great-grandson ˌgreɪtˈgrænd.sʌn **-s**
Greatham *in Durham:* ˈgriː.təm US ˈgriː.t̬əm *in Northamptonshir[e,] Hampshire, and West Sussex:* ˈgret.əm US ˈgreɪ.t̬əm
Greathead ˈgreɪt.hed
Greatheart ˈgreɪt.hɑːt US -hɑːrt
greathearted ˌgreɪtˈhɑː.tɪd US -ˈhɑːr.t̬ɪd *stress shift:* ˌgreathearted ˈwarrior
greatly ˈgreɪt.li
Greatorex ˈgreɪ.tə.reks US -t̬ə-
Greats greɪts
great-uncle ˌgreɪtˈʌŋ.kl̩, ˈ-ˌ-- **-s** -z *stress shift:* ˌgreat-uncle ˈJohn
Great Yarmouth ˌgreɪtˈjɑː.məθ US -ˈjɑːr-
greave griːv **-s** -z
Greaves griːvz, greɪvz
grebe griːb **-s** -z
Grecian ˈgriː.ʃᵊn **-s** -z
Grecism ˈgriː.sɪ.zᵊm
Greco- ˈgriː.kəʊ-, ˈgrek.əʊ- US ˈgrek.oʊ-, ˈgriː.koʊ-
Greece griːs
greed griːd
greed|y ˈgriː.d|i **-ier** -i.əʳ US -i.ɚ **-ie[st]** -i.ɪst, -i.əst **-ily** -ɪ.li, -ᵊl.i **-iness** -ɪ.nəs, -ɪ.nɪs ˈ**greedy** ˌ**guts**
Greek griːk **-s** -s ˌ**Greek** ˌ**Orthodox** ˈ**Church**
Greel(e)y ˈgriː.li
green (G) griːn **-s** -z **-er** -əʳ US -ɚ **-e[st]** -ɪst, -əst **-ly** -li **-ness** -nəs, -nɪs **-i[ng]** -ɪŋ **-ed** -d ˌ**green** ˈ**bean** US ˈ**gree[n]** ˌ**bean;** ˌ**Green Be**ˈ**ret;** ˈ**green** ˌ**ca[rd]** ˌ**green cross** ˈ**code;** ˈ**Green** ˌ**Part[y]**
Greenall ˈgriː.nɔːl **-s** -z
Greenaway ˈgriː.nə.weɪ
greenback ˈgriːn.bæk, ˈgriːm- US ˈgriːn- **-s** -s

greenbelt (G) ˈgriːn.belt, ˈgriːm- (US) ˈgriːn- -s -s

Green(e) griːn

greenery ˈgriː.nᵊr.i

green-eyed ˌgriːnˈaɪd (US) ˈgriːn.aɪd *stress shift, British only:* ˌgreen-eyed ˈmonster

jreenfield (G) ˈgriːn.fiːld

jreenfinch ˈgriːn.fɪntʃ -es -ɪz

jreen|fly ˈgriːn|.flaɪ -flies -flaɪz

ɜreenford ˈgriːn.fəd (US) -fɚd

jreengag|e ˈgriːn.geɪdʒ, ˈgriːŋ- (US) ˈgriːn- -es -ɪz

reengrocer ˈgriːnˌgrəʊ.səʳ, ˈgriːŋ- (US) ˈgriːnˌgroʊ.sɚ -s -z

ireenhalgh ˈgriːn.hælʃ, -hældʒ, -hɔː

ɜreenham ˈgriː.nəm ˌGreenham ˈCommon

ireenhaulgh ˈgriːn.hɔː

reenhill ˈgriːn.hɪl

ireenhithe ˈgriːn.haɪð

reenhorn ˈgriːn.hɔːn (US) -hɔːrn -s -z

reenhou|se ˈgriːn.haʊ|s -ses -zɪz ˈgreenhouse efˌfect; ˌgreenhouse ˈgas

reenish (G) ˈgriː.nɪʃ

reenland ˈgriːn.lənd, -lænd -er/s -əʳ/z

reenleaf ˈgriːn.liːf

eenmarket ˈgriːnˌmɑː.kɪt, ˈgriːm- (US) ˈgriːnˌmɑːr.kɪt -s -s

reenock ˈgriː.nək, ˈgrɪn.ək, ˈgren-

eenore ˈgriː.nɔːʳ (US) -nɔːr

eenough ˈgriː.nəʊ (US) -noʊ

eenpeace ˈgriːn.piːs, ˈgriːm- (US) ˈgriːn-

eenpoint ˈgriːn.pɔɪnt, ˈgriːm- (US) ˈgriːn-

eenport ˈgriːn.pɔːt, ˈgriːm- (US) ˈgriːn.pɔːrt

eenroom ˈgriːn.rʊm, -ruːm (US) -ruːm, -rʊm -s -z

eensand ˈgriːn.sænd

eenshank ˈgriːn.ʃæŋk -s -s

eenslade ˈgriːn.sleɪd

eensleeves ˈgriːn.sliːvz

eenspan ˈgriːn.spæn

eenstick ˈgriːn.stɪk -s -z ˌgreenstick ˈfracture

eenstone ˈgriːn.stəʊn (US) -stoʊn

eensward ˈgriːn.swɔːd (US) -swɔːrd

enville ˈgriːn.vɪl

eenway ˈgriːn.weɪ

enwell ˈgriːn.wᵊl, -wel

enwich ˈgren.ɪdʒ, ˈgrɪn-, -ɪtʃ (US) ˈgren.ɪdʒ, ˈgrɪn-, -nɪtʃ, -wɪtʃ ˌGreenwich ˈMean Time, ˌGreenwich Mean ˈTime

enwood (G) ˈgriːn.wʊd -s -z

er grɪəʳ (US) grɪr

et (G) griːt -s -s -ing/s -ɪŋ/z (US) ˈgriː.t̬ɪŋ/z -ed -ɪd (US) ˈgriː.t̬ɪd greetings ˌcard (US) ˈgreeting ˌcard

Greetland ˈgriːt.lənd

gregarious grɪˈgeə.ri.əs, grə- (US) -ˈger.i- -ly -li -ness -nəs, -nɪs

Greg(g) greg

Gregor ˈgreg.əʳ (US) -ɚ

Gregorian grɪˈgɔː.ri.ən, grə-, gregˈɔː- -s -z GreˌGorian ˈchant

Gregory ˈgreg.ᵊr.i

Greig greg

greige greɪʒ

greisen ˈgraɪ.zᵊn

gremlin ˈgrem.lɪn -s -z

grenache grenˈæʃ

Grenada grəˈneɪ.də, grɪ-, grenˈeɪ-

grenade grəˈneɪd, grɪ-, grenˈeɪd -s -z

grenadier (G) ˌgren.əˈdɪəʳ (US) -ˈdɪr -s -z

grenadine ˈgren.ə.diːn, ˌgren.əˈdiːn

Grenadines ˌgren.əˈdiːnz

Grendel ˈgren.dᵊl

Grenfell ˈgren.fel, -fᵊl

Grenoble grəˈnəʊ.bl̩, grɪˈnəʊ- (US) grəˈnoʊ-

Grenville ˈgren.vɪl, -vᵊl

Gresham ˈgreʃ.əm

Gresley ˈgrez.li

Greswell ˈgrez.wᵊl, -wel

Greta ˈgriː.tə, ˈgret.ə, ˈgreɪ.tə (US) ˈgret̬.ə, ˈgriː.t̬ə, ˈgreɪ.t̬ə

Gretchen ˈgretʃ.ᵊn

Gretel ˈgret.ᵊl

Gretna ˈgret.nə ˌGretna ˈGreen

Greuz|e grɜːz (US) grɜːz -es -ɪz

Greville ˈgrev.ɪl, -ᵊl

grew *(from* grow*)* (G) gruː

grey (G) greɪ -s -z -er -əʳ (US) -ɚ -est -ɪst, -əst -ness -nəs, -nɪs -ing -ɪŋ

greybeard ˈgreɪ.bɪəd (US) -bɪrd -s -z

greycoat (G) ˈgreɪ.kəʊt (US) -koʊt -s -s

grey-haired ˌgreɪˈheəd (US) -ˈherd *stress shift:* ˌgrey-haired ˈperson

greyhound ˈgreɪ.haʊnd -s -z ˌGreyhound ˈbus®

greyish ˈgreɪ.ɪʃ

greylag ˈgreɪ.læg -s -z

Greylock ˈgreɪ.lɒk (US) -lɑːk

Greyson ˈgreɪ.sᵊn

Greystoke ˈgreɪ.stəʊk (US) -stoʊk

Gribbin ˈgrɪb.ɪn

gribble (G) ˈgrɪb.l̩ -s -z

Grice graɪs

grid grɪd -s -z

griddl|e ˈgrɪd.l̩ -es -z -ing -ɪŋ -ed -d

gridiron ˈgrɪd.aɪən (US) -aɪɚn -s -z

Gridley ˈgrɪd.li

gridlock ˈgrɪd.lɒk (US) -lɑːk -s -s -ed -t

grief griːf -s -z ˈgrief-ˌstricken

Grieg griːg

Grierson ˈgrɪə.sᵊn (US) ˈgrɪr-

grievanc|e ˈgriː.vᵊnts -es -ɪz

griev|e (G) griːv -es -z -ing -ɪŋ -ed -d -er/s -əʳ/z (US) -ɚ/z

grievous ˈgriː.vəs -ly -li -ness -nəs, -nɪs ˌgrievous ˌbodily ˈharm

griffin (G) ˈgrɪf.ɪn -s -z

Griffith ˈgrɪf.ɪθ -s -s

griffon ˈgrɪf.ᵊn -s -z

grift grɪft -s -s -ing -ɪŋ -ed -ɪd

grifter ˈgrɪf.təʳ (US) -tɚ -s -z

grig grɪg -s -z

Grigg grɪg -s -z

Grigson ˈgrɪg.sᵊn

grill grɪl -s -z -ing -ɪŋ -ed -d -er/s -əʳ/z (US) -ɚ/z

grillag|e ˈgrɪl.ɪdʒ -es -ɪz

grille grɪl -s -z

grillroom ˈgrɪl.rʊm, -ruːm (US) -ruːm, -rʊm -s -z

grilse grɪls

grim grɪm -mer -əʳ (US) -ɚ -mest -ɪst, -əst -ly -li -ness -nəs, -nɪs ˌGrim ˈReaper

grimac|e ˈgrɪm.əs, grɪˈmeɪs (US) ˈgrɪm.əs; grɪˈmeɪs -es -ɪz -ing -ɪŋ -ed -t

Grimald ˈgrɪm.ᵊld

Grimaldi grɪˈmɔːl.di, grə-, -ˈmɒl-, -ˈmæl- (US) -ˈmɑːl-, -ˈmɔːl-

grimalkin grɪˈmæl.kɪn, -ˈmɔːl- -s -z

grim|e graɪm -es -z -ing -ɪŋ -ed -d

Grimes graɪmz

Grimethorpe ˈgraɪm.θɔːp (US) -θɔːrp

Grimké ˈgrɪm.ki

Grimm grɪm

Grimond ˈgrɪm.ənd

Grimsby ˈgrɪmz.bi

Grimshaw ˈgrɪm.ʃɔː (US) -ʃɑː, -ʃɔː

Grimwood ˈgrɪm.wʊd

grim|y ˈgraɪ.m|i -ier -i.əʳ (US) -i.ɚ -iest -i.ɪst, -i.əst -ily -ɪ.li, -ᵊl.i -iness -ɪ.nəs, -ɪ.nɪs

grin grɪn -s -z -ning -ɪŋ -ned -d

Grinch grɪntʃ

grind graɪnd -s -z -ing -ɪŋ ground graʊnd grinder/s ˈgraɪn.dəʳ/z (US) -dɚ/z

Grindal ˈgrɪnd.ᵊl

Grindelwald ˈgrɪn.dᵊl.vɑːld, -væld (US) -vɑːld, -væld, -wɔːld

Grindon ˈgrɪn.dən

grindstone ˈgraɪnd.stəʊn (US) -stoʊn -s -z ˌkeep one's ˌnose to the ˈgrindstone

gringo ˈgrɪŋ.gəʊ (US) -goʊ -s -z

Grinnell grɪˈnel

Grinstead ˈgrɪn.stɪd, -sted (US) -sted

grip grɪp -s -s -ping -ɪŋ -ped -t

grip|e graɪp -es -s -ing -ɪŋ -ed -t ˈgripe ˌwater

gripes graɪps

grippe griːp, grɪp (US) grɪp

grisaille grɪˈzeɪl, grə-, griː-, -ˈzaɪ, -ˈzaɪl (US) -ˈzaɪ, -ˈzeɪl

Griselda grɪˈzel.də, grə-

grisette grɪˈzet -s -s

Grisewood 'graɪz.wʊd
Grisham 'grɪʃ.ᵊm
griskin 'grɪs.kɪn
grisl|y 'grɪz.l|i **-ier** -i.əʳ (US) -i.ɚ **-iest** -i.ɪst, -i.əst **-iness** -ɪ.nəs, -ɪ.nɪs
Grisons griː'zɔ̃ːŋ, -'zɔːŋ (US) griː'zɔ̃ːŋ, -'zɔːŋ
Grissel 'grɪs.ᵊl
grist grɪst
gristle 'grɪs.l̩
gristly 'grɪs.l̩.i, 'grɪs.li
Griswold 'grɪz.wəʊld, -wᵊld (US) -wɔːld, -wᵊld
grit grɪt **-s** -s **-ting** -ɪŋ (US) 'grɪt̬.ɪŋ **-ted** -ɪd (US) 'grɪt̬.ɪd
gritter 'grɪt.əʳ (US) 'grɪt̬.ɚ **-s** -z
Gritton 'grɪt.ᵊn
gritt|y 'grɪt|.i (US) 'grɪt̬|.i **-ier** -i.əʳ (US) -i.ɚ **-iest** -i.ɪst, -i.əst **-ily** -ɪ.li, -ᵊl.i **-iness** -ɪ.nəs, -ɪ.nɪs
Grizedale 'graɪz.deɪl
Grizel grɪ'zel
grizzl|e 'grɪz.l̩ **-es** -z **-ing** -ɪŋ, '-lɪŋ **-ed** -d
grizzl|y 'grɪz.l|i **-ies** -iz **-ier** -i.əʳ (US) -i.ɚ **-iest** -i.ɪst, -i.əst **'grizzly ˌbear**
Gro grəʊ, gruː, grɔː (US) groʊ, grɔː
groan grəʊn (US) groʊn **-s** -z **-ing/s** -ɪŋ/z **-ed** -d
groat grəʊt (US) groʊt **-s** -s
grocer 'grəʊ.səʳ (US) 'groʊ.sɚ **-s** -z
grocer|y 'grəʊ.sᵊr|.i (US) 'groʊ- **-ies** -iz
grockle 'grɒk.l̩ (US) 'grɑː.kl̩ **-s** -z
Grocott 'grɒk.ət, 'grəʊ.kɒt (US) 'grɑː.kət, 'groʊ-
Grocyn 'grəʊ.sɪn (US) 'groʊ-
grog grɒg (US) grɑːg, grɔːg
grogg|y 'grɒg|.i (US) 'grɑː.g|i, 'grɔː- **-ier** -i.əʳ (US) -i.ɚ **-iest** -i.ɪst, -i.əst **-ily** -ɪ.li, -ᵊl.i **-iness** -ɪ.nəs, -ɪ.nɪs
grogram 'grɒg.rəm (US) 'grɑː.grəm
groin grɔɪn **-s** -z
grommet 'grɒm.ɪt, 'grʌm- (US) 'grɑː.mɪt **-s** -s
gromwell 'grɒm.wᵊl, -wel (US) 'grɑːm-
Gromyko grə'miː.kəʊ (US) -koʊ
Grongar 'grɒŋ.gəʳ (US) 'grɑːŋ.gɚ, 'grɔːŋ
Groningen 'grəʊ.nɪŋ.ən, 'grɒn.ɪŋ- (US) 'groʊ-
groom (G) gruːm, grʊm **-s** -z **-ing** -ɪŋ **-ed** -d
grooms|man 'gruːmz|.mən, 'grʊmz- **-men** -mən, -men
groov|e gruːv **-es** -z **-ing** -ɪŋ **-ed** -d
groov|y 'gruː.v|i **-ier** -i.əʳ (US) -i.ɚ **-iest** -i.ɪst, -i.əst **-iness** -ɪ.nəs, -ɪ.nɪs
grop|e grəʊp (US) groʊp **-es** -s **-ing/ly** -ɪŋ/li **-ed** -t **-er/s** -əʳ/z (US) -ɚ/z
Gropius 'grəʊ.pi.əs (US) 'groʊ-
Grosart 'grəʊ.zɑːt (US) 'groʊ.zɑːrt
grosbeak 'grəʊs.biːk, 'grɒs-, 'grɒz- (US) 'groʊs- **-s** -s
groschen 'grɒʃ.ᵊn, 'grəʊʃ.ᵊn (US) 'groʊ.ʃᵊn
Grose grəʊs, grəʊz (US) groʊs, groʊz
grosgrain 'grəʊ.greɪn (US) 'groʊ-
Grosmont *in North Yorkshire:* 'grəʊ.mənt, -mɒnt *locally also:* 'grəʊs.mənt (US) 'groʊ.mɑːnt, 'groʊs- *in Gwent:* 'grɒs.mənt (US) 'grɑːs-
gros point ˌgrəʊ'pɔɪnt (US) 'groʊ.pɔɪnt
gross grəʊs (US) groʊs **-er** -əʳ (US) -ɚ **-est** -ɪst, -əst **-ly** -li **-ness** -nəs, -nɪs **-es** -ɪz **-ing** -ɪŋ **-ed** -t **ˌgross doˌmestic 'product; ˌgross ˌnational 'product**
Gross *surname:* grɒs, grəʊs (US) grɑːs, groʊs
Grosseteste 'grəʊs.test (US) 'groʊs-
Grossmith 'grəʊ.smɪθ (US) 'groʊ-
grosso modo ˌgrɒs.əʊ'mɒd.əʊ, -'məʊ.dəʊ (US) ˌgroʊ.soʊ'moʊ.doʊ
Grosvenor 'grəʊv.nəʳ (US) 'groʊv.nɚ
grosz grɔːʃ (US) grɑːʃ, grɔːʃ **groszy** 'grɔː.ʃi (US) 'grɑː-, 'grɔː-
Grote grəʊt (US) groʊt
grotesque grəʊ'tesk (US) groʊ- **-ly** -li **-ness** -nəs, -nɪs
Grotius 'grəʊ.ti.əs (US) 'groʊ.ʃəs, -ʃi.əs
grotto 'grɒt.əʊ (US) 'grɑː.t̬oʊ **-(e)s** -z
grott|y 'grɒt|.i (US) 'grɑː.t̬|i **-ier** -i.əʳ (US) -i.ɚ **-iest** -i.ɪst, -i.əst **-ily** -ɪ.li, -ᵊl.i **-iness** -ɪ.nəs, -ɪ.nɪs
grouch graʊtʃ **-es** -ɪz **-ing** -ɪŋ **-ed** -t
Groucho 'graʊ.tʃəʊ (US) -tʃoʊ
grouch|y 'graʊ.tʃ|i **-ier** -i.əʳ (US) -i.ɚ **-iest** -i.ɪst, -i.əst **-ily** -ɪ.li, -ᵊl.i **-iness** -ɪ.nəs, -ɪ.nɪs
ground graʊnd **-s** -z **-ing** -ɪŋ **-ed** -ɪd **-er/s** -əʳ/z (US) -ɚ/z **'ground ˌplan; 'ground ˌrule; 'ground ˌstroke; 'ground ˌswell; ˌsuit someone ˌdown to the 'ground**
groundbreaking 'graʊndˌbreɪ.kɪŋ
ground|cloth 'graʊnd|.klɒθ, 'graʊŋ- (US) 'graʊnd|.klɑːθ **-cloths** -klɒθs, -klɒðz (US) -klɑːθs, -klɑːðz
groundcover 'graʊndˌkʌv.əʳ, 'graʊŋ- (US) 'graʊndˌkʌv.ɚ
groundhog 'graʊnd.hɒg (US) -hɑːg, -hɔːg **-s** -z **'Groundhog ˌDay**
groundless 'graʊnd.ləs, -lɪs **-ly** -li **-ness** -nəs, -nɪs
groundling 'graʊnd.lɪŋ **-s** -z
groundnut 'graʊnd.nʌt **-s** -s
groundout 'graʊnd.aʊt **-s** -s
groundsel 'graʊnd.sᵊl
groundsheet 'graʊnd.ʃiːt **-s** -s
grounds|man 'graʊndz|.mən **-men** -mən, -men
groundspeed 'graʊnd.spiːd **-s** -z
groundstroke 'graʊnd.strəʊk (US) -stroʊk **-s** -s
groundwater 'graʊndˌwɔː.təʳ (US) -ˌwɑː.t̬ɚ, -ˌwɔː-
groundwork 'graʊnd.wɜːk (US) -wɝːk
group gruːp **-s** -s **-ing/s** -ɪŋ/z **-ed** -t
grouper 'gruː.pəʳ (US) -pɚ **-s** -z
groupie 'gruː.pi **-s** -z
grous|e (G) graʊs **-es** -ɪz **-ing** -ɪŋ **-ed** -t **-er/s** -əʳ/z (US) -ɚ/z
grout graʊt **-s** -s **-ing** -ɪŋ (US) 'graʊ.t̬ɪŋ **-ed** -ɪd (US) 'graʊ.t̬ɪd **-er/s** -əʳ/z (US) 'graʊ.t̬ɚ/z
grove (G) grəʊv (US) groʊv **-s** -z
grovel 'grɒv.ᵊl (US) 'grɑː.vᵊl, 'grʌv.ᵊl **-s** -z **-(l)ing** -ɪŋ **-(l)ed** -d **-(l)er/s** -əʳ/z (US) -ɚ/z
Grover 'grəʊ.vəʳ (US) 'groʊ.vɚ
grow grəʊ (US) groʊ **-s** -z **-ing** -ɪŋ **grew** gruː **grown** grəʊn (US) groʊn **'grow ˌbag; 'growing ˌpains**
grow-bag 'grəʊ.bæg (US) 'groʊ- **-s** -z
grower 'grəʊ.əʳ (US) 'groʊ- **-s** -z
growl graʊl **-s** -z **-ing** -ɪŋ **-ed** -d **-er/s** -əʳ/z (US) -ɚ/z
grown *(from* **grow***)* grəʊn (US) groʊn
grown-up *(n.)* 'grəʊn.ʌp (US) 'groʊn- **-s** -s *stress shift:* ˌgrown-up 'languag
grown-up *(adj.)* ˌgrəʊn'ʌp (US) ˌgroʊn'-
growth grəʊθ (US) groʊθ **-s** -s
groyne grɔɪn **-s** -z
Grozny 'grɒz.ni (US) 'grɑːz-
grub grʌb **-s** -z **-bing** -ɪŋ **-bed** -d **-ber/s** -əʳ/z (US) -ɚ/z
grubb|y 'grʌb|.i **-ier** -i.əʳ (US) -i.ɚ **-iest** -i.ɪst, -i.əst **-iness** -ɪ.nəs, -ɪ.nɪs
grubstak|e 'grʌb.steɪk **-es** -s **-ing** -ɪŋ **-ed** -t
grudg|e grʌdʒ **-es** -ɪz **-ing/ly** -ɪŋ/li **-ed** -
gruel grʊəl, 'gruː.əl (US) 'gruː.əl
gruel(l)ing 'grʊə.lɪŋ, 'gruː.ᵊl.ɪŋ (US) 'gruː.lɪŋ, -ᵊl.ɪŋ
Gruenther 'grʌn.θəʳ (US) -θɚ
gruesome 'gruː.səm **-ly** -li **-ness** -nəs, -nɪs
gruff grʌf **-er** -əʳ (US) -ɚ **-est** -ɪst, -əst **-ly** -li **-ness** -nəs, -nɪs
grumbl|e 'grʌm.bl̩ **-es** -z **-ing** -ɪŋ, '-bl **-ed** -d **-er/s** -əʳ/z, '-bləʳ/z (US) '-bl̩.ɚ/z, '-blɚ/z
grummet 'grʌm.ɪt, -ət **-s** -s
grump grʌmp **-s** -s
grump|y 'grʌm.p|i **-ier** -i.əʳ (US) -i.ɚ **-ie** -i.ɪst, -i.əst **-ily** -ɪ.li, -ᵊl.i **-iness** -ɪ.nəs, -ɪ.nɪs
Grundig® 'grʌn.dɪg, 'grʊn-
Grundtvig 'grʊnt.vɪg
Grundy 'grʌn.di
grunge grʌndʒ
grung|y 'grʌn.dʒ|i **-ier** -i.əʳ (US) -i.ɚ **-i** -i.ɪst, -i.əst
grunt grʌnt **-s** -s **-ing** -ɪŋ (US) 'grʌn.t̬ɪŋ **-ed** -ɪd (US) 'grʌn.t̬ɪd **-er/s** -əʳ/z (US) 'grʌn.t̬ɚz
Gruyère 'gruː.jeəʳ, -jəʳ; gru'jeəʳ (US) gru'jer

Pronouncing the letters G U

At the beginning of words, the consonant digraph **gu** is usually realised as /g/, e.g.:

guest /gest/

Word-finally, **gu** is usually followed by **e** in nouns and is pronounced /g/, e.g.:

fatigue /fəˈtiːg/

gu may also be pronounced as /gw/, e.g.:

language /ˈlæŋ.gwɪdʒ/

Gryll grɪl
gryphon ˈgrɪf.ᵊn **-s** -z
G-seven ˌdʒiːˈsev.ᵊn
g-spot ˈdʒiː.spɒt (US) -spɑːt
Gstaad kʃtɑːd; gəˈʃtɑːd (US) gəˈʃtɑːt, -ˈʃtɑːd
G-string ˈdʒiː.strɪŋ **-s** -z
GTech® ˈdʒiː.tek
GTI ˌdʒiː.tiːˈaɪ **-s** -z
guacamole ˌgwɑː.kəˈməʊ.li, ˌgwæk-, -leɪ (US) ˌgwɑː.kəˈmoʊ.li
Guadalajara ˌgwɑː.dᵊl.əˈhɑː.rə, ˌgwæd.ᵊl- (US) ˌgwɑː.dᵊl.əˈhɑːr.ə
Guadalquivir ˌgwɑː.dᵊl.kwɪˈvɪəʳ, ˌgwæd.ᵊl-, -kɪˈ- (US) ˌgwɑː.dᵊlˈkwɪ.vɚ, -kɪˈvɪr
Guadeloupe ˌgwɑː.dəˈluːp, -dᵊlˈuːp, ˈ---
Guam gwɑːm
Guangdong ˌgwæŋˈdɒŋ, ˌgwɒŋ-, -ˈdʊŋ (US) ˌgwɑːŋˈdɑːŋ, -ˈdʊŋ
Guangzhou ˌgwæŋˈʒəʊ, ˌgwɒŋ- (US) ˌgwɑːŋˈdʒoʊ
guano ˈgwɑː.nəʊ (US) -noʊ **-s** -z
Guantánamo gwænˈtæn.ə.məʊ, gwɑːn- (US) gwɑːnˈtɑː.nə.moʊ
Guarani, **Guaraní** ˌgwɑː.rəˈniː, ˈgwɑː.rᵊn.i **-s** -z
guarantee ˌgær.ᵊnˈtiː (US) ˌger-, ˌgær-, ˈ--- **-s** -z **-ing** -ɪŋ **-d** -d
guarantor ˌgær.ᵊnˈtɔːʳ (US) ˈger.ᵊn.tɔːr, ˈgær-, ˌ--ˈ- **-s** -z
guarant|y ˈgær.ᵊn.t|i (US) ˈger.ᵊn.t̬|i, ˈgær- **-ies** -iz
guard **(G)** gɑːd (US) gɑːrd **-s** -z **-ing** -ɪŋ **-ed/ly** -ɪd/li **-edness** -ɪd.nəs, -nɪs **ˈguard's ˌvan**
guardian **(G)** ˈgɑː.di.ən (US) ˈgɑːr- **-s** -z **-ship** -ʃɪp
guardrail ˈgɑːd.reɪl (US) ˈgɑːrd- **-s** -z
guardroom ˈgɑːd.rʊm, -ruːm (US) ˈgɑːrd.ruːm, -rʊm **-s** -z
guards|man ˈgɑːdz|.mən, -mæn (US) ˈgɑːrdz- **-men** -mən, -men
Guarneri gwɑːˈneə.ri (US) gwɑːrˈner.i
Guatemal|a ˌgwæ.təˈmɑː.l|ə, ˌgwɑː.tə-, -ɪmˈɑː- (US) ˌgwɑː.t̬əˈ- **-an/s** -ən/z
guava ˈgwɑː.və **-s** -z

Guayaquil ˌgwaɪ.əˈkiːl, -ˈkɪl
Guayra ˈgwaɪ.rə
gubbins **(G)** ˈgʌb.ɪnz
gubernatorial ˌguː.bᵊn.əˈtɔː.ri.əl, ˌgjuː- (US) ˌguː.bɚ.nəˈtɔːr.i-
Gucci® ˈguː.tʃi
gudgeon ˈgʌdʒ.ᵊn **-s** -z
Gudrun ˈgʊd.ruːn, gʊˈdruːn
Gue gjuː
guelder-ros|e ˈgel.də.rəʊz, ˌ--ˈ- (US) ˈgel.dɚ.roʊz, ˌ--ˈ- **-es** -ɪz
Guelph, **Guelf** gwelf **-s** -s
Guenevere ˈgwɪn.ɪ.vɪəʳ, ˈgwen-, ˈ-ə- (US) -vɪr
guerdon ˈgɜː.dᵊn (US) ˈgɝː- **-s** -z
guerilla gəˈrɪl.ə, gjə-, gɜː- (US) gə- **-s** -z
Guernica ˈgɜː.nɪk.ə, ˈgwɜː-; (US) ˈgwer.nɪk-
guernsey **(G)** ˈgɜːn.zi (US) ˈgɝːn- **-s** -z
guerrilla gəˈrɪl.ə, gjə-, gɜː- (US) gə- **-s** -z
guess ges **-es** -ɪz **-ing** -ɪŋ **-ed** -t **-er/s** -əʳ/z (US) -ɚ/z **-able** -ə.bl̩ **ˈguessing ˌgame**
guesstimate (*n.*) ˈges.tɪ.mət, -tə-, -mɪt, -meɪt **-s** -s
guessti|mate (*v.*) ˈges.tɪ|.meɪt, -tə- (US) -tə- **-mates** -meɪts **-mating** -meɪ.tɪŋ (US) -meɪ.t̬ɪŋ **-mated** -meɪ.tɪd (US) -meɪ.t̬ɪd
guesswork ˈges.wɜːk (US) -wɝːk
guest **(G)** gest **-s** -s **-ing** -ɪŋ **-ed** -ɪd **ˈguest ˌnight; ˈguest ˌroom**
guesthou|se ˈgest.haʊ|s **-ses** -zɪz
Guevara gəˈvɑː.rə, gɪ-, gevˈɑː-
guff gʌf
guffaw gʌfˈɔː, gəˈfɔː (US) gʌfˈɑː, -ˈɔː, gəˈfɑː, -ˈfɔː **-s** -z **-ing** -ɪŋ **-ed** -d
Guggenheim ˈgʊg.ᵊn.haɪm, ˈguː.gᵊn-
Guggisberg ˈgʌg.ɪs.bɜːg (US) -bɝːg
Guiana gaɪˈæn.ə, giˈɑː.nə (US) giˈæn.ə, gaɪ-, -ˈɑː.nə **-s** -z
Guianese ˌgaɪ.əˈniːz (US) ˌgiː.əˈniːz, ˌgaɪ-, -ˈniːs *stress shift:* ˌGuianese ˈpeople
guidance ˈgaɪ.dᵊnts
guid|e gaɪd **-es** -z **-ing** -ɪŋ **-ed** -ɪd **ˈguide ˌdog**
guidebook ˈgaɪd.bʊk **-s** -s

guideline ˈgaɪd.laɪn **-s** -z
guidepost ˈgaɪd.pəʊst (US) -poʊst **-s** -s
Guido ˈgwiː.dəʊ, ˈgiː- (US) -doʊ
guidon ˈgaɪ.dᵊn **-s** -z
guild gɪld **-s** -z
Guildenstern ˈgɪl.dᵊn.stɜːn (US) -stɝːn
guilder ˈgɪl.dəʳ (US) -dɚ **-s** -z
Guildford ˈgɪl.fəd (US) -fɚd
guildhall **(G)** ˈgɪldˌhɔːl, ˌ-ˈ- (US) -hɔːl, -hɑːl **-s** -z
Guilding ˈgɪl.dɪŋ
guile gaɪl
guileful ˈgaɪl.fᵊl, -fʊl **-ly** -i **-ness** -nəs, -nɪs
guileless ˈgaɪl.ləs, -lɪs **-ly** -li **-ness** -nəs, -nɪs
Guilford ˈgɪl.fəd (US) -fɚd
guillemot ˈgɪl.ɪ.mɒt, ˈ-ə- (US) -ə.mɑːt **-s** -s
Guillim ˈgwɪl.ɪm
guillotin|e ˈgɪl.ə.tiːn, ˌ--ˈ- **-es** -z **-ing** -ɪŋ **-ed** -d
Note: Some people use /ˈgɪl.ə.tiːn/ for the noun and /ˌgɪl.əˈtiːn/ for the verb.
guilt gɪlt
guiltless ˈgɪlt.ləs, -lɪs **-ly** -li **-ness** -nəs, -nɪs
guilt|y ˈgɪl.t|i (US) -t̬|i **-ier** -i.əʳ (US) -i.ɚ **-iest** -i.ɪst, -i.əst **-ily** -ɪ.li, -ᵊl.i **-iness** -ɪ.nəs, -ɪ.nɪs
guimpe gɪmp, gæmp **-s** -s
guinea **(G)** ˈgɪn.i **-s** -z **ˈguinea ˌfowl; ˈguinea ˌpig**
Guinea-Bissau ˌgɪn.i.bɪˈsaʊ
Guiness ˈgɪn.ɪs
Guinevere ˈgwɪn.ɪ.vɪəʳ, ˈgɪn-, ˈ-ə- (US) ˈgwɪn.ɪ.vɪr, ˈ-ə-
Guinness ˈgɪn.ɪs, -əs; gɪˈnes
Note: The beer is called /ˈgɪn.ɪs/.
guipure gɪˈpjʊəʳ (US) -ˈpjʊr, -ˈpʊr
Guisborough ˈgɪz.bᵊr.ə (US) -bɚ.oʊ, -bɚ.ə
guis|e gaɪz **-es** -ɪz
Guise giːz, gwiːz
Guiseley ˈgaɪz.li
guitar gɪˈtɑːʳ (US) -ˈtɑːr **-s** -z
guitarist gɪˈtɑː.rɪst, gə- (US) -ˈtɑːr.ɪst **-s** -s

Gujarat ˌgʊdʒ.əˈrɑːt, ˌguː.dʒəˈ-
Gujarati ˌgʊdʒ.əˈrɑː.ti, ˌguː.dʒəˈ- (US) -t̬i
Gujranwala guːdʒˈrɑːn.wʌl.ə (US) -rənˈwɑː.lə
gulag (G) ˈguː.læg, -lɑːg (US) -lɑːg **-s** -z
Gulbenkian gʊlˈbeŋ.ki.ən
gulch gʌltʃ **-es** -ɪz
gulden ˈgʊl.dən, ˈguːl- **-s** -z
gules gjuːlz, dʒuːlz
gulf gʌlf **-s** -s **-y** -i ˌ**Gulf** ˈ**States**; ˈ**Gulf** ˌ**Stream**; ˈ**Gulf** ˌ**War** ˌ**Gulf** ˈ**War**
gull (G) gʌl **-s** -z **-ing** -ɪŋ **-ed** -d
gullet ˈgʌl.ɪt, -ət **-s** -s
gulley ˈgʌl.i **-s** -z
gullibility ˌgʌl.ɪˈbɪl.ə.ti, -əˈ-, -ɪ.ti (US) -əˈbɪl.ə.t̬i
gullible ˈgʌl.ɪ.bl̩, ˈ-ə- (US) ˈ-ə-
Gullit ˈhʊl.ɪt *as if Dutch* ˈxʊl.ɪt
Gulliver ˈgʌl.ɪ.vəʳ, ˈ-ə- (US) -ə.vɚ
gull|y (G) ˈgʌl|.i **-ies** -iz
gulp gʌlp **-s** -s **-ing** -ɪŋ **-ed** -t
gum gʌm **-s** -z **-ming** -ɪŋ **-med** -d **-mer/s** -əʳ/z (US) -ɚ/z
gumball ˈgʌm.bɔːl (US) -bɔːl, -bɑːl **-s** -z
Gumbley ˈgʌm.bli
gumbo (G) ˈgʌm.bəʊ (US) -boʊ **-s** -z
gumboil ˈgʌm.bɔɪl **-s** -z
gumboot ˈgʌm.buːt **-s** -s
gumdrop ˈgʌm.drɒp (US) -drɑːp **-s** -s
Gummidge ˈgʌm.ɪdʒ
gumm|y ˈgʌm|.i **-ier** -i.əʳ (US) -i.ɚ **-iest** -i.ɪst, -i.əst **-iness** -ɪ.nəs, -ɪ.nɪs
gumption ˈgʌmp.ʃᵊn
gumshield ˈgʌm.ʃiːld **-s** -z
gumshoe ˈgʌm.ʃuː **-s** -z **-ing** -ɪŋ **-d** -d
gumtree ˈgʌm.triː **-s** -z
gun gʌn **-s** -z **-ning** -ɪŋ **-ned** -d **-ner/s** -əʳ/z (US) -ɚ/z ˈ**gun** ˌ**carriage**; ˈ**gun** ˌ**dog**; ˈ**gun** ˌ**room**; ˌ**jump the** ˈ**gun**
gunboat ˈgʌn.bəʊt, ˈgʌm- (US) ˈgʌn.boʊt **-s** -s
Gunby Hadath ˌgʌn.biˈhæd.əθ, ˌgʌm- (US) ˌgʌn-
guncatcher ˈgʌnˌkætʃ.əʳ, ˈgʌŋ- (US) ˈgʌnˌkætʃ.ɚ
guncotton ˈgʌn.kɒt.ᵊn, ˈgʌŋ- (US) ˈgʌn.kɑː.tᵊn
gunfight ˈgʌn.faɪt **-s** -s **-er/s** -əʳ/z (US) ɚ/z
gunfire ˈgʌn.faɪəʳ (US) -faɪɚ
Gunga Din ˌgʌŋ.gəˈdɪn
gung|e gʌndʒ **-y** -i
gung ho ˌgʌŋˈhəʊ (US) -ˈhoʊ
gunk gʌŋk **-y** -i
gun|man ˈgʌn|.mən, ˈgʌm-, -mæn (US) ˈgʌn- **-men** -mən, -men
gunmetal ˈgʌnˌmet.ᵊl, ˈgʌm- (US) ˈgʌnˌmet̬.ᵊl
Gunn gʌn
Gunnar ˈgʊn.ɑːʳ (US) -ɑːr
gunnel (G) ˈgʌn.ᵊl **-s** -z
Gunnell ˈgʌn.əl
Gunner ˈgʌn.əʳ (US) -ɚ
Gunnersbury ˈgʌn.əz.bᵊr.i (US) -ɚzˌber-, -bᵊr-
gunnery ˈgʌn.ᵊr.i
Gunning ˈgʌn.ɪŋ
Gunnison ˈgʌn.ɪ.sᵊn
gunny ˈgʌn.i
gunnysack ˈgʌn.i.sæk **-s** -s
gunpoint ˈgʌn.pɔɪnt, ˈgʌm- (US) ˈgʌn-
gunpowder ˈgʌnˌpaʊ.dəʳ, ˈgʌm- (US) ˈgʌnˌpaʊ.dɚ ˌ**Gunpowder** ˈ**Plot** (US) ˈ**Gunpowder** ˌ**Plot**
gunrunn|er ˈgʌnˌrʌn|.əʳ (US) -ɚ **-ers** -əz (US) -ɚz **-ing** -ɪŋ
gunship ˈgʌn.ʃɪp **-s** -s
gunshot ˈgʌn.ʃɒt (US) -ʃɑːt **-s** -s
gunslinger ˈgʌn.slɪŋ.əʳ **-s** -z
gunsmith ˈgʌn.smɪθ **-s** -s
Gunter ˈgʌn.təʳ (US) -tɚ
Guntram ˈgʌn.trəm
gunwale ˈgʌn.ᵊl **-s** -z
gupp|y (G) ˈgʌp|.i **-ies** -iz
Gupta ˈgʊp.tə, ˈgʌp.tə
gurgl|e ˈgɜː.gl̩ (US) ˈgɝː- **-es** -z **-ing** -ɪŋ, ˈ-glɪŋ **-ed** -d
Gurkha ˈgɜː.kə (US) ˈgɝː- **-s** -z
Gurkhali ˌgɜːˈkɑː.li, ˌgʊə- (US) ˌgɝː-
Gurley ˈgɜː.li (US) ˈgɝː-
Gurnall ˈgɜː.nᵊl (US) ˈgɝː-
gurnard (G) ˈgɜː.nəd (US) ˈgɝː.nɚd **-s** -z
gurnet ˈgɜː.nɪt, -nət (US) ˈgɝː- **-s** -s
gurney (G) ˈgɜː.ni (US) ˈgɝː-
Gurton ˈgɜː.tᵊn (US) ˈgɝː-
guru ˈgʊr.uː, ˈguː.ruː, ˈgʊə- (US) ˈguː.ruː **-s** -z
Gus gʌs
gush gʌʃ **-es** -ɪz **-ing/ly** -ɪŋ/li **-ed** -t **-er/s** -əʳ/z (US) -ɚ/z
Gushington ˈgʌʃ.ɪŋ.tən
gusset ˈgʌs.ɪt **-s** -s **-ing** -ɪŋ **-ed** -ɪd
Gussie, Gussy ˈgʌs.i
gust gʌst **-s** -s **-ing** -ɪŋ **-ed** -ɪd
Gustafson ˈgʊs.tæf.sᵊn (US) ˈgʌs.təf-, -tɑːf-
gustation gʌsˈteɪ.ʃᵊn
gustatory ˈgʌs.tə.tᵊr.i; gʌsˈteɪ- (US) ˈgʌs.tə.tɔːr-
Gustav, Gustave ˈgʊs.tɑːv, ˈgʌs- (US) ˈgʌs-
Gustavus gʊsˈtɑː.vəs, gʌs-, gəˈstɑː- (US) gʌsˈteɪ.vəs, -ˈtɑː-
gusto ˈgʌs.təʊ (US) -toʊ
gust|y ˈgʌs.t|i **-ier** -i.əʳ (US) -i.ɚ **-iest** -i.ɪst, -i.əst **-ily** -ɪ.li, -ᵊl.i **-iness** -ɪ.nəs, -ɪ.nɪs
gut gʌt **-s** -s **-ting** -ɪŋ (US) ˈgʌt̬.ɪŋ **-ted** -ɪd (US) ˈgʌt̬.ɪd
Gutenberg ˈguː.tᵊn.bɜːg (US) -bɝːg
Guthrie ˈgʌθ.ri
Gutierrez guːˈtjer.ez
gutless ˈgʌt.ləs, -lɪs **-ly** -li **-ness** -nəs, -nɪs
guts|y ˈgʌt.s|i **-ier** -i.əʳ (US) -i.ɚ **-iest** -i.ɪst, -i.əst **-ily** -ɪ.li, -ᵊl.i **-iness** -ɪ.nəs, -ɪ.nɪs
gutt|a ˈgʌt|.ə (US) ˈgʌt̬|.ə **-ae** -iː
gutta-percha ˌgʌt.əˈpɜː.tʃə (US) ˌgʌt̬.əˈpɝː-
gutt|er ˈgʌt|.əʳ (US) ˈgʌt̬|.ɚ **-ers** -əz (US) -ɚz **-ering** -ᵊr.ɪŋ **-ered** -əd (US) -ɚd ˌ**gutter** ˈ**press** (US) ˈ**gutter** ˌ**press**
guttersnipe ˈgʌt.ə.snaɪp (US) ˈgʌt̬.ɚ- **-s** -s
guttural ˈgʌt.ᵊr.ᵊl (US) ˈgʌt̬- **-s** -z **-ly** -i
guv gʌv
guvnor ˈgʌv.nəʳ (US) -nɚ **-s** -z
guy (G) gaɪ **-s** -z
Guyana gaɪˈɑːn.ə, giˈɑː.nə (US) giˈæn.ə, gaɪ-, -ˈɑː.nə
Guyanese ˌgaɪ.əˈniːz (US) ˌgiː.əˈniːz, ˌgaɪ-, -ˈniːs *stress shift:* ˌGuyanese ˈpeople
Guy Fawkes ˌgaɪˈfɔːks, ˈ-- (US) -ˈfɔːks, -ˈfɑːks *stress shift, see compound:* ˈ**Guy Fawkes** ˌ**night**
Guylian ˈgiː.li.ən
Guysborough ˈgaɪz.bᵊr.ə (US) -bɚ.oʊ
guzzl|e ˈgʌz.l̩ **-es** -z **-ing** -ɪŋ, ˈ-lɪŋ **-ed** -d **-er/s** -əʳ/z, ˈ-ləʳ/z (US) ˈ-l̩.ɚ/z, ˈ-lɚ/z
Gwalia ˈgwɑː.li.ə
Gwalior ˈgwɑː.li.ɔːʳ (US) -ɔːr
Gwatkin ˈgwɒt.kɪn (US) ˈgwɑːt-
Gwaun-Cae-Gurwen ˌgwaɪn.kəˈgɜː.wən, ˌgwaɪŋ- (US) -ˈgɝː-
Gwen gwen
Gwenda ˈgwen.də
Gwendol|en ˈgwen.də.l|ɪn, -dᵊl.|ɪn -ən, -iːn **-yn** -ɪn
Gwent gwent
Gwersyllt ˌgweəˈsɪlt (US) ˌgwer-
Gwinnett gwɪˈnet
Gwladys ˈglæd.ɪs
Gwrych gʊˈriːk, -ˈriːx
Gwydion ˈgwɪd.i.ən
Gwydyr ˈgwɪd.ɪəʳ, -əʳ; (US) ˈgwɪd.ɪr
Gwynedd ˈgwɪn.əð, -ɪð, -eð
Gwyneth ˈgwɪn.əθ, -ɪθ, -eθ
gwyniad ˈgwɪn.i.æd **-s** -z
Gwyn(ne) gwɪn
gyb|e dʒaɪb **-es** -z **-ing** -ɪŋ **-ed** -d
Gye dʒaɪ, gaɪ
Gyges ˈgaɪ.dʒiːz
Gyle gaɪl
Gyles gaɪlz
gym dʒɪm **-s** -z
gymkhana dʒɪmˈkɑː.nə **-s** -z
gymnas|ium dʒɪmˈneɪ.z|i.əm **-iums** -i.əmz **-ia** -i.ə
gymnast ˈdʒɪm.næst (US) -næst, -nəst **-s** -s
gymnastic dʒɪmˈnæs.tɪk **-s** -s **-al** -ᵊl **-ally** -ᵊl.i, -li

gymnosophist dʒɪmˈnɒs.ə.fɪst (US) -ˈnɑː.sə- **-s** -s
gymnosperm ˈdʒɪm.nəʊ.spɜːm, ˈgɪm- (US) -nə.spɝːm **-s** -z
gymnospermous ˌdʒɪm.nəʊˈspɜː.məs, ˌgɪm- (US) -nəˈspɝː-
Gympie ˈgɪm.pi
gymslip ˈdʒɪm.slɪp **-s** -s
gyn(a)ecological ˌgaɪ.nə.kəˈlɒdʒ.ɪ.kəl, -nɪ- (US) -ˈlɑː.dʒɪ- **-li** -i
gyn(a)ecolog|y ˌgaɪ.nəˈkɒl.ə.dʒ|i, -ɪˈ- (US) -ˈkɑː.lə- **-ist/s** -ɪst/s
gyneci|um ˌdʒaɪˈniː.si|əm, ˌgaɪ- **-a** -ə
Gyngell ˈgɪn.dʒəl
gynoeci|um ˌdʒaɪˈniː.si|.əm, ˌgaɪ- **-a** -ə
Györ djɜːʳ (US) djɝː, djɔːr
gyp dʒɪp **-s** -s **-ping** -ɪŋ **-ped** -t
Gyp *nickname:* dʒɪp *French novelist:* ʒiːp
gypsophila dʒɪpˈsɒf.ɪ.lə, -əl.ə (US) -ˈsɑː.fɪ- **-s** -z
gypsum ˈdʒɪp.səm
gyps|y ˈdʒɪp.s|i **-ies** -iz
gyrate (*adj.*) ˈdʒaɪə.rət, -reɪt, -rɪt (US) ˈdʒaɪ.reɪt
gy|rate (*v.*) dʒaɪə|ˈreɪt (US) ˈdʒaɪ|.reɪt **-rates** -ˈreɪts (US) -reɪts **-rating** -ˈreɪ.tɪŋ (US) -reɪ.t̬ɪŋ **-rated** -ˈreɪ.tɪd (US) -reɪ.t̬ɪd
gyration dʒaɪəˈreɪ.ʃən (US) dʒaɪ- **-s** -z
gyratory ˈdʒaɪə.rə.tər.i; dʒaɪəˈreɪ- (US) ˈdʒaɪ.rə.tɔːr-
gyr|e dʒaɪəʳ (US) dʒaɪɚ **-es** -z **-ing** -ɪŋ **-ed** -d
gyrfalcon ˈdʒɜːˌfɔːl.kən, ˈdʒɪə-, -ˌfɔː- (US) ˈdʒɝː.fæl-, -fɔːl- **-s** -z
gyro- dʒaɪə.rəʊ- (US) dʒaɪ.roʊ-, -rə-
Note: Prefix. Normally takes either primary or secondary stress on the first syllable, e.g. **gyroscope** /ˈdʒaɪə.rə.skəʊp (US) ˈdʒaɪ.rə.skoʊp/, **gyroscopic** /ˌdʒaɪə.rəˈskɒp.ɪk (US) ˌdʒaɪ.rəˈskɑː.pɪk/.
gyro ˈdʒaɪə.rəʊ (US) ˈdʒaɪ.roʊ, ˈgɪr.oʊ **-s** -z
gyrocompass ˈdʒaɪə.rəʊˌkʌm.pəs (US) ˈdʒaɪ.roʊ- **-es** -ɪz
gyromagnetic ˌdʒaɪə.rəʊ.mægˈnet.ɪk, -məgˈ- (US) ˌdʒaɪ.roʊ.mægˈnet̬.ɪk
gyron ˈdʒaɪə.rən, -rɒn (US) ˈdʒaɪ.rən, -rɑːn **-s** -z
gyroscope ˈdʒaɪə.rə.skəʊp (US) ˈdʒaɪ.rə.skoʊp **-s** -s
gyroscopic ˌdʒaɪə.rəˈskɒp.ɪk (US) ˌdʒaɪ.rəˈskɑː.pɪk **-ally** -əl.i, -li
gyrostat ˈdʒaɪə.rəʊ.stæt (US) ˈdʒaɪ.rə-, -roʊ- **-s** -s
gyrostatic ˌdʒaɪə.rəʊˈstæt.ɪk (US) ˌdʒaɪ.rəˈstæt̬- **-s** -s
gyv|e dʒaɪv **es**-z **-ing** -ɪŋ **-ed** -d

Pronouncing the letter H

There are two main pronunciations for the consonant letter **h**: /h/ and silent.

The usual pronunciation is /h/, e.g.:

head /hed/

h has a silent realisation at the end of a word, e.g.:

oh /əʊ/ (US) /oʊ/
loofah /ˈluː.fə/

There is a group of words in which it is also silent initially: *heir, honest, honour* and *hour*, and their derivatives, and *herb* for American English.

Following an initial **r**, **h** is silent, e.g.:

rhythm /ˈrɪð.ᵊm/

In weak forms, **h** is often not pronounced, e.g.:

him /ɪm/
have /əv/

h (H) eɪtʃ **-'s** -ɪz
H_2O ˌeɪtʃ.tuːˈəʊ (US) -ˈoʊ
ha *exclamation:* hɑː
ha *(abbrev. for* **hectare***)* ˈhek.teəʳ, -tɑːʳ, -təʳ (US) -ter
Haagen Dazs® ˌhɑː.gənˈdɑːz (US) ˈhɑː.gənˌdæs
Haakon ˈhɔː.kɒn, ˈhɑː-, -kᵊn (US) ˈhɔː.kʊn, ˈhɑː-, -kɑːn, -kən
Haarlem ˈhɑː.ləm, -lem (US) ˈhɑːr-
Habacuc, Habakkuk ˈhæb.ə.kək, -kʌk; həˈbæk.ək
Habberton ˈhæb.ə.tən (US) -ɚ.t̬ən
habeas corpus ˌheɪ.bi.əsˈkɔː.pəs, -æsˈ- (US) -ˈkɔːr-
haberdasher ˈhæb.ə.dæʃ.əʳ (US) -ɚ.dæʃ.ɚ **-s** -z
haberdasher|y ˌhæb.əˈdæʃ.ᵊr|.i, ˈhæb.ə.dæʃ- (US) ˈhæb.ɚ.dæʃ- **-ies** -iz
Habgood ˈhæb.gʊd
Habibie həˈbiː.bi, hæbˈiː-
habiliment həˈbɪl.ɪ.mənt, hæbˈɪl-, ˈ-ə- (US) həˈbɪl.ə- **-s** -s
habili|tate həˈbɪl.ɪ|teɪt, hæbˈɪl-, ˈ-ə- (US) həˈbɪl.ə- **-tates** -teɪts **-tating** -teɪ.tɪŋ (US) -teɪ.t̬ɪŋ **-tated** -teɪ.tɪd (US) -teɪ.t̬ɪd
habilitation həˌbɪl.ɪˈteɪ.ʃᵊn, hæbˌɪl-, -əˈ- (US) həˌbɪl.əˈ-
Habington ˈhæb.ɪŋ.tən
habit ˈhæb.ɪt **-s** -s
habitab|le ˈhæb.ɪ.tə.b|l̩ (US) -t̬ə- **-ly** -li **-leness** -l̩.nəs, -nɪs
habitant *inhabitant:* ˈhæb.ɪ.tᵊnt (US) -t̬ᵊnt **-s** -s
habitant *in Canada and Louisiana:* ˈhæb.ɪ.tɔ̃ːŋ, ˈæb-, -tɒŋ (US) ˈhæb.ɪ.tɑːnt, -tənt; ˌæb.iˈtɑːn **-s** -z
habitat (H®) ˈhæb.ɪ.tæt, ˈ-ə- **-s** -s
habitation ˌhæb.ɪˈteɪ.ʃᵊn, -əˈ- **-s** -z
habit-forming ˈhæb.ɪtˌfɔː.mɪŋ (US) -ˌfɔːr-
habit|ual həˈbɪtʃ|.u.əl, hæbˈɪtʃ-, -ˈbɪt.j|u- (US) həˈbɪtʃ|.u.əl **-ually** -ʊ.li, -ə.li
habitu|ate həˈbɪtʃ.u|.eɪt, hæbˈɪtʃ-, -ˈbɪt.ju- (US) həˈbɪtʃ.u- **-ates** -eɪts **-ating** -eɪ.tɪŋ (US) -eɪ.t̬ɪŋ **-ated** -eɪ.tɪd (US) -eɪ.t̬ɪd
habitude ˈhæb.ɪ.tjuːd, -tʃuːd (US) -tuːd, -tjuːd **-s** -z
habitué həˈbɪt.ju.eɪ, hæbˈɪt-, -ˈbɪtʃ.u.eɪ (US) həˌbɪtʃ.uˈeɪ, həˈbɪtʃ.u.eɪ **-s** -z
Note: Also occasionally /əˈbɪt.ju.eɪ/ in British English, when not initial.
Habsburg ˈhæps.bɜːg (US) -bɝːg
hacek ˈhɑː.tʃek, ˈhætʃ.ek
hachure hæʃˈjʊəʳ, -ˈʊəʳ (US) hæʃˈʊr, -ˈjʊr, ˈhæʃ.ʊr **-s** -z
hacienda ˌhæs.iˈen.də (US) ˌhɑː.siˈ- **-s** -z
hack (H) hæk **-s** -s **-ing** -ɪŋ **-ed** -t
hackamore ˈhæk.ə.mɔːʳ (US) -mɔːr **-s** -z
hackberr|y ˈhækˌber|.i, -bᵊr|.i (US) -ˌber- **-ies** -iz
hacker (H) ˈhæk.əʳ (US) -ɚ **-s** -z
Hackett ˈhæk.ɪt
hackl|e ˈhæk.l̩ **-es** -z **-ing** -ɪŋ, ˈhæk.lɪŋ **-ed** -d
hackney (H) ˈhæk.ni **-s** -z **-ed** -d
hacksaw ˈhæk.sɔː (US) -sɑː, -sɔː **-s** -z
hackwork ˈhæk.wɜːk (US) -wɝːk
had *(from* **have***) strong form:* hæd *weak forms:* həd, əd, d
Note: The strong form is used when **had** is used as a full verb rather than an auxiliary, e.g. 'We had some tea.' The auxiliary verb is a weak form word: the strong form /hæd/ is used contrastively, e.g. 'I don't know if she had or she hadn't', in final position, e.g. 'I'd read as much as he had' and quite frequently in initial position, e.g. 'Had anyone seen it before?'. It is also used for emphasis, e.g. 'It had to break down when it was raining'. Elsewhere, the weak form is usually /həd/ or /əd/. The form /d/ is usually used only after vowels.
Hadar ˈheɪ.dɑːʳ (US) -dɑːr
hadarim *(plur. of* **heder***)* ˌhæd.ɑːˈriːm (US) ˌhɑː- *as if Hebrew:* ˌxæd- (US) ˌxɑː-
Hadden ˈhæd.ᵊn
Haddington ˈhæd.ɪŋ.tən
haddock (H) ˈhæd.ək **-s** -s
Haddon ˈhæd.ᵊn
had|e heɪd **-es** -z **-ing** -ɪŋ **-ed** -ɪd
Haden ˈheɪ.dᵊn
Hades ˈheɪ.diːz
Hadfield ˈhæd.fiːld
hadj hædʒ, hɑːdʒ (US) hædʒ **-es** -ɪz
hadji ˈhædʒ.i, ˈhɑː.dʒi, -dʒiː (US) ˈhædʒ.iː **-s** -z
Hadleigh, Hadley ˈhæd.li
Hadlow ˈhæd.ləʊ (US) -loʊ
hadn't ˈhæd.ᵊnt
Hadrian ˈheɪ.dri.ən ˌ**Hadrian's** ˈ**Wall**
hadst *strong form:* hædst *weak form:* hədst
Note: Weak form word, rarely used. See the note for **had**.
haecceity hekˈsiː.ə.ti, hiːk-, haɪk-, -ɪ. (US) hekˈsiː.ə.t̬i, hiːk-
haem hiːm
haematite ˈhiː.mə.taɪt, ˈhem.ə- (US) ˈhiː.mə-
haematologic ˌhiː.mə.təˈlɒdʒ.ɪk (US) -t̬əˈlɑːdʒ- **-al** -ᵊl
haematolog|y ˌhiː.məˈtɒl.ə.dʒ|i (US) -ˈtɑː.lə- **-ist/s** -ɪst/s
haematoma ˌhiː.məˈtəʊ.mə, ˌhem.ə- (US) ˌhiː.məˈtoʊ- **-s** -əz **-ta** -tə
haemoglobin ˌhiː.məʊˈgləʊ.bɪn, ˌhem.əʊˈ- (US) ˈhiː.mə.gloʊ-, -mə-
haemophili|a ˌhiː.məˈfɪl.i|.ə, ˌhem.ə- (US) ˌhiː.moʊˈ-, -məˈ-, -ˈfiːl.j|ə **-ac/s** -æk/s
haemorrhag|e ˈhem.ᵊr.ɪdʒ (US) -ɚ.ɪdʒ, ˈ-rɪdʒ **-es** -ɪz **-ing** -ɪŋ **-ed** -d
haemorrhoid ˈhem.ᵊr.ɔɪd (US) -ə.rɔɪd, ˈ-rɔɪd **-s** -z
haemosta|sis ˌhiː.məˈsteɪ|.sɪs, ˌhem.əˈ- (US) ˌhiː.məˈ- **-ses** -siːz
hafnium ˈhæf.ni.əm
haft hɑːft (US) hæft **-s** -s
hag hæg **-s** -s

Hag® hɑːg
Hagan ˈheɪ.gᵊn ⓤⓢ ˈheɪ-, ˈhɑː-
Hagar *biblical name:* ˈheɪ.gɑːʳ, -gəʳ ⓤⓢ -gɑːr *modern personal name:* ˈheɪ.gəʳ ⓤⓢ -gɑːr, -gɚ
Hagarene ˈhæg.ᵊr.iːn, ˈheɪ.gᵊr-, ˌ--ˈ- ⓤⓢ ˈhæg.ə.riːn, ˈheɪ.gə- **-s** -z
Hagerstown ˈheɪ.gəz.taʊn ⓤⓢ -gɚz-
Haggada(h) hægˈʌd.ə, -ˈɒd- ⓤⓢ həˈgɑː.dɑː, -də; ˌhɑː.gɑːˈdɑː
Haggai ˈhæg.eɪ.aɪ, -i.aɪ, ˈhæg.aɪ; hægˈeɪ.aɪ ⓤⓢ ˈhæg.i.aɪ, ˈhæg.aɪ
Haggar ˈhæg.ɑːʳ, -əʳ ⓤⓢ -ɑːr, -ɚ
haggard (H) ˈhæg.əd ⓤⓢ -ɚd **-ly** -li **-ness** -nəs, -nɪs
Hagger ˈhæg.əʳ ⓤⓢ -ɚ
Haggerston ˈhæg.ə.stᵊn ⓤⓢ ˈ-ɚ-
haggis ˈhæg.ɪs **-es** -ɪz
haggl|e ˈhæg.l̩ **-es** -z **-ing** -ɪŋ, ˈhæg.lɪŋ **-ed** -d **-er/s** -əʳ/z ⓤⓢ -ɚ/z, ˈhæg.ləʳ/z ⓤⓢ -lɚ/z
hagiograph|y ˌhæg.iˈɒg.rə.f|i, ˌheɪ.dʒiˈ- ⓤⓢ -ˈɑː.grə- **-er/s** -əʳ/z ⓤⓢ -ɚ/z
hagiolatry ˌhæg.iˈɒl.ə.tri, ˌheɪ.dʒiˈ- ⓤⓢ -ˈɑː.lə-
hagiolog|y ˌhæg.iˈɒl.ə.dʒ|i, ˌheɪ.dʒiˈ- ⓤⓢ -ˈɑː.lə- **-ist/s** -ɪst/s
hagioscope ˈhæg.i.ə.skəʊp, ˈheɪ.dʒi- ⓤⓢ -skoʊp **-s** -s
Hagley ˈhæg.li
Hagman ˈhæg.mən
hagridden ˈhægˌrɪd.ᵊn
Hague heɪg
ha-ha (*interj.*) hɑːˈhɑː, ˈ--
ha-ha *sunken fence:* ˈhɑː.hɑː **-s** -z
Hahn hɑːn
hahnium ˈhɑː.ni.əm
Haider ˈhaɪ.dəʳ ⓤⓢ -dɚ
Haifa ˈhaɪ.fə
Haig heɪg
Haigh heɪg, heɪ
Haight-Ashbury ˌheɪtˈæʃ.bᵊr.i ⓤⓢ -ˌber-
haiku ˈhaɪ.kuː
hail heɪl **-s** -z **-ing** -ɪŋ **-ed** -d ˌ**Hail** ˈ**Mary**
Hailes heɪlz
Haile Selassie ˌhaɪ.li.səˈlæs.i, -sɪˈ- ⓤⓢ -ˈlæs.i, -ˈlɑː.si
Hailey ˈheɪ.li
Haileybury ˈheɪ.lɪ.bᵊr.i ⓤⓢ -ˌber-
hail-fellow-well-met ˌheɪlˌfel.əʊˌwelˈmet ⓤⓢ -oʊˌ-
Hailsham ˈheɪl.ʃəm
hailstone ˈheɪl.stəʊn ⓤⓢ -stoʊn **-s** -z
hailstorm ˈheɪl.stɔːm ⓤⓢ -stɔːrm **-s** -z
Hain heɪn
Hainan ˌhaɪˈnæn
Hainault ˈheɪ.nɔːt, -nɔːlt, -nɒlt ⓤⓢ -nɑːlt, -nɔːlt
Haines heɪnz
Haiphong ˌhaɪˈfɒŋ ⓤⓢ -ˈfɑːŋ
hair heəʳ ⓤⓢ her **-s** -z ˈ**hair** ˌ**gel**; ˈ**hair's** ˌ**breadth**; ˈ**hair** ˌ**piece**; ˌ**hair** ˈ**shirt**; ˈ**hair** ˌ**slide**; ˌ**hair** ˈ**trigger**; **let one's** ˈ**hair** ˌ**down**; ˌ**make someone's** ˈ**hair stand on** ˌ**end**
hairball ˈheə.bɔːl ⓤⓢ ˈher-, -bɑːl **-s** -z
hairband ˈheə.bænd ⓤⓢ ˈher- **-s** -z
hairbreadth ˈheə.bretθ, -bredθ ⓤⓢ ˈher- **-s** -s
hairbrush ˈheə.brʌʃ ⓤⓢ ˈher- **-es** -ɪz
haircloth ˈheə.klɒθ ⓤⓢ ˈher.klɑːθ
haircut ˈheə.kʌt ⓤⓢ ˈher- **-s** -s
haircutt|er ˈheəˌkʌt|.əʳ ⓤⓢ ˈherˌkʌt̬|.ɚ **-ers** -əz ⓤⓢ -ɚz **-ing** -ɪŋ
hairdo ˈheə.duː ⓤⓢ ˈher- **-s** -z
hairdress|er ˈheəˌdres|.əʳ ⓤⓢ ˈherˌdres|.ɚ **-ers** -əz ⓤⓢ -ɚz **-ing** -ɪŋ
hairdryer, hairdrier ˈheəˌdraɪ.əʳ ⓤⓢ ˈherˌdraɪ.ɚ **-s** -z
-haired -ˈheəd ⓤⓢ -herd
Note: Suffix. Compounds ending **-haired** normally carry primary stress on the suffix in British English, but there is a stress shift when such words are used attributively, e.g. ˌ**goldenhaired** ˈ**child**. In American English, compounds ending **-haired** are normally stressed on the first element, e.g. **goldenhaired** /ⓤⓢ ˈgoʊl.dᵊn.herd/.
hairgrass ˈheə.grɑːs ⓤⓢ ˈher.græs
hairgrip ˈheə.grɪp ⓤⓢ ˈher- **-s** -s
hairless ˈheə.ləs, -lɪs ⓤⓢ ˈher- **-ness** -nəs, -nɪs
hairline ˈheə.laɪn ⓤⓢ ˈher- **-s** -z
hairnet ˈheə.net ⓤⓢ ˈher- **-s** -s
hairpiec|e ˈheə.piːs ⓤⓢ ˈher- **-es** -ɪz
hairpin ˈheə.pɪn ⓤⓢ ˈher- **-s** -z ˌ**hairpin** ˈ**bend**; ˌ**hairpin** ˈ**turn**
hair-raising ˈheəˌreɪ.zɪŋ ⓤⓢ ˈher-
hairsplitting ˈheəˌsplɪt.ɪŋ ⓤⓢ ˈherˌsplɪt̬-
hairspray ˈheə.spreɪ ⓤⓢ ˈher- **-s** -z
hairspring ˈheə.sprɪŋ ⓤⓢ ˈher- **-s** -z
hairstyle ˈheə.staɪl ⓤⓢ ˈher- **-s** -z
hairstylist ˈheəˌstaɪ.lɪst ⓤⓢ ˈher- **-s** -s
hair|y ˈheə.r|i ⓤⓢ ˈher|.i **-ier** -i.əʳ ⓤⓢ -i.ɚ **-iest** -i.ɪst, -i.əst **-iness** -ɪ.nəs, -ɪ.nɪs
Haiti ˈheɪ.ti, ˈhaɪ-; haɪˈiː.ti, hɑː- ⓤⓢ ˈheɪ.t̬i, -ti
Haitian ˈheɪ.ʃᵊn, -ʃi.ən, -ti-; haɪˈiː.ʃᵊn, hɑː-, -ʃi.ən ⓤⓢ ˈheɪ.ʃᵊn, -ti.ən **-s** -z
Haitink ˈhaɪ.tɪŋk
hajj hædʒ, hɑːdʒ ⓤⓢ hædʒ
hajji ˈhædʒ.i, ˈhɑː.dʒi, -dʒiː ⓤⓢ ˈhædʒ.iː **-s** -z
haka ˈhɑː.kə **-s** -z
hake heɪk **-s** -s
hakim *doctor:* hɑːˈkiːm, hə-, hækˈiːm ⓤⓢ hɑːˈkiːm **-s** -z *ruler:* ˈhɑː.kiːm, -ˈ- ⓤⓢ ˈhɑː.kiːm, -kɪm
Hakkinen ˈhæk.ɪ.nən
Hakluyt ˈhæk.luːt
Hakodate ˌhæk.əʊˈdɑː.ti ⓤⓢ ˌhɑː.koʊˈdɑː.teɪ
Hal hæl
Halakah hælˈʌk.ə ⓤⓢ ˌhɑː.lɑːˈkɑː, -ˈxɑː; həˈlɑː.kə, -xə
halal hælˈæl; həˈlɑːl
halala, halalah həˈlæl.ə, hælˈæl.ə ⓤⓢ həˈlɑː.lə **-s** -z
halation həˈleɪ.ʃᵊn, hælˈeɪ- ⓤⓢ həˈleɪ- **-s** -z
halberd ˈhæl.bəd, ˈhɔːl-, -bɜːd ⓤⓢ ˈhæl.bɚd, ˈhɑːl- **-s** -z
halberdier ˌhæl.bəˈdɪəʳ ⓤⓢ -bɚˈdɪr **-s** -z
halcyon ˈhæl.si.ən **-s** -z
Halcyone hælˈsaɪə.ni
Haldane ˈhɔːl.deɪn, ˈhɒl- ⓤⓢ ˈhɔːl-, ˈhɑːl-
Haldon ˈhɔːl.dᵊn
hal|e (H) (*adj. v.*) heɪl **-er** -əʳ ⓤⓢ -ɚ **-est** -ɪst, -əst **-es** -z **-ing** -ɪŋ **-ed** -d
haler ˈhɑː.ləʳ ⓤⓢ -lɚ, -ler **-s** -z **-u** -uː
Hales heɪlz
Halesowen ˌheɪlzˈəʊ.ɪn, -ən ⓤⓢ -ˈoʊ-
Halesworth ˈheɪlz.wəθ, -wɜːθ ⓤⓢ -wɝːθ, -wɚθ
Halex® ˈheɪ.leks
Haley ˈheɪ.li
hal|f hɑː|f ⓤⓢ hæ|f **-ves** -vz ˌ**half a** ˈ**dozen**; ˌ**half an** ˈ**hour**; ˌ**half** ˈ**cock**; ˌ**half** ˈ**measures**; ˌ**half** ˈ**nelson**; ˌ**half** ˈ**pay**; ˌ**half** ˈ**term**
Note: Compound words beginning with **half-** usually have secondary stress on this syllable and primary stress later in the compound word (e.g. **half-baked** has the stress pattern ˌ-ˈ-); however, the word is liable to undergo stress shift when a strongly stressed syllable follows (e.g. **half-baked plan** often has the pattern ˈ--ˌ-). Since there are many such words, notes about this stress shift for individual words are not given.
half-a-crown ˌhɑːf.əˈkraʊn ⓤⓢ ˌhæf-
halfback ˈhɑːf.bæk ⓤⓢ ˈhæf- **-s** -s
half-baked ˌhɑːfˈbeɪkt ⓤⓢ ˌhæf-
half-blood ˈhɑːf.blʌd ⓤⓢ ˈhæf-
half-board ˌhɑːfˈbɔːd ⓤⓢ ˌhæfˈbɔːrd
half-bred ˈhɑːf.bred ⓤⓢ ˈhæf-
half-breed ˈhɑːf.briːd ⓤⓢ ˈhæf- **-s** -z
half-brother ˈhɑːfˌbrʌð.əʳ ⓤⓢ ˈhæfˌbrʌð.ɚ **-s** -z
half-caste ˈhɑːf.kɑːst ⓤⓢ ˈhæf.kæst **-s** -s
half-crown ˌhɑːfˈkraʊn ⓤⓢ ˌhæf- **-s** -z
half-dozen ˌhɑːfˈdʌz.ᵊn ⓤⓢ ˌhæf- **-s** -z
half-hardy ˌhɑːfˈhɑː.di ⓤⓢ ˌhæfˈhɑːr-
half-hearted ˌhɑːfˈhɑː.tɪd ⓤⓢ ˌhæfˈhɑːr.t̬ɪd
half-hearted|ly ˌhɑːfˈhɑː.tɪd|.li ⓤⓢ ˌhæfˈhɑːr.t̬ɪd- **-ness** -nəs, -nɪs

half-holiday ˌhɑːfˈhɒl.ə.deɪ, ˈ-ɪ-, -di ⓤⓢ ˌhæfˈhɑː.lə.deɪ **-s** -z
half-hour ˌhɑːfˈaʊəʳ ⓤⓢ ˌhæfˈaʊr, -ˈaʊɚ **-s** -z
half-hourly ˌhɑːfˈaʊə.li ⓤⓢ ˌhæfˈaʊr-, -ˈaʊɚ-
half-length ˌhɑːfˈleŋθ, -ˈleŋkθ ⓤⓢ ˌhæf- **-s** -s
half-li|fe ˈhɑːf.laɪ|f ⓤⓢ ˈhæf- **-ves** -vz
half-mast ˌhɑːfˈmɑːst ⓤⓢ ˌhæfˈmæst
half-moon ˌhɑːfˈmuːn ⓤⓢ ˌhæf- **-s** -z
Halford ˈhæl.fəd, ˈhɔːl-, ˈhɒl- ⓤⓢ ˈhæl.fɚd, ˈhɔːl-, ˈhɑːl-
halfpence ˈheɪ.pᵊnts
halfpenn|y ˈheɪp.n|i, ˈheɪ.pᵊn|.i **-ies** -iz
Halfpenny ˈhɑːf.pen.i, -pə.ni ⓤⓢ ˈhæf-
halfpennyworth ˈheɪp.ni.wəθ, ˈheɪ.pᵊn.i-, -wɜːθ; ˌhɑːfˈpen.əθ ⓤⓢ ˈheɪ.pᵊn.i.wɝːθ **-s** -s
half-pint ˌhɑːfˈpaɪnt ⓤⓢ ˌhæf- **-s** -s
half-price ˌhɑːfˈpraɪs ⓤⓢ ˌhæf-
half-sister ˈhɑːfˌsɪs.təʳ ⓤⓢ ˈhæfˌsɪs.tɚ **-s** -z
half-size ˌhɑːfˈsaɪz ⓤⓢ ˈhæf.saɪz
half-time ˌhɑːfˈtaɪm ⓤⓢ ˈhæf.taɪm
halftone ˌhɑːfˈtəʊn ⓤⓢ ˈhæf.toʊn **-s** -z
half-tru|th ˌhɑːfˈtruː|θ ⓤⓢ ˈhæf.truː|θ **-ths** -ðz
half-volley ˌhɑːfˈvɒl.i ⓤⓢ ˈhæfˌvɑː.li **-s** -z
halfway ˌhɑːfˈweɪ ⓤⓢ ˌhæf- ˌ**halfway ˈhouse** ⓤⓢ ˈ**halfway** ˌ**house**
half-wit ˈhɑːf.wɪt ⓤⓢ ˈhæf- **-s** -s
half-witted ˌhɑːfˈwɪt.ɪd ⓤⓢ ˌhæfˈwɪt̬-
half-year ˌhɑːfˈjɪəʳ ⓤⓢ ˌhæfˈjɪr **-s** -z **-ly** -li
Haliburton ˌhæl.ɪˈbɜː.tᵊn ⓤⓢ ˈhæl.ɪ.bɝː-
halibut ˈhæl.ɪ.bət, -bʌt **-s** -s
Halicarnassus ˌhæl.ɪ.kɑːˈnæs.əs ⓤⓢ -kɑːr'-
halidom ˈhæl.ɪ.dəm
Halidon ˈhæl.ɪ.dᵊn
Halifax ˈhæl.ɪ.fæks
halitosis ˌhæl.ɪˈtəʊ.sɪs ⓤⓢ -ˈtoʊ-
Halkett ˈhɔːl.kɪt, ˈhæl.kɪt, ˈhæk.ɪt
hall (H) hɔːl ⓤⓢ hɔːl, hɑːl **-s** -z ˌ**Hall of ˈFame**; ˌ**hall of ˈresidence**; ˈ**residence** ˌ**hall**
hallal hælˈæl, həˈlɑːl
Hallam ˈhæl.əm
Hallé ˈhæl.eɪ, -i ⓤⓢ ˈhæl.eɪ
Halle ˈhæl.ə ⓤⓢ ˈhɑː.lə
hallelujah (H) ˌhæl.ɪˈluː.jə, -əˈ- **-s** -z
Haller ˈhæl.əʳ ⓤⓢ -ɚ
Hallett ˈhæl.ɪt
Halley ˈhæl.i, ˈhɔː.li ⓤⓢ ˈhæl.i, ˈheɪ.li ˌ**Halley's ˈComet**
Note: Halley's Comet is usually referred to as /ˈhæl.iz/, with the popular variant /ˈheɪ.liz/ in the US.
halliard ˈhæl.jəd, -i.əd ⓤⓢ -jɚd **-s** -z

Halliday ˈhæl.ɪ.deɪ, ˈ-ə-
Halliwell ˈhæl.ɪ.wel
hallmark ˈhɔːl.mɑːk ⓤⓢ -mɑːrk, ˈhɑːl- **-s** -s **-ing** -ɪŋ **-ed** -t
hallo(a) həˈləʊ, hælˈəʊ, helˈ-, ˈhʌl.əʊ ⓤⓢ həˈloʊ
halloo həˈluː, hælˈuː ⓤⓢ həˈluː **-s** -z **-ing** -ɪŋ **-ed** -d
hallow ˈhæl.əʊ ⓤⓢ -oʊ **-s** -z **-ing** -ɪŋ **-ed** -d
Halloween, Hallowe'en ˌhæl.əʊˈiːn ⓤⓢ ˌhæl.oʊˈ-, ˌhɑː.loʊˈ-, -ləˈwiːn
Hallowmas ˈhæl.əʊ.mæs, -məs ⓤⓢ -oʊ- **-es** -ɪz
Hallows ˈhæl.əʊz ⓤⓢ -oʊz
hallstand ˈhɔːl.stænd ⓤⓢ ˈhɔːl-, ˈhɑːl- **-s** -z
halluci|nate həˈluː.sɪ|.neɪt, -ˈljuː-, -sə- ⓤⓢ -ˈluː- **-nates** -neɪts **-nating** -neɪ.tɪŋ ⓤⓢ -neɪ.t̬ɪŋ **-nated** -neɪ.tɪd ⓤⓢ -neɪ.t̬ɪd
hallucination həˌluː.sɪˈneɪ.ʃᵊn, -ˌljuː-, -səˈ- ⓤⓢ -ˌluː- **-s** -z
hallucinatory həˈluː.sɪ.nə.tᵊr.i, -ˈljuː-, -sᵊn.ə-, -tri; həˌluː.sɪˈneɪ-, -ˌljuː-, -sᵊnˈeɪ- ⓤⓢ həˈluː.sɪ.nə.tɔːr.i
hallucinogen həˈluː.sɪ.nə.dʒen, -dʒᵊn; ˌhæl.uːˈsɪn- ⓤⓢ həˈluː.sɪ.nə.dʒen; ˌhæl.juːˈsɪn.ə-, -jəˈ- **-s** -z
hallucinogenic həˌluː.sɪ.nəʊˈdʒen.ɪk, -ˌljuː-, -sᵊn.əˈ- ⓤⓢ -ˌluː.sɪ.noʊˈ-
hallway ˈhɔːl.weɪ ⓤⓢ ˈhɔːl-, ˈhɑːl- **-s** -z
halma ˈhæl.mə
halo ˈheɪ.ləʊ ⓤⓢ -loʊ **-(e)s** -z **-ing** -ɪŋ **-ed** -d
halogen ˈhæl.ə.dʒen, ˈheɪ.lə-, -dʒən ⓤⓢ ˈhæl.oʊ-, ˈ-ə- **-s** -z
halogenous həˈlɒdʒ.ɪ.nəs, -ᵊn.əs ⓤⓢ -ˈlɑː.dʒə.nəs
Halper ˈhæl.pəʳ ⓤⓢ -pɚ
Halpern ˈhæl.pən ⓤⓢ -pɚn
Hals hæls, hælz ⓤⓢ hɑːls, hɑːlz
Halsbury ˈhɔːlz.bᵊr.i, ˈhɒlz- ⓤⓢ ˈhɔːlzˌber-, ˈhɑːlz-
Halsey ˈhɔːl.si, ˈhæl-, -zi ⓤⓢ ˈhɔːl.zi, ˈhɑːl-
Halstead ˈhɔːl.sted, ˈhɒl-, ˈhæl-, -stɪd ⓤⓢ ˈhɔːl-, ˈhɑːl-, ˈhæl-
halt hɒlt, hɔːlt ⓤⓢ hɔːlt, hɑːlt **-s** -s **-ing/ly** -ɪŋ/li ⓤⓢ ˈhɔːl.t̬ɪŋ/li, ˈhɑːl- **-ed** -ɪd ⓤⓢ ˈhɔːl.t̬ɪd, ˈhɑːl-
halter ˈhɔːl.təʳ, ˈhɒl- ⓤⓢ ˈhɔːl.t̬ɚ, ˈhɑːl- **-s** -z
halterneck ˈhɒl.tə.nek, ˈhɔːl- ⓤⓢ ˈhɔːl.t̬ɚ-, ˈhɑːl- **-s** -s
halva(h) ˈhæl.və, -vɑː ⓤⓢ hɑːlˈvɑː; ˈ--, -və
halv|e hɑːv ⓤⓢ hæv **-es** -z **-ing** -ɪŋ **-ed** -d
Halvergate ˈhæl.və.geɪt ⓤⓢ -vɚ-
halves *(plur. of* **half***)* hɑːvz ⓤⓢ hævz
halyard ˈhæl.jəd ⓤⓢ -jɚd **-s** -z
ham (H) hæm **-s** -z **-ming** -ɪŋ **-med** -d

hamadryad ˌhæm.əˈdraɪ.əd, -ˈdraɪ.æd **-s** -z
Hamah ˈhæm.ə ⓤⓢ ˈhɑː.mɑː
Haman *biblical name:* ˈheɪ.mæn, -mən ⓤⓢ -mən *modern surname:* ˈheɪ.mən
Hamar ˈheɪ.mɑːʳ ⓤⓢ -mɑːr
hamartia ˌhɑː.mɑːˈtiː.ə ⓤⓢ -mɑːrˈ-
Hamas hæmˈæs, ˈ--
Hamble ˈhæm.bl̩
Hambleden ˈhæm.bl̩.dən
Hambledon ˈhæm.bl̩.dən
Hambleton ˈhæm.bl̩.tən
Hamblin ˈhæmb.lɪn
Hambro ˈhæm.brəʊ, -brə ⓤⓢ ˈhæm.brə, -broʊ
Hamburg ˈhæm.bɜːg ⓤⓢ -bɝːg, ˈhɑːm.bʊrg
hamburger ˈhæmˌbɜː.gəʳ ⓤⓢ -ˌbɝː.gɚ **-s** -z
Hamed ˈhæm.ed ⓤⓢ ˈhɑːməd
Hamelin ˈhæm.lɪn, -ᵊl.ɪn, -ɪ.lɪn
Hamer ˈheɪ.məʳ ⓤⓢ -mɚ
Hamerton ˈhæm.ə.tᵊn ⓤⓢ ˈ-ɚ-
ham-fisted ˌhæmˈfɪs.tɪd ⓤⓢ ˈ--- **-ly** -li **-ness** -nəs, -nɪs *stress shift, British only:* ˌham-fisted ˈeffort
ham-handed ˌhæmˈhæn.dɪd ⓤⓢ ˈhæmˌhæn- **-ly** -li **-ness** -nəs, -nɪs *stress shift, British only:* ˌham-handed ˈgesture
Hamhung ˌhɑːmˈhʊŋ
Hamilcar hæmˈɪl.kɑːʳ, həˈmɪl-; ˈhæm.ɪl-, -ᵊl- ⓤⓢ -kɑːr
Hamill ˈhæm.ᵊl
Hamilton ˈhæm.ᵊl.tən, -ɪl-
Hamiltonian ˌhæm.ᵊlˈtəʊ.ni.ən, -ɪlˈ- ⓤⓢ -ˈtoʊ-
Hamish ˈheɪ.mɪʃ
Hamite ˈhæm.aɪt **-s** -s
Hamitic hæmˈɪt.ɪk, həˈmɪt- ⓤⓢ hæmˈɪt̬-, həˈmɪt̬-
hamlet (H) ˈhæm.lət, -lɪt **-s** -s
Hamley ˈhæm.li
Hamlin, Hamlyn ˈhæm.lɪn
hammam ˈhæm.æm, -əm, ˈhʌm.ʌm; həˈmɑːm ⓤⓢ ˈhæm.əm **-s** -z
Hammarskjöld ˈhæm.ə.ʃəʊld ⓤⓢ -ɚ.ʃoʊld, ˈhɑː.mɚ-
hamm|er (H) ˈhæm|.əʳ ⓤⓢ -ɚ **-ers** -əz ⓤⓢ -ɚz **-ering** -ᵊr.ɪŋ **-ered** -əd ⓤⓢ -ɚd ˌ**go at it** ˌ**hammer and ˈtongs**
Hammerfest ˈhæm.ə.fest ⓤⓢ ˈ-ɚ-
hammerhead ˈhæm.ə.hed ⓤⓢ ˈ-ɚ- **-s** -z
hammerlock ˈhæm.ə.lɒk ⓤⓢ -ɚ.lɑːk **-s** -s
Hammersmith ˈhæm.ə.smɪθ ⓤⓢ ˈ-ɚ-
Hammerstein ˈhæm.ə.staɪn, -stiːn ⓤⓢ ˈ-ɚ-
Hammett ˈhæm.ɪt
hammock ˈhæm.ək **-s** -s
Ham(m)ond ˈhæm.ənd

Hammurabi ˌhæm.ʊˈrɑː.bi US ˌhɑː.mʊˈ-, ˌhæm.əˈ-
hamm|y ˈhæm|.i **-ier** -i.əʳ US -i.ɚ **-iest** -i.ɪst, -i.əst **-ily** -ɪ.li, -ᵊl.i **-iness** -ɪ.nəs, -ɪ.nɪs
Hampden ˈhæmp.dən
hamp|er ˈhæm.p|əʳ US -p|ɚ **-ers** -əz US -ɚz **-ering** -ᵊr.ɪŋ **-ered** -əd US -ɚd
Hampshire ˈhæmp.ʃəʳ, -ˌʃɪəʳ US -ʃɚ, -ˌʃɪr
Hampstead ˈhæmp.sted, -stɪd ˌ**Hampstead** ˈ**Heath**
Hampton ˈhæmp.tən ˌ**Hampton** ˈ**Court**
Hamshaw ˈhæm.ʃɔː US -ʃɑː, -ʃɔː
hamster ˈhæmp.stəʳ US -stɚ **-s** -z
ham|string ˈhæm|.strɪŋ **-strings** -strɪŋz **-stringing** -strɪŋ.ɪŋ **-strung** -strʌŋ
hamza ˈhæm.zə **-s** -z
Han hæn US hɑːn
Hanan ˈhæn.ən
Hananiah ˌhæn.əˈnaɪ.ə
Hanbury ˈhæn.bᵊr.i, ˈhæm- US ˈhænˌber-
Hancock ˈhæn.kɒk, ˈhæŋ- US ˈhæn.kɑːk
Hancox ˈhæn.kɒks, ˈhæŋ- US ˈhæn.kɑːks
hand (H) hænd **-s** -z **-ing** -ɪŋ **-ed** -ɪd **-er/s** -əʳ/z US -ɚ/z **-edness** -ɪd.nəs, -nɪs ˈ**hand** ˌ**cream**; ˈ**hand gre**ˌ**nade**; ˌ**know somewhere like the** ˌ**back of one's** ˈ**hand**; ˌ**bite the** ˌ**hand that** ˈ**feeds** ˌ**one**; ˌ**force someone's** ˈ**hand**; ˌ**hand in** ˈ**glove (with)**; ˌ**wait on someone** ˌ**hand and** ˈ**foot**
andbag ˈhænd.bæg, ˈhæm- US ˈhænd- **-s** -z **-ging** -ɪŋ **-ged** -d
andball ˈhænd.bɔːl, ˈhæm- US ˈhænd.bɔːl, -bɑːl **-s** -z
andbarrow ˈhændˌbær.əʊ, ˈhæm- US ˈhændˌber.oʊ, -ˌbær- **-s** -z
andbasin ˈhændˌbeɪ.sᵊn, ˈhæm-, -sɪn US ˈhænd- **-s** -z
andbell ˈhænd.bel, ˈhæm- US ˈhænd- **-s** -z
ndbill ˈhænd.bɪl, ˈhæm- US ˈhænd- **-s** -z
ndbook ˈhænd.bʊk, ˈhæm- US ˈhænd- **-s** -s
ndbrake ˈhænd.breɪk, ˈhæm- US ˈhænd- **-s** -s
ndcart ˈhænd.kɑːt, ˈhæŋ- US ˈhænd.kɑːrt **-s** -s
ndclap ˈhænd.klæp, ˈhæŋ- US ˈhænd- **-s** -s
ndcock ˈhænd.kɒk US -kɑːk
ndcraft ˈhænd.krɑːft, ˈhæŋ- US ˈhænd.kræft **-s** -s
ndcuff ˈhænd.kʌf **-s** -s **-ing** -ɪŋ **-ed** -t
ndel ˈhæn.dᵊl
ndelian hænˈdiː.li.ən US -ˈdel.i-, -ˈdiː.li-
handful ˈhænd.fʊl **-s** -z
handgrip ˈhænd.grɪp, ˈhæŋ- US ˈhænd- **-s** -s
handgun ˈhænd.gʌn, ˈhæŋ- US ˈhænd- **-s** -z
hand-held ˌhændˈheld US ˌ-ˈ-, ˈ-- *stress shift, British only:* ˌhand-held ˈcamera
handhold ˈhænd.həʊld US -hoʊld **-s** -z
hand-holding ˈhændˌhəʊl.dɪŋ US -ˌhoʊl-
handicap ˈhæn.dɪ.kæp US ˈ-dɪ-, ˈ-di- **-s** -s **-ping** -ɪŋ **-ped** -t **-per/s** -əʳ/z US -ɚ/z
handicraft ˈhæn.dɪ.krɑːft US ˈ-dɪ.kræft, ˈ-di- **-s** -s
handiwork ˈhæn.dɪ.wɜːk US ˈ-dɪ.wɝːk, ˈ-di-
handkerchie|f ˈhæŋ.kə.tʃiː|f, -tʃɪ|f US -kɚ.tʃɪ|f, -tʃiː|f **-fs** -fs **-ves** -vz
handknit ˌhændˈnɪt **-s** -ˈnɪts **-ting** -ˈnɪt.ɪŋ US -ˈnɪt̬.ɪŋ **-ted** -ˈnɪt.ɪd US -ˈnɪt̬.ɪd *stress shift:* ˌhandknit ˈsweater
handl|e ˈhæn.dl̩ **-es** -z **-ing** -ɪŋ, -ˈhænd.lɪŋ **-ed** -d **-er/s** -əʳ/z US -ɚ/z, ˈhænd.ləʳ/z US -lɚ/z
handlebar ˈhæn.dl̩.bɑːʳ US -bɑːr **-s** -z
Handley ˈhænd.li
handmade ˌhændˈmeɪd, ˌhæm- US ˌhænd- *stress shift:* ˌhandmade ˈsweets
handmaid ˈhænd.meɪd, ˈhæm- US ˈhænd- **-s** -z
handmaiden ˈhændˌmeɪ.dᵊn, ˈhæm- US ˈhænd- **-s** -z
hand-me-down ˈhænd.mi.daʊn, ˈhæm- US ˈhænd- **-s** -z
handout ˈhænd.aʊt **-s** -s
handover ˈhænˌdəʊ.vəʳ US -ˌdoʊ.vɚ **-s** -z
hand-pick ˌhændˈpɪk, ˌhæm- US ˌhænd- **-s** -s **-ing** -ɪŋ **-ed** -t
handrail ˈhænd.reɪl **-s** -z
Hands hændz
handsaw ˈhænd.sɔː US -sɑː, -sɔː **-s** -z
handsel ˈhænd.sᵊl **-s** -z **-ling** -ɪŋ **-led** -d
handset ˈhænd.set **-s** -s
handsful *(plur. of* **handful***)* ˈhændz.fʊl
handshak|e ˈhænd.ʃeɪk **-es** -s **-ing** -ɪŋ
hands-off ˌhændzˈɒf US -ˈɑːf, -ˈɔːf *stress shift:* ˌhands-off ˈmanner
handsom|e ˈhænd.səm **-er** -əʳ US -ɚ **-est** -ɪst, -əst **-ely** -li **-eness** -nəs, -nɪs
hands-on ˌhændzˈɒn US -ˈɑːn *stress shift:* ˌhands-on ˈpractice
handspring ˈhænd.sprɪŋ **-s** -z
handstand ˈhænd.stænd **-s** -z
hand-to-hand ˌhænd.təˈhænd *stress shift:* ˌhand-to-hand ˈfighting
hand-to-mouth ˌhænd.təˈmaʊθ *stress shift:* ˌhand-to-mouth ˈliving
handwork ˈhænd.wɜːk US -wɝːk
handwriting ˈhændˌraɪ.tɪŋ US -t̬ɪŋ **-s** -z
handwritten ˌhændˈrɪt.ᵊn *stress shift:* ˌhandwritten ˈnote
hand|y (H) ˈhæn.d|i **-ier** -i.əʳ US -i.ɚ **-iest** -i.ɪst, -i.əst **-ily** -ɪ.li, -ᵊl.i **-iness** -ɪ.nəs, -ɪ.nɪs
handy|man ˈhæn.di|.mæn, -mən **-men** -men
hang hæŋ **-s** -z **-ing/s** -ɪŋ/z **-ed** -d **hung** hʌŋ
hangar ˈhæŋ.gəʳ, -əʳ US -ɚ **-s** -z
hangdog ˈhæŋ.dɒg US -dɑːg, -dɔːg **-s** -z
hanger (H) ˈhæŋ.əʳ US -ɚ **-s** -z
hanger-on ˌhæŋ.əʳˈɒn US -ɚˈɑːn **hangers-on** ˌhæŋ.əzˈɒn US -ɚz-
hang-glid|er ˈhæŋˌglaɪ.d|əʳ US -ɚ **-ers** -əz US -ɚz **-ing** -ɪŋ
hang|man ˈhæŋ|.mən, -mæn **-men** -mən
hangnail ˈhæŋ.neɪl **-s** -z
hangout ˈhæŋ.aʊt **-s** -s
hangover ˈhæŋ.əʊ.vəʳ US -oʊ.vɚ **-s** -z
hang-up ˈhæŋ.ʌp **-s** -s
hank (H) hæŋk **-s** -s
hank|er ˈhæŋ.k|əʳ US -k|ɚ **-ers** -əz US -ɚz **-ering** -ᵊr.ɪŋ **-ered** -əd US -ɚd
hankie ˈhæŋ.ki **-s** -z
Hankow ˌhænˈkaʊ, ˌhæŋ- US ˌhæn-, ˌhɑːn-, -ˈkoʊ
Hanks hæŋks
hank|y ˈhæŋ.k|i **-ies** -iz
hanky-panky ˌhæŋ.kiˈpæŋ.ki US ˌhæŋ.kiˈpæŋ-, ˈhæŋ.kiˌpæŋ-
Hanley ˈhæn.li
Hanna(h) ˈhæn.ə
Hannay ˈhæn.eɪ
Hannen ˈhæn.ən
Hannibal ˈhæn.ɪ.bᵊl, ˈ-ə-
Hannington ˈhæn.ɪŋ.tən
Hanoi hænˈɔɪ, həˈnɔɪ US hænˈɔɪ, hɑːˈnɔɪ, hə- *stress shift:* ˌHanoi ˈRocks
Hanover ˈhæn.əʊ.vəʳ US -oʊ.vɚ
Hanoverian ˌhæn.əʊˈvɪə.ri.ən, -ˈveə- US -əˈvɪr.i-, -ˈver **-s** -z
Hansa ˈhænt.sə, ˈhæn.zə
Hansard ˈhænt.sɑːd, -səd US -sɚd
Hansberry ˈhænz.bᵊr.i US -ˌber-
Hans|e hænts **-es** -ɪz
Hanseatic ˌhænt.siˈæt.ɪk, ˌhæn.ziˈ- US -ˈæt̬-
hansel (H) ˈhænt.sᵊl **-s** -z **-(l)ing** -ɪŋ **-(l)ed** -d
Hänsel ˈhænt.sᵊl, ˈhent-
Hansell ˈhænt.sᵊl
Hansen ˈhænt.sen
hansom (H) ˈhænt.səm **-s** -z ˈ**hansom** ˌ**cab**
Hanson ˈhænt.sᵊn
Hants. *(abbrev. for* **Hampshire***)* hænts
Hanuk(k)ah ˈhʌn.ʊ.kə, ˈhæn- US ˈhɑː.nə.kə, ˈxɑː-, -nuː-, -kɑː

Hanuman ˌhʌn.ʊˈmɑːn (US) ˌhɑː.nʊˈmɑːn, ˈ---
Hanway ˈhæn.weɪ
Hanwell ˈhæn.wəl, -wel
hào haʊ
hap hæp **-s** -s **-ping** -ɪŋ **-ped** -t
haphazard ˌhæpˈhæz.əd (US) -ɚd **-ly** -li **-ness** -nəs, -nɪs
hapless ˈhæp.ləs, -lɪs **-ly** -li **-ness** -nəs, -nɪs
haploid ˈhæp.lɔɪd **-s** -z
haplology hæpˈlɒl.ə.dʒi (US) -ˈlɑː.lə-
haply ˈhæp.li
hap'orth ˈheɪ.pəθ (US) -pɚθ **-s** -s
happ|en ˈhæp|.^{ə}n **-ens** -^{ə}nz **-ening/s** -^{ə}n.ɪŋ/z, ˈhæp.nɪŋ/z **-ened** -^{ə}nd
happenstance ˈhæp.^{ə}n.stæn*t*s, -^{ə}m-, -stɑːn*t*s (US) -^{ə}n.stæn*t*s
Happisburgh ˈheɪz.b^{ə}r.ə
happ|y ˈhæp|.i **-ier** -i.ə^{r} (US) -i.ɚ **-iest** -i.ɪst, -i.əst **-ily** -ɪ.li, -^{ə}l.i **-iness** -ɪ.nəs, -ɪ.nɪs ˈ**happy** ˌ**hour**; ˌ**happy** ˈ**medium**
happy-go-lucky ˌhæp.i.gəʊˈlʌk.i (US) -goʊˈ- *stress shift:* ˌhappy-go-lucky ˈfellow
Hapsburg ˈhæps.bɜːg (US) -bɝːg
hara-kiri ˌhær.əˈkɪr.i, -ˈkɪə.ri (US) ˌhɑːr.əˈkɪr.i, ˌhær-
harangu|e həˈræŋ **-es** -z **-ing** -ɪŋ **-ed** -d **-er/s** -ə^{r}/z (US) -ɚ/z
Harare həˈrɑː.ri, -reɪ (US) hɑːˈrɑːr.i, hə-, -eɪ
harass ˈhær.əs; həˈræs (US) həˈræs; ˈher.əs, ˈhær- **-es** -ɪz **-ing** -ɪŋ **-ed** -t **-er/s** -ə^{r}/z (US) -ɚ/z **-ment** -mənt
Harben ˈhɑː.b^{ə}n (US) ˈhɑːr-
Harberton ˈhɑː.bə.t^{ə}n (US) ˈhɑːr.bɚ.t̬^{ə}n
Harbin hɑːˈbiːn, -ˈbɪn (US) ˈhɑːr.bɪn
harbinger ˈhɑː.bɪn.dʒə^{r} (US) ˈhɑːr.bɪn.dʒɚ **-s** -z
harb|or ˈhɑː.b|ə^{r} (US) ˈhɑːr.b|ɚ **-ors** -əz (US) -ɚz **-oring** -^{ə}r.ɪŋ **-ored** -əd (US) -ɚd **-orage** -^{ə}r.ɪdʒ **-orless** -ə.ləs, -lɪs (US) -ɚ.ləs, -lɪs ˈ**harbor** ˌ**master**
Harborough ˈhɑː.b^{ə}r.ə (US) ˈhɑːr.bə.roʊ
harb|our ˈhɑː.b|ə^{r} (US) ˈhɑːr.b|ɚ **-ours** -əz (US) -ɚz **-ouring** -^{ə}r.ɪŋ **-oured** -əd (US) -ɚd **-ourage** -^{ə}r.ɪdʒ **-ourless** -ə.ləs, -lɪs (US) -ɚ.ləs, -lɪs ˈ**harbour** ˌ**master**
Harcourt ˈhɑː.kət, -kɔːt (US) ˈhɑːr.kɔːrt, -kɚt
hard (H) hɑːd (US) hɑːrd **-er** -ə^{r} (US) -ɚ **-est** -ɪst, -əst **-ness** -nəs, -nɪs ˌ**hard** ˈ**copy** ˈ**hard** ˌ**copy**; ˌ**hard** ˈ**currency**; ˌ**hard** ˈ**disk**; ˌ**no** ˌ**hard** ˈ**feelings**; ˌ**hard** ˈ**labour**; ˌ**hard** ˈ**luck**; ˌ**hard** ˈ**luck** ˌ**story**; ˌ**hard of** ˈ**hearing**; ˌ**hard** ˈ**sell**; ˌ**hard** ˈ**shoulder**
hardback ˈhɑːd.bæk (US) ˈhɑːrd- **-s** -s
hardbake ˈhɑːd.beɪk (US) ˈhɑːrd-
hard-baked ˌhɑːdˈbeɪkt (US) ˌhɑːrd- *stress shift:* ˌhard-baked ˈcharacter
hard-bitten ˌhɑːdˈbɪt.^{ə}n (US) ˌhɑːrd- *stress shift:* ˌhard-bitten ˈcynic
hardboard ˈhɑːd.bɔːd (US) ˈhɑːrd.bɔːrd
hard-boiled ˌhɑːdˈbɔɪld (US) ˌhɑːrd- *stress shift:* ˌhard-boiled ˈegg
Hardcastle ˈhɑːdˌkɑː.sl̩ (US) ˈhɑːrdˌkæs-
hard-core (*adj.*) ˌhɑːdˈkɔː^{r}, ˈ-- (US) ˌhɑːrdˈkɔːr *stress shift:* ˌhard-core ˈporn
hard core (*n.*) (*nucleus:*) ˌhɑːdˈkɔː (US) ˌhɑːrdˈkɔːr
hardcore (*n.*) *rubble:* ˈhɑːd.kɔː^{r} (US) ˈhɑːrd.kɔːr
hardcover ˈhɑːdˌkʌv.ə^{r} (US) ˈhɑːrdˌkʌv.ɚ **-s** -z
hard-earned ˌhɑːdˈɜːnd (US) ˌhɑːrdˈɝːnd *stress shift:* ˌhard-earned ˈcash
harden (H) ˈhɑː.d^{ə}n (US) ˈhɑːr- **-s** -z **-ing** -ɪŋ, ˈhɑːd.nɪŋ (US) ˈhɑːrd- **-ed** -d
Hardern ˈhɑː.d^{ə}n (US) ˈhɑːr.dɚn
hard-fought ˌhɑːdˈfɔːt (US) ˌhɑːrdˈfɑːt, -ˈfɔːt *stress shift:* ˌhard-fought ˈbattle
hardheaded ˌhɑːdˈhed.ɪd (US) ˌhɑːrd- **-ness** -nəs, -nɪs *stress shift:* ˌhardheaded ˈbargaining
hardhearted ˌhɑːdˈhɑː.tɪd (US) ˌhɑːrdˈhɑːr.t̬ɪd **-ly** -li **-ness** -nəs, -nɪs *stress shift:* ˌhardhearted ˈvillain
hard-hit ˌhɑːdˈhɪt (US) ˌhɑːrd- **-ting** -ɪŋ *stress shift:* ˌhard-hit ˈregion
Hardicanute ˈhɑː.dɪ.kəˌnjuːt, -də-; ˌhɑː.dɪ.kəˈnjuːt (US) ˌhɑːr.dɪ.kəˈnuːt, -ˈnjuːt
Hardie ˈhɑː.di (US) ˈhɑːr-
hardihood ˈhɑː.di.hʊd (US) ˈhɑːr-
Harding ˈhɑː.dɪŋ (US) ˈhɑːr-
Hardinge ˈhɑː.dɪŋ, -dɪndʒ (US) ˈhɑːr-
hardline ˌhɑːdˈlaɪn (US) ˌhɑːrd- *stress shift:* ˌhardline ˈleader
hardliner ˌhɑːdˈlaɪ.nə^{r}, ˈ-ˌ-- (US) ˌhɑːrdˈlaɪ.nɚ, ˈ-ˌ-- **-s** -z
hardly ˈhɑːd.li (US) ˈhɑːrd-
hard-nosed ˌhɑːdˈnəʊzd (US) ˌhɑːrdˈnoʊzd *stress shift:* ˌhard-nosed ˈpolicy
hard-on ˈhɑːd.ɒn (US) ˈhɑːrd.ɑːn
hard-pressed ˌhɑːdˈprest (US) ˌhɑːrd- *stress shift:* ˌhard-pressed ˈleader
hardship ˈhɑːd.ʃɪp (US) ˈhɑːrd- **-s** -s
hardtop ˈhɑːd.tɒp (US) ˈhɑːrd.tɑːp **-s** -s
hard-up ˌhɑːdˈʌp (US) ˌhɑːrd- *stress shift:* ˌhard-up ˈpensioner
hardware ˈhɑːd.weə^{r} (US) ˈhɑːrd.wer
hard-wearing ˌhɑːdˈweə.rɪŋ (US) ˌhɑːrdˈwer.ɪŋ *stress shift:* ˌhard-wearing ˈcarpet
Hardwick(e) ˈhɑːd.wɪk (US) ˈhɑːrd-
hardwood ˈhɑːd.wʊd (US) ˈhɑːrd- **-s** -z
hard-working ˌhɑːdˈwɜː.kɪŋ (US) ˌhɑːrdˈwɝː- *stress shift:* ˌhard-working ˈsecretary
hard|y (H) ˈhɑː.d|i (US) ˈhɑːr- **-ier** -i.ə^{r} (US) -i.ɚ **-iest** -i.ɪst, -i.əst **-ily** -ɪ.li, -^{ə}l.i **-iness** -ɪ.nəs, -ɪ.nɪs
har|e (H) heə^{r} (US) her **-es** -z **-ing** -ɪŋ **-ed** -
harebell ˈheə.bel (US) ˈher- **-s** -z
harebrained ˈheə.breɪnd (US) ˈher-
Harefield ˈheə.fiːld (US) ˈher-
Hare Krishna ˌhær.iˈkrɪʃ.nə, ˌhɑː.riˈ- (US) ˌhɑː.riˈ- **-s** -z
harelip ˌheəˈlɪp (US) ˌher- **-s** -s **-ped** -t
harem ˈhɑː.riːm, ˈheə-, -rəm; həˈriːm, hɑː- (US) ˈher.əm, ˈhær- **-s** -z
Harewood ˈhɑː.wʊd, ˈheə.wʊd (US) ˈhɑːr-, ˈher-

Note: The Earl of Harewood pronounces /ˈhɑː.wʊd (US) ˈhɑːr-/, and his house is called /ˌhɑː.wʊdˈhaʊs (US) ˌhɑːr-/. The village in West Yorkshire is now generally pronounced /ˈheə.wʊd (US) ˈher-/, though /ˈhɑː.wʊd (US) ˈhɑːr-/ may sometimes be heard from old people there. Other peop[le] with the surname **Harewood** pronounce /ˈheə.wʊd (US) ˈher-/.

Harford ˈhɑː.fəd (US) ˈhɑːr.fɚd
Hargraves ˈhɑː.greɪvz (US) ˈhɑːr-
Hargreaves ˈhɑː.griːvz, -greɪvz (US) ˈhɑːr-
haricot ˈhær.ɪ.kəʊ (US) ˈher.ɪ.koʊ, ˈhæ **-s** -z ˌ**haricot** ˈ**bean**, ˈ**haricot** ˌ**bean**
Haringey ˈhær.ɪŋ.geɪ (US) ˈher-, ˈhær-
Harington ˈhær.ɪŋ.tən (US) ˈher-, ˈhær
Hariot ˈhær.i.ət (US) ˈher-, ˈhær-, -ɑːt
hark hɑːk (US) hɑːrk **-s** -s **-ing** -ɪŋ **-ed** -
Harker ˈhɑː.kə^{r} (US) ˈhɑːr.kɚ
Harkin ˈhɑː.kɪn (US) ˈhɑːr-
Harkinson ˈhɑː.kɪn*t*.s^{ə}n (US) ˈhɑːr-
Harkness ˈhɑːk.nəs, -nɪs (US) ˈhɑːrk-
Harland ˈhɑː.lənd (US) ˈhɑːr-
Harlech ˈhɑː.lek, -lex, -lək, -ləx (US) ˈhɑːr.lek
Harleian hɑːˈliː.ən; ˈhɑː.li- (US) ˈhɑːr. hɑːrˈliː-
Harlem ˈhɑː.ləm, -lem (US) ˈhɑːr- ˌ**Harlem** ˈ**Globetrotters**
harlequin ˈhɑː.lɪ.kwɪn, -lə-, -kɪn (US) ˈhɑːr.lɪ- **-s** -z
harlequinade ˌhɑː.lɪ.kwɪˈneɪd, -lə-, -kɪˈ- (US) ˌhɑːr.lɪ- **-s** -z
Harlesden ˈhɑːlz.dən (US) ˈhɑːrlz-
Harley ˈhɑː.li (US) ˈhɑːr- ˈ**Harley** ˌ**Stre**
Harley Davidson® ˌhɑː.liˈdeɪ.vɪd.s (US) ˌhɑːr-
Harlock ˈhɑː.lɒk (US) ˈhɑːr.lɑːk
harlot ˈhɑː.lət (US) ˈhɑːr- **-s** -s **-ry** -ri
Harlow(e) ˈhɑː.ləʊ (US) ˈhɑːr.loʊ
harm hɑːm (US) hɑːrm **-s** -z **-ing** -ɪŋ **-e** ˌ**out of** ˌ**harm's** ˈ**way**

Harman 'hɑː.mən (US) 'hɑːr-
Harmer 'hɑː.məʳ (US) 'hɑːr.mɚ
harmful 'hɑːm.fəl, -fʊl (US) 'hɑːrm- **-ly** -i **-ness** -nəs, -nɪs
harmless 'hɑːm.ləs, -lɪs (US) 'hɑːrm- **-ly** -li **-ness** -nəs, -nɪs
Harmon 'hɑː.mən (US) 'hɑːr-
Harmondsworth 'hɑː.məndz.wəθ, -wɜːθ (US) 'hɑːr.məndz.wɝːθ
Harmonia hɑː'məʊ.ni.ə (US) hɑːr'moʊ-
harmonic hɑː'mɒn.ɪk (US) hɑːr'mɑː.nɪk **-s** -s **-al** -əl **-ally** -əl.i, -li
harmonica hɑː'mɒn.ɪ.kə (US) hɑːr'mɑː.nɪ- **-s** -z
harmonious hɑː'məʊ.ni.əs (US) hɑːr'moʊ- **-ly** -li **-ness** -nəs, -nɪs
harmonist 'hɑː.mə.nɪst (US) 'hɑːr- **-s** -s
harmonium hɑː'məʊ.ni.əm (US) hɑːr'moʊ- **-s** -z
harmonization, -isa- ˌhɑː.mə.naɪ'zeɪ.ʃən, -nɪ'- (US) ˌhɑːr.mə.nɪ'- **-s** -z
harmoniz|e, -is|e 'hɑː.mə.naɪz (US) 'hɑːr- **-es** -ɪz **-ing** -ɪŋ **-ed** -d **-er/s** -əʳ/z (US) -ɚ/z
harmon|y 'hɑː.mə.n|i (US) 'hɑːr- **-ies** -iz
Harmsworth 'hɑːmz.wəθ, -wɜːθ (US) 'hɑːrmz.wɝːθ
Harnack 'hɑː.næk (US) 'hɑːr-
harness (H) 'hɑː.nɪs, -nəs (US) 'hɑːr- **-es** -ɪz **-ing** -ɪŋ **-ed** -t **-er/s** -əʳ/z (US) -ɚ/z
Harold 'hær.əld (US) 'her-, 'hær-
harp hɑːp (US) hɑːrp **-s** -s **-ing** -ɪŋ **-ed** -t
Harpenden 'hɑː.pən.dən (US) 'hɑːr-
Harper 'hɑː.pəʳ (US) 'hɑːr.pɚ
Harpham 'hɑː.pəm (US) 'hɑːr-
Harpic® 'hɑː.pɪk (US) 'hɑːr-
harpist 'hɑː.pɪst (US) 'hɑːr- **-s** -s
harpoon ˌhɑː'puːn (US) ˌhɑːr- **-s** -z **-ing** -ɪŋ **-ed** -d **-er/s** -əʳ/z (US) -ɚ/z
harpsichord 'hɑːp.sɪ.kɔːd (US) 'hɑːrp.sɪ.kɔːrd **-s** -z
harp|y (H) 'hɑː.p|i (US) 'hɑːr- **-ies** -iz
harquebus 'hɑː.kwɪ.bəs, -kwə- (US) 'hɑːr.kwə- **-es** -ɪz
Harraden 'hær.ə.dən, -den (US) 'her-, 'hær-
Harrap 'hær.əp (US) 'her-, 'hær-
Harrell 'hær.əl (US) 'her-, 'hær-
harridan 'hær.ɪ.dən, '-ə- (US) 'her-, 'hær- **-s** -z
Harrie 'hær.i (US) 'her-, 'hær-
harrier 'hær.i.əʳ (US) 'her.i.ɚ, 'hær- **-s** -z
Harries 'hær.ɪs, -iz (US) 'her-, 'hær-
Harriet 'hær.i.ət (US) 'her-, 'hær-
Harriman 'hær.ɪ.mən (US) 'her-, 'hær-
Harrington 'hær.ɪŋ.tən (US) 'her-, 'hær-
Harriot 'hær.i.ət (US) 'her-, 'hær-
Harris 'hær.ɪs (US) 'her-, 'hær- ˌ**Harris** '**Tweed**
Harrisburg 'hær.ɪs.bɜːg (US) 'her.ɪs.bɝːg, 'hær-
Harris(s)on 'hær.ɪ.sən (US) 'her-, 'hær-
Harrod 'hær.əd (US) 'her-, 'hær- **-s** -z
Harrogate 'hær.ə.gət, -geɪt, -gɪt (US) 'her-, 'hær-
Harrop 'hær.əp (US) 'her-, 'hær-
Harrovian hær'əʊ.vi.ən, hə'rəʊ- (US) hə'roʊ- **-s** -z
harrow (H) 'hær.əʊ (US) 'her.oʊ, 'hær- **-s** -z **-ing/ly** -ɪŋ/li **-ed** -d
Harrowby 'hær.əʊ.bi (US) 'her.oʊ-, 'hær-
harrumph hə'rʌmpf **-s** -s **-ing** -ɪŋ **-ed** -t
harr|y (H) 'hær|.i (US) 'her-, 'hær- **-ies** -iz **-ying** -i.ɪŋ **-ied** -id
harsh hɑːʃ (US) hɑːrʃ **-er** -əʳ (US) -ɚ **-est** -ɪst, -əst **-ly** -li **-ness** -nəs, -nɪs
hart (H) hɑːt (US) hɑːrt **-s** -s
Harte hɑːt (US) hɑːrt
hartebeest 'hɑː.tɪ.biːst, -tə- (US) 'hɑːr.t̬ə-, -tə- **-s** -s
Hartford 'hɑːt.fəd (US) 'hɑːrt.fɚd
Harthan 'hɑː.ðən, 'hɑː.θən (US) 'hɑːr-
Hartington 'hɑː.tɪŋ.tən (US) 'hɑːr.t̬ɪŋ-
Hartland 'hɑːt.lənd (US) 'hɑːrt-
Hartlepool 'hɑːt.lɪ.puːl, -lə- (US) 'hɑːrt-
Hartley 'hɑːt.li (US) 'hɑːrt-
Hartman 'hɑːt.mən (US) 'hɑːrt-
Hartnell 'hɑːt.nəl (US) 'hɑːrt-
Hartshill 'hɑːts.hɪl (US) 'hɑːrts-
hartshorn (H) 'hɑːts.hɔːn (US) 'hɑːrts.hɔːrn
hart's-tongue 'hɑːts.tʌŋ (US) 'hɑːrts- **-s** -z
Hartz hɑːts (US) hɑːrts
harum-scarum ˌheə.rəm'skeə.rəm (US) ˌher.əm'sker.əm, ˌhær-, -'skær-
Harun-al-Rashid hærˌuːn.æl.ræʃ'iːd, hɑːˌruːn-; ˌhær.uːn.æl'ræʃ.iːd, ˌhɑː.ruːn-, -ɪd (US) hɑːˌruːn.ɑːl.rɑː'ʃiːd
haruspex hə'rʌs.peks, hær'ʌs-; 'hær.ə.speks **haruspices** hə'rʌs.pɪ.siːz, hær'ʌs-
Harvard 'hɑː.vəd (US) 'hɑːr.vɚd
Harverson 'hɑː.və.sən (US) 'hɑːr.vɚ-
harvest 'hɑː.vɪst, -əst (US) 'hɑːr- **-s** -s **-ing** -ɪŋ **-ed** -ɪd **-er/s** -əʳ/z (US) -ɚ/z ˌ**harvest** '**festival**; '**harvest** ˌ**mite**; ˌ**harvest** '**moon**; '**harvest** ˌ**mouse**
Harvey 'hɑː.vi (US) 'hɑːr-
Harwich 'hær.ɪtʃ, -ɪdʒ (US) 'hær-, 'her-
Harwood 'hɑː.wʊd (US) 'hɑːr-
Harworth 'hɑː.wəθ (US) 'hɑːr.wɚθ
Haryana ˌhær.i'ɑː.nə (US) ˌhɑːr'jɑː-
Harz hɑːts (US) hɑːrts
has *(from* **have***) strong form:* hæz *weak forms:* həz, əz, z, s
Note: The strong form is used when **has** is used as a full verb rather than as an auxiliary, e.g. 'He has some money'. The auxiliary verb is a weak form word: the strong form /hæz/ is used contrastively, e.g. 'I don't know if she has or she hasn't', in final position, e.g. 'I've read as much as he has' and quite frequently in initial position, e.g. 'Has anyone seen my glasses?'. It is also used for emphasis, e.g. 'She **has** to have one'. Elsewhere, the weak form is usually /həz/ or /əz/. The shortest weak forms are /s/ and /z/: the form /s/ is used only after voiceless consonants other than /s, ʃ, tʃ/, while the form /z/ is used only after a vowel or a voiced consonant other than /z, ʒ, dʒ/. After /s, z, ʃ, ʒ, tʃ, dʒ/, the weak form is usually /əz/.
has-been 'hæz.biːn, -bɪn (US) -bɪn **-s** -z
Hasdrubal 'hæz.drʊ.bəl, -druː-, -bæl
Haselden 'hæz.əl.dən, 'heɪz-
hash hæʃ **-es** -ɪz **-ing** -ɪŋ **-ed** -t ˌ**hash** '**brown**
Hashemite 'hæʃ.ɪ.maɪt, -ə-
Hashimoto ˌhæʃ.ɪ'məʊ.təʊ (US) -'moʊ.t̬oʊ, ˌhɑːʃ-, -toʊ
hashish 'hæʃ.ɪʃ, -iːʃ; hæs'iːʃ
Hasid hæs'iːd, hɑː'siːd **-im** -ɪm
Hasidic hæs'ɪd.ɪk, hɑː'sɪd- (US) hæs'ɪd-, hə'sɪd-, hɑː-
Hasidism hæs'ɪd.ɪ.zəm, 'hæs- (US) 'hæs.ɪ.dɪ-, 'hɑː.sɪ-; hæs'ɪd.ɪ-, hə'sɪd-, hɑː-
Haslam 'hæz.ləm
Haslemere 'heɪ.zl̩.mɪəʳ (US) -mɪr
haslet 'hæz.lət, 'heɪz-, -lɪt (US) 'hæs-, 'heɪz-
Haslett 'hæz.lət, 'heɪz.lət, -lɪt
Haslingden 'hæz.lɪŋ.dən
Hasluck 'hæz.lʌk, -lək
hasn't 'hæz.ənt
hasp hɑːsp, hæsp (US) hæsp **-s** -s **-ing** -ɪŋ **-ed** -t
Hassall 'hæs.əl
Hassan *district in India:* 'hʌs.ən, 'hæs- *Arabic name:* hə'sɑːn, hæs'ɑːn; 'hæs.ən, 'hʌs- (US) 'hɑː.sɑːn; hə'sɑːn
Hasselhoff 'hæs.əl.hɒf (US) -hɑːf
hassl|e 'hæs.l̩ **-es** -z **-ing** -ɪŋ, 'hæs.lɪŋ **-ed** -d
hassock (H) 'hæs.ək **-s** -s
hast (H) *(from* **have***) strong form:* hæst *weak forms:* həst, əst, st
Note: This weak form word is little used. See the note for **have** for guidance on when to use the strong form.
hast|e heɪst **-es** -s **-ing** -ɪŋ **-ed** -ɪd
hasten 'heɪ.sən **-s** -z **-ing** -ɪŋ, 'heɪs.nɪŋ **-ed** -d
Hastie 'heɪ.sti
Hastings 'heɪ.stɪŋz
hast|y 'heɪ.st|i **-ier** -i.əʳ (US) -i.ɚ **-iest** -i.ɪst, -i.əst **-ily** -ɪ.li, -əl.i **-iness** -ɪ.nəs, -ɪ.nɪs

hat hæt **-s** -s ˈ**hat** ˌ**rack** ˈ**hat** ˌ**stand**; ˈ**hat** ˌ**trick**; **at the** ˌ**drop of a** ˈ**hat**; ˌ**keep something** ˌ**under one's** ˈ**hat**; **I'll** ˌ**eat my** ˈ**hat**
hatband ˈhæt.bænd **-s** -z
hatbox ˈhæt.bɒks ⓤⓢ -bɑːks **-es** -ɪz
hatch (H) *(n. v.)* hætʃ **-es** -ɪz **-ing** -ɪŋ **-ed** -t
hatchback ˈhætʃ.bæk **-s** -s
hatcher|y ˈhætʃ.ər|.i **-ies** -iz
hatchet ˈhætʃ.ɪt **-s** -s ˈ**hatchet** ˌ**job**; ˌ**bury the** ˈ**hatchet**
hatchling ˈhætʃ.lɪŋ **-s** -z
hatchment ˈhætʃ.mənt **-s** -s
hatchway (H) ˈhætʃ.weɪ **-s** -z
hat|e heɪt **-es** -s **-ing** -ɪŋ ⓤⓢ ˈheɪ.t̬ɪŋ **-ed** -ɪd ⓤⓢ ˈheɪ.t̬ɪd **-er/s** -əʳ/z ⓤⓢ ˈheɪ.t̬ɚ/z
hateful ˈheɪt.fəl, -fʊl **-ly** -i **-ness** -nəs, -nɪs
Hatfield ˈhæt.fiːld
hath *(from* **have***) strong form:* hæθ *weak forms:* həθ, əθ
Note: This weak form word is little used. See the note for **has** for guidance on when to use the strong form.
hatha ˈhæθ.ə, ˈhʌθ-
Hathaway ˈhæθ.ə.weɪ
Hatherell ˈhæð.ər.əl
Hatherleigh ˈhæð.ə.li ⓤⓢ ˈ-ɚ-
Hatherley ˈhæð.ə.li ⓤⓢ ˈ-ɚ-
Hathersage ˈhæð.ə.seɪdʒ, -sɪdʒ, -sedʒ ⓤⓢ ˈ-ɚ-
Hatherton ˈhæð.ə.tən ⓤⓢ -ɚ.t̬ən
Hathorn(e) ˈhɔː.θɔːn ⓤⓢ ˈhɑː.θɔːrn, ˈhɔː-
Hathway ˈhæθ.weɪ
hatless ˈhæt.ləs, -lɪs, -les
hatpin ˈhæt.pɪn **-s** -z
hatred ˈheɪ.trɪd, -trəd
hatter ˈhæt.əʳ ⓤⓢ ˈhæt̬.ɚ **-s** -z **as** ˌ**mad as a** ˈ**hatter**
Hatteras ˈhæt.ər.əs ⓤⓢ ˈhæt̬.ɚ-
Hattersley ˈhæt.əz.li ⓤⓢ ˈhæt̬.ɚz-
Hattie ˈhæt.i ⓤⓢ ˈhæt̬-
Hatton ˈhæt.ən
hauberk ˈhɔː.bɜːk ⓤⓢ ˈhɑː.bɝːk, ˈhɔː- **-s** -s
haugh hɔː ⓤⓢ hɑː, hɔː **-s** -z
Haughey ˈhɔː.hi, ˈhɒ- ⓤⓢ ˈhɑː-, ˈhɔː-
Haughton ˈhɔː.tən ⓤⓢ ˈhɑː-, ˈhɔː-
haught|y ˈhɔː.t|i ⓤⓢ ˈhɑː.t̬|i, ˈhɔː- **-ier** -i.əʳ ⓤⓢ -i.ɚ **-iest** -i.ɪst, -i.əst **-ily** -ɪ.li, -əl.i **-iness** -ɪ.nəs, -ɪ.nɪs
haul hɔːl ⓤⓢ hɑːl, hɔːl **-s** -z **-ing** -ɪŋ **-ed** -d **-er/s** -əʳ/z ⓤⓢ -ɚ/z
haulage ˈhɔː.lɪdʒ ⓤⓢ ˈhɑː-, ˈhɔː-
haulier ˈhɔː.li.əʳ ⓤⓢ ˈhɑːl.jɚ, ˈhɔː- **-s** -z
haulm hɔːm ⓤⓢ hɔːm, hɑːm **-s** -z
haunch hɔːntʃ ⓤⓢ hɑːntʃ, hɔːntʃ **-es** -ɪz
haunt hɔːnt ⓤⓢ hɑːnt, hɔːnt **-s** -s **-ing/ly** -ɪŋ/li ⓤⓢ ˈhɑːn.t̬ɪŋ/li, ˈhɔːn- **-ed** -ɪd ⓤⓢ ˈhɑːn.t̬ɪd, ˈhɔːn-
Hausa ˈhaʊ.sə, -zə **-s** -z
hausfrau ˈhaʊs.fraʊ **-s** -z **-en** -ən
Haussmann ˈhaʊs.mæn ⓤⓢ -mæn, -mən
hautbois *(sing.)* ˈəʊ.bɔɪ, ˈhəʊ-, ˈhɔːt- ⓤⓢ ˈhoʊ-, ˈoʊ- ˈəʊ.bɔɪz, ˈhəʊ-, ˈhɔːt- ⓤⓢ ˈhoʊ-, ˈoʊ-
hautboy ˈəʊ.bɔɪ, ˈhəʊ-, ˈhɔːt- ⓤⓢ ˈhoʊ-, ˈoʊ- **-s** -z
haute couture ˌəʊt.kʊˈtjʊəʳ, -kuːˈ-, -ˈtʊəʳ ⓤⓢ ˌoʊt.kuːˈtʊr
haute cuisine ˌəʊt.kwɪˈziːn, -kwəˈ- ⓤⓢ ˌoʊt-
hauteur əʊˈtɜːʳ, ˈ-- ⓤⓢ hoʊˈtɝː, oʊˈ-
Havana həˈvæn.ə, hævˈæn-, -ˈvɑː.nə ⓤⓢ -ˈvæn.ə **-s** -z
Havant ˈhæv.ənt
Havard ˈhæv.ɑːd, -əd ⓤⓢ -ɑːrd, -ɚd
Havarti həˈvɑː.ti ⓤⓢ -ˈvɑːr-
have *one who has:* hæv **-s** -z
Note: This word usually occurs only in conjunction with **have-not**, in expressions such as 'There's a conflict between the haves and have-nots'.
have *(v.) strong form:* hæv *weak forms:* həv, əv, v **hast** *strong form:* hæst *weak forms:* həst, əst, st *strong form:* **has** hæz *weak forms:* həz, əz, z, s **having** ˈhæv.ɪŋ **had** *strong form:* hæd *weak forms:* həd, əd, d
Note: When **have** occurs as a full verb, e.g. 'to have and to hold', the strong form is used. As an auxiliary verb, it is a weak form word: the strong form is used contrastively, e.g. 'I don't know if you have or haven't', for emphasis, e.g. 'You **have** to see it', and also in final position, e.g. 'I've got as much as you have'. It is also quite often used in initial position, e.g. 'Have you seen my book?'. Elsewhere the weak form is commonly used; the form /v/ is only found after vowels. For **hast**, **has**, **had** and **hadst**, see notes provided for those word entries.
Havel ˈhɑː.vəl ⓤⓢ -fəl
Havell ˈhæv.əl
Havelo(c)k ˈhæv.lɒk, -lək ⓤⓢ -lɑːk, -lək
haven ˈheɪ.vən **-s** -z
have-not ˈhæv.nɒt, ˌ-ˈ- ⓤⓢ ˈhæv.nɑːt, ˌ-ˈ- **-s** -s
haven't ˈhæv.ənt
hav|er ˈheɪ.v|əʳ ⓤⓢ -v|ɚ **-ers** -əz ⓤⓢ -ɚz **-ering** -ər.ɪŋ **-ered** -əd ⓤⓢ -ɚd
Haverford ˈhæv.ə.fəd ⓤⓢ -ɚ.fɚd
Haverfordwest ˌhæv.ə.fədˈwest, ˌhɑː.fədˈwest ⓤⓢ ˌhæv.ɚ.fɚdˈ-, ˌhɑː.fɚdˈ-
Havergal ˈhæv.ə.gəl ⓤⓢ ˈ-ɚ-
Haverhill ˈheɪ.vər.ɪl, -əl; ˈheɪ.və.hɪl ⓤⓢ -vɚ-
Havering ˈheɪ.vər.ɪŋ
Havers ˈheɪ.vəz ⓤⓢ -vɚz
haversack ˈhæv.ə.sæk ⓤⓢ ˈ-ɚ- **-s** -s
haversian canal (H) həˌvɜː.ʃən.kəˈnæl, hævˌɜː-, -ʒən- ⓤⓢ həˌvɝː.ʒən
Haverstock ˈhæv.ə.stɒk ⓤⓢ -ɚ.stɑːk
Havilah ˈhæv.ɪ.lə ⓤⓢ -lə, -lɑː
Haviland ˈhæv.ɪ.lænd, ˈ-ə-, -lənd
Havisham ˈhæv.ɪ.ʃəm
havoc ˈhæv.ək
Havre *place in France:* ˈhɑː.vrə, -vəʳ ⓤⓢ -vrə, -vɚ *place in Maryland:* ˈhɑː.vəʳ ⓤⓢ -vɚ, ˈhæv.ɚ *place in Montana:* ˈhæv.əʳ ⓤⓢ -ɚ
Havre de Grace ˌhɑː.və.dəˈgrɑːs, ˌhæv.ə-, -ˈgræs, -ˈgreɪs ⓤⓢ ˌhɑː.vɚ-, ˌhæv.ɚ-
haw hɔː ⓤⓢ hɑː, hɔː **-s** -z **-ing** -ɪŋ **-ed** -d
Hawaii həˈwaɪ.iː, hɑː-, -i ⓤⓢ həˈwɑː-, -ˈwaɪ-
Hawaiian həˈwaɪ.ən, hɑː-, ˈ-i.ən ⓤⓢ həˈwɑː.jən **-s** -z
Haward ˈheɪ.wəd, ˈhɔː.əd, hɑːd, hɔːd ⓤⓢ ˈheɪ.wɚd, ˈhɔː.ɚd, hɑːrd, hɔːrd
Hawarden *in Clwyd:* ˈhɑː.dən, ˈhɔː- ⓤⓢ ˈhɑːr-, ˈhɔːr *Viscount:* ˈheɪˌwɔː.dən ⓤⓢ -ˌwɔːr- *town in US:* ˈheɪˌwɑː.dən ⓤⓢ -ˌwɑːr-
Haweis ˈhɔː.ɪs ⓤⓢ ˈhɔː.ɪs, hɔɪs
Hawes hɔːz ⓤⓢ hɑːz, hɔːz
hawfinch ˈhɔː.fɪntʃ ⓤⓢ ˈhɑː-, ˈhɔː- **-es** -ɪz
haw-haw ˈhɔːˌhɔː, ˌ-ˈ- ⓤⓢ ˈhɑː.hɑː, ˈhɔː.hɔː, ˌ-ˈ- **-s** -z
Hawick ˈhɔː.ɪk, hɔɪk ⓤⓢ ˈhɑː.ɪk, ˈhɔː-, hɔɪk
hawk hɔːk ⓤⓢ hɑːk, hɔːk **-s** -s **-ing** -ɪŋ **-ed** -t **-er/s** -əʳ/z ⓤⓢ -ɚ/z
Hawke hɔːk ⓤⓢ hɑːk, hɔːk **-s** -s
Hawker-Siddeley® ˌhɔː.kəˈsɪd.əl.i, ˈ-li ⓤⓢ ˌhɑː.kɚˈ-, ˌhɔː-
Hawkeye ˈhɔːk.aɪ ⓤⓢ ˈhɑːk-, ˈhɔːk-
hawk-eyed ˈhɔːk.aɪd ⓤⓢ ˈhɑːk-, ˈhɔːk-
Hawking ˈhɔː.kɪŋ ⓤⓢ ˈhɑː-, ˈhɔː-
Hawkins ˈhɔː.kɪnz ⓤⓢ ˈhɑː-, ˈhɔː-
hawkish ˈhɔː.kɪʃ ⓤⓢ ˈhɑː-, ˈhɔː- **-ly** -li **-ness** -nes, -nɪs
hawkmoth ˈhɔːk.mɒθ ⓤⓢ ˈhɑːk.mɑːθ, ˈhɔːk- **-s** -s
Hawks hɔːks ⓤⓢ hɑːks, hɔːks
hawksbill ˈhɔːks.bɪl ⓤⓢ ˈhɑːks-, ˈhɔːks- **-s** -z
Hawkshaw ˈhɔːk.ʃɔː ⓤⓢ ˈhɑːk.ʃɑː, ˈhɔːk-, -ʃɔː
Hawksley ˈhɔːk.sli ⓤⓢ ˈhɑːks-, ˈhɔːks-
Hawksmoor ˈhɔːks.mɔːʳ ⓤⓢ ˈhɑːks.mɔːr, ˈhɔːks-, -mʊr
hawkweed ˈhɔːk.wiːd ⓤⓢ ˈhɑːk-, ˈhɔːk-
Hawkwood ˈhɔːk.wʊd ⓤⓢ ˈhɑːk-, ˈhɔːk-
Hawley ˈhɔː.li ⓤⓢ ˈhɑː-, ˈhɔː-

Hawn hɔːn (US) hɑːn, hɔːn
Haworth *place in Yorkshire:* ˈhaʊ.əθ, ˈhɔː.əθ (US) ˈhɔː.wɚθ *surname:* ˈhaʊ.əθ (US) ˈheɪ.wɚθ, ˈhaʊ.ɚθ, ˈhoʊ-; hɑːrθ *place in New Jersey:* ˈhɔː.wəθ (US) -wɚθ
haws|e hɔːz (US) hɑːz, hɔːz **-es** -ɪz
hawser ˈhɔː.zəʳ (US) ˈhɑː.zɚ, ˈhɔː- **-s** -z
hawthorn ˈhɔː.θɔːn (US) ˈhɑː.θɔːrn, ˈhɔː- **-s** -z
Hawthornden ˈhɔː.θɔːn.dən (US) ˈhɑː.θɔːrn-, ˈhɔː-
Hawthorne ˈhɔː.θɔːn (US) ˈhɑː.θɔːrn, ˈhɔː-
Haxby ˈhæks.bi
hay (H) heɪ **ˈhay ˌfever**
haybox ˈheɪ.bɒks (US) -bɑːks **-es** -ɪz
haycart ˈheɪ.kɑːt (US) -kɑːrt **-s** -s
haycock (H) ˈheɪ.kɒk (US) -kɑːk **-s** -s
Hayden ˈheɪ.dᵊn
Haydn *English surname:* ˈheɪ.dᵊn *Austrian composer:* ˈhaɪ.dᵊn
Haydock ˈheɪ.dɒk (US) -dɑːk
Haydon ˈheɪ.dᵊn
Hayes heɪz
Hayesford ˈheɪz.fəd (US) -fɚd
Hayhurst ˈhaɪ.əst, ˈheɪ.hɜːst (US) ˈhaɪ.ɚst, ˈheɪ.hɝːst
Hayle heɪl
Hayles heɪlz
Hayley ˈheɪ.li
Hayling Island ˌheɪ.lɪŋˈaɪ.lənd, ˈheɪ.lɪŋˌaɪ-
Hayloft ˈheɪ.lɒft (US) -lɑːft **-s** -s
haymak|er ˈheɪˌmeɪ.k|əʳ (US) -k|ɚ **-ers** -əz (US) -ɚz **-ing** -ɪŋ
Haymarket ˈheɪˌmɑː.kɪt (US) -ˌmɑːr-
Haynes heɪnz
Hayrick ˈheɪ.rɪk **-s** -s
Hays heɪz
hayseed ˈheɪ.siːd **-s** -z
haystack ˈheɪ.stæk **-s** -s
Hayter, Haytor ˈheɪ.təʳ (US) -t̬ɚ
Hayward (H) ˈheɪ.wəd (US) -wɚd **-s** -z
haywire ˈheɪ.waɪəʳ (US) -waɪr
Haywood ˈheɪ.wʊd
Hazara həˈzɑː.rə (US) -ˈzɑːr.ə
hazard (H) ˈhæz.əd (US) -ɚd **-s** -z **-ing** -ɪŋ **-ed** -ɪd
hazardous ˈhæz.ə.dəs (US) ˈ-ɚ- **-ly** -li **-ness** -nəs, -nɪs
haz|e heɪz **-es** -ɪz **-ing** -ɪŋ **-ed** -d
hazel ˈheɪ.zᵊl **-s** -z
Hazelhurst ˈheɪ.zᵊl.hɜːst (US) -hɝːst
hazelnut ˈheɪ.zᵊl.nʌt **-s** -s
Hazen ˈheɪ.zᵊn
Hazledean ˈheɪ.zl̩.diːn
Hazlemere ˈheɪ.zl̩.mɪəʳ (US) -mɪr
Hazlett ˈheɪz.lɪt, ˈhæz-, -lət
Hazlitt ˈheɪz.lɪt, ˈhæz-
Note: William Hazlitt, the essayist, called himself /ˈheɪz.lɪt/, and the present members of his family pronounce the name thus. He is, however, commonly referred to as /ˈhæz.lɪt/. In the **Hazlitt Gallery** in London the pronunciation is /ˈhæz.lɪt/.
Hazor ˈheɪ.zɔːʳ (US) -zɔːr
haz|y ˈheɪ.z|i **-ier** -i.əʳ (US) -i.ɚ **-iest** -i.ɪst, -i.əst **-ily** -ɪ.li, -ᵊl.i **-iness** -ɪ.nəs, -ɪ.nɪs
Hazzard ˈhæz.əd (US) -ɚd
H-Block ˈeɪtʃ.blɒk (US) -blɑːk
H-bomb ˈeɪtʃ.bɒm (US) -bɑːm **-s** -z
HDTV ˌeɪtʃ.diː.tiːˈviː
he *strong form:* hiː *weak forms:* hi, i
Note: Weak form word. The strong form /hiː/ is usually used contrastively, e.g. 'I'm not interested in what **he** says, it's **her** I'm listening to' or for emphasis, e.g. '**he**'s the one'. The weak form is /hi/ in careful speech, e.g. 'Does he live here?' /ˌdʌz.hi.lɪvˈhɪə (US) -ˈhɪr/; in rapid speech it may be pronounced /i/ when following a consonant, e.g. 'What does he want?' /ˌwɒt.dəz.iˈwɒnt/ (US) ˌwɑːt.dəz.iˈwɑːnt/.
head (H) hed **-s** -z **-ing** -ɪŋ **-ed** -ɪd **ˌhead of ˈstate; ˌhead ˈstart; ˌhead ˈteacher; ˌbite someone's ˈhead off; have ˌeyes in the ˌback of one's ˈhead; ˌbang one's ˌhead against a ˌbrick ˈwall; ˌbury one's ˌhead in the ˈsand; ˌhave one's ˈhead screwed on; ˌhead over ˈheels; keep one's ˌhead above ˈwater; make ˌhead or ˈtail of; ˌhold one's ˌhead ˈhigh**
head|ache ˈhed|.eɪk **-aches** -eɪks **-achy** -ˌeɪ.ki
headband ˈhed.bænd **-s** -z
headbang ˈhed.bæŋ **-s** -z **-ing** -ɪŋ **-ed** -d **-er/s** -əʳ/z (US) -ɚ/z
headboard ˈhed.bɔːd (US) -bɔːrd **-s** -z
headcas|e ˈhed.keɪs, ˈheg- (US) ˈhed- **-es** -ɪz
headcheese ˈhed.tʃiːz
headdress ˈhed.dres **-es** -ɪz
header ˈhed.əʳ (US) -ɚ **-s** -z
headfirst ˌhedˈfɜːst (US) -ˈfɝːst *stress shift:* ˌheadfirst ˈleap
headgear ˈhed.gɪəʳ (US) -gɪr **-s** -z
headhun|t ˈhed.hʌn|t **-ts** -ts **-ting** -tɪŋ (US) -t̬ɪŋ **-ted** -tɪd (US) -t̬ɪd
headhunt|er ˈhedˌhʌn.t|əʳ (US) -t̬|ɚ **-ers** -əz (US) -ɚz **-ing** -ɪŋ
heading (H) ˈhed.ɪŋ **-s** -z
Headingl(e)y ˈhed.ɪŋ.li
Headlam ˈhed.ləm
headlamp ˈhed.læmp **-s** -s
headland ˈhed.lənd, -lænd **-s** -z
headless ˈhed.ləs, -lɪs **-ness** -nəs, -nɪs
headlight ˈhed.laɪt **-s** -s
headlin|e ˈhed.laɪn **-es** -z **-ing** -ɪŋ **-ed** -d
headlock ˈhed.lɒk (US) -lɑːk
headlong ˈhed.lɒŋ (US) -lɑːŋ, -lɔːŋ
headman *of group of workers:* ˌhedˈmæn, ˈ-- **headmen** ˌhedˈmen, ˈ-- *of tribe:* ˈhed|.mæn, -mən **-men** -men, -mən
headmaster ˌhedˈmɑː.stəʳ, ˈ-ˌ-- (US) ˈhedˌmæs.tɚ **-s** -z
headmistress ˌhedˈmɪs.trəs, -trɪs, ˈ-ˌ-- (US) ˈhedˌ- **-es** -ɪz
headnote ˈhed.nəʊt (US) -noʊt **-s** -s
head-on ˌhedˈɒn (US) -ˈɑːn *stress shift:* ˌhead-on ˈimpact
headphones ˈhed.fəʊnz (US) -foʊnz
headpiec|e ˈhed.piːs **-es** -ɪz
headquarters ˌhedˈkwɔː.təz, ˈ--- (US) ˈhedˌkwɔːr.t̬ɚz
headrest ˈhed.rest **-s** -s
headroom ˈhed.rʊm, -ruːm (US) -ruːm, -rʊm
headscar|f ˈhed.skɑː|f (US) -skɑːr|f **-ves** -vz
headset ˈhed.set **-s** -s
headship ˈhed.ʃɪp **-s** -s
heads|man ˈhedz|.mən **-men** -mən
headstand ˈhed.stænd **-s** -z
headstone (H) ˈhed.stəʊn (US) -stoʊn **-s** -z
headstrong ˈhed.strɒŋ (US) -strɑːŋ
headteacher ˌhedˈtiː.tʃəʳ (US) -tʃɚ **-s** -z
headwater ˈhedˌwɔː.təʳ (US) -ˌwɑː.t̬ɚ, -ˌwɔː- **-s** -z
headway ˈhed.weɪ
headwind ˈhed.wɪnd **-s** -z
headword ˈhed.wɜːd (US) -wɝːd **-s** -z
headwork ˈhed.wɜːk (US) -wɝːk
head|y ˈhed|.i **-ier** -i.əʳ (US) -i.ɚ **-iest** -i.ɪst, -i.əst **-ily** -ɪ.li, -ᵊl.i **-iness** -ɪ.nəs, -ɪ.nɪs
Heagerty ˈheg.ə.ti (US) -ɚ.t̬i
heal (H) hiːl **-s** -z **-ing** -ɪŋ **-ed** -d **-er/s** -əʳ/z (US) -ɚ/z
Healey ˈhiː.li
health helθ **ˌhealth and ˈsafety; ˈhealth ˌfarm; ˈhealth ˌfood; ˈhealth ˌservice; ˈhealth ˌvisitor**
healthcare ˈhelθ.keəʳ (US) -ker
healthful ˈhelθ.fᵊl, -fʊl **-ly** -i **-ness** -nəs, -nɪs
health-giving ˈhelθˌgɪv.ɪŋ
health|y ˈhel.θ|i **-ier** -i.əʳ (US) -i.ɚ **-iest** -i.ɪst, -i.əst **-ily** -ɪ.li, -ᵊl.i **-iness** -ɪ.nəs, -ɪ.nɪs
Healy ˈhiː.li
Heaney ˈhiː.ni
Heanor ˈhiː.nəʳ (US) -nɚ
heap hiːp **-s** -s **-ing** -ɪŋ **-ed** -t
hear hɪəʳ (US) hɪr **-s** -z **-ing/s** -ɪŋ/z **heard** hɜːd (US) hɝːd **hearer/s** ˈhɪə.rəʳ/z (US) ˈhɪr.ɚ/z **ˈhearing ˌaid; ˌhard of ˈhearing**

heard (H) *(from* **hear***)* hɜːd (US) hɝːd
hearing-impaired ˈhɪə.rɪŋ.ɪmˌpeəd (US) ˈhɪr.ɪŋ.ɪmˌperd
hearken ˈhɑː.kᵊn (US) ˈhɑːr- **-s** -z **-ing** -ɪŋ, ˈhɑːk.nɪŋ (US) ˈhɑːr.kᵊn.ɪŋ, ˈhɑːrk.nɪŋ **-ed** -d
Hearn(e) hɜːn (US) hɝːn
hearsay ˈhɪə.seɪ (US) ˈhɪr-
hears|e hɜːs (US) hɝːs **-es** -ɪz
Hearsey ˈhɜː.si (US) ˈhɝː-
Hearst hɜːst (US) hɝːst
heart hɑːt (US) hɑːrt **-s** -s ˈ**heart atˌtack**; ˈ**heart ˌfailure**; ˌ**eat one's** ˈ**heart out**; **have one's** ˌ**heart in the** ˌ**right** ˈ**place**; **in one's** ˌ**heart of** ˈ**hearts**; ˌ**set one's** ˈ**heart on something**; ˌ**wear one's** ˌ**heart on one's** ˈ**sleeve**
heartache ˈhɑːt.eɪk (US) ˈhɑːrt-
heartbeat ˈhɑːt.biːt (US) ˈhɑːrt- **-s** -s
heartbreak ˈhɑːt.breɪk (US) ˈhɑːrt-
heartbreaking ˈhɑːtˌbreɪ.kɪŋ (US) ˈhɑːrt- **-ly** -li
heartbroken ˈhɑːtˌbrəʊ.kᵊn (US) ˈhɑːrtˌbroʊ-
heartburn ˈhɑːt.bɜːn (US) ˈhɑːrt.bɝːn **-ing** -ɪŋ
-hearted -ˈhɑː.tɪd (US) -ˈhɑːr.t̬ɪd
Note: Suffix. Compounds containing **-hearted** are normally stressed on the suffix as shown, but a stress shift occurs when the word is used attributively, e.g. ˈ**brokenhearted** ˌ**lover**.
hearten ˈhɑː.tᵊn (US) ˈhɑːr- **-s** -z **-ing/ly** -ɪŋ/li, ˈhɑːt.nɪŋ/li (US) ˈhɑːrt- **-ed** -d
heartfelt ˈhɑːt.felt (US) ˈhɑːrt-
hear|th hɑː|θ (US) hɑːr|θ **-ths** -θs, -ðz ˈ**hearth** ˌ**rug**
hearthstone ˈhɑːθ.stəʊn (US) ˈhɑːrθ.stoʊn **-s** -z
heartland ˈhɑːt.lænd (US) ˈhɑːrt- **-s** -z
heartless ˈhɑːt.ləs, -lɪs (US) ˈhɑːrt- **-ly** -li **-ness** -nəs, -nɪs
heart-rending ˈhɑːtˌren.dɪŋ (US) ˈhɑːrt- **-ly** -li
heart-searching ˈhɑːtˌsɜː.tʃɪŋ (US) ˈhɑːrtˌsɝː- **-s** -z
heart's-ease ˈhɑːts.iːz (US) ˈhɑːrts-
heart-shaped ˈhɑːt.ʃeɪpt (US) ˈhɑːrt-
heartsick ˈhɑːt.sɪk (US) ˈhɑːrt- **-ness** -nəs, -nɪs
heartsore ˈhɑːt.sɔːʳ (US) ˈhɑːrt.sɔːr
heartstrings ˈhɑːt.strɪŋz (US) ˈhɑːrt-
heart-throb ˈhɑːt.θrɒb (US) ˈhɑːrt.θrɑːb **-s** -z
heart-to-heart ˌhɑːt.təˈhɑːt (US) ˌhɑːrt.tuːˈhɑːrt, -təˈ- **-s** -s *stress shift:* ˌheart-to-heart ˈtalk
heart-warming ˈhɑːtˌwɔː.mɪŋ (US) ˈhɑːrtˌwɔːr- **-ly** -li
heartwood ˈhɑːt.wʊd (US) ˈhɑːrt-
heart|y ˈhɑː.t|i (US) ˈhɑːr.t̬|i **-ier** -i.əʳ (US) -i.ɚ **-iest** -i.ɪst, -i.əst **-ily** -ɪ.li, -ᵊl.i **-iness** -ɪ.nəs, -ɪ.nɪs
heat hiːt **-s** -s **-ing** -ɪŋ (US) ˈhiː.t̬ɪŋ **-ed/ly** -ɪd/li (US) ˈhiː.t̬ɪd/li ˈ**heat** ˌ**rash**; ˈ**heat** ˌ**spot**; ˈ**heat** ˌ**wave**
heater ˈhiː.təʳ (US) -t̬ɚ **-s** -z
heath (H) hiːθ **-s** -s ˌ**Heath** ˈ**Robinson**
Heathcliff(e) ˈhiːθ.klɪf
Heathcoat ˈhiːθ.kəʊt (US) -koʊt
Heathcote ˈheθ.kət, ˈhiːθ.kət (US) ˈhiːθ.koʊt, -kət
heathen ˈhiː.ðᵊn **-s** -z **-ish** -ɪʃ **-dom** -dəm
heathenism ˈhiː.ðᵊn.ɪ.zᵊm
heathenız|e, -is|e ˈhiː.ðᵊn.aɪz **-es** -ɪz **-ing** -ɪŋ **-ed** -d
heath|er (H) *shrub, girl's name:* ˈheð|.əʳ (US) -ɚ **-ers** -əz (US) -ɚz **-ery** -ᵊr.i
Heather *place in Leicestershire:* ˈhiː.ðəʳ (US) -ðɚ
Heathfield ˈhiːθ.fiːld
heathland ˈhiːθ.lənd, -lænd
Heathrow ˌhiːθˈrəʊ, ˈ-- (US) -roʊ ˌ**Heathrow** ˈ**Airport**
Heath-Stubbs ˌhiːθˈstʌbz
heath|y ˈhiː.θ|i **-ier** -i.əʳ (US) -i.ɚ **-iest** -i.ɪst, -i.əst
Heaton ˈhiː.tᵊn
heat-seeking ˈhiːtˌsiː.kɪŋ
heatstroke ˈhiːt.strəʊk (US) -stroʊk
heav|e hiːv **-es** -z **-ing** -ɪŋ **-ed** -d **hove** həʊv (US) hoʊv **heaver/s** ˈhiː.vəʳ/z (US) -vɚ/z
heave-ho ˌhiːvˈhəʊ (US) -hoʊ
heaven (H) ˈhev.ᵊn **-s** -z **move** ˌ**heaven and** ˈ**earth**
heavenl|y ˈhev.ᵊn.l|i **-iness** -ɪ.nəs, -ɪ.nɪs
heaven-sent ˌhev.ᵊnˈsent (US) ˈ--- *stress shift, British only:* ˌheaven-sent ˈchance
heavenward ˈhev.ᵊn.wəd (US) -wɚd **-s** -z
Heaviside ˈhev.ɪ.saɪd
heav|y ˈhev|.i **-ier** -i.əʳ (US) -i.ɚ **-iest** -i.ɪst, -i.əst **-ily** -ɪ.li, -ᵊl.i **-iness** -ɪ.nəs, -ɪ.nɪs ˌ**heavy** ˈ**breather**; ˌ**heavy** ˈ**cream**; ˌ**heavy** ˈ**metal**
heavy-duty ˌhev.iˈdjuː.ti (US) -ˈduː.t̬i, -ˈdjuː- *stress shift:* ˌheavy-duty ˈbattery
heavy-handed ˌhev.iˈhæn.dɪd **-ly** -li **-ness** -nəs, -nɪs *stress shift:* ˌheavy-handed ˈcriticism
heavy-hearted ˌhev.iˈhɑː.tɪd (US) -ˈhɑːr.t̬ɪd **-ly** -li **-ness** -nəs, -nɪs *stress shift:* ˌheavy-hearted ˈlover
heavyweight ˈhev.i.weɪt **-s** -s
Heazell ˈhiː.zᵊl
Hebburn ˈheb.ɜːn, -ən (US) -ɝːn, -ɚn
Hebden ˈheb.dən
hebdomadal hebˈdɒm.ə.dᵊl (US) -ˈdɑː.mə- **-ly** -li
Hebe ˈhiː.bi
Heber ˈhiː.bəʳ (US) -bɚ
Heberden ˈheb.ə.dᵊn (US) ˈ-ɚ-
Hebraic hiːˈbreɪ.ɪk, hɪˈbreɪ-, hebˈreɪ- (US) hiːˈbreɪ-, hɪ- **-al** -ᵊl **-ally** -ᵊl.i, -li
Hebra|ism ˈhiː.breɪ|.ɪ.zᵊm, -bri- **-isms** -ɪ.zᵊmz **-ist/s** -ɪst/s
Hebraistic ˌhiː.breɪˈɪst.ɪk, -briˈ-
hebraiz|e, -is|e ˈhiː.breɪ.aɪz, -bri- **-es** -ɪz **-ing** -ɪŋ **-ed** -d
Hebrew ˈhiː.bruː **-s** -z
Hebridean ˌheb.rɪˈdiː.ən, -rəˈ- **-s** -z *stress shift:* ˌHebridean ˈcattle
Hebrides ˈheb.rɪ.diːz, -rə-
Hebron *biblical place-name:* ˈheb.rɒn, ˈhiː.brɒn, -brən (US) ˈhiː.brən, ˈheb- *modern surname:* ˈheb.rən, -rɒn (US) -rən, -rɑːn
Hecate ˈhek.ə.ti *in Shakespeare sometimes:* ˈhek.ət
hecatomb ˈhek.ə.tuːm, -təʊm, -təm (US) -toʊm, -tʊm **-s** -z
Hecht hekt
heck hek
heckl|e ˈhek.l̩ **-es** -z **-ing** -ɪŋ, ˈhek.lɪŋ **-ed** -d **-er/s** -əʳ/z (US) -ɚ/z, ˈhek.ləʳ/z (US) -lɚ/z
Heckmondwike ˈhek.mənd.waɪk
Hecla ˈhek.lə
hectare ˈhek.teəʳ, -tɑːʳ, -təʳ (US) -ter **-s** -z
hectic ˈhek.tɪk **-ally** -ᵊl.i, -li
hectogram, hectogramme ˈhek.təʊ.græm (US) -toʊ-, -tə- **-s** -z
hectograph ˈhek.təʊ.grɑːf, -græf (US) -toʊ.græf, -tə- **-s** -s **-ing** -ɪŋ **-ed** -t
hectographic ˌhek.təʊˈgræf.ɪk (US) -toʊˈ-, -təˈ-
hectolitre, hectoliter ˈhek.təʊˌliː.təʳ (US) -toʊˌliː.t̬ɚ, -təˌ- **-s** -z
hectometre, hectometer ˈhek.təʊˌmiː.təʳ (US) -toʊˌmiː.t̬ɚ, -təˌ- **-s** -z
hector (H) ˈhek.təʳ (US) -tɚ **-s** -z **-ing** -ɪŋ **-ed** -d
Hecuba ˈhek.jə.bə, -jʊ-
heder ˈheɪ.dəʳ (US) ˈheɪ.dɚ *as if Hebrew:* ˈxeɪ- **-s** -z **hadarim** ˌhæd.ɑːˈriːm (US) ˌhɑː- *as if Hebrew:* ˌxæd- (US) ˌxɑː-
Hedgcock ˈhedʒ.kɒk (US) -kɑːk
hedg|e hedʒ **-es** -ɪz **-ing** -ɪŋ **-ed** -d **-er/s** -əʳ/z (US) -ɚ/z ˈ**hedge** ˌ**sparrow**; ˌ**hedge one's** ˈ**bets**
hedgehog ˈhedʒ.hɒg (US) -hɑːg, -hɔːg **-s** -z
hedgehop ˈhedʒ.hɒp (US) -hɑːp **-s** -s **-ping** -ɪŋ **-ped** -t
Hedgeley ˈhedʒ.li
Hedger ˈhedʒ.əʳ (US) -ɚ
Hedgerley ˈhedʒ.ə.li (US) ˈ-ɚ-

hedgerow ˈhedʒ.rəʊ US -roʊ **-s** -z
Hedges ˈhedʒ.ɪz
Hedley ˈhed.li
hedon|ism ˈhiː.dᵊn|.ɪ.zᵊm, ˈhed.ᵊn- US ˈhiː.dᵊn- **-ist/s** -ɪst/s
hedonistic ˌhiː.dᵊnˈɪs.tɪk, ˌhed.ᵊnˈ- US ˌhiː.dᵊnˈ- **-ally** -ᵊl.i, -li
heebie-jeebies ˌhiː.biˈdʒiː.biz
heed hiːd **-s** -z **-ing** -ɪŋ **-ed** -ɪd
heedful ˈhiːd.fᵊl, -fʊl **-ly** -i **-ness** -nəs, -nɪs
heedless ˈhiːd.ləs, -lɪs **-ly** -li **-ness** -nəs, -nɪs
heehaw ˈhiː.hɔː, ˌ-ˈ- US ˈhiː.hɑː, -hɔː, ˌ-ˈ- **-s** -z **-ing** -ɪŋ **-ed** -d
heel hiːl **-s** -z **-ing** -ɪŋ **-ed** -d **ˌcool one's ˈheels; ˌdig one's ˈheels in; ˌdrag one's ˈheels; ˌhard on the ˈheels of; ˌkick one's ˈheels**
heeler ˈhiː.ləʳ US -lɚ **-s** -z
Heeley ˈhiː.li
Heenan ˈhiː.nən
Heep hiːp
Heffer ˈhef.əʳ US -ɚ
Hefner ˈhef.nəʳ US -nɚ
heft heft **-s** -s **-ing** -ɪŋ **-ed** -tɪd
heft|y ˈhef.t|i **-ier** -i.əʳ US -i.ɚ **-iest** -i.ɪst, -i.əst **-ily** -ɪ.li, -ᵊl.i **-iness** -ɪ.nəs, -ɪ.nɪs
Hegarty ˈheg.ə.ti US -ɚ.t̬i
Hegel ˈheɪ.gᵊl
Hegelian hɪˈgeɪ.li.ən, hegˈeɪ-; heɪˈgiː-, hegˈiː- **-ism** -ɪ.zᵊm
hegemonic ˌheg.ɪˈmɒn.ɪk, ˌhiː.gɪˈ-, ˌhedʒ.ɪˈ-, -əˈ- US ˌhedʒ.ɪˈmɑː.nɪk
hegemony hɪˈgem.ə.ni, hiːˈgem-, -ˈdʒem-; ˈheg.ɪ.mə-, ˈhedʒ- US hɪˈdʒem.ə-; ˈhedʒ.ə.moʊ-
hegira (H) ˈhedʒ.ɪ.rə, -ᵊr.ə, hɪˈdʒaɪᵊ.rə, hedʒˈaɪᵊ- US ˈhedʒ.ɪ.rə, -ɚ.ə, hɪˈdʒaɪ-, hedʒˈaɪ- **-s** -z
Hegley ˈheg.li
Heidegger ˈhaɪ.deg.əʳ, -dɪ.gəʳ US -dɪ.gɚ
Heidelberg ˈhaɪ.dᵊl.bɜːg US -bɝːg
Heidi ˈhaɪ.di
heifer ˈhef.əʳ US -ɚ **-s** -z
heigh heɪ
heigh-ho ˌheɪˈhəʊ US -ˈhoʊ
Heighington ˈheɪ.ɪŋ.tən, ˈhiː-
height haɪt **-s** -s
heighten ˈhaɪ.tᵊn **-s** -z **-ing** -ɪŋ, ˈhaɪt.nɪŋ **-ed** -d
Heighton ˈheɪ.tᵊn
Heighway ˈhaɪ.weɪ, ˈheɪ-
Heimlich manoeuvre, Heimlich maneuver ˈhaɪm.lɪk.məˌnuː.vəʳ, -lɪx- US -vɚ
Heineken® ˈhaɪ.nɪ.kᵊn, -nə-
Heinekey ˈhaɪ.nɪ.ki
Heinemann ˈhaɪ.nə.mən, -mæn
Heinlein ˈhaɪn.laɪn
heinous ˈheɪ.nəs, ˈhiː- US ˈheɪ- **-ly** -li **-ness** -nəs, -nɪs
Heinz haɪnts, haɪnz
Note: The trademark is always pronounced /haɪnz/.
heir eəʳ US er **-s** -z **-dom** -dəm **-less** -ləs, -lɪs, -les **ˌheir apˈparent; ˌheir preˈsumptive**
heiress ˈeə.res, -rɪs, -rəs; eəˈres US ˈer.ɪs **-es** -ɪz
heirloom ˈeə.luːm US ˈer- **-s** -z
heirship ˈeə.ʃɪp US ˈer-
heist haɪst **-s** -s **-ing** -ɪŋ **-ed** -ɪd
heister ˈhaɪ.stəʳ US -stɚ **-s** -z
hejira (H) ˈhedʒ.ɪ.rə, -ᵊr.ə; hɪˈdʒaɪᵊ.rə, hə- **-s** -z
Hekla ˈhek.lə
Hel hel
held *(from* **hold***)* held
Helen ˈhel.ən, -ɪn
Helena ˈhel.ɪ.nə, ˈ-ə-; helˈiː.nə, hɪˈliː-, hə-
Note: /ˈhel.ɪ.nə, ˈhel.ə.nə/ are the more usual pronunciations, except in the name of the island **St. Helena**; the city in Montana is normally /ˈhel-/.
Helene helˈeɪn, hɪˈleɪn, hə-, -ˈliːn
Helensburgh ˈhel.ənzˌbᵊr.ə, -ɪnzˌ-, -ˌbʌr- US -bɝːg
Helenus ˈhel.ɪ.nəs, ˈ-ə-
Helga ˈhel.gə
heliacal hɪˈlaɪə.kᵊl, hiː-, helˈaɪə- **-ly** -i
Heliades helˈaɪə.diːz, hɪˈlaɪə-
helianth|us ˌhiː.liˈænt.θ|əs, ˌhel.iˈ- **-i** -aɪ **-uses** -ə.sɪz
helical ˈhel.ɪ.kᵊl, ˈhiː.lɪ- **-ly** -i
helices *(plur. of* **helix***)* ˈhiː.lɪ.siːz, ˈhel.ɪ-, -lə-
Helicon ˈhel.ɪ.kᵊn, ˈ-ə-, -ɪ.kɒn US -kɑːn, -kᵊn
helicopter ˈhel.ɪ.kɒp.təʳ, ˈ-əˌ- US -kɑːp.tɚ **-s** -z
Heligoland ˈhel.ɪ.gəʊ.lænd, ˈ-ə- US -goʊ-
heliocentric ˌhiː.li.əʊˈsen.trɪk US -oʊˈ-, -əˈ- **-al** -ᵊl **-ally** -ᵊl.i, -li *stress shift:* ˌheliocentric ˈforce
Heliogabalus ˌhiː.li.əʊˈgæb.ᵊl.əs US -oʊˈ-, -əˈ-
heliogram ˈhiː.li.əʊ.græm US -oʊ-, -ə- **-s** -z
heliograph ˈhiː.li.əʊ.grɑːf, -græf US -oʊ.græf, -ə- **-s** -s
heliograph|er ˌhiː.liˈɒg.rə.f|əʳ US -ˈɑː.grə.f|ɚ **-ers** -əz US -ɚz **-y** -i
heliographic ˌhiː.li.əʊˈgræf.ɪk US -oʊˈ-, -əˈ- **-al** -ᵊl
heliometer ˌhiː.liˈɒm.ɪ.təʳ, ˈ-ə- US -ˈɑː.mə.t̬ɚ **-s** -z
heliometric ˌhiː.li.əʊˈmet.rɪk US -oʊˈ- **-ally** -ᵊl.i, -li
Heliopolis ˌhiː.liˈɒp.ᵊl.ɪs US -ˈɑː.pᵊl-
Helios ˈhiː.li.ɒs US -ɑːs
helioscope ˈhiː.li.əʊ.skəʊp US -oʊ.skoʊp, -ə- **-s** -s
heliostat ˈhiː.li.əʊ.stæt US -oʊ-, -ə- **-s** -s
heliotrope ˈhiː.li.ə.trəʊp, ˈhel.i- US ˈhiː.li.ə.troʊp **-s** -s
heliotropic ˌhiː.li.əˈtrɒp.ɪk US -ˈtrɑː.pɪk **-ally** -ᵊl.i, -li
heliotropism ˌhiː.liˈɒt.rə.pɪ.zᵊm; ˈhiː.li.əˌtrəʊ-, ˌhiː.li.əˈtrəʊ- US ˌhiː.liˈɑː.trə-
helipad ˈhel.ɪ.pæd **-s** -z
heliport ˈhel.ɪ.pɔːt US -pɔːrt **-s** -s
helium ˈhiː.li.əm
helix ˈhiː.lɪks **-es** -ɪz **helices** ˈhiː.lɪ.siːz, ˈhel.ɪ-, -lə-
hell (H) hel **-s** -z **ˌHell's ˈAngel; come ˌhell or ˌhigh ˈwater**
he'll *(=* **he will***)* hiːl
hellacious helˈeɪ.ʃəs
Hellas ˈhel.æs US -æs, -əs
hellbent ˌhelˈbent US ˈ-ˌ-
hellebore ˈhel.ɪ.bɔːʳ, ˈ-ə- US -bɔːr
helleborine ˈhel.ɪ.bə.raɪn, ˈ-ə-, -riːn; ˌhel.ɪˈbɔː.riːn, -əˈ- US ˌhel.əˈbɔːr.ɪn, -iːn
Hellene ˈhel.iːn **-s** -z
Hellenic helˈiː.nɪk, hɪˈliː-, hə-, -ˈlen- US həˈlen-
Hellen|ism ˈhel.ɪ.n|ɪ.zᵊm, ˈ-ə- **-isms** -ɪ.zᵊmz **-ist/s** -ɪst/s
Hellenistic ˌhel.ɪˈnɪs.tɪk, -əˈ- **-al** -ᵊl **-ally** -ᵊl.i, -li
helleniz|e, -is|e ˈhel.ɪ.naɪz, ˈ-ə- **-es** -ɪz **-ing** -ɪŋ **-ed** -d
Heller ˈhel.əʳ US -ɚ
Hellespont ˈhel.ɪ.spɒnt, ˈ-ə- US -spɑːnt
hellfire ˌhelˈfaɪəʳ, ˈ-- US ˈhel.faɪr
hellhole ˈhel.həʊl US -hoʊl **-s** -z
hellhound ˈhel.haʊnd **-s** -z
Hellingly ˌhel.ɪŋˈlaɪ
hellish ˈhel.ɪʃ **-ly** -li **-ness** -nəs, -nɪs
Hellman ˈhel.mən
hello helˈəʊ, həˈləʊ US helˈoʊ, həˈloʊ, ˈhel.oʊ **-(e)s** -z **-ing** -ɪŋ **-ed** -d
helluva ˈhel.ə.və
hellward ˈhel.wəd US -wɚd
helm helm **-s** -z
helme|t ˈhel.mə|t, -mɪ|t **-ts** -ts **-ted** -tɪd US -t̬ɪd
Helmholtz ˈhelm.həʊlts US -hoʊlts
helminth ˈhel.mɪntθ **-s** -s
helminthiasis ˌhel.mɪntˈθaɪə.sɪs
Helmsley ˈhelmz.li *locally:* ˈhemz-
helms|man ˈhelmz|.mən **-men** -mən, -men
Helmut ˈhel.mʊt
Héloïse ˌel.əʊˈiːz US -oʊˈ-; ˈel.ə.wiːz
hel|ot ˈhel|.ət **-ots** -əts **-otage** -ə.tɪdʒ US -ə.t̬ɪdʒ **-otism** -ə.tɪ.zᵊm US -ə.t̬ɪ.zᵊm **-otry** -ət.ri

help help **-s** -s **-ing/s** -ɪŋ/s **-ed** -t **-er/s** -əʳ/z ⓊⓈ -ɚ/z
helpful 'help.fəl, -fʊl **-ly** -i **-ness** -nəs, -nɪs
helpless 'help.ləs, -lɪs **-ly** -li **-ness** -nəs, -nɪs
helpline 'help.laɪn **-s** -z
helpmate 'help.meɪt **-s** -s
helpmeet 'help.miːt **-s** -s
Helsingborg 'hel.sɪŋ.bɔːg ⓊⓈ -bɔːrg
Helsinki hel'sɪŋ.ki, '--- ⓊⓈ 'hel.siŋ.ki, -'--
Helston(e) 'hel.stən
helter-skelter ˌhel.tə'skel.təʳ ⓊⓈ -t̬ɚ'skel.t̬ɚ **-s** -z
helve helv **-s** -z
Helvellyn hel'vel.ɪn
Helveti|a hel'viː.ʃ|ə, -ʃi|.ə **-an/s** -ən/z
Helvetic hel'vet.ɪk ⓊⓈ -'vet̬-
Helvétius hel'viː.ʃəs, -ʃi.əs ⓊⓈ -'viː-, -'veɪ-
Hely 'hiː.li
hem (*n. v.*) hem **-s** -z **-ming** -ɪŋ **-med** -d
hemal 'hiː.məl
he|-man 'hiː|.mæn **-men** -men
Hemans 'hem.ənz
hematite 'hiː.mə.taɪt, 'hem.ə- ⓊⓈ 'hiː.mə-
hematologic ˌhiː.mə.tə'lɒdʒ.ɪk ⓊⓈ -'lɑː.dʒɪk **-al** -əl
hematolog|y ˌhiː.mə'tɒl.ə.dʒ|i ⓊⓈ -'tɑː.lə- **-ist/s** -ɪst/s
hematoma ˌhiː.mə'təʊ.mə, ˌhem.ə'- ⓊⓈ ˌhiː.mə'toʊ- **-s** -z **-ta** -tə
heme hiːm
Hemel Hempstead ˌhem.əl'hemp.stɪd, -stəd, -sted
hemicycle 'hem.iˌsaɪ.kl̩ **-s** -z
hemidemisemiquaver ˌhem.iˌdem.i'sem.iˌkweɪ.vəʳ ⓊⓈ -vɚ **-s** -z
Heming 'hem.ɪŋ
Hemingway 'hem.ɪŋ.weɪ
hemipleg|ia ˌhem.i'pliː.dʒ|i.ə, -dʒ|ə **-ic** -ɪk
hemisphere 'hem.ɪ.sfɪəʳ, '-ə- ⓊⓈ -sfɪr **-s** -z
hemispheric ˌhem.ɪ'sfer.ɪk, -ə'- ⓊⓈ -'sfɪr-, -'sfer- **-al** -əl **-ally** -əl.i, -li
hemistich 'hem.i.stɪk **-s** -s
hemline 'hem.laɪn **-s** -z
hemlock 'hem.lɒk ⓊⓈ -lɑːk **-s** -s
Hemming 'hem.ɪŋ
Hemmings 'hem.ɪŋz
hemoglobin ˌhiː.məʊ'gləʊ.bɪn, ˌhem.əʊ'- ⓊⓈ 'hiː.moʊ.gloʊ-, '-ə-
hemophili|a ˌhiː.mə'fɪl.i|.ə, ˌhem.ə'- ⓊⓈ ˌhiː.moʊ'-, -mə'- **-ac/s** -æk/s
hemorrhag|e 'hem.ər.ɪdʒ ⓊⓈ -ɚ.ɪdʒ, '-rɪdʒ **-es** -ɪz **-ing** -ɪŋ **-ed** -d
hemorrhoid 'hem.ər.ɔɪd ⓊⓈ -ə.rɔɪd, '-rɔɪd **-s** -z
hemosta|sis ˌhiː.mə'steɪ|.sɪs, ˌhem.ə'- ⓊⓈ ˌhiː.mə'- **-ses** -siːz
hemp hemp **-en** -ən
Hemp(e)l 'hem.pəl
hemstitch 'hem.stɪtʃ **-es** -ɪz **-ing** -ɪŋ **-ed** -t
Hemy 'hem.i
hen hen **-s** -z **'hen ˌparty**
henbane 'hen.beɪn, 'hem- ⓊⓈ 'hen-
hence hen*t*s
henceforth ˌhen*t*s'fɔːθ ⓊⓈ 'hen*t*s.fɔːrθ
henceforward ˌhen*t*s'fɔː.wəd ⓊⓈ -'fɔːr.wɚd
Henchard 'hen.tʃɑːd, -tʃəd ⓊⓈ -tʃɚd, -tʃɑːrd
hench|man 'hen*t*ʃ|.mən **-men** -mən
hencoop 'hen.kuːp **-s** -s
hendecagon hen'dek.ə.gən ⓊⓈ -gɑːn **-s** -z
hendecagonal ˌhen.dɪ'kæg.ən.əl, -dek'æg-
hendecasyllabic henˌdek.ə.sɪ'læb.ɪk, -sə'- **-s** -s
hendecasyllable ˌhen.dek.ə'sɪl.ə.bəl **-s** -z
Henderson 'hen.də.sən ⓊⓈ -dɚ-
hendiadys hen'daɪə.dɪs
Hendon 'hen.dən
Hendricks 'hen.drɪks
Hendrickson 'hen.drɪk.sən
Hendrix 'hen.drɪks
Hendry 'hen.dri
Heneage 'hen.ɪdʒ
heng|e hendʒ **-es** -ɪz
Hengist 'heŋ.gɪst
Henley 'hen.li
Henlow 'hen.ləʊ ⓊⓈ -loʊ
Henman 'hen.mən
henna 'hen.ə **-s** -z **-ing** -ɪŋ **-ed** -d
henner|y 'hen.ər|.i **-ies** -iz
Henness(e)y 'hen.ə.si, '-ɪ-
Henniker 'hen.ɪ.kəʳ ⓊⓈ -kɚ
Henning 'hen.ɪŋ
henpeck 'hen.pek, 'hem- ⓊⓈ 'hen- **-s** -s **-ing** -ɪŋ **-ed** -t
Henri *French name:* 'ɑ̃ː*n*.riː, -'- ⓊⓈ ɑ̃ːn'riː *US surname:* 'hen.ri
Henrietta ˌhen.ri'et.ə ⓊⓈ -'et̬-
Henriques hen'riː.kɪz
henr|y (H) 'hen.r|i **-ys** -iz **-ies** -iz
Henryson 'hen.rɪ.sən
Hensen 'hen*t*.sən
Hensley 'henz.li
Henslow(e) 'henz.ləʊ ⓊⓈ -loʊ
Henson 'hen*t*.sən
Henty 'hen.ti ⓊⓈ -t̬i
Hentzau 'hent.zaʊ
hepatic hɪ'pæt.ɪk, hep'æt- ⓊⓈ hɪ'pæt̬-
hepatica hɪ'pæt.ɪ.kə, hep'æt- ⓊⓈ hɪ'pæt̬- **-s** -z
hepatite 'hep.ə.taɪt
hepati|tis ˌhep.ə'taɪ|.tɪs, -təs ⓊⓈ -t̬ɪs **-tides** -tɪ.diːz
Hepburn 'heb.ɜːn, -bən; 'hep.bɜːn ⓊⓈ 'hep.bɝːn, -bɚn
Note: The names of Katharine and Audrey Hepburn are usually pronounced /'hep.bɜːn ⓊⓈ -bɜːrn/.
Hephaestus hɪ'fiː.stəs, hef'iː-, hə'fiː- ⓊⓈ hɪ'fes.təs
Hephzibah 'hef.sɪ.bɑː, 'hep-, -sə-
Hepplewhite 'hep.l̩.*h*waɪt
hepta- 'hep.tə-; hep'tæ-
Note: Prefix. Normally takes either primary or secondary stress on the first syllable, e.g. **heptagon** /'hep.tə.gən ⓊⓈ -gɑːn/, **heptahedron** /ˌhep.tə'hiː.drən/, or primary stress on the second syllable, e.g. **heptathlete** /hep'tæθ.liːt/.
heptagon 'hep.tə.gən, -gɒn ⓊⓈ -gɑːn **-s** -z
heptagonal hep'tæg.ən.əl
heptahedr|on ˌhep.tə'hiː.dr|ən, -'hed.r|ən, -r|ɒn; 'hep.təˌhiː.dr|ən, -ˌhed.r|ən, -r|ɒn ⓊⓈ ˌhep.tə'hiː.dr|ən **-ons** -ənz **-a** -ə **-al** -əl
heptameter hep'tæm.ɪ.təʳ, '-ə- ⓊⓈ -ə.t̬ɚ **-s** -z
heptarch 'hep.tɑːk ⓊⓈ -tɑːrk **-s** -s **-y** -i **-ies** -iz
Heptateuch 'hep.tə.tjuːk ⓊⓈ -tuːk, -tjuːk
heptathlete hep'tæθ.liːt **-s** -s
heptathlon hep'tæθ.lɒn, -lən ⓊⓈ -lɑːn **-s** -z
Hepworth 'hep.wəθ, -wɜːθ ⓊⓈ -wɝːθ, -wɚθ
her *strong form:* hɜːʳ ⓊⓈ hɝː *weak forms:* həʳ, əʳ ⓊⓈ hɚ, ɚ **-s** -z
Note: Weak form word. The strong form /hɜːʳ ⓊⓈ hɜːr/ is used for emphasis, e.g. 'it was **her** fault' or contrast, e.g. 'his or her bank'. There is a weak form /həʳ ⓊⓈ hɚ/ which is used at the beginning of sentences, e.g. 'Her train was late' /hə'treɪn.wəzˌleɪt ⓊⓈ hɚ-/ and elsewhere in slow, careful speech, e.g. 'I admired her skill', /aɪ.ədˌmaɪəd.hə'skɪl ⓊⓈ -ˌmaɪrd.hɚ'-/. In rapid speech the weak form is likely to be /əʳ ⓊⓈ ɚ/, e.g. 'Let her through', /ˌlet.ə'θruː ⓊⓈ ˌlet̬.ɚ'-/.
Hera 'hɪə.rə ⓊⓈ 'hɪr.ə, 'hiː.rə
Heraclean ˌher.ə'kliː.ən
Heracles 'her.ə.kliːz, 'hɪə.rə- ⓊⓈ 'her.ə-
Heraclitus ˌher.ə'klaɪ.təs ⓊⓈ -t̬əs
Heraklion her'æk.li.ən
herald 'her.əld **-s** -z **-ing** -ɪŋ **-ed** -ɪd

heraldic hɪˈræl.dɪk, həˈræl-, herˈæl- (US) həˈræl-, herˈæl- **-ally** -ᵊl.i, -li
heraldr|y ˈher.ᵊl.dr|i **-ies** -iz
Herat herˈæt, hɪˈræt, həˈræt, -ˈrɑːt (US) herˈɑːt
herb (H) hɜːb (US) ɝːb, hɝːb **-s** -z **-age** -ɪdʒ **-y** -i
Note: The US pronunciation for the name **Herb** is always /hɜːrb/.
herbaceous hɜːˈbeɪ.ʃəs, hə- (US) hɚˈ-, ɚˈ- **herˌbaceous ˈborder**
herbal ˈhɜː.bᵊl (US) ˈhɝː-, ˈɝː-
herbal|ism ˈhɜː.bᵊl|.ɪ.zᵊm (US) ˈhɝː-, ˈɝː- **-ist/s** -ɪst/s
herbarium hɜːˈbeə.ri.əm (US) hɝːˈber.i-, ɝː- **-s** -z
Herbert ˈhɜː.bət (US) ˈhɝː.bɚt
herbicidal ˌhɜː.bɪˈsaɪ.dᵊl (US) ˌhɝː-, ˌɝː-
herbicide ˈhɜː.bɪ.saɪd (US) ˈhɝː-, ˈɝː- **-s** -z
Herbie ˈhɜː.bi (US) ˈhɝː-
herbivore ˈhɜː.bɪ.vɔːʳ (US) ˈhɝː.bə.vɔːr, ˈɝː- **-s** -z
herbivorous hɜːˈbɪv.ᵊr.əs, hə- (US) hɝː-, hɚ-, ɝː-, ɚ-
herboriz|e, -is|e ˈhɜː.bᵊr.aɪz (US) ˈhɝː-, ˈɝː- **-es** -ɪz **-ing** -ɪŋ **-ed** -d
Herbst hɜːbst (US) hɝːpst
Herculaneum ˌhɜː.kjəˈleɪ.ni.əm, -kjʊˈ- (US) ˌhɝː.kjəˈ-
Hercule ˈeə.kjuːl, ˈɜː-, ˌ-ˈ- (US) erˈkjuːl, ɝː- **ˌHercule ˈPoirot, ˌHercule Poiˈrot**
herculean (H) ˌhɜː.kjəˈliː.ən, -kjʊˈ-; hɜːˈkjuː.li- (US) ˌhɝː.kjuːˈliː-; hɚˈkjuː.li-
Hercules ˈhɜː.kjə.liːz, -kjʊ- (US) ˈhɝː.kjə-
herd (H) hɜːd (US) hɝːd **-s** -z **-ing** -ɪŋ **-ed** -ɪd **ˌherd ˈinstinct**
herds|man ˈhɜːdz|.mən (US) ˈhɝːdz- **-men** -mən
here hɪəʳ (US) hɪr **ˌhere, ˌthere, and ˈeverywhere; ˌneither ˌhere nor ˈthere**
hereabouts ˌhɪər.əˈbaʊts, ˈ--- (US) ˌhɪr.əˈbaʊts, ˈ---
hereafter ˌhɪərˈɑːf.təʳ (US) ˌhɪrˈæf.tɚ
hereby ˌhɪəˈbaɪ, ˈ-- (US) ˌhɪrˈbaɪ, ˈ--
hereditable hɪˈred.ɪ.tə.bl̩, hə-, herˈed-, ˈ-ə- (US) həˈred.ɪ.t̬ə-
hereditament ˌher.ɪˈdɪt.ə.mənt, -əˈ-, ˈ-ɪ- (US) -əˈdɪt̬.ə- **-s** -s
hereditar|y hɪˈred.ɪ.tᵊr|.i, hə-, herˈed-, ˈ-ə- (US) həˈred.ɪ.ter- **-ily** -ᵊl.i, -ɪ.li **-iness** -ɪ.nəs, -ɪ.nɪs
heredity hɪˈred.ə.ti, hə-, herˈed-, -ɪ.ti (US) həˈred.ɪ-
Hereford *place in UK:* ˈher.ɪ.fəd, -ə.fəd (US) -ə.fɚd **-shire** -ʃəʳ, -ˌʃɪəʳ (US) -ʃɚ, -ˌʃɪr *in US:* ˈhɜː.fəd (US) ˈhɝː.fɚd
herein ˌhɪəʳˈɪn (US) ˌhɪr-
hereinabove ˌhɪəʳ.ɪn.əˈbʌv (US) ˌhɪr-
hereinafter ˌhɪəʳ.ɪnˈɑːf.təʳ (US) ˌhɪr.ɪnˈæf.tɚ
hereinbefore ˌhɪəʳ.ɪn.bɪˈfɔːʳ, -bəˈfɔːʳ (US) ˌhɪr.ɪn.bɪˈfɔːr, -bəˈ-
hereinbelow ˌhɪəʳ.ɪn.bɪˈləʊ, -bəˈ- (US) ˌhɪr.ɪn.bɪˈloʊ, -bəˈ-
hereof ˌhɪəʳˈɒv (US) ˌhɪrˈɑːv
hereon ˌhɪəʳˈɒn (US) ˌhɪrˈɑːn
Herero həˈreə.rəʊ, herˈeə-, -ˈɪə-; ˈhɪə.rə.rəʊ, ˈher.ə- (US) həˈrer.oʊ; ˈher.ə.roʊ **-s** -z
heresiarch həˈriː.zi.ɑːk, hɪ-, herˈiː-; -si-, ˈher.ə.si- (US) həˈriː.zi.ɑːrk; ˈher.ə.si- **-s** -s
heres|y ˈher.ə.s|i, ˈ-ɪ- **-ies** -iz
heretic ˈher.ə.tɪk, -ɪ.tɪk (US) ˈ-ə- **-s** -s
heretic|al həˈret.ɪ.k|ᵊl, hɪˈ-, herˈet- (US) həˈret̬- **-ally** -ᵊl.i, -li
hereto ˌhɪəˈtuː (US) ˌhɪr-
heretofore ˌhɪə.tuːˈfɔːʳ (US) ˌhɪr.tuːˈfɔːr, ˈ---
hereunder ˌhɪəʳˈʌn.dəʳ (US) ˌhɪrˈʌn.dɚ, ˈ---
hereunto ˌhɪəʳ.ʌnˈtuː, -ˈʌn.tuː (US) ˌhɪr-, ˈ---
hereupon ˌhɪəʳ.əˈpɒn (US) ˌhɪr.əˈpɑːn, ˈ---
Hereward ˈher.ɪ.wəd, -ə- (US) -wɚd
herewith ˌhɪəˈwɪð, -ˈwɪθ (US) ˌhɪrˈwɪð, ˈ--
Herford ˈhɜː.fəd, ˈhɑː- (US) ˈhɝː.fɚd
Hergé eəˈʒeɪ (US) er-
heriot (H) ˈher.i.ət, -ɒt (US) -ət **-s** -s
Heriot-Watt ˌher.i.ətˈwɒt (US) -ˈwɑːt
heritable ˈher.ɪ.tə.bl̩, ˈ-ə- (US) -ɪ.t̬ə-
heritag|e ˈher.ɪ.tɪdʒ, ˈ-ə- (US) -ɪ.t̬ɪdʒ **-es** -ɪz
heritor ˈher.ɪ.təʳ, ˈ-ə- (US) -ɪ.t̬ɚ **-s** -z
Herkomer ˈhɜː.kə.məʳ (US) ˈhɝː.kə.mɚ **-s** -z
Herman ˈhɜː.mən (US) ˈhɝː-
hermaphrodite hɜːˈmæf.rə.daɪt, hə- (US) hɚˈmæf.roʊ-, -rə- **-s** -s
hermaphroditic hɜːˌmæf.rəˈdɪt.ɪk, hə- (US) hɚˌmæf.roʊˈdɪt̬-, -rəˈ- **-ally** -ᵊl.i, -li
hermeneutic ˌhɜː.mɪˈnjuː.tɪk, -məˈ- (US) ˌhɝː.məˈnuː.t̬ɪk, -ˈnjuː- **-s** -s **-al** -ᵊl **-ally** -ᵊl.i, -li
Hermes ˈhɜː.miːz (US) ˈhɝː-
Hermès® eəˈmes (US) er-
Hermesetas® ˌhɜː.mɪˈsiː.təz, -məˈ-, -təs (US) ˌhɝː.məˈsiː.t̬əz, -təs
hermetic hɜːˈmet.ɪk, hə- (US) hɚˈmet̬- **-al** -ᵊl **-ally** -ᵊl.i, -li
Hermia ˈhɜː.mi.ə (US) ˈhɝː-
Hermione hɜːˈmaɪə.ni, hə- (US) hɚ-
Hermiston ˈhɜː.mɪ.stᵊn (US) ˈhɝː-
hermit ˈhɜː.mɪt (US) ˈhɝː- **-s** -s **ˈhermit ˌcrab**
hermitag|e (H) ˈhɜː.mɪ.tɪdʒ, -mə- *as if French:* ˌeə.mɪˈtɑːʒ (US) ˈhɝː.mɪ.t̬ɪdʒ **-es** -ɪz
hermitic hɜːˈmɪt.ɪk, hə- (US) hɚˈmɪt̬-
Hermocrates hɜːˈmɒk.rə.tiːz, hə- (US) hɚˈmɑː.krə-
Hermogenes hɜːˈmɒdʒ.ɪ.niːz, hə-, -ən.iːz (US) hɚˈmɑː.dʒə.niːz
Hermon ˈhɜː.mən (US) ˈhɝː-
hern hɜːn (US) hɝːn **-s** -z
Hernandez hɜːˈnæn.dez (US) hɚ-; erˈnɑːn.des
Herne hɜːn (US) hɝːn
herni|a ˈhɜː.ni|.ə (US) ˈhɝː- **-as** -əz **-ae** -iː **-al** -əl
herni|ate ˈhɜː.ni|.eɪt (US) ˈhɝː- **-ates** -eɪts **-ating** -eɪ.tɪŋ (US) -t̬ɪŋ **-ated** -eɪ.tɪd (US) -t̬ɪd
herniation ˌhɜː.niˈeɪ.ʃᵊn (US) ˌhɝː- **-s** -z
hero (H) ˈhɪə.rəʊ (US) ˈhɪr.oʊ, ˈhiː.roʊ **-es** -z **ˈhero ˌworship**
Herod ˈher.əd **ˌHerod ˈAntipas**
Herodian herˈəʊ.di.ən, həˈrəʊ-, hɪ- (US) həˈroʊ- **-s** -z
Herodias herˈəʊ.di.æs, həˈrəʊ-, hɪ-, -əs (US) həˈroʊ-
Herodotus herˈɒd.ə.təs, həˈrɒd-, hɪ- (US) həˈrɑː.də.t̬əs
heroic hɪˈrəʊ.ɪk, hə-, herˈəʊ- (US) hɪˈroʊ-, hiː- **-s** -s **-al** -ᵊl **-ally** -ᵊl.i, -li **heˌroic ˈverse**
heroin ˈher.əʊ.ɪn (US) -oʊ-
heroine ˈher.əʊ.ɪn (US) -oʊ- **-s** -z
heroism ˈher.əʊ.ɪ.zᵊm (US) -oʊ-
heron (H) ˈher.ᵊn **-s** -z **-ry** -ri **-ries** -riz
herpes ˈhɜː.piːz (US) ˈhɝː-
herpetologic ˌhɜː.pɪ.təˈlɒdʒ.ɪk, -pə- (US) ˌhɝː.pə.t̬əˈlɑː.dʒɪk **-al** -ᵊl **-ally** -ᵊl.i, -li
herpetolog|y ˌhɜː.pɪˈtɒl.ə.dʒ|i, -pəˈ- (US) -pəˈtɑː.lə- **-ist/s** -ɪst/s
Herr heəʳ (US) her
Herrick ˈher.ɪk
Herries ˈher.ɪs, -ɪz
herring (H) ˈher.ɪŋ **-s** -z
herringbone ˈher.ɪŋ.bəʊn (US) -boʊn **-s** -z
Herriot ˈher.i.ət
Herron ˈher.ən
hers hɜːz (US) hɝːz
Herschel(l) ˈhɜː.ʃᵊl (US) ˈhɝː-
herself həˈself (US) hɚ- *when not initial:* ə- (US) ɚ-
Hershey ˈhɜː.ʃi (US) ˈhɝː-
Herstmonceux ˌhɜːst.mənˈzuː, -mɒn-, -ˈsjuː, -ˈsuː (US) ˌhɝːst.mənˈ-, -mɑːnˈ-
Hertford *in England:* ˈhɑːt.fəd, ˈhɑː- (US) ˈhɑːrt.fɚd, ˈhɑːr- **-shire** -ʃəʳ, -ˌʃɪəʳ (US) -ʃɚ, -ʃɪr
Hertford *in US:* ˈhɜːt.fəd (US) ˈhɝːt.fɚd
Herts. *(abbrev. for* **Hertfordshire***)* hɑːts; ˈhɑːt.fəd.ʃəʳ, ˈhɑː-, -ˌʃɪəʳ (US) hɑːrts; ˈhɑːrt.fɚd.ʃɚ, ˈhɑːr-, -ˌʃɪr

Hertslet 'hɜːt.slɪt (US) 'hɝːt-

hertz hɜːts (US) hɝːts

Hertz hɜːts, heəts (US) hɝːts, herts **-ian** -i.ən

Note: The trademark is pronounced /hɜːts (US) hɜːrts/.

Hertzog 'hɜːt.sɒg (US) 'hɝːt.sɑːg, -sɔːg

Hervey 'hɑː.vi, 'hɜː.vi (US) 'hɝː-

Herzegovina ˌhɜːt.sə.gəʊ'viː.nə, ˌheət-, -sɪ.gəʊ'-; -sɪ'gɒv.ɪ.nə (US) ˌhɝːt.sə.goʊ'viː.nə

Herzog 'hɜːt.sɒg (US) 'hɝːt.sɑːg, -sɔːg

he's *(***he is** *or* **he has***) strong form:* hiːz *occasional weak forms:* hiz, iz

Note: See note for **he**.

Hesba 'hez.bə

Heseltine 'hes.ᵊl.taɪn, 'hez-

Heshbon 'heʃ.bɒn (US) -bɑːn

Hesiod 'hiː.si.əd, 'hes.i-, -ɒd (US) -əd

hesitan|ce 'hez.ɪ.tᵊnt|s, '-ə- **-cy** -si

hesitant 'hez.ɪ.tᵊnt, '-ə- **-ly** -li

hesi|tate 'hez.ɪ|.teɪt, '-ə- **-tates** -teɪts **-tating/ly** -teɪ.tɪŋ/li (US) -teɪ.t̬ɪŋ/li **-tated** -teɪ.tɪd (US) -teɪ.t̬ɪd

hesitation ˌhez.ɪ'teɪ.ʃᵊn, -ə'- **-s** -z

Hesketh 'hes.kəθ, -kɪθ

Heskey 'hes.ki

Hesperian hes'pɪə.ri.ən (US) -'pɪr.i-

Hesperides hes'per.ɪ.diːz, hɪ'sper-, hə-, '-ə- (US) hes'per.ɪ-

Hesperus 'hes.pᵊr.əs

Hess hes

Hessayon 'hes.i.ən

Hesse 'hes.ə, hes

hessian (H) 'hes.i.ən (US) 'heʃ.ᵊn **-s** -z

Hester 'hes.təʳ (US) -tɚ

Heston 'hes.tᵊn

Heswall 'hez.wəl (US) 'hes.wɔːl

Hesychius hes'ɪk.i.əs

hetero 'het.ᵊr.əʊ (US) 'het̬.ə.roʊ **-s** -z

heteroclite 'het.ᵊr.əʊ.klaɪt (US) 'het.ɚ.ə- **-s** -s

heterodox 'het.ᵊr.əʊ.dɒks (US) 'het̬.ɚ.ə.dɑːks **-y** -i

heterodyne 'het.ᵊr.əʊ.daɪn (US) 'het̬.ɚ.ə-

heterogeneity ˌhet.ᵊr.əʊ.dʒə'niː.ə.ti, -dʒɪ'-, -ɪ.ti (US) ˌhet̬.ə.roʊ.dʒə'niː.ə.t̬i, '-ɚ.ə-

heterogeneous ˌhet.ᵊr.əʊ'dʒiː.ni.əs (US) ˌhet̬.ə.roʊ'-, -ɚ.ə'- **-ly** -li **-ness** -nəs, -nɪs

heterogenesis ˌhet.ᵊr.əʊ'dʒen.ə.sɪs, '-ɪ- (US) ˌhet̬.ə.roʊ'dʒen.ə.sɪs, -ɚ.ə'-

heteronym 'het.ᵊr.əʊ.nɪm (US) 'het̬.ə.roʊ-, -ɚ.ə- **-s** -z

heteronym|ous ˌhet.ə'rɒn.ɪ.m|əs, '-ə- (US) ˌhet̬.ə'rɑː.nɪ- **-y** -i

heterosex|ism ˌhet.ᵊr.əʊ'sek.s|ɪ.zᵊm (US) ˌhet̬.ə.roʊ'-, -ɚ.ə'- **-ist/s** -ɪst/s

heterosexual ˌhet.ᵊr.əʊ'sek.ʃu.ᵊl, '-sju-, -ʃᵊl (US) ˌhet̬.ə.roʊ'sek.ʃu.ᵊl, -ɚ.ə'- **-s** -z **-ly** -i

heterosexuality ˌhet.ᵊr.əʊˌsek.ʃu'æl.ə.ti, -sju'- (US) ˌhet̬.ə.roʊˌsek.ʃu'æl.ə.t̬i, -ɚ.əˌ-

heterozygous ˌhet.ᵊr.əʊ'zaɪ.gəs (US) ˌhet̬.ə.roʊ'-, -ɚ.ə'-

Hetherington 'heð.ᵊr.ɪŋ.tən

Hetton-le-Hole ˌhet.ᵊn.lə'həʊl, -lɪ'- (US) ˌhet̬.ᵊn.lə'hoʊl

Hetty 'het.i (US) 'het̬-

het up ˌhet'ʌp (US) ˌhet̬- *stress shift:* ˌhet up 'teenager

Heugh *place:* hjuːf *surname:* hjuː

heuristic hjʊə'rɪs.tɪk (US) hjuː'- **-s** -s **-ally** -ᵊl.i, -li

Hever 'hiː.vəʳ (US) -vɚ

hew hjuː **-s** -z **-ing** -ɪŋ **-ed** -d **-n** -n **-er/s** -əʳ/z (US) -ɚ/z

Heward 'hjuː.əd (US) -ɚd

Hewart 'hjuː.ət (US) -ɚt

Hewetson 'hjuː.ɪt.sᵊn

Hewett, Hewitt 'hjuː.ɪt

Hewke hjuːk

Hewlett 'hjuː.lɪt, -lət

Hewlettson 'hjuː.lɪt.sᵊn, -lət-

hewn *(from* **hew***)* hjuːn

hex heks **-es** -ɪz **-ing** -ɪŋ **-ed** -t

hexa- 'hek.sə-; hek'sæ-

Note: Prefix. Normally either takes primary or secondary stress on the first syllable, e.g. **hexagon** /'hek.sə.gᵊn (US) -gɑːn/, **hexahedron** /ˌhek.sə'hiː.drᵊn/, or primary stress on the second syllable, e.g. **hexagonal** /hek'sæg.ᵊn.ᵊl/.

hexachord 'hek.sə.kɔːd (US) -kɔːrd **-s** -z

hexagon 'hek.sə.gən (US) -gɑːn **-s** -z

hexagonal hek'sæg.ᵊn.ᵊl **-ly** -i

hexagram 'hek.sə.græm **-s** -z

hexahedr|on ˌhek.sə'hiː.dr|ən, -'hed.r|ən (US) -'hiː.dr|ən **-ons** -ənz **-a** -ə **-al** -əl

Hexam 'hek.səm

hexameter hek'sæm.ɪ.təʳ, hɪk'-, '-ə- (US) -ə.t̬ɚ **-s** -z

Hexateuch 'hek.sə.tjuːk (US) -tuːk, -tjuːk

Hexham 'hek.səm

Hextable 'hek.stə.bl̩

hey heɪ

Heycock 'heɪ.kɒk (US) -kɑːk

heyday 'heɪ.deɪ

Heyer heɪəʳ (US) heɪɚ

Heyerdahl 'heɪə.dɑːl (US) 'heɪɚ-, 'haɪɚ-

hey presto ˌheɪ'pres.təʊ (US) -toʊ

Heysham 'hiː.ʃᵊm

Heyward 'heɪ.wəd (US) -wɚd

Heywood 'heɪ.wʊd

Hezbollah ˌhɪz.bɒl'ɑː, 'hez- (US) ˌhez.bə'lɑː

Hezekiah ˌhez.ɪ'kaɪə, -ə'-

Hezlewood 'hez.l̩.wʊd

HGV ˌeɪtʃ.dʒiː'viː

hi haɪ

hiatus haɪ'eɪ.təs, hi- (US) haɪ'eɪ.t̬əs **-es** -ɪz

Hiawatha ˌhaɪ.ə'wɒθ.ə (US) -'wɑː.θə

hibachi hɪ'bɑː.tʃi, hiː- **-s** -z

Hibbert 'hɪb.ət, -ɜːt (US) -ɚt, -ɝːt

hibernal haɪ'bɜː.nᵊl (US) -'bɝː-

hiber|nate 'haɪ.bə|.neɪt (US) -bɚ- **-nates** -neɪts **-nating** -neɪ.tɪŋ (US) -neɪ.t̬ɪŋ **-nated** -neɪ.tɪd (US) -neɪ.t̬ɪd

hibernation ˌhaɪ.bə'neɪ.ʃᵊn (US) -bɚ'- **-s** -z

Hibernia haɪ'bɜː.ni.ə, hɪ- (US) -'bɝː-

Hibernian *(n. adj.)* haɪ'bɜː.ni.ən (US) -'bɝː- **-s** -z *in name of football club:* hɪ'bɜː.ni.ən (US) -'bɝː- **-s** -z

Hibernicism haɪ'bɜː.nɪ.sɪ.zᵊm, -nə- (US) -'bɝː- **-s** -z

hibiscus hɪ'bɪs.kəs, haɪ- (US) haɪ-, hɪ-

hiccough 'hɪk.ʌp, -əp **-s** -s **-ing** -ɪŋ **-ed** -t

hiccup 'hɪk.ʌp, -əp **-s** -s **-(p)ing** -ɪŋ **-(p)ed** -t

hick hɪk **-s** -s

hickey 'hɪk.i **-s** -z

Hickman 'hɪk.mən

Hickok 'hɪk.ɒk (US) -ɑːk

hickory (H) 'hɪk.ᵊr.i (US) -ɚ.i, '-ri

Hicks hɪks

Hickson 'hɪk.sᵊn

hid *(from* **hide***)* hɪd

hidalgo (H) hɪ'dæl.gəʊ (US) -goʊ **-s** -z

hid|e haɪd **-es** -z **-ing/s** -ɪŋ/z **hid** hɪd **hidden** 'hɪd.ᵊn ˌ**hide-and-'seek**; '**hiding** ˌ**place**

hideaway 'haɪd.ə.weɪ **-s** -z

hidebound 'haɪd.baʊnd

hideous 'hɪd.i.əs **-ly** -li **-ness** -nəs, -nɪs

hideout 'haɪd.aʊt **-s** -s

hid(e)y-hole 'haɪ.di.həʊl (US) -hoʊl **-s** -z

hie haɪ **-s** -z **-ing** -ɪŋ **-d** -d

Hierapolis ˌhaɪə'ræp.ᵊl.ɪs (US) ˌhaɪ'ræp.ə.lɪs

hierarch 'haɪə.rɑːk (US) 'haɪ.rɑːrk **-s** -s

hierarchal ˌhaɪə'rɑː.kᵊl (US) ˌhaɪ'rɑːr-

hierarchic ˌhaɪə'rɑː.kɪk (US) ˌhaɪ'rɑːr- **-al** -ᵊl **-ally** -ᵊl.i, -li

hierarch|y 'haɪə.rɑː.k|i (US) 'haɪ.rɑːr- **-ies** -iz

hieratic ˌhaɪə'ræt.ɪk (US) ˌhaɪ'ræt̬-

hieroglyph 'haɪə.rəʊ.glɪf (US) 'haɪ.roʊ- **-s** -s

hieroglyphic ˌhaɪə.rəʊ'glɪf.ɪk (US) ˌhaɪ.roʊ'- **-s** -s **-al** -ᵊl **-ally** -ᵊl.i, -li

Hieronimo hɪə'rɒn.ɪ.məʊ (US) hɪ'rɑː.nɪ.moʊ

Hieronymus hɪə'rɒn.ɪ.məs, haɪə'- (US) haɪ'rɑː.nɪ-

hierophant 'hɪə.rəʊ.fænt, 'haɪə- (US) 'haɪ.roʊ- **-s** -s

hifalutin ˌhaɪ.fəˈluː.tɪn, -tᵊn *stress shift:* ˌhifalutin ˈattitude
hi-fi ˈhaɪ.faɪ, ˌ-ˈ- **-s** -z
Higginbotham ˈhɪg.ɪnˌbɒt.əm, -ᵊnˌ-, -ᵊmˌ-, -ˌbɒθ.əm US -ˌbɑː.t̬əm, -θəm
Higginbottom ˈhɪg.ɪnˌbɒt.əm, -ᵊnˌ-, -ᵊmˌ- US -ˌbɑː.t̬əm
Higgins ˈhɪg.ɪnz
Higginson ˈhɪg.ɪn.sᵊn
higgl|e ˈhɪg.l̩ **-es** -z **-ing** -ɪŋ, ˈhɪg.lɪŋ **-ed** -d **-er/s** -əʳ/z US -ɚ/z, ˈhɪg.ləʳ/z US -lɚ/z
higgledy-piggledy ˌhɪg.l̩.diˈpɪg.l̩.di
Higgs hɪgz
high haɪ **-er** -əʳ US -ɚ **-est** -ɪst, -əst **-s** -z **-ly** -li **-ness** -nəs, -nɪs ˌ**High** ˈ**Court** *stress shift, British only:* ˌHigh Court ˌjudge; ˈ**high** ˌ**chair**; ˌ**high** ˈ**church**; ˌ**high** ˈ**churchman**; ˈ**high** ˌ**day**; ˌ**high** ˈ**frequency**; ˌ**high** ˈ**heels**; ˌ**high** ˈ**horse**; ˈ**high** ˌ**jump**; ˌ**high** ˈ**roller**; ˈ**high** ˌ**school**; ˈ**high** ˌ**street**; ˌ**high** ˈ**tide**; ˌ**high** ˈ**water**; ˌ**high** ˈ**water mark**; ˌ**high and** ˈ**dry**; ˌ**high and** ˈ**low**; ˌ**higher eduˈcation**
Higham ˈhaɪ.əm **-s** -z
high-and-mighty ˌhaɪ.ənˈmaɪ.ti, -əmˈ- US -ənˈmaɪ.t̬i *stress shift:* ˌhigh-and-mighty ˈmanners
highball ˈhaɪ.bɔːl US -bɔːl, -bɑːl **-s** -z **-ing** -ɪŋ **-ed** -d
highborn ˌhaɪˈbɔːn US ˈhaɪ.bɔːrn *stress shift, British only:* ˌhighborn ˈlady
highboy ˈhaɪ.bɔɪ **-s** -z
Highbridge ˈhaɪ.brɪdʒ
highbrow ˈhaɪ.braʊ **-s** -z
Highbury ˈhaɪ.bᵊr.i US -ber.i, -bɚ-
highchair ˈhaɪ.tʃeəʳ, ˌ-ˈ- US -tʃer **-s** -z
High Church ˌhaɪˈtʃɜːtʃ US -ˈtʃɝːtʃ **-man** -mən **-men** -mən, -men *stress shift:* ˌHigh Church ˈmannerism
high-class ˌhaɪˈklɑːs US -ˈklæs *stress shift:* ˌhigh-class ˈbutcher
Highclere ˈhaɪ.klɪəʳ US -klɪr
highfalut|in ˌhaɪ.fəˈluː.t|ɪn, -t|ᵊn **-ing** -ɪŋ *stress shift:* ˌhighfalutin ˈattitude
Highfield ˈhaɪ.fiːld
highflier, highflyer ˌhaɪˈflaɪ.əʳ US -ɚ **-s** -z
highflown ˌhaɪˈfləʊn US -ˈfloʊn *stress shift:* ˌhigh-flown ˈrhetoric
Highgate ˈhaɪ.geɪt, -gɪt, -gət
Highgrove ˈhaɪ.grəʊv US -groʊv
high-handed ˌhaɪˈhæn.dɪd **-ly** -li **-ness** -nəs, -nɪs *stress shift:* ˌhigh-handed ˈruler
high-heeled ˌhaɪˈhiːld *stress shift:* ˌhigh-heeled ˈshoes
highjack ˈhaɪ.dʒæk **-s** -s **-ing** -ɪŋ **-ed** -t **-er/s** -əʳ/z US -ɚ/z
highjinks ˈhaɪ.dʒɪŋks
highland (H) ˈhaɪ.lənd **-s** -z **-er/s** -əʳ/z US -ɚ/z ˌ**Highland** ˈ**fling**
high-level ˌhaɪˈlev.ᵊl *stress shift:* ˌhigh-level ˈlanguage
high|light ˈhaɪ|.laɪt **-lights** -laɪts **-lighting** -ˌlaɪ.tɪŋ US -ˌlaɪ.t̬ɪŋ **-lighted** -ˌlaɪ.tɪd US -ˌlaɪ.t̬ɪd
highlighter ˈhaɪˌlaɪ.təʳ US -t̬ɚ **-s** -z
highly ˈhaɪ.li
high-minded ˌhaɪˈmaɪn.dɪd **-ness** -nəs, -nɪs *stress shift:* ˌhigh-minded ˈthinker
Highness ˈhaɪ.nəs, -nɪs **-es** -ɪz
high-octane ˌhaɪˈɒk.teɪn US -ˈɑːk- *stress shift:* ˌhigh-octane ˈfuel
high-pitched ˌhaɪˈpɪtʃt *stress shift:* ˌhigh-pitched ˈvoice
high-powered ˌhaɪˈpaʊəd US -ˈpaʊ.ɚd *stress shift:* ˌhigh-powered ˈengine
high-pressure ˌhaɪˈpreʃ.əʳ US -ɚ *stress shift:* ˌhigh-pressure ˈsalesman
high-priced ˌhaɪˈpraɪst *stress shift:* ˌhigh-priced ˈgoods
high-priest ˌhaɪˈpriːst **-s** -s **-hood/s** -hʊd/z
high-priestess ˌhaɪ.priːˈstes, ˌ-ˈ-- US ˌhaɪˈpriː- **-es** -ɪz
high-profile ˌhaɪˈprəʊ.faɪl US -ˈproʊ- *stress shift:* ˌhigh-profile ˈmission
high-ranking ˌhaɪˈræŋ.kɪŋ, ˈ--- *stress shift:* ˌhigh-ranking ˈofficer
high-ris|e ˌhaɪˈraɪz, ˈ-- US ˈ-- **-s** -ɪz *stress shift:* ˌhigh-rise ˈflats
high-risk ˌhaɪˈrɪsk *stress shift:* ˌhigh-risk ˈstrategy
highroad ˈhaɪ.rəʊd US -roʊd **-s** -z
high-speed ˌhaɪˈspiːd *stress shift:* ˌhigh-speed ˈchase
high-spirited ˌhaɪˈspɪr.ɪ.tɪd US -t̬ɪd **-ly** -li **-ness** -nəs, -nɪs
highspot ˈhaɪ.spɒt US -spɑːt **-s** -s
high-strung ˌhaɪˈstrʌŋ *stress shift:* ˌhigh-strung ˈhorse
hightail ˈhaɪ.teɪl **-s** -z **-ing** -ɪŋ **-ed** -d
high-tech ˌhaɪˈtek *stress shift:* ˌhigh-tech ˈoffice
Highton ˈhaɪ.tᵊn
high-up ˌhaɪˈʌp **-s** -s *stress shift:* ˌhigh-up ˈsource
highway ˈhaɪ.weɪ **-s** -z ˌ**Highway** ˈ**Code**, ˈ**Highway** ˌ**Code**; ˌ**highway** ˈ**robbery**
highway|man ˈhaɪ.weɪ|.mən **-men** -mən
Highworth ˈhaɪ.wəθ, -wɜːθ US -wɚθ
High Wycombe ˌhaɪˈwɪk.əm
hijack ˈhaɪ.dʒæk **-s** -s **-ing** -ɪŋ **-ed** -t **-er/s** -əʳ/z US -ɚ/z
hijinks ˈhaɪ.dʒɪŋks
hik|e haɪk **-es** -s **-ing** -ɪŋ **-ed** -t **-er/s** -əʳ/z US -ɚ/z
Hilaire hɪˈleəʳ; ˈhɪl.eəʳ US hɪˈler; ˈhɪl.er
hilarious hɪˈleə.ri.əs, hə- US hɪˈler.i-, -ˈlær- **-ly** -li **-ness** -nəs, -nɪs
hilarity hɪˈlær.ə.ti, hə-, -ɪ.ti US hɪˈler.ə.t̬i, -ˈlær-
Hilary ˈhɪl.ᵊr.i
Hilda ˈhɪl.də
Hildebrand ˈhɪl.də.brænd, -dɪ-
Hildegard(e) ˈhɪl.də.gɑːd, -dɪ- US -gɑːrd
hill (H) hɪl **-s** -z ˌ**over the** ˈ**hill**; **as** ˌ**old as the** ˈ**hills**
Hillary ˈhɪl.ᵊr.i
hillbill|y ˈhɪlˌbɪl|.i **-ies** -iz
Hillborn ˈhɪl.bɔːn US -bɔːrn
Hillel ˈhɪl.el, -əl; hɪˈlel
Hillhead hɪlˈhed, ˈ--
Note: The pronunciation in Scotland is /-ˈ-/.
Hilliard ˈhɪl.i.əd, -ɑːd US ˈ-jɚd
Hillingdon ˈhɪl.ɪŋ.dən
hill|man ˈhɪl|.mæn, -mən **-men** -men
Hillman ˈhɪl.mən **-s** -z
hillock ˈhɪl.ək **-s** -s
Hillsboro ˈhɪlz.bᵊr.ə US -oʊ
Hillsborough ˈhɪlz.bᵊr.ə US -oʊ
hillside (H) ˈhɪl.saɪd, ˌ-ˈ- **-s** -z
hilltop ˈhɪl.tɒp US -tɑːp **-s** -s
hill|y ˈhɪl|.i **-ier** -i.əʳ US -i.ɚ **-iest** -i.ɪst, -i.əst **-iness** -ɪ.nəs, -ɪ.nɪs
Hillyard ˈhɪl.jəd, -jɑːd US -jɚd
Hillyer ˈhɪl.i.əʳ US ˈ-jɚ
hilt hɪlt **-s** -s **-ed** -ɪd US ˈhɪl.t̬ɪd
Hilton ˈhɪl.tᵊn
hil|um ˈhaɪ.l|əm **-ums** -əmz **-a** -ə **-i** -aɪ **-us** -əs
Hilversum ˈhɪl.və.sʊm, -sᵊm US -vɚ-
him *strong form:* hɪm *weak form:* ɪm
Note: Weak form word. The strong form is mainly used for contrastive purposes, e.g. 'The gift is for **him**, not **her**'.
Himachal Pradesh hɪˌmɑː.tʃᵊl.prɑːˈdeʃ US -prə-
Himalaya ˌhɪm.əˈleɪə, hɪˈmɑː.li.ə, -lə.jə **-as** -əz **-an** -ən
Himes haɪmz
Himmler ˈhɪm.ləʳ US -lɚ
himself hɪmˈself *when not initial:* ɪm-
Himyaritic ˌhɪm.jəˈrɪt.ɪk US -ˈrɪt̬-
Hinayana ˌhiː.nəˈjɑː.nə, ˌhɪn.əˈ- US ˌhiː.nəˈ-
Hinchcliffe ˈhɪntʃ.klɪf
Hinchingbrooke ˈhɪn.tʃɪŋ.brʊk
Hinchliffe ˈhɪntʃ.lɪf
Hinckley ˈhɪŋ.kli
hind (H) haɪnd **-s** -z
Hinde haɪnd
Hindemith ˈhɪnd.ə.mɪt, -mɪθ
Hindenburg ˈhɪn.dən.bɜːg, -dəm- US -bɝːg
hinder *(adj.)* ˈhaɪn.dəʳ US -dɚ **-most** -məʊst US -moʊst

hind|er (*v.*) 'hɪn.d|əʳ ⓤⓢ -d|ɚ **-ers** -əz ⓤⓢ -ɚz **-ering** -ᵊr.ɪŋ **-ered** -əd ⓤⓢ -ɚd **-erer/s** -ᵊr.əʳ/z ⓤⓢ -ɚ.ɚ/z
Hinderwell 'hɪn.də.wel, -wəl ⓤⓢ -dɚ-
Hindhead 'haɪnd.hed
Hindi 'hɪn.diː, -di
Hindle 'hɪn.dl̩
Hindley *surname:* 'hɪnd.li, 'haɪnd- *town in Greater Manchester:* 'hɪnd.li
Hindlip 'hɪnd.lɪp
hindmost 'haɪn*d*.məʊst ⓤⓢ -moʊst
hindquarters ˌhaɪn*d*'kwɔː.təz, ˌhaɪŋ-, '--- ⓤⓢ 'haɪndˌkwɔːr.t̬ɚz
hindranc|e 'hɪn.drən*t*s **-es** -ɪz
hindsight 'haɪnd.saɪt
Hindu 'hɪn.duː ⓤⓢ 'hɪn.duː **-s** -z
Hinduism 'hɪn.duː.ɪ.zᵊm, ˌhɪn'duː- ⓤⓢ 'hɪn.duː-
Hinduja hɪn'duː.dʒə
Hindu Kush ˌhɪn.duː'kuːʃ, -'kʊʃ
Hindustan ˌhɪn.dʊ'stɑːn, -'stæn **-i** -i
Hines haɪnz
hing|e hɪndʒ **-es** -ɪz **-ing** -ɪŋ **-ed** -d
Hingis 'hɪŋ.gɪs
Hingston 'hɪŋ*k*.stən
Hinkley 'hɪŋ.kli
Hinkson 'hɪŋk.sən
hinn|y 'hɪn|.i **-ies** -iz **-ying** -i.ɪŋ **-ied** -id
hint hɪnt **-s** -s **-ing** -ɪŋ ⓤⓢ 'hɪn.t̬ɪŋ **-ed** -ɪd ⓤⓢ 'hɪn.t̬ɪd
hinterland 'hɪn.tə.lænd, -lənd ⓤⓢ -t̬ɚ-
Hinton 'hɪn.tən
hip hɪp **-s** -s **-ped** -t **-per** -əʳ ⓤⓢ -ɚ **-pest** -ɪst, -əst **'hip ˌbath; 'hip ˌjoint**
hipbone 'hɪp.bəʊn ⓤⓢ -boʊn **-s** -z
hip-hop 'hɪp.hɒp ⓤⓢ -hɑːp
Hipomenes haɪ'pɒm.ɪ.niːz ⓤⓢ -'pɑː.mɪ-
Hipparchus hɪ'pɑː.kəs ⓤⓢ -'pɑːr-
Hippias 'hɪp.i.æs ⓤⓢ -æs, -əs
hippie 'hɪp.i **-s** -z
hippo 'hɪp.əʊ ⓤⓢ -oʊ **-s** -z
hippocamp|us ˌhɪp.əʊ'kæm.p|əs ⓤⓢ -oʊ'- **-i** -aɪ
Hippocrates hɪ'pɒk.rə.tiːz ⓤⓢ -'pɑː.krə-
Hippocratic ˌhɪp.əʊ'kræt.ɪk ⓤⓢ -ə'kræt̬- **ˌHippocratic 'oath**
Hippocrene ˌhɪp.əʊ'kriː.niː, -ni *also in poetry:* 'hɪp.əʊ.kriːn ⓤⓢ 'hɪp.oʊ.kriːn, ˌhɪp.oʊ'kriː.ni
hippodrome (H) 'hɪp.ə.drəʊm ⓤⓢ -droʊm **-s** -z
Hippolyta hɪ'pɒl.ɪ.tə, '-ə- ⓤⓢ -'pɑː.lɪ.tə
Hippolyte hɪ'pɒl.ɪ.tiː, '-ə- ⓤⓢ -'pɑː.lɪ.tiː
Hippolytus hɪ'pɒl.ɪ.təs, '-ə- ⓤⓢ -'pɑː.lɪ.təs
hippopotam|us ˌhɪp.ə'pɒt.ə.m|əs ⓤⓢ -'pɑː.t̬ə- **-uses** -ə.sɪz **-i** -aɪ
hipp|y 'hɪp|.i **-ies** -iz
hipster 'hɪp.stəʳ ⓤⓢ -stɚ **-s** -z
Hiram *biblical name:* 'haɪə.rəm, -ræm ⓤⓢ 'haɪ.rəm *modern names:* 'haɪə.rəm ⓤⓢ 'haɪ-
hircine 'hɜː.saɪn ⓤⓢ 'hɝː-, -sɪn
Hird hɜːd ⓤⓢ hɝːd
hir|e haɪəʳ ⓤⓢ haɪr **-es** -z **-ing** -ɪŋ **-ed** -d **-er/s** -əʳ/z ⓤⓢ -ɚ/z **-eling/s** -lɪŋ/z **ˌhire 'purchase; ˌhired 'hand**
hireling 'haɪə.lɪŋ ⓤⓢ 'haɪr- **-s** -z
Hirohito ˌhɪr.əʊ'hiː.təʊ ⓤⓢ -oʊ'hiː.toʊ
Hiroshima hɪ'rɒʃ.ɪ.mə, hə-, '-ə-; ˌhɪr.ɒʃ'iː-, -ə'ʃiː- ⓤⓢ ˌhɪr.ə'ʃiː-, hɪ'roʊ.ʃɪ-
Hirst hɜːst ⓤⓢ hɝːst
hirsute 'hɜː.sjuːt, -suːt, -'- ⓤⓢ 'hɝː.suːt, 'hɪr-; hɚ'suːt **-ness** -nəs, -nɪs
hirsutism 'hɜː.sjuː.tɪ.zᵊm, -suː-; hɜː'sjuː-, -'suː- ⓤⓢ 'hɝː.suː.t̬ɪ-, 'hɪr-; hɚ'suː-
his *strong form:* hɪz *weak form:* ɪz
Note: Weak form word. The strong form /hɪz/ is always used when the word occurs contrastively, e.g. 'It's **his**, not **hers**' and when it is in final position, e.g. 'He said it was **his**'. When the word is unstressed the weak pronuciation is usually /ɪz/, e.g. 'on his back', /ɒn.ɪz'bæk ⓤⓢ ɑːn-/, though /hɪz/ occurs when it is the first word in a sentence, e.g. 'His shoes were wet', /hɪz'ʃuːz.wəˌwet ⓤⓢ -wɚ-/, and when the style of speech is slow and careful.
Hislop 'hɪz.lɒp, -ləp ⓤⓢ -lɑːp
his'n'hers ˌhɪz.ᵊn'hɜːz ⓤⓢ -'hɝːz
Hispanic hɪ'spæn.ɪk **-s** -s
Hispanic|ism hɪ'spæn.ɪ.s|ɪ.zᵊm, '-ə- **-ist/s** -ɪst/s
Hispaniola ˌhɪs.pæn.i'əʊ.lə; -pæn'jəʊ-; hɪˌspæn- ⓤⓢ ˌhɪs.pən'joʊ-
hiss (H) hɪs **-es** -ɪz **-ing** -ɪŋ **-ed** -t **-er/s** -əʳ/z ⓤⓢ -ɚ/z
hist sːt, hɪst
Note: This spelling is used to represent the hissing sound made to attract someone's attention; it has a connotation of secrecy.
histamine 'hɪs.tə.miːn, -mɪn **-s** -z
histogram 'hɪs.tə.græm ⓤⓢ -toʊ-, -tə- **-s** -z
histological ˌhɪs.tə'lɒdʒ.ɪ.kᵊl ⓤⓢ -toʊ'lɑː.dʒɪ-, -tə'- **-ly** -li
histolog|y hɪ'stɒl.ə.dʒ|i ⓤⓢ 'tɑː.lə- **-ist/s** -ɪst/s
Histon 'hɪs.tᵊn
historian hɪ'stɔː.ri.ən ⓤⓢ -'stɔːr.i- **-s** -z
historic hɪ'stɒr.ɪk ⓤⓢ hɪ'stɔːr.ɪk **-al** -ᵊl **-ally** -ᵊl.i, -li
Note: In British English, the pronunciation /ɪs'tɒr.ɪk/ is sometimes used, though only after 'an' /ən/.
historicism hɪ'stɒr.ɪ.sɪ.zᵊm, '-ə- ⓤⓢ -'stɔːr.ə-
historicity ˌhɪs.tɒr'ɪs.ə.ti, -tə'rɪs-, -ɪ.ti ⓤⓢ -tə'rɪs.ə.t̬i
historiograph|y hɪˌstɒr.i'ɒg.rə.f|i ⓤⓢ -ˌstɔːr.i'ɑː.grə- **-er/s** -əʳ/z ⓤⓢ -ɚ/z
histor|y 'hɪs.tᵊr|.i **-ies** -iz
histrionic ˌhɪs.tri'ɒn.ɪk ⓤⓢ -'ɑː.nɪk **-s** -s **-al** -ᵊl **-ally** -ᵊl.i, -li
histrionism 'hɪs.tri.ə.nɪ.zᵊm
hit hɪt **-s** -s **-ting** -ɪŋ ⓤⓢ 'hɪt̬.ɪŋ **-ter/s** -əʳ/z ⓤⓢ 'hɪt̬.ɚ/z **'hit ˌlist; 'hit paˌrade**
Hitachi® hɪ'tɑː.tʃi, -'tætʃ.i ⓤⓢ -'tɑː.tʃi
hit-and-miss ˌhɪt.ᵊn'mɪs, -ᵊm'- ⓤⓢ -ᵊn'-
hit-and-run ˌhɪt.ᵊn'rʌn, -ᵊm'- ⓤⓢ -ᵊn'- *stress shift, see compound:* **ˌhit-and-run 'driver**
hitch hɪtʃ **-es** -ɪz **-ing** -ɪŋ **-ed** -t
Hitchcock 'hɪtʃ.kɒk ⓤⓢ -kɑːk
Hitchens 'hɪtʃ.ɪnz
hitchhik|e 'hɪtʃ.haɪk **-es** -s **-ing** -ɪŋ **-ed** -t **-er/s** -əʳ/z ⓤⓢ -ɚ/z
Hitchin 'hɪtʃ.ɪn **-s** -z
Hite haɪt
hi-tech ˌhaɪ'tek *stress shift:* ˌhi-tech 'product
hither (H) 'hɪð.əʳ ⓤⓢ -ɚ
hithermost 'hɪð.ə.məʊst ⓤⓢ -ɚ.moʊst
hitherto ˌhɪð.ə'tuː ⓤⓢ -ɚ'- *stress shift:* ˌhitherto 'named
hitherwards 'hɪð.ə.wədz ⓤⓢ -ɚ.wɚdz
Hitler 'hɪt.ləʳ ⓤⓢ -lɚ
Hitlerian hɪt'lɪə.ri.ən ⓤⓢ -'lɪr.i-
Hitlerism 'hɪt.ləʳ.ɪ.zᵊm ⓤⓢ -lɚ-
Hitlerite 'hɪt.ləʳ.aɪt ⓤⓢ -lɚ.aɪt **-s** -s
hit|man 'hɪt|.mæn **-men** -men
Hittite 'hɪt.aɪt ⓤⓢ 'hɪt̬- **-s** -s
HIV ˌeɪtʃ.aɪ'viː *stress shift, see compound:* **ˌHIV 'positive**
hiv|e (*n. v.*) haɪv **-es** -z **-ing** -ɪŋ **-ed** -d
Hivite 'haɪ.vaɪt **-s** -s
Hizbollah ˌhɪz.bɒl'ɑː ⓤⓢ ˌhez.bə'lɑː
Hizbullah ˌhɪz.bʊ'lɑː, -bə'-
HMO ˌeɪtʃ.em'əʊ ⓤⓢ -'oʊ
HMS ˌeɪtʃ.em'es
HNC ˌeɪtʃ.en'siː
HND ˌeɪtʃ.en'diː
ho həʊ ⓤⓢ hoʊ
Hoadl(e)y 'həʊd.li ⓤⓢ 'hoʊd-
hoag|ie, hoag|y 'həʊ.g|i ⓤⓢ 'hoʊ- **-ies** -iz
hoar (H) hɔːʳ ⓤⓢ hɔːr
hoard hɔːd ⓤⓢ hɔːrd **-s** -z **-ing** -ɪŋ **-ed** -ɪd **-er/s** -əʳ/z ⓤⓢ -ɚ/z
hoarding 'hɔː.dɪŋ ⓤⓢ 'hɔːr- **-s** -z
Hoare hɔːʳ ⓤⓢ hɔːr
hoarfrost 'hɔː.frɒst, ˌ-'- ⓤⓢ 'hɔːr.frɑːst **-s** -s
hoars|e hɔːs ⓤⓢ hɔːrs **-er** -əʳ ⓤⓢ -ɚ **-est** -ɪst, -əst **-ely** -li **-eness** -nəs, -nɪs
hoar|y 'hɔː.r|i ⓤⓢ 'hɔːr|.i **-ier** -i.əʳ ⓤⓢ -i.ɚ **-iest** -i.ɪst, -i.əst **-ily** -ᵊl.i, -ɪ.li **-iness** -ɪ.nəs, -ɪ.nɪs

hoax həʊks ⓤⓢ hoʊks **-es** -ɪz **-ing** -ɪŋ **-ed** -t **-er/s** -əʳ/z ⓤⓢ -ɚ/z
hob hɒb ⓤⓢ hɑːb **-s** -z
Hoban ˈhəʊ.bən ⓤⓢ ˈhoʊ-
Hobart ˈhəʊ.bɑːt, -bət; ˈhʌb.ət ⓤⓢ ˈhoʊ.bɑːrt, -bɚt; ˈhʌb.ɚt
Hobbema ˈhɒb.ɪ.mə ⓤⓢ ˈhɑː.bə.mɑː, -mə **-s** -z
Hobbes hɒbz ⓤⓢ hɑːbz
hobbit (H) ˈhɒb.ɪt ⓤⓢ ˈhɑː.bɪt **-s** -s
hobbl|e ˈhɒb.l̩ ⓤⓢ ˈhɑː.b|l̩ **-es** -z **-ing** -ɪŋ, ˈhɒb.lɪŋ ⓤⓢ ˈhɑː.blɪŋ **-ed** -d **-er/s** -əʳ/z ⓤⓢ -ɚ/z, ˈhɒb.ləʳ/z ⓤⓢ ˈhɑː.blɚ/z
hobbledehoy ˌhɒb.l̩.diˈhɔɪ, ˈhɒb.l̩.di.hɔɪ ⓤⓢ ˈhɑː.bl̩.di.hɔɪ **-s** -z
Hobbs hɒbz ⓤⓢ hɑːbz
hobb|y ˈhɒb|.i ⓤⓢ ˈhɑː.b|i **-ies** -iz
hobbyhors|e ˈhɒb.i.hɔːs ⓤⓢ ˈhɑː.bi.hɔːrs **-es** -ɪz
Hobday ˈhɒb.deɪ ⓤⓢ ˈhɑːb-
hobgoblin ˌhɒbˈgɒb.lɪn, ˈ-ˌ-- ⓤⓢ ˈhɑːbˌgɑːb- **-s** -z
Hobhouse ˈhɒb.haʊs ⓤⓢ ˈhɑːb-
hobnail ˈhɒb.neɪl ⓤⓢ ˈhɑːb- **-s** -z **-ed** -d ˌ**hobnail** ˈ**boots**
hobnob ˈhɒb.nɒb, ˌ-ˈ- ⓤⓢ ˈhɑːb.nɑːb **-s** -z **-bing** -ɪŋ **-bed** -d
hobo ˈhəʊ.bəʊ ⓤⓢ ˈhoʊ.boʊ **-(e)s** -z
Hoboken ˈhəʊ.bəʊ.kən ⓤⓢ ˈhoʊ.boʊ-
Hobsbaum ˈhɒbz.baʊm ⓤⓢ ˈhɑːbz-
Hobsbawm ˈhɒbz.bɔːm ⓤⓢ ˈhɑːbz.bɑːm, -bɔːm
Hobson ˈhɒb.sən ⓤⓢ ˈhɑːb- ˌ**Hobson's** ˈ**choice**
Hobson-Jobson ˌhɒb.sənˈdʒɒb.sən ⓤⓢ ˌhɑːb.sənˈdʒɑːb-
Hoby ˈhəʊ.bi ⓤⓢ ˈhoʊ-
Hoccleve ˈhɒk.liːv ⓤⓢ ˈhɑːk-
Ho Chi Minh ˌhəʊ.tʃiːˈmɪn ⓤⓢ ˌhoʊ-
Ho Chi Minh City ˌhəʊ.tʃiː.mɪnˈsɪt.i ⓤⓢ ˌhoʊ.tʃiː.mɪnˈsɪt̬-
hock hɒk ⓤⓢ hɑːk **-s** -s **-ing** -ɪŋ **-ed** -t
hockey ˈhɒk.i ⓤⓢ ˈhɑː.ki ˈ**hockey** ˌ**stick**
Hockin ˈhɒk.ɪn ⓤⓢ ˈhɑː.kɪn
Hocking ˈhɒk.ɪŋ ⓤⓢ ˈhɑː.kɪŋ
Hockley ˈhɒk.li ⓤⓢ ˈhɑːk-
Hockney ˈhɒk.ni ⓤⓢ ˈhɑːk-
hockshop ˈhɒk.ʃɒp ⓤⓢ ˈhɑːk.ʃɑːp **-s** -s
hocus ˈhəʊ.kəs ⓤⓢ ˈhoʊ- **-es** -ɪz **-(s)ing** -ɪŋ **-(s)ed** -t
hocus-pocus ˌhəʊ.kəsˈpəʊ.kəs ⓤⓢ ˌhoʊ.kəsˈpoʊ-
hod hɒd ⓤⓢ hɑːd **-s** -z
Hodder ˈhɒd.əʳ ⓤⓢ ˈhɑː.dɚ
Hoddesdon ˈhɒdz.dən ⓤⓢ ˈhɑːdz-
Hoddinott ˈhɒd.ɪ.nɒt, -ən.ɒt ⓤⓢ ˈhɑː.dən.ɑːt
hoddle ˈhɒd.l̩ ⓤⓢ ˈhɑː.dl̩
Hodge hɒdʒ ⓤⓢ hɑːdʒ
hodgepodge ˈhɒdʒ.pɒdʒ ⓤⓢ ˈhɑːdʒ.pɑːdʒ
Hodges ˈhɒdʒ.ɪz ⓤⓢ ˈhɑː.dʒɪz
Hodgetts ˈhɒdʒ.ɪts ⓤⓢ ˈhɑː.dʒɪts
Hodgins ˈhɒdʒ.ɪnz ⓤⓢ ˈhɑː.dʒɪnz
Hodgkin ˈhɒdʒ.kɪn ⓤⓢ ˈhɑːdʒ- ˈ**Hodgkin's di**ˌ**sease**
Hodgkins ˈhɒdʒ.kɪnz ⓤⓢ ˈhɑːdʒ-
Hodgkinson ˈhɒdʒ.kɪn.sən ⓤⓢ ˈhɑːdʒ-
Hodgkiss ˈhɒdʒ.kɪs ⓤⓢ ˈhɑːdʒ-
Hodgson ˈhɒdʒ.sən *in the North of England also:* ˈhɒdʒ.ən ⓤⓢ ˈhɑːdʒ.sən
hodometer hɒdˈɒm.ɪ.təʳ, -ə.təʳ ⓤⓢ hɑːˈdɑː.mə.t̬ɚ **-s** -z
Hodson ˈhɒd.sən ⓤⓢ ˈhɑːd-
hoe (H) həʊ ⓤⓢ hoʊ **-s** -z **-ing** -ɪŋ **-d** -d
hoedown ˈhəʊ.daʊn ⓤⓢ ˈhoʊ- **-s** -z
Hoey hɔɪ, ˈhəʊ.i ⓤⓢ ˈhoʊ.i
Hoffa ˈhɒf.ə ⓤⓢ ˈhɑː.fə
Hoffman(n) ˈhɒf.mən ⓤⓢ ˈhɑːf-
Hofmannsthal ˈhɒf.mən.stɑːl ⓤⓢ ˈhɑːf.mɑːn-, ˈhɔːf-
Hofmeister ˈhɒfˌmaɪ.stəʳ ⓤⓢ ˈhɑːfˌmaɪ.stɚ
hog hɒg ⓤⓢ hɑːg, hɔːg **-s** -z **-ging** -ɪŋ **-ged** -d
Hogan ˈhəʊ.gən ⓤⓢ ˈhoʊ-
Hogarth ˈhəʊ.gɑːθ, ˈhɒg.ət ⓤⓢ ˈhoʊ.gɑːrθ
Hogarthian həʊˈgɑː.θi.ən ⓤⓢ hoʊˈgɑːr-
Hogben ˈhɒg.bən, -ben ⓤⓢ ˈhɑːg-, ˈhɔːg
Hogg hɒg ⓤⓢ hɑːg, hɔːg
Hoggart ˈhɒg.ət ⓤⓢ ˈhɑː.gɚt, ˈhɔː-
hogget (H) ˈhɒg.ɪt ⓤⓢ ˈhɑː.gɪt, ˈhɔː- **-s** -s
hoggish ˈhɒg.ɪʃ ⓤⓢ ˈhɑː.gɪʃ, ˈhɔː- **-ly** -li **-ness** -nəs, -nɪs
hogmanay (H) ˈhɒg.mə.neɪ, ˌ--ˈ- ⓤⓢ ˈhɑːg.mə.neɪ, ˈhɔːg-
hogshead ˈhɒgz.hed ⓤⓢ ˈhɑːgz-, ˈhɔːgz- **-s** -z
Hogwarts ˈhɒg.wɔːts
hogwash ˈhɒg.wɒʃ ⓤⓢ ˈhɑːg.wɑːʃ, ˈhɔːg-, -wɔːʃ
hogweed ˈhɒg.wiːd ⓤⓢ ˈhɑːg-, ˈhɔːg- **-s** -z
Hohenlinden ˌhəʊ.ənˈlɪn.dən ⓤⓢ ˌhoʊ.ənˈ-, ˈhoʊ.ənˌlɪn-
Hohenzollern ˌhəʊ.ənˈzɒl.ən ⓤⓢ ˈhoʊ.ənˌzɑː.lɚn **-s** -z
hoi(c)k hɔɪk **-s** -s **-ing** -ɪŋ **-ed** -t
hoi polloi ˌhɔɪ.pəˈlɔɪ, -pɒlˈɔɪ; -ˈpɒl.ɔɪ ⓤⓢ ˌhɔɪ.pəˈlɔɪ
hoisin ˈhɔɪ.sɪn, -ˈ- ˌ**hoisin** ˈ**sauce**
hoist hɔɪst **-s** -s **-ing** -ɪŋ **-ed** -ɪd
hoity-toity ˌhɔɪ.tiˈtɔɪ.ti ⓤⓢ ˌhɔɪ.t̬iˈtɔɪ.t̬i
hokey ˈhəʊ.ki ⓤⓢ ˈhoʊ- ˌ**hokey** ˈ**cokey**
hokey-pokey ˌhəʊ.kiˈpəʊ.ki ⓤⓢ ˌhoʊ.kiˈpoʊ-
Hokkaido hɒkˈaɪ.dəʊ ⓤⓢ hɑːˈkaɪ.doʊ
hokum ˈhəʊ.kəm ⓤⓢ ˈhoʊ-
Holbeach ˈhɒl.biːtʃ, ˈhəʊl- ⓤⓢ ˈhɑːl-, ˈhoʊl-
Holbech ˈhəʊl.biːtʃ, ˈhɒl- ⓤⓢ ˈhoʊl-
Holbeck ˈhɒl.bek, ˈhəʊl- ⓤⓢ ˈhoʊl-
Holbein ˈhɒl.baɪn ⓤⓢ ˈhoʊl- **-s** -z
Holborn ˈhəʊ.bən, ˈhəʊl-, ˈhɒl- ⓤⓢ ˈhoʊl.bɚn, ˈhoʊ-
Holbrook(e) ˈhəʊl.brʊk, ˈhɒl- ⓤⓢ ˈhoʊl-
Holburn ˈhɒl.bɜːn, ˈhəʊl- ⓤⓢ ˈhoʊl.bɝːn
Holcroft ˈhəʊl.krɒft ⓤⓢ ˈhoʊl.krɑːft
hold həʊld ⓤⓢ hoʊld **-s** -z **-ing/s** -ɪŋ/z **held** held ˌ**no** ˌ**holds** ˈ**barred**; ˈ**holding** ˌ**company**; ˌ**hold one's** ˈ**own**
holdall ˈhəʊld.ɔːl ⓤⓢ ˈhoʊld-, -ɑːl **-s** -z
Holden ˈhəʊl.dən ⓤⓢ ˈhoʊl-
holder (H) ˈhəʊl.dəʳ ⓤⓢ ˈhoʊl.dɚ **-s** -z
Holderness ˈhəʊl.də.nəs, -nɪs, -nes ⓤⓢ ˈhoʊl.dɚ-
holdover ˈhəʊldˌəʊ.vəʳ ⓤⓢ ˈhoʊldˌoʊ.vɚ **-s** -z
Holdsworth ˈhəʊldz.wəθ, -wɜːθ ⓤⓢ ˈhoʊldz.wɚθ, -wɝːθ
holdup ˈhəʊld.ʌp ⓤⓢ ˈhoʊld- **-s** -s
hol|e (H) həʊl ⓤⓢ hoʊl **-es** -z **-ing** -ɪŋ **-ed** -d ˌ**hole in** ˈ**one** ⓤⓢ ˈ**hole in** ˌ**one**; ˌ**need something like a** ˌ**hole in the** ˈ**head** ⓤⓢ ˌ**need something like a** ˈ**hole in the** ˌ**head**
hole-and-corner ˌhəʊl.əndˈkɔː.nəʳ, -əŋˈ- ⓤⓢ ˌhoʊl.əndˈkɔːr.nɚ
hole-in-the-wall ˌhəʊl.ɪn.ðəˈwɔːl ⓤⓢ ˌhoʊl.ɪn.ðəˈwɔːl, -wɑːl
Holford ˈhəʊl.fəd, ˈhɒl- ⓤⓢ ˈhoʊl.fɚd
holiday (H) ˈhɒl.ə.deɪ, ˈ-ɪ-, -di ⓤⓢ ˈhɑː.lə.deɪ **-s** -z **-ing** -ɪŋ **-ed** -d ˈ**holiday** ˌ**camp**
holidaymaker ˈhɒl.ə.diˌmeɪ.kəʳ, ˈ-ɪ-, -deɪˌ- ⓤⓢ ˈhɑː.lə.deɪˌmeɪ.kɚ **-s** -z
holier-than-thou ˌhəʊ.li.ə.ðənˈðaʊ ⓤⓢ ˌhoʊ.li.ɚ- *stress shift:* ˌholier-than-thou ˈattitude
Holies ˈhəʊ.lɪz ⓤⓢ ˈhoʊ-
Holifield ˈhɒl.ɪ.fiːld ⓤⓢ ˈhoʊ.lɪ-, ˈhɑː-
Holinshed ˈhɒl.ɪn.ʃed ⓤⓢ ˈhɑː.lɪn-
holism ˈhəʊ.lɪ.zəm, ˈhɒl.ɪ- ⓤⓢ ˈhoʊ.lɪ-
holistic həʊˈlɪs.tɪk, hɒlˈɪs- ⓤⓢ hoʊˈlɪs- **-ally** -əl.i, -li
Holland, holland ˈhɒl.ənd ⓤⓢ ˈhɑː.lənd **-s** -z
hollandaise ˌhɒl.ənˈdeɪz ⓤⓢ ˌhɑː.lənˈ- *stress shift, see compound:* ˌ**hollandaise** ˈ**sauce** ⓤⓢ ˈ**hollandaise** ˌ**sauce**
Hollander ˈhɒl.ən.dəʳ ⓤⓢ ˈhɑː.lən.dɚ **-s** -z
holl|er ˈhɒl|.əʳ ⓤⓢ ˈhɑː.l|ɚ **-ers** -əz ⓤⓢ -ɚz **-ering** -ər.ɪŋ **-ered** -əd ⓤⓢ -ɚd
Holles ˈhɒl.ɪs ⓤⓢ ˈhɑː.lɪs
Hollick ˈhɒl.ɪk ⓤⓢ ˈhɑː.lɪk
Holliday ˈhɒl.ɪ.deɪ, ˈ-ə-, -di ⓤⓢ ˈhɑː.lə-
Hollings ˈhɒl.ɪŋz ⓤⓢ ˈhɑː.lɪŋz
Hollingsworth ˈhɒl.ɪŋz.wəθ, -wɜːθ ⓤⓢ ˈhɑː.lɪŋz.wɚθ, -wɝːθ

Hollingworth 'hɒl.ɪŋ.wəθ, -wɜːθ US 'hɑː.lɪŋ.wɚθ, -wɝːθ
Hollins 'hɒl.ɪnz US 'hɑː.lɪnz
Hollis 'hɒl.ɪs US 'hɑː.lɪs
hollo 'hɒl.əʊ US 'hɑː.loʊ; hə'loʊ **-es** -z **-ing** -ɪŋ **-ed** -d
hollo(a) 'hɒl.əʊ US 'hɑː.loʊ; hə'loʊ **-s** -z **-ing** -ɪŋ **-ed** -d
Hollom 'hɒl.əm US 'hɑː.ləm
hollow 'hɒl.əʊ US 'hɑː.loʊ **-s** -z **-er** -əʳ US -ɚ **-est** -ɪst, -əst **-ly** -li **-ness** -nəs, -nɪs **-ing** -ɪŋ **-ed** -d
Holloway 'hɒl.ə.weɪ US 'hɑː.lə-
holl|y (H) 'hɒl|.i US 'hɑː.l|i **-ies** -iz
hollyhock 'hɒl.i.hɒk US 'hɑː.li.hɑːk **-s** -s
Hollywood 'hɒl.i.wʊd US 'hɑː.li-
holm (H) həʊm US hoʊlm **-s** -z **'holm ˌoak**
Holman 'həʊl.mən, 'hɒl- US 'hoʊl-
Holmby 'həʊm.bi US 'hoʊlm-
Holmer 'həʊl.məʳ, 'həʊ- US 'hoʊl.mɚ
Holmes həʊmz US hoʊlmz
Holmesdale 'həʊmz.deɪl US 'hoʊlmz-
Holmfirth 'həʊm.fəθ, -fɜːθ US 'hoʊlm.fɚθ, -fɝːθ
holmium 'həʊl.mi.əm, 'hɒl- US 'hoʊl-
holo- hɒl.əʊ-; hɒl'ɒ- US hɑː.loʊ-, hoʊ-, -lə-; hoʊ'lɑː-

Note: Prefix. Normally either takes primary or secondary stress on the first syllable, e.g. **holograph** /'hɒl.ə.grɑːf US 'hɑː.lə.græf/, **holographic** /ˌhɒl.ə'græf.ɪk US ˌhɑː.lə'-/, or primary stress on the second syllable, e.g. **holography** /hɒl'ɒg.rə.fi US hoʊ'lɑː.grə-/.

holocaust (H) 'hɒl.ə.kɔːst, -kɒst US 'hɑː.lə.kɑːst, 'hoʊ-, -kɔːst **-s** -s
Holofernes ˌhɒl.əʊ'fɜː.niːz, hə'lɒf.ə- US ˌhɑː.lə'fɝː-
hologram 'hɒl.ə.græm US 'hɑː.lə-, 'hoʊ- **-s** -z
holograph 'hɒl.ə.grɑːf, -græf US 'hɑː.lə.græf, 'hoʊ- **-s** -s
holographic ˌhɒl.ə'græf.ɪk US ˌhɑː.lə-, ˌhoʊ- **-ally** -əl.i, -li
holography hɒl'ɒg.rə.fi US hoʊ'lɑː.grə-
Holon 'hɒl.ən US 'hɑː.lən; 'hoʊ.lɑːn
holophras|e 'hɒl.ə.freɪz US 'hɑː.lə-, 'hoʊ- **-es** -ɪz
holophrastic ˌhɒl.ə'fræs.tɪk US ˌhɑː.lə'-, ˌhoʊ-
Holroyd 'hɒl.rɔɪd, 'həʊl- US 'hɑːl-
Holst həʊlst US hoʊlst
holstein (H) 'hɒl.staɪn, 'həʊl- US 'hoʊl.staɪn, -stiːn
holster 'həʊl.stəʳ US 'hoʊl.stɚ **-s** -z **-ed** -d
holt (H) həʊlt US hoʊlt **-s** -s
Holtby 'həʊlt.bi US 'hoʊlt-
Holtham 'həʊl.θəm, 'hɒl-, 'həʊ- US 'hoʊl-
holus-bolus ˌhəʊ.ləs'bəʊ.ləs US ˌhoʊ.ləs'boʊ-
hol|y (H) 'həʊ.l|i US 'hoʊ- **-ier** -i.əʳ US -i.ɚ **-iest** -i.ɪst, -i.əst **-iness** -ɪ.nəs, -ɪ.nɪs ˌ**Holy 'Bible;** ˌ**Holy Com'munion;** ˌ**Holy 'Ghost;** ˌ**Holy 'Grail;** '**Holy** ˌ**Land;** ˌ**Holy** ˌ**Roman 'Empire;** ˌ**Holy 'Spirit;** '**Holy** ˌ**Week**
Holycross 'həʊ.li.krɒs US 'hoʊl.i.krɑːs
Holyfield 'həʊl.ɪ.fiːld US 'hɑː.lɪ-
Holyhead ˌhɒl.i'hed, '--- US 'hɑː.li-
Holyoake *place in Massachusetts:* 'həʊl.jəʊk US 'hoʊl.joʊk *all other senses:* 'həʊ.li.əʊk US 'hoʊ.li.oʊk
Holyrood 'hɒl.i.ruːd US 'hɑː.li-
holyston|e 'həʊl.i.stəʊn US 'hoʊl.i.stoʊn **-es** -z **-ing** -ɪŋ **-ed** -d
Holywell 'hɒl.i.wəl, -wel US 'hɑː.li-
homage 'hɒm.ɪdʒ US 'hɑː.mɪdʒ, 'ɑː-
hombre 'ɒm.breɪ, -bri US 'ɑːm- **-s** -z
homburg (H) 'hɒm.bɜːg US 'hɑːm.bɝːg **-s** -z
home həʊm US hoʊm **-s** -z ˌ**home 'brew;** ˌ**Home 'Counties;** ˌ**home eco'nomics;** ˌ**home 'free;** ˌ**home 'front** US '**home** ˌ**front;** ˌ**home 'help;** '**Home** ˌ**Office;** '**home** ˌ**page;** ˌ**home 'rule;** ˌ**Home 'Secretary;** ˌ**home 'truth;** ˌ**close to 'home;** ˌ**home from 'home**
Home həʊm, hjuːm US hoʊm, hjuːm

Note: /hjuːm/ in **Milne-Home, Douglas-Home,** and **Baron Home of the Hirsel.**

Homebase® 'həʊm.beɪs US 'hoʊm-
homeboy 'həʊm.bɔɪ US 'hoʊm- **-s** -z
homebred ˌhəʊm'bred US ˌhoʊm- *stress shift:* ˌhomebred 'livestock
homecoming 'həʊmˌkʌm.ɪŋ US 'hoʊm- **-s** -z
homegrown ˌhəʊm'grəʊn US ˌhoʊm'groʊn *stress shift:* ˌhomegrown 'food
homeland (H) 'həʊm.lænd, -lənd US 'hoʊm- **-s** -z
homeless 'həʊm.ləs, -lɪs US 'hoʊm- **-ness** -nəs, -nɪs
homelike 'həʊm.laɪk US 'hoʊm-
homel|y 'həʊm.l|i US 'hoʊm- **-ier** -i.əʳ US -i.ɚ **-iest** -i.ɪst, -i.əst **-iness** -ɪ.nəs, -ɪ.nɪs
homemade ˌhəʊm'meɪd US ˌhoʊm- *stress shift:* ˌhomemade 'jam
homemaker 'həʊmˌmeɪ.kəʳ US 'hoʊmˌmeɪ.kɚ **-s** -z
homeo- 'həʊ.mi.əʊ-, 'hɒm.i.əʊ-; ˌhəʊ.mi'ɒ-, ˌhɒm.i'ɒ- US 'hoʊ.mi.oʊ-, -ə-; ˌhoʊ.mi'ɑː-

Note: Prefix. Normally ether takes primary or secondary stress on the first syllable, e.g. **homeopath** /'həʊ.mi.əʊ.pæθ US 'hoʊ.mi.oʊ-/, **homeopathic** /ˌhəʊ.mi.əʊ'pæθ.ɪk US ˌhoʊ.mi.oʊ'-/, or primary stress on the third syllable with secondary stress on the first, e.g. **homeopathy** /ˌhəʊ.mi'ɒp.ə.θi US ˌhoʊ.mi'ɑː.pə-/.

homeopath 'həʊ.mi.əʊ.pæθ, 'hɒm.i- US 'hoʊ.mi.oʊ-, -ə- **-s** -s
homeopathic ˌhəʊ.mi.əʊ'pæθ.ɪk, ˌhɒm.i- US ˌhoʊ.mi.oʊ'-, -ə- **-al** -əl **-ally** -əl.i, -li
homeopathy ˌhəʊ.mi'ɒp.ə.θi, ˌhɒm. US ˌhoʊ.mi'ɑː.pə-
homeostasis ˌhəʊ.mi.əʊ'steɪ.sɪs, ˌhɒm.i-, ˌ--'ɒs.tə- US ˌhoʊ.mi.oʊ'- -'stæs.ɪs
homeostatic ˌhəʊ.mi.əʊ'stæt.ɪk, ˌhɒm.i- US ˌhoʊ.mi.oʊ'stæt̬- **-ally** -əl.i, -li
homeowner 'həʊmˌəʊ.nəʳ US 'hoʊmˌoʊ.nɚ **-s** -z
homepag|e 'həʊm.peɪdʒ US 'hoʊm- **-es** -ɪz
Homer 'həʊ.məʳ US 'hoʊ.mɚ
homer 'həʊ.məʳ US 'hoʊ.mɚ **-s** -z
Homeric *relating to Homer:* həʊ'mer US hoʊ- *name of ship:* 'həʊ.mər.ɪ US 'hoʊ-
Homerton 'hɒm.ə.tən US 'hɑː.mɚ-
homesick 'həʊm.sɪk US 'hoʊm- **-ness** -nəs, -nɪs
homespun 'həʊm.spʌn US 'hoʊm- **-s** -z
homestead 'həʊm.sted, -stɪd US 'hoʊm- **-s** -z
homesteader 'həʊmˌsted.əʳ US 'hoʊmˌsted.ɚ **-s** -z
homestretch ˌhəʊm'stretʃ, '-- US ˌhoʊm'stretʃ, '-- **-es** -ɪz
homeward 'həʊm.wəd US 'hoʊm.w **-s** -z
homework 'həʊm.wɜːk US 'hoʊm.wɝːk
homey 'həʊ.mi US 'hoʊ-
homicidal ˌhɒm.ɪ'saɪ.dəl, -ə'- US ˌhɑː.mə'-, ˌhoʊ- *stress shift:* ˌhomicidal 'maniac
homicide 'hɒm.ɪ.saɪd, '-ə- US 'hɑː. 'hoʊ- **-s** -z
homil|y 'hɒm.ɪ.l|i, '-ə- US 'hɑː.mə- **-ies** -iz
homing 'həʊ.mɪŋ US 'hoʊ- '**homing deˌvice;** '**homing** ˌ**pigeon**
hominid 'hɒm.ɪ.nɪd, '-ə- US 'hɑː.m -mə- **-s** -z
hominoid 'hɒm.ɪ.nɔɪd, -ə- US 'hɑː. -mə- **-s** -z
hominy 'hɒm.ɪ.ni, '-ə- US 'hɑː.mɪ-, -mə-
homo 'həʊ.məʊ, 'hɒm.əʊ US 'hoʊ. **-s** -z

Homographs

When two lexical items have the same form in spelling, these are known as homographs. Homographs can be pronounced the same as or different to each other.

Examples

Here are some examples of homographs with the same pronunciation:

- bank /bæŋk/
  (*e.g. financial institution; area of ground by a river*)
- well /wel/
  (*e.g. source of water; healthy; adv.*)

Other homographs differ in their pronunciation, but usually only in the vowel sound used, e.g.:

- bow
  — (*e.g. a slip knot with a double loop; a device for shooting arrows*) /bəʊ/ ⓊⓈ /boʊ/
  — (*e.g. incline the head or trunk; submit*) /baʊ/
- dove
  — (*pigeon*) /dʌv/
  — (*past tense of* dive) /dəʊv/ ⓊⓈ /doʊv/

Homographs also appear in noun/verb, noun/adjective and verb/adjective pairs. The difference in pronunciation indicates which part of speech is being used, e.g.:

insert	(*n.*)	/ˈɪn.sɜːt/	ⓊⓈ /-sɝːt/
	(*v.*)	/ɪnˈsɜːt/	ⓊⓈ /-ˈsɝːt/
deliberate	(*adj.*)	/dɪˈlɪb.ər.ət/	
	(*v.*)	/dɪˈlɪb.ər.eɪt/	ⓊⓈ /ˈ-ə.reɪt/
arithmetic	(*n.*)	/əˈrɪθ.mə.tɪk/	
	(*adj.*)	/ˌær.ɪθˈmet.ɪk/	ⓊⓈ /ˌer.ɪθˈmet̬-/

Pronunciation tip

In most cases it is necessary to check the pronunciation of a word individually, as the correct realisation is not obvious from the form of the word. However, some rules are available. For example, the pronunciation of word pairs ending with *–ate* is predictable depending on the part of speech. In two-syllable words where the stress moves to show the difference between a noun and a verb (e.g. *insert, export*), the noun is almost always stressed on the first syllable and the verb on the second.

homo- həʊ.məʊ-, hɒm.əʊ-; həˈmɒ-, hɒmˈɒ- ⓊⓈ hoʊ.moʊ-, hɑː-, -mə-; həˈmɑː-, hoʊ-
Note: Prefix. Normally either takes primary or secondary stress on the first syllable, e.g. **homonym** /ˈhɒm.ə.nɪm ⓊⓈ ˈhɑː.mə-/, **homophobia** /ˌhɒm.əˈfəʊ.bi.ə ⓊⓈ ˌhoʊ.məˈfoʊ-/, or primary stress on the second syllable, e.g. **homonymy** /həˈmɒn.ɪ.mi ⓊⓈ hoʊˈmɑː.nə-/.

homoeopath ˈhəʊ.mi.əʊ.pæθ, ˈhɒm.i- ⓊⓈ ˈhoʊ.mi.oʊ- **-s** -s

homoeopathic ˌhəʊ.mi.əʊˈpæθ.ɪk, ˌhɒm.i- ⓊⓈ ˌhoʊ.mi.oʊˈ- **-al** -əl **-ally** -əl.i, -li

homoeopathy ˌhəʊ.miˈɒp.ə.θi, ˌhɒm.iˈ- ⓊⓈ ˌhoʊ.miˈɑː.pə-

homoeostasis ˌhəʊ.mi.əʊˈsteɪ.sɪs, ˌ--ˈɒs.tə- ⓊⓈ ˌhoʊ.mi.oʊˈ-, -ˈstæs.ɪs

homoeostatic ˌhəʊ.mi.əʊˈstæt.ɪk ⓊⓈ ˌhoʊ.mi.oʊˈstæt̬- **-ally** -əl.i, -li

homoerotic ˌhəʊ.məʊ.ɪˈrɒt.ɪk, ˌhɒm.əʊ-, -əˈ- ⓊⓈ ˌhoʊ.moʊ.ɪˈrɑː.t̬ɪk, -əˈ-

homoeroticism ˌhəʊ.məʊ.ɪˈrɒt.ɪ.sɪ.z.əm, ˌhɒm.əʊ-, -əˈ-, ˈ-ə- ⓊⓈ ˌhoʊ.moʊ.ɪˈrɑː.t̬ə-, -əˈ-

homogeneity ˌhəʊ.məʊ.dʒəˈneɪ.ə.ti, ˌhɒm.əʊ-, -dʒenˈeɪ-, -dʒɪˈneɪ-, -ɪ.ti ⓊⓈ ˌhoʊ.moʊ.dʒəˈniː.ə.t̬i, ˌhɑː-, -mə-, -ˈneɪ-

homogeneous ˌhɒm.əˈdʒiː.ni.əs, ˌhəʊ.mə- ⓊⓈ ˌhoʊ.moʊˈdʒiː-, ˌhɑː-, -məˈ- **-ly** -li **-ness** -nəs, -nɪs

homogeniz|e, -is|e həˈmɒdʒ.ə.naɪz, hɒmˈɒdʒ-, ˈ-ɪ- ⓊⓈ həˈmɑː.dʒə- **-es** -ɪz **-ing** -ɪŋ **-ed** -d

homograph ˈhɒm.ə.grɑːf, ˈhəʊ.mə-, -græf ⓊⓈ ˈhɑː.mə.græf, ˈhoʊ- **-s** -s

homographic ˌhɒm.əˈgræf.ɪk, ˌhəʊ.məˈ- ⓊⓈ ˌhɑː.məˈ-, ˌhoʊ-

homoiotherm həˈmɔɪ.ə.θɜːm, hɒmˈɔɪ- ⓊⓈ hoʊˈmɔɪ.oʊ.θɝːm, -ə.θɝːm **-s** -z

homoiothermic həˌmɔɪ.əˈθɜː.mɪk, hɒmˌɔɪ- ⓊⓈ hoʊˌmɔɪ.oʊˈθɝː-, -əˈθɝː-

homolog ˈhɒm.ə.lɒg ⓊⓈ ˈhɑː.mə.lɑːg, ˈhoʊ-, -lɔːg **-s** -z

homologous həˈmɒl.ə.gəs, hɒmˈɒl- ⓊⓈ hoʊˈmɑː.lə-, hə-

homologue ˈhɒm.ə.lɒg ⓊⓈ ˈhɑː.mə.lɑːg, ˈhoʊ-, -lɔːg **-s** -z

homolog|y həˈmɒl.ə.dʒ|i, hɒmˈɒl- ⓊⓈ hoʊˈmɑː.lə-, hə- **-ies** -iz

homonym ˈhɒm.ə.nɪm ⓊⓈ ˈhɑː.mə- **-s** -z

homonymous həˈmɒn.ɪ.məs, hɒmˈɒn-, -ə.məs ⓊⓈ hoʊˈmɑː.nə-, hə- **-ly** -li

homonymy həˈmɒn.ɪ.mi, hɒmˈɒn-, -ə.mi ⓊⓈ hoʊˈmɑː.nə-, hə-

homophobe ˈhəʊ.mə.fəʊb ⓊⓈ ˈhoʊ.mə.foʊb **-s** -z

homophobia ˌhəʊ.məˈfəʊ.bi.ə ⓊⓈ ˌhoʊ.məˈfoʊ-

homophobic ˌhəʊ.məˈfəʊ.bɪk ⓊⓈ ˌhoʊ.məˈfoʊ-

homophone ˈhɒm.ə.fəʊn, ˈhəʊ.mə- ⓊⓈ ˈhɑː.mə.foʊn, ˈhoʊ- **-s** -z

homophonic ˌhɒm.əˈfɒn.ɪk, ˌhəʊ.məˈ- ⓊⓈ ˌhɑː.məˈfɑː.nɪk, ˌhoʊ- **-ally** -əl.i, -li

homophon|ous həˈmɒf.ən|.əs, hɒmˈɒf- ⓊⓈ hoʊˈmɑː.fən-, hə- **-y** -i

homorganic ˌhɒm.ɔːˈgæn.ɪk ⓊⓈ ˌhoʊ.mɔːrˈ-, ˌhɑː-

homo sapiens ˌhəʊ.məʊˈsæp.i.enz, -ənz ⓊⓈ ˌhoʊ.moʊˈ-

homosexual ˌhəʊ.məʊˈsek.ʃu.əl, ˌhɒm.əʊˈ-, ˈ-sju-, -ʃəl ⓊⓈ ˌhoʊ.moʊˈsek.ʃu.əl, -məˈ- **-s** -z **-ist/s** -ɪst/s

homosexuality ˌhəʊ.məʊˌsek.ʃuˈæl.ə.ti, ˌhɒm.əʊ-, -sjuˈ-, -ɪ.ti ⓊⓈ ˌhoʊ.moʊ.sek.ʃuˈæl.ə.t̬i, -mə-

homozygous ˌhɒm.əˈzaɪ.gəs ⓊⓈ ˌhoʊ.məˈ-, ˌhɑː-

Homs hɒmz ⓊⓈ hɔːmz

homuncul|us hɒmˈʌŋ.kjə.l|əs, həˈmʌŋ-, -kjʊ- ⓊⓈ hoʊˈmʌŋ.kjə-, hə- **-i** -aɪ

hon. (H) (*abbrev. for* **honourable**) ˈɒn.ər.ə.bl̩ ⓊⓈ ˈɑː.nɚ- (*abbrev. for* **honorary**) ˈɒn.ər.ə.ri, ˈ-ər.i ⓊⓈ ˈɑː.nɚ.er.i

honcho ˈhɒn.tʃəʊ ⓊⓈ ˈhɑːn.tʃoʊ **-s** -z **-ing** -ɪŋ **-ed** -d

Honda® ˈhɒn.də ⓊⓈ ˈhɑːn.də

Hondur|as hɒnˈdjʊə.r|əs, -ˈdʊə-, -ˈdjɔː-, -r|æs ⓊⓈ hɑːnˈdʊr|.əs, -ˈdjʊr- **-an/s** -ən/z

hon|e (H) həʊn US hoʊn **-es** -z **-ing** -ɪŋ **-ed** -d
Honecker ˈhɒn.ɪ.kəʳ, -ek.əʳ US ˈhɑː.nɪ.kɚ
Honegger ˈhɒn.ɪ.gəʳ, -eg.əʳ US ˈhɑː.nɪ.gɚ, ˈhoʊ-
honest ˈɒn.ɪst, -əst US ˈɑː.nɪst **-ly** -li
honest-to-goodness ˌɒn.ɪs*t*.təˈgʊd.nəs, -əs*t*-, -nɪs US ˌɑː.nɪst.təˈ-
honesty ˈɒn.ɪ.sti, ˈ-ə- US ˈɑː.nɪ-
hon|ey ˈhʌn|.i **-eyed** -id **-ied** -id
honeybee ˈhʌn.i.biː **-s** -z
Honeybourne ˈhʌn.i.bɔːn US -bɔːrn
honeybun ˈhʌn.i.bʌn **-s** -z
honeybunch ˈhʌn.i.bʌn*t*ʃ **-es** -ɪz
Honeychurch ˈhʌn.i.tʃɜːtʃ US -tʃɝːtʃ
honeycomb (H) ˈhʌn.i.kəʊm US -koʊm **-s** -z **-ed** -d
honeydew ˈhʌn.i.djuː US -duː, -djuː **ˌhoneydew ˈmelon**
honeyeater ˈhʌn.iˌiː.təʳ US -t̬ɚ **-s** -z
honeymoon ˈhʌn.i.muːn **-s** -z **-ing** -ɪŋ **-ed** -d **-er/s** -əʳ/z US -ɚ/z
honeysucker ˈhʌn.iˌsʌk.əʳ US -ɚ **-s** -z
honeysuckle ˈhʌn.iˌsʌk.l̩ **-s** -z
hong hɒŋ US hɑːŋ **-s** -z
Hong Kong ˌhɒŋˈkɒŋ US ˈhɑːŋˌkɑːŋ, ˈhɔːŋ-, -ˌkɔːŋ, ˌ-ˈ-
Honiara ˌhəʊ.niˈɑː.rə US ˌhoʊ.niˈɑːr.ə
Honi soit qui mal y pense ˌɒn.iˌswɑː.kiːˌmæl.iˈpɑ̃ː*nt*s US ˌɔː.ni-
Honiton ˈhɒn.ɪ.tᵊn *locally:* ˈhʌn- US ˈhɑː.nə.t̬ən
honk hɒŋk US hɑːŋk, hɔːŋk **-s** -s **-ing** -ɪŋ **-ed** -t
honk|ie, honk|y ˈhɒŋ.k|i US ˈhɑːŋ-, ˈhɔːŋ- **-ies** -iz
honky-tonk ˈhɒŋ.ki.tɒŋk, ˌ--ˈ- US ˈhɑːŋ.ki.tɑːŋk, ˈhɔːŋ-, -tɔːŋk
Honolulu ˌhɒn.ᵊlˈuː.luː US ˌhɑː.nəˈluː-
hon|or (H) ˈɒn|.əʳ US ˈɑː.n|ɚ **-ors** -əz US -ɚz **-oring** -ᵊr.ɪŋ **-ored** -əd US -ɚd
honorab|le ˈhɒn.ᵊr.ə.b|l̩ US ˈɑː.nɚ- **-ly** -li **-leness** -l̩.nəs, -nɪs
honorarium ˌɒn.əˈreə.ri.əm, -ˈrɑː- US ˌɑː.nəˈrer.i- **-s** -z
honorary ˈɒn.ᵊr.ə.ri, ˈ-ᵊr.i US ˈɑː.nə.rer.i
honorific ˌɒn.ᵊrˈɪf.ɪk US ˌɑː.nəˈrɪf- **-s** -s
Honorius həˈnɔː.ri.əs, hɒnˈɔː- US hoʊˈnɔːr.i-, hə-
hon|our ˈɒn|.əʳ US ˈɑː.n|ɚ **-ours** -əz US -ɚz **-ouring** -ᵊr.ɪŋ **-oured** -əd US -ɚd **ˈhonours ˌlist**
honourab|le (H) ˈɒn.ᵊr.ə.b|l̩ US ˈɑː.nɚ- **-ly** -li **-leness** -l̩.nəs, -nɪs
Honshu ˈhɒn.ʃuː US ˈhɑːn-
Honyman ˈhʌn.i.mən
Hoo huː
hooch huːtʃ
hood (H) hʊd **-s** -z **-ing** -ɪŋ **-ed** -ɪd **-less** -ləs, -lɪs
-hood -hʊd
Note: Suffix. Normally unstressed, e.g. **womanhood** /ˈwʊm.ən.hʊd/.
hoodlum ˈhuːd.ləm, ˈhʊd- **-s** -z
hoodwink ˈhʊd.wɪŋk **-s** -s **-ing** -ɪŋ **-ed** -t
hooey ˈhuː.i
hoo|f huː|f US hʊ|f, huː|f **-fs** -fs **-ves** -vz **-fing** -fɪŋ **-fed** -ft **-fer/s** -fəʳ/z US -fɚ/z
Hoog(h)ly ˈhuː.gli
hook (H) hʊk **-s** -s **-ing** -ɪŋ **-ed** -t **ˌhook and ˈeye; ˌHook of ˈHolland; by ˌhook or by ˈcrook; ˌhook, ˌline, and ˈsinker**
hookah ˈhʊk.ə, -ɑː US ˈhʊk.ə, ˈhuː.kə, -kɑː **-s** -z
Hooke hʊk
hooker (H) ˈhʊk.əʳ US -ɚ **-s** -z
hookey ˈhʊk.i
hookup ˈhʊk.ʌp **-s** -s
hookworm ˈhʊk.wɜːm US -wɝːm **-s** -z
hooky ˈhʊk.i
Hooley ˈhuː.li
hooligan (H) ˈhuː.lɪ.gᵊn, -lə- US -lɪ- **-s** -z **-ism** -ɪ.zᵊm
Hoon huːn
hoop huːp US huːp, hʊp **-s** -s **-ing** -ɪŋ **-ed** -t
hooper (H) ˈhuː.pəʳ US -pɚ **-s** -z
hoopla ˈhuːp.lɑː, ˈhʊp-
hoopoe ˈhuː.puː **-s** -z
hoorah hʊˈrɑː, hə-, ˌhuː- **-s** -z
hooray hʊˈreɪ, hə-, ˌhuː-
hooray Henr|y ˌhuː.reɪˈhen.r|i **-ies** -iz
hoot huːt **-s** -s **-ing** -ɪŋ US ˈhuː.t̬ɪŋ **-ed** -ɪd US ˈhuː.t̬ɪd
hootch huːtʃ
hootenan|ny ˈhuː.tᵊn.æn|.i **-nies** -iz
hooter ˈhuː.təʳ US -t̬ɚ **-s** -z
hoov|er (H®) ˈhuː.v|əʳ US -v|ɚ **-ers** -əz US -ɚz **-ering** -ᵊr.ɪŋ **-ered** -əd US -ɚd
hooves *(from* **hoof)** huːvz US hʊvz, huːvz
hop hɒp US hɑːp **-s** -s **-ping** -ɪŋ **-ped** -t **ˌhopping ˈmad**
Hopcraft ˈhɒp.krɑːft US ˈhɑːp.kræft
hop|e (H) həʊp US hoʊp **-es** -s **-ing** -ɪŋ **-ed** -t **ˈhope ˌchest**
hopeful (H) ˈhəʊp.fᵊl, -fʊl US ˈhoʊp- **-s** -z **-ly** -i **-ness** -nəs, -nɪs
hopeless ˈhəʊp.ləs, -lɪs US ˈhoʊp- **-ly** -li **-ness** -nəs, -nɪs
Hopi ˈhəʊ.pi US ˈhoʊ-
Hopkins ˈhɒp.kɪnz US ˈhɑːp-
Hopkinson ˈhɒp.kɪn.sən US ˈhɑːp-
hoplite ˈhɒp.laɪt US ˈhɑː.plaɪt **-s** -s
hopper (H) ˈhɒp.əʳ US ˈhɑː.pɚ **-s** -z
hop-pick|er ˈhɒpˌpɪk|.əʳ US ˈhɑːpˌpɪk|.ɚ **-ers** -əz US -ɚz **-ing** -ɪŋ
Hoppner ˈhɒp.nəʳ US ˈhɑːp.nɚ **-s** -z
hopscotch ˈhɒp.skɒtʃ US ˈhɑːp.skɑːtʃ
Hopton ˈhɒp.tən US ˈhɑːp-
Hor hɔːʳ US hɔːr
Horace ˈhɒr.ɪs, -əs US ˈhɔːr.ɪs
Horae ˈhɔː.riː US ˈhoʊ.riː, ˈhɔːr.iː
Horatian həˈreɪ.ʃᵊn, hɒrˈeɪ-, -ʃi.ən US hɔːˈreɪ-, hə-
Horatio həˈreɪ.ʃi.əʊ, hɒrˈeɪ- US hɔːˈreɪ-, hə-
Horati|us həˈreɪ.ʃ|əs, hɒrˈeɪ-, -ʃi|.əs US hɔːˈreɪ-, hə-
Horbury ˈhɔː.bᵊr.i US ˈhɔːrˌber-
horde hɔːd US hɔːrd **-s** -z
Horeb ˈhɔː.reb US ˈhɔːr.eb
horehound ˈhɔː.haʊnd US ˈhɔːr- **-s** -z
horizon həˈraɪ.zᵊn **-s** -z
horizontal ˌhɒr.ɪˈzɒn.tᵊl, -əˈ- US ˌhɔːr.ɪˈzɑːn- **-ly** -i
Horley ˈhɔː.li US ˈhɔːr-
Horlick ˈhɔː.lɪk US ˈhɔːr-
Horlicks® ˈhɔː.lɪks US ˈhɔːr-
hormonal hɔːˈməʊ.nᵊl US hɔːrˈmoʊ-
hormone ˈhɔː.məʊn US ˈhɔːr.moʊn **-s** -z **ˌhormone reˈplacement ˌtherapy**
Hormuz ˌhɔːˈmuːz, ˈhɔː.məz US ˈhɔːr.mʌz, -muːz
horn (H) hɔːn US hɔːrn **-s** -z **ˌHorn of ˈAfrica; ˌhorn of ˈplenty; take the ˌbull by the ˈhorns**
hornbeam ˈhɔːn.biːm, ˈhɔːm- US ˈhɔːrn- **-s** -z
hornbill ˈhɔːn.bɪl, ˈhɔːm- US ˈhɔːrn- **-s** -z
hornblende ˈhɔːn.blend, ˈhɔːm- US ˈhɔːrn-
Hornblower ˈhɔːnˌbləʊ.əʳ, ˈhɔːm- US ˈhɔːrnˌbloʊ.ɚ
hornbook ˈhɔːn.bʊk, ˈhɔːm- US ˈhɔːrn- **-s** -s
Hornby ˈhɔːn.bi, ˈhɔːm- US ˈhɔːrn-
Horncastle ˈhɔːnˌkɑː.sᵊl, ˈhɔːŋ- US ˈhɔːrnˌkæs.ᵊl
Hornchurch ˈhɔːn.tʃɜːtʃ US ˈhɔːrn.tʃɝːtʃ
Horne hɔːn US hɔːrn
horned *of cattle, birds, etc.:* hɔːnd US hɔːrnd *poetic:* ˈhɔː.nɪd US ˈhɔːr-
Hornell hɔːˈnel US hɔːr-
Horner ˈhɔː.nəʳ US ˈhɔːr.nɚ
hornet ˈhɔː.nɪt, -nət US ˈhɔːr- **-s** -s **ˈhornet's ˌnest, ˌhornet's ˈnest**
Horniman ˈhɔː.nɪ.mən US ˈhɔːr-
hornpipe ˈhɔːn.paɪp, ˈhɔːm- US ˈhɔːrn- **-s** -s
horn-rimmed ˌhɔːnˈrɪmd US ˈhɔːrn.rɪmd *stress shift, British only:* ˌhorn-rimmed ˈspectacles
Hornsea ˈhɔːn.siː US ˈhɔːrn-
Hornsey ˈhɔːn.zi US ˈhɔːrn-
hornswoggl|e ˈhɔːnˌswɒg.l̩ US ˈhɔːrnˌswɑː.gl̩ **-es** -z **-ing** -ɪŋ **-ed** -d
Hornung ˈhɔː.nəŋ US ˈhɔːr-
hornwork ˈhɔːn.wɜːk US ˈhɔːrn.wɝːk **-s** -s

horn|y ˈhɔː.n|i US ˈhɔːr- **-ier** -i.əʳ US -i.ɚ **-iest** -i.ɪst, -i.əst **-iness** -ɪ.nəs, -ɪ.nɪs
horography hɒrˈɒg.rə.fi, hɔːˈrɒg-, hə- US hɔːˈrɑːg-
horologe ˈhɒr.ə.lɒdʒ, ˈhɔː.rə-, -ləʊdʒ US ˈhɔːr.ə.loʊdʒ **-es** -ɪz
horologic ˌhɒr.əˈlɒdʒ.ɪk, ˌhɔː.rəˈ- US ˌhɔːr.əˈlɑː.dʒɪk **-al** -ᵊl
horological ˌhɒr.əˈlɒdʒ.ɪ.kᵊl, ˌhɔː.rəˈ- US ˌhɔːr.əˈlɑː.dʒɪ-
horolog|y hɒrˈɒl.ə.dʒ|i, hɔːˈrɒl-, hə- US hɔːrˈɑː.lə- **-er/s** -əʳ/z US -ɚ/z **-ist/s** -ɪst/s
horoscope ˈhɒr.ə.skəʊp US ˈhɔːr.ə.skoʊp **-s** -s
horoscopic ˌhɒr.əˈskɒp.ɪk US ˌhɔːr.əˈskɑː.pɪk
Horovitz ˈhɒr.ə.vɪts US ˈhɔːr-
Horowitz ˈhɒr.ə.vɪts, -wɪts US ˈhɔːr.ə.wɪts
horrendous hɒrˈen.dəs, həˈren- US hɔːˈren-, hə- **-ly** -li **-ness** -nəs, -nɪs
horrib|le ˈhɒr.ə.b|l̩, ˈ-ɪ- US ˈhɔːr- **-ly** -li **-leness** -l̩.nəs, -nɪs
horrid ˈhɒr.ɪd US ˈhɔːr- **-er** -əʳ US -ɚ **-est** -ɪst, -əst **-ly** -li **-ness** -nəs, -nɪs
horrific hɒrˈɪf.ɪk, həˈrɪf- US hɔːˈrɪf-, hə- **-ally** -ᵊl.i, -li
horri|fy ˈhɒr.ɪ|.faɪ, ˈ-ə- US ˈhɔːr- **-fies** -faɪz **-fying/ly** -faɪ.ɪŋ/li **-fied** -faɪd
horripilation hɒrˌɪp.ɪˈleɪ.ʃᵊn, -əˈ-; ˌhɒr.ɪ.pɪˈ-, ˌ-ə- US ˌhɔːr.ɪ.pəˈleɪ-
Horrocks ˈhɒr.əks US ˈhɔːr-
horror ˈhɒr.əʳ US ˈhɔːr.ɚ **-s** -z
horror|-stricken ˈhɒr.ə|ˌstrɪk.ᵊn US ˈhɔːr.ɚ|ˌ- **-struck** -strʌk
Horsa ˈhɔː.sə US ˈhɔːr-
hors de combat ˌhɔː.dəˈkɔ̃ːm.bɑː, -ˈkɔːm-, -ˈkɒm-, -bæt US ˌɔːr.də.kɔ̃ːmˈbɑː
hors d'oeuvre ˌɔːˈdɜːv, -ˈdɜːv.rə US ˌɔːrˈdɝːv, -ˈdɝːv.rə **-s** -z
hors|e hɔːs US hɔːrs **-es** -ɪz **-ing** -ɪŋ **-ed** -t ˌ**horse ˈchestnut**; ˈ**horse ˌopera**; ˈ**horse ˌsense**; ˈ**horse ˌshow**; ˈ**horse ˌtrials**; ˌ**flog a ˌdead ˈhorse**; ˌ**hold your ˈhorses**; (ˌ**straight) from the ˌhorse's ˈmouth**
horse-and-buggy ˌhɔːs.ᵊndˈbʌg.i, -ᵊmˈ- US ˌhɔːrs-
horseback ˈhɔːs.bæk US ˈhɔːrs- ˈ**horseback ˌriding**
horsebox ˈhɔːs.bɒks US ˈhɔːrs.bɑːks **-es** -ɪz
horseflesh ˈhɔːs.fleʃ US ˈhɔːrs-
horsefl|y ˈhɔːs.fl|aɪ US ˈhɔːrs- **-ies** -aɪz
Horseguard ˈhɔːs.gɑːd US ˈhɔːrs.gɑːrd **-s** -z
horsehair ˈhɔːs.heəʳ US ˈhɔːrs.her **-s** -z
horselaugh ˈhɔːs.lɑːf US ˈhɔːrs.læf **-s** -s
horse|man (H) ˈhɔːs|.mən US ˈhɔːrs- **-men** -mən, -men **-manship** -mən.ʃɪp
horseplay ˈhɔːs.pleɪ US ˈhɔːrs-
horsepower ˈhɔːsˌpaʊəʳ US ˈhɔːrsˌpaʊr
horseradish ˈhɔːsˌræd.ɪʃ US ˈhɔːrs- **-es** -ɪz
horseshoe ˈhɔːs.ʃuː, ˈhɔːʃ- US ˈhɔːrs-, ˈhɔːrʃ- **-s** -z
horsetail ˈhɔːs.teɪl US ˈhɔːrs- **-s** -z
horsetrad|e ˈhɔːs.treɪd US ˈhɔːrs- **-es** -z **-ing** -ɪŋ **-ed** -ɪd **-er/s** -əʳ/z US -ɚ/z
horse-trading ˈhɔːsˌtreɪ.dɪŋ US ˈhɔːrs-
horsewhip ˈhɔːs.*h*wɪp US ˈhɔːrs- **-s** -s **-ping** -ɪŋ **-ped** -t
horse|woman ˈhɔːs|ˌwʊm.ən US ˈhɔːrs- **-women** -ˌwɪm.ɪn
hors|ey ˈhɔː.s|i US ˈhɔːr- **-ier** -i.əʳ US -i.ɚ **-iest** -i.ɪst, -i.əst **-ily** -ɪ.li, -ᵊl.i **-iness** -ɪ.nəs, -ɪ.nɪs
Horsfall ˈhɔːs.fɔːl US ˈhɔːrs.fɔːl, -fɑːl
Horsforth ˈhɔːs.fəθ US ˈhɔːrs.fɚθ
Horsham ˈhɔː.ʃᵊm US ˈhɔːr-
Horsley ˈhɔːz.li, ˈhɔːs- US ˈhɔːrz-, ˈhɔːrs-
Horsmonden *in Kent:* ˌhɔːz.mənˈden *old-fashioned local pronunciation:* ˌhɔː.sᵊn- US ˌhɔːrz.mᵊnˈ-
hors|y ˈhɔː.s|i US ˈhɔːr- **-ier** -i.əʳ US -i.ɚ **-iest** -i.ɪst, -i.əst **-ily** -ɪ.li, -ᵊl.i **-iness** -ɪ.nəs, -ɪ.nɪs
horta|tive ˈhɔː.tə|.tɪv US ˈhɔːr.t̬ə|.t̬ɪv **-tory** -tᵊr.i US -tɔːr.i
Hortensi|a hɔːˈten*t*.si|.ə, -ˈten.*t*ʃi|.ə, -*t*ʃ|ə US hɔːrˈten.*t*ʃi- **-us** -əs
horticultural ˌhɔː.tɪˈkʌl.tʃᵊr.ᵊl, -təˈ-, -tʃʊ.rᵊl US ˌhɔːr.t̬əˈkʌl.tʃɚ.ᵊl **-ist/s** -ɪst/s
horticulture ˈhɔː.tɪ.kʌl.tʃəʳ, -tə- US ˈhɔːr.t̬ə.kʌl.tʃɚ
Horton ˈhɔː.tᵊn US ˈhɔːr-
Horus ˈhɔː.rəs US ˈhɔːr.əs
Horwich ˈhɒr.ɪtʃ US ˈhɔːr.ɪtʃ
Hosack ˈhɒs.ək US ˈhɑː.sək
hosanna həʊˈzæn.ə US hoʊ- **-s** -z
hos|e həʊz US hoʊz **-es** -ɪz **-ing** -ɪŋ **-ed** -d
Hosea həʊˈzɪə US hoʊˈzeɪ.ə, -ˈziː-
hosepipe ˈhəʊz.paɪp US ˈhoʊz- **-s** -s
hoser ˈhəʊ.zəʳ US ˈhoʊ.zɚ **-s** -z
hosier (H) ˈhəʊ.zi.əʳ, -ʒəʳ US ˈhoʊ.ʒɚ **-s** -z
hosiery ˈhəʊ.zi.ə.ri, -ʒᵊr.i US ˈhoʊ.ʒɚ.i
Hoskins ˈhɒs.kɪnz US ˈhɑː.skɪnz
Hosmer ˈhɒz.məʳ US ˈhɑːz.mɚ
hospic|e ˈhɒs.pɪs US ˈhɑː.spɪs **-es** -ɪz
hospitab|le hɒsˈpɪt.ə.b|l̩, həˈspɪt-; ˈhɒs.pɪ.tə- US ˈhɑː.spɪ.t̬ə-; hɑːˈspɪt̬.ə- **-ly** -li **-leness** -l̩.nəs, -nɪs
hospital ˈhɒs.pɪ.tᵊl US ˈhɑː.spɪ.t̬ᵊl **-s** -z
Hospitaler ˈhɒs.pɪ.tᵊl.əʳ US ˈhɑː.spɪ.t̬ᵊl.ɚ **-s** -z
hospitalit|y ˌhɒs.pɪˈtæl.ə.t|i, -pəˈ-, -ɪ.t|i US ˌhɑː.spɪˈtæl.ə.t̬|i **-ies** -iz
hospitalization, -isa- ˌhɒs.pɪ.tᵊl.aɪˈzeɪ.ʃᵊn, -pə-, -ɪˈ- US ˌhɑː.spɪ.t̬ᵊl.ɪˈ-
hospitaliz|e, -is|e ˈhɒs.pɪ.tᵊl.aɪz, -pə- US ˈhɑː.spɪ.t̬ᵊl- **-es** -ɪz **-ing** -ɪŋ **-ed** -d
Hospitaller ˈhɒs.pɪ.tᵊl.əʳ US ˈhɑː.spɪ.t̬ᵊl.ɚ **-s** -z
host (H) həʊst US hoʊst **-s** -s **-ing** -ɪŋ **-ed** -ɪd
hosta ˈhɒs.tə, ˈhəʊ.stə US ˈhɑː-, ˈhoʊ- **-s** -z
hostag|e ˈhɒs.tɪdʒ US ˈhɑː.stɪdʒ **-es** -ɪz
hostel ˈhɒs.tᵊl US ˈhɑː.stᵊl **-s** -z
hostell|er ˈhɒs.tᵊl|.əʳ US ˈhɑː.stᵊl|.ɚ **-ers** -əz US -ɚz **-ing** -ɪŋ
hostelr|y ˈhɒs.tᵊl.r|i US ˈhɑː.stᵊl- **-ies** -iz
hostess ˈhəʊ.stɪs, -stes, -stəs; ˌhəʊˈstes US ˈhoʊ.stɪs, -stəs **-es** -ɪz
hostile ˈhɒs.taɪl US ˈhɑː.stᵊl, -staɪl **-ly** -li
hostilit|y hɒsˈtɪl.ə.t|i, -ɪ.t|i US hɑːˈstɪl.ə.t̬|i **-ies** -iz
hostler ˈɒs.ləʳ, ˈhɒs- US ˈhɑː.slɚ, ˈɑː- **-s** -z
hot hɒt US hɑːt **-ter** -əʳ US ˈhɑː.t̬ɚ **-test** -ɪst, -əst US ˈhɑː.t̬ɪst, -t̬əst **-ly** -li **-ness** -nəs, -nɪs **-s** -s **-ting** -ɪŋ US ˈhɑː.t̬ɪŋ **-ted** -ɪd US ˈhɑː.t̬ɪd ˌ**hot ˈair**; ˌ**hot cross ˈbun**; ˈ**hot ˌdog**; ˌ**hot ˈdog** ˈ**hot ˌpants**; ˌ**hot poˈtato**; ˈ**hot ˌseat**, ˌ**hot ˈseat**; ˌ**hot ˈstuff**; ˌ**hot ˈticket**; ˌ**hot ˈwater**; ˌ**blow ˌhot and ˈcold**; ˌ**sell like ˌhot ˈcakes**; US ˌ**sell like ˈhot ˌcakes**
hotbed ˈhɒt.bed US ˈhɑːt- **-s** -z
hot-blooded ˌhɒtˈblʌd.ɪd US ˌhɑːt- *stress shift:* ˌhot-blooded ˈyouth
Hotchkiss ˈhɒtʃ.kɪs US ˈhɑːtʃ-
hotchpot ˈhɒtʃ.pɒt US ˈhɑːtʃ.pɑːt **-s** -s
hotchpotch ˈhɒtʃ.pɒtʃ US ˈhɑːtʃ.pɑːtʃ **-es** -ɪz
hotdog ˈhɒt.dɒg US ˈhɑːt.dɑːg, -dɔːg **-s** -z **-ging** -ɪŋ **-ged** -d
hotel həʊˈtel, əʊ- US hoʊ- **-s** -z
Note: Some British speakers use the form /əʊˈtel/ always; others use it occasionally when the word is not initial, with 'an' as preceding indefinite article.
hotelier həʊˈtel.i.eɪ, əʊ-, -əʳ US ˌhoʊ.tᵊlˈjeɪ, ˌoʊ-; hoʊˈtel.jɚ **-s** -z
hotfoo|t ˌhɒtˈfʊ|t, ˈ-- US ˈhɑːt.fʊ|t **-ts** -ts **-ting** -tɪŋ US -t̬ɪŋ **-ted** -tɪd US -t̬ɪd
Hotham ˈhʌð.əm
hothead ˈhɒt.hed US ˈhɑːt- **-s** -z
hotheaded ˌhɒtˈhed.ɪd, ˈ-ˌ-- US ˈhɑːtˌhed.ɪd, ˌ-ˈ-- **-ly** -li **-ness** -nəs, -nɪs
hothou|se ˈhɒt.haʊ|s US ˈhɑːt- **-ses** -zɪz
hotline ˈhɒt.laɪn US ˈhɑːt- **-s** -z
Hotol ˈhɒt.ɒl, ˈhoʊ.tɒl US ˈhɑː.tɑːl, ˈhoʊ-
hotplate ˈhɒt.pleɪt US ˈhɑːt- **-s** -s

Hotpoint® 'hɒt.pɔɪnt ⓤⓢ 'hɑːt-
hotpot 'hɒt.pɒt ⓤⓢ 'hɑːt.pɑːt **-s** -s
hotrod 'hɒt.rɒd ⓤⓢ 'hɑːt.rɑːd **-s** -z **-ding** -ɪŋ **-ded** -ɪd **-der/s** -əʳ/z ⓤⓢ -ɚ/z
hotshot 'hɒt.ʃɒt ⓤⓢ 'hɑːt.ʃɑːt **-s** -s
hotspot 'hɒt.spɒt ⓤⓢ 'hɑːt.spɑːt **-s** -s
hotspur (H) 'hɒt.spɜːʳ, -spəʳ ⓤⓢ 'hɑːt.spɝː, -spɚ **-s** -z
hot-tempered ˌhɒt'tem.pəd ⓤⓢ ˌhɑːt'tem.pɚd *stress shift:* ˌhot-tempered 'fighter
Hottentot 'hɒt.ən.tɒt ⓤⓢ 'hɑː.tən.tɑːt **-s** -s
hot-water bottle ˌhɒt'wɔː.tə,bɒt.l̩ ⓤⓢ ˌhɑːt'wɑː.t̬ɚ,bɑː.t̬l̩, -'wɔː- **-s** -z
Houdini huː'diː.ni
hough hɒk ⓤⓢ hɑːk **-s** -s **-ing** -ɪŋ **-ed** -t
Hough hʌf, hɒf, haʊ ⓤⓢ hʌf, hɔːf, hɑːf
Houghall 'hɒf.əl ⓤⓢ 'hɑː.fəl
Hougham 'hʌf.əm
Houghton 'hɔː.tən, 'haʊ-, 'həʊ- ⓤⓢ 'hoʊ-, 'hɔː-, 'hɑː-, 'haʊ-
Note: /'hɔː.tən, 'haʊ.tən/ are more usual in British English when the word is a surname. The city in Michigan is /'həʊ- ⓤⓢ 'hoʊ-/.
Houghton-le-Spring ˌhəʊ.tən.lə'sprɪŋ, ˌhaʊ-, -li'- ⓤⓢ ˌhoʊ-, ˌhaʊ-
Houllier '*h*uː.li.eɪ
Houltby 'həʊlt.bi ⓤⓢ 'hoʊlt-
houm(o)us 'huː.mʊs, 'hʊm.ʊs, -əs ⓤⓢ 'hʌm.əs, 'hʊm-
hound haʊnd **-s** -z **-ing** -ɪŋ **-ed** -ɪd
Houndsditch 'haʊn*dz*.dɪtʃ
houndstooth 'haʊn*dz*.tuːθ, ˌ-'- ⓤⓢ '--
Hounslow 'haʊnz.ləʊ ⓤⓢ -loʊ
hour aʊəʳ ⓤⓢ aʊr, aʊɚ **-s** -z **-ly** -li
hourglass 'aʊə.glɑːs ⓤⓢ 'aʊr.glæs, 'aʊɚ- **-es** -ɪz
houri 'hʊə.ri ⓤⓢ 'hʊr.i, 'huːr- **-s** -z
Housden 'haʊz.dən
hou|se (H) *(n.)* haʊ|s **-ses** -zɪz ˌ**house ar'rest; 'house ˌhusband; 'house ˌmartin; 'house ˌmusic; ˌHouse of 'Commons; ˌHouse of 'Lords; ˌHouse of Repre'sentatives; ˌHouses of 'Parliament; 'house ˌparty; 'house ˌsparrow; ˌeat one out of ˌhouse and 'home; ˌbring the 'house ˌdown; get ˌon like a 'house on ˌfire; ˌset one's 'house in ˌorder**
hous|e *(v.)* haʊz **-es** -ɪz **-ing** -ɪŋ **-ed** -d
houseboat 'haʊs.bəʊt ⓤⓢ -boʊt **-s** -s
housebound 'haʊs.baʊnd
housebreak|er 'haʊsˌbreɪ.k|əʳ ⓤⓢ -k|ɚ **-ers** -əz ⓤⓢ -ɚz **-ing** -ɪŋ
house-broken 'haʊsˌbrəʊ.kən ⓤⓢ -ˌbroʊ-
housebuy|er 'haʊsˌbaɪ|.əʳ ⓤⓢ -ɚ **-ers** -z **-ing** -ɪŋ
housecoat 'haʊs.kəʊt ⓤⓢ -koʊt **-s** -s
housefather 'haʊsˌfɑː.ðəʳ ⓤⓢ -ðɚ **-s** -z
housefl|y 'haʊs.fl|aɪ **-ies** -aɪz
houseful 'haʊs.fʊl **-s** -z
houseguest 'haʊs.gest **-s** -s
household (H) 'haʊs.*h*əʊld ⓤⓢ -*h*oʊld **-s** -z **-er/s** -əʳ/z ⓤⓢ -ɚ/z
housekeeper 'haʊsˌkiː.pəʳ ⓤⓢ -pɚ **-s** -z ⓤⓢ -z
housekeeping 'haʊsˌkiː.pɪŋ
Housel 'haʊ.zəl
houseleek 'haʊs.liːk **-s** -s
housemaid 'haʊs.meɪd **-s** -z
house|man 'haʊs|.mən, -mæn **-men** -mən, -men
housemaster 'haʊsˌmɑː.stəʳ ⓤⓢ -ˌmæs.tɚ **-s** -z
housemate 'haʊs.meɪt **-s** -s
housemother 'haʊsˌmʌð.əʳ ⓤⓢ -ɚ **-s** -z
houseplant 'haʊs.plɑːnt ⓤⓢ -plænt **-s** -s
houseproud 'haʊs.praʊd
houseroom 'haʊs.rʊm, -ruːm ⓤⓢ -ruːm, -rʊm
house|sit 'haʊs|.sɪt **-sits** -sɪts **-sitting** -ˌsɪt.ɪŋ ⓤⓢ -ˌsɪt̬.ɪŋ **-sat** -sæt **-sitter/s** -ˌsɪt.əʳ/z ⓤⓢ -ˌsɪt̬.ɚ/z
Housestead's Fort ˌhaʊs.stedz'fɔːt ⓤⓢ -'fɔːrt
house-to-house ˌhaʊs.tə'haʊs *stress shift:* ˌhouse-to-house 'search
housetop 'haʊs.tɒp ⓤⓢ -tɑːp **-s** -s
housewares 'haʊs.weəz ⓤⓢ -werz
housewarming 'haʊsˌwɔː.mɪŋ ⓤⓢ -ˌwɔːr- **-s** -z
housewife *woman:* 'haʊs.waɪf; *old-fashioned:* 'hʌz.ɪf **housewives** 'haʊs.waɪvz; *old-fashioned:* -ɪvz **housewifes** *old-fashioned:* 'hʌz.ɪfs
housewi|fe *needle-case:* 'hʌz.ɪ|f **-fes** -fs **-ves** -vz
housewifel|y 'haʊsˌwaɪf.l|i **-iness** -ɪ.nəs, -ɪ.nɪs
housewifery 'haʊsˌwɪf.ər.i; *old-fashioned:* 'hʌz.ɪ.fri ⓤⓢ 'haʊsˌwaɪ.fɚ.i, ˌ-fri
housework 'haʊs.wɜːk ⓤⓢ -wɝːk
housey-housey, housie-housie ˌhaʊ.si'haʊ.si, -zi'haʊ.zi
housing 'haʊ.zɪŋ **'housing asˌsociation; 'housing deˌvelopment; 'housing eˌstate; 'housing ˌlist**
Housman 'haʊs.mən
Houston *English surname:* 'huː.stən, 'haʊ- *Scottish surname:* 'huː.stən *in US:* 'hjuː.stən
Houyhnhnm 'huː.ɪ.nəm ⓤⓢ 'hwɪn.əm, hu'ɪn- **-s** -z
hove (H) *(from* **heave***)* həʊv ⓤⓢ hoʊv
hovel 'hɒv.əl, 'hʌv- ⓤⓢ 'hʌv-, 'hɑː.vəl **-s** -z
Hovell 'həʊ.vəl, 'hɒv.əl, həʊ'vel ⓤⓢ 'hoʊ.vəl, 'hɑː-, hoʊ'vel
Hovenden 'hɒv.ən.dən ⓤⓢ 'hoʊ.vən-
hov|er 'hɒv|.əʳ ⓤⓢ 'hʌv|.ɚ, 'hɑː.v|ɚ **-ers** -əz ⓤⓢ -ɚz **-ering** -ər.ɪŋ **-ered** -əd ⓤⓢ -ɚd
hovercraft 'hɒv.ə.krɑːft ⓤⓢ 'hʌv.ɚ.kræft, 'hɑː.vɚ- **-s** -s
hoverfl|y 'hɒv.ə.fl|aɪ ⓤⓢ 'hʌv.ɚ-, 'hɑː.vɚ- **-ies** -aɪz
hoverport 'hɒv.ə.pɔːt ⓤⓢ 'hʌv.ɚ.pɔːrt, 'hɑː.vɚ- **-s** -s
Hovis® 'həʊ.vɪs ⓤⓢ 'hoʊ-
how (H) haʊ
Howard haʊəd ⓤⓢ haʊɚd
Howarth haʊəθ ⓤⓢ haʊɚθ
howdah 'haʊ.də **-s** -z
Howden 'haʊ.dən
how-do-you-do ˌhaʊ.djʊ'duː, -djə'-, -dʒʊ'-, -dʒə'-, '--- ⓤⓢ 'haʊ.də.juː.duː, '-djə.duː
howdy 'haʊ.di
howdy-do ˌhaʊ.di'duː **-s** -z
Howe haʊ
Howell haʊəl **-s** -z
Howerd haʊəd ⓤⓢ haʊɚd
Howers haʊəz ⓤⓢ haʊɚz
Howes haʊz
however haʊ'ev.əʳ ⓤⓢ -ɚ
Howick 'haʊ.ɪk
Howie 'haʊ.i
Howitt 'haʊ.ɪt
howitzer 'haʊ.ɪt.səʳ ⓤⓢ -sɚ **-s** -z
howl haʊl **-s** -z **-ing** -ɪŋ **-ed** -d
howler 'haʊ.ləʳ ⓤⓢ -lɚ **-s** -z
Howlett 'haʊ.lɪt
Howley 'haʊ.li
Howorth haʊəθ ⓤⓢ haʊɚθ
Howse haʊz
howsoever ˌhaʊ.səʊ'ev.əʳ ⓤⓢ -soʊ'ev.ɚ
Howson 'haʊ.sən
Howth həʊθ ⓤⓢ hoʊθ
how-to 'haʊ.tuː **-s** -z
Hoxha 'hɒdʒ.ə ⓤⓢ 'hɔː.dʒɑː
Hoxton 'hɒk.stən ⓤⓢ 'hɑːk-
hoy (H) hɔɪ **-s** -z
hoyden (H) 'hɔɪ.dən **-s** -z
Hoylake 'hɔɪ.leɪk
Hoyland Nether ˌhɔɪ.lən*d*'neð.əʳ ⓤⓢ -ɚ
HP ˌeɪtʃ'piː
HQ ˌeɪtʃ'kjuː
HRH ˌeɪtʃ.ɑːʳ'eɪtʃ ⓤⓢ -ɑːr'-
HRT ˌeitʃ.ɑː'tiː ⓤⓢ -ɑːr'-
HSBC ˌeɪtʃ.esˌbiː'siː
Huang Ho ˌhwæŋ'həʊ ⓤⓢ ˌhwɑːŋ'hoʊ, ˌhwæŋ-
hub hʌb **-s** -z
Hubbard 'hʌb.əd ⓤⓢ -ɚd
Hubble 'hʌb.l̩
hubble-bubble 'hʌb.l̩ˌbʌb.l̩ **-s** -z
hubbub 'hʌb.ʌb, -əb ⓤⓢ -ʌb **-s** -z
hubb|y 'hʌb|.i **-ies** -iz
hubcap 'hʌb.kæp **-s** -s
Hubert 'hjuː.bət ⓤⓢ -bɚt
hubris 'hjuː.brɪs, 'huː- ⓤⓢ 'hjuː-

ubristic hjuːˈbrɪs.tɪk, huː- (US) hjuː-
uckaback ˈhʌk.ə.bæk **-s** -s
uckle ˈhʌk.l̩
uckleberr|y **(H)** ˈhʌk.l̩.bər|.i, -ˌber|.i (US) -ˈber- **-ies** -iz
ucknall, **Hucknell** ˈhʌk.nəl
uckster ˈhʌk.stər (US) -stɚ **-s** -z
uddersfield ˈhʌd.əz.fiːld (US) -ɚz-
uddl|e ˈhʌd.l̩ **-es** -z **-ing** -ɪŋ, ˈhʌd.lɪŋ **-ed** -d
ud(d)leston(e) ˈhʌd.l̩.stən
udibras ˈhjuː.dɪ.bræs, -də-
udnott ˈhʌd.nɒt, -nət (US) -nɑːt
udson ˈhʌd.sən
ue hjuː **-s** -z ˌ**hue and** ˈ**cry**
ueffer ˈhef.ər (US) -ɚ
uelva ˈwel.və (US) -və, -vɑː
uevos rancheros ˌweɪ.vɒs.rænˈtʃeə.rɒs (US) -voʊs.rænˈtʃer.oʊs
uff **(H)** hʌf **-s** -s **-ing** -ɪŋ **-ed** -t
uffish ˈhʌf.ɪʃ **-ly** -li **-ness** -nəs, -nɪs
uffman ˈhʌf.mən
uff|y ˈhʌf|.i **-ier** -i.ər (US) -i.ɚ **-iest** -i.ɪst, -i.əst **-ily** -ɪ.li, -əl.i **-iness** -ɪ.nəs, -ɪ.nɪs
ug hʌg **-s** -z **-ging** -ɪŋ **-ged** -d
ugall ˈhjuː.gəl
ug|e hjuːdʒ **-er** -ər (US) -ɚ **-est** -ɪst, -əst **-ely** -li **-eness** -nəs, -nɪs
ugger-mugger ˈhʌg.əˌmʌg.ər, ˌhʌg.əˈmʌg- (US) ˈhʌg.ɚˌmʌg.ɚ
uggin ˈhʌg.ɪn **-s** -z
ugh hjuː
ughenden ˈhjuː.ən.dən
ughes hjuːz
ugo ˈhjuː.gəʊ (US) -goʊ
ugon ˈhjuː.gən, -gɒn (US) -gɑːn
uguenot ˈhjuː.gə.nəʊ, ˈhuː-, -nɒt (US) ˈhjuː.gə.nɑːt **-s** -z
ish ˈhjuː.ɪʃ
la ˈhuː.lə **-s** -z
la-Hoop® ˈhuː.lə.huːp **-s** -s
lbert ˈhʌl.bət (US) -bɚt
lk hʌlk **-s** -s **-ing** -ɪŋ
ll **(H)** hʌl **-s** -z **-ing** -ɪŋ **-ed** -d
llabaloo ˌhʌl.ə.bəˈluː **-s** -z
llah ˈhʌl.ə
llbridge ˈhʌl.brɪdʒ
llo həˈləʊ, hʌlˈəʊ (US) həˈloʊ, hʌlˈoʊ **-s** -z
lme hjuːm, huːm
lse hʌls
lsean hʌlˈsiː.ən
m *(n. v.)* hʌm **-s** -z **-ming** -ɪŋ **-med** -d ˈ**humming** ˌ**top**
man **(H)** ˈhjuː.mən **-s** -z **-ly** -li ˌ**human** ˈ**being**; ˌ**human** ˈ**nature**; ˌ**human** ˈ**race**; ˌ**human** ˈ**rights**
man|e hjuːˈmeɪn **-er** -ər (US) -ɚ **-est** -ɪst, -əst **-ely** -li **-eness** -nəs, -nɪs
man|ism ˈhjuː.mə.n|ɪ.zəm **-ist/s** -ɪst/s

humanistic ˌhjuː.məˈnɪs.tɪk
humanitarian hjuːˌmæn.ɪˈteə.ri.ən, -əˈ-; ˌhjuː.mæn- (US) hjuːˌmæn.əˈter.i- **-s** -z **-ism** -ɪ.zəm
humanit|y hjuːˈmæn.ə.t|i, -ɪ.t|i (US) -ə.t̬|i **-ies** -iz
humanization, **-isa-** ˌhjuː.mə.naɪˈzeɪ.ʃən, -nɪˈ- (US) -nɪˈ-
humaniz|e, **-is|e** ˈhjuː.mə.naɪz **-es** -ɪz **-ing** -ɪŋ **-ed** -d
humankind ˌhjuː.mənˈkaɪnd, -məŋˈ- (US) -mənˈ-
humanoid ˈhjuː.mə.nɔɪd **-s** -z
Humber ˈhʌm.bər (US) -bɚ **-s** -z **-side** -saɪd
Humberston ˈhʌm.bə.stən (US) -bɚ-
Humbert ˈhʌm.bət (US) -bɚt
humb|le ˈhʌm.b|l̩ **-ler** -lər (US) -lɚ **-lest** -lɪst, -ləst **-ly** -li **-leness** -l̩.nəs, -nɪs **-les** -l̩z **-ling** -l̩.ɪŋ (US) -lɪŋ **-led** -l̩d **eat** ˌ**humble** ˈ**pie**
Humblethwaite ˈhʌm.bl̩.θweɪt
Humboldt ˈhʌm.bəʊlt, ˈhʊm- (US) -boʊlt
Humbrol® ˈhʌm.brɒl (US) -brɑːl
humbug ˈhʌm.bʌg **-s** -z **-ging** -ɪŋ **-ged** -d
humdinger ˌhʌmˈdɪŋ.ər (US) -ɚ **-s** -z
humdrum ˈhʌm.drʌm
Hume hjuːm
humectant hjuːˈmek.tənt **-s** -s
humer|us ˈhjuː.mər|.əs **-i** -aɪ **-al** -əl
Humian ˈhjuː.mi.ən
humid ˈhjuː.mɪd **-ness** -nəs, -nɪs
humidification hjuːˌmɪd.ɪ.fɪˈkeɪ.ʃən, ˌ-ə-
humidifier hjuːˈmɪd.ɪ.faɪ.ər, ˈ-ə- **-s** -z
humidif|y hjuːˈmɪd.ɪ.f|aɪ, ˈ-ə- **-ies** -aɪz **-ying** -aɪ.ɪŋ **-ied** -aɪd **-ier/s** -aɪ.ər/z (US) -aɪ.ɚ/z
humidity hjuːˈmɪd.ə.ti, -ɪ.ti (US) -ə.t̬i
humili|ate hjuːˈmɪl.i|.eɪt **-ates** -eɪts **-ating/ly** -eɪ.tɪŋ/li (US) -eɪ.t̬ɪŋ/li **-ated** -eɪ.tɪd (US) -eɪ.t̬ɪd
humiliation hjuːˌmɪl.iˈeɪ.ʃən, ˌhjuː.mɪ.liˈ- (US) hjuːˌmɪl.iˈ- **-s** -z
humility hjuːˈmɪl.ə.ti, -ɪt.i (US) -ə.t̬i
hummingbird ˈhʌm.ɪŋ.bɜːd (US) -bɝːd **-s** -z
hummock ˈhʌm.ək **-s** -s **-y** -i
hummus ˈhʊm.ʊs, ˈhʌm-, -əs, ˈhuː.məs (US) ˈhʌm.əs, ˈhʊm-
humongous hjuːˈmʌŋ.gəs
hum|or ˈhjuː.m|ər (US) -m|ɚ **-ors** -əz (US) -ɚz **-oring** -ər.ɪŋ **-ored** -əd (US) -ɚd **-orless/ly** -ə.ləs/li, -ɚ.lɪs/li
humoral ˈhjuː.mər.əl
humoresque ˌhjuː.mərˈesk (US) -məˈresk **-s** -s
humorist ˈhjuː.mər.ɪst **-s** -s
humoristic ˌhjuː.mərˈɪs.tɪk
humorous ˈhjuː.mər.əs **-ly** -li **-ness** -nəs, -nɪs

hum|our ˈhjuː.m|ər (US) -m|ɚ **-ours** -əz (US) -ɚz **-ouring** -ər.ɪŋ **-oured** -əd (US) -ɚd **-ourless/ly** -ə.ləs/li, -ɚ.lɪs/li
humoursome ˈhjuː.mə.səm (US) -mɚ- **-ly** -li **-ness** -nəs, -nɪs
hump hʌmp **-s** -s **-ing** -ɪŋ **-ed** -t
humpback ˈhʌmp.bæk **-s** -s **-ed** -t ˌ**humpbacked** ˈ**bridge**
Humperdinck ˈhʌm.pə.dɪŋk (US) -pɚ-
humph *(interj.)* ˌm̥m, hə̃h, hʌmf
Note: Interjection indicating annoyance or disapproval, with rapid fall in pitch. The transcriptions reflect a wide range of possible pronunciations. The small circle uncer the /m/ symbol indicates a voiceless consonant.
Humphr(e)y ˈhʌmp.fri **-s** -z
Humphries ˈhʌmp.friz
Humpty Dumpty ˌhʌmp.tiˈdʌmp.ti
hump|y ˈhʌm.p|i **-ier** -i.ər (US) -i.ɚ **-iest** -i.ɪst, -i.əst **-iness** -ɪ.nəs, -ɪ.nɪs
humus ˈhjuː.məs
Hun hʌn **-s** -z
hunch hʌntʃ **-es** -ɪz **-ing** -ɪŋ **-ed** -t
hunchback ˈhʌntʃ.bæk **-s** -s **-ed** -t
hundred ˈhʌn.drəd, -drɪd **-s** -z
hundredfold ˈhʌn.drəd.fəʊld, -drɪd- (US) -foʊld
hundredth ˈhʌn.drədθ, -drɪdθ, -drətθ, -drɪtθ **-s** -s
hundredweight ˈhʌn.drəd.weɪt, -drɪd- **-s** -s
hung *(from* **hang***)* hʌŋ ˌ**hung** ˈ**jury**; ˌ**hung** ˈ**parliament**
Hungarian hʌŋˈgeə.ri.ən (US) -ˈger.i- **-s** -z
Hungary ˈhʌŋ.gər.i
hung|er ˈhʌŋ.g|ər (US) -g|ɚ **-ers** -əz (US) -ɚz **-ering** -ər.ɪŋ **-ered** -əd (US) -ɚd ˈ**hunger** ˌ**strike**; ˈ**hunger** ˌ**striker**
Hungerford ˈhʌŋ.gə.fəd (US) -gɚ.fɚd
hungerstrik|e ˈhʌŋ.gə.straɪk (US) -gɚ- **-es** -s **-ing** -ɪŋ **hungerstruck** ˈhʌŋ.gə.strʌk (US) -gɚ-
hungover ˌhʌŋˈəʊ.vər (US) -ˈoʊ.vɚ
hungr|y ˈhʌŋ.gr|i **-ier** -i.ər (US) -i.ɚ **-iest** -i.ɪst, -i.əst **-ily** -əl.i, -ɪ.li **-iness** -ɪ.nəs, -ɪ.nɪs
hunk hʌŋk **-s** -s
hunk|y ˈhʌŋ.k|i **-ier** -i.ər (US) -i.ɚ **-iest** -i.ɪst, -i.əst
hunky-dory ˌhʌŋ.kiˈdɔː.ri (US) -ˈdɔːr.i
hunnish **(H)** ˈhʌn.ɪʃ
Hunslet ˈhʌnz.lət, -lɪt, ˈhʌn.slɪt, -slət
Hunstanton hʌnˈstæn.tən *locally:* ˈhʌn.stən-
Hunsworth ˈhʌnz.wəθ (US) -wɚθ
hunt **(H)** hʌnt **-s** -s **-er/s** -ər/z (US) -ɚ/z **-ing** -ɪŋ (US) ˈhʌn.t̬ɪŋ **-ed** -ɪd (US) ˈhʌn.t̬ɪd ˈ**hunting** ˌ**ground**; ˈ**hunting** ˌ**horn**; ˈ**hunting** ˌ**knife**

hunter-gatherer ˌhʌn.tə'gæð.ər.ər (US) -t̬ɚ'gæð.ɚ.ɚ **-s** -z
Hunterian hʌn'tɪə.ri.ən (US) -'tɪr.i-
Huntingdon 'hʌn.tɪŋ.dən **-shire** -ʃər, -ˌʃɪər (US) -ʃɚ, -ˌʃɪr
Huntingdonian ˌhʌn.tɪŋ'dəʊ.ni.ən (US) -'doʊ- **-s** -z
Huntingford 'hʌn.tɪŋ.fəd (US) -fɚd
Huntington 'hʌn.tɪŋ.tən ˌ**Huntington's cho'rea**
Huntl(e)y 'hʌnt.li
Hunton 'hʌn.tən (US) -tən
huntress 'hʌn.trəs, -trɪs **-es** -ɪz
Hunts. *(abbrev. for* **Huntingdonshire***)* hʌnts; 'hʌn.tɪŋ.dən.ʃər, -ˌʃɪər (US) hʌnts; 'hʌn.tɪŋ.dən.ʃɚ, -ˌʃɪr
hunts|man 'hʌnts|.mən **-men** -mən, -men **-manship** -mən.ʃɪp
Huntsville 'hʌnts.vɪl
Hunyadi 'hʊn.jɑː.di, 'hʌn-, -'-- (US) 'hʊn.jɑː.di
Hurd hɜːd (US) hɝːd
hurdl|e 'hɜː.dl̩ **-es** -z **-ing** -ɪŋ, 'hɜːd.lɪŋ (US) 'hɝːd- **-ed** -d **-er/s** -ər/z (US) -ɚ/z
hurdy-gurd|y 'hɜː.diˌgɜː.d|i, ˌhɜː.di'gɜː- (US) ˌhɝː.di'gɝː.d|i, 'hɝː.diˌgɝː- **-ies** -iz
Hurford 'hɜː.fəd (US) 'hɝː.fɚd
hurl hɜːl (US) hɝːl **-s** -z **-ing** -ɪŋ **-ed** -d **-er/s** -ər/z (US) -ɚ/z
hurley (H) 'hɜː.li (US) 'hɝː- **-s** -z
hurling 'hɜː.lɪŋ (US) 'hɝː-
Hurlingham 'hɜː.lɪŋ.əm (US) 'hɝː-
Hurlstone 'hɜːl.stən (US) 'hɝːl-
hurly-burly 'hɜː.liˌbɜː.li, ˌhɜː.li'bɜː- (US) 'hɝː.liˌbɝː-, ˌhɝː.li'bɝː-
Huron 'hjʊə.rən, -rɒn (US) 'hjʊr.ɑːn, -ən
hurrah hə'rɑː, hʊ- (US) -'rɑː, -'rɔː **-s** -z **-ing** -ɪŋ **-ed** -d
hurray hə'reɪ, hʊ- **-s** -z
Hurrell 'hʌr.əl, 'hʊə.rəl (US) 'hɝː.əl
hurricane 'hʌr.ɪ.kən, '-ə-, -keɪn (US) 'hɝː.ɪ.keɪn, -kən **-s** -z '**hurricane** ˌ**lamp**
hurried 'hʌr.id (US) 'hɝː- **-ly** -li
hurr|y (H) 'hʌr|.i (US) 'hɝː- **-ies** -i.z **-ying** -i.ɪŋ
hurry-scurry ˌhʌr.i'skʌr.i (US) ˌhɝː.i'skɝː-
hurst (H) hɜːst (US) hɝːst **-s** -s
Hurstmonceux ˌhɜːst.mən'zuː, -mɒn'-, -'sjuː, -'suː (US) 'hɝːst.mən.suː, ˌ--'-
Hurston 'hɜː.stən (US) 'hɝː-
Hurstpierpoint ˌhɜːst.pɪə'pɔɪnt (US) ˌhɝːst.pɪr'-
hurt (H) hɜːt (US) hɝːt **-s** -s **-ing** -ɪŋ (US) 'hɝː.t̬ɪŋ
hurtful 'hɜːt.fəl, -fʊl (US) 'hɝːt- **-ly** -i **-ness** -nəs, -nɪs
hurtl|e 'hɜː.tl̩ (US) -t̬l̩ **-es** -z **-ing** -ɪŋ, 'hɜːt.lɪŋ (US) 'hɝːt- **-ed** -d
husband 'hʌz.bənd **-s** -z **-ing** -ɪŋ **-ed** -ɪd **-ly** -li
husband|man 'hʌz.bənd|.mən **-men** -mən, -men
husbandry 'hʌz.bən.dri
hush hʌʃ **-es** -ɪz **-ing** -ɪŋ **-ed** -t '**hush** ˌ**money**
hushaby 'hʌʃ.ə.baɪ
hush-hush ˌhʌʃ'hʌʃ *stress shift:* ˌhush-hush 'service
Hush Puppies® 'hʌʃˌpʌp.iz
husk (H) hʌsk **-s** -s
Huskisson 'hʌs.kɪ.sən, -kə-
husk|y 'hʌs.k|i **-ier** -i.ər (US) -i.ɚ **-iest** -i.ɪst, -i.əst **-ily** -ɪ.li, -əl.i **-iness** -ɪ.nəs, -ɪ.nɪs
Hussain hʊ'seɪn (US) huː-
hussar hʊ'zɑːr, hə- (US) -'zɑːr **-s** -z
Hussein hʊ'seɪn (US) huː-
Hussey 'hʌs.i
Hussite 'hʌs.aɪt, 'hʊs- (US) 'hʌs- **-s** -s
huss|y (H) 'hʌs|.i, 'hʌz- **-ies** -iz
hustings 'hʌs.tɪŋz
hustl|e 'hʌs.l̩ **-es** -z **-ing** -ɪŋ, 'hʌs.lɪŋ **-ed** -d **-er/s** -ər/z (US) -ɚ/z, 'hʌs.lər/z (US) -lɚ/z
Huston 'hjuː.stən
hut hʌt **-s** -s
hutch hʌtʃ **-es** -ɪz
Hutchence 'hʌtʃ.ənts, -ents
Hutcheson 'hʌtʃ.ɪ.sən, '-ə-
Hutchings 'hʌtʃ.ɪŋz
Hutchinson 'hʌtʃ.ɪn.sən
Hutchinsonian ˌhʌtʃ.ɪn'səʊ.ni.ən (US) -'soʊ- **-s** -z
Hutchison 'hʌtʃ.ɪ.sən
Huth huːθ
Huthwaite 'huːθ.weɪt
hutment 'hʌt.mənt **-s** -s
Hutton 'hʌt.ən
Hutu 'huː.tuː **-s** -z
hutzpah 'hʊt.spɑː, 'xʊt-, -spə
Huw hjuː
Huxley 'hʌk.sli
Huxtable 'hʌk.stə.bl̩
Huygens 'haɪ.gənz
Huyton 'haɪ.tən
huzza(h) hʊ'zɑː, hʌz'ɑː-, hə'zɑː (US) hə'zɑː, -'zɔː **-s** -z
Hwang-ho ˌhwæŋ'həʊ (US) ˌhwɑːŋ'hoʊ
hwyl 'huː.ɪl, -əl
hyacinth (H) 'haɪə.sɪntθ **-s** -s
hyacinthine ˌhaɪə'sɪnt.θaɪn (US) -θaɪn, -θɪn
Hyades 'haɪ.ə.diːz
hyaena haɪ'iː.nə **-s** -z
hyalin 'haɪ.ə.lɪn
hyaline 'haɪə.lɪn, -liːn, -laɪn
hyalite 'haɪə.laɪt
hyaloid 'haɪə.lɔɪd
Hyam haɪəm
Hyamson 'haɪəm.sən
Hyannis haɪ'æn.ɪs
hybrid 'haɪ.brɪd **-s** -z **-ism** -ɪ.zəm
hybridity haɪ'brɪd.ə.ti, -ɪ.ti (US) -ə.t̬i
hybridization, -isa- ˌhaɪ.brɪ.daɪ'zeɪ.ʃən, ˌ-brə-, -dɪ'- (US) -dɪ'-
hybridiz|e, -is|e 'haɪ.brɪ.daɪz, -brə- **-es** -ɪz **-ing** -ɪŋ **-ed** -d **-er/s** -ər/z (US) -ɚ/z
Hyde haɪd ˌ**Hyde 'Park**; ˌ**Hyde** ˌ**Park 'Corner**
Hyder® 'haɪ.dər (US) -dɚ
Hyderabad 'haɪ.dər.ə.bæd, -bɑːd, ˌhaɪ.dər.ə'bæd, -'bɑːd (US) 'haɪ.dɚ.ə.bæd, -bɑːd, '-drə.bæ[d], -bɑːd
hydra (H) 'haɪ.drə **-s** -z
hydrangea haɪ'dreɪn.dʒə, -dʒi.ə (US) -'dreɪn-, -'dræn- **-s** -z
hydrant 'haɪ.drənt **-s** -s
hydrate *(n.)* 'haɪ.dreɪt, -drɪt **-s** -s
hydra|te *(v.)* haɪ'dreɪ|t, '-- (US) '-- **-tes** [-ts] **-ting** -tɪŋ (US) -t̬ɪŋ **-ted** -tɪd (US) -t̬ɪd
hydration haɪ'dreɪ.ʃən
hydraulic haɪ'drɔː.lɪk, -'drɒl.ɪk (US) -'drɑː-, -'drɔː- **-s** -s
hydrazine 'haɪ.drə.ziːn, -zɪn
hydro- haɪ.drəʊ-; haɪ'drɒ- (US) haɪ.droʊ-, -drə-; haɪ'drɑː-

Note: Prefix. Normally either takes primary or secondary stress on t[he] first syllable, e.g. **hydrofoil** /'haɪ.drəʊ.fɔɪl (US) -droʊ-/, **hydrochloric** /ˌhaɪ.drəʊ'klɒr.ɪk (US) -droʊ'klɔːr-/, or primary stres[s] on the second syllable, e.g. **hydrogenate** /haɪ'drɒdʒ.ɪ.neɪt (US) -'drɑː.dʒə-/.

hydro 'haɪ.drəʊ (US) -droʊ **-s** -z
hydrocarbon ˌhaɪ.drəʊ'kɑː.bən (US) -droʊ'kɑːr-, -drə'- **-s** -z
hydrocephalus ˌhaɪ.drəʊ'sef.əl.əs, -'kef- (US) -droʊ'sef-
hydrochloric ˌhaɪ.drəʊ'klɒr.ɪk, -'klɔː.rɪk (US) -droʊ'klɔːr.ɪk, -drə'- *stress shift, see compound:* ˌ**hydrochloric 'acid**
hydrodynamic ˌhaɪ.drəʊ.daɪ'næm.[ɪk], -dɪ'- (US) -droʊ.daɪ'-, -drə- **-al** -əl **-[ally]** -əl.i, -li **-s** -s
hydroelectric ˌhaɪ.drəʊ.ɪ'lek.trɪk, (US) -droʊ- **-s** -s *stress shift:* ˌhydroelectric 'power
hydroelectricity ˌhaɪ.drəʊ.ɪ.lek'trɪs.ɪ.ti, -ə- (US) -droʊ.ɪ.lek'trɪs.ɪ.t̬i, -ə.t̬i
hydrofoil 'haɪ.drəʊ.fɔɪl (US) -droʊ-, -drə- **-s** -z
hydrogen 'haɪ.drə.dʒən, -drɪ-, -dʒ[ɪn] (US) -drə.dʒən '**hydrogen** ˌ**bomb**; ˌ**hydrogen 'chloride**; ˌ**hydrogen 'fluoride**; ˌ**hydrogen pe'roxide**

hydroge|nate haɪˈdrɒdʒ.ɪ|.neɪt, ˈ-ə-; ˈhaɪ.drə.dʒɪ-, -dʒə- (US) haɪˈdrɑː.dʒə-; ˈhaɪ.drə- **-nates** -neɪts **-nating** -neɪ.tɪŋ (US) -neɪ.t̬ɪŋ **-nated** -neɪ.tɪd (US) -neɪ.t̬ɪd
hydrogenation ˌhaɪ.drə.dʒəˈneɪ.ʃən, -dʒɪˈ- (US) haɪˌdrɑː.dʒəˈ-
hydrogenous haɪˈdrɒdʒ.ɪ.nəs, ˈ-ə- (US) -ˈdrɑː.dʒɪ-, -dʒə-
hydrographic ˌhaɪ.drəʊˈgræf.ɪk (US) -droʊˈgræf- **-al** -əl **-ally** -əl.i, -li
hydrograph|y haɪˈdrɒg.rə.f|i (US) -ˈdrɑː.grə- **-er/s** -əʳ/z (US) -ɚ/z
hydrology haɪˈdrɒl.ə.dʒi (US) -ˈdrɑː.lə-
hydrolysis haɪˈdrɒl.ə.sɪs, ˈ-ɪ- (US) -ˈdrɑː.lɪ-
hydrolytic ˌhaɪ.drəˈlɪt.ɪk (US) -ˈlɪt̬- **-ally** -əl.i, -li
hydrolyz|e, -ys|e ˈhaɪ.drə.laɪz **-es** -ɪz **-ing** -ɪŋ **-ed** -d
hydromechanics ˌhaɪ.drəʊ.mɪˈkæn.ɪks, -məˈ- (US) -droʊ.məˈ-
hydrometer haɪˈdrɒm.ɪ.təʳ, ˈ-ə- (US) -ˈdrɑː.mə.t̬ɚ **-s** -z
hydrometric ˌhaɪ.drəʊˈmet.rɪk (US) -droʊˈ-, -drəˈ- **-al** -əl **-ally** -əl.i, -li
hydrometry haɪˈdrɒm.ə.tri, ˈ-ɪ- (US) -ˈdrɑː.mə-
hydropathic ˌhaɪ.drəʊˈpæθ.ɪk (US) -droʊˈ-, -drəˈ- **-s** -s **-al** -əl **-ally** -əl.i, -li
hydropath|y haɪˈdrɒp.ə.θ|i (US) -ˈdrɑː.pə- **-ist/s** -ɪst/s
hydrophilic ˌhaɪ.drəʊˈfɪl.ɪk (US) -droʊˈ-, -drəˈ-
hydrophobia ˌhaɪ.drəʊˈfəʊ.bi.ə (US) -droʊˈfoʊ-, -drəˈ-
hydrophobic ˌhaɪ.drəʊˈfəʊ.bɪk (US) -droʊˈfoʊ-, -drəˈ-
hydrophyte ˈhaɪ.drəʊ.faɪt (US) -droʊ-, -drə- **-s** -s
hydroplan|e ˈhaɪ.drəʊ.pleɪn (US) -droʊ-, -drə- **-es** -z **-ing** -ɪŋ **-ed** -d
hydroponic ˌhaɪ.drəʊˈpɒn.ɪk (US) -droʊˈpɑː.nɪk, -drəˈ- **-s** -s **-ally** -əl.i, -li
hydroscope ˈhaɪ.drəʊ.skəʊp (US) -droʊ.skoʊp, -drə- **-s** -s
hydrostat ˈhaɪ.drəʊ.stæt (US) -droʊ-, -drə- **-s** -s
hydrostatic ˌhaɪ.drəʊˈstæt.ɪk (US) -droʊˈstæt̬-, -drəˈ- **-al** -əl **-ally** -əl.i, -li **-s** -s
hydrotherapy ˌhaɪ.drəʊˈθer.ə.pi (US) -droʊˈ-, -drəˈ-
hydrotropism haɪˈdrɒt.rə.pɪ.zəm (US) -ˈdrɑː.trə-
hydrous ˈhaɪ.drəs
hydroxide haɪˈdrɒk.saɪd (US) -ˈdrɑːk- **-s** -z
hydroxyl haɪˈdrɒk.sɪl (US) -ˈdrɑːk-
hyena haɪˈiː.nə **-s** -z
Hygeia haɪˈdʒiː.ə
hygiene ˈhaɪ.dʒiːn
hygienic haɪˈdʒiː.nɪk (US) ˌhaɪ.dʒiˈen.ɪk; haɪˈdʒen-, -ˈdʒiː.nɪk **-ally** -əl.i, -li
hygienist ˈhaɪ.dʒiː.nɪst (US) ˈhaɪ.dʒiː.nɪst; -ˈ--, -ˈdʒen.ɪst **-s** -s
hygrometric ˌhaɪ.grəʊˈmet.rɪk (US) -groʊˈ-, -grəˈ- **-al** -əl **-ally** -əl.i, -li
hygromet|ry haɪˈgrɒm.ə.t|ri (US) -ˈgrɑː.mə- **-er/s** -əʳ/z (US) -ɚ/z
hygroscope ˈhaɪ.grəʊ.skəʊp (US) -groʊ.skoʊp, -grə- **-s** -s
hygroscopic ˌhaɪ.grəʊˈskɒp.ɪk (US) -groʊˈskɑː.pɪk, -grəˈ- **-ally** -əl.i, -li
Hyksos ˈhɪk.sɒs (US) -sɑːs
Hylas ˈhaɪ.læs, -ləs
Hylton ˈhɪl.tən
Hyman ˈhaɪ.mən
hymen (H) ˈhaɪ.men, -mən (US) -mən **-s** -z
hymene|al ˌhaɪ.menˈiː|.əl, -məˈniː-, -mɪˈ- (US) -məˈ- **-an** -ən
Hymettus haɪˈmet.əs (US) -ˈmet̬-
hymn hɪm **-s** -z **-ing** -ɪŋ **-ed** -d ˈ**hymn** ˌ**book**
hymnal ˈhɪm.nəl **-s** -z
hymnar|y ˈhɪm.nər|.i **-ies** -iz
hymnic ˈhɪm.nɪk
hymnody ˈhɪm.nə.di
hymnolog|y hɪmˈnɒl.ə.dʒi (US) -nɑː.lə- **-ist/s** -ɪst/s
Hyndley ˈhaɪnd.li
Hyndman ˈhaɪnd.mən
Hynes haɪnz
hyoid ˈhaɪ.ɔɪd
hyoscine ˈhaɪ.əʊ.siːn (US) -ə.siːn, -sɪn
hypallage haɪˈpæl.ə.gi, -dʒi (US) haɪ-, hə-; ˌhaɪ.pəˈlædʒ.i, ˌhɪp.əˈ-
Hypatia haɪˈpeɪ.ʃə, -ʃi.ə
hyp|e haɪp **-es** -s **-ing** -ɪŋ **-ed** -t ˌ**hyped** ˈ**up**
hyper- haɪ.pəʳ-; haɪˈpɜː- (US) haɪ.pɚ-; haɪˈpɝː-

Note: Prefix. Normally either takes primary or secondary stress on the first syllable, e.g. **hypermarket** /ˈhaɪ.pəˌmɑː.kɪt (US) -pɚˌmɑːr-/, **hyperactive** /ˌhaɪ.pəʳˈæk.tɪv (US) -pɚˈ-/, or primary stress on the second syllable, e.g. **hyperbole** /haɪˈpɜː.bəl.i (US) -ˈpɝːr-/. Note also that, although /r/ is normally assigned to a following strong syllable in US transcriptions, in **hyper-** it is perceived to be morphemically linked to that morpheme and is retained in the prefix as /ɚ/.

hyper ˈhaɪ.pəʳ (US) -pɚ
hyperactive ˌhaɪ.pəʳˈæk.tɪv (US) -pɚˈ- *stress shift* ˌhyperactive ˈchild
hyperactivity ˌhaɪ.pər.ækˈtɪv.ə.ti, -ɪ.ti (US) -pɚ.ækˈtɪv.ə.t̬i
hyperacute ˌhaɪ.pəʳ.əˈkjuːt (US) -pɚ- **-ness** -nəs, -nɪs
hyperbol|a haɪˈpɜː.bəl|.ə (US) -ˈpɝː- **-ae** -iː **-as** -əz
hyperbole haɪˈpɜː.bəl.i (US) -ˈpɝː- **-s** -z
hyperbolic ˌhaɪ.pəˈbɒl.ɪk (US) -pɚˈbɑː.lɪk **-al** -əl **-ally** -əl.i, -li
hyperbol|ism haɪˈpɜː.bəl|.ɪ.zəm (US) -ˈpɝː- **-ist/s** -ɪst/s
hyperboliz|e, -is|e haɪˈpɜː.bəl.aɪz (US) -ˈpɝː- **-es** -ɪz **-ing** -ɪŋ **-ed** -d
hyperboloid haɪˈpɜː.bəl.ɔɪd (US) -ˈpɝː- **-s** -z
hyperborean ˌhaɪ.pəˈbɔː.ri.ən; -bɔːˈriː.ən, -bɒrˈiː.ən (US) -pɚ.bɔːˈriː-, -bəˈ- **-s** -z
hypercorrect ˌhaɪ.pə.kəˈrekt (US) -pɚ.kəˈrekt **-ly** -li **-ness** -nəs, -nɪs
hypercorrection ˌhaɪ.pə.kəˈrek.ʃən (US) -pɚ.kəˈrek- **-s** -z
hypercritic|al ˌhaɪ.pəˈkrɪt.ɪ.k|əl (US) -pɚˈkrɪt̬- **-ally** -əl.i (US) -li
hypercriticism ˌhaɪ.pəˈkrɪt.ɪ.sɪ.zəm (US) -pɚˈkrɪt̬.ɪ-
hypercriticiz|e, -is|e ˌhaɪ.pəˈkrɪt.ɪ.saɪz (US) -pɚˈkrɪt̬- **-es** -ɪz **-ing** -ɪŋ **-ed** -d
hyperglycaem|ia ˌhaɪ.pə.glaɪˈsiː.m|i.ə (US) -pɚ- **-ic** -ɪk
hypericum haɪˈper.ɪ.kəm **-s** -z
Hyperides haɪˈper.ɪ.diːz; ˌhaɪ.pəˈraɪ- (US) haɪˈper.ɪ-, hɪ-
hyperinflation ˌhaɪ.pər.ɪnˈfleɪ.ʃən (US) -pɚ-
Hyperion haɪˈpɪə.ri.ən, -ˈper.i- (US) -ˈpɪr-
hyperlink ˈhaɪ.pə.lɪŋk (US) -pɚ- **-s** -s
hypermarket ˈhaɪ.pəˌmɑː.kɪt (US) -pɚˌmɑːr- **-s** -s
hypernym ˈhaɪ.pə.nɪm (US) -pɚ- **-s** -z
hypersensitive ˌhaɪ.pəˈsent.sə.tɪv, -sɪ- (US) -pɚˈsent.sə.t̬ɪv
hypersensitivity ˌhaɪ.pəˌsent.səˈtɪv.ə.ti, -sɪˈ-, -ɪ.ti (US) -pɚˌsent.səˈtɪv.ə.t̬i
hyperspace ˈhaɪ.pə.speɪs (US) -pɚ-
hypertension ˌhaɪ.pəˈten.tʃən, ˈhaɪ.pəˌten- (US) ˌhaɪ.pɚˈtent.ʃən
hypertext ˈhaɪ.pə.tekst (US) -pɚ-
hyperthyroid ˌhaɪ.pəˈθaɪ.rɔɪd (US) -pɚˈ- **-ism** -ɪ.zəm
hypertroph|y haɪˈpɜː.trə.f|i (US) -ˈpɝː- **-ied** -id
hyperventi|late ˌhaɪ.pəˈven.tɪ|.leɪt, -tə- (US) -pɚˈven.t̬ə- **-lates** -leɪts **-lating** -leɪ.tɪŋ (US) -leɪ.t̬ɪŋ **-lated** -leɪ.tɪd (US) -leɪ.t̬ɪd
hyperventilation ˌhaɪ.pəˌven.tɪˈleɪ.ʃən, -təˈ- (US) -pɚˌven.t̬əˈ-
hyph|a ˈhaɪ.f|ə **-ae** -iː
hyphal ˈhaɪ.fəl

hyphen 'haɪ.fᵊn **-s** -z **-ing** -ɪŋ **-ed** -d
hyphen|ate 'haɪ.fᵊn|.eɪt, -fɪ.n|eɪt (US) -fə- **-ates** -eɪts **-ating** -eɪ.tɪŋ (US) -eɪ.t̬ɪŋ **-ated** -eɪ.tɪd (US) -eɪ.t̬ɪd
hyphenation ˌhaɪ.fᵊn'eɪ.ʃᵊn
hypno- 'hɪp.nəʊ-; hɪp'nɒ-, -'nəʊ- (US) 'hɪp.noʊ-, -nə-; hɪp'nɑː-, -'noʊ-
Note: Prefix. Normally either takes primary or secondary stress on the first syllable, e.g. **hypnotism** /'hɪp.nə.tɪ.zᵊm/, **hypnotherapy** /ˌhɪp.nəʊ'θer.ə.pi (US) -noʊ'-/, or primary stress on the second syllable, e.g. **hypnotic** /hɪp'nɒt.ɪk (US) -'nɑː.t̬ɪk/.
hypnosis hɪp'nəʊ.sɪs (US) -'noʊ-
hypnotherapist ˌhɪp.nəʊ'θer.ə.pɪst (US) -noʊ'- **-s** -s
hypnotherapy ˌhɪp.nəʊ'θer.ə.pi (US) -noʊ'-
hypnotic hɪp'nɒt.ɪk (US) -'nɑː.t̬ɪk
hypnot|ism 'hɪp.nə.t|ɪ.zᵊm **-ist/s** -ɪst/s
hypnotization, -isa- ˌhɪp.nə.taɪ'zeɪ.ʃᵊn, -tɪ'- (US) -tɪ'-
hypnotiz|e, -is|e 'hɪp.nə.taɪz **-es** -ɪz **-ing** -ɪŋ **-ed** -d **-er/s** -əʳ/z (US) -ɚ/z
hypo- 'haɪ.pəʊ-; haɪ'pɒ- (US) 'haɪ.poʊ-, -pə-; haɪ'pɑː-, hɪ-
Note: Prefix. Normally either takes primary or secondary stress on the first syllable, e.g. **hypocaust** /'haɪ.pəʊ.kɔːst (US) -poʊ-/, **hypothetic** /ˌhaɪ.pəʊ'θet.ɪk (US) -poʊ'θet̬-/, or primary stress on the second syllable, e.g. **hypotenuse** /haɪ'pɒt.ᵊn.juːz (US) -'pɑː.tᵊn.uːs/.
hypo 'haɪ.pəʊ (US) -poʊ **-s** -z
hypoallergenic ˌhaɪ.pəʊˌæl.ə'dʒen.ɪk, -ɜː'- (US) -poʊˌæl.ɚ'-
hypocaust 'haɪ.pəʊ.kɔːst, -kɒst (US) -poʊ.kɔːst, -pə-, -kɑːst **-s** -s
hypochondri|a ˌhaɪ.pəʊ'kɒn.dri|.ə (US) -poʊ'kɑːn-, -pə'- **-ac/s** -æk/s
hypochondriacal ˌhaɪ.pəʊ.kɒn'draɪ.ə.kᵊl, -kən'- (US) -poʊ.kɑːn'-, -pə-
hypochondriasis ˌhaɪ.pəʊ.kɒn'draɪ.ə.sɪs, -kən'- (US) -poʊ.kɑːn'-, -pə-
hypocotyl ˌhaɪ.pə'kɒt.ɪl (US) -poʊ'kɑː.t̬ᵊl
hypocris|y hɪ'pɒk.rə.s|i, -rɪ- (US) -'pɑː.krə- **-ies** -iz
hypocrite 'hɪp.ə.krɪt **-s** -s
hypocritic|al ˌhɪp.əʊ'krɪt.ɪ.k|ᵊl (US) -ə'krɪt̬- **-ally** -ᵊl.i, -li
hypocycloid ˌhaɪ.pəʊ'saɪ.klɔɪd (US) -poʊ'-, -pə'- **-s** -z
hypodermic ˌhaɪ.pəʊ'dɜː.mɪk (US) -poʊ'dɝː-, -pə'- *stress shift, see compounds:* ˌ**hypodermic 'needle**; *stress shift, see compounds:* ˌ**hypodermic sy'ringe**
hypodermis ˌhaɪ.pəʊ'dɜː.mɪs (US) -poʊ'dɝː-, -pə'-
hypogeal ˌhaɪ.pəʊ'dʒiː.əl (US) -poʊ'-
hypoglyc(a)em|ia ˌhaɪ.pəʊ.glaɪ'siː.m|i.ə (US) -poʊ- **-ic** -ɪk
hypophosphate ˌhaɪ.pəʊ'fɒs.feɪt, -fɪt (US) -poʊ'fɑːs-, -pə'- **-s** -s
hyposta|sis haɪ'pɒs.tə|.sɪs (US) -'pɑː.stə-, hɪ- **-ses** -siːz
hypostatiz|e, -is|e haɪ'pɒs.tə.taɪz (US) -'pɑː.stə-, hɪ- **-es** -ɪz **-ing** -ɪŋ **-ed** -d
hypostyle 'haɪ.pəʊ.staɪl (US) -poʊ-
hyposulphite ˌhaɪ.pəʊ'sʌl.faɪt (US) -poʊ'-, -pə'- **-s** -s
hypotactic ˌhaɪ.pəʊ'tæk.tɪk (US) -poʊ'-, -pə'-
hypotax|is ˌhaɪ.pəʊ'tæk.s|ɪs, 'haɪ.pəʊ.tæk- (US) ˌhaɪ.poʊ'tæk-, -pə'- **-es** -iːz
hypotension ˌhaɪ.pəʊ'ten.tʃᵊn (US) 'haɪ.poʊˌten-, -pəˌ-
hypotenus|e haɪ'pɒt.ᵊn.juːz, -ɪ.njuːz, -juːs (US) -'pɑː.tᵊn.uːs, -tɪ.nuːs, -njuːs **-es** -ɪz
hypothalamus ˌhaɪ.pəʊ'θæl.ə.məs (US) -poʊ'-, -pə'-
hypothe|cate haɪ'pɒθ.ə|.keɪt, '-ɪ- (US) -'pɑː.θə-, hɪ- **-cates** -keɪts **-cating** -keɪ.tɪŋ (US) -keɪ.t̬ɪŋ **-cated** -keɪ.tɪd (US) -keɪ.t̬ɪd
hypothecation haɪˌpɒθ.ə'keɪ.ʃᵊn, -ɪ'- (US) -pɑː.θə'-, hɪ- **-s** -z
hypothermal ˌhaɪ.pəʊ'θɜː.mᵊl (US) -poʊ'θɝː-, -pə'-
hypothermia ˌhaɪ.pəʊ'θɜː.mi.ə (US) -poʊ'θɝː-, -pə'-
hypothes|is haɪ'pɒθ.ə.s|ɪs, '-ɪ- (US) -'pɑː.θə-, hɪ- **-es** -iːz
hypothesiz|e, -is|e haɪ'pɒθ.ə.saɪz (US) -'pɑː.θə-, hɪ- **-es** -ɪz **-ing** -ɪŋ **-ed** -
hypothetic ˌhaɪ.pəʊ'θet.ɪk (US) -poʊ'θet̬-, -pə'- **-al** -ᵊl **-ally** -ᵊl.i, -
hypothyroid ˌhaɪ.pəʊ'θaɪ.rɔɪd (US) -poʊ'- **-ism** -ɪ.zᵊm
hypoxia haɪ'pɒk.si.ə (US) -'pɑːk-, hɪ-
hypoxic haɪ'pɒk.sɪk (US) -'pɑːk-, hɪ-
hypsome|try hɪp'sɒm.ə|.tri (US) -'sɑː.mə- **-ter/s** -təʳ/z (US) -t̬ɚ/z
hyrax 'haɪ.ræks **-es** -ɪz
Hyslop 'hɪz.ləp, -lɒp (US) -lɑːp, -ləp
hyson (H) 'haɪ.sᵊn
hyssop 'hɪs.əp
hysterectom|y ˌhɪs.tᵊr'ek.tə.m|i (US) -tə'rek- **-ies** -iz
hysteria hɪ'stɪə.ri.ə (US) -'ster.i-, -'stɪ
hysteric hɪ'ster.ɪk **-s** -s **-al** -ᵊl **-ally** -ᵊl.i, -li
hysteron proteron ˌhɪs.tə.rɒn'prɒt.ə.rɒn, -rɒm'-, -'prəʊ.tə- (US) -rɑːn'prɑː.t̬ə.rɑːn
hythe (H) haɪð **-s** -z
Hytner 'haɪt.nəʳ (US) -nɚ
Hyundai® 'haɪ.ʌn.daɪ, -ən-, 'hjɒn-, 'hjɒn.deɪ (US) 'hjʌn.deɪ, 'hʌn-
Hywel haʊəl
Hz *(abbrev. for* **Hertz***)* hɜːts, heəts (US) hɜːrts, herts

Pronouncing the letter I

See also IE, IEU, IO

The vowel letter **i** has two main strong pronunciations linked to spelling: a 'short' pronunciation /ɪ/ and a 'long' pronunciation /aɪ/. In the 'short' pronunciation, the **i** is generally followed by a consonant which closes the syllable, or a double consonant before another vowel, e.g.:

ship /ʃɪp/
shipping /ˈʃɪp.ɪŋ/

The 'long' pronunciation is usually found when the **i** is followed by a single consonant and then a vowel, although it should be noted that this spelling does not regularly predict a 'long' pronunciation, e.g.:

pipe /paɪp/
piping /ˈpaɪ.pɪŋ/

In many cases, the 'short' pronunciation results from the above kind of spelling, e.g.:

give /gɪv/
living /ˈlɪv.ɪŋ/

Also, the 'long' pronunciation appears in some words where the vowel is followed by two consonants, e.g.:

mind /maɪnd/
wild /waɪld/

Preceding the letters **gh**, **i** is pronounced /aɪ/, except in some names such as *Brigham* and *Brighouse* e.g.:

high /haɪ/
light /laɪt/
Brigham /ˈbrɪg.əm/

When **i** is followed by **r**, the strong pronunciation is one of two possibilities: /aɪə (US) aɪɚ/ or /ɜː (US) ɝː/. E.g., in:

fire /faɪəʳ/ (US) /faɪɚ/
fir /fɜːʳ/ (US) /fɝː/

Another vowel sound associated with the letter **i** is /iː/, e.g.:

/iː/ machine /məˈʃiːn/

In weak syllables

The vowel letter **i** is realised with the vowels /ɪ/ and /ə/ in weak syllables, and may also be elided in British English, e.g.:

divide /dɪˈvaɪd, də-/
medicine /ˈmed.sᵊn/ (US) /ˈ-ɪ.sən/

aɪ -'s -z
(*abbrev. for* **Iowa**) ˈaɪ.əʊə; ˈaɪə.wə (US) ˈaɪə.wə; ˈaɪ.oʊ-
c i.æk, iː-, -ək
te: Suffix. Does not normally affect stress patterning, e.g. **mania** /ˈmeɪ.ni.ə/, **maniac** /ˈmeɪ.ni.æk/.
himo iˈæk.ɪ.məʊ, aɪ- (US) -moʊ
o iˈɑː.gəʊ (US) -goʊ
n ˈiː.ən
-i.əl, -əl
e: Suffix. Normally stressed on the syllable before the prefix, e.g. **facial** ˈfeɪ.ʃᵊl/.
b ˈaɪ.æmb -s -z
b|ic aɪˈæm.b|ɪk -us/es -əs/ɪz
ˈiː.ən
-i.ən
e: Suffix. Words ending **-ian** are tressed in a similar way to those nding **-ial**; see above.
son aɪˈænt.sən
he aɪˈænt.θi
aɪˈɑː.tə, iː- (US) ˌaɪˌeɪˌtiːˈeɪ, aɪˈɑː.t̬ə
ogenic aɪˌæt.rəʊˈdʒen.ɪk, ˌaɪ.æt- (US) aɪˌæt.roʊˈ-, iː-, -rəˈ- **-ally** -ᵊl.i, -li
lan ɪˈbæd.ᵊn (US) iːˈbɑː.dɑːn, -dᵊn
rtson ˈɪb.ət.sᵊn (US) -ɚt-
tson ˈɪb.ɪt.sᵊn, -ət-
am ˈaɪ.biːm -s -z

Iberi|a aɪˈbɪə.ri|.ə (US) -ˈbɪr.i- **-an/s** -ən/z
iberis aɪˈbɪə.rɪs (US) -ˈbɪr.ɪs
Iberus aɪˈbɪə.rəs (US) -ˈbɪr.əs
ibex ˈaɪ.beks **-es** -ɪz
ibid ɪˈbɪd, ˈɪb.ɪd
ibidem ˈɪb.ɪ.dem, ˈ-ə-; ɪˈbaɪ.dem (US) ˈɪb.ɪ.dem, ˈ-ə-; ɪˈbiː.dem, -ˈbaɪ-
-ibility -ɪˈbɪl.ɪ.ti, -əˈ-, -ə.ti (US) -ə.t̬i
Note: Suffix. Words containing **-ibility** always exhibit primary stress as shown above, e.g. **eligibility** /ˌel.ɪ.dʒəˈbɪl.ə.ti (US) -t̬i/.
ibis ˈaɪ.bɪs **-es** -ɪz
Ibiza ɪˈbiː.θə, iː- (US) ɪˈbiː.zə, -sə; -ˈviː.θə, -θɑː
-ible -ə.bl̩, -ɪ-
Note: Suffix. Words containing **-ible** are normally stressed either on the antepenultimate syllable, e.g. **susceptible** /səˈsep.tə.bl̩/, or two syllables preceding the suffix, e.g. **eligible** /ˈel.ɪ.dʒə.bl̩/.
IBM® ˌaɪ.biːˈem
Ibo ˈiː.bəʊ (US) -boʊ **-s** -z
iBook® ˈaɪ.bʊk
Ibrahim ˈɪb.rə.hiːm, -hɪm, ˌ--ˈ-
Ibrox ˈaɪ.brɒks (US) -brɑːks
Ibsen ˈɪb.sᵊn
Ibstock ˈɪb.stɒk (US) -stɑːk

ibuprofen ˌaɪ.bjuːˈprəʊ.fen, -fᵊn; aɪˈbjuː.prəʊ- (US) ˌaɪ.bjuːˈproʊ.fᵊn
IC ˌaɪˈsiː **-s** -z
-ic -ɪk
Note: Suffix. Words containing **-ic** are normally stressed on the penultimate syllable, e.g. **music** /ˈmjuː.zɪk/.
-ic|al -ɪ.k|ᵊl **-ally** -ᵊl.i, -li
Note: Suffix. Words containing **-ical** are normally stressed on the antepenultimate syllable, e.g. **musical** /ˈmjuː.zɪ.kᵊl/.
Icari|a ɪˈkeə.ri|.ə, aɪ- (US) -ˈker.i- **-an** -ən
Icarus ˈɪk.ᵊr.əs, ˈaɪ.kᵊr- (US) ˈɪk.ɚ-
ICBM ˌaɪ.siː.biːˈem
ic|e aɪs **-es** -ɪz **-ing** -ɪŋ **-ed** -t ˈ**ice** ˌ**age**; ˈ**ice** ˌ**axe**; ˈ**ice** ˌ**bucket**; ˈ**ice** ˌ**cap**; ˈ**ice** ˌ**field**; ˈ**ice** ˌ**floe**; ˈ**ice** ˌ**hockey**, ˌ**ice** ˈ**hockey**; ˈ**ice** ˌ**lolly** ˌ**ice** ˈ**lolly**; ˈ**ice** ˌ**pack**; ˈ**ice** ˌ**rink**; ˌ**break the** ˈ**ice**; ˌ**skate on** ˌ**thin** ˈ**ice**
iceberg ˈaɪs.bɜːg (US) -bɝːg **-s** -z ˌ**iceberg** ˈ**lettuce**
icebound ˈaɪs.baʊnd
icebox ˈaɪs.bɒks (US) -bɑːks **-es** -ɪz
icebreaker ˈaɪsˌbreɪ.kəʳ (US) -kɚ **-s** -z
ice cream ˌaɪsˈkriːm, ˈ-- (US) ˈ-- **-s** -z ˌ**ice** ˈ**cream** ˌ**parlo(u)r**; ˌ**ice cream** ˈ**soda**
icefall ˈaɪs.fɔːl (US) -fɔːl, -fɑːl **-s** -z

icehou|se 'aɪs.haʊ|s **-ses** -zɪz
Iceland 'aɪs.lənd
Icelander 'aɪs.lən.dəʳ, -læn- US -dɚ **-s** -z
Icelandic aɪs'læn.dɪk
icemaker 'aɪsˌmeɪ.kəʳ US -kɚ **-s** -z
ice|man 'aɪs|.mæn, -mən **-men** -men, -mən
Iceni aɪ'siː.naɪ, -ni
icepick 'aɪs.pɪk **-s** -s
ice|skate 'aɪs|.skeɪt **-skates** -skeɪts **-skating** -ˌskeɪ.tɪŋ US -ˌskeɪ.t̬ɪŋ **-skated** -ˌskeɪ.tɪd US -ˌskeɪ.t̬ɪd **-skater/s** -ˌskeɪ.təʳ/z US -ˌskeɪ.t̬ɚ/z
Ichabod 'ɪk.ə.bɒd, 'ɪx- US ɪk-, -bɑːd
ich dien ˌɪx'diːn
I Ching ˌiː'tʃɪŋ, ˌaɪ-, -'dʒɪŋ US ˌiː-
ich-laut 'ɪx.laut, 'ɪk-
ichneumon ɪk'njuː.mən US -'nuː-, -'njuː- **-s** -z
ichnographic ˌɪk.nəʊ'græf.ɪk US -noʊ'- **-al** -ᵊl **-ally** -ᵊl.i, -li
ichnography ɪk'nɒg.rə.fi US -'nɑː.grə-
ichnological ˌɪk.nəʊ'lɒdʒ.ɪ.kᵊl US -noʊ'lɑː.dʒɪ-
ichnology ɪk'nɒl.ə.dʒi US -'nɑː.lə-
ichor 'aɪ.kɔːʳ US -kɔːr, -kɚ
ichthyologic|al ˌɪk.θi.ə'lɒdʒ.ɪ.k|ᵊl US -'lɑː.dʒɪ- **-ally** -ᵊl.i, -li
ichthyolog|y ˌɪk.θi'ɒl.ə.dʒ|i US -'ɑː.lə- **-ist/s** -ɪst/s
ichthyosaur 'ɪk.θi.ə.sɔːʳ US -sɔːr **-s** -z
ichthyosaur|us ˌɪk.θi.əʊ'sɔː.r|əs US -oʊ'sɔːr|.əs, -ə'- **-i** -aɪ **-uses** -ə.sɪz
ICI® ˌaɪ.siː'aɪ
-ician -'ɪʃ.ᵊn
Note: Suffix. Normally carries primary stress as shown above, e.g. **musician** /mjuː'zɪʃ.ᵊn/, **technician** /tek'nɪʃ.ᵊn/.
icicle 'aɪ.sɪ.kl̩, -sə- **-s** -z
icing 'aɪ.sɪŋ **'icing ˌsugar**
Icke aɪk, ɪk
Icknield 'ɪk.niːld
ick|y 'ɪk|.i **-ier** -i.əʳ US -i.ɚ **-iest** -i.ɪst, -i.əst
icon 'aɪ.kɒn, -kən US -kɑːn, -kən **-s** -z
iconic aɪ'kɒn.ɪk US -'kɑː.nɪk
Iconium aɪ'kəʊ.ni.əm, ɪ- US aɪ'koʊ-
iconoclasm aɪ'kɒn.əʊˌklæz.ᵊm US -'kɑː.nə-
iconoclast aɪ'kɒn.əʊ.klæst, -klɑːst US -'kɑː.nə.klæst **-s** -s
iconoclastic aɪˌkɒn.əʊ'klæs.tɪk, ˌaɪ.kɒn- US aɪˌkɑː.nə'- **-ally** -ᵊl.i, -li
iconographic ˌaɪ.kə.nəʊ'græf.ɪk US -noʊ-
iconograph|y ˌaɪ.kə'nɒg.rə.f|i, -kɒn'ɒg- US -kə'nɑː.grə- **-er/s** -əʳ/z US -ɚ/z
iconoscope aɪ'kɒn.ə.skəʊp US -'kɑː.nə.skoʊp **-s** -s
icosahedr|on ˌaɪ.kɒs.ə'hiː.dr|ən, -kə.sə'-; aɪˌkɒs- US ˌaɪ.koʊ.sə'-; aɪˌkɑː- **-ons** -ənz **-a** -ə **-al** -əl
ictus 'ɪk.təs **-es** -ɪz
ICU ˌaɪ.siː'juː
ic|y 'aɪ.s|i **-ier** -i.əʳ US -i.ɚ **-iest** -i.ɪst, -i.əst **-ily** -ɪ.li, -ᵊl.i **-iness** -ɪ.nəs, -ɪ.nɪs
id ɪd
'Id iːd
ID ˌaɪ'diː ˌ**I'D** ˌ**card**
I'd (= **I would, I should** *or* **I had**) aɪd
Ida 'aɪ.də
Ida. (*abbrev. for* **Idaho**) 'aɪ.də.həʊ US -hoʊ
Idaho 'aɪ.də.həʊ US -hoʊ
Iddesleigh 'ɪdz.li
Ide iːd
-ide -aɪd
Note: Suffix. Words containing **-ide** are normally stressed on the penultimate or antepenultimate syllable, e.g. **hydroxide** /haɪ'drɒk.saɪd US -'drɑːk-/.
idea aɪ'dɪə US -'diː.ə **-s** -z
Note: In British English, the pronunciation /'aɪ.dɪə/ is also sometimes heard, especially when a stress immediately follows, e.g. "I thought of the 'idea ˌfirst".
ideal (*n.*) aɪ'dɪəl, -'diː.əl US -'diː- **-s** -z
stress shift: ˌideal 'home
ideal (*adj.*) aɪ'dɪəl, -'diː.əl, '-- US -'diː-
ideal|ism aɪ'dɪə.l|ɪ.zᵊm; 'aɪ.dɪə- US aɪ'diː.ə.l|ɪ- **-ist/s** -ɪst/s
idealistic aɪˌdɪə'lɪs.tɪk; ˌaɪ.dɪə- US ˌaɪ.di.ə'- **-ally** -ᵊl.i, -li
ideality ˌaɪ.di'æl.ə.ti, -ɪ.ti US -ə.t̬i
idealization, -isa- aɪˌdɪə.laɪ'zeɪ.ʃᵊn, -lɪ'-; ˌaɪ.dɪə- US aɪˌdiː.ə.lə'- **-s** -z
idealiz|e, -is|e aɪ'dɪə.laɪz US -'diː.ə- **-es** -ɪz **-ing** -ɪŋ **-ed** -d **-er/s** -əʳ/z US -ɚ/z
ideally aɪ'dɪə.li, -'dɪəl.li US -'diː.li, -ə.li
ide|ate 'aɪ.di|.eɪt **-ates** -eɪts **-ating** -eɪ.tɪŋ US -t̬ɪŋ **-ated** -eɪ.tɪd US -t̬ɪd
ideational ˌaɪ.di'eɪ.ʃᵊn.ᵊl, -'eɪʃ.nᵊl
idée fixe ˌiː.deɪ'fiːks **idées fixes** ˌiː.deɪ'fiːks, -deɪz'-
idée reçue ˌiː.deɪ.rə'suː **idées reçues** ˌiː.deɪ.rə'suː, -deɪz-
idem 'ɪd.em, 'iː.dem, 'aɪ- US 'aɪ-, 'iː-, 'ɪd.em
idempotent ˌɪd.əm'pəʊ.tənt, ˌiː.dəm-, ˌaɪ-, -dem'- US ˌaɪ.dem'poʊ-, ˌiː-, ˌɪd.em'-
identic|al aɪ'den.tɪ.k|ᵊl, ɪ- US -t̬ə- **-ally** -ᵊl.i, -li **-alness** -ᵊl.nəs, -ᵊl.nɪs
identifiable aɪ'den.tɪ.faɪ.ə.bl̩, -tə'-, aɪˌden.tɪ'faɪ-, -tə- US aɪˌden.t̬ə'-
identification aɪˌden.tɪ.fɪ'keɪ.ʃᵊn, -tə- US -t̬ə- **-s** -z
identi|fy aɪ'den.tɪ|.faɪ, -tə- US -t̬ə- **-f**-faɪz **-fying** -faɪ.ɪŋ **-fied** -faɪd **-fier**-faɪ.əʳ/z US -faɪ.ɚ/z
identikit (I) aɪ'den.tɪ.kɪt US -t̬ə- **-s** -s
identit|y aɪ'den.tə.t|i, -ɪ.t|i US -t̬ə.t̬ **-ies** -iz **i'dentity ˌcard; i'dentity ˌcrisis; i'dentity paˌrade; i'dentity ˌlineup**
ideogram 'ɪd.i.əʊ.græm, 'aɪ.di- US -oʊ-, -ə- **-s** -z
ideograph 'ɪd.i.əʊ.grɑːf, 'aɪ.di-, -gr US -oʊ.græf, -ə- **-s** -s
ideographic ˌɪd.i.əʊ'græf.ɪk, ˌaɪ.di- US -oʊ'-, -ə'- **-al** -ᵊl **-ally** -ᵊl.i, -li
ideography ˌɪd.i'ɒg.rə.fi, ˌaɪ.di'- US -'ɑː.grə-
ideologic|al ˌaɪ.di.ə'lɒdʒ.ɪ.k|ᵊl, ˌɪd. US -'lɑː.dʒɪ- **-ally** -ᵊl.i, -li
ideologue 'aɪ.di.əʊ.lɒg, 'ɪd.i- US -ə.lɑːg **-s** -z
ideolog|y ˌaɪ.di'ɒl.ə.dʒ|i, ˌɪd.i'- US -'ɑː.lə- **-ies** -iz **-ist/s** -ɪst/s
ides (I) aɪdz ˌ**Ides of 'March**
Idi Amin ˌiː.diˌɑː'miːn
idio- ɪd.i.əʊ-; ˌɪd.i'ɒ- US ɪd.i.oʊ-, -ə-, ˌɪd.i'ɑː-
Note: Prefix. Normally takes either primary or secondary stress on first syllable, e.g. **idiolect** /'ɪd.i.əʊ.lekt US -oʊ-/, **idiomati** /ˌɪd.i.əʊ'mæt.ɪk US -ə'mæt̬-/, or secondary stress on the first syll and primary stress on the third, **idiotic** /ˌɪd.i'ɒt.ɪk US -'ɑː.t̬ɪk/.
idioc|y 'ɪd.i.ə.s|i **-ies** -iz
idiolect 'ɪd.i.əʊ.lekt US -oʊ-, -ə- **-s** -ᵊl
idiom 'ɪd.i.əm **-s** -z
idiomatic ˌɪd.i.əʊ'mæt.ɪk US -ə'mæ **-al** -ᵊl **-ally** -ᵊl.i, -li
idiophone 'ɪd.i.əʊ.fəʊn US -oʊ.foʊ -ə- **-s** -z
idiosyncras|y ˌɪd.i.əʊ'sɪŋ.krə.s|i US -oʊ'sɪn-, -ə'-, -'sɪŋ- **-ies** -iz
idiosyncratic ˌɪd.i.əʊ.sɪŋ'kræt.ɪk US -oʊ.sɪn'kræt̬-, -ə-, -sɪŋ'- **-ally** -li
idiot 'ɪd.i.ət **-s** -s **'idiot ˌbox**
idiotic ˌɪd.i'ɒt.ɪk US -'ɑː.t̬ɪk **-al** -ᵊl -ᵊl.i, -li
idiotism 'ɪd.i.ə.tɪ.zᵊm US -t̬ɪ- **-s** -z
idiot-proof 'ɪd.i.ətˌpruːf
idiot(s) savant(s) ˌiː.di.əʊ.sæv'ɑ̃ː, ˌɪd.i.ət'sæv.ᵊnt US ˌiː.diː.oʊ.sæv'ɑːnt, -'ænt
Idist 'iː.dɪst **-s** -s
id|le (I) 'aɪ.d|l̩ **-ly** -li **-lest** -lɪst, -ləst **-leness** -l̩.nəs, -nɪs **-les** -l̩z **-ling** **-led** -l̩d **-ler/s** -ləʳ/z US -lɚ/z
Ido 'iː.dəʊ US -doʊ
idol 'aɪ.dᵊl **-s** -z
idolater aɪ'dɒl.ə.təʳ US -'dɑː.lə.t̬

Pronouncing the letters IE

There are several pronunciation possibilities for the vowel digraph **ie**. One of the most common is /iː/:

achieve /ə'tʃiːv/
piece /piːs/

Another common pronunciation is /aɪ/, e.g.:

pie /paɪ/
magnifies /'mæg.nɪ.faɪz/

When followed by an **r** in the spelling, **ie** is pronounced as /ɪə, Ⓤⓢ ɪr/, e.g.:

pier /pɪəʳ/ Ⓤⓢ /pɪr/
fierce /fɪəs/ Ⓤⓢ /fɪrs/

In addition

Other vowel sounds are associated with the digraph **ie**, e.g.:

/ɪ/ handkerchief /'hæŋ.kə.tʃɪf/ Ⓤⓢ /-kɚ-/
/aɪə/ diet /daɪət/
/e/ friend /frend/
/i.e/ conscientious /ˌkɒn.tʃi'en.tʃəs/ Ⓤⓢ /ˌkɑːn.tʃi'ent.ʃəs/
/i.iː/ medieval /ˌmed.i'iː.vᵊl/ Ⓤⓢ /ˌmiː.di'-/

In weak syllables

The vowel digraph **ie** is realised with the vowel /ə/ in weak syllables, or can cause the following consonant to be realised as syllabic, e.g.:

patient /'peɪ.ʃᵊnt/

Pronouncing the letters IEU

The vowel letter combination **ieu** has a number of possible pronunciations, but most are associated with particular words, e.g.:

lieutenant /lef'ten.ənt/ Ⓤⓢ /luː-/
lieu /ljuː, luː/ Ⓤⓢ /luː/

olatrous aɪ'dɒl.ə.trəs Ⓤⓢ -'dɑː.lə- **-ly** -li **-ness** -nəs, -nɪs
olatr|y aɪ'dɒl.ə.tr|i Ⓤⓢ -'dɑː.lə- **-ies** -iz
olization, -isa- ˌaɪ.dᵊl.aɪ'zeɪ.ʃᵊn, -ɪ'- Ⓤⓢ -ɪ'-
oliz|e, -is|e 'aɪ.dᵊl.aɪz **-es** -ɪz **-ing** -ɪŋ **-ed** -d **-er/s** -əʳ/z Ⓤⓢ -ɚ/z
omeneus aɪ'dɒm.ɪ.njuːs, ɪ'-, '-ə-; ɪˌdɒm.ɪ'niː.əs, aɪˌ-, -ə'- Ⓤⓢ -'dɑː.mə.nuːs, -njuːs
is 'ɪd.rɪs, 'aɪ.drɪs
umea ˌaɪ.djʊ'miː.ə, ˌɪd.jʊ'- Ⓤⓢ ˌɪd.juː'miː.ə, ˌiː.djuː'-, ˌiː.dʒuː'-
ll 'ɪd.ᵊl, 'aɪ.dᵊl, -dɪl Ⓤⓢ 'aɪ.dᵊl **-s** -z
llic ɪ'dɪl.ɪk, aɪ- Ⓤⓢ aɪ- **-ally** -ᵊl.i, -li
llist 'ɪd.ᵊl.ɪst, 'aɪ.dᵊl-, -dɪl- Ⓤⓢ 'aɪ.dᵊl- **-s** -s
ˌaɪ'iː
f
surname: aɪf *town in Nigeria:* 'iː.feɪ
ey 'ɪf.li
y 'ɪf.i
r 'aɪ.vəʳ, -fəʳ, 'iː.vɔːʳ Ⓤⓢ 'aɪ.vɚ, 'iː-
y -ɪ.faɪ, -ə-
te: Suffix. Words containing **-ify** normally carry stress on the antepenultimate syllable, e.g. **person** /'pɜː.sᵊn Ⓤⓢ 'pɜːr-/, **personify** /pə'sɒn.ɪ.faɪ Ⓤⓢ pɚ'sɑː.nɪ-/. Exceptions exist; see individual entries.

Igbo 'iː.bəʊ Ⓤⓢ -boʊ **-s** -z
Ightham 'aɪ.təm Ⓤⓢ -t̬əm
Iglesias ɪ'gleɪ.si.æs, -əs, -zi- Ⓤⓢ -əs
igloo 'ɪg.luː **-s** -z
Ignatieff ɪg'næt.i.ef Ⓤⓢ -'næt̬-
Ignatius ɪg'neɪ.ʃəs
igneous 'ɪg.ni.əs
ignis fatu|us ˌɪg.nɪs'fæt.ju|.əs Ⓤⓢ -'fætʃ.uː- **-i** -iː
ig|nite ɪg|'naɪt **-nites** -'naɪts **-niting** -'naɪ.tɪŋ Ⓤⓢ -'naɪ.t̬ɪŋ **-nited** -'naɪ.tɪd Ⓤⓢ -'naɪ.t̬ɪd **-nitable** -'naɪ.tə.bl̩ Ⓤⓢ -'naɪ.t̬ə.bl̩
ignition ɪg'nɪʃ.ᵊn **-s** -z
ignobility ˌɪg.nəʊ'bɪl.ə.ti, -ɪ.ti Ⓤⓢ -noʊ'bɪl.ə.t̬i, -nə'-
ignob|le ɪg'nəʊ.b|l̩ Ⓤⓢ -'noʊ- **-ly** -li **-leness** -l̩.nəs, -nɪs
ignominious ˌɪg.nəʊ'mɪn.i.əs Ⓤⓢ -nə'- **-ly** -li **-ness** -nəs, -nɪs
ignominy 'ɪg.nə.mɪ.ni, -mə.ni Ⓤⓢ -nə.mɪ-
ignoramus ˌɪg.nə'reɪ.məs **-es** -ɪz
ignorance 'ɪg.nᵊr.ᵊnts
ignorant 'ɪg.nᵊr.ᵊnt **-ly** -li
ignor|e ɪg'nɔːʳ Ⓤⓢ -'nɔːr **-es** -z **-ing** -ɪŋ **-ed** -d **-able** -ə.bl̩

Igoe 'aɪ.gəʊ Ⓤⓢ -goʊ
Igor 'iː.gɔːʳ Ⓤⓢ -gɔːr
Igorot ˌiː.gə'rəʊt, ˌɪg.ə'- Ⓤⓢ ˌiː.goʊ'roʊt, ˌɪg.oʊ'- **-s** -s
Igraine ɪ'greɪn, iː-
Iguaçú ˌiː.gwɑː'suː
iguana ɪ'gwɑː.nə, ˌɪg.ju'ɑː- Ⓤⓢ ɪ'gwɑː-, iː- **-s** -z
iguanodon ɪ'gwɑː.nə.dɒn, ˌɪg.ju'ɑː-, -'æn.ə-, -dən Ⓤⓢ ɪ'gwɑː.nə.dɑːn, iː- **-s** -z
Iguazú ˌiː.gwɑː'suː
ikat 'iː.kɑːt
IKBS ˌaɪ.keɪ.biː'es
Ike aɪk
Ikea® aɪ'kiː.ə *as if Swedish:* ɪ'keɪ.ə
ikon 'aɪ.kɒn, -kən Ⓤⓢ -kɑːn, -kən **-s** -z
Ilchester 'ɪl.tʃɪs.təʳ Ⓤⓢ -tɚ
ILEA 'ɪl.i.ə, ˌaɪ.el.iː'eɪ
ilea *(plur. of* **ileum***)* 'ɪl.i.ə
ileostom|y ˌɪl.i'ɒs.tə.m|i Ⓤⓢ -'ɑː.stə- **-ies** -iz
ile|um 'ɪl.i|.əm **-a** -ə **-al** -əl
ilex 'aɪ.leks **-es** -ɪz
Ilford 'ɪl.fəd Ⓤⓢ -fɚd
Ilfracombe 'ɪl.frə.kuːm
ilia *(plur. of* **ilium***)* 'ɪl.i.ə
iliac 'ɪl.i.æk
Iliad 'ɪl.i.æd, -əd Ⓤⓢ -əd, -æd

Iliffe 'aɪ.lɪf
ili|um 'ɪl.i|.əm **-a** -ə
Ilium 'ɪl.i.əm, 'aɪ.li-
ilk ɪlk
Ilkeston(e) 'ɪl.kɪ.stᵊn, -kə-
Ilkley 'ɪl.kli
ill ɪl **-s** -z ˌ**ill at 'ease**; ˌ**ill 'will**
I'll *(=* **I will** *or* **I shall***)* aɪl
Ill. *(abbrev. for* **Illinois***)* ˌɪl.ɪ'nɔɪ, -ə'-
ill-advised ˌɪl.əd'vaɪzd *stress shift:* ˌill-advised 'plan
ill-advisedly ˌɪl.əd'vaɪ.zɪd.li
ill-assorted ˌɪl.ə'sɔː.tɪd ⓤⓢ -'sɔːr.t̬ɪd *stress shift:* ˌill-assorted 'candidates
illative ɪ'leɪ.tɪv, 'ɪl.ə.tɪv ⓤⓢ -t̬ɪv **-ly** -li
ill-bred ˌɪl'bred *stress shift:* ˌill-bred 'lout
ill-breeding ˌɪl'briː.dɪŋ
ill-conceived ˌɪl.kən'siːvd *stress shift:* ˌill-conceived 'plan
ill-conditioned ˌɪl.kən'dɪʃ.ᵊnd *stress shift:* ˌill-conditioned 'crew
ill-considered ˌɪl.kən'sɪd.əd ⓤⓢ -ɚd *stress shift:* ˌill-considered 'action
ill-disposed ˌɪl.dɪ'spəʊzd ⓤⓢ -'spoʊzd *stress shift:* ˌill-disposed 'patient
illegal ɪ'liː.gᵊl ⓤⓢ ɪ'liː-, ˌɪl- **-ly** -i **ilˌlegal 'alien; ilˌlegal 'immigrant**
illegalit|y ˌɪl.iː'gæl.ə.t|i, -ɪ'-, -ɪ.t|i ⓤⓢ -ə.t̬|i **-ies** -iz
illegibility ɪˌledʒ.ə'bɪl.ə.ti, ˌɪl.ledʒ-, -ɪ'-, -ɪ.ti ⓤⓢ -ə.t̬i
illegib|le ɪ'ledʒ.ə.b|l̩, ˌɪl'ledʒ-, '-ɪ- **-ly** -li **-leness** -l̩.nəs, -nɪs
illegitimacy ˌɪl.ɪ'dʒɪt.ə.mə.si, -ə'-, '-ɪ- ⓤⓢ -'dʒɪt̬.ə-
illegitimate ˌɪl.ɪ'dʒɪt.ə.mət, -ə'-, '-ɪ-, -mɪt ⓤⓢ -'dʒɪt̬.ə- **-ly** -li
ill-equipped ˌɪl.ɪ'kwɪpt *stress shift:* ˌill-equipped 'project
ill-fated ˌɪl'feɪ.tɪd ⓤⓢ -t̬ɪd *stress shift:* ˌill-fated 'lovers
ill-favoured ˌɪl'feɪ.vəd ⓤⓢ -vɚd **-ly** -li **-ness** -nəs, -nɪs *stress shift:* ˌill-favoured 'couple
ill-feeling ˌɪl'fiː.lɪŋ
ill-founded ˌɪl'faʊn.dɪd *stress shift:* ˌill-founded 'rumo(u)r
ill-gotten ˌɪl'gɒt.ᵊn ⓤⓢ -'gɑː.tᵊn *stress shift, see compound:* ˌ**ill-gotten 'gains**
illiberal ɪ'lɪb.ᵊr.ᵊl, ˌɪl- **-ly** -i **-ness** -nəs, -nɪs
illiberalism ɪ'lɪb.ᵊr.ᵊl.ɪ.zᵊm, ˌɪl-
illiberality ɪˌlɪb.ə'ræl.ə.ti, ˌɪl-, -ɪ.ti ⓤⓢ -ə.t̬i
illicit ɪ'lɪs.ɪt, ˌɪl- **-ly** -li **-ness** -nəs, -nɪs
illimitab|le ɪ'lɪm.ɪ.tə.b|l̩, ˌɪl- ⓤⓢ -t̬ə- **-ly** -li **-leness** -l̩.nəs, -nɪs
Illingworth 'ɪl.ɪŋ.wəθ, -wɜːθ ⓤⓢ -wɚθ, -wɝːθ
Illinois ˌɪl.ɪ'nɔɪ, -ə'-
illiteracy ɪ'lɪt.ᵊr.ə.si, ˌɪl- ⓤⓢ -'lɪt̬-
illiterate ɪ'lɪt.ᵊr.ət, ˌɪl-, -ɪt ⓤⓢ -'lɪt̬- **-s** -s **-ly** -li **-ness** -nəs, -nɪs
ill-judged ˌɪl'dʒʌdʒd *stress shift:* ˌill-judged 'move
ill-mannered ˌɪl'mæn.əd ⓤⓢ -ɚd *stress shift:* ˌill-mannered 'man
ill-natured ˌɪl'neɪ.tʃəd ⓤⓢ -tʃɚd **-ly** -li *stress shift:* ˌill-natured 'dog
illness 'ɪl.nəs, -nɪs **-es** -ɪz
illocution ˌɪl.ə'kjuː.ʃᵊn **-s** -z **-ary** -ᵊr.i ⓤⓢ -er-
Illogan ɪ'lʌg.ən
illogic|al ɪ'lɒdʒ.ɪ.k|ᵊl, ˌɪl- ⓤⓢ -'lɑː.dʒɪ- **-ally** -ᵊl.i, -li **-alness** -ᵊl.nəs, -nɪs
illogicalit|y ɪˌlɒdʒ.ɪ'kæl.ə.t|i, ˌɪl-, -ɪ.t|i ⓤⓢ -ˌlɑː.dʒɪ'kæl.ə.t̬|i **-ies** -iz
ill-omened ˌɪl'əʊ.mend, -mənd, -mɪnd ⓤⓢ -'oʊ- *stress shift:* ˌill-omened 'voyage
ill-starred ˌɪl'stɑːd ⓤⓢ -'stɑːrd *stress shift:* ˌill-starred 'love
ill-tempered ˌɪl'tem.pəd ⓤⓢ -pɚd *stress shift:* ˌill-tempered 'customer
ill-timed ˌɪl'taɪmd *stress shift:* ˌill-timed 'entrance
ill|-treat ˌɪl|'triːt, ɪl- **-treats** -'triːts **-treating** -'triː.tɪŋ ⓤⓢ -'triː.t̬ɪŋ **-treated** -'triː.tɪd ⓤⓢ -'triː.t̬ɪd **-treatment** -'triːt.mənt
illum|e ɪ'ljuːm, -'luːm ⓤⓢ -'luːm **-es** -z **-ing** -ɪŋ **-ed** -d
illuminant ɪ'luː.mɪ.nənt, -'ljuː-, -mə- ⓤⓢ -'luː.mə- **-s** -s
illumi|nate ɪ'luː.mɪ|.neɪt, -'ljuː-, -mə- ⓤⓢ -'luː.mə- **-nates** -neɪts **-nating** -neɪ.tɪŋ ⓤⓢ -neɪ.t̬ɪŋ **-nated** -neɪ.tɪd ⓤⓢ -neɪ.t̬ɪd **-nator/s** -neɪ.təʳ/z ⓤⓢ -neɪ.t̬ɚ/z
illuminati (I) ɪˌluː.mɪ'nɑː.tiː, -mə'- ⓤⓢ -'nɑː.t̬i
illumination ɪˌluː.mɪ'neɪ.ʃᵊn, -ˌljuː-, -mə'- ⓤⓢ -ˌluː- **-s** -z
illuminative ɪ'luː.mɪ.nə.təv, -'ljuː-, -mə-, -neɪ- ⓤⓢ -'luː.mɪ.neɪ.t̬ɪv, -mə-
illumin|e ɪ'ljuː.mɪn, -'luː- ⓤⓢ -'luː- **-es** -z **-ing** -ɪŋ **-ed** -d
ill-usage ˌɪl'juː.zɪdʒ, -sɪdʒ ⓤⓢ -sɪdʒ, -zɪdʒ **-s** -ɪz
ill-used ˌɪl'juːzd *stress shift:* ˌill-used 'servant
illusion ɪ'luː.ʒᵊn, -'ljuː- ⓤⓢ -'luː- **-s** -z
illusion|ism ɪ'luː.ʒᵊn|.ɪ.zᵊm, -'ljuː- ⓤⓢ -'luː- **-ist/s** -ɪst/s
illusive ɪ'luː.sɪv, -'ljuː- ⓤⓢ -'luː- **-ly** -li **-ness** -nəs, -nɪs
illusor|y ɪ'luː.sᵊr|.i, -'ljuː-, -zᵊr- ⓤⓢ -'luː- **-ily** -ᵊl.i, -ɪ.li **-iness** -ɪ.nəs, -ɪ.nɪs
illu|strate 'ɪl.ə|.streɪt **-strates** -streɪts **-strating** -streɪ.tɪŋ ⓤⓢ -streɪ.t̬ɪŋ **-strated** -streɪ.tɪd ⓤⓢ -streɪ.t̬ɪd **-strator/s** -streɪ.təʳ/z ⓤⓢ -streɪ.t̬ɚ/z
illustration ˌɪl.ə'streɪ.ʃᵊn **-s** -z
illustrative 'ɪl.ə.strə.tɪv, -streɪ-; ɪ'lʌs.trə.tɪv ⓤⓢ ɪ'lʌs.trə.t̬ɪv; 'ɪl.ə.streɪ- **-ly** -li
illustrious ɪ'lʌs.tri.əs **-ly** -li **-ness** -nəs -nɪs
illuvi|um ɪ'luː.vi|.əm **-ums** -əmz **-a** -ə **-al** -əl
Illyri|a ɪ'lɪr.i|.ə **-an/s** -ən/z
Illyricum ɪ'lɪr.ɪ.kəm
Ilminster 'ɪl.mɪn.stəʳ ⓤⓢ -stɚ
Ilorin ɪ'lɒr.ɪn ⓤⓢ -'lɔːr-
Ilyushin ɪ'ljuː.ʃɪn, -ʃᵊn ⓤⓢ ɪl'juː-, ɪ'luː
im- ɪm-

Note: Prefix. The form of **in-** where t[he] stem begins with /p/, /b/, or /m/. When a negative prefix, **im-** does [not] affect the stress pattern of the ste[m], e.g. **balance** /'bæl.ənts/, **imbalan[ce]** /ɪm'bæl.ənts/. In other cases, the prefix is normally stressed in nou[ns] but not in verbs, e.g. **imprint**, nou[n] /'ɪm.prɪnt/, verb /ɪm'prɪnt/.

I'm *(=* **I am***)* aɪm
imag|e 'ɪm.ɪdʒ **-es** -ɪz **-ing** -ɪŋ **-ed** -d
imager|y 'ɪm.ɪ.dʒᵊr|.i, '-ə- **-ies** -iz
imaginab|le ɪ'mædʒ.ɪ.nə.b|l̩, -ᵊn.ə- **-ly** -li **-leness** -l̩.nəs, -nɪs
imaginar|y ɪ'mædʒ.ɪ.nᵊr|.i, -ᵊn.ᵊr-, -'-nᵊr|.i ⓤⓢ -ə.ner- **-ily** -ᵊl.i, -ɪ.li **-in[ess]** -ɪ.nəs, -ɪ.nɪs
imagination ɪˌmædʒ.ɪ'neɪ.ʃᵊn, -ə'- -[s]
imaginative ɪ'mædʒ.ɪ.nə.tɪv, '-ə- ⓤⓢ -nə.t̬ɪv, -neɪ- **-ly** -li **-ness** -nəs, -[nɪs]
imagin|e ɪ'mædʒ.ɪn, -ᵊn **-es** -z **-ing/s** -ɪŋ/z **-ed** -d
imagines *(plur. of* **imago***)* ɪ'meɪ.dʒɪ.niːz, ɪ'mɑː-, -neɪz ⓤⓢ -n[iːz]
imagism 'ɪm.ɪ.dʒɪ.zᵊm
ima|go ɪ'meɪ|.gəʊ, ɪ'mɑː- ⓤⓢ -goʊ **-g[oes]** -gəʊz ⓤⓢ -goʊz **-gines** -dʒɪ.niːz, -neɪz ⓤⓢ -niːz
imam ɪ'mɑːm, 'iː.mɑːm ⓤⓢ ɪ'mɑːm -[s]
imbalanc|e ˌɪm'bæl.ənts **-es** -ɪz
imbecile 'ɪm.bə.siːl, -bɪ-, -saɪl ⓤⓢ -s[ɪl], -səl **-s** -z
imbecilic ˌɪm.bə'sɪl.ɪk, -bɪ'-
imbecilit|y ˌɪm.bə'sɪl.ə.t|i, -bɪ'-, -ɪ.t[|i] ⓤⓢ -ə.t̬|i **-ies** -iz
imbed ɪm'bed **-s** -z **-ding** -ɪŋ **-ded** -ɪ[d]
Imbert 'ɪm.bət ⓤⓢ -bɚt
imbib|e ɪm'baɪb **-es** -z **-ing** -ɪŋ **-ed** -[d] **-er/s** -əʳ/z ⓤⓢ -ɚ/z
imbroglio ɪm'brəʊ.li.əʊ ⓤⓢ -'broʊ.[ljoʊ] **-s** -z
imbru|e ɪm'bruː **-es** -z **-ing** -ɪŋ **-ed** -[d]
imbu|e ɪm'bjuː **-es** -z **-ing** -ɪŋ **-ed** -d
Imelda ɪ'mel.də
Imeson 'aɪ.mɪ.sᵊn
IMF ˌaɪ.em'ef
imitability ˌɪm.ɪ.tə'bɪl.ə.ti, ˌ-ə-, -ɪ. ⓤⓢ -ə.t̬i

imitable 'ɪm.ɪ.tə.bl̩, '-ə- US -ə.t̬ə-

imi|tate 'ɪm.ɪ|.teɪt, '-ə- **-tates** -teɪts **-tating** -teɪ.tɪŋ US -teɪ.t̬ɪŋ **-tated** -teɪ.tɪd US -teɪ.t̬ɪd **-tator/s** -teɪ.təʳ/z US -teɪ.t̬ɚ/z

imitation ˌɪm.ɪ'teɪ.ʃᵊn, -ə'- **-s** -z **-al** -ᵊl

imitative 'ɪm.ɪ.tə.tɪv, '-ə-, -teɪ- US -teɪ.t̬ɪv **-ly** -li **-ness** -nəs, -nɪs

Imlay 'ɪm.leɪ

immaculate ɪ'mæk.jə.lət, -jʊ-, -lɪt **-ly** -li **-ness** -nəs, -nɪs **Imˌmaculate Con'ception**

immanen|ce 'ɪm.ə.nən|*t*s **-t** -t

Immanuel ɪ'mæn.ju.əl US -el, -ᵊl

immaterial ˌɪm.ə'tɪə.ri.əl US -'tɪr.i- **-ly** -i **-ness** -nəs, -nɪs

immaterial|ism ˌɪm.ə'tɪə.ri.ᵊl|.ɪ.zᵊm US -'tɪr.i- **-ist/s** -ɪst/s

immateriality ˌɪm.əˌtɪə.ri'æl.ə.ti, -ɪ.ti US -ˌtɪr.i'æl.ə.t̬i

immaterializ|e, -is|e ˌɪm.ə'tɪə.ri.ᵊl.aɪz US -'tɪr.i- **-es** -ɪz **-ing** -ɪŋ **-ed** -d

immature ˌɪm.ə'tjʊəʳ, -'tʃʊəʳ, -'tjɔːʳ, -'tʃɔːʳ US -'tʊr, -'tjʊr, -'tʃʊr **-ly** -li **-ness** -nəs, -nɪs

immaturit|y ˌɪm.ə'tjʊə.rə.t|i, -'tʃʊə-, -'tjɔː-, -'tʃɔː-, -rɪ- US -'tʊr.ə.t̬|i, -'tjʊr-, -'tʃʊr- **-ies** -iz

immeasurab|le ɪ'meʒ.ᵊr.ə.b|l̩, ˌɪm- **-ly** -li **-leness** -l̩.nəs, -nɪs

immediacy ɪ'miː.di.ə.si

immediate ɪ'miː.di.ət, -ɪt, -dʒət US -di.ɪt **-ly** -li

immemorial ˌɪm.ɪ'mɔː.ri.əl, -ə'- US -'mɔːr.i- **-ly** -li

immense ɪ'men*t*s **-ly** -li **-ness** -nəs, -nɪs

immensit|y ɪ'men*t*.sə.t|i, -sɪ- US -sə.t̬|i **-ies** -iz

immers|e ɪ'mɜːs US -'mɝːs **-es** -ɪz **-ing** -ɪŋ **-ed** -t

immersion ɪ'mɜː.ʃᵊn, -ʒᵊn US -'mɝː- **-s** -z **im'mersion ˌheater**

immigrant 'ɪm.ɪ.grənt, '-ə- **-s** -s

immi|grate 'ɪm.ɪ|.greɪt, '-ə- **-grates** -greɪts **-grating** -greɪ.tɪŋ US -greɪ.t̬ɪŋ **-grated** -greɪ.tɪd US -greɪ.t̬ɪd

immigration ˌɪm.ɪ'greɪ.ʃᵊn, -ə'- **-s** -z

imminence 'ɪm.ɪ.nən*t*s, '-ə-

imminent 'ɪm.ɪ.nənt, '-ə- **-ly** -li

Immingham 'ɪm.ɪŋ.əm US -hæm, -həm, -əm

immiscibility ɪˌmɪs.ɪ'bɪl.ə.ti, ˌɪm-, -ə'-, -ɪ.ti US -ə.t̬i

immiscib|le ɪ'mɪs.ə.b|l̩, ˌɪm-, '-ɪ- **-ly** -li

immobile ɪ'məʊ.baɪl, ɪm- US -'moʊ.bᵊl, -bɪl, -baɪl

immobility ˌɪm.əʊ'bɪl.ə.ti, -ɪ.ti US -moʊ'bɪl.ə.t̬i

immobilization, -isa- ɪˌməʊ.bᵊl.aɪ'zeɪ.ʃᵊn, ˌɪm-, -bɪ.laɪ'-, -lɪ'- US -ˌmoʊ.bə.lɪ'-

immobiliz|e, -is|e ɪ'məʊ.bᵊl.aɪz, ˌɪm-, -bɪ.laɪz US -'moʊ- **-es** -ɪz **-ing** -ɪŋ **-ed** -d

immobilizer, -ise- ɪ'məʊ.bᵊl.aɪ.zəʳ US -zɚ **-s** -z

immoderate ɪ'mɒd.ᵊr.ət, ˌɪm-, -ɪt US -'mɑː.dɚ- **-ly** -li **-ness** -nəs, -nɪs

immoderation ɪˌmɒd.ə'reɪ.ʃᵊn, ˌɪm- US -ˌmɑː.də'-

immodest ɪ'mɒd.ɪst, ˌɪm- US -'mɑː.dɪst **-ly** -li

immodesty ɪ'mɒd.ə.sti, ˌɪm-, '-ɪ- US -'mɑː.də-

immo|late 'ɪm.əʊ|.leɪt US '-ə- **-lates** -leɪts **-lating** -leɪ.tɪŋ US -leɪ.t̬ɪŋ **-lated** -leɪ.tɪd US -leɪ.t̬ɪd **-lator/s** -leɪ.təʳ/z US -leɪ.t̬ɚ/z

immolation ˌɪm.əʊ'leɪ.ʃᵊn US -ə'- **-s** -z

immoral ɪ'mɒr.ᵊl, ˌɪm- US -'mɔːr- **-ly** -i

immoralit|y ˌɪm.ə'ræl.ə.t|i, -ɒr'æl-, -ɪ.t|i US -mɔː'ræl.ə.t̬|i, -mə'- **-ies** -iz

immortal ɪ'mɔː.tᵊl, ˌɪm- US -'mɔːr.t̬ᵊl **-s** -z **-ly** -i

immortality ˌɪm.ɔː'tæl.ə.ti, -ɪ.ti US -ɔːr'tæl.ə.t̬i

immortaliz|e, -is|e ɪ'mɔː.tᵊl.aɪz, ˌɪm- US -'mɔːr.t̬ᵊl- **-es** -ɪz **-ing** -ɪŋ **-ed** -d

immortelle ˌɪm.ɔː'tel US -ɔːr'- **-s** -z

immovability ɪˌmuː.və'bɪl.ə.ti, ˌɪm-, -ɪ.ti US -ə.t̬i

immovab|le ɪ'muː.və.b|l̩, ˌɪm- **-ly** -li **-leness** -l̩.nəs, -nɪs

immune ɪ'mjuːn **im'mune ˌsystem**

immunit|y ɪ'mjuː.nə.t|i, -nɪ- US -nə.t̬|i **-ies** -iz

immunization, -isa- ˌɪm.jə.naɪ'zeɪ.ʃᵊn, -jʊ-, -nɪ'- US -nɪ'- **-s** -z

immuniz|e, -is|e 'ɪm.jə.naɪz, -jʊ- **-es** -ɪz **-ing** -ɪŋ **-ed** -d

immuno- ˌɪm.jə.nəʊ-, -jʊ-; ɪˌmjuː.nəʊ- US -noʊ-

immunodeficiency ˌɪm.jə.nəʊ.dɪ'fɪʃ.ᵊn*t*.si, -jʊ-; ɪˌmjuː- US -noʊ-

immunologic|al ˌɪm.jə.nəʊ'lɒdʒ.ɪ.k|ᵊl, -jʊ-; ɪˌmjuː.nəʊ'- US ˌɪm.jə.noʊ'lɑː.dʒɪ-, -jʊ- **-ally** -ᵊl.i, -li

immunolog|y ˌɪm.jə'nɒl.ə.dʒ|i, -jʊ'- US -'nɑː.lə- **-ist/s** -ɪst/s

immunosuppress|ant ˌɪm.jə.nəʊ.sə'pres|.ᵊnt, -jʊ-; ɪˌmjuː- US -noʊ- **-ive** -ɪv

immunosuppression ˌɪm.jə.nəʊ.sə'preʃ.ᵊn, -jʊ-; ɪˌmjuː- US -noʊ-

immur|e ɪ'mjʊəʳ, -'mjɔːʳ US -'mjʊr **-es** -z **-ing** -ɪŋ **-ed** -d **-ement** -mənt

immutability ɪˌmjuː.tə'bɪl.ə.ti, -ɪ.ti; ˌɪm.jə-, -jʊ- US ɪˌmjuː.t̬ə'bɪl.ə.t̬i

immutab|le ɪ'mjuː.tə.b|l̩ US -t̬ə- **-ly** -li **-leness** -l̩.nəs, -nɪs

Imogen 'ɪm.ə.dʒᵊn, -dʒen, -dʒɪn US -dʒen, -dʒᵊn

Imogene 'ɪm.ə.dʒiːn

Imola 'ɪm.əʊ.lə US -ə-, -ˌoʊ-

imp ɪmp **-s** -s **-ing** -ɪŋ **-ed** -t

impact (*n.*) 'ɪm.pækt **-s** -s

impact (*v.*) ɪm'pækt, '-- **-s** -s **-ing** -ɪŋ **-ed** -ɪd

impair ɪm'peəʳ US -'per **-s** -z **-ing** -ɪŋ **-ed** -d

impairment ɪm'peə.mənt US -'per- **-s** -s

impala ɪm'pɑː.lə US -'pɑː.lə, -'pæl.ə **-s** -z

impal|e ɪm'peɪl **-es** -z **-ing** -ɪŋ **-ed** -d **-ement** -mənt

impalpab|le ɪm'pæl.pə.b|l̩, ˌɪm- **-ly** -li

impanel ɪm'pæn.ᵊl **-s** -z **-(l)ing** -ɪŋ **-(l)ed** -d

imparisyllabic ɪmˌpær.ɪ.sɪ'læb.ɪk, ˌɪm.pær-, ˌ-ə- US ɪmˌper-, -ˌpær-

im|part ɪm|'pɑːt US -'pɑːrt **-parts** -'pɑːts US -'pɑːrts **-parting** -'pɑː.tɪŋ US -'pɑːr.t̬ɪŋ **-parted** -'pɑː.tɪd US -'pɑːr.t̬ɪd

impartation ˌɪm.pɑː'teɪ.ʃᵊn US -pɑːr'-

impartial ɪm'pɑː.ʃᵊl, ˌɪm- US -'pɑːr- **-ly** -i **-ness** -nəs, -nɪs

impartiality ɪmˌpɑː.ʃi'æl.ə.ti, ˌɪm.pɑː-, ˌɪmˌpɑː-, -ɪ.ti US ɪmˌpɑːr-, ˌɪm-

impassability ɪmˌpɑː.sə'bɪl.ə.ti, ˌɪm.pɑː-, ˌɪmˌpɑː-, -ɪ.ti US ɪmˌpæs.ə'bɪl.ə.t̬i, ˌɪm-

impassable ɪm'pɑː.sə.bl̩, ˌɪm- US -'pæs.ə- **-ness** -nəs, -nɪs

impasse '*æ̃m*.pɑːs, 'æm-, 'ɪm-, -pæs, -'- US 'ɪm.pæs, -'- **-es** -ɪz

impassibility ɪmˌpæs.ə'bɪl.ə.ti, ˌɪm.pæs-, -sɪ'-, -ɪ.ti US ɪmˌpæs-

impassible ɪm'pæs.ə.bl̩, '-ɪ-

impassioned ɪm'pæʃ.ᵊnd

impassive ɪm'pæs.ɪv **-ly** -li **-ness** -nəs, -nɪs

impassivity ˌɪm.pæs'ɪv.ə.ti, -ɪ.ti US -ə.t̬i

impasto ɪm'pæs.təʊ US -toʊ, -'pɑː.stoʊ **-ed** -d

impatience ɪm'peɪ.ʃᵊn*t*s

impatiens ɪm'peɪ.ʃi.enz, -'pæt.i-

impatient ɪm'peɪ.ʃᵊnt **-ly** -li

impeach ɪm'piːtʃ **-es** -ɪz **-ing** -ɪŋ **-ed** -t **-er/s** -əʳ/z US -ɚ/z **-ment/s** -mənt/s **-able** -ə.bl̩

impeccability ɪmˌpek.ə'bɪl.ə.ti, ˌɪm.pek-, -ɪ.ti US ɪmˌpek.ə'bɪl.ə.t̬i

impeccab|le ɪm'pek.ə.b|l̩ **-ly** -li

impecunious ˌɪm.pɪ'kjuː.ni.əs, -pə'- **-ly** -li **-ness** -nəs, -nɪs

impedanc|e ɪm'piː.dᵊn*t*s **-es** -ɪz

imped|e ɪm'piːd **-es** -z **-ing** -ɪŋ **-ed** -ɪd

impediment ɪm'ped.ɪ.mənt, '-ə- **-s** -s

impedimenta ɪmˌped.ɪ'men.tə, ˌɪm.ped-

impel ɪmˈpel **-s** -z **-ling** -ɪŋ **-led** -d **-ler/s** -əʳ/z ⓤⓢ -ɚ/z **-lent** -ənt
impend ɪmˈpend **-s** -z **-ing** -ɪŋ **-ed** -ɪd
impenetrability ɪmˌpen.ɪ.trəˈbɪl.ə.ti, ˌɪm.pen-, ˌ-ə-, -ɪ.ti ⓤⓢ ɪmˌpen.ɪ.trəˈbɪl.ə.t̬i, ˌ-ə-
impenetrab|le ɪmˈpen.ɪ.trə.b|l̩, ˌɪm-, ˈ-ə- **-ly** -li **-leness** -l̩.nəs, -nɪs
impenitence ɪmˈpen.ɪ.tᵊnts, ˌɪm- ⓤⓢ ˈ-ə-
impenitent ɪmˈpen.ɪ.tᵊnt, ˌɪm- ⓤⓢ ˈ-ə- **-ly** -li
imperative ɪmˈper.ə.tɪv ⓤⓢ -t̬ɪv **-s** -z **-ly** -li **-ness** -nəs, -nɪs
imperator ˌɪm.pəˈrɑː.tɔːʳ, -ˈreɪ-, -təʳ ⓤⓢ -ˈreɪ.tɔːr, -ˈrɑː-, -t̬ɚ **-s** -z
imperatorial ɪmˌper.əˈtɔː.ri.əl; ˌɪm.per-, -pᵊr- ⓤⓢ ˌɪm.pɚ.əˈtɔːr.i.əl
imperceptibility ˌɪm.pəˌsep.təˈbɪl.ə.ti, -tɪˈ-, -ɪ.ti ⓤⓢ -pɚˌsep.təˈbɪl.ə.t̬i
imperceptib|le ˌɪm.pəˈsep.tə.b|l̩, -tɪ- ⓤⓢ -pɚˈsep.tə- **-ly** -li **-leness** -l̩.nəs, -nɪs
imperceptive ˌɪm.pəˈsep.tɪv ⓤⓢ -pɚˈ- **-ness** -nəs, -nɪs
imperfect ɪmˈpɜː.fɪkt, ˌɪm-, -fekt ⓤⓢ -ˈpɝː- **-s** -s **-ly** -li **-ness** -nəs, -nɪs
imperfection ˌɪm.pəˈfek.ʃᵊn ⓤⓢ -pɚˈ- **-s** -z
imperfective ˌɪm.pəˈfek.tɪv ⓤⓢ -pɚˈ-
imperforat|e ɪmˈpɜː.fᵊr.ət, ˌɪm-, -ɪt ⓤⓢ -ˈpɝː- **-ed** -ɪd **-s** -s
imperial ɪmˈpɪə.ri.əl ⓤⓢ -ˈpɪr- **-s** -z **-ly** -i
imperial|ism ɪmˈpɪə.ri.ə.l|ɪ.zᵊm ⓤⓢ -ˈpɪr.i- **-ist/s** -ɪst/s
imperialist ɪmˈpɪə.ri.ə.lɪst ⓤⓢ -ˈpɪr.i-
imperialistic ɪmˌpɪə.ri.əˈlɪs.tɪk ⓤⓢ -ˈpɪr.i-
imperil ɪmˈper.ᵊl, -ɪl ⓤⓢ -ᵊl **-s** -z **-(l)ing** -ɪŋ **-(l)ed** -d
imperious ɪmˈpɪə.ri.əs ⓤⓢ -ˈpɪr.i- **-ly** -li **-ness** -nəs, -nɪs
imperishab|le ɪmˈper.ɪ.ʃə.b|l̩, ˌɪm- **-ly** -li **-leness** -l̩.nəs, -nɪs
impermanence ɪmˈpɜː.mə.nənts, ˌɪm- ⓤⓢ -ˈpɝː-
impermanent ɪmˈpɜː.mə.nənt, ˌɪm- ⓤⓢ -ˈpɝː- **-ly** -li
impermeability ɪmˌpɜː.mi.əˈbɪl.ə.ti, ˌɪm-, -ɪ.ti ⓤⓢ -ˌpɝː.mi.əˈbɪl.ə.t̬i
impermeable ɪmˈpɜː.mi.ə.b|l̩, ˌɪm- ⓤⓢ -ˈpɝː- **-ly** -li **-leness** -l̩.nəs, -nɪs
impermissibility ˌɪm.pəˌmɪs.əˈbɪl.ə.ti, -ɪˈ-, -ɪ.ti ⓤⓢ -pɚˌmɪs.əˈbɪl.ə.t̬i, -ɪˈ-
impermissib|le ˌɪm.pəˈmɪs.ə.b|l̩, ˈ-ɪ- ⓤⓢ -pɚˈ- **-ly** -li
impers|onal ɪmˈpɜː.s|ᵊn.ᵊl, ˌɪm- ⓤⓢ -ˈpɝː- **-onally** -nə.li, -ᵊn.ᵊl.i
impersonality ɪmˌpɜː.sᵊnˈæl.ə.ti, ˌɪm-, -ɪ.ti ⓤⓢ -ˌpɝː.sᵊnˈæl.ə.t̬i
imperson|ate ɪmˈpɜː.sᵊn|.eɪt ⓤⓢ -ˈpɝː- **-ates** -eɪts **-ating** -eɪ.tɪŋ ⓤⓢ -eɪ.t̬ɪŋ **-ated** -eɪ.tɪd ⓤⓢ -eɪ.t̬ɪd **-ator/s** -eɪ.təʳ/z ⓤⓢ -eɪ.t̬ɚ/z
impersonation ɪmˌpɜː.sᵊnˈeɪ.ʃᵊn ⓤⓢ -ˌpɝː- **-s** -z
impertinence ɪmˈpɜː.tɪ.nənts, ˌɪm-, -tᵊn.ənts ⓤⓢ -ˈpɝː.t̬ᵊn-
impertinent ɪmˈpɜː.tɪ.nənt, ˌɪm-, -tᵊn.ənt ⓤⓢ -ˈpɝː.t̬ᵊn- **-ly** -li
imperturbability ˌɪm.pəˌtɜː.bəˈbɪl.ə.ti, -ɪ.ti ⓤⓢ -pɚˌtɝː.bəˈbɪl.ə.t̬i
imperturbab|le ˌɪm.pəˈtɜː.bə.b|l̩ ⓤⓢ -pɚˈtɝː- **-ly** -li **-leness** -l̩.nəs, -nɪs
impervious ɪmˈpɜː.vi.əs, ˌɪm- ⓤⓢ -ˈpɝː- **-ly** -li **-ness** -nəs, -nɪs
impetigo ˌɪm.pɪˈtaɪ.gəʊ, -pəˈ-, -petˈaɪ- ⓤⓢ -pəˈtaɪ.goʊ
impetuosity ɪmˌpet.juˈɒs.ə.ti ⓤⓢ ˌɪm-, -ˌpetʃ.uˈ-, -ɪ.ti ⓤⓢ ɪmˌpetʃ.uˈɑː.sə.t̬i
impetuous ɪmˈpetʃ.u.əs, ˌɪm-, -ˈpet.ju- ⓤⓢ -ˈpetʃ.u- **-ly** -li **-ness** -nəs, -nɪs
impetus ˈɪm.pɪ.təs, -pə- ⓤⓢ -t̬əs
Impey ˈɪm.pi
impiet|y ɪmˈpaɪ.ə.t|i, ˌɪm-, -ɪ.t|i ⓤⓢ -ə.t̬|i **-ies** -iz
imping|e ɪmˈpɪndʒ **-es** -ɪz **-ing** -ɪŋ **-ed** -d **-ement/s** -mənt/s
impious ˈɪm.pi.əs; ɪmˈpaɪ-, ˌɪm- ⓤⓢ ˈɪm.pi-; ɪmˈpaɪ- **-ly** -li **-ness** -nəs, -nɪs
impish ˈɪm.pɪʃ **-ly** -li **-ness** -nəs, -nɪs
implacability ɪmˌplæk.əˈbɪl.ə.ti, ˌɪm-, -ɪ.ti ⓤⓢ -ə.t̬i
implacab|le ɪmˈplæk.ə.b|l̩ **-ly** -li **-leness** -l̩.nəs, -nɪs
implant (*n.*) ˈɪm.plɑːnt ⓤⓢ -plænt **-s** -s
implan|t (*v.*) ɪmˈplɑːn|t ⓤⓢ -ˈplæn|t **-ts** -ts **-ting** -tɪŋ ⓤⓢ -t̬ɪŋ **-ted** -tɪd ⓤⓢ -t̬ɪd **-ter/s** -təʳ/z ⓤⓢ -t̬ɚ/z
implantation ˌɪm.plɑːnˈteɪ.ʃᵊn, -plænˈ- ⓤⓢ -plænˈ-
implausibilit|y ɪmˌplɔː.zəˈbɪl.ə.t|i, ˌɪm.plɔː-, ˌɪmˌplɔː-, -zɪˈ-, -ɪ.t|i ⓤⓢ ɪmˌplɑː.zəˈbɪl.ə.t̬|i, ˌɪm-, -ˌplɔː- **-ies** -iz
implausib|le ɪmˈplɔː.zə.b|l̩, ˌɪm-, -zɪ- ⓤⓢ -ˈplɑː-, -ˈplɔː- **-ly** -li **-leness** -l̩.nəs, -nɪs
impleader ɪmˈpliː.dəʳ ⓤⓢ -dɚ **-s** -z
implement (*n.*) ˈɪm.plɪ.mənt, -plə- **-s** -s
implemen|t (*v.*) ˈɪm.plɪ.men|t, -plə-, -mən|t ⓤⓢ -men|t **-ts** -ts **-ting** -tɪŋ ⓤⓢ -t̬ɪŋ **-ted** -tɪd ⓤⓢ -t̬ɪd
implementation ˌɪm.plɪ.menˈteɪ.ʃᵊn, -plə-, -mənˈ- **-s** -z
impli|cate ˈɪm.plɪ|.keɪt, -plə- **-cates** -keɪts **-cating** -keɪ.tɪŋ ⓤⓢ -keɪ.t̬ɪŋ **-cated** -keɪ.tɪd ⓤⓢ -keɪ.t̬ɪd
implication ˌɪm.plɪˈkeɪ.ʃᵊn, -pləˈ- **-s** -z
implicative ɪmˈplɪk.ə.tɪv; ˈɪm.plɪ.keɪ.tɪv, -plə- ⓤⓢ ˈɪm.plɪ.keɪ.t̬ɪv; ɪmˈplɪk.ə- **-ly** -li
implicature ɪmˈplɪk.ə.tʃəʳ, -tjʊəʳ ⓤⓢ -tʃɚ **-s** -z
implicit ɪmˈplɪs.ɪt **-ly** -li **-ness** -nəs, -nɪ
implod|e ɪmˈpləʊd ⓤⓢ -ˈploʊd **-es** -z **-ing** -ɪŋ **-ed** -ɪd
implor|e ɪmˈplɔːʳ ⓤⓢ -ˈplɔːr **-es** -z **-ing/** -ɪŋ/li **-ed** -d **-er/s** -əʳ/z ⓤⓢ -ɚ/z
implosion ɪmˈpləʊ.ʒᵊn ⓤⓢ -ˈploʊ- **-s** -z
implosive ɪmˈpləʊ.sɪv, ˌɪm-, -zɪv ⓤⓢ -ˈploʊ.sɪv **-s** -z
impl|y ɪmˈpl|aɪ **-ies** -aɪz **-ying** -aɪ.ɪŋ **-ie** -aɪd
impolic|y ɪmˈpɒl.ə.s|i, ˌɪm-, ˈ-ɪ- ⓤⓢ -ˈpɑː.lə- **-ies** -iz
impolite ˌɪm.pᵊlˈaɪt ⓤⓢ -pəˈlaɪt **-ly** -li **-ness** -nəs, -nɪs
impolitic ɪmˈpɒl.ə.tɪk, ˌɪm-, ˈ-ɪ- ⓤⓢ -ˈpɑː.lə-
imponderab|le ɪmˈpɒn.dᵊr.ə.b|l̩, ˌɪm- ⓤⓢ -ˈpɑːn- **-les** -l̩z **-ly** -li **-leness** -l̩.nə -nɪs
import (*n.*) ˈɪm.pɔːt ⓤⓢ -pɔːrt **-s** -s
impor|t (*v.*) ɪmˈpɔː|t, ˌɪm-, ˈ-- ⓤⓢ ɪmˈpɔːr|t, ˈ-- **-ts** -ts **-ting** -tɪŋ ⓤⓢ -t̬ɪŋ **-ted** -tɪd ⓤⓢ -t̬ɪd **-ter/s** -təʳ/ ⓤⓢ -t̬ɚ/z
importable ɪmˈpɔː.tə.bl̩, ˌɪm- ⓤⓢ -ˈpɔːr.t̬ə-
importance ɪmˈpɔː.tᵊnts ⓤⓢ -ˈpɔːr-
important ɪmˈpɔː.tᵊnt ⓤⓢ -ˈpɔːr- **-ly**
importation ˌɪm.pɔːˈteɪ.ʃᵊn ⓤⓢ -pɔːr **-s** -z
importunate ɪmˈpɔː.tjʊ.nət, -tʃʊ-, -tʃə-, -ɪt ⓤⓢ -ˈpɔːr.tʃə.nɪt **-ly** -li **-ne** -nəs, -nɪs
importun|e ˌɪm.pəˈtjuːn, -ˈtʃuːn; ɪmˈpɔː.tjuːn, -tʃuːn ⓤⓢ ˌɪm.pɔːrˈtuːn, -ˈtjuːn, ɪmˈpɔːr.tʃən **-es** -z **-ing** -ɪŋ **-ed** -d
importunit|y ˌɪm.pɔːˈtjuː.nə.t|i, -nɪ ⓤⓢ -pɔːrˈtuː.nə.t̬|i, -ˈtjuː- **-ies** -iz
impos|e ɪmˈpəʊz ⓤⓢ -ˈpoʊz **-es** -ɪz **-i** -ɪŋ **-ed** -d **-er/s** -əʳ/z ⓤⓢ -ɚ/z **-able** -ə.bl̩
imposing ɪmˈpəʊ.zɪŋ ⓤⓢ -ˈpoʊ- **-ly** **-ness** -nəs, -nɪs
imposition ˌɪm.pəˈzɪʃ.ᵊn **-s** -z
impossibilit|y ɪmˌpɒs.əˈbɪl.ə.t|i, ˌɪm.pɒs-, ˌɪmˌpɒs-, -ɪˈ-, -ɪ.t|i ⓤⓢ ɪmˌpɑː.səˈbɪl.ə.t̬|i, ˌɪm- **-ies** -i
impossib|le ɪmˈpɒs.ə.b|l̩, ˌɪm-, ˈ-ɪ- ⓤⓢ -ˈpɑː.sə- **-ly** -li
impost ˈɪm.pəʊst, -pɒst ⓤⓢ -poʊst -
impostor, imposter ɪmˈpɒs.təʳ ⓤⓢ -ˈpɑː.stɚ **-s** -z
imposture ɪmˈpɒs.tjəʳ, -tʃəʳ ⓤⓢ -ˈpɑːs.tʃɚ **-s** -z
impoten|ce ˈɪm.pə.tən|ts ⓤⓢ -t̬ən|ts **-cy** -si
impotent ˈɪm.pə.tənt ⓤⓢ -t̬ənt **-ly** -
impound ɪmˈpaʊnd **-s** -z **-ing** -ɪŋ **-ed** -ɪd

impoverish ɪmˈpɒv.ᵊr.ɪʃ (US) -ˈpɑː.vɚ-, -ˈpɑːv.rɪʃ **-es** -ɪz **-ing** -ɪŋ **-ed** -t **-ment** -mənt

impracticabilit|y ɪmˌpræk.tɪ.kəˈbɪl.ə.t|i, ˌɪm-, -ɪ.t|i (US) -ə.t̬|i **-ies** -iz

impracticab|le ɪmˈpræk.tɪ.kə.b|l̩, ˌɪm- **-ly** -li **-leness** -l̩.nəs, -nɪs

impractic|al ɪmˈpræk.tɪ.k|ᵊl, ˌɪm- **-ally** -ᵊl.i (US) -li **-alness** -ᵊl.nəs, -nɪs

impracticalit|y ɪmˌpræk.tɪˈkæl.ə.t|i, ˌɪm.præk-, ˌɪmˌpræk-, -ɪ.t|i (US) ɪmˌpræk.tɪˈkæl.ə.t̬|i, ˌɪm- **-ies** -iz

impre|cate ˈɪm.prɪ|.keɪt, -prə- **-cates** -keɪts **-cating** -keɪ.tɪŋ (US) -keɪ.t̬ɪŋ **-cated** -keɪ.tɪd (US) -keɪ.t̬ɪd **-cator/s** -keɪ.təʳ/z (US) -keɪ.t̬ɚ/z

imprecation ˌɪm.prɪˈkeɪ.ʃᵊn, -prəˈ-, -prekˈeɪ- (US) -prɪˈkeɪ- **-s** -z

imprecatory ˈɪm.prɪ.keɪ.tᵊr.i, ˌɪm.prɪˈkeɪ-; ɪmˈprek.ə- (US) ˈɪm.prɪ.kə.tɔːr.i

imprecise ˌɪm.prɪˈsaɪs, -prəˈ- **-ly** -li **-ness** -nəs, -nɪs

imprecision ˌɪm.prɪˈsɪʒ.ᵊn, -prəˈ-

impregnability ɪmˌpreg.nəˈbɪl.ə.ti, ˌɪm-, -ɪ.ti (US) -ə.t̬i

impregnab|le ɪmˈpreg.nə.b|l̩ **-ly** -li

impregnate (*adj.*) ɪmˈpreg.nɪt, -nət, -neɪt

impregna|te (*v.*) ˈɪm.preg.neɪ|t, -ˈ-- (US) ɪmˈpreg.neɪ|t **-tes** -ts **-ting** -tɪŋ (US) -t̬ɪŋ **-ted** -tɪd (US) -t̬ɪd

impregnation ˌɪm.pregˈneɪ.ʃᵊn, -prɪgˈ- (US) -pregˈ- **-s** -z

impresario ˌɪm.prɪˈsɑː.ri.əʊ, -prəˈ-, -presˈɑː-, -ˈɑː- (US) ˌɪm.prəˈsɑːr.i.oʊ, -ˈser- **-s** -z

imprescriptible ˌɪm.prɪˈskrɪp.tə.bl̩

impress (*n.*) ˈɪm.pres **-es** -ɪz

impress (*v.*) ɪmˈpres **-es** -ɪz **-ing** -ɪŋ **-ed** -t

impressibility ɪmˌpres.ɪˈbɪl.ə.ti, -əˈ-, -ɪ.ti (US) -ə.t̬i

impressib|le ɪmˈpres.ə.b|l̩, ˈ-ɪ- **-ly** -li **-leness** -l̩.nəs, -nɪs

impression ɪmˈpreʃ.ᵊn **-s** -z

impressionability ɪmˌpreʃ.ᵊn.əˈbɪl.ə.ti, -ˌpreʃ.nəˈ-, -ɪ.ti (US) -ə.t̬i

impressionab|le ɪmˈpreʃ.ᵊn.ə.b|l̩, -ˈpreʃ.nə- **-ly** -li

impression|ism (I) ɪmˈpreʃ.ᵊn|.ɪ.zᵊm **-ist/s** -ɪst/s

impressionistic ɪmˌpreʃ.ᵊnˈɪs.tɪk **-ally** -ᵊl.i, -li

impressive ɪmˈpres.ɪv **-ly** -li **-ness** -nəs, -nɪs

impressment ɪmˈpres.mənt **-s** -s

imprest ˈɪm.prest, -ˈ- **-s** -s

imprimatur ˌɪm.prɪˈmeɪ.təʳ, -praɪˈ-, -ˈmɑː-, -tʊəʳ, -tɜːʳ (US) -prɪˈmɑː.t̬ɚ, -ˈmeɪ-, -tʊr **-s** -z

imprint (*n.*) ˈɪm.prɪnt **-s** -s

im|print (*v.*) ɪm|ˈprɪnt, ˌɪm- **-prints** -ˈprɪnts **-printing** -ˈprɪn.tɪŋ (US) -ˈprɪn.t̬ɪŋ **-printed** -ˈprɪn.tɪd (US) -ˈprɪn.t̬ɪd

imprison ɪmˈprɪz.ᵊn, ˌɪm- **-s** -z **-ing** -ɪŋ, -ˈprɪz.nɪŋ **-ed** -d

imprisonment ɪmˈprɪz.ᵊn.mənt, -ᵊm- (US) -ᵊn-

improbabilit|y ɪmˌprɒb.əˈbɪl.ə.t|i, ˌɪm.prɒb-, ˌɪmˌprɒb-, -ɪ.ti (US) ˌɪm.prɑː.bəˈbɪl.ə.t̬|i **-ies** -iz

improbab|le ɪmˈprɒb.ə.b|l̩, ˌɪm- (US) -ˈprɑː.bə- **-ly** -li

improbity ɪmˈprəʊ.bə.ti, ˌɪm-, -bɪ- (US) -ˈproʊ.bə.t̬i

impromptu ɪmˈprɒm*p*.tjuː, -tʃuː (US) -ˈprɑːm*p*.tuː, -tjuː **-s** -z

improper ɪmˈprɒp.əʳ, ˌɪm- (US) -ˈprɑː.pɚ **-ly** -li ˌ**improper** ˈ**fraction, im**ˌ**proper** ˈ**fraction**

impropri|ate ɪmˈprəʊ.pri|.eɪt (US) -ˈproʊ- **-ates** -eɪts **-ating** -eɪ.tɪŋ (US) -eɪ.t̬ɪŋ **-ated** -eɪ.tɪd (US) -eɪ.t̬ɪd **-ator/s** -eɪ.təʳ/z (US) -eɪ.t̬ɚ/z

impropriation ɪmˌprəʊ.priˈeɪ.ʃᵊn, ˌɪm.prəʊ-, ˌɪmˌprəʊ- (US) ɪmˌproʊ-, ˌɪm- **-s** -z

impropriet|y ˌɪm.prəˈpraɪ.ə.t|i (US) -t̬|i **-ies** -iz

improvability ɪmˌpruː.vəˈbɪl.ə.ti, -ɪ.ti (US) -ə.t̬i

improvab|le ɪmˈpruː.və.b|l̩ **-ly** -li **-leness** -l̩.nəs, -nɪs

improv|e ɪmˈpruːv **-es** -z **-ing** -ɪŋ **-ed** -d **-er/s** -əʳ/z (US) -ɚ/z

improvement ɪmˈpruːv.mənt **-s** -s

improvidence ɪmˈprɒv.ɪ.dᵊn*t*s, ˌɪm-, ˈ-ə- (US) -ˈprɑː.və-

improvident ɪmˈprɒv.ɪ.dᵊnt, ˌɪm- (US) -ˈprɑː.və- **-ly** -li

improvisation ˌɪm.prə.vaɪˈzeɪ.ʃᵊn (US) ɪmˌprɑː.vɪˈ-; ˌɪm.prə- **-s** -z

improvisatory ˌɪm.prə.vaɪˈzeɪ.tᵊr.i; -ˈvaɪ.zə- (US) ɪmˈprɑː.və.zə.tɔːr-; ˌɪm.prəˈvaɪ-

improvis|e ˈɪm.prə.vaɪz **-es** -ɪz **-ing** -ɪŋ **-ed** -d **-er/s** -əʳ/z (US) -ɚ/z **-or/s** -əʳ/z (US) -ɚ/z

imprudence ɪmˈpruː.dᵊn*t*s, ˌɪm-

imprudent ɪmˈpruː.dᵊnt, ˌɪm- **-ly** -li

impudence ˈɪm.pjə.dᵊn*t*s, -pjʊ-

impudent ˈɪm.pjə.dᵊnt, -pjʊ- **-ly** -li

impugn ɪmˈpjuːn **-s** -z **-ing** -ɪŋ **-ed** -d **-er/s** -əʳ/z (US) -ɚ/z **-able** -ə.bl̩ **-ment** -mənt

impuissan|ce ɪmˈpjuː.ɪ.sᵊn|*t*s (US) -ˈpjuː.ɪ-, -ˈpwɪ.sᵊn*t*s; ˌɪm.pjuːˈɪs.ᵊn*t*s **-t** -t

impuls|e ˈɪm.pʌls **-es** -ɪz ˈ**impulse** ˌ**buying**

impulsion ɪmˈpʌl.ʃᵊn **-s** -z

impulsive ɪmˈpʌl.sɪv **-ly** -li **-ness** -nəs, -nɪs

impunit|y ɪmˈpjuː.nə.t|i, -nɪ- (US) -t̬|i **-ies** -iz

impure ɪmˈpjʊəʳ, ˌɪm-, -ˈpjɔːʳ (US) -ˈpjʊr **-ly** -li **-ness** -nəs, -nɪs

impurit|y ɪmˈpjʊə.rə.t|i, ˌɪm-, -ˈpjɔː-, -rɪ- (US) -ˈpjʊr.ə.t̬|i **-ies** -iz

imputability ɪmˌpjuː.təˈbɪl.ə.ti, ˌɪm.pjuː-, ˌɪmˌpjuː-, -ɪ.ti (US) ɪmˌpjuː.t̬əˈbɪl.ə.t̬i, ˌɪm-

imputation ˌɪm.pjʊˈteɪ.ʃᵊn **-s** -z

im|pute ɪm|ˈpjuːt **-putes** -ˈpjuːts **-puting** -ˈpjuː.tɪŋ (US) -ˈpjuː.t̬ɪŋ **-puted** -ˈpjuː.tɪd (US) -ˈpjuː.t̬ɪd **-putable** -ˈpjuː.tə.bl̩ (US) -ˈpjuː.t̬ə.bl̩

Imray ˈɪm.reɪ

Imrie ˈɪm.ri

IMRO ˈɪm.rəʊ (US) -roʊ

in- ɪn-

Note: Prefix. When the meaning of the prefix is "in", it often carries secondary stress, e.g. **inbuilt** /ˌɪnˈbɪlt/. The resulting compounds may undergo stress-shift (see entry for **inbuilt**). As a negative prefix, **in-** does not normally affect the stress pattern of the stem to which it is added, e.g. **active** /ˈæk.tɪv/, **inactive** /ɪnˈæk.tɪv/. In other cases, the prefix is normally stressed in nouns but not in verbs, e.g. **increase** noun /ˈɪn.kriːs /, verb /ɪnˈkriːs/.

in ɪn ˌ**ins and** ˈ**outs**

in. (*abbrev. for* **inch/es**) *singular:* ɪn*t*ʃ *plural:* -ɪz

Ina ˈiː.nə, ˈaɪ- (US) ˈaɪ-

inabilit|y ˌɪn.əˈbɪl.ə.t|i, -ɪ.t|i (US) -ə.t̬|i **-ies** -iz

in absentia ˌɪn.æbˈsen.ti.ə, -*t*ʃi-, -ɑː (US) -ˈsen.*t*ʃə, -*t*ʃi.ə

inaccessibility ˌɪn.əkˌses.əˈbɪl.ə.ti, -ækˌ-, -ɪˈ-, -ɪ.ti (US) -ə.t̬i

inaccessib|le ˌɪn.əkˈses.ə.b|l̩, -ækˈ-, ˈ-ɪ- **-ly** -li **-leness** -l̩.nəs, -nɪs

inaccurac|y ɪnˈæk.jə.rə.s|i, ˌɪn-, -jʊ-, -rɪ.s|i (US) -jɚ.ə- **-ies** -iz

inaccurate ɪnˈæk.jə.rət, ˌɪn-, -jʊ-, -rɪt (US) -jɚ.ət **-ly** -li

inaction ɪnˈæk.ʃᵊn, ˌɪn-

inacti|vate ɪnˈæk.tɪ|.veɪt, ˌɪn-, -tə- **-vates** -veɪts **-vating** -veɪ.tɪŋ (US) -veɪ.t̬ɪŋ **-vated** -veɪ.tɪd (US) -veɪ.t̬ɪd

inactive ɪnˈæk.tɪv, ˌɪn- **-ly** -li

inactivity ˌɪn.ækˈtɪv.ə.ti, -ɪ.ti (US) -ə.t̬i

inadequac|y ɪˈnæd.ɪ.kwə.s|i, ˌɪnˈæd-, ˈ-ə- **-ies** -iz

inadequate ɪˈnæd.ɪ.kwət, ˌɪnˈæd-, -kwɪt **-ly** -li **-ness** -nəs, -nɪs

inadmissibility ˌɪn.ədˌmɪs.əˈbɪl.ə.ti, -ɪˈ-, -ɪ.ti (US) -ə.t̬i

inadmissib|le ˌɪn.əd'mɪs.ə.bl̩, '-ɪ- **-ly** -li

inadverten|ce ˌɪn.əd'vɜː.tᵊnt|s US -'vɝː- **-cy** -si

inadvertent ˌɪn.əd'vɜː.tᵊnt US -'vɝː- **-ly** -li

inadvisability ˌɪn.ədˌvaɪ.zə'bɪl.ə.ti, -ɪ.ti US -ə.t̬i

inadvisable ˌɪn.əd'vaɪ.zə.bl̩

inalienability ɪˌneɪ.li.ə.nə'bɪl.ə.ti, ˌɪnˌeɪ-, -ɪ.ti US -ə.t̬i

inalienab|le ɪ'neɪ.li.ə.nə.bl|l̩, ˌɪn'eɪ- **-ly** -li **-leness** -l̩.nəs, -nɪs

inamora|ta ɪˌnæm.ə'rɑː|.tə, ˌɪn.æm- US -'rɑː|.t̬ə, -ˌnæm- **-as** -təz US -t̬əz **-o/s** -təʊ/z US -toʊ/z

inane ɪ'neɪn **-ly** -li **-ness** -nəs, -nɪs

inanimate ɪ'næn.ɪ.mət, ˌɪn'æn-, -mɪt **-ly** -li **-ness** -nəs, -nɪs

inanition ˌɪn.ə'nɪʃ.ᵊn, -æn'ɪʃ-

inanit|y ɪ'næn.ə.t|i, -ɪ.t|i US -ə.t̬|i **-ies** -iz

inappeasable ˌɪn.ə'piː.zə.bl̩

inapplicability ɪˌnæp.lɪ.kə'bɪl.ə.ti, ˌɪnˌæp-, -ɪ.ti; ˌɪn.əˌplɪk.ə'- US ɪˌnæp.lɪ.kə'bɪl.ə.t̬i, ˌɪnˌæp-; ˌɪn.ə.plɪ.kə'bɪl.ə.ti

inapplicable ˌɪn.ə'plɪk.ə.bl̩; ɪ'næp.lɪ.kə-, ˌɪn'æp- US ɪ'næp-, ˌɪn'æp-; ˌɪn.ə'plɪk.ə- **-ness** -nəs, -nɪs

inapposite ɪ'næp.ə.zɪt, ˌɪn'æp- **-ly** -li **-ness** -nəs, -nɪs

inappreciab|le ˌɪn.ə'priː.ʃi.ə.bl|l̩, -ʃə- **-ly** -li

inapprehensible ɪnˌæp.rɪ'hent.sə.bl̩, '-sɪ-

inapproachab|le ˌɪn.ə'prəʊ.tʃə.bl|l̩ US -'proʊ- **-ly** -li

inappropriate ˌɪn.ə'prəʊ.pri.ət, -ɪt US -'proʊ- **-ly** -li **-ness** -nəs, -nɪs

inapt ɪ'næpt, ˌɪn'æpt **-ly** -li **-ness** -nəs, -nɪs

inaptitude ɪ'næp.tɪ.tjuːd, ˌɪn'æp- US -tə.tuːd, -tjuːd

inarguab|le ɪ'nɑː.gju.ə.bl|l̩, ˌɪn'ɑː- US ˌɪn'ɑːr- **-ly** -li

inarticulate ˌɪn.ɑː'tɪk.jə.lət, -jʊ-, -lɪt US -ɑːr'- **-ly** -li **-ness** -nəs, -nɪs

inartistic ˌɪn.ɑː'tɪs.tɪk US -ɑːr'- **-al** -ᵊl **-ally** -ᵊl.i, -li

inasmuch ˌɪn.əz'mʌtʃ

inattention ˌɪn.ə'ten.tʃᵊn

inattentive ˌɪn.ə'ten.tɪv US -t̬ɪv **-ly** -li **-ness** -nəs, -nɪs

inaudibility ɪˌnɔː.də'bɪl.ə.ti, ˌɪn.ɔː-, -dɪ'-, -ɪ.ti US ɪˌnɑː.dɪ'bɪl.ə.t̬i, ˌɪnˌɑː-, ɪˌnɔː-, ˌɪnˌɔː-

inaudib|le ɪ'nɔː.də.bl|l̩, ˌɪn.ɔː-, -dɪ- US ɪ'nɑː-, ˌɪn'ɑː-, ɪ'nɔː-, ˌɪn'ɔː- **-ly** -li **-leness** -l̩.nəs, -nɪs

inaugural ɪ'nɔː.gjə.rᵊl, -jʊ- US ɪ'nɑː.gjʊr.ᵊl, -'nɔː.g-, -jɚ-, '-ɚ-

inaugu|rate ɪ'nɔː.gjə|.reɪt, -jʊ- US ɪ'nɑː.g.jʊ|.reɪt, ɪ'nɔː.g-, -jə-, '-ə- **-rates** -reɪts **-rating** -reɪ.tɪŋ US -reɪ.t̬ɪŋ **-rated** -reɪ.tɪd US -reɪ.t̬ɪd **-rator/s** -reɪ.təʳ/z US -reɪ.t̬ɚ/z

inauguration ɪˌnɔː.gjə'reɪ.ʃᵊn, -jʊ'- US ɪˌnɑː.gjʊ'-, -ˌnɔː.g-, -jə'-, -ə'- **-s** -z

inauspicious ˌɪn.ɔː'spɪʃ.əs, -ɒs'pɪʃ- US -ɑː'spɪʃ-, -ɔː'- **-ly** -li **-ness** -nəs, -nɪs

inboard ˌɪn'bɔːd, ˌɪm- US 'ɪn.bɔːrd *stress shift, British only:* ˌinboard 'motor

inborn ˌɪn'bɔːn, ˌɪm- US 'ɪn.bɔːrn *stress shift, British only:* ˌinborn 'talent

inbox 'ɪn.bɒks, 'ɪm- US 'ɪn.bɑːks **-es** -ɪz

inbreath|e ˌɪn'briːð, ˌɪm- US ˌɪn- **-es** -z **-ing** -ɪŋ **-ed** -d

inbreed ˌɪn'briːd, ˌɪm- US 'ɪn.briːd **-s** -z **-ing** -ɪŋ **inbred** ˌɪn'bred, ˌɪm- US 'ɪn.bred *stress shift, British only:* ˌinbred 'trait

inbuilt ˌɪn'bɪlt, ˌɪm-, '-- US 'ɪn.bɪlt *stress shift, British only:* ˌinbuilt 'hazard

inc. *(abbrev. for* **incorporated***)* ɪŋ'kɔː.pᵊr.eɪ.tɪd, ɪŋk US ɪn'kɔːr.pə.reɪ.t̬ɪd, ɪŋk

Inca 'ɪŋ.kə **-s** -z

incalculability ɪnˌkæl.kjə.lə'bɪl.ə.ti, ˌɪn-, ɪŋ-, ˌɪŋ-, -kjʊ-, -ɪ.ti US ɪnˌkæl.kjə.lə'bɪl.ə.t̬i, ˌɪn-, -kjʊ-

incalculab|le ɪn'kæl.kjə.lə.bl|l̩, ˌɪn-, ɪŋ-, ˌɪŋ-, -kjʊ- US ɪn'kæl-, ˌɪn- **-ly** -li **-leness** -l̩.nəs, -nɪs

in camera ˌɪn'kæm.ᵊr.ə, ˌɪŋ-, '-rə US ˌɪn-

incandescence ˌɪn.kæn'des.ᵊnts, ˌɪŋ-, -kən'- US ˌɪn.kən'-

incandescent ˌɪn.kæn'des.ᵊnt, ˌɪŋ-, -kən'- US ˌɪn.kən'- **-ly** -li

incantation ˌɪn.kæn'teɪ.ʃᵊn, ˌɪŋ- US ˌɪn- **-s** -z

incapabilit|y ɪnˌkeɪ.pə'bɪl.ə.t|i, ˌɪn-, ɪŋ-, ˌɪŋ-, -ɪ.t|i US ɪnˌkeɪ.pə'bɪl.ə.t̬|i, ˌɪn- **-ies** -iz

incapab|le ɪn'keɪ.pə.bl|l̩, ˌɪn-, ɪŋ-, ˌɪŋ- US ɪn'keɪ-, ˌɪn- **-ly** -li **-leness** -l̩.nəs, -nɪs

incapaci|tate ˌɪn.kə'pæs.ɪ|.teɪt, ˌɪŋ-, '-ə- US ˌɪn- **-tates** -teɪts **-tating** -teɪ.tɪŋ US -teɪ.t̬ɪŋ **-tated** -teɪ.tɪd US -teɪ.t̬ɪd

incapacitation ˌɪn.kəˌpæs.ɪ'teɪ.ʃᵊn, ˌɪŋ-, -ə'- US ˌɪn- **-s** -z

incapacit|y ˌɪn.kə'pæs.ə.t|i, ˌɪŋ-, -ɪ.t|i US ˌɪn.kə'pæs.ə.t̬|i **-ies** -iz

in capite ˌɪn'kæp.ɪ.teɪ US -teɪ, -ti

incarcer|ate ɪn'kɑː.sᵊr|.eɪt, ɪŋ- US ɪn'kɑːr.sə.r|eɪt **-ates** -eɪts **-ating** -eɪ.tɪŋ US -eɪ.t̬ɪŋ **-ated** -eɪ.tɪd US -eɪ.t̬ɪd

incarceration ɪnˌkɑː.sᵊr'eɪ.ʃᵊn, ˌɪn.kɑː-, ˌɪnˌkɑː-, ɪŋˌkɑː-, ˌɪŋ.kɑː- US ɪnˌkɑːr.sə'reɪ-, ˌɪn- **-s** -z

incarnadine ɪn'kɑː.nə.daɪn, ɪŋ- US ɪn'kɑːr-, -diːn, -dɪn

incarnate *(adj.)* ɪn'kɑː.nət, ɪŋ-, -neɪt, -nɪt US ɪn'kɑːr-

incar|nate *(v.)* 'ɪn.kɑː|.neɪt, 'ɪŋ-, -'-- US ɪn'kɑːr- **-nates** -neɪts **-nating** -neɪ.tɪŋ US -neɪ.t̬ɪŋ **-nated** -neɪ.tɪd US -neɪ.t̬ɪd

incarnation (I) ˌɪn.kɑː'neɪ.ʃᵊn, ˌɪŋ- US ˌɪn.kɑːr'- **-s** -z

incautious ɪn'kɔː.ʃəs, ˌɪn-, ɪŋ-, ˌɪŋ- US ɪn'kɑː-, ˌɪn-, -'kɔː- **-ly** -li **-ness** -nəs, -nɪs

Ince ɪnts

Ince-in-Makerfield ˌɪnts.ɪn'meɪ.kə.fiːld US -kɚ-

incendiar|y ɪn'sen.di.ᵊr|.i, -djᵊr- US -di.er|.i, -ɚ|.i **-ies** -iz **-ism** -ɪ.zᵊm

incense *(n.)* 'ɪn.sents

incens|e *(v.) enrage:* ɪn'sents **-es** -ɪz **-ing** -ɪŋ **-ed** -t

incens|e *(v.) burn incense:* 'ɪn.sents **-es** -ɪz **-ing** -ɪŋ **-ed** -t

incentive ɪn'sen.tɪv US -t̬ɪv **-s** -z

incept ɪn'sept **-s** -s **-ing** -ɪŋ **-ed** -ɪd **-or/s** -əʳ/z US -ɚ/z **-ive** -ɪv

inception ɪn'sep.ʃᵊn **-s** -z

incertitude ɪn'sɜː.tɪ.tjuːd, ˌɪn- US -'sɝː.t̬ɪ.tuːd, -tjuːd **-s** -z

incessant ɪn'ses.ᵊnt **-ly** -li

incest 'ɪn.sest

incestuous ɪn'ses.tju.əs, -tʃu- US - **-ly** -li **-ness** -nəs, -nɪs

inch (I) ɪntʃ **-es** -ɪz **-ing** -ɪŋ **-ed** -t **,give him an ˌinch and he'll ˌtake a 'mi[le]**; **not ˌbudge an 'inch**

Inchcape 'ɪntʃ.keɪp, ˌ-'-

Inchinnan ɪn'ʃɪn.ən

inchoate *(adj.)* ɪn'kəʊ.eɪt, ɪŋ-, -ɪt, US ɪn'koʊ- **-ly** -li

incho|ate *(v.)* 'ɪn.kəʊ|.eɪt, 'ɪŋ- US 'ɪn.koʊ- **-ates** -eɪts **-ating** -eɪ[.tɪŋ] US -eɪ.t̬ɪŋ **-ated** -eɪ.tɪd US -eɪ.t̬[ɪd]

inchoation ˌɪn.kəʊ'eɪ.ʃᵊn, ˌɪŋ- US ˌɪn.koʊ'-

inchoative 'ɪn.kəʊ.eɪ.tɪv, 'ɪŋ-; ɪn'kəʊ.ə.tɪv, ɪŋ- US ɪn'koʊ.ə.t̬[ɪv]

Inchon ˌɪn'tʃɒn US 'ɪn.tʃɑːn

inchworm 'ɪntʃ.wɜːm US -wɝːm

incidence 'ɪnt.sɪ.dᵊnts

incident 'ɪnt.sɪ.dᵊnt **-s** -s

incident|al ˌɪnt.sɪ'den.t|ᵊl US -t̬|ᵊl **-ally** -ᵊl.i, -li **-ness** -nəs, -nɪs **-s** -z *stre[ss] shift:* ˌincidental 'music

inciner|ate ɪn'sɪn.ᵊr|.eɪt US -ə.r|e[ɪt] **-ates** -eɪts **-ating** -eɪ.tɪŋ US -eɪ.[t̬ɪŋ] **-ated** -eɪ.tɪd US -eɪ.t̬ɪd

incineration ɪnˌsɪn.ᵊr'eɪ.ʃᵊn US -[ə'reɪ-]

incinerator ɪn'sɪn.ᵊr.eɪ.təʳ US -ə.reɪ.t̬ɚ **-s** -z

incipien|ce ɪn'sɪp.i.ənt|s **-cy** -si

incipient ɪn'sɪp.i.ənt **-ly** -li

incis|e ɪnˈsaɪz **-es** -ɪz **-ing** -ɪŋ **-ed** -d

incision ɪnˈsɪʒ.ən **-s** -z

incisive ɪnˈsaɪ.sɪv **-ly** -li **-ness** -nəs, -nɪs

incisor ɪnˈsaɪ.zər (US) -zɚ **-s** -z

incitation ˌɪn*t*.saɪˈteɪ.ʃən, -sɪˈ- (US) -səˈ- **-s** -z

in|cite ɪnˈsaɪt **-cites** -ˈsaɪts **-citing** -ˈsaɪ.tɪŋ (US) -ˈsaɪ.t̬ɪŋ **-cited** -ˈsaɪ.tɪd (US) -ˈsaɪ.t̬ɪd

incitement ɪnˈsaɪt.mənt **-s** -s

incivilit|y ˌɪn.sɪˈvɪl.ə.t|i, -səˈ-, -ɪ.t|i (US) -ə.t̬|i **-ies** -iz

incl. *(abbrev. for* **including***)* ɪnˈkluː.dɪŋ, ɪŋ- (US) ɪn- *(abbrev. for* **inclusive***)* ɪnˈkluː.sɪv, ɪŋ- (US) ɪn-

Incledon ˈɪŋ.kl̩.dən

inclemency ɪnˈklem.ən*t*.si, ˌɪn-, ɪŋ-, ˌɪŋ- (US) ɪnˈklem-, ˌɪn-

inclement ɪnˈklem.ənt, ˌɪn-, ɪŋ-, ˌɪŋ- (US) ɪnˈklem-, ˌɪn- **-ly** -li

inclination ˌɪn.klɪˈneɪ.ʃən, ˌɪŋ-, -kləˈ- (US) ˌɪn- **-s** -z

incline *(n.)* ˈɪn.klaɪn, ˈɪŋ-, ˌ-ˈ- (US) ˈɪn.klaɪn, ˌ-ˈ- **-s** -z

inclin|e *(v.)* ɪnˈklaɪn, ɪŋ- (US) ɪn- **-es** -z **-ing** -ɪŋ **-ed** -d **-able** -ə.bl̩

inclos|e ɪnˈkləʊz, ɪŋ- (US) ɪnˈkloʊz **-es** -ɪz **-ing** -ɪŋ **-ed** -d

inclosure ɪnˈkləʊ.ʒər, ɪŋ- (US) ɪnˈkloʊ.ʒɚ **-s** -z

includ|e ɪnˈkluːd, ɪŋ- (US) ɪn- **-es** -z **-ing** -ɪŋ **-ed** -ɪd

inclusion ɪnˈkluː.ʒən, ɪŋ- (US) ɪn- **-s** -z

inclusive ɪnˈkluː.sɪv, ɪŋ- (US) ɪn- **-ly** -li **-ness** -nəs, -nɪs

incognito ˌɪn.kɒgˈniː.təʊ, ˌɪŋ-; ɪnˈkɒg.nɪ.təʊ, ɪŋ-, -nə- (US) ˌɪn.kɑːgˈniː.toʊ; ɪnˈkɑːg.nɪ-, -t̬oʊ **-s** -z

incognizan|ce ɪnˈkɒg.nɪ.zən|*t*s, ɪŋ- (US) ɪnˈkɑːg- **-t** -t

incoherence ˌɪn.kəʊˈhɪə.rən*t*s, ˌɪŋ- (US) ˌɪn.koʊˈhɪr.ən*t*s, -ˈher-

incoherent ˌɪn.kəʊˈhɪə.rənt, ˌɪŋ- (US) ˌɪn.koʊˈhɪr.ənt, -ˈher- **-ly** -li

incombustibility ˌɪn.kəmˌbʌs.təˈbɪl.ə.ti, ˌɪŋ-, -tɪˈ-, -ɪ.ti (US) ˌɪn.kəmˌbʌs.təˈbɪl.ə.t̬i, -tɪˈ-

incombustible ˌɪn.kəmˈbʌs.tə.bl̩, ˌɪŋ-, -tɪ- (US) ˌɪn- **-ness** -nəs, -nɪs

income ˈɪŋ.kʌm, ˈɪn-, -kəm (US) ˈɪn- **-s** -z
ˌincome supˈport, ˈincome supˌport; ˈincome ˌtax

incomer ˈɪnˌkʌm.ər, ˈɪŋ- (US) ˈɪnˌkʌm.ɚ **-s** -z

incoming ˈɪnˌkʌm.ɪŋ, ˈɪŋ- (US) ˈɪnˌkʌm- **-s** -z

incommensurability ˌɪn.kəˌmen.*t*ʃər.əˈbɪl.ə.ti, ˌɪŋ-, -*t*ʃʊr-, -ɪ.ti (US) ˌɪn.kəˌmen*t*.sɚ.əˈbɪl.ə.t̬i, -ʃɚ-

incommensurab|le ˌɪn.kəˈmen.*t*ʃər.ə.b|l̩, ˌɪŋ-, -*t*ʃʊr- (US) ˌɪn.kəˈmen*t*.sɚ-, -ʃɚ- **-les** -l̩z **-ly** -li **-leness** -l̩.nəs, -nɪs

incommensurate ˌɪn.kəˈmen.*t*ʃər.ət, ˌɪŋ-, -*t*ʃʊr-, -ɪt (US) ˌɪn.kəˈmen*t*.sɚ-, -ʃɚ- **-ly** -li **-ness** -nəs, -nɪs

incommod|e ˌɪn.kəˈməʊd, ˌɪŋ- (US) ˌɪn.kəˈmoʊd **-es** -z **-ing** -ɪŋ **-ed** -ɪd

incommodious ˌɪn.kəˈməʊ.di.əs, ˌɪŋ- (US) ˌɪn.kəˈmoʊ- **-ly** -li **-ness** -nəs, -nɪs

incommunicab|le ˌɪn.kəˈmjuː.nɪ.kə.b|l̩, ˌɪŋ- (US) ˌɪn- **-ly** -li **-leness** -l̩.nəs, -nɪs

incommunicado ˌɪn.kəˌmjuː.nɪˈkɑː.dəʊ, ˌɪŋ-, -nəˈ- (US) ˌɪn.kəˌmjuː.nɪˈkɑː.doʊ, -nəˈ-

incommutab|le ˌɪn.kəˈmjuː.tə.b|l̩, ˌɪŋ- (US) ˌɪn.kəˈmjuː.t̬ə.b|l̩ **-ly** -li **-leness** -l̩.nəs, -nɪs

incomparability ɪnˌkɒm.pər.əˈbɪl.ə.ti, ɪŋ-, -ɪ.ti (US) ɪnˌkɑːm.pɚ.əˈbɪl.ə.t̬i

incomparab|le ɪnˈkɒm.pər.ə.b|l̩, ɪŋ- (US) ɪnˈkɑːm- **-ly** -li **-leness** -l̩.nəs, -nɪs

incompatibilit|y ˌɪn.kəmˌpæt.əˈbɪl.ə.t|i, ˌɪŋ-, -ɪˈ-, -ɪ.t|i (US) ˌɪn.kəmˌpæt̬.əˈbɪl.ə.t̬|i **-ies** -iz

incompatib|le ˌɪn.kəmˈpæt.ə.b|l̩, ˌɪŋ-, ˈ-ɪ- (US) ˌɪn.kəmˈpæt̬- **-ly** -li **-leness** -l̩.nəs, -nɪs

incompeten|ce ɪnˈkɒm.pɪ.tən*t*|s, ˌɪn-, ɪŋ-, ˌɪŋ-, -pə- (US) ɪnˈkɑːm.pə.t̬ən*t*|s, ˌɪn- **-cy** -si

incompetent ɪnˈkɒm.pɪ.tənt, ˌɪn-, ɪŋ-, ˌɪŋ-, -pə- (US) ɪnˈkɑːm.pə.t̬ənt, ˌɪn- **-ly** -li

incomplete ˌɪn.kəmˈpliːt, ˌɪŋ- (US) ˌɪn- **-ly** -li **-ness** -nəs, -nɪs

incompletion ˌɪn.kəmˈpliː.ʃən, ˌɪŋ- (US) ˌɪn-

incomprehensibility ɪnˌkɒm.prɪˌhen*t*.səˈbɪl.ə.ti, ˌɪn-, ɪŋ-, ˌɪŋ-, -prəˌ-, -sɪˈ-, -ɪ.ti (US) ˌɪn.kɑːm.prɪ.hen*t*.səˈbɪl.ə.t̬i

incomprehensib|le ɪnˌkɒm.prɪˈhen*t*.sə.b|l̩, ˌɪn-, ɪŋ-, ˌɪŋ-, -sɪ- (US) ˌɪn.kɑːm- **-ly** -li **-leness** -l̩.nəs, -nɪs

incomprehension ɪnˌkɒm.prɪˈhen.*t*ʃən, ˌɪn-, ɪŋ-, ˌɪŋ-, -prəˈ- (US) ˌɪn.kɑːm-

incompressibility ˌɪn.kəmˌpres.əˈbɪl.ə.ti, ˌɪŋ-, -ɪˈ-, -ɪ.ti (US) ˌɪn.kəmˌpres.əˈbɪl.ə.t̬i

incompressible ˌɪn.kəmˈpres.ə.bl̩, ˌɪŋ-, ˈ-ɪ- (US) ˌɪn- **-ness** -nəs, -nɪs

incomputab|le ˌɪn.kəmˈpjuː.tə.b|l̩, ˌɪŋ-; ɪnˈkɒm.pjə.tə.b|l̩, ˌɪn-, ɪŋ-, ˌɪŋ-, -pjʊ- (US) ˌɪn.kəmˈpjuː.t̬ə- **-ly** -li

inconceivability ˌɪn.kənˌsiː.vəˈbɪl.ə.ti, ˌɪŋ-, -ɪ.ti (US) ˌɪn.kənˌsiː.vəˈbɪl.ə.t̬i

inconceivab|le ˌɪn.kənˈsiː.və.b|l̩, ˌɪŋ- (US) ˌɪn- **-ly** -li **-leness** -l̩.nəs, -nɪs

inconclusive ˌɪn.kənˈkluː.sɪv, ˌɪŋ-, -kəŋˈ- (US) ˌɪn.kənˈ- **-ly** -li **-ness** -nəs, -nɪs

incondite ɪnˈkɒn.dɪt, ɪŋ-, -daɪt (US) ɪnˈkɑːn-

incongruent ɪnˈkɒŋ.gru.ənt, ɪŋ- (US) ɪnˈkɑːŋ-; ˌɪn.kənˈgruː- **-ly** -li

incongruit|y ˌɪn.kɒŋˈgruː.ə.t|i, ˌɪŋ-, -ɪ.t|i (US) ˌɪn.kənˈgruː.ə.t̬|i **-ies** -iz

incongruous ɪnˈkɒŋ.gru.əs, ɪŋ- (US) ɪnˈkɑːŋ- **-ly** -li **-ness** -nəs, -nɪs

inconsequenc|e ɪnˈkɒn*t*.sɪ.kwən*t*s, ɪŋ-, -sə- (US) ɪnˈkɑːn*t*- **-es** -ɪz

inconsequent ɪnˈkɒn*t*.sɪ.kwənt, ɪŋ-, -sə- (US) ɪnˈkɑːn*t*- **-ly** -li

inconsequential ɪnˌkɒn*t*.sɪˈkwen.*t*ʃəl, ˌɪn-, ɪŋ-, ˌɪŋ-, -səˈ- (US) ɪnˌkɑːn*t*- **-ly** -i

inconsiderab|le ˌɪn.kənˈsɪd.ər.ə.b|l̩, ˌɪŋ- (US) ˌɪn- **-ly** -li **-leness** -l̩.nəs, -nɪs

inconsiderate ˌɪn.kənˈsɪd.ər.ət, ˌɪŋ-, -ɪt (US) ˌɪn- **-ly** -li **-ness** -nəs, -nɪs

inconsideration ˌɪn.kənˌsɪd.əˈreɪ.ʃən, ˌɪŋ- (US) ˌɪn-

inconsistenc|y ˌɪn.kənˈsɪs.tən*t*.s|i, ˌɪŋ- (US) ˌɪn- **-ies** -iz

inconsistent ˌɪn.kənˈsɪs.tənt, ˌɪŋ- (US) ˌɪn- **-ly** -li

inconsolab|le ˌɪn.kənˈsəʊ.lə.b|l̩, ˌɪŋ- (US) ˌɪn.kənˈsoʊ- **-ly** -li **-leness** -l̩.nəs, -nɪs

inconsonant ɪnˈkɒn*t*.sə.nənt, ɪŋ- (US) ɪnˈkɑːn*t*-

inconspicuous ˌɪn.kənˈspɪk.ju.əs, ˌɪŋ- (US) ˌɪn- **-ly** -li **-ness** -nəs, -nɪs

inconstanc|y ɪnˈkɒn*t*.stən*t*.s|i, ˌɪn-, ɪŋ-, ˌɪŋ- (US) ɪnˈkɑːn*t*-, ˌɪn- **-ies** -iz

inconstant ɪnˈkɒn*t*.stənt, ˌɪn-, ɪŋ-, ˌɪŋ- (US) ɪnˈkɑːn*t*-, ˌɪn- **-ly** -li

incontestability ˌɪn.kənˌtes.təˈbɪl.ə.ti, ˌɪŋ-, -ɪ.ti (US) ˌɪn.kənˌtes.təˈbɪl.ə.t̬i

incontestab|le ˌɪn.kənˈtes.tə.b|l̩, ˌɪŋ- (US) ˌɪn- **-ly** -li

incontinence ɪnˈkɒn.tɪ.nən*t*s, ˌɪn-, ɪŋ-, ˌɪŋ-, -tə- (US) ɪnˈkɑːn.tən.ən*t*s, ˌɪn-

incontinent ɪnˈkɒn.tɪ.nənt, ˌɪn-, ɪŋ-, ˌɪŋ-, -tə- (US) ɪnˈkɑːn.tən.ənt, ˌɪn- **-ly** -li

incontrollab|le ˌɪn.kənˈtrəʊ.lə.b|l̩, ˌɪŋ- (US) ˌɪn.kənˈtroʊ- **-ly** -li

incontrovertibility ˌɪnˌkɒn.trəˌvɜː.təˈbɪl.ə.ti, ˌɪŋ-, -tɪˈ-, -ɪ.ti (US) ˌɪn.kɑːn.trəˌvɝː.t̬əˈbɪl.ə.t̬i

incontrovertib|le ˌɪnˌkɒn.trəˈvɜː.tə.b|l̩, ˌɪŋ-, -tɪ- (US) ˌɪnˌkɑːn.trəˈvɝː.t̬ə- **-ly** -li

inconvenienc|e ˌɪn.kənˈviː.ni.ən*t*s, ˌɪŋ- (US) ˌɪn-, ˈ-njən*t*s **-es** -ɪz **-ing** -ɪŋ **-ed** -t

inconvenient ˌɪn.kənˈviː.ni.ənt, ˌɪŋ- (US) ˌɪn-, ˈ-njənt **-ly** -li

inconvertibility ˌɪn.kənˌvɜː.təˈbɪl.ə.ti, ˌɪŋ-, -tɪˈ-, -ɪ.ti (US) ˌɪn.kənˌvɝː.t̬əˈbɪl.ə.t̬i
inconvertib|le ˌɪn.kənˈvɜː.tə.b|l̩, ˌɪŋ-, -tɪ- (US) ˌɪn.kənˈvɝː.t̬ə- **-ly** -li
incorporate (*adj.*) ɪnˈkɔː.pᵊr.ət, ˌɪn-, ɪŋ-, ˌɪŋ-, -ɪt (US) ɪnˈkɔːr-, ˌɪn-
incorpor|ate (*v.*) ɪnˈkɔː.pᵊr|.eɪt, ɪŋ- (US) ɪnˈkɔːr.pə.r|eɪt **-ates** -eɪts **-ating** -eɪ.tɪŋ (US) -eɪ.t̬ɪŋ **-ated** -eɪ.tɪd (US) -eɪ.t̬ɪd
incorporation ɪnˌkɔː.pᵊrˈeɪ.ʃᵊn, ɪŋ- (US) ɪnˌkɔːr.pəˈreɪ- **-s** -z
incorporeal ˌɪn.kɔːˈpɔː.ri.əl, ˌɪŋ- (US) ˌɪn.kɔːrˈpɔːr.i- **-ly** -i
incorrect ˌɪn.kᵊrˈekt, ˌɪŋ- (US) ˌɪn.kəˈrekt **-ly** -li **-ness** -nəs, -nɪs
incorrigibility ɪnˌkɒr.ɪ.dʒəˈbɪl.ə.ti, ɪŋ-, -dʒɪˈ-, -ɪ.ti (US) ɪnˌkɔːr.ə.dʒəˈbɪl.ə.t̬i
incorrigib|le ɪnˈkɒr.ɪ.dʒə.b|l̩, ɪŋ-, -dʒɪ- (US) ɪnˈkɔːr.ə.dʒə- **-ly** -li **-leness** -l̩.nəs, -nɪs
incorruptibility ˌɪn.kəˌrʌp.təˈbɪl.ə.ti, ˌɪŋ-, -tɪˈ-, -ɪ.ti (US) ˌɪn.kəˌrʌp.təˈbɪl.ə.t̬i
incorruptib|le ˌɪn.kəˈrʌp.tə.b|l̩, ˌɪŋ-, -tɪ- (US) ˌɪn- **-ly** -li **-leness** -l̩.nəs, -nɪs
incorruption ˌɪn.kəˈrʌp.ʃᵊn, ˌɪŋ- (US) ˌɪn-
increas|e (*n.*) ˈɪn.kriːs, ˈɪŋ-, -ˈ- (US) ˈɪn.kriːs, -ˈ- **-es** -ɪz
increas|e (*v.*) ɪnˈkriːs, ɪŋ-, ˈ-- (US) ɪnˈkriːs, ˈ-- **-es** -ɪz **-ing/ly** -ɪŋ/li **-ed** -t
incredibility ɪnˌkred.ɪˈbɪl.ə.ti, ɪŋ-, -əˈ-, -ɪ.ti (US) ɪnˌkred.ɪˈbɪl.ə.t̬i, -əˈ-
incredib|le ɪnˈkred.ɪ.b|l̩, ɪŋ-, ˈ-ə- (US) ˌɪn- **-ly** -li **-leness** -l̩.nəs, -nɪs
incredulity ˌɪn.krəˈdjuː.lə.ti, ˌɪŋ-, -krɪˈ-, -kredˈjuː-, -ɪ.ti (US) ˌɪn.krəˈduː.lə.t̬i, -ˈdjuː-
incredulous ɪnˈkred.jə.ləs, ɪŋ-, -jʊ-, -ˈkredʒ.ə-, ˈ-ʊ- (US) ɪnˈkredʒ.ʊ- **-ly** -li **-ness** -nəs, -nɪs
increment ˈɪn.krə.mənt, ˈɪŋ-, -krɪ- (US) ˈɪn- **-s** -s
incremental ˌɪn.krəˈmen.tᵊl, ˌɪŋ-, -krɪˈ- (US) ˌɪn.krəˈmen.t̬ᵊl **-ly** -i
incrimi|nate ɪnˈkrɪm.ɪ|.neɪt, ɪŋ-, ˈ-ə- (US) ɪn- **-nates** -neɪts **-nating** -neɪ.tɪŋ (US) -neɪ.t̬ɪŋ **-nated** -neɪ.tɪd (US) -neɪ.t̬ɪd
incrimination ɪnˌkrɪm.ɪˈneɪ.ʃᵊn, ɪŋ-, -əˈ- (US) ɪn-
incriminatory ɪnˈkrɪm.ɪ.nə.tᵊr.i, ɪŋ-, -ᵊn.ə-, -neɪ.tᵊr-; ɪnˌkrɪm.ɪˈneɪ-, ˌɪn-, ɪŋ-, ˌɪŋ- (US) ɪnˈkrɪm.ɪ.nə.tɔːr.i
incrust ɪnˈkrʌst, ɪŋ- (US) ɪn- **-s** -s **-ing** -ɪŋ **-ed** -ɪd
incrustation ˌɪn.krʌsˈteɪ.ʃᵊn, ˌɪŋ- (US) ˌɪn- **-s** -z
incu|bate ˈɪŋ.kjʊ|.beɪt, ˈɪn-, -kjə- **-bates** -beɪts **-bating** -beɪ.tɪŋ (US) -beɪ.t̬ɪŋ **-bated** -beɪ.tɪd (US) -beɪ.t̬ɪd **-bative** -beɪ.tɪv (US) -beɪ.t̬ɪv
incubation ˌɪŋ.kjʊˈbeɪ.ʃᵊn, ˌɪn-, -kjəˈ- **-s** -z
incubator ˈɪŋ.kjʊ.beɪ.təʳ, ˈɪn-, -kjə- (US) -t̬ɚ **-s** -z
incubatory ˈɪŋ.kjʊ.beɪ.tᵊr.i, ˈɪn-, -kjə- (US) -bə.tɔːr-, ˌɪŋ.kjʊˈbeɪ.t̬ɚ-, ˌɪn-, -kjə-
incub|us ˈɪŋ.kjʊ.b|əs, ˈɪn-, -kjə- **-uses** -ə.sɪz **-i** -aɪ
incul|cate ˈɪn.kʌl|.keɪt, ˈɪŋ-, -kəl-; ɪnˈkʌl-, ɪŋ- (US) ˈɪn.kʌl-, -kəl-; ɪnˈkʌl- **-cates** -keɪts **-cating** -keɪ.tɪŋ (US) -keɪ.t̬ɪŋ **-cated** -keɪ.tɪd (US) -keɪ.t̬ɪd **-cator/s** -keɪ.təʳ/z (US) -keɪ.t̬ɚ/z
inculcation ˌɪn.kʌlˈkeɪ.ʃᵊn, ˌɪŋ-, -kəlˈ- (US) ˌɪn-
incul|pate ˈɪn.kʌl|.peɪt, ˈɪŋ-, -kəl-; ɪnˈkʌl-, ɪŋ- (US) ˈɪn.kʌl-, -kəl-; ɪnˈkʌl- **-pates** -peɪts **-pating** -peɪ.tɪŋ (US) -peɪ.t̬ɪŋ **-pated** -peɪ.tɪd (US) -peɪ.t̬ɪd
inculpation ˌɪn.kʌlˈpeɪ.ʃᵊn, ˌɪŋ-, -kəlˈ- (US) ˌɪn-
inculpatory ɪnˈkʌl.pə.tᵊr.i, ɪŋ-; ˈɪn.kʌl.peɪ-, ˈɪŋ-, -kəl-, ˌɪn.kʌlˈpeɪ-, ˌɪŋ-, -kəlˈ- (US) ɪnˈkʌl.pə.tɔːr.i
incumbenc|y ɪnˈkʌm.bənt.s|i, ɪŋ- (US) ɪn- **-ies** -iz
incumbent ɪnˈkʌm.bənt, ɪŋ- (US) ɪn- **-s** -s **-ly** -li
incumbranc|e ɪnˈkʌm.brənts, ɪŋ- (US) ɪn- **-es** -ɪz
incunabul|um ˌɪn.kjuːˈnæb.jə.l|əm, ˌɪŋ-, -jʊ- (US) -kjəˈ-, -kjʊˈ- **-a** -ə
incur ɪnˈkɜːʳ, ɪŋ- (US) ɪnˈkɝː **-s** -z **-ring** -ɪŋ **-red** -d **-rable** -ə.bl̩
incurability ɪnˌkjʊə.rəˈbɪl.ə.ti, ˌɪn-, ɪŋ-, ˌɪŋ-, -ˌkjɔː-, -ɪ.ti (US) ɪnˌkjʊr.əˈbɪl.ə.t̬i
incurab|le ɪnˈkjʊə.rə.b|l̩, ˌɪn-, ɪŋ-, ˌɪŋ-, -ˈkjɔː- (US) ɪnˈkjʊr.ə- **-ly** -li **-leness** -l̩.nəs, -nɪs
incurious ɪnˈkjʊə.ri.əs, ˌɪn-, ɪŋ-, ˌɪŋ-, -ˈkjɔː- (US) ɪnˈkjʊr.i- **-ly** -li **-ness** -nəs, -nɪs
incursion ɪnˈkɜː.ʃᵊn, ɪŋ-, -ʒᵊn (US) ɪnˈkɝː- **-s** -z
incursive ɪnˈkɜː.sɪv, ɪŋ- (US) ɪnˈkɝː-
incurvate (*adj.*) ɪnˈkɜː.veɪt, ɪŋ-, -vət, -vɪt (US) ɪnˈkɝː-
incur|vate (*v.*) ˈɪn.kɜː|.veɪt, ˈɪŋ- (US) ɪnˈkɝː-, ˈɪn.kɝː- **-vates** -veɪts **-vating** -veɪ.tɪŋ (US) -veɪ.t̬ɪŋ **-vated** -veɪ.tɪd (US) -veɪ.t̬ɪd
incurvation ˌɪn.kɜːˈveɪ.ʃᵊn, ˌɪŋ- (US) ˌɪn.kɝːˈ-
incurv|e ˌɪnˈkɜːv, ˌɪŋ- (US) ˌɪnˈkɝːv **-es** -z **-ing** -ɪŋ **-ed** -d *stress shift:* ˌincurved ˈsurface
incus|e ɪnˈkjuːz, ɪŋ- (US) ɪnˈkjuːz, -ˈkjuːs **-es** -ɪz **-ing** -ɪŋ **-ed** -d
Ind *surname:* ɪnd *India:* ɪnd, aɪnd
Ind. (*abbrev. for* **Indiana**) ˌɪn.diˈæn.ə, -ˈɑː.nə (US) -ˈæn.ə
ind. (*abbrev. for* **independent**) ˌɪn.dɪˈpen.dənt, -dəˈ- (*abbrev. for* **indicative**) ɪnˈdɪk.ə.tɪv (US) -t̬ɪv (*abbrev. for* **industrial**) ɪnˈdʌs.tri.ə
Indaur ɪnˈdɔːʳ (US) -ˈdɔːr
Ind Coope® ˌɪndˈkuːp
indebted ɪnˈdet.ɪd (US) -ˈdet̬- **-ness** -nəs, -nɪs
indecenc|y ɪnˈdiː.sᵊnt.s|i, ˌɪn- **-ies** -iz
indecent ɪnˈdiː.sᵊnt, ˌɪn- **-ly** -li inˌdecent asˈsault; inˌdecent exˈposure
indecipherable ˌɪn.dɪˈsaɪ.fᵊr.ə.bl̩, -də
indecision ˌɪn.dɪˈsɪʒ.ᵊn, -dəˈ-
indecisive ˌɪn.dɪˈsaɪ.sɪv, -dəˈ- **-ly** -li **-ness** -nəs, -nɪs
indeclinable ˌɪn.dɪˈklaɪ.nə.bl̩, -dəˈ- **-s**
indecomposable ɪnˌdiː.kəmˈpəʊ.zə.b, ˌɪn- (US) -ˈpoʊ-
indecorous ɪnˈdek.ᵊr.əs, ˌɪn- **-ly** -li **-ness** -nəs, -nəs
indecorum ˌɪn.dɪˈkɔː.rəm, -dəˈ- (US) -ˈkɔːr.əm
indeed (*adv.*) ɪnˈdiːd (*interj.*) ɪnˈdiːd, ˌɪn.diːd
indefatigab|le ˌɪn.dɪˈfæt.ɪ.gə.b|l̩, -də (US) -ˈfæt̬- **-ly** -li **-leness** -l̩.nəs, -nɪs
indefeasibility ˌɪn.dɪˌfiː.zəˈbɪl.ə.ti, -dəˌ-, -zɪˈ-, -ɪ.ti (US) -ə.t̬i
indefeasib|le ˌɪn.dɪˈfiː.zə.b|l̩, -dəˈ-, - **-ly** -li
indefensibility ˌɪn.dɪˌfent.səˈbɪl.ə.ti, -dəˌ-, -sɪˈ-, -ɪ.ti (US) -ə.t̬i
indefensib|le ˌɪn.dɪˈfent.sə.b|l̩, -dəˈ-, -sɪ- **-ly** -li
indefinab|le ˌɪn.dɪˈfaɪ.nə.b|l̩, -dəˈ- **-ly**
indefinite ɪnˈdef.ɪ.nət, ˌɪn-, -ᵊn.ət, ˈ-nət, -nɪt (US) -ə.nət, ˈ-nət **-ly** -li **-ness** -nəs, -nɪs inˌdefinite ˈarticle
indelibility ɪnˌdel.ɪˈbɪl.ə.ti, ˌɪn-, -əˈ-, -ɪ.ti (US) -ə.t̬i
indelib|le ɪnˈdel.ə.b|l̩, ˌɪn-, ˈ-ɪ- **-ly** -li
indelicac|y ɪnˈdel.ɪ.kə.s|i, ˌɪn-, ˈ-ə- **-ies** -iz
indelicate ɪnˈdel.ɪ.kət, ˌɪn-, ˈ-ə-, -kɪt **-ly** -li
in delicto ˌɪn.delˈɪk.təʊ, -dɪˈlɪk- (US) -dəˈlɪk.toʊ
indemnification ɪnˌdem.nɪ.fɪˈkeɪ.ʃ -nə- **-s** -z
indemni|fy ɪnˈdem.nɪ|.faɪ, -nə- **-fies** -faɪz **-fying** -faɪ.ɪŋ **-fied** -faɪd
indemnit|y ɪnˈdem.nə.t|i, -nɪ- (US) -t̬ **-ies** -iz
indemonstrab|le ɪnˈdem.ənt.strə.b ˌɪn-; ˌɪn.dɪˈmɒnt.strə-, -dəˈ- (US) ˌɪn.dɪˈmɑːnt.strə-; ɪnˈdem.ən ˌɪn- **-ly** -li

indent (*n.*) ˈɪn.dent, -ˈ- **-s** -s
in|dent (*v.*) ɪn|ˈdent, ˌɪn- **-dents** -ˈdents **-denting** -ˈden.tɪŋ ⓤⓢ -ˈden.t̬ɪŋ **-dented** -ˈden.tɪd ⓤⓢ -ˈden.t̬ɪd
indentation ˌɪn.denˈteɪ.ʃᵊn **-s** -z
indenture ɪnˈden.tʃəʳ ⓤⓢ -tʃɚ **-s** -z **-d** -d
independen|ce ˌɪn.dɪˈpen.dənt|s, -dəˈ- **-cy** -si **Indeˈpendence ˌDay**
independent (I) ˌɪn.dɪˈpen.dənt, -dəˈ- **-s** -s **-ly** -li
in-depth ˌɪnˈdepθ *stress shift:* ˌin-depth ˈtreatment
ndescribab|le ˌɪn.dɪˈskraɪ.bə.b|l̩, -dəˈ- **-ly** -li
ndestructibility ˌɪn.dɪˌstrʌk.təˈbɪl.ə.ti, -tɪˈ-, -ɪ.ti ⓤⓢ -ə.t̬i
ndestructib|le ˌɪn.dɪˈstrʌk.tə.b|l̩, -tɪ- **-ly** -li **-leness** -l̩.nəs, -l̩.nɪs
ndetectab|le, -ib|le ˌɪn.dɪˈtek.tə.b|l̩, -dəˈ- **-ly** -li
ndeterminab|le ˌɪn.dɪˈtɜː.mɪ.nə.b|l̩, -dəˈ- ⓤⓢ -ˈtɝː- **-ly** -li **-leness** -l̩.nəs, -l̩.nɪs
ndeterminacy ˌɪn.dɪˈtɜː.mɪ.nə.si, -dəˈ-, -mᵊn.ə- ⓤⓢ -ˈtɝː-
ndeterminate ˌɪn.dɪˈtɜː.mɪ.nət, -dəˈ-, -nɪt ⓤⓢ -ˈtɝː- **-ly** -li **-ness** -nəs, -nɪs
ndetermination ˌɪn.dɪˌtɜː.mɪˈneɪ.ʃᵊn, -dəˌ-, -məˈ- ⓤⓢ -ˌtɝː-
d|ex ˈɪn.d|eks **-exes** -ek.sɪz **-exing** -eks.ɪŋ **-exed** -ekst **-ices** -ɪ.siːz, -ə- ˈ**index ˌcard**; ˌ**index ˈfinger**, ˈ**index ˌfinger**; ˈ**index ˌnumber**
dexer ˈɪn.dek.səʳ ⓤⓢ -sɚ **-s** -z
dex-linked ˌɪn.deksˈlɪŋkt
di|a ˈɪn.di|.ə **-an/s** -ən/z ˌ**Indian ˈOcean**; ˌ**India ˈrubber**; ˌ**Indian ˈsummer**
diana ˌɪn.diˈæn.ə, -ˈɑː.nə ⓤⓢ -ˈæn.ə
dianapolis ˌɪn.di.əˈnæp.ᵊl.ɪs ⓤⓢ -ə.lɪs
dic ˈɪn.dɪk
di|cate ˈɪn.dɪ|.keɪt, -də- **-cates** -keɪts **-cating** -keɪ.tɪŋ ⓤⓢ -keɪ.t̬ɪŋ **-cated** -keɪ.tɪd ⓤⓢ -keɪ.t̬ɪd
dication ˌɪn.dɪˈkeɪ.ʃᵊn, -dəˈ- **-s** -z
dicative (*n. adj.*) *in grammar:* ɪnˈdɪk.ə.tɪv ⓤⓢ -t̬ɪv **-s** -z **-ly** -li
dicative (*adj.*) *indicating:* ɪnˈdɪk.ə.tɪv; ˈɪn.dɪ.keɪ- ⓤⓢ ɪnˈdɪk.ə.t̬ɪv **-ly** -li
licator ˈɪn.dɪ.keɪ.təʳ, -də- ⓤⓢ -t̬ɚ **-s** -z
licatory ɪnˈdɪk.ə.tᵊr.i; ˈɪn.dɪ.keɪ-, ˌɪn.dɪˈkeɪ- ⓤⓢ ˈɪn.dɪ.kə.tɔːr-; ɪnˈdɪk.ə-
lices (*plur. of* **index**) ˈɪn.dɪ.siːz, -də-
licia ɪnˈdɪʃ.i.ə ⓤⓢ -ˈdɪʃ.ə, -i.ə
dict ɪn|ˈdaɪt **-dicts** -ˈdaɪts **-dicting** -ˈdaɪ.tɪŋ ⓤⓢ -ˈdaɪ.t̬ɪŋ **-dicted** -ˈdaɪ.tɪd ⓤⓢ -ˈdaɪ.t̬ɪd **-dicter/s** -ˈdaɪ.təʳ/z ⓤⓢ -ˈdaɪ.t̬ɚ/z **-dictable** -ˈdaɪ.tə.bl̩ ⓤⓢ -ˈdaɪ.t̬ə.bl̩

indiction ɪnˈdɪk.ʃᵊn **-s** -z
indictment ɪnˈdaɪt.mənt **-s** -s
indie ˈɪn.di **-s** -z
Indies ˈɪn.diz
indifference ɪnˈdɪf.ᵊr.ᵊnts, ˈ-rᵊnts
indifferent ɪnˈdɪf.ᵊr.ᵊnt, ˈ-rᵊnt **-ly** -li
indigen ˈɪn.dɪ.dʒən, -də- **-s** -z
indigence ˈɪn.dɪ.dʒənts
indigene ˈɪn.dɪ.dʒiːn **-s** -z
indigenous ɪnˈdɪdʒ.ɪ.nəs, -ᵊn.əs **-ly** -li **-ness** -nəs, -nɪs
indigent ˈɪn.dɪ.dʒənt **-s** -s **-ly** -li
indigestibility ˌɪn.dɪˌdʒes.təˈbɪl.ə.ti, -tɪˈ-, -ɪ.ti ⓤⓢ -dɪˌdʒes.təˈbɪl.ə.t̬i, -daɪˌ-
indigestib|le ˌɪn.dɪˈdʒes.tə.b|l̩, -dəˈ-, -tɪ- ⓤⓢ -dɪˈ-, -daɪˈ- **-leness** -l̩.nəs, -nɪs **-ly** -li
indigestion ˌɪn.dɪˈdʒes.tʃᵊn, -dəˈ-, -ˈdʒeʃ- ⓤⓢ -dɪˈdʒes-, -daɪˈ-
indignant ɪnˈdɪg.nənt **-ly** -li
indignation ˌɪn.dɪgˈneɪ.ʃᵊn
indignit|y ɪnˈdɪg.nə.t|i, -nɪ- ⓤⓢ -nə.t̬|i **-ies** -iz
indigo ˈɪn.dɪ.gəʊ ⓤⓢ -goʊ **-(e)s** -z
Indira ˈɪn.dɪ.rə, -dᵊr.ə; ɪnˈdɪə.rə ⓤⓢ ɪnˈdɪr.ə
indirect ˌɪn.dɪˈrekt, -daɪˈ-, -dəˈ- **-ly** -li **-ness** -nəs, -nɪs ˌ**indirect ˈobject**; ˌ**indirect ˈspeech**
indiscernib|le ˌɪn.dɪˈsɜː.nə.b|l̩, -ˈzɜː-, -nɪ- ⓤⓢ -ˈsɝː-, -ˈzɝː- **-ly** -li
indisciplin|e ɪnˈdɪs.ə.plɪn, ˌɪn-, ˈ-ɪ- **-ed** -d **-able** -ə.bl̩
indiscreet ˌɪn.dɪˈskriːt, -dəˈ- **-ly** -li **-ness** -nəs, -nɪs
indiscrete ˌɪn.dɪˈskriːt, -dəˈ-
indiscretion ˌɪn.dɪˈskreʃ.ᵊn, -dəˈ- **-s** -z
indiscriminate ˌɪn.dɪˈskrɪm.ɪ.nət, -dəˈ-, ˈ-ə-, -nɪt **-ly** -li **-ness** -nəs, -nɪs
indiscrimination ˌɪn.dɪˌskrɪm.ɪˈneɪ.ʃᵊn, -dəˌ-, -əˈ-
indispensability ˌɪn.dɪˌspent.səˈbɪl.ə.ti, -dəˌ-, -ɪ.ti ⓤⓢ -ə.t̬i
indispensab|le, -ib|le ˌɪn.dɪˈspent.sə.b|l̩, -dəˈ- **-ly** -li **-leness** -nəs, -nɪs
indispos|e ˌɪn.dɪˈspəʊz, -dəˈ- ⓤⓢ -ˈspoʊz **-es** -ɪz **-ing** -ɪŋ **-ed** -d
indisposition ˌɪn.dɪ.spəˈzɪʃ.ᵊn; ɪnˌdɪs.pəˈ- ⓤⓢ ˌɪn.dɪ.spəˈ- **-s** -z
indisputability ˌɪn.dɪˌspjuː.təˈbɪl.ə.ti; ɪnˌdɪs.pjuː-, -ɪ.ti ⓤⓢ ˌɪn.dɪˌspjuː.təˈbɪl.ə.t̬i
indisputab|le ˌɪn.dɪˈspjuː.tə.b|l̩; ɪnˈdɪs.pjuː- ⓤⓢ ˌɪn.dɪˈspjuː.t̬ə-; ɪnˈdɪs.pjuː-, -pjə- **-ly** -li **-leness** -l̩.nəs, -nɪs
indissociable ˌɪn.dɪˈsəʊ.ʃi.ə.bl̩, -ʃə.bl̩ ⓤⓢ -ˈsoʊ-

indissolubility ˌɪn.dɪˌsɒl.jəˈbɪl.ə.ti, -dəˌ-, -jʊˈ-, -ɪ.ti ⓤⓢ -ˌsɑːl.jəˈbɪl.ə.t̬i
indissolub|le ˌɪn.dɪˈsɒl.jə.b|l̩, -dəˈ-, -jʊ- ⓤⓢ -ˈsɑːl- **-ly** -li **-leness** -l̩.nəs, -nɪs
indistinct ˌɪn.dɪˈstɪŋkt, -dəˈ- **-ly** -li **-ness** -nəs, -nɪs
indistinctive ˌɪn.dɪˈstɪŋk.tɪv, -dəˈ- **-ly** -li **-ness** -nəs, -nɪs
indistinguishab|le ˌɪn.dɪˈstɪŋ.gwɪ.ʃə.b|l̩, -dəˈ- **-ly** -li **-leness** -l̩.nəs, -nɪs
in|dite ɪn|ˈdaɪt **-dites** -ˈdaɪts **-diting** -ˈdaɪ.tɪŋ ⓤⓢ -ˈdaɪ.t̬ɪŋ **-dited** -ˈdaɪ.tɪd ⓤⓢ -ˈdaɪ.t̬ɪd **-diter/s** -ˈdaɪ.təʳ/z ⓤⓢ -ˈdaɪ.t̬ɚ/z
indium ˈɪn.di.əm
individual ˌɪn.dɪˈvɪdʒ.u.əl, -dəˈ-, -ˈvɪd.ju- ⓤⓢ -ˈvɪdʒ.u-, -ˈvɪdʒ.ᵊl **-s** -z **-ly** -i
individual|ism ˌɪn.dɪˈvɪdʒ.u.ə.l|ɪ.zᵊm, -dəˈ-, -ˈvɪd.ju.ə.l|ɪz- ⓤⓢ -ˈvɪdʒ.u-, -ˈvɪdʒ.ᵊl|.ɪ- **-ist/s** -ɪst/s
individualistic ˌɪn.dɪˌvɪdʒ.u.əˈlɪs.tɪk, -dəˌ-, -ˌvɪd.ju- ⓤⓢ -ˌvɪdʒ.u-, -ˌvɪdʒ.ᵊlˈɪs- **-ally** -ᵊl.i, -li
individualit|y ˌɪn.dɪˌvɪdʒ.uˈæl.ə.t|i, -dəˌ-, -ˌvɪd.juˈ-, -ɪ.t|i ⓤⓢ -ˌvɪdʒ.uˈæl.ə.t̬|i **-ies** -iz
individualization, -isa- ˌɪn.dɪˌvɪdʒ.u.ᵊl.aɪˈzeɪ.ʃᵊn, -dəˌ-, -ˌvɪd.ju-, -ɪˈ- ⓤⓢ -ˌvɪdʒ.u.ᵊl.ɪˈ-, -ˌvɪdʒ.ᵊl-
individualiz|e, -is|e ˌɪn.dɪˈvɪdʒ.u.ə.laɪz, -dəˈ-, -ˈvɪd.ju- ⓤⓢ -ˈvɪdʒ.u-, -ˈvɪdʒ.ᵊl.aɪz **-es** -ɪz **-ing** -ɪŋ **-ed** -d
individu|ate ˌɪn.dɪˈvɪdʒ.u|.eɪt, -dəˈ-, -ˈvɪd.ju- ⓤⓢ -ˈvɪdʒ.u- **-ates** -eɪts **-ating** -eɪ.tɪŋ ⓤⓢ -eɪ.t̬ɪŋ **-ated** -eɪ.tɪd ⓤⓢ -eɪ.t̬ɪd
individuation ˌɪn.dɪˌvɪdʒ.uˈeɪ.ʃᵊn, -dəˌ-, -ˌvɪd.juˈ- ⓤⓢ -ˌvɪdʒ.uˈ- **-s** -s
indivisibility ˌɪn.dɪˌvɪz.ɪˈbɪl.ə.ti, -əˈ-, -ɪ.ti ⓤⓢ -ə.t̬i
indivisib|le ˌɪn.dɪˈvɪz.ə.b|l̩, ˈ-ɪ- **-ly** -li **-leness** -l̩.nəs, -nɪs
Indo-China ˌɪn.dəʊˈtʃaɪ.nə ⓤⓢ -doʊˈ-
Indo-Chinese ˌɪn.dəʊ.tʃaɪˈniːz ⓤⓢ -doʊ-
indocile ɪnˈdəʊ.saɪl, ˌɪn- ⓤⓢ -ˈdɑː.səl
indocility ˌɪn.dəʊˈsɪl.ə.ti, -ɪ.ti ⓤⓢ -dɑːˈsɪl.ə.t̬i, -doʊˈ-
indoctri|nate ɪnˈdɒk.trɪ|.neɪt, -trə- ⓤⓢ -ˈdɑːk- **-nates** -neɪts **-nating** -neɪ.tɪŋ ⓤⓢ -neɪ.t̬ɪŋ **-nated** -neɪ.tɪd ⓤⓢ -neɪ.t̬ɪd **-nator/s** -neɪ.təʳ/z ⓤⓢ -neɪ.t̬ɚ/z
indoctrination ɪnˌdɒk.trɪˈneɪ.ʃᵊn, ˌɪn-, -trəˈ- ⓤⓢ -ˌdɑːk- **-s** -z
Indo-European ˌɪn.dəʊˌjʊə.rəˈpiː.ən, -ˌjɔː- ⓤⓢ -doʊ.jʊr.əˈ- **-s** -z
Indo-Germanic ˌɪn.dəʊ.dʒɜːˈmæn.ɪk, -dʒəˈ- ⓤⓢ -doʊ.dʒɝːˈ-

indolence ˈɪn.dᵊl.ənts

indolent ˈɪn.dᵊl.ənt **-ly** -li

indomitab|le ɪnˈdɒm.ɪ.tə.b|l̩, ˈ-ə- (US) -ˈdɑː.mə.t̬ə- **-ly** -li **-leness** -l̩.nəs, -nɪs

Indonesi|a ˌɪn.dəʊˈniː.ʒ|ə, -zi|.ə, -si|.ə, -ˈniː.ʃ|ə (US) -dəˈniː.ʒ|ə, -ʃ|ə **-an/s** -ən/z

indoor ˌɪnˈdɔːʳ (US) -ˈdɔːr *stress shift:* ˌindoor ˈgames

indoors ˌɪnˈdɔːz (US) -ˈdɔːrz

Indore ˌɪnˈdɔːʳ (US) -ˈdɔːr

indors|e ɪnˈdɔːs (US) -ˈdɔːrs **-es** -ɪz **-ing** -ɪŋ **-ed** -t

indorsement ɪnˈdɔːs.mənt (US) -ˈdɔːrs- **-s** -s

Indra ˈɪn.drə

indrawn ˌɪnˈdrɔːn (US) ˈɪn.drɑːn, -drɔːn *stress shift, British only:* ˌindrawn ˈbreath

indubitab|le ɪnˈdjuː.bɪ.tə.b|l̩, ˌɪn- (US) -ˈduː.bɪ.t̬ə-, -ˈdjuː- **-ly** -li **-leness** -l̩.nəs, -nɪs

induc|e ɪnˈdjuːs (US) -ˈduːs, -ˈdjuːs **-es** -ɪz **-ing** -ɪŋ **-ed** -t **-er/s** -əʳ/z (US) -ɚ/z

inducement ɪnˈdjuːs.mənt (US) -ˈduːs-, -ˈdjuːs- **-s** -s

induct ɪnˈdʌkt **-s** -s **-ing** -ɪŋ **-ed** -ɪd **-or/s** -əʳ/z (US) -ɚ/z

inductanc|e ɪnˈdʌk.tᵊnts **-es** -ɪz

inductee ˌɪn.dʌkˈtiː **-s** -z

inductile ɪnˈdʌk.taɪl, ˌɪn- (US) -tɪl

inductility ˌɪn.dʌkˈtɪl.ə.ti, -ɪ.ti (US) -ə.t̬i

induction ɪnˈdʌk.ʃᵊn **-s** -z **inˈduction ˌcoil**

inductive ɪnˈdʌk.tɪv **-ly** -li

indulg|e ɪnˈdʌldʒ **-es** -ɪz **-ing** -ɪŋ **-ed** -d **-er/s** -əʳ/z (US) -ɚ/z

indulgenc|e ɪnˈdʌl.dʒənts **-es** -ɪz

indulgent ɪnˈdʌl.dʒənt **-ly** -li

indur|ate ˈɪn.djʊə.r|eɪt, -djʊr|.eɪt (US) -dʊ.r|eɪt, -djʊ-, -də-, -djə- **-ates** -eɪts **-ating** -eɪ.tɪŋ (US) -eɪ.t̬ɪŋ **-ated** -eɪ.tɪd (US) -eɪ.t̬ɪd **-ative** -ə.tɪv (US) -t̬ɪv

induration ɪn.djʊəˈreɪ.ʃᵊn, -djʊˈ- (US) -dʊˈ-, -djʊˈ-, -dəˈ-, -djəˈ-

Indus ˈɪn.dəs

industrial ɪnˈdʌs.tri.əl **-ly** -i **inˌdustrial ˈaction; inˌdustrial disˈpute, inˌdustrial ˈdispute; inˌdustrial ˈespionage; inˌdustrial esˈtate; inˈdustrial ˌpark; inˌdustrial reˈlations; Inˌdustrial Revoˈlution; inˌdustrial triˈbunal**

industrial|ism ɪnˈdʌs.tri.əl|.ɪ.zᵊm **-ist/s** -ɪst/z

industrialization, -isa- ɪnˌdʌs.tri.ə.laɪˈzeɪ.ʃᵊn, -lɪˈ- (US) -lɪˈ-

industrializ|e, -is|e ɪnˈdʌs.tri.ə.laɪz **-es** -ɪz **-ing** -ɪŋ **-ed** -d

industrious ɪnˈdʌs.tri.əs **-ly** -li **-ness** -nəs, -nɪs

industr|y ˈɪn.də.str|i **-ies** -iz

industrywide ˌɪn.də.striˈwaɪd *stress shift:* ˌindustrywide ˈslump

indwel|l ˌɪnˈdwel, ˈ-- **-ls** -z **-ling** -ɪŋ **-t** -t

indweller ˈɪnˌdwel.əʳ (US) -ɚ **-s** -z

-ine -aɪn, -iːn, -ɪn

inebriate (*n. adj.*) ɪˈniː.bri.ət, -ɪt, -eɪt **-s** -s

inebri|ate (*v.*) ɪˈniː.bri|.eɪt **-ates** -eɪts **-ating** -eɪ.tɪŋ (US) -eɪ.t̬ɪŋ **-ated** -eɪ.tɪd (US) -eɪ.t̬ɪd

inebriation ɪˌniː.briˈeɪ.ʃᵊn

inebriety ˌɪn.iːˈbraɪ.ə.ti, -ɪˈ-, -ɪ.ti (US) -ə.t̬i

inedible ɪˈned.ɪ.bl̩, ˌɪnˈed-, ˈ-ə- (US) ˌɪnˈed-, ɪˈned-

inedited ɪˈned.ɪ.tɪd, ˌɪnˈed-, ˈ-ə- (US) ˌɪnˈed.ɪ.t̬ɪd, ɪˈned-, ˈ-ə-

ineducable ɪˈned.jə.kə.bl̩, ˌɪnˈed-, -ˈedʒ.ə-, ˈ-ʊ- (US) ˌɪnˈedʒ.ʊ-, ɪˈnedʒ-, ˈ-ə-

ineffab|le ɪˈnef.ə.b|l̩, ˌɪnˈef- (US) ˌɪnˈef-, ɪˈnef- **-ly** -li **-leness** -l̩.nəs, -nɪs

ineffaceab|le ˌɪn.ɪˈfeɪ.sə.b|l̩, -efˈeɪ-, -əˈfeɪ- **-ly** -li

ineffective ˌɪn.ɪˈfek.tɪv, -əˈ- **-ly** -li **-ness** -nəs, -nɪs

ineffectual ˌɪn.ɪˈfek.tʃu.ᵊl, -əˈ-, -tju- (US) -tʃu- **-ly** -i **-ness** -nəs, -nɪs

inefficacious ˌɪn.ef.ɪˈkeɪ.ʃəs, ɪˌnef- **-ly** -li

inefficacy ɪˈnef.ɪ.kə.si, ˌɪnˈef- (US) ˌɪnˈef-, ɪˈnef-

inefficiency ˌɪn.ɪˈfɪʃ.ᵊnt.si, -əˈ-

inefficient ˌɪn.ɪˈfɪʃ.ᵊnt, -əˈ- **-ly** -li

inelastic ˌɪn.ɪˈlæs.tɪk, -əˈ-, -ˈlɑː.stɪk (US) -iːˈlæs-, -ɪˈ-

inelasticity ˌɪn.ɪ.læsˈtɪs.ə.ti, ˌ-ə-, -ˌiː.læsˈ-, -lɑːˈstɪs-, -ɪ.ti (US) -iː.læsˈtɪs.ə.t̬i, ˌ-ɪ-

inelegance ɪˈnel.ɪ.gənts, ˌɪnˈel-, ˈ-ə- (US) ˌɪnˈel-, ɪˈnel-

inelegant ɪˈnel.ɪ.gənt, ˌɪnˈel-, ˈ-ə- (US) ˌɪnˈel-, ɪˈnel- **-ly** -li

ineligibility ɪˌnel.ɪ.dʒəˈbɪl.ə.ti, ˌɪn.el-, -dʒɪˈ-, -ɪ.ti (US) ˌɪn.el.ɪ.dʒəˈbɪl.ə.t̬i, ɪˌnel-, -dʒɪˈ-

ineligib|le ɪˈnel.ɪ.dʒə.b|l̩, ˌɪnˈel-, -dʒɪ- (US) ˌɪnˈel-, ɪˈnel- **-ly** -li

ineluctab|le ˌɪn.ɪˈlʌk.tə.b|l̩, -əˈ- **-ly** -li

inept ɪˈnept, ˌɪnˈept (US) ˌɪnˈept, ɪˈnept **-ly** -li **-ness** -nəs, -nɪs

ineptitude ɪˈnep.tɪ.tjuːd, ˌɪnˈep-, -tə- (US) ˌɪnˈep.tɪ.tuːd, ɪˈnep-, -tə-, -tjuːd

inequab|le ɪˈnek.wə.b|l̩, ˌɪnˈek- (US) ˌɪnˈek-, ɪˈnek- **-ly** -li

inequalit|y ˌɪn.ɪˈkwɒl.ə.t|i, -iːˈ-, -əˈ-, -ɪ.t|i (US) -ˈkwɑː.lə.t̬|i **-ies** -iz

inequitab|le ɪˈnek.wɪ.tə.b|l̩, ˌɪnˈek- (US) ˌɪnˈek.wə.t̬ə-, ɪˈnek- **-ly** -li

inequit|y ɪˈnek.wə.t|i, ˌɪnˈek-, -wɪ- (US) ˌɪnˈek.wə.t̬|i, ɪˈnek- **-ies** -iz

ineradicab|le ˌɪn.ɪˈræd.ɪ.kə.b|l̩, -əˈ- **-ly** -li

inert ɪˈnɜːt (US) ˌɪnˈɝːt, ɪˈnɝːt **-ly** -li **-ne** -nəs, -nɪs

inertia ɪˈnɜː.ʃə, -ʃi.ə (US) ˌɪnˈɝː-, ɪˈnɝː-

inescapab|le ˌɪn.ɪˈskeɪ.pə.b|l̩, -əˈ- **-ly** -li

inessential ˌɪn.ɪˈsen.tʃᵊl, -əˈ-

inessive ɪˈnes.ɪv, ˌɪnˈes- (US) ˌɪnˈes-, ɪˈnes-

inestimab|le ɪˈnes.tɪ.mə.b|l̩, ˌɪnˈes-, -tə- (US) ˌɪnˈes-, ɪˈnes- **-ly** -li

inevitability ɪˌnev.ɪ.təˈbɪl.ə.ti, ˌɪn.ev ˌ-ə-, -ɪ.ti (US) ˌɪn.ev.ɪ.t̬əˈbɪl.ə.t̬i, ɪˌnev-, ˌ-ə-

inevitab|le ɪˈnev.ɪ.tə.b|l̩, ˌɪnˈev-, ˈ-ə- (US) ˌɪnˈev.ɪ.t̬ə-, ɪˈnev-, ˈ-ə- **-ly** -li **-leness** -l̩.nəs, -nɪs

inexact ˌɪn.ɪgˈzækt, -egˈ-; -ɪkˈsækt, -ekˈ- (US) -ɪgˈzækt, -egˈ- **-ly** -li **-ness** -nəs, -nɪs

inexactitude ˌɪn.ɪgˈzæk.tɪ.tjuːd, -eg -tə-; -ɪkˈsæk-, -ekˈ- (US) -ɪgˈzæk.tə.tuːd, -egˈ- **-s** -z

inexcusab|le ˌɪn.ɪkˈskjuː.zə.b|l̩, -ek **-ly** -li **-leness** -l̩.nəs, -nɪs

inexhaustibility ˌɪn.ɪgˌzɔː.stəˈbɪl.ə -egˌ-, -stɪˈ-, -ɪ.ti; -ɪkˌsɔː-, -ekˌ- (US) -ɪgˌzɑː.stəˈbɪl.ə.t̬i, -egˌ-, -ˌzɔː

inexhaustib|le ˌɪn.ɪgˈzɔː.stə.b|l̩, -eg -stɪ-; -ɪkˈsɔː-, -ekˈ- (US) -ɪgˈzɑː.stə -egˈ-, -ˈzɔː- **-ly** -li **-leness** -l̩.nəs, -n

inexisten|t ˌɪn.ɪgˈzɪs.tᵊn|t, -ekˈ-; -ɪkˈsɪs-, -ekˈ- (US) -ɪgˈzɪs-, -egˈ- **-ce**

inexorability ɪˌnek.sᵊr.əˈbɪl.ə.ti, ˌɪn.ek-, -ɪ.ti (US) ˌɪn.ek.sɚ.əˈbɪl.ə. ɪˌnek-

inexorab|le ɪˈnek.sᵊr.ə.b|l̩, ˌɪnˈek- (US) ˌɪnˈek-, ɪˈnek- **-ly** -li **-leness** -l̩. -nɪs

inexpedien|ce ˌɪn.ɪkˈspiː.di.ən|ts, - **-cy** -si

inexpedient ˌɪn.ɪkˈspiː.di.ənt, -ekˈ- **-ly** -li

inexpensive ˌɪn.ɪkˈspent.sɪv, -ekˈ- **-ly** -li **-ness** -nəs, -nɪs

inexperience ˌɪn.ɪkˈspɪə.ri.ənts, -e (US) -ˈspɪr.i- **-d** -t

inexpert ɪˈnek.spɜːt, ˌɪnˈek- (US) ˌɪnˈek.spɝːt, ɪˈnek-; ˌɪn.ɪkˈsp -ekˈ- **-ly** -li **-ness** -nəs, -nɪs

inexpiab|le ɪˈnek.spi.ə.b|l̩, ˌɪnˈek- (US) ˌɪnˈek-, ɪˈnek- **-ly** -li **-leness** -l̩. -nɪs

inexplicability ˌɪn.ɪkˌsplɪk.əˈbɪl.ə -ekˌ-, -ɪ.ti; ɪnˌek.splɪk.əˈ-, ˌɪn- (US) ɪˌnek.splɪ.kəˈbɪl.ə.t̬i, ˌɪn.ek-

inexplicab|le ˌɪn.ɪkˈsplɪk.ə.b|l̩, -ek ɪˈnek.splɪ.kə-, ˌɪnˈek-, -splə- (US) ˌɪnˈek.splɪ.kə-, ɪˈnek-, -splə-; ˌɪn.ɪkˈsplɪk.ə- **-ly** -li **-leness** -l̩.nə -nɪs

inexplicit ˌɪn.ɪk'splɪs.ɪt, -ek'- **-ly** -li **-ness** -nəs, -nɪs
inexplorable ˌɪn.ɪk'splɔː.rə.bl̩, -ek'- ⓤⓢ -'splɔːr.ə-
inexpressib|le ˌɪn.ɪk'spres.ə.b|l̩, -ek'-, '-ɪ- **-ly** -li
inexpressive ˌɪn.ɪk'spres.ɪv, -ek'- **-ly** -li **-ness** -nəs, -nɪs
inexpugnab|le ˌɪn.ɪk'spʌg.nə.b|l̩, -ek'- ⓤⓢ -'spʌg-, -'spjuː- **-ly** -li **-leness** -l̩.nəs, -nɪs
nextensible ˌɪn.ɪk'stent.sə.bl̩, -ek'-, -sɪ-
nextinguishab|le ˌɪn.ɪk'stɪŋ.gwɪ.ʃə.b|l̩, -ek'-, -wɪ- **-ly** -li
n extremis ˌɪn.ɪk'striː.mɪs ⓤⓢ -ɪk'-, -ek'-
nextricab|le ˌɪn.ɪk'strɪk.ə.b|l̩, -ek'-; ɪ'nek.strɪ.kə-, ˌɪn'ek- **-ly** -li **-leness** -l̩.nəs, -nɪs
nez 'iː.nez, 'aɪ- ⓤⓢ iː'nez, ɪ-, aɪ-, 'iː.nez, 'aɪ-, -nes
ıfallibility ɪnˌfæl.ə'bɪl.ə.ti, ˌɪn-, -ɪ'-, -ɪ.ti ⓤⓢ -ə.t̬i
ıfallib|le ɪn'fæl.ə.b|l̩, '-ɪ- **-ly** -li
ıfamous 'ɪn.fə.məs **-ly** -li **-ness** -nəs, -nɪs
ıfam|y 'ɪn.fə.m|i **-ies** -iz
ıfanc|y 'ɪn.fənt.s|i **-ies** -iz
ıfant 'ɪn.fənt **-s** -s 'infant ˌschool; ˌinfant mor'tality ˌrate
ıfanta ɪn'fæn.tə ⓤⓢ -t̬ə, -'fɑːn- **-s** -z
ıfante ɪn'fæn.ti ⓤⓢ -teɪ, -'fɑːn- **-s** -z
ıfanticide ɪn'fæn.tɪ.saɪd, -tə- ⓤⓢ -t̬ə- **-s** -z
fant|ile 'ɪn.fən.t|aɪl ⓤⓢ -t|aɪl, -t|ɪl **-ine** -aɪn ˌinfantile pa'ralysis
fantilism ɪn'fæn.tɪ.lɪ.zəm, -tə- ⓤⓢ 'ɪn.fən.t̬ə-, -taɪ-; ɪn'fæn.t̬ə-
fantry 'ɪn.fən.tri **-man** -mən, -mæn **-men** -mən, -men
farct 'ɪn.fɑːkt, ˌ-'- ⓤⓢ 'ɪn.fɑːrkt, ˌ-'- **-s** -s
farction ɪn'fɑːk.ʃən ⓤⓢ -'fɑːrk- **-s** -z
fatu|ate ɪn'fæt.ju|.eɪt, -'fætʃ.u- ⓤⓢ -'fætʃ.u- **-ates** -eɪts **-ating** -eɪ.tɪŋ ⓤⓢ -eɪ.t̬ɪŋ **-ated** -eɪ.tɪd ⓤⓢ -eɪ.t̬ɪd
fatuation ɪnˌfæt.ju'eɪ.ʃən, -ˌfætʃ.u'- ⓤⓢ -ˌfætʃ.u'- **-s** -z
ect ɪn'fekt **-s** -s **-ing** -ɪŋ **-ed** -ɪd
ection ɪn'fek.ʃən **-s** -z
ectious ɪn'fek.ʃəs **-ly** -li **-ness** -nəs, -nɪs
ecundity ˌɪn.fɪ'kʌn.də.ti, -fiː'-, -fek'ʌn-, -dɪ- ⓤⓢ -fiː'kʌn.də.t̬i, -fɪ'-
elicitous ˌɪn.fə'lɪs.ɪ.təs, -fɪ'-, -fel'ɪs-, '-ə- ⓤⓢ -fə'lɪs.ə.t̬əs **-ly** -li
elicit|y ˌɪn.fə'lɪs.ə.t|i, -fɪ'-, -fel'ɪs-, -ɪ- ⓤⓢ -ə.t̬|i **-ies** -iz
er ɪn'fɜːʳ ⓤⓢ -'fɝː **-s** -z **-ring** -ɪŋ **-red** -d **-able** -ə.bl̩

inferenc|e 'ɪn.fər.ənts, '-frənts **-es** -ɪz
inferential ˌɪn.fər'en.tʃəl ⓤⓢ -fə'ren- **-ly** -i
inferior ɪn'fɪə.ri.əʳ, ˌɪn- ⓤⓢ -'fɪr.i.ɚ **-s** -z
inferiority ɪnˌfɪə.ri'ɒr.ə.ti, ˌɪn-, -ɪ.ti ⓤⓢ -ˌfɪr.i'ɔːr.ə.t̬i inferi'ority ˌcomplex
infernal ɪn'fɜː.nəl ⓤⓢ -'fɝː- **-ly** -i
inferno (I) ɪn'fɜː.nəʊ ⓤⓢ -'fɝː.noʊ **-s** -z
infertile ɪn'fɜː.taɪl, ˌɪn- ⓤⓢ -'fɝː.t̬əl
infertility ˌɪn.fə'tɪl.ə.ti, -fɜː'-, -ɪ.ti ⓤⓢ -fɚ'tɪl.ə.t̬i
infest ɪn'fest **-s** -s **-ing** -ɪŋ **-ed** -ɪd
infestation ˌɪn.fes'teɪ.ʃən **-s** -z
infibu|late ɪn'fɪb.jə|.leɪt, -jʊ- **-lates** -leɪts **-lating** -leɪ.tɪŋ ⓤⓢ -leɪ.t̬ɪŋ **-lated** -leɪ.tɪd ⓤⓢ -leɪ.t̬ɪd
infibulation ɪnˌfɪb.jə'leɪ.ʃən, -jʊ'-
infidel 'ɪn.fɪ.dəl, -fə-, -del ⓤⓢ -fə.del, -dəl **-s** -z
infidelit|y ˌɪn.fɪ'del.ə.t|i, -fə'-, -ɪ.t|i ⓤⓢ -fə'del.ə.t̬|i **-ies** -iz
infield 'ɪn.fiːld **-s** -z
infielder 'ɪnˌfiːl.dəʳ ⓤⓢ -dɚ **-s** -z
infighting 'ɪnˌfaɪ.tɪŋ
infill 'ɪn.fɪl **-s** -z **-ing** -ɪŋ **-ed** -d
infilling 'ɪnˌfɪl.ɪŋ
infil|trate 'ɪn.fɪl|.treɪt, -fəl- ⓤⓢ ɪn'fɪl|.treɪt, 'ɪn.fɪl- **-trates** -treɪts **-trating** -treɪ.tɪŋ ⓤⓢ -treɪ.t̬ɪŋ **-trated** -treɪ.tɪd ⓤⓢ -treɪ.t̬ɪd **-trator/s** -treɪ.təʳ/z ⓤⓢ -treɪ.t̬ɚ/z
infiltration ˌɪn.fɪl'treɪ.ʃən, -fəl'- **-s** -z
in fine ˌɪn'faɪ.ni, -'fiː-, -neɪ
infinite *in non-technical sense:* 'ɪn.fɪ.nət, -fən.ət, -ɪt *in church music:* 'ɪn.fɪ.naɪt, -faɪ- ⓤⓢ 'ɪn.fə.nɪt **-ly** -li **-ness** -nəs, -nɪs *in grammar:* ˌɪn'faɪ.naɪt *in mathematics:* 'ɪn.fɪ.nət, -fən.ət, -ɪt, -ˌfaɪ.naɪt
infinitesimal ˌɪn.fɪ.nɪ'tes.ɪ.məl, -fən.ɪ'-, -ə'-, -əm.əl ⓤⓢ -'tes-, -'tez- **-ly** -i
infinitival ɪnˌfɪn.ɪ'taɪ.vəl, -ə'-; ˌɪn.fɪ.nɪ'-, -nə'- ⓤⓢ ɪnˌfɪn.ɪ'taɪ-
infinitive ɪn'fɪn.ə.tɪv, '-ɪ- ⓤⓢ -t̬ɪv **-s** -z **-ly** -li
infinitude ɪn'fɪn.ɪ.tjuːd, '-ə- ⓤⓢ -tuːd, -tjuːd **-s** -z
infinit|y ɪn'fɪn.ə.t|i, -ɪ.t|i ⓤⓢ -ə.t̬|i **-ies** -iz
infirm ɪn'fɜːm, ˌɪn- ⓤⓢ -'fɝːm **-ly** -li
infirmar|y ɪn'fɜː.mər|.i ⓤⓢ -'fɝː- **-ies** -iz
infirmit|y ɪn'fɜː.mə.t|i, -mɪ- ⓤⓢ -'fɝː.mə.t̬|i **-ies** -iz
infix *(n.)* 'ɪn.fɪks **-es** -ɪz
infix *(v.)* 'ɪn.fɪks, ˌ-'- **-es** -ɪz **-ing** -ɪŋ **-ed** -t
in flagrante delicto ɪn.fləˌgræn.teɪ.dɪ'lɪk.təʊ, -ti-, -də'-, -diː'-, -deɪ'- ⓤⓢ -ˌgrɑːn.teɪ.dɪ'lɪk.toʊ, -ˌgræn-, -ti-, -də'-, -diː'-, -deɪ'-
inflam|e ɪn'fleɪm **-es** -z **-ing** -ɪŋ **-ed** -d
inflammability ɪnˌflæm.ə'bɪl.ə.ti, -ɪ.ti ⓤⓢ -ə.t̬i
inflammable ɪn'flæm.ə.bl̩ **-ness** -nəs, -nɪs
inflammation ˌɪn.flə'meɪ.ʃən **-s** -z
inflammatory ɪn'flæm.ə.tər.i ⓤⓢ -tɔːr-
inflatable ɪn'fleɪ.tə.bl̩ ⓤⓢ -t̬ə- **-s** -z
in|flate ɪn|'fleɪt **-flates** -'fleɪts **-flating** -'fleɪ.tɪŋ ⓤⓢ -'fleɪ.t̬ɪŋ **-flated** -'fleɪ.tɪd ⓤⓢ -'fleɪ.t̬ɪd **-flator/s** -'fleɪ.təʳ/z ⓤⓢ -'fleɪ.t̬ɚ/z
inflation ɪn'fleɪ.ʃən **-s** -z **-ary** -ər.i
inflationism ɪn'fleɪ.ʃən.ɪ.zəm
inflect ɪn'flekt **-s** -s **-ing** -ɪŋ **-ed** -ɪd
inflection ɪn'flek.ʃən **-s** -z
inflectional ɪn'flek.ʃən.əl
inflective ɪn'flek.tɪv
inflexibility ɪnˌflek.sə'bɪl.ə.ti, ˌɪn-, -sɪ'-, -ɪ.ti ⓤⓢ -ə.t̬i
inflexib|le ɪn'flek.sə.b|l̩, -sɪ- **-ly** -li **-leness** -l̩.nəs, -nɪs
inflexion ɪn'flek.ʃən **-s** -z
inflexional ɪn'flek.ʃən.əl
inflict ɪn'flɪkt **-s** -s **-ing** -ɪŋ **-ed** -ɪd
infliction ɪn'flɪk.ʃən **-s** -z
in-flight ˌɪn'flaɪt ⓤⓢ '--, ˌ-'- *stress shift, British only:* ˌin-flight 'service
inflorescence ˌɪn.flɔː'res.ənts, -flɒr'es-, -flə'res- ⓤⓢ -flə'res-, -flɔː-, -floʊ-
inflow 'ɪn.fləʊ ⓤⓢ -floʊ **-s** -z
influenc|e 'ɪn.flu.ənts, -flʊənts ⓤⓢ -flu.ənts **-es** -ɪz **-ing** -ɪŋ **-ed** -t
influent 'ɪn.flu.ənt, -flʊənt ⓤⓢ -flu.ənt **-s** -s
influential ˌɪn.flu'en.tʃəl **-ly** -i
influenza ˌɪn.flu'en.zə
influx 'ɪn.flʌks **-es** -ɪz
influxion ɪn'flʌk.ʃən
info 'ɪn.fəʊ ⓤⓢ -foʊ
infomercial ˌɪn.fəʊ'mɜː.ʃəl ⓤⓢ 'ɪn.foʊ.mɝː- **-s** -z
inform ɪn'fɔːm ⓤⓢ -'fɔːrm **-s** -z **-ing** -ɪŋ **-ed** -d inˌformed o'pinion
informal ɪn'fɔː.məl, ˌɪn- ⓤⓢ -'fɔːr- **-ly** -i
informalit|y ˌɪn.fɔː'mæl.ə.t|i, -ɪ.t|i ⓤⓢ -fɔːr'mæl.ə.t̬|i **-ies** -iz
informant ɪn'fɔː.mənt ⓤⓢ -'fɔːr- **-s** -s
in forma pauperis ɪnˌfɔː.mə'paʊ.pər.ɪs ⓤⓢ ɪnˌfɔːr.mə'pɑː.pɚ-, -'pɔː-
informatics ˌɪn.fə'mæt.ɪks, -fɔː'- ⓤⓢ -fɚ'mæt̬-
information ˌɪn.fə'meɪ.ʃən, -fɔː'- ⓤⓢ -fɚ'- **-s** -z inforˌmation tech'nology ⓤⓢ inforˌmation tech'nology, infor'mation techˌnology

informa|tive ɪnˈfɔː.mə|.tɪv **-tory** -tᵊr.i ⓤⓢ -tɔːr.i ⓤⓢ -ˈfɔːr.mə|.t̬ɪv
informer ɪnˈfɔː.məʳ ⓤⓢ -ˈfɔːr.mɚ **-s** -z
infotainment ˌɪn.fəʊˈteɪn.mənt ⓤⓢ ˈɪn.foʊ.teɪn-, ˌɪn.foʊˈteɪn-
infra ˈɪn.frə ˌ**infra** ˈ**dig**
infract ɪnˈfrækt **-s** -s **-ing** -ɪŋ **-ed** -ɪd
infraction ɪnˈfræk.ʃᵊn **-s** -z
infralapsarian ˌɪn.frə.læpˈseə.ri.ən ⓤⓢ -ˈser.i- **-s** -z
infrangibility ɪnˌfræn.dʒɪˈbɪl.ə.ti, ˌɪn-, -dʒəˈ-, -ɪ.ti ⓤⓢ -ə.t̬i
infrangib|le ɪnˈfræn.dʒɪ.b|l̩, ˌɪn-, -dʒə- **-ly** -li **-leness** -l̩.nəs, -nɪs
infrared ˌɪn.frəˈred *stress shift:* ˌinfrared ˈcamera
infrastructure ˈɪn.frəˌstrʌk.tʃəʳ ⓤⓢ -tʃɚ **-s** -z
infrequency ɪnˈfriː.kwənt.si, ˌɪn-
infrequent ɪnˈfriː.kwənt, ˌɪn- **-ly** -li
infring|e ɪnˈfrɪndʒ **-es** -ɪz **-ing** -ɪŋ **-ed** -d **-er/s** -əʳ/z ⓤⓢ -ɚ/z
infringement ɪnˈfrɪndʒ.mənt **-s** -s
infuri|ate ɪnˈfjʊə.ri|.eɪt, -ˈfjɔː- ⓤⓢ -ˈfjʊr.i- **-ates** -eɪts **-ating/ly** -eɪ.tɪŋ/li ⓤⓢ -eɪ.t̬ɪŋ/li **-ated** -eɪ.tɪd ⓤⓢ -eɪ.t̬ɪd
infus|e ɪnˈfjuːz **-es** -ɪz **-ing** -ɪŋ **-ed** -d **-er/s** -əʳ/z ⓤⓢ -ɚ/z
infusible *capable of being infused:* ɪnˈfjuː.zə.bl̩, -zɪ- *not fusible:* ɪnˈfjuː.zə.bl̩, ˌɪn-, -zɪ-
infusion ɪnˈfjuː.ʒᵊn **-s** -z
infusori|an ˌɪn.fjʊˈzɔː.ri|.ən, -ˈsɔː- ⓤⓢ -ˈsɔːr.i- **-al** -əl
infusory ɪnˈfjuː.zᵊr.i, -sᵊr- ⓤⓢ -sɚ-, -zɚ-
in futuro ˌɪn.fjuːˈtjʊə.rəʊ ⓤⓢ -ˈtʊr.oʊ, -ˈtjʊr-
-ing -ɪŋ
Note: Suffix. Normally unstressed, e.g. **shopping** /ˈʃɒp.ɪŋ ⓤⓢ ˈʃɑː.pɪŋ/.
Inga ˈɪŋ.ə, -gə ⓤⓢ -gə
Ingall ˈɪŋ.gɔːl ⓤⓢ -gəl
Ingalls ˈɪŋ.gɔːlz ⓤⓢ -gəlz
Ingatestone ˈɪn.gət.stəʊn, ˈɪŋ- ⓤⓢ -stoʊn
ingathering ˈɪnˌgæð.ᵊr.ɪŋ **-s** -z
Inge *surname:* ɪŋ, ɪndʒ
Note: The American playwright is pronounced /ɪndʒ/. *girl's name:* ˈɪŋ.ə, -gə ⓤⓢ -gə
Ingelow ˈɪn.dʒɪ.ləʊ ⓤⓢ -loʊ
in genere ˌɪnˈdʒen.ᵊr.eɪ ⓤⓢ -ɚ.i
ingenious ɪnˈdʒiː.ni.əs, ˌɪn- ⓤⓢ -ˈnjəs, -ni.əs **-ly** -li **-ness** -nəs, -nɪs
ingénue, ingenue ˈæ̃n.ʒeɪ.njuː, ˈæn-, -ʒə-, -ʒen.juː, ˌ--ˈ- ⓤⓢ ˈæn.ʒə.nuː, ˈɑːn-, -dʒə-, -njuː **-s** -z
ingenuit|y ˌɪn.dʒɪˈnjuː.ə.t|i, -dʒəˈ-, -ɪ.t|i ⓤⓢ -ə.t̬|i **-ies** -iz
ingenuous ɪnˈdʒen.ju.əs **-ly** -li **-ness** -nəs, -nɪs

Ingersoll® ˈɪŋ.gə.sɒl ⓤⓢ -gɚ.sɑːl, -sɔːl **-s** -z
ingest ɪnˈdʒest **-s** -s **-ing** -ɪŋ **-ed** -ɪd **-ible** -ə.bl̩, -ɪ-
inges|tion ɪnˈdʒes|.tʃᵊn **-tive** -tɪv
Ingham ˈɪŋ.əm
ingle (I) ˈɪŋ.gl̩ **-s** -z
Ingleborough ˈɪŋ.gl̩.bᵊr.ə ⓤⓢ -oʊ
Ingleby ˈɪŋ.gl̩.bi
inglenook ˈɪŋ.gl̩.nʊk **-s** -s
Inglewood ˈɪŋ.gl̩.wʊd
Inglis ˈɪŋ.gᵊlz, -glɪs
inglorious ɪnˈglɔː.ri.əs, ˌɪn-, ɪŋ-, ˌɪŋ- ⓤⓢ -ˈglɔːr.i- **-ly** -li **-ness** -nəs, -nɪs
Ingmar ˈɪŋ.mɑːʳ ⓤⓢ -mɑːr
ingoing ˈɪnˌgəʊ.ɪŋ, ˈɪŋ- ⓤⓢ ˈɪnˌgoʊ-
Ingold ˈɪŋ.gəʊld ⓤⓢ -goʊld
Ingoldsby ˈɪn.gᵊldz.bi
ingot ˈɪŋ.gət, -gɒt ⓤⓢ -gət **-s** -s
Ingraham ˈɪŋ.grə.həm, -grɪəm ⓤⓢ ˈɪŋ.grəm
ingrain ɪnˈgreɪn, ˌɪn-, ɪŋ-, ˌɪŋ- ⓤⓢ ɪn-, ˌɪn- **-s** -z **-ing** -ɪŋ **-ed** -d *stress shift:* ˌingrained ˈhabits
Ingram ˈɪŋ.grəm
Ingrams ˈɪŋ.grəmz
ingrate ˈɪn.greɪt, ˈɪŋ-, -ˈ- ⓤⓢ ˈɪn.greɪt, -ˈ- **-s** -s **-ly** -li
ingrati|ate ɪnˈgreɪ.ʃi|.eɪt, ɪŋ- ⓤⓢ ɪn- **-ates** -eɪts **-ating** -eɪ.tɪŋ ⓤⓢ -eɪ.t̬ɪŋ **-ated** -eɪ.tɪd ⓤⓢ -eɪ.t̬ɪd
ingratitude ɪnˈgræt.ɪ.tjuːd, ˌɪn-, ɪŋ-, ˌɪŋ-, ˈ-ə- ⓤⓢ ɪnˈgræt̬.ə.tuːd, ˌɪn-, -tjuːd
Ingrebourne ˈɪŋ.grɪ.bɔːn ⓤⓢ -bɔːrn
ingredient ɪnˈgriː.di.ənt, ɪŋ- ⓤⓢ ɪn- **-s** -s
Ingres ˈæŋ.grə, ˈæ̃ŋ- ⓤⓢ ˈæŋ-, ˈæ̃ŋ, ˈæn-
ingress ˈɪn.gres, ˈɪŋ- ⓤⓢ ˈɪn-
ingressive ɪnˈgres.ɪv, ɪŋ- ⓤⓢ ɪn-
Ingrey ˈɪŋ.gri
Ingrid ˈɪŋ.grɪd
in-group ˈɪn.gruːp, ˈɪŋ- ⓤⓢ ˈɪn- **-s** -s
ingrow|ing ɪnˈgrəʊ|.ɪŋ, ˌɪn-, ɪŋ-, ˌɪŋ-, ˈ-ˌ-- ⓤⓢ ˈɪn.groʊ- ˌ**ingrowing** ˈ**toenail**
ingrown ɪnˈgrəʊn, ˌɪn-, ɪŋ-, ˌɪŋ ⓤⓢ ˈɪn.groʊn *stress shift, British only:* ˌingrown ˈtoenail
ingrowth ˈɪn.grəʊθ, -ˈɪŋ- ⓤⓢ -groʊθ **-s** -s
inguinal ˈɪŋ.gwɪ.nᵊl, -gwə-
Ingushetia ˌɪŋ.gʊˈʃet.i.ə
inhab|it ɪnˈhæb|.ɪt **-its** -ɪts **-iting** -ɪ.tɪŋ ⓤⓢ -ɪ.t̬ɪŋ **-ited** -ɪ.tɪd ⓤⓢ -ɪ.t̬ɪd **-iter/s** -ɪ.təʳ/z ⓤⓢ -ɪ.t̬ɚ/z **-itable** -ɪ.tə.bl̩ ⓤⓢ -ɪ.t̬ə.bl̩
inhabitant ɪnˈhæb.ɪ.tᵊnt **-s** -s
inhabitation ɪnˌhæb.ɪˈteɪ.ʃᵊn
inhalation ˌɪn.həˈleɪ.ʃᵊn **-s** -z
inhal|e ɪnˈheɪl **-es** -z **-ing** -ɪŋ **-ed** -d **-ant/s** -ənt/s **-er/s** -əʳ/z ⓤⓢ -ɚ/z
inharmonious ˌɪn.hɑːˈməʊ.ni.əs ⓤⓢ -hɑːrˈmoʊ- **-ly** -li **-ness** -nəs, -nɪs

inher|e ɪnˈhɪəʳ ⓤⓢ -ˈhɪr **-es** -z **-ing** -ɪŋ **-ed** -d
inheren|ce ɪnˈher.ᵊnt|s, -ˈhɪə.rᵊnt|s ⓤⓢ -ˈhɪr.ᵊnt|s, -ˈher- **-cy** -si
inherent ɪnˈher.ᵊnt, -ˈhɪə.rᵊnt ⓤⓢ -ˈhɪr.ᵊnt, -ˈher- **-ly** -li
inher|it ɪnˈher|.ɪt **-its** -ɪts **-iting** -ɪ.tɪŋ ⓤⓢ -ɪ.t̬ɪŋ **-ited** -ɪ.tɪd ⓤⓢ -ɪ.t̬ɪd **-itor/s** -ɪ.təʳ/z ⓤⓢ -ɪ.t̬ɚ/z **-itable** -ɪ.tə.bl̩ ⓤⓢ -ɪ.t̬ə.bl̩
inheritanc|e ɪnˈher.ɪ.tᵊnts **-es** -ɪz
inheritrix ɪnˈher.ɪ.trɪks **-es** -ɪz
inhib|it ɪnˈhɪb|.ɪt **-its** -ɪts **-iting** -ɪ.tɪŋ ⓤⓢ -ɪ.t̬ɪŋ **-ited** -ɪ.tɪd ⓤⓢ -ɪ.t̬ɪd **-itor/s** -ɪ.təʳ/z ⓤⓢ -ɪ.t̬ɚ/z **-itory** -ɪ.tᵊr.i ⓤⓢ -ɪ.tɔːr.i
inhibition ˌɪn.hɪˈbɪʃ.ᵊn **-s** -z
inhospitab|le ˌɪn.hɒsˈpɪt.ə.b|l̩; ɪnˈhɒs.pɪ.tə-, ˌɪn-, -pə- ⓤⓢ ɪnˈhɑː.spɪ.t̬ə-, ˌɪn-; ˌɪn.hɑːˈspɪt̬.ə- **-ly** -li **-leness** -l̩.nəs, -nɪs
inhospitality ɪnˌhɒs.pɪˈtæl.ə.ti, ˌɪn-, -ɪ.ti ⓤⓢ -ˌhɑː.spəˈtæl.ə.t̬i
in-house ˌɪnˈhaʊs *stress shift:* ˌin-hous[e] proˈduction
inhuman ɪnˈhjuː.mən, ˌɪn- **-ly** -li
inhumane ˌɪn.hjuːˈmeɪn, -hjʊˈ- **-ly** -li
inhumanit|y ˌɪn.hjuːˈmæn.ə.t|i, -hjʊˈ- -ɪ.t|i ⓤⓢ -ə.t̬|i **-ies** -iz
inhumation ˌɪn.hjuːˈmeɪ.ʃᵊn, -hjʊˈ- **-s** -z
inhum|e ɪnˈhjuːm **-es** -z **-ing** -ɪŋ **-ed** -d
Inigo ˈɪn.ɪ.gəʊ ⓤⓢ -goʊ
inimic|al ɪˈnɪm.ɪ.k|ᵊl **-ally** -ᵊl.i, -li
inimitability ɪˌnɪm.ɪ.təˈbɪl.ə.ti, ˌ-ə-, -ɪ.ti ⓤⓢ -t̬əˈbɪl.ə.t̬i
inimitab|le ɪˈnɪm.ɪ.tə.b|l̩, ˈ-ə- ⓤⓢ -t̬ə- **-ly** -li **-leness** -l̩.nəs, -nɪs
iniquitous ɪˈnɪk.wɪ.təs, -wə- ⓤⓢ -t̬əs **-ly** -li
iniquit|y ɪˈnɪk.wə.t|i, -wɪ- ⓤⓢ -t̬|i **-ies** -iz
initial ɪˈnɪʃ|.ᵊl **-s** -ᵊlz **-ly** -ᵊl.i, -li **-(l)ing** -ᵊl.ɪŋ, -lɪŋ **-(l)ed** -ᵊld
initialization, -isa- ɪˌnɪʃ.ᵊl.aɪˈzeɪ.ʃᵊn, -ɪˈ- ⓤⓢ -ɪˈ-
initializ|e, -is|e ɪˈnɪʃ.ᵊl.aɪz **-es** -ɪz **-ing** -ɪŋ **-ed** -d
initiate (*n.*) ɪˈnɪʃ.i.ət, -eɪt, -ɪt **-s** -s
initi|ate (*v.*) ɪˈnɪʃ.i|.eɪt **-ates** -eɪts **-ating** -eɪ.tɪŋ ⓤⓢ -eɪ.t̬ɪŋ **-ated** -eɪ.tɪd ⓤⓢ -eɪ.t̬ɪd **-ator/s** -eɪ.təʳ/z ⓤⓢ -eɪ.t̬ɚ/z
initiation ɪˌnɪʃ.iˈeɪ.ʃᵊn **-s** -z
initiative ɪˈnɪʃ.ə.tɪv, -i.ə- ⓤⓢ -t̬ɪv **-s** -[z]
initiatory ɪˈnɪʃ.ə.tᵊr.i, -i.ə-, -eɪ- ⓤⓢ -ə.tɔːr.i
initio ɪˈnɪʃ.i.əʊ, -ˈnɪt-, -ˈnɪs- ⓤⓢ -oʊ
inject ɪnˈdʒekt **-s** -s **-ing** -ɪŋ **-ed** -ɪd **-[or/s]** -əʳ/z ⓤⓢ -ɚ/z **-able** -ə.bl̩
injection ɪnˈdʒek.ʃᵊn **-s** -z

injudicious ˌɪn.dʒuːˈdɪʃ.əs **-ly** -li **-ness** -nəs, -nɪs
Injun ˈɪn.dʒən **-s** -z
injunction ɪnˈdʒʌŋk.ʃᵊn **-s** -z
injurant ˈɪn.dʒʊ.rənt, -dʒə.rənt **-s** -s
inj|ure ˈɪn.dʒ|əʳ (US) -dʒ|ɚ **-ures** -əz (US) -ɚz **-uring** -ᵊr.ɪŋ **-ured** -əd (US) -ɚd **-urer/s** -ᵊr.əʳ/z (US) -ɚ.ɚ/z
injuria absque damno ɪnˌdʒʊə.ri.əˌæb.skweɪˈdæm.nəʊ (US) -ˌdʒʊr.i.əˌæb.skweɪˈdæm.noʊ
injurious ɪnˈdʒʊə.ri.əs, -ˈdʒɔː- (US) -ˈdʒʊr.i- **-ly** -li **-ness** -nəs, -nɪs
injur|y ˈɪn.dʒᵊr|.i **-ies** -iz ˈ**injury** ˌ**time**
injustic|e ɪnˈdʒʌs.tɪs, ˌɪn- **-es** -ɪz
ink ɪŋk **-s** -s **-ing** -ɪŋ **-ed** -t **-er/s** -əʳ/z (US) -ɚ/z
Inkatha ɪnˈkɑː.tə, ɪŋˈ-
inkblot ˈɪŋk.blɒt (US) -blɑːt **-s** -s
Inkerman ˈɪŋ.kə.mən (US) -kɚ-
inkhorn ˈɪŋk.hɔːn (US) -hɔːrn **-s** -z
inkjet ˈɪŋk.dʒet **-s** -s
inkling ˈɪŋk.lɪŋ **-s** -z
inkpen ˈɪŋk.pen
inkpot ˈɪŋk.pɒt (US) -pɑːt **-s** -s
ink-stain ˈɪŋk.steɪn **-s** -z
inkstand ˈɪŋk.stænd **-s** -z
inkwell ˈɪŋk.wel **-s** -z
ink|y ˈɪŋ.k|i **-ier** -i.əʳ (US) -i.ɚ **-iest** -i.ɪst, -i.əst **-iness** -ɪ.nəs, -ɪ.nɪs
INLA ˌaɪ.en.elˈeɪ
inlaid *(from* **inlay***)* ɪnˈleɪd (US) ˈ-- *stress shift, British only:* ˌinlaid ˈgold
inland *(n. adj.)* ˈɪn.lənd, -lænd **-s** -z ˌ**Inland** ˈ**Revenue**
inland *(adv.)* ˈɪn.lænd, -ˈ-
inlander ˈɪn.lən.dəʳ (US) -dɚ, -læn- **-s** -z
in-law ˈɪn.lɔː (US) -lɑː, -lɔː **-s** -z
inlay *(n.)* ˈɪn.leɪ
in|lay *(v.)* ɪn|ˈleɪ, ˌɪn- (US) ɪn|ˈleɪ, ˌɪn-, ˈɪn|.leɪ **-lays** -ˈleɪz (US) -ˈleɪz, -leɪz **-laying** -ˈleɪ.ɪŋ (US) -ˈleɪ-, -ˌleɪ-
inlet ˈɪn.let, -lət, -lɪt **-s** -s
in loco parentis ɪnˌləʊ.kəʊ.pəˈren.tɪs, -ˌlɒk.əʊ- (US) -ˌloʊ.koʊ.pəˈren.t̬ɪs
inly ˈɪn.li
inman ˈɪn.mən, ˈɪm- (US) ˈɪn-
inmate ˈɪn.meɪt, ˈɪm- (US) ˈɪn- **-s** -s
in medias res ɪnˌmiː.di.æsˈreɪs, ɪm-, -ˌmeɪ-, -ˌmed.i-, -ɑːsˈ-, -əsˈ-, -ˈreɪz (US) ɪnˌmiː.di.əsˈreɪs, -ˌmed.i-, -ˈreɪz
in memoriam ˌɪn.mɪˈmɔː.ri.əm, ˌɪm-, -məˈ-, -æm (US) ˌɪn.mɪˈmɔːr.i-, -məˈ-
inmost ˈɪn.məʊst, ˈɪm- (US) ˈɪn.moʊst
inn ɪn **-s** -z
innards ˈɪn.ədz (US) -ɚdz
innate ɪˈneɪt, ˌɪnˈeɪt **-ly** -li **-ness** -nəs, -nɪs
innavigable ɪnˈnæv.ɪ.gə.bl̩, ˌɪnˈnæv-, ˈ-ə-
inner ˈɪn.əʳ (US) -ɚ ˌ**inner** ˈ**city**; ˈ**inner** ˌ**tube**
inner-city ˈɪn.əˌsɪt.i (US) -ɚˌsɪt̬-
innermost ˈɪn.ə.məʊst (US) -ɚ.moʊst
inner|vate ˈɪn.ə|.veɪt; ɪˈnɜː-, ˌɪnˈɜː- (US) ɪˈnɝː-, ˌɪnˈɝː-; ˈɪn.ɚ- **-vates** -veɪts **-vating** -veɪ.tɪŋ (US) -veɪ.t̬ɪŋ **-vated** -veɪ.tɪd (US) -veɪ.t̬ɪd
innervation ˌɪn.əˈveɪ.ʃᵊn (US) -ɚˈ-
Innes(s) ˈɪn.ɪs
inning ˈɪn.ɪŋ **-s** -z **-ses** -zɪz
innings ˈɪn.ɪŋz **-es** -ɪz
Innisfail ˌɪn.ɪsˈfeɪl, -əsˈ-
Innisfree ˌɪn.ɪsˈfriː, -əsˈ-
innit ˈɪn.ɪt
innkeeper ˈɪnˌkiː.pəʳ, ˈɪŋ- (US) -pɚ **-s** -z
innocen|ce ˈɪn.ə.sᵊnt|s **-cy** -si
innocent (I) ˈɪn.ə.sᵊnt **-s** -s **-ly** -li
innocuous ɪˈnɒk.ju.əs (US) -ˈnɑːk- **-ly** -li **-ness** -nəs, -nɪs
innominate ɪˈnɒm.ɪ.nət, ˈ-ə-, -nɪt, -neɪt (US) -ˈnɑːm.ə-
inno|vate ˈɪn.əʊ|.veɪt (US) ˈ-ə- **-vates** -veɪts **-vating** -veɪ.tɪŋ (US) -veɪ.t̬ɪŋ **-vated** -veɪ.tɪd (US) -veɪ.t̬ɪd **-vator/s** -veɪ.təʳ/z (US) -veɪ.t̬ɚ/z
innovation ˌɪn.əʊˈveɪ.ʃᵊn (US) -əˈ- **-s** -z
innovative ˈɪn.ə.və.tɪv, -veɪ-; ɪˈnəʊ.və.tɪv (US) ˈɪn.ə.veɪ.t̬ɪv
innovatory ˈɪn.əʊ.veɪ.tᵊr.i, -və- (US) ˈɪn.ə.və.tɔːr.i
innoxious ɪˈnɒk.ʃəs (US) -ˈnɑːk- **-ly** -li **-ness** -nəs, -nɪs
Innsbruck ˈɪnz.brʊk
Innsworth ˈɪnz.wəθ, -wɜːθ (US) -wɚθ, -wɝːθ
innuendo ˌɪn.juˈen.dəʊ (US) -doʊ **-(e)s** -z
Innuit ˈɪn.u.ɪt, -ju- (US) ˈ-u- **-s** -s
innumerability ɪˌnjuː.mᵊr.əˈbɪl.ə.ti, ˌɪnˌjuː-, -ɪ.ti (US) ɪˌnuː.mɚ.əˈbɪl.ə.t̬i, ˌɪnˌuː-, -ˌjuː-
innumerab|le ɪˈnjuː.mᵊr.ə.b|l̩, ˌɪnˈjuː- (US) ɪˈnuː-, ˌɪnˈuː-, -ˈjuː- **-ly** -li **-leness** -l̩.nəs, -nɪs
innumeracy ɪˈnjuː.mᵊr.ə.si, ˌɪnˈjuː- (US) ɪˈnuː-, ˌɪnˈuː-, -ˈjuː-
innumerate ɪˈnjuː.mᵊr.ət, ˌɪnˈjuː- (US) ɪˈnuː.mɚ-, ˌɪnˈuː-, -ˈjuː- **-s** -s
innutriti|on ˌɪn.njuːˈtrɪʃ|.ᵊn (US) -nuːˈ-, -njuːˈ- **-ous** -əs
inobservan|ce ˌɪn.əbˈzɜː.vᵊn|ts (US) -ˈzɝː- **-t** -t
inoccupation ɪˌnɒk.jʊˈpeɪ.ʃᵊn, ˌɪnˌɒk- (US) ɪˌnɑː.kjəˈ-, ˌɪnˌɑː-
inocu|late ɪˈnɒk.jə|.leɪt, -jʊ- (US) -ˈnɑː.kjə- **-lates** -leɪts **-lating** -leɪ.tɪŋ (US) -leɪ.t̬ɪŋ **-lated** -leɪ.tɪd (US) -leɪ.t̬ɪd **-lator/s** -leɪ.təʳ/z (US) -leɪ.t̬ɚ/z
inoculation ɪˌnɒk.jəˈleɪ.ʃᵊn, -jʊˈ- (US) -ˌnɑː.kjəˈ- **-s** -z
inodorous ɪˈnəʊ.dᵊr.əs, ˌɪnˈəʊ- (US) ˌɪnˈoʊ-, ɪˈnoʊ-
inoffensive ˌɪn.əˈfent.sɪv **-ly** -li **-ness** -nəs, -nɪs
inofficious ˌɪn.əˈfɪʃ.əs
in omnibus ˌɪnˈɒm.nɪ.bəs, -bʊs (US) -ˈɑːm.nɪ-, -niː-
inoperable ɪˈnɒp.ᵊr.ə.bl̩, ˌɪnˈɒp- (US) ˌɪnˈɑː.pɚ-, ɪˈnɑː-
inoperative ɪˈnɒp.ᵊr.ə.tɪv, ˌɪnˈɒp- (US) ˌɪnˈɑː.pɚ.ə.t̬ɪv, ɪˈnɑː-
inopportune ɪˈnɒp.ə.tjuːn, ˌɪnˈɒp-, -tʃuːn; ˌɪn.ɒp.əˈtjuːn, -ˈtʃuːn (US) ˌɪnˌɑː.pɚˈtuːn, ɪˌnɑː-, -ˈtjuːn **-ly** -li **-ness** -nəs, -nɪs
inordinate ɪˈnɔː.dɪ.nət, ˌɪnˈɔː-, -dᵊn.ət, -ɪt (US) ˌɪnˈɔːr.dᵊn.ɪt, ɪˈnɔːr- **-ly** -li **-ness** -nəs, -nɪs
inorganic ˌɪn.ɔːˈgæn.ɪk (US) -ɔːrˈ- **-ally** -ᵊl.i, -li
inoscu|late ɪˈnɒs.kjə|.leɪt, -kjʊ- (US) -ˈnɑː.skjuː-, ˌɪnˈɑː- **-lates** -leɪts **-lating** -leɪ.tɪŋ (US) -leɪ.t̬ɪŋ **-lated** -leɪ.tɪd (US) -leɪ.t̬ɪd
inosculation ɪˌnɒs.kjəˈleɪ.ʃᵊn (US) -ˌnɑː.skjuːˈ-, ˌɪnˌɑː-
in pais ˌɪnˈpeɪs (US) ˌɪnˈpeɪ
in pari delicto ɪnˌpær.i.dɪˈlɪk.təʊ (US) -dəˈlɪk.toʊ, -ˌpɑːr-
in pari materia ɪnˌpær.i.məˈtɪə.ri.ə (US) -ˈtɪr.i.ə, -ˌpɑːr-
inpatient ˈɪnˌpeɪ.ʃᵊnt **-s** -s
in personam ˌɪn.pɜːˈsəʊ.næm, ˌɪm-, -pəˈ-, -nəm (US) ˌɪn.pɚˈsoʊ.næm
in praesenti ˌɪn.praɪˈsen.tiː (US) -prɪˈzen.tiː
in|put ˈɪn|.pʊt, ˈɪm- **-puts** -pʊts **-putting** -ˌpʊt.ɪŋ (US) -ˌpʊt̬.ɪŋ **-putted** -ˌpʊt.ɪd (US) -ˌpʊt̬.ɪd **-putter/s** -ˌpʊt.əʳ/z (US) -ˌpʊt̬.ɚ/z
input-output ˌɪn.pʊtˈaʊt.pʊt, ˌɪm-
inquest ˈɪŋ.kwest, ˈɪn- (US) ˈɪn- **-s** -s
inquietude ɪnˈkwaɪə.tjuːd, ɪŋ-, -ˈkwaɪ.ɪ- (US) ɪnˈkwaɪə.tuːd, -ˈkwaɪ.ɪ-, -tjuːd
inquiline ˈɪŋ.kwɪ.laɪn, ˈɪn- (US) ˈɪn.kwɪ.laɪn, -lɪn **-s** -z
inquir|e ɪnˈkwaɪəʳ, ɪŋ- (US) ɪnˈkwaɪr **-es** -z **-ing/ly** -ɪŋ/li **-ed** -d **-er/s** -əʳ/z (US) -ɚ/z
inquir|y ɪnˈkwaɪə.r|i, ɪŋ- (US) ɪnˈkwaɪ-; ˈɪn.kwɚ|.i **-ies** -iz
inquisition (I) ˌɪŋ.kwɪˈzɪʃ.ᵊn, ˌɪn- (US) ˌɪn- **-s** -z
inquisitional ˌɪŋ.kwɪˈzɪʃ.ᵊn.ᵊl, ˌɪn- (US) ˌɪn-
inquisitive ɪnˈkwɪz.ə.tɪv, ɪŋ-, ˈ-ɪ- (US) ɪnˈkwɪz.ə.t̬ɪv, ˈ-ɪ- **-ly** -li **-ness** -nəs, -nɪs
inquisitor ɪnˈkwɪz.ɪ.təʳ, ɪŋ- (US) ɪnˈkwɪz.ɪ.t̬ɚ **-s** -z
inquisitorial ɪnˌkwɪz.ɪˈtɔː.ri.əl, ɪŋ-; ˌɪn.kwɪ.zɪˈ-, ˌɪŋ- (US) ɪnˌkwɪz.ɪˈtɔːr.i- **-ly** -i
inquorate ˌɪnˈkwɔː.reɪt, ˌɪŋ-, -rət, -rɪt (US) ɪnˈkwɔːr.eɪt, -ət, -ɪt

in re ˌɪn'reɪ
in rem ˌɪn'rem
inroad 'ɪn.rəʊd (US) -roʊd **-s** -z
inrush 'ɪn.rʌʃ **-es** -ɪz
INS ˌaɪ.en'es
insalubr|ious ˌɪn.sə'luː.br|i.əs, -'ljuː- (US) -'luː- **-ity** -ə.ti, -ɪ.ti (US) -ə.ṭi
insane ɪn'seɪn, ˌɪn- **-ly** -li **-ness** -nəs, -nɪs
insanitar|y ɪn'sæn.ɪ.tᵊr|.i, ˌɪn-, '-ə-, -tr|i (US) -ter|.i **-iness** -ɪ.nəs, -nɪs
insanity ɪn'sæn.ə.ti, ˌɪn-, -ɪ.ti (US) -ə.ṭi
insatiability ɪnˌseɪ.ʃə'bɪl.ə.ti, -ʃi.ə'-, -ɪ.ti (US) -ə.ṭi
insatiab|le ɪn'seɪ.ʃə.b|l̩, -ʃi.ə- **-ly** -li **-leness** -l̩.nəs, -nɪs
insatiate ɪn'seɪ.ʃi.ət, -ɪt, -eɪt
inscape 'ɪn.skeɪp
inscrib|e ɪn'skraɪb **-es** -z **-ing** -ɪŋ **-ed** -d **-er/s** -əʳ/z (US) -ɚ/z
inscription ɪn'skrɪp.ʃᵊn **-s** -z
inscrutability ɪnˌskruː.tə'bɪl.ə.ti, ˌɪn-, -ɪ.ti (US) -ˌskruː.ṭə'bɪl.ə.ṭi
inscrutab|le ɪn'skruː.tə.b|l̩, ˌɪn- (US) -ṭə- **-ly** -li **-leness** -l̩.nəs, -nɪs
inseam 'ɪn.siːm
insect 'ɪn.sekt **-s** -s
insectari|um ˌɪn.sek'teə.ri|.əm (US) -'ter.i- **-ums** -əmz **-a** -ə
insecticidal ɪnˌsek.tɪ'saɪ.dᵊl, -tə'- **-ly** -i
insecticide ɪn'sek.tɪ.saɪd, -tə- **-s** -z
insectivore ɪn'sek.tɪ.vɔːʳ, -tə- (US) -vɔːr **-s** -z
insectivorous ˌɪn.sek'tɪv.ᵊr.əs
insecure ˌɪn.sɪ'kjʊəʳ, -sə'-, -'kjɔːʳ (US) -'kjʊr **-ly** -li
insecurit|y ˌɪn.sɪ'kjʊə.rə.t|i, -sə'-, -'kjɔː-, -rɪ- (US) -'kjʊr.ə.ṭ|i **-ies** -iz
insemi|nate ɪn'sem.ɪ|.neɪt, '-ə- **-nates** -neɪts **-nating** -neɪ.tɪŋ (US) -neɪ.ṭɪŋ **-nated** -neɪ.tɪd (US) -neɪ.ṭɪd **-nator/s** -neɪ.təʳ/z (US) -neɪ.ṭɚ/z
insemination ɪnˌsem.ɪ'neɪ.ʃᵊn, ˌɪn-, -ə'-
insensate ɪn'sent.seɪt, ˌɪn-, -sət, -sɪt **-ly** -li **-ness** -nəs, -nɪs
insensibility ɪnˌsent.sə'bɪl.ə.ti, ˌɪn-, -sɪ'-, -ɪ.ti (US) -ə.ṭi
insensib|le ɪn'sent.sə.b|l̩, ˌɪn-, -sɪ- **-ly** -li **-leness** -l̩.nəs, -nɪs
insensitive ɪn'sent.sə.tɪv, ˌɪn-, -sɪ- (US) -ṭɪv **-ness** -nəs, -nɪs
insensitivity ɪnˌsent.sə'tɪv.ə.ti, ˌɪn-, -sɪ'-, -ɪ.ti (US) -ə.ṭi
insentien|t ˌɪn'sen.tʃᵊn|t, -tʃi.ən|t **-ce** -ts
inseparability ɪnˌsep.ᵊr.ə'bɪl.ə.ti, ˌɪn-, ˌ-rə'-, -ɪ.ti (US) -ə.ṭi
inseparab|le ɪn'sep.ᵊr.ə.b|l̩, ˌɪn-, '-rə- **-ly** -li **-leness** -l̩.nəs, -nɪs
insert (*n.*) 'ɪn.sɜːt (US) -sɝːt **-s** -s
in|sert (*v.*) ɪn|'sɜːt (US) -'sɝːt **-serts** -'sɜːts (US) -'sɝːts **-serting** -'sɜː.tɪŋ (US) -'sɝː.ṭɪŋ **-serted** -'sɜː.tɪd (US) -'sɝː.ṭɪd
insertion ɪn'sɜː.ʃᵊn (US) -'sɝː- **-s** -z
in-service ˌɪn'sɜː.vɪs (US) 'ɪnˌsɝː- *stress shift, British only:* ˌin-service 'training
inset (*n.*) 'ɪn.set **-s** -s
inse|t (*v.*) ˌɪn'se|t (US) ɪn'se|t, '-- **-ts** -ts **-tting** -tɪŋ (US) -ṭɪŋ
inseverable ɪn'sev.ᵊr.ə.bl̩, ˌɪn-
inshore ˌɪn'ʃɔːʳ (US) -'ʃɔːr *stress shift:* ˌinshore 'rescue
inside ˌɪn'saɪd, '-- **-s** -z ˌ**inside 'job** (US) '**inside ˌjob**; ˌ**inside 'out**
insider ɪn'saɪ.dəʳ, ˌɪn- (US) 'ɪnˌsaɪ.dɚ, -'-- **-s** -z **inˌsider 'dealing** (US) ˌ**insider 'dealing**; **inˌsider 'trading** (US) ˌ**insider 'trading**
insidious ɪn'sɪd.i.əs **-ly** -li **-ness** -nəs, -nɪs
insight 'ɪn.saɪt **-s** -s
insightful 'ɪn.saɪt.fᵊl, -fʊl (US) 'ɪn.saɪt.fᵊl, -'-- **-ly** -li
insignia ɪn'sɪg.ni.ə **-s** -z
insignifican|ce ˌɪn.sɪg'nɪf.ɪ.kᵊnt|s **-cy** -si
insignificant ˌɪn.sɪg'nɪf.ɪ.kᵊnt **-ly** -li
insincere ˌɪn.sɪn'sɪəʳ, -sᵊn'- (US) -'sɪr **-ly** -li
insincerit|y ˌɪn.sɪn'ser.ə.t|i, -sᵊn'-, -ɪ.t|i (US) -ə.ṭ|i **-ies** -iz
insinu|ate ɪn'sɪn.ju|.eɪt **-ates** -eɪts **-ating/ly** -eɪ.tɪŋ/li (US) -eɪ.ṭɪŋ/li **-ated** -eɪ.tɪd (US) -eɪ.ṭɪd **-ator/s** -eɪ.təʳ/z (US) -eɪ.ṭɚ/z
insinuation ɪnˌsɪn.ju'eɪ.ʃᵊn, ˌɪn- **-s** -z
insipid ɪn'sɪp.ɪd **-ly** -li **-ness** -nəs, -nɪs
insipidity ˌɪn.sɪ'pɪd.ə.ti, -ɪ.ti (US) -ɪ.ṭi
insipien|ce ɪn'sɪp.i.ən|ts **-t** -t
insist ɪn'sɪst **-s** -s **-ing** -ɪŋ **-ed** -ɪd
insisten|ce ɪn'sɪs.tᵊnt|s **-cy** -si
insistent ɪn'sɪs.tᵊnt **-ly** -li
in situ ˌɪn'sɪt.juː, -'sɪtʃ.uː, -'saɪ.tjuː, -tʃuː (US) -'saɪ.tuː, -'siː-, -'sɪt.uː, -juː
Inskip 'ɪn.skɪp
insobriety ˌɪn.səʊ'braɪ.ə.ti, -'braɪ.ɪ- (US) -soʊ'braɪ.ə.ṭi
insofar ˌɪn.səʊ'fɑːʳ (US) -soʊ'fɑːr
insolation ˌɪn.səʊ'leɪ.ʃᵊn (US) -soʊ'-
insole 'ɪn.səʊl (US) -soʊl **-s** -z
insolence 'ɪnt.sᵊl.ənts
insolent 'ɪnt.sᵊl.ənt **-ly** -li
insolubility ɪnˌsɒl.jə'bɪl.ə.ti, ˌɪn-, -jʊ'-, -ɪ.ti (US) -ˌsɑːl.jə'bɪl.ə.ṭi
insolub|le ɪn'sɒl.jə.b|l̩, ˌɪn-, -jʊ- (US) -'sɑːl.jə- **-ly** -li **-leness** -l̩.nəs, -nɪs
insolvable ɪn'sɒl.və.bl̩, ˌɪn- (US) -'sɑːl-
insolven|cy ɪn'sɒl.vᵊn|t.si, ˌɪn- (US) -'sɑːl- **-t** -t
insomnia ɪn'sɒm.ni.ə (US) -'sɑːm-
insomniac ɪn'sɒm.ni.æk (US) -'sɑːm- **-s** -s
insomuch ˌɪn.səʊ'mʌtʃ (US) -soʊ'-
insouciance ɪn'suː.si.ənts (US) -si.ənts, -ʃənts
insouciant ɪn'suː.si.ənt (US) -si.ənt, -ʃənt **-ly** -li
in specie ˌɪn'spes.i.eɪ (US) ˌɪn'spiː.ʃi, -si
inspect ɪn'spekt **-s** -s **-ing** -ɪŋ **-ed** -ɪd
inspection ɪn'spek.ʃᵊn **-s** -z
inspector ɪn'spek.təʳ **-s** -z
inspectorate ɪn'spek.tᵊr.ət, -ɪt **-s** -s
inspectorship ɪn'spek.tə.ʃɪp (US) -tɚ- **-s** -s
inspiration ˌɪnt.spᵊr'eɪ.ʃᵊn, -spɪ'reɪ- (US) -spə'reɪ- **-s** -z
inspirational ˌɪnt.spᵊr'eɪ.ʃᵊn.əl, -spɪ'reɪ- (US) -spə'reɪ- **-ly** -i
inspirator 'ɪnt.spᵊr.eɪ.təʳ, -spɪ.reɪ- (US) -spə.reɪ.ṭɚ **-s** -z
inspiratory ɪn'spaɪə.rə.tᵊr.i, -'spɪr.ə- (US) -'spaɪ.rə.tɔːr-
inspir|e ɪn'spaɪəʳ (US) -'spaɪr **-es** -z **-ing/ly** -ɪŋ/li **-ed** -d **-er/s** -əʳ/z (US) -ɚ/z
inspir|it ɪn'spɪr|.ɪt **-its** -ɪts **-iting** -ɪ.tɪŋ (US) -ɪ.ṭɪŋ **-ited** -ɪ.tɪd (US) -ɪ.ṭɪd
inspiss|ate ɪn'spɪs|.eɪt; 'ɪn.spɪ.s|eɪt (US) ɪn'spɪs|.eɪt **-ates** -eɪts **-ating** -eɪ.tɪŋ (US) -eɪ.ṭɪŋ **-ated** -eɪ.tɪd (US) -eɪ.ṭɪd
inst. (*abbrev. for* **instant**) ɪntst, 'ɪnt.stᵊnt
inst. (**I**) (*abbrev. for* **institute**) ɪntst, 'ɪnt.stɪ.tjuːt, -stə-, -tʃuːt (US) -tuːt, -tjuːt
instabilit|y ˌɪn.stə'bɪl.ə.t|i, -ɪ.t|i (US) -ə.ṭ|i **-ies** -iz
instal ɪn'stɔːl (US) -'stɔːl, -'stɑːl **-s** -z **-ling** -ɪŋ **-led** -d
install ɪn'stɔːl (US) -'stɔːl, -'stɑːl **-s** -z **-ing** -ɪŋ **-ed** -d **-able** -ə.bl̩
installation ˌɪn.stə'leɪ.ʃᵊn **-s** -z
installer ɪn'stɔː.ləʳ (US) -'stɔː.lɚ, -'stɑː- **-s** -z
instal(l)ment ɪn'stɔːl.mənt (US) -'stɔːl-, -'stɑːl- **-s** -s **in'stallment ˌplan**
instanc|e 'ɪnt.stənts **-es** -ɪz **-ing** -ɪŋ **-ed**
instant 'ɪnt.stənt **-s** -s **-ly** -li
instantaneous ˌɪnt.stən'teɪ.ni.əs **-ly** -**ness** -nəs, -nɪs
instanter ɪn'stæn.təʳ (US) -ṭɚ
in statu quo ɪnˌstæt.juː'kwəʊ (US) -ˌsteɪ.tuː'kwoʊ, -ˌstɑː-
instead ɪn'sted
instep 'ɪn.step **-s** -s
insti|gate 'ɪnt.stɪ|.geɪt, -stə- **-gates** -geɪts **-gating** -geɪ.tɪŋ (US) -geɪ.ṭɪŋ **-gated** -geɪ.tɪd (US) -geɪ.ṭɪd **-gator/s** -geɪ.təʳ/z (US) -geɪ.ṭɚ/z
instigation ˌɪnt.stɪ'geɪ.ʃᵊn, -stə'- **-s**
instil ɪn'stɪl **-s** -z **-ling** -ɪŋ **-led** -d **-ment** -mənt
instill ɪn'stɪl **-s** -z **-ing** -ɪŋ **-ed** -d **-ment** -mənt

instillation ˌɪnt.stɪˈleɪ.ʃᵊn, -stəˈ-

instinct ˈɪnt.stɪŋkt -s -s

instinctive ɪnˈstɪŋk.tɪv -ly -li

institu|te ˈɪnt.stɪ.tjuː|t, -stə-, -tʃuː|t (US) -tuː|t, -tjuː|t -tes -ts -ting -tɪŋ (US) -t̬ɪŋ -ted -tɪd (US) -t̬ɪd -tor/s -təʳ/z (US) -t̬ɚ/z

institution ˌɪnt.stɪˈtjuː.ʃᵊn, -stəˈ-, -ˈtʃuː- (US) -ˈtuː-, -ˈtjuː- -s -z

institutional ˌɪnt.stɪˈtjuː.ʃᵊn.ᵊl, -stəˈ-, -ˈtʃuː- (US) -ˈtuː-, -ˈtjuː- -ly -li

institutionalization, -isa- ˌɪnt.stɪˌtjuː.ʃᵊn.ᵊl.aɪˈzeɪ.ʃᵊn, -stəˌ-, -ˌtʃuː-, -ɪˈ- (US) -ˌtuː.ʃᵊn.ᵊl.ɪˈ-, -ˌtjuː-

institutionaliz|e, -is|e ˌɪnt.stɪˈtjuː.ʃᵊn.ə.laɪz, -stəˈ-, -ˈtʃuː- (US) -ˈtuː-, -ˈtjuː- -es -ɪz -ing -ɪŋ -ed -d

in-store ˌɪnˈstɔːʳ (US) -ˈstɔːr *stress shift:* ˌin-store ˈrestaurant

instress ˌɪnˈstres

instruct ɪnˈstrʌkt -s -s -ing -ɪŋ -ed -ɪd

instruction ɪnˈstrʌk.ʃᵊn -s -z

instructional ɪnˈstrʌk.ʃᵊn.ᵊl -ly -i

instructive ɪnˈstrʌk.tɪv -ly -li -ness -nəs, -nɪs

instructor ɪnˈstrʌk.təʳ (US) -tɚ -s -z

instrument ˈɪnt.strə.mənt, -strʊ- (US) -strə- -s -s

instrumental ˌɪnt.strəˈmen.tᵊl, -strʊˈ- (US) -strəˈmen.t̬ᵊl -s -z -ly -i -ist/s -ɪst/s

instrumentality ˌɪnt.strə.menˈtæl.ə.ti, -strʊ-, -mənˈ-, -ɪ.ti (US) -strə.menˈtæl.ə.t̬i, -mənˈ-

instrumentation ˌɪnt.strə.menˈteɪ.ʃᵊn, -strʊ-, -mənˈ- (US) -strə-

insubordinate ˌɪn.səˈbɔː.dᵊn.ət, -dɪ.nət, -nɪt (US) -ˈbɔːr.dᵊn.ɪt -s -s

insubordination ˌɪn.səˌbɔː.dɪˈneɪ.ʃᵊn, -dəˈ- (US) -ˌbɔːr-

insubstantial ˌɪn.səbˈstæn.tʃᵊl, -ˈstɑːn- (US) -ˈstæn- -ly -i

insufferab|le ɪnˈsʌf.ᵊr.ə.b|l̩ -ly -li

insufficien|ce ˌɪn.səˈfɪʃ.ᵊnt|s -cy -si

insufficient ˌɪn.səˈfɪʃ.ᵊnt -ly -li

insular ˈɪnt.sjə.ləʳ, -sjʊ- (US) -sə.lɚ, -sjə- -ly -li -ism -ɪ.zᵊm

insularity ˌɪnt.sjəˈlær.ə.ti, -sjʊˈ-, -ɪ.ti (US) -səˈler.ə.t̬i, -sjəˈ-, -ˈlær-

insu|late ˈɪnt.sjə|.leɪt, -sjʊ- (US) -sə-, -sjə- -lates -leɪts -lating -leɪ.tɪŋ (US) -leɪ.t̬ɪŋ -lated -leɪ.tɪd (US) -leɪ.t̬ɪd -lator/s -leɪ.təʳ/z (US) -leɪ.t̬ɚ/z ˈinsulating ˌtape

insulation ˌɪnt.sjəˈleɪ.ʃᵊn, -sjʊˈ- (US) -səˈ-, -sjəˈ-

insulin ˈɪnt.sjə.lɪn, -sjʊ- (US) -sə-

insult (*n.*) ˈɪn.sʌlt -s -s add ˌinsult to ˈinjury

in|sult (*v.*) ɪn|ˈsʌlt -sults -ˈsʌlts -sulting/ly -ˈsʌl.tɪŋ/li (US) -ˈsʌl.t̬ɪŋ/li -sulted -ˈsʌl.tɪd (US) -ˈsʌl.t̬ɪd -sulter/s -ˈsʌl.təʳ/z (US) -ˈsʌl.t̬ɚ/z

insuperability ɪnˌsuː.pᵊr.əˈbɪl.ə.ti, ˌɪn-, -ˌsjuː-, -ɪ.ti (US) -ˌsuː.pɚ.əˈbɪl.ə.t̬i

insuperab|le ɪnˈsuː.pᵊr.ə.b|l̩, ˌɪn-, -ˈsjuː- (US) -ˈsuː- -ly -li

insupportab|le ˌɪn.səˈpɔː.tə.b|l̩ (US) -ˈpɔːr.t̬ə- -ly -li -leness -l̩.nəs, -nɪs

insuppressib|le ˌɪn.səˈpres.ə.b|l̩, ˈ-ɪ- -ly -li

insuranc|e ɪnˈʃʊə.rᵊnts, -ˈʃɔː- (US) -ˈʃʊr.ᵊnts -es -ɪz inˈsurance ˌbroker; inˈsurance ˌpolicy

insur|e ɪnˈʃʊəʳ, -ʃɔːʳ (US) -ˈʃʊr -es -z -ing -ɪŋ -ed -d -er/s -əʳ/z (US) -ɚ/z -able -ə.bl̩

insurgen|ce ɪnˈsɜː.dʒᵊnt|s (US) -ˈsɝː- -cy -si

insurgent ɪnˈsɜː.dʒᵊnt (US) -ˈsɝː- -s -s

insurmountability ˌɪn.səˌmaʊn.təˈbɪl.ə.ti, -ɪ.ti (US) -sɚˌmaʊn.t̬əˈbɪl.ə.t̬i

insurmountab|le ˌɪn.səˈmaʊn.tə.b|l̩ (US) -sɚˈmaʊn.t̬ə- -ly -li

insurrection ˌɪn.sᵊrˈek.ʃᵊn (US) -səˈrek- -s -z

insurrectional ˌɪn.sᵊrˈek.ʃᵊn.ᵊl (US) -səˈrek-

insurrectionar|y ˌɪn.sᵊrˈek.ʃᵊn.ᵊr|.i (US) -səˈrek.ʃᵊn.er- -ies -iz

insurrection|ism ˌɪn.sᵊrˈek.ʃᵊn|.ɪ.zᵊm (US) -səˈrek- -ist/s -ɪst/s

insusceptibility ˌɪn.səˌsep.təˈbɪl.ə.ti, -tɪˈ-, -ɪ.ti (US) -ə.t̬i

insusceptib|le ˌɪn.səˈsep.tə.b|l̩, -tɪ- -ly -li

intact ɪnˈtækt, ˌɪn- -ness -nəs, -nɪs

intaglio ɪnˈtɑː.li.əʊ, -ˈtæl.i- (US) -ˈtæl.joʊ, -ˈtɑːl- -s -z

intake ˈɪn.teɪk -s -s

intangibility ɪnˌtæn.dʒəˈbɪl.ə.ti, ˌɪn-, -dʒɪˈ-, -ɪ.ti (US) -ə.t̬i

intangib|le ɪnˈtæn.dʒə.b|l̩, ˌɪn-, -dʒɪ- -ly -li -leness -l̩.nəs, -nɪs

integer ˈɪn.tɪ.dʒəʳ, -tə- (US) -dʒɚ, -t̬ə- -s -z

integral (*n.*) ˈɪn.tɪ.grəl, -tə- (US) -t̬ə- -s -z

integral (*adj.*) ˈɪn.tɪ.grəl, -tə-; ɪnˈteg.rəl (US) ˈɪn.t̬ə.grəl; ɪnˈteg.rəl -ly -i

Note: As a mathematical term always /ˈɪn.tɪ.grəl (US) -t̬ə-/.

inte|grate ˈɪn.tɪ|.greɪt, -tə- (US) -t̬ə- -grates -greɪts -grating -greɪ.tɪŋ (US) -greɪ.t̬ɪŋ -grated -greɪ.tɪd (US) -greɪ.t̬ɪd -grator/s -greɪ.təʳ/z (US) -greɪ.t̬ɚ/z ˌintegrated ˈcircuit

integration ˌɪn.tɪˈgreɪ.ʃᵊn, -təˈ- (US) -t̬əˈ- -s -z

integrity ɪnˈteg.rə.ti, -rɪ- (US) -t̬i

integument ɪnˈteg.jə.mənt, -jʊ- -s -s

Intel® ˈɪn.tel

intellect ˈɪn.tᵊl.ekt, -tɪ.lekt (US) -t̬ə.lekt -s -s

intellection ˌɪn.tᵊlˈek.ʃᵊn, -tɪˈlek- (US) -t̬əˈlek-

intellective ˌɪn.tᵊlˈek.tɪv, -tɪˈlek- (US) -t̬əˈlek-

intellectual ˌɪn.tᵊlˈek.tju.əl, -tɪˈlek-, -tʃu- (US) -t̬ᵊlˈek.tʃu- -s -z -ly -i

intellectual|ism ˌɪn.tᵊlˈek.tju.ə.l|ɪ.zᵊm, -tɪˈlek-, -tʃu- (US) -t̬ᵊlˈek.tʃu- -ist/s -ɪst/s

intellectuality ˌɪn.tᵊlˌek.tjuˈæl.ə.ti, -tɪˌlek-, -tʃuˈ-, -ɪ.ti (US) -tʃuˈæl.ə.t̬i

intellectualiz|e, -is|e ˌɪn.tᵊlˈek.tju.ə.laɪz, -tɪˈlek-, -tʃu- (US) -t̬ᵊlˈek.tʃu- -es -ɪz -ing -ɪŋ -ed -d

intelligence ɪnˈtel.ɪ.dʒᵊnts, ˈ-ə- -es -ɪz -er/s -əʳ/z (US) -ɚ/z inˈtelligence ˌtest

intelligent ɪnˈtel.ɪ.dʒᵊnt, ˈ-ə- -ly -li

intelligentsia ɪnˌtel.ɪˈdʒent.si.ə, ˌɪn- (US) -ˈdʒent-, -ˈgent-

intelligibility ɪnˌtel.ɪ.dʒəˈbɪl.ə.ti, ˌ-ə-, -dʒɪˈ-, -ɪ.ti (US) -ə.t̬i

intelligib|le ɪnˈtel.ɪ.dʒə.b|l̩, ˈ-ə-, -dʒɪ- -ly -li -leness -l̩.nəs, -nɪs

intemperance ɪnˈtem.pᵊr.ᵊnts, ˌɪn-, ˈ-prᵊnts

intemperate ɪnˈtem.pᵊr.ət, ˌɪn-, -ɪt, ˈ-prət (US) -prɪt -ly -li -ness -nəs, -nɪs

intend ɪnˈtend -s -z -ing -ɪŋ -ed -ɪd

intendan|ce ɪnˈten.dən|ts -cy -tsi -t/s -t/s

intens|e ɪnˈtents -er -əʳ -est -ɪst, -əst -ely -li -eness -nəs, -nɪs

intensification ɪnˌtent.sɪ.fɪˈkeɪ.ʃᵊn, -sə- -s -z

intensi|fy ɪnˈtent.sɪ|.faɪ, -sə- -fies -faɪz -fying -faɪ.ɪŋ -fied -faɪd -fier/s -faɪ.əʳ/z (US) -faɪ.ɚ/z

intension ɪnˈten.tʃᵊn

intensit|y ɪnˈtent.sə.t|i, -sɪ- (US) -sə.t̬|i -ies -iz

intensive ɪnˈtent.sɪv -ly -li -ness -nəs, -nɪs inˌtensive ˈcare

in|tent ɪn|ˈtent -tents -ˈtents -tenter -ˈten.təʳ (US) -ˈten.t̬ɚ -tentest -ˈten.tɪst, -ˈten.təst (US) -ˈten.t̬ɪst, -ˈten.t̬əst -tently -ˈtent.li -tentness -ˈtent.nəs, -ˈtent.nɪs

intention ɪnˈten.tʃᵊn -s -z -ed -d

intentional ɪnˈten.tʃᵊn.ᵊl -ly -i

inter- ɪn.təʳ- (US) ɪn.t̬ɚ-

Note: Prefix. Normally takes either primary stress or secondary stress on the first syllable, with nouns often receiving front stress, e.g. **intercom** (noun) /ˈɪn.tə.kɒm (US) -t̬ɚ.kɑːm/, **interact** (verb) /ˌɪn.təʳˈækt (US) -t̬ɚˈækt/. Exceptions exist; see individual entries. Note also that, although /r/ is normally assigned to a following strong syllable in US transcriptions, in **inter-** it is perceived to be morphemically linked to that morpheme and is retained in the prefix as /ɚ/.

inter (*v.*) ɪnˈtɜːʳ (US) -ˈtɝː **-s** -z **-ring** -ɪŋ **-red** -d

inter (*Latin prep., in such phrases as* **inter alia, inter se**) ˈɪn.təʳ (US) -t̬ɚ

interact (*n.*) ˈɪn.təʳ.ækt (US) -t̬ɚˈækt **-s** -s

interact (*v.*) ˌɪn.təʳˈækt (US) -t̬ɚˈækt **-s** -s **-ing** -ɪŋ **-ed** -ɪd

interaction ˌɪn.təʳˈæk.ʃən (US) -t̬ɚˈæk- **-s** -z

interactive ˌɪn.təʳˈæk.tɪv (US) -t̬ɚˈæk- **-ly** -li

interactivity ˌɪn.təʳ.ækˈtɪv.ə.ti, -ɪ.ti (US) -t̬ɚ.ækˈtɪv.ə.t̬i

Interahamwe ˌɪn.tər.əˈhæm.weɪ (US) -t̬ɚ-

inter alia ˌɪn.təʳˈeɪ.li.ə, -ˈæl.i- (US) -t̬ɚˈɑː-, -ˈeɪ-, -ɑː

interblend ˌɪn.təˈblend (US) -t̬ɚˈ- **-s** -z **-ing** -ɪŋ **-ed** -ɪd

inter|breed ˌɪn.tə|ˈbriːd (US) -t̬ɚˈ- **-breeds** -ˈbriːdz **-breeding** -ˈbriː.dɪŋ **-bred** -ˈbred

intercalary ɪnˈtɜː.kəl.ər.i; ˌɪn.təˈkæl- (US) ɪnˈtɝː.kə.ler-, ˌɪn.t̬ɚˈkæl.ɚ.i

interca|late ɪnˈtɜː.kə|.leɪt, ˈɪn.tə.kə- (US) -ˈtɝː- **-lates** -leɪts **-lating** -leɪ.tɪŋ (US) -leɪ.t̬ɪŋ **-lated** -leɪ.tɪd (US) -leɪ.t̬ɪd

intercalation ɪnˌtɜː.kəˈleɪ.ʃən (US) -ˌtɝː- **-s** -z

interced|e ˌɪn.təˈsiːd (US) -t̬ɚˈ- **-es** -z **-ing** -ɪŋ **-ed** -ɪd **-er/s** -əʳ/z (US) -ɚ/z

intercept (*n.*) ˈɪn.tə.sept (US) -t̬ɚ- **-s** -s

intercept (*v.*) ˌɪn.təˈsept (US) -t̬ɚˈ- **-s** -s **-ing** -ɪŋ **-ed** -ɪd **-er/s** -əʳ/z (US) -ɚ/z **-or/s** -əʳ/z (US) -ɚ/z

interception ˌɪn.təˈsep.ʃən (US) -t̬ɚˈ- **-s** -z

interceptive ˌɪn.təˈsep.tɪv (US) -t̬ɚˈ-

intercession ˌɪn.təˈseʃ.ən (US) -t̬ɚˈ- **-s** -z

intercessional ˌɪn.təˈseʃ.ən.əl (US) -t̬ɚˈ-

intercessor ˌɪn.təˈses.əʳ, ˈɪn.tə.ses- (US) ˌɪn.t̬ɚˈses.ɚ, ˈɪn.t̬ɚ.ses- **-s** -z

intercessory ˌɪn.təˈses.ər.i (US) -t̬ɚˈ-

interchang|e (*n.*) ˈɪn.tə.tʃeɪndʒ (US) -t̬ɚ- **-es** -ɪz

interchang|e (*v.*) ˌɪn.təˈtʃeɪndʒ (US) -t̬ɚˈ- **-es** -ɪz **-ing** -ɪŋ **-ed** -d

interchangeability ˌɪn.təˌtʃeɪn.dʒəˈbɪl.ə.ti, -ɪ.ti (US) -t̬ɚˌtʃeɪn.dʒəˈbɪl.ə.t̬i

interchangeab|le ˌɪn.təˈtʃeɪn.dʒə.b|l̩ (US) -t̬ɚˈ- **-ly** -li **-leness** -l̩.nəs, -nɪs

intercity (I) ˌɪn.təˈsɪt.i (US) -t̬ɚˈsɪt̬- *stress shift:* ˌintercity ˈtrain

intercollegiate ˌɪn.tə.kəˈliː.dʒət, -kɒlˈiː-, -dʒi.ət, -ɪt (US) -t̬ɚ.kəˈliː.dʒɪt

intercolonial ˌɪn.tə.kəˈləʊ.ni.əl (US) -t̬ɚ.kəˈloʊ-

intercom ˈɪn.tə.kɒm (US) -t̬ɚ.kɑːm **-s** -z

intercommuni|cate ˌɪn.tə.kəˈmjuː.nɪ|.keɪt, -nə- (US) -t̬ɚ- **-cates** -keɪts **-cating** -keɪ.tɪŋ (US) -keɪ.t̬ɪŋ **-cated** -keɪ.tɪd (US) -keɪ.t̬ɪd **-cator/s** -keɪ.təʳ/z (US) -keɪ.t̬ɚ/z

intercommunication ˌɪn.tə.kəˌmjuː.nɪˈkeɪ.ʃən, -nəˈ- (US) -t̬ɚ-

intercommunion ˌɪn.tə.kəˈmjuː.ni.ən (US) -t̬ɚ.kəˈmjuː.njən

intercommunity ˌɪn.tə.kəˈmjuː.nə.ti, -nɪ- (US) -t̬ɚ.kəˈmjuː.nə.t̬i

interconnect ˌɪn.tə.kəˈnekt (US) -t̬ɚ- **-s** -s **-ing** -ɪŋ **-ed** -ɪd

interconnection ˌɪn.tə.kəˈnek.ʃən (US) -t̬ɚ- **-s** -z

intercontinental ˌɪn.təˌkɒn.tɪˈnen.təl, -təˈ- (US) -t̬ɚˌkɑːn.təˈnen.t̬əl

intercostal ˌɪn.təˈkɒs.təl (US) -t̬ɚˈkɑː.stəl

intercourse ˈɪn.tə.kɔːs (US) -t̬ɚ.kɔːrs

intercurrent ˌɪn.təˈkʌr.ənt (US) -t̬ɚˈkɝː- **-ly** -li

interdenominational ˌɪn.tə.dɪˌnɒm.ɪˈneɪ.ʃən.əl, -dəˌ-, -əˈ- (US) -t̬ɚ.dɪˌnɑː.məˈ-, -diˌ- **-ism** -ɪ.zəm **-ly** -i

interdental ˌɪn.təˈden.təl (US) -t̬ɚˈden.t̬əl

interdepartmental ˌɪn.təˌdiː.pɑːtˈmen.təl; ˌɪn.tə.dɪˌpɑːtˈ-, -dəˌ- (US) -t̬ɚˌdiː.pɑːrtˈmen.t̬əl, -dɪ-

interdependence ˌɪn.tə.dɪˈpen.dənts, -dəˈ- (US) -t̬ɚ.diːˈ-, -dɪˈ-

interdependent ˌɪn.tə.dɪˈpen.dənt, -dəˈ- (US) -t̬ɚ.diːˈ-, -dɪˈ- **-ly** -li

interdict (*n.*) ˈɪn.tə.dɪkt, -daɪt (US) -t̬ɚ.dɪkt **-s** -s

interdict (*v.*) ˌɪn.təˈdɪkt, -ˈdaɪt (US) -t̬ɚˈdɪkt **-s** -s **-ing** -ɪŋ **-ed** -ɪd

interdiction ˌɪn.təˈdɪk.ʃən (US) -t̬ɚˈ- **-s** -z

interdigi|tate ˌɪn.təˈdɪdʒ.ɪ|.teɪt, ˈ-ə- (US) -t̬ɚˈ- **-tates** -teɪts **-tating** -teɪ.tɪŋ (US) -teɪ.t̬ɪŋ **-tated** -teɪ.tɪd (US) -teɪ.t̬ɪd

interdisciplinary ˌɪn.təˈdɪs.ɪ.plɪ.nər.i, ˈ-ə-; ˌɪn.təˌdɪs.ɪˈplɪn.ər-, -əˈ- (US) -t̬ɚˈdɪs.ə.plɪ.ner-

interest ˈɪn.trəst, -trest, -trɪst; -tər.əst, -est, -ɪst (US) ˈɪn.trɪst, -trəst, -trest; -t̬ɚ.ɪst, -əst, -est **-s** -s **-ing** -ɪŋ **-ed/ly** -ɪd/li ˈ**interest** ˌ**rate**

interesting ˈɪn.trə.stɪŋ, -tres.tɪŋ, -trɪ.stɪŋ, -tər.ə-, -es.tɪŋ, -ɪ.stɪŋ (US) ˈɪn.trɪ.stɪŋ, -trə-, -tres.tɪŋ, -t̬ɚ.ɪ.stɪŋ, -es.tɪŋ **-ly** -li

interfac|e (*n.*) ˈɪn.tə.feɪs (US) -t̬ɚ- **-es** -ɪz

interfac|e (*v.*) ˌɪn.təˈfeɪs, ˈ--- (US) ˈɪn.t̬ɚ.feɪs **-es** -ɪz **-ing** -ɪŋ **-ed** -t

Note: The computer world uses first-syllable stress for both noun and verb.

interfaith ˌɪn.təˈfeɪθ (US) ˈɪn.t̬ɚ.feɪθ *stress shift, British only:* ˌinterfaith ˈservice

interfer|e ˌɪn.təˈfɪəʳ (US) -t̬ɚˈfɪr **-es** -z **-ing** -ɪŋ **-ed** -d **-er/s** -əʳ/z (US) -ɚ/z

interferenc|e ˌɪn.təˈfɪə.rənts (US) -t̬ɚˈfɪr.ənts **-es** -ɪz

interferon ˌɪn.təˈfɪə.rɒn (US) -t̬ɚˈfɪr.ɑː **-s** -z

Interflora® ˌɪn.təˈflɔː.rə (US) -t̬ɚˈflɔːr

interfus|e ˌɪn.təˈfjuːz (US) -t̬ɚˈ- **-es** -ɪz **-ing** -ɪŋ **-ed** -d

interfusion ˌɪn.təˈfjuː.ʒən (US) -t̬ɚˈ-

intergalactic ˌɪn.tə.gəˈlæk.tɪk (US) -t̬ɚ

interglacial ˌɪn.təˈgleɪ.si.əl, -ʃi-, -ʃəl (US) -t̬ɚˈgleɪ.ʃəl

intergovernmental ˌɪn.tə.gʌv.ənˈmen.təl, -əmˈ- (US) -t̬ɚˌgʌv.ɚnˈmen.t̬əl

interim ˈɪn.tər.ɪm (US) -t̬ɚ-

interior ɪnˈtɪə.ri.əʳ (US) -ˈtɪr.i.ɚ **-s** -z **inˌterior ˈdecorator; inˌterior deˈsigner**

interioriz|e, -is|e ɪnˈtɪə.ri.ə.raɪz (US) -ˈtɪr.i- **-es** -ɪz **-ing** -ɪŋ **-ed** -d

interject ˌɪn.təˈdʒekt (US) -t̬ɚˈ- **-s** -s **-i** -ɪŋ **-ed** -ɪd **-or/s** -əʳ/z (US) -ɚ/z

interjection ˌɪn.təˈdʒek.ʃən (US) -t̬ɚˈ- **-s** -z **-al/ly** -əl/i

inter|knit ˌɪn.tə|ˈnɪt (US) -t̬ɚˈ- **-knits** -ˈnɪts **-knitting** -ˈnɪt.ɪŋ (US) -ˈnɪt̬.ɪŋ **-knitted** -ˈnɪt.ɪd (US) -ˈnɪt̬.ɪd

interlac|e ˌɪn.təˈleɪs (US) -t̬ɚˈ- **-es** -ɪz **-ing** -ɪŋ **-ed** -t **-ement** -mənt

Interlaken ˈɪn.tə.lɑː.kən, ˌɪn.təˈlɑː- (US) ˈɪn.t̬ɚ.lɑː-, ˌɪn.t̬ɚˈlɑː, -t̬ɚ-

interlanguage ˈɪn.təˌlæŋ.gwɪdʒ (US) -t̬ɚ-

interlard ˌɪn.təˈlɑːd (US) -t̬ɚˈlɑːrd **-s** - **-ing** -ɪŋ **-ed** -ɪd

interlea|f ˈɪn.tə.liː|f (US) -t̬ɚ- **-ves** -vz

interleav|e ˌɪn.təˈliːv (US) -t̬ɚˈ- **-es** -z **-ing** -ɪŋ **-ed** -d

interlin|e ˌɪn.təˈlaɪn (US) -t̬ɚˈ- **-es** -z **-ing** -ɪŋ **-ed** -d

interlinear ˌɪn.təˈlɪn.i.əʳ (US) -t̬ɚˈlɪn.

interlineation ˌɪn.təˌlɪn.iˈeɪ.ʃən (US) -t̬ɚ- **-s** -z

interlink ˌɪn.təˈlɪŋk (US) -t̬ɚˈ- **-s** -s **-ing** -ɪŋ **-ed** -t

interlock ˌɪn.təˈlɒk (US) -t̬ɚˈlɑːk **-s** -s **-ing** -ɪŋ **-ed** -t

interlocution ˌɪn.tə.ləˈkjuː.ʃən, -lɒkˈjuː- (US) -t̬ɚ.loʊˈkjuː- **-s** -z

interlocutor ˌɪn.təˈlɒk.jə.təʳ, -jʊ- (US) -t̬ɚˈlɑː.kjə.t̬ɚ, -kjʊ- **-s** -z **-y** -i

interlocu|tress ˌɪn.təˈlɒk.jə|.trəs, -trɪs (US) -t̬ɚˈlɑː.kjʊ|.trɪs, -kjə- **-t** -trɪs **-trix** -trɪks

interlop|e ˌɪn.təˈləʊp US ˈɪn.t̬ɚ.loʊp **-es** -s **-ing** -ɪŋ **-ed** -t
interloper ˈɪn.təˌləʊ.pəʳ, ˌɪn.təˈləʊ.pəʳ US ˈɪn.t̬ɚˌloʊ.pɚ **-s** -z
interlude ˈɪn.tə.luːd, -ljuːd US -t̬ɚ.luːd **-s** -z
intermarriag|e ˌɪn.təˈmær.ɪdʒ US -t̬ɚˈmer-, -ˈmær- **-es** -ɪz
intermarr|y ˌɪn.təˈmær|.i US ˈɪn.t̬ɚˌmer-, -ˈmær- **-ies** -iz **-ying** -i.ɪŋ **-ied** -id
intermeddl|e ˌɪn.təˈmed.l̩ US -t̬ɚˈ- **-es** -z **-ing** -ɪŋ, -ˈmed.lɪŋ **-ed** -d **-er/s** -əʳ/z, -ˈmed.ləʳ/z US -lɚ/z
intermediar|y ˌɪn.təˈmiː.di.ə.r|i US -t̬ɚˈmiː.di.er-, -ɚ- **-ies** -iz
intermediate ˌɪn.təˈmiː.di.ət, -ɪt US -t̬ɚˈ- **-s** -s **-ly** -li
interment ɪnˈtɜː.mənt US -ˈtɝː- **-s** -s
intermezz|o ˌɪn.təˈmet.s|əʊ, -ˈmed.z|əʊ US -t̬ɚˈmet.s|oʊ, -ˈmed.z|oʊ **-os** -əʊz US -oʊz **-i** -i, -iː
interminab|le ɪnˈtɜː.mɪ.nə.b|l̩, ˌɪn-, -mᵊn.ə- US -ˈtɝː- **-ly** -li **-leness** -l̩.nəs, -nɪs
intermingl|e ˌɪn.təˈmɪŋ.gl̩ US -t̬ɚˈ- **-es** -z **-ing** -ɪŋ, -ˈmɪŋ.glɪŋ **-ed** -d
intermission ˌɪn.təˈmɪʃ.ᵊn US -t̬ɚˈ- **-s** -z
inter|mit ˌɪn.tə|ˈmɪt US -t̬ɚˈ- **-mits** -ˈmɪts **-mitting/ly** -ˈmɪt.ɪŋ/li US -ˈmɪt̬.ɪŋ/li **-mitted** -ˈmɪt.ɪd US -ˈmɪt̬.ɪd
intermittent ˌɪn.təˈmɪt.ᵊnt US -t̬ɚˈmɪt- **-ly** -li
intermix ˌɪn.təˈmɪks US -t̬ɚˈ- **-es** -ɪz **-ing** -ɪŋ **-ed** -t
intermixture ˌɪn.təˈmɪks.tʃəʳ US -t̬ɚˈmɪks.tʃɚ **-s** -z
intermodal ˌɪn.təˈməʊ.dᵊl US -t̬ɚˈmoʊ-
intern (*n.*) ˈɪn.tɜːn, -ˈ- US ˈɪn.tɝːn **-s** -z
intern (*v.*) ɪnˈtɜːn US ɪnˈtɝːn, ˈ-- **-s** -z **-ing** -ɪŋ **-ed** -d
internal ɪnˈtɜː.nᵊl, ˌɪn- US -ˈtɝː- **-ly** -i **inˌternal comˈbustion; inˌternal comˈbustion ˌengine** US **inˌternal comˌbustion ˈengine; Inˌternal ˈRevenue ˌService**
internalization ɪnˌtɜː.nᵊl.aɪˈzeɪ.ʃᵊn, ˌɪn-, -ɪˈ- US -ˌtɝː.nᵊl.ɪˈ-
internaliz|e, -is|e ɪnˈtɜː.nᵊl.aɪz US -ˈtɝː- **-es** -ɪz **-ing** -ɪŋ **-ed** -d
international ˌɪn.təˈnæʃ.ᵊn.ᵊl, -təˈnæʃ.nᵊl US -t̬ɚˈ- **-s** -z **-ly** -i
internationale ˌɪn.təˌnæʃ.əˈnɑːl, -ˌnæʃ.i.əˈnɑːl US -t̬ɚˌnæʃ.əˈnæl, -ˈnɑːl
internationalism ˌɪn.təˈnæʃ.ᵊn.ᵊl|.ɪ.zᵊm, -ˈnæʃ.nᵊl- US -t̬ɚˈ- **-ist/s** -ɪst/s
internationalization, -isa- ˌɪn.təˌnæʃ.ᵊn.ᵊl.aɪˈzeɪ.ʃᵊn, ˌ-nᵊl-, -ɪˈ- US -t̬ɚˌnæʃ.ᵊn.ᵊl.ɪˈ-, ˌ-nᵊl-
internationaliz|e, -is|e ˌɪn.təˈnæʃ.ᵊn.ᵊl.aɪz, -ˈnæʃ.nᵊl- US -t̬ɚˈ- **-es** -ɪz **-ing** -ɪŋ **-ed** -d
interne ˈɪn.tɜːn US -tɝːn **-s** -z
internecine ˌɪn.təˈniː.saɪn, -tɜːˈ- US -t̬ɚˈniː.sɪn, -siːn, -ˈnes.ɪn, -iːn
internee ˌɪn.tɜːˈniː US -tɝːˈ- **-s** -z
Internet ˈɪn.tə.net US -t̬ɚ-
internist ˈɪn.tɜː.nɪst, -ˈ-- US ˈɪn.tɝː-, -ˈ-- **-s** -s
internment ɪnˈtɜːn.mənt, -ˈtɜːm- US -ˈtɝːn- **-s** -s
internodal ˌɪn.təˈnəʊ.dᵊl US -t̬ɚˈnoʊ-
internode ˈɪn.tə.nəʊd US -t̬ɚ.noʊd **-s** -z
internship ˈɪn.tɜːn.ʃɪp, -ˈ-- US ˈɪn.tɝːn-, -ˈ-- **-s** -s
interoceanic ˌɪn.təʳˌəʊ.ʃiˈæn.ɪk US -t̬ɚˌoʊ-
inter pares ˌɪn.təˈpɑː.riːz, -ˈpeə-, -reɪs US -təˈpɑː.res
inter partes ˌɪn.təˈpɑː.tiːz, -teɪs US ˌɪn.tɚˈpɑːr.tes
interpellant ˌɪn.təˈpel.ənt US -t̬ɚˈ- **-s** -s
interpell|ate ɪnˈtɜː.pə.l|eɪt, -pɪ-, -pel|.eɪt; ˌɪn.təˈpel|.eɪt US ˌɪn.t̬ɚˈpel-; ɪnˈtɜː.pə.l|eɪt **-ates** -eɪts **-ating** -eɪ.tɪŋ US -eɪ.t̬ɪŋ **-ated** -eɪ.tɪd US -eɪ.t̬ɪd
interpellation ɪnˌtɜː.pəˈleɪ.ʃᵊn, -pɪˈ-, -pelˈeɪ-; ˌɪn.tə.pəˈleɪ- US ˌɪn.tɚ.pəˈleɪ-; ɪnˌtɝː- **-s** -z
interpene|trate ˌɪn.təˈpen.ɪ|.treɪt, ˈ-ə- US -t̬ɚˈ- **-trates** -treɪts **-trating** -treɪ.tɪŋ US -treɪ.t̬ɪŋ **-trated** -treɪ.tɪd US -treɪ.t̬ɪd
interpenetration ˌɪn.təˌpen.ɪˈtreɪ.ʃᵊn, -əˈ- US -t̬ɚˌ-
interpersonal ˌɪn.təˈpɜː.sᵊn.ᵊl US -t̬ɚˈpɝː- **-ly** -i
interplanetary ˌɪn.təˈplæn.ɪ.tᵊr.i, ˈ-ə- US -t̬ɚˈplæn.ə.ter-
interplay ˈɪn.tə.pleɪ US -t̬ɚ-
interpleader ˌɪn.təˈpliː.dəʳ US -t̬ɚˈpliː.dɚ **-s** -z
Interpol ˈɪn.tə.pɒl US -t̬ɚ.pɑːl, -poʊl
interpo|late ɪnˈtɜː.pə|.leɪt US -ˈtɝː- **-lates** -leɪts **-lating** -leɪ.tɪŋ US -leɪ.t̬ɪŋ **-lated** -leɪ.tɪd US -leɪ.t̬ɪd **-lator/s** -leɪ.təʳ/z US -leɪ.t̬ɚ/z
interpolation ɪnˌtɜː.pəˈleɪ.ʃᵊn US -ˌtɝː- **-s** -z
interposal ˌɪn.təˈpəʊ.zᵊl US -t̬ɚˈpoʊ- **-s** -z
interpos|e ˌɪn.təˈpəʊz US -t̬ɚˈpoʊz **-es** -ɪz **-ing** -ɪŋ **-ed** -d **-er/s** -əʳ/z US -ɚ/z
interposition ˌɪn.tə.pəˈzɪʃ.ᵊn; ɪnˌtɜː- US ˌɪn.t̬ɚ.pəˈ- **-s** -z
interpre|t ɪnˈtɜː.prɪ|t, -prə|t US -ˈtɝː.prə|t **-ts** -ts **-ting** -tɪŋ US -t̬ɪŋ **-ted** -tɪd US -t̬ɪd **-table** -tə.bl̩ US -t̬ə.bl̩
interpretation ɪnˌtɜː.prɪˈteɪ.ʃᵊn, -prəˈ- US -ˌtɝː.prəˈ- **-s** -z **-al** -ᵊl
interpretative ɪnˈtɜː.prɪ.tə.tɪv, -prə-, -teɪ- US -ˈtɝː.prə.teɪ.t̬ɪv, -t̬ə- **-ly** -li
interpreter ɪnˈtɜː.prɪ.təʳ, -prə- US -ˈtɝː.prə.t̬ɚ **-s** -z
interpretive ɪnˈtɜː.prɪ.tɪv, -prə- US -ˈtɝː.prə.t̬ɪv **-ly** -li
interquartile ˌɪn.təˈkwɔː.taɪl US -t̬ɚˈkwɔːr-, -tɪl, -t̬ᵊl
interracial ˌɪn.təˈreɪ.ʃᵊl, -ʃi.əl US -t̬ɚˈreɪ.ʃᵊl
interregn|um ˌɪn.təˈreg.n|əm US -t̬ɚˈ- **-ums** -əmz **-a** -ə
interre|late ˌɪn.tə.rɪ|ˈleɪt, -rəˈ- US -t̬ɚ.riˈ-, -rɪˈ- **-lates** -ˈleɪts **-lating** -ˈleɪ.tɪŋ US -ˈleɪ.t̬ɪŋ **-lated** -ˈleɪ.tɪd US -ˈleɪ.t̬ɪd
interrelation ˌɪn.tə.rɪˈleɪ.ʃᵊn, -rəˈ- US -t̬ɚ.riˈ-, -rɪˈ- **-s** -z
interrelationship ˌɪn.tə.rɪˈleɪ.ʃᵊn.ʃɪp
interro|gate ɪnˈter.ə|.geɪt **-gates** -geɪts **-gating** -geɪ.tɪŋ US -geɪ.t̬ɪŋ **-gated** -geɪ.tɪd US -geɪ.t̬ɪd **-gator/s** -geɪ.təʳ/z US -geɪ.t̬ɚ/z
interrogation ɪnˌter.əˈgeɪ.ʃᵊn **-s** -z
interrogative ˌɪn.təˈrɒg.ə.tɪv US -t̬ɚˈrɑː.gə.t̬ɪv **-s** -z **-ly** -li
interrogator|y ˌɪn.təˈrɒg.ə.tᵊr|.i US -t̬ɚˈrɑː.gə.tɔːr- **-ies** -iz
interrupt (*v.*) ˌɪn.təˈrʌpt US -t̬ɚˈ- **-s** -s **-ing** -ɪŋ **-ed** -ɪd **-er/s** -əʳ/z US -ɚ/z
interrupt (*n.*) ˈɪn.tə.rʌpt US -t̬ɚ-
interruption ˌɪn.təˈrʌp.ʃᵊn US -t̬ɚˈ- **-s** -z
intersect ˌɪn.təˈsekt US -t̬ɚˈ- **-s** -s **-ing** -ɪŋ **-ed** -ɪd **-or/s** -əʳ/z US -ɚ/z
intersection ˌɪn.təˈsek.ʃᵊn, ˈɪn.təˌsek- US ˌɪn.t̬ɚˈsek-, ˈɪn.t̬ɚˌsek- **-s** -z
Note: /ˈɪn.t̬ɚˌsek.ʃᵊn/ is the common US pronunciation for a place where streets meet.
interspac|e (*n.*) ˈɪn.tə.speɪs, ˌ--ˈ- US ˈɪn.t̬ɚ.speɪs **-es** -ɪz
interspac|e (*v.*) ˌɪn.təˈspeɪs US -t̬ɚˈ-, ˈ--- **-es** -ɪz **-ing** -ɪŋ **-ed** -t
interspers|e ˌɪn.təˈspɜːs US -t̬ɚˈspɝːs **-es** -ɪz **-ing** -ɪŋ **-ed** -t
interspersion ˌɪn.təˈspɜː.ʃᵊn, -ʒᵊn US -t̬ɚˈspɝː-
interstate (I) ˌɪn.təˈsteɪt US ˈɪn.t̬ɚ.steɪt *stress shift, British only:* ˌinterstate ˈhighway
interstellar ˌɪn.təˈstel.əʳ US -t̬ɚˈstel.ɚ *stress shift:* ˌinterstellar ˈtravel
interstic|e ɪnˈtɜː.stɪs US -ˈtɝː- **-es** -ɪz, -iːz
interstitial ˌɪn.təˈstɪʃ.ᵊl US -t̬ɚˈ-
intertribal ˌɪn.təˈtraɪ.bᵊl US -t̬ɚˈ-
intertwin|e ˌɪn.təˈtwaɪn US -t̬ɚˈ- **-es** -z **-ing** -ɪŋ **-ed** -d

intertwist ˌɪn.təˈtwɪst ⓤⓢ -t̬ɚˈ- **-s** -s **-ing** -ɪŋ **-ed** -ɪd
interurban ˌɪn.təʳˈɜː.bᵊn ⓤⓢ -t̬ɚˈɝː-
interval ˈɪn.tə.vᵊl ⓤⓢ -t̬ɚ- **-s** -z
interven|e ˌɪn.təˈviːn ⓤⓢ -t̬ɚˈ- **-es** -z **-ing** -ɪŋ **-ed** -d **-er/s** -əʳ/z ⓤⓢ -ɚ/z
intervention ˌɪn.təˈven.*t*ʃᵊn ⓤⓢ -t̬ɚˈ- **-s** -z
intervention|ism ˌɪn.təˈven.*t*ʃᵊn|.ɪ.zᵊm ⓤⓢ -t̬ɚˈ- **-ist/s** -ɪst/s
interventionist ˌɪn.təˈven.tʃᵊn.ɪst ⓤⓢ -t̬ɚˈ-
interview ˈɪn.tə.vjuː ⓤⓢ -t̬ɚ- **-s** -z **-ing** -ɪŋ **-ed** -d **-er/s** -əʳ/z ⓤⓢ -ɚ/z
interviewee ˌɪn.tə.vjuˈiː ⓤⓢ -t̬ɚ- **-s** -z
inter vivos ˌɪn.təˈviː.vəʊs ⓤⓢ -tɚˈviː.voʊs, -ˈvaɪ-
intervocalic ˌɪn.tə.vəʊˈkæl.ɪk ⓤⓢ -t̬ɚ.voʊˈ-
interweav|e ˌɪn.təˈwiːv ⓤⓢ -t̬ɚˈ-, ˈ--- **-es** -z **-ing** -ɪŋ **-ed** -d **interwove** ˌɪn.təˈwəʊv ⓤⓢ -t̬ɚˈwoʊv, ˈ--- **interwoven** ˌɪn.təˈwəʊ.vᵊn ⓤⓢ -t̬ɚˈwoʊ.vᵊn, ˈɪn.t̬ɚˌwoʊ-
intestac|y ɪnˈtes.tə.s|i **-ies** -iz
intestate ɪnˈtes.teɪt, -tɪt, -tət **-s** -s
intestinal ɪnˈtes.tɪ.nᵊl, -tᵊn.ᵊl, ˌɪn.tesˈtaɪ.nᵊl ⓤⓢ ɪnˈtes.tɪ-
intestine ɪnˈtes.tɪn, -tiːn ⓤⓢ -tɪn, -tən **-s** -z
inthral(l) ɪnˈθrɔːl ⓤⓢ -ˈθrɑːl, -ˈθrɔːl **-s** -z **-ing** -ɪŋ **-ed** -d
intifada ˌɪn.tɪˈfɑː.də **-s** -z
intimac|y ˈɪn.tɪ.mə.s|i, -tə- ⓤⓢ -t̬ə-, -t̬ɪ- **-ies** -iz
intimate (*n. adj.*) ˈɪn.tɪ.mət, -tə-, -mɪt ⓤⓢ -t̬ə.mət, -t̬ɪ- **-s** -s **-ly** -li
inti|mate (*v.*) ˈɪn.tɪ|.meɪt, -tə- ⓤⓢ -t̬ə-, -t̬ɪ- **-mates** -meɪts **-mating** -meɪ.tɪŋ ⓤⓢ -meɪ.t̬ɪŋ **-mated** -meɪ.tɪd ⓤⓢ -meɪ.t̬ɪd **-mater/s** -meɪ.təʳ/z ⓤⓢ -meɪ.t̬ɚ/z
intimation ˌɪn.tɪˈmeɪ.ʃᵊn, -təˈ- ⓤⓢ -t̬əˈ-, -t̬ɪˈ- **-s** -z
intimi|date ɪnˈtɪm.ɪ|.deɪt, ˈ-ə- **-dates** -deɪts **-dating** -deɪ.tɪŋ ⓤⓢ -deɪ.t̬ɪŋ **-dated** -deɪ.tɪd ⓤⓢ -deɪ.t̬ɪd **-dator/s** -deɪ.təʳ/z ⓤⓢ -deɪ.t̬ɚ/z
intimidation ɪnˌtɪm.ɪˈdeɪ.ʃᵊn, -əˈ-
intituled ɪnˈtɪt.juːld
into ˈɪn.tə, -tu, -tuː ⓤⓢ -tə, -tu
Note: In British English, the pronunciation /ˈɪn.tuː/ is sometimes used in final position (e.g. 'That's the wall he walked into'), though the /u/ vowel is more usual. Elsewhere the pronunciation /ˈɪn.tə/ is used before consonants (e.g. 'into debt' /ˌɪn.təˈdet/) and /ˈɪn.tu/ before vowels (e.g. 'into each' /ɪn.tuˈiːtʃ/). In American English the schwa form is usual before consonants and also vowels (e.g. 'into each' /ˌɪn.təˈiːtʃ/).
intolerab|le ɪnˈtɒl.ᵊr.ə.b|l̩, ˌɪn- ⓤⓢ -ˈtɑː.lɚ- **-ly** -li **-leness** -l̩.nəs, -nɪs
intolerance ɪnˈtɒl.ᵊr.ᵊn*t*s, ˌɪn- ⓤⓢ -ˈtɑː.lɚ-
intolerant ɪnˈtɒl.ᵊr.ᵊnt, ˌɪn- ⓤⓢ -ˈtɑː.lɚ- **-ly** -li
into|nate ˈɪn.təʊ|.neɪt ⓤⓢ -toʊ-, -tə- **-nates** -neɪts **-nating** -neɪ.tɪŋ ⓤⓢ -neɪ.t̬ɪŋ **-nated** -neɪ.tɪd ⓤⓢ -neɪ.t̬ɪd
intonation ˌɪn.təʊˈneɪ.ʃᵊn ⓤⓢ -toʊˈ-, -təˈ- **-s** -z
intonational ˌɪn.təʊˈneɪ.ʃᵊn.ᵊl ⓤⓢ -toʊˈ-, -təˈ-
inton|e ɪnˈtəʊn ⓤⓢ -ˈtoʊn **-es** -z **-ing** -ɪŋ **-ed** -d **-er/s** -əʳ/z ⓤⓢ -ɚ/z
in toto ɪnˈtəʊ.təʊ ⓤⓢ -ˈtoʊ.toʊ
Intourist® ˈɪnˌtʊə.rɪst, -ˌtɔː- ⓤⓢ -ˌtʊr-

Intonation

The use of the pitch of the voice to convey linguistic information. The word is used with two rather different meanings. In a restricted sense, it is the variations in the pitch of a speaker's voice used to convey or alter meaning. In a broader and more popular sense, intonation is equivalent to 'prosody', where variations in such things as voice quality, tempo and loudness are included.

Examples for English

Intonation is said to convey emotions and attitudes. Other linguistic functions have also been claimed: interesting relationships exist in English between intonation and grammar, for example. In a few extreme cases a perceived difference in grammatical meaning may depend on the pitch movement, e.g.:

- ▶ she didn't go because of her ˇ timetable (meaning 'she did go, but it was not because of her timetable')
- ▶ she didn't go because of her ˋ timetable (meaning 'she didn't go, the reason being her timetable').

Other 'meanings' of intonation include things like the difference between statement and question, e.g.:

- ▶ it was ˋ cold (meaning "it was cold")
- ▶ it was ˊ cold (meaning "was it cold?)

the contrast between 'open' and 'closed' lists, e.g.:

- ▶ would you like ˊ wine, ˊ sherry or ˊ beer ('open', implying other things are also on offer)
- ▶ would you like ˊ wine, ˊ sherry or ˋ beer ('closed', implying no further choices are available)

and the indication of whether a relative clause is restrictive or non-restrictive, e.g.:

- ▶ the students who were ˇ nervous ˋ failed (restrictive relative clause: only students who were nervous failed)
- ▶ the ˇ students, who were ˇ nervous, ˋ failed (non-restrictive relative clause: all students were nervous and all failed)

Another approach to intonation is to concentrate on its role in conversational discourse: this involves such aspects as indicating whether the particular thing being said constitutes new information or old, the regulation of turn-taking in conversation, the establishment of dominance and the elicitation of co-operative responses. As with the signalling of attitudes, it seems that though analysts concentrate on pitch movements there are many other prosodic factors being used to create these effects.

intoxicant ɪn'tɒk.sɪ.kᵊnt, -sə- (US) -'tɑːk.sɪ- -s -s
intoxi|cate ɪn'tɒk.sɪ|.keɪt, -sə- (US) -'tɑːk.sɪ- -cates -keɪts -cating -keɪ.tɪŋ (US) -keɪ.t̬ɪŋ -cated -keɪ.tɪd (US) -keɪ.t̬ɪd -cator/s -keɪ.təʳ/z (US) -keɪ.t̬ɚ/z
intoxication ɪnˌtɒk.sɪ'keɪ.ʃᵊn, -sə'- (US) -ˌtɑːk.sɪ'-
intra- ˌɪn.trə-
Note: Prefix. Normally takes secondary stress on the first syllable, e.g. **intravenous** /ˌɪn.trə'viː.nəs/.
ntractability ɪnˌtræk.tə'bɪl.ə.ti, ˌɪn-, -ɪ.ti (US) -ə.t̬i
ntractab|le ɪn'træk.tə.b|l̩, ˌɪn- -ly -li -leness -l̩.nəs, -nɪs
ntradepartmental ˌɪn.trəˌdiː.pɑːt'men.tᵊl (US) -pɑːrt'men.t̬ᵊl
ntrados ɪn'treɪ.dɒs (US) -dɑːs; 'ɪn.trə.dɑːs, -doʊs -es -ɪz
ntramural ˌɪn.trə'mjʊə.rᵊl, -'mjɔː- (US) -'mjʊr.ᵊl
ntramuscular ˌɪn.trə'mʌs.kjə.ləʳ, -kjʊ- (US) -lɚ -ly -li
ntranet 'ɪn.trə.net -s -s
ntransigence ɪn'træn*t*.sɪ.dʒᵊn*t*s, -'trɑːn*t*-, -sə-; -'træn.zɪ-, -'trɑːn-, -zə- (US) -'træn*t*.sə-
ntransigent ɪn'træn*t*.sɪ.dʒᵊnt, -'trɑːn*t*-, -sə-; -'træn.zɪ-, -'trɑːn-, -zə- (US) -'træn*t*.sə- -s -s -ly -li
transitive ɪn'træn*t*.sə.tɪv, ˌɪn-, -'trɑːn*t*-, -sɪ-; -'træn.zə-, -'trɑːn-, -zɪ- (US) -'træn*t*.sə.t̬ɪv -s -z -ly -li
transitivity ɪnˌtræn*t*.sə'tɪv.ə.ti, ˌɪn-, -ˌtrɑːn*t*-, -sɪ'-; -ˌtræn.zə'-, -ˌtrɑːn-, -zɪ'-, -ɪ.ti (US) -ˌtræn*t*.sə'tɪv.ə.t̬i
trapersonal ˌɪn.trə'pɜː.sᵊn.ᵊl (US) -'pɝː-
trauterine ˌɪn.trə'juː.tᵊr.aɪn (US) -t̬ɚ.ɪn, -t̬ə.raɪn ˌ**intraˌuterine de'vice**
travenous ˌɪn.trə'viː.nəs -ly -li
-tray 'ɪn.treɪ -s -z
trench ɪn'tren*t*ʃ -es -ɪz -ing -ɪŋ -ed -t -ment/s -mənt/s
trepid ɪn'trep.ɪd -ly -li
trepidity ˌɪn.trə'pɪd.ə.ti, -trɪ'-, -trep'ɪd-, -ɪ.ti (US) ˌɪn.trə'pɪd.ə.t̬i, -trɪ'-
tricac|y 'ɪn.trɪ.kə.s|i, -trə- -ies -iz
tricate 'ɪn.trɪ.kət, -trə-, -kɪt -ly -li -ness -nəs, -nɪs
trigue (*n.*) 'ɪn.triːg, ˌ-'-
trigu|e (*v.*) ɪn'triːg -es -z -ing/ly -ɪŋ/li -ed -d -er/s -əʳ/z (US) -ɚ/z
trinsic ɪn'trɪn*t*.sɪk; -'trɪn.zɪk -ally -ᵊl.i, -li
ro- ɪn.trəʊ- (US) ɪn.troʊ-, -trə-
Note: Prefix. Normally takes either primary or secondary stress on the first syllable, e.g. **introvert** (noun), /'ɪn.trəʊ.vɜːt (US) -troʊ.vɝːrt/, **introspect** /ˌɪn.trəʊ'spekt (US) -troʊ'-/.
intro 'ɪn.trəʊ (US) -troʊ -s -z
introduc|e ˌɪn.trə'djuːs, -'dʒuːs (US) -'duːs, -'djuːs -es -ɪz -ing -ɪŋ -ed -t -er/s -əʳ/z (US) -ɚ/z
introduction ˌɪn.trə'dʌk.ʃᵊn -s -z
introductor|y ˌɪn.trə'dʌk.tᵊr|.i -ily -ᵊl.i, -ɪ.li -iness -ɪ.nəs, -nɪs
introit 'ɪn.trɔɪt, -trəʊ.ɪt; ɪn'trəʊ.ɪt (US) ɪn'troʊ.ɪt; 'ɪn.trɔɪt -s -s
intromission ˌɪn.trəʊ'mɪʃ.ᵊn (US) -troʊ'-, -trə'- -s -z
intro|mit ˌɪn.trəʊ|'mɪt (US) -troʊ'-, -trə'- -mits -'mɪts -mitting -'mɪt.ɪŋ (US) -'mɪt̬.ɪŋ -mitted -'mɪt.ɪd (US) -'mɪt̬.ɪd
introspect ˌɪn.trəʊ'spekt (US) -troʊ'-, -trə'- -s -s -ing -ɪŋ -ed -ɪd
introspection ˌɪn.trəʊ'spek.ʃᵊn (US) -troʊ'-, -trə'- -ist/s -ɪst/s -al -ᵊl
introspective ˌɪn.trəʊ'spek.tɪv (US) -troʊ'-, -trə'- -ly -li -ness -nəs, -nɪs
introversion ˌɪn.trəʊ'vɜː.ʃᵊn, -ʒᵊn (US) -troʊ'vɝː-, -trə'-
introvert (*n.*) 'ɪn.trəʊ.vɜːt (US) -troʊ.vɝːt, -trə- -s -s
introver|t (*v.*) ˌɪn.trəʊ'vɜː|t (US) -troʊ'vɝː|t, -trə'-, '--- -ts -ts -ting -tɪŋ (US) -t̬ɪŋ -ted -tɪd (US) -t̬ɪd
intrud|e ɪn'truːd -es -z -ing -ɪŋ -ed -ɪd -er/s -əʳ/z (US) -ɚ/z
intrusion ɪn'truː.ʒᵊn -s -z
intrusive ɪn'truː.sɪv -ly -li -ness -nəs, -nɪs
intu|it ɪn'tjuː|.ɪt (US) ɪn'tuː-, -'tjuː-, 'ɪn.tu|.ɪt -its -ɪts -iting -ɪ.tɪŋ (US) -ɪ.t̬ɪŋ -ited -ɪ.tɪd (US) -ɪ.t̬ɪd -itable -ɪ.tə.bl̩
intuition ˌɪn.tju'ɪʃ.ᵊn (US) -tu'-, -tju'- -s -z -al -ᵊl
intuitive ɪn'tjuː.ɪ.tɪv, '-ə- (US) -'tuː.ɪ.t̬ɪv, -'tjuː- -ly -li -ness -nəs, -nɪs
intumescen|ce ˌɪn.tjuː'mes.ᵊn|*t*s (US) -tuː'-, -tjuː'- -t -t
Inuit 'ɪn.u.ɪt, -ju- (US) '-u- -s -s
inun|date 'ɪn.ʌn|.deɪt, -ən- (US) -ən- -dates -deɪts -dating -deɪ.tɪŋ (US) -deɪ.t̬ɪŋ -dated -deɪ.tɪd (US) -deɪ.t̬ɪd
inundation ˌɪn.ʌn'deɪ.ʃᵊn, -ən'- (US) -ən'- -s -z
inur|e ɪ'njʊəʳ, -'njɔːʳ (US) -'njʊr, -'nʊr -es -z -ing -ɪŋ -ed -d -ement -mənt
in utero ɪn'juː.tᵊr.əʊ (US) -t̬ɚ.oʊ
inutility ˌɪn.juː'tɪl.ə.ti, -ɪ.ti (US) -ə.t̬i
invad|e ɪn'veɪd -es -z -ing -ɪŋ -ed -ɪd -er/s -əʳ/z (US) -ɚ/z
invalid (*n. v. adj.*) *infirm through illness, etc.:* 'ɪn.və.lɪd, -liːd (US) -lɪd -s -z -ing -ɪŋ -ed -ɪd
invalid (*adj.*) *not valid:* ɪn'væl.ɪd, ˌɪn-
invali|date ɪn'væl.ɪ|.deɪt, ˌɪn-, '-ə- -dates -deɪts -dating -deɪ.tɪŋ (US) -deɪ.t̬ɪŋ -dated -deɪ.tɪd (US) -deɪ.t̬ɪd
invalidation ɪnˌvæl.ɪ'deɪ.ʃᵊn, ˌɪn-, -ə'-
invalidity ˌɪn.və'lɪd.ə.ti, -ɪ.ti (US) -ə.t̬i **inva'lidity ˌbenefit**
invaluab|le ɪn'væl.ju.ə.b|l̩, -jə.b|l̩, -jʊ- (US) -ju.ə- -ly -li
Invar® ɪn'vɑːʳ, '--, 'ɪn.vəʳ (US) 'ɪn.vɑːr
invariability ɪnˌveə.ri.ə'bɪl.ə.ti, ˌɪn-, -ɪ.ti (US) -ˌver.i.ə'bɪl.ə.t̬i
invariab|le ɪn'veə.ri.ə.b|l̩, ˌɪn- (US) -'ver.i- -ly -li -leness -l̩.nəs, -nɪs
invariance ɪn'veə.ri.ən*t*s, ˌɪn- (US) -'ver.i-
invasion ɪn'veɪ.ʒᵊn -s -z
invasive ɪn'veɪ.sɪv, -zɪv (US) -zɪv, -sɪv -ly -li -ness -nəs, -nɪs
invective ɪn'vek.tɪv -s -z
inveigh ɪn'veɪ -s -z -ing -ɪŋ -ed -d
inveigl|e ɪn'veɪ.gl̩, -'viː- -es -z -ing -ɪŋ, -'veɪ.glɪŋ, -'viː- -ed -əd -ement/s -mənt/s
in|vent ɪn|'vent -vents -'vents -venting -'ven.tɪŋ (US) -'ven.t̬ɪŋ -vented -'ven.tɪd (US) -'ven.t̬ɪd
invention ɪn'ven.*t*ʃᵊn -s -z
inventive ɪn'ven.tɪv (US) -t̬ɪv -ly -li -ness -nəs, -nɪs
inventor ɪn'ven.təʳ (US) -t̬ɚ -s -z
inventor|y 'ɪn.vᵊn.tr|i, -tᵊr|.i, ɪn'ven.tᵊr|.i (US) -tɔːr- -ies -iz
Inverary ˌɪn.vᵊr'eə.ri, -rə (US) -və'rer.i
Invercargill *in Scotland:* ˌɪn.və'kɑː.gɪl, -gᵊl; -kɑː'gɪl (US) -vɚ'kɑːr.gɪl *in New Zealand:* ˌɪn.və'kɑː.gɪl (US) -vɚ'kɑːr-
Invergordon ˌɪn.və'gɔː.dᵊn (US) -vɚ'gɔːr-
Inverkeithing ˌɪn.və'kiː.ðɪŋ (US) -vɚ'-
Inverness, inverness ˌɪn.və'nes (US) -vɚ'- -es -ɪz *stress shift:* ˌInverness 'train
Inverness-shire ˌɪn.və'nes.ʃəʳ, -'neʃ-, -ˌʃɪəʳ (US) -vɚ'nes.ʃɚ, -ˌʃɪr
inverse ɪn'vɜːs, '-- (US) -'vɝːs, '-- -s -ɪz -ly -li
inversion ɪn'vɜː.ʃᵊn, -ʒᵊn (US) -'vɝː.ʒᵊn, -ʃᵊn -s -z
invert (*n. adj.*) 'ɪn.vɜːt (US) -vɝːt -s -s
in|vert (*v.*) ɪn|'vɜːt (US) -'vɝːt -verts -'vɜːts (US) -'vɝːts -verting -'vɜː.tɪŋ (US) -'vɝː.t̬ɪŋ -verted -'vɜː.tɪd (US) -'vɝː.t̬ɪd **inˌverted 'comma; inˌverted 'snob; inˌverted 'snobbery**
invertase ɪn'vɜː.teɪz (US) -'vɝː.teɪs, -teɪz, '---

invertebrate ɪnˈvɜː.tɪ.breɪt, ˌɪn-, ˈ-tə-, -brət, -brɪt (US) -ˈvɝː.t̬ə.brɪt, -breɪt **-s** -s

Inverurie ˌɪn.vᵊrˈʊə.ri (US) -vəˈrʊr.i

invest ɪnˈvest **-s** -s **-ing** -ɪŋ **-ed** -ɪd

investi|gate ɪnˈves.tɪ|.geɪt, -tə- **-gates** -geɪts **-gating** -geɪ.tɪŋ (US) -geɪ.t̬ɪŋ **-gated** -geɪ.tɪd (US) -geɪ.t̬ɪd **-gator/s** -geɪ.təʳ/z (US) -geɪ.t̬ɚ/z

investigation ɪnˌves.tɪˈgeɪ.ʃᵊn, -təˈ- **-s** -z

investigative ɪnˈves.tɪ.gə.tɪv, -tə-, -geɪ- (US) -geɪ.t̬ɪv

investigatory ɪnˈves.tɪ.gə.tᵊr.i, -tə-, -geɪ-; ɪnˌves.tɪˈgeɪ-, -təˈ- (US) ɪnˈves.tɪ.gə.tɔːr-, -tə-

investiture ɪnˈves.tɪ.tʃəʳ, -tə-, -tjʊəʳ (US) -tʃɚ **-s** -z

investment ɪnˈves*t*.mənt **-s** -s **inˈvestment ˌbond**

investor ɪnˈves.təʳ (US) -tɚ **-s** -z

inveteracy ɪnˈvet.ᵊr.ə.si (US) -ˈvet̬-

inveterate ɪnˈvet.ᵊr.ət, -ɪt (US) -ˈvet̬- **-ly** -li **-ness** -nəs, -nɪs

invidious ɪnˈvɪd.i.əs **-ly** -li **-ness** -nəs, -nɪs

invigi|late ɪnˈvɪdʒ.ə|.leɪt, ˈ-ɪ- **-lates** -leɪts **-lating** -leɪ.tɪŋ (US) -leɪ.t̬ɪŋ **-lated** -leɪ.tɪd (US) -leɪ.t̬ɪd **-lator/s** -leɪ.təʳ/z (US) -leɪ.t̬ɚ/z

invigilation ɪnˌvɪdʒ.əˈleɪ.ʃᵊn, -ɪˈ- **-s** -z

invigor|ate ɪnˈvɪg.ᵊr|.eɪt (US) -ə.r|eɪt **-ates** -eɪts **-ating** -eɪ.tɪŋ (US) -eɪ.t̬ɪŋ **-ated** -eɪ.tɪd (US) -eɪ.t̬ɪd **-ator/s** -eɪ.təʳ/z (US) -eɪ.t̬ɚ/z

invigoration ɪnˌvɪg.ᵊrˈeɪ.ʃᵊn (US) -əˈreɪ-

invincibility ɪnˌvɪn*t*.səˈbɪl.ə.ti, -sɪˈ-, -ɪ.ti (US) -ə.t̬i

invincib|le ɪnˈvɪn*t*.sə.b|l̩, -sɪ- **-ly** -li **-leness** -l̩.nəs, -nɪs

inviolability ɪnˌvaɪə.ləˈbɪl.ə.ti, ˌɪn-, -ɪ.ti (US) -ə.t̬i

inviolab|le ɪnˈvaɪə.lə.b|l̩ **-ly** -li **-leness** -l̩.nəs, -nɪs

inviolate ɪnˈvaɪə.lət, -lɪt, -leɪt **-ly** -li **-ness** -nəs, -nɪs

invisibility ɪnˌvɪz.əˈbɪl.ə.ti, ˌɪn-, -ɪˈ-, -ɪ.ti (US) -ə.t̬i

invisib|le ɪnˈvɪz.ə.b|l̩, ˌɪn-, ˈ-ɪ- **-ly** -li **-leness** -l̩.nəs, -nɪs

invitation ˌɪn.vɪˈteɪ.ʃᵊn, -vəˈ- **-s** -z **-al/s** -ᵊl/z

in|vite (*v.*) ɪn|ˈvaɪt **-vites** -ˈvaɪts **-viting/ly** -ˈvaɪ.tɪŋ/li (US) -ˈvaɪ.t̬ɪŋ/li **-vited** -ˈvaɪ.tɪd (US) -ˈvaɪ.t̬ɪd **-viter/s** -ˈvaɪ.təʳ/z (US) -ˈvaɪ.t̬ɚ/z

invite (*n.*) ˈɪn.vaɪt **-s** -s

invitee ˌɪn.vaɪˈtiː, -vɪˈ- (US) -vaɪˈ-, -vəˈ-

in vitro ˌɪnˈviː.trəʊ, -ˈvɪt.rəʊ (US) -ˈviː.troʊ, -ˈvɪt.roʊ **in ˌvitro fertiliˈzation**

in vivo ˌɪnˈviː.vəʊ (US) -voʊ

invo|cate ˈɪn.və*ʊ*|.keɪt (US) -və- **-cates** -keɪts **-cating** -keɪ.tɪŋ (US) -keɪ.t̬ɪŋ **-cated** -keɪ.tɪd (US) -keɪ.t̬ɪd

invocation ˌɪn.və*ʊ*ˈkeɪ.ʃᵊn (US) -vəˈ- **-s** -z **-al** -ᵊl

invoic|e ˈɪn.vɔɪs **-es** -ɪz **-ing** -ɪŋ **-ed** -t

invok|e ɪnˈvəʊk (US) -ˈvoʊk **-es** -s **-ing** -ɪŋ **-ed** -t

involucre ˈɪn.və.luː.kəʳ, -ljuː-, ˌɪn.vəˈluː.kəʳ, -ˈljuː- (US) ˌɪn.voʊˈluː.kɚ, -vəˈ- **-s** -z

involuntar|y ɪnˈvɒl.ən.tᵊr|.i, ˌɪn-, -ᵊn-, -tr|i (US) -ˈvɑː.lən.ter|.i **-ily** -ᵊl.i, -ɪ.li **-iness** -ɪ.nəs, -ɪ.nɪs

involu|te ˈɪn.və.luː|t, -ljuː|t, ˌ--ˈ- (US) ˈɪn.və.luː|t **-tes** -ts **-ting** -tɪŋ (US) -t̬ɪŋ **-ted** -tɪd (US) -t̬ɪd

involution ˌɪn.vəˈluː.ʃᵊn, -ˈljuː- (US) -ˈluː- **-s** -z

involv|e ɪnˈvɒlv (US) -ˈvɑːlv, -ˈvɔːlv **-es** -z **-ing** -ɪŋ **-ed** -d

involvement ɪnˈvɒlv.mənt (US) -ˈvɑːlv-, -ˈvɔːlv- **-s** -s

invulnerability ɪnˌvʌl.nᵊr.əˈbɪl.ə.ti, ˌɪn-, -ˌvʌn.ᵊr-, -ɪ.ti (US) -ˌvʌl.nɚ.əˈbɪl.ə.t̬i

invulnerab|le ɪnˈvʌl.nᵊr.ə.b|l̩, ˌɪn-, -ˈvʌn.ᵊr- (US) -ˈvʌl.nɚ- **-ly** -li **-leness** -l̩.nəs, -nɪs

inward ˈɪn.wəd (US) -wɚd **-s** -z **-ly** -li **-ness** -nəs, -nɪs

Inwards ˈɪn.wədz (US) -wɚdz

inweav|e ɪnˈwiːv **-es** -z **-ing** -ɪŋ **-ed** -d **inwove** ɪnˈwəʊv (US) -ˈwoʊv **inwoven** ɪnˈwəʊ.vᵊn (US) -ˈwoʊ-

Inwood ˈɪn.wʊd

inwov|e (*from* **inweave**) ɪnˈwəʊv (US) -ˈwoʊv **-en** -ᵊn

inwrought ɪnˈrɔːt (US) -ˈrɑːt, -ˈrɔːt

io (I) ˈaɪ.əʊ (US) -oʊ **-s** -z

io|date ˈaɪ.əʊ|.deɪt (US) ˈ-ə- **-dates** -deɪts **-dating** -deɪ.tɪŋ (US) -deɪ.t̬ɪŋ **-dated** -deɪ.tɪd (US) -deɪ.t̬ɪd

iodic aɪˈɒd.ɪk (US) -ˈɑː.dɪk

iodide ˈaɪ.ə*ʊ*.daɪd (US) ˈ-ə- **-s** -z

iodine ˈaɪ.ə.diːn, -daɪn (US) -daɪn, -dɪn, -diːn

iodiz|e, -is|e ˈaɪ.ə.daɪz **-es** -ɪz **-ing** -ɪŋ **-ed** -d

iodoform aɪˈɒd.ə.fɔːm (US) -ˈoʊ.də.fɔːrm, -ˈɑː-

Iolanthe ˌaɪ.ə*ʊ*ˈlæn*t*.θi (US) ˌaɪəˈ-, ˌaɪ.o-

iolite ˈaɪ.ə*ʊ*.laɪt (US) ˈ-oʊ-

Iolo ˈjəʊ.ləʊ (US) ˈjoʊ.loʊ

ion ˈaɪ.ən, -ɒn (US) -ən, -ɑːn **-s** -z

Iona aɪˈəʊ.nə (US) -ˈoʊ-

Ione aɪˈəʊ.ni (US) -ˈoʊ-

Ionesco jɒnˈes.kəʊ, ˌiː.ɒnˈ-, ˌiː.əˈnes-kuː (US) jəˈnes.koʊ, ˌiː.əˈ-

Ioni|a aɪˈəʊ.ni|.ə (US) -ˈoʊ- **-an/s** -ən/z

ionic (I) aɪˈɒn.ɪk (US) -ˈɑː.nɪk **-s** -s

Ionica® aɪˈɒn.ɪ.kə (US) -ˈɑː.nɪ-

ionization, -isa- ˌaɪə.naɪˈzeɪ.ʃᵊn, -nɪˈ- (US) -nɪˈ- **-s** -z

ioniz|e, -is|e ˈaɪə.naɪz **-es** -ɪz **-ing** -ɪŋ **-ed** -d **-er/s** -əʳ/z (US) -ɚ/z **-able** -ə.bl̩

Pronouncing the letters IO

There are several pronunciation possibilities for the vowel digraph **io**, e.g.:

/aɪə/	lion	/laɪən/
/i.əʊ (US) i.oʊ/	radio	/ˈreɪ.di.əʊ/ (US) /-oʊ/
/aɪ.ɒ (US) aɪ.ɑː, aɪ.ɔː/	priority	/praɪˈɒr.ə.ti/ (US) /-ˈɔːr.ə.t̬i/
/i.ɒ (US) i.ɑː/	curiosity	/ˌkjʊə.riˈɒs.ə.ti/ (US) /ˌkjʊr.iˈɑː.sə.t̬i/

In weak syllables

In weak syllables where it is preceded by the letters **s** and **t**, the vowel digraph **io** is realised with the vowel /ə/, and may result in a syllabic consonant, e.g.:

station	/ˈsteɪ.ʃᵊn/
invasion	/ɪnˈveɪ.ʒᵊn/

In other weak syllable contexts, **io** is realised with /i.ə/ or /jə/, e.g.:

million	/ˈmɪl.jən, -i.ən/	(US) /-jən/
patriot	/ˈpæt.ri.ət/	(US) /ˈpeɪ.tri-/

onosphere aɪˈɒn.ə.sfɪəʳ US -ˈɑː.nə.sfɪr -s -z
ota aɪˈəʊ.tə US -ˈoʊ.t̬ə -s -z
otacism aɪˈəʊ.tə.sɪ.zəm US -ˈoʊ.t̬ə- -s -z
OU ˌaɪ.əʊˈjuː US -oʊˈ- -s -z
owa ˈaɪ.əʊə, ˈaɪə.wə US ˈaɪə.wə **ˌIowa ˈCity**
PA ˌaɪ.piːˈeɪ
pecac ˈɪp.ɪ.kæk, ˈ-ə-
pecacuanha ˌɪp.ɪˌkæk.juˈæn.ə, -əˌ-, -ˈɑː.nə US -juˈæn.ə
phicrates ɪˈfɪk.rə.tiːz
phigenia ˌɪf.ɪ.dʒɪˈnaɪə, ˌaɪ.fɪ-, -dʒəˈ-; ɪˌfɪdʒ.ɪˈ-, -əˈ- US ˌɪf.ə.dʒəˈ-
poh ˈiː.pəʊ US -poʊ
pse dixit ˌɪp.siˈdɪk.sɪt, -seɪˈ- US -siˈ-
pso facto ˌɪp.səʊˈfæk.təʊ US -soʊˈfæk.toʊ
pso jure ˌɪp.səʊˈjʊə.reɪ, -ri US -soʊˈdʒʊr.i
pswich ˈɪp.swɪtʃ
Q ˌaɪˈkjuː **IˈQ ˌtest**
qbal ˈɪk.bæl, ˈɪg-, -bɑːl US ɪkˈbɑːl
quique ɪˈkiː.ki, -keɪ US iːˈkiː.keɪ
quitos ɪˈkiː.tɒs US iːˈkiː.toʊs, -tɔːs
a ˈaɪə.rə US ˈaɪ-
A ˌaɪ.ɑːʳˈeɪ US -ɑːrˈ-
abu ɪˈrɑː.bu, ˈɪr.ə.buː
ak ɪˈrɑːk, -ˈræk US ɪ-, iː- **-i/s** -i/z
an ɪˈrɑːn, -ˈræn US -ˈræn
anian ɪˈreɪ.ni.ən, -ˈrɑː- US ɪ- **-s** -z
aq ɪˈrɑːk, -ˈræk US ɪ- **-i/s** -i/z
ascibility ɪˌræs.əˈbɪl.ə.ti, -ɪˈ-, -ɪ.ti US -ə.t̬i
ascib|le ɪˈræs.ə.b|l̩, ˈ-ɪ- **-ly** -li **-leness** -l̩.nəs, -nɪs
ate aɪˈreɪt, ˌaɪ- US aɪˈreɪt, ˈ-- **-ly** -li
bid ˈɪə.bɪd US ˈɪr-
e aɪəʳ US aɪr
edell ˈaɪə.del US ˈaɪr-
eful ˈaɪə.fəl, -fʊl US ˈaɪr **-ly** -i **-ness** -nəs, -nɪs
eland ˈaɪə.lənd US ˈaɪr-
emonger ˈaɪəˌmʌŋ.gəʳ US ˈaɪrˌmʌŋ.gɚ, -ˌmɑːŋ-
ne ˈaɪ.riːn, -ˈ-; -ˈriː.ni US -ˈriːn; -ˈriː.ni
nic aɪˈriː.nɪk, -ˈren.ɪk US -ˈren-, -ˈriː.nɪk **-al** -əl
ton ˈaɪə.tən US ˈaɪr-
an ˈɪr.i.ən, -ɑːn US -ɑːn, -ən
an Jaya ˌɪr.i.ɑːnˈdʒɑː.jə, -ənˈ-, -jɑː
des *(plur. of* **iris***)* ˈaɪə.rɪ.diːz, ˈɪr.ɪ- US ˈaɪ.rɪ-, ˈɪr.ɪ-
descence ˌɪr.ɪˈdes.ənts, -əˈ-
descent ˌɪr.ɪˈdes.ənt, -əˈ- **-ly** -li
dium ɪˈrɪd.i.əm, aɪ-
dolog|y ˌɪr.ɪˈdɒl.ə.dʒ|i US -ˈdɑː.lə- **-ist/s** -ɪst/s
on ˈɪr.i.ən, -ɒn US -ɑːn, -ən

iris (I) ˈaɪə.rɪs US ˈaɪ- **irises** ˈaɪə.rɪ.sɪz US ˈaɪ- **irides** ˈaɪə.rɪ.diːz, ˈɪr.ɪ- US ˈaɪ.rɪ-, ˈɪr.ɪ-
Irish ˈaɪə.rɪʃ US ˈaɪ- **-ism/s** -ɪ.zəm/z **ˌIrish ˈcoffee; ˌIrish ReˈpubIic; ˌIrish ReˌpublicanˈArmy; ˌIrish ˈSea; ˌIrish ˈstew**
Irish|man ˈaɪə.rɪʃ|.mən US ˈaɪ- **-men** -mən, -men
Irishry ˈaɪə.rɪʃ.ri US ˈaɪ-
Irish|woman ˈaɪə.rɪʃ|ˌwʊm.ən US ˈaɪ- **-women** -ˌwɪm.ɪn
irk ɜːk US ɝːk **-s** -s **-ing** -ɪŋ **-ed** -t
irksome ˈɜːk.səm US ˈɝːk- **-ly** -li **-ness** -nəs, -nɪs
Irkutsk ɜːˈkʊtsk, ɪə- US ɪr-
Irlam ˈɜː.ləm US ˈɝː-
Irma ˈɜː.mə US ˈɝː-
iron (I) aɪən US ˈaɪ.ɚn, aɪrn **-s** -z **-ing** -ɪŋ **-ed** -d **ˈIron ˌAge; ˈironing ˌboard; ˌIron ˈCurtain; ˌiron ˈlung; ˈiron ˌmould; ˌstrike while the ˌiron's ˈhot**
ironbark ˈaɪən.bɑːk US ˈaɪ.ɚn.bɑːrk, ˈaɪrn- **-s** -s
ironbound ˈaɪən.baʊnd US ˈaɪ.ɚn-, ˈaɪrn-
Ironbridge ˈaɪən.brɪdʒ, -ˈ- US ˈaɪ.ɚn-, ˈaɪrn-
ironclad ˈaɪən.klæd US ˈaɪ.ɚn-, ˈaɪrn- **-s** -z
irongray, irongrey ˌaɪənˈgreɪ, ˌaɪəŋ- US ˌaɪ.ɚnˈ-, ˌaɪrn- *stress shift:* ˌirongray ˈbattleship
ironic aɪəˈrɒn.ɪk US aɪˈrɑː.nɪk **-al** -əl **-ally** -əl.i, -li
ironmonger ˈaɪənˌmʌŋ.gəʳ, ˈaɪəm- US ˈaɪ.ɚnˌmʌŋ.gɚ, ˈaɪrn-, -ˌmɑːŋ- **-s** -z
ironmongery ˈaɪənˌmʌŋ.gər.i, ˈaɪəm- US ˈaɪ.ɚnˌ-, ˈaɪrn-, -ˌmɑːŋ-
ironside (I) ˈaɪən.saɪd US ˈaɪ.ɚn-, ˈaɪrn- **-s** -z
ironstone ˈaɪən.stəʊn US ˈaɪ.ɚn.stoʊn, ˈaɪrn-
Ironton ˈaɪən.tən US ˈaɪ.ɚn-, ˈaɪrn-
ironware ˈaɪən.weəʳ US ˈaɪ.ɚn.wer, ˈaɪrn-
ironwood (I) ˈaɪən.wʊd US ˈaɪ.ɚn-, ˈaɪrn-
ironwork ˈaɪən.wɜːk US ˈaɪ.ɚn.wɝːk, ˈaɪrn- **-s** -s
iron|y *(n.) sarcasm, etc.:* ˈaɪə.rən|.i US ˈaɪ- **-ies** -iz
irony *(adj.) like iron:* ˈaɪə.ni US ˈaɪ.ɚ-, ˈaɪr-
Iroquoian ˌɪr.əʊˈkwɔɪ.ən US -əˈ-
Iroquois *(sing.)* ˈɪr.ə.kwɔɪ, -kwɔɪ *(plur.)* ˈɪr.ə.kwɔɪz, -kwɔɪ
irradian|ce ɪˈreɪ.di.ənt|s US ɪrˈ- **-cy** -si
irradi|ate ɪˈreɪ.di|.eɪt US ɪrˈ- **-ates** -eɪts **-ating** -eɪ.tɪŋ US -eɪ.t̬ɪŋ **-ated** -eɪ.tɪd US -eɪ.t̬ɪd

irradiation ɪˌreɪ.diˈeɪ.ʃən, ˌɪr.eɪ- US ɪrˈ-, ɪˌreɪ- **-s** -z
irradicab|le ɪˈræd.ɪ.kə.b|l̩ US ɪrˈ- **-ly** -li
irrational ɪˈræʃ.ən.əl, ˌɪrˈæʃ-, -ˈræʃ.nəl **-ly** -i
irrationality ɪˌræʃ.ənˈæl.ə.ti, ˌɪrˌæʃ-, -ɪ.ti US -ə.t̬i
Irrawaddy ˌɪr.əˈwɒd.i US -ˈwɑː.di, -ˈwɔː-
irrebuttable ˌɪr.ɪˈbʌt.ə.bl̩ US -ˈbʌt̬-
irreceptive ˌɪr.ɪˈsep.tɪv
irreclaimab|le ˌɪr.ɪˈkleɪ.mə.b|l̩ **-ly** -li
irrecognizable, -isa- ɪˌrek.əgˈnaɪ.zə.bl̩, ˌɪrˌek-
irreconcilability ɪˌrek.ənˌsaɪ.ləˈbɪl.ə.ti, ˌɪrˌek-, -ɪ.ti US -ə.t̬i
irreconcilab|le ˌɪr.ek.ənˈsaɪ.lə.b|l̩, ɪˌrek- **-ly** -li **-leness** -l̩.nəs, -nɪs
irrecoverab|le ˌɪr.ɪˈkʌv.ər.ə.b|l̩, -əˈ- **-ly** -li **-leness** -l̩.nəs, -nɪs
irredeemab|le ˌɪr.ɪˈdiː.mə.b|l̩, -əˈ- **-ly** -li **-leness** -l̩.nəs, -nɪs
irredent|ism ˌɪr.ɪˈden.t|ɪ.zəm, -əˈ- **-ist/s** -ɪst/s
irreducib|le ˌɪr.ɪˈdjuː.sə.b|l̩, -əˈ-, -sɪ- US -ˈduː-, -ˈdjuː- **-ly** -li **-leness** -l̩.nəs, -nɪs
irrefutability ɪˌref.jə.təˈbɪl.ə.ti, -jʊ-, -ɪ.ti; ˌɪr.ɪˌfjuː.təˈ-, -əˌ- US -t̬əˈbɪl.ə.t̬i
irrefutab|le ˌɪr.ɪˈfjuː.tə.b|l̩, -əˈ-; ɪˈref.jə-, -jʊ- US ɪˈref.jə.t̬ə-; ˌɪr.ɪˈfjuː-, -əˈ- **-ly** -li **-leness** -l̩.nəs, -nɪs
irregardless ˌɪr.ɪˈgɑːd.ləs, -əˈ-, -lɪs US -iˈgɑːrd-
irregular ɪˈreg.jə.ləʳ, -jʊ- US -lɚ **-ly** -li
irregularit|y ɪˌreg.jəˈlær.ə.t|i, ˌɪrˌeg-, -jʊˈ-, -ɪ.t|i US ɪˌreg.jəˈler.ə.t̬|i, -ˈlær- **-ies** -iz
irrelevan|ce ɪˈrel.ə.vənt|s, ˈ-ɪ- US ɪrˈ- **-cy** -si **-cies** -siz
irrelevant ɪˈrel.ə.vənt, ˈ-ɪ- US ɪrˈ- **-ly** -li
irreligion ˌɪr.ɪˈlɪdʒ.ən, -əˈ-
irreligious ˌɪr.ɪˈlɪdʒ.əs, -əˈ- **-ly** -li **-ness** -nəs, -nɪs
irremediab|le ˌɪr.ɪˈmiː.di.ə.b|l̩ **-ly** -li
irremovability ˌɪr.ɪˌmuː.vəˈbɪl.ə.ti, -əˌ-, -ɪ.ti US -ə.t̬i
irremovab|le ˌɪr.ɪˈmuː.və.b|l̩, -əˈ- **-ly** -li
irreparability ɪˌrep.ər.əˈbɪl.ə.ti, ˌɪrˌep-, -ɪ.ti US -ə.t̬i
irreparab|le ɪˈrep.ər.ə.b|l̩ **-ly** -li **-leness** -l̩.nəs, -nɪs
irreplaceable ˌɪr.ɪˈpleɪ.sə.bl̩
irrepressib|le ˌɪr.ɪˈpres.ə.b|l̩, -əˈ-, ˈ-ɪ- **-ly** -li **-leness** -l̩.nəs, -nɪs
irreproachability ˌɪr.ɪˌprəʊ.tʃəˈbɪl.ə.ti, -əˌ-, -ɪ.ti US -ˌproʊ.tʃəˈbɪl.ə.t̬i
irreproachab|le ˌɪr.ɪˈprəʊ.tʃə.b|l̩, -əˈ- US -ˈproʊ- **-ly** -li **-leness** -l̩.nəs, -nɪs

irresistibility ˌɪr.ɪˌzɪs.təˈbɪl.ə.ti, -əˌ-, -tɪˈ-, -ɪ.ti (US) -ə.t̬i
irresistib|le ˌɪr.ɪˈzɪs.tə.b|l̩, -əˈ-, -tɪ- **-ly** -li **-leness** -l̩.nəs, -nɪs
irresoluble ɪˈrez.əl.jə.bl̩, -jʊ- (US) ˌɪr.ɪˈzɑːl.jə-
irresolute ɪˈrez.əl.uːt, ˌɪrˈez-, -juːt (US) -uːt **-ly** -li **-ness** -nəs, -nɪs
irresolution ɪˌrez.əlˈuː.ʃən, -ˈljuː- (US) -ˈuː-
irresolvability ˌɪr.ɪˌzɒl.vəˈbɪl.ə.ti, -əˌ-, -ɪ.ti (US) -ˌzɑːl.vəˈbɪl.ə.t̬i
irresolvab|le ˌɪr.ɪˈzɒl.və.b|l̩ (US) -ˈzɑːl.və- **-ly** -li **-leness** -l̩.nəs, -nɪs
irrespective ˌɪr.ɪˈspek.tɪv, -əˈ- **-ly** -li
irresponsibility ˌɪr.ɪˌspɒnt.səˈbɪl.ə.ti, -əˌ-, -sɪˈ-, -ɪ.ti (US) -ˌspɑːnt.səˈbɪl.ə.t̬i
irresponsib|le ˌɪr.ɪˈspɒnt.sə.b|l̩, -əˈ-, -sɪ- (US) -ˈspɑːnt- **-ly** -li **-leness** -l̩.nəs, -nɪs
irresponsive ˌɪr.ɪˈspɒnt.sɪv, -əˈ- (US) -ˈspɑːnt- **-ly** -li **-ness** -nəs, -nɪs
irretentive ˌɪr.ɪˈten.tɪv, -əˈ- (US) -t̬ɪv
irretrievability ˌɪr.ɪˌtriː.vəˈbɪl.ə.ti, -əˌ-, -ɪ.ti (US) -ə.t̬i
irretrievab|le ˌɪr.ɪˈtriː.və.b|l̩, -əˈ- **-ly** -li **-leness** -l̩.nəs, -nɪs
irreverence ɪˈrev.ər.ənts, ˌɪrˈev-
irreverent ɪˈrev.ər.ənt, ˌɪrˈev- **-ly** -li
irreversibility ˌɪr.ɪˌvɜː.səˈbɪl.ə.ti, -əˌ-, -sɪˈ-, -ɪ.ti (US) -ˌvɝː.səˈbɪl.ə.t̬i, -sɪˈ-
irreversib|le ˌɪr.ɪˈvɜː.sə.b|l̩, -əˈ-, -sɪ- (US) -ˈvɝː- **-ly** -li **-leness** -l̩.nəs, -nɪs
irrevocability ɪˌrev.ə.kəˈbɪl.ə.ti, -ɪ.ti (US) -ə.t̬i
irrevocab|le ɪˈrev.ə.kə.b|l̩ **-ly** -li *when applied to letters of credit:* ˌɪr.ɪˈvəʊ.kə.bl̩, -əˈ- (US) ɪˈrev.ə.kə-; ˌɪr.ɪˈvoʊ-
irrigable ˈɪr.ɪ.gə.bl̩, ˈ-ə-
irri|gate ˈɪr.ɪ|.geɪt, ˈ-ə- **-gates** -geɪts **-gating** -geɪ.tɪŋ (US) -geɪ.t̬ɪŋ **-gated** -geɪ.tɪd (US) -geɪ.t̬ɪd **-gator/s** -geɪ.təʳ/z (US) -geɪ.t̬ɚ/z
irrigation ˌɪr.ɪˈgeɪ.ʃən, -əˈ- **-s** -z
irritability ˌɪr.ɪ.təˈbɪl.ə.ti, ˈ-ə-, -ɪ.ti (US) -t̬əˈbɪl.ə.t̬i
irritab|le ˈɪr.ɪ.tə.b|l̩, ˈ-ə- (US) -t̬ə- **-ly** -li **-leness** -l̩.nəs, -nɪs ˌ**irritable ˈbowel ˌsyndrome**
irritant ˈɪr.ɪ.tənt, ˈ-ə- (US) -t̬ənt **-s** -s
irri|tate ˈɪr.ɪ|.teɪt, ˈ-ə- **-tates** -teɪts **-tating/ly** -teɪ.tɪŋ/li (US) -teɪ.t̬ɪŋ/li **-tated** -teɪ.tɪd (US) -teɪ.t̬ɪd **-tative** -teɪ.tɪv (US) -teɪ.t̬ɪv **-tator/s** -teɪ.təʳ/z (US) -teɪ.t̬ɚ/z
irritation ˌɪr.ɪˈteɪ.ʃən, -əˈ- **-s** -z
irrupt ɪˈrʌpt **-s** -s **-ing** -ɪŋ **-ed** -ɪd **-ive/ly** -ɪv/li
irruption ɪˈrʌp.ʃən **-s** -z
Irvine *name:* ˈɜː.vɪn, -vaɪn (US) ˈɝː- *US city:* ˈɜː.vaɪn (US) ˈɝː-
Irvinestown ˈɜː.vɪnz.taʊn (US) ˈɝː-
Irving ˈɜː.vɪŋ (US) ˈɝː-
Irwin ˈɜː.wɪn (US) ˈɝː-
is *(from* **be**) *strong form:* ɪz *weak forms:* z, s
Note: /z/ is used only when the preceding word ends in a vowel or a voiced consonant other than /z/ or /ʒ/. /s/ is used only when the preceding word ends in a voiceless consonant other than /s/ or /ʃ/.
ISA, Isa ˈaɪ.sə **-s** -z
Isaac ˈaɪ.zək **-s** -s
Isaacson ˈaɪ.zək.sən
Isabel ˈɪz.ə.bel
Isabella ˌɪz.əˈbel.ə
Isabelle ˈɪz.ə.bel
Isaiah aɪˈzaɪə (US) aɪˈzeɪə, -ˈzaɪə
Isambard ˈɪz.əm.bɑːd (US) -bɑːrd
Isard ˈɪz.ɑːd (US) -ɑːrd
-isation -aɪˈzeɪ.ʃən, -ɪˈ- (US) -ɪˈ-
Note: Suffix. Words containing **-isation** alway carry primary stress as shown above, e.g. **decimalisation** /ˌdes.ɪ.məl.aɪˈzeɪ.ʃən (US) -ɪˈ-/.
ISBN ˌaɪ.es.biːˈen
Iscariot ɪsˈkær.i.ət (US) -ˈker-, -ˈkær-
Ischia ˈɪs.ki.ə
-ise -aɪz, -iːz
Note: Suffix. Where **-ise** forms a verb, the pronunciation is /-aɪz/. See note for **-ize**. Where **-ise** forms a noun, it usually carries primary stress (e.g. **experˈtise**) and is pronounced /-iːz/.
Iseult iˈzuːlt, -ˈsuːlt (US) -ˈsuːlt
-ish -ɪʃ
Note: Suffix. When forming an adjective, **-ish** does not affect the stress pattern of the word, e.g. **yellowish** /ˈjel.əʊ.ɪʃ (US) -oʊ-/. When forming a verb, the antepenultimate syllable is stressed, e.g. **demolish** /dɪˈmɒl.ɪʃ (US) -ˈmɑː.lɪʃ/.
Isham ˈaɪ.ʃəm
Isherwood ˈɪʃ.ə.wʊd (US) ˈ-ɚ-
Ishiguro ˌɪʃ.ɪˈgʊər.əʊ (US) -ˈgʊr.oʊ
Ishmael ˈɪʃ.meɪəl, -mi.əl
Ishmae|lite ˈɪʃ.mi.ə|.laɪt, -meɪə|.laɪt, -mə|.laɪt **-lites** -laɪts **-litish** -laɪ.tɪʃ (US) -laɪ.t̬ɪʃ
Ishtar ˈɪʃ.tɑːʳ (US) -tɑːr
Isidore ˈɪz.ɪ.dɔːʳ, ˈ-ə- (US) -ə.dɔːr
Isidorian ˌɪz.ɪˈdɔː.ri.ən, -əˈ- (US) -ːˈdɔːr.i-
isinglass ˈaɪ.zɪŋ.glɑːs (US) -zɪn.glæs, -zɪŋ-
Isis ˈaɪ.sɪs
Isla ˈaɪ.lə
Islam ˈɪz.lɑːm, ˈɪs-, -læm, -ləm; ɪzˈlɑːm, ɪs-
Islamabad ɪzˈlɑː.mə.bæd, ɪs-, -ˈlæm.ə-, -bɑːd (US) -ˈlɑː.mə.bɑːd
Islamic ɪzˈlæm.ɪk, ɪs-, -ˈlɑː.mɪk (US) -ˈlɑː-, -ˈlæm.ɪk **-s** -s
Islam|ism ˈɪz.lə.m|ɪ.zəm, ˈɪs- **-ist/s** -ɪst/s
island ˈaɪ.lənd **-s** -z **-er/s** -əʳ/z (US) -ɚ/z
Islay ˈaɪ.leɪ *locally:* ˈaɪ.lə
isle aɪl **-s** -z
Isle of Dogs ˌaɪl.əvˈdɒgz (US) -ˈdɑːgz, -ˈdɔːgz
Isle of Man ˌaɪl.əvˈmæn
Isle of Wight ˌaɪl.əvˈwaɪt
islet ˈaɪ.lət, -lɪt, -let (US) -lɪt **-s** -s
Isleworth ˈaɪ.zəl.wəθ, -wɜːθ (US) -wɝːθ, -wɚθ
Islington ˈɪz.lɪŋ.tən
Islip *archbishop:* ˈɪz.lɪp *in Oxfordshire:* ˈaɪ.slɪp
Islwyn ˈɪs.lu.ɪn; ɪzˈluː.ɪn, ɪs-
-ism -ɪ.zəm **-s** -z
Note: Suffix. When added to a free stem, **-ism** does not normally affect the stress pattern of the word, e.g. **absentee** /ˌæb.sənˈtiː/, **absenteeism** /ˌæb.sənˈtiː.ɪ.zəm/. When added to a bound stem, the word is normally stressed two syllables before the suffix, e.g. **exorcism** /ˈek.sɔː.sɪ.zəm (US) -sɔːr-/. Exceptions exist; see individual entries.
Ismail ˌɪz.mɑːˈiːl, ˌɪs-; ˈɪz.maɪl, -meɪl
Ismailiya ˌɪz.maɪˈliː.ə, ˌɪs- (US) ˌɪs.meɪ.əˈ-, ˌɪz-
Ismay ˈɪz.meɪ
isn't ˈɪz.ənt
iso- aɪ.səʊ-; aɪˈsɒ- (US) aɪ.soʊ-, -sə-; aɪˈsɑː-
Note: Prefix. Normally takes either primary or secondary stress on the first syllable, e.g. **isotope** /ˈaɪ.sə.təʊp (US) -toʊp/, **isotopic** /ˌaɪ.səˈtɒp.ɪk (US) -ˈtɑː.pɪk/, or primary stress on the second syllable, e.g. **isotropy** /aɪˈsɒt.rə.pi (US) -ˈsɑː.trə-/.
ISO ˌaɪ.esˈəʊ (US) -ˈoʊ
isobar ˈaɪ.səʊ.bɑːʳ (US) -soʊ.bɑːr, -sə- **-s** -z
Isobel ˈɪz.ə.bel
isochromatic ˌaɪ.səʊ.krəʊˈmæt.ɪk (US) -soʊ.kroʊˈmæt̬.ɪk, -sə-
isochronal aɪˈsɒk.rə.nəl (US) -ˈsɑː.krə- **-ly** -i
isochronous aɪˈsɒk.rə.nəs (US) -ˈsɑː.krə- **-ly** -li
Isocrates aɪˈsɒk.rə.tiːz (US) -ˈsɑː.krə-
isogloss ˈaɪ.səʊ.glɒs (US) -soʊ.glɑːs, -glɔːs **-es** -ɪz
isolate *(n.)* ˈaɪ.səl.ət, -ɪt, -eɪt (US) -sə- **-s** -s

iso|late (*v.*) ˈaɪ.sə l.leɪt **-lates** -leɪts **-lating** -leɪ.tɪŋ (US) -leɪ.t̬ɪŋ **-lated** -leɪ.tɪd (US) -leɪ.t̬ɪd **-lator/s** -leɪ.təʳ/z (US) -leɪ.t̬ɚ/z

isolation ˌaɪ.sᵊlˈeɪ.ʃᵊn

isolation|ism ˌaɪ.sᵊlˈeɪ.ʃᵊn l.ɪ.zᵊm **-ist/s** -ɪst/s

isolative ˈaɪ.sᵊl.ə.tɪv, -eɪ.tɪv (US) -sə.leɪ.t̬ɪv, -soʊ- **-ly** -li

Isolda ɪˈzɒl.də (US) -ˈsoʊl-, -ˈzoʊl-

Isolde ɪˈzɒl.də (US) -ˈsoʊl-, -ˈzoʊl-; -ˈsoʊld, -ˈzoʊld

isomer ˈaɪ.sə.məʳ (US) -soʊ.mɚ, -sə- **-s** -z

isomeric ˌaɪ.səʊˈmer.ɪk (US) -soʊˈ-, -səˈ-

isomer|ism aɪˈsɒm.ᵊr l.ɪ.zᵊm (US) -ˈsɑː.mɚ- **-ous** -əs

isometric ˌaɪ.səʊˈmet.rɪk (US) -soʊˈ-, -səˈ- **-al** -ᵊl **-ally** -ᵊl.i, -li

isomorph ˈaɪ.səʊ.mɔːf (US) -soʊ.mɔːrf, -sə- **-s** -s

isomorph|ism ˌaɪ.səʊˈmɔː.f l.ɪ.zᵊm (US) -soʊˈmɔːr- **-ic** -ɪk **-ous** -əs

ison ˈaɪ.sᵊn

isophone ˈaɪ.səʊ.fəʊn (US) -soʊ.foʊn, -sə- **-s** -z

isosceles aɪˈsɒs.ᵊl.iːz, -ɪ.liːz (US) -ˈsɑː.sᵊl.iːz

isotherm ˈaɪ.səʊ.θɜːm (US) -soʊ.θɝːm, -sə- **-s** -z

isothermal ˌaɪ.səˈθɜː.mᵊl (US) -ˈθɝː- **-ly** -i

isotonic ˌaɪ.səˈtɒn.ɪk (US) -ˈtɑː.nɪk

isotope ˈaɪ.sə.təʊp (US) -toʊp **-s** -s

isotopic ˌaɪ.səˈtɒp.ɪk (US) -ˈtɑː.pɪk **-ally** -ᵊl.i, -li

isotropic ˌaɪ.səˈtrɒp.ɪk (US) -ˈtrɑː.pɪk **-ally** -ᵊl.i, -li

isotropy aɪˈsɒt.rə.pi (US) -ˈsɑː.trə-

ISP ˌaɪ.esˈpiː

I-spy ˌaɪˈspaɪ

Israel ˈɪz.reɪəl, -ri.əl, -reɪ.el (US) -ri.əl, -reɪ-, -rᵊl

Israeli ɪzˈreɪ.li **-s** -z

Israelite ˈɪz.ri.ə.laɪt, -reɪ-, -rə.laɪt, -rɪ- (US) -ri.ə-, -reɪ- **-s** -s

Issachar ˈɪs.ə.kəʳ, -kɑːʳ (US) -kɑːr

iss|ue ˈɪʃ l.uː, ˈɪs.j luː (US) ˈɪʃ l.uː **-ues** -uːz **-uing** -uː.ɪŋ **-ued** -uːd **-uer/s** -uː.əʳ/z (US) -uː.ɚ/z **-uable** -u.ə.bl̩ **-uance** -u.ᵊnts

-ist -ɪst

Note: Suffix. When attached to a free stem, **-ist** does not normally affect the stress pattern of the stem, e.g. **modern** /ˈmɒd.ᵊn (US) ˈmɑː.dɚn/, **modernist** /ˈmɒd.ᵊn.ɪst (US) ˈmɑː.dɚ.nɪst/. When attached to a bound stem, the word is normally stressed on the penultimate syllable, e.g. **Baptist** /ˈbæp.tɪst/. Exceptions exist; see individual entries.

Istanbul ˌɪs.tænˈbʊl, -tɑːnˈ-, -tæmˈ-, -tɑːmˈ- (US) -tɑːnˈ-, -tænˈ-, -ˈbuːl

isthmi (*plur. of* **isthmus**) ˈɪs.maɪ, ˈɪsθ-, ˈɪst- (US) ˈɪs-

isthmian (I) ˈɪsθ.mi.ən, ˈɪst-, ˈɪs- (US) ˈɪs-

isthmus ˈɪs.məs, ˈɪsθ-, ˈɪst- (US) ˈɪs- **-es** -ɪz

-istic -ˈɪs.tɪk

Note: Suffix. Normally takes primary stress as shown, e.g. **impressionistic** /ɪmˌpreʃ.ᵊnˈɪs.tɪk/.

istle ˈɪst.li

Istria ˈɪs.tri.ə

it ɪt

IT ˌaɪˈtiː

Italian ɪˈtæl.i.ən (US) ˈ-jən **-s** -z

italianate ɪˈtæl.i.ə.neɪt, -nət, -nɪt (US) ˈ-jə.nɪt

italianism ɪˈtæl.i.ə.nɪ.zᵊm (US) ˈ-jə- **-s** -z

italianiz|e, -is|e ɪˈtæl.i.ə.naɪz (US) ˈ-jə- **-es** -ɪz **-ing** -ɪŋ **-ed** -d

italic (I) ɪˈtæl.ɪk **-s** -s

italicization, -isa- ɪˌtæl.ɪ.saɪˈzeɪ.ʃᵊn, ˌ-ə-, -sɪˈ- (US) -sɪˈ-

italiciz|e, -is|e ɪˈtæl.ɪ.saɪz, ˈ-ə- **-es** -ɪz **-ing** -ɪŋ **-ed** -d

Italy ˈɪt.ᵊl.i (US) ˈɪt̬-

itch ɪtʃ **-es** -ɪz **-ing** -ɪŋ **-ed** -t

Itchen ˈɪtʃ.ɪn, -ᵊn

itch|y ˈɪtʃ l.i **-ier** -i.əʳ (US) -i.ɚ **-iest** -i.ɪst, -i.əst **-iness** -ɪ.nəs, -ɪ.nɪs

it'd ˈɪt.əd (US) ˈɪt̬-

item ˈaɪ.təm, -tɪm, -tem (US) -t̬əm **-s** -z

itemiz|e, -is|e ˈaɪ.tə.maɪz, -tɪ- (US) -t̬ə- **-es** -ɪz **-ing** -ɪŋ **-ed** -d

iter|ate ˈɪt.ᵊr l.eɪt (US) ˈɪt̬.ə.r l eɪt **-ates** -eɪts **-ating** -eɪ.tɪŋ (US) -eɪ.t̬ɪŋ **-ated** -eɪ.tɪd (US) -eɪ.t̬ɪd

iteration ˌɪt.ᵊrˈeɪ.ʃᵊn (US) ˌɪt̬.əˈreɪ- **-s** -z

iterative ˈɪt.ᵊr.ə.tɪv, -eɪ- (US) ˈɪt̬.ə.reɪ.t̬ɪv, -ɚ.ə- **-ly** -li **-ness** -nəs, -nɪs

Ithaca ˈɪθ.ə.kə

itinerancy aɪˈtɪn.ᵊr.ᵊnt.si, ɪ-

itinerant aɪˈtɪn.ᵊr.ᵊnt, ɪ- **-s** -s

itinerar|y aɪˈtɪn.ᵊr.ᵊr l.i, ɪ- (US) -ə.rer- **-ies** -iz

itiner|ate aɪˈtɪn.ᵊr l.eɪt, ɪ- (US) -ə.r l eɪt **-ates** -eɪts **-ating** -eɪ.tɪŋ (US) -eɪ.t̬ɪŋ **-ated** -eɪ.tɪd (US) -eɪ.t̬ɪd

-ition -ˈɪʃ.ᵊn

Note: Suffix. Always stressed as shown, e.g. **edition** /ɪˈdɪʃ.ᵊn/.

-itious -ˈɪʃ.əs

Note: Suffix. Always stressed as shown, e.g. **surreptitious** /ˌsʌr.əpˈtɪʃ.əs (US) ˌsɜːr.əpˈ-/.

-itis -ˈaɪ.tɪs (US) -ˈaɪ.t̬ɪs, -t̬əs

Note: Suffix. Always stressed as shown, e.g. **tonsilitis** /ˌtɒnt.sᵊlˈaɪ.tɪs (US) ˌtɑːnt.səˈlaɪ.t̬ɪs/.

-itive -ɪ.tɪv, -ə- (US) -ə.t̬ɪv, -ɪ-

Note: Suffix. Words containing **-itive** are normally stressed on the antepenultimate syllable, e.g. **competitive** /kəmˈpet.ɪ.tɪv (US) -ə.t̬ɪv/. Exceptions exist; see individual entries.

it'll (= **it will, it shall**) ˈɪt.ᵊl (US) ˈɪt̬-

ITN ˌaɪ.tiːˈen

-itory -ə.tᵊr.i, -ɪ-, -tri (US) -ə.tɔːr.i, -ɪ-

Note: Suffix. Words containing **-itory** are normally stressed on the syllable preceding the prefix, e.g. **territory** /ˈter.ɪ.tᵊr.i (US) ˈter.ɪ.tɔːr.i/. Exceptions exist; see individual entries.

its ɪts

it's (= **it is, it has**) ɪts

itself ɪtˈself

itsy-bitsy ˌɪt.siˈbɪt.si

itty-bitty ˌɪt.iˈbɪt.i (US) ˌɪt̬.iˈbɪt̬-

ITV ˌaɪ.tiːˈviː

-ity -ə.ti, -ɪ.ti (US) -ə.t̬i

Note: Suffix. Words containing **-ity** are normally stressed on the antepenultimate syllable, e.g. **conformity** /kənˈfɔː.mə.ti (US) -ˈfɔːr.mə.t̬i/.

IUD ˌaɪ.juːˈdiː

Ivan ˈaɪ.vᵊn; (US) ˈaɪ.vən *foreign name:* iːˈvæn, ɪ-, -ˈvɑːn (US) -ˈvɑːn

Ivanhoe ˈaɪ.vᵊn.həʊ (US) -hoʊ

Ivanoff ɪˈvɑː.nəf, iː-, -nɒf (US) ˈiː.və.nɑːf; iːˈvɑː-

Ivanov ˈaɪ.və.nɒf, ɪˈvɑː.nɒf (US) iː.vəˈnɑːf, aɪ-

Ivatt ˈaɪ.vət, -væt **-s** -s

I've (= **I have**) aɪv

-ive -ɪv

Note: Suffix. Words containing **-ive** are either stressed on the penultimate syllable, e.g. **expensive** /ɪkˈspent.sɪv/, or on the antepenultimate syllable, e.g. **executive** /ɪɡˈzek.jə tɪv (US) -t̬ɪv/.

Iveagh ˈaɪ.və, -veɪ

Iveco® ɪˈveɪ.kəʊ, aɪˈ-, -ˈviː- (US) -ˈveɪ.koʊ

Ivens ˈaɪ.vᵊnz

Iver ˈaɪ.vəʳ (US) -vɚ

Ives *surname, and towns* **St. Ives** *in Cornwall and Cambridgeshire: aɪvz in Stevenson's 'St. Ives': iːvz*

Ivey ˈaɪ.vi

IVF ˌaɪ.viːˈef

Ivor ˈaɪ.vəʳ (US) -vɚ, ˈiː-

ivor|y (I) ˈaɪ.vᵊr l.i **-ies** -iz ˌ**Ivory** ˈ**Coast**; ˌ**ivory** ˈ**tower**

ivory-black ˌaɪ.vᵊr.iˈblæk

iv|y (I) ˈaɪ.v l i **-ies** -iz **-ied** -id ˈ**Ivy** ˌ**League**

Ivybridge ˈaɪ.vi.brɪdʒ

ixia ˈɪk.si.ə **-s** -z

Ixion ɪkˈsaɪən (US) -ˈsaɪən, -ˈsaɪ.ɑːn

Iza ˈaɪ.zə

Izaby 'ɪz.ə.bi
Izal® 'aɪ.zᵊl
izard 'ɪz.əd ⓤⓢ -ɚd **-s** -z
Izard 'aɪ.zɑːd, -zəd; 'ɪz.əd ⓤⓢ 'aɪ.zɑːrd, -zɚd; 'ɪz.ɚd
-ization -aɪ'zeɪ.ʃᵊn, -ɪ'- ⓤⓢ -ɪ'-
Note: Suffix. Words containing **-ization** always carry primary stress as shown above, e.g. **decimalization** /ˌdes.ɪ.mᵊl.aɪ'zeɪ.ʃᵊn ⓤⓢ -ɪ'-/.
-ize, -ise -aɪz
Note: Suffix. When attached to a free stem, **-ize** does not normally affect the stress pattern of the stem, e.g. **decimal** /'des.ɪ.mᵊl/, **decimalize** /'des.ɪ.mᵊl.aɪz ⓤⓢ -mə.laɪz/. When attached to a bound stem, the word is normally stressed on the antepenultimate syllable, e.g. **recognize** /'rek.əg.naɪz/. Exceptions exist; see individual entries.
Izmir 'ɪz.mɪəʳ, -'- ⓤⓢ ɪz'mɪr
Izzard 'ɪz.əd, -ɑːd ⓤⓢ -ɚd, -ɑːrd

Pronouncing the letter J

In general, the consonant letter **j** is pronounced /dʒ/, e.g.:

jam /dʒæm/
raj /rɑːdʒ/

(The latter can also be pronounced /rɑːʒ/ in British English.)

In some exceptional cases, **j** is pronounced /j/, e.g.:
hallelujah /ˌhæl.ɪˈluː.jə/

(J) dʒeɪ **-'s** -z
ab dʒæb **-s** -z **-bing** -ɪŋ **-bed** -d
abb|er ˈdʒæb|.ə^r (US) -ɚ **-ers** -əz (US) -ɚz **-ering** -^{ə}r.ɪŋ **-ered** -əd (US) -ɚd **-erer/s** -^{ə}r.ə^r/z (US) -ɚ.ɚ/z
abberwock ˈdʒæb.ə.wɒk (US) -ɚ.wɑːk **-y** -i
abberwocky (J) ˈdʒæb.ə.wɒk.i (US) -ɚ.wɑː.ki, -wɔː.ki
abez ˈdʒeɪ.bez, -bɪz
abiru ˌdʒæb.əˈruː, -ɪˈ-, ˈ--- (US) ˈdʒæb.ə.ruː, ˌ--ˈ- **-s** -z
aborandi ˌdʒæb.əˈræn.di, ˌʒæb-, -ɔːˈ-; -rænˈdiː (US) ˌdʒæb.əˈræn.di; -rænˈdiː
abot ˈʒæb.əʊ (US) ʒæbˈoʊ **-s** -z
acamar ˈdʒæk.ə.mɑː^r, ˈʒæk- (US) ˈdʒæk.ə.mɑːr **-s** -z
acaranda ˌdʒæk.əˈræn.də **-s** -z
acinta dʒəˈsɪn.tə, hə-
acinth (J) ˈdʒæs.ɪn*t*θ, ˈdʒeɪ.sɪn*t*θ **-s** -s
acintha dʒəˈsɪn*t*.θə, dʒæsˈɪn*t*-
ack (J) dʒæk **-s** -s **-ing** -ɪŋ **-ed** -t **ˌJack ˈFrost; ˌJack ˈRobinson; ˌJack ˈRussell; ˌjack ˈtar; ˌJack the ˈlad**
ackal ˈdʒæk.ɔːl, -^{ə}l (US) -^{ə}l **-s** -z
ackanapes ˈdʒæk.ə.neɪps **-es** -ɪz
ackaroo ˌdʒæk.^{ə}rˈuː (US) -əˈruː **-s** -z
ackass ˈdʒæk.æs **-es** -ɪz
ackboot ˈdʒæk.buːt **-s** -s **-ed** -ɪd
ackdaw ˈdʒæk.dɔː (US) -dɑː, -dɔː **-s** -z
ackeroo ˌdʒæk.^{ə}rˈuː (US) -əˈruː **-s** -z
ack|et ˈdʒæk|.ɪt **-ets** -ɪts **-eting** -ɪ.tɪŋ (US) -ɪ.t̬ɪŋ **-eted** -ɪ.tɪd (US) -ɪ.t̬ɪd
ackhammer ˈdʒækˌhæm.ə^r (US) -ɚ **-s** -z
ackie ˈdʒæk.i
ack-in-office ˈdʒæk.ɪnˌɒf.ɪs (US) -ˌɑː.fɪs **jacks-in-office** ˈdʒæks-
ack-in-the-box ˈdʒæk.ɪn.ðə.bɒks (US) -bɑːks **-es** -ɪz
ack-kni|fe (*n.*) ˈdʒæk.naɪ|f **-ves** -vz
ackknif|e (*v.*) ˈdʒæk.naɪf **-es** -s **-ing** -ɪŋ **-ed** -t
acklin ˈdʒæk.lɪn
acklyn ˈdʒæk.lɪn
ackman ˈdʒæk.mən
ack-of-all-trades ˌdʒæk.əvˈɔːl.treɪdz, -ɔːlˈtreɪdz (US) -ˈɔːl-, -ˈɑːl- **jacks-of-all-trades** ˌdʒæks-
ack-o'-lantern ˌdʒæk.əʊˈlæn.tən, ˈdʒæk.əʊˌlæn.tən (US) ˈdʒæk.əˌlæn.tɚn **-s** -z

jackpot ˈdʒæk.pɒt (US) -pɑːt **-s** -s **ˌhit the ˈjackpot**
jackrabbit ˈdʒækˌræb.ɪt **-s** -s
Jackson ˈdʒæk.s^{ə}n
Jacksonian ˌdʒækˈsəʊ.ni.ən (US) -ˈsoʊ-
Jacksonville ˈdʒæk.s^{ə}n.vɪl
jack-tar ˌdʒækˈtɑː^r, ˈ-- (US) ˌdʒækˈtɑːr, ˈ-- **-s** -z
Jacob ˈdʒeɪ.kəb **ˌJacob's ˈladder**
jacobean (J) ˌdʒæk.əʊˈbiː.ən (US) -əˈ-, -oʊˈ- **-s** -z
Jacobi ˈdʒæk.ə.bi; dʒəˈkəʊ- (US) -ˈkoʊ-
jacobian (J) dʒəˈkəʊ.bi.ən (US) -ˈkoʊ- **-s** -z
Jacobin ˈdʒæk.əʊ.bɪn (US) ˈ-ə- **-s** -z **-ism** -ɪ.z^{ə}m
Jacobit|e ˈdʒæk.əʊ.baɪt (US) ˈ-ə- **-es** -s **-ism** -ɪ.z^{ə}m
Jacobs ˈdʒeɪ.kəbz
Jacobson ˈdʒæk.əb.s^{ə}n, ˈjæk- (US) ˈdʒeɪ.kəb-
jacobus (J) dʒəˈkəʊ.bəs (US) -ˈkoʊ- **-es** -ɪz
Jacoby dʒəˈkəʊ.bi; ˈdʒæk.ə- (US) dʒəˈkoʊ-; ˈdʒæk.ə-
Jacquard ˈdʒæk.ɑːd, dʒəˈkɑːd (US) dʒəˈkɑːrd
Jacqueline ˈdʒæk.ə.liːn, ˈʒæk-, -lɪn; ˈdʒæk.liːn, -lɪn (US) ˈdʒæk.ə.lɪn, -liːn; ˈ-wə.lɪn
Jacques *English surname:* dʒeɪks, dʒæks *French name:* ʒæk (US) ʒɑːk
Jacqui ˈdʒæk.i
jactitation ˌdʒæk.tɪˈteɪ.ʃ^{ə}n **-s** -z
jacuzzi (J®) dʒəˈkuː.zi, dʒækˈuː- (US) dʒəˈkuː- **-s** -z
jad|e (J) dʒeɪd **-es** -z **-ing** -ɪŋ **-ed** -ɪd
jaeger (J®) ˈjeɪ.gə^r, ˈdʒeɪ- (US) -gɚ **-s** -z
Jael dʒeɪəl, dʒeɪl, ˈdʒeɪ.el (US) dʒeɪəl
Jaffa ˈdʒæf.ə (US) ˈdʒæf-, ˈdʒɑː.fə, ˈjɑː- **-s** -z
Jaffna ˈdʒæf.nə
Jaffrey ˈdʒæf.ri
jag dʒæg **-s** -z **-ging** -ɪŋ **-ged** -d
Jaggard ˈdʒæg.əd (US) -ɚd
jagged ˈdʒæg.ɪd **-ly** -li **-ness** -nəs, -nɪs
jagger (J) ˈdʒæg.ə^r (US) -ɚ **-s** -z
jagg|y ˈdʒæg|.i **-ier** -i.ə^r (US) -i.ɚ **-iest** -i.ɪst, -i.əst **-iness** -ɪ.nəs, -ɪ.nɪs
Jago ˈdʒeɪ.gəʊ (US) -goʊ
jaguar (J) ˈdʒæg.ju.ə^r (US) ˈdʒæg.wɑːr, ˈ-ju.ɑːr **-s** -z

Jah dʒɑː, jɑː
Jahveh ˈjɑː.veɪ, ˌjɑːˈveɪ, ˈdʒɑː.veɪ, ˈjɑː.və (US) ˈjɑː.veɪ
jai alai ˌhaɪ.əˈlaɪ, ˈ---, ˌhaɪˈlaɪ, ˈ-- (US) ˈhaɪˌlaɪ, -əˌlaɪ; ˌhaɪ.əˈlaɪ
jail dʒeɪl **-s** -z **-ing** -ɪŋ **-ed** -d
jailbait ˈdʒeɪl.beɪt
jailbird ˈdʒeɪl.bɜːd (US) -bɝːd **-s** -z
jailbreak ˈdʒeɪl.breɪk **-s** -s
jailer, jailor ˈdʒeɪ.lə^r (US) -lɚ **-s** -z
jailhou|se ˈdʒeɪl.haʊ|s **-ses** -zɪz
Jaime *English name:* ˈdʒeɪ.mi *Spanish name:* ˈhaɪ.mi
Jain dʒaɪn, dʒeɪn (US) dʒaɪn **-s** -z **-ism** -ɪ.z^{ə}m
Jaipur ˌdʒaɪˈpʊə^r, -ˈpɔː^r (US) -ˈpʊr
Jairus ˈdʒaɪə.rəs, dʒeɪˈaɪə- (US) ˈdʒaɪ-, dʒeɪˈaɪ-
Jaish-e-Mohamed dʒɑːˌiːʃ.ɪ.məʊˈhæm.ɪd, ˌ-eɪ-, -əd, -ɪd (US) dʒaɪ.iːʃ.ə.moʊˈhɑː.mɪd, -ˈhæm-
Jakarta dʒəˈkɑː.tə (US) -ˈkɑːr.t̬ə
Jake dʒeɪk
Jakes dʒeɪks
Jalalabad dʒəˈlɑː.lə.bɑːd, -ˈlæl.ə-, -bæd; dʒəˌlɑː.ləˈbɑːd, -ˌlæl.əˈ-, -ˈbæd
jalap ˈdʒæl.əp
jalapeño ˌhæl.əˈpeɪ.njəʊ (US) ˌhɑː.ləˈpeɪ.njoʊ, ˌhæl.əˈ- **-s** -z
Jalisco hɑːˈles.kəʊ (US) -ˈliːs.koʊ
jalop|y dʒəˈlɒp|.i (US) -ˈlɑː.p|i **-ies** -iz
jalousie ˈʒæl.u.ziː, ˌ--ˈ-, dʒəˈluː.si (US) ˈdʒæl.ə.si **-s** -z
jam dʒæm **-s** -z **-ming** -ɪŋ **-med** -d **ˈjam ˌjar; ˌjam ˈtart; ˈjam ˌsession**
Jam *Indian title:* dʒɑːm **-s** -z
Jamaic|a dʒəˈmeɪ.k|ə **-an/s** -ən/z
Jamal dʒəˈmɑːl
jamb dʒæm*b* **-s** -z
jambalaya ˌdʒæm.bəˈlaɪ.ə, ˌdʒʌm- **-s** -z
jamboree ˌdʒæm.b^{ə}rˈiː, ˈ--- (US) ˌdʒæm.bəˈriː **-s** -z
James dʒeɪmz
Jameson ˈdʒeɪm.s^{ə}n, ˈdʒɪm-, ˈdʒem-, ˈdʒæm-; ˈdʒeɪ.mɪ.s^{ə}n, ˈdʒɪm.ɪ-, ˈdʒem-, ˈdʒæm-, ˈ-ə- (US) ˈdʒeɪm.s^{ə}n; ˈdʒeɪ.mɪ-
James's ˈdʒeɪm.zɪz
Jamestown ˈdʒeɪmz.taʊn
Jamia ˈdʒʌm.i.ə, ˈdʒæm-

Jamie 'dʒeɪ.mi
Jamieson 'dʒeɪ.mɪ.sᵊn, 'dʒæm.ɪ-, 'dʒem-, 'dʒɪm-, '-ə- (US) 'dʒeɪ.mɪ-
jam-jar 'dʒæm.dʒɑːʳ (US) -dʒɑːr
Jammu 'dʒæm.uː, 'dʒʌm- (US) 'dʒʌm-
jamm|y 'dʒæm|.i **-ier** -i.əʳ (US) -i.ɚ **-iest** -i.ɪst, -i.əst **-iness** -ɪ.nəs, -ɪ.nɪs
jam-pot 'dʒæm.pɒt (US) -pɑːt **-s** -s
Jamy 'dʒeɪ.mi
Jan *female first name:* dʒæn *male first name:* jæn
Jan. *(abbrev. for* **January***)* dʒæn, 'dʒæn.ju.ᵊr.i, -jʊə.ri, -jʊ- (US) -ju.er.i
Jana 'dʒæn.ə, 'dʒeɪ.nə *as if Czech or Polish:* 'jɑː.nə (US) 'dʒæn.ə
Janácek 'jæn.ə.tʃek, '-ɑː- (US) 'jɑː.nə-
Jane dʒeɪn ˌ**Jane 'Doe**
Janeiro dʒə'nɪə.rəʊ, -'neə- (US) ʒə'ner.oʊ, dʒə-, -'nɪr-
Janet 'dʒæn.ɪt, -ət
jangl|e 'dʒæŋ.gl̩ **-es** -z **-ing** -ɪŋ, 'dʒæŋ.glɪŋ **-ed** -d **-er/s** -əʳ/z (US) -ɚ/z, 'dʒæŋ.gləʳ/z (US) -glɚ/z
Janice 'dʒæn.ɪs
Janine dʒə'niːn
janissar|y 'dʒæn.ɪ.sᵊr|.i (US) -ə.ser- **-ies** -iz
janitor 'dʒæn.ɪ.təʳ (US) -ə.t̬ɚ **-s** -z
Jan(n)ette dʒə'net, dzæn'et
Jansen 'dʒænt.sᵊn
Jansen|ism 'dʒænt.sᵊn|.ɪ.zᵊm **-ist/s** -ɪst/s
Jantzen® 'jænt.sᵊn, 'dʒænt- (US) 'dʒænt-
Januarius ˌdʒæn.ju'eə.ri.əs (US) -'er.i-
Januar|y 'dʒæn.ju.ᵊr|.i, -jʊə.r|i, -jʊ- (US) -ju.er|.i **-ies** -iz
Janus 'dʒeɪ.nəs
Jap dʒæp **-s** -s
Japan, japan dʒə'pæn **-s** -z **-ning** -ɪŋ **-ned** -d **-ner/s** -əʳ/z (US) -ɚ/z
Japanese ˌdʒæp.ᵊn'iːz (US) -'iːz, -'iːs
jap|e dʒeɪp **-es** -s **-ing** -ɪŋ **-ed** -t
Japhet 'dʒeɪ.fet, -fɪt
Japheth 'dʒeɪ.feθ, -fɪθ
japhetic dʒeɪ'fet.ɪk, dʒə- (US) dʒə'fet̬-
japonica dʒə'pɒn.ɪ.kə (US) -'pɑː.nɪ- **-s** -z
Jaques *name:* dʒeɪks, dʒæks *Shakespearian character:* 'dʒeɪ.kwɪz (US) -kwɪz, -kiːz; dʒeɪks, dʒæks
jar dʒɑːʳ (US) dʒɑːr **-s** -z **-ring/ly** -ɪŋ/li **-red** -d
Jardine 'dʒɑː.diːn, -'- (US) 'dʒɑːr.diːn, -'-
jardinière ˌʒɑː.dɪ.ni'eəʳ, ˌdʒɑː-, -dɪ'njeəʳ (US) ˌdʒɑːr.dᵊn'ɪr, ˌʒɑːr-, -'jer **-s** -z
Jared 'dʒær.əd (US) 'dʒer-, 'dʒær-
jarful 'dʒɑː.fʊl (US) 'dʒɑːr- **-s** -z
jargon 'dʒɑː.gən (US) 'dʒɑːr- **-s** -z
jargonelle ˌdʒɑː.gə'nel (US) ˌdʒɑːr- **-s** -z
Jarley 'dʒɑː.li (US) 'dʒɑːr-
Jarlsberg® 'jɑːlz.bɜːg (US) 'jɑːrlz.bɝːg
Jarlshof 'jɑːlz.hɒf (US) 'jɑːrlz.hɑːf
Jarmaine dʒɑː'meɪn (US) dʒɑːr-
Jarman 'dʒɑː.mən (US) 'dʒɑːr-
Jarndyce 'dʒɑːn.daɪs (US) 'dʒɑːrn-
Jarratt 'dʒær.ət (US) 'dʒer-, 'dʒær-
Jarrell dʒə'rel (US) dʒə'rel; 'dʒer.ᵊl, 'dʒær-
Jarrett 'dʒær.ət (US) 'dʒer-, 'dʒær-
Jarrod 'dʒær.əd (US) 'dʒer-, 'dʒær-
Jarrold 'dʒær.ᵊld (US) 'dʒer-, 'dʒær-
Jarrow 'dʒær.əʊ (US) 'dʒer.oʊ, 'dʒær-
Jarry 'ʒær.i (US) ʒɑː'riː
Jaruzelski ˌjær.u'zel.ski (US) ˌjɑː.ruː'-
jarvey 'dʒɑː.vi (US) 'dʒɑːr- **-s** -z
Jarvie 'dʒɑː.vi (US) 'dʒɑːr-
Jarvis 'dʒɑː.vɪs (US) 'dʒɑːr-
Jas. *(abbrev. for* **James***)* dʒeɪmz, dʒæs (US) dʒeɪmz
jasey 'dʒeɪ.zi **-s** -z
Jasher 'dʒæʃ.əʳ (US) -ɚ
jasmine (J) 'dʒæz.mɪn, 'dʒæs-
Jason 'dʒeɪ.sᵊn
jasper (J) 'dʒæs.pəʳ (US) 'dʒæs.pɚ **-s** -z
Jaspers 'jæs.pəz (US) 'jɑː.spɚz
Jassy 'dʒæs.i
jaundice 'dʒɔːn.dɪs (US) 'dʒɑːn-, 'dʒɔːn- **-d** -t
jaun|t dʒɔːn|t (US) dʒɑːn|t, dʒɔːn|t **-ts** -ts **-ting/ly** -tɪŋ/li (US) -t̬ɪŋ/li **-ted** -tɪd (US) -t̬ɪd
jaunt|y 'dʒɔːn.t|i (US) 'dʒɑːn.t̬|i, 'dʒɔːn- **-ier** -i.əʳ (US) -i.ɚ **-iest** -i.ɪst, -i.əst **-ily** -ɪ.li, -ᵊl.i **-iness** -ɪ.nəs, -ɪ.nɪs
Java 'dʒɑː.və (US) 'dʒɑː-, 'dʒæv.ə
Note: **Java coffee** is more likely to be /'dʒæv.ə/ in the US.
Javan *of Java:* 'dʒɑː.vᵊn (US) 'dʒɑː-, 'dʒæv.ᵊn *biblical name:* 'dʒeɪ.væn
Javanese ˌdʒɑː.vᵊn'iːz (US) -'iːz, -'iːs *stress shift:* ˌJavanese 'people
javelin (J) 'dʒæv.ᵊl.ɪn, -lɪn **-s** -z
jaw dʒɔː (US) dʒɑː, dʒɔː **-s** -z **-ing** -ɪŋ **-ed** -d
jawbone 'dʒɔː.bəʊn (US) 'dʒɑː.boʊn, 'dʒɔː- **-s** -z
jawboning 'dʒɔːˌbəʊ.nɪŋ (US) 'dʒɑːˌboʊ-, 'dʒɔː-
jawbreak|er 'dʒɔːˌbreɪ.k|ə (US) 'dʒɑːˌbreɪ.k|ɚ, 'dʒɔː- **-ers** -əz (US) -ɚz **-ing** -ɪŋ
jay (J) dʒeɪ **-s** -z
Jayne dʒeɪn
jaywalk 'dʒeɪ.wɔːk (US) -wɑːk, -wɔːk **-s** -s **-ing** -ɪŋ **-ed** -t **-er/s** -əʳ/z (US) -ɚ/z
jazz dʒæz **'jazz ˌband**
jazz|y 'dʒæz|.i **-ier** -i.əʳ (US) -i.ɚ **-iest** -i.ɪst, -i.əst **-ily** -ɪ.li, -ᵊl.i **-iness** -ɪ.nəs, -ɪ.nɪs
JCB ˌdʒeɪ.siː'biː
JD ˌdʒeɪ'diː
Jeakes dʒeɪks
jealous 'dʒel.əs **-ly** -li **-ness** -nəs, -nɪs
jealous|y 'dʒel.ə.s|i **-ies** -iz
Jean *female name:* dʒiːn *French name:* ʒɑ̃ːn (US) ʒɑ̃ːn
jean *cotton fabric:* dʒeɪn (US) dʒiːn
Jeanette dʒə'net, dʒɪ-
Jeanne *English name:* dʒiːn *French name:* ʒæn (US) ʒɑ̃ːn
Jeannie 'dʒiː.ni
jeans dʒiːnz
Jeavons 'dʒev.ᵊnz
Jebb dʒeb
Jebusite 'dʒeb.ju.zaɪt (US) -jə.saɪt **-s** -s
Jed dʒed
Jedburgh 'dʒed.bᵊr.ə (US) -bɝːg
Jeddah 'dʒed.ə
Jedediah ˌdʒed.ɪ'daɪ.ə
Jeep® dʒiːp **-s** -s
jeepers 'dʒiː.pəz (US) -pɚz
jeer dʒɪəʳ (US) dʒɪr **-s** -z **-ing/ly** -ɪŋ/li **-ed** -d **-er/s** -əʳ/z (US) -ɚ/z
Jeeves dʒiːvz
jeez dʒiːz
Jeff dʒef
Jefferies 'dʒef.riz
Jeffers 'dʒef.əz (US) -ɚz
Jefferson 'dʒef.ə.sᵊn (US) '-ɚ-
Jeffersonian ˌdʒef.ə'səʊ.ni.ən (US) -ɚ'soʊ-
Jeffery 'dʒef.ri **-s** -z
Jeffrey 'dʒef.ri **-s** -z
Jeffries 'dʒef.riz
Jehoiachin dʒɪ'hɔɪ.ə.kɪn, dʒə-
Jehoiakim dʒɪ'hɔɪ.ə.kɪm, dʒə-
Jehoram dʒɪ'hɔː.rəm, dʒə-, -ræm (US) -'hɔːr.əm, -æm
Jehoshaphat dʒɪ'hɒʃ.ə.fæt, dʒə-, -'hɒs- (US) -'hɑː.ʃə-, -sə-
Jehovah dʒɪ'həʊ.və, dʒə- (US) -'hoʊ- **Jeˌhovah's 'witness**
jehu (J) 'dʒiː.hjuː (US) -hjuː, -huː **-s** -z
jejune dʒɪ'dʒuːn, dʒə- **-ly** -li **-ness** -nəs, -nɪs
jejunum dʒɪ'dʒuː.nəm, dʒə- **-s** -z
Jekyll 'dʒek.ᵊl, -ɪl, 'dʒiː.kɪl
jell dʒel **-s** -z **-ing** -ɪŋ **-ed** -d
jellaba(h) 'dʒel.ə.bə **-s** -z
Jellicoe 'dʒel.ɪ.kəʊ (US) -koʊ
jello 'dʒel.əʊ (US) -oʊ **-s** -z
Jell-O® 'dʒel.əʊ (US) -oʊ
jell|y 'dʒel|.i **-ies** -iz **-ying** -i.ɪŋ **-ied** -id **'jelly ˌbag; 'jelly ˌbaby, ˌjelly 'baby; 'jelly ˌbean**
jellyfish 'dʒel.i.fɪʃ **-es** -ɪz
jellygraph 'dʒel.i.grɑːf, -græf (US) -græf **-s** -s **-ing** -ɪŋ **-ed** -t
jellyroll 'dʒel.i.rəʊl (US) -roʊl **-s** -z
Jemima dʒɪ'maɪ.mə, dʒə-
Jemma 'dʒem.ə
jemm|y 'dʒem|.i **-ies** -iz **-ying** -i.ɪŋ **-ied** -id

Jena ˈjeɪ.nə US -nɑː
Je ne sais quoi ˌʒə.nə.seɪˈkwɑː US -seɪˈ-, -seˈ-
Jenkin ˈdʒeŋ.kɪn **-s** -z
Jenkinson ˈdʒeŋ.kɪn.sᵊn
Jenna ˈdʒen.ə
Jenner ˈdʒen.əʳ US -ɚ
Jennet ˈdʒen.ɪt **-s** -s
Jennifer ˈdʒen.ɪ.fəʳ, ˈ-ə- US -fɚ
Jennings ˈdʒen.ɪŋz
Jenny *female name:* ˈdʒen.i, ˈdʒɪn- US ˈdʒen-
jenn|y *in machinery:* ˈdʒen|.i *in billiards:* ˈdʒɪn|.i, ˈdʒen- **-ies** -iz
Jensen ˈdʒent.sᵊn **-s** -z
jeopardiz|e, -is|e ˈdʒep.ə.daɪz US ˈ-ɚ- **-es** -ɪz **-ing** -ɪŋ **-ed** -d
jeopardy ˈdʒep.ə.di US ˈ-ɚ-
Jephthah ˈdʒef.θə
jerboa dʒɜːˈbəʊ.ə, dʒə- US dʒɚˈboʊ- **-s** -z
jeremiad ˌdʒer.ɪˈmaɪ.əd, -əˈ-, -æd US -əˈ- **-s** -z
Jeremiah ˌdʒer.ɪˈmaɪ.ə, -əˈ- US -əˈ-
Jeremy ˈdʒer.ə.mi, ˈ-ɪ-
Jerez həˈrez *as if Spanish:* herˈeθ US -ˈres, -ˈreθ
Jericho ˈdʒer.ɪ.kəʊ US -koʊ
jerk dʒɜːk US dʒɝːk **-s** -s **-ing** -ɪŋ **-ed** -t
jerkin ˈdʒɜː.kɪn US ˈdʒɝː- **-s** -z
jerkwater ˈdʒɜːkˌwɔː.təʳ US ˈdʒɝːkˌwɑː.t̬ɚ, -ˌwɔː- ˈ**jerkwater** ˌ**town**
jerk|y ˈdʒɜː.k|i US ˈdʒɝː- **-ier** -i.əʳ US -i.ɚ **-iest** -i.ɪst, -i.əst **-ily** -ɪ.li, -ᵊl.i **-iness** -ɪ.nəs, -ɪ.nɪs
Jermaine dʒɜːˈmeɪn, dʒə-, dʒɜːr- US dʒɚ-
Jermyn ˈdʒɜː.mɪn US ˈdʒɝː-
Jeroboam (J) ˌdʒer.əˈbəʊ.əm US -ˈboʊ- **-s** -z
Jerome *Saint:* dʒəˈrəʊm, dʒerˈəʊm, dʒɪˈrəʊm US dʒəˈroʊm, dʒerˈoʊm, dʒɪˈroʊm *surname:* dʒəˈrəʊm, dʒerˈəʊm, dʒɪˈrəʊm, ˈdʒer.əm US dʒəˈroʊm, dʒerˈoʊm, dʒɪˈroʊm, ˈdʒer.əm
Note: Jerome K. Jerome, the author, is pronounced /dʒəˈrəʊm US -roʊm/.
Jerram ˈdʒer.əm
Jerrold ˈdʒer.ᵊld
jerr|y (J) ˈdʒer|.i **-ies** -iz ˈ**jerry** ˌ**can**
jerry-build ˈdʒer.i.bɪld **-s** -z **-ing** -ɪŋ **jerry-built** ˈdʒer.i.bɪlt **jerry-builder/s** ˈdʒer.iˌbɪl.dəʳ/z US -dɚ/z
jersey (J) ˈdʒɜː.zi US ˈdʒɝː- **-s** -z
Jerusalem dʒəˈruː.sᵊl.əm, dʒɪ-, -lem **Je**ˌ**rusalem** ˈ**artichoke**
Jervaulx ˈdʒɜː.vəʊ, ˈdʒɑː-, -vɪs, -vəs US ˈdʒɝː.voʊ, -vɪs, -vəs
Jervis ˈdʒɑː.vɪs, ˈdʒɜː.vɪs US ˈdʒɝː-
Jervois ˈdʒɜː.vɪs US ˈdʒɝː-
Jespersen ˈjes.pə.sᵊn US -pɚ-
jess (J) dʒes **-es** -ɪz **-ing** -ɪŋ **-ed** -t
jessamine (J) ˈdʒes.ə.mɪn
Jesse ˈdʒes.i
Jessel ˈdʒes.ᵊl
Jessica ˈdʒes.ɪ.kə
Jessie ˈdʒes.i
Jessop ˈdʒes.əp
jest dʒest **-s** -s **-ing/ly** -ɪŋ/li **-ed** -ɪd
jester ˈdʒes.təʳ US -tɚ **-s** -z
Jesu ˈdʒiː.zjuː US ˈdʒiː.zjuː, ˈdʒeɪ-, ˈjeɪ-, -suː, -zuː
Jesu|it ˈdʒez.ju|.ɪt, ˈ-u-, ˈdʒeʒ.u|.ɪt **-its** -ɪts **-itism** -ɪ.tɪ.zᵊm US -ɪ.t̬ɪ-
jesuitic ˌdʒez.juˈɪt.ɪk, -uˈ-, ˌdʒeʒ.uˈ- US -ˈɪt- **-al** -ᵊl **-ally** -ᵊl.i, -li
Jesus ˈdʒiː.zəs ˌ**Jesus** ˈ**Christ**
jet dʒet **-s** -s **-ting** -ɪŋ US ˈdʒet̬.ɪŋ **-ted** -ɪd US ˈdʒet̬.ɪd ˌ**jet** ˈ**engine**; ˈ**jet** ˌ**lag**; ˈ**jet** ˌ**set**; ˈ**jet** ˌ**setter**; ˈ**jet** ˌ**stream**
jeté ʒəˈteɪ **-s** -z
jetfoil ˈdʒet.fɔɪl **-s** -z
Jethro ˈdʒeθ.rəʊ US -roʊ
jetliner ˈdʒetˌlaɪ.nəʳ US -nɚ **-s** -z
jetsam ˈdʒet.səm, -sæm US -səm
jettison ˈdʒet.ɪ.sᵊn, -zᵊn US ˈdʒet̬.ə- **-s** -z **-ing** -ɪŋ **-ed** -d
jett|y ˈdʒet|.i US ˈdʒet̬- **-ies** -iz
Jetway® ˈdʒet.weɪ
jeu ʒɜː **-s** -z
jeunesse dorée ˌʒɜː.nes.dɔːˈreɪ US ʒɜːˌnes.dɔːˈ-
Jevons ˈdʒev.ᵊnz
Jew dʒuː **-s** -z ˌ**Jew's** ˈ**harp** US ˈ**Jew's** ˌ**harp**
jewel (J) ˈdʒuː.əl, dʒʊəl US ˈdʒuː.əl **-s** -z **-(l)ing** -ɪŋ **-(l)ed** -d
Jewell ˈdʒuː.əl, dʒʊəl US ˈdʒuː.əl
jewel(l)er ˈdʒuː.ə.ləʳ, ˈdʒʊə.ləʳ US ˈdʒuː.ə.lɚ, ˈdʒuː.lɚ **-s** -z
jewellery, jewelry ˈdʒuː.əl.ri, ˈdʒʊəl- US ˈdʒuː.əl-
Jewess ˈdʒuː.es, -ɪs, -əs; dʒuːˈes US ˈdʒuː.ɪs **-es** -ɪz
Jewett ˈdʒuː.ɪt
Jewish ˈdʒuː.ɪʃ **-ness** -nəs, -nɪs
Jewry ˈdʒʊə.ri, ˈdʒuː- US ˈdʒuː.ri
Jewsbury ˈdʒuːz.bᵊr.i US -ˌber-
Jeyes dʒeɪz
Jezebel ˈdʒez.ə.bel, ˈ-ɪ-, -bᵊl
Jezreel ˈdʒez.ri.əl, ˌdʒezˈriːl
Jhabvala ˌdʒɑːbˈvɑː.lə
Jiang Qing ˌdʒæŋˈtʃɪŋ
jiao dʒaʊ
jib dʒɪb **-s** -z **-bing** -ɪŋ **-bed** -d
jib-boom dʒɪbˈbuːm, ˈ-- **-s** -z
jib|e dʒaɪb **-es** -z **-ing** -ɪŋ **-ed** -d **-er/s** -əʳ/z US -ɚ/z
Jif® dʒɪf
jiff dʒɪf
jiff|y ˈdʒɪf|.i **-ies** -iz ˈ**Jiffy** ˌ**bag®**
jig dʒɪg **-s** -z **-ging** -ɪŋ **-ged** -d
jigger ˈdʒɪg.əʳ US -ɚ **-s** -z **-ing** -ɪŋ **-ed** -d
jiggered ˈdʒɪg.əd US -ɚd
jiggery-pokery ˌdʒɪg.ᵊr.iˈpəʊ.kᵊr.i US -ˈpoʊ-
jiggl|e ˈdʒɪg.l̩ **-es** -z **-ing** -ɪŋ, ˈdʒɪg.lɪŋ **-ed** -d
jigsaw ˈdʒɪg.sɔː US -sɑː, -sɔː **-s** -z ˈ**jigsaw** ˌ**puzzle**
jihad dʒɪˈhæd, dʒə-, -ˈhɑːd US dʒɪˈhɑːd, dʒiː-
Jill dʒɪl
jillaroo ˌdʒɪl.əˈruː **-s** -z
Jillian ˈdʒɪl.i.ən
jilt dʒɪlt **-s** -s **-ing** -ɪŋ US ˈdʒɪl.t̬ɪŋ **-ed** -ɪd US ˈdʒɪl.t̬ɪd
Jim dʒɪm **-my** -i
jim-dandy ˌdʒɪmˈdæn.di
jimjams ˈdʒɪm.dʒæmz
jimm|y (J) ˈdʒɪm.i **-ies** -iz **-ying** -i.ɪŋ **-ied**-id
jimsonweed ˈdʒɪmp.sᵊn.wiːd
jingl|e (J) ˈdʒɪŋ.gl̩ **-es** -z **-ing** -ɪŋ, ˈdʒɪŋ.glɪŋ **-ed** -d **-y** -i **-er/s** -əʳ/z US -ɚ/z
jingo (J) ˈdʒɪŋ.gəʊ US -goʊ **-es** -z
jingo|ism ˈdʒɪŋ.gəʊ|.ɪ.zᵊm US -goʊ- **-ist/s** -ɪst/s
jingoistic ˌdʒɪŋ.gəʊˈɪs.tɪk US -goʊˈ- **-ally** -ᵊl.i, -li
jink dʒɪŋk **-s** -s **-ing** -ɪŋ **-ed** -t
jinks (J) dʒɪŋks
jinn dʒɪn **-s** -z
Jinnah ˈdʒɪn.ə
jinrick|sha ˌdʒɪnˈrɪk|.ʃə US -ʃɑː, -ʃɔː **-shas** -ʃəz US -ʃɑːz, -ʃɔːz **-shaw/s** -ʃɔː/z US -ʃɑː/z, -ʃɔː/z
jinx dʒɪŋks **-es** -ɪz **-ing** -ɪŋ **-ed** -t
jitney ˈdʒɪt.ni **-s** -z
jitter ˈdʒɪt.əʳ US ˈdʒɪt̬.ɚ **-s** -z **-ing** -ɪŋ **-ed** -d
jitterbug ˈdʒɪt.ə.bʌg US ˈdʒɪt̬.ɚ- **-s** -z **-ging** -ɪŋ **-ged** -d
jitters ˈdʒɪt.əz US ˈdʒɪt̬.ɚz
jitter|y ˈdʒɪt.ᵊr|.i US ˈdʒɪt̬- **-iness** -ɪ.nəs, -ɪ.nɪs
jiujitsu ˌdʒjuːˈdʒɪt.suː
jiv|e dʒaɪv **-es** -z **-ing** -ɪŋ **-ed** -d
jnr (J) *(abbrev. for* **junior***)* ˈdʒuː.ni.əʳ US ˈ-njɚ
jo (J) dʒəʊ US dʒoʊ **-es** -z
Joab ˈdʒəʊ.æb US ˈdʒoʊ-
Joachim ˈjəʊ.ə.kɪm US ˈjoʊ-
Joan dʒəʊn US dʒoʊn
Joanna dʒəʊˈæn.ə US dʒoʊ-
Joanne dʒəʊˈæn US dʒoʊ-
Joash ˈdʒəʊ.æʃ US ˈdʒoʊ-
job dʒɒb US dʒɑːb **-s** -z **-bing** -ɪŋ **-bed** -d ˈ**Job** ˌ**Centre**; ˈ**job des**ˌ**cription**, ˌ**job des**ˈ**cription**; ˌ**job** ˈ**lot** US ˈ**job** ˌ**lot**; ˈ**job** ˌ**share**; ˌ**give something** ˌ**up as a** ˌ**bad** ˈ**job**;
Job dʒəʊb US dʒoʊb
jobber ˈdʒɒb.əʳ US ˈdʒɑː.bɚ **-s** -z

jobbery ˈdʒɒb.ᵊr.i (US) ˈdʒɑː.bɚ-
job-hop ˈdʒɒb.hɒp (US) ˈdʒɑːb.hɑːp **-s** -s **-ping** -ɪŋ **-ped** -t **-per/s** -əʳ/z (US) -ɚ/z
jobhunting ˈdʒɒbˌhʌn.tɪŋ (US) ˈdʒɑːbˌhʌn.t̬ɪŋ
jobless ˈdʒɒb.ləs, -lɪs (US) ˈdʒɑːb- **-ness** -nəs, -nɪs
jobmaster ˈdʒɒbˌmɑː.stəʳ (US) ˈdʒɑːbˌmæs.tɚ **-s** -z
jobseeker ˈdʒɒbˌsiː.kəʳ, ˈdʒɑːbˌsiː.kɚ **-s** -z
jobsharing ˈdʒɒbˌʃeə.rɪŋ (US) ˈdʒɑːbˌʃer.ɪŋ
Jobson ˈdʒɒb.sᵊn, ˈdʒəʊb- (US) ˈdʒɑːb-, ˈdʒoʊb-
Jocasta dʒəʊˈkæs.tə (US) dʒoʊ-
Jocelyn ˈdʒɒs.lɪn, ˈ-ᵊl.ɪn (US) ˈdʒɑː.sᵊl.ɪn, ˈ-slɪn
jock (J) dʒɒk (US) dʒɑːk
jockey ˈdʒɒk.i (US) ˈdʒɑː.ki **-s** -z **-ing** -ɪŋ **-ed** -d **-ship** -ʃɪp **ˈJockey ˌClub**
jockstrap ˈdʒɒk.stræp (US) ˈdʒɑːk- **-s** -s
jocose dʒəʊˈkəʊs (US) dʒoʊˈkoʊs **-ly** -li **-ness** -nəs, -nɪs
jocosity dʒəʊˈkɒs.ə.ti, -ɪ.ti (US) dʒoʊˈkɑː.sə.t̬i
jocular ˈdʒɒk.jə.ləʳ, -jʊ- (US) ˈdʒɑː.kjə.lɚ **-ly** -li
jocularity ˌdʒɒk.jəˈlær.ə.ti, -jʊˈ-, -ɪ.ti (US) ˌdʒɑː.kjəˈler.ə.t̬i, -ˈlær-
jocund ˈdʒɒk.ənd, ˈdʒəʊ.kənd, -kʌnd (US) ˈdʒɑː.kənd, ˈdʒoʊ- **-ly** -li **-ness** -nəs, -nɪs
jocundity dʒəʊˈkʌn.də.ti, dʒɒkˈʌn-, -dɪ- (US) dʒoʊˈkʌn.də.t̬i
jod jɒd (US) jɑːd *as if Hebrew:* jʊd **-s** -z
jodhpurs ˈdʒɒd.pəz, -pɜːz (US) ˈdʒɑːd.pɚz
Jodi ˈdʒəʊ.di (US) ˈdʒoʊ-
Jodie ˈdʒəʊ.di (US) ˈdʒoʊ-
Jodrell ˈdʒɒd.rᵊl (US) ˈdʒɑː.drᵊl **ˌJodrell ˈBank**
Jody ˈdʒəʊ.di (US) ˈdʒoʊ-
Joe dʒəʊ (US) dʒoʊ **ˌJoe ˈBloggs**; **ˌJoe ˈBlow**; **ˌJoe ˈPublic**
Joel ˈdʒəʊ.əl, -el (US) ˈdʒoʊ-
Joely ˈdʒəʊ.li, ˈdʒəʊ.ə.li (US) ˈdʒoʊ-
joey (J) ˈdʒəʊ.i (US) ˈdʒoʊ- **-s** -z
Joffe ˈdʒɒf.i (US) ˈdʒɑː.fi
jog dʒɒg (US) dʒɑːg **-s** -z **-ging** -ɪŋ **-ged** -d **-ger/s** -əʳ/z (US) -ɚ/z **ˈjog ˌtrot**
joggl|e ˈdʒɒg.l̩ (US) ˈdʒɑː.gl̩ **-es** -z **-ing** -ɪŋ, ˈdʒɒg.lɪŋ (US) ˈdʒɑː.glɪŋ **-ed** -d **-er/s** -əʳ/z (US) -ɚ/z
johannes *coin:* dʒəʊˈæn.ɪs (US) dʒoʊˈhæn.iːz **-es** -ɪz
Johannes *personal name:* jəʊˈhæn.ɪs (US) joʊˈhɑː.nɪs
Johannesburg dʒəʊˈhæn.ɪs.bɜːg, -ɪz-, -əs-, -əz- (US) dʒoʊˈhæn.ɪs.bɝːg, joʊˈhɑː.nɪs-
Note: There exists also a local pronunciation /dʒəˈhɒn.ɪs.bɜːg/, which is used by many English-speaking South Africans.
Johannine dʒəʊˈhæn.aɪn (US) dʒoʊˈhæn.ɪn, -aɪn
Johannisburger jəʊˈhæn.ɪsˌbɜː.gəʳ, -ɪz-, -əs-, -əz- (US) dʒoʊˈhæn.ɪsˌbɝː.gɚ, joʊˈhɑː.nɪs-
john (J) dʒɒn (US) dʒɑːn **-s** -z **ˌJohn ˈBull**; **ˌJohn ˈDoe**; **ˌJohn ˈDory**
Johnes dʒəʊnz, dʒɒnz (US) dʒoʊnz, dʒɑːnz
Johnian ˈdʒəʊ.ni.ən (US) ˈdʒoʊ- **-s** -z
johnn|y (J) ˈdʒɒn|.i (US) ˈdʒɑː.n|i **-ies** -iz
Johnny-come-latel|y ˌdʒɒn.i.kʌmˈleɪt.l|i (US) ˌdʒɑː.ni- **-ies** -z
John o' Groat's ˌdʒɒn.əˈgrəʊts (US) ˌdʒɑːn.əˈgroʊts
Johns dʒɒnz (US) dʒɑːnz
Johnson ˈdʒɒn*t*.sᵊn (US) ˈdʒɑːn*t*-
Johnsonese ˌdʒɒn*t*.sᵊnˈiːz (US) ˌdʒɑːn*t*-
Johnsonian dʒɒnˈsəʊ.ni.ən (US) dʒɑːnˈsoʊ-
Johnston(e) ˈdʒɒn*t*.stᵊn, -sᵊn (US) ˈdʒɑːn*t*-
Johore dʒəʊˈhɔːʳ (US) dʒəˈhɔːr
Johor(e) Baharu ˌdʒəʊ.hɔːˈbɑː.ruː (US) dʒəˌhɔːrˈbɑːr.uː
joie de vivre ˌʒwɑː.dəˈviː.vrə, -ˈviːv
join dʒɔɪn **-s** -z **-ing** -ɪŋ **-ed** -d
joinder ˈdʒɔɪn.dəʳ (US) -dɚ
joiner ˈdʒɔɪ.nəʳ (US) -nɚ **-s** -z
joinery ˈdʒɔɪ.nᵊr.i
joint dʒɔɪnt **-s** -s **-ly** -li **-ing** -ɪŋ (US) ˈdʒɔɪn.t̬ɪŋ **-ed** -ɪd (US) ˈdʒɔɪn.t̬ɪd **-er/s** -əʳ/z (US) ˈdʒɔɪn.t̬ɚ/z
joint-stock ˌdʒɔɪntˈstɒk (US) -ˈstɑːk *stress shift:* ˌjoint-stock ˈbank
jointure ˈdʒɔɪn.tʃəʳ (US) -tʃɚ **-s** -z
Joinville ˈʒwæ̃*n*.viːl (US) -ˈ-
joist dʒɔɪst **-s** -s
jojoba həʊˈhəʊ.bə (US) hoʊˈhoʊ-, hə-
jok|e dʒəʊk (US) dʒoʊk **-es** -s **-ing/ly** -ɪŋ/li **-ed** -t **-(e)y** -i
joker ˈdʒəʊ.kəʳ (US) ˈdʒoʊ.kɚ **-s** -z
Jolie ˈdʒəʊ.li, dʒəʊˈliː, ʒəʊ-
Jolley ˈdʒɒl.i (US) ˈdʒɑː.li
Jolliffe ˈdʒɒl.ɪf (US) ˈdʒɑː.lɪf
jollification ˌdʒɒl.ɪ.fɪˈkeɪ.ʃᵊn, ˌ-ə- (US) ˌdʒɑː.lə- **-s** -z
jolli|fy ˈdʒɒl.ɪ|.faɪ (US) ˈdʒɑː.lɪ- **-fies** -faɪz **-fying** -faɪ.ɪŋ **-fied** -faɪd
jollit|y ˈdʒɒl.ə.t|i, -ɪ.t|i (US) ˈdʒɑː.lə.t̬|i **-ies** -iz
joll|y (J) ˈdʒɒl|.i (US) ˈdʒɑː.l|i **-ier** -i.əʳ (US) -i.ɚ **-iest** -i.ɪst, -i.əst **-ily** -ɪ.li, -ᵊl.i **-iness** -ɪ.nəs, -ɪ.nɪs **-ies** -ɪz **-ying** -i.ɪŋ **-ied** -ɪd **ˌJolly ˈRoger**
jollyboat ˈdʒɒl.i.bəʊt (US) ˈdʒɑː.li.boʊt **-s** -s
Jolson ˈdʒɒl.sᵊn, ˈdʒəʊl- (US) ˈdʒoʊl-
jolt dʒəʊlt (US) dʒoʊlt **-s** -s **-ing/ly** -ɪŋ/li (US) ˈdʒoʊl.t̬ɪŋ/li **-ed** -ɪd (US) ˈdʒoʊl.t̬ɪ
jolt|y ˈdʒəʊl.t|i (US) ˈdʒoʊl.t̬|i **-ier** -i.əʳ (US) -i.ɚ **-iest** -i.ɪst, -i.əst **-ily** -ɪ.li, -ᵊl. **-iness** -ɪ.nəs, -ɪ.nɪs
Jolyon ˈdʒəʊ.li.ən, ˈdʒɒl.i- (US) ˈdʒoʊ.li-, ˈdʒɑː-
Jon dʒɒn (US) dʒɑːn
Jonah ˈdʒəʊ.nə (US) ˈdʒoʊ-
Jonas ˈdʒəʊ.nəs, -næs (US) ˈdʒoʊ.nəs
Jonathan, Jonathon ˈdʒɒn.ə.θᵊn (US) ˈdʒɑː.nə-
Jones dʒəʊnz (US) dʒoʊnz
Jonesboro ˈdʒəʊnz.bᵊr.ə (US) ˈdʒoʊnz.bɚ.oʊ
jongleur ʒɔ̃ː*ŋ*ˈglɜːʳ, ʒɔːŋ-, ʒɒŋ- (US) ˈdʒɑːŋ.glɚ **-s** -z
jonquil ˈdʒɒŋ.kwɪl, -kwᵊl (US) ˈdʒɑːŋ.kwɪl, ˈdʒɑːn- **-s** -z
Jonson ˈdʒɒn*t*.sᵊn (US) ˈdʒɑːn*t*-
Jonty ˈdʒɒn.ti (US) ˈdʒɑːn-
Joplin ˈdʒɒp.lɪn (US) ˈdʒɑːp-
Joppa ˈdʒɒp.ə (US) ˈdʒɑː.pə
Jopson ˈdʒɒp.sᵊn (US) ˈdʒɑːp-
Joram ˈdʒɔː.rəm, -ræm (US) ˈdʒɔːr.əm
Jordan ˈdʒɔː.dᵊn (US) ˈdʒɔːr- **-s** -z
Jordanian dʒɔːˈdeɪ.ni.ən (US) dʒɔːr- **-s** -
Jorge dʒɔːdʒ *as if Spanish:* ˈhɔː.heɪ, ˈxɔː.xeɪ (US) ˈhɔːr.heɪ
jorum ˈdʒɔː.rəm (US) ˈdʒɔːr.əm, ˈdʒoʊ.rəm **-s** -z
Josceline ˈdʒɒs.lɪn, ˈ-ᵊl.ɪn (US) ˈdʒɑː.sᵊl.ɪn, ˈ-slɪn
José, Jose həʊˈzeɪ, -ˈseɪ (US) hoʊ-
joseph (J) ˈdʒəʊ.zɪf, -zəf (US) ˈdʒoʊ- **-s** -s
Josephine ˈdʒəʊ.zə.fiːn, -zɪ- (US) ˈdʒoʊ-
Josephus dʒəʊˈsiː.fəs (US) dʒoʊ-
josh (J) dʒɒʃ (US) dʒɑːʃ **-es** -ɪz **-ing/ly** -ɪŋ/li **-ed** -t **-er/s** -əʳ/z (US) -ɚ/z
Joshua ˈdʒɒʃ.ju.ə, ˈ-u- (US) ˈdʒɑːʃ-
Josiah dʒəʊˈsaɪ.ə, -ˈzaɪ- (US) dʒoʊ-
Josias dʒəʊˈsaɪ.əs, -ˈzaɪ- (US) dʒoʊ-
Josie ˈdʒəʊ.zi, -si (US) ˈdʒoʊ-
Jospin ˈʒɒs.pæ̃, -ˈ-, dʒɑːsˈpæ̃*n*
joss dʒɒs (US) dʒɑːs **-es** -ɪz **ˈjoss ˌhouse**; **ˈjoss ˌstick**
Jost jəʊst (US) joʊst
jostl|e ˈdʒɒs.l̩ (US) ˈdʒɑː.sl̩ **-es** -z **-ing** -ɪŋ ˈdʒɒs.lɪŋ (US) ˈdʒɑː.slɪŋ **-ed** -d **-er/s** -əʳ/z (US) -ɚ/z
jot dʒɒt (US) dʒɑːt **-s** -s **-ting/s** -ɪŋ/z (US) ˈdʒɑː.t̬ɪŋ/z **-ted** -ɪd (US) ˈdʒɑː.t̬ɪd
jotter ˈdʒɒt.əʳ (US) ˈdʒɑː.t̬ɚ **-s** -z
joule *unit of energy:* dʒuːl, dʒaʊl **-s** -z
Joule *English surname:* dʒuːl, dʒəʊl, dʒaʊl (US) dʒuːl, dʒoʊl, dʒaʊl
jounc|e dʒaʊn*t*s **-es** -ɪz **-ing** -ɪŋ **-ed** -t
journal ˈdʒɜː.nᵊl (US) ˈdʒɝː- **-s** -z

ournalese ˌdʒɜː.nəlˈiːz ⓤⓢ ˌdʒɝː-
ournal|ism ˈdʒɜː.nəl|.ɪ.zəm ⓤⓢ ˈdʒɝː- -ist/s -ɪst/s
ournalistic ˌdʒɜː.nəlˈɪs.tɪk ⓤⓢ ˌdʒɝː- -ally -əl.i, -li
ournaliz|e, -is|e ˈdʒɜː.nəl.aɪz ⓤⓢ ˈdʒɝː- -es -ɪz -ing -ɪŋ -ed -d
ourney ˈdʒɜː.ni ⓤⓢ ˈdʒɝː- -s -z -ing/s -ɪŋ/z -ed -d
ourney|man ˈdʒɜː.ni|.mən ⓤⓢ ˈdʒɝː- -men -mən
oust dʒaʊst -s -s -ing -ɪŋ -ed -ɪd -er/s -əʳ/z ⓤⓢ -ɚ/z
ove dʒəʊv ⓤⓢ dʒoʊv
ovial ˈdʒəʊ.vi.əl ⓤⓢ ˈdʒoʊ- -ly -i -ness -nəs, -nɪs
oviality ˌdʒəʊ.viˈæl.ə.ti, -ɪ.ti ⓤⓢ ˌdʒoʊ.viˈæl.ə.t̬i
owell dʒaʊəl, dʒəʊəl ⓤⓢ dʒaʊəl, dʒoʊəl
owett, Jowitt ˈdʒaʊ.ɪt, ˈdʒəʊ- ⓤⓢ ˈdʒaʊ-, ˈdʒoʊ-
owl dʒaʊl -s -z
oy (J) dʒɔɪ -s -z -ing -ɪŋ -ed -d
oyce dʒɔɪs
oyful ˈdʒɔɪ.fəl, -fʊl -lest -ɪst, -əst -ly -i -ness -nəs, -nɪs
oyless ˈdʒɔɪ.ləs, -lɪs -ly -li -ness -nəs, -nɪs
oyous ˈdʒɔɪ.əs -ly -li -ness -nəs, -nɪs
oy|ride ˈdʒɔɪ|.raɪd -rides -raɪdz -riding -ˌraɪ.dɪŋ -rode -rəʊd ⓤⓢ -roʊd -ridden -rɪd.ən -rider/s -ˌraɪ.dəʳ/z ⓤⓢ -dɚ/z
oystick ˈdʒɔɪ.stɪk -s -s
PEG ˈdʒeɪ.peg
r (J) *(abbrev. for* **junior***)* ˈdʒuː.ni.əʳ ⓤⓢ ˈ-njɚ
uan hwɑːn; ˈdʒuː.ən *as if Spanish:* xwɑːn, xwæn ⓤⓢ hwɑːn
Note: In Byron's Don Juan, the pronunciation is /ˈdʒuː.ən/ in both British and American English.
uan Carlos ˌhwɑːnˈkɑː.lɒs, ˌhwɑːŋ- *as if Spanish:* ˌxwɑːn-, ˌxwæn- ⓤⓢ ˌhwɑːnˈkɑːr.loʊs
uan Fernandez ˌhwɑːn.fəˈnæn.dez, -des *as if Spanish:* ˌxwɑːn.fəˈnæn.dez, ˌxwæn- ⓤⓢ ˌhwɑːn.fɚˈnɑːn.des
uanita ˌdʒuː.əˈniː.tə; hwɑːˈniː.tə, hwænˈiː ⓤⓢ hwɑːˈniː.t̬ə, hwə-
ubilant ˈdʒuː.bɪ.lənt, -bəl.ənt -ly -li
ubi|late *(v.)* ˈdʒuː.bɪ|.leɪt, -bə- -lates -leɪts -lating -leɪ.tɪŋ ⓤⓢ -leɪ.t̬ɪŋ -lated -leɪ.tɪd ⓤⓢ -leɪ.t̬ɪd
ubilate *(n.)* ˌdʒuː.bɪˈlɑː.teɪ, ˌjuː-, -bəˈ-, -ti ⓤⓢ ˌjuː.biːˈlɑː.teɪ -s -z
ubilation ˌdʒuː.bɪˈleɪ.ʃən, -bəˈ- -s -z
ubilee ˈdʒuː.bɪ.liː, -bə-, ˌ--ˈ- -s -z
udae|a dʒuːˈdiː|.ə -an/s -ən/z
Juda(h) ˈdʒuː.də
Judaic dʒuːˈdeɪ.ɪk -al -əl -ally -əl.i, -li
Juda|ism ˈdʒuː.deɪ|.ɪ.zəm, -di- ⓤⓢ -deɪ-, -di-, -də- -ist/s -ɪst/s
judaiz|e, -is|e ˈdʒuː.deɪ.aɪz ⓤⓢ -deɪ-, -di-, -də- -es -ɪz -ing -ɪŋ -ed -d -er/s -əʳ/z ⓤⓢ -ɚ/z
Judas ˈdʒuː.dəs -es -ɪz ˈJudas ˌtree
Judd dʒʌd
judder ˈdʒʌd.əʳ ⓤⓢ -ɚ -s -z -ing -ɪŋ -ed -d
Jude dʒuːd
Jude|a dʒuːˈdiː|.ə -an/s -ən/z
judg|e (J) dʒʌdʒ -es -ɪz -ing -ɪŋ -ed -d
judg(e)ment ˈdʒʌdʒ.mənt -s -s ˈJudgement ˌDay
judgeship ˈdʒʌdʒ.ʃɪp, ˈdʒʌd- -s -s
judgmental dʒʌdʒˈmen.təl ⓤⓢ -t̬əl -ly -i
judicator|y ˈdʒuː.dɪ.kə.tər|.i ⓤⓢ -tɔːr- -ies -iz
judicature ˈdʒuː.dɪ.kə.tʃəʳ, -tjʊəʳ ⓤⓢ -tʃɚ
judicial dʒuːˈdɪʃ.əl -ly -i juˌdicial reˈview
judiciar|y dʒuːˈdɪʃ.ər|.i, -i.ər- ⓤⓢ -i.er-, -ˈdɪʃ.ɚ-, -i.ɚ- -ies -iz
judicious dʒuːˈdɪʃ.əs -ly -li -ness -nəs, -nɪs
Judith ˈdʒuː.dɪθ
judo ˈdʒuː.dəʊ ⓤⓢ -doʊ
Judson ˈdʒʌd.sən
Judy ˈdʒuː.di
jug dʒʌg -s -z -ging -ɪŋ -ged -d
jugful ˈdʒʌg.fʊl -s -z
juggernaut (J) ˈdʒʌg.ə.nɔːt ⓤⓢ -ɚ.nɑːt, -nɔːt -s -s
juggins (J) ˈdʒʌg.ɪnz -es -ɪz
juggl|e ˈdʒʌg.l̩ -es -z -ing -ɪŋ, ˈdʒʌg.lɪŋ -ed -d -er/s -əʳ/z, ˈdʒʌg.ləʳ/z ⓤⓢ -ɚ/z, ˈdʒʌg.lɚ/z
jugglery ˈdʒʌg.lər.i
Jugoslav ˈjuː.gəʊ.slɑːv, ˌ--ˈ- ⓤⓢ ˈjuː.goʊ.slɑːv -s -z
Jugoslavi|a ˌjuː.gəʊˈslɑː.vi|.ə ⓤⓢ -goʊˈ- -an -ən
jugular ˈdʒʌg.jə.ləʳ, -jʊ- ⓤⓢ -lɚ ˌjugular ˈvein ˈjugular ˌvein ⓤⓢ ˈjugular ˌvein
Jugurtha dʒʊˈgɜː.θə, jʊ- ⓤⓢ dʒuːˈgɝː-
juic|e dʒuːs -es -ɪz -ing -ɪŋ -ed -t -er/s -əʳ/z ⓤⓢ -ɚ/z
juic|y ˈdʒuː.s|i -ier -i.əʳ ⓤⓢ -i.ɚ -iest -i.ɪst, -i.əst -ily -ɪ.li, -əl.i -iness -ɪ.nəs, -ɪ.nɪs
Juilliard ˈdʒuː.li.ɑːd ⓤⓢ -ɑːrd
jujitsu dʒuːˈdʒɪt.suː
jujube ˈdʒuː.dʒuːb -s -z
jukebox ˈdʒuːk.bɒks ⓤⓢ -bɑːks -es -ɪz
Jukes dʒuːks
Jul. *(abbrev. for* **July***)* dʒʊˈlaɪ, dʒə-, dʒuː-
julep ˈdʒuː.lɪp, -lep, -ləp ⓤⓢ -ləp -s -s
Julia ˈdʒuː.li.ə ⓤⓢ ˈdʒuːl.jə
Julian ˈdʒuː.li.ən ⓤⓢ ˈdʒuːl.jən
Juliana ˌdʒuː.liˈɑː.nə ⓤⓢ -ˈæn.ə, -ˈɑː.nə
Julie ˈdʒuː.li
julienne ˌdʒuː.liˈen, ˌʒuː- ⓤⓢ ˌdʒuː-
Juliet ˈdʒuː.li.ət; ˌdʒuː.liˈet ⓤⓢ ˈdʒuː.li.et, -ɪt; ˌdʒuː.liˈet; ˈdʒuːl.jɪt
Juliette ˌdʒuː.liˈet, ˈ---
Julius ˈdʒuː.li.əs ⓤⓢ ˈdʒuːl.jəs
Julius Caesar ˌdʒuː.li.əsˈsiː.zəʳ ⓤⓢ ˌdʒuːl.jəsˈsiː.zɚ
Jul|y dʒʊˈl|aɪ, dʒə-, ˌdʒuː- -ies -aɪz
Julyan ˈdʒuː.li.ən ⓤⓢ ˈdʒuːl.jən
jumbl|e ˈdʒʌm.bl̩ -es -z -ing -ɪŋ, ˈdʒʌm.blɪŋ -ed -d ˈjumble ˌsale
Jumbl|y ˈdʒʌm.bl|i -ies -iz
jumbo (J) ˈdʒʌm.bəʊ ⓤⓢ -boʊ -s -z ˌjumbo ˈjet, ˈjumbo ˌjet
Jumna ˈdʒʌm.nə
jump dʒʌmp -s -s -ing -ɪŋ -ed -t -er/s -əʳ/z ⓤⓢ -ɚ/z ˈjumper ˌcables; ˌjumping ˈjack ⓤⓢ ˈjumping ˌjack; ˈjump ˌleads; ˈjump ˌrope; ˌjump the ˈgun
jumped-up ˌdʒʌmptˈʌp *stress shift:* ˌjumped-up ˈtyrant
jumper ˈdʒʌm.pəʳ ⓤⓢ -pɚ -s -z
jump-jet ˈdʒʌmp.dʒet -s -s
jump-off ˈdʒʌmp.ɒf ⓤⓢ -ɑːf -s -s
jump|-start ˈdʒʌmp|.stɑːt ⓤⓢ -stɑːrt -starts -stɑːts ⓤⓢ -stɑːrts -starting -ˌstɑː.tɪŋ ⓤⓢ -ˌstɑːr.t̬ɪŋ -started -ˌstɑː.tɪd ⓤⓢ -ˌstɑːr.t̬ɪd
jumpsuit ˈdʒʌmp.suːt, -sjuːt ⓤⓢ -suːt -s -s
jump|y ˈdʒʌm.p|i -ier -i.əʳ ⓤⓢ -i.ɚ -iest -i.ɪst, -i.əst -ily -ɪ.li, -əl.i -iness -ɪ.nəs, -ɪ.nɪs
Jun. *(abbrev. for* **junior***)* ˈdʒuː.ni.əʳ ⓤⓢ ˈ-njɚ
Jun. *(abbrev. for* **June***)* dʒuːn
junction ˈdʒʌŋk.ʃən -s -z ˈjunction ˌbox
juncture ˈdʒʌŋk.tʃəʳ ⓤⓢ -tʃɚ -s -z
June dʒuːn -s -z
Juneau ˈdʒuː.nəʊ, -ˈ- ⓤⓢ ˈdʒuː.noʊ
Jung jʊŋ
Jungfrau ˈjʊŋ.fraʊ
Jungian ˈjʊŋ.i.ən -s -z
jungl|e ˈdʒʌŋ.gl̩ -es -z -y -i ˈjungle ˌfowl; ˈjungle ˌgym ˌjungle ˈgym
junior ˈdʒuː.ni.əʳ ⓤⓢ ˈ-njɚ -s -z
juniority ˌdʒuː.niˈɒr.ə.ti, -ɪ.ti ⓤⓢ -ˈɔːr.ə.t̬i
juniper ˈdʒuː.nɪ.pəʳ, -nə- ⓤⓢ -pɚ -s -z
Junius ˈdʒuː.ni.əs ⓤⓢ -njəs
junk dʒʌŋk -s -s -ing -ɪŋ -ed -t ˈjunk ˌbond; ˈjunk ˌfood, ˌjunk ˈfood; ˈjunk ˌmail, ˌjunk ˈmail; ˈjunk ˌshop
junker (J) ˈjʊŋ.kəʳ ⓤⓢ -kɚ *old car:* ˈdʒʌŋ.kəʳ ⓤⓢ -kɚ -s -z
jun|ket ˈdʒʌŋ|.kɪt -kets -kɪts -keting -kɪ.tɪŋ ⓤⓢ -kɪ.t̬ɪŋ -keted -kɪ.tɪd ⓤⓢ -t̬ɪd

junkie 'dʒʌŋ.ki **-s** -z
junkyard 'dʒʌŋk.jɑːd (US) -jɑːrd **-s** -z
Juno 'dʒuː.nəʊ (US) -noʊ
Junoesque ˌdʒuː.nəʊ'esk (US) -noʊ'-
junta 'dʒʌn.tə, 'dʒʊn-, 'hʊn- (US) 'hʊn-, 'dʒʊn-, 'dʒʌn-, 'hʌn- **-s** -z
junto 'dʒʌn.təʊ, 'dʒʊn-, 'hʊn (US) -toʊ **-s** -z
jupe ʒuːp (US) dʒuːp **-s** -s
Jupiter 'dʒuː.pɪ.təʳ, -pə- (US) -t̬ɚ
jupon 'ʒuː.pɒn, 'dʒuː-, -pɔ̃ːŋ, -pɒŋ (US) 'dʒuː.pɑːn, -'- **-s** -z
Jura 'dʒʊə.rə (US) 'dʒʊr.ə
Jurassic dʒʊə'ræs.ɪk (US) dʒʊ-, dʒə-
jurat 'dʒʊə.ræt (US) 'dʒʊr.æt **-s** -s
Jürgen 'jɜː.gᵊn, 'jʊə- (US) 'jɝː-
juridic|al dʒʊə'rɪd.ɪ.k|ᵊl (US) dʒʊ- **-ally** -ᵊl.i, -li
jurisdiction ˌdʒʊə.rɪs'dɪk.ʃᵊn, -rəs'-, -rɪz'-, -rəz'- (US) ˌdʒʊr.ɪs'- **-s** -z **-al** -ᵊl
jurisprudence ˌdʒʊə.rɪs'pruː.dᵊn*ts*, -rəs-; 'dʒʊə.rɪsˌpruː-, -rəs- (US) ˌdʒʊr.ɪs'pruː-
jurist 'dʒʊə.rɪst (US) 'dʒʊr.ɪst **-s** -s
juror 'dʒʊə.rəʳ (US) 'dʒʊr.ɚ, -ɔːr **-s** -z
jur|y 'dʒʊə.r|i (US) 'dʒʊr.|i **-ies** -iz **'jury ˌbox; 'jury ˌservice**
jury|man 'dʒʊə.ri|.mən (US) 'dʒʊr.i- **-men** -mən, -men
jury-mast 'dʒʊə.ri.mɑːst (US) 'dʒʊr.i.mæst *nautical pronunciation:* -məst **-s** -s
just (J) *(adj.)* dʒʌst **-er** -əʳ (US) -ɚ **-est** -ɪst, -əst **-ly** -li **-ness** -nəs, -nɪs
just *(adv.) strong form:* dʒʌst *weak form:* dʒəst
jus tertii ˌjʊs'tɜː.ti.iː (US) ˌdʒʌs'tertiː, ˌjuːs-
justic|e 'dʒʌs.tɪs **-es** -ɪz **ˌjustice of the 'peace**
justiciable dʒʌs'tɪʃ.i.ə.bl̩, -'tɪʃ.ə- (US) -i.ə-
justiciar dʒʌs'tɪʃ.i.ɑːʳ, -'tɪs- (US) -'tɪʃ.i.ɚ **-s** -z
justiciar|y dʒʌs'tɪʃ.i.ᵊr|.i, -'tɪʃ.ᵊr-, -'tɪs.i- (US) -'tɪʃ.i.er- **-ies** -iz
justifiab|le 'dʒʌs.tɪ.faɪ.ə.b|l̩, -tə'-; ˌdʒʌs.tɪ'faɪ-, -tə'- (US) 'dʒʌs.tə.faɪ-, -tɪ- **-ly** -li **-leness** -l̩.nəs, -nɪs
justification ˌdʒʌs.tɪ.fɪ'keɪ.ʃᵊn, -tə- (US) -tə-, -tɪ- **-s** -z
justificatory 'dʒʌs.tɪ.fɪ.keɪ.tᵊr.i, -tə-; ˌdʒʌs.tɪ.fɪ'keɪ-; ˌdʒʌs.tɪ'fɪk.ə- (US) dʒə'stɪf.ɪ.kə.tɔːr-; 'dʒʌs.tə.fɪ.keɪ.tɚ-
justi|fy 'dʒʌs.tɪ|.faɪ, -tə- **-fies** -faɪz **-fying** -faɪ.ɪŋ **-fied** -faɪd **-fier/s** -faɪ.əʳ/z (US) -faɪ.ɚ/z
Justin 'dʒʌs.tɪn
Justine dʒʌs'tiːn, '--
Justinian dʒʌs'tɪn.i.ən
Justus 'dʒʌs.təs
jut dʒʌt **-s** -s **-ting** -ɪŋ (US) 'dʒʌt̬.ɪŋ **-ted** -ɪd (US) 'dʒʌt̬.ɪd
Juta 'dʒuː.tə
jute (J) dʒuːt **-s** -s
Jutland 'dʒʌt.lənd
Juvenal 'dʒuː.vᵊn.ᵊl, -vɪ.nᵊl
juvenescen|ce ˌdʒuː.vᵊn'es.ᵊn|*ts*, -vɪ'nes- **-t** -t
juvenile 'dʒuː.vᵊn.aɪl, -vɪ.naɪl (US) -və.nᵊl, -naɪl **-s** -z **ˌjuvenile de'linquent**
juvenilia ˌdʒuː.və'nɪl.i.ə, -vɪ'-, -'niː.l- (US) -və'nɪl.i-, '-jə
juvenility ˌdʒuː.və'nɪl.ə.ti, -vɪ'-, -ɪ.t (US) -ə.t̬i
Juventus juː'ven.təs
juxtapos|e ˌdʒʌk.stə'pəʊz, '--- (US) 'dʒʌk.stə.poʊz, ˌ--'- **-es** -ɪz **-ing** -ɪŋ **-ed** -d
juxtaposition ˌdʒʌk.stə.pə'zɪʃ.ᵊn **-s** **-al** -ᵊl

Pronouncing the letter K

In general, the consonant letter **k** is pronounced /k/, e.g.:

Kate /keɪt/

This is also the case in the digraph **kh**, e.g.:

khaki /ˈkɑː.ki/ (US) /ˈkæk.i/

In words beginning **kn**, **k** is usually silent, e.g.:

knack /næk/

However, where the **k** appears before an **n** at a morpheme boundary, it is pronounced, e.g.:

sickness /ˈsɪk.nəs/

(K) keɪ -'s -z
2 ˌkeɪˈtuː
aba ˈkɑː.bə, ˈkɑː.ə.bɑː (US) -bə
baka (K) kəˈbɑː.kə -s -z
bbadi kɑːˈbɑː.di
b(b)ala kəˈbɑː.lə, kæbˈɑː- (US) ˈkæb.ə-; kəˈbɑː-
bila kəˈbiː.lə, kæbˈiː- (US) kɑːˈbiːlə
bob kəˈbɒb (US) -ˈbɑːb
buki kəˈbuː.ki, kæbˈuː- (US) kə-, kɑː-
bul ˈkɑː.bəl, ˈkɔː-, -bʊl; kəˈbʊl (US) ˈkɑː.bʊl; kəˈbʊl
bwe ˈkæb.weɪ (US) ˈkɑːb-
byle kəˈbaɪl, kæbˈaɪl, -iːl -s -z
china (K) kəˈtʃiː.nə -s -z
czynski kəˈzɪnt.ski
ddish ˈkæd.ɪʃ (US) ˈkɑː.dɪʃ -im -ɪm, -iːm
f(f)ir (K) ˈkæf.əʳ -s -z
fka ˈkæf.kə (US) ˈkɑːf-
fkaesque ˌkæf.kəˈesk (US) ˌkɑːf-
ftan ˈkæf.tæn (US) -tən, -tæn -s -z
goule kəˈguːl -s -z
hn kɑːn
lyard ˈkeɪl.jɑːd (US) -jɑːrd -s -z
ser ˈkaɪ.zəʳ (US) -zɚ -s -z
serslautern ˈkaɪ.zəzˌlaʊ.tɜːn, -tən (US) ˌkaɪ.zɚzˈlaʊ.tɚn
tlin, **Kaitlyn** ˈkeɪt.lɪn
kadu ˈkæk.ə.duː, --ˈ-
kemono ˌkæk.iˈməʊ.nəʊ (US) ˌkɑː.kəˈmoʊ.noʊ -s -z
ahari ˌkæl.əˈhɑː.ri (US) ˌkɑː.lɑːˈhɑːr.i, ˌkæl-
amazoo ˌkæl.ə.məˈzuː
ashnikov® kəˈlæʃ.nɪ.kɒf, -nə- (US) -ˈlɑːʃ.nɪ.kɑːf -s -s
at kəˈlɑːt
e keɪl
eidoscope kəˈlaɪ.də.skəʊp (US) -skoʊp -s -s
eidoscopic kəˌlaɪ.dəˈskɒp.ɪk (US) -ˈskɑː.pɪk
nds ˈkæl.endz, -ɪndz, -əndz (US) -əndz, ˈkeɪ.ləndz
evala ˌkɑː.ləˈvɑː.lə (US) -lə, -lɑː
goorlie kælˈgʊə.li (US) -ˈgʊr- ˈkɑː.li

kalif ˈkeɪ.lɪf, ˈkæl.ɪf, ˈkɑː.lɪf; kəˈlɪf (US) ˈkeɪ.lɪf, ˈkæl.ɪf -s -s
Kalimantan ˌkæl.ɪˈmæn.tən (US) ˌkɑː.liːˈmɑːn.tɑːn
Kam|a *Hindu god:* ˈkɑː.m|ə -ic -ɪk *Russian river:* ˈkɑː.mə
Kamasutra ˌkɑː.məˈsuː.trə
Kamchatka kæmˈtʃæt.kə (US) kæmˈtʃæt-, kɑːmˈtʃɑːt-
kamikaze ˌkæm.ɪˈkɑː.zi (US) ˌkɑː.məˈkɑː.zi -s -z
Kampala kæmˈpɑː.lə (US) kɑːm-
kampong ˈkæm.pɒŋ, -ˈ- (US) ˈkɑːm.pɔːŋ, -pɑːŋ
Kampuche|a ˌkæm.pʊˈtʃiː|.ə (US) -puːˈ- -an/s -ən/z
kana ˈkɑː.nə (US) -nə, -nɑː
Kananga kəˈnæŋ.gə (US) -ˈnɑːŋ-
Kanarese ˌkæn.əʳˈiːz (US) ˌkɑː.nəˈriːz, -ˈriːs
Kanchenjunga ˌkæn.tʃənˈdʒʊŋ.gə, -ˈdʒʌŋ- (US) ˌkɑːn.tʃənˈdʒʊŋ-
Kandahar ˌkæn.dəˈhɑːʳ (US) ˌkɑːn.dəˈhɑːr
Kandinsky kænˈdɪnt.ski
Kandy ˈkæn.di (US) ˈkæn-, ˈkɑːn-
Kane keɪn
Kanga ˈkæŋ.gə
kangaroo ˌkæŋ.gəʳˈuː *sometimes in Australia:* ˈ--- (US) ˌkæŋ.gəˈruː -s -z *stress shift, see compound:* ˌ**kangaroo ˈcourt**
Kangchenjunga ˌkæn.tʃənˈdʒʊŋ.gə, -ˈdʒʌŋ- (US) ˌkɑːn.tʃənˈdʒʊŋ-
kanji ˈkæn.dʒi, ˈkɑːn- (US) ˈkɑːn.dʒi -s -z
Kano ˈkɑː.nəʊ, ˈkeɪ- (US) ˈkɑː.noʊ
Kanpur kɑːnˈpʊəʳ (US) ˈkɑːn.pʊr
Kans. *(abbrev. for* **Kansas***)* ˈkæn.zəs
Kansas ˈkæn.zəs ˌ**Kansas ˈCity**; ˌ**Kansas ˌCity ˈsteak**
Kant kænt (US) kænt, kɑːnt
Kantian ˈkæn.ti.ən (US) ˈkæn.ţi-, ˈkɑːn-
Kant|ism ˈkæn.t|ɪ.zəm (US) ˈkæn.t|ɪ-, ˈkɑːn- -ist/s -ɪst/s
Kaohsiung ˌkaʊ.ʃiˈʊŋ (US) -ˈʃʊŋ
Kaolak ˈkɑː.əʊ.læk, ˈkaʊ.læk (US) ˈkɑː.oʊ-, ˈkaʊ.læk
kaolin ˈkeɪ.ə.lɪn

kapellmeister kəˈpel.maɪ.stəʳ, kæpˈel- (US) kɑːˈpel.maɪ.stɚ, kə- -s -z
Kaplan ˈkæp.lən
kapok ˈkeɪ.pɒk (US) -pɑːk
Kaposi kəˈpəʊ.zi, kæpˈəʊ-, -si; ˈkɑː.pə.ʃi, ˈkæp.ə- (US) kəˈpoʊ.zi, -si; ˈkæp.ə- **Kaˌposi's sarˈcoma**
kappa ˈkæp.ə
kaput(t) kəˈpʊt, kæpˈʊt (US) kəˈpʊt, -ˈpuːt
Kara ˈkɑː.rə (US) ˈkɑːr.ə
Karachi kəˈrɑː.tʃi
Karadzic ˈkær.ə.dʒɪtʃ, -dɪtʃ (US) kəˈrɑː.dʒɪtʃ
Karaganda ˌkær.əˈgæn.də (US) ˌkɑːr.əˈgɑːn-
Karajan ˈkær.ə.jɑːn (US) ˈkɑːr-, -jən
karaoke ˌkær.iˈəʊ.ki (US) ˌker.iˈoʊ.ki, ˌkær- -s -z
karat ˈkær.ət (US) ˈker-, ˈkær- -s -z
karate kəˈrɑː.ti, kærˈɑː- (US) kəˈrɑː.ţi
Kareli|a kəˈreɪ.li|.ə, -ˈriː- (US) -li|.ə, -lj|ə -ans -ənz
Karen *female name:* ˈkær.ən (US) ˈker-, ˈkær- *of Burma:* kəˈren -s -z
Karenina kəˈren.ɪ.nə
Karl kɑːl (US) kɑːrl
Karla ˈkɑː.lə (US) ˈkɑːr-
Karl-Marx-Stadt ˌkɑːlˈmɑːksˌʃtæt (US) ˌkɑːrˈmɑːrksˌʃtɑːt
Karloff ˈkɑː.lɒf (US) ˈkɑːr.lɑːf
Karlsbad ˈkɑːlz.bæd (US) ˈkɑːrlz-
Karlsruhe ˈkɑːlz.ruː.ə (US) ˈkɑːrlz-
karm|a ˈkɑː.m|ə, ˈkɜː- (US) ˈkɑːr-, ˈkɝː- -ik -ɪk
Karnak ˈkɑː.næk (US) ˈkɑːr-
Karnataka kəˈnɑː.tə.kə (US) kɑːrˈnɑː.ţə-
Karpov ˈkɑː.pɒf (US) ˈkɑːr.pɑːf
karroo kəˈruː -s -z
Kars kɑːz (US) kɑːrz
Karsh kɑːʃ (US) kɑːrʃ
kart kɑːt (US) kɑːrt -s -s -ing -ɪŋ (US) ˈkɑːr.ţɪŋ
Karzai ˈkɑː.zaɪ (US) ˈkɑːr-
Kasakhstan ˌkæz.ækˈstɑːn, ˌkɑː.zækˈ-, -zɑːkˈ-, -ˈstæn (US) ˌkɑː.zɑːkˈstɑːn
kasbah (K) ˈkæz.bɑː, -bə (US) -bɑː, ˈkɑːz- -s -z

Kasey 'keɪ.si
kasha 'kæʃ.ə, 'kɑː.ʃə ⓤⓢ 'kɑː.ʃə
Kashgar 'kæʃ.gɑːʳ ⓤⓢ 'kɑːʃ.gɑːr
Kashmir ˌkæʃ'mɪəʳ ⓤⓢ 'kæʃ.mɪr, -'- **-i/s** -i/z *stress shift, British only:* ˌKashmir 'border
Kaspar 'kæs.pəʳ, -pɑːʳ ⓤⓢ -pɚ, -pɑːr
Kasparov kæs'pɑː.rɒf; 'kæs.pə- ⓤⓢ kæs'pɑːr.ɔːf, kə'spɑːr-; 'kæs.pə.rɔːf
Kassala kə'sɑː.lə ⓤⓢ kə-, kɑː-
Kassel 'kæs.əl ⓤⓢ 'kɑː.səl, 'kæs.əl
Kasur kʌs'ɔːʳ ⓤⓢ -'ʊr
katakana ˌkæt.ə'kɑː.nə ⓤⓢ ˌkɑː.t̬ə'-
Kate keɪt
Katelyn 'keɪt.lɪn
Kater 'keɪ.təʳ ⓤⓢ -t̬ɚ
Katerina ˌkæt.əʳr'iː.nə ⓤⓢ ˌkæt̬.ə'riː-
Kath kæθ
Katharina ˌkæθ.əʳr'iː.nə ⓤⓢ -ə'riː-
Katharine, Katherine 'kæθ.rɪn, -əʳr.ɪn
Kathie 'kæθ.i
Kathleen 'kæθ.liːn, ˌ-'-
Kathmandu ˌkæt.mæn'duː, ˌkɑːt-, -mən'-, -mɑːn'- ⓤⓢ ˌkɑːt.mɑːn'-, ˌkæt-
Kathryn 'kæθ.rɪn
Kathy 'kæθ.i
Katie 'keɪ.ti ⓤⓢ -t̬i
Katin 'keɪ.tɪn ⓤⓢ -t̬ɪn
Katmandu ˌkæt.mæn'duː, ˌkɑːt-, -mən'-, -mɑːn'- ⓤⓢ ˌkɑːt.mɑːn'-, ˌkæt-
Katowice ˌkæt.əʊ'vɪt.seɪ, -'viːt- ⓤⓢ -tə'viːt.sə, -tɔː'viːt.seɪ
Katrina kə'triː.nə
Katrine 'kæt.rɪn
Kattegat ˌkæt.i'gæt, '--- ⓤⓢ 'kæt̬-
Katty 'kæt.i ⓤⓢ 'kæt̬-
Katy 'keɪ.ti ⓤⓢ -t̬i
katydid 'keɪ.ti.dɪd ⓤⓢ -t̬i- **-s** -z
Katz kæts, keɪts
katzenjammer 'kæt.sənˌdʒæm.əʳ ⓤⓢ -ɚ
Kaufman 'kɔːf.mən, 'kaʊf- ⓤⓢ 'kɑːf-, 'kɔːf-
Kaunas 'kaʊ.nəs ⓤⓢ -nɑːs
Kaunda kɑː'ʊn.də, -'uːn-
Kaur kaʊəʳ ⓤⓢ kaʊr
Kavanagh 'kæv.ən.ə; kə'væn.ə ⓤⓢ 'kæv.ə.nɑː, -nɔː
Note: In Ireland always /'kæv.ən.ə/.
Kawasaki® ˌkaʊ.ə'sɑː.ki, ˌkɑː.wə'-, -'sæk.i ⓤⓢ ˌkɑː.wə'sɑː.ki
Kay keɪ
kayak 'kaɪ.æk **-s** -s **-ing** -ɪŋ **-ed** -t
Kaye keɪ **-s** -z
Kayla 'keɪ.lə
Kayleigh 'keɪ.li
Kayseri 'keɪ.sər.i
Kazakh 'kæ.zæk, -'zɑːk; ⓤⓢ kə'zɑːk, kɑː-, -'zæk **-s** -s
Kazakhstan, Kazakstan ˌkæz.æk'stɑːn, ˌkɑː.zæk'-, -zɑːk'-, -'stæn ⓤⓢ kə'zɑːk.stɑːn, kɑː-, -'zæk-, -stæn
Kazan kə'zæn, -'zɑːn ⓤⓢ kə'zæn, kɑː-, -'zɑːn
kazi 'kɑː.zi **-s** -z
kazoo kə'zuː **-s** -z
kcal *(abbrev. for* **kilocalorie***)* 'kɪl.əʊˌkæl.ər.i ⓤⓢ '-oʊ-, '-ə-
kea 'keɪ.ə, 'kiː- **-s** -z
Keady 'kiː.di ⓤⓢ 'keɪ-
Kean(e) kiːn
Kearn(e)y 'kɜː.ni, 'kɑː- ⓤⓢ 'kɑːr-, 'kɝː-
Kearsley 'kɪəz.li *locally:* 'kɜːz- ⓤⓢ 'kɪrz-
Kearsney 'kɜːz.ni ⓤⓢ 'kɝːz-
Kearton 'kɪə.tən, 'kɜː- ⓤⓢ 'kɪr-, 'kɝː-
Keary 'kɪə.ri ⓤⓢ 'kɪr.i
Keating(e) 'kiː.tɪŋ ⓤⓢ -t̬ɪŋ
Keaton 'kiː.tən
Keats kiːts
kebab kɪ'bæb, kə- ⓤⓢ -'bɑːb **-s** -z
Keble 'kiː.bl̩
kebob kə'bɒb ⓤⓢ -'bɑːb **-s** -z
kedg|e kedʒ **-es** -ɪz **-ing** -ɪŋ **-ed** -d
kedgeree ˌkedʒ.ər'iː; 'kedʒ.ər.i ⓤⓢ 'kedʒ.ər-; ˌkedʒ.ə'riː **-s** -z
Kedleston 'ked.l̩.stən
Kedron 'ked.rɒn, 'kiː.drɒn ⓤⓢ 'kiː.drɑːn, -drən
Keeble 'kiː.bl̩
Keegan 'kiː.gən
keel kiːl **-s** -z **-ing** -ɪŋ **-ed** -d **on an ˌeven 'keel**
Keele kiːl
Keeler 'kiː.ləʳ ⓤⓢ -lɚ
keelhaul 'kiːl.hɔːl ⓤⓢ -hɑːl, -hɔːl **-s** -z **-ing** -ɪŋ **-ed** -d
Keeling 'kiː.lɪŋ
keelson 'kel.sən, 'kiːl- **-s** -z
keen kiːn **-er** -əʳ ⓤⓢ -ɚ **-est** -ɪst, -əst **-s** **-ing** **-ed** **-ly** -li **-ness** -nəs, -nɪs **as ˌkeen as 'mustard**
Keenan 'kiː.nən
Keen(e) kiːn
keep kiːp **-s** -s **-ing** -ɪŋ **kept** kept **keeper/s** 'kiː.pəʳ/z ⓤⓢ -pɚ/z
keepnet 'kiːp.net **-s** -s
keepsake 'kiːp.seɪk **-s** -s
Kefauver 'kiːˌfɔː.vəʳ, -ˌfəʊ- ⓤⓢ -ˌfɑː.vɚ, -ˌfɔː-
Keflavik 'kef.lə.vɪk
keg keg **-s** -z
Kegan 'kiː.gən
Keig kiːg
Keighley *in West Yorkshire:* 'kiːθ.li *surname:* 'kiːθ.li, 'kiː-, 'kaɪ-
Keightley 'kiːt.li, 'kaɪt-
Keigwin 'keg.wɪn
Keiller, Keillor 'kiː.ləʳ ⓤⓢ -lɚ
Keir kɪəʳ ⓤⓢ kɪr
Keisha 'kiː.ʃə
Keitel ˌkaɪ'tel
Keith kiːθ
Kelland 'kel.ənd
Kellas 'kel.æs
Keller 'kel.əʳ ⓤⓢ -ɚ
Kelley, Kellie 'kel.i
Kellogg 'kel.ɒg ⓤⓢ -ɑːg, -ɔːg
Kelly 'kel.i
kelly-green ˌkel.i'griːn *stress shift:* ˌkelly-green 'fabric
Kelman 'kel.mən
kelp kelp
kelpie 'kel.pi **-s** -z
Kelsey 'kel.si, -zi
Kelso 'kel.səʊ ⓤⓢ -soʊ
kelson 'kel.sən **-s** -z
Kelt kelt **-s** -s **-ic** -ɪk
Kelty 'kel.ti ⓤⓢ -t̬i
kelvin (K) 'kel.vɪn
Kelway 'kel.wi, -weɪ
Kemal kem'ɑːl, kə'mɑːl ⓤⓢ kə'mɑːl
Kemble 'kem.bl̩
kemp kemp **-y** -i
Kemp(e) kemp
Kempenfelt 'kem.pən.felt
Kempis 'kem.pɪs
Kempson 'kemp.sən
Kempston 'kemp.stən
kempt kem*p*t
Kempton 'kem*p*.tən
Kemsing 'kem.zɪŋ
ken (K) ken **-s** -z **-ning** -ɪŋ **-ned** -d
Ken. *(abbrev. for* **Kentucky***)* ken'tʌ kən- ⓤⓢ kən-
Kendal(l) 'ken.dəl
kendo 'ken.dəʊ ⓤⓢ -doʊ
Kendra 'ken.drə
Kendrick 'ken.drɪk
Keneal(l)y kɪ'niː.li, kə-, ken'iː-
Kenelm 'ken.elm
Kenilworth 'ken.əl.wəθ, -ɪl-, -wɜːθ ⓤⓢ -wɚθ, -wɝːθ
Kenite 'kiː.naɪt **-s** -s
Kénitra 'keɪ.niː.trə; ken'iː-
Kenmare ken'meəʳ ⓤⓢ -'mer
Kenmore 'ken.mɔːʳ ⓤⓢ -mɔːr
Kennaird kə'neəd, ken'eəd ⓤⓢ ken' kə'nerd
Kennan 'ken.ən
Kennard 'ken.ɑːd; kɪ'nɑːd ⓤⓢ 'ken.ɑːrd, kɪ'nɑːrd
Kennedy 'ken.ə.di, '-ɪ-
kennel (K) 'ken.əl **-s** -z **-(l)ing** -ɪŋ **-(l)ed** -d
Kennerley 'ken.əl.i ⓤⓢ -ɚ.li
Kennet 'ken.ɪt, -ət
Kenneth 'ken.ɪθ, -əθ
Kenney 'ken.i
Kennicot 'ken.ɪ.kət ⓤⓢ -kət, -kɑːt
Kennington 'ken.ɪŋ.tən
Kennish 'ken.ɪʃ
Kennoway 'ken.ə.weɪ

Kenny 'ken.i
keno 'kiː.nəʊ US -noʊ
Kenosha kiː'nəʊ.ʃə, kə- US kə'noʊ-
Kenrick 'ken.rɪk
Kensal 'ken.sᵊl
Kensington 'ken.zɪŋ.tən
Kensit 'ken.zɪt, -sɪt
Kent kent **-s** -s **-ish** -ɪʃ
Kentucky ken'tʌk.i, kən- US kən-
Kenˌtucky 'Derby; Kenˌtucky ˌFried 'Chicken
Kenwood® 'ken.wʊd
Kenya 'ken.jə, 'kiː.njə **-n/s** -n/z
Note: Both pronunciations are heard locally.
Kenyatta ken'jæt.ə US -'jɑː.t̬ə
Kenyon 'ken.jən
Keogh kjəʊ; 'kiː.əʊ US 'kiː.oʊ
Keown kjəʊn; ki'oʊn; 'kiː.əʊn; US kjoʊn; ki'oʊn; 'kiː.oʊn;
kepi 'keɪ.pi US 'keɪ-, 'kep.i **-s** -z
Kepler 'kep.ləʳ US -lɚ
Keppel 'kep.ᵊl
kept *(from* **keep***)* kept
Ker kɑːʳ, keəʳ, kɜːʳ *in Scotland* kɛr US kɝː
Kerala 'ker.ᵊl.ə, kə'rɑː.lə US 'ker.ə.lə
Kerans 'ker.ənz
keratin 'ker.ə.tɪn US -t̬ɪn
keratitis ˌker.ə'taɪ.tɪs US -t̬ɪs
kerb kɜːb US kɝːb **-s** -z
kerbside 'kɜːb.saɪd US 'kɝːb-
kerbstone 'kɜːb.stəʊn US 'kɝːb.stoʊn **-s** -z
ker|chief 'kɜː|.tʃɪf, -tʃiːf, -tʃəf US 'kɝː|.tʃɪf, -tʃiːf **-chiefs** -tʃɪfs, -tʃiːfs **-chieves** -tʃɪvz, -tʃiːvz **-chiefed** -tʃɪft **-chieft** -tʃiːft
Kerensky kə'rent.ski
kerfuffl|e kə'fʌf.l̩ US kɚ- **-es** -z **-ing** -ɪŋ **-ed** -d
Kerguelen 'kɜː.gɪ.lɪn, -gᵊl.ɪn, -ən US 'kɝː.gᵊl.ən
Keri 'ker.i
Kerith 'kɪə.rɪθ, 'ker.ɪθ US 'kɪr-, 'ker-
Kermes 'kɜː.mɪz, -miːz US 'kɝː.miːz
Kermit 'kɜː.mɪt US 'kɝː-
Kermode 'kɜː.məʊd, -'- US 'kɝː.moʊd, -'-
kern (K) kɜːn US kɝːn **-s** -z **-ing** -ɪŋ **-ed** -d
Kernahan 'kɜː.nə.hən, -ni.ən US 'kɝː-, -nə.hæn
kernel 'kɜː.nᵊl US 'kɝː- **-s** -z
Kernohan 'kɜː.nə.hən US 'kɝː-, -hæn
kerosene 'ker.ə.siːn, ˌ--'-
Kerouac 'ker.u.æk US 'ker.u.æk, '-ə-
Kerr kɜːʳ, keəʳ, kɑːʳ US kɝː, kɑːr
Kerri 'ker.i
Kerria 'ker.i.ə **-s** -z
Kerridge 'ker.ɪdʒ
Kerry 'ker.i

Kerse kɜːs US kɝːs
kersey (K) 'kɜː.zi US 'kɝː- **-s** -z
kerseymere (K) 'kɜː.zi.mɪəʳ US 'kɝː.zi.mɪr
Kershaw 'kɜː.ʃɔː US 'kɝː.ʃɑː, -ʃɔː
Kes kes, kez
Kesey 'kes.i, 'kiː.si, -zi US 'kiː.si, -zi
Kesteven *Barony:* 'kes.tɪ.vᵊn *Lincolnshire:* kes'tiː.vᵊn, kə'stiː-
Keston 'kes.tᵊn
kestrel 'kes.trᵊl **-s** -z
Keswick 'kez.ɪk
ketch (K) ketʃ **-es** -ɪz
ketchup 'ketʃ.ʌp, -əp US -əp **-s** -s
Ketteridge 'ket.ᵊr.ɪdʒ US 'ket̬-
Kettering 'ket.ᵊr.ɪŋ US 'ket̬-
kettle (K) 'ket.l̩ US 'ket̬- **-s** -z **a 'pretty ˌkettle of ˌfish**
kettledrum 'ket.l̩.drʌm US 'ket̬- **-s** -z
Kevin 'kev.ɪn
Kevlar® 'kev.lɑːʳ US -lɑːr
Kevorkian kə'vɔː.ki.ən, kev'- US -'vɔːr-
Kew kjuː **ˌKew 'Gardens**
kewpie 'kjuː.pi **-s** -z
key (K) kiː **-s** -z **-ing** -ɪŋ **-ed** -d **'key ˌring; 'key ˌsignature; ˌKey 'West**
keyboard 'kiː.bɔːd US -bɔːrd **-s** -z **-ing** -ɪŋ **-ed** -ɪd **-er/s** -əʳ/z US -ɚ/z **-ist/s** -ɪst/s
keycard 'kiː.kɑːd US -kɑːrd **-s** -z
Keyes kiːz, kaɪz
keyhole 'kiː.həʊl US -hoʊl **-s** -z **ˌkeyhole 'surgery**
Key Largo ˌkiː'lɑː.gəʊ US -'lɑːr.goʊ
Keymer 'kiː.məʳ, 'kaɪ- US -mɚ
Keymour 'kiː.məʳ US -mɚ
Keyne kiːn
Keynes *in Milton Keynes:* kiːnz *surname, other places:* keɪnz
Keynesian 'keɪn.zi.ən **-ism** -ɪ.zᵊm
keynote 'kiː.nəʊt, ˌ-'- US 'kiː.noʊt **-s** -s
Keynsham 'keɪn.ʃᵊm
keypad 'kiː.pæd **-s** -z
keypunch 'kiː.pʌntʃ **-es** -ɪz
Keyser 'kiː.zəʳ, 'kaɪ.zəʳ US 'kaɪ.zɚ
keystone (K) 'kiː.stəʊn US -stoʊn **-s** -z
keystroke 'kiː.strəʊk US -stroʊk **-s** -s
keyword 'kiː.wɜːd US -wɝːd **-s** -z
Keyworth 'kiː.wəθ, -wɜːθ US -wɚθ, -wɝːθ
kg *(abbrev. for* **kilogram/s***) singular:* 'kɪl.ə.græm *plural:* 'kɪl.ə.græmz
KGB ˌkeɪ.dʒiː'biː
Khabarovsk kɑː'bɑː.rɒfsk US -rɔːfsk
Khachaturian ˌkætʃ.ə'tʊə.ri.ən, ˌkɑː.tʃə'-, -'tjʊə- US -'tʊr.i-
khaki 'kɑː.ki US 'kæk.i, 'kɑː.ki **-s** -z
khalif 'keɪ.lɪf US 'kɑː-, 'kæl.ɪf, 'kɑː.lɪf; kæl'ɪf US 'keɪ.lɪf, 'kæl.ɪf **-s** -s
Khalifa kɑː'liː.fə, kə'liː- **-s** -z
khalifate 'kæl.ɪ.feɪt, 'keɪ.lɪ-, -lə- US 'kæl.ɪ-, '-ə- **-s** -s

Khan kɑːn US kɑːn, kæn
Khanpur ˌkɑːn'pʊəʳ, ˌkɑːm'-, '-- US ˌkɑːn'pʊr
Kharkov 'kɑː.kɒf US 'kɑːr.kɔːf
Khartoum ˌkɑː'tuːm, kɑː- US kɑːr-
Khatami kə'tɑː.mi, kæt'- US 'kɑː.tɑː.mi, kə'-, hɑː.tɑː'miː
Khayyam kaɪ'æm, -'ɑːm US -'jɑːm, -'jæm
khazi 'kɑː.zi **-s** -z
khedival kɪ'diː.vᵊl, ked'iː-, kə'diː- US kə'diː-
khedive kɪ'diːv, ked'iːv, kə'diːv US kə'diːv **-s** -z
khedivial kɪ'diː.vi.əl, ked'iː-, kə'diː- US kə'diː-
Khmer kmeəʳ, kə'meəʳ US kə'mer **Khˌmer 'Rouge**
Khomeini kɒm'eɪ.ni, kəʊ'meɪ- US koʊ-, kə-
khoums kuːmz
Khrus(h)chev 'krʊs.tʃɒf, 'krʊʃ-, ˌ-'- US 'kruː.tʃef, -tʃɔːf; kruːʃ'tʃɔːf
Khyber 'kaɪ.bəʳ US -bɚ **ˌKhyber 'Pass**
kHz *(abbrev. for* **kilohertz***)* 'kɪl.əʊ.hɜːts US -ə.hɝːts
Kia Ora® ˌkɪə'ɔː.rə, ˌkiː.ə'- US ˌkiː.ə'ɔːr.ə
kibbl|e 'kɪb.l̩ **-es** -z **-ing** -ɪŋ, 'kɪb.lɪŋ **-ed** -d
kibbutz kɪ'bʊts US -'bʊts, -'buːts **-nik/s** -nɪk **-es** -ɪz **kibbutzim** ˌkɪb.ʊt'siːm; kɪ'bʊt.siːm US ˌkiː.buːt'siːm
kibe kaɪb **-s** -z
kibitz 'kɪb.ɪts **-es** -ɪz **-ing** -ɪŋ **-ed** -t **-er/s** -əʳ/z US -ɚ/z
kibosh 'kaɪ.bɒʃ US 'kaɪ.bɑːʃ; kɪ'bɑːʃ **-es** -ɪz **-ing** -ɪŋ **-ed** -t
kick kɪk **-s** -s **-ing** -ɪŋ **-ed** -t **-er/s** -əʳ/z US -ɚ/z
kickabout 'kɪk.ə.baʊt **-s** -s
kickback 'kɪk.bæk **-s** -s
Kickham 'kɪk.əm
kick-off 'kɪk.ɒf US -ɑːf **-s** -s
kickshaw 'kɪk.ʃɔː US -ʃɑː, -ʃɔː **-s** -z
kick|-start 'kɪk|.stɑːt US -stɑːrt **-starts** -stɑːts US -stɑːrts **-starting** -ˌstɑː.tɪŋ US -ˌstɑːr.t̬ɪŋ **-started** -ˌstɑː.tɪd US -ˌstɑːr.t̬ɪd **-starter/s** -ˌstɑː.təʳ/z US -ˌstɑːr.t̬ɚ/z
kid kɪd **-s** -z **-ding** -ɪŋ **-ded** -ɪd **ˌkid 'glove**
Kidd kɪd
Kidderminster 'kɪd.ə.mɪnt.stəʳ US -ɚ.mɪnt.stɚ
kiddie 'kɪd.i **-s** -z
kiddle (K) 'kɪd.l̩ **-s** -z
kidd|y 'kɪd|.i **-ies** -iz
Kidlington 'kɪd.lɪŋ.tən
Kidman 'kɪd.mən
kidnap 'kɪd.næp **-s** -s **-(p)ing/s** -ɪŋ/z **-(p)ed** -t **-(p)er/s** -əʳ/z US -ɚ/z

kidney 'kɪd.ni **-s** -z **'kidney ˌbean; 'kidney maˌchine**
Kidsgrove 'kɪdz.grəʊv ⓤⓢ -groʊv
Kiel kiːl
kielbas(s)a kiːl'bæs.ə ⓤⓢ -'bɑː.sə, kɪl-
Kielder 'kiːl.dəʳ ⓤⓢ -dɚ
kier (K) kɪəʳ ⓤⓢ kɪr **-s** -z
Kieran 'kɪə.rᵊn ⓤⓢ 'kɪr.ᵊn
Kierkegaard 'kɪə.kə.gɑːd, -gɔːd ⓤⓢ 'kɪr.kə.gɑːrd, -gɔːrd
Kiev 'kiː.ev, -ef, ˌ-'-
Kigali kɪ'gɑː.li ⓤⓢ kə-
Kikuyu kɪ'kuː.juː ⓤⓢ kiː-
Kilbirnie kɪl'bɜː.ni ⓤⓢ -'bɝː-
Kilbride kɪl'braɪd ⓤⓢ 'kɪl.braɪd, -'-
Kilburn 'kɪl.bən, -bɜːn ⓤⓢ -bɚn, -bɝːn
Kilby 'kɪl.bi
Kildale 'kɪl.deɪl
Kildare kɪl'deəʳ ⓤⓢ -'der
kilderkin 'kɪl.də.kɪn ⓤⓢ -dɚ- **-s** -z
Kilen 'kaɪ.lən
Kiley 'kaɪ.li
Kilfoyle kɪl'fɔɪl
Kilham 'kɪl.əm
kilim (K) kɪ'liːm **-s** -z
Kilimanjaro ˌkɪl.ɪ.mən'dʒɑː.rəʊ, ˌ-ə-, -mæn'- ⓤⓢ -ə.mən'dʒɑːr.oʊ
Kilkeel kɪl'kiːl
Kilkenny kɪl'ken.i
kill kɪl **-s** -z **-ing/s** -ɪŋ/z **-ed** -d **ˌdressed to 'kill**
Killaloe ˌkɪl.ə'luː ⓤⓢ kɪ'læl.oʊ
Killamarsh 'kɪl.ə.mɑːʃ ⓤⓢ -mɑːrʃ
Killarney kɪ'lɑː.ni ⓤⓢ -'lɑːr-
Killearn kɪ'lɜːn ⓤⓢ -'lɝːn
killer 'kɪl.əʳ ⓤⓢ -ɚ **-s** -z **'killer ˌinstinct; 'killer ˌwhale**
Killick 'kɪl.ɪk
Killiecrankie ˌkɪl.ɪ'kræŋ.ki
Killigrew 'kɪl.ɪ.gruː
Killin 'kɪl.ɪn
Killingworth 'kɪl.ɪŋ.wəθ, -wɜːθ ⓤⓢ -wɚθ, -wɝːθ
killjoy 'kɪl.dʒɔɪ **-s** -z
Killwick 'kɪl.wɪk
Kilmainham kɪl'meɪ.nəm
Kilmarnock kɪl'mɑː.nək, -nɒk ⓤⓢ -'mɑːr.nək, -nɑːk
kiln kɪln, kɪl **-s** -z
Note: The pronunciation /kɪl/ appears to be used only by those concerned with the working of kilns.
Kilnsey 'kɪln.zi
kilo- kɪl.əʊ-; kɪ'lɒ- ⓤⓢ kɪl.oʊ-, -ə-; kɪ'lɑː-
Note: Prefix. Normally carries primary stress on the first syllable, e.g. **kilometre** /'kɪl.əʊˌmiː.təʳ ⓤⓢ -əˌmiː.t̬ɚ-/.
kilo 'kiː.ləʊ ⓤⓢ -loʊ **-s** -z
kilobyte 'kɪl.əʊ.baɪt ⓤⓢ '-oʊ-, '-ə- **-s** -s
kilocalorie 'kɪl.əʊˌkæl.ᵊr.i ⓤⓢ '-oʊ-, '-ə- **-s** -z
kilocycle 'kɪl.əʊˌsaɪ.kl̩ ⓤⓢ -oʊˌ-, -əˌ- **-s** -z
kilogram, kilogramme 'kɪl.əʊ.græm ⓤⓢ '-oʊ-, '-ə- **-s** -z
kilohertz 'kɪl.əʊ.hɜːts, -heəts ⓤⓢ -oʊ.herts, '-ə-, -hɝːts
kilojoule 'kɪl.əʊ.dʒuːl ⓤⓢ '-oʊ-, '-ə- **-s** -z
kilolitre, kiloliter 'kɪl.əʊˌliː.təʳ ⓤⓢ -oʊˌliː.t̬ɚ, -əˌ- **-s** -z
kilometre, kilometer kɪ'lɒm.ɪ.təʳ, '-ə-; 'kɪl.əʊˌmiː- ⓤⓢ kɪ'lɑː.mə.t̬ɚ; 'kɪl.əˌmiː- **-s** -z
kiloton 'kɪl.əʊ.tʌn ⓤⓢ '-oʊ-, '-ə- **-s** -z
kilovolt 'kɪl.əʊ.vəʊlt ⓤⓢ -oʊ.voʊlt, '-ə- **-s** -s
kilowatt 'kɪl.əʊ.wɒt ⓤⓢ -oʊ.wɑːt, '-ə- **-s** -s
Kilpatrick kɪl'pæt.rɪk
Kilrush kɪl'rʌʃ
Kilsyth kɪl'saɪθ
kilt kɪlt **-s** -s **-ing** -ɪŋ ⓤⓢ 'kɪl.t̬ɪŋ **-ed** -ɪd ⓤⓢ 'kɪl.t̬ɪd
kilter 'kɪl.təʳ ⓤⓢ -t̬ɚ
Kilvert 'kɪl.vət ⓤⓢ -vɚt
Kilwarden kɪl'wɔː.dᵊn ⓤⓢ -'wɔːr-
Kilwinning kɪl'wɪn.ɪŋ
Kim kɪm
Kimball 'kɪm.bᵊl
Kimberl(e)y 'kɪm.bəl.i ⓤⓢ -bɚ.li
Kimbolton kɪm'bəʊl.tᵊn ⓤⓢ -'boʊl-
Kimmeridge 'kɪm.ᵊr.ɪdʒ
Kimmins 'kɪm.ɪnz
kimono kɪ'məʊ.nəʊ ⓤⓢ kə'moʊ.nə, -noʊ **-s** -z
kin kɪn
kina 'kiː.nə
kinaesthetic ˌkɪn.iːs'θet.ɪk, ˌkaɪ.niːs'-, -nɪs'- ⓤⓢ ˌkɪn.es'θet̬.ɪk
Kincardine kɪn'kɑː.dɪn, kɪŋ-, -dᵊn ⓤⓢ kɪn'kɑːr- **-shire** -ʃəʳ, -ˌʃɪəʳ ⓤⓢ -ʃɚ, -ˌʃɪr
Kinchinjunga ˌkɪn.tʃɪn'dʒʌŋ.gə ⓤⓢ -tʃɪn'dʒʊŋ-
kind kaɪnd **-s** -z **-er** -əʳ ⓤⓢ -ɚ **-est** -ɪst, -əst **-ly** -li **-ness/es** -nəs/ɪz, -nɪs/ɪz
kinda 'kaɪn.də
kindergarten 'kɪn.dəˌgɑː.tᵊn ⓤⓢ -dɚˌgɑːr- **-s** -z
Kinder Scout ˌkɪn.də'skaʊt ⓤⓢ -dɚ-
Kindersley 'kɪn.dəz.li ⓤⓢ -dɚz-
kind-hearted ˌkaɪnd'hɑː.tɪd ⓤⓢ -'hɑːr.t̬ɪd **-ly** -li **-ness** -nəs, -nɪs *stress shift:* ˌkindhearted 'person
kindl|e 'kɪn.dl̩ **-es** -z **-ing** -ɪŋ, 'kɪnd.lɪŋ **-ed** -d **-er/s** -əʳ/z, 'kɪnd.ləʳ/z ⓤⓢ -ɚ/z, 'kɪnd.lɚ/z
kindling 'kɪnd.lɪŋ, 'kɪn.dl̩.ɪŋ
kindl|y 'kaɪnd.l|i **-ier** -i.əʳ ⓤⓢ -i.ɚ **-iest** -i.ɪst, -i.əst **-iness** -ɪ.nəs, -ɪ.nɪs
kindred 'kɪn.drəd, -drɪd **ˌkindred 'spirit**
kine kaɪn
kinema 'kɪn.ɪ.mə, '-ə- **-s** -z
kinematic ˌkɪn.ɪ'mæt.ɪk, ˌkaɪ.nɪ'-, -nə'- ⓤⓢ ˌkɪn.ə'mæt̬- **-al** -ᵊl **-ally** -ᵊl.i, -li **-s** -s
kinematograph ˌkɪn.ɪ'mæt.ə.grɑːf, ˌkaɪ.nɪ'-, -nə'-, -græf ⓤⓢ ˌkɪn.ə'mæt̬.ə.græf **-s** -s
kinesics kɪ'niː.sɪks, kaɪ- ⓤⓢ -sɪks, -zɪks
kinesis kɪ'niː.sɪs, kaɪ- ⓤⓢ -sɪs, -zɪs
kinesthetic ˌkɪn.iːs'θet.ɪk, ˌkaɪ.niːs'-, -nɪs'- ⓤⓢ ˌkɪn.ɪs'θet̬-
kinetic kɪ'net.ɪk, kaɪ- ⓤⓢ kɪ'net̬- **-ally** -ᵊl.i, -li **-s** -s
kinfolk 'kɪn.fəʊk ⓤⓢ -foʊk **-s** -s
king (K) kɪŋ **-s** -z **ˌKing's 'Bench; ˌKing Charles 'spaniel; ˌKing's 'Counsel; ˌKing's 'English; ˌking's 'evidence; ˌKing's 'Lynn; ˌking 'prawn; 'king-ˌsize**
king-at-arms ˌkɪŋ.ət'ɑːmz ⓤⓢ -'ɑːrmz **kings-at-arms** ˌkɪŋz-
kingcraft 'kɪŋ.krɑːft ⓤⓢ -kræft
kingcup 'kɪŋ.kʌp **-s** -s
kingdom (K) 'kɪŋ.dəm **-s** -z **ˌkingdom 'come; ˌKingdom 'Hall**
Kingdon 'kɪŋ.dən
kingfisher 'kɪŋˌfɪʃ.əʳ ⓤⓢ -ɚ **-s** -z
Kinghorn 'kɪŋ.hɔːn ⓤⓢ -hɔːrn
Kinglake 'kɪŋ.leɪk
kingless 'kɪŋ.ləs, -lɪs
kinglet 'kɪŋ.lət, -lɪt **-s** -s
kinglike 'kɪŋ.laɪk
kingl|y 'kɪŋ.l|i **-ier** -i.əʳ ⓤⓢ -i.ɚ **-iest** -i.ɪst, -i.əst **-iness** -ɪ.nəs, -ɪ.nɪs
kingmaker (K) 'kɪŋˌmeɪ.kəʳ ⓤⓢ -kɚ **-s**
kingpin 'kɪŋ.pɪn, ˌ-'- ⓤⓢ 'kɪŋ.pɪn **-s** -z
Kingsborough 'kɪŋz.bᵊr.ə ⓤⓢ -oʊ
Kingsbury 'kɪŋz.bᵊr.i ⓤⓢ -ˌber-
Kingscote -kəʊt ⓤⓢ -kət, -koʊt
Kings Cross ˌkɪŋz'krɒs ⓤⓢ -'krɑːs *stress shift:* ˌKings Cross 'Station
kingship 'kɪŋ.ʃɪp
king-size 'kɪŋ.saɪz **-d** -d
Kingsley 'kɪŋz.li
Kings|man 'kɪŋz|.mən, -mæn **-men** -mən, -men
Kingsteignton kɪŋ'steɪn.tən ⓤⓢ -tᵊn
Kingston(e) 'kɪŋ.stən, 'kɪŋk-, 'kɪŋz.tən
Kingstown 'kɪŋz.taʊn, 'kɪŋ.stən, 'kɪŋk-
Kingsway 'kɪŋz.weɪ
Kingswinford kɪŋ'swɪn.fəd ⓤⓢ -fɚd
Kingswood 'kɪŋz.wʊd
Kington 'kɪŋ.tən, 'kɪŋk-
Kingussie kɪŋ'juː.si
kink kɪŋk **-s** -s **-ing** -ɪŋ **-ed** -t
kinkajou 'kɪŋ.kə.dʒuː **-s** -z
Kinkel 'kɪŋ.kᵊl
kink|y 'kɪŋ.k|i **-ier** -i.əʳ ⓤⓢ -i.ɚ **-iest** -i.ɪst, -i.əst **-iness** -ɪ.nəs, -ɪ.nɪs
kinless 'kɪn.ləs, -lɪs

Kinnaird kɪˈneəd (US) -ˈnerd
Kinnear kɪˈnɪəʳ, -ˈneəʳ (US) -ˈnɪr, -ˈner
Kinnock ˈkɪn.ək
Kinnoull kɪˈnuːl
kino ˈkiː.nəʊ (US) -noʊ
Kinros|s kɪnˈrɒs (US) -ˈrɑːs -shire -ʃəʳ, -ˌʃɪəʳ (US) -ʃɚ, -ˌʃɪr
Kinsale kɪnˈseɪl
Kinsella kɪnˈsel.ə, ˈkɪnt.sel.ə
Kinsey ˈkɪn.zi
kinsfolk ˈkɪnz.fəʊk (US) -foʊk
Kinshasa kɪnˈʃɑː.sə, -ˈʃæs.ə (US) -ˈʃɑː.sə, -sɑː
kinship ˈkɪn.ʃɪp
Kinski ˈkɪnt.ski
kins|man ˈkɪnz|.mən -men -mən, -men
kins|woman ˈkɪnz|ˌwʊm.ən -women -ˌwɪm.ɪn
Kintore kɪnˈtɔːʳ (US) -ˈtɔːr
Kintyre kɪnˈtaɪəʳ (US) -ˈtaɪr
kiosk ˈkiː.ɒsk (US) -ɑːsk, kiˈɑːsk -s -s
kip kɪp -s -s -ping -ɪŋ -ped -t
Kipling ˈkɪp.lɪŋ
Kippax ˈkɪp.æks, -əks
kipp|er ˈkɪp|.əʳ (US) -ɚ -ers -əz (US) -ɚz -ering -ᵊr.ɪŋ -ered -əd (US) -ɚd
Kipps kɪps
kir kɪəʳ (US) kɪr -s -z
Kirby ˈkɜː.bi (US) ˈkɝː-
Kircaldie kɜːˈkɔːl.di, kə- (US) kɝː-, kɚ-
Kirchner ˈkɜːk.nəʳ (US) ˈkɪrk.nɚ *US family name:* ˈkɜːtʃ.nəʳ, ˈkɜːʃ- (US) ˈkɝːtʃ.nɚ, ˈkɝːʃ-
Kirghiz ˈkɜː.gɪz, ˈkɪə- (US) kɪrˈgiːz
Kirghizia kɜːˈgɪz.i.ə, kɪə- (US) kɪrˈgiː.ʒə, -ʒi.ə
Kiribati ˌkɪr.əˈbæs, ˌkɪə.rəˈ-, -rɪˈ-; ˌkɪr.iˈbɑː.ti (US) ˌkɪr.iˈbɑː.ti; ˈkɪr.ə.bæs
Kiri Te Kanawa ˌkɪr.i.tɪˈkæn.ə.wə, ˌkɪə.ri-, -ˈkɑː.nə-, -teɪ- (US) ˌkɪr.i.təˈkɑː.nə.wɑː
Kiriyenko ˌkɪr.iˈjeŋ.kəʊ (US) -koʊ
Kirk kɜːk (US) kɝːk -s -s
Kirkby *surname:* ˈkɜː.bi, ˈkɜːk.bi (US) ˈkɝː-, ˈkɝːk- *place:* ˈkɜː.bi (US) ˈkɝː-
Kirkcaldy *place:* kɜːˈkɔː.di, kəˈkɒd.i, -ˈkɔː.di (US) kɝː-, kɚ- *surname:* kɜːˈkɔː.di, kə- (US) kɝː-, kɚ-
Kirkcudbright kɜːˈkuː.bri, kə- (US) kɝː-, kɚ- -shire -ʃəʳ, -ˌʃɪəʳ (US) -ʃɚ, -ˌʃɪr
Kirkdale ˈkɜːk.deɪl (US) ˈkɝːk-
Kirk(e) kɜːk (US) kɝːk
Kirkham ˈkɜː.kəm (US) ˈkɝː-
Kirkintilloch ˌkɜː.kɪnˈtɪl.ək *as if Scots:* -əx (US) ˌkɝː.kɪnˈtɪl.ək
Kirkland ˈkɜːk.lənd (US) ˈkɝːk-
Kirklees ˌkɜːkˈliːz (US) ˌkɝːk-
Kirkman ˈkɜːk.mən (US) ˈkɝːk-
Kirkness ˌkɜːkˈnes (US) ˌkɝːk-
Kirkpatrick ˌkɜːkˈpæt.rɪk (US) ˌkɝːk-
Kirkstall ˈkɜːk.stɔːl *locally also:* -stᵊl (US) ˈkɝːk-
Kirkuk kɜːˈkʊk, ˈ-- (US) kɪrˈkuːk
Kirkwall ˈkɜːk.wɔːl (US) ˈkɝːk-
Kirkwood ˈkɜːk.wʊd (US) ˈkɝːk-
Kirov ˈkɪə.rɒf, -rɒv (US) ˈkiː.rɔːf
Kirovabad kɪəˈrɒv.ə.bæd, kɪ- (US) kiːˈroʊ.və-, kɪ-
Kirriemuir ˌkɪr.iˈmjʊəʳ, -ˈmjɔːʳ (US) -ˈmjʊɚ
kirsch kɪəʃ, kɜːʃ (US) kɪrʃ
kirschwasser ˈkɪəʃˌvæs.əʳ, -ˌvɑː.səʳ (US) ˈkɪrʃˌvɑː.sɚ
Kirsten ˈkɜː.stɪn, ˈkɪə-, -stᵊn (US) ˈkɝː-, ˈkɪr-
Kirstie, **Kirsty** ˈkɜː.sti (US) ˈkɝː-
kirtle ˈkɜː.tl̩ (US) ˈkɝː.t̬l̩ -s -z
Kisangani ˌkɪs.æŋˈgɑː.ni (US) ˌkiː.sɑːnˈgɑː-
kish kɪʃ
Kishinev ˈkɪʃ.ɪ.nɒf, -nef (US) -nev, -nef, -nɔːf
Kishon ˈkaɪ.ʃɒn *with some Jews:* ˈkiː.ʃɒn (US) ˈkaɪ.ʃɑːn, -ʃᵊn
kismet ˈkɪz.met, ˈkɪs-, -mɪt, -mət (US) -met, -mɪt
kiss kɪs -es -ɪz -ing -ɪŋ -ed -t -er/s -əʳ/z (US) -ɚ/z ˌkiss of ˈdeath; ˌkiss of ˈlife
kissagram, **kiss-a-gram, kissogram** ˈkɪs.ə.græm -s -z
kiss-and-tell ˌkɪs.ᵊndˈtel
Kissinger ˈkɪs.ɪn.dʒəʳ, -ɪŋ.əʳ (US) -ən.dʒɚ, -ɪn-
kiss-off ˈkɪs.ɒf (US) -ɑːf
Kisumu kɪˈsuː.muː (US) kiː-
kit (K) kɪt -s -s -ting -ɪŋ (US) ˈkɪt̬.ɪŋ -ted -ɪd (US) ˈkɪt̬.ɪd ˌkit and caˈboodle; ˈkit ˌbag; ˈkit ˌcar
kitbag ˈkɪt.bæg -s -z
kit-cat (K) ˈkɪt.kæt -s -s
kitchen (K) ˈkɪtʃ.ɪn, -ᵊn -s -z ˌkitchen ˈcabinet; ˌkitchen ˈgarden; ˌkitchen ˈsink; ˌkitchen ˈunit
kitchener (K) ˈkɪtʃ.ɪ.nəʳ, -ᵊn.əʳ (US) -ə.nɚ -s -z
kitchenette ˌkɪtʃ.ɪˈnet, -əˈ- -s -s
kitchenmaid ˈkɪtʃ.ɪn.meɪd, -ᵊn- -s -z
kitchenware ˈkɪtʃ.ɪn.weəʳ, -ᵊn- (US) -wer
Kitchin ˈkɪtʃ.ɪn
Kitching ˈkɪtʃ.ɪŋ
kit|e kaɪt -es -s -ing -ɪŋ -ed -əd
Kit-E-Kat® ˈkɪt.i.kæt
kitemark ˈkaɪt.mɑːk (US) -mɑːrk
kith kɪθ
Kithnos ˈkɪθ.nɒs (US) -nɑːs
Kit-Kat® ˈkɪt.kæt
kitsch kɪtʃ -y -i
Kitson ˈkɪt.sᵊn
kitten ˈkɪt.ᵊn -s -z
kittenish ˈkɪt.ᵊn.ɪʃ -ly -li
kittiwake ˈkɪt.ɪ.weɪk (US) ˈkɪt̬- -s -s
Kitto ˈkɪt.əʊ (US) ˈkɪt̬.oʊ
Kittredge ˈkɪt.rɪdʒ
Kitts kɪts
Kittson ˈkɪt.sᵊn
kitt|y (K) ˈkɪt|.i (US) ˈkɪt̬- -ies -iz ˈKitty ˌHawk
Kitwe ˈkɪt.weɪ
Kitzbuhel, **Kitzbühel** ˈkɪts.bjuː.əl, -buː-, -bjuːl, -buːl
kiwi (K®) ˈkiː.wiː, -wi -s -z ˈkiwi ˌfruit
kJ *(abbrev. for* **kilojoule***)* ˈkɪl.əʊˌdʒuːl (US) ˈ-oʊ, ˈ-ə-
KKK *(abbrev. for* **Ku Klux Klan***)* ˌkeɪ.keɪˈkeɪ
kl *(abbrev. for* **kilolitre/s***) singular:* ˈkɪl.əʊˌliː.təʳ (US) -oʊˌliː.t̬ɚ, ˈ-ə- *plural:* ˈkɪl.əʊˌliː.təz (US) -oʊˌliː.t̬ɚz, ˈ-ə-
Klagenfurt ˈklɑː.gᵊn.fɜːt (US) -fɝːt
Klan klæn
Klans|man ˈklænz|.mən, -mæn -men -mən, -men
klatch klætʃ (US) klætʃ, klɑːtʃ -es -ɪz
klaxon ˈklæk.sᵊn -s -z
Klee kleɪ
Kleenex® ˈkliː.neks
Klein klaɪn
Kleinwort ˈkleɪn.wɔːt (US) -wɔːrt
Kleist klaɪst
Klemperer ˈklem.pᵊr.əʳ (US) -ɚ
kleptomani|a ˌklep.təʊˈmeɪ.ni|.ə (US) -toʊˈ-, -təˈ- -ac/s -æk/s
Kline klaɪn
Klondike ˈklɒn.daɪk (US) ˈklɑːn-
Kluge *English name:* kluːdʒ *German name:* ˈkluː.gə
klutz klʌts -es -ɪz
klutz|y ˈklʌt.s|i -iness -ɪ.nəs, -ɪ.nɪs
km *(abbrev. for* **kilometre/s***) singular:* kɪˈlɒm.ɪ.təʳ, ˈ-ə-; ˈkɪl.əʊˌmiː- (US) kɪˈlɑː.mə.t̬ɚ; ˈkɪl.əˌmiː- *plural:* kɪˈlɒm.ɪ.təz, ˈ-ə-; ˈkɪl.əʊˌmiː.təz (US) kɪˈlɑː.mɪ.t̬ɚz; ˈkɪl.əˌmiː.t̬ɚz
K Mart® ˈkeɪˌmɑːt (US) -ˌmɑːrt
knack næk -s -s
knack|er ˈnæk|.əʳ (US) -ɚ -ers -əz (US) -ɚz -ering -ᵊr.ɪŋ -ered -əd (US) -ɚd
knacker|y ˈnæk.ᵊr|.i -ies -iz
knag næg -s -z -gy -i
knap næp -s -s -ping -ɪŋ -ped -t
Knapp næp
knapsack ˈnæp.sæk -s -s
knar nɑːʳ (US) nɑːr -s -z
Knaresborough ˈneəz.bᵊr.ə, ˈ-brə (US) ˈnerz.bɚ.oʊ, ˈ-brə
knave neɪv -s -z
knaver|y ˈneɪ.vᵊr|.i -ies -iz
knavish ˈneɪ.vɪʃ -ly -li -ness -nəs, -nɪs
knead niːd -s -z -ing -ɪŋ -ed -ɪd
Knebworth ˈneb.wəθ, -wɜːθ (US) -wɚθ, -wɝːθ

knee niː **-s** -z **-ing** -ɪŋ **-d** -d ˌ**knee-ˈdeep; ˌweak at the ˈknees**
knee-breeches ˈniːˌbrɪtʃ.ɪz
kneecap ˈniː.kæp **-s** -s **-ping** -ɪŋ **-ped** -t
knee-high *(adj.)* ˌniːˈhaɪ *stress shift:* ˌknee-high ˈsocks
kneehigh *(n.)* ˈniː.haɪ **-s** -z
knee-jerk ˈniː.dʒɜːk ⓤⓢ -dʒɝːk
knee-joint ˈniː.dʒɔɪnt **-s** -s
kneel niːl **-s** -z **-ing** -ɪŋ **-ed** -d **knelt** nelt
knees-up ˈniːz.ʌp
knell nel **-s** -z **-ing** -ɪŋ **-ed** -d
Kneller ˈnel.əʳ ⓤⓢ -ɚ **-s** -z
knelt *(from* **kneel***)* nelt
Knesset ˈknes.et, kəˈnes-, -ɪt
knew *(from* **know***)* njuː, nuː ⓤⓢ nuː, njuː
knicker ˈnɪk.əʳ ⓤⓢ -ɚ **-s** -z
knickerbocker (K) ˈnɪk.əˌbɒk.əʳ ⓤⓢ -ɚˌbɑː.kɚ **-s** -z ˌ**knickerbocker ˈglory**
knick-knack ˈnɪk.næk **-s** -s **-ery** -ᵊr.i
kni|fe *(n.)* naɪ|f **-ves** -vz
knif|e *(v.)* naɪf **-es** -s **-ing** -ɪŋ **-ed** -t
knight (K) naɪt **-s** -s **-ing** -ɪŋ ⓤⓢ ˈnaɪ.t̬ɪŋ **-ed** -ɪd ⓤⓢ ˈnaɪ.t̬ɪd
knight-errant ˌnaɪtˈer.ᵊnt **knights-errant** ˌnaɪtsˈer.ᵊnt
knighthood ˈnaɪt.hʊd **-s** -z
Knightley ˈnaɪt.li
knightl|y ˈnaɪt.l|i **-ier** -i.əʳ ⓤⓢ -i.ɚ **-iest** -i.ɪst, -i.əst **-iness** -ɪ.nəs, -ɪ.nɪs
Knighton ˈnaɪ.tᵊn
Knightsbridge ˈnaɪts.brɪdʒ
knish kəˈnɪʃ **-es** -ɪz
knit nɪt **-s** -s **-ting** -ɪŋ ⓤⓢ ˈnɪt̬.ɪŋ **-ted** -ɪd ⓤⓢ ˈnɪt̬.ɪd **-ter/s** -əʳ/z ⓤⓢ ˈnɪt̬.ɚ/z **ˈknitting maˌchine; ˈknitting ˌneedle**
knitwear ˈnɪt.weəʳ ⓤⓢ -wer
knob nɒb ⓤⓢ nɑːb **-s** -z
knobbly ˈnɒb.l̩.i, ˈ-li ⓤⓢ ˈnɑː.bl̩.i, ˈ-bli
knobb|y ˈnɒb|.i ⓤⓢ ˈnɑː.b|i **-ier** -i.əʳ ⓤⓢ -i.ɚ **-iest** -i.ɪst, -i.əst **-iness** -ɪ.nəs, -ɪ.nɪs
knock nɒk ⓤⓢ nɑːk **-s** -s **-ing/s** -ɪŋ/z **-ed** -t **-er/s** -əʳ/z ⓤⓢ -ɚ/z
knockabout ˈnɒk.əˌbaʊt ⓤⓢ ˈnɑːk- **-s** -s
Knockbreda nɒkˈbreɪ.də ⓤⓢ nɑːk-
knock-down ˈnɒk.daʊn ⓤⓢ ˈnɑːk.daʊn
knock-down-drag-out ˌnɒk.daʊnˈdræg.aʊt ⓤⓢ ˌnɑːk- *stress shift:* ˌknock-down-ˌdrag-out ˈfight
knock-kneed ˌnɒkˈniːd ⓤⓢ ˈnɑːk.niːd *stress shift:* ˌknock-kneed ˈchild
knockoff ˈnɒk.ɒf ⓤⓢ ˈnɑːk.ɑːf **-s** -s
knock-on *(adj.)* ˌnɒkˈɒn ⓤⓢ ˌnɑːkˈɑːn *stress shift, see compound:* **ˈknock-on efˌfect**
knock-on *(n.) (in rugby)* ˌnɒkˈɒn, ˈ-- ⓤⓢ ˌnɑːkˈɑːn, ˈ--
knock-out ˈnɒk.aʊt ⓤⓢ ˈnɑːk- **-s** -s **ˈknockout ˌdrops**
knock-up ˈnɒk.ʌp ⓤⓢ ˈnɑːk- **-s** -s
knockwurst ˈnɒk.wɜːst ⓤⓢ ˈnɑːk.wɝːst, -wʊrst
Knole nəʊl ⓤⓢ noʊl
knoll nəʊl ⓤⓢ noʊl **-s** -z
Knolles, Knollys nəʊlz ⓤⓢ noʊlz
knop nɒp ⓤⓢ nɑːp **-s** -s
Knopfler ˈnɒp.fləʳ ⓤⓢ ˈnɑːp.flɚ
Knossos ˈknɒs.ɒs, ˈknəʊ.sɒs, -səs ⓤⓢ ˈnɑː.səs
knot nɒt ⓤⓢ nɑːt **-s** -s **-ting** -ɪŋ ⓤⓢ ˈnɑː.t̬ɪŋ **-ted** -ɪd ⓤⓢ ˈnɑː.t̬ɪd **at a ˌrate of ˈknots**
knotgrass ˈnɒt.grɑːs ⓤⓢ ˈnɑːt.græs
knothole ˈnɒt.həʊl ⓤⓢ ˈnɑːt.hoʊl **-s** -z
Knott nɒt ⓤⓢ nɑːt
Knottingley ˈnɒt.ɪŋ.li ⓤⓢ ˈnɑː.t̬ɪŋ-
knott|y ˈnɒt|.i ⓤⓢ ˈnɑː.t̬|i **-ier** -i.əʳ ⓤⓢ -i.ɚ **-iest** -i.ɪst, -i.əst **-ily** -ɪ.li, -ᵊl.i **-iness** -ɪ.nəs, -ɪ.nɪs
Knotty Ash ˌnɒt.iˈæʃ ⓤⓢ ˌnɑː.t̬i-
knout naʊt **-s** -s **-ing** -ɪŋ ⓤⓢ ˈnaʊ.t̬ɪŋ **-ed** -ɪd ⓤⓢ ˈnaʊ.t̬ɪd
know nəʊ ⓤⓢ noʊ **-s** -z **-ing** -ɪŋ **knew** njuː ⓤⓢ nuː **known** nəʊn ⓤⓢ noʊn **knower/s** ˈnəʊ.əʳ/z ⓤⓢ ˈnoʊ.ɚ/z **knowable** ˈnəʊ.ə.bl̩ ⓤⓢ ˈnoʊ-
know-all ˈnəʊ.ɔːl ⓤⓢ ˈnoʊ-, -ɑːl **-s** -z
know-how ˈnəʊ.haʊ ⓤⓢ ˈnoʊ-
knowing ˈnəʊ.ɪŋ ⓤⓢ ˈnoʊ- **-ly** -li **-ness** -nəs, -nɪs
know-it-all ˈnəʊ.ɪt.ɔːl ⓤⓢ ˈnoʊ.ɪt̬-, -ɑːl **-s** -z
Knowle nəʊl ⓤⓢ noʊl
knowledg|e ˈnɒl.ɪdʒ ⓤⓢ ˈnɑː.lɪdʒ **-es** -ɪz
knowledgeab|le ˈnɒl.ɪ.dʒə.b|l̩ ⓤⓢ ˈnɑː.lɪ- **-ly** -li
Knowles nəʊlz ⓤⓢ noʊlz
known *(from* **know***)* nəʊn ⓤⓢ noʊn
know-nothing ˈnəʊˌnʌθ.ɪŋ ⓤⓢ ˈnoʊ- **-s** -z
Knox nɒks ⓤⓢ nɑːks
Knoxville ˈnɒks.vɪl ⓤⓢ ˈnɑːks-, -vᵊl
knuckl|e ˈnʌk.l̩ **-es** -z **-ing** -ɪŋ, ˈ-lɪŋ **-ed** -d **-y** -i, ˈ-li ˌ**knuckle ˈsandwich**
knuckleball ˈnʌk.l̩.bɔːl ⓤⓢ -bɔːl, -bɑːl
knucklebone ˈnʌk.l̩.bəʊn ⓤⓢ -boʊn **-s** -z
knuckle-duster ˈnʌk.l̩ˌdʌs.təʳ ⓤⓢ -tɚ **-s** -z
knucklehead ˈnʌk.l̩.hed **-ed** -ɪd
knurled nɜːld ⓤⓢ nɝːld
Knutsford ˈnʌts.fəd ⓤⓢ -fɚd
KO, k.o. ˌkeɪˈəʊ ⓤⓢ -ˈoʊ **-ˈs** -z **-ˈing** -ɪŋ **-ˈd** -d
koala kəʊˈɑː.lə ⓤⓢ koʊ- **-s** -z
Kobe ˈkəʊ.beɪ, -bi ⓤⓢ ˌkoʊˈbeɪ, ˈkoʊ.bi
Koblenz kəʊˈblents ⓤⓢ ˈkoʊ.blents
kobo ˈkɒb.əʊ ⓤⓢ ˈkɑː.boʊ, ˈkoʊ-; ˈkɔː.bɔː
kobold ˈkɒb.əʊld, ˈkəʊ.bəʊld, -bᵊld ⓤⓢ ˈkoʊ.bɔːld, -bɑːld **-s** -z
Koch kəʊk, kɒtʃ *as if German:* kɒx ⓤⓢ koʊk, kɑːk, kɑːtʃ *as if German:* kɔːx, koʊx
Köchel ˈkɜː.kᵊl *as if German:* -xᵊl ⓤⓢ ˈkɝː- **ˈKöchel ˌnumber**
Kodak® ˈkəʊ.dæk ⓤⓢ ˈkoʊ- **-s** -s
Kodály ˈkəʊ.daɪ, -dɑː.i ⓤⓢ ˈkoʊ-; koʊˈdɑː.i
Kodiak ˈkəʊ.di.æk ⓤⓢ ˈkoʊ-
Koestler ˈkɜːst.ləʳ ⓤⓢ ˈkest.lɚ
Koh-i-noor ˌkəʊ.iˈnʊəʳ, -ˈnɔəʳ, -ˈnɔːʳ, ˈ--- ⓤⓢ ˈkoʊ.ɪ.nʊr
kohl kəʊl ⓤⓢ koʊl
Kohl kəʊl ⓤⓢ koʊl
kohlrab|i ˌkəʊlˈrɑː.b|i ⓤⓢ ˌkoʊl-, ˈ--- **-ies** -iz
koine (K) ˈkɔɪ.neɪ, -niː, -ni ⓤⓢ kɔɪˈneɪ; ˈkɔɪ.neɪ, -niː
Kojak ˈkəʊ.dʒæk ⓤⓢ ˈkoʊ-
kola (K) ˈkəʊ.lə ⓤⓢ ˈkoʊ-
kolkhoz ˌkɒlˈkɒz, -ˈkɔːz, -ˈhɔːz ⓤⓢ ˌkɑːlˈkɔːz **-es** -ɪz
Kolnai ˈkɒl.naɪ ⓤⓢ ˈkɑːl-
Komodo kəˈməʊ.dəʊ ⓤⓢ -ˈmoʊ.doʊ
Kongo ˈkɒŋ.gəʊ ⓤⓢ ˈkɑːŋ.goʊ
Konica® ˈkɒn.ɪ.kə, ˈkəʊ.nɪ- ⓤⓢ ˈkɑː.nɪ-
Königsberg ˈkɜː.nɪgz.bɜːg, -beəg ⓤⓢ ˈkɝː.nɪgz.bɝːrg, -berg
Konrad ˈkɒn.ræd ⓤⓢ ˈkɑːn-
Konya ˈkɔː.njɑː
koodoo ˈkuː.duː **-s** -z
kook kuːk **-s** -s
kookaburra ˈkʊk.əˌbʌr.ə ⓤⓢ -ˌbɝː-, -ˌbʌr- **-s** -z
kook|y ˈkuː.k|i **-ier** -i.əʳ ⓤⓢ -i.ɚ **-iest** -i.ɪst, -i.əst **-iness** -ɪ.nəs, -ɪ.nɪs
Kool-Aide® ˈkuːl.eɪd
Koori(e) ˈkʊə.ri, ˈkɔː- ⓤⓢ ˈkʊr.i
Kop kɒp ⓤⓢ kɑːp
kope(c)k ˈkəʊ.pek, ˈkɒp.ek ⓤⓢ ˈkoʊ.pek **-s** -s
kopje ˈkɒp.i ⓤⓢ ˈkɑː.pi **-s** -z
Kops kɒps ⓤⓢ kɑːps
Korah ˈkɔː.rə ⓤⓢ ˈkɔːr.ə
Koran kɒrˈɑːn, kɔːˈrɑːn, kʊ-, kə- ⓤⓢ kəˈræn, -ˈrɑːn; ˈkɔːr.æn, -ɑːn
Koranic kɒrˈæn.ɪk, kɔːˈræn-, kʊ-, kə- ⓤⓢ kəˈræn.ɪk, -ˈrɑː.nɪk; ˈkɔːr.æn.ɪk -ɑː.nɪk
Kore|a kəˈriːl.ə, kɒrˈiː- ⓤⓢ kəˈriː-, kɔː- **-an/s** -ᵊn/z
korma ˈkɔː.mə ⓤⓢ ˈkɔːr-
koruna kɒrˈuː.nə, kəˈruː- ⓤⓢ ˈkɔːr.uː- **-s** -z
koruny *(plur. of* **koruna***)* kɒrˈuː.ni, kəˈruː- ⓤⓢ ˈkɔːr.uː-
kosher ˈkəʊ.ʃəʳ *occasionally, by non-Jews:* ˈkɒʃ.əʳ ⓤⓢ ˈkoʊ.ʃɚ
Kosice kɒʃˈɪt.sə ⓤⓢ ˈkɔː.ʃiː.t.seɪ, -ʃɪt-
Kosov|o ˈkɒs.ə.v|əʊ ⓤⓢ ˈkoʊ.sə.v|oʊ, ˈkɑː-, ˈkɔː- **-an** -ən **-ar/s** -ɑːʳ/z ⓤⓢ -ɑːr/z

Kostunica kɒsˈtuː.nɪt.sə
(US) kɑːs.tuː.ˈnit.sə
Kosygin kəˈsiː.gɪn (US) kə-, koʊ-
Kotex® ˈkəʊ.teks (US) ˈkoʊ-
kotow ˌkəʊˈtaʊ (US) ˌkoʊ- **-s** -z **-ing** -ɪŋ **-ed** -d **-er/s** -əʳ/z (US) -ɚ/z
Kough kjəʊ, kəʊ (US) kjoʊ, koʊ
koumiss ˈkuː.mɪs, -məs
Kournikova ˌkɔː.nɪˈkəʊ.və, -nəˈ-
(US) ˌkɔːr.nɪˈkoʊ-, -nəˈ-
Kowasaki kəʊ.əˈsɑː.ki, -ˈsæk.i (US) koʊ-
Kowloon ˌkaʊˈluːn
kowtow ˌkaʊˈtaʊ (US) ˌkaʊˈtaʊ, ˈ-- **-s** -z **-ing** -ɪŋ **-ed** -d **-er/s** -əʳ/z (US) -ɚ/z
kraal krɑːl, krɔːl **-s** -z
Note: Usually pronounced /krɑːl/ in England, but /krɔːl/ in South Africa.
Kraft® krɑːft (US) kræft
Kragujevac krægˈuː.jə.væts
(US) ˈkrɑː.guː.jə.vɑːts
krait kraɪt **-s** -s
Krajicek ˈkraɪ.tʃek, ˈkrɑː.jɪ.tʃek, ˈkraɪ.ə.tʃek
Krakatoa ˌkræk.əˈtəʊ.ə (US) -ˈtoʊ-
kraken ˈkrɑː.kᵊn, ˈkreɪ- (US) ˈkrɑː- **-s** -z
Krakow ˈkræk.ɒv, -ɒf, -aʊ
(US) ˈkrɑː.kaʊ, ˈkræk.aʊ, ˈkreɪ.kaʊ; ˈkrɑː.kʊf
Kramer ˈkreɪ.məʳ (US) -mɚ
krantz (K) krænts
Krasnodar ˌkrɑːs.nəʊˈdɑːʳ
(US) -noʊˈdɑːr
Krasnoyarsk ˌkrɑːs.nəʊˈjɑːsk
(US) -noʊˈjɑːrsk
Kravchuk krævˈtʃʊk
Kray kreɪ
kremlin (K) ˈkrem.lɪn **-s** -z
Kremlinolog|y ˌkrem.lɪˈnɒl.ə.dʒ|i
(US) -ˈnɑː.lə- **-ist/s** -ɪst/s
kreu(t)zer (K) ˈkrɔɪt.səʳ (US) -sɚ **-s** -z
krill krɪl
kris kriːs **-es** -ɪz
Krishna ˈkrɪʃ.nə
Kris Kringle, Kriss Kringle ˌkrɪsˈkrɪŋ.gl̩
Krista ˈkrɪs.tə
Kristen ˈkrɪs.tᵊn, -tɪn
Kristi ˈkrɪs.ti
Kristiansand ˈkrɪs.tʃᵊn.sænd
Kristie ˈkrɪs.ti
Kristin ˈkrɪs.tɪn
Kristina krɪˈstiː.nə
Kristine krɪˈstiːn
Kristopher ˈkrɪs.tə.fəʳ (US) -fɚ
kro|na ˈkrəʊ|.nə (US) ˈkroʊ- **-nor** -nɔːʳ
(US) -nɔːr
kró|na ˈkrəʊ|.nə (US) ˈkroʊ- **-nur** -nʊəʳ
(US) -nɚ

kro|ne ˈkrəʊ|.nə (US) ˈkroʊ- **-nes** -nəz **-ner** -nəʳ **-nen** -nən
Kronin ˈkrəʊ.nɪn (US) ˈkroʊ-
Krons(h)tadt ˈkrɒnt.ʃtæt
(US) ˈkrɔːnt.ʃtɑːt
kroon kruːn
Krug kruːg
Kruger ˈkruː.gəʳ (US) -gɚ
krugerrand (K) ˈkruː.gᵊr.ænd (US) -gɚ- **-s** -z
Krupp krʊp, krʌp
Krushchev ˈkrʊs.tʃɒf, ˈkrʊʃ-, ˌ-ˈ-
(US) ˈkruː.tʃef, -tʃɔːf, -tʃev, kruːʃˈtʃɔːf
krypton ˈkrɪp.tɒn, -tən (US) -tɑːn
kryptonite ˈkrɪp.tᵊn.aɪt (US) -tə.naɪt
Krystal ˈkrɪs.tᵊl
Krystle ˈkrɪs.tl̩
Kuala Lumpur ˌkwɑː.ləˈlʊm.pʊəʳ, ˌkwɒl-, -ˈlʌm-, -pəʳ
(US) ˌkwɑː.ləˈlʊm.pʊr
Kubla Khan ˌkuː.bləˈkɑːn, ˌkʊb.ləˈ-
(US) ˌkuː.bləˈ-
Kubrick ˈkjuː.brɪk, ˈkuː-
kudos ˈkjuː.dɒs (US) ˈkuː.doʊz, ˈkjuː-, -doʊs, -dɑːs
Kudrow ˈkʊd.rəʊ (US) ˈkuːdroʊ
kudu ˈkuː.duː **-s** -z
Ku Klux Klan ˌkuː.klʌksˈklæn, ˌkjuː-
kulak ˈkuː.læk (US) kuːˈlɑːk, ˈ-- **-s** -s
kultur (K) kʊlˈtʊəʳ (US) -ˈtʊr
Kumanovo ˌkuː.məˈnəʊ.vəʊ
(US) ˈkʊm.əˌnoʊ.voʊ
Kumar kuːˈmɑːʳ (US) ˈkuː.mɑːr
Kumasi kʊˈmæs.i, -ˈmɑː.si (US) -ˈmɑː.si
Kumin ˈkjuː.mɪn, ˈkuː- (US) ˈkuː-
kümmel ˈkʊm.ᵊl, ˈkɪm- (US) ˈkɪm-
kumquat ˈkʌm.kwɒt (US) -kwɑːt **-s** -s
Kundera ˈkʊn.də.rə (US) -dɚ.ə
kung fu ˌkʊŋˈfuː, ˌkʌŋ- (US) ˌkʌŋ-, ˌkʊŋ-, ˌgʊŋ-
Kunitz ˈkjuː.nɪts, ˈkuː- (US) ˈkuː-
Kuomintang ˌkwəʊ.mɪnˈtæŋ, ˌgwəʊ-
(US) ˌkwoʊ-
Kuoni® kuˈəʊ.ni (US) -ˈoʊ-
Kurath ˈkjʊə.ræθ (US) ˈkʊr.ɑːt, ˈkjʊr-
(US) -ɑːθ
Kurd kɜːd (US) kɝːd, kʊrd **-s** -z **-ish** -ɪʃ
Kurdistan ˌkɜː.dɪˈstɑːn, -dəˈ-, -ˈstæn
(US) ˌkɝː.dɪˈstæn, ˌkʊr-, -dəˈ-, -ˈstɑːn
Kureishi kʊˈreʃ.i, -ˈreɪ.ʃi, -ˈriː-
Kuril(e) kʊˈriːl, kjuː- (US) ˈkuː.rɪl; kuːˈriːl **-s** -z
Kurosawa ˌkʊə.rəʊˈsɑː.wə (US) ˌkʊr.əˈ-
kursaal ˈkʊə.zɑːl, ˈkɜː-, -sɑːl, -sᵊl
(US) ˈkʊr-, ˈkɝː- **-s** -z
Kursk kɜːsk, kʊəsk (US) kɝːsk
Kurt kɜːt (US) kɝːt

Kurtis ˈkɜː.tɪs (US) ˈkɝː.t̬ɪs
Kurtz kɜːts (US) kɝːts
kurus kʊˈrʊʃ, -ˈruːʃ (US) -ˈruːʃ
Kutaisi kʊˈtaɪ.si (US) kʊˈtaɪ.si, ˌkuː.təˈjiː.si
Ku|wait kuː|ˈweɪt, kjuː-, kə-
(US) kuː|ˈweɪt, -ˈwaɪt **-waiti/s** -ˈweɪ.ti/z (US) -ˈweɪ.t̬i/z, -ˈwaɪ.t̬i/z
Kuyper ˈkaɪ.pəʳ (US) -pɚ
kvas(s) kvɑːs, kvæs (US) kvɑːs, kəˈvɑːs
kvetch kvetʃ, kəˈvetʃ **-es** -ɪz **-ing** -ɪŋ **-ed** -t
kW *(abbrev. for* **kilowatt***)* ˈkɪl.əʊ.wɒt
(US) -oʊ.wɑːt, ˈ-ə-
kwacha ˈkwɑː.tʃɑː
Kwangtung ˌkwænˈtʌŋ, ˌkwæŋ-
(US) ˌkwɑːŋˈtʊŋ, ˌgwɑːŋ-
Kwantung ˌkwænˈtʌŋ (US) ˌkwɑːŋˈtʊŋ, ˌgwɑːŋ-
kwanza ˈkwæn.zə (US) ˈkwɑːn.zɑː, -zə **-s** -z
Kwanzaa ˈkwɑːn.zə, ˈkwæn-, -zɑː
(US) ˈkwɑːn- **-s** -z
kwashiorcor ˌkwæʃ.iˈɔː.kɔːʳ, -kəʳ
(US) ˌkwɑː.ʃiːˈɔːr.kɔːr
KwaZulu kwɑːˈzuː.luː
KwaZulu-Natal kwɑːˌzuː.luː.nəˈtæl, -ˈtɑːl
kwela ˈkweɪ.lə
KWIC kwɪk
Ky. *(abbrev. for* **Kentucky***)* kenˈtʌk.i, kən- (US) kən-
kyat kiˈɑːt (US) tʃɑːt, kjɑːt
Kyd kɪd
Kyla ˈkaɪ.lə
kyle (K) kaɪl **-s** -z
Kylie ˈkaɪ.li
kylin ˈkaɪ.lɪn **-s** -z
Kyllachy ˈkaɪ.lə.ki, -xi (US) -ki
kyloe ˈkaɪ.ləʊ (US) -loʊ **-s** -z
kymogram ˈkaɪ.məʊ.græm (US) -moʊ-, -mə-
kymograph ˈkaɪ.məʊ.grɑːf, -græf
(US) -moʊ.græf, -mə- **-s** -s
kymographic ˌkaɪ.məʊˈgræf.ɪk
(US) -moʊˈ-, -məˈ-
Kynance ˈkaɪ.nænts
Kynaston ˈkɪn.ə.stᵊn
Kyoto ˈkjəʊ.təʊ, kiˈəʊ.təʊ
(US) kiːˈoʊ.toʊ, ˈkjoʊ-
Kyrgyzstan ˌkɜː.gɪˈstɑːn
(US) ˈkɪr.gɪ.stɑːn, -stæn, ˌ--ˈ-
kyrie ˈkɪr.i.eɪ, ˈkɪə.ri-, -iː (US) ˈkɪr.i.eɪ **-s** -z
Kyrle kɜːl (US) kɝːl
Kythe ˈkaɪ.θi
Kyushu ˈkjuː.ʃuː, kiˈuː-
Kyzyl-Kum kəˌzɪlˈkuːm, -ˈkʊm

Pronouncing the letter L

See also LL

In general, the consonant letter l is pronounced /l/, e.g.:

like /laɪk/
wool /wʊl/

However, l is frequently silent, particularly when preceded by an a, e.g.:

calf /kɑːf/ ⓤⓢ /kæf/
calm /kɑːm/ ⓤⓢ /kɑːlm/

In the past tense form of modal verbs spelt **ould**, l is also silent, e.g.:

could /kʊd/
would /wʊd/

l (L) el **-'s** -z
l *(abbrev. for* **litre/s***) singular:* 'liː.təʳ ⓤⓢ -t̬ɚ *plural:* 'liː.təz ⓤⓢ -t̬ɚz
la lɑː **-s** -z
La. *(abbrev. for* **Louisiana***)* luˌiː.zi'æn.ə, -'ɑː.nə; ˌluː.i.zi'- ⓤⓢ luˌiː.zi'æn.ə; ˌluː.zi'-
LA ˌel'eɪ *stress shift:* ˌLA 'Law
laager 'lɑː.gəʳ ⓤⓢ -gɚ **-s** -z
laari 'lɑː.ri ⓤⓢ 'lɑːr.i **-s** -z
lab læb **-s** -z
Laban *biblical character:* 'leɪ.bən, -bæn ⓤⓢ -bən *US family name:* lə'bæn
label 'leɪ.bəl **-s** -z **-(l)ing** -ɪŋ, 'leɪ.blɪŋ **-(l)ed** -d
labia *(from* **labium***)* 'leɪ.bi.ə
labial 'leɪ.bi.əl **-s** -z **-ly** -i
labialization, -isa- ˌleɪ.bi.əl.aɪ'zeɪ.ʃən, -ɪ'- ⓤⓢ -ɪ'-
labializ|e, -is|e 'leɪ.bi.əl.aɪz **-es** -ɪz **-ing** -ɪŋ **-ed** -d
labia majora ˌleɪ.bi.ə.mə'dʒɔː.rə, -maɪ'ɔː- ⓤⓢ -mə'dʒɔːr.ə
labia minora ˌleɪ.bi.ə.mɪ'nɔː.rə ⓤⓢ -'nɔːr.ə
labiate 'leɪ.bi.eɪt, -ət, -ɪt **-s** -s
Labienus ˌlæb.i'iː.nəs, -'eɪ-
labile 'leɪ.baɪl ⓤⓢ -baɪl, -bəl
labiodental ˌleɪ.bi.əʊ'den.təl ⓤⓢ -oʊ'den.t̬əl **-s** -z
labiopalatal ˌleɪ.bi.əʊ'pæl.ə.təl ⓤⓢ -oʊ'pæl.ə.t̬əl **-s** -z **-ly** -li
labiovelar ˌleɪ.bi.əʊ'viː.ləʳ ⓤⓢ -oʊ'viː.lɚ **-s** -z
labiovelariz|e, -is|e ˌleɪ.bi.əʊ'viː.lər.aɪz ⓤⓢ -oʊ'viː.lə.raɪz **-es** -ɪz **-ing** -ɪŋ **-ed** -d
labi|um 'leɪ.bi|.əm **-a** -ə
La Bohème ˌlɑː.bəʊ'em, ˌlæ-, -'eɪm ⓤⓢ ˌlɑː.boʊ'-
lab|or (L) 'leɪ.b|əʳ ⓤⓢ -b|ɚ **-ors** -əz ⓤⓢ -ɚz **-oring** -ər.ɪŋ **-ored** -əd ⓤⓢ -ɚd **-orer/s** -ər.əʳ/z ⓤⓢ -ɚ.ɚ/z ˌ**labor of** '**love**; '**labor** ˌ**union**
laborator|y lə'bɒr.ə.tər|.i, -tr|i ⓤⓢ 'læb.rə.tɔːr|.i, 'læb.ɚ.ə- **-ies** -iz
labor-intensive ˌleɪ.bər.ɪn'tent.sɪv ⓤⓢ -bɚ- *stress shift:* ˌlabor-intensive 'work
laborious lə'bɔː.ri.əs ⓤⓢ -'bɔːr.i- **-ly** -li **-ness** -nəs, -nɪs
laborite (L) 'leɪ.bər.aɪt ⓤⓢ -bə.raɪt **-s** -s
labor-saving 'leɪ.bəˌseɪ.vɪŋ ⓤⓢ -bɚˌ- *stress shift:* ˌlabor-saving 'gadget
Labouchere ˌlæb.uː'ʃeəʳ, -ʊ'-, '--- ⓤⓢ ˌlæb.uː'ʃer
lab|our (L) 'leɪ.b|əʳ ⓤⓢ -b|ɚ **-ours** -əz ⓤⓢ -ɚz **-ouring** -ər.ɪŋ **-oured** -əd ⓤⓢ -ɚd **-ourer/s** '-ər.əʳ/z '**labour exˌchange**; ˌ**labour of** '**love**; '**Labour** ˌ**Party**
labour-intensive ˌleɪ.bər.ɪn'tent.sɪv ⓤⓢ -bɚ- *stress shift:* ˌlabour-intensive 'work
labourite (L) 'leɪ.bər.aɪt ⓤⓢ -bə.raɪt **-s** -s
labour-saving 'leɪ.bəˌseɪ.vɪŋ ⓤⓢ -bɚˌ- *stress shift:* ˌlabour-saving 'gadget
Labrador 'læb.rə.dɔːʳ ⓤⓢ -dɔːr **-s** -z
Labuan lə'buː.ən ⓤⓢ ˌlɑː.buː'ɑːn, lə'buː.ən
laburnum lə'bɜː.nəm ⓤⓢ -'bɝː- **-s** -z
labyrinth 'læb.ər.ɪntθ, -ɪ.rɪntθ ⓤⓢ -ɚ.ɪntθ, '-əntθ **-s** -s
labyrinth|ian ˌlæb.ə'rɪnt.θ|i.ən, -ɪ'- ⓤⓢ -ə'rɪnt- **-ine** -aɪn ⓤⓢ -ɪn, -iːn, -aɪn
lac læk **-s** -s
Laccadive 'læk.ə.dɪv, 'lɑː.kə-, -diːv, -daɪv ⓤⓢ 'læk.ə.daɪv; 'lɑː.kə.diːv **-s** -z
laccolith 'læk.ə.lɪθ
lac|e leɪs **-es** -ɪz **-ing** -ɪŋ **-ed** -t **-er/s** -əʳ/z ⓤⓢ -ɚ/z
Lacedaemon ˌlæs.ə'diː.mən, -ɪ'- ⓤⓢ -ə'-
Lacedaemonian ˌlæs.ə.dɪ'məʊ.ni.ən, ˌ-ɪ-, -də'- ⓤⓢ -ə.dɪ'moʊ.ni- **-s** -z
lacer|ate 'læs.ər|.eɪt ⓤⓢ -ə.r|eɪt **-ates** -eɪts **-ating** -eɪ.tɪŋ ⓤⓢ -eɪ.t̬ɪŋ **-ated** -eɪ.tɪd ⓤⓢ -eɪ.t̬ɪd
laceration ˌlæs.ər'eɪ.ʃən ⓤⓢ -ə'reɪ- **-s** -z
Lacert|a lə'sɜː.t|ə ⓤⓢ -'sɝː.t̬|ə **-ae** -iː
Lacey 'leɪ.si
laches 'lætʃ.ɪz, 'leɪ.tʃɪz, -tʃəz ⓤⓢ 'lætʃ.ɪz, 'leɪ.tʃɪz
Lachesis 'læk.ə.sɪs, -ɪ- ⓤⓢ 'læk-, 'lætʃ-
Lachish 'leɪ.kɪʃ
Lachlan 'læk.lən, 'lɒk.lən ⓤⓢ 'lɑːk-
lachrymal 'læk.rɪ.məl
lachrymatory ˌlæk.rɪ'meɪ.tər.i; 'læk.rɪ.mə-, -meɪ- ⓤⓢ 'læk.rɪ.mə.tɔːr-
lachrymose 'læk.rɪ.məʊs, -rə-, -məʊz ⓤⓢ -rɪ.moʊs **-ly** -li
lack læk **-s** -s **-ing** -ɪŋ **-ed** -t
lackadaisic|al ˌlæk.ə'deɪ.zɪ.k|əl **-ally** -əl.i, -li **-alness** -nəs, -nɪs
lackaday 'læk.ə.deɪ, ˌ--'-
lackey 'læk.i **-s** -z **-ing** -ɪŋ **-ed** -d
lacklustre, lackluster 'lækˌlʌs.təʳ, ˌ-'-- ⓤⓢ 'lækˌlʌs.tɚ
Lacon 'leɪ.kən
Laconi|a lə'kəʊ.ni|.ə ⓤⓢ -'koʊ- **-an/s** -ən/z
laconic (L) lə'kɒn.ɪk ⓤⓢ -'kɑː.nɪk **-al** -əl **-ally** -əl.i, -li
lacqu|er 'læk|.əʳ ⓤⓢ -ɚ **-ers** -əz ⓤⓢ -ɚz **-ering** -ər.ɪŋ **-ered** -əd ⓤⓢ -ɚd **-erer/s** -ər.əʳ/z ⓤⓢ -ɚ.ɚ/z
lacquey 'læk.i **-s** -z **-ing** -ɪŋ **-ed** -d
Lacroix læk'rwɑː ⓤⓢ lə'kwɑː, -'krɔɪ
lacrosse lə'krɒs ⓤⓢ -'krɑːs
lactase 'læk.teɪs, -teɪz ⓤⓢ -teɪs
lactate *(n.)* 'læk.teɪt
lacta|te *(v.)* læk'teɪ|t ⓤⓢ '-- **-tes** -ts **-ting** -tɪŋ ⓤⓢ -t̬ɪŋ **-ted** -tɪd ⓤⓢ -t̬ɪd
lactation læk'teɪ.ʃən
lacteal 'læk.ti.əl
lactic 'læk.tɪk ˌ**lactic** '**acid**
lactometer læk'tɒm.ɪ.təʳ, -ə.təʳ ⓤⓢ -'tɑː.mə.t̬ɚ **-s** -z
lactose 'læk.təʊs, -təʊz ⓤⓢ -toʊs
lacun|a lə'kjuː.n|ə, læk'juː- ⓤⓢ lə'kjuː- **-ae** -iː **-as** -əz
lacy (L) 'leɪ.si
lad læd **-s** -z
Lada® 'lɑː.də **-s** -z
Ladakh lə'dɑːk, -'dɔːk ⓤⓢ -'dɑːk
Ladbroke 'læd.brʊk, -brəʊk ⓤⓢ -brʊk, -broʊk
Ladbrokes 'læd.brəʊks, -brʊks ⓤⓢ -broʊks, -brʊks

Labiodental

A consonant articulated with contact between the lips and the teeth.

Examples for English

By far the most common type of labiodental articulation is one where the lower surface of the lower lip touches the upper front teeth, as in the fricatives [f] (voiceless) and [v] (voiced); these two occur in English, e.g.:

fine	/faɪn/	safe	/seɪf/
vine	/vaɪn/	save	/seɪv/

The fricative noise made by /f/ and /v/ is very weak. In final position, as /f/ is FORTIS and /v/ is LENIS, 'pre-fortis clipping' of the vowel occurs. This has the effect of shortening the vowel in *safe*, making it much shorter than the one in *save*.

ladd|er ˈlæd|.əʳ US -ɚ **-ers** -əz US -ɚz **-ering** -ᵊr.ɪŋ **-ered** -əd US -ɚd
ladderback ˈlæd.ə.bæk US ˈ-ɚ-
laddie ˈlæd.i **-s** -z
laddish ˈlæd.ɪʃ **-ly** -li **-ness** -nəs, -nɪs
lad|e leɪd **-es** -z **-ing** -ɪŋ **-ed** -ɪd **-en** -ᵊn
Ladefoged ˈlæd.ɪ.fəʊ.gɪd, ˈ-ə-, -gəd US -ə.foʊ.gəd
laden *(from* **lade***)* ˈleɪ.dᵊn
la-di-da, **lah-di-dah** ˌlɑː.dɪˈdɑː US -diːˈ- *stress shift:* ˌla-di-da ˈvoice
ladies ˈleɪ.diz **ˈladies' ˌman; ˈladies' ˌroom**
ladieswear ˈleɪ.diz.weəʳ US -wer
Ladislaus ˈlæd.ɪ.slɔːs US -slɔːs, -slɑːs
Ladislaw ˈlæd.ɪ.slɔː US -slɔː, -slɑː
ladl|e ˈleɪ.dl̩ **-es** -z **-ing** -ɪŋ, ˈleɪd.lɪŋ **-ed** -d
ladleful ˈleɪ.dl̩.fʊl **-s** -z
Ladoga ˈlæd.əʊ.gə, ˈlɑː.dəʊ-; ləˈdəʊ- US ˈlɑː.dɔː.gɑː, -də.gə
a dolce vita lɑːˌdɒl.tʃeɪˈviː.tə US -ˌdoʊl.tʃeɪˈ-, -tʃəˈ-, -t̬ə
adrone ləˈdrəʊn US -ˈdroʊn
ad|y (L) ˈleɪ.d|i **-ies** -iz **ˌLady ˈBountiful; ˈlady ˌchapel; ˈLady ˌDay; ˈlady ˌfriend**
adybird (L®) ˈleɪ.di.bɜːd US -bɝːd **-s** -z
adybug ˈleɪ.di.bʌg **-s** -z
adyfinger ˈleɪ.diˌfɪŋ.gəʳ US -gɚ **-s** -z
ady-in-waiting ˌleɪ.di.ɪnˈweɪ.tɪŋ US -t̬ɪŋ **ladies-in-waiting** ˌleɪ.diz-
ady-killer ˈleɪ.diˌkɪl.əʳ US -ɚ **-s** -z
adylike ˈleɪ.di.laɪk
adylove ˈleɪ.di.lʌv **-s** -z
adyship ˈleɪ.di.ʃɪp **-s** -s
adysmith ˈleɪ.di.smɪθ
aertes leɪˈɜː.tiːz US -ˈɝː-, -ˈer-
aestrygones liːˈstraɪ.gə.niːz US lesˈtrɪg.ə-
aetitia lɪˈtɪʃ.i.ə, liː-, lə-, -ˈtiː.ʃi-, ˈ-ʃə US ləˈtɪʃ.ə, -ˈtiː.ʃə
afarge ləˈfɑːʒ US -ˈɑːrʒ
afayette *French name:* ˌlɑː.faɪˈet, ˌlæf-, -feɪˈ- US ˌlæf.iːˈ-, ˌlɑː.fiːˈ-, -faɪˈ- *in Louisiana:* ˌlɑːˈfeɪt, lə-
afcadio læfˈkɑː.di.əʊ US lɑːfˈkɑː.di.oʊ
Laffan ˈlæf.ən; ləˈfæn
Laf(f)itte læfˈiːt, lɑːˈfiːt, lə- US lɑːˈfiːt, lə-
Lafontaine ˌlæf.ɒnˈten, ˌlɑːfɒn-, -ˈteɪn US ˌlɑː.fɔːn-, -foʊnˈ-
lag læg **-s** -z **-ging** -ɪŋ **-ged** -d **-ger/s** -əʳ/z US -ɚ/z
Lagan ˈlæg.ᵊn
lager *beer:* ˈlɑː.gəʳ US -gɚ **-s** -z **ˈlager ˌlout**
Lager *English surname:* ˈleɪ.gəʳ US -gɚ
Lagerfeld ˈlɑː.gə.felt US -gɚ-
laggard ˈlæg.əd US -ɚd **-s** -z **-ly** -li
lagn(i)appe ˈlæn.jæp, ˌ-ˈ-
lagoon ləˈguːn **-s** -z
Lagos ˈleɪ.gɒs US -gɑːs; ˈlɑː.goʊs
Lagrange lægˈrɑ̃ːnʒ, ləˈ-, -ˈgreɪndʒ US lɑːˈgrɑ̃ːndʒ, lə-
La Guardia ləˈgwɑː.di.ə US -ˈgwɑːr-
Laguna Beach ləˌguː.nəˈbiːtʃ
lah lɑː **-s** -z
Lahore ləˈhɔːʳ, lɑː- US -ˈhɔːr
laic ˈleɪ.ɪk **-al** -ᵊl
laid *(from* **lay***)* leɪd
laid-back ˌleɪdˈbæk *stress shift:* ˌlaid-back ˈattitude
Laidlaw ˈleɪd.lɔː US -lɑː, -lɔː
lain *(from* **lie***)* leɪn
Laindon ˈleɪn.dən
Laing læŋ, leɪŋ
lair leəʳ US ler **-s** -z
laird (L) leəd US lerd **-s** -z **-ship** -ʃɪp
laissez-faire, **laisser-faire** ˌleɪ.seɪˈfeəʳ, ˌles.eɪˈ- US ˌles.eɪˈfer, ˌleɪ.seɪˈ- *stress shift:* ˌlaissez-faire ˈattitude
laity ˈleɪ.ə.ti, -ɪ.ti US -ti, -t̬i
Laius ˈlaɪ.əs, ˈleɪ- US ˈleɪ-, ˈlaɪ-
lake (L) leɪk **-s** -s
Lakeland ˈleɪk.lənd, -lænd
Lakenheath ˈleɪ.kᵊn.hiːθ
Lake Placid ˌleɪkˈplæs.ɪd
Laker ˈleɪ.kəʳ US -kɚ
lakeside (L) ˈleɪk.saɪd **-s** -z
lakh lɑːk, læk **-s** -s
Lakin ˈleɪ.kɪn
Lalage ˈlæl.ə.gi, -dʒi
Lalique® lælˈiːk, ləˈliːk US lɑːˈliːk, lə-
lam læm **-s** -z **-ming** -ɪŋ **-med** -d
lama (L) ˈlɑː.mə **-s** -z
Lamarr ləˈmɑːʳ US -ˈmɑːr
lamaser|y ˈlɑː.mə.sᵊr|.i, ˈlæm.ə- US ˈlɑː.mə.ser- **-ies** -iz
Lamaze ləˈmɑːz **Laˈmaze ˌmethod**
lamb (L) læm **-s** -z **-ing** -ɪŋ **-ed** -d **ˌlamb's ˈlettuce; ˈlamb's ˌwool; ˌmutton dressed as ˈlamb**
lambada læmˈbɑː.də US lɑːm- **-s** -z **-ing** -ɪŋ **-ed** -d
lambast læmˈbæst US -ˈbeɪst, -ˈbæst **-s** -s **-ing** -ɪŋ **-ed** -ɪd
lambast|e læmˈbeɪst US -ˈbeɪst, -ˈbæst **-es** -s **-ing** -ɪŋ **-ed** -ɪd
lambda ˈlæm.də **-s** -z
lambdacism ˈlæm.də.sɪ.zᵊm **-s** -z
Lambe læm
lamben|cy ˈlæm.bən|*t*.si **-t** -t
Lambert ˈlæm.bət US -bɚt
Lambeth ˈlæm.bəθ
lambkin ˈlæm.kɪn **-s** -z
lamblike ˈlæm.laɪk
Lamborghini® ˌlæm.bɔːˈgiː.ni, -bəˈ- US ˌlɑːm.bɔːrˈ-, ˌlæm-, -bɚˈ-
Lambretta® læmˈbret.ə US -ˈbret̬-
lambrusco (L) læmˈbrʊs.kəʊ US -ˈbruː.skoʊ, lɑːm-, -ˈbrʊs.koʊ
lambskin ˈlæm.skɪn **-s** -z
Lambton ˈlæm*p*.tən
lam|e leɪm **-er** -əʳ US -ɚ **-est** -ɪst, -əst **-ely** -li **-eness** -nəs, -nɪs **-es** -z **-ing** -ɪŋ **-ed** -d **ˌlame ˈduck**
lamé ˈlɑː.meɪ US læmˈeɪ, lɑːˈmeɪ
lamebrain ˈleɪm.breɪn **-s** -z
Lamech ˈleɪ.mek, ˈlɑː-, -mex US ˈleɪ.mek
lamell|a ləˈmel|.ə **-ae** -iː **-as** -əz **-ar** -əʳ US -ɚ
la|ment lə|ˈment **-ments** -ˈments **-menting** -ˈmen.tɪŋ US -ˈmen.t̬ɪŋ **-mented** -ˈmen.tɪd US -ˈmen.t̬ɪd
lamentab|le ˈlæm.ən.tə.b|l̩, -ɪn-; ləˈmen- US ləˈmen.t̬ə-; ˈlæm.ən.t̬ə- **-ly** -li
lamentation (L) ˌlæm.enˈteɪ.ʃᵊn, -ənˈ-, -ɪnˈ- US -ənˈ- **-s** -z

Lamia *Greek town:* læm'iː.ə ⓤⓢ lə'miː- *literary title, Keats:* 'lɑː.mi.ə, 'leɪ- ⓤⓢ 'leɪ-
lamin|a 'læm.ɪ.n|ə, '-ə- **-al** -əl **-ae** -iː **-as** -əz **-ar** -ər ⓤⓢ -ɚ
lami|nate (*v.*) 'læm.ɪ|.neɪt, '-ə- **-nates** -neɪts **-nating** -neɪ.tɪŋ ⓤⓢ -neɪ.t̬ɪŋ **-nated** -neɪ.tɪd ⓤⓢ -neɪ.t̬ɪd
laminate (*n.*) 'læm.ɪ.nət, '-ə-, -nɪt, -neɪt ⓤⓢ -nɪt
lamination ˌlæm.ɪ'neɪ.ʃən, -ə'-
lamington (L) 'læm.ɪŋ.tən
Lammas 'læm.əs **-tide** -taɪd
lammergeier, lammergeyer 'læm.ə.gaɪər ⓤⓢ -ɚ.gaɪɚ **-s** -z
Lammermoor 'læm.ə.mʊər, -mɔːr, ˌ--'- ⓤⓢ 'læm.ɚ.mʊr, -mɔːr, ˌ--'-
Lammermuir 'læm.ə.mjʊər, -mjɔːr ⓤⓢ -ɚ.mjʊr, -mjʊɚ
Lamond 'læm.ənd
Lamont *surname:* lə'mɒnt; 'læm.ənt ⓤⓢ lə'mɑːnt *in US:* lə'mɒnt ⓤⓢ -'mɑːnt
lamp læmp **-s** -s
lampas *silk material:* 'læm.pəs *swelling in horse's mouth:* 'læm.pəz
lampblack 'læmp.blæk
Lampedusa ˌlæm.pɪ'djuː.zə ⓤⓢ -pə'duː.sə, -zə
Lampet 'læm.pɪt
Lampeter 'læm.pɪ.tər, -pə- ⓤⓢ -t̬ɚ
lampion 'læm.pi.ən **-s** -z
lamp|light 'læmp|.laɪt **-lighter/s** -ˌlaɪ.tər/z ⓤⓢ -ˌlaɪ.t̬ɚ/s
Lamplough 'læm.pluː, -plʌf
Lamplugh 'læm.pluː, -plə
lampoon læm'puːn **-s** -z **-ing** -ɪŋ **-ed** -d **-er/s** -ər/z ⓤⓢ -ɚ/z
lamp-post 'læmp.pəʊst ⓤⓢ -poʊst **-s** -s
lamprey 'læm.pri **-s** -z
lampshade 'læmp.ʃeɪd **-s** -z
Lampson 'læm*p*.sən
lampstand 'læmp.stænd **-s** -z
LAN læn **-s** -z
Lana 'lɑː.nə ⓤⓢ 'læn.ə, 'lɑː.nə
Lanagan 'læn.ə.gən
Lanark 'læn.ək ⓤⓢ -ɚk **-shire** -ʃər, -ˌʃɪər ⓤⓢ -ʃɚ, -ˌʃɪr
Lancashire 'læŋ.kə.ʃər, -ˌʃɪər ⓤⓢ -ʃɚ, -ˌʃɪr
Lancaster 'læŋ.kə.stər, -kæs.tər ⓤⓢ 'læŋ.kə.stɚ, 'læn-, -kæs.tɚ
Lancasterian ˌlæŋ.kæs'tɪə.ri.ən, -kə'stɪə- ⓤⓢ ˌlæŋ.kæs'tɪr.i-, ˌlæn-, -kə'stɪr- **-s** -z
Lancastrian læŋ'kæs.tri.ən ⓤⓢ læŋ-, læn- **-s** -z
lanc|e (L) lɑːnts ⓤⓢ lænts **-es** -ɪz **-ing** -ɪŋ **-ed** -t ˌ**lance 'corporal**
Lancelot 'lɑːnt.sə.lɒt, -səl.ɒt, -ət ⓤⓢ 'lænt.sə.lɑːt, 'lɑːnt-, -lət
lancer 'lɑːnt.sər ⓤⓢ 'lænt.sɚ **-s** -z
lancet (L) 'lɑːnt.sɪt ⓤⓢ 'lænt- **-s** -s
Lancia® 'lɑːnt.si.ə, 'lænt- **-s** -z
Lancing 'lɑːnt.sɪŋ ⓤⓢ 'lænt-
Lancôme®, Lancome 'lɑ̃ːŋ.kəʊm, -'- ⓤⓢ 'læn.koʊm, -kəm, ˌlæn'koʊm
Lancs. *(abbrev. for* **Lancashire***)* læŋks
land (L) lænd **-s** -z **-ing** -ɪŋ **-ed** -ɪd
landau 'læn.dɔː, -daʊ **-s** -z
Lander 'læn.dər ⓤⓢ -dɚ
landfall 'lænd.fɔːl ⓤⓢ -fɔːl, -fɑːl **-s** -z
landfill 'lænd.fɪl **-s** -z
landforc|e 'lænd.fɔːs ⓤⓢ -fɔːrs **-es** -ɪz
landgrabb|er 'lænd,græb|.ər, 'læŋ- ⓤⓢ 'lænd,græb|.ɚ **-ers** -əz ⓤⓢ -ɚz **-ing** -ɪŋ
landgrave 'lænd.greɪv, 'læŋ- ⓤⓢ 'lænd- **-s** -z
landholder 'lænd,həʊl.dər ⓤⓢ -ˌhoʊl.dɚ **-s** -z
landing 'læn.dɪŋ **-s** -z '**landing** ˌ**gear**; '**landing** ˌ**net**; '**landing** ˌ**stage**; '**landing** ˌ**strip**
landlad|y 'lænd,leɪ.d|i **-ies** -iz
landlocked 'lænd.lɒkt ⓤⓢ -lɑːkt
landlord 'lænd.lɔːd ⓤⓢ -lɔːrd **-s** -z **-ism** -ɪ.zəm
landlubber 'lænd,lʌb.ər ⓤⓢ -ɚ **-s** -z
landmark 'lænd.mɑːk, 'læm- ⓤⓢ 'lænd.mɑːrk **-s** -s
landmass 'lænd.mæs, 'læm- ⓤⓢ 'lænd- **-es** -ɪz
landmine 'lænd.maɪn, 'læm- ⓤⓢ 'lænd- **-s** -z
Landon 'læn.dən
Landor 'læn.dɔːr, -dər ⓤⓢ -dɚ, -dɔːr
land-own|er 'lænd,əʊ.n|ər ⓤⓢ -ˌoʊ.n|ɚ **-ers** -əz ⓤⓢ -ɚz **-ing** -ɪŋ
landrail 'lænd.reɪl **-s** -z
Land Rover® 'lænd,rəʊ.vər ⓤⓢ -ˌroʊ.vɚ **-s** -z
landscap|e 'lænd.skeɪp **-es** -s **-ing** -ɪŋ **-ed** -t **-er/s** -ər/z ⓤⓢ -ɚ/z ˌ**landscape 'gardener** ⓤⓢ '**landscape** ˌ**gardener**; '**landscape** ˌ**mode**
Landseer 'lænd,siː.ər, -sɪər ⓤⓢ -ˌsiː.ɚ, -ˌsɪr
Land's End ˌlæn*dz*'end
landslide 'lænd.slaɪd **-s** -z
landslip 'lænd.slɪp **-s** -s
lands|man 'læn*dz*|.mən **-men** -mən
landward 'lænd.wəd ⓤⓢ -wɚd
landwehr 'lænd.veər ⓤⓢ -veɪr
landwind 'lænd.wɪnd **-s** -z
lane (L) leɪn **-s** -z **in the 'fast** ˌ**lane**
Lanfranc 'læn.fræŋk
Lang læŋ
Langbaine 'læŋ.beɪn
Langbourne 'læŋ.bɔːn ⓤⓢ -bɔːrn
Langdale 'læŋ.deɪl
Langer 'læŋ.ər ⓤⓢ -ɚ
Langerhans 'læŋ.ə.hænz, -hænts ⓤⓢ 'læŋ.ɚ.hænz, 'lɑːŋ.ɚ.hɑːnz
Langford 'læŋ.fəd ⓤⓢ -fɚd
Langham, Langholm(e) 'læŋ.əm
Langhorne 'læŋ.hɔːn ⓤⓢ -hɔːrn
Langland 'læŋ.lənd
langlauf 'lɑːŋ.laʊf **-s** -s
Langley 'læŋ.li
Langmere 'læŋ.mɪər ⓤⓢ -mɪr
langoustine ˌlɑ̃ŋ.gu'stiːn, ˌlæn- ⓤⓢ ˌlæŋ.gə'- **-s** -z
Langridge 'læŋ.grɪdʒ
Langside 'læŋ.saɪd, ˌ-'-
lang syne ˌlæŋ'saɪn ⓤⓢ -'zaɪn, -'saɪn
Langton 'læŋ*k*.tən
Langtry 'læŋ*k*.tri
languag|e 'læŋ.gwɪdʒ **-es** -ɪz
langue lɑ̃ːŋg ⓤⓢ lɑ̃ːŋg, lɑːŋ
langue de chat ˌlɑ̃ːŋ.də'ʃɑː ⓤⓢ ˌlɑ̃ːŋg-, ˌlɑːŋ-
Languedoc 'lɑ̃ːŋ.gə.dɒk, ˌ--'- ⓤⓢ lɑ̃ːŋg'dɔːk, lɑːŋ-
languid 'læŋ.gwɪd **-ly** -li **-ness** -nəs, -nɪs
languish (L) 'læŋ.gwɪʃ **-es** -ɪz **-ing/ly** -ɪŋ/li **-ed** -t **-ment** -mənt
languor 'læŋ.gər ⓤⓢ -gɚ **-ous/ly** -əs/li
langur 'læŋ.gər, 'lʌŋ-, -gʊər ⓤⓢ lɑːŋ'gʊ **-s** -z
Lanier 'læn.jər; lə'nɪər ⓤⓢ lə'nɪr
Lanigan 'læn.ɪ.gən, '-ə-
lank læŋk **-er** -ər ⓤⓢ -ɚ **-est** -ɪst, -əst **-ly** -li **-ness** -nəs, -nɪs
Lankester 'læŋ.kɪ.stər, -kə- ⓤⓢ -stɚ
lank|y 'læŋ.k|i **-ier** -i.ər ⓤⓢ -i.ɚ **-iest** -i.ɪst, -i.əst **-ily** -ɪ.li, -əl.i **-iness** -ɪ.nəs, -ɪ.nɪs
lanolin(e) 'læn.əl.ɪn, -ə.liːn ⓤⓢ -ə.lɪn
Lansbury 'lænz.bər.i ⓤⓢ -ber.i
Lansdown(e) 'lænz.daʊn
Lansing 'lɑːnt.sɪŋ, 'lænt- ⓤⓢ 'lænt-
Lansley 'læn*dz*.li
Lantau 'læn.taʊ
lantern 'læn.tən ⓤⓢ -t̬ɚn **-s** -z
lanthanum 'lænt.θə.nəm
lanyard 'læn.jəd, -jɑːd ⓤⓢ -jɚd, -jɑːr **-s** -z
Lanzarote ˌlæn.zə'rɒt.i ⓤⓢ ˌlɑːnt.sə'roʊ.t̬i, -teɪ
Laocoön leɪ'ɒk.əʊ.ɒn, -ən ⓤⓢ -'ɑː.koʊ.ɑːn
Laodamia ˌleɪ.əʊ.də'maɪə, -'miː.ə ⓤⓢ leɪˌɑː.də'maɪ.ə
Laodice|a ˌleɪ.əʊ.dɪ'siː|.ə, -də'- ⓤⓢ leɪˌɑː.dɪ'-; ˌleɪ.ə.də'- **-an/s** -ən/
Laois liːʃ
Laomedon leɪ'ɒm.ɪ.dən, '-ə- ⓤⓢ -'ɑː.mə.dɑːn
Laos 'leɪ.ɒs, 'lɑː-; laʊs, laʊz ⓤⓢ laʊs; 'leɪ.ɑːs, -oʊs
Laotian leɪ'əʊ.ʃən; 'laʊ.ʃi.ən, -ʃən; lɑː'ɒʃ.ən ⓤⓢ leɪ'oʊ.ʃən; 'laʊ.ʃən
Lao-tsze ˌlɑː.əʊ'tseɪ, ˌlaʊ'tseɪ, -'tsiː ⓤⓢ ˌlaʊ'dzuː, -'tseɪ

Larynx

The larynx is located in the throat and its main biological function is to act as a valve that can stop air entering or escaping from the lungs and also (usually) prevents food and other solids from entering the lungs. It consists of a rigid framework or box made of cartilage and, inside, the vocal folds, which are two small lumps of muscular tissue like a very small pair of lips with the division between them (the 'glottis') running from front to back of the throat. There is a complex set of muscles inside the larynx that can open and close the vocal folds as well as changing their length and tension.

In speech the larynx has many important functions including the following:

i) the distinction between voiced and voiceless sounds
ii) the control of pitch
iii) the production of the glottal fricative [h] and the glottal stop [ʔ]
iv) producing variation in voice quality.

lap læp **-s** -s **-ping** -ɪŋ **-ped** -t **-per/s** -əʳ/z US -ɚ/z **in the ˌlap of ˈluxury**
laparoscop|y ˌlæp.əʳˈɒs.kə.p|i **-ies** -iz
laparotom|y ˌlæp.əʳˈɒt.ə.m|i US -əˈrɑː.t̬ə- **-ies** -iz
La Paz lɑːˈpæz, læ- US ləˈpɑːz, lɑː-, -ˈpɑːs
lapdog ˈlæp.dɒg US -dɑːg, -dɔːg **-s** -z
lapel ləˈpel **-s** -z
lapful ˈlæp.fʊl **-s** -z
lapidar|y ˈlæp.ɪ.dəʳr|.i, ˈ-ə- US -ə.der- **-ies** -iz
lapis lazuli ˌlæp.ɪsˈlæz.jʊ.li, -jə-, -laɪ US -ˈlæz.ə.li, -ˈlæʒ-, -jʊ-
Lapithae ˈlæp.ɪ.θiː
Lapland ˈlæp.lænd **-er/s** -əʳ/z US -ɚ/z
La Porte ləˈpɔːt US -ˈpɔːrt
Lapp læp **-s** -s **-ish** -ɪʃ
lapp|et ˈlæp|.ɪt **-ets** -ɪts **-eted** -ɪ.tɪd US -ɪ.t̬ɪd
Lappin ˈlæp.ɪn
Lapsang ˈlæp.sæŋ
Lapsang Souchong ˌlæp.sæŋ.suːˈʃɒŋ, -ˈtʃɒŋ US -tʃɔːŋ, -ʃɔːŋ
laps|e læps **-es** -ɪz **-ing** -ɪŋ **-ed** -t
lapsus linguae ˌlæp.səsˈlɪŋ.gwaɪ, -sʊsˈ-, -gweɪ US -səsˈlɪŋ.gwiː, -gwaɪ
laptop ˈlæp.tɒp US -tɑːp **-s** -s
laput|a ləˈpjuː.t|ə US -t̬|ə **-an/s** -ən/z
lapwing ˈlæp.wɪŋ **-s** -z
lar (L) lɑːʳ US lɑːr **lares** ˈleə.riːz, ˈlɑː.reɪz US ˈler.iːz, ˈlɑːr.iːz
Lara ˈlɑː.rə US ˈlɑːr.ə, ˈler.ə
Laramie ˈlær.ə.mi US ˈler-, ˈlær-
Larbert ˈlɑː.bət, -bɜːt US ˈlɑːr.bɚt, -bɝːt
larboard ˈlɑː.bəd, -bɔːd US -bɚd, -bɔːrd
larcenous ˈlɑː.sən.əs, -sɪ.nəs US ˈlɑːr.sə- **-ly** -li
larcen|y ˈlɑː.sən|.i, -sɪ.n|i US ˈlɑːr.sə- **-ies** -iz
larch lɑːtʃ US lɑːrtʃ **-es** -ɪz
lard lɑːd US lɑːrd **-s** -z **-ing** -ɪŋ **-ed** -ɪd
larder ˈlɑː.dəʳ US ˈlɑːr.dɚ **-s** -z
Lardner ˈlɑːd.nəʳ US ˈlɑːrd.nɚ
lardon ˈlɑː.dən US ˈlɑːr- **-s** -z
Laredo ləˈreɪ.dəʊ US -doʊ
lares (*plur. of* **lar**) ˈleə.riːz, ˈlɑː.reɪz US ˈler.iːz, ˈlɑːr.iːz
Largactil® lɑːˈgæk.tɪl, -təl US lɑːr-
larg|e lɑːdʒ US lɑːrdʒ **-er** -əʳ US -ɚ **-est** -ɪst, -əst **-ely** -li **-eness** -nəs, -nɪs **as ˌlarge as ˈlife**
largehearted ˌlɑːdʒˈhɑː.tɪd US ˌlɑːrʒˈhɑːr.t̬ɪd **-ness** -nəs, -nɪs *stress shift:* ˌlargehearted ˈperson
large-scale ˌlɑːdʒˈskeɪl US ˌlɑːrdʒ- *stress shift:* ˌlarge-scale ˈchanges
largess|(e) lɑːˈʒes, -ˈdʒes; ˈ-- US lɑːrˈdʒes, -ˈʒes; ˈlɑːr.dʒəs **-es** -ɪz
larghetto lɑːˈget.əʊ US lɑːrˈget̬.oʊ **-s** -z
largish ˈlɑː.dʒɪʃ US ˈlɑːr-
largo ˈlɑː.gəʊ US ˈlɑːr.goʊ **-s** -z
Largs lɑːgz US lɑːrgz
Larham ˈlɑː.rəm US ˈlɑːr-
lari|at ˈlær.i|.ət US ˈler-, ˈlær- **-ats** -əts **-ating** -ə.tɪŋ US -ə.t̬ɪŋ **-ated** -ə.tɪd US -ə.t̬ɪd
Larisa, Larissa ləˈrɪs.ə
lark lɑːk US lɑːrk **-s** -s **-ing** -ɪŋ **-ed** -t
Larkhall ˈlɑːk.hɔːl US ˈlɑːrk-, -hɑːl
Larkin ˈlɑː.kɪn US ˈlɑːr-
larkspur ˈlɑːk.spɜːʳ, -spəʳ US ˈlɑːrk.spɝː, -spɚ **-s** -z
lark|y ˈlɑː.k|i US ˈlɑːr- **-ier** -i.əʳ US -i.ɚ **-iest** -i.ɪst, -i.əst **-iness** -ɪ.nəs, -ɪ.nɪs
Larmor, Larmour ˈlɑː.məʳ US ˈlɑːr.mɚ, -mɔːr
Larne lɑːn US lɑːrn
Larousse lærˈuːs US lɑːˈruːs
larrikin ˈlær.ɪ.kɪn, ˈ-ə- US ˈler-, ˈlær- **-s** -z
larrup ˈlær.əp US ˈler-, ˈlær- **-s** -s **-ping** -ɪŋ **-ped** -t
Larry ˈlær.i US ˈler-, ˈlær-
Larsen, Larson ˈlɑː.sən US ˈlɑːr-
Lars Porsena ˌlɑːzˈpɔː.sɪ.nə, -sə- US ˌlɑːrzˈpɔːr-
larum ˈlær.əm US ˈler-, ˈlær-; ˈlɑːr.ʊm **-s** -z
larv|a ˈlɑː.v|ə US ˈlɑːr- **-ae** -iː **-al** -əl
laryngal ləˈrɪŋ.gəl, lærˈɪŋ- US ləˈrɪŋ-, lerˈɪŋ-, lær-
laryngeal ləˈrɪn.dʒi.əl, lærˈɪn-, -dʒəl; ˌlær.ɪnˈdʒiː.əl, -ənˈ- US ləˈrɪn.dʒi.əl, -dʒəl
laryngectom|y ˌlær.ɪnˈdʒek.tə.m|i, -ənˈ- US ˌler-, ˌlær- **-ies** -iz
larynges (*plur. of* **larynx**) lærˈɪn.dʒiːz, ləˈrɪn- US lə-, lerˈɪn-, lær-
laryngitis ˌlær.ɪnˈdʒaɪ.tɪs, -ənˈ- US ˌler.ɪnˈdʒaɪ.t̬ɪs, ˌlær-
laryngolog|y ˌlær.ɪŋˈgɒl.ə.dʒ|i, -əŋˈ- US ˌler.ɪŋˈgɑː.lə-, ˌlær-, -ɪnˈdʒɑː- **-ist/s** -ɪst/s
laryngoscope ləˈrɪŋ.gə.skəʊp, lærˈɪŋ-; ˈlær.ɪŋ- US ləˈrɪŋ.goʊ.skoʊp, -gə-, -ˈrɪn.dʒə- **-s** -s
laryngoscopic ləˌrɪŋ.gəˈskɒp.ɪk, lærˌɪŋ-; ˌlær.ɪŋ- US ləˌrɪŋ.goʊˈskɑː.pɪk, -gəˈ-, -ˌrɪn.dʒəˈ-
laryngoscop|y ˌlær.ɪŋˈgɒs.kə.p|i, -əŋˈ- US ˌler.ɪŋˈgɑː.skə-, ˌlær-, -ɪnˈdʒɑː- **-ist/s** -ɪst/s
larynx ˈlær.ɪŋks US ˈler-, ˈlær- **-es** -ɪz **larynges** lærˈɪn.dʒiːz, ləˈrɪn- US lə-, lerˈɪn-, lær-
lasagne, lasagna ləˈzæn.jə, -ˈsæn-, -ˈzɑː.njə, -ˈsɑː- US -ˈzɑː.njə, -ˈsɑː-
Lascar ˈlæs.kəʳ US -kɚ **-s** -z
Lascaux ˈlæs.kəʊ, -ˈ- US læsˈkoʊ
Lascelles ˈlæs.əlz, ləˈselz
lascivious ləˈsɪv.i.əs **-ly** -li **-ness** -nəs, -nɪs
laser ˈleɪ.zəʳ US -zɚ **-s** -z **ˈlaser ˌdisk; ˈlaser ˌprinter**
laserjet ˈleɪ.zə.dʒet US -zɚ- **-s** -s
lash læʃ **-es** -ɪz **-ing/s** -ɪŋ/z **-ed** -t **-er/s** -əʳ/z US -ɚ/z
Lasham ˈlæʃ.əm *locally also:* ˈlæs.əm
Las Palmas ˌlæsˈpæl.məs, -ˈpɑːl- US ˌlɑːsˈpɑːl-, -mɑːs
lass læs **-es** -ɪz
Lassa ˈlæs.ə, ˈlɑː.sə US ˈlɑː.sə, ˈlæs.ə **ˌLassa ˈfever**
Lassalle ləˈsæl

Lateral

A lateral consonant is one where there is obstruction to the passage of air in the centere (mid-line) of the air-passage and the air flows to the side of the obstruction.

Examples for English

In English the /l/ phoneme is lateral both in its "clear" and its "dark" allophones (see CLEAR L and DARK L): the blade of the tongue is in contact with the alveolar ridge as for /t d n/ but the sides of the tongue are lowered to allow the passage of air, e.g.:

lip	/lɪp/	pill	/pɪl/

When an alveolar plosive precedes a lateral consonant in English it is usual for it to have a 'lateral release'. This means that to go from /t/ or /d/ to /l/ we simply lower the sides of the tongue to release the compressed air, rather than lowering and then raising the tongue blade. A syllabic /l/ is the usual result of this in word final position (see SYLLABIC CONSONANT), e.g.:

bottle	/ˈbɒt.l̩/	puddle	/ˈpʌd.l̩/

Most laterals are produced with the air passage to both sides of the obstruction (they are 'bilateral'), but sometimes we find air passing to one side only ('unilateral').

In other languages

Other lateral consonants are found in other languages: the Welsh ll sound is a voiceless lateral fricative [ɬ], and Xhosa and Zulu have a voiced lateral fricative [ɮ]. Several Southern African languages have lateral clicks (where the plosive occlusion is released laterally) and at least one language (of Papua New Guinea) has a contrast between alveolar and velar lateral.

Lassell læsˈel, ləˈsel
lassie (L) ˈlæs.i **-s** -z
lassitude ˈlæs.ɪ.tjuːd, ˈ-ə- (US) -tuːd, -tjuːd
lasso *(n.)* læsˈuː; ˈlæs.əʊ (US) ˈlæs.oʊ, -uː **-(e)s** -z
lasso *(v.)* læsˈuː, ləˈsuː (US) ˈlæs.oʊ, -uː **-(e)s** -z **-ing** -ɪŋ **-ed** -d
last (L) lɑːst (US) læst **-s** -s **-ing/ly** -ɪŋ/li **-ed** -ɪd **-ly** ˈlɑːs*t*.li (US) ˈlæs*t*.li ˌ**Last ˈJudgment**; ˌ**last ˈstraw**; ˌ**Last ˈSupper**; ˌ**last ˈword**; **at the ˌlast ˈminute**
last-ditch ˌlɑːs*t*ˈdɪtʃ (US) ˌlæs*t*- *stress shift, see compound:* ˌ**last-ditch atˈtempt**
last-minute ˌlɑːs*t*ˈmɪn.ɪt (US) ˌlæs*t*- *stress shift:* ˌlast-minute ˈplans
Las Vegas ˌlæsˈveɪ.gəs, ˌlɑːs- (US) ˌlɑːs-
lat læt **-s** -s
Latakia ˌlæt.əˈkiː.ə (US) ˌlɑː.t̬əˈ-, ˌlæt̬.əˈ-
latch lætʃ **-es** -ɪz **-ing** -ɪŋ **-ed** -t
latchet ˈlætʃ.ɪt, -ət **-s** -s
latchkey ˈlætʃ.kiː **-s** -z ˈ**latchkey ˌchild**, ˌ**latchkey ˈchild**
lat|e leɪt **-er** -əʳ (US) ˈleɪ.t̬ɚ **-est** -ɪst, -əst (US) ˈleɪ.t̬ɪst, -t̬əst **-ely** -li **-eness** -nəs, -nɪs
latecomer ˈleɪtˌkʌm.əʳ (US) -ɚ **-s** -z
lateen ləˈtiːn (US) lætˈiːn, ləˈtiːn **-s** -z
latency ˈleɪ.tᵊn*t*.si
late-night ˈleɪtˌnaɪt ˌ**late-ˌnight ˈshopping**
latent ˈleɪ.tᵊnt **-ly** -li
lateral ˈlæt.ᵊr.ᵊl, ˈ-rᵊl (US) ˈlæt̬.ɚ.ᵊl **-s** -z **-ly** -i ˌ**lateral ˈthinking**
Lateran ˈlæt.ᵊr.ᵊn (US) ˈlæt̬-
laterite ˈlæt.ᵊr.aɪt (US) ˈlæt̬.ə.raɪt
latex ˈleɪ.teks **-es** -ɪz **latices** ˈlæt.ɪ.siːz, ˈleɪ.tɪ- (US) ˈlæt̬.ɪ-, ˈleɪ.t̬ɪ-
lath læθ, lɑːθ (US) læθ **-s** -s, lɑːðz (US) -s, læðz
Latham ˈleɪ.θəm, -ðəm
Note: Generally /ˈleɪ.θəm/ in S. of England; always /ˈleɪ.ðəm/ in N.
Lathbury ˈlæθ.bᵊr.i (US) -ber-
lath|e leɪð **-es** -z **-ing** -ɪŋ **-ed** -d
lath|er ˈlɑː.ðləʳ, ˈlæðl.əʳ (US) ˈlæðl.ɚ **-ers** -əz (US) -ɚz **-ering** -ᵊr.ɪŋ **-ered** -əd (US) -ɚd
lathi ˈlɑː.ti **-s** -z
Lathom ˈleɪ.θəm, -ðəm
Lathrop ˈleɪ.θrəp
latices *(plur. of* **latex***)* ˈlæt.ɪ.siːz, ˈleɪ.tɪ- (US) ˈlæt̬.ɪ-, ˈleɪ.t̬ɪ-
Latimer ˈlæt.ɪ.məʳ, ˈ-ə- (US) ˈlæt̬.ə.mɚ
Latin ˈlæt.ɪn (US) -ᵊn **-ate** -eɪt ˌ**Latin Aˈmerica**
latin|ism ˈlæt.ɪ.nl.ɪ.zᵊm (US) -ᵊnl.ɪ- **-isms** -ɪ.zᵊmz **-ist/s** -ɪst/s
latinity ləˈtɪn.ə.ti, lætˈɪn-, -ɪ.ti (US) lætˈɪn.ə.t̬i
latiniz|e, -is|e ˈlæt.ɪ.naɪz (US) -ᵊn.aɪz **-es** -ɪz **-ing** -ɪŋ **-ed** -d
latin|o (L) ləˈtiː.nləʊ, lætˈiː- (US) -nloʊ **-os** -əʊz (US) -oʊz **-a/s** -ə/z (US) -ɑː/z
Latinus ləˈtaɪ.nəs
latish ˈleɪ.tɪʃ (US) -t̬ɪʃ
latitude ˈlæt.ɪ.tjuːd, ˈ-ə-, -tʃuːd (US) ˈlæt̬.ə.tuːd, -tjuːd **-s** -z
latitudinal ˌlæt.ɪˈtjuː.dɪ.nᵊl, -əˈ-, -ˈtʃuː-, -dᵊn.ᵊl (US) ˌlæt̬.əˈtuː-, -ˈtjuː-
latitudinarian ˌlæt.ɪˌtjuː.dɪˈneə.ri.ən, -əˌ-, -ˌtʃuː- (US) ˌlæt̬.əˌtuː.dɪˈner.i-, -ˌtjuː- **-s** -z **-ism** -ɪ.zᵊm
Latium ˈleɪ.ʃi.əm, ˈlæt.i- (US) ˈleɪ.ʃᵊm, -ʃi.əm
latke ˈlɑːt.kə **-s** -z
Latoya ləˈtɔɪ.ə
latria ləˈtraɪə
latrine ləˈtriːn **-s** -z
Lattakia ˌlæt.əˈkiː.ə (US) ˌlɑː.t̬əˈ-, ˌlæt̬.ə
latte ˈlæt.eɪ (US) ˈlɑː.teɪ
latter ˈlæt.əʳ (US) ˈlæt̬.ɚ **-ly** -li
latter-day ˈlæt.ə.deɪ (US) ˈlæt̬.ɚ- ˌ**Latter-Day ˈSaint**
lattic|e ˈlæt.ɪs (US) ˈlæt̬- **-es** -ɪz **-ed** -t
latticework ˈlæt.ɪs.wɜːk (US) ˈlæt̬.ɪs.wɝːk
Latvi|a ˈlæt.vil.ə **-an/s** -ən/z
laud (L) lɔːd (US) lɑːd, lɔːd **-s** -z **-ing** -ɪŋ **-ed** -ɪd
Lauda ˈlaʊ.də
laudab|le ˈlɔː.də.bl̩ (US) ˈlɑː-, ˈlɔː- **-ly** - **-leness** -l̩.nəs, -nɪs
laudanum ˈlɔː.dᵊn.əm (US) ˈlɑː-, ˈlɔː-
laudatory ˈlɔː.də.tᵊr.i (US) ˈlɑː.də.tɔːr ˈlɔː-
Lauder ˈlɔː.dəʳ (US) ˈlɑː.dɚ, ˈlɔː-
Lauderdale ˈlɔː.də.deɪl (US) ˈlɑː.dɚ-, ˈl
laugh lɑːf (US) læf **-s** -s **-ing/ly** -ɪŋ/li **-ed** **-er/s** -əʳ/z (US) -ɚ/z ˈ**laughing ˌgas**; ˌ**laughing ˈjackass**; **no ˌlaughing ˈmatter, no ˈlaughing ˌmatter**; **have the ˌlast ˈlaugh**
laughab|le ˈlɑː.fə.bl̩ (US) ˈlæf.ə- **-ly** -li **-leness** -l̩.nəs, -nɪs
Laugharne lɑːn (US) lɑːrn
laughingstock ˈlɑː.fɪŋ.stɒk (US) ˈlæf.ɪŋ.stɑːk **-s** -s
Laughland ˈlɒk.lənd (US) ˈlɑːk-
Laughlin ˈlɒk.lɪn, ˈlɒx-, ˈlɒf-, ˈlɑː.flɪ (US) ˈlɑː-, ˈlɔː-

Latin words and phrases

Words, names and phrases from Latin have entered the English language at many different times. Some words and names are in relatively common use and have been completely anglicised, while others are used in particular types of discourse which to some extent determine their pronunciation. The pronunciation used by academic scholars of Latin has tended to be based on a reconstruction of what was supposed to be the pronunciation in Roman times. Ecclesiastical Latin, previously used in the Roman Catholic church and closely similar to the pronunciation of Italian, has largely disappeared, but phrases such as *Gloria in excelsis* or *Humanae Vitae* are still heard. Legal Latin is also now much less widely used than it used to be, but some phrases survive, such as *habeas corpus, ultra vires* (usual pronunciation /ˌheɪ.bi.əsˈkɔː.pəs, ⓤⓢ -ˈkɔːr-/ and /ˌʌl.trəˈvaɪə.riːz, ˌʊl.trɑːˈvɪə.reɪz, ⓤⓢ ˌʌl.trəˈvaɪ.riːz/). Most of the Latin words, phrases and names in this dictionary are ones that have been fully anglicized, but there is no set of rules to determine exactly how this is done.

Examples

Words, e.g.:

accidia /ækˈsɪd.i.ə/
flamen /ˈfleɪ.men/
vale /ˈvɑː.leɪ, ˈveɪ.li, ˈvæl.eɪ/ ⓤⓢ /ˈveɪ.li, ˈvɑː.leɪ/

Names, e.g.:

Aeneas /ˈiː.ni.əs, iːˈniː-, -æs/
Flaminius /fləˈmɪn.i.əs, flæmˈɪn-/ ⓤⓢ /fləˈmɪn-/

Phrases, e.g.:

ad hoc /ˌædˈhɒk, -ˈhəʊk/ ⓤⓢ /-ˈhɑːk, -ˈhoʊk/
ex voto /ˌeksˈvəʊ.təʊ/ ⓤⓢ /-ˈvoʊ.t̬oʊ/
flagrante delicto /fləˌgræn.teɪ.dɪˈlɪk.təʊ/, /flægˌræn-, -ti-, -dəˈ-, -deɪˈ-/ ⓤⓢ /fləˌgræn.ti.diːˈlɪk.toʊ/

laughter ˈlɑːf.təʳ ⓤⓢ ˈlæf.tɚ
Laughton ˈlɔː.tᵊn ⓤⓢ ˈlɑː-, ˈlɔː-
launc|e lɑːnts ⓤⓢ lænts, lɑːnts, lɔːnts **-es** -ɪz
Launce lɑːnts, lɔːnts ⓤⓢ lænts, lɑːnts, lɔːnts
Launcelot ˈlɑːnt.sᵊl.ɒt, ˈlɔːnt-, -ət ⓤⓢ ˈlænt.sə.lɑːt, ˈlɑːnt-, ˈlɔːnt-, -lət
Launceston *in Cornwall:* ˈlɔːnt.stən, -sᵊn *locally:* ˈlɑːnt- *in Tasmania:* ˈlɔːnt.səs.tᵊn *locally:* ˈlɒnt- ⓤⓢ ˈlɑːnt-, ˈlɔːnt-
launch lɔːntʃ ⓤⓢ lɑːntʃ, lɔːntʃ **-es** -ɪz **-ing** -ɪŋ **-ed** -t **-er/s** -əʳ/z ⓤⓢ -ɚ/z
launchpad ˈlɔːntʃ.pæd ⓤⓢ ˈlɑːntʃ-, ˈlɔːntʃ- **-s** -z
laund|er ˈlɔːn.d|əʳ ⓤⓢ ˈlɑːn.d|ɚ, ˈlɔːn- **-ers** -əz ⓤⓢ -ɚz **-ering** -ᵊr.ɪŋ **-ered** -əd ⓤⓢ -ɚd
launderette ˌlɔːn.dᵊrˈet, ˌ-ˈdret ⓤⓢ ˌlɑːn.dəˈret, ˌlɔːn-, ˌ-ˈdret **-s** -s
laundress ˈlɔːn.dres, -drəs, -drɪs ⓤⓢ ˈlɑːn.drɪs, ˈlɔːn- **-es** -ɪz
laundrette ˌlɔːnˈdret ⓤⓢ ˌlɑːn-, ˌlɔːn- **-s** -s
Laundromat® ˈlɔːn.drə.mæt ⓤⓢ ˈlɔːn.droʊ-, ˈlɑːn-, -drə- **-s** -s
laundr|y ˈlɔːn.dr|i ⓤⓢ ˈlɑːn-, ˈlɔːn- **-ies** -iz **ˈlaundry ˌbasket**; **ˈlaundry ˌlist**
laundry|man ˈlɔːn.dri|.mæn, -mən ⓤⓢ ˈlɑːn-, ˈlɔːn- **-men** -mən, -men **-woman** -ˌwʊm.ən **-women** -ˌwɪm.ɪn
Laundy ˈlɔːn.di ⓤⓢ ˈlɑːn-, ˈlɔːn-
Laura ˈlɔː.rə ⓤⓢ ˈlɔːr.ə
laureate (*n. adj.*) ˈlɔː.ri.ət, ˈlɒr.i-, -ɪt ⓤⓢ ˈlɔːr.i.ɪt, ˈlɑːr- **-s** -s **-ship/s** -ʃɪp/s
laure|ate (*v.*) ˈlɔː.ri|.eɪt, ˈlɒr.i- ⓤⓢ ˈlɔːr.i-, ˈlɑːr- **-ates** -eɪts **-ating** -eɪ.tɪŋ ⓤⓢ -eɪ.t̬ɪŋ **-ated** -eɪ.tɪd ⓤⓢ -eɪ.t̬ɪd
laurel (L) ˈlɒr.ᵊl ⓤⓢ ˈlɔːr-, ˈlɑːr- **-s** -z
Lauren ˈlɔː.rən, ˈlɒr.ən ⓤⓢ ˈlɔːr.ən, ˈlɑːr-
Laurence ˈlɒr.ᵊnts ⓤⓢ ˈlɔːr-, ˈlɑːr-
Laurent lɔːˈrɑ̃ːŋ, lə- ⓤⓢ lɑːˈrɑːnt, lə-
Laurie ˈlɒr.i, ˈlɔː.ri ⓤⓢ ˈlɔːr.i, ˈlɑːr-
Laurier *English name:* ˈlɒr.i.əʳ ⓤⓢ ˈlɔːr.i.ɚ, ˈlɑːr- *Canadian name:* ˈlɒr.i.eɪ ⓤⓢ ˈlɔːr.i.eɪ
Lauriston ˈlɒr.ɪ.stᵊn, ˈ-ə- ⓤⓢ ˈlɔːr-, ˈlɑːr-
laurustinus ˌlɒr.əˈstaɪ.nəs, ˌlɔː.rəˈ- ⓤⓢ ˌlɑːr-, ˌlɔːr- **-es** -ɪz
Lausanne ləʊˈzæn ⓤⓢ loʊ-, -ˈzɑːn
Lauterbrunnen ˈlaʊ.tə.brʊn.ən ⓤⓢ -t̬ɚ-
Lautrec ləʊˈtrek ⓤⓢ loʊ-, lə-
lav læv **-s** -z
lava ˈlɑː.və ⓤⓢ ˈlɑː-, ˈlæv.ə
lavabo *ritual:* ləˈvɑː.bəʊ, lævˈɑː-, -ˈeɪ- ⓤⓢ ləˈvɑː.boʊ, -ˈveɪ- **-s** -z *basin:* ləˈveɪ.bəʊ; ˈlæv.ə.bəʊ ⓤⓢ ləˈvɑː.boʊ, -ˈveɪ- **-s** -z
lavage lævˈɑːʒ, ləˈvɑːʒ, -ˈvɑːdʒ; ˈlæv.ɪdʒ, -ɑːʒ ⓤⓢ ləˈvɑːʒ; ˈlæv.ɪdʒ
Lavater lɑːˈvɑː.təʳ, ˈ--- ⓤⓢ -t̬ɚ
lavatorial ˌlæv.əˈtɔː.ri.əl ⓤⓢ -ˈtɔːr.i-
lavator|y ˈlæv.ə.tᵊr|.i, -tr|i ⓤⓢ -tɔːr.i **-ies** -iz
lav|e leɪv **-es** -z **-ing** -ɪŋ **-ed** -d
lavender (L) ˈlæv.ᵊn.dəʳ, -ɪn- ⓤⓢ -dɚ **ˈlavender ˌwater**
Lavengro ləˈveŋ.grəʊ, lævˈeŋ- ⓤⓢ -groʊ
Lavenham ˈlæv.ᵊn.əm
laver *seaweed:* ˈlɑː.vəʳ ⓤⓢ ˈleɪ.vɚ, ˈlɑː- **-s** -z *all other senses:* ˈleɪ.vəʳ ⓤⓢ -vɚ **-s** -z
Laver *name:* ˈleɪ.vəʳ ⓤⓢ -vɚ
Laverty ˈlæv.ə.ti ⓤⓢ -ɚ.t̬i
Lavery ˈleɪ.vᵊr.i, ˈlæv.ᵊr-
Lavin ˈlæv.ɪn
Lavington ˈlæv.ɪŋ.tən
Lavini|a ləˈvɪn.i|.ə **-an** -ən
lavish ˈlæv.ɪʃ **-ly** -li **-ness** -nəs, -nɪs **-es** -ɪz **-ing** -ɪŋ **-ed** -t
Lavoisier ləˈvwɑː.zi.eɪ, lævˈwɑː-, -ˈwæz.i- ⓤⓢ ləˈvwɑː.zi-
law (L) lɔː ⓤⓢ lɑː, lɔː **-s** -z ˈ**law** ˌ**lord**; **be a ˌlaw unto oneˈself**; **take the ˌlaw into one's ˌown ˈhands**
law-abiding ˈlɔː.əˌbaɪ.dɪŋ ⓤⓢ ˈlɑː-, ˈlɔː-
lawbreak|er ˈlɔːˌbreɪ.k|əʳ ⓤⓢ ˈlɑːˌbreɪ.k|ɚ, ˈlɔː- **-ers** -əz ⓤⓢ -ɚz **-ing** -ɪŋ
Lawes lɔːz ⓤⓢ lɑːz, lɔːz
Lawesford ˈlɔːz.fəd ⓤⓢ ˈlɑːz.fɚd, ˈlɔːz-
lawful ˈlɔː.fᵊl, -fʊl ⓤⓢ ˈlɑː-, ˈlɔː- **-ly** -i **-ness** -nəs, -nɪs
lawgiv|er ˈlɔːˌgɪv|.əʳ ⓤⓢ ˈlɑːˌgɪv|.ɚ, ˈlɔː- **-ers** -əz ⓤⓢ -ɚz **-ing** -ɪŋ
lawks lɔːks ⓤⓢ lɑːks, lɔːks
lawless (L) ˈlɔː.ləs, -lɪs ⓤⓢ ˈlɑː-, ˈlɔː- **-ly** -li **-ness** -nəs, -nɪs
Lawley, Lawly ˈlɔː.li ⓤⓢ ˈlɑː-, ˈlɔː-
lawmak|er ˈlɔːˌmeɪ.k|əʳ ⓤⓢ ˈlɑːˌmeɪ.k|ɚ, ˈlɔː- **-ers** -əz ⓤⓢ -ɚz **-ing** -ɪŋ

Lax

A lax sound is produced with relatively little articulatory energy. Since there is no established standard for measuring articulatory energy, this concept only has meaning if it is used relative to some other sounds that are felt to be articulated with a comparatively greater amount of energy (i.e. TENSE).

Examples for English

It is mainly American phonologists who use the terms lax and tense in describing English vowels; the short vowels /ɪ e æ ʌ ɒ ʊ ə/ are classed as lax, while what are referred to in our description of BBC pronunciation as the long vowels and the diphthongs are tense. The terms can also be used of consonants as equivalent to FORTIS (tense) and LENIS (lax), though this is not commonly done in present-day descriptions.

lawn lɔːn (US) lɑːn, lɔːn **-s** -z **ˈlawn ˌmower; ˌlawn ˈtennis** (US) **ˈlawn ˌtennis**
Lawrence, Lawrance ˈlɒr.ənts (US) ˈlɔːr-, ˈlɑːr-
lawrencium ləˈrent.si.əm, lɔː-, lɒrˈent- (US) lɔːˈrent-, lɑː-
Lawrenson ˈlɒr.ənt.sən (US) ˈlɔːr.ənt-, ˈlɑːr-
Lawrentian ləˈren.ʃi.ən, lɒrˈen-, -ʃən (US) ləˈrent-, lɔː-, lɑː-
Lawson ˈlɔː.sən (US) ˈlɑː-, ˈlɔː-
lawsuit ˈlɔː.suːt, -sjuːt (US) ˈlɑː.suːt, ˈlɔː- **-s** -s
Lawton ˈlɔː.tən (US) ˈlɑː-, ˈlɔː-
lawyer ˈlɔɪ.əʳ, ˈlɔː.jəʳ (US) ˈlɑː.jɚ, ˈlɔː-, ˈlɔɪ- **-s** -z
lax læks **-er** -əʳ (US) -ɚ **-est** -ɪst, -əst **-ly** -li **-ness** -nəs, -nɪs
laxative ˈlæk.sə.tɪv (US) -t̬ɪv **-s** -z
laxity ˈlæk.sə.ti, -sɪ- (US) -sə.t̬i
lay (L) leɪ **-s** -z **-ing** -ɪŋ **laid** leɪd **ˌlay ˈreader** (US) **ˈlay ˌreader; ˌlay of the ˈland**
layabout ˈleɪ.əˌbaʊt **-s** -s
Layamon ˈlaɪ.ə.mən, -mɒn (US) ˈleɪ.ə.mən, ˈlaɪ-
Layard ˈleɪ.ɑːd, leəd (US) ˈleɪ.ɑːrd, lerd
layaway ˈleɪ.ə.weɪ
lay-by ˈleɪ.baɪ **-s** -z
Laycock ˈleɪ.kɒk (US) -kɑːk
layer leɪəʳ, leəʳ (US) ˈleɪ.ɚ **-s** -z **-ing** -ɪŋ **-ed** -d
layette leɪˈet **-s** -s
lay|man ˈleɪ|.mən **-men** -mən
layoff ˈleɪ.ɒf (US) -ɑːf **-s** -s
layout ˈleɪ.aʊt **-s** -s
layover ˈleɪˌəʊ.vəʳ (US) -ˌoʊ.vɚ
lay|person ˈleɪˌpɜː.sən (US) -ˌpɝː- **-people** -ˌpiː.pl̩
Layton ˈleɪ.tən
layup ˈleɪ.ʌp **-s** -s
lay|woman ˈleɪ|ˌwʊm.ən **-women** -ˌwɪm.ɪn
lazar ˈlæz.əʳ (US) ˈleɪ.zɚ, ˈlæz.ɚ **-s** -z
lazaretto ˌlæz.əˈret.əʊ, -ərˈet- (US) -ˈret̬.oʊ **-s** -z
Lazarus ˈlæz.ər.əs
laz|e leɪz **-es** -ɪz **-ing** -ɪŋ **-ed** -d
Lazenby ˈleɪ.zən.bi, -zəm- (US) -zən-
Lazio ˈlæt.si.əʊ (US) ˈlɑːt.si.oʊ
lazuli ˈlæz.jə.liː, -jʊ-, ˈlæʒ.ə-, ˈ-ʊ-, -laɪ (US) ˈlæʒ.juː-, ˈlæz-, ˈ-ə-
lazulite ˈlæz.jə.laɪt, -jʊ-, ˈlæʒ.ə-, -ˈʊ- (US) ˈlæʒ.juː-, ˈlæz-, ˈ-ə-
laz|y ˈleɪ.z|i **-ier** -i.əʳ (US) -i.ɚ **-iest** -i.ɪst, -i.əst **-ily** -ɪ.li, -əl.i **-iness** -ɪ.nəs, -ɪ.nɪs
lazybones ˈleɪ.ziˌbəʊnz (US) -ˌboʊnz
lb *(abbrev. for* **pound/s***) singular:* paʊnd *plural:* paʊndz
lbw ˌel.biːˈdʌb.l̩.juː
LCD ˌel.siːˈdiː
L-dopa ˌelˈdəʊ.pə (US) -ˈdoʊ-
lea (L) liː **-s** -z
LEA ˌel.iːˈeɪ
leach (L) liːtʃ **-es** -ɪz **-ing** -ɪŋ **-ed** -t
Leachman ˈliːtʃ.mən
Leacock ˈliː.kɒk, ˈleɪ- (US) -kɑːk
lead *metal:* led **-s** -z **-ing** -ɪŋ **-ed** -ɪd **ˌlead ˈpencil;** (US) **ˈlead ˌpencil; ˌlead ˈpoisoning**
lead *cable, flex:* liːd **-s** -z
lead *guide:* liːd **-s** -z **-ing** -ɪŋ **led** led **ˌleading ˈlight; ˈleading ˌrein; ˈlead ˌtime**
Lead *surname:* liːd
Leadbetter ˈledˌbet.əʳ, -ˈ-- (US) ˈledˌbet̬.ɚ, -ˈ--
leaden ˈled.ən **-ly** -li **-ness** -nəs, -nɪs
Leadenhall ˈled.ən.hɔːl (US) -hɔːl, -hɑːl
leader (L) ˈliː.dəʳ (US) -dɚ **-s** -z **ˌleader of the ˌoppoˈsition**
leaderboard ˈliː.də.bɔːd (US) -dɚ.bɔːrd **-s** -z
leaderette ˌliː.dərˈet **-s** -s
leadership ˈliː.də.ʃɪp (US) -dɚ- **-s** -s
lead-in ˈliːd.ɪn **-s** -z
lead-off ˈliːd.ɒf (US) -ɑːf **-s** -s
leads *(n.) roofing:* ledz
lea|f *(n.)* liː|f **-ves** -vz **ˈleaf ˌmould; take a ˌleaf out of ˌsomeone's ˈbook; ˌturn over a ˌnew ˈleaf**
leaf *(v.)* liːf **-s** -s **-ing** -ɪŋ **-ed** -t
leafless ˈliːf.ləs, -lɪs
leafle|t ˈliː.flə|t, -flɪ|t **-ts** -ts **-(t)ting** -tɪŋ (US) -t̬ɪŋ **-(t)ted** -tɪd (US) -t̬ɪd
leaf|y ˈliː.f|i **-ier** -i.əʳ (US) -i.ɚ **-iest** -i.ɪst, -i.əst **-iness** -ɪ.nəs, -ɪ.nɪs
leagu|e liːg **-es** -z **-ing** -ɪŋ **-ed** -d **ˈleague ˌtable**
leaguer (L) ˈliː.gəʳ (US) -gɚ **-s** -z
Leah ˈliː.ə; lɪə (US) ˈliː.ə
Leahy ˈliː.hi (US) ˈleɪ-
leak liːk **-s** -s **-ing** -ɪŋ **-ed** -t
leakag|e ˈliː.kɪdʒ **-es** -ɪz
Leake liːk
Leakey ˈliː.ki
leak|y ˈliː.k|i **-ier** -i.əʳ (US) -i.ɚ **-iest** -i.ɪst, -i.əst **-iness** -ɪ.nəs, -ɪ.nɪs
Leamington ˈlem.ɪŋ.tən **ˌLeamington ˈSpa**
lean liːn **-er** -əʳ (US) -ɚ **-est** -ɪst, -əst **-ly** -li **-ness** -nəs, -nəs **-s** -z **-ing/s** -ɪŋ/z **leaned** -d, lent **leant** lent
Leander liˈæn.dəʳ (US) -dɚ
Leanne liˈæn
lean-to ˈliːn.tuː **-s** -z
leap liːp **-s** -s **-ing** -ɪŋ **-ed** lept, liːpt **-t** lept **-er/s** -əʳ/z (US) -ɚ/z **ˈleap ˌyear; by ˌleaps and ˈbounds**
leapfrog ˈliːp.frɒg (US) -frɑːg, -frɔːg **-s** -z **-ging** -ɪŋ **-ged** -d
Lear lɪəʳ (US) lɪr
learn lɜːn (US) lɝːn **-s** -z **-ing** -ɪŋ **-ed** -d, **-t** -t **-er/s** -əʳ/z (US) -ɚ/z **ˈlearning ˌcurve; ˈlearning disaˌbility**
learned *scholarly:* ˈlɜː.nɪd (US) ˈlɝː- **-ly** **-ness** -nəs, -nɪs
Learney ˈleə.ni (US) ˈler-
leas|e liːs **-es** -ɪz **-ing** -ɪŋ **-ed** -t **a ˌnew ˌlease of ˈlife; a ˌnew ˌlease on ˈlife**
leaseback ˈliːs.bæk
leasehold ˈliːs.həʊld (US) -hoʊld **-s** -z **-er/s** -əʳ/z (US) -ɚ/z
lease-|lend ˌliːs|ˈlend **-lends** -ˈlendz **-lending** -ˈlen.dɪŋ **-lent** -ˈlent

leash liːʃ **-es** -ɪz **-ing** -ɪŋ **-ed** -t
least liːst
leastways ˈliːst.weɪz
leastwise ˈliːst.waɪz
leat liːt **-s** -s
Leatham ˈliː.θəm, -ðəm
Leathart ˈliː.θɑːt (US) -θɑːrt
leath|er ˈleð|.əʳ (US) -ɚ **-ers** -əz (US) -ɚz **-ering** -ər.ɪŋ **-ered** -əd (US) -ɚd
leatherback ˈleð.ə.bæk (US) ˈ-ɚ-
Leatherette® ˌleð.ərˈet
Leatherhead ˈleð.ə.hed (US) ˈ-ɚ-
leatherjacket ˈleð.əˌdʒæk.ɪt (US) -ɚˌ- **-s** -s
leathern ˈleð.ən (US) -ɚn
leatherneck ˈleð.ə.nek (US) ˈ-ɚ- **-s** -s
leather|y ˈleð.ər|.i **-iness** -ɪ.nəs, -ɪ.nɪs
Leathes liːðz
leave *(n.)* liːv **-s** -z
Note: Formerly, the pronunciation /liːf/ was used in the British army (plural: /liːfs/).
leav|e *(v.)* liːv **-es** -z **-ing/s** -ɪŋ/z **left** left **-er/s** -əʳ/z (US) -ɚ/z
leaved liːvd
leaven ˈlev.ən **-s** -z **-ing** -ɪŋ, ˈlev.nɪŋ **-ed** -d
Leavenworth ˈlev.ən.wəθ, -wɜːθ (US) -wɚθ, -wɝːθ
leaves *(plur. of* **leaf***)* liːvz
leave-taking ˈliːvˌteɪ.kɪŋ
Leavis ˈliː.vɪs
Leavisite ˈliː.vɪ.saɪt **-s** -s
Leavitt ˈlev.ɪt
Lebanese ˌleb.əˈniːz *stress shift:* ˌLebanese ˈcapital
Lebanon ˈleb.ə.nən, -nɒn (US) -nɑːn, -nən
Le Beau ləˈbəʊ (US) -ˈboʊ
Lebed ˈleb.jed, -ed, -ˈ- (US) -ed
Lebensraum (L) ˈleɪ.bənz.raʊm, -bəmz- (US) -bənz-
Le Bon ləˈbɒn (US) -ˈbɔːn
Lebowa ləˈbəʊ.ə (US) -ˈboʊ-
Lebrun ləˈbrɜ̃ːŋ (US) -ˈbrɜ̃n
Leburn ˈliː.bɜːn (US) -bɝːn
Lec® lek
Le Carré, le Carré ləˈkær.eɪ (US) -ˈkær.eɪ; -kɑːˈreɪ
lech letʃ **-es** -ɪz **-ing** -ɪŋ **-ed** -t
Lech lek *as if Polish:* lex
lecher ˈletʃ.əʳ (US) -ɚ **-s** -z
lecherous ˈletʃ.ər.əs **-ly** -li **-ness** -nəs, -nɪs
lechery ˈletʃ.ər.i
Lechlade ˈletʃ.leɪd
Lechmere ˈleʃ.mɪəʳ, ˈletʃ- (US) -mɪr
lecithin ˈles.ɪ.θɪn, ˈ-ə-, -θən (US) -ɪ.θɪn
Leckhampton ˈlekˌhæmp.tən
Leckie ˈlek.i
Lecky ˈlek.i
Leclanché ləˈklɑ̃ːn.ʃeɪ
Leconfield ˈlek.ən.fiːld
Leconte ləˈkɒnt, ləˈkɔ̃ːt, -ˈkɑːnt
Le Corbusier lə.kɔːˈbuː.zi.eɪ, -ˈbjuː- (US) -kɔːr.buːˈzjeɪ, -ziˈeɪ
lect lekt **-al** -əl
lectern ˈlek.tən, -tɜːn (US) -tɚn, -tɝːn **-s** -z
lection ˈlek.ʃən **-s** -z
lectionar|y ˈlek.ʃən.ər|.i (US) -er- **-ies** -iz
lector ˈlek.tɔːʳ (US) -tɚ, -tɔːr **-s** -z
lect|ure ˈlek.tʃ|əʳ (US) -tʃ|ɚ **-ures** -əz (US) -ɚz **-uring** -ər.ɪŋ **-ured** -əd (US) -ɚd
lecturer ˈlek.tʃər.əʳ (US) -ɚ **-s** -z
lectureship ˈlek.tʃə.ʃɪp (US) -tʃɚ- **-s** -s
led *(from* **lead***)* led
LED ˌel.iːˈdiː
Leda ˈliː.də
Ledbury ˈled.bər.i (US) ˈled.ber-
lederhosen ˈleɪ.dəˌhəʊ.zən (US) -dɚˌhoʊ-
ledg|e ledʒ **-es** -ɪz
ledger ˈledʒ.əʳ (US) -ɚ **-s** -z ˈ**ledger** ˌ**line**
Ledi ˈled.i
Lediard ˈled.i.əd, -ɑːd, ˈ-jəd (US) ˈled.jɚd, ˈ-i.ɚd, -ɑːrd
Ledward ˈled.wəd (US) -wɚd
Ledyard ˈled.jəd (US) -jɚd
lee (L) liː **-s** -z
leech (L) liːtʃ **-es** -ɪz
Leeds liːdz
Lee-Enfield ˌliːˈen.fiːld
leek (L) liːk **-s** -s
leer lɪəʳ (US) lɪr **-s** -z **-ing/ly** -ɪŋ/li **-ed** -d
leer|y ˈlɪə.r|i (US) ˈlɪr|.i **-ier** -i.əʳ (US) -i.ɚ **-iest** -i.ɪst, -i.əst **-ily** -ɪ.li, -əl.i **-iness** -ɪ.nəs, -ɪ.nɪs
lees (L) liːz
leeson liː.sən
leet liːt **-s** -s
leeward ˈliː.wəd (US) -wɚd *nautical pronunciation:* ˈluː.əd, ˈljuː.əd (US) ˈluː.ɚd
Leeward *islands:* ˈliː.wəd (US) -wɚd
leeway ˈliː.weɪ
Lefanu, Le Fanu ˈlef.ə.njuː, -nuː; ləˈfɑː.nuː (US) ˈlef.ə.nuː, ləˈfɑː-
Lefevre ləˈfiː.vəʳ, -ˈfeɪ-, -ˈfɛː.v.rə (US) -ˈfiː.vɚ
Note: /ləˈfiː.vəʳ (US) -vɚ/ in Sterne's 'Sentimental Journey'.
Lefroy ləˈfrɔɪ
left left ˌ**Left** ˈ**Bank** *stress shift:* ˌLeft Bank ˈartist
left|ie ˈlef.t|i **-ies** -iz
left-hand ˌleftˈhænd, ˈ--
left-hand|ed ˌleftˈhæn.d|ɪd **-edness** -ɪd.nəs, -nɪs **-er/s** -əʳ/z (US) -ɚ/z *stress shift:* ˌleft-handed ˈscissors
leftist ˈlef.tɪst **-s** -s
left-luggage office ˌleftˈlʌg.ɪdʒˌɒf.ɪs (US) -ˌɑː.fɪs
leftover ˈleftˌəʊ.vəʳ (US) -ˌoʊ.vɚ **-s** -z
leftward ˈleft.wəd (US) -wɚd **-s** -z
left-wing ˌleftˈwɪŋ **-er/s** -əʳ/z (US) -ɚ/z *stress shift:* ˌleft-wing ˈtendencies
left|y ˈlef.t|i **-ies** -iz
leg leg **-s** -z **-ging** -ɪŋ **-ged** -d ˌ**leg before** ˈ**wicket;** ˌ**leg** ˈ**bye; on one's** ˌ**last** ˈ**legs; not have a** ˌ**leg to** ˈ**stand on**
legac|y ˈleg.ə.s|i **-ies** -iz
legal ˈliː.gəl **-ly** -i ˌ**legal** ˈ**aid;** ˌ**legal** ˈ**tender**
legalese ˌliː.gəlˈiːz
legal|ism ˈliː.gəl|.ɪ.zəm **-ist/s** -ɪst/s
legalistic ˌliː.gəlˈɪs.tɪk **-ally** -əl.i, -li
legalit|y liːˈgæl.ə.t|i, lɪ-, -ɪ.t|i (US) -ə.ţ|i **-ies** -iz
legalization, -isa- ˌliː.gəl.aɪˈzeɪ.ʃən, -ɪˈ- (US) -ɪˈ-
legaliz|e, -is|e ˈliː.gəl.aɪz **-es** -ɪz **-ing** -ɪŋ **-ed** -d
legal-size ˈliː.gəlˌsaɪz
legate ˈleg.ət, -ɪt, -eɪt (US) -ɪt **-s** -s
legatee ˌleg.əˈtiː **-s** -z
legation lɪˈgeɪ.ʃən, lə-, legˈeɪ- (US) lɪˈgeɪ- **-s** -z
legatissimo ˌleg.ɑːˈtɪs.ɪ.məʊ, -əˈ- (US) -ɪ.moʊ
legato lɪˈgɑː.təʊ, lə-, legˈɑː- (US) -toʊ **-s** -z
legend ˈledʒ.ənd **-s** -z
legendary ˈledʒ.ən.dər.i, -ɪn- (US) -der-
Leger ˈledʒ.əʳ (US) -ɚ
Léger leɪˈʒeɪ
legerdemain ˌledʒ.ə.dəˈmeɪn *as if French:* ˌleʒ.ə.dəˈmæ̃ŋ (US) ˌ-ɚ-
Leggatt ˈleg.ət
Legge leg
-legged -ˈleg.ɪd, -ˈlegd
Note: Suffix. Normally carries primary stress on the penultimate syllable, e.g. **three-legged** /ˌθriːˈleg.ɪd/, but when a strong stress follows closely it undergoes stress shift, e.g. ˈ**three-legged** ˌ**stool**. However, the phrase "three-legged race" is usually ˈ**three-**ˌ**legged** ˈ**race**.
Leggett ˈleg.ɪt, -ət
Leggetter ˈleg.ɪ.təʳ, ˈ-ə- (US) -ţɚ
legging ˈleg.ɪŋ **-s** -z
leggy ˈleg.i
Legh liː
leghorn *fowl:* legˈɔːn, lɪˈgɔːn; ˈleg.ɔːn, ˈlɪg- (US) ˈleg.hɔːrn, -ɚn **-s** -z
leghorn *straw hat:* ˈleg.hɔːn; legˈɔːn, lɪˈgɔːn, lə- (US) ˈleg.hɔːrn, -ɚn **-s** -z
Leghorn *place:* ˈleg.hɔːn, -ˈ- (US) -hɔːrn, ˌ-ˈ-
legibility ˌledʒ.əˈbɪl.ə.ti, -ɪˈ-, -ɪ.ti (US) -ə.ţi
legib|le ˈledʒ.ə.b|l̩, ˈ-ɪ- **-ly** -li **-leness** -l̩.nəs, -nɪs

legion (L) ˈliː.dʒən **-s** -z ˌ**Legion of ˈHonour**
legionar|y ˈliː.dʒə.nᵊr|.i ⓤⓢ -er- **-ies** -iz
legionnaire (L) ˌliː.dʒəˈneəʳ ⓤⓢ -ˈner **-s** -z **Legionˈnaire's diˌsease**
legi|slate ˈledʒ.ɪ|.sleɪt, ˈ-ə- **-slates** -sleɪts **-slating** -sleɪ.tɪŋ ⓤⓢ -sleɪ.t̬ɪŋ **-slated** -sleɪ.tɪd ⓤⓢ -sleɪ.t̬ɪd
legislation ˌledʒ.ɪˈsleɪ.ʃᵊn, -əˈ-
legislative ˈledʒ.ɪ.slə.tɪv, ˈ-ə-, -sleɪ- ⓤⓢ -sleɪ.t̬ɪv
legislator ˈledʒ.ɪ.sleɪ.təʳ, ˈ-ə- ⓤⓢ -t̬ɚ **-s** -z
legislature ˈledʒ.ɪ.slə.tʃəʳ, -sleɪ-, -tjʊəʳ, -tʃʊəʳ ⓤⓢ -sleɪ.tʃɚ **-s** -z
legit ləˈdʒɪt, lɪ-
legitimacy lɪˈdʒɪt.ə.mə.si, lə-, ˈ-ɪ- ⓤⓢ ləˈdʒɪt̬.ə-
legitimate *(adj.)* lɪˈdʒɪt.ə.mət, lə-, ˈ-ɪ-, -mɪt ⓤⓢ ləˈdʒɪt̬.ə- **-ly** -li **-ness** -nəs, -nɪs
legiti|mate *(v.)* lɪˈdʒɪt.ə|.meɪt, lə-, ˈ-ɪ- ⓤⓢ ləˈdʒɪt̬.ə- **-mates** -meɪts **-mating** -meɪ.tɪŋ ⓤⓢ -meɪ.t̬ɪŋ **-mated** -meɪ.tɪd ⓤⓢ -meɪ.t̬ɪd
legitimation lɪˌdʒɪt.əˈmeɪ.ʃᵊn, lə-, -ɪˈ- ⓤⓢ ləˌdʒɪt̬.əˈ-
legitimatiz|e, -is|e lɪˈdʒɪt.ə.mə.taɪz, lə-, ˈ-ɪ- ⓤⓢ ləˈdʒɪt̬.ə- **-es** -ɪz **-ing** -ɪŋ **-ed** -d
legitimist lɪˈdʒɪt.ə.mɪst, lə-, ˈ-ɪ- ⓤⓢ ləˈdʒɪt̬.ə- **-s** -s
legitimiz|e, -is|e lɪˈdʒɪt.ə.maɪz, lə-, ˈ-ɪ- ⓤⓢ ləˈdʒɪt̬.ə- **-es** -ɪz **-ing** -ɪŋ **-ed** -d
legless ˈleg.ləs, -lɪs
Lego® ˈleg.əʊ ⓤⓢ -oʊ
Legoland® ˈleg.əʊ.lænd ⓤⓢ -oʊ-
leg-pull ˈleg.pʊl **-s** -z **-ing** -ɪŋ **-ed** -d
Legree lɪˈgriː, lə-
legroom ˈleg.rʊm, -ruːm ⓤⓢ -ruːm, -rʊm
Legros ləˈgrəʊ ⓤⓢ -ˈgroʊ
legume ˈleg.juːm; lɪˈgjuːm, lə- **-s** -z
leguminous lɪˈgjuː.mɪ.nəs, lə-, legˈjuː-, -mə- ⓤⓢ ləˈgjuː-
leg-warmer ˈlegˌwɔː.məʳ ⓤⓢ -ˌwɔːr.mɚ **-s** -z
legwork ˈleg.wɜːk ⓤⓢ -wɝːk
Lehar, Lehàr leɪˈhɑːʳ, lɪ-, lə-; ˈleɪ.hɑːʳ ⓤⓢ ˈleɪ.hɑːr
Le Havre ləˈ*h*ɑː.vrə, -vəʳ ⓤⓢ -ˈhɑː.vrə, -vɚ
Lehigh ˈliː.haɪ
Lehman(n) ˈleɪ.mən, ˈliː-
lehr lɪəʳ, leəʳ ⓤⓢ lɪr, ler **-s** -z
lei ˈleɪ.iː **-s** -z
lei *(plur. of* **leu)** leɪ
Leibni(t)z ˈlaɪb.nɪts, ˈliːb-
Leica® ˈlaɪ.kə
Leicester ˈles.təʳ ⓤⓢ -tɚ **-shire** -ʃəʳ, -ˌʃɪəʳ ⓤⓢ -ʃɚ, -ˌʃɪr
Leics. *(abbrev. for* **Leicestershire)** ˈles.tə.ʃəʳ, -ˌʃɪəʳ ⓤⓢ -ʃɚ, -ˌʃɪr
Leiden ˈlaɪ.dᵊn, ˈleɪ- ⓤⓢ ˈlaɪ-
Leigh *surname:* liː *place name:* liː, laɪ
Leighton ˈleɪ.tᵊn
Leila ˈliː.lə, ˈleɪ-
Leinster *Irish province:* ˈlen*t*.stəʳ ⓤⓢ -stɚ *Duke of:* ˈlɪn*t*.stəʳ ⓤⓢ -stɚ *square in London:* ˈlen*t*.stəʳ, ˈlɪn*t*- ⓤⓢ -stɚ
Leipzig ˈlaɪp.sɪg, -sɪk
Leishman ˈliːʃ.mən, ˈlɪʃ-
leishmania ˌliːʃˈmeɪ.ni.ə
leishmaniasis ˌliːʃ.məˈnaɪ.ə.sɪs
leishmaniosis ˌleɪʃ.mə.niˈəʊ.sɪs, -meɪ- ⓤⓢ -meɪ.niˈoʊ-
leister ˈliː.stəʳ ⓤⓢ -stɚ **-s** -z
Leister ˈles.təʳ ⓤⓢ -tɚ
Leiston ˈleɪ.stᵊn
leisure ˈleʒ.əʳ ⓤⓢ ˈliː.ʒɚ, ˈleʒ.ɚ **-d** -d **-ly** -li **-liness** -lɪ.nəs, -nɪs
Leith liːθ
leitmotif, leitmotiv ˈlaɪt.məʊˌtiːf, -ˌməʊ.tɪv ⓤⓢ -moʊˌtiːf **-s** -s, -z ⓤⓢ -s
Leitrim ˈliː.trɪm
Leix liːʃ
lek lek **-s** -s **-king** -ɪŋ **-ked** -t
lekker ˈlek.əʳ ⓤⓢ -ɚ
Leland ˈliː.lənd
Lelean ləˈliːn
Lely ˈliː.li, ˈlɪl.i
leman ˈlem.ən, ˈliː.mən **-s** -z
Leman *lake:* ˈlem.ən, ˈliː.mən; lɪˈmæn, ləˈmæn, ləˈmɑ̃ː*ŋ* ⓤⓢ ˈliː.mən; ləˈmæn *surname:* ˈle.mən, ˈliː.mən *street in London:* ˈlem.ən *formerly:* ˈlɪm.æn
Le Mans ləˈmɑ̃ː*ŋ* ⓤⓢ -ˈmɑːn, -ˈmɑ̃ː*n*
Le Marchant ləˈmɑː.tʃᵊnt ⓤⓢ -ˈmɑːr-
Lemare ləˈmeəʳ ⓤⓢ -ˈmer
Lemberg ˈlem.bɜːg ⓤⓢ -bɝːg
Lemesurier, Le Mesurier ləˈmeʒ.ᵊr.əʳ; lə.məˈʒʊə.ri.eɪ ⓤⓢ ləˈmeʒ.ɚ.ɚ; lə.məˈʒʊr.i.eɪ
lemma ˈlem.ə **-s** -z
lemmatization, -isa- ˌlem.ə.taɪˈzeɪ.ʃᵊn, -tɪˈ- ⓤⓢ -t̬ɪˈ-
lemmatiz|e, -is|e ˈlem.ə.taɪz **-es** -ɪz **-ing** -ɪŋ **-ed** -d **-er/s** -əʳ/z ⓤⓢ -ɚ/z
lemme ˈlem.i
lemming ˈlem.ɪŋ **-s** -z
Lemmon ˈlem.ən
lemnis|cus lemˈnɪs|.kəs **-ci** -aɪ, -kaɪ, -iː, -kiː ⓤⓢ -aɪ, -kaɪ
Lemnos ˈlem.nɒs ⓤⓢ -nɑːs, -noʊs
Lemoine ləˈmɔɪn
lemon (L) ˈlem.ən **-s** -z ˈ**lemon** ˌ**grass;** ˈ**lemon** ˌ**juice;** ˌ**lemon** ˈ**sole;** ˌ**lemon** ˈ**squash;** ˌ**lemon me**ˌ**ringue** ˈ**pie**
lemonade ˌlem.əˈneɪd **-s** -z
Le Morte D'Arthur ləˌmɔːtˈdɑː.θəʳ ⓤⓢ -ˌmɔːrtˈdɑːr.θɚ
lempira lemˈpɪə.rə ⓤⓢ -ˈpɪr.ə **-s** -z
Lempriere ˈlem.pri.eəʳ ⓤⓢ -er
Lemsip® ˈlem.sɪp
Lemuel ˈlem.jʊəl, -ju.əl ⓤⓢ -ju.əl, -jʊl
lemur ˈliː.məʳ ⓤⓢ -mɚ **-s** -z
Len len
Lena *first name:* ˈliː.nə *Siberian river:* ˈleɪ.nə
lend lend **-s** -z **-ing** -ɪŋ **lent** lent **lender/s** ˈlen.dəʳ/z ⓤⓢ -dɚ/z ˈ**lending** ˌ**library**
lenes *(plur. of* **lenis)** ˈliː.neɪz, ˈleɪ- ⓤⓢ ˈliː.niːz, ˈleɪ-
length leŋ*k*θ **-s** -s
lengthen ˈleŋ*k*.θən **-s** -z **-ing** -ɪŋ, ˈleŋ*k*θ.nɪŋ **-ed** -d
length|man ˈleŋ*k*θ|.mən **-men** -mən
lengthways ˈleŋ*k*θ.weɪz
lengthwise ˈleŋ*k*θ.waɪz
length|y ˈleŋ*k*.θ|i **-ier** -i.əʳ ⓤⓢ -i.ɚ **-iest** -i.ɪst, -i.əst **-ily** -ɪ.li, -ᵊl.i **-iness** -ɪ.nəs, -ɪ.nɪs
lenien|ce ˈliː.ni.ən*t*|s **-cy** -si
lenient ˈliː.ni.ənt **-ly** -li
Lenin ˈlen.ɪn **-ism** -ɪ.zᵊm **-ist/s** -ɪst/s **-ite/s** -aɪt/s
Leningrad ˈlen.ɪn.græd, -ɪŋ-, -grɑːd ⓤⓢ -græd
lenis ˈliː.nɪs, ˈleɪ- ⓤⓢ ˈliː.nɪs, ˈleɪ- **lenes** ˈliː.niːz, ˈleɪ-, -neɪz
lenition lɪˈnɪʃ.ᵊn, lə-
lenitive ˈlen.ɪ.tɪv ⓤⓢ -ə.t̬ɪv **-s** -z
lenity ˈlen.ə.ti, ˈliː.nə-, -nɪ- ⓤⓢ ˈlen.ə.
Lennie ˈlen.i
Lennon ˈlen.ən
Lennox ˈlen.əks
Lenny ˈlen.i
leno ˈliː.nəʊ ⓤⓢ -noʊ ˈlen.əʊ, ˈliː.nəʊ ⓤⓢ ˈlen.oʊ, ˈliː.noʊ
Lenoir *surname:* ləˈnwɑːʳ ⓤⓢ -ˈnwɑːr *town in US:* ləˈnɔːʳ ⓤⓢ -ˈnɔːr
Lenor® lɪˈnɔːʳ, lə- ⓤⓢ -ˈnɔːr
Lenore lɪˈnɔːʳ, lə- ⓤⓢ -ˈnɔːr
Lenox ˈlen.əks
lens lenz **-es** -ɪz
lent *(from* **lend)** lent
Lent lent **-en** -ən
Lenthall *surname:* ˈlen.tɔːl *place in Yorkshire:* ˈlen.θɔːl, -θᵊl
Lenthéric®, Lentheric ˈlɒn*t*.θᵊr.ɪk, ˈlɑ̃ː*n*- ⓤⓢ ˈlɑːn*t*-
lenticel ˈlen.tɪ.sel ⓤⓢ -t̬ɪ- **-s** -z
lenticular lenˈtɪk.jə.ləʳ, -jʊ- ⓤⓢ -jə.l
lentil ˈlen.tᵊl, -tɪl ⓤⓢ -t̬ᵊl **-s** -z
lentivirus ˈlen.tɪ.vaɪə.rəs ⓤⓢ -t̬ɪ.va **-es** -ɪz
lento ˈlen.təʊ ⓤⓢ -toʊ
Lenton ˈlen.tən
Lentulus ˈlen.tjə.ləs, -tjʊ- ⓤⓢ -tuː-,
Lenz lents
Leo ˈliː.əʊ ⓤⓢ -oʊ
Leofric ˈleɪ.əʊ.frɪk, ˈlef.rɪk ⓤⓢ leɪˈɑː.frɪk, -ˈoʊ-
Leominster *place in Britain:* ˈlemp ⓤⓢ -stɚ *place in US:* ˈlem.ɪn*t*.stə ⓤⓢ -stɚ

Length

A term used in phonetics to refer to a subjective impression of how much time a sound takes; it is distinct from physically measurable 'duration'. Usually, however, the term is used as synonymous with duration.

Examples for English

Length is important in many ways in speech: in English and most other languages, stressed syllables tend to be longer than unstressed (see RHYTHM, STRESS and WEAK FORM). Some languages have phonemic differences between long and short sounds, and BBC English is claimed by some writers to be of this type, contrasting short vowels /ɪ e æ ʌ ɒ ʊ ə/ with long vowels /iː ɜː ɑː ɔː uː/ (though other, equally valid analyses have been put forward). However, the context in which these sounds occur must be taken into account. For example, the vowel /iː/ is said to be longer than /ɪ/ as well as having a different quality, but the vowel in *beat* is unlikely to be longer than the vowel in *bid* as the phonetic environment in *beat* causes the vowel to be shorter.

In other languages

When languages have long/short consonant differences, as does Arabic, for example, it is usual to treat the long consonants as **geminate**; it is odd that this is not done equally regularly in the case of vowels. Perhaps the most interesting example of length differences comes from Estonian, which has traditionally been said to have a three-way distinction between short, long and extra-long consonants and vowels.

Lenis

A lenis sound is weakly articulated (the word comes from Latin, where it means 'smooth, gentle'). The opposite term is FORTIS.

Examples for English

In general, the term lenis is used of voiced consonants (which are supposed to be less strongly articulated than their corresponding voiceless ones), and is resorted to for languages such as German, Russian and English where voiced PHONEMES like /b d g/ are not always voiced. (See the entry at FORTIS for examples.) However, it is claimed that the language which most clearly shows a distinction between fortis and lenis consonants is Korean.

eon 'liː.ɒn, 'leɪ-, -ən (US) -ɑːn
eón leɪ'ɒn (US) -'oʊn
eonard 'len.əd (US) -ɚd **-s** -z
eonardo ˌliː.ə'nɑː.dəʊ, ˌleɪ- (US) ˌliː.ə'nɑːr.doʊ **-s** -z
one (L) li'əʊ.ni (US) -'oʊ- **-s** -z
eonid 'liː.əʊ.nɪd, 'leɪ- (US) '-ə- **-s** -z
eonidas li'ɒn.ɪ.dæs, '-ə- (US) -'ɑː.nə.dəs
eonie li'əʊ.ni (US) -'oʊ-
onine 'liː.əʊ.naɪn (US) '-ə-
onora ˌliː.ə'nɔː.rə (US) -'nɔːr.ə
eontes li'ɒn.tiːz, leɪ- (US) li'ɑːn-
opard 'lep.əd (US) -ɚd **-s** -z **-ess/es** -es/ɪz, -ɪs/ɪz, -əs/ɪz
opardstown 'lep.ədz.taʊn (US) -ɚrdz-
opold 'liː.ə.pəʊld, 'lɪə.pəʊld (US) 'liː.ə.poʊld
otard 'liː.ə.tɑːd (US) -tɑːrd **-s** -z
panto lɪ'pæn.təʊ, lə- (US) lɪ'pæn.toʊ, -'pɑːn-
er 'lep.ə^{r} (US) -ɚ **-s** -z
idopter|an ˌlep.ɪ'dɒp.t^{ə}r|.ən (US) -'dɑːp- **-ans** -ənz **-a** -ə
idopterist ˌlep.ɪ'dɒp.t^{ə}r.ɪst (US) -'dɑːp- **-s** -s
lepidopterology ˌlep.ɪˌdɒp.t^{ə}r'ɒl.ə.dʒi (US) -ˌdɑːp.tə'rɑː.lə-
lepidopter|on ˌlep.ɪ'dɒp.t^{ə}r|.ən (US) -'dɑːp- **-ons** -ənz **-a** -ə
Lepidus 'lep.ɪ.dəs
Le Play lə'pleɪ
leprechaun 'lep.rə.kɔːn, -rɪ-, -hɔːn (US) -rə.kɑːn, -kɔːn **-s** -z
leprosy 'lep.rə.si
leprous 'lep.rəs **-ly** -li **-ness** -nəs, -nɪs
Lepsius 'lep.si.əs
lept|on 'lep.t|ɒn, -t|ən (US) -t|ɑːn **-a** -ə
Lepus 'liː.pəs, 'lep.əs (US) 'liː.pəs
Lermontov 'leə.mɒn.tɒf, -mən-, -təf (US) 'ler.mɑːn.tɔːf
Lerner 'lɜː.nə^{r} (US) 'lɝː.nɚ
Leroy 'liː.rɔɪ, lə'rɔɪ
Lerwick 'lɜː.wɪk (US) 'lɝː-
les *in French phrases:* leɪ, leɪz
Note: The form /leɪz/ only occurs when the following word begins with a vowel.
Les *first name:* lez (US) les
Lesbi|a 'lez.bi|.ə **-an** -ən
lesbian 'lez.bi.ən **-s** -z **-ism** -ɪ.z^{ə}m
Lesbos 'lez.bɒs (US) -bɑːs, -boʊs
lèse-majesté, **lese-majesty** ˌleɪz'mædʒ.ə.steɪ, ˌliːz-, '-ɪ-, -sti (US) ˌliːzˌmæʒ.es'teɪ; -'mædʒ.ɪ.sti
lesion 'liː.ʒ^{ə}n **-s** -z
Leskovac 'les.kəʊ.vɑːts, -væts (US) -kɔː-
Leslie, **Lesley** 'lez.li (US) 'les-, 'lez-
Lesmahagow ˌles.mə'heɪ.gəʊ (US) -goʊ
Lesotho lə'suː.tuː, lɪ-, leɪ-, -'səʊ-, -təʊ (US) lə'soʊ.toʊ, -'suː.tuː
less les **-er** -ə^{r} (US) -ɚ
lessee les'iː **-s** -z
lessen 'les.^{ə}n **-s** -z **-ing** -ɪŋ, 'les.nɪŋ **-ed** -d
Lesseps 'les.əps, -eps; les'eps (US) 'les.əps
Lessing 'les.ɪŋ
lesson 'les.^{ə}n **-s** -z ˌ**learn one's** '**lesson**
lessor les'ɔː^{r}, '-- (US) 'les.ɔːr, -'- **-s** -z
lest lest
Lester 'les.tə^{r} (US) -tɚ
L'Estrange lə'streɪndʒ, lɪ-
Le Sueur lə'suː.ə^{r} (US) -'sʊr
let let **-s** -s **-ting** -ɪŋ (US) 'leṭ.ɪŋ
letch letʃ **-es** -ɪz **-ing** -ɪŋ **-ed** -t
Letchworth 'letʃ.wəθ, -wɜːθ (US) -wɚθ, -wɝːθ
letdown 'let.daʊn **-s** -z
lethal 'liː.θ^{ə}l **-ly** -i

lethargic lə'θɑː.dʒɪk, lɪ-, leθ'ɑː- (US) lɪ'θɑːr-, lə- **-ally** -əl.i, -li
lethargy 'leθ.ə.dʒi (US) '-ɚ-
Lethe 'liː.θi, -θiː
Letheby 'leθ.ə.bi
Lethem 'leθ.əm
Letitia lɪ'tɪʃ.i.ə, liː-, lə-, -'tiː.ʃi-, '-ʃə (US) lə'tɪʃ.ə, -'tiː.ʃə
Letraset® 'let.rə.set
Lett let **-s** -s
lett|er 'let|.əʳ (US) 'leţ|.ɚ **-ers** -əz (US) -ɚz **-ering** -ər.ɪŋ **-ered** -əd (US) -ɚd **'letter ˌbomb; 'letter ˌbox; 'letter ˌcarrier; 'letter ˌopener**
letterhead 'let.ə.hed (US) 'leţ.ɚ- **-s** -z
Letterman 'let.ə.mən (US) 'leţ.ɚ-
letter-perfect ˌlet.ə'pɜː.fɪkt, -fekt (US) ˌleţ.ɚ'pɝː.fɪkt
letterpress 'let.ə.pres (US) 'leţ.ɚ-
letter-quality 'let.əˌkwɒl.ə.ti, -ɪ.ti (US) 'leţ.ɚˌkwɑː.lə.ţi
letter-size 'let.ə.saɪz (US) 'leţ.ɚ-
Lettice 'let.ɪs (US) 'leţ-
Lettish 'let.ɪʃ (US) 'leţ-
lettuc|e 'let.ɪs, -əs (US) 'leţ- **-es** -ɪz
Letty 'let.i (US) 'leţ-
letup 'let.ʌp (US) 'leţ- **-s** -s
leu 'leɪ.uː **lei** leɪ
Leuchars *place in Scotland:* 'luː.kəz, 'ljuː-, -xəz (US) 'luː.kɚz *surname:* 'luː.kəs, 'ljuː- (US) 'luː.kɚs
leucine 'ljuː.siːn, 'luː-, -saɪn (US) 'luː-
leucite 'ljuː.saɪt, 'luː- (US) 'luː-
leucocyte 'ljuː.kəʊ.saɪt, 'luː- (US) 'luː.koʊ-, -kə- **-s** -s
leucotom|y ljuː'kɒt.ə.m|i, luː- (US) luː'kɑː.ţə- **-ies** -iz
Leuctra 'ljuːk.trə (US) 'luːk-
leuk(a)emia ljuː'kiː.mi.ə, luː- (US) luː-
lev lev (US) lef **leva** 'lev.ə
le|vant (L) *(n.v.)* lə|'vænt, lɪ- (US) lə- **-vants** -'vænts **-vanting** -'væn.tɪŋ (US) -'væn.ţɪŋ **-vanted** -'væn.tɪd (US) -'væn.ţɪd
levant *(adj.)* 'lev.ənt
levanter (L) lə'væn.təʳ, lɪ- (US) lə'væn.ţɚ **-s** -z
Levantine 'lev.ən.taɪn, -tiːn (US) 'lev.ən.tiːn, -taɪn; lɪ'væn-
levee *royal reception:* 'lev.i, -eɪ (US) 'lev.i; lə'viː, -'veɪ **-s** -z
levee *embankment:* 'lev.i **-s** -z
level 'lev.əl **-s** -z **-(l)ing** -ɪŋ, 'lev.lɪŋ **-(l)ed** -d **-(l)er/s** -əʳ/z (US) -ɚ/z **-ness** -nəs, -nɪs **-ly** -li **ˌlevel 'crossing**
level-headed ˌlev.əl'hed.ɪd (US) 'lev.əlˌhed.ɪd *stress shift, British only:* ˌlevel-headed 'person
Leven *loch:* 'liː.vən *surname:* 'lev.ən, 'liː.vən
Note: The Earl pronounces /'liː.vən/
lev|er *(n. v.) on machine:* 'liː.v|əʳ (US) 'lev.|ɚ, 'liː.v|ɚ **-ers** -əz (US) -ɚz **-ering** -ər.ɪŋ **-ered** -əd (US) -ɚd
Lever *surname:* 'liː.vəʳ (US) -vɚ
leverag|e 'liː.vər.ɪdʒ (US) 'lev.ɚ-, 'liː.vɚ- **-ing** -ɪŋ **-ed** -d
leveret 'lev.ər.ɪt, -ət **-s** -s
Leverett 'lev.ər.ɪt
Leverhulme 'liː.və.hjuːm (US) -vɚ-
Levertov 'lev.ə.tɒf (US) -ɚ.tɑːf
Leveson 'lev.ɪ.sən
Leveson-Gower ˌluː.sən'gɔːʳ, ˌljuː-, -sən'- (US) ˌluː.sən'gɔːr
Levett 'lev.ɪt
Levey 'liː.vi, 'lev.i
Levi 'liː.vaɪ, 'lev.i, 'liː.vi
leviable 'lev.i.ə.bl̩
leviathan (L) lɪ'vaɪə.θən, lə- **-s** -z
Levin 'lev.ɪn
Levine lə'viːn, -'vaɪn
levirate 'liː.vɪ.rət, 'lev.ɪ-, -rɪt (US) 'lev.ə.rɪt, 'liː.və-, -reɪt
Levis *in Quebec:* 'lev.i
Levis *trademark, jeans brand:* 'liː.vaɪz
Lévi-Strauss ˌlev.i'straʊs (US) ˌleɪ.vi-, ˌlev.i'-
levi|tate 'lev.ɪ|.teɪt, '-ə- **-tates** -teɪts **-tating** -teɪ.tɪŋ (US) -teɪ.ţɪŋ **-tated** -teɪ.tɪd (US) -teɪ.ţɪd
levitation ˌlev.ɪ'teɪ.ʃən, -ə'- **-s** -z
Levite 'liː.vaɪt **-s** -s
levitic lə'vɪt.ɪk, lɪ- (US) lə'vɪţ- **-al** -əl **-ally** -əl.i, -li
Leviticus lə'vɪt.ɪ.kəs, lɪ- (US) lə'vɪţ-
Levitt 'lev.ɪt
levit|y 'lev.ə.t|i, -ɪ.t|i (US) -ə.ţ|i **-ies** -iz
lev|y *(n. v.)* 'lev|.i **-ies** -iz **-ying** -i.ɪŋ **-ied** -id **-ier/s** -i.əʳ/z (US) -i.ɚ/z
Levy *surname:* 'liː.vi, 'lev.i
lewd ljuːd, luːd (US) luːd **-er** -əʳ (US) -ɚ **-est** -ɪst, -əst **-ly** -li **-ness** -nəs, -nɪs
Lewes 'luː.ɪs
Lewin 'luː.ɪn
Lewinsky lə'wɪnt.ski (US) luː'wɪn.ski
lewis (L) 'luː.ɪs **-es** -ɪz
Lewisham 'luː.ɪ.ʃəm
Lewison 'luː.ɪ.sən
Lewsey 'ljuː.si (US) 'luː-
lexeme 'lek.siːm **-s** -z
lexic|al 'lek.sɪ.k|əl **-ally** -əl.i, -li
lexicographic ˌlek.sɪ.kəʊ'græf.ɪk (US) -koʊ'-, -kə'- **-al** -əl **-ally** -əl.i, -li
lexicograph|y ˌlek.sɪ'kɒg.rə.f|i (US) -kɑː'grə- **-er/s** -əʳ/z (US) -ɚ/z
lexicological ˌlek.sɪ.kə'lɒdʒ.ɪ.kəl (US) -'lɑː.dʒɪ-
lexicolog|y ˌlek.sɪ'kɒl.ə.dʒ|i (US) -'kɑː.lə- **-ist/s** -ɪst/s
lexicon 'lek.sɪ.kən, -kɒn (US) -kɑːn, -kən **-s** -z
Lexington 'lek.sɪŋ.tən
lexis 'lek.sɪs
lex loci contractus ˌleksˌləʊ.saɪ.kɒn'træk.təs, -ˌləʊ.k… (US) -ˌloʊ.saɪ.kɑːn'-, -kiː-, -siː-
lex loci delicti ˌleksˌləʊ.saɪ.del'ɪk.tiː, -ˌləʊ.kiː-, -taɪ (US) -ˌloʊ.saɪ.də'lɪk-, -kiː-, -siː-
ley (L) leɪ, liː **'ley ˌline**
Leybourne 'leɪ.bɔːn (US) -bɔːrn
Leyburn 'leɪ.bɜːn (US) -bɝːn
Leyden jar ˌleɪ.dən'dʒɑːʳ (US) 'laɪ.dənˌdʒɑːr **-s** -z
Leyland 'leɪ.lənd
Leys liːz
Leyton 'leɪ.tən
Lhasa 'lɑː.sə, 'læs.ə
li liː **-s** -z
liabilit|y ˌlaɪ.ə'bɪl.ə.t|i, -ɪ.t|i (US) -ə.ţ|i **-ies** -iz
liable 'laɪ.ə.bl̩
liais|e li'eɪz **-es** -ɪz **-ing** -ɪŋ **-ed** -d
liaison li'eɪ.zən, -zɒn *as if French:* -zɔ̃ːŋ (US) 'liː.ə.zɑːn; li'eɪ-, -zən **-s** -z
Note: In military use always /li'eɪ.zən/ (US) -zɑːn, -zən/.
Liam 'liː.əm
liana li'ɑː.nə, -'æn.ə
liar 'laɪ.əʳ (US) -ɚ **-s** -z
Lias 'laɪ.əs
Liassic laɪ'æs.ɪk, li-
lib lɪb **ˌwomen's 'lib**
Libanus 'lɪb.ə.nəs
libation laɪ'beɪ.ʃən, lɪ- (US) laɪ- **-s** -z
libber 'lɪb.əʳ (US) -ɚ **-s** -z **ˌwomen's 'lib…**
Libby 'lɪb.i
Libdem ˌlɪb'dem **-s** -z *stress shift:* ˌLibdem 'vote
libel 'laɪ.bəl **-s** -z **-(l)ing** -ɪŋ **-(l)ed** -d **-(l)er/s** -əʳ/z (US) -ɚ/z
libel(l)ous 'laɪ.bəl.əs **-ly** -li
Liber 'laɪ.bəʳ (US) -bɚ
Liberace ˌlɪb.ər'ɑː.tʃi (US) -ə'rɑː-
liberal (L) 'lɪb.ər.əl, '-rəl **-s** -z **-ly** -i
Liberal Democrat ˌlɪb.ər.əl'dem.ə.kræt, -rəl'- **-s** -s
liberalism (L) 'lɪb.ər.əl.ɪ.zəm, '-rəl-
liberality ˌlɪb.ər'æl.ə.ti, lɪ'bræl- (US) ˌlɪb.ə'ræl-, -ɪ.ti (US) -ə.ţi
liberalization, -isa- ˌlɪb.ər.əl.aɪ'zeɪ…, -rəl-, -ɪ'- (US) -ɪ'-
liberaliz|e, -is|e 'lɪb.ər.əl.aɪz, '-rəl- **-es** -ɪz **-ing** -ɪŋ **-ed** -d
liber|ate 'lɪb.ər|.eɪt (US) -ə.r|eɪt **-ate…** -eɪts **-ating** -eɪ.tɪŋ (US) -eɪ.ţɪŋ **-at…** -eɪ.tɪd (US) -eɪ.ţɪd **-ator/s** -eɪ.təʳ/… (US) -eɪ.ţɚ/z
liberation ˌlɪb.ər'eɪ.ʃən (US) -ə'reɪ-
Liberi|a laɪ'bɪə.ri|.ə (US) -'bɪr.i- **-an/…** -ən/z
libertarian ˌlɪb.ə'teə.ri.ən (US) -ɚ't… **-s** -z **-ism** -ɪ.zəm
libertine 'lɪb.ə.tiːn, -taɪn (US) -ɚ.ti… -tɪn **-s** -z
Liberton 'lɪb.ə.tən (US) '-ɚ-

Liaison

The linking or joining together of sounds.

Examples for English

In English the best-known case of liaison is the 'linking r': there are many words in English (e.g. *car, here, tyre*) which in a RHOTIC accent such as US English or Scots would be pronounced with a final /r/, but which in BBC pronunciation end in a vowel when they are pronounced before a pause or before a consonant. When they are followed by a vowel, British English speakers pronounce /r/ at the end, e.g.:

the car stopped	/ðə kɑː stɒpt/
	(US) /ðə kɑːr stɑːpt/
the car is blue	/ðə kɑːr ɪz bluː/
	(US) /ðə kɑːr ɪz bluː/

In BBC English there is also 'intrusive r' – an /r/ inserted between two vowels at word boundaries where there is none in the spelling. This does not occur after close vowels (/iː uː/), or diphthongs which end with a close element (/eɪ aɪ ɔɪ aʊ əʊ/), e.g.:

China and Japan	tʃaɪnə r ən dʒə'pæn
	(US) tʃaɪnə ən dʒə'pæn
law and order	lɔː r ən 'ɔː.də
	(US) lɑː ən 'ɔːr.dɚ

It is said that liaison is done to link the words without sliding the two vowels together though many languages do run vowels together.

Another aspect of liaison in English is the movement of a single consonant at the end of an unstressed word to the beginning of the next if that is strongly stressed. A well-known example in British English is *none at all*, where the /t/ of *at* becomes initial (and therefore strongly aspirated) in the final syllable for many speakers.

ibert|y (L) 'lɪb.ə.t|i (US) -ɚ.t̬|i **-ies** -iz ˌ**Liberty 'Island**
ibidinous lɪ'bɪd.ɪ.nəs, lə-, -ᵊn.əs (US) lə'bɪd.ᵊn.əs **-ly** -li **-ness** -nəs, -nɪs
bido lɪ'biː.dəʊ, lə- (US) -doʊ **-s** -z
ibr|a *pound:* 'liː.br|ə, 'laɪ- (US) 'liː- **-ae** -iː, -eɪ, -aɪ
ibr|a *constellation:* 'liː.br|ə, 'lɪb.r|ə, 'laɪ.br|ə (US) 'liː-, 'laɪ- **-an/s** -ən/z
ibrarian laɪ'breə.ri.ən (US) -'brer.i- **-s** -z **-ship** -ʃɪp
brar|y 'laɪ.brᵊr|.i, -br|i (US) -brer|.i **-ies** -iz
bration laɪ'breɪ.ʃᵊn **-s** -z
brettist lɪ'bret.ɪst, lə- (US) lɪ'bret̬- **-s** -s
brett|o lɪ'bret|.əʊ, lə- (US) lɪ'bret̬|.oʊ **-os** -əʊz (US) -oʊz **-i** -iː
ibreville 'liː.brə.vɪl (US) -viːl, -vɪl
ibrium® 'lɪb.ri.əm
by|a 'lɪb.i|.ə **-an/s** -ən/z
ce (*plur. of* **louse**) laɪs
cenc|e 'laɪ.sᵊnts **-es** -ɪz **-ed** -t
cens|e 'laɪ.sᵊnts **-es** -ɪz **-ing** -ɪŋ **-ed** -t **-er/s** -əʳ/z (US) -ɚ/z **-or/s** -əʳ/z (US) -ɚ/z **'license ˌplate**
censee ˌlaɪ.sᵊnt'siː **-s** -z
centiate laɪ'sen.tʃi.ət, lɪ-, -tʃət, -tʃi.ɪt (US) -ʃi.ɪt, -ʃi.eɪt, -ʃət **-s** -s
centious laɪ'sen.tʃəs **-ly** -li **-ness** -nəs, -nɪs
chee ˌlaɪ'tʃiː; 'laɪ.tʃiː, 'liː- (US) 'liː.tʃiː **-s** -z
chen 'laɪ.kən, -kɪn, 'lɪtʃ.ən, -ɪn (US) 'laɪ.kən **-s** -z **-ed** -d
chenous 'laɪ.kə.nəs, -kɪ-, 'lɪtʃ.ə-, '-ɪ- (US) 'laɪ.kə-
chfield 'lɪtʃ.fiːld
chgate 'lɪtʃ.geɪt **-s** -s

Lichtenstein 'lɪx.tən.staɪn, 'lɪk- (US) lɪk-
Licini|an laɪ'sɪn.i|.ən, lɪ- **-us** -əs
licit 'lɪs.ɪt **-ly** -li **-ness** -nəs, -nɪs
lick lɪk **-s** -s **-ing/s** -ɪŋ/z **-ed** -t
lickety-split ˌlɪk.ə.ti'splɪt, ˌ-ɪ- (US) -ə.t̬i'-
licorice 'lɪk.ᵊr.ɪs, -ɪʃ, 'lɪk.rɪs, -rɪʃ (US) 'lɪk.ɚ.ɪʃ, '-rɪʃ, 'lɪk.ɚ.ɪs
lictor 'lɪk.təʳ, -tɔːʳ (US) -tɚ **-s** -z
lid lɪd **-s** -z **-ded** -ɪd
Liddell 'lɪd.ᵊl, lɪ'del
Liddesdale 'lɪdz.deɪl
Liddiment 'lɪd.ɪ.mənt
Liddle 'lɪd.l̩
Liddon 'lɪd.ᵊn
Lidell lɪ'del
Lidgate 'lɪd.geɪt, -gɪt
lido (L) 'liː.dəʊ, 'laɪ- (US) 'liː.doʊ **-s** -z
lie (*n. v.*) *falsehood:* laɪ **-s** -z **lying/ly** 'laɪ.ɪŋ/li **lied** laɪd ˌ**lie through one's 'teeth**
lie (*v.*) *recline:* laɪ **-s** -z **lying** 'laɪ.ɪŋ **lay** leɪ **lain** leɪn
lie-abed 'laɪ.ə.bed **-s** -z
Lieberman 'liː.bə.mən (US) -bɚ-
liebfraumilch (L) 'liːb.fraʊ.mɪltʃ *as if German:* -mɪlx (US) -mɪlk, 'liːp-
Liebig 'liː.bɪg *as if German:* -bɪx (US) -bɪg *as if German:* -bɪx
Liebknecht 'liːb.knekt *as if German:* -knext
Liechtenstein 'lɪk.tᵊn.staɪn *as if German:* 'lɪx-
lied *German song:* liːd *as if German:* liːt **lieder** 'liː.dəʳ (US) -dɚ
lief liːf **-er** -əʳ (US) -ɚ
lieg|e liːdʒ **-es** -ɪz
Liège li'eɪʒ, -'eʒ
lie-in ˌlaɪ'ɪn, '-- **-s** -z

lien 'liː.ən, liːn (US) liːn, 'liː.ən **-s** -z
Liepaja lɪ'pɑː.jə (US) li'ep.ə-, lɪ'pɑː-
lieu ljuː, luː (US) luː
lieutenanc|y lef'ten.ənt.s|i, ləf- (US) luː- **-ies** -iz
lieutenant lef'ten.ənt, ləf- (US) luː- **-s** -s **lieuˌtenant 'colonel; lieuˌtenant com'mander; lieuˌtenant 'general; lieuˌtenant 'governor**
li|fe laɪ|f **-ves** -vz **'life ˌcycle; 'life exˌpectancy; 'life inˌsurance; ˌlife 'savings; ˌlife 'sentence**
life-and-death ˌlaɪf.ən'deθ *stress shift:* ˌlife-and-death 'issue
lifebelt 'laɪf.belt **-s** -s
lifeblood 'laɪf.blʌd
lifeboat 'laɪf.bəʊt (US) -boʊt **-s** -s
life-buoy 'laɪf.bɔɪ (US) -bɔɪ, -ˌbuː.i **-s** -z
life-giving 'laɪfˌgɪv.ɪŋ
lifeguard 'laɪf.gɑːd (US) -gɑːrd **-s** -z
lifejacket 'laɪfˌdʒæk.ɪt **-s** -s
lifeless 'laɪf.ləs, -lɪs **-ly** -li **-ness** -nəs, -nɪs
lifelike 'laɪf.laɪk
lifeline 'laɪf.laɪn **-s** -z
lifelong ˌlaɪf'lɒŋ (US) ˌlaɪf'lɑːŋ, -'lɔːŋ *stress shift:* ˌlifelong 'dream
life of Riley ˌlaɪf.əv'raɪ.li
life-or-death ˌlaɪf.ɔː'deθ (US) -ɔːr'- *stress shift:* ˌlife-or-death 'issue
life-preserver 'laɪf.prɪˌzɜː.vəʳ, -prəˌ- (US) -priːˌzɝː.vɚ, -prɪˌ- **-s** -z
lifer 'laɪ.fəʳ (US) -fɚ **-s** -z
lifesaver 'laɪfˌseɪ.vəʳ (US) -vɚ **-s** -z
life-saving 'laɪfˌseɪ.vɪŋ *stress shift:* ˌlife-saving 'medicine
life-size 'laɪf.saɪz, ˌ-'-
lifespan 'laɪf.spæn **-s** -z
lifestyle 'laɪf.staɪl **-s** -z

life-support 'laɪf.sə,pɔːt, ,--'- ⓤⓢ 'laɪf.sə,pɔːrt **,life-sup'port ,system, 'life-sup,port ,system** ⓤⓢ **'life-sup,port ,system**
life-threatening 'laɪf,θret.ən.ɪŋ
lifetime 'laɪf.taɪm **-s** -z
lifework ,laɪf'wɜːk, '-- ⓤⓢ ,laɪf'wɝːk, '-- **-s** -s
Liffe laɪf
Liffey 'lɪf.i
Lifford 'lɪf.əd ⓤⓢ -ɚd
lift lɪft **-s** -s **-ing** -ɪŋ **-ed** -ɪd **-er/s** -əʳ/z ⓤⓢ -ɚ/z
lift-off 'lɪft.ɒf ⓤⓢ -ɑːf
ligament 'lɪg.ə.mənt **-s** -s
ligament|al ,lɪg.ə'men.t|əl ⓤⓢ -t̬|əl **-ous** -əs
ligature 'lɪg.ə.tʃəʳ, -tjʊəʳ, -tʃʊəʳ ⓤⓢ -tʃɚ **-s** -z **-d** -d
liger 'laɪ.gəʳ ⓤⓢ -gɚ **-s** -z
Ligeti 'lɪg.et.i
Liggett 'lɪg.ɪt, -ət
light laɪt **-s** -s **-er** -əʳ ⓤⓢ 'laɪ.t̬ɚ **-est** -ɪst, -əst ⓤⓢ 'laɪ.t̬ɪst, -t̬əst **-ly** -li **-ness** -nəs, -nɪs **-ing** -ɪŋ ⓤⓢ 'laɪ.t̬ɪŋ **-ed** -ɪd ⓤⓢ 'laɪ.t̬ɪd **lit** lɪt **,light 'aircraft; 'light ,bulb; 'light ,meter**
lighten 'laɪ.tən **-s** -z **-ing** -ɪŋ, 'laɪt.nɪŋ **-ed** -d
lighter 'laɪ.təʳ ⓤⓢ -t̬ɚ **-s** -z
lighterage 'laɪ.tər.ɪdʒ ⓤⓢ -t̬ɚ-
light-fingered ,laɪt'fɪŋ.gəd ⓤⓢ -gɚd *stress shift:* ,light-fingered 'thief
lightfoot (L) 'laɪt.fʊt
light-headed ,laɪt'hed.ɪd **-ly** -li **-ness** -nəs, -nɪs *stress shift:* ,light-headed 'daze
light-hearted ,laɪt'hɑː.tɪd ⓤⓢ -'hɑːr.t̬ɪd **-ly** -li **-ness** -nəs, -nɪs *stress shift:* ,light-hearted 'comment
lighthou|se 'laɪt.haʊ|s **-ses** -zɪz
lighthousekeeper 'laɪt.haʊs,kiː.pəʳ ⓤⓢ -pɚ **-s** -z
lighting-up time ,laɪ.tɪŋ'ʌp,taɪm ⓤⓢ -t̬ɪŋ'-
lightning 'laɪt.nɪŋ **-s** -z
lightning-conductor 'laɪt.nɪŋ.kən,dʌk.təʳ ⓤⓢ -t̬ɚ **-s** -z
lightship 'laɪt.ʃɪp **-s** -s
lightweight 'laɪt.weɪt **-s** -s
light-year 'laɪt.jɪəʳ ⓤⓢ -jɪr **-s** -z
ligneous 'lɪg.ni.əs
lignite 'lɪg.naɪt
lignum 'lɪg.nəm
Liguri|a lɪg'jʊə.ri|.ə, -'jɔː- ⓤⓢ -'jʊr.i- **-an/s** -ən/z
likable 'laɪ.kə.bl̩ **-ness** -nəs, -nɪs
lik|e laɪk **-es** -s **-ing** -ɪŋ **-ed** -t
likeable 'laɪ.kə.bl̩ **-ness** -nəs, -nɪs
likelihood 'laɪ.kli.hʊd
likel|y 'laɪ.kl|i **-ier** -i.əʳ ⓤⓢ -i.ɚ **-iest** -i.ɪst, -i.əst **-iness** -ɪ.nəs, -ɪ.nɪs
likeminded ,laɪk'maɪn.dɪd ⓤⓢ '-,--, ,-'-- *stress shift, British only:* ,likeminded 'friend
liken 'laɪ.kən **-s** -z **-ing** -ɪŋ **-ed** -d
likeness 'laɪk.nəs, -nɪs **-es** -ɪz
likewise 'laɪk.waɪz
liking 'laɪ.kɪŋ **-s** -z
Likud lɪ'kʊd, -'kuːd ⓤⓢ -'kuːd
likuta liː'kuː.tɑː
lilac 'laɪ.lək ⓤⓢ -lɑk, -læk, -lɑːk **-s** -s
liliaceous ,lɪl.i'eɪ.ʃəs
Lilian 'lɪl.i.ən
Lilias 'lɪl.i.əs
Liliburlero ,lɪl.i.bə'leə.rəʊ ⓤⓢ -bɚ'ler.oʊ
Lilith 'lɪl.ɪθ
Lilla 'lɪl.ə
Lille liːl
Lillehammer 'lɪl.ɪ.hæm.əʳ, -ə,- ⓤⓢ -ə.hɑː.mɚ, -hæm.ɚ
Lil-lets® lɪ'lets
Lilley 'lɪl.i
Lillian 'lɪl.i.ən
Lilliput 'lɪl.ɪ.pʌt, '-ə-, -pʊt, -pət ⓤⓢ -ə.pʌt, -pət, -pʊt
lilliputian (L) ,lɪl.ɪ'pjuː.ʃən, -ə'-, -ʃi.ən ⓤⓢ -ə'pjuː.ʃən **-s** -z
Lilly 'lɪl.i
Lillywhite 'lɪl.i.*h*waɪt
Lilo® 'laɪ.ləʊ ⓤⓢ -loʊ **-s** -z
Lilongwe lɪ'lɒŋ.weɪ ⓤⓢ -'lɔːŋ-, -'lɑːŋ-
lilt lɪlt **-s** -s **-ing** -ɪŋ ⓤⓢ 'lɪl.t̬ɪŋ **-ed** -ɪd ⓤⓢ 'lɪl.t̬ɪd
lil|y (L) 'lɪl|.i **-ies** -iz **,lily of the 'valley**
lily-livered ,lɪl.i'lɪv.əd ⓤⓢ -ɚd *stress shift:* ,lily-livered 'scoundrel
lily-white ,lɪl.i'*h*waɪt *stress shift:* ,lily-white 'hands
Lima *in Peru:* 'liː.mə *in US:* 'laɪ.mə
lima *bean:* 'liː.mə ⓤⓢ 'laɪ-
Limavady ,lɪm.ə'væd.i
limb lɪm **-s** -z **-ed** -d **,out on a 'limb**
limber *(n. adj.)* 'lɪm.bəʳ ⓤⓢ -bɚ **-s** -z
limbo (L) 'lɪm.bəʊ ⓤⓢ -boʊ **-s** -z **-ing** -ɪŋ **-ed** -d
Limburg 'lɪm.bɜːg ⓤⓢ -bɝːg
lim|e *(n. v.)* laɪm **-es** -z **-ing** -ɪŋ **-ed** -d **,lime 'green**
limeade ,laɪ'meɪd ⓤⓢ ,-'-, 'laɪ.meɪd
Limehouse 'laɪm.haʊs
limekiln 'laɪm.kɪln, -kɪl **-s** -z
limelight 'laɪm.laɪt **-s** -s
limen 'laɪ.men, -mən ⓤⓢ -mən
limerick (L) 'lɪm.ər.ɪk ⓤⓢ -ɚ.ɪk, '-rɪk **-s** -s
limescale 'laɪm.skeɪl
limestone 'laɪm.stəʊn ⓤⓢ -stoʊn
limewash 'laɪm.wɒʃ ⓤⓢ -wɑːʃ, -wɔːʃ **-es** -ɪz **-ing** -ɪŋ **-ed** -t
limewater 'laɪm,wɔː.təʳ ⓤⓢ -,wɑː.t̬ɚ, -,wɔː-
limey 'laɪ.mi **-s** -z
liminal 'lɪm.ɪ.nəl
lim|it *(n. v.)* 'lɪm|.ɪt **-its** -ɪts **-iting** -ɪ.tɪŋ ⓤⓢ -ɪ.t̬ɪŋ **-ited/ness** -ɪ.tɪd/nəs, -nɪs ⓤⓢ -ɪ.t̬ɪd/nəs, -nɪs **-itable** -ɪ.tə.bl̩ ⓤⓢ -ɪ.t̬ə.bl̩
limitation ,lɪm.ɪ'teɪ.ʃən, -ə'- **-s** -z
limitless 'lɪm.ɪt.ləs, -lɪs
limn lɪm **-s** -z **-ing** -ɪŋ, -nɪŋ **-ed** -d **-er/s** -nəʳ/z ⓤⓢ -ɚ/z, -nɚ/z
limo 'lɪm.əʊ ⓤⓢ -oʊ **-s** -z
Limoges lɪ'məʊʒ ⓤⓢ liː'moʊʒ
Limousin ,lɪm.uː'zæn *as if French:* -'zæ̃ŋ ⓤⓢ ,liː.muː'zæn
limousine ,lɪm.ə'ziːn, -ʊ'-, '--- ⓤⓢ 'lɪm.ə.ziːn, ,--'- **-s** -z
limp lɪmp **-s** -s **-er** -əʳ ⓤⓢ -ɚ **-est** -ɪst, -əst **-ly** -li **-ness** -nəs, -nɪs **-ing/ly** -ɪŋ/li **-ed** -t
limpet 'lɪm.pɪt **-s** -s
limpid 'lɪm.pɪd **-ly** -li **-ness** -nəs, -nɪs
limpidity lɪm'pɪd.ə.ti, -ɪ.ti ⓤⓢ -ə.t̬i
Limpopo lɪm'pəʊ.pəʊ ⓤⓢ -'poʊ.poʊ
limp-wristed ,lɪmp'rɪs.tɪd ⓤⓢ ,-'--, 'lɪmp,rɪs-
limy 'laɪ.mi
Linacre 'lɪn.ə.kəʳ, '-ɪ- ⓤⓢ -kɚ
linag|e 'laɪ.nɪdʒ **-es** -ɪz
Linares lɪ'nɑː.rɪs ⓤⓢ lɪ'ner.ɪs
linchpin 'lɪntʃ.pɪn **-s** -z
Lincoln 'lɪŋ.kən **-shire** -ʃəʳ, -,ʃɪəʳ ⓤⓢ -ʃɚ, -,ʃɪr
Lincs. *(abbrev. for* **Lincolnshire***)* lɪŋks lɪŋ.kən.ʃəʳ, -ʃɪəʳ ⓤⓢ -ʃɚ, -,ʃɪr
linctus 'lɪŋk.təs **-es** -ɪz
Lind lɪnd
Linda 'lɪn.də
Lindbergh 'lɪn*d*.bɜːg ⓤⓢ -bɝːg
linden (L) 'lɪn.dən **-s** -z
Lindisfarne 'lɪn.dɪs.fɑːn, -dəs- ⓤⓢ -fɑːrn
Lindley 'lɪn*d*.li
Lindon 'lɪn.dən
Lindsay, Lindsey 'lɪn*d*.zi
lin|e (L) laɪn **-es** -z **-ing** -ɪŋ **-ed** -d **'line ,drawing; ,read be,tween the 'lines**
lineag|e *family:* 'lɪn.i.ɪdʒ ⓤⓢ '-ɪdʒ, -i.ɪdʒ **-es** -ɪz
lineag|e *alternative spelling of* **linage** 'laɪ.nɪdʒ **-es** -ɪz
lineal 'lɪn.i.əl **-ly** -i
lineament 'lɪn.i.ə.mənt **-s** -s
linear 'lɪn.i.əʳ ⓤⓢ -ɚ **-ly** -li
lineation ,lɪn.i'eɪ.ʃən **-s** -z
linebacker 'laɪn,bæk.əʳ, 'laɪm- ⓤⓢ 'laɪn,bæk.ɚ **-s** -z
line-engraving 'laɪn.ɪn,greɪ.vɪŋ, -ɪŋ,- ⓤⓢ -ɪn,- **-s** -z
Lineker 'lɪn.ɪ.kəʳ, '-ə- ⓤⓢ -kɚ
line|man 'laɪn|.mən, 'laɪm- ⓤⓢ 'laɪn- **-men** -mən, -men
linen 'lɪn.ɪn, -ən **-s** -z
lineout 'laɪn.aʊt **-s** -s

iner 'laɪ.nəʳ US -nɚ **-s** -z
nes|man 'laɪnz|.mən **-men** -mən, -men
ineup 'laɪn.ʌp **-s** -s
inford 'lɪn.fəd US -fɚd
ng (L) lɪŋ **-s** -z
ngam 'lɪŋ.gəm, -æm
ingay 'lɪŋ.gi
ingen 'lɪŋ.ən
ing|er 'lɪŋ.g|əʳ US -g|ɚ **-ers** -əz US -ɚz **-ering/ly** -ᵊr.ɪŋ/li **-ered** -əd US -ɚd **-erer/s** -ᵊr.əʳ/z US -ɚ.ɚ/z
ngerie 'læ̃n.ʒᵊr.i, 'lɒn-, -dʒᵊr-, -ri, -reɪ US ˌlɑːn.ʒə'reɪ; ˌlæn.ʒə'riː, -dʒə'-
ingfield 'lɪŋ.fiːld
ngo 'lɪŋ.gəʊ US -goʊ **-s** -z
ngua franca ˌlɪŋ.gwə'fræŋ.kə
ngual 'lɪŋ.gwəl **-ly** -i
inguaphone® 'lɪŋ.gwə.fəʊn US -foʊn
inguarama® ˌlɪŋ.gwə'rɑː.mə US -'ræm.ə, -'rɑː.mə
nguine, linguini lɪŋ'gwiː.ni
nguist 'lɪŋ.gwɪst **-s** -s
nguistic lɪŋ'gwɪs.tɪk **-s** -s **-al** -ᵊl **-ally** -ᵊl.i, -li
nguistician ˌlɪŋ.gwɪ'stɪʃ.ᵊn **-s** -z
niment 'lɪn.ɪ.mənt, '-ə- **-s** -s
ning 'laɪ.nɪŋ **-s** -z
nk (*n. v.*) lɪŋk **-s** -s **-ing** -ɪŋ **-ed** -t
nkag|e 'lɪŋ.kɪdʒ **-es** -ɪz
nklater 'lɪŋkˌleɪ.təʳ US -t̬ɚ
nks lɪŋks
nkup 'lɪŋk.ʌp
nley 'lɪn.li
nlithgow lɪn'lɪθ.gəʊ US -goʊ **-shire** -ʃəʳ, -ˌʃɪəʳ US -ʃɚ, -ˌʃɪr
nnaean lɪ'niː.ən, -'neɪ-
nnaeus lɪ'niː.əs, -'neɪ-
nnean lɪ'niː.ən, -'neɪ-
net (L) 'lɪn.ɪt **-s** -s
o 'laɪ.nəʊ US -noʊ **-s** -z
ocut 'laɪ.nəʊ.kʌt US -noʊ-, -nə- **-s** -s
oleum lɪ'nəʊ.li.əm US -'noʊ- **-s** -z
otype® 'laɪ.nəʊ.taɪp US -nə- **-s** -s
seed 'lɪn.siːd **'linseed ˌoil ˌlinseed 'oil**
sey (L) 'lɪn.zi
sey-woolsey (L) ˌlɪn.zi'wʊl.zi
t lɪnt
tel 'lɪn.tᵊl US -t̬ᵊl **-s** -z
thwaite 'lɪn.θweɪt
ton 'lɪn.tən
tot(t) 'lɪn.tɒt US -tɑːt
us 'laɪ.nəs
ux 'lɪn.əks, 'laɪ.nəks, -nʌks US 'lɪn.əks
z lɪnts
n laɪən **-s** -z **'lion ˌtamer**
nel 'laɪə.nᵊl
ness 'laɪə.nes, -nɪs; ˌlaɪə'nes US 'laɪə.nes, -nɪs **-es** -ɪz
nheart 'laɪən.hɑːt US -hɑːrt

lion-hearted ˌlaɪən'hɑː.tɪd US 'laɪənˌhɑːr.t̬ɪd *stress shift, British only:* ˌlion-hearted 'warrior
lionization, -isa- ˌlaɪə.naɪ'zeɪ.ʃᵊn, -nɪ'- US -nɪ'-
lioniz|e, -is|e 'laɪə.naɪz **-es** -ɪz **-ing** -ɪŋ **-ed** -d
lip lɪp **-s** -s **-ping** -ɪŋ **-ped** -t **'lip ˌservice**
Lipari 'lɪp.ᵊr.i, 'liː.pær-
lipas|e 'laɪ.peɪz, 'lɪp.eɪz, -eɪs US 'lɪp.eɪs, 'laɪ.peɪs **-es** -ɪz
lipbrush 'lɪp.brʌʃ **-es** -ɪz
lipid(e) 'lɪp.ɪd, 'laɪ.pɪd US 'lɪp.ɪd **-s** -z
Lipman 'lɪp.mən
lipoid 'lɪp.ɔɪd, 'laɪ.pɔɪd
lipoprotein ˌlɪp.əʊ'prəʊ.tiːn, ˌlaɪ.pəʊ'- US ˌlɪp.oʊ'pro.tiːn, ˌlaɪ.poʊ'-, -pə'-, -tiː.ɪn **-s** -z
liposome 'lɪp.əʊ.səʊm US -ə.soʊm, 'laɪ.pə- **-s** -z
liposuction 'lɪp.əʊˌsʌk.ʃᵊn US 'lɪp.oʊˌ-, 'laɪ.poʊˌ-, -pəˌ-
Lippi 'lɪp.i
Lippincott 'lɪp.ɪŋ.kət, -kɒt US -ɪn.kɑːt, -kət
Lippizaner ˌlɪp.ɪt'sɑː.nəʳ, -ət'- US -nɚ **-s** -z
Lippmann 'lɪp.mən
lipp|y 'lɪp|.i **-ier** -i.əʳ US -i.ɚ **-iest** -i.ɪst, -i.əst **-iness** -ɪ.nəs, -ɪ.nɪs
lip|-read 'lɪp|.riːd **-reads** -riːdz **-reading** -ˌriː.dɪŋ *past tense:* **-read** -red **-readers** -ˌriː.dəʳ/z US -ˌriː.dɚ/z
lip-salve 'lɪp.sælv, -sɑːlv US -sæv, -sɑːv **-s** -z
Lipscomb(e) 'lɪp.skəm
Lipstadt 'lɪp.stæt
lipstick 'lɪp.stɪk **-s** -s
lip-synch 'lɪp.sɪŋk **-s** -s **-ing** -ɪŋ **-ed** -t
Lipton 'lɪp.tən
liquefaction ˌlɪk.wɪ'fæk.ʃᵊn, -wə'-
lique|fy 'lɪk.wɪ|.faɪ, -wə- **-fies** -faɪz **-fying** -faɪ.ɪŋ **-fied** -faɪd **-fier/s** -faɪ.əʳ/z US -faɪ.ɚ/z **-fiable** -faɪ.ə.bl̩
liqueur lɪ'kjʊəʳ, lə-, -'kjɔːʳ, -'kjɜːʳ US lɪ'kɝː, -'kʊr, -'kjʊr **-s** -z
liquid 'lɪk.wɪd **-s** -z **-ly** -li **-ness** -nəs, -nɪs
liqui|date 'lɪk.wɪ|.deɪt, -wə- **-dates** -deɪts **-dating** -deɪ.tɪŋ US -deɪ.t̬ɪŋ **-dated** -deɪ.tɪd US -deɪ.t̬ɪd **-dator/s** -deɪ.təʳ/z US -deɪ.t̬ɚ/z
liquidation ˌlɪk.wɪ'deɪ.ʃᵊn, -wə'- **-s** -z
liquidity lɪ'kwɪd.ə.ti, lə-, -ɪ.ti US -ə.t̬i
liquidiz|e, -is|e 'lɪk.wɪ.daɪz, -wə- **-es** -ɪz **-ing** -ɪŋ **-ed** -d
liquidizer, -iser 'lɪk.wɪ.daɪ.zəʳ, -wə- US -zɚ **-s** -z
liquif|y 'lɪk.wɪ.f|aɪ, -wə- **-ies** aɪz **-ying** aɪ.ɪŋ **-ied** -aɪd
liqu|or 'lɪk|.əʳ US -ɚ **-ors** -əz US -ɚz **-oring** -ᵊr.ɪŋ **-ored** -əd US -ɚd

liquorice 'lɪk.ᵊr.ɪs, -ɪʃ, 'lɪk.rɪs, -rɪʃ US 'lɪk.ɚ.ɪʃ, '-rɪʃ, 'lɪk.ɚ.ɪs
lir|a 'lɪə.r|ə US 'lɪr|.ə **-as** -əz **-e** -i, -eɪ
Lisa 'liː.sə, -zə
Lisbet 'lɪz.bət, -bet, -bɪt
Lisbeth 'lɪz.bəθ, -beθ, -bɪθ
Lisbon 'lɪz.bən
Lisburn 'lɪz.bɜːn US -bɝːn
lisente lɪ'sen.teɪ US -ti
Lisette lɪ'zet, 'liː.zet
Liskeard 'lɪs.kɑːd US -kɑːrd
lisle *thread:* laɪl
Lisle laɪl, liːl
Note: Baron Lisle pronounces /laɪl/.
Lismore *in Scotland and Ireland:* lɪz'mɔːʳ US -'mɔːr *in Australia:* 'lɪz.mɔːʳ US -mɔːr
lisp, LISP lɪsp **-s** -s **-ing/ly** -ɪŋ/li **-ed** -t **-er/s** -əʳ/z US -ɚ/z
lis pendens ˌlɪs'pen.denz
Liss lɪs
lissom(e) 'lɪs.əm **-ness** -nəs, -nɪs
Lisson 'lɪs.ᵊn
list lɪst **-s** -s **-ing/s** -ɪŋ/z **-ed** -ɪd
listen 'lɪs.ᵊn **-s** -z **-ing** -ɪŋ, 'lɪs.nɪŋ **-ed** -d **-er/s** -əʳ/z, 'lɪs.nəʳ/z **-er/z** US 'lɪs.ᵊn.ɚ/z **-er/s** US 'lɪs.nɚ/z
Lister 'lɪs.təʳ US -tɚ
listeria lɪ'stɪə.ri.ə US -'stɪr.i-
listeriasis ˌlɪs.tə'riː.ə.sɪs
Listerine® 'lɪs.tᵊr.iːn US ˌlɪs.tə'riːn
listeriosis lɪˌstɪə.ri'əʊ.sɪs, ˌlɪs.tɪə- US lɪˌstɪr.i'oʊ-
listless 'lɪst.ləs, -lɪs **-ly** -li **-ness** -nəs, -nɪs
Liston 'lɪs.tᵊn
Listowel lɪ'stəʊəl US -'stoʊəl, -'staʊl
Liszt lɪst
lit *(from* **light***)* lɪt
litan|y 'lɪt.ᵊn|.i **-ies** -iz
Litchfield 'lɪtʃ.fiːld
litchi ˌlaɪ'tʃiː; 'laɪ.tʃiː, 'liː- US 'liː.tʃiː **-s** -z
lite laɪt
liter 'liː.təʳ US -t̬ɚ **-s** -z
literacy 'lɪt.ᵊr.ə.si, '-rə.si US 'lɪt̬.ɚ.ə-
literal 'lɪt.ᵊr.ᵊl, '-rᵊl US 'lɪt̬.ɚ.ᵊl **-ly** -i **-ness** -nəs, -nɪs
literal|ism 'lɪt.ᵊr.ᵊl|.ɪ.zᵊm, '-rᵊl- US 'lɪt̬.ɚ.ᵊl- **-ist/s** -ɪst/s
literality ˌlɪt.ᵊr'æl.ə.ti, -ɪ.ti US -ə'ræl.ə.t̬i
literar|y 'lɪt.ᵊr.ᵊr|.i, '-ᵊr|.i US 'lɪt̬.ə.rer- **-ily** -ᵊl.i, -ɪ.li **-iness** -ɪ.nəs, -ɪ.nɪs
literate 'lɪt.ᵊr.ət, -ɪt, '-rət, -rɪt US 'lɪt̬.ɚ.ət **-s** -s
literati ˌlɪt.ᵊr'ɑː.tiː US ˌlɪt̬.ə'rɑː.t̬iː
literatim ˌlɪt.ᵊr'ɑː.tɪm US ˌlɪt̬.ə'reɪ.t̬ɪm, -'rɑː-
literature 'lɪt.rə.tʃəʳ, -rɪ-, '-ᵊr.ə-, -ɪ- US 'lɪt̬.ɚ.ə.tʃɚ, -tʃʊr **-s** -z
litharge 'lɪθ.ɑːdʒ US -ɑːrdʒ; lɪ'θɑːrdʒ

lith|e laɪð **-er** -əʳ ⓤⓢ -ɚ **-est** -ɪst, -əst **-ely** -li **-eness** -nəs, -nɪs
Litheby 'lɪð.ɪ.bi, '-ə-
Litherland 'lɪð.ə.lænd ⓤⓢ '-ɚ-
lithesome 'laɪð.səm **-ness** -nəs, -nɪs
Lithgow 'lɪθ.gəʊ ⓤⓢ -goʊ
lithia 'lɪθ.i.ə
lithic 'lɪθ.ɪk
lithium 'lɪθ.i.əm
litho 'lɪθ.əʊ, 'laɪ.θəʊ ⓤⓢ 'lɪθ.oʊ **-s** -z
lithograph 'lɪθ.əʊ.grɑːf, -græf ⓤⓢ -ə.græf, '-oʊ- **-s** -s **-ing** -ɪŋ **-ed** -t
Note: In British printers' usage /'laɪ.θəʊ-/. So also with derived words (**lithographer**, etc.).
lithographer lɪ'θɒg.rə.fəʳ ⓤⓢ -'θɑː.grə.fɚ **-s** -z
lithographic ˌlɪθ.əʊ'græf.ɪk ⓤⓢ -oʊ'-, -ə'- **-al** -ᵊl **-ally** -ᵊl.i, -li
lithography lɪ'θɒg.rə.fi ⓤⓢ -'θɑː.grə-
lithosphere 'lɪθ.əʊˌsfɪəʳ ⓤⓢ -oʊˌsfɪr, -əˌ- **-s** -z
Lithuani|a ˌlɪθ.ju'eɪ.ni|.ə, -u'- ⓤⓢ -u'eɪ-, -ə'weɪ- **-an/s** -ən/z
litigant 'lɪt.ɪ.gənt, '-ə- ⓤⓢ 'lɪţ- **-s** -s
liti|gate 'lɪt.ɪ|.geɪt, '-ə- ⓤⓢ 'lɪţ- **-gates** -geɪts **-gating** -geɪ.tɪŋ ⓤⓢ -geɪ.ţɪŋ **-gated** -geɪ.tɪd ⓤⓢ -geɪ.ţɪd **-gator/s** -geɪ.təʳ/z ⓤⓢ -geɪ.ţɚ/z
litigation ˌlɪt.ɪ'geɪ.ʃᵊn, -ə'- ⓤⓢ ˌlɪţ- **-s** -z
litigious lɪ'tɪdʒ.əs, lə- ⓤⓢ lɪ- **-ly** -li **-ness** -nəs, -nɪs
litmus 'lɪt.məs **'litmus ˌpaper; 'litmus ˌtest**
litotes laɪ'təʊ.tiːz; 'laɪ.təʊ- ⓤⓢ 'laɪ.tə.tiːz; laɪ'toʊ-; 'lɪt.oʊ-
litre 'liː.təʳ ⓤⓢ -ţɚ **-s** -z
Littel lɪ'tel
litt|er 'lɪt|.əʳ ⓤⓢ 'lɪţ|.ɚ **-ers** -əz ⓤⓢ -ɚz **-ering** -ᵊr.ɪŋ **-ered** -əd ⓤⓢ -ɚd
litterbug 'lɪt.ə.bʌg ⓤⓢ 'lɪţ.ɚ- **-s** -z
littl|e (L) 'lɪt.l̩ ⓤⓢ 'lɪţ.l̩ **-er** -əʳ ⓤⓢ -ɚ **-est** -ɪst, -əst **-eness** -nəs, -nɪs
Littleborough 'lɪt.l̩.bᵊr.ə, -ˌbʌr.ə ⓤⓢ 'lɪţ.l̩.bɚ.oʊ
Littlechild 'lɪt.l̩.tʃaɪld
little-englander ˌlɪt.l̩'ɪŋ.glən.dəʳ ⓤⓢ ˌlɪţ.l̩'ɪŋ.glən.dɚ **-s** -z
little-go 'lɪt.l̩.gəʊ ⓤⓢ 'lɪţ.l̩.goʊ **-es** -z
Littlehampton 'lɪt.l̩ˌhæmp.tən, ˌlɪt.l̩'hæmp- ⓤⓢ ˌlɪţ.l̩'-, 'lɪţ.l̩ˌ-
Littlejohn 'lɪt.l̩.dʒɒn ⓤⓢ 'lɪţ.l̩.dʒɑːn
littleneck 'lɪt.l̩.nek ⓤⓢ 'lɪţ- **-s** -s
Littler 'lɪt.l̩.əʳ, '-ləʳ ⓤⓢ 'lɪt.lɚ, 'lɪţ.l̩.ɚ
Littleton 'lɪt.l̩.tᵊn ⓤⓢ 'lɪţ-
Littlewoods 'lɪt.l̩.wʊdz
Litton 'lɪt.ᵊn
littoral 'lɪt.ᵊr.ᵊl ⓤⓢ 'lɪţ- **-s** -z
liturgic lɪ'tɜː.dʒɪk, lə- ⓤⓢ lɪ'tɝː- **-s** -s **-al** -ᵊl **-ally** -ᵊl.i, -li
liturgist 'lɪt.ə.dʒɪst, '-ɜː- ⓤⓢ 'lɪţ.ɚ- **-s** -s
liturg|y 'lɪt.ə.dʒ|i, '-ɜː- ⓤⓢ 'lɪţ.ɚ- **-ies** -iz
livable 'lɪv.ə.bl̩
live *(adj.)* laɪv
liv|e *(v.)* lɪv **-es** -z **-ing** -ɪŋ **-ed** -d **-er/s** -əʳ/z ⓤⓢ -ɚ/z ˌ**living 'will**
live-circuit ˌlaɪv'sɜː.kɪt ⓤⓢ -'sɝː- **-s** -s
live-in ˌlɪv'ɪn, '-- ˌ**live-in 'lover**
livelihood 'laɪv.li.hʊd **-s** -z
livelong 'lɪv.lɒŋ, 'laɪv- ⓤⓢ 'lɪv.lɑːŋ, -lɔːŋ
livel|y (L) 'laɪv.l|i **-ier** -i.əʳ ⓤⓢ -i.ɚ **-iest** -i.ɪst, -i.əst **-iness** -ɪ.nəs, -ɪ.nɪs
liven 'laɪ.vᵊn **-s** -z **-ing** -ɪŋ, 'laɪv.nɪŋ **-ed** -d
Livens 'lɪv.ᵊnz
liv|er 'lɪv|.əʳ ⓤⓢ -ɚ **-ers** -əz ⓤⓢ -ɚz **-erish** -ᵊr.ɪʃ
Livermore 'lɪv.ə.mɔːʳ ⓤⓢ -ɚ.mɔːr
Liverpool 'lɪv.ə.puːl ⓤⓢ '-ɚ-
Liverpudlian ˌlɪv.ə'pʌd.li.ən ⓤⓢ -ɚ'- **-s** -z
Liversedge 'lɪv.ə.sedʒ ⓤⓢ '-ɚ-
liverwort 'lɪv.ə.wɜːt ⓤⓢ -ɚ.wɝːt, -wɔːrt **-s** -s
liverwurst 'lɪv.ə.wɜːst ⓤⓢ -ɚ.wɝːst
liver|y 'lɪv.ᵊr|.i, '-r|i **-ies** -iz **-ied** -id
livery|man 'lɪv.ᵊr.i|.mən ⓤⓢ '-ri-, -mæn **-men** -mən, -men
livery-stable 'lɪv.ᵊr.iˌsteɪ.bl̩ ⓤⓢ '-riˌ- **-s** -z
lives *(plur. of* **life***)* laɪvz *(from* **live** *v.)* lɪvz
Livesey 'lɪv.si, -zi
livestock 'laɪv.stɒk ⓤⓢ -stɑːk
live wire ˌlaɪv'waɪəʳ ⓤⓢ -'waɪr, '-- **-s** -
Livia 'lɪv.i.ə
livid 'lɪv.ɪd **-ly** -li **-ness** -nəs, -nɪs
lividity lɪ'vɪd.ə.ti, -ɪ.ti ⓤⓢ -ə.ţi
living 'lɪv.ɪŋ **-s** -z
living-room 'lɪv.ɪŋ.rʊm, -ruːm ⓤⓢ -ruːm, -rʊm **-s** -z
Livingston(e) 'lɪv.ɪŋ.stᵊn
Livoni|a lɪ'vəʊ.ni|.ə ⓤⓢ -'voʊ-, '-nj|ə **-an/s** -ən/z
Livorno lɪ'vɔː.nəʊ ⓤⓢ lə'vɔːr.noʊ
Livy 'lɪv.i
lixivi|ate lɪk'sɪv.i|.eɪt **-ates** -eɪts **-ati**[ng] -eɪ.tɪŋ ⓤⓢ -eɪ.ţɪŋ **-ated** -eɪ.tɪd ⓤⓢ -eɪ.ţɪd
Liz lɪz
Liza 'laɪ.zə, 'liː- ⓤⓢ 'laɪ-
lizard (L) 'lɪz.əd ⓤⓢ -ɚd **-s** -z
Lizzie 'lɪz.i
Ljubljana ˌlʊb.li'ɑː.nə *as if Slovene:* ˌljuːb'ljɑː.nə ⓤⓢ ˌluː.bli'ɑː.nə
llama (L) 'lɑː.mə ⓤⓢ 'lɑː-, 'jɑː- **-s** -z
Llanberis *h*læn'ber.ɪs, θlæn- ⓤⓢ *h*læ[n-]
Llandaff '*h*læn.dəf, 'θlæn-; læn'dæf, θlæn- ⓤⓢ *h*læn'dɑːf
Llandeilo *h*læn'daɪ.ləʊ, θlæn- ⓤⓢ *h*læn'daɪ.loʊ
Llandovery *h*læn'dʌv.ᵊr.i, θlæn- ⓤⓢ *h*læn-
Llandrindod Wells *h*lænˌdrɪn.dɒd'welz, θlæn- ⓤⓢ *h*lænˌdrɪn.dɑːd'-
Llandudno *h*læn'dɪd.nəʊ, θlæn-, -'d[ʌd-] ⓤⓢ *h*læn'dɪd.noʊ, -'dʌd-
Llanelli *h*læn'eθ.li, lə'neθ-, θlæn'eθ-, θlə'neθ- ⓤⓢ *h*læn'el.i
Llanfair *h*læn'feəʳ, θlæn-, -'vaɪəʳ ⓤⓢ *h*læn'fer
Llanfairfechan ˌ*h*læn.feə'fek.ən, ˌθlæn-, -vaɪə'-, -'vek-, -'vex- ⓤⓢ ˌ*h*læn.fer'fek-
Llanfair PG ˌ*h*læn.feəˌpiː'dʒiː, ˌθlæ[n-], -vaɪə,- ⓤⓢ ˌ*h*læn.fer-
Note: This is the accepted abbrevia of the following entry.

Pronouncing the letters LL

In general, the consonant digraph ll is pronounced /l/, e.g.:

fall	/fɔːl/	ⓤⓢ /fɑːl/
illustrate	/'ɪl.ə.streɪt/	

Where the ll is produced by adding the suffix *–ly* or *–less* to a word ending in a single l, the pronunciation reflects this, e.g.:

coolly	/'kuːl.li/	
soulless	/'səʊl.ləs/	ⓤⓢ /'soʊl-/

In addition

In Welsh words, ll may be pronounced by English speakers in a variety of different ways. In this dictionary, we suggest /*h*l[-]/ which stands both for the phonetic [ɬ] used in Welsh and for the English approximation of either a voiceless or voiced [l], and also the variant /θl/ for British English speakers, e.g.:

Llanberis	/*h*læn'ber.ɪs, θlæn-/	ⓤⓢ /*h*læn-/

lanfairpwllgwyngyllgogerychwyrnd robwllllantysiliogogogoch ˌhlæn.feə.pʊlˌgwɪŋ.gɪl.gəʊˌger.əˌk wɜːnˌdrəʊ.bʊlˌhlæn.dəˌsɪl.i.əʊˌgəʊ. gəʊ'gɒf, ˌθlæn-, ˌ-vaɪə-, -ˌθlæn- *as if Welsh:* -xwɜːn-, -'gɒx (US) ˌhlæn.fer.pʊlˌgwɪn.gɪl.goʊˌger.ə .kwɝːnˌdroʊ.bʊlˌhlæn.dəˌsɪl.i.oʊˌg oʊ.goʊ'gɑːf

langattock hlæn'gæt.ək, θlæn-, læŋ-, θlæŋ- (US) hlæn'gæt̬.ək

langollen hlæn'gɒθ.lən, θlæn-, læŋ-, θlæŋ-, -len (US) hlæn'gɑː.lən

lanharan hlæn'hær.ən, θlæn- (US) hlæn'hɑːr.ən

anrwst hlæn'ruːst, θlæn- (US) hlæn-

antrisant hlæn'trɪs.ənt

antwit Major ˌhlæn.twɪt'meɪ.dʒəʳ (US) -dʒɚ

anuwchllyn hlæn'juːx.klɪn, θlæn-, -'juːx.lɪn (US) hlæn'juː.klɪn

anwern hlæn'weən (US) -'wern

echwedd hlek'wed

ewel(l)yn *English name:* luː'el.ɪn, lə'wel- *Welsh name:* hluː'el.ɪn, θluː- (US) hluː-

eyn hliːn, θliːn, hleɪn, θleɪn (US) hliːn, hleɪn

w hluː

oyd lɔɪd **'s** -z

oyd Webber ˌlɔɪd'web.əʳ (US) -ɚ

yn Tegid ˌhlɪn'teg.ɪd, ˌθlɪn- (US) ˌhlɪn-

ywelyn hlə'wel.ɪn, θlə- (US) hlə-

ləʊ (US) loʊ

ach ləʊtʃ (US) loʊtʃ

ad ləʊd (US) loʊd **-s** -z **-ing** -ɪŋ **-ed** -ɪd **-er/s** -əʳ/z (US) -ɚ/z

adstone 'ləʊd.stəʊn (US) 'loʊd.stoʊn **-s** -z

a|f *(n.)* ləʊ|f (US) loʊ|f **-ves** -vz

af *(v.)* ləʊf (US) loʊf **-s** -s **-ing** -ɪŋ **-ed** -t

afer 'ləʊ.fəʳ (US) 'loʊ.fɚ **-s** -z

am ləʊm (US) loʊm

am|y 'ləʊ.m|i (US) 'loʊ.m|i **-ier** -i.əʳ (US) -i.ɚ **-iest** -i.ɪst, -i.əst **-iness** -ɪ.nəs, -ɪ.nɪs

an ləʊn (US) loʊn **-s** -z **-ing** -ɪŋ **-ed** -d **-er/s** -əʳ/z (US) -ɚ/z **'loan ˌshark**

anhead ˌləʊn'hed (US) ˌloʊn-

anword 'ləʊn.wɜːd (US) 'loʊn.wɝːd **-s** -z

ath ləʊθ, ləʊð (US) loʊð **-ness** -nəs, -nɪs

ath|e ləʊð (US) loʊð **-es** -z **-ing/ly** -ɪŋ/li **-ed** -d

athsome 'ləʊð.səm, 'ləʊθ- (US) 'loʊð-, 'loʊθ- **-ly** -li **-ness** -nəs, -nɪs

aves *(plur. of* **loaf***)* ləʊvz (US) loʊvz

(L) lɒb (US) lɑːb **-s** -z **-bing** -ɪŋ **-bed** -d **-ber/s** -əʳ/z (US) -ɚ/z

b|y 'lɒb|.i (US) 'lɑː.b|i **-ies** -iz **-ying** -i.ɪŋ **-ied** -id

byist 'lɒb.i.ɪst (US) 'lɑː.bi- **-s** -s

lobe ləʊb (US) loʊb **-s** -z **-d** -d

lobelia ləʊ'biː.li.ə (US) loʊ'biːl.jə, -'biː.li.ə **-s** -z

lobotomiz|e, -is|e ləʊ'bɒt.ə.maɪz (US) loʊ'bɑː.t̬ə-, lə- **-es** -ɪz **-ing** -ɪŋ **-ed** -d

lobotom|y ləʊ'bɒt.ə.m|i (US) loʊ'bɑː.t̬ə-, lə- **-ies** -iz

lobster 'lɒb.stəʳ (US) 'lɑːb.stɚ **-s** -z

lobular 'lɒb.jə.ləʳ, -jʊ- (US) 'lɑː.bjə.lɚ

lobule 'lɒb.juːl (US) 'lɑː.bjuːl **-s** -z

local 'ləʊ.kᵊl (US) 'loʊ- **-s** -z **-ly** -i **ˌlocal 'colo(u)r; 'local ˌtime, ˌlocal 'time**

locale ləʊ'kɑːl (US) loʊ'kæl **-s** -z

localism 'ləʊ.kᵊl.ɪ.zᵊm (US) 'loʊ-

localit|y ləʊ'kæl.ə.t|i, -ɪ.t|i (US) loʊ'kæl.ə.t̬|i **-ies** -iz

localization, -isa- ˌləʊ.kᵊl.aɪ'zeɪ.ʃᵊn, -ɪ'- (US) ˌloʊ.kᵊl.ɪ'-

localiz|e, -is|e 'ləʊ.kᵊl.aɪz (US) 'loʊ- **-es** -ɪz **-ing** -ɪŋ **-ed** -d **-er/s** -əʳ/z (US) -ɚ/z

Locarno ləʊ'kɑː.nəʊ, lɒk'ɑː- (US) loʊ'kɑːr.noʊ

loca|te ləʊ'keɪ|t (US) 'loʊ.keɪ|t, -'- **-tes** -ts **-ting** -tɪŋ (US) -t̬ɪŋ **-ted** -tɪd (US) -t̬ɪd

location ləʊ'keɪ.ʃᵊn (US) loʊ- **-s** -z

locative 'lɒk.ə.tɪv (US) 'lɑː.kə.t̬ɪv **-s** -z

loc. cit. ˌlɒk'sɪt, ˌlɒk.əʊ.sɪ'tɑː.təʊ *old-fashioned:* ˌləʊ.kəʊ.sɪ'teɪ.təʊ (US) ˌlɑːk'sɪt

loch (L) lɒk *as if Scots:* lɒx (US) lɑːk *as if Scots:* lɑːx **-s** -s

Lochaber lɒk'ɑː.bəʳ, -'æb.əʳ *as if Scots:* lɒx- (US) lɑː'kɑː.bɚ *as if Scots:* -'xɑː-

Lochgelly lɒk'gel.i *as if Scots:* lɒx- (US) lɑːk- *as if Scots:* lɑːx-

Lochhead 'lɒk.hed *as if Scots:* 'lɒx- (US) 'lɑːk- *as if Scots:* 'lɑːx-

Lochiel lɒk'iːl *as if Scots:* lɒx- (US) lɑː'kiːl *as if Scots:* -'xiːl

Lochinvar ˌlɒk.ɪn'vɑːʳ *as if Scots:* ˌlɒx- (US) ˌlɑː.kɪn'vɑːr *as if Scots:* -xɪn'-

Lochleven lɒk'liː.vᵊn *as if Scots:* lɒx- (US) lɑːk- *as if Scots:* lɑːx-

Lochnagar ˌlɒk.nə'gɑːʳ *as if Scots:* ˌlɒx- (US) ˌlɑːk.nə'gɑːr *as if Scots:* ˌlɑːx-

loci *(plur. of* **locus***)* 'ləʊ.saɪ, -kaɪ, -kiː; 'lɒk.aɪ, 'lɒs- (US) 'loʊ.saɪ, -kaɪ, -ki

lock (L) lɒk (US) lɑːk **-s** -s **-ing** -ɪŋ **-ed** -t **ˌlock, ˌstock, and 'barrel; under ˌlock and 'key**

Locke lɒk (US) lɑːk

locker (L) 'lɒk.əʳ (US) 'lɑː.kɚ **-s** -z **'locker ˌroom**

Lockerbie 'lɒk.ə.bi (US) 'lɑː.kɚ-

locket 'lɒk.ɪt (US) 'lɑː.kɪt **-s** -s

Lockhart 'lɒk.ət, -hɑːt (US) 'lɑːk.hɑːrt, 'lɑː.kɚt

Note: The Bruce-Lockhart family pronounce /'lɒk.ət/ (or in the Scottish manner /'lɒk.ərt/).

Lockheed 'lɒk.hiːd (US) 'lɑːk-

Lockie 'lɒk.i (US) 'lɑː.ki

lockjaw 'lɒk.dʒɔː (US) 'lɑːk.dʒɑː, -dʒɔː

lock-keeper 'lɒkˌkiː.pəʳ (US) 'lɑːkˌkiː.pɚ **-s** -z

locknut 'lɒk.nʌt (US) 'lɑːk- **-s** -s

lockout 'lɒk.aʊt (US) 'lɑːk- **-s** -s

Locksley 'lɒk.sli (US) 'lɑːk-

locksmith 'lɒk.smɪθ (US) 'lɑːk- **-s** -s

lockstep 'lɒk.step (US) 'lɑːk-

lockstitch 'lɒk.stɪtʃ (US) 'lɑːk- **-es** -ɪz

lockup 'lɒk.ʌp (US) 'lɑːk- **-s** -s

Lockwood 'lɒk.wʊd (US) 'lɑːk-

Lockyer 'lɒk.jəʳ (US) 'lɑː.kjɚ

loco 'ləʊ.kəʊ (US) 'loʊ.koʊ **-s** -z

locomotion ˌləʊ.kə'məʊ.ʃᵊn (US) ˌloʊ.kə'moʊ-

locomotive ˌləʊ.kə'məʊ.tɪv, 'ləʊ.kəˌməʊ- (US) ˌloʊ.kə'moʊ.t̬ɪv **-s** -z

locomotor ˌləʊ.kə'məʊ.təʳ, 'ləʊ.kəˌməʊ- (US) ˌloʊ.kə'moʊ.t̬ɚ *stress shift, see compound:* **ˌlocoˌmotor a'taxia**

Locri|a 'ləʊ.kri|.ə (US) 'loʊ- **-an/s** -ən/z

Locrine 'lɒk.raɪn (US) 'lɑː.kraɪn

Locris 'ləʊ.krɪs (US) 'loʊ-

Loctite® 'lɒk.taɪt (US) 'lɑːk-

locum 'ləʊ.kəm (US) 'loʊ- **-s** -z

locum-tenens ˌləʊ.kəm'ten.enz, -'tiː.nenz (US) ˌloʊ.kəm'tiː.nenz, -'ten.enz

locus 'ləʊ.kəs, 'lɒk.əs (US) 'loʊ.kəs **-es** -ɪz **loci** 'ləʊ.saɪ, -kaɪ, -kiː; 'lɒk.aɪ, 'lɒs- (US) 'loʊ.saɪ

locus delicti ˌləʊ.kəs.del'ɪk.taɪ (US) ˌloʊ.kəs.də'lɪk.ti, -taɪ

locus in quo ˌləʊ.kəs.ɪn'kwəʊ, -ˌɪŋ'- (US) ˌloʊ.kəs.ɪn'kwoʊ

locust 'ləʊ.kəst (US) 'loʊ- **-s** -s

locution ləʊ'kjuː.ʃᵊn, lɒk'juː- (US) loʊ'kjuː- **-s** -z

locutionary ləʊ'kjuː.ʃᵊn.ᵊr.i, lɒk'juː- (US) loʊ'kjuː-

locutor|y 'lɒk.jə.tᵊr|.i, -jʊ- (US) 'lɑː.kjə.tɔːr- **-ies** -iz

lode ləʊd (US) loʊd **-s** -z

loden 'ləʊ.dᵊn (US) 'loʊ-

lodestar 'ləʊd.stɑːʳ (US) 'loʊd.stɑːr **-s** -z

lodestone 'ləʊd.stəʊn (US) 'loʊd.stoʊn **-s** -z

lodg|e (L) lɒdʒ (US) lɑːdʒ **-es** -ɪz **-ing/s** -ɪŋ/z **-ed** -d

lodg(e)ment 'lɒdʒ.mənt (US) 'lɑːdʒ- **-s** -s

lodger 'lɒdʒ.əʳ (US) 'lɑː.dʒɚ **-s** -z

lodging-hou|se 'lɒdʒ.ɪŋ.haʊ|s (US) 'lɑː.dʒɪŋ- **-ses** -zɪz

Lodore ləʊ'dɔːʳ (US) loʊ'dɔːr

Lódz wʊdʒ, wuːdʒ (US) luːdʒ, lɑːdʒ, loʊdz, wuːdʒ

Loe luː

Loeb lɜːb, ləʊb (US) loʊb

loess 'ləʊ.es, -ɪs, -əs; lɜːs ⓊⓈ 'loʊ.es, less, lɜːs
Loewe 'ləʊ.i ⓊⓈ loʊ
Lofoten ləʊ'fəʊ.tᵊn; 'lɒ.fəʊ- ⓊⓈ 'loʊ.fʊ-, -foʊ-
loft lɒft ⓊⓈ lɑːft **-s** -s **-ing** -ɪŋ **-ed** -ɪd **-er/s** -əʳ/z ⓊⓈ -ɚ/z
Lofthouse 'lɒf.təs, 'lɒft.haʊs ⓊⓈ 'lɑːf.təs, 'lɑːft.haʊs
Lofting 'lɒf.tɪŋ ⓊⓈ 'lɑːf-
Loftus 'lɒf.təs ⓊⓈ 'lɑːf-
loft|y 'lɒf.t|i ⓊⓈ 'lɑːf- **-ier** -i.əʳ ⓊⓈ -i.ɚ **-iest** -i.ɪst, -i.əst **-ily** -ɪ.li, -ᵊl.i **-iness** -ɪ.nəs, -ɪ.nɪs
log lɒg ⓊⓈ lɑːg, lɔːg **-s** -z **-ging** -ɪŋ **-ged** -d **-ger/s** -əʳ/z ⓊⓈ -ɚ/z **ˌlog 'cabin; ˌsleep like a 'log**
-log -lɒg ⓊⓈ -lɑːg, -lɔːg
Logan 'ləʊ.gən ⓊⓈ 'loʊ-
loganberr|y 'ləʊ.gᵊn.bᵊr.|i, -gəm-, -ˌber- ⓊⓈ 'loʊ.gənˌber- **-ies** -iz
logarithm 'lɒg.ᵊr.ɪ.ðᵊm, -θᵊm ⓊⓈ 'lɑː.gɚ.ɪ.ðᵊm, 'lɔː- **-s** -z
logarithmic ˌlɒg.ᵊr'ɪð.mɪk, -'rɪθ- ⓊⓈ ˌlɑː.gə'rɪθ-, ˌlɔː- **-al** -ᵊl **-ally** -ᵊl.i, -li
logbook 'lɒg.bʊk ⓊⓈ 'lɑːg-, 'lɔːg- **-s** -s
logger 'lɒg.əʳ ⓊⓈ 'lɑː.gɚ, 'lɔː- **-s** -z
loggerhead 'lɒg.ə.hed ⓊⓈ 'lɑː.gɚ-, 'lɔː- **-s** -z
loggia 'ləʊ.dʒə, 'lɒdʒ.ə, -i.ə ⓊⓈ 'lɑː.dʒə, -dʒi.ə **-s** -z
Logia 'lɒg.i.ə ⓊⓈ 'loʊ.gi-, 'lɑː-
logic 'lɒdʒ.ɪk ⓊⓈ 'lɑː.dʒɪk **-al** -ᵊl **-ally** -ᵊl.i, -li
Logica® 'lɒdʒ.ɪ.kə ⓊⓈ 'lɑː.dʒɪ-
logician lɒdʒ'ɪʃ.ᵊn ⓊⓈ loʊ'dʒɪ- **-s** -z
Logie 'ləʊ.gi ⓊⓈ 'loʊ-
-logist -lə.dʒɪst
Note: Suffix. Words containing **-logist** are normally stressed on the syllable preceding the suffix, e.g. **sociologist** /ˌsəʊ.ʃi'ɒl.ə.dʒɪst ⓊⓈ ˌsoʊ.si'ɑː.lə-/.
logistic lə'dʒɪs.tɪk, lɒdʒ'ɪs- ⓊⓈ loʊ'dʒɪs- **-s** -s **-al** -ᵊl **-ally** -ᵊl.i, -li
logjam 'lɒg.dʒæm ⓊⓈ 'lɑːg-, 'lɔːg- **-s** -z
logo 'ləʊ.gəʊ, 'lɒg.əʊ ⓊⓈ 'loʊ.goʊ **-s** -z
logogram 'lɒg.əʊ.græm ⓊⓈ 'lɑː.goʊ-, 'lɔː-, 'loʊ-, -gə- **-s** -z
logograph 'lɒg.əʊ.grɑːf, -græf ⓊⓈ 'lɑː.goʊ.græf, 'lɔː-, 'loʊ-, -gə- **-s** -s
logographic ˌlɒg.əʊ'græf.ɪk ⓊⓈ ˌlɑː.goʊ-, ˌlɔː-, ˌloʊ-, -gə- **-al** -ᵊl **-ally** -ᵊl.i, -li
Logos 'lɒg.ɒs, 'ləʊ.gɒs ⓊⓈ 'loʊ.goʊs, 'lɔː-, 'lɑː-, -gɔːs, -gɑːs
logotype 'lɒg.əʊ.taɪp ⓊⓈ 'lɑː.gə-, 'lɔː- **-s** -s
logroll 'lɒg.rəʊl ⓊⓈ 'lɑːg.roʊl, 'lɔːg- **-s** -z **-ing** -ɪŋ **-ed** -d **-er/s** -əʳ/z ⓊⓈ -ɚ/z

Logue ləʊg ⓊⓈ loʊg
-logue -lɒg ⓊⓈ -lɑːg, -lɔːg
-logy -lə.dʒi
Note: Suffix. Words containing **-logy** are normally stressed on the syllable preceding the suffix, e.g. **biology** /baɪ'ɒl.ə.dʒi ⓊⓈ -'ɑː.lə-/.
Lohengrin 'ləʊ.ən.grɪn, -ɪn-, -əŋ-, -ɪŋ- ⓊⓈ 'loʊ.ən-
loin lɔɪn **-s** -z
loin|cloth 'lɔɪn|.klɒθ ⓊⓈ -klɑːθ **-cloths** -klɒθs ⓊⓈ -klɑːθs
Loire lwɑːʳ ⓊⓈ lwɑːr
Lois 'ləʊ.ɪs ⓊⓈ 'loʊ-
loit|er 'lɔɪ.t|əʳ ⓊⓈ -t̬|ɚ **-ers** -əz ⓊⓈ -ɚz **-ering** -ᵊr.ɪŋ **-ered** -əd ⓊⓈ -ɚd **-erer/s** -ᵊr.əʳ/z ⓊⓈ -ɚ.ɚ/z
Loki 'ləʊ.ki ⓊⓈ 'loʊ-
Lola 'ləʊ.lə ⓊⓈ 'loʊ-
Lolita lɒl'iː.tə, ləʊ'liː- ⓊⓈ loʊ'liː.t̬ə
loll lɒl ⓊⓈ lɑːl **-s** -z **-ing** -ɪŋ **-ed** -d
Lollard 'lɒl.əd, -ɑːd ⓊⓈ 'lɑː.lɚd **-s** -z
lollipop 'lɒl.i.pɒp ⓊⓈ 'lɑː.li.pɑːp **-s** -s
lollop 'lɒl.əp ⓊⓈ 'lɑː.ləp **-s** -s **-ing** -ɪŋ **-ed** -t
lollo rosso ˌlɒl.əʊ'rɒs.əʊ ⓊⓈ ˌlɑː.loʊ'rɑː.soʊ, ˌloʊ-, '-roʊ-
loll|y 'lɒl|.i ⓊⓈ 'lɑː.l|i **-ies** -iz
lollypop 'lɒl.i.pɒp ⓊⓈ 'lɑː.li.pɑːp **-s** -s
Loman 'ləʊ.mən ⓊⓈ 'loʊ-
Lomas 'ləʊ.mæs, -məs ⓊⓈ 'loʊ.mæs
Lomax 'ləʊ.mæks, -məks ⓊⓈ 'loʊ.mæks
Lombard 'lɒm.bəd, -bɑːd ⓊⓈ 'lɑːm.bɑːrd, -bɚd, 'lʌm- **-s** -z
Lombardy 'lɒm.bə.di ⓊⓈ 'lɑːm.bɚ-, 'lʌm-
Lombok 'lɒm.bɒk ⓊⓈ 'lɑːm.bɑːk
Lomé 'ləʊ.meɪ ⓊⓈ loʊ'meɪ
Lomond 'ləʊ.mənd ⓊⓈ 'loʊ-
Londesborough 'lɒnz.bᵊr.ə ⓊⓈ 'lɑːndz.bɚ.oʊ
London 'lʌn.dən **-er/s** -əʳ/z ⓊⓈ -ɚ/z **ˌLondon 'Bridge; ˌLondon 'pride; ˌLondon 'weighting**
Londonderry *place:* 'lʌn.dən.der.i, ˌlʌn.dən'der- ⓊⓈ 'lʌn.dən.der- *Lord:* 'lʌn.dən.dᵊr.i ⓊⓈ -der-
lone ləʊn ⓊⓈ loʊn
lonel|y 'ləʊn.l|i ⓊⓈ 'loʊn- **-ier** -i.əʳ ⓊⓈ -i.ɚ **-iest** -i.ɪst, -i.əst **-iness** -ɪ.nəs, -ɪ.nɪs **ˌlonely 'hearts**
loner 'ləʊ.nəʳ ⓊⓈ 'loʊ.nɚ **-s** -z
lonesome 'ləʊn.səm ⓊⓈ 'loʊn- **-ness** -nəs, -nɪs
long (L) (*n. adj.*) lɒŋ ⓊⓈ lɑːŋ, lɔːŋ **-er** -gəʳ ⓊⓈ -gɚ **-est** -gɪst, -gəst **ˌLong 'Island; 'long ˌjump; 'long ˌshot; 'long ˌwave; ˌlong week'end;** ⓊⓈ **ˌlong 'weekend the ˌlong and the 'short of it; in the 'long ˌrun**
long (*v.*) lɒŋ ⓊⓈ lɑːŋ, lɔːŋ **-s** -z **-ing/ly** -ɪŋ/li **-ed** -d **-er/s** -əʳ/z ⓊⓈ -ɚ/z

Longannet lɒŋ'æn.ɪt, -ət ⓊⓈ lɑːŋ-, lɔː
long-awaited ˌlɒŋ.ə'weɪ.tɪd ⓊⓈ ˌlɑːŋ.ə'weɪ.t̬ɪd, ˌlɔːŋ- *stress shi* ˌlong-awaited 'moment
longboat 'lɒŋ.bəʊt ⓊⓈ 'lɑːŋ.boʊt, 'lɔːŋ- **-s** -s
longbow (L) 'lɒŋ.bəʊ ⓊⓈ 'lɑːŋ.boʊ, 'lɔːŋ- **-s** -z
Longbridge 'lɒŋ.brɪdʒ ⓊⓈ 'lɑːŋ-, 'lɔːŋ
Longdendale 'lɒŋ.ən.deɪl ⓊⓈ 'lɑːŋ-, 'lɔːŋ-
long-distance ˌlɒŋ'dɪs.tᵊnts ⓊⓈ ˌlɑːŋ-, ˌlɔːŋ- *stress shift:* ˌlong-distance 'driver
long-drawn-out ˌlɒŋ.drɔːn'aʊt ⓊⓈ ˌlɑːŋ.drɑːn'-, ˌlɔːŋ-, -drɔːn'- *str shift:* ˌlong-drawn-out 'sigh
longeron 'lɒn.dʒᵊr.ᵊn ⓊⓈ 'lɑːn.dʒə.rɑːn, -dʒɚ.ən **-s** -z
longevity lɒn'dʒev.ə.ti, 'lɒŋ-, -ɪ.ti ⓊⓈ lɑːn'dʒev.ə.t̬i, lɑːŋ-, lɔːŋ-
Longfellow 'lɒŋˌfel.əʊ ⓊⓈ 'lɑːŋˌfel.o 'lɔːŋ-
Longfield 'lɒŋ.fiːld ⓊⓈ 'lɑːŋ-, 'lɔːŋ-
Longford 'lɒŋ.fəd ⓊⓈ 'lɑːŋ.fɚd, 'lɔːŋ
longhand 'lɒŋ.hænd ⓊⓈ 'lɑːŋ-, 'lɔːŋ-
long-haul ˌlɒŋ'hɔːl, '-- ⓊⓈ ˌlɑːŋ'hɑːl, ˌlɔːŋ-, -hɔːl, '-- *stress shift:* ˌlong-h 'jet
longheaded ˌlɒŋ'hed.ɪd ⓊⓈ ˌlɑːŋ-, ˌlɔːŋ- *stress shift:* ˌlongheaded 'eld
longhorn 'lɒŋ.hɔːn ⓊⓈ 'lɑːŋ.hɔːrn, 'lɔːŋ- **-s** -z
Longines® 'lɒn.dʒiːn, -'- ⓊⓈ ˌlɑːn'dʒ
longing 'lɒŋ.ɪŋ ⓊⓈ 'lɑːŋ-, 'lɔːŋ- **-s** -z
Longinus lɒn'dʒaɪ.nəs, lɒŋ'giː- ⓊⓈ lɑːn'dʒaɪ-
longish 'lɒŋ.ɪʃ ⓊⓈ 'lɑːŋ-, 'lɔːŋ-
longitude 'lɒn.dʒɪ.tjuːd, 'lɒŋ.gɪ- ⓊⓈ 'lɑːn.dʒə.tuːd, -tjuːd **-s** -z
longitudinal ˌlɒn.dʒɪ'tjuː.dɪ.nᵊl, -dʒə'-, ˌlɒŋ.gɪ'-, -gə'-, -də- ⓊⓈ ˌlɑːn.dʒə'tuː-, -'tjuː- **-ly** -i
long johns 'lɒŋ.dʒɒnz, ˌ-'- ⓊⓈ 'lɑːŋ.dʒɑːnz, 'lɔːŋ-, ˌ-'-
Longland 'lɒŋ.lənd ⓊⓈ 'lɑːŋ-, 'lɔːŋ-
Longleat 'lɒŋ.liːt ⓊⓈ 'lɑːŋ-, 'lɔːŋ-
long-lived ˌlɒŋ'lɪvd ⓊⓈ ˌlɑːŋ-, ˌlɔːŋ-, -laɪvd *stress shift:* ˌlong-lived 'per
Longman 'lɒŋ.mən ⓊⓈ 'lɑːŋ-, 'lɔːŋ-
long-range ˌlɒŋ'reɪndʒ ⓊⓈ ˌlɑːŋ-, ˌlɔ *stress shift:* ˌlong-range 'missile
Longridge 'lɒŋ.rɪdʒ ⓊⓈ 'lɑːŋ-, 'lɔːŋ-
long-running ˌlɒŋ'rʌn.ɪŋ ⓊⓈ ˌlɑːŋ-, ˌlɔːŋ- *stress shift:* ˌlong-running 'problems
longshore|man 'lɒŋ.ʃɔː|.mən ⓊⓈ 'lɑːŋ.ʃɔːr-, 'lɔːŋ- **-men** -mən, -
long-sighted ˌlɒŋ'saɪ.tɪd ⓊⓈ ˌlɑːŋ'saɪ.t̬ɪd, ˌlɔːŋ-, '-ˌ-- **-ness** -nəs, -nɪs *stress shift, British only* ˌlong-sighted 'person

ngstaff ˈlɒŋ.stɑːf ⓤⓢ ˈlɑːŋ.stæf, ˈlɔːŋ-

ng-standing ˌlɒŋˈstæn.dɪŋ ⓤⓢ ˌlɑːŋ-, ˌlɔːŋ- *stress shift:* ˌlong-standing ˈfeud

ngstreet ˈlɒŋ.striːt ⓤⓢ ˈlɑːŋ-, ˈlɔːŋ-

ng-suffering ˌlɒŋˈsʌf.ər.ɪŋ ⓤⓢ ˌlɑːŋ-, ˌlɔːŋ- *stress shift:* ˌlong-suffering ˈfamily

ng-term ˌlɒŋˈtɜːm ⓤⓢ ˌlɑːŋˈtɝːm, ˌlɔːŋ- *stress shift:* ˌlong-term ˈgoal

ng-time ˈlɒŋ.taɪm ⓤⓢ ˈlɑːŋ-, ˈlɔːŋ-

ngton ˈlɒŋ*k*.tən ⓤⓢ ˈlɑːŋ-, ˈlɔːŋ-

ngtown ˈlɒŋ.taʊn ⓤⓢ ˈlɑːŋ-, ˈlɔːŋ-

ngueur lɔ̃ːŋˈgɜːʳ, lɔːŋ-, lɒŋ- ⓤⓢ lɔːŋˈgɝː **-s** -z

ngus ˈlɒŋ.gəs ⓤⓢ ˈlɑːŋ-, ˈlɔːŋ-

ngways ˈlɒŋ.weɪz ⓤⓢ ˈlɑːŋ-, ˈlɔːŋ-

ng-winded ˌlɒŋˈwɪn.dɪd ⓤⓢ ˌlɑːŋ-, ˌlɔːŋ- **-ness** -nəs, -nɪs *stress shift:* ˌlong-winded ˈstory

ngwise ˈlɒŋ.waɪz ⓤⓢ ˈlɑːŋ-, ˈlɔːŋ-

nicera lɒnˈɪs.ər.ə, ləˈnɪs- ⓤⓢ loʊ-; ˌlɑː.nɪˈsɪr.ə **-s** -z

onrho® ˈlɒn.rəʊ, ˈlʌn- ⓤⓢ ˈlɑːn.roʊ

onsdale ˈlɒnz.deɪl ⓤⓢ ˈlɑːnz-

o luː **-s** -z

oob|y ˈluː.b|i **-ies** -iz

ooe luː

oofah ˈluː.fə **-s** -z

ook lʊk **-s** -s **-ing** -ɪŋ **-ed** -t **-er/s** -əʳ/z ⓤⓢ -ɚ/z

ookalike ˈlʊk.ə.laɪk **-s** -s

ooker-on ˌlʊk.əʳˈɒn ⓤⓢ -kɚˈɑːn **lookers-on** ˌlʊk.əzˈɒn ⓤⓢ -kɚzˈɑːn

ooking-glass ˈlʊk.ɪŋ.glɑːs ⓤⓢ -glæs **-es** -ɪz

ookout ˈlʊk.aʊt **-s** -s

ook-see ˈlʊk.siː

oom luːm **-s** -z **-ing** -ɪŋ **-ed** -d

oon luːn **-s** -z

oonie ˈluː.ni **-s** -z

oon|y ˈluː.n|i **-ies** -iz ˈ**loony** ˌ**bin**; ˌ**loony** ˈ**left**

oop luːp **-s** -s **-ing** -ɪŋ **-ed** -t

oophol|e ˈluːp.həʊl ⓤⓢ -hoʊl **-es** -z **-ing** -ɪŋ **-ed** -d

oop|y ˈluː.p|i **-ier** -i.əʳ ⓤⓢ -i.ɚ **-iest** -i.ɪst, -i.əst

oos ləʊs, luːs ⓤⓢ luːs

oos|e luːs **-er** -əʳ ⓤⓢ -ɚ **-est** -ɪst, -əst **-eness** -nəs, -nɪs **-es** -ɪz **-ing** -ɪŋ **-ed** -t ˌ**let someone** ˈ**loose on**

ooseleaf ˌluːsˈliːf *stress shift:* ˌlooseleaf ˈfolder

oosely ˈluː.sli

oosen ˈluː.sən **-s** -z **-ing** -ɪŋ, ˈluːs.nɪŋ **-ed** -d

oosestrife ˈluːs.straɪf

oot luːt **-s** -s **-ing** -ɪŋ ⓤⓢ ˈluː.t̬ɪŋ **-ed** -ɪd ⓤⓢ ˈluː.t̬ɪd **-er/s** -əʳ/z ⓤⓢ ˈluː.t̬ɚ/z

op lɒp ⓤⓢ lɑːp **-s** -s **-ping** -ɪŋ **-ped** -t

lop|e ləʊp ⓤⓢ loʊp **-es** -s **-ing** -ɪŋ **-ed** -t

lop-eared ˌlɒpˈɪəd ⓤⓢ ˈlɑːp.ɪrd *stress shift, British only:* ˌlop-eared ˈrabbit

Lopez ˈləʊ.pez ⓤⓢ ˈloʊ-

lopping ˈlɒp.ɪŋ ⓤⓢ ˈlɑː.pɪŋ **-s** -z

lop-sided ˌlɒpˈsaɪ.dɪd ⓤⓢ ˌlɑːp- **-ness** -nəs, -nɪs *stress shift:* ˌlop-sided ˈsmile

loquacious ləʊˈkweɪ.ʃəs, lɒkˈweɪ- ⓤⓢ loʊˈkweɪ- **-ly** -li **-ness** -nəs, -nɪs

loquacity ləʊˈkwæs.ə.ti, lɒkˈwæs-, -ɪ.ti ⓤⓢ loʊˈkwæs.ə.t̬i

loquat ˈləʊ.kwɒt, ˈlɒk.wɒt, -wæt ⓤⓢ ˈloʊ.kwɑːt, -kwæt **-s** -s

lor lɔːʳ ⓤⓢ lɔːr

Loraine ləˈreɪn, lɒrˈeɪn ⓤⓢ ləˈreɪn

Loral ˈlɔː.ræl, ˈlɒr.æl ⓤⓢ ˈlɔːr.æl

Loram ˈlɔː.rəm ⓤⓢ ˈlɔːr.əm

Lorca ˈlɔː.kə ⓤⓢ ˈlɔːr-

lord (L) lɔːd ⓤⓢ lɔːrd **-s** -z **-ing** -ɪŋ **-ed** -ɪd ˌ**Lord's** ˈ**Prayer**

Note: British lawyers addressing a judge in court sometimes pronounce **my lord** as /mɪˈlʌd/ instead of the normal /mɪˈlɔːd/.

lordling ˈlɔːd.lɪŋ ⓤⓢ ˈlɔːrd- **-s** -z

lordl|y ˈlɔːd.l|i ⓤⓢ ˈlɔːrd- **-ier** -i.əʳ ⓤⓢ -i.ɚ **-iest** -i.ɪst, -i.əst **-iness** -ɪ.nəs, -ɪ.nɪs

lordship (L) ˈlɔːd.ʃɪp ⓤⓢ ˈlɔːrd- **-s** -s

lore lɔːʳ ⓤⓢ lɔːr

L'Oréal® ˈlɒr.i.æl ⓤⓢ ˌlɔːr.iˈæl

Lorelei ˈlɔː.rə.laɪ, ˈlɒr.ə- ⓤⓢ ˈlɔːr-

Loren ˈlɔː.ren, -rən; lɔːˈren ⓤⓢ ˈlɔːr.ən

Lorenzo ləˈren.zəʊ, lɒrˈen- ⓤⓢ ləˈren.zoʊ, lɔː-

Loretto ləˈret.əʊ, lɔː- ⓤⓢ ləˈret̬.oʊ, lɔː-

lorgnette lɔːˈnjet ⓤⓢ lɔːr- **-s** -s

Lori(e) ˈlɒr.i ⓤⓢ ˈlɔːr-

lorikeet ˈlɒr.ɪ.kiːt, ˈ-ə- ⓤⓢ ˈlɔːr.ɪ- **-s** -s

lorimer (L) ˈlɒr.ɪ.məʳ ⓤⓢ ˈlɔːr.ɪ.mɚ **-s** -z

loris ˈlɔː.rɪs ⓤⓢ ˈlɔːr.ɪs **-es** -ɪz

lorn lɔːn ⓤⓢ lɔːrn

Lorna ˈlɔː.nə ⓤⓢ ˈlɔːr-

Lorne lɔːn ⓤⓢ lɔːrn

Lorraine ləˈreɪn, lɒrˈeɪn ⓤⓢ ləˈreɪn, lɔː-

lorr|y ˈlɒr|.i ⓤⓢ ˈlɔːr- **-ies** -iz

lor|y ˈlɔː.r|i ⓤⓢ ˈlɔːr|.i **-ies** -iz

losable ˈluː.zə.bl̩

Los Alamos ˌlɒsˈæl.ə.mɒs, -məʊs ⓤⓢ ˌlɑːsˈæl.ə.moʊs, ˌlɔːs-

Los Angeles lɒsˈæn.*d*ʒɪ.liːz, -*d*ʒə-, -lɪz, -lɪs ⓤⓢ lɑːsˈæn.dʒə.ləs, lɔːs-, -gə-, -liːz

los|e luːz **-es** -ɪz **-ing** -ɪŋ **lost** lɒst ⓤⓢ lɑːst

loser ˈluː.zəʳ ⓤⓢ -zɚ **-s** -z

Losey ˈləʊ.zi ⓤⓢ ˈloʊ-

loss lɒs ⓤⓢ lɑːs **-es** -ɪz ˈ**loss** ˌ**leader**

Lossiemouth ˌlɒs.iˈmaʊθ, ˈlɒs.i.maʊθ ⓤⓢ ˌlɑː.siˈ-

lost *(from* **lose***)* lɒst ⓤⓢ lɑːst ˌ**lost** ˈ**property**

Lostwithiel lɒs*t*ˈwɪθ.i.əl, -ˈwɪð- ⓤⓢ lɑːs*t*-

lot (L) lɒt ⓤⓢ lɑːt **-s** -s **-ting** -ɪŋ ⓤⓢ ˈlɑː.t̬ɪŋ **-ted** -ɪd ⓤⓢ ˈlɑː.t̬ɪd

loth ləʊθ ⓤⓢ loʊθ, loʊð

Lothair ləʊˈθeəʳ ⓤⓢ loʊˈθer

Lothario ləʊˈθɑː.ri.əʊ, lɒθˈɑː-, -ˈeə- ⓤⓢ loʊˈθer.i.oʊ, -ˈθɑːr-

Lothbury ˈləʊθ.bər.i, ˈlɒθ- ⓤⓢ ˈloʊθ.ber-, ˈlɑːθ-, -bɚ-

Lothian ˈləʊ.ði.ən ⓤⓢ ˈloʊ-

loti ˈləʊ.ti ⓤⓢ ˈloʊ-

lotion ˈləʊ.ʃən ⓤⓢ ˈloʊ- **-s** -z

lotta ˈlɒt.ə ⓤⓢ ˈlɑː.t̬ə

lotter|y ˈlɒt.ər|.i ⓤⓢ ˈlɑː.t̬ɚ- **-ies** -iz

Lottie ˈlɒt.i ⓤⓢ ˈlɑː.t̬i

lotto (L) ˈlɒt.əʊ ⓤⓢ ˈlɑː.t̬oʊ

lotus ˈləʊ.təs ⓤⓢ ˈloʊ.t̬əs **-es** -ɪz ˈ**lotus po**ˌ**sition**

Lou luː

louche luːʃ **-ly** -li **-ness** -nəs, -nɪs

loud laʊd **-er** -əʳ ⓤⓢ -ɚ **-est** -ɪst, -əst **-ly** -li **-ness** -nəs, -nɪs

loud-hailer ˌlaʊdˈheɪ.ləʳ ⓤⓢ -lɚ **-s** -z

loud|mouth ˈlaʊd|.maʊθ **-mouths** -maʊðz **-mouthed** -maʊθt

Loudo(u)n ˈlaʊ.dən

loudspeaker ˌlaʊdˈspiː.kəʳ ⓤⓢ ˈlaʊdˌspiː.kɚ **-s** -z

Loudwater ˈlaʊdˌwɔː.təʳ ⓤⓢ -ˌwɑː.t̬ɚ, -ˌwɔː-

lough *lake:* lɒk *as if Irish:* lɒx ⓤⓢ lɑːk *as if Irish:* lɑːx **-s** -s

Lough *surname:* lʌf, ləʊ ⓤⓢ lʌf, loʊ

Loughborough ˈlʌf.bər.ə ⓤⓢ -bɚ.oʊ, -ə

Loughlin ˈlɒk.lɪn, -lən *as if Irish:* ˈlɒx- ⓤⓢ ˈlɑːks- *as if Irish:* ˈlɑːx-

Loughman ˈlʌf.mən

Loughran *as if Irish:* ˈlɒx.rən *as if Irish:* ⓤⓢ ˈlɑːx-

Loughrea lɒkˈreɪ *as if Irish:* lɒx- ⓤⓢ lɑːk- *as if Irish:* lɑːx-

Loughrey *as if Irish:* ˈlɒx.ri ⓤⓢ ˈlɑːk-, ˈlɑːf- *as if Irish:* ˈlɑːx-

Loughton ˈlaʊ.tən

Louie ˈluː.i

Louis *English name:* ˈluː.i, -ɪs *French name:* ˈluː.i, -iː, luˈi

Louisa luˈiː.zə

Louisburg ˈluː.ɪs.bɜːg ⓤⓢ -bɝːg

louis-d'or ˌluː.iˈdɔːʳ ⓤⓢ -ˈdɔːr **-s** -z

Louise luˈiːz

Louisiana luˌiː.ziˈæn.ə, -ˈɑː.nə; ˌluː.ɪ.ziˈ- ⓤⓢ luˌiː.ziˈæn.ə; ˌluː.ziˈ-

Louis Quatorze ˌluː.i.kætˈɔːz ⓤⓢ -ˈɔːrz

Louis Quinze ˌluː.iˈkæ̃nz

Louisville ˈluː.i.vɪl ⓤⓢ -ɪ.vɪl *locally:* ˈluː.ə.vəl

loung|e laʊndʒ **-es** -ɪz **-ing** -ɪŋ **-ed** -d **-er/s** -əʳ/z ⓤⓢ -ɚ/z ˈ**lounge** ˌ**bar**; ˈ**lounge** ˌ**lizard**; ˈ**lounge** ˌ**suit**

Lounsbury ˈlaʊnz.bər.i ⓤⓢ -ber-, -bɚ-

lour laʊəʳ ⓊⓈ laʊr **-s** -z **-ing** -ɪŋ **-ed** -d
Lourdes lʊəd, lʊədz, lɔːdz ⓊⓈ lʊrd, lʊrdz
Lourenço Marques ləˌrent.səʊˈmɑː.kez, -kes ⓊⓈ -soʊˈmɑːr.kes
louse *(n.)* laʊs **lice** laɪs
lous|e *(v.)* laʊz, laʊs ⓊⓈ laʊs, laʊz **-es** -ɪz **-ing** -ɪŋ **-ed** -d, laʊst
lous|y ˈlaʊ.z|i **-ier** -i.əʳ ⓊⓈ -i.ɚ **-iest** -i.ɪst, -i.əst **-ily** -ɪ.li, -əl.i **-iness** -ɪ.nəs, -ɪ.nɪs
lout laʊt **-s** -s
Louth *in Ireland:* laʊð *in Lincolnshire:* laʊθ
loutish ˈlaʊ.tɪʃ ⓊⓈ -t̬ɪʃ **-ly** -li **-ness** -nəs, -nɪs
Louvain ˈluː.vɛ̃ŋ, -veɪn; lʊˈvɛ̃ŋ, -ˈvæn ⓊⓈ luːˈvæn, -ˈvɛ̃n
louver, louvre ˈluː.vəʳ ⓊⓈ -vɚ **-s** -z
Louvre ˈluː.vrə ⓊⓈ -vrə, luːv
lovab|le ˈlʌv.ə.b|l̩ **-ly** -li **-leness** -l̩.nəs, -nɪs
lovage ˈlʌv.ɪdʒ
Lovat ˈlʌv.ət
lov|e (L) lʌv **-es** -z **-ing/ly** -ɪŋ/li **-ed** -d **ˈlove afˌfair; ˈlove ˌletter; ˌmake ˈlove; ˈlove song; ˈlove ˌstory; not for ˌlove nor ˈmoney**
loveab|le ˈlʌv.ə.b|l̩ **-ly** -li **-leness** -l̩.nəs, -nɪs
lovebird ˈlʌv.bɜːd ⓊⓈ -bɝːd **-s** -z
lovebite ˈlʌv.baɪt **-s** -s
love|-child ˈlʌv|.tʃaɪld **-children** -ˌtʃɪl.drən
Loveday ˈlʌv.deɪ
Lovejoy ˈlʌv.dʒɔɪ
Lovel ˈlʌv.əl
Lovelace ˈlʌv.leɪs
loveless ˈlʌv.ləs, -lɪs **-ly** -li **-ness** -nəs, -nɪs
Lovell ˈlʌv.əl
lovelorn ˈlʌv.lɔːn ⓊⓈ -lɔːrn
lovel|y ˈlʌv.l|i **-ies** -i.z **-ier** -i.əʳ ⓊⓈ -i.ɚ **-iest** -i.ɪst, -i.əst **-iness** -ɪ.nəs, -ɪ.nɪs
lovemaking ˈlʌvˌmeɪ.kɪŋ
love-match ˈlʌv.mætʃ **-es** -ɪz
love-potion ˈlʌvˌpəʊ.ʃən ⓊⓈ -ˌpoʊ- **-s** -z
lover ˈlʌv.əʳ ⓊⓈ -ɚ **-s** -z
Loveridge ˈlʌv.rɪdʒ, -ər.ɪdʒ
lovesick ˈlʌv.sɪk **-ness** -nəs, -nɪs
love-stor|y ˈlʌvˌstɔː.r|i ⓊⓈ -ˌstɔːr|.i **-ies** -ɪz
Lovett ˈlʌv.ɪt
lovey-dovey ˌlʌv.iˈdʌv.i, ˈlʌv.iˌdʌv-
Loveys ˈlʌv.ɪs
Lovibond ˈlʌv.ɪ.bɒnd ⓊⓈ -bɑːnd
Lovick ˈlʌv.ɪk
loving-cup ˈlʌv.ɪŋ.kʌp **-s** -s
low (L) ləʊ ⓊⓈ loʊ **-er** -əʳ ⓊⓈ -ɚ **-est** -ɪst, -əst **-ness** -nəs, -nɪs **-s** -z **-ing** -ɪŋ **-ed** -d **ˌLow ˈChurch; ˌlow ˈprofile; ˈlow ˌseason**
lowborn ˌləʊˈbɔːn ⓊⓈ ˈloʊ.bɔːrn *stress shift, British only:* ˌlowborn ˈperson
lowbred ˌləʊˈbred ⓊⓈ ˈloʊ.bred *stress shift, British only:* ˌlowbred ˈperson
lowbrow ˈləʊ.braʊ ⓊⓈ ˈloʊ-
lowdown *(n.)* ˈləʊ.daʊn ⓊⓈ ˈloʊ- *stress shift:* ˌlow-down ˈscoundrel
low-down *(adj.)* ˌləʊˈdaʊn ⓊⓈ ˌloʊ-
Lowe ləʊ ⓊⓈ loʊ
Lowell ˈləʊ.əl ⓊⓈ ˈloʊ-
low|er *(v. adj.) cause to descend:* ˈləʊ|.əʳ ⓊⓈ ˈloʊ|.ɚ **-ers** -əz, -ɚs **-ering** -ər.ɪŋ **-ered** -əd ⓊⓈ -ɚd
lower *(v.) look threatening:* laʊəʳ ⓊⓈ laʊr, laʊɚ **-s** -z **-ing/ly** -ɪŋ/li **-ed** -d
lower-case ˌləʊ.əˈkeɪs ⓊⓈ ˌloʊ.ɚˈ- *stress shift:* ˌlower-case ˈletter
lowermost ˈləʊ.ə.məʊst, -məst ⓊⓈ ˈloʊ.ɚ.moʊst
Lowery ˈlaʊə.ri ⓊⓈ ˈlaʊ.ri
Lowes ləʊz ⓊⓈ loʊz
Lowestoft ˈləʊ.stɒft, ˈləʊ.ɪ-, -stəft ⓊⓈ ˈloʊ.stɑːft, ˈloʊ.ɪ- *locally:* ˈləʊ.stəf ⓊⓈ ˈloʊ-
Lowick ˈləʊ.ɪk ⓊⓈ ˈloʊ-
Lowis ˈlaʊ.ɪs
lowkey ˌləʊˈkiː ⓊⓈ ˌloʊ-
lowland (L) ˈləʊ.lənd ⓊⓈ ˈloʊ- **-s** -z **-er/s** -əʳ/z ⓊⓈ -ɚ/z
low-life ˈləʊ.laɪf, ˌ-ˈ- ⓊⓈ ˈloʊ-, ˌ-ˈ- **-s** -s
low-loader ˌləʊˈləʊ.dəʳ ⓊⓈ ˈloʊˌloʊ.dɚ **-s** -z
lowl|y ˈləʊ.l|i ⓊⓈ ˈloʊ- **-ier** -i.əʳ ⓊⓈ -i.ɚ **-iest** -i.ɪst, -i.əst **-iness** -ɪ.nəs, -ɪ.nɪs
low-lying ˌləʊˈlaɪ.ɪŋ ⓊⓈ ˌloʊ- *stress shift:* ˌlow-lying ˈcloud
Lowndes laʊndz
low-necked ˌləʊˈnekt ⓊⓈ ˌloʊ- *stress shift:* ˌlow-necked ˈsweater
Lowood ˈləʊ.wʊd ⓊⓈ ˈloʊ-
Lowries ˈlaʊə.rɪz, ˈlaʊ- ⓊⓈ ˈlaʊ-
Lowry ˈlaʊə.ri, ˈlaʊ- ⓊⓈ ˈlaʊ-
Lowsley ˈləʊz.li ⓊⓈ ˈloʊz-
Lowson ˈləʊ.sən, ˈlaʊ- ⓊⓈ ˈloʊ-, ˈlaʊ-
Lowth laʊθ
Lowther ˈlaʊ.ðəʳ ⓊⓈ -ðɚ
Lowton ˈləʊ.tən ⓊⓈ ˈloʊ-
Lowville ˈlaʊ.vɪl
lox lɒks ⓊⓈ lɑːks
Loxley ˈlɒk.sli ⓊⓈ ˈlɑːk-
loyal lɔɪəl ⓊⓈ ˈlɔɪ.əl **-ly** -i
loyalist ˈlɔɪə.lɪst ⓊⓈ ˈlɔɪ.ə.lɪst **-s** -s
loyalt|y ˈlɔɪəl.t|i ⓊⓈ ˈlɔɪ.əl.t̬|i **-ies** -iz
Loyd lɔɪd
Loyola ˈlɔɪ.əʊ.lə; lɔɪˈəʊ- ⓊⓈ lɔɪˈoʊ-
lozeng|e ˈlɒz.ɪndʒ, -əndʒ ⓊⓈ ˈlɑː.zəndʒ **-es** -ɪz
LP ˌelˈpiː
L-plate ˈel.pleɪt **-s** -s
LPN ˌel.piːˈen
LSD ˌel.esˈdiː
LSE ˌel.esˈiː
Ltd. ˈlɪm.ɪ.tɪd, ˈ-ə- ⓊⓈ -ə.t̬ɪd
Luanda luˈæn.də ⓊⓈ -ˈæn-, -ˈɑːn-
luau ˈluː.aʊ
Lubavitcher ˈluː.bə.vɪ.tʃəʳ ⓊⓈ -tʃɚ **-s**
lubber ˈlʌb.əʳ ⓊⓈ -ɚ **-s** -z
Lubbock ˈlʌb.ək
lube luːb **-s** -z
Lübeck ˈluː.bek, ˈljuː- ⓊⓈ ˈluː-
Lubin ˈluː.bɪn
Lublin ˈluː.blɪn
lubricant ˈluː.brɪ.kənt, ˈljuː-, -brə- ⓊⓈ ˈluː- **-s** -s
lubri|cate ˈluː.brɪ|.keɪt, ˈljuː-, -brə- ⓊⓈ ˈluː- **-cates** -keɪts **-cating** -keɪ.tɪ ⓊⓈ -keɪ.t̬ɪŋ **-cated** -keɪ.tɪd ⓊⓈ -keɪ.t̬ɪd **-cator/s** -keɪ.təʳ/z ⓊⓈ -keɪ.t̬ɚ/z
lubrication ˌluː.brɪˈkeɪ.ʃən, ˌljuː-, -brəˈ- ⓊⓈ ˌluː- **-s** -z
lubricious luːˈbrɪʃ.əs, ljuː- ⓊⓈ luː- **-ly** **-ness** -nəs, -nɪs
lubricity luːˈbrɪs.ə.ti, ljuː-, -ɪ.ti ⓊⓈ luːˈbrɪs.ə.t̬i
Lubumbashi ˌluː.bʊmˈbæʃ.i ⓊⓈ -ˈbɑː.
Luca ˈluː.kə
Lucan ˈluː.kən, ˈljuː- ⓊⓈ ˈluː-
Lucania luːˈkeɪ.ni.ə, ljuː- ⓊⓈ luː-
lucarne luːˈkɑːn, ljuː- ⓊⓈ luːˈkɑːrn **-s** -z
Lucas ˈluː.kəs
Luce luːs
lucen|t ˈluː.sən|t, ˈljuː- ⓊⓈ ˈluː- **-cy** *-t*.s
lucern(e) luːˈsɜːn, ljuː-, ˈ-- ⓊⓈ luːˈsɝːn
Lucerne luːˈsɜːn, ljuː- ⓊⓈ luːˈsɝːn
luces *(plur. of* **lux***)* ˈluː.siːz
Lucia ˈluː.si.ə, ˈ-ʃə; luːˈtʃiː.ə
Lucian ˈluː.si.ən, ˈ-ʃən, -ʃi.ən ⓊⓈ ˈluː.ʃən
Luciana ˌluː.siˈɑː.nə, ˌljuː- ⓊⓈ ˌluː-, -ˈæn.ə
Lucianus ˌluː.siˈɑː.nəs, ˌljuː-, -ˈeɪ- ⓊⓈ ˌluː.siˈɑː-
lucid ˈluː.sɪd, ˈljuː- ⓊⓈ ˈluː- **-ly** -li **-ness** -nəs, -nɪs
lucidity luːˈsɪd.ə.ti, ljuː-, -ɪ.ti ⓊⓈ luːˈsɪd.ə.t̬i
Lucie ˈluː.si, ˈljuː- ⓊⓈ ˈluː-
Lucien ˈluː.si.ən, ˈljuː- ⓊⓈ ˈluː-
Lucie-Smith ˌluː.siˈsmɪθ, ˌljuː- ⓊⓈ ˌluː-
lucifer (L) ˈluː.sɪ.fəʳ, ˈljuː-, -sə- ⓊⓈ ˈluː.sə.fɚ **-s** -z
Lucilius luːˈsɪl.i.əs, ljuː- ⓊⓈ luː-
Lucille luːˈsiːl
Lucina luːˈsiː.nə, ljuː-, -ˈsaɪ-, -ˈtʃiː- ⓊⓈ luːˈsaɪ-, -ˈsiː-
Lucinda luːˈsɪn.də, ljuː- ⓊⓈ luː-
Lucite® ˈluː.saɪt, ˈljuː- ⓊⓈ ˈluː-
Lucius ˈluː.si.əs, ˈljuː-, ˈ-ʃəs, -ʃi.əs ⓊⓈ ˈluː.ʃəs
luck (L) lʌk **to be ˌdown on one's ˈluck**

ckless 'lʌk.ləs, -lɪs -ly -li -ness -nəs, -nɪs
cknow 'lʌk.naʊ, ,-'- (US) 'lʌk.naʊ
ck|y 'lʌk|.i -ier -i.əʳ (US) -i.ɚ -iest -i.ɪst, -i.əst -ily -ɪ.li, -ᵊl.i -iness -ɪ.nəs, -ɪ.nɪs
cock 'luː.kɒk, 'ljuː- (US) 'luː.kɑːk
cozade® 'luː.kə.zeɪd
crative 'luː.krə.tɪv, 'ljuː- (US) 'luː.krə.t̬ɪv -ly -li -ness -nəs, -nɪs
cre 'luː.kəʳ, 'ljuː- (US) 'luː.kɚ
crece luː'kriːs, ljuː- (US) luː-
cretia luː'kriː.ʃə, ljuː-, -ʃi.ə (US) luː'kriː.ʃə
cretius luː'kriː.ʃəs, ljuː-, -ʃi.əs (US) luː'kriː.ʃəs
cu|brate 'luː.kjə|.breɪt, -kjʊ-, 'ljuː- (US) 'luː- -brates -breɪts -brating -breɪ.tɪŋ (US) -breɪ.t̬ɪŋ -brated -breɪ.tɪd (US) -breɪ.t̬ɪd
ubration ,luː.kjə'breɪ.ʃᵊn, -kjʊ'-, ,ljuː- (US) ,luː- -s -z
cullus luː'kʌl.əs, ljuː-, -'sʌl- (US) luː'kʌl-
cy 'luː.si
d lʌd
ddite 'lʌd.aɪt -s -s
dgate 'lʌd.gət, -gɪt, -geɪt
licrous 'luː.dɪ.krəs, 'ljuː-, -də- (US) 'luː- -ly -li -ness -nəs, -nɪs
dlow 'lʌd.ləʊ (US) -loʊ
dmilla lʊd'mɪl.ə, lʌd-
o 'luː.dəʊ (US) -doʊ
lovic 'luː.də.vɪk
dwig 'lʊd.vɪg, 'luːd- (US) 'lʊd-, 'luːd-, 'lʌd-, -wɪg
f (L) lʌf -s -s -ing -ɪŋ -ed -t
thansa® 'lʊft,hænt.sə, -,hæn.zə (US) lʊf'tɑːn.zə
twaffe 'lʊft,wæf.ə, -,væf-, -,wɑː.fə, -,vɑː- (US) -,vɑː-, -,wɑː-
lʌg -s -z -ging -ɪŋ -ged -d
ano luː'gɑː.nəʊ, lə- (US) luː'gɑː.noʊ
ard 'luː.gɑːd, -'- (US) 'luː.gɑːrd, -'-
e luːʒ, luːdʒ (US) luːʒ -es -ɪz -(e)ing -ɪŋ -ed -d
er® 'luː.gəʳ (US) -gɚ
gable 'lʌg.ə.bl̩
gage 'lʌg.ɪdʒ **'luggage ,label; 'luggage ,rack**
ger 'lʌg.əʳ (US) -ɚ -s -z
hole 'lʌg.həʊl, -əʊl (US) -hoʊl -s -z
osi luː'gəʊ.si (US) -'goʊ-
sail 'lʌg.seɪl *nautical pronunciation:* -sᵊl -s -z
ubrious luː'guː.bri.əs, ljuː-, lə- (US) lə'guː-, luː- -ly -li -ness -nəs, -nɪs
worm 'lʌg.wɜːm (US) -wɝːm -s -z
'luː.ɪs
a 'luː.kə
acs, **Lukács** 'luː.kætʃ (US) -kɑːtʃ
e luːk

lukewarm ,luːk'wɔːm, '-- (US) 'luːk.wɔːrm, ,-'- -ly -li -ness -nəs, -nɪs
lull lʌl -s -z -ing -ɪŋ -ed -d
lullab|y 'lʌl.ə.b|aɪ -ies -aɪz
Lully 'lʊl.i; *as if French:* luː'liː (US) luː'liː
lulu (L) 'luː.luː
lumbago lʌm'beɪ.gəʊ (US) -goʊ
lumbar 'lʌm.bəʳ, -bɑːʳ (US) -bɑːr, -bɚ
lumb|er 'lʌm.b|əʳ (US) -b|ɚ -ers -əz (US) -ɚz -ering -ᵊr.ɪŋ -ered -əd (US) -ɚd -erer/s -ᵊr.əʳ/z (US) -ɚ.ɚ/z -erman -ə.mən (US) -ɚ.mən -ermen -ə.mən, -ə.men (US) -ɚ.mən, -ɚ.men
lumberjack 'lʌm.bə.dʒæk (US) -bɚ- -s -s
lumberyard 'lʌm.bə.jɑːd (US) -bɚ.jɑːrd -s -z
lumiere, lumière 'luː.mi.eəʳ, ,--'- (US) ,luː.mi'er
luminar|y 'luː.mɪ.nᵊr|.i, 'ljuː-, -mə- (US) 'luː.mə.ner- -ies -iz
luminesc|e ,luː.mɪ'nes, ,ljuː-, -mə'- (US) ,luː.mə'- -es -ɪz -ing -ɪŋ -ed -t
luminescen|ce ,luː.mɪ'nes.ᵊn|*t*s, ,ljuː-, -mə'- (US) ,luː.mə'- -t -t
luminiferous ,luː.mɪ'nɪf.ᵊr.əs, ,ljuː-, -mə'- (US) ,luː.mə'-
luminosity ,luː.mɪ'nɒs.ə.ti, ,ljuː-, -mə'-, -ɪ.ti (US) ,luː.mə'nɑː.sə.t̬i
luminous 'luː.mɪ.nəs, 'ljuː-, -mə- (US) 'luː.mə- -ly -li -ness -nəs, -nɪs
Lumley 'lʌm.li
lumme 'lʌm.i
lummox 'lʌm.əks -es -ɪz
lump lʌmp -s -s -ing -ɪŋ -ed -t
lumpectom|y lʌm'pek.tə.m|i -ies -iz
lumpen 'lʌm.pən, 'lʊm-
lumpenproletariat ,lʌm.pən,prəʊ.lə'teə.ri.ət, ,lʊm-, -pəm,-, -lɪ'-, -æt (US) -pən,proʊ.lə'ter.i.ət
lumpfish 'lʌmp.fɪʃ -es -ɪz
lumpish 'lʌm.pɪʃ -ly -li -ness -nəs, -nɪs
Lumpkin 'lʌmp.kɪn
lump|y 'lʌm.p|i -ier -i.əʳ (US) -i.ɚ -iest -i.ɪst, -i.əst -iness -ɪ.nəs, -ɪ.nɪs
Lumsden 'lʌmz.dən
Luna 'luː.nə, 'ljuː- (US) 'luː-
lunacy 'luː.nə.si, 'ljuː- (US) 'luː-
lunar 'luː.nəʳ, 'ljuː- (US) 'luː.nɚ
lunate 'luː.neɪt, 'ljuː-, -nət, -nɪt (US) 'luː.neɪt, -nɪt
lunatic 'luː.nə.tɪk, 'ljuː- (US) 'luː- -s -s **'lunatic a,sylum; ,lunatic 'fringe**
lunation luː'neɪ.ʃᵊn, ljuː- (US) luː- -s -z
Luncarty 'lʌŋ.kə.ti (US) -kɚ.t̬i
lunch lʌn*t*ʃ -es -ɪz -ing -ɪŋ -ed -t
lunchbox 'lʌn*t*ʃ.bɒks (US) -bɑːks -es -ɪz
luncheon 'lʌn.*t*ʃən -s -z **'luncheon ,meat; 'luncheon ,voucher**
luncheonette ,lʌn.*t*ʃə'net -s -s

lunchroom 'lʌn*t*ʃ.ruːm, -rʊm -s -z
lunchtime 'lʌn*t*ʃ.taɪm -s -z
Lund *place in Sweden:* lʊnd (US) lʊnd, lʌnd *family name:* lʌnd
Lundy 'lʌn.di
lune (L) luːn, ljuːn (US) luːn -s -z
Lüneburg 'luː.nə.bɜːg (US) -bɝːg
lunette luː'net, ljuː- (US) luː- -s -s
lung lʌŋ -s -z
lung|e lʌndʒ -es -ɪz -ing -ɪŋ -ed -d -er/s -əʳ/z (US) -ɚ/z
lungfish 'lʌŋ.fɪʃ -es -ɪz
lunkhead 'lʌŋk.hed -s -z
Lunn lʌn
lunul|a 'luː.njə.l|ə, 'ljuː- (US) -njʊ-, 'luː.njə- -ae -iː
lunule 'luː.njuːl, 'ljuː- (US) 'luː- -s -z
Lupercal 'luː.pə.kæl, 'ljuː-, -pɜː- (US) 'luː.pɚ.kæl
Lupercalia ,luː.pə'keɪ.li.ə, ,ljuː-, -pɜː'- (US) ,luː.pɚ'keɪl.jə
lupin(e) *flower:* 'luː.pɪn -s -z
lupine *(adj.) wolfish:* 'luː.paɪn, 'ljuː- (US) 'luː-
lupus (L) 'luː.pəs, 'ljuː- (US) 'luː-
lurch lɜːtʃ (US) lɝːtʃ -es -ɪz -ing -ɪŋ -ed -t -er/s -əʳ/z (US) -ɚ/z **,leave someone in the 'lurch**
lur|e lʊəʳ, ljʊəʳ, ljɔːʳ (US) lʊr -es -z -ing -ɪŋ -ed -d
Lurex® 'ljʊə.reks, 'lʊə-, 'ljɔː- (US) 'lʊr.eks
Lurgan 'lɜː.gᵊn (US) 'lɝː-
lurg|y 'lɜː.g|i (US) 'lɝː- -ies -iz
lurid 'lʊə.rɪd, 'ljʊə-, 'ljɔː- (US) 'lʊr.ɪd -ly -li -ness -nəs, -nɪs
lurk lɜːk (US) lɝːk -s -s -ing -ɪŋ -ed -t -er/s -əʳ/z (US) -ɚ/z
Lurpak® 'lɜː.pæk (US) 'lɝː-
Lusaka luː'sɑː.kə, lʊ-, -'zɑː- (US) luː'sɑː.kɑː
Lusardi luː'sɑː.di (US) -'sɑːr-
Lusati|a luː'seɪ.ʃ|ə, -ʃi|.ə -an/s -ən/z
luscious 'lʌʃ.əs -ly -li -ness -nəs, -nɪs
lush (L) lʌʃ -es -ɪz -er -əʳ (US) -ɚ -est -ɪst, -əst -ing -ɪŋ -ed -t -ness -nəs, -nɪs
Lushington 'lʌʃ.ɪŋ.tən
Lusiad 'luː.si.æd, 'ljuː- (US) 'luː- -s -z
Lusitania ,luː.sɪ'teɪ.ni.ə, ,ljuː-, -sə'- (US) ,luː-
lust lʌst -s -s -ing -ɪŋ -ed -ɪd
luster 'lʌs.təʳ (US) -tɚ -s -z -less -ləs, -lɪs
lustful 'lʌst.fᵊl, -fʊl -ly -i -ness -nəs, -nɪs
lustral 'lʌs.trᵊl
lustration lʌs'treɪ.ʃᵊn -s -z
lustre 'lʌs.təʳ (US) -tɚ -s -z -less -ləs, -lɪs
lustrous 'lʌs.trəs -ly -li -ness -nəs, -nɪs
lustr|um 'lʌs.tr|əm -ums -əmz -a -ə
lust|y 'lʌs.t|i -ier -i.əʳ (US) -i.ɚ -iest -i.ɪst, -i.əst -ily -ɪ.li, -ᵊl.i -iness -ɪ.nəs, -ɪ.nɪs

lutanist 'luː.tᵊn.ɪst, 'ljuː- US 'luː-
lute luːt, ljuːt US luːt **-s** -s
lutein 'luː.ti.ɪn, 'ljuː-, -tiːn, 'luː.ti.ɪn
luteiniz|e, -is|e 'luː.ti.ɪ.naɪz, 'ljuː-, -ə-; -tɪ.naɪz, -tə-, -tiː-, -tᵊn.aɪz US 'luː.ti.ə.naɪz, -ə- **-es** -ɪz **-ing** -ɪŋ **-ed** -d
lutenist 'luː.tᵊn.ɪst, 'ljuː- US 'luː- **-s** -s
lutetium luː'tiː.ʃəm, ljuː-, -ʃi.əm US luː'tiː.ʃi.əm
Luth|er 'luː.θ|əʳ US 'luː.θ|ɚ **-eran/s** -ᵊr.ᵊn/z **-eranism** -ᵊr.ᵊn.ɪ.zᵊm **-erism** -ᵊr.ɪ.zᵊm
Lutine luː'tiːn, '--
lutist 'luː.tɪst, 'ljuː- US 'luː.t̬ɪst **-s** -s
Luton 'luː.tᵊn
Lutterworth 'lʌt.ə.wəθ, -wɜːθ US 'lʌt̬.ɚ.wəθ, -wɝːθ
Lutton 'lʌt.ᵊn
Luttrell 'lʌt.rəl
Lutyens 'lʌt.jənz, 'lʌtʃ.ənz
luv lʌv **-s** -z
luvv|ie, luvv|y 'lʌv|.i **-ies** -ɪz
lux lʌks **luxes** 'lʌk.sɪz
Lux® lʌks
luxe lʌks, luːks, lʊks
Luxemb(o)urg 'lʌk.sᵊm.bɜːg US -bɝːg
Luxor 'lʌk.sɔːʳ US -sɔːr, 'lʊk-
luxuriance lʌg'ʒʊə.ri.ənts, ləg-, -'ʒɔː-, -'zjʊə-, -'zjɔː-; lʌk'sjʊə-, lək-, -'sjɔː- US lʌg'ʒʊr.i-, -'zjʊr-; lʌk'ʃʊr-, -'sjʊr-
luxuriant lʌg'ʒʊə.ri.ənt, ləg-, -'ʒɔː-, -'zjʊə-, -'zjɔː-; lʌk'sjʊə-, lək-, -'sjɔː- US lʌg'ʒʊr.i-, -'zjʊr-; lʌk'ʃʊr-, -'sjʊr- **-ly** -li
luxuri|ate lʌg'ʒʊə.ri|.eɪt, ləg-, -'ʒjɔː-, -'zjʊə-, -'zjɔː-; lʌk'sjʊə-, lək-, -'sjɔː- US lʌg'ʒʊr.i-, -'ʒjʊr-; lʌk'ʃʊr-, -'sjʊr- **-ates** -eɪts **-ating** -eɪ.tɪŋ US -eɪ.t̬ɪŋ **-ated** -eɪ.tɪd US -eɪ.t̬ɪd
luxurious lʌg'ʒʊə.ri.əs, ləg-, -'ʒɔː-, -'zjʊə-, -'zjɔː-; lʌk'sjʊə-, lək-, -'sjɔː- US lʌg'ʒʊr.i-, -'zjʊr-; lʌk'ʃʊr-, -'sjʊr- **-ly** -li **-ness** -nəs, -nɪs
luxur|y 'lʌk.ʃᵊr|.i US 'lʌk.ʃɚ|.i, -ʃʊr-; 'lʌg.ʒɚ-, -ʒʊr- **-ies** -iz **in the ˌlap of 'luxury**
Luzon luː'zɒn US -'zɑːn
Lvov lə'vɒf US -'vɑːf
lwei lə'weɪ **-s** -z
-ly -li
Note: Suffix. Does not alter the stress pattern of the stem to which it is added, e.g. **rapid** /'ræp.ɪd/, **rapidly** /'ræp.ɪd.li/.
Lyall 'laɪ.əl, laɪəl
lycanthrope 'laɪ.kᵊn.θrəʊp; laɪ'kænt.θrəʊp US -θroʊp **-s** -s
lycanthropic ˌlaɪ.kᵊn'θrɒp.ɪk US -'θrɑː.pɪk
lycanthropy laɪ'kænt.θrə.pi
lycée 'liː.seɪ US liː'seɪ **-s** -z
Lycett 'laɪ.sɪt, -set
lyceum (L) laɪ'siː.əm, 'laɪ- **-s** -z
lychee ˌlaɪ'tʃiː; 'laɪ.tʃiː, 'liː- US 'liː.tʃiː **-s** -z
lychgate 'lɪtʃ.geɪt **-s** -s
lychnis 'lɪk.nɪs
Lyci|a 'lɪs.i|.ə, 'lɪʃ-, 'lɪʃ|.ə US 'lɪʃ|.ə, -i|.ə **-an/s** -ən/z
Lycidas 'lɪs.ɪ.dæs US -dæs, -dəs
Lycoming laɪ'kɒm.ɪŋ US -'kʌm-
lycopodium ˌlaɪ.kəʊ'pəʊ.di.əm US -koʊ'poʊ- **-s** -z
Lycra® 'laɪ.krə
Lycurgus laɪ'kɜː.gəs US -'kɝː-
Lydall 'laɪ.dᵊl
Lydd lɪd
lyddite 'lɪd.aɪt
Lydekker laɪ'dek.əʳ US -ɚ
Lydgate *fifteenth century poet, place in Greater Manchester:* 'lɪd.geɪt, -gɪt *place in Yorkshire:* 'lɪd.gɪt, 'lɪ.gɪt *lane in Sheffield:* 'lɪdʒ.ɪt
Lydi|a 'lɪd.i|.ə **-an/s** -ən/z
Lydiate 'lɪd.i.ət
Lydney 'lɪd.ni
Lydon 'laɪ.dᵊn
lye (L) laɪ
Lyell 'laɪ.əl; laɪəl
Lygon 'lɪg.ən
lying *(from* **lie***)* 'laɪ.ɪŋ **ˌtake something ˌlying 'down**
Lyle laɪl
Lyly 'lɪl.i
Lyme laɪm **'Lyme diˌsease**
Lyme Regis ˌlaɪm'riː.dʒɪs
Lymeswold® 'laɪmz.wəʊld US -woʊld
Lymington 'lɪm.ɪŋ.tən
Lymm lɪm
Lympany 'lɪm.pə.ni
lymph lɪmpf **-s** -s
lymphatic lɪm'fæt.ɪk US -'fæt̬- **-s** -s **-ally** -ᵊl.i, -li
lymphocyte 'lɪmp.fəʊ.saɪt US -foʊ-, -fə- **-s** -s
lymphoid 'lɪmp.fɔɪd
lymphoma lɪm'fəʊ.mə US -'foʊ- **-s** …
Lympne lɪm
Lyn lɪn
Lynam 'laɪ.nəm
Lynas 'laɪ.nəs
lynch (L) lɪntʃ US lɪntʃ **-es** -ɪz **-ing** -ɪ… **-ed** -t
Lynchburg 'lɪntʃ.bɜːg US -bɝːg
lynchpin 'lɪntʃ.pɪn **-s** -z
Lynda 'lɪn.də
Lyndhurst 'lɪnd.hɜːst US -hɝːst
Lyndon 'lɪn.dən
Lyndsay, Lyndsey 'lɪnd.zi
Lyness 'laɪ.nɪs, -nəs, -nes
Lynette lɪ'net
Lynmouth 'lɪn.məθ
Lynn(e) lɪn
Lynton 'lɪn.tən
lynx lɪŋks **-es** -ɪz
Lyon laɪən
lyonnaise ˌlaɪə'neɪz, ˌliː.ə'-
Lyons laɪənz *French city:* 'liː.ɔ̃ːŋ, -ɒ… laɪənz *as if French:* li'ɔ̃ŋ US li'õʊ…
Lyr|a 'laɪə.r|ə US 'laɪ- **-ae** -iː
lyrate 'laɪə.rɪt, -reɪt, -rət US 'laɪ.re…
lyre laɪəʳ US laɪr **-s** -z
lyrebird 'laɪə.bɜːd US 'laɪr.bɝːd **-s** …
lyric (L) 'lɪr.ɪk **-s** -s **-al** -ᵊl **-ally** -ᵊl.i, …
lyricism 'lɪr.ɪ.sɪ.zᵊm, '-ə-
lyricist 'lɪr.ɪ.sɪst, '-ə- **-s** -s
lyrist *player on the lyre:* 'laɪə.rɪst, 'lɪr.ɪst US 'laɪr.ɪst **-s** -s
lyrist *lyric poet:* 'lɪr.ɪst **-s** -s
Lysander laɪ'sæn.dəʳ US -dɚ
lysergic laɪ'sɜː.dʒɪk, lɪ- US laɪ'sɝː-
Lysias 'lɪs.i.æs
Lysicrates laɪ'sɪk.rə.tiːz
Lysippus laɪ'sɪp.əs
-lysis -lə.sɪs, -lɪ-
Note: Suffix. Words containing **-ly…** are normally stressed on the syllable preceding the suffix, e.… **paralysis** /pə'ræl.ə.sɪs/.
Lysistrata laɪ'sɪs.trə.tə US ˌlɪs.ɪ'st… laɪ'sɪs.trə-
Lysol® 'laɪ.sɒl US -sɑːl
Lystra 'lɪs.trə
Lyte laɪt
Lytham 'lɪð.əm
Lythe laɪð
Lyttelton 'lɪt.ᵊl.tən US 'lɪt̬-
Lyttle 'lɪt.l̩ US 'lɪt̬-
Lytton 'lɪt.ᵊn

Pronouncing the letter M

See also MN

The consonant letter **m** is always realised as /m/.

(M) em **-'s** -z
(abbrev. for **metre/s***) singular:* 'miː.tər ⓤⓢ -t̬ɚ *plural:* -z
a *(mother)* mɑː **-s** -z
A ˌem'eɪ
a'am *(abbrev. for* **madam***)* mæm, mɑːm, məm, m ⓤⓢ mæm
ote: /mɑːm/, or alternatively /mæm/, is used in addressing members of the royal family.
aas mɑːs
aastricht 'mɑː.strɪkt, -strɪxt; *as if Dutch:* mɑː'strɪxt ⓤⓢ 'mɑː.strɪkt, -strɪxt
ab mæb
abel 'meɪ.bəl
abinogion ˌmæb.ɪ'nɒg.i.ɒn, -ə'-, -ən ⓤⓢ -'nɔː.gi.ɑːn, -'nɑː-, -ən
ablethorpe 'meɪ.bl̩.θɔːp ⓤⓢ -θɔːrp
abley 'mæb.li ⓤⓢ 'mæb-, 'meɪb-
abs mæbz
ac mæk
c, mack mæk **-s** -s
acabre mə'kɑː.brə, mæk'ɑː-, -bər ⓤⓢ mə'kɑː.brə, -'kɑːb, -'kɑː.bɚ
cadam mə'kæd.əm
cAdam mə'kæd.əm
cadamia ˌmæk.ə'deɪ.mi.ə **-s** -z
ˌmaca'damia ˌnut
cadamization, -isa- məˌkæd.ə.maɪ'zeɪ.ʃən, -mɪ'- ⓤⓢ -mə'-
cadamiz|e, -is|e mə'kæd.ə.maɪz **-es** -ɪz **-ing** -ɪŋ **-ed** -d
calister mə'kæl.ɪ.stər ⓤⓢ -stɚ
can mə'kæn
cao mə'kaʊ, mæk'aʊ ⓤⓢ mə'kaʊ
caque mə'kɑːk, -'kæk; 'mæk.æk ⓤⓢ mə'kɑːk **-s** -s
caroni ˌmæk.ər'əʊ.ni ⓤⓢ -ə'roʊ- **(e)s** -z *stress shift, see compound:* **macaroni 'cheese**
caroon ˌmæk.ər'uːn ⓤⓢ -ə'ruːn **-s** -z
cArthur mə'kɑː.θər ⓤⓢ -'kɑːr.θɚ
cassar (M) mə'kæs.ər ⓤⓢ -ɚ
ma'cassar ˌoil
cau mə'kaʊ, mæk'aʊ ⓤⓢ mə'kaʊ
caulay mə'kɔː.li ⓤⓢ -'kɑː.li, -'kɔː-
cavity mə'kæv.ə.ti, -ɪ.ti ⓤⓢ -ə.t̬i
:Avoy 'mæk.ə.vɔɪ
:aw mə'kɔː ⓤⓢ -'kɑː, -'kɔː **-s** -z
:Bain mək'beɪn
:beth mək'beθ, mæk-
e: In Scotland always /mək-/.

Maccabaeus ˌmæk.ə'biː.əs, -'beɪ- ⓤⓢ -'biː-
Maccabean ˌmæk.ə'biː.ən, -'beɪ- ⓤⓢ -'biː-
Maccabees 'mæk.ə.biːz
Maccabeus ˌmæk.ə'biː.əs, -'beɪ- ⓤⓢ -'biː-
MacCaig mə'keɪg
MacCall mə'kɔːl ⓤⓢ -'kɔːl, -'kɑːl
MacCallum mə'kæl.əm
MacCarthy mə'kɑː.θi ⓤⓢ -'kɑːr-
Macclesfield 'mæk.l̩z.fiːld, -l̩s-
MacCunn mə'kʌn
MacDaire mək'dɑː.rə ⓤⓢ mək'der
MacDiarmid mək'dɜː.mɪd, -'deə- ⓤⓢ -'dɝː-
Macdonald, MacDonald mək'dɒn.əld, mæk- ⓤⓢ -'dɑː.nəld
MacDonaugh mək'dɒn.ə ⓤⓢ -'dɑː.nə
MacDon(n)ell mək'dɒn.əl ⓤⓢ -'dɑː.nəl
MacDougal mək'duː.gəl
MacDuff mək'dʌf, mæk-
Note: In Scotland always /mək-/.
mace meɪs **-s** -ɪz
macedoine, macédoine ˌmæs.ɪ'dwɑːn, -ə'-, '--- ⓤⓢ ˌmæs.ɪ'dwɑːn **-s** -z
Macedon 'mæs.ɪ.dən, '-ə- ⓤⓢ -ə.dɑːn, -dən
Macedoni|a ˌmæs.ɪ'dəʊ.ni|.ə ⓤⓢ -ə'doʊ.ni-, '-nj|ə **-an/s** -ən/z
MacElder(r)y ˌmæk.əl'der.i, mə'kel.dər- ⓤⓢ mə'kel.dɚ-
MacElwain 'mæk.əl.weɪn, mə'kel.weɪn
MacElwin 'mæk.əl.wɪn
macer|ate 'mæs.ər|.eɪt ⓤⓢ -ə.r|eɪt **-ates** -eɪts **-ating** -eɪ.tɪŋ ⓤⓢ -eɪ.t̬ɪŋ **-ated** -eɪ.tɪd ⓤⓢ -eɪ.t̬ɪd
maceration ˌmæs.ər'eɪ.ʃən ⓤⓢ -ə'reɪ- **-s** -z
macerator 'mæs.ər.eɪ.tər ⓤⓢ -ə.reɪ.t̬ɚ **-s** -z
MacFarlane mək'fɑː.lən ⓤⓢ -'fɑːr-
Macfarren mək'fær.ən ⓤⓢ -'fer-, -'fær-
Macgillicuddy, MacGillicuddy mə'gɪl.i.kʌd.i; 'mæg.li-, 'mæk.ɪl- ⓤⓢ mə'gɪl.i-
Note: **Macgillicuddy's Reeks** is pronounced /məˌgɪl.i.kʌd.iz'riːks/.
Macgregor, MacGregor mə'greg.ər ⓤⓢ -ɚ
Mach mæk, mɑːk ⓤⓢ mɑːk, mæk
Machakos mə'tʃɑː.kɒs ⓤⓢ -kɑːs
Macheath mək'hiːθ ⓤⓢ mæk-, mək-

Machen 'meɪ.tʃɪn, -tʃən; 'mæk.ɪn *as if Welsh:* 'mæx- ⓤⓢ 'mæk.ɪn
machete mə'tʃet.i, mætʃ'et-, -'eɪ.ti ⓤⓢ mə'tʃet̬.i **-s** -z
Machiavelli ˌmæk.i.ə'vel.i, ˌ-jə'-
Machiavellian ˌmæk.i.ə'vel.i.ən, ˌmæk.jə- **-s** -z **-ism** -ɪ.zəm
machico|late mə'tʃɪk.əʊ|.leɪt, mætʃ'ɪk- ⓤⓢ mə'tʃɪk.oʊ-, '-ə- **-lates** -leɪts **-lating** -leɪ.tɪŋ ⓤⓢ -leɪ.t̬ɪŋ **-lated** -leɪ.tɪd ⓤⓢ -leɪ.t̬ɪd
machicolation məˌtʃɪk.əʊ'leɪ.ʃən, mætʃˌɪk- ⓤⓢ məˌtʃɪk.oʊ'-, -ə'- **-s** -z
Machin 'meɪ.tʃɪn
machi|nate 'mæk.ɪ|.neɪt, 'mæʃ-, '-ə- ⓤⓢ -ə|.neɪt **-nates** -neɪts **-nating** -neɪ.tɪŋ ⓤⓢ -neɪ.t̬ɪŋ **-nated** -neɪ.tɪd ⓤⓢ -neɪ.t̬ɪd **-nator/s** -neɪ.tər/z ⓤⓢ -neɪ.t̬ɚ/s
machination ˌmæk.ɪ'neɪ.ʃən, ˌmæʃ-, -ə'- ⓤⓢ -ə'- **-s** -z
machin|e mə'ʃiːn **-es** -z **-ing** -ɪŋ **-ed** -d
ma'chine ˌcode; ma'chine ˌtool
machine-gun mə'ʃiːnˌgʌn, -'ʃiːŋ,- ⓤⓢ -'ʃiːn,- **-s** -z **-ning** -ɪŋ **-ned** -d **-ner/s** -ər/z ⓤⓢ -ɚ/z
machine-made mə'ʃiːn.meɪd
machine-readable məˌʃiːn'riː.də.bl̩ *stress shift:* maˌchine-readable 'dictionary
machiner|y mə'ʃiː.nər.i **-ies** -ɪz
machine-washable məˌʃiːn'wɒʃ.ə.bl̩ ⓤⓢ -'wɑː.ʃə- *stress shift:* maˌchine-washable 'wool
machinist mə'ʃiː.nɪst **-s** -s
machismo mætʃ'ɪz.məʊ, mə'tʃɪz-, -'kɪz- ⓤⓢ mɑː'tʃiːz.moʊ, mə'kɪz-
macho 'mætʃ.əʊ ⓤⓢ 'mɑː.tʃoʊ **-s** -z
macho-|man 'mætʃ.əʊ|ˌmæn ⓤⓢ 'mɑː.tʃoʊ- **-men** -men
Machu Picchu ˌmɑː.tʃuː'piːk.tʃuː
Machynlleth mə'kʌn.*h*ləθ
MacIlwain 'mæk.əl.weɪn, -ɪl-
MacIlwraith 'mæk.ɪl.reɪθ
Macindoe, MacIndoe 'mæk.ɪn.dəʊ, -ən- ⓤⓢ -doʊ
MacInnes, MacInnis mə'kɪn.ɪs
macintosh 'mæk.ɪn.tɒʃ ⓤⓢ -tɑːʃ **-es** -ɪz
MacIntyre 'mæk.ɪn.taɪər, -ən- ⓤⓢ -taɪɚ
MacIver mə'kaɪ.vər, -'kɪv.ər ⓤⓢ -vɚ
MacIvor mə'kaɪ.vər ⓤⓢ -vɚ
Mack mæk
Mackay(e), MacKay(e) mə'kaɪ, mə'keɪ
Note: /mə'keɪ/ mainly in U.S.A.
Mackenzie mə'ken.zi
mackerel 'mæk.rəl, 'mæk.ər.əl **-s** -z
Mackerras mə'ker.əs
Mackeson 'mæk.ɪ.sən, '-ə-
Mackie 'mæk.i
Mackin 'mæk.ɪn
mackinaw 'mæk.ɪ.nɔː ⓤⓢ -nɑː, -nɔː **-s** -z

Mackinlay, Mackinley mə'kɪn.li
mackintosh (M) 'mæk.ɪn.tɒʃ (US) -tɑːʃ **-es** -ɪz
Mackowie, MacKowie mə'kaʊ.i
MacLachlan mə'klɒk.lən, -'klɒx-, -'klæk-, -'klæx- (US) -'klɑː.klən
MacLagan mə'klæg.^{ə}n (US) mək'lɑː.ken, -'glɑː.kən
MacLaglan mə'klæg.lən (US) -'klæg-, -'klɑːg-
Maclaren mə'klær.^{ə}n (US) -'kler-, -'klær-
MacLaverty mə'klæv.ə.ti (US) -ɚ.ţi
Maclean mə'kleɪn, -'kliːn (US) -'kliːn
Macleans® mə'kliːnz
MacLeish mə'kliːʃ
MacLeod mə'klaʊd
Maclise mə'kliːs
MacManus mək'mæn.əs, -meɪ.nəs
Macmillan mək'mɪl.ən, mæk-
Macmorran mək'mɒr.ən, mæk- (US) -'mɔːr-
MacNab mək'næb
Macnamara ˌmæk.nə'mɑː.rə (US) 'mæk.nə.mer.ə, -mær-
MacNaught mək'nɔːt (US) -nɑːt, -nɔːt
MacNeice mək.niːs
Mâcon 'mɑː.kɔ̃ːŋ, 'mæk.ɔ̃ːŋ, -ɒn, -ən (US) mɑː'koʊn
Macon 'meɪ.k^{ə}n
Maconchy mə'kɒŋ.ki (US) -'kɑːŋ-, -'kɔːŋ-
Maconochie mə'kɒn.ə.ki, -xi (US) -'kɑː.nə-
MacPhee mək'fiː
MacPherson, Macpherson mək'fɜː.s^{ə}n, mæk-, -'fɪə- (US) -'fɝː-, -'fɪr-
Macquarie mə'kwɒr.i (US) -'kwɑːr-, -'kwɔːr-
macrame, macramé mə'krɑː.meɪ, -mi (US) 'mæk.rə.meɪ
Macready mə'kriː.di
macro- 'mæk.rəʊ- (US) 'mæk.roʊ-, -rə-
macro 'mæk.rəʊ (US) -roʊ **-s** -z
macrobiotic ˌmæk.rəʊ.baɪ'ɒt.ɪk (US) -roʊ.baɪ'ɑː.ţɪk, -rə- **-s** -s
macroclimate 'mæk.rəʊˌklaɪ.mɪt, -mət (US) -roʊˌ- **-s** -s
macroclimatic ˌmæk.rəʊ.klaɪ'mæt.ɪk (US) -roʊ.klaɪ'mæţ-, -rə-
macrocosm 'mæk.rəʊˌkɒz.^{ə}m (US) -roʊˌkɑː.z^{ə}m, -rə- **-s** -z
macroeconomic ˌmæk.rəʊ.iː.kə'nɒm.ɪk, -ek.ə'- (US) -roʊˌek.ə'nɑː.mɪk, -ˌiː.kə'- **-s** -s
macron 'mæk.rɒn (US) 'meɪ.krɑːn, 'mæk.rɑːn, -rən **-s** -z
macrophag|e 'mæk.rəʊ.feɪdʒ (US) -roʊ- **-es** -ɪz
macrophagic ˌmæk.rəʊ'feɪ.dʒɪk (US) -roʊ'fædʒ.ɪk
macroscopic ˌmæk.rəʊ'skɒp.ɪk (US) -roʊ'skɑː.pɪk **-al** -^{ə}l
Macrow mə'krəʊ (US) -'kroʊ
MacSwiney mək'swiː.ni, -'swɪn-
MacTavish mək'tæv.ɪʃ
macul|a 'mæk.jʊ.l|ə, -jə- (US) -jə-, -juː- **-as** -əz **-ae** -iː
Macy® 'meɪ.si 'meɪ.siz
mad mæd **-der** -ə^{r} (US) -ɚ **-dest** -ɪst, -əst **-ly** -li **-ness** -nəs, -nɪs **as ˌmad as a 'hatter**; **ˌmad 'cow diˌsease**
Madagasc|ar ˌmæd.ə'gæs.k|ə^{r} (US) -k|ɚ **-an/s** -ən/z
madam 'mæd.əm **-s** -z
madame (M) 'mæd.əm, mə'dæm, -'dɑːm; **-s** -z
Madan 'mæd.^{ə}n, 'meɪ.d^{ə}n
madcap 'mæd.kæp **-s** -s
Maddalo 'mæd.^{ə}l.əʊ (US) -oʊ
madden (M) 'mæd.^{ə}n **-s** -z **-ing** -ɪŋ **-ed** -d
madder 'mæd.ə^{r} (US) -ɚ **-s** -z
Maddie 'mæd.i
madding 'mæd.ɪŋ
Maddison 'mæd.ɪ.s^{ə}n, '-ə-
Maddox 'mæd.əks
made *(from* **make***)* meɪd
Madeira mə'dɪə.rə (US) -'dɪr.ə **-s** -z **Ma'deira ˌcake**
Madeleine 'mæd.^{ə}l.ɪn, -eɪn
Madeley 'meɪd.li
Madeline 'mæd.^{ə}l.ɪn, -eɪn
mademoiselle (M) ˌmæd.ə.m*w*ə'zel, ˌmæm.*w*ə'-, ˌmæm'zel (US) ˌmæd.ə.mə'-, ˌmæm'- **-s** -z
made-to-measure ˌmeɪd.tə'meʒ.ə^{r} (US) -ɚ *stress shift:* ˌmade-to-measure 'suit
made-to-order ˌmeɪd.tu'ɔː.də^{r} (US) -'ɔːr.dɚ *stress-shift:* **ˌmade-to-order 'suit**
Madge mædʒ
madhou|se 'mæd.haʊ|s **-ses** -zɪz
Madhya Pradesh ˌmʌd.jə.prɑː'deʃ, ˌmɑːd- (US) -'prɑː.deʃ
Madingley 'mæd.ɪŋ.li
Madison 'mæd.ɪ.s^{ə}n, '-ə- **ˌMadison 'Avenue**
mad|man 'mæd|.mən (US) -mən, -mæn **-men** -mən, -men **-woman** -ˌwʊm.ən **-women** -ˌwɪm.ɪn
Madoc 'mæd.ək
madonna (M) mə'dɒn.ə (US) -'dɑː.nə **-s** -z
Madras *in India:* mə'drɑːs, -dræs
madras *fabric:* 'mæd.rəs (US) 'mæd.rəs, mə'dræs, -'drɑːs
madrepore ˌmæd.rɪ'pɔː^{r}, -rə'-, '--- (US) 'mæd.rə.pɔːr **-s** -z
Madrid mə'drɪd
madrigal 'mæd.rɪ.g^{ə}l, -rə- **-s** -z
madrigalist 'mæd.rɪ.g^{ə}l.ɪst, -rə- **-s** -s
Madura mə'djʊə.rə, -'dʒʊə-, -'dʊə- (US) mɑː'dʊr.ə
madwort 'mæd.wɜːt (US) -wɝːt, -wɔː
Mae meɪ
Maecenas maɪ'siː.næs, miː'-, -nəs (US) miː'-, mɪ-
maelstrom (M) 'meɪl.strɒm, -strəʊn (US) -strəm **-s** -z
maenad 'miː.næd **-s** -z
Maerdy 'mɑː.di, 'meə- (US) 'mɑːr-, 'm
Maesteg ˌmaɪ'steɪg
maestoso ˌmɑː.es'təʊ.zəʊ, maɪ'stə -səʊ (US) maɪ'stoʊ.zoʊ
maestr|o (M®) 'maɪ.str|əʊ (US) -str|o **-os** -əʊz (US) -oʊz **-i** -i
Maeterlinck 'meɪ.tə.lɪŋk (US) 'meɪ.t 'met.ɚ-
Maev(e) meɪv
Mae West ˌmeɪ'west **-s** -s
Mafeking 'mæf.ɪ.kɪŋ, '-ə-
MAFF, Maff mæf
maffick 'mæf.ɪk **-s** -s **-ing** -ɪŋ **-ed** -t -ə^{r}/z (US) -ɚ/z
mafia (M) 'mæf.i.ə, 'mɑː.fi- (US) 'mɑ
Mafikeng 'mæf.ɪ.keŋ, '-ə-
mafios|o (M) ˌmæf.i'əʊ.s|əʊ, ˌmɑː.f -z|əʊ (US) ˌmɑː.fi'oʊ.s|oʊ **-os** -əʊz (US) -oʊz **-i** -iː
mag (M) mæg **-s** -z
magalog 'mæg.ə.lɒg (US) -lɑːg **-s** -z
Magan 'meɪ.g^{ə}n, mə'gæn
magazine ˌmæg.ə'ziːn, '--- (US) 'mæg.ə.ziːn, ˌ--'- **-s** -z
Note: The stressing /'---/ is usual in north of England, but uncommo the south.
Magdala 'mæg.d^{ə}l.ə, ˌmæg'dɑː.lə (US) 'mæg.d^{ə}l.ə
Magdalen *biblical name, modern fi name, Canadian islands:* 'mæg.d^{ə}l.ɪn, -ən (US) -ən, -ɪn *Oxfo college and bridge:* 'mɔːd.lɪn (US) 'mɑːd-, 'mɔːd- *Oxford street:* 'mæg.d^{ə}l.ɪn, -ən (US) -ən, -ɪn
Magdalene *biblical name:* ˌmæg.də'liː.ni; 'mæg.d^{ə}l.iːn, -ɪr (US) 'mæg.d^{ə}l.iːn, -ən, -ɪn; ˌmæg.də'liː.nə *modern first nar* 'mæg.d^{ə}l.iːn, -ɪn (US) -iːn, -ən, -ɪn *Cambridge college and street:* 'mɔːd.lɪn (US) 'mɑːd-, 'mɔːd-
Magdalenian ˌmæg.d^{ə}l'iː.ni.ən
Magdeburg 'mæg.də.bɜːg, '-dɪ- (US) 'mæg.də.bɝːg, 'mɑːg.də.bʊ
mag|e meɪdʒ **-es** -ɪz
Magee mə'giː
Magellan mə'gel.ən (US) -'dʒel-
magenta (M) mə'dʒen.tə (US) -ţə
Maggie 'mæg.i
Maggiore ˌmædʒ'ɔː.reɪ, -ri; ˌ-i'-, mə'dʒɔː- (US) mə'dʒɔːr.i
magg|ot 'mæg|.ət **-ots** -əts **-oty** -ə (US) -ə.ţi
Maghera ˌmæk.ə'rɑː, ˌmæ.hə'-

agherafelt ˌmæk.ᵊr.əˈfelt, ˌmæ.hᵊr-
aghreb, **Maghrib** ˈmɑː.greb, ˈmʌg.reb, ˈmæg.reb, -rɪb, -rəb; məˈgreb, mɑː- (US) ˈmʌg.rəb
aghull məˈgʌl
agi *(plur. of* **Magus***)* ˈmeɪ.dʒaɪ, -gaɪ (US) -dʒaɪ
agic ˈmædʒ.ɪk **-al** -ᵊl **-ally** -ᵊl.i, -li ˌ**magic** ˈ**carpet**; ˌ**magic** ˈ**eye**; ˌ**magic** ˈ**lantern**; ˌ**magic** ˈ**mushroom**; ˌ**magic** ˈ**wand**
agician məˈdʒɪʃ.ᵊn **-s** -z
aginot ˈmæʒ.ɪ.nəʊ, ˈmædʒ-, ˈ-ə- (US) -ə.noʊ ˈ**Maginot** ˌ**Line**
agisterial ˌmædʒ.ɪˈstɪə.ri.əl, -əˈ- (US) -ɪˈstɪr.i- **-ly** -i
agistrac|y ˈmædʒ.ɪ.strə.s|i, ˈ-ə- (US) ˈ-ɪ- **-ies** -iz
agistral məˈdʒɪs.trᵊl, mædʒˈɪs-; ˈmædʒ.ɪ.strᵊl, ˈ-ə- (US) ˈmædʒ.ɪ.strᵊl
agistrate ˈmædʒ.ɪ.streɪt, ˈ-ə-, -strɪt, -strət (US) -ɪ.streɪt, -strɪt **-s** -s
agistrature ˈmædʒ.ɪ.strə.tʃəʳ, ˈ-ə-, -ˌtjʊəʳ, -ˌtʃʊəʳ (US) -ɪ.streɪ.tʃɚ, -strə.tʃʊr **-s** -z
agma ˈmæg.mə
agmatic mægˈmæt.ɪk (US) -ˈmæt̬-
agna Carta ˌmæg.nəˈkɑː.tə (US) -ˈkɑːr.t̬ə
agna cum laude ˌmæg.nɑː.kʊmˈlaʊ.deɪ
agnanimity ˌmæg.nəˈnɪm.ə.ti, -nænˈɪm-, -ɪ.ti (US) -nəˈnɪm.ə.t̬i
agnanimous mægˈnæn.ɪ.məs, məg- (US) mægˈnæn.ə- **-ly** -li
gnate ˈmæg.neɪt, -nɪt **-s** -s
gnesia *substance:* mægˈniː.zi.ə, məg-, ˈ-si.ə, -ʒi.ə, -ʒə (US) mægˈniː.ʒə, -ʃə
gnesia *city:* mægˈniː.zi.ə, -ʒi.ə, -ʒə (US) -zi.ə, -ʒi.ə, -ʒə, -ʃə
gnesium mægˈniː.zi.əm, məg-, -si-, -ʒi- (US) mægˈniː.zi-, -ʒi-, ˈ-ʒᵊm
gnet ˈmæg.nət, -nɪt **-s** -s
gnetic mægˈnet.ɪk, məg- (US) mægˈnet̬- **-al** -ᵊl **-ally** -ᵊl.i, -li **mag**ˌ**netic** ˈ**field**; **mag**ˌ**netic** ˈ**north**; **mag**ˌ**netic** ˈ**storm**; **mag**ˌ**netic** ˈ**tape**
gnetism ˈmæg.nə.tɪ.zᵊm, -nɪ- (US) -t̬ɪ-
gnetiz|e, **-is|e** ˈmæg.nə.taɪz, -nɪ- **-es** -ɪz **-ing** -ɪŋ **-ed** -d **-er/s** -əʳ/z (US) -ɚ/z
gneto mægˈniː.təʊ, məg- (US) mægˈniː.t̬oʊ **-s** -z
gnetron ˈmæg.nə.trɒn, -nɪ- (US) -trɑːn **-s** -z
gnificat mægˈnɪf.ɪ.kæt, məg-, ˈ-ə- (US) mægˈnɪf-; mɑːˈnjɪ.fɪ.kɑːt **-s** -s
gnification ˌmæg.nɪ.fɪˈkeɪ.ʃᵊn, -nə- **-s** -z
gnificence mægˈnɪf.ɪ.sᵊnts, məg-, -ə- (US) mæg-

magnificent mægˈnɪf.ɪ.sᵊnt, məg-, ˈ-ə- (US) mæg- **-ly** -li
magnifico mægˈnɪf.ɪ.kəʊ, ˈ-ə- (US) -koʊ **-(e)s** -z
magni|fy ˈmæg.nɪ|.faɪ, -nə- **-fies** -faɪz **-fying** -faɪ.ɪŋ **-fied** -faɪd **-fier/s** -faɪ.əʳ/z (US) -faɪ.ɚ/z **-fiable** -faɪ.ə.bl̩ ˈ**magnifying** ˌ**glass**
magniloquen|ce mægˈnɪl.ə.kwən|*t*s **-t** -t
magnitude ˈmæg.nɪ.tjuːd, -nə-, -tʃuːd (US) -tuːd, -tjuːd **-s** -z
magnolia mægˈnəʊ.li.ə, məg- (US) mægˈnoʊl.jə, -ˈnoʊ.li.ə **-s** -z
Magnox ˈmæg.nɒks (US) -nɑːks
magnum ˈmæg.nəm **-s** -z
magnum bonum ˌmæg.nəmˈbəʊ.nəm, -ˈbɒn.əm (US) -ˈboʊ.nəm **-s** -z
magnum opus ˌmæg.nəmˈəʊ.pəs, -ˈɒp.əs (US) -ˈoʊ.pəs
Magnus ˈmæg.nəs
Magnyficence mægˈnɪf.ɪ.sᵊn*t*s, ˈ-ə-
Magog ˈmeɪ.gɒg (US) -gɑːg, -gɔːg
magpie ˈmæg.paɪ **-s** -z
Magrath məˈgrɑː, -ˈgrɑːθ, -ˈgræθ (US) -ˈgræθ
Magritte mægˈriːt, məˈgriːt (US) mɑː-
Magruder məˈgruː.dəʳ (US) -dɚ
Maguiness məˈgɪn.ɪs, -əs
Maguire məˈgwaɪəʳ (US) -ˈgwaɪɚ
ma|gus (M) ˈmeɪ|.gəs **-gi** -dʒaɪ, -gaɪ (US) -dʒaɪ
Magwitch ˈmæg.wɪtʃ
Magyar ˈmæg.jɑːʳ (US) -jɑːr **-s** -z
Mahabharata məˌhɑːˈbɑː.rə.tə, ˌmɑː.həˈ- (US) məˌhɑːˈbɑːr.ə-, ˌmɑː-, -ˈrɑː.tɑː
Mahaffy məˈhæf.i
Mahan məˈhæn; mɑːn (US) məˈhæn
Mahany ˈmɑː.ni
maharaja(h) ˌmɑː.*h*əˈrɑː.dʒə (US) -həˈ- **-s** -z
maharani, maharanee ˌmɑː.*h*əˈrɑː.ni (US) -həˈ- **-s** -z
Maharashtra ˌmɑː.*h*əˈræʃ.trə, -ˈrɑːʃ- (US) -hɑːˈrɑːʃ-
maharishi (M) ˌmɑː.*h*əˈriː.ʃi (US) -həˈ- **-s** -z
mahatma (M) məˈhɑːt.mə, -ˈhæt- **-s** -z
Mahayana məˌhɑːˈjɑː.nə, ˌmɑː.həˈ- (US) ˌmɑː.həˈ-
Mahdi ˈmɑː.diː, -di **-s** -z
Mahé ˈmɑː.*h*eɪ (US) mɑːˈheɪ
Mahican məˈ*h*iː.kᵊn, mɑː- **-s** -z
mah-jong(g) ˌmɑːˈdʒɒŋ (US) -ˈdʒɔːŋ, -ˈdʒɑːŋ, -ˈʒɔːŋ, -ˈʒɑːŋ
Mahler ˈmɑː.ləʳ (US) -lɚ
mahlstick ˈmɔːl.stɪk (US) ˈmɑːl-, ˈmɔːl- **-s** -s
Mahmud mɑːˈmuːd
mahogany məˈhɒg.ᵊn.i (US) -ˈhɑː.gᵊn-

Mahomet, Mahomed məˈhɒm.ɪt, -et (US) məˈhɑː.mɪt
Mahometan məˈhɒm.ɪ.tᵊn, ˈ-ə- (US) -ˈhɑː.mə.t̬ən **-s** -z
Mahommed məˈhɒm.ɪd, -ed (US) -ˈhɑː.mɪd
Mahommedan məˈhɒm.ɪ.dᵊn (US) -ˈhɑː.mə- **-s** -z
Mahon mɑːn; ˈmæ.hən; məˈhuːn, -ˈhəʊn (US) mæn; məˈhoʊn, -ˈhuːn
Mahon(e)y ˈmɑː.ə.nɪ, ˈmɑː.ni, məˈhəʊ.ni (US) məˈhoʊ-
mahonia məˈhəʊ.ni.ə, mɑː- (US) məˈhoʊ- **-s** -z
mahout məˈhaʊt, mɑː-, -ˈhuːt (US) məˈhoʊt **-s** -s
Mahratta məˈræt.ə (US) -ˈrɑː.t̬ə **-s** -z
Maia ˈmaɪ.ə, ˈmeɪ-
maid meɪd **-s** -z
Maida ˈmeɪ.də
maidan (M) maɪˈdɑːn, mædˈɑːn **-s** -z
maiden ˈmeɪ.dᵊn **-s** -z **-ly** -li ˌ**maiden** ˈ**name**
maidenhair ˈmeɪ.dᵊn.heəʳ (US) -her **-s** -z
maidenhead (M) ˈmeɪ.dᵊn.hed
maidenhood ˈmeɪ.dᵊn.hʊd
Maidens ˈmeɪ.dᵊnz
maid-servant ˈmeɪdˌsɜː.vᵊnt (US) -ˌsɝː- **-s** -s
Maidstone ˈmeɪd.stᵊn, -stəʊn (US) -stoʊn, -stᵊn
maieutic meɪˈuː.tɪk, maɪ- (US) -ˈjuː.t̬ɪk
Maigret ˈmeɪ.greɪ (US) ˌ-ˈ-
mail meɪl **-s** -z **-ing** -ɪŋ **-ed** -d **-er/s** -əʳ/z (US) -ɚ/z ˈ**mail** ˌ**drop**; ˈ**mailing** ˌ**list**;
mailbag ˈmeɪl.bæg **-s** -z
mailbox ˈmeɪl.bɒks (US) -bɑːks **-es** -ɪz
Mailer ˈmeɪ.ləʳ (US) -lɚ
Mailgram® ˈmeɪl.græm
Maillard ˈmeɪ.ləd (US) -lɚd
mail|man ˈmeɪl|.mæn **-men** -men, -mən
mail-order ˌmeɪlˈɔː.dəʳ (US) ˈmeɪlˌɔːr.dɚ *stress shift, British English:* ˌmail-order ˈcatalogue
mailroom ˈmeɪl.rʊm, -ruːm (US) -ruːm, -rʊm **-s** -z
mailshot ˈmeɪl.ʃɒt (US) -ʃɑːt **-s** -s
maim meɪm **-s** -z **-ing** -ɪŋ **-ed** -d
main meɪn **-s** -z ˌ**main** ˈ**drag**; ˌ**main** ˈ**line**; ˈ**Main** ˌ**Street**
Main *German river:* maɪn, meɪn
mainbrac|e ˈmeɪn.breɪs, ˈmeɪm- (US) ˈmeɪn- **-es** -ɪz
Maine meɪn
mainframe ˈmeɪn.freɪm **-s** -z
mainland ˈmeɪn.lənd, -lænd
Mainland ˈmeɪn.lænd
mainlin|e ˈmeɪn.laɪn, ˌ-ˈ- (US) ˈ-- **-es** -z **-ing** -ɪŋ **-ed** -d **-er/s** -əʳ/z (US) -ɚ/z
mainly ˈmeɪn.li

mainmast 'meɪn.mɑːst, 'meɪm- Ⓤⓢ 'meɪn.mæst *nautical pronunciation:* -məst **-s** -s
mainsail 'meɪn.seɪl *nautical pronunciation:* -sᵊl **-s** -z
mainspring 'meɪn.sprɪŋ **-s** -z
mainstay 'meɪn.steɪ **-s** -z
mainstream 'meɪn.striːm, ,-'- Ⓤⓢ '--
mainstreaming 'meɪn,striː.mɪŋ
maintain meɪn'teɪn, mən-, men- Ⓤⓢ meɪn- **-s** -z **-ing** -ɪŋ **-ed** -d **-able** -ə.bl̩ **-er/s** -əʳ/z Ⓤⓢ -ɚ/z
maintenance 'meɪn.tᵊn.ənts, -tɪ.nənts Ⓤⓢ -tᵊn.ənts
Mainwaring *surname:* 'mæn.ᵊr.ɪŋ *in Wales:* 'meɪn.wə.rɪŋ, -weə-; ,meɪn'weə- Ⓤⓢ 'meɪn.wɚ.ɪŋ, -wer-; ,meɪn'wer-
Mainz maɪnts
Maisie 'meɪ.zi
maisonette ,meɪ.zᵊn'et, -sᵊn'- **-s** -s
Maitland 'meɪt.lənd
maître d', maitre d' ,meɪ.trə'diː, ,met.rə'- Ⓤⓢ ,meɪ.trə'-, -t̬ɚ'- **-s** -z
maître(s) d'hôtel ,meɪ.trə.dəʊ'tel, ,met.rə- Ⓤⓢ ,meɪ.trə.doʊ'-, -t̬ɚ-
maize meɪz
majestic (M) mə'dʒes.tɪk **-al** -ᵊl **-ally** -ᵊl.i, -li
majest|y (M) 'mædʒ.ə.st|i, '-ɪ- **-ies** -iz
majolica mə'jɒl.ɪ.kə, -'dʒɒl- Ⓤⓢ -'dʒɑː.lɪ-
maj|or (M) 'meɪ.dʒ|əʳ Ⓤⓢ -dʒ|ɚ **-ors** -əz Ⓤⓢ -ɚz **-oring** -ᵊr.ɪŋ **-ored** -əd Ⓤⓢ -ɚd
Majorca mə'jɔː.kə, maɪ'ɔː-, -'dʒɔː- Ⓤⓢ -'jɔːr-, -'dʒɔːr-
majordomo ,meɪ.dʒə'dəʊ.məʊ Ⓤⓢ -dʒɚ'doʊ.moʊ **-s** -z
majorette ,meɪ.dʒᵊr'et **-s** -s
major-general ,meɪ.dʒə'dʒen.ᵊr.ᵊl, '-rᵊl Ⓤⓢ -dʒɚ'- **-s** -z
majorit|y mə'dʒɒr.ə.t|i, -ɪ.t|i Ⓤⓢ -'dʒɔːr.ə.t̬|i **-ies** -iz
major-league ,meɪ.dʒə'liːg Ⓤⓢ ,meɪ.dzɚ'liːg *stress shift:* ,major-league 'player
majuscule 'mædʒ.ə.skjuːl Ⓤⓢ mə'dʒʌs.kjuːl; 'mædʒ.ə.skjuːl **-s** -z
Makarios mə'kɑː.ri.ɒs, -'kær.i- Ⓤⓢ mə'kɑːr.i.oʊs, -'kær.i-, -ɑːs, -əs
mak|e meɪk **-es** -s **-ing** -ɪŋ **made** meɪd **maker/s** 'meɪ.kəʳ/z Ⓤⓢ -kɚ/z
Makeba mə'keɪ.bə
make-believe 'meɪk.bɪ,liːv, -bə,-, ,--'-
Makeham 'meɪ.kəm
make-or-break ,meɪk.ɔː'breɪk Ⓤⓢ -ɔːr'-, -ɚ'- *stress shift:* ,make-or-break 'deal
makeover 'meɪk,əʊ.vəʳ Ⓤⓢ -,oʊ.vɚ **-s** -z
Makepeace 'meɪk.piːs
Makerere mə'ker.ᵊr.i
makeshift 'meɪk.ʃɪft
make-up 'meɪk.ʌp **-s** -s
makeweight 'meɪk.weɪt **-s** -s
makings 'meɪ.kɪŋz
Makins 'meɪ.kɪnz
Makower mə'kaʊəʳ Ⓤⓢ -'kaʊɚ
makuta *(plur. of* **likuta)** mɑː'kuː.tɑː
mal- mæl-
Note: Prefix. In verbs or adjectives, **mal-** usually carries secondary stress, e.g. **malfunction** /,mæl'fʌnk.ʃᵊn/, **maladjusted** /,mæl.ə'dʒʌs.tɪd/. Nouns containing **mal-** normally carry stress on the first syllable, e.g. **malcontent** /'mæl.kən.tent/. Exceptions exist: see individual entries.
Malabar 'mæl.ə.bɑːʳ, ,--'- Ⓤⓢ 'mæl.ə.bɑːr
Malabo mə'lɑː.bəʊ Ⓤⓢ -boʊ; 'mæl.ə-
malabsorption ,mæl.əb'zɔːp.ʃᵊn, -'sɔːp- Ⓤⓢ -'sɔːrp-, -'zɔːrp-
Malacca mə'læk.ə Ⓤⓢ -'læk-, -'lɑː.kə
Malachi 'mæl.ə.kaɪ
malachite 'mæl.ə.kaɪt
maladjusted ,mæl.ə'dʒʌs.tɪd *stress shift:* ,maladjusted 'person
maladjustment ,mæl.ə'dʒʌst.mənt **-s** -s
maladministration ,mæl.əd,mɪn.ɪ'streɪ.ʃᵊn Ⓤⓢ -ə'-
maladroit ,mæl.ə'drɔɪt, '--- **-ly** -li **-ness** -nəs, -nɪs *stress shift:* ,maladroit 'tactics
malad|y 'mæl.ə.d|i **-ies** -iz
mala fide ,meɪ.lə'faɪ.di, ,mæl.ə'fɪd.i, -eɪ Ⓤⓢ ,meɪ.lə'fiː.di, ,mæl.ə'fiː.deɪ
Malaga, Málaga 'mæl.ə.gə Ⓤⓢ 'mɑː.lɑː.gɑː, 'mæl.ə.gə
Malagasy ,mæl.ə'gæs.i, -'gɑː.zi Ⓤⓢ -'gæs.i
Malahide 'mæl.ə.haɪd
malaise mə'leɪz, mæl'eɪz
Malamud 'mæl.ə.mʊd Ⓤⓢ -məd, -mʊd
Malan *English surname:* 'mæl.ən *South African name:* mə'læn, -'lɑːn
malaprop (M) 'mæl.ə.prɒp Ⓤⓢ -prɑːp **-s** -s
malapropism 'mæl.ə.prɒp.ɪ.zᵊm Ⓤⓢ -prɑː.pɪ- **-s** -z
malapropos ,mæl,æp.rə'pəʊ, ,-'--- Ⓤⓢ ,mæl.æp.rə'poʊ
malari|a mə'leə.ri|.ə Ⓤⓢ -'ler.i- **-al** -əl **-an** -ən
malark(e)y mə'lɑː.ki Ⓤⓢ -'lɑːr-
Malawi mə'lɑː.wi Ⓤⓢ mɑː-, mə- **-an/s** -ən/z
Malay mə'leɪ Ⓤⓢ 'meɪ.leɪ, mə'leɪ **-s** -z
Malay|a mə'leɪ|.ə **-an/s** -ən/z
Malayalam ,mæl.i'ɑː.ləm, -eɪ'-; -ə'j… Ⓤⓢ ,mæl.ə'jɑː.ləm
Malaysi|a mə'leɪ.zi|.ə, -ʒi-, '-ʒ|ə Ⓤⓢ -ʒ|ə, -ʃ|ə **-an/s** -ən/z
Malchus 'mæl.kəs
Malcolm 'mæl.kəm
malcontent 'mæl.kən,tent **-s** -s
Malden 'mɔːl.dᵊn, 'mɒl- Ⓤⓢ 'mɔːl-, 'mɑːl-
Maldive 'mɔːl.diːv, 'mɒl-, -dɪv, -daɪ… Ⓤⓢ 'mæl.daɪv, 'mɑːl-, -diːv **-s** -z
Maldivian mɔːl'dɪv.i.ən, mɒl-, mɑːl… Ⓤⓢ mæl'daɪ.vi-, mɑːl-, -'diː- **-s** -z
Maldon 'mɔːl.dᵊn, 'mɒl- Ⓤⓢ 'mɔːl-, 'mɑːl-
male meɪl **-s** -z **-ness** -nəs, -nɪs ,**male 'chauvinist; ,male ,chauvinist 'pig**
Malé 'mɑː.liː, -leɪ Ⓤⓢ -liː
malediction ,mæl.ɪ'dɪk.ʃᵊn, -ə'- Ⓤⓢ … **-s** -z
maledictory ,mæl.ɪ'dɪk.tᵊr.i, -ə'- Ⓤⓢ …
malefaction ,mæl.ɪ'fæk.ʃᵊn, -ə'- Ⓤⓢ … **-s** -z
malefactor 'mæl.ɪ.fæk.təʳ, '-ə- Ⓤⓢ -ə.fæk.tɚ **-s** -z
malefic mə'lef.ɪk
maleficen|ce mə'lef.ɪ.sᵊn|ts, mæl'e… Ⓤⓢ mə'lef.ə- **-t** -t
Malet 'mæl.ɪt
malevolence mə'lev.ᵊl.ənts, mæl'e… Ⓤⓢ mə'lev-
malevolent mə'lev.ᵊl.ənt, mæl'ev- Ⓤⓢ mə'lev- **-ly** -li
malfeasance mæl'fiː.zᵊnts
Malfi 'mæl.fi
malformation ,mæl.fɔː'meɪ.ʃᵊn, -f… Ⓤⓢ -fɔːr'- **-s** -z
malformed ,mæl'fɔːmd Ⓤⓢ -'fɔːrm…
malfunction ,mæl'fʌŋk.ʃᵊn **-s** -z **-in…** -ɪŋ **-ed** -d
Malham 'mæl.əm
Mali 'mɑː.li
Malibu 'mæl.ɪ.buː, '-ə-
malic 'mæl.ɪk, 'meɪ-
malice 'mæl.ɪs
malicious mə'lɪʃ.əs **-ly** -li **-ness** -nə… -nɪs
Malick 'mæl.ɪk
malign mə'laɪn **-ly** -li **-s** -z **-ing** -ɪŋ **-e…** **-er/s** -əʳ/z Ⓤⓢ -ɚ/z
malignancy mə'lɪg.nənt.si
malignant mə'lɪg.nənt **-ly** -li
malignity mə'lɪg.nə.ti, -nɪ- Ⓤⓢ -nə…
Malik 'mæl.ɪk
Malin 'mæl.ɪn, 'meɪ.lɪn
Malines mæl'iːn
maling|er mə'lɪŋ.g|əʳ Ⓤⓢ -g|ɚ **-ers** -əz Ⓤⓢ -ɚz **-ering** -ᵊr.ɪŋ **-ered** -əd Ⓤⓢ … **-erer/s** -ᵊr.əʳ/z Ⓤⓢ -ɚ.ɚ/z
Malins 'meɪ.lɪnz, 'mæl.ɪnz
malkin 'mɔː.kɪn, 'mɔːl-, 'mɒl- Ⓤⓢ '… 'mɔːl- **-s** -z

Malkin 'mæl.kɪn
Malkovich 'mæl.kə.vɪtʃ
mall mɔːl, mæl US mɔːl, mɑːl **-s** -z
Mall *(in* **The Mall, Chiswick Mall, Pall Mall***)* mæl
mallard (M) 'mæl.ɑːd, -ləd US -ɚd **-s** -z
Mallarmé 'mæl.ɑː.meɪ US ˌmæl.ɑːr'meɪ
Malle mæl, mɑːl US mɑːl
malleability ˌmæl.i.ə'bɪl.ə.ti, ˌmæl.ə'bɪl-, -ɪ.ti US ˌmæl.i.ə'bɪl.ə.t̬i
malleable 'mæl.i.ə.bl̩, '-ə.bl̩ US '-i.ə- **-ness** -nəs, -nɪs
Mallee 'mæl.i
malleolar mə'liː.ə.ləʳ US -lɚ
malleo|lus mə'liː.ə|.ləs **-li** -laɪ
Mallet (M) 'mæl.ɪt, -ət **-s** -s
Mallett 'mæl.ɪt, -ət
malle|us 'mæl.i|.əs **-i** -aɪ
Malling 'mɔː.lɪŋ US 'mɔː-, 'mɑː-
Mallon 'mæl.ən
Mallorca mə'jɔː.kə, -'ljɔː-, -'lɔː- US mɑː'jɔːr.kɑː, mɑːl-, mə-, -kə
Mallory 'mæl.ᵊr.i
mallow (M) 'mæl.əʊ US -oʊ **-s** -z
Malmaison ˌmæl'meɪ.zɔ̃ːŋ, -zɒn, ˌ--'- US -'zɑːn, -'zɔ̃ːn **-s** -z
Malmesbury 'mɑːmz.bᵊr.i US -ber-, -bɚ-
Malmö 'mæl.məʊ, -mɜː US -moʊ
Malmsey (M) 'mɑːm.zi
malnourished ˌmæl'nʌr.ɪʃt US -'nɝː-
malnutrition ˌmæl.njuː'trɪ.ʃᵊn US -nuː'-
malodor ˌmæl'əʊ.dəʳ US -'oʊ.dɚ **-s** -z
malodorous ˌmæl'əʊ.dᵊr.əs US -'oʊ- **-ly** -li **-ness** -nəs, -nɪs
Malone mə'ləʊn US -'loʊn
Maloney mə'ləʊ.ni US -'loʊ-
Malory 'mæl.ᵊr.i
Malpas *near Truro:* 'məʊ.pəs US 'moʊ- *in Gwent:* 'mæl.pəs *in Cheshire:* 'mɔːl.pəs, 'mɔː-, 'mæl-
Note: Viscount Malpas pronounces /'mɔːl.pəs/
Malpighi mæl'piː.gi US mɑːl-, mæl-
Malpighian mæl'pɪg.i.ən, -'piː.gi- US mɑːl'pɪg.i-, mæl- **Mal**ˌ**pighian** '**layer**
Malplaquet 'mæl.plə.keɪ, ˌ--'- US ˌmæl.plæk'eɪ, -plə'keɪ
malpractic|e ˌmæl'præk.tɪs **-es** -ɪz
Malraux 'mæl.rəʊ US 'mæl.roʊ, mɑːl'roʊ
mal|t mɔːl|t, mɒl|t US mɔːl|t, mɑːl|t **-ts** -ts **-ting** -tɪŋ US -t̬ɪŋ **-ted** -tɪd US -t̬ɪd ˌ**malted** '**milk**
Malta 'mɔːl.tə, 'mɒl- US 'mɔːl.t̬ə, 'mɑːl-
Maltase 'mɔːl.teɪz, 'mɒl- US 'mɔːl.teɪs, 'mɑːl-
Maltby 'mɔːlt.bi, 'mɒlt- US 'mɔːlt-, 'mɑːlt-
Maltese ˌmɔːl'tiːz, ˌmɒl- US ˌmɔːl'tiːz, ˌmɑːl-, -'tiːs *stress shift, see compounds:* ˌ**Maltese** '**cross**; ˌ**Maltese** '**falcon**
Maltesers® mɔːl'tiː.zəz, mɒl- US mɔːl'tiː.zɚz, mɑːl-
Malthus 'mæl.θəs
Malthusian mæl'θjuː.zi.ən, mɔːl-, mɒl-, -'θuː- US mæl'θuː.ʒᵊn, -zi.ən **-s** -z **-ism** -ɪ.zᵊm
maltings 'mɔːl.tɪŋz, 'mɒl- US 'mɔːl.t̬ɪŋz, 'mɑːl-
Malton 'mɔːl.tᵊn, 'mɒl- US 'mɔːl-, 'mɑːl-
maltose 'mɔːl.təʊz, 'mɒl- US 'mɔːl.toʊz, 'mɑːl-, -toʊs
Maltravers mæl'træv.əz US -ɚz
mal|treat ˌmæl|'triːt **-treats** -'triːts **-treating** -'triː.tɪŋ US -'triː.t̬ɪŋ **-treated** -'triː.tɪd US -'triː.t̬ɪd **-treatment** -'triːt.mənt **-treater/s** -'triː.təʳ/z US -'triː.t̬ɚ/z
maltster 'mɔːlt.stəʳ, 'mɒlt- US 'mɔːlt.stɚ, 'mɑːlt- **-s** -z
Maltz mɔːlts, mɒlts US mɔːlts, mɑːlts
malum in se ˌmɑː.lʊm.ɪn'seɪ US ˌmɑː.ləm.ɪn'seɪ
malum prohibitum ˌmɑː.lʊm.prəʊ'hɪb.ɪ.tʊm US ˌmɑː.ləm.proʊ'hɪb.ɪ.təm
Malvasia ˌmæl.və'siː.ə
Malvern *in UK:* 'mɔːl.vᵊn, 'mɒl-, -vɜːn *locally also:* 'mɔː.vᵊn US 'mɔːl.vɚn *in US:* 'mæl.vən US -vɚn
malversation ˌmæl.vɜː'seɪ.ʃᵊn, -və'- US -vɚ'-
Malvinas mæl'viː.nəs
Malvolio mæl'vəʊ.li.əʊ US -'voʊ.li.oʊ, -'voʊl.joʊ
Malyon 'mæl.jən
mam mæm **-s** -z
mama mə'mɑː; 'mæm.ə US 'mɑː.mə; mə'mɑː **-s** -z
mamba 'mæm.bə US 'mɑːm- **-s** -z
mambo 'mæm.bəʊ US 'mɑːm.boʊ **-es** -z **-ing** -ɪŋ **-ed** -d
Mameluke 'mæm.ɪ.luːk, '-ə-, -ljuːk US -ə.luːk **-s** -s
Mamet 'mæm.ɪt US -ət
Mamie 'meɪ.mi
Mamilius mə'mɪl.i.əs, mæm'ɪl-
mamma *mother:* mə'mɑː US 'mɑː.mə, mə'mɑː **-s** -z
mamm|a *milk-secreting organ:* 'mæm|.ə **-ae** -iː
mammal 'mæm.ᵊl **-s** -z
mammalian mæm'eɪ.li.ən, mə'meɪ-
mammary 'mæm.ᵊr.i '**mammary** ˌ**gland**
mammogram 'mæm.ə.græm **-s** -z
mammograph 'mæm.əʊ.grɑːf, -græf US -græf, -ə-, -oʊ- **-s** -s
mammography mæm'ɒg.rə.fi, mə'mɒg- US mə'mɑː.grə-, mæm'ɑːg-
mammon (M) 'mæm.ən
mammoth 'mæm.əθ **-s** -s
mamm|y 'mæm|.i **-ies** -iz
man (M) *(n.)* mæn **men** men ˌ**man** '**Friday**; ˌ**man of the** '**world**
man *(v.)* mæn **-s** -z **-ning** -ɪŋ **-ned** -d
manacl|e 'mæn.ə.kl̩ **-es** -z **-ing** -ɪŋ, 'mæn.ə.klɪŋ **-ed** -d
manag|e 'mæn.ɪdʒ, -ədʒ **-es** -ɪz **-ing** -ɪŋ **-ed** -d ˌ**managing di**'**rector**
manageability ˌmæn.ɪ.dʒə'bɪl.ə.ti, ˌ-ə-, -ɪ.ti US -ə.t̬i
manageab|le 'mæn.ɪ.dʒə.b|l̩, '-ə- **-ly** -li **-leness** -l̩.nəs, -nɪs
management 'mæn.ɪdʒ.mənt, -ədʒ- **-s** -s
manager 'mæn.ɪ.dʒəʳ, '-ə- US -dʒɚ **-s** -z
manageress ˌmæn.ɪ.dʒᵊr'es, ˌ-ə-; 'mæn.ɪ.dʒᵊr.es, '-ə- US 'mæn- **-es** -ɪz
managerial ˌmæn.ə'dʒɪə.ri.əl US -'dʒɪr.i- **-ly** -i
Managua mə'næg.wə, mæn'æg-, -'ɑː.gwə US mə'nɑː.gwɑː, mɑː-, -gwə
Manama mə'nɑː.mə US -'næm.ə
mañana mæn'jɑː.nə, mə'njɑː- US mə'njɑː-, mɑː-
Manassas mə'næs.əs
Manasseh mə'næs.i, -ə US -ə
Manasses mə'næs.ɪz, -iːz
manatee (M) ˌmæn.ə'tiː US 'mæn.ə.ti, ˌmæn.ə'tiː **-s** -z
Manáus mə'naʊs US mə-, mɑː-
Manchester 'mæn.tʃɪs.təʳ, -tʃes-, -tʃəs- US -tʃes.tɚ, -tʃɪ.stɚ
Manchu ˌmæn'tʃuː **-s** -z *stress shift:* ˌManchu 'dynasty
Manchukuo ˌmænˌtʃuː'kwəʊ US -'kwoʊ
Manchuri|a mæn'tʃʊə.ri|.ə, -'tʃɔː- US -'tʃʊr.i- **-an/s** -ən/z
Mancini mæn'siː.ni
manciple 'mænt.sɪ.pl̩, -sə- **-s** -z
Mancunian mæŋ'kjuː.ni.ən, mæn- US mæn- **-s** -z
mandala 'mæn.dᵊl.ə, 'mʌn-; mən'dɑː.lə, mæn- US 'mʌn.də- **-s** -z
Mandalay ˌmæn.dᵊl'eɪ, '---
mandamus mæn'deɪ.məs **-es** -ɪz
mandarin (M) 'mæn.dᵊr.ɪn, ˌ--'- US 'mæn.dɚ.ɪn **-s** -z
mandate *(n.)* 'mæn.deɪt, -dɪt, -dət US -deɪt **-s** -s
manda|te *(v.)* mæn'deɪ|t, '-- US '-- **-tes** -ts **-ting** -tɪŋ US -t̬ɪŋ **-ted** -tɪd US -t̬ɪd **-tor/s** -təʳ/z US -t̬ɚ/z
mandator|y 'mæn.də.tᵊr|.i, -tr|i; mæn'deɪ- US 'mæn.də.tɔːr|.i **-ies** -iz
Mandela mæn'del.ə, -'deɪ.lə US -'del.ə
Mandelson 'mæn.dᵊl.sᵊn US -sᵊn, -soʊn

Mandelstam 'mæn.dᵊl.stæm, -stəm
Mander 'mɑːn.dəʳ, 'mæn- ⓤⓢ -dɚ
Mandeville 'mæn.də.vɪl, -dɪ-
mandible 'mæn.dɪ.bl̩, -də- **-s** -z
Mandingo mæn'dɪŋ.gəʊ ⓤⓢ -goʊ **-(e)s** -z
mandolin ˌmæn.dᵊl'ɪn, '--- **-s** -z
mandoline ˌmæn.dᵊl'iːn **-s** -z
mandragora mæn'dræg.ᵊr.ə, mən- ⓤⓢ mæn-
mandrake 'mæn.dreɪk **-s** -s
mandrax (M®) 'mæn.dræks **-es** -ɪz
mandrill 'mæn.drɪl, -drᵊl ⓤⓢ -drɪl **-s** -z
Mandy 'mæn.di
mane meɪn **-s** -z **-d** -d
man-eater 'mænˌiː.təʳ ⓤⓢ -t̬ɚ **-s** -z
manège, manege mæn'eɪʒ, -'eʒ, '-- ⓤⓢ mæn'eʒ, mə'neʒ, -'neɪʒ **-s** -ɪz
manes (M) 'mɑː.neɪz, -neɪs, 'meɪ.niːz ⓤⓢ 'meɪ.niːz, 'mɑː.neɪs
Manet 'mæn.eɪ ⓤⓢ mæn'eɪ, mə'neɪ
Manette mæn'et
maneuv|er mə'nuː.v|əʳ ⓤⓢ -v|ɚ **-ers** -əz ⓤⓢ -ɚz **-ering/s** -ᵊr.ɪŋ/z **-ered** -əd ⓤⓢ -ɚd **-erer/s** -ᵊr.əʳ/z ⓤⓢ -ɚ.ɚ/z
maneuverability məˌnuː.vᵊr.ə'bɪl.ə.ti, -ɪ.ti ⓤⓢ -ə.t̬i
maneuverable mə'nuː.vᵊr.ə.bl̩
Manfred 'mæn.fred, -frɪd
manful 'mæn.fᵊl, -fʊl **-ly** -i **-ness** -nəs, -nɪs
Mangan 'mæŋ.gən
manganate 'mæŋ.gə.neɪt **-s** -s
manganese 'mæŋ.gə.niːz, ˌ--'- ⓤⓢ '---, -niːs
manganic mæŋ'gæn.ɪk, mæn- ⓤⓢ mæn-
mange meɪndʒ
mangel-wurzel 'mæŋ.gᵊlˌwɜː.zᵊl, ˌmæŋ.gᵊl'wɜː- ⓤⓢ 'mæŋ.gᵊlˌwɝː-, -ˌwɝː.t.sᵊl **-s** -z
manger 'meɪn.dʒəʳ ⓤⓢ -dʒɚ **-s** -z
mangetout ˌmɑ̃ːnʒ'tuː ⓤⓢ ˌmɑ̃ːndʒ- **-s** -z
mangl|e 'mæŋ.gl̩ **-es** -z **-ing** -ɪŋ, 'mæŋ.glɪŋ **-ed** -d **-er/s** -əʳ/z ⓤⓢ -ɚ/z
mango 'mæŋ.gəʊ ⓤⓢ -goʊ **-(e)s** -z
mangold (M) 'mæŋ.gəʊld ⓤⓢ -goʊld **-s** -z
mangosteen 'mæŋ.gəʊ.stiːn ⓤⓢ -gə- **-s** -z
Mangotsfield 'mæŋ.gəts.fiːld
mangrove 'mæŋ.grəʊv ⓤⓢ 'mæn.groʊv, 'mæŋ- **-s** -z
mang|y 'meɪn.dʒ|i **-ier** -i.əʳ ⓤⓢ -i.ɚ **-iest** -i.ɪst, -i.əst **-ily** -ɪ.li, -ᵊl.i **-iness** -ɪ.nəs, -ɪ.nɪs
manhandl|e 'mænˌhæn.dl̩, ˌ-'-- ⓤⓢ '--- **-es** -z **-ing** -ɪŋ, -ˌhænd.lɪŋ **-ed** -d
manhattan (M) mæn'hæt.ᵊn ⓤⓢ mæn-, mən-
manhole 'mæn.həʊl ⓤⓢ -hoʊl **-s** -z
manhood (M) 'mæn.hʊd
manhour 'mæn.aʊəʳ ⓤⓢ -aʊr, -aʊɚ **-s** -z
manhunt 'mæn.hʌnt **-s** -s
mania 'meɪ.ni.ə ⓤⓢ -ni.ə, '-njə **-s** -z
maniac 'meɪ.ni.æk **-s** -s
maniac|al mə'naɪə.k|ᵊl **-ally** -ᵊl.i ⓤⓢ -li
manic 'mæn.ɪk **-s** -s ˌ**manic de'pression**
manic-depressive ˌmæn.ɪk.dɪ'pres.ɪv, -də'- **-s** -z
Manich(a)ean ˌmæn.ɪ'kiː.ən, -ə'- **-s** -z
manicur|e 'mæn.ɪ.kjʊəʳ, '-ə-, -kjɔːʳ ⓤⓢ -kjʊr **-es** -z **-ing** -ɪŋ **-ed** -d **-ist/s** -ɪst/s
manifest 'mæn.ɪ.fest, '-ə- **-ly** -li **-s** -s **-ing** -ɪŋ **-ed** -ɪd **-ness** -nəs, -nɪs
manifestation ˌmæn.ɪ.fes'teɪ.ʃᵊn, ˌ-ə-, -fə'steɪ- **-s** -z
manifesto ˌmæn.ɪ'fes.təʊ, -ə'- ⓤⓢ -toʊ **-(e)s** -z
manifold 'mæn.ɪ.fəʊld, '-ə- ⓤⓢ -foʊld **-ness** -nəs, -nɪs
manikin 'mæn.ɪ.kɪn, '-ə- **-s** -z
manila (M) mə'nɪl.ə **-s** -z
manilla mə'nɪl.ə **-s** -z
Manilow 'mæn.ɪ.ləʊ, '-ə- ⓤⓢ -loʊ
manioc 'mæn.i.ɒk ⓤⓢ -ɑːk
maniple 'mæn.ɪ.pl̩, '-ə- **-s** -z
manipu|late mə'nɪp.jə|.leɪt, -jʊ- ⓤⓢ -jə-, -juː- **-lates** -leɪts **-lating** -leɪ.tɪŋ ⓤⓢ -leɪ.t̬ɪŋ **-lated** -leɪ.tɪd ⓤⓢ -leɪ.t̬ɪd **-lator/s** -leɪ.təʳ/z ⓤⓢ -leɪ.t̬ɚ/z
manipulation məˌnɪp.jə'leɪ.ʃᵊn, -jʊ'- ⓤⓢ -jə'-, -juː'- **-s** -z
manipulative mə'nɪp.jə.lə.tɪv, -jʊ- ⓤⓢ -jə.leɪ.t̬ɪv, -juː-, -lə- **-ly** -li **-ness** -nəs, -nɪs
Manitoba ˌmæn.ɪ'təʊ.bə, -ə'- ⓤⓢ -ə'toʊ-
manit(o)u 'mæn.ɪ.tuː ⓤⓢ '-ə- **-s** -z
mankind *general use:* mæn'kaɪnd, mæŋ- ⓤⓢ mæn-
mank|y 'mæŋ.k|i **-ier** -i.əʳ ⓤⓢ -i.ɚ **-iest** -i.ɪst, -i.əst
Manley 'mæn.li
manlike 'mæn.laɪk
Manlius 'mæn.li.əs
manl|y (M) 'mæn.l|i **-ier** -i.əʳ ⓤⓢ -i.ɚ **-iest** -i.ɪst, -i.əst **-iness** -ɪ.nəs, -ɪ.nɪs
man-made ˌmæn'meɪd, ˌmæm- ⓤⓢ ˌmæn- *stress shift:* ˌman-made 'fibre
Mann mæn
manna 'mæn.ə
mannequin 'mæn.ɪ.kɪn, '-ə- **-s** -z
manner 'mæn.əʳ ⓤⓢ -ɚ **-s** -z **-ed** -d
mannerism (M) 'mæn.ᵊr.ɪ.zᵊm **-s** -z
mannerist (M) 'mæn.ᵊr.ɪst
mannerl|y 'mæn.ᵊl|.i ⓤⓢ -ɚ.l|i **-iness** -ɪ.nəs, -ɪ.nɪs
Manners 'mæn.əz ⓤⓢ -ɚz
Mannesmann 'mæn.ə.smæn, -smən
Mannheim 'mæn.haɪm
mannikin 'mæn.ɪ.kɪn, '-ə- **-s** -z
Manning 'mæn.ɪŋ
mannish 'mæn.ɪʃ **-ly** -li **-ness** -nəs, -nɪ
Manns mænz
Manny 'mæn.i
Mannyng of Brunne ˌmæn.ɪŋ.əv'brʊ
manoeuvrability məˌnuː.vᵊr.ə'bɪl.ə.-ɪ.ti ⓤⓢ -ə.t̬i
manoeuvrable mə'nuː.vᵊr.ə.bl̩
manoeuv|re mə'nuː.v|əʳ ⓤⓢ -v|ɚ **-res** -əz ⓤⓢ -ɚz **-ring/s** -ᵊr.ɪŋ/z **-red** -əd ⓤⓢ -ɚd **-rer/s** -ᵊr.əʳ/z ⓤⓢ -ɚ.ɚ/z
man-of-war ˌmæn.əv'wɔːʳ ⓤⓢ -'wɔːr **men-of-war** ˌmen-
manometer mə'nɒm.ɪ.təʳ, mæn'ɒm- '-ə- ⓤⓢ mə'nɑː.mə.t̬ɚ **-s** -z
manometric ˌmæn.əʊ'met.rɪk ⓤⓢ -ə **-al** -ᵊl **-ally** -ᵊl.i, -li
manor 'mæn.əʳ ⓤⓢ -ɚ **-s** -z
manor-hou|se 'mæn.ə.haʊ|s ⓤⓢ '-ɚ- **-ses** -zɪz
manorial mə'nɔː.ri.əl, mæn'ɔː- ⓤⓢ mə'nɔːr.i-
manpower 'mænˌpaʊəʳ, 'mæm- ⓤⓢ 'mænˌpaʊɚ
manqué 'mɑ̃ːŋ.keɪ ⓤⓢ mɑ̃ːŋ'keɪ
Manresa mæn'reɪ.sə, -zə ⓤⓢ mɑːn'reɪ.sə, mæn-
Mansa 'mænt.sə
mansard 'mænt.sɑːd ⓤⓢ -sɑːrd **-s** -z
mans|e mænts **-es** -ɪz
Mansel(l) 'mænt.sᵊl
Mansergh *surname:* 'mæn.zəʳ, 'mænt.səʳ, -sɜːdʒ ⓤⓢ 'mæn.zɚ, 'mænt.sɚ, -sɝːdʒ *place in Cumb.* 'mæn.zəʳ ⓤⓢ -zɚ
manservant 'mænˌsɜː.vᵊnt ⓤⓢ -ˌsɝː **menservants** 'menˌsɜː.vᵊnts ⓤⓢ -ˌsɝː-
Mansfield 'mænts.fiːld ⓤⓢ 'mænz-
-manship -mən.ʃɪp
mansion (M) 'mæn.tʃᵊn **-s** -z
mansion-hou|se (M) 'mæn.tʃᵊn.ha **-ses** -zɪz
manslaughter 'mænˌslɔː.təʳ ⓤⓢ -ˌslɑː.t̬ɚ, -ˌslɔː-
Manson 'mænt.sᵊn
Manston 'mænt.stᵊn
mansuetude 'mæn.swɪ.tjuːd ⓤⓢ -t -tjuːd
Manta 'mæn.tə
Mantegna mæn'ten.jə ⓤⓢ mɑːn'ten.jɑː, -jə
mantel 'mæn.tᵊl **-s** -z
mantelpiec|e 'mæn.tᵊl.piːs **-es** -ɪz
mantelshel|f 'mæn.tᵊl.ʃel|f **-ves** -v
-mantic -'mæn.tɪk
mantilla mæn'tɪl.ə ⓤⓢ -'tɪl-, -'tiː.jə
mantis 'mæn.tɪs ⓤⓢ -t̬ɪs **-es** -ɪz
mantissa mæn'tɪs.ə **-s** -z
mantl|e 'mæn.tl̩ **-es** -z **-ing** -ɪŋ, 'mænt.lɪŋ **-ed** -d
Mantovani ˌmæn.tə'vɑː.ni ⓤⓢ ˌmɑ

mantra ˈmæn.trə, ˈmʌn- (US) ˈmæn-, ˈmɑːn-, ˈmʌn- **-s** -z
mantrap ˈmæn.træp **-s** -s
Mantu|a (M) ˈmæn.tju|.ə, -tu-, -tʃu- (US) -tʃu.w|ə, -tu- **-an/s** -ən z
manual ˈmæn.ju.əl **-s** -z **-ly** -i
Manuel *surname:* ˈmæn.ju.el, -əl
Manuel *first name:* mænˈwel; ˌmæn.uˈel, -juˈ- (US) mænˈwel, mɑːn-
manufact|ure ˌmæn.jəˈfæk.tʃ|əʳ, -jʊˈ-, -əˈ- (US) -jəˈfæk.tʃ|ɚ, -juːˈ- **-ures** -əz (US) -ɚz **-uring** -ᵊr.ɪŋ **-ured** -əd (US) -ɚd **-urer/s** -ᵊr.əʳ/z (US) -ɚ.ɚ/z
manumission ˌmæn.jəˈmɪʃ.ᵊn, -jʊˈ- (US) -jəˈ-, -juː- **-s** -z
manu|mit ˌmæn.jə|ˈmɪt, -jʊˈ- (US) -jəˈ-, -juːˈ- **-mits** -ˈmɪts **-mitting** -ˈmɪt.ɪŋ (US) -ˈmɪt̬.ɪŋ **-mitted** -ˈmɪt.ɪd (US) -ˈmɪt̬.ɪd
manur|e məˈnjʊəʳ, -njɔːʳ (US) -ˈnʊr, -ˈnjʊr **-es** -z **-ing** -ɪŋ **-ed** -d
manuscript ˈmæn.jə.skrɪpt, -jʊ- **-s** -s
Manutius məˈnjuː.ʃi.əs, ˈ-ʃəs (US) -ˈnuː.ʃi.əs, -ˈnjuː-
Manwaring ˈmæn.ᵊr.ɪŋ
Manx mæŋks ˌ**Manx** ˈ**cat**
Manx|man ˈmæŋks|.mæn, -mən **-men** -men, -mən **-woman** -ˌwʊm.ən **-women** -ˌwɪm.ɪn
many ˈmen.i
manyfold ˈmen.i.fəʊld (US) -foʊld
many-sided ˌmen.iˈsaɪ.dɪd **-ness** -nəs, -nɪs *stress shift:* ˌmany-sided ˈshape
manzanilla (M) ˌmæn.zəˈnɪl.ə, -jə (US) -ˈniːl.jə, -ˈniː-, -ˈnɪl.ə
Manzoni mænˈzəʊ.ni (US) mɑːnˈzoʊ-
Mao maʊ
Mao|ism ˈmaʊ|.ɪ.zᵊm **-ist/s** -ɪst/s
Maori ˈmaʊə.ri (US) ˈmaʊ.ri; ˈmɑː.oʊ.ri **-s** -z
Mao Tse-tung ˌmaʊ.tseɪˈtʊŋ, ˌmaʊ.dzeɪˈdʊŋ (US) -tsəˈdʊŋ
Mao Zedong ˌmaʊ.dʒeɪˈdʊŋ, ˌmaʊ.tseɪˈtʊŋ (US) -dʒəˈ-, -ˈdɑːŋ
map mæp **-s** -s **-ping** -ɪŋ **-ped** -t
maple (M) ˈmeɪ.pl̩ **-s** -z ˈ**Maple** ˌ**Leaf**; ˌ**maple** ˈ**syrup**
Maplin Sands ˌmæp.lɪnˈsændz, -lənˈ-
mapmak|er/s ˈmæp.meɪ.k|əʳ/z, -k|ɚ/z **-ing** -ɪŋ
Mappin ˈmæp.ɪn
Mapplethorpe ˈmæp.l̩.θɔːp (US) ˈmeɪ.pl̩.θɔːrp
Maputo məˈpuː.təʊ (US) -toʊ
maquillage ˌmæk.iːˈɑːʒ, -ˈjɑːʒ (US) ˌmɑː.kiˈɑːʒ
maquis mækˈiː, ˈ-- (US) mɑːˈkiː, mækˈiː
mar (M) mɑːʳ (US) mɑːr **-s** -z **-ring** -ɪŋ **-red** -d
Mar. *(abbrev. for* **March***)* mɑːtʃ (US) mɑːrtʃ

marabou ˈmær.ə.buː (US) ˈmer-, ˈmær- **-s** -z
maraca məˈræk.ə (US) -ˈrɑː.kə **-s** -z
Maracaibo ˌmær.əˈkaɪ.bəʊ (US) ˌmer.əˈkaɪ.boʊ, ˌmær-
Maradona ˌmær.əˈdɒn.ə (US) ˌmer.əˈdɑː.nə, ˌmær-
maraschino (M) ˌmær.əˈʃiː.nəʊ, -ˈskiː- (US) ˌmer.əˈʃiː.noʊ, ˌmær-, -ˈskiː- **-s** -z ˌ**mara**ˌ**schino** ˈ**cherry**
Marat ˈmær.ɑː (US) mɑːˈrɑː, mə-
Marathi məˈrɑː.ti **-s** -z
marathon (M) ˈmær.ə.θᵊn (US) ˈmer.ə.θɑːn, ˈmær- **-s** -z
maraud məˈrɔːd (US) -ˈrɑːd, -ˈrɔːd **-s** -z **-ing** -ɪŋ **-ed** -ɪd **-er/s** -əʳ/z (US) -ɚ/z
Marazion ˌmær.əˈzaɪən (US) ˌmer-, ˌmær-
Marbella mɑːˈbeɪ.ə, -jə (US) mɑːr-
marbl|e ˈmɑː.bl̩ (US) ˈmɑːr- **-es** -z **-ing** -ɪŋ, ˈmɑː.blɪŋ (US) ˈmɑːr- **-ed** -d
Marburg ˈmɑː.bʊəg, -bɜːg (US) ˈmɑːr.bɝːg, -bʊrg
Marc mɑːk (US) mɑːrk
marcasite ˈmɑː.kə.saɪt (US) ˈmɑːr-
Marceau ˌmɑːˈsəʊ, ˈ-- (US) mɑːrˈsoʊ
Marcel mɑːˈsel (US) mɑːr-
Marcella mɑːˈsel.ə (US) mɑːr-
Marcelle mɑːˈsel (US) mɑːr-
Marcellus mɑːˈsel.əs (US) mɑːr-
march (M) mɑːtʃ (US) mɑːrtʃ **-es** -ɪz **-ing** -ɪŋ **-ed** -t **-er/s** -əʳ/z (US) -ɚ/z
Marchant ˈmɑː.tʃᵊnt (US) ˈmɑːr-
Marchbank ˈmɑːtʃ.bæŋk (US) ˈmɑːrtʃ- **-s** -s
marchioness ˌmɑː.ʃᵊnˈes, -ˈɪs; ˈmɑː.ʃᵊn.əs (US) ˈmɑːr.ʃᵊn.ɪs; ˌmɑːr.ʃᵊnˈes **-es** -ɪz
Marchmain ˈmɑːtʃ.meɪn (US) ˈmɑːrtʃ-
Marchmont ˈmɑːtʃ.mənt (US) ˈmɑːrtʃ-
Marcia ˈmɑː.si.ə, ˈ-ʃə (US) ˈmɑːr.ʃə
Marciano ˌmɑː.siˈɑː.nəʊ, -ʃiˈ- (US) ˌmɑːr.siˈæn.oʊ, -ʃiˈ-, -ˈɑː.noʊ
Marco ˈmɑː.kəʊ (US) ˈmɑːr.koʊ
Marconi mɑːˈkəʊ.ni (US) mɑːrˈkoʊ-
marconigram mɑːˈkəʊ.ni.græm (US) mɑːrˈkoʊ- **-s** -z
Marcos ˈmɑː.kɒs (US) ˈmɑːr.koʊs
Marcus ˈmɑː.kəs (US) ˈmɑːr-
Marcuse mɑːˈkuː.zə; mɑːˈkjuːz (US) mɑːrˈkuː.zə
Mar del Plata ˌmɑː.delˈplɑː.tə (US) ˌmɑːr.delˈplɑː.tə
Marden *in Kent:* ˈmɑː.dᵊn; mɑːˈden (US) ˈmɑːr.dᵊn; mɑːrˈden *other places:* ˈmɑː.dᵊn (US) ˈmɑːr-
Mardi Gras ˌmɑː.diˈgrɑː (US) ˈmɑːr.diˌgrɑː, ˌ--ˈ-
Marduk ˈmɑː.dʊk (US) ˈmɑːr-
mare *female horse:* meəʳ (US) mer **-s** -z
mare *lunar plain:* ˈmɑː.reɪ (US) ˈmɑːr.eɪ **maria** ˈmɑː.ri.ə (US) ˈmɑːr.i-

Marengo məˈreŋ.gəʊ (US) -goʊ
mare's-nest ˈmeəz.nest, ˌ-ˈ- (US) ˈmerz.nest **-s** -s
mare's-tail ˈmeəz.teɪl, ˌ-ˈ- (US) ˈmerz- **-s** -z
Margaret ˈmɑː.gᵊr.ət, -ɪt, ˈ-grət, -grɪt (US) ˈmɑːr.grət
margarine ˌmɑː.dʒəˈriːn, -gəˈ-, ˈ--- (US) ˈmɑːr.dʒɚ.ɪn
margarita (M) ˌmɑː.gᵊrˈiː.tə (US) -gəˈriː.t̬ə **-s** -z
Margate ˈmɑː.geɪt, -gɪt (US) ˈmɑːr-
marge mɑːdʒ (US) mɑːrdʒ
Margerison mɑːˈdʒer.ɪ.sᵊn, ˈ-ə-; ˈmɑː.dʒᵊr- (US) mɑːrˈdʒer-; ˈmɑːr.dʒə.rɪ-, -rə-
Margery ˈmɑː.dʒᵊr.i (US) ˈmɑːr-
Margetts ˈmɑː.gɪts (US) ˈmɑːr-
margin ˈmɑː.dʒɪn (US) ˈmɑːr- **-s** -z
marginal ˈmɑː.dʒɪ.nᵊl, -dʒᵊn.ᵊl (US) ˈmɑːr- **-s** -z **-ly** -i
marginalia ˌmɑː.dʒɪˈneɪ.li.ə, -dʒəˈ- (US) ˌmɑːr-, -ˈneɪl.jə
marginalization, -isa- ˌmɑː.dʒɪ.nᵊl.aɪˈzeɪ.ʃᵊn, -dʒᵊn.ᵊl-, -ɪˈ- (US) ˌmɑːr.dʒɪ.nᵊl.ɪˈ-, -dʒᵊn.ᵊl-
marginaliz|e, -is|e ˈmɑː.dʒɪ.nᵊl.aɪz, -dʒᵊn.ᵊl- (US) ˈmɑːr- **-es** -ɪz **-ing** -ɪŋ **-ed** -d
Margolis mɑːˈgəʊ.lɪs (US) mɑːrˈgoʊ-
Margot ˈmɑː.gəʊ (US) ˈmɑːr.goʊ
margrave (M) ˈmɑː.greɪv (US) ˈmɑːr- **-s** -z
margravine ˈmɑː.grə.viːn (US) ˈmɑːr- **-s** -z
marguerite (M) ˌmɑː.gᵊrˈiːt (US) ˌmɑːr.gəˈriːt **-s** -s
Margulies ˈmɑː.gʊ.lɪs (US) ˈmɑːrˈguː.lɪz
Marham *in Norfolk:* ˈmær.əm, ˈmɑː.rəm (US) ˈmær.əm, ˈmɑːr-
Note: The pronunciation of the local residents is /ˈmær.əm/.
Marhamchurch ˈmær.əm.tʃɜːtʃ (US) -tʃɝːtʃ
Maria *first name:* məˈriː.ə, məˈraɪ.ə
maria *(plur. of* **mare***)* ˈmɑː.ri.ə (US) ˈmɑːr.i-
Marian *first name:* ˈmær.i.ən (US) ˈmer-, ˈmær-
Marian *(n. adj.) of Mary, or person devoted to Mary:* ˈmeə.ri.ən (US) ˈmer.i-, ˈmær-
Mariana *English name:* ˌmær.iˈæn.ə, ˌmeə.riˈ-, -ˈɑː.nə (US) ˌmer.iˈæn.ə, ˌmær- *Spanish historian:* ˌmɑː.riˈɑː.nə (US) ˌmɑːr.iˈɑː-
Marianne ˌmær.iˈæn (US) ˌmer.iˈæn, ˌmær-
Maribor ˈmær.i.bɔːʳ (US) ˈmɑːr.i.bɔːr
Marie məˈriː, ˈmɑː.ri, ˈmær.i (US) məˈriː
Marie Antoinette ˌmær.iˌæn.twəˈnet, -ˌɑ̃ːn- (US) məˌriː.æn-

Marienbad 'mær.i.ən.bæd, -əm-; mə'riː- (US) 'mer.i.ən-, 'mær-

marigold (M) 'mær.ɪ.gəʊld (US) 'mer.ɪ.goʊld, 'mær- **-s** -z

marijuana, marihuana ˌmær.ɪ'wɑː.nə, -ə'- (US) ˌmer.ɪ'-, ˌmær-

Marilla mə'rɪl.ə

Marilyn 'mær.ɪ.lɪn, '-ə- (US) 'mer-, 'mær-

marimba mə'rɪm.bə **-s** -z

marina (M) mə'riː.nə **-s** -z

marinad|e ˌmær.ɪ'neɪd, '--- (US) ˌmer.ɪ'neɪd, ˌmær-, '--- **-es** -z **-ing** -ɪŋ **-ed** -ɪd

marinara ˌmær.ɪ'nɑː.rə, -ə'- (US) ˌmer.ɪ'ner.ə, -nær.ə, -nɑː.rə

marinat|e 'mær.ɪ.neɪt, '-ə- (US) 'mer-, 'mær- **-es** -s **-ing** -ɪŋ **-ed** -ɪd

marination ˌmær.ɪ'neɪ.ʃᵊn, -ə'- (US) ˌmer-, ˌmær-

marine mə'riːn **-s** -z

mariner 'mær.ɪ.nəʳ, '-ə- (US) 'mer.ɪ.nɚ, 'mær-, '-ə- **-s** -z

Marino Faliero məˌriː.nəʊ.fə'lɪə.rəʊ (US) -noʊ.fə'lɪr.oʊ

Mario 'mær.i.əʊ, 'mɑː.ri- (US) 'mɑːr.i.oʊ, 'mer-, 'mær-

Marion 'mær.i.ən, 'meə.ri- (US) 'mer.i-, 'mær-

marionette ˌmær.i.ə'net (US) ˌmer-, ˌmær- **-s** -s

Marisa mə'rɪs.ə

Marischal 'mɑː.ʃᵊl (US) 'mɑːr.ɪ.ʃɑːl, '-ʃɑːl, '-ʃəl

Marissa mə'rɪs.ə

marital 'mær.ɪ.tᵊl, '-ə- (US) 'mer.ɪ.t̬ᵊl, 'mær- **-ly** -i

maritime (M) 'mær.ɪ.taɪm, '-ə- (US) 'mer-, 'mær-

Marius 'mær.i.əs, 'meə.ri-, 'mɑː- (US) 'mer.i-, 'mær-

Marivaux 'mær.i.vəʊ, --'-

marjoram 'mɑː.dʒᵊr.əm (US) 'mɑːr.dʒɚ.əm

Marjoribanks 'mɑːtʃ.bæŋks (US) 'mɑːrtʃ-

Marjorie, Marjory 'mɑː.dʒᵊr.i (US) 'mɑːr-

mark (M) mɑːk (US) mɑːrk **-s** -s **-ing/s** -ɪŋ/z **-ed** -t **-edly** -ɪd.li **-er/s** -əʳ/z (US) -ɚ/z ˌ**Mark 'Antony**

Markby 'mɑːk.bi (US) 'mɑːrk-

markdown 'mɑːk.daʊn (US) 'mɑːrk-

mar|ket (M) 'mɑː|.kɪt (US) 'mɑːr- **-kets** -kɪts **-keting** -kɪ.tɪŋ (US) -kɪ.t̬ɪŋ **-keted** -kɪ.tɪd **-keter/s** -kɪ.təʳ/z (US) -kɪ.t̬ɚ/z **-keted** (US) -kɪ.t̬ɪd **-ketable** -kɪ.tə.bl̩ (US) -kɪ.t̬ə.bl̩ ˌ**market e'conomy;** ˌ**market 'gardening;** ˌ**market re'search;** (US) **'market ˌresearch,** **'market reˌsearch; 'market ˌtown,** ˌ**market 'town**

marketability ˌmɑː.kɪ.tə'bɪl.ə.ti, -ɪ.ti (US) ˌmɑːr.kɪ.t̬ə'bɪl.ə.t̬i

Market Deeping ˌmɑː.kɪt'diː.pɪŋ (US) ˌmɑːr-

marketeer ˌmɑː.kɪ'tɪəʳ, -kə'- (US) ˌmɑːr.kə'tɪr **-s** -z

market-plac|e 'mɑː.kɪt.pleɪs (US) 'mɑːr- **-es** -ɪz

Market Rasen ˌmɑː.kɪt'reɪ.zᵊn (US) ˌmɑːr-

Markham 'mɑː.kəm (US) 'mɑːr-

markk|a 'mɑː.k|ɑː, -k|ə (US) 'mɑːr- **-aa** -ɑː

Markov 'mɑː.kɒf, -kɒv (US) 'mɑːr.kɔːf

Markova mɑː'kəʊ.və (US) mɑːr'koʊ-

Marks mɑːks (US) mɑːrks

Marks and Spencer® ˌmɑːks.ᵊnd'spent.səʳ (US) ˌmɑːrks.ᵊnd'spent.sɚ

marks|man 'mɑːks|.mən (US) 'mɑːrks- **-men** -mən, -men **-woman** -ˌwʊm.ən **-women** -ˌwɪm.ɪn

marksmanship 'mɑːks.mən.ʃɪp (US) 'mɑːrks-

markup 'mɑːk.ʌp (US) 'mɑːrk- **-s** -s

marl mɑːl (US) mɑːrl

Marlboro® 'mɑːl.bᵊr.ə, 'mɔːl- (US) 'mɑːrl-

Marlborough *town in Wiltshire, family name:* 'mɔːl.bᵊr.ə (US) 'mɑːrl.bə.roʊ *London streets, town in US, New Zealand district:* 'mɑːl.bᵊr.ə (US) 'mɑːrl.bɚ-

Marlene *English name:* 'mɑː.liːn, -'- (US) mɑːr'- *German name:* mɑː'leɪ.nə (US) mɑːr-

Marler 'mɑː.ləʳ (US) 'mɑːr.lɚ

Marley 'mɑː.li (US) 'mɑːr-

marlin 'mɑː.lɪn (US) 'mɑːr- **-s** -z

Marling 'mɑː.lɪŋ (US) 'mɑːr-

Marlovian mɑː'ləʊ.vi.ən (US) mɑːr'loʊ-

Marlow(e) 'mɑː.ləʊ (US) 'mɑːr.loʊ

Marmaduke 'mɑː.mə.djuːk (US) 'mɑːr.mə.duːk, -djuːk

marmalade 'mɑː.mᵊl.eɪd (US) 'mɑːr- **-s** -z

Marmion 'mɑː.mi.ən (US) 'mɑːr-

marmite (M®) 'mɑː.maɪt (US) 'mɑːr-

Marmora 'mɑː.mᵊr.ə (US) 'mɑːr-

marmoreal mɑː'mɔː.ri.əl (US) mɑːr'mɔːr.i- **-ly** -i

marmoset 'mɑː.mə.set, -zet, ˌ--'- (US) 'mɑːr.mə- **-s** -s

marmot 'mɑː.mət (US) 'mɑːr- **-s** -s

Marne mɑːn (US) mɑːrn

Marner 'mɑː.nəʳ (US) 'mɑːr.nɚ

marocain 'mær.ə.keɪn, ˌ--'- (US) 'mer-, 'mær-

maroon mə'ruːn **-s** -z **-ing** -ɪŋ **-ed** -d

Marple 'mɑː.pl̩ (US) 'mɑːr-

Marprelate 'mɑː.prel.ət, -ɪt (US) 'mɑːr-

Marquand 'mɑː.kwənd (US) 'mɑːr-

marque mɑːk (US) mɑːrk **-s** -s

marquee mɑː'kiː (US) mɑːr- **-s** -z

Marquesas mɑː'keɪ.səs, -zəs, -sæs, -zæs (US) mɑːr'keɪ.zəs, -səs

marquess 'mɑː.kwɪs, -kwəs (US) 'mɑːr- **-es** -ɪz

marquetr|y 'mɑː.kɪ.tr|i, -kə- (US) 'mɑːr- **-ies** -iz

marquis (M) 'mɑː.kwɪs, -kwəs; mɑː'kiː (US) 'mɑːr.kwɪs, -kwəs; mɑːr'kiː **marquises** 'mɑː.kwɪ.sɪz, -kwə- (US) 'mɑːr.kwɪ- *(alternative plur. of* **marquis***)* mɑː'kiːz (US) mɑːr-

marquis|e mɑː'kiːz (US) mɑːr- **-es** -ɪz

Marr mɑːʳ (US) mɑːr

Marrakesh, Marrakech ˌmær.ə'keʃ, mə'ræk.eʃ (US) 'mer.ə.keʃ, 'mær-; ˌmə'rɑː.keʃ

marram grass 'mær.əm.grɑːs (US) 'mer.əm.græs, 'mær-

marriag|e 'mær.ɪdʒ (US) 'mer-, 'mær- **-es** -ɪz **-eable** -ə.bl̩

Marriner 'mær.ɪ.nəʳ (US) 'mer.ɪ.nɚ, 'mær-

Marriott 'mær.i.ət (US) 'mer-, 'mær-, -ɑːt

marron 'mær.ᵊn, -ɔ̃ːŋ (US) 'mer.ᵊn, 'mær-; mə'roʊn **-s** -z

marrons glacés ˌmær.ᵊn'glæs.eɪ, -ᵊŋ'-, -ɔ̃ːŋ'- (US) məˌroʊn.glɑː'seɪ

marrow 'mær.əʊ (US) 'mer.oʊ, 'mær- **-s** -z **-y** -i

marrowbone 'mær.əʊ.bəʊn (US) 'mer.oʊ.boʊn, 'mær- **-s** -z

marrowfat 'mær.əʊ.fæt (US) 'mer.oʊ-, 'mær- **-s** -s

marr|y 'mær|.i (US) 'mer-, 'mær- **-ies** -iz **-ying** -i.ɪŋ **-ied** -id **-ier/s** -i.əʳ/z (US) -i.ɚ/z

Marryat 'mær.i.ət (US) 'mer-, 'mær-

Mars mɑːz (US) mɑːrz **'Mars ˌbar®**

Marsala mɑː'sɑː.lə (US) mɑːr'sɑː.lɑː

Marsalis mɑː'sɑː.lɪs (US) mɑːr.sæ-

Marsden 'mɑːz.dᵊn (US) 'mɑːrz-

Marseillaise ˌmɑː.seɪ'jeɪz, -'eɪz, -sᵊl'eɪz (US) ˌmɑːr.sᵊl'eɪz, -seɪ'ez

Marseilles, Marseille ˌmɑː'seɪ (US) ˌmɑːr-

marsh (M) mɑːʃ (US) mɑːrʃ **-es** -ɪz

Marsha 'mɑː.ʃə (US) 'mɑːr-

marshal 'mɑː.ʃᵊl (US) 'mɑːr- **-s** -z **-(l)ing** -ɪŋ **-(l)ed** -d **-(l)er/s** -əʳ/z (US) -ɚ/z

Marshall 'mɑː.ʃᵊl (US) 'mɑːr-

marshland 'mɑːʃ.lænd, -lənd (US) 'mɑːrʃ-

marshmallow ˌmɑːʃ'mæl.əʊ (US) 'mɑːrʃ.mel.oʊ, -mæl- **-s** -z

marsh|y 'mɑː.ʃ|i (US) 'mɑːr- **-ier** -i.əʳ (US) -i.ɚ **-iest** -i.ɪst, -i.əst **-iness** -ɪ.nəs, -ɪ.nɪs

Marske mɑːsk (US) mɑːrsk

Marsland 'mɑːz.lənd (US) 'mɑːrz-

Marston 'mɑː.stᵊn (US) 'mɑːr-

marsupial mɑː'suː.pi.əl, -'sjuː- (US) mɑːr'suː- **-s** -z

mart mɑːt (US) mɑːrt **-s** -s
Martel(l) mɑːˈtel (US) mɑːr-
Martello tower mɑːˌtel.əʊˈtaʊəʳ (US) mɑːrˌtel.oʊˈtaʊɚ **-s** -z
marten ˈmɑː.tɪn (US) ˈmɑːr.tᵊn **-s** -z
Martens ˈmɑː.tɪnz; mɑːˈtenz (US) ˈmɑːr.tᵊnz; mɑːrˈtenz
Martha ˈmɑː.θə (US) ˈmɑːr- ˌ**Martha's** ˈ**Vineyard**
martial (M) ˈmɑː.ʃᵊl (US) ˈmɑːr- **-ly** -i ˌ**martial** ˈ**law**
Martian ˈmɑː.ʃᵊn (US) ˈmɑːr- **-s** -z
martin (M) ˈmɑː.tɪn (US) ˈmɑːr.tᵊn **-s** -z
Martina mɑːˈtiː.nə (US) mɑːr-
Martine mɑːˈtiːn (US) mɑːr-
Martineau ˈmɑː.tɪ.nəʊ, -tə- (US) ˈmɑːr.tə.noʊ
martinet (M) ˌmɑː.tɪˈnet, -təˈ-, -ˈneɪ (US) ˌmɑːr.tᵊnˈet, -ˈeɪ, ˈ--- **-s** -s
Martinez mɑːˈtiː.nez (US) mɑːr-, -nəs
martingale ˈmɑː.tɪŋ.geɪl (US) ˈmɑːr.tᵊn- **-s** -z
martini (M®) mɑːˈtiː.ni (US) mɑːr- **-s** -z
Martinique ˌmɑː.tɪˈniːk, -təˈ- (US) ˌmɑːr.tᵊnˈiːk
Martinmas ˈmɑː.tɪn.məs, -tɪm-, -mæs (US) ˈmɑːr.tᵊn.məs
Martyn ˈmɑː.tɪn (US) ˈmɑːr.tᵊn
martyr (M) ˈmɑː.t|əʳ (US) ˈmɑːr.t̬|ɚ **-yrs** -əz (US) -ɚz **-yring** -ᵊr.ɪŋ **-yred** -əd (US) -ɚd
martyrdom ˈmɑː.tə.dəm (US) ˈmɑːr.t̬ɚ- **-s** -z
martyriz|e, -is|e ˈmɑː.tᵊr.aɪz, -tɪ.raɪz (US) ˈmɑːr.t̬ə.raɪz **-es** -ɪz **-ing** -ɪŋ **-ed** -d
marvel ˈmɑː.vᵊl (US) ˈmɑːr- **-s** -z **-(l)ing** -ɪŋ, ˈmɑːv.lɪŋ **-(l)ed** -d
Marvell ˈmɑː.vᵊl (US) ˈmɑːr-
marvel(l)ous ˈmɑː.vᵊl.əs; ˈmɑːv.ləs (US) ˈmɑːr.vᵊl.əs; ˈmɑːrv.ləs **-ly** -li **-ness** -nəs, -nɪs
Marvin ˈmɑː.vɪn (US) ˈmɑːr-
Marx mɑːks (US) mɑːrks ˈ**Marx** ˌ**Brothers**
Marxian ˈmɑːk.si.ən (US) ˈmɑːrk-
Marx|ism ˈmɑːk.s|ɪ.zᵊm (US) ˈmɑːrk- **-ist/s** -ɪst/s
Marxism-Leninism ˌmɑːk.sɪ.zᵊmˈlen.ɪ.nɪ.zᵊm (US) ˌmɑːrk-
Marxist-Leninist ˌmɑːk.sɪstˈlen.ɪ.nɪst (US) ˌmɑːrk- **-s** -s
Mary ˈmeə.ri (US) ˈmer.i
Maryborough ˈmeə.ri.bᵊr.ə, -ˌbʌr.ə (US) ˈmer.i.bə.roʊ
Maryland ˈmeə.ri.lænd, ˈmer.ɪ-, -lənd (US) ˈmer.ə.lənd
Marylebone *road, district:* ˈmær.ᵊl.ə.bən, -bəʊn; ˈ-ə.bən, ˈ-ɪ-; ˈmɑː.lɪ- (US) ˈmer.ᵊl.ə.bən, -boʊn; -ə.bən, ˈ-ɪ-; ˈmɑːr.lɪ-
Mary-le-Bone *preceded by 'St.':* ˈmær.ɪ.lə.bən, -ᵊl.ə- (US) ˈmer-
Maryport ˈmeə.ri.pɔːt (US) ˈmer.i.pɔːrt
marzipan ˈmɑː.zɪ.pæn, -zə-, ˌ--ˈ- (US) ˈmɑːr.zɪ.pæn, ˈmɑːrt.sɪ-, -pɑːn
Masaccio məˈzɑː.tʃəʊ, -ˈzætʃ.əʊ, -tʃi.əʊ (US) -ˈsɑː.tʃi.oʊ
Masada məˈsɑː.də, mæsˈɑː- (US) məˈsɑː.də; ˌmɑː.sɑːˈdɑː
Masai ˈmɑː.saɪ; -ˈ-, məˈ- (US) mɑːˈsaɪ, məˈ-
masala məˈsɑː.lə, mɑː-
Masaryk ˈmæs.ə.rɪk, ˈmæz- (US) ˈmæs.ɚ.ɪk
Mascagni mæsˈkɑː.nji, -ˈkæn.ji (US) mɑːs-
mascara məˈskɑː.rə, mæsˈkɑː- (US) mæsˈker.ə, -ˈkær- **-s** -z
mascarpone ˌmæs.kɑːˈpəʊ.neɪ (US) ˌmɑːs.kɑːrˈpoʊ-, ˌmæs-
mascot ˈmæs.kɒt, -kət (US) -kɑːt, -kət **-s** -s
masculine ˈmæs.kjə.lɪn, -kjʊ- (US) ˈmæs.kjə-, -kjuː- **-s** -z
masculinity ˌmæs.kjəˈlɪn.ə.ti, -kjʊˈ-, -ɪ.ti (US) ˌmæs.kjəˈlɪn.ə.t̬i, -kjuːˈ-
Masefield ˈmeɪs.fiːld
Masekela ˌmæs.əˈkeɪ.lə
maser ˈmeɪ.zəʳ (US) -zɚ **-s** -z
Maserati® ˌmæz.ᵊrˈɑː.ti (US) ˌmɑː.səˈrɑː.t̬i, ˌmæz.əˈ- **-s** -z
Maseru məˈsɪə.ruː, -ˈseə- (US) ˈmæz.ə.ruː, ˌmɑː.səˈruː
mash (M) mæʃ **-es** -ɪz **-ing** -ɪŋ **-ed** -t
MASH mæʃ
Masham *in North Yorkshire:* ˈmæs.əm *surname:* ˈmæs.əm, ˈmæʃ-
masher ˈmæʃ.əʳ (US) -ɚ **-s** -z
mashie ˈmæʃ.i **-s** -z
Mashona məˈʃɒn.ə, -ˈʃəʊ.nə (US) -ˈʃɑː-, -ˈʃoʊ- **-s** -z **-land** -lænd
mash|y ˈmæʃ|.i **-ies** -iz
Masie ˈmeɪ.zi
mask mɑːsk (US) mæsk **-s** -s **-ing** -ɪŋ **-ed** -t ˈ**masking** ˌ**tape**
Maskell ˈmæs.kᵊl
Maskelyne ˈmæs.kɪ.lɪn, -kᵊl.ɪn (US) -ɪn, -aɪn
masoch|ism ˈmæs.ə.k|ɪ.zᵊm, ˈmæz- **-ist/s** -ɪst/s
masochistic ˌmæs.əˈkɪs.tɪk, ˌmæz- **-ally** -ᵊl.i, -li
mason (M) ˈmeɪ.sᵊn **-s** -z ˈ**mason** ˌ**jar**
Mason-Dixon ˌmeɪ.sᵊnˈdɪk.sᵊn ˌ**Mason-**ˈ**Dixon** ˌ**line**
masonic (M) məˈsɒn.ɪk (US) -ˈsɑː.nɪk
Masonite® ˈmeɪ.sᵊn.aɪt
masonr|y (M) ˈmeɪ.sᵊn.r|i **-ies** -iz
masque mɑːsk, mæsk (US) mæsk **-s** -s
masquerad|e ˌmæs.kᵊrˈeɪd, ˌmɑː.skᵊrˈ- (US) ˌmæs.kəˈreɪd **-es** -z **-ing** -ɪŋ **-ed** -ɪd **-er/s** -əʳ/z (US) -ɚ/z
mass mæs **-es** -ɪz **-ing** -ɪŋ **-ed** -t ˌ**mass** ˈ**media**; ˌ**mass pro**ˈ**duction**
mass (M) *(n.) religious service:* mæs, mɑːs (US) mæs **-es** -ɪz
Mass. *(abbrev. for* **Massachusetts***)* mæs
Massachusetts ˌmæs.əˈtʃuː.sɪts, -səts (US) -sɪts
massac|re ˈmæs.ə.k|əʳ, ˈ-ɪ- (US) -k|ɚ **-res** -əz (US) -ɚz **-ring** -ᵊr.ɪŋ **-red** -əd (US) -ɚd
massag|e ˈmæs.ɑːdʒ (US) məˈsɑːdʒ **-es** -ɪz **-ing** -ɪŋ **-ed** -d **-er/s** -əʳ/z **-er/z** (US) -ɚ/z **-ist/s** -ɪst/s ˈ**massage** ˌ**parlour** (US) **mas**ˈ**sage** ˌ**parlor**
Massawa məˈsɑː.wə (US) mɑːˈsɑː.wɑː, məˈsɑː.wə
Massenet ˈmæs.ᵊn.eɪ (US) ˌ--ˈ-
masseur mæsˈɜːʳ, məˈsɜːʳ (US) -ˈsɝː, -ˈsuːr, -ˈsʊr **-s** -z
masseus|e mæsˈɜːz, məˈsɜːz (US) -ˈsɜːz, -ˈsuːz, -ˈsʊz **-es** -ɪz
Massey ˈmæs.i
massif mæsˈiːf, ˈ-- (US) mæsˈiːf **-s** -s
Massif Central ˌmæs.iːf.sɑ̃ːnˈtrɑːl
Massinger ˈmæs.ɪn.dʒəʳ (US) -dʒɚ
massive ˈmæs.ɪv **-ly** -li **-ness** -nəs, -nɪs
mass-market ˌmæsˈmɑː.kɪt (US) -ˈmɑːr- **-s** -s **-ing** -ɪŋ **-ed** -ɪd
mass-meeting ˌmæsˈmiː.tɪŋ, ˈ-ˌ-- (US) -t̬ɪŋ **-s** -z
Masson ˈmæs.ᵊn (US) ˈmæs.ɑːn, -ˈ-
Massow ˈmæs.əʊ (US) -oʊ
mass-produc|e ˌmæs.prəˈdjuːs, -ˈdʒuːs (US) ˌmæs.prəˈduːs, -proʊˈ-, -ˈdjuːs **-es** -ɪz **-ing** -ɪŋ **-ed** -t **-er/s** -əʳ/z (US) -ɚ/z *stress shift:* ˌmass-produced ˈgoods
mass-production ˌmæs.prəˈdʌk.ʃᵊn, ˈmæs.prə,- (US) ˌmæs.prəˈdʌk-, -proʊˈ-
mass|y ˈmæs|.i **-iness** -ɪ.nəs, -ɪ.nɪs
mast mɑːst (US) mæst **-s** -s
mastectom|y mæsˈtek.tə.m|i (US) məˈstek-, mæsˈtek- **-ies** -iz
mast|er ˈmɑː.st|əʳ (US) ˈmæs.t|ɚ **-ers** -əz (US) -ɚz **-ering** -ᵊr.ɪŋ **-ered** -əd (US) -ɚd ˌ**master** ˈ**bedroom**; ˈ**master** ˌ**class**; ˌ**master of** ˈ**ceremonies**; ˈ**master** ˌ**key**; ˈ**master** ˌ**race**
master-at-arms ˌmɑː.stᵊr.ətˈɑːmz (US) ˌmæs.tɚ.ətˈɑːrmz **masters-at-arms** ˌmɑː.stəz- (US) ˌmæs.tɚz-
Mastercard® ˈmɑː.stə.kɑːd (US) ˈmæs.tɚ.kɑːrd
masterclass ˈmɑː.stə.klɑːs (US) ˈmæs.tɚ.klæs **-es** -ɪz
masterful ˈmɑː.stə.fᵊl, -fʊl (US) ˈmæs.tɚ- **-ly** -i **-ness** -nəs, -nɪs
masterl|y ˈmɑː.stə.l|i (US) ˈmæs.tɚ- **-iness** -ɪ.nəs, -ɪ.nɪs
Masterman ˈmɑː.stə.mən (US) ˈmæs.tɚ-
mastermind ˈmɑː.stə.maɪnd (US) ˈmæs.tɚ- **-s** -z **-ing** -ɪŋ **-ed** -ɪd

masterpiec|e ˈmɑː.stə.piːs US ˈmæs.tɚ- **-es** -ɪz
Masters ˈmɑː.stəz US ˈmæs.tɚz
mastership ˈmɑː.stə.ʃɪp US ˈmæs.tɚ-
master-stroke ˈmɑː.stə.strəʊk US ˈmæs.tɚ.stroʊk **-s** -s
masterwork ˈmɑː.stə.wɜːk US ˈmæs.tɚ.wɝːk **-s** -s
master|y ˈmɑː.stər|.i US ˈmæs.tɚ- **-ies** -iz
masthead ˈmɑːst.hed US ˈmæst- **-s** -z
mastic ˈmæs.tɪk
masti|cate ˈmæs.tɪ|.keɪt, -tə- **-cates** -keɪts **-cating** -keɪ.tɪŋ US -keɪ.t̬ɪŋ **-cated** -keɪ.tɪd US -keɪ.t̬ɪd **-cator/s** -keɪ.tər/z US -keɪ.t̬ɚ/z
mastication ˌmæs.tɪˈkeɪ.ʃən, -təˈ-
masticatory ˈmæs.tɪ.kə.tər.i, -keɪ-; ˌmæs.tɪˈkeɪ-, -təˈ- US ˈmæs.tɪ.kə.tɔːr-, -tə-
mastiff ˈmæs.tɪf, ˈmɑː.stɪf US ˈmæs.tɪf **-s** -s
mastitis mæsˈtaɪ.tɪs, məˈstaɪ- US mæsˈtaɪ.t̬ɪs, məˈstaɪ- **mastitides** mæsˈtɪt.ə.diːz, məˈstɪt- US mæsˈtɪt̬.ə-, məˈstɪt̬-
mastodon ˈmæs.tə.dɒn, -dən US -dɑːn **-s** -z
mastoid ˈmæs.tɔɪd **-s** -z
Mastroianni ˌmæs.trəʊˈjɑː.ni, ˌmɑːs.trəʊ-, -ˈjæn.i US -troʊˈ-
mastur|bate ˈmæs.tə|.beɪt US -tɚ- **-bates** -beɪts **-bating** -beɪ.tɪŋ US -beɪ.t̬ɪŋ **-bated** -beɪ.tɪd US -beɪ.t̬ɪd **-bator/s** -beɪ.tər/z US -beɪ.t̬ɚ/z
masturbation ˌmæs.təˈbeɪ.ʃən US -tɚˈ- **-s** -z
masturbatory ˌmæs.təˈbeɪ.tər.i, ˈmæs.tə.beɪ- US ˈmæs.tɚ.bə.tɔːr-
Masur məˈzʊər US -ˈzʊr
mat mæt **-s** -s **-ting** -ɪŋ US ˈmæt̬.ɪŋ **-ted** -ɪd US ˈmæt̬.ɪd
Matabel|e ˌmæt.əˈbiː.li US ˌmæt̬- **-ies** -iz **-ie** -i
Matabeleland ˌmæt.əˈbiː.li.lænd US ˌmæt̬-
matador ˈmæt.ə.dɔːr US ˈmæt̬.ə.dɔːr **-s** -z
Mata Hari ˌmɑː.təˈhɑː.ri US ˌmɑː.t̬əˈhɑːr.i, ˌmæt̬.əˈher-, -ˈhær-
match mætʃ **-es** -ɪz **-ing** -ɪŋ **-ed** -t **-er/s** -ər/z US -ɚ/z ˌ**match** ˈ**point**
matchboard ˈmætʃ.bɔːd US -bɔːrd
matchbook ˈmætʃ.bʊk **-s** -s
matchbox ˈmætʃ.bɒks US -bɑːks **-es** -ɪz
matchless ˈmætʃ.ləs, -lɪs **-ly** -li **-ness** -nəs, -nɪs
matchlock ˈmætʃ.lɒk US -lɑːk **-s** -s
matchmaker ˈmætʃˌmeɪ.kər US -kɚ **-s** -z
matchmaking ˈmætʃˌmeɪ.kɪŋ
matchplay ˈmætʃ.pleɪ
matchstick ˈmætʃ.stɪk **-s** -s
matchwood ˈmætʃ.wʊd
mat|e meɪt **-es** -s **-ing** -ɪŋ US ˈmeɪ.t̬ɪŋ **-ed** -ɪd US ˈmeɪ.t̬ɪd
maté ˈmɑː.teɪ, ˈmæt.eɪ
matelot ˈmæt.ləʊ, ˈ-əl.əʊ US -əl.oʊ **-s** -z
mater ˈmeɪ.tər, ˈmɑː- US -t̬ɚ **-s** -z
materfamilias ˌmæt.ə.fəˈmɪl.i.æs US ˌmeɪ.t̬ɚ.fəˈmɪl.i.əs, ˌmɑː-
material məˈtɪə.ri.əl US -ˈtɪr.i- **-s** -z **-ly** -i
material|ism məˈtɪə.ri.ə.l|ɪ.zəm US -ˈtɪr.i- **-ist/s** -ɪst/s
materialistic məˌtɪə.ri.əˈlɪs.tɪk US -ˌtɪr.i-
materialization, -isa- məˌtɪə.ri.əl.aɪˈzeɪ.ʃən, -ɪˈ- US -ˌtɪr.i.əl.ɪˈ- **-s** -z
materializ|e, -is|e məˈtɪə.ri.ə.laɪz US -ˈtɪr.i- **-es** -ɪz **-ing** -ɪŋ **-ed** -d
matériel, materiel məˌtɪə.riˈel, mætˌɪə-; məˈtɪə.ri.əl US məˌtɪr.iˈel; məˈtɪr.i.əl
maternal məˈtɜː.nəl US -ˈtɝː- **-ly** -i
maternit|y məˈtɜː.nə.t|i, -ɪ.t|i US -ˈtɝː.nə.t̬|i **-ies** -iz **maˈternity** ˌ**leave; maˈternity** ˌ**ward**
matey ˈmeɪ.ti US -t̬i **-ness** -ɪ.nəs, -ɪ.nɪs
math mæθ
mathematic ˌmæθ.əmˈæt.ɪk, -ɪˈmæt-, mæθˈmæt- US ˌmæθ.əˈmæt̬-, mæθˈmæt̬-
mathematic|al ˌmæθ.əmˈæt.ɪ.k|əl, -ɪˈmæt, mæθˈmæt- US ˌmæθ.əˈmæt̬-, mæθˈmæt̬- **-ally** -əl.i, -li
mathematician ˌmæθ.əm.əˈtɪʃ.ən, -ɪ.məˈ-, ˌmæθ.məˈ- US ˌmæθ.ə.məˈ-, ˌmæθ.məˈ- **-s** -z
mathematics mæθ.əmˈæt.ɪks, -ɪˈmæt-, mæθˈmæt- US ˌmæθ.əˈmæt̬-, mæθˈmæt̬-
Mather ˈmeɪ.ðər, -θər; ˈmæð.ər US ˈmæð.ɚ **-s** -z
Matheson ˈmæθ.ɪ.sən, ˈ-ə-
Mathew ˈmæθ.juː, ˈmeɪ.θjuː
Mathews ˈmæθ.juːz, ˈmeɪ.θjuːz
Mathias məˈθaɪəs
Mathilda məˈtɪl.də
Mathis ˈmæθ.ɪs
maths mæθs
Matilda məˈtɪl.də
matinée, matinee ˈmæt.ɪ.neɪ, -ən.eɪ US ˌmæt.ənˈeɪ **-s** -z ˈ**matinée** ˌ**idol** **matinˈée** ˌ**idol**
matins ˈmæt.ɪnz US -ənz
Matisse məˈtiːs US mə-, mɑː-
Matlock ˈmæt.lɒk US -lɑːk
Mato Grosso ˌmæt.əʊˈgrəʊ.səʊ, ˌmɑː.təʊˈ- US ˌmæt̬.əˈgroʊ.soʊ, ˌmɑː.tuːˈgroʊ.suː, -ˈgrɔː-
Maton ˈmeɪ.tən
Matravers məˈtræv.əz US -ɚz
matriarch ˈmeɪ.tri.ɑːk, ˈmæt.ri- US ˈmeɪ.tri.ɑːrk **-y** -i
matriarchal ˌmeɪ.triˈɑː.kəl, ˌmæt.riˈ- US ˌmeɪ.triˈɑːr-
matric məˈtrɪk
matrices (*plur. of* **matrix**) ˈmeɪ.trɪ.siːz, -trə, ˈmæt.rɪ-, -rə- US ˈmeɪ.trɪ-
matricidal ˌmæt.rɪˈsaɪ.dəl, ˌmeɪ.trɪˈ-, -trəˈ-
matricide ˈmæt.rɪ.saɪd, ˈmeɪ.trɪ-, -trə- **-s** -z
matricu|late məˈtrɪk.jə|.leɪt, -jʊ- US -jə-, -juː- **-lates** -leɪts **-lating** -leɪ.tɪŋ US -leɪ.t̬ɪŋ **-lated** -leɪ.tɪd US -leɪ.t̬ɪd **-lator/s** -leɪ.tər/z US -leɪ.t̬ɚ/z
matriculation məˌtrɪk.jəˈleɪ.ʃən, -jʊˈ- US -jəˈ-, -juːˈ- **-s** -z
matrilineal ˌmæt.rɪˈlɪn.i.əl, ˌmeɪ.trɪˈ-, -trəˈ- US -trəˈ- **-ly** -i
matrimonial ˌmæt.rɪˈməʊ.ni.əl, -rəˈ- US -rəˈmoʊ- **-ly** -i
matrimon|y ˈmæt.rɪ.mə.n|i, -rə- US -rə.moʊ- **-ies** -iz
mat|rix ˈmeɪ.t|rɪks, ˈmæt|.rɪks US ˈmeɪ.t|rɪks **-rixes** -rɪk.sɪz **-rices** -rɪ.siːz, -rə-

Note: British doctors generally pronounce /ˈmeɪ.trɪks/ when talking about the cell type. Those connected with the printing trade pronounce /ˈmæt.rɪks/.

matron ˈmeɪ.trən **-s** -z **-ly** -li ˌ**matron** ˈ**honour**
Matrûh mætˈruː
Matsui® mætˈsuː.i
Matsushita® ˌmæt.suˈʃiː.tə US -t̬ə
matt(e) mæt
matt|er ˈmæt|.ər US ˈmæt̬|.ɚ **-ers** -əz US -ɚz **-ering** -ər.ɪŋ **-ered** -əd US -ɚ
as a ˌ**matter of** ˈ**fact**
Matterhorn ˈmæt.ə.hɔːn US ˈmæt̬.ɚ.hɔːrn
matter-of-fact ˌmæt.ər.əvˈfækt US ˌmæt̬.ɚ-
Matthau ˈmæθ.aʊ, ˈmæt-
Matthes ˈmæθ.əs
Matthew ˈmæθ.juː
Matthews ˈmæθ.juːz
Matthias məˈθaɪəs
Matthiessen ˈmæθ.ɪ.sən
matting ˈmæt.ɪŋ US ˈmæt̬-
mattins ˈmæt.ɪnz US -ənz
mattock ˈmæt.ək US ˈmæt̬- **-s** -s
mattress ˈmæt.rəs, -trɪs **-es** -ɪz
matur|ate ˈmæt.jər|.eɪt, -jʊ.r|eɪt; ˈmætʃ.ər|.eɪt US ˈmætʃ.ə.r|eɪt, - **-ates** -eɪts **-ating** -eɪ.tɪŋ US -eɪ.t **-ated** -eɪ.tɪd US -eɪ.t̬ɪd

maturation ˌmæt.jəˈreɪ.ʃən, -jʊˈreɪ-; ˌmætʃ.əˈreɪ- ⓤⓢ ˌmætʃ.əˈreɪ-, -ʊˈ-
matur|e (M) məˈtjʊəʳ, -ˈtjɔːʳ, -ˈtʃʊəʳ, -ˈtʃɔːʳ ⓤⓢ -ˈtʊr, -ˈtjʊr, -ˈtʃʊr **-ely** -li **-eness** -nəs, -nɪs **-es** -z **-ing** -ɪŋ **-ed** -d
Maturin *surname:* ˈmæt.jʊə.rɪn, -jəˈ- ⓤⓢ ˌmɑː.tuːˈriːn, -təˈ-
Maturin *in Venezuela:* ˌmæt.jʊəˈrɪn, -jəˈ- ⓤⓢ ˌmɑː.tuːˈriːn, -t̬əˈ-
maturity məˈtjʊə.rə.ti, -ˈtjɔː-, -ˈtʃʊə-, -ˈtʃɔː-, -rɪ- ⓤⓢ -ˈtʊr.ə.t̬i, -ˈtjʊr-, -ˈtʃʊr-
matutinal ˌmæt.jʊˈtaɪ.nᵊl; məˈtjuː.tɪ-, -tə- ⓤⓢ məˈtuː.tᵊn.ᵊl, -ˈtjuː-
matzo(h) ˈmɒt.sə, ˈmæt-, ˈmɑːt-, -səʊ ⓤⓢ ˈmɑːt.sə, -soʊ **-s** -z **matzoth** ˈmɒt.sət, ˈmæt-, ˈmɑːt-, -səʊθ ⓤⓢ -soʊt
maud (M) mɔːd ⓤⓢ mɑːd, mɔːd **-s** -z
Maude mɔːd ⓤⓢ mɑːd, mɔːd
maudlin ˈmɔːd.lɪn ⓤⓢ ˈmɑːd-, ˈmɔːd-
Maudsley ˈmɔːdz.li ⓤⓢ ˈmɑːdz-, ˈmɔːdz-
Mauger ˈmeɪ.dʒəʳ, ˈmɔː.gəʳ ⓤⓢ ˈmɑː.gɚ, ˈmɔː-, ˈmeɪ.dʒɚ
Maugham mɔːm; ˈmɒf.əm ⓤⓢ mɑːm, mɔːm
Note: The author Somerset Maugham is pronounced /mɔːm/.
Maughan mɔːn ⓤⓢ mɑːn, mɔːn
maugre ˈmɔː.gəʳ ⓤⓢ ˈmɑː.gɚ, ˈmɔː-
Maui ˈmaʊ.i
maul mɔːl ⓤⓢ mɑːl, mɔːl **-s** -z **-ing** -ɪŋ **-ed** -d **-er/s** -əʳ/z ⓤⓢ -ɚ/z
Mauleverer mɔːˈlev.ᵊr.əʳ, mə- ⓤⓢ mɑːˈlev.ɚ.ɚ, mɔː-, mə-
maulstick ˈmɔːl.stɪk ⓤⓢ ˈmɑːl-, ˈmɔːl- **-s** -s
Mau Mau ˈmaʊˌmaʊ, ˌ-ˈ-
Mauna Kea ˌmaʊ.nəˈkeɪ.ə ⓤⓢ ˌmaʊ-, ˌmɑː-, ˌmɔː-
Mauna Loa ˌmaʊ.nəˈləʊ.ə ⓤⓢ -ˈloʊ-, ˌmɑː-, ˌmɔː-
maunder ˈmɔːn.dəʳ ⓤⓢ ˈmɑːn.dɚ, ˈmɔːn- **-s** -z **-ing** -ɪŋ **-ed** -d
maundy (M) ˈmɔːn.di ⓤⓢ ˈmɑːn-, ˈmɔːn- ˌ**Maundy** ˈ**Thursday**
Maunsell ˈmæn*t*.sᵊl
Maupassant ˈməʊ.pæs.ɑ̃ːŋ ⓤⓢ ˈmoʊ.pə.sɑːnt
Maupin ˈmɔː.pɪn, -pæ̃ ⓤⓢ ˈmɑː-
Maureen ˈmɔː.riːn, -ˈ- ⓤⓢ mɔːˈriːn, mə-
Mauretani|a ˌmɒr.ɪˈteɪ.ni|.ə, ˌmɔː.rɪˈ- ⓤⓢ ˌmɔːr.ɪˈ-, ˌmɑːr-, -ˈnj|ə **-an/s** -ən/z
Mauriac ˈmɒr.i.æk, ˈmɔː.ri- ⓤⓢ ˈmɔːr-, ˈmɑːr-
Maurice ˈmɒr.ɪs, mɒrˈiːs ⓤⓢ mɔːˈriːs, mɑː-, mə-; ˈmɑːr.ɪs, ˈmɔːr-
Mauritani|a ˌmɒr.ɪˈteɪ.ni|.ə, ˌmɔː.rɪˈ- ⓤⓢ ˌmɔːr.ɪˈ-, ˌmɑːr-, -ˈnj|ə **-an/s** -ən/z
Maurit|ius məˈrɪʃ|.əs, mɔː-, mɒrˈɪʃ- ⓤⓢ mɔːˈrɪʃ.i|.əs, mɑː-, ˈ-əs **-ian/s** -ən/z

Mauser ˈmaʊ.zəʳ ⓤⓢ -zɚ **-s** -z
mausoleum ˌmɔː.səˈliː.əm, ˌmaʊ-, -zəˈ-, -ˈleɪ- ⓤⓢ ˌmɑː.səˈliː-, ˌmɔː-, -zəˈ- **-s** -z
mauve məʊv ⓤⓢ moʊv, mɑːv, mɔːv **-s** -z
maven ˈmeɪ.vᵊn **-s** -z
maverick ˈmæv.ᵊr.ɪk ⓤⓢ ˈmæv.ɚ-, ˈ-rɪk **-s** -s
mavis (M) ˈmeɪ.vɪs
maw (M) mɔː ⓤⓢ mɑː, mɔː **-s** -z
Mawer ˈmɔː.əʳ, mɔːʳ ⓤⓢ ˈmɔː.ɚ
Mawhinney, Mawhinny məˈ*h*wɪn.i
mawkish ˈmɔː.kɪʃ ⓤⓢ ˈmɑː-, ˈmɔː- **-ly** -li **-ness** -nəs, -nɪs
max (M) mæks
Maxey ˈmæk.si
Max Factor® ˌmæksˈfæk.təʳ ⓤⓢ -tɚ
maxi ˈmæk.si **-s** -z
maxill|a mækˈsɪl|.ə **-ae** -iː **-as** -əz **-ary** -ᵊr.i
maxim (M) ˈmæk.sɪm **-s** -z
maximal ˈmæk.sɪ.mᵊl, -sə- **-ly** -i
maximalist ˈmæk.sɪ.mᵊl.ɪst, -sə- **-s** -s
Maximilian ˌmæk.sɪˈmɪl.i.ən, -səˈ- ⓤⓢ ˈ-jən, ˈ-i.ən
maximization, -isa- ˌmæk.sɪ.maɪˈzeɪ.ʃᵊn, -sə-, -mɪˈ- ⓤⓢ -mɪˈ- **-s** -z
maximiz|e, -is|e ˈmæk.sɪ.maɪz, -sə- **-es** -ɪz **-ing** -ɪŋ **-ed** -d **-er/s** -əʳ/z ⓤⓢ -ɚ/z
maxim|um ˈmæk.sɪ.m|əm, -sə- **-ums** -əmz **-a** -ə
Maximus ˈmæk.sɪ.məs, -sə-
Maxine mækˈsiːn, ˈ-- ⓤⓢ mækˈsiːn
Maxse ˈmæk.si
Maxwell ˈmæk.swəl, -swel
may *(auxil. v.)* meɪ
May meɪ ˈ**May** ˌ**Day**
May|a ˈmaɪ|.ə ⓤⓢ ˈmɑː.j|ə, ˈmaɪ|.ə **-as** -əz **-an/s** -ən/z
Mayall ˈmeɪ.ɔːl, -əl ⓤⓢ -ɔːl, -ɑːl, -əl
mayapple ˈmeɪˌæp.l̩ **-s** -z
maybe ˈmeɪ.bi, -biː, ˌ-ˈ-
maybug ˈmeɪ.bʌg **-s** -z
mayday (M) ˈmeɪ.deɪ **-s** -z
Mayer ˈmeɪ.əʳ ⓤⓢ -ɚ
mayest ˈmeɪ.ɪst, -əst; meɪst
Mayfair ˈmeɪ.feəʳ ⓤⓢ -fer
Mayfield ˈmeɪ.fiːld
mayflower (M) ˈmeɪ.flaʊəʳ ⓤⓢ -flaʊɚ **-s** -z
mayfl|y ˈmeɪ.fl|aɪ **-ies** -aɪz
mayhap ˈmeɪ.hæp
mayhem ˈmeɪ.hem
Mayhew ˈmeɪ.hjuː
maying ˈmeɪ.ɪŋ
Maynard ˈmeɪ.nɑːd, -nəd ⓤⓢ -nɚd
Maynooth məˈnuːθ, meɪ-
mayn't meɪnt; ˈmeɪ.ᵊnt
Maynwaring ˈmæn.ᵊr.ɪŋ

Mayo *in Ireland, surname:* ˈmeɪ.əʊ, -ˈ- ⓤⓢ -oʊ, -ˈ- **-s** -z *American Indian:* ˈmaɪ.əʊ ⓤⓢ -oʊ **-s** -z
mayo *(abbrev. for* **mayonnaise***)* ˈmeɪ.əʊ ⓤⓢ -oʊ
mayonnaise ˌmeɪ.əˈneɪz ⓤⓢ ˈmeɪ.ə.neɪz, ˌ--ˈ-
mayor (M) meəʳ ⓤⓢ meɪɚ, mer **-s** -z
mayoral ˈmeə.rᵊl ⓤⓢ ˈmeɪ.ɔːr.ᵊl
mayoralt|y ˈmeə.rᵊl.t|i ⓤⓢ ˈmeɪɚ.ᵊl.t̬|i, ˈmer- **-ies** -iz
mayoress (M) ˌmeəˈres; ˈmeə.res, -rɪs, -rəs ⓤⓢ ˈmeɪɚ.ɪs, ˈmer-, -əs **-es** -ɪz
mayorship ˈmeə.ʃɪp ⓤⓢ ˈmeɪɚ-, ˈmer- **-s** -s
Mayotte maɪˈjɒt ⓤⓢ mɑːˈjɑːt
Mayou ˈmeɪ.uː
maypole ˈmeɪ.pəʊl ⓤⓢ -poʊl **-s** -z
mayst meɪst
Mazda® ˈmæz.də ⓤⓢ ˈmɑːz- **-s** -z
maz|e meɪz **-es** -ɪz
Mazeppa məˈzep.ə
Mazo de la Roche ˌmæz.əʊ.də.lɑːˈrɒʃ, ˌmeɪ.zəʊ- ⓤⓢ ˌmɑː.zoʊ.də.lɑːˈroʊʃ
mazourka məˈzɜː.kə ⓤⓢ -ˈzɝː-, -ˈzʊr- **-s** -z
mazuma məˈzuː.mə
mazurka məˈzɜː.kə ⓤⓢ -ˈzɝː-, -ˈzʊr- **-s** -z
mazuzah məˈzuː.zə
maz|y ˈmeɪ.z|i **-ier** -i.əʳ ⓤⓢ -i.ɚ **-iest** -i.ɪst, -i.əst **-ily** -ɪ.li, -ᵊl.i **-iness** -ɪ.nəs, -ɪ.nɪs
MBA ˌem.biːˈeɪ
Mbabane ᵊm.bɑːˈbɑː.neɪ ⓤⓢ ˌem-
MBE ˌem.biːˈiː
Mbeki əmˈbek.i
Mbuji-Mayi ᵊmˈbuː.dʒi.maɪ.i ⓤⓢ emˌbuː.dʒiˈmaɪ.ji, -ˈmɑː-
Mc mək, mæk
MC ˌemˈsiː
McAdam məˈkæd.əm
McAfee məˈkæf.i; ˌmæk.əˈfiː ⓤⓢ ˈmæk.ə.fiː; məˈkæf.i
McAiley məˈkeɪ.li
McAleer ˌmæk.əˈlɪəʳ ⓤⓢ -ˈlɪr
McAleese ˌmæk.əˈliːs
McAlinden ˌmæk.əˈlɪn.dən
McAlister məˈkæl.ɪ.stəʳ ⓤⓢ -stɚ
McAll məˈkɔːl ⓤⓢ -ˈkɔːl, -ˈkɑːl
McAl(l)ister məˈkæl.ɪ.stəʳ, ˈ-ə- ⓤⓢ -stɚ
McAlpine məˈkæl.pɪn, -paɪn
McAnally ˌmæk.əˈnæl.i ⓤⓢ ˈmæk.ᵊn.æl.i
McArdle məˈkɑː.dl̩ ⓤⓢ -ˈkɑːr-
McArthur məˈkɑː.θəʳ ⓤⓢ -ˈkɑːr.θɚ
McAteer ˌmæk.əˈtɪəʳ, ˈ--- ⓤⓢ ˌmæk.əˈtɪr, ˈ---
McAulay məˈkɔː.li ⓤⓢ -ˈkɔː-, -ˈkɑː-
McAvoy ˈmæk.ə.vɔɪ
McBain məkˈbeɪn
McBeal məkˈbiːl

McBean mək'beɪn, -'biːn
McBeth mək'beθ
McBrain mək'breɪn
McBride mək'braɪd
MCC ˌem.siː'siː
McCabe mə'keɪb
McCaffrey mə'kæf.ri
McCain® mə'keɪn
McCall mə'kɔːl (US) -'kɔːl, -'kɑːl
McCallie mə'kɔː.li (US) -'kɑː.li, -'kɔː-
McCallion mə'kæl.i.ən
McCallum mə'kæl.əm
McCann mə'kæn
McCartan, McCarten mə'kɑː.tᵊn (US) -'kɑːr-
McCarthy mə'kɑː.θi (US) -'kɑːr- **-ism** -ɪ.zᵊm **-ite/s** -aɪt/s
McCartney mə'kɑːt.ni (US) -'kɑːrt-
McCaughey mə'kæx.i, -'kæ.hi, -'kɒf.i (US) -'kæ.hi, -'kɑː.fi
McCausland mə'kɔːz.lənd (US) -'kɑːz-, -'kɔːz-
McClain mə'kleɪn
McClean mə'kleɪn, -'kliːn
McClear mə'klɪəʳ (US) -'klɪr
McClellan mə'klel.ən
McClelland mə'klel.ənd
McClintock mə'klɪn.tək, -tɒk (US) -t̬ək, -tɑːk
McCloskey mə'klɒs.ki (US) -'klɑː.ski, -'klʌs.ki
McClure mə'klʊəʳ, -'klɔːʳ (US) -'klʊr
McColl mə'kɒl (US) -'kɑːl, -'kɔːl
McCollum mə'kɒl.əm (US) -'kɑː.ləm
McComb mə'kəʊm (US) -'koʊm
McConnell mə'kɒn.əl (US) -'kɑː.nəl
McConochie mə'kɒn.ə.ki, -xi (US) -'kɑː.nə-
McConville mə'kɒn.vɪl (US) -'kɑːn-
McCormack mə'kɔː.mək (US) -'kɔːr-
McCormick mə'kɔː.mɪk (US) -'kɔːr-
McCorquodale mə'kɔː.kə.deɪl (US) -'kɔːr-
McCorry mə'kɒr.i (US) -'kɔːr-
McCourt mə'kɔːt (US) -'kɔːrt
McCoy mə'kɔɪ
McCrae, McCrea mə'kreɪ
McCready mə'kriː.di
McCrory mə'krɔː.ri (US) -'krɔːr.i
McCullagh mə'kʌl.ə
McCullam mə'kʌl.əm
McCullers mə'kʌl.əz (US) -ɚz
McCulloch mə'kʌl.ək, -əx
McCusker mə'kʌs.kəʳ (US) -kɚ
McDade mək'deɪd
McDaniels mək'dæn.jəlz
McDermot(t) mək'dɜː.mət (US) -'dɝː-
McDiarmid mək'dɜː.mɪd, -'deə- (US) -'dɝː-
McDonald mək'dɒn.ᵊld, mæk- (US) -'dɑː.nᵊld
McDonaugh mək'dɒn.ə (US) -'dɑː.nə
McDon(n)ell mək'dɒn.ᵊl, ˌmæk.də'nel (US) -'dɑː.nəl
McDono(u)gh mək'dʌn.ə, -'dɒn- (US) -'dɑː.nə, -'dʌn-
McDougal mək'duː.gᵊl
McDougall mək'duː.gᵊl
McDougall's® mək'duː.gᵊlz, mæk-
McDowell, McDowall mək'daʊəl, -'dəʊəl (US) -'daʊəl, -'doʊəl
McDuff mək'dʌf, mæk-
Note: In Scotland always /mək-/.
McElder(r)y 'mæk.ᵊlˌder.i, ˌmæk.ᵊl'der-
McEldowney ˌmæk.ᵊl'daʊ.ni, 'mæk.ᵊlˌdaʊ-
McElroy 'mæk.ᵊl.rɔɪ
McElwain mə'kel.weɪn; 'mæk.ᵊl.weɪn
McElwin mə'kel.wɪn
McEnroe 'mæk.ɪn.rəʊ, -ᵊn- (US) -roʊ
McEwen, McEwan mə'kjuː.ən, -ɪn
McFadzean mək'fæd.i.ən
McFarland mək'fɑː.lənd (US) -'fɑːr-
McFarlane mək'fɑː.lɪn, -lən (US) -'fɑːr-
McGahey mə'gæx.i, -'gæ.hi (US) -'geɪ.hi
McGee mə'giː
McGillicuddy 'mæg.li.kʌd.i, 'mæk.ɪl-; mə'gɪl.i- (US) mə'gɪl.i-
McGillivray mə'gɪl.ɪ.vri, -'gɪl.vri, -'glɪv.ri, -reɪ
McGoldrick mə'gəʊl.drɪk (US) -goʊl-
McGough mə'gɒf (US) -'gɑːf
McGovern mə'gʌv.ən (US) -ɚn
McGowan mə'gaʊən
McGrath mə'grɑː, -'grɑːθ, -'græθ (US) -'græθ
McGraw mə'grɔː (US) -'grɑː, -'grɔː
McGregor mə'greg.əʳ (US) -ɚ
McGuane mə'gweɪn
McGuigan mə'gwɪg.ən
McGuinness mə'gɪn.ɪs, -əs
McGuire mə'gwaɪəʳ (US) -'gwaɪɚ
McIlrath 'mæk.ᵊl.rɑːθ, -ɪl- (US) -ræθ
McIlroy 'mæk.ᵊl.rɔɪ, -ɪl-, ˌ--'-
McIlvanney ˌmæk.ᵊl'væn.i, -ɪl'-
McIlwraith 'mæk.ᵊl.reɪθ, -ɪl-
McInlay, McInley mə'kɪn.li (US) mək'ɪn.li
McInroy 'mæk.ɪn.rɔɪ, -ᵊn-
McIntosh 'mæk.ɪn.tɒʃ, -ᵊn- (US) -tɑːʃ
McIntyre 'mæk.ɪn.taɪəʳ, -ᵊn- (US) -taɪɚ
McIver mə'kaɪ.vəʳ, -'kɪv.əʳ (US) -vɚ
McIvor mə'kiː.vəʳ, -'kaɪ.vəʳ (US) -vɚ
McKee mə'kiː
McKellen mə'kel.ᵊn
McKenna mə'ken.ə
McKenzie mə'ken.zi
McKeown mə'kjəʊn, -'kjʊən (US) -'kjoʊn
McKerras mə'ker.əs
McKie mə'kaɪ, -'kiː
McKinlay, McKinley mə'kɪn.li
McKinnon mə'kɪn.ən
McKinny mə'kɪn.i
McKnight mək'naɪt
McLachlan mə'klɒk.lən, -'klɒx-, -'klæk-, -'klæx- (US) -'klɑː.klən
McLagan mə'klæg.ᵊn
McLaine mə'kleɪn
McLaren mə'klær.ᵊn (US) -'kler-, -'klær-, -ən
McLaughlin mə'klɒk.lɪn, -'klɒx- (US) -'klɑː.klɪn, -'klɑːf-, -'klɔːf-
McLay mə'kleɪ
McLean mə'kleɪn, -'kliːn (US) -'kliːn
McLeish mə'kliːʃ
McLeod mə'klaʊd
McMahon mək'mɑːn (US) -'mæn, -'meɪən, -'mɑːn
McManaman mək'mæn.ə.mən
McManus mək'mæn.əs, -'meɪ.nəs
McMaster mək'mɑː.stəʳ (US) -'mæs.tɚ
McMenem(e)y mək'men.ə.mi
McMichael mək'maɪ.kᵊl
McMillan mək'mɪl.ən
McMullen mək'mʌl.ən
McMurdo mək'mɜː.dəʊ (US) -'mɝː.doʊ
McNab mək'næb
McNaghten, McNachton mək'nɔː.tᵊn (US) -'nɑː-, -'nɔː-
McNally mək'næl.i
McNamara ˌmæk.nə'mɑː.rə (US) 'mæk.nə.mer.ə, -mær-
McNaught mək'nɔːt (US) -'nɑːt, -'nɔːt **-on** -ᵊn **-en** -ᵊn
McNeice mək'niːs
McNeil mək'niːl
McPhee mək'fiː
McQuarie mə'kwɒr.i, -'kwɑːr-, -'kwɔːr- (US) mə'kwɑː.ri
McQueen mə'kwiːn
McRae mə'kreɪ
McReady mə'kriː.di
McShane mək'ʃeɪn
McShea mək'ʃeɪ
McSwiney mək'swiː.ni, -'swɪn-
McTaggart mək'tæg.ət (US) -ɚt
McTavish mək'tæv.ɪʃ
McTeague mək'tiːg
McVay mək'veɪ
McVeagh mək'veɪ
McVean mək'veɪn, -viːn
McVeigh mək'veɪ
McVey mək'veɪ
McVicar mək'vɪk.əʳ (US) -ɚ
McVitie's® mək'vɪt.iz (US) -'vɪt̬-
McVit(t)ie mək'vɪt.i (US) -'vɪt̬-
McWhirter mək'*h*wɜː.təʳ (US) -'*h*wɝː.t̬ɚ
McWilliams mək'wɪl.jəmz, -i.əmz (US) '-jəmz
MD ˌem'di
Md. *(abbrev. for* **Maryland***)* 'meə.rɪ.lænd, 'mer.ɪ-, -lənd (US) 'mer.ɪ.lənd

me *note in Tonic Sol-fa:* miː -s -z
me *(pron.) normal form:* miː *freq. weak form:* mi
Me. *(abbrev. for* **Maine***)* meɪn
ME ˌem'iː
Meacher 'miː.tʃəʳ (US) -tʃɚ
mea culpa ˌmeɪ.ə'kʊl.pə, -ɑː'-, -'kʌl-, -pɑː (US) -ɑː'kʊl.pɑː, miː-, -ə'kʌl.pə
mead (M) miːd -s -z
Meaden 'miː.dᵊn
meadow 'med.əʊ (US) -oʊ -s -z -y -i
meadowlark 'med.əʊ.lɑːk (US) -oʊ.lɑːrk -s -s
Meadows 'med.əʊz (US) -oʊz
meadowsweet 'med.əʊ.swiːt (US) -oʊ-
Meagan 'miː.gᵊn
meag|er 'miː.g|əʳ (US) -g|ɚ -erer -ᵊr.əʳ (US) -ɚ.ɚ -erest -ᵊr.ɪst, -əst -erly -ᵊl.i (US) -ɚ.li -erness -ə.nəs, -nɪs (US) -ɚ-
Meagher mɑːʳ (US) mɑːr
meag|re 'miː.g|əʳ (US) -gɚ -rer -ᵊr.əʳ (US) -ɚ.ɚ -rest -ᵊr.ɪst, -əst -rely -ᵊl.i (US) -ɚ.li -reness -ə.nəs, -nɪs (US) -ɚ-
Meaker 'miː.kəʳ (US) -kɚ
meal miːl -s -z ˌmeals on 'wheels; 'meal ˌticket
mealie 'miː.li -s -z
mealtime 'miːl.taɪm -s -z
meal|y 'miː.l|i -ier -i.əʳ (US) -i.ɚ -iest -i.ɪst, -i.əst -iness -ɪ.nəs, -ɪ.nɪs
mealybug 'miː.li.bʌg
mealy-mouthed ˌmiː.li'maʊðd (US) 'miː.li.maʊðd, -maʊθt, ˌ--'- *stress shift, British only:* ˌmealy-mouthed 'person
mean miːn -s -z -er -əʳ (US) -ɚ -est -ɪst, -əst -ly -li -ness -nəs, -nɪs -ing -ɪŋ meant ment 'means ˌtest
meand|er (M) mi'æn.d|əʳ (US) -d|ɚ -ers -əz (US) -ɚz -ering/s -ᵊr.ɪŋ -ered -əd (US) -ɚd
meanie 'miː.ni -s -z
meaning 'miː.nɪŋ -s -z -ly -li
meaningful 'miː.nɪŋ.fᵊl, -fʊl -ly -i -ness -nəs, -nɪs
meaningless 'miː.nɪŋ.ləs, -lɪs -ly -li -ness -nəs, -nɪs
means-test 'miːnz.test -s -s -ing -ɪŋ -ed -ɪd
meant *(from* **mean***)* ment
meantime ˌmiːn'taɪm, '-- (US) 'miːn-
meanwhile ˌmiːn'*h*waɪl, '-- (US) 'miːn-
mean|y 'miː.n|i -ies -iz
Meany 'miː.ni
Mearns mɜːnz, meənz, mɪənz (US) mɝːnz, mernz, mɪrnz
Mears mɪəz (US) mɪrz
measles 'miː.zl̩z
measly 'miːz.li
measurab|le 'meʒ.ᵊr.ə.b|l̩ -ly -li -leness -l̩.nəs, -nɪs
meas|ure 'meʒ|.əʳ (US) -ɚ -ures -əz (US) -ɚz -uring -ᵊr.ɪŋ -ured -əd (US) -ɚd -urer/s -ᵊr.əʳ/z (US) -ɚ.ɚ/z
measureless 'meʒ.ə.ləs, -lɪs (US) '-ɚ- -ly -li -ness -nəs, -nɪs
measurement 'meʒ.ə.mənt (US) '-ɚ- -s -s
meat miːt -s -s
meat-and-potatoes ˌmiːt.ᵊn*d*.pə'teɪ.təʊz, -ᵊm- (US) -ᵊn*d*.pə'teɪ.t̬oʊz
meatball 'miːt.bɔːl (US) -bɔːl, -bɑːl -s -z
Meates miːts
Meath *Irish county:* miːð
Note: Often pronounced /miːθ/ by English people.
meathead 'miːt.hed -s -z
meatless 'miːt.ləs, -lɪs
meatloa|f 'miːt.ləʊ|f (US) -loʊ|f -ves -vz
meatpacking 'miːtˌpæk.ɪŋ
meatus mi'eɪ.təs (US) -t̬əs -es -ɪz
meat|y 'miː.t|i (US) -t̬|i -ier -i.əʳ (US) -i.ɚ -iest -i.ɪst, -i.əst -iness -ɪ.nəs, -ɪ.nɪs
mecca (M) 'mek.ə
Meccano® mɪ'kɑː.nəʊ, mek'ɑː-, mə'kɑː- (US) -noʊ
mechanic mɪ'kæn.ɪk, mə- -s -s -al -ᵊl -ally -ᵊl.i, -li
mechanician ˌmek.ə'nɪʃ.ᵊn -s -z
mechanism 'mek.ə.nɪ.zᵊm -s -z
mechanistic ˌmek.ə'nɪs.tɪk -ally -ᵊl.i, -li
mechanization, -isa- ˌmek.ə.naɪ'zeɪ.ʃᵊn, -nɪ'- (US) -nɪ'-
mechaniz|e, -is|e 'mek.ə.naɪz -es -ɪz -ing -ɪŋ -ed -d
Mecklenburg 'mek.lɪn.bɜːg, -lən-, -lɪm-, -ləm- (US) -lɪn.bɝːg, -lən-
MEd ˌem'ed
Med med
medal 'med.ᵊl -s -z
medalist 'med.ᵊl.ɪst -s -s
medallion mɪ'dæl.i.ən, med'æl-, mə'dæl- (US) mə'dæl.jən -s -z
medallist 'med.ᵊl.ɪst -s -s
Medan 'med.ɑːn, 'meɪ.dɑːn, -'- (US) meɪ'dɑːn, '--
Medawar 'med.ə.wəʳ (US) -wɚ
meddl|e 'med.l̩ -es -z -ing -ɪŋ, '-lɪŋ -ed -d -er/s -əʳ/z (US) -ɚ/z, '-ləʳ/z (US) '-l̩.ɚ/z, '-lɚ/z
meddlesome 'med.l̩.səm -ness -nəs, -nɪs
Mede miːd -s -z
Medea mɪ'dɪə, mə-, -'diː.ə (US) mɪ'diː-, mə-
Medellin ˌmed.ᵊl'ɪn, -'iːn *as if Spanish:* ˌmed.eɪ'jin (US) -'iːn
medfl|y 'med.fl|aɪ -ies -aɪz
media *(plur. of* **medium***)* 'miː.di.ə
mediaeval (M) ˌmed.i'iː.vᵊl, med'iː- (US) ˌmiː.di'-, ˌmed.i'-; mə'diː- -ism -ɪ.zᵊm -ist/s -ɪst/s
medial 'miː.di.əl
median 'miː.di.ən -s -z 'median ˌstrip
mediant 'miː.di.ənt -s -s
mediastin|um ˌmiː.di.ə'staɪ.n|əm (US) -æs'taɪ- -a -ə
mediate *(adj.)* 'miː.di.ət, -ɪt -ly -li -ness -nəs, -nɪs
medi|ate *(v.)* 'miː.di|.eɪt -ates -eɪts -ating -eɪ.tɪŋ (US) -eɪ.t̬ɪŋ -ated -eɪ.tɪd (US) -eɪ.t̬ɪd
mediation ˌmiː.di'eɪ.ʃᵊn -s -z
mediative 'miː.di.ə.tɪv (US) -t̬ɪv
mediator 'miː.di.eɪ.təʳ (US) -t̬ɚ -s -z
mediatorial ˌmiː.di.ə'tɔː.ri.əl (US) -'tɔːr.i- -ly -i
mediatory 'miː.di.ə.tᵊr.i, -tri (US) -tɔːr.i
medic 'med.ɪk -s -s
Medicaid 'med.ɪ.keɪd
medic|al 'med.ɪ.k|ᵊl -als -ᵊlz -ally -ᵊl.i, -li
medicament mə'dɪk.ə.mənt, mɪ-, med'ɪk-; 'med.ɪ.kə- (US) mə'dɪk.ə-; 'med.ɪ.kə- -s -s
Medicare 'med.ɪ.keəʳ (US) -ker
medi|cate 'med.ɪ|.keɪt -cates -keɪts -cating -keɪ.tɪŋ (US) -keɪ.t̬ɪŋ -cated -keɪ.tɪd (US) -keɪ.t̬ɪd
medication ˌmed.ɪ'keɪ.ʃᵊn -s -z
Medici 'med.ɪ.tʃiː, -tʃi; med'iː.tʃi, mə'diː-, mɪ- (US) 'med.ə.tʃiː
medicinal mə'dɪs.ɪ.nᵊl, mɪ-, med'ɪs-, -ᵊn.ᵊl (US) mə'dɪs- -ly -i
medicine 'med.sᵊn, -sɪn, '-ɪ.sᵊn, '-ə-, -sɪn (US) 'med.ɪ.sən -s -z 'medicine ˌball; 'medicine ˌchest; ˌgive someone a ˌtaste of their ˌown 'medicine
medico 'med.ɪ.kəʊ (US) -koʊ -s -z
medico- ˌmed.ɪ.kəʊ- (US) -koʊ-
medieval (M) ˌmed.i'iː.vᵊl, med'iː- (US) ˌmiː.di'-, ˌmed.i'-; mə'diː- -ism -ɪ.zᵊm -ist/s -ɪst/s
Medill mə'dɪl
Medina *in Saudi Arabia:* med'iː.nə, mɪ'diː-, mə- (US) mə- *in US:* med'aɪ.nə, mɪ'daɪ-, mə- (US) mə-
mediocre ˌmiː.di'əʊ.kəʳ, 'miː.di.əʊ- (US) ˌmiː.di'oʊ.kɚ, 'miː.di.oʊ-
mediocrit|y ˌmiː.di'ɒk.rə.t|i, ˌmed.i'-, -ɪ.t|i (US) ˌmiː.di'ɑː.krə.t̬|i -ies -iz
medi|tate 'med.ɪ|.teɪt, '-ə- -tates -teɪts -tating -teɪ.tɪŋ (US) -teɪ.t̬ɪŋ -tated -teɪ.tɪd (US) -teɪ.t̬ɪd -tator/s -teɪ.təʳ/z (US) -teɪ.t̬ɚ/z
meditation ˌmed.ɪ'teɪ.ʃᵊn, -ə'- -s -z
meditative 'med.ɪ.tə.tɪv, '-ə-, -teɪ- (US) -teɪ.t̬ɪv -ly -li -ness -nəs, -nɪs
Mediterranean ˌmed.ɪ.tᵊr'eɪ.ni.ən, ˌ-ə- (US) -tə'reɪ-
medi|um 'miː.di|.əm -a -ə -ums -əmz 'medium ˌwave
Medjugorje 'met.jʊ.gɔː.tʃə (US) -gɔːr-

medlar 'med.ləʳ (US) -lɚ **-s** -z
medley (M) 'med.li **-s** -z
Medlock 'med.lɒk (US) -lɑːk
Médoc 'meɪ.dɒk, 'med.ɒk, -'- (US) 'meɪ.dɑːk, -'- **-s** -s
medulla med'ʌl.ə, mɪ'dʌl-, mə- (US) mɪ- **-s** -z
medus|a (M) mɪ'djuː.z|ə, mə-, med'juː-, -s|ə (US) mə'duː-, -'djuː- **-as** -əz **-ae** -iː
Medway 'med.weɪ
Mee miː
meed miːd **-s** -z
meek (M) miːk **-er** -əʳ (US) -ɚ **-est** -ɪst, -əst **-ly** -li **-ness** -nəs, -nɪs
meerkat 'mɪə.kæt (US) 'mɪr- **-s** -s
meerschaum 'mɪə.ʃəm, -ʃaʊm (US) 'mɪr-, -ʃɑːm, -ʃɔːm **-s** -z
Meerut 'mɪə.rət (US) 'miː-
meet miːt **-s** -s **-ness** -nəs, -nɪs **-ing** -ɪŋ, 'miː.t̬ɪŋ **met** met
meeting 'miː.tɪŋ (US) -t̬ɪŋ **-s** -z
Meg meg
mega- 'meg.ə-, ˌmeg.ə'-
Note: Prefix. May carry primary or secondary stress on the first syllable, e.g. **megalith** /'meg.ə.lɪθ/, **megalithic** /ˌmeg.ə'lɪθ.ɪk/.
megabit 'meg.ə.bɪt **-s** -s
megabucks 'meg.ə.bʌks
megabyte 'meg.ə.baɪt **-s** -s
megacycle 'meg.əˌsaɪ.kl̩ **-s** -z
megadeath 'meg.ə.deθ **-s** -s
megahertz 'meg.ə.hɜːts (US) -hɝːts, -herts
megalith 'meg.ə.lɪθ **-s** -s
megalithic ˌmeg.ə'lɪθ.ɪk
megalomania ˌmeg.əl.əʊ'meɪ.ni.ə (US) -oʊ'meɪ-, -ə'-, '-njə
megalomaniac ˌmeg.əl.əʊ'meɪ.ni.æk (US) -oʊ'-, -ə'- **-s** -s
megalomaniacal ˌmeg.əl.əʊ.mə'naɪ.ə.kəl
megalopolis ˌmeg.əl'ɒp.ə.lɪs (US) -'ɑː.pə-
Megan 'meg.ən (US) 'meg-, 'miː.gən
megaphone 'meg.ə.fəʊn (US) -foʊn **-s** -z
megaplex 'meg.ə.pleks **-es** -ɪz
megastar 'meg.ə.stɑːʳ (US) -stɑːr **-s** -z
megastore 'meg.ə.stɔːʳ (US) -stɔːr **-s** -z
megatheri|um ˌmeg.ə'θɪə.ri|.əm (US) -'θɪr.i- **-a** -ə
megaton 'meg.ə.tʌn **-s** -z
megavolt 'meg.ə.vəʊlt, -vɒlt (US) -voʊlt **-s** -s
megawatt 'meg.ə.wɒt (US) -wɑːt **-s** -s
Meghan 'meg.ən (US) 'meg-, 'miː.gən
megilp mə'gɪlp, mɪ- (US) mə-
megrim 'miː.grɪm, -grəm (US) -grɪm **-s** -z
Mehta 'meɪ.tə
Meier 'maɪ.əʳ (US) -ɚ
Meikle 'miː.kl̩
Meiklejohn 'mɪk.l̩.dʒɒn, 'miː.kl̩- (US) -dʒɑːn
meios|is maɪ'əʊ.s|ɪs (US) -'oʊ- **-es** -iːz
Meir *English surname:* mɪəʳ (US) mɪr *Israeli surname:* meɪ'ɪəʳ (US) meɪ'ɪr, maɪ.ɚ
Meirionnydd mer.i.ɒn.ɪð (US) -ɑː.nɪθ
Meissen 'maɪ.sən
Meistersinger 'maɪ.stəˌsɪŋ.əʳ, -ˌzɪŋ- (US) -stɚˌsɪŋ.ɚ, -ˌzɪŋ- **-s** -z
Mekka 'mek.ə
Meknès mek'nes
Mekong ˌmiː'kɒŋ, ˌmeɪ- (US) ˌmeɪ'kɑːŋ, -kɔːŋ *stress shift:* ˌMekong 'River
Mel mel
melamine 'mel.ə.miːn, -mɪn (US) -miːn
melancholia ˌmel.ən'kəʊ.li.ə, -əŋ'- (US) -ən'koʊ-
melancholic ˌmel.ən'kɒl.ɪk, -əŋ'- (US) -ən'kɑː.lɪk *stress shift:* ˌmelancholic 'mood
melancholy 'mel.ən.kəl.i, -əŋ-, -kɒl- (US) -ən.kɑː.li
Melanchthon mə'læŋk.θɒn, mɪ-, mel'æŋk-, -θən (US) mə'læŋk.θən
Melanesi|a ˌmel.ə'niː.zi|.ə, -ʒi-, '-ʒ|ə (US) -ʒ|ə, -ʃ|ə **-an/s** -ən/z
mélang|e meɪ'lɑ̃ːnʒ, '-- (US) meɪ'lɑ̃ːʒ, -'lɔ̃ːʒ, -'lɑːndʒ, -'lɔːndʒ **-es** -ɪz
Melanie 'mel.ə.ni
mela|nin 'mel.ə|.nɪn **-nism** -nɪ.zəm
melanom|a ˌmel.ə'nəʊ.m|ə (US) -'noʊ- **-as** -əz **-ata** -ə.tə (US) -t̬ə
Melanthius mə'lænt.θi.əs, mɪ-, mel'ænt-, -ɒs (US) mə'lænt.θi.əs
Melba 'mel.bə ˌ**Melba 'toast**
Melbourne 'mel.bən, -bɔːn (US) -bɚn, -bɔːrn
Note: In Australia always /'mel.bən/.
Melchett 'mel.tʃɪt
Melchior 'mel.ki.ɔːʳ (US) -ɔːr
Melchizedek mel'kɪz.ə.dek
Melcombe 'mel.kəm
meld meld **-s** -z **-ing** -ɪŋ **-ed** -ɪd
Meldrew 'mel.druː
Meleager ˌmel.i'eɪ.gəʳ (US) -dʒɚ
mêlée, melee 'mel.eɪ, 'meɪ.leɪ, -'- (US) 'meɪ.leɪ, -'- **-s** -z
Melhuish 'mel.ɪʃ, 'mel.ju.ɪʃ, -hju-; mel'juː.ɪʃ, -'hjuː-
Melibeus ˌmel.ɪ'biː.əs, -ə'- (US) -ə'-
Melincourt 'mel.ɪn.kɔːt, -ɪŋ- (US) -ɪn.kɔːrt
Melinda mə'lɪn.də, mɪ-, mel'ɪn- (US) mə'lɪn-
melinite 'mel.ɪ.naɪt
meliorable 'miː.li.ər.ə.bl̩ (US) 'miːl.jɚ.ə-
melior|ate 'miː.li.ər|.eɪt (US) 'miːl.jə.r|eɪt, 'miː.li.ə- **-ates** -eɪts **-ating** -eɪ.tɪŋ (US) -eɪ.t̬ɪŋ **-ated** -eɪ.tɪd (US) -eɪ.t̬ɪd
melioration ˌmiː.li.ər'eɪ.ʃən (US) ˌmiːl.jə'reɪ-, ˌmiː.li.ə'- **-s** -z
meliorative 'miː.li.ər.ə.tɪv (US) 'miːl.jɚ-
meliorator 'miː.li.ər.eɪ.təʳ (US) 'miːl.jə.reɪ.t̬ɚ **-s** -z
Melissa mə'lɪs.ə, mɪ-, mel'ɪs- (US) mə'lɪs-
Melita mə'liː.tə; 'mel.ɪ- (US) 'mel.ɪ.t̬ə; mə'liː-, -'lɪt̬.ə
Melksham 'melk.ʃəm
mellifluen|t mɪ'lɪf.lu.ən|t, mə-, mel'ɪf- (US) mə'lɪf- **-ce** -*t*s
mellifluous mɪ'lɪf.lu.əs, mə-, mel'ɪf- (US) mə'lɪf- **-ly** -li **-ness** -nəs, -nɪs
Mellin 'mel.ɪn
Mellor 'mel.əʳ, -ɔːʳ (US) -ɚ, -ɔːr
Mellors 'mel.əz, -ɔːz (US) -ɚz, -ɔːrz
mellow 'mel.əʊ (US) -oʊ **-er** -əʳ (US) -ɚ **-est** -ɪst, -əst **-ness** -nəs, -nɪs **-s** -z **-ing** -ɪŋ **-ed** -d
Melmoth 'mel.məθ
Melmotte 'mel.mɒt, -'- (US) 'mel.mɑːt
melodic mə'lɒd.ɪk, mɪ-, mel'ɒd- (US) mə'lɑː.dɪk **-ally** -əl.i, -li
melodious mə'ləʊ.di.əs, mɪ-, mel'əʊ- (US) mə'loʊ- **-ly** -li **-ness** -nəs, -nɪs
melodist 'mel.ə.dɪst **-s** -s
melodrama 'mel.əʊˌdrɑː.mə (US) -oʊˌdrɑː.mə, -əˌ-, -ˌdræm.ə **-s** -z
melodramatic ˌmel.əʊ.drə'mæt.ɪk (US) -oʊ.drə'mæt̬-, ˌ-ə- **-s** -s **-ally** -əl.i, -li
melodramatist ˌmel.əʊ'dræm.ə.tɪst (US) -oʊ'drɑː.mə.t̬ɪst, -ə'-, -'dræm.ə- **-s** -s
melod|y (M) 'mel.ə.d|i **-ies** -iz
Meloids® 'mel.ɔɪdz
melon 'mel.ən **-s** -z
Melos 'miː.lɒs, 'mel.ɒs (US) 'miː.lɑːs
Melpomene mel'pɒm.ə.ni, '-ɪ-, -niː (US) -'pɑː.mə-
Melrose 'mel.rəʊz (US) -roʊz
melt melt **-s** -s **-ing/ly** -ɪŋ/li (US) 'mel.t̬ɪŋ/li **-ed** -ɪd (US) 'mel.t̬ɪd **'melting ˌpot**
meltdown 'melt.daʊn **-s** -z
Meltham 'mel.θəm
Melton 'mel.tən
Meltonian® mel'təʊ.ni.ən (US) -'toʊ-
Melton Mowbray ˌmel.tən'məʊ.breɪ, -təm'-, -bri (US) -tən'moʊ-
meltwater 'meltˌwɔː.təʳ (US) -ˌwɑː.t̬ɚ, -ˌwɔː- **-s** -z
Melville 'mel.vɪl
Melvin, Melvyn 'mel.vɪn
member 'mem.bəʳ (US) -bɚ **-s** -z **-ship/s** -ʃɪp/s ˌ**Member of 'Parliament**
membrane 'mem.breɪn **-s** -z
membraneous mem'breɪ.ni.əs
membranous 'mem.brə.nəs
Memel 'meɪ.məl
memento mɪ'men.təʊ, mem'en-, mə'men- (US) mə'men.toʊ **-(e)s** -z

memento mori mɪˌmen.təʊˈmɒr.i, memˌen-, məˌmen-, -ˈmɔː.raɪ (US) məˌmen.toʊˈmɔːr.iː, -aɪ
Memnon ˈmem.nɒn, -nən (US) -nɑːn
memo ˈmem.əʊ (US) -oʊ **-s** -z
memoir ˈmem.wɑːʳ (US) -wɑːr, -wɔːr **-s** -z
memorabilia ˌmem.ᵊr.əˈbɪl.i.ə, -ˈbiː.li- (US) -ˈbɪl.i-, ˈ-jə, -ˈbiː.li-, -ˈbiːl.jə
memorab|le ˈmem.ᵊr.ə.b|l̩ **-ly** -li
memorand|um ˌmem.ᵊrˈæn.d|əm (US) -əˈræn- **-a** -ə **-ums** -əmz
memorial məˈmɔː.ri.əl, mɪˈ-, memˈɔː- (US) məˈmɔːr.i- **-s** -z
memorializ|e, -is|e məˈmɔː.ri.ə.laɪz, mɪˈ-, memˈɔː- (US) məˈmɔːr.i- **-es** -ɪz **-ing** -ɪŋ **-ed** -d
memoriz|e, -is|e ˈmem.ᵊr.aɪz (US) -ə.raɪz **-es** -ɪz **-ing** -ɪŋ **-ed** -d
memor|y ˈmem.ᵊr|.i, ˈ-r|i **-ies** -iz
Memphis ˈmemp.fɪs
memsahib ˈmemˌsɑː.hɪb, ˈ-sɑːb (US) ˈmemˌsɑː.hɪb, ˈ-sɑːb; ˌmem.sɑːˈhiːb, -ˈɪb **-s** -z
men *(plur. of* **man***)* men **ˈmen's ˌroom**
menac|e ˈmen.ɪs, -əs (US) -əs **-es** -ɪz **-ing/ly** -ɪŋ/li **-ed** -t
ménag|e menˈɑːʒ, meɪˈnɑːʒ, mə-, mɪ-, -ˈnæʒ, ˈ-- (US) meɪˈnɑːʒ, mə- **-es** -ɪz
ménage à trois menˌɑːʒ.ɑːˈtrwɑː, meɪˌnɑːz-, mə-, mɪ-, -ˌnæʒ, ˌmen.ɑːz-, ˌmeɪ.nɑːʒ-, -ˌnæʒ (US) meɪˌnɑːʒ-, mə-
menagerie məˈnædʒ.ᵊr.i, mɪ-, menˈædʒ-, -ˈæʒ- (US) məˈnædʒ-, -ˈnæʒ- **-s** -z
Menai ˈmen.aɪ
Menander məˈnæn.dəʳ, mɪ-, menˈæn- (US) məˈnæn.dɚ
menarche menˈɑː.ki, mɪˈnɑː-, mə-; ˈmen.ɑːk (US) məˈnɑːr.ki, men-
Mencap ˈmen.kæp, ˈmeŋ- (US) ˈmen-
Mencken ˈmeŋ.kən
mend mend **-s** -z **-ing** -ɪŋ **-ed** -ɪd **-er/s** -əʳ/z (US) -ɚ/z
mendacious menˈdeɪ.ʃəs **-ly** -li **-ness** -nəs, -nɪs
mendacity menˈdæs.ə.ti, -ɪ.ti (US) -ə.t̬i
Mendel ˈmen.dᵊl
Mendeleev ˌmen.dᵊlˈeɪ.ev, -dɪˈleɪ-, -ef, -əf (US) -dəˈleɪ.əf
mendelevium ˌmen.dᵊlˈiː.vi.əm, -dɪˈliː- (US) -dəˈliː-
Mendeleyev ˌmen.dᵊlˈeɪ.ev, -dɪˈleɪ-, -ef, -əf (US) -dəˈleɪ.əf
Mendelian menˈdiː.li.ən
Mendelssohn *English surname:* ˈmen.dᵊl.sᵊn *German composer:* ˈmen.dᵊl.sᵊn, -səʊn (US) -sᵊn, -soʊn, -zoʊn
Mendes ˈmen.dez, -des (US) -ˈ-
mendican|cy ˈmen.dɪ.kən|t.si **-t/s** -t/s
mendicity menˈdɪs.ə.ti, -ɪ.ti (US) -ə.t̬i
Mendip ˈmen.dɪp **-s** -s
Mendoza menˈdəʊ.zə (US) -ˈdoʊ-, -sɑː
mene ˈmiː.ni
Menelaus ˌmen.ɪˈleɪ.əs, -ᵊlˈeɪ-
Menem ˈmen.em (US) ˈmeɪn-
menfolk ˈmen.fəʊk (US) -foʊk **-s** -s
menhir ˈmen.hɪəʳ (US) -hɪr **-s** -z
menial ˈmiː.ni.əl, ˈ-njəl **-s** -z **-ly** -i
Ménière ˈmen.i.eəʳ, ˈmeɪ.ni-, ˌ--ˈ-; ˈmeɪ.njeəʳ, -ˈ- (US) meɪˈnjer
meningeal menˈɪn.dʒi.əl, məˈnɪn-, mɪ-; ˌmen.ɪnˈdʒiː.əl, -ənˈ- (US) məˈnɪn.dʒi-
meninges *(plur. of* **meninx***)* məˈnɪn.dʒiːz, mɪ-, menˈɪn- (US) məˈnɪn-
meningitis ˌmen.ɪnˈdʒaɪ.tɪs, -ənˈ- (US) -t̬ɪs
meningococcal məˌnɪn.dʒəʊˈkɒk.ᵊl, -ˌnɪŋ.gəʊˈ- (US) -ˌnɪŋ.goʊˈkɑː.kᵊl
meningo|coccus məˌnɪn.dʒəʊ|ˈkɒk.əs, -ˌnɪŋ.gəʊˈ- (US) -ˌnɪŋ.goʊ|ˈkɑː.kəs **-cocci** -ˈkɒk.saɪ, -aɪ, -iː (US) -ˈkɑːk.saɪ, -ˈkɑː.kaɪ, -kiː
meninx ˈmen.ɪnks (US) ˈmiː.nɪŋks, ˈmen.ɪŋks **meninges** məˈnɪn.dʒiːz, mɪ-, menˈɪn- (US) məˈnɪn-
menisc|us məˈnɪs.k|əs, mɪ-, menˈɪs- (US) məˈnɪs- **-uses** -ə.sɪz **-i** -aɪ, -iː
Menlo Park ˌmen.ləʊˈpɑːk (US) -loʊˈpɑːrk
Mennonite ˈmen.ə.naɪt **-s** -s
Meno ˈmiː.nəʊ (US) -noʊ
men-of-war *(plur. of* **man-of-war***)* ˌmen.əvˈwɔːʳ (US) -ˈwɔːr
menopausal ˌmen.əʊˈpɔː.zᵊl, ˌmiː.nəʊˈ- (US) ˈmen.ə.pɑː.zᵊl, -pɔː-
menopause ˈmen.əʊ.pɔːz, ˈmiː.nəʊ- (US) ˈmen.ə.pɑːz, -pɔːz
menorah mɪˈnɔː.rə, mə- (US) -ˈnɔːr.ə **-s** -z
Menorca menˈɔː.kə, məˈnɔː-, mɪ- (US) məˈnɔːr.kə
Mensa ˈment.sə
menservants *(plur. of* **manservant***)* ˈmenˌsɜː.vᵊnts (US) -ˌsɝː-
menses ˈment.siːz
Menshevik ˈmen.ʃə.vɪk, -ʃɪ- (US) -ʃə.vɪk **-s** -s
mens rea ˌmenzˈreɪ.ə (US) -ˈriː.ə
menstrual ˈment.struəl, -stru.əl (US) -strəl, -stru.əl
menstru|ate ˈment.stru|.eɪt (US) -stru-, -str|eɪt **-ates** -eɪts **-ating** -eɪ.tɪŋ (US) -eɪ.t̬ɪŋ **-ated** -eɪ.tɪd (US) -eɪ.t̬ɪd
menstruation ˌment.struˈeɪ.ʃᵊn (US) -struˈeɪ-, -ˌstreɪ-
mensual ˈment.sju.əl, sjʊəl (US) -ʃu.əl
mensurability ˌment.ʃᵊr.əˈbɪl.ə.ti, -ʃʊ.rəˈ-, -sjᵊr.əˈ-, -sjʊ.rəˈ-, -ɪ.ti (US) -ʃɚ.əˈbɪl.ə.t̬i, -sɚ-
mensurable ˈment.ʃᵊr.ə.bl̩, -ʃʊ.rə-, -sjᵊr.ə-, -sjʊ.rə- (US) -ʃɚ.ə-, -sɚ-
mensuration ˌment.ʃᵊrˈeɪ.ʃᵊn, -ʃʊˈreɪ-, -sjᵊrˈeɪ-, -sjʊˈreɪ- (US) -ʃəˈreɪ-, -səˈ-
menswear ˈmenz.weəʳ (US) -wer
-ment -mənt
mental ˈmen.tᵊl (US) -t̬ᵊl **-ly** -i **ˌmental ˈage; ˈmental ˌhospital**
mentalism ˈmen.tᵊl.ɪ.zᵊm (US) -t̬ᵊl-
mentalistic ˌmen.tᵊlˈɪs.tɪk (US) -t̬ᵊlˈ- **-ally** -ᵊl.i, -li
mentalit|y menˈtæl.ə.t|i, -ɪ.t|i (US) -ə.t̬|i **-ies** -iz
Menteith menˈtiːθ, mən-
menthol ˈment.θɒl, -θᵊl (US) -θɔːl, -θɑːl, -θᵊl, -θoʊl
mentholated ˈment.θᵊl.eɪ.tɪd (US) -t̬ɪd
mention ˈmen.tʃᵊn **-s** -z **-ing** -ɪŋ **-ed** -d **-able** -ə.bl̩, ˈmentʃ.nə-
Mentone menˈtəʊ.neɪ, -ni (US) -ˈtoʊ.ni
mentor ˈmen.tɔːʳ, -təʳ (US) -tɚ, -tɔːr **-s** -z **-ing** -ɪŋ
menu ˈmen.juː **-s** -z
menu-driven ˈmen.juːˌdrɪv.ᵊn, ˌmen.juːˈdrɪv- (US) ˈmen.juːˌdrɪv-
Menuhin ˈmen.ju.ɪn, -hɪn (US) -ɪn
Menzies ˈmen.zɪz, ˈmeŋ.ɪs, ˈmɪŋ- (US) ˈmen.ziːz
Meopham ˈmep.əm
meow miːˈaʊ **-s** -z **-ing** -ɪŋ **-ed** -d
MEP ˌem.iːˈpiː **-s** -z
Mepham ˈmef.əm
Mephisto məˈfɪs.təʊ, mɪ-, mefˈɪs- (US) məˈfɪs.toʊ
Mephistophelean, -lian ˌmef.ɪ.stəˈfiː.li.ən, ˌ-ə-, -stɒfˈɪl-; məˌfɪs.təˈ-, mɪ-, mefˌɪs-; ˌmef.ɪˌstɒf.əˈliː- (US) ˌmef.ɪ.stəˈfiː.li-; məˌfɪs.təˈ-; ˌmef.əˌstɑː.fəˈliː-, -ˌstoʊ-
Mephistopheles ˌmef.ɪˈstɒf.ɪ.liːz, -ᵊl.iːz (US) -əˈstɑː.fə.liːz
mephitic mɪˈfɪt.ɪk, mefˈɪt- (US) məˈfɪt̬-
mephitis mɪˈfaɪ.tɪs, mefˈaɪ- (US) məˈfaɪ.t̬ɪs
Merc mɜːk (US) mɝːk **-s** -s
mercantile ˈmɜː.kᵊn.taɪl (US) ˈmɝː-, -tiːl, -taɪl, -tɪl
mercantilism ˈmɜː.kᵊn.tɪ.lɪ.zᵊm, -taɪ-, -tᵊl.ɪ- (US) ˈmɝː.kən.tiː-, -tɪ-, -taɪ-
Mercator mɜːˈkeɪ.təʳ, -tɔːʳ (US) mɚˈkeɪ.t̬ɚ
Mercedes *English female name:* ˈmɜː.sɪ.diːz (US) ˈmɝː-; mɚˈseɪ.diːz *trademark:* məˈseɪ.diːz, mɜː- (US) mɚ-, mɝː-
Mercedes-Benz məˌseɪ.diːzˈbents, mɜː-, -ˈbenz (US) mɚˌseɪ.diːzˈbenz, mɝː-, -ˈbents
mercenar|y ˈmɜː.sᵊn.ᵊr|.i, -sɪ.nᵊr-, -sᵊn.r|i (US) ˈmɝː.sə.ner.i **-ies** -iz
mercer (M) ˈmɜː.səʳ (US) ˈmɝː.sɚ **-s** -z
merceriz|e, -is|e ˈmɜː.sᵊr.aɪz (US) ˈmɝː- **-es** -ɪz **-ing** -ɪŋ **-ed** -d

merchandise *(n.)* 'mɜː.tʃən.daɪs, -daɪs (US) 'mɝː-
merchandiz|e, -ise *(v.)* 'mɜː.tʃən.daɪz (US) 'mɝː- **-es** -ɪz **-ing** -ɪŋ **-ed** -d **-er/s** -ər/z (US) -ɚ/z
merchant 'mɜː.tʃənt (US) 'mɝː- **-s** -s **-able** -ə.bl̩ ˌ**merchant 'bank;** ˌ**merchant 'navy**
merchant|man 'mɜː.tʃənt|.mən (US) 'mɝː- **-men** -mən, -men
Merchison 'mɜː.kɪ.sən (US) 'mɝː-
Merchiston 'mɜː.tʃɪ.stən (US) 'mɝː-
Merci|a 'mɜː.si|.ə, -ʃi|.ə (US) 'mɝː.ʃ|ə, '-ʃi|.ə, -si- **-an** -ən
merciful 'mɜː.sɪ.fəl, -fʊl (US) 'mɝː- **-ly** -i **-ness** -nəs, -nɪs
merciless 'mɜː.sɪ.ləs, -lɪs (US) 'mɝː- **-ly** -li **-ness** -nəs, -nɪs
mercurial mɜː'kjʊə.ri.əl, -'kjɔː- (US) mɝː'kjʊr.i- **-s** -z **-ly** -i
mercuric mɜː'kjʊə.rɪk, -'kjɔː- (US) mɝː'kjʊr.ɪk
Mercurochrome® mɜː'kjʊə.rə.krəʊm, -'kjɔː- (US) mɝː'kjʊr.ə.kroʊm
mercurous 'mɜː.kjər.əs, -kjʊ.rəs (US) 'mɝː.kjʊr.əs, -kjɚ-
mercury (M) 'mɜː.kjər.i, -kjʊ.ri (US) 'mɝː.kjə.ri, -kjɚ-
Mercutio mɜː'kjuː.ʃi.əʊ (US) mɝː'kjuː.ʃi.oʊ
merc|y (M) 'mɜː.s|i (US) 'mɝː- **-ies** -iz 'mercy ˌkilling
mere mɪər (US) mɪr **-s** -z
Meredith 'mer.ə.dɪθ, '-ɪ- *as if Welsh:* mer'ed.ɪθ
merely 'mɪə.li (US) 'mɪr-
merest 'mɪə.rɪst, -rəst (US) 'mɪr.ɪst, -əst
meretricious ˌmer.ɪ'trɪʃ.əs, -ə'- (US) -ə'- **-ly** -li **-ness** -nəs, -nɪs
merganser mɜː'gænt.sər, -'gæn.zər (US) mɝː'gænt.sɚ **-s** -z
merg|e mɜːdʒ (US) mɝːdʒ **-es** -ɪz **-ing** -ɪŋ **-ed** -d
merger 'mɜː.dʒər (US) 'mɝː.dʒɚ **-s** -z
Meribel 'mer.i.bel
Mérida 'mer.ɪ.də (US) -iː.dɑː
meridian mə'rɪd.i.ən, mɪ- (US) mə'rɪd- **-s** -z
meridional mə'rɪd.i.ə.nəl, mɪ- (US) mə'rɪd- **-ly** -i
Mérimée 'mer.ɪ.meɪ (US) ˌmeɪ.riː'meɪ
meringue mə'ræŋ **-s** -z
merino mə'riː.nəʊ (US) -noʊ **-s** -z
Merioneth ˌmer.i'ɒn.ɪθ, -neθ, -nəθ (US) -'ɑː.nɪθ **-shire** -ʃər, -ʃɪər (US) -ʃɚ, -ˌʃɪr
meristem 'mer.i.stem, '-ə- (US) '-ə- **-s** -z
meristematic ˌmer.i.stɪ'mæt.ɪk, ˌ-ə-, -stə'- (US) -ə.stə'mæţ- **-ally** -əl.i, -li
mer|it 'mer|.ɪt **-its** -ɪts **-iting** -ɪ.tɪŋ (US) -ɪ.ţɪŋ **-ited** -ɪ.tɪd (US) -ɪ.ţɪd
meritocrac|y ˌmer.ɪ'tɒk.rə.s|i, -ə'- (US) -ə'tɑː.krə- **-ies** -iz
meritocratic ˌmer.ɪ.tə'kræt.ɪk
meritorious ˌmer.ɪ'tɔː.ri.əs, -ə'- (US) -ə'tɔːr.i- **-ly** -li **-ness** -nəs, -nɪs
Merivale 'mer.ɪ.veɪl
merl mɜːl (US) mɝːl **-s** -z
merle (M) mɜːl (US) mɝːl **-s** -z
merlin (M) 'mɜː.lɪn (US) 'mɝː- **-s** -z
merlot (M) 'meə.ləʊ, -'- (US) mɝː'loʊ, mer- **-s** -z
mermaid 'mɜː.meɪd (US) 'mɝː- **-s** -z
mer|man (M) 'mɜː|.mæn (US) 'mɝː- **-men** -men
Meroe 'mer.əʊ.i (US) -oʊ-
Merope 'mer.ə.pi
Merovingian ˌmer.əʊ'vɪn.dʒi.ən, '-dʒən (US) -oʊ'-, -ə'-
Merrick 'mer.ɪk
Merrilies 'mer.ɪ.liz, -əl.iz
Merrill 'mer.əl, -ɪl
Merrimac 'mer.ɪ.mæk, '-ə-
Merriman 'mer.i.mən
merriment 'mer.i.mənt
Merritt 'mer.ɪt
Merrivale 'mer.i.veɪl
merr|y (M) 'mer|.i **-ier** -i.ər (US) -i.ɚ **-iest** -i.ɪst, -i.əst **-ily** -əl.i, -ɪ.li **-iness** -ɪ.nəs, -ɪ.nɪs
merry-andrew ˌmer.i'æn.druː **-s** -z
Merrydown® 'mer.i.daʊn
merry-go-round 'mer.i.gəʊˌraʊnd (US) -goʊˌ- **-s** -z
merrymak|er 'mer.iˌmeɪ.k|ər (US) -k|ɚ **-ers** -əz (US) -ɚz **-ing** -ɪŋ
Merryweather 'mer.iˌweð.ər (US) -ɚ
Mersey 'mɜː.zi (US) 'mɝː- **-side** -saɪd **-sider/s** -ˌsaɪ.dər/z
Merson 'mɜː.sən (US) 'mɝː-
Merthyr 'mɜː.θər (US) 'mɝː.θɚ
Merthyr Tydfil ˌmɜː.θə'tɪd.vɪl (US) ˌmɝː.θɚ'-
Merton 'mɜː.tən (US) 'mɝː-
Mervyn 'mɜː.vɪn (US) 'mɝː-
Meryl 'mer.əl, -ɪl
mesa 'meɪ.sə **-s** -z
mésallianc|e mez'æl.i.ənts, meɪ'zæl-, -ɑ̃ːns *as if French:* ˌmez.æl.i.'ɑ̃ːns (US) meɪ'zæl.i.ənts; ˌmeɪ.zə'liː- **-es** -ɪz
mescal 'mes.kæl, -'- (US) -'- **-s** -z
mescalin(e) 'mes.kəl.ɪn, -iːn
mesdames (M) *(plur. of* **madame***)* meɪ'dæm, -dæmz, '-- (US) -'dɑːm, -'dæm
mesdemoiselles (M) *(plur. of* **mademoiselle***)* ˌmeɪ.dəm.wə'zel, -'zelz (US) ˌmeɪd.mwɑː'zel
meseems mɪ'siːmz
mesembryanthemum məˌzem.bri'ænt.θɪ.məm, mɪ-, -θəm.əm (US) mesˌem-, mez- **-s** -z
mesh meʃ **-es** -ɪz **-ing** -ɪŋ **-ed** -t
Meshach, Meschak 'miː.ʃæk
Meshed 'meʃ.ed
mesial 'miː.zi.əl (US) 'miː-, 'mez.i-, 'mes-
Mesmer 'mez.mər (US) -mɚ
mesmeric mez'mer.ɪk
mesmer|ism 'mez.mər|.ɪ.zəm **-ist/s** -ɪst/s
mesmeriz|e, -is|e 'mez.mər.aɪz **-es** -ɪz **-ing** -ɪŋ **-ed** -d **-er/s** -ər/z (US) -ɚ/z
mesne miːn
meso- mes.əʊ-, mez-, miː.səʊ-, -zəʊ- (US) mez.oʊ-, mes-, -ə-, miː.soʊ-, -sə-
Note: Prefix. May carry either primary or secondary stress on the first syllable, e.g. **mesoderm** /'mes.əʊ.dɜːm (US) 'mez.oʊ.dɜːrm/, **mesodermal** /ˌmes.əʊ'dɜː.məl (US) ˌmez.oʊ'dɜːr-/.
mesoderm 'mes.əʊ.dɜːm, 'mez-, 'miː.səʊ-, -zəʊ- (US) 'mez.oʊ.dɝːm, 'mes-, '-ə-
mesodermal ˌmes.əʊ'dɜː.məl, ˌmez-, ˌmiː.səʊ'-, -zəʊ'- (US) ˌmez.oʊ'dɝː-, ˌmes-, -ə'-
mesodermic ˌmes.əʊ'dɜː.mɪk, ˌmez-, ˌmiː.səʊ'-, -zəʊ'- (US) ˌmez.oʊ'dɝː-, ˌmes-, -ə'-
mesolect 'mes.əʊ.lekt, 'mez-, 'miː.səʊ-, -zəʊ- (US) 'mez.oʊ-, 'mes-, -ə- **-s** -s
mesolectal ˌmes.əʊ'lek.təl, ˌmez-, ˌmiː.səʊ'-, -zəʊ'- (US) ˌmez.oʊ'-, ˌmes-, -ə-
mesomorph 'mes.əʊ.mɔːf, 'mez-, 'miː.səʊ-, -zəʊ- (US) 'mez.oʊ.mɔːrf, 'mes-, '-ə- **-s** -s
meson 'miː.zɒn, 'meɪ-, -sɒn, 'mes.ɒn, 'mez- (US) 'mez.ɑːn, 'mes-, 'meɪ.sɑːn, 'miː-, -zɑːn **-s** -z
Mesopotami|a ˌmes.ə.pə'teɪ.mi|.ə **-an/s** -ən/z
mesotron 'mes.əʊ.trɒn, 'mez-, 'miː.səʊ-, -zəʊ- (US) 'mez.oʊ.trɑːn, 'mes-, '-ə- **-s** -z
Mesozoic ˌmes.əʊ'zəʊ.ɪk, ˌmiː.səʊ'- (US) ˌmez.oʊ'zoʊ-, ˌmes-, -ə'-
mesquite (M) mes'kiːt, mə'skiːt, mɪ-, 'mes.kɪt (US) mə'skiːt, mes'kiːt
mess mes **-es** -ɪz **-ing** -ɪŋ **-ed** -t
messag|e 'mes.ɪdʒ **-es** -ɪz **-ing** -ɪŋ **-ed**
messeigneurs *(plur. of* **monseigneur***)* ˌmes.eɪ'njɜː
messenger 'mes.ɪn.dʒər, -ən- (US) -dʒ[illegible] **-s** -z
Messerschmitt® 'mes.ə.ʃmɪt (US) '-ɚ-
Messiaen 'mes.jɑ̃ːŋ, -i.ɑ̃ːŋ *as if French:* mes'jɑ̃ːŋ (US) mes'jɑ̃ːn
messiah (M) mə'saɪ.ə, mɪ-, mes'aɪ- (US) mə'saɪ- **-s** -z
messianic ˌmes.i'æn.ɪk

messieurs meɪˈsjɜːz, mesˈjɜːz, ˈmes.əz *as if French:* mesˈjɜː (US) -ɚz
Messina mesˈiː.nə, məˈsiː-, mɪ- (US) mə-, mesˈiː-
messmate ˈmes.meɪt **-s** -s
Messrs. *(plur. of* **Mr***)* ˈmes.əz (US) -ɚz
messuag|e ˈmes.wɪdʒ, -ju.ɪdʒ (US) ˈ-wɪdʒ **-es** -ɪz
mess|y ˈmes|.i **-ier** -i.əʳ (US) -i.ɚ **-iest** -i.ɪst, -i.əst **-ily** -ɪ.li, -ᵊl.i **-iness** -ɪ.nəs, -ɪ.nɪs
mestiz|o mesˈtiː.z|əʊ, məˈstiː-, mɪ- (US) mesˈtiː.z|oʊ **-a** -ə **-os** -əʊz (US) -oʊz **-as** -əz
Mestre ˈmes.treɪ
met *(from* **meet***)* met
meta- met.ə-; məˈtæ-, metˈæ-, mɪˈtæ- (US) meţ.ə-; məˈtæ-, metˈæ-
Note: Prefix. Normally carries primary or secondary stress on the first syllable, e.g. **metaplasm** /ˈmet.əˌplæz.ᵊm (US) ˈmeţ-/, **metabolic** /ˌmet.əˈbɒl.ɪk (US) ˌmeţ.əˈbɑː.lɪk/, or primary stress on the second syllable, e.g. **metabolism** /məˈtæb.ᵊl.ɪ.zᵊm/.
metabolic ˌmet.əˈbɒl.ɪk (US) ˌmeţ.əˈbɑː.lɪk **-ally** -ᵊl.i, -li
metabolism məˈtæb.ᵊl.ɪ.zᵊm, mɪ-, metˈæb- (US) məˈtæb- **-s** -z
metaboliz|e, -is|e məˈtæb.ᵊl.aɪz, mɪ-, metˈæb- (US) məˈ- **-es** -ɪz **-ing** -ɪŋ **-ed** -d
metacarp|al ˌmet.əˈkɑː.p|ᵊl (US) ˌmeţ.əˈkɑːr- **-us** -əs
metacentre, -center ˈmet.əˌsen.təʳ (US) ˈmeţ.əˌsen.ţɚ **-s** -z
metagalax|y ˈmet.əˌgæl.ək.s|i (US) ˈmeţ- **-ies** -iz
metal ˈmet.ᵊl (US) ˈmeţ- **-s** -z **-ling** -ɪŋ **-led** -d ˈ**metal deˌtector**
metalanguage ˈmet.ᵊlˌæŋ.gwɪdʒ (US) ˈmeţ-
metallic məˈtæl.ɪk, mɪ-, metˈæl- (US) məˈtæl- **-ally** -ᵊl.i, -li
Metallica metˈæl.ɪ.kə, məˈtæl-, mɪ-, -lə-
metalliferous ˌmet.ᵊlˈɪf.ᵊr.əs (US) ˌmeţ-
metallography ˌmet.ᵊlˈɒg.rə.fi (US) ˌmeţ.ᵊlˈɑː.grə-
metalloid ˈmet.ᵊl.ɔɪd (US) ˈmeţ-
metallurgic|al ˌmet.ᵊlˈɜː.dʒɪ.k|ᵊl (US) ˌmeţ.ᵊlˈɝː- **-ally** -ᵊl.i, -li
metallurgist metˈæl.ə.dʒɪst, məˈtæl-, mɪ-; ˈmet.ᵊl.ɜː- (US) ˈmeţ.ᵊl.ɝː- **-s** -s
metallurgy metˈæl.ə.dʒi, məˈtæl, mɪ-; ˈmet.ᵊl.ɜː- (US) ˈmeţ.ᵊl.ɝː-
metalwork ˈmet.ᵊl.wɜːk (US) ˈmeţ.ᵊl.wɝːk **-er/s** -əʳ/z (US) -ɚ/z
metamorphic ˌmet.əˈmɔː.fɪk (US) ˌmeţ.əˈmɔːr-
metamorphism ˌmet.əˈmɔː.fɪ.zᵊm (US) ˌmeţ.əˈmɔːr- **-s** -z
metamorphos|e ˌmet.əˈmɔː.fəʊz (US) ˌmeţ.əˈmɔːr.foʊz **-es** -ɪz **-ing** -ɪŋ **-ed** -d
metamorphos|is ˌmet.əˈmɔː.fə.s|ɪs; -mɔːˈfəʊ- (US) ˌmeţ.əˈmɔːr.fə-; -mɔːrˈfoʊ- **-es** -iːz
metaphor ˈmet.ə.fəʳ, -fɔːʳ (US) ˈmeţ.ə.fɔːr, -fɚ **-s** -z
metaphoric ˌmet.əˈfɒr.ɪk (US) ˌmeţ.əˈfɔːr.ɪk **-al** -ᵊl **-ally** -ᵊl.i, -li
metaphysic|al ˌmet.əˈfɪz.ɪ.k|ᵊl (US) ˌmeţ- **-ally** -ᵊl.i, -li
metaphysician ˌmet.ə.fɪˈzɪʃ.ᵊn (US) ˌmeţ- **-s** -z
metaphysics ˌmet.əˈfɪz.ɪks (US) ˌmeţ-, ˈmeţ.əˌfɪz-
metaplasm ˈmet.əˌplæz.ᵊm (US) ˈmeţ-
metastas|is metˈæs.tə.s|ɪs, mɪˈtæs-, məˈtæs- (US) məˈtæs- **-es** -iːz
metatarsal ˌmet.əˈtɑː.sᵊl (US) ˌmeţ.əˈtɑːr- **-s** -z
metatars|us ˌmet.əˈtɑː.s|əs (US) ˌmeţ.əˈtɑːr- **-i** -aɪ
metathes|is metˈæθ.ə.s|ɪs, mɪˈtæθ-, mə-, ˈ-ɪ- (US) məˈtæθ.ə- **-es** -iːz
Metaxa® metˈæk.sə, mɪˈtæk-, mə- (US) mə-
Metayers mɪˈteɪəz, mə- (US) -ˈteɪɚz
Metcalfe ˈmet.kɑːf, -kəf (US) -kæf
met|e miːt **-es** -s **-ing** -ɪŋ (US) ˈmiː.ţɪŋ **-ed** -ɪd (US) ˈmiː.ţɪd
Metellus mɪˈtel.əs, metˈel- (US) mɪˈtel-
metempsychosis ˌmet.emp.saɪˈkəʊ.sɪs, -əmp-, -sɪˈ-; metˌemp- (US) mɪˌtemp.sɪˈkoʊ-; ˌmet.əmp.saɪˈ-
meteor ˈmiː.ti.əʳ, -ɔːʳ (US) -ţi.ɚ, -ɔːr **-s** -z
meteoric ˌmiː.tiˈɒr.ɪk (US) -ţiˈɔːr- **-ally** -ᵊl.i, -li
meteorite ˈmiː.ti.ᵊr.aɪt (US) -ţi.ə.raɪt **-s** -s
meteorologic ˌmiː.ti.ᵊr.əˈlɒdʒ.ɪk (US) -ţi.ɚ.əˈlɑː.dʒɪ- **-al** -ᵊl **-ally** -ᵊl.i, -li
meteorologist ˌmiː.ti.ᵊrˈɒl.ə.dʒɪst (US) -ţi.əˈrɑːl- **-s** -s
meteorology ˌmiː.ti.ᵊrˈɒl.ə.dʒi (US) -əˈrɑː.lə-
met|er ˈmiː.t|əʳ (US) -ţ|ɚ **-ers** -əz (US) -ɚz **-ering** -ᵊr.ɪŋ **-ered** -əd (US) -ɚd
methadone ˈmeθ.ə.dəʊn (US) -doʊn
methane ˈmiː.θeɪn (US) ˈmeθ.eɪn
methanol ˈmeθ.ə.nɒl, ˈmiː.θə- (US) ˈmeθ.ə.nɑːl, -noʊl
metheglin meθˈeg.lɪn, mɪˈθeg-, mə- (US) məˈθeg-
Metheny məˈθiː.ni
methinks mɪˈθɪŋks
method ˈmeθ.əd **-s** -z
méthode champenoise meɪˌtɒd.ʃɑ̃ːm.pᵊnˈwɑːz (US) -toʊd.ʃɑːm-
methodic məˈθɒd.ɪk, mɪ-, meθˈɒd- (US) məˈθɑː.dɪk **-al** -ᵊl **-ally** -ᵊl.i, -li
Method|ism ˈmeθ.ə.d|ɪ.zᵊm **-ist/s** -ɪst/s
methodologi|cal ˌmeθ.ə.dᵊlˈɒdʒ.ɪ|kᵊl (US) -dᵊlˈɑː.dʒɪ- **-ally** -kᵊl.i, -kli
methodolog|y ˌmeθ.əˈdɒl.ə.dʒ|i (US) -ˈdɑː.lə- **-ies** -iz
methought mɪˈθɔːt (US) -ˈθɑːt, -ˈθɔːt
meths meθs
Methuen *surname:* ˈmeθ.ju.ən, -ɪn (US) mɪˈθjuː.ɪn, mə-, -ˈθuː-, -ən; ˈmeθ.juː-, -uː- *US town:* mɪˈθjuː.ɪn, mə-, -ˈθuː-, -ən
Methuselah məˈθjuː.zᵊl.ə, mɪ-, -ˈθuː- (US) məˈθuː-, -ˈθjuː-
Methven ˈmeθ.vən, -ven
methyl *commercial and general pronunciation:* ˈmeθ.ᵊl, -ɪl (US) -aɪl *chemists' pronunciation:* ˈmiː.θaɪl (US) ˈmeθ.aɪl
methylated ˈmeθ.ᵊl.eɪ.tɪd, -ɪ.leɪ- (US) -ɪ.leɪ.ţɪd ˌ**methylated** ˈ**spirits**
methylene ˈmeθ.ᵊl.iːn, -ɪ.liːn (US) ˈ-ɪ-
meti|cal ˌmet.ɪ|ˈkæl (US) ˌmeţ- **-cais** -ˈkaɪʃ
meticulous məˈtɪk.jə.ləs, mɪ-, metˈɪk-, -jʊ- (US) məˈtɪk.jə-, -juː- **-ly** -li **-ness** -nəs, -nɪs
métier ˈmet.i.eɪ, ˈmeɪ.ti- (US) meɪˈtjeɪ **-s** -z
metonym ˈmet.ə.nɪm (US) ˈmeţ- **-s** -z
metonymy metˈɒn.ə.mi, mɪˈtɒn-, mə-, ˈ-ɪ- (US) məˈtɑː.nə-
me-too ˌmiːˈtuː **-ism** -ɪ.zᵊm
metope ˈmet.əʊp; -əʊ.pi (US) ˈmeţ.ə.pi; ˈ-oʊp **-s** -s
metre ˈmiː.təʳ (US) -ţɚ **-s** -z
metric ˈmet.rɪk **-al** -ᵊl **-ally** -ᵊl.i, -li
metrication ˌmet.rɪˈkeɪ.ʃᵊn, -rəˈ-
metrics ˈmet.rɪks
metro (M) ˈmet.rəʊ (US) -roʊ **-s** -z
metro- ˈmet.rəʊ-, metˈrɒ- (US) ˈmet.roʊ-, -rə-; məˈtrɑː-
Metro-Goldwyn-Mayer ˌmet.rəʊˌgəʊld.wɪnˈmeɪ.əʳ (US) -roʊˌgoʊld.wɪnˈmeɪ.ɚ
Metroland ˈmet.rəʊ.lænd (US) -roʊ-
metronome ˈmet.rə.nəʊm (US) -noʊm **-s** -z
metronomic ˌmet.rəˈnɒm.ɪk (US) -ˈnɑː.mɪk **-al** -ᵊl **-ally** -ᵊl.i, -li
Metropole ˈmet.rə.pəʊl (US) -poʊl
metropolis məˈtrɒp.ə.lɪs, mɪ-, metˈrɒp-, -ᵊl.ɪs (US) məˈtrɑː.pᵊl- **-es** -ɪz
metropolitan ˌmet.rəˈpɒl.ɪ.tᵊn, ˈ-ə- (US) -ˈpɑː.lə- **-s** -z
-metry -mə.tri
mettle ˈmet.l̩ (US) ˈmeţ- **-some** -səm
Metz mets *as if French:* mes
meunière, meuniere ˌmɜː.niˈeəʳ, -ˈnjeəʳ, məˈ-, ˈ--- (US) məˈnjer

Meursault ˈmɜː.səʊ ⓤⓢ məˈsoʊ
Meuse mɜːz ⓤⓢ mjuːz, mɜːz
Meux mjuːz, mjuːks, mjuː
Mevagissey ˌmev.əˈgɪs.i
mew (M) mjuː **-s** -z **-ing** -ɪŋ **-ed** -d
mewl mjuːl **-s** -z **-ing** -ɪŋ **-ed** -d
mews mjuːz
Mexborough ˈmeks.bᵊr.ə ⓤⓢ -oʊ
Mexicali ˌmek.sɪˈkɑː.li, -ˈkæl.i ⓤⓢ -ˈkæl.i
Mexican ˈmek.sɪ.kᵊn ˌ**Mexican** ˈ**wave**
Mexico ˈmek.sɪ.kəʊ ⓤⓢ -koʊ ˌ**Mexico** ˈ**City**
Mey meɪ
Meyer ˈmaɪ.əʳ, ˈmeɪ-, meəʳ ⓤⓢ ˈmaɪ.ɚ
Meyerbeer ˈmaɪ.ə.bɪəʳ, -beəʳ ⓤⓢ -ɚ.bɪr, -ber
Meyers ˈmaɪ.əz, ˈmeɪ.əz, meəz ⓤⓢ ˈmaɪ.ɚz
Meynell ˈmen.ᵊl, ˈmeɪ.nᵊl; meɪˈnel
Meyrick ˈmer.ɪk, ˈmeɪ.rɪk
mezzanine ˈmet.sə.niːn, ˈmez.ə- ⓤⓢ ˈmez-, ˌ--ˈ- **-s** -z
mezzo ˈmet.səʊ, ˈmed.zəʊ ⓤⓢ ˈmet.soʊ, ˈmed.zoʊ, ˈmez.oʊ **-s** -z
mezzo-soprano ˌmet.səʊ.səˈprɑː.nəʊ, ˌmed.zəʊ- ⓤⓢ ˌmet.soʊ.səˈpræn.oʊ, -ˈprɑː.noʊ, ˌmed.zoʊ-, ˌmez.oʊ- **-s** -z
mezzotint ˈmet.səʊ.tɪnt, ˈmed.zəʊ- ⓤⓢ ˈmet.soʊ-, ˈmed.zoʊ-, ˈmez.oʊ- **-s** -s
mg *(abbrev. for* **milligram/s)** *singular:* ˈmɪl.ɪ.græm *plural:* ˈmɪl.ɪ.græmz
MGM® ˌem.dʒiːˈem
Mgr. *(abbrev. for* **Monseigneur, Monsignor)** mɒnˈsiː.njəʳ, -njɔːʳ ⓤⓢ mɑːnˈsiː.njɚ **-s.** -z
MHz *(abbrev. for* **megahertz)** ˈmeg.ə.hɜːts ⓤⓢ -hɝːts
mi miː **-s** -z
MI5 ˌem.aɪˈfaɪv
MI6 ˌem.aɪˈsiks
Mia ˈmiː.ə
MIA ˌem.aɪˈeɪ
Miami maɪˈæm.i ⓤⓢ -i, -ə
miaow ˌmiːˈaʊ, miˈaʊ ⓤⓢ miˈaʊ, mjaʊ **-s** -z **-ing** -ɪŋ **-ed** -d
miasm|a miˈæz.m|ə, maɪ- ⓤⓢ maɪ-, mi- **-as** -əz **-ata** -ə.tə ⓤⓢ -ə.t̬ə **-al** -ᵊl
mic maɪk **-s** -s
mica ˈmaɪ.kə
micaceous maɪˈkeɪ.ʃəs
Micah ˈmaɪ.kə
Micawber mɪˈkɔː.bəʳ, mə- ⓤⓢ -ˈkɑː.bɚ, -ˈkɔː-
mice *(plur. of* **mouse)** maɪs
Mich. *(abbrev. for* **Michigan)** ˈmɪʃ.ɪ.gən, ˈ-ə- ⓤⓢ ˈ-ɪ-
Michael ˈmaɪ.kᵊl
Michaela mɪˈkaɪ.lə
Michaelmas ˈmɪk.ᵊl.məs
Michelangelo ˌmaɪ.kᵊlˈæn.dʒə.ləʊ, -dʒɪ- ⓤⓢ -loʊ, ˌmɪk.ᵊl-
Micheldever ˈmɪtʃ.ᵊl.dev.əʳ ⓤⓢ -ɚ
Michele, Michèle mɪˈʃel, miː-
Michelin® ˈmɪtʃ.ᵊl.ɪn, ˈmɪʃ- *as if French:* miːʃˈlæ̃ŋ ⓤⓢ ˈmɪʃ.ə.lɪn, ˈmɪtʃ- **-s** -z
Note: In the UK, /miːʃˈlæ̃ŋ/ is used for the Guide, but not the tyres.
Michelle mɪˈʃel, miː-
Michelmore ˈmɪtʃ.ᵊl.mɔːʳ ⓤⓢ -mɔːr
Michelson ˈmɪtʃ.ᵊl.sᵊn, ˈmɪk.ᵊl-, ˈmaɪ.kᵊl- ⓤⓢ ˈmaɪ-, ˈmɪk.ᵊl-
Michie ˈmɪx.i, ˈmiː.xi, ˈmɪk.i ⓤⓢ ˈmɪk.i
Michigan ˈmɪʃ.ɪ.gən, ˈ-ə- ⓤⓢ ˈ-ɪ-
Michmash ˈmɪk.mæʃ
Michoacán ˌmɪtʃ.əʊ.əˈkæn ⓤⓢ -ə.wɑːˈkɑːn
mick (M) mɪk
mickey (M) ˈmɪk.i ˌ**Mickey** ˈ**Finn**; ˌ**Mickey** ˈ**Mouse** ⓤⓢ ˈ**Mickey** ˌ**Mouse**
mickey-mouse *(adj.)* ˌmɪk.iˈmaʊs ⓤⓢ ˈ--ˌ- *stress shift, British only:* ˌmickey-mouse ˈjob
micra *(plur. of* **micron)** ˈmaɪ.krə
Micra® ˈmaɪ.krə
micro- maɪ.krəʊ- ⓤⓢ maɪ.kroʊ-, maɪ.krə-
Note: Prefix. May carry primary or secondary stress, e.g. **microfiche** /ˈmaɪ.krəʊ.fiːʃ ⓤⓢ -kroʊ-/, **microbiology** /ˌmaɪ.krəʊ.baɪˈɒl.ə.dʒi ⓤⓢ -kroʊ.baɪˈɑː.lə-/.
micro ˈmaɪ.krəʊ ⓤⓢ -kroʊ **-s** -z
microbe ˈmaɪ.krəʊb ⓤⓢ -kroʊb **-s** -z
microbiologic|al ˌmaɪ.krəʊˌbaɪ.əˈlɒdʒ.ɪ.k|ᵊl ⓤⓢ -kroʊˌbaɪ.əˈlɑː.dʒɪ- **-ally** -ᵊl.i ⓤⓢ -li
microbiologist ˌmaɪ.krəʊ.baɪˈɒl.ə.dʒɪst ⓤⓢ -kroʊ.baɪˈɑː.lə- **-s** -s
microbiolog|y ˌmaɪ.krəʊ.baɪˈɒl.ə.dʒ|i ⓤⓢ -kroʊ.baɪˈɑː.lə- **-ist/s** -ɪst/s
microbrewer|y ˈmaɪ.krəʊˌbruː.ᵊr|.i ⓤⓢ -kroʊ-, ˌ-r|i **-ies** -iz
microcephalic ˌmaɪ.krəʊ.sefˈæl.ɪk, -sɪˈfæl-, -kefˈæl-, -kɪˈfæl- ⓤⓢ -kroʊ.səˈfæl-
microcephalous ˌmaɪ.krəʊˈsef.ᵊl.əs, -ˈkef- ⓤⓢ -kroʊˈsef-
microchip ˈmaɪ.krəʊ.tʃɪp ⓤⓢ -kroʊ-, -krə- **-s** -s
microcircuit ˈmaɪ.krəʊˌsɜː.kɪt ⓤⓢ -kroʊˌsɝː- **-s** -s
microclimate ˈmaɪ.krəʊˌklaɪ.mɪt, -mət ⓤⓢ -mɪt, -kroʊ- **-s** -s
microcomputer ˈmaɪ.krəʊ.kəmˌpjuː.təʳ ⓤⓢ -kroʊ.kəmˌpjuː.t̬ɚ **-s** -z
microcop|y ˈmaɪ.krəʊˌkɒp|.i ⓤⓢ -kroʊˌkɑː.p|i **-ies** -iz
microcosm ˈmaɪ.krəʊˌkɒz.ᵊm ⓤⓢ -kroʊˌkɑː.zᵊm, -krəˌ- **-s** -z
microdot ˈmaɪ.krəʊ.dɒt ⓤⓢ -kroʊ.dɑːt, -krə- **-s** -s
microeconomic ˌmaɪ.krəʊ.iː.kəˈnɒm.ɪk, -ek.əˈ- ⓤⓢ -kroʊˌek.əˈnɑː.mɪk, -krəˌ-, -ˌiː.kəˈ- **-s** -s
microelectronics ˌmaɪ.krəʊˌɪl.ekˈtrɒn.ɪks, -ˌel-, -ˌel.ɪkˈ-, -ˌiː.lekˈ- ⓤⓢ -kroʊ.ɪˌlekˈtrɑː.nɪks, -ˌiː.lekˈ-
microfich|e ˈmaɪ.krəʊ.fiːʃ ⓤⓢ -kroʊ-, -krə- **-es** -ɪz
microfilm ˈmaɪ.krəʊ.fɪlm ⓤⓢ -kroʊ-, -krə- **-s** -z **-ing** -ɪŋ **-ed** -d
microgram, microgramme ˈmaɪ.krəʊ.græm ⓤⓢ -kroʊ- **-s** -z
microgroove ˈmaɪ.krəʊ.gruːv ⓤⓢ -kroʊ- **-s** -z
microlight, microlite ˈmaɪ.krəʊ.laɪt ⓤⓢ -kroʊ- **-s** -s
micromesh ˈmaɪ.krəʊ.meʃ ⓤⓢ -kroʊ-
micrometer *measuring device:* maɪˈkrɒm.ɪ.təʳ, ˈ-ə- ⓤⓢ -ˈkrɑː.mə.t̬ɚ
micrometre, micrometer *unit of measurement:* ˈmaɪ.krəʊˌmiː.təʳ ⓤⓢ -kroʊˌmiː.t̬ɚ **-s** -z
micr|on ˈmaɪ.kr|ɒn, -kr|ᵊn ⓤⓢ -kr|ɑːn **-ons** -ɒnz, -ᵊnz ⓤⓢ -ɑːnz **-a** -ə
Micronesi|a ˌmaɪ.krəʊˈniː.zi|.ə, -ʒi|.ə, -ʒ|ə, -si|.ə, -ʃi|.ə, -ʃ|ə ⓤⓢ -kroʊˈniː.ʒ|ə, -ʃ|ə **-an/s** -ən/z
microorganism ˌmaɪ.krəʊˈɔː.gᵊn.ɪ.zᵊm, ˈmaɪ.krəʊˌɔː- ⓤⓢ ˌmaɪ.kroʊˈɔːr- **-s** -z
microphone ˈmaɪ.krə.fəʊn ⓤⓢ -foʊn **-s** -z
microprocessor ˌmaɪ.krəʊˈprəʊ.ses.əʳ, ˈmaɪ.krəʊˌprəʊ- ⓤⓢ ˈmaɪ.kroʊˌprɑː.ses.ɚ **-s** -z
micropyle ˈmaɪ.krəʊ.paɪl ⓤⓢ -kroʊ-
microscope ˈmaɪ.krə.skəʊp ⓤⓢ -skoʊp **-s** -s
microscopic ˌmaɪ.krəˈskɒp.ɪk ⓤⓢ -ˈskɑː.pɪk **-al** -ᵊl **-ally** -ᵊl.i ⓤⓢ -li
microscopy maɪˈkrɒs.kə.pi ⓤⓢ -ˈkrɑː.skə-
microsecond ˈmaɪ.krəʊˌsek.ᵊnd ⓤⓢ -kroʊˌ-, -krəˌ- **-s** -z
Microsoft® ˈmaɪ.krəʊ.sɒft ⓤⓢ -kroʊ.sɑːft, -krə-
microsurgery ˌmaɪ.krəʊˈsɜː.dʒᵊr.i ⓤⓢ -kroʊˈsɝː-, ˈmaɪ.kroʊˌsɝː-
microsurgical ˌmaɪ.krəʊˈsɜː.dʒɪ.kᵊl ⓤⓢ -kroʊˈsɝː- *stress shift:* ˌmicrosurgical ˈgraft
microwav|e ˈmaɪ.krəʊ.weɪv ⓤⓢ -kroʊ-, -krə- **-es** -z **-ing** -ɪŋ **-ed** -d **-eable** -ə.bl̩ ˌ**microwave** ˈ**oven**

mictur|ate 'mɪk.tjᵊr|.eɪt, -tjʊ.reɪt (US) -tʃuː-, -tʃə-, -tə- **-ates** -eɪts **-ating** -eɪ.tɪŋ (US) -eɪ.t̬ɪŋ **-ated** -eɪ.tɪd (US) -eɪ.t̬ɪd
micturation ˌmɪk.tjᵊr'eɪ.ʃᵊn, -tjʊ'reɪ- (US) -tʃuː'reɪ-, -tʃə'-, -tə'- **-s** -z
micturition ˌmɪk.tjᵊr'ɪʃ.ᵊn, -tjʊ'rɪʃ- (US) -tʃuː'-, -tʃə'-, -tə'-
mid mɪd
midair ˌmɪd'eəʳ, mɪ'deəʳ (US) ˌmɪd'er *stress shift:* ˌmidair 'crash
Midas 'maɪ.dəs, -dæs (US) -dəs
midday ˌmɪd'deɪ **-s** -z *stress shift:* ˌmidday 'sun
midden 'mɪd.ᵊn **-s** -z
middle 'mɪd.l̩ **-s** -z ˌ**middle** ˈ**age**; ˌ**Middle** ˈ**Ages**; ˌ**middle** ˈ**class**; ˌ**Middle** ˈ**East**; ˌ**middle** ˈ**management**; ˌ**middle** ˈ**name**; ˌ**middle of** ˈ**nowhere**; ˈ**middle** ˌ**school**
middle-aged ˌmɪd.l̩'eɪdʒd *stress shift, see compound:* ˌ**middle-aged** ˈ**spread**
middlebrow 'mɪd.l̩.braʊ **-s** -z
middle-class ˌmɪd.l̩'klɑːs (US) -'klæs *stress shift:* ˌmiddle-class 'values
middle distance (*n.*) ˌmɪd.l̩'dɪs.tᵊn*t*s
middle-distance (*adj.*) 'mɪd.l̩ˌdɪs.tᵊn*t*s
Middle-Earth ˌmɪd.l̩'ɜːθ (US) -'ɝːθ
Middle East ˌmɪd.l̩'iːst **-ern** -ən *stress shift:* ˌMiddle Eastern 'customs
Middleham 'mɪd.l̩.əm
middle|man 'mɪd.l̩|.mæn **-men** -men
Middlemarch 'mɪd.l̩.mɑːtʃ (US) -mɑːrtʃ
Middlemast 'mɪd.l̩.mɑːst, -mæst (US) -mæst
middlemost 'mɪd.l̩.məʊst (US) -moʊst
middle-of-the-road ˌmɪd.l̩.əv.ðə'rəʊd (US) -'roʊd
Middlesbro(ugh) 'mɪd.l̩z.brə
Middlesex 'mɪd.l̩.seks
Middleton 'mɪd.l̩.tən
middleweight 'mɪd.l̩.weɪt **-s** -s
Middlewich 'mɪd.l̩.wɪtʃ
middling 'mɪd.l̩.ɪŋ, 'mɪd.lɪŋ
Middx. (*abbrev. for* **Middlesex**) 'mɪd.l̩.seks
midd|y 'mɪd|.i **-ies** -iz
Mideast ˌmɪd'iːst *stress shift:* ˌMideast 'town
midfield 'mɪd.fiːld, -'-
midfielder 'mɪdˌfiːl.dəʳ, ˌ-'-- (US) 'mɪdˌfiːl.dɚ, ˌ-'-- **-s** -z
Midgard 'mɪd.gɑːd (US) -gɑːrd
midg|e mɪdʒ **-es** -ɪz
midget 'mɪdʒ.ɪt **-s** -s
Midhurst 'mɪd.hɜːst (US) -hɝːst
MIDI *computer interface:* 'mɪd.i
midi *style of clothes:* 'mɪd.i **-s** -z
Midi *in France:* miː'diː, mɪd'iː (US) miː'di
Midian 'mɪd.i.ən **-ite/s** -aɪt/s
midland **(M)** 'mɪd.lənd **-s** -z

Midler 'mɪd.ləʳ (US) -lɚ
mid-life ˌmɪd'laɪf *stress shift, see compound:* ˌ**mid-life** ˈ**crisis**
Midlothian ˌmɪd'ləʊ.ði.ən (US) -'loʊ-
midmorning ˌmɪd'mɔː.nɪŋ (US) -'mɔːr-
midnight 'mɪd.naɪt
mid-off ˌmɪd'ɒf (US) -'ɑːf **-s** -s
mid-on ˌmɪd'ɒn (US) -'ɑːn **-s** -z
midpoint 'mɪd.pɔɪnt **-s** -s
midriff 'mɪd.rɪf **-s** -s
midsection 'mɪd.sek.ʃᵊn
midship|man 'mɪdˌʃɪp|.mən (US) 'mɪdˌ-, ˌmɪd'ʃɪp- **-men** -mən
midships 'mɪd.ʃɪps
midst mɪdst, mɪtst
midstream ˌmɪd'striːm
midsummer **(M)** ˌmɪd'sʌm.əʳ, '--- (US) -ɚ **-'s** -z *stress shift, see compounds:* ˌ**Midsummer** ˈ**Day**; ˌ**midsummer** ˈ**madness**; ˌ**Midsummer** ˌ**Night's** ˈ**Dream**
midterm (*n.*) 'mɪd.tɜːm (US) -tɝːm *stress shift:* ˌmid-term 'crisis
mid-term (*adj.*) ˌmɪd'tɜːm (US) -'tɝːm
midtown 'mɪd.taʊn
midway ˌmɪd'weɪ, '--
Midway *island:* 'mɪd.weɪ
midweek ˌmɪd'wiːk *stress shift:* ˌmidweek 'news
Midwest ˌmɪd'west *stress shift:* ˌMidwest 'town
midwi|fe 'mɪd.waɪ|f **-ves** -vz
midwifery mɪd'wɪf.ᵊr.i, 'mɪdˌwɪf.ᵊr- (US) ˌmɪd'wɪf.ɚ-; 'mɪdˌwaɪf.ɚ-
midwinter ˌmɪd'wɪn.təʳ (US) -t̬ɚ *stress shift:* ˌmidwinter 'holiday
mien miːn **-s** -z
Miers maɪəz (US) maɪɚz
Mies van der Rohe ˌmiːz.væn.də'rəʊ.ə, ˌmiːs- (US) -dɚ'roʊ.ə
miff mɪf **-s** -s **-ing** -ɪŋ **-ed** -t
MiG, MIG mɪg **-s** -z
might maɪt
mightn't 'maɪ.tᵊnt
might|y 'maɪ.t|i (US) -t̬|i **-ier** -i.əʳ (US) -i.ɚ **-iest** -i.ɪst, -i.əst **-ily** -ɪ.li, -ᵊl.i **-iness** -ɪ.nəs, -ɪ.nɪs
mignon 'miː.njɒn, ˌ-'- *as if French:* mɪ'njɔ̃ːŋ (US) ˌmiː'njɑːn, -'njɔ̃ːn
mignonette **(M)** ˌmɪn.jə'net, '--- (US) ˌ--'- **-s** -s
mignonne 'miː.njɒn, ˌ-'- *as if French:* mi'njɔːn (US) ˌmiː'njɑːn, -'njɔːn
migraine 'miː.greɪn, 'maɪ-, 'mɪg.reɪn (US) 'maɪ.greɪn **-s** -z
migrant 'maɪ.grᵊnt **-s** -s
migra|te maɪ'greɪ|t, '-- (US) 'maɪ.greɪ|t **-tes** -ts **-ting** -tɪŋ (US) -t̬ɪŋ **-ted** -tɪd (US) -t̬ɪd **-tor/s** -təʳ/z (US) -t̬ɚ/z
migration maɪ'greɪ.ʃᵊn **-s** -z

migratory 'maɪ.grə.tᵊr.i; maɪ'greɪ- (US) 'maɪ.grə.tɔːr-
Miguel mɪ'gel, miː-
mikado **(M)** mɪ'kɑː.dəʊ, mə- (US) mɪ'kɑː.doʊ **-s** -z
Mikardo mɪ'kɑː.dəʊ, mə- (US) mɪ'kɑːr.doʊ
mike **(M)** maɪk **-s** -s
Mikonos 'mɪk.ə.nɒs, -ɒn.ɒs (US) 'miː.kɑː.nɑːs
mil mɪl **-s** -z
milady mɪ'leɪ.di, mə-
Milan *in Italy:* mɪ'læn, mə-, -'lɑːn, 'mɪl.ən (US) mɪ'læn, -'lɑːn *in US:* 'maɪ.lən
Note: /'mɪl.ən/ is used for rhythm in Shakespeare's 'The Tempest'.
Milanese *from Milan:* ˌmɪl.ə'niːz, -'neɪz (US) -'niːz, -'niːs
Milanese *cookery term: as if Italian:* ˌmɪl.ə'neɪ.zeɪ, -æn'eɪ-, -zi (US) -ə'neɪz
Milburn 'mɪl.bɜːn, -bən (US) -bɝːn
milch mɪl*t*ʃ (US) mɪltʃ
mild maɪld **-er** -əʳ (US) -ɚ **-est** -ɪst, -əst **-ly** -li **-ness** -nəs, -nɪs
Mildenhall 'mɪl.dᵊn.hɔːl (US) 'mɪl.dᵊn.hɔːl, -hɑːl
mildew 'mɪl.djuː (US) -duː, -djuː **-s** -z **-ing** -ɪŋ **-ed** -d
Mildmay 'maɪld.meɪ
Mildred 'mɪl.drəd, -drɪd, -dred
mile maɪl **-s** -z
mileag|e 'maɪ.lɪdʒ **-es** -ɪz
mileometer maɪ'lɒm.ɪ.təʳ, '-ə- (US) -'lɑː.mə.t̬ɚ **-s** -z
Miles maɪlz
Milesian maɪ'liː.zi.ən, mɪ-, -ʒi.ən, -ʒᵊn (US) -ʒᵊn, -ʃᵊn **-s** -z
milestone 'maɪl.stəʊn (US) -stoʊn **-s** -z
Miletus maɪ'liː.təs, mɪ- (US) maɪ-
milfoil 'mɪl.fɔɪl **-s** -z
Milford 'mɪl.fəd (US) -fɚd
Milhaud 'miː.jəʊ, -əʊ *as if French:* miː'jəʊ (US) miː'joʊ
milieu 'miː.ljɜː, -'- (US) miːl'jɜː, mɪl-, -'juː, '-- **-s** -z
milieux (*alternative plur. of* **milieu**) 'miː.ljɜː, -ljɜːz, -'- (US) miːl'jɜː, mɪl-, -'juː, -'jɜːz, -'juːz, '--
militancy 'mɪl.ɪ.tᵊn*t*.si, '-ə- (US) -tən*t*-
militant 'mɪl.ɪ.tᵊnt, '-ə- (US) -tənt **-s** -s **-ly** -li
militarily 'mɪl.ɪ.tᵊr.ᵊl.i, -ə-, ˌmɪl.ɪ'ter-, ˌmɪl.ɪ'tær-, -ə'- (US) ˌmɪl.ə'ter-
militar|ism 'mɪl.ɪ.tᵊr|.ɪ.zᵊm, '-ə- (US) -tɚ- **-ist/s** -ɪst/s
militaristic ˌmɪl.ɪ.tᵊr'ɪs.tɪk, ˌ-ə- (US) -tə'rɪs- **-ally** -ᵊl.i, -li
militarization, -isa- ˌmɪl.ɪ.tᵊr.aɪ'zeɪ.ʃᵊn, ˌ-ə-, -ɪ'- (US) -tɚ.ɪ'-

militariz|e, -is|e ˈmɪl.ɪ.tᵊr.aɪz, ˈ-ə- ⓤⓢ -tə.raɪz **-es** -ɪz **-ing** -ɪŋ **-ed** -d
military ˈmɪl.ɪ.tri, ˈ-ə-, -tᵊr.i ⓤⓢ -ter- ˌ**military poˈlice**
mili|tate ˈmɪl.ɪ|.teɪt, ˈ-ə- **-tates** -teɪts **-tating** -teɪ.tɪŋ ⓤⓢ -teɪ.t̬ɪŋ **-tated** -teɪ.tɪd ⓤⓢ -teɪ.t̬ɪd
militia mɪˈlɪʃ.ə, mə- **-s** -z **-man** -mən **-men** -mən, -men
milk mɪlk **-s** -s **-ing** -ɪŋ **-ed** -t **-er/s** -əʳ/z ⓤⓢ -ɚ/z ˌ**milk ˈchocolate** ⓤⓢ **ˈmilk ˌchocolate; ˈmilk ˌfloat; ˌmilk of magˈnesia; ˈmilk ˌround; ˈmilk ˌrun; ˈmilk ˌshake; ˈmilk ˌtooth; ˈmilking maˌchine; it's ˌno good ˌcrying over ˌspilt ˈmilk**
milkfish ˈmɪlk.fɪʃ **-es** -ɪz
milkmaid ˈmɪlk.meɪd **-s** -z
milk|man ˈmɪlk|.mən ⓤⓢ -mæn, -mən **-men** -mən, -men
milksop ˈmɪlk.sɒp ⓤⓢ -sɑːp **-s** -s
milkwort ˈmɪlk.wɜːt ⓤⓢ -wɝːt, -wɔːrt **-s** -s
milk|y ˈmɪl.k|i **-ier** -i.əʳ ⓤⓢ -i.ɚ **-iest** -i.ɪst, -i.əst **-ily** -ɪ.li, -ᵊl.i **-iness** -ɪ.nəs, -ɪ.nɪs ˌ**Milky ˈWay**
mill (M) mɪl **-s** -z **-ing** -ɪŋ **-ed** -d
Millais ˈmɪl.eɪ, -ˈ- ⓤⓢ mɪˈleɪ
Millar ˈmɪl.əʳ ⓤⓢ -ɚ
Millard ˈmɪl.əd, -ɑːd ⓤⓢ -ɚd
Millay mɪˈleɪ
Millbank ˈmɪl.bæŋk
millboard ˈmɪl.bɔːd ⓤⓢ -bɔːrd
millefeuille(s) ˌmiːlˈfɔɪ, -ˈfɜː.jə ⓤⓢ -ˈfɜː.jə
millenarian ˌmɪl.əˈneə.ri.ən, -ɪˈ- ⓤⓢ -əˈner.i- **-s** -z
millenarianism ˌmɪl.əˈneə.ri.ə.nɪ.zᵊm, -ɪˈ- ⓤⓢ -əˈner.i-
millenary mɪˈlen.ᵊr.i, mə- ⓤⓢ ˈmɪl.ə.ner-
millenni|um mɪˈlen.i|.əm, mə- ⓤⓢ mɪ- **-ums** -əmz **-a** -ə **-al** -əl
millepede ˈmɪl.ɪ.piːd, ˈ-ə- **-s** -z
miller (M) ˈmɪl.əʳ ⓤⓢ -ɚ **-s** -z
millesimal mɪˈles.ɪ.mᵊl, mə-, ˈ-ə- ⓤⓢ mɪˈles.ə- **-ly** -i
millet (M) ˈmɪl.ɪt
milliard ˌmɪl.iˈɑːd; mɪlˈjɑːd ⓤⓢ ˈmɪl.jɚd, -jɑːrd **-s** -z
millibar ˈmɪl.ɪ.bɑːʳ ⓤⓢ -bɑːr **-s** -z
Millicent ˈmɪl.ɪ.sᵊnt, ˈ-ə-
milligram(me) ˈmɪl.ɪ.græm **-s** -z
millilitre, milliliter ˈmɪl.ɪˌliː.təʳ, ˈ-ə- ⓤⓢ -t̬ɚ **-s** -z
millimetre, millimeter ˈmɪl.ɪˌmiː.təʳ, ˈ-ə- ⓤⓢ -t̬ɚ **-s** -z
milliner ˈmɪl.ɪ.nəʳ, ˈ-ə- ⓤⓢ -nɚ **-s** -z
millinery ˈmɪl.ɪ.nᵊr.i, ˈ-ə- ⓤⓢ -ner-
Millington ˈmɪl.ɪŋ.tən
million ˈmɪl.jən, -i.ən ⓤⓢ ˈ-jən **-s** -z **a ˌchance in a ˈmillion**
millionaire ˌmɪl.jəˈneəʳ, -i.əˈ- ⓤⓢ ˌ-jəˈner, ˈmɪl.jə.ner **-s** -z
millionairess ˌmɪl.jə.neəˈres, ˌ-i.ə-; -ˈneə.rɪs, -res ⓤⓢ -jəˈner.ɪs **-es** -ɪz
millionfold ˈmɪl.jən.fəʊld, -i.ən- ⓤⓢ -jən.foʊld
millionth ˈmɪl.jəntθ, -i.əntθ ⓤⓢ ˈ-jəntθ **-s** -s
millipede ˈmɪl.ɪ.piːd, ˈ-ə- **-s** -z
millisecond ˈmɪl.ɪˌsek.ənd, ˈ-ə- **-s** -z
Millom ˈmɪl.əm
millpond ˈmɪl.pɒnd ⓤⓢ -pɑːnd **-s** -z
millrac|e ˈmɪl.reɪs **-es** -ɪz
Mills mɪlz
millstone ˈmɪl.stəʊn ⓤⓢ -stoʊn **-s** -z
Milltimber ˈmɪlˌtɪm.bəʳ ⓤⓢ -bɚ
Millwall ˈmɪl.wɔːl, -wəl; mɪlˈwɔːl
Millward ˈmɪl.wɔːd, -wəd ⓤⓢ -wɚd
Milman ˈmɪl.mən
Milne mɪln, mɪl
Milner ˈmɪl.nəʳ ⓤⓢ -nɚ
Milnes mɪlz, mɪlnz
Milngavie mɪlˈgaɪ, mʌl-
Milnrow ˈmɪln.rəʊ ⓤⓢ -roʊ
Milo ˈmaɪ.ləʊ, ˈmiː- ⓤⓢ ˈmaɪ.loʊ
milometer maɪˈlɒm.ɪ.təʳ, ˈ-ə- ⓤⓢ -ˈlɑː.mə.t̬ɚ **-s** -z
milord mɪˈlɔːd, mə- ⓤⓢ -ˈlɔːrd **-s** -z
Milos ˈmiː.lɒs ⓤⓢ -lɑːs
Milosevic mɪˈlɒs.ə.vɪtʃ ⓤⓢ -ˈlɑː.sə-
Milosz ˈmiː.lɒʃ ⓤⓢ -lɑːʃ
milquetoast ˈmɪlk.təʊst ⓤⓢ -toʊst **-s** -s
Milton ˈmɪl.tᵊn
Miltonic mɪlˈtɒn.ɪk ⓤⓢ -ˈtɑː.nɪk
Milton Keynes ˌmɪl.tᵊnˈkiːnz
Milwaukee mɪlˈwɔː.ki, -iː ⓤⓢ -ˈwɑː-, -ˈwɔː-
mim|e maɪm **-es** -z **-ing** -ɪŋ **-ed** -d **-er/s** -əʳ/z ⓤⓢ -ɚ/z
mimeo ˈmɪm.i.əʊ ⓤⓢ -oʊ **-s** -z **-ing** -ɪŋ **-ed** -d
mimeograph ˈmɪm.i.əʊ.grɑːf, -græf ⓤⓢ -ə.græf **-s** -s **-ing** -ɪŋ **-ed** -t
mimesis mɪˈmiː.sɪs, maɪ-
mimetic mɪˈmet.ɪk, maɪ-
mimic ˈmɪm.ɪk **-s** -s **-king** -ɪŋ **-ked** -t **-ker/s** -əʳ/z ⓤⓢ -ɚ/z
mimicry ˈmɪm.ɪ.kri
mimosa mɪˈməʊ.zə, -sə ⓤⓢ -ˈmoʊ.sə, -zə **-s** -z
mimulus ˈmɪm.jə.ləs, -jʊ- ⓤⓢ -jə-, -juː- **-es** -ɪz
mina ˈmaɪ.nə **-s** -z
minaret ˌmɪn.əˈret, ˈ--- **-s** -s
minatory ˈmɪn.ə.tᵊr.i, ˈmaɪ- ⓤⓢ ˈmɪn.ə.tɔːr-
minc|e mɪnts **-es** -ɪz **-ing/ly** -ɪŋ/li **-ed** -t **-er/s** -əʳ/z ⓤⓢ -ɚ/z ˌ**mince ˈpie**
mincemeat ˈmɪnts.miːt **make ˈmincemeat of ˌsomeone**
Minch mɪntʃ **-es** -ɪz
mind maɪnd **-s** -z **-ing** -ɪŋ **-ed** -ɪd **ˈmind ˌreader; ˌmind's ˈeye; ˌgive someone a ˌpiece of one's ˈmind**
Mindanao ˌmɪn.dəˈnaʊ ⓤⓢ -ˈnaʊ, -ˈnɑː.oʊ
mind-blowing ˈmaɪndˌbləʊ.ɪŋ ⓤⓢ -ˌbloʊ- **-ly** -li
mind-boggling ˈmaɪndˌbɒg.l̩.ɪŋ, ˈmaɪm-, -ˌbɒg.lɪŋ ⓤⓢ ˈmaɪndˌbɑː.glɪŋ, -ˌbɑː.gl̩.ɪŋ **-ly** -li
minder ˈmaɪn.dəʳ ⓤⓢ -dɚ **-s** -z
mind-expanding ˈmaɪnd.ɪkˌspæn.dɪŋ, -ekˌ- ⓤⓢ -ekˌ-, -ɪkˌ-
mindful ˈmaɪnd.fᵊl, -fʊl **-ly** -i **-ness** -nəs, -nɪs
mindless ˈmaɪnd.ləs, -lɪs **-ly** -li **-ness** -nəs, -nɪs
mind-set ˈmaɪnd.set
Mindy ˈmɪn.di
min|e maɪn **-es** -z **-ing** -ɪŋ **-ed** -d
minefield ˈmaɪn.fiːld **-s** -z
Minehead ˈmaɪn.hed, ˌ-ˈ-
Minelli mɪˈnel.i, mə-
miner ˈmaɪ.nəʳ ⓤⓢ -nɚ **-s** -z
mineral ˈmɪn.ᵊr.ᵊl **-s** -z **ˈmineral ˌwater**
mineraliz|e, -is|e ˈmɪn.ᵊr.ᵊl.aɪz **-es** -ɪz **-ing** -ɪŋ **-ed** -d
mineralogical ˌmɪn.ᵊr.əˈlɒdʒ.ɪ.kᵊl ⓤⓢ -ˈlɑː.dʒɪ- **-ly** -i
mineralog|y ˌmɪn.ᵊrˈæl.ə.dʒ|i ⓤⓢ -əˈrɑː.lə-, -ˈræl.ə- **-ist/s** -ɪst/s
Minerva mɪˈnɜː.və ⓤⓢ məˈnɝː-
minestrone ˌmɪn.ɪˈstrəʊ.ni, -əˈ- ⓤⓢ -əˈstroʊ-
minesweep|er ˈmaɪnˌswiː.p|əʳ ⓤⓢ -p|ɚ **-ers** -əz ⓤⓢ -ɚz **-ing** -ɪŋ
Ming mɪŋ
Minghella mɪŋˈgel.ə
mingl|e ˈmɪŋ.gl̩ **-es** -z **-ing** -ɪŋ, ˈmɪŋ.glɪŋ **-ed** -d
mingogram ˈmɪŋ.gəʊ.græm, -əʊ- ⓤⓢ -gə- **-s** -z
mingograph® ˈmɪŋ.gəʊ.grɑːf, -əʊ-, -græf ⓤⓢ -gə.græf **-s** -s
Mingus ˈmɪŋ.gəs
ming|y ˈmɪn.dʒ|i **-ier** -i.əʳ ⓤⓢ -i.ɚ **-iest** -i.ɪst, -i.əst
mini (M®) ˈmɪn.i **-s** -z
miniature ˈmɪn.ə.tʃəʳ, ˈ-ɪ- ⓤⓢ ˈ-i.ə.tʃɚ, ˈ-ə.tʃɚ **-s** -z
miniaturist ˈmɪn.ə.tʃᵊr.ɪst, ˈ-ɪ-, -tjʊə.rɪst ⓤⓢ ˈ-i.ə.tʃɚ.ɪst, ˈ-ə.tʃɚ- **-s** -s
miniaturization, -isa- ˌmɪn.ə.tʃᵊr.aɪˈzeɪ.ʃᵊn, ˌ-ɪ- ⓤⓢ -i.ə.tʃɚ.ɪˈ-, -ə.tʃɚ- **-s** -z
miniaturiz|e, -is|e ˈmɪn.ə.tʃᵊr.aɪz, ˈ-ɪ- ⓤⓢ ˈ-i.ə.tʃɚ-, ˈ-ə.tʃɚ- **-es** -ɪz **-ing** -ɪŋ **-ed** -d
minibus ˈmɪn.ɪ.bʌs ⓤⓢ mɪn.i- **-es** -ɪz
minicab ˈmɪn.ɪ.kæb ⓤⓢ mɪn.i- **-s** -z
minicam ˈmɪn.ɪ.kæm ⓤⓢ mɪn.i- **-s** -z
minicomputer ˈmɪn.ɪ.kəmˌpjuː.təʳ,

ˌmɪn.ɪ.kəmˈpjuː- (US) mɪn.i-, -ˈpjuː.t̬ɚ -s -z
minim (M) ˈmɪn.ɪm -s -z
minimal ˈmɪn.ɪ.məl, ˈ-ə- -ly -i
minimal|ism ˈmɪn.ɪ.məl|.ɪ.zəm, ˈ-ə- -ist/s -ɪst/s
minimization ˌmɪn.ɪ.maɪˈzeɪ.ʃən, ˌ-ə-, -mɪˈ- (US) -mɪˈ-
minimiz|e, -is|e ˈmɪn.ɪ.maɪz, ˈ-ə- -es -ɪz -ing -ɪŋ -ed -d
minim|um ˈmɪn.ɪ.m|əm -a -ə -ums ˌminimum ˈwage
mining ˈmaɪ.nɪŋ
minion ˈmɪn.jən -s -z
minipill ˈmɪn.ɪ.pɪl
miniseries ˈmɪn.ɪˌsɪə.rɪz, -riːz (US) mɪn.i-, -ˌsɪr.iːz
minish ˈmɪn.ɪʃ -es -ɪz -ing -ɪŋ -ed -t
miniskirt ˈmɪn.ɪ.skɜːt (US) mɪn.i-, -skɝːt -s -s -ed -ɪd
minist|er ˈmɪn.ɪ.st|əʳ, ˈ-ə- (US) -st|ɚ -ers -əz (US) -ɚz -ering -ər.ɪŋ -ered -əd (US) -ɚd
ministerial ˌmɪn.ɪˈstɪə.ri.əl, -əˈ- (US) -ˈstɪr.i- -ly -i
ministration ˌmɪn.ɪˈstreɪ.ʃən, -əˈ- -s -z
ministr|y ˈmɪn.ɪ.str|i, ˈ-ə- -ies -iz
minivan ˈmɪn.i.væn (US) -i- -s -z
miniver (M) ˈmɪn.ɪ.vəʳ, ˈ-ə- (US) -vɚ
mink mɪŋk -s -s
minke ˈmɪŋ.ki, -kə (US) -kə -s -z
Minn. *(abbrev. for* **Minnesota***)* ˌmɪn.ɪˈsəʊ.tə, -əˈ- (US) -ˈsoʊ.t̬ə
Minneapolis ˌmɪn.iˈæp.əl.ɪs
Minnehaha ˌmɪn.iˈhɑː.hɑː
Minnelli mɪˈnel.i, mə-
minneola ˌmɪn.iˈəʊ.lə (US) -ˈoʊ- -s -z
minnesinger ˈmɪn.ɪˌsɪŋ.əʳ, -əˌ-, -gəʳ (US) -sɪŋ.ɚ -s -z
Minnesot|a ˌmɪn.ɪˈsəʊ.t|ə, -əˈ- (US) -ˈsoʊ.t̬|ə -an/s -ən/z
Minnie ˈmɪn.i
minnow ˈmɪn.əʊ (US) -oʊ -s -z
Minoan mɪˈnəʊ.ən, mə-, maɪ- (US) mɪ-
Minogue mɪˈnəʊg, mə- (US) -ˈnoʊg
Minolta® mɪˈnɒl.tə, mə-, -ˈnəʊl- (US) -ˈnoʊl-, -ˈnɑːl-
minor ˈmaɪ.nəʳ (US) -nɚ -s -z -ing -ɪŋ -ed -d
Minorca mɪˈnɔː.kə, mə- (US) -ˈnɔːr-
Minories ˈmɪn.ər.iz
minorit|y maɪˈnɒr.ə.t|i, mɪ-, mə-, -ɪ.t|i (US) maɪˈnɔːr.ə.t̬|i, mɪ- -ies -iz
Minos ˈmaɪ.nɒs (US) -nɑːs, -nəs
Minotaur ˈmaɪ.nə.tɔːʳ (US) ˈmɪn.ə.tɔːr -s -z
Minsk mɪntsk
Minsmere ˈmɪnz.mɪəʳ (US) -mɪr
minster (M) ˈmɪn.stəʳ (US) -stɚ -s -z
minstrel ˈmɪnt.strəl -s -z
minstrel|sy ˈmɪnt.strəl|.si -sies -siz
mint mɪnt -s -s -ing -ɪŋ (US) ˈmɪn.t̬ɪŋ -ed -ɪd (US) ˈmɪn.t̬ɪd -age -ɪdʒ (US) ˈmɪn.t̬ɪdʒ ˌmint conˈdition; ˌmint ˈjulep; ˌmint ˈsauce (US) ˈmint ˌsauce
Mintel ˈmɪn.tel
Minto ˈmɪn.təʊ (US) -toʊ
Mintoff ˈmɪn.tɒf (US) -tɑːf
minuet ˌmɪn.juˈet -s -s
minus ˈmaɪ.nəs -es -ɪz
minuscule ˈmɪn.ə.skjuːl, ˈ-ɪ- (US) ˈ-ɪ-; mɪˈnʌs.kjuːl -s -z
minu|te *very small:* maɪˈnjuː|t (US) -ˈnuː|t, -ˈnjuː|t -test -tɪst, -təst (US) -t̬ɪst, -t̬əst -tely -t.li -teness -t.nəs, -t.nɪs
minute *(n.) division of time, angle, memorandum:* ˈmɪn.ɪt -s -s
min|ute *(v.)* ˈmɪn|.ɪt -utes -ɪts -uting -ɪ.tɪŋ (US) -ɪ.t̬ɪŋ -uted -ɪ.tɪd (US) -ɪ.t̬ɪd
minute-gun ˈmɪn.ɪt.gʌn -s -z
minute-hand ˈmɪn.ɪt.hænd -s -z
minute|man (M) ˈmɪn.ɪt|.mæn -men -men
minuti|a maɪˈnjuː.ʃi|.ə, mɪ-, mə-, -ˈnuː-, -ti- (US) mɪˈnuː.ʃi-, -ˈnjuː-, ˈ-ʃ|ə -ae -iː, -aɪ
minx mɪŋks -es -ɪz
Miocene ˈmaɪ.əʊ.siːn (US) ˈ-oʊ-, ˈ-ə-
mios|is maɪˈəʊ.s|ɪs (US) -ˈoʊ- -es -iːz
miotic maɪˈɒt.ɪk (US) -ˈɑː.t̬ɪk -s -s
mips, MIPS mɪps
Mir mɪəʳ (US) mɪr
Mira ˈmaɪə.rə, ˈmɪr.ə (US) ˈmaɪ.rə
Mirabell ˈmɪr.ə.bel
miracle ˈmɪr.ə.kl, ˈ-ɪ- -s -z
miraculous mɪˈræk.jə.ləs, mə-, -jʊ- (US) mɪˈræk.jə.ləs, -juː- -ly -li -ness -nəs, -nɪs
mirag|e ˈmɪr.ɑːʒ; məˈrɑːʒ, mɪˈ- (US) mɪˈrɑːʒ, mə- -es -ɪz
Miramax ˈmɪr.ə.mæks
Miranda mɪˈræn.də (US) mə-, mɪ-
MIRAS ˈmaɪə.rəs, -ræs (US) ˈmaɪ-
mir|e maɪəʳ (US) maɪr -es -ing -ed
Mirfield ˈmɜː.fiːld (US) ˈmɝː-
Miriam ˈmɪr.i.əm
mirk|y ˈmɜː.k|i (US) ˈmɝː- -ier -i.əʳ (US) -i.ɚ -iest -i.ɪst, -i.əst -ily -ɪ.li, -əl.i -iness -ɪ.nəs, -ɪ.nɪs
Miró mɪˈrəʊ (US) miːˈroʊ
Mirren ˈmɪr.ən
mirr|or ˈmɪr|.əʳ (US) -ɚ -ors -əz (US) -ɚz -oring -ər.ɪŋ -ored -əd (US) -ɚd ˌmirror ˈimage
mirth mɜːθ (US) mɝːθ
mirthful ˈmɜːθ.fəl, -fʊl (US) ˈmɝːθ- -ly -i -ness -nəs, -nɪs
mirthless ˈmɜːθ.ləs, -lɪs (US) ˈmɝːθ- -ly -li -ness -nəs, -nɪs
MIRV mɜːv (US) mɝːv -s -z -ing -ɪŋ -ed -d
mir|y ˈmaɪə.r|i -ier -i.əʳ (US) -i.ɚ -iest -i.ɪst, -i.əst -iness -ɪ.nəs, -ɪ.nɪs
mis- mɪs-
Note: Prefix. In words containing **mis-**, the prefix may either be unstressed, e.g. **misdeal** /mɪsˈdiːl/, or receive secondary stress, especially if the stem is stressed on its second syllable, e.g. **align** /əˈlaɪn/, **misalign** /ˌmɪs.əˈlaɪn/. There is sometimes a difference between nouns and verbs, e.g. **miscount**, noun /ˈmɪs.kaʊnt/, verb /mɪˈskaʊnt/. There are exceptions; see individual entries.
misadventure ˌmɪs.ədˈven.tʃəʳ (US) -tʃɚ -s -z
misalign ˌmɪs.əˈlaɪn -s -z -ing -ɪŋ -d -d
misalignment ˌmɪs.əˈlaɪn.mənt, -ˈlaɪm- (US) -ˈlaɪn- -s -s
misallianc|e ˌmɪs.əˈlaɪ.ənts -es -ɪz
misandry mɪˈsæn.dri; ˈmɪs.ən- (US) ˈmɪs.æn-
misanthrope ˈmɪs.ən.θrəʊp, ˈmɪz-, -æn- (US) -ən.θroʊp -s -s
misanthropic ˌmɪs.ənˈθrɒp.ɪk, ˌmɪz-, -ænˈ- (US) -ənˈθrɑː.pɪk -al -əl -ally -əl.i, -li
misanthrop|y mɪˈsæn.θrə.p|i, -ˈzæn- -ist/s -ɪst/s
misapplication ˌmɪs.æp.lɪˈkeɪ.ʃən, -ləˈ- -s -z
misappl|y ˌmɪs.əˈpl|aɪ -ies -aɪz -ying -aɪ.ɪŋ -ied -aɪd
misapprehend ˌmɪs.æp.rɪˈhend, -rəˈ- -s -z -ing -ɪŋ -ed -ɪd
misapprehension ˌmɪs.æp.rɪˈhen.tʃən, -rəˈ- -s -z
misappropri|ate ˌmɪs.əˈprəʊ.pri|.eɪt (US) -ˈproʊ- -ates -eɪts -ating -eɪ.tɪŋ (US) -eɪ.t̬ɪŋ -ated -eɪ.tɪd (US) -eɪ.t̬ɪd
misappropriation ˌmɪs.əˌprəʊ.priˈeɪ.ʃən (US) -ˌproʊ- -s -z
misbecoming ˌmɪs.bɪˈkʌm.ɪŋ, -bəˈ-
misbegotten ˌmɪs.bɪˈgɒt.ən, -bəˈ-, ˈmɪs.bɪˌgɒt-, -bəˌ- (US) ˌmɪs.bɪˈgɑː.tən
misbehav|e ˌmɪs.bɪˈheɪv, -bəˈ- -es -z -ing -ɪŋ -ed -d
misbehavio(u)r ˌmɪs.bɪˈheɪ.vjəʳ, -bəˈ- (US) -vjɚ -s -z
misbelief ˌmɪs.bɪˈliːf, -bəˈ-, ˈ--- (US) ˌ--ˈ-
misbeliev|e ˌmɪs.bɪˈliːv, -bəˈ-, ˈ--- (US) ˌ--ˈ- -es -z -ing -ɪŋ -ed -d -er/s -əʳ/z (US) -ɚ/z
misc. *(abbrev. for* **miscellaneous***)* ˌmɪs.əlˈeɪ.ni.əs
miscalcu|late mɪsˈkæl.kjə|.leɪt, -kjʊ-; ˌmɪsˈkæl- (US) -kjə-, -kjuː- -lates -leɪts -lating -leɪ.tɪŋ (US) -leɪ.t̬ɪŋ -lated -leɪ.tɪd (US) -leɪ.t̬ɪd
miscalculation ˌmɪs.kæl.kjəˈleɪ.ʃən, -kjʊˈ- (US) -kjəˈ-, -kjuːˈ- -s -z
miscall mɪˈskɔːl; ˌmɪsˈkɔːl (US) mɪsˈkɔːl, -ˈkɑːl; ˌmɪsˈkɔːl, -ˈkɑːl -s -z -ing -ɪŋ -ed -d

miscarriag|e 'mɪsˌkær.ɪdʒ; -'-- ⓤⓢ 'mɪsˌker-, -ˌkær-; mɪ'sker-, -'skær-; ˌmɪs'ker-, -'kær- **-es** -ɪz
miscarr|y mɪ'skær|.i; ˌmɪs'kær- ⓤⓢ 'mɪsˌker-, -ˌkær-; mɪ'sker-, -'skær-; ˌmɪs'ker-, -'kær- **-ies** -iz **-ying** -i.ɪŋ **-ied** -id
miscast mɪ'skɑːst; ˌmɪs'kɑːst ⓤⓢ mɪ'skæst; ˌmɪs'kæst **-s** -s **-ing** -ɪŋ
miscegenation ˌmɪs.ɪ.dʒɪ'neɪ.ʃᵊn, ˌ-ə-, ˌ-e-, -dʒə'- ⓤⓢ -edʒ.ə'-; -ɪ.dʒə'- **-al** -ᵊl
miscellanea ˌmɪs.ᵊl'eɪ.ni.ə
miscellaneous ˌmɪs.ᵊl'eɪ.ni.əs, -ɪ'leɪ- **-ly** -li **-ness** -nəs, -nɪs
miscellan|y mɪ'sel.ə.n|i ⓤⓢ 'mɪs.ə.leɪ- **-ies** -iz
mischanc|e mɪs'tʃɑːnts, ˌmɪs-, '-- ⓤⓢ mɪs'tʃænts, ˌmɪs-, '-- **-es** -ɪz
mischief 'mɪs.tʃɪf, -tʃiːf ⓤⓢ -tʃɪf **-s** -s
mischief-mak|er 'mɪs.tʃɪfˌmeɪ.k|əʳ ⓤⓢ -k|ɚ **-ers** -əz ⓤⓢ -ɚz **-ing** -ɪŋ
mischievous 'mɪs.tʃɪ.vəs, -tʃə- ⓤⓢ -tʃə- **-ly** -li **-ness** -nəs, -nɪs
miscibility ˌmɪs.ɪ'bɪl.ɪ.ti, -ə'-, '-ə- ⓤⓢ -ə'bɪl.ə.t̬i
miscible 'mɪs.ɪ.bl̩, '-ə- ⓤⓢ '-ə-
misconceiv|e ˌmɪs.kən'siːv **-es** -z **-ing** -ɪŋ **-ed** -d
misconception ˌmɪs.kən'sep.ʃᵊn **-s** -z
misconduct (*n.*) mɪ'skɒn.dʌkt; ˌmɪs'kɒn-, -dəkt ⓤⓢ mɪ'skɑːn.dʌkt; ˌmɪs'kɑːn-
misconduct (*v.*) ˌmɪs.kən'dʌkt **-s** -s **-ing** -ɪŋ **-ed** -ɪd
misconstruction ˌmɪs.kən'strʌk.ʃᵊn **-s** -z
misconstru|e ˌmɪs.kən'struː, -kɒn'- ⓤⓢ -kən'- **-es** -z **-ing** -ɪŋ **-ed** -d
miscount (*n.*) 'mɪs.kaʊnt **-s** -s
miscoun|t (*v.*) mɪ'skaʊn|t; **-ts** -ts **-ting** -tɪŋ ⓤⓢ -t̬ɪŋ **-ted** -tɪd ⓤⓢ -t̬ɪd
miscreant 'mɪs.kri.ənt **-s** -s
miscu|e mɪ'skjuː; ˌmɪs'kjuː ⓤⓢ mɪ'skjuː; ˌmɪs'kjuː, '-- **-es** -z **-ing** -ɪŋ **-ed** -d
misdeal mɪs'diːl, ˌ-'- ⓤⓢ mɪs'diːl, ˌ-'-, '-- **-s** -z **-ing** -ɪŋ **misdealt** -'delt, ˌ-'- ⓤⓢ -'-, ˌ-'-, '--
misdeed mɪs'diːd, ˌ-'-, '-- **-s** -z
misdemeano(u)r ˌmɪs.dɪ'miː.nəʳ, -də'- ⓤⓢ -nɚ, '-ˌ--- **-s** -z
misdiagnos|e mɪs'daɪəg.nəʊz, ˌ-'--- ⓤⓢ ˌmɪs.daɪ.əg'noʊs, -'noʊz; -'---, ˌ-'---, -noʊz **-es** -ɪz **-ing** -ɪŋ **-ed** -d
misdiagnos|is ˌmɪs.daɪəg'nəʊ.s|ɪs ⓤⓢ -'noʊ-
misdirect ˌmɪs.dɪ'rekt, -də'-, -daɪə'- ⓤⓢ -də'-, -daɪ'- **-s** -s **-ing** -ɪŋ **-ed** -ɪd
misdirection ˌmɪs.dɪ'rek.ʃᵊn, -də'-, -daɪə'- ⓤⓢ -də'-, -daɪ'-
misdoing mɪs'duː.ɪŋ, ˌmɪs- **-s** -z
mise-en-scène ˌmiːz.ɑ̃ːn'seɪn, -'sen ⓤⓢ -ɑ̃ːn'sen **mise-en-scènes** ˌmiːz.ɑ̃ːn'seɪn, -'sen, -z ⓤⓢ -ɑ̃ːn'sen, -z
miser 'maɪ.zəʳ ⓤⓢ -zɚ **-s** -z
miserab|le 'mɪz.ᵊr.ə.b|l̩, 'mɪz.rə- **-ly** -li **-leness** -l̩.nəs, -nɪs
miserere ˌmɪz.ᵊr'eə.ri, -'ɪə-, -reɪ ⓤⓢ -'rer.eɪ **-s** -z
misericord mɪ'zer.ɪ.kɔːd, mə-, '-ə-; 'mɪz.ᵊr.ɪ- ⓤⓢ -kɔːrd **-s** -z
miserl|y 'maɪ.zᵊl|.i ⓤⓢ -zɚ.l|i **-iness** -ɪ.nəs, -ɪ.nɪs
miser|y 'mɪz.ᵊr|.i ⓤⓢ '-r|i, '-ɚ|.i **-ies** -iz
misfeasance mɪs'fiː.zᵊnts ⓤⓢ ˌmɪs-
misfire (*n.*) mɪs'faɪəʳ, ˌmɪs-, '-- ⓤⓢ 'mɪs.faɪɚ
misfir|e (*v.*) mɪs'faɪəʳ, ˌmɪs- ⓤⓢ -'faɪɚ **-es** -z **-ing** -ɪŋ **-ed** -d
misfit (*n.*) 'mɪs.fɪt **-s** -s
misfortune mɪs'fɔː.tʃuːn, ˌmɪs-, -tʃən, -tjuːn ⓤⓢ -'fɔːr.tʃən **-s** -z
misgiving mɪs'gɪv.ɪŋ, ˌmɪs- **-s** -z
misgovern mɪs'gʌv.ᵊn, ˌmɪs- ⓤⓢ -ɚn **-s** -z **-ing** -ɪŋ **-ed** -d **-ment** -mənt
misguided mɪs'gaɪ.dɪd, ˌmɪs- **-ly** -li **-ness** -nəs, -nɪs
mishandl|e mɪs'hæn.dl̩, ˌmɪs- **-es** -z **-ing** -ɪŋ, -'hænd.lɪŋ **-ed** -d
mishap 'mɪs.hæp, -'-, ˌ-'- ⓤⓢ 'mɪs.hæp **-s** -s
mis|hear mɪs|'hɪəʳ, ˌmɪs- ⓤⓢ -'hɪr **-hears** -'hɪəz ⓤⓢ -'hɪrz **-hearing** -'hɪə.rɪŋ ⓤⓢ -'hɪr.ɪŋ **-heard** -'hɜːd ⓤⓢ -'hɝːd
Mishima 'mɪʃ.ɪ.mə; mɪ'ʃiː- ⓤⓢ 'mɪʃ.ɪ-, 'miː.ʃɪ-
mis|hit mɪs|'hɪt, ˌmɪs- **-hits** -'hɪts **-hitting** -'hɪt.ɪŋ ⓤⓢ -'hɪt̬.ɪŋ
mishmash 'mɪʃ.mæʃ
misinform ˌmɪs.ɪn'fɔːm ⓤⓢ -'fɔːrm **-s** -z **-ing** -ɪŋ **-ed** -d **-ant/s** -ənt/s **-er/s** -əʳ/z ⓤⓢ -ɚ/z
misinformation ˌmɪs.ɪn.fə'meɪ.ʃᵊn ⓤⓢ -fɚ'-
misinter|pret ˌmɪs.ɪn'tɜː|.prɪt ⓤⓢ -'tɝː- **-prets** -prɪts **-preting** -prɪ.tɪŋ ⓤⓢ -prɪ.t̬ɪŋ **-preted** -prɪ.tɪd ⓤⓢ -prɪ.t̬ɪd
misinterpretation ˌmɪs.ɪnˌtɜː.prɪ'teɪ.ʃᵊn, -prə'- ⓤⓢ -ˌtɝː.prɪ'- **-s** -z
misjoinder mɪs'dʒɔɪn.dəʳ, ˌmɪs- ⓤⓢ -dɚ
misjudg|e mɪs'dʒʌdʒ, ˌmɪs- **-es** -ɪz **-ing** -ɪŋ **-ed** -d
misjudg(e)ment mɪs'dʒʌdʒ.mənt, ˌmɪs- **-s** -s
Miskolc 'mɪʃ.kəʊlts ⓤⓢ -kɔːlts
mislay mɪ'sleɪ, ˌmɪs'leɪ **-s** -z **-ing** -ɪŋ **mislaid** mɪ'sleɪd, ˌmɪs'leɪd
mislead mɪ'sliːd, ˌmɪs'liːd **-s** -z **-ing/ly** -ɪŋ/li **misled** mɪ'sled, ˌmɪs'led
mismanag|e ˌmɪs'mæn.ɪdʒ **-es** -ɪz **-ing** -ɪŋ **-ed** -d **-ement** -mənt
mismatch (*n.*) 'mɪs.mætʃ; -'-, ˌ-'- **-es** -ɪ[…]
mismatch (*v.*) mɪ'smætʃ; ˌmɪs'mætʃ, '- ⓤⓢ mɪ'smætʃ; ˌmɪs'mætʃ **-es** -ɪs **-ing** -ɪŋ **-ed** -t
misnomer mɪ'snəʊ.məʳ; ˌmɪs'nəʊ- ⓤⓢ mɪ'snoʊ.mɚ, ˌmɪs'noʊ- **-s** -z
miso 'miː.səʊ ⓤⓢ -soʊ
misogynist mɪ'sɒdʒ.ᵊn.ɪst, maɪ-, mə- ⓤⓢ -'sɑːdʒ- **-s** -s
misogynistic mɪˌsɒdʒ.ᵊn'ɪs.tɪk, maɪ-, mə-, -dʒɪ'nɪs- ⓤⓢ -ˌɑː.dʒɪ'-
misogyn|y mɪ'sɒdʒ.ɪ.n|i, maɪ-, mə- ⓤⓢ -sɑːdʒ-
misplac|e mɪ'spleɪs, ˌmɪs'pleɪs **-es** -ɪz **-ing** -ɪŋ **-ed** -t **-ement** -mənt *stress shift:* ˌmisplaced 'trust
misprint (*n.*) 'mɪs.prɪnt **-s** -s
misprin|t (*v.*) mɪ'sprɪn|t; ˌmɪs'prɪn|t **-t[s]** -ts **-ting** -tɪŋ ⓤⓢ -t̬ɪŋ **-ted** -tɪd ⓤⓢ -t̬ɪ[d]
misprision mɪ'sprɪʒ.ᵊn
mispronounc|e ˌmɪs.prə'naʊnts ⓤⓢ -prə'-, -proʊ'- **-es** -ɪz **-ing** -ɪŋ **-ed**
mispronunciation ˌmɪs.prəˌnʌnt.si'eɪ.ʃən ⓤⓢ -prəˌ-, -proʊˌ- **-s** -z
misquotation ˌmɪs.kwəʊ'teɪ.ʃᵊn ⓤⓢ -kwoʊ'- **-s** -z
misquo|te mɪ'skwəʊ|t; ˌmɪs'kwəʊ|t ⓤⓢ mɪ'skwoʊ|t; ˌmɪs'kwoʊ|t **-tes** -t[s] **-ting** -tɪŋ ⓤⓢ -t̬ɪŋ **-ted** -tɪd ⓤⓢ -t̬ɪd
Misratah 'mɪs.ræt.ɑː
misread mɪs'riːd, ˌmɪs- **-s** -z **-ing** -ɪŋ *past tense:* mɪs'red, ˌmɪs-
misrememb|er ˌmɪs.rɪ'mem.b|əʳ, -rə[…] ⓤⓢ -b|ɚ **-ers** -əz ⓤⓢ -ɚz **-ering** -ᵊr.ɪŋ **-ered** -əd ⓤⓢ -ɚd
misre|port ˌmɪs.rɪ|'pɔːt ⓤⓢ -'pɔːrt **-ports** -'pɔːts ⓤⓢ -'pɔːrts **-porting** -'pɔː.tɪŋ ⓤⓢ -'pɔːr.t̬ɪŋ **-ported** -'pɔː.tɪd ⓤⓢ -'pɔːr.t̬ɪd
misrepre|sent ˌmɪs.rep.rɪ|'zent **-sen[ts]** -'zents **-senting** -'zen.tɪŋ ⓤⓢ -'zen.t̬ɪŋ **-sented** -'zen.tɪd ⓤⓢ -'zen.t̬ɪd
misrepresentation ˌmɪs.rep.rɪ.zen'teɪ.ʃᵊn, -zᵊn'- ⓤⓢ -zen'- **-s** -z
misrule mɪs'ruːl, ˌmɪs-
miss (M) mɪs **-es** -ɪz **-ing** -ɪŋ **-ed** -t
Miss. (*abbrev. for* **Mississippi**) ˌmɪs.ɪ'sɪp.i ⓤⓢ -ə'-, -ɪ'-
missal 'mɪs.ᵊl **-s** -z
missel thrush 'mɪz.ᵊlˌθrʌʃ, 'mɪs-
Missenden 'mɪs.ᵊn.dən
misshapen mɪs'ʃeɪ.pᵊn, ˌmɪs-, mɪʃ-, ˌmɪʃ- **-ly** -li
missile 'mɪs.aɪl ⓤⓢ -ᵊl **-s** -z
missing 'mɪs.ɪŋ
mission 'mɪʃ.ᵊn **-s** -z
missionar|y 'mɪʃ.ᵊn.ᵊr|.i, 'mɪʃ.nᵊr- ⓤⓢ '-ᵊn.er- **-ies** -iz '**missionary** poˌ**sition**

missioner 'mɪʃ.ᵊn.əʳ (US) -ɚ -s -z
missis 'mɪs.ɪz
Mississippi ˌmɪs.ɪ'sɪp.i (US) -ə'-, -ɪ'- -an/s -ən/z
missive 'mɪs.ɪv -s -z
Missoula mɪ'zuː.lə
Missouri mɪ'zʊə.ri, -'sʊə- (US) -'zʊr.i *locally:* -ə
misspell mɪs'spel, ˌmɪs- -s -z -ing/s -ɪŋ/z -ed -t, -d misspelt mɪs'spelt (US) ˌmɪs-
misspend mɪs'spend, ˌmɪs -s -z -ing -ɪŋ misspent mɪs'spent, ˌmɪs- ˌmisspent 'youth
mis|state mɪs|'steɪt, ˌmɪs- -states -'steɪts -stating -'steɪ.tɪŋ (US) -'steɪ.t̬ɪŋ -stated -'steɪ.tɪd (US) -'steɪ.t̬ɪd -statement/s -'steɪt.mənt/s
missus 'mɪs.ɪz, -ɪs
miss|y 'mɪs|.i -ies -iz
mist mɪst -s -s -ing -ɪŋ -ed -ɪd -er/s -əʳ/z, -ɚ/z
mistak|e mɪ'steɪk -es -s -ing -ɪŋ mistook mɪ'stʊk
mistak(e)able mɪ'steɪ.kə.bl̩
mistaken mɪ'steɪ.kᵊn -ly -li
mister (M) 'mɪs.təʳ (US) -tɚ
mistim|e mɪs'taɪm; ˌmɪs- -es -z -ing -ɪŋ -ed -d
mistle thrush 'mɪs.l̩ˌθrʌʃ, 'mɪz- (US) 'mɪs-
mistletoe 'mɪs.l̩.təʊ, 'mɪz- (US) 'mɪs.l̩.toʊ
mistook *(from* **mistake***)* mɪ'stʊk
mistral (M) 'mɪs.trᵊl, -trɑːl; mɪ'strɑːl (US) mɪ'strɑːl; 'mɪs.trᵊl -s -z
mistransla|te ˌmɪs.træn'sleɪ|t, -trɑːn-, -trᵊn-; -trænz'leɪ|t, -trɑːnz'-, -trᵊnz'- (US) ˌmɪs'træn.sleɪ|t, -'trænz.leɪ|t; mɪs.træn'sleɪ|t; -trænz'leɪ|t -tes -ts -ting -tɪŋ (US) -t̬ɪŋ -ted -tɪd (US) -t̬ɪd
mistranslation ˌmɪs.træn'sleɪ.ʃᵊn, -trɑːn'-, -trᵊn'-; -trænz'leɪ-, -trænz'-, -trᵊnz'- (US) -træn'sleɪ-; -trænz'leɪ- -s -z
mistrea|t mɪs'triː|t; ˌmɪs- -ts -ts -ting -tɪŋ (US) -t̬ɪŋ -ted -tɪd (US) -t̬ɪd
mistreatment mɪs'triːt.mənt; ˌmɪs-
mistress 'mɪs.trəs, -trɪs (US) -trɪs -es -ɪz
mistrial mɪ'straɪəl; ˌmɪs'traɪ- (US) 'mɪsˌtraɪ-; mɪ'straɪ-; ˌmɪs'traɪ- -s -z
mistrust mɪ'strʌst; ˌmɪs'trʌst (US) ˌmɪs'trʌst; mɪ'strʌst; 'mɪs.trʌst -s -s -ing -ɪŋ -ed -ɪd
mistrustful mɪ'strʌst*.*fᵊl, ˌmɪs'trʌst- -ly -li
mist|y (M) 'mɪs.t|i -ier -i.əʳ (US) -i.ɚ -iest -i.ɪst, -i.əst -ily -ɪ.li, -ᵊl.i -iness -ɪ.nəs, -ɪ.nɪs
misunder|stand ˌmɪs.ʌn.də|'stænd (US) -dɚ'- -stands -'stændz -standing/s -'stæn.dɪŋ/z -stood -'stʊd
misuse *(n.)* ˌmɪs'juːs
misus|e *(v.)* ˌmɪs'juːz -es -ɪz -ing -ɪŋ -ed -d
MIT ˌem.aɪ'tiː *stress shift:* ˌMIT 'graduate
Mitcham 'mɪtʃ.əm
Mitchel(l) 'mɪtʃ.ᵊl
Mitchison 'mɪtʃ.ɪ.sᵊn
Mitchum 'mɪtʃ.əm
mite maɪt -s -s
mit|er 'maɪ.t|əʳ (US) -t̬|ɚ -ers -əz (US) -ɚz -ering -ᵊr.ɪŋ -ered -əd (US) -ɚd 'miter ˌbox; 'miter ˌjoint
Mitford 'mɪt.fəd (US) -fɚd
Mithr|a 'mɪθ.r|ə -as -æs (US) -əs, -æs
Mithraic mɪ'θreɪ.ɪk
Mithra|ism 'mɪθ.reɪ|.ɪ.zᵊm; mɪ'θreɪ- (US) 'mɪθ.reɪ-, -rə- -ist/s -ɪst/s
Mithridates ˌmɪθ.rɪ'deɪ.tiːz (US) -rə'-
mitigable 'mɪt.ɪ.gə.bl̩ (US) 'mɪt̬-
miti|gate 'mɪt.ɪ|.geɪt (US) 'mɪt̬- -gates -geɪts -gating -geɪ.tɪŋ (US) -geɪ.t̬ɪŋ -gated -geɪ.tɪd (US) -geɪ.t̬ɪd -gator/s -geɪ.təʳ/z (US) -geɪ.t̬ɚ/z
mitigation ˌmɪt.ɪ'geɪ.ʃᵊn (US) ˌmɪt̬-
mitigatory 'mɪt.ɪ.geɪ.tᵊr.i (US) 'mɪt̬.ɪ.gə.tɔːr-
mitochondrial ˌmaɪ.təʊ'kɒn.dri.əl (US) -toʊ'kɑːn-, -t̬ə'-
mitochondri|on ˌmaɪ.təʊ'kɒn.dri|.ən (US) -toʊ'kɑːn-, -t̬ə'- -a -ə
mitosis maɪ'təʊ.sɪs (US) -'toʊ-
mitrailleus|e ˌmɪt.raɪ'ɜːz (US) ˌmiː.treɪ'jɜːz -es -ɪz
mitral 'maɪ.trᵊl
mit|re 'maɪ.t|əʳ (US) -t̬|ɚ -res -əz (US) -ɚz -ring -ᵊr.ɪŋ -red -əd (US) -ɚd 'mitre ˌbox; 'mitre ˌjoint
Mitrovice ˌmɪt.rəʊ'vɪt.sə, 'mɪt.rəʊ.vɪt.sə (US) mɪt.rə'viːt.sə, -roʊ'-
Mitsubishi® ˌmɪt.sʊ'bɪʃ.i, -suː'- (US) -suː'-
mitt mɪt -s -s
mitten 'mɪt.ᵊn -s -z
Mitterand, **Mitterrand** 'miː.tə.rɑ̃ːŋ (US) 'miːt.ə.rɑːnd, 'mɪt-
Mitylene ˌmɪt.ᵊl'iː.ni, -ɪ'liː- (US) ˌmɪt̬.ə'liː-
mitz|vah 'mɪts|.və (US) 'mɪts-; mɪts'vɑː -vahs -əz (US) 'mɪts.vəs; mɪts'vɑːz -voth -vɒt (US) 'mɪts.voʊt, -voʊs
Mivart 'maɪ.vət, -vɑːt (US) -vɚt, -vɑːrt
mix *(n. v.)* mɪks -es -ɪz -ing -ɪŋ -ed -t ˌmixed 'bag; ˌmixed 'blessing; ˌmixed 'doubles; ˌmixed 'farming; ˌmixed 'grill; ˌmixed 'marriage; ˌmixed 'metaphor
mix-and-match ˌmɪks.ᵊnd'mætʃ, -ᵊm'- (US) -ᵊnd'- *stress shift:* ˌmix-and-match 'clothes
mixed-ability ˌmɪkst.ə'bɪl.ə.ti, -ɪ.ti (US) -ə.t̬i *stress shift:* ˌmixed-ability 'students
mixed blessing ˌmɪkst'bles.ɪŋ
mixed-up ˌmɪkst'ʌp *stress shift:* ˌmixed-up 'kid
mixer 'mɪk.səʳ (US) -sɚ -s -z
mixture 'mɪks.tʃəʳ (US) -tʃɚ -s -z
mix-up 'mɪks.ʌp -s -s
Mizpah 'mɪz.pə
mizzen 'mɪz.ᵊn -s -z
mizzen-mast 'mɪz.ᵊnˌmɑːst, -ᵊmˌ-, -ᵊnˌmæst *nautical pronunciation:* -məst (US) -ᵊn.mæst -s -s
mizzl|e 'mɪz.l̩ -es -z -ing -ɪŋ, 'mɪz.lɪŋ -ed -d -y -i
ml *(abbrev. for* **millilitre/s***) singular:* 'mɪl.ɪˌliː.təʳ, '-ə- (US) -t̬ɚ *plural:* -z
Mladic 'mlæd.ɪtʃ (US) mə'læd.ɪtʃ
mm *(abbrev. for* **millimetre/s***) singular:* 'mɪl.ɪˌmiː.təʳ, '-ə- (US) -t̬ɚ *plural:* -z
MMR ˌem.em'ɑːʳ (US) -ɑːr
mnemonic nɪ'mɒn.ɪk, nə-, niː-, mnɪ-, mnə-, mniː- (US) nɪ'mɑː.nɪk, niː- -s -s -ally -ᵊl.i, -li

Pronouncing the letters MN

The consonant digraph **mn** is word or morpheme final and usually realised as /m/, that is, the **n** is silent, e.g.:

hymn	/hɪm/
condemning	/kən'dem.ɪŋ/

However, in some cases the **n** is pronounced, particularly (as in the case of *condemnation*) where the vowel following the **n** is in a stressed syllable, e.g.:

hymnal	/'hɪm.nᵊl/	
condemnation	/ˌkɒn.dem'neɪ.ʃᵊn/	(US) /ˌkɑːn-/

Mnemosyne nɪˈmɒz.ɪ.ni, nə-, niː-, mnɪ-, mnə-, mniː-, -ˈmɒs-, -ᵊn.i (US) nɪˈmɑː.sɪ-, niː-, -zɪ-
mo, mo' məʊ (US) moʊ
Mo. *(abbrev. for* **Missouri***)* mɪˈzʊə.ri, -ˈsʊə- (US) -ˈzʊr.i *locally:* -ə
Mo məʊ (US) moʊ
moa məʊə (US) moʊə **-s** -z
Moab ˈməʊ.æb (US) ˈmoʊ-
Moabite ˈməʊ.ə.baɪt (US) ˈmoʊ- **-s** -s
moan məʊn (US) moʊn **-s** -z **-ing/s** -ɪŋ/z **-ed** -d
moat (M) məʊt (US) moʊt **-s** -s **-ing** -ɪŋ (US) ˈmoʊ.t̬ɪŋ **-ed** -ɪd (US) ˈmoʊ.t̬ɪd
mob mɒb (US) mɑːb **-s** -z **-bing** -ɪŋ **-bed** -d
mobcap ˈmɒb.kæp (US) ˈmɑːb- **-s** -s
Moberly ˈməʊ.bᵊl.i (US) ˈmoʊ.bɚ.li
Mobil® ˈməʊ.bɪl, -bᵊl (US) ˈmoʊ.bᵊl, -bɪl
mobile *(adj.)* ˈməʊ.baɪl (US) ˈmoʊ.bᵊl, -bɪl, -baɪl **ˌmobile ˈphone; ˌmobile ˈhome**
mobile *(n.)* ˈməʊ.baɪl (US) ˈmoʊ.biːl **-s** -z
mobility məʊˈbɪl.ə.ti, -ɪ.ti (US) moʊˈbɪl.ə.t̬i
mobilization, -isa- ˌməʊ.bɪ.laɪˈzeɪ.ʃᵊn, -bᵊl.aɪˈ-, -ɪˈ- (US) -bᵊl.ɪˈ- **-s** -z
mobiliz|e, -is|e ˈməʊ.bɪ.laɪz, -bᵊl.aɪz (US) -bə.laɪz **-es** -ɪz **-ing** -ɪŋ **-ed** -d
mobius, möbius (M) ˈməʊ.bi.əs *as if German:* ˈmɜː- (US) ˈmeɪ.bi.əs, ˈmoʊ-, ˈmiː- *as if German:* ˈmɜː- **ˌMobius ˈstrip**
mobster ˈmɒb.stəʳ (US) ˈmɑːb.stɚ **-s** -z
Mobutu məˈbuː.tuː
Moby Dick ˌməʊ.biˈdɪk (US) ˌmoʊ-
moccasin ˈmɒk.ə.sɪn (US) ˈmɑː.kə.sən, -sɪn **-s** -z
mocha *coffee, leather, etc.:* ˈmɒk.ə, ˈməʊ.kə (US) ˈmoʊ.kə
Mocha *Arabian seaport:* ˈməʊ.kə, ˈmɒk.ə (US) ˈmoʊ.kə
mock mɒk (US) mɑːk **-s** -s **-ing/ly** -ɪŋ/li **-ed** -t **-er/s** -əʳ/z (US) -ɚ/z
mockers ˈmɒk.əz (US) ˈmɑː.kɚz **put the ˈmockers on ˌsomething**
mocker|y ˈmɒk.ᵊr|.i (US) ˈmɑː.kɚ- **-ies** -iz
Mockett ˈmɒk.ɪt (US) ˈmɑː.kɪt
mockingbird ˈmɒk.ɪŋ.bɜːd (US) ˈmɑː.kɪŋ.bɝːd **-s** -z
mock-turtle ˌmɒkˈtɜː.tl̩ (US) ˌmɑːkˈtɝː.t̬l̩ *stress shift:* ˌmock-turtle ˈsoup
mock-up ˈmɒk.ʌp (US) ˈmɑːk- **-s** -s
mod (M) mɒd (US) mɑːd **-s** -z
MoD ˌem.əʊˈdiː (US) -oʊˈ- *stress shift:* ˌMoD ˈcuts
modal ˈməʊ.dᵊl (US) ˈmoʊ- **-s** -z **-ly** -i **ˌmodal ˈverb**
modality məʊˈdæl.ə.ti, -ɪ.ti (US) moʊˈdæl.ə.t̬i
mod con ˌmɒdˈkɒn (US) ˌmɑːdˈkɑːn, ˈ-- **-s** -z
mode məʊd (US) moʊd **-s** -z
model ˈmɒd.ᵊl (US) ˈmɑː.dᵊl **-s** -z **-(l)ing** -ɪŋ, ˈmɒd.lɪŋ (US) ˈmɑːd- **-(l)ed** -d **-(l)er/s** -əʳ/z (US) -ɚ/z, ˈmɒd.ləʳ/z (US) ˈmɑːd.lɚ/z
modem ˈməʊ.dem, -dəm (US) ˈmoʊ.dəm, -dem **-s** -z
Modena ˈmɒd.ɪ.nə; mɒdˈeɪ.nə, məˈdeɪ- (US) ˈmoʊ.dᵊn.ə, ˈmɔː-, -ɑː
moderate *(n. adj.)* ˈmɒd.ᵊr.ət, -ɪt (US) ˈmɑː.dɚ- **-s** -s **-ly** -li **-ness** -nəs, -nɪs
moder|ate *(v.)* ˈmɒd.ᵊr|.eɪt (US) ˈmɑː.də.r|eɪt **-ates** -eɪts **-ating** -eɪ.tɪŋ (US) -eɪ.t̬ɪŋ **-ated** -eɪ.tɪd (US) -eɪ.t̬ɪd **-ator/s** -eɪ.təʳ/z (US) -eɪ.t̬ɚ/z
moderation ˌmɒd.ᵊrˈeɪ.ʃᵊn (US) ˌmɑː.dəˈreɪ- **-s** -z
moderato ˌmɒd.ᵊrˈɑː.təʊ (US) ˌmɑː.dəˈrɑː.t̬oʊ **-s** -z
modern ˈmɒd.ᵊn (US) ˈmɑː.dɚn **-s** -z **-ly** -li **-ness** -nəs, -nɪs **ˌmodern ˈlanguages**
modern|ism (M) ˈmɒd.ᵊn|.ɪ.zᵊm (US) ˈmɑːd.ɚ.n|ɪ- **-ist/s** -ɪst/s
modernistic ˌmɒd.ᵊnˈɪs.tɪk (US) ˌmɑː.dɚˈnɪs- **-ally** -ᵊl.i, -li
modernity mɒdˈɜː.nə.ti, məˈdɜː-, -ɪ.ti (US) mɑːˈdɝː.nə.t̬i, mə-, moʊ-
modernization, -isa- ˌmɒd.ᵊn.aɪˈzeɪ.ʃᵊn, -ɪˈ- (US) ˌmɑː.dɚ.nɪˈ- **-s** -z
moderniz|e, -is|e ˈmɒd.ᵊn.aɪz (US) ˈmɑː.dɚ.naɪz **-es** -ɪz **-ing** -ɪŋ **-ed** -d **-er/s**
modest ˈmɒd.ɪst (US) ˈmɑː.dɪst **-ly** -li **-y** -i
modicum ˈmɒd.ɪ.kəm, ˈ-ə- (US) ˈmɑː.dɪ- **-s** -z
modification ˌmɒd.ɪ.fɪˈkeɪ.ʃᵊn, ˌ-ə- (US) ˌmɑː.dɪ- **-s** -z
modi|fy ˈmɒd.ɪ|.faɪ (US) ˈmɑː.dɪ- **-fies** -faɪz **-fying** -faɪ.ɪŋ **-fied** -faɪd **-fier/s** -faɪ.əʳ/z (US) -faɪ.ɚ/z **-fiable** -faɪ.ə.bl̩
Modigliani ˌmɒd.ɪˈljɑː.ni (US) ˌmoʊ.diːlˈjɑː-
modish ˈməʊ.dɪʃ (US) ˈmoʊ- **-ly** -li **-ness** -nəs, -nɪs
modiste məʊˈdiːst (US) moʊ- **-s** -s
Modred ˈməʊ.drɪd (US) ˈmoʊ-
modular ˈmɒd.jə.ləʳ, ˈmɒdʒ-, -jʊ- (US) ˈmɑː.dʒə.lɚ
modularity ˌmɒd.jəˈlær.ə.ti, ˌmɒdʒ-, -jʊˈ-, -ɪ.ti (US) ˌmɑː.dʒəˈler.ə.t̬i, -ˈlær-
modu|late ˈmɒd.jə|.leɪt, ˈmɒdʒ-, -jʊ- (US) ˈmɑː.dʒə- **-lates** -leɪts **-lating** -leɪ.tɪŋ (US) -leɪ.t̬ɪŋ **-lated** -leɪ.tɪd (US) -leɪ.t̬ɪd **-lator/s** -leɪ.təʳ/z (US) -leɪ.t̬ɚ/z
modulation ˌmɒd.jəˈleɪ.ʃᵊn, ˌmɒdʒ-, -jʊˈ- (US) ˌmɑː.dʒəˈ- **-s** -z
module ˈmɒd.juːl, ˈmɒdʒ- (US) ˈmɑː.dʒuːl **-s** -z
modul|us ˈmɒd.jə.l|əs, -jʊ- (US) ˈmɑː.dʒə- **-uses** -ə.sɪz **-i** -aɪ
modus ˈməʊ.dəs (US) ˈmoʊ-
modus operandi ˌməʊ.dəsˌɒp.əˈræn.diː, ˌmɒd.əs-, -daɪ (US) ˌmoʊ.dəsˌoʊ.pəˈrɑːn.di, -ɑː-, -ˈræn-
modus vivendi ˌməʊ.dəs.vɪˈven.diː, ˌmɒd.əs-, -viːˈ-, -daɪ (US) ˌmoʊ.dəs.viːˈven.di
Moesia ˈmiː.si.ə, -ʃə, -zi.ə, -ʒə (US) -ʃi.ə, -ʃə
Moffat ˈmɒf.ət (US) ˈmɑː.fət
Moffett ˈmɒf.ət, -ɪt (US) ˈmɑː.fət
Mogadishu ˌmɒg.əˈdɪʃ.uː (US) ˌmoʊ.gɑːˈdiː.ʃuː, ˌmɑː-, -gəˈ-, -ˈdɪʃ.uː
Mogadon® ˈmɒg.ə.dɒn (US) ˈmɑː.gə.dɑːn
Mogador ˌmɒg.əˈdɔːʳ, ˈ--- (US) ˈmɑː.gə.dɔːr, ˌ--ˈ-
Moggach ˈmɒg.ək, -əx (US) ˈmɑː.gək
mogg|y, mogg|ie ˈmɒg|.i (US) ˈmɑː.g|i **-ies** -z
mogul (M) ˈməʊ.gᵊl, -gʊl, -gʌl (US) ˈmoʊ.gʌl, -gᵊl; moʊˈgʌl **-s** -z
mohair ˈməʊ.heəʳ (US) ˈmoʊ.her
Moham(m)ed məʊˈhæm.ɪd, -əd, -ed (US) moʊ-
Mohammedan məʊˈhæm.ɪ.dᵊn, ˈ-ə- (US) moʊ- **-s** -z **-ism** -ɪ.zᵊm
Mohave məʊˈhɑː.vi (US) moʊ-
Mohawk ˈməʊ.hɔːk (US) ˈmoʊ.hɑːk, -hɔːk **-s** -s
Mohegan məʊˈhiː.gᵊn, mə- (US) moʊ- **-s** -z
Mohican məʊˈhiː.kᵊn; ˈməʊ.ɪ- (US) moʊˈhiː- **-s** -z
Mohun məʊən; ˈməʊ.hən; muːn (US) muːn, ˈmoʊ.hən
moidore ˌmɔɪˈdɔːʳ, ˌməʊ.ɪˈ-; ˈmɔɪ.dɔ (US) ˈmɔɪ.dɔːr **-s** -z
Note: In John Masefield's poem 'Cargoes' the stress is on the last syllable.
moiet|y ˈmɔɪ.ə.t|i, ˈ-ɪ- (US) -ə.t̬|i **-ies**
moil mɔɪl **-s** -z **-ing** -ɪŋ **-ed** -d
Moir mɔɪəʳ (US) mɔɪɚ
Moira ˈmɔɪə.rə (US) ˈmɔɪ-
moire mwɑːʳ, mwɔːʳ (US) mwɑːr, mɔː **-s** -z
moiré ˈmwɑː.reɪ, ˈmwɔː- (US) mwɑːˈr mɔː-; ˈmɔː.reɪ
moist mɔɪst **-er** -əʳ (US) -ɚ **-est** -ɪst, -ə **-ly** -li **-ness** -nəs, -nɪs
moisten ˈmɔɪ.sᵊn **-s** -z **-ing** -ɪŋ, ˈmɔɪs.nɪŋ **-ed** -d
moisture ˈmɔɪs.tʃəʳ (US) -tʃɚ

oisturiz|e, -is|e 'mɔɪs.tʃᵊr.aɪz (US) -tʃə.raɪz **-es** -ɪz **-ing** -ɪŋ **-ed** -d **-er/s** -əʳ/z (US) -ɚ/z
oivre 'mɔɪ.vəʳ (US) -vɚ
ojave məʊ'hɑː.vi (US) moʊ-
oke məʊk (US) moʊk **-s** -s
olar 'məʊ.ləʳ (US) 'moʊ.lɚ **-s** -z
olasses məʊ'læs.ɪz, -əz (US) mə-
olassine 'mɒl.ə.siːn, 'məʊ.lə- (US) 'mɑː.lə-, 'moʊ-
old məʊld (US) moʊld
old məʊld (US) moʊld **-s** -z **-ing/s** -ɪŋ **-ed** -ɪd
oldavi|a mɒl'deɪ.vi|.ə (US) mɑːl-, '-vj|ə **-an/s** -ən/z
old|er 'məʊl.d|əʳ (US) 'moʊl.d|ɚ **-ers** -əz (US) -ɚz **-ering** -ᵊr.ɪŋ **-ered** -əd (US) -ɚd
oldov|a mɒl'dəʊ.v|ə (US) mɑːl'doʊ- **-an/s** -ən/z
old|y 'məʊl.d|i (US) 'moʊl- **-ier** -i.əʳ (US) -i.ɚ **-iest** -i.ɪst, -i.əst **-iness** -ɪ.nəs, -ɪ.nɪs
ole (M) məʊl (US) moʊl **-s** -z
olech 'məʊ.lek (US) 'moʊ-
olecular məʊ'lek.jə.ləʳ, mɒl'ek-, -jʊ- (US) mə'lek.jə.lɚ, moʊ-, -juː-
olecule 'mɒl.ɪ.kjuːl, 'məʊ.lɪ-, -lə- (US) 'mɑː.lɪ.kjuːl **-s** -z
olehill 'məʊl.hɪl (US) 'moʊl- **-s** -z **make a ˌmountain out of a 'mole-hill**
olesey 'məʊl.zi (US) 'moʊl-
oleskin 'məʊl.skɪn (US) 'moʊl- **-s** -z
olest məʊ'lest (US) mə-, moʊ- **-s** -s **-ing** -ɪŋ **-ed** -ɪd **-er/s** -əʳ/z (US) -ɚ/z
olestation ˌmɒl.es'teɪ.ʃən, ˌməʊ.les'- (US) ˌmoʊ.les'-, ˌmɑː- **-s** -z
olester məʊ'les.təʳ (US) mə'les.tɚ, moʊ- **-s** -z
olesworth 'məʊlz.wəθ, -wɜːθ (US) 'moʊlz.wɚθ, -wɝːθ
olière 'mɒl.i.eəʳ, 'məʊ.li- (US) ˌmoʊl'jer
oline məʊ'liːn (US) moʊ-
oll (M) mɒl (US) mɑːl
ollification ˌmɒl.ɪ.fɪ'keɪ.ʃᵊn, ˌ-ə- (US) ˌmɑː.lə-
olli|fy 'mɒl.ɪ|.faɪ, '-ə- (US) 'mɑː.lə- **-fies** -faɪz **-fying** -faɪ.ɪŋ **-fied** -faɪd
ollusc 'mɒl.əsk, -ʌsk (US) 'mɑː.ləsk **-s** -s
olluscan mɒl'ʌs.kᵊn, mə'lʌs- (US) mə-
olluscoid mɒl'ʌs.kɔɪd, mə'lʌs- (US) mə-
oll|y (M) 'mɒl|.i (US) 'mɑː.l|i **-ies** -iz
ollycoddl|e 'mɒl.iˌkɒd.l̩ (US) 'mɑː.liˌkɑː.dl̩ **-es** -z **-ing** -ɪŋ, ˌkɒd.lɪŋ (US) -ˌkɑːd.lɪŋ **-ed** -d
oloch 'məʊ.lɒk (US) 'moʊ.lɑːk, mɑː.lək
olony mə'ləʊ.ni (US) -'loʊ-
Molotov 'mɒl.ə.tɒf (US) 'mɑː.lə.tɔːf, 'moʊ-, -tɔːv **ˌMolotov 'cocktail**
molt məʊlt (US) moʊlt **-s** -s **-ing** -ɪŋ (US) 'moʊl.t̬ɪŋ **-ed** -ɪd (US) 'moʊl.t̬ɪd **-er/s** -əʳ/z (US) 'moʊl.t̬ɚ/z
molten 'məʊl.tᵊn (US) 'moʊl-
molto 'mɒl.təʊ (US) 'moʊl.toʊ
Molton 'məʊl.tᵊn (US) 'moʊl-
Moluccas məʊ'lʌk.əz (US) moʊ-, mə-
moly 'məʊ.li (US) 'moʊ-
molybdenum mə'lɪb.də.nəm, -dɪ-, mɒl'ɪb-, məʊ'lɪb-; ˌmɒl.ɪb'diː.nəm (US) mə'lɪb.də-
Molyneux 'mɒl.ɪ.njuːks, 'mʌl-, '-ə-, -njuː (US) 'mʌl.ɪ.nuːks, -njuː, -nuː
mom (M) mɒm (US) mɑːm **-s** -z
Mombasa mɒm'bæs.ə, -'bɑː.sə (US) mɑːm'bɑː.sə, -'bæs.ə
moment 'məʊ.mənt (US) 'moʊ- **-s** -s **ˌmoment of 'truth**
momenta *(plur. of* **momentum***)* məʊ'men.tə (US) moʊ'men.t̬ə, mə-
momentarily 'məʊ.mən.tᵊr.ᵊl.i, -ɪ.li; ˌməʊ.mən'ter- (US) ˌmoʊ.mən'ter-, 'moʊ.mən.ter-
momentar|y 'məʊ.mən.tᵊr|.i (US) 'moʊ.mən.ter- **-iness** -ɪ.nəs, -ɪ.nɪs
momentous məʊ'men.təs (US) moʊ'men.t̬əs, mə- **-ly** -li **-ness** -nəs, -nɪs
moment|um məʊ'men.t|əm (US) moʊ'men.t̬|əm, mə- **-ums** -əmz **-a** -ə
momma (M) 'mɒm.ə (US) 'mɑː.mə **-s** -z
momm|y 'mɒm|.i (US) 'mɑː.m|i **-ies** -iz
Mon *language:* məʊn, mɒn (US) moʊn
Mon. *(abbrev. for* **Monday***)* 'mʌn.deɪ, -di
Note: Can be pronounced /mʌn/ in British English.
mona (M) 'məʊ.nə (US) 'moʊ- **-s** -z **ˌMona 'Lisa**
Monaco 'mɒn.ə.kəʊ, mə'nɑː- (US) 'mɑː.nə.koʊ, mə'nɑː-
monad 'mɒn.æd, 'məʊ.næd (US) 'moʊ-, 'mɑː.næd **-s** -z
Monadhliath ˌməʊ.nə'liː.ə (US) ˌmoʊ-
monadic mɒn'æd.ɪk, məʊ'næd- (US) mə-, moʊ-
Monaghan 'mɒn.ə.hən, -kən *as if Irish:* -xən (US) 'mɑː.nə.gən
monarch 'mɒn.ək (US) 'mɑː.nɚk, -nɑːrk **-s** -s
monarch|al mɒn'ɑː.k|ᵊl, mə'nɑː- (US) mə'nɑːr-, moʊ- **-ic** -ɪk **-ical** -ɪ.kᵊl
monarch|ism 'mɒn.ə.k|ɪ.zᵊm (US) 'mɑː.nɚ-, -nɑːr- **-ist/s** -ɪst/s
monarchiz|e, -is|e 'mɒn.ə.kaɪz (US) 'mɑː.nɚ-, -nɑːr- **-es** -ɪz **-ing** -ɪŋ **-ed** -d
monarch|y 'mɒn.ə.k|i (US) 'mɑː.nɚ-, -nɑːr- **-ies** -iz
Monash 'mɒn.æʃ (US) 'mɑː.næʃ
monaster|y 'mɒn.ə.stᵊr|.i, -str|i (US) 'mɑː.nə.ster|.i **-ies** -iz
monastic mə'næs.tɪk, mɒn'æs- (US) mə-, moʊ- **-al** -ᵊl **-ally** -ᵊl.i, -li
monasticism mə'næs.tɪ.sɪ.zᵊm, mɒn'æs- (US) mə'næs-, moʊ-
monatomic ˌmɒn.ə'tɒm.ɪk (US) ˌmɑː.nə'tɑː.mɪk
monaural mɒn'ɔː.rᵊl (US) mɑː'nɔːr.ᵊl
Monbiot 'mɒn.bi.əʊ (US) -oʊ, 'mɑːn.bi.oʊ
Monchen-Gladbach, Mönchen-Gladbach ˌmɜːn.ʃən'glæd.bæk, ˌmʊn-, -kəŋ'- (US) -kən'glɑːt.bɑːk
Monck mʌŋk
Monckton 'mʌŋk.tən
Moncrieff mən'kriːf, məŋ-, mɒn-, mɒŋ- (US) mɑːn-, mən-; 'mɑːn.kriːf
Mond mɒnd (US) mɑːnd
Mondale 'mɒn.deɪl (US) 'mɑːn-
Monday 'mʌn.deɪ, -di **-s** -z
Mondeo® ˌmɒn'deɪ.əʊ (US) ˌmɑːn'deɪ.oʊ
Mondrian 'mɒn.dri.æn, -ən (US) 'mɑːn.dri.ɑːn, -ən
Monegasque ˌmɒn.ɪ'gæsk, -ə'- (US) ˌmɑː.neɪ'-
Monet 'mɒn.eɪ *as if French:* -'- (US) moʊ'neɪ, mə-
monetar|ism 'mʌn.ɪ.tᵊr|.ɪ.zᵊm, '-ə- (US) 'mɑː.nə-, 'mʌn.ə- **-ist/s** -ɪst/s
monetary 'mʌn.ɪ.tᵊr.i, '-ə-, -tri (US) 'mɑː.nə.ter.i, 'mʌn.ə-
monetiz|e, -is|e 'mʌn.ɪ.taɪz, '-ə- (US) 'mɑː.nə-, 'mʌn.ə- **-es** -ɪz **-ing** -ɪŋ **-ed** -d
mon|ey (M) 'mʌn|.i **-eys** -z **-ies** -iz **-eyed** -id **-ied** -id **'money ˌbox; 'money ˌchanger; 'money ˌmarket; 'money ˌorder; 'money ˌsupply; ˌthrow good ˌmoney after 'bad**
moneybag 'mʌn.i.bæg **-s** -z
moneygrabb|ing 'mʌn.iˌgræb|.ɪŋ **-er/s** -əʳ/z (US) -ɚ/z
money-grubb|er 'mʌn.iˌgrʌb|.əʳ (US) -ɚ **-ers** -əz (US) -ɚz **-ing** -ɪŋ
moneylend|er 'mʌn.iˌlen.d|əʳ (US) -d|ɚ **-ers** -əz (US) -ɚz **-ing** -ɪŋ
money-market 'mʌn.iˌmɑː.kɪt (US) -ˌmɑːr- **-s** -s
money-off ˌmʌn.i'ɒf (US) -'ɑːf
Moneypenny 'mʌn.iˌpen.i
money-spinner 'mʌn.iˌspɪn.əʳ (US) -ɚ **-s** -z
monger 'mʌŋ.gəʳ (US) -gɚ, 'mɑːŋ- **-s** -z
mongo 'mɒŋ.gəʊ (US) 'mɑːŋ.goʊ **-s** -z
mongol (M) 'mɒŋ.gəl, -gɒl (US) 'mɑːŋ-, 'mɑːn-, -gəl, -goʊl **-s** -z **-oid** -ɔɪd
Mongoli|a mɒŋ'gəʊ.li|.ə (US) mɑːŋ'goʊ-, mɑːn-, -'goʊl.j|ə **-an/s** -ən/z

mongolism (M) ˈmɒŋ.gəl.ɪ.zəm, -gɒl- US ˈmɑːŋ.gəl-, ˈmɑːn-
mongoos|e ˈmɒŋ.guːs, ˈmʌŋ- US ˈmɑːŋ-, ˈmɑːn- **-es** -ɪz
mongrel ˈmʌŋ.grəl US ˈmɑːŋ-, ˈmʌŋ- **-s** -z
Monica ˈmɒn.ɪ.kə US ˈmɑː.nɪ-
monicker ˈmɒn.ɪ.kər US ˈmɑː.nɪ.kɚ **-s** -z
Monier ˈmʌn.i.ər, ˈmɒn- US ˈmɑː.ni.ɚ, ˈmʌn.i-
moniker ˈmɒn.ɪ.kər US ˈmɑː.nɪ.kɚ **-s** -z
Monique mɒnˈiːk US moʊ-, mə-
mon|ism ˈmɒn|.ɪ.zəm, ˈməʊ.n|ɪ- US ˈmoʊ-, ˈmɑː- **-ist/s** -ɪst/s
monistic mɒnˈɪs.tɪk, məˈnɪs- US moʊ-, mə- **-al** -əl
monition məʊˈnɪʃ.ən, mɒnˈɪʃ- US moʊˈnɪʃ-, mə- **-s** -z
monit|or ˈmɒn.ɪ.t|ər, -ə- US ˈmɑː.nə.t̬|ɚ **-ors** -əz US -ɚz **-oring** -ər.ɪŋ **-ored** -əd US -ɚd
monitorial ˌmɒn.ɪˈtɔː.ri.əl, -əˈ- US ˌmɑː.nɪˈtɔːr.i-
monitory ˈmɒn.ɪ.tər.i, ˈ-ə- US ˈmɑː.nɪ.tɔːr-
monk (M) mʌŋk **-s** -s **-ish** -ɪʃ
monkey ˈmʌŋ.ki **-s** -z **-ing** -ɪŋ **-ed** -d ˈ**monkey** ˌ**bars**; ˈ**monkey** ˌ**business**; ˈ**monkey** ˌ**wrench**
monkey-puzzle ˈmʌŋ.kiˌpʌz.l̩ **-s** -z
monkfish ˈmʌŋk.fɪʃ **-es** -ɪz
Monkhouse ˈmʌŋk.haʊs
Monkton ˈmʌŋk.tən
Monmouth ˈmɒn.məθ US ˈmɑːn- **-shire** -ʃər, -ˌʃɪər US -ʃɚ, -ˌʃɪr
mono- mɒn.əʊ-; məˈnɒ- US mɑː.noʊ-, -nə-; məˈnɑː-

Note: Prefix. Normally either takes primary or secondary stress on the first syllable, e.g. **monotone** /ˈmɒn.ə.təʊn US ˈmɑː.nə.toʊn/, **monotonic** /ˌmɒn.əˈtɒn.ɪk US ˌmɑː.nəˈtɑː.nɪk/, or primary stress on the second syllable, e.g. **monotony** /məˈnɒt.ən.i US -ˈnɑː.tən-/.

mono *monotype:* ˈməʊ.nəʊ, ˈmɒn.əʊ US ˈmɑː.noʊ **-s** -z *in sound recording:* ˈmɒn.əʊ US ˈmɑː.noʊ **-s** -z
monobasic ˌmɒn.əʊˈbeɪ.sɪk US ˌmɑː.nəˈ-
monoceros məˈnɒs.ər.ɒs, mɒnˈɒs- US məˈnɑː.sɚ-
monochloride ˌmɒn.əʊˈklɔː.raɪd US ˌmɑː.noʊˈklɔːr.aɪd, -əˈ- **-s** -z
monochord ˈmɒn.əʊ.kɔːd US ˈmɑː.nə.kɔːrd **-s** -z
monochromatic ˌmɒn.ə.krəʊˈmæt.ɪk US ˌmɑː.nə.kroʊˈmæt̬-, -krə-
monochrome ˈmɒn.ə.krəʊm US ˈmɑː.nə.kroʊm **-s** -z
monocle ˈmɒn.ə.kl̩ US ˈmɑː.nə- **-s** -z
monoclonal ˌmɒn.əʊˈkləʊ.nəl US ˌmɑː.nəˈkloʊ-, -noʊˈ-
monocotyledon ˌmɒn.əʊˌkɒt.ɪˈliː.dən, -əlˈiː- US ˌmɑː.nəˌkɑː.təlˈiː-, -noʊˌ- **-s** -z
monoculture ˈmɒn.əʊˌkʌl.tʃər US ˈmɑː.nəˌkʌl.tʃɚ, -noʊˌ-
monod|y ˈmɒn.ə.d|i US ˈmɑː.nə- **-ies** -iz
monogamist məˈnɒg.ə.mɪst, mɒnˈɒg- US məˈnɑː.gə- **-s** -s
monogamous məˈnɒg.ə.məs, mɒnˈɒg- US məˈnɑː.gə-
monogamy məˈnɒg.ə.mi, mɒnˈɒg- US məˈnɑː.gə-
monoglot ˈmɒn.ə.glɒt US ˈmɑː.nə.glɑːt **-s** -s
monogram ˈmɒn.ə.græm US ˈmɑː.nə- **-s** -z **-ming** -ɪŋ **-med** -d
monograph ˈmɒn.ə.grɑːf, -græf US ˈmɑː.nə.græf **-s** -s
monographic ˌmɒn.əʊˈgræf.ɪk US ˌmɑː.nəˈ-
monolingual ˌmɒn.əʊˈlɪŋ.gwəl US ˌmɑː.nəˈ-, -noʊˈ- **-s** -z **-ly** -i
monolinguist ˌmɒn.əʊˈlɪŋ.gwɪst US ˌmɑː.nəˈ-, -noʊˈ- **-s** -s
monolith ˈmɒn.əʊ.lɪθ US ˈmɑː.nə- **-s** -s
monolithic ˌmɒn.əʊˈlɪθ.ɪk US ˌmɑː.nəˈ-
monologue, monolog ˈmɒn.əl.ɒg US ˈmɑː.nə.lɑːg, -lɔːg **-s** -z

monolog(u)ist ˈmɒn.əl.ɒg.ɪst, -ɒdʒ-; məˈnɒl.ə.gɪst, -dʒɪst US ˈmɑː.nə.lɑːg.ɪst, -lɔːg.ɪst, məˈnɑː.lə.dʒɪst **-s** -s
monomani|a ˌmɒn.əʊˈmeɪ.ni|.ə US ˌmɑː.noʊˈ-, -nəˈ- **-ac/s** -æk/s
mononuclear ˌmɒn.əʊˈnjuː.kli.ər US ˌmɑː.noʊˈnuː.kli.ɚ, -ˈnjuː-
mononucleosis ˌmɒn.əʊˌnjuː.kliˈəʊ. US ˌmɑː.noʊˌnuː.kliˈoʊ-, -ˌnjuː-
monophonic ˌmɒn.əʊˈfɒn.ɪk US ˌmɑː.nəˈfɑː.nɪk, -noʊˈ-
monophthong ˈmɒn.əf.θɒŋ, ˈ-ə- US ˈmɑː.nəf.θɑːŋ, -θɔːŋ **-s** -z
monophthong|al ˌmɒn.əfˈθɒŋ.g|əl, - US ˌmɑː.nəfˈθɑːŋ|.əl, -ˈθɔːŋ-, -g|əl **-ic** -ɪk
monophthongiz|e, -is|e ˈmɒn.əf.θɒŋ.gaɪz, ˈ-ə-, -aɪz US ˈmɑː.nəf.θɑːŋ-, -θɔːŋ- **-es** -ɪz **-i** -ɪŋ **-ed** -d
monoplane ˈmɒn.əʊ.pleɪn US ˈmɑː. **-s** -z
monopole ˈmɒn.ə.pəʊl US ˈmɑː.nə.poʊl
monopolism məˈnɒp.əl.ɪ.zəm US məˈnɑː.pə.lɪ-
monopolist məˈnɒp.əl.ɪst US -ˈnɑː.pə.lɪst **-s** -s
monopolistic məˌnɒp.əlˈɪs.tɪk US -ˌnɑː.pəˈlɪs- **-ally** -əl.i, -li
monopoliz|e, -is|e məˈnɒp.əl.aɪz US -ˈnɑː.pə.laɪz **-es** -ɪz **-ing** -ɪŋ **-e** **-er/s** -ər/z
monopol|y məˈnɒp.əl|.i US -ˈnɑː.pəl **-ies** -iz
monorail ˈmɒn.əʊ.reɪl US ˈmɑː.nə-, -noʊ- **-s** -z
monosaccharide ˌmɒn.əʊˈsæk.ər.a US ˌmɑː.noʊˈsæk.ə.raɪd, -nəˈ- **-s**
monosodium ˌmɒn.əʊˈsəʊ.di.əm US ˌmɑː.noʊˈsoʊ-, -nəˈ- *stress sh* *see compound:* ˌ**monosodium** ˈ**glutamate**
monosyllabic ˌmɒn.əʊ.sɪˈlæb.ɪk US ˌmɑː.nə-, -noʊ- *stress shift:* ˌmonosyllabic ˈword **-ally** -əl.i, -l

Monophthong

A single vowel. The term is used only in contrast with the word DIPHTHONG, which originally meant a 'double sound'.

Examples for English

British English has 12 vowel monophthongs /ɪ e æ ʌ ɒ ʊ ə iː ɑː ɔː ɜː uː/, and US English has 11, or 12 if r-coloured SCHWA /ɚ/ is taken into account. In British English these are traditionally divided into short and long, with a length mark [ː] used to show that there is a difference in length as well as vowel quality. This convention is extend in this dictionary to US English vowels. Long vowels are permitted to appear in a stressed syllable without a CODA, whereas short vowels are not. It should be noted that the schwa vowel, /ə/, never appears in stressed syllable and has a different distribution to the other short vowels.

monosyllable 'mɒn.əʊˌsɪl.ə.bl̩ (US) 'mɑː.nəˌ-, -noʊˌ- **-s** -z
monothe|ism 'mɒn.əʊ.θiː.ɪ.zəm, ˌmɒn.əʊ'θiː- (US) 'mɑː.noʊˌθiː-, -nəˌ- **-ist/s** -ɪst/s
monotheistic ˌmɒn.əʊ.θi'ɪs.tɪk (US) ˌmɑː.noʊ- *stress shift:* ˌmonotheistic 'culture
monoton|e 'mɒn.ə.təʊn (US) 'mɑː.nə.toʊn **-es** -z **-ing** -ɪŋ **-ed** -d
monotonic ˌmɒn.ə'tɒn.ɪk (US) ˌmɑː.nə'tɑː.nɪk *stress shift:* ˌmonotonic 'function
monotonous mə'nɒt.ən.əs (US) -'nɑː.tən- **-ly** -li **-ness** -nəs, -nɪs
monotony mə'nɒt.ən.i (US) -'nɑː.tən-
monotype (M®) 'mɒn.əʊ.taɪp, 'məʊ.nəʊ- (US) 'mɑː.noʊ-, -nə- **-s** -s
monovalen|ce ˌmɒn.əʊ'veɪ.lən|ts, 'mɒn.əʊˌveɪ- (US) ˌmɑː.noʊ'veɪ-, 'mɑː.noʊˌveɪ-, -nə'- **-t** -t
monoxide mə'nɒk.saɪd, mɒn'ɒk- (US) mə'nɑːk- **-s** -z
Monro(e) mən'rəʊ, mʌn'rəʊ, 'mʌn.rəʊ (US) mən'roʊ
Monrovia mɒn'rəʊ.vi.ə, mən- (US) mən'roʊ-
Mons mɒnz *as if French:* mɔ̃ːns (US) mõʊns
Monsanto® mɒn'sæn.təʊ
Monsarrat 'mɒnt.sər.æt, ˌ--'- (US) ˌmɑːnt.sə'rɑːt, -'ræt
monseigneur ˌmɒn.sen'jɜːr (US) ˌmɑːn.sən'jɝː **-s** -z **messeigneurs** ˌmes.eɪ'njɜː (US) 'jɝː
monsieur (M) mə'sjɜːr, -'sjər (US) -'sjɝː, -'sjɜː

Note: /mə'sjɜːr/ is the form of address in isolation. When attached to the surname /mə'sjər/ is unstressed.

monsignor (M) mɒn'siː.njər (US) mɑːn'siː.njɚ
Monson 'mʌnt.sən
monsoon mɒn'suːn, mən- (US) mɑːn- **-s** -z
monster 'mɒnt.stər (US) 'mɑːnt.stɚ **-s** -z
monstranc|e 'mɒnt.strənts (US) 'mɑːnt- **-es** -ɪz
monstrosit|y mɒn'strɒs.ə.t|i, mən-, -ɪ.t|i (US) mɑːn'strɑː.sə.t̬|i **-ies** -iz
monstrous 'mɒnt.strəs (US) 'mɑːnt- **-ly** -li **-ness** -nəs, -nɪs
Mont. *(abbrev. for* **Montana***)* mɒn'tæn.ə, -'tɑː.nə (US) mɑːn'tæn.ə
montag|e mɒn'tɑːʒ, '--, -tɪdʒ (US) 'mɑːn.tɑːʒ; moʊn'tɑːʒ **-es** -ɪz
Montagu(e) 'mɒn.tə.gjuː, -tɪ-, 'mʌn- (US) 'mɑːn-
Montaigne mɒn'teɪn (US) mɑːn-
Montana mɒn'tæn.ə, -'tɑː.nə (US) mɑːn'tæn.ə
Mont Blanc *as if French:* ˌmɔ̃ːm'blɑ̃ːŋ *as if French:* (US) mõʊm'blɑ̃ːŋ
montbretia mɒn'briː.ʃə, mɒm-, -ʃi.ə (US) mɑːnt'- **-s** -z
Mont Cenis ˌmɔ̃ːn.sə'niː (US) ˌmõʊn-
monte (M) 'mɒn.teɪ, -ti (US) 'mɑːn.t̬i
Monte Carlo ˌmɒnt.i'kɑː.ləʊ (US) ˌmɑːn.t̬i'kɑːr.loʊ
Montefiore ˌmɒn.ti.fi'ɔː.reɪ, -ri, -tə-, -'fjɔː- (US) ˌmɑːn.t̬i.fi'ɔːr.i
Montego® mɒn'tiː.gəʊ (US) mɑːn'tiː.goʊ
Montego Bay mɒnˌtiː.gəʊ'beɪ (US) mɑːnˌtiː.goʊ'-
monteith mɒn'tiːθ (US) mɑːn- **-s** -s
Monteith mən'tiːθ, mɒn- (US) mɑːn-
Montenegr|o ˌmɒn.tɪ'niː.gr|əʊ, -tə'-, -'neɪ- (US) ˌmɑːn.t̬ə'niː.gr|oʊ, -'neg.r|oʊ **-an/s** -ən/z
Monte Rosa ˌmɒn.tɪ'rəʊ.zə, -tə'- (US) ˌmɑːn.t̬ə'roʊ-
Monterrey ˌmɒn.tər.eɪ, -tɪ'reɪ (US) ˌmɑːn.t̬ə'reɪ
Montesquieu ˌmɒn.tes'kjuː, -'kjɜː, '--- (US) 'mɑːn.t̬ə.skjuː
Montessori ˌmɒn.tes'ɔː.ri, -tɪ'sɔː- (US) ˌmɑːn.t̬ə'sɔːr.i
Monteverdi ˌmɒn.tɪ'vɜː.di, -tə'-, -'veə- (US) ˌmɑːn.t̬ə'ver
Montevideo ˌmɒn.tɪ.vɪ'deɪ.əʊ, -tə- (US) ˌmɑːn.t̬ə.və'deɪ.oʊ, -'vɪd.i.oʊ
Montezuma ˌmɒn.tɪ'zuː.mə, -tə'-, -'zjuː- (US) ˌmɑːn.t̬ə'zuː-
Montfort 'mɒnt.fət, -fɔːt (US) 'mɑːnt.fɚt, -fɔːrt
Montgomerie mənt'gʌm.ər.i, mɒnt-, -'gɒm-, '-ri (US) mɑːnt'gʌm.ri, mənt-, '-ɚ.i
Montgomery mənt'gʌm.ər.i, mɒnt-, -'gɒm-, -'ri (US) mɑːnt'gʌm.ri, mənt-, '-ɚ.i **-shire** -ʃər, -ˌʃɪər (US) -ʃɚ, -ˌʃɪr
month mʌntθ **-s** -s **-ly** -li **in a** ˌ**month of** '**Sundays**
Monticello ˌmɒn.tɪ'tʃel.əʊ (US) ˌmɑːn.tɪ'tʃel.oʊ, -'sel-
Montmorency ˌmɒnt.mər'ent.si (US) ˌmɑːnt-
Montpelier *in US, London street:* mɒnt'piː.li.ər (US) mɑːnt'piːl.jɚ
Montpellier *in France:* mɔ̃ːm'pel.i.eɪ (US) ˌmõʊn.pəl'jeɪ *in names of streets, etc.:* mɒnt'pel.i.ər, mənt- (US) mɑːnt'pel.i.ɚ
Montreal ˌmɒn.tri'ɔːl (US) ˌmɑːn.tri'ɔːl, ˌmʌn-, -'ɑːl
Montreux mɒn'trɜː *as if French:* mɔ̃ːn- (US) mɑːn-
Montrose mɒn'trəʊz, mən- (US) mɑːn'troʊz
Mont-Saint-Michel ˌmɒntˌsæn.mɪ'ʃel, -ˌsæm- *as if French:* ˌmɔ̃ːn- *as if French:* (US) ˌmõʊnˌsæn.miː'ʃel
Montserrat *island in West Indies:* ˌmɒnt.sə'ræt, -ser'æt (US) ˌmɑːnt.sə'ræt *monastery in Spain:* ˌmɒnt.sə'rɑːt, -ser'ɑːt (US) ˌmɑːnt.sə'rɑːt
Monty 'mɒn.ti (US) 'mɑːn.t̬i, -ti
monument 'mɒn.jə.mənt, -jʊ- (US) 'mɑːn.jə-, -juː- **-s** -s
monumental ˌmɒn.jə'men.təl, -jʊ'- (US) ˌmɑːn.jə'men.t̬əl, -juː'- **-ly** -i
Monza 'mɒn.zə (US) 'mɔːnt.sɑː, 'moʊnt-, 'mɑː-
Monzie mə'niː, mɒn'iː (US) mɔːn'ziː, mɑːn-, '--
moo muː **-s** -z **-ing** -ɪŋ **-ed** -d
mooch muːtʃ **-es** -ɪz **-ing** -ɪŋ **-ed** -t **-er/s** -ər/z (US) -ɚ/z
moo-cow 'muː.kaʊ **-s** -z
mood muːd **-s** -z
mood|y (M) 'muː.d|i **-ier** -i.ər (US) -i.ɚ **-iest** -i.ɪst, -i.əst **-ily** -ɪ.li, -əl.i **-iness** -ɪ.nəs, -ɪ.nɪs
Moog® məʊg, muːg (US) moʊg, muːg
moola(h) 'muː.lə
mooli 'muː.li
moon (M) muːn **-s** -z **-ing** -ɪŋ **-ed** -d ˌ**over the** '**moon**
moonbeam 'muːn.biːm, 'muːm- (US) 'muːn- **-s** -z
mooncal|f 'muːn.kɑː|f, 'muːŋ- (US) 'muːn.kæ|f **-ves** -vz
Mooney 'muː.ni
moonie (M) 'muː.ni **-s** -z
moon|light 'muːn|.laɪt **-lit** -lɪt **-lights** -laɪts **-lighting** -ˌlaɪ.tɪŋ (US) -ˌlaɪ.t̬ɪŋ **-lighted** -ˌlaɪ.tɪd (US) -ˌlaɪ.t̬ɪd
moonscape 'muːn.skeɪp **-s** -s
moonshine 'muːn.ʃaɪn
moonstone 'muːn.stəʊn (US) -stoʊn **-s** -z
moonstruck 'muːn.strʌk
moony 'muː.ni
moor (M) mɔːr, mʊər (US) mʊr **-s** -z **-ing** -ɪŋ/z **-ed** -d
Moorall 'mɔː.rɔːl (US) 'mɔːr.ɔːl, -əl
moorcock (M) 'mɔː.kɒk, 'mʊə- (US) 'mʊr.kɑːk **-s** -z
Moorcroft 'mɔː.krɒft, 'mʊə- (US) 'mʊr.kræːft
Moore mɔːr, mʊər (US) mʊr, mɔːr
Moorends 'mɔː.rendz, 'mʊə- (US) 'mʊr.endz
Moorfoot 'mɔː.fʊt, 'mʊə- (US) 'mʊr-
Moorgate 'mɔː.geɪt, 'mʊə-, -gɪt (US) 'mʊr-
Moorhead 'mɔː.hed, 'mʊə- (US) 'mʊr-, 'mɔːr-
moorhen 'mɔː.hen, 'mʊə- (US) 'mʊr- **-s** -z
Moorhouse 'mɔː.haʊs, 'mʊə- (US) 'mʊr-, 'mɔːr-
mooring 'mɔː.rɪŋ, 'mʊə- (US) 'mʊr.ɪŋ **-s** -z
Moorish 'mʊə.rɪʃ, 'mɔː- (US) 'mʊr.ɪʃ
moorland 'mɔː.lənd, 'mʊə-, -lænd (US) 'mʊr- **-s** -z

Note: The variant /-lænd/ is not used when the word is attributive.
moos|e muːs **-es** -ɪz
moot muːt **-s** -s **-ing** -ɪŋ US ˈmuː.t̬ɪŋ **-ed** -ɪd US ˈmuː.t̬ɪd
mop mɒp US mɑːp **-s** -s **-ping** -ɪŋ **-ped** -t
mop|e məʊp US moʊp **-es** -s **-ing/ly** -ɪŋ/li **-ed** -t
moped (*n.*) ˈməʊ.ped US ˈmoʊ- **-s** -z
mopoke ˈməʊ.pəʊk US ˈmoʊ.poʊk **-s** -s
moppet (M) ˈmɒp.ɪt US ˈmɑː.pɪt **-s** -s
Mopsy ˈmɒp.si US ˈmɑːp-
moquette mɒkˈet, məʊˈket US moʊ-
mor|a ˈmɔː.r|ə US ˈmɔːr|.ə, ˈmoʊ.r|ə **-ae** -iː, -aɪ **-as** -əz
Morag ˈmɔː.ræg US ˈmɔːr.æg
moraine mɒrˈeɪn, məˈreɪn US mə-, mɔː- **-s** -z
moral ˈmɒr.ᵊl US ˈmɔːr- **-s** -z **-ly** -i
morale məˈrɑːl, mɒrˈɑːl US məˈræl, mɔː-
Morales mɒrˈɑː.lez, -les US məˈræl.ɪs, mɔːˈrɑː.lɪs
moralist ˈmɒr.ᵊl.ɪst US ˈmɔːr- **-s** -s
moralistic ˌmɒr.ᵊlˈɪs.tɪk US ˌmɔːr- **-ally** -ᵊl.i, -li
morality məˈræl.ə.ti, mɒrˈæl-, -ɪ.ti US mɔːˈræl.ə.t̬i, mə- **moˈrality ˌplay**
moraliz|e, -is|e ˈmɒr.ᵊl.aɪz US ˈmɔːr- **-es** -ɪz **-ing** -ɪŋ **-ed** -d **-er/s** -əʳ/z US -ɚ/z
Moran ˈmɔː.rən, ˈmɒr.ən; məˈræn, mɒrˈæn US mɔːˈræn, mə-; ˈmɔːr.ən
Morant məˈrænt, mɒrˈænt US mɔːˈrænt, mə-
Morar ˈmɔː.rəʳ US ˈmɔːr.ɚ
morass məˈræs, mɒrˈæs US məˈræs, mɔː- **-es** -ɪz
moratori|um ˌmɒr.əˈtɔː.ri|.əm, ˌmɔː.rəˈ- US ˌmɔːr.əˈtɔːr.i- **-ums** -əmz **-a** -ə
Moravi|a məˈreɪ.vi|.ə, mɒrˈeɪ- US mɔːˈreɪ-, mə- **-an/s** -ən/z
moray *eel:* ˈmɒr.eɪ, ˈmɔː.reɪ; məˈreɪ US ˈmɔːr.eɪ; mɔːˈreɪ, mə- **-s** -z
Moray ˈmʌr.i US ˈmɝː-
morbid ˈmɔː.bɪd US ˈmɔːr- **-ly** -li **-ness** -nəs, -nɪs
morbidity mɔːˈbɪd.ə.ti, -ɪ.ti US mɔːrˈbɪd.ə.t̬i
mordant ˈmɔː.dᵊnt US ˈmɔːr- **-s** -s **-ly** -li
Mordaunt ˈmɔː.dᵊnt, -daʊnt US ˈmɔːr-
Mordecai ˌmɔː.dɪˈkeɪ.aɪ, -dəˈ-, -ˈkaɪ.iː; ˈmɔː.dɪ.kaɪ, -də- US ˈmɔːr.də.kaɪ, ˈkeɪ.aɪ
Morden ˈmɔː.dᵊn US ˈmɔːr-
mordent ˈmɔː.dᵊnt US ˈmɔːr- **-s** -s
Mordor ˈmɔː.dɔːʳ US ˈmɔːr.dɔːr
Mordred ˈmɔː.drɪd, -drəd, -dred US ˈmɔːr.dred, -drəd
more (M) mɔːʳ US mɔːr
Morea mɒrˈiː.ə, məˈriː.ə, mɔː- US mɔːˈriː.ə
Moreau mɒrˈəʊ, məˈrəʊ US mɑːˈroʊ, mə-
Morecambe ˈmɔː.kəm US ˈmɔːr-
moreish ˈmɔː.rɪʃ US ˈmɔːr.ɪʃ
morel (M) mɒrˈel, məˈrel US mɔː-, mə- **-s** -z
morello məˈrel.əʊ, mɒrˈel- US məˈrel.oʊ **-s** -z
Morelos məˈrel.ɒs, mɔː- US mɔːˈrel.ɑːs
Moreno məˈriː.nəʊ, mɒrˈiː- US məˈriː.noʊ, mɔː-, -ˈren.oʊ
moreover mɔːˈrˈəʊ.vəʳ, məʳ- US mɔːrˈoʊ.vɚ, ˈ-ˌ--
mores ˈmɔː.reɪz, -riːz US ˈmɔːr.eɪz, -iːz
Moresby *surname:* ˈmɔːz.bi US ˈmɔːrz- *in Cumbria:* ˈmɒr.ɪs.bi US ˈmɔːr.ɪs-
Moreton ˈmɔː.tᵊn US ˈmɔːr-
Morgan ˈmɔː.gᵊn US ˈmɔːr-
morganatic ˌmɔː.gəˈnæt.ɪk US ˌmɔːr.gəˈnæt̬- **-ally** -ᵊl.i US -li
Morgan le Fay ˌmɔː.gᵊn.ləˈfeɪ US ˌmɔːr-
morgue mɔːg US mɔːrg **-s** -z
MORI ˈmɔː.ri, ˈmɒr.i US ˈmɔːr.i
Moriah mɒrˈaɪ.ə, mɔːˈraɪ.ə, mə- US mə-, mɔː-, moʊ-
Moriarty ˌmɒr.iˈɑː.ti US ˌmɔːr.iˈɑːr.t̬i
moribund ˈmɒr.ɪ.bʌnd, ˈmɔː.rɪ-, -bənd US ˈmɔːr.ɪ.bʌnd
Morison ˈmɒr.ɪ.sᵊn, ˈ-ə- US ˈmɔːr.ɪ-
Morley ˈmɔː.li US ˈmɔːr-
Morlock ˈmɔː.lɒk US ˈmɔːr.lɑːk **-s** -s
Mormon ˈmɔː.mən US ˈmɔːr- **-s** -z **-ism** -ɪ.zᵊm
morn mɔːn US mɔːrn **-s** -z
mornay ˈmɔː.neɪ US mɔːrˈneɪ
morning ˈmɔː.nɪŋ US ˈmɔːr- **-s** -z **ˈmorning ˌcoat; ˈmorning ˌdress, ˌmorning ˈdress; ˈmorning ˌroom; ˈmorning ˌsickness; ˌmorning ˈstar**
morning-after ˌmɔː.nɪŋˈɑːf.təʳ US ˌmɔːr.nɪŋˈæf.tɚ **ˌmorning-ˈafter ˌpill**
Mornington ˈmɔː.nɪŋ.tən US ˈmɔːr-
Moroccan məˈrɒk.ən US -ˈrɑː.kən **-s** -z
Morocco, morocco məˈrɒk.əʊ US -ˈrɑː.koʊ **-s** -z
moron ˈmɔː.rɒn US ˈmɔːr.ɑːn **-s** -z
Moroni məˈrəʊ.ni US -ˈroʊ-, mɔː-
moronic mɔːˈrɒn.ɪk, mə-, mɒrˈɒn- US mɔːˈrɑː.nɪk, mə- **-ally** -ᵊl.i, -li
morose məˈrəʊs, mɒrˈəʊs US məˈroʊs, mɔː- **-ly** -li **-ness** -nəs, -nɪs
Morpeth ˈmɔː.peθ, -pəθ US ˈmɔːr-
-morph -mɔːf US -mɔːrf
Note: Suffix. Normally not stressed, e.g. **ectomorph** /ˈek.təʊ.mɔːf US -tə.mɔːrf/.
morph mɔːf US mɔːrf **-s** -s **-ing** -ɪŋ **-ed** -t
morpheme ˈmɔː.fiːm US ˈmɔːr- **-s** -z
morphemic mɔːˈfiː.mɪk US mɔːr- **-ally** -ᵊl.i, -li
morphemics mɔːˈfiː.mɪks US mɔːr-
Morpheus ˈmɔː.fi.əs, ˈ-fjəs US ˈmɔːr.fi.əs, ˈ-fjuːs
morphia ˈmɔː.fi.ə US ˈmɔːr-
morphine ˈmɔː.fiːn US ˈmɔːr-
morpho- mɔː.fəʊ-; mɔːˈfɒ- US mɔːr.foʊ-, -fə-; mɔːrˈfɑː-
Note: Prefix. Normally takes secondary stress on the first syllable, e.g. **morphologic** /ˌmɔː.fəˈlɒdʒ.ɪk US ˌmɔːr.fəˈlɑː.dʒɪk/, or primary stress on the second syllable, e.g **morphology** /mɔːˈfɒl.ə.dʒi US mɔːrˈfɑː.lə-/.
morphologic ˌmɔː.fəˈlɒdʒ.ɪk US ˌmɔːr.fəˈlɑː.dʒɪk **-al** -ᵊl **-ally** -ᵊl.i, -li
morpholog|y mɔːˈfɒl.ə.dʒ|i US mɔːrˈfɑː.lə- **-ies** -iz **-ist/s** -ɪst/s
morphophoneme ˌmɔː.fəʊˈfəʊ.niːm US ˌmɔːr.foʊˈfoʊ- **-s** -z
morphophonemic ˌmɔː.fəʊ.fəˈniː.m[ɪk] US ˌmɔːr.foʊ- **-s** -s
morphophonology ˌmɔː.fəʊ.fəˈnɒl.ə.dʒi US ˌmɔːr.foʊ.fəˈnɑː.lə-
morphosyntactic ˌmɔː.fəʊ.sɪnˈtæk[.tɪk] US ˌmɔːr.foʊ- **-ally** -ᵊl.i, -li
morphosyntax ˌmɔː.fəʊˈsɪn.tæks US ˌmɔːr.foʊ-
Morphy ˈmɔː.fi US ˈmɔːr-
Morrell ˈmʌr.ᵊl, məˈrel
Morrill ˈmɒr.ɪl, -ᵊl US ˈmɔːr-
morris (M) ˈmɒr.ɪs US ˈmɔːr- **-es** -ɪz **ˈmorris ˌdancing; ˈmorris ˌman**
Morrison ˈmɒr.ɪ.sᵊn, ˈ-ə- US ˈmɔːr-
Morrissey ˈmɒr.ɪ.si, -ə- US ˈmɔːr-, ˈmɑːr-
Morristown ˈmɒr.ɪs.taʊn US ˈmɔːr-
morrow (M) ˈmɒr.əʊ US ˈmɑːr.oʊ, ˈmɔːr- **-s** -z
mors|e (M) mɔːs US mɔːrs **-es** -ɪz **ˌM[orse] ˈcode, ˈMorse ˌcode**
morsel ˈmɔː.sᵊl US ˈmɔːr- **-s** -z
Morshead ˈmɔːz.hed US ˈmɔːrz-
mort (M) mɔːt US mɔːrt **-s** -s
mortadella ˌmɔː.təˈdel.ə US ˌmɔːr-
mortal ˈmɔː.tᵊl US ˈmɔːr.t̬ᵊl **-s** -z **-ly** [-i] **ˌmortal ˈsin**
mortalit|y (M) mɔːˈtæl.ə.t|i, -ɪ.t|i US mɔːrˈtæl.ə.t̬|i **-ies** -iz
mort|ar ˈmɔː.t|əʳ US ˈmɔːr.t|ɚ **-ars** [-əz] US -ɚz **-aring** -ᵊr.ɪŋ **-ared** -əd US [-ɚd]
mortarboard ˈmɔː.tə.bɔːd US ˈmɔːr.t̬ɚ.bɔːrd **-s** -z
Morte d'Arthur(e) ˌmɔːtˈdɑː.θəʳ US ˌmɔːrtˈdɑːr.θɚ
mortgag|e ˈmɔː.gɪdʒ US ˈmɔːr- **-es** [-ɪz] **-ing** -ɪŋ **-ed** -d
mortgagee ˌmɔː.gɪˈdʒiː, -gəˈ- US ˌmɔːr- **-s** -z

nortgagor ˌmɔː.gɪˈdʒɔːʳ, -gəˈ-; ˈmɔː.gɪ.dʒəʳ, -gə- (US) ˈmɔːr.gɪ.dʒɚ **-s** -z

nortic|e ˈmɔː.tɪs (US) ˈmɔːr.t̬ɪs **-es** -ɪz **-ing** -ɪŋ **-ed** -t

nortician mɔːˈtɪʃ.ən (US) mɔːr- **-s** -z

nortification ˌmɔː.tɪ.fɪˈkeɪ.ʃən, -tə- (US) ˌmɔːr.t̬ə.fɪˈ-

norti|fy ˈmɔː.tɪ|.faɪ, -tə- (US) ˈmɔːr.t̬ə- **-fies** -faɪz **-fying** -faɪ.ɪŋ **-fied** -faɪd

Aortimer ˈmɔː.tɪ.məʳ, -tə- (US) ˈmɔːr.t̬ə.mɚ

nortis|e ˈmɔː.tɪs (US) ˈmɔːr.t̬ɪs **-es** -ɪz **-ing** -ɪŋ **-ed** -t **ˈmortise ˌlock**

lortlake ˈmɔːt.leɪk (US) ˈmɔːrt-

lortlock ˈmɔːt.lɒk (US) ˈmɔːrt.lɑːk

ıortmain ˈmɔːt.meɪn (US) ˈmɔːrt-

lorton ˈmɔː.tən (US) ˈmɔːr-

ıortuar|y ˈmɔː.tʃu.ər|.i, -tjʊ-, -tjʊ.r|i, -tʃər|.i (US) ˈmɔːr.tʃu.er|.i **-ies** -iz

lorwenna mɔːˈwen.ə (US) mɔːr-

ıosaic (M) məʊˈzeɪ.ɪk (US) moʊ- **-s** -s

losborough ˈmɒz.brə, -bər.ə (US) ˈmɑːz.bɚ.oʊ, -bər.ə

losby ˈmɒz.bi (US) ˈmoʊz-

losca ˈmɒs.kə (US) ˈmɑːs-

loscow ˈmɒs.kəʊ (US) ˈmɑː.skaʊ, -skoʊ

loseley ˈməʊz.li (US) ˈmoʊz-

oselle (M) məʊˈzel (US) moʊ- **-s** -z

oses ˈməʊ.zɪz (US) ˈmoʊ- **ˈMoses ˌbasket**

osey ˈməʊ.zi (US) ˈmoʊ- **-s** -z **-ing** -ɪŋ **-ed** -d

osimann ˈmɒs.ɪ.mən (US) ˈmɑː.sɪ-

oslem ˈmɒz.ləm, ˈmʊz-, -lem, -lɪm (US) ˈmɑːz.lem, ˈmɑːs- **-s** -z

osley ˈməʊz.li, ˈmɒz- (US) ˈmoʊz-

osque mɒsk (US) mɑːsk **-s** -s

osquito (M) mɒsˈkiː.təʊ, məˈskiː- (US) məˈskiː.t̬oʊ **-(e)s** -z **mosˈquito ˌnet**

oss (M) mɒs (US) mɑːs **-es** -ɪz

ossad ˈmɒs.æd (US) moʊˈsɑːd

oss-grown ˈmɒs.grəʊn (US) ˈmɑːs.groʊn

ossley ˈmɒs.li (US) ˈmɑːs-

ossman *area of Sydney:* ˈmɒz.mən (US) ˈmɑːz- *other senses:* ˈmɒs.mən (US) ˈmɑːs-

ossmorran mɒsˈmɒr.ən (US) mɑːsˈmɔːr-

oss|y ˈmɒs|.i (US) ˈmɑː.s|i **-ier** -i.əʳ (US) -i.ɚ **-iest** -i.ɪst, -i.əst **-iness** -ɪ.nəs, -ɪ.nɪs

os|t məʊs|t (US) moʊs|t **-tly** -tli

ostar ˈmɒs.tɑːʳ (US) ˈmɑː.stɑːr

ostyn ˈmɒs.tɪn (US) ˈmɑː.stɪn

osul ˈməʊ.səl (US) moʊˈsuːl; ˈmoʊ.səl

ot məʊ (US) moʊ **-s** -z

oT, MOT ˌem.əʊˈtiː (US) -oʊˈ- **-s** -z **-ˈs** -z **-ˈd** -d **-ˈing** -ɪŋ **ˌMoT cerˈtificate, ˌMoˈT cerˌtificate; ˌMoT ˈtest, ˌMoˈT ˌtest**

mote məʊt (US) moʊt **-s** -s

motel məʊˈtel (US) moʊ- **-s** -z

motet məʊˈtet (US) moʊ- **-s** -s

moth mɒθ (US) mɑːθ **-s** -s

Mothaks® ˈmɒθ.æks (US) ˈmɑː.θæks

mothball ˈmɒθ.bɔːl (US) ˈmɑːθ-, -bɑːl **-s** -z **-ing** -ɪŋ **-ed** -d

moth-eaten ˈmɒθˌiː.tən (US) ˈmɑːθˌiː-

moth|er (M) ˈmʌð|.əʳ (US) -ɚ **-ers** -əz (US) -ɚz **-ering** -ər.ɪŋ **-ered** -əd (US) -ɚd **-erless** -ə.ləs, -les, -lɪs (US) -ɚ- **ˈmother ˌcountry; ˌmother ˈhen; ˌmother ˈnature; ˌmother suˈperior; ˈMother's ˌDay; ˌmother ˈtongue**

motherboard ˈmʌð.ə.bɔːd (US) -ɚ.bɔːrd **-s** -z

Mothercare® ˈmʌð.ə.keəʳ (US) -ɚ.ker

motherfucker ˈmʌð.əˌfʌk.əʳ (US) -ɚˌfʌk.ɚ **-s** -z

mother-fucking ˈmʌð.əˌfʌk.ɪŋ (US) -ɚˌ-

motherhood ˈmʌð.ə.hʊd (US) ˈ-ɚ-

mother-in-law ˈmʌð.ər.ɪnˌlɔː (US) -ɚ.ɪnˌlɑː, -ˌlɔː **mothers-in-law** ˈmʌð.əz- (US) -ɚz-

motherland ˈmʌð.ə.lænd (US) ˈ-ɚ- **-s** -z

motherl|y ˈmʌð.əl|.i (US) -ɚ.l|i **-iness** -ɪ.nəs, -ɪ.nɪs

mother-of-pearl ˌmʌð.ər.əvˈpɜːl (US) -ɚ.əvˈpɝːl

mothersill ˈmʌð.ə.sɪl (US) ˈ-ɚ-

Motherwell ˈmʌð.ə.wel (US) ˈ-ɚ-

motif məʊˈtiːf (US) moʊ- **-s** -s

motile ˈməʊ.taɪl (US) ˈmoʊ.t̬əl, -taɪl

motion (M) ˈməʊ.ʃən (US) ˈmoʊ- **-s** -z **-ing** -ɪŋ, ˈməʊʃ.nɪŋ (US) ˈmoʊʃ- **-ed** -d **-less** -ləs, -lɪs **ˌmotion ˈpicture; ˈmotion ˌsickness**

moti|vate ˈməʊ.tɪ|.veɪt, -tə- (US) ˈmoʊ.t̬ə- **-vates** -veɪts **-vating** -veɪ.tɪŋ (US) -veɪ.t̬ɪŋ **-vated** -veɪ.tɪd (US) -veɪ.t̬ɪd **-vator/s** -veɪ.təʳ/z (US) -veɪ.t̬ɚ/z

motivation ˌməʊ.tɪˈveɪ.ʃən, -təˈ- (US) ˌmoʊ.t̬əˈ- **-al** -əl

motive ˈməʊ.tɪv (US) ˈmoʊ.t̬ɪv **-s** -z **-less** -ləs, -lɪs

mot juste ˌməʊˈʒuːst (US) ˌmoʊ-

motley (M) ˈmɒt.li (US) ˈmɑːt-

motocross ˈməʊ.təʊ.krɒs (US) ˈmoʊ.t̬oʊ.krɑːs

mot|or ˈməʊ.t|əʳ (US) ˈmoʊ.t̬|ɚ **-ors** -əz (US) -ɚz **-oring** -ər.ɪŋ **-ored** -əd (US) -ɚd **ˈmotor ˌcar; ˈmotor ˌhome; ˈmotor ˌlodge; ˈmotor ˌscooter; ˈmotor ˌvehicle**

Motorail® ˈməʊ.tər.eɪl (US) ˈmoʊ.t̬ə.reɪl

motorbike ˈməʊ.tə.baɪk (US) ˈmoʊ.t̬ɚ- **-s** -s

motorboat ˈməʊ.tə.bəʊt (US) ˈmoʊ.t̬ɚ.boʊt **-s** -s

motorcade ˈməʊ.tə.keɪd (US) ˈmoʊ.t̬ɚ- **-s** -z

motorcycle ˈməʊ.təˌsaɪ.kl̩ (US) ˈmoʊ.t̬ɚ- **-s** -z

motorcyclist ˈməʊ.təˌsaɪ.klɪst, -kl̩.ɪst (US) ˈmoʊ.t̬ɚ- **-s** -s

motorhome ˈməʊ.tə.həʊm (US) ˈmoʊ.t̬ɚ.hoʊm **-s** -z

motorist ˈməʊ.tər.ɪst (US) ˈmoʊ.t̬ɚ- **-s** -s

motoriz|e, -is|e ˈməʊ.tər.aɪz (US) ˈmoʊ.t̬ə.raɪz **-es** -ɪz **-ing** -ɪŋ **-ed** -d

motor|man ˈməʊ.tə|.mæn (US) ˈmoʊ.t̬ɚ-, -mən **-men** -men

motormou|th ˈməʊ.tə.maʊ|θ (US) ˈmoʊ.t̬ɚ- **-ths** -ðz

Motorola ˌməʊ.təˈrəʊ.lə (US) ˌmoʊ.t̬əˈroʊ.lə

motor-scooter ˈməʊ.təˌskuː.təʳ (US) ˈmoʊ.t̬ɚˌskuː.t̬ɚ **-s** -z

motorway ˈməʊ.tə.weɪ (US) ˈmoʊ.t̬ɚ- **-s** -z

Motown® ˈməʊ.taʊn (US) ˈmoʊ-

Mott mɒt (US) mɑːt

motte mɒt (US) mɑːt **-s** -s

Mottistone ˈmɒt.ɪ.stən, -stəʊn (US) ˈmɑː.t̬ɪ.stən, -stoʊn

mottl|e ˈmɒt.l̩ (US) ˈmɑː.t̬l̩ **-es** -z **-ing** -ɪŋ **-ed** -d

motto ˈmɒt.əʊ (US) ˈmɑː.t̬oʊ **-(e)s** -z

Mottram ˈmɒt.rəm (US) ˈmɑː.trəm

moue muː **-s** -z

mouf(f)lon ˈmuː.flɒn (US) -flɑːn **-s** -z

Moughton ˈməʊ.tən (US) ˈmoʊ-

Mouland ˈmuː.lænd, mʊˈlænd

mould məʊld (US) moʊld **-s** -z **-ing/s** -ɪŋ/z **-ed** -ɪd

mould|er ˈməʊl.d|əʳ (US) ˈmoʊl.d|ɚ **-ers** -əz (US) -ɚz **-ering** -ər.ɪŋ **-ered** -əd (US) -ɚd

mould|y ˈməʊl.d|i (US) ˈmoʊl- **-ier** -i.əʳ (US) -i.ɚ **-iest** -i.ɪst, -i.əst **-iness** -ɪ.nəs, -ɪ.nɪs

Moule məʊl, muːl (US) moʊl, muːl

Moulinex® ˈmuː.lɪ.neks, -lə-

Moulin Rouge ˌmuː.læ̃*n*ˈruːʒ

Moulmein ˈmaʊl.meɪn (US) mʊlˈmeɪn, moʊl-

Moulsford ˈməʊls.fəd, ˈməʊlz- (US) ˈmoʊls.fɚd, ˈmoʊlz-

moult məʊlt (US) moʊlt **-s** -s **-ing** -ɪŋ (US) ˈmoʊl.t̬ɪŋ **-ed** -ɪd (US) ˈmoʊl.t̬ɪd

Moulton ˈməʊl.tən (US) ˈmoʊl-

Moultrie ˈmɔːl.tri, ˈmuː-

mound (M) maʊnd **-s** -z

Mounsey ˈmaʊn.zi

mount (M) maʊnt **-s** -s **-ing** -ɪŋ (US) ˈmaʊn.t̬ɪŋ **-ed** -ɪd (US) ˈmaʊn.t̬ɪd

mountain ˈmaʊn.tɪn, -tən (US) -tən **-s** -z **ˈmountain ˌbike; ˈmountain ˌlion; make a ˌmountain out of a ˈmole-hill**

mountain-ash ˌmaʊn.tɪnˈæʃ, -tənˈ- (US) -tᵊnˈ- **-es** -ɪz

mountaineer ˌmaʊn.tɪˈnɪəʳ, -təˈ- (US) -tᵊnˈɪr **-s** -z **-ing** -ɪŋ

mountainous ˈmaʊn.tɪ.nəs, -tə- (US) -tᵊn.əs

mountainside ˈmaʊn.tɪn.saɪd, -tən- (US) -tᵊn- **-s** -z

mountaintop ˈmaʊn.tɪn.tɒp, -tən- (US) -tᵊn.tɑːp **-s** -s

mountant ˈmaʊn.tənt **-s** -s

Mountbatten maʊntˈbæt.ᵊn

mountebank ˈmaʊn.tɪ.bæŋk, -tə- (US) -t̬ə- **-s** -s

Mount Everest ˌmaʊntˈev.ᵊr.ɪst, -est

Mountford ˈmaʊnt.fəd (US) -fɚd

Mountie ˈmaʊn.ti (US) -t̬i **-s** -z

Mountjoy ˌmaʊntˈdʒɔɪ, ˈ--

Mountsorrel ˌmaʊntˈsɒr.əl (US) -ˈsɔːr-

Mount Vernon ˌmaʊntˈvɜː.nən (US) -ˈvɝː-

Mount|y ˈmaʊn.t|i (US) -t̬|i **-ies** -iz

Moura ˈmʊə.rə (US) ˈmʊr.ə

mourn mɔːn (US) mɔːrn **-s** -z **-ing** -ɪŋ **-ed** -d **-er/s** -əʳ/z (US) -ɚ/z

Mourne mɔːn (US) mɔːrn

mournful ˈmɔːn.fᵊl, -fʊl (US) ˈmɔːrn- **-ly** -i **-ness** -nəs, -nɪs

Mousa ˈmuː.zə

mouse (*n.*) maʊs **mice** maɪs

mous|e (*v.*) maʊs, maʊz (US) maʊz **-es** -ɪz **-ing** -ɪŋ **-ed** -d

Mousehole ˈmaʊ.zᵊl

mouser ˈmaʊ.səʳ, -zəʳ (US) -zɚ **-s** -z

mouse-trap ˈmaʊs.træp **-s** -s

mous|ey ˈmaʊ.s|i **-ier** -i.əʳ (US) -i.ɚ **-iest** -i.ɪst, -i.əst

moussaka muˈsɑː.kə, ˈmuː.sæk.ə (US) ˌmuˈsɑː.kə; ˌmuː.sɑːˈkɑː

mousse muːs

Moussec® ˌmuːˈsek

mousseline ˈmuː.slɪn, ˌmuːˈsliːn (US) ˌmuːˈsliːn

Moussorgsky mʊˈsɔːg.ski, muː- (US) muːˈsɔːrg-, mə-, -ˈzɔːrg-, -ˈsɔːrk-, -ˈzɔːrk-

moustach|e məˈstɑːʃ, mʊ- (US) ˈmʌs.tæʃ; məˈstæʃ **-es** -ɪz

mous|y ˈmaʊ.s|i **-ier** -i.əʳ (US) -i.ɚ **-iest** -i.ɪst, -i.əst

mou|th (*n.*) maʊ|θ **-ths** -ðz ˈ**mouth organ; from the** ˌ**horse's** ˈ**mouth;** ˌ**down in the** ˈ**mouth**

mouth (*v.*) maʊð **-s** -z **-ing** -ɪŋ **-ed** -d

mouthful ˈmaʊθ.fʊl **-s** -z

mouthpiec|e ˈmaʊθ.piːs **-es** -ɪz

mouth-to-mouth ˌmaʊθ.təˈmaʊθ *stress shift, see compound:* ˌ**mouth-to-mouth re**ˌ**susci**ˈ**tation**

mouthwash ˈmaʊθ.wɒʃ (US) -wɑːʃ, -wɔːʃ **-es** -ɪz

mouthwatering ˈmaʊθˌwɔː.tᵊr.ɪŋ (US) -ˌwɑː.t̬ɚ-, -ˌwɔː- **-ly** -li

mouth|y ˈmaʊ.ð|i, -θ|i **-ier** -i.əʳ (US) -i.ɚ **-iest** -i.ɪst, -i.əst

movability ˌmuː.vəˈbɪl.ə.ti, -ɪ.ti (US) -ə.t̬i

movable ˈmuː.və.bl̩ **-s** -z **-ness** -nəs, -nɪs

movant ˈmuː.vənt **-s** -s

mov|e muːv **-es** -z **-ing/ly** -ɪŋ/li **-ed** -d **-er/s** -əʳ/z (US) -ɚ/z **-eable** -ə.bl̩

movement ˈmuːv.mənt **-s** -s

movie ˈmuː.vi **-s** -z

moviegoer ˈmuː.viˌgəʊ.əʳ (US) -ˌgoʊ.ɚ **-s** -z

moviegoing ˈmuː.viˌgəʊ.ɪŋ (US) -ˌgoʊ-

moviemak|er ˈmuː.viˌmeɪ.k|əʳ (US) -ɚ **-ers** -əz (US) -ɚz **-ing** -ɪŋ

mow (*v.*) *cut down and stack:* məʊ (US) moʊ **-s** -z **-ing** -ɪŋ **-ed** -d **-n** -n **-er/s** -əʳ/z (US) -ɚ/z

mow (*n.*) *stack:* maʊ **-s** -z

mow (*n.*) *grimace:* maʊ (US) moʊ, maʊ **-s** -z

Mowat, Mowatt maʊət, məʊət (US) maʊət, moʊət

Mowbray ˈməʊ.breɪ, -bri (US) ˈmoʊ-

Mowgli ˈmaʊ.gli

Mowlam ˈməʊ.ləm (US) ˈmoʊ-

mown (*from* **mow** *v.*) məʊn (US) moʊn

Moxon ˈmɒk.sᵊn (US) ˈmɑːk-

moya (M) ˈmɔɪ.ə **-s** -z

Moyes mɔɪz

Moygashel *place:* mɔɪˈgæʃ.ᵊl *linen:* ˈmɔɪ.gə.ʃᵊl

Moynahan ˈmɔɪ.nə.hæn, -hən (US) ˈmɔɪ.nə.hæn

Moynihan ˈmɔɪ.ni.ən, -hæn; -nə.hæn (US) ˈmɔɪ.nɪ.hæn, -nə-

Mozambique ˌməʊ.zæmˈbiːk, -zəmˈ- (US) ˌmoʊ-

Mozart ˈməʊt.sɑːt (US) ˈmoʊt.sɑːrt

Mozartian ˌməʊtˈsɑː.ti.ən (US) ˌmoʊtˈsɑːr.t̬i- **-s** -z

mozzarella ˌmɒt.səˈrel.ə (US) ˌmɑːt-, ˌmoʊt-

MP ˌemˈpiː

mph ˌem.piːˈeɪtʃ

MPhil ˌemˈfɪl

Mr ˈmɪs.təʳ (US) -tɚ

Mrs ˈmɪs.ɪz

ms, MS *(abbrev. for* **manuscript***)* ˌemˈes, ˈmæn.jə.skrɪpt, -jʊ-

MS *(abbrev. for* **multiple sclerosis***)* ˌemˈes

Ms mɪz, məz (US) mɪz

Note: Used to avoid indicating a woman's marital status. The pronunciation is unstable in Britain.

MSc ˌem.esˈsiː

MS-DOS® ˌem.esˈdɒs (US) -ˈdɑːs

MSS *(abbrev. for* **manuscripts***)* ˌem.esˈes, ˈmæn.jə.skrɪpts, -jʊ-

MTV ˌem.tiːˈviː

mu mjuː (US) mjuː, muː

Mubarak mʊˈbɑː.rək, -ˈbær.æk, -ək (US) muːˈbɑːr.ək

much mʌtʃ **-ly** -li

Muchalls ˈmʌk.ᵊlz, ˈmʌx-

muchness ˈmʌtʃ.nəs, -nɪs

mucilag|e ˈmjuː.sɪ.lɪdʒ, -sᵊl.ɪdʒ (US) -sə.lɪdʒ **-es** -ɪz

mucilaginous ˌmjuː.sɪˈlædʒ.ɪ.nəs, -sᵊlˈædʒ-, ˈ-ə- (US) -sɪˈlædʒ.ə-

muck mʌk **-s** -s **-ing** -ɪŋ **-ed** -t

muck|er ˈmʌk|.əʳ (US) -ɚ **-ers** -əz (US) -ɚz **-ering** -ᵊr.ɪŋ **-ered** -əd (US) -ɚd

Muckle Flugga ˌmʌk.l̩ˈflʌg.ə

muckrak|e ˈmʌk.reɪk **-es** -s **-ing** -ɪŋ **-ed** -t **-er/s** -əʳ/z (US) -ɚ/z

muck|y ˈmʌk|.i **-ier** -i.əʳ (US) -i.ɚ **-iest** -i.ɪst, -i.əst **-iness** -ɪ.nəs, -ɪ.nɪs

muc(o)us ˈmjuː.kəs ˌ**mucous** ˈ**membrane**

mud mʌd **-s** -z

mudba|th ˈmʌd.bɑː|θ (US) -bæ|θ **-ths** -ð…

Mud(d)eford ˈmʌd.ɪ.fəd (US) -fɚd

muddl|e ˈmʌd.l̩ **-es** -z **-ing** -ɪŋ, ˈmʌd.l… **-ed** -d **-er/s** -əʳ/z (US) -ɚ/z, ˈmʌd.ləʳ/z (US) -lɚ/z

muddleheaded ˌmʌd.l̩ˈhed.ɪd, ˈmʌd.l̩ˌhed- (US) ˈmʌd.l̩ˌhed- **-ness** -nəs, -nɪs

mudd|y ˈmʌd|.i **-ier** -i.əʳ (US) -i.ɚ **-iest** -i.ɪst, -i.əst **-ily** -ɪ.li, -ᵊl.i **-iness** -ɪ.nəs, -ɪ.nɪs **-ies** -iz **-ying** -i.ɪŋ **-ied** -id

mudflap ˈmʌd.flæp **-s** -s

mudguard ˈmʌd.gɑːd (US) -gɑːrd **-s** -z

Mudie ˈmjuː.di

mudlark ˈmʌd.lɑːk (US) -lɑːrk **-s** -s

mudpack ˈmʌd.pæk **-s** -s

mudslide ˈmʌd.slaɪd **-s** -z

Mueller ˈmjuː.ləʳ, ˈmʊl.əʳ (US) -ɚ

muesli ˈmjuːz.li, ˈmuːz- (US) ˈmjuːz-, ˈmjuːs- **-s** -z

muezzin muˈez.ɪn, mju- (US) mju-, mu… **-s** -z

muff mʌf **-s** -s **-ing** -ɪŋ **-ed** -t

muffin ˈmʌf.ɪn **-s** -z

muffl|e ˈmʌf.l̩ **-es** -z **-ing** -ɪŋ, ˈmʌf.lɪŋ **-ed** -d

muffler ˈmʌf.ləʳ (US) -lɚ **-s** -z

mufti ˈmʌf.ti

mug mʌg **-s** -z **-ging/s** -ɪŋ/z **-ged** -d ˈ**m…** ˌ**shot**

Mugabe mʊˈgɑː.beɪ, -bi

mugger ˈmʌg.əʳ (US) -ɚ **-s** -z

muggins (M) ˈmʌg.ɪnz **-es** -ɪz

Muggins ˈmʌg.ɪnz, ˈmjuː.gɪnz

Muggleton ˈmʌg.l̩.tᵊn (US) -tən

Muggletonian ˌmʌg.l̩ˈtəʊ.ni.ən (US) -ˈtoʊ- **-s** -z

muggl|y ˈmʌɡl.i -ier -i.əʳ US -i.ɚ -iest -i.ɪst, -i.əst -iness -ɪ.nəs, -ɪ.nɪs
mugwump ˈmʌɡ.wʌmp -s -s
Muhhamad mʊˈhæm.əd, mə-, -ɪd, -ed
Muir mjʊəʳ, mjɔːʳ US mjʊr
Muirhead ˈmjʊə.hed, ˈmjɔː- US ˈmjʊr-
mujahideen (M) ˌmuː.dʒə.hedˈiːn, ˈmʊdʒ.ə-, ˈmuː.ʒə-, -ʒɑː-, -həˈdiːn US muːˌdʒɑː.həˈdiːn
Muji ˈmuː.dʒi
Mukden ˈmʊk.dən
Mukle ˈmjuː.kli
mukluk ˈmʌk.lʌk -s -s
mulatto mjuːˈlæt.əʊ, mjə-, mjʊ-, mə- US məˈlæt̬.oʊ, mjuː-, -ˈlɑː.t̬oʊ -(e)s -z
mulberr|y ˈmʌl.bᵊr|.i US -ˌber- -ies -iz
Mulcaster ˈmʌl.kæs.təʳ US -tɚ
mulch mʌltʃ -es -ɪz -ing -ɪŋ -ed -t
Mulciber ˈmʌl.sɪ.bəʳ US -bɚ
mulct mʌlkt -s -s -ing -ɪŋ -ed -ɪd
Mulder ˈmʌl.dəʳ US -dɚ
Muldoon mʌlˈduːn
mule mjuːl -s -z
muleteer ˌmjuː.lɪˈtɪəʳ, -ləˈ- US -ləˈtɪr -s -z
Mulga ˈmʊl.ɡə -s -z
Mulgrave ˈmʌl.ɡreɪv
Mulholland mʌlˈhɒl.ənd US -ˈhɑː.lənd
mulish ˈmjuː.lɪʃ -ly -li -ness -nəs, -nɪs
mull (M) mʌl -s -z -ing -ɪŋ -ed -d
mullah (M) ˈmʊl.ə, ˈmʌl.ə -s -z
Mullan, Mullen ˈmʌl.ən
mullein ˈmʌl.ɪn, -eɪn US -ɪn
mullet (M) ˈmʌl.ɪt, -ət -s -s
Mulligan ˈmʌl.ɪ.ɡən, ˈ-ə-
mulligatawny ˌmʌl.ɪ.ɡəˈtɔː.ni, ˌ-ə- US -ˈtɑː.ni, -ˈtɔː-
Mullinar, Mulliner ˈmʌl.ɪ.nəʳ US -nɚ
Mullinger ˈmʌl.ɪn.dʒəʳ, -ᵊn- US -dʒɚ
Mullins ˈmʌl.ɪnz
mullion (M) ˈmʌl.jən, ˈ-i.ən US ˈ-jən -s -z -ed -d
Mullock ˈmʌl.ək
Mulready mʌlˈred.i
Mulroney mʌlˈrəʊ.ni US -ˈroʊ-
Multan ˌmʌlˈtɑːn US ˌmʊl-
multi- mʌl.ti-, -tɪ-, -tə- US mʌl.t̬i-, -t̬ə-, -taɪ-
Note: Prefix. Normally carries primary or secondary stress on the first syllable, e.g. **multiform** /ˈmʌl.ti.fɔːm US -t̬i.fɔːrm/, **multilingual** /ˌmʌl.tiˈlɪŋ.ɡwᵊl US -t̬iˈ-/.
multicolo(u)red ˌmʌl.tiˈkʌl.əd, ˈmʌl.tiˌkʌl- US ˌmʌl.t̬ɪˈkʌl.ɚd, ˈmʌl.t̬iˌkʌl-
multicultural ˌmʌl.tiˈkʌl.tʃᵊr.ᵊl US -t̬iˈ-, -taɪˈ- -ly -i -ism -ɪ.zᵊm *stress shift:* ˌmulticultural ˈfestival
multiethnic ˌmʌl.tiˈeθ.nɪk US -t̬iˈ- *stress shift:* ˌmultiethnic ˈbackground
multifarious ˌmʌl.tɪˈfeə.ri.əs US -t̬əˈfer.i- -ly -li -ness -nəs, -nɪs *stress shift:* ˌmultifarious ˈinfluences
multiform ˈmʌl.ti.fɔːm US -t̬i.fɔːrm
multigym ˈmʌl.ti.dʒɪm US -t̬i- -s -z
multilateral ˌmʌl.tiˈlæt.ᵊr.ᵊl US -t̬iˈlæt̬-, -taɪˈ- -ly -i *stress shift:* ˌmultilateral ˈtalks
multilingual ˌmʌl.tiˈlɪŋ.ɡwəl US -t̬iˈ- -ly -i *stress shift:* ˌmultilingual ˈpeople
multimedia ˌmʌl.tiˈmiː.di.ə US -t̬iˈ-
multimillionaire ˌmʌl.tiˌmɪl.jəˈneəʳ, -i.əˈ- US -t̬iˌmɪl.jəˈner, -taɪˌ-, ˌmʌl.t̬iˈmɪl.jə.ner, -taɪˈ- -s -z
multinational ˌmʌl.tiˈnæʃ.ᵊn.ᵊl, -ˈnæʃ.nᵊl US -t̬iˈ-, -taɪˈ- -s -z *stress shift:* ˌmultinational ˈcompany
multipartite ˌmʌl.tiˈpɑː.taɪt US -t̬iˈpɑːr- *stress shift:* ˌmultipartite ˈtreaty
multiplayer ˈmʌl.tɪˌpleɪ.əʳ, -tə- US -t̬iˌpleɪ.ɚ -s -z
multiple ˈmʌl.tɪ.pl̩, -tə- US -t̬ə- -s -z ˌmultiple scleˈrosis
multiple-choice ˌmʌl.tɪ.pl̩ˈtʃɔɪs, -tə- US -t̬ə- *stress shift:* ˌmultiple-choice ˈpaper
multiplex ˈmʌl.tɪ.pleks, -tə- US -t̬ə- -es -ɪz
multiplicand ˌmʌl.tɪ.plɪˈkænd, -tə- US -t̬ə- -s -z
multiplication ˌmʌl.tɪ.plɪˈkeɪ.ʃᵊn, -tə- US -t̬ə- -s -z
multiplicative ˌmʌl.tɪˈplɪk.ə.tɪv, -təˈ-; ˈmʌl.tɪ.plɪ.keɪ.tɪv US ˈmʌl.t̬ə.plɪ.keɪ.t̬ɪv; ˌmʌl.təˈplɪk.ə-
multiplicator ˈmʌl.tɪ.plɪ.keɪ.təʳ US -t̬ɚ -s -z
multiplicit|y ˌmʌl.tɪˈplɪs.ə.t|i, -təˈ-, -ɪ.t|i US -t̬əˈplɪs.ə.t̬|i -ies -iz
multipl|y ˈmʌl.tɪ.pl|aɪ, -tə- US -t̬ə- -ies -aɪz -ying -aɪ.ɪŋ -ied -aɪd -ier/s -aɪ.əʳ/z US -aɪ.ɚ/z
multiprocessing ˌmʌl.tiˈprəʊ.ses.ɪŋ US -t̬iˈprɑː-
multiprocessor ˌmʌl.tiˈprəʊ.ses.əʳ US -t̬iˈprɑː.ses.ɚ -s -z
multipurpose ˌmʌl.tiˈpɜː.pəs US -t̬iˈpɝː- *stress shift:* ˌmultipurpose ˈtool
multiracial ˌmʌl.tiˈreɪ.ʃᵊl, -ʃi.əl US -t̬iˈreɪ.ʃᵊl, -taɪˈ- *stress shift:* ˌmultiracial ˈarea
multiscreen ˌmʌl.tiˈskriːn *stress shift:* ˌmultiscreen ˈcinema
multi-storey ˌmʌl.tiˈstɔː.ri US -t̬iˈstɔːr.i *stress shift, see compound:* ˌ**multi-storey ˈcar park**
multi-tasking ˌmʌl.tiˈtɑː.skɪŋ, ˈmʌl.tiˌtɑː- US ˈmʌl.t̬iˌtæs.kɪŋ
multitude ˈmʌl.tɪ.tjuːd, -tə-, -tʃuːd US -t̬ə.tuːd, -tjuːd -s -z
multitudinous ˌmʌl.tɪˈtjuː.dɪ.nəs, -təˈ-, -ˈtʃuː-, -dᵊn.əs US -t̬əˈtuː.dᵊn-, -ˈtjuː- -ly -li -ness -nəs, -nɪs
multivalen|t ˌmʌl.tiˈveɪ.lən|t US -t̬iˈ- -ce -ts
multivitamin ˌmʌl.tiˈvɪt.ə.mɪn, -ˈvaɪ.tə- US -ˈvaɪ.t̬ə- -s -z
multum in parvo ˌmʊl.təm.ɪnˈpɑː.vəʊ, ˌmʌl- US -ˈpɑːr.voʊ
mum (M) mʌm -s -z
Mum and the Sothsegger ˌmʌm.ənd.ðəˈsɒθ.seɡ.əʳ, -ˈsəʊθ- US -ænd.ðəˈsɑːθ.seɡ.ɚ
mumbl|e ˈmʌm.bl̩ -es -z -ing/ly -ɪŋ/li, ˈ-blɪŋ/li -ed -d -er/s -əʳ/z US ˈ-bləʳ/z, ˈ-bl̩.ɚ/z US ˈ-blɚ/z
Mumbles ˈmʌm.bl̩z
mumbo-jumbo ˌmʌm.bəʊˈdʒʌm.bəʊ US -boʊˈdʒʌm.boʊ
Mumm mʌm *as if French:* mʊm
mumm|er ˈmʌm|.əʳ US -ɚ -ers -əz, -ɚz -ery -ᵊr.i
mummification ˌmʌm.ɪ.fɪˈkeɪ.ʃᵊn, ˌ-ə-
mummi|fy ˈmʌm.ɪ|.faɪ US ˈ-ə- -fies -faɪz -fying -faɪ.ɪŋ -fied -faɪd
mumm|y (M) ˈmʌm|.i -ies -iz
mump mʌmp -s -s -ing -ɪŋ -ed -t
mumpish ˈmʌm.pɪʃ -ly -li -ness -nəs, -nɪs
mumps mʌmps
mums|y ˈmʌm.z|i -ily -ɪ.li, -ᵊl.i -iness -ɪ.nəs, -ɪ.nɪs
Munby ˈmʌn.bi, ˈmʌm- US ˈmʌn-
munch mʌntʃ -es -ɪz -ing -ɪŋ -ed -t -er/s -əʳ/z US -ɚ/z
Munch mʊŋk -s -s
Munchausen, Münchausen, Münchhausen ˈmʌn.tʃaʊ.zᵊn, ˈmʊntʃ-, -haʊ-; mʌnˈtʃɔː.zᵊn US ˈmʌn.tʃaʊ.zᵊn, ˈmʊn-, -tʃɔː-
munchies (M®) ˈmʌn.tʃiz
munchkin ˈmʌntʃ.kɪn -s -z
Muncie ˈmʌn.tsi
mundane mʌnˈdeɪn, ˈ-- -ly -li
Munera Pulveris ˌmjuː.nᵊr.əˈpʊl.vᵊr.ɪs
mung mʌŋ ˈmung ˌbean
mungo (M) ˈmʌŋ.ɡəʊ US -ɡoʊ -s -z
Munich ˈmjuː.nɪk
municipal mjuːˈnɪs.ɪ.pᵊl, ˈ-ə- US ˈ-ə-
municipalit|y mjuːˌnɪs.ɪˈpæl.ə.t|i, -əˈ-, -ɪ.t|i; ˌmjuː.nɪ.sɪˈ-, -səˈ- US mjuːˌnɪs.əˈpæl.ə.t̬|i -ies -iz
municipaliz|e, -is|e mjuːˈnɪs.ɪ.pᵊl.aɪz, ˈ-ə- US ˈ-ə.pə.laɪz -es -ɪz -ing -ɪŋ -ed -d

munificen|ce mjuːˈnɪf.ɪ.sᵊn|ts, ˈ-ə- US ˈ-ə- **-t/ly** -t/li
muniment ˈmjuː.nɪ.mənt, -nə- US -nə- **-s** -s
munition mjuːˈnɪʃ.ᵊn **-s** -z
Munro mʌnˈrəʊ, mənˈ-; ˈmʌn.rəʊ US mənˈroʊ
Munsey ˈmʌn.zi
Munster *in Ireland:* ˈmʌn*t*.stəʳ US -stɚ
Münster *in Germany:* ˈmʊn*t*.stəʳ US -stɚ, ˈmʌn*t*-
muntjak, muntjac ˈmʌnt.dʒæk, ˈmʌn*t*.ʃæk US ˈmʌnt.dʒæk **-s** -s
Muppet ˈmʌp.ɪt **-s** -s
mural ˈmjʊə.rᵊl, ˈmjɔː- US ˈmjʊr.ᵊl **-s** -z
Murchie ˈmɜː.ki *in S. England also:* -tʃi US ˈmɝː-
Murchison ˈmɜː.tʃɪ.sᵊn, -kɪ- US ˈmɝː.tʃɪ-
Murcia ˈmɜː.ʃi.ə *as if Spanish:* ˈmʊə.θi.ə US ˈmɝː.ʃə, -ʃi.ə
Murcott ˈmɜː.kət US ˈmɝː-
murd|er ˈmɜː.d|əʳ US ˈmɝː.d|ɚ **-ers** -əz US -ɚz **-ering** -ᵊr.ɪŋ **-ered** -əd US -ɚd
murderer ˈmɜː.dᵊr.əʳ US ˈmɝː.dɚ.ɚ **-s** -z
murderess ˈmɜː.dᵊr.ɪs, -es, -əs; ˌmɜː.dəˈres US ˈmɝː.dɚ.əs; ˌmɝː.dɚˈes **-es** -ɪz
murderous ˈmɜː.dᵊr.əs US ˈmɝː- **-ly** -li
Murdo ˈmɜː.dəʊ US ˈmɝː.doʊ
Murdoch, Murdock ˈmɜː.dɒk US ˈmɝː.dɑːk
Murdstone ˈmɜːd.stᵊn US ˈmɝːd-
Mure mjʊəʳ, mjɔːʳ US mjʊr
muriate ˈmjʊə.ri.ət, ˈmjɔː-, -ɪt, -eɪt US ˈmjʊr.i.eɪt, -ɪt
muriatic ˌmjʊə.riˈæt.ɪk, ˌmjɔː-, ˈmjʊə.ri.æt-, ˈmjɔː- US ˌmjʊr.iˈæt̬-
Muriel ˈmjʊə.ri.əl, ˈmjɔː- US ˈmjʊr.i-
Murillo mjʊˈrɪl.əʊ, mjʊə-, -jəʊ *as if Spanish:* mʊˈriː.jəʊ US mjʊˈrɪl.oʊ, mə- **-s** -z
Murison ˈmjʊə.rɪ.sᵊn, ˈmjɔː- US ˈmjʊr.ɪ-
murk mɜːk US mɝːk
murk|y ˈmɜː.k|i US ˈmɝː- **-ier** -i.əʳ US -i.ɚ **-iest** -i.ɪst, -i.əst **-ily** -ɪ.li, -ᵊl.i **-iness** -ɪ.nəs, -ɪ.nɪs
Murmansk mɜːˈmæn*t*sk, mə- US mʊrˈmɑːn*t*sk; ˈmɝː.mæn*t*sk
murm|ur ˈmɜː.m|əʳ US ˈmɝː.m|ɚ **-urs** -əz US -ɚz **-uring/ly** -ᵊr.ɪŋ/li **-ured** -əd US -ɚd **-urer/s** -ᵊr.əʳ/z US -ɚ.ɚ/z
murph|y (M) ˈmɜː.f|i US ˈmɝː- **-ies** -iz ˈ**Murphy's** ˌ**law**
murrain ˈmʌr.ɪn, -eɪn US ˈmɝː.ɪn
Murray ˈmʌr.i US ˈmɝː-, ˈmʌr-
Murrayfield ˈmʌr.i.fiːld
Murree ˈmʌr.i US ˈmɝː-
Murrell ˈmʌr.ᵊl; mʌrˈel, məˈrel US ˈmɝː.ᵊl; məˈrel
Murrie ˈmjʊə.ri US ˈmjʊr.i
Murrumbidgee ˌmʌr.əmˈbɪdʒ.i US ˌmɝː-
Murry ˈmʌr.i US ˈmɝː-
Murtagh ˈmɜː.tə US ˈmɝː.tɑː
Murtle ˈmɜː.tḷ US ˈmɝː.t̬ḷ
Murton ˈmɜː.tᵊn US ˈmɝː-
Mururoa mʊ.rʊˈrəʊ.ə US ˌmuː.ruːˈroʊ-
muscadet (M) ˈmʌs.kə.deɪ, ˌ--ˈ- US ˈmʌs.kə.deɪ **-s** -z
muscat (M) ˈmʌs.kət, -kæt **-s** -s
muscatel ˌmʌs.kəˈtel **-s** -z
muscl|e ˈmʌs.ḷ **-es** -z **-ing** -ɪŋ, ˈmʌs.lɪŋ **-ed** -d
muscle-bound ˈmʌs.ḷˌbaʊnd
muscle|man ˈmʌs.ḷ|.mæn **-men** -men
muscl|y ˈmʌs.l|i, ˈmʌs.ḷ|.i **-ier** -i.əʳ US -i.ɚ **-iest** -i.ɪst, -i.əst
muscovado ˌmʌs.kəˈvɑː.dəʊ, -ˈveɪ- US -doʊ
Muscovite ˈmʌs.kə.vaɪt **-s** -s
Muscovy ˈmʌs.kə.vi
muscular ˈmʌs.kjə.ləʳ, -kjʊ- US -kjə.lɚ, -kjuː- **-ly** -li ˌ**muscular** ˈ**dystrophy**
muscularity ˌmʌs.kjəˈlær.ə.ti, -kjʊˈ-, -ɪ.ti US -kjəˈler.ə.t̬i, -kjuːˈ-, -ˈlær-
musculature ˈmʌs.kjə.lə.tʃəʳ, -kjʊ-, -tjʊəʳ, -tʃʊəʳ US -kjə.lə.tʃɚ, -kjuː- **-s** -z
mus|e (M) mjuːz **-es** -ɪz **-ing/s** -ɪŋ/z **-ingly** -ɪŋ.li **-ed** -d
musette mjuːˈzet **-s** -s
museum mjuːˈziː.əm, mjʊ- **-s** -z
Museveni ˌmuː.səˈveɪ.ni
Musgrave ˈmʌz.greɪv
mush mʌʃ **-es** -ɪz **-ing** -ɪŋ **-ed** -t
Musharraf mʊˈʃær.æf US -ˈʃɑːr.əf
mushroom ˈmʌʃ.rʊm, -ruːm US -ruːm, -rʊm **-s** -z **-ing** -ɪŋ **-ed** -d
mush|y ˈmʌʃ|.i **-ier** -i.əʳ US -i.ɚ **-iest** -i.ɪst, -i.əst **-iness** -ɪ.nəs, -ɪ.nɪs
music ˈmjuː.zɪk ˈ**music** ˌ**centre**; ˈ**music** ˌ**hall**; ˈ**music** ˌ**stand**; ˈ**music** ˌ**stool**; ˈ**music** ˌ**video**; ˌ**face the** ˈ**music**
music|al ˈmjuː.zɪ.k|ᵊl, -zə- **-als** -ᵊlz **-ally** -ᵊl.i, -li **-alness** -ᵊl.nəs, -nɪs ˈ**musical** ˌ**box**; ˌ**musical** ˈ**chairs**
musicale ˌmjuː.zɪˈkɑːl, -ˈkæl US -ˈkæl **-s** -z
musicality ˌmjuː.zɪˈkæl.ə.ti, -ɪ.ti US -ə.t̬i
musician mjuːˈzɪʃ.ᵊn **-s** -z **-ly** -li **-ship** -ʃɪp
musicolog|y ˌmjuː.zɪˈkɒl.ə.dʒ|i US -ˈkɑː.lə- **-ist/s** -ɪst/s
Musil ˈmuː.zɪl, -sɪl
musk mʌsk **-y** -i ˈ**musk** ˌ**deer**; ˈ**musk** ˌ**rose**
musket ˈmʌs.kɪt **-s** -s **-ry** -ri
musketeer ˌmʌs.kɪˈtɪəʳ, -kəˈ- US -kəˈtɪr **-s** -z
Muskett ˈmʌs.kɪt
Muskie ˈmʌs.ki
musk-ox ˈmʌsk.ɒks, ˌ-ˈ- US ˈmʌsk.ɑː **-en** -ᵊn
muskrat ˈmʌsk.ræt, ˌ-ˈ- US ˈ-- **-s** -s
Muslim ˈmʊz.lɪm, ˈmʊs-, -ləm US ˈmʌz.ləm, ˈmʌs-, ˈmʊz-, ˈmʊs-, ˈmuːz-, ˈmuːz-, -lɪm **-s** -z
muslin ˈmʌz.lɪn **-s** -z
musquash ˈmʌs.kwɒʃ US -kwɑːʃ
muss mʌs **-es** -ɪz **-ing** -ɪŋ **-ed** -t
mussel ˈmʌs.ᵊl **-s** -z
Musselburgh ˈmʌs.l.bᵊr.ə, -ˌbʌr.ə
Mussolini ˌmʊs.əˈliː.ni, ˌmʌs- US ˌmuː.səˈ-
Mussorgsky mʊˈsɔːg.ski, mə-, -ˈzɔːg US məˈsɔːrg-, -ˈsɔːrk-, -ˈzɔːrg-, -ˈzɔːrk-
Mussulman ˈmʌs.ᵊl.mən, -mæn **-s** -z
must (*n. adj.*) mʌst
must (*v.*) *strong form:* mʌst *weak for* məst, məs
Note: Weak form word. There are tw senses of **must**: one is concerned with supposition, or making deductions, and in this sense it is usual for the strong form to be us (e.g. 'If he's late, he must be ill') T other sense is related to obligatic the word may be stressed, in whi case it has the strong form (e.g. 'Y must try harder'), or unstressed, which case the pronunciation is either /məs/ before a consonant, /məst/ before a vowel (e.g. 'Each us must buy some' /ˈiːtʃ.əv.əs.məsˌbaɪ.sʌm/; 'You must always look first' /jʊ.məstˌɔːl.wɪz.lʊkˈfɜːst US -ɑːl.weɪz.lʊkˈfɜːrst/).
mustach|e məˈstɑːʃ, mʊ- US ˈmʌs.t məˈstæʃ **-es** -ɪz **-ed** -t
mustachio məˈstɑː.ʃi.əʊ, -ˈstæʃ.i- US -ˈstæʃ.i.oʊ, -ˈstɑː.ʃi- **-s** -z **-ed** -d
mustang ˈmʌs.tæŋ **-s** -z
Mustapha ˈmʊs.tə.fə, ˈmʌs-, -fɑː, mʊˈstɑː.fə, mə- US ˈmʊs.tɑː.fɑː *Egyptian:* mʊˈstɑː.fə, mə- US ˈmʊs.tɑː.fɑː
Mustapha Kemal ˌmʊs.tə.fə.kemˈ -kɪˈmɑːl US ˌmʊs.tɑː.fɑː.kemˈɑː
mustard (M) ˈmʌs.təd US -tɚd ˈ**mus** ˌ**gas**; ˈ**mustard** ˌ**plaster**; **as** ˌ**keen** ˈ**mustard**
Mustel ˈmʌs.tᵊl
must|er ˈmʌs.t|əʳ US -t|ɚ **-ers** -əz US -ɚz **-ering** -ᵊr.ɪŋ **-ered** -əd US -ɚd
musth mʌst
Mustique muːˈstiːk
mustn't ˈmʌs.ᵊnt

nust|y 'mʌs.t|i -ier -i.əʳ (US) -i.ɚ -iest -i.ɪst, -i.əst -ily -ɪ.li, -əl.i -iness -ɪ.nəs, -ɪ.nɪs
Mut muːt
nutability ˌmjuː.tə'bɪl.ə.ti, -ɪ.ti (US) -t̬ə'bɪl.ə.t̬i
nutable 'mjuː.tə.bl̩ (US) -t̬ə-
nutant 'mjuː.tənt -s -s
nuta|te mjuː'teɪ|t (US) '-- -tes -ts -ting -tɪŋ (US) -t̬ɪŋ -ted -tɪd (US) -t̬ɪd
nutation mjuː'teɪ.ʃən -s -z
mutatis mutandis muːˌtɑː.tiːs.muː'tæn.diːs, mjuːˌteɪ.tiːs.mjuː'- (US) muːˌtɑː.t̬ɪs.muː'tɑːn.dɪs, mjuːˌteɪ.t̬ɪs.mjuː'tæn.dɪs
mut|e mjuːt -es -s -ely -li -eness -nəs, -nɪs -ing -ɪŋ (US) 'mjuː.t̬ɪŋ -ed -ɪd (US) 'mjuː.t̬ɪd
mutil|ate 'mjuː.tɪ.l|eɪt, -təl|.eɪt (US) -t̬əl- -ates -eɪts -ating -eɪ.tɪŋ (US) -eɪ.t̬ɪŋ -ated -eɪ.tɪd (US) -eɪ.t̬ɪd -ator/s -eɪ.təʳ/z (US) -eɪ.t̬ɚ/z
mutilation ˌmjuː.tɪ'leɪ.ʃən, -təl'eɪ- (US) -t̬əl'- -s -z
mutineer ˌmjuː.tɪ'nɪəʳ, -tən.ɪəʳ (US) -tən'ɪr -s -z
mutinous 'mjuː.tɪ.nəs, -tən.əs (US) -tən- -ly -li -ness -nəs, -nɪs
mutin|y 'mjuː.tɪ.n|i, -tən.i -ies -iz -ying -i.ɪŋ -ied -id
mutism 'mjuː.tɪ.zəm
mutt mʌt -s -s
mutt|er 'mʌt|.əʳ (US) 'mʌt̬|.ɚ -ers -əz (US) -ɚz -ering/ly -ər.ɪŋ/li -ered -əd (US) -ɚd -erer/s -ər.əʳ/z (US) -ɚ.ɚ/z -erings -ər.ɪŋz (US) -ɚ.ɪŋz
mutton (M) 'mʌt.ən ˌmutton ˌdressed as 'lamb
muttonchops 'mʌt.ən.tʃɒps (US) -tʃɑːps
muttonhead 'mʌt.ən.hed -s -z
mutual 'mjuː.tʃu.əl, -tʃəl, -tju.əl (US) -tʃu.əl -s -z -ly -i ˌmutual ˌfund
mutuality ˌmjuː.tju'æl.ə.ti, -ɪ.ti (US) -tʃu'æl.ə.t̬i
muzak® 'mjuː.zæk
muzzl|e 'mʌz.l̩ -es -z -ing -ɪŋ, 'mʌz.l.ɪŋ -ed -d
muzzle-load|er 'mʌz.l̩ˌləʊ.d|əʳ (US) -ˌloʊ.d|ɚ -ers -əz (US) -ɚz -ing -ɪŋ

muzz|y 'mʌz|.i -ier -i.əʳ (US) -i.ɚ -iest -i.ɪst, -i.əst -iness -ɪ.nəs, -ɪ.nɪs
Mwanza mə'wæn.zə (US) 'mwɑːn.zɑː
my *normal form:* maɪ *occasional weak form:* mɪ
Note: Occasional weak form word. The strong form is used contrastively (e.g. 'My friends and your friends') or for emphasis (e.g. 'It's my turn'). Many speakers do not have a special weak form, and simply produce a brief, weakened pronunciation of /maɪ/. However, some speakers do use a weak form of **my** in common phrases. British English speakers may have the pronunciation /mi/ before a vowel (e.g. 'On my own' /ˌɒn.mi'əʊn/) and /mə/ before a consonant (e.g. 'On my back' /ˌɒn.mə'bæk/). For American English, the variant /mə/ may be used before a consonant, but /mi/ is not acceptable. In British English, there is also a special form of **my** used by lawyers in court, in phrases such as 'my Lord' or 'my learned friend', pronounced /mɪ/ or /mə/.
myalg|ia maɪ'æl.dʒ|ə, -i.ə -ic -ɪk
Myanmar 'mjæn.mɑːʳ (US) mjɑːn'mɑːr
Myatt maɪət
myceli|um maɪ'siː.li|.əm -a -ə
Mycenae maɪ'siː.ni, -niː
Mycenaean ˌmaɪ.sɪ'niː.ən, -sən'iː- (US) -sə'niː-
mycolog|ist maɪ'kɒl.ə.dʒ|ɪst (US) -'kɑː.lə- -ists -ɪsts -y -i
mycolog|y maɪ'kɒl.ə.dʒ|i (US) -'kɑː.lə-
myelitis ˌmaɪə'laɪ.tɪs, ˌmaɪ.ɪ'-, maɪ'- (US) ˌmaɪ.ə'laɪ.t̬ɪs
Myers maɪəz (US) maɪɚz
Myerscough 'maɪə.skəʊ (US) 'maɪɚ.skoʊ
Myfanwy mə'væn.wi, mɪ-, -'fæn-
Myingyan mjɪŋ'jɑːn
Mylar® 'maɪ.lɑːʳ (US) -lɑːr
myna(h) 'maɪ.nə -s -z 'myna(h) ˌbird
mynheer maɪn'hɪəʳ, -'heəʳ (US) mɪ'ner, -'nɪr; maɪn'her, -hɪr -s -z
Mynheer *form of address in S Africa:* mə'nɪəʳ (US) -'ner, -'nɪr

Mynott 'maɪ.nət
myoelastic ˌmaɪ.əʊ.ɪ'læs.tɪk, -'lɑː.stɪk (US) -oʊ.ɪ'læs.tɪk
myope 'maɪ.əʊp (US) -oʊp -s -s
myopia maɪ'əʊ.pi.ə (US) -'oʊ-
myopic maɪ'ɒp.ɪk (US) -'ɑː.pɪk
myosin 'maɪ.əʊ.sɪn (US) -oʊ-
myosis maɪ'əʊ.sɪs (US) -'oʊ-
myosotis ˌmaɪ.əʊ'səʊ.tɪs (US) -oʊ'soʊ.t̬ɪs
Myra 'maɪə.rə (US) 'maɪ-
myriad 'mɪr.i.əd -s -z
myrmidon (M) 'mɜː.mɪ.dən, -dɒn (US) 'mɝː.mə.dɑːn, -dən -s -z
myrrh mɜːʳ (US) mɝː
Myrrha 'mɪr.ə
myrrhic 'mɜː.rɪk, 'mɪr.ɪk (US) 'mɝː-
myrrhine 'mɜː.raɪn, 'mɪr.aɪn (US) 'mɝː.iːn, -ɪn
myrtle (M) 'mɜː.tl̩ (US) 'mɝː.t̬l̩ -s -z
myself maɪ'self, mɪ- (US) maɪ-, mə-
Mysia 'mɪs.i.ə, 'mɪʃ.ə
Mysore 'maɪ.sɔːʳ (US) -sɔːr
mysterious mɪ'stɪə.ri.əs (US) -'stɪr.i- -ly -li -ness -nəs, -nɪs
myster|y 'mɪs.tər|.i, '-tr|i -ies -iz 'mystery ˌplay
mystic 'mɪs.tɪk -s -s
mystic|al 'mɪs.tɪ.k|əl -ally -əl.i, -li -alness -əl.nəs, -nɪs
mysticism 'mɪs.tɪ.sɪ.zəm, -tə-
mystification ˌmɪs.tɪ.fɪ'keɪ.ʃən, -tə-
mysti|fy 'mɪs.tɪ|.faɪ -fies -faɪz -fying/ly -faɪ.ɪŋ/li -fied -faɪd
mystique mɪ'stiːk
myth mɪθ -s -s
mythic 'mɪθ.ɪk -al -əl -ally -əl.i, -li
Mytholmroyd ˌmaɪ.ðəm'rɔɪd
mythologic ˌmɪθ.əl'ɒdʒ.ɪk, ˌmaɪ.θəl'- (US) ˌmɪθ.ə'lɑː.dʒɪk -al -əl -ally -əl.i, -li
mythologist mɪ'θɒl.ə.dʒɪst, maɪ- (US) mɪ'θɑː.lə- -s -s
mythologiz|e, -is|e mɪ'θɒl.ə.dʒaɪz, maɪ- (US) mɪ'θɑː.lə- -es -ɪz -ing -ɪŋ -ed -d
mytholog|y mɪ'θɒl.ə.dʒ|i, maɪ- (US) -'θɑː.lə- -ies -iz
Mytilene ˌmɪt.ɪ'liː.ni, ˌmaɪ.tɪ'-, -təl'iː-, -niː (US) ˌmɪt.əl'iː-
myxomatosis ˌmɪk.sə.mə'təʊ.sɪs (US) -'toʊ-

Pronouncing the letter N

See also NG

The consonant letter **n** has two pronunciations: /n/ and /ŋ/.

In most contexts, it is realised as /n/, e.g.:

nail /neɪl/
mine /maɪn/

Preceding the letters **k, qu, x** and **c** realised as /k/, **n** is pronounced /ŋ/, e.g.:

bank /bæŋk/
anxious /ˈæŋ*k*.ʃəs/

However, when **k** is silent, **n** is pronounced as /n/, e.g.:

unknown /ʌnˈnəʊn/ ⓤⓢ /-ˈnoʊn/

n (N) en **-'s** -z
N *(abbrev. for* **North***)* nɔːθ ⓤⓢ nɔːrθ *(abbrev. for* **Northerly***)* ˈnɔː.ðəl.i ⓤⓢ ˈnɔːr.ðɚ.li *(abbrev. for* **Northern***)* ˈnɔː.ðən ⓤⓢ ˈnɔːr.ðɚn
'n', 'n ən ˌ**fish 'n' 'chips**; ˌ**rock 'n' 'roll**
NAACP ˌen.dʌb.l̩ˌeɪ.siːˈpiː
NAAFI, Naafi ˈnæf.i
Naaman ˈneɪə.mən
naan nɑːn, næn ⓤⓢ nɑːn **-s** -z
Naas neɪs ⓤⓢ neɪs, nɑːs
nab næb **-s** -z **-bing** -ɪŋ **-bed** -d
nabe neɪb **-s** -z
Nabisco® nəˈbɪs.kəʊ, næbˈɪs- ⓤⓢ -koʊ
nablab ˈnæb.læb **-s** -z
Nablus ˈnɑː.bləs, ˈnæb.ləs ⓤⓢ ˈnɑː.bləs, ˈnæb.ləs ⓤⓢ -lʊs
nabob ˈneɪ.bɒb ⓤⓢ -bɑːb **-s** -z
nabobess ˌneɪ.bɒbˈes ⓤⓢ -bɑːˈbes **-es** -ɪz
Nabokov ˈnæb.ə.kɒf; nəˈbəʊ- ⓤⓢ nəˈbɑː.kɑːf; ˈnɑː.bə-, ˈnæb.ə-
Naboth ˈneɪ.bɒθ ⓤⓢ -bɑːθ
nacelle nəˈsel, næsˈel ⓤⓢ nəˈsel **-s** -z
nacho ˈnɑː.tʃəʊ, ˈnætʃ.əʊ ⓤⓢ ˈnɑː.tʃoʊ **-s** -z
NACNE ˈnæk.niː
NACODS ˈneɪ.kɒdz ⓤⓢ -kɑːdz
nacre ˈneɪ.kəʳ ⓤⓢ -kɚ
nacreous ˈneɪ.kri.əs
nacrite ˈneɪ.kraɪt
NACRO, Nacro ˈnæk.rəʊ ⓤⓢ -roʊ
Nader ˈneɪ.dəʳ ⓤⓢ -dɚ
Nadia ˈnɑː.di.ə, ˈneɪ- ⓤⓢ ˈnɑː-, ˈ-djə
Nadine neɪˈdiːn, nə-; ˈneɪ.diːn ⓤⓢ nəˈdiːn, neɪ-
nadir ˈneɪ.dɪəʳ, -dəʳ; ˈnæd.ɪəʳ ⓤⓢ ˈneɪ.dɚ, -dɪr **-s** -z
Nadir nædˈɪəʳ ⓤⓢ -ɪr
naev|us ˈniː.v|əs **-uses** -ə.sɪz **-i** -aɪ
naff næf
NAFTA, Nafta ˈnæf.tə
nag næg **-s** -z **-ging** -ɪŋ **-ged** -d **-ger/s** -əʳ/z ⓤⓢ -ɚ/z
Naga ˈnɑː.gə **-s** -z
Nagano ˈnæg.ə.nəʊ, ˈnɑː.gə- ⓤⓢ ˈnɑː.gə.noʊ
Nagasaki ˌnæg.əˈsɑː.ki, -ˈsæk.i ⓤⓢ ˌnɑː.gəˈsɑː.ki
Nagorno-Karabakh nəˌgɔː.nəʊˌkær.əˈbæk ⓤⓢ -ˌgɔːr.noʊ.kɑː.rɑːˈbɑːk
Nagoya nəˈgɔɪ.ə ⓤⓢ nɑːˈgɔː.jɑː, -ˈgɔɪ.ə
Nagpur ˌnægˈpʊəʳ ⓤⓢ ˌnɑːgˈpʊr
nah næː ⓤⓢ næː, nɑː
Note: This is an informal pronunciation of **no**; in the British accent described, its usage is often semi-comical.
Nahuatl ˈnɑː.wɑː.tl̩, -ˈ-- ⓤⓢ ˈnɑː.wɑː.t̬l̩ **-s** -z
Nahuatlan ˈnɑː.wɑː.tlən, nɑːˈwɑː- ⓤⓢ ˈnɑː.wɑː.t̬lən **-s** -z
Nahum ˈneɪ.həm, -hʌm ⓤⓢ -həm, -əm
naiad ˈnaɪ.æd ⓤⓢ ˈneɪ-, ˈnaɪ-, -əd **-s** -z
naif, naïf naɪˈiːf, nɑː- ⓤⓢ nɑː- **-s** -s
nail neɪl **-s** -z **-ing** -ɪŋ **-ed** -d ˈ**nail** ˌ**file**; ˈ**nail** ˌ**polish**; ˈ**nail** ˌ**scissors**; ˈ**nail** ˌ**varnish**; ˌ**hit the** ˌ**nail on the** ˈ**head**
nailbiting ˈneɪlˌbaɪ.tɪŋ ⓤⓢ -t̬ɪŋ **-ly** -li
nailbrush ˈneɪl.brʌʃ **-es** -ɪz
nailclipper ˈneɪlˌklɪp.əʳ ⓤⓢ -ɚ **-s** -z
Nailsea ˈneɪl.siː
Nailsworth ˈneɪlz.wəθ, -wɜːθ ⓤⓢ -wɚθ, -wɝːθ
Nain ˈneɪ.ɪn; neɪn
Naipaul ˈnaɪ.pɔːl ⓤⓢ -pɑːl, -pɔːl
naira ˈnaɪ.rə **-s** -z
Nairn(e) neən ⓤⓢ nern
Nairnshire ˈneən.ʃəʳ, -ˌʃɪəʳ ⓤⓢ ˈnern.ʃɚ, -ˌʃɪr
Nairobi naɪˈrəʊ.bi ⓤⓢ -ˈroʊ-
Naish næʃ, neɪʃ
naiv|e, naïv|e naɪˈiːv, nɑː- ⓤⓢ nɑː-, naɪ- **-ely** -li **-eness** -nəs, -nɪs
naiveté, naïveté nɑːˈiː.və.teɪ, naɪ-, -ˈiːv.teɪ ⓤⓢ ˌnɑː.iːvˈteɪ, ˌnaɪ-, -ˈ--
naivety, naïvety naɪˈiː.və.ti, nɑː- ⓤⓢ nɑːˈiː.və.t̬i, naɪ-
Nakasone ˌnæk.əˈsəʊ.neɪ, -ni ⓤⓢ ˌnɑː.k.əˈsoʊ-
naked ˈneɪ.kɪd **-ly** -li **-ness** -nəs, -nɪs **the** ˌ**naked** ˈ**eye**
naker ˈneɪ.kəʳ, ˈnæk.əʳ ⓤⓢ ˈneɪ.kɚ **-s** -z
Nakhon Ratchasima nəˌkɒn.rɑː.tʃɑːˈsiː.mə ⓤⓢ -ˌkɑːn-
NALGO ˈnæl.gəʊ ⓤⓢ -goʊ
Nam, 'Nam *(abbrev. for* **Vietnam***)* nɑːm, næm
Namangan ˌnæm.æŋˈgɑːn ⓤⓢ ˌnɑː.mən-, nə-
namby-pamby ˌnæm.biˈpæm.bi **-ism** -ɪ.zəm
nam|e neɪm **-es** -z **-ing** -ɪŋ **-ed** -d **-eless** -ləs, -lɪs
name-brand ˈneɪm.brænd **-s** -z
namedrop ˈneɪm.drɒp ⓤⓢ -drɑːp **-s** -s **-ping** -ɪŋ **-ped** -t **-per/s** -əʳ/z ⓤⓢ -ɚ/z
namely ˈneɪm.li
nameplate ˈneɪm.pleɪt **-s** -s
namesake ˈneɪm.seɪk **-s** -s
nametag ˈneɪm.tæg **-s** -z
Namibi|a nəˈmɪb.i|.ə, næmˈɪb- ⓤⓢ nəˈmɪb- **-an/s** -ən/z
Namier ˈneɪ.mɪəʳ, -mi.əʳ ⓤⓢ -mi.ɚ
Nampula næmˈpuː.lə
Namur næmˈʊəʳ ⓤⓢ -ˈʊr, nɑːˈmʊr
nan *bread:* nɑːn, næn ⓤⓢ næn, nɑːn **-s**
Nan *name:* næn
nana ˈnæn.ə ⓤⓢ ˈnæn.ə, ˈnɑː.nə, -nɑː **-s** -z
Nanaimo nəˈnaɪ.məʊ, nænˈaɪ- ⓤⓢ nəˈnaɪ.moʊ
Nanak ˈnɑː.nək
nance (N) næn*t*s
nancy (N) *female name or effeminate man:* ˈnæn*t*.si ˈ**nancy** ˌ**boy**
Nancy *in France:* ˈnɑ̃ː*n*.si; *as if Frenc[h]* nɑ̃ː*n*ˈsiː ⓤⓢ ˈnɑ̃ː*n*.si, ˈnæn*t*-
NAND nænd
nandrolone ˈnæn.drə.ləʊn
Nanette nænˈet, nəˈnet
Nanjing nænˈdʒɪŋ
nankeen næŋˈkiːn, næn- ⓤⓢ næn-
Nank|in ˌnænˈk|ɪn, ˌnæŋ- ⓤⓢ ˌnæn-, ˌnɑːn- **-ing** -ɪŋ *stress shift:* ˌNankin ˈhighway
Nannie ˈnæn.i
nann|y (N) ˈnæn|.i **-ies** -iz ˈ**nanny** ˌ**goa[t]**
nanometre, nanometer ˈnæn.əʊˌmiː.təʳ; nænˈɒm.ɪ- ⓤⓢ ˈnæn.oʊˌmiː.t̬ɚ; nænˈɑː.mɪ-
Nanook ˈnæn.uːk ⓤⓢ -ʊk
nanosecond ˈnæn.əʊˌsek.ənd ⓤⓢ -o[ʊ]-, -əˌ- **-s** -z

Names of people and places

It can be difficult to work out the pronunciation of some English words, and something like between ten to thirty percent of words in any text will have irregular spellings. Proper nouns for people and places can have really unexpected pronunciations. Here, we look at a few of the most interesting ones.

Examples

Family names are well known for having interesting realisations. This can be because some letters are not pronounced, but, in some cases, the way a word is written looks almost entirely different to the pronunciation, e.g.:

Cholmondeley /ˈtʃʌm.li/
Colquhoun /kəˈhuːn/
Dalziel /diːˈel; ˈdæl.ziːl/
Featherstonehawe /ˈfeð.ə.stᵊn.hɔː; ˈfæn.ʃɔː/ (US) /ˈfeð.ɚ.stᵊn.hɑː; ˈfæn.ʃɑː/
Quesnel /ˈkeɪ.nᵊl/

It is a similar situation for place names, e.g.:

Alnwick /ˈæn.ɪk/
Cirencester /ˈsaɪə.rᵊn.ses.təʳ; ˈsɪs.ɪ.təʳ/ (US) /ˈsaɪ.rᵊn.ses.tɚ/
Lympne /lɪm/
Woolfardisworthy /ˈwʊl.zᵊr.i; wʊlˈfɑː.dɪˌswɜː.ði/ (US) /ˈwʊl.zɚ.i; wʊlˈfɑːr.dɪˌswɝː.ði/
Worcester /ˈwʊs.təʳ/ (US) /-ɚ/

Welsh place names can be very difficult to decipher for people who do not know the rules that govern the spelling of Welsh. Although Welsh is written using the same alphabet as English, the values of the letters are frequently different, e.g.:

Llanrwst /*h*lænˈruːst/
Penmaenmawr /ˌpen.mənˈmaʊəʳ, -ˈmɔːʳ/ (US) /-ˈmaʊɚ, -ˈmɔːr/

There is some regularity amongst suffixes in some place names. The suffix *–ham* in British place names, for example, is usually pronounced /-əm/, as in *Birmingham*. However, in the North American place name *Birmingham*, *-ham* is pronounced /-hæm/. Another common suffix in British place names, *–cester*, is usually pronounced /-stəʳ (US) -stɚ/, e.g. as in *Worcester* above (although note also *Cirencester*, in which one possible realisation is /-ses.təʳ (US) –ses.tɚ/). Finally, the suffix *–wick* in e.g. *Warwick* is usually pronounced /-ɪk/ in British place names, although there are exceptions.

notechnology ˌnæn.əʊ.tekˈnɒl.ə.dʒi (US) -oʊ.tekˈnɑː.lə-
nsen ˈnæn*t*.sᵊn
ntes nɑ̃ː*n*t (US) nɑ̃ː*n*t, nænts
ntucket nænˈtʌk.ɪt
ntwich ˈnænt.wɪtʃ *locally also:* -waɪtʃ
oise ˈniː.ʃə (US) -si, ˈneɪ-
omi ˈneɪ.ə.mi; neɪˈəʊ- (US) -ˈoʊ-; ˈneɪ.oʊ-
p næp **-s** -s **-ping** -ɪŋ **-ped** -t
palm ˈneɪ.pɑːm, ˈnæp.ɑːm (US) ˈneɪ.pɑːm **-s** -z **-ing** -ɪŋ **-ed** -d
pa Valley ˌnæp.əˈvæl.i
pe neɪp **-s** -s
pery ˈneɪ.pᵊr.i
phtali ˈnæf.tə.laɪ
phtha ˈnæf.θə, ˈnæp-
phthalene ˈnæf.θə.liːn, ˈnæp-
phthol ˈnæf.θɒl, ˈnæp- (US) -θɑːl
pier ˈneɪ.pi.əʳ, nəˈpɪəʳ (US) ˈneɪ.pi.ɚ, nəˈpɪr
pierian nəˈpɪə.ri.ən, neɪ- (US) -ˈpɪr.i-
kin ˈnæp.kɪn **-s** -z **ˈnapkin ˌring**
ples ˈneɪ.pl̩z
poleon (N) nəˈpəʊ.li.ən (US) -ˈpoʊ- **-s** -z
poleonic nəˌpəʊ.liˈɒn.ɪk (US) -ˌpoʊ.liˈɑː.nɪk
pp|y ˈnæp|.i **-ies** -iz **ˈnappy ˌrash**

Napster ˈnæp.stəʳ (US) -stɚ
Narayan nəˈraɪ.ən (US) nɑːˈrɑː.jən
Narbonne nɑːˈbɒn (US) nɑːrˈbɑːn
Narborough ˈnɑː.bᵊr.ə (US) ˈnɑːr.bə.roʊ
narc nɑːk (US) nɑːrk **-s** -s
narcissi *(plur. of* **narcissus***)* nɑːˈsɪs.aɪ (US) nɑːr-
narcissism ˈnɑː.sɪ.sɪ.zᵊm; nɑːˈsɪs.ɪ- (US) ˈnɑːr.sə.sɪ-
narcissist ˈnɑː.sɪ.sɪst; nɑːˈsɪs.ɪst (US) ˈnɑːr.sɪ- **-s** -s
narcissistic ˌnɑː.sɪˈsɪs.tɪk (US) ˌnɑːr-
narciss|us (N) nɑːˈsɪs|.əs (US) nɑːr- **-uses** -ə.sɪz **-i** -aɪ
narcolepsy ˈnɑː.kə*ʊ*.lep.si (US) ˈnɑːr.kə-, -koʊ-
narcoleptic ˌnɑː.kə*ʊ*ˈlep.tɪk (US) ˌnɑːr.kəˈ-, -koʊ- **-s** -s
narcos|is nɑːˈkəʊ.s|ɪs (US) nɑːrˈkoʊ- **-es** -iːz
narcotic nɑːˈkɒt.ɪk (US) nɑːrˈkɑːt̬- **-s** -s
nard nɑːd (US) nɑːrd
nares ˈneə.riːz (US) ˈner.iːz
Nares neəz (US) nerz
narghile, nargileh ˈnɑː.gɪ.leɪ, -gə-, -li (US) ˈnɑːr.gə- **-s** -z
nark nɑːk (US) nɑːrk **-s** -s **-ing** -ɪŋ **-ed** -t
nark|y ˈnɑː.k|i (US) ˈnɑːr- **-ier** -i.əʳ (US) -i.ɚ **-iest** -i.ɪst, -i.əst

Narnia ˈnɑː.ni.ə (US) ˈnɑːr-
Narragansett ˌnær.əˈgæn.sɪt (US) ˌnær-, ˌner-
narra|te nəˈreɪ|t, nærˈeɪ|t (US) ˈner.eɪ|t, ˈnær-; nəˈreɪ|t, nærˈeɪ|t **-tes** -ts **-ting** -tɪŋ (US) -t̬ɪŋ **-ted** -tɪd (US) -t̬ɪd
narration nəˈreɪ.ʃᵊn, nærˈeɪ- (US) nerˈeɪ-, nær- **-s** -z
narrative ˈnær.ə.tɪv (US) ˈner.ə.t̬ɪv, ˈnær- **-s** -z
narrator nəˈreɪ.təʳ, nærˈeɪ- (US) ˈner.eɪ.t̬ɚ, ˈnær-; nəˈreɪ-, nærˈeɪ- **-s** -z
narrow ˈnær.əʊ (US) ˈner.oʊ, ˈnær- **-s** -z **-er** -əʳ (US) -ɚ **-est** -ɪst, -əst **-ly** -li **-ness** -nəs, -nɪs **-ing** -ɪŋ **-ed** -d **ˈnarrow ˌboat; ˌnarrow ˈgauge;** *stress shift:* ˌnarrow gauge ˈrailway
narrowcast ˈnær.əʊˌkɑːst (US) ˈner.oʊˌkæst, ˈnær- **-s** -s **-ing** -ɪŋ **-ed** -ɪd **-er/s** -əʳ/z (US) -ɚ/z
narrow-minded ˌnær.əʊˈmaɪn.dɪd (US) ˌner.oʊˈ-, ˌnær- **-ly** -li **-ness** -nəs, -nɪs *stress shift:* ˌnarrow-minded ˈperson
narw(h)al ˈnɑː.wəl (US) ˈnɑːr- **-s** -z
nary ˈneə.ri (US) ˈner.i
NASA ˈnæs.ə

Nasal consonant

A consonant in which the air escapes only through the nose. For this to happen, two articulatory actions are necessary: firstly, the 'soft palate' (or 'velum') must be lowered to allow air to escape past it and, secondly, a closure must be made in the oral cavity to prevent air from escaping through it. The closure may be at any place of articulation from **BILABIAL** at the front of the oral cavity to 'uvular' at the back (in the latter case there is contact between the tip of the lowered soft palate and the raised back of the tongue).

Examples for English

English has three commonly found nasal consonants: bilabial, alveolar and velar, for which the symbols /m n ŋ/ are used. /ŋ/ cannot occur at the beginning of a syllable, e.g.:

map	/mæp/
nap	/næp/
sang	/sæŋ/

There is disagreement over the phonemic status of the velar nasal: some claim that it must be a phoneme since it can be placed in contrastive contexts like *sum/sun/sung*, while others state that the velar nasal is an **ALLOPHONE** of /n/ which occurs before /k/ and /g/.

In English we find 'nasal release' of **PLOSIVE** consonants: when a plosive is followed by a nasal consonant the usual articulation is to release the compressed air by lowering the soft palate. This is particularly noticeable when the plosive and the nasal are 'homorganic' (share the same place of articulation), as for example in *topmost, Putney*. The result is that no plosive release is heard from the speaker's mouth before the nasal consonant, e.g.:

topmost	ˈtɒp.məʊst	ⓤⓢ ˈtɑːp.moʊst
Putney	ˈpʌt.ni	

Nasal release can also result in a **SYLLABIC CONSONANT**, e.g.:

button	ˈbʌt.n̩

Nasalisation

The addition of nasal escape of air to a sound which would not normally have it.

Examples for English

The best known examples of nasalisation in English are nasalised vowels. In most vowels the airflow escapes entirely through the mouth, but often, in a vowel preceding or following a nasal consonant, we find air escaping also through the nose.

This is a kind of coarticulation, e.g.:

pin	/pɪn/	[pʰɪ̃n]
man	/mæn/	[mæ̃n]
sing	/sɪŋ/	[sɪ̃ŋ]

Nasalised vowels are not phonemically contrastive in Englis[h]

In other languages

Nasalised vowels are phonemically contrastive in a number of languages, such as French, which has pairs of words such *beau – bon* /bo – bõ/ and *mais – main* /mɛ – mɛ̃/.

nasal ˈneɪ.zəl **-s** -z **-ly** -i
nasalism ˈneɪ.zəl.ɪ.zəm
nasality neɪˈzæl.ə.ti, nə-, -ɪ.ti ⓤⓢ neɪˈzæl.ə.t̬i
nasalization, -isa- ˌneɪ.zəl.aɪˈzeɪ.ʃən, -ɪˈ- ⓤⓢ -ɪˈ- **-s** -z
nasaliz|e, -is|e ˈneɪ.zəl.aɪz **-es** -ɪz **-ing** -ɪŋ **-ed** -d
Nasby ˈnæz.bi
nascen|t ˈnæs.ənǀt, ˈneɪ.sənǀt **-ce** -ts **-cy** -t.si
Nasdaq ˈnæz.dæk
Naseby ˈneɪz.bi
Nash(e) næʃ
Nashville ˈnæʃ.vɪl *locally:* -vəl
nasi goreng ˌnɑː.si.gəˈreŋ, -zi-, ˌnæs.i-
Nasmyth *name:* ˈneɪz.mɪθ, ˈneɪ.smɪθ, ˈnæz.mɪθ, ˈnæs- *in US:* ˈneɪ.smɪθ
nasopharyngeal ˌneɪ.zəʊ.fær.ɪnˈdʒiː.əl, -ən-; -fərˈɪn.dʒi.əl, -færˈ- ⓤⓢ -zoʊ.fəˈrɪn- *stress shift:* ˌnasopharyngeal ˈport
nasopharynx ˌneɪ.zəʊˈfær.ɪŋks ⓤⓢ -zoʊˈfer-, -ˈfær-
Nassau *in Bahamas and US:* ˈnæs.ɔː ⓤⓢ -ɔː, -ɑː *German province:* ˈnæs.aʊ ⓤⓢ ˈnɑː.saʊ *princely family:* ˈnæs.ɔː, -aʊ ⓤⓢ ˈnɑː.saʊ
Nasser ˈnæs.əʳ, ˈnɑː.səʳ ⓤⓢ ˈnæs.ɚ, ˈnɑː.sɚ
Nastase næsˈtɑː.zi, nəˈstɑː-, -zeɪ
nasturtium nəˈstɜː.ʃəm ⓤⓢ -ˈstɝː-, næsˈtɝː- **-s** -z
nast|y ˈnɑː.stǀi ⓤⓢ ˈnæs.tǀi **-ies** -iz **-ier** -i.əʳ ⓤⓢ -i.ɚ **-iest** -i.ɪst, -i.əst **-ily** -ɪ.li, -əl.i **-iness** -ɪ.nəs, -ɪ.nɪs
natal (*adj.*) ˈneɪ.təl ⓤⓢ -t̬əl
Natal nəˈtæl, -ˈtɑːl
Natalie ˈnæt.əl.i ⓤⓢ ˈnæt̬-
Natasha nəˈtæʃ.ə
natation nəˈteɪ.ʃən, neɪ- ⓤⓢ neɪ-, nætˈeɪ-
natch nætʃ
NATFHE, Natfhe ˈnæt.fiː
Nathan ˈneɪ.θən, -θæn ⓤⓢ -θən
Nathaniel nəˈθæn.jəl
nation ˈneɪ.ʃən **-s** -z
national ˈnæʃ.ən.əl, ˈnæʃ.nəl **-s** -z **ˌnational ˈanthem; ˌnational curˈriculum; ˌnational ˈdebt; ˌNational ˈFront; ˌNational ˈGua[rd]; ˌNational ˈHealth ˌService; ˌnati[onal] ˈpark; ˌnational seˈcurity; ˌnatio[nal] ˈservice; ˌNational ˈTrust**
national|ism ˈnæʃ.ən.əlǀɪ.zəm, ˈnæʃ.nəl- **-ist/s** -ɪst/s
nationalistic ˌnæʃ.ən.əlˈɪs.tɪk, ˌnæʃ.nəlˈ- **-ally** -əl.i, -li
nationalit|y ˌnæʃ.ənˈæl.ə.tǀi, ˌnæʃˈnæl-, -ɪ.tǀi **-ies** -iz

ationalization, -isa-
ˌnæʃ.ən.əl.aɪˈzeɪ.ʃən, ˌnæʃ.nəl-, -ɪˈ-
US -ɪˈ-
ationaliz|e, -is|e ˈnæʃ.ən.əl.aɪz, ˈnæʃ.nəl- -es -ɪz -ing -ɪŋ -ed -d
ationhood ˈneɪ.ʃən.hʊd
ation-state ˌneɪ.ʃənˈsteɪt US ˈ--- -s -s
ationwide ˌneɪ.ʃənˈwaɪd *stress shift:* ˌnationwide ˈsearch
ative ˈneɪ.tɪv US -t̬ɪv -s -z -ly -li ˌNative Aˈmerican; ˌnative ˈspeaker
ativit|y (N) nəˈtɪv.ə.t|i, -ɪ.t|i US -ə.t̬|i -ies -iz naˈtivity ˌplay
ATO, Nato ˈneɪ.təʊ US -t̬oʊ
atron ˈneɪ.trən, -trɒn US -trɑːn
ATSOPA nætˈsəʊ.pə US -ˈsoʊ-
att|er ˈnæt|.ər US ˈnæt̬|.ɚ -ers -əz US -ɚz -ering -ər.ɪŋ US -ɚ.ɪŋ -ered -əd US -ɚd -erer/s -ər.ər/z, -ɚ.ɚ/z
atterjack ˈnæt.ə.dʒæk US ˈnæt̬.ɚ- -s -s
att|y ˈnæt|.i US ˈnæt̬|.i -ier -i.ər US -i.ɚ -iest -i.ɪst, -i.əst -ily -ɪ.li, -əl.i -iness -ɪ.nəs, -ɪ.nɪs
atural ˈnætʃ.ər.əl, -ʊ.rəl US -ɚ.əl, ˈ-rəl -s -z -ly -i -ness -nəs, -nɪs ˌnatural ˈchildbirth; ˌnatural ˈgas; ˌnatural ˈhistory; ˌnatural reˈsources; US ˌnatural ˈresources; ˌnatural seˈlection
atural|ism ˈnætʃ.ər.əl|.ɪ.zəm, -ʊr- US -ɚ.əl-, ˈ-rəl- -ist/s -ɪst/s
aturalistic ˌnætʃ.ər.əlˈɪs.tɪk, -ʊr- US -ɚ.əlˈ-, ˌ-rəlˈ- -ally -əl.i, -li
aturalization, -isa- ˌnætʃ.ər.əl.aɪˈzeɪ.ʃən, -ʊr-, -ɪˈ- US -ɚ.əl.ɪˈ-, ˌ-rəl-
aturaliz|e, -is|e ˈnætʃ.ər.əl.aɪz, -ʊr- US -ɚ.əl-, ˈ-rəl- -es -ɪz -ing -ɪŋ -ed -d
ature ˈneɪ.tʃər US -tʃɚ -s -z -d -d ˈnature reˌserve
atur|ism ˈneɪ.tʃər|.ɪ.zəm -ist/s -ɪst/s
aturopath ˈneɪ.tʃər.əʊ.pæθ, -tʃʊr-, ˈnætʃ.ər-, -ʊr- US ˈneɪ.tʃɚ.ə- -s -s
aturopathic ˌneɪ.tʃər.əʊˈpæθ.ɪk, -tʃʊr-, ˌnætʃ.ər- US ˌneɪ.tʃɚ.əˈ- -ally -əl.i, -li
aturopathy ˌneɪ.tʃərˈɒp.ə.θi, -tʃʊr-, ˌnætʃ.ərˈ-, -ʊrˈ- US ˌneɪ.tʃəˈrɑː.pə-
atWest® ˌnætˈwest *stress shift:* ˌNatWest ˈBank
augahyde® ˈnɔː.gə.haɪd US ˈnɑː.gə-, ˈnɔː-
aught nɔːt US nɑːt, nɔːt -s -s
aughtie ˈnɒx.ti US ˈnɑːk-, ˈnɑːx-
aught|y ˈnɔː.t|i US ˈnɑː.t̬|i, ˈnɔː- -ier -i.ər US -i.ɚ -iest -i.ɪst, -i.əst -ily -ɪ.li, -əl.i -iness -ɪ.nəs, -ɪ.nɪs
auru nɑːˈuː.ruː; naʊˈruː, nɑː-, ˈ-- US nɑːˈuː.ruː
auruan nɑːˈuː.ruː.ən; naʊˈruː-, nɑː- US nɑːˈuː.ruː- -s -z

nausea ˈnɔː.si.ə, -zi-, ˈ-ʒə US ˈnɑː.zi.ə, ˈnɔː-, ˈ-ʒə, ˈ-ʃə, ˈ-si.ə
nause|ate ˈnɔː.si|.eɪt, -zi-, ˈ-ʒ|eɪt US ˈnɑː.zi-, ˈnɔː-, -ʒi-, -ʃi-, -si- -ates -eɪts -ating -eɪ.tɪŋ US -eɪ.t̬ɪŋ -ated -eɪ.tɪd US -eɪ.t̬ɪd
nauseating ˈnɔː.si.eɪ.tɪŋ, -zi- US ˈnɑː.zi-, ˈnɔː-, -ʒi-, -ʃi-, -si- -ly -li
nauseous ˈnɔː.si.əs, -zi-, ˈ-ʃəs, ˈ-ʒəs US ˈnɑː.ʃəs, ˈnɔː-, ˈ-zi.əs -ly -li -ness -nəs, -nɪs
Nausicaa, Nausicaä nɔːˈsɪk.i.ə, -eɪ.ə US nɑː-, nɔː-
nautch nɔːtʃ US nɑːtʃ, nɔːtʃ -es -ɪz
nautic|al ˈnɔː.tɪ.k|əl US ˈnɑː.t̬ɪ-, ˈnɔː- -ally -əl.i ˌnautical ˈmile
nautil|us ˈnɔː.tɪ.l|əs, ˈ-təl- US ˈnɑː.t̬ɪ-, ˈnɔː- -uses -ə.sɪz -i -aɪ, -iː
Navajo, Navaho ˈnæv.ə.həʊ US -hoʊ, ˈnɑː.və- -s -z
naval ˈneɪ.vəl
Navan ˈneɪ.vən
navarin ˈnæv.ər.ɪn -s -z
Navarino ˌnæv.ərˈiː.nəʊ US -əˈriː.noʊ
Navarre nəˈvɑːr US -ˈvɑːr
nave neɪv -s -z
navel ˈneɪ.vəl -s -z
navicular nəˈvɪk.jə.lər, -jʊ- US -lɚ
navigability ˌnæv.ɪ.gəˈbɪl.ə.ti, -ɪ.ti US -ə.t̬i
navigable ˈnæv.ɪ.gə.bl̩ -ness -nəs, -nɪs
navi|gate ˈnæv.ɪ|.geɪt -gates -geɪts -gating -geɪ.tɪŋ US -geɪ.t̬ɪŋ -gated -geɪ.tɪd US -geɪ.t̬ɪd
navigation ˌnæv.ɪˈgeɪ.ʃən -al -əl
navigator ˈnæv.ɪ.geɪ.tər US -t̬ɚ -s -z
Navratilova næv.ræt.ɪˈləʊ.və, ˌnæv.rə- US ˌnæv.rə.tɪˈloʊ.və, ˌnɑːv-
navv|y ˈnæv|.i -ies -iz
nav|y ˈneɪ.v|i -ies -iz ˌnavy ˈblue
nawab (N) nəˈwɑːb US -ˈwɑːb, -ˈwɔːb -s -z
Nawanagar nəˈwɑː.nə.gər US ˌnɑː.wəˈnʌg.ɚ; nəˈwɑː.nə.gɚ
Naxos ˈnæk.sɒs US -sɑːs, -soʊs
nay neɪ
Nayarit ˈnɑː.jɑː.rɪt
Naylor ˈneɪ.lər US -lɚ
naysayer ˈneɪˌseɪ.ər US -ɚ -s -z
Nazarene ˌnæz.ərˈiːn, ˈ--- US ˌnæz.əˈriːn, ˈ--- -s -z
Nazareth ˈnæz.ər.əθ, -ɪθ
Nazarite ˈnæz.ər.aɪt US -ə.raɪt -s -s
Naze neɪz
Nazeing ˈneɪ.zɪŋ
nazi (N) ˈnɑːt.si US ˈnɑːt-, ˈnæt- -s -z
nazism (N) ˈnɑːt.sɪ.zəm US ˈnɑːt-, ˈnæt-
NB ˌenˈbiː; ˌnəʊ.təˈbiː.ni, -tɑːˈben.eɪ US ˌenˈbiː; ˌnoʊ.t̬əˈben.eɪ, -tɑːˈ-, -ˈbiː.ni
NBA ˌen.biːˈeɪ, ˌem- US ˌen-

NBC ˌen.biːˈsiː, ˌem- US ˌen-
N.C. ˌenˈsiː
NCO ˌen.siːˈəʊ US -ˈoʊ -s -z
NCT ˌen.siːˈtiː
N.D. ˌenˈdiː
Ndebele ən.dɪˈbel.i, -dəˈ-, -ˈbeɪ.li, -ˈbiː-, -leɪ US ən.dəˈbel.eɪ, -ˈbiː.li -s -z
N'Djamena ən.dʒɑːˈmeɪ.nə, -dʒæmˈeɪ- US -ˈdʒɑː.mə-
Ndola ənˈdəʊ.lə US -ˈdoʊ-
NE (*abbrev. for* **northeast**) ˌenˈiː, ˌnɔːθˈiːst US ˌenˈiː, ˌnɔːrθˈiːst
Neagh neɪ
Neagle ˈniː.gl̩
Neal(e) niːl
Neanderthal niˈæn.də.tɑːl, -θɔːl, -təl US -dɚ.θɔːl, -tɑːl
neap niːp -s -s
Neapolis niˈæp.ə.lɪs
neapolitan (N) ˌniː.əˈpɒl.ɪ.tən, nɪəˈ-, ˈ-ə- US ˌniː.əˈpɑː.lə- -s -z
near nɪər US nɪr -er -ər US -ɚ -est -ɪst, -əst -ness -nəs, -nɪs -s -z -ing -ɪŋ -ed -d ˌNear ˈEast; ˌnear ˈmiss; ˌnearest and ˈdearest
nearby ˌnɪəˈbaɪ US ˌnɪr- *stress shift:* ˌnearby ˈtown
nearly ˈnɪə.li US ˈnɪr-
nearside ˌnɪəˈsaɪd US ˌnɪr- *stress shift:* ˌnearside ˈlane
nearsighted ˌnɪəˈsaɪ.tɪd US ˌnɪrˈsaɪ.t̬ɪd -ness -nəs, -nɪs *stress shift:* ˌnearsighted ˈvision
Neasden ˈniːz.dən
neat niːt -er -ər US ˈniː.t̬ɚ -est -ɪst, -əst US ˈniː.t̬ɪst, -t̬əst -ly -li -ness -nəs, -nɪs
neaten ˈniː.tən -s -z -ing -ɪŋ -ed -d
ˈneath niːθ
Neath niːθ
Nebo ˈniː.bəʊ US -boʊ
Nebr. (*abbrev. for* **Nebraska**) nɪˈbræs.kə, nebˈræs-, nəˈbræs- US nəˈbræs-
Nebrask|a nɪˈbræs.k|ə, nebˈræs-, nəˈbræs- US nəˈbræs- -an -ən
Nebuchadnezzar ˌneb.jə.kədˈnez.ər, -jʊ- US -ə.kədˈnez.ɚ, ˌneb.jə-
nebul|a ˈneb.jə.l|ə, -jʊ- US -jə- -ae -iː -as -əz -ar -ər US -ɚ -ous -əs
nebuliz|e, -is|e ˈneb.jə.laɪz, -jʊ- US -jə- -es -ɪs -ing -ɪŋ -ed -d -er/s -ər/z US -ɚ/z
nebulosity ˌneb.jəˈlɒs.ə.ti, -jʊˈ-, -ɪ.ti US -jəˈlɑː.sə.t̬i
nebulous ˈneb.jə.ləs, -jʊ- -ly -li -ness -nəs, -nɪs
NEC ˌen.iːˈsiː
necessarily ˈnes.ə.sər.əl.i, ˈ-ɪ-, -ɪ.li; ˌnes.əˈser-, -ɪˈ- US ˌnes.əˈser-; ˈnes.ə.ser-

necessar|y 'nes.ə.sər|.i, '-ɪ-, -ser- US -ser- **-ies** -iz **-iness** -ɪ.nəs, -ɪ.nɪs
necessi|tate nə'ses.ɪ|.teɪt, nɪ-, '-ə- US nə- **-tates** -teɪts **-tating** -teɪ.tɪŋ US -teɪ.t̬ɪŋ **-tated** -teɪ.tɪd US -teɪ.t̬ɪd
necessitous nə'ses.ɪ.təs, nɪ-, '-ə- US nə'ses.ə.t̬əs **-ly** -li **-ness** -nəs, -nɪs
necessit|y nə'ses.ə.t|i, nɪ-, -ɪ.t|i US nə'ses.ə.t̬|i **-ies** -iz
neck nek **-s** -s **-ing** -ɪŋ **-ed** -t **,neck and 'neck; ,neck of the 'woods; ,pain in the 'neck; ,up to one's 'neck**
Neckar 'nek.əːr *as if German:* -ɑːr US -ɚ *as if German:* -ɑːr
neckband 'nek.bænd **-s** -z
neck|cloth 'nek|.klɒθ US -klɑːθ **-cloths** -klɒθs, -klɒðz US -klɑːθs, -klɑːðz
necker|chief 'nek.əl.tʃɪf, -tʃiːf US '-ɚ- **-chiefs** -tʃɪfs **-chieves** -tʃiːvz
necklac|e 'nek.ləs, -lɪs **-es** -ɪz **-ing** -ɪŋ **-ed** -t
necklet 'nek.lət, -lɪt **-s** -s
neckline 'nek.laɪn **-s** -z
necktie 'nek.taɪ **-s** -z
neckwear 'nek.weər US -wer
necro- nek.rəʊ-; nek'rɒ- US nek.roʊ-, -rə-; nek'rɑː-, nə'krɑː-
Note: Prefix. Normally takes either primary or secondary stress on the first syllable, e.g. **necrophile** /'nek.rəʊ.faɪl US -rə-/, **necrophilia** /,nek.rəʊ'fɪl.i.ə US -ə'-/, or primary stress on the second syllable, e.g. **necrology** /nek'rɒl.ə.dʒi US -'rɑː.lə-/.
necrolatry nek'rɒl.ə.tri US -'rɑː.lə-, nə'krɑː-
necrological ,nek.rə'lɒdʒ.ɪ.kəl US -'lɑː.dʒɪ-
necrolog|y nek'rɒl.ə.dʒ|i US -'rɑː.lə-, nə'krɑː- **-ies** -iz **-ist/s** -ɪst/s
necromanc|er 'nek.rəʊ.mænt.s|ər US -rə.mænt.s|ɚ **-ers** -əz US -ɚz **-y** -i
necromantic ,nek.rəʊ'mæn.tɪk US -rə- **-ally** -əl.i, -li
necrophile 'nek.rəʊ.faɪl US -rə- **-s** -z
necrophili|a ,nek.rəʊ'fɪl.i|.ə US -ə'-, -'fɪl.i|.ə, -'fiːl.j|ə **-ac/s** -æk/s
necrophilism nek'rɒf.ɪ.lɪ.zəm, nɪ'krɒf-, '-ə- US nek'rɑː.fə-, nə'krɑː-
necropol|is nek'rɒp.əl|.ɪs, nɪ'krɒp- US nek'rɑː-, nə'krɑː- **-ises** -ɪ.sɪz **-i** -aɪ
necrops|y 'nek.rɒp.s|i US -rɑːp- **-ies** -iz
necrosis nek'rəʊ.sɪs, nɪ'krəʊ- US nek'roʊ-, nə'kroʊ-
nectar 'nek.tər US -tɚ **-ous** -əs
nectarial nek'teə.ri.əl US -'ter.i-
nectarine 'nek.tər.iːn, -ɪn US ,nek.tə'riːn, '--- **-s** -z
nectar|y 'nek.tər|.i **-ies** -iz
Ned ned
Nedd|y 'ned|.i **-ies** -iz
Neden 'niː.dən
née, nee neɪ
need niːd **-s** -z **-ing** -ɪŋ **-ed** -ɪd
needful 'niːd.fəl, -fʊl **-ly** -i **-ness** -nəs, -nɪs
Needham 'niː.dəm
needl|e (N) 'niː.dl̩ **-es** -z **-ing** -ɪŋ, 'niːd.lɪŋ **-ed** -d
needlecord 'niː.dl̩.kɔːd US -kɔːrd
needlecraft 'niː.dl̩.krɑːft US -kræft **-s** -s
needlepoint 'niː.dl̩.pɔɪnt
needless 'niːd.ləs, -lɪs **-ly** -li **-ness** -nəs, -nɪs
needle|woman 'niː.dl̩|,wʊm.ən **-women** -,wɪm.ɪn
needlework 'niː.dl̩.wɜːk US -wɝːk
needn't 'niː.dənt
needs (N) niːdz
need|y 'niː.d|i **-ier** -i.ər US -i.ɚ **-iest** -i.ɪst, -i.əst **-ily** -ɪ.li, -əl.i **-iness** -ɪ.nəs, -ɪ.nɪs
neep niːp **-s** -s
ne'er neər US ner
ne'er-do-well 'neə.du,wel US 'ner- **-s** -z
Neeson 'niː.sən
nefarious nɪ'feə.ri.əs, nə-, nef'eə- US nə'fer.i- **-ly** -li **-ness** -nəs, -nɪs
Nefertiti ,nef.ə'tiː.ti US -ɚ'-
Neff® nef
neg. *(abbrev. for* **negative***)* neg, 'neg.ə.tɪv US neg, 'neg.ə.t̬ɪv
nega|te nɪ'geɪ|t, nə-, neg'eɪ|t US nɪ'geɪ|t **-tes** -ts **-ting** -tɪŋ US -t̬ɪŋ **-ted** -tɪd US -t̬ɪd
negation nɪ'geɪ.ʃən, nə-, neg'eɪ- US nɪ'geɪ- **-s** -z
negativ|e 'neg.ə.tɪv US -t̬ɪv **-es** -z **-ely** -li **-eness** -nəs, -nɪs **-ing** -ɪŋ **-ed** -d **,negative 'feedback**
negativ|ism 'neg.ə.tɪ.v|ɪ.zəm US -t̬ɪ- **-ist/s** -ɪst/s
negativity ,neg.ə'tɪv.ə.ti, -ɪ.ti US -ə.t̬i
Negeb 'neg.eb
Negev 'neg.ev
neglect nɪ'glekt, nə- US nɪ- **-s** -s **-ing** -ɪŋ **-ed** -ɪd
neglectful nɪ'glekt.fəl, nə-, -fʊl US nɪ- **-ly** -i **-ness** -nəs, -nɪs
negligé(s), negligee(s) 'neg.lɪ.ʒeɪ, -lə-, -liː-, ,--'- US ,neg.lə'ʒeɪ, '---
negligenc|e 'neg.lɪ.dʒənts, -lə- **-es** -ɪz
negligent 'neg.lɪ.dʒənt, -lə- **-ly** -li
negligibility ,neg.lɪ.dʒə'bɪl.ə.ti, -lə-, -ɪ.ti US -t̬i
negligi|ble 'neg.lɪ.dʒə|bl̩, -lə-, -dʒɪ- US -dʒə- **-bly** -bli
negotiability nɪ,gəʊ.ʃi.ə'bɪl.ə.ti, nə-, ,-ʃə'-, -ɪ.ti US nɪ,goʊ.ʃi.ə'bɪl.ə.t̬i, ,-ʃə'-
negotiable nɪ'gəʊ.ʃi.ə.bl̩, nə-, '-ʃə- US nɪ'goʊ.ʃi.ə-, '-ʃə-
negoti|ate nɪ'gəʊ.ʃi|.eɪt, nə-, -si- US nɪ'goʊ- **-ates** -eɪts **-ating** -eɪ.tɪŋ US -eɪ.t̬ɪŋ **-ated** -eɪ.tɪd US -eɪ.t̬ɪd **ne'gotiating ,table**
negotiation nɪ,gəʊ.ʃi'eɪ.ʃən, nə-, -si US nɪ,goʊ- **-s** -z
negotiator nɪ'gəʊ.ʃi.eɪ.tər, nə-, -si- US nɪ'goʊ.ʃi.eɪ.t̬ɚ, -si- **-s** -z
negotiatory nɪ'gəʊ.ʃi.eɪ.tər.i, nə-, -s US nɪ'goʊ.ʃi.eɪ.t̬ɚ-
negress (N) 'niː.grəs, -grɪs, -gres US -grɪs **-es** -ɪz
Negrillo nɪ'grɪl.əʊ, nə-, neg'rɪl- US nə'grɪl.oʊ **-(e)s** -z
Negrito nɪ'griː.təʊ, nə-, neg'riː- US nə'griː.t̬oʊ **-(e)s** -z
negritude 'neg.rɪ.tjuːd, 'niː.grɪ-, -g US -tuːd, -tjuːd
negro (N) *person:* 'niː.grəʊ US -groʊ **-es** -z
Negro *river:* 'neɪ.grəʊ, 'neg.rəʊ US 'neɪ.groʊ
negroid 'niː.grɔɪd
negus (N) 'niː.gəs **-es** -ɪz
Nehemiah ,niː.*h*ɪ'maɪ.ə, ,neɪ-, -*h*ə'- US ,niː.ə'-, -hɪ'-
Nehru 'neə.ruː US 'neɪ-
neigh neɪ **-s** -z **-ing** -ɪŋ **-ed** -d
neighb|o(u)r 'neɪ.b|ər US -bɚ **-o(u)rs** US -ɚz **-o(u)ring** -ər.ɪŋ
neighbo(u)rhood 'neɪ.bə.hʊd US -b **-s** -z **,neighbourhood 'watch**
neighbo(u)ring 'neɪ.bər.ɪŋ
neighbo(u)rl|y 'neɪ.bəl|.i US -bɚ.l|i **-iness** -ɪ.nəs, -ɪ.nɪs
Neil(l) niːl
Neilson 'niːl.sən
Neisse 'naɪ.sə
neither 'naɪ.ðər, 'niː- US 'niː.ðɚ, 'na
nekton 'nek.tən US -tɑːn, -tən
Nell nel
Nellie 'nel.i
nelly (N) 'nel.i
Nelson 'nel.sən
Nelsonian nel'səʊ.ni.ən US -'soʊ-
nematode 'nem.ə.təʊd US -toʊd **-s** -z
Nembutal® 'nem.bjə.tæl, -bjʊ-, -t US -bjə.tɑːl, -bjʊ-, -tɔːl
nem. con. ,nem'kɒn US -'kɑːn
Neme|a nɪ'miː|.ə, nə-, nem'iː-; 'ner 'niː.mi- US 'niː.mi- **-an** -ən
nemesis (N) 'nem.ə.sɪs, '-ɪ- US '-ə- **nemeses** 'nem.ə.siːz
Nemo 'niː.məʊ US -moʊ
nemophila nə'mɒf.ɪ.lə, nɪ-, -əl.ə US niː'mɑː.fəl.ə, nə- **-s** -z
Nemtsov 'nempt.sɒf US -sɑːv, -sɑ
Nen nen
Nene *river:* niːn, nen
nene *goose:* 'neɪ.neɪ
Nennius 'nen.i.əs

eo-, Neo- niː.əʊ-; ni'ɒ- (US) ni.oʊ-, -ə-; ni'ɑː-
ote: Prefix. Normally either takes primary or secondary stress on the first syllable, e.g. **neonate** /'niː.əʊ.neɪt (US) -oʊ-/, **neonatal** /ˌniː.əʊ'neɪ.tᵊl (US) -oʊ'neɪ.t̬ᵊl/, or primary stress on the second syllable, e.g. **neologize** /ni'ɒl.ə.dʒaɪz ⁻-'ɑː.lə-/.
eoclassic ˌniː.əʊ'klæs.ɪk (US) -oʊ'- **-al** -ᵊl
eoclassic|ism ˌniː.əʊ'klæs.ɪ.s|ɪ.zᵊm (US) -oʊ'- **-ist/s** -ɪst/s
eocolonial|ism ˌniː.əʊ.kə'ləʊ.ni.ᵊl|ɪ.zᵊm, '-njᵊl- (US) -oʊ.kə'loʊ- **-ist/s** -ɪst/s
eodymium ˌniː.əʊ'dɪm.i.əm (US) -oʊ'-
eoimpressionism ˌniː.əʊ.ɪm'preʃ.ᵊnɪ.zᵊm (US) -oʊ-
eoimpressionist ˌniː.əʊ.ɪm'preʃ.ᵊn.ɪst (US) -oʊ- **-s** -s
eo-Latin ˌniː.əʊ'læt.ɪn (US) -oʊ'læt.ᵊn
eolithic (N) ˌniː.əʊ'lɪθ.ɪk (US) -oʊ'-, -ə'-
eolog|ism ni'ɒl.ə.dʒ|ɪ.zᵊm (US) -'ɑː.lə- **-isms** -ɪ.zᵊmz **-y** -i
eologiz|e, -is|e ni'ɒl.ə.dʒaɪz (US) -'ɑː.lə- **-es** -ɪz **-ing** -ɪŋ **-ed** -d
eon 'niː.ɒn (US) -ɑːn ˌ**neon** '**light**
eonatal ˌniː.əʊ'neɪ.tᵊl (US) -oʊ'neɪ.t̬ᵊl, -ə'- **-ly** -i
eonate 'niː.əʊ.neɪt (US) -oʊ-, '-ə- **-s** -s
eophyte 'niː.əʊ.faɪt (US) -oʊ-, '-ə- **-s** -s
eoprene 'niː.əʊ.priːn (US) -oʊ-, '-ə-
epal nɪ'pɔːl, nə-, nep'ɔːl, -ɑːl (US) nə'pɔːl, -'pɑːl
epalese ˌnep.ᵊl'iːz, -ɔː'liːz (US) -ə'liːz, -'liːs
epali nɪ'pɔː.li, nə-, nep'ɔː-, -'ɑː- (US) nɪ'pɔː-, nep'ɔː-, -'ɑː- **-s** -z
penthe nɪ'pent.θi, nə-, nep'ent- (US) nɪ'pent-
phew 'nef.juː, 'nev- (US) 'nef- **-s** -z
phrite 'nef.raɪt
phritic nɪ'frɪt.ɪk, nə-, nef'rɪt- (US) nɪ'frɪt̬-, nef'rɪt̬-
phritis nɪ'fraɪ.tɪs, nə-, nef'raɪ- (US) nɪ'fraɪ.t̬ɪs, nef'raɪ-
phthys 'nef.tɪs (US) -θɪs
plus ultra ˌneɪ.plʊs'ʊl.trɑː, ˌniː-, -plʌs'-, -'ʌl-, -trə (US) -plʌs'ʌl.trə, -plʊs'-, -'ʊl-
pos 'niː.pɒs, 'nep.ɒs (US) 'niː.pɑːs, 'nep.ɑːs
potism 'nep.ə.tɪ.zᵊm, -ɒt.ɪ- (US) -ə.tɪ- **-ist/s** -ɪst/s
potistic nep.ə'tis.tik
ptune 'nep.tjuːn, -tʃuːn (US) -tuːn, -tjuːn
ptunian (N) nep'tjuː.ni.ən, -'tʃuː- (US) -'tuː-, -'tjuː-
ptunium nep'tjuː.ni.əm, -'tʃuː- (US) -'tuː-, -'tjuː-

nerd nɜːd (US) nɝːd **-s** -z **-y** -i
nereid (N) 'nɪə.ri.ɪd (US) 'nɪr.i- **-s** -z
Nereus 'nɪə.ri.uːs, -əs (US) 'nɪr.i.əs, '-juːs
Neri 'nɪə.ri (US) 'nɪr.i, 'ner-, 'neɪ.ri
Nero 'nɪə.rəʊ (US) 'nɪr.oʊ, 'niː.roʊ
Neruda nə'ruː.də, ner'uː-
nerv|e nɜːv (US) nɝːv **-es** -z **-ing** -ɪŋ **-ed** -d '**nerve** ˌ**cell**; '**nerve** ˌ**centre**; '**nerve** ˌ**gas**; ˌ**get on** ˌ**someone's** '**nerves**
nerveless 'nɜːv.ləs, -lɪs (US) 'nɝːv- **-ly** -li **-ness** -nəs, -nɪs
nerve-racking, nerve-wracking 'nɜːvˌræk.ɪŋ (US) 'nɝːv-
nerves nɜːvz (US) nɝːvz
nervine 'nɜː.viːn (US) 'nɝː-, -vaɪn
nervous 'nɜː.vəs (US) 'nɝː- **-ly** -li **-ness** -nəs, -nɪs ˌ**nervous** '**breakdown**; '**nervous** ˌ**system**
nerv|y 'nɜː.v|i (US) 'nɝː- **-ier** -i.əʳ (US) -i.ɚ **-iest** -i.ɪst, -i.əst **-ily** -ɪ.li, -ᵊl.i **-iness** -ɪ.nəs, -ɪ.nɪs
Nesbit(t) 'nez.bɪt
Nescafé® 'nes.kə.feɪ, -kæf.eɪ (US) 'nes.kə.feɪ, -kæf.eɪ, ˌ--'-
nescien|ce 'nes.i.ən|*t*s (US) 'neʃ.ən|*t*s, '-i.ən|*t*s **-t** -t
Nesfield 'nes.fiːld
Nesquik® 'nes.kwɪk
ness (N) nes **-es** -ɪz
-ness *noun-forming suffix:* -nəs, -nɪs
Note: Suffix. When added to a stem to form a noun, **-ness** does not change the existing stress pattern, e.g. **happy** /'hæp.i/, **happiness** /'hæp.ɪ.nəs/.
-ness *in place names:* -'ness
Note: In place names, the suffix **-ness** normally takes primary stress, e.g. **Inverness** /ˌɪn.və'nes (US) -vɚ'-/. However, placenames containing **-ness** are subject to stress shift; see individual entries.
Nessie 'nes.i
nest nest **-s** -s **-ing** -ɪŋ **-ed** -ɪd '**nest** ˌ**egg**
Nesta 'nes.tə
nestl|e 'nes.l̩ **-es** -z **-ing** -ɪŋ, 'nes.lɪŋ **-ed** -d
Nestlé® 'nes.leɪ, -li, -l̩ (US) 'nes.li
nestling 'nes*t*.lɪŋ **-s** -z
Neston 'nes.tᵊn
Nestor 'nes.tɔːʳ, -təʳ (US) -tɚ, -tɔːr
Nestorian nes'tɔː.ri.ən (US) -'tɔːr.i- **-s** -z
net (N) net **-s** -s **-ting** -ɪŋ (US) 'net̬.ɪŋ **-ted** -ɪd (US) 'net̬.ɪd
Netanyahu ˌnet.ən'jɑː.hu, -æn'- (US) ˌnet.ɑːn'jɑː.hu, -ən'-
netball 'net.bɔːl (US) -bɔːl, -bɑːl
netcronym 'net.krəʊ.nɪm, 'nek- (US) 'net.krə- **-s** -z
nether 'neð.əʳ (US) -ɚ **-most** -məʊst (US) -moʊst

Nether|land 'neð.ə|lənd, -ᵊl|.ənd (US) -ɚ|lənd **-lands** -ləndz **-lander/s** -lən.dəʳ/z (US) -lən.dɚ/z
netherworld 'neð.ə.wɜːld (US) -ɚ.wɝːld **-s** -z
netizen 'net.ɪ.zᵊn, -ə- (US) 'net̬- **-s** -z
Netley 'net.li
Netscape® 'net.skeɪp
netsuke 'net.skeɪ, -ski, '-sʊ.ki, -keɪ (US) -sʊ.ki, -sə.keɪ **-s** -z
Nettie, Netty 'net.i (US) 'net̬-
netting 'net.ɪŋ (US) 'net̬-
nettl|e 'net.l̩ (US) 'net̬- **-es** -z **-ing** -ɪŋ, 'net.lɪŋ **-ed** -d '**nettle** ˌ**rash**; ˌ**grasp the** '**nettle**
Nettlefold 'net.l̩.fəʊld (US) 'net̬.l̩.foʊld
nettlerash 'net.l̩.ræʃ (US) 'net̬-
Nettleship 'net.l̩.ʃɪp (US) 'net̬-
nettlesome 'net.l̩.səm (US) 'net̬-
network 'net.wɜːk (US) -wɝːk **-s** -s **-ing** -ɪŋ **-ed** -t
Neuchâtel ˌnɜː.ʃæt'el, -ʃə'tel; (US) ˌnuː.ʃə'tel, ˌnɜː-
Neufchâtel ˌnɜː.ʃæt'el, -ʃə'tel (US) ˌnuː.ʃə'tel, ˌnɜː-
neum(e) njuːm (US) nuːm, njuːm **-s** -z
neural 'njʊə.rᵊl, 'njɔː- (US) 'nʊr.əl, 'njʊr-, 'nɝː- ˌ**neural** '**network**
neuralg|ia njʊə'ræl.dʒ|ə, njɔː-, njᵊr'æl-, njʊ'ræl- (US) nʊ'ræl-, njʊ-, nə- **-ic** -ɪk
neurasthenia ˌnjʊə.rəs'θiː.ni.ə, ˌnjɔː- (US) ˌnʊr.æs'-, ˌnjʊr-
neurasthenic ˌnjʊə.rəs'θen.ɪk, ˌnjɔː- (US) ˌnʊr.æs'-, ˌnjʊr- **-s** -s
neuritis njʊə'raɪ.tɪs, njɔː-, njᵊr'aɪ-, njʊ'raɪ- (US) nʊ'raɪ.t̬ɪs, njʊ-
neuro- ˌnjʊə.rəʊ-, ˌnjɔː-, njʊə'rɒ-, njɔː'- (US) ˌnʊr.oʊ-, ˌnjʊr-, ˌ-ə-
Note: Prefix. Normally either takes primary or secondary stress on the first syllable, e.g. **neuron** /'njʊə.rɒn (US) 'nʊr.ɑːn/, **neurological** /ˌnjʊə.rə'lɒdʒ.ɪ.kᵊl (US) ˌnʊr.ə'lɑː.dʒɪ-/, or primary stress on the second syllable, e.g. **neurologist** /njʊə'rɒl.ə.dʒɪst (US) nʊ'rɑː.lə-/.
neurologi|cal ˌnjʊə.rə'lɒdʒ.ɪ|.kᵊl, ˌnjɔː- (US) ˌnʊr.ə'lɑː.dʒɪ-, ˌnjʊr- **-cally** -kᵊl.i, -kli
neurolog|ist njʊə'rɒl.ə.dʒ|ɪst, njɔː-, njᵊr'ɒl-, njʊ'rɒl- (US) nʊ'rɑː.lə-, njʊ- **-ist/s** -ɪst/s **-y** -i
neuron 'njʊə.rɒn, 'njɔː- (US) 'nʊr.ɑːn, 'njʊr- **-s** -z
neurone 'njʊə.rəʊn, 'njɔː- (US) 'nʊr.oʊn, 'njʊr- **-s** -z
neuroscien|ce ˌnjʊə.rəʊ'saɪ.ən|*t*s, ˌnjɔː-, 'njʊə.rəʊˌ-, 'njɔː- (US) ˌnʊr.oʊ'saɪ-, ˌnjʊr-, 'nʊr.oʊˌsaɪ-, 'njʊr- **-ces** -*t*sɪz **-tist/s** -tɪst/s

Neutral

A term used to describe lip configuration in speech sounds, in which the lips are neither rounded nor spread (see ROUNDING and SPREADING). The term 'unrounded' is also commonly used but can apply equally to spread lips.

Examples for English

The English vowels /ə/and /ɜː/are thought of as having a neutral lip configuration.

Neutralisation

The loss of contrast between PHONEMES.

Examples for English

In its simple form, the theory of the phoneme implies that two sounds that are in opposition to each other (e.g. /t/ and /d/ in English) are in this relationship in all contexts throughout the language. Closer study of phonemes has, however, shown that there are some contexts where the opposition no longer functions: for example, in a word like *still* /stɪl/, the /t/ is in a position (following /s/ and preceding a vowel) where voiced (LENIS) PLOSIVES do not occur. There is no possibility in English of the existence of a pair of words such as /stɪl/ and */sdɪl/, so in this context the opposition between /t/ and /d/ is 'neutralised'. One consequence of this is that one could equally well claim that the plosive in this word is a /d/, not a /t/. (See also ASPIRATION.)

neuros|is njʊəˈrəʊ.s|ɪs, njɔː-, njᵊrˈəʊ-, njʊˈrəʊ- (US) nʊˈroʊ-, njʊ-, nə- **-es** -iːz

neurosurgeon ˈnjʊə.rəʊ,sɜː.dʒᵊn, ˌnjɔː-, ˌ--ˈ-- (US) ˌnʊr.oʊˈsɝː-, ˌnjʊr- **-s** -z

neurosurg|ery ˌnjʊə.rəʊˈsɜː.dʒ|ᵊr.i, ˌnjɔː- (US) ˌnʊr.oʊˈsɝː-, ˌnjʊr- **-ical** -ɪ.kᵊl

neurotic njʊəˈrɒt.ɪk, njɔː-, njᵊrˈɒt-, njʊˈrɒt- (US) nʊˈrɑː.t̬ɪk, njʊ-, nə- **-s** -s **-ally** -ᵊl.i, -li

neurotransmitter ˌnjʊə.rəʊ.trænzˈmɪt.əʳ, ˈ---,--, ˌnjɔː- (US) ˌnʊr.oʊ.trænˈsmɪt̬.ɚ, ˌnjʊr-, -trænzˈmɪt̬- **-s** -z

neut|er ˈnjuː.t|əʳ (US) ˈnuː.t̬|ɚ, ˈnjuː- **-ers** -əz (US) -ɚz **-ering** -ᵊr.ɪŋ **-ered** -əd (US) -ɚd

neutral ˈnjuː.trᵊl (US) ˈnuː-, ˈnjuː- **-s** -z **-ly** -i **-ness** -nəs, -nɪs

neutralism ˈnjuː.trᵊl.ɪ.zᵊm (US) ˈnuː-, ˈnjuː-

neutralist ˈnjuː.trᵊl.ɪst (US) ˈnuː-, ˈnjuː- **-s** -s

neutrality njuːˈtræl.ə.ti, -ɪ.ti (US) nuːˈtræl.ə.t̬i, njuː-

neutralization, -isa- ˌnjuː.trᵊl.aɪˈzeɪ.ʃᵊn, -ɪˈ- (US) ˌnuː.trᵊl.ɪˈ-, ˌnjuː-

neutraliz|e, -is|e ˈnjuː.trᵊl.aɪz (US) ˈnuː-, ˈnjuː- **-es** -ɪz **-ing** -ɪŋ **-ed** -d

neutrino njuːˈtriː.nəʊ (US) nuːˈtriː.noʊ, njuː- **-s** -z

neutron ˈnjuː.trɒn (US) ˈnuː.trɑːn, ˈnjuː- **-s** -z **ˈneutron ˌbomb**

Nev. *(abbrev. for* **Nevada***)* nəˈvɑː.də, nɪ-, nevˈɑː- (US) nəˈvæd.ə, -ˈvɑː.də

Neva ˈneɪ.və, ˈniː- (US) ˈniː-

Nevada nəˈvɑː.də, nɪ-, nevˈɑː- (US) nəˈvæd.ə, -ˈvɑː.də

Neve niːv

névé ˈnev.eɪ (US) neɪˈveɪ, ˈ--

never ˈnev.əʳ (US) -ɚ

never-ending ˌnev.ᵊrˈen.dɪŋ (US) ˈ-ɚ-

nevermore ˌnev.əˈmɔːʳ (US) -ɚˈmɔːr

never-never ˌnev.əˈnev.əʳ (US) ˌ-ɚˈnev.ɚ **on the ˌnever-ˈnever**; **ˌnever-ˈnever ˌland**

nevertheless ˌnev.ə.ðəˈles (US) ˌ-ɚ-

Nevey ˈnev.i

Nevil ˈnev.ᵊl, -ɪl (US) -ᵊl

Nevill(e) ˈnev.ᵊl, -ɪl (US) -ᵊl

Nevin ˈnev.ɪn

Nevinson ˈnev.ɪn.sᵊn

Nevis *in Scotland:* ˈnev.ɪs *in West Indies:* ˈniː.vɪs

nev|us ˈniː.v|əs **-uses** -ə.sɪz **-i** -aɪ

new njuː (US) nuː, njuː **-er** -əʳ (US) -ɚ **-est** -ɪst, -əst **-ish** -ɪʃ **-ly** -li **-ness** -nəs, -nɪs **ˌNew ˈAge**; *stress shift:* ˌNew Age ˈtraveller; **ˌnew ˈbroom**; **ˌNew ˈBrunswick**; **ˌNew Caleˈdonia**; **ˌNew ˈDeal**; **ˌNew ˈDelhi**; **ˌNew ˈEngland** *stress shift:* ˌNew England ˈcoast; **ˌNew ˈForest** *stress shift:* ˌNew Forest ˈponies; **ˌNew ˈHampshire** *stress shift:* ˌNew Hampshire ˈprimary; **ˌNew ˈJersey** *stress shift:* ˌNew Jersey ˈturnpike; **ˌnew ˈman**; **ˌNew ˈMexico**; **ˌNew ˈQuay** *stress shift:* ˌNew Quay ˈharbour; **ˌNew ˌSouth ˈWales**; **ˌNew ˈTestament**; **ˌNew ˈWave** *stress shift:* ˌNew Wav[e] ˈband; **ˌNew ˈWorld** *stress shift:* ˌN[ew] World ˈSymphony; **ˌNew ˈYear** *stre[ss] shift:* ˌNew Year ˈparty; **ˌNew ˌYea[r's] ˈDay**; **ˌNew ˌYear's ˈEve**

Newark ˈnjuː.ək (US) ˈnuː.ɚk, ˈnjuː-

Newbery ˈnjuː.bᵊr.i (US) ˈnuː.ber-, ˈnjuː-

newbie ˈnjuː.bi (US) ˈnuː-, ˈnjuː- **-s** -z

Newbiggin *place:* ˈnjuː.bɪ.gɪn (US) ˈn[uː-], ˈnjuː- *surname:* ˈnjuː.bɪ.gɪn, -ˈbɪg.ɪn (US) ˈnuː-, ˈnjuː-, -ˈbɪg.ɪn

Newbold ˈnjuː.bəʊld (US) ˈnuː.boʊld, ˈnjuː-

Newbolt ˈnjuː.bəʊlt (US) ˈnuː.boʊlt, ˈnjuː-

newborn ˌnjuːˈbɔːn (US) ˈnuː.bɔːrn, ˈnjuː- *stress shift, British only:* ˌnewborn ˈbaby

Newbridge ˈnjuː.brɪdʒ (US) ˈnuː-, ˈnjuː-

Newburg(h) *in the UK:* ˈnjuː.bᵊr.ə (US) ˈnuː-, ˈnjuː- *in the US:* ˈnjuː.bɜ[ːg] (US) ˈnuː.bɝːg, ˈnjuː-

Newburn ˈnjuː.bɜːn (US) ˈnuː.bɝːn, ˈnjuː-

Newbury ˈnjuː.bᵊr.i (US) ˈnuː.ber-, ˈnjuː-, -bɚ-

Newby ˈnjuː.bi (US) ˈnuː-, ˈnjuː-

Newcastle ˈnjuːˌkɑː.sḷ (US) ˈnuːˌkæs ˈnjuː-

ewcastle-under-Lyme ˌnjuː.kɑː.sl̩ˌʌn.dəˈlaɪm US ˌnuː.kæs.l̩ˌʌn.dɚˈ-, ˌnjuː-

ewcastle upon Tyne ˌnjuː.kɑː.sl̩.ə.pɒnˈtaɪn US ˌnuː.kæs.l̩.ə.pɑːn-, ˌnjuː-

ote: /njuːˈkæs.l̩/ is the local form.

ewcome ˈnjuː.kəm US ˈnuː-, ˈnjuː- **-s** -z

ewcomer ˈnjuːˌkʌm.əʳ US ˈnuːˌkʌm.ɚ, ˈnjuː- **-s** -z

ewdigate ˈnjuː.dɪ.geɪt, -gɪt, -gət US ˈnuː.dɪ.geɪt, ˈnjuː-, -gət

ewe njuː US nuː, njuː

ewel ˈnjuː.əl US ˈnuː.əl, ˈnjuː- **-s** -z **ˈnewel ˌpost**

ewell ˈnjuː.əl US ˈnuː.əl, ˈnjuː-

ewey ˈnjuː.i US ˈnuː-, ˈnjuː-

ewfangled ˌnjuːˈfæŋ.gl̩d US ˌnuː-, ˌnjuː- *stress shift:* ˌnewfangled ˈways

ew-fashioned ˌnjuːˈfæʃ.ᵊnd US ˈnuːˌfæʃ-, ˈnjuː-

ew-found ˌnjuːˈfaʊnd US ˌnuː-, ˌnjuː- *stress shift:* ˌnew-found ˈlove

ewfoundland *place:* ˈnjuː.fᵊnd.lənd, -lænd; njuːˈfaʊnd-; ˌnjuː.fᵊndˈlænd US ˈnuː.fənd.lənd, ˈnjuː-, -lænd; ˌnuː.faʊndˈlænd, ˌnjuː-; nuːˈfaʊnd.lənd, njuː-, -lænd **-er/s** -əʳ/z US -ɚ/z

ote: /ˌnjuː.fᵊndˈlænd/ is the local form; it is also the nautical pronunciation in England.

ewfoundland *dog:* njuːˈfaʊnd.lənd US ˈnuː.fənd.lənd, ˈnjuː-, -lænd; nuːˈfaʊnd-, njuː- **-s** -z

ewgate ˈnjuː.geɪt, -gɪt, -gət US ˈnuː.geɪt, ˈnjuː-

wham ˈnjuː.əm; njuːˈhæm US ˈnuː.əm, ˈnjuː-; nuːˈhæm, njuː-

whaven ˈnjuː.heɪ.vᵊn, -ˈ-- US ˈnuː.heɪ-, ˈnjuː-, -ˈ--

wington ˈnjuː.ɪŋ.tən US ˈnuː-, ˈnjuː-

w-laid ˌnjuːˈleɪd US ˌnuː-, ˌnjuː- *stress shift:* ˌnew-laid ˈeggs

wlands ˈnjuː.ləndz US ˈnuː-, ˈnjuː-

wlywed ˈnjuː.li.wed US ˈnuː-, ˈnjuː- **-s** -z

Newman ˈnjuː.mən US ˈnuː-, ˈnjuː-

Newmarket ˈnjuː.mɑː.kɪt US ˈnuː.mɑːr-, ˈnjuː-

Newnes njuːnz US nuːnz, njuːnz

Newnham ˈnjuː.nəm US ˈnuː-, ˈnjuː-

New Orleans ˌnjuːˈɔː.li.ənz, ˈ-lɪənz, ˈ-lənz; -ɔːˈliːnz US ˌnuːˈɔːr.li.ənz, ˌnjuː-, ˈ-lənz; -ɔːrˈliːnz

Newport ˈnjuː.pɔːt US ˈnuː.pɔːrt, ˈnjuː-

Newport Pagnell ˌnjuː.pɔːtˈpæg.nᵊl US ˌnuː.pɔːrtˈ-, ˌnjuː-

Newquay ˈnjuː.ki US ˈnuː-, ˈnjuː-

New Rossington ˌnjuːˈrɒs.ɪŋ.tən US ˌnuːˈrɑː.sɪŋ-, ˌnjuː-

Newry ˈnjʊə.ri US ˈnʊr.i, ˈnjʊr-

news njuːz US nuːz, njuːz **ˈnews ˌagency; ˈnews ˌconference**

newsagent ˈnjuːzˌeɪ.dʒᵊnt US ˈnuːz-, ˈnjuːz- **-s** -s

newsboy ˈnjuːz.bɔɪ US ˈnuːz-, ˈnjuːz- **-s** -z

newsbreak ˈnjuːz.breɪk US ˈnuːz-, ˈnjuːz- **-s** -s

newscast ˈnjuːz.kɑːst US ˈnuːz.kæst, ˈnjuːz- **-s** -s **-ing** -ɪŋ **-er/s** -əʳ/z US -ɚ/z

newscopy ˈnjuːzˌkɒp.i US ˈnuːzˌkɑː.pi, ˈnjuːz-

newsdealer ˈnjuːzˌdiː.ləʳ US ˈnuːzˌdiː.lɚ, ˈnjuːz- **-s** -z

newsflash ˈnjuːz.flæʃ US ˈnuːz-, ˈnjuːz- **-es** -ɪz

newsgroup ˈnjuːz.gruːp US ˈnuːz-, ˈnjuːz- **-s** -s

newshound ˈnjuːz.haʊnd US ˈnuːz-, ˈnjuːz- **-s** -z

newsletter ˈnjuːzˌlet.əʳ US ˈnuːzˌleṭ.ɚ, ˈnjuːz- **-s** -z

news|man ˈnjuːz|.mən, -mæn US ˈnuːz-, ˈnjuːz- **-men** -men, -mən

newsmonger ˈnjuːzˌmʌŋ.gəʳ US ˈnuːzˌmʌŋ.gɚ, ˈnjuːz-, -ˌmɑːŋ- **-s** -z

newspaper ˈnjuːsˌpeɪ.pəʳ, ˈnjuːz- US ˈnuːzˌpeɪ.pɚ, ˈnjuːz- **-s** -z

newspeak **(N)** ˈnjuː.spiːk US ˈnuː-, ˈnjuː-

news|person ˈnjuːz|ˌpɜː.sᵊn US ˈnuːz|ˌpɝː-, ˈnjuːz- **-people** -ˌpiː.pl̩

newsprint ˈnjuːz.prɪnt US ˈnuːz-, ˈnjuːz-

newsreader ˈnjuːzˌriː.dəʳ US ˈnuːzˌriː.dɚ, ˈnjuːz- **-s** -z

newsreel ˈnjuːz.riːl US ˈnuːz-, ˈnjuːz- **-s** -z

newsroom ˈnjuːz.rʊm, -ruːm US ˈnuːz.ruːm, ˈnjuːz-, -rʊm **-s** -z

news-sheet ˈnjuːz.ʃiːt, ˈnjuːʒ- US ˈnuːz-, ˈnjuːz- **-s** -s

newsstand ˈnjuːz.stænd US ˈnuːz-, ˈnjuːz- **-s** -z

Newstead ˈnjuː.stɪd, -sted US ˈnuː-, ˈnjuː-

newsvendor ˈnjuːzˌven.dəʳ US ˈnuːzˌven.dɚ, ˈnjuːz- **-s** -z

news|woman ˈnjuːz|ˌwʊm.ən US ˈnuːz-, ˈnjuːz- **-women** -ˌwɪm.ɪn

newsworthy ˈnjuːzˌwɜː.ði US ˈnuːzˌwɝː-, ˈnjuːz-

news|y ˈnjuː.z|i US ˈnuː-, ˈnjuː- **-iness** -ɪ.nəs, -ɪ.nɪs

newt njuːt US nuːt, njuːt **-s** -s

New Testament ˌnjuːˈtes.tə.mənt US ˌnuː-, ˌnjuː-

newton **(N)** ˈnjuː.tᵊn US ˈnuː-, ˈnjuː-

Newtonian njuːˈtəʊ.ni.ən US nuːˈtoʊ-, njuː-

Newton-le-Willows ˌnjuː.tᵊn.liˈwɪl.əʊz US ˌnuː.tᵊn.liˈwɪl.oʊz, ˌnjuː-

Newtown ˈnjuː.taʊn US ˈnuː-, ˈnjuː-

Newtownabbey ˌnjuː.tᵊnˈæb.i US ˌnuː-, ˌnjuː-

Newtownards ˌnjuː.tᵊnˈɑːdz US ˌnuː.tᵊnˈɑːrdz, ˌnjuː-

Newtown St Boswells ˌnjuː.tᵊn.sᵊntˈbɒz.welz US ˌnuː.tᵊn.sᵊntˈbɑːz-, ˌnjuː-

New York ˌnjuːˈjɔːk US ˌnuːˈjɔːrk, ˌnjuː- **-er/s** -əʳ/z US -ɚ/z *stress shift, see compound:* **ˌNew York ˈCity**

New Zealand ˌnjuːˈziː.lənd US ˌnuː-, ˌnjuː- **-er/s** -əʳ/z US -ɚ/z

next nekst **ˌnext ˈdoor** *stress shift:* ˌnext door ˈneighbours; **ˌnext of ˈkin**

nexus ˈnek.səs **-es** -ɪz

Ng ɪŋ, əŋ, eŋ

Ngaio ˈnaɪ.əʊ *as if Maori:* ˈŋaɪ- US -oʊ

Pronouncing the letters NG

The main realisation for the consonant digraph **ng** is /ŋ/, e.g.:

sing	/sɪŋ/
ringing	/ˈrɪŋ.ɪŋ/

Other pronunciations are possible, one being /ŋg/, e.g.:

finger	/ˈfɪŋ.gəʳ/	US /-gɚ/
English	/ˈɪŋ.glɪʃ/	

In addition

In many words spelt **nge**, or where **ng** is followed by **i** or **y**, the pronunciation is /ndʒ/, e.g.:

change	/tʃeɪndʒ/
engine	/ˈen.dʒɪn/

Ngami ᵊŋ'gɑː.mi (US) ᵊn-, ᵊŋ-
ngultrum ᵊŋ'guːl.trəm (US) -'ʊl.trʊm; ən'gʌl.trəm, əŋ- **-s** -z
ngwee ᵊŋ'gweɪ (US) -'gwiː
N.H. ˌen'eɪtʃ
NHS ˌen.eɪtʃ'es
NI ˌen'aɪ
niacin 'naɪə.sɪn
Niagara naɪ'æg.ᵊr.ə (US) '-rə, '-ɚ.ə **Niˌagara 'Falls**
Niall 'naɪ.əl, naɪl, niːl
Niamey ni'ɑː.meɪ; nɪə'meɪ (US) ni'ɑː.meɪ; njɑː'meɪ
Niamh niːv, nɪəv
nib nɪb **-s** -z
nibbl|e 'nɪb.l̩ **-es** -z **-ing** -ɪŋ, 'nɪb.lɪŋ **-ed** -d **-er/s** -əʳ/z, -ɚ/z
Nibelung 'niː.bə.lʊŋ, -bɪ- (US) -bə- **-s** -z **-en** -ən
Nibelungenlied ˌniː.bə'lʊŋ.ən.liːt, -ˌliːd
niblick 'nɪb.lɪk **-s** -s
NiCad® 'naɪ.kæd
Nicaea naɪ'siː.ə
NICAM 'naɪ.kæm
Nicaragu|a ˌnɪk.ᵊr'æg.ju|.ə, -'ɑː.gju-; -'ɑː.gw|ə, -'æg.w|ə (US) -ə'rɑː.gw|ə **-an/s** -ən/z
nic|e (*adj.*) naɪs **-er** -əʳ (US) -ɚ **-est** -ɪst, -əst **-ely** -li **-eness** -nəs, -nɪs
Nice *in France:* niːs
nicely 'naɪs.li
Nicene 'naɪ.siːn, -'- ˌ**Nicene 'Creed**
nicet|y 'naɪ.sə.t|i, -sɪ- (US) -sə.t̬|i **-ies** -iz
nich|e niːʃ (US) nɪtʃ, niːʃ **-es** -ɪz **-ed** -t
Nicholas 'nɪk.ᵊl.əs
Nichol(l) 'nɪk.ᵊl **-s** -z
Nicholson 'nɪk.ᵊl.sᵊn
nick (N) nɪk **-s** -s **-ing** -ɪŋ **-ed** -t **in the ˌnick of 'time**
nickel 'nɪk.l̩ **-s** -z **-(l)ing** -ɪŋ **-(l)ed** -d
nickel-and-dime ˌnɪk.ᵊl.ᵊnd'daɪm **-s** -z **-ing** -ɪŋ **-ed** -d
nickelodeon ˌnɪk.l̩'əʊ.di.ən (US) -'oʊ- **-s** -z
nicker 'nɪk.əʳ (US) -ɚ
Nicklaus 'nɪk.laʊs, -ləs (US) -ləs
Nickleby 'nɪk.l̩.bi
Nicklin 'nɪk.lɪn
nicknack 'nɪk.næk **-s** -s
nicknam|e 'nɪk.neɪm **-es** -z **-ing** -ɪŋ **-ed** -d
Nicobar 'nɪk.əʊ.bɑːʳ (US) -oʊ.bɑːr, ˌ--'-
Nicodemus ˌnɪk.əʊ'diː.məs (US) -ə'-
nicoise, niçoise niː'swɑːz, nɪ-
Nicola 'nɪk.ᵊl.ə
Nicolas 'nɪk.ᵊl.əs
Nicole nɪ'kəʊl, niː- (US) -'koʊl
Nicol(l) 'nɪk.ᵊl **-s** -z
Nicolson 'nɪk.ᵊl.sᵊn
Nicomachean ˌnaɪ.kɒm.ə'kiː.ən, naɪˌkɒm- (US) ˌnɪk.oʊ.mə'-; ˌnaɪ.kɑː.mə'-
Nicomachus naɪ'kɒm.ə.kəs (US) nɪ'kɑː.mə.kəs; ˌnaɪ.koʊ'mæk.əs
Nicosia ˌnɪk.əʊ'siː.ə (US) -ə'-, -oʊ'-
nicotine 'nɪk.ə.tiːn, ˌ--'-
nic|tate 'nɪk|.teɪt **-tates** -teɪts **-tating** -teɪ.tɪŋ (US) -teɪ.t̬ɪŋ **-tated** -teɪ.tɪd (US) -teɪ.t̬ɪd
nictation nɪk'teɪ.ʃᵊn
nicti|tate 'nɪk.tɪ|.teɪt (US) -tə- **-tates** -teɪts **-tating** -teɪ.tɪŋ (US) -teɪ.t̬ɪŋ **-tated** -teɪ.tɪd (US) -teɪ.t̬ɪd
nictitation ˌnɪk.tɪ'teɪ.ʃᵊn (US) -tə'-
niec|e niːs **-es** -ɪz
Niedersachsen 'niː.dəˌzæk.sᵊn *as if German:* -ˌzæx- (US) -dɚˌzɑːk-
Nielsen 'niːl.sᵊn
Niersteiner 'nɪə.staɪ.nəʳ *as if German:* -ʃtaɪ- (US) 'nɪr.staɪ.nɚ *as if German:* -ʃtaɪ-
Nietzsche 'niː.tʃə (US) -tʃə, -tʃi
niff nɪf **-s** -s **-ing** -ɪŋ **-ed** -t **-y** -i
nift|y 'nɪf.t|i **-ier** -i.əʳ (US) -i.ɚ **-iest** -i.ɪst, -i.əst **-ies** -iz **-ily** -ɪ.li
Nige naɪdʒ
Nigel 'naɪ.dʒᵊl
Nigella naɪ'dʒel.ə
Niger *river:* 'naɪ.dʒəʳ (US) -dʒɚ *country:* niː'ʒeəʳ (US) 'naɪ.dʒɚ **-ien/s** -i.ən/z
Nigeri|a naɪ'dʒɪə.ri|.ə (US) -'dʒɪr.i- **-an/s** -ən/z
niggard 'nɪg.əd (US) -ɚd **-s** -z
niggardl|y 'nɪg.əd.l|i (US) -ɚd- **-iness** -ɪ.nəs, -ɪ.nɪs
nigger 'nɪg.əʳ (US) -ɚ **-s** -z
niggl|e 'nɪg.l̩ **-es** -z **-ing** -ɪŋ, 'nɪg.lɪŋ **-ed** -d
niggl|y 'nɪg.l|i, 'nɪg.l̩|.i **-iness** -ɪ.nəs, -ɪ.nɪs
nigh naɪ
night naɪt **-s** -s ˌ**night 'blindness** (US) **'night ˌblindness; 'night ˌowl; ˌnight 'porter** (US) **'night ˌporter; 'night ˌschool; 'night ˌshift; ˌnight 'watchman**
nightcap 'naɪt.kæp **-s** -s
nightclothes 'naɪt.kləʊðz (US) -kloʊðz
nightclub 'naɪt.klʌb **-s** -z **-bing** -ɪŋ **-ber/s** -əʳ/z (US) -ɚ/z
nightdress 'naɪt.dres **-es** -ɪz
nightfall 'naɪt.fɔːl (US) -fɔːl, -fɑːl
nightgown 'naɪt.gaʊn **-s** -z
nighthawk 'naɪt.hɔːk (US) -hɑːk, -hɔːk **-s** -s
nightie 'naɪ.ti (US) -t̬i **-s** -z
nightingale (N) 'naɪ.tɪŋ.geɪl (US) -tᵊn-, -t̬ɪŋ- **-s** -z
nightjar 'naɪt.dʒɑːʳ (US) -dʒɑːr **-s** -z
nightlife 'naɪt.laɪf
night-light 'naɪt.laɪt **-s** -s
nightlong ˌnaɪt'lɒŋ (US) -'lɑːŋ, -'lɔːŋ *stress shift:* ˌnightlong 'vigil
nightly 'naɪt.li
nightmar|e 'naɪt.meəʳ (US) -mer **-es** -z **-ish** -ɪʃ **-ishly** -ɪʃ.li **-ishness** -ɪʃ.nəs, -ɪʃ.nɪs
nightshade 'naɪt.ʃeɪd
nightshirt 'naɪt.ʃɜːt (US) -ʃɝːt **-s** -s
nightspot 'naɪt.spɒt (US) -spɑːt **-s** -s
nightstand 'naɪt.stænd **-s** -z
nightstick 'naɪt.stɪk **-s** -s
nighttime 'naɪt.taɪm
nightwatch 'naɪt.wɒtʃ, ˌ-'- (US) 'naɪt.wɑːtʃ, -wɔːtʃ **-es** -ɪz
nightwear 'naɪt.weəʳ (US) -wer
nihil 'niː.hɪl, 'naɪ-, -hᵊl (US) 'naɪ.hɪl, 'ni
nihil|ism 'niː.ɪ.l|ɪ.zᵊm, 'naɪ-, '-hɪ-, -ᵊl|.ɪ-, -hᵊl- (US) 'naɪ.ə.l|ɪ-, 'niː- **-ist/s** -ɪst/s **-istic** ˌ--'ɪs.tɪk
Nijinsky nɪ'dʒɪnt.ski, nə-, -'ʒɪnt- (US) nə'dʒɪnt-
Nijmegen 'naɪ.meɪ.gən, -'-- (US) '---
Nike *goddess:* 'naɪ.kiː *trademark:* 'naɪ.ki; naɪk (US) 'naɪ.ki
Nikita nɪ'kiː.tə (US) -t̬ə
Nikkei nɪ'keɪ (US) 'niː.keɪ *stress shift,* *compound:* ˌ**Nikkei 'index**
Nikki 'nɪk.i
Nikon® 'nɪk.ɒn (US) 'naɪ.kɑːn, 'niː-
nil nɪl
nil desperandum ˌnɪl.des.pə'ræn.də -pᵊr'æn-, -dʊm (US) -pə'ræn.dəm; -'rɑːn.dʊm
Nile naɪl
Nilgiri 'nɪl.gɪ.ri **-s** -z
nilometer naɪ'lɒm.ɪ.təʳ, -ə.təʳ (US) -'lɑː.mə.t̬ɚ **-s** -z
Nilotic naɪ'lɒt.ɪk (US) -'lɑː.t̬ɪk
Nilsen 'niːl.sᵊn, 'nɪl-
Nilsson 'niːl.sᵊn, 'nɪl-
nimbi *(plur. of* **nimbus***)* 'nɪm.baɪ
nimb|le 'nɪm.b|l̩ **-ler** -ləʳ, -l̩.əʳ (US) -lɚ, -l̩.ɚ **-lest** -lɪst, -ləst, -l̩.ɪst, -l̩.əst **-ly** -li **-leness** -l̩.nəs, -l̩.nɪs
nimb|us 'nɪm.b|əs **-uses** -ə.sɪz **-i** -aɪ
nimb|y, NIMB|Y 'nɪm.b|i **-ies** -iz
Nîmes niːm
nimiety nɪ'maɪə.ti, -'maɪ.ɪ.ti (US) -t̬i
nimini-piminy, niminy-piminy ˌnɪm.ɪ.ni'pɪm.ɪ.ni, ˌ-ə-, '-ə- (US) -ə.ni'pɪm.ə-
Nimmo 'nɪm.əʊ (US) -oʊ
Nimrod 'nɪm.rɒd (US) -rɑːd
Nin nɪn (US) nɪn, niːn
Nina 'niː.nə (US) 'niː-, 'naɪ-
nincompoop 'nɪŋ.kəm.puːp, 'nɪn- (US) 'nɪn-, 'nɪŋ- **-s** -s
nine naɪn **-s** -z **-fold** -fəʊld (US) -foʊld ˌ**dressed ˌup to the 'nines; ˌnine-to-'five; ˌnine days' 'wonde**
ninepenc|e 'naɪn.pənts, 'naɪm- (US) 'naɪn- **-es** -ɪz
Note: See note under **penny**.
ninepenny 'naɪn.pᵊn.i, 'naɪm- (US) 'naɪn-

ninepin ˈnaɪn.pɪn, ˈnaɪm- (US) ˈnaɪn- **-s** -z
nineteen ˌnaɪnˈtiːn **-s** -z **-th/s** -tθ/s
stress shift: ˌnineteen ˈyears
ˌnineteen to the ˈdozen
ninetieth ˈnaɪn.ti.əθ, -ɪθ (US) -t̬i- **-s** -s
Ninette nɪˈnet, niː-
ninet|y ˈnaɪn.t|i (US) -t̬|i **-ies** -iz
ninetyfold ˈnaɪn.ti.fəʊld (US) -t̬i.foʊld
ninety-nine ˌnaɪn.tiˈnaɪn (US) -t̬iˈ- *stress shift:* ˌninety-nine ˈdays
Nineveh ˈnɪn.ɪ.və, ˈ-ə- (US) ˈ-ə-
ninish ˈnaɪ.nɪʃ
ninja ˈnɪn.dʒə **-s** -z **ˌNinja ˈwarriors**
ninn|y ˈnɪn|.i **-ies** -iz
Nintendo® nɪnˈten.dəʊ (US) -doʊ
ninth naɪntθ **-s** -s **-ly** -li
Ninus ˈnaɪ.nəs
Niobe ˈnaɪ.əʊ.bi (US) -oʊ-, ˈ-ə-
niobium naɪˈəʊ.bi.əm (US) -ˈoʊ-
nip (N) nɪp **-s** -s **-ping** -ɪŋ **-ped** -t **ˌnip and ˈtuck**
nipper ˈnɪp.əʳ (US) -ɚ **-s** -z
nipple ˈnɪp.l̩ **-s** -z
Nippon ˈnɪp.ɒn (US) -ɑːn; nɪˈpɑːn **-ese** --ˈiːz
nipp|y ˈnɪp|.i **-ier** -i.əʳ (US) -i.ɚ **-iest** -i.ɪst, -i.əst **-ily** -ɪ.li, -əl.i **-iness** -ɪ.nəs, -ɪ.nɪs
IREX, Nirex® ˈnaɪə.reks (US) ˈnaɪ-
irvana (N) nɪəˈvɑː.nə, nɜː- (US) nɪr-, nɚ- **-s** -z
is, Nish niːʃ
isan ˈnaɪ.sæn *Jewish pronunciation:* ˈnɪs.ɑːn (US) niːˈsɑːn; ˈnɪs.ən
isbet(t) ˈnɪz.bɪt, -bət
isei niːˈseɪ (US) niːˈseɪ, ˈ-- **-s** -z
ish nɪʃ
isi ˈnaɪ.saɪ, ˈniː-, -si (US) ˈnaɪ.saɪ
isi prius ˌnaɪ.saɪˈpraɪ.əs, ˌniː-, -siˈ-, -ˈpriː- (US) ˌnaɪ.saɪˈpraɪ-
issan® ˈnɪs.æn (US) ˈniː.sɑːn
issen ˈnɪs.ən **ˈNissen ˌhut**
isus ˈnaɪ.səs
it nɪt **-s** -s
iter ˈnaɪ.təʳ (US) -t̬ɚ
ith nɪθ
it-pick ˈnɪt.pɪk **-s** -s **-ing** -ɪŋ **-ed** -t **-er/s** -əʳ/z (US) -ɚ/z
itrate ˈnaɪ.treɪt, -trɪt (US) -treɪt **-s** -s
itre ˈnaɪ.təʳ (US) -t̬ɚ
itric ˈnaɪ.trɪk **ˌnitric ˈacid**
itrite ˈnaɪ.traɪt
itro- ˌnaɪ.trəʊ- (US) ˌnaɪ.troʊ-, -trə-
itrochalk ˈnaɪ.trəʊ.tʃɔːk, ˌ--ˈ- (US) ˈnaɪ.troʊ.tʃɔːk, -tʃɑːk
trogen ˈnaɪ.trə.dʒən, -trɪ- (US) -trə-
trogenous naɪˈtrɒdʒ.ɪ.nəs, -ən.əs (US) -ˈtrɑː.dʒə.nəs
troglycerine, nitroglycerin ˌnaɪ.trəʊˈglɪs.ər.iːn, -ɪn (US) -troʊˈ-, -trəˈ-
trous ˈnaɪ.trəs

nitty-gritty ˌnɪt.iˈgrɪt.i (US) ˌnɪt̬.iˈgrɪt̬-
nitwit ˈnɪt.wɪt **-s** -s
Niue ˈnjuː.eɪ, niˈuː- (US) niˈuː- **-an/s** -ən/z
Nivea® ˈnɪv.i.ə
Niven ˈnɪv.ən
nix nɪks **-es** -ɪz **-ing** -ɪŋ **-ed** -t
Nixdorf® ˈnɪks.dɔːf (US) -dɔːrf
nixie ˈnɪk.si **-s** -z
Nixon ˈnɪk.sən
nizam (N) naɪˈzæm, nɪ-, -ˈzɑːm (US) nɪˈzɑːm; naɪˈzæm **-ate** -eɪt **-s** -z
Nizhni Novgorod ˌnɪʒ.niˈnɒv.gər.ɒd (US) -ˈnɑːv.gə.rɑːd
N.J. ˌenˈdʒeɪ
Nkomo əŋˈkəʊ.məʊ (US) -ˈkoʊ.moʊ, ən-
Nkrumah əŋˈkruː.mə (US) əŋ-, ən-
N.M. *(abbrev. for* **New Mexico***)* ˌenˈem
NME ˌen.emˈiː
N.Mex. *(abbrev. for* **New Mexico***)* ˌenˈmeks
NNE *(abbrev. for* **north-northeast***)* ˌnɔːθ.nɔːθˈiːst (US) ˌnɔːrθ.nɔːrθˈ- *nautical pronunciation:* ˌnɔː.nɔːrˈiːst (US) ˌnɔːr.nɔːrˈiːst
NNW *(abbrev. for* **north-northwest***)* ˌnɔːθ.nɔːθˈwest (US) ˌnɔːrθ.nɔːrθˈ- *nautical pronunciation:* ˌnɔː.nɔːˈ- (US) ˌnɔːr.nɔːrˈ-
no *(n. interj.)* nəʊ (US) noʊ **-es** -z
no *(adj.) normal form:* nəʊ (US) noʊ *weak form:* nə

Note: Occasional weak form word. The pronunciation of **no** is nearly always /nəʊ (US) noʊ/, but, particularly in British English, there is a weak form /nə/ in a few common expressions such as "no more do I" /nə.mɔː.duːˈaɪ (US) -ˌmɔːr-/.

no. (N) *(abbrev. for* **number***)* ˈnʌm.bəʳ (US) -bɚ **nos.** -z
no-account ˈnəʊ.əˌkaʊnt (US) ˈnoʊ-
Noah ˈnəʊ.ə (US) ˈnoʊ- **ˌNoah's ˈark**
Noakes nəʊks (US) noʊks
Noam ˈnəʊ.əm, nəʊm (US) ˈnoʊ.əm, noʊm
nob nɒb (US) nɑːb **-s** -z
no-ball ˌnəʊˈbɔːl (US) ˈnoʊ-, -bɑːl **-s** -z **-ing** -ɪŋ **-ed** -d
nobbl|e ˈnɒb.l̩ (US) ˈnɑː.bl̩ **-es** -z **-ing** -ɪŋ, ˈnɒb.lɪŋ (US) ˈnɑː.blɪŋ **-ed** -d
nobb|y ˈnɒb|.i (US) ˈnɑː.b|i **-ier** -i.əʳ (US) -i.ɚ **-iest** -i.ɪst, -i.əst **-ily** -ɪ.li, -əl.i **-iness** -ɪ.nəs, -ɪ.nɪs
Nobel nəʊˈbel (US) noʊ- *stress shift, see compound:* **ˌNobel ˈprize**
nobelium nəʊˈbiː.li.əm (US) noʊˈbel.i-
nobilit|y nəʊˈbɪl.ə.t|i, -ɪ.t|i (US) noʊˈbɪl.ə.t̬|i **-ies** -iz
nob|le (N) ˈnəʊ.b|l̩ (US) ˈnoʊ- **-les** -l̩z **-ler** -ləʳ, -l̩.əʳ **-lest** -lɪst, -ləst, -l̩.ɪst, -l̩.əst **-ly** -li **-leness** -l̩.nəs, -l̩.nɪs

noble|man ˈnəʊ.bl̩|.mən (US) ˈnoʊ- **-men** -mən
noble-minded ˌnəʊ.bl̩ˈmaɪn.dɪd (US) ˌnoʊ- **-ness** -nəs, -nɪs *stress shift:* ˌnoble-minded ˈperson
noblesse nəʊˈbles (US) noʊ-
noblesse oblige nəʊˌbles.əʊˈbliːʒ, ˌnəʊ.bles- (US) noʊˌbles.oʊˈ-
noble|woman ˈnəʊ.bl̩|ˌwʊm.ən (US) ˈnoʊ- **-women** -ˌwɪm.ɪn
nobod|y ˈnəʊ.bə.d|i, -bɒd|.i (US) ˈnoʊ.bɑː.d|i, -bʌd|.i, -bə.d|i **-ies** -iz
nock (N) nɒk (US) nɑːk
no-claim bonus ˌnəʊˈkleɪmˌbəʊ.nəs, ˌnəʊˌkleɪmˈbəʊ- (US) ˌnoʊˈkleɪmˌboʊ-, ˌnoʊˌkleɪmˈboʊ- **-es** -ɪz
no-claims bonus ˌnəʊˈkleɪmzˌbəʊ.nəs, ˌnəʊˌkleɪmzˈbəʊ- (US) ˌnoʊˈkleɪmzˌboʊ-, ˌnoʊˌkleɪmzˈboʊ- **-es** -ɪz
no-confidence ˌnəʊˈkɒn.fɪ.dənts (US) ˌnoʊˈkɑːn-
noctambul|ism nɒkˈtæm.bjə.l|ɪ.zəm, -bjʊ- (US) nɑːkˈtæm.bjuː-, -bjə- **-ist/s** -ɪst/s
Noctes Ambrosianae ˌnɒk.teɪsˌæm.brəʊ.ziˈɑː.naɪ, -brɒs.iˈ- (US) ˌnɑːk.tiːz.æm.broʊ.siˈeɪ.ni
nocturnal nɒkˈtɜː.nəl (US) nɑːkˈtɝː- **-ly** -i
nocturn(e) ˈnɒk.tɜːn, ˌ-ˈ- (US) ˈnɑːk.tɝːn **-s** -z
nocuous ˈnɒk.ju.əs (US) ˈnɑːk- **-ly** -li
nod (N) nɒd (US) nɑːd **-s** -z **-ding** -ɪŋ **-ded** -ɪd
nodal ˈnəʊ.dəl (US) ˈnoʊ- **-ly** -i
nodding ˈnɒd.ɪŋ (US) ˈnɑː.dɪŋ
noddle ˈnɒd.l̩ (US) ˈnɑː.dl̩ **-s** -z
nodd|y (N) ˈnɒd|.i (US) ˈnɑː.d|i **-ies** -iz
node nəʊd (US) noʊd **-s** -z
nodul|ar ˈnɒd.jə.l|əʳ, -jʊ- (US) ˈnɑː.djuː.l|ɚ, -djə- **-ous** -əs
nodule ˈnɒd.juːl (US) ˈnɑː.djuːl **-s** -z
Noel, Noël *personal name:* nəʊəl (US) noʊəl *Christmas:* nəʊˈel (US) noʊ-
no-fault ˈnəʊ.fɔːlt, -fɒlt (US) ˈnoʊ.fɔːlt, -fɑːlt
no-fly ˌnəʊˈflaɪ (US) ˌnoʊ- *stress shift:* ˌno-fly ˈzone
no-frills ˌnəʊˈfrɪlz (US) ˌnoʊ- *stress shift:* ˌno-frills ˈservice
noggin ˈnɒg.ɪn (US) ˈnɑː.gɪn **-s** -z
no-go ˌnəʊˈgəʊ (US) ˌnoʊˈgoʊ *stress shift, see compound:* **ˌno-go ˈarea**
no-good ˌnəʊˈgʊd (US) ˌnoʊ- *stress shift:* ˌno-good ˈcheat
Noh nəʊ (US) noʊ
no-holds-barred ˌnəʊˌhəʊldzˈbɑːd (US) ˌnoʊˌhoʊldzˈbɑːrd *stress shift:* ˌno-holds-barred ˈcontest

no-hoper ˌnəʊˈhəʊ.pəʳ ⓤⓢ ˌnoʊˈhoʊ.pɚ **-s** -z
nohow ˈnəʊ.haʊ ⓤⓢ ˈnoʊ-
noir nwɑːʳ ⓤⓢ nwɑːr
nois|e nɔɪz **-es** -ɪz **-ing** -ɪŋ **-ed** -d
noiseless ˈnɔɪz.ləs, -lɪs **-ly** -li **-ness** -nəs, -nɪs
noisemaker ˈnɔɪzˌmeɪ.kəʳ ⓤⓢ -kɚ **-s** -z
noisette nwɑːˈzet **-s** -s
noisettes *(alternative plur. of* **noisette***)* nwɑːˈzet
noisome ˈnɔɪ.səm **-ly** -li **-ness** -nəs, -nɪs
nois|y ˈnɔɪ.z|i **-ier** -i.əʳ ⓤⓢ -i.ɚ **-iest** -i.ɪst, -i.əst **-ily** -ɪ.li, -əl.i **-iness** -ɪ.nəs, -ɪ.nɪs
Nokes nəʊks ⓤⓢ noʊks
Nokia ˈnɒk.i.ə ⓤⓢ ˈnoʊ.ki-
Nokomis nəʊˈkəʊ.mɪs ⓤⓢ noʊˈkoʊ-
Nolan ˈnəʊ.lən ⓤⓢ ˈnoʊ-
noli me tangere ˌnəʊ.liˌmeɪˈtæŋ.gə.reɪ, ˈ-dʒə- ⓤⓢ ˌnoʊ-
Noll nɒl ⓤⓢ nɑːl
nolo contendere ˌnəʊ.ləʊ.kɒnˈten.dər.i, -eɪ ⓤⓢ ˌnoʊ.loʊ.kənˈ-
Nolte ˈnɒl.ti ⓤⓢ ˈnoʊl.ti
noma ˈnəʊ.mə ⓤⓢ ˈnoʊ- **-s** -z
nomad ˈnəʊ.mæd ⓤⓢ ˈnoʊ- **-s** -z **-ism** -ɪ.zəm
nomadic nəʊˈmæd.ɪk ⓤⓢ noʊ- **-ally** -əl.i, -li
no-man's-land ˈnəʊ.mænz.lænd ⓤⓢ ˈnoʊ-
nom(s) de guerre ˌnɔ̃ːn.dəˈgeəʳ, ˌnɒm- ⓤⓢ ˌnɑːm.dəˈger
nom(s) de plume ˌnɔ̃ːn.dəˈpluːm, ˌnɒm- ⓤⓢ ˌnɑːm.dəˈ-
-nome -nəʊm, -noʊm
Note: Suffix. Normally unstressed, e.g. **metronome** /ˈmet.rə.nəʊm ⓤⓢ -noʊm/.
nomenclature nəʊˈmeŋ.klə.tʃəʳ; ˈnəʊ.men.kleɪ-, -mən- ⓤⓢ ˈnoʊ.men.kleɪ.tʃɚ, -mən-; noʊˈmen.klə- **-s** -z
-nomic -ˈnɒm.ɪk, -ˈnəʊ.mɪk ⓤⓢ -ˈnɑː.mɪk, -ˈnoʊ- **-s** -s
Note: Suffix. Words containing **-nomic** normally carry primary stress on the penultimate syllable, e.g. **ergonomic** /ˌɜː.gəˈnɒm.ɪk ⓤⓢ ˌɜːr.gəˈnɑː.mɪk/.
nominal ˈnɒm.ɪ.nəl, -ən.əl ⓤⓢ ˈnɑː.mə.nəl **-ly** -i
nomi|nate ˈnɒm.ɪ|.neɪt, ˈ-ə- ⓤⓢ ˈnɑː.mə- **-nates** -neɪts **-nating** -neɪ.tɪŋ ⓤⓢ -neɪ.t̬ɪŋ **-nated** -neɪ.tɪd ⓤⓢ -neɪ.t̬ɪd **-nator/s** -neɪ.təʳ/z ⓤⓢ -neɪ.t̬ɚ/z
nomination ˌnɒm.ɪˈneɪ.ʃən, -əˈ- ⓤⓢ ˌnɑː.məˈ- **-s** -z
nominative ˈnɒm.ɪ.nə.tɪv, -ən.ə- ⓤⓢ ˈnɑː.mə.nə.t̬ɪv **-s** -z
nominee ˌnɒm.ɪˈniː, -əˈ- ⓤⓢ ˌnɑː.məˈ- **-s** -z
Nomura nəʊˈmʊə.rə, -ˈmjʊə- ⓤⓢ noʊˈmuː.rə
-nomy -nə.mi
Note: Suffix. Words containing **-nomy** normally carry stress on the syllable preceding the suffix, e.g. **astronomy** /əˈstrɒn.ə.mi ⓤⓢ -ˈstrɑː.nə-/.
non- ˌnɒn- ⓤⓢ ˌnɑːn-
Note: Prefix. In words containing **non-**, the stress pattern of the stem to which it is added does not normally change, e.g. **verbal** /ˈvɜː.bəl ⓤⓢ ˈvɜːr-/, **nonverbal** /ˌnɒnˈvɜː.bəl ⓤⓢ ˌnɑːnˈvɜːr-/.
non nɒn ⓤⓢ nɑːn
non-acceptance ˌnɒn.əkˈsep.tənts, -ækˈ- ⓤⓢ ˌnɑː.nəkˈ-
nonage ˈnəʊ.nɪdʒ, ˈnɒn.ɪdʒ ⓤⓢ ˈnɑː.nɪdʒ, ˈnoʊ-, -neɪdʒ
nonagenarian ˌnəʊ.nə.dʒəˈneə.ri.ən, ˌnɒn.ə-, -dʒɪˈ- ⓤⓢ ˌnɑː.nə.dʒəˈner.i-, ˌnoʊ- **-s** -z
nonaggression ˌnɒn.əˈgreʃ.ən ⓤⓢ ˌnɑː.nəˈ-
nonagon ˈnɒn.ə.gɒn, ˈnəʊ.nə- ⓤⓢ ˈnɑː.nə.gɑːn, ˈnoʊ- **-s** -z
nonalcoholic ˌnɒn.æl.kəˈhɒl.ɪk ⓤⓢ ˌnɑː.næl.kəˈhɑː.lɪk
nonalign|ed ˌnɒn.əlˈaɪn|d ⓤⓢ ˌnɑː.nəˈlaɪn|d **-ment** -mənt
non-appearance ˌnɒn.əˈpɪə.rənts ⓤⓢ ˌnɑː.nəˈpɪr.ənts
nonary ˈnəʊ.nər.i, ˈnɒn.ər- ⓤⓢ ˈnoʊ.nɚ-, ˈnɑː-
non-attendance ˌnɒn.əˈten.dənts ⓤⓢ ˌnɑː.nəˈ-
nonbeliever ˌnɒn.bɪˈliː.vəʳ, ˌnɒm-, -bəˈ- ⓤⓢ ˌnɑːn.bɪˈliː.vɚ, -bəˈ- **-s** -z
non-biological ˌnɒnˌbaɪəˈlɒdʒ.ɪ.kəl ⓤⓢ ˌnɑːn.baɪəˈlɑː.dʒɪ-
nonc|e nɒnts ⓤⓢ nɑːnts **-es** -ɪz ˈ**nonce ˌword**
non-certifiable ˌnɒnˌsɜː.tɪˈfaɪ.ə.bl̩, -təˈ- ⓤⓢ ˌnɑːnˌsɝː.t̬əˈ-
nonchalance ˈnɒn.tʃəl.ənts ⓤⓢ ˌnɑːn.ʃəˈlɑːnts
nonchalant ˈnɒn.tʃəl.ənt ⓤⓢ ˌnɑːn.ʃəˈlɑːnt **-ly** -li
non-collegiate ˌnɒn.kəlˈiː.dʒi.ət, ˌnɒŋ-, -kɒlˈ-, ˈ-dʒət ⓤⓢ ˌnɑːn.kəˈliː.dʒɪt, -dʒi.ɪt **-s** -s
non-combatant ˌnɒnˈkɒm.bə.tənt, ˌnɒŋ-, -ˈkʌm-; -kəmˈbæt.ənt ⓤⓢ ˌnɑːn.kəmˈbæt.ənt; ˌnɑːnˈkɑːm.bə.tənt **-s** -s
noncommercial ˌnɒn.kəˈmɜː.ʃəl, ˌnɒŋ- ⓤⓢ ˌnɑːn.kəˈmɝː-
non-commissioned ˌnɒn.kəˈmɪʃ.ənd, ˌnɒŋ- ⓤⓢ ˌnɑːn- *stress shift, see compound:* ˌ**non-commissioned ˈofficer**
noncommitt|al ˌnɒn.kəˈmɪt|.əl, ˌnɒŋ- ⓤⓢ ˌnɑːn.kəˈmɪt̬- **-ally** -əl.i *stress shift:* ˌnoncommittal ˈanswer
noncompetitive ˌnɒn.kəmˈpet.ə.tɪv, ˈnɒŋ-, ˈ-ɪ- ⓤⓢ ˌnɑːn.kəmˈpet̬.ə.t̬ɪv **-ly** -li *stress shift:* ˌnoncompetitive ˈgames
non-compliance ˌnɒn.kəmˈplaɪ.ənts, ˌnɒŋ- ⓤⓢ ˌnɑːn-
non compos mentis ˌnɒnˌkɒm.pəsˈmen.tɪs, ˌnɒŋ-, -pɒs ⓤⓢ ˌnɑːnˌkɑːm.poʊsˈmen.t̬ɪs, -pəs
non-conducting ˌnɒn.kənˈdʌk.tɪŋ, ˌnɒŋ- ⓤⓢ ˌnɑːn- *stress shift:* ˌnon-conducting ˈsubstance
nonconductor ˌnɒn.kənˈdʌk.təʳ, ˌnɒŋ- ⓤⓢ ˌnɑːn.kənˈdʌk.tɚ **-s** -z
nonconform|ist ˌnɒn.kənˈfɔː.m|ɪst, ˌnɒŋ- ⓤⓢ ˌnɑːn.kənˈfɔːr- **-ists** -ɪsts **-ism** -ɪ.zəm *stress shift:* ˌnonconformist ˈstance
nonconformity ˌnɒn.kənˈfɔː.mə.ti, ˌnɒŋ-, -mɪ- ⓤⓢ ˌnɑːn.kənˈfɔːr.mə.t̬
noncontiguous ˌnɒn.kənˈtɪg.ju.əs, ˌnɒŋ-, -kɒnˈ- ⓤⓢ ˌnɑːn.kənˈ- **-ly** -li *stress shift:* ˌnoncontiguous ˈboundaries
noncontributory ˌnɒn.kənˈtrɪb.jə.tər.i, ˌnɒŋ-, -jʊ- ⓤⓢ ˌnɑːn.kənˈtrɪb.juː.tɔːr-, -jə- *stress shift:* ˌnoncontributory ˈaction
noncooperation ˌnɒn.kəʊˌɒp.ərˈeɪ.ʃ, ˌnɒŋ- ⓤⓢ ˌnɑːn.koʊˌɑː.pəˈreɪ-
noncooperationist ˌnɒn.kəʊˌɒp.ərˈeɪ.ʃən.ɪst, ˌnɒŋ- ⓤⓢ ˌnɑːn.koʊˌɑː.pəˈreɪ- **-s** -s *stress shift:* ˌnon-cooperationist ˈstance
noncorrosive ˌnɒn.kərˈəʊ.sɪv, ˌnɒŋ-, -zɪv ⓤⓢ ˌnɑːn.kəˈroʊ- *stress shift:* ˌnoncorrosive ˈacid
non-custodial ˌnɒn.kʌsˈtəʊ.di.əl, ˌnɒŋ- ⓤⓢ ˌnɑːn.kʌsˈtoʊ- *stress shift:* ˌnon-custodial ˈsentence
nondairy ˌnɒnˈdeə.ri ⓤⓢ ˌnɑːnˈder.i *stress shift:* ˌnondairy ˈproduct
non-delivery ˌnɒn.dɪˈlɪv.ər.i, -dəˈ- ⓤⓢ ˌnɑːn.dəˈ-, ˈ-ri
nondenominational ˌnɒn.dɪˌnɒm.ɪˈneɪ.ʃən.əl, -dəˌ-, -ˈneɪʃ.nəl ⓤⓢ ˌnɑːn.dəˌnɑː.məˈ- *stress shift:* ˌnondenominational ˈpolicy
nondescript ˈnɒn.dɪ.skrɪpt, -də- ⓤⓢ ˈnɑːn.dɪ-, ˌ--ˈ- **-s** -s
nondriver ˌnɒnˈdraɪ.vəʳ ⓤⓢ ˌnɑːnˈdraɪ.vɚ **-s** -z
none *(adj. pron. adv.) not any:* nʌn

none **(N)** *(n.) church service:* nəʊn (US) noʊn **-s** -z
nonentit|y ˌnɒnˈen.tə.t|i, nəˈnen-, -ɪ.t|i (US) ˌnɑːˈnen.t̬ə.t̬|i **-ies** -iz
nones **(N)** nəʊnz (US) noʊnz
non-essential ˌnɒn.ɪˈsen.tʃəl (US) ˌnɑː.nɪˈ- **-s** -z *stress shift:* ˌnon-essential ˈitem
nonesuch ˈnʌn.sʌtʃ **-es** -ɪz
nonet nəʊˈnet, nɒnˈet (US) noʊˈnet **-s** -s
nonetheless ˌnʌn.ðəˈles
non-event ˌnɒn.ɪˈvent, ˈ--- (US) ˌnɑː.nɪˈvent **-s** -s
non-existen|t ˌnɒn.ɪgˈzɪs.tən|t, -egˈ-, -ɪkˈsɪs-, -ekˈ- (US) ˌnɑː.nɪgˈzɪs-, -negˈ- **-ce** -*t*s *stress shift:* ˌnonexistent ˈmeans
nonfat ˌnɒnˈfæt (US) ˌnɑːn- *stress shift:* ˌnonfat ˈsubstance
non-feasance ˌnɒnˈfiː.zən*t*s (US) ˌnɑːn-
nonfiction ˌnɒnˈfɪk.ʃən (US) ˌnɑːn-
nonflammab|le ˌnɒnˈflæm.ə.b|l (US) ˌnɑːn- *stress shift:* ˌnonflammable ˈclothing
nonillion nəʊˈnɪl.jən, nɒnˈɪl-, ˈ-i.ən (US) noʊˈnɪl.jən **-s** -z
non-intervention ˌnɒn.ɪn.təˈven.*t*ʃən (US) ˌnɑː.nɪn.t̬ɚˈven*t*.ʃən
non-interventionist ˌnɒn.ɪn.təˈven.*t*ʃən.ɪst (US) ˌnɑː.nɪn.t̬ɚˈven*t*.ʃən- **-s** -s *stress shift:* ˌnon-interventionist ˈpolicy
nonjudgmental ˌnɒn.dʒʌdʒˈmen.təl (US) ˌnɑːn.dʒʌdʒˈmen.t̬əl **-ly** -i *stress shift:* ˌnonjudgmental ˈview
nonjuror ˌnɒnˈdʒʊə.rər (US) ˌnɑːnˈdʒʊr.ɚ, -ɔːr **-s** -z
nonlinear ˌnɒnˈlɪn.i.ər (US) ˌnɑːnˈlɪn.i.ɚ *stress shift:* ˌnonlinear ˈtheory
non-member ˌnɒnˈmem.bər, ˈ--- (US) ˌnɑːnˈmem.bɚ, ˈ--- **-s** -z
non-nuclear ˌnɒnˈnjuː.kli.ər (US) ˌnɑːnˈnuː.kli.ɚ, -ˈnjuː- *stress shift:* ˌnon-nuclear ˈpower
no-no ˈnəʊ.nəʊ (US) ˈnoʊ.noʊ **-s** -z
non-observance ˌnɒn.əbˈzɜː.vən*t*s (US) ˌnɑː.nəbˈzɝː-
non obstante ˌnɒn.ɒbˈstæn.teɪ (US) ˌnɑːn.əbˈstæn.ti, -ˈstɑːn-
non obstante verdicto ˌnɒn.ɒbˌstæn.teɪ.vəˈdɪk.təʊ (US) ˌnɑːn.əbˌstæn.ti.verˈdɪk.toʊ, -ˌstɑːn-
nonoccurrence ˌnɒn.əˈkʌr.ən*t*s (US) ˌnɑː.nəˈkɝː-
no-nonsense ˌnəʊˈnɒn*t*.sən*t*s (US) ˌnoʊˈnɑːn*t*.sen*t*s *stress shift:* ˌno-nonsense ˈattitude
nonoperational ˌnɒn.ɒp.əˈreɪ.ʃən.əl, -ˈreɪʃ.nəl (US) ˌnɑː.nɑː.pəˈreɪ.ʃən.əl, -ˈreɪʃ.nəl *stress shift:* ˌnonoperational ˈforces
nonpareil ˌnɒn.pəˈreɪl, ˌnɒm-, -ˈeɪ (US) ˌnɑːn.pəˈrel
non-payment ˌnɒnˈpeɪ.mənt, ˌnɒm- (US) ˌnɑːn-
nonplaying ˌnɒnˈpleɪ.ɪŋ, ˌnɒm- (US) ˌnɑːn- *stress shift:* ˌnonplaying ˈteam
nonplus ˌnɒnˈplʌs, ˌnɒm- (US) ˌnɑːn- **-ses** -ɪz **-sing** -ɪŋ **-sed** -t
non-profit-making ˌnɒnˈprɒf.ɪtˌmeɪ.kɪŋ, ˌnɒm- (US) ˌnɑːnˈprɑː.fɪt- *stress shift, see compound:* **ˌnon-profit-making ˌorganiˈsation**
nonproliferation ˌnɒn.prəˌlɪf.əˈreɪ.ʃən, ˌnɒm- (US) ˌnɑːn-
nonrefundable ˌnɒn.rɪˈfʌnd.ə.bl̩, -riːˈ- (US) ˌnɑːn- *stress shift:* ˌnonrefundable ˈmoney
nonresident ˌnɒnˈrez.ɪ.dənt, ˈ-ə- (US) ˌnɑːn- **-s** -s
nonrestrictive ˌnɒn.rɪˈstrɪk.tɪv, -rəˈ- (US) ˌnɑːn- *stress shift:* ˌnonrestrictive ˈclause
nonreturnable ˌnɒn.rɪˈtɜː.nə.bl̩, -rəˈ- (US) ˌnɑːn.rɪˈtɝː- *stress shift:* ˌnonreturnable ˈgoods
nonsectarian ˌnɒn.sekˈteə.ri.ən (US) ˌnɑːn.sekˈter.i- *stress shift:* ˌnonsectarian ˈviolence
nonsense ˈnɒn.sən*t*s (US) ˈnɑːn.sen*t*s, -sən*t*s **ˈnonsense ˌverse**
nonsensical ˌnɒnˈsen*t*.sɪ.kl̩ (US) ˌnɑːn- **-ly** -i **-ness** -nəs, -nɪs
non sequitur ˌnɒnˈsek.wɪ.tər, ˌnəʊn-, -wə- (US) ˌnɑːnˈsek.wɪ.t̬ɚ **-s** -z
nonskid ˌnɒnˈskɪd (US) ˌnɑːn- *stress shift:* ˌnonskid ˈsurface
nonslip ˌnɒnˈslɪp (US) ˌnɑːn- *stress shift:* ˌnonslip ˈsurface
nonsmok|er ˌnɒnˈsməʊ.k|ər (US) ˌnɑːnˈsmoʊ.k|ɚ **-ers** -əz (US) -ɚz **-ing** -ɪŋ
nonspecific ˌnɒn.spəˈsɪf.ɪk, -spɪˈ- (US) ˌnɑːn- *stress shift:* ˌnonspecific ˈorder
nonstandard ˌnɒnˈstæn.dəd (US) ˌnɑːnˈstæn.dɚd *stress shift:* ˌnonstandard ˈfitting
nonstarter ˌnɒnˈstɑː.tər (US) ˌnɑːnˈstɑːr.t̬ɚ **-s** -z
nonstick ˌnɒnˈstɪk (US) ˌnɑːn- *stress shift:* ˌnonstick ˈcoating
non-stop ˌnɒnˈstɒp (US) ˌnɑːnˈstɑːp *stress shift:* ˌnon-stop ˈmusic
nonsuch **(N)** ˈnʌn.sʌtʃ
nonsui|t ˌnɒnˈsuː|t, -ˈsjuː|t (US) ˌnɑːnˈsuː|t **-ts** -ts **-ting** -tɪŋ (US) -t̬ɪŋ **-ted** -tɪd (US) -t̬ɪd
nonswimmer ˌnɒnˈswɪm.ər (US) ˌnɑːnˈswɪm.ɚ **-s** -z
nontrivial ˌnɒnˈtrɪv.i.əl (US) ˌnɑːn- *stress shift:* ˌnontrivial ˈproblem
non-U ˌnɒnˈjuː (US) ˌnɑːn- *stress shift:* ˌnon-U ˈaccent
nonunion ˌnɒnˈjuː.njən, ˈ-ni.ən (US) ˌnɑːnˈjuː.njən *stress shift:* ˌnonunion ˈmembers
non-user ˌnɒnˈjuː.zər (US) ˌnɑːnˈjuː.zɚ *stress shift:* ˌnon-user ˈguide
nonverbal ˌnɒnˈvɜː.bəl (US) ˌnɑːnˈvɝː- *stress shift:* ˌnonverbal ˈmessage
non-violen|t ˌnɒnˈvaɪə.lən|t (US) ˌnɑːn- **-ly** -li **-ce** -*t*s *stress shift:* ˌnon-violent ˈpolicy
nonvoter ˌnɒnˈvəʊ.tər (US) ˌnɑːnˈvoʊ.t̬ɚ **-s** -z
nonwhite ˌnɒnˈwaɪt (US) ˌnɑːn- *stress shift:* ˌnonwhite ˈprejudice
noodle ˈnuː.dl̩ **-s** -z
nook nʊk **-s** -s **ˌnook and ˈcranny**
nooky, nookie ˈnʊk.i
noon nuːn **-s** -z
Noonan ˈnuː.nən
noonday ˈnuːn.deɪ
no one ˈnəʊ.wʌn (US) ˈnoʊ-
noontide ˈnuːn.taɪd
noos|e nuːs **-es** -ɪz **-ing** -ɪŋ **-ed** -t
nope nəʊp (US) noʊp
noplace ˈnəʊ.pleɪs (US) ˈnoʊ-
nor *normal form:* nɔːr (US) nɔːr *weak form:* nər (US) nɚ
Note: Occasional weak form word. The pronunciation is normally /nɔːr (US) nɔːr/, but, particularly in British English, there is a weak form /nər (US) nɚ/, as in "no use to man nor beast" /nəʊˌjuːs.təˌmæn.nəˈbiːst (US) noʊˌjuːs.təˌmæn.nɚˈ-/.
NORAD ˈnɔː.ræd (US) ˈnɔːr.æd
noradrenalin(e) ˌnɔː.rəˈdren.əl.ɪn, ˌnɒr.əˈ-, -iːn (US) ˌnɔːr.əˈdren.ə.lɪn
Nora(h) ˈnɔː.rə (US) ˈnɔːr.ə
Noraid ˈnɔː.reɪd (US) ˈnɔːr.eɪd
Norden ˈnɔː.dən (US) ˈnɔːr-
Nordenfelt ˈnɔː.dən.felt (US) ˈnɔːr-
Nordic ˈnɔː.dɪk (US) ˈnɔːr-
Nore nɔːr (US) nɔːr
Norf. *(abbrev. for* **Norfolk***)* ˈnɔː.fək (US) ˈnɔːr-, -fɔːk, -foʊk
Norfolk ˈnɔː.fək (US) ˈnɔːr-, -fɔːk, -foʊk **ˌNorfolk ˈBroads**
Norgate ˈnɔː.geɪt, -gɪt (US) ˈnɔːr-
Norham ˈnɒr.əm, ˈnɔː.rəm (US) ˈnɔːr.əm
nori ˈnɒr.i, ˈnɔː.ri (US) ˈnɔːr.i
Noriega ˌnɒr.iˈeɪ.gə (US) ˌnɔːr-
Norland ˈnɔː.lənd (US) ˈnɔːr-
norm nɔːm (US) nɔːrm **-s** -z
Norma ˈnɔː.mə (US) ˈnɔːr-
normal ˈnɔː.məl (US) ˈnɔːr- **-ly** -i
normalcy ˈnɔː.məl.si (US) ˈnɔːr-
normality nɔːˈmæl.ə.ti, -ɪ.ti (US) nɔːrˈmæl.ə.t̬i

normalization, -isa- ˌnɔː.mᵊl.aɪˈzeɪ.ʃᵊn, -ɪˈ- US ˌnɔːr.mᵊl.ɪˈ-

normaliz|e, -is|e ˈnɔː.mᵊl.aɪz US ˈnɔːr- **-es** -ɪz **-ing** -ɪŋ **-ed** -d

normally ˈnɔː.mᵊl.i US ˈnɔːr-

Norman ˈnɔː.mən US ˈnɔːr- **-s** -z **ˌNorman ˈconquest**

Normanby ˈnɔː.mən.bi, -məm- US ˈnɔːr-

Normandy *in France:* ˈnɔː.mən.di US ˈnɔːr- *in Surrey:* ˈnɔː.mən.di US ˈnɔːr- *also locally:* nɔːˈmæn.di US nɔːr-

Normanton ˈnɔː.mən.tən US ˈnɔːr-

normative ˈnɔː.mə.tɪv US ˈnɔːr.mə.t̬ɪv **-ly** -li

Norn nɔːn US nɔːrn **-s** -z

Norodom Sihanouk ˌnɒr.ə.dɒmˈsiː.jæn.ʊk US ˌnɔːr.ə.dɑːm-, -jɑː.nʊk

Norris ˈnɒr.ɪs US ˈnɔːr-

Norrköping ˈnɔː.tʃɜː.pɪŋ US ˈnɔːr-

Norroy ˈnɒr.ɔɪ US ˈnɔːr- **-s** -z

Norse nɔːs US nɔːrs **-man** -mən **-men** -mən, -men

north (N) nɔːθ US nɔːrθ **ˌNorth Aˈmerica; ˌNorth Atˈlantic; ˌNorth Caroˈlina; ˌNorth Daˈkota; ˈNorth ˌIsland; ˌNorth Koˈrea; ˌnorth ˈpole; ˌNorth ˈSea**

Northallerton ˌnɔːˈθæl.ə.tᵊn US ˌnɔːrθˈæl.ɚ.t̬ən

Northampton ˌnɔːˈθæm*p*.tən, ˌnɔːθˈhæm*p*- *locally:* nəˈθæm*p*- US ˌnɔːrˈθæm*p*-, ˌnɔːrθˈhæm*p*- **-shire** -ʃəʳ US -ʃɚ, -ˌʃɪəʳ US -ˌʃɪr

Northanger nɔːˈθæŋ.gəʳ, -əʳ; ˈnɔː.θæŋ-, ˈnɔːθ.hæŋ- US nɔːrˈθæŋ.gɚ, -ɚ; ˈnɔːr.θæŋ-, ˈnɔːrθ.hæŋ-

Northants. *(abbrev. for* **Northamptonshire***)* ˈnɔː.θænts, -ˈ- US ˈnɔːr.θænts, -ˈ-

North Baddesley ˌnɔːθˈbædz.li US ˌnɔːrθ-

northbound ˈnɔːθ.baʊnd US ˈnɔːrθ-

Northbrook ˈnɔːθ.brʊk US ˈnɔːrθ-

Northcliffe ˈnɔːθ.klɪf US ˈnɔːrθ-

Northcote ˈnɔːθ.kət, -kəʊt US ˈnɔːrθ.kət, -koʊt

northeast (N) ˌnɔːθˈiːst US ˌnɔːrθ- *nautical pronunciation:* ˌnɔːˈriːst US ˌnɔːrˈiːst **-wards** -wədz US -wɚdz *stress shift:* ˌnortheast ˈwind

northeaster ˌnɔːθˈiː.stəʳ US ˌnɔːrθˈiː.stɚ *in nautical usage also:* ˌnɔːˈriː- US ˌnɔːrˈiː- **-s** -z

northeasterl|y ˌnɔːθˈiː.stᵊl.li US ˌnɔːrθˈiː.stɚ.l|i *in nautical usage also:* ˌnɔːˈriː- US ˌnɔːrˈiː- **-ies** -iz

northeastern (N) ˌnɔːθˈiː.stən US ˌnɔːrθˈiː.stɚn *in nautical usage also:* ˌnɔːˈriː- US ˌnɔːrˈiː- **-er/s** -əʳ/z US -ɚ/z

northeastward ˌnɔːθˈiːst.wəd US ˌnɔːrθˈiːst.wɚd *in nautical usage also:* ˌnɔːˈriː- US ˌnɔːrˈiː- **-s** -z

Northen ˈnɔː.ðᵊn US ˈnɔːr-

northerl|y ˈnɔː.ðᵊl.|i US ˈnɔːr.ðɚ.l|i **-ies** -iz

northern (N) ˈnɔː.ðᵊn US ˈnɔːr.ðɚn **-most** -məʊst, -məst US -moʊst, -məst **ˌNorthern ˈIreland; ˌnorthern ˈlights; ˌNorthern ˈTerritory**

northerner (N) ˈnɔː.ðᵊn.əʳ US ˈnɔːr.ðɚ.nɚ **-s** -z

Northfield ˈnɔːθ.fiːld US ˈnɔːrθ-

Northfleet ˈnɔːθ.fliːt US ˈnɔːrθ-

northing ˈnɔː.θɪŋ US ˈnɔːr-

Northland ˈnɔːθ.lənd US ˈnɔːrθ.lænd, -lənd

North|man ˈnɔːθ|.mən US ˈnɔːrθ- **-men** -mən, -men

north-northeast ˌnɔːθ.nɔːθˈiːst US ˌnɔːrθ.nɔːrθˈ- *in nautical usage also:* ˌnɔː.nɔːˈriːst US ˌnɔːr.nɔːrˈiːst

north-northwest ˌnɔːθ.nɔːθˈwest US ˌnɔːrθ.nɔːrθˈ- *in nautical usage also:* ˌnɔː.nɔːˈ- US ˌnɔːr.nɔːrˈ-

Northolt ˈnɔː.θəʊlt US ˈnɔːr.θoʊlt

North-South ˌnɔːθˈsaʊθ US ˌnɔːrθ- **ˌNorth-ˌSouth diˈvide**

Northumberland nɔːˈθʌmb.ᵊl.ənd, nə- US nɔːrˈθʌm.bɚ.lənd

Northumbri|a nɔːˈθʌm.bri|.ə US nɔːr- **-an/s** -ən/z

northward ˈnɔːθ.wəd US ˈnɔːrθ.wɚd **-s** -z **-ly** -li

northwest (N) ˌnɔːθˈwest US ˌnɔːrθ- *nautical pronunciation:* ˌnɔːˈwest US ˌnɔːr- **-wards** -wədz US -wɚdz *stress shift, see compound:* **ˌNorthwest ˈTerritories**

northwesterl|y ˌnɔːθˈwes.tᵊl.|i US ˌnɔːrθˈwes.tɚ.l|i *in nautical usage also:* ˌnɔː- US ˌnɔːr- **-ies** -iz

northwestern (N) ˌnɔːθˈwes.tən US ˌnɔːrθˈwes.tɚn *in nautical usage also:* ˌnɔː- US ˌnɔːr- **-er/s** -əʳ/z US -ɚ/z

northwestward ˌnɔːθˈwest.wəd US ˌnɔːrθˈwest.wɚd *in nautical usage also:* ˌnɔː- US ˌnɔːr-

Northwich ˈnɔːθ.wɪtʃ US ˈnɔːrθ-

Northwood ˈnɔːθ.wʊd US ˈnɔːrθ-

Norton ˈnɔː.tᵊn US ˈnɔːr-

Norton Radstock ˌnɔː.tᵊnˈræd.stɒk US ˌnɔːr.tᵊnˈræd.stɑːk

Norway ˈnɔː.weɪ US ˈnɔːr-

Norwegian nɔːˈwiː.dʒᵊn US nɔːr- **-s** -z

Norwich *in England:* ˈnɒr.ɪdʒ, -ɪtʃ US ˈnɔːr.ɪtʃ, -wɪtʃ *in US:* ˈnɔː.wɪtʃ US ˈnɔːr-

Norwood ˈnɔː.wʊd US ˈnɔːr-

nos. (N) *(abbrev. for* **numbers***)* ˈnʌm.bəz US -bɚz

nos|e nəʊz US noʊz **-es** -ɪz **-ing** -ɪŋ **-ed** -d **ˈnose ˌring; ˌcut off one's ˌnose to ˌspite one's ˈface; ˌkeep one's ˌnose to the ˈgrindstone; ˌlook down one's ˈnose at; ˌpay through the ˈnose (for); ˌpoke one's ˈnose (into)**

nosebag ˈnəʊz.bæg US ˈnoʊz- **-s** -z

nosebleed ˈnəʊz.bliːd US ˈnoʊz- **-s** -z

nosediv|e ˈnəʊz.daɪv US ˈnoʊz- **-es** -z **-ing** -ɪŋ **-ed** -d

no-see-um ˌnəʊˈsiː.əm US ˌnoʊ- **-s** -z

nosegay ˈnəʊz.geɪ US ˈnoʊz- **-s** -z

nos|ey ˈnəʊ.z|i US ˈnoʊ- **-ier** -i.əʳ US -i.ɚ **-iest** -i.ɪst, -i.əst **-ily** -ɪ.li, -ᵊl.i **-iness** -ɪ.nəs, -ɪ.nɪs

Nosferatu ˌnɒs.fəˈrɑː.tuː US ˌnɑːs-

nosh nɒʃ US nɑːʃ **-es** -ɪz **-ing** -ɪŋ **-ed** -t

no-show ˌnəʊˈʃəʊ US ˈnoʊˌʃoʊ *stress shift, British only:* ˌno-show ˈpassenger

nosh-up ˈnɒʃ.ʌp US ˈnɑːʃ- **-s** -s

nostalg|ia nɒsˈtæl.dʒ|ə, -dʒ|i.ə US nɑːˈstæl.dʒ|ə, nə-, nɔː-, -dʒ|i.ə **-ic** -ɪk **-ically** -ɪ.kᵊl.i, -ɪ.kli

Nostradamus ˌnɒs.trəˈdeɪ.məs, -ˈdɑː- US ˌnoʊ.strəˈdɑː-, ˌnɑː.strəˈdeɪ-

nostril ˈnɒs.trᵊl, -trɪl US ˈnɑː.strᵊl **-s** -z

Nostromo nɒsˈtrəʊ.məʊ US nɑːˈstroʊ.moʊ

nostrum ˈnɒs.trəm US ˈnɑː.strəm **-s** -z

nos|y ˈnəʊ.z|i US ˈnoʊ- **-ier** -i.əʳ US -i.ɚ **-iest** -i.ɪst, -i.əst **-ily** -ɪ.li, -ᵊl.i **-iness** -ɪ.nəs, -ɪ.nɪs

nosy parker ˌnəʊ.ziˈpɑː.kəʳ US ˌnoʊ.ziˈpɑːr.kɚ **-s** -z

not nɒt US nɑːt

nota bene ˌnəʊ.tɑːˈben.eɪ, -təˈbiː.ni US ˌnoʊ.t̬əˈben.eɪ, -tɑːˈ-, -ˈbiː.ni

notabilit|y ˌnəʊ.təˈbɪl.ə.t|i, -ɪ.t|i US ˌnoʊ.t̬əˈbɪl.ə.t̬|i **-ies** -iz

notab|le ˈnəʊ.tə.b|l̩ US ˈnoʊ.t̬ə- **-ly** -li **-leness** -l̩.nəs, -nɪs

notarial nəʊˈteə.ri.əl US noʊˈter.i- **-ly**

notariz|e, -is|e ˈnəʊ.tᵊr.aɪz US ˈnoʊ.t̬ə.raɪz **-es** -ɪz **-ing** -ɪŋ **-ed**

notar|y ˈnəʊ.tᵊr|.i US ˈnoʊ.t̬ɚ- **-ies** -iz

nota|te nəʊˈteɪ|t US ˈnoʊ.teɪ|t **-tes** -ts **-ting** -tɪŋ US -t̬ɪŋ **-ted** -tɪd US -t̬ɪd

notation nəʊˈteɪ.ʃᵊn US noʊ- **-s** -z

notch nɒtʃ US nɑːtʃ **-es** -ɪz **-ing** -ɪŋ **-ed** -t

not|e nəʊt US noʊt **-es** -s **-ing** -ɪŋ US ˈnoʊ.t̬ɪŋ **-ed** -ɪd US ˈnoʊ.t̬ɪd

notebook ˈnəʊt.bʊk US ˈnoʊt- **-s** -s

notelet ˈnəʊt.lət, -lɪt US ˈnoʊt- **-s** -s

notepad ˈnəʊt.pæd US ˈnoʊt- **-s** -z

notepaper ˈnəʊtˌpeɪ.pəʳ US ˈnoʊtˌpeɪ.pɚ

noteworth|y ˈnəʊtˌwɜː.ð|i

(US) ˈnoʊtˌwɝː- **-ily** -ɪ.li, -ᵊl.i **-iness** -ɪ.nəs, -ɪ.nɪs
not-for-profit ˌnɒt.fəˈprɒf.ɪt (US) ˌnɑːt.fɚˈprɑː.fɪt
nothing ˈnʌθ.ɪŋ **-s** -z **-ness** -nəs, -nɪs
notic|e ˈnəʊ.tɪs (US) ˈnoʊ.t̬ɪs **-es** -ɪz **-ing** -ɪŋ **-ed** -t
noticeab|le ˈnəʊ.tɪ.sə.b|l̩ (US) ˈnoʊ.t̬ɪ- **-ly** -li
notice-board ˈnəʊ.tɪs.bɔːd (US) ˈnoʊ.t̬ɪs.bɔːrd **-s** -z
notifiable ˈnəʊ.tɪ.faɪ.ə.bl̩, -tə-, ˌnəʊ.tɪˈfaɪ-, -təˈ- (US) ˈnoʊ.t̬ə.faɪ-
notification ˌnəʊ.tɪ.fɪˈkeɪ.ʃᵊn, -tə- (US) ˌnoʊ.t̬ə- **-s** -z
noti|fy ˈnəʊ.tɪ|.faɪ, -tə- (US) ˈnoʊ.t̬ə- **-fies** -faɪz **-fying** -faɪ.ɪŋ **-fied** -faɪd
notion ˈnəʊ.ʃᵊn (US) ˈnoʊ- **-s** -z
notional ˈnəʊ.ʃᵊn.ᵊl, ˈnəʊʃ.nᵊl (US) ˈnoʊ.ʃᵊn.ᵊl, ˈnoʊʃ.nᵊl **-ly** -i
notoriety ˌnəʊ.tᵊrˈaɪ.ə.ti (US) ˌnoʊ.t̬əˈraɪ.ə.t̬i
notorious nəʊˈtɔː.ri.əs (US) noʊˈtɔːr.i- **-ly** -li **-ness** -nəs, -nɪs
Notre Dame *in France:* ˌnəʊ.trəˈdɑːm, ˌnɒt.rəˈ- (US) ˌnoʊ.trəˈ-, ˌnoʊ.t̬ɚˈ-, -ˈdeɪm *in the US:* ˌnəʊ.trəˈdeɪm (US) ˌnoʊ.t̬ɚˈ-
Nottingham ˈnɒt.ɪŋ.əm (US) ˈnɑː.t̬ɪŋ- **-shire** -ʃəʳ, -ˌʃɪəʳ (US) -ʃɚ, -ˌʃɪr
Notting Hill ˌnɒt.ɪŋˈhɪl (US) ˌnɑː.t̬ɪŋˈ- *stress shift, see compound:* ˌ**Notting Hill** ˈ**Gate**
Notts. *(abbrev. for* **Nottinghamshire***)* nɒts (US) nɑːts
notwithstanding ˌnɒt.wɪθˈstæn.dɪŋ, -wɪðˈ- (US) ˌnɑːt-
Nouakchott nuˈɑːk.ʃɒt (US) ˈnwɑːk.ʃɑːt, -ˈ-
nougat ˈnuː.gɑː, ˈnʌg.ət (US) ˈnuː.gət **nougats** ˈnuː.gɑːz, ˈnʌg.əts (US) ˈnuː.gəts
nought nɔːt (US) nɑːt, nɔːt **-s** -s ˌ**noughts and** ˈ**crosses**
noumen|on ˈnuː.mə.n|ən, ˈnaʊ-, -mɪ-, -n|ɒn (US) ˈnuː.mə.n|ɑːn **-a** -ə **-al** -ᵊl
noun naʊn **-s** -z
nourish ˈnʌr.ɪʃ (US) ˈnɝː- **-es** -ɪz **-ing** -ɪŋ **-ed** -t **-ment** -mənt
nourishing ˈnʌr.ɪ.ʃɪŋ (US) ˈnɝː-
nous naʊs (US) nuːs, naʊs
nouveau(x) ˈnuː.vəʊ, -ˈ- (US) nuːˈvoʊ, ˈ--
nouveau(x) riche(s) ˌnuː.vəʊˈriːʃ (US) -voʊˈ-
nouveau roman ˌnuː.vəʊ.rəʊˈmɑ̃ːŋ (US) -voʊ.roʊˈmɑːn
nouvelle cuisine ˌnuː.vel.kwɪˈziːn, nuːˌvel-, -kwəˈ-, -kwiː- (US) nuːˌvel-
nouvelle vague (N) ˌnuː.velˈvɑːg
Nov. *(abbrev. for* **November***)* nɒv, nəʊˈvem.bəʳ (US) noʊˈvem.bɚ

nov|a (N) ˈnəʊ.v|ə (US) ˈnoʊ- **-ae** -iː **-as** -əz
Nova Scotia ˌnəʊ.vəˈskəʊ.ʃə (US) ˌnoʊ.vəˈskoʊ-
novation nəʊˈveɪ.ʃᵊn (US) noʊ-
Novaya Zemlya ˌnɒv.ə.jə.zemˈljɑː, -ɑː- (US) ˌnɔː.vɑː.jɑː-, ˌnoʊ-
novel ˈnɒv.ᵊl (US) ˈnɑː.vᵊl **-istic** --ˈɪs.tɪk **-s** -z
novelette ˌnɒv.ᵊlˈet (US) ˌnɑː.vᵊlˈ- **-s** -s
novelist ˈnɒv.ᵊl.ɪst (US) ˈnɑː.və- **-s** -s
novelization, -isation ˌnɒv.ᵊl.aɪˈzeɪ.ʃᵊn, -ɪˈ- (US) ˌnɑː.vᵊl.ɪˈ- **-s** -z
noveliz|e, -is|e ˈnɒv.ᵊl.aɪz (US) ˈnɑː.və.laɪz **-es** -ɪz **-ing** -ɪŋ **-ed** -d
novel|la nəʊˈvel|.ə (US) noʊ- **-las** -z **-le** -eɪ
Novello nəˈvel.əʊ (US) -oʊ
novelt|y ˈnɒv.ᵊl.t|i (US) ˈnɑː.vᵊl.t̬|i **-ies** -iz
November nəʊˈvem.bəʳ (US) noʊˈvem.bɚ **-s** -z
novena nəʊˈviː.nə (US) noʊ- **-s** -z
Novgorod ˈnɒv.gə.rɒd (US) ˈnɔːv.gə.rɑːd, ˈnɑːv-, -rɑːt
Novial ˈnəʊ.vi.əl (US) ˈnoʊ-
novic|e ˈnɒv.ɪs (US) ˈnɑː.vɪs **-es** -ɪz
novitiate nəʊˈvɪʃ.i.ət, nɒvˈɪʃ-, -eɪt, -ɪt (US) noʊˈvɪʃ.ɪt, ˈ-i.ɪt, -eɪt **-s** -s
Novocaine® ˈnəʊ.vəʊ.keɪn, ˈnɒv.əʊ- (US) ˈnoʊ.və-
Novosibirsk ˌnəʊ.vəʊ.sɪˈbɪəsk, ˌnɒv.əʊ-, -səˈ- (US) ˌnoʊ.və.sɪˈbɪrsk, -səˈ-
Novotna nəʊˈvɒt.nə, ˈnɒv.ɒt.nə (US) nəˈvɑːt.nə
Novum Organum ˌnəʊ.vəmˈɔː.gə.nəm, -ɔːˈgɑː.nəm (US) ˌnoʊ.vəmˈɔːr.gə.nəm; -ɔːrˈgæn-
now naʊ
NOW naʊ
nowadays ˈnaʊ.ə.deɪz, ˈnaʊə-
Nowell *personal name:* nəʊəl; ˈnəʊ.el (US) noʊəl; ˈnoʊ.el *Christmas:* nəʊˈel (US) noʊ-
nowhere ˈnəʊ.*h*weəʳ (US) ˈnoʊ.*h*wer
no-win ˌnəʊˈwɪn (US) ˌnoʊ- *stress shift, see compound:* ˌ**no-win situ**ˈ**ation**
nowise ˈnəʊ.waɪz (US) ˈnoʊ-
nowt naʊt
noxious ˈnɒk.ʃəs (US) ˈnɑːk- **-ly** -li **-ness** -nəs, -nɪs
Noye nɔɪ
Noyes nɔɪz
nozzle ˈnɒz.l̩ (US) ˈnɑː.zl̩ **-s** -z
nr *(abbrev. for* **near***)* nɪəʳ (US) nɪr
NSPCC ˌen.esˌpiː.siːˈsiː
-n't -ᵊnt
Note: Weak form suffix. This spelling represents a weak form of **not** which occurs after auxiliary verbs.

nth enθ
nu njuː (US) nuː, njuː
nuanc|e ˈnjuː.ɑːnts, -ɑ̃ːns, -ˈ- (US) ˈnuː.ɑːnts, ˈnjuː-, -ˈ- **-es** -ɪz
nub nʌb
nubble ˈnʌb.l̩ **-s** -z
nubbly ˈnʌb.li, -l̩.i
Nubi|a ˈnjuː.bi|.ə (US) ˈnuː-, ˈnjuː- **-an/s** -ən/z
nubile ˈnjuː.baɪl (US) ˈnuː.bɪl, ˈnjuː-, -baɪl, -bᵊl
nubility njuːˈbɪl.ə.ti, -ɪ.ti (US) nuːˈbɪl.ə.t̬i, njuː-
nuclear ˈnjuː.kli.əʳ (US) ˈnuː.kli.ɚ, ˈnjuː- ˌ**nuclear dis**ˈ**armament**; ˌ**nuclear** ˈ**energy**; ˌ**nuclear** ˈ**family**; ˌ**nuclear** ˈ**fusion**; ˌ**nuclear** ˈ**industry**; ˌ**nuclear re**ˈ**actor**; ˌ**nuclear** ˈ**winter**
nuclear-free ˌnjuː.kli.əˈfriː (US) ˌnuː.kli.ɚˈ-, ˌnjuː- *stress shift, British only, see compound:* ˌ**nuclear-free** ˈ**zone** (US) ˌ**nuclear-**ˈ**free** ˌ**zone**
nucleic njuːˈkliː.ɪk, -ˈkleɪ- (US) nuːˈkliː-, njuː-, -ˈkleɪ- **nu**ˌ**cleic** ˈ**acid**
nucleo- ˌnjuː.kli.əʊ- (US) ˌnuː.kli.oʊ-, ˌnjuː-, -ə-
nucleol|us njuːˈkliː.ᵊl|.əs; ˌnjuː.kliˈəʊ.l|əs (US) nuːˈkliː.ᵊl|.əs, njuː- **-i** -aɪ
nucleotide ˈnjuː.kli.əʊ.taɪd (US) ˈnuː.kli.oʊ-, ˈnjuː- **-s** -z
nucle|us ˈnjuː.kli|.əs (US) ˈnuː-, ˈnjuː- **-uses** -əs.ɪz **-i** -aɪ
nuclide ˈnjuː.klaɪd (US) ˈnuː-, ˈnjuː- **-s** -z
nude njuːd (US) nuːd, njuːd **-s** -z
nudg|e nʌdʒ **-es** -ɪz **-ing** -ɪŋ **-ed** -d
nud|ism ˈnjuː.dɪ|.zᵊm (US) ˈnuː-, ˈnjuː- **-ist/s** -ɪst/s
nudit|y ˈnjuː.də.t|i, -ɪ.t|i (US) ˈnuː.də.t̬|i, ˈnjuː-
Nuevo Leon nweɪ.vəʊ.leɪˈɒn (US) nuːˈeɪ.voʊ.leɪˈɑːn
Nuffield ˈnʌf.iːld
nugatory ˈnjuː.gə.tᵊr.i; njuːˈgeɪ- (US) ˈnuː.gə.tɔːr-, ˈnjuː-
Nugent ˈnjuː.dʒᵊnt (US) ˈnuː-, ˈnjuː-
nugg|et ˈnʌg|.ɪt **-ets** -ɪts **-ety** -ɪ.ti (US) -ɪ.t̬i
nuisanc|e ˈnjuː.sᵊnts (US) ˈnuː-, ˈnjuː- **-es** -ɪz
Nuit nʌt (US) nʌt, nuːt
NUJ ˌen.juːˈdʒeɪ
nuk|e njuːk (US) nuːk, njuːk **-es** -s **-ing** -ɪŋ **-ed** -t
Nuku'alofa ˌnuː.kuː.əˈlɔː.fə
null nʌl ˌ**null and** ˈ**void**
nullah ˈnʌl.ə **-s** -z
Nullarbor ˈnʌl.ə.bɔːʳ (US) -ɚ.bɔːr ˌ**Nullarbor** ˈ**Plains**
nullification ˌnʌl.ɪ.fɪˈkeɪ.ʃᵊn, ˌ-ə-

nulli|fy 'nʌl.ɪ|.faɪ, '-ə- **-fies** -faɪz **-fying** -faɪ.ɪŋ **-fied** -faɪd

nullipar|a nʌl'ɪp.ər|.ə US nʌl-, nə'lɪp- **-ae** -iː **-as** -əz **-ous** -əs

nullit|y 'nʌl.ə.t|i, -ɪ.t|i US -ə.ţ|i **-ies** -iz

NUM ˌen.juː'em

Numa Pompilius ˌnjuː.mə.pɒm'pɪl.i.əs US ˌnuː.mə.pɑːm'-, ˌnjuː-

numb nʌm **-ly** -li **-ness** -nəs, -nɪs **-s** -z **-ing** -ɪŋ **-ed** -d

numbat 'nʌm.bæt **-s** -s

numb|er 'nʌm.b|əʳ US -b|ɚ **-ers** -əz US -ɚz **-ering** -ər.ɪŋ **-ered** -əd US -ɚd **-erless** -əl.əs, -ɪs US -ɚ.ləs, -lɪs **ˌnumber 'one** *stress shift:* ˌnumber one 'fan; **ˌNumber '10/Ten** *stress shift:* ˌNumber 10/Ten 'Downing Street

number-crunch 'nʌm.bə.krʌntʃ US -bɚ- **-es** -ɪz **-ing** -ɪŋ **-ed** -t **-er/s** -əʳ/z US -ɚ/z

numberplate 'nʌm.bə.pleɪt US -bɚ- **-s** -s

Numbers 'nʌm.bəz US -bɚz

numbing 'nʌm.ɪŋ **-ly** -li

numbskull 'nʌm.skʌl **-s** -z

numerable 'njuː.mər.ə.bl̩ US 'nuː-, 'njuː-

numeracy 'njuː.mər.ə.si US 'nuː-, 'njuː-

numeral 'njuː.mər.əl US 'nuː-, 'njuː- **-s** -z

numerate *(adj.)* 'njuː.mər.ət, -ɪt US 'nuː-, 'njuː-

numer|ate *(v.)* 'njuː.mər|.eɪt US 'nuː.mə.r|eɪt, 'njuː- **-ates** -eɪts **-ating** -eɪ.tɪŋ US -eɪ.ţɪŋ **-ated** -eɪ.tɪd US -eɪ.ţɪd

numeration ˌnjuː.mər'eɪ.ʃən US ˌnuː.mə'reɪ-, ˌnjuː-

numerative 'njuː.mər.ə.tɪv US 'nuː.mɚ.ə.ţɪv, 'njuː- **-s** -z

numerator 'njuː.mər.eɪ.təʳ US 'nuː.mə.reɪ.ţɚ, 'njuː- **-s** -z

numeric njuː'mer.ɪk US nuː-, njuː- **-s** -s

numerical njuː'mer.ɪ.kl̩ US nuː-, njuː- **-ly** -i

numerologic|al ˌnjuː.mər.ə'lɒdʒ.ɪ.k|əl US ˌnuː.mɚ.ə'lɑː.dʒɪ-, ˌnjuː- **-ally** -əl.i, -li

numerolog|y ˌnjuː.mər'ɒl.ə.dʒ|i US ˌnuː.mə'rɑː.lə-, ˌnjuː- **-ist** -ɪst/s

numero uno ˌnuː.mər.əʊ'uː.nəʊ US ˌnuː.mə.roʊ'uː.noʊ, ˌnjuː-

numerous 'njuː.mər.əs US 'nuː-, 'njuː- **-ly** -li **-ness** -nəs, -nɪs

Numidi|a njuː'mɪd.i|.ə US nuː-, njuː- **-an/s** -ən/z

numinous 'njuː.mɪ.nəs US 'nuː-, 'njuː-

numismatic ˌnjuː.mɪz'mæt.ɪk US ˌnuː.mɪz'mæţ.ɪk, ˌnjuː- **-s** -s **-ally** -əl.i, -li

numismatist njuː'mɪz.mə.tɪst US nuː-, njuː- **-s** -s

numnah 'nʌm.nə **-s** -z

numskull 'nʌm.skʌl **-s** -z

nun (N) nʌn **-s** -z

Nunc Dimittis ˌnʊŋk.dɪ'mɪt.ɪs, ˌnʌŋk-, -daɪ'-, -də'- US ˌnʊŋk.dɪ'mɪţ- **-es** -ɪz

nunciature 'nʌnt.si.ə.tjʊəʳ, -tʃəʳ US -tjʊr, -tʃɚ

nuncio 'nʌn.ʃi.əʊ, -ʃəʊ, 'nʌnt.si- US 'nʌnt.si.oʊ, 'nʊnt- **-s** -z

Nuneaton nʌn'iː.tən

Nuneham 'njuː.nəm US 'nuː-, 'njuː-

Nunn nʌn

nunner|y 'nʌn.ər|.i **-ies** -iz

NUPE *trades union:* 'njuː.pi US 'nuː-, 'njuː-

Nupe *language and people:* 'nuː.peɪ **-s** -z

nuptial 'nʌp.ʃəl, -tʃəl **-s** -z

Nuremberg 'njʊə.rəm.bɜːg, 'njɔː- US 'nʊr.əm.bɝːg, 'njʊr-

Nureyev 'njʊə.ri.ef; -reɪ-, njʊə'reɪ-, -ev US 'nʊr.i.ef, nʊ'reɪ.jef

Nurofen® 'njʊə.rəʊ.fen, 'njɔː- US nuː'roʊ.fən, njʊ'-

nurs|e nɜːs US nɝːs **-es** -ɪz **-ing** -ɪŋ **-ed** -t

nurs(e)ling 'nɜːs.lɪŋ US 'nɝːs- **-s** -z

nursemaid 'nɜːs.meɪd US 'nɝːs- **-s** -z

nurser|y 'nɜː.sər|.i US 'nɝː- **-ies** -iz **'nursery ˌrhyme; 'nursery ˌschool; 'nursery ˌslope**

nurserymaid 'nɜː.sər.i.meɪd US 'nɝː- **-s** -z

nursery|man 'nɜː.sər.i|.mən US 'nɝː- **-men** -mən

nursing 'nɜː.sɪŋ US 'nɝː- **'nursing ˌhome; ˌnursing 'mother**

nurt|ure 'nɜː.tʃ|əʳ US 'nɝː.tʃ|ɚ **-ures** -əz US -ɚz **-uring** -ər.ɪŋ **-ured** -əd US -ɚd

NUS ˌen.juː'es

nut *food:* nʌt **-s** -s **-ting** -ɪŋ **-ted** -ɪd

Nut *Egyptian goddess:* nʌt US nʌt, nuːt

NUT *trades union:* ˌen.juː'tiː

nu|tate njuː|'teɪt US nuː-, njuː- **-tates** -'teɪts **-tating** -'teɪ.tɪŋ US -'teɪ.ţɪŋ **-tated** -'teɪ.tɪd US -'teɪ.ţɪd

nutation njuː'teɪ.ʃən US nuː-, njuː- **-al** **-s** -z

nut-brown ˌnʌt'braʊn *stress shift:* ˌnut-brown 'hair

nutcas|e 'nʌt.keɪs **-es** -ɪz

nutcracker 'nʌtˌkræk.əʳ US -ɚ **-s** -z

nuthatch 'nʌt.hætʃ **-es** -ɪz

nuthou|se 'nʌt.haʊ|s **-ses** -zɪz

Nutkin 'nʌt.kɪn

nutmeg 'nʌt.meg **-s** -z

nutraceutical ˌnjuː.trə'sjuː.tɪ.kəl, -'suː-, -'kjuː- US ˌnuː.trə'suː.ţɪ-, ˌnjuː-, -'sjuː- **-s** -z

Nutrasweet® 'njuː.trəˌswiːt US 'nuː-, 'njuː

nutria 'njuː.tri.ə US 'nuː-, 'njuː-

nutrient 'njuː.tri.ənt US 'nuː-, 'njuː-

nutriment 'njuː.trə.mənt, -trɪ- US 'nuː-, 'njuː- **-s** -s

nutrition njuː'trɪʃ.ən US nuː-, njuː- **-al** -əl **-ally** -əl.i

nutritionist njuː'trɪʃ.ən.ɪst, -'trɪʃ.nɪs US nuː-, njuː- **-s** -s

nutritious njuː'trɪʃ.əs US nuː-, njuː- - -li **-ness** -nəs, -nɪs

nutritive 'njuː.trə.tɪv, -trɪ- US 'nuː.trə.ţɪv, 'njuː-

nuts nʌts **ˌnuts and 'bolts**

nutshell 'nʌt.ʃel **-s** -z

Nutt nʌt

Nuttall 'nʌt.ɔːl

nutter (N) 'nʌt.əʳ US 'nʌţ.ɚ

nutt|y 'nʌt|.i US 'nʌţ|.i **-ily** -ɪ.li **-iness** -ɪ.nəs, -ɪ.nɪs

nux vomica ˌnʌks'vɒm.ɪ.kə US -'vɑː.mɪ-

nuzzl|e 'nʌz.l̩ **-es** -z **-ing** -ɪŋ, 'nʌz.lɪŋ **-ed** -d

NVQ ˌen.viː'kjuː

NW *(abbrev. for* **northwest***)* ˌen'dʌb.l̩.juː; ˌnɔːθ'west US ˌen'dʌb.l̩.juː; ˌnɔːrθ-

NY *(abbrev. for* **New York***)* ˌen'waɪ

Nyanja 'njæn.dʒə

Nyanza ni'æn.zə, naɪ-; 'njæn- US 'njæn-, ni'æn-, naɪ-

Nyasa naɪ'æs.ə, ni-; 'njæs- US naɪ'æs 'njɑː.sɑː

Nyasaland naɪ'æs.ə.lænd, ni-; 'njæs- US naɪ'æs-; 'njɑː.sɑː.lænd

Nyerere njə'reə.ri, nɪə-, -'rer.i US njə'rer-, ˌni.ə'-

nylon 'naɪ.lɒn US -lɑːn **-s** -z

Nyman 'naɪ.mən

Nymex 'naɪ.meks

nymph nɪmpf **-s** -s **-al** -əl

nymphet, nymphette nɪmp'fet; 'nɪmp.fɪt, -fət, -fet US 'nɪmp.fət; nɪmp'fet

nympho 'nɪmp.fəʊ US -foʊ **-s** -z

nymphomani|a ˌnɪmp.fəʊ'meɪ.ni|.ə US -foʊ'-, -fə'-, '-nj|ə **-ac/s** -æk

Nyree 'naɪə.riː, -ri US 'naɪ-

nystagmus nɪ'stæg.məs

NZ *(abbrev. for* **New Zealand***)* ˌen'ze US -'ziː

Pronouncing the letter O

See also OA, OEU, OI/OY, OO, OU, OW

The vowel letter **o** has several pronunciations. The two most predictable strong pronunciations linked to spelling are: a monophthongal pronunciation, sometimes described as 'short' in British English /ɒ (US) ɑː ɔː/ and a diphthongal pronunciation, sometimes described as 'long' /əʊ (US) oʊ/. In the monophthongal pronunciation, the **o** is generally followed by a consonant which closes the syllable, or a double consonant before another vowel, e.g.:

cod	/kɒd/	(US) /kɑːd/
robbing	/ˈrɒb.ɪŋ/	(US) /ˈrɑː.bɪŋ/

The diphthongal pronunciation usually means the **o** is followed by a single consonant and then a vowel, e.g.:

code	/kəʊd/	(US) /koʊd/
robing	/ˈrəʊ.bɪŋ/	(US) /ˈroʊ.bɪŋ/

In many cases, the monophthongal pronunciation results from the above kind of spelling, e.g.:

gone	/gɒn/	(US) /gɑːn/
copy	/ˈkɒp.i/	(US) /ˈkɑː.pi/

Also, the 'long' pronunciation occasionally appears in words where the vowel is followed by a single consonant and no vowel, e.g.:

control	/kənˈtrəʊl/	(US) /-ˈtroʊl/

When **r** is followed by **o**, the strong pronunciation is one of several possibilities: /ɒ (US) ɔːr/, /ɔː (US) ɔːr/, /ʌ (US) ɝː/ or /ɜː (US) ɝː/, e.g.:

forest	/ˈfɒr.ɪst/	(US) /ˈfɔːr-/
foremost	/ˈfɔː.məʊst/	(US) /ˈfɔːr.moʊst/
borough	/ˈbʌr.ə/	(US) /ˈbɝː-/
word	/wɜːd/	(US) /wɝːd/

And exceptionally, /ʊ/, e.g.:

Worcester	/ˈwʊs.təʳ/	(US) /-tɚ/

In addition

There are other vowel sounds associated with the letter **o**, e.g.:

/ʌ/	colour	/ˈkʌl.əʳ/	(US) /-ɚ/
/uː/	move	/muːv/	
/ʊ/	woman	/ˈwʊm.ən/	
/wʌ/	once	/wʌnts/	
/ɜː (US) ɝː/	colonel	/ˈkɜː.nəl/	(US) /ˈkɝː-/

And, exceptionally:

/ɪ/	women	/ˈwɪm.ɪn/

In weak syllables

The vowel letter **o** is realised with the vowel /ə/ in weak syllables, /ɚ/ in American English when followed by an **r**, and may also be elided in British English, due to compression or realisation as a syllabic consonant, e.g.:

observe	/əbˈzɜːv/	(US) /-ˈzɝːv/
forget	/fəˈget/	(US) /fɚ-/
factory	/ˈfæk.tər.i/, /-tri/	

the letter: əʊ (US) oʊ **-'s** -z **-es** -z

(interjection) əʊ (US) oʊ

' *(abbrev. for* **of***) weak form only:* ə

Note: This spelling is used to represent a weak form of **of** in archaic and slang expressions and names, for example "pint o' bitter" /ˌpaɪnt.əˈbɪt.əʳ (US) -ˈbɪt̬.ɚ/, "will-o'-the-wisp" /ˌwɪl.ə.ðəˈwɪsp/.

. *(abbrev. of* **Ohio***)* əʊ; əʊˈhaɪ.əʊ (US) oʊ; oʊˈhaɪ.oʊ, ə-

adby ˈəʊd.bi (US) ˈoʊd-

af əʊf (US) oʊf **-s** -s

afish ˈəʊ.fɪʃ (US) ˈoʊ- **-ly** -li **-ness** -nəs, -nɪs

ahu əʊˈɑː.huː (US) oʊ-

ak əʊk (US) oʊk **-s** -s **-en** -ən **-y** -i

ak-apple ˈəʊkˌæp.l̩ (US) ˈoʊk- **-s** -z

akdale ˈəʊk.deɪl (US) ˈoʊk-

akeley ˈəʊk.li (US) ˈoʊk-

akengates ˈəʊ.kən.geɪts, -kəŋ-, ˌ--ˈ- (US) ˈoʊk.ən.geɪts, ˌ--ˈ-

akes əʊks (US) oʊks

akey ˈəʊ.ki (US) ˈoʊ-

Oakham ˈəʊ.kəm (US) ˈoʊ-

Oakhampton ˌəʊkˈhæmp.tən (US) ˈoʊkˌhæmp- *stress shift, British only:* ˌOakhampton ˈcentre

Oakland ˈəʊk.lənd (US) ˈoʊk- **-s** -z

Oakleigh, Oakley ˈəʊk.li (US) ˈoʊk-

Oaks əʊks (US) oʊks

oakum ˈəʊ.kəm (US) ˈoʊ-

Oakworth ˈəʊk.wəθ, -wɜːθ (US) ˈoʊk.wɚθ, -wɝːθ

OAP ˌəʊ.eɪˈpiː (US) ˌoʊ- **-s** -z

OAPEC ˌəʊˈeɪ.pek (US) ˌoʊ-

oar ɔːʳ (US) ɔːr **-s** -z **-ing** -ɪŋ **-ed** -d **ˌstick one's ˈoar in**

oarlock ˈɔː.lɒk (US) ˈɔːr.lɑːk **-s** -s

oars|man ˈɔːz|.mən (US) ˈɔːrz- **-men** -mən **-woman** -ˌwʊm.ən **-women** -ˌwɪm.ɪn

OAS ˌəʊ.eɪ.ˈes (US) ˌoʊ-

oas|is (O) əʊˈeɪ.s|ɪs (US) oʊ- **-es** -iːz

oast əʊst (US) oʊst **-s** -s

oasthou|se ˈəʊst.haʊ|s (US) ˈoʊst- **-ses** -zɪz

oat əʊt (US) oʊt **-s** -s

oatcake ˈəʊt.keɪk (US) ˈoʊt- **-s** -s

oaten ˈəʊ.tən (US) ˈoʊ-

Oates əʊts (US) oʊts

oa|th əʊ|θ (US) oʊ|θ **-ths** -ðz, -θs

Oatlands ˈəʊt.ləndz (US) ˈoʊt-

oatmeal ˈəʊt.miːl (US) ˈoʊt-

oats əʊts (US) oʊts

Oaxaca wəˈhɑː.kə, wɑː- (US) wɑːˈhɑː.kɑː, wə-, -kə

Ob ɒb (US) ɑːb, ɑːp

Obadiah ˌəʊ.bəˈdaɪə (US) ˌoʊ-

Oban ˈəʊ.bən (US) ˈoʊ-

obbligat|o ˌɒb.lɪˈgɑː.t|əʊ, -ləˈ- (US) ˌɑː.blɪˈgɑː.t̬|oʊ **-os** -əʊz (US) -oʊz **-i** -iː

obduracy ˈɒb.djər.ə.si, -djʊ.rə- (US) ˈɑːb.dʊr.ə-, -djʊr-

obdurate ˈɒb.djər.ət, -djʊ.rət, -rɪt, -reɪt (US) ˈɑːb.dʊr.ɪt, -djʊr- **-ly** -li **-ness** -nəs, -nɪs

obduration ˌɒb.djərˈeɪ.ʃən, -djʊˈreɪ- (US) ˌɑːb.dʊrˈeɪ, -djʊrˈ-

OBE ˌəʊ.biːˈiː (US) ˌoʊ- **-s** -z

obeah (O) ˈəʊ.bi.ə (US) ˈoʊ-

obedience əʊˈbiː.di.ənts (US) oʊ-, ə-, ˈ-djənts

Pronouncing the letters OA

The vowel digraph **oa** has two main strong pronunciations: /əʊ ⓤⓢ oʊ/ and /ɔː ⓤⓢ ɑː/, e.g.:

road	/rəʊd/	ⓤⓢ /roʊd/
broad	/brɔːd/	ⓤⓢ /brɑːd/

When the digraph is followed by an **r** in the spelling, the strong pronunciation is /ɔː ⓤⓢ ɔːr/, e.g.:

board	/bɔːd/	ⓤⓢ /bɔːrd/
soar	/sɔːʳ/	ⓤⓢ /sɔːr/

In addition

Another vowel sound associated with the digraph **oa** is /əʊə, ⓤⓢ oʊə/, e.g.:

coalescence	/kəʊə'les.ᵊnts/	ⓤⓢ /koʊə-/

In weak syllables

The vowel digraph **oa** is realised with the vowel /ə/ in weak syllables and with /ɚ/ in American English when followed by an r, e.g.:

cupboard	/'kʌb.əd/	ⓤⓢ /-ɚd/

obedient əʊ'biː.di.ənt ⓤⓢ oʊ-, ə-, '-djənt **-ly** -li

obeisanc|e əʊ'beɪ.sᵊnts ⓤⓢ oʊ-, -'biː- **-es** -ɪz

obelisk 'ɒb.ᵊl.ɪsk, -ɪ.lɪsk ⓤⓢ 'ɑː.bᵊl.ɪsk **-s** -s

obel|us 'ɒb.ᵊl|.əs, -ɪ.l|əs ⓤⓢ 'ɑː.bᵊl|.əs, 'oʊ- **-i** -aɪ

Oberammergau ˌəʊ.bə'ræm.ə.gaʊ ⓤⓢ ˌoʊ.bɚ'ɑː.mɚ-

Oberland 'əʊ.bə.lænd ⓤⓢ 'oʊ.bɚ-

Oberlin 'əʊ.bə.lɪn ⓤⓢ 'oʊ.bɚ-

Oberon 'əʊ.bᵊr.ɒn, -ᵊn ⓤⓢ 'oʊ.bə.rɑːn, -bɚ.ən

obese əʊ'biːs ⓤⓢ oʊ- **-ness** -nəs, -nɪs

obesity əʊ'biː.sə.ti, -sɪ- ⓤⓢ oʊ'biː.sə.ţi

obey əʊ'beɪ ⓤⓢ oʊ-, ə- **-s** -z **-ing** -ɪŋ **-ed** -d **-er/s** -əʳ/z ⓤⓢ -ɚ/z

obfus|cate 'ɒb.fʌs|.keɪt, -fə.s|keɪt ⓤⓢ 'ɑːb.fə-; ɑːb'fʌs|.keɪt **-cates** -keɪts **-cating** -keɪ.tɪŋ ⓤⓢ -keɪ.ţɪŋ **-cated** -keɪ.tɪd ⓤⓢ -keɪ.ţɪd

obfuscation ˌɒb.fʌs'keɪ.ʃᵊn, -fə'skeɪ- ⓤⓢ ˌɑːb.fə'skeɪ- **-s** -z

obfuscatory ˌɒb.fʌs'keɪ.tᵊr.i, -fə'skeɪ- ⓤⓢ ɑːb'fʌs.kə.tɔːr-, əb-

obi 'əʊ.bi ⓤⓢ 'oʊ- **-s** -z

Obi *river in Siberia:* 'əʊ.bi ⓤⓢ 'oʊ-

Obie 'əʊ.bi ⓤⓢ 'oʊ- **-s** -z

obit 'ɒb.ɪt; əʊ'bɪt ⓤⓢ 'oʊ-, -'- **-s** -s

obiter dict|um ˌɒb.ɪ.tə'dɪk.t|ʊm, ˌəʊ.bɪ-, -təm ⓤⓢ ˌoʊ.bɪ.ţɚ'dɪk-, ˌɑː- **-a** -ə

obituarist əʊ'bɪtʃ.ʊə.rɪst, ɒb'ɪtʃ-, -'ɪt.jʊə-, -jə-, -jʊ- ⓤⓢ oʊ'bɪtʃ.u.ɚ.ɪst, ə- **-s** -s

obituar|y əʊ'bɪtʃ.ʊə.r|i, ɒb'ɪtʃ-, -'ɪt.jʊə-, -jə-, -jʊ- ⓤⓢ oʊ'bɪtʃ.u.er|.i, ə- **-ies** -iz

object (*n.*) 'ɒb.dʒɪkt, -dʒekt ⓤⓢ 'ɑːb- **-s** -s **'object ˌlesson**

object (*v.*) əb'dʒekt **-s** -s **-ing** -ɪŋ **-ed** -ɪd **-or/s** -əʳ/z ⓤⓢ -ɚ/z

objecti|fy əb'dʒek.tɪ|.faɪ, ɒb-, -tə- ⓤⓢ əb'dʒek.tə- **-fies** -faɪz **-fying** -faɪ.ɪŋ **-fied** -faɪd

objection əb'dʒek.ʃᵊn **-s** -z

objectionab|le əb'dʒek.ʃᵊn.ə.b|l̩, -'dʒekʃ.nə- **-ly** -li

objective əb'dʒek.tɪv, ɒb- ⓤⓢ əb- **-s** -z **-ly** -li **-ness** -nəs, -nɪs

objectivism əb'dʒek.tɪ.vɪ.zᵊm, ɒb- ⓤⓢ əb'dʒek.tə-

objectivity ˌɒb.dʒɪk'tɪv.ə.ti, -dʒek-, -ɪ.ti ⓤⓢ ˌɑːb.dʒek'tɪv.ə.ţi

objectless 'ɒb.dʒɪkt.ləs, -dʒekt-, -lɪs ⓤⓢ 'ɑːb.dʒɪkt-

objet(s) d'art ˌɒb.ʒeɪ'dɑːʳ ⓤⓢ ˌɑːb.ʒeɪ'dɑːr

objet(s) trouvé(s) ˌɒb.ʒeɪ.truː'veɪ ⓤⓢ ˌɑːb-

objur|gate 'ɒb.dʒə|.geɪt, -dʒɜː- ⓤⓢ 'ɑːb.dʒɚ-, əb'dʒɜː- **-gates** -geɪts **-gating** -geɪ.tɪŋ ⓤⓢ -geɪ.ţɪŋ **-gated** -geɪ.tɪd ⓤⓢ -geɪ.ţɪd

objurgation ˌɒb.dʒə'geɪ.ʃᵊn, -dʒɜː'- ⓤⓢ ˌɑːb.dʒɚ'- **-s** -z

objurgatory ɒb'dʒɜː.gə.tᵊr.i, əb-; ˌɒb.dʒə'geɪ-, -dʒɜː'- ⓤⓢ əb'dʒɝː.gə.tɔːr-

oblate (*adj.*) 'ɒb.leɪt; -'-, əʊ'bleɪt ⓤⓢ 'ɑː.bleɪt, -'- **-ly** -li **-ness** -nəs, -nɪs

oblate (*n.*) 'ɒb.leɪt ⓤⓢ 'ɑː.bleɪt **-s** -s

oblation əʊ'bleɪ.ʃᵊn, ɒb'leɪ- ⓤⓢ ə'bleɪ-, oʊ-, ɑː- **-s** -z

obligat|e 'ɒb.lɪ.geɪt ⓤⓢ 'ɑː.blɪ- **-es** -s **-ing** -ɪŋ **-ed** -ɪd

obligation ˌɒb.lɪ'geɪ.ʃᵊn, -lə'- ⓤⓢ ˌɑː.blə'- **-s** -z

obligat|o ˌɒb.lɪ'gɑː.t|əʊ, -lə'- ⓤⓢ ˌɑː.blɪ'gɑː.ţ|oʊ **-os** -əʊz ⓤⓢ -oʊz **-i** -iː

obligator|y ə'blɪg.ə.tᵊr|.i, ɒb'lɪg-; ˌɒb.lɪ'geɪ-, -lə'- ⓤⓢ ə'blɪg.ə.tɔːr-; 'ɑː.blə.gə- **-ily** -ᵊl.i, -ɪ.li **-iness** -ɪ.nəs, -ɪ.nɪs

oblig|e ə'blaɪdʒ ⓤⓢ ə-, oʊ- **-es** -ɪz **-ing/ly** -ɪŋ/li **-ingness** -ɪŋ.nəs, -nɪs **-ed** -d

obliged ə'blaɪdʒd ⓤⓢ ə-, oʊ-

obligee ˌɒb.lɪ'dʒiː, -lə'- ⓤⓢ ˌɑː.blə'- **-s** -z

obliging ə'blaɪ.dʒɪŋ ⓤⓢ ə-, oʊ-

obligor ˌɒb.lɪ'gɔːʳ, -lə'- ⓤⓢ ˌɑː.blə'gɔːr, '--- **-s** -z

oblique əʊ'bliːk ⓤⓢ oʊ-, ə-, -'blaɪk **-ly** -li **-ness** -nəs, -nɪs

Note: The US form /-'blaɪk/ is associated with military usage.

obliquit|y əʊ'blɪk.wə.t|i, -wɪ- ⓤⓢ ə'blɪk.wə.ţ|i **-ies** -iz

obliter|ate ə'blɪt.ᵊr|.eɪt ⓤⓢ -'blɪţ.ə.r|eɪt, oʊ- **-ates** -eɪts **-ating** -eɪ.tɪŋ ⓤⓢ -eɪ.ţɪŋ **-ated** -eɪ.tɪd ⓤⓢ -eɪ.ţɪd

obliteration əˌblɪt.ᵊr'eɪ.ʃᵊn ⓤⓢ -ˌblɪţ.ə'reɪ-, oʊ- **-s** -z

oblivion ə'blɪv.i.ən

oblivious ə'blɪv.i.əs **-ly** -li **-ness** -nəs, -nɪs

oblong 'ɒb.lɒŋ ⓤⓢ 'ɑːb.lɑːŋ, -lɔːŋ **-s** -z

obloquy 'ɒb.lə.kwi ⓤⓢ 'ɑːb-

obnoxious əb'nɒk.ʃəs, ɒb- ⓤⓢ əb'nɑːk-, ɑːb- **-ly** -li **-ness** -nəs, -nɪs

oboe 'əʊ.bəʊ ⓤⓢ 'oʊ.boʊ **-s** -z

oboe d'amore ˌəʊ.bəʊ.dæm'ɔː.reɪ, -də'mɔː-, -riː ⓤⓢ ˌoʊ.boʊ.də'mɔːr.eɪ

oboist 'əʊ.bəʊ.ɪst ⓤⓢ 'oʊ.boʊ- **-s** -s

obol 'ɒb.ɒl, 'əʊ.bɒl, -bᵊl ⓤⓢ 'ɑː.bᵊl, 'oʊ- **-s** -z

Obote əʊ'bəʊ.teɪ, ɒb'əʊ-, -ti ⓤⓢ oʊ'boʊ-

O'Boyle əʊ'bɔɪl ⓤⓢ oʊ-

O'Brady əʊ'breɪ.di, -'brɔː- ⓤⓢ oʊ'breɪ-

O'Brien, O'Bryan əʊ'braɪən ⓤⓢ oʊ-

obscene əb'siːn, ɒb- ⓤⓢ əb-, ɑːb- **-ly** -li **-ness** -nəs, -nɪs

obscenit|y əb'sen.ə.t|i, ɒb-, -ɪ.t|i ⓤⓢ əb'sen.ə.ţ|i, ɑːb- **-ies** -iz

obscurant ɒb'skjʊə.rᵊnt, əb- ⓤⓢ ɑːb'skjʊr.ᵊnt, əb-

obscurant|ism ˌɒb.skjʊə'ræn.t|ɪ.zᵊm;

ɒb'skjʊə.rən-, əb- (US) ɑːb'skjʊr.ən-, əb- **-ist/s** -ɪst/s
›bscuration ˌɒb.skjʊə'reɪ.ʃᵊn, -skjə'- (US) ˌɑːb.skjʊ'- **-s** -z
›bscur|e əb'skjʊəʳ, -'skjɔːʳ (US) əb'skjʊr, ɑːb- **-er** -əʳ (US) -ɚ **-est** -ɪst, -əst **-ely** -li **-eness** -nəs, -nɪs **-es** -z **-ing** -ɪŋ **-ed** -d
›bscurit|y əb'skjʊə.rə.t|i, -'skjɔː-, -rɪ- (US) əb'skjʊr.ə.t̬|i, ɑːb- **-ies** -iz
›bse|crate 'ɒb.sɪ|.kreɪt, -sə- (US) 'ɑːb.sɪ- **-crates** -kreɪts **-crating** -kreɪ.tɪŋ (US) -kreɪ.t̬ɪŋ **-crated** -kreɪ.tɪd (US) -kreɪ.t̬ɪd
bsecration ˌɒb.sɪ'kreɪ.ʃᵊn, -sə'- (US) ˌɑːb.sə'- **-s** -z
bsequies 'ɒb.sɪ.kwiz, -sə-; ɒb'siː- (US) 'ɑːb.sɪ-
bsequious əb'siː.kwi.əs, ɒb- (US) əb-, ɑːb- **-ly** -li **-ness** -nəs, -nɪs
bservab|le əb'zɜː.və.b|l̩ (US) -'zɝː- **-ly** -li **-leness** -l̩.nəs, -nɪs
bservanc|e əb'zɜː.vᵊn*t*s (US) -'zɝː- **-es** -ɪz
bservant əb'zɜː.vᵊnt (US) -'zɝː- **-ly** -li
bservation ˌɒb.zə'veɪ.ʃᵊn (US) ˌɑːb.zɚ'-, -sɚ'- **-s** -z
bservational ˌɒb.zə'veɪ.ʃᵊn.ᵊl, -veɪʃ.nᵊl (US) ˌɑːb.zɚ'-, -sɚ'- **-ly** -i
bservator|y əb'zɜː.və.tr|i, -tᵊr|.i (US) -'zɝː.və.tɔːr- **-ies** -iz
bserv|e əb'zɜːv (US) -'zɝːv **-es** -z **-ing/ly** -ɪŋ/li **-ed** -d
bserver (O) əb'zɜː.vəʳ (US) -'zɝː.vɚ **-s** -z
›sess əb'ses, ɒb- (US) əb- **-es** -ɪz **-ing** -ɪŋ **-ed** -t
›session əb'seʃ.ᵊn, ɒb- (US) əb- **-s** -s **-al** -ᵊl
›sessive əb'ses.ɪv, ɒb- (US) əb- **-s** -s **-ly** -li **-ness** -nəs, -nɪs
›sidian ɒb'sɪd.i.ən, əb- (US) əb-, ɑːb-
›solescence ˌɒb.sə'les.ᵊn*t*s, -sᵊl'es- (US) ˌɑːb-
›solescent ˌɒb.sə'les.ᵊnt, -sᵊl'es- (US) ˌɑːb- **-ly** -li
›solete 'ɒb.sᵊl.iːt (US) ˌɑːb.sᵊl'iːt **-ly** -li **-ness** -nəs, -nɪs
›stacle 'ɒb.stə.kl̩, -stɪ- (US) 'ɑːb.stə- **-s** -z **'obstacle ˌcourse**
stetric ɒb'stet.rɪk, əb- (US) əb-, ɑːb- **-al** -ᵊl **-s** -s
stetrician ˌɒb.stə'trɪʃ.ᵊn, -stɪ'-, -stet'rɪʃ- (US) ˌɑːb.stə'trɪʃ- **-s** -z
stinac|y 'ɒb.stɪ.nə.s|i, -stᵊn.ə- (US) 'ɑːb.stə.nə- **-ies** -iz
stinate 'ɒb.stɪ.nət, -stᵊn.ət, -ɪt (US) 'ɑːb.stə.nət **-ly** -li **-ness** -nəs, -nɪs
streperous əb'strep.ᵊr.əs, ɒb- (US) əb-, ɑːb- **-ly** -li **-ness** -nəs, -nɪs
struct əb'strʌkt **-s** -s **-ing** -ɪŋ **-ed** -ɪd **-or/s** -əʳ/z (US) -ɚ/z

obstruction əb'strʌk.ʃᵊn **-s** -z
obstructionism əb'strʌk.ʃᵊn.ɪ.zᵊm
obstructionist əb'strʌk.ʃᵊn.ɪst **-s** -s
obstructive əb'strʌk.tɪv **-ly** -li **-ness** -nəs, -nɪs
obstruent 'ɒb.stru.ənt (US) 'ɑːb- **-s** -s
obtain əb'teɪn **-s** -z **-ing** -ɪŋ **-ed** -d **-er/s** -əʳ/z (US) -ɚ/z **-able** -ə.bl̩
obtrud|e əb'truːd, ɒb- (US) əb-, ɑːb- **-es** -z **-ing** -ɪŋ **-ed** -ɪd **-er/s** -əʳ/z (US) -ɚ/z
obtrusion əb'truː.ʒᵊn, ɒb- (US) əb-, ɑːb- **-s** -z
obtrusive əb'truː.sɪv, ɒb-, -zɪv (US) əb-, ɑːb- **-ly** -li **-ness** -nəs, -nɪs
obtu|rate 'ɒb.tjʊə|.reɪt, -tjə- (US) 'ɑːb.tə-, -tjə-, -tʊ-, -tjʊ- **-rates** -reɪts **-rating** -reɪ.tɪŋ (US) -reɪ.t̬ɪŋ **-rated** -reɪ.tɪd (US) -reɪ.t̬ɪd **-rator/s** -reɪ.təʳ/z (US) -reɪ.t̬ɚ/z
obturation ˌɒb.tjʊə'reɪ.ʃᵊn, -tjə'- (US) ˌɑːb.tə'-, -tjə'-, -tʊ'-, -tjʊ'- **-s** -z
obtuse əb'tjuːs, ɒb- (US) ɑːb'tuːs, əb-, -'tjuːs **-ly** -li **-ness** -nəs, -nɪs
obvers|e *(adj.)* 'ɒb.vɜːs (US) ɑːb'vɝːs, əb-; 'ɑːb.vɝːs
obvers|e *(n.)* 'ɒb.vɜːs (US) 'ɑːb.vɝːs **-es** -ɪz
obversely 'ɒb.vɜː.sli (US) ɑːb'vɝː-
ob|vert ɒb|'vɜːt, əb- (US) ɑːb|'vɝːt, əb- **-verts** -'vɜːts (US) -'vɝːts **-verting** -'vɜː.tɪŋ (US) -'vɝː.t̬ɪŋ **-verted** -'vɜː.tɪd (US) -'vɝː.t̬ɪd
obvi|ate 'ɒb.vi|.eɪt (US) 'ɑːb- **-ates** -eɪts **-ating** -eɪ.tɪŋ (US) -eɪ.t̬ɪŋ **-ated** -eɪ.tɪd (US) -eɪ.t̬ɪd
obviative 'ɒb.vi.ə.tɪv (US) 'ɑːb.vi.eɪ.t̬ɪv
obvious 'ɒb.vi.əs (US) 'ɑːb- **-ly** -li **-ness** -nəs, -nɪs
O'Byrne əʊ'bɜːn (US) oʊ'bɝːn
O'Callaghan əʊ'kæl.ə.hən, -gən, -hæn (US) oʊ'kæl.ə.hən, -hæn
ocarina ˌɒk.ᵊr'iː.nə (US) ˌɑː.kə'riː- **-s** -z
O'Casey əʊ'keɪ.si (US) oʊ-
occam (O) 'ɒk.əm (US) 'ɑː.kəm
occasion ə'keɪ.ʒᵊn **-s** -z **-ing** -ɪŋ **-ed** -d **ˌrise to the oc'casion**
occasional ə'keɪ.ʒᵊn.ᵊl, -'keɪʒ.nᵊl **-ly** -i
occasional|ism ə'keɪ.ʒᵊn.ᵊl|.ɪ.zᵊm, -'keɪʒ.nᵊl- **-ist/s** -ɪst/s
occident (O) 'ɒk.sɪ.dᵊnt, -sə- (US) 'ɑːk.sə.dənt, -sɪ-, -dent
occidental (O) ˌɒk.sɪ'den.tᵊl, -sə'- (US) ˌɑːk.sə'den.t̬ᵊl, -sɪ'- **-s** -z
occidental|ism (O) ˌɒk.sɪ'den.tᵊl|.ɪ.zᵊm, -sə'- (US) ˌɑːk.sə'den.t̬ᵊl-, -sɪ'- **-ist/s** -ɪst/s
occidentaliz|e, -is|e ˌɒk.sɪ'den.tᵊl.aɪz, -sə'- (US) ˌɑːk.sə'den.t̬ᵊl-, -si'- **-es** -ɪz **-ing** -ɪŋ **-ed** -d
occipita *(from* **occiput***)* ɒk'sɪp.ɪ.tə (US) ɑːk'sɪp.ɪ.t̬ə

occipital ɒk'sɪp.ɪ.tᵊl, '-ə- (US) ɑːk'sɪp.ɪ.t̬ᵊl **-ly** -i
occiput 'ɒk.sɪ.pʌt, -pət (US) ɑːk- **-s** -s **occipita** ɒk'sɪp.ɪ.tə (US) ɑːk'sɪp.ɪ.t̬ə
Occleve 'ɒk.liːv (US) 'ɑːk-
occlud|e ə'kluːd, ɒk'luːd (US) ə'kluːd, ɑː- **-es** -z **-ing** -ɪŋ **-ed** -ɪd
occlusal ə'kluː.zᵊl, ɒk'luː- (US) ə'kluː-, ɑː-
occlusion ə'kluː.ʒᵊn, ɒk'luː- (US) ə'kluː-, ɑː- **-s** -z
occlusive ə'kluː.sɪv, ɒk'luː- (US) ə'kluː-, ɑː- **-s** -z
occult *(adj.)* 'ɒk.ʌlt; ə'kʌlt, ɒk'ʌlt (US) ə'kʌlt; 'ɑː.kʌlt **-ly** -li **-ness** -nəs, -nɪs
occul|t *(v.)* ɒk'ʌl|t, ə'kʌl|t (US) ə- **-ts** -ts **-ting** -tɪŋ (US) -t̬ɪŋ **-ted** -tɪd (US) -t̬ɪd
occultation ˌɒk.ᵊl'teɪ.ʃᵊn, -ʌl'- (US) ˌɑː.kʌl'- **-s** -z
occult|ism 'ɒk.ᵊl.t|ɪ.zᵊm, -ʌl-; ɒk'ʌl-, ə'kʌl- (US) ə'kʌl-; 'ɑː.kʌl- **-ist/s** -ɪst/s
occupancy 'ɒk.jə.pən*t*.si, -jʊ- (US) 'ɑː.kjə-, -kjʊ-
occupant 'ɒk.jə.pənt, -jʊ- (US) 'ɑː.kjə-, -kjʊ- **-s** -s
occupation ˌɒk.jə'peɪ.ʃᵊn, -jʊ'- (US) ˌɑː.kjə'-, -kjʊ'- **-s** -z
occupational ˌɒk.jə'peɪ.ʃᵊn.ᵊl, -jʊ'-, -'peɪʃ.nᵊl (US) ˌɑː.kjə'-, -kjʊ'- **-ly** -i *stress shift, see compound:* **ˌoccupational 'therapy**
occupier 'ɒk.jə.paɪ.əʳ, -jʊ- (US) 'ɑː.kjə.paɪ.ɚ, -kjʊ- **-s** -z
occup|y 'ɒk.jə.p|aɪ, -jʊ- (US) 'ɑː.kjuː-, -kjə- **-ies** -aɪz **-ying** -aɪ.ɪŋ **-ied** -aɪd
occur ə'kɜːʳ (US) -'kɝː **-s** -z **-ring** -ɪŋ **-red** -d
occurrenc|e ə'kʌr.ᵊn*t*s (US) -'kɝː- **-es** -ɪz
ocean 'əʊ.ʃᵊn (US) 'oʊ- **-s** -z **a ˌdrop in the 'ocean**
oceanfront 'əʊ.ʃᵊn.frʌnt (US) 'oʊ- **-s** -s
ocean-going 'əʊ.ʃᵊnˌgəʊ.ɪŋ (US) 'oʊ.ʃᵊnˌgoʊ-
Oceani|a ˌəʊ.ʃi'eɪ.ni|.ə, -si'-, -'ɑː- (US) ˌoʊ.ʃi'æn.i-, -'ɑː.ni-, -'eɪ- **-an/s** -ən/z
oceanic (O) ˌəʊ.ʃi'æn.ɪk, -si'- (US) ˌoʊ.ʃi'-
oceanographic ˌəʊ.ʃᵊn.əʊ'græf.ɪk, -ʃi.ᵊn- (US) ˌoʊ.ʃə.noʊ'-, -ʃi.ə- **-ally** -ᵊl.i, -li
oceanograph|y ˌəʊ.ʃᵊn'ɒg.rə.f|i, -ʃi.ᵊn'- (US) ˌoʊ.ʃə'nɑː.grə-, -ʃi.ə'- **-er/s** -əʳ/z (US) -ɚ/z
oceanolog|y ˌəʊ.ʃᵊn'ɒl.ə.dʒ|i, -ʃi.ᵊn'- (US) ˌoʊ.ʃə'nɑː.lə-, -ʃi.ə'- **-ist/s** -ɪst/s
Oceanus əʊ'siː.ə.nəs, -'ʃiː- (US) oʊ'siː-
ocell|us əʊ'sel|.əs (US) oʊ- **-i** -aɪ, -iː
ocelot 'ɒs.ᵊl.ɒt, 'əʊ.sᵊl-, -sɪ.lɒt (US) 'ɑː.sə.lɑːt, 'oʊ-, -lət **-s** -s
och ɒx (US) ɑːk *as if Scots:* ɑːx

oche ˈɒk.i (US) ˈɑː.ki **-s** -z
ocher ˈəʊ.kəʳ (US) ˈoʊ.kɚ **-ous** -əs
Ochil(l) ˈəʊ.kᵊl, -xᵊl (US) ˈoʊ.tʃɪl, ˈɑː-, -kᵊl
Ochiltree *in Scott's 'Antiquary':* ˈəʊ.kɪl.triː, -xɪl-, ˈɒk.ɪl-, ˈɒx-, -ᵊl- (US) ˈoʊ.kɪl-, ˈɑː-, -tʃɪl- *in US:* ˈəʊ.kɪl.triː (US) ˈoʊ-
och|re ˈəʊ.k|əʳ (US) ˈoʊ.k|ɚ **-res** -əz (US) -ɚz **-reing** -ᵊr.ɪŋ **-red** -əd (US) -ɚd
ochreous ˈəʊ.kri.əs, -kᵊr- (US) ˈoʊ-
ochry ˈəʊ.kᵊr.i (US) ˈoʊ-
Ochterlony ˌɒk.təˈləʊ.ni, ˌɒx- (US) ˌɑːk.tɚˈloʊ-
ocker, okker ˈɒk.əʳ (US) ˈɑː.kɚ **-s** -z
Ockham ˈɒk.əm (US) ˈɑː.kəm
Ockley ˈɒk.li (US) ˈɑːk-
O'Clery əʊˈklɪə.ri (US) oʊˈklɪr.i
o'clock əˈklɒk (US) -ˈklɑːk
O'Connell əʊˈkɒn.ᵊl (US) oʊˈkɑː.nᵊl
O'Connor əʊˈkɒn.əʳ (US) oʊˈkɑː.nɚ
Ocracoke ˈəʊ.krə.kəʊk (US) ˈoʊ.krə.koʊk
Oct. *(abbrev. for* **October***)* ɒkt; ɒkˈtəʊ.bəʳ (US) ɑːkˈtoʊ.bɚ
octa- ɒk.tə-; ɒkˈtæ- (US) ɑːk-; ɑːkˈtæ-
Note: Prefix. Normally either takes primary or secondary stress on the first syllable, e.g. **octagon** /ˈɒk.tə.gən (US) ˈɑːk.tə.gɑːn/, **octahedron** /ˌɒk.təˈhiː.drən (US) ˌɑːk.təˈhiː.drən/, or primary stress on the second syllable, e.g. **octagonal** /ɒkˈtæg.ᵊn.ᵊl ˉɑːk-/.
octagon ˈɒk.tə.gən (US) ˈɑːk.tə.gɑːn **-s** -z
octagonal ɒkˈtæg.ᵊn.ᵊl (US) ɑːk- **-ly** -i
octahedr|on ˌɒk.təˈhiː.dr|ᵊn, -ˈhed.r|ᵊn (US) ˈɑːk.təˈhiː.dr|ᵊn **-ons** -ᵊnz **-a** -ə **-al** -ᵊl
octal ˈɒk.tᵊl (US) ˈɑːk-
octane ˈɒk.teɪn (US) ˈɑːk-
octant ˈɒk.tənt (US) ˈɑːk- **-s** -s
Octateuch ˈɒk.tə.tjuːk (US) ˈɑːk.tə.tuːk, -tjuːk
octave *musical term:* ˈɒk.tɪv, -teɪv (US) ˈɑːk- **-s** -z
octave *ecclesiastical term:* ˈɒk.teɪv, -tɪv (US) ˈɑːk.tɪv, -teɪv **-s** -z
Octavi|a ɒkˈteɪ.vi|.ə, -ˈtɑː- (US) ɑːkˈteɪ- **-an** -ən
Octavius ɒkˈteɪ.vi.əs, -ˈtɑː- (US) ɑːkˈteɪ-
octavo ɒkˈtɑː.vəʊ, -ˈteɪ- (US) ɑːkˈteɪ.voʊ, -ˈtɑː- **-s** -z
octennial ɒkˈten.i.əl (US) ɑːk- **-ly** -i
octet(te) ɒkˈtet (US) ɑːk- **-s** -s
octillion ɒkˈtɪl.jən, -i.ən (US) ɑːkˈtɪl.jən **-s** -z
octo- ɒk.təʊ- (US) ɑːk.toʊ-, -tə-
Note: Prefix. Normally takes primary or secondary stress on the first syllable, e.g. **octosyllable** /ˈɒk.təʊˌsɪl.ə.bl̩ (US) ˈɑːk.toʊ-/, **octosyllabic** /ˌɒk.təʊ.sɪˈlæb.ɪk (US) ˌɑːk.toʊ-/.
October ɒkˈtəʊ.bəʳ (US) ɑːkˈtoʊ.bɚ **-s** -z
octodecimo ˌɒk.təʊˈdes.ɪ.məʊ (US) ˌɑːk.toʊˈdes.ɪ.moʊ **-s** -z
octogenarian ˌɒk.təʊ.dʒəˈneə.ri.ən, -dʒɪˈ- (US) ˌɑːk.toʊ.dʒɪˈner.i-, -tə- **-s** -z
octop|us ˈɒk.tə.p|əs, -p|ʊs (US) ˈɑːk.tə.p|əs **-uses** -ə.sɪz, -ʊ.sɪz (US) -ə.sɪz **-i** -aɪ
octoroon ˌɒk.təˈruːn (US) ˌɑːk- **-s** -z
octosyllabic ˌɒk.təʊ.sɪˈlæb.ɪk, -səˈ- (US) ˌɑːk.toʊ-, -tə- *stress shift:* ˌoctosyllabic ˈmeter
octosyllable ˈɒk.təʊˌsɪl.ə.bl̩ (US) ˈɑːk.toʊˌ-, -təˌ- **-s** -z
octroi ˈɒk.trwɑː, -trɔɪ (US) ˈɑːk.trɔɪ **-s** -z
octuple ˈɒk.tjə.pl̩, -tjʊ-; ɒkˈtjuː- (US) ˈɑːk.tə-; ɑːkˈtuː-
ocular ˈɒk.jə.ləʳ, -jʊ- (US) ˈɑː.kjə.lɚ, -kjʊ- **-ly** -li
oculist ˈɒk.jə.lɪst, -jʊ- (US) ˈɑː.kjə-, -kjʊ- **-s** -s
O'Curry əʊˈkʌr.i (US) oʊˈkɝː-
od (O) ɒd (US) ɑːd **-s** -z
OD ˌəʊˈdiː (US) ˌoʊ- **-'s** -z **-'ing** -ɪŋ **-'d** -d
odalisque, odalisk ˈɒd.ᵊl.ɪsk, ˈəʊ.dᵊl- (US) ˈoʊ.dᵊl- **-s** -s
O'Daly əʊˈdeɪ.li (US) oʊ-
Odam ˈəʊ.dəm (US) ˈoʊ-
odd ɒd (US) ɑːd **-er** -əʳ (US) -ɚ **-est** -ɪst, -əst **-ly** -li **-ness** -nəs, -nɪs ˌ**odd man ˈout**
oddball ˈɒd.bɔːl (US) ˈɑːd-, -bɑːl **-s** -z
Oddbins® ˈɒd.bɪnz (US) ˈɑːd-
odd bod ˈɒd.bɒd (US) ˈɑːd.bɑːd **-s** -z
Oddfellow ˈɒdˌfel.əʊ (US) ˈɑːdˌfel.oʊ **-s** -z
Oddie ˈɒd.i (US) ˈɑː.di
oddish ˈɒd.ɪʃ (US) ˈɑː.dɪʃ
oddit|y ˈɒd.ɪ.t|i, -ə.t|i (US) ˈɑː.də.t̬|i **-ies** -iz
odd-job |man ˌɒdˈdʒɒb|.mæn (US) ˈɑːd.dʒɑːb- **-men** -men
oddment ˈɒd.mənt (US) ˈɑːd- **-s** -s
odds ɒdz (US) ɑːdz ˌ**odds and ˈends**
odds-on ˌɒdzˈɒn (US) ˌɑːdzˈɑːn *stress shift:* ˌodds-on ˈfavourite
ode əʊd (US) oʊd **-s** -z
O'Dea əʊˈdeɪ (US) oʊ-
Odell əʊˈdel; ˈəʊ.dᵊl (US) oʊˈdel
Odense ˈəʊ.dᵊnt.sə (US) ˈoʊ.dənt-, -θənt-
Odeon® ˈəʊ.di.ən (US) ˈoʊ-
Oder ˈəʊ.dəʳ (US) ˈoʊ.dɚ
Oder-Neisse Line ˌəʊ.dəˈnaɪ.səˌlaɪn (US) ˌoʊ.dɚˈ-
Odessa əʊˈdes.ə (US) oʊ-
Odets əʊˈdets (US) oʊ-
Odette əʊˈdet (US) oʊ-
ode|um əʊˈdiː|.əm; ˈəʊ.di- (US) oʊˈdiː-; ˈoʊ.di- **-a** -ə **-ums** -əmz
Odgers ˈɒdʒ.əz (US) ˈɑː.dʒɚz
Odham ˈɒd.əm (US) ˈɑː.dəm
Odiham ˈəʊ.dɪ.əm, -həm (US) ˈoʊ-
Odile əʊˈdiːl (US) oʊ-
Odin ˈəʊ.dɪn (US) ˈoʊ-
odious ˈəʊ.di.əs (US) ˈoʊ- **-ly** -li **-ness** -nəs, -nɪs
odium ˈəʊ.di.əm (US) ˈoʊ-
Odling ˈɒd.lɪŋ (US) ˈɑːd-
Odlum ˈɒd.ləm (US) ˈɑːd-
Odo ˈəʊ.dəʊ (US) ˈoʊ.doʊ
Odoacer ˌɒd.əʊˈeɪ.səʳ, ˌəʊ.dəʊˈ- (US) ˌoʊ.doʊˈeɪ.sɚ
O'Doherty əʊˈdəʊ.ə.ti, -ˈdɒ.hə.ti, -ˈdɒx.ə- (US) oʊˈdɔːr.t̬i, -ˈdɑː.hɚ-
odometer əʊˈdɒm.ɪ.təʳ, ɒdˈɒm-, -ə.təʳ (US) oʊˈdɑː.mə.t̬ɚ **-s** -z
O'Donnell əʊˈdɒn.ᵊl (US) oʊˈdɑː.nᵊl
odontolog|y ˌɒd.ɒnˈtɒl.ə.dʒ|i, ˌəʊ.dɒnˈ- (US) ˌoʊ.dɑːnˈtɑː.lə- **-ist/s** -ɪst/s
odor ˈəʊ.dəʳ (US) ˈoʊ.dɚ **-s** -z **-ed** -d **-less** -ləs, -lɪs
odoriferous ˌəʊ.dᵊrˈɪf.ᵊr.əs, ˌɒd.ᵊrˈ- (US) ˌoʊ.dəˈrɪf.ɚ.əs **-ly** -li **-ness** -nəs, -nɪs
odorous ˈəʊ.dᵊr.əs (US) ˈoʊ- **-ly** -li **-ness** -nəs, -nɪs
odour ˈəʊ.dəʳ (US) ˈoʊ.dɚ **-s** -z **-ed** -d **-less** -ləs, -lɪs
O'Dowd əʊˈdaʊd (US) oʊ-
odsbodikins ˌɒdzˈbɒd.ɪ.kɪnz (US) ˌɑːdzˈbɑːd-
O'Dwyer əʊˈdwaɪəʳ (US) oʊˈdwaɪɚ
Ody ˈəʊ.di (US) ˈoʊ-
Odysseus əˈdɪs.juːs, ɒdˈɪs-, əʊˈdɪs-, ˈ-i.əs (US) oʊˈdɪs.i.əs, ˈ-juːs
odyssey (O) ˈɒd.ɪ.si, ˈ-ə- (US) ˈɑː.dɪ-
OECD ˌəʊ.iː.siːˈdiː (US) ˌoʊ-
oecumenic ˌiː.kjʊˈmen.ɪk (US) ˌek.jəˈ-, -jʊˈ- **-al** -ᵊl *stress shift:* ˌoecumenic ˈservice
oedema ɪˈdiː.mə, iː- (US) ɪ- **-ta** -tə (US) -t̬
oedematous ɪˈdiː.mə.təs, iː-, -ˈdem.ə- (US) ɪˈdem.ə.t̬əs
oedipal (O) ˈiː.dɪ.pᵊl, -də- (US) ˈed.ɪ-, ˈiː.dɪ-
Oedipus ˈiː.dɪ.pəs, -də- (US) ˈed.ɪ-, ˈiː.d… ˈ**Oedipus** ˌ**complex**
OEEC ˌəʊ.iː.iːˈsiː (US) ˌoʊ-
Oenomaus ˌiː.nəʊˈmeɪ.əs (US) -nəˈ-, -noʊˈ-
Oenone iːˈnəʊ.niː, ɪ-, -ni (US) iːˈnoʊ-
oenophile ˈiː.nəʊ.faɪl (US) -nə- **-s** -z
o'er *(contracted form of* **over***)* ɔəʳ, ɔːʳ, əʊəʳ (US) ɔːr, oʊɚ
oes *(plur. of* **O***)* əʊz (US) oʊz
oesophageal ɪˌsɒf.əˈdʒiː.əl, iː-, ə-; ˌiː.sɒf- (US) ɪˌsɑː.fəˈ-; ˌiː.sɑː-
oesopha|gus iːˈsɒf.ə|l.gəs, ɪ-, ə- (US) ɪˈsɑː.fə-, iː- **-guses** -gə.sɪz **-gi** -gaɪ, -dʒaɪ

Pronouncing the letters OEU

The vowel letter combination **oeu** (a chiefly British spelling) has two possible pronunciations: /uː/ and /ɜː/, e.g.:

manoeuvre	/məˈnuː.vəʳ/	ⓊⓈ /-vɚ/
oeuvre	/ˈɜː.vrə/	

It should be noted that more recent borrowings from French, like *oeuvre* above, usually have the latter pronunciation (see, for example, *cri de coeur*, *hors d'oeuvre*).

estrogen ˈiː.strəʊ.dʒᵊn, ˈes.trəʊ- ⓊⓈ ˈes.trə-, -dʒen
estrus ˈiː.strəs ⓊⓈ ˈes.trəs **-es** -ɪz
euvre ˈɜː.vrə **-s** -z
f *strong form:* ɒv ⓊⓈ ɑːv *weak form:* əv
ote: Weak form word. The strong form is usually found only in final position (e.g. "She's the one I'm fond of"), though it can occur initially in some forms such as "Of the ten who set out, only three returned". Elsewhere the weak form /əv/ is used.
'Faolain, O'Faoláin əʊˈfeɪ.lən, -ˈfæl.ən ⓊⓈ oʊ-
ff ɒf ⓊⓈ ɑːf
ffa ˈɒf.ə ⓊⓈ ˈɑː.fə ˌ**Offa's** ˈ**Dyke**
ffal ˈɒf.ᵊl ⓊⓈ ˈɑː.fᵊl
ffaly ˈɒf.ᵊl.i ⓊⓈ ˈɑː.fᵊl.i
ff-bail ˌɒfˈbeɪl ⓊⓈ ˌɑːf- **-s** -z
ote: Also ˈ-- when in contrast with **leg-bail**.
ffbeat *(adj.)* ˌɒfˈbiːt ⓊⓈ ˌɑːfˈbiːt
ffbeat *(n.)* ˈɒf.biːt ⓊⓈ ˈɑːf- **-s** -s
ff-bye ˌɒfˈbaɪ ⓊⓈ ˌɑːf- **-s** -z
ote: Also ˈ-- when in contrast with **leg-bye**.
ff-chance ˈɒf.tʃɑːnts ⓊⓈ ˈɑːf.tʃænts ˌ**on the** ˈ**off-**ˌ**chance**
ff-colo(u)r ˌɒfˈkʌl.əʳ ⓊⓈ ˌɑːfˈkʌl.ɚ
ffcut ˈɒf.kʌt ⓊⓈ ˈɑːf- **-s** -s
ff-drive ˈɒf.draɪv ⓊⓈ ˈɑːf- **-s** -z
ffenbach ˈɒf.ᵊn.bɑːk, -ᵊm- ⓊⓈ ˈɑː.fᵊn.bɑːk, ˈɔː-
fenc|e əˈfents **-es** -ɪz **-eless** -ləs, -lɪs
fend əˈfend **-s** -z **-ing** -ɪŋ **-ed** -ɪd **-er/s** -əʳ/z ⓊⓈ -ɚ/z
fens|e əˈfents ⓊⓈ ə-; *especially in sport:* ˈɑː.fents **-es** -ɪz **-eless** -ləs, -lɪs
fensive əˈfent.sɪv ⓊⓈ ə-; *especially in sport:* ˈɑː-, ˈʌf.ent- **-s** -z **-ly** -li **-ness** -nəs, -nɪs
f|er ˈɒf|.əʳ ⓊⓈ ˈɑː.f|ɚ **-ers** -əz ⓊⓈ -ɚz **-ering/s** -ᵊr.ɪŋ/z **-ered** -əd ⓊⓈ -ɚd **-erer/s** -ᵊr.əʳ/z ⓊⓈ -ɚ.ɚ/z **-erable** -ᵊr.ə.bl
fertor|y ˈɒf.ə.tᵊr|.i ⓊⓈ ˈɑː.fɚ.tɔːr-, ˈɔː- **-ies** -iz
f-hand ˌɒfˈhænd ⓊⓈ ˌɑːf-
f-handed ˌɒfˈhæn.dɪd ⓊⓈ ˌɑːf- **-ly** -li **-ness** -nəs, -nɪs
offic|e ˈɒf.ɪs ⓊⓈ ˈɑː.fɪs **-es** -ɪz ˈ**office** ˌ**block**; ˈ**office** ˌ**hours**, ˌ**office** ˈ**hours**
office-bearer ˈɒf.ɪsˌbeə.rəʳ ⓊⓈ ˈɑː.fɪsˌber.ɚ **-s** -z
office-boy ˈɒf.ɪsˌbɔɪ ⓊⓈ ˈɑː.fɪs- **-s** -z
officer ˈɒf.ɪ.səʳ ⓊⓈ ˈɑː.fɪ.sɚ **-s** -z
official əˈfɪʃ|.ᵊl ⓊⓈ ə-, oʊ- **-s** -z **-ly** -i **-ism** -ɪ.zᵊm **of**ˌ**ficial re**ˈ**ceiver**; **Of**ˌ**ficial** ˈ**Secrets** ˌ**Act**
officialdom əˈfɪʃ.ᵊl.dəm ⓊⓈ ə-
officialese əˌfɪʃ.ᵊlˈiːz, əˈfɪʃ.ᵊl.iːz ⓊⓈ əˌfɪʃ.ᵊlˈiːz
officiant əˈfɪʃ.i.ənt, ɒfˈɪʃ- ⓊⓈ əˈfɪʃ.ᵊnt, -i.ənt **-s** -s
offici|ate əˈfɪʃ.i|.eɪt **-ates** -eɪts **-ating** -eɪ.tɪŋ ⓊⓈ -eɪ.t̬ɪŋ **-ated** -eɪ.tɪd ⓊⓈ -eɪ.t̬ɪd
officinal ˌɒf.ɪˈsaɪ.nᵊl; ɒfˈɪs.ɪ.nᵊl ⓊⓈ əˈfɪs.ɪ-; ˌɑː.fɪˈsaɪ-
officious əˈfɪʃ.əs **-ly** -li **-ness** -nəs, -nɪs
offing ˈɒf.ɪŋ ⓊⓈ ˈɑː.fɪŋ **-s** -z
offish ˈɒf.ɪʃ ⓊⓈ ˈɑː.fɪʃ
off-key ˌɒfˈkiː ⓊⓈ ˌɑːf- *stress shift:* ˌoff-key ˈsinging
off-licenc|e ˈɒfˌlaɪ.sᵊnts ⓊⓈ ˌɑːfˈlaɪ- **-es** -ɪz
offline ˌɒfˈlaɪn ⓊⓈ ˌɑːf- *stress shift:* ˌoff-line ˈprinter
off-load ˌɒfˈləʊd ⓊⓈ ˈɑːf.loʊd **-s** -z **-ing** -ɪŋ **-ed** -ɪd
Offor ˈɒf.əʳ ⓊⓈ ˈɑː.fɚ
off-peak ˌɒfˈpiːk ⓊⓈ ˌɑːf- *stress shift:* ˌoff-peak ˈtravel
off-piste ˌɒfˈpiːst ⓊⓈ ˌɑːf- *stress shift:* ˌoff-piste ˈskiing
off-print ˈɒf.prɪnt ⓊⓈ ˈɑːf- **-s** -s
off-putting ˌɒfˈpʊt.ɪŋ ⓊⓈ ˈɑːfˌpʊt̬- *stress shift, British only:* ˌoff-putting ˈhabit
offscreen ˌɒfˈskriːn ⓊⓈ ˌɑːf- *stress shift:* ˌoffscreen ˈlife
off|set *(v.) compensate:* ˌɒf|ˈset ⓊⓈ ˌɑːf- **-sets** -ˈsets **-setting** -ˈset.ɪŋ ⓊⓈ -ˈset̬.ɪŋ
offse|t *(n. v.)* ˈɒf.se|t ⓊⓈ ˈɑːf-, -ˈ- **-ts** -ts **-tting** -tɪŋ ⓊⓈ -t̬ɪŋ
offshoot ˈɒf.ʃuːt ⓊⓈ ˈɑːf- **-s** -s
offshore ˌɒfˈʃɔːʳ ⓊⓈ ˌɑːfˈʃɔːr *stress shift:* ˌoffshore ˈsavings
offside ˌɒfˈsaɪd ⓊⓈ ˌɑːf- *stress shift:* ˌoffside ˈrule
offspring ˈɒf.sprɪŋ ⓊⓈ ˈɑːf- **-s** -z
offstage ˌɒfˈsteɪdʒ ⓊⓈ ˌɑːf- *stress shift:* ˌoffstage ˈwhisper
off-street ˌɒfˈstriːt ⓊⓈ ˌɑːf- *stress shift:* ˌoff-street ˈshops
off-the-cuff ˌɒf.ðəˈkʌf ⓊⓈ ˌɑːf- *stress shift:* ˌoff-the-cuff ˈcomment
off-the-peg ˌɒf.ðəˈpeg ⓊⓈ ˌɑːf- *stress shift:* ˌoff-the-peg ˈsuit
off-the-rack ˌɒf.ðəˈræk ⓊⓈ ˌɑːf- *stress shift:* ˌoff-the-rack ˈsuit
off-the-record ˌɒf.ðəˈrek.ɔːd ⓊⓈ ˌɑːf.ðəˈrek.ɔːrd, -ˈrek.ɚd *stress shift:* ˌoff-the-record ˈquote
off-the-shelf ˌɒf.ðəˈʃelf ⓊⓈ ˌɑːf- *stress shift:* ˌoff-the-shelf ˈgoods
off-the-wall ˌɒf.ðəˈwɔːl ⓊⓈ ˌɑːf.ðəˈwɔːl, -ˈwɔːl *stress shift:* ˌoff-the-wall ˈcomedy
off-white ˌɒfˈ*h*waɪt ⓊⓈ ˌɑːf- *stress shift:* ˌoff-white ˈdrapes
Ofgas, OFGAS ˈɒf.gæs ⓊⓈ ˈɑːf-
O'Flaherty əʊˈfleə.ti, -ˈflæ.hə-, -ˈflɑː.ə-, -ˈflɑː- ⓊⓈ oʊˈfler.t̬i, -ˈflæ.hɚ-
O'Flynn əʊˈflɪn ⓊⓈ oʊ-
Ofsted ˈɒf.sted ⓊⓈ ˈɑːf-
oft ɒft ⓊⓈ ɑːft
Oftel, OFTEL ˈɒf.tel ⓊⓈ ˈɑːf-
often ˈɒf.ᵊn, -tᵊn ⓊⓈ ˈɑː.fᵊn, ˈɑːf.tᵊn **-times** -taɪmz **as** ˌ**often as** ˈ**not**
often|er ˈɒf.ᵊn|.əʳ, -tᵊn-, ˈɒf.n|əʳ ⓊⓈ ˈɑː.fᵊn|.ɚ, ˈɑːf.tᵊn-, ˈɑːf.n|ɚ **-est** -ɪst
ofttimes ˈɒft.taɪmz ⓊⓈ ˈɑːft-
Ofwat, OFWAT ˈɒf.wɒt ⓊⓈ ˈɑːf.wɑːt
Og ɒg ⓊⓈ ɑːg, ɔːg
ogam ˈɒg.əm ⓊⓈ ˈɑː.gəm
ogamic ɒgˈæm.ɪk ⓊⓈ ɑːˈgæm-, ɔː-, oʊ-
Ogbomosho ˌɒg.bəˈməʊ.ʃəʊ ⓊⓈ ˌɑːg.bəˈmoʊ.ʃoʊ
Ogden ˈɒg.dən ⓊⓈ ˈɑːg-, ˈɔːg-
ogee ˈəʊ.dʒiː, -ˈ- ⓊⓈ ˈoʊ.dʒiː, -ˈ- **-s** -z
ogham ˈɒg.əm ⓊⓈ ˈɑː.gəm, ˈɔː-
oghamic ɒgˈæm.ɪk ⓊⓈ ɑːˈgæm-, ɔː-, oʊ-
Ogilby ˈəʊ.gᵊl.bi ⓊⓈ ˈoʊ-
Ogilvie, Ogilvy ˈəʊ.gᵊl.vi ⓊⓈ ˈoʊ-
ogival əʊˈdʒaɪ.vᵊl, -ˈgaɪ- ⓊⓈ oʊˈdʒaɪ-
ogive ˈəʊ.dʒaɪv, -gaɪv, -ˈ- ⓊⓈ ˈoʊ.dʒaɪv, -gaɪv, -ˈ- **-s** -z

Pronouncing the letters OI, OY

The vowel letter digraphs **oi** and **oy** are similar in that their most common pronunciation is /ɔɪ/, e.g.:

boy /bɔɪ/
boil /bɔɪl/

When followed by an **r** in the spelling, **oi** is pronounced as /waɪə, (US) waɪɚ/ or /wɑː, (US) wɑːr/, e.g.:

choir /kwaɪəʳ/ (US) /kwaɪɚ/
reservoir /ˈrez.əv.wɑːʳ/ (US) /-ɚv.wɑːr/

In addition

There are other vowel sounds associated with the digraph **oi**. In the following examples, the pronunciation is due to the addition of the inflection -ing to words ending in **o**, e.g.:

/əʊ.ɪ (US) oʊ.ɪ/ going /ˈɡəʊ.ɪŋ/ (US) /ˈɡoʊ-/
/uː.ɪ/ doing /ˈduː.ɪŋ/

In words borrowed from French, the pronunciation of **oi** may be /wɑː/, e.g.:

Bois /bɔɪs, bwɑː/
foie gras /ˌfwɑːˈɡrɑː/

In weak syllables

The vowel digraph **oi** is realised with the vowel /ə/ in weak syllables, e.g.:

tortoise /ˈtɔː.təs/ (US) /ˈtɔːr.t̬əs/
connoisseur /ˌkɒn.əˈsɜːʳ/ (US) /ˌkɑː.nəˈsɝː/

ogl|e (O) ˈəʊ.ɡl̩ (US) ˈoʊ-, ˈɑː- **-es** -z **-ing** -ɪŋ, ˈəʊ.ɡlɪŋ (US) ˈoʊ-, ˈɑː- **-ed** -d **-er/s** -əʳ/z (US) -ɚ/z, ˈəʊ.ɡləʳ/z (US) ˈoʊ.ɡlɚ/z, ˈɑː-
Ogleby ˈəʊ.ɡl̩.bi (US) ˈoʊ-
Oglethorpe ˈəʊ.ɡl̩.θɔːp (US) ˈoʊ.ɡl̩.θɔːrp
Ogmore ˈɒɡ.mɔːʳ (US) ˈɑːɡ.mɔːr, ˈɔːɡ-
Ogoni əˈɡəʊ.ni, ɒɡˈ- (US) oʊˈ- **-land** -lænd
Ogpu ˈɒɡ.puː (US) ˈɑːɡ-, ˈɔːɡ-
O'Grady əʊˈɡreɪ.di (US) oʊ-
og|re ˈəʊ.ɡləʳ (US) ˈoʊ.ɡlɚ **-res** -əz (US) -ɚz **-reish** -ər.ɪʃ
ogress ˈəʊ.ɡrəs, -rɪs (US) ˈoʊ- **-es** -ɪz
Ogwr ˈɒɡ.ʊəʳ (US) ˈɑː.ɡʊr
oh əʊ (US) oʊ
O'Hagan əʊˈheɪ.ɡən (US) oʊ-
O'Halloran əʊˈhæl.ər.ən (US) oʊ-
O'Hanlon əʊˈhæn.lən (US) oʊ-
O'Hara əʊˈhɑː.rə (US) oʊˈher.ə, -ˈhær-
O'Hare əʊˈheəʳ (US) oʊˈher
O'Hea əʊˈheɪ (US) oʊ-
Ohio əʊˈhaɪ.əʊ (US) oʊˈhaɪ.oʊ, ə- **-an/s** -ən/z
ohm (O) əʊm (US) oʊm **-s** -z
OHMS ˌəʊ.eɪtʃ.emˈes (US) ˌoʊ-
oho əʊˈhəʊ (US) oʊˈhoʊ
oick ɔɪk **-s** -s
-oid -ɔɪd
Note: Suffix. Does not normally change the stress pattern of the stem, e.g. **human** /ˈhjuː.mən/, **humanoid** /ˈhjuː.mə.nɔɪd/.
oik ɔɪk **-s** -s
oil ɔɪl **-s** -z **-ing** -ɪŋ **-ed** -d **-er/s** -əʳ/z (US) -ɚ/z **ˈoil ˌcan; ˈoil ˌfield; ˈoil ˌpaint; ˈoil ˌpainting; ˈoil ˌslick; ˈoil ˌwell; ˌpour ˌoil on ˌtroubled ˈwaters; ˌburn the ˌmidnight ˈoil**
oil|cloth ˈɔɪl.klɒθ (US) -klɑːθ **-cloths** -klɒθs, -klɒðz (US) -klɑːθs, -klɑːðz
oil|man ˈɔɪl.mæn (US) -mæn, -mən **-men** -men
oil-rig ˈɔɪl.rɪɡ **-s** -z
oilseed ˈɔɪl.siːd
oilskin ˈɔɪl.skɪn **-s** -z
oil|y ˈɔɪ.l|i **-ier** -i.əʳ (US) -i.ɚ **-iest** -i.ɪst, -i.əst **-iness** -ɪ.nəs, -ɪ.nɪs
oink ɔɪnk **-s** -s **-ing** -ɪŋ **-ed** -t
ointment ˈɔɪnt.mənt **-s** -s
Oisin ˈɔɪ.zɪn (US) ˈɑː.ʃən, ə.ˈʃiːn
Oistrakh ˈɔɪ.strɑːk *as if Russian:* -strɑːx
Ojai ˈəʊ.haɪ (US) ˈoʊ-
Ojibwa(y) əʊˈdʒɪb.weɪ, ɒdʒˈɪb-, -wə (US) oʊˈdʒɪb.weɪ, -wə **-s** -z
OK əʊˈkeɪ (US) oʊ-, ə- **-s** -z **-ing** -ɪŋ **-ed** -d *stress shift:* ˌOK ˈperson
O'Kane əʊˈkeɪn (US) oʊ-
okapi əʊˈkɑː.pi (US) oʊ- **-s** -z
Okara ɒkˈɑː.rə (US) əˈkɑːr.ə
Okavango, Okovango ˌɒk.əˈvæŋ.ɡəʊ (US) ˌoʊ.kəˈvæŋ.ɡoʊ
okay əʊˈkeɪ (US) oʊ-, ə- **-s** -z **-ing** -ɪŋ **-ed** -d *stress shift:* ˌokay ˈperson
Okeechobee ˌəʊ.kɪˈtʃəʊ.bi, -kiːˈ- (US) ˌoʊ.kɪˈtʃoʊ-, -kiːˈ-
O'Keef(f)e əʊˈkiːf (US) oʊ-
Okehampton ˌəʊkˈhæmp.tən (US) ˈoʊkˌhæmp- *stress shift, British only:* ˌOkehampton ˈcentre
O'Kelly əʊˈkel.i (US) oʊ-
okeydoke ˌəʊ.kiˈdəʊk (US) ˌoʊ.kiˈdoʊk **-y** -i
Okhotsk əʊˈkɒtsk, ɒkˈɒtsk (US) oʊˈkɑːtsk
Okie ˈəʊ.ki (US) ˈoʊ- **-s** -z
Okinawa ˌɒk.ɪˈnɑː.wə, ˌəʊ.kɪˈ- (US) ˌoʊ.kəˈnɑː.wə, -kɪ-
okker, ocker ˈɒk.əʳ (US) ˈɑː.kɚ **-s** -z
Okla. *(abbrev. for* **Oklahoma***)* ˌəʊ.kləˈhəʊ.mə (US) ˌoʊ.kləˈhoʊ-
Oklahom|a ˌəʊ.kləˈhəʊ.m|ə (US) ˌoʊ.kləˈhoʊ- **-an/s** -ən/z
Okovango, Okavango ˌɒk.əˈvæŋ.ɡəʊ (US) ˌoʊ.kəˈvæŋ.ɡoʊ
okra ˈɒk.rə, ˈəʊ.krə (US) ˈoʊ-
Okri ˈɒk.ri (US) ˈɑː.kri
Olaf, Olav ˈəʊ.læf, -ləf (US) ˈoʊ.ləf, -lɑːf
Olave ˈɒl.ɪv, -əv, -eɪv (US) ˈoʊ.ləf, -lɑːf, -ləv
Olcott ˈɒl.kət (US) ˈɑːl-
old əʊld (US) oʊld **-er** -əʳ (US) -ɚ **-est** -ɪst **-ness** -nəs, -nɪs **ˌOld ˈBailey; ˈold bo… ˌOld ˈEnglish; ˌOld ˌEnglish ˈsheepdog; ˌOld ˈFaithful; ˌOld ˈGlor… ˌold ˈguard; ˌold ˈhand; ˌold ˈhat; ˌo… ˈlady; ˌold ˈmaid; ˌold ˈman; ˌold ˈmaster; ˈold ˌschool; ˌOld ˈTestament; as ˌold as the ˈhills**
old-age *(adj.)* ˈəʊld,eɪdʒ (US) ˈoʊld- *(n.)* ˌəʊldˈeɪdʒ (US) ˌoʊld-
old-age pension ˌəʊld.eɪdʒˈpen.tʃən (US) ˌoʊld- **-s** -z **-er/s** -əʳ/z (US) -ɚ/z
Oldbuck ˈəʊl*d*.bʌk (US) ˈoʊl*d*-
Oldbury ˈəʊl*d*.bər.i (US) ˈoʊl*d*ˌber-, -bɚ.i
Oldcastle ˈəʊl*d*ˌkɑː.sl̩ (US) ˈoʊl*d*ˌkæs.l̩
olden ˈəʊl.dən (US) ˈoʊl-
Oldenburg ˈəʊl.dən.bɜːɡ, -dəm- (US) ˈoʊl.dən.bɝːɡ
olde worlde ˌəʊl.diˈwɜːl.di (US) ˌoʊl.diˈwɝːl-
Note: Joking imitation of spelling.
old-fashioned ˌəʊl*d*ˈfæʃ.ənd (US) ˌoʊl… *stress shift:* ˌold-fashioned ˈways
Oldfield ˈəʊl*d*.fiːld (US) ˈoʊl*d*-
old-fog(e)yish ˌəʊl*d*ˈfəʊ.ɡi.ɪʃ (US) ˌoʊl*d*ˈfoʊ-
Oldham ˈəʊl.dəm (US) ˈoʊl-
oldie ˈəʊl.di (US) ˈoʊl- **-s** -z
oldish ˈəʊl.dɪʃ (US) ˈoʊl-
Oldrey ˈəʊl.dri (US) ˈoʊl-

Oldsmobile® ˈəʊldz.mə.biːl ⓤⓢ ˈoʊldz-
oldster ˈəʊld.stəʳ ⓤⓢ ˈoʊld.stɚ **-s** -z
old-time ˌəʊldˈtaɪm ⓤⓢ ˌoʊld- *stress shift:* ˌold-time ˈdancing
old-timer ˌəʊldˈtaɪ.məʳ ⓤⓢ ˈoʊldˌtaɪ.mɚ **-s** -z
old wives' tale ˌəʊldˈwaɪvzˌteɪl ⓤⓢ ˌoʊld-
old-world ˌəʊldˈwɜːld ⓤⓢ ˌoʊldˈwɝːld *stress shift:* ˌold-world ˈvalues
olé əʊˈleɪ ⓤⓢ oʊ-
oleaginous ˌəʊ.liˈædʒ.ɪ.nəs, ˈ-ə- ⓤⓢ ˌoʊ- **-ly** -li **-ness** -nəs, -nɪs
oleander (O) ˌəʊ.liˈæn.dəʳ ⓤⓢ ˌoʊ.liˈæn.dɚ, ˈoʊ.liˌæn- **-s** -z
O'Leary əʊˈlɪə.ri ⓤⓢ oʊˈlɪr.i
oleaster ˌəʊ.liˈæs.təʳ ⓤⓢ ˌoʊ.liˈæs.tɚ **-s** -z
oleograph ˈəʊ.li.əʊ.grɑːf, ˈɒl.i-, -græf ⓤⓢ ˈoʊ.li.oʊ.græf, -ə- **-s** -s
O level ˈəʊˌlev.əl ⓤⓢ ˈoʊ- **-s** -z
olfactory ɒlˈfæk.tər.i ⓤⓢ ɑːl-, oʊl-
Olga ˈɒl.gə ⓤⓢ ˈɑːl-, ˈɔːl-, ˈoʊl-
Oliffe ˈɒl.ɪf ⓤⓢ ˈɑː.lɪf
oligarch ˈɒl.ɪ.gɑːk ⓤⓢ ˈɑː.lɪ.gɑːrk, ˈoʊ- **-s** -s
oligarchal ˌɒl.ɪˈgɑː.kəl ⓤⓢ ˌɑː.lɪˈgɑːr-, ˌoʊ- *stress shift:* ˌoligarchal ˈstate
oligarchic ˌɒl.ɪˈgɑː.kɪk ⓤⓢ ˌɑː.lɪˈgɑːr-, ˌoʊ- *stress shift:* ˌoligarchic ˈstate
oligarch|y ˈɒl.ɪ.gɑː.k|i ⓤⓢ ˈɑː.lɪ.gɑːr-, ˈoʊ- **-ies** -iz
Oligocene ˈɒl.ɪ.gəʊ.siːn; ɒlˈɪg.əʊ- ⓤⓢ ˈɑː.lɪ.goʊ-, ˈoʊ-
oligopol|y ˌɒl.ɪˈgɒp.əl|.i ⓤⓢ ˌɑː.lɪˈgɑː.pəl-, ˌoʊ- **-ies** -iz
olio ˈəʊ.li.əʊ ⓤⓢ ˈoʊ.li.oʊ **-s** -z
Oliphant ˈɒl.ɪ.fənt, ˈ-ə- ⓤⓢ ˈɑː.lɪ-
olivaceous ˌɒl.ɪˈveɪ.ʃəs ⓤⓢ ˌɑː.lɪˈ-
olive (O) ˈɒl.ɪv; ⓤⓢ ˈɑː.lɪv **-s** -z ˈ**olive** ˌ**branch**; ˌ**olive** ˈ**green**; ˌ**olive** ˈ**oil**, ˈ**olive** ˌ**oil**
Oliver (O) ˈɒl.ɪ.vəʳ, ˈ-ə- ⓤⓢ ˈɑː.lɪ.vɚ **-s** -z
Oliverian ˌɒl.ɪˈvɪə.ri.ən, -əˈ- ⓤⓢ ˌɑː.lɪˈver.i-
Olivet ˈɒl.ɪ.vet, ˈ-ə-, -vɪt, -vət ⓤⓢ ˈɑː.lɪ.vet, -lə-
Olivetti® ˌɒl.ɪˈvet.i, -əˈ- ⓤⓢ ˌɑː.ləˈvet̬.i
Olivia ɒlˈɪv.i.ə, əˈlɪv-, əʊ- ⓤⓢ oʊ-, ə-
Olivier əˈlɪv.i.eɪ, ɒlˈɪv-, -ə ⓤⓢ oʊˈlɪv.i.eɪ
Olivine ˈɒl.ɪ.viːn, ˈ-ə-, ˌ--ˈ- ⓤⓢ ˈɑː.lə.viːn **-s** -z
olla podrida ˌɒl.jə.pɒdˈriː.də, -pəˈdriː- ⓤⓢ ˌɑː.lə.poʊˈ-, -pəˈ- **-s** -z
Ollendorf ˈɒl.ən.dɔːf, -ɪn- ⓤⓢ ˈɑː.lən.dɔːrf
Ollerton ˈɒl.ə.tən ⓤⓢ ˈɑː.lɚ-
Olley, Ollie ˈɒl.i ⓤⓢ ˈɑː.li
Olliffe ˈɒl.ɪf ⓤⓢ ˈɑː.lɪf
Ollivant ˈɒl.ɪ.vənt, -vænt ⓤⓢ ˈɑː.lɪ-
Olmstead ˈɒm.sted ⓤⓢ ˈoʊm-, ˈɑːm-, -stəd

Olney ˈəʊl.ni, ˈəʊ- ⓤⓢ ˈoʊl-, ˈoʊ-, ˈɑːl-
-olog|y -ˈɒl.ə.dʒ|i ⓤⓢ -ˈɑː.lə.dʒ|i **-ies** -iz
Note: Suffix. Normally takes primary stress as shown, e.g. **biology** /baɪˈɒl.ə.dʒi ⓤⓢ -ˈɑː.lə-/, **pharmacology** /ˌfɑː.məˈkɒl.ə.dʒi ⓤⓢ ˌfɑːr.məˈkɑː.lə-/.
oloroso ˌɒl.əˈrəʊ.səʊ, ˌəʊ.ləˈ-, -zəʊ ⓤⓢ ˌoʊ.loʊˈroʊ.soʊ, -ləˈ- **-s** -z
Olsen, Olson ˈəʊl.sən ⓤⓢ ˈoʊl-
Olver ˈɒl.vəʳ, ˈəʊl- ⓤⓢ ˈɑː.lvɚ
Olwen ˈɒl.wen, -wɪn ⓤⓢ ˈɑːl-
Olympi|a əʊˈlɪm.pi|.ə ⓤⓢ oʊ-, ə- **-an** -ən
Olympiad əʊˈlɪm.pi.æd ⓤⓢ oʊ-, ə- **-s** -z
Olympic əʊˈlɪm.pɪk ⓤⓢ oʊ-, ə- **-s** -s **O**ˌ**lympic** ˈ**Games**
Olympus əʊˈlɪm.pəs ⓤⓢ oʊ-, ə-
Olynthus əʊˈlɪnt.θəs ⓤⓢ oʊ-, ə-
om (O) əʊm, ɒm ⓤⓢ oʊm
Omagh ˈəʊ.mə, -mɑː ⓤⓢ ˈoʊ-
Omaha ˈəʊ.mə.hɑː ⓤⓢ ˈoʊ-, -hɔː
O'Malley əʊˈmæl.i, -ˈmeɪ.li ⓤⓢ oʊ-
Oman əʊˈmɑːn ⓤⓢ oʊ-
Omar ˈəʊ.mɑːʳ ⓤⓢ ˈoʊ.mɑːr
Omar Khayyám ˌəʊ.mɑː.kaɪˈæm, -ˈɑːm ⓤⓢ ˌoʊ.mɑːr.kaɪˈjɑːm, -ˈæm
ombre ˈɒm.bəʳ ⓤⓢ ˈɑːm.bɚ
ombuds|man ˈɒm.bʊdz|.mən, -bʌdz-, -bədz-, -mæn ⓤⓢ ˈɑːm.bədz-, -bʌdz-; ɑːmˈbʌdz- **-men** -mən, -men
Omdurman ˌɒm.dɜːˈmɑːn, -dəˈ-, -ˈmæn; ˈɒm.də.mən ⓤⓢ ˌɑːm.dʊrˈmɑːn
O'Meara əʊˈmɑː.rə, -ˈmɪə- ⓤⓢ oʊˈmɪr.ə, -ˈmɑːr-
omega (O) ˈəʊ.mɪ.gə, -meg.ə ⓤⓢ oʊˈmeɪ.gə, -ˈmeg.ə, -ˈmiː.gə; ˈoʊ.meg- **-s** -z
omelet, omelette ˈɒm.lət, -lɪt, -let ⓤⓢ ˈɑːm.lət, -lɪt; ˈɑː.mə- **-s** -s
omen ˈəʊ.mən, -men ⓤⓢ ˈoʊ- **-s** -z **-ed** -d
omer (O) ˈəʊ.məʳ ⓤⓢ ˈoʊ.mɚ **-s** -z
omertà ˌəʊ.məˈtɑː ⓤⓢ ˌoʊ.merˈtɑː
omicron əʊˈmaɪ.krɒn, -krən; ˈɒm.ɪ- ⓤⓢ ˈoʊ.mɪ.krɑːn, ˈɑː- **-s** -z
ominous ˈɒm.ɪ.nəs, ˈəʊ.mɪ-, -mə- ⓤⓢ ˈɑː.mə- **-ly** -li **-ness** -nəs, -nɪs
omissible əʊˈmɪs.ɪ.bl̩, ˈ-ə- ⓤⓢ oʊ-
omission əʊˈmɪʃ.ən ⓤⓢ oʊ- **-s** -z
o|mit əʊ|ˈmɪt ⓤⓢ oʊ- **-mits** -ˈmɪts **-mitting** -ˈmɪt.ɪŋ ⓤⓢ -ˈmɪt̬.ɪŋ **-mitted** -ˈmɪt.ɪd ⓤⓢ -ˈmɪt̬.ɪd
ommatidi|um ˌɒm.əˈtɪd.i|.əm ⓤⓢ ˌɑː.məˈ- **-a** -ə **-al** -əl
omni- ɒm.nɪ-, -nə-, -ni-; ɒmˈnɪ- ⓤⓢ ɑːm.nɪ-, -nə-, -ni-; ɑːmˈnɪ-
Note: Prefix. Normally takes either primary or secondary stress on the first syllable, e.g. **omnibus** /ˈɒm.nɪ.bəs ⓤⓢ ˈɑːm-/, **omnipresent** /ˌɒm.nɪˈpres.ənt ⓤⓢ ˌɑːm-/, or primary stress on the second syllable, e.g. **omnipotent** /ɒmˈnɪp.ə.tənt ⓤⓢ ɑːmˈnɪ.pə.t̬ənt/.
omnibus ˈɒm.nɪ.bəs, -nə-, -bʌs ⓤⓢ ˈɑːm- **-es** -ɪz
omnifarious ˌɒm.nɪˈfeə.ri.əs ⓤⓢ ˌɑːm.nɪˈfer.i-
omnificent ɒmˈnɪf.ɪ.sənt ⓤⓢ ɑːm-
omnipotence ɒmˈnɪp.ə.tənts ⓤⓢ ɑːmˈnɪp.ə.t̬ənts
omnipotent ɒmˈnɪp.ə.tənt ⓤⓢ ɑːmˈnɪp.ə.t̬ənt **-ly** -li
omnipresen|t ˌɒm.nɪˈprez.ən|t, -nəˈ- ⓤⓢ ˌɑːm.nɪˈ- **-ce** -ts
omniscience ɒmˈnɪs.i.ənts, -ˈnɪʃ-, -ˈnɪʃ.ənts ⓤⓢ ɑːmˈnɪʃ.ənts
omniscient ɒmˈnɪs.i.ənt, -ˈnɪʃ-, -ˈnɪʃ.ənt ⓤⓢ ɑːmˈnɪʃ.ənt **-ly** -li
omnium (O) ˈɒm.ni.əm ⓤⓢ ˈɑːm- **-s** -z
omnium gatherum ˌɒm.ni.əmˈgæð.ər.əm ⓤⓢ ˌɑːm- **-s** -z
omnivore ˈɒm.nɪ.vɔːʳ, -nə- ⓤⓢ ˈɑːm.nɪ.vɔːr **-s** -z
omnivorous ɒmˈnɪv.ər.əs ⓤⓢ ɑːm- **-ly** -li
Omond ˈəʊ.mənd ⓤⓢ ˈoʊ-
omphalos ˈɒmp.fəl.ɒs ⓤⓢ ˈɑːmp.fəl.əs, -ɑːs
Omri ˈɒm.raɪ ⓤⓢ ˈɑːm-
Omsk ɒmsk ⓤⓢ ɔːmsk, ɑːmsk
on (*n. adj. adv. prep.*) ɒn ⓤⓢ ɑːn, ɔːn
onager ˈɒn.ə.gəʳ ⓤⓢ ˈɑː.nə.gɚ **-s** -z
Onan ˈəʊ.næn, -nən ⓤⓢ ˈoʊ-
onan|ism ˈəʊ.nə.n|ɪ.zəm, -næn|.ɪ- ⓤⓢ ˈoʊ- **-ist/s** -ɪst/s
onanistic ˌəʊ.nəˈnɪs.tɪk, -nænˈɪst- ⓤⓢ ˌoʊ-
Onassis əʊˈnæs.ɪs ⓤⓢ oʊ-, -ˈnɑː.sɪs
on-board (*adj.*) ˈɒn.bɔːd ⓤⓢ ˈɑːn.bɔːrd
once wʌnts ˌ**once and for** ˈ**all**
once-over ˈwʌntsˌəʊ.vəʳ, ˌ-ˈ-- ⓤⓢ ˈwʌntsˌoʊ.vɚ
oncer ˈwʌnt.səʳ ⓤⓢ -sɚ **-s** -z
onco- ɒŋ.kəʊ-; ɒŋˈkɒ- ⓤⓢ ɑːn.koʊ-, ɑːŋ-, -kə-; ɑːnˈkɑː-, ɑːŋ-
Note: Prefix. Normally either takes primary or secondary stress on the first syllable, e.g. **oncogene** /ˈɒŋ.kəʊ.dʒiːn ⓤⓢ ˈɑːŋ.kə-/, **oncogenic** /ˌɒŋ.kəʊˈdʒen.ɪk ⓤⓢ ˌɑːŋ.kə-/, or primary stress on the second syllable, e.g. **oncology** /ɒŋˈkɒl.ə.dʒi ⓤⓢ ɑːŋˈkɑː.lə-/.
oncogene ˈɒŋ.kəʊ.dʒiːn ⓤⓢ ˈɑːn.kə-, ˈɑːŋ- **-s** -z
oncogenic ˌɒŋ.kəʊˈdʒen.ɪk ⓤⓢ ˌɑːn.kəˈ-, ˌɑːŋ-
oncologic ˌɒŋ.kəʊˈlɒdʒ.ɪk ⓤⓢ ˌɑːn.kəˈlɑː.dʒɪk, ˌɑːŋ-
oncological ˌɒŋ.kəʊˈlɒdʒ.ɪ.kəl ⓤⓢ ˌɑːn.kəˈlɑː.dʒɪ-, ˌɑːŋ-
oncologist ɒŋˈkɒl.ə.dʒɪst ⓤⓢ ɑːnˈkɑː.lə-, ɑːŋ- **-s** -s

Onset

In the analysis of syllable structure (and occasionally in other areas), the first part of a syllable.

Examples for English

In English the onset may be zero (when no consonant precedes the vowel in a syllable), one consonant, or two, or three, e.g.:

in	/ɪn/	spin	/spɪn/
pin	/pɪn/	spring	/sprɪŋ/

There are many restrictions on what clusters of consonants may occur in onsets: for example, if an English syllable has a three-consonant onset, the first consonant must be /s/ and the last one must be one of /l r j w/.

oncology ɒŋˈkɒl.ə.dʒi ⓊⓈ ɑːnˈkɑː.lə-, ɑːŋ-
oncoming ˈɒn,kʌm.ɪŋ, ˈɒŋ- ⓊⓈ ˈɑːn-, ˈɔːn-
Ondaatje ɒnˈdɑː.tʃə ⓊⓈ ɑːnˈdɑː.tʃe
on-drive ˈɒn.draɪv ⓊⓈ ˈɑːn-, ˈɔːn- **-s** -z
one wʌn **-s** -z
O'Neal əʊˈniːl ⓊⓈ oʊ-
one-armed ,wʌnˈɑːmd ⓊⓈ -ˈɑːrmd **,one-armed ˈbandit**
one-eyed ,wʌnˈaɪd *stress shift:* ,one-eyed ˈpirate
Onega ɒnˈeɪ.gə, əʊˈneɪ-, -ˈnjeg.ə; *old fashioned:* ˈəʊ.nɪ.gə ⓊⓈ oʊnˈjeg.ə, -neɪ-
Onegin ɒnˈjeɪ.gɪn ⓊⓈ ɑːn-
one-horse ,wʌnˈhɔːs ⓊⓈ -ˈhɔːrs *stress shift, see compound:* **,one-horse ˈtown**
O'Neil(l) əʊˈniːl ⓊⓈ oʊ-
one-legged ,wʌnˈleg.ɪd, -ˈlegd *stress shift:* ,one-legged ˈtable
one-liner ,wʌnˈlaɪ.nəʳ ⓊⓈ -nɚ **-s** -z
one-man ,wʌnˈmæn, ,wʌm- ⓊⓈ ,wʌn- *stress shift, see compound:* **,one-man ˈband**
oneness ˈwʌn.nəs, -nɪs
one-night stand ,wʌn.naɪtˈstænd
one-off ,wʌnˈɒf, ˈ-- ⓊⓈ ˈwʌn.ɑːf **-s** -s
one-parent family ,wʌn.peə.rᵊntˈfæm.ᵊl.i, ,wʌm-, -ɪ.li ⓊⓈ ,wʌn.per.ᵊntˈ-, -pær-
one-piece ˈwʌn.piːs, ˈwʌm- ⓊⓈ ˈwʌn-
oner ˈwʌn.əʳ ⓊⓈ -ɚ **-s** -z
onerous ˈəʊ.nᵊr.əs, ˈɒn.ᵊr- ⓊⓈ ˈɑː.nɚ-, ˈoʊ- **-ly** -li **-ness** -nəs, -nɪs
oneself wʌnˈself **,keep one,self to oneˈself**
onesided ,wʌnˈsaɪ.dɪd **-ly** -li **-ness** -nəs, -nɪs *stress shift:* ,onesided ˈargument
Onesimus əʊˈnes.ɪ.məs, -ˈniː.sɪ-, -sə- ⓊⓈ oʊ-
one-stop ,wʌnˈstɒp ⓊⓈ -ˈstɑːp *stress shift:* ,one-stop ˈshop
onetime ˈwʌn.taɪm
one-to-one ,wʌn.təˈwʌn, -tuˈ- ⓊⓈ -ţəˈ-
one-track mind ,wʌn.trækˈmaɪnd **-s** -z
one-upmanship ,wʌnˈʌp.mən.ʃɪp
one-way ,wʌnˈweɪ *stress shift, see compound:* **,one-way ˈstreet**
ongoing ˈɒn,gəʊ.ɪŋ, ˈɒŋ-, ,-ˈ-- ⓊⓈ ˈɑːn,goʊ- **-s** -z
Onians əˈnaɪənz, əʊ- ⓊⓈ oʊ-
Onich ˈəʊ.nɪk, -nɪx ⓊⓈ ˈoʊ-
onion ˈʌn.jən **-s** -z **-y** -i
Onions ˈʌn.jənz, əʊˈnaɪənz ⓊⓈ ˈʌn.jənz
online ,ɒnˈlaɪn ⓊⓈ ,ɑːn-, ,ɔːn- *stress shift:* ,online ˈchat
onlook|er ˈɒn,lʊk|.əʳ ⓊⓈ ˈɑːn,lʊk|.ɚ, ˈɔːn- **-ers** -əz ⓊⓈ -ɚz **-ing** -ɪŋ
only ˈəʊn.li ⓊⓈ ˈoʊn-
Ono ˈəʊ.nəʊ ⓊⓈ ˈoʊ.noʊ
onomasiological ,ɒn.əʊ,meɪ.si.əˈlɒdʒ.ɪ.kᵊl, -zi- ⓊⓈ ,ɑː.noʊ,meɪ.si.əˈlɑː.dʒɪ-, -nə,-
onomasiology ,ɒn.əʊ,meɪ.siˈɒl.ə.dʒi, -ziˈ- ⓊⓈ ,ɑː.noʊ,meɪ.siˈɑː.lə-, -nə,-
onomastic ,ɒn.əʊˈmæs.tɪk ⓊⓈ ,ɑː.noʊˈ-, -nəˈ- **-s** -s
onomatopoe|ia ,ɒn.əʊ,mæt.əˈpiː|.ə ⓊⓈ ,ɑː.noʊ,mæţ.oʊˈ-, -nə,- **-ias** -əz **-ic** -ɪk
onrush ˈɒn.rʌʃ ⓊⓈ ˈɑːn-, ˈɔːn- **-ing** -ɪŋ
onscreen ,ɒnˈskriːn ⓊⓈ ,ɑːn-, ,ɔːn- *stress shift* ,onscreen ˈdaughter
onset ˈɒn.set ⓊⓈ ˈɑːn-, ˈɔːn- **-s** -s
onshore ,ɒnˈʃɔːʳ ⓊⓈ ˈɑːn.ʃɔːr, ˈɔːn- *stress shift, British only:* ,onshore ˈwind
onside ,ɒnˈsaɪd ⓊⓈ ˈɑːn.saɪd, ˈɔːn- *stress shift, British only:* ,onside ˈplayer
onslaught ˈɒn.slɔːt ⓊⓈ ˈɑːn.slɑːt, ˈɔːn-, -slɔːt **-s** -s
Onslow ˈɒnz.ləʊ ⓊⓈ ˈɑːnz.loʊ
onstage ,ɒnˈsteɪdʒ ⓊⓈ ,ɑːn-, ,ɔːn- *stress shift:* ,onstage ˈson
onstream ,ɒnˈstriːm ⓊⓈ ,ɑːn-, ,ɔːn- *stress shift:* ,onstream ˈoilfield
Ontario ɒnˈteə.ri.əʊ ⓊⓈ ɑːnˈter.i.oʊ
onto ˈɒn.tuː, -tə, -tu ⓊⓈ ˈɑːn.tuː, ˈɔːn-, -tə, -tu
Note: The pronunciation /ˈɒn.tuː ⓊⓈ ˈɑːn-/ is only rarely heard. The usual pronunciation is /ˈɒn.tə ⓊⓈ ɑːn.tə/ before consonants, e.g. "onto ships" /,ɒn.təˈʃɪps ⓊⓈ ɑːn.təˈ-/ and /ˈɒn.tu ⓊⓈ ˈɑːn-/ before vowels, e.g. "onto aircraft" /,ɒn.tuˈeə.krɑːft ⓊⓈ ,ɑːn.tuˈer.kræft/.
ontogenesis ,ɒn.təʊˈdʒen.ə.sɪs, ˈ-ɪ- ⓊⓈ ,ɑːn.toʊˈdʒen.ə-
ontogenetic ,ɒn.təʊ.dʒəˈnet.ɪk, -dʒɪˈ- ⓊⓈ ,ɑːn.toʊ.dʒəˈneţ- **-ally** -ᵊl.i, -li
ontogeny ɒnˈtɒdʒ.ə.ni, ˈ-ɪ- ⓊⓈ ɑːnˈtɑː.dʒə-
ontologic ,ɒn.təˈlɒdʒ.ɪk ⓊⓈ ,ɑːn.toʊˈlɑː.dʒɪk **-al** -ᵊl **-ally** -ᵊl.i, -li
ontolog|y ɒnˈtɒl.ə.dʒ|i ⓊⓈ ɑːnˈtɑː.lə- **-ist/s** -ɪst/s
onus ˈəʊ.nəs ⓊⓈ ˈoʊ-
onward ˈɒn.wəd ⓊⓈ ˈɑːn.wɚd, ˈɔːn- **-s** -z
onyx ˈɒn.ɪks ⓊⓈ ˈɑː.nɪks **-es** -ɪz
oodles ˈuː.dl̩z
oof uːf
ooh uː
oolite ˈəʊ.əʊ.laɪt ⓊⓈ ˈoʊ.ə- **-s** -s
oolitic ,əʊ.əʊˈlɪt.ɪk ⓊⓈ ,oʊ.əˈlɪţ-
oolog|y əʊˈɒl.ə.dʒ|i ⓊⓈ oʊˈɑː.lə- **-ist/s** -ɪst/s
Oolong ˈuː.lɒŋ, ,-ˈ- ⓊⓈ ˈuː.lɑːŋ, -lɔːŋ
oompah ˈʊm.pɑː, ˈuːm-
oomph ʊmpf, uːmpf
oops uːps, ʊps
oops-a-daisy ,ʊps.əˈdeɪ.zi, ,uːps-, ,wʊps-, ˈʊps.ə,deɪ-, ˈuːps-, ˈwʊps-
ooz|e uːz **-es** -ɪz **-ing** -ɪŋ **-ed** -d
ooz|y ˈuː.z|i **-ier** -i.əʳ ⓊⓈ -i.ɚ **-iest** -i.ɪst, -i.əst **-ily** -ɪ.li, -ᵊl.i **-iness** -ɪ.nəs, -ɪ.nɪs
op ɒp ⓊⓈ ɑːp **-s** -s
opacity əʊˈpæs.ə.ti, -ɪ.ti ⓊⓈ oʊˈpæs.ə.ţi
opal ˈəʊ.pᵊl ⓊⓈ ˈoʊ- **-s** -z
opalescen|t ,əʊ.pᵊlˈes.ᵊn|t ⓊⓈ ,oʊ- **-ce** -*t*s
opaline (*adj.*) ˈəʊ.pᵊl.aɪn ⓊⓈ ˈoʊ.pᵊl.iːn, -aɪn, -ɪn
opaline (*n.*) ˈəʊ.pᵊl.iːn, -aɪn ⓊⓈ ˈoʊ- **-s** -z

Pronouncing the letters OO

The most common pronunciation for the vowel digraph **oo** is /uː/, e.g.:

boom /buːm/

The realisation /ʊ/ is also quite common, e.g.:

book /bʊk/
stood /stʊd/

When followed by an r in the spelling, **oo** is pronounced as either /ɔː (US) ɔːr/ or /ʊə (US) ʊr/ e.g

door /dɔːʳ/ (US) /dɔːr/
moor /mɔːʳ, mʊəʳ/ (US) /mʊr/

It should be noted that, for many speakers, the form /mʊəʳ/ has dropped out of use in favour of /mɔːʳ/.

In addition

There are other vowel sounds associated with the digraph **oo**, e.g.:

/ʌ/ blood /blʌd/
/əʊ (US) oʊ/ brooch /brəʊtʃ/ (US) /broʊtʃ/

opaque əʊ'peɪk (US) oʊ- **-ly** -li **-ness** -nəs, -nɪs
op art 'ɒp,ɑːt (US) 'ɑːp,ɑːrt
op. cit. ,ɒp'sɪt (US) ,ɑːp-
op|e əʊp (US) oʊp **-es** -s **-ing** -ɪŋ **-ed** -t
OPEC, Opec 'əʊ.pek (US) 'oʊ-
Opel® 'əʊ.pᵊl (US) 'oʊ-
open 'əʊ.pᵊn (US) 'oʊ- **-er** -əʳ (US) -ɚ **-est** -ɪst (US) -əst **-s** -z **-ing** -ɪŋ, 'əʊp.nɪŋ (US) 'oʊp- **-ed** -d **,open 'book; 'open ,day; ,open 'house; ,open 'market; ,open 'prison; ,open 'sesame; ,Open Uni'versity; ,open 'verdict**
open-air (*adj.*) ,əʊ.pᵊn'eəʳ (US) ,oʊ.pᵊn'er *stress shift:* ,open-air 'concert (*n.*) **open air** ,əʊ.pᵊn'eəʳ (US) ,oʊ.pᵊn'er
open-and-shut ,əʊ.pᵊn.ənd'ʃʌt (US) ,oʊ- *stress shift:* ,open-and-shut 'case
opencast 'əʊ.pᵊn.kɑːst, -pᵊŋ- (US) 'oʊ.pᵊn.kæst
open-ended ,əʊ.pᵊn'end.ɪd (US) ,oʊ- *stress shift:* ,open-ended 'verdict
opener 'əʊ.pᵊn.əʳ (US) 'oʊ.pᵊn.ɚ **-s** -z
open-eyed ,əʊ.pᵊn'aɪd (US) ,oʊ- *stress shift:* ,open-eyed 'onlooker
open-handed ,əʊ.pᵊn'hæn.dɪd, 'əʊ.pᵊn,hæn- (US) 'oʊ.pᵊn,hæn-, ,oʊ.pᵊn'hæn- **-ness** -nəs, -nɪs *stress shift, British only:* ,open-handed 'benefactor
open-heart ,əʊ.pᵊn'hɑːt (US) ,oʊ.pᵊn'hɑːrt *stress shift, see compound:* **,open-heart 'surgery**
open-hearted ,əʊ.pᵊn'hɑː.tɪd, 'əʊ.pᵊn,hɑː- (US) 'oʊ.pᵊn,hɑːr.t̬ɪd, ,oʊ.pᵊn'hɑːr- **-ly** -li **-ness** -nəs, -nɪs *stress shift, British only:* ,open-hearted 'person
opening 'əʊp.nɪŋ, 'əʊ.pᵊn.ɪŋ (US) 'oʊp.nɪŋ, 'oʊ.pᵊn.ɪŋ **-s** -z
opening time 'əʊp.nɪŋ,taɪm, 'əʊ.pᵊn.ɪŋ,- (US) 'oʊp.nɪŋ,-, 'oʊ.pᵊn.ɪŋ,-
openly 'əʊ.pᵊn.li (US) 'oʊ-
open-minded ,əʊ.pᵊn'maɪn.dɪd, -pᵊm'-, 'əʊ.pᵊn,maɪn-, -pᵊm,- (US) ,oʊ.pᵊn'maɪn-, 'oʊ.pᵊn,maɪn- **-ly** -li **-ness** -nəs, -nɪs *stress shift, British only:* ,open-minded 'person
open-mouthed ,əʊ.pᵊn'maʊðd, -pᵊm'-, 'əʊ.pᵊn,maʊðd (US) 'oʊ.pᵊn,maʊðd, -,maʊθt, ,--'- *stress shift, British only:* ,open-mouthed 'children
openness 'əʊ.pᵊn.nəs, -nɪs (US) 'oʊ-
open-plan ,əʊ.pᵊn'plæn, -pᵊm'- (US) ,oʊ.pᵊn- *stress shift:* ,open-plan 'offices
open sesame ,əʊ.pᵊn'ses.ə.mi (US) ,oʊ-
Openshaw 'əʊ.pᵊn.ʃɔː (US) 'oʊ.pᵊn.ʃɑː, -ʃɔː
open-work 'əʊ.pᵊn.wɜːk (US) 'oʊ.pᵊn.wɝːk
opera 'ɒp.ᵊr.ə, 'ɒp.rə (US) 'ɑː.pᵊr.ə, 'ɑː.prə **-s** -z **'opera ,house**
operability ,ɒp.ᵊr.ə'bɪl.ɪ.ti, -ə.ti (US) ,ɑː.pᵊr.ə'bɪl.ə.t̬i, ,ɑː.prə'-
operab|le 'ɒp.ᵊr.ə.b|l̩ (US) 'ɑː.pᵊr.ə-, 'ɑː.prə- **-ly** -li
opéra bouffe ,ɒp.ᵊr.ə'buːf (US) ,ɑː.pᵊr-, ,ɑː.prə'-
opera buffa ,ɒp.ᵊr.ə'buː.fə (US) ,ɑː.pᵊr.ə'-, ,ɑː.prə'-
opéra comique ,ɒp.ᵊr.ə.kɒm'iːk (US) ,ɑː.pᵊr.ə.kɑː'miːk, ,ɑː.prə-
operant 'ɒp.ᵊr.ᵊnt (US) 'ɑː.pᵊr- **-s** -s
oper|ate 'ɒp.ᵊr|.eɪt (US) 'ɑː.pᵊr- **-ates** -eɪts **-ating** -eɪ.tɪŋ (US) -eɪ.t̬ɪŋ **-ated** -eɪ.tɪd (US) -eɪ.t̬ɪd **-ator/s** -eɪ.təʳ/z (US) -eɪ.t̬ɚ/z **'operating ,system; 'operating ,table**
operatic ,ɒp.ᵊr'æt.ɪk (US) ,ɑː.pə'ræt̬- **-s** -s **-ally** -ᵊl.i, -li
operation ,ɒp.ᵊr'eɪ.ʃᵊn (US) ,ɑː.pə'reɪ- **-s** -z
operational ,ɒp.ᵊr'eɪ.ʃᵊn.ᵊl, -'eɪʃ.nᵊl (US) ,ɑː.pə'reɪ.ʃᵊn.ᵊl, -'reɪʃ.nᵊl **-ly** -i
operative 'ɒp.ᵊr.ə.tɪv, -eɪ- (US) 'ɑː.pɚ.ə.t̬ɪv, -pə.reɪ- **-ly** -li **-ness** -nəs, -nɪs
operetta ,ɒp.ᵊr'et.ə (US) ,ɑː.pə'ret̬- **-s** -z
operettist ,ɒp.ᵊr'et.ɪst (US) ,ɑː.pə'ret̬- **-s** -s
Ophelia əʊ'fiː.li.ə, ɒf'iː- (US) oʊ'fiːl.jə
ophicleide 'ɒf.ɪ.klaɪd (US) 'ɑː.fɪ- **-s** -z
ophidian ɒf'ɪd.i.ən, əʊ'fɪd- (US) oʊ-
Ophir 'əʊ.fəʳ (US) 'oʊ.fɚ
Ophiuchus ɒf'juː.kəs, ,ɒf.i'uː- (US) ,ɑː.fi'juː.kəs, ,oʊ-
ophthalmia ɒf'θæl.mi.ə, ɒp- (US) ɑːf-, ɑːp-
ophthalmic ɒf'θæl.mɪk, ɒp- (US) ɑːf-, ɑːp-
ophthalmo- ɒf,θæl.məʊ-, ɒp- (US) ɑːf,θæl.moʊ-, ɑːp-, -mə-
ophthalmolog|y ,ɒf.θæl'mɒl.ə.dʒ|i, ɒp- (US) ,ɑːf.θæl'mɑː.lə-, ,ɑːp- **-ist/s** -ɪst/s
ophthalmoscope ɒf'θæl.mə.skəʊp, ɒp- (US) ɑːf'θæl.mə.skoʊp, ɑːp- **-s** -s
ophthalmoscopy ,ɒf.θæl'mɒs.kə.pi, ɒp- (US) ,ɑːf.θæl'mɑː.skə-, ,ɑːp-
opiate 'əʊ.pi.ət, -ɪt, -eɪt (US) 'oʊ.pi.ɪt, -eɪt **-s** -s
opiated 'əʊ.pi.eɪ.tɪd (US) 'oʊ.pi.eɪ.t̬ɪd
Opie 'əʊ.pi (US) 'oʊ-
opin|e əʊ'paɪn (US) oʊ- **-es** -z **-ing** -ɪŋ **-ed** -d
opinion ə'pɪn.jən (US) ə-, oʊ- **-s** -z **o'pinion ,poll**
opinionated ə'pɪn.jə.neɪ.tɪd (US) -t̬ɪd, oʊ-
opium 'əʊ.pi.əm (US) 'oʊ- **'opium ,den**
Oporto əʊ'pɔː.təʊ (US) oʊ'pɔːr.toʊ
opossum ə'pɒs.əm (US) -'pɑː.səm **-s** -z
Oppenheim 'ɒp.ᵊn.haɪm (US) 'ɑː.pᵊn- **-er** -əʳ (US) -ɚ
oppidan 'ɒp.ɪ.dᵊn (US) 'ɑː.pɪ- **-s** -z
opponent ə'pəʊ.nənt (US) -'poʊ- **-s** -s

opportune ˈɒp.ə.tjuːn, -tʃuːn, ˌ--ˈ- ⓤⓢ ˌɑː.pɚˈtuːn, -ˈtjuːn **-ly** -li **-ness** -nəs, -nɪs
opportun|ism ˌɒp.əˈtjuː.n|ɪ.zᵊm, -ˈtʃuː-, ˈɒp.ə.tjuː-, -tʃuː- ⓤⓢ ˌɑː.pɚˈtuː-, -ˈtjuː- **-ist/s** -ɪst/s
opportunistic ˌɒp.ə.tjuːˈnɪs.tɪk, -tʃuːˈ- ⓤⓢ ˌɑː.pɚ.tuːˈ-, -tjuːˈ- **-ally** -ᵊl.i, -li
opportunit|y ˌɒp.əˈtjuː.nə.t|i, -ˈtʃuː-, -nɪ- ⓤⓢ ˌɑː.pɚˈtuː.nə.t̬|i, -ˈtjuː- **-ies** -iz
oppos|e əˈpəʊz ⓤⓢ -ˈpoʊz **-es** -ɪz **-ing** -ɪŋ **-ed** -d **-er/s** -əʳ/z ⓤⓢ -ɚ/z **-able** -ə.bl̩
opposite ˈɒp.ə.zɪt, -sɪt ⓤⓢ ˈɑː.pə- **-s** -s **-ly** -li **-ness** -nəs, -nɪs ˌ**opposite** ˈ**number**
opposition ˌɒp.əˈzɪʃ.ᵊn ⓤⓢ ˌɑː.pəˈ- **-s** -z
oppress əˈpres **-es** -ɪz **-ing** -ɪŋ **-ed** -t
oppression əˈpreʃ.ᵊn **-s** -z
oppressive əˈpres.ɪv **-ly** -li **-ness** -nəs, -nɪs
oppressor əˈpres.əʳ ⓤⓢ -ɚ **-s** -z
opprobrious əˈprəʊ.bri.əs ⓤⓢ -ˈproʊ- **-ly** -li **-ness** -nəs, -nɪs
opprobrium əˈprəʊ.bri.əm ⓤⓢ -ˈproʊ-
oppugn əˈpjuːn **-s** -z **-ing** -ɪŋ **-ed** -d **-er/s** -əʳ/z ⓤⓢ -ɚ/z
Oprah ˈəʊ.prə ⓤⓢ ˈoʊ-
Opren® ˈɒp.rᵊn, -ren ⓤⓢ ˈɑː.prᵊn, -pren
opt ɒpt ⓤⓢ ɑːpt **-s** -s **-ing** -ɪŋ **-ed** -ɪd
optative ˈɒp.tə.tɪv; ɒpˈteɪ- ⓤⓢ ˈɑːp.tə.t̬ɪv **-s** -z
optic ˈɒp.tɪk ⓤⓢ ˈɑːp- **-s** -s
optical ˈɒp.tɪ.kᵊl ⓤⓢ ˈɑːp- **-ly** -i ˌ**optical** ˈ**fibre**; ˌ**optical il**ˈ**lusion**
optician ɒpˈtɪʃ.ᵊn ⓤⓢ ɑːp- **-s** -z
optimal ˈɒp.tɪ.mᵊl ⓤⓢ ˈɑːp- **-ly** -i
optime ˈɒp.tɪ.meɪ ⓤⓢ ˈɑːp- **-s** -z
optim|ism ˈɒp.tɪ.m|ɪ.zᵊm, -tə- ⓤⓢ ˈɑːp.tə- **-ist/s** -ɪst/s
optimistic ˌɒp.tɪˈmɪs.tɪk, -təˈ- ⓤⓢ ˌɑːp.təˈ- **-al** -ᵊl **-ally** -ᵊl.i, -li
optimization ˌɒp.tɪ.maɪˈzeɪ.ʃᵊn, -tə-, -mɪˈ- ⓤⓢ ˌɑːp.tə.mɪˈzeɪ- **-s** -z
optimiz|e, -is|e ˈɒp.tɪ.maɪz, -tə- ⓤⓢ ˈɑːp.tə- **-es** -ɪz **-ing** -ɪŋ **-ed** -d
optim|um ˈɒp.tɪ.m|əm, -tə- ⓤⓢ ˈɑːp.tə- **-ums** -əmz **-a** -ə
option ˈɒp.ʃᵊn ⓤⓢ ˈɑːp- **-s** -z **-ing** -ɪŋ **-ed** -d
optional ˈɒp.ʃᵊn.ᵊl ⓤⓢ ˈɑːp.ʃᵊn.ᵊl **-ly** -i
optometric ˌɒp.təʊˈmet.rɪk ⓤⓢ ˌɑːp.təˈmet- **-s** -s
optometrist ɒpˈtɒm.ə.trɪst, ˈ-ɪ- ⓤⓢ ɑːpˈtɑː.mə- **-s** -s
optometry ɒpˈtɒm.ɪ.tri, ˈ-ə- ⓤⓢ ɑːpˈtɑː.mə-
Optrex® ˈɒp.treks ⓤⓢ ˈɑːp-
opulence ˈɒp.jə.lən*t*s, -jʊ- ⓤⓢ ˈɑːp-
opulent ˈɒp.jə.lənt, -jʊ- ⓤⓢ ˈɑːp- **-ly** -li
opus ˈəʊ.pəs, ˈɒp.əs ⓤⓢ ˈoʊ.pəs **-es** -ɪz
opera ˈɒp.ᵊr.ə ⓤⓢ ˈoʊ.pɚ.ə, ˈɑː-, ˈ-prə
opuscule ɒpˈʌs.kjuːl, əʊˈpʌs- ⓤⓢ oʊˈpʌs.kjuːl **-s** -z
or (*n.*) ɔːʳ ⓤⓢ ɔːr
or (*conj.*) *normal form:* ɔːʳ ⓤⓢ ɔːr *weak form:* əʳ ⓤⓢ ɚ
Note: Occasional weak form word. The weak form /əʳ ⓤⓢ ɚ/ is used in phrases such as "two or three pounds" /ˌtuː.əˌθriːˈpaʊndz ⓤⓢ -ɚˌ-/.
orach|(e) ˈɒr.ɪtʃ ⓤⓢ ˈɔːr.ətʃ **-es** -ɪz
oracle ˈɒr.ə.kl̩, ˈ-ɪ- ⓤⓢ ˈɔːr.ə- **-s** -z
oracular ɒrˈæk.jə.ləʳ, ɔːˈræk-, ə-, -jʊ- ⓤⓢ ɔːˈræk.juː.lɚ, ə-, -jə- **-ly** -li **-ness** -nəs, -nɪs
oracy ˈɔː.rə.si ⓤⓢ ˈɔːr.ə-
Oradea ɒrˈɑː.di.ə ⓤⓢ ɔːˈrɑː.djɑː
oral ˈɔː.rᵊl ⓤⓢ ˈɔːr.əl **-s** -z **-ly** -i ˌ**oral** ˈ**sex**
Oran ɔːˈrɑːn, ə-, ɒrˈɑːn, -ˈæn ⓤⓢ oʊˈrɑːn, -ˈræn
orang|e (O) ˈɒr.ɪndʒ, -əndʒ ⓤⓢ ˈɔːr.ɪndʒ **-es** -ɪz ˌ**Orange** ˈ**Free** ˌ**State**; ˈ**orange** ˌ**juice**
orangeade ˌɒr.ɪndʒˈeɪd, -əndʒˈ- ⓤⓢ ˌɔːr.ɪndʒˈ-
orange-blossom ˈɒr.ɪndʒˌblɒs.əm, -əndʒˌ- ⓤⓢ ˈɔːr.ɪndʒˌblɑː.səm **-s** -z
Orange|man ˈɒr.ɪndʒ|.mən, -əndʒ-, -mæn ⓤⓢ ˈɔːr.ɪndʒ **-men** -mən, -men
oranger|y ˈɒr.ɪn.dʒᵊr|.i, -ən-, ˈ-ɪndʒ.r|i ⓤⓢ ˈɔːr.ɪndʒ.ri **-ies** -iz
orangoutan, orangutan, orangutang ɔːˌræŋ.uːˈtæn, ɒrˌæŋ-, əˌræŋ-, -əˈ-, -juːˈ-, -ˈtɑːn, -ˈtæŋ, ɔːˈræŋ.uː.tæn, ɒrˈæŋ-, əˈræŋ-, ˈ-ə-, ˈ-juː-, -tɑːn, -tæŋ ⓤⓢ ɔːˈræŋ.ə.tæn, ə-, oʊ-, -tæŋ **-s** -s
ora|te ɔːˈreɪ|t, ɒrˈeɪ|t, əˈreɪ|t ⓤⓢ ˈɔːr.eɪt; ɔːˈreɪ|t **-tes** -ts **-ting** -tɪŋ ⓤⓢ -t̬ɪŋ **-ted** -tɪd ⓤⓢ -t̬ɪd
oration ɔːˈreɪ.ʃᵊn, ɒr- ⓤⓢ ɔː- **-s** -z
orator ˈɒr.ə.təʳ ⓤⓢ ˈɔːr.ə.t̬ɚ **-s** -z
oratorical ˌɒr.əˈtɒr.ɪ.kᵊl ⓤⓢ ˌɔːr.əˈtɔːr- **-ly** -i
oratorio ˌɒr.əˈtɔː.ri.əʊ ⓤⓢ ˌɔːr.əˈtɔːr.i.oʊ **-s** -z
orator|y (O) ˈɒr.ə.tᵊr|.i ⓤⓢ ˈɔːr.ə.tɔːr- **-ies** -iz
orb ɔːb ⓤⓢ ɔːrb **-s** -z **-ing** -ɪŋ **-ed** -d
Orbach ˈɔː.bæk ⓤⓢ ˈɔːr-
orbed ɔːbd ⓤⓢ ɔːrbd *in poetry generally:* ˈɔː.bɪd ⓤⓢ ˈɔːr.bɪd
orbicular ɔːˈbɪk.jə.ləʳ, -jʊ- ⓤⓢ ɔːrˈbɪk.juː.lɚ, -jə- **-ly** -li
Orbison ˈɔː.bɪ.sᵊn, -bə- ⓤⓢ ˈɔːr-
or|bit ˈɔː|.bɪt ⓤⓢ ˈɔːr- **-bits** -bɪts **-biting** -bɪ.tɪŋ ⓤⓢ -bɪ.t̬ɪŋ **-bited** -bɪ.tɪd ⓤⓢ -bɪ.t̬ɪd **-bital** -bɪ.tᵊl ⓤⓢ -t̬ᵊl
orc ɔːk ⓤⓢ ɔːrk **-s** -s
Orcadian ɔːˈkeɪ.di.ən ⓤⓢ ɔːr- **-s** -z
orchard (O) ˈɔː.tʃəd ⓤⓢ ˈɔːr.tʃɚd **-s** -z
Orchardson ˈɔː.tʃəd.sᵊn ⓤⓢ ˈɔːr.tʃɚd-
Orchehill ˈɔː.tʃɪl ⓤⓢ ˈɔːr-
orchestra ˈɔː.kɪ.strə, -kə-, -kes.trə ⓤⓢ ˈɔːr.kɪ.strə, -kes.trə **-s** -z
orchestral ɔːˈkes.trᵊl ⓤⓢ ɔːr-
orchest|rate ˈɔː.kɪ.st|reɪt, -kə-, -kes.t|reɪt ⓤⓢ ˈɔːr.kɪ.st|reɪt, -kes.t|reɪt **-rates** -reɪts **-rating** -reɪ.tɪŋ ⓤⓢ -reɪ.t̬ɪŋ **-rated** -reɪ.tɪd ⓤⓢ -reɪ.t̬ɪd
orchestration ˌɔː.kɪˈstreɪ.ʃᵊn, -kəˈ-, -kesˈtreɪ- ⓤⓢ ˌɔːr.kɪˈstreɪ-, -kesˈtreɪ- **-s** -z
orchestrion ɔːˈkes.tri.ən ⓤⓢ ɔːr- **-s** -z
orchid ˈɔː.kɪd ⓤⓢ ˈɔːr- **-s** -z
orchidaceous ˌɔː.kɪˈdeɪ.ʃəs ⓤⓢ ˌɔːr-
orchil ˈɔː.tʃɪl, -kɪl ⓤⓢ ˈɔːr-
orchis ˈɔː.kɪs ⓤⓢ ˈɔːr- **-es** -ɪz
Orczy ˈɔːk.si, ˈɔːt- ⓤⓢ ˈɔːrk-, ˈɔːrt-
Ord ɔːd ⓤⓢ ɔːrd
ordain ɔːˈdeɪn ⓤⓢ ɔːr- **-s** -z **-ing** -ɪŋ **-ed** -d **-er/s** -əʳ/z ⓤⓢ -ɚ/z
Orde ɔːd ⓤⓢ ɔːrd
ordeal ɔːˈdiːl, ˈ-- ⓤⓢ ɔːrˈdiːl, ˈ-- **-s** -z
ord|er ˈɔː.d|əʳ ⓤⓢ ˈɔːr.d|ɚ **-ers** -əz ⓤⓢ -ɚz **-ering** -ᵊr.ɪŋ **-ered** -əd ⓤⓢ -ɚd **-erless** -ᵊl.əs, -ɪs ⓤⓢ -ɚ.ləs, -lɪs
orderl|y ˈɔː.dᵊl|.i ⓤⓢ ˈɔːr.dɚ.l|i **-ies** -iz **-iness** -ɪ.nəs, -ɪ.nɪs
ordinaire ˌɔː.dɪˈneəʳ, -dᵊn.eəʳ, ˈ--- ⓤⓢ ˌɔːr.dɪˈner
ordinal ˈɔː.dɪ.nᵊl, -dᵊn.ᵊl ⓤⓢ ˈɔːr.dᵊn-, ˈɔːrd.nᵊl **-s** -z ˌ**ordinal** ˈ**number**
ordinanc|e ˈɔː.dɪ.nən*t*s, -dᵊn.ən*t*s ⓤⓢ ˈɔːr.dᵊn-, ˈɔːrd.nᵊn*t*s **-es** -ɪz
ordinand ˈɔː.dɪ.nænd, -dᵊn.ænd, ˌ--ˈ- ⓤⓢ ˈɔːr.dᵊn.ænd **-s** -z
ordinarily ˈɔː.dᵊn.ᵊr.ᵊl.i, -dɪ.nᵊr-, -ɪ.li; ˌɔː.dᵊnˈer.ɪ- ⓤⓢ ˈɔːr.dᵊn.er.ᵊl.i, ˌɔːr.dᵊnˈer-
ordinariness ˈɔː.dᵊn.ᵊr.ɪ.nəs, -dɪ.nᵊr-, -nɪs ⓤⓢ ˌɔːr.dᵊnˈer-
ordinar|y ˈɔː.dᵊn.ᵊr|.i, -dɪ.nᵊr- ⓤⓢ ˈɔːr.dᵊn.er- **-ies** -iz
ordinate ˈɔː.dᵊn.ət, -dɪ.nət, -nɪt ⓤⓢ ˈɔːr.dᵊn.ɪt, -eɪt **-s** -s
ordination ˌɔː.dɪˈneɪ.ʃᵊn, -dᵊnˈeɪ- ⓤⓢ ˌɔːr.dᵊnˈeɪ- **-s** -z
ordnance ˈɔːd.nən*t*s ⓤⓢ ˈɔːrd- ˌ**Ordnance** ˈ**Survey**
ordure ˈɔː.djʊəʳ, -djəʳ ⓤⓢ ˈɔːr.dʒɚ, -djʊr
Ore. (*abbrev. for* **Oregon**) ˈɒr.ɪ.gən, ˈ-ə-, -gɒn ⓤⓢ ˈɔːr.ɪ.gən, -gɑːn
ore (O) ɔːʳ ⓤⓢ ɔːr **-s** -z
öre, ore ˈɜː.rə ⓤⓢ ˈɝː.ə
oread ˈɔː.ri.æd ⓤⓢ ˈɔːr.i- **-s** -z
Örebro ˈɜː.rə.bruː ⓤⓢ ˈɝː.ə-
O'Regan əʊˈriː.gən ⓤⓢ oʊ-
oregano ˌɒr.ɪˈgɑː.nəʊ, -əˈ- ⓤⓢ ɔːˈreg.ə.noʊ, ə-

regon ˈɒr.ɪ.gən, ˈ-ə-, -gɒn (US) ˈɔːr.ɪ.gən, -gɑːn
'Reilly əʊˈraɪ.li (US) oʊ-
reo® ˈɔː.ri.əʊ (US) ˈɔːr.i.oʊ **-s** -z
resteia ˌɒr.ɪˈstaɪə, ˌɔː.rɪˈ-, -rəˈ-, -ˈsteɪə (US) ˌɔːr.esˈtiː.ə, -əˈstiː-
restes ɒrˈes.tiːz, ɔːˈres-, ə- (US) ɔː-
rfe ɔːf (US) ɔːrf
rfeo ˈɔː.fi.əʊ *as if Italian:* ɔːˈfeɪ.əʊ (US) ˈɔːr.fi.oʊ, -feɪ-
rff ɔːf (US) ɔːrf
rford ˈɔː.fəd (US) ˈɔːr.fɚd
rgan ˈɔː.gən (US) ˈɔːr- **-s** -z
rgand|y, -|ie ˈɔː.gᵊn.d|i, ɔːˈgæn- (US) ˈɔːr.gən- **-ies** -iz
rganelle ˌɔː.gᵊnˈel (US) ˌɔːr- **-s** -z
rgan-grinder ˈɔː.gᵊnˌgraɪn.dəʳ, -gᵊŋˌ- (US) ˈɔːr.gᵊnˌgraɪn.dɚ **-s** -z
rganic ɔːˈgæn.ɪk (US) ɔːr- **-s** -s **-al** -ᵊl **-ally** -ᵊl.i, -li
rganism ˈɔː.gᵊn.ɪ.zᵊm (US) ˈɔːr- **-s** -z
rganist ˈɔː.gᵊn.ɪst (US) ˈɔːr- **-s** -s
rganizability, -isa- ˌɔː.gᵊnˌaɪ.zəˈbɪl.ə.ti, -ɪ.ti (US) ˌɔːr.gᵊnˌaɪ.zəˈbɪl.ə.t̬i
ganization, -isa- ˌɔː.gᵊn.aɪˈzeɪ.ʃᵊn, -ɪˈ- (US) ˌɔːr.gᵊn.ɪˈ- **-s** -z
ganizational, -isa- ˌɔː.gᵊn.aɪˈzeɪ.ʃᵊn.ᵊl, -ɪˈ- (US) ˌɔːr.gᵊn.ɪˈ- **-ly** -i
ganiz|e, -is|e ˈɔː.gᵊn.aɪz (US) ˈɔːr- **-es** -ɪz **-ing** -ɪŋ **-ed** -d **-er/s** -əʳ/z (US) -ɚ/z **-able** -ə.bl̩
gan|on ˈɔː.gə.n|ɒn (US) ˈɔːr.gə.n|ɑːn **-ons** -ɒnz (US) -ɑːnz **-a** -ə
ganophosphate ɔːˌgæn.əʊˈfɒs.feɪt, -fɪt, -fət; ˌɔːr.gᵊn.əʊ- (US) ɔːrˌgæn.oʊˈfɑːs.feɪt, -əˈ-; ˌɔːr.gᵊn.oʊ- **-s** -s
ganum ˈɔː.gə.nəm (US) ˈɔːr- **-s** -z
ganza ɔːˈgæn.zə (US) ɔːr-
gasm ˈɔː.gæz.ᵊm (US) ˈɔːr- **-s** -z
gasmic ɔːˈgæz.mɪk (US) ɔːr- **-ally** -ᵊl.i, -li
giastic ˌɔː.dʒiˈæs.tɪk (US) ˌɔːr- **-ally** -ᵊl.i, -li
g|y ˈɔː.dʒ|i (US) ˈɔːr- **-ies** -iz
iana ˌɒr.iˈɑː.nə, ˌɔː.riˈ- (US) ˌɔːr.iˈæn.ə
el (O) ˈɔː.ri.əl (US) ˈɔːr.i- **-s** -z
ent (O) (*n. adj.*) ˈɔː.ri.ənt, ˈɒr.i- (US) ˈɔːr.i- ˌ**Orient Ex**ˈ**press**
ent (*v.*) ˈɔː.ri|.ent, ˈɒr.i- (US) ˈɔːr.i- **-ents** -ents **-enting** -en.tɪŋ (US) -en.t̬ɪŋ **-ented** -en.tɪd (US) -en.t̬ɪd
ental (O) ˌɔː.riˈen.tᵊl, ˌɒr.iˈ- (US) ˌɔːr.iˈ- **-s** -z
ental|ism ˌɔː.riˈen.tᵊl|.ɪ.zᵊm, ˌɒr.iˈ- (US) ˌɔːr.iˈen.t̬ᵊl- **-ist/s** -ɪst/s
entaliz|e, -is|e ˌɔː.riˈen.tᵊl.aɪz, ˌɒr.iˈ- (US) ˌɔːr.iˈen.t̬ᵊl- **-es** -ɪz **-ing** -ɪŋ **-ed** -d

orien|tate ˈɔː.ri.ən|.teɪt, ˈɒr.i-, -en- (US) ˈɔːr.i.en-, ˌɔːr.iˈen- **-tates** -teɪts **-tating** -teɪ.tɪŋ (US) -teɪ.t̬ɪŋ **-tated** -teɪ.tɪd (US) -teɪ.t̬ɪd
orientation ˌɔː.ri.enˈteɪ.ʃᵊn, ˌɒr.i- (US) ˌɔːr.i.enˈ- **-s** -z
orienteer ˌɔː.ri.ənˈtɪəʳ, ˌɒr.i-, -enˈ- (US) ˌɔːr.i.enˈtɪr **-s** -z
orienteering ˌɔː.ri.ənˈtɪə.rɪŋ, ˌɒr.i-, -enˈ- (US) ˌɔːr.i.enˈtɪr.ɪŋ
orific|e ˈɒr.ɪ.fɪs, ˈ-ə- (US) ˈɔːr.ə- **-es** -ɪz
oriflamme ˈɒr.ɪ.flæm, ˈ-ə- (US) ˈɔːr.ɪ- **-s** -z
origami ˌɒr.ɪˈgɑː.mi, -ˈgæm.i (US) ˌɔːr.ɪˈgɑː.mi
Origen ˈɒr.ɪ.dʒen, ˈ-ə- (US) ˈɔːr.ɪ.dʒən, -dʒen
origin ˈɒr.ɪ.dʒɪn, ˈ-ə-, -dʒən (US) ˈɔːr.ə.dʒɪn **-s** -z
original əˈrɪdʒ.ᵊn.ᵊl, ɒrˈɪdʒ-, -ɪ.nᵊl (US) əˈrɪdʒ.ɪ- **-s** -z **-ness** -nəs, -nɪs
oˌ**riginal** ˈ**sin**
originalit|y əˌrɪdʒ.ᵊnˈæl.ə.t|i, ɒrˌɪdʒ-, -ɪˈnæl-, -ɪ.t|i (US) əˌrɪdʒ.ɪˈnæl.ə.t̬|i **-ies** -iz
originally əˈrɪdʒ.ᵊn.ᵊl.i, ɒrˈɪdʒ-, -ɪ.nᵊl- (US) əˈrɪdʒ.ɪ-
origi|nate əˈrɪdʒ.ᵊn|.eɪt, ɒrˈɪdʒ-, -ɪ.n|eɪt (US) əˈrɪdʒ.ɪ- **-nates** -neɪts **-nating** -neɪ.tɪŋ (US) -neɪ.t̬ɪŋ **-nated** -neɪ.tɪd (US) -neɪ.t̬ɪd **-nator/s** -neɪ.təʳ/z (US) -neɪ.t̬ɚ/z **-native** -neɪ.tɪv (US) -neɪ.t̬ɪv
origination əˌrɪdʒ.ᵊnˈeɪ.ʃᵊn, ɒrˌɪdʒ-, -ɪˈneɪ- (US) əˌrɪdʒ.ɪˈ-
Orinoco ˌɒr.ɪˈnəʊ.kəʊ, -əˈ- (US) ˌɔːr.əˈnoʊ.koʊ
oriole ˈɔː.ri.əʊl (US) ˈɔːr.i.oʊl **-s** -z
Orion əˈraɪən, ɒrˈaɪən-, ɔːˈraɪən (US) oʊ-, ə-
O'Riordan əʊˈrɪə.dᵊn, -ˈraɪə- (US) oʊˈrɪr-
orison ˈɒr.ɪ.zᵊn, -ə- (US) ˈɔːr.ɪ.zᵊn, -sᵊn **-s** -z
Orissa ɒrˈɪs.ə, ɔːˈrɪs-, ə- (US) oʊ-, ɔː-
Oriya ɒrˈiː.ə (US) ɔːˈriː.ə
ork ɔːk (US) ɔːrk **-s** -s
Orkney ˈɔːk.ni (US) ˈɔːrk- **-s** -z
Orlan® ˈɔː.lᵊn, -læn (US) ˈɔːr.lɑːn
Orlando ɔːˈlæn.dəʊ (US) ɔːrˈlæn.doʊ
Orléans *in France:* ɔːˈlɪənz, ˈ-- *as if French:* ˌɔː.leɪˈɑ̃ːŋ (US) -ˈliː.ənz *as if French:* ˌɔːr.leɪˈɑ̃ːn
Orleans *in US:* ˈɔː.li.ənz, ˈ-lɪənz, ˈ-lənz; ɔːˈliːnz (US) ˈɔːr.li.ənz, ˈ-lənz; ɔːrˈliːnz
Orlon® ˈɔː.lɒn (US) ˈɔːr.lɑːn
Orly ˈɔː.li (US) ˈɔːr-
Orm(e) ɔːm (US) ɔːrm
ormer ˈɔː.məʳ (US) ˈɔːr.mɚ **-s** -z
Ormes ɔːmz (US) ɔːrmz
Ormiston ˈɔː.mɪ.stᵊn (US) ˈɔːr-

ormolu ˈɔː.mə.luː, -ljuː, ˌ--ˈ- (US) ˈɔːr.mə.luː
Ormond(e) ˈɔː.mənd (US) ˈɔːr-
Ormsby ˈɔːmz.bi (US) ˈɔːrmz-
Ormulum ˈɔː.mjə.ləm, -mjʊ- (US) ˈɔːr.mjuː-, -mjə-
ornament (*n.*) ˈɔː.nə.mənt (US) ˈɔːr- **-s** -s
orna|ment ˈɔː.nə|.ment (US) ˈɔːr- **-ments** -ments **-menting** -men.tɪŋ (US) -men.t̬ɪŋ **-mented** -men.tɪd (US) -men.t̬ɪd
ornamental ˌɔː.nəˈmen.tᵊl (US) ˌɔːr.nəˈmen.t̬ᵊl **-ly** -i
ornamentation ˌɔː.nə.menˈteɪ.ʃᵊn (US) ˌɔːr- **-s** -z
ornate ɔːˈneɪt (US) ɔːr- **-ly** -li **-ness** -nəs, -nɪs
ornery ˈɔː.nᵊr.i (US) ˈɔːr.nɚ-
ornithologic|al ˌɔː.nɪ.θəˈlɒdʒ.ɪ.k|ᵊl, -θᵊlˈɒdʒ-, -nə- (US) ˌɔːr.nə.θəˈlɑː.dʒɪ- **-ally** -ᵊl.i, -li
ornitholog|y ˌɔː.nɪˈθɒl.ə.dʒ|i, -nəˈ- (US) ˌɔːr.nəˈθɑː.lə- **-ist/s** -ɪst/s
orographic ˌɒr.əʊˈgræf.ɪk, ˌɔː.rəʊˈ- (US) ˌɔːr.oʊˈ- **-al** -ᵊl
orography ɒrˈɒg.rə.fi, ɔːˈrɒg- (US) ɔːˈrɑː.grə-
orological ˌɒr.əˈlɒdʒ.ɪ.kᵊl, ˌɔː.rəˈ- (US) ˌɔːr.əˈlɑː.dʒɪ-
orology ɒrˈɒl.ə.dʒi, ɔːˈrɒl- (US) ɔːˈrɑː.lə-
Oronsay ˈɒr.ᵊn.seɪ, -zeɪ (US) ˈɔːr-, -ɑːn-
Orontes ɒrˈɒn.tiːz, əˈrɒn- (US) oʊˈrɑːn-
Oroonoko ˌɒr.ʊˈnəʊ.kəʊ (US) ˌɔːr.ʊˈnoʊ.koʊ
Orosius əˈrəʊ.si.əs, ɒrˈəʊ- (US) ɔːˈroʊ.ʒi.əs
orotund ˈɒr.əʊ.tʌnd, ˈɔː.rəʊ- (US) ˈɔːr.ə-, -oʊ-, ˈ-ə-
O'Rourke əʊˈrɔːk (US) oʊˈrɔːrk
orphan ˈɔː.fᵊn (US) ˈɔːr- **-s** -z **-ing** -ɪŋ **-ed** -d
orphanag|e ˈɔː.fᵊn.ɪdʒ (US) ˈɔːr- **-es** -ɪz
Orphean ɔːˈfiː.ən; ˈɔː.fi- (US) ˈɔːr.fi.ən
Orpheus ˈɔː.fi.əs, -fjuːs (US) ˈɔːr.fi.əs, ˈ-fjuːs
orpiment ˈɔː.pɪ.mənt (US) ˈɔːr-
Orpington ˈɔː.pɪŋ.tən (US) ˈɔːr- **-s** -z
Orr ɔːʳ (US) ɔːr
Orrell ˈɒr.ᵊl (US) ˈɔːr-
orrer|y (O) ˈɒr.ᵊr|.i (US) ˈɔːr- **-ies** -iz
orris ˈɒr.ɪs (US) ˈɔːr-
Orsino ɔːˈsiː.nəʊ (US) ɔːrˈsiː.noʊ
Orson ˈɔː.sᵊn (US) ˈɔːr-
Ortega ɔːˈteɪ.gə (US) ɔːr-; ˌɔːr.t̬əˈgɑː
ortho- ɔː.θəʊ-; ɔːˈθɒ- (US) ɔːr.θoʊ-, -θə-; ɔːrˈθɑː-

Note: Prefix. Normally either takes primary or secondary stress on the first syllable, e.g. **orthodox** /ˈɔː.θə.dɒks (US) ˈɔːr.θə.dɑːks/, **orthogenic** /ˌɔː.θəʊˈdʒen.ɪk (US) ˌɔːr.θoʊ-/, or primary stress on

the second syllable, e.g. **orthography** /ɔː'θɒg.rə.fi ⓤⓢ ɔːr'θɑː.grə-/.
orthochromatic ˌɔː.θəʊ.krəʊ'mæt.ɪk ⓤⓢ ˌɔːr.θoʊ.kroʊ'mæţ-, -θə-
orthodontic ˌɔː.θəʊ'dɒn.tɪk ⓤⓢ ˌɔːr.θoʊ'dɑːn.ţɪk, -θə'-
orthodontist ˌɔː.θəʊ'dɒn.tɪst ⓤⓢ ˌɔːr.θoʊ'dɑːn.ţɪst, -θə'- **-s** -s
orthodox 'ɔː.θə.dɒks ⓤⓢ 'ɔːr.θə.dɑːks
orthodox|y 'ɔː.θə.dɒk.s|i ⓤⓢ 'ɔːr.θə.dɑːk- **-ies** -iz
orthoep|y 'ɔː.θəʊ.ep|.i; ɔː'θəʊ.ɪ.p|i; ˌɔː.θəʊ'ep|.i; ⓤⓢ ɔːr'θoʊ.ə.p|i, 'ɔːr.θoʊ-, -ep|.i **-ist/s** -ɪst/s
orthogenic ˌɔː.θəʊ'dʒen.ɪk ⓤⓢ ˌɔːr.θoʊ'-, -θə'-
orthogonal ɔː'θɒg.ᵊn.ᵊl ⓤⓢ ɔːr'θɑː.gᵊn-
orthographer ɔː'θɒg.rə.fəʳ ⓤⓢ ɔːr'θɑː.grə.fɚ **-s** -z
orthographic ˌɔː.θəʊ'græf.ɪk ⓤⓢ ˌɔːr.θoʊ'-, -θə'- **-al** -ᵊl **-ally** -ᵊl.i, -li
orthograph|y ɔː'θɒg.rə.f|i ⓤⓢ ɔː'θɑː.grə- **-ist/s** -ɪst/s
orthop(a)edic ˌɔː.θəʊ'piː.dɪk ⓤⓢ ˌɔːr.θoʊ'-, -θə'- **-s** -s **-ally** -ᵊl.i, -li
orthop(a)ed|y ˌɔː.θəʊ'piː.d|i ⓤⓢ ˌɔːr.θoʊ'-, -θə'- **-ist/s** -ɪst/s
orthopterous ɔː'θɒp.tᵊr.əs ⓤⓢ ɔːr'θɑːp-
orthoptic ɔː'θɒp.tɪk ⓤⓢ ɔːr'θɑːp-
Ortiz 'ɔː.tɪz, ɔː'tɪz, -'tiːz, -'tiːs ⓤⓢ ɔːr'tiːz, -'tiːs
Ortler 'ɔːt.ləʳ ⓤⓢ 'ɔːrt.lɚ
ortolan 'ɔː.tᵊl.ən, -æn ⓤⓢ 'ɔːr.ţə.lən **-s** -z
Orton 'ɔː.tᵊn ⓤⓢ 'ɔːr-
Oruro ɒr'ʊə.rəʊ ⓤⓢ ɔː'rʊr.oʊ, -'ruː.roʊ
Orville 'ɔː.vɪl ⓤⓢ 'ɔːr-
Orwell 'ɔː.wel, -wəl ⓤⓢ 'ɔːr-
Orwellian ɔː'wel.i.ən ⓤⓢ ɔːr-
-ory -ᵊr.i, -ri ⓤⓢ -ɔːr.i, -ᵊr.i
Note: Suffix. When added to a free stem, **-ory** does not change the stress pattern of the word, e.g. **promise** /'prɒ.mɪs ⓤⓢ 'prɑː.mɪs/, **promissory** /'prɒm.ɪs.ᵊr.i ⓤⓢ 'prɑː.mɪ.sɔːr.i/. When added to a bound stem, stress may be one or two syllables before thesuffix, e.g. **olfactory** /ɒl'fæk.tᵊr.i ⓤⓢ ɑːl-/.
oryx 'ɒr.ɪks ⓤⓢ 'oʊ.rɪks, 'ɔːr.ɪks **-es** -ɪz
Osage ˌəʊ'seɪdʒ, '-- ⓤⓢ ˌoʊ'seɪdʒ, '--
Osaka əʊ'sɑː.kə, 'ɔː.sə.kə ⓤⓢ 'oʊ.sɑː.kɑː, oʊ'sɑː.kɑː
Osama əʊ'sɑː.mə, ɒs'-, ʊs'-
Osbaldiston(e) ˌɒz.bᵊl'dɪs.tᵊn ⓤⓢ ˌɑːz-
Osbert 'ɒz.bət, -bɜːt ⓤⓢ 'ɑːz.bɚt, -bɝːt
Osborn(e), Osbourne 'ɒz.bɔːn, -bən ⓤⓢ 'ɑːz.bɔːrn, -bɚn
Oscan 'ɒs.kən ⓤⓢ 'ɑːs- **-s** -z
Oscar 'ɒs.kəʳ ⓤⓢ 'ɑː.skɚ **-s** -z
oscill|ate 'ɒs.ɪ.l|eɪt, -ᵊl|.eɪt ⓤⓢ 'ɑː.sᵊl- **-ates** -eɪts **-ating** -eɪ.tɪŋ ⓤⓢ -eɪ.ţɪŋ **-ated** -eɪ.tɪd ⓤⓢ -eɪ.ţɪd **-ator/s** -eɪ.təʳ/z ⓤⓢ -eɪ.ţɚ/z
oscillation ˌɒs.ɪ'leɪ.ʃᵊn, -ᵊl'eɪ- ⓤⓢ ˌɑː.sᵊl'- **-s** -z
oscillatory 'ɒs.ɪ.lə.tᵊr.i, -ᵊl.eɪ-, -leɪ-; ˌɒs.ɪ'leɪ-, -ᵊl'eɪ- ⓤⓢ 'ɑː.sᵊl.ə.tɔːr-
oscillogram ə'sɪl.ə.græm, ɒs'ɪl- ⓤⓢ ə'sɪl- **-s** -z
oscillograph ə'sɪl.ə.grɑːf, ɒs'ɪl-, -græf ⓤⓢ ə'sɪl.ə.græf **-s** -s
oscilloscope ə'sɪl.ə.skəʊp, ɒs'ɪl- ⓤⓢ ə'sɪl.ə.skoʊp **-s** -s
osculant 'ɒs.kjə.lənt, -kjʊ- ⓤⓢ 'ɑː.skjuː-, -skjə-
oscular 'ɒs.kjə.ləʳ, -kjʊ- ⓤⓢ 'ɑː.skjuː.lɚ, -skjə-
oscu|late 'ɒs.kjə|.leɪt, -kjʊ- ⓤⓢ 'ɑː.skjuː-, -skjə- **-lates** -leɪts **-lating** -leɪ.tɪŋ ⓤⓢ -leɪ.ţɪŋ **-lated** -leɪ.tɪd ⓤⓢ -leɪ.ţɪd
osculation ˌɒs.kjə'leɪ.ʃᵊn, -kjʊ'- ⓤⓢ ˌɑː.skjuː'-, -skjə'- **-s** -z
osculator|y 'ɒs.kjə.lə.tᵊr|.i, -kjʊ-; ˌɒs.kjə'leɪ-, -kjʊ'- ⓤⓢ 'ɑː.skjuː.lə.tɔːr-, -skjə- **-ies** -iz
Osgood 'ɒz.gʊd ⓤⓢ 'ɑːz-
O'Shaughnessy əʊ'ʃɔː.nɪ.si, -nə- ⓤⓢ oʊ'ʃɑː.nə-, -'ʃɔː-
O'Shea əʊ'ʃeɪ ⓤⓢ oʊ-
Oshkosh 'ɒʃ.kɒʃ ⓤⓢ 'ɑːʃ.kɑːʃ
Oshogbo ə'ʃɒg.bəʊ ⓤⓢ oʊ'ʃɑːg.boʊ
osier 'əʊ.zi.əʳ, -ʒəʳ ⓤⓢ 'oʊ.ʒɚ **-s** -z
Osijek 'ɒs.i.ek ⓤⓢ ɔː'siː.ek
Osirian əʊ'saɪə.ri.ən, ɒs'aɪə- ⓤⓢ oʊ'saɪ- **-s** -z
Osiris əʊ'saɪə.rɪs, ɒs'aɪə- ⓤⓢ oʊ'saɪ-
-osis -ə.sɪs; -'əʊ.sɪs ⓤⓢ -ə.sɪs; -'oʊ.sɪs
Note: Suffix. Words containing **-osis** either carry primary stress on the syllable preceeding the suffix, or on the suffix itself e.g. **metamorphosis** /ˌmet.ə'mɔː.fə.sɪs; -mɔː'fəʊ- ⓤⓢ ˌmeţ.ə'mɔːr.fə-; -mɔːr'foʊ-/. See individual entries.
-osity -'ɒs.ə.ti, -ɪ.ti ⓤⓢ -'ɑː.sə.ţi
Note: Suffix. Normally takes primary stress as shown, e.g. **curious** /'kjʊə.ri.əs ⓤⓢ 'kjʊr.i-/, **curiosity** /ˌkjʊə.ri'ɒs.ə.ti ⓤⓢ ˌkjʊr.i'ɑː.sə.ţi/.
Osler 'əʊz.ləʳ, 'əʊ.sləʳ ⓤⓢ 'oʊz.lɚ, 'oʊ.slɚ
Oslo 'ɒz.ləʊ, 'ɒs- ⓤⓢ 'ɑː.sloʊ, 'ɑːz-
Osman ɒz'mɑːn, ɒs-; '--, -mən ⓤⓢ 'ɑːz.mən, 'ɑːs-
Osmanli ɒz'mæn.li, ɒs-, -'mɑːn- ⓤⓢ ɑːs'mæn-, ɑːz- **-s** -z
osmium 'ɒz.mi.əm ⓤⓢ 'ɑːz-
Osmond 'ɒz.mənd ⓤⓢ 'ɑːz-
osmosis ɒz'məʊ.sɪs ⓤⓢ ɑːz'moʊ-, ɑːs-
osmotic ɒz'mɒt.ɪk ⓤⓢ ɑːz'mɑː.ţɪk, ɑːs- **-ally** -ᵊl.i, -li
osmund (O) 'ɒz.mənd ⓤⓢ 'ɑːz-, 'ɑːs- **-s** -z
osmunda ɒz'mʌn.də ⓤⓢ ɑːz-, ɑːs- **-s** -z
Osnaburg(h) 'ɒz.nə.bɜːg ⓤⓢ 'ɑːz.nə.bɝːg
osprey 'ɒs.preɪ, -pri ⓤⓢ 'ɑː.spri, -spreɪ **-s** -z
Ossa 'ɒs.ə ⓤⓢ 'ɑː.sə
osseous 'ɒs.i.əs ⓤⓢ 'ɑː.si-
Ossett 'ɒs.ɪt ⓤⓢ 'ɑː.sɪt
Ossian 'ɒs.i.ən ⓤⓢ 'ɑː.si-
ossicle 'ɒs.ɪ.kl̩ ⓤⓢ 'ɑː.sɪ- **-s** -z
ossicular ɒs'ɪk.jə.ləʳ, -jʊ- ⓤⓢ ɑː'sɪk.jə.lɚ, -jʊ-
ossification ˌɒs.ɪ.fɪ'keɪ.ʃᵊn, ˌ-ə- ⓤⓢ ˌɑː.sə.fɪ'-
ossifrag|e 'ɒs.ɪ.frɪdʒ, '-ə-, -freɪdʒ ⓤⓢ 'ɑː.sə- **-es** -ɪz
ossi|fy 'ɒs.ɪ|.faɪ, '-ə- ⓤⓢ 'ɑː.sə- **-fies** -faɪz **-fying** -faɪ.ɪŋ **-fied** -faɪd
Ossining 'ɒs.ɪn.ɪŋ ⓤⓢ 'ɑː.sɪn-
osso buc(c)o ˌɒs.əʊ'buː.kəʊ ⓤⓢ ˌɑː.soʊ'buː.koʊ, ˌoʊ-
Ossory 'ɒs.ᵊr.i ⓤⓢ 'ɑː.sɚ-
ossuar|y 'ɒs.jʊə.r|i ⓤⓢ 'ɑː.sjuː.er|.i **-ies** -iz
osteitis ˌɒs.ti'aɪ.tɪs ⓤⓢ ˌɑː.sti'aɪ.ţɪs
Ostend ɒs'tend ⓤⓢ ɑː'stend, '--
ostensibility ɒsˌtent.sɪ'bɪl.ə.ti, -sə'-, -ɪ.ti ⓤⓢ ɑːˌstent.sə'bɪl.ə.ţi
ostensib|le ɒs'tent.sɪ.b|l̩, -sə- ⓤⓢ ɑː'stent.sə- **-ly** -li
ostentation ˌɒs.ten'teɪ.ʃᵊn, -tən'- ⓤⓢ ˌɑː.stən'-
ostentatious ˌɒs.ten'teɪ.ʃəs, -tən'- ⓤⓢ ˌɑː.stən'- **-ly** -li **-ness** -nəs, -nɪs
osteo- ˌɒs.ti.əʊ- ⓤⓢ ˌɑː.sti.oʊ-, -ə-
osteoarthritis ˌɒs.ti.əʊ.ɑː'θraɪ.tɪs ⓤⓢ ˌɑː.sti.oʊ.ɑːr'θraɪ.ţɪs
osteologic|al ˌɒs.ti.ə'lɒdʒ.ɪ.k|ᵊl ⓤⓢ ˌɑː.sti.oʊ'lɑː.dʒɪ- **-ally** -ᵊl.i, -li
osteolog|y ˌɒs.ti'ɒl.ə.dʒ|i ⓤⓢ ˌɑː.sti'ɑː.lə- **-ist/s** -ɪst/s
osteomyelitis ˌɒs.ti.əʊ.maɪ.ᵊl'aɪ.tɪs ⓤⓢ ˌɑː.sti.oʊ.maɪ.ə'laɪ.ţɪs
osteopath 'ɒs.ti.əʊ.pæθ ⓤⓢ 'ɑː.sti.o -ə- **-s** -s
osteopathic ˌɒs.ti.əʊ'pæθ.ɪk ⓤⓢ ˌɑː.sti.oʊ'-
osteopathy ˌɒs.ti'ɒp.ə.θi ⓤⓢ ˌɑː.sti'ɑː.pə-
osteoporosis ˌɒs.ti.əʊ.pə'rəʊ.sɪs, -pɔː'- ⓤⓢ ˌɑː.sti.oʊ.pə'roʊ-
Osterley 'ɒs.tᵊl.i ⓤⓢ 'ɑː.stɚ.li
Ostia 'ɒs.ti.ə ⓤⓢ 'ɑː.sti-
ostiar|y 'ɒs.ti.ər|.i ⓤⓢ 'ɑː.sti.er- **-ies**
osti|um (O) 'ɒs.ti|.əm ⓤⓢ 'ɑː.sti- **-a** -ə
ostler 'ɒs.ləʳ ⓤⓢ 'ɑː.slɚ **-s** -z
ostracism 'ɒs.trə.sɪ.zᵊm ⓤⓢ 'ɑː.strə-

Pronouncing the letters OU

There are several pronunciation possibilities for the strong pronunciation of the vowel digraph **ou**, e.g.:

/aʊ/	cloud	/klaʊd/	
/əʊ (US) oʊ/	though	/ðəʊ/	(US) /ðoʊ/
/ʌ/	country	/ˈkʌn.tri/	
/ɔː (US) ɑː/	bought	/bɔːt/	(US) /bɑːt/
/uː/	soup	/suːp/	
/ʊ/	could	/kʊd/	

When followed by a **gh** in the spelling which is realised as /f/, it is usually pronounced /ɒ (US) ɑː/ or /ʌ/, e.g.:

cough	/kɒf/	(US) /kɑːf/
enough	/ɪˈnʌf/	

When followed by an **r** in the spelling, **ou** is pronounced as /ɔː (US) ɔːr/, /aʊə (US) aʊɚ/, /ɜː (US) ɝː/, /ʌ (US) ɝː/, and /ʊə (US) ʊr/, e.g.:

four	/fɔːʳ/	(US) /fɔːr/
flour	/flaʊəʳ/	(US) /flaʊɚ/
journey	/ˈdʒɜː.ni/	(US) /ˈdʒɝː-/
flourish	/ˈflʌr.ɪʃ/	(US) /ˈflɝː-/
tour	/tʊəʳ, stɔːʳ/	(US) /tʊr/

In weak syllables

The vowel digraph **ou** is realised with the vowel /ə/ in weak syllables, and may also not be pronounced at all in British English, due to compression, e.g.:

famous	/ˈfeɪ.məs/
favourite	/ˈfeɪ.vᵊr.ɪt, ˈfeɪv.rɪt/

straciz|e, -is|e ˈɒs.trə.saɪz (US) ˈɑː.strə- **-es** -ɪz **-ing** -ɪŋ **-ed** -d

strava ˈɒs.trə.və (US) ˈɔː.strɑː.vɑː, ˈɑː-

strich ˈɒs.trɪtʃ (US) ˈɑː.strɪtʃ **-es** -ɪz

strogoth ˈɒs.trəʊ.gɒθ (US) ˈɑː.strə.gɑːθ **-s** -s

'Sullivan əʊˈsʌl.ɪ.vən, ˈ-ə- (US) oʊ-

swald ˈɒz.wəld (US) ˈɑːz-, -wɔːld

swaldtwistle ˈɒz.wəldˌtwɪs.l̩ (US) ˈɑːz.wɔːld-

swego ɒzˈwiː.gəʊ, ɒs- (US) ɑːˈswiː.goʊ **-s** -z

swestry ˈɒz.wə.stri, -wɪ- (US) ˈɑːz-

tago əʊˈtɑː.gəʊ, ɒtˈɑː- (US) əˈtɑː.go, oʊ-

taheite ˌəʊ.tɑːˈheɪ.ti, -təˈ- (US) ˌoʊ.t̬əˈhiː.t̬i, -ˈheɪ-

tar|y ˈəʊ.tᵊr|.i (US) ˈoʊ.t̬ɚ- **-ies** -iz

TB ˌəʊ.tiːˈbiː (US) ˌoʊ-

tford ˈɒt.fəd (US) ˈɑːt.fɚd

tfried ˈɒt.friːd (US) ˈɑːt-

thello əʊˈθel.əʊ, ɒθˈel- (US) oʊˈθel.oʊ, ə-

her ˈʌð.əʳ (US) -ɚ **-s** -z **-ness** -nəs, -nɪs

herwise ˈʌð.ə.waɪz (US) ˈ-ɚ-

herworld|ly ˌʌð.əˈwɜːld|.li (US) -ɚˈwɝːld- **-liness** -lɪ.nəs, -nɪs

thman ɒθˈmɑːn, ˈ-- (US) ˈɑːθ.mən, ʊθˈmɑːn

thniel ˈɒθ.ni.əl (US) ˈɑːθ-

ho ˈəʊ.θəʊ (US) ˈoʊ.θoʊ

tic -ˈɒt.ɪk (US) -ˈɑː.t̬ɪk

ote: Suffix. Normally takes primary stress as shown, e.g **idiot** /ˈɪd.i.ət/, **idiotic** /ˌɪd.iˈɒt.ɪk (US) -ˈɑː.t̬ɪk/.

iose ˈəʊ.ti.əʊz, -ʃi-, -əʊs (US) ˈoʊ.ʃi.oʊs, -t̬i- **-ly** -li **-ness** -nəs, -nɪs

otiosity ˌəʊ.tiˈɒs.ə.ti, -ʃiˈ-, -ɪ.ti (US) ˌoʊ.ʃiˈɑː.sə.t̬i, -t̬iˈ-

Otis ˈəʊ.tɪs (US) ˈoʊ.t̬ɪs

otitis əʊˈtaɪ.tɪs (US) oʊˈtaɪ.t̬ɪs

Otley ˈɒt.li (US) ˈɑːt-

otolaryngolog|y ˌəʊ.təʊˌlær.ɪŋˈgɒl.ə.dʒ|i, -ˌleə.rɪŋˈ- (US) ˌoʊ.t̬oʊˌler.ɪŋˈgɑː.lə-, -ˌlær- **-ist/s** -ɪst/s

otological ˌəʊ.təˈlɒdʒ.ɪ.kᵊl (US) ˌoʊ.t̬əˈlɑː.dʒɪ-

otolog|y əʊˈtɒl.ə.dʒ|i (US) oʊˈtɑː.lə- **-ist/s** -ɪst/s

otoscope ˈəʊ.tə.skəʊp (US) ˈoʊ.t̬oʊ.skoʊp, -t̬ə- **-s** -s

Otranto ɒtˈræn.təʊ, ˈɒt.rᵊn- (US) oʊˈtrɑːn.toʊ

O'Trigger əʊˈtrɪg.əʳ (US) oʊˈtrɪg.ɚ

OTT ˌəʊ.tiːˈtiː (US) ˌoʊ- *stress shift:* ˌOTT ˈspeech

Note: The letters OTT stand for "over-the-top"; see also that entry.

ottava rima ɒtˈɑː.vəˌriː.mə (US) oʊˈtɑː-

Ottaw|a ˈɒt.ə.w|ə (US) ˈɑː.t̬ə.w|ə, -w|ɑː, -w|ɔː **-as** -əz (US) -əz, -ɑːz, -ɔːz **-an/s** -ən/z

Ottaway ˈɒt.ə.weɪ (US) ˈɑː.t̬ə-

otter ˈɒt.əʳ (US) ˈɑː.t̬ɚ **-s** -z

Otterburn ˈɒt.ə.bɜːn (US) ˈɑː.t̬ɚ.bɝːn

Ottery ˈɒt.ᵊr.i (US) ˈɑː.t̬ɚ-

Ottley ˈɒt.li (US) ˈɑːt-

otto (O) ˈɒt.əʊ (US) ˈɑː.t̬oʊ

ottoman (O) ˈɒt.əʊ.mən (US) ˈɑː.t̬ə.mən **-s** -z

Ottoway ˈɒt.ə.weɪ (US) ˈɑː.t̬ə-

Otuel ˈɒt.juəl (US) ɔːˈtʊl, -ˈtuː.əl

Otway ˈɒt.weɪ (US) ˈɑːt-

Ouagadougou ˌwɑː.gəˈduː.guː, ˌwæg.əˈ- (US) ˌwɑː.gəˈ-

oubliette ˌuː.bliˈet **-s** -s

ouch aʊtʃ

Oudenarde ˈuː.də.nɑːd, -dɪ- (US) -dᵊn.ɑːrd; ˌuː.dəˈnɑːr.də

Oudh aʊd

Ougham ˈɔː.əm

ought ɔːt (US) ɑːt, ɔːt **-n't** -ᵊnt

Oughtershaw ˈaʊ.tə.ʃɔː (US) -t̬ɚ.ʃɑː, -ʃɔː

Oughterside ˈaʊ.tə.saɪd (US) -t̬ɚ-

Oughton ˈaʊ.tᵊn, ˈɔː.tᵊn

Oughtred ˈɔː.tred, -trɪd (US) ˈɔː-, ˈɑː-

ouguiya uːˈgwiː.ə, -ˈgiː-

Ouida ˈwiː.də

Ouija® ˈwiː.dʒə, -dʒɑː, -dʒi (US) -dʒə, -dʒi

Oujda uːdʒˈdɑː

Ould əʊld (US) oʊld

ounc|e aʊnts **-es** -ɪz

Oundle ˈaʊn.dl̩

our aʊəʳ, ɑːʳ (US) aʊɚ, aʊr, ɑːr **-s** -z

oursel|f ˌaʊəˈsel|f, ˌɑː- (US) ˌaʊɚ-, ˌaʊr-, ˌɑːr- **-ves** -vz

Ouse uːz

ousel ˈuː.zl̩ **-s** -z

Ouseley ˈuːz.li

Ousey ˈuː.zi

Ousley ˈaʊ.sli

oust aʊst **-s** -s **-ing** -ɪŋ **-ed** -ɪd **-er/s** -əʳ/z (US) -ɚ/z

Ouston ˈaʊ.stᵊn

out- aʊt-

Note: Prefix. Many compounds with beginning with **out-** have the stress pattern **ˈout**,-; these are likely to undergo stress shift when a stressed syllable follows closely, especially in adjectives derived from verbs.

out aʊt **-s** -s **-ing** -ɪŋ US ˈaʊ.t̬ɪŋ **-ed** -ɪd US ˈaʊ.t̬ɪd
outag|e ˈaʊ.tɪdʒ US -t̬ɪdʒ **-es** -ɪz
out-and-out ˌaʊt.ənˈdaʊt *stress shift:* ˌout-and-out ˈscoundrel
outback ˈaʊt.bæk
outbalanc|e ˌaʊtˈbæl.ənts, aʊt- **-es** -ɪz **-ing** -ɪŋ **-ed** -t
outbid ˌaʊtˈbɪd, aʊt- **-s** -z **-ding** -ɪŋ
outboard ˈaʊt.bɔːd US -bɔːrd
outbound ˈaʊt.baʊnd
outbox ˈaʊt.bɒks US -bɑːks **-es** -ɪz
outbrav|e ˌaʊtˈbreɪv, aʊt- **-es** -z **-ing** -ɪŋ **-ed** -d
outbreak ˈaʊt.breɪk **-s** -s
outbuilding ˈaʊtˌbɪl.dɪŋ **-s** -z
outburst ˈaʊt.bɜːst US -bɝːst **-s** -s
outcast ˈaʊt.kɑːst US -kæst **-s** -s
outcast|e ˈaʊt.kɑːst US -kæst **-es** -s **-ing** -ɪŋ **-ed** -ɪd
outclass ˌaʊtˈklɑːs, aʊt- US -ˈklæs **-es** -ɪz **-ing** -ɪŋ **-ed** -t
outcome ˈaʊt.kʌm **-s** -z
outcrop ˈaʊt.krɒp US -krɑːp **-s** -s **-ping** -ɪŋ **-ped** -t
outcr|y ˈaʊt.kr|aɪ **-ies** -aɪz
out|date ˌaʊt|ˈdeɪt, aʊt- **-dates** -ˈdeɪts **-dating** -ˈdeɪ.tɪŋ US -ˈdeɪ.t̬ɪŋ **-dated** -ˈdeɪ.tɪd US -ˈdeɪ.t̬ɪd
outdated ˌaʊtˈdeɪ.tɪd, aʊt- US -t̬ɪd *stress shift:* ˌoutdated ˈclothes
outdistanc|e ˌaʊtˈdɪs.tənts, aʊt- **-es** -ɪz **-ing** -ɪŋ **-ed** -t
out|do ˌaʊt|ˈduː, aʊt- **-does** -ˈdʌz **-doing** -ˈduː.ɪŋ **-did** -ˈdɪd **-done** -ˈdʌn
outdoor ˌaʊtˈdɔːʳ, aʊt- US -ˈdɔːr **-s** -z *stress shift:* ˌoutdoor ˈsports
outer ˈaʊ.təʳ US -t̬ɚ **-most** -məʊst US -məst, -moʊst ˌ**outer** ˈ**space**
outerwear ˈaʊ.tə.weəʳ US -t̬ɚ.wer
outfac|e ˌaʊtˈfeɪs, aʊt- **-s** -ɪz **-ing** -ɪŋ **-ed** -t
outfall ˈaʊt.fɔːl **-s** -z
outfield ˈaʊt.fiːld **-s** -z **-er/s** -əʳ/z US -ɚ/z
out|fit ˈaʊt|.fɪt **-fits** -fɪts **-fitting** -ˌfɪt.ɪŋ US -ˌfɪt̬.ɪŋ **-fitted** -ˌfɪt.ɪd US -ˌfɪt̬.ɪd **-fitter/s** -ˌfɪt.əʳ/z US -ˌfɪt̬.ɚ/z
outflank ˌaʊtˈflæŋk, aʊt- **-s** -s **-ing** -ɪŋ **-ed** -t
outflow (*n.*) ˈaʊt.fləʊ US -floʊ **-s** -z
outflow (*v.*) ˌaʊtˈfləʊ, aʊt- US -ˈfloʊ **-s** -z **-ing** -ɪŋ **-ed** -d
outfox ˌaʊtˈfɒks, aʊt- US -ˈfɑːks **-es** -ɪz **-ing** -ɪŋ **-ed** -t
outgeneral ˌaʊtˈdʒen.ər.əl, aʊt- **-s** -z **-(l)ing** -ɪŋ **-(l)ed** -d
outgo (*n.*) ˈaʊt.gəʊ US -goʊ **-es** -z
out|go (*v.*) ˌaʊt|ˈgəʊ, aʊt- US -ˈgoʊ **-goes** -ˈgəʊz US -ˈgoʊz **-going** -ˈgəʊ.ɪŋ US -ˈgoʊ.ɪŋ **-went** -ˈwent **-gone** -ˈgɒn US -ˈgɑːn
outgoer ˈaʊtˌgəʊ.əʳ US -ˌgoʊ.ɚ **-s** -z
outgoing ˌaʊtˈgəʊ.ɪŋ, aʊt-, ˈ--- US ˈaʊt.goʊ- **-s** -z
out|grow (*v.*) ˌaʊt|ˈgrəʊ, aʊt- US -ˈgroʊ **-grows** -ˈgrəʊz US -ˈgroʊz **-growing** -ˈgrəʊ.ɪŋ US -ˈgroʊ.ɪŋ **-grew** -ˈgruː **-grown** -ˈgrəʊn US -ˈgroʊn
outgrowth ˈaʊt.grəʊθ US -groʊθ **-s** -s
outguess ˌaʊtˈges, aʊt- **-es** -ɪz **-ing** -ɪŋ **-ed** -t
outgun ˌaʊtˈgʌn, aʊt- **-s** -z **-ning** -ɪŋ **-ned** -d
out-Herod ˌaʊtˈher.əd, aʊt- **-s** -z **-ing** -ɪŋ **-ed** -ɪd
outhou|se ˈaʊt.haʊ|s **-ses** -zɪz
Outhwaite ˈuː.θweɪt, ˈəʊ-, ˈaʊ- US ˈuː-, ˈoʊ-, ˈaʊ-
outing ˈaʊ.tɪŋ US -t̬ɪŋ **-s** -z
Outlander ˈaʊtˌlæn.dəʳ US -dɚ **-s** -z
outlandish ˌaʊtˈlæn.dɪʃ, aʊt- **-ly** -li **-ness** -nəs, -nɪs
outlast ˌaʊtˈlɑːst, aʊt- US -ˈlæst **-s** -s **-ing** -ɪŋ **-ed** -ɪd
outlaw ˈaʊt.lɔː US -lɑː, -lɔː **-s** -z **-ing** -ɪŋ **-ed** -d **-ry** -ri
outlay (*n.*) ˈaʊt.leɪ **-s** -z
out|lay (*v.*) ˌaʊt|ˈleɪ, aʊt- **-lays** -ˈleɪz **-laying** -ˈleɪ.ɪŋ **-laid** -ˈleɪd
outlet ˈaʊt.let, -lət, -lɪt US -let, -lət **-s** -s
outlier ˈaʊtˌlaɪ.əʳ US -ɚ **-s** -z
outline (*n.*) ˈaʊt.laɪn **-s** -z
outlin|e (*v.*) ˈaʊt.laɪn, ˌ-ˈ-, aʊt- US ˈ-- **-es** -z **-ing** -ɪŋ **-ed** -d
outliv|e ˌaʊtˈlɪv, aʊt- **-es** -z **-ing** -ɪŋ **-ed** -d
outlook ˈaʊt.lʊk **-s** -s
outlying ˈaʊtˌlaɪ.ɪŋ, ˌ-ˈ--, aʊt- US ˈ-ˌ--
outmaneuv|er ˌaʊt.məˈnuː.v|əʳ US -v|ɚ **-ers** -əz US -ɚz **-ering** -ər.ɪŋ **-ered** -əd US -ɚd
outmanoeuv|re ˌaʊt.məˈnuː.v|əʳ US -v|ɚ **-res** -əz US -ɚz **-ring** -ər.ɪŋ **-red** -əd US -ɚd
outmarch ˌaʊtˈmɑːtʃ, aʊt- US -ˈmɑːrtʃ **-es** -ɪz **-ing** -ɪŋ **-ed** -t
outmatch ˌaʊtˈmætʃ, aʊt- **-es** -ɪz **-ing** -ɪŋ **-ed** -t
outmoded ˌaʊtˈməʊ.dɪd, aʊt- US -ˈmoʊ- *stress shift:* ˌoutmoded ˈclothes
outmost ˈaʊt.məʊst US -moʊst
outnumb|er ˌaʊtˈnʌm.b|əʳ, aʊt- US -b|ɚ **-ers** -əz US -ɚz **-ering** -ər.ɪŋ **-ered** -əd US -ɚd
out-of-date ˌaʊt.əvˈdeɪt US ˌaʊt̬- *stress shift:* ˌout-of-date ˈfoodstuffs
out-of-door ˌaʊt.əvˈdɔːʳ US ˌaʊt̬.əvˈdɔːr **-s** -z *stress shift:* ˌout-of-door ˈsports
out-of-pocket ˌaʊt.əvˈpɒk.ɪt US ˌaʊt̬.əvˈpɑː.kɪt *stress shift:* ˌout-of-pocket ˈpayment
out-of-state ˌaʊt.əvˈsteɪt US ˌaʊt̬- *stress shift:* ˌout-of-state ˈvisitors
out-of-the-way ˌaʊt.əv.ðəˈweɪ US ˌaʊt̬.əv.ðəˈ- *stress shift:* ˌout-of-the-way ˈplaces
outpac|e ˌaʊtˈpeɪs, aʊt- **-es** -ɪz **-ing** -ɪ[ŋ] **-ed** -t
outpatient ˈaʊtˌpeɪ.ʃənt **-s** -s
outperform ˌaʊt.pəˈfɔːm US -pɚˈfɔː[rm] **-s** -z **-ing** -ɪŋ **-ed** -d
outplacement ˈaʊtˌpleɪs.mənt
outplay ˌaʊtˈpleɪ, aʊt- **-s** -z **-ing** -ɪŋ **-ed** -d
outport ˈaʊt.pɔːt US -pɔːrt **-s** -s
outpost ˈaʊt.pəʊst US -poʊst **-s** -s
outpour (*n.*) ˈaʊt.pɔːʳ US -pɔːr **-s** -z
outpour (*v.*) ˌaʊtˈpɔːʳ, aʊt- US -ˈpɔːr **-s** -z **-ing** -ɪŋ **-ed** -d
outpouring ˈaʊtˌpɔː.rɪŋ, ˌ-ˈ--, aʊt- US ˈaʊtˌpɔːr.ɪŋ **-s** -z
out|put ˈaʊt|.pʊt **-puts** -pʊts **-putting** -ˌpʊt.ɪŋ US -ˌpʊt̬.ɪŋ **-putted** -ˌpʊt.ɪd US -ˌpʊt̬.ɪd
outrage (O) (*n.*) ˈaʊt.reɪdʒ
outrag|e (*v.*) ˈaʊt.reɪdʒ, ˌ-ˈ-, aʊt- US ˈ[--] **-es** -ɪz **-ing** -ɪŋ **-ed** -d
outrageous ˌaʊtˈreɪ.dʒəs, aʊt- **-ly** -li **-ness** -nəs, -nɪs
Outram ˈuː.trəm
outrang|e ˌaʊtˈreɪndʒ, aʊt- **-es** -ɪz **-i[ng]** -ɪŋ **-ed** -d
outrank ˌaʊtˈræŋk, aʊt- **-s** -s **-ing** -ɪŋ **-ed** -t
outré ˈuː.treɪ US -ˈ-
outreach (*n.*) ˈaʊt.riːtʃ **-es** -ɪz
outreach (*v.*) ˌaʊtˈriːtʃ, aʊt- **-es** -ɪz **-i[ng]** -ɪŋ **-ed** -t
out|ride ˌaʊt|ˈraɪd, aʊt- **-rides** -ˈraɪd[z] **-riding** -ˈraɪ.dɪŋ **-rode** -ˈrəʊd US -ˈroʊd **-ridden** -ˈrɪd.ən
outrider ˈaʊtˌraɪ.dəʳ US -dɚ **-s** -z
outrigger ˈaʊtˌrɪg.əʳ US -ɚ **-s** -z
outright (*adj.*) ˈaʊt.raɪt (*adv.*) ˌaʊtˈr[aɪt], aʊt-
outrival ˌaʊtˈraɪ.vəl, aʊt- **-s** -z **-ling** -[ɪŋ] **-led** -d
out|run ˌaʊt|ˈrʌn, aʊt- **-runs** -ˈrʌnz **-running** -ˈrʌn.ɪŋ **-ran** -ˈræn
outrush ˈaʊt.rʌʃ **-es** -ɪz
out|sell ˌaʊt|ˈsel, aʊt- **-sells** -ˈselz **-selling** -ˈsel.ɪŋ **-sold** -ˈsəʊld US -ˈsoʊld
outset ˈaʊt.set **-s** -s
out|shine ˌaʊt|ˈʃaɪn, aʊt- **-shines** -ˈʃaɪnz **-shining** -ˈʃaɪ.nɪŋ **-shined** -ˈʃaɪnd **-shone** -ˈʃɒn US -ˈʃoʊn
outside ˌaʊtˈsaɪd, aʊt- **-s** -z *stress sh[ift:]* ˌoutside ˈtoilet
outsider ˌaʊtˈsaɪ.dəʳ, aʊt- US aʊtˈsaɪ.dɚ, ˈ--- **-s** -z *stress shi[ft:]* *British only:* ˌoutsider ˈdealing

utsiz|e ˌaʊtˈsaɪz, aʊt- **-es** -ɪz **-ed** -d *stress shift:* ˌoutsize ˈclothes
utskirts ˈaʊt.skɜːts (US) -skɝːts
ut|smart ˌaʊtˈsmɑːt, aʊt- (US) -ˈsmɑːrt **-smarts** -ˈsmɑːts (US) -ˈsmɑːrts **-smarting** -ˈsmɑː.tɪŋ (US) -ˈsmɑːr.t̬ɪŋ **-smarted** -ˈsmɑː.tɪd (US) -ˈsmɑːr.t̬ɪd
utsourc|e ˈaʊt.sɔːs (US) -sɔːrs **-es** -ɪz **-ing** -ɪŋ **-ed** -t
utspan® ˈaʊt.spæn **-s** -z
utspan ˌaʊtˈspæn, aʊt- **-s** -z **-ning** -ɪŋ **-ned** -d
utspend ˌaʊtˈspend, aʊt- **-s** -z **-ing** -ɪŋ **outspent** ˌaʊtˈspent, aʊt-
utspoken ˌaʊtˈspəʊ.kᵊn, aʊt- (US) -ˈspoʊ- **-ly** -li **-ness** -nəs, -nɪs *stress shift:* ˌoutspoken ˈperson
utspread ˌaʊtˈspred (US) aʊt- **-s** -z **-ing** -ɪŋ *stress shift:* ˌoutspread ˈarms
utstanding *very good:* ˌaʊtˈstæn.dɪŋ, aʊt- **-ly** -li *sticking out:* ˈaʊtˌstæn.dɪŋ
utstar|e ˌaʊtˈsteəʳ, aʊt- (US) -ˈster **-es** -z **-ing** -ɪŋ **-ed** -d
utstation ˈaʊt.steɪ.ʃᵊn **-s** -z **-ed** -d
utstay ˌaʊtˈsteɪ, aʊt- **-s** -z **-ing** -ɪŋ **-ed** -d
utstretch ˌaʊtˈstretʃ, aʊt- **-es** -ɪz **-ing** -ɪŋ **-ed** -t *stress shift:* ˌoutstretched ˈarms
utstrip ˌaʊtˈstrɪp, aʊt- **-s** -s **-ping** -ɪŋ **-ped** -t
utta ˈaʊ.t̬ə
ote: This is a form of **out of**, and is only used by British speakers when imitating American speakers.
ttake ˈaʊt.teɪk **-s** -s
t|vote ˌaʊtˈvəʊt, aʊt- (US) -ˈvoʊt **-votes** -ˈvəʊts (US) -ˈvoʊts **-voting** -ˈvəʊ.tɪŋ (US) -ˈvoʊ.t̬ɪŋ **-voted** -ˈvəʊ.tɪd (US) -ˈvoʊ.t̬ɪd
tward ˈaʊt.wəd (US) -wɚd **-s** -z **-ly** -li **-ness** -nəs, -nɪs
tward-bound ˌaʊt.wədˈbaʊnd (US) -wɚdˈ- ˌ**Outward** ˈ**Bound** ˌ**course**
t|wear ˌaʊtˈweəʳ, aʊt- (US) -ˈwer **-wears** -ˈweəz (US) -ˈwers **-wearing** -ˈweə.rɪŋ (US) -ˈwer.ɪŋ **-worn** -ˈwɔːn (US) -ˈwɔːrn
tweigh ˌaʊtˈweɪ, aʊt- **-s** -z **-ing** -ɪŋ **-ed** -d
twent *(from* **outgo***)* ˌaʊtˈwent, aʊt-
t|wit ˌaʊtˈwɪt, aʊt- **-wits** -ˈwɪts **-witting** -ˈwɪt.ɪŋ (US) -ˈwɪt̬.ɪŋ **-witted** -ˈwɪt.ɪd (US) -ˈwɪt̬.ɪd
twith ˌaʊtˈwɪθ, aʊt, -ˈwɪð
twork *(n.)* ˈaʊt.wɜːk (US) -wɝːk **-s** -s
twork *(v.)* ˌaʊtˈwɜːk, aʊt- (US) -ˈwɝːk **-s** -s **-ing** -ɪŋ **-ed** -t
t-worker ˈaʊtˌwɜː.kəʳ (US) -ˌwɝː.kɚ **-s** -z
tworn ˌaʊtˈwɔːn, aʊt- (US) -ˈwɔːrn
el ˈuː.zᵊl **-s** -z

ouzo ˈuː.zəʊ (US) -zoʊ
ova *(plur. of* **ovum***)* ˈəʊ.və (US) ˈoʊ-
oval (O) ˈəʊ.vᵊl (US) ˈoʊ- **-s** -z **-ly** -i ˈ**Oval** ˌ**Office,** ˌ**Oval** ˈ**Office**
Ovaltine® ˈəʊ.vᵊl.tiːn (US) ˈoʊ-
ovari|an əʊˈveə.ri.ən (US) oʊˈver.i- **-al** -əl
ovariectomy əʊˌveə.riˈek.tə.mi (US) oʊˌver.iˈ-
ovariotomy əʊˌveə.riˈɒt.ə.mi (US) oʊˌver.iˈɑː.t̬ə-
ovar|y ˈəʊ.vᵊr.i (US) ˈoʊ- **-ies** -iz
ovate *(n.) Welsh title:* ˈɒv.ət, -ɪt; ˈəʊ.veɪt (US) ˈoʊ.veɪt; ˈɑː.vət **-s** -s
ovate *(adj.) egg-shaped:* ˈəʊ.veɪt, -vɪt, -vət (US) ˈoʊ.veɪt
ovation əʊˈveɪ.ʃᵊn (US) oʊ- **-s** -z ˌ**standing** **o**ˈ**vation**
oven ˈʌv.ᵊn **-s** -z ˈ**oven** ˌ**glove**
ovenbird ˈʌv.ᵊn.bɜːd, -ᵊm- (US) -ᵊn.bɝːd **-s** -s
ovenproof ˈʌv.ᵊn.pruːf, -ᵊm- (US) -ᵊn-
oven-ready ˌʌv.ᵊnˈred.i *stress shift:* ˌoven-ready ˈchicken
ovenware ˈʌv.ᵊn.weəʳ (US) -wer
over- əʊ.vəʳ-, oʊ.vɚ-
Note: Prefix. Many compounds with **over-** have the stress pattern ˌ**over**ˈ-; these are likely to undergo stress shift when a stressed syllable follows, especially in adjectives derived from verbs.
over ˈəʊ.vəʳ (US) ˈoʊ.vɚ **-s** -z ˌ**over and** ˈ**done** ˌ**with**
over-abundan|ce ˌəʊ.vᵊr.əˈbʌn.dən|ts (US) ˌoʊ.vɚ- **-t** -t
over-achiever ˌəʊ.vᵊr.əˈtʃiː.vəʳ (US) ˌoʊ.vɚ.əˈtʃiː.vɚ, ˈoʊ.vɚ.əˌtʃiː- **-s** -z
overact ˌəʊ.vᵊrˈækt (US) ˌoʊ.vɚˈ- **-s** -s **-ing** -ɪŋ **-ed** -ɪd
overactive ˌəʊ.vᵊrˈæk.tɪv (US) ˌoʊ.vɚˈ- *stress shift:* ˌoveractive ˈgland
over-age ˌəʊ.vᵊrˈeɪdʒ (US) ˌoʊ.vɚˈ- *stress shift:* ˌover-age ˈapplicant
overall (O) *(n. adj.)* ˈəʊ.vᵊr.ɔːl (US) ˈoʊ- **-s** -z
overall *(adv.)* ˌəʊ.vᵊrˈɔːl (US) ˌoʊ.vɚˈ-, -ˈɑːl
over-ambitious ˌəʊ.vᵊr.æmˈbɪʃ.əs (US) ˌoʊ.vɚ- *stress shift:* ˌover-ambitious ˈpartner
over-anxiety ˌəʊ.vᵊr.æŋˈzaɪ.ə.ti (US) ˌoʊ.vɚ.æŋˈzaɪ.ə.t̬i
over-anxious ˌəʊ.vᵊrˈæŋk.ʃəs (US) ˌoʊ.vɚˈ- **-ly** -li *stress shift:* ˌover-anxious ˈparent
overarching ˌəʊ.vᵊrˈɑː.tʃɪŋ (US) ˌoʊ.vɚˈɑːr-
overarm ˈəʊ.vᵊr.ɑːm (US) ˈoʊ.vɚ.ɑːrm
overaw|e ˌəʊ.vᵊrˈɔː (US) ˌoʊ.vɚˈɑː, -ˈɔː **-es** -z **-ing** -ɪŋ **-ed** -d

overbalanc|e ˌəʊ.vəˈbæl.ənts (US) ˌoʊ.vɚˈ- **-es** -ɪz **-ing** -ɪŋ **-ed** -t
overbear ˌəʊ.vəˈbeəʳ (US) ˌoʊ.vɚˈber **-s** -z **-ing** -ɪŋ **over|bore** ˌəʊ.vəˈbɔːʳ (US) ˌoʊ.vɚˈbɔːr **-borne** -ˈbɔːn (US) -ˈbɔːrn
overbearing ˌəʊ.vəˈbeə.rɪŋ (US) ˌoʊ.vɚˈber.ɪŋ **-ly** -li **-ness** -nəs, -nɪs *stress shift:* ˌoverbearing ˈrelatives
overbid ˌəʊ.vəˈbɪd (US) ˌoʊ.vɚ- **-s** -z **-ding** -ɪŋ
overbid ˈəʊ.və.bɪd (US) ˈoʊ.vɚ- **s** -z
overbite ˈəʊ.və.baɪt (US) ˈoʊ.vɚ-
over|blow ˌəʊ.vəˈbləʊ (US) ˌoʊ.vɚˈbloʊ, ˈ--ˌ- **-blows** -ˈbləʊz (US) -ˈbloʊz, -bloʊz **-blowing** -ˈbləʊ.ɪŋ (US) -ˈbloʊ.ɪŋ, -ˌbloʊ.ɪŋ **-blew** -ˈbluː (US) -ˈbluː, -bluː **-blown** -ˈbləʊn (US) -ˈbloʊn, -bloʊn
overboard ˈəʊ.və.bɔːd, ˌ--ˈ- (US) ˈoʊ.vɚ.bɔːrd
overbook ˌəʊ.vəˈbʊk (US) ˌoʊ.vɚˈ- **-s** -s **-ing** -ɪŋ **-ed** -t
overbreadth ˌəʊ.vəˈbredθ, -ˈbretθ (US) ˌoʊ.vɚˈ-
overbrim ˌəʊ.vəˈbrɪm (US) ˌoʊ.vɚˈ- **-s** -z **-ming** -ɪŋ **-med** -d
overbuild ˌəʊ.vəˈbɪld (US) ˌoʊ.vɚˈ-, ˈ--- **-s** -z **-ing** -ɪŋ **overbuilt** ˌəʊ.vəˈbɪlt (US) ˌoʊ.vɚˈ-, ˈ---
overburden ˌəʊ.vəˈbɜː.dᵊn (US) ˌoʊ.vɚˈbɝː- **-s** -z **-ing** -ɪŋ **-ed** -d
Overbury ˈəʊ.və.bᵊr.i (US) ˈoʊ.vɚˌber-, -bɚ-
overcapacity ˌəʊ.və.kəˈpæs.ə.ti, -ɪ.ti (US) ˌoʊ.vɚ.kəˈpæs.ə.t̬i
over-careful ˌəʊ.vəˈkeə.fᵊl, -fʊl (US) ˌoʊ.vɚˈker- **-ly** -i **-ness** -nəs, -nɪs
overcast ˈəʊ.və.kɑːst, ˌ--ˈ- (US) ˈoʊ.vɚ.kæst, ˌoʊ.vɚˈkæst
over-cautious ˌəʊ.vəˈkɔː.ʃəs (US) ˌoʊ.vɚˈkɑː-, -ˈkɔː- *stress shift:* ˌover-cautious ˈperson
overcharg|e *(v.)* ˌəʊ.vəˈtʃɑːdʒ (US) ˌoʊ.vɚˈtʃɑːrdʒ, ˈ--- **-es** -ɪz **-ing** -ɪŋ **-ed** -d
overcloud ˌəʊ.vəˈklaʊd (US) ˌoʊ.vɚˈklaʊd **-s** -z **-ing** -ɪŋ **-ed** -ɪd
overcoat ˈəʊ.və.kəʊt (US) ˈoʊ.vɚ.koʊt **-s** -s
over|come ˌəʊ.vəˈkʌm (US) ˌoʊ.vɚˈ- **-comes** -ˈkʌmz **-coming** -ˈkʌm.ɪŋ **-came** -ˈkeɪm
overcompen|sate ˌəʊ.vəˈkɒm.pən.seɪt, -pen- (US) ˌoʊ.vɚˈkɑːm.pən- **-sates** -seɪts **-sating** -seɪ.tɪŋ (US) -seɪ.t̬ɪŋ **-sated** -seɪ.tɪd (US) -seɪ.t̬ɪd
overcompensation ˌəʊ.vəˌkɒm.pənˈseɪ.ʃᵊn, -penˈ- (US) ˌoʊ.vɚˌkɑːm.pənˈ-

over-confidence ˌəʊ.vəˈkɒn.fɪ.dᵊnts, -fə- US ˌoʊ.vɚˈkɑːn.fə-

over-confident ˌəʊ.vəˈkɒn.fɪ.dᵊnt, -fə- US ˌoʊ.vɚˈkɑːn.fə- **-ly** -li *stress shift:* ˌover-confident ˈcandidate

over-cook ˌəʊ.vəˈkʊk US ˌoʊ.vɚˈ- **-s** -s **-ing** -ɪŋ **-ed** -t

overcrowd ˌəʊ.vəˈkraʊd US ˌoʊ.vɚˈ- **-s** -z **-ing** -ɪŋ **-ed** -ɪd *stress shift:* ˌovercrowded ˈroom

over-develop ˌəʊ.və.dɪˈvel.əp, -dəˈ- US ˌoʊ.vɚ.dɪˈ- **-s** -s **-ing** -ɪŋ **-ed** -t **-ment** -mənt *stress shift:* ˌoverdeveloped ˈmuscles

over|do ˌəʊ.və|ˈduː US ˌoʊ.vɚˈ- **-does** -ˈdʌz **-doing** -ˈduː.ɪŋ **-did** -ˈdɪd **-done** -ˈdʌn

overdone *over-cooked:* ˌəʊ.vəˈdʌn US ˌoʊ.vɚˈ- *stress shift:* ˌoverdone ˈchicken

overdos|e (*n.*) ˈəʊ.və.dəʊs US ˈoʊ.vɚ.doʊs **-es** -ɪz

overdos|e (*v.*) ˌəʊ.vəˈdəʊs US ˌoʊ.vɚˈdoʊs, ˈ--- **-es** -ɪz **-ing** -ɪŋ **-ed** -t

overdraft ˈəʊ.və.drɑːft US ˈoʊ.vɚ.dræft **-s** -s

overdraught ˈəʊ.və.drɑːft US ˈoʊ.vɚ.dræft **-s** -s

overdraw ˌəʊ.vəˈdrɔː US ˌoʊ.vɚˈdrɑː, -ˈdrɔː, ˈ--- **-s** -z **-ing** -ɪŋ **overdrew** ˌəʊ.vəˈdruː US ˌoʊ.vɚ-, ˈ--- **overdrawn** ˌəʊ.vəˈdrɔːn US ˌoʊ.vɚˈdrɑːn, -ˈdrɔːn, ˈ---

overdress (*v.*) ˌəʊ.vəˈdres US ˌoʊ.vɚˈ-, ˈ--- **-es** -ɪz **-ing** -ɪŋ **-ed** -t

overdress (*n.*) ˈəʊ.və.dres US ˈoʊ.vɚ- **-es** -ɪz

overdrive (*n.*) ˈəʊ.və.draɪv US ˈoʊ.vɚ-

over|drive (*v.*) ˌəʊ.və|ˈdraɪv US ˌoʊ.vɚˈ- **-drives** -ˈdraɪvz **-driving** -ˈdraɪ.vɪŋ **-drove** -ˈdrəʊv US -ˈdroʊv **-driven** -ˈdrɪv.ᵊn

overdue ˌəʊ.vəˈdjuː US ˌoʊ.vɚˈduː, -ˈdjuː *stress shift:* ˌoverdue ˈpayment

over|eat ˌəʊ.vᵊr|ˈiːt US ˌoʊ.vɚˈ- **-eats** -ˈiːts **-eating** -ˈiː.tɪŋ US -ˈiː.t̬ɪŋ **-eaten** -ˈiː.tᵊn **-ate** -ˈet, -ˈeɪt US -ˈeɪt

over-emphasis ˌəʊ.vᵊrˈemp.fə.sɪs US ˌoʊ.vɚˈ-

over-emphasiz|e, -is|e ˌəʊ.vᵊrˈemp.fə.saɪz US ˌoʊ.vɚˈ- **-es** -ɪz **-ing** -ɪŋ **-ed** -d

overestimate (*n.*) ˌəʊ.vᵊrˈes.tɪ.mət, -tə-, -mɪt, -meɪt US ˌoʊ.vɚˈes.tɪ.mɪt **-s** -s

overesti|mate (*v.*) ˌəʊ.vᵊrˈes.tɪ|.meɪt, -tə- US ˌoʊ.vɚˈes.tə- **-mates** -meɪts **-mating** -meɪ.tɪŋ US -meɪ.t̬ɪŋ **-mated** -meɪ.tɪd US -meɪ.t̬ɪd

over-estimation ˌəʊ.vᵊrˌes.tɪˈmeɪ.ʃᵊn, -təˈ- US ˌoʊ.vɚˌes.təˈ-

overex|cite ˌəʊ.vᵊr.ɪk|ˈsaɪt, -ekˈ- US ˌoʊ.vɚ- **-cites** -ˈsaɪts **-citing** -ˈsaɪ.tɪŋ US -ˈsaɪ.t̬ɪŋ **-cited** -ˈsaɪ.tɪd US -ˈsaɪ.t̬ɪd **-citement** -ˈsaɪt.mənt

overexer|t ˌəʊ.vᵊr.ɪgˈzɜː|t, -egˈ- US ˌoʊ.vɚ.ɪgˈzɝː|t, -egˈ- **-ts** -ts **-ting** -tɪŋ US -t̬ɪŋ **-ted** -tɪd US -t̬ɪd

overexertion ˌəʊ.vᵊr.ɪgˈzɜː.ʃᵊn, -egˈ- US ˌoʊ.vɚ.ɪgˈzɝː-, -egˈ-

overexpos|e ˌəʊ.vᵊr.ɪkˈspəʊz, -ekˈ- US ˌoʊ.vɚ.ɪkˈspoʊz, -ekˈ- **-es** -ɪz **-ing** -ɪŋ **-ed** -d

over-exposure ˌəʊ.vᵊr.ɪkˈspəʊ.ʒəʳ, -ekˈ- US ˌoʊ.vɚ.ɪkˈspoʊ.ʒɚ, -ekˈ-

overfatigu|e ˌəʊ.və.fəˈtiːg US ˌoʊ.vɚ- **-es** -z **-ing** -ɪŋ **-ed** -d

overfeed ˌəʊ.vəˈfiːd US ˌoʊ.vɚˈ- **-s** -z **-ing** -ɪŋ **overfed** ˌəʊ.vəˈfed US ˌoʊ.vɚˈ- *stress shift:* ˌoverfed ˈpets

overflow (*n.*) ˈəʊ.və.fləʊ US ˈoʊ.vɚ.floʊ **-s** -z

overflow (*v.*) ˌəʊ.vəˈfləʊ US ˌoʊ.vɚˈfloʊ **-s** -z **-ing** -ɪŋ **-ed** -d

over|fly ˌəʊ.və|ˈflaɪ US ˌoʊ.vɚˈ-, ˈ--- **-flies** -ˈflaɪz US -ˈflaɪz, -flaɪz **-flying** -ˈflaɪ.ɪŋ US -ˈflaɪ.ɪŋ, -flaɪ.ɪŋ **-flew** -ˈfluː US -ˈfluː, -fluː **-flown** -ˈfləʊn US -ˈfloʊn, -floʊn

over-fond ˌəʊ.vəˈfɒnd US ˌoʊ.vɚˈfɑːnd

over-generalization, -isa- ˌəʊ.vəˌdʒen.ᵊr.ᵊl.aɪˈzeɪ.ʃᵊn, -ɪˈ- US ˌoʊ.vɚˌdʒen.ɚ.ᵊl.ɪˈ-

overground ˈəʊ.və.graʊnd, ˌ--ˈ- US ˈoʊ.vɚ.graʊnd, ˌ--ˈ-

over|grow ˌəʊ.və|ˈgrəʊ US ˌoʊ.vɚˈgroʊ **-grows** -ˈgrəʊz US -ˈgroʊz **-growing** -ˈgrəʊ.ɪŋ US -ˈgroʊ.ɪŋ **-grew** -ˈgruː **-grown** -ˈgrəʊn US -ˈgroʊn

overgrowth ˈəʊ.və.grəʊθ US ˈoʊ.vɚ.groʊθ **-s** -s

overhand (*n. adj.*) ˈəʊ.və.hænd US ˈoʊ.vɚ- **-s** -z

overhang (*n.*) ˈəʊ.və.hæŋ US ˈoʊ.vɚ- **-s** -z

overhang (*v.*) ˌəʊ.vəˈhæŋ US ˌoʊ.vɚˈ-, ˈ--- **-s** -z **-ing** -ɪŋ **overhung** ˌəʊ.vəˈhʌŋ US ˌoʊ.vɚˈ-, ˈ---

over-hasty ˌəʊ.vəˈheɪ.sti US ˌoʊ.vɚˈ- *stress shift:* ˌover-hasty ˈchoice

overhaul (*n.*) ˈəʊ.və.hɔːl US ˈoʊ.vɚ.hɑːl, -hɔːl **-s** -z

overhaul (*v.*) ˌəʊ.vəˈhɔːl US ˌoʊ.vɚˈhɑːl, -ˈhɔːl, ˈ--- **-s** -z **-ing** -ɪŋ **-ed** -d

overhead (*n. adj.*) ˈəʊ.və.hed US ˈoʊ.vɚ- **-s** -z **ˌoverhead proˈjector**

overhead (*adv.*) ˌəʊ.vəˈhed US ˌoʊ.vɚˈ-

overhear ˌəʊ.vəˈhɪəʳ US ˌoʊ.vɚˈhɪr **-s** -z **-ing** -ɪŋ **overheard** ˌəʊ.vəˈhɜːd US ˌoʊ.vɚˈhɝːd

over|heat ˌəʊ.və|ˈhiːt US ˌoʊ.vɚˈ- **-heats** -ˈhiːts **-heating** -ˈhiː.tɪŋ US -ˈhiː.t̬ɪŋ **-heated** -ˈhiː.tɪd US -ˈhiː.t̬ɪd

over-impress|ed ˌəʊ.vᵊr.ɪmˈpres|t US ˌoʊ.vɚ- **-ive** -ɪv

over-indulg|e ˌəʊ.vᵊr.ɪnˈdʌldʒ US ˌoʊ.vɚ- **-es** -ɪz **-ing** -ɪŋ **-ed** -d **-ence** -ᵊnts

overjoyed ˌəʊ.vəˈdʒɔɪd US ˌoʊ.vɚˈ- *stress shift:* ˌoverjoyed ˈwinner

overkill ˈəʊ.və.kɪl US ˈoʊ.vɚ-

overladen ˌəʊ.vəˈleɪ.dᵊn US ˌoʊ.vɚˈ- *stress shift:* ˌoverladen ˈbasket

overlaid ˌəʊ.vəˈleɪd US ˌoʊ.vɚˈ-

overland (*adj.*) ˈəʊ.və.lænd US ˈoʊ.v

overland (*adv.*) ˌəʊ.vəˈlænd, ˈ--- US ˌoʊ.vɚˈlænd, ˈ---

overlap (*n.*) ˈəʊ.və.læp US ˈoʊ.vɚ- **-s**

overlap (*v.*) ˌəʊ.vəˈlæp US ˌoʊ.vɚˈ- **-s** **-ping** -ɪŋ **-ped** -t

overlay (*n.*) ˈəʊ.vᵊl.eɪ US ˈoʊ.vɚ.leɪ **-s** -z

overlay (*v.*) ˌəʊ.vᵊlˈeɪ US ˌoʊ.vɚˈleɪ **-s** -z **-ing** -ɪŋ **overlaid** ˌəʊ.vᵊlˈeɪd US ˌoʊ.vɚˈleɪd

overleaf ˌəʊ.vᵊlˈiːf US ˈoʊ.vɚ.liːf

overload (*n.*) ˈəʊ.vᵊl.əʊd US ˈoʊ.vɚ.loʊd **-s** -z

overload (*v.*) ˌəʊ.vᵊlˈəʊd US ˌoʊ.vɚˈloʊd, ˈ--- **-s** -z **-ing** -ɪŋ **-ed** -ɪd

overlock ˈəʊ.vᵊl.ɒk US ˈoʊ.vɚ.lɑːk - **-ing** -ɪŋ **-ed** -t

overlong ˌəʊ.vəˈlɒŋ US ˌoʊ.vɚˈlɑːŋ, -ˈlɔːŋ

overlook (*v.*) ˌəʊ.vəˈlʊk US ˌoʊ.vɚˈ- -s **-ing** -ɪŋ **-ed** -t

overlook (*n.*) ˈəʊ.və.lʊk US ˈoʊ.vɚ- **-s** -s

overlord ˈəʊ.və.lɔːd US ˈoʊ.vɚ.lɔːrd **-s** -z

overly ˈəʊ.vᵊl.i US ˈoʊ.vɚ.li

overlying ˌəʊ.vᵊlˈaɪ.ɪŋ US ˌoʊ.vɚˈla *stress shift:* ˌoverlying ˈstructure

overman (*v.*) ˌəʊ.vəˈmæn US ˌoʊ.vɚ -z **-ning** -ɪŋ **-ned** -d

over|man (*n.*) ˈəʊ.və|.mæn US ˈoʊ.v **-men** -men

overmantel ˈəʊ.vəˌmæn.tᵊl US ˈoʊ.vɚˌmæn.t̬ᵊl **-s** -z

overmast|er ˌəʊ.vəˈmɑː.st|əʳ US ˌoʊ.vɚˈmæs.tɚ **-ers** -əz US -ɚz **-ering** -ᵊr.ɪŋ **-ered** -əd US -ɚd

overmatch ˌəʊ.vəˈmætʃ US ˌoʊ.vɚ- ˈ--- **-es** -ɪz **-ing** -ɪŋ **-ed** -t

overmuch ˌəʊ.vəˈmʌtʃ, ˈ--- US ˌoʊ.vɚˈ-, ˈ---

overnight ˌəʊ.vəˈnaɪt US ˌoʊ.vɚˈ- *stress shift:* ˌovernight ˈsleeper

overoptimistic ˌəʊ.vᵊrˌɒp.tɪˈmɪs.t -təˈ- US ˌoʊ.vɚˌɑːp.təˈ- **-ally** -ᵊl.i, *stress shift:* ˌoveroptimistic ˈoutl

verpass (*n.*) ˈəʊ.və.pɑːs US ˈoʊ.vɚ.pæs **-es** -ɪz
ver|pay ˌəʊ.və|ˈpeɪ US ˌoʊ.vɚˈ-, ˈ--|- **-pays** -ˈpeɪz **-paying** -ˈpeɪ.ɪŋ **-paid** -ˈpeɪd **-payment/s** -ˈpeɪ.mənt/s
verplay ˌəʊ.vəˈpleɪ US ˌoʊ.vɚ- **-s** -z **-ing** -ɪŋ **-ed** -d
verplus ˈəʊ.və.plʌs US ˈoʊ.vɚ- **-es** -ɪz
verpopu|late ˌəʊ.vəˈpɒp.jə|.leɪt, -jʊ- US ˌoʊ.vɚˈpɑː.pjə-, -pjʊ- **-lates** -leɪts **-lating** -leɪ.tɪŋ US -leɪ.t̬ɪŋ **-lated** -leɪ.tɪd US -leɪ.t̬ɪd
verpopulation ˌəʊ.vəˌpɒp.jəˈleɪ.ʃᵊn, -jʊˈ- US ˌoʊ.vɚˌpɑː.pjəˈ-, -pjʊˈ-
verpower ˌəʊ.vəˈpaʊəʳ US ˌoʊ.vɚˈpaʊɚ **-s** -z **-ing/ly** -ɪŋ/li **-ed** -d
verpriced ˌəʊ.vəˈpraɪst US ˌoʊ.vɚ- *stress shift:* ˌoverpriced ˈgoods
verprint (*n.*) ˈəʊ.və.prɪnt US ˈoʊ.vɚ- **-s** -s
verprin|t (*v.*) ˌəʊ.vəˈprɪn|t, ˈ--- US ˌoʊ.vɚˈ-, ˈ--- **-ts** -ts **-ting** -tɪŋ US -t̬ɪŋ **-ted** -tɪd US -t̬ɪd
verproduc|e ˌəʊ.və.prəˈdjuːs US ˌoʊ.vɚ.proʊˈduːs, -ˈdjuːs, ˈoʊ.vɚ.proʊˌduːs, -ˌdjuːs **-es** -ɪz **-ing** -ɪŋ **-ed** -t
verproduction ˌəʊ.və.prəˈdʌk.ʃᵊn US ˌoʊ.vɚ-
erprotect ˌəʊ.və.prəˈtekt US ˌoʊ.vɚ- **-s** -s **-ing** -ɪŋ **-ed** -ɪd
erprotective ˌəʊ.və.prəˈtek.tɪv US ˌoʊ.vɚ- *stress shift:* ˌoverprotective ˈparent
erqualified ˌəʊ.vəˈkwɒl.ɪ.faɪd, ˈ-ə- US ˌoʊ.vɚˈkwɑː.lɪ-, ˈoʊ.vɚˌkwɑː.lɪ- *stress shift, British only:* ˌoverqualified ˈapplicant
erra|te ˌəʊ.vᵊrˈeɪ|t US ˌoʊ.vɚˈreɪ|t, ˈ--- **-tes** -ts **-ting** -tɪŋ US -t̬ɪŋ **-ted** -tɪd US -t̬ɪd
erreach (*n.*) ˈəʊ.vᵊrˈiːtʃ US ˈoʊ.vɚ.riːtʃ **-es** -ɪz
erreach (*v.*) ˌəʊ.vᵊrˈiːtʃ US ˌoʊ.vɚˈriːtʃ, ˈ--- **-es** -ɪz **-ing** -ɪŋ **-ed** -t
erreact ˌəʊ.vᵊr.iˈækt US ˌoʊ.vɚ.riˈ- **-s** -s **-ing** -ɪŋ **-ed** -ɪd
erreaction ˌəʊ.vᵊr.iˈæk.ʃᵊn US -oʊ.vɚ.riˈ-
errid|e ˌəʊ.vᵊrˈaɪd US ˌoʊ.vɚˈraɪd **-es** -z **-ing** -ɪŋ **overrode** ˌəʊ.vᵊrˈəʊd US ˌoʊ.vɚˈroʊd **overridden** ˌəʊ.vᵊrˈɪd.ᵊn US ˌoʊ.vɚˈrɪd-
errider ˈəʊ.vᵊrˌaɪ.dəʳ US ˈoʊ.vɚˌraɪ.dɚ **-s** -z
erripe ˌəʊ.vᵊrˈaɪp US ˌoʊ.vɚˈraɪp **-ness** -nəs, -nɪs *stress shift:* ˌoverripe ˈfruit
erripen ˌəʊ.vᵊrˈaɪ.pᵊn US ˌoʊ.vɚˈraɪ- **-s** -z **-ing** -ɪŋ, -vᵊrˈaɪp.nɪŋ US -vɚˈraɪp- **-ed** -d
overrul|e ˌəʊ.vᵊrˈuːl US ˌoʊ.vɚˈruːl **-es** -z **-ing** -ɪŋ **-ed** -d
overrun (*v.*) ˌəʊ.vᵊrˈʌn US ˌoʊ.vɚˈrʌn **-s** -z **-ning** -ɪŋ **overran** ˌəʊ.vᵊrˈæn US ˌoʊ.vɚˈræn
overrun (*n.*) ˈəʊ.vᵊr.ʌn US ˈoʊ.vɚ- **-s** -z
over-scrupulous ˌəʊ.vəˈskruː.pjə.ləs, -pjʊ- US ˌoʊ.vɚˈskruː.pjə- **-ly** -li **-ness** -nəs, -nɪs *stress shift:* ˌover-scrupulous ˈperson
oversea ˌəʊ.vəˈsiː US ˌoʊ.vɚˈ-, ˈoʊ.vɚ.siː **-s** -z *stress shift:* ˌoverseas ˈapplicant
over|see ˌəʊ.və|ˈsiː US ˌoʊ.vɚˈ- **-sees** -ˈsiːz **-seeing** -ˈsiː.ɪŋ **-saw** -ˈsɔː US -ˈsɑː, -ˈsɔː **-seen** -ˈsiːn
overseer ˈəʊ.vəˌsiː.əʳ US ˈoʊ.vɚˌsiː.ɚ, -ˌsɪr **-s** -z
over|sell ˌəʊ.və|ˈsel US -vɚ- **-sells** -selz **-selling** -sel.ɪŋ **-sold** -səʊld US -soʊld
oversensitive ˌəʊ.vəˈsent.sɪ.tɪv, -sə- US ˌoʊ.vɚˈsent.sə.t̬ɪv *stress shift:* ˌoversensitive ˈperson
oversensitivity ˌəʊ.vəˌsent.sɪˈtɪv.ə.ti, -səˈ-, -ɪ.ti US ˌoʊ.vɚˌsent.səˈtɪv.ə.t̬i
oversew ˈəʊ.və.səʊ, ˌ--ˈ- US ˈoʊ.vɚ.soʊ, ˌ--ˈ- **-s** -z **-ing** -ɪŋ **-ed** -d **-n** -n
oversexed ˌəʊ.vəˈsekst US ˌoʊ.vɚˈ- *stress shift:* ˌoversexed ˈperson
overshadow ˌəʊ.vəˈʃæd.əʊ US ˌoʊ.vɚˈʃæd.oʊ **-s** -z **-ing** -ɪŋ **-ed** -d
overshoe ˈəʊ.və.ʃuː US ˈoʊ.vɚ- **-s** -z
overshoot (*n.*) ˈəʊ.və.ʃuːt US ˈoʊ.vɚ-
overshoot (*v.*) ˌəʊ.vəˈʃuːt US ˌoʊ.vɚˈ- **-s** -s **-ing** -ɪŋ **overshot** ˌəʊ.vəˈʃɒt US ˌoʊ.vɚˈʃɑːt
overside (*adv.*) ˈəʊ.və.saɪd US ˈoʊ.vɚ-
oversight ˈəʊ.və.saɪt US ˈoʊ.vɚ- **-s** -s
oversimplification ˌəʊ.vəˌsɪm.plɪ.fɪˈkeɪ.ʃᵊn, -plə- US ˌoʊ.vɚˌsɪm.plə- **-s** -z
oversimpli|fy ˌəʊ.vəˈsɪm.plɪ|.faɪ, -plə- US ˌoʊ.vɚˈsɪm.plə-, ˈ--ˌ--- **-fies** -faɪz **-fying** -faɪ.ɪŋ **-fied** -faɪd
oversize ˌəʊ.vəˈsaɪz US ˌoʊ.vɚˈ-, ˈ--- **-d** -d *stress shift:* ˌoversize ˈclothes
oversleep ˌəʊ.vəˈsliːp US ˌoʊ.vɚˈ- **-s** -s **-ing** -ɪŋ **overslept** ˌəʊ.vəˈslept US ˌoʊ.vɚˈ-
oversold (*from* **oversell**) ˌəʊ.vəˈsəʊld US ˌoʊ.vɚˈsoʊld *stress shift:* ˌoversold ˈconcept
overspend ˌəʊ.vəˈspend US ˌoʊ.vɚˈ-, ˈ--- **-s** -z **-ing** -ɪŋ **overspent** ˌəʊ.vəˈspent US ˌoʊ.vɚˈ-, ˈ---
overspill ˈəʊ.və.spɪl US ˈoʊ.vɚ-
overspread ˌəʊ.vəˈspred US ˌoʊ.vɚˈ-, ˈ--- **-s** -z **-ing** -ɪŋ
overstaff ˌəʊ.vəˈstɑːf US ˌoʊ.vɚˈstæf **-s** -s **-ing** -ɪŋ **-ed** -t
over|state ˌəʊ.və|ˈsteɪt US ˌoʊ.vɚˈ- **-states** -ˈsteɪts **-stating** -ˈsteɪ.tɪŋ US -ˈsteɪ.t̬ɪŋ **-stated** -ˈsteɪ.tɪd US -ˈsteɪ.t̬ɪd *stress shift:* ˌoverstated ˈargument
overstatement ˌəʊ.vəˈsteɪt.mənt, ˈəʊ.vəˌsteɪt- US ˌoʊ.vɚˈsteɪt, ˈoʊ.vɚˌsteɪt **-s** -s
overstay ˌəʊ.vəˈsteɪ US ˌoʊ.vɚˈ-, ˈ--- **-s** -z **-ing** -ɪŋ **-ed** -d
overstep ˌəʊ.vəˈstep US ˌoʊ.vɚˈ- **-s** -s **-ping** -ɪŋ **-ped** -t
overstimu|late ˌəʊ.vəˈstɪm.jə|.leɪt, -jʊ- US ˌoʊ.vɚˈstɪm.jə-, -jʊ- **-lates** -leɪts **-lating** -leɪ.tɪŋ US -leɪ.t̬ɪŋ **-lated** -leɪ.tɪd US -leɪ.t̬ɪd
overstock ˌəʊ.vəˈstɒk US ˌoʊ.vɚˈstɑːk **-s** -s **-ing** -ɪŋ **-ed** -t
overstrain (*n.*) ˈəʊ.və.streɪn, ˌ--ˈ- US ˌoʊ.vɚˈ-, ˈ---
overstrain (*v.*) ˌəʊ.vəˈstreɪn US ˌoʊ.vɚˈ- **-s** -z **-ing** -ɪŋ **-ed** -d
Overstrand ˈəʊ.və.strænd US ˈoʊ.vɚ-
overstretch ˌəʊ.vəˈstretʃ US ˌoʊ.vɚˈ- **-es** -ɪz **-ing** -ɪŋ **-ed** -t
overstrung *in state of nervous tension:* ˌəʊ.vəˈstrʌŋ US ˌoʊ.vɚˈ- *of piano:* ˈəʊ.və.strʌŋ US ˈoʊ.vɚ-
oversubscrib|e ˌəʊ.və.səbˈskraɪb US ˌoʊ.vɚ- **-es** -z **-ing** -ɪŋ **-ed** -d
oversubscription ˌəʊ.və.səbˈskrɪp.ʃᵊn US ˌoʊ.vɚ-
oversupp|ly ˌəʊ.və.səˈpl|aɪ US ˌoʊ.vɚ- **-ies** -aɪz
overt əʊˈvɜːt; ˈəʊ.vɜːt US oʊˈvɝːt, ˈ-- **-ly** -li **-ness** -nəs, -nɪs
over|take ˌəʊ.və|ˈteɪk US ˌoʊ.vɚˈ- **-takes** -ˈteɪks **-taking** -ˈteɪ.kɪŋ **-took** -ˈtʊk **-taken** -ˈteɪ.kᵊn, -kᵊŋ US -kᵊn
overtask ˌəʊ.vəˈtɑːsk US ˌoʊ.vɚˈtæsk **-s** -s **-ing** -ɪŋ **-ed** -t
overtax ˌəʊ.vəˈtæks US ˌoʊ.vɚˈ- **-es** -ɪz **-ing** -ɪŋ **-ed** -t
over-the-counter ˌəʊ.və.ðəˈkaʊn.təʳ US ˌoʊ.vɚ.ðəˈkaʊn.t̬ɚ *stress shift:* ˌover-the-counter ˈsales
over-the-top ˌəʊ.və.ðəˈtɒp US ˌoʊ.vɚ.ðəˈtɑːp *stress shift:* ˌover-the-top ˈspeech
Note: See also **OTT**.
overthrow (*n.*) ˈəʊ.və.θrəʊ US ˈoʊ.vɚ.θroʊ **-s** -z
overthrow (*v.*) ˌəʊ.vəˈθrəʊ US ˌoʊ.vɚˈθroʊ, ˈ--- **-s** -z **-ing** -ɪŋ **overthrew** ˌəʊ.vəˈθruː US ˌoʊ.vɚˈ-, ˈ--- **overthrown** ˌəʊ.vəˈθrəʊn US ˌoʊ.vɚˈθroʊn, ˈ---

Pronouncing the letters OW

There are two common pronunciations of the vowel digraph ow: /əʊ US oʊ/ and /aʊ/, e.g.:

blow	/bləʊ/	US /bloʊ/
brown	/braʊn/	

In addition

A less common realisation is /ɒ US ɑː/, e.g.:

knowledge	/ˈnɒl.ɪdʒ/	US /ˈnɑː.lɪdʒ/

overthrust ˈəʊ.və.θrʌst US ˈoʊ.vɚ- **-s** -s
overtime ˈəʊ.və.taɪm US ˈoʊ.vɚ-
overtir|e ˌəʊ.vəˈtaɪəʳ US ˌoʊ.vɚˈtaɪɚ **-es** -z **-ing** -ɪŋ **-ed** -d
overtone ˈəʊ.və.təʊn US ˈoʊ.vɚ.toʊn **-s** -z
overtop ˌəʊ.vəˈtɒp US ˌoʊ.vɚˈtɑːp **-s** -s **-ping** -ɪŋ **-ped** -t
Overtoun ˈəʊ.və.tᵊn US ˈoʊ.vɚ-
Overtown ˈəʊ.və.tᵊn US ˈoʊ.vɚ-
over-trump ˌəʊ.vəˈtrʌmp US ˌoʊ.vɚˈ- **-s** -s **-ing** -ɪŋ **-ed** -t
overture ˈəʊ.və.tjʊəʳ, -tjəʳ, -tʃʊəʳ, -tʃəʳ US ˈoʊ.vɚ.tʃɚ, -tʃʊr **-s** -z
overturn (*n.*) ˈəʊ.və.tɜːn US ˈoʊ.vɚ.tɝːn **-s** -z
overturn (*v.*) ˌəʊ.vəˈtɜːn US ˌoʊ.vɚˈtɝːn **-s** -z **-ing** -ɪŋ **-ed** -d
overus|e (*v.*) ˌəʊ.vəˈjuːz US ˌoʊ.vɚˈ- **-es** -ɪz **-ing** -ɪŋ **-ed** -d
overuse (*n.*) ˌəʊ.vəˈjuːs US ˌoʊ.vɚˈ-
overval|ue ˌəʊ.vəˈvæl|.juː US ˌoʊ.vɚˈ- **-ues** -juːz **-uing** -juː.ɪŋ **-ued** -juːd
overview ˈəʊ.və.vjuː US ˈoʊ.vɚ- **-s** -z
overweening ˌəʊ.vəˈwiː.nɪŋ US ˌoʊ.vɚˈ-, ˈoʊ.vɚˌwiː- **-ly** -li *stress shift:* ˌoverweening ˈpride
overweight (*n.*) ˈəʊ.və.weɪt US ˈoʊ.vɚ- **-s** -s
overweight (*adj.*) ˌəʊ.vəˈweɪt US ˌoʊ.vɚˈ-, ˈ--- *stress shift, British only:* ˌoverweight ˈperson
overweigh|t (*v.*) ˌəʊ.vəˈweɪ|t US ˌoʊ.vɚˈ-, ˈ--- **-ts** -ts **-ting** -tɪŋ US -t̬ɪŋ **-ted** -tɪd US -t̬ɪd
overwhelm ˌəʊ.vəˈhwelm US ˌoʊ.vɚˈ- **-s** -z **-ing/ly** -ɪŋ/li **-ed** -d
overwind ˌəʊ.vəˈwaɪnd US ˌoʊ.vɚˈ-, ˈ--- **-s** -z **-ing** -ɪŋ **overwound** ˌəʊ.vəˈwaʊnd US ˌoʊ.vɚˈ-, ˈ---
overwint|er ˌəʊ.vəˈwɪn.t|əʳ US ˌoʊ.vɚˈwɪn.t̬|ɚ **-ers** -əz US -ɚz **-ering** -ᵊr.ɪŋ **-ered** -əd US -ɚd
overwork (*n.*) ˈəʊ.və.wɜːk US ˈoʊ.vɚ.wɝːk
overwork (*v.*) ˌəʊ.vəˈwɜːk US ˌoʊ.vɚˈwɝːk, ˈ--- **-s** -s **-ing** -ɪŋ **-ed** -t **-er/s** -əʳ/z US -ɚ/z *stress shift:* ˌoverworked ˈeditor
overwrit|e ˌəʊ.vᵊrˈaɪt US ˌoʊ.vɚˈraɪt **-es** -s **-ing** -ɪŋ **overwrote** ˌəʊ.vᵊrˈəʊt US ˌoʊ.vɚˈroʊt **overwritten** ˌəʊ.vᵊrˈɪt.ᵊn US ˌoʊ.vɚˈrɪt-
overwrought ˌəʊ.vᵊrˈɔːt US ˌoʊ.vɚˈrɑːt, -ˈrɔːt *stress shift:* ˌoverwrought ˈperson
overzealous ˌəʊ.vəˈzel.əs US ˌoʊ.vɚˈ- *stress shift:* ˌoverzealous ˈfollower
Ovett ˈəʊ.vet, -ˈ- US ˈoʊ.vet, -ˈ-
Ovid *Latin poet:* ˈɒv.ɪd US ˈɑː.vɪd *US surname:* ˈəʊ.vɪd US ˈoʊ-
Ovidian əʊˈvɪd.i.ən, ɒvˈɪd- US oʊˈvɪd-
Oviedo ˌɒv.iˈeɪ.dəʊ US oʊˈvjeɪ.doʊ, -ðoʊ
oviform ˈəʊ.vɪ.fɔːm US ˈoʊ.vɪ.fɔːrm
ovine ˈəʊ.vaɪn US ˈoʊ-
Ovingdean ˈɒv.ɪŋ.diːn US ˈɑː.vɪŋ-
Ovingham ˈɒv.ɪn.dʒəm US ˈɑː.vɪn-
Ovington *in North Yorkshire, street in London:* ˈɒv.ɪŋ.tən US ˈɑː.vɪŋ- *in Norfolk, surname:* ˈəʊ.vɪŋ.tən US ˈoʊ-
oviparous əʊˈvɪp.ᵊr.əs US oʊ- **-ly** -li **-ness** -nəs, -nɪs
ovoid ˈəʊ.vɔɪd US ˈoʊ- **-s** -z
ovular ˈɒv.jə.ləʳ, ˈəʊ.vjə-, -vjʊ- US ˈɑː.vjuː.lɚ, ˈoʊ-, -vjə-
ovu|late ˈɒv.jə|.leɪt, ˈəʊ.vjə- US ˈɑː.vjuː-, ˈoʊ-, -vjə- **-lates** -leɪts **-lating** -leɪ.tɪŋ US -leɪ.t̬ɪŋ **-lated** -leɪ.tɪd US -leɪ.t̬ɪd
ovulation ˌɒv.jəˈleɪ.ʃᵊn, ˌəʊ.vjəˈ-, -vjʊˈ- US ˌɑː.vjuːˈ-, ˌoʊ-, -vjəˈ-
ovule ˈɒv.juːl, ˈəʊ.vjuːl US ˈɑː-, ˈoʊ- **-s** -z
ov|um ˈəʊ.v|əm US ˈoʊ- **-a** -ə
Owbridge ˈəʊ.brɪdʒ US ˈoʊ-
ow|e əʊ US oʊ **-es** -z **-ing** -ɪŋ **-ed** -d
Owen ˈəʊ.ɪn US ˈoʊ- **-s** -z
Ower aʊəʳ US aʊɚ
Owers əʊəz, aʊəz US oʊɚz, aʊɚz
owing *(from* **owe***)* ˈəʊ.ɪŋ US ˈoʊ-
owl aʊl **-s** -z
owler|y ˈaʊ.lᵊr|.i **-ies** -iz
Owles əʊlz, aʊlz, uːlz US oʊlz, aʊlz, uːlz
owlet ˈaʊ.lət, -lɪt, -let US -lɪt **-s** -s
Owlett ˈaʊ.lɪt, -let US -lɪt
owlish ˈaʊ.lɪʃ **-ly** -li **-ness** -nəs, -nɪs
own əʊn US oʊn **-s** -z **-ing** -ɪŋ **-ed** -d **-er/s** -əʳ/z US -ɚ/z ˌ**own** ˈ**goal**
own-brand ˌəʊnˈbrænd, ˌəʊm-, ˈ-- US ˌoʊnˈ-, ˈ-- **-s** -z **-ing** -ɪŋ
owner-driver ˌəʊ.nəˈdraɪ.vəʳ US ˌoʊ.nɚˈdraɪ.vɚ **-s** -z *stress shi*[ft:] ˌowner-driver ˈtaxi
owner-occup|ier ˌəʊ.nəʳˈɒk.jə.pla[ɪəʳ], -jʊ- US ˌoʊ.nɚˈɑː.kjuː.plaɪ.ɚ, -k[jə-] **-iers** -aɪ.əz US -aɪ.ɚz **-ied** -aɪd
ownership ˈəʊ.nə.ʃɪp US ˈoʊ.nɚ-
own-label ˌəʊnˈleɪ.bᵊl US ˌoʊn-
Owsley ˈaʊz.li
owt aʊt, əʊt US aʊt, oʊt
ox ɒks US ɑːks **-en** -ᵊn
oxalate ˈɒk.sə.leɪt, -lɪt, -lət US ˈɑːk.sə.leɪt **-s** -s
oxalic ɒkˈsæl.ɪk US ɑːkˈ-
oxalis ɒkˈsɑː.lɪs, -ˈsæl.ɪs, -ˈseɪ.lɪs; ˈɒk.sə.lɪs US ˈɑːk.sə.lɪs; ɑːkˈsæl[.ɪs]
oxbow ˈɒks.bəʊ US ˈɑːks.boʊ **-s** -z
Oxbridge ˈɒks.brɪdʒ US ˈɑːks-
Oxbrow ˈɒks.braʊ US ˈɑːks-
oxen *(plur. of* **ox***)* ˈɒk.sᵊn US ˈɑːk-
Oxenden ˈɒk.sᵊn.dən US ˈɑːk-
Oxenford ˈɒk.sᵊn.fɔːd, -fəd US ˈɑːk.sən.fɔːrd, -fɚd
Oxenham ˈɒk.sᵊn.əm US ˈɑːk-
Oxenhope ˈɒk.sᵊn.həʊp US ˈɑːk.sᵊn.hoʊp
oxer ˈɒk.səʳ US ˈɑːk.sɚ **-s** -z
oxeye ˈɒks.aɪ US ˈɑːk.saɪ **-s** -z **-d** -d
Oxfam ˈɒks.fæm US ˈɑːks-
Oxford ˈɒks.fəd US ˈɑːks.fɚd **-shir**[e] -ʃəʳ, -ˌʃɪəʳ US -ʃɚ, -ˌʃɪr
oxidant ˈɒk.sɪ.dᵊnt, -sə- US ˈɑːk.sɪ[-]
oxi|date ˈɒk.sɪ|.deɪt, -sə- US ˈɑːk.s[ɪ-] **-dates** -deɪts **-dating** -deɪ.tɪŋ US -deɪ.t̬ɪŋ **-dated** -deɪ.tɪd US -deɪ.t̬ɪd
oxidation ˌɒk.sɪˈdeɪ.ʃᵊn, -səˈ- US ˌɑːk.sɪˈ-
oxide ˈɒk.saɪd US ˈɑːk- **-s** -z
oxidization, -isa- ˌɒk.sɪ.daɪˈzeɪ.ʃᵊ[n], -sə-, -dɪˈ- US ˌɑːk.sɪ.dɪˈ-
oxidiz|e, -is|e ˈɒk.sɪ.daɪz, -sə- US ˈɑːk.sɪ- **-es** -ɪz **-ing** -ɪŋ **-ed** -d **-er/s** -əʳ/z US -ɚ/z **-able** -ə.bl̩
Oxley ˈɒk.sli US ˈɑːk-
oxlip ˈɒk.slɪp US ˈɑːk- **-s** -s
oxo (O®) ˈɒk.səʊ US ˈɑːk.soʊ
Oxon. ˈɒk.sᵊn, -sɒn US ˈɑːk.sᵊn, -s[ɑːn]

Oxonian ɒk'səʊ.ni.ən (US) ɑːk'soʊ- **-s** -z
Oxshott 'ɒk.ʃɒt (US) 'ɑːk.ʃɑːt
oxtail 'ɒks.teɪl (US) 'ɑːks- **-s** -z ˌ**oxtail** '**soup**
Oxted 'ɒk.stɪd (US) 'ɑːk-
ox-tongue 'ɒks.tʌŋ (US) 'ɑːks- **-s** -z
Oxus 'ɒk.səs (US) 'ɑːk-
oxy- ɒk.sɪ-, -si-; ɒk'sɪ (US) ɑːk.sɪ-, -si-; ɑːk'sɪ-
Note: Prefix. Normally either takes primary or secondary stress on the first syllable, e.g. **oxygen** /'ɒk.sɪ.dʒən (US) 'ɑːk-/, **oxychloride** /ˌɒk.sɪ'klɔː.raɪd (US) ˌɑːk.sɪ'klɔːr.aɪd/, or primary stress on the second syllable, e.g. **oxygenous** /ɒk'sɪdʒ.ən.əs (US) ɑːk-/.
oxyacetylene ˌɒk.si.ə'set.əl.iːn, -ɪ.liːn, -lɪn (US) ˌɑːk.si.ə'set̬.əl.iːn, -ɪn
oxychloride ˌɒk.sɪ'klɔː.raɪd (US) ˌɑːk.sɪ'klɔːr.aɪd **-s** -z
oxygen 'ɒk.sɪ.dʒən, -sə- (US) 'ɑːk.sɪ-
oxyge|nate 'ɒk.sɪ.dʒə|.neɪt, -sə-, -dʒɪ-; (US) 'ɑːk.sɪ.dʒə- **-nates** -neɪts **-nating** -neɪ.tɪŋ (US) -neɪ.t̬ɪŋ **-nated** -neɪ.tɪd (US) -neɪ.t̬ɪd
oxygenation ˌɒk.sɪ.dʒə'neɪ.ʃən, -sə-, -dʒɪ'-; (US) ˌɑːk.sɪ.dʒə'-
oxygeniz|e, -is|e 'ɒk.sɪ.dʒə.naɪz, -sə- (US) 'ɑːk.sɪ- **-es** -ɪz **-ing** -ɪŋ **-ed** -d
oxygenous ɒk'sɪdʒ.ən.əs, -ɪ.nəs (US) ɑːk-
oxyhaemoglobin ˌɒk.siˌhiː.məʊ'gləʊ.bɪn (US) ˌɑːk.siˌhiː.mə'gloʊ-, -moʊ'-
oxyhydrogen ˌɒk.si'haɪ.drə.dʒən, -drɪ- (US) ˌɑːk.si'haɪ.drə-
oxymoron ˌɒk.sɪ'mɔː.rɒn, -rən (US) ˌɑːk.sɪ'mɔːr.ɑːn **-s** -z
oxytone 'ɒk.sɪ.təʊn (US) 'ɑːk.sɪ.toʊn **-s** -z
oyer 'ɔɪ.əʳ (US) -ɚ ˌ**oyer and** '**terminer**
oyes, oyez əʊ'jes, -'jez, -'jeɪ, '-- (US) 'oʊ.jes, -jez, -jeɪ
oyster (O) 'ɔɪ.stəʳ (US) -stɚ **-s** -z
oyster-catcher 'ɔɪ.stəˌkætʃ.əʳ (US) -stɚˌkætʃ.ɚ **-s** -z
Oystermouth 'ɔɪ.stə.maʊθ (US) -stɚ-
oz. *(abbrev. for* **ounce/s***) singular:* aʊnts *plural:* 'aʊnt.sɪz
Oz ɒz (US) ɑːz
Ozalid® 'əʊ.zəl.ɪd, 'ɒz.əl- (US) 'ɑː.zəl- **-s** -z
Ozanne əʊ'zæn (US) oʊ-
Ozarks 'əʊ.zɑːks (US) 'oʊ.zɑːrks
ozokerite əʊ'zəʊ.kər.ɪt, ɒz'əʊ-, ə'zəʊ- (US) oʊ'zoʊ.kə.raɪt; ˌoʊ.zoʊ'kɪr.aɪt
ozone 'əʊ.zəʊn (US) 'oʊ.zoʊn '**ozone** ˌ**layer**
ozone-friendly ˌəʊ.zəʊn'frend.li (US) ˌoʊ.zoʊn'- *stress shift:* ˌozone-friendly 'chemicals
ozonic əʊ'zɒn.ɪk (US) oʊ'zɑː.nɪk
ozoniferous ˌəʊ.zəʊ'nɪf.ər.əs (US) ˌoʊ.zə'-
ozonosphere əʊ'zɒn.ə.sfɪəʳ, -'zəʊ.nə- (US) oʊ'zoʊ.nə.sfɪr
Ozymandias ˌɒz.ɪ'mæn.di.əs, -æs (US) ˌɑː.zi-
Ozzie 'ɒz.i (US) 'ɑː.zi

Pronouncing the letter P

See also PH

The consonant letter **p** is most often realised as /p/, e.g.:

pen /pen/

In addition

p can be silent. There are three combinations in which this can occur: **pn**, **ps** and **pt**.

p is silent in **pn** and **ps** when word initial, e.g.:

pneumatic /njuːˈmæt.ɪk/ (US) /nuːˈmæt̬-/
psalm /sɑːm/

pt can be silent word initially and word finally, e.g.:

pterodactyl /ˌter.əʊˈdæk.tɪl/ (US) /ˌter.əˈdæk.təl/
receipt /rɪˈsiːt/

In addition

p can be silent in other instances, e.g.:

corps /kɔːʳ/ (US) /kɔːr/
cupboard /ˈkʌb.əd/ (US) /-ɚd/
raspberry /ˈrɑːz.bᵊr.i/ (US) /ˈræzˌber.i/

p (P) piː **-'s** -z ˌ**p's and 'q's**
pa pɑː **-s** -z
PA ˌpiːˈeɪ
Pa. *(abbrev. for* **Pennsylvania***)* ˌpent.sɪlˈveɪ.ni.ə, -sᵊlˈ-, ˈ-njə (US) -sᵊlˈveɪ.njə, ˈ-ni.ə
pa'anga pɑːˈæŋ.gə, -ə (US) -ˈɑːŋ.gə, ˈpɑːŋ-
pabulum ˈpæb.jə.ləm, -jʊ-
pac|e *(n. v.)* peɪs **-es** -ɪz **-ing** -ɪŋ **-ed** -t **-er/s** -əʳ/z (US) -ɚ/z ˌ**put someone** ˌ**through their 'paces**
pace *(prep.)* ˈpeɪ.si, ˈpɑː.tʃeɪ, -keɪ
pacemaker ˈpeɪsˌmeɪ.kəʳ (US) -kɚ **-s** -z
pace|man ˈpeɪ.smæn, -smən **-men** -men
pace-setter ˈpeɪsˌset.əʳ (US) -ˌset̬.ɚ **-s** -z
Pachmann ˈpɑːk.mən, -mɑːn
pachyderm ˈpæk.ɪ.dɜːm (US) -ə.dɝːm **-s** -z
pachydermatous ˌpæk.ɪˈdɜː.mə.təs (US) -əˈdɝː.mə.t̬əs
pacific (P) pəˈsɪf.ɪk **-ally** -ᵊl.i, -li
pacification ˌpæs.ɪ.fɪˈkeɪ.ʃᵊn, ˌ-ə- (US) ˌ-ə- **-s** -z
pacificatory pəˈsɪf.ɪ.kə.tᵊr.i, pæsˈɪf-, ˌpæs.ɪ.fɪˈkeɪ-, ˌ-ə-; ˈ-ə- (US) pəˈsɪf.ɪ.kə.tɔːr-
pacificist pəˈsɪf.ɪ.sɪst, pæsˈɪf- (US) pəˈsɪf- **-s** -s
pacifism ˈpæs.ɪ.fɪ.zᵊm, ˈ-ə- (US) ˈ-ə-
pacifist ˈpæs.ɪ.fɪst, ˈ-ə- (US) ˈ-ə- **-s** -s
paci|fy ˈpæs.ɪ|.faɪ, ˈ-ə- (US) ˈ-ə- **-fies** -faɪz **-fying** -faɪ.ɪŋ **-fied** -faɪd **-fier/s** -faɪ.əʳ/z (US) -faɪ.ɚ/z
Pacino pəˈtʃiː.nəʊ (US) -noʊ
pack pæk **-s** -s **-ing** -ɪŋ **-ed** -t **-er/s** -əʳ/z (US) -ɚ/z ˈ**pack** ˌ**ice**; ˈ**packing** ˌ**case**
packag|e ˈpæk.ɪdʒ **-es** -ɪz **-ing** -ɪŋ **-ed** -d ˌ**package** ˈ**holiday**; ˈ**package** ˌ**store**
Packard ˈpæk.ɑːd (US) -ɚd
packed pækt
Packer ˈpæk.əʳ (US) -ɚ
packet ˈpæk.ɪt **-s** -s
packhors|e ˈpæk.hɔːs (US) -hɔːrs **-es** -ɪz
packing|house ˈpæk.ɪŋ|.haʊs **-houses** -haʊ.zɪz
pack|man ˈpæk|.mən, -mæn **-men** -mən (US) -mən, -men
Pac-man® ˈpæk.mæn
pact pækt **-s** -s
pactum ˈpæk.təm
pac|y ˈpeɪ.s|i **-ier** -i.əʳ (US) -i.ɚ **-iest** -i.ɪst
pad pæd **-s** -z **-ding** -ɪŋ **-ded** -ɪd ˌ**padded** ˈ**cell**
Padang ˈpɑː.dɑːŋ (US) pɑːˈdɑːŋ
Paddington ˈpæd.ɪŋ.tən
paddl|e ˈpæd.l̩ **-es** -z **-ing** -ɪŋ, ˈpæd.lɪŋ **-ed** -d **-er/s** -əʳ/z, ˈpæd.ləʳ/z (US) ˈpæd.l̩.ɚ/z, ˈpæd.lɚ/z ˈ**paddle** ˌ**steamer**; ˈ**paddle** ˌ**wheel**
paddleboard ˈpæd.l̩.bɔːd (US) -bɔːrd **-s** -z
paddling-pool ˈpæd.l̩.ɪŋ.puːl, ˈ-lɪŋ-
paddock (P) ˈpæd.ək **-s** -s
padd|y (P) ˈpæd|.i **-ies** -iz
paddyfield ˈpæd.i.fiːld **-s** -z
paddywagon ˈpæd.iˌwæg.ᵊn
Paderewski ˌpæd.ᵊrˈef.ski, -ᵊrˈev- (US) ˌpæd.əˈ-, ˌpɑː.dəˈ-
Padiham ˈpæd.i.əm
padlock ˈpæd.lɒk (US) -lɑːk **-s** -s **-ing** -ɪŋ **-ed** -t
Padraic ˈpɑː.drɪk, ˈpæt.rɪk (US) ˈpɑː.drɪk, -drɪg
Padraic Colum ˌpɑː.drɪkˈkɒl.əm, ˌpæt.rɪk- (US) ˌpɑː.drɪkˈkɑː.ləm, -drɪgˈ-
Padraig ˈpɑː.drɪg
padre ˈpɑː.dreɪ, -dri **-s** -z
padrone pædˈrəʊ.neɪ, pəˈdrəʊ-, -ni (US) pəˈdroʊ- **-s** -z
Padstow ˈpæd.stəʊ (US) -stoʊ
Padu|a ˈpæd.ju|.ə (US) ˈpædʒ.uː-, ˈpæd.juː- **-an/s** -ən/z
paean ˈpiː.ən **-s** -z
paederast ˈpiː.dᵊr.æst, ˈped.ᵊr- (US) ˈped.ə.ræst **-s** -s **-y** -i
paediatric ˌpiː.diˈæt.rɪk **-s** -s
paediatrician ˌpiː.di.əˈtrɪʃ.ᵊn **-s** -z
paedophile ˈpiː.dəʊ.faɪl (US) ˈped.oʊ-, ˈpiː.doʊ-, -də- **-s** -z
paedophili|a ˌpiː.dəʊˈfɪl.i|.ə (US) ˌped.oʊˈfiː.li-, ˌpiː.doʊˈ-, -dəˈ-, -ˈfiːl.j|ə **-ac/s** -æk/s
paella paɪˈel.ə (US) pɑːˈjel-, -ˈeɪ.jɑː **-s** -
paeon ˈpiː.ən **-s** -z
paeonic piːˈɒn.ɪk (US) -ˈɑː.nɪk
paeon|y ˈpiː.ə.n|i **-ies** -iz
pagan ˈpeɪ.gᵊn **-s** -z
Pagani pəˈgɑː.ni (US) pə-, pɑː-
Paganini ˌpæg.əˈniː.ni
paganism ˈpeɪ.gᵊn.ɪ.zᵊm
paganiz|e, -is|e ˈpeɪ.gᵊn.aɪz **-es** -ɪz **-in**[g] -ɪŋ **-ed** -d
pag|e (P) peɪdʒ **-es** -ɪz **-ing** -ɪŋ **-ed** -d
pageant ˈpædʒ.ənt **-s** -s
pageantry ˈpædʒ.ən.tri
pageboy ˈpeɪdʒ.bɔɪ
pager ˈpeɪ.dʒəʳ (US) -dʒɚ **-s** -z
Paget ˈpædʒ.ɪt
paginal ˈpædʒ.ɪ.nᵊl, ˈpeɪ.dʒɪ- (US) ˈpædʒ.ə-
pagin|ate ˈpædʒ.ɪ.n|eɪt, ˈpeɪ.dʒɪ-, -dʒᵊn|.eɪt (US) ˈpædʒ.ᵊn- **-ates** -eɪts **-ating** -eɪ.tɪŋ (US) -eɪ.t̬ɪŋ **-ated** -eɪ.t[ɪd] (US) -eɪ.t̬ɪd
pagination ˌpædʒ.ɪˈneɪ.ʃᵊn, ˌpeɪ.dʒ[ɪ-], -dʒᵊnˈeɪ- (US) ˌpædʒ.ᵊnˈeɪ- **-s** -z
Paglia pɑː.li.ə (US) ˈpæg.liː.ə, ˈpeɪg.li[ː-]
Pagliacci ˌpæl.iˈɑː.tʃi, -ˈætʃ.i (US) pɑːˈjɑː.tʃi
Pagnell ˈpæg.nəl
pagoda pəˈgəʊ.də (US) -ˈgoʊ- **-s** -z
Pagones pəˈgəʊ.nez (US) -ˈgoʊ-
pah pɑː
Pahang pəˈhʌŋ, -ˈhæŋ (US) -ˈhɑːŋ, pɑː[-]
Note: Usually pronounced /pəˈhʌŋ/ i[n] Malaya.

Palatal

A palatal consonant is one in which the tongue makes contact with or approaches the highest part of the hard palate. The hard palate is mainly composed of a thin layer of bone and is dome-shaped, as you can feel by exploring it with the tip of your tongue.

Examples for English

In English, the only phoneme described as palatal is /j/, e.g.:

yes	/jes/	
beautiful	/ˈbjuː.tɪ.fəl/	(US) /-t̬ə-/

However, phonetically a voiceless palatal fricative [ç] can also occur for the consonants in the sequence /hjuː/, e.g.:

huge	/hjuːdʒ/	[çʉːd̥ʒ̊]
Hugh, Huw	/hjuː/	[çʉː]

aid (*from* **pay**) peɪd

aige peɪdʒ

aignton ˈpeɪn.tən (US) -tᵊn

ail peɪl **-s** -z **-ful/s** -fʊl/z

aillass|e ˈpæl.i.æs, ˌ--ˈ- (US) pælˈjæs, ˈ-- **-es** -ɪz

aillette pælˈjet, ˌpæl.iˈet (US) ˌpælˈjet, ˈpɑː.jet **-s** -s

ain peɪn **-s** -z **-ing** -ɪŋ **-ed** -d **ˌpain in the ˈneck; be at ˌpains to ˈdo something**

ain(e) peɪn

ainful ˈpeɪn.fᵊl, -fʊl **-ly** -i **-ness** -nəs, -nɪs

ainkill|er ˈpeɪnˌkɪl|.əʳ, ˈpeɪŋ- (US) ˈpeɪnˌkɪl|.ɚ **-ers** -əz (US) -ɚz **-ing** -ɪŋ

ainless ˈpeɪn.ləs, -lɪs **-ly** -li **-ness** -nəs, -nɪs

ainstaking ˈpeɪnzˌteɪ.kɪŋ, ˈpeɪns- (US) ˈpeɪnz- **-ly** -li

ainswick ˈpeɪnz.wɪk

aint peɪnt **-s** -s **-ing/s** -ɪŋ/z (US) ˈpeɪn.t̬ɪŋ **-ed** -ɪd (US) ˈpeɪn.t̬ɪd **-er/s** -əʳ/z (US) ˈpeɪn.t̬ɚ/z **ˌpainted ˈlady**

aintball ˈpeɪnt.bɔːl (US) -bɔːl, -bɑːl **-ing** -ɪŋ **-er/s** -əʳ/z (US) -ɚ/z

aintbox ˈpeɪnt.bɒks (US) -bɑːks **-es** -ɪz

aintbrush ˈpeɪnt.brʌʃ **-es** -ɪz

inter ˈpeɪn.təʳ (US) -t̬ɚ

interly ˈpeɪn.tᵊl.i (US) -t̬ɚ.li

intwork ˈpeɪnt.wɜːk (US) -wɝːk

int|y ˈpeɪn.t|i (US) -t̬|i **-ier** -i.əʳ (US) -i.ɚ **-iest** -i.ɪst, -i.əst

ir peəʳ (US) per **-s** -z **-ing** -ɪŋ **-ed** -d

is|a ˈpaɪ.s|ɑː **-e** -eɪ **-as** -ɑːz

isley (P) ˈpeɪz.li

jama pəˈdʒɑː.mə (US) -ˈdʒɑː-, -ˈdʒæm.ə **-s** -z

k-choi ˌpækˈtʃɔɪ, ˌbɒk-, ˌpɑːk- (US) ˌbɑːkˈtʃɔɪ

keman ˈpeɪk.mən

kenham ˈpæk.ᵊn.əm

ki ˈpæk.i **-s** -z

kistan ˌpɑː.kɪˈstɑːn, ˌpæk.ɪˈ-, -ˈstæn (US) ˈpæk.ɪ.stæn, ˈpɑː.kɪ.stɑːn; ˌpæk.ɪˈstæn, ˌpɑː.kɪˈstɑːn

Pakistani ˌpɑː.kɪˈstɑː.ni, ˌpæk.ɪˈ- **-s** -z

pakora pəˈkɔː.rə (US) -ˈkɔːr.ə

pal pæl **-s** -z

palac|e ˈpæl.ɪs, -əs (US) -əs **-es** -ɪz

paladin ˈpæl.ə.dɪn **-s** -z

palaeo- ˌpæl.i.əʊ-, ˌpeɪ.li.əʊ- (US) ˌpeɪ.li.oʊ-, -ə-

palaeobotany ˌpæl.i.əʊˈbɒt.ᵊn.i, ˌpeɪ.li- (US) ˌpeɪ.li.oʊˈbɑː.tᵊn-

Palaeocene ˈpæl.i.əʊ.siːn, ˈpeɪ.li- (US) ˈpeɪ.li.oʊ-, -ə-

palaeographic ˌpæl.i.əʊˈgræf.ɪk, ˌpeɪ.li- (US) ˌpeɪ.li.oʊˈ-, -əˈ-

palaeograph|y ˌpæl.iˈɒg.rə.f|i, ˌpeɪ.li- (US) ˌpeɪ.liˈɑː.grə- **-er/s** -əʳ/z (US) -ɚ/z

palaeolithic (P) ˌpæl.i.əʊˈlɪθ.ɪk, ˌpeɪ.li- (US) ˌpeɪ.li.oʊˈ-, -əˈ-

palaeontological ˌpæl.iˌɒn.təˈlɒdʒ.ɪ.kᵊl, ˌpeɪ.li- (US) ˌpeɪ.liˌɑːn.təˈlɑː.dʒɪ-

palaeontolog|y ˌpæl.i.ɒnˈtɒl.ə.dʒ|i, ˌpeɪ.li- (US) ˌpeɪ.li.ɑːnˈtɑː.lə- **-ist/s** -ɪsts

palaeotype ˈpæl.i.əʊ.taɪp, ˈpeɪ.li- (US) ˈpeɪ.li.oʊ-, -ə-

Palaeozoic ˌpæl.i.əʊˈzəʊ.ɪk, ˌpeɪ.li- (US) ˌpeɪ.li.oʊˈzoʊ-, -ə-

Palamedes ˌpæl.əˈmiː.diːz

palamino ˌpæl.əˈmiː.nəʊ (US) -noʊ **-s** -z

Palamon ˈpæl.ə.mən, -mɒn (US) -mən, -mɑːn

palanquin ˌpæl.əŋˈkiːn (US) -ənˈ- **-s** -z

palatab|le ˈpæl.ə.tə.b|l̩, ˈ-ɪ- (US) -ə.t̬ə- **-ly** -li **-leness** -l̩.nəs, -nɪs

palatal ˈpæl.ə.tᵊl (US) -t̬ᵊl **-s** -z

palatalization, -isa- ˌpæl.ə.tᵊl.aɪˈzeɪ.ʃᵊn, pəˌlæt.ᵊl-, -ɪˈ- (US) ˌpæl.ə.t̬ᵊl.ɪˈ- **-s** -z

palataliz|e, -is|e ˈpæl.ə.tᵊl.aɪz, pəˈlæt.ᵊl- (US) ˈpæl.ə.t̬ə.laɪz **-es** -ɪz **-ing** -ɪŋ **-ed** -d

palate ˈpæl.ət, -ɪt (US) -ət **-s** -s

palatial pəˈleɪ.ʃᵊl (US) -ʃᵊl **-ly** -i

palatinate (P) pəˈlæt.ɪ.nət, -ᵊn.ət, -ɪt (US) -ᵊn.eɪt, -ɪt **-s** -s

palatine (P) ˈpæl.ə.taɪn (US) -taɪn, -tɪn **-s** -z

palatogram ˈpæl.ə.təʊ.græm, pəˈlæt.əʊ- (US) ˈpæl.ə.toʊ-, -t̬ə- **-s** -z

palatography ˌpæl.əˈtɒg.rə.fi (US) -ˈtɑː.grə-

palav|er pəˈlɑː.v|əʳ (US) -ˈlæv|.ɚ, -ˈlɑː.v|ɚ **-ers** -əz (US) -ɚz **-ering** -ᵊr.ɪŋ **-ered** -əd (US) -ɚd

palazzo pəˈlæt.səʊ, -sə; -ˈlæd.zəʊ, -zə (US) pəˈlɑːt.soʊ, pɑː- **paˌlazzo ˈpants**

pal|e peɪl **-er** -əʳ (US) -ɚ **-est** -ɪst, -əst **-ely** -li **-eness** -nəs, -nɪs **-es** -z **-ing** -ɪŋ **-ed** -d **ˌpale ˈale; beˌyond the ˈpale**

palefac|e ˈpeɪl.feɪs **-es** -ɪz

paleo- ˌpæl.i.əʊ-, ˌpeɪ.li.əʊ- (US) ˈpeɪ.li.oʊ-, -ə-

paleobotany ˌpæl.i.əʊˈbɒt.ᵊn.i, ˌpeɪ.li- (US) ˌpeɪ.li.oʊˈbɑː.tᵊn-

Paleocene ˈpæl.i.əʊ.siːn, ˈpeɪ.li- (US) ˈpeɪ.li.oʊ-, -ə-

paleographic ˌpæl.i.əʊˈgræf.ɪk, ˌpeɪ.li- (US) ˌpeɪ.li.oʊˈ-, -əˈ-

paleograph|y ˌpæl.iˈɒg.rə.f|i, ˌpeɪ.li- (US) ˌpeɪ.liˈɑː.grə- **-er/s** -əʳ/z (US) -ɚ/z

paleolithic (P) ˌpæl.i.əʊˈlɪθ.ɪk, ˌpeɪ.li- (US) ˌpeɪ.li.oʊˈ-, -əˈ-

paleontological ˌpæl.iˌɒn.təˈlɒdʒ.ɪ.kᵊl, ˌpeɪ.li- (US) ˌpeɪ.liˌɑːn.təˈlɑː.dʒɪ-

paleontolog|y ˌpæl.i.ɒnˈtɒl.ə.dʒ|i, ˌpeɪ.li- (US) ˌpeɪ.li.ɑːnˈtɑː.lə- **-ist/s** -ɪst/s

paleotype ˈpæl.i.əʊ.taɪp, ˈpeɪ.li- (US) ˈpeɪ.li.oʊ-, -ə-

Palermo pəˈlɜː.məʊ, -ˈleə- (US) -ˈler.moʊ

Palestine ˈpæl.ə.staɪn, ˈ-ɪ- (US) -ə.staɪn

Palestinian ˌpæl.əˈstɪn.i.ən, -ɪˈ- (US) -əˈstɪn- **-s** -z

Palestrina ˌpæl.əˈstriː.nə, -ɪˈ- (US) -əˈstriː-

palette ˈpæl.ət, -ɪt, -et (US) -ɪt **-s** -s **ˈpalette ˌknife**

Paley ˈpeɪ.li

palfrey (P) ˈpɔːl.fri, ˈpɒl- (US) ˈpɔːl-, ˈpɑːl- **-s** -z

Palato-alveolar

Palato-aleolar sounds are made between the upper teeth and the front part of the palate.

In the description of English, this term has been largely replaced by POST-ALVEOLAR.

In other languages

It has been proposed that there is a difference between palato-alveolar and 'alveolo-patatal' that can be reliably distinguished, though others argue that factors other than place of articulation are usually involved. The latter sounds are placed further forward in the mouth than the former: an example of an alveolo-palatal consonant is that of Polish /ɕ/ in *Kasia* (compare /ʃ/ in *kasza*).

Palgrave ˈpɔːl.ɡreɪv, ˈpæl- (US) ˈpæl-, ˈpɔːl-
Pali ˈpɑː.li
palimony ˈpæl.ɪ.mə.ni, ˈ-ə- (US) -ə.moʊ-
palimpsest ˈpæl.ɪmp.sest, -əmp- (US) -ɪmp- **-s** -s
Palin ˈpeɪ.lɪn
palindrome ˈpæl.ɪn.drəʊm, -ən- (US) -ɪn.droʊm **-s** -z
palindromic ˌpæl.ɪnˈdrɒm.ɪk, -ənˈ- (US) -ɪnˈdrɑː.mɪk, -ˈdroʊ-
paling ˈpeɪ.lɪŋ **-s** -z
palingenesis ˌpæl.ɪnˈdʒen.ə.sɪs, ˈ-ɪ- (US) ˈ-ə-
palinode ˈpæl.ɪ.nəʊd, ˈ-ə- (US) -ə.noʊd **-s** -z
palisad|e (P) ˌpæl.ɪˈseɪd, -əˈ- (US) -əˈ-, ˈ--- **-es** -z **-ing** -ɪŋ **-ed** -ɪd
palish ˈpeɪ.lɪʃ
Palk pɔːlk, pɒlk (US) pɔːlk, pɔːk
pall pɔːl **-s** -z **-ing** -ɪŋ **-ed** -d
palladi|an (P) pəˈleɪ.di|.ən **-um/s** -əm/z
Pallas ˈpæl.əs, -æs
pall-bearer ˈpɔːlˌbeə.rəʳ (US) -ˌber.ɚ, ˈpɑːl- **-s** -z
pallet ˈpæl.ɪt, -ət (US) -ɪt **-s** -s
palliass|e ˈpæl.i.æs, ˌ--ˈ- (US) pælˈjæs, ˈ-- **-es** -ɪz
palli|ate ˈpæl.i|.eɪt **-ates** -eɪts **-ating** -eɪ.tɪŋ (US) -eɪ.t̬ɪŋ **-ated** -eɪ.tɪd (US) -eɪ.t̬ɪd
palliation ˌpæl.iˈeɪ.ʃᵊn
palliative ˈpæl.i.ə.tɪv (US) -t̬ɪv **-s** -z
pallid ˈpæl.ɪd **-est** -ɪst, -əst **-ly** -li **-ness** -nəs, -nɪs
Palliser ˈpæl.ɪ.səʳ (US) -sɚ
palli|um ˈpæl.i|.əm **-ums** -əmz **-a** -ə
Pall Mall ˌpælˈmæl, ˌpelˈmel (US) ˌpælˈmæl, ˌpelˈmel, ˌpɔːlˈmɔːl *stress shift:* ˌPall Mall ˈClub
pall-mall ˌpælˈmæl (US) ˌpælˈmæl, ˌpelˈmel, ˌpɑːlˈmɑːl
pallor ˈpæl.əʳ (US) -ɚ
pally ˈpæl.i
palm pɑːm **-s** -z **-ing** -ɪŋ **-ed** -d **ˌPalm ˈBeach; ˌPalm ˈSprings; ˌPalm ˈSunday; ˌgrease one's ˈpalm**
Palma ˈpæl.mə, ˈpɑː-, ˈpɑːl- (US) ˈpɑːl.mɑː
palmar ˈpæl.məʳ, -mɑːʳ (US) -mɚ, ˈpɑːl-
palma|te ˈpæl.meɪ|t, ˈpɑː-, -mɪ|t (US) ˈpæl.meɪ|t, ˈpɑːl-, ˈpɑː- **-ted** -tɪd (US) -t̬ɪd
palmer (P) ˈpɑː.məʳ (US) -mɚ **-s** -z
Palmerston ˈpɑː.mə.stᵊn (US) -mɚ-
palmist ˈpɑː.mɪst **-s** -s
palmistry ˈpɑː.mɪ.stri
palm-oil ˈpɑːm.ɔɪl, ˌ-ˈ- (US) ˈpɑːm.ɔɪl
Palmolive® pɑːˈmɒl.ɪv (US) -ˈmɑː.lɪv
palmtop ˈpɑːm.tɒp (US) -tɑːp **-s** -s
palm|y ˈpɑː.m|i **-ier** -i.əʳ (US) -i.ɚ **-iest** -i.ɪst, -i.əst
palmyra (P) pælˈmaɪə.rə -ˈmɪə.rə (US) -ˈmaɪ- **-s** -z
Palo Alto ˌpæl.əʊˈæl.təʊ (US) -oʊˈæl.t̬oʊ
Palomar ˈpæl.əʊ.mɑːʳ (US) -ə.mɑːr
palomino ˌpæl.əˈmiː.nəʊ (US) -noʊ, -oʊˈ- **-s** -z
palooka pəˈluː.kə **-s** -z
palpability ˌpæl.pəˈbɪl.ə.ti, ˈ-ɪ- (US) -ə.t̬i
palpab|le ˈpæl.pə.b|l̩ **-ly** -li **-leness** -l̩.nəs, -nɪs
palpa|te (*v.*) pælˈpeɪ|t (US) ˈ-- **-tes** -ts **-ting** -tɪŋ (US) -t̬ɪŋ **-ted** -tɪd (US) -t̬ɪd
palpate (*adj.*) ˈpæl.peɪt (US) -peɪt, -pɪt
palpation pælˈpeɪ.ʃᵊn
palpi|tate ˈpæl.pɪ.teɪt (US) -pə- **-tates** -teɪts **-tating** -teɪ.tɪŋ (US) -teɪ.t̬ɪŋ **-tated** -teɪ.tɪd (US) -teɪ.t̬ɪd
palpitation ˌpæl.pɪˈteɪ.ʃᵊn (US) -pəˈ- **-s** -z
palsgrave (P) ˈpɔːlz.ɡreɪv (US) ˈpɔːlz-, ˈpælz- **-s** -z
pals|y ˈpɔːl.z|i, ˈpɒl- (US) ˈpɔːl-, ˈpɑːl- **-ies** -iz **-ied** -id
palt|er ˈpɔːl.t|əʳ, ˈpɒl- (US) ˈpɔːl.t̬|ɚ, ˈpɑːl- **-ers** -əz (US) -ɚz **-ering** -ᵊr.ɪŋ **-ered** -əd (US) -ɚd **-erer/s** -ᵊr.əʳ/z (US) -ɚ.ɚ/z
Paltrow ˈpæl.trəʊ, ˈpɒl- (US) ˈpæl.troʊ, ˈpɑːl-
paltr|y ˈpɔːl.tr|i, ˈpɒl- (US) ˈpɔːl-, ˈpɑːl- **-ier** -i.əʳ (US) -i.ɚ **-iest** -i.ɪst, -i.əst **-ily** -ɪ.li, -ᵊl.i **-iness** -ɪ.nəs, -ɪ.nɪs
Pam pæm
Pamela ˈpæm.ᵊl.ə, -ɪ.lə (US) -ᵊl.ə
Pamir pəˈmɪəʳ (US) pɑːˈmɪr **-s** -z
Pampa ˈpæm.pə **-s** -z
pampas ˈpæm.pəs (US) ˈpæm.pəz, ˈpɑːm-, -pəs **ˈpampas ˌgrass**
pamp|er ˈpæm.p|əʳ (US) -p|ɚ **-ers** -əz (US) -ɚz **-ering** -ᵊr.ɪŋ **-ered** -əd (US) -ɚd **-erer/s** -ᵊr.əʳ/z (US) -ɚ.ɚ/z
Pampers® ˈpæm.pəz (US) -pɚz
pamphlet ˈpæm.flɪt, -flət (US) -flɪt **-s** -s
pamphleteer ˌpæm.fləˈtɪəʳ, -flɪˈ- (US) -flɪˈtɪr **-s** -z **-ing** -ɪŋ
Pamphyli|a pæmˈfɪl.i|.ə **-an/s** -ən/z
Pamplona pæmˈpləʊ.nə (US) pæmˈploʊ.nə, pɑːm-, -nɑː
pan (P) pæn **-s** -z **-ning** -ɪŋ **-ned** -d
panacea ˌpæn.əˈsiː.ə **-s** -z
panach|e pəˈnæʃ, pænˈæʃ-, -ˈɑːʃ (US) pəˈnæʃ, -ˈnɑːʃ **-es** -ɪz
Panadol® ˈpæn.ə.dɒl (US) -dɑːl
panama (P) ˌpæn.əˈmɑː, ˈ--- (US) ˈ---, -mɔː **-s** -z **ˌPanama Caˈnal; ˌPanama ˈCity; ˌpanama ˈhat**
Panamanian ˌpæn.əˈmeɪ.ni.ən **-s** -z
Pan-American ˌpæn.əˈmer.ɪ.kən **-ism** -ɪ.zᵊm
Panasonic ˌpæn.əˈsɒn.ɪk (US) -ˈsɑː.nɪk
panatel(l)a ˌpæn.əˈtel.ə **-s** -z
pancake ˈpæn.keɪk, ˈpæŋ- (US) ˈpæn- **-s** -s **ˈPancake ˌDay**
pancetta pænˈtʃet.ə (US) -ˈtʃet̬-
panchromatic ˌpæn.krəʊˈmæt.ɪk, ˌpæŋ- (US) ˌpæn.kroʊˈmæt̬-
Pancras ˈpæŋ.krəs
pancreas ˈpæŋ.kri.əs, -æs (US) ˈpæn.kri.əs, ˈpæŋ- **-es** -ɪz
pancreatic ˌpæŋ.kriˈæt.ɪk (US) ˌpæn.kriˈæt̬-, ˌpæŋ-
panda ˈpæn.də **-s** -z **ˈpanda ˌcar**
pandanus pænˈdeɪ.nəs, -ˈdæn.əs **-es** -ɪz
pandect ˈpæn.dekt **-s** -s
pandemic pænˈdem.ɪk **-s** -s
pandemonium (P) ˌpæn.dəˈməʊ.ni.ə[m] -dɪˈ- (US) -dəˈmoʊ- **-s** -z
pand|er ˈpæn.d|əʳ (US) -ɚ **-ers** -əz (US) -[ɚz] **-ering** -ᵊr.ɪŋ **-ered** -əd (US) -ɚd

pandialectal ˌpæn.daɪəˈlek.təl

pandit (P) ˈpæn.dɪt -s -s

andora (P) pænˈdɔː.rə (US) -ˈdɔːr.ə -s -z
Panˌdora's ˈbox

andowd|y pænˈdaʊ.d|i -ies -iz

ane peɪn -s -z

anegyric ˌpæn.əˈdʒɪr.ɪk, -ɪˈ- (US) -əˈ-, -ˈdʒaɪ.rɪk -s -s -al -əl

anegyrist ˌpæn.əˈdʒɪr.ɪst, -ɪˈ-, ˈpæn.ə.dʒɪr-, ˈ-ɪ- (US) ˌpæn.əˈdʒɪr-, -ˈdʒaɪ.rɪst -s -s

anegyriz|e, -is|e ˈpæn.ə.dʒɪ.raɪz, ˈ-ɪ-, -dʒər.aɪz (US) -dʒə.raɪz -es -ɪz -ing -ɪŋ -ed -d

anel ˈpæn.əl -s -z -(l)ing/s -ɪŋ/z -(l)ed -d
ˈpanel ˌbeater

anel(l)ist ˈpæn.əl.ɪst -s -s

anettone ˌpæn.əˈtəʊ.neɪ, -ni (US) -ɪˈtoʊ- -s -z

an-|fry ˈpæn|.fraɪ -fries -fraɪz -frying -fraɪ.ɪŋ -fried -fraɪd

anful ˈpæn.fʊl -s -z

ang pæŋ -s -z

anga ˈpæŋ.gə -s -z

angbourne ˈpæŋ.bɔːn, -bən (US) -bɔːrn

angloss ˈpæŋ.glɒs, ˈpæn- (US) ˈpæn.glɑːs

anglossian (P) pæŋˈglɒs.i.ən, pæn- (US) pænˈglɑː.si-

angolin ˈpæŋ.gəʊ.lɪn; pæŋˈgəʊ- (US) ˈpæn.goʊ-, ˈpæŋ-, -gə-; pænˈgoʊ-, pæŋ- -s -z

anhandl|e ˈpænˌhæn.dl̩ -es -z -ing -ɪŋ, -ˌhænd.lɪŋ -ed -d -er/s -əʳ/z (US) -ɚ/z, -ˌhænd.ləʳ/z (US) -lɚ/z

anic ˈpæn.ɪk -s -s -king -ɪŋ -ked -t
ˈpanic ˌbutton; ˈpanic ˌstations

anicky ˈpæn.ɪ.ki

anicle ˈpæn.ɪ.kl̩ -s -z

nic-stricken ˈpæn.ɪkˌstrɪk.ən

nini ˈpɑː.nɪ.niː, -ni (US) pɑːˈniː.ni

njandr|um pænˈdʒæn.dr|əm, pən- (US) pæn- -ums -əmz -a -ə

nkhurst ˈpæŋk.hɜːst (US) -hɝːst

nlectal ˌpænˈlek.təl

nne pæn

nnier ˈpæn.i.əʳ (US) ˈ-jɚ, ˈ-i.ɚ -s -z

nnikin ˈpæn.ɪ.kɪn, ˈ-ə- (US) ˈ-ɪ- -s -z

nnill ˈpæn.ɪl

nopl|y ˈpæn.ə.pl|i -ies -iz -ied -id

norama ˌpæn.ərˈɑː.mə (US) -əˈræm.ə, -ˈrɑː.mə -s -z

noramic ˌpæn.ərˈæm.ɪk, -ˈɑː.mɪk (US) -əˈræm.ɪk, -ˈrɑː.mɪk -ally -əl.i (US) -li

npipe ˈpæn.paɪp, ˈpæm- (US) ˈpæn- -s -s

n-Slavism ˌpænˈslɑː.vɪ.zəm, -ˈslæv.ɪ-

ns|y ˈpæn.z|i -ies -iz

nt pænt -s -s -ing/ly -ɪŋ/li (US) ˈpæn.t̬ɪŋ/li -ed -ɪd (US) ˈpæn.t̬ɪd

Pantagruel ˌpæn.tə.gruˈel; ˈpæn.tə.gru.əl, pænˈtæg.ru.əl (US) ˌpæn.t̬ə.gruˈel; -ˈgruː.əl; pænˈtæg.ru.el

pantaloon ˌpæn.təlˈuːn, ˈ--- (US) ˌpæn.t̬əlˈuːn, ˈ--- -s -z

pantechnicon pænˈtek.nɪ.kən -s -z

panthe|ism ˈpænt.θi|.ɪ.zəm -ist/s -ɪst/s

pantheistic ˌpænt.θiˈɪs.tɪk -al -əl

pantheon (P) ˈpænt.θi.ən (US) -ɑːn, -ən -s -z

panther ˈpænt.θəʳ (US) -θɚ -s -z

pantie girdle ˈpæn.tiˌgɜː.dl̩ (US) -t̬iˌgɝː- -s -z

panties ˈpæn.tiz (US) -t̬iz

pantihose ˈpæn.ti.həʊz (US) -t̬i.hoʊz

pantile ˈpæn.taɪl -s -z

panto ˈpæn.təʊ (US) -toʊ -s -z

pantograph ˈpæn.təʊ.grɑːf, -græf (US) -t̬ə.græf -s -s

pantographic ˌpæn.təʊˈgræf.ɪk (US) -t̬əˈ- -al -əl

pantomim|e ˈpæn.tə.maɪm (US) -t̬ə- -es -z -ist/s -ɪst/s

pantomimic ˌpæn.təʊˈmɪm.ɪk (US) -t̬əˈ- -al -əl -ally -əl.i, -li

pantr|y ˈpæn.tr|i -ies -iz

pants pænts

pantsuit ˈpænt.suːt, -sjuːt (US) -suːt -s -s

pantyhose ˈpæn.ti.həʊz (US) -t̬i.hoʊz

pantyliner ˈpæn.tiˌlaɪ.nəʳ (US) -t̬iˌlaɪ.nɚ -s -z

Panza ˈpæn.zə

panzer ˈpænt.səʳ, ˈpæn.zəʳ (US) ˈpæn.zɚ, ˈpɑːnt.sɚ -s -z

pap pæp -s -s

papa pəˈpɑː (US) ˈpɑː.pə; pəˈpɑː -s -z

papac|y (P) ˈpeɪ.pə.s|i -ies -iz

papal ˈpeɪ.pəl

papal|ism ˈpeɪ.pəl|.ɪ.zəm -ist/s -ɪst/s

Papandreou ˌpæp.ænˈdreɪ.uː

paparazz|o ˌpæp.ərˈæt.s|əʊ (US) ˌpɑː.pɑːˈrɑːt.s|oʊ -i -i

papaw ˈpɔː.pɔː, pəˈpɔː (US) pɔːˈpɑː, -ˈɔː, ˈpɑː-, ˈpɔː- -s -z

papaya pəˈpaɪ.ə (US) -ˈpaɪ.ə, -ˈpɑː.jə -s -z

Papeete ˌpɑː.piˈeɪ.ti, -ˈiː-; pəˈpiː.ti (US) ˌpɑː.piˈeɪ.teɪ; pəˈpiː.ti

pap|er ˈpeɪ.p|əʳ (US) -ɚ -ers -əz (US) -ɚz -ering -ər.ɪŋ -ered -əd (US) -ɚd -erer/s -ər.əʳ/z (US) -ɚ.ɚ/z -ery -ər.i **ˌpaper ˈbag; ˈpaper ˌboy; ˈpaper ˌchase; ˈpaper ˌclip; ˈpaper ˌknife; ˌpaper ˈmoney; ˈpaper ˌround; ˌpaper ˈtiger; ˈpaper ˌtrail**

paperback ˈpeɪ.pə.bæk (US) -pɚ- -s -s

paperbark ˈpeɪ.pə.bɑːk (US) -pɚ.bɑːrk -s -s

paperhang|er ˈpeɪ.pəˌhæŋ|.əʳ (US) -pɚˌhæŋ|.ɚ -ers -əz (US) -ɚz -ing -ɪŋ

paperless ˈpeɪ.pə.ləs, -lɪs (US) -pɚ-

paperweight ˈpeɪ.pə.weɪt (US) -pɚ- -s -s

paperwork ˈpeɪ.pə.wɜːk (US) -pɚ.wɝːk

Paphlagoni|a ˌpæf.ləˈgəʊ.ni|.ə (US) -ˈgoʊ- -an/s -ən/z

Paphos ˈpæf.ɒs (US) ˈpeɪ.fɑːs

papier-mâché ˌpæp.i.eɪˈmæʃ.eɪ, ˌpeɪ.pəˈ- (US) ˌpeɪ.pɚ.məˈʃeɪ, ˌpæp.jeɪ-

papill|a pəˈpɪl|.ə -ae -iː

papillary pəˈpɪl.ər.i (US) ˈpæp.ə.ler-; pəˈpɪl.ɚ-

papillote ˈpæp.ɪ.lɒt, -ləʊt, -jɒt (US) -ə.loʊt, ˈpɑː.pə-, -joʊt -s -s

papist (P) ˈpeɪ.pɪst -s -s

papistry ˈpeɪ.pɪ.stri

papoos|e pəˈpuːs (US) pæpˈuːs, pəˈpuːs -es -ɪz

Papp pæp

papp|us (P) ˈpæp|.əs -i -aɪ

pappy ˈpæp.i

paprika ˈpæp.rɪ.kə; pəˈpriː- (US) pæpˈriː-, pəˈpriː-

Papu|a ˈpæp.u|.ə, ˈpɑː.pu-, -pju- (US) ˈpæp.ju|.ə, pɑːˈpuː- -an/s -ən/z
ˌPapua New ˈGuinea

Papworth ˈpæp.wəθ, -wɜːθ (US) -wɚθ, -wɝːθ

papyr|us pəˈpaɪə.r|əs (US) -ˈpaɪ- -i -aɪ -uses -ə.sɪz

par (P) pɑːʳ (US) pɑːr

para- pær.ə-; pəˈræ- (US) per.ə-, pær.ə-; pəˈræ-

Note: Prefix. Normally either carries primary or secondary stress on the first syllable, e.g. **parachute** /ˈpær.ə.ʃuːt (US) ˈper-/, **parabolic** /ˌpær.əˈbɒl.ɪk (US) ˌper.əˈbɑː.lɪk/, or primary stress on the second syllable, e.g. **paraboloid** /pəˈræb.əl.ɔɪd (US) -ə.lɔɪd/.

para *paratrooper, paramilitary:* ˈpær.ə (US) ˈper.ə, ˈpær- -s -z

para *Turk or Yugoslav monetary unit:* ˈpɑː.rə (US) ˈpɑː.rɑː, -ˈ- -s -z

Pará *Brazilian river:* pəˈrɑː

parable ˈpær.ə.bl̩ (US) ˈper-, ˈpær- -s -z

parabola pəˈræb.əl.ə -s -z

parabolic ˌpær.əˈbɒl.ɪk (US) ˌper.əˈbɑː.lɪk, ˌpær- -al -əl -ally -əl.i, -li

paraboloid pəˈræb.əl.ɔɪd (US) -ə.lɔɪd -s -z

Paracelsus ˌpær.əˈsel.səs (US) ˌper-, ˌpær-

paracetamol ˌpær.əˈsiː.tə.mɒl, -ˈset.ə- (US) ˌper.əˈsiː.t̬ə.mɑːl, ˌpær-, -ˈset̬.ə-, -moʊl -s -z

para|chute ˈpær.ə|.ʃuːt (US) ˈper-, ˈpær- -chutes -ʃuːts -chuting -ˌʃuː.tɪŋ (US) -ˌʃuː.t̬ɪŋ -chuted -ˌʃuː.tɪd (US) -ˌʃuː.t̬ɪd

parachutist ˈpær.əˌʃuː.tɪst (US) ˈper.əˌʃuː.t̬ɪst, ˈpær- -s -s

Paraclete 'pær.ə.kliːt (US) 'per-, 'pær-
parad|e pə'reɪd **-es** -z **-ing** -ɪŋ **-ed** -ɪd **pa'rade ˌground**
paradigm 'pær.ə.daɪm (US) 'per-, 'pær-, -dɪm **-s** -z
paradigmatic ˌpær.ə.dɪg'mæt.ɪk (US) ˌper.ə.dɪg'mæt̬-, ˌpær- **-al** -ᵊl **-ally** -ᵊl.i, -li
paradisal ˌpær.ə'daɪ.sᵊl, -zᵊl (US) ˌper.ə'daɪ-, ˌpær-
paradis|e (P) 'pær.ə.daɪs (US) 'per-, 'pær-, -daɪz **-es** -ɪz
paradisiac ˌpær.ə'dɪs.i.æk, -'dɪz- (US) ˌper.ə'dɪs-, ˌpær-
paradisiacal ˌpær.ə.dɪ'saɪ.ə.kᵊl, -də'-, -'zaɪ- (US) ˌper.ə.dɪ'-, ˌpær-
Paradiso ˌpær.ə'diː.səʊ (US) ˌper.ə'diː.soʊ, ˌpær-
parador 'pær.ə.dɔːʳ (US) 'per.ə.dɔːr, 'pær- **paradores** ˌpær.ə'dɔː.reɪs, -rɪs (US) ˌper.ə'dɔːr.əs, ˌpær-, -'dɔːrz
parados 'pær.ə.dɒs (US) 'per.ə.dɑːs, 'pær- **-es** -ɪz
paradox 'pær.ə.dɒks (US) 'per.ə.dɑːks, 'pær- **-es** -ɪz
paradoxic|al ˌpær.ə'dɒk.sɪ.k|ᵊl (US) ˌper.ə'dɑːk-, ˌpær- **-ally** -ᵊl.i, -li **-alness** -ᵊl.nəs, -nɪs
paraffin 'pær.ə.fɪn, -fiːn, ˌ--'- (US) 'per.ə.fɪn, 'pær-
paraffine ˌpær.ə'fiːn (US) 'per.ə.fɪn, 'pær-, -fiːn
paragliding 'pær.əˌglaɪ.dɪŋ (US) 'per.ə-, 'pær-
paragoge ˌpær.ə'gəʊ.dʒi (US) 'per.ə.goʊ-, 'pær- **-s** -z
paragogic ˌpær.ə'gɒdʒ.ɪk (US) ˌper.ə'gɑː.dʒɪk, ˌpær-
paragon 'pær.ə.gən (US) 'per.ə.gɑːn, 'pær-, -gən **-s** -z
paragraph 'pær.ə.grɑːf, -græf (US) 'per.ə.græf, 'pær- **-s** -s **-ing** -ɪŋ **-ed** -t
Paraguay 'pær.ə.gwaɪ, -gweɪ, ˌ--'- (US) 'per.ə.gweɪ, 'pær-, -gwaɪ
Paraguayan ˌpær.ə'gwaɪ.ən, -'gweɪ- (US) ˌper.ə'gweɪ-, ˌpær-, -'gwaɪ-
parakeet ˌpær.ə'kiːt, '--- (US) 'per.ə.kiːt, 'pær- **-s** -s
paraldehyde pə'ræl.dɪ.haɪd, pær'æl-, -də- (US) pə'ræl.də-
paralexia ˌpær.ə'lek.si.ə (US) ˌper-, ˌpær-
paralinguistic ˌpær.ə.lɪŋ'gwɪs.tɪk (US) ˌper-, ˌpær- **-s** -s **-ally** -ᵊl.i, -li
parallax 'pær.ə.læks (US) 'per-, 'pær- **-es** -ɪz
parallel 'pær.ə.lel, -ᵊl.əl (US) 'per-, 'pær- **-s** -z **-ing** -ɪŋ **-ed** -d **-ism** -ɪ.zᵊm **ˌparallel 'bars**
parallelepiped ˌpær.ə.lel'ep.ɪ.ped, -ᵊl.ə'lep-; ˌpær.əˌlel.ə'paɪ- (US) ˌper.əˌlel.ə'paɪ-, ˌpær-, -'pɪp.əd, -ed **-s** -z
parallelogram ˌpær.ə'lel.ə.græm (US) ˌper-, ˌpær- **-s** -z
Paralympics ˌpær.ə'lɪm.pɪks (US) ˌper-, ˌpær-
paralys|e, -lyz|e 'pær.ᵊl.aɪz (US) 'per-, 'pær- **-es** -ɪz **-ing** -ɪŋ **-ed** -d **-er/s** -əʳ/z (US) -ɚ/z
paralys|is pə'ræl.ə.s|ɪs, pᵊr'æl-, '-ɪ- (US) '-ə- **-es** -iːz
paralytic ˌpær.ə'lɪt.ɪk (US) ˌper.ə'lɪt̬-, ˌpær- **-s** -s
paralyzation ˌpær.ᵊl.aɪ'zeɪ.ʃᵊn (US) ˌper.ə.lɪ'-, ˌpær-
Paramaribo ˌpær.ə'mær.ɪ.bəʊ (US) ˌper.ə'mer.ɪ.boʊ, ˌpær-, -'mær-
paramatta (P) ˌpær.ə'mæt.ə (US) ˌper.ə'mæt̬-, ˌpær-
paramecium ˌpær.ə'miː.si.əm (US) ˌper-, ˌpær-, -ʃi-
paramedic ˌpær.ə'med.ɪk (US) ˌper.ə'med-, ˌpær-, 'per.əˌmed-, 'pær- **-s** -s **-al** -ᵊl
parameter pə'ræm.ɪ.təʳ, pᵊr'æm-, '-ə- (US) -ə.t̬ɚ **-s** -z
parametric ˌpær.ə'met.rɪk (US) ˌper-, ˌpær- **-ally** -ᵊl.i, -li
paramilitar|y ˌpær.ə'mɪl.ɪ.tᵊr|.i, '-ə- (US) ˌper.ə'mɪl.ə.ter-, ˌpær- **-ies** -iz
paramount (P) 'pær.ə.maʊnt (US) 'per-, 'pær- **-ly** -li
paramour 'pær.ə.mʊəʳ, -mɔːʳ (US) 'per.ə.mʊr, 'pær- **-s** -z
Paraná pær.æn'ɑː
paranoi|a ˌpær.ə'nɔɪ|.ə (US) ˌper-, ˌpær- **-ac** -æk
paranoid 'pær.ᵊn.ɔɪd (US) 'per.ə.nɔɪd, 'pær-
paranormal ˌpær.ə'nɔː.mᵊl (US) ˌper.ə'nɔːr-, ˌpær- **-ly** -i
parape|t 'pær.ə.pɪ|t, -pe|t, -pə|t (US) 'per.ə.pe|t, 'pær-, -pə|t **-ts** -ts **-ted** -tɪd (US) -t̬ɪd
paraphernalia ˌpær.ə.fə'neɪ.li.ə (US) ˌper.ə.fɚ'neɪl.jə, ˌpær-, -'neɪ.li.ə
paraphras|e 'pær.ə.freɪz (US) 'per-, 'pær- **-es** -ɪz **-ing** -ɪŋ **-ed** -d
paraphrastic ˌpær.ə'fræs.tɪk (US) ˌper-, ˌpær- **-ally** -ᵊl.i, -li
parapleg|ia ˌpær.ə'pliː.dʒ|ə, -dʒi|.ə (US) ˌper-, ˌpær- **-ic/s** -ɪk
paraprax|is ˌpær.ə'præk.s|ɪs (US) ˌper-, ˌpær- **-es** -ɪz
parapsychologic ˌpær.əˌsaɪ.kə'lɒdʒ.ɪk, -kᵊl'ɒdʒ- (US) ˌper.ə.saɪ.kə'lɑː.dʒɪk, ˌpær- **-al** -ᵊl **-ally** -ᵊl.i, -li
parapsycholog|y ˌpær.ə.saɪ'kɒl.ə.dʒ|i, -psaɪ'- (US) ˌper.ə.saɪ'kɑː.lə-, ˌpær- **-ist/s** -ɪst/s
Paraquat® 'pær.ə.kwɒt, -kwæt (US) 'per.ə.kwɑːt, 'pær-
parasang 'pær.ə.sæŋ (US) 'per-, 'pær- **-s** -z
parascend|ing 'pær.əˌsen.d|ɪŋ (US) 'p[…] 'pær- **-er/s** -əʳ/z (US) -ɚ/z
parasite 'pær.ə.saɪt (US) 'per-, 'pær- […]
parasitic ˌpær.ə'sɪt.ɪk (US) ˌper.ə'sɪt̬-[…] ˌpær- **-al** -ᵊl **-ally** -ᵊl.i, -li **-alness** -ᵊl.nəs, -nɪs
parasitolog|y ˌpær.ə.saɪ'tɒl.ə.dʒ|i, -sɪ'- (US) ˌper.ə.saɪ'tɑː.lə-, ˌpær-, -s[…] **-ist/s** -ɪst/s
parasol 'pær.ə.sɒl, ˌ--'- (US) 'per.ə.sɔ[…] 'pær-, -sɑːl **-s** -z
paratactic ˌpær.ə'tæk.tɪk (US) ˌper-, ˌpær-
parataxis ˌpær.ə'tæk.sɪs (US) ˌper-, ˌp[…]
parathyroid ˌpær.ə'θaɪə.rɔɪd (US) ˌper.ə'θaɪ-, ˌpær-
paratone 'pær.ə.təʊn (US) 'per.ə.to[…] 'pær- **-s** -z
paratroop 'pær.ə.truːp (US) 'per-, 'p[…] **-s** -s **-er/s** -əʳ/z (US) -ɚ/z
paratyphoid ˌpær.ə'taɪ.fɔɪd (US) ˌpe[…] ˌpær-
paravane 'pær.ə.veɪn (US) 'per-, 'pæ[…] **-s** -z
parboil 'pɑː.bɔɪl (US) 'pɑːr **-s** -z **-ing** […] **-ed** -d
parcel 'pɑː.sᵊl (US) 'pɑːr- **-s** -z **-(l)ing** […] **-(l)ed** -d **'parcel ˌpost**
parch pɑːtʃ (US) pɑːrtʃ **-es** -ɪz **-ing** -ɪ[…] -t **-edness** -t.nəs, -nɪs
Parcheesi® pɑː'tʃiː.zi (US) pɑːr-
parchment (P) 'pɑːtʃ.mənt (US) 'pɑː[…] **-s** -s
pard pɑːd (US) pɑːrd **-s** -z
pardner 'pɑːd.nəʳ (US) 'pɑːd.nəʳ, 'pɑːrd.nɚ **-s**
Pardoe 'pɑː.dəʊ (US) 'pɑːr.doʊ
pardon 'pɑː.dᵊn (US) 'pɑːr- **-s** -z **-ing** […] **-ed** -d **-er/s** -əʳ/z (US) -ɚ/z
pardonab|le 'pɑː.dᵊn.ə.b|l̩ (US) 'pɑː[…] -li **-leness** -l̩.nəs, -nɪs
par|e peəʳ (US) per **-es** -z **-ing** -ɪŋ **-ed** […]
paregoric ˌpær.ɪ'gɒr.ɪk, -ə'- (US) ˌper.ə'gɔːr.ɪk, ˌpær-
paren|t 'peə.rᵊn|t (US) 'per.ᵊn|t, 'pæ[…] -ts **-tage** -tɪdʒ (US) -t̬ɪdʒ
parental pə'ren.tᵊl (US) -t̬ᵊl **-ly** -i
parenthes|is pə'ren*t*.θə.s|ɪs, -θɪ- (US) -θə- **-es** -iːz
parenthesiz|e, -is|e pə'ren*t*.θə.sa[…] -θɪ- (US) -θə- **-es** -ɪz **-ing** -ɪŋ **-ed** -d[…]
parenthetic ˌpær.ᵊn'θet.ɪk, -en'- (US) ˌper.ᵊn'θet̬-, ˌpær- **-al** -ᵊl **-all[…]** -li
parenthood 'peə.rᵊnt.hʊd (US) 'per[…] 'pær-
parenting 'peə.rᵊn.tɪŋ (US) 'per.ᵊn.[…] 'pær-

parentless ˈpeə.rənt.ləs, -lɪs (US) ˈper.ənt-, ˈpær-
parent-teacher ˌpeə.rəntˈtiː.tʃəʳ (US) ˌper.əntˈtiː.tʃɚ, ˌpær- **ˌparent-ˈteacher associˌation**
pareo pɑːˈreɪ.əʊ (US) -oʊ **-s** -z
paresis pəˈriː.sɪs; ˈpær.ə- (US) pəˈriː-; ˈper.ə-, ˈpær-
paretic pəˈret.ɪk (US) -ˈret̬-, -ˈriː.t̬ɪk
pareu pɑːˈreɪ.uː **-s** -z
par excellence ˌpɑːrˈek.səl.ɑ̃ːns, -sel-, -ɑːnts, ˌpɑːr.ek.səlˈɑ̃ːns, -selˈ-, -ˈɑːnts (US) ˌpɑːrˌek.səˈlɑːnts
parfait ˌpɑːˈfeɪ, ˈ-- (US) pɑːrˈfeɪ **-s** -z
arfitt ˈpɑː.fɪt (US) ˈpɑːr-
arfum ˈpɑː.fʌm (US) pɑːrˈfʌm
ar|get ˈpɑː|.dʒɪt (US) ˈpɑːr- **-gets** -dʒɪts **-get(t)ing** -dʒɪ.tɪŋ (US) -dʒɪ.t̬ɪŋ **-get(t)ed** -dʒɪ.tɪd (US) -dʒɪ.t̬ɪd
argiter ˈpɑː.dʒɪ.təʳ (US) ˈpɑːr.dʒɪ.t̬ɚ
arheli|on pɑːˈhiː.li|.ən, -ɒn (US) pɑːrˈhiː-, -ˈhiːl.j|ən **-a** -ə
ariah pəˈraɪə, ˈpær.i.ə (US) pəˈraɪə **-s** -z
arian ˈpeə.ri.ən (US) ˈper.i-, ˈpær- **-s** -z
arietal pəˈraɪə.təl, -ˈraɪ.ɪ- (US) -ˈraɪə-
aring ˈpeə.rɪŋ (US) ˈper.ɪŋ, ˈpær- **-s** -z
aris ˈpær.ɪs (US) ˈper-, ˈpær-
arish **(P)** ˈpær.ɪʃ (US) ˈper-, ˈpær- **-es** -ɪz **ˌparish ˈpriest**
arishioner pəˈrɪʃ.ən.əʳ (US) -ɚ **-s** -z
arisian pəˈrɪz.i.ən, -ˈrɪʒ.ən (US) -ˈrɪʒ-, -ˈriː.ʒən **-s** -z
arisyllabic ˌpær.ɪ.sɪˈlæb.ɪk, ˌ-ə-, -səlˈæb- (US) ˌper-, ˌpær-
arity ˈpær.ə.ti, -ɪ.ti (US) ˈper.ə.t̬i, ˈpær-
ark **(P)** pɑːk (US) pɑːrk **-s** -s **-ing** -ɪŋ **-ed** -t **ˈparking ˌlot**; **ˈparking ˌmeter**; **ˈparking ˌspace**; **ˈparking ˌticket**; **ˌpark-and-ˈride**
arka ˈpɑː.kə (US) ˈpɑːr- **-s** -z
arke pɑːk (US) pɑːrk **-s** -s
rker ˈpɑː.kəʳ (US) ˈpɑːr.kɚ
rkestone ˈpɑːk.stən (US) ˈpɑːrk-
rkhurst ˈpɑːk.hɜːst (US) ˈpɑːrk.hɝːst
rkin **(P)** ˈpɑː.kɪn (US) ˈpɑːr-
rking meter ˈpɑː.kɪŋˌmiː.təʳ (US) ˈpɑːr.kɪŋˌmiː.t̬ɚ **-s** -z
rkinson ˈpɑː.kɪn.sən (US) ˈpɑːr- **-ism** -ɪ.zəm **ˈParkinson's diˌsease**
rkland ˈpɑːk.lænd (US) ˈpɑːrk-
rkman ˈpɑːk.mən (US) ˈpɑːrk-
rks pɑːks (US) pɑːrks
rkstone ˈpɑːk.stən (US) ˈpɑːrk-
rkway ˈpɑːk.weɪ (US) ˈpɑːrk- **-s** -z
rk|y ˈpɑː.k|i (US) ˈpɑːr- **-ier** -i.əʳ (US) -i.ɚ **-iest** -i.ɪst, -i.əst
lance ˈpɑː.lənts (US) ˈpɑːr-
lay (*v.*) ˈpɑː.li (US) ˈpɑːr.leɪ, -li; pɑːrˈleɪ **-s** -z **-ing** -ɪŋ **-ed** -d
lay (*n.*) ˈpɑː.li (US) ˈpɑːr.leɪ, -li **-s** -z
lement of Foules pɑː.lə.mənt.əvˈfuːlz (US) ˌpɑːr-

parley **(P)** ˈpɑː.li (US) ˈpɑːr- **-s** -z **-ing** -ɪŋ **-ed** -d
parliament **(P)** ˈpɑː.lə.mənt, -lɪ-, -li.ə- (US) ˈpɑːr.lə- **-s** -s
parliamentarian **(P)** ˌpɑː.lə.menˈteə.ri.ən, -lɪ-, -li.ə-, -mənˈ- (US) ˌpɑːr.lə.menˈter.i- **-s** -z
parliamentary ˌpɑː.ləˈmen.tər.i, -lɪˈ-, -li.əˈ- (US) ˌpɑːr.ləˈmen.t̬ɚ-, ˈ-tri
parlo(u)r ˈpɑː.ləʳ (US) ˈpɑːr.lɚ **-s** -z **ˈparlo(u)r ˌcar**; **ˈparlo(u)r ˌgame**; **ˈparlo(u)r ˌmaid**
parlous ˈpɑː.ləs (US) ˈpɑːr- **-ly** -li
Parma ˈpɑː.mə (US) ˈpɑːr- **ˌParma ˈham**
Parmar ˈpɑː.məʳ (US) ˈpɑːr.mɚ
Parmenter ˈpɑː.mɪn.təʳ, -mən- (US) ˈpɑːr.mən.t̬ɚ
Parmesan ˈpɑː.mɪˌzæn, ˌ--ˈ-, -əˈ- (US) ˈpɑːr.mə.zɑːn, -zən, -zæn, -ʒɑːn
Parminter ˈpɑː.mɪn.təʳ (US) ˈpɑːr.mɪn.t̬ɚ
Parmiter ˈpɑː.mɪ.təʳ (US) ˈpɑːr.mɪ.t̬ɚ
Parnassian pɑːˈnæs.i.ən (US) pɑːr-
Parnassus pɑːˈnæs.əs (US) pɑːr-
Parnell pɑːˈnel; ˈpɑː.nəl (US) pɑːrˈnel; ˈpɑːr.nəl
parochial pəˈrəʊ.ki.əl (US) -ˈroʊ- **-ly** -i **-ism** -ɪ.zəm
parodist ˈpær.ə.dɪst (US) ˈper-, ˈpær- **-s** -s
parod|y ˈpær.ə.d|i (US) ˈper-, ˈpær- **-ies** -iz **-ying** -i.ɪŋ **-ied** -id
parol ˈpær.əl; pəˈrəʊl (US) -ˈroʊl, ˈper.əl, ˈpær-
parol|e pəˈrəʊl (US) -ˈroʊl **-es** -z **-ing** -ɪŋ **-ed** -d
Parolles pəˈrɒl.ɪz, -ɪs, -iːz, -es, -ez (US) pəˈrɑː.ləs
paronomazia, **-sia** ˌpær.ə.nəˈmeɪ.zi.ə, -si.ə, ˈ-ʒə (US) ˌper.ə.noʊˈmeɪ.ʒə, ˌpær-, ˈ-ʒi.ə
paronym ˈpær.ə.nɪm (US) ˈper-, ˈpær- **-s** -z
paronymy pəˈrɒn.ɪ.mi, pærˈɒn-, ˈ-ə- (US) pəˈrɑːn-
Paros ˈpær.ɒs (US) ˈper.ɑːs, ˈpær-, ˈpɑːr-
parotid pəˈrɒt.ɪd (US) -ˈrɑː.t̬ɪd **-s** -z
paroxysm ˈpær.ək.sɪ.zəm, -ɒk-; pəˈrɒk- (US) ˈper.ək-, ˈpær- **-s** -z
paroxysmal ˌpær.əkˈsɪz.məl, -ɒkˈ- (US) ˌper.əkˈ-, ˌpær-
paroxytone pəˈrɒk.sɪ.təʊn, pærˈɒk- (US) perˈɑːk.sɪ.toʊn, pær- **-s** -z
parquet ˈpɑː.keɪ, -ki (US) pɑːrˈkeɪ **-s** -z
parquetry ˈpɑː.kɪ.tri, -kə- (US) ˈpɑːr.kə-
parr **(P)** pɑːʳ (US) pɑːr
parrakeet ˌpær.əˈkiːt, ˈ--- (US) ˈper.ə.kiːt, ˈpær- **-s** -s
Parramatta ˌpær.əˈmæt.ə (US) ˌper.əˈmæt̬-, ˌpær-
Parratt ˈpær.ət (US) ˈper-, ˈpær-
Parret ˈpær.ɪt (US) ˈper-, ˈpær-

parricidal ˌpær.ɪˈsaɪ.dəl, -əˈ- (US) ˌper.əˈ-, ˌpær-
parricide ˈpær.ɪ.saɪd, ˈ-ə- (US) ˈper.ə-, ˈpær- **-s** -z
Parrish ˈpær.ɪʃ (US) ˈper-, ˈpær-
parrot **(P)** ˈpær.ət (US) ˈper-, ˈpær- **-s** -s **-ing** -ɪŋ **-ed** -ɪd
parrot-fashion ˈpær.ətˌfæʃ.ən (US) ˈper-, ˈpær-
parr|y **(P)** ˈpær|.i (US) ˈper-, ˈpær- **-ies** -iz **-ying** -i.ɪŋ **-ied** -id
pars|e pɑːz (US) pɑːrs **-es** -ɪz **-ing** -ɪŋ **-ed** -d **-er/s** -əʳ/z (US) -ɚ/z
Parsi, **Parsee** ˌpɑːˈsiː, ˈ-- (US) ˈpɑːr.siː, -ˈ- **-s** -z
Parsifal ˈpɑː.sɪ.fəl, -sə-, -fɑːl, -fæl (US) ˈpɑːr.sə.fəl, -fɑːl
parsimonious ˌpɑː.sɪˈməʊ.ni.əs, -səˈ- (US) ˌpɑːr.səˈmoʊ- **-ly** -li **-ness** -nəs, -nɪs
parsimony ˈpɑː.sɪ.mə.ni, -sə- (US) ˈpɑːr.sə.moʊ-
parsley ˈpɑː.sli (US) ˈpɑːr-
parsnip ˈpɑː.snɪp (US) ˈpɑːr- **-s** -z
parson ˈpɑː.sən (US) ˈpɑːr- **-s** -z **ˌparson's ˈnose**
parsonag|e ˈpɑː.sən.ɪdʒ (US) ˈpɑːr- **-es** -ɪz
Parsons ˈpɑː.sənz (US) ˈpɑːr-
part pɑːt (US) pɑːrt **-s** -s **-ing** -ɪŋ (US) ˈpɑːr.t̬ɪŋ **-ed** -ɪd (US) ˈpɑːr.t̬ɪd **ˌpart and ˈparcel**; **ˌpart exˈchange**; **ˌparting ˈshot** (US) **ˈparting ˌshot**; **ˌpart of ˈspeech**
partak|e pɑːˈteɪk (US) pɑːr- **-es** -s **-ing** -ɪŋ **partook** pɑːˈtʊk (US) pɑːr- **partak|en** pɑːˈteɪ.k|ən (US) pɑːr- **-er/s** -əʳ/z (US) -ɚ/z
parterre pɑːˈteəʳ (US) pɑːrˈter **-s** -z
Parthenia pɑːˈθiː.ni.ə (US) pɑːr-
parthenogenesis ˌpɑː.θə.nəʊˈdʒen.ɪ.sɪs, -θɪ-, ˈ-ə- (US) ˌpɑːr.θə.noʊˈdʒen.ə-
Parthenon ˈpɑː.θən.ən, -θɪ.nən, -nɒn (US) ˈpɑːr.θə.nɑːn, -nən **-s** -z
Parthenope pɑːˈθen.ə.pi (US) pɑːr-
Parthi|a ˈpɑː.θi|.ə (US) ˈpɑːr- **-an/s** -ən/z
partial ˈpɑː.ʃəl (US) ˈpɑːr- **-ly** -i
partiality ˌpɑː.ʃiˈæl.ə.ti, -ɪ.ti (US) ˌpɑːr.ʃiˈæl.ə.t̬i
participant pɑːˈtɪs.ɪ.pənt, ˈ-ə- (US) pɑːrˈtɪs.ə-, pɚ- **-s** -s
partici|pate pɑːˈtɪs.ɪ|.peɪt, ˈ-ə- (US) pɑːrˈtɪs.ə-, pɚ- **-pates** -peɪts **-pating** -peɪ.tɪŋ (US) -peɪ.t̬ɪŋ **-pated** -peɪ.tɪd (US) -peɪ.t̬ɪd **-pator/s** -peɪ.təʳ/z (US) -peɪ.t̬ɚ/z
participation pɑːˌtɪs.ɪˈpeɪ.ʃən, ˌpɑː.tɪ.sɪˈ-, -səˈ- (US) pɑːrˌtɪs.əˈ-, pɚ- **-s** -z
participatory pɑːˈtɪs.ɪ.pə.tər.i, ˈ-ə-; ˌpɑː.tɪ.sɪˈpeɪ-, -səˈ- (US) pɑːrˈtɪs.ə.pəˌtɔːr-, pɚ-

participial ˌpɑː.tɪˈsɪp.i.əl, -təˈ- US ˌpɑːr.tɪˈ- **-ly** -i
participle pɑːˈtɪs.ɪ.pl̩, ˈ-ə- US ˈpɑːr.tɪ.sɪ- **-s** -z
particle ˈpɑː.tɪ.kl̩, -tə- US ˈpɑːr.t̬ə- **-s** -z
particleboard ˈpɑː.tɪ.kl̩ˌbɔːd US ˈpɑːr.t̬ɪ.kl̩ˌbɔːrd
particolo(u)red ˈpɑː.tiˌkʌl.əd, ˌpɑː.tiˈkʌl- US ˈpɑːr.t̬iˌkʌl.ɚd
particular pəˈtɪk.jə.ləʳ, -jʊ- US pɚˈtɪk.jə.lɚ, -juː- **-s** -z **-ly** -li
particularit|y pəˌtɪk.jəˈlær.ə.t|i, -jʊˈ-, -ɪ.t|i US pɚˌtɪk.jəˈler.ə.t̬|i, -juːˈ-, -ˈlær- **-ies** -iz
particulariz|e, -is|e pəˈtɪk.jə.lᵊr.aɪz, -jʊ- US pɚˈtɪk.jə.lə.raɪz, -juː- **-es** -ɪz **-ing** -ɪŋ **-ed** -d
parting ˈpɑː.tɪŋ US ˈpɑːr.t̬ɪŋ **-s** -z
Partington ˈpɑː.tɪŋ.tən US ˈpɑːr.t̬ɪŋ-
partisan ˌpɑː.tɪˈzæn, -təˈ-, ˈ--- US ˈpɑːr.t̬ɪ.zən, -zæn **-s** -z **-ship/s** -ʃɪp/s
partita pɑːˈtiː.tə US pɑːrˈtiː.t̬ə
partite ˈpɑː.taɪt US ˈpɑːr-
partition pɑːˈtɪʃ.ᵊn, pə- US pɑːr- **-s** -z **-ing** -ɪŋ **-ed** -d
partitive ˈpɑː.tɪ.tɪv, -tə- US ˈpɑːr.t̬ə.t̬ɪv **-ly** -li
partly ˈpɑːt.li US ˈpɑːrt-
partn|er ˈpɑːt.n|əʳ US ˈpɑːrt.n|ɚ **-ers** -əz US -ɚz **-ering** -ᵊr.ɪŋ **-ered** -əd US -ɚd
partnership ˈpɑːt.nə.ʃɪp US ˈpɑːrt.nɚ- **-s** -s
Parton ˈpɑː.tᵊn US ˈpɑːr-
partook *(from* **partake***)* pɑːˈtʊk US pɑːr-
partridg|e (P) ˈpɑː.trɪdʒ US ˈpɑːr- **-es** -ɪz
part-singing ˈpɑːtˌsɪŋ.ɪŋ US ˈpɑːrt-
part-song ˈpɑːt.sɒŋ US ˈpɑːrt.sɑːŋ, -sɔːŋ **-s** -z
part-tim|e ˌpɑːtˈtaɪm US ˌpɑːrt-, ˈ-- **-er/s** -əʳ/z US -ɚ/z *stress shift, British only:* ˌpart-time ˈjob
parturition ˌpɑː.tjʊəˈrɪʃ.ᵊn, -tjᵊrˈɪʃ- US ˌpɑːr.tuːˈrɪʃ-, -tjuːˈ-, -t̬əˈ-, -tʃəˈ- **-s** -z
partway ˌpɑːtˈweɪ US ˌpɑːrt- *stress shift:* ˌpartway ˈthere
part|y ˈpɑː.t|i US ˈpɑːr.t̬|i **-ies** -iz **-ying** -i.ɪŋ **-ied** -id ˈ**party** ˌ**piece**; ˌ**party** ˈ**wall**
partygoer ˈpɑː.tiˌgəʊ.əʳ US ˈpɑːr.t̬iˌgoʊ.ɚ **-s** -z
party line *in politics:* ˌpɑː.tiˈlaɪn US ˌpɑːr.t̬iˈ-
party line *telephone:* ˈpɑː.ti.laɪn US ˈpɑːr.t̬i-
party poop|er ˈpɑː.tiˌpuː.p|əʳ US ˈpɑːr.t̬iˌpuː.p|ɚ **-ers** -əz US -ɚz **-ing** -ɪŋ
party-spirit ˌpɑː.tiˈspɪr.ɪt US ˌpɑːr.t̬iˈ-
parvenu(e) ˈpɑː.və.njuː, -nuː US ˈpɑːr.və.nuː, -njuː **-s** -z
Parzival ˈpɑːt.sɪ.fɑːl US ˈpɑːrt-
pas *singular:* pɑː *plural:* pɑːz, pɑː
Pasadena ˌpæs.əˈdiː.nə
Pascal, PASCAL pæsˈkæl, -ˈkɑːl; US pæsˈkæl, pɑːˈskæl, ˈ--
paschal ˈpæs.kᵊl, ˈpɑː.skᵊl US ˈpæs.kᵊl
pas de deux ˌpɑː.dəˈdɜː
pasha (P) ˈpɑː.ʃə, ˈpæʃ.ə; pəˈʃɑː **-s** -z
pashmina pæʃˈmiː.nə **-s** -z
Pashtun pæʃˈtuːn, ˈpɑːʃ-
Pasiphae pəˈsɪf.i.iː, -eɪ US ˈ-ə.i
paso doble ˌpæs.əʊˈdəʊ.bleɪ US ˌpɑː.soʊˈdoʊ-
Pasolini ˌpæs.əʊˈliː.ni US -oʊˈ-
pasquinade ˌpæs.kwɪˈneɪd, -kwəˈ- US -kwɪˈ- **-s** -z
pass pɑːs US pæs **-es** -ɪz **-ing** -ɪŋ **-ed** -t **-er/s** -əʳ/z US -ɚ/z ˈ**pass de**ˌ**gree**; ˈ**pass** ˌ**law**
passab|le ˈpɑː.sə.b|l̩ US ˈpæs.ə- **-ly** -li **-leness** -l̩.nəs, -nɪs
passacaglia ˌpæs.əˈkɑː.li.ə, -ˈkæl.jə US ˌpɑː.səˈkɑːl.jə, ˌpæs.əˈ-, -ˈkæl- **-s** -z
passag|e ˈpæs.ɪdʒ **-es** -ɪz **-ing** -ɪŋ **-ed** -d
passageway ˈpæs.ɪdʒ.weɪ
passant *in heraldry:* ˈpæs.ᵊnt *in chess:* pæsˈɑ̃ːŋ, pɑːˈsɑːŋ US ˈpæs.ənt
Passat® pæsˈæt, -ɑːt US pəˈsɑːt, pæsˈɑːt
passbook ˈpɑːs.bʊk US ˈpæs- **-s** -s
Passe pæs
passé(e) pæsˈeɪ, pɑːˈseɪ, ˈ-- US pæsˈeɪ, ˈ--; pɑːˈseɪ
passenger ˈpæs.ᵊn.dʒəʳ, -ɪn- US -ᵊn.dʒɚ **-s** -z
passe-partout ˌpæs.pəˈtuː, ˌpɑːs-, -pɑːˈ-, ˈ--- US ˌpæs.pɑːrˈ-, ˌpɑːs- **-s** -z
passer-by ˌpɑː.səˈbaɪ US ˌpæs.ɚˈ- **passers-by** ˌpɑː.səzˈbaɪ US ˌpæs.ɚzˈ-
passerine ˈpæs.ə.raɪn, -riːn US -ə.raɪn, -ɚ.ɪn
Passfield ˈpæs.fiːld, ˈpɑːs- US ˈpæs-
passibility ˌpæs.ɪˈbɪl.ə.ti, -əˈ-, -ɪ.ti US -ɪˈbɪl.ə.t̬i
passible ˈpæs.ɪ.bl̩, ˈ-ə- US ˈ-ɪ-
passim ˈpæs.ɪm
passing note ˈpɑː.sɪŋˌnəʊt US ˈpæs.ɪŋˌnoʊt **-s** -s
passion (P) ˈpæʃ.ᵊn **-s** -z ˈ**passion** ˌ**play**
passionate ˈpæʃ.ᵊn.ət, -ɪt US -ə.nɪt **-ly** -li **-ness** -nəs, -nɪs
passionflower ˈpæʃ.ᵊnˌflaʊəʳ US -ˌflaʊɚ **-s** -z
passionfruit ˈpæʃ.ᵊn.fruːt **-s** -s
Passiontide ˈpæʃ.ᵊn.taɪd
passive ˈpæs.ɪv **-ly** -li **-ness** -nəs, -nɪs ˌ**passive** ˈ**smoking**
passivity pæsˈɪv.ə.ti, pəˈsɪv-, -ɪ.ti US pæsˈɪv.ə.t̬i
passivization, -isa- ˌpæs.ɪ.vaɪˈzeɪ.ʃᵊn, ˌ-ə-, -vɪˈ- US -ɪ.vɪˈ-
passiviz|e, -is|e ˈpæs.ɪ.vaɪz, ˈ-ə- US ˈ-ɪ- **-es** -ɪz **-ing** -ɪŋ **-ed** -d
pass-key ˈpɑːs.kiː US ˈpæs- **-s** -z
Passmore ˈpɑːs.mɔːʳ, ˈpæs- US ˈpæs.mɔːr
Passover ˈpɑːsˌəʊ.vəʳ US ˈpæsˌoʊ.vɚ **-s** -z
passport ˈpɑːs.pɔːt US ˈpæs.pɔːrt **-s** -
password ˈpɑːs.wɜːd US ˈpæs.wɝːd **-s** -z
past pɑːst US pæst ˌ**past par**ˈ**ticiple**; US ˌ**past** ˈ**participle**; ˌ**past** ˈ**perfect**; ˌ**past** ˈ**tense**
pasta ˈpæs.tə, ˈpɑː.stə US ˈpɑː.stə
past|e peɪst **-es** -s **-ing** -ɪŋ **-ed** -ɪd
pasteboard ˈpeɪs*t*.bɔːd US -bɔːrd
pastel ˈpæs.tᵊl, -tel; pæsˈtel US pæsˈt **-s** -z
pastelist ˈpæs.tᵊl.ɪst US pæsˈtel-; ˈpæs.tᵊl- **-s** -s
pastern ˈpæs.tɜːn, -tən US -tɚn **-s** -z
Pasternak ˈpæs.tə.næk US -tɚ-
paste-up ˈpeɪst.ʌp **-s** -s
Pasteur pæsˈtɜːʳ, pɑːˈstɜːʳ US pæsˈtɝ pɑːˈstɝː
pasteurization, -isa- ˌpæs.tʃᵊr.aɪˈzeɪ.ʃᵊn, ˌpɑːs-, -tjᵊr-, -tᵊr-, -ɪˈ- US ˌpæs.tʃɚ.ɪˈ-, -tɚ-
pasteuriz|e, -is|e ˈpæs.tʃᵊr.aɪz, ˈpɑːs -tjᵊr-, -tᵊr- US ˈpæs.tʃə.raɪz, -tə- -ɪz **-ing** -ɪŋ **-ed** -d
pastich|e pæsˈtiːʃ, ˈ-- US pæsˈtiːʃ, pɑːˈstiːʃ **-es** -ɪz
pastille ˈpæs.tᵊl, -tɪl, -tiːl; pæsˈtiːl US pæsˈtiːl **-s** -z
pastime ˈpɑːs.taɪm US ˈpæs- **-s** -z
pastis pæsˈtiːs
past-master ˌpɑːstˈmɑː.stəʳ, ˈ-ˌ-- US ˈpæstˌmæs.tɚ, ˌ-ˈ-- **-s** -z
Paston ˈpæs.tᵊn
pastor ˈpɑː.stəʳ US ˈpæs.tɚ **-s** -z
pastoral ˈpɑː.stᵊr.ᵊl, ˈpæs.tᵊr- US ˈp **-s** -z
pastorale ˌpæs.tᵊrˈɑːl, -ˈæl, -ˈɑː.leɪ US -təˈrɑːl, -ˈræl, -ˈrɑː.leɪ **-s** -z
pastoralism ˈpɑː.stᵊr.ᵊl.ɪ.zᵊm, ˈpæs.tᵊr- US ˈpæs-
pastorate ˈpɑː.stᵊr.ət, -ɪt US ˈpæs.tɚ.ɪt **-s** -s
pastrami pæsˈtrɑː.mi, pəˈstrɑː- US pə-
pastr|y ˈpeɪ.str|i **-ies** -iz
pastrycook ˈpeɪ.stri.kʊk **-s** -s
pasturage ˈpɑː.stjʊ.rɪdʒ, -tjᵊr.ɪdʒ, -tʃᵊr- US ˈpæs.tʃɚ.ɪdʒ, -tjɚ-
past|ure ˈpɑːs.tʃ|əʳ US ˈpæs.tʃ|ɚ, - **-ures** -əz US -ɚz **-uring** -ᵊr.ɪŋ **-ure** -əd US -ɚd

pastureland ˈpɑː.stʃə.lænd (US) ˈpæs.tʃɚ-, -tjɚ-

past|y (n.) ˈpæs.t|i *for the Cornish kind also:* ˈpɑː.st|i (US) ˈpæs.t|i -ies -iz

past|y (adj.) ˈpeɪ.st|i -ier -i.əʳ (US) -i.ɚ -iest -i.ɪst, -i.əst -ily -ɪ.li, -ᵊl.i -iness -ɪ.nəs, -ɪ.nɪs

pat (P) pæt -s -s -ting -ɪŋ (US) ˈpæt̬.ɪŋ -ted -ɪd (US) ˈpæt̬.ɪd

pat-a-cake ˈpæt.ə.keɪk (US) ˈpæt̬- -s -s

Patagoni|a ˌpæt.əˈgəʊ.ni|.ə (US) ˌpæt̬.əˈgoʊ-, ˈ-nj|ə -an/s -ən/z

Pataki pəˈtɑːk.i, -ˈtæk-

Patara ˈpæt.ᵊr.ə

patch pætʃ -es -ɪz -ing -ɪŋ -ed -t

patchouli, patchouly pəˈtʃuː.li; ˈpætʃ.ʊ.li, -ᵊl.i (US) ˈpætʃ.uː.li; pəˈtʃuː-

patchwork ˈpætʃ.wɜːk (US) -wɝːk -s -s ˌpatchwork ˈquilt

patch|y ˈpætʃ|.i -ier -i.əʳ (US) -i.ɚ -iest -i.ɪst, -i.əst -ily -ɪ.li, -ᵊl.i -iness -ɪ.nəs, -ɪ.nɪs

pate peɪt -s -s

pâté ˈpæt.eɪ, -ˈ- (US) pɑːˈteɪ, pætˈeɪ

pâté de foie ˌpæt.eɪ.dəˈfwɑː (US) pɑːˌteɪ-, pætˌeɪ-

pâté de foie gras ˌpæt.eɪ.dəˌfwɑːˈgrɑː (US) pɑːˌteɪ-, pætˌeɪ-

patel pəˈtel, -ˈteɪl

Pateley ˈpeɪt.li

patell|a pəˈtel|.ə -as -əz -ae -iː -ar -əʳ (US) -ɚ

paten ˈpæt.ᵊn -s -z

paten|t ˈpeɪ.tᵊn|t, ˈpæt.ᵊn|t (US) ˈpæt-, ˈpeɪ.tᵊn|t -ts -ts -ting -tɪŋ (US) -t̬ɪŋ -ted -tɪd (US) -t̬ɪd -table -tə.bl̩ (US) -t̬ə.bl̩ ˌpatent ˈleather

Note: For British English, /ˈpæt.ᵊnt/ in **letters patent**; otherwise /ˈpeɪ.tᵊnt/ seems the more usual. For American English, the usual pronunciation is /ˈpæt.ᵊnt/, except for the meanings **open, obvious**, where /ˈpeɪ.tᵊnt/ is the normal form.

patentee ˌpeɪ.tᵊnˈtiː, ˌpæt.ᵊnˈ- (US) ˌpæt.ᵊnˈtiː -s -z

patently ˈpeɪ.tᵊnt.li (US) ˈpeɪ-, ˈpæt.ᵊnt-

pater (P) ˈpeɪ.təʳ, ˈpɑː- (US) ˈpɑː.t̬ɚ -s -z

Note: This word is never used to mean **father** in the U.S..

paterfamilias ˌpeɪ.tə.fəˈmɪl.i.æs, ˌpæt.ə-, -əs (US) ˌpeɪ.t̬ɚ.fəˈmɪl.i.əs, ˌpɑː.t̬ɚ-, ˌpæt̬.ɚ-

paternal pəˈtɜː.nᵊl (US) -ˈtɝː- -ly -li

paternal|ism pəˈtɜː.nᵊl|.ɪ.zᵊm (US) -ˈtɝː- -ist/s -ɪst/s

paternalistic pəˌtɜː.nᵊlˈɪs.tɪk (US) -ˌtɝː- -ally -ᵊl.i, -li

paternity pəˈtɜː.nə.ti, -nɪ- (US) -ˈtɝː.nə.t̬i paˈternity ˌleave; paˈternity ˌsuit; paˈternity ˌtest

Paternoster *Lord's prayer:* ˌpæt.əˈnɒs.təʳ (US) ˌpɑː.t̬ɚˈnɔː.stɚ, -ˈnoʊ- -s -z

Paternoster *Square:* ˈpæt.əˌnɒs.təʳ (US) ˌpɑː.t̬ɚˈnɔː.stɚ, ˌpæt.ɚˈ-, ˌpeɪ.tɚˈ-, -ˈnɑː-

Paterson ˈpæt.ə.sᵊn (US) ˈpæt̬.ɚ-

Pateshall ˈpæt.ə.ʃᵊl, ˈ-ɪ- (US) ˈpæt̬-

Patey ˈpeɪ.ti (US) -t̬i

pa|th pɑː|θ (US) pæ|θ -ths -ðz (US) -θs, -ðz ˌlead someone ˌup/ˌdown the ˌgarden ˈpath

path. pæθ

-path -pæθ

Note: Suffix. Normally unstressed, e.g. **psychopath** /ˈsaɪ.kəʊ.pæθ (US) -kə-/.

Pathan pəˈtɑːn (US) pəˈtɑːn, pətˈhɑːn -s -z

Pathé ˈpæθ.eɪ

pathetic pəˈθet.ɪk (US) -ˈθet̬- -ally -ᵊl.i, -li

pathfinder (P) ˈpɑːθˌfaɪn.dəʳ (US) ˈpæθˌfaɪn.dɚ -s -z

-pathic -ˈpæθ.ɪk

Note: Suffix. Words containing **-pathic** normally carry primary stress on the penultimate syllable, e.g. **psychopathic** /ˌsaɪ.kəʊˈpæθ.ɪk (US) -kəˈ-/.

pathless ˈpɑːθ.ləs, -lɪs (US) ˈpæθ-

patho- pæθ.əʊ-; pəˈθɒ-, pæθˈɒ- (US) pæθ.ə-; pəˈθɑː-, pæθˈɑː-

Note: Prefix. Normally either carries primary or secondary stress on the first syllable, e.g. **pathogen** /ˈpæθ.əʊ.dʒen (US) -ə-/, **pathogenic** /ˌpæθ.əʊˈdʒen.ɪk (US) -əˈ-/, or primary stress on the second syllable, e.g. **pathology** /pəˈθɒl.ə.dʒi (US) -ˈθɑː.lə-/.

pathogen ˈpæθ.əʊ.dʒən, -dʒen (US) -ə.dʒən -s -z

pathogenesis ˌpæθ.əʊˈdʒen.ə.sɪs, ˈ-ɪ- (US) ˈ-ə-

pathogenic ˌpæθ.əʊˈdʒen.ɪk (US) -əˈ- -ally -ᵊl.i, -li

pathologic ˌpæθ.əˈlɒdʒ.ɪk (US) -ˈlɑː.dʒɪk -al -ᵊl -ally -ᵊl.i, -li

patholog|y pəˈθɒl.ə.dʒ|i, pæθˈɒl- (US) pəˈθɑː.lə- -ist/s -ɪst/s

pathos ˈpeɪ.θɒs (US) -θɑːs

pathway ˈpɑːθ.weɪ (US) ˈpæθ- -s -z

-pathy -pə.θi

Note: Suffix. Normally unstressed, e.g. **telepathy** /təˈlep.ə.θi/.

patience (P) ˈpeɪ.ʃᵊnts

patient ˈpeɪ.ʃᵊnt -s -s -ly -li

patina ˈpæt.ɪ.nə, -ᵊn.ə; pəˈtiː.nə (US) ˈpæt.ᵊn.ə; pəˈtiː.nə

patio ˈpæt.i.əʊ (US) ˈpæt̬.i.oʊ, ˈpɑː.t̬i- -s -z

patisserie pəˈtiː.sᵊr.i, pætˈɪs- -s -z

Patman ˈpæt.mən

Patmore ˈpæt.mɔːʳ (US) -mɔːr

Patmos ˈpæt.mɒs (US) -məs, ˈpɑːt-, -mɑːs

Patna ˈpæt.nə, ˈpʌt- (US) ˈpʌt-, ˈpæt-

patois *singular:* ˈpæt.wɑː *plural:* -z

Paton ˈpeɪ.tᵊn

Patou ˈpæt.uː *as if French:* -ˈ-

Patras pəˈtræs; ˈpæt.rəs

patrial ˈpeɪ.tri.əl, ˈpæt.ri- (US) ˈpeɪ.tri-

patriarch ˈpeɪ.tri.ɑːk, ˈpæt.ri- (US) ˈpeɪ.tri.ɑːrk -s -s -y -i -ies -iz

patriarch|al ˌpeɪ.triˈɑː.k|ᵊl, ˌpæt.riˈ- (US) ˌpeɪ.triˈɑːr- -ic -ɪk

patriarchate ˈpeɪ.tri.ɑː.kɪt, ˈpæt.ri-, -keɪt, -kət (US) ˈpeɪ.tri.ɑːr.kɪt, -keɪt -s -s

Patricia pəˈtrɪʃ.ə (US) -ˈtrɪʃ-, -ˈtriː.ʃə

patrician pəˈtrɪʃ.ᵊn -s -z

patriciate pəˈtrɪʃ.i.ət, -ˈtrɪʃ.ət (US) -ˈtrɪs.i-, -ɪt, -eɪt (US) -trɪʃ.i.ɪt, -eɪt; -ˈtrɪʃ.ɪt

patricide ˈpæt.rɪ.saɪd, ˈpeɪ.trɪ-, -trə- (US) ˈpæt.rə- -s -z

Patrick ˈpæt.rɪk

patrilineal ˌpæt.rɪˈlɪn.i.əl, -rəˈ- (US) ˌpæt.rəˈ-

patrimonial ˌpæt.rɪˈməʊ.ni.əl, -rəˈ- (US) ˌpæt.rəˈmoʊ- -ly -i

patrimon|y ˈpæt.rɪ.mə.n|i, -rə- (US) -rə.moʊ- -ies -iz

patriot ˈpeɪ.tri.ət, ˈpæt.ri- (US) ˈpeɪ-, -ɑːt -s -s

patriotic ˌpæt.riˈɒt.ɪk, ˌpeɪ.triˈ- (US) ˌpeɪ.triˈɑː.t̬ɪk -ally -ᵊl.i, -li

patriotism ˈpeɪ.tri.ə.tɪ.zᵊm, ˈpæt.ri- (US) ˈpeɪ.tri-

patristic pəˈtrɪs.tɪk -s -s -al -ᵊl

Patroclus pəˈtrɒk.ləs (US) -ˈtroʊ.kləs; ˈpæt.roʊ-

patrol pəˈtrəʊl (US) -ˈtroʊl -s -z -ling -ɪŋ -led -d

patrolcar pəˈtrəʊl.kɑːʳ (US) -ˈtroʊl.kɑːr -s -z

patrol|man pəˈtrəʊl|.mən, -mæn (US) -ˈtroʊl- -men -mən, -men

patron ˈpeɪ.trᵊn, ˈpæt.rᵊn (US) ˈpeɪ.trᵊn -s -z

patronage ˈpæt.rᵊn.ɪdʒ, ˈpeɪ.trᵊn- (US) ˈpeɪ.trᵊn-, ˈpæt.rᵊn-

patronal pəˈtrəʊ.nᵊl, pætˈrəʊ- (US) ˈpeɪ.trᵊn.ᵊl, ˈpæt.rᵊn-; pəˈtroʊ.nᵊl

patroness ˌpeɪ.trəˈnes, ˌpæt.rəˈ-; ˈpeɪ.trᵊn.es, ˈpæt.rᵊn-, -ɪs, -əs (US) ˈpeɪ.trə.nɪs -es -ɪz

patroniz|e, -is|e ˈpæt.rᵊn.aɪz (US) ˈpeɪ.trᵊn-, ˈpæt.rᵊn- -es -ɪz -ing/ly -ɪŋ/li -ed -d

patronymic ˌpæt.rəˈnɪm.ɪk (US) -rəˈ-, -roʊˈ- -s -s

patroon pəˈtruːn -s -z

pats|y (P) ˈpæt.s|i -ies -iz

patten (P) ˈpæt.ən **-s** -z
patt|er ˈpæt|.əʳ ⓤⓢ ˈpæţ|.ɚ **-ers** -əz ⓤⓢ -ɚz **-ering** -ər.ɪŋ **-ered** -əd ⓤⓢ -ɚd
Patterdale ˈpæt.ə.deɪl ⓤⓢ ˈpæţ.ɚ-
pattern ˈpæt.ən ⓤⓢ ˈpæţ.ɚn **-s** -z **-ing** -ɪŋ **-ed** -d
Patterson ˈpæt.ə.sən ⓤⓢ ˈpæţ.ɚ-
Patteson ˈpæt.ɪ.sən, ˈ-ə- ⓤⓢ ˈpæţ-
Patti(e) ˈpæt.i ⓤⓢ ˈpæţ-
Pattison ˈpæt.ɪ.sən ⓤⓢ ˈpæţ-
Patton ˈpæt.ən
patt|y ˈpæt|.i ⓤⓢ ˈpæţ- **-ies** -iz
paucity ˈpɔː.sə.ti, -sɪ- ⓤⓢ ˈpɑː.sə.ţi, ˈpɔː-
Paul pɔːl ⓤⓢ pɔːl, pɑːl **-'s** -z ˌ**Paul** ˈ**Jones**
Paula ˈpɔː.lə ⓤⓢ ˈpɑː-, ˈpɔː-
Paulding ˈpɔːl.dɪŋ ⓤⓢ ˈpɑːl-, ˈpɔːl-
Paulette pɔːˈlet ⓤⓢ pɑː-, pɔː-
Pauley ˈpɔː.li ⓤⓢ ˈpɑː-, ˈpɔː-
Pauli ˈpɔː.li, ˈpaʊ- ⓤⓢ ˈpaʊ-, ˈpɔː-
Paulin ˈpɔː.lɪn ⓤⓢ ˈpɑː-, ˈpɔː-
Pauline *scholar of St Paul's school, relating to St Paul:* ˈpɔː.laɪn ⓤⓢ ˈpɑː.laɪn, ˈpɔː-, -liːn **-s** -z
Pauline *female name:* ˈpɔː.liːn, -ˈ- ⓤⓢ pɑːˈliːn, pɔː-
Pauling ˈpɔː.lɪŋ ⓤⓢ ˈpɑː-, ˈpɔː-
Paulinus pɔːˈlaɪ.nəs ⓤⓢ pɑː-, pɔː-
Paulus ˈpɔː.ləs ⓤⓢ ˈpɑː-, ˈpɔː-
Pauncefote ˈpɔːnts.fʊt, -fət ⓤⓢ ˈpɑːnts-, ˈpɔːnts-
paunch pɔːntʃ ⓤⓢ pɑːntʃ, pɔːntʃ **-es** -ɪz **-y** -i **-iness** -ɪ.nəs, -ɪ.nɪs
pauper ˈpɔː.pəʳ ⓤⓢ ˈpɑː.pɚ, ˈpɔː- **-s** -z
pauperism ˈpɔː.pər.ɪ.zəm ⓤⓢ ˈpɑː-, ˈpɔː-
pauperization, -isa- ˌpɔː.pər.aɪˈzeɪ.ʃən, -ɪˈ- ⓤⓢ ˌpɑː.pɚ.ɪˈ-, ˌpɔː-
pauperiz|e, -is|e ˈpɔː.pər.aɪz ⓤⓢ ˈpɑː-, ˈpɔː- **-es** -ɪz **-ing** -ɪŋ **-ed** -d
Pausanias pɔːˈseɪ.ni.æs, -əs ⓤⓢ pɑːˈseɪ.ni.əs, pɔː-
paus|e pɔːz ⓤⓢ pɑːz, pɔːz **-es** -ɪz **-ing** -ɪŋ **-ed** -d
pavan(e) ˈpæv.ən; pəˈvæn, -ˈvɑːn ⓤⓢ pəˈvɑːn, -ˈvæn **-s** -z
Pavarotti ˌpæv.əˈrɒt.i ⓤⓢ -ˈrɔː.ţi, ˌpɑː.vəˈ-
pav|e peɪv **-es** -z **-ing** -ɪŋ **-ed** -d **-er/s** -əʳ/z ⓤⓢ -ɚ/z ˈ**paving** ˌ**stone**
pavé ˈpæv.eɪ, -ˈ- ⓤⓢ pævˈeɪ, ˈ-- **-s** -z
pavement ˈpeɪv.mənt **-s** -s
Pavia pəˈviː.ə, pɑː-, pɑːˈviː.ɑː
pavid ˈpæv.ɪd
pavilion pəˈvɪl.jən, ˈ-i.ən ⓤⓢ ˈ-jən **-s** -z **-ing** -ɪŋ **-ed** -d
pavio(u)r ˈpeɪ.vjəʳ ⓤⓢ -vjɚ **-s** -s
Pavitt ˈpæv.ɪt
Pavlov ˈpæv.lɒf, -lɒv ⓤⓢ -lɔːv, -lɔːf
pavlova pævˈləʊ.və ⓤⓢ pɑːvˈloʊ-, pæv- **-s** -z
Pavlova ˈpæv.lə.və, ˈpɑːv-; pævˈləʊ- ⓤⓢ pɑːvˈloʊ-, pæv-
Pavlovian pævˈləʊ.vi.ən ⓤⓢ pɑːvˈloʊ-, pæv-
paw (*n. v.*) pɔː ⓤⓢ pɑː, pɔː **-s** -z **-ing** -ɪŋ **-ed** -d
pawk|y ˈpɔː.k|i ⓤⓢ ˈpɑː-, ˈpɔː- **-ier** -i.əʳ ⓤⓢ -i.ɚ **-iest** -i.ɪst, -i.əst **-ily** -ɪ.li, -əl.i **-iness** -ɪ.nəs, -ɪ.nɪs
pawl pɔːl ⓤⓢ pɑːl, pɔːl **-s** -z
pawn pɔːn ⓤⓢ pɑːn, pɔːn **-s** -z **-ing** -ɪŋ **-ed** -d
pawnbrok|er ˈpɔːnˌbrəʊ.k|əʳ, ˈpɔːm- ⓤⓢ ˈpɑːnˌbroʊ.k|ɚ, ˈpɔːn- **-ers** -əz ⓤⓢ -ɚz **-ing** -ɪŋ
Pawnee ˌpɔːˈniː ⓤⓢ ˌpɑː-, ˌpɔː- **-s** -z
pawnshop ˈpɔːn.ʃɒp ⓤⓢ ˈpɑːn.ʃɑːp, ˈpɔːn- **-s** -s
pawpaw ˈpɔː.pɔː ⓤⓢ ˈpɑː.pɑː; ˈpɔː.pɔː **-s** -z
Pawtucket pɔːˈtʌk.ɪt ⓤⓢ pɑː-, pɔː-
pax pæks
Paxman ˈpæk.smən
Paxo® ˈpæk.səʊ ⓤⓢ -soʊ
Paxos ˈpæk.sɒs ⓤⓢ -sɑːs
Paxton ˈpæk.stən
pay peɪ **-s** -z **-ing** -ɪŋ **paid** peɪd **payer/s** ˈpeɪ.əʳ/z ⓤⓢ -ɚ/z ˈ**pay** ˌ**packet**
payable ˈpeɪ.ə.bl̩
payback ˈpeɪ.bæk
paybed ˈpeɪ.bed
paycheck, -cheque ˈpeɪ.tʃek
payday ˈpeɪ.deɪ **-s** -z
PAYE ˌpiː.eɪ.waɪˈiː
payee peɪˈiː **-s** -z
payload ˈpeɪ.ləʊd ⓤⓢ -loʊd **-s** -z
paymaster ˈpeɪˌmɑː.stəʳ ⓤⓢ -ˌmæs.tɚ **-s** -z ˌ**paymaster** ˈ**general**
payment ˈpeɪ.mənt **-s** -s
Payne peɪn
paynim (P) ˈpeɪ.nɪm
Paynter ˈpeɪn.təʳ ⓤⓢ -ţɚ
payoff ˈpeɪ.ɒf ⓤⓢ -ɑːf **-s** -s
payola peɪˈəʊ.lə ⓤⓢ -ˈoʊ-
payout ˈpeɪ.aʊt **-s** -s
payphone ˈpeɪ.fəʊn ⓤⓢ -foʊn
payroll ˈpeɪ.rəʊl ⓤⓢ -roʊl **-s** -z
payslip ˈpeɪ.slɪp
paytrain ˈpeɪ.treɪn **-s** -z
Paz pæz ⓤⓢ pɑːz, pɑːs
pazazz pəˈzæz
PBS ˌpiː.biːˈes
PC ˌpiːˈsiː
PE ˌpiːˈiː
pea piː **-s** -z
Peabody ˈpiːˌbɒd.i ⓤⓢ -ˌbɑː.di
peac|e (P) piːs **-es** -ɪz ˈ**Peace** ˌ**Corps**; ˈ**peace** ˌ**offering**; ˈ**peace** ˌ**pipe**
peaceab|le ˈpiː.sə.b|l̩ **-ly** -li **-leness** -l̩.nəs, -nɪs
peaceful ˈpiːs.fəl, -fʊl **-ly** -i **-ness** -nəs, -nɪs
Peacehaven ˈpiːsˌheɪ.vən
peacekeep|er ˈpiːsˌkiː.p|əʳ ⓤⓢ -ɚ **-ers** -əz ⓤⓢ -ɚz **-ing** -ɪŋ
peacekeeping ˈpiːsˌkiː.pɪŋ
peacemaker ˈpiːsˌmeɪ.kəʳ ⓤⓢ -kɚ **-s** -z
peacenik ˈpiːs.nɪk **-s** -s
peacetime ˈpiːs.taɪm
Peacey ˈpiː.si
peach piːtʃ **-es** -ɪz **-ing** -ɪŋ **-ed** -t **-er/s** -əʳ/z ⓤⓢ -ɚ/z
Peachey ˈpiː.tʃi
Peachum ˈpiː.tʃəm
peach|y ˈpiː.tʃ|i **-ier** -i.əʳ ⓤⓢ -i.ɚ **-iest** -i.ɪst, -i.əst **-iness** -ɪ.nəs, -ɪ.nɪs
peacock (P) ˈpiː.kɒk ⓤⓢ -kɑːk **-s** -s
pea-green ˌpiːˈgriːn *stress shift:* ˌpea-green ˈboat
peahen ˈpiː.hen, ˌ-ˈ- ⓤⓢ ˈ-- **-s** -z
pea-jacket ˈpiːˌdʒæk.ɪt **-s** -s
peak (P) piːk **-s** -s **-ing** -ɪŋ **-ed** -t ˈ**Peak** ˌ**District**; ˌ**peak** ˈ**time** *stress shift:* ˌpeak time ˈtraffic
Peake piːk
peaky ˈpiː.ki
peal piːl **-s** -z **-ing** -ɪŋ **-ed** -d
Peall piːl
pean *alternative spelling of* **paean**: ˈpiː.ən **-s** -z
pean *in heraldry:* piːn
peanut ˈpiː.nʌt **-s** -s ˌ**peanut** ˈ**butter** ⓤⓢ ˈ**peanut** ˌ**butter**
pear peəʳ ⓤⓢ per **-s** -z
Pear *surname:* pɪəʳ ⓤⓢ pɪr
Pearce pɪəs ⓤⓢ pɪrs
Peard pɪəd ⓤⓢ pɪrd
pearl (P) pɜːl ⓤⓢ pɝːl **-s** -z **-ing** -ɪŋ **-ed** ˌ**Pearl** ˈ**Harbor**
pearlite ˈpɜː.laɪt ⓤⓢ ˈpɝː-
pearly ˈpɜː.li ⓤⓢ ˈpɝː- ˌ**pearly** ˈ**gates**; ˌ**pearly** ˈ**king**; ˌ**pearly** ˈ**queen**
pearmain ˈpɜː.meɪn, ˈpeə- ⓤⓢ ˈper- **-s** -z
Pearman ˈpɪə.mən ⓤⓢ ˈpɪr-
Pears pɪəz, peəz ⓤⓢ pɪrs, perz
Note: /peəz ⓤⓢ perz/ in **Pears' soap**; /pɪəz ⓤⓢ pɪrz/ for the singer.
Pearsall ˈpɪə.sɔːl, -səl ⓤⓢ ˈpɪr-, -sɑːl
Pearse pɪəs ⓤⓢ pɪrs
pear-shaped ˈpeə.ʃeɪpt ⓤⓢ ˈper-
Pearson ˈpɪə.sən ⓤⓢ ˈpɪr-
Peart pɪət ⓤⓢ pɪrt
Peary ˈpɪə.ri ⓤⓢ ˈpɪr.i
peasant ˈpez.ənt **-s** -s
peasantry ˈpez.ən.tri
Peascod ˈpes.kəd ⓤⓢ -kəd, -kɑːd
pease (P) piːz
Peaseblossom ˈpiːzˌblɒs.əm ⓤⓢ -ˌblɑː.səm
peasecod ˈpiːz.kɒd ⓤⓢ -kɑːd **-s** -z
pease-pudding ˌpiːzˈpʊd.ɪŋ, ˌpiːs-
peashooter ˈpiːˌʃuː.təʳ ⓤⓢ -ţɚ **-s** -z

pea-souper ˌpiːˈsuː.pəʳ ⓤⓢ ˈpiːˌsuː.pɚ, ˌ-ˈ-- -s -z
peat piːt ˈpeat ˌbog
peat|y ˈpiː.t|i ⓤⓢ -t̬|i -ier -i.əʳ ⓤⓢ -i.ɚ -iest -i.ɪst, -i.əst -iness -ɪ.nəs, -ɪ.nɪs
pebble ˈpeb.l̩ -s -z
pebbledash ˈpeb.l̩.dæʃ -es -ɪz -ing -ɪŋ -ed -t
pebbly ˈpeb.l̩.i, ˈpeb.li
pecan ˈpiː.kæn, -kən; pɪˈkæn ⓤⓢ pɪˈkɑːn, piː-, -ˈkæn; ˈpiː.kɑːn, -kæn -s -z ˌpecan ˈpie
peccability ˌpek.əˈbɪl.ə.ti, -ɪ.ti ⓤⓢ -ə.t̬i
peccable ˈpek.ə.bl̩
peccadillo ˌpek.əˈdɪl.əʊ ⓤⓢ -oʊ -(e)s -z
peccant ˈpek.ənt -ly -li
peccar|y ˈpek.ər|.i -ies -iz
peccavi pekˈɑː.viː *old-fashioned:* -ˈkeɪ.vaɪ ⓤⓢ peɪˈkɑː.vi -s -z
Pechey ˈpiː.tʃi
Pechili ˈpetʃ.ɪ.li
peck (P) pek -s -s -ing -ɪŋ -ed -t -er/s -əʳ/z ⓤⓢ -ɚ/z ˈpecking ˌorder
Peckham ˈpek.əm
Peckinpah ˈpek.ɪn.pɑː
peckish ˈpek.ɪʃ -ly -li -ness -nəs, -nɪs
Peckitt ˈpek.ɪt
Pecksniff ˈpek.snɪf
Pecock ˈpek.ɒk ⓤⓢ -ɑːk
pecorino (P) ˌpek.ərˈiː.nəʊ ⓤⓢ -əˈriː.noʊ
Pecos ˈpeɪ.kəs, -kɒs ⓤⓢ -kəs, -koʊs
Pécs petʃ ⓤⓢ peɪtʃ
pect|in ˈpek.t|ɪn -ic -ɪk -inous -ɪ.nəs
pectoral ˈpek.tər.əl -s -z ˈpectoral ˌmuscle
pecul|ate ˈpek.jə|.leɪt -lates -leɪts -lating -leɪ.tɪŋ ⓤⓢ -leɪ.t̬ɪŋ -lated -leɪ.tɪd ⓤⓢ -leɪ.t̬ɪd -lator/s -leɪ.təʳ/z ⓤⓢ -leɪ.t̬ɚ/z
peculation ˌpek.jəˈleɪ.ʃən, -jʊˈ- -s -z
peculiar pɪˈkjuː.li.əʳ, pə- ⓤⓢ pɪˈkjuːl.jɚ, piː- -s -z -ly -li
peculiarit|y pɪˌkjuː.liˈær.ə.t|i, pə-, -ɪ.t|i ⓤⓢ pɪˌkjuː.liˈer.ə.t̬|i, piː-, -ˈær- -ies -iz
pecuniar|y pɪˈkjuː.njər|.i, -ni.ə.r|i ⓤⓢ pɪˈkjuː.ni.er-, piː- -ily -əl.i, -ɪ.li
pedagogic ˌped.əˈgɒdʒ.ɪk, -ˈgɒg-, -ˈgəʊ.dʒɪk ⓤⓢ -ˈgɑː-, -ˈgoʊ- -s -s -al -əl -ally -əl.i, -li *stress shift:* ˌpedagogic ˈfunction
pedagogue ˈped.ə.gɒg ⓤⓢ -gɑːg, -gɔːg -s -z
pedagogy ˈped.ə.gɒdʒ.i, -gɒg-, -gəʊ.dʒi ⓤⓢ -gɑː.dʒi, -goʊ-
pedal *(n. v.)* ˈped.əl -s -z -(l)ing -ɪŋ -(l)ed -d ˈpedal ˌpushers
pedal *(adj.) of the foot:* ˈpiː.dəl, ˈped.əl *in geometry:* ˈped.əl
pedalo ˈped.əl.əʊ ⓤⓢ -oʊ -(e)s -z
pedant ˈped.ənt -s -s

pedantic pɪˈdæn.tɪk, pə-, pedˈæn-, pəˈdæn- ⓤⓢ pedˈæn- -al -əl -ally -əl.i, -li
pedantism ˈped.ən.tɪ.zəm, pɪˈdæn-, pedˈæn-
pedantr|y ˈped.ən.tr|i -ies -iz
peddl|e ˈped.l̩ -es -z -ing -ɪn, ˈped.lɪŋ -ed -d -er/s -əʳ/z ⓤⓢ -ɚ/z, ˈped.ləʳ/z -er/z ⓤⓢ -ɚ/z
Peden ˈpiː.dən ⓤⓢ ˈpiː.dən, ˈpeɪ-
pederast ˈped.ər.æst, ˈpiː.dər- ⓤⓢ ˈped.ə.ræst -s -s -y -i
pedestal ˈped.ɪ.stəl, ˈ-ə- -s -z
pedestrian pɪˈdes.tri.ən, pə- ⓤⓢ pə- -s -z -ism -ɪ.zəm peˌdestrian ˈcrossing
pedestrianiz|e, -is|e pɪˈdes.tri.ə.naɪz, pə- ⓤⓢ pə- -es -ɪz -ing -ɪŋ -ed -d
pediatric ˌpiː.diˈæt.rɪk -s -s
pediatrician ˌpiː.di.əˈtrɪʃ.ən -s -z
pedicel ˈped.ɪ.sel, ˈ-ə- -s -z
pedicle ˈped.ɪ.kl̩, ˈ-ə- -s -z
pedicure ˈped.ɪ.kjʊəʳ, ˈ-ə-, -kjɔːʳ ⓤⓢ -ɪ.kjʊr -s -z
pedigree ˈped.ɪ.griː, ˈ-ə- -s -z -d -d
pediment ˈped.ɪ.mənt, ˈ-ə- -s -s
pedimental ˌped.ɪˈmen.təl, -əˈ- ⓤⓢ -t̬əl
pedimented ˈped.ɪ.men.tɪd, ˈ-ə-, -mən- ⓤⓢ -men.t̬ɪd
pedlar ˈped.ləʳ ⓤⓢ -lɚ -s -z
pedometer pɪˈdɒm.ɪ.təʳ, pə-, pedˈɒm-, ˈ-ə- ⓤⓢ pɪˈdɑː.mə.t̬ɚ, pə- -s -z
pedophile ˈpiː.dəʊ.faɪl ⓤⓢ ˈped.oʊ-, ˈpiː.doʊ-, -də- -s -z
pedophili|a ˌpiː.dəʊˈfɪl.i|.ə ⓤⓢ ˌped.oʊˈfiː.li-, ˌpiː.doʊˈ-, -dəˈ-, -ˈfiːl.j|ə -ac/s -æk
Pedro ˈped.rəʊ, ˈpiː.drəʊ ⓤⓢ ˈpeɪ.droʊ, ˈped.roʊ
Note: The pronunciation /ˈpiː.drəʊ/ is generally used in Shakespeare's 'Much Ado.'
peduncle pɪˈdʌŋ.kl̩, pə-, pedˈʌŋ- ⓤⓢ pɪˈdʌŋ-; ˈpiː.dʌŋ- -s -z
pee piː -s -z -ing -ɪŋ -d -d
Peeb|les ˈpiː.bl̩|z -les-shire -l̩z.ʃəʳ, -l̩ʒ.ʃəʳ, -l̩.ʃəʳ, -ˌʃɪəʳ ⓤⓢ -ʃɚ, -ˌʃɪr
peek (P) piːk -s -s -ing -ɪŋ -ed -t
peekaboo ˈpiː.kə.buː
peel (P) piːl -s -z -ing/s -ɪŋ/z -ed -d
Peele piːl
peeler ˈpiː.ləʳ ⓤⓢ -lɚ -s -z
peep (P) piːp -s -s -ing -ɪŋ -ed -t -er/s -əʳ/z ⓤⓢ -ɚ/z
peepal ˈpiː.pəl -s -z
peep-bo ˈpiːp.bəʊ, -əʊ, ˌ-ˈ- ⓤⓢ ˈpiːp.boʊ, -oʊ, ˌ-ˈ-
peep-hole ˈpiːp.həʊl ⓤⓢ -hoʊl -s -z
peeping Tom ˌpiː.pɪŋˈtɒm ⓤⓢ -ˈtɑːm -s -z
peepshow ˈpiːp.ʃəʊ ⓤⓢ -ʃoʊ -s -z
peep-toe ˈpiːp.təʊ ⓤⓢ -toʊ -d -d
peepul ˈpiː.pəl -s -z

peer pɪəʳ ⓤⓢ pɪr -s -z -ing -ɪŋ -ed -d
peerag|e ˈpɪə.rɪdʒ ⓤⓢ ˈpɪr.ɪdʒ -es -ɪz
peeress pɪəˈres; ˈpɪə.rəs, -rɪs, -res ⓤⓢ ˈpɪr.ɪs -es -ɪz
peergroup ˈpɪə.gruːp ⓤⓢ ˈpɪr- -s -s
peerless (P) ˈpɪə.ləs, -lɪs ⓤⓢ ˈpɪr- -ly -li -ness -nəs, -nɪs
peev|e piːv -es -z -ing -ɪŋ -ed -d
peevish ˈpiː.vɪʃ -ly -li -ness -nəs, -nɪs
peewee ˈpiː.wiː -s -z
peewit ˈpiː.wɪt -s -s
peg (P) peg -s -z -ging -ɪŋ -ged -d
Pegasus ˈpeg.ə.səs
Pegeen pegˈiːn
Pegge peg
Peggotty ˈpeg.ə.ti ⓤⓢ -t̬i
Peggy ˈpeg.i
Pegram, Pegrum ˈpiː.grəm
Pegu pegˈuː
Pei peɪ
peignoir ˈpeɪ.nwɑːʳ, -nwɔːʳ ⓤⓢ peɪnˈwɑːr, pen-, ˈ-- -s -z
Peile piːl
Peiping ˌpeɪˈpɪŋ
Peirce pɪəs ⓤⓢ pɪrs, pɝːs
pejoration ˌpiː.dʒərˈeɪ.ʃən, ˌpedʒ.ərˈ- ⓤⓢ ˌpedʒ.əˈreɪ-, ˌpiː.dʒəˈ-
pejorative pɪˈdʒɒr.ə.tɪv, pə-, ˈpiː.dʒər- ⓤⓢ pɪˈdʒɔːr.ə.t̬ɪv; ˈpedʒ.ə.reɪ-, ˈpiː.dʒə- -s -z -ly -li
peke piːk -s -s
Pekin ˌpiːˈkɪn ⓤⓢ ˈ--
pekines|e (P) ˌpiː.kɪˈniːz, -kənˈiːz ⓤⓢ ˌpiː.kəˈniːz, -ˈniːs -es -ɪz
Peking ˌpiːˈkɪŋ *stress shift, see compound:* ˌPeking ˈduck
pekinges|e (P) ˌpiː.kɪŋˈiːz, -kɪˈniːz, -kənˈiːz ⓤⓢ -kɪŋˈiːz, -ˈiːs -es -ɪz
pekoe ˈpiː.kəʊ ⓤⓢ -koʊ
pelagic pəˈlædʒ.ɪk, pɪ-, pelˈædʒ- ⓤⓢ pəˈlædʒ-, pɪ-
pelargonium ˌpel.əˈgəʊ.ni.əm, -ɑːˈ- ⓤⓢ -ɑːrˈgoʊ- -s -z
Pelasgian pelˈæz.gi.ən, pɪˈlæz-, pə-, -dʒi- ⓤⓢ pəˈlæz.dʒi- -s -z
Pelé ˈpel.eɪ, -ˈ- ⓤⓢ ˈpel.eɪ
pelerine ˈpel.ər.iːn ⓤⓢ -ə.riːn -s -z
Peleus ˈpiː.ljuːs, ˈpel.juːs, -jəs, -i.əs ⓤⓢ ˈpiː.li.əs, ˈpiːl.juːs
pelf pelf
pelham (P) ˈpel.əm
Pelias ˈpiː.li.æs, ˈpel.i-, -əs ⓤⓢ -əs
pelican ˈpel.ɪ.kən, ˈ-ə- -s -z ˌpelican ˈcrossing
peliss|e pelˈiːs, pɪˈliːs, pə- ⓤⓢ pəˈliːs -es -ɪz
pellagr|a pəˈlæg.r|ə, pelˈæg- ⓤⓢ pəˈleɪ.gr|ə, -ˈlæg.r|ə -ous -əs
Pelleas, Pelléas ˈpel.eɪ.æs, ˈ-i- ⓤⓢ ˈ-i-
Pelles ˈpel.iːz
pellet ˈpel.ɪt, -ət -s -s
Pelley ˈpel.i

pellicle ˈpel.ɪ.kl̩, ˈ-ə- **-s** -z
pellitory ˈpel.ɪ.tᵊr.i, ˈ-ə- (US) -tɔːr-
pell-mell ˌpelˈmel
pellucid pɪˈluː.sɪd, pə-, pelˈuː-, -ˈjuː- (US) pəˈluː.sɪd **-ly** -li **-ness** -nəs, -nɪs
Pelman ˈpel.mən **-ism** -ɪ.zᵊm
pelmet ˈpel.mɪt, -mət **-s** -s
Peloponnese ˈpel.ə.pə.niːz, -niːs, ˌpel.ə.pəˈniːs, -ˈniːz (US) ˌpel.ə.pəˈniːz, -ˈniːs
Peloponnesian ˌpel.ə.pəˈniː.ʃᵊn, -ʃi.ən, ˈ-ʒᵊn (US) -ʒən, -ʃən **-s** -z
Peloponnesus ˌpel.ə.pəˈniː.səs
Pelops ˈpiː.lɒps (US) -lɑːps
pelota pəˈlɒt.ə, pɪ-, pelˈɒt-, -ˈəʊ.tə (US) pəˈloʊ.t̬ə
Pelsall ˈpel.sɔːl
pelt pelt **-s** -s **-ing** -ɪŋ (US) ˈpel.t̬ɪŋ **-ed** -ɪd (US) ˈpel.t̬ɪd
Peltier effect ˈpel.ti.eɪ.ɪˌfekt (US) ˈpel.tjeɪ.ɪˌ-, -əˌ-, -iːˌ-
pelv|is ˈpel.v|ɪs **-ises** -ɪ.sɪz **-es** -iːz **-ic** -ɪk
Pemba ˈpem.bə
Pemberton ˈpem.bə.tᵊn (US) -bɚ-
Pembridge ˈpem.brɪdʒ
Pembroke ˈpem.brʊk, -brək (US) -brʊk, -broʊk **-shire** -ʃəʳ, -ˌʃɪəʳ (US) -ʃɚ, -ˌʃɪr
Pembury ˈpem.bᵊr.i
pemmican ˈpem.ɪ.kən
pen (P) pen **-s** -z **-ning** -ɪŋ **-ned** -d ˈ**pen ˌfriend**; ˈ**pen ˌname**; ˈ**pen ˌpal**; ˈ**pen ˌpusher**
penal ˈpiː.nᵊl **-ly** -i ˈ**penal ˌcolony**
penaliz|e, -is|e ˈpiː.nᵊl.aɪz (US) ˈpiː-, ˈpen.ᵊl- **-es** -ɪz **-ing** -ɪŋ **-ed** -d
penalt|y ˈpen.ᵊl.t|i (US) -t̬|i **-ies** -iz ˈ**penalty ˌbox**
penanc|e ˈpen.ənts **-es** -ɪz
pen-and-ink ˌpen.ənˈdɪŋk *stress shift:* ˌpen-and-ink ˈdrawing
Penang penˈæŋ, pɪˈnæŋ, pə- (US) pɪˈnæŋ, penˈæŋ
Penarth penˈɑːθ, pəˈnɑːθ (US) penˈɑːrθ
penates penˈɑː.teɪz, pɪˈnɑː-, pə-, -ˈneɪ-, -tiːz (US) pəˈneɪ.t̬iːz, -ˈnɑː-
pence *(plur. of* **penny**) pents
Note: See **penny**.
penchant ˈpɑ̃ː.ŋ.ʃɑ̃ːŋ (US) ˈpen.tʃənt **-s** -z
pencil ˈpent.sᵊl **-s** -z **-(l)ing** -ɪŋ **-(l)ed** -d ˈ**pencil ˌcase**; ˈ**pencil ˌsharpener**
Pencoed penˈkɔɪd, peŋ- (US) pen-
pendant ˈpen.dənt **-s** -s
penden|cy ˈpen.dən|t.si **-t** -t
Pendennis penˈden.ɪs
pendente lite penˌden.tiˈlaɪ.ti
Pender ˈpen.dəʳ (US) -dɚ
Pendine penˈdaɪn
pending ˈpen.dɪŋ
Pendle ˈpen.dl̩
Pendlebury ˈpen.dl̩.bᵊr.i (US) -ˌber-, -bɚ-
Pendleton ˈpen.dl̩.tən
pendragon (P) penˈdræg.ən **-s** -z
pendulous ˈpen.djᵊl.əs, -dʒʊ.ləs, -dʒᵊl.əs (US) -dʒə.ləs, -djə-, -də-, -dʒʊ- **-ly** -li **-ness** -nəs, -nɪs
pendulum ˈpen.djᵊl.əm, -djʊ.ləm, -dʒᵊl.əm (US) -dʒə.ləm, -djə-, -də-, -dʒʊ- **-s** -z
Penelope pəˈnel.ə.pi, pɪ- (US) pə-
penetrability ˌpen.ɪ.trəˈbɪl.ə.ti, ˌ-ə-, -ɪ.ti (US) -ə.t̬i
penetrab|le ˈpen.ɪ.trə.b|l̩, ˈ-ə- **-ly** -li **-leness** -l̩.nəs, -nɪs
penetralia ˌpen.ɪˈtreɪ.li.ə, -əˈ-
pene|trate ˈpen.ɪ|.treɪt, ˈ-ə- **-trates** -treɪts **-trating/ly** -treɪ.tɪŋ/li (US) -treɪ.t̬ɪŋ/li **-trated** -treɪ.tɪd (US) -treɪ.t̬ɪd
penetration ˌpen.ɪˈtreɪ.ʃᵊn, -əˈ- **-s** -z
penetrative ˈpen.ɪ.trə.tɪv, ˈ-ə-, -treɪ- (US) -treɪ.t̬ɪv **-ly** -li **-ness** -nəs, -nɪs
Penfold ˈpen.fəʊld (US) -foʊld
penful ˈpen.fʊl **-s** -z
Penge pendʒ
penguin ˈpeŋ.gwɪn (US) ˈpeŋ-, ˈpen- **-s** -z
Penhaligon penˈhæl.ɪ.gᵊn
penholder ˈpenˌhəʊl.dəʳ (US) -ˌhoʊl.dɚ **-s** -z
penicillin ˌpen.ɪˈsɪl.ɪn, -əˈ-
penicillium ˌpen.ɪˈsɪl.i.əm, -əˈ-
Penicuik ˈpen.ɪ.kʊk
penile ˈpiː.naɪl (US) -naɪl, -nɪl
peninsul|a (P) pəˈnɪnt.sjə.l|ə, pɪ-, penˈɪnt-, -sjʊ-, -ʃə-, -ʃʊ- (US) pəˈnɪnt.sə-, -sjə-, -ˈnɪn.tʃə- **-as** -əz **-ar** -əʳ (US) -ɚ
penis ˈpiː.nɪs **-es** -ɪz ˈ**penis ˌenvy**
Penistone ˈpen.ɪ.stᵊn
penitence ˈpen.ɪ.tᵊnts, ˈ-ə-
penitent ˈpen.ɪ.tᵊnt, ˈ-ə- **-s** -s **-ly** -li
penitential ˌpen.ɪˈten.tʃᵊl, -əˈ- (US) -ʃᵊl **-ly** -i
penitentiar|y ˌpen.ɪˈten.tʃᵊr|.i, -əˈ- (US) -tʃə.ri: **-ies** -iz
penkni|fe ˈpen.naɪ|f **-ves** -vz
Penkridge ˈpeŋ.krɪdʒ
penlight ˈpen.laɪt **-s** -s
Penmaenmawr ˌpen.mənˈmaʊəʳ, -ˈmɔːʳ (US) -ˈmaʊɚ, -ˈmɔːr
pen|man ˈpen|.mən, ˈpem- (US) ˈpen- **-men** -mən
Penman ˈpen.mən, ˈpem- (US) ˈpen-
penmanship ˈpen.mən.ʃɪp, ˈpem- (US) ˈpen-
Penn pen
Penn. *(abbrev. for* **Pennsylvania**) pen, ˌpent.sɪlˈveɪ.ni.ə, -sᵊlˈ-, ˈ-njə (US) ˌpent.sᵊlˈveɪ.njə, ˈ-ni.ə, pen
Note: The form /pen/ is especially used when referring to university names.
pennant (P) ˈpen.ənt **-s** -s
penne ˈpen.eɪ, -i (US) -i, -eɪ
penn|i ˈpen|.i **-is** -ɪs **-ia** -i.ə
penniless ˈpen.i.ləs, -lɪs
Pennine ˈpen.aɪn **-s** -z
Pennington ˈpen.ɪŋ.tən
pennon ˈpen.ən **-s** -z
Pennsylvani|a ˌpent.sɪlˈveɪ.ni|.ə, -sᵊlˈ-njə (US) -sᵊlˈveɪ.nj|ə, ˈ-ni.ə **-an/s** -ən/z ˌ**Pennsylˌvania ˈDutch**
penn|y (P) ˈpen|.i **-ies** -iz **pence** pents ˌ**penny arˈcade**; ˌ**penny ˈblack**; ˌ**penny ˈdreadful**; ˌ**penny ˈfarthing**
Note: After decimalization of the currency in Britain, the pronunciation of compounds with **penny, pence** (now abbreviated to **p**) changed. Formerly, compounds from **1/2d** to **11d** invariably had /-pᵊn.i, -pᵊnts/, e.g. see entries under **half-penny,** fourpence**, etc.** With the extension of **-pence** compounds beyond **11p**, e.g. **12p**, the reduced forms have more or less disappeared. Instead, the full forms /ˈpen.i/ and /pents/, or commonly /piː/, are used, e.g. **4p** (/ˈfɔː.pᵊnts/) is /ˌfɔːˈpents/ or /-ˈpiː/; **12p** is /ˌtwelvˈpents/ or /-ˈpiː/.
penny-pinch|ing ˈpen.iˌpɪn.tʃ|ɪŋ **-er/s** -əʳ/z (US) -ɚ/z
pennyroyal ˌpen.iˈrɔɪəl (US) ˈpen.iˌrɔɪ.əl, ˌpen.iˈrɔɪ-
pennyweight ˈpen.i.weɪt **-s** -s
pennywort ˈpen.i.wɜːt (US) -wɝːt, -wɔːrt
pennyworth ˈpen.i.wəθ, -wɜːθ, ˈpen.əθ (US) ˈpen.i.wɚθ, -wɝːθ **-s** -s
Penobscot penˈɒb.skɒt, pəˈnɒb- (US) pəˈnɑːb.skɑːt, penˈɑːb-, -skət
penological ˌpiː.nəˈlɒdʒ.ɪ.kᵊl (US) -ˈlɑː.dʒɪ-
penolog|y piːˈnɒl.ə.dʒ|i, pɪ- (US) piːˈnɑː.lə- **-ist/s** -ɪst/s
Penrhyn penˈrɪn
Penrith *town in Cumbria:* penˈrɪθ, ˈ- *surname:* ˈpen.rɪθ
Penrose *surname:* ˈpen.rəʊz, -ˈ- (US) ˈpen.roʊz, -ˈ- *place in Cornwall:* penˈrəʊz (US) -ˈroʊz
Penryn penˈrɪn
Pensacola ˌpent.səˈkəʊ.lə (US) -ˈkoʊ-
Pensarn penˈsɑːn (US) -ˈsɑːrn
penseroso ˌpent.səˈrəʊ.zəʊ, -səʊ (US) -ˈroʊ.soʊ
Penshurst ˈpenz.hɜːst (US) -hɝːst
pension *(n. v.) monetary allowance:* ˈpen.tʃᵊn **-s** -z **-ing** -ɪŋ **-ed** -d
pension *(n.) boarding house, board:* ˈpɑ̃ːn.sjɔ̃ːŋ, -ˈ- (US) pɑ̃ːnˈsjõʊŋ, ˌpɑːnˈsjoʊn **-s** -z
pensionable ˈpen.tʃᵊn.ə.bl̩ (US) -ʃᵊn-
pensioner ˈpen.tʃᵊn.əʳ (US) -ʃᵊn.ɚ **-s**

pensive ˈpent.sɪv **-ly** -li **-ness** -nəs, -nɪs

penta- pen.tə-; penˈtæ- (US) pen.t̬ə-; penˈtæ-

Note: Prefix. Normally either takes primary or secondary stress on the first syllable, e.g. **pentagon** /ˈpen.tə.gᵊn (US) -t̬ə.gɑːn/, **pentatonic** /ˌpen.təˈtɒn.ɪk (US) -t̬əˈtɑː.nɪk/, or primary stress on the second syllable, e.g. **pentagonal** /penˈtæg.ᵊn.ᵊl/.

pentad ˈpen.tæd **-s** -z

pentagon (P) ˈpen.tə.gᵊn, -gɒn (US) -t̬ə.gɑːn **-s** -z

pentagonal penˈtæg.ᵊn.ᵊl **-ly** -i

pentagram ˈpen.tə.græm (US) -t̬ə- **-s** -z

pentahedr|on ˌpen.təˈhiː.dr|ən, -dr|ɒn (US) -t̬əˈhiː.dr|ən **-ons** -ənz, -ɒnz (US) -ənz **-a** -ə **-al** -ᵊl

pentameter penˈtæm.ɪ.təʳ, ˈ-ə- (US) -ə.t̬ɚ **-s** -z

pentangle ˈpen.tæŋ.gl̩ **-s** -z

Pentateuch ˈpen.tə.tjuːk (US) -t̬ə.tuːk, -tjuːk

pentathlete penˈtæθ.liːt **-s** -s

pentathlon penˈtæθ.lɒn, -lən (US) -lɑːn, -lən

pentatonic ˌpen.təˈtɒn.ɪk (US) -t̬əˈtɑː.nɪk *stress shift:* ˌpentatonic ˈscale

Pentax® ˈpen.tæks

Pentecost ˈpen.tɪ.kɒst, -tə- (US) -t̬ɪ.kɑːst **-s** -s

Pentecostal ˌpen.tɪˈkɒs.tᵊl, -təˈ- (US) -t̬ɪˈkɑː.stᵊl **-ism** -ɪ.zᵊm **-ist/s** -ɪst/s *stress shift:* ˌPentecostal ˈfeast

Pentel® ˈpen.tel

Penthesilea ˌpent.θes.ɪˈliː.ə, -θə.sɪˈ-, -səˈ-, -ˈleɪ- (US) -θə.səˈliː-

penthou|se (P) ˈpent.haʊ|s **-ses** -zɪz

pentiment|o ˌpen.tɪˈmen.t|əʊ (US) -t̬ɪˈmen.t|oʊ **-i** -iː

Pentium® ˈpen.ti.əm (US) -t̬i-

Pentland ˈpent.lənd **-s** -z

Pentonville ˈpen.tən.vɪl

Pentothal® ˈpen.tə.θæl, -θɔːl (US) -t̬ə.θɔːl, -θɑːl

pentstemon pentˈstem.ən, pen-, -ˈstiː.mən; ˈpent.stɪ.mən, -stə- (US) pentˈstiː-; ˈpent.stə-

pent-up ˌpentˈʌp *stress shift:* ˌpent-up ˈanger

pentyl ˈpen.taɪl, -tɪl (US) -tɪl, -t̬ᵊl

penult pəˈnʌlt, pɪ-, penˈʌlt (US) ˈpiː.nʌlt; pɪˈnʌlt **-s** -s

penultimate pəˈnʌl.tɪ.mət, pɪ-, penˈʌl-, -tə-, -mɪt (US) pɪˈnʌl.t̬ə.mət **-s** -s **-ly** -li

penumbr|a pəˈnʌm.br|ə, pɪ-, penˈʌm- (US) pɪˈnʌm- **-as** -əz **-ae** -iː **-al** -ᵊl

penurious pəˈnjʊə.ri.əs, pɪ-, penˈjʊə-, -ˈjɔː- (US) pəˈnʊr.i-, penˈʊr-, -ˈjʊr- **-ly** -li **-ness** -nəs, -nɪs

penury ˈpen.jə.ri, -jʊ- (US) -jʊ.ri, -jɚ.i

Pen-y-Ghent ˌpen.iˈgent

Penzance penˈzænts, pən- *locally:* pənˈzɑːnts (US) penˈzænts

peon *Indian servant:* pjuːn; ˈpiː.ən; peɪˈɒn (US) ˈpiː.ɑːn, ˈpeɪ-, -ən **-s** -z *in US:* ˈpiː.ən (US) -ɑːn, -ən **-s** -z

peon|y ˈpiː.ə.n|i **-ies** -iz

peopl|e ˈpiː.pl̩ **-es** -z **-ing** -ɪŋ, ˈpiːp.lɪŋ **-ed** -d

Peoria piːˈɔː.ri.ə (US) -ˈɔːr.i-

Peover ˈpiː.vəʳ (US) -vɚ

pep pep **-s** -s **-ping** -ɪŋ **-ped** -t ˈ**pep** ˌ**pill**; ˈ**pep** ˌ**talk**

PEP pep, ˌpiː.iːˈpiː

Pepin ˈpep.ɪn

peplum ˈpep.ləm **-s** -z

pepp|er (P) ˈpep|.əʳ (US) -ɚ **-ers** -əz (US) -ɚz **-ering** -ᵊr.ɪŋ **-ered** -əd (US) -ɚd ˈ**pepper** ˌ**pot**

pepperbox ˈpep.ə.bɒks (US) -ɚ.bɑːks **-es** -ɪz

peppercorn ˈpep.ə.kɔːn (US) -ɚ.kɔːrn **-s** -z

peppermint ˈpep.ə.mɪnt (US) -ɚ-, -mənt **-s** -s

pepperoni ˌpep.əˈrəʊ.ni (US) -ˈroʊ-

pepper|y ˈpep.ᵊr|.i **-iness** -ɪ.nəs, -ɪ.nɪs

pepp|y ˈpep|.i **-ier** -i.əʳ (US) -i.ɚ **-iest** -i.ɪst, -i.əst **-iness** -ɪ.nəs, -ɪ.nɪs **-ily** -ɪ.li, -ᵊl.i

Pepsi® ˈpep.si

Pepsi-Cola® ˌpep.siˈkəʊ.lə (US) -ˈkoʊ-

pepsin ˈpep.sɪn

Pepsodent® ˈpep.səʊ.dent, -sə.dᵊnt (US) -soʊ.dent, -sə-

peptic ˈpep.tɪk

Pepto-Bismol® ˌpep.təʊˈbɪz.mɒl (US) -toʊˈbɪz.mɑːl, -tə-

peptone ˈpep.təʊn (US) -toʊn **-s** -z

Pepys ˈpep.ɪs; piːps, peps

Note: The pronunciation in the family of the present Lord Cottenham is /ˈpep.ɪs/. Samuel Pepys is generally referred to as /piːps/.

per *strong form:* pɜːʳ (US) pɝː *weak form:* pəʳ (US) pɚ

Note: This word has a weak form /pəʳ (US) pɚ/, which is almost always used in the phrases **per cent**, **per annum**. It is also used in phrases such as **per capita**, **per centimetre**, **per head**, but the strong form /pɜːʳ (US) pɜːr/ is more usual.

peradventure pə.rədˈven.tʃəʳ, ˌpɜː.rədˈ-, ˌper.ədˈ- (US) ˌpɝː.ədˈven.tʃɚ, ˌper-

Perak ˈpeə.rə, ˈpɪə.rə; pəˈræk, pɪ-, perˈæk (US) ˈpeɪ.ræk, -rɑːk; ˈper.ə, ˈpɪr-

Note: English speakers who have lived in Malaysia pronounce /ˈpeə.rə (US) ˈper.ə/ or /ˈpɪə.rə (US) ˈpɪr.ə/.

perambu|late pəˈræm.bjə|.leɪt, -bjʊ- **-lates** -leɪts **-lating** -leɪ.tɪŋ (US) -leɪ.t̬ɪŋ **-lated** -leɪ.tɪd (US) -leɪ.t̬ɪd

perambulation pəˌræm.bjəˈleɪ.ʃᵊn, -bjʊˈ- **-s** -z

perambulator pəˈræm.bjə.leɪ.təʳ, -bjʊ- (US) -t̬ɚ **-s** -z

per annum pəʳˈæn.əm (US) pɚ-

percale pəˈkeɪl, -ˈkɑːl (US) pɚˈkeɪl

per capita pəˈkæp.ɪ.tə, ˌpɜː- (US) pɚˈkæp.ɪ.t̬ə

perceivab|le pəˈsiː.və.b|l̩, pɜː- (US) pɚ- **-ly** -li

perceiv|e pəˈsiːv (US) pɚ- **-es** -z **-ing** -ɪŋ **-ed** -d

percener ˈpɜː.sᵊn.əʳ (US) ˈpɝː.sᵊn.ɚ **-s** -z

per cent, percent pəˈsent (US) pɚ-

percentag|e pəˈsen.tɪdʒ (US) pɚˈsen.t̬ɪdʒ **-es** -ɪz

percentile pəˈsen.taɪl (US) pɚˈsen-, -t̬ᵊl **-s** -z

percept ˈpɜː.sept (US) ˈpɝː- **-s** -s

perceptibility pəˌsep.təˈbɪl.ə.ti, -tɪˈ-, -ɪ.ti (US) pɚˌsep.təˈbɪl.ə.t̬i

perceptib|le pəˈsep.tə.b|l̩, -tɪ- (US) pɚˈsep.tə- **-ly** -li **-leness** -l̩.nəs, -nɪs

perception pəˈsep.ʃᵊn (US) pɚ- **-s** -z

perceptive pəˈsep.tɪv (US) pɚ- **-ly** -li **-ness** -nəs, -nɪs

perceptual pəˈsep.tʃu.əl, -tju- (US) -tʃu-, pɚˈsep.tju- **-ly** -i

Perceval ˈpɜː.sɪ.vᵊl, -sə- (US) ˈpɝː-

perch pɜːtʃ (US) pɝːtʃ **-es** -ɪz **-ing** -ɪŋ **-ed** -t

perchance pəˈtʃɑːnts, ˌpɜː- (US) pɚˈtʃænts

Percheron ˈpɜː.ʃə.rɒn (US) ˈpɝː.tʃə.rɑːn **-s** -z

percipien|t pəˈsɪp.i.ən|t (US) pɚ- **-ce** -ts

Percival(e) ˈpɜː.sɪ.vᵊl, -sə- (US) ˈpɝː-

percol|ate ˈpɜː.kᵊl|.eɪt (US) ˈpɝː- **-ates** -eɪts **-ating** -eɪ.tɪŋ (US) -eɪ.t̬ɪŋ **-ated** -eɪ.tɪd (US) -eɪ.t̬ɪd

percolation ˌpɜː.kᵊlˈeɪ.ʃᵊn (US) ˌpɝː- **-s** -z

percolator ˈpɜː.kᵊl.eɪ.təʳ (US) ˈpɝː.kᵊl.eɪ.t̬ɚ **-s** -z

per contra ˌpɜːˈkɒn.trə (US) pɚˈkɑːn-

per curiam ˌpɜːˈkjʊə.ri.æm, -ˈkjɔː- (US) pɚˈkjʊr.i-

percuss pəˈkʌs, pɜː- (US) pɚ- **-es** -ɪz **-ing** -ɪŋ **-ed** -t

percussion pəˈkʌʃ.ᵊn, pɜː- (US) pɚ- **-s** -z **-ist/s** -ɪst/s

percussive pəˈkʌs.ɪv, pɜː- (US) pɚ-

percutaneous ˌpɜː.kjuːˈteɪ.ni.əs, -kjʊˈ- (US) ˌpɝː.kjuːˈ- **-ly** -li

Percy ˈpɜː.si (US) ˈpɝː-

per diem ˌpɜː'diː.em, -'daɪ- ⓤⓢ ˌpɝː-
Perdita 'pɜː.dɪ.tə ⓤⓢ 'pɝː.dɪ.t̬ə; pɚ'diː-
perdition pə'dɪʃ.ən, pɜː- ⓤⓢ pɚ-
perdu(e) 'pɜː.djuː ⓤⓢ pɚ'duː, -'djuː
père, pere peər ⓤⓢ per
peregrin 'per.ɪ.grɪn, '-ə- **-s** -z
peregri|nate 'per.ɪ.grɪ|.neɪt, '-ə-, -grə- ⓤⓢ -ə.grɪ- **-nates** -neɪts **-nating** -neɪ.tɪŋ ⓤⓢ -neɪ.t̬ɪŋ **-nated** -neɪ.tɪd ⓤⓢ -neɪ.t̬ɪd
peregrination ˌper.ɪ.grɪ'neɪ.ʃən, ˌ-ə-, -grə'- ⓤⓢ -ə.grɪ'- **-s** -z
peregrine (P) (*n. adj.*) 'per.ɪ.grɪn, '-ə-, -griːn ⓤⓢ -grɪn, -griːn, -graɪn **-s** -z **ˌperegrine 'falcon**
Perelman 'per.əl.mən, 'pɜːl- ⓤⓢ 'pɝːl-
peremptor|y pə'remp.tər|.i, pɪ-; 'per.əmp- ⓤⓢ pə'remp- **-ily** -əl.i, -ɪ.li **-iness** -ɪ.nəs, -ɪ.nɪs
Note: /'per.əmp-/ is more usual in British English when the word is used as a legal term. Otherwise /pə'remp-/ and /pɪ-/ are commoner.
perennial pər'en.i.əl, pɪ'ren- ⓤⓢ pə'ren- **-s** -z **-ly** -i
Peres 'per.ez
perestroika ˌper.ə'strɔɪ.kə, -ɪ'-
Perez 'per.es ⓤⓢ 'per.ez, -es, -əz, -əs
Pérez de Cuéllar ˌper.es.də'kweɪ.jɑː ⓤⓢ ˌper.ez.deɪ'kweɪ.jɑːr, ˌ-əz-, ˌ-es-
perfec|t (*n. adj.*) 'pɜː.fɪk|t ⓤⓢ 'pɝː- **-ts** -ts **-tly** -t.li **-tness** -t.nəs, -nɪs **ˌperfect 'pitch; ˌperfect 'tense**
perfect (*v.*) pə'fekt, pɜː- ⓤⓢ pɝː-, pɚ- **-s** -s **-ing** -ɪŋ **-ed** -ɪd
perfectibility pəˌfek.tɪ'bɪl.ə.ti, pɜː-, -tə'-, -ɪ.ti ⓤⓢ pɚˌfek.tə'bɪl.ə.t̬i
perfectible pə'fek.tə.bəl, pɜː-, -tɪ- ⓤⓢ pɚ-
perfection pə'fek.ʃən ⓤⓢ pɚ- **-s** -z **-ist/s** -ɪst/s **-ism** -ɪ.zəm
perfective pə'fek.tɪv ⓤⓢ pɚ- **-ly** -li **-ness** -nəs, -nɪs
perfervid pɜː'fɜː.vɪd, pə- ⓤⓢ pɚ'fɝː-
perfidious pə'fɪd.i.əs, pɜː- ⓤⓢ pɚ- **-ly** -li **-ness** -nəs, -nɪs
perfid|y 'pɜː.fɪ.d|i, -fə- ⓤⓢ 'pɝː.fə- **-ies** -iz
perforable 'pɜː.fər.ə.bl̩ ⓤⓢ 'pɝː-
perforate (*adj.*) 'pɜː.fər.ɪt, -ət, -eɪt ⓤⓢ 'pɝː.fɚ.ɪt, -fə.reɪt
perfor|ate (*v.*) 'pɜː.fər|.eɪt ⓤⓢ 'pɝː.fə.r|eɪt **-ates** -eɪts **-ating** -eɪ.tɪŋ ⓤⓢ -eɪ.t̬ɪŋ **-ated** -eɪ.tɪd ⓤⓢ -eɪ.t̬ɪd **-ator/s** -eɪ.tər/z ⓤⓢ -eɪ.t̬ɚ/z
perforation ˌpɜː.fər'eɪ.ʃən ⓤⓢ ˌpɝː.fə'reɪ- **-s** -z
perforce pə'fɔːs, pɜː- ⓤⓢ pɚ'fɔːrs
perform pə'fɔːm ⓤⓢ pɚ'fɔːrm **-s** -z **-ing** -ɪŋ **-ed** -d **-er/s** -ər/z ⓤⓢ -ɚ/z **-able** -ə.bl̩
performanc|e pə'fɔː.mənts ⓤⓢ pɚ'fɔːr- **-es** -ɪz **per'formance ˌart, perˌformance 'art; perˌformance re'lated; perˌformance reˌlated 'pay**
performative pə'fɔː.mə.tɪv ⓤⓢ pɚ'fɔːr.mə.t̬ɪv **-s** -z
perfume (*n.*) 'pɜː.fjuːm ⓤⓢ 'pɝː-, -'- **-s** -z
perfum|e (*v.*) pə'fjuːm, pɜː-; 'pɜː.fjuːm ⓤⓢ pɚ'fjuːm **-es** -z **-ing** -ɪŋ **-ed** -d
perfumed 'pɜː.fjuːmd ⓤⓢ pɚ'fjuːmd
perfum|er pə'fjuː.m|ər, pɜː- ⓤⓢ pɚ'fjuː.m|ɚ **-ers** -əz ⓤⓢ -ɚz **-ery** -ər.i
perfunctor|y pə'fʌŋk.tər|.i, pɜː- ⓤⓢ pɚ- **-ily** -əl.i, -ɪ.li **-iness** -ɪ.nəs, -ɪ.nɪs
Pergam|um 'pɜː.gə.m|əm ⓤⓢ 'pɝː- **-us** -əs
pergola 'pɜː.gəl.ə ⓤⓢ 'pɝː- **-s** -z
Pergolese ˌpɜː.gəʊ'leɪ.zi, ˌpeə-, -zeɪ ⓤⓢ ˌper.goʊ'leɪ.zi, -si
Perham 'per.əm
perhaps pə'hæps; præps ⓤⓢ pɚ'hæps, -'æps
Note: In British English, /pə'hæps/ is more usual in formal speech, and colloquially when the word is said in isolation or used parenthetically (as in **You know, perhaps, ...**). /præps/ is common in other situations, especially initially (e.g. in **Perhaps we shall, perhaps it is a mistake**).
peri- per.ɪ-, -i-; pə'rɪ-, per'ɪ-
Note: Prefix. Normally either takes primary or secondary stress on the first syllable, e.g. **periscope** /'per.ɪ.skəʊp ⓤⓢ -skoʊp/, **periscopic** /ˌper.ɪ'skɒp.ɪk ⓤⓢ -'skɑː.pɪk/, or primary stress on the second syllable, e.g. **peripheral** /pə'rɪf.ər.əl/.
peri 'pɪə.ri ⓤⓢ 'piː-, 'pɪr.i **-s** -z
perianth 'per.i.æntθ **-s** -s
pericarditis ˌper.ɪ.kɑː'daɪ.tɪs ⓤⓢ -kɑːr'daɪ.t̬ɪs
pericardi|um ˌper.ɪ'kɑː.di|.əm ⓤⓢ -'kɑːr- **-a** -ə
pericarp 'per.ɪ.kɑːp, '-ə- ⓤⓢ -ɪ.kɑːrp **-s** -s
Pericles 'per.ɪ.kliːz, '-ə- ⓤⓢ -ɪ.kliːz
peridot 'per.ɪ.dɒt ⓤⓢ -dɑːt **-s** -s
perigee 'per.ɪ.dʒiː, '-ə- ⓤⓢ '-ɪ- **-s** -z
periheli|on ˌper.ɪ'hiː.li|.ən ⓤⓢ -'hiː.li.ən, -'hiːl.jən **-a** -ə
peril 'per.əl, -ɪl ⓤⓢ -əl **-s** -z
perilous 'per.əl.əs, -ɪ.ləs ⓤⓢ -əl.əs **-ly** -li **-ness** -nəs, -nɪs
perilune 'per.ɪ.luːn, -ljuːn ⓤⓢ -luːn **-s** -z
Perim 'per.ɪm ⓤⓢ pə'rɪm
perimeter pə'rɪm.ɪ.tər, pɪ-, per'ɪm-, '-ə- ⓤⓢ pə'rɪm.ə.t̬ɚ **-s** -z
perinatal ˌper.ɪ'neɪ.təl ⓤⓢ -t̬əl
perine|um ˌper.ɪ'niː|.əm **-a** -ə **-al** -əl
period 'pɪə.ri.əd ⓤⓢ 'pɪr.i- **-s** -z **'period ˌpiece**
periodic ˌpɪə.ri'ɒd.ɪk ⓤⓢ ˌpɪr.i'ɑː.dɪk *stress shift, see compound:* **ˌperiodic 'table**
periodic|al ˌpɪə.ri'ɒd.ɪ.k|əl ⓤⓢ ˌpɪr.i'ɑː.dɪ- **-als** -əlz **-ally** -əl.i, -li
periodicit|y ˌpɪə.ri.ə'dɪs.ə.t|i, -ɒd'ɪs-, -ɪ.t|i ⓤⓢ ˌpɪr.i.oʊ'dɪs.ə.t̬|i, -ə'- **-ies** -iz
periodontal ˌper.i.əʊ'dɒn.təl ⓤⓢ -oʊ'dɑːn.t̬əl, -ə'- **-ly** -i
periodont|ic ˌper.i.əʊ'dɒn.t|ɪk ⓤⓢ -oʊ'dɑːn.t̬|ɪk, -ə'- **-ics** -ɪks **-ist/s** -ɪst/s
peripatetic ˌper.ɪ.pə'tet.ɪk, ˌ-ə- ⓤⓢ -'tet̬- **-ally** -əl.i, -li *stress shift:* ˌperipatetic 'teacher
peripheral pə'rɪf.ər.əl, pɪ-, per'ɪf- ⓤⓢ pə'rɪf- **-s** -z **-ly** -i
peripher|y pə'rɪf.ər|.i, pɪ-, per'ɪf- ⓤⓢ pə'rɪf- **-ies** -iz
periphras|is pə'rɪf.rə.s|ɪs, pɪ-, per'ɪf- ⓤⓢ pə'rɪf **-es** -iːz
periphrastic ˌper.ɪ'fræs.tɪk, -ə'- **-ally** -əl.i, -li
periscope 'per.ɪ.skəʊp, '-ə- ⓤⓢ -ɪ.skoʊp **-s** -s
periscopic ˌper.ɪ'skɒp.ɪk, -ə'- ⓤⓢ -ɪ'skɑː.pɪk
perish 'per.ɪʃ **-es** -ɪz **-ing/ly** -ɪŋ/li **-ed** -t **-er/s** -ər/z ⓤⓢ -ɚ/z
perishability ˌper.ɪ.ʃə'bɪl.ə.ti, -ɪ.ti ⓤⓢ -ə.t̬i
perishab|le 'per.ɪ.ʃə.bl̩ **-ly** -li **-leness** -l̩.nəs, -nɪs
perispomenon ˌper.ɪ'spəʊ.mɪ.nən, -mə-, -nɒn ⓤⓢ -'spoʊ.mɪ.nɑːn
peristalsis ˌper.ɪ'stæl.sɪs, -ə'- ⓤⓢ -ɪ'stɑːl-, -'stæl-
peristaltic ˌper.ɪ'stæl.tɪk, -ə'- ⓤⓢ -ɪ'stɑːl.t̬ɪk, -'stæl-
peristyle 'per.ɪ.staɪl, '-ə- ⓤⓢ '-ɪ- **-s** -z
peritone|um ˌper.ɪ.təʊ'niː|.əm, ˌ-ə- ⓤⓢ -'toʊ.ni-, -tə- **-ums** -əmz **-a** -ə
peritonitis ˌper.ɪ.təʊ'naɪ.tɪs, ˌ-ə- ⓤⓢ -ɪ.toʊ'naɪ.t̬ɪs
Perivale 'per.ɪ.veɪl, '-ə- ⓤⓢ '-ɪ-
periwig 'per.ɪ.wɪg, '-ə- ⓤⓢ '-ɪ- **-s** -z
periwinkle 'per.ɪˌwɪŋ.kl̩, '-ə- ⓤⓢ -ɪˌ- **-s** -z
perj|ure 'pɜː.dʒ|ər ⓤⓢ 'pɝː.dʒ|ɚ **-ures** -əz ⓤⓢ -ɚz **-uring** -ər.ɪŋ **-ured** -əd ⓤⓢ -ɚd **-urer/s** -ər.ər/z ⓤⓢ -ɚ.ɚ/z
perjur|y 'pɜː.dʒər|.i ⓤⓢ 'pɝː- **-ies** -iz
perk pɜːk ⓤⓢ pɝːk **-s** -s **-ing** -ɪŋ **-ed** -t
Perkin 'pɜː.kɪn ⓤⓢ 'pɝː- **-s** -z
Perks pɜːks ⓤⓢ pɝːks
perk|y 'pɜː.k|i ⓤⓢ 'pɝː- **-ier** -i.ər ⓤⓢ -i.ɚ **-iest** -i.ɪst, -i.əst **-ily** -ɪ.li, -əl.i **-iness** -ɪ.nəs, -ɪ.nɪs

Perlis ˈpɜː.lɪs (US) ˈpɝː-

perlite ˈpɜː.laɪt (US) ˈpɝː-

Perlman ˈpɜːl.mən (US) ˈpɝːl-

perlocutionary ˌpɜː.ləˈkjuː.ʃᵊn.ᵊr.i, -lɒkˈjuː- (US) ˌpɝː.loʊˈkjuː-

perm pɜːm (US) pɝːm **-s** -z **-ing** -ɪŋ **-ed** -d

Perm *city in Eastern Europe:* pɜːm, peəm (US) perm

permafrost ˈpɜː.mə.frɒst (US) ˈpɝː.mə.frɑːst

permanenc|e ˈpɜː.mᵊn.ənts (US) ˈpɝː- **-es** -ɪz **-y** -i **-ies** -iz

permanent ˈpɜː.mᵊn.ənt (US) ˈpɝː- **-ly** -li

permanganate pɜːˈmæŋ.gə.neɪt, pə-, -nɪt, -nət (US) pɚˈmæŋ.gə.neɪt

permeability ˌpɜː.mi.əˈbɪl.ə.ti, -ɪ.ti (US) ˌpɝː.mi.əˈbɪl.ə.t̬i

permeab|le ˈpɜː.mi.ə.bl̩ (US) ˈpɝː- **-ly** -li **-leness** -l̩.nəs, -nɪs

perme|ate ˈpɜː.mi|.eɪt (US) ˈpɝː- **-ates** -eɪts **-ating** -eɪ.tɪŋ (US) -eɪ.t̬ɪŋ **-ated** -eɪ.tɪd (US) -eɪ.t̬ɪd

permeation ˌpɜː.miˈeɪ.ʃᵊn (US) ˌpɝː-

permissib|le pəˈmɪs.ə.bl̩, ˈ-ɪ- (US) pɚˈmɪs.ə- **-ly** -li **-leness** -l̩.nəs, -nɪs

permission pəˈmɪʃ.ᵊn (US) pɚ- **-s** -z

permissive pəˈmɪs.ɪv (US) pɚ- **-ly** -li **-ness** -nəs, -nɪs **perˌmissive soˈciety**

permit (*n.*) ˈpɜː.mɪt (US) ˈpɝː-; pɚˈmɪt **-s** -s

per|mit (*v.*) pə|ˈmɪt (US) pɚ- **-mits** -ˈmɪts **-mitting** -ˈmɪt.ɪŋ (US) -ˈmɪt̬.ɪŋ **-mitted** -ˈmɪt.ɪd (US) -ˈmɪt̬.ɪd

permutation ˌpɜː.mjʊˈteɪ.ʃᵊn, -mjuːˈ-, -mjəˈ- (US) ˌpɝː.mjuːˈ- **-s** -z

per|mute pə|ˈmjuːt (US) pɚ- **-mutes** -ˈmjuːts **-muting** -ˈmjuː.tɪŋ (US) -ˈmjuː.t̬ɪŋ **-muted** -ˈmjuː.tɪd (US) -ˈmjuː.t̬ɪd **-mutable** -ˈmjuː.tə.bl̩ (US) -ˈmjuː.t̬ə.bl̩

Pernambuco ˌpɜː.næmˈbuː.kəʊ, -nəmˈ-, -ˈbjuː- (US) ˌpɝː.nəmˈbuː.koʊ

pernicious pəˈnɪʃ.əs, pɜː- (US) pɚ- **-ly** -li **-ness** -nəs, -nɪs

pernicket|y pəˈnɪk.ə.t|i, -ɪ.t|i (US) pɚˈnɪk.ə.t̬|i **-iness** -ɪ.nəs, -ɪ.nɪs

Pernod® ˈpɜː.nəʊ, ˈpeə- (US) perˈnoʊ

Perón, **Peron** pəˈrɒn, perˈɒn, pɪˈrɒn (US) perˈoʊn, pəˈroʊn

peror|ate ˈper.ᵊr|.eɪt, -ɒr- (US) -ə.r|eɪt, -oʊ- **-ates** -eɪts **-ating** -eɪ.tɪŋ (US) -eɪ.t̬ɪŋ **-ated** -eɪ.tɪd (US) -eɪ.t̬ɪd

peroration ˌper.ᵊrˈeɪ.ʃᵊn, -ɒrˈ- (US) ˌper.əˈreɪ-, -oʊˈ- **-s** -z

Perot pəˈrəʊ, perˈəʊ (US) pəˈroʊ

Perowne pəˈrəʊn, pɪ-, perˈəʊn (US) pəˈroʊn

peroxide pəˈrɒk.saɪd (US) pəˈrɑːk- **-s** -z

perpend (*v.*) pəˈpend, pɜː- (US) pɚ- **-s** -z **-ing** -ɪŋ **-ed** -ɪd

perpend (*n.*) ˈpɜː.pənd (US) ˈpɝː- **-s** -z

perpendicular ˌpɜː.pᵊnˈdɪk.jʊ.ləʳ, -kjə- (US) ˌpɝː.pənˈdɪk.juː.lɚ, -jə- **-s** -z **-ly** -li

perpendicularity ˌpɜː.pᵊnˌdɪk.jəˈlær.ə.ti, -jʊˈ-, -ɪ.ti (US) ˌpɝː.pənˌdɪk.juːˈler.ə.t̬i, -jəˈ-, -ˈlær-

perpe|trate ˈpɜː.pɪ|.treɪt, -pə- (US) ˈpɝː.pə|.treɪt **-trates** -treɪts **-trating** -treɪ.tɪŋ (US) -treɪ.t̬ɪŋ **-trated** -treɪ.tɪd (US) -treɪ.t̬ɪd **-trator/s** -treɪ.təʳ/z (US) -treɪ.t̬ɚ/z

perpetration ˌpɜː.pɪˈtreɪ.ʃᵊn, -pəˈ- (US) ˌpɝː.pəˈ- **-s** -z

perpetual pəˈpetʃ.u.əl, -ˈpet.ju- (US) pɚˈpetʃ.u- **-ly** -i

perpetu|ate pəˈpetʃ.u|.eɪt, pɜː-, -ˈpet.ju- (US) pɚˈpetʃ.u- **-ates** -eɪts **-ating** -eɪ.tɪŋ (US) -eɪ.t̬ɪŋ **-ated** -eɪ.tɪd (US) -eɪ.t̬ɪd

perpetuation pəˌpetʃ.uˈeɪ.ʃᵊn, pɜː-, -ˌpet.juˈ- (US) ˌpɚ.petʃ.uˈ- **-s** -z

perpetuit|y ˌpɜː.pɪˈtjuː.ə.t|i, -pəˈ-, -ɪ.t|i (US) ˌpɝː.pəˈtuː.ə.t̬|i, -ˈtjuː- **-ies** -iz

perpetuum mobile pəˌpetʃ.u.ʊmˈməʊ.bɪ.leɪ, pɜː-, -ˌpet.ju-, -əmˈ- (US) pɚˌpetʃ.ə.wəmˈmoʊ-

Perpignan ˈpɜː.piː.njɑ̃ŋ, ˈpeə-, ˌ--ˈ- (US) ˌper.piːˈnjɑ̃ːŋ

perplex pəˈpleks (US) pɚ- **-es** -ɪz **-ing/ly** -ɪŋ/li **-ed** -t **-edly** -ɪd.li, -t.li **-edness** -ɪd.nəs, -t.nəs, -nɪs

perplexit|y pəˈplek.sə.t|i, -ɪ.t|i (US) pɚˈplek.sə.t̬|i **-ies** -iz

perquisite ˈpɜː.kwɪ.zɪt, -kwə- (US) ˈpɝː.kwɪ- **-s** -s

per quod ˌpɜːˈkwɒd (US) ˌpɝːˈkwɑːd

Perrault ˈper.əʊ, -ˈ- (US) perˈoʊ

Perrett ˈper.ɪt

Perrier® ˈper.i.eɪ (US) -eɪ, ˌ--ˈ-

perrin **(P)** ˈper.ɪn

perr|y **(P)** ˈper|.i **-ies** -iz

Perse pɜːs (US) pɝːs

per se ˌpɜːˈseɪ (US) ˌpɝː-

perse|cute ˈpɜː.sɪ|.kjuːt, -sə- (US) ˈpɝː.sɪ- **-cutes** -kjuːts **-cuting** -kjuː.tɪŋ (US) -kjuː.t̬ɪŋ **-cuted** -kjuː.tɪd (US) -kjuː.t̬ɪd **-cutor/s** -kjuː.təʳ/z (US) -kjuː.t̬ɚ/z

persecution ˌpɜː.sɪˈkjuː.ʃᵊn, -səˈ- (US) ˌpɝː.sɪˈ- **-s** -z

Persephone pɜːˈsef.ᵊn.i, pə- (US) pɚ-

Persepolis pɜːˈsep.ᵊl.ɪs, pə- (US) pɚ-

Perseus ˈpɜː.si.əs, ˈ-sjuːs (US) ˈpɝː-

persever|ate pəˈsev.ᵊr|.eɪt, pɜː- (US) pɚˈsev.ə.r|eɪt **-ates** -eɪts **-ating** -eɪ.tɪŋ (US) -eɪ.t̬ɪŋ **-ated** -eɪ.tɪd (US) -eɪ.t̬ɪd

perseveration pəˌsev.ᵊrˈeɪ.ʃᵊn, pɜː- (US) pɚˌsev.əˈreɪ-

persever|e ˌpɜː.sɪˈvɪəʳ, -səˈ- (US) ˌpɝː.səˈvɪr **-es** -z **-ing/ly** -ɪŋ/li **-ed** -d **-ance** -ᵊnts

Pershing ˈpɜː.ʃɪŋ (US) ˈpɝː-

Pershore ˈpɜː.ʃɔːʳ (US) ˈpɝː.ʃɔːr

Persi|a ˈpɜː.ʒ|ə, -ʃ|ə (US) ˈpɝː.ʒ|ə, -ʃ|ə **-an/s** -ən/z

persiflage ˈpɜː.sɪ.flɑːʒ, ˈpeə-, -sə-, ˌ--ˈ- (US) ˈpɝː.sɪ-

Persil® ˈpɜː.sɪl, -sᵊl (US) ˈpɝː-

persimmon **(P)** pəˈsɪm.ən, pɜː- (US) pɚ- **-s** -z

persist pəˈsɪst (US) pɚ- **-s** -s **-ing/ly** -ɪŋ/li **-ed** -ɪd

persisten|ce pəˈsɪs.tᵊnt|s (US) pɚ- **-cy** -si

persistent pəˈsɪs.tᵊnt (US) pɚ- **-ly** -li

persnickety pəˈsnɪk.ə.ti, -ɪ.ti (US) pɚˈsnɪk.ə.t̬i

person ˈpɜː.sᵊn (US) ˈpɝː- **-s** -z

person|a pəˈsəʊ.n|ə, pɜː- (US) pɚˈsoʊ- **-ae** -iː, -aɪ

personable ˈpɜː.sᵊn.ə.bl̩ (US) ˈpɝː-

personag|e ˈpɜː.sᵊn.ɪdʒ (US) ˈpɝː- **-es** -ɪz

personal ˈpɜː.sᵊn.ᵊl, ˈpɜːs.nᵊl (US) ˈpɝː.sᵊn.ᵊl, ˈpɝːs.nᵊl **-ly** -i **ˌpersonal asˈsistant; ˈpersonal ˌcolumn; ˌpersonal comˈputer; ˌpersonal ˈhygiene; ˌpersonal ˈstereo**

personalit|y ˌpɜː.sᵊnˈæl.ə.t|i, -ɪ.t|i (US) ˌpɝː.sᵊnˈæl.ə.t̬i **-ies** -iz

personalization, **-isa-** ˌpɜː.sᵊn.ᵊl.aɪˈzeɪ.ʃᵊn, -ɪˈ- (US) ˌpɝː.sᵊn.ᵊlˈɪ-

personaliz|e, **is|e** ˈpɜː.sᵊn.ᵊl.aɪz (US) ˈpɝː- **-es** -ɪz **-ing** -ɪŋ **-ed** -d

personalt|y ˈpɜː.sᵊn.ᵊl.t|i (US) ˈpɝː.sᵊn.ᵊl.t̬|i **-ies** -iz

persona non grata pəˌsəʊ.nə.nɒnˈgrɑː.tə, pɜː-, -nəʊnˈ- (US) pɚˌsoʊ.nə.nɑːnˈgrɑː.t̬ə, -ˈgræt̬.ə

person|ate ˈpɜː.sᵊn|.eɪt (US) ˈpɝː- **-ates** -eɪts **-ating** -eɪ.tɪŋ (US) -eɪ.t̬ɪŋ **-ated** -eɪ.tɪd (US) -eɪ.t̬ɪd **-ator/s** -eɪ.təʳ/z (US) -eɪ.t̬ɚ/z

personation ˌpɜː.sᵊnˈeɪ.ʃᵊn (US) ˌpɝː- **-s** -s

personification pəˌsɒn.ɪ.fɪˈkeɪ.ʃᵊn, pɜː-, ˌ-ə- (US) pɚˌsɑː.nɪ- **-s** -z

personi|fy pəˈsɒn.ɪ|.faɪ, pɜː-, ˈ-ə- (US) pɚˈsɑː.nɪ- **-fies** -faɪz **-fying** -faɪ.ɪŋ **-fied** -faɪd

personnel ˌpɜː.sᵊnˈel (US) ˌpɝː- **-s** -z **personˈnel ˌmanager**

perspective pəˈspek.tɪv, pɜː- (US) pɚ- **-s** -z **-ly** -li

Perspex® ˈpɜː.speks (US) ˈpɝː-

perspicacious ˌpɜː.spɪˈkeɪ.ʃəs, -spəˈ- (US) ˌpɝː.spɪˈ- **-ly** -li **-ness** -nəs, -nɪs

perspicacity ˌpɜː.spɪˈkæs.ə.ti, -spəˈ-, -ɪ.ti (US) ˌpɝː.spɪˈkæs.ə.t̬i

perspicuity ˌpɜː.spɪˈkjuː.ə.ti, -ɪ.ti (US) ˌpɝː.spɪˈkjuː.ə.t̬i

perspicuous pə'spɪk.ju.əs, pɜː- ⓊⓈ pɚ- **-ly** -li **-ness** -nəs, -nɪs
perspiration ˌpɜː.spᵊr'eɪ.ʃᵊn ⓊⓈ ˌpɝː.spə'reɪ-
perspir|e pə'spaɪəʳ ⓊⓈ pɚ'spaɪɚ **-es** -z **-ing** -ɪŋ **-ed** -d
per stirpes ˌpɜː'stɜː.piːz ⓊⓈ pɚ'stɝː-
persuad|e pə'sweɪd ⓊⓈ pɚ- **-es** -z **-ing** -ɪŋ **-ed** -ɪd **-er/s** -əʳ/z ⓊⓈ -ɚ/z
persuasion pə'sweɪ.ʒᵊn ⓊⓈ pɚ- **-s** -z
persuasive pə'sweɪ.sɪv, -zɪv ⓊⓈ pɚ'sweɪ.sɪv **-ly** -li **-ness** -nəs, -nɪs
pert pɜːt ⓊⓈ pɝːt **-er** -əʳ ⓊⓈ 'pɝː.t̬ɚ **-est** -ɪst, -əst ⓊⓈ 'pɝː.t̬ɪst, -t̬əst **-ly** -li **-ness** -nəs, -nɪs
pertain pə'teɪn, pɜː- ⓊⓈ pɚ- **-s** -z **-ing** -ɪŋ **-ed** -d
Perth pɜːθ ⓊⓈ pɝːθ **-shire** -ʃəʳ, -ˌʃɪəʳ ⓊⓈ -ʃɚ, -ˌʃɪr
pertinacious ˌpɜː.tɪ'neɪ.ʃəs, -tə'- ⓊⓈ ˌpɝː.tᵊn'eɪ- **-ly** -li **-ness** -nəs, -nɪs
pertinacity ˌpɜː.tɪ'næs.ə.ti, -tə'-, -ɪ.ti ⓊⓈ ˌpɝː.tᵊn'æs.ə.t̬i
pertinen|ce 'pɜː.tɪ.nənt|s, -tə- ⓊⓈ 'pɝː.tᵊn.ᵊnt|s **-cy** -si
pertinent 'pɜː.tɪ.nənt, -tə- ⓊⓈ 'pɝː.tᵊn.ᵊnt **-ly** -li
perturb pə'tɜːb, pɜː- ⓊⓈ pɚ'tɝːb **-s** -z **-ing** -ɪŋ **-ed** -d **-er/s** -əʳ/z **-able** -ə.bl̩
perturbation ˌpɜː.tə'beɪ.ʃᵊn, -tɜː'- ⓊⓈ ˌpɝː.t̬ɚ'- **-s** -z
pertussis pə'tʌs.ɪs, pɜː- ⓊⓈ pɚ-
Pertwee 'pɜː.twiː ⓊⓈ 'pɝː-
Peru pə'ruː, pɪ- ⓊⓈ pə-
Perugia pə'ruː.dʒə, pɪ-, per'uː-, -dʒi.ə ⓊⓈ per'uː.dʒɑː, -dʒi.ə
Perugino ˌper.u'dʒiː.nəʊ ⓊⓈ -noʊ
peruke pə'ruːk, pɪ-, per'uːk ⓊⓈ pə'ruːk **-s** -s
perusal pə'ruː.zᵊl, pɪ- ⓊⓈ pə'ruː- **-s** -z
perus|e pə'ruːz, pɪ- ⓊⓈ pə'ruːz **-es** -ɪz **-ing** -ɪŋ **-ed** -d **-er/s** -əʳ/z ⓊⓈ -ɚ/z
Peruvian pə'ruː.vi.ən, pɪ-, per'uː- ⓊⓈ pə'ruː- **-s** -z
pervad|e pə'veɪd, pɜː- ⓊⓈ pɚ- **-es** -z **-ing** -ɪŋ **-ed** -ɪd
pervasion pə'veɪ.ʒᵊn, pɜː- ⓊⓈ pɚ-
pervasive pə'veɪ.sɪv, pɜː-, -zɪv ⓊⓈ pɚ'veɪ.sɪv **-ly** -li **-ness** -nəs, -nɪs
perverse pə'vɜːs, pɜː- ⓊⓈ pɚ'vɝːs **-ly** -li **-ness** -nəs, -nɪs
perversion pə'vɜː.ʃᵊn, pɜː-, -ʒᵊn ⓊⓈ pɚ'vɝː.ʒᵊn, -ʃᵊn **-s** -z
perversit|y pə'vɜː.sə.t|i, pɜː-, -ɪ.t|i ⓊⓈ pɚ'vɝː.sə.t̬|i **-ies** -iz
pervert *(n.)* 'pɜː.vɜːt ⓊⓈ 'pɝː.vɝːt **-s** -s
per|vert *(v.)* pə|'vɜːt, pɜː- ⓊⓈ pɚ|'vɝːt **-verts** -'vɜːts ⓊⓈ -'vɝːts **-verting** -'vɜː.tɪŋ ⓊⓈ -'vɝː.t̬ɪŋ **-verted** -'vɜː.tɪd ⓊⓈ -'vɝː.t̬ɪd **-verter/s** -'vɜː.təʳ/z ⓊⓈ -'vɝː.t̬ɚ/z
pervious 'pɜː.vi.əs ⓊⓈ 'pɝː- **-ly** -li **-ness** -nəs, -nɪs
pesante pez'æn.teɪ ⓊⓈ pes'ɑːn-
Pescadores ˌpes.kə'dɔː.rɪz ⓊⓈ -'dɔːr.iːz, -ɪs
peseta pə'seɪ.tə, pɪ-, pes'eɪ- ⓊⓈ pə'seɪ.t̬ə **-s** -z
pesewa pɪ'seɪ.wɑː ⓊⓈ 'pes.ə.wɑː; peɪ'seɪ- **-s** -z
Peshawar pə'ʃɔː.əʳ, peʃ'ɔː-, -'ɑː-, -wə ⓊⓈ peʃ'ɑː.wɚ, pə'ʃɑː-
peshwari peʃ'wɑː.ri
pesk|y 'pes.k|i **-ier** -i.əʳ ⓊⓈ -i.ɚ **-iest** -i.ɪst, -i.əst **-ily** -ɪ.li, -ᵊl.i **-iness** -ɪ.nəs, -ɪ.nɪs
peso 'peɪ.səʊ ⓊⓈ -soʊ **-s** -z
pessar|y 'pes.ᵊr|.i **-ies** -iz
pessim|ism 'pes.ɪ.m|ɪ.zᵊm, '-ə- ⓊⓈ '-ə- **-ist/s** -ɪst/s
pessimistic ˌpes.ɪ'mɪs.tɪk, -ə'- ⓊⓈ -ə'- **-al** -ᵊl **-ally** -ᵊl.i, -li
pest (P) pest **-s** -s
Pestalozzi ˌpes.tə'lɒt.si ⓊⓈ -'lɑːt-
pest|er 'pes.t|əʳ ⓊⓈ -t|ɚ **-ers** -əz ⓊⓈ -ɚz **-ering/ly** -ᵊr.ɪŋ/li **-ered** -əd ⓊⓈ -ɚd **-erer/s** -ᵊr.əʳ/z ⓊⓈ -ɚ.ɚ/z
pesticide 'pes.tɪ.saɪd ⓊⓈ -tə- **-s** -z
pestiferous pes'tɪf.ᵊr.əs **-ly** -li **-ness** -nəs, -nɪs
pestilenc|e 'pes.tɪ.lənts, -tᵊl.ənts ⓊⓈ -tᵊl- **-es** -ɪz
pestilent 'pes.tɪ.lənt, -tᵊl.ənt ⓊⓈ -tᵊl- **-ly** -li
pestilential ˌpes.tɪ'len.*t*ʃᵊl, -tə'- ⓊⓈ -tə'len*t*.ʃᵊl **-ly** -i
pestl|e 'pes.l̩, -tl̩ **-es** -z **-ing** -ɪŋ, 'pes.lɪŋ, 'pest.lɪŋ **-ed** -d
pesto 'pes.təʊ ⓊⓈ -toʊ
pestolog|y pes'tɒl.ə.dʒ|i ⓊⓈ -'tɑː.lə- **-ist/s** -ɪst/s
pet pet **-s** -s **-ting** -ɪŋ ⓊⓈ 'pet̬.ɪŋ **-ted** -ɪd ⓊⓈ 'pet̬.ɪd
petal 'pet.ᵊl ⓊⓈ 'pet̬- **-s** -z **-(l)ed** -d
pétanque peɪ'tɑ̃ːŋk
petard pet'ɑːd, pɪ'tɑːd, pə-; 'pet.ɑːd ⓊⓈ pɪ'tɑːrd **-s** -z **ˌhoist by one's ˌown pe'tard**
Pete piːt
pet|er (P) 'piː.t|əʳ ⓊⓈ -t̬|ɚ **-ers** -əz ⓊⓈ -ɚz **-ering** -ᵊr.ɪŋ **-ered** -əd ⓊⓈ -ɚd **ˌPeter 'Pan**
Peterborough, -boro' 'piː.tə.bᵊr.ə, -ˌbʌr.ə ⓊⓈ -t̬ɚˌbɝ.oʊ, -ə
Peterhead ˌpiː.tə'hed ⓊⓈ -t̬ɚ'- *stress shift:* ˌPeterhead 'resident
Peterhouse 'piː.tə.haʊs ⓊⓈ -t̬ɚ-
Peterlee ˌpiː.tə'liː, '--- ⓊⓈ ˌpiː.t̬ɚ'liː, '---
Peters 'piː.təz ⓊⓈ -t̬ɚz
Petersburg 'piː.təz.bɜːg ⓊⓈ -t̬ɚz.bɝːg
Petersfield 'piː.təz.fiːld ⓊⓈ -t̬ɚz-
petersham (P) 'piː.tə.ʃᵊm ⓊⓈ -t̬ɚ- **-s** -z
Peterson, Petersen 'piː.tə.sᵊn ⓊⓈ -t̬ɚ-
Pethick 'peθ.ɪk
petiole 'pet.i.əʊl, 'piː.ti- ⓊⓈ 'pet̬.i.oʊl **-s** -z
petit(s) bourgeois ˌpet.i'bɔː.ʒwɑː, -'bʊə- ⓊⓈ pəˌtiː.bʊr'ʒwɑː; ˌpet̬.i-
petite bourgeoisie pəˌtiːtˌbɔː.ʒwɑː'zi -ˌbʊə- ⓊⓈ -ˌbʊr-
petit bourgeoisie ˌpet.iˌbɔː.ʒwɑː'ziː, -ˌbʊə- ⓊⓈ pəˌtiː.bʊr-; ˌpet̬.i-
petite pə'tiːt
petit four ˌpet.i'fɔːʳ, -fʊəʳ ⓊⓈ ˌpet̬.i'fɔːr **-s** -z
petition pə'tɪʃ.ᵊn, pɪ- ⓊⓈ pə- **-s** -z **-ing** -ɪŋ **-ed** -d **-er/s** -əʳ/z
petit mal ˌpet.i'mæl ⓊⓈ pəˌtiː'mɑːl, -'mæl; ˌpet̬.i'-
petit point ˌpet.i'pɔɪnt ⓊⓈ 'pet̬.iˌpɔɪnt
petit(s) pois ˌpet.i'pwɑː ⓊⓈ pəˌtiː'-, ˌpet̬.i'-
Peto 'piː.təʊ ⓊⓈ -toʊ
Petra 'pet.rə ⓊⓈ 'piː.trə, 'pet.rə
Petrarch 'pet.rɑːk ⓊⓈ 'piː.trɑːrk, 'pet.rɑːrk
Petrarchan pet'rɑː.kᵊn, pə'trɑː-, pɪ- ⓊⓈ pɪ'trɑːr-
Petre 'piː.təʳ ⓊⓈ -t̬ɚ
petrel 'pet.rᵊl **-s** -z
petri dish 'pet.riˌdɪʃ ⓊⓈ 'piː.tri- **-es** -ɪz
Petrie 'piː.tri
petrifaction ˌpet.rɪ'fæk.ʃᵊn, -rə'-
petrification ˌpet.rɪ.fɪ'keɪ.ʃᵊn, -rə-
petri|fy 'pet.rɪ|.faɪ, -rə- **-fies** -faɪz **-fying** -faɪ.ɪŋ **-fied** -faɪd
petrochem|ical ˌpet.rəʊ'kem|.ɪ.kᵊl **-istry** -ɪ.stri
petrodollar 'pet.rəʊˌdɒl.əʳ ⓊⓈ -roʊˌdɑː.lɚ **-s** -z
Petrograd 'pet.rə*ʊ*.græd, -grɑːd ⓊⓈ -rə.græd
petrol 'pet.rᵊl **'petrol ˌpump; 'petrol ˌstation**
petrolatum ˌpet.rə'leɪ.təm ⓊⓈ -t̬əm
petrol-bomb 'pet.rᵊl.bɒm ⓊⓈ -bɑːm **-s** -z **-ing** -ɪŋ **-ed** -d
petroleum pə'trəʊ.li.əm, pɪ- ⓊⓈ pə'troʊ- **peˌtroleum 'jelly**
petrolog|y pet'rɒl.ə.dʒ|i, pə'trɒl-, pɪ- ⓊⓈ pə'trɑː.lə- **-ist/s** -ɪst/s
Petruchio pɪ'truː.ki.əʊ, pə-, pet'ruː-, -tʃi- ⓊⓈ pɪ'truː.ki.oʊ, pə-, -tʃi-
Petrushka pɪ'truːʃ.kə, pə-, pet'ruːʃ-
Pett pet
petticoat 'pet.ɪ.kəʊt ⓊⓈ 'pet̬.ɪ.koʊt **-s** -s
pettifogg|ing 'pet.ɪˌfɒg|.ɪŋ ⓊⓈ 'pet̬.ɪˌfɑː.g|ɪŋ, -ˌfɔː- **-er/s** -əʳ/z ⓊⓈ -ɚ/z
Pettigrew 'pet.ɪ.gruː ⓊⓈ 'pet̬-
pettish 'pet.ɪʃ ⓊⓈ 'pet̬- **-ly** -li **-ness** -nəs, -nɪs
Pettit 'pet.ɪt ⓊⓈ 'pet̬-

Pronouncing the letters PH

The consonant digraph **ph** is usually pronounced as /f/, e.g.:

photo /ˈfəʊ.təʊ/ (US) /ˈfoʊ.t̬oʊ/
alphabet /ˈæl.fə.bet/

However, the realisation /v/ can occur in some words, e.g.:

nephew /ˈnef.juː, ˈnev-/
Stephen /ˈstiː.vᵊn/

In addition

A much less common realisation of the consonant digraph **ph** is /p/, e.g.:

shepherd /ˈʃep.əd/ (US) /-ɚd/

Pharyngeal

Descriptive of a sound made by constricting the muscles of the pharynx (and usually also some of the LARYNX muscles) to create an obstruction to the airflow from the lungs.

Examples for English

English does not have any pharyngeal phonemes.

In other languages

The best known language that has pharyngeal consonants is Arabic, most dialects of which have voiced and voiceless fricatives.

pettitoes ˈpet.ɪ.təʊz (US) ˈpet̬.ɪ.toʊz
pett|y ˈpet|.i (US) ˈpet̬- **-ier** -i.əʳ (US) -i.ɚ **-iest** -i.ɪst, -i.əst **-ily** -ɪ.li, -ᵊl.i **-iness/es** -ɪ.nəs/ɪz, -ɪ.nɪs/ɪz ˌ**petty ˈcash**; ˌ**petty ˈofficer**
petty bourgeois ˌpet.iˈbɔː.ʒwɑː, -ˈbʊə- (US) ˌpet̬.i.bʊrˈʒwɑː
petty bourgeoisie ˌpet.iˌbɔː.ʒwɑːˈzi, -ˌbʊə- (US) ˌpet̬.iˌbʊr-
Petula pɪˈtjuː.lə, pə-, petˈjuː- (US) pəˈtuː-, -ˈtjuː-
petulan|ce ˈpet.jə.lənt|s, -jʊ-, ˈpetʃ.ə-, ˈ-ʊ- (US) ˈpetʃ.ə- **-cy** -si
petulant ˈpet.jə.lənt, -jʊ-, ˈpetʃ.ə-, ˈ-ʊ- (US) ˈpetʃ.ə- **-ly** -li
petunia pɪˈtjuː.ni.ə, pə- (US) pəˈtuː.njə, -ˈtjuː-, ˈ-ni.ə **-s** -z
Petworth ˈpet.wəθ, -wɜːθ (US) -wɚθ, -wɝːθ
Peugeot® ˈpɜː.ʒəʊ (US) pɜːˈʒoʊ, puː-, pjuː- **-s** -z
Pevensey ˈpev.ᵊn.zi
Peveril ˈpev.ᵊr.ɪl
Pevsner ˈpevz.nəʳ (US) -nɚ
pew pjuː **-s** -z
pewit ˈpiː.wɪt (US) ˈpiː-, ˈpjuː.ɪt **-s** -s
pewter ˈpjuː.təʳ (US) -t̬ɚ
Peynell ˈpeɪ.nᵊl, -nel
peyote peɪˈəʊ.ti (US) -ˈoʊ.t̬i **-s** -z
Peyton ˈpeɪ.tᵊn
Pfeiffer ˈfaɪ.fəʳ, ˈpfaɪ- (US) -fɚ
Pfennig ˈpfen.ɪg (US) ˈfen- **-s** -z
PH ˌpiːˈeɪtʃ
Phaedo ˈfiː.dəʊ, ˈfaɪ- (US) ˈfiː.doʊ
Phaedra ˈfiː.drə, ˈfaɪ- (US) ˈfiː-, ˈfed.rə
Phaedrus ˈfiː.drəs, ˈfaɪ- (US) ˈfiː-
Phaer feɪəʳ (US) feɪɚ, fer
Phaethon ˈfeɪ.ə.θən, ˈ-ɪ- (US) -ə.θɑːn, -θən
phaeton *carriage:* ˈfeɪ.tᵊn, -tɒn (US) ˈfeɪ.ə.t̬ən, ˈfeɪ.tᵊn **-s** -z
Phaeton *Greek mythology:* ˈfeɪ.ə.tᵊn, ˈ-ɪ- (US) -ə.tɑːn
phagocyte ˈfæg.əʊ.saɪt (US) -oʊ-, -ə- **-s** -s
phagocytosis ˌfæg.əʊ.saɪˈtəʊ.sɪs (US) -oʊ.saɪˈtoʊ-, ˌ-ə-
phalang|e ˈfæl.ændʒ; fəˈlændʒ (US) feɪˈlændʒ, fə-; ˈfæl.əndʒ **-es** -ɪz
phalanges *(alternative plur. of* **phalanx**) fælˈæn.dʒiːz, fəˈlæn- (US) fə-, feɪ-
phalangist (P) fælˈæn.dʒɪst, fəˈlæn- (US) fə-, feɪ- **-s** -s
phalanster|y ˈfæl.ən.stᵊr|.i (US) -ster- **-ies** -iz
phalanx ˈfæl.æŋ*k*s (US) ˈfeɪ.læŋks, ˈfæl.æŋks **-es** -ɪz **phalanges** fælˈæn.dʒiːz, fəˈlæn- (US) fə-, feɪ-
Phalaris ˈfæl.ə.rɪs
phalarope ˈfæl.ə.rəʊp (US) -roʊp **-s** -s
phallic ˈfæl.ɪk
phallicism ˈfæl.ɪ.sɪ.zᵊm
phall|us ˈfæl|.əs **-uses** -ə.sɪz **-i** -aɪ
phanerogam ˈfæn.ᵊr.əʊ.gæm, fəˈner- (US) ˈfæn.ə.roʊ-, -ɚ.ə-; fəˈner.oʊ-, ˈ-ə- **-s** -z
phanerogamic ˌfæn.ᵊr.əʊˈgæm.ɪk, fəˌner- (US) ˌfæn.ə.roʊˈ-, -ɚ.əˈ-, fəˌner.oʊˈ-, -əˈ-
phanerogamous ˌfæn.ᵊrˈɒg.ə.məs (US) -əˈrɑː.gə-
phantasm ˈfæn.tæz.ᵊm **-s** -z
phantasmagoria ˌfæn.tæz.məˈgɔː.ri.ə, -təz-, -ˈgɒr.i- (US) -ˈgɔːr.i-
phantasmagoric ˌfæn.tæz.məˈgɒr.ɪk, -təz- (US) -ˈgɔːr.ɪk **-al** -ᵊl
phantasm|al fænˈtæz.m|ᵊl **-ally** -ᵊl.i **-ic** -ɪk
phantas|y ˈfæn.tə.s|i (US) -t̬ə- **-ies** -iz
phantom ˈfæn.təm (US) -t̬əm **-s** -z
pharaoh (P) ˈfeə.rəʊ (US) ˈfer.oʊ, ˈfær-, ˈfeɪ.roʊ **-s** -z
pharisaic (P) ˌfær.ɪˈseɪ.ɪk, -əˈ- (US) ˌfer.ɪˈ-, ˌfær- **-al** -ᵊl **-ally** -ᵊl.i, -li **-alness** -ᵊl.nəs, -nɪs
pharisaism (P) ˈfær.ɪ.seɪ.ɪ.zᵊm, ˈ-ə- (US) ˈfer.ɪ-, ˈfær-
pharisee (P) ˈfær.ɪ.siː, ˈ-ə- (US) ˈfer.ɪ-, ˈfær- **-s** -z
pharmaceutic ˌfɑː.məˈsjuː.tɪk, -ˈsuː-, -ˈkjuː- (US) ˌfɑːr.məˈsuː.t̬ɪ-, -ˈsjuː- **-al/s** -ᵊl/z **-ally** -ᵊl.i, -li **-s** -s
pharmacist ˈfɑː.mə.sɪst (US) ˈfɑːr- **-s** -s
pharmacolog|y ˌfɑː.məˈkɒl.ə.dʒ|i (US) ˌfɑːr.məˈkɑː.lə- **-ist/s** -ɪst/s
pharmacop(o)ei|a ˌfɑː.mə.kəˈpiː|.ə, -kəʊˈ- (US) ˌfɑːr.məˈkoʊ- **-as** -əz **-al** -ᵊl
pharmac|y ˈfɑː.mə.s|i (US) ˈfɑːr- **-ies** -iz
Pharos ˈfeə.rɒs, ˈfær.ɒs (US) ˈfer.ɑːs
pharyngal fəˈrɪŋ.gᵊl, færˈɪŋ- (US) fəˈrɪŋ-
pharyngeal ˌfær.ɪnˈdʒiː.əl; fəˈrɪn.dʒi.əl, færˈɪn- (US) fəˈrɪn.dʒi-; ˌfer.ɪnˈdʒiː-, ˌfær-

pharynges *(plur. of* **pharynx)** færˈɪn.dʒiːz, fəˈrɪn- US fə-
pharyngitis ˌfær.ɪnˈdʒaɪ.tɪs US ˌfer.ɪnˈdʒaɪ.t̬ɪs, ˌfær-
pharynx ˈfær.ɪŋks **-es** -ɪz **pharynges** færˈɪn.dʒiːz, fəˈrɪn- US fə-
phas|e feɪz **-es** -ɪz **-ing** -ɪŋ **-ed** -d
phas|is ˈfeɪ.s|ɪs US -s|ɪs, -z|ɪs **-es** -iːz
phatic ˈfæt.ɪk US ˈfæt̬-
PhD ˌpiː.eɪtʃˈdiː **-'s** -z
pheasant ˈfez.ᵊnt **-s** -s
Phebe ˈfiː.bi
Phelps felps
phenacetin fɪˈnæs.ɪ.tɪn, fə-, fenˈæs-, ˈ-ə- US fɪˈnæs.ə-, -tən
Phenic|ia fɪˈnɪʃ|.ə, fə-, fiː-, -ˈniː.ʃ|ə, -i|.ə US fəˈnɪʃ|.ə, -ˈniː.ʃ|ə **-ian/s** -ᵊn/z
pheno- ˌfiː.nəʊ- US ˌfiː.noʊ-, -nə-
phenobarbitone ˌfiː.nəʊˈbɑː.bɪ.təʊn, -bə- US -noʊˈbɑːr.bɪ.toʊn, -nəˈ-
phenol ˈfiː.nɒl US -noʊl, -nɔːl, -nɑːl
phenolphthalein ˌfiː.nɒlfˈθæl.iːn, -nɒlˈ-, -ˈθeɪ.li-, -i.ɪn US -noʊlˈθæl.iːn, -noʊlfˈ-, -iː.ɪn
phenom fɪˈnɒm, fə- US -ˈnɑːm **-s** -z
phenomenologic|al fɪˌnɒm.ɪ.nəˈlɒdʒ.ɪ.k|ᵊl, fə-, ˌ-ə- US fəˌnɑː.mə.nəˈlɑː.dʒɪ- **-ally** -ᵊl.i, -li
phenomenology fɪˌnɒm.ɪˈnɒl.ə.dʒi, fə-, -əˈ- US fəˌnɑː.məˈnɑː.lə-
phenomen|on fɪˈnɒm.ɪ.n|ən, fə-, ˈ-ə- US fəˈnɑː.mə.n|ɑːn, -n|ən **-a** -ə **-al** -ᵊl **-ally** -ᵊl.i
phenotype ˈfiː.nəʊ.taɪp US -noʊ-, -nə-
pheromonal ˈfer.ə.məʊ.nᵊl US ˌfer.əˈmoʊ-
pheromon|e ˈfer.ə.məʊn US -moʊn **-es** -s
phew ɸː, pɸː, fjuː
Note: Expression of surprise, or exclamation indicating that the speaker is hot. It may be a non-verbal exclamation, or have a spelling-based pronunciation /fjuː/.
phi faɪ **-s** -z
phial faɪəl **-s** -z
Phi Beta Kappa ˌfaɪˌbiː.təˈkæp.ə US -ˌbeɪ.t̬əˈ-, -ˌbiː-
Phidias ˈfaɪ.di.æs, ˈfɪd.i- US ˈfɪd.i.əs
Phidippides faɪˈdɪp.ɪ.diːz
Phil fɪl
Philadelphi|a ˌfɪl.əˈdel.fi|.ə US -fi|.ə, -fj|ə **-an/s** -ən/z
philand|er fɪˈlæn.d|əʳ, fə- US fɪˈlæn.d|ɚ **-ers** -əz US -ɚz **-ering** -ᵊr.ɪŋ **-ered** -əd US -ɚd **-erer/s** -ᵊr.əʳ/z US -ɚ.ɚ/z
philanthrope ˈfɪl.ən.θrəʊp, -æn- US -ən.θroʊp **-s** -s
philanthropic ˌfɪl.ənˈθrɒp.ɪk US -ænˈ-, -ənˈθrɑː.pɪk **-al** -ᵊl **-ally** -ᵊl.i, -li
philanthrop|y fɪˈlænt.θrə.p|i, fə- US fə-, fɪ-, -θroʊ- **-ist/s** -ɪst/s
Philaster fɪˈlæs.təʳ US -tɚ
philatelic ˌfɪl.əˈtel.ɪk *stress shift:* ˌphilatelic ˈclub
philatel|y fɪˈlæt.ᵊl|.i, fə- US -ˈlæt̬- **-ist/s** -ɪst/s
Philbrick ˈfɪl.brɪk
Philby ˈfɪl.bi
-phile, -phil -faɪl US -faɪl, -fɪl
Note: Suffix. Normally unstressed, e.g. **francophile** /ˈfræŋ.kəʊ.faɪl US -koʊ-/.
Philemon fɪˈliː.mɒn, faɪ-, fə-, -mən US fɪˈliː.mən, faɪ-
Philharmonia ˌfɪl.hɑːˈməʊ.ni.ə, -əˈ- US -hɑːrˈmoʊ-, -ɚˈ-
philharmonic (P) ˌfɪl.hɑːˈmɒn.ɪk, -əˈ- US -hɑːrˈmɑː.nɪk, -ɚˈ- **-s** -s *stress shift:* ˌphilharmonic ˈorchestra
philhellene fɪlˈhel.iːn, ˈ--- US fɪlˈhel- **-s** -z
philhellenic ˌfɪl.helˈiː.nɪk, -həˈliː-, -ˈlen.ɪk US -həˈlen-
philhellenism fɪlˈhel.ɪ.nɪ.zᵊm, ˈ-ə- US ˈ-ə-
-philia -ˈfɪl.i.ə US -ˈfɪl.i.ə, ˈ-jə
Note: Suffix. Words containing **-philia** are normally stressed on /-ˈfɪl-/, e.g. **haemophilia** /ˌhiː.məˈfɪl.i.ə US -moʊˈ-/.
-philiac -ˈfɪl.i.æk
Note: Suffix. Words containing **-philiac** are normally stressed on the antepenultimate syllable, e.g. **haemophiliac** /ˌhiː.məˈfɪl.i.æk US -moʊˈ-/.
Philip ˈfɪl.ɪp **-s** -s
Philippa ˈfɪl.ɪ.pə, ˈ-ə-
Philippi fɪˈlɪp.aɪ, fə-; ˈfɪl.ɪ.paɪ, ˈ-ə- US fɪˈlɪp.aɪ
Philippian fɪˈlɪp.i.ən, fə- **-s** -z
philippic fɪˈlɪp.ɪk, fə- **-s** -s
Philippine ˈfɪl.ɪ.piːn, ˈ-ə-, -paɪn, ˌ--ˈ- US ˈfɪl.ə.piːn **-s** -z
Philippoussis ˌfɪl.ɪˈpuː.sɪs, -əˈ-
Philipps ˈfɪl.ɪps
Philistia fɪˈlɪs.ti.ə, fə- US fə-
philistine (P) ˈfɪl.ɪ.staɪn, ˈ-ə- US ˈfɪl.ɪ.stiːn, -staɪn; fɪˈlɪs.tɪn, -tiːn **-s** -z
philistinism ˈfɪl.ɪ.stɪ.nɪ.zᵊm, ˈ-ə- US ˈfɪl.ɪ.stiː-, -staɪ-; fɪˈlɪs.tɪ-
Phillimore ˈfɪl.ɪ.mɔːʳ US -mɔːr
Phillip(p)s ˈfɪl.ɪps
Phillpot ˈfɪl.pɒt US -pɑːt **-s** -s
phillumenist fɪˈluː.mə.nɪst, fə-, -ˈljuː-, -mɪ- US -ˈluː.mə- **-s** -s
philo- fɪl.əʊ-; fɪˈlɒ-, fə- US fɪl.oʊ-, -ə-; fɪˈlɑː-, fə-
Note: Prefix. Normally either takes primary or secondary stress on the first syllable, e.g. **philosophic** /ˌfɪl.əˈsɒf.ɪk US -ˈsɑː.fɪk/, or primary stress on the second syllable, e.g. **philosophy** /fɪˈlɒs.ə.fi US -ˈlɑː.sə-/.
Philoctetes ˌfɪl.əkˈtiː.tiːz, -ɒkˈ- US -əkˈ-, -ɑːkˈ-
philodendron ˌfɪl.əˈden.drən **-s** -z
philologic ˌfɪl.əˈlɒdʒ.ɪk US -ˈlɑː.dʒɪk **-al** -ᵊl **-ally** -ᵊl.i, -li
philolog|y fɪˈlɒl.ə.dʒ|i, fə- US fɪˈlɑː.lə- **-ist/s** -ɪst/s
Philomel ˈfɪl.əʊ.mel US -oʊ- **-s** -z
Philomela ˌfɪl.əʊˈmiː.lə US -oʊˈ-
Philomena ˌfɪl.əʊˈmiː.nə US -oʊˈ-
philosopher fɪˈlɒs.ə.fəʳ, fə- US -ˈlɑː.sə.fɚ **-s** -z
philosophic ˌfɪl.əˈsɒf.ɪk US -əˈsɑː.fɪk, -oʊˈ- **-al** -ᵊl **-ally** -ᵊl.i, -li *stress shift:* ˌphilosophic ˈview
philosoph|ism fɪˈlɒs.ə.f|ɪ.zᵊm, fə- US -ˈlɑː.sə- **-ist/s** -ɪst/s
philosophiz|e, -is|e fɪˈlɒs.ə.faɪz, fə- US -ˈlɑː.sə- **-es** -ɪz **-ing** -ɪŋ **-ed** -d
philosoph|y fɪˈlɒs.ə.f|i, fə- US -ˈlɑː.sə- **-ies** -iz
Philostratus fɪˈlɒs.trə.təs, fə- US fɪˈlɑː.strə.t̬əs
Philotas ˈfɪl.ə.tæs
Philpot ˈfɪl.pɒt US -pɑːt
Philpotts ˈfɪl.pɒts US -pɑːts
philtre, philter ˈfɪl.təʳ US -t̬ɚ **-s** -z
Phineas ˈfɪn.i.əs, -æs US -əs
Phipps fɪps
phiz (P) fɪz
Phizackerley fɪˈzæk.ᵊl.i, fə- US -ɚ.li
phizog ˈfɪz.ɒg US -ɑːg
phlebitic flɪˈbɪt.ɪk, flebˈɪt- US fliːˈbɪt̬.ɪk, flɪ-
phlebitis flɪˈbaɪ.tɪs, flebˈaɪ- US fliːˈbaɪ.t̬ɪs, flɪ-
phlebotomy flɪˈbɒt.ə.mi, flebˈɒt- US fliːˈbɑː.t̬ə-, flɪ-
Phlegethon ˈfleg.ɪ.θɒn, ˈ-ə-, -θən US -ɪ.θɑːn, ˈfledʒ-
phlegm flem **-s** -z
phlegmatic flegˈmæt.ɪk US -ˈmæt̬- **-al** -ᵊl **-ally** -ᵊl.i, -li
phloem ˈfləʊ.em, -ɪm US ˈfloʊ.em
phlogistic flɒdʒˈɪs.tɪk, flɒg-, fləˈdʒɪs-, fləˈgɪs- US floʊˈdʒɪs-
phlogiston flɒdʒˈɪs.tən, flɒg-, fləˈdʒɪs-, fləˈgɪs-, -tɒn US floʊˈdʒɪs.tɑːn, -tən
phlox flɒks US flɑːks **-es** -ɪz
Phnom Penh ˌnɒmˈpen, pəˌnɒm- US ˌnɑːm-
-phobe -fəʊb US -foʊb
Note: Suffix. Normally unstressed, e.g. **technophobe** /ˈtek.nəʊ.fəʊb US -nə.foʊb/.
phob|ia ˈfəʊ.b|i.ə US ˈfoʊ- **-ias** -i.əz **-ic** -ɪk
-phobia -ˈfəʊ.bi.ə US -ˈfoʊ.bi.ə

Phone

A unit at the phonetic level in the study of speech. The term PHONEME is very widely used for a contrastive unit of sound in language. However, a term is also needed for a unit at the phonetic level, since there is not always a one-to-one correspondence between units at the two levels.

Examples for English

The English word *can't* is phonemically /kɑːnt/ in British English and /kænt/ in US English (4 phonemic units), but may be pronounced [kɑ̃ːt] or [kæ̃t] with the nasal consonant phoneme absorbed into the preceding vowel as NASALISATION (3 phonetic units).

Phoneme

A fundamental unit of phonology, usually said to be the smallest unit of speech. It has been defined and used in many different ways.

Examples for English

Virtually all theories of phonology hold that spoken language can be broken down into a string of sound units (phonemes), and that each language has a small, relatively fixed set of these phonemes. Most phonemes can be put into groups; for example, in English we can identify a group of PLOSIVE phonemes /p t k b d g/, a group of voiceless FRICATIVES /f θ s ʃ h/, and so on.

An important question in phoneme theory is how the analyst can establish what the phonemes of a language are.

The most widely accepted view is that phonemes are 'contrastive' and one must find cases where the difference between two words is dependent on the difference between two phonemes. For example, we can prove that the difference between *pin* and *pan* depends on the vowel, and that /ɪ/ and /æ/ are different phonemes.

Pairs of words that differ in just one phoneme are known as 'minimal pairs'. We can establish the same fact about /p/ and /b/ by citing *pin* and *bin*.

Tests like these are called 'commutation tests' and can only be carried out when a provisional list of possible phonemes has been established, so some basic phonetic analysis must precede this stage.

Note: Suffix. Words containing -**phobia** are normally stressed on the antepenultimate syllable, e.g. **arachnophobia** /əˌræk.nəʊˈfəʊ.bi.ə (US) -ˈfoʊ-/.

-phobic -ˈfəʊ.bɪk (US) -ˈfoʊ.bɪk

Note: Suffix. Words containing -**phobic** are normally stressed on the penultimate syllable, e.g. **claustrophobic** /ˌklɔː.strəˈfəʊ.bɪk (US) ˌklɑː.strəˈfoʊ-/.

Phocian ˈfəʊ.ʃi.ən, -si- (US) ˈfoʊ.si- **-s** -z

Phocion ˈfəʊ.si.ən, -ɒn (US) ˈfoʊ.si.ɑːn

Phocis ˈfəʊ.sɪs (US) ˈfoʊ-

Phoebe ˈfiː.bi

Phoebus ˈfiː.bəs

Phoenic|ia fɪˈnɪʃ|.ə, fə-, fiː-, -ˈniː.ʃ|ə, -i|.ə (US) fəˈnɪʃ|.ə, -ˈniː.ʃ|ə **-ian/s** -ᵊn/z

phoenix (P) ˈfiː.nɪks **-es** -ɪz

phon fɒn (US) fɑːn **-s** -z

phonaesthesia ˌfəʊ.nɪsˈθiː.zi.ə, -niːsˈ-, -nəsˈ-, -ʒi.ə, -ʒə (US) ˌfoʊ.nɪsˈθiː.ʒə, -niːsˈ-, -nəsˈ-

pho|nate fəʊ|ˈneɪt (US) ˈfoʊ|.neɪt **-nates** -ˈneɪts (US) -neɪt **-nating** -ˈneɪ.tɪŋ (US) -neɪ.t̬ɪŋ **-nated** -ˈneɪ.tɪd (US) -neɪ.t̬ɪd

phonation fəʊˈneɪ.ʃᵊn (US) foʊ-

phonatory ˈfəʊ.nə.tᵊr.i, fəʊˈneɪ- (US) ˈfoʊ.nə.tɔːr-

phon|e fəʊn (US) foʊn **-es** -z **-ing** -ɪŋ **-ed** -d **ˈphone ˌbook**; **ˈphone ˌbooth**; **ˈphone ˌbox**; **ˈphone ˌcall**

phonecard ˈfəʊn.kɑːd, ˈfəʊŋ- (US) ˈfoʊn.kɑːrd **-s** -z

phone-in ˈfəʊn.ɪn (US) ˈfoʊn- **-s** -z

phonematic ˌfəʊ.nɪˈmæt.ɪk, -niːˈ- (US) ˌfoʊ.nɪˈmæt̬- **-s** -s **-ally** -ᵊl.i, -li

phoneme ˈfəʊ.niːm (US) ˈfoʊ- **-s** -z

phonemic fəʊˈniː.mɪk (US) foʊ-, fə- **-s** -s **-ally** -ᵊl.i, -li

phonemicist fəʊˈniː.mɪ.sɪst, -mə- (US) foʊ-, fə- **-s** -s

phone-tapping ˈfəʊnˌtæp.ɪŋ (US) ˈfoʊn-

phonetic fəʊˈnet.ɪk (US) foʊˈnet̬-, fə- **-ally** -ᵊl.i, -li **-s** -s

phonetician ˌfəʊ.nɪˈtɪʃ.ᵊn, ˌfɒn.ɪˈ-, -əˈ- (US) ˌfoʊ.nəˈ- **-s** -z

phoneticiz|e, -is|e fəʊˈnet.ɪ.saɪz, ˈ-ə- (US) foʊˈnet̬-, fə- **-es** -ɪz **-ing** -ɪŋ **-ed** -d

phonetist ˈfəʊ.nɪ.tɪst, -nə-, -net.ɪst (US) ˈfoʊ.nə.t̬ɪst **-s** -s

phon|ey ˈfəʊ.n|i (US) ˈfoʊ- **-ier** -i.əʳ (US) -i.ɚ **-iest** -i.ɪst, -i.əst **-ily** -ɪ.li, -ᵊl.i **-eys** -iz **-iness** -ɪ.nəs, -ɪ.nɪs

phonic ˈfɒn.ɪk (US) ˈfɑː.nɪk

phonics ˈfɒn.ɪks (US) ˈfɑː.nɪks

phono- fəʊ.nəʊ-, fɒn.əʊ-; fəʊˈnɒ- (US) foʊ.nə-, fɑː-, -noʊ-; foʊˈnɑː-, fə-

Note: Prefix. Normally either takes primary or secondary stress on the first syllable, e.g. **phonogram** /ˈfəʊ.nə.græm (US) ˈfoʊ.nə-/, **phonographic** /ˌfəʊ.nəˈgræf.ɪk (US) ˌfoʊ.nəˈ-/, or primary stress on the second syllable, e.g. **phonology** /fəʊˈnɒl.ə.dʒi ˉfəˈnɑː.lə-/.

phonogram ˈfəʊ.nə.græm (US) ˈfoʊ- **-s** -z

phonograph ˈfəʊ.nə.grɑːf, -græf (US) ˈfoʊ.nə.græf **-s** -s

phonographer fəʊˈnɒg.rə.fəʳ (US) foʊˈnɑː.grə.fɚ, fə- **-s** -z

phonographic ˌfəʊ.nəˈgræf.ɪk (US) ˌfoʊˈ- **-al** -ᵊl **-ally** -ᵊl.i, -li *stress shift:* ˌphonographic ˈsystem

phonographist fəʊˈnɒg.rə.fɪst (US) foʊˈnɑː.grə-, fə- **-s** -s

phonography fəʊˈnɒg.rə.fi (US) foʊˈnɑː.grə-, fə-

phonological ˌfəʊ.nəˈlɒdʒ.ɪ.kᵊl, ˌfɒn.əˈ-, -ᵊlˈɒdʒ- (US) ˌfoʊ.nəˈlɑː.dʒɪ-, -noʊˈ- **-ly** -i *stress shift:* ˌphonological ˈtheory

Phonetics

The scientific study of speech. It has a long history, going back certainly to well over two thousand years ago. The central concerns in phonetics are the discovery of how speech sounds are produced, how they are used in spoken language, how we can record speech sounds with written symbols and how we hear and recognise different sounds.

In the first of these areas, when we study the production of speech sounds we can observe what speakers do ('articulatory' observation) and we can try to feel what is going on inside our vocal tract ('kinaesthetic' observation). The second area is where phonetics overlaps with PHONOLOGY: usually in phonetics we are only interested in sounds that are used in meaningful speech, and phoneticians are interested in discovering the range and variety of sounds used in this way in all the known languages of the world. This is sometimes known as 'linguistic phonetics'. Thirdly, there has always been a need for agreed conventions for using phonetic symbols that represent speech sounds; the International Phonetic Association has played a very important role in this. Finally, the 'auditory' aspect of speech is very important. The ear is capable of making fine discrimination between different sounds, and sometimes it is not possible to define in articulatory terms precisely what the difference is. A good example of this is in vowel classification. While it is important to know the position and shape of the tongue and lips, it is often very important to have been trained in an agreed set of standard auditory qualities that vowels can be reliably related to (see CARDINAL VOWEL). Another important area is acoustic phonetics which studies the physical properties of speech sounds.

Phonology

The study of the sound systems of languages.

The most basic activity in phonology is 'phonemic analysis', in which the objective is to establish what the PHONEMES are and arrive at the 'phonemic inventory' of the language. Very few phonologists have ever believed that this would be an adequate analysis of the sound system of a language: it is necessary to go beyond this. One can look at 'suprasegmental' phonology – the study of STRESS, RHYTHM and INTONATION. One can go beyond the phoneme and look into the detailed characteristics of each unit in terms of 'distinctive features'. The way in which sounds can combine in a language is studied in 'phonotactics' and in the analysis of syllable structure.

For some phonologists the most important area is the relationships between the different phonemes – how they form groups, the nature of the contrasts between them and how those oppositions may be neutralised (see NEUTRALISATION). For others, the most important activity is to discover the rules which affect the phonemes of the language and the way they are produced, and to express these rules as economically as possible.

phonologist fəʊ'nɒl.ə.dʒɪst (US) fə'nɑː.lə-, foʊ- **-s** -s

phonolog|y fəʊ'nɒl.ə.dʒ|i (US) fə'nɑː.lə-, foʊ- **-ies** -iz

phonotactic ˌfəʊ.nəʊ'tæk.tɪk, ˌfɒn.əʊ'- (US) ˌfoʊ.nə'-, -noʊ'- **-s** -s **-ally** -ᵊl.i, -li *stress shift:* ˌphonotactic 'rules

phonotype 'fəʊ.nəʊ.taɪp (US) 'foʊ.nə-, -noʊ- **-s** -s

phon|y 'fəʊ.n|i (US) 'foʊ- **-ier** -i.əʳ (US) -i.ɚ **-iest** -i.ɪst, -i.əst **-ily** -ɪ.li, -ᵊl.i **-ies** -iz **-iness** -ɪ.nəs, -ɪ.nɪs

phosgene 'fɒz.dʒiːn, 'fɒs- (US) 'fɑːs-, 'fɑːz-

phosphate 'fɒs.feɪt, -fɪt, -fət (US) 'fɑːs.feɪt **-s** -s

phosphene 'fɒs.fiːn (US) 'fɑːs-, 'fɑːz- **-s** -z

phosphide 'fɒs.faɪd (US) 'fɑːs- **-s** -z

phosphite 'fɒs.faɪt (US) 'fɑːs- **-s** -s

phospho- ˌfɒs.fəʊ- (US) ˌfɑːs.foʊ-, -fə-

phosphor 'fɒs.fəʳ (US) 'fɑːs.fɚ, -fɔːr **-s** -z

phosphoresc|e ˌfɒs.fᵊr'es (US) ˌfɑːs.fə'res **-es** -ɪz **-ing** -ɪŋ **-ed** -t

phosphorescence ˌfɒs.fᵊr'es.ᵊnts (US) ˌfɑːs.fə'res-

phosphorescent ˌfɒs.fᵊr'es.ᵊnt (US) ˌfɑːs.fə'res- *stress shift:* ˌphosphorescent 'ink

phosphoric fɒs'fɒr.ɪk (US) fɑːs'fɔːr-

phosphorous 'fɒs.fᵊr.əs (US) 'fɑːs-; fɑːs'fɔːr-

phosphorus 'fɒs.fᵊr.əs (US) 'fɑːs-

phossy 'fɒs.i (US) 'fɑː.si

photic 'fəʊ.tɪk (US) 'foʊ.t̬ɪk

photo 'fəʊ.təʊ (US) 'foʊ.t̬oʊ **-s** -z ˌ**photo** '**finish**

photocall 'fəʊ.təʊ.kɔːl (US) 'foʊ.t̬oʊ- **-s** -z

photocell 'fəʊ.təʊ.sel (US) 'foʊ.t̬oʊ- **-s** -z

photochemical ˌfəʊ.təʊ'kem.ɪ.kᵊl (US) ˌfoʊ.t̬oʊ-

photochrome 'fəʊ.təʊ.krəʊm (US) 'foʊ.t̬oʊ.kroʊm **-s** -z

photocompos|e ˌfəʊ.təʊ.kəm'pəʊz (US) ˌfoʊ.t̬oʊ.kəm'poʊz **-es** -ɪz **-ing** -ɪŋ **-ed** -d

photocomposition ˌfəʊ.təʊˌkɒm.pə'zɪʃ.ᵊn (US) ˌfoʊ.t̬oʊˌkɑːm.pə'- **-s** -z

photocopier 'fəʊ.təʊˌkɒp.i.əʳ, ˌfəʊ.təʊ'kɒp.i.əʳ (US) 'foʊ.t̬oʊˌkɑː.pi.ɚ, -t̬əˌ- **-s** -z

photocop|y 'fəʊ.təʊˌkɒp|.i (US) 'foʊ.t̬oʊˌkɑː.p|i, -t̬əˌ- **-ies** -iz **-ying** -i.ɪŋ **-ied** -id

photoelectric ˌfəʊ.təʊ.ɪ'lek.trɪk (US) ˌfoʊ.t̬oʊ- *stress shift:* ˌphotoelectric 'cell

photo-essay 'fəʊ.təʊˌes.eɪ (US) ˌfoʊ.t̬oʊ- **-s** -z

Photofit® 'fəʊ.təʊ.fɪt (US) 'foʊ.t̬oʊ-

photogenic ˌfəʊ.təʊˈdʒen.ɪk, -ˈdʒiː.nɪk (US) ˌfoʊ.t̬oʊˈdʒen.ɪk, -t̬əˈ- *stress shift:* ˌphotogenic ˈperson

photogrammetr|ist ˌfəʊ.təʊˈɡræm.ə.tr|ɪst, ˈ-ɪ- (US) ˌfoʊ.t̬oʊ- **-ists** -ɪsts **-y** -i

photograph ˈfəʊ.tə.ɡrɑːf, -ɡræf (US) ˈfoʊ.t̬oʊ.ɡræf, -t̬ə- **-s** -s **-ing** -ɪŋ **-ed** -t

photographer fəˈtɒɡ.rə.fəʳ (US) -ˈtɑː.ɡrə.fɚ **-s** -z

photographic ˌfəʊ.təˈɡræf.ɪk (US) ˌfoʊ.t̬əˈ- **-al** -əl **-ally** -əl.i, -li *stress shift:* ˌphotographic ˈmodel

photography fəˈtɒɡ.rə.fi (US) -ˈtɑː.ɡrə-

photogravure ˌfəʊ.təʊ.ɡrəˈvjʊəʳ, -ˈvjɔːʳ (US) ˌfoʊ.t̬oʊ.ɡrəˈvjʊr, -t̬ə- **-s** -z

photojournal|ism ˌfəʊ.təʊˈdʒɜː.nəl|.ɪ.zəm (US) ˌfoʊ.t̬oʊˈdʒɝː- **-ist/s** -ɪst/s

photomontag|e ˌfəʊ.təʊ.mɒnˈtɑːʒ (US) ˌfoʊ.t̬oʊ.mɑːnˈ- **-es** -ɪz

photon ˈfəʊ.tɒn (US) ˈfoʊ.tɑːn **-s** -z

photo-opportunit|y ˌfəʊ.təʊˌɒp.əˈtjuː.nə.t|i, -ˈtʃuː-, -nɪ- (US) ˌfoʊ.t̬oʊˌɑː.pɚˈtuː.nə.t̬|i, -ˈtjuː- **-ies** -iz

photosensitive ˌfəʊ.təʊˈsent.sɪ.tɪv, -sə- (US) ˌfoʊ.t̬oʊˈsent.sə-

photosensitivity ˌfəʊ.təʊˌsent.sɪˈtɪv.ə.ti, -səˈ-, -ə.ti (US) ˌfoʊ.t̬oʊˌsent.səˈtɪv.ə.t̬i

photosensitiz|e, -is|e ˌfəʊ.təʊˈsent.sɪ.taɪz (US) ˌfoʊ.t̬oʊˈsent.sə- **-es** -ɪz **-ing** -ɪŋ **-ed** -d

photosphere ˈfəʊ.təʊ.sfɪəʳ (US) ˈfoʊ.t̬oʊ.sfɪr **-s** -z

photo|stat® ˈfəʊ.təʊ|.stæt (US) ˈfoʊ.t̬oʊ-, -t̬ə- **-stats** -stæts **-statting** -stæt.ɪŋ (US) -stæt̬.ɪŋ **-statted** -stæt.ɪd (US) -stæt̬.ɪd

photostatic ˌfəʊ.təʊˈstæt.ɪk (US) ˌfoʊ.t̬oʊˈstæt̬.ɪk, -t̬əˈ- *stress shift:* ˌphotostatic ˈcopy

photosynthesis ˌfəʊ.təʊˈsɪnt.θə.sɪs, -θɪ- (US) ˌfoʊ.t̬oʊˈ-, -t̬əˈ-

photosynthesiz|e, -is|e ˌfəʊ.təʊˈsɪnt.θə.saɪz, -θɪ- (US) ˌfoʊ.t̬oʊˈ-, -t̬əˈ- **-es** -ɪz **-ing** -ɪŋ **-ed** -d

photosynthetic ˌfəʊ.təʊ.sɪnˈθet.ɪk (US) ˌfoʊ.t̬oʊ.sɪnˈθet̬-, -t̬ə- **-ally** -əl.i, -li

phototropic ˌfəʊ.təʊˈtrɒp.ɪk (US) ˌfoʊ.t̬oʊˈtrɑː.pɪk, -t̬əˈ-, -ˈtroʊ- **-ally** -əl.i (US) -li

phototropism fəʊˈtɒt.rə.pɪ.zəm; ˌfəʊ.təʊˈtrəʊ- (US) foʊˈtɑː.trə- **-s** -z

phrasal ˈfreɪ.zəl **-s** -z ˌ**phrasal** ˈ**verb**

phras|e freɪz **-es** -ɪz **-ing** -ɪŋ **-ed** -d ˈ**phrase** ˌ**book**

phraseologic ˌfreɪ.zi.əˈlɒdʒ.ɪk (US) -ˈlɑː.dʒɪk **-al** -əl **-ally** -əl.i, -li

phraseolog|y ˌfreɪ.ziˈɒl.ə.dʒ|i (US) -ˈɑː.lə- **-ies** -iz

phrenetic frəˈnet.ɪk, frɪ-, frenˈet- (US) frɪˈnet̬-, frə- **-al** -əl **-ally** -əl.i, -li

phrenic ˈfren.ɪk

phrenologic|al ˌfren.əlˈɒdʒ.ɪ.k|əl (US) -əˈlɑː.dʒɪ- **-ally** -əl.i, -li

phrenolog|y frɪˈnɒl.ə.dʒ|i, frə-, frenˈɒl- (US) frɪˈnɑː.lə-, frə- **-ist/s** -ɪst/s

Phryg|ia ˈfrɪdʒ|.i.ə **-ian/s** -i.ən/z (US) -i.ən/z, -jən/z

Phryne ˈfraɪ.ni

phthalic ˈθæl.ɪk, ˈfθæl-, ˈθeɪ.lɪk (US) ˈθæl-, ˈfθæl-

phthisis ˈθaɪ.sɪs, ˈfθaɪ- (US) ˈθaɪ-, ˈtaɪ-, ˈfθaɪ-

Phuket ˌpuːˈket

phut fʌt

phylacter|y fɪˈlæk.tər|.i **-ies** -iz

Phyllis ˈfɪl.ɪs

phyllo ˈfaɪ.ləʊ, ˈfiː-, ˈfɪl.əʊ (US) ˈfiː.loʊ, ˈfaɪ- ˌ**phyllo** ˈ**pastry** (US) ˈ**phyllo** ˌ**pastry**

phylloxer|a fɪˈlɒk.sər|.ə; ˌfɪl.ɒkˈsɪə.r|ə (US) fɪˈlɑːk.sɚ|.ə; ˌfɪl.ɑːkˈsɪr- **-ae** -iː **-as** -əz

phyl|um ˈfaɪ.l|əm **-a** -ə

physiatric ˌfɪz.iˈæt.rɪk **-s** -s **-al** -əl

physiatricist ˌfɪz.iˈæt.rɪ.sɪst, -rə- **-s** -s

physic ˈfɪz.ɪk **-s** -s **-king** -ɪŋ **-ked** -t

physic|al ˈfɪz.ɪ.k|əl **-als** -əlz **-ally** -əl.i, -li ˌ**physical edu**ˈ**cation**; ˌ**physical** ˈ**therapy**

physicality ˌfɪz.ɪˈkæl.ə.ti, -ɪ.ti (US) -ə.t̬i

physician fɪˈzɪʃ.ən, fə- (US) fɪ- **-s** -z

physicist ˈfɪz.ɪ.sɪst, ˈ-ə- (US) ˈ-ɪ- **-s** -s

physio- fɪz.i.əʊ-; ˌfɪz.iˈɒ- (US) fɪz.i.oʊ-, -ə-; ˌfɪz.iˈɑː-

Note: Prefix. Normally either takes primary or secondary stress on the first syllable, e.g. **physiologic** /ˌfɪz.i.əˈlɒdʒ.ɪk (US) -ˈlɑː.dʒɪk/, or secondary stress on the first syllable with primary stress on the third syllable, e.g. **physiology** /ˌfɪz.iˈɒl.ə.dʒi (US) -ˈɑː.lə-/.

physio ˈfɪz.i.əʊ (US) -oʊ **-s** -z

physiognomic ˌfɪz.i.əˈnɒm.ɪk (US) -ɑːɡˈnɑː.mɪk, -əˈ- **-al** -əl **-ally** -əl.i, -li

physiognomist ˌfɪz.iˈɒn.ə.mɪst (US) -ˈɑːɡ.nə- **-s** -s

physiognom|y ˌfɪz.iˈɒn.ə.m|i (US) -ˈɑːɡ.nə- **-ies** -iz

physiographic ˌfɪz.i.əʊˈɡræf.ɪk (US) -oʊˈ-, -əˈ- **-al** -əl

physiograph|y ˌfɪz.iˈɒɡ.rə.f|i (US) -ˈɑː.ɡrə- **-er/s** -əʳ/z (US) -ɚ/z

physiologic ˌfɪz.i.əˈlɒdʒ.ɪk (US) -ˈlɑː.dʒɪk **-al** -əl **-ally** -əl.i, -li

physiolog|y ˌfɪz.iˈɒl.ə.dʒ|i (US) -ˈɑː.lə- **-ist/s** -ɪst/s

physiotherap|y ˌfɪz.i.əʊˈθer.ə.p|i (US) -oʊˈ-, -əˈ- **-ist/s** -ɪst/s

physique fɪˈziːk, fə- (US) fɪ-

phytoplankton ˌfaɪ.təʊˈplæŋk.tən, -tɒn (US) -t̬oʊˈplæŋk.tən

pi paɪ **-s** -z

Piaf ˈpiː.æf, -ˈ- (US) ˈpiː.ɑːf, -ˈ-

piaff|e piˈæf, pjæf (US) pjæf **-es** -s **-ing** -ɪŋ **-ed** -t

Piaget piˈæʒ.eɪ, -ˈɑː.ʒeɪ (US) ˌpiː.əˈʒeɪ, pjɑːˈ-

pia mater ˌpaɪ.əˈmeɪ.təʳ, ˌpiː- (US) -ˈmeɪ.t̬ɚ, -ˈmɑː-

pianissimo ˌpiː.əˈnɪs.ɪ.məʊ, -ænˈɪs-, pjɑːˈnɪs-, ˌpiː.ɑːˈ-, pjænˈɪs-, pjəˈnɪs- (US) ˌpiː.əˈnɪs.ɪ.moʊ **-s** -z

Note: Among British professional musicians, /pjɑːˈnɪs-, ˌpɪ.ɑːˈ-, ˌpiː.əˈ-/ appear to be the most frequently used forms.

pianist ˈpiː.ə.nɪst, ˈpjɑː.nɪst, ˈpjæn.ɪst, piˈæn- (US) ˈpiː.ən.ɪst; piˈæn-, ˈpjæn- **-s** -s

Note: British professional musicians generally pronounce /ˈpiː.ə.nɪst/.

piano *instrument:* piˈæn.əʊ, ˈpjæn-, ˈpjɑː.nəʊ, piˈɑː- (US) piˈæn.oʊ, ˈpjæn- **-s** -z **pi**ˌ**ano ac**ˈ**cordion**; **pi**ˈ**ano** ˌ**bar**; **pi**ˈ**ano** ˌ**stool**

Note: The forms /ˈpjɑː.nəʊ, piˈɑː-/ are frequent among British professional musicians.

piano *softly:* ˈpjɑː.nəʊ, piˈɑː- (US) -noʊ **-s** -z

pianoforte piˌæn.əʊˈfɔː.teɪ, ˌpjæn-, ˌpjɑː.nəʊˈ-, piˌɑː-, -ti (US) piˌæn.oʊˈfɔːr.teɪ, -ti; -ˈæn.oʊ.fɔːrt **-s** -z

Pianola® ˌpiː.əˈnəʊ.lə, pjænˈəʊ-, ˌpiː.ænˈ- (US) ˌpiː.əˈnoʊ-, -ænˈoʊ- **-s** -z

piastre, piaster piˈæs.təʳ, -ˈɑː.stəʳ (US) -ˈæs.tɚ **-s** -z

piazza piˈæt.sə, -ˈɑːt- (US) -ˈɑːt.sə, -sɑː, -ˈɑː.zə, -ˈæt.sə, -ˈæz.ə **-s** -z

pibroch ˈpiː.brɒk, -brɒx (US) -brɑːk **-s** -s

pica ˈpaɪ.kə

picador ˈpɪk.ə.dɔːʳ (US) -dɔːr **-s** -z

picadores *(alternative plur. of* **picador***)* ˌpɪk.əˈdɔː.riːz (US) -ˈdɔːr.iːz

picaninn|y ˌpɪk.əˈnɪn|.i, ˈpɪk.ə.nɪ.n|i (US) ˈpɪk- **-ies** -iz

Picardy ˈpɪk.ə.di, ˈ-ɑː- (US) ˈ-ɚ-, ˈ-ɑːr-

picaresque ˌpɪk.ərˈesk (US) -ɚˈ-

picaroon ˌpɪk.əˈruːn **-s** -z **-ing** -ɪŋ **-ed** -d

Picasso pɪˈkæs.əʊ (US) -ˈkɑː.soʊ, -ˈkæs.oʊ

picayun|e ˌpɪk.əˈjuːn, -eɪˈ-, -iˈ- (US) ˈpɪk.ə.juːn, ˌ--ˈ- **-es** -z **-ish** -ɪʃ

Piccadilly ˌpɪk.əˈdɪl.i *stress shift, see compound:* ˌ**Piccadilly** ˈ**Circus**

piccalilli ˌpɪk.ə'lɪl.i US 'pɪk.ə.lɪl-
piccaninn|y ˌpɪk.ə'nɪn|.i, 'pɪk.ə.nɪ.n|i US 'pɪk- **-ies** -iz
piccolo 'pɪk.ə.ləʊ US -loʊ **-s** -z
pick pɪk **-s** -s **-ing** -ɪŋ **-ed** -t **-er/s** -əʳ/z US -ɚ/z
pickaback 'pɪk.ə.bæk
pickaninn|y ˌpɪk.ə'nɪn|.i, 'pɪk.ə.nɪ.n|i US 'pɪk- **-ies** -iz
pickax|(e) 'pɪk.æks **-es** -ɪz **-ing** -ɪŋ **-ed** -t
pickerel 'pɪk.ᵊr.ᵊl **-s** -z
Pickering 'pɪk.ᵊr.ɪŋ
pick|et 'pɪk|.ɪt **-ets** -ɪts **-eting** -ɪ.tɪŋ US -ɪ.ţɪŋ **-eted** -ɪ.tɪd US -ɪ.ţɪd **-er/s** -ɪ.təʳ/z US -ɪ.ţɚ/z **'picket ˌline**
Pickford 'pɪk.fəd US -fɚd
pickings 'pɪk.ɪŋz
pickl|e 'pɪk.ḷ **-es** -z **-ing** -ɪŋ, 'pɪk.lɪŋ **-ed** -d
Pickles 'pɪk.ḷz
picklock 'pɪk.lɒk US -lɑːk **-s** -s
pick-me-up 'pɪk.mi.ʌp **-s** -s
pickpocket 'pɪkˌpɒk.ɪt US -ˌpɑː.kɪt **-s** -s
pickup 'pɪk.ʌp **-s** -s **'pick-up ˌtruck**
Pickwick 'pɪk.wɪk **ˌPickwick 'Papers** US **'Pickwick ˌPapers**
Pickwickian pɪk'wɪk.i.ən
pick|y 'pɪk|.i **-ier** -i.əʳ US -i.ɚ **-iest** -i.ɪst, -i.əst **-iness** -ɪ.nəs, -ɪ.nɪs
picnic 'pɪk.nɪk **-s** -s **-king** -ɪŋ **-ked** -t **-ker/s** -əʳ/z US -ɚ/z
picot 'piː.kəʊ; -'-, pɪ'kəʊ US 'piː.koʊ, -'-
picotee ˌpɪk.ə'tiː US ˌpɪk.ə'tiː, '--- **-s** -z
picric 'pɪk.rɪk
Pict pɪkt **-s** -s
Pictish 'pɪk.tɪʃ
pictogram 'pɪk.təʊ.græm US -toʊ-, -tə- **-s** -z
pictograph 'pɪk.təʊ.grɑːf, -græf US -toʊ.græf, -tə- **-s** -s
Picton 'pɪk.tən
pictorial pɪk'tɔː.ri.əl US -'tɔːr.i- **-ly** -i
pict|ure 'pɪk.tʃ|əʳ US -tʃ|ɚ **-ures** -əz US -ɚz **-uring** -ᵊr.ɪŋ **-ured** -əd US -ɚd **'picture ˌbook; ˌpicture 'postcard; ˌpicture 'window**
picturesque ˌpɪk.tʃᵊr'esk **-ly** -li **-ness** -nəs, -nɪs
piddl|e 'pɪd.ḷ **-es** -z **-ing** -ɪŋ, 'pɪd.lɪŋ **-ed** -d **-er/s** -əʳ/z US -ɚ/z, 'pɪd.ləʳ/z US -lɚ/z
piddling (*adj.*) 'pɪd.ḷ.ɪŋ, 'pɪd.lɪŋ
pidgin (P) 'pɪdʒ.ɪn **-s** -z
Pidsley 'pɪdz.li
pie paɪ **-s** -z **'pie ˌchart; as ˌeasy as 'pie; have a ˌfinger in ˌevery 'pie; to ˌeat ˌhumble 'pie; ˌpie in the 'sky**
piebald 'paɪ.bɔːld US -bɔːld, -bɑːld **-s** -z
piec|e piːs **-es** -ɪz **-ing** -ɪŋ **-ed** -t **'piece ˌrate; ˌpiece of 'cake**
pièce(s) de résistance piˌes.də.rez.ɪ'stɑ̃ns, ˌpjes-, -rɪ.zɪ'-, -rə- US ˌpjes.dəˌreɪ.ziː'stɑ̃ːns
piecemeal 'piːs.miːl
piecework 'piːs.wɜːk US -wɝːk
piecrust 'paɪ.krʌst **-s** -s
pied paɪd **ˌpied 'piper**
pied(s)-à-terre ˌpjeɪd.ɑː'teəʳ, ˌpjed- US -'ter
piedmont (P) 'piːd.mənt, -mɒnt US -mɑːnt
piedmontese (P) ˌpiːd.mən'tiːz, -mɒn'- US -mɑːn'-
pie-eyed ˌpaɪ'aɪd *stress shift:* ˌpie-eyed 'reveller
pier pɪəʳ US pɪr **-s** -z
pierc|e (P) pɪəs US pɪrs **-es** -ɪz **-ing/ly** -ɪŋ/li **-ed** -t **-er/s** -əʳ/z US -ɚ/z **-eable** -ə.bḷ
Piercy 'pɪə.si US 'pɪr-
pierglass 'pɪə.glɑːs US 'pɪr.glæs **-es** -ɪz
pierhead 'pɪə.hed US 'pɪr- **-s** -z
Pierian paɪ'er.i.ən, -'ɪə.ri-, pi- US paɪ'ɪr.i-
Pierpoint 'pɪə.pɔɪnt US 'pɪr-
Pierpont 'pɪə.pɒnt, -pənt US 'pɪr.pɑːnt
Pierre *name:* pi'eəʳ US piː'er
Pierre *place in US:* pɪəʳ US pɪr
Pierrepont 'pɪə.pɒnt, -pənt US 'pɪr.pɑːnt
pierrot (P) 'pɪə.rəʊ, 'pjer.əʊ US ˌpiː.ə'roʊ **-s** -z
Piers pɪəz US pɪrz
Pierson 'pɪə.sᵊn US 'pɪr-
Piesporter 'piːz.pɔː.təʳ US -pɔːr.ţɚ
pietà ˌpiː.et'ɑː, -eɪ'tɑː, '--- US ˌpiː.eɪ'tɑː, ˌpjeɪ'- **-s** -z
Pietermaritzburg ˌpiː.tə'mær.ɪts.bɜːg US -ţɚ'mer.ɪts.bɝːg
piet|ism 'paɪə.t|ɪ.zᵊm, 'paɪ.ɪ- US 'paɪə- **-ist/s** -ɪst/s
pietistic ˌpaɪə'tɪs.tɪk
piet|y 'paɪə.t|i, 'paɪ.ɪ- US 'paɪə.ţ|i **-ies** -iz
piezoelectric piˌet.səʊ.ɪ'lek.trɪk; ˌpiː.zəʊ-; paɪˌiː.zəʊ-; ˌpaɪ.ɪ- US paɪˌiː.zoʊ-; piːˌeɪ- **-al** -ᵊl
piezoelectricity piˌet.səʊˌel.ɪk'trɪs.ə.ti; ˌpiː.zəʊ-; paɪˌiː.zəʊ-; ˌpaɪ.ɪ-; -ˌiː.lek'-; -ɪˌlek'-; -ɪ.ti; US paɪˌiː.zoʊˌiː.lek'trɪs.ə.ţi, -iːˌlek'-; piˌeɪ-
piffl|e 'pɪf.ḷ **-es** -z **-ing** -ɪŋ, 'pɪf.lɪŋ **-ed** -d
pig pɪg **-s** -z **-ging** -ɪŋ **-ged** -d **'pig ˌiron; ˌmake a ˌpig's 'ear of**
pigeon 'pɪdʒ.ən, -ɪn US -ən **-s** -z
pigeonhol|e (*n. v.*) 'pɪdʒ.ən.həʊl, -ɪn- US -ən.hoʊl **-es** -z **-ing** -ɪŋ **-ed** -d
pigeon-toed ˌpɪdʒ.ən'təʊd, -ɪn- US 'pɪdʒ.ən.toʊd *stress shift, British only:* ˌpigeon-toed 'walk
pigger|y 'pɪg.ᵊr|.i **-ies** -iz
piggish 'pɪg.ɪʃ **-ly** -li **-ness** -nəs, -nɪs
Piggott 'pɪg.ət
piggl|y 'pɪg|.i **-ies** -iz **-ier** -i.əʳ US -i.ɚ **-iest** -i.ɪst, -i.əst
piggyback 'pɪg.i.bæk
piggybank 'pɪg.i.bæŋk **-s** -s
pigheaded ˌpɪg'hed.ɪd **-ly** -li **-ness** -nə... -nɪs *stress shift:* ˌpigheaded 'person
piglet 'pɪg.lət, -lɪt US -lɪt **-s** -s
pigment (*n.*) 'pɪg.mənt **-s** -s
pigmen|t (*v.*) pɪg'men|t, 'pɪg.mən|t US 'pɪg.mən|t **-ts** -ts **-ting** -tɪŋ US -ţɪŋ **-ted** -tɪd US -ţɪd
pigmentation ˌpɪg.mən'teɪ.ʃᵊn, -men... **-s** -z
pigm|y 'pɪg.m|i **-ies** -iz
pignut 'pɪg.nʌt **-s** -s
Pigott 'pɪg.ət
pigpen 'pɪg.pen **-s** -z
pigskin 'pɪg.skɪn **-s** -z
pig-sticking 'pɪgˌstɪk.ɪŋ
pigst|y 'pɪg.st|aɪ **-ies** -aɪz
pigswill 'pɪg.swɪl
pigtail 'pɪg.teɪl **-s** -z
Pikachu 'pɪk.ə.tʃuː US 'piː.kə-
pike (P) paɪk **-s** -s **ˌPike's 'Peak**
pikelet 'paɪ.klət, -klɪt US -lɪt **-s** -s
piker 'paɪ.kəʳ US -kɚ **-s** -z
pikestaff 'paɪk.stɑːf US -stæf **-s** -s
pilaf(f) 'pɪl.æf, 'piː.læf, -'- US piː'lɑːf '-- **-s** -s
pilaster pɪ'læs.təʳ, pə- US pɪ'læs.tɚ **-s** -z
Pilate 'paɪ.lət
Pilatus pɪ'lɑː.təs US pɪ-; piː'lɑː.tʊs
pilau 'pɪl.aʊ, 'piː.laʊ, -'- US pɪ'lɔː, piː-'laʊ, -'lɑː **-s** -z
pilchard 'pɪl.tʃəd US -tʃɚd **-s** -z
pil|e paɪl **-es** -z **-ing** -ɪŋ **-ed** -d
pile-driv|er 'paɪlˌdraɪ.v|əʳ US -v|ɚ **-e...** -əz US -ɚz **-ing** -ɪŋ
pile-up 'paɪl.ʌp **-s** -s
pilf|er 'pɪl.f|əʳ US -f|ɚ **-ers** -əz US -ɚz **-ering** -ᵊr.ɪŋ **-ered** -əd US -ɚd **-erer...** -ᵊr.əʳ/z US -ɚ.ɚ/z
pilferage 'pɪl.fᵊr.ɪdʒ
pilferous 'pɪl.fᵊr.əs
Pilger 'pɪl.dʒəʳ US -dʒɚ
pilgrim 'pɪl.grɪm **-s** -z **ˌPilgrim 'Fathe...**
pilgrimag|e 'pɪl.grɪ.mɪdʒ, -grə- **-es** ...
piling 'paɪ.lɪŋ **-s** -z
Pilkington 'pɪl.kɪŋ.tən
pill pɪl **-s** -z **-ing** -ɪŋ **-ed** -d
pillag|e 'pɪl.ɪdʒ **-es** -ɪz **-ing** -ɪŋ **-ed** -d **-er/s** -əʳ/z US -ɚ/z
pillar 'pɪl.əʳ US -ɚ **-s** -z **-ed** -d **from ˌpillar to 'post**
pillar-box 'pɪl.ə.bɒks US -ɚ.bɑːks **-es** -ɪz
pillbox 'pɪl.bɒks US -bɑːks **-es** -ɪz
pillion 'pɪl.i.ən US '-jən **-s** -z
pillock 'pɪl.ək **-s** -s

pillor|y ˈpɪl.ər|.i **-ies** -iz **-ying** -i.ɪŋ **-ied** -id
pillow ˈpɪl.əʊ US -oʊ **-s** -z **-ing** -ɪŋ **-ed** -d **ˈpillow ˌslip; ˈpillow ˌtalk**
pillowcas|e ˈpɪl.əʊ.keɪs US -oʊ- **-es** -ɪz
Pillsbury ˈpɪlz.bər.i US -ˌber-
pilocarpine ˌpaɪ.ləʊˈkɑː.pɪn, -paɪn US ˌpaɪ.loʊˈkɑːr.piːn, ˌpɪl.oʊˈ-, -pɪn
pi|lot ˈpaɪ|.lət **-lots** -ləts **-loting** -lə.tɪŋ US -lə.t̬ɪŋ **-loted** -lə.tɪd US -lə.t̬ɪd **-lotage** -lə.tɪdʒ US -lə.t̬ɪdʒ **ˈpilot ˌlight**
Pilsen ˈpɪl.zən, -sən
pilsener (P) ˈpɪlz.nər, ˈpɪl.snər, -sən.ər US ˈpɪlz.nɚ, ˈpɪl.snɚ
Pilsworth ˈpɪlz.wəθ, -wɜːθ US -wɚθ, -wɝːθ
Piltdown ˈpɪlt.daʊn
pilule ˈpɪl.juːl **-s** -z
pimento pɪˈmen.təʊ US -toʊ **-s** -z
pimiento pɪˈmjen.təʊ, -ˈmen- US -toʊ **-s** -z
Pimlico ˈpɪm.lɪ.kəʊ US -koʊ
Pimm pɪm **-'s** -z
pimp pɪmp **-s** -s **-ing** -ɪŋ **-ed** -t
pimpernel ˈpɪm.pə.nel, -nəl US -pɚ- **-s** -z
pimple ˈpɪm.pl̩ **-s** -z **-d** -d
pimpl|y ˈpɪm.pl̩|.i, ˈ-pl|i US ˈ-pl|i **-iness** -ɪ.nəs, -ɪ.nɪs
pin pɪn **-s** -z **-ning** -ɪŋ **-ned** -d **ˈpin ˌmoney; ˈpin ˌtuck; ˌpins and ˈneedles**
PIN pɪn **ˈPIN ˌnumber**
piña colada ˌpiː.nə.kəʊˈlɑː.də, -njə- US -njə.koʊˈ- **-s** -z
pinafore (P) ˈpɪn.ə.fɔːr US -fɔːr **-s** -z **ˈpinafore ˌdress**
piñata pɪnˈjɑː.tə US -t̬ə **-s** -z
pinball ˈpɪn.bɔːl, ˈpɪm- US ˈpɪn-, -bɑːl **-s** -z **ˈpinball maˌchine**
pince-nez *singular:* ˌpæ̃nsˈneɪ, ˌpænts-, ˌpɪnts-, ˈ-ˌ- *plural:* -ˈneɪz
pincer ˈpɪnt.sər US -sɚ **-s** -z
pinch pɪntʃ **-es** -ɪz **-ing** -ɪŋ **-ed** -t **-er/s** -ər/z US -ɚ/z **ˌtake something with a ˌpinch of ˈsalt**
pinchbeck ˈpɪntʃ.bek **-s** -s
Pinches ˈpɪn.tʃɪz
pinch-hit ˈpɪntʃ.hɪt **-s** -s **-ting** -ɪŋ US -ˌhɪt̬.ɪŋ
Pinckney ˈpɪŋk.ni
pincushion ˈpɪnˌkʊʃ.ən, ˈpɪŋ- US ˈpɪn- **-s** -z
Pindar ˈpɪn.dər US -dɚ
Pindaric pɪnˈdær.ɪk US -ˈdær-, -ˈder- **-s** -s
Pindus ˈpɪn.dəs
pin|e paɪn **-es** -z **-ing** -ɪŋ **-ed** -d **ˈpine ˌcone; ˈpine ˌkernel; ˈpine ˌmarten; ˈpine ˌneedle; ˈpine ˌnut**
pineal ˈpɪn.i.əl; paɪˈniː- US ˈpɪn.i-
pineapple ˈpaɪ.næp.l̩ **-s** -z
Pinel pɪˈnel US pɪ-, ˌpiː-
Pinero pɪˈnɪə.rəʊ, -ˈneə- US -ˈnɪr.oʊ
piner|y ˈpaɪ.nər|.i **-ies** -iz
pinetum paɪˈniː.təm US -t̬əm
pinewood (P) ˈpaɪn.wʊd **-s** -z
ping pɪŋ **-s** -z **-ing** -ɪŋ **-ed** -d **-er/s** -ər/z US -ɚ/z
ping-pong ˈpɪŋˌpɒŋ US -ˌpɑːŋ, -ˌpɔːŋ
pinhead ˈpɪn.hed **-s** -z **-ed** -ɪd
pinhole ˈpɪn.həʊl US -hoʊl **-s** -z **ˌpinhole ˈcamera**
pinion ˈpɪn.jən **-s** -z **-ing** -ɪŋ **-ed** -d
pink (P) pɪŋk **-s** -s **-ing** -ɪŋ **-ed** -t **-er -est ˌpink ˈgin; ˌpink ˈslip; ˈpinking ˌshears**
Pinker ˈpɪŋ.kər US -kɚ
Pinkerton ˈpɪŋ.kə.tən US -kɚ.t̬ən
pink-eye ˈpɪŋk.aɪ **-d** -d
pinkie ˈpɪŋ.ki **-s** -z
pinkish ˈpɪŋ.kɪʃ
pinko ˈpɪŋ.kəʊ US -koʊ **-(e)s** -z
pink|y ˈpɪŋ.k|i **-ies** -iz
pinnac|e ˈpɪn.ɪs, -əs **-es** -ɪz
pinnacl|e ˈpɪn.ə.kl̩, ˈ-ɪ- **-es** -z **-ing** -ɪŋ, ˈpɪn.ə.klɪŋ, ˈ-ɪ- **-ed** -d
pinnate ˈpɪn.eɪt, -ɪt, -ət US -eɪt, -ɪt
pinner (P) ˈpɪn.ər US -ɚ **-s** -z
pinn|y ˈpɪn|.i **-ies** -iz
Pinocchio pɪˈnəʊ.ki.əʊ, -ˈnɒk.i- US pəˈnoʊ.ki.oʊ, pɪ-
Pinochet ˈpɪn.əʊ.ʃeɪ US ˈpiː.noʊ.ʃet, -ʃeɪ
pinoc(h)le ˈpiː.nʌk.l̩, -nɒk- US -nʌk-, -nɑː.kl̩
pinot ˈpiː.nəʊ, -ˈ- US piːˈnoʊ **-s** -z
Pinot Blanc ˌpiː.nəʊˈblɑ̃ːŋ US -noʊˈ-
Pinot Noir ˌpiː.nəʊˈnwɑːr US -noʊˈnwɑːr
pin|point ˈpɪn|.pɔɪnt, ˈpɪm- US ˈpɪn- **-points** -pɔɪnts **-pointing** -ˌpɔɪn.tɪŋ US -ˌpɔɪn.t̬ɪŋ **-pointed** -ˌpɔɪn.tɪd US -ˌpɔɪn.t̬ɪd
pinprick ˈpɪn.prɪk, ˈpɪm- US ˈpɪn- **-s** -s
Pinsent ˈpɪnt.sənt
pinstripe ˈpɪn.straɪp **-s** -s **-d** -t
pint paɪnt **-s** -s
pinta *pint of milk:* ˈpaɪn.tə US -t̬ə **-s** -z
pinta (P) *disease:* ˈpɪn.tə, ˈpiːn- US ˈpɪn.t̬ə, -tɑː
pintado pɪnˈtɑː.dəʊ US -doʊ **-(e)s** -z
pintail ˈpɪn.teɪl **-s** -z
Pinter ˈpɪn.tər US -t̬ɚ
Pinteresque ˌpɪn.tərˈesk US -t̬ɚˈ-
pinto ˈpɪn.təʊ US -t̬oʊ **-(e)s** -z **ˈpinto bean**
pint-pot ˈpaɪnt.pɒt, ˌ-ˈ- US ˈpaɪnt.pɑːt **-s** -s
pint-size ˈpaɪnt.saɪz **-d** -d
pin-up ˈpɪn.ʌp **-s** -s
pinwheel ˈpɪn.*h*wiːl **-s** -z
pinxit ˈpɪŋk.sɪt
Pinxton ˈpɪŋk.stən
Pioline ˌpiː.əʊˈliːn US ˌpiː.oʊˈliːn
pioneer (P) ˌpaɪəˈnɪər US -ˈnɪr **-s** -z **-ing** -ɪŋ **-ed** -d
pious ˈpaɪ.əs **-ly** -li **-ness** -nəs, -nɪs
pip (P) pɪp **-s** -s **-ping** -ɪŋ **-ped** -t
pipal ˈpiː.pəl **-s** -z
pip|e (P) paɪp **-es** -s **-ing** -ɪŋ **-ed** -t **-er/s** -ər/z US -ɚ/z **ˈpipe ˌcleaner; ˈpipe ˌdream; ˌpipe of ˈpeace**
pipeclay ˈpaɪp.kleɪ
pipeline ˈpaɪp.laɪn **-s** -z
Piper ˈpaɪ.pər US -pɚ
pipette pɪˈpet US paɪ-, pɪ- **-s** -s
piping ˈpaɪ.pɪŋ
pipistrel(le) ˌpɪp.ɪˈstrel, -əˈ-, ˈ--- US ˌpɪp.ɪˈstrel **-s** -z
pipit ˈpɪp.ɪt **-s** -s
pipkin ˈpɪp.kɪn **-s** -z
Pippa ˈpɪp.ə
pippin ˈpɪp.ɪn **-s** -z
pipsqueak ˈpɪp.skwiːk **-s** -s
piquancy ˈpiː.kən*t*.si
piquant ˈpiː.kənt, -kɑːnt **-ly** -li
piqu|e piːk **-es** -s **-ing** -ɪŋ **-ed** -t
piqué ˈpiː.keɪ US -ˈ-
piquet *card game:* piːˈket, -ˈkeɪ; ˈpɪk.et, -eɪ US piːˈkeɪ, -ˈket
piquet *soldiers:* ˈpɪk.ɪt **-s** -s
Piquet *racing driver:* ˈpiː.keɪ
pirac|y ˈpaɪə.rə.s|i US ˈpaɪ- **-ies** -iz
Piraeus paɪˈriː.əs, pɪˈreɪ-, pə- US paɪˈriː-
Pirandello ˌpɪr.ənˈdel.əʊ US -oʊ
piranha pɪˈrɑː.nə, pə-, -njə US pəˈrɑː.njə, pɪ-, -nə **-s** -z
pira|te ˈpaɪə.rə|t, -rɪ|t US ˈpaɪ.rə|t **-tes** -ts **-ting** -tɪŋ US -t̬ɪŋ **-ted** -tɪd US -t̬ɪd
piratical paɪəˈræt.ɪ.kəl, pə-, pɪ- US paɪˈræt̬- **-ly** -i
Pirbright ˈpɜː.braɪt US ˈpɝː-
Pirelli® pɪˈrel.i, pə-
Pirie ˈpɪr.i
pirogue pɪˈrəʊg, pə- US -ˈroʊg **-s** -z
pirou|ette ˌpɪr.u|ˈet **-ettes** -ˈets **-etting** -ˈet.ɪŋ US -ˈet̬.ɪŋ **-etted** -ˈet.ɪd US -ˈet̬.ɪd *stress shift:* ˌpirouetting ˈdancer
Pisa ˈpiː.zə
pis aller ˌpiːzˈæl.eɪ, ˌ--ˈ- US -ælˈeɪ **-s** -z
Piscator pɪˈskeɪ.tər US -ˈskɑː.tɔːr
piscatorial ˌpɪs.kəˈtɔː.ri.əl US -ˈtɔːr.i-
piscatory ˈpɪs.kə.tər.i US -tɔːr-
Piscean ˈpaɪ.si.ən, ˈpɪs.i-, ˈpɪs.ki-; pɪˈsiː- US ˈpaɪ.si-, ˈpɪs.i-
Pisces ˈpaɪ.siːz, ˈpɪs.iːz, ˈpɪs.kiːz US ˈpaɪ.siːz, ˈpɪs.iːz
pisciculture ˈpɪs.ɪˌkʌl.tʃər US -tʃɚ
piscin|a pɪˈsiː.n|ə **-as** -əz **-ae** -iː
piscine ˈpɪs.aɪn, ˈpɪsk-, ˈpaɪ.saɪn US ˈpaɪ.siːn, ˈpɪs.iːn-, -aɪn, -ɪn
Piscis| Austrinus ˌpɪs.ɪs|.ɒsˈtraɪ.nəs, ˌ-kɪs-, -ɔːˈstraɪ- US ˌpaɪ.sɪs|.ɔːˈ-, ˌpɪs.ɪs-, -ɑːˈ- **-Australis** -ɒsˈtrɑː.lɪs, -ɔːˈstrɑː- US -ɔːˈstreɪ-, -ɑːˈ-

Pitch

An auditory sensation which places sounds on a scale from low to high.

When we hear a regularly vibrating sound such as a note played on a musical instrument, or a vowel produced by the human voice, we hear a high pitch if the rate of vibration is high and a low pitch if the rate of vibration is low. Many speech sounds are voiceless (e.g. [s]), and cannot give rise to a sensation of pitch in this way. The pitch sensation that we receive from a voiced sound corresponds quite closely to the frequency of vibration of the vocal folds. However, we usually refer to this vibration frequency as 'fundamental frequency' (which we can measure) in order to distinguish it from the subjective impression of pitch.

Pitch is used in many languages as an essential component of the pronunciation of a word, so that a change of pitch may cause a change in meaning: these are called 'tone languages'. In most languages (whether or not they are tone languages) pitch plays a central role in INTONATION.

Pisgah 'pɪz.gə, -gɑː ⓊⓈ -gə
pish pɪʃ
Pisidia paɪ'sɪd.i.ə ⓊⓈ pɪ-
Pisistratus paɪ'sɪs.trə.təs, pɪ-
pismire 'pɪs.maɪəʳ ⓊⓈ -maɪɚ, 'pɪz- **-s** -z
piss pɪs **-es** -ɪz **-ing** -ɪŋ **-ed** -t **'piss ˌartist -er/s** -əʳ/z ⓊⓈ -ɚ/z
pissant 'pɪs.ᵊnt ⓊⓈ -ænt **-s** -s
Pissarro pɪ'sɑː.rəʊ ⓊⓈ -'sɑːr.oʊ
pissed pɪst **ˌpissed as a 'newt**; **ˌpissed as a 'fart**
pissoir 'pɪs.wɑːʳ, 'piː.swɑːʳ ⓊⓈ piː'swɑːr **-s** -z
pisspot 'pɪs.pɒt ⓊⓈ -pɑːt **-s** -s
piss-take 'pɪs.teɪk **-s** -s
piss-up 'pɪs.ʌp **-s** -s
pistachio pɪ'stɑː.ʃi.əʊ, -'stæʃ.i- ⓊⓈ -'stæʃ.i.oʊ, -'stɑː.ʃi- **-s** -z
piste piːst **-s** -s
pistil 'pɪs.tɪl, -tᵊl **-s** -z
pistol 'pɪs.tᵊl **-s** -z
pistole pɪ'stəʊl; 'pɪs.təʊl ⓊⓈ pɪ'stoʊl **-s** -z
pistol-whip 'pɪs.tᵊl.*h*wɪp **-s** -s **-ping** -ɪŋ **-ped** -t
piston 'pɪs.tᵊn **-s** -z **'piston ˌrod**
pit pɪt **-s** -s **-ting** -ɪŋ ⓊⓈ 'pɪt̬.ɪŋ **-ted** -ɪd ⓊⓈ 'pɪt̬.ɪd **ˌpit bull 'terrier**; **'pit ˌpony**; **'pit ˌstop**
pita 'pɪt.ə ⓊⓈ 'piː.t̬ə **'pita ˌbread**
pit-a-pat ˌpɪt.ə'pæt, '--- ⓊⓈ 'pɪt̬.ə.pæt
Pitcairn *surname:* pɪt'keən ⓊⓈ -'kern *island:* pɪt'keən, '-- ⓊⓈ pɪt'kern, '--
pitch pɪtʃ **-es** -ɪz **-ing** -ɪŋ **-ed** -t **'pitch ˌpipe**
pitch-and-putt ˌpɪtʃ.ᵊnd'pʌt
pitch-and-toss ˌpɪtʃ.ᵊnd'tɒs ⓊⓈ -'tɑːs
pitch-black ˌpɪtʃ'blæk *stress shift:* ˌpitch-black 'night
pitchblende 'pɪtʃ.blend
pitch-dark ˌpɪtʃ'dɑːk ⓊⓈ -'dɑːrk *stress shift:* ˌpitch-dark 'night
pitcher (P) 'pɪtʃ.əʳ ⓊⓈ -ɚ **-s** -z **'pitcher ˌplant**
pitchfork 'pɪtʃ.fɔːk ⓊⓈ -fɔːrk **-s** -s **-ing** -ɪŋ **-ed** -t
pitch|man 'pɪtʃ|.mən, -mæn **-men** -mən, -men
pitchpine 'pɪtʃ.paɪn **-s** -z
pitchy 'pɪtʃ.i
piteous 'pɪt.i.əs ⓊⓈ 'pɪt̬- **-ly** -li **-ness** -nəs, -nɪs
pitfall 'pɪt.fɔːl ⓊⓈ -fɔːl, -fɑːl **-s** -z
pith pɪθ **-s** -s **-ing** -ɪŋ **-ed** -t **-less** -ləs, -lɪs **ˌpith 'helmet** ⓊⓈ **'pith ˌhelmet**
pithead 'pɪt.hed **-s** -z
pithecanthrop|us ˌpɪθ.ɪ.kæn'θrəʊ.p|əs; -'kænt.θrə- ⓊⓈ -'kænt.θroʊ-, -θrə-; -kæn'θroʊ- **-i** -aɪ
Pither 'paɪ.θəʳ, -ðəʳ ⓊⓈ -θɚ, -ðɚ
pith|y 'pɪθ|.i **-ier** -i.əʳ ⓊⓈ -i.ɚ **-iest** -i.ɪst, -i.əst **-ily** -ɪ.li, -ᵊl.i **-iness** -ɪ.nəs, -ɪ.nɪs
pitiab|le 'pɪt.i.ə.b|l̩ ⓊⓈ 'pɪt̬- **-ly** -li **-leness** -l̩.nəs, -nɪs
pitiful 'pɪt.i.fᵊl, -fʊl ⓊⓈ 'pɪt̬- **-ly** -i **-ness** -nəs, -nɪs
pitiless 'pɪt.i.ləs, -lɪs ⓊⓈ 'pɪt̬- **-ly** -li **-ness** -nəs, -nɪs
Pitlochry pɪt'lɒk.ri, -'lɒx- ⓊⓈ -'lɑː.kri
pit|man (P) 'pɪt|.mən **-men** -mən, -men
piton 'piː.tɒn, -tɔ̃ːŋ ⓊⓈ -tɑːn **-s** -z
Pitsea 'pɪt.siː, -si
Pitt pɪt
pitta 'pɪt.ə ⓊⓈ 'pɪt̬- **'pitta ˌbread**
pittanc|e 'pɪt.ᵊnts ⓊⓈ 'pɪt- **-es** -ɪz
Pittaway 'pɪt.ə.weɪ ⓊⓈ 'pɪt̬-
pitted 'pɪt.ɪd ⓊⓈ 'pɪt̬-
pitter-patter 'pɪt.əˌpæt.əʳ, ˌpɪt.ə'pæt- ⓊⓈ 'pɪt̬.ɚˌpæt̬.ɚ
Pittman 'pɪt.mən
Pitts pɪts
Pittsburgh 'pɪts.bɜːg ⓊⓈ -bɝːg
pituitary pɪ'tjuː.ɪ.tᵊr.i, '-ə- ⓊⓈ -'tuː.ə.ter-, pə-, -'tjuː- **pi'tuitary ˌgland**
pit|y 'pɪt|.i ⓊⓈ 'pɪt̬- **-ies** -iz **-ying/ly** -i.ɪŋ/li **-ied** -id
pityriasis ˌpɪt.ɪ'raɪə.sɪs, -ə'- ⓊⓈ ˌpɪt̬.ɪ'-
Pius paɪəs
piv|ot 'pɪv|.ət **-ots** -əts **-oting** -ə.tɪŋ ⓊⓈ -ə.t̬ɪŋ **-oted** -ə.tɪd ⓊⓈ -ə.t̬ɪd
pivotal 'pɪv.ə.tᵊl ⓊⓈ -t̬ᵊl **-ly** -i
pix pɪks
pixel 'pɪk.sᵊl, -sel **-s** -z
pix|ie, -|y 'pɪk.s|i **-ies** -iz
pixilated 'pɪk.sɪ.leɪ.tɪd, -sə- ⓊⓈ -t̬ɪd
Pizarro pɪ'zɑː.rəʊ ⓊⓈ -'zɑːr.oʊ
pizazz pɪ'zæz, pə- ⓊⓈ pɪ-
pizza 'piːt.sə, 'pɪt- ⓊⓈ 'piːt- **-s** -z
pizzazz pɪ'zæz, pə- ⓊⓈ pɪ-
pizzeria ˌpiːt.sə'riː.ə, ˌpɪt- ⓊⓈ ˌpiːt- **-s** -z
Pizzey 'pɪt.si; 'pɪz.i
pizzicat|o ˌpɪt.sɪ'kɑː.t|əʊ ⓊⓈ -t|oʊ **-os** -əʊz ⓊⓈ -oʊz **-i** -iː
placability ˌplæk.ə'bɪl.ə.ti, -ɪ.ti ⓊⓈ -ə.t̬i, ˌpleɪ.kə'-
placab|le 'plæk.ə.b|l̩ ⓊⓈ 'plæk.ə-, 'pleɪ.kə- **-ly** -li **-leness** -l̩.nəs, -nɪs
placard (*n.*) 'plæk.ɑːd ⓊⓈ -ɑːrd, -ɚd
placard (*v.*) 'plæk.ɑːd ⓊⓈ -ɑːrd, -ɚd; plə'kɑːrd, plæk'ɑːrd **-s** -z **-ing** -ɪŋ **-ed** -ɪd
placa|te plə'keɪ|t, pleɪ- ⓊⓈ 'pleɪ.keɪ|t, 'plæk.eɪ|t; pleɪ'keɪ|t **-tes** -ts **-ting** -tɪŋ ⓊⓈ -t̬ɪŋ **-ted** -tɪd ⓊⓈ -t̬ɪd
placatory plə'keɪ.tᵊr.i, pleɪ'- ⓊⓈ 'pleɪ.kə.tɔːr-, 'plæk.ə-
plac|e pleɪs **-es** -ɪz **-ing** -ɪŋ **-ed** -t **-er/s** -əʳ/z ⓊⓈ -ɚ/z **'place ˌsetting**
placebo plə'siː.bəʊ, plæs'iː- ⓊⓈ plə'siː.boʊ **-s** -z **pla'cebo efˌfect**
placekick 'pleɪs.kɪk **-s** -s **-ing** -ɪŋ **-ed** -t
place|man 'pleɪs|.mən **-men** -mən
placement 'pleɪs.mənt **-s** -s
placent|a plə'sen.t|ə, plæs'en- ⓊⓈ plə'sen.t̬|ə **-as** -əz **-ae** -iː
placet 'pleɪ.set, -sɪt **-s** -s
placid (P) 'plæs.ɪd **-ly** -li **-ness** -nəs, -nɪs
placidity plə'sɪd.ə.ti, plæs'ɪd-, -ɪ.ti ⓊⓈ plə'sɪd.ə.t̬i
placket 'plæk.ɪt **-s** -s
plagal 'pleɪ.gᵊl
plag|e plɑːʒ **-es** -ɪz
plagiarism 'pleɪ.dʒᵊr.ɪ.zᵊm, -dʒi.ə.rɪ- ⓊⓈ -dʒɚ.ɪ-, -dʒi.ɚ- **-s** -z
plagiarist 'pleɪ.dʒᵊr.ɪst, -dʒi.ə.rɪst ⓊⓈ -dʒɚ.ɪst, -dʒi.ɚ- **-s** -s

plagiaristic ˌpleɪ.dʒəʳˈɪs.tɪk, -dʒi.əˈrɪs- (US) -dʒəˈrɪs-, -dʒi.ə'-
plagiariz|e, -is|e ˈpleɪ.dʒəʳr.aɪz, -dʒi.ə.raɪz (US) -dʒə.raɪz, -dʒi.ə- **-es** -ɪz **-ing** -ɪŋ **-ed** -d
plagiar|y ˈpleɪ.dʒəʳr|.i, -dʒi.ə.r|i (US) -dʒɚ|.i, -dʒi.ɚ- **-ies** -iz
plagu|e pleɪg **-es** -z **-ing** -ɪŋ **-ed** -d **-er/s** -əʳ/z (US) -ɚ/z
plagu|y ˈpleɪ.g|i **-ily** -ɪ.li, -əl.i **-iness** -ɪ.nəs, -ɪ.nɪs
plaice pleɪs
plaid plæd **-s** -z **-ed** -ɪd
Plaid Cymru ˌplaɪdˈkʌm.ri
plain pleɪn **-s** -z **-er** -əʳ (US) -ɚ **-est** -ɪst, -əst **-ly** -li **-ness** -nəs, -nɪs ˌ**plain** ˈ**clothes**; ˌ**plain** ˈ**sailing**
plainchant ˈpleɪn.tʃɑːnt (US) -tʃænt **-s** -s **-ing** -ɪŋ **-ed** -ɪd
plainsong ˈpleɪn.sɒŋ (US) -sɑːŋ, -sɔːŋ
plain-spoken ˌpleɪnˈspəʊ.kən (US) -ˈspoʊ-, ˈ-ˌ-- **-ness** -nəs, -nɪs *stress shift:* ˌplain-spoken ˈperson
plaint pleɪnt **-s** -s
plaintiff ˈpleɪn.tɪf (US) -t̬ɪf **-s** -s
plaintive ˈpleɪn.tɪv (US) -t̬ɪv **-ly** -li **-ness** -nəs, -nɪs
Plaistow ˈplæs.təʊ, ˈplɑː.stəʊ (US) ˈplæs.toʊ, ˈplɑː.stoʊ
Note: The local pronunciation is /ˈplɑː.stəʊ/.
plait plæt **-s** -s **-ing** -ɪŋ (US) ˈplæt̬.ɪŋ **-ed** -ɪd (US) ˈplæt̬.ɪd
plan plæn **-s** -z **-ning** -ɪŋ **-ned** -d **-ner/s** -əʳ/z (US) -ɚ/z ˈ**planning per**ˌ**mission**
planchet ˈplɑːn.tʃɪt (US) ˈplæn-, -tʃet **-s** -s
planchette plɑ̃ːnˈʃet, plɑːn- (US) plænˈʃet **-s** -s
Planck plæŋk
plan|e pleɪn **-es** -z **-ing** -ɪŋ **-ed** -d ˈ**plane** ˌ**tree**
planer (P) ˈpleɪ.nəʳ (US) -nɚ **-s** -z
planet ˈplæn.ɪt **-s** -s
planetari|um ˌplæn.ɪˈteə.ri|.əm, -əˈ- (US) -ɪˈter.i- **-ums** -əmz **-a** -ə
planetary ˈplæn.ɪ.tər.i, ˈ-ə- (US) -ɪ.ter-
planet ˈplæn.dʒənt **-ly** -li
planimeter plænˈɪm.ɪ.təʳ, pləˈnɪm-, ˈ-ə- (US) pləˈnɪm.ə.t̬ɚ, pleɪ- **-s** -z
planimetric ˌplæn.ɪˈmet.rɪk (US) ˌpleɪ.nɪˈ-, ˌplæn.ɪˈ-
planimetry plænˈɪm.ɪ.tri, pləˈnɪm-, ˈ-ə- (US) pləˈnɪm-, pleɪ-
plank plæŋk **-s** -s **-ing** -ɪŋ **-ed** -t
plankton ˈplæŋk.tən, -tɒn (US) -tən
plant (P) (*n. v.*) plɑːnt (US) plænt **-s** -s **-ing** -ɪŋ (US) ˈplæn.t̬ɪŋ **-ed** -ɪd (US) ˈplæn.t̬ɪd **-er/s** -əʳ/z (US) ˈplæn.t̬ɚ/z
Plantagenet plænˈtædʒ.ən.ɪt, -ɪn-, -ət, -et (US) -ə.nɪt **-s** -s
plantain ˈplæn.teɪn, ˈplɑːn-, -tɪn (US) ˈplæn.tɪn, -tən **-s** -z
plantation plænˈteɪ.ʃən, plɑːn- (US) plæn- **-s** -z
Plantin ˈplæn.tɪn, ˈplɑːn- (US) ˈplɑː.n.tæn, ˈplæn-
plantocrac|y plɑːnˈtɒk.rə.s|i (US) plænˈtɑː.krə- **-ies** -iz
plaque plɑːk, plæk (US) plæk **-s** -s
plash plæʃ **-es** -ɪz **-ing** -ɪŋ **-ed** -t **-y** -i
plasm ˈplæz.əm
plasm|a ˈplæz.m|ə **-ic** -ɪk
plasmolysis plæzˈmɒl.ə.sɪs, ˈ-ɪ- (US) -ˈmɑː.lɪ-
Plassey ˈplæs.i
plast|er ˈplɑː.st|əʳ (US) ˈplæs.t|ɚ **-ers** -əz (US) -ɚz **-ering** -ər.ɪŋ **-ered** -əd (US) -ɚz **-erer/s** -ər.əʳ/z (US) -ɚ.ɚ/z ˌ**plaster** ˈ**cast**; ˌ**plaster of** ˈ**Paris**
plasterboard ˈplɑː.stə.bɔːd (US) ˈplæs.tɚ.bɔːrd
plastic ˈplæs.tɪk, ˈplɑː.stɪk (US) ˈplæs.tɪk **-s** -s ˌ**plastic** ˈ**bullet**; ˌ**plastic** ˈ**money**; ˌ**plastic** ˈ**surgeon**; ˌ**plastic** ˈ**surgery**
Plasticine® ˈplæs.tə.siːn, ˈplɑː.stə-, -stɪ- (US) ˈplæs.tɪ-
plasticity plæsˈtɪs.ə.ti, plɑːˈstɪs-, -ɪ.ti (US) plæsˈtɪs.ə.t̬i
plasticiz|e, -is|e ˈplæs.tɪ.saɪz, ˈplɑː.stɪ-, -stə- (US) ˈplæs.tɪ- **-es** -ɪs **-ing** -ɪŋ **-ed** -d **-er/s** -əʳ/z (US) -ɚ/z
plastid ˈplæs.tɪd **-s** -z
Plata ˈplɑː.tə (US) -tɑː
Plataea pləˈtiː.ə
platan ˈplæt.ən **-s** -z
plat(s) du jour ˌplɑː.djuˈʒʊəʳ, -dʊˈ-, -dəˈ- (US) -ˈʒʊr
plat|e (P) (*n. v.*) pleɪt **-es** -s **-ing** -ɪŋ (US) ˈpleɪ.t̬ɪŋ **-ed** -ɪd (US) ˈpleɪ.t̬ɪd ˌ**plate tec**ˈ**tonics**
plateau ˈplæt.əʊ; -ˈ-, pləˈtəʊ (US) plætˈoʊ **-s** -z **-x** -z **-ing** **-ed**
plateful ˈpleɪt.fʊl **-s** -z
plate-glass ˌpleɪtˈglɑːs (US) -ˈglæs ˌ**plate-glass** ˈ**window**
platelayer ˈpleɪtˌleɪ.əʳ (US) -ɚ **-s** -z
platelet ˈpleɪt.lət, -lɪt **-s** -s
platen ˈplæt.ən **-s** -z
platform ˈplæt.fɔːm (US) -fɔːrm **-s** -z **-ing** -ɪŋ **-ed** -d ˌ**platform** ˈ**shoes**
Plath plæθ
Platignum® plætˈɪg.nəm, pləˈtɪg- (US) plə-
platiniz|e, -is|e ˈplæt.ɪ.naɪz, -ən.aɪz (US) -ən- **-es** -ɪz **-ing** -ɪŋ **-ed** -d
platinum ˈplæt.ɪ.nəm, -ən.əm (US) ˈplæt.nəm ˌ**platinum** ˈ**blond(e)**
platitude ˈplæt.ɪ.tjuːd, ˈ-ə-, -tʃuːd (US) ˈplæt̬.ə.tuːd, -tjuːd **-s** -z
platitudinarian ˌplæt.ɪˌtjuː.dɪˈneə.ri.ən, -əˌ-, -ˌtʃuː-, -dəˈ- (US) ˌplæt̬.əˌtuː.dɪˈner.i-, -ˌtjuː- **-s** -z
platitudinous ˌplæt.ɪˈtjuː.dɪ.nəs, -əˈ-, -ˈtʃuː-, -dən.əs (US) ˌplæt̬.əˈtuː.dən-, -ˈtjuː- **-ly** -li
Plato ˈpleɪ.təʊ (US) -t̬oʊ
platonic pləˈtɒn.ɪk, plætˈɒn- (US) pləˈtɑː.nɪk, pleɪ- **-al** -əl **-ally** -əl.i, -li
Platon|ism ˈpleɪ.tən|.ɪ.zəm **-ist/s** -ɪst/s
platoon pləˈtuːn **-s** -z
Platt plæt **-s** -s
platter ˈplæt.əʳ (US) ˈplæt̬.ɚ **-s** -z
platyp|us ˈplæt.ɪ.p|əs, ˈ-ə- (US) ˈplæt̬.ɪ- **-uses** -ə.sɪz **-i** -aɪ
plaudit ˈplɔː.dɪt (US) ˈplɑː-, ˈplɔː- **-s** -s
plausibility ˌplɔː.zɪˈbɪl.ə.ti, -zəˈ-, -ɪ.ti (US) ˌplɑː.zəˈbɪl.ə.t̬i, ˌplɔː-
plausib|le ˈplɔː.zɪ.b|l, -zə- (US) ˈplɑː.zə-, ˈplɔː- **-ly** -li **-leness** -l.nəs, -nɪs
Plautus ˈplɔː.təs (US) ˈplɑː.t̬əs, ˈplɔː-
play pleɪ **-s** -z **-ing** -ɪŋ **-ed** -d **-er/s** -əʳ/z (US) -ɚ/z ˌ**play on** ˈ**words**; ˌ**play the** ˈ**field**; ˈ**playing** ˌ**card**; ˈ**playing** ˌ**field**
playable ˈpleɪ.ə.bl
play-act ˈpleɪ.ækt **-s** -z **-ing** -ɪŋ **-ed** -ɪd **-or/s** -əʳ/z (US) -ɚ/z
playback ˈpleɪ.bæk
playbill ˈpleɪ.bɪl **-s** -z
playboy ˈpleɪ.bɔɪ **-s** -z
Play-Doh® ˈpleɪ.dəʊ (US) -doʊ
player (P) ˈpleɪ.əʳ (US) -ɚ **-s** -z
Playfair ˈpleɪ.feəʳ (US) -fer
playfellow ˈpleɪˌfel.əʊ (US) -oʊ **-s** -z
playful ˈpleɪ.fəl, -fʊl **-ly** -i **-ness** -nəs, -nɪs
playgoer ˈpleɪˌgəʊ.əʳ (US) -ˌgoʊ.ɚ **-s** -z
playground ˈpleɪ.graʊnd **-s** -z
playgroup ˈpleɪ.gruːp **-s** -s
playhou|se ˈpleɪ.haʊ|s **-ses** -zɪz
playlet ˈpleɪ.lət, -lɪt **-s** -s
playlist ˈpleɪ.lɪst **-s** -s
playmate ˈpleɪ.meɪt **-s** -s
play-off ˈpleɪ.ɒf (US) -ɑːf **-s** -s
playpen ˈpleɪ.pen **-s** -z
playroom ˈpleɪ.rʊm, -ruːm (US) -ruːm, -rʊm **-s** -z
playschool ˈpleɪ.skuːl **-s** -z
PlayStation® ˈpleɪˌsteɪ.ʃən **-s** -z
playsuit ˈpleɪ.suːt, -sjuːt (US) -suːt **-s** -s
Playtex® ˈpleɪ.teks
plaything ˈpleɪ.θɪŋ **-s** -z
playtime ˈpleɪ.taɪm **-s** -z
playwright ˈpleɪ.raɪt **-s** -s
plaza (P) ˈplɑː.zə (US) ˈplɑː-, ˈplæz.ə **-s** -z
plc ˌpiː.elˈsiː
plea pliː **-s** -z
plea-bargain ˈpliːˌbɑː.gɪn, -gən (US) -ˌbɑːr.gən **-s** -z **-ing** -ɪŋ **-ed** -d
plead pliːd **-s** -z **-ing/ly** -ɪŋ/li **-ed** -ɪd **pled** pled **pleader/s** ˈpliː.dəʳ/z (US) -dɚ/z
pleading ˈpliː.dɪŋ **-s** -z

Plosive

A sound produced by forming a complete obstruction to the flow of air out of the mouth and nose. Normally, this results in a build-up of compressed air inside the chamber formed by the closure. When the closure is released, there is a small explosion that causes a sharp noise.

Examples for English

British English and US English have six plosive consonants, /p t k/ (voiceless) and /b d g/ (voiced).

In syllable-initial position, sounds in the voiceless group /p t k/ are strongly aspirated (see ASPIRATION), and in final position GLOTTALISATION of these sounds causes a shortening of the preceding vowel. Sounds in the voiced group /b d g/ tend to be 'devoiced' at the beginning and ends of words. At the ends of words, the pairs of sounds /p b/, /t d/ and /k g/ can sound very similar due to this, and one must listen to the length of the vowel to work out which consonant is being produced.

The basic plosive consonant type can be of many different forms: plosives may have any place of articulation, may be voiced or voiceless and may have an 'egressive' (breathing out) or 'ingressive' (breathing in) airflow. The airflow may be from the lungs ('pulmonic'), from the larynx ('glottalic') or generated in the mouth ('velaric'). We find great variation in the release of the plosive.

pleasance (P) 'plez.ᵊnts
pleas|ant 'plez|.ᵊnt **-anter** -ᵊn.təʳ ⓤⓢ -ᵊn.t̬ɚ **-antest** -ᵊn.tɪst, -ᵊn.təst ⓤⓢ -ᵊn.t̬ɪst, -ᵊn.t̬əst **-antly** -ᵊnt.li **-antness** -ᵊnt.nəs, -ᵊnt.nɪs
pleasantr|y 'plez.ᵊn.tr|i **-ies** -iz
pleas|e pliːz **-es** -ɪz **-ing/ly** -ɪŋ/li **-ed** -d
pleasurab|le 'pleʒ.ᵊr.ə.b|l̩ **-ly** -li **-leness** -l̩.nəs, -nɪs
pleasure 'pleʒ.əʳ ⓤⓢ -ɚ **-s** -z **-ing** -ɪŋ **-ed** -d **'pleasure ˌprinciple**
pleat pliːt **-s** -s **-ing** -ɪŋ ⓤⓢ 'pliː.t̬ɪŋ **-ed** -ɪd ⓤⓢ 'pliː.t̬ɪd
pleb pleb **-s** -z **-by** -i
plebe pliːb **-s** -z
plebeian plə'biː.ən, plɪ- ⓤⓢ plɪ-, plə- **-s** -z
plebiscite 'pleb.ɪ.sɪt, '-ə-, -saɪt ⓤⓢ -ə.saɪt, -sɪt **-s** -s
plectr|um 'plek.tr|əm **-ums** -əmz **-a** -ə
pled *(past of* **plead***)* pled
pledg|e pledʒ **-es** -ɪz **-ing** -ɪŋ **-ed** -d **-er/s** -əʳ/z ⓤⓢ -ɚ/z
Pledger 'pledʒ.əʳ ⓤⓢ -ɚ
-plegia -'pliː.dʒi.ə, -dʒə
Note: Suffix. Words containing **-plegia** are always stressed on the syllable **-ple-**, e.g. **paraplegia** /ˌpær.ə'pliː.dʒə ⓤⓢ ˌper-/.
-plegic -'pliː.dʒɪk
Note: Suffix. Words containing **-plegic** are always stressed on the penultimate syllable, e.g. **paraplegic** /ˌpær.ə'pliː.dʒɪk ⓤⓢ ˌper-/.
Pleiad 'plaɪ.æd, -əd, 'pliː-, 'pleɪ- ⓤⓢ 'pliː.æd, 'plaɪ-, -jæd, -əd **-s** -z **-es** -iːz
Pléiade 'pleɪ.ɑːd, -æd, -'- **-s** -z
Pleistocene 'plaɪ.stəʊ.siːn ⓤⓢ -stoʊ-, -stə-
plenar|y 'pliː.nᵊr|.i ⓤⓢ 'pliː-, 'plen.ɚ- **-ily** -ᵊl.i, -ɪ.li
plenipotentiar|y ˌplen.ɪ.pəʊ'tent.ʃᵊr|.i, -ʃi.ᵊr- ⓤⓢ ˌplen.ɪ.poʊ'tent.ʃi.er-, -pə'-, '-ʃɚ- **-ies** -iz
plenitude 'plen.ɪ.tjuːd ⓤⓢ -tuːd, -tjuːd
plenteous 'plen.ti.əs ⓤⓢ -t̬i- **-ly** -li **-ness** -nəs, -nɪs
plentiful 'plen.tɪ.fᵊl, -fʊl ⓤⓢ -t̬ɪ- **-ly** -i **-ness** -nəs, -nɪs
plenty 'plen.ti ⓤⓢ -t̬i
plen|um 'pliː.n|əm ⓤⓢ 'pliː-, 'plen|.əm **-ums** -əmz **-a** -ə
pleonasm 'pliː.əʊ.næz.ᵊm ⓤⓢ -oʊ-, '-ə- **-s** -z
pleonastic ˌpliː.əʊ'næs.tɪk ⓤⓢ -oʊ'-, -ə'- **-al** -ᵊl **-ally** -ᵊl.i, -li
plesiosaur 'pliː.si.əʊ.sɔːʳ ⓤⓢ -oʊ.sɔːr, -ə- **-s** -z
Plessey® 'ples.i
plethora 'pleθ.ᵊr.ə; pleθ'ɔː.rə, plə'θɔː-, plɪ- ⓤⓢ 'pleθ.ɚ.ə
plethoric pleθ'ɒr.ɪk, plə-, plɪ- ⓤⓢ plə'θɔːr-
pleur|a 'plʊə.r|ə, 'plɔː- ⓤⓢ 'plʊr|.ə **-ae** -iː **-as** -əz **-al** -ᵊl
pleurisy 'plʊə.rə.si, 'plɔː-, -rɪ- ⓤⓢ 'plʊr.ə-
pleuritic plʊə'rɪt.ɪk, plɔː- ⓤⓢ plʊ'rɪt̬-
pleuro-pneumonia ˌplʊə.rəʊ.njuː'məʊ.ni.ə, ˌplɔː- ⓤⓢ ˌplʊr.oʊ.nuː'moʊ.njə, -njuː'-
plexiglass (P®)'plek.si.glɑːs ⓤⓢ -sɪ.glæs
plexus 'plek.səs **-es** -ɪz
Pleyel 'pleɪ.el, 'plaɪ- ⓤⓢ 'plaɪ- **-s** -z
pliability ˌplaɪ.ə'bɪl.ə.ti, -ɪ.ti ⓤⓢ -ə.t̬i
pliab|le 'plaɪ.ə.b|l̩ **-ly** -li **-leness** -l̩.nəs, -nɪs
pliancy 'plaɪ.ᵊnt.si
pliant 'plaɪ.ᵊnt **-ly** -li **-ness** -nəs, -nɪs
plié 'pliː.eɪ, -'- ⓤⓢ -'- **-s** -z
pliers plaɪəz ⓤⓢ plaɪɚz
plight plaɪt **-s** -s **-ing** -ɪŋ ⓤⓢ 'plaɪ.t̬ɪŋ **-ed** -ɪd ⓤⓢ 'plaɪ.t̬ɪd
plimsoll (P) 'plɪmp.sᵊl, -sɒl ⓤⓢ -səl, -sɑːl, -sɔːl **-s** -z **'Plimsoll ˌline**
Plinlimmon plɪn'lɪm.ən
plinth plɪntθ **-s** -s
Pliny 'plɪn.i
Pliocene 'plaɪ.əʊ.siːn ⓤⓢ -oʊ-, '-ə-
PLO ˌpiː.el'əʊ ⓤⓢ -'oʊ
plod plɒd ⓤⓢ plɑːd **-s** -z **-ding** -ɪŋ **-ded** -ɪd **-der/s** -əʳ/z ⓤⓢ -ɚ/z
Ploesti, Ploiesti pləʊ'jeʃ.ti ⓤⓢ plɔː-, -'jeʃt.i
Plomer 'pluː.məʳ, 'plʌm.əʳ ⓤⓢ -ɚ
Plomley 'plʌm.li
plonk *(n. v.)* plɒŋk ⓤⓢ plʌŋk, plɑːŋk **-s** -s **-ing** -ɪŋ **-ed** -t
plonker 'plɒŋ.kəʳ ⓤⓢ 'plʌŋ.kɚ **-s** -z
plop plɒp ⓤⓢ plɑːp **-s** -s **-ping** -ɪŋ **-ped** -t
plosion 'pləʊ.ʒᵊn ⓤⓢ 'ploʊ- **-s** -z
plosive 'pləʊ.sɪv, -zɪv ⓤⓢ 'ploʊ.sɪv **-s** -z
plot plɒt ⓤⓢ plɑːt **-s** -s **-ting** -ɪŋ ⓤⓢ 'plɑː.t̬ɪŋ **-ted** -ɪd ⓤⓢ 'plɑː.t̬ɪd **-ter/s** -əʳ/z ⓤⓢ 'plɑː.t̬ɚ/z
plough (P) plaʊ **-s** -z **-ing** -ɪŋ **-ed** -d **-er/s** -əʳ/z ⓤⓢ -ɚ/z **-able** -ə.bl̩
ploughboy 'plaʊ.bɔɪ **-s** -z
plough|man 'plaʊ|.mən **-men** -mən, -men ˌ**ploughman's 'lunch**
ploughshare 'plaʊ.ʃeəʳ ⓤⓢ -ʃer **-s** -z
Plovdiv 'plɒv.dɪv, -dɪf ⓤⓢ 'plɔːv.dɪf
plover 'plʌv.əʳ ⓤⓢ -ɚ **-s** -z
plow plaʊ **-s** -z **-ing** -ɪŋ **-ed** -d **-er/s** -əʳ/z ⓤⓢ -ɚ/z **-able** -ə.bl̩
plowboy 'plaʊ.bɔɪ **-s** -z
Plowden 'plaʊ.dᵊn
plow|man (P) 'plaʊ|.mən **-men** -mən, -men
Plowright 'plaʊ.raɪt
plowshare 'plaʊ.ʃeəʳ ⓤⓢ -ʃer **-s** -z
ploy plɔɪ **-s** -z
pluck (P) plʌk **-s** -s **-ing** -ɪŋ **-ed** -t

pluck|y ˈplʌk|.i -ier -i.əʳ ⓊⓈ -i.ɚ -iest -i.ɪst, -i.əst -ily -ɪ.li, -ᵊl.i -iness -ɪ.nəs, -ɪ.nɪs
plug plʌg -s -z -ging -ɪŋ -ged -d
plughole ˈplʌg.həʊl ⓊⓈ -hoʊl -s -z
plug-in ˈplʌg.ɪn -s -z
plum plʌm -s -z ˌplum ˈpudding
plumag|e ˈpluː.mɪdʒ -es -ɪz
plumb (P) plʌm -s -z -ing -ɪŋ -ed -d
plumbago plʌmˈbeɪ.gəʊ ⓊⓈ -goʊ -s -z
Plumbe plʌm
plumber ˈplʌm.əʳ ⓊⓈ -ɚ -s -z
plumbic ˈplʌm.bɪk
plumbing ˈplʌm.ɪŋ
plumb-line ˈplʌm.laɪn -s -z
plumbous ˈplʌm.bəs
plum|e pluːm -es -z -ing -ɪŋ -ed -d
Plummer ˈplʌm.əʳ ⓊⓈ -ɚ
plumm|et ˈplʌm|.ɪt -ets -ɪts -eting -ɪ.tɪŋ ⓊⓈ -ɪ.t̬ɪŋ -eted -ɪ.tɪd ⓊⓈ -ɪ.t̬ɪd
plummy ˈplʌm.i
plump plʌmp -er -əʳ ⓊⓈ -ɚ -est -ɪst, -əst -ly -li -ness -nəs, -nɪs -s -z -ing -ɪŋ -ed -t
Plumpton ˈplʌmp.tən
Plum(p)tre ˈplʌmp.triː
Plumridge ˈplʌm.rɪdʒ
Plumstead ˈplʌmp.stɪd, -sted
plumule ˈpluː.mjuːl -s -z
plund|er ˈplʌn.d|əʳ ⓊⓈ -d|ɚ -ers -əz ⓊⓈ -ɚz -ering -ᵊr.ɪŋ -ered -əd ⓊⓈ -ɚd -erer/s -ᵊr.əʳ/z ⓊⓈ -ɚ.ɚ/z -erous -ᵊr.əs
plung|e plʌndʒ -es -ɪz -ing -ɪŋ -ed -d
plunger ˈplʌn.dʒəʳ ⓊⓈ -dʒɚ -s -z
plunk plʌŋk -s -s -ing -ɪŋ -ed -t
Plunket(t) ˈplʌŋ.kɪt
pluperfect ˌpluːˈpɜː.fɪkt, -fekt ⓊⓈ ˈpluːˌpɝː.fɪkt, ˌ-ˈ-- -s -s *stress shift, British only:* ˌpluperfect ˈtense
plural ˈplʊə.rᵊl, ˈplɔː- ⓊⓈ ˈplʊr.ᵊl -s -z -ly -i
plural|ism ˈplʊə.rᵊl|.ɪ.zᵊm, ˈplɔː- ⓊⓈ ˈplʊr.ᵊl- -ist/s -ɪst/s
pluralistic ˌplʊə.rᵊlˈɪs.tɪk ⓊⓈ ˌplʊr.ᵊlˈ- -ally -ᵊl.i, -li *stress shift:* ˌpluralistic ˈsystem
pluralit|y plʊəˈræl.ə.t|i, plɔː-, -ɪ.t|i ⓊⓈ plʊˈræl.ə.t̬|i -ies -iz
pluraliz|e, -is|e ˈplʊə.rᵊl.aɪz, ˈplɔː- ⓊⓈ ˈplʊr.ᵊl- -es -ɪz -ing -ɪŋ -ed -d
plurisegmental ˌplʊə.rɪ.segˈmen.tᵊl, ˌplɔː- ⓊⓈ ˌplʊr.ɪ.segˈmen.t̬ᵊl *stress shift:* ˌplurisegmental ˈitem
plus plʌs -(s)es -ɪz
plus-fours ˌplʌsˈfɔːz ⓊⓈ -ˈfɔːrz
plush plʌʃ -er -est -es -ɪz -y -i
Plutarch ˈpluː.tɑːk ⓊⓈ -tɑːrk
Pluto ˈpluː.təʊ ⓊⓈ -t̬oʊ
plutocracy pluːˈtɒk.rə.si ⓊⓈ -ˈtɑː.krə-
plutocrat ˈpluː.təʊ.kræt ⓊⓈ -t̬ə-, -toʊ- -s -s
plutocratic ˌpluː.təʊˈkræt.ɪk ⓊⓈ -toʊˈkræt̬-, -t̬əˈ- -ally -ᵊl.i, -li *stress shift:* ˌplutocratic ˈgovernment
plutonian (P) pluːˈtəʊ.ni.ən ⓊⓈ -ˈtoʊ-
plutonic (P) pluːˈtɒn.ɪk ⓊⓈ -ˈtɑː.nɪk
plutonium pluːˈtəʊ.ni.əm ⓊⓈ -ˈtoʊ-
pluvi|al ˈpluː.vi|.əl -ous -əs
pluviometer ˌpluː.viˈɒm.ɪ.təʳ, ˈ-ə- ⓊⓈ -ˈɑː.mə.t̬ɚ -s -z
pl|y pl|aɪ -ies -aɪz -ying -aɪ.ɪŋ -ied -aɪd
Plymouth ˈplɪm.əθ ˌPlymouth ˈBrethren; ˌPlymouth ˈRock
Plynlimon Fawr plɪnˌlɪm.ənˈvaʊəʳ ⓊⓈ -ˈvaʊr
plywood ˈplaɪ.wʊd
p.m. ˌpiːˈem
PM ˌpiːˈem
PMS ˌpiː.emˈes
PMT ˌpiː.emˈtiː
pneumatic njuːˈmæt.ɪk ⓊⓈ nuːˈmæt̬-, njuː- -s -s -al -ᵊl -ally -ᵊl.i, -li pneuˌmatic ˈdrill
pneumatolog|y ˌnjuː.məˈtɒl.ə.dʒ|i ⓊⓈ ˌnuː.məˈtɑː.lə-, ˌnjuː- -ist/s -ɪst/s
pneumoconios|is ˌnjuː.məʊˌkəʊ.niˈəʊ.s|ɪs, -ˌkɒn.iˈ- ⓊⓈ ˌnuː.moʊˌkoʊ.niˈoʊ-, ˌnjuː-, -məˌ- -es -iːz
pneumonia njuːˈməʊ.ni.ə ⓊⓈ nuːˈmoʊ.njə, njuː-
pneumonic njuːˈmɒn.ɪk ⓊⓈ nuːˈmɑː.nɪk, njuː-
Pnom Penh ˌnɒmˈpen, pəˌnɒm- ⓊⓈ ˌnɑːm-
po (P) pəʊ ⓊⓈ poʊ -es -z
PO ˌpiːˈəʊ ⓊⓈ -ˈoʊ ˈPO ˌbox
poach pəʊtʃ ⓊⓈ poʊtʃ -es -ɪz -ing -ɪŋ -ed -t -er/s -əʳ/z ⓊⓈ -ɚ/z
Pocahontas ˌpɒk.əˈhɒn.təs, -tæs ⓊⓈ ˌpoʊ.kəˈhɑːn.t̬əs
pochard ˈpəʊ.tʃəd, ˈpɒtʃ.əd ⓊⓈ ˈpoʊ.tʃɚd, -kɚd -s -z
pochette pɒʃˈet ⓊⓈ poʊˈʃet -s -s
pock pɒk ⓊⓈ pɑːk -s -s -ed -t
pock|et ˈpɒk|.ɪt ⓊⓈ ˈpɑː.k|ɪt -ets -ɪts -eting -ɪ.tɪŋ ⓊⓈ -ɪ.t̬ɪŋ -eted -ɪ.tɪd ⓊⓈ -ɪ.t̬ɪd -etable -ɪ.tə.bl̩ ⓊⓈ -ɪ.t̬ə.bl̩ -etful/s -ɪt.fʊl/z ˈpocket ˌmoney
pocketbook ˈpɒk.ɪt.bʊk ⓊⓈ ˈpɑː.kɪt- -s -s
pocket-handkerchie|f ˌpɒk.ɪtˈhæŋ.kə.tʃiː|f, -tʃɪ|f ⓊⓈ ˌpɑː.kɪtˈhæŋ.kɚ- -fs -fs -ves -vz
pocketknif|e ˈpɒk.ɪt.naɪ|f ⓊⓈ ˈpɑː.kɪt- -ves -vz
pocket-size ˈpɒk.ɪt.saɪz ⓊⓈ ˈpɑː.kɪt- -d -d
Pocklington ˈpɒk.lɪŋ.tən ⓊⓈ ˈpɑː.klɪŋ-
pockmark ˈpɒk.mɑːk ⓊⓈ ˈpɑːk.mɑːrk -s -s -ing -ɪŋ -ed -t
poco ˈpəʊ.kəʊ ⓊⓈ ˈpoʊ.koʊ
Pocock ˈpəʊ.kɒk ⓊⓈ ˈpoʊ.kɑːk
pococurante ˌpəʊ.kəʊ.kjʊəˈræn.teɪ, -ti ⓊⓈ ˌpoʊ.koʊ.kuːˈræn.t̬i, -kjuːˈ-, -ˈrɑːn- -s -z
pod pɒd ⓊⓈ pɑːd -s -z -ding -ɪŋ -ded -ɪd
podagra pəʊˈdæg.rə, pɒdˈæg-, ˈpɒd.ə.grə ⓊⓈ pəˈdæg.rə; ˈpɑː.də.grə
podg|y ˈpɒdʒ|.i ⓊⓈ ˈpɑː.dʒ|i -ier -i.əʳ ⓊⓈ -i.ɚ -iest -i.ɪst, -i.əst -ily -ɪ.li, -ᵊl.i -iness -ɪ.nəs, -ɪ.nɪs
podiatric ˌpəʊ.diˈæt.rɪk, ˌpɒd.iˈ- ⓊⓈ ˌpoʊ-
podiatr|y pəʊˈdaɪ.ə.tr|i, pɒdˈaɪ- ⓊⓈ pəˈdaɪ-, poʊ- -ist/s -ɪst/s
podi|um ˈpəʊ.di|.əm ⓊⓈ ˈpoʊ- -ums -əmz -a -ə
Podunk ˈpəʊ.dʌŋk ⓊⓈ ˈpoʊ-
Poe pəʊ ⓊⓈ poʊ
Poel pəʊəl; ˈpəʊ.el, -ɪl ⓊⓈ poʊəl; ˈpoʊ.el, -ɪl
poem ˈpəʊ.ɪm, -em; pəʊəm ⓊⓈ poʊəm -s -z
Poema Morale pəʊˌeɪ.mə.mɒrˈɑː.leɪ, -mɔːˈrɑː- ⓊⓈ poʊˌeɪ.mə.mɔːrˈɑː-
poesy ˈpəʊ.ɪ.zi, -ez.i; ˈpəʊə.zi ⓊⓈ ˈpoʊə.si, -zi
poet ˈpəʊ.ɪt, -et; pəʊət ⓊⓈ poʊət -s -s ˌpoet ˈlaureate
poetaster ˌpəʊ.ɪˈtæs.təʳ, ˌpəʊəˈ- ⓊⓈ ˈpoʊə.tæs.tɚ -s -z
poetess ˌpəʊ.ɪˈtes, ˌpəʊəˈ-; ˈpəʊ.ɪ.tɪs, ˈpəʊə.tɪs, -tes ⓊⓈ ˈpoʊ.ɪ.t̬ɪs -es -ɪz
poetic pəʊˈet.ɪk ⓊⓈ poʊˈet̬- -al -ᵊl -ally -ᵊl.i, -li poˌetic ˈjustice
poeticism pəʊˈet.ɪ.sɪ.zᵊm, ˈ-ə- ⓊⓈ poʊˈet̬.ə-
poeticiz|e, -is|e pəʊˈet.ɪ.saɪz, ˈ-ə- ⓊⓈ poʊˈet̬.ə- -es -ɪz -ing -ɪŋ -ed -d -er/s -əʳ/z ⓊⓈ -ɚ/z
poetiz|e, -is|e ˈpəʊ.ɪ.taɪz, ˈpəʊə.taɪz ⓊⓈ ˈpoʊə- -es -ɪz -ing -ɪŋ -ed -d -er/s -əʳ/z ⓊⓈ -ɚ/z
poetry ˈpəʊ.ɪ.tri, ˈpəʊə.tri ⓊⓈ ˈpoʊə-
po-faced ˌpəʊˈfeɪst ⓊⓈ ˌpoʊ- *stress shift:* ˌpo-faced ˈperson
Pogner ˈpəʊg.nəʳ ⓊⓈ ˈpoʊg.nɚ
pogo ˈpəʊ.gəʊ ⓊⓈ ˈpoʊ.goʊ -s -z -ing -ɪŋ -ed -d ˈpogo ˌstick
pogrom ˈpɒg.rəm, -rɒm ⓊⓈ ˈpoʊ.grəm, -grɑːm; pəˈgrɑːm -s -z
poignancy ˈpɔɪ.njənt.si, -nənt- ⓊⓈ -njənt.si
poignant ˈpɔɪ.njənt, -nənt ⓊⓈ -njənt -ly -li
poikilotherm pɔɪˈkɪl.əʊ.θɜːm ⓊⓈ -ə.θɝːm, ˈ-oʊ-
poikilotherm|ic ˌpɔɪ.kɪ.ləʊˈθɜː.m|ɪk ⓊⓈ -ləˈθɝː-, -loʊˈ- -al -ᵊl -ism -ɪ.zᵊm
Poindexter ˈpɔɪn.dek.stəʳ ⓊⓈ -stɚ
poinsettia ˌpɔɪntˈset.i.ə ⓊⓈ -ˈset̬-, ˈ-ə -s -z

point pɔɪnt **-s** -s **-ing** -ɪŋ (US) ˈpɔɪn.t̬ɪŋ **-ed** -ɪd (US) ˈpɔɪn.t̬ɪd **-er/s** -əʳ/z (US) ˈpɔɪn.t̬ɚ/z **ˌpoint of ˌno reˈturn; ˌpoint of ˈorder; ˌpoint of ˈview**
point-blank ˌpɔɪntˈblæŋk *stress shift:* ˌpoint-blank ˈrange
point-duty ˈpɔɪntˌdjuː.ti (US) -ˌduː.t̬i, -ˌdjuː-
pointed ˈpɔɪn.tɪd (US) -t̬ɪd **-ly** -li **-ness** -nəs, -nɪs
Pointe-Noire ˌpwɑ̃ːntˈnwɑːʳ (US) -ˈnwɑːr
pointill|ism ˈpɔɪn.tɪ.l|ɪ.zᵊm, ˈpwæ̃n.tiː.j|ɪ.zᵊm (US) ˈpwæn.tə.l|ɪ-, -tiː.j|ɪ- **-ist/s** -ɪst/s
pointless ˈpɔɪnt.ləs, -lɪs **-ly** -li **-ness** -nəs, -nɪs
point-of-sale ˌpɔɪnt.əvˈseɪl
Pointon ˈpɔɪn.tən (US) -tᵊn
points|man ˈpɔɪnts|.mən **-men** -mən, -men
point-to-point ˌpɔɪnt.təˈpɔɪnt *stress shift:* ˌpoint-to-point ˈchampion
point|y ˈpɔɪn.t|i (US) -t̬|i **-ier** -i.əʳ (US) -i.ɚ **-iest** -i.ɪst, -i.əst
Poirot ˈpwɑː.rəʊ, -ˈ- (US) pwɑːˈroʊ
pois|e pɔɪz **-es** -ɪz **-ing** -ɪŋ **-ed** -d
poison ˈpɔɪ.zᵊn **-s** -z **-ing** -ɪŋ **-ed** -d **-er/s** -əʳ/z (US) -ɚ/z **ˌpoison ˈivy; ˌpoison ˈoak; ˈpoison ˌpill**
poisonous ˈpɔɪ.zᵊn.əs **-ly** -li **-ness** -nəs, -nɪs
poison-pen letter ˌpɔɪ.zᵊnˈpenˌlet.əʳ (US) -ˌlet̬.ɚ **-s** -z
Poitier ˈpwɒt.i.eɪ, ˈpwæt-, ˈpwɑː.ti- (US) ˈpwɑː.ti.eɪ, -tjeɪ
Poitiers ˈpwɑː.ti.eɪ, ˈpwɒt.i-, ˈpwæt.i-, ˌ--ˈ- (US) pwɑːˈtjeɪ, -tiˈeɪ
pok|e pəʊk (US) poʊk **-es** -s **-ing** -ɪŋ **-ed** -t
Pokémon® ˈpəʊ.kə.mɒn, -kɪ-, ˈpɒk- (US) ˈpoʊ.keɪ.mɑːn, -kiː-
poker ˈpəʊ.kəʳ (US) ˈpoʊ.kɚ **-s** -z **ˈpoker ˌface**
pok|ey ˈpəʊ.k|i (US) ˈpoʊ- **-eys** -iz **-ies** -iz
pokie ˈpəʊ.ki (US) ˈpoʊ- **-s** -z
pok|y ˈpəʊ.k|i (US) ˈpoʊ- **-ier** -i.əʳ (US) -i.ɚ **-iest** -i.ɪst, -i.əst **-ily** -ɪ.li, -ᵊl.i **-iness** -ɪ.nəs, -ɪ.nɪs
Pola(c)k ˈpəʊ.læk (US) ˈpoʊ- **-s** -s
Poland ˈpəʊ.lənd (US) ˈpoʊ-
Polanski pəʊˈlænt.ski, pɒlˈænt- (US) pəˈlænt-, poʊ-
polar ˈpəʊ.ləʳ (US) ˈpoʊ.lɚ **-s** -z **ˌpolar ˈbear, ˈpolar ˌbear** (US) **ˈpolar ˌbear**
Polaris pəʊˈlɑː.rɪs, -ˈlær.ɪs, -ˈleə.rɪs (US) pəˈler.ɪs, poʊ-, -ˈlær-
Note: In British English, the rocket and submarine are usually pronounced with /-ˈlɑː-/.
polariscope pəʊˈlær.ɪ.skəʊp, ˈ-ə- (US) poʊˈler.ɪ.skoʊp, -ˈlær- **-s** -s
polarity pəʊˈlær.ə.ti, -ɪ.ti (US) poʊˈler.ə.t̬i, -ˈlær-
polarization, -isa- ˌpəʊ.lᵊr.aɪˈzeɪ.ʃᵊn, -ɪˈ- (US) ˌpoʊ.lɚ.ɪˈ-
polariz|e, -is|e ˈpəʊ.lᵊr.aɪz (US) ˈpoʊ.lə.raɪz **-es** -ɪz **-ing** -ɪŋ **-ed** -d **-er/s** -əʳ/z (US) -ɚ/z
Polaroid® ˈpəʊ.lᵊr.ɔɪd (US) ˈpoʊ.lə.rɔɪd **-s** -z
polder ˈpɒl.dəʳ, ˈpəʊl- (US) ˈpoʊl.dɚ **-s** -z
pole pəʊl (US) poʊl **-s** -z **ˈPole ˌStar; ˈpole ˌvault**
Pole *inhabitant of Poland:* pəʊl (US) poʊl **-s** -z
Pole *surname:* pəʊl, puːl (US) poʊl, puːl
poleax|(e) ˈpəʊl.æks (US) ˈpoʊl- **-es** -ɪz **-ing** -ɪŋ **-ed** -t
polecat ˈpəʊl.kæt (US) ˈpoʊl- **-s** -s
polemic pəˈlem.ɪk, pɒlˈem- (US) pəˈlem- **-s** -s **-al** -ᵊl **-ally** -ᵊl.i, -li
polemicist pəˈlem.ɪ.sɪst, pɒlˈem- (US) pəˈlem- **-s** -s
polemiciz|e, -is|e pəˈlem.ɪ.saɪz, pɒlˈem- (US) pəˈlem.ɪ.saɪz **-es** -ɪz **-ing** -ɪŋ **-ed** -d
polenta pəʊˈlen.tə (US) poʊˈlen.t̬ə, pə-
polestar ˈpəʊl.stɑːʳ (US) ˈpoʊl.stɑːr **-s** -z
Polesworth ˈpəʊlz.wəθ, -wɜːθ (US) ˈpoʊlz.wɚθ, -wɝːθ
pole-vaul|t ˈpəʊl.vɔː|lt, -vɒ|lt (US) ˈpoʊl.vɑː|lt, -vɔː|lt **-ts** -ts **-ting** -tɪŋ (US) -t̬ɪŋ **-ted** -tɪd (US) -t̬ɪd **-ter/s** -təʳ/z (US) -t̬ɚ/z
polic|e pəˈliːs, pliːs (US) pəˈliːs, poʊ-, pliːs **-es** -ɪz **-ing** -ɪŋ **-ed** -t **poˈlice ˌcar; poˌlice ˈconstable; poˈlice ˌforce; poˈlice ˌofficer, poˌlice ˈofficer; poˌlice ˈstate** (US) **poˈlice ˌstate; poˈlice ˌstation**
police|man pəˈliːs|.mən, ˈpliːs- (US) pəˈliːs-, poʊ-, pliːs- **-men** -mən
police|woman pəˈliːs|ˌwʊm.ən, ˈpliːs- (US) pəˈliːs-, poʊ-, pliːs- **-women** -ˌwɪm.ɪn
polic|y ˈpɒl.ə.s|i, ˈ-ɪ- (US) ˈpɑː.lə- **-ies** -iz
policyholder ˈpɒl.ə.siˌhəʊl.dəʳ, ˈ-ɪ- (US) ˈpɑː.lə.siˌhoʊl.dɚ **-s** -z
policymaker ˈpɒl.ə.siˌmeɪ.kəʳ, -ɪ- (US) ˈpɑː.lə.siˌmeɪ.kɚ **-s** -z
polio ˈpəʊ.li.əʊ (US) ˈpoʊ.li.oʊ
poliomyelitis ˌpəʊl.i.əʊ.maɪəˈlaɪ.tɪs, -maɪ.ɪˈ-, -elˈaɪ- (US) ˌpoʊ.li.oʊˌmaɪəˈlaɪ.t̬ɪs
polish (*n. v.*) ˈpɒl.ɪʃ (US) ˈpɑː.lɪʃ **-es** -ɪz **-ing** -ɪŋ **-ed** -t **-er/s** -əʳ/z (US) -ɚ/z
Polish (*adj.*) *of Poland:* ˈpəʊ.lɪʃ (US) ˈpoʊ-
politburo (P) ˈpɒl.ɪtˌbjʊə.rəʊ, pɒlˈɪt-, -ˌbjɔː-; -bjəˌrəʊ, -bjʊˌ- (US) ˈpɑː.lɪtˌbjʊr.oʊ, ˈpoʊ-; poʊˈlɪt-, pə- **-s** -z
po|lite pə|ˈlaɪt (US) pə-, poʊ- **-litest** -ˈlaɪ.tɪst, -ˈlaɪ.təst (US) -ˈlaɪ.t̬ɪst, -ˈlaɪ.t̬əst **-litely** -ˈlaɪt.li **-liteness** -ˈlaɪt.nəs, -ˈlaɪt.nɪs
politic ˈpɒl.ə.tɪk, ˈ-ɪ- (US) ˈpɑː.lə- **-s** -s
politic|al pəˈlɪt.ɪ.k|ᵊl, ˈ-ə- (US) -ˈlɪt̬.ə-, poʊ- **-ally** -ᵊl.i, -li **poˌlitical ˈprisoner; poˌlitical ˈscience**
politician ˌpɒl.ɪˈtɪʃ.ᵊn, -əˈ- (US) ˌpɑː.ləˈ- **-s** -z
politiciz|e, -cis|e pəˈlɪt.ɪ.saɪz, ˈ-ə- (US) -ˈlɪt̬.ə-, poʊ- **-es** -ɪz **-ing** -ɪŋ **-ed** -d
politick ˈpɒl.ə.tɪk, ˈ-ɪ- (US) ˈpɑː.lə- **-s** -s **-ing** -ɪŋ **-ed** -t **-er/s** -əʳ/z (US) -ɚ/z
politico- pəˌlɪt.ɪ.kəʊ- (US) pəˌlɪt̬.ɪ.koʊ-, poʊ-, -kə-
politico pəˈlɪt.ɪ.kəʊ (US) -ˈlɪt̬.ɪ.koʊ, poʊ- **-s** -z
polity ˈpɒl.ə.ti, -ɪ.ti (US) ˈpɑː.lə.t̬i
Polixenes pɒlˈɪk.sə.niːz, pəˈlɪk-, -sɪ- (US) pəˈlɪk.sə-
Polk pəʊk (US) poʊk
polka ˈpɒl.kə (US) ˈpoʊl- **-s** -z **ˈpolka ˌdot**
poll (*n. v.*) pəʊl (US) poʊl **-s** -z **-ing** -ɪŋ **-ed** -d **ˈpoll ˌtax; ˈpolling ˌbooth; ˈpolling ˌstation**
pollard ˈpɒl.əd, -ɑːd (US) ˈpɑː.lɚd **-s** -z **-ing** -ɪŋ **-ed** -ɪd
Pollard ˈpɒl.ɑːd (US) ˈpɑː.lɚd
pollen (P) ˈpɒl.ən, -ɪn (US) ˈpɑː.lən **-s** -z **ˈpollen ˌcount**
polli|nate ˈpɒl.ə|.neɪt, ˈ-ɪ- (US) ˈpɑː.lə- **-nates** -neɪts **-nating** -neɪ.tɪŋ (US) -neɪ.t̬ɪŋ **-nated** -neɪ.tɪd (US) -neɪ.t̬ɪd
pollination ˌpɒl.əˈneɪ.ʃᵊn, -ɪˈ- (US) ˌpɑː.ləˈ-
Pollock ˈpɒl.ək (US) ˈpɑː.lək
pollster ˈpəʊl.stəʳ (US) ˈpoʊl.stɚ **-s** -z
pollutant pəˈluː.tᵊnt, -ˈljuː- (US) -ˈluː- **-s** -s
pollu|te pəˈluː|t, -ˈljuː|t (US) -luː|t **-tes** -ts **-ting** -tɪŋ (US) -t̬ɪŋ **-ted** -tɪd (US) -t̬ɪd **-ter/s** -təʳ/z (US) -t̬ɚ/z
pollution pəˈluː.ʃᵊn, -ˈljuː- (US) -ˈluː- **-s**
Pollux ˈpɒl.əks (US) ˈpɑː.ləks
Polly ˈpɒl.i (US) ˈpɑː.li
pollyanna (P) ˌpɒl.iˈæn.ə (US) ˌpɑː.liˈ- **-s** -z
Polmont ˈpəʊl.mənt (US) ˈpoʊl.mɑːnt
polo (P) ˈpəʊ.ləʊ (US) ˈpoʊ.loʊ **ˈpolo ˌneck**
polonais|e ˌpɒl.əˈneɪz (US) ˌpɑː.ləˈ-, ˌpoʊ- **-es** -ɪz
polonium pəˈləʊ.ni.əm (US) -ˈloʊ-
Polonius pəˈləʊ.ni.əs, pɒlˈəʊ- (US) pəˈloʊ-
polon|y pəˈləʊ.n|i (US) -ˈloʊ- **-ies** -iz
Pol Pot ˌpɒlˈpɒt (US) ˌpɑːlˈpɑːt
Polson ˈpəʊl.sᵊn (US) ˈpoʊl-
poltergeist ˈpɒl.tə.gaɪst, ˈpəʊl- (US) ˈpoʊl.t̬ɚ- **-s** -s
poltroon pɒlˈtruːn (US) pɑːl- **-s** -z **-ery** -ᵊr.i

Polwarth *in Scotland:* ˈpəʊl.wəθ (US) ˈpoʊl.wɚθ *surname:* ˈpɒl.wəθ (US) ˈpɑːl.wɚθ
poly- pɒl.i-, -ɪ-; pəˈlɪ- (US) pɑː.li-, -lɪ-, -lə-; pəˈlɪ-
Note: Prefix. Many compounds with **poly-** have the stress pattern ˈ**poly**,-; these are likely to undergo stress shift when a stressed syllable follows. The prefix may also be stressed on the second syllable, e.g. **polygonal** /pəˈlɪg.ᵊn.ᵊl/.
poly ˈpɒl.i (US) ˈpɑː.li **-s** -z
polyamide ˌpɒl.iˈæm.aɪd, -ˈeɪ.maɪd (US) ˌpɑː.liˈ- **-s** -z
polyandrous ˌpɒl.iˈæn.drəs (US) ˌpɑː.liˈ-
polyandry ˈpɒl.i.æn.dri, ˌpɒl.iˈæn- (US) ˈpɑː.li.æn-, ˌpɑː.liˈæn-
polyanth|us ˌpɒl.iˈænt.θ|əs (US) ˌpɑː.liˈ- **-uses** -ə.sɪz **-i** -aɪ
polybag ˈpɒl.i.bæg, ˌ--ˈ- (US) ˈpɑː.li.bæg **-s** -z
Polybius pəˈlɪb.i.əs, pɒlˈɪb- (US) pəˈlɪb-, poʊ-
polycarbonate ˌpɒl.ɪˈkɑː.bə.neɪt, -iˈ-, -nət, -nɪt (US) ˌpɑː.lɪˈkɑːr.bə.nɪt, -liˈ-, -neɪt **-s** -s
Polycarp ˈpɒl.ɪ.kɑːp, -i- (US) ˈpɑː.lɪ.kɑːrp, -li-
Polycell® ˈpɒl.ɪ.sel, -i- (US) ˈpɑː.lɪ-, -li-
polyclinic ˌpɒl.ɪˈklɪn.ɪk (US) ˌpɑː.lɪˈ- **-s** -s
polycotton ˌpɒl.ɪˈkɒt.ᵊn, -iˈ- (US) ˌpɑː.lɪˈkɑː.tᵊn, -liˈ-
Polycrates pəˈlɪk.rə.tiːz, pɒlˈɪk- (US) pəˈlɪk-
Polydor® ˈpɒl.i.dɔːʳ (US) ˈpɑː.lɪ.dɔːr, -li-
polyester ˌpɒl.iˈes.təʳ (US) ˌpɑː.liˈes.tɚ, ˈpɑː.li.es-
polyethylene ˌpɒl.iˈeθ.ɪ.liːn, ˈ-ə- (US) ˌpɑː.liˈeθ.ə-
Polyfilla® ˈpɒl.ɪˌfɪl.ə, -i- (US) ˈpɑː.lɪˌ-, -liˌ-
polygam|y pəˈlɪg.ə.m|i, pɒlˈɪg- (US) pəˈlɪg-, -li- **-ist/s** -ɪst/s **-ous** -əs
polyglot ˈpɒl.ɪ.glɒt, -i- (US) ˈpɑː.lɪ.glɑːt, -li- **-s** -s
polygon ˈpɒl.ɪ.gɒn, -gən (US) ˈpɑː.lɪ.gɑːn **-s** -z
polygonal pəˈlɪg.ᵊn.ᵊl, pɒlˈɪg- (US) pəˈlɪg- **-ly** -i
polygonum pəˈlɪg.ᵊn.əm, pɒlˈɪg- (US) pəˈlɪg-
polygram® ˈpɒl.i.græm (US) ˈpɑː.lɪ-
polygraph ˈpɒl.ɪ.grɑːf, -i-, -græf (US) ˈpɑː.lɪ.græf, -li- **-s** -s
polyhedr|on ˌpɒl.ɪˈhiː.dr|ᵊn, -iˈ-, -ˈhed.r|ᵊn (US) ˌpɑː.lɪˈhiː-, -li- **-ons** -ᵊnz **-a** -ə **-al** -ᵊl
polylectal ˌpɒl.ɪˈlek.tᵊl, -iˈ- (US) ˌpɑː.lɪˈ-, -liˈ-
polymath ˈpɒl.ɪ.mæθ, -i- (US) ˈpɑː.lɪ-, -li- **-s** -s
polymer ˈpɒl.ɪ.məʳ (US) ˈpɑː.lɪ.mɚ **-s** -z
polymeras|e ˈpɒl.ɪ.mᵊr.eɪs, -eɪz (US) ˈpɑː.lɪ.mə.reɪz, -reɪs **-es** -ɪz
polymeric ˌpɒl.ɪˈmer.ɪk (US) ˌpɑː.lɪ- **-ally** -ᵊl.i, -li
polymerism pəˈlɪm.ᵊr.ɪ.zᵊm, pɒlˈɪm-; ˈpɒl.ɪ.mᵊr- (US) pəˈlɪm.ɚ-; ˈpɑː.lɪ.mɚ-
polymerization, -isa- ˌpɒl.ɪ.mᵊr.aɪˈzeɪ.ʃᵊn, -lə-, -ɪˈ- (US) ˌpɑː.lɪ.mɚ.ɪˈ-
polymeriz|e, -is|e ˈpɒl.ɪ.mᵊr.aɪz, ˈ-ə- (US) ˈpɑː.lɪ.mə.raɪz **-es** -ɪz **-ing** -ɪŋ **-ed** -d
polymerous pəˈlɪm.ᵊr.əs, pɒlˈɪm- (US) pəˈlɪm-
polymorph|ic ˌpɒl.ɪˈmɔː.f|ɪk, -i- (US) ˌpɑː.lɪˈmɔːr-, -iˈ- **-ism** -ɪ.zᵊm **-ous** -əs
Polynesi|a ˌpɒl.ɪˈniː.ʒ|ə, -zi|.ə, -ʒi|.ə, -si|.ə, -ʃi|.ə, -ʃ|ə (US) ˌpɑː.ləˈniː.ʒ|ə, -ʃ|ə **-an/s** -ən/z
polynomial ˌpɒl.ɪˈnəʊ.mi.əl (US) ˌpɑː.liˈnoʊ- **-s** -z
Poly-Olbion ˌpɒl.iˈɒl.bi.ən (US) ˌpɑː.liˈɑːl-
polyp ˈpɒl.ɪp (US) ˈpɑː.lɪp **-s** -s **-ous** -əs
polypeptide ˌpɒl.ɪˈpep.taɪd, -i- (US) ˌpɑː.lɪˈ-, -liˈ- **-s** -z
Polyphemus ˌpɒl.ɪˈfiː.məs, -əˈ- (US) ˌpɑː.lɪˈ-
polyphon|ic ˌpɒl.ɪˈfɒn|.ɪk, -əˈ-, -iˈ- (US) ˌpɑː.lɪˈfɑː.n|ɪk, -liˈ- **-ous** -əs
polyphony pəˈlɪf.ᵊn.i, pɒlˈɪf- (US) pəˈlɪf-
polypody ˈpɒl.ɪ.pəʊ.di, -i- (US) ˈpɑː.lɪ.poʊ-, -li-
polyp|us ˈpɒl.ɪ.p|əs, ˈ-ə- (US) ˈpɑː.lɪ- **-i** -aɪ
polysaccharide ˌpɒl.ɪˈsæk.ᵊr.aɪd, -i-, -ɪd (US) ˌpɑː.lɪˈsæk.ə.raɪd, -liˈ-
polysemous pəˈlɪs.ɪ.məs, pɒlˈɪs-; ˌpɒl.ɪˈsiː- (US) ˌpɑː.lɪˈsiː-; pəˈlɪs.ə-
polysemy pəˈlɪs.ɪ.mi; ˌpɒl.ɪˈsiː.mi, ˈpɒl.ɪ.siː- (US) ˈpɑː.lɪ.siː-; pəˈlɪs.ə-
polystyrene ˌpɒl.ɪˈstaɪə.riːn, -iˈ- (US) ˌpɑː.lɪˈstaɪ-, -liˈ-
polysyllabic ˌpɒl.ɪ.sɪˈlæb.ɪk, -i-, -səˈ- (US) ˌpɑː.lɪ.sɪˈ-, -li- **-al** -ᵊl **-ally** -ᵊl.i, -li
polysyllable ˌpɒl.ɪˈsɪl.ə.bl̩, ˈpɒl.ɪˌsɪl-, -i- (US) ˈpɑː.lɪˌsɪl-, -liˌ- **-s** -z
polysyndeton ˌpɒl.ɪˈsɪn.də.tən, -iˈ-, -dɪ- (US) ˌpɑː.lɪˈsɪn.də.tɑːn, -liˈ-, -tən
polysynthesis ˌpɒl.ɪˈsɪnt.θə.sɪs, -iˈ-, -θɪ- (US) ˌpɑː.lɪˈ-, -liˈ-
polysynthetic ˌpɒl.ɪ.sɪnˈθet.ɪk, -i- (US) ˌpɑː.lɪ.sɪnˈθeţ.ɪk, -li-
polysystemic ˌpɒl.ɪ.sɪˈstiː.mɪk, -i-, -səˈ- (US) ˌpɑː.lɪ-, -li-
polytechnic ˌpɒl.ɪˈtek.nɪk (US) -iˈ-, ˌpɑː.lɪˈ-, -liˈ- **-s** -s
polythe|ism ˈpɒl.ɪ.θiː|.ɪ.zᵊm, ˌpɒl.ɪˈθiː-, -i- (US) ˈpɑː.lɪ.θiː-, ˌpɑː.liˈθiː, -li- **-ist/s** -ɪst/s
polytheistic ˌpɒl.ɪ.θiˈɪs.tɪk; -ˈθiː.ɪ.stɪk, -i- (US) ˌpɑː.lɪ.θiˈɪs.tɪk, -li-
polythene ˈpɒl.ɪ.θiːn, ˈ-ə- (US) ˈpɑː.lɪ-
polyunsaturate ˌpɒl.i.ʌnˈsætʃ.ᵊr.eɪt, -ˈsæt.jᵊr-, -ət (US) ˌpɑː.li.ʌnˈsætʃ.ə.reɪt **-s** -s
polyunsaturated ˌpɒl.i.ʌnˈsætʃ.ᵊr.eɪ.tɪd, -ˈsæt.jᵊr- (US) ˌpɑː.li.ʌnˈsætʃ.ə.reɪ.ţɪd
polyurethane ˌpɒl.ɪˈjʊə.rə.θeɪn, -ˈjɔː-, -iˈ-, -rɪ- (US) ˌpɑː.lɪˈjʊr.ə-, -liˈ-
polyvalent ˌpɒl.ɪˈveɪ.lənt, -iˈ- (US) ˌpɑː.lɪˈ-, ˈpɑː.lɪ.veɪ-, -liˈ-
polyvinyl ˌpɒl.ɪˈvaɪ.nᵊl, -iˈ-, -nɪl (US) ˌpɑː.lɪˈvaɪ.nəl, -liˈ-
Polyxen|a pəˈlɪk.sɪ.n|ə, pɒlˈɪk-, -sə- (US) pəˈlɪk-; ˌpoʊ.lɪkˈsiː- **-us** -əs
Polzeath pɒlˈzeθ (US) pɑːl-
pom (P) pɒm (US) pɑːm **-s** -z
pomace ˈpʌm.ɪs (US) ˈpʌm-, ˈpɑː.mɪs
pomade pəʊˈmeɪd, pɒmˈeɪd, -ˈɑːd (US) pɑːˈmeɪd, poʊ-, ˈpɑː.meɪd, -mɑːd **-s** -z
Pomagne® pəˈmeɪn, pɒmˈeɪn (US) pɑːˈmeɪn, pə-
pomander pəˈmæn.dəʳ, pɒmˈæn- (US) ˈpoʊ.mæn.dɚ; -ˈ--, pə- **-s** -z
pomatum pəˈmeɪ.təm, -ˈmɑː- (US) -ţəm, poʊ- **-s** -z
pome pəʊm (US) poʊm **-s** -z
pomegranate ˈpɒm.ɪˌgræn.ɪt, -əˌ- (US) ˈpɑːmˌgræn-, ˈpʌmˌ-, ˈpɑː.məˌ-, ˈpʌm.əˌ- **-s** -s
pomelo ˈpɒm.ɪ.ləʊ, ˈ-ə-; pəˈmel.oʊ (US) ˈpɑː.mə.loʊ **-s** -z
Pomerania ˌpɒm.əˈreɪ.ni.ə (US) ˌpɑː.məˈ-
Pomeranian ˌpɒm.əˈreɪ.ni.ən (US) ˌpɑː.məˈ- *stress shift:* ˌPomeranian ˈdog
Pomeroy ˈpɒm.ə.rɔɪ, ˈpəʊm.rɔɪ (US) ˈpɑː.mə.rɔɪ, ˈpɑːm.rɔɪ
pomfret *fish:* ˈpɒm.frɪt (US) ˈpɑːm-, ˈpʌm- **-s** -s
Pomfret ˈpʌm.frɪt, ˈpɒm- (US) ˈpʌm-, ˈpɑːm- ˈ**Pomfret** ˌ**cake**
pommel *(n.)* ˈpɒm.ᵊl (US) ˈpʌm.ᵊl, ˈpɑː.mᵊl **-s** -z
pommel *(v.)* ˈpʌm.ᵊl, ˈpɒm- (US) ˈpʌm-, ˈpɑː.mᵊl **-s** -z **-(l)ing** -ɪŋ **-(l)ed** -d
pomm|ie, pomm|y (P) ˈpɒm|.i (US) ˈpɑː.m|i **-ies** -iz
Pomona pəˈməʊ.nə, pɒmˈəʊ- (US) pəˈmoʊ-
pomp pɒmp (US) pɑːmp **-s** -s
pompadour (P) ˈpɒm.pə.dʊəʳ, ˈpɔ̃ːm-, -dɔːʳ (US) ˈpɑːm.pə.dɔːr, -dʊr **-s** -z
Pompeian pɒmˈpeɪ.ən, -ˈpiː- (US) pɑːmˈpeɪ-
Pompeii pɒmˈpeɪ.i, -ˈpeɪ (US) pɑːm-
Pompey ˈpɒm.pi (US) ˈpɑːm-, -peɪ
Pompidou ˈpɒm.pɪ.duː (US) ˈpɑːm- ˈ**Pompidou** ˌ**Centre**

pompom ˈpɒm.pɒm (US) ˈpɑːm.pɑːm **-s** -z
pompon ˈpɒm.pɒn, -pɒŋ, ˈpɔ̃ːm.pɔ̃ːŋ (US) ˈpɑːm.pɑːn **-s** -z
pomposity pɒmˈpɒs.ə.ti, -ɪ.ti (US) pɑːmˈpɑː.sə.t̬i
pompous ˈpɒm.pəs (US) ˈpɑːm- **-ly** -li **-ness** -nəs, -nɪs
ponc|e pɒnts (US) pɑːnts **-es** -ɪz **-(e)y** -i
poncho ˈpɒn.tʃəʊ (US) ˈpɑːn.tʃoʊ **-s** -z
pond (P) pɒnd (US) pɑːnd **-s** -z
pond|er ˈpɒn.d|əʳ (US) ˈpɑːn.d|ɚ **-ers** -əz (US) -ɚz **-ering/ly** -ᵊr.ɪŋ/li **-ered** -əd (US) -ɚd
ponderability ˌpɒn.dᵊr.əˈbɪl.ə.ti, -ɪ.ti (US) ˌpɑːn.dɚ.əˈbɪl.ə.t̬i
ponderable ˈpɒn.dᵊr.ə.bl̩ (US) ˈpɑːn.dɚ- **-ness** -nəs, -nɪs
ponderous ˈpɒn.dᵊr.əs (US) ˈpɑːn- **-ly** -li **-ness** -nəs, -nɪs
Ponders ˈpɒn.dəz (US) ˈpɑːn.dɚz
Pondicherry ˌpɒn.dɪˈtʃer.i, -ˈʃer- (US) ˌpɑːn.dɪˈtʃer-
pondweed ˈpɒnd.wiːd (US) ˈpɑːnd-
pong pɒŋ (US) pɑːŋ, pɔːŋ **-s** -z **-ing** -ɪŋ **-ed** -d
pongee ˌpɒnˈdʒiː, ˌpʌn- (US) ˌpɑːnˈdʒiː; ˈpɑːn.dʒi
poniard ˈpɒn.jəd, -jɑːd (US) ˈpɑː.njɚd **-s** -z **-ing** -ɪŋ **-ed** -ɪd
pons asinorum ˌpɒnzˌæs.ɪˈnɔː.rəm, -rʊm (US) ˌpɑːnzˌæs.ɪˈnɔːr.əm
Ponsonby ˈpʌnt.sᵊn.bi, ˈpɒnt-, -sᵊm- (US) ˈpɑːnt.sᵊn-, ˈpʌnt-
Pontardawe ˌpɒn.təˈdaʊ.i, -eɪ (US) ˌpɑːn.t̬ɚ'-
Pontardulais ˌpɒn.təˈdɪl.əs, -ˈdʌl-, -aɪs (US) ˌpɑːn.t̬ɚ'-
Pontefract ˈpɒn.tɪ.frækt (US) ˈpɑːn.t̬ɪ- **ˈPontefract ˌcake**
Ponteland pɒnˈtiː.lənd (US) pɑːn-
Pontiac ˈpɒn.ti.æk (US) ˈpɑːn.t̬i- **-s** -s
pontifex (P) ˈpɒn.tɪ.feks (US) ˈpɑːn.t̬ɪ- **pontifices** pɒnˈtɪf.ɪ.siːz (US) pɑːn-
pontiff ˈpɒn.tɪf (US) ˈpɑːn.t̬ɪf **-s** -s
pontific pɒnˈtɪf.ɪk (US) pɑːn- **-al/s** -ᵊl/z **-ally** -ᵊl.i, -li
pontificate *(n.) pope:* pɒnˈtɪf.ɪ.kət, ˈ-ə-, -kɪt, -keɪt (US) pɑːnˈtɪf.ɪ.kət, -keɪt **-s** -s
pontifi|cate *(v.) give opinions:* pɒnˈtɪf.ɪ|.keɪt, ˈ-ə- (US) pɑːn- **-cates** -keɪts **-cating** -keɪ.tɪŋ, -keɪ.t̬ɪŋ **-cated** -keɪ.tɪd (US) -keɪ.t̬ɪd
pontification ˌpɒn.tɪ.fɪˈkeɪ.ʃᵊn, -tə- (US) ˌpɑːn.tɪ-, -t̬ə- **-s** -z
Pontine ˈpɒn.taɪn (US) ˈpɑːn.tiːn, -taɪn
Ponting ˈpɒn.tɪŋ (US) ˈpɑːn.t̬ɪŋ
Pontins® ˈpɒn.tɪnz (US) ˈpɑːn-
Pontius ˈpɒn.ti.əs, -tʃi.əs, ˈ-ʃəs (US) ˈpɑːn.tʃəs, ˈ-t̬i.əs **ˌPontius ˈPilate**
Pont l'Évêque ˌpɔ̃ːn.leɪˈvek (US) ˌpɑ̃ːnt.ləˈvek
Pontllanfraith ˌpɒnt.hlænˈvraɪθ, -θlæn'- (US) ˌpɑːnt.θlæn'-
pontoon pɒnˈtuːn (US) pɑːn- **-s** -z
Pont|us ˈpɒn.t|əs (US) ˈpɑːn.t̬|əs **-ic** -ɪk
Pontyclun ˌpɒn.tɪˈklɪn, -tə'- (US) ˌpɑːn.t̬ɪ'-
Pontypool ˌpɒn.tɪˈpuːl, -tə'- (US) ˌpɑːn.t̬ɪ'-
Pontypridd ˌpɒn.tɪˈpriːð, -tə'- (US) ˌpɑːn.t̬ɪ'-
pon|y ˈpəʊ.n|i (US) ˈpoʊ- **-ies** -iz **ˈpony ˌtrekking**
ponytail ˈpəʊ.ni.teɪl (US) ˈpoʊ- **-s** -z
pooch puːtʃ **-es** -ɪz
pood puːd **-s** -z
poodle ˈpuː.dl̩ **-s** -z
poof pʊf, puːf (US) puːf, pʊf **-s** -s
poofter ˈpʊf.təʳ, ˈpuːf- (US) ˈpuːf.tɚ **-s** -z
poofy ˈpʊf.i, ˈpuː.fi (US) ˈpuː.fi
poo(h) (P) *exclamation:* pˌu, phuː, puː *other senses:* puː
Note: /puː/ is the pronunciation for A.A. Milne's character "Winnie the Pooh".
Pooh-Bah ˌpuːˈbɑː, ˈ-- (US) ˈ--
pooh-pooh ˌpuːˈpuː **-s** -z **-ing** -ɪŋ **-ed** -d
Pook puːk
pool puːl **-s** -z **-ing** -ɪŋ **-ed** -d
Poole puːl
Pooley ˈpuː.li
poolroom ˈpuːl.rʊm, -ruːm (US) -ruːm, -rʊm **-s** -z
poon puːn **-s** -z
Poona ˈpuː.nə, -nɑː (US) -nə
poontang ˈpuːn.tæŋ
poop puːp **-s** -s **-ing** -ɪŋ **-ed** -t **ˈpoop ˌdeck**
pooper ˈpuː.pəʳ (US) -pɚ **-s** -z
pooper-scooper ˈpuː.pəˌskuː.pəʳ (US) -pɚˌskuː.pɚ **-s** -z
poop-scoop ˈpuːp.skuːp **-s** -s
poor (P) pɔːʳ, pʊəʳ (US) pʊr **-er** -əʳ (US) -ɚ **-est** -ɪst, -əst **-ly** -li **-ness** -nəs, -nɪs **ˈpoor ˌbox; ˈpoor ˌlaw; ˌpoor reˈlation; ˌpoor ˈwhite**
Poore pɔːʳ, pʊəʳ (US) pʊr
poorhou|se ˈpɔː.haʊ|s, ˈpʊə- (US) ˈpʊr- **-ses** -zɪz
poorly ˈpɔː.li, ˈpʊə- (US) ˈpʊr-
Pooter ˈpuː.təʳ (US) -t̬ɚ **-ish** -ɪʃ
poove puːv **-s** -z
pop pɒp (US) pɑːp **-s** -s **-ping** -ɪŋ **-ped** -t **-per/s** -əʳ/z (US) -ɚ/z **ˈpop ˌart; ˈpop ˌmusic** (US) **ˌpop ˈmusic; ˈpop ˌstar**
popadom, -dum ˈpɒp.ə.dəm (US) ˈpɑː.pə- **-s** -z
popcorn ˈpɒp.kɔːn (US) ˈpɑːp.kɔːrn
pop-down ˈpɒp.daʊn (US) ˈpɑːp-
pope (P) pəʊp (US) poʊp **-s** -s **-dom/s** -dəm/z
popery ˈpəʊ.pᵊr.i (US) ˈpoʊ-
Popeye ˈpɒp.aɪ (US) ˈpɑː.paɪ
pop-eyed ˌpɒpˈaɪd (US) ˈpɑːpˌaɪd *stress shift, British only:* ˌpop-eyed ˈmonst…
pop-gun ˈpɒp.gʌn (US) ˈpɑːp- **-s** -z
Popham ˈpɒp.əm (US) ˈpɑː.pəm
popinjay ˈpɒp.ɪn.dʒeɪ (US) ˈpɑː.pɪn- **-s**
popish ˈpəʊ.pɪʃ (US) ˈpoʊ- **-ly** -li **-ness** -nəs, -nɪs
poplar (P) ˈpɒp.ləʳ (US) ˈpɑː.plɚ **-s** -z
poplin ˈpɒp.lɪn (US) ˈpɑː.plɪn **-s** -z
Popocatépetl ˌpɒp.əʊˌkæt.ɪˈpet.l̩, ˌpəʊ.pəʊ-, -ə'-, ˌpəʊ.pəʊˈkæt.ɪ.pet…, ˌpɒp.əʊ'-, ˈ-ə- (US) ˌpoʊ.pəˈkæt.ə.pet̬.l̩; ˌpɑː.pɑː.kɑːˈteɪ-
popover ˈpɒpˌəʊ.vəʳ (US) ˈpɑːˌpoʊ.vɚ **-s** -z
poppa ˈpɒp.ə (US) ˈpɑː.pə **-s** -z
poppadom, -dum ˈpɒp.ə.dəm (US) ˈpɑː.pə- **-s** -z
popper (P) ˈpɒp.əʳ (US) ˈpɑː.pɚ **-s** -z
Popperian pɒpˈɪə.ri.ən (US) pɑːˈpɪr.i-
poppet ˈpɒp.ɪt (US) ˈpɑː.pɪt **-s** -s
popping creas|e ˈpɒp.ɪŋˌkriːs (US) ˈpɑː.pɪŋˌ- **-es** -ɪz
poppl|e ˈpɒp.l̩ (US) ˈpɑː.pl̩ **-es** -z **-ing** -ɪ… ˈpɒp.lɪŋ (US) ˈpɑː.plɪŋ **-ed** -d
Popplewell ˈpɒp.l̩.wel (US) ˈpɑː.pl̩-
popp|y (P) ˈpɒp|.i (US) ˈpɑː.p|i **-ies** -iz **ˈPoppy ˌDay**
poppycock ˈpɒp.ɪ.kɒk (US) ˈpɑː.pɪ.kɑ…
popsicle (P®) ˈpɒp.sɪ.kl̩ (US) ˈpɑːp- **-s** …
pop|sy, pop|sie ˈpɒp|.si (US) ˈpɑːp- **-sie…** -siz
populace ˈpɒp.jə.ləs, -jʊ-, -lɪs (US) ˈpɑː.pjə.lɪs, -pjʊ-, -ləs
popular ˈpɒp.jə.ləʳ, -jʊ- (US) ˈpɑː.pjə.lɚ, -pjʊ- **-ly** -li
popularity ˌpɒp.jəˈlær.ə.ti, -jʊ'-, -ɪ.t… (US) ˌpɑː.pjəˈler.ə.t̬i, -pjʊ'-, -ˈlær-
popularization, -isa- ˌpɒp.jə.lᵊr.aɪˈzeɪ.ʃᵊn, -jə-, -ɪ'- (US) ˌpɑː.pjə.lɚ.ɪ'-, -pjʊ-
populariz|e, -is|e ˈpɒp.jə.lᵊr.aɪz, -jʊ- (US) ˈpɑː.pjə.lə.raɪz, -pjʊ- **-es** -ɪz **-i…** -ɪŋ **-ed** -d
popu|late ˈpɒp.jə|.leɪt, -jʊ- (US) ˈpɑː.pjə-, -pjʊ- **-lates** -leɪts **-lating** -leɪ.tɪŋ (US) -leɪ.t̬ɪŋ **-lated** -leɪ.tɪd (US) -leɪ.t̬ɪd
population ˌpɒp.jəˈleɪ.ʃᵊn, -jʊ'- (US) ˌpɑː.pjə'-, -pjʊ'- **-s** -z **popuˈlati… exˌplosion**
popul|ism ˈpɒp.jə.l|ɪ.zᵊm, -jʊ- (US) ˈpɑː.pjə-, -pjʊ- **-ist/s** -ɪst/s
populous ˈpɒp.jə.ləs, -jʊ- (US) ˈpɑː.p… -pjʊ- **-ly** -li **-ness** -nəs, -nɪs
pop-up ˈpɒp.ʌp (US) ˈpɑːp-
porcelain ˈpɔː.sᵊl.ɪn (US) ˈpɔːr-, ˈ-slɪn …
porch pɔːtʃ (US) pɔːrtʃ **-es** -ɪz
Porchester ˈpɔː.tʃɪ.stəʳ, -tʃə- (US) ˈpɔːr.tʃɪ.stɚ, -tʃə-
porcine ˈpɔː.saɪn (US) ˈpɔːr-, -sɪn

porcin|o pɔːˈtʃiː.n|əʊ US pɔːrˈtʃiː.n|oʊ -i -iː
porcupine ˈpɔː.kjə.paɪn, -kjʊ- US ˈpɔːr- -s -z
por|e pɔːʳ US pɔːr -es -z -ing -ɪŋ -ed -d
porg|y fish: ˈpɔː.dʒ|i US ˈpɔːr.g|i -ies -iz
Porgy name: ˈpɔː.gi US ˈpɔːr-
pork pɔːk US pɔːrk -er/s -əʳ/z US -ɚ/z -y -i ˌpork ˈpie
porkpie hat ˌpɔːk.paɪˈhæt US ˌpɔːrk- -s -s
Porlock ˈpɔː.lɒk US ˈpɔːr.lɑːk
porn pɔːn US pɔːrn
porno ˈpɔː.nəʊ US ˈpɔːr.noʊ
pornographic ˌpɔː.nəˈgræf.ɪk US ˌpɔːr-
pornograph|y pɔːˈnɒg.rə.f|i US pɔːrˈnɑː.grə- -er/s -əʳ/z US -ɚ/z
porosity pɔːˈrɒs.ə.ti, -ɪ.ti US pɔːˈrɑː.sə.t̬i, pə-
porous ˈpɔː.rəs US ˈpɔːr.əs -ly -li -ness -nəs, -nɪs
porphyria pɔːˈfɪr.i.ə, -ˈfaɪ.ri- US pɔːrˈfɪr.i-
porphyrin ˈpɔː.fᵊr.ɪn, -fɪ.rɪn US ˈpɔːr.fɚ.ɪn
porphyry (P) ˈpɔː.fᵊr.i, -fɪ.ri US ˈpɔːr.fɚ.i
porpois|e ˈpɔː.pəs US ˈpɔːr- -es -ɪz
porridge ˈpɒr.ɪdʒ US ˈpɔːr-
porringer ˈpɒr.ɪn.dʒəʳ US ˈpɔːr.ɪn.dʒɚ -s -z
Porritt ˈpɒr.ɪt US ˈpɔːr-
Porsch|e® pɔːʃ, ˈpɔː.ʃ|ə US pɔːrʃ, ˈpɔːr.ʃ|ə -es -iz, -əz
Porsena ˈpɔː.sɪ.nə, -sᵊn.ə US ˈpɔːr-
Porson ˈpɔː.sᵊn US ˈpɔːr-
port pɔːt US pɔːrt -s -s -ing -ɪŋ US ˈpɔːr.t̬ɪŋ -ed -ɪd US ˈpɔːr.t̬ɪd ˌPort ˈMoresby; ˌport of ˈcall; ˌport of ˈentry; ˌPort ˈStanley; ˌPort ˈTalbot
portability ˌpɔː.təˈbɪl.ə.ti, -ɪ.ti US ˌpɔːr.t̬əˈbɪl.ə.t̬i
portable ˈpɔː.tə.bl̩ US ˈpɔːr.t̬ə- -ness -nəs, -nɪs
portadown ˌpɔː.təˈdaʊn US ˌpɔːr.t̬əˈ-
portage ˈpɔː.tɪdʒ US ˈpɔːr.t̬ɪdʒ
Portakabin® ˈpɔː.təˌkæb.ɪn US ˈpɔːr.t̬əˌ- -s -z
portal (P) ˈpɔː.tᵊl US ˈpɔːr.t̬ᵊl -s -z
portament|o ˌpɔː.təˈmen.t|əʊ US ˌpɔːr.t̬əˈmen.t|oʊ -i -iː
Port-au-Prince ˌpɔː.təʊˈprɪnts US ˌpɔːr.toʊˈ-
Portchester ˈpɔː.tʃɪ.stəʳ, -tʃə- US ˈpɔːr.tʃə.stɚ, -tʃɪ-
portcullis ˌpɔːtˈkʌl.ɪs US ˌpɔːrt- -es -ɪz
Porte pɔːt US pɔːrt
portend pɔːˈtend US pɔːr- -s -z -ing -ɪŋ -ed -ɪd
portent ˈpɔː.tent, -tᵊnt US ˈpɔːr.tent -s -s
portentous pɔːˈten.təs US pɔːrˈten.t̬əs -ly -li -ness -nəs, -nɪs
Porteous ˈpɔː.ti.əs US ˈpɔːr.t̬i-
porter (P) ˈpɔː.təʳ US ˈpɔːr.t̬ɚ -s -z -age -ɪdʒ
porterhou|se ˈpɔː.tə.haʊ|s US ˈpɔːr.t̬ɚ- -ses -zɪz
Porteus ˈpɔː.ti.əs US ˈpɔːr.t̬i-
portfolio ˌpɔːtˈfəʊ.li.əʊ US ˌpɔːrtˈfoʊ.li.oʊ -s -z
Porthcawl ˌpɔːθˈkɔːl, -ˈkaʊl US ˌpɔːrθˈkɑːl, -ˈkɔːl, -ˈkaʊl
porthole ˈpɔːt.həʊl US ˈpɔːrt.hoʊl -s -z
Portia ˈpɔː.ʃə, -ʃi.ə US ˈpɔːr.ʃə
portico ˈpɔː.tɪ.kəʊ US ˈpɔːr.t̬ɪ.koʊ -(e)s -z
portière ˌpɔː.tiˈeəʳ US ˌpɔːrˈtjer, -tiˈer, ˌ-ˈtɪr -s -z
Portillo pɔːˈtɪl.əʊ US pɔːrˈtɪl.oʊ
portion ˈpɔː.ʃᵊn US ˈpɔːr- -s -z -ing -ɪŋ -ed -d
Portishead ˈpɔː.tɪs.hed US ˈpɔːr.t̬ɪs-
Portland ˈpɔːt.lənd US ˈpɔːrt- ˌPortland ceˈment; ˌPortland ˈstone
portl|y ˈpɔːt.l|i US ˈpɔːrt- -ier -i.əʳ US -i.ɚ -iest -i.ɪst, -i.əst -iness -ɪ.nəs, -ɪ.nɪs
Portmadoc ˌpɔːtˈmæd.ək US ˌpɔːrt-
Portman ˈpɔːt.mən US ˈpɔːrt-
portmanteau pɔːtˈmæn.təʊ US pɔːrtˈmæn.toʊ, ˌ--ˈ- -s -z -x -z
Portmeirion ˌpɔːtˈmer.i.ən US ˌpɔːrt-
Pôrto Alegre ˌpɔː.təʊ.əˈleg.ri US ˌpɔːr.tu.əˈleg.rə
Portobello ˌpɔː.təˈbel.əʊ US ˌpɔːr.t̬əˈbel.oʊ, -t̬oʊˈ- *stress shift, see compound:* ˌPortobello ˈRoad
Porto-Novo ˌpɔː.təʊˈnəʊ.vəʊ US ˌpɔːr.t̬oʊˈnoʊ.voʊ
Porto Rico ˌpɔː.təʊˈriː.kəʊ US ˌpɔːr.t̬oʊˈriː.koʊ, -t̬əˈ-
portrai|t ˈpɔː.trɪ|t, -trə|t, -treɪ|t US ˈpɔːr.trɪ|t, -treɪ|t -ts -ts -tist/s -tɪst/s US -t̬ɪst/s
portraiture ˈpɔː.trɪ.tʃə, -trə-, -tjʊəʳ US ˈpɔːr.trɪ.tʃɚ
portray pɔːˈtreɪ, pə- US pɔːr- -s -z -ing -ɪŋ -ed -d -er/s -əʳ/z US -ɚ/z
portrayal pɔːˈtreɪ.əl, pə- US pɔːr- -s -z
Portrush ˌpɔːtˈrʌʃ US ˌpɔːrt-
Port Said ˌpɔːtˈsaɪd, -sɑːˈiːd US ˌpɔːrt.sɑːˈiːd, -ɪd
Port Salut ˌpɔː.səˈluː, -sælˈuː US ˌpɔːr.sælˈuː
Portsea ˈpɔːt.si, -siː US ˈpɔːrt-
Portslade ˌpɔːtˈsleɪd US ˌpɔːrt-
Portsmouth ˈpɔːt.sməθ US ˈpɔːrt-
Portstewart ˌpɔːtˈstjuː.ət US ˌpɔːrtˈstuː.ɚt, -ˈstjuː-
Portugal ˈpɔː.tʃə.gᵊl, -tʃʊ-, -tjə-, -tjʊ- US ˈpɔːr.tʃə-
Portuguese ˌpɔː.tʃəˈgiːz, -tʃʊˈ-, -tjəˈ-, -tjʊˈ- US ˌpɔːr.tʃəˈ-, -ˈgiːs, ˈ--- *stress shift, British only, see compound:* ˌPortuguese ˌman-of-ˈwar
pos|e pəʊz US poʊz -es -ɪz -ing -ɪŋ -ed -d
Poseidon pəˈsaɪ.dᵊn, pɒsˈaɪ- US poʊˈsaɪ-, pə-
poser ˈpəʊ.zəʳ US ˈpoʊ.zɚ -s -z
poseur pəʊˈzɜːʳ US poʊˈzɝː -s -z
posh pɒʃ US pɑːʃ -er -əʳ US -ɚ -est -ɪst, -əst
pos|it ˈpɒz|.ɪt US ˈpɑː.z|ɪt -its -ɪts -iting -ɪ.tɪŋ US -ɪ.t̬ɪŋ -ited -ɪ.tɪd US -ɪ.t̬ɪd
position pəˈzɪʃ.ᵊn -s -z -ing -ɪŋ -ed -d
positional pəˈzɪʃ.ᵊn.ᵊl
positive ˈpɒz.ə.tɪv, ˈ-ɪ- US ˈpɑː.zə.t̬ɪv -s -z -ly -li -ness -nəs, -nɪs ˌpositive discrimiˈnation
positiv|ism ˈpɒz.ɪ.tɪ.v|ɪ.zᵊm, ˈ-ə- US ˈpɑː.zɪ.t̬ɪ- -ist/s -ɪst/s
positron ˈpɒz.ɪ.trɒn, -trən US ˈpɑː.zɪ.trɑːn -s -z
posse ˈpɒs.i US ˈpɑː.si -s -z
possess pəˈzes -es -ɪz -ing -ɪŋ -ed -t -or/s -əʳ/z US -ɚ/z
possession pəˈzeʃ.ᵊn -s -z
possessive pəˈzes.ɪv -s -z -ly -li -ness -nəs, -nɪs posˌsessive ˈadjective; posˌsessive ˈpronoun
possessory pəˈzes.ᵊr.i
posset ˈpɒs.ɪt US ˈpɑː.sɪt -s -s
possibilit|y ˌpɒs.əˈbɪl.ə.t|i, -ɪˈ-, -ɪ.t|i US ˌpɑː.səˈbɪl.ə.t̬|i -ies -iz
possib|le ˈpɒs.ə.b|l̩, ˈ-ɪ- US ˈpɑː.sə- -ly -li
possum ˈpɒs.əm US ˈpɑː.səm -s -z
post pəʊst US poʊst -s -s -ing -ɪŋ -ed -ɪd ˈpost ˌoffice
postag|e ˈpəʊ.stɪdʒ US ˈpoʊ- -es -ɪz ˈpostage ˌstamp; ˌpostage and ˈpacking
postal ˈpəʊ.stᵊl US ˈpoʊ- ˈpostal ˌorder
postbag ˈpəʊst.bæg US ˈpoʊst- -s -z
postbellum ˌpəʊstˈbel.əm US ˌpoʊst- *stress shift:* ˌpostbellum ˈbuilding
postbox ˈpəʊst.bɒks US ˈpoʊst.bɑːks -es -ɪz
postcard ˈpəʊst.kɑːd US ˈpoʊst.kɑːrd -s -z
post-chaise ˈpəʊst.ʃeɪz, ˌ-ˈ- US ˈpoʊst.ʃeɪz, ˌ-ˈ- -s -ɪz
postcode ˈpəʊst.kəʊd US ˈpoʊst.koʊd -s -z
postda|te ˌpəʊstˈdeɪ|t, ˈ-- US ˌpoʊstˈdeɪ|t, ˈ-- -tes -ts -ting -tɪŋ US -t̬ɪŋ -ted -tɪd US -t̬ɪd
post-diluvian ˌpəʊst.dɪˈluː.vi.ən, -daɪˈ-, -ˈljuː- US ˌpoʊst.dɪˈluː-
postdoctoral ˌpəʊstˈdɒk.tᵊr.ᵊl US ˌpoʊstˈdɑːk- *stress shift:* ˌpostdoctoral ˈcontract
poster ˈpəʊ.stəʳ US ˈpoʊs.tɚ -s -z ˈposter ˌpaint

Postalveolar

Descriptive of sounds made between the upper teeth and the front part of the palate.

Examples for English

British and US English have two sets of sounds referred to postalveolar, the fricatives /ʃ ʒ/ and the affricates /tʃ dʒ/.

These are also referred to as PALATO-ALVEOLAR, e.g.:

pressure	/ˈpreʃ.əʳ/	(US) /-ɚ/
pleasure	/ˈpleʒ.əʳ/	(US) /-ɚ/
church	/tʃɜːtʃ/	(US) /tʃɝːtʃ/
judge	/dʒʌdʒ/	

poste restante ˌpəʊst.resˈtɑ̃ːⁿt, ˌ-ˈ-- (US) ˌpoʊst.resˈtɑːnt

posterior pɒsˈtɪə.ri.əʳ (US) pɑːˈstɪr.i.ɚ, poʊ-, pə- **-ly** -li

posteriority pɒsˌtɪə.riˈɒr.ə.ti, ˌpɒs.tɪə-, -ɪ.ti (US) pɑːˌstɪr.iˈɔːr.ə.t̬i, poʊ-

posterit|y pɒsˈter.ə.t|i, -ɪ.t|i (US) pɑːˈster.ə- **-ies** -iz

postern ˈpɒs.tən, ˈpəʊ.stən, -stɜːn (US) ˈpoʊ.stɚn, ˈpɑː- **-s** -z

post-free ˌpəʊstˈfriː (US) ˌpoʊst- *stress shift:* ˌpost-free ˈsystem

Postgate ˈpəʊst.geɪt, -gɪt (US) ˈpoʊst.geɪt

postglacial ˌpəʊstˈgleɪ.si.əl, -ʃəl, -ˈglæs.i.əl (US) ˌpoʊstˈgleɪ.ʃəl *stress shift:* ˌpostglacial ˈperiod

postgraduate ˌpəʊstˈgrædʒ.u.ət, -ˈgræd.ju-, -ɪt (US) ˌpoʊstˈgrædʒ.u.wɪt, ˈ-ə-; ˈ-u.eɪt **-s** -s *stress shift:* ˌpostgraduate ˈstudent

posthaste ˌpəʊstˈheɪst (US) ˌpoʊst-

post hoc ˌpəʊstˈhɒk (US) ˌpoʊstˈhɑːk, -ˈhoʊk

posthumous ˈpɒs.tjə.məs, -tjʊ- (US) ˈpɑːs.tʃə.məs, -tʃʊ- **-ly** -li

Posthumus ˈpɒs.tjʊ.məs, ˈpɒst.hjʊ- (US) ˈpɑːs.tjuː-, -tʃuː-

postich|e pɒsˈtiːʃ (US) pɑːˈstiːʃ, pɔː- **-es** -ɪz

postie ˈpəʊ.sti (US) ˈpoʊ- **-s** -z

postil ˈpɒs.tɪl (US) ˈpɑː.stɪl **-s** -z

postil(l)ion pəˈstɪl.i.ən, pɒsˈtɪl-, ˈ-jən (US) poʊˈstɪl.jən, pɑː- **-s** -z

Post-impression|ism ˌpəʊst.ɪmˈpreʃ.ən|.ɪ.zəm (US) ˌpoʊst- **-ist/s** -ɪst/s

posting ˈpəʊ.stɪŋ (US) ˈpoʊ- **-s** -z

Post-it® ˈpəʊst.ɪt (US) ˈpoʊst-

Postlethwaite ˈpɒs.l̩.θweɪt (US) ˈpɑː.sl̩-

post|man ˈpəʊst|.mən (US) ˈpoʊst- **-men** -mən **-woman** -ˌwʊm.ən **-women** -ˌwɪm.ɪn ˌ**postman's** ˈ**knock**

postmark ˈpəʊst.mɑːk (US) ˈpoʊst.mɑːrk **-s** -s **-ing** -ɪŋ **-ed** -t

postmaster ˈpəʊstˌmɑː.stəʳ (US) ˈpoʊstˌmæs.tɚ **-s** -z ˌ**Postmaster** ˈ**General**

post-meridian ˌpəʊst.məˈrɪd.i.ən (US) ˌpoʊst-

postmistress ˈpəʊst.mɪs.trəs, -trɪs (US) ˈpoʊst- **-es** -ɪz

postmodern ˌpəʊstˈmɒd.ən (US) ˌpoʊstˈmɑː.dɚn **-ism** -ɪ.zəm **-ist/s** -ɪst/s *stress shift:* ˌpostmodern ˈartists

postmortem ˌpəʊstˈmɔː.tem, -təm (US) ˌpoʊstˈmɔːr.t̬əm **-s** -z

postnatal ˌpəʊstˈneɪ.təl (US) ˌpoʊstˈneɪ.t̬əl *stress shift, see compound:* ˌ**postnatal deˈpression**

postoperative ˌpəʊstˈɒp.ər.ə.tɪv (US) ˌpoʊstˈɑː.pɚ.ə.t̬ɪv

postpaid ˌpəʊstˈpeɪd (US) ˌpoʊst- *stress shift:* ˌpostpaid ˈenvelope

post partum ˌpəʊstˈpɑː.təm (US) ˌpoʊstˈpɑːr.t̬əm

postpon|e pəʊstˈpəʊn, pəs- (US) poʊstˈpoʊn **-es** -z **-ing** -ɪŋ **-ed** -d **-ement/s** -mənt/s

postposition ˌpəʊst.pəˈzɪʃ.ən, ˈpəʊst.pəˌzɪʃ- (US) ˌpoʊst.pəˈzɪʃ- **-s** -z

postpositional ˌpəʊst.pəˈzɪʃ.ən.əl (US) ˌpoʊst- *stress shift:* ˌpostpositional ˈparticle

postpositive ˌpəʊstˈpɒz.ə.tɪv, ˈ-ɪ- (US) ˌpoʊstˈpɑː.zə.t̬ɪv *stress shift:* ˌpostpositive ˈadjective

postscript ˈpəʊst.skrɪpt (US) ˈpoʊst- **-s** -s

post-structuralism ˌpəʊstˈstrʌk.tʃər.əl.ɪ.zəm, -tʃʊ.rəl- (US) ˌpoʊstˈstrʌk.tʃɚ-

post-traumatic stress disorder ˌpəʊst.trɔːˌmæt.ɪkˈstres.dɪˌsɔː.dəʳ, -ˌzɔː- (US) ˌpoʊst.trɑːˌmæt̬.ɪkˈstres.dɪˌsɔːr.dɚ, -trɔːˌ-

postulant ˈpɒs.tjə.lənt, -tjʊ- (US) ˈpɑːs.tʃə-, ˈpɑː.stjə- **-s** -s

postulate (*n.*) ˈpɒs.tjə.lət, -tjʊ-, -lɪt, -leɪt (US) ˈpɑːs.tʃə.lɪt, -tʃʊ-, ˈpɑː.stjə-, -stjʊ-, -leɪt **-s** -s

postu|late (*v.*) ˈpɒs.tjə|.leɪt, -tjʊ- (US) ˈpɑːs.tʃə-, ˈpɑː.stjə- **-lates** -leɪts **-lating** -leɪ.tɪŋ (US) -leɪ.t̬ɪŋ **-lated** -leɪ.tɪd (US) -leɪ.t̬ɪd

postulation ˌpɒs.tjəˈleɪ.ʃən, -tjʊˈ- (US) ˌpɑːs.tʃəˈ-, ˌpɑː.stjəˈ- **-s** -z

post|ure ˈpɒs.tʃ|əʳ (US) ˈpɑːs.tʃ|ɚ **-ur** -əz (US) -ɚz **-uring** -ər.ɪŋ **-ured** -əd (US) -ɚd

postviral ˌpəʊstˈvaɪə.rəl (US) ˌpoʊstˈ *stress shift, see compound:* ˌ**postvi faˈtigue** ˌ**syndrome**

post-war ˌpəʊstˈwɔːʳ (US) ˌpoʊstˈwɔ *stress shift:* ˌpost-war ˈpolitics

pos|y ˈpəʊ.z|i (US) ˈpoʊ- **-ies** -iz

pot pɒt (US) pɑːt **-s** -s **-ting** -ɪŋ (US) ˈpɑː.t̬ɪŋ **-ted** -ɪd (US) ˈpɑː.t̬ɪd **-e** -əʳ/z (US) ˈpɑː.t̬ɚ/z ˌ**pot** ˈ**luck**; ˈ**pot** ˌ**plant**; ˌ**potted** ˈ**plant**; ˈ**potting** ˌ**sh**

potable ˈpəʊ.tə.bl̩ (US) ˈpoʊ.t̬ə- **-s** -z

potag|e pɒtˈɑːʒ, pəʊˈtɑːʒ, ˈ-- (US) poʊˈtɑːʒ **-es** -ɪz

potash ˈpɒt.æʃ (US) ˈpɑːt-

potassium pəˈtæs.i.əm (US) pə-, poʊ

potation pəʊˈteɪ.ʃən (US) poʊ- **-s** -z

potato pəˈteɪ.təʊ (US) -t̬oʊ **-es** -z **po**ˈ ˌ**chip**; **po**ˌ**tato** ˈ**crisp**

pot-au-feu ˌpɒt.əʊˈfɜː (US) ˌpɑːt.oʊˈ

pot-bell|y pɒtˈbel|.i, ˈ-ˌ-- (US) ˈpɑːtˌb **-ied** -id

potboiler ˈpɒtˌbɔɪ.ləʳ (US) ˈpɑːtˌbɔɪ. **-s** -z

potbound (*adj.*) ˈpɒt.baʊnd (US) ˈpɑ

poteen pɒtˈiːn, pəʊˈtiːn, -ˈtʃiːn (US) poʊˈtiːn

Potemkin pəˈtemp.kɪn, pɒtˈemp-, pəˈtjɒm.kɪn (US) poʊˈtemp-, pə-

potency ˈpəʊ.tənt.si (US) ˈpoʊ-

potent ˈpəʊ.tənt (US) ˈpoʊ- **-ly** -li

potentate ˈpəʊ.tən.teɪt (US) ˈpoʊ- **-s**

potential pəʊˈten.tʃəl (US) poʊ-, pə- **-ly** -i

potentialit|y pəʊˌten.tʃiˈæl.ə.t|i, - (US) poʊˌten.tʃiˈæl.ə.t̬|i, pə- **-ies**

potentilla ˌpəʊ.tənˈtɪl.ə (US) ˌpoʊ- -

potentiometer pəʊˌten.tʃiˈɒm.ɪ.t ˈ-ə- (US) poʊˌten.tʃiˈɑː.mə.t̬ɚ, pə **-s** -z

potheen pɒtˈiːn, pəʊˈtiːn, -tʃiːn, - ˈpɒθ.iːn (US) poʊˈθiːn, -ˈtiːn

poth|er ˈpɒð|.əʳ (US) ˈpɑː.ð|ɚ **-ers** -ə (US) -ɚz **-ering** -ər.ɪŋ **-ered** -əd (US)

pot-herb ˈpɒt.hɜːb (US) ˈpɑːt.hɝːb

pothole ˈpɒt.həʊl (US) ˈpɑːt.hoʊl -s -z
pothol|ing ˈpɒtˌhəʊ.l|ɪŋ (US) ˈpɑːtˌhoʊ- -er/s -əʳ/z (US) -ɚ/z
pothook ˈpɒt.hʊk (US) ˈpɑːt- -s -s
pothou|se ˈpɒt.haʊ|s (US) ˈpɑːt- -ses -zɪz
pot-hunter ˈpɒtˌhʌn.təʳ (US) ˈpɑːtˌhʌn.t̬ɚ -s -z
potion ˈpəʊ.ʃᵊn (US) ˈpoʊ- -s -z
Potiphar ˈpɒt.ɪ.fɑːʳ, ˈ-ə-, -fəʳ (US) ˈpɑː.t̬ə.fɚ
Potomac pəˈtəʊ.mæk, -mək (US) -ˈtoʊ.mək
potometer pəʊˈtɒm.ɪ.təʳ, ˈ-ə- (US) pəˈtɑː.mə.t̬ɚ
Potosi *in Bolivia:* ˌpɒt.əʊˈsiː (US) ˌpɔː.tɔːˈ-
Potosi *in US:* pəˈtəʊ.si (US) -ˈtoʊ-
potpourri ˌpəʊ.pəˈriː, -pʊˈ- (US) ˌpoʊ.pʊˈriː, -pəˈ-; ˈpoʊ.pʊr.i, -pɚ- -s -z
pot-roast ˈpɒt.rəʊst (US) ˈpɑːt.roʊst -s -s -ing -ɪŋ -ed -ɪd
Potsdam ˈpɒts.dæm (US) ˈpɑːts-
potsherd ˈpɒt.ʃɜːd (US) ˈpɑːt.ʃɝːd -s -z
potshot ˈpɒt.ʃɒt, ˌ-ˈ- (US) ˈpɑːt.ʃɑːt -s -s
Pott pɒt (US) pɑːt
pottage ˈpɒt.ɪdʒ (US) ˈpɑː.t̬ɪdʒ
potted ˈpɒt.ɪd (US) ˈpɑː.t̬ɪd
pott|er (P) ˈpɒt|.əʳ (US) ˈpɑː.t̬|ɚ -ers -əz (US) -ɚz -ering -ᵊr.ɪŋ -ered -əd (US) -ɚd -erer/s -ᵊr.əʳ/z (US) -ɚ.ɚ/z
potter|y (P) ˈpɒt.ᵊr|.i (US) ˈpɑː.t̬ɚ- -ies -iz
pottle ˈpɒt.l̩ (US) ˈpɑː.t̬l̩ -s -z
Potts pɒts (US) pɑːts
pott|y ˈpɒt|.i (US) ˈpɑː.t̬|i -ier -i.əʳ (US) -i.ɚ -iest -i.ɪst, -i.əst -iness -ɪ.nəs, -ɪ.nɪs
pouch paʊtʃ -es -ɪz -ing -ɪŋ -ed -t
pouf *(derog. for homosexual)* pʊf, puːf (US) puːf -s -s
pouffe, pouf, pouff *(seat, headdress)* puːf -s -s
Poughill ˈpɒf.ɪl, ˈpʌf-, ˈpaʊ- (US) ˈpɑː.fɪl, ˈpʌf.ɪl, ˈpaʊ-
Poughkeepsie pəˈkɪp.si (US) pə-, poʊ-
Poulenc ˈpuː.læ̃ŋk (US) puːˈlæ̃ŋk
Poulson ˈpəʊl.sᵊn, ˈpuːl- (US) ˈpoʊl-, ˈpuːl-
poult *chicken:* pəʊlt (US) poʊlt -s -s
poult *silk material:* puːlt (US) puːlt, puː
poulter ˈpəʊl.təʳ (US) ˈpoʊl.t̬ɚ
poulterer ˈpəʊl.tᵊr.əʳ (US) ˈpoʊl.t̬ɚ.ɚ -s -z
poultic|e ˈpəʊl.tɪs (US) ˈpoʊl.t̬ɪs -es -ɪz -ing -ɪŋ -ed -t
Poultney ˈpəʊlt.ni (US) ˈpoʊlt-
Poulton ˈpəʊl.tᵊn (US) ˈpoʊl-
Poulton-le-Fylde ˌpəʊl.tᵊn.ləˈfaɪld, -lɪˈ- (US) ˌpoʊl-
poultry ˈpəʊl.tri (US) ˈpoʊl-
poultry|man ˈpəʊl.tri|.mən, -mæn (US) ˈpoʊl- -men -mən, -men
pounc|e paʊn*t*s -es -ɪz -ing -ɪŋ -ed -t
Pouncefoot ˈpaʊn*t*s.fʊt
pound (P) paʊnd -s -z -ing -ɪŋ -ed -ɪd -er/s -əʳ/z (US) -ɚ/z ˌpound ˈsterling
poundag|e ˈpaʊn.dɪdʒ -es -ɪz
Pounds paʊndz
Pount(e)ney ˈpaʊnt.ni
Poupart ˈpəʊ.pɑːt, ˈpuː- (US) ˌpuːˈpɑːrt
Pouparts ˈpuː.pɑːts (US) ˌpuːˈpɑːrts
pour pɔːʳ (US) pɔːr -s -z -ing -ɪŋ -ed -d -er/s -əʳ/z (US) -ɚ/z
pourboire ˈpʊə.bwɑːʳ, ˈpɔː- (US) pʊrˈbwɑːr -s -z
pourparler ˌpʊəˈpɑː.leɪ, ˌpɔː- (US) ˌpʊr.pɑːrˈleɪ -s -z
poussin (P) ˈpuː.sæ̃ŋ (US) puːˈsæ̃n -s -z
pout paʊt -s -s -ing -ɪŋ (US) ˈpaʊ.t̬ɪŋ -ed -ɪd (US) ˈpaʊ.t̬ɪd
poverty ˈpɒv.ə.ti (US) ˈpɑː.vɚ.t̬i ˈpoverty ˌtrap
poverty-stricken ˈpɒv.ə.tiˌstrɪk.ᵊn (US) ˈpɑː.vɚ.t̬iˌ-
Povey ˈpəʊ.vi; pəˈveɪ (US) ˈpoʊ.vi; pəˈveɪ
Pow paʊ
POW ˌpiː.əʊˈdʌb.l̩.juː (US) -oʊˈ- -ˈs -z
powd|er ˈpaʊ.d|əʳ (US) -d|ɚ -ers -əz (US) -ɚz -ering -ᵊr.ɪŋ -ered -əd (US) -ɚd ˌpowder ˈblue; ˈpowder ˌkeg; ˈpowder ˌpuff; ˈpowder ˌroom
powder|y ˈpaʊ.dᵊr|.i -iness -ɪ.nəs, -ɪ.nɪs
Powell paʊəl, pəʊəl; ˈpaʊ.ɪl, ˈpəʊ-, -el (US) paʊəl, poʊəl
power (P) paʊəʳ (US) paʊɚ -s -z -ing -ɪŋ -ed -d ˈpower ˌbase; ˈpower ˌcut; ˌpower of atˈtorney; ˌpower ˈpolitics; ˈpower ˌstation; ˌpower ˈsteering
powerboat ˈpaʊə.bəʊt (US) ˈpaʊɚ.boʊt -s -s
powerful ˈpaʊə.fᵊl, -fʊl (US) ˈpaʊɚ- -ly -i -ness -nəs, -nɪs
Powergen ˈpaʊə.dʒen (US) ˈpaʊɚ-
powerhou|se ˈpaʊə.haʊ|s (US) ˈpaʊɚ- -ses -zɪz
powerless ˈpaʊə.ləs, -lɪs (US) ˈpaʊɚ- -ly -li -ness -nəs, -nɪs
powerpack ˈpaʊə.pæk (US) ˈpaʊɚ- -s -s
powerpoint ˈpaʊə.pɔɪnt (US) ˈpaʊɚ- -s -s
Powerscourt ˈpɔːz.kɔːt, ˈpaʊəz- (US) ˈpaʊɚz.kɔːrt
Powicke ˈpəʊ.ɪk (US) ˈpoʊ-
Powis *place in Scotland, square in London:* ˈpaʊ.ɪs *surname:* ˈpəʊ.ɪs, ˈpaʊ- (US) ˈpoʊ-, ˈpaʊ-
Powles pəʊlz (US) poʊlz
Powlett ˈpɔː.lɪt (US) ˈpɑː-, ˈpɔː-
Pownall ˈpaʊ.nᵊl
powwow *(n. v.)* ˈpaʊ.waʊ -s -z -ing -ɪŋ -ed -d
Powys ˈpəʊ.ɪs, ˈpaʊ.ɪs (US) ˈpoʊ-, ˈpaʊ-
pox pɒks (US) pɑːks
poxy ˈpɒk.si (US) ˈpɑːk-
Poyner ˈpɔɪ.nəʳ (US) -nɚ
Poynings ˈpɔɪ.nɪŋz
Poynter ˈpɔɪn.təʳ (US) -t̬ɚ
Poynton ˈpɔɪn.tən
Poznan ˈpɒz.næn (US) ˈpoʊz-, -nɑːn
PR ˌpiːˈɑːʳ (US) -ˈɑːr
practicability ˌpræk.tɪ.kəˈbɪl.ə.ti, -ɪ.ti (US) -ə.t̬i
practicab|le ˈpræk.tɪ.kə.b|l̩ -ly -li -leness -l̩.nəs, -nɪs
practical ˈpræk.tɪ.kᵊl -ness -nəs, -nɪs ˌpractical ˈjoke
practicalit|y ˌpræk.tɪˈkæl.ə.t|i, -ɪ.t|i (US) -ə.t̬|i -ies -iz
practically ˈpræk.tɪ.kᵊl.i (US) -tɪ.kli
practic|e ˈpræk.tɪs -es -ɪz -ing -ɪŋ -ed -t
practician prækˈtɪʃ.ᵊn -s -z
practis|e ˈpræk.tɪs -es -ɪz -ing -ɪŋ -ed -t ˌpractise what one ˈpreaches
practitioner prækˈtɪʃ.ᵊn.əʳ (US) -ɚ -s -z
Prada® ˈprɑː.də
Prado ˈprɑː.dəʊ (US) -doʊ
praecox ˈpriː.kɒks, ˈpraɪ- (US) ˈpriː.kɑːks
Praed preɪd
prae|nomen ˌpriː|ˈnəʊ.men, ˌpraɪ- (US) ˌpriː|ˈnoʊ- -nomens -ˈnəʊ.mənz (US) -ˈnoʊ- -nomina -ˈnɒm.ɪ.nə, -ˈnəʊ.mɪ- (US) -ˈnɑː-, -ˈnoʊ-
praepostor ˌpriːˈpɒs.təʳ (US) -ˈpɑː.stɚ -s -z
praesidi|um prɪˈsɪd.i|.əm, prə-, praɪ- -ums -əmz -a -ə
Praeterita ˌpriːˈter.ɪ.tə, prɪ-, praɪ- (US) prɪˈter.ɪ.t̬ə
praetor ˈpriː.təʳ, ˈpraɪ-, -tɔːʳ (US) ˈpriː.t̬ɚ -s -z -ship/s -ʃɪp/s
praetori|al priːˈtɔː.ri|.əl, praɪˈ- (US) -ˈtɔːr- -an -ən
pragmatic prægˈmæt.ɪk (US) -ˈmæt̬- -s -s -al -ᵊl -ally -ᵊl.i, -li
pragmat|ism ˈpræg.mə.t|ɪ.zᵊm -ist/s -ɪst/s
Prague prɑːg
Praia ˈpraɪ.ə (US) ˈprɑː.jə
prairie (P) ˈpreə.ri (US) ˈprer.i -s -z ˈprairie ˌdog; ˌprairie ˈoyster
prais|e preɪz -es -ɪz -ing -ɪŋ -ed -d -er/s -əʳ/z
praiseworth|y ˈpreɪzˌwɜː.ð|i (US) -ˌwɝː- -iness -ɪ.nəs, -ɪ.nɪs
Prakrit ˈprɑː.krɪt
praline ˈprɑː.liːn (US) ˈprɑː-, ˈpreɪ- -s -z
Prall prɔːl (US) prɔːl, prɑːl
pram *baby carriage:* præm -s -z
pram *flat-bottomed boat:* prɑːm -s -z
pranc|e (P) prɑːn*t*s (US) præn*t*s -es -ɪz -ing -ɪŋ -ed -t -er/s -əʳ/z (US) -ɚ/z
prandial ˈpræn.di.əl
prang præŋ -s -z -ing -ɪŋ -ed -d
prank præŋk -s -s -ing -ɪŋ -ed -t

prank|ish 'præŋ.klɪʃ **-some** -səm
prankster 'præŋk.stəʳ ⓤⓢ -stɚ **-s** -z
praseodymium ˌpreɪ.zi.əʊ'dɪm.i.əm, ˌpraɪ.zəʊ'- ⓤⓢ ˌpreɪ.zi.oʊ'-, -si-
prat præt **-s** -s
Pratchett 'prætʃ.ɪt
prat|e preɪt **-es** -s **-ing** -ɪŋ **-ed** -ɪd **-er/s** -əʳ/z ⓤⓢ -ɚ/z
pratfall 'præt.fɔːl **-s** -z
pratincole 'præt.ɪŋ.kəʊl, 'preɪ.tɪŋ- ⓤⓢ 'præt.ɪn.koʊl, 'preɪ.tɪn-, -tən-, -ɪŋ- **-s** -z
pratique 'præt.iːk, -ɪk, præt'iːk ⓤⓢ præt'iːk; 'præţ.ɪk **-s** -s
Pratt præt
prattl|e 'præt.l̩ ⓤⓢ 'præţ- **-es** -z **-ing** -ɪŋ, 'præt.lɪŋ **-ed** -d **-er/s** -əʳ/z, 'præt.ləʳ/z ⓤⓢ 'præţ.l̩.ɚ/z, 'præt.lɚ/z
Pravda 'prɑːv.də
prawn prɔːn ⓤⓢ prɑːn, prɔːn **-s** -z **ˌprawn 'cocktail**; **ˌprawn 'cracker**
prax|is 'præk.s|ɪs **-es** -iːz
Praxiteles præk'sɪt.əl.iːz, -tɪ.liːz ⓤⓢ -'sɪţ.əl.iːz
pray (P) preɪ **-s** -z **-ing** -ɪŋ **-ed** -d
prayer *person who prays:* 'preɪ.əʳ ⓤⓢ -ɚ **-s** -z
prayer *supplication:* preəʳ ⓤⓢ prer **-s** -z **'prayer ˌmat**; **'prayer ˌmeeting**; **'prayer ˌrug**; **'prayer ˌwheel**
prayer-book 'preə.bʊk ⓤⓢ 'prer- **-s** -s
prayerful 'preə.fəl, -fʊl ⓤⓢ 'prer- **-ly** -i **-ness** -nəs, -nɪs
prayerless 'preə.ləs, -lɪs ⓤⓢ 'prer- **-ly** -li **-ness** -nəs, -nɪs
praying mant|is ˌpreɪ.ɪŋ'mæn.t|ɪs ⓤⓢ -ţ|ɪs **-ises** -ɪ.sɪz **-es** -iːz
pre- priː-, prɪ-, pri-, prə-
Note: Prefix. In words containing **pre-** where the stem is free, and the meaning is **beforehand**, it generally takes secondary stress, e.g. **pre-eminence** /ˌpriː'em.ɪ.nənts/. Attached to bound stems the pronunciation is normally /prɪ-/ or /prə-/ for British English and /prɪ-/ or /priː-/ for American English, e.g. **prefer** /prɪ'fɜː ⓤⓢ priː'fɜːr/. There are exceptions; see individual entries.
preach priːtʃ **-es** -ɪz **-ing** -ɪŋ **-ed** -t **-er/s** -əʳ/z ⓤⓢ -ɚ/z **ˌpreach to the con'verted**
preachi|fy 'priː.tʃɪ|.faɪ **-fies** -faɪz **-fying** -faɪ.ɪŋ **-fied** -faɪd
preach|y 'priː.tʃ|i **-ily** -ɪ.li, -əl.i **-iness** -ɪ.nəs, -ɪ.nɪs
Preager 'preɪ.gəʳ ⓤⓢ -gɚ
preamble 'priː.æm.bl̩, pri'æm- **-s** -z
preamplifier pri'æm.plɪ.faɪ.əʳ ⓤⓢ -plə.faɪ.ɚ **-s** -z
prearrang|e ˌpriː.ə'reɪndʒ **-es** -ɪz **-ing** -ɪŋ **-ed** -d
Prebble 'preb.l̩
prebend 'preb.ənd **-s** -z
prebendar|y 'preb.ən.dər|.i, -əm-, -ən.der- **-ies** -ɪz
Precambrian ˌpriː'kæm.bri.ən
precancerous ˌpriː'kænt.sər.əs *stress shift:* ˌprecancerous 'tissue
precarious prɪ'keə.ri.əs, prə- ⓤⓢ prɪ'ker.i-, priː- **-ly** -li **-ness** -nəs, -nɪs
precast ˌpriː'kɑːst ⓤⓢ 'priː.kæst, ˌ-'- *stress shift, British only:* ˌprecast 'concrete
preca|tory 'prek.ə|.tər.i ⓤⓢ -tɔːr- **-tive** -tɪv ⓤⓢ -ţɪv
precaution prɪ'kɔː.ʃən, prə- ⓤⓢ prɪ'kɑː-, priː-, -'kɔː- **-s** -z
precautionary prɪ'kɔː.ʃən.ər.i, prə- ⓤⓢ prɪ'kɑː.ʃən.er-, priː-, -'kɔː-
preced|e priː'siːd, prɪ- ⓤⓢ prɪ-, priː- **-es** -z **-ing** -ɪŋ **-ed** -ɪd
precedenc|e 'pres.ɪ.dənts, 'priː.sɪ- ⓤⓢ 'pres.ə.dents; prɪ'siː.dənts, priː- **-y** -i
precedent (*n.*) 'pres.ɪ.dənt ⓤⓢ '-ə- **-s** -s **-ed** -ɪd
precedent (*adj.*) prɪ'siː.dənt, 'pres.ɪ.dənt ⓤⓢ prɪ'siː.dənt, priː-, 'pres.ə.dənt **-ly** -li
precentor ˌpriː'sen.təʳ, prɪ- ⓤⓢ priː'sen.ţɚ **-s** -z
precept 'priː.sept **-s** -s
preceptor prɪ'sep.təʳ ⓤⓢ priː'sep.tɚ, prɪ- **-s** -z
preceptor|y prɪ'sep.tər|.i ⓤⓢ prɪ-, priː- **-ies** -iz
precession prɪ'seʃ.ən, prə- ⓤⓢ prɪ-, priː- **-s** -z
precinct 'priː.sɪŋkt **-s** -s
preciosity ˌpres.i'ɒs.ə.ti, ˌpreʃ-, -ɪ.ti ⓤⓢ ˌpreʃ.i'ɑː.sə.ţi, ˌpres-
precious (P) 'preʃ.əs **-ly** -li **-ness** -nəs, -nɪs **ˌprecious 'metal**; **ˌprecious 'stone**
precipic|e 'pres.ɪ.pɪs, '-ə- ⓤⓢ '-ə- **-es** -ɪz
precipitanc|e prɪ'sɪp.ɪ.tənts, prə-, '-ə- ⓤⓢ prɪ-, priː- **-y** -i
precipitate (*n.*) prɪ'sɪp.ɪ.teɪt, prə-, '-ə-, -tət, -tɪt ⓤⓢ prɪ'sɪp.ɪ.tɪt, priː-, -teɪt **-s** -s
precipitate (*adj.*) prɪ'sɪp.ɪ.tət, prə-, '-ə-, -tɪt ⓤⓢ prɪ'sɪp.ɪ.tɪt, priː-, -teɪt **-ly** -li **-ness** -nəs, -nɪs
precipi|tate (*v.*) prɪ'sɪp.ɪ|.teɪt, prə-, '-ə- ⓤⓢ prɪ'sɪp.ɪ-, priː- **-tates** -teɪts **-tating** -teɪ.tɪŋ ⓤⓢ -teɪ.ţɪŋ **-tated** -teɪ.tɪd ⓤⓢ -teɪ.ţɪd
precipitation prɪˌsɪp.ɪ'teɪ.ʃən, prə-, -ə'- ⓤⓢ prɪˌsɪp.ɪ'-, priː- **-s** -z
precipitous prɪ'sɪp.ɪ.təs, prə-, '-ə- ⓤⓢ prɪ'sɪp.ɪ.ţəs, priː- **-ly** -li **-ness** -nəs, -nɪs
précis *singular:* 'preɪ.siː ⓤⓢ 'preɪ.siː, -'- **-ing** -ɪŋ **-ed** -d *plural:* -z
precise prɪ'saɪs, prə- ⓤⓢ prɪ-, priː- **-ly** -li **-ness** -nəs, -nɪs
precision prɪ'sɪʒ.ən, prə- ⓤⓢ prɪ-, priː-
preclassical ˌpriː'klæs.ɪ.kəl *stress shift:* ˌpreclassical 'music
preclud|e prɪ'kluːd ⓤⓢ prɪ-, priː- **-es** -z **-ing** -ɪŋ **-ed** -ɪd
preclu|sion prɪ'kluː|.ʒən ⓤⓢ prɪ-, priː- **-sive** -sɪv
precocious prɪ'kəʊ.ʃəs, prə- ⓤⓢ prɪ'koʊ-, priː- **-ly** -li **-ness** -nəs, -nɪs
precocity prɪ'kɒs.ə.ti, prə-, -ɪ.ti ⓤⓢ prɪ'kɑː.sə.ţi, priː-
precognition ˌpriː.kɒg'nɪʃ.ən ⓤⓢ -kɑːg'-
preconceiv|e ˌpriː.kən'siːv **-es** -z **-ing** -ɪŋ **-ed** -d
preconception ˌpriː.kən'sep.ʃən **-s** -z
precon|cert ˌpriː.kən|'sɜːt ⓤⓢ -'sɝːt **-certs** -'sɜːts ⓤⓢ -'sɝːts **-certing** -'sɜː.tɪŋ ⓤⓢ -'sɝː.ţɪŋ **-certed** -'sɜː.tɪd ⓤⓢ -'sɝː.ţɪd
precondition ˌpriː.kən'dɪʃ.ən **-s** -z **-ing** -ɪŋ **-ed** -d
precook ˌpriː'kʊk **-s** -s **-ing** -ɪŋ **-ed** -t
precursor ˌpriː'kɜː.səʳ, prɪ- ⓤⓢ prɪ'kɝː.sɚ, priː- **-s** -z **-y** -i
preda|te ˌpriː'deɪ|t ⓤⓢ ˌpriː'deɪ|t, '-- **-tes** -ts **-ting** -tɪŋ ⓤⓢ -ţɪŋ **-ted** -tɪd ⓤⓢ -ţɪd *stress shift:* ˌpredated 'cheque
predation prɪ'deɪ.ʃən, prə- ⓤⓢ prɪ-, priː- **-s** -z
predator 'pred.ə.təʳ, '-ɪ- ⓤⓢ -də.ţɚ
predator|y 'pred.ə.tər|.i ⓤⓢ -tɔːr- **-ily** -əl.i, -ɪ.li **-iness** -ɪ.nəs, -ɪ.nɪs
predeceas|e ˌpriː.dɪ'siːs, -də'- ⓤⓢ -diː-, -dɪ'- **-es** -ɪz **-ing** -ɪŋ **-ed** -t
predecessor 'priː.dɪˌses.əʳ, -də-, ˌpriː.dɪ'ses-, -də'- ⓤⓢ 'pred.ə.ses.ɚ, 'priː.də-; ˌpred.ə'ses- **-s** -z
predesti|nate (*v.*) ˌpriː'des.tɪ|.neɪt, prɪ-, -tə- ⓤⓢ ˌpriː'des.tə- **-nates** -neɪts **-nating** -neɪ.tɪŋ ⓤⓢ -neɪ.ţɪŋ **-nated** -neɪ.tɪd ⓤⓢ -neɪ.ţɪd
predestinate (*adj.*) ˌpriː'des.tɪ.nət, prɪ-, -tə- ⓤⓢ ˌpriː'des.tə.nɪt
predestination ˌpriː.des.tɪ'neɪ.ʃən, prɪˌdes- ⓤⓢ priː-, -tə'-, priːˌdes.tə'-
predestin|e ˌpriː'des.tɪn, prɪ- ⓤⓢ ˌpriː- **-es** -z **-ing** -ɪŋ **-ed** -d
predetermination ˌpriː.dɪˌtɜː.mɪ'neɪ.ʃən, -dəˌ-, -mə'- ⓤⓢ -dɪˌtɝː.mə'-
predetermin|e ˌpriː.dɪ'tɜː.mɪn, -də'-, -mən ⓤⓢ -dɪ'tɝː.mən **-es** -z **-ing** -ɪŋ **-ed** -d *stress shift:* ˌpredetermined 'path

Prefixes

A prefix is an element placed at the beginning of a word to modify or alter its meaning. In general, prefixes do not alter the original pronunciation of the word stem on to which they are affixed, though they may attract secondary stress.

A narrow definition of *prefix* would apply only in the case of words where removal of the prefix would leave a free-standing word (for example, 'unfit' is 'un' + 'fit'), but many treatments of English word stress also treat as prefixes such elements as 'con' in 'contain' or 'in' in 'insert', where 'tain' and 'sert' do not exist independently as words.

Examples

Some examples of words containing unstressed prefixes follow, e.g.:

admire	/ədˈmaɪəʳ/	(US) /-ˈmaɪɚ/
contain	/kənˈteɪn/	
desist	/dɪˈsɪst/	
undo	/ʌnˈduː/	

A prefix may attract secondary stress if it is affixed to a word beginning with an unstressed syllable (e.g. another prefix), e.g.:

undivided	/ˌʌn.dɪˈvaɪ.dɪd/	
unforseen	/ˌʌn.fɔːˈsiːn/	(US) /-fɔːrˈ-/

A prefix may be stressed to avoid a clash of two stressed syllables in stress-shift situations, e.g.:

unfair dismissal /ˌʌn.feə dɪˈsmɪs.əl/ (US) /-fer-/

In homographic noun/verb pairs containing prefixes, the prefix is usually stressed in the nominal form and unstressed in the verbal form (see the panel on HOMOGRAPHS), e.g.:

insert	(*n.*)	/ˈɪn.sɜːt/	(US) /-sɝːt/
	(*v.*)	/ɪnˈsɜːt/	(US) /-ˈsɝːt/
record	(*n.*)	/ˈrek.ɔːd/	(US) /-ɚd/
	(*v.*)	/rɪˈkɔːd/	(US) /-ˈkɔːrd/

predeterminer ˌpriː.dɪˈtɜː.mɪ.nəʳ, -dəˈ-, -mə- (US) -dɪˈtɝː.mə.nɚ

predicability ˌpred.ɪ.kəˈbɪl.ə.ti, -ɪ.ti (US) -ə.t̬i

predicable ˈpred.ɪ.kə.bl̩

predicament prɪˈdɪk.ə.mənt, prə- (US) prɪ-, priː- **-s** -s

predicate (*n.*) ˈpred.ɪ.kət, ˈpriː.dɪ-, -də-, -kɪt, -keɪt (US) ˈpred.ɪ.kɪt, ˈ-ə- **-s** -s

predi|cate (*v.*) ˈpred.ɪ|.keɪt, ˈ-ə- (US) ˈ-ɪ- **-cates** -keɪts **-cating** -keɪ.tɪŋ (US) -keɪ.t̬ɪŋ **-cated** -keɪ.tɪd (US) -keɪ.t̬ɪd

predication ˌpred.ɪˈkeɪ.ʃᵊn, -əˈ- (US) -ɪˈ- **-s** -z

predicative prɪˈdɪk.ə.tɪv, prə- (US) prɪˈdɪk.ə.t̬ɪv, priː- **-ly** -li

predicatory ˈpred.ɪ.keɪ.tᵊr.i, ˈ-ə-, ˌpred.ɪˈkeɪ-, -əˈ- (US) ˈpred.ɪ.kə.tɔːr-

predict prɪˈdɪkt, prə- (US) prɪ-, priː- **-s** -s **-ing** -ɪŋ **-ed** -ɪd **-or/s** -əʳ/z (US) -ɚ/z

predictability prɪˌdɪk.təˈbɪl.ɪ.ti, prə- (US) prɪˌdɪk.təˈbɪl.ə.t̬i, priː-

predictab|le prɪˈdɪk.tə.b|l̩, prə- (US) prɪ-, priː- **-ly** -li

prediction prɪˈdɪk.ʃᵊn, prə- (US) prɪ-, priː- **-s** -z

predictive prɪˈdɪk.tɪv **-ly** -li

predilection ˌpriː.dɪˈlek.ʃᵊn, -dəˈ- (US) ˌpred.ᵊlˈek-, ˌpriː.dᵊlˈ- **-s** -z

predispos|e ˌpriː.dɪˈspəʊz, -dəˈ- (US) -dɪˈspoʊz **-es** -ɪz **-ing** -ɪŋ **-ed** -d

predisposition ˌpriː.dɪ.spəˈzɪʃ.ᵊn, priːˌdɪs.pəˈ- **-s** -z

predominance prɪˈdɒm.ɪ.nənts, prə-, ˈ-ə- (US) prɪˈdɑː.mə-, priː-

predominant prɪˈdɒm.ɪ.nənt, prə-, ˈ-ə- (US) prɪˈdɑː.mə-, priː- **-ly** -li

predomi|nate prɪˈdɒm.ɪ|.neɪt, prə-, ˈ-ə- (US) prɪˈdɑː.mə-, priː- **-nates** -neɪts **-nating** -neɪ.tɪŋ (US) -neɪ.t̬ɪŋ **-nated** -neɪ.tɪd (US) -neɪ.t̬ɪd

predomination prɪˌdɒm.ɪˈneɪ.ʃᵊn, prə-, -əˈ- (US) prɪˌdɑː.məˈ-, priː-

Preece priːs

pre-eclampsia ˌpriː.ɪˈklæmp.si.ə

preemie ˈpriː.mi **-s** -z

pre-eminence ˌpriːˈem.ɪ.nənts, pri-, ˈ-ə-

pre-eminent ˌpriːˈem.ɪ.nənt, pri-, ˈ-ə- **-ly** -li

pre-empt ˌpriːˈempt, pri- **-s** -s **-ing** -ɪŋ **-ed** -ɪd

pre-emption ˌpriːˈemp.ʃᵊn, pri-

pre-emptive ˌpriːˈemp.tɪv, pri- **preˌemptive ˈstrike**

preen priːn **-s** -z **-ing** -ɪŋ **-ed** -d

pre-exist ˌpriː.ɪgˈzɪst, -egˈ-; -ɪkˈsɪst, -ekˈ- (US) -ɪgˈzɪst, -egˈ- **-s** -s **-ing** -ɪŋ **-ed** -ɪd **-ence** -ᵊnts **-ent** -ᵊnt *stress shift:* ˌpre-existing ˈrule

prefab ˈpriː.fæb **-s** -z

prefabri|cate ˌpriːˈfæb.rɪ|.keɪt, -rə- **-cates** -keɪts **-cating** -keɪ.tɪŋ (US) -keɪ.t̬ɪŋ **-cated** -keɪ.tɪd (US) -keɪ.t̬ɪd

pre-fabrication ˌpriː.fæb.rɪˈkeɪ.ʃᵊn, priːˌfæb-, -rəˈ- (US) ˌpriː.fæb-

prefac|e ˈpref.ɪs, -əs (US) -ɪs **-es** -ɪz **-ing** -ɪŋ **-ed** -t

prefatorial ˌpref.əˈtɔː.ri.əl (US) -ˈtɔːr.i- **-ly** -i

prefatory ˈpref.ə.tᵊr.i (US) -tɔːr-

prefect ˈpriː.fekt **-s** -s

prefecture ˈpriː.fek.tʃəʳ, -tʃʊəʳ, -tjʊəʳ (US) -tʃɚ **-s** -z

prefer prɪˈfɜːʳ, prə- (US) priːˈfɝː, prɪ- **-s** -z **-ring** -ɪŋ **-red** -d

preferability ˌpref.ᵊr.əˈbɪl.ə.ti, -ɪ.ti (US) -ə.t̬i

preferab|le ˈpref.ᵊr.ə.b|l̩ **-ly** -li **-leness** -l̩.nəs, -nɪs

preferenc|e ˈpref.ᵊr.ᵊnts **-es** -ɪz

preferential ˌpref.ᵊrˈen.tʃᵊl **-ly** -i

preferment prɪˈfɜː.mənt, prə- (US) priːˈfɝː-, prɪ- **-s** -s

prefigurative priːˈfɪg.ᵊr.ə.tɪv (US) -jɚ- **-ly** -li **-ness** -nəs, -nɪs

prefig|ure priːˈfɪg|.əʳ (US) -j|ɚ **-ures** -əz (US) -ɚz **-uring** -ᵊr.ɪŋ **-ured** -əd (US) -ɚd

prefigurement priːˈfɪg.ə.mənt (US) -jɚ-, -jʊr- **-s** -s

prefix (*n.*) ˈpriː.fɪks **-es** -ɪz

prefix (*v.*) ˌpriːˈfɪks, ˈ-- (US) ˈpriː.fɪks, ˌ-ˈ- **-es** -ɪz **-ing** -ɪŋ **-ed** -t

preggers ˈpreg.əz (US) -ɚz

pregnable ˈpreg.nə.bl̩

pregnanc|y ˈpreg.nənt.s|i **-ies** -iz

pregnant ˈpreg.nənt **-ly** -li

pre|heat ˌpriː|ˈhiːt **-heats** -ˈhiːts **-heating** -ˈhiː.tɪŋ (US) -ˈhiː.t̬ɪŋ **-heated** -ˈhiː.tɪd (US) -ˈhiː.t̬ɪd *stress shift:* ˌpreheated ˈmeal

prehensible prɪˈhent.sə.bl̩, -sɪ- (US) priː-

prehensile prɪˈhent.saɪl, ˌpriː- (US) priːˈhent.sɪl, -sᵊl

prehistoric ˌpriː.hɪˈstɒr.ɪk (US) -hɪˈstɔːr-

-ally -ᵊl.i, -li *stress shift:* ˌprehistoric ˈmonster

prehistory ˌpriːˈhɪs.tᵊr.i

prejudg|e ˌpriːˈdʒʌdʒ **-es** -ɪz **-ing** -ɪŋ **-ed** -d **-(e)ment** -mənt

prejudic|e ˈpredʒ.ə.dɪs, ˈ-ʊ- **-es** -ɪz **-ing** -ɪŋ **-ed** -t

prejudicial ˌpredʒ.əˈdɪʃ.ᵊl, -ʊˈ- **-ly** -i

prelac|y ˈprel.ə.s|i **-ies** -iz

prelate ˈprel.ɪt, -ət ⓤⓢ -ɪt **-s** -s

preliminar|y prɪˈlɪm.ɪ.nᵊr|.i, prə-, -ᵊn.ᵊr- ⓤⓢ prɪˈlɪm.ə.ner-, priː- **-ies** -iz **-ily** -ᵊl.i, -ɪ.li

prelims ˈpriː.lɪmz, ˌ-ˈ-; prɪ- ⓤⓢ ˈpriː.lɪms; ˌpriːˈlɪmz, prɪ-

prelud|e ˈprel.juːd ⓤⓢ ˈprel-, -uːd; ˈpreɪ.luːd, ˈpriː- **-es** -z **-ing** -ɪŋ **-ed** -ɪd

premarital ˌpriːˈmær.ɪ.tᵊl ⓤⓢ -ˈmer.ə.t̬ᵊl, -ˈmær- **-ly** -i *stress shift, see compound:* ˌ**premarital ˈsex**

premature ˈprem.ə.tʃəʳ, ˈpriː.mə-, -tjʊəʳ, -tʃʊəʳ, -tjɔːʳ, -tʃɔːʳ; ˌ--ˈ- ⓤⓢ ˌpriː.məˈtʊr, -ˈtjʊr, -ˈtʃʊr **-ly** -li **-ness** -nəs, -nɪs *stress shift, British only:* ˌpremature ˈaging

premed ˌpriːˈmed **-s** -z *stress shift:* ˌpremed ˈscience

premedical ˌpriːˈmed.ɪ.kᵊl, ˈ-ə- *stress shift:* ˌpremedical ˈscience

premedication ˌpriː.med.ɪˈkeɪ.ʃᵊn, -əˈ-

premedi|tate ˌpriːˈmed.ɪ|.teɪt, prɪ-, ˈ-ə- ⓤⓢ priːˈmed.ɪ- **-tates** -teɪts **-tating** -teɪ.tɪŋ ⓤⓢ -teɪ.t̬ɪŋ **-tated/ly** -teɪ.tɪd/li ⓤⓢ -teɪ.t̬ɪd/li

premeditation ˌpriː.med.ɪˈteɪ.ʃᵊn, prɪˌmed-, priː-, -əˈ- ⓤⓢ priː-

premenstrual ˌpriːˈment.stru.əl ⓤⓢ -strəl **-ly** -i *stress shift, see compounds:* ˌ**premenstrual ˈtension**; ˌ**premenstrual ˈsyndrome**

premier ˈprem.i.əʳ, ˈpriː.mi- ⓤⓢ prɪˈmɪr, -ˈmjɪr; ˈpriː.miː.ɚ **-s** -z **-ship/s** -ʃɪp/s

premièr|e ˈprem.i.eəʳ, ˌ--ˈ- ⓤⓢ prɪˈmɪr, premˈɪr, -ˈjer, -ˈjɪr **-es** -z **-ing** **-ed**

Preminger ˈprem.ɪn.dʒəʳ, ˈpreɪ.mɪŋ.əʳ ⓤⓢ ˈprem.ɪn.dʒɚ

premis|e (*n.*) ˈprem.ɪs **-s** -ɪz

premis|e (*v.*) prɪˈmaɪz, ˈprem.ɪs ⓤⓢ ˈprem.ɪs **-es** -ɪz **-ing** -ɪŋ **-ed** prɪˈmaɪzd, ˈprem.ɪst ⓤⓢ ˈprem.ɪst

premium ˈpriː.mi.əm **-s** -z ˈ**premium ˌbond**

premmie ˈprem.i **-s** -z

premodification ˌpriː.mɒd.ɪ.fɪˈkeɪ.ʃᵊn, priːˌmɒd-, -ə- ⓤⓢ ˌpriː.mɑː.dɪ.fɪˈ-

premodif|y priːˈmɒd.ɪ.f|aɪ ⓤⓢ -ˈmɑː.dɪ- **-ies** -aɪz **-ying** -aɪ.ɪŋ **-ied** -aɪd

premolar ˌpriːˈməʊ.ləʳ ⓤⓢ -ˈmoʊ.lɚ **-s** -z *stress shift:* ˌpremolar ˈteeth

premonition ˌprem.əˈnɪʃ.ᵊn, ˌpriː.məˈ- **-s** -z

premonitorily prɪˈmɒn.ɪ.tᵊr.ᵊl.i, -ɪ.li ⓤⓢ priːˈmɑː.nə.tɔːr-, -ˌmɑː.nəˈtɔːr-

premonitory prɪˈmɒn.ɪ.tᵊr.i ⓤⓢ priːˈmɑː.nə.tɔːr-

prenatal ˌpriːˈneɪ.tᵊl ⓤⓢ -t̬ᵊl **-ly** -i *stress shift:* ˌprenatal ˈcare

Prendergast ˈpren.də.gɑːst, -gæst ⓤⓢ -dɚ.gæst

prentic|e (P) ˈpren.tɪs ⓤⓢ -t̬ɪs **-es** -ɪz

Prentis(s) ˈpren.tɪs ⓤⓢ -t̬ɪs

prenuptial ˌpriːˈnʌp.*t*ʃᵊl *stress shift, see compound:* ˌ**prenuptial aˈgreement**

preoccupation priːˌɒk.jəˈpeɪ.ʃᵊn, prɪ-, ˌpriː.ɒk-, -jʊˈ- ⓤⓢ priːˌɑː.kjuːˈ-, -kjəˈ- **-s** -z

preoccup|y ˌpriːˈɒk.jə.p|aɪ, pri- ⓤⓢ priːˈɑː.kjuː-, -kjə- **-ies** -aɪz **-ying** -aɪ.ɪŋ **-ied** -aɪd

preordain ˌpriː.ɔːˈdeɪn ⓤⓢ -ɔːrˈ- **-s** -z **-ing** -ɪŋ **-ed** -d *stress shift:* ˌpreordained ˈdestiny

prep prep **-s** -s **-ping** -ɪŋ **-ped** -t ˈ**prep ˌschool**

prepackag|e ˌpriːˈpæk.ɪdʒ **-es** -ɪz **-ing** -ɪŋ **-ed** -d *stress shift:* ˌprepackaged ˈgoods

prepaid *(from* **prepay***)* ˌpriːˈpeɪd *stress shift:* ˌprepaid ˈpostage

preparation ˌprep.ᵊrˈeɪ.ʃᵊn ⓤⓢ -əˈreɪ- **-s** -z

preparative prɪˈpær.ə.tɪv, prə- ⓤⓢ prɪˈper.ə.t̬ɪv, priː-, -ˈpær- **-ly** -li

preparator|y prɪˈpær.ə.tᵊr|.i, prə- ⓤⓢ prɪˈper.ə.tɔːr-, priː-, -ˈpær-; ˈprep.ɚ.ə- **-ily** -ᵊl.i, -ɪ.li **preˈparatory ˌschool**

prepar|e prɪˈpeəʳ, prə- ⓤⓢ prɪˈper, priː- **-es** -z **-ing** -ɪŋ **-ed** -d **-edly** -d.li, -ɪd.li **-edness** -d.nəs, -nɪs, -ɪd.nəs, -nɪs **-er/s** -əʳ/z ⓤⓢ -ɚ/z

prepay ˌpriːˈpeɪ **-s** -z **-ing** -ɪŋ **prepaid** ˌpriːˈpeɪd *stress shift:* ˌprepaid ˈpostage

prepayment ˌpriːˈpeɪ.mənt **-s** -s

prepense prɪˈpen*t*s **-ly** -li

preponderance prɪˈpɒn.dᵊr.ᵊn*t*s, prə- ⓤⓢ prɪˈpɑːn-, priː-

preponderant prɪˈpɒn.dᵊr.ᵊnt, prə- ⓤⓢ prɪˈpɑːn-, priː- **-ly** -li

preponder|ate prɪˈpɒn.dᵊr|.eɪt, prə- ⓤⓢ prɪˈpɑːn.də.r|eɪt, priː- **-ates** -eɪts **-ating/ly** -eɪ.tɪŋ/li ⓤⓢ -eɪ.t̬ɪŋ/li **-ated** -eɪ.tɪd ⓤⓢ -eɪ.t̬ɪd

preponderation prɪˌpɒn.dᵊrˈeɪ.ʃᵊn, prə-, priː- ⓤⓢ prɪˌpɑːn.dəˈreɪ-, priː-

preposition ˌprep.əˈzɪʃ.ᵊn **-s** -z

prepositional ˌprep.əˈzɪʃ.ᵊn.ᵊl, ˈ-nᵊl ⓤⓢ -əˈ- **-ly** -i *stress shift, see compound:* ˌ**prepositional ˈphrase**

prepositive prɪˈpɒz.ə.tɪv, priː-, ˈ-ɪ- ⓤⓢ prɪˈpɑː.zə.t̬ɪv, priː- *stress shift:* ˌprepositive ˈadjective

prepossess ˌpriː.pəˈzes **-es** -ɪz **-ing/ly** -ɪŋ/li **-ed** -t

prepossession ˌpriː.pəˈzeʃ.ᵊn **-s** -z

preposterous prɪˈpɒs.tᵊr.əs, prə- ⓤⓢ prɪˈpɑː.stɚ-, priː- **-ly** -li **-ness** -nəs, -nɪs

prepp|y, prepp|ie ˈprep|.i **-ies** -iz **-ier** -i.əʳ ⓤⓢ -i.ɚ **-iest** -i.ɪst, -i.əst **-iness** -ɪ.nəs, -ɪ.nɪs

prepubescen|t ˌpriː.pjuːˈbes.ᵊn|t **-ce** -*t*s

prepuc|e ˈpriː.pjuːs **-es** -ɪz

prequel ˈpriː.kwəl **-s** -z

Pre-Raphaelite ˌpriːˈræf.i.ᵊl.aɪt, -eɪ-, -ˈræf.ᵊl-, -ɪ.laɪt ⓤⓢ -ˈræf.i.ᵊl-, -ˈreɪ. **-s** -s ˌ**Pre-ˌRaphaelite ˈBrotherhood**

prerecord ˌpriː.rɪˈkɔːd, -rəˈ- ⓤⓢ -rɪˈkɔːrd **-s** -z **-ing** -ɪŋ **-ed** -ɪd

prerequisite ˌpriːˈrek.wɪ.zɪt, -wə- **-s**

prerogative prɪˈrɒg.ə.tɪv, prə- ⓤⓢ -ˈrɑː.gə.t̬ɪv **-s** -z

presag|e (*n.*) ˈpres.ɪdʒ **-es** -ɪz

presag|e (*v.*) ˈpres.ɪdʒ; prɪˈseɪdʒ, prə ⓤⓢ prɪˈseɪdʒ; ˈpres.ɪdʒ **-es** -ɪz **-ing** **-ed** -d

presbyopia ˌprez.biˈəʊ.pi.ə ⓤⓢ -ˈoʊ-, ˌpres-

presbyter ˈprez.bɪ.təʳ ⓤⓢ -t̬ɚ, ˈpres- **-s** -z

presbyterian (P) ˌprez.bɪˈtɪə.ri.ən, -bəˈ- ⓤⓢ -bɪˈtɪr.i-, ˌpres- **-s** -z **-ism** -ɪ.zᵊm

presbyter|y ˈprez.bɪ.tᵊr|.i, -bə- ⓤⓢ -bɪ.ter-, ˈpres- **-ies** -iz

Prescel(l)y prɪˈsel.i, prə-, presˈel-

preschool ˈpriː.skuːl, ˌ-ˈ- ⓤⓢ ˈ--

preschooler ˈpriːˌskuː.ləʳ ⓤⓢ -lɚ **-s** -z

prescience ˈpres.i.ən*t*s, ˈpreʃ- ⓤⓢ ˈpreʃ.ᵊn*t*s, ˈpriː.ʃᵊn*t*s, -ʃi.ən*t*s

prescient ˈpres.i.ənt, ˈpreʃ- ⓤⓢ ˈpreʃ.ᵊnt, ˈpriː.ʃᵊnt, -ʃi.ənt **-ly**

prescind prɪˈsɪnd, prə-, priː- ⓤⓢ prɪ-, priː- **-s** -z **-ing** -ɪŋ **-ed** -ɪd

Prescot(t) ˈpres.kət, -kɒt ⓤⓢ -kət, -k

prescrib|e prɪˈskraɪb, prə- ⓤⓢ prɪ-, p **-es** -z **-ing** -ɪŋ **-ed** -d **-er/s** -əʳ/z ⓤⓢ -

prescript ˈpriː.skrɪpt **-s** -s

prescription prɪˈskrɪp.ʃᵊn, prə- ⓤⓢ p priː- **-s** -z

prescriptive prɪˈskrɪp.tɪv, prə-, priː ⓤⓢ prɪ-, priː- **-ly** -li

prescriptiv|ism prɪˈskrɪp.tɪ.v|ɪ.zᵊm prə-, priː- ⓤⓢ prɪ-, priː- **-ist/s** -ɪst/s

pre-season ˌpriːˈsiː.zᵊn *stress shift:* ˌpre-season ˈsale

Preseli prɪˈsel.i, prə-, priː-

presenc|e ˈprez.ᵊn*t*s **-es** -ɪz ˌ**presenc of ˈmind**

present (*n.*) *ordinary senses:* ˈprez.ᵊ **-s** -s

present *(n.) military term:* prɪˈzent, prə- **-s** -s
present *(adj.)* ˈprez.ᵊnt **-ly** -li ˌ**present parˈticiple** US ˌ**present ˈparticiple**; ˌ**present ˈperfect**; ˌ**present ˈtense**
pre|sent *(v.)* prɪ|ˈzent, prə- US prɪ-, priː- **-sents** -ˈzents **-senting** -ˈzen.tɪŋ US -ˈzen.t̬ɪŋ **-sented** -ˈzen.tɪd US -ˈzen.t̬ɪd
presentab|le prɪˈzen.tə.b|l̩, prə- US prɪˈzen.t̬ə-, priː- **-ly** -li **-leness** -l̩.nəs, -nɪs
presentation ˌprez.ᵊnˈteɪ.ʃᵊn, -enˈ- US -ᵊnˈ-, ˌpriː.zᵊnˈ- **-s** -z **-al**
present-day ˌprez.ᵊntˈdeɪ *stress shift:* ˌpresent-day ˈfashions
presenter prɪˈzen.təʳ, prə- US prɪˈzen.t̬ɚ, priː- **-s** -z
presentient prɪˈsen*t*.ʃi.ənt, -ʃᵊnt US priː-, prɪ-
presentiment prɪˈzen.tɪ.mənt US prɪ-, priː- **-s** -s
presently ˈprez.ᵊnt.li
preservation ˌprez.əˈveɪ.ʃᵊn US -ɚˈ- **-s** -z **-ist/s** -ɪst/s **preserˈvation** ˌ**order**
preservative prɪˈzɜː.və.tɪv, prə- US prɪˈzɝː.və.t̬ɪv, priː- **-s** -z
preserv|e prɪˈzɜːv, prə- US prɪˈzɝːv, priː- **-es** -z **-ing** -ɪŋ **-ed** -d **-er/s** -əʳ/z US -ɚ/z **-able** -ə.bl̩
pre|set priː|ˈset **-sets** -ˈsets **-setting** -ˈset.ɪŋ US -ˈset̬.ɪŋ *stress shift:* ˌpreset ˈchannel
pre|shrink ˌpriːˈʃrɪŋk **-shrinks** -ˈʃrɪŋks **-shrinking** -ˈʃrɪŋ.kɪŋ **-shrank** -ˈʃræŋk **-shrunk** -ˈʃrʌŋk **-shrunken** -ˈʃrʌŋ.kᵊn *stress shift:* ˌpreshrunk ˈjeans
presid|e prɪˈzaɪd, prə- US prɪ-, priː- **-es** -z **-ing** -ɪŋ **-ed** -ɪd
presidenc|y ˈprez.ɪ.dᵊn*t*.s|i **-ies** -iz
president ˈprez.ɪ.dᵊnt **-s** -s
presidential ˌprez.ɪˈden.*t*ʃᵊl *stress shift:* ˌpresidential ˈsuite
presidi|um prɪˈsɪd.i|.əm, prə- **-ums** -əmz **-a** -ə
Presley ˈprez.li US ˈpres-, ˈprez-
pre|sort ˌpriː|ˈsɔːt US -ˈsɔːrt **-sorts** -ˈsɔːts US -ˈsɔːrts **-sorting** -ˈsɔː.tɪŋ US -ˈsɔːr.t̬ɪŋ **-sorted** -ˈsɔː.tɪd US -ˈsɔːr.t̬ɪd
press pres **-es** -ɪz **-ing/ly** -ɪŋ/li **-ed** -t **-er/s** -əʳ/z US -ɚ/z ˈ**press** ˌ**agent**; ˈ**press** ˌ**baron**; ˈ**press** ˌ**conference**; ˈ**press** ˌ**cutting**; ˈ**press** ˌ**office**; ˈ**press reˌlease**
pressgang ˈpres.gæŋ **-s** -z **-ing** -ɪŋ **-ed** -d
pressie ˈprez.i **-s** -z
pression ˈpreʃ.ᵊn
press|man ˈpres|.mæn, -mən **-men** -mən, -men
pressrun ˈpres.rʌn
press-stud ˈpres.stʌd **-s** -s
press-up ˈpres.ʌp **-s** -s
pressur|e ˈpreʃ.əʳ US -ɚ **-es** -z **-ing** -ɪŋ **-ed** -d ˈ**pressure** ˌ**cooker**; ˈ**pressure** ˌ**group**
pressuriz|e, -is|e ˈpreʃ.ᵊr.aɪz US -ə.raɪz **-es** -ɪz **-ing** -ɪŋ **-ed** -d
Prestage ˈpres.tɪdʒ
Prestatyn presˈtæt.ɪn, prɪˈstæt-
Presteign presˈtiːn
Prestel® ˈpres.tel
prestidigitation ˌpres.tɪˌdɪdʒ.ɪˈteɪ.ʃᵊn US -təˌ-
prestidigitator ˌpres.tɪˈdɪdʒ.ɪ.teɪ.təʳ US -təˈdɪdʒ.ə.teɪ.t̬ɚ **-s** -z
prestige presˈtiːʒ US -ˈtiː*d*ʒ
Prestige *surname:* ˈpres.tɪdʒ
prestigious presˈtɪdʒ.əs, prɪˈstɪdʒ-, prə-, -i.əs US presˈtɪdʒ.əs, -ˈtiː.dʒəs **-ly** -li **-ness** -nəs, -nɪs
prestissimo presˈtɪs.ɪ.məʊ, ˈ-ə- US -ə.moʊ
presto (P) ˈpres.təʊ US -toʊ **-s** -z
Preston ˈpres.tᵊn
Prestonpans ˌpres.tᵊnˈpænz, -tᵊmˈ- US -tᵊnˈ-
prestressed ˌpriːˈstrest
Prestwich ˈpres.twɪtʃ
Prestwick ˈpres.twɪk
Prestwood ˈpres.twʊd
presumab|ly prɪˈzjuː.mə.b|li, prə-, -ˈzuː- US prɪˈzuː.mə-, priː- **-le** -l̩
presum|e prɪˈzjuːm, prə-, -ˈzuːm US prɪˈzuːm, priː- **-es** -z **-ing/ly** -ɪŋ/li **-ed** -d
presumption prɪˈzʌmp.ʃᵊn, prə- US prɪ-, priː- **-s** -z
presumptive prɪˈzʌmp.tɪv, prə- US prɪ-, priː- **-ly** -li
presumptuous prɪˈzʌmp.tʃu.əs, prə-, -tju-, -tʃəs US prɪˈzʌmp.tʃuː.əs, priː-, -tʃə.wəs **-ly** -li **-ness** -nəs, -nɪs
presuppos|e ˌpriː.səˈpəʊz US -ˈpoʊz **-es** -ɪz **-ing** -ɪŋ **-ed** -d
presupposition ˌpriː.sʌp.əˈzɪʃ.ᵊn **-s** -z
prêt-à-porter ˌpret.ɑːˈpɔː.teɪ US -pɔːrˈteɪ
pre-tax ˌpriːˈtæks *stress shift:* ˌpretax ˈprofit
preteen ˌpriːˈtiːn **-s** -z *stress shift:* ˌpreteen ˈyears
pretenc|e prɪˈten*t*s, prə- US ˈpriː.ten*t*s; prɪˈten*t*s **-es** -ɪz
pretend prɪˈtend, prə- US prɪ-, priː- **-s** -z **-ing** -ɪŋ **-ed** -ɪd **-er/s** -əʳ/z US -ɚ/z
pretens|e prɪˈten*t*s, prə- US ˈpriː.ten*t*s; prɪˈten*t*s **-es** -ɪz
pretension prɪˈten.*t*ʃᵊn, prə- US prɪ-, priː- **-s** -z
pretentious prɪˈten.*t*ʃəs, prə- US prɪ-, priː- **-ly** -li **-ness** -nəs, -nɪs
preterit(e) ˈpret.ᵊr.ɪt, -ət US ˈpret̬.ɚ.ɪt **-s** -s
pretermission ˌpriː.təˈmɪʃ.ᵊn US -t̬ɚˈ-
preter|mit ˌpriː.tə|ˈmɪt US -t̬ɚˈ- **-mits** -ˈmɪts **-mitting** -ˈmɪt.ɪŋ US -ˈmɪt̬.ɪŋ **-mitted** -ˈmɪt.ɪd US -ˈmɪt̬.ɪd
preternatural ˌpriː.təˈnætʃ.ᵊr.ᵊl, -ʊ.rᵊl US -t̬ɚˈnætʃ.ɚ.ᵊl, ˈ-rᵊl **-ly** -i **-ness** -nəs, -nɪs *stress shift:* ˌpreternatural ˈhappening
pretext ˈpriː.tekst **-s** -s
pretor ˈpriː.təʳ US -t̬ɚ **-s** -z **-ship/s** -ʃɪp/s
Pretori|a prɪˈtɔː.ri|.ə, prə- US prɪˈtɔːr.i-, priː- **-us** -əs
pretori|al prɪˈtɔː.ri|.əl, prə- US prɪˈtɔːr.i-, priː- **-an** -ən
prettification ˌprɪt.ɪ.fɪˈkeɪ.ʃᵊn, ˌ-ə- US ˌprɪt̬-
prettif|y ˈprɪt.ɪ.f|aɪ US ˈprɪt̬- **-ies** -aɪz **-ying** -aɪ.ɪŋ **-ied** -aɪd
prett|y *(adj. adv.)* ˈprɪt|.i US ˈprɪt̬- **-ier** -i.əʳ US -i.ɚ **-iest** -i.ɪst, -i.əst **-ily** -ɪ.li, -ᵊl.i **-iness** -ɪ.nəs, -ɪ.nɪs
Pretty *surname:* ˈprɪt.i, ˈpret- US ˈprɪt̬-, ˈpret̬-
Pret(t)yman ˈprɪt.ɪ.mən US ˈprɪt̬-
pretty-pretty ˈprɪt.iˌprɪt.i US ˈprɪt̬.iˌprɪt̬.i
pretzel ˈpret.sᵊl **-s** -z
prevail prɪˈveɪl, prə- US prɪ-, priː- **-s** -z **-ing** -ɪŋ **-ed** -d
prevalence ˈprev.ᵊl.ən*t*s US -ə.lən*t*s
prevalent ˈprev.ᵊl.ənt US -ə.lənt **-ly** -li
prevari|cate prɪˈvær.ɪ|.keɪt, prə-, ˈ-ə- US prɪˈver.ɪ-, -ˈvær- **-cates** -keɪts **-cating** -keɪ.tɪŋ US -keɪ.t̬ɪŋ **-cated** -keɪ.tɪd US -keɪ.t̬ɪd **-cator/s** -keɪ.təʳ/z US -keɪ.t̬ɚ/z
prevarication prɪˌvær.ɪˈkeɪ.ʃᵊn, prə-, -əˈ- US prɪˌver-, -ˌvær- **-s** -z
pre|vent *hinder:* prɪ|ˈvent, prə- US prɪ-, priː- **-vents** -ˈvents **-venting** -ˈven.tɪŋ US -ˈven.t̬ɪŋ **-vented** -ˈven.tɪd US -ˈven.t̬ɪd **-venter/s** -ˈven.təʳ/z US -ˈven.t̬ɚ/z **-ventable** -ˈven.tə.bl̩ US -ˈven.t̬ə.bl̩
pre|vent *go before:* ˌpriː|ˈvent, prɪ- US priː-, prɪ- **-vents** -ˈvents **-venting** -ˈven.tɪŋ US -ˈven.t̬ɪŋ **-vented** -ˈven.tɪd US -ˈven.t̬ɪd
preventability prɪˌven.təˈbɪl.ə.ti, prə-, -ɪ.ti US prɪˌven.t̬əˈbɪl.ə.t̬i, priː-
preventative prɪˈven.tə.tɪv, prə- US prɪˈven.t̬ə.t̬ɪv, priː- **-s** -z
prevention prɪˈven.*t*ʃᵊn, prə- US prɪ-, priː-
preventive prɪˈven.tɪv, prə- US prɪˈven.t̬ɪv, priː- **-ly** -li **-ness** -nəs, -nɪs
preverbal ˌpriːˈvɜː.bᵊl US -ˈvɝː- *stress shift:* ˌpreverbal ˈstate
preview ˈpriː.vjuː **-s** -z **-ing** -ɪŋ **-ed** -d
Previn ˈprev.ɪn

previous ˈpriː.vi.əs, ˈ-vjəs US -vi.əs **-ly** -li **-ness** -nəs, -nɪs

prevision ˌpriːˈvɪʒ.ᵊn, prɪ- US priː-

prevocalic ˌpriː.vəʊˈkæl.ɪk US -voʊˈ- **-ally** -ᵊl.i, -li *stress shift:* ˌprevocalic ˈconsonant

Prevost ˈprev.əʊ, ˈprev.əʊst, prevˈəʊ US ˈpreɪ.voʊ, ˈprev.oʊ

pre-war ˌpriːˈwɔːʳ US -ˈwɔːr *stress shift:* ˌpre-war ˈpolitics

Prewett ˈpruː.ɪt

prey preɪ **-s** -z **-ing** -ɪŋ **-ed** -d

prezzie ˈprez.i **-s** -z

Priam praɪəm, ˈpraɪ.æm

priapic praɪˈæp.ɪk, -ˈeɪ.pɪk

priapism ˈpraɪ.ə.pɪ.zᵊm

priapus (P) praɪˈeɪ.pəs; ˈpraɪ.ə.pəs **-es** -ɪz

pric|e (P) praɪs **-es** -ɪz **-ing** -ɪŋ **-ed** -t **ˈprice ˌtag; ˈprice ˌwar**

price-cutting ˈpraɪsˌkʌt.ɪŋ US -ˌkʌt̬-

priceless ˈpraɪ.sləs, -slɪs **-ness** -nəs, -nɪs

pric|ey ˈpraɪ.s|i **-ier** -i.əʳ US -i.ɚ **-iest** -i.ɪst, -i.əst **-ily** -ɪ.li, -ᵊl.i **-iness** -ɪ.nəs, -ɪ.nɪs

prick prɪk **-s** -s **-ing/s** -ɪŋ/z **-ed** -t **-er/s** -əʳ/z US -ɚ/z

prickl|e ˈprɪk.l̩ **-es** -z **-ing** -ɪŋ, ˈprɪk.lɪŋ **-ed** -d

prickl|y ˈprɪk.l|i, -l̩|.i US ˈ-li **-ier** -i.əʳ US -i.ɚ **-iest** -ɪ.ɪst, -i.əst **-iness** -ɪ.nəs, -ɪ.nɪs **ˌprickly ˈpear**

prid|e (P) praɪd **-es** -z **-ing** -ɪŋ **-ed** -ɪd **ˌpride of ˈplace**

Prideaux ˈprɪd.əʊ, ˈpriː.dəʊ US ˈprɪd.oʊ

Pridham ˈprɪd.əm

prie-dieu ˌpriːˈdjɜː, ˈ-- US ˈpriː.djɜː **prie-dieus** ˌpriːˈdjɜːz, -ˈdjɜː, ˈ-- US ˈpriː.djɜːz

prie-dieux *(alternative plur. of* **prie-dieu***)* ˌpriːˈdjɜːz, -ˈdjɜː, ˈ-- US ˈpriː.djɜːz

priest (P) priːst **-s** -s

priestess ˌpriːˈstes; ˈpriː.stəs, -stɪs US ˈpriː.stɪs **-es** -ɪz

priesthood ˈpriːst.hʊd

Priestland ˈpriːs*t*.lənd

Priestley ˈpriːs*t*.li

priestl|y ˈpriːs*t*.l|i **-iness** -ɪ.nəs, -ɪ.nɪs

prig prɪg **-s** -z **-gery** -ᵊr.i

priggish ˈprɪg.ɪʃ **-ly** -li **-ness** -nəs, -nɪs

prim (P) prɪm **-mer** -əʳ US -ɚ **-mest** -ɪst, -əst **-ly** -li **-ness** -nəs, -nɪs **-s** -z **-ming** -ɪŋ **-med** -d

prima ballerina ˌpriː.mə.bæl.ᵊrˈiː.nə US -əˈriː- **-s** -z

primac|y ˈpraɪ.mə.s|i **-ies** -iz

prima donna ˌpriː.məˈdɒn.ə US -ˈdɑː.nə, ˌprɪm.əˈ- **-s** -z

primaeval ˌpraɪˈmiː.vᵊl

prima facie ˌpraɪ.məˈfeɪ.ʃi, -ʃiː, ˈ-ʃi.iː, ˈ-si, -siː, ˈ-si.iː US ˈ-ʃi.ː, ˈ-ʃiː, -ʃə

Primakov ˈpriː.mə.kɒf, ˌ--ˈ- US ˈpriː.mə.kɔːf, -kɑːf

primal ˈpraɪ.mᵊl **ˌprimal ˈtherapy**

primarily praɪˈmer.ᵊl.i, -ˈmeə.rᵊl-, -ɪ.li; ˈpraɪ.mᵊr.ᵊl-, -ɪ.li US praɪˈmer.ᵊl.i, ˈpraɪ.mer-

primar|y ˈpraɪ.mᵊr|.i US -mer-, -mɚ- **-ies** -iz **-iness** -ɪ.nəs, -ɪ.nɪs **ˌprimary ˈcolour** US **ˈprimary ˌcolor; ˈprimary ˌschool; ˌprimary ˈstress**

primate *archbishop:* ˈpraɪ.meɪt, -mɪt, -mət US -mɪt **-s** -s

primate *higher mammal:* ˈpraɪ.meɪt **-s** -s

primateship ˈpraɪ.mət.ʃɪp, -mɪt-, -meɪt- US -mɪt- **-s** -s

prim|e (P) praɪm **-es** -z **-ing** -ɪŋ **-ed** -d **ˌprime ˈminister; ˌprime ˈmover; ˈprime ˌtime, ˌprime ˈtime**

primer *thing that primes:* ˈpraɪ.məʳ US -mɚ **-s** -z *elementary school book:* ˈpraɪ.məʳ, ˈprɪm.əʳ US ˈprɪm.ɚ **-s** -z

primer *printing type:* ˈprɪm.əʳ US -ɚ

primetime ˈpraɪm.taɪm

primeval praɪˈmiː.vᵊl

primipar|a praɪˈmɪp.ᵊr|.ə **-as** -əz **-ae** -iː

primiparous praɪˈmɪp.ᵊr.əs

primitive ˈprɪm.ɪ.tɪv, ˈ-ə- US -ɪ.t̬ɪv **-ly** -li **-ness** -nəs, -nɪs

primitiv|ism ˈprɪm.ɪ.tɪ.v|ɪ.zᵊm, ˈ-ə- US -ɪ.t̬ɪ- **-ist/s** -ɪst/s

primo ˈpriː.məʊ US -moʊ

primogenitor ˌpraɪ.məʊˈdʒen.ɪ.təʳ, ˌpriː-, ˈ-ə- US ˌpraɪ.moʊˈdʒen.ɪ.tɚ, -məˈ- **-s** -z

primogeniture ˌpraɪ.məʊˈdʒen.ɪ.tʃəʳ, ˈ-ə-, -tʃʊəʳ, -tjʊəʳ US ˌpraɪ.moʊˈdʒen.ɪ.tʃɚ, -məˈ-

primordial praɪˈmɔː.di.əl US -ˈmɔːr- **-s** -z **-ly** -i

primp prɪmp **-s** -s **-ing** -ɪŋ **-ed** -t, prɪmt

primros|e (P) ˈprɪm.rəʊz US -roʊz **-es** -ɪz **ˌprimrose ˈpath**

primula ˈprɪm.jə.lə, -jʊ- **-s** -z

primum mobile ˌpraɪ.məmˈməʊ.bɪ.li, ˌpriː-, -mʊmˈ-, -bᵊl.i, -eɪ US ˌpraɪ.məmˈmoʊ.bᵊl.i, ˌpriː-, -eɪ **-s** -z

primus (P®) ˈpraɪ.məs **-es** -ɪz

princ|e (P) prɪn*t*s **-es** -ɪz **ˌprince ˈcharming; ˌprince ˈconsort; ˌPrince ˈEdward ˌIsland** US **ˌPrince ˌEdward ˈIsland; ˌPrince of ˈWales; ˌprince ˈregent**

princedom ˈprɪn*t*s.dəm **-s** -z

princeling ˈprɪn*t*s.lɪŋ **-s** -z

princel|y ˈprɪn*t*s.l|i **-ier** -i.əʳ US -i.ɚ **-iest** -i.ɪst, -i.əst **-iness** -ɪ.nəs, -ɪ.nɪs

Princes Risborough ˌprɪn*t*.sɪzˈrɪz.bᵊr.ə US -bɚ.oʊ

princess (P) prɪnˈses, ˈprɪn*t*.ses, -ɪs, -əs US ˈprɪn*t*.sɪs, -ses **-es** -ɪz **ˌprincess ˈroyal**

Princeton ˈprɪn*t*.stən

Princetown ˈprɪn*t*s.taʊn

princip|al (P) ˈprɪn*t*.sə.p|ᵊl, -sɪ- US -sə- **-als** -ᵊlz **-ally** -ᵊl.i, -li **-alness** -ᵊl.nəs, -nɪs **ˌprincipal ˈboy**

principalit|y ˌprɪn*t*.sɪˈpæl.ə.t|i, -səˈ-, -ɪ.t|i US -səˈpæl.ə.t̬|i **-ies** -iz

principalship ˈprɪn*t*.sə.pᵊl.ʃɪp, -sɪ- US -sə- **-s** -s

principate ˈprɪn*t*.sɪ.pət, -sə-, -pɪt, -peɪt US -sə.peɪt, -pɪt **-s** -s

Principia prɪnˈsɪp.i.ə

principle ˈprɪn*t*.sə.pl̩, -sɪ- US -sə- **-s** -z **-d** -d

Pring prɪŋ

Pringle ˈprɪŋ.gl̩

Prinknash ˈprɪn.ɪdʒ

Prinsep ˈprɪn*t*.sep

print prɪnt **-s** -s **-ing/s** -ɪn/z US ˈprɪn.t̬ɪŋ/z **-ed** -ɪd US ˈprɪn.t̬ɪd **ˈprint ˌrun; ˈprinting ˌpress**

printable ˈprɪn.tə.bl̩ US -t̬ə-

printer ˈprɪn.təʳ US -t̬ɚ **-s** -z

printmak|ing ˈprɪntˌmeɪ.k|ɪŋ **-er/s** -əʳ/z US -ɚ/z

printout ˈprɪnt.aʊt **-s** -s

printwheel ˈprɪnt.*h*wiːl **-s** -z

prior (P) praɪəʳ US praɪɚ **-s** -z

prioress ˈpraɪə.rəs, -rɪs, -res; ˌpraɪəˈres US ˈpraɪɚ.ɪs **-es** -ɪz

prioritiz|e, -is|e praɪˈɒr.ɪ.taɪz, ˈ-ə- US -ˈɔːr.ə- **-es** -ɪz **-ing** -ɪŋ **-ed** -d

priorit|y praɪˈɒr.ə.t|i, -ɪ.t|i US -ˈɔːr.ə.t̬|i **-ies** -iz

prior|y ˈpraɪə.r|i **-ies** -iz

Priscian ˈprɪʃ.i.ən US ˈ-ən, -i.ən

Priscilla prɪˈsɪl.ə, prə- US prɪ-

pris|e praɪz **-es** -ɪz **-ing** -ɪŋ **-ed** -d

prism ˈprɪz.ᵊm **-s** -z

prismatic prɪzˈmæt.ɪk US -ˈmæt̬- **-al** **-ally** -ᵊl.i, -li

prison ˈprɪz.ᵊn **-s** -z **ˈprison ˌcamp; ˌprison ˈvisitor**

prisoner ˈprɪz.ᵊn.əʳ, ˈ-nəʳ US ˈprɪz.ᵊn.ɚ, ˈ-nɚ **-s** -z **ˌprisoner of ˈconscience; ˌprisoner of ˈwar**

priss|y ˈprɪs|.i **-ier** -i.əʳ US -i.ɚ **-iest** -i.ɪst, -i.əst **-ily** -ɪ.li, -ᵊl.i **-iness** -ɪ.nəs, -ɪ.nɪs

Pristina ˈprɪʃ.tɪ.nə

pristine ˈprɪs.tiːn, -taɪn US -tiːn; prɪˈstiːn

Pritchard ˈprɪtʃ.əd, -ɑːd US -ɚd

Pritchett ˈprɪtʃ.ɪt, -ət

prithee ˈprɪð.i, -iː

privacy ˈprɪv.ə.si, ˈpraɪ.və- US ˈpraɪ-

private ˈpraɪ.vɪt, -vət US -vət **-s** -s **-ly** **-ness** -nəs, -nɪs **ˌprivate deˈtective; ˌprivate ˈenterprise; ˌprivate ˈeye;**

,private 'member's ,bill; ,private 'sector (US) 'private ,sector; ,private 'school
privateer ,praɪ.və'tɪəʳ, -vɪ'- (US) -və'tɪr **-s** -z
privation praɪ'veɪ.ʃᵊn **-s** -z
privative 'prɪv.ə.tɪv **-ly** -li
privatization, -isa- ,praɪ.vɪ.taɪ'zeɪ.ʃᵊn, -və-, -tɪ'- (US) -və.tɪ'- **-s** -z
privatiz|e, -is|e 'praɪ.vɪ.taɪz, -və- (US) -və- **-es** -ɪz **-ing** -ɪŋ **-ed** -d
privet 'prɪv.ɪt **-s** -s 'privet ,hedge, ,privet 'hedge
privileg|e 'prɪv.ᵊl.ɪdʒ, -ɪ.lɪdʒ (US) -ᵊl.ɪdʒ, '-lɪdʒ **-es** -ɪz **-ed** -d
privity 'prɪv.ə.ti, -ɪ.ti (US) -ə.t̬i
priv|y 'prɪv|.i **-ies** -iz **-ily** -ɪ.li, -ᵊl.i ,Privy 'Council; ,Privy 'Purse; ,Privy 'Seal
priz|e praɪz **-es** -ɪz **-ing** -ɪŋ **-ed** -d 'prize ,day
prize|-fight 'praɪz|.faɪt **-fights** -faɪts **-fighter/s** -,faɪ.təʳ/z (US) -,faɪ.t̬ɚ/z
prizewinn|er 'praɪz,wɪn|.əʳ (US) -ɚ **-ers** -əz (US) -ɚz **-ing** -ɪŋ
Prizren 'prɪz.rɪn (US) 'priːz.rən
pro- prəʊ- (US) proʊ-, prə-
Note: Prefix. In words containing **pro-** where the stem is free and the meaning is **in favour of**, it generally takes secondary stress, e.g. **pro-choice** /,prəʊ'tʃɔɪs (US) ,proʊ-/. Attached to bound stems, the pron is normally /prəʊ- (US) proʊ-, prə-/, e.g.**probation** /prəʊ'beɪ.ʃᵊn (US) proʊ-/. There are exceptions; see individual entries.
PRO ,piː.ɑː'rəʊ (US) -ɑːr'oʊ
pro prəʊ (US) proʊ **-s** -z ,pros and 'cons
proactive ,prəʊ'æk.tɪv (US) ,proʊ- **-ly** -li
pro-am ,prəʊ'æm (US) ,proʊ-
probabilistic ,prɒb.ə.bᵊl'ɪs.tɪk, -bɪ'lɪs- (US) ,prɑː.bə.bᵊl'ɪs-
probabilit|y ,prɒb.ə'bɪl.ə.t|i, -ɪ.t|i (US) ,prɑː.bə'bɪl.ə.t̬|i **-ies** -iz
probab|le 'prɒb.ə.b|l̩ (US) 'prɑː.bə- **-ly** -li
proba|te 'prəʊ.beɪ|t, -bɪ|t (US) 'proʊ.beɪ|t **-tes** -ts **-ting** -tɪŋ (US) -t̬ɪŋ **-ted** -tɪd (US) -t̬ɪd
probation prəʊ'beɪ.ʃᵊn (US) proʊ- **-s** -z pro'bation ,officer
probationary prəʊ'beɪ.ʃᵊn.ᵊr.i, -'beɪʃ.nᵊr- (US) proʊ'beɪ.ʃᵊn.er-
probationer prəʊ'beɪ.ʃᵊn.əʳ, -'beɪʃ.nəʳ (US) proʊ'beɪ.ʃᵊn.ɚ, -'beɪʃ.nɚ **-s** -z
probative 'prəʊ.bə.tɪv (US) 'proʊ.bə.t̬ɪv
prob|e prəʊb (US) proʊb **-es** -z **-ing** -ɪŋ **-ed** -d
Probert 'prəʊ.bət, 'prɒb.ət (US) 'proʊ.bɚt, 'prɑː.bɚt
probity 'prəʊ.bə.ti, -ɪ.ti (US) 'proʊ.bə.t̬i
problem 'prɒb.ləm, -lem, -lɪm (US) 'prɑː.bləm **-s** -z 'problem ,child; 'problem ,page
problematic ,prɒb.lə'mæt.ɪk, -lɪ'-, -lem'æt- (US) ,prɑː.blə'mæt̬- **-al** -ᵊl **-ally** -ᵊl.i, -li *stress shift:* ,problematic 'state
pro bono ,prəʊ'bəʊ.nəʊ (US) ,proʊ'boʊ.noʊ
proboscis prəʊ'bɒs.ɪs (US) proʊ'bɑː.sɪs **-es** -iːz
Probus 'prəʊ.bəs (US) 'proʊ-
Probyn 'prəʊ.bɪn (US) 'proʊ-
procedural prə'siː.dʒᵊr.ᵊl, prəʊ-, -djʊ.rᵊl, -djᵊr.ᵊl (US) prə'siː.dʒɚ.ᵊl, proʊ-
procedure prəʊ'siː.dʒəʳ, -djəʳ (US) prə'siː.dʒɚ, proʊ- **-s** -z
proceed (*v.*) prəʊ'siːd (US) proʊ-, prə- **-s** -z **-ing/s** -ɪŋ/z **-ed** -ɪd
proceeds (*n.*) 'prəʊ.siːdz (US) 'proʊ-
pro-celebrity ,prəʊ.sə'leb.rɪ.ti, -sɪ'-, -rə- (US) ,proʊ.sə'leb.rə.t̬i *stress shift:* ,pro-celebrity 'golf
proc|ess (*n.*) 'prəʊ.s|es, -s|ɪs (US) 'prɑː.s|es, -s|əs **-esses** -es.ɪz, -ɪ.sɪz (US) -es.ɪz, -ə.sɪz
process (*v.*) *go in a procession:* prəʊ'ses (US) prə-, proʊ- **-es** -ɪz **-ing** -ɪŋ **-ed** -t
process (*v.*) *treat by a process:* 'prəʊ.ses, -sɪs (US) 'prɑː.ses, -səs **-es** -ɪz **-ing** -ɪŋ **-ed** -t **-or/s** -əʳ/z (US) -ɚ/z
procession prə'seʃ.ᵊn (US) prə-, proʊ- **-s** -z
processional prə'seʃ.ᵊn.ᵊl (US) prə-, proʊ- **-s** -z
pro-choice ,prəʊ'tʃɔɪs (US) ,proʊ-
proclaim prəʊ'kleɪm (US) proʊ-, prə- **-s** -z **-ing** -ɪŋ **-ed** -d **-er/s** -əʳ/z (US) -ɚ/z
proclamation ,prɒk.lə'meɪ.ʃᵊn (US) ,prɑː.klə'- **-s** -z
proclitic prəʊ'klɪt.ɪk (US) proʊ'klɪt̬- **-s** -s
proclivit|y prəʊ'klɪv.ə.t|i, -ɪ.t|i (US) proʊ'klɪv.ə.t̬|i **-ies** -iz
proconsul prəʊ'kɒnt.sᵊl (US) proʊ'kɑːnt- **-s** -z
proconsul|ar prəʊ'kɒnt.sjə.l|əʳ, -sjʊ- (US) proʊ'kɑːnt.sᵊl|.ɚ **-ate/s** -ət/s, -ɪt/s, -eɪt/s (US) -ɪt/s
proconsulship prəʊ'kɒnt.sᵊl.ʃɪp (US) proʊ'kɑːnt- **-s** -s
procrasti|nate prəʊ'kræs.tɪ|.neɪt (US) proʊ'kræs.tə-, prə- **-nates** -neɪts **-nating** -neɪ.tɪŋ (US) -neɪ.t̬ɪŋ **-nated** -neɪ.tɪd (US) -neɪ.t̬ɪd **-nator/s** -neɪ.təʳ/z (US) -neɪ.t̬ɚ/z
procrastination prəʊ,kræs.tɪ'neɪ.ʃᵊn (US) proʊ,kræs.tə'-, prə- **-s** -z
procreant 'prəʊ.kri.ənt (US) 'proʊ-
procrea|te 'prəʊ.kri.eɪ|t, ,--'- (US) 'proʊ.kri.eɪ|t **-tes** -ts **-ting** -tɪŋ (US) -t̬ɪŋ **-ted** -tɪd (US) -t̬ɪd
procreation ,prəʊ.kri'eɪ.ʃᵊn (US) ,proʊ-
procreative 'prəʊ.kri.eɪ.tɪv, -ə-, ,prəʊ.kri'eɪ- (US) 'proʊ.kri.eɪ.t̬ɪv
Procrust|es prəʊ'krʌs.t|iːz (US) proʊ- **-ean** -i.ən
Procter 'prɒk.təʳ (US) 'prɑːk.tɚ
proctor (P) 'prɒk.təʳ (US) 'prɑːk.tɚ **-s** -z **-ing** -ɪŋ **-ed** -d
proctorial prɒk'tɔː.ri.əl (US) prɑːk'tɔːr.i-
procumbent prəʊ'kʌm.bənt (US) proʊ-
procuration ,prɒk.jʊə'reɪ.ʃᵊn, -jə'- (US) ,prɑːk.juː'-, -jə'- **-s** -z
procurator 'prɒk.jʊə.reɪ.təʳ, -jə- (US) 'prɑː.kjə.reɪ.t̬ɚ, -kjʊ- **-s** -z
procurator-fiscal, (PF) ,prɒk.jʊə.reɪ.tə'fɪs.kᵊl, -jə- (US) ,prɑː.kjə.reɪ.t̬ɚ'-, -kjʊ- **-s** -z
procur|e prə'kjʊəʳ, -kjɔːʳ (US) proʊ'kjʊr, prə- **-es** -z **-ing** -ɪŋ **-ed** -d **-er/s** -əʳ/z (US) -ɚ/z **-able** -ə.bl̩
procurement prə'kjʊə.mənt, -'kjɔː- (US) proʊ'kjʊr-, prə-
procuress prə'kjʊə.res, -'kjɔː-, -rɪs; 'prɒk.jə-, -jʊ- (US) proʊ'kjʊr.ɪs, prə- **-es** -ɪz
Procyon 'prəʊ.si.ən (US) 'proʊ.si.ɑːn
prod prɒd (US) prɑːd **-s** -z **-ding** -ɪŋ **-ded** -ɪd
prodd|y 'prɒd|.i (US) 'prɑː.d|i **-ies** -iz
Prodi 'prəʊ.di (US) 'proʊ-
prodigal 'prɒd.ɪ.gᵊl (US) 'prɑː.dɪ- **-s** -z **-ly** -i **-ness** -nəs, -nɪs ,prodigal 'son
prodigality ,prɒd.ɪ'gæl.ə.ti, -ɪ.ti (US) ,prɑː.dɪ'gæl.ə.t̬i
prodigaliz|e, -is|e 'prɒd.ɪ.gᵊl.aɪz (US) 'prɑː.dɪ- **-es** -ɪz **-ing** -ɪŋ **-ed** -d
prodigious prə'dɪdʒ.əs (US) prə-, proʊ- **-ly** -li **-ness** -nəs, -nɪs
prodig|y 'prɒd.ɪ.dʒ|i, '-ə- (US) 'prɑː.də- **-ies** -iz
produce (*n.*) 'prɒd.juːs, 'prɒdʒ.uːs (US) 'prɑː.duːs, 'proʊ-, -djuːs
produc|e (*v.*) prə'djuːs, -'dʒuːs (US) -'duːs, proʊ-, -'djuːs **-es** -ɪz **-ing** -ɪŋ **-ed** -t **-er/s** -əʳ/z (US) -ɚ/z
producible prə'djuː.sə.bl̩, -sɪ- (US) -'duː.sə-, proʊ-, -'djuː-
product 'prɒd.ʌkt, -əkt (US) 'prɑː.dʌkt, -dəkt **-s** -s
production prə'dʌk.ʃᵊn (US) prə-, proʊ- **-s** -z pro'duction ,line
productional prə'dʌk.ʃᵊn.ᵊl (US) prə-, proʊ-
productive prə'dʌk.tɪv (US) prə-, proʊ- **-ly** -li **-ness** -nəs, -nɪs
productivity ,prɒd.ʌk'tɪv.ə.ti, -ək'-, -ɪ.ti (US) ,proʊ.dək'tɪv.ə.t̬i, ,prɑː-; proʊ,dʌk'-, prə-
proem 'prəʊ.em (US) 'proʊ- **-s** -z
prof prɒf (US) prɑːf **-s** -s

profanation ˌprɒf.əˈneɪ.ʃən (US) ˌprɑː.fəˈ- **-s** -z
profan|e prəˈfeɪn (US) proʊ-, prə- **-est** -ɪst, -əst **-ely** -li **-eness** -nəs, -nɪs **-es** -z **-ing** -ɪŋ **-ed** -d **-er/s** -əʳ/z (US) -ɚ/z
profanit|y prəˈfæn.ə.t|i, -ɪ.t|i (US) proʊˈfæn.ə.ţ|i, prə- **-ies** -iz
profess prəˈfes (US) prə-, proʊ- **-es** -ɪz **-ing** -ɪŋ **-ed** -t **-edly** -ɪd.li
profession prəˈfeʃ.ən (US) prə-, proʊ- **-s** -z
professional prəˈfeʃ.ən.əl (US) prə-, proʊ- **-s** -z
professionalism prəˈfeʃ.ən.əl.ɪ.zəm (US) prə-, proʊ-
professionally prəˈfeʃ.ən.əl.i, ˈ-nəl.i (US) prə-, proʊ-
professor prəˈfes.əʳ (US) -ɚ, proʊ- **-s** -z
professorate prəˈfes.ər.ət, -eɪt (US) -ɚ.ət, proʊ- **-s** -s
professorial ˌprɒf.ɪˈsɔː.ri.əl, -əˈ-, -esˈɔː- (US) ˌproʊ.fəˈsɔːr.i-, ˌprɑː- **-ly** -i *stress shift:* ˌprofessorial ˈduties
professoriat(e) ˌprɒf.ɪˈsɔː.ri.ət, -əˈ-, -esˈɔː-, -ɪt (US) ˌproʊ.fəˈsɔːr.i.ət, ˌprɑː- **-s** -s
professorship prəˈfes.ə.ʃɪp (US) ˈ-ɚ-, proʊ- **-s** -s
proff|er ˈprɒf|.əʳ (US) ˈprɑː.f|ɚ **-ers** -əz (US) -ɚz **-ering** -ər.ɪŋ **-ered** -əd (US) -ɚd
proficiency prəˈfɪʃ.ən*t*.si (US) prə-, proʊ-
proficient prəˈfɪʃ.ənt (US) prə-, proʊ- **-ly** -li
profil|e ˈprəʊ.faɪl (US) ˈproʊ- **-es** -z **-ing** -ɪŋ **-ed** -d
prof|it (*n. v.*) ˈprɒf|.ɪt (US) ˈprɑː.f|ɪt **-its** -ɪts **-iting** -ɪ.tɪŋ (US) -ɪ.ţɪŋ **-ited** -ɪ.tɪd (US) -ɪ.ţɪd **ˌprofit and ˈloss; ˈprofit ˌmargin**
profitability ˌprɒf.ɪ.təˈbɪl.ɪ.ti, ˌ-ə-, -ə.ti (US) ˌprɑː.fɪ.ţəˈbɪl.ə.ţi
profitab|le ˈprɒf.ɪ.tə.b|l̩, ˈ-ə- (US) ˈprɑː.fɪ.ţə- **-ly** -li **-leness** -l̩.nəs, -nɪs
profiteer ˌprɒf.ɪˈtɪəʳ, -əˈ- (US) ˌprɑː.fɪˈtɪr **-s** -z **-ing** -ɪŋ **-ed** -d
profiterole prɒfˈɪt.ər.əʊl, prəˈfɪt-; ˈprɒf.ɪ.tər-, ˌprɒf.ɪ.tərˈəʊl (US) prəˈfɪt.ə.roʊl **-s** -z
profitless ˈprɒf.ɪt.ləs, -lɪs (US) ˈprɑː.fɪt-
profitmaking ˈprɒf.ɪtˌmeɪ.kɪŋ (US) ˈprɑː.fɪt-
profit-sharing ˈprɒf.ɪtˌʃeə.rɪŋ (US) ˈprɑː.fɪtˌʃer.ɪŋ
profligacy ˈprɒf.lɪ.gə.si (US) ˈprɑː.flɪ-
profligate ˈprɒf.lɪ.gət, -gɪt (US) ˈprɑː.flɪ.gɪt **-s** -s **-ly** -li **-ness** -nəs, -nɪs
pro forma ˌprəʊˈfɔː.mə (US) ˌproʊˈfɔːr-
profound prəˈfaʊnd (US) prə-, proʊ- **-er** -əʳ (US) -ɚ **-est** -ɪst, -əst **-ly** -li **-ness** -nəs, -nɪs
Profumo prəˈfjuː.məʊ (US) -moʊ
profundit|y prəˈfʌn.də.t|i, -ɪ.t|i (US) proʊ-, prə- **-ies** -iz
profus|e prəˈfjuːs (US) prə-, proʊ- **-est** -ɪst, -əst **-ely** -li **-eness** -nəs, -nɪs
profusion prəˈfjuː.ʒən (US) prə-, proʊ- **-s** -z
prog prɒg (US) prɑːg, prɔːg **-s** -z **-ging** -ɪŋ **-ged** -d
progenitor prəʊˈdʒen.ɪ.təʳ, ˈ-ə- (US) proʊˈdʒen.ə.ţɚ, prə- **-s** -z
progeniture prəʊˈdʒen.ɪ.tʃəʳ, ˈ-ə-, -tjʊəʳ, -tjəʳ (US) proʊˈdʒen.ə.tʃɚ, prə-
progen|y ˈprɒdʒ.ə.n|i, ˈ-ɪ- (US) ˈprɑː.dʒə- **-ies** -iz
progesterone prəʊˈdʒes.tər.əʊn (US) proʊˈdʒes.tə.roʊn
progestogen prəʊˈdʒes.tə.dʒɪn, -dʒən (US) proʊˈdʒes.tə.dʒən, -dʒen **-s** -z
prognathic prɒgˈnæθ.ɪk (US) prɑːg-, -ˈneɪ.θɪk
prognathism ˈprɒg.nə.θɪ.zəm; prɒgˈnæθ.ɪ- (US) ˈprɑːg.nə.θɪ-; prɑːgˈneɪ-
prognathous prɒgˈneɪ.θəs; ˈprɒg.nə.θəs (US) ˈprɑːg.nə-; prɑːgˈneɪ-
prognos|is prɒgˈnəʊ.s|ɪs (US) prɑːgˈnoʊ- **-es** -iːz
prognostic prɒgˈnɒs.tɪk, prəg- (US) prɑːgˈnɑː.stɪk
prognosti|cate prɒgˈnɒs.tɪ|.keɪt, prəg- (US) prɑːgˈnɑː.stɪ- **-cates** -keɪts **-cating** -keɪ.tɪŋ (US) -keɪ.ţɪŋ **-cated** -keɪ.tɪd (US) -keɪ.ţɪd **-cator/s** -keɪ.təʳ/z (US) -keɪ.ţɚ/z
prognostication prəgˌnɒs.tɪˈkeɪ.ʃən, prɒg- (US) prɑːgˌnɑː.stɪˈ- **-s** -z
program ˈprəʊ.græm (US) ˈproʊ-, -grəm **-s** -z **-ing** -ɪŋ **-ed** -d **-er/s** -əʳ/z (US) -ɚ/z
programmable prəʊˈgræm.ə.bl̩; ˈprəʊ.græm- (US) ˈproʊ.græm.ə-, -grə.mə-
programmatic ˌprəʊ.grəˈmæt.ɪk (US) ˌproʊ.grəˈmæţ-
programm|e ˈprəʊ.græm (US) ˈproʊ-, -grəm **-es** -z **-ing** -ɪŋ **-ed** -d **-er/s** -əʳ/z (US) -ɚ/z
progress (*n.*) ˈprəʊ.gres (US) ˈprɑː- **ˈprogress reˌport**
progress (*v.*) prəʊˈgres (US) prə-, proʊ- **-es** -ɪz **-ing** -ɪŋ **-ed** -t
progression prəʊˈgreʃ.ən (US) prə-, proʊ- **-s** -z
progressional prəʊˈgreʃ.ən.əl, ˈ-nəl (US) prə-, proʊ-
progressionist prəʊˈgreʃ.ən.ɪst (US) prə-, proʊ- **-s** -s
progressist prəʊˈgres.ɪst (US) ˈprɑː.gres-, ˈproʊ-; prəˈgres- **-s** -s
progressive prəʊˈgres.ɪv (US) prə-, proʊ- **-s** -z **-ly** -li **-ness** -nəs, -nɪs
progressiv|ism prəʊˈgres.ɪ.v|ɪ.zəm (US) prə-, proʊ- **-ist/s** -ɪst/s
prohib|it prəʊˈhɪb|.ɪt (US) proʊ-, prə- **-its** -ɪts **-iting** -ɪ.tɪŋ (US) -ɪ.ţɪŋ **-ited** -ɪ.tɪd (US) -ɪ.ţɪd
prohibition (P) ˌprəʊ.*h*ɪˈbɪʃ.ən (US) ˌproʊ- **-s** -z
prohibition|ism ˌprəʊ.*h*ɪˈbɪʃ.ən|.ɪ.zəm (US) ˌproʊ- **-ist/s** -ɪst/s
prohibitive prəʊˈhɪb.ə.tɪv (US) proʊˈhɪb.ə.ţɪv, prə- **-ly** -li
prohibitory prəʊˈhɪb.ɪ.tər.i (US) proʊˈhɪb.ə.tɔːr-, prə-
project (*n.*) ˈprɒdʒ.ekt, -ɪkt (US) ˈprɑː.dʒekt, -dʒɪkt **-s** -s
project (*v.*) prəʊˈdʒekt (US) prə-, proʊ- **-s** -s **-ing** -ɪŋ **-ed** -ɪd
projectile prəʊˈdʒek.taɪl (US) prəˈdʒek.təl, proʊ- **-s** -z
projection prəʊˈdʒek.ʃən (US) prə-, proʊ- **-s** -z **-ist/s** -ɪst/s
projective prəʊˈdʒek.tɪv (US) prə-, proʊ- **-ly** -li
projector prəʊˈdʒek.təʳ (US) prəˈdʒek.tɚ, proʊ- **-s** -z
Prokofiev prəˈkɒf.i.ef (US) proʊˈkɔː.fi.ef, prə-, -ˈkoʊ-
prolactin prəʊˈlæk.tɪn (US) proʊ-
prolaps|e ˈprəʊ.læps, -ˈ- (US) ˈproʊ- **-es** -ɪz **-ing** -ɪŋ **-ed** -t
prolate ˈprəʊ.leɪt, ˌ-ˈ- (US) ˈproʊ.leɪt
prole prəʊl (US) proʊl **-s** -z
prolegomen|on ˌprəʊ.lɪˈgɒm.ɪ.n|ən, -ləˈ-, -legˈɒm-, ˈ-ə-, -ɒn (US) ˌproʊ.lɪˈgɑː.mə.n|ɑːn, -n|ən **-a** -ə
proleps|is prəʊˈlep.s|ɪs, -ˈliːp- (US) proʊˈlep- **-es** -iːz
proleptic prəʊˈlep.tɪk, -ˈliːp- (US) proʊˈlep- **-ally** -əl.i, -li
proletarian ˌprəʊ.lɪˈteə.ri.ən, -ləˈ-, -letˈeə- (US) ˌproʊ.ləˈter.i-, -ˈtær- **-s** -z **-ism** -ɪ.zəm
proletariat ˌprəʊ.lɪˈteə.ri.ət, -ləˈ-, -letˈeə-, -æt (US) ˌproʊ.ləˈter.i.ət, -ˈtær-
pro-life ˌprəʊˈlaɪf (US) ˌproʊ-
prolifer|ate prəʊˈlɪf.ər|.eɪt (US) proʊˈlɪf.ə.r|eɪt, prə- **-ates** -eɪts **-ating** -eɪ.tɪŋ (US) -eɪ.ţɪŋ **-ated** -eɪ.tɪd (US) -eɪ.ţɪd
proliferation prəʊˌlɪf.ərˈeɪ.ʃən (US) proʊˌlɪf.əˈreɪ-, prə- **-s** -z
prolific prəʊˈlɪf.ɪk (US) proʊ-, prə- **-ally** -əl.i, -li **-ness** -nəs, -nɪs
prolix ˈprəʊ.lɪks (US) proʊˈlɪks, ˈ--
prolixity prəʊˈlɪk.sə-, -sɪ- (US) proʊˈlɪk.sə.ţi, prə-
prolix|ly prəʊˈlɪk.s|li, ˈ--- (US) proʊˈlɪk.s|li, prə- **-ness** -nəs, -nɪs

prolocutor prəʊˈlɒk.jə.tə^r, -jʊ- (US) proʊˈlɑː.kjə.t̬ɚ, -kjʊ- -s -z

prolog, PROLOG ˈprəʊ.lɒg (US) ˈproʊ.lɑːg, -lɔːg -s -z

prologu|e ˈprəʊ.lɒg (US) ˈproʊ.lɑːg, -lɔːg -es -z -ing -ɪŋ -ed -d

prolong prəʊˈlɒŋ (US) proʊˈlɑːŋ, prə-, -ˈlɔːŋ -s -z -ing -ɪŋ -ed -d

prolongation ˌprəʊ.lɒŋˈgeɪ.ʃ^{ə}n, ˌprɒl.ɒŋˈ- (US) ˌproʊ.lɑːŋˈ-, -lɔːŋˈ- -s -z

prom (P) prɒm (US) prɑːm -s -z

promenad|e ˌprɒm.əˈnɑːd, -ɪˈ- (US) ˌprɑː.məˈneɪd, -ˈnɑːd -es -z -ing -ɪŋ -ed -ɪd -er/s -ə^r/z (US) -ɚ/z *stress shift:* ˌpromenade ˈconcert

Note: A British pronunciation /ˌprɒm.əˈneɪd, -ɪˈ-/ also exists, used chiefly in square dancing.

Promethean prəʊˈmiː.θi.ən (US) proʊ-, prə-

Prometheus prəʊˈmiː.θi.uːs, -əs (US) proʊˈmiː.θi.əs, prə-, -uːs

promethium prəʊˈmiː.θi.əm (US) proʊ-

prominenc|e ˈprɒm.ɪ.nənts, ˈ-ə- (US) ˈprɑː.mə- -es -ɪz

prominent ˈprɒm.ɪ.nənt, ˈ-ə- (US) ˈprɑː.mə- -ly -li

promiscuity ˌprɒm.ɪˈskjuː.ə.ti, -əˈ-, -ɪ.ti (US) ˌprɑː.mɪˈskjuː.ə.t̬i, ˌproʊ-

promiscuous prəˈmɪs.kju.əs, prɒmˈɪs- (US) prəˈmɪs-, proʊ- -ly -li -ness -nəs, -nɪs

promis|e ˈprɒm.ɪs (US) ˈprɑː.mɪs -es -ɪz -ing/ly -ɪŋ/li -ed -t ˌpromised ˈland (US) ˈpromised ˌland

promissory ˈprɒm.ɪ.s^{ə}r.i; prəˈmɪs.^{ə}r- (US) ˈprɑː.mɪ.sɔːr- ˌpromissory ˈnote (US) ˈpromissory ˌnote

promo ˈprəʊ.məʊ (US) ˈproʊ.moʊ -s -z

promontor|y ˈprɒm.ən.t^{ə}r|.i (US) ˈprɑː.mən.tɔːr- -ies -iz

pro|mote prə|ˈməʊt (US) -ˈmoʊt -motes -ˈməʊts (US) -ˈmoʊts -moting -ˈməʊ.tɪŋ (US) -ˈmoʊ.t̬ɪŋ -moted -ˈməʊ.tɪd (US) -ˈmoʊ.t̬ɪd -moter/s -ˈməʊ.tə^r/z (US) -ˈmoʊ.t̬ɚ/z

promotion prəˈməʊ.ʃ^{ə}n (US) -ˈmoʊ-, proʊ- -s -z

promotional prəˈməʊ.ʃ^{ə}n.^{ə}l (US) -ˈmoʊ-, proʊ- -ly -i

promotive prəˈməʊ.tɪv (US) -ˈmoʊ.t̬ɪv, proʊ-

prompt prɒmpt (US) prɑːmpt -s -s -est -ɪst, -əst -ly -li -ness -nəs, -nɪs -ing/s -ɪŋ/z -ed -ɪd -er/s -ə^r/z (US) -ɚ/z

promptitude ˈprɒmp.tɪ.tjuːd (US) ˈprɑːmp.tɪ.tuːd

promul|gate ˈprɒm.^{ə}l|.geɪt, -ʌl- (US) ˈprɑː.m^{ə}l-; proʊˈmʌl- -gates -geɪts -gating -geɪ.tɪŋ (US) -geɪ.t̬ɪŋ -gated -geɪ.tɪd (US) -geɪ.t̬ɪd -gator/s -geɪ.tə^r/z (US) -geɪ.t̬ɚ/z

promulgation ˌprɒm.^{ə}lˈgeɪ.ʃ^{ə}n, -ʌlˈ- (US) ˌprɑː.məlˈ- -s -z

prone prəʊn (US) proʊn -ly -li -ness -nəs, -nɪs

prong prɒŋ (US) prɑːŋ, prɔːŋ -s -z -ing -ɪŋ -ed -d

pronghorn ˈprɒŋ.hɔːn (US) ˈprɑːŋ.hɔːrn, ˈprɔːŋ- -s -z

pronominal prəʊˈnɒm.ɪ.n^{ə}l, -^{ə}n.^{ə}l (US) proʊˈnɑː.mə- -ly -i

pronominalization prəʊˌnɒm.ɪ.n^{ə}l.aɪˈzeɪ.ʃ^{ə}n, -^{ə}n.^{ə}l-, -ɪˈ- (US) proʊˌnɑː.mɪ.n^{ə}l.ɪˈ- -s -z

pronominaliz|e, -is|e prəʊˈnɒm.ɪ.n^{ə}l.aɪz, -^{ə}n.^{ə}l- (US) proʊˈnɑː.mɪ.n^{ə}l- -es -ɪz -ing -ɪŋ -ed -d

pronoun ˈprəʊ.naʊn (US) ˈproʊ- -s -z

pronounc|e prəˈnaʊnts (US) prə-, proʊ- -es -ɪz -ing -ɪŋ -ed -t -edly -t.li, -ɪd.li -er/s -ə^r/z (US) -ɚ/z -eable/ness -ə.bl̩/nəs, -nɪs

pronouncement prəʊˈnaʊnt.smənt (US) prə-, proʊ- -s -s

pronto ˈprɒn.təʊ (US) ˈprɑːn.t̬oʊ

pronunciamento prəʊˌnʌnt.si.əˈmen.təʊ, -ʃi- (US) proʊˌnʌnt.si.əˈmen.toʊ, prə- -(e)s -z

pronunciation prəˌnʌnt.siˈeɪ.ʃ^{ə}n (US) prə-, proʊ- -s -z

proof pruːf -s -s -ing -ɪŋ -ed -t

proofread ˈpruːf.riːd -s -z -ing -ɪŋ -er/s -ə^r/z (US) -ɚ/z *past tense:* ˈpruːf.red

Proops pruːps

prop prɒp (US) prɑːp -s -s -ping -ɪŋ -ped -t

propaedeutic ˌprəʊ.piːˈdjuː.tɪk (US) ˌproʊ.pɪˈduː.t̬ɪk, -ˈdjuː- -al -^{ə}l -s -s

propaganda ˌprɒp.əˈgæn.də (US) ˌprɑː.pəˈ-

propagand|ism ˌprɒp.əˈgæn.d|ɪ.z^{ə}m (US) ˌprɑː.pəˈ- -ist/s -ɪst/s

propagandiz|e, -is|e ˌprɒp.əˈgæn.daɪz (US) ˌprɑː.pəˈ- -es -ɪz -ing -ɪŋ -ed -d

propa|gate ˈprɒp.ə|.geɪt (US) ˈprɑː.pə- -gates -geɪts -gating -geɪ.tɪŋ (US) -geɪ.t̬ɪŋ -gated -geɪ.tɪd (US) -geɪ.t̬ɪd -gator/s -geɪ.tə^r/z (US) -geɪ.t̬ɚ/z

propagation ˌprɒp.əˈgeɪ.ʃ^{ə}n (US) ˌprɑː.pəˈ-

propane ˈprəʊ.peɪn (US) ˈproʊ-

proparoxytone ˌprəʊ.p^{ə}rˈɒk.sɪ.təʊn, -pærˈ-, ˈ-ə-, -tən (US) ˌproʊ.pəˈrɑːk.sɪ.toʊn, -pærˈ- -s -z

propel prəˈpel -s -z -ling -ɪŋ -led -d proˌpelling ˈpencil

propellant, propellent prəˈpel.ənt -s -s

propeller, propellor prəˈpel.ə^r (US) -ɚ -s -z

propene ˈprəʊ.piːn (US) ˈproʊ-

propensit|y prəʊˈpent.sə.t|i, -ɪ.t|i (US) prəˈpent.sə.t̬|i, proʊ- -ies -iz

proper ˈprɒp.ə^r (US) ˈprɑː.pɚ ˌproper ˈnoun

properly ˈprɒp.^{ə}l.i, ˈ-li (US) ˈprɑː.pɚ.li

Propertius prəʊˈpɜː.ʃəs, -ʃi.əs (US) proʊˈpɝː-

propert|y ˈprɒp.ə.t|i (US) ˈprɑː.pɚ.t̬|i -ies -iz -ied -id

prophec|y (*n.*) ˈprɒf.ə.s|i, ˈ-ɪ- (US) ˈprɑː.fə- -ies -iz

prophes|y (*v.*) ˈprɒf.ə.s|aɪ, ˈ-ɪ- (US) ˈprɑː.fə- -ies -aɪz -ying -aɪ.ɪŋ -ied -aɪd -ier/s -aɪ.ə^r/z (US) -aɪ.ɚ/z

prophet ˈprɒf.ɪt (US) ˈprɑː.fɪt -s -s

prophetess ˌprɒf.ɪˈtes; ˈprɒf.ɪ.tɪs, -tes (US) ˈprɑː.fɪ.t̬əs -es -ɪz

prophetic prəʊˈfet.ɪk (US) prə-, proʊ- -al -^{ə}l -ally -^{ə}l.i, -li

prophylactic ˌprɒf.ɪˈlæk.tɪk, -əˈ- (US) ˌproʊ.fəˈ-, ˌprɑː- -s -s -ally -^{ə}l.i, -li *stress shift:* ˌprophylactic ˈmedicine

prophylax|is ˌprɒf.ɪˈlæk.s|ɪs, -əˈ- (US) ˌproʊ.fəˈ-, ˌprɑː- -es -iːz

propinquity prəʊˈpɪŋ.kwə.ti, prɒpˈɪŋ-, -kwɪ- (US) proʊˈpɪŋ.kwə.t̬i, -ˈpɪn-

propiti|ate prəˈpɪʃ.i|.eɪt (US) proʊ-, prə- -ates -eɪts -ating -eɪ.tɪŋ (US) -eɪ.t̬ɪŋ -ated -eɪ.tɪd (US) -eɪ.t̬ɪd -ator/s -eɪ.tə^r/z (US) -eɪ.t̬ɚ/z

propitiation prəˌpɪʃ.iˈeɪ.ʃ^{ə}n (US) proʊ-, prə- -s -z

propitiatory prəˈpɪʃ.i.ə.t^{ə}r.i, -ˈpɪʃ.ə-, -eɪ.t^{ə}r-; prəʊˌpɪʃ.iˈeɪ- (US) proʊˈpɪʃ.i.ə.tɔːr-, prə-

propitious prəˈpɪʃ.əs (US) prə-, proʊ- -ly -li -ness -nəs, -nɪs

propjet ˈprɒp.dʒet (US) ˈprɑːp- -s -s

Pro-Plus® ˌprəʊˈplʌs (US) ˌproʊ-

proponent prəʊˈpəʊ.nənt (US) prəˈpoʊ-, proʊ- -s -s

proportion prəˈpɔː.ʃ^{ə}n (US) -ˈpɔːr- -s -z -ing -ɪŋ -ed -d

proportionab|le prəˈpɔː.ʃ^{ə}n.ə.b|l̩ (US) -ˈpɔːr- -ly -li -leness -l̩.nəs, -nɪs

proportional prəˈpɔː.ʃ^{ə}n.^{ə}l, -ˈpɔːʃ.n^{ə}l (US) -ˈpɔːr.ʃ^{ə}n.^{ə}l, -ˈpɔːrʃ.n^{ə}l -ly -i proˌportional ˌrepresenˈtation

proportionality prəˌpɔː.ʃ^{ə}nˈæl.ə.ti, -ɪ.ti (US) -ˌpɔːr.ʃ^{ə}nˈæl.ə.t̬i

proportionate prəˈpɔː.ʃ^{ə}n.ət, -ˈpɔːʃ.nət, -nɪt (US) -ˈpɔːr.ʃ^{ə}n.ɪt, -ˈpɔːrʃ.nɪt -ly -li -ness -nəs, -nɪs

proposal prəˈpəʊ.z^{ə}l (US) -ˈpoʊ- -s -z

propos|e prəˈpəʊz (US) -ˈpoʊz -es -ɪz -ing -ɪŋ -ed -d -er/s -ə^r/z (US) -ɚ/z

proposition ˌprɒp.əˈzɪʃ.^{ə}n (US) ˌprɑː.pəˈ- -s -z -ing -ɪŋ -ed -d

propound prəˈpaʊnd (US) prə-, proʊ- -s -z -ing -ɪŋ -ed -ɪd -er/s -ə^r/z (US) -ɚ/z

propranolol prəʊ'præn.ə.lɒl (US) proʊ'præn.oʊ.lɔːl, '-ə-, -loʊl
proprietary prə'praɪə.tᵊr.i (US) -ter-
proprietor prə'praɪə.təʳ (US) proʊ'praɪə.t̬ɚ, prə- **-s** -z **-ship/s** -ʃɪp/s
proprietorial prə,praɪə'tɔː.ri.əl (US) -'tɔːr.i-, proʊ- **-ly** -i
proprietress prə'praɪə.trɪs, -tres (US) proʊ-, -trɪs, -trəs **-es** -ɪz
propriet|y prə'praɪə.t|i (US) -t̬|i, proʊ- **-ies** -iz
propriocep|tion ,prəʊ.pri.əʊ'sep|.ʃᵊn, ,prɒp.ri- (US) ,proʊ.pri.oʊ'-, -ə'- **-tive** -tɪv
propul|sion prə'pʌl|.ʃᵊn (US) prə-, proʊ- **-sive** -sɪv
propylae|um (P) ,prɒp.ɪ'liː|.əm, -ə'- (US) ,prɑː.pə'- **-a** -ə
propylene 'prɒp.ɪ.liːn, '-ə- (US) 'proʊ.pə-
pro rata ,prəʊ'rɑː.tə, -'reɪ- (US) ,proʊ'reɪ.t̬ə, -'rɑː-
prorogation ,prəʊ.rəʊ'geɪ.ʃᵊn, ,prɒr.əʊ'- (US) ,proʊ.roʊ'- **-s** -z
prorogu|e prəʊ'rəʊg (US) proʊ'roʊg **-es** -z **-ing** -ɪŋ **-ed** -d
prosaic prəʊ'zeɪ.ɪk (US) proʊ- **-al** -ᵊl **-ally** -ᵊl.i, -li **-ness** -nəs, -nɪs
prosceni|um prəʊ'siː.ni|.əm (US) proʊ- **-ums** -əmz **-a** -ə **pro,scenium 'arch**
prosciutto prəʊ'ʃuː.təʊ (US) proʊ'ʃuː.t̬oʊ
proscrib|e prəʊ'skraɪb (US) proʊ- **-es** -z **-ing** -ɪŋ **-ed** -d **-er/s** -əʳ/z (US) -ɚ/z
proscription prəʊ'skrɪp.ʃᵊn (US) proʊ- **-s** -z
proscriptive prəʊ'skrɪp.tɪv (US) proʊ-
pro se ,prəʊ'seɪ (US) ,proʊ-
pros|e prəʊz (US) proʊz **-es** -ɪz **-ing** -ɪŋ **-ed** -d **-er/s** -əʳ/z (US) -ɚ/z
prose|cute 'prɒs.ɪ|.kjuːt, '-ə- (US) 'prɑː.sɪ- **-cutes** -kjuːts **-cuting** -kjuː.tɪŋ (US) -kjuː.t̬ɪŋ **-cuted** -kjuː.tɪd (US) -kjuː.t̬ɪd **,prosecuting at'torney**
prosecution ,prɒs.ɪ'kjuː.ʃᵊn, -ə'- (US) ,prɑː.sɪ'- **-s** -z *stress shift:* ,prosecution 'witness
prosecutor 'prɒs.ɪ.kjuː.təʳ, '-ə- (US) 'prɑː.sɪ.kjuː.t̬ɚ **-s** -z
prosecutorial ,prɒs.ɪ.kjuː'tɔː.ri.əl (US) ,prɑː.sɪ.kjuː'tɔːr.i-
prosecutrix 'prɒs.ɪ.kjuː.trɪks, '-ə-; ,prɒs.ɪ'kjuː-, -ə'- (US) 'prɑː.sɪ.kjuː-, ,prɑː.sɪ'kjuː- **-es** -ɪz
proselyte 'prɒs.ə.laɪt, '-ɪ- (US) 'prɑː.sə- **-s** -s
proselytism 'prɒs.ᵊl.ɪ.tɪ.zᵊm, -ɪ.lɪ-, -lə- (US) 'prɑː.sə.lɪ-, -laɪ-
proselytiz|e, -is|e 'prɒs.ᵊl.ɪ.taɪz, -ɪ.lɪ-, -lə- (US) 'prɑː.sə.lɪ- **-es** -ɪz **-ing** -ɪŋ **-ed** -d

Proserpina prə'sɜː.pɪ.nə, prɒs'ɜː- (US) proʊ'sɝː-
Proserpine 'prɒs.ə.paɪn (US) 'prɑː.sɚ-; proʊ'sɝː.pɪ.niː
prosit 'prəʊ.zɪt, -sɪt; prəʊst (US) 'proʊ.sɪt, -zɪt; proʊst
prosodic prə'sɒd.ɪk (US) proʊ'sɑː.dɪk, prə- **-al** -ᵊl **-ally** -ᵊl.i, -li
prosodist 'prɒs.ə.dɪst, 'prɒz- (US) 'prɑː.sə-, -zə- **-s** -s
prosod|y 'prɒs.ə.d|i, 'prɒz- (US) 'prɑː.sə-, -zə- **-ies** -iz
prospect (P) (*n.*) 'prɒs.pekt (US) 'prɑː.spekt **-s** -s
prospect (*v.*) prə'spekt, prɒs'pekt; 'prɒs.pekt (US) 'prɑː.spekt **-s** -s **-ing** -ɪŋ **-ed** -ɪd
prospective prə'spek.tɪv, prɒs'pek- (US) prə'spek-, proʊ-, prɑː- **-ly** -li **-ness** -nəs, -nɪs
prospector prə'spek.təʳ, prɒs'pek- (US) 'prɑː.spek.tɚ **-s** -z
prospectus prə'spek.təs (US) prə-, proʊ-, prɑː- **-es** -ɪz
prosp|er 'prɒs.p|əʳ (US) 'prɑː.sp|ɚ **-ers** -əz (US) -ɚz **-ering** -ᵊr.ɪŋ **-ered** -əd (US) -ɚd
prosperity prɒs'per.ə.ti, prə'sper-, -ɪ.ti (US) prɑː'sper.ə.t̬i
Prospero 'prɒs.pᵊr.əʊ (US) 'prɑː.spə.roʊ
prosperous 'prɒs.pᵊr.əs (US) 'prɑː.spɚ- **-ly** -li **-ness** -nəs, -nɪs
Prosser 'prɒs.əʳ (US) 'prɑː.sɚ
Prost prɒst (US) proʊst
prostaglandin ,prɒs.tə'glæn.dɪn (US) ,prɑː.stə'- **-s** -z
prostate 'prɒs.teɪt (US) 'prɑː.steɪt **-s** -s **'prostate ,gland**
prostatic prɒs'tæt.ɪk, prə'stæt- (US) proʊ'stæt̬.ɪk, prɑː-
prosthes|is *grammatical term:* 'prɒs.θɪ.s|ɪs, -θə-; 'prɑːs.θə- **-es** -iːz *medical term:* 'prɒs.θə.s|ɪs, -θɪ-; prɒs'θiː- (US) 'prɑːs.θə.s|ɪs; prɑːs'θiː- **-es** (US) -iːz
prosthetic prɒs'θet.ɪk (US) prɑːs'θet̬- **-s** -s
prosthetist prɒs'θiː.tɪst, prəs- (US) 'prɑːs.θɪ.tɪst **-s** -s
prostitu|te 'prɒs.tɪ.tjuː|t, -tə-, -tʃuː|t (US) 'prɑː.stə.tuː|t, -tjuː|t **-tes** -ts **-ting** -tɪŋ (US) -t̬ɪŋ **-ted** -tɪd (US) -t̬ɪd
prostitution ,prɒs.tɪ'tjuː.ʃᵊn, -tə'-, -'tʃuː.ʃᵊn (US) -'tʃuː-, ,prɑː.stə'tuː- **-s** -z
prostrate (*adj.*) 'prɒs.treɪt, -'- (US) 'prɑː.streɪt
prostra|te (*v.*) prɒs'treɪ|t, prə'streɪ|t (US) 'prɑː.streɪ|t **-tes** -ts **-ting** -tɪŋ (US) -t̬ɪŋ **-ted** -tɪd (US) -t̬ɪd
prostration prɒs'treɪ.ʃᵊn, prə'streɪ- (US) prɑː'streɪ- **-s** -z

pros|y 'prəʊ.z|i (US) 'proʊ- **-ier** -i.əʳ (US) -i.ɚ **-iest** -i.ɪst, -i.əst **-ily** -ɪ.li, -ᵊl.i **-iness** -ɪ.nəs, -ɪ.nɪs
protactinium ,prəʊ.tæk'tɪn.i.əm (US) ,proʊ-
protagonist prəʊ'tæg.ᵊn.ɪst (US) proʊ- **-s** -s
Protagoras prəʊ'tæg.ᵊr.æs, -ɒr-, -əs (US) proʊ'tæg.ɚ.əs
pro tanto ,prəʊ'tæn.təʊ (US) ,proʊ'tæn.toʊ, -'tɑːn-
protas|is 'prɒt.ə.s|ɪs (US) 'prɑː.t̬ə- **-es** -iːz
protean prəʊ'tiː.ən; 'prəʊ.ti- (US) 'proʊ-; proʊ'tiː-
protease 'prəʊ.ti.eɪz, -eɪs (US) 'proʊ.t̬ **-s** -z
protect prə'tekt (US) prə-, proʊ- **-s** -s **-ing/ly** -ɪŋ/li **-ed** -ɪd **-or/s** -əʳ/z (US) -ɚ
protection prə'tek.ʃᵊn (US) prə-, proʊ **-s** -z
protection|ism prə'tek.ʃᵊn|.ɪ.zᵊm (US) prə-, proʊ- **-ist/s** -ɪst/s
protective prə'tek.tɪv (US) prə-, proʊ- **-ly** -li **-ness** -nəs, -nɪs
protectorate prə'tek.tᵊr.ət, -ɪt (US) -ɪ proʊ- **-s** -s
protectress prə'tek.trəs, -trɪs (US) -trɪ proʊ- **-es** -ɪz
protégé(e), protege(e) 'prɒt.ɪ.ʒeɪ, 'prəʊ.tɪ-, -tə-, -teʒ.eɪ, -teɪ.ʒeɪ (US) 'proʊ.t̬ə.ʒeɪ, ,--'- **-s** -z
protein 'prəʊ.tiːn (US) 'proʊ- **-s** -z
pro tem ,prəʊ'tem (US) ,proʊ'tem
protest (*n.*) 'prəʊ.test (US) 'proʊ.test **-s** -s
protest (*v.*) prəʊ'test (US) proʊ'test, prə-; 'proʊ.test **-s** -s **-ing/ly** -ɪŋ/li -ɪd **-er/s** -əʳ/z (US) -ɚ/z **-or/s** -əʳ/z (US) -ɚ/z
protestant (P) 'prɒt.ɪ.stᵊnt, '-ə- (US) 'prɑː.t̬ə- **-s** -s **-ism** -ɪ.zᵊm
protestantiz|e, -is|e 'prɒt.ɪ.stən.ta '-ə- (US) 'prɑː.t̬ə- **-es** -ɪz **-ing** -ɪŋ **-e**
protestation ,prɒt.es'teɪ.ʃᵊn; ,prəʊ.tes'-, -tɪ'steɪ-, -tə'- (US) ,prɑː.t̬es'teɪ-, ,proʊ-, -t̬ə'steɪ **-s** -z
Proteus 'prəʊ.ti.uːs, -əs (US) 'proʊ.t̬i
prothalami|on ,prəʊ.θᵊl'eɪ.mi|.ən (US) ,proʊ.θə'leɪ-, -ɑːn **-um** -əm **-a**
Protheroe 'prɒð.ᵊr.əʊ (US) 'prɑː.ðə.
prothes|is 'prɒθ.ɪ.s|ɪs, '-ə- (US) 'prɑː. **-es** -iːz
protium 'prəʊ.ti.əm (US) 'proʊ.t̬i-
proto- prəʊ.təʊ- (US) proʊ.t̬oʊ-, -t̬ə-
Note: Prefix. Normally takes prima or secondary stress on the first syllable, e.g. **prototype** /'prəʊ.təʊ.taɪp (US) 'proʊ.tə-/, **prototypic** /,prəʊ.təʊ'tɪp.ɪk (US) ,proʊ.t̬ə'-/.

protocol ˈprəʊ.tə.kɒl (US) ˈproʊ.t̬ə.kɔːl, -t̬oʊ-, -kɑːl **-s** -z
proton (P®) ˈprəʊ.tɒn (US) ˈproʊ.tɑːn **-s** -z
protoplasm ˈprəʊ.təʊ.plæz.əm (US) ˈproʊ.t̬ə-, -t̬oʊ-
prototype ˈprəʊ.təʊ.taɪp (US) ˈproʊ.t̬ə-, -t̬oʊ- **-s** -s
prototypic ˌprəʊ.təʊˈtɪp.ɪk (US) ˌproʊ.t̬əˈ-, -t̬oʊˈ- **-al** -əl
protozo|a ˌprəʊ.təʊˈzəʊ|.ə (US) ˌproʊ.t̬əˈzoʊ-, -t̬oʊˈ- **-an/s** -ən/z **-on** -ɒn (US) -ɑːn **-ic** -ɪk
protract prəʊˈtrækt (US) proʊ-, prə- **-s** -s **-ing** -ɪŋ **-ed/ly** -ɪd/li **-ile** -aɪl (US) -əl
protraction prəʊˈtræk.ʃən (US) proʊ-, prə- **-s** -z
protractor prəʊˈtræk.təʳ (US) proʊ-, prə- **-s** -z
protrud|e prəʊˈtruːd (US) proʊ-, prə- **-es** -z **-ing** -ɪŋ **-ed** -ɪd
protrusion prəʊˈtruː.ʒən (US) proʊ-, prə- **-s** -z
protrusive prəʊˈtruː.sɪv (US) proʊ-, prə- **-ly** -li **-ness** -nəs, -nɪs
protuberanc|e prəʊˈtjuː.bər.ənts (US) proʊˈtuː-, prə-, -ˈtjuː- **-es** -ɪz
protuberant prəʊˈtjuː.bər.ənt (US) proʊˈtuː-, prə-, -ˈtjuː- **-ly** -li
proud praʊd **-er** -əʳ (US) -ɚ **-est** -ɪst, -əst **-ly** -li **-ness** -nəs, -nɪs
Proudfoot ˈpraʊd.fʊt
Proudhon ˈpruː.dɒn (US) -dɑːn, -doʊn
Proudie ˈpraʊ.di
Proulx pruː
Proust pruːst
Proustian ˈpruː.sti.ən
Prout praʊt
provab|le ˈpruː.və.b|l **-ly** -li **-leness** -l̩.nəs, -nɪs
prov|e pruːv **-es** -z **-ing** -ɪŋ **-ed** -d **-er/s** -əʳ/z (US) -ɚ/z
proven ˈpruː.vən, ˈprəʊ- (US) ˈpruː-
provenance ˈprɒv.ən.ənts, -ɪ.nənts (US) ˈprɑː.vən.ənts
Provençal(e), Provencal(e) ˌprɒv.ɑ̃ːnˈsɑːl, -ɔ̃ːn-, -vəntˈ- (US) ˌproʊ.vɑːnˈ-, ˌprɑː-, -vənˈ-
Provence prɒvˈɑ̃ːns, prəˈvɑ̃ːns, -ˈvɔ̃ːns, -ˈvɑːnts (US) prɑːˈvɑ̃ːnts, proʊ-
provender ˈprɒv.ɪn.dəʳ, -ən- (US) ˈprɑː.vən.dɚ
proverb (P) ˈprɒv.ɜːb (US) ˈprɑː.vɝːb **-s** -z
proverbial prəʊˈvɜː.bi.əl (US) prəˈvɝː-, proʊ- **-ly** -i
provid|e prəʊˈvaɪd (US) prə-, proʊ- **-es** -z **-ing** -ɪŋ **-ed** -ɪd **-er/s** -əʳ/z (US) -ɚ/z
providen|ce (P) ˈprɒv.ɪ.dən|ts (US) ˈprɑː.və- **-t/ly** -t/li
providential ˌprɒv.ɪˈden.tʃəl (US) ˌprɑː.vəˈ- **-ly** -i
provinc|e ˈprɒv.ɪnts (US) ˈprɑː.vɪnts **-es** -ɪz
provincial prəʊˈvɪn.tʃəl (US) prəˈvɪnt.ʃəl, proʊ- **-s** -z **-ly** -i
provincialism prəʊˈvɪn.tʃəl.ɪ.zəm (US) prəˈvɪnt.ʃəl-, proʊ- **-s** -z
provinciality prəʊˌvɪn.tʃiˈæl.ə.ti, -ɪ.ti (US) prəˌvɪnt.ʃiˈæl.ə.t̬i, proʊ-
provincializ|e, -is|e prəʊˈvɪn.tʃəl.aɪz (US) prəˈvɪnt.ʃəl-, proʊ- **-es** -ɪz **-ing** -ɪŋ **-ed** -d
provision prəʊˈvɪʒ.ən (US) prə-, proʊ- **-s** -z **-ing** -ɪŋ **-ed** -d
provisional prəʊˈvɪʒ.ən.əl, ˈ-nəl (US) prə-, proʊ-, prəˈvɪʒ.ən.əl **-ly** -i
proviso prəʊˈvaɪ.zəʊ (US) prəˈvaɪ.zoʊ, proʊ- **-(e)s** -z
provisor prəʊˈvaɪ.zəʳ (US) prəˈvaɪ.zɚ, proʊ- **-s** -z
provisor|y prəʊˈvaɪ.zər|.i (US) prə-, proʊ- **-ily** -əl.i, -ɪ.li
Provo ˈprəʊ.vəʊ (US) ˈproʊ.voʊ **-s** -z
provocation ˌprɒv.əˈkeɪ.ʃən (US) ˌprɑː.vəˈ- **-s** -z
provocative prəˈvɒk.ə.tɪv (US) -ˈvɑː.kə.t̬ɪv, proʊ- **-ly** -li
provok|e prəˈvəʊk (US) -ˈvoʊk, proʊ- **-es** -s **-ing/ly** -ɪŋ/li **-ed** -t
provost ˈprɒv.əst (US) ˈproʊ.voʊst, -vəst; ˈprɑː.vəst; *also in the US military:* ˈproʊ.voʊ **-s** -s ˌ**provost** ˈ**marshal**
provostship ˈprɒv.əst.ʃɪp (US) ˈproʊ.voʊst-, -vəst-; ˈprɑː.vəst- **-s** -s
prow praʊ **-s** -z
prowess ˈpraʊ.ɪs, -es; praʊˈes (US) ˈpraʊ.ɪs
prowl praʊl **-s** -z **-ing** -ɪŋ **-ed** -d **-er/s** -əʳ/z (US) -ɚ/z
Prowse praʊs, praʊz
prox. prɒks, ˈprɒk.sɪ.məʊ, -sə- (US) ˈprɑːk.sə.moʊ
proximal ˈprɒk.sɪ.məl, -sə- (US) ˈprɑːk.sə- **-ly** -i
proximate ˈprɒk.sɪ.mət, -sə-, -mɪt (US) ˈprɑːk.sə.mət **-ly** -li
proxime access|it ˌprɒk.sɪ.meɪ.ækˈses|.ɪt, -əkˈ-, -əˈkes- (US) ˌprɑːk.səm.ækˈses.ət, -sɪm- **-erunt** -ə.rʊnt
proximit|y prɒkˈsɪm.ə.t|i, -ɪ.t|i (US) prɑːkˈsɪm.ə.t̬|i **-ies** -iz
proximo ˈprɒk.sɪ.məʊ, -sə- (US) ˈprɑːk.sə.moʊ
prox|y ˈprɒk.s|i (US) ˈprɑːk- **-ies** -iz
Prozac® ˈprəʊ.zæk (US) ˈproʊ-
prud|e pruːd **-es** -z **-ery** -ər.i
prudence (P) ˈpruː.dənts
prudent ˈpruː.dənt **-ly** -li
prudential pruːˈden.tʃəl (US) -ˈdent.ʃəl **-ly** -i
Prudhoe ˈprʌd.həʊ, ˈpruː.dəʊ, ˈpruːd.həʊ (US) ˈpruːd.hoʊ, ˈpruː.doʊ, ˈprʌd.hoʊ
prudish ˈpruː.dɪʃ **-ly** -li **-ness** -nəs, -nɪs
Prufrock ˈpruː.frɒk (US) -frɑːk
prun|e pruːn **-es** -z **-ing** -ɪŋ **-ed** -d
prunella (P) pruːˈnel.ə **-s** -z
prurience ˈprʊə.ri.ənts (US) ˈprʊr.i-
prurient ˈprʊə.ri.ənt (US) ˈprʊr.i- **-ly** -li
prurigo prʊəˈraɪ.gəʊ (US) prʊˈraɪ.goʊ
pru|ritus prʊə|ˈraɪ.təs (US) prʊ|ˈraɪ.t̬əs **-ritic** -ˈrɪt.ɪk (US) -ˈrɪt̬-
Prussia ˈprʌʃ.ə
Prussian ˈprʌʃ.ən **-s** -z ˌ**Prussian** ˈ**blue**
prussiate ˈprʌʃ.i.ət, ˈprʌʃ.ət, -ɪt (US) ˈprʌs.i.eɪt, ˈprʌʃ-, -ɪt **-s** -s
prussic acid ˌprʌs.ɪkˈæs.ɪd
Pruth pruːt
pr|y pr|aɪ **-ies** -aɪz **-ying/ly** -aɪ.ɪŋ/li **-ied** -aɪd **-yer/s** -aɪ.əʳ/z (US) -aɪ.ɚ/z
Pryce praɪs
Pryde praɪd
Pryke praɪk
Prynne prɪn
Pryor praɪəʳ (US) praɪɚ
Przewalski pʃəˈvæl.ski, -ˈvɑːl- (US) pʃəˈvɑːl- **Prze**ˌ**walski's** ˈ**horse**
PS ˌpiːˈes **-'s** -ɪz
psalm (P) sɑːm **-s** -z **-ist/s** -ɪst/s
psalmodic sælˈmɒd.ɪk (US) sɑːˈmɑː.dɪk, sæl-
psalmod|y ˈsæl.mə.d|i, ˈsɑː.mə- (US) ˈsɑː-, ˈsæl- **-ist/s** -ɪst/s
psalter ˈsɔːl.təʳ, ˈsɒl- (US) ˈsɔːl.t̬ɚ, ˈsɑːl- **-s** -z
psalt(e)r|y ˈsɔːl.tər|.i, ˈsɒl- (US) ˈsɔːl.tɚ-, ˈsɑːl- **-ies** -iz
Note: In the following words beginning with **ps-**, the form with /p/ is rare.
psepholog|y psɪˈfɒl.ə.dʒ|i, psə-, psefˈɒl- (US) siːˈfɑː.lə- **-ist/s** -ɪst/s
pseud sjuːd, suːd (US) suːd **-s** -z
pseudo- ˌsjuː.dəʊ-, ˌsuː- (US) ˌsuː.doʊ-
pseudo ˈsjuː.dəʊ, ˈsuː- (US) ˈsuː.doʊ **-s** -z
pseudonym ˈsjuː.də.nɪm, ˈsuː- (US) ˈsuː.dən.ɪm **-s** -z
pseudonymity ˌsjuː.dəˈnɪm.ə.ti, ˌsuː-, -ɪ.ti (US) ˌsuː.dənˈɪm.ə.t̬i
pseudonymous sjuːˈdɒn.ɪ.məs, suː- (US) suːˈdɑː.nɪ-
pseudopodi|um ˌsjuː.dəˈpəʊ.di|.əm, ˌsuː- (US) ˌsuː.doʊˈpoʊ- **-a** -ə
Pseudoxia Epidemica sjuːˌdɒk.si.ə.ep.ɪˈdem.ɪ.kə, suː- (US) suːˌdɑːk.si-
pshaw (*interj.*) pɸː, pʃɔː (US) pʃɔː, pʃɑː
Note: Sound of derision or protest: the spelling was probably originally intended to represent a voiceless bilabial affricate (a more polite version of the bilabial trill known as a “raspberry” in British English

and also as a "Bronx Cheer" in American English), but it is usually now given a spelling-based pronunciation.

psi psaɪ, saɪ US saɪ, psiː

Psion ˈ*p*saɪ.ɒn US -ɑːn

psittacosis ˌ*p*sɪt.əˈkəʊ.sɪs US ˌsɪt.əˈkoʊ-

Psmith smɪθ

psoriasis *p*səˈraɪə.sɪs, *p*sɒrˈaɪə-, *p*sɔːˈraɪə-, *p*sʊ- US səˈraɪə-, soʊ-

psych saɪk **-s** -s **-ing** -ɪŋ **-ed** -t

psych|e (*v.*) saɪk **-es** -s **-ing** -ɪŋ **-ed** -t

psyche (*n.*) ˈsaɪ.ki, -kiː **-s** -s

psychedelia ˌsaɪ.kɪˈdiː.li.ə, -kəˈ- US -kəˈdiː.li.ə, -ˈdiːl.jə

psychedelic ˌsaɪ.kɪˈdel.ɪk, -kəˈ- US -kəˈ- **-ally** -əl.i, -li *stress shift:* ˌpsychedelic ˈcolours

psychiatric ˌsaɪ.kiˈæt.rɪk **-al** -əl **-ally** -əl.i, -li *stress shift:* ˌpsychiatric ˈnurse

psychiatr|y saɪˈkaɪə.tr|i, sɪ-, sə- US saɪ-, sɪ- **-ist/s** -ɪst/s

psychic ˈsaɪ.kɪk **-al** -əl **-ally** -əl.i, -li

psycho- saɪ.kəʊ-; saɪˈkɒ- US saɪ.koʊ-, -kə-; saɪˈkɑː-

Note: Prefix. Normally either takes primary or secondary stress on the first syllable, e.g. **psychodrama** /ˈsaɪ.kəʊˌdrɑː.mə US -koʊˌ-/, **psychodramatic** /ˌsaɪ.kəʊ.drəˈmæt.ɪk US -koʊ.drəˈmæt̬.ɪk/, or primary stress on the second syllable, e.g. **psychotic** /saɪˈkɒt.ɪk US -ˈkɑː.t̬ɪk/.

psycho ˈsaɪ.kəʊ US -koʊ **-s** -z

psychoanalys|e ˌsaɪ.kəʊˈæn.əl.aɪz US -koʊˈæn.ə.laɪz **-es** -ɪz **-ing** -ɪŋ **-ed** -d

psychoanalysis ˌsaɪ.kəʊ.əˈnæl.ə.sɪs, ˈ-ɪ- US -koʊ-

psychoanalyst ˌsaɪ.kəʊˈæn.əl.ɪst US -koʊˈæn.ə.lɪst **-s** -s

psychoanalytic ˌsaɪ.kəʊˌæn.əlˈɪt.ɪk US -koʊˌæn.əˈlɪt̬.ɪk **-al** -əl **-ally** -əl.i, -li *stress shift:* ˌpsychoanalytic ˈcounselling

psychoanalyz|e ˌsaɪ.kəʊˈæn.əl.aɪz US -koʊˈæn.ə.laɪz **-es** -ɪz **-ing** -ɪŋ **-ed** -d

psychobabble ˈsaɪ.kəʊˌbæb.l̩ US -koʊˌ-

psychodrama ˈsaɪ.kəʊˌdrɑː.mə US -koʊˌ-, -ˌdræm.ə **-s** -z

psychodramatic ˌsaɪ.kəʊ.drəˈmæt.ɪk US -koʊ.drəˈmæt̬-

psychokinesis ˌsaɪ.kəʊ.kaɪˈniː.sɪs, -kɪˈ- US -koʊ.kɪˈ-, -kaɪˈ-

psychokinetic ˌsaɪ.kəʊ.kɪˈnet.ɪk, -kaɪˈ- US -koʊ- *stress shift:* ˌpsychokinetic ˈpowers

psycholinguist ˌsaɪ.kəʊˈlɪŋ.gwɪst US -koʊˈ- **-s** -s

psycholinguistic ˌsaɪ.kəʊ.lɪŋˈgwɪs.tɪk US -koʊ- **-s** -s **-ally** -əl.i, -li *stress shift:* ˌpsycholinguistic ˈprocess

psychologic ˌsaɪ.kəˈlɒdʒ.ɪk US -ˈlɑː.dʒɪk *stress shift:* ˌpsychologic ˈwarfare

psychological ˌsaɪ.kəlˈɒdʒ.ɪ.kəl US -kəˈlɑː.dʒɪ- **-ly** -i *stress shift, see compound:* ˌ**psychological ˈwarfare**

psychologiz|e, -is|e saɪˈkɒl.ə.dʒaɪz US -ˈkɑː.lə- **-es** -ɪz **-ing** -ɪŋ **-ed** -d

psycholog|y saɪˈkɒl.ə.dʒ|i US -ˈkɑː.lə- **-ist/s** -ɪst/s

psychometric ˌsaɪ.kəʊˈmet.rɪk US -koʊˈ- **-s** -s *stress shift:* ˌpsychometric ˈmeasurement

psychometr|y saɪˈkɒm.ɪ.tr|i, ˈ-ə- US -ˈkɑː.mə- **-ist/s** -ɪst/s

psychopath ˈsaɪ.kəʊ.pæθ US -kə-, -koʊ- **-s** -s

psychopathic ˌsaɪ.kəʊˈpæθ.ɪk US -kəˈ-, -koʊˈ- **-ally** -əl.i, -li *stress shift:* ˌpsychopathic ˈtendencies

psychopatholog|y ˌsaɪ.kəʊ.pæθˈɒl.ə.dʒ|i US -koʊ.pæθˈɑː.lə- **-ist/s** -ɪst/s

psychophysical ˌsaɪ.kəʊˈfɪz.ɪ.kəl, ˈ-ə- US -koʊˈ- **-ly** -li *stress shift:* ˌpsychophysical ˈstimulus

psychosexual ˌsaɪ.kəʊˈsek.ʃʊəl, -sjʊəl US -ʃu.əl **-ly** -i *stress shift:* ˌpsychosexual ˈaspects

psychos|is saɪˈkəʊ.s|ɪs US -ˈkoʊ- **-es** -iːz

psychosocial ˌsaɪ.kəʊˈsəʊ.ʃəl US -koʊˈsoʊ- *stress shift:* ˌpsychosocial ˈproblems

psychosomatic ˌsaɪ.kəʊ.səʊˈmæt.ɪk US -koʊ.soʊˈmæt̬- **-ally** -əl.i, -li *stress shift:* ˌpsychosomatic ˈsymptoms

psychotherap|y ˌsaɪ.kəʊˈθer.ə.p|i US -koʊˈ- **-ist/s** -ɪst/s

psychotic saɪˈkɒt.ɪk US -ˈkɑː.t̬ɪk **-ally** -əl.i, -li

pt *(abbrev. for* **pint***)* paɪnt

PTA ˌpiː.tiːˈeɪ

Ptah tɑː, ptɑː, pəˈtɑː US pəˈtɑː

ptarmigan ˈtɑː.mɪ.gən, -mə- US ˈtɑːr-

pterodactyl ˌter.əʊˈdæk.tɪl, -təl US -əˈdæk.təl, -oʊˈ- **-s** -z

pterosaur ˈter.əʊ.sɔːr US -ə.sɑːr, -oʊ-, -sɔːr **-s** -z

PTO ˌpiː.tiːˈəʊ US -ˈoʊ

Ptolemaeus ˌtɒl.əˈmiː.əs, -ɪˈ-, -ˈmeɪ- US ˌtɑː.ləˈmeɪ-, -ˈmiː-

Ptolema|ic ˌtɒl.əˈmeɪ|.ɪk, -ɪˈ- US ˌtɑː.ləˈ- **-ist** -ɪst

Ptolemy ˈtɒl.ə.mi, ˈ-ɪ- US ˈtɑː.lə-

ptomaine ˈtəʊ.meɪn; təʊˈmeɪn US ˈtoʊ.meɪn

Pty *(abbrev. for* **Proprietary***)* prəˈpraɪə.tər.i US proʊ-, prə-

ptyalin ˈtaɪə.lɪn

pub pʌb **-s** -z **-by** -i

pub-crawl ˈpʌb.krɔːl US -krɑːl, -krɔːl **-s** -z **-ing** -ɪŋ **-ed** -d **-er/s** -ər/z US -ɚ/z

puberty ˈpjuː.bə.ti US -bɚ.t̬i

pubes *slang for pubic hair:* pjuːbz

pubes *plural of* **pubis**: ˈpjuː.biːz

pubescen|ce pjuːˈbes.ən|ts, pjʊ- **-t** -t

pubic ˈpjuː.bɪk ˌ**pubic ˈhair** US ˈ**pubic ˌhair**

pub|is ˈpjuː.b|ɪs **-es** -iːz

public ˈpʌb.lɪk **-ly** -li ˌ**public conˈvenience**; ˌ**public ˈenemy**; ˌ**publi ˈhouse**; ˌ**public oˈpinion**; ˌ**public reˈlations**; ˌ**public ˈschool**; ˌ**public ˈsector** US ˈ**public ˌsector**; *stress shif British only:* ˌpublic sector ˈservice ˌ**public ˈspeaking**; ˌ**public ˈtransport**

public-address system ˌpʌb.lɪk.əˈdresˌsɪs.təm **-s** -z

publican ˈpʌb.lɪ.kən **-s** -z

publication ˌpʌb.lɪˈkeɪ.ʃən, -ləˈ- **-s** -z

publicist ˈpʌb.lɪ.sɪst, -lə- **-s** -s

publicity pʌbˈlɪs.ə.ti, pəˈblɪs-, -ɪ.ti US -ə.t̬i

publiciz|e, -is|e ˈpʌb.lɪ.saɪz, -lə- **-es** -ɪ **-ing** -ɪŋ **-ed** -d

public-spirited ˌpʌb.lɪkˈspɪr.ɪ.tɪd, ˈ-ə US -ə.t̬ɪd **-ness** -nəs, -nɪs *stress shif* ˌpublic-spirited ˈpolicies

publish ˈpʌb.lɪʃ **-es** -ɪz **-ing** -ɪŋ **-ed** -t **-er/s** -ər/z US -ɚ/z

Publius ˈpʌb.li.əs

Puccini pʊˈtʃiː.ni US puː-

puce pjuːs

puck (P) pʌk **-s** -s

puck|er ˈpʌk|.ər US -ɚ **-ers** -əz US -ɚz **-ering** -ər.ɪŋ **-ered** -d US -ɚd

puckish ˈpʌk.ɪʃ **-ly** -li **-ness** -nəs, -nɪs

pud pʊd **-s** -z

pudding ˈpʊd.ɪŋ **-s** -z **the ˌproof of th ˌpudding is ˌin the ˈeating**

puddl|e ˈpʌd.l̩ **-es** -z **-ing** -ɪŋ, ˈpʌd.lɪŋ **-ed** -d **-er/s** -ər/z US -ɚ/z, ˈpʌd.lər/z US -lɚ/z

pudend|um pjuːˈden.d|əm, pjʊ- US pjuː- **-a** -ə

pudg|y ˈpʌdʒ|.i **-ier** -i.ər US -i.ɚ **-iest** -i.ɪst, -i.əst **-iness** -ɪ.nəs, -ɪ.nɪs

Pudsey ˈpʌd.zi *locally:* ˈpʊt.si

Puebla ˈpweb.lə, puˈeb- US ˈpweb.lə

pueblo (P) ˈpweb.ləʊ, puˈeb- US ˈpweb.loʊ **-s** -z

puerile ˈpjʊə.raɪl, ˈpjɔː- US ˈpjuː.ɚ. ˈpjʊr.ɪl, -aɪl **-ly** -li

puerilit|y pjʊəˈrɪl.ə.t|i, pjɔː-, -ɪ.t|i US ˌpjuː.əˈrɪl.ə.t̬|i, pjʊˈ- **-ies** -iz

puerperal pjuˈɜː.pər.əl US -ˈɝː-

Puerto Ric|o ˌpwɜː.təʊˈriː.k|əʊ, ˌpw US ˌpwer.t̬əˈriː.koʊ, -toʊˈ-, ˌpɔːr.t̬əˈ- **-an/s** -ən/z

Puerto Vallarta ˌpwɜː.təʊ.væl'ɑː.tə *as if Spanish:* ˌpweə.təʊ.vaɪ'- (US) ˌpwer.toʊ.vɑː'jɑːr.t̬ə, -tɑː
puff pʌf **-s** -s **-ing** -ɪŋ **-ed** -t **-er/s** -əʳ/z (US) -ɚ/z ˈ**puff** ˌ**adder**; ˌ**puff** ˈ**pastry**
puffball 'pʌf.bɔːl (US) -bɔːl, -bɑːl **-s** -z ˌ**puffball** ˈ**skirt**
puffed sleeve ˌpʌf*t*'sliːv **-s** -z
puffery 'pʌf.ᵊr.i (US) -ɚ-
puffin (P) 'pʌf.ɪn **-s** -z
puff|y 'pʌf|.i **-ier** -i.əʳ (US) -i.ɚ **-iest** -i.ɪst, -i.əst **-ily** -ɪ.li, -ᵊl.i **-iness** -ɪ.nəs, -ɪ.nɪs
pug pʌg **-s** -z
pug(g)aree 'pʌg.ᵊr.i **-s** -z
puggree 'pʌg.ri **-s** -z
Pugh pjuː
pugil|ism 'pjuː.dʒɪ.l|ɪ.zᵊm, -dʒə- **-ist/s** -ɪst/s
pugilistic ˌpjuː.dʒɪ'lɪs.tɪk, -dʒə'- **-ally** -ᵊl.i, -li *stress shift:* ˌpugilistic 'attitude
Pugin 'pjuː.dʒɪn
pugnacious pʌg'neɪ.ʃəs **-ly** -li **-ness** -nəs, -nɪs
pugnacity pʌg'næs.ə.ti, -ɪ.ti (US) -ə.t̬i
pug-nos|e ˌpʌg'nəʊz (US) 'pʌg.noʊz **-es** -ɪz **-ed** -d *stress shift, British only:* ˌpug-nose 'face
puisne 'pjuː.ni
puissan|ce *power:* 'pjuː.ɪ.sᵊn|*t*s, 'pwɪs.ᵊn|*t*s *sometimes in poetry:* pju'ɪ.sᵊn|*t*s **-t** -t
puissance *in show-jumping:* 'pwiː.sɑ̃ːns, -sɑːn*t*s, -sᵊn*t*s
puk|e pjuːk **-es** -s **-ing** -ɪŋ **-ed** -t
pukka 'pʌk.ə
pul puːl **-s** -z **-i** -iː
pula 'pjuː.lə, 'puː- (US) 'puː.lɑː
Pulaski pə'læs.ki, pjuː- (US) pə-, pʊl'æs-
pulchritude 'pʌl.krɪ.tjuːd, -krə- (US) -tuːd, -tjuːd
pulchritudinous ˌpʌl.krɪ'tjuː.dɪ.nəs, -krə'-, -dᵊn.əs (US) -'tuː.dᵊn-, -'tjuː-
pul|e pjuːl **-es** -z **-ing** -ɪŋ **-ed** -d
Puleston 'pʊl.ɪ.stᵊn *locally also:* 'pɪl.sᵊn
Pulham 'pʊl.əm
Pulitzer *US publisher:* 'pʊl.ɪt.səʳ (US) 'pʊl.ɪt.sɚ, 'pjuː.lɪt- *prize at Columbia University:* 'pjuː.lɪt.səʳ (US) 'pʊl.ɪt.sɚ, 'pjuː.lɪt- ˈ**Pulitzer** ˌ**prize**, ˌ**Pulitzer** ˈ**prize**
pull pʊl **-s** -z **-ing** -ɪŋ **-ed** -d **-er/s** -əʳ/z (US) -ɚ/z
pullback 'pʊl.bæk **-s** -s
pull-down 'pʊl.daʊn
pullet 'pʊl.ɪt, -ət **-s** -s
pulley 'pʊl.i **-s** -z
Pullman (P) 'pʊl.mən **-s** -z
pullout 'pʊl.aʊt **-s** -s
pullover 'pʊl.əʊ.vəʳ (US) -oʊ.vɚ **-s** -z
pullu|late 'pʌl.jə|.leɪt, -jʊ- **-lates** -leɪts **-lating** -leɪ.tɪŋ (US) -leɪ.t̬ɪŋ **-lated** -leɪ.tɪd (US) -leɪ.t̬ɪd
pullulation ˌpʌl.jə'leɪ.ʃᵊn, -jʊ'-
pull-up 'pʊl.ʌp **-s** -s
pulmonary 'pʌl.mə.nᵊr.i, 'pʊl- (US) -ner-
pulmonic pʌl'mɒn.ɪk, pʊl- (US) -'mɑː.nɪk
pulp pʌlp **-s** -s **-ing** -ɪŋ **-ed** -t
pulpi|fy 'pʌl.pɪ|.faɪ **-fies** -faɪz **-fying** -faɪ.ɪŋ **-fied** -faɪd
pulpit 'pʊl.pɪt (US) 'pʊl-, 'pʌl- **-s** -s
pulp|y 'pʌl.p|i **-ier** -i.əʳ (US) -i.ɚ **-iest** -i.ɪst, -i.əst **-iness** -ɪ.nəs, -ɪ.nɪs
pulsar 'pʌl.sɑːʳ, -səʳ (US) -sɑːr, -sɚ **-s** -z
pul|sate pʌl|'seɪt (US) '-- **-sates** -'seɪts (US) -seɪts **-sating** -'seɪ.tɪŋ (US) -seɪ.t̬ɪŋ **-sated** -'seɪ.tɪd (US) -seɪ.t̬ɪd
pulsatile 'pʌl.sə.taɪl (US) -tɪl, -taɪl
pulsation pʌl'seɪ.ʃᵊn **-s** -z
pulsative 'pʌl.sə.tɪv (US) -t̬ɪv
pulsatory 'pʌl.sə.tᵊr.i, pʌl'seɪ- (US) 'pʌl.sə.tɔːr-
puls|e pʌls **-es** -ɪz **-ing** -ɪŋ **-ed** -t
Pulteney *surname:* 'pʌlt.ni, 'pəʊlt-, 'pʊlt- (US) 'pʌlt-, 'poʊlt-, 'pʊlt-
Pulteney *bridge in Bath:* 'pʌlt.ni
pulverization, -isa- ˌpʌl.vᵊr.aɪ'zeɪ.ʃᵊn, -ɪ'- (US) -ɪ'- **-s** -z
pulveriz|e, -is|e 'pʌl.vᵊr.aɪz (US) -və.raɪz **-es** -ɪz **-ing** -ɪŋ **-ed** -d
puma 'pjuː.mə (US) 'pjuː-, 'puː- **-s** -z
Pumblechook 'pʌm.bl̩.tʃʊk
pumic|e 'pʌm.ɪs **-es** -ɪz **-ing** -ɪŋ **-ed** -t ˈ**pumice** ˌ**stone**
pummel 'pʌm.ᵊl **-s** -z **-(l)ing** -ɪŋ **-(l)ed** -d
pump pʌmp **-s** -s **-ing** -ɪŋ **-ed** -t **-er/s** -əʳ/z (US) -ɚ/z ˈ**pump** ˌ**room**
pumpernickel 'pʌm.pə.nɪk.l̩ (US) -pɚˌ-
pumpkin 'pʌmp.kɪn **-s** -z ˌ**pumpkin** ˈ**pie**
pun pʌn **-s** -z **-ning** -ɪŋ **-ned** -d **-ner/s** -əʳ/z (US) -ɚ/z
punch (P) pʌn*t*ʃ (US) pʌntʃ **-es** -ɪz **-ing** -ɪŋ **-ed** -t **-er/s** -əʳ/z (US) -ɚ/z
Punch-and-Judy ˌpʌn*t*ʃ.ᵊn*d*'dʒuː.di (US) ˌpʌntʃ- ˌ**Punch-and-**ˈ**Judy** ˌ**show**
punchbag 'pʌn*t*ʃ.bæg (US) 'pʌntʃ- **-s** -z
punchball 'pʌn*t*ʃ.bɔːl (US) 'pʌntʃ.bɔːl, -bɑːl **-s** -z
punchbowl 'pʌn*t*ʃ.bəʊl (US) 'pʌntʃ.boʊl **-s** -z
punch-drunk 'pʌn*t*ʃ.drʌŋk (US) 'pʌntʃ-
puncheon 'pʌn.*t*ʃᵊn (US) -tʃᵊn **-s** -z
punchinello (P) ˌpʌn.*t*ʃɪ'nel.əʊ, -*t*ʃə'- (US) -tʃə'nel.oʊ
punchline 'pʌn*t*ʃ.laɪn (US) 'pʌntʃ- **-s** -z
punch-up 'pʌn*t*ʃ.ʌp (US) 'pʌntʃ- **-s** -s
punch|y 'pʌn.*t*ʃ|i (US) -tʃ|i **-ier** -i.əʳ (US) -i.ɚ **-iest** -i.ɪst, -i.əst **-ily** -ɪ.li, -ᵊl.i **-iness** -ɪ.nəs, -ɪ.nɪs
punctilio pʌŋk'tɪl.i.əʊ (US) -oʊ **-s** -z
punctilious pʌŋk'tɪl.i.əs **-ly** -li **-ness** -nəs, -nɪs
punctual 'pʌŋk.tʃu.əl, -tʃʊəl, -tju.əl, -tjʊəl (US) 'pʌŋk.tʃu.əl **-ly** -i
punctuality ˌpʌnk.tʃu'æl.ə.ti, -tju'-, -ɪ.ti (US) -ə.t̬i
punctu|ate 'pʌŋk.tʃu|.eɪt, -tju- (US) -tʃu- **-ates** -eɪts **-ating** -eɪ.tɪŋ (US) -eɪ.t̬ɪŋ **-ated** -eɪ.tɪd (US) -eɪ.t̬ɪd **-ator/s** -eɪ.təʳ/z (US) -eɪ.t̬ɚ/z
punctuation ˌpʌŋk.tʃu'eɪ.ʃᵊn, -tju'- (US) -tʃu'- **-s** -z
punct|ure 'pʌŋk.tʃ|əʳ (US) -tʃ|ɚ **-ures** -əz (US) -ɚz **-uring** -ᵊr.ɪŋ **-ured** -əd (US) -ɚd
pundit 'pʌn.dɪt **-s** -s
Pune pjuːn
pungency 'pʌn.dʒᵊn*t*.si
pungent 'pʌn.dʒᵊnt **-ly** -li
Punic 'pjuː.nɪk
puniness 'pjuː.nɪ.nəs, -nɪs (US) -ni-
punish 'pʌn.ɪʃ **-es** -ɪz **-ing/ly** -ɪŋ/li **-ed** -t **-er/s** -əʳ/z (US) -ɚ/z **-able/ness** -ə.bl̩/nəs, -nɪs
punishment 'pʌn.ɪʃ.mənt **-s** -s
puni|tive 'pjuː.nə|.tɪv, -nɪ- (US) -nə|.t̬ɪv **-tively** -tɪv.li (US) -t̬ɪv.li **-tory** -tᵊr.i (US) -tɔːr.i
Punjab ˌpʌn'dʒɑːb, ˌpʊn-, '-- (US) pʌn'dʒɑːb; 'pʌn.dʒɑːb, -dʒæb **-i** -iː, -i
Punjabi pʌn'dʒɑː.biː, pʊn-, -bi (US) pʌn-
punk pʌŋk **-s** -s **-y** -i **-ier** -i.əʳ (US) -i.ɚ **-iest** -i.ɪst, -i.əst ˌ**punk** ˈ**rock**; ˌ**punk** ˈ**rocker**
punkah 'pʌŋ.kə **-s** -z
punnet 'pʌn.ɪt **-s** -s
Punshon 'pʌn.ʃᵊn
punster 'pʌn.stəʳ (US) -stɚ **-s** -z
punt *boat:* pʌnt **-s** -s **-ing** -ɪŋ (US) 'pʌn.t̬ɪŋ **-ed** -ɪd (US) 'pʌn.t̬ɪd
punt *currency:* pʊnt **-s** -s
punter 'pʌn.təʳ (US) -t̬ɚ **-s** -z
Punto® 'pʊn.təʊ, 'pʌn- (US) -toʊ
pun|y 'pjuː.n|i **-ier** -i.əʳ (US) -i.ɚ **-iest** -i.ɪst, -i.əst **-iness** -ɪ.nəs, -ɪ.nɪs
pup pʌp **-s** -s **-ping** -ɪŋ **-ped** -t
pup|a 'pjuː.p|ə **-ae** -iː **-as** -əz **-al** -ᵊl
pupil 'pjuː.pᵊl, -pɪl (US) -pᵊl **-s** -z
pupil(l)age 'pjuː.pɪ.lɪdʒ, -pᵊl.ɪdʒ (US) -pᵊl.ɪdʒ
pupillary 'pjuː.pɪ.lᵊr.i, -pᵊl.ᵊr- (US) -pᵊl.er-
puppet 'pʌp.ɪt **-s** -s ˌ**puppet** ˈ**government**
puppeteer ˌpʌp.ɪ'tɪəʳ, -ə'- (US) -ə'tɪr **-s** -z
pupp|y 'pʌp|.i **-ies** -iz ˈ**puppy** ˌ**dog**; ˈ**puppy** ˌ**fat**; ˈ**puppy** ˌ**love**
Purbeck 'pɜː.bek (US) 'pɝː-
purblind 'pɜː.blaɪnd (US) 'pɝː- **-ness** -nəs, -nɪs
Purcell 'pɜː.sel, -sᵊl; pɜː'sel (US) 'pɝː.sᵊl, -'-
purchas|e 'pɜː.tʃəs, -tʃɪs (US) 'pɝː.tʃəs

-es -ɪz -ing -ɪŋ -ed -t -er/s -əʳ/z US -ɚ/z -able -ə.bl̩
purdah 'pɜː.də, -dɑː US 'pɝː.də
Purdie, Purdy 'pɜː.di US 'pɝː-
pur|e pjʊəʳ, pjɔːʳ US pjʊr -er -əʳ US -ɚ -est -ɪst, -əst -ely -li -eness -nəs, -nɪs
purebred 'pjʊə.bred, 'pjɔː- US 'pjʊr- -s -z
purée, puree 'pjʊə.reɪ, 'pjɔː- US pjʊ'reɪ; 'pjʊr.eɪ -s -z -ing -ɪŋ -d -d
purfl|e 'pɜː.fl̩ US 'pɝː- -es -z -ing -ɪŋ, '-flɪŋ -ed -d
purfling 'pɜː.flɪŋ US 'pɝː- -s -z
purgation pɜː'geɪ.ʃᵊn US pɝː- -s -z
purgative 'pɜː.gə.tɪv US 'pɝː.gə.t̬ɪv -s -z
purgatorial ˌpɜː.gə'tɔː.ri.əl US ˌpɝː.gə'tɔːr.i-
Purgatorio ˌpɜː.gə'tɔː.ri.əʊ US ˌpɝː.gə'tɔːr.i.oʊ
purgator|y (P) 'pɜː.gə.tᵊr|.i, -tr|i US 'pɝː.gə.tɔːr- -ies -iz
purg|e pɜːdʒ US pɝːdʒ -es -ɪz -ing -ɪŋ -ed -d
purification ˌpjʊə.rɪ.fɪ'keɪ.ʃᵊn, ˌpjɔː-, -rə- US ˌpjʊr.ə- -s -z
purificatory ˌpjʊə.rɪ.fɪ'keɪ.tᵊr.i, ˌpjɔː-, -rə-; US pjʊ'rɪf.ɪ.kəˌtɔːr-
puri|fy 'pjʊə.rɪ|.faɪ, 'pjɔː-, -rə- US 'pjʊr.ə- -fies -faɪz -fying -faɪ.ɪŋ -fied -faɪd -fier/s -faɪ.əʳ/z US -faɪ.ɚ/z
Purim 'pʊə.rɪm, 'pjʊə- US 'pʊr.ɪm; puː'riːm
purism 'pjʊə.rɪ.zᵊm, 'pjɔː- US 'pjʊr.ɪ-
purist 'pjʊə.rɪst, 'pjɔː- US 'pjʊr.ɪst -s -s
puristic pjʊə'rɪs.tɪk, pjɔː- US pjʊ- -al -ᵊl
puritan (P) 'pjʊə.rɪ.tᵊn, 'pjɔː- US 'pjʊr.ɪ- -s -z -ism -ɪ.zᵊm
puritanic ˌpjʊə.rɪ'tæn.ɪk, ˌpjɔː- US ˌpjʊr.ɪ'- -al -ᵊl -ally -ᵊl.i, -li
purity 'pjʊə.rə.ti, 'pjɔː-, -rɪ- US 'pjʊr.ɪ.t̬i, '-ə-
Purkinje pɜː'kɪn.ji US pɝː-
Purkiss 'pɜː.kɪs US 'pɝː-
purl pɜːl US pɝːl -s -z -ing -ɪŋ -ed -d
Purley 'pɜː.li US 'pɝː-
purlieu 'pɜː.ljuː US 'pɝːl.juː, 'pɝː.luː -s -z
purlin(e) 'pɜː.lɪn US 'pɝː- -s -z
purloin pɜː'lɔɪn, '-- US pɚ'lɔɪn; 'pɝː.lɔɪn -s -z -ing -ɪŋ -ed -d
purloiner pɜː'lɔɪ.nəʳ US pɚ'lɔɪ.nɚ -s -z
Purnell pɜː'nel US pɝː-
purpl|e 'pɜː.pl̩ US 'pɝː- -er -əʳ, 'pɜː.pləʳ US 'pɝː.plɚ -est -ɪst, -əst, 'pɜː.plɪst, -pləst, -pləst US 'pɝː- -es -z -ing -ɪŋ, 'pɜː.plɪŋ US 'pɝː- -ed -d ˌPurple 'Heart
purplish 'pɜː.pl̩.ɪʃ, -plɪʃ US 'pɝː-
purpor|t pə'pɔː|t, pɜː-; 'pɜː.pə|t, -pɔː|t US pɝː'pɔːr|t, '-- -ts -ts -ting -tɪŋ US -t̬ɪŋ -ted/ly -tɪd/li US -t̬ɪd/li
purpos|e 'pɜː.pəs US 'pɝː- -es -ɪz -ing -ɪŋ -ed -t
purpose-built ˌpɜː.pəs'bɪlt US ˌpɝː- *stress shift:* ˌpurpose-built 'residence
purposeful 'pɜː.pəs|.fᵊl, -fʊl US 'pɝː- -ly -i -ness -nəs, -nɪs
purposeless 'pɜː.pəs.ləs, -lɪs US 'pɝː- -ly -li -ness -nəs, -nɪs
purposely 'pɜː.pə.sli US 'pɝː-
purposive 'pɜː.pə.sɪv US 'pɝː- -ly -li -ness -nəs, -nɪs
purpura 'pɜː.pjʊ.rə, -pjə- US 'pɝː.pɚ.ə, -pjɚ-, -pʊ.rə
purr pɜːʳ US pɝː -s -z -ing -ɪŋ -ed -d
purs|e pɜːs US pɝːs -es -ɪz -ing -ɪŋ -ed -t
purser 'pɜː.səʳ US 'pɝː.sɚ -s -z
purse-string 'pɜːs.strɪŋ US 'pɝːs- -s -z
purslane 'pɜː.slɪn, -slən, -sleɪn US 'pɝː.slɪn, -sleɪn
pursuance pə'sjuː.ənts, pɜː-, -'su- US pɚ'suː-
pursuant pə'sjuː.ənt, pɜː-, -'su- US pɚ'suː- -ly -li
pursu|e pə'sjuː, pɜː-, -'suː US pɚ'suː -es -z -ing -ɪŋ -ed -d -er/s -əʳ/z US -ɚ/z
pursuit pə'sjuːt, pɜː-, -'suːt US pɚ'suːt -s -s
pursuivant 'pɜː.sɪ.vənt, -sə- US 'pɝː.sɪ-, -swɪ- -s -s
Purton 'pɜː.tᵊn US 'pɝː-
purulency 'pjʊə.rʊ.lənt.si, -rjʊ-, -rə- US 'pjʊr.ə-, -jə-
purulent 'pjʊə.rʊ.lənt, -rjʊ-, -rə- US 'pjʊr.ə-, -rjə- -ly -li
Purver 'pɜː.vəʳ US 'pɝː.vɚ
Purves 'pɜː.vɪs US 'pɝː-
purvey pə'veɪ, pɜː- US pɚ- -s -z -ing -ɪŋ -ed -d
purvey|ance pə'veɪ|.ənts, pɜː- US pɚ- -or/s -əʳ/z US -ɚ/z
purview 'pɜː.vjuː US 'pɝː- -s -z
pus pʌs
Pusan ˌpuː'sæn US -'sɑːn
Pusey 'pjuː.zi -ism -ɪ.zᵊm -ite/s -aɪt/s
push pʊʃ -es -ɪz -ing -ɪŋ/li -ed -t -er/s -əʳ/z US -ɚ/z
pushball 'pʊʃ.bɔːl US -bɔːl, -bɑːl
pushbike 'pʊʃ.baɪk -s -s
push-button 'pʊʃˌbʌt.ᵊn -s -z
push-cart 'pʊʃ.kɑːt US -kɑːrt -s -s
pushchair 'pʊʃ.tʃeəʳ US -tʃer -s -z
pushdown 'pʊʃ.daʊn
pushful 'pʊʃ.fᵊl, -fʊl -ness -nəs, -nɪs
Pushkin 'pʊʃ.kɪn
pushover 'pʊʃˌəʊ.vəʳ US -ˌoʊ.vɚ -s -z
pushpin 'pʊʃ.pɪn -s -z
push|-start 'pʊʃ|.stɑːt US -stɑːrt -starts -stɑːts US -stɑːrts -starting -ˌstɑː.tɪŋ US -ˌstɑːr.t̬ɪŋ -started -ˌstɑː.tɪd US -ˌstɑːr.t̬ɪd
Pushtu 'pʌʃ.tuː, ˌ-'- US 'pʌʃ.tuː
pushup 'pʊʃ.ʌp -s -s
push|y 'pʊʃ|.i -ier -i.əʳ US -i.ɚ -iest -i.ɪst, -i.ɪst -iness -ɪ.nəs, -ɪ.nɪs
pusillanimity ˌpjuː.sɪ.lə'nɪm.ə.ti, -zɪ -læn'ɪm-, -ɪ.ti US -sɪ.lə'nɪm.ə.t̬i
pusillanimous ˌpjuː.sɪ'læn.ɪ.məs, -zɪ '-ə- US -sɪ'læn.ə- -ly -li -ness -nəs, -n
puss pʊs -es -ɪz
puss|y 'pʊs|.i -ies -iz ˌpussy 'willow
pussycat 'pʊs.i.kæt -s -s
pussy|foot 'pʊs.i|.fʊt -foots -fʊts -footing -ˌfʊt.ɪŋ US -ˌfʊt̬.ɪŋ -foote -ˌfʊt.ɪd US -ˌfʊt̬.ɪd -footer/s -ˌfʊt.əʳ/z US -ˌfʊt̬.ɚ/z
pustular 'pʌs.tjə.ləʳ, -tjʊ- US -tʃə.lɚ -tjə-, -tjʊ-
pustu|late 'pʌs.tjə|.leɪt, -tjʊ- US -tju -tjə-, -tʃə- -lated -leɪ.tɪd US -leɪ.t̬ɪ
pustulation ˌpʌs.tjə'leɪ.ʃᵊn, -tjʊ'- US -tʃə'-, -tjə'-, -tjʊ'- -s -z
pustule 'pʌs.tjuːl US -tʃuːl, -tjuːl -s -
pustulous 'pʌs.tjə.ləs, -tjʊ- US -tʃə-, -tjə-, -tjʊ-
put pʊt -s -s -ting -ɪŋ US 'pʊt̬.ɪŋ
putative 'pjuː.tə.tɪv US -t̬ə.t̬ɪv -ly -li
put-down 'pʊt.daʊn -s -z
Putin 'puː.tɪn, 'pjuː- US 'puː.tɪn, 'puː
Putnam 'pʌt.nəm
Putney 'pʌt.ni
put-on 'pʊt.ɒn US -ɑːn -s -z
putrefaction ˌpjuː.trɪ'fæk.ʃᵊn, -trə'- US -trə'-
putre|fy 'pjuː.trɪ|.faɪ, -trə- US -trə- -fies -faɪz -fying -faɪ.ɪŋ -fied -faɪd
putrescenc|e pjuː'tres.ᵊn|ts -t -t
putrid 'pjuː.trɪd -ly -li -ness -nəs, -n
putridity pjuː'trɪd.ə.ti, -ɪ.ti US -ə.t̬i
putsch pʊtʃ -es -ɪz
putt (P) pʌt -s -s -ing -ɪŋ US 'pʌt̬.ɪŋ -e -ɪd US 'pʌt̬.ɪd -er/s -əʳ/z US 'pʌt̬.ɚ 'putting ˌgreen
puttee 'pʌt.i, -iː-; pʌt'iː US pʌt'iː, '- -s -z
Puttenham 'pʌt.ᵊn.əm
putter *(from* **putt***)* 'pʌt.əʳ US 'pʌt̬.ɚ -z -ing -ed
putter *(from* **put***)* 'pʊt.əʳ US 'pʊt̬.ɚ -s -z
putti *(plur. of* **putto***)* 'pʊt.i, -iː US 'puː.ti, -tiː
Puttick 'pʌt.ɪk US 'pʌt̬-
Puttnam 'pʌt.nəm
putt|o 'pʊt|.əʊ US 'puː.t|oʊ -i -i, -iː
putt|y 'pʌt|.i US 'pʌt̬- -ies -iz -ying -i -ied -id
putz pʌts -es -ɪz
puzzl|e 'pʌz.l̩ -es -z -ing/ly -ɪŋ/li, '-lɪ -ed -d
puzzlement 'pʌz.l̩.mənt

puzzler 'pʌz.ləʳ, -l̩.əʳ (US) '-lɚ, -l̩.ɚ **-s** -z
PVC ˌpiː.viː'siː
Pwllheli pʊθ'lel.i *as if Welsh:* pʊ'hlel.i
PWR ˌpiːˌdʌb.l̩.juˈɑːʳ (US) -'ɑːr
pya pjɑː, pi'ɑː (US) pjɑː **-s** -z
pyaemia paɪ'iː.mi.ə
Pybus 'paɪ.bəs
Pye paɪ
pygmaean pɪg'miː.ən
Pygmalion pɪg'meɪ.li.ən (US) -'meɪl.jən, -'meɪ.li.ən
pygm|y 'pɪg.m|i **-ies** -iz
pyjama pɪ'dʒɑː.mə, pə- (US) pə'dʒɑː-, -'dʒæm.ə **-s** -z
Pyke paɪk
Pylades 'pɪl.ə.diːz, 'paɪ.lə-
Pyle paɪl
pylon 'paɪ.lɒn, -lən (US) -lɑːn, -lən **-s** -z
pylor|us paɪ'lɔː.r|əs (US) -'lɔːr|.əs, pɪ- **-i** -aɪ **-ic** -ɪk
Pym pɪm
Pynchon 'pɪn.tʃən (US) 'pɪn.tʃən
Pyongyang ˌpjɒŋ'jæŋ (US) ˌpjʌŋ'jɑːŋ, ˌpjɑːŋ-, -'jæŋ
pyorrhoea ˌpaɪə'rɪə (US) -'riː.ə
pyracantha ˌpaɪə.rə'kænt.θə (US) ˌpaɪ-, ˌpɪr.ə'- **-s** -z
pyramid 'pɪr.ə.mɪd **-s** -z **'pyramid ˌselling, ˌpyramid 'selling**
pyramidal pɪ'ræm.ɪ.dəl, pə-, '-ə- (US) pɪ'ræm.ɪ-, pə-, '-ə-; ˌpɪr.ə'mɪd.əl **-ly** -i
Pyramus 'pɪr.ə.məs
pyre paɪəʳ (US) paɪɚ **-s** -z
Pyrene paɪə'riː.ni (US) paɪ'riːn
Pyren|ees ˌpɪr.ə'n|iːz, -ɪ'- (US) -ə'- **-ean** -iː.ən
pyrethrin paɪə'riː.θrɪn (US) paɪ-, -'reθ.rɪn
pyrethrum paɪə'riː.θrəm (US) paɪ-, -'reθ.rəm **-s** -z
pyretic paɪə'ret.ɪk, pɪ- (US) paɪ'ret̬-
Pyrex® 'paɪə.reks (US) 'paɪ-
pyriform 'pɪr.ɪ.fɔːm (US) -fɔːrm
pyrite 'paɪə.raɪt (US) 'paɪ-
pyrites paɪə'raɪ.tiːz, pɪ-, pə- (US) paɪ'raɪ.tiːz, pɪ-; 'paɪ.raɪts
pyritic paɪə'rɪt.ɪk (US) paɪ'rɪt̬-
pyro- paɪə.rəʊ-; paɪə'rɒ-; (US) paɪ.roʊ-, -rə-; paɪ'rɑː-
Note: Prefix. Normally either takes primary or secondary stress on the first syllable, e.g. **pyromania** /ˌpaɪə.rəʊ'meɪ.ni.ə (US) ˌpaɪ.roʊ'-/, or primary stress on the second syllable, e.g. **pyrolysis** /paɪə'rɒl.ə.sɪs (US) paɪ'rɑː.lə-/.
pyrocanthus ˌpaɪə.rəʊ'kæn.θəs (US) ˌpaɪ.roʊ-
pyrogallic ˌpaɪə.rəʊ'gæl.ɪk (US) ˌpaɪ.roʊ'-, -'gɑː.lɪk
pyrolysis **(P)** paɪə'rɒl.ə.sɪs, '-ə- (US) paɪ'rɑː.lə-
pyromani|a ˌpaɪə.rəʊ'meɪ.ni|.ə (US) ˌpaɪ.roʊ'-, '-nj|ə **-ac** -æk
pyromet|er paɪə'rɒm.ɪ.t|əʳ, '-ə- (US) paɪ'rɑː.mə.t̬|ɚ **-ers** -əz (US) -ɚz **-ry** -ri
pyrometric ˌpaɪə.rəʊ'met.rɪk (US) ˌpaɪ.roʊ'-, -rə'- **-ally** -əl.i, -li *stress shift:* ˌpyrometric 'measurement
pyrotechnic ˌpaɪə.rəʊ'tek.nɪk (US) ˌpaɪ.roʊ'-, -rə'- **-al** -əl **-ally** -əl.i, -li **-s** -s *stress shift:* ˌpyrotechnic 'substance
Pyrrh|a 'pɪr|.ə **-us** -əs
pyrrhic **(P)** 'pɪr.ɪk **-s** -s **ˌPyrrhic 'victory**
Pytchley 'paɪtʃ.li
Pythagoras paɪ'θæg.ər.əs, -ɒr-, -æs (US) pɪ'θæg.ɚ.əs **Pyˌthagoras' 'theorem**
Pythagorean paɪˌθæg.ər'iː.ən, ˌpaɪ.θæg-, -ɒr'- (US) pɪˌθæg.ə'riː- **-s** -z
Pythian 'pɪθ.i.ən
Pythias 'pɪθ.i.æs (US) -əs
python 'paɪ.θən (US) -θɑːn, -θən **-s** -z
Pythonesque ˌpaɪ.θən'esk
pythoness 'paɪ.θən.es, -ɪs (US) 'paɪ-, 'pɪθ.ən-, -ɪs **-es** -ɪz
pythonic paɪ'θɒn.ɪk (US) -'θɑː.nɪk, pɪ-
pyx pɪks **-es** -ɪz

Pronouncing the letter Q

In general, the consonant letter **q** is followed by **u** and pronounced /kw/ or /k/, e.g.:

queen	/kwiːn/	
antiquated	/ˈæn.tɪ.kweɪ.tɪd/	US /ˈæn.t̬ə.kweɪ.t̬ɪd/
quay	/kiː/	
antique	/ænˈtiːk/	

In words borrowed from Arabic, **q** is not always followed by **u**, e.g.:

Qatar	/ˈkʌt.ɑːʳ, kəˈtɑːʳ/	US /ˈkɑː.tɑːr, kəˈtɑːr/

q (Q) kjuː **-'s** -z

Qaddafi, Qadhafi gəˈdɑː.fi, -ˈdæf.i US kəˈdɑː-

Qantas® ˈkwɒn.təs, -tæs US ˈkwɑːn.təs

Qatar ˈkʌt.ɑːʳ, ˈkæt-, ˈgæt-; kəˈtɑːʳ, gætˈɑːʳ, kæt- US ˈkɑː.tɑːr; kəˈtɑːr

QC ˌkjuːˈsiː **-'s** -z

q.e.d., QED ˌkjuː.iːˈdiː

qintar kɪnˈtɑːʳ, ˈ-- US kɪnˈtɑːr **-s** -z

qt ˌkjuːˈtiː

Q-Tip® ˈkjuː.tɪp **-s** -s

qua kweɪ, kwɑː

quack kwæk **-s** -s **-ing** -ɪŋ **-ed** -t **-ery** -ᵊr.i **-ish** -ɪʃ

quad kwɒd US kwɑːd **-s** -z

Quadragesim|a ˌkwɒd.rəˈdʒes.ɪ.m|ə, ˈ-ə- US ˌkwɑː.drəˈ-, -ˈdʒeɪ.zɪ- **-al** -ᵊl

quadrangle ˈkwɒd.ræŋ.gl̩, kwɒdˈræŋ- US ˈkwɑː.dræŋ- **-s** -z

quadrangular kwɒdˈræŋ.gjə.ləʳ, kwəˈdræŋ-, -gjʊ- US kwɑːˈdræŋ.gjə.lɚ, -gjʊ-

quadrant ˈkwɒd.rᵊnt US ˈkwɑː.drᵊnt **-s** -s

quadraphonic ˌkwɒd.rəˈfɒn.ɪk US ˌkwɑː.drəˈfɑː.nɪk **-ally** -ᵊl.i, -li **-s** -s *stress shift:* ˌquadraphonic ˈsound

quadraphony kwɒdˈrɒf.ᵊn.i, kwəˈdrɒf-, -ˈdræf-; ˈkwɒd.rə.fɒn- US kwɑːˈdræf.ᵊn-

quadrate *(n. adj.)* ˈkwɒd.rət, -rɪt, -reɪt US ˈkwɑː.drɪt, -dreɪt **-s** -s

quadra|te *(v.)* kwɒdˈreɪ|t, kwəˈdreɪ|t US kwɑːˈdreɪ|t **-tes** -ts **-ting** -tɪŋ US -t̬ɪŋ **-ted** -tɪd US -t̬ɪd

quadratic kwɒdˈræt.ɪk, kwəˈdræt- US kwɑːˈdræt̬- **-s** -s **quadˌratic eˈquation**

quadrature ˈkwɒd.rə.tʃəʳ, -rɪ-, -tjʊəʳ US ˈkwɑː.drə.tʃɚ

quadric ˈkwɒd.rɪk US ˈkwɑː.drɪk **-s** -s

quadri|ga kwɒdˈriː|.gə, kwəˈdriː-, -ˈdraɪ- US kwɑːˈdraɪ- **-gae** -dʒiː US -giː, -dʒiː **-gas** -gəz

quadrilateral ˌkwɒd.rɪˈlæt.ᵊr.ᵊl, -rəˈ-, ˈ-rᵊl US ˌkwɑː.drɪˈlæt̬- **-s** -z *stress shift:* ˌquadrilateral ˈshape

quadrilingual ˌkwɒd.rɪˈlɪŋ.gwəl, -rəˈ- US ˌkwɑː.drɪˈ- *stress shift:* ˌquadrilingual ˈnation

quadrille kwəˈdrɪl, kwɒdˈrɪl US kwəˈdrɪl, kwɑː- **-s** -z

quadrillion kwɒdˈrɪl.jən, kwəˈdrɪl-, ˈ-i.ən US kwɑːˈdrɪl.jən **-s** -z

quadriplegia ˌkwɒd.rɪˈpliː.dʒə, -rəˈ-, ˈ-dʒi.ə US ˌkwɑː.drɪˈpliː-

quadriplegic ˌkwɒd.rɪˈpliː.dʒɪk, -rəˈ- US ˌkwɑː.drɪˈ- **-s** -s *stress shift:* ˌquadriplegic ˈstate

quadrisyllabic ˌkwɒd.rɪ.sɪˈlæb.ɪk, -rə-, -səˈ- US ˌkwɑː.drɪ- *stress shift:* ˌquadrisyllabic ˈword

quadrisyllable ˌkwɒd.rɪˈsɪl.ə.bl̩ US ˈkwɑː.drɪˌsɪl- **-s** -z

quadroon kwɒdˈruːn, kwəˈdruːn US kwɑːˈdruːn **-s** -z

quadrophonic ˌkwɒd.rəˈfɒn.ɪk US ˌkwɑː.drəˈfɑː.nɪk **-ally** -ᵊl.i, -li **-s** -s *stress shift:* ˌquadrophonic ˈsound

quadrophony kwɒdˈrɒf.ᵊn.i, kwəˈdrɒf-; ˈkwɒd.rə.fɒn- US kwɑːˈdræf.ᵊn-

quadrumana kwɒdˈruː.mə.nə, kwəˈdruː- US kwɑːˈdruː-

quadrumanous kwɒdˈruː.mə.nəs, kwəˈdruː- US kwɑːˈdruː-

quadruped ˈkwɒd.rə.ped, -rʊ- US ˈkwɑː.drʊ-, -drə- **-s** -z

quadrupl|e ˈkwɒd.rʊp.l̩, -ruː.pl̩; kwɒdˈruː.pl̩, kwəˈdruː- US kwɑːˈdruː.pl̩, kwə-, -ˈdrʊp.l̩; ˈkwɑː.druː.pl̩, -drʊ-, -drə- **-es** -z **-y** -i **-ing** -ɪŋ **-ed** -d

quadruplet kwɒdˈrʊ.plət, -plɪt, -plet; ˈkwɒd.ruː- US kwɑːˈdruː.plɪt; ˈkwɑː.druː-, -drə-; kwɑːˈdrʌp.lɪt **-s** -s

quadruplicate *(n. adj.)* kwɒdˈruː.plɪ.kət, kwəˈdruː-, -plə-, -kɪt, -keɪt US kwɑːˈdruː.plɪ.kɪt, -keɪt **-s** -s

quadrupli|cate *(v.)* kwɒdˈruː.plɪ|.keɪt, kwəˈdruː- US kwɑːˈdruː- **-cates** -keɪts **-cating** -keɪ.tɪŋ US -keɪ.t̬ɪŋ **-cated** -keɪ.tɪd US -keɪ.t̬ɪd

quaestor ˈkwiː.stəʳ, ˈkwaɪ-, -stɔːʳ US ˈkwes.tɚ, ˈkwiː.stɚ **-s** -z

quaff kwɒf, kwɑːf US kwɑːf, kwæf, kwɔːf **-s** -s **-ing** -ɪŋ **-ed** -t **-er/s** -əʳ/z US -ɚ/z

quag kwɒg, kwæg US kwæg, kwɑːg **-s** -z

quagga ˈkwæg.ə, ˈkwɒg- US ˈkwæg-, ˈkwɑː.gə **-s** -z

Quaglino's® kwægˈliː.nəʊz US -noʊz

quagmire ˈkwɒg.maɪəʳ, ˈkwæg- US ˈkwæg.maɪɚ, ˈkwɑːg- **-s** -z

quail (Q) kweɪl **-s** -z **-ing** -ɪŋ **-ed** -d

Quain kweɪn

quaint kweɪnt **-er** -əʳ US ˈkweɪn.t̬ɚ **-est** -ɪst, -əst US ˈkweɪn.t̬ɪst, -t̬əst **-ly** -li **-ness** -nəs, -nɪs

quak|e kweɪk **-es** -s **-ing** -ɪŋ **-ed** -t

Quaker ˈkweɪ.kəʳ US -kɚ **-s** -z

qualification ˌkwɒl.ɪ.fɪˈkeɪ.ʃᵊn, ˌ-ə- US ˌkwɑː.lɪ- **-s** -z

qualificative ˈkwɒl.ɪ.fɪ.kə.tɪv, ˈ-ə- US ˈkwɑː.lɪ.fɪ.keɪ.t̬ɪv **-s** -z

qualificatory ˌkwɒl.ɪ.fɪˈkeɪ.tᵊr.i, ˌ-ə- US ˈkwɑː.lɪ.fə.kə.tɔːr-

quali|fy ˈkwɒl.ɪ|.faɪ, ˈ-ə- US ˈkwɑː.lɪ- **-fies** -faɪz **-fying** -faɪ.ɪŋ **-fied** -faɪd **-fier/s** -faɪ.əʳ/z US -faɪ.ɚ/z

qualitative ˈkwɒl.ɪ.tə.tɪv, -teɪ- US ˈkwɑː.lɪ.teɪ.t̬ɪv **-ly** -li

qualit|y ˈkwɒl.ə.t|i, -ɪ.t|i US ˈkwɑː.lə.t̬|i **-ies** -iz **ˈquality conˌtrol**; **ˈquality ˌtime**

qualm kwɑːm, kwɔːm US kwɑːm **-s** -z

qualmish ˈkwɑː.mɪʃ, ˈkwɔː- US ˈkwɑː- **-ly** -li **-ness** -nəs, -nɪs

quandar|y (Q) ˈkwɒn.dᵊr|.i, -dr|i US ˈkwɑːn- **-ies** -iz

quango ˈkwæŋ.gəʊ US -goʊ **-s** -z

Quant kwɒnt US kwɑːnt

quanta *(plur. of* **quantum***)* ˈkwɒn.tə US ˈkwɑːn.t̬ə

quantal ˈkwɒn.tᵊl US ˈkwɑːn.t̬ᵊl

quantic ˈkwɒn.tɪk US ˈkwɑːn.t̬ɪk **-s** -s

quantifiable ˈkwɒn.tɪ.faɪ.ə.bl̩, -tə-, ˌkwɒn.tɪˈfaɪ-, -təˈ- US ˈkwɑːn.t̬ə.faɪ-

quantification ˌkwɒn.tɪ.fɪˈkeɪ.ʃᵊn, -tə- US ˌkwɑːn.t̬ə-

quanti|fy ˈkwɒn.tɪ|.faɪ, -tə- US ˈkwɑːn.t̬ə- **-fies** -faɪz **-fying**

-faɪ.ɪŋ **-fied** -faɪd **-fier/s** -faɪ.əʳ/z US -faɪ.ɚ/z

quantitative 'kwɒn.tɪ.tə.tɪv, -teɪ- US 'kwɑːn.t̬ə.teɪ.t̬ɪv **-ly** -li

quantit|y 'kwɒn.tə.t|i, -tɪ- US 'kwɑːn.t̬ə.t̬|i **-ies** -iz ˌ**quantity sur'veyor,** '**quantity sur**ˌ**veyor**

quantiz|e, -is|e 'kwɒn.taɪz US 'kwɑːn- **-es** -ɪz **-ing** -ɪŋ **-ed** -d

Quantock 'kwɒn.tək, -tɒk US 'kwɑːn.t̬ək, -tɑːk

quant|um *amount:* 'kwɒn.t|əm US 'kwɑːn.t̬|əm **-a** -ə ˌ**quantum 'jump;** ˌ**quantum 'leap;** ˌ**quantum me'chanics;** '**quantum** ˌ**theory**

quantum *in Latin phrases:* 'kwæn.tʊm, 'kwɒn-, -təm US 'kwɑːn.t̬əm, -tʊm

quantum meruit ˌkwæn.tʊm'mer.u.ɪt, ˌkwɒn-, -təm'- US ˌkwɑːn.tʊm'-, -t̬əm'-

quarantin|e 'kwɒr.ən.tiːn, -taɪn US 'kwɔːr.ən.tiːn, 'kwɑːr- **-es** -z **-ing** -ɪŋ **-ed** -d

quare clausim fregit ˌkwɑː.reɪˌklaʊ.səm'freɪ.gɪt US ˌkwɑːr.iˌklaʊ.səm'freɪ.gət, -gɪt

Quaritch 'kwɒr.ɪtʃ US 'kwɑːr-

quark *in physics:* kwɑːk, kwɔːk US kwɑːrk, kwɔːrk **-s** -s

quark *soft cheese:* kwɑːk US kwɑːrk, kwɔːrk

Quarles kwɔːlz US kwɔːrlz, kwɑːrlz

Quarmby 'kwɔːm.bi US 'kwɔːrm-

quarrel 'kwɒr.əl US 'kwɔːr-, 'kwɑːr- **-s** -z **-(l)ing** -ɪŋ **-(l)ed** -d **-(l)er/s** -əʳ/z US -ɚ/z

quarrelsome 'kwɒr.əl.səm US 'kwɔːr-, 'kwɑːr- **-ly** -li **-ness** -nəs, -nɪs

quarr|y 'kwɒr|.i US 'kwɔːr-, 'kwɑːr- **-ies** -iz **-ying** -i.ɪŋ **-ied** -id '**quarry** ˌ**tile,** ˌ**quarry 'tile**

quarry|man 'kwɒr.i|.mən, -mæn US 'kwɔːr-, 'kwɑːr- **-men** -mən, -men

quart *measurement:* kwɔːt, kɔː- US kwɔːrt **-s** -s

quart *in card games, fencing:* kɑːt US kɑːrt **-s** -s **-ing** -ɪŋ US 'kɑːr.t̬ɪŋ **-ed** -ɪd US 'kɑːr.t̬ɪd

quartan 'kwɔː.tən US 'kwɔːr-

quarte *(n. v.) in card games, fencing:* kɑːt US kɑːrt **-s** -s **-ing** -ɪŋ US 'kɑːr.t̬ɪŋ **-ed** -ɪd US 'kɑːr.t̬ɪd

quart|er 'kwɔː.t|əʳ, kɔː- US 'kwɔːr.t̬|ɚ **-ers** -əz US -ɚz **-ering/s** -ər.ɪŋ/z **-ered** -əd US -ɚd **-erage** -ər.ɪdʒ '**quarter** ˌ**day;** '**quarter** ˌ**note;** '**Quarter** ˌ**Sessions;** '**quarter** ˌ**tone**

quarterback 'kwɔː.tə.bæk US 'kwɔːr.t̬ɚ- **-s** -s

quarterdeck 'kwɔː.tə.dek US 'kwɔːr.t̬ɚ- **-s** -s

quarterfinal ˌkwɔː.tə'faɪ.nəl US ˌkwɔːr.t̬ɚ'- **-s** -z

quarterfinalist ˌkwɔː.tə'faɪ.nəl.ɪst US ˌkwɔːr.t̬ɚ'- **-s** -s

quarterl|y 'kwɔː.təl|.i US 'kwɔːr.t̬ɚ.l|i **-ies** -iz

Quartermain(e) 'kwɔː.tə.meɪn US 'kwɔːr.t̬ɚ-

quartermaster 'kwɔː.təˌmɑː.stəʳ US 'kwɔːr.t̬ɚˌmæs.tɚ **-s** -z

quartern 'kwɔː.tən US 'kwɔːr.t̬ɚn **-s** -z

quarter|staff 'kwɔː.tə|.stɑːf US 'kwɔːr.t̬ɚ|.stæf **-aves** -steɪvz

quartet(te) kwɔː'tet US kwɔːr- **-s** -s

quartic 'kwɔː.tɪk US 'kwɔːr.t̬ɪk **-s** -s

quartile 'kwɔː.taɪl US 'kwɔːr-, -t̬ɪl, -t̬əl **-s** -z

quarto 'kwɔː.təʊ US 'kwɔːr.t̬oʊ **-s** -z

quartus (Q) 'kwɔː.təs US 'kwɔːr.t̬əs

quartz 'kwɔːts US 'kwɔːrts

quasar 'kweɪ.zɑːʳ, -sɑːʳ US -zɑːr, -sɑːr **-s** -z

quash kwɒʃ US kwɑːʃ, kwɔːʃ **-es** -ɪz **-ing** -ɪŋ **-ed** -t

quasi- kweɪ.zaɪ-, kwɑː-, -saɪ-, -zi- US kweɪ.saɪ-, -zaɪ-; kwɑː.zi-, -si-

Note: Prefix. Words beginning with **quasi-** are normally hyphenated, with **quasi-** taking secondary stress on the first syllable, e.g. **quasi-stellar** /ˌkweɪ.zaɪ'stel.əʳ US -saɪ'stel.ɚ/.

quasi 'kweɪ.zaɪ, 'kwɑː-, -saɪ, -zi US 'kweɪ.saɪ, -zaɪ; 'kwɑː.zi, -si

quasi in rem ˌkweɪ.zi.ɪn'rem US ˌkwɑː-, -ən'-

Quasimodo ˌkwɑː.zi'məʊ.dəʊ, ˌkwɒz.i'-, ˌkwæz- US ˌkwɑː.zi'moʊ.doʊ

quassia 'kwɒʃ.ə, -i.ə US 'kwɑː.ʃə, '-ʃi.ə

quatercentenar|y ˌkwæt.ə.sen'tiː.nər|.i, ˌkwɔː.tə-, ˌkwɒt.ə-, ˌkweɪ.tə-, -'ten.ər- US ˌkwɑː.t̬ɚ.sen'ten.ɚ|.i; -'sen.tən.er- **-ies** -iz

Quatermain 'kwɔː.tə.meɪn US 'kwɑː.t̬ɚ-

quaternar|y (Q) kwə'tɜː.nər|.i, kwɒt'ɜː- US 'kwɑː.t̬ɚ.ner-; kwə'tɝː.nɚ- **-ies** -iz

quaternion kwə'tɜː.ni.ən, kwɒt'ɜː- US kwə'tɝː-, kwɑː- **-s** -z

quatorzain kə'tɔː.zeɪn, kæt'ɔː-; 'kæt.ə- US kə'tɔːr-, kæt'ɔːr-; 'kæt̬.ɚ- **-s** -z

quatrain 'kwɒt.reɪn, -rən US 'kwɑː.treɪn, -'- **-s** -z

quatrefoil 'kæt.rə.fɔɪl, '-ə- US 'kæt̬.ɚ.fɔɪl, -rə- **-s** -z

quatrillion kwɒt'rɪl.jən, kwə'trɪl-, '-i.ən US kwɑː'trɪl-, kwə- **-s** -z

quattrocento (Q) ˌkwæt.rəʊ'tʃen.təʊ, ˌkwɒt- US ˌkwɑː.troʊ'tʃen.toʊ

quav|er 'kweɪ.v|əʳ US -v|ɚ **-ers** -əz US -ɚz **-ering/ly** -ər.ɪŋ/li **-ered** -əd US -ɚd

quay kiː US kiː, keɪ, kweɪ **-s** -z **-age** -ɪdʒ

Quay *place name:* kiː *surname:* kweɪ

Quayle kweɪl

quayside 'kiː.saɪd

quean kwiːn **-s** -z

queas|y 'kwiː.z|i **-ier** **-iest** **-ily** -ɪ.li **-iness** -ɪ.nəs, -ɪ.nɪs

Quebec kwɪ'bek, kwə-, kɪ-, kə- *as if French:* keb'ek US kwiː'bek, kwɪ-, kɪ- *as if French:* keb'ek

Quebecois, Québecois ˌkeɪ.bek'wɑː, ˌkeb.ek'-, -ɪ'kwɑː, -ə'- US ˌkeɪ.bek'wɑː

Quechu|a 'ketʃ.u|.ə, -w|ə US -w|ɑː, -w|ə **-an/s** -ən/z

queen kwiːn **-s** -z **-ing** -ɪŋ **-ed** -d ˌ**Queen's 'Counsel;** ˌ**Queen's 'English;** ˌ**queen's 'evidence;** ˌ**Queen 'Mother**

Queenborough 'kwiːn.bər.ə, 'kwiːm- US 'kwiːn.bɚ.oʊ

Queenie 'kwiː.ni

queenlike 'kwiːn.laɪk

queenl|y 'kwiːn.l|i **-ier** -i.əʳ US -i.ɚ **-iest** -i.ɪst, -i.əst **-iness** -ɪ.nəs, -ɪ.nɪs

Queens kwiːnz

Queensberry 'kwiːnz.bər.i US -ˌber.i, -bɚ- ˌ**Queensberry 'rules**

Queensbury 'kwiːnz.bər.i

Queensferry 'kwiːnzˌfer.i

Queensland 'kwiːnz.lənd, -lænd

Queenstown 'kwiːnz.taʊn

Queensway 'kwiːnz.weɪ

queer kwɪəʳ US kwɪr **-s** -z **-ing** -ɪŋ **-ed** -d **-er** -əʳ US -ɚ **-est** -ɪst US -əst **-ly** -li **-ness** -nəs, -nɪs **-ish** -ɪʃ '**queer** ˌ**street**

quell kwel **-s** -z **-ing** -ɪŋ **-ed** -d

quench kwentʃ **-es** -ɪz **-ing** -ɪŋ **-ed** -t **-er/s** -əʳ/z US -ɚ/z **-able** -ə.bl̩

quenelle kə'nel, kɪ- US kə- **-s** -z

Quen(n)ell kwɪ'nel, kwə-, 'kwen.əl US kwə'nel, 'kwen.əl

Quentin 'kwen.tɪn US -tən

Querétaro kə'reɪ.tər.əʊ US -'ret.ə.roʊ; kɚ.ə'tɑːr.oʊ

quern kwɜːn US kwɝːn **-s** -z

querulous 'kwer.ʊ.ləs, -jʊ-, '-ə- US 'kwer.jə.ləs, -jʊ-, '-ə-, '-ʊ- **-ly** -li **-ness** -nəs, -nɪs

quer|y 'kwɪə.r|i US 'kwɪr|.i **-ies** -iz **-ying** -i.ɪŋ **-ied** -id

quesadilla ˌkeɪ.sə'diː.jə, -ljə US -jə **-s** -z

Quesnel 'keɪ.nəl

quest kwest **-s** -s **-ing** -ɪŋ **-ed** -ɪd

Quested 'kwes.tɪd

question 'kwes.tʃən, 'kweʃ- US 'kwes.tʃən, -tjən **-s** -z **-ing/ly** -ɪŋ/li **-ed** -d **-er/s** -əʳ/z US -ɚ/z '**question** ˌ**mark;** '**question** ˌ**time;** ˌ**out of the 'question**

questionab|le 'kwes.tʃə.nə.bl̩, 'kweʃ- US 'kwes.tʃə-, -tjə- **-ly** -li **-leness** -l̩.nəs, -nɪs
questionar|y 'kwes.tʃə.nᵊr|.i, 'kweʃ- US 'kwes.tʃə.ner-, -tjə- **-ies** -iz
question-master 'kwes.tʃən,mɑː.stəʳ, 'kweʃ-, -tʃəm,- US 'kwes.tʃən,mæs.tɚ, -tjən,- **-s** -z
questionnaire ,kwes.tʃə'neəʳ, ,kweʃ-, ,kes-, '---- US ,kwes.tʃə'ner, -tjə'- **-s** -z
Quetta 'kwet.ə US 'kwet̬-
quetzal 'kwet.sᵊl US ket'sɑːl **-s** -z **quetzales** kwet'sɑː.les US ket-
Quetzalcoatl ,ket.sᵊl.kəʊ'æt.ᵊl US -sɑːl.koʊ'ɑː.t̬ᵊl
queue kjuː **-s** -z **-ing** -ɪŋ **-d** -d
queue-jump 'kjuː.dʒʌmp **-s** -s **-ing** -ɪŋ **-ed** -t **-er/s** -əʳ/z US -ɚ/z
Quex kweks
Quezon City ,keɪ.zɒn'sɪt.i, -sɒn'- US ,keɪ.sɑːn'sɪt̬-
quibbl|e 'kwɪb.l̩ **-es** -z **-ing** -ɪŋ, 'kwɪb.lɪŋ **-ed** -d **-er/s** -əʳ/z, 'kwɪb.ləʳ/z US 'kwɪb.l̩.ɚ/z, '-lɚ/z
Quibell 'kwaɪ.bᵊl, 'kwɪb.ᵊl; kwɪ'bel, kwaɪ'bel
Note: Baron Quibell of Scunthorpe pronounced /'kwaɪ.bᵊl/.
quich|e kiːʃ **-es** -ɪz
quick (Q) kwɪk **-er** -əʳ US -ɚ **-est** -ɪst, -əst **-ly** -li **-ness** -nəs, -nɪs ,**quick** '**march**; '**quick** ,**time**
quick-change ,kwɪk'tʃeɪndʒ *stress shift:* ,quick-change 'tyres
Quicke kwɪk
quicken 'kwɪk.ᵊn **-s** -z **-ing** -ɪŋ **-ed** -d
quickfire 'kwɪk.faɪəʳ US -faɪɚ
quick-freez|e ,kwɪk'friːz, '-- US 'kwɪk.friːz **-es** -ɪz **-ing** -ɪŋ **quick-froze** ,kwɪk'frəʊz, '-- US 'kwɪk.froʊz **quick frozen** -ən **quick-freezer/s** ,kwɪk'friː.zəʳ/z, '-,-- US 'kwɪk,friː.zɚ/z
quickie 'kwɪk.i **-s** -z
quicklime 'kwɪk.laɪm
Quickly 'kwɪk.li
quicksand 'kwɪk.sænd **-s** -z
quickset 'kwɪk.set
quicksilver 'kwɪk,sɪl.vəʳ US -vɚ
quickstep 'kwɪk.step **-s** -s
quick-tempered ,kwɪk'tem.pəd US -pɚd, '-,-- *stress shift, British only:* ,quick-tempered 'person
quick-witted ,kwɪk'wɪt.ɪd US -'wɪt̬-, '-,-- **-ly** -li **-ness** -nəs, -nɪs *stress shift, British only:* ,quick-witted 'person
quid kwɪd **-s** -z
quidditch 'kwɪd.ɪtʃ
quiddit|y 'kwɪd.ɪ.t|i, -ə.t|i US -ə.t̬|i **-ies** -iz
quid pro quo ,kwɪd.prəʊ'kwəʊ US -proʊ'kwoʊ **-s** -z

quiescence kwi'es.ᵊnts US kwaɪ-, kwi-
quiescent kwi'es.ᵊnt US kwaɪ-, kwi- **-ly** -li
quiet kwaɪət **-er** -əʳ US 'kwaɪə.t̬ɚ **-est** -ɪst, -əst US 'kwaɪə.t̬ɪst, -əst **-ly** -li **-ness** -nəs, -nɪs **-s** -s **-ing** -ɪŋ US 'kwaɪə.t̬ɪŋ **-ed** -ɪd US 'kwaɪə.t̬ɪd
quieten 'kwaɪə.tᵊn **-s** -z **-ing** -ɪŋ **-ed** -d
quiet|ism 'kwaɪə.t|ɪ.zᵊm, 'kwaɪ.ɪ- US 'kwaɪə.t|ɪ- **-ist/s** -ɪst/s
quietude 'kwaɪə.tjuːd, 'kwaɪ.ɪ- US 'kwaɪə.tuːd, -tjuːd
quietus kwaɪ'iː.təs, -'eɪ- US -'iː.t̬əs
quiff kwɪf **-s** -s
Quigg kwɪg
Quiggin 'kwɪg.ɪn
Quigley 'kwɪg.li
quill kwɪl **-s** -z **-ing** -ɪŋ **-ed** -d
Quiller-Couch ,kwɪl.ə'kuːtʃ US -ɚ'-
Quilliam 'kwɪl.i.əm
Quilp kwɪlp
quilt kwɪlt **-s** -s **-ing** -ɪŋ US 'kwɪl.t̬ɪŋ **-ed** -ɪd US 'kwɪl.t̬ɪd
Quilter 'kwɪl.təʳ US -t̬ɚ
quin (Q) kwɪn **-s** -z
Quinault *North American people:* 'kwɪn.ᵊlt, -ɔːlt US kwɪ'nɑːlt *French dramatist:* 'kiː.nəʊ US kɪ'noʊ
quinc|e (Q) kwɪnts **-es** -ɪz
quincentenar|y ,kwɪn.sen'tiː.nᵊr|.i, -'ten.ᵊr-, -'tɪn- US kwɪn'sen.tə.ner|.i; ,kwɪn.sen'ten.ɚ- **-ies** -iz
Quincey 'kwɪnt.si
quincunx 'kwɪn.kʌŋks, 'kwɪŋ- US 'kwɪn- **-es** -ɪz
Quincy 'kwɪnt.si
quindecagon kwɪn'dek.ə.gᵊn US -gɑːn **-s** -z
quinella kwɪ'nel.ə
quingentenar|y ,kwɪn.dʒen'tiː.nᵊr|.i, -'ten.ᵊr-, -'tɪn- **-ies** -iz
quinine 'kwɪn.iːn, -'-; kwə- US 'kwaɪ.naɪn
Quink® kwɪŋk
Quinn kwɪn
Quinney 'kwɪn.i
quinquagenarian ,kwɪŋ.kwə.dʒə'neə.ri.ən, -kwɪ-, -dʒɪ'- US ,kwɪn.kwə.dʒə'ner.i-, ,kwɪŋ- **-s** -z
Quinquagesima ,kwɪŋ.kwə'dʒes.ɪ.mə, -kwɪ'-, '-ə- US ,kwɪn.kwə'dʒeɪ.zɪ-, ,kwɪŋ-, -'dʒes.ɪ-
quinquennial kwɪŋ'kwen.i.əl US kwɪn-, kwɪŋ-
quinquennium kwɪŋ'kwen.i.əm US kwɪn-, kwɪŋ- **-s** -z
quinsy 'kwɪn.zi
quint *organ stop:* kwɪnt **-s** -s *in piquet:* kɪnt, kwɪnt *old fashioned:* kent **-s** -s *US for quintuplet:* kwɪnt **-s** -s

quintain 'kwɪn.tɪn **-s** -z
quintal 'kwɪn.tᵊl US -t̬ᵊl **-s** -z
Quintana Roo kɪn,tɑː.nə'rəʊ.əʊ US -'roʊ.oʊ
quintessence kwɪn'tes.ᵊnts
quintessential ,kwɪn.tɪ'sen.tʃᵊl, -tə'- US -te'sent.ʃəl **-ly** -i
quintet, quintette kwɪn'tet **-s** -s
quintic 'kwɪn.tɪk US -t̬ɪk **-s** -s
Quintilian kwɪn'tɪl.i.ən US '-jən, -i.ən
quintillion kwɪn'tɪl.jən, '-i.ən US '-jən **-s** -z
Quintin 'kwɪn.tɪn US -tɪn, -tᵊn
Quinton 'kwɪn.tən US -tᵊn
quintupl|e 'kwɪn.tjʊ.pl̩, -tjuː-; kwɪn'tjuː- US kwɪn'tuː-, -'tjuː-; 'kwɪn.t̬ə- **-es** -z **-ing** -ɪŋ **-ed** -d
quintuplet 'kwɪn.tjʊ.plət, -plɪt, -plet; kwɪn'tjuː- US kwɪn'tʌp.lɪt, -'tuː.plɪt, -'tjuː-; 'kwɪn.tə.plet **-s** -s
quintus (Q) 'kwɪn.təs US -t̬əs
quip kwɪp **-s** -s **-ping** -ɪŋ **-ped** -t
quire kwaɪəʳ US kwaɪɚ **-s** -z
Quirey *in England, surname:* 'kwaɪə.ri US 'kwaɪ- *in Ireland:* 'kwɪə.ri US 'kwɪr.i
Quirinal 'kwɪr.ɪ.nᵊl, -ᵊn.ᵊl US 'kwɪr.ɪ.nᵊl; kwɪ'raɪ-
Quirinus kwɪ'raɪ.nəs
quirk (Q) kwɜːk US kwɝːk **-s** -s
quirk|y 'kwɜː.k|i US 'kwɝː- **-ier** -i.əʳ US -i.ɚ **-iest** -i.ɪst, -i.əst **-ily** -ɪ.li, -ᵊl.i **-iness** -ɪ.nəs, -ɪ.nɪs
quisling 'kwɪz.lɪŋ **-s** -z
quit kwɪt **-s** -s **-ting** -ɪŋ US 'kwɪt̬.ɪŋ **-ted** -ɪd US 'kwɪt̬.ɪd
quitclaim 'kwɪt.kleɪm **-s** -s
quite kwaɪt
Quito 'kiː.təʊ US -t̬oʊ, -toʊ
quit-rent 'kwɪt.rent **-s** -s
quits kwɪts
quittanc|e 'kwɪt.ᵊnts **-es** -ɪz
quitter 'kwɪt.əʳ US 'kwɪt̬.ɚ **-s** -z
quiv|er 'kwɪv|.əʳ US -ɚ **-ers** -əz US -ɚz **-ering/ly** -ᵊr.ɪŋ/li **-ered** -əd US -ɚd
Quiverful 'kwɪv.ə.fʊl US '-ɚ-
qui vive ,kiː'viːv
Quixote 'kwɪk.sət, -səʊt; kɪ'həʊ.ti, -teɪ US kɪ'hoʊ.t̬i, -teɪ; 'kwɪk.sət
quixotic kwɪk'sɒt.ɪk US -'sɑː.t̬ɪk **-ally** -ᵊl.i, -li
quiz kwɪz **-zes** -ɪz **-zing** -ɪŋ **-zed** -d
quiz-master 'kwɪz,mɑː.stəʳ US -,mæs.tɚ **-s** -z
quizzic|al 'kwɪz.ɪ.k|ᵊl **-ally** -ᵊl.i, -li
quod kwɒd US kwɑːd **-s** -z **-ding** -ɪŋ **-ded** -ɪd
quod erat demonstrandum ,kwɒd,er.æt,dem.ən'stræn.dəm US ,kwɑːd-, -'strɑːn-
quodlibet 'kwɒd.lɪ.bet US 'kwɑːd.lə- **-s** -s

quoin kɔɪn, kwɔɪn **-s** -z **-ing** -ɪŋ **-ed** -d
quoit kɔɪt, kwɔɪt **-s** -s
quokka ˈkwɒk.ə (US) ˈkwɑː.kə **-s** -z
quondam ˈkwɒn.dæm, -dəm
(US) ˈkwɑːn.dəm, -dæm
Quonset® ˈkwɒnt.sɪt, -sət, -set
(US) ˈkwɑːnt- ˈ**Quonset** ˌ**hut**
quorate ˈkwɔː.reɪt, -rət, -rɪt
(US) ˈkwɔːr.ɪt, -eɪt
Quorn® kwɔːn (US) kwɔːrn
quorum ˈkwɔː.rəm (US) ˈkwɔːr.əm **-s** -z
quota ˈkwəʊ.tə (US) ˈkwoʊ.t̬ə **-s** -z **-ing** -ɪŋ **-ed** -d
quotable ˈkwəʊ.tə.bl̩ (US) ˈkwoʊ.t̬ə-
quotation kwəʊˈteɪ.ʃən (US) kwoʊ- **-s** -z
quoˈtation ˌ**mark**
quot|e kwəʊt (US) kwoʊt **-es** -s **-ing** -ɪŋ
(US) ˈkwoʊ.t̬ɪŋ **-ed** -ɪd
(US) ˈkwoʊ.t̬ɪd
quoth kwəʊθ (US) kwoʊθ **-a** -ə
quotidian kwəʊˈtɪd.i.ən, kwɒtˈɪd-
(US) kwoʊˈtɪd-
quotient ˈkwəʊ.ʃənt (US) ˈkwoʊ- **-s** -s
quo warranto ˌkwəʊ.wɒrˈæn.təʊ
(US) ˌkwoʊ.wəˈræn.toʊ, -ˈrɑːn-,
-wɔːˈ-
Qur'an, Quran kɒrˈɑːn, kɔːˈrɑːn, kʊ-,
kə- (US) kəˈrɑːn, kɔː-, kʊ-, -ˈræn
qursh ˈkuː.əʃ; kʊəʃ (US) ˈkuː.ɚʃ; kʊrʃ
Quy kwaɪ
q.v. ˌkjuːˈviː, ˌwɪtʃˈsiː, ˌkwɒdˈvɪd.eɪ
(US) ˌkjuːˈviː, ˌwɪtʃˈsiː, ˌkwɑːdˈvɪd.eɪ
qwerty, QWERTY ˈkwɜː.ti (US) ˈkwɝː.t̬i

Pronouncing the letter R

See also RRH

In British English, **r** is pronounced only where it appears before a vowel. In American English, **r** is pronounced in all positions, e.g.:

red	/red/	
bore	/bɔːʳ/	(US) /bɔːr/
boring	/ˈbɔː.rɪŋ/	/ˈbɔːr.ɪŋ/

See the discussion at LIAISON for comments concerning 'linking r' in British English.

In addition

In the word *iron*, **r** is not pronounced in British English but colours the vowel in the second syllable in US English, e.g.:

iron	/aɪən/	(US) /ˈaɪ.ɚn, aɪrn/

r (R) ɑːʳ (US) ɑːr **-'s** -z
Ra rɑː
Rabat rəˈbɑːt, rɑː-, -ˈbæt (US) rəˈbɑːt, rɑː-
rabbet ˈræb.ɪt **-s** -s **-ing** -ɪŋ **-ed** -ɪd
rabbi ˈræb.aɪ **-s** -z
rabbinate ˈræb.ɪ.nət, ˈ-ə-, -nɪt, -neɪt (US) -ɪ.nɪt, -neɪt **-s** -s
rabbinic rəˈbɪn.ɪk, ræbˈɪn- (US) rəˈbɪn- **-al** -əl **-ally** -əl.i, -li
rabb|it ˈræb|.ɪt **-its** -ɪts **-iting** -ɪ.tɪŋ (US) -ɪ.t̬ɪŋ **-ited** -ɪ.tɪd (US) -ɪ.t̬ɪd **ˈrabbit ˌhole; ˈrabbit ˌhutch; ˈrabbit ˌwarren**
rabble ˈræb.l̩ **-s** -z
rabble-rous|er ˈræb.l̩ˌraʊ.z|əʳ (US) -z|ɚ **-ers** -əz (US) -ɚz **-ing** -ɪŋ
Rabelais ˈræb.əl.eɪ (US) ˌræb.əˈleɪ, ˈ---
Rabelaisian ˌræb.əlˈeɪ.zi.ən, -ʒən (US) -əˈleɪ.ʒən, ˈ-zi.ən
rabid ˈræb.ɪd, ˈreɪ.bɪd (US) ˈræb.ɪd **-ly** -li **-ness** -nəs, -nɪs
rabies ˈreɪ.biːz, -biz
Rabin ˈreɪ.bɪn *Israeli politician:* ræbˈiːn (US) rɑːˈbiːn
Rabindranath Tagore rəˌbɪn.drə.nɑːt.təˈgɔːʳ, -nɑːθ- (US) -ˌben.drə.nɑːt.təˈgɔːr, -nɑːθ-
Rabinowitz rəˈbɪn.ə.wɪts, ræbˈɪn-, -vɪts
Raby ˈreɪ.bi
RAC ˌɑːʳ.eɪˈsiː (US) ˌɑːr-
Racal® ˈreɪ.kəl, -kɔːl
raccoon rəˈkuːn, rækˈuːn (US) rækˈuːn, rəˈkuːn **-s** -z
rac|e reɪs **-es** -ɪz **-ing** -ɪŋ **-ed** -t **-er/s** -əʳ/z (US) -ɚ/z **ˌrace reˈlations** (US) **ˈrace ˌrelations**
racecar ˈreɪs.kɑːʳ (US) -kɑːr **-s** -z
racecours|e ˈreɪs.kɔːs (US) -kɔːrs **-es** -ɪz
racegoer ˈreɪsˌgəʊ.əʳ (US) -ˌgoʊ.ɚ **-s** -z
racehors|e ˈreɪs.hɔːs (US) -ˌhɔːrs **-es** -ɪz
raceme ˈræs.iːm, ˈreɪ.siːm; rəˈsiːm, ræsˈiːm (US) reɪˈsiːm, rə- **-s** -z
race-meeting ˈreɪsˌmiː.tɪŋ (US) -t̬ɪŋ **-s** -z
racemic rəˈsiː.mɪk, ræsˈiː-, reɪˈsiː-, -ˈsem.ɪk (US) reɪˈsiː-, rə-
racetrack ˈreɪs.træk **-s** -s
Rachael, Rachel ˈreɪ.tʃəl
Rachelle rəˈʃel; ˈreɪ.tʃəl
rachitis rəˈkaɪ.tɪs, rækˈaɪ- (US) -t̬ɪs
Rachman ˈræk.mən
Rachmaninoff, Rachmaninov rækˈmæn.ɪ.nɒf, ræxˈ- (US) rɑːkˈmɑːn.ɪ.nɔːf
rachmanism (R) ˈræk.mə.nɪ.zəm
racial ˈreɪ.ʃəl, -ʃi.əl (US) ˈ-ʃəl **-ly** -i
racial|ism ˈreɪ.ʃəl|.ɪ.zəm, -ʃi.əl- (US) ˈ-ʃəl- **-ist/s** -ɪst/s
Racine *English personal name, city in US:* rəˈsiːn (US) rə-, reɪ- *French author:* ræsˈiːn, rəˈsiːn (US) rɑːˈsiːn, rə-
rac|ism ˈreɪ.s|ɪ.zəm **-ist/s** -ɪst/s
rack ræk **-s** -s **-ing** -ɪŋ **-ed** -t
rack|et ˈræk|.ɪt **-ets** -ɪts **-eting** -ɪ.tɪŋ (US) -ɪ.t̬ɪŋ **-eted** -ɪ.tɪd (US) -ɪ.t̬ɪd **-ety** -ə.ti, -ɪ.ti (US) -ə.t̬i
racketball ˈræk.ɪt.bɔːl (US) -bɔːl, -bɑːl
racketeer ˌræk.ɪˈtɪəʳ, -əˈ- (US) -əˈtɪr **-s** -z **-ing** -ɪŋ **-ed** -d
Rackham ˈræk.əm
rack|-rent ˈræk|.rent **-rents** -rents **-renter/s** -ˌren.təʳ/z (US) -ˌren.t̬ɚ/z
raclette rækˈlet
raconteur ˌræk.ɒnˈtɜːʳ, -ɔ̃ːnˈ- (US) -ɑːnˈtɝː, -ənˈ- **-s** -z
racoon rəˈkuːn, rækˈuːn (US) rækˈuːn, rəˈkuːn **-s** -z
racquet ˈræk.ɪt **-s** -s
racquetball ˈræk.ɪt.bɔːl (US) -bɔːl, -bɑːl
rac|y ˈreɪ.s|i **-ier** -i.əʳ (US) -i.ɚ **-iest** -i.ɪst, -i.əst **-ily** -ɪ.li, -əl.i **-iness** -ɪ.nəs, -ɪ.nɪs
rad ræd **-s** -z
RADA ˈrɑː.də
radar ˈreɪ.dɑːʳ (US) -dɑːr
Radcliffe ˈræd.klɪf
raddled ˈræd.l̩d
Radetzky rəˈdet.ski, rædˈet- (US) rɑːˈdet-, rə-
Radford ˈræd.fəd (US) -fɚd
radial ˈreɪ.di.əl **-ly** -i
radian ˈreɪ.di.ən **-s** -z
radianc|e ˈreɪ.di.ənts **-es** -ɪz
radiant ˈreɪ.di.ənt **-s** -s **-ly** -li
radi|ate ˈreɪ.di|.eɪt **-ates** -eɪts **-ating** -eɪ.tɪŋ (US) -eɪ.t̬ɪŋ **-ated** -eɪ.tɪd (US) -eɪ.t̬ɪd
radiation ˌreɪ.diˈeɪ.ʃən **-s** -z **radiˈation ˌsickness**
radiator ˈreɪ.di.eɪ.təʳ (US) -t̬ɚ **-s** -z
radic|al ˈræd.ɪ.k|əl **-als** -əlz **-ally** -əl.i, -li **-alness** -əl.nəs, -əl.nɪs **-alism** -əl.ɪ.zəm **ˌradical ˈchic; ˌradical ˈsign**
radicaliz|e, -is|e ˈræd.ɪ.kəl.aɪz **-es** -ɪz **-ing** -ɪŋ **-ed** -d
radicchio rəˈdɪk.i.əʊ, rædˈɪk- (US) rəˈdiː.ki.oʊ, rɑː-, ˈ-kjoʊ **-s** -z
Radice rəˈdiː.tʃi, -tʃeɪ
radicle ˈræd.ɪ.kl̩ **-s** -z
radii *(plur. of* **radius***)* ˈreɪ.di.aɪ
radio *(n.v.)* ˈreɪ.di.əʊ (US) -oʊ **-s** -z **-ing** -ɪŋ **-ed** -d **ˌradio aˈlarm; ˈradio ˌcar; ˌradio ˈtelescope; ˈradio ˌwave**
radioactive ˌreɪ.di.əʊˈæk.tɪv (US) -oʊˈ- **-ly** -li *stress shift:* ˌradioactive ˈwaste
radioactivity ˌreɪ.di.əʊ.ækˈtɪv.ə.ti, -ɪ.ti (US) -oʊ.ækˈtɪv.ə.t̬i
radiocarbon ˌreɪ.di.əʊˈkɑː.bən (US) -oʊˈkɑːr-
radiogenic ˌreɪ.di.əʊˈdʒen.ɪk (US) -oʊˈ- *stress shift:* ˌradiogenic ˈoutput
radiogram ˈreɪ.di.əʊ.græm (US) -oʊ- **-s** -z
radiograph ˈreɪ.di.əʊ.grɑːf, -græf (US) -oʊ.græf **-s** -s
radiograph|y ˌreɪ.diˈɒg.rə.f|i (US) -ˈɑː.grə- **-er/s** -əʳ/z (US) -ɚ/z
Radiohead ˈreɪ.di.əʊ.hed (US) -oʊ-
radioisotope ˌreɪ.di.əʊˈaɪ.sə.təʊp (US) -oʊˈaɪ.sə.toʊp **-s** -s
radiolo|cate ˌreɪ.di.əʊ.ləʊ|ˈkeɪt (US) -oʊ.loʊˈ- **-cates** -ˈkeɪts **-cating** -ˈkeɪ.tɪŋ (US) -ˈkeɪ.t̬ɪŋ **-cated** -ˈkeɪ.tɪd (US) -ˈkeɪ.t̬ɪd
radiolocation ˌreɪ.di.əʊ.ləʊˈkeɪ.ʃən (US) -oʊ.loʊˈ-
radiolog|y ˌreɪ.diˈɒl.ə.dʒ|i (US) -ˈɑː.lə- **-ist/s** -ɪst/s
radiometer ˌreɪ.diˈɒm.ɪ.təʳ, ˈ-ə- (US) -ˈɑː.mə.t̬ɚ **-s** -z

radionics ˌreɪ.di'ɒn.ɪks (US) -'ɑː.nɪks
radiopag|e ˌreɪ.di.əʊ'peɪdʒ, 'reɪ.di.əʊ.peɪdʒ (US) 'reɪ.di.oʊ- **-es** -ɪz **-ing** -ɪŋ **-ed** -d **-er/s** -əʳ/z (US) -ɚ/z
radiophone 'reɪ.di.əʊ.fəʊn (US) -oʊ.foʊn **-s** -z
radiophonic ˌreɪ.di.əʊ'fɒn.ɪk (US) -oʊ'fɑː.nɪk
radiotelegram ˌreɪ.di.əʊ'tel.ɪ.græm, '-ə- (US) -oʊ'tel.ə- **-s** -z
radiotelegraph ˌreɪ.di.əʊ'tel.ɪ.grɑːf, '-ə-, -græf (US) -oʊ'tel.ə.græf **-s** -s
radiotelephone ˌreɪ.di.əʊ'tel.ɪ.fəʊn, '-ə- (US) -oʊ'tel.ə.foʊn **-s** -z
radiotherap|y ˌreɪ.di.əʊ'θer.ə.p|i (US) -oʊ'- **-ist/s** -ɪst/s
radish 'ræd.ɪʃ **-es** -ɪz
radium 'reɪ.di.əm
radi|us 'reɪ.di|.əs **-i** -aɪ
rad|ix 'reɪ.d|ɪks, 'ræd- **-ixes** -ɪk.sɪz **-ices** -ɪ.siːz (US) 'ræd.ə.siːz, 'reɪ.də-
Radlett 'ræd.lɪt, -lət
Radley 'ræd.li
Radnor 'ræd.nəʳ, -nɔːʳ (US) -nɚ, -nɔːr **-shire** -ʃəʳ, -ˌʃɪəʳ (US) -ʃɚ, -ˌʃɪr
radon 'reɪ.dɒn (US) -dɑːn
Radovan 'ræd.ə.væn
Radox® 'reɪ.dɒks (US) -dɑːks
Rae reɪ
Raeburn 'reɪ.bɜːn (US) -bɝːn **-s** -z
Raf ræf
RAF ˌɑːʳ.eɪ'ef; ræf (US) ˌɑːr-
Rafferty 'ræf.ə.ti (US) -ɚ.t̬i
raffia 'ræf.i.ə
raffish 'ræf.ɪʃ **-ly** -li **-ness** -nəs, -nɪs
raffl|e 'ræf.l̩ **-es** -z **-ing** -ɪŋ, 'ræf.lɪŋ **-ed** -d **'raffle ˌticket**
Raffles 'ræf.l̩z
Rafsanjani ˌræf.sɑːn'dʒɑː.ni, -sæn'-, -'dʒæn.i; -dʒɑː'niː (US) ˌrɑːf.sɑːn'dʒɑː.ni; ˌrʌf.sən'dʒæn.i
raft rɑːft (US) ræft **-s** -s **-ing** -ɪŋ **-ed** -ɪd
rafter 'rɑːf.təʳ (US) 'ræf.tɚ **-s** -z **-ed** -d
rag ræg **-s** -z **-ging** -ɪŋ **-ged** -d ˌ**rag 'doll;** **'rag ˌtrade**
raga 'rɑː.gə; rɑːg (US) 'rɑː.gə **-s** -z
ragamuffin 'ræg.əˌmʌf.ɪn **-s** -z
rag-and-bone|-man ˌræg.ᵊnd'bəʊn|.mæn, -ᵊm'- (US) -ᵊnd'boʊn- **-men** -men
ragbag 'ræg.bæg **-s** -z
rag|e reɪdʒ **-es** -ɪz **-ing/ly** -ɪŋ/li **-ed** -d
ragga 'ræg.ə
ragged 'ræg.ɪd **-er** -əʳ (US) -ɚ **-est** -ɪst, -əst **-ly** -li **-ness** -nəs, -nɪs **-y** -i
raggle-taggle 'ræg.l̩ˌtæg.l̩, ˌræg.l̩'tæg-
raglan (R) 'ræg.lən ˌ**raglan 'sleeve**
ragout ræg'uː, '-- (US) ræg'uː **-s** -z
ragtag 'ræg.tæg
ragtime 'ræg.taɪm
ragweed 'ræg.wiːd
ragwort 'ræg.wɜːt (US) -wɝːt, -wɔːrt **-s** -s
Rahman 'rɑː.mən
rah-rah 'rɑː.rɑː
raid reɪd **-s** -z **-ing** -ɪŋ **-ed** -ɪd **-er/s** -əʳ/z (US) -ɚ/z
Raikes reɪks
rail reɪl **-s** -z **-ing** -ɪŋ **-ed** -d
railcard 'reɪl.kɑːd (US) -kɑːrd **-s** -z
railhead 'reɪl.hed **-s** -z
railing 'reɪ.lɪŋ **-s** -z
railler|y 'reɪ.lᵊr|.i **-ies** -iz
railroad 'reɪl.rəʊd (US) -roʊd **-s** -z **-ing** -ɪŋ **-ed** -ɪd
Railtrack® 'reɪl.træk
railway 'reɪl.weɪ **-s** -z
railway|man 'reɪl.weɪ|.mən, -mæn **-men** -mən, -men
raiment 'reɪ.mənt
rain reɪn **-s** -z **-ing** -ɪŋ **-ed** -d **-less** -ləs, -lɪs **'rain ˌforest; ˌtake a 'rain ˌcheck; come ˌrain or 'shine**
rainbow 'reɪn.bəʊ, 'reɪm- (US) 'reɪn.boʊ **-s** -z ˌ**rainbow 'trout**
rainbow-colo(u)red 'reɪn.bəʊˌkʌl.əd, 'reɪm- (US) 'reɪn.boʊˌkʌl.ɚd
raincoat 'reɪn.kəʊt, 'reɪŋ- (US) 'reɪn.koʊt **-s** -s
raindrop 'reɪn.drɒp (US) -drɑːp **-s** -s
Raine reɪn
Rainey 'reɪ.ni
rainfall 'reɪn.fɔːl (US) -fɔːl, -fɑːl
Rainford 'reɪn.fəd (US) -fɚd
rainforest 'reɪnˌfɒr.ɪst (US) -ˌfɔːr- **-s** -s
rain-gaug|e 'reɪn.geɪdʒ, 'reɪŋ- (US) 'reɪn- **-es** -ɪz
Rainier *prince of Monaco:* 'reɪ.ni.eɪ (US) reɪ'nɪr, rə-; ren'jeɪ
Rainier *Mount:* 'reɪ.ni.əʳ; reɪ'nɪəʳ, rə- (US) rə'nɪr, reɪ-
rainmak|ing 'reɪnˌmeɪ.k|ɪŋ, 'reɪm- (US) 'reɪn- **-er/s** -əʳ/z (US) -ɚ/z
rainproof 'reɪn.pruːf, 'reɪm- (US) 'reɪn-
rainstorm 'reɪn.stɔːm (US) -stɔːrm **-s** -z
rainwater 'reɪnˌwɔː.təʳ (US) -ˌwɑː.t̬ɚ, -ˌwɔː-
Rainworth 'reɪn.wəθ, -wɜːθ (US) -wɝːθ, -wɚθ
rain|y 'reɪ.n|i **-ier** -i.əʳ (US) -i.ɚ **-iest** -i.ɪst, -i.əst **-iness** -ɪ.nəs, -ɪ.nɪs ˌ**save something for a ˌrainy 'day**
Raisa raɪ'iː.sə, rɑː- (US) rɑː-
rais|e reɪz **-es** -ɪz **-ing** -ɪŋ **-ed** -d
raisin 'reɪ.zᵊn **-s** -z
raison d'être ˌreɪ.zɔ̃ːŋ'de.trə, -zɒn'- (US) ˌreɪ.zoʊn'det, ˌrez.ɑːn'-, -'det.rə
raj (R) rɑːdʒ, rɑːʒ (US) rɑːdʒ
raja(h) (R) 'rɑː.dʒə (US) -dʒə, -dʒɑː **-s** -z
Rajasthan ˌrɑː.dʒə'stɑːn (US) -dʒɑː'-
Rajasthani ˌrɑː.dʒə'stɑː.ni (US) -dʒɑː'-
Rajiv rɑː'dʒiːv *stress shift:* ˌRajiv 'Ghandi
Rajput 'rɑː.dʒ.pʊt (US) -puːt
Rajputana ˌrɑː.dʒ.pʊ'tɑː.nə (US) -puː'-
rak|e reɪk **-es** -s **-ing** -ɪŋ **-ed** -t
rakee 'rɑː.ki, 'ræk.i; rɑː'kiː
rake-off 'reɪk.ɒf (US) -ɑːf **-s** -s
raki 'rɑː.ki, 'ræk.i; rɑː'kiː
rakish 'reɪ.kɪʃ **-ly** -li **-ness** -nəs, -nɪs
rale rɑːl, ræl (US) rɑːl **-s** -z
Rale(i)gh 'rɔː.li, 'rɑː-, 'ræl.i (US) 'rɑː.li, 'rɔː-
Note: The family of the late Sir Walter Raleigh pronounced /'rɔː.li (US) 'rɑː-, rɔː-/. Raleigh bicycles are generally called /'ræl.i/ in Britain and /'rɑː.li/ in the United States. When used as the name of a ship, the British English pronunciation is /'ræl.i/.
rallentand|o ˌræl.en'tæn.d|əʊ, -ən'-, -ɪn'- (US) ˌrɑː.lən'tɑːn.d|oʊ **-os** -əʊz (US) -oʊz **-i** -i
rall|y 'ræl|.i **-ies** -iz **-ying** -i.ɪŋ **-ied** -id **'rally ˌdriver**
rallycross 'ræl.i.krɒs (US) -krɑːs
Ralph rælf, reɪf
Ralph Cross ˌrɑːlf'krɒs, ˌrælf- (US) ˌrælf'krɑːs
Ralston 'rɔːl.stᵊn
ram (R) ræm **-s** -z **-ming** -ɪŋ **-med** -d **-mer/s** -əʳ/z (US) -ɚ/z
RAM ræm
Ramad(h)an ˌræm.ə'dæn, ˌrɑː.mə'-, -'dɑːn, '--- (US) ˌræm.ə'dɑːn, ˌrɑː.mə'-
Ramage 'ræm.ɪdʒ
Rama(h) 'rɑː.mə
Ramallah rə'mɑː.lə, -'mæl-
Ramaphosa ˌræm.ə'pəʊ.zə (US) -'poʊ-
Ramayana rɑː'maɪ.ə.nə, rə-, -'mɑː- (US) rɑː'mɑː.jə-
Rambert 'rɑ̃ːm.beə, -'- (US) rɑːm'ber
rambl|e 'ræm.bl̩ **-es** -z **-ing** -ɪŋ, 'ræm.blɪŋ **-ed** -d
rambler (R) 'ræm.bləʳ (US) -blɚ **-s** -z
rambling 'ræm.blɪŋ, -bl̩.ɪŋ **-s** -z **-ly** -li
Rambo 'ræm.bəʊ (US) -boʊ
Ramboesque ˌræm.bəʊ'esk (US) -boʊ'-
Rambouillet ˌrɑ̃ːm.buː'jeɪ, -'-- (US) ˌræm.bui'jeɪ
rambunctious ræm'bʌŋk.ʃəs **-ly** -li **-ness** -nəs, -nɪs
rambutan ræm'buː.tᵊn; ˌræm.bʊ'tæn, -'tɑːn (US) ræm'buː.tᵊn **-s** -z
ramekin, ramequin 'ræm.ɪ.kɪn, '-ə-, '-kɪn (US) '-ə.kɪn **-s** -z
Rameses 'ræm.ɪ.siːz, '-ə-
ramification ˌræm.ɪ.fɪ'keɪ.ʃᵊn, ˌ-ə- **-s** -z
rami|fy 'ræm.ɪ|.faɪ, '-ə- **-fies** -faɪz **-fying** -faɪ.ɪŋ **-fied** -faɪd
Ramillies 'ræm.ɪ.liz
Ramirez rə'mɪə.rez (US) -'mɪr.ez, -'miː.reɪs, rɑː'mɪr.ez, -'miː.reθ
ramjet 'ræm.dʒet **-s** -s

Ramos 'rɑː.mɒs (US) 'reɪ.moʊs, rɑː'moʊs
ramp ræmp **-s** -s **-ing** -ɪŋ **-ed** -t
rampag|e (*n.*) 'ræm.peɪdʒ, -'- (US) 'ræm.peɪdʒ **-es** -ɪz (*v.*) ræm'peɪdʒ, '-- **-es** -ɪz **-ing** -ɪŋ **-ed** -d
rampageous ræm'peɪ.dʒəs **-ly** -li **-ness** -nəs, -nɪs
rampant 'ræm.pənt **-ly** -li
rampart 'ræm.pɑːt, -pət (US) -pɑːrt, -pɚt **-s** -s
rampion 'ræm.pi.ən **-s** -z
Rampling 'ræm.plɪŋ
Ramprakash 'ræm.prə.kæʃ
Rampton 'ræm*p*.tən
ram-raid 'ræm.reɪd **-s** -z **-er/s** -əʳ/z (US) -ɚ/z **-ing** -ɪŋ
ramrod 'ræm.rɒd (US) -rɑːd **-s** -z
Ramsaran 'rɑːm*p*.sᵊr.ən
Ramsay 'ræm.zi
Ramsbottom 'ræmzˌbɒt.əm (US) -ˌbɑː.t̬əm
Ramsden 'ræmz.dən
Ramses 'ræm.siːz
Ramsey 'ræm.zi
Ramsgate 'ræmz.geɪt, -gɪt
ramshackle 'ræmˌʃæk.l̩
ran (*from* **run**) ræn
Ranariddh ˌræn.ə'rɪt
rance ræn*t*s
Rance *surname:* rɑːn*t*s (US) ræn*t*s
ranch rɑːn*t*ʃ, ræn*t*ʃ (US) ræn*t*ʃ **-es** -ɪz **-ing** -ɪŋ **-ed** -t **-er/s** -əʳ/z (US) -ɚ/z **'ranch ˌhouse**
ranchero rɑːn'tʃeə.rəʊ, ræn- (US) ræn'tʃer.oʊ **-s** -z
rancid 'ræn*t*.sɪd **-ness** -nəs, -nɪs
rancidity ræn'sɪd.ə.ti, -ɪ.ti (US) -ə.t̬i
rancorous 'ræŋ.kᵊr.əs **-ly** -li
ranco(u)r 'ræŋ.kəʳ (US) -kɚ
rand (R) *South African money and region:* rænd, rɑːnd, rɑːnt, rɒnt (US) rænd, rɑːnd, rɑːnt *strip, border:* rænd **-s** -z
Randall, Randell 'ræn.dᵊl
Randalstown 'ræn.dᵊlz.taʊn
R and B ˌɑːʳ.ᵊn*d*'biː, -ᵊm'- (US) ˌɑːr-
R and D ˌɑːʳ.ᵊn*d*'diː (US) ˌɑːr-
Randi 'ræn.di
Randle 'ræn.dl̩
Randolph 'ræn.dɒlf, -dᵊlf (US) -dɑːlf, -dᵊlf
random 'ræn.dəm **-ly** -li **-ness** -nəs, -nɪs
random-access ˌræn.dəm'æk.ses *stress shift:* ˌrandom-access 'memory
randomization, -isa- ˌræn.dəm.aɪ'zeɪ.ʃᵊn, -ɪ'- (US) -ɪ'-
randomiz|e, -is|e 'ræn.də.maɪz **-es** -ɪz **-ing** -ɪŋ **-ed** -d
R and R ˌɑːʳ.ᵊn*d*'ɑːʳ (US) ˌɑːr.ᵊn*d*'ɑːr
rand|y (R) 'ræn.d|i **-ier** -i.əʳ (US) -i.ɚ **-iest** -i.ɪst, -i.əst **-ily** -ɪ.li, -ᵊl.i **-iness** -ɪ.nəs, -ɪ.nɪs
ranee (R) 'rɑː.niː, ˌ-'- (US) 'rɑː.niː **-s** -z
Ranelagh 'ræn.ɪ.lə, -ᵊl.ə, -ɔː (US) -ᵊl.ə
rang (*from* **ring**) ræŋ
rang|e reɪndʒ **-es** -ɪz **-ing** -ɪŋ **-ed** -d
range-finder 'reɪndʒˌfaɪn.dəʳ (US) -dɚ **-s** -z
ranger (R) 'reɪn.dʒəʳ (US) -dʒɚ **-s** -z
Rangoon ˌræŋ'guːn (US) ˌræn-, ˌræŋ- *stress shift:* ˌRangoon 'streets
rang|y 'reɪn.dʒ|i **-ier** -i.əʳ (US) -i.ɚ **-iest** -i.ɪst, -i.əst **-iness** -ɪ.nəs, -ɪ.nɪs
rani 'rɑː.niː, ˌ-'- (US) 'rɑː.niː **-s** -z
rank (R) ræŋk **-s** -s **-ing** -ɪŋ **-ed** -t **-ly** -li **-ness** -nəs, -nɪs ˌ**rank and 'file**
Rankin(e) 'ræŋ.kɪn
rankl|e 'ræŋ.kl̩ **-es** -z **-ing** -ɪŋ, 'ræŋ.klɪŋ **-ed** -d
Rannoch 'ræn.ək, -əx (US) -ək
Ranoe 'rɑː.nəʊ (US) -noʊ
ransack 'ræn.sæk **-s** -s **-ing** -ɪŋ **-ed** -t **-er/s** -əʳ/z (US) -ɚ/z
ransom (R) 'ræn*t*.sᵊm **-s** -z **-ing** -ɪŋ **-ed** -d **-er/s** -əʳ/z (US) -ɚ/z
Ransome 'ræn*t*.səm
rant rænt **-s** -s **-ing/ly** -ɪŋ/li (US) 'ræn.t̬ɪŋ/li **-ed** -ɪd (US) 'ræn.t̬ɪd **-er/s** -əʳ/z (US) 'ræn.t̬ɚ/z
Rantzen 'rænt.sᵊn
Ranulph 'ræn.ʌlf, -ᵊlf
ranuncul|us rə'nʌŋ.kjə.l|əs, ræn'ʌŋ-, -kjʊ- (US) rə'nʌŋ- **-uses** -ə.sɪz **-i** -aɪ
Ranworth 'ræn.wəθ, -wɜːθ (US) -wɚθ, -wɜːθ
rap ræp **-s** -s **-ping** -ɪŋ **-ped** -t **-per/s** -əʳ/z (US) -ɚ/z
rapacious rə'peɪ.ʃəs **-ly** -li **-ness** -nəs, -nɪs
rapacity rə'pæs.ə.ti, -ɪ.ti (US) -ə.t̬i
rap|e reɪp **-es** -s **-ing** -ɪŋ **-ed** -t **-ist/s** -ɪst/s
Raphael *angel:* 'ræf.eɪ.əl; ˌræf.ɑː'el; 'ræf.eɪl; 'reɪ.fi.əl; *and in Jewish usage:* 'reɪ.fᵊl (US) 'ræf.i.əl; ˌrɑː.fi'el; 'reɪ.fi.el *modern name:* 'reɪ.fᵊl, 'ræf.eɪl *Italian artist:* 'ræf.eɪ.əl, -fi.əl, -feɪl (US) 'ræf.i.əl; ˌrɑː.fi'el; 'reɪ.fi.el
rapid 'ræp.ɪd **-est** -ɪst, -əst **-ly** -li **-ness** -nəs, -nɪs **-s** -z ˌ**rapid 'eye ˌmovement**; ˌ**rapid 'transit**
rapid-fire ˌræp.ɪd'faɪəʳ (US) -'faɪɚ *stress shift:* ˌrapid-fire 'shooting
rapidity rə'pɪd.ə.ti, ræp'ɪd-, -ɪ.ti (US) rə'pɪd.ə.t̬i
rapier 'reɪ.pi.əʳ (US) -pi.ɚ, '-pjɚ **-s** -z
rapine 'ræp.aɪn, -ɪn (US) -ɪn
rapparee ˌræp.ᵊr'iː (US) -ə'riː **-s** -z
rappel (US) ræp'el **-s** (US) -z **-ling** (US) -ɪŋ **-led** (US) -d
rapport ræp'ɔːʳ, rə'pɔːʳ; 'ræp.ɔːʳ (US) ræp'ɔːr, rə'pɔːr
rapporteur ˌræp.ɔː'tɜːʳ (US) -ɔːr'tɜː **-s** -z
rapprochement ræp'rɒʃ.mɑ̃ːŋ, -'rəʊʃ- (US) ˌræp.rɔːʃ'mɑ̃ːŋ, -roʊʃ'- **-s** -z
rapscallion ræp'skæl.jən, '-i.ən (US) '-jən **-s** -z
rapt ræpt
rapture 'ræp.tʃəʳ (US) -tʃɚ **-s** -z **-d** -d
rapturous 'ræp.tʃᵊr.əs **-ly** -li
Rapunzel rə'pʌn.zᵊl
Raquel rə'kel, ræk'el
rara avis ˌrɑː.rə'æv.ɪs, ˌreə-, -'eɪ.vɪs (US) ˌrer.ə'eɪ.vɪs
rare reəʳ (US) rer **-r** -əʳ (US) -ɚ **-st** -ɪst, -əst **-ly** -li **-ness** -nəs, -nɪs ˌ**rare 'earth**
rarebit 'reə.bɪt (US) 'rer- **-s** -s
Note: The pronunciation /'ræb.ɪt/ is very often used in British English in the phrase **Welsh rarebit**.
rarefaction ˌreə.rɪ'fæk.ʃᵊn, -rə'- (US) ˌrer.ə'-
rarefication ˌreə.rɪ.fɪ'keɪ.ʃᵊn, -rə- (US) ˌrer.ə-
rare|fy 'reə.rɪ|.faɪ, -rə- (US) 'rer.ə- **-fies** -faɪz **-fying** -faɪ.ɪŋ **-fied** -faɪd
raring (*adj.*) 'reə.rɪŋ (US) 'rer.ɪŋ
rarit|y 'reə.rə.t|i, -ɪ.t|i (US) 'rer.ə.t̬|i **-ies** -iz
Rarotonga ˌreə.rəʊ'tɒŋ.gə, ˌrær.əʊ'- (US) ˌrɑːr.oʊ'tɔːŋ.gə, ˌrer.ə'-
Ras al Khaimah ˌrɑːs.æl'kaɪ.mə
rascal 'rɑː.skᵊl (US) 'ræs.kᵊl **-s** -z
rascalit|y rɑː'skæl.ə.t|i, -ɪ.t|i (US) ræs'kæl.ə.t̬|i **-ies** -iz
rascally 'rɑː.skᵊl.i (US) 'ræs.kᵊl-
ras|e reɪz **-es** -ɪz **-ing** -ɪŋ **-ed** -d
rash ræʃ **-es** -ɪz **-er** -əʳ (US) -ɚ **-est** -ɪst, -əst **-ly** -li **-ness** -nəs, -nɪs
rasher 'ræʃ.əʳ (US) -ɚ **-s** -z
Rashid ræʃ'iːd (US) ræʃ-, rɑː'ʃiːd
rasp rɑːsp (US) ræsp **-s** -s **-ing** -ɪŋ **-ed** -t
raspberr|y 'rɑːz.bᵊr|.i, 'rɑːs- (US) 'ræzˌber|.i, -bɚ- **-ies** -iz
Rasputin ræs'pjuː.tɪn, -'puː- (US) -'pjuː-
rasp|y 'rɑː.sp|i (US) 'ræsp|.i **-iness** -ɪ.nəs, -ɪ.nɪs
Rasselas 'ræs.ɪ.ləs (US) '-ə-, -læs
Rasta 'ræs.tə (US) 'rɑː.stə, 'ræs.tə **-s** -z
Rastafarian ˌræs.tə'feə.ri.ən (US) ˌrɑː.stə'fer.i-, ˌræs.tə'-, -'fɑːr- **-s** -z **-ism** -ɪ.zᵊm
Rasta|man 'ræs.tə|.mæn (US) 'rɑː.stə-, 'ræs.tə- **-men** -men
rat ræt **-s** -s **-ting** -ɪŋ (US) 'ræt̬.ɪŋ **-ted** -ɪd (US) 'ræt̬.ɪd **'rat ˌrace**; **'rat ˌtrap**
rata 'reɪ.tə (US) 'rɑː.t̬ə **-s** -z
rata (*in* **pro rata**) 'rɑː.tə, 'reɪ- (US) -t̬ə
ratability ˌreɪ.tə'bɪl.ə.ti, -ɪ.ti (US) -t̬ə'bɪl.ə.t̬i
ratab|le 'reɪ.tə.b|l̩ (US) -t̬ə- **-ly** -li
ratafia ˌræt.ə'fiː.ə **-s** -z
rataplan ˌræt.ə'plæn (US) 'ræt̬.ə.plæn
rat-a-tat ˌræt.ə'tæt, '--- (US) ˌræt̬-, '---

ratatouille ˌræt.əˈtwiː, -ˈtuː.i (US) -ˈtuː.i, ˌrɑː.tɑːˈ-
ratbag ˈræt.bæg **-s** -z
rat-catcher ˈrætˌkætʃ.əʳ (US) -ɚ **-s** -z
ratchet ˈrætʃ.ɪt **-s** -s **-ing -ed**
Ratcliff(e) ˈræt.klɪf
rat|e reɪt **-es** -s **-ing** -ɪŋ (US) ˈreɪ.t̬ɪŋ **-ed** -ɪd (US) ˈreɪ.t̬ɪd ˌ**rate of ex**ˈ**change**
rateab|le ˈreɪ.tə.b|l̩ (US) -t̬ə- **-ly** -li ˌ**rateable** ˈ**value**
rate-cap ˈreɪt.kæp **-s** -s **-ping** -ɪŋ **-ped** -t
ratel ˈreɪ.tᵊl, ˈrɑː-, -tel (US) ˈreɪ.t̬ᵊl, ˈrɑː- **-s** -z
ratepayer ˈreɪtˌpeɪ.əʳ (US) -ɚ **-s** -z
Rath ræθ
Rathbone ˈræθ.bəʊn, -bən (US) -boʊn, -bən
rather (*adv.*) ˈrɑː.ðəʳ (US) ˈræð.ɚ *British only, old-fashioned:* ˌrɑːˈðɜːʳ
Rather ˈræð.əʳ (US) ˈræð.ɚ
Rathfarnham ræθˈfɑː.nəm (US) -ˈfɑːr-
Rathlin ˈræθ.lɪn
ratification ˌræt.ɪ.fɪˈkeɪ.ʃᵊn, ˌ-ə- (US) ˌræt̬.ə- **-s** -z
rati|fy ˈræt.ɪ|.faɪ, ˈ-ə- (US) ˈræt̬.ə- **-fies** -faɪz **-fying** -faɪ.ɪŋ **-fied** -faɪd **-fier/s** -faɪ.əʳ/z (US) -faɪ.ɚ/z
rating ˈreɪ.tɪŋ (US) -t̬ɪŋ **-s** -z
ratio ˈreɪ.ʃi.əʊ (US) -oʊ, ˈ-ʃoʊ **-s** -z
ratioci|nate ˌræt.iˈɒs.ɪ|.neɪt, ˌræʃ-, -ˈəʊ.sɪ-, -sə- (US) ˌræʃ.iˈɑː.sə- **-nates** -neɪts **-nating** -neɪ.tɪŋ (US) -neɪ.t̬ɪŋ **-nated** -neɪ.tɪd (US) -neɪ.t̬ɪd
ratiocination ˌræt.i.ɒs.ɪˈneɪ.ʃᵊn, ˌræʃ-, -əʊ.sɪˈ-, -səˈ- (US) ˌræʃ.i.ɑː.səˈ- **-s** -z
ratio decidendi ˌræt.i.əʊˌdeɪ.sɪˈden.di (US) ˌræt̬.i.oʊˌ-, ˌrɑː.t̬i-
ratio legis ˌræt.i.əʊˈleɪ.gɪs (US) ˌræt̬.i.oʊˈleg.ɪs, ˌrɑː.t̬i-
ration ˈræʃ.ᵊn (US) ˈræʃ.ᵊn, ˈreɪ- **-s** -z **-ing** -ɪŋ **-ed** -d
rational ˈræʃ.ᵊn.ᵊl, ˈ-nᵊl **-ly** -i
rationale ˌræʃ.əˈnɑːl, -ˈnæl, -ˈnɑː.leɪ (US) -əˈnæl **-s** -z
rational|ism ˈræʃ.ᵊn.ᵊl|.ɪ.zᵊm, ˈ-nᵊl- **-ist/s** -ɪst/s
rationalistic ˌræʃ.ᵊn.ᵊlˈɪs.tɪk, ˌ-nᵊlˈ- **-ally** -ᵊl.i, -li
rationality ˌræʃ.ᵊnˈæl.ə.ti, -ɪ.ti (US) -ə.t̬i
rationalization, -isa- ˌræʃ.ᵊn.ᵊl.aɪˈzeɪ.ʃᵊn, ˌ-nᵊl-, -ɪˈ- (US) -ɪˈ-
rationaliz|e, -is|e ˈræʃ.ᵊn.ᵊl.aɪz, ˈ-nᵊl- (US) -ᵊn.ᵊ.laɪz, ˈ-nə- **-es** -ɪz **-ing** -ɪŋ **-ed** -d
Ratisbon ˈræt.ɪz.bɒn, -ɪs-, -əz-, -əs- (US) -ɪz.bɑːn, -ɪs-
ratline ˈræt.lɪn **-s** -z
Ratner ˈræt.nəʳ (US) -nɚ **-'s** -z
rat-race ˈræt.reɪs
rat-tail ˈræt.teɪl **-s** -z **-ed** -d
rattan rəˈtæn, rætˈæn **-s** -z
Rattigan ˈræt.ɪ.gən, ˈ-ə- (US) ˈræt̬-
rattl|e (R) ˈræt.l̩ (US) ˈræt̬- **-es** -z **-ing** -ɪŋ, ˈræt.lɪŋ **-ed** -d **-er/s** -əʳ/z (US) -ɚ/z, ˈræt.ləʳ/z (US) -lɚ/z
rattlesnake ˈræt.l̩.sneɪk (US) ˈræt̬- **-s** -s
rattling ˈræt.lɪŋ, -l̩.ɪŋ (US) ˈræt.lɪŋ, ˈræt̬.l̩.ɪŋ
ratt|y (R) ˈræt|.i (US) ˈræt̬- **-ier** -i.əʳ (US) -i.ɚ **-iest** -i.ɪst, -i.əst **-ily** -ɪ.li, -ᵊl.i **-iness** -ɪ.nəs, -ɪ.nɪs
raucous ˈrɔː.kəs (US) ˈrɑː-, ˈrɔː- **-ly** -li **-ness** -nəs, -nɪs
raunch|y ˈrɔːn.tʃ|i (US) ˈrɑːn.tʃ|i, ˈrɔːn- **-ier** -i.əʳ (US) -i.ɚ **-iest** -i.ɪst, -i.əst **-ily** -ɪ.li, -ᵊl.i **-iness** -ɪ.nəs, -ɪ.nɪs
Raunds rɔːn*d*z (US) rɑːn*d*z, rɔːn*d*z
Rauschenberg ˈraʊ.ʃᵊn.bɜːg (US) -bɝːg
ravag|e ˈræv.ɪdʒ **-es** -ɪz **-ing** -ɪŋ **-ed** -d **-er/s** -əʳ/z (US) -ɚ/z
Ravana rəˈvɑː.nə (US) ˈrɑː.və-; rəˈvɑː-
rav|e reɪv **-es** -z **-ing/s** -ɪŋ/z **-ed** -d
ravel ˈræv.ᵊl **-s** -z **-(l)ing** -ɪŋ **-(l)ed** -d
Ravel *French composer:* rævˈel (US) rəˈvel, rɑː-
ravelin ˈræv.ᵊl.ɪn **-s** -z
raven (R) (*n.*) ˈreɪ.vᵊn **-s** -z
raven (*v.*) ˈræv.ᵊn **-s** -z **-ing** -ɪŋ **-ed** -d
Ravening ˈreɪ.vᵊn.ɪŋ, ˈræv.ᵊn-
Ravenna rəˈven.ə, rævˈen- (US) rə-, rɑː-
ravenous ˈræv.ᵊn.əs, -ɪ.nəs (US) -ᵊn.əs **-ly** -li **-ness** -nəs, -nɪs
Ravensbourne ˈreɪ.vᵊnz.bɔːn (US) -bɔːrn
Ravenshead ˈreɪ.vᵊnz.hed
Ravenshoe ˈreɪ.vᵊnz.həʊ (US) -hoʊ
raver ˈreɪ.vəʳ (US) -vɚ **-s** -z
Raverat ˈrɑː.vᵊr.ɑː (US) -və.rɑː
rave-up ˈreɪv.ʌp **-s** -s
ravin ˈræv.ɪn
ravine rəˈviːn **-s** -z
raving ˈreɪ.vɪŋ **-s** -z
ravioli ˌræv.iˈəʊ.li (US) -ˈoʊ-
ravish ˈræv.ɪʃ **-es** -ɪz **-ing/ly** -ɪŋ/li **-ed** -t **-er/s** -əʳ/z (US) -ɚ/z **-ment** -mənt
raw rɔː (US) rɑː, rɔː **-er** -əʳ (US) -ɚ **-est** -ɪst, -əst **-ly** -li **-ness** -nəs, -nɪs ˌ**raw** ˈ**deal**; ˌ**raw ma**ˈ**terial**
Rawalpindi ˌrɑː.wəlˈpɪn.di, ˌrɔːlˈpɪn- (US) ˌrɑː.wəlˈ-
Rawdon ˈrɔː.dᵊn (US) ˈrɑː-, ˈrɔː-
rawhid|e ˈrɔː.haɪd (US) ˈrɑː-, ˈrɔː- **-es** -z **-ing** -ɪŋ **-ed** -ɪd
Rawlings ˈrɔː.lɪŋz (US) ˈrɑː-, ˈrɔː-
Rawlins ˈrɔː.lɪnz (US) ˈrɑː-, ˈrɔː-
Rawlinson ˈrɔː.lɪn.sᵊn (US) ˈrɑː-, ˈrɔː-
Rawlplug® ˈrɔːl.plʌg (US) ˈrɑːl-, ˈrɔːl-
Rawmarsh ˈrɔː.mɑːʃ (US) ˈrɑː.mɑːrʃ, ˈrɔː-
Rawnsley ˈrɔːnz.li (US) ˈrɑːnz-, ˈrɔː-
Rawtenstall ˈrɒt.ᵊn.stɔːl, ˈrɔː.tᵊn- (US) ˈrɑː.tᵊn-, ˈrɔː-
ray (R) reɪ **-s** -z
Ray-Bans® ˈreɪ.bænz
Raybould ˈreɪ.bəʊld (US) -boʊld
Rayburn ˈreɪ.bɜːn (US) -bɝːn
Rayleigh ˈreɪ.li
Rayment ˈreɪ.mənt
Raymond ˈreɪ.mənd
Rayner ˈreɪ.nəʳ (US) -nɚ
Raynes reɪnz
Raynsford ˈreɪnz.fəd (US) -fɚd
rayon ˈreɪ.ɒn, -ən (US) -ɑːn
raz|e reɪz **-es** -ɪz **-ing** -ɪŋ **-ed** -d
razoo rəˈzuː (US) rə-, rɑː-
razor ˈreɪ.zəʳ (US) -zɚ **-s** -z ˈ**razor** ˌ**blade**
razorback ˈreɪ.zə.bæk (US) -zɚ- **-s** -s
razorbill ˈreɪ.zə.bɪl (US) -zɚ- **-s** -z
razor-blade ˈreɪ.zə.bleɪd (US) -zɚ- **-s** -z
razor-shell ˈreɪ.zə.ʃel (US) -zɚ- **-s** -z
razzamat(t)azz ˌræz.ə.məˈtæz, ˈræz.ə.mə.tæz (US) ˈræz.ə.mə.tæz
razzia ˈræz.i.ə **-s** -z
razzle ˈræz.l̩ ˌ**on the** ˈ**razzle**
razzle-dazzle ˌræz.l̩ˈdæz.l̩, ˈræz.l̩ˌdæz- (US) ˌræz.l̩ˈdæz-
razzmatazz ˌræz.məˈtæz, ˈ--- (US) ˈræz.mə.tæz
RC *(abbrev. for* **Roman Catholic***)* ˌɑːˈsiː; ˌrəʊ.mənˈkæθ.ᵊl.ɪk, -mənˈ-, ˈ-lɪk (US) ˌɑːr-; ˌroʊ.mənˈkæθ.ᵊl.ɪk, ˈ-lɪk
Rd *(abbrev. for* **Road***)* rəʊd (US) roʊd
re- *prefix denoting repetition:* ˌriː-, rɪ-, ri-, rə-

Note: Prefix. In compounds containing **re-** where the stem is free and the meaning is "again", it is normally pronounced /ˌriː-/, e.g. **re-read** /ˌriːˈriːd/. Many such compounds are likely to undergo stress shift, especially in adjectives derived from verbs, e.g. ˈ**rear**ˌ**range**, ˈ**rearranged** ˌ**furniture**. Attached to bound stems the pronunciation is normally /rɪ-, ri-/ or /rə-/, e.g. **refer** /rɪˈfɜːʳ (US) -ˈfɜːr/. There are exceptions; see individual entries.

re *note in Tonic Sol-fa:* reɪ **-s** -z
re (prep.) *with regard to:* riː
RE *(abbrev. for* **Religious Education***)* ˌɑːʳˈiː (US) ˌɑːr-
Rea reɪ, rɪə, riː
reach riːtʃ **-es** -ɪz **-ing** -ɪŋ **-ed** -t
reach-me-down ˈriːtʃ.mi.daʊn **-s** -z
react riˈækt **-s** -s **-ing** -ɪŋ **-ed** -ɪd
reactant riˈæk.tᵊnt (US) -tənt **-s** -s
reaction riˈæk.ʃᵊn **-s** -z
reactionar|y riˈæk.ʃᵊn.ᵊr|.i (US) -er- **-ies** -iz
reacti|vate riˈæk.tɪ|.veɪt, ˌriː-, -tə- (US) -tə- **-vates** -veɪts **-vating** -veɪ.tɪŋ (US) -veɪ.t̬ɪŋ **-vated** -veɪ.tɪd (US) -veɪ.t̬ɪd
reactivation ˌriː.æk.tɪˈveɪ.ʃᵊn, riˌæk-, -təˈ- (US) riˌæk-

reactive ri'æk.tɪv **-ly** -li
reactor ri'æk.təʳ (US) -tɚ **-s** -z
read (R) *present tense:* riːd **-s** -z **-ing** -ɪŋ *past tense:* red
readability ˌriː.də'bɪl.ə.ti, -ɪ.ti (US) -ə.t̬i
readab|le 'riː.də.b|l̩ **-ly** -li **-leness** -l̩.nəs, -nɪs
re-address ˌriː.ə'dres **-es** -ɪz **-ing** -ɪŋ **-ed** -t
Reade riːd
reader (R) 'riː.dəʳ (US) -dɚ **-s** -z
readership 'riː.də.ʃɪp (US) -dɚ- **-s** -s
readies 'red.iz
reading (*n.*) 'riː.dɪŋ **-s** -z
Reading 'red.ɪŋ
readjust ˌriː.ə'dʒʌst **-s** -s **-ing** -ɪŋ **-ed** -ɪd
readjustment ˌriː.ə'dʒʌst.mənt **-s** -s
readmission ˌriː.əd'mɪʃ.ᵊn **-s** -z
read|mit ˌriː.əd'mɪt **-mits** -'mɪts **-mitting** -'mɪt.ɪŋ (US) -'mɪt̬.ɪŋ **-mitted** -'mɪt.ɪd (US) -'mɪt̬.ɪd **-mittance** -'mɪt.ᵊnts
readout 'riː.daʊt **-s** -s
read|y 'red|.i **-ier** -i.əʳ (US) -i.ɚ **-iest** -i.ɪst, -i.əst **-ily** -ɪ.li, -ᵊl.i **-iness** -ɪ.nəs, -ɪ.nɪs **-ies** -iz **-ying** -i.ɪŋ **-ied** -id ˌ**ready 'money**
ready-made ˌred.i'meɪd *stress shift:* ˌready-made 'meal
ready-to-wear ˌred.i.tə'weəʳ (US) -'wer, 'red.i.təˌwer *stress shift, British only:* ˌready-to-wear 'suit
reaffirm ˌriː.ə'fɜːm (US) -'fɝːm **-s** -z **-ing** -ɪŋ **-ed** -d
reafforest ˌriː.ə'fɒr.ɪst (US) -'fɔːr.ɪst **-s** -s **-ing** -ɪŋ **-ed** -ɪd
reafforestation ˌriː.əˌfɒr.ɪ'steɪ.ʃᵊn, -ə'- (US) -ˌfɔːr.ɪ'-
Reagan 'reɪ.gᵊn, 'riː-
Note: The former US president is normally /'reɪ-/.
Reaganomics ˌreɪ.gᵊn'ɒm.ɪks (US) -'ɑː.mɪks
reagent ˌriː'eɪ.dʒənt **-s** -s
real (*adj.*) rɪəl (US) riːl, 'riː.əl '**real eˌstate**; ˌ**real 'life**
real *monetary unit:* reɪ'ɑːl (US) reɪ'ɑːl; 'reɪ.əl **-s** -z
realia ri'eɪ.li.ə, -'ɑː- (US) ri'eɪ-; reɪ'ɑː-
realign ˌriː.ə'laɪn **-s** -z **-ing** -ɪŋ **-ed** -d **-ment/s** -mənt/s
real|ism 'rɪə.l|ɪ.zᵊm (US) 'riː-, 'riː.ə- **-ist/s** -ɪst/s
realistic ˌrɪə'lɪs.tɪk (US) ˌriː.ə'- **-ally** -ᵊl.i, -li
realit|y ri'æl.ə.t|i, -ɪ.t|i (US) -ə.t̬|i **-ies** -iz
realization, -isa- ˌrɪə.laɪ'zeɪ.ʃᵊn, -lɪ'- (US) ˌriː.ə.lɪ'- **-s** -z
realiz|e, -is|e 'rɪə.laɪz (US) 'riː.ə- **-es** -ɪz **-ing** -ɪŋ **-ed** -d **-able** -ə.bl̩
real-life ˌrɪəl'laɪf (US) ˌriː.əl'- *stress shift:* ˌreal-life 'drama
reallo|cate ri'æl.əl.keɪt **-cates** -keɪts **-cating** -keɪ.tɪŋ (US) -keɪ.t̬ɪŋ **-cated** -keɪ.tɪd (US) -keɪ.t̬ɪd
reallocation ˌriː.æl.ə'keɪ.ʃᵊn, riˌæl- (US) ˌriː.æl-
really 'rɪə.li (US) 'riː.ə-, 'riː.li
realm relm **-s** -z
realpolitik reɪ'ɑːl.pɒl.ɪˌtiːk, -ə- (US) -poʊ.lɪˌ- **-s** -s
real-time 'rɪəl.taɪm (US) 'riː.əl-
realtor (R®) 'riːl.təʳ, 'rɪəl-, -tɔːʳ (US) 'riː.əl.t̬ɚ, -tɔːr **-s** -z
realty 'rɪəl.ti (US) 'riː.əl.t̬i
ream riːm **-s** -z **-ing** -ɪŋ **-ed** -d
reamer 'riː.məʳ (US) -mɚ **-s** -z
reap riːp **-s** -s **-ing** -ɪŋ **-ed** -t **-er/s** -əʳ/z (US) -ɚ/z
reappear ˌriː.ə'pɪəʳ (US) -'pɪr **-s** -z **-ing** -ɪŋ **-ed** -d
reappearanc|e ˌriː.ə'pɪə.rᵊnts (US) -'pɪr.ᵊnts **-es** -ɪz
reapplication ˌriː.æp.lɪ'keɪ.ʃᵊn, riˌæp-, -lə'- (US) ˌriː.æp- **-s** -z
reappl|y ˌriː.ə'pl|aɪ **-ies** -aɪz **-ying** -aɪ.ɪŋ **-ied** -aɪd
reap|point ˌriː.ə|'pɔɪnt **-points** -'pɔɪnts **-pointing** -'pɔɪn.tɪŋ (US) -'pɔɪn.t̬ɪŋ **-pointed** -'pɔɪn.tɪd (US) -'pɔɪn.t̬ɪd **-pointment/s** -'pɔɪnt.mənt/s
reappraisal ˌriː.ə'preɪ.zᵊl **-s** -z
reapprais|e ˌriː.ə'preɪz **-es** -ɪz **-ing** -ɪŋ **-ed** -d
rear rɪəʳ (US) rɪr **-s** -z **-ing** -ɪŋ **-ed** -d ˌ**bring up the 'rear**
rear-admiral ˌrɪəʳ'æd.mᵊr.ᵊl, -mɪ.rᵊl (US) ˌrɪr- **-s** -z
rearguard 'rɪə.gɑːd (US) 'rɪr.gɑːrd **-s** -z ˌ**rearguard 'action**
rearm ˌriː'ɑːm (US) -'ɑːrm **-s** -z **-ing** -ɪŋ **-ed** -d
rearmament ri'ɑː.mə.mənt, ˌriː- (US) -'ɑːr-
rearmost 'rɪə.məʊst (US) 'rɪr.moʊst
rearrang|e ˌriː.ə'reɪndʒ **-es** -ɪz **-ing** -ɪŋ **-ed** -d **-ement/s** -mənt/s
rearview ˌrɪə'vjuː (US) ˌrɪr- *stress shift, see compound:* ˌ**rearview 'mirror**
rearward 'rɪə.wəd (US) 'rɪr.wɚd **-s** -z
reason 'riː.zᵊn **-s** -z **-ing/s** -ɪŋ/z **-ed** -d **-er/s** -əʳ/z (US) -ɚ/z
reasonab|le 'riː.zᵊn.ə.b|l̩ **-ly** -li **-leness** -l̩.nəs, -nɪs
reassembl|e ˌriː.ə'sem.bl̩ **-es** -z **-ing** -ɪŋ, ˌriː.ə'sem.blɪŋ **-ed** -d
reas|sert ˌriː.ə|'sɜːt (US) -'sɝːt **-serts** -'sɜːts (US) -'sɝːts **-serting** -'sɜː.tɪŋ (US) -'sɝː.t̬ɪŋ **-serted** -'sɜː.tɪd (US) -'sɝː.t̬ɪd
reassess ˌriː.ə'ses **-es** -ɪz **-ing** -ɪŋ **-ed** -t **-ment/s** -mənt/s
reassign ˌriː.ə'saɪn **-s** -z **-ing** -ɪŋ **-ed** -d
reassuranc|e ˌriː.ə'ʃʊə.rᵊnts, -'ʃɔː- (US) -'ʃʊr.ᵊnts, -'ʃɝː- **-es** -ɪz
reassur|e ˌriː.ə'ʃʊəʳ, -'ʃɔːʳ (US) -'ʃʊr, -'ʃɝː **-es** -z **-ing/ly** -ɪŋ/li **-ed** -d
Réaumur 'reɪ.əʊ.mjʊəʳ, -məʳ (US) -ə.mjʊr, '-oʊ-
reawaken ˌriː.ə'weɪ.kᵊn **-s** -z **-ing** -ɪŋ **-ed** -d
Reay reɪ
rebarbative rɪ'bɑː.bə.tɪv, rə- (US) rɪ'bɑːr.bə.t̬ɪv **-ly** -li
rebate (*n.*) *discount:* 'riː.beɪt; rɪ'beɪt, rə- (US) 'riː.beɪt **-s** -s
reba|te (*v.*) *deduct:* rɪ'beɪ|t, rə-; 'riː.beɪ|t (US) 'riː.beɪ|t, rɪ'beɪ|t **-tes** -t[s] **-ting** -tɪŋ (US) -t̬ɪŋ **-ted** -tɪd (US) -t̬ɪd
reba|te (*v.*) *in masonry and woodworking:* 'ræb.ɪ|t, 'riː.beɪ|t (US) 'riː.beɪ|t, 'ræb.ɪ|t **-tes** -ts **-ting** -tɪŋ (US) -t̬ɪŋ **-ted** -tɪd (US) -t̬ɪd
Rebecca rɪ'bek.ə, rə-
rebec(k) 'riː.bek, 'reb.ek **-s** -s
Rebekah rɪ'bek.ə, rə-
rebel (*n.*) 'reb.ᵊl **-s** -z
rebel (*v.*) rɪ'bel, rə- **-s** -z **-ling** -ɪŋ **-led** -d
rebellion rɪ'bel.i.ən, rə-, '-jən (US) '-jən **-s** -z
rebellious rɪ'bel.i.əs, rə- (US) rɪ'bel.jəs **-ly** -li **-ness** -nəs, -nɪs
rebirth ˌriː'bɜːθ (US) -'bɝːθ **-s** -s
rebirthing ˌriː'bɜː.θɪŋ (US) -'bɝː-
reborn ˌriː'bɔːn (US) -'bɔːrn
rebound (*n.*) 'riː.baʊnd **-s** -z ˌ**on the 'rebound**
rebound (*adj.*) *of books, etc.:* ˌriː'baʊn[d]
rebound (*v.*) rɪ'baʊnd, ˌriː- (US) 'riː.baʊnd-; ˌriː'baʊnd, rɪ- **-s** -z **-ing** -ɪŋ **-ed** -ɪd
rebrand ˌriː'brænd **-s** -z **-ing** -ɪŋ **-ed** -ɪ[d]
Rebuck 'riː.bʌk
rebuff rɪ'bʌf, rə- **-s** -s **-ing** -ɪŋ **-ed** -t
rebuild ˌriː'bɪld **-s** -z **-ing** -ɪŋ **rebuilt** ˌriː'bɪlt
rebuk|e rɪ'bjuːk, rə- **-es** -s **-ing/ly** -ɪŋ/[li] **-ed** -t
rebus 'riː.bəs **-es** -ɪz
re|but rɪ|'bʌt **-buts** -'bʌts **-butting** -'bʌt.ɪŋ (US) -'bʌt̬.ɪŋ **-butted** -'bʌt.ɪ[d] (US) -'bʌt̬.ɪd
rebuttable rɪ'bʌt|.ə.bl̩ (US) -'bʌt̬-
rebutt|al rɪ'bʌt|.ᵊl (US) -'bʌt̬- **-er/s** -əʳ/[z] (US) -ɚ/z
recalcitran|t rɪ'kæl.sɪ.trən|t, rə-, -sə- (US) -sɪ- **-ts** -ts **-ce** -ts
recall (*v.*) rɪ'kɔːl, rə- (US) rɪ-, rə-; 'riː.kɔ[ːl] -kɑːl **-s** -z **-ing** -ɪŋ **-ed** -d
recall (*n.*) rɪ'kɔːl, rə-; 'riː.kɔːl (US) 'riː.kɔːl, -kɑːl **-s** -z
re|cant rɪ|'kænt **-cants** -'kænts **-canti[ng]** -'kæn.tɪŋ (US) -'kæn.t̬ɪŋ **-canted** -'kæn.tɪd (US) -'kæn.t̬ɪd
recantation ˌriː.kæn'teɪ.ʃᵊn **-s** -z

recap (*n.*) *recapitulation:* ˈriː.kæp **-s** -s
recap (*v.*) *recapitulate:* ˈriː.kæp; ˌriːˈkæp, rɪ-, rə- (US) ˈriː.kæp **-s** -s **-ping** -ɪŋ **-ped** -t
recap (*n.*) *a recapped tyre:* ˈriː.kæp **-s** -s
recap (*v.*) *retread a tyre:* ˌriːˈkæp (US) ˌriːˈkæp, ˈ-- **-s** -s **-ping** -ɪŋ **-ped** -t
recapitu|late ˌriː.kəˈpɪt.jə|.leɪt, -jʊ-, -ˈpɪtʃ.ə-, ˈ-ʊ- (US) -ˈpɪtʃ.ə- **-lates** -leɪts **-lating** -leɪ.tɪŋ (US) -leɪ.t̬ɪŋ **-lated** -leɪ.tɪd (US) -leɪ.t̬ɪd
recapitulation ˌriː.kəˌpɪt.jəˈleɪ.ʃᵊn, -jʊˈ-, -ˌpɪtʃ.əˈ-, -ʊˈ- (US) -ˌpɪtʃ.əˈ- **-s** -z
recapitulatory ˌriː.kəˈpɪt.jə.lə.tᵊr.i, -jʊ-, -ˈpɪtʃ.ə-, ˈ-ʊ-, -leɪ- (US) -ˈpɪtʃ.ə.lə.tɔːr-
recapt|ure ˌriːˈkæp.tʃ|əʳ (US) -tʃ|ɚ **-ures** -əz (US) -ɚz **-uring** -ᵊr.ɪŋ **-ured** -əd (US) -ɚd
recast ˌriːˈkɑːst (US) -ˈkæst **-s** -s **-ing** -ɪŋ
recce (R) ˈrek.i **-s** -z **-ing** -ɪŋ **-(e)d** -d
reced|e rɪˈsiːd, rə-, ˌriː- **-es** -z **-ing** -ɪŋ **-ed** -ɪd
re|ceipt rɪ|ˈsiːt, rə- **-ceipts** -ˈsiːts **-ceipting** -ˈsiː.tɪŋ (US) -ˈsiː.t̬ɪŋ **-ceipted** -ˈsiː.tɪd (US) -ˈsiː.t̬ɪd
receiv|e rɪˈsiːv, rə- **-es** -z **-ing** -ɪŋ **-ed** -d **-er/s** -əʳ/z (US) -ɚ/z **-able** -ə.bl̩
Reˌceived pronunciˈation; ˌon the reˈceiving ˌend (of)
receivership rɪˈsiː.və.ʃɪp, rə- (US) -vɚ-
recency ˈriː.sᵊnt.si
recension rɪˈsent.ʃᵊn, rə- **-s** -z
recent ˈriː.sᵊnt **-ly** -li **-ness** -nəs, -nɪs
receptacle rɪˈsep.tə.kl̩, rə- **-s** -z
reception rɪˈsep.ʃᵊn, rə- **-s** -z
receptionist rɪˈsep.ʃᵊn.ɪst, rə- **-s** -s
receptive rɪˈsep.tɪv, rə- **-ly** -li **-ness** -nəs, -nɪs
receptivity ˌriː.sepˈtɪv.ə.ti, ˌrɪs.epˈ-, ˌres.epˈ-, -ɪ.ti (US) riːˌsepˈtɪv.ə.t̬i, rɪ-
receptor rɪˈsep.təʳ, rə- (US) -tɚ **-s** -z
recess rɪˈses, rə-; ˈriː.ses (US) ˈriː.ses; rɪˈses **-es** -ɪz
recession rɪˈseʃ.ᵊn, rə- **-s** -z
recessional rɪˈseʃ.ᵊn.ᵊl, rə- **-s** -z
recessive rɪˈses.ɪv, rə- **-ly** -li **-ness** -nəs, -nɪs
Rechabite ˈrek.ə.baɪt
recharg|e (*v.*) ˌriːˈtʃɑːdʒ, rɪ- (US) ˌriːˈtʃɑːrdʒ **-es** -ɪz **-ing** -ɪŋ **-ed** -d **-able** -ə.bl̩ **-er/s** -əʳ/z (US) -ɚ/z
recharge (*n.*) ˈriː.tʃɑːdʒ (US) -tʃɑːrdʒ
recherché rəˈʃeə.ʃeɪ (US) -ˈʃer-, --ˈ-
rechristen ˌriːˈkrɪs.ᵊn **-s** -z **-ing** -ɪŋ **-ed** -d
recidivism rɪˈsɪd.ɪ.vɪ.zᵊm, rə-, ˈ-ə- (US) ˈ-ə-
recidivist rɪˈsɪd.ɪ.vɪst, rə-, ˈ-ə- (US) ˈ-ə- **-s** -s
Recife resˈiː.fə (US) rəˈsiː-, resˈiː
recipe ˈres.ɪ.pi, ˈ-ə-, -piː **-s** -z
recipient rɪˈsɪp.i.ənt, rə- **-s** -s
reciproc|al rɪˈsɪp.rə.k|ᵊl, rə- **-als** -ᵊlz **-ally** -ᵊl.i, -li **-alness** -ᵊl.nəs, -nɪs
recipro|cate rɪˈsɪp.rə|.keɪt, rə- **-cates** -keɪts **-cating** -keɪ.tɪŋ (US) -keɪ.t̬ɪŋ **-cated** -keɪ.tɪd (US) -keɪ.t̬ɪd
reciprocation rɪˌsɪp.rəˈkeɪ.ʃᵊn, rə-
reciprocity ˌres.ɪˈprɒs.ə.ti, -ɪ.ti (US) -ˈprɑː.sə.t̬i
recis(s)ion rɪˈsɪʒ.ᵊn, rə-
recital rɪˈsaɪ.tᵊl, rə- (US) -t̬ᵊl **-s** -z
recitation ˌres.ɪˈteɪ.ʃᵊn **-s** -z
recitative (*adj.*) *relating to* **recital**: rɪˈsaɪ.tə.tɪv (US) ˈres.ɪ.teɪ.t̬ɪv; rɪˈsaɪ.t̬ə-
recitative (*n. adj.*) *in music:* ˌres.ɪ.təˈtiːv (US) -t̬əˈ- **-s** -z
re|cite rɪ|ˈsaɪt, rə- **-cites** -ˈsaɪts **-citing** -ˈsaɪ.tɪŋ (US) -ˈsaɪ.t̬ɪŋ **-cited** -ˈsaɪ.tɪd (US) -ˈsaɪ.t̬ɪd **-citer/s** -ˈsaɪ.təʳ/z (US) -ˈsaɪ.t̬ɚ/z
reck rek **-s** -s **-ing** -ɪŋ **-ed** -t
reckless ˈrek.ləs, -lɪs **-ly** -li **-ness** -nəs, -nɪs
reckon ˈrek.ᵊn **-s** -z **-ing/s** -ɪŋ/z **-ed** -d **-er/s** -əʳ/z (US) -ɚ/z
reclaim rɪˈkleɪm, ˌriː- **-s** -z **-ing** -ɪŋ **-ed** -d
reclaimable rɪˈkleɪ.mə.bl̩, ˌriː-
reclamation ˌrek.ləˈmeɪ.ʃᵊn **-s** -z
reclin|e rɪˈklaɪn, rə- **-es** -z **-ing** -ɪŋ **-ed** -d
recliner rɪˈklaɪ.nəʳ, rə- (US) -nɚ **-s** -z
reclus|e rɪˈkluːs, rə- (US) ˈrek.luːs; rɪˈkluːs **-es** -ɪz **-ive** -ɪv
recognition ˌrek.əgˈnɪʃ.ᵊn **-s** -z
recognizab|le, -isa- ˈrek.əg.naɪ.zə.b|l̩, ˌrek.əgˈnaɪ- (US) ˈrek.əg.naɪ- **-ly** -li
recognizanc|e, -isa- rɪˈkɒg.nɪ.zᵊnts, rə-, -ˈkɒn.ɪ- (US) -ˈkɑːg.nɪ-, -ˈkɑː- **-es** -ɪz
recogniz|e, -is|e ˈrek.əg.naɪz **-es** -ɪz **-ing** -ɪŋ **-ed** -d
recoil (*n.*) ˈriː.kɔɪl; rɪˈkɔɪl, rə- **-s** -z
recoil (*v.*) rɪˈkɔɪl, rə- **-s** -z **-ing** -ɪŋ **-ed** -d
recollect ˌrek.ᵊlˈekt, ˈ--- (US) ˌrek.əˈlekt **-s** -s **-ing** -ɪŋ **-ed** -ɪd
recollection ˌrek.ᵊlˈek.ʃᵊn (US) -əˈlek- **-s** -z
recombinant ˌriːˈkɒm.bɪ.nənt, rɪ-, rə-, -bə- (US) -ˈkɑːm.bə-
recommenc|e ˌriː.kəˈments, ˌrek.əˈ- **-es** -ɪz **-ing** -ɪŋ **-ed** -t
recommend ˌrek.əˈmend **-s** -z **-ing** -ɪŋ **-ed** -ɪd **-able** -ə.bl̩
recommendation ˌrek.ə.menˈdeɪ.ʃᵊn, -mənˈ- (US) -mənˈ- **-s** -z
recompens|e ˈrek.əm.pents **-es** -ɪz **-ing** -ɪŋ **-ed** -t
recompos|e ˌriː.kəmˈpəʊz (US) -ˈpoʊz **-es** -ɪz **-ing** -ɪŋ **-ed** -d
recon ˈriː.kɒn (US) -kɑːn
reconcilab|le ˈrek.ᵊn.saɪ.lə.b|l̩, ˌrek.ᵊnˈsaɪ- (US) ˌrek.ᵊnˈsaɪ- **-ly** -li
reconcil|e ˈrek.ᵊn.saɪl **-es** -z **-ing** -ɪŋ **-ed** -d **-er/s** -əʳ/z (US) -ɚ/z
reconciliation ˌrek.ᵊnˌsɪl.iˈeɪ.ʃᵊn **-s** -z
recondite ˈrek.ᵊn.daɪt; rɪˈkɒn-, rə- (US) ˈrek.ᵊn-; rɪˈkɑːn-, rə-
recondition ˌriː.kᵊnˈdɪʃ.ᵊn **-s** -z **-ing** -ɪŋ **-ed** -d
reconduct ˌriː.kᵊnˈdʌkt **-s** -s **-ing** -ɪŋ **-ed** -ɪd
reconnaissanc|e rɪˈkɒn.ɪ.sᵊnts, rə-, ˈ-ə- (US) -ˈkɑː.nə-, -zᵊnts **-es** -ɪz
reconnoit|er ˌrek.əˈnɔɪ.t|əʳ (US) ˌriː.kəˈnɔɪ.t̬|ɚ, ˌrek.əˈ- **-ers** -əz (US) -ɚz **-ering** -ᵊr.ɪŋ **-ered** -əd (US) -ɚd
reconnoit|re ˌrek.əˈnɔɪ.t|əʳ (US) ˌriː.kəˈnɔɪ.t̬|ɚ, ˌrek.əˈ- **-res** -əz (US) -ɚz **-ring** -ᵊr.ɪŋ **-red** -əd (US) -ɚd
reconqu|er ˌriːˈkɒŋ.k|əʳ (US) -ˈkɑːŋ.k|ɚ **-ers** -əz (US) -ɚz **-ering** -ᵊr.ɪŋ **-ered** -əd (US) -ɚd
reconquest ˌriːˈkɒŋ.kwest (US) -ˈkɑːŋ- **-s** -s
reconsid|er ˌriː.kᵊnˈsɪd|.əʳ (US) -ɚ **-ers** -əz (US) -ɚz **-ering** -ᵊr.ɪŋ **-ered** -əd (US) -ɚz
reconsideration ˌriː.kᵊnˌsɪd.ᵊrˈeɪ.ʃᵊn (US) -əˈreɪ-
reconstitu|te ˌriːˈkɒn.stɪ.tjuː|t, -stə-, -tʃuː|t (US) -ˈkɑːn.stə.tuː|t, -tjuː|t **-tes** -ts **-ting** -tɪŋ (US) -t̬ɪŋ **-ted** -tɪd (US) -t̬ɪd
reconstitution ˌriːˌkɒnt.stɪˈtjuː.ʃᵊn, -stəˈ-, -ˈtʃuː- (US) -ˌkɑːnt.stəˈtuː-, -ˈtjuː- **-s** -z
reconstruct ˌriː.kᵊnˈstrʌkt **-s** -s **-ing** -ɪŋ **-ed** -ɪd **-ive** -ɪv
reconstruction ˌriː.kᵊnˈstrʌk.ʃᵊn **-s** -z
reconven|e ˌriː.kənˈviːn **-es** -z **-ing** -ɪŋ **-ed** -d
reconversion ˌriː.kᵊnˈvɜː.ʃᵊn, -ʒᵊn (US) -ˈvɝː.ʒᵊn, -ʃᵊn **-s** -z
recon|vert ˌriː.kᵊn|ˈvɜːt (US) -ˈvɝːt **-verts** -ˈvɜːts (US) -ˈvɝːts **-verting** -ˈvɜː.tɪŋ (US) -ˈvɝː.t̬ɪŋ **-verted** -ˈvɜː.tɪd (US) -ˈvɝː.t̬ɪd
reconvey ˌriː.kᵊnˈveɪ **-s** -z **-ing** -ɪŋ **-ed** -d
record (*n.*) ˈrek.ɔːd (US) -ɚd **-s** -z ˈ**record ˌplayer**
record (*v.*) rɪˈkɔːd, rə- (US) -ˈkɔːrd **-s** -z **-ing/s** -ɪŋ/z **-ed** -ɪd **-able** -ə.bl̩ **reˌcorded deˈlivery**
record-break|ing ˈrek.ɔːdˌbreɪ.k|ɪŋ (US) -ɚdˌ- **-er/s** -əʳ/z (US) -ɚ/z
recorder rɪˈkɔː.dəʳ, rə- (US) -ˈkɔːr.dɚ **-s** -z
recordist rɪˈkɔː.dɪst, rə- (US) -ˈkɔːr- **-s** -s
recount (*n.*) ˈriː.kaʊnt, ˌ-ˈ- (US) ˈriː.kaʊnt **-s** -s
re|count (*v.*) *count again:* ˌriː|ˈkaʊnt **-counts** -ˈkaʊnts **-counting** -ˈkaʊn.tɪŋ (US) -ˈkaʊn.t̬ɪŋ **-counted** -ˈkaʊn.tɪd (US) -ˈkaʊn.t̬ɪd

re|count (*v.*) *narrate:* rɪˈkaʊnt, rə- **-counts** -ˈkaʊnts **-counting** -ˈkaʊn.tɪŋ (US) -ˈkaʊn.t̬ɪŋ **-counted** -ˈkaʊn.tɪd (US) -ˈkaʊn.t̬ɪd
recoup rɪˈkuːp, rə-, ˌriː- (US) rɪ-, rə- **-s** -s **-ing** -ɪŋ **-ed** -t **-ment** -mənt
recourse rɪˈkɔːs, rə- (US) ˈriː.kɔːrs; rɪˈkɔːrs
recov|er *get back, come back to health, etc.:* rɪˈkʌv|.əʳ, rə- (US) -ɚ **-ers** -əz (US) -ɚz **-ering** -ᵊr.ɪŋ **-ered** -əd (US) -ɚd **-erable** -ᵊr.ə.bl̩
recov|er *cover again:* ˌriːˈkʌv|.əʳ (US) -ɚ **-ers** -əz (US) -ɚz **-ering** -ᵊr.ɪŋ **-ered** -əd (US) -ɚd
recover|y rɪˈkʌv.ᵊr|.i, rə- (US) -ɚ|.i, ˈ-r|i **-ies** -iz
recreant ˈrek.ri.ənt **-s** -s **-ly** -li
recre|ate *create anew:* ˌriː.kriˈ|eɪt **-ates** -ˈeɪts **-ating** -ˈeɪ.tɪŋ (US) -ˈeɪ.t̬ɪŋ **-ated** -ˈeɪ.tɪd (US) -ˈeɪ.t̬ɪd
recre|ate *refresh:* ˈrek.ri.|eɪt **-ates** -eɪts **-ating** -eɪ.tɪŋ (US) -eɪ.t̬ɪŋ **-ated** -eɪ.tɪd (US) -eɪ.t̬ɪd **-ative** -eɪ.tɪv (US) -eɪ.t̬ɪv
recreation *creating anew:* ˌriː.kriˈeɪ.ʃᵊn **-s** -z
recreation *refreshment, amusement:* ˌrek.riˈeɪ.ʃᵊn **-s** -z **-al** -ᵊl
recrimi|nate rɪˈkrɪm.ɪ|.neɪt, rə-, ˈ-ə- (US) ˈ-ə- **-nates** -neɪts **-nating** -neɪ.tɪŋ (US) -neɪ.t̬ɪŋ **-nated** -neɪ.tɪd (US) -neɪ.t̬ɪd **-nator/s** -neɪ.təʳ/z (US) -neɪ.t̬ɚ/z
recrimination rɪˌkrɪm.ɪˈneɪ.ʃᵊn, rə-, -əˈ- (US) -əˈ- **-s** -z
recriminatory rɪˈkrɪm.ɪ.nə.tᵊr.i, rə-, ˈ-ə- (US) -ə.nə.tɔːr-
recross ˌriːˈkrɒs (US) -ˈkrɑːs **-es** -ɪz **-ing** -ɪŋ **-ed** -t
recrudesc|e ˌriː.kruːˈdes, ˌrek.ruːˈ- (US) ˌriː.kruːˈ- **-es** -ɪz **-ing** -ɪŋ **-ed** -t
recrudescen|ce ˌriː.kruːˈdes.ᵊn|ts, ˌrek.ruːˈ- (US) ˌriː.kruːˈ- **-t** -t
re|cruit rɪ|ˈkruːt, rə- **-cruits** -ˈkruːts **-cruiting** -ˈkruː.tɪŋ (US) -ˈkruː.t̬ɪŋ **-cruited** -ˈkruː.tɪd (US) -ˈkruː.t̬ɪd **-cruiter/s** -ˈkruː.təʳ/z (US) -ˈkruː.t̬ɚ/z **-cruitment** -ˈkruːt.mənt
rectal ˈrek.tᵊl **-ly** -i
rectangle ˈrek.tæŋ.gl̩ **-s** -z
rectangular rekˈtæŋ.gjə.ləʳ, -gjʊ- (US) -gjə.lɚ **-ly** -li
rectification ˌrek.tɪ.fɪˈkeɪ.ʃᵊn, -tə- (US) -tə- **-s** -z
recti|fy ˈrek.tɪ|.faɪ, -tə- (US) -tə- **-fies** -faɪz **-fying** -faɪ.ɪŋ **-fied** -faɪd **-fier/s** -faɪ.əʳ/z (US) -faɪ.ɚ/z **-fiable** -faɪ.ə.bl̩
rectiline|al ˌrek.tɪˈlɪn.i|.əl, -təˈ- (US) -təˈ- **-ar** -əʳ (US) -ɚ
rectitude ˈrek.tɪ.tjuːd, -tə-, -tʃuːd (US) -tə.tuːd, -tjuːd
recto ˈrek.təʊ (US) -toʊ
rector ˈrek.təʳ (US) -tɚ **-s** -z
rectorate ˈrek.tᵊr.ət, -ɪt, -eɪt (US) -ɪt **-s** -s
rectorial rekˈtɔː.ri.əl (US) -ˈtɔːr.i-
rectorship ˈrek.tə.ʃɪp (US) -tɚ- **-s** -s
rector|y ˈrek.tᵊr|.i **-ies** -ɪz
rect|um ˈrek.t|əm **-ums** -əmz **-a** -ə
rect|us ˈrek.t|əs **-i** -aɪ
Reculver rɪˈkʌl.vəʳ, rə- (US) -vɚ **-s** -z
recumben|ce rɪˈkʌm.bən|ts, rə- **-cy** -si
recumbent rɪˈkʌm.bənt, rə- **-ly** -li
recuper|ate rɪˈkjuː.pᵊr|.eɪt, rə-, -ˈkuː- (US) -ˈkuː.pə.r|eɪt, -ˈkjuː- **-ates** -eɪts **-ating** -eɪ.tɪŋ (US) -eɪ.t̬ɪŋ **-ated** -eɪ.tɪd (US) -eɪ.t̬ɪd
recuperation rɪˌkjuː.pᵊrˈeɪ.ʃᵊn, rə-, -ˌkuː- (US) -ˌkuː.pəˈreɪ-, -ˌkjuː-
recuperative rɪˈkjuː.pᵊr.ə.tɪv, rə-, -ˈkjuː- (US) -ˈkuː.pɚ.ə.t̬ɪv, -ˈkjuː-
recur rɪˈkɜːʳ, rə- (US) -ˈkɝː **-s** -z **-ring** -ɪŋ **-red** -d
recurrenc|e rɪˈkʌr.ᵊnts, rə- (US) -ˈkɝː- **-es** -ɪz
recurrent rɪˈkʌr.ənt, rə- (US) -ˈkɝː- **-ly** -li
recursive rɪˈkɜː.sɪv, ˌriː- (US) -ˈkɝː- **-s** -z **-ly** -li
recurved ˌriːˈkɜːvd, rɪ-, rə- (US) -ˈkɝːvd
recusan|cy ˈrek.jʊ.zᵊnt|.si, -jə-; rɪˈkjuː-, rə- (US) ˈrek.jʊ-; rɪˈkjuː-, rə- **-ce** -s
recusant ˈrek.jʊ.zᵊnt, -jə-; rɪˈkjuː-, rə- (US) ˈrek.jʊ-; rɪˈkjuː-, rə- **-s** -s
recycl|e ˌriːˈsaɪ.kl̩ **-es** -z **-ing** -ɪŋ, ˈ-klɪŋ **-ed** -d **-able** -ə.bl̩, ˈ-klə.bl̩
red (R) red **-s** -z **-der** -əʳ (US) -ɚ **-dest** -ɪst, -əst **-ness** -nəs, -nɪs **ˌred aˈlert; ˌred ˈcard; ˌred ˈcarpet; ˌRed ˈCrescent; ˌRed ˈCross; ˌred ˈherring; ˌRed ˈIndian; ˌRed ˈSea; ˌred ˈtape; in the ˈred; ˌsee ˈred; ˌnot worth a ˌred ˈcent; ˌreds under the ˈbed**
redact rɪˈdækt, rə- **-s** -s **-ing** -ɪŋ **-ed** -ɪd **-or/s** -əʳ/z (US) -ɚ/z
redaction rɪˈdæk.ʃᵊn, rə- **-s** -z
red-blooded ˌredˈblʌd.ɪd **-ness** -nəs, -nɪs *stress shift:* ˌred-blooded ˈmale
Redbourn ˈred.bɔːn (US) ˈred.bɔːrn
redbreast ˈred.brest **-s** -s
redbrick ˈred.brɪk, ˌ-ˈ- (US) ˈred.brɪk **ˌredbrick uniˈversity**
Redbridge ˈred.brɪdʒ
redbud ˈred.bʌd **-s** -z
redcap ˈred.kæp **-s** -s
Redcar ˈred.kɑːʳ *locally:* -kə (US) ˈred.kɑːr
Redcliffe, Redclyffe ˈred.klɪf
redcoat ˈred.kəʊt (US) -koʊt **-s** -s
redcurrant ˈredˌkʌr.ənt **-s** -s
Reddaway ˈred.ə.weɪ
redden ˈred.ᵊn **-s** -z **-ing** -ɪŋ **-ed** -d
Redding ˈred.ɪŋ
reddish ˈred.ɪʃ **-ness** -nəs, -nɪs
Redditch ˈred.ɪtʃ
reddle ˈred.l̩
redecor|ate ˌriːˈdek.ᵊr|.eɪt (US) -ə.r|eɪt **-ates** -eɪts **-ating** -eɪ.tɪŋ (US) -eɪ.t̬ɪŋ **-ated** -eɪ.tɪd (US) -eɪ.t̬ɪd
redeem rɪˈdiːm, rə- **-s** -z **-ing** -ɪŋ **-ed** -d **-able** -ə.bl̩
redeemer (R) rɪˈdiː.məʳ, rə- (US) -mɚ **-s** -z
redefin|e ˌriː.dɪˈfaɪn, -dəˈ- **-es** -z **-ing** -ɪŋ **-ed** -d
redeliv|er ˌriː.dɪˈlɪv|.əʳ, -dəˈ- (US) -ɚ **-ers** -əz (US) -ɚz **-ering** -ᵊr.ɪŋ **-ered** -əd (US) -ɚd **-ery** -ᵊr.i
redemption (R) rɪˈdemp.ʃᵊn, rə- **-s** -z
redemptive rɪˈdemp.tɪv, rə-
re-deploy ˌriː.dɪˈplɔɪ, -dəˈ- **-s** -z **-ing** -ɪŋ **-ed** -d **-ment/s** -mənt/s
redesign ˌriː.dɪˈzaɪn, -dəˈ- **-s** -z **-ing** -ɪŋ **-ed** -d
redevelop ˌriː.dɪˈvel.əp, -dəˈ- **-s** -s **-ing** -ɪŋ **-ed** -t **-ment/s** -mənt/s
red-eye ˈred.aɪ **-s** -z
Redfern ˈred.fɜːn (US) -fɝːn
Redfield ˈred.fiːld
Redford ˈred.fəd (US) -fɚd
Redgrave ˈred.greɪv, ˈreg- (US) ˈred-
red-handed ˌredˈhæn.dɪd
redhead (R) ˈred.hed **-s** -z
Redheugh ˈred.hjuːf, -juːf, -jəf
Redhill ˌredˈhɪl, ˈ--
red-hot ˌredˈhɒt (US) -ˈhɑːt *stress shift:* ˌred-hot ˈpoker
re-dial ˌriːˈdaɪəl (US) -ˈdaɪəl **-s** -z **-ling** -ɪŋ **-led** -d
Rediffusion® ˌriː.dɪˈfjuː.ʒᵊn, -dəˈ-
redintegration rɪˌdɪn.tɪˈgreɪ.ʃᵊn, redˌɪn-, -təˈ- (US) redˌɪn.t̬əˈ-, rɪˌdɪn-
redirect ˌriː.dɪˈrekt, -daɪ-, -də- (US) -dɪˈ-, -daɪˈ- **-s** -s **-ing** -ɪŋ **-ed** -ɪd
rediscov|er ˌriː.dɪˈskʌv|.əʳ (US) -ɚ **-ers** -əz (US) -ɚz **-ering** -ᵊr.ɪŋ **-ered** -əd (US) -ɚd **-ery** -ᵊr.i
redistribu|te ˌriː.dɪˈstrɪb.juː|t, -jʊ|t, -dəˈ-; -strɪˈbjuː|t, -stəˈ- (US) ˌriː.dɪˈstrɪb.juː|t, -jʊ|t **-tes** -ts **-ting** -tɪŋ (US) -t̬ɪŋ **-ted** -tɪd (US) -t̬ɪd
redistribution ˌriː.dɪ.strɪˈbjuː.ʃᵊn, -strəˈ- **-s** -z
redivid|e ˌriː.dɪˈvaɪd, -dəˈ- **-es** -z **-ing** -ɪŋ **-ed** -ɪd
redivivus ˌred.ɪˈvaɪ.vəs, -əˈ-, -ˈviː-
Redknapp ˈred.næp
red-letter day ˌredˈlet.əˌdeɪ (US) -ˈlet̬.ɚˌ- **-s** -z
red-light district ˌredˈlaɪtˌdɪs.trɪkt (US) ˈred.laɪtˌ- **-s** -s
Redman ˈred.mən, ˈreb- (US) ˈred.mæn
Redmond ˈred.mənd
redneck ˈred.nek **-s** -s
re|-do ˌriː|ˈduː **-does** -ˈdʌz **-doing** -ˈduː.ɪŋ **-did** -ˈdɪd **-done** -ˈdʌn
redolen|t ˈred.ᵊl.ən|t, -əʊ.lən|t (US) -ᵊl.ən|t **-ce** -ts

redoubl|e ˌriːˈdʌb.l̩, rɪ- **-es** -z **-ing** -ɪŋ, ˌriːˈdʌb.lɪŋ, rɪˈdʌb- **-ed** -d
redoubt rɪˈdaʊt, rə- **-s** -s
redoubtab|le rɪˈdaʊ.tə.b|l̩, rə- (US) -t̬ə- **-ly** -li
redound rɪˈdaʊnd, rə- **-s** -z **-ing** -ɪŋ **-ed** -ɪd
Redpath ˈred.pɑːθ, ˈreb- (US) ˈred.pæθ
redraft ˌriːˈdrɑːft (US) -ˈdræft **-s** -s **-ing** -ɪŋ **-ed** -ɪd
re-draw ˌriːˈdrɔː (US) -ˈdrɑː, -ˈdrɔː **-s** -z **-ing** -ɪŋ **re-drew** ˌriːˈdruː **re-drawn** ˌriːˈdrɔːn (US) -ˈdrɑːn, -ˈdrɔːn
redress (*v.*) rɪˈdres, rə- **-es** -ɪz **-ing** -ɪŋ **-ed** -t
redress (*n.*) rɪˈdres, rə-; ˈriː.dres (US) ˈriː.dres
Redriff ˈred.rɪf
Redruth ˌredˈruːθ, ˈ--
redshank ˈred.ʃæŋk **-s** -s
redskin **(R)** ˈred.skɪn **-s** -z
redstart ˈred.stɑːt (US) -stɑːrt **-s** -s
reduc|e rɪˈdjuːs, rə- (US) -ˈduːs, -ˈdjuːs **-es** -ɪz **-ing** -ɪŋ **-ed** -t **-er/s** -əʳ/z (US) -ɚ/z
reducibility rɪˌdjuː.səˈbɪl.ə.ti, rə-, -sɪˈ-, -ɪ.ti (US) -ˌduː.səˈbɪl.ə.t̬i, -ˌdjuː-
reducible rɪˈdjuː.sə.bl̩, rə-, -sɪ- (US) -ˈduː.sə-, -ˈdjuː-
reductio ad absurdum rɪˌdʌk.ti.əʊ.æd.æbˈsɜː.dəm, rə-, -ʃi-, -əbˈ- (US) -ti.oʊ.æd.æbˈsɝː-, ˈ-ʃi-
reduction rɪˈdʌk.ʃən, rə- **-s** -z
reduction|ism rɪˈdʌk.ʃən|.ɪ.zəm **-ist/s** -ɪst/s
reductionistic rɪˌdʌk.ʃənˈɪs.tɪk, rə-
reductive rɪˈdʌk.tɪv, rə-
redundan|cy rɪˈdʌn.dənt|.si, rə- **-cies** -siz **-ce** -s
redundant rɪˈdʌn.dənt, rə- **-ly** -li
redupli|cate rɪˈdjuː.plɪ|.keɪt, rə-, ˌriː-, -ˈdʒuː-, -plə- (US) -ˈduː.plə-, -ˈdjuː- **-cates** -keɪts **-cating** -keɪ.tɪŋ (US) -keɪ.t̬ɪŋ **-cated** -keɪ.tɪd (US) -keɪ.t̬ɪd
reduplication rɪˌdjuː.plɪˈkeɪ.ʃən, rə-, ˌriː-, -ˌdʒuː-, -pləˈ- (US) -ˌduː.pləˈ-, -ˌdjuː- **-s** -z
reduplicative rɪˈdjuː.plɪ.kə.tɪv, rə-, -ˈdʒuː-, -plə-, -keɪ- (US) -ˈduː.plə.keɪ.t̬ɪv, -ˈdju-
redwing ˈred.wɪŋ **-s** -z
redwood **(R)** ˈred.wʊd **-s** -z
Reebok® ˈriː.bɒk (US) -bɑːk **-s** -s
Reece riːs
re-echo ˌriːˈek.əʊ, ri- (US) -oʊ **-es** -z **-ing** -ɪŋ **-ed** -d
reed **(R)** riːd **-s** -z
re-ed|it ˌriːˈed|.ɪt **-its** -ɪts **-iting** -ɪ.tɪŋ (US) -ɪ.t̬ɪŋ **-ited** -ɪ.tɪd (US) -ɪ.t̬ɪd
re-edition ˌriː.ɪˈdɪʃ.ən, -əˈ- **-s** -z
re-edu|cate ˌriːˈedʒ.ʊ|.keɪt, ˈ-ə-, -ˈed.jʊ-, -jə- (US) -ˈedʒ.ʊ-, ˈ-ə- **-cates** -keɪts **-cating** -keɪ.tɪŋ (US) -keɪ.t̬ɪŋ **-cated** -keɪ.tɪd (US) -keɪ.t̬ɪd
re-education ˌriːˌedʒ.ʊˈkeɪ.ʃən, -əˈ-, -ˌed.jʊˈ-, -jəˈ- (US) -ˌedʒ.ʊˈ-, -əˈ-
reed-warbler ˈriːdˌwɔː.bləʳ, ˌ-ˈ-- (US) ˈriːdˌwɔːr.blɚ **-s** -z
reed|y ˈriː.d|i **-ier** -i.əʳ (US) -i.ɚ **-iest** -i.ɪst, -i.əst **-iness** -ɪ.nəs, -ɪ.nɪs
reef riːf **-s** -s **-ing** -ɪŋ **-ed** -t **ˈreef ˌknot**
reefer ˈriː.fəʳ (US) -fɚ **-s** -z
reek riːk **-s** -s **-ing** -ɪŋ **-ed** -t
Reekie ˈriː.ki
reel riːl **-s** -z **-ing** -ɪŋ **-ed** -d
re-elect ˌriː.ɪˈlekt, -əˈ- **-s** -s **-ing** -ɪŋ **-ed** -ɪd
re-election ˌriː.ɪˈlek.ʃən, -əˈ- **-s** -z
reel-to-reel ˌriːl.təˈriːl, -tʊˈ-
re-embark ˌriː.ɪmˈbɑːk, -emˈ- (US) -ˈbɑːrk **-s** -s **-ing** -ɪŋ **-ed** -t
re-embarkation ˌriː.ɪm.bɑːˈkeɪ.ʃən, -em-; riˌem- (US) ˌriː.ɪm.bɑːrˈ-, -em- **-s** -z
re-enact ˌriː.ɪˈnækt, -əˈ-, -enˈækt **-s** -s **-ing** -ɪŋ **-ed** -ɪd **-ment/s** -mənt/s
reenforc|e ˌriː.ɪnˈfɔːs, -ənˈ- (US) -ˈfɔːrs **-es** -ɪz **-ing** -ɪŋ **-ed** -t
re-engag|e ˌriː.ɪŋˈgeɪdʒ, -eŋˈ-, -ɪnˈ-, -enˈ- (US) -ɪnˈ-, -enˈ- **-es** -ɪz **-ing** -ɪŋ **-ed** -d **-ement/s** -mənt/s
re-enlist ˌriː.ɪnˈlɪst, -enˈ- **-s** -s **-ing** -ɪŋ **-ed** -ɪd
re-ent|er ˌriːˈen.t|əʳ, ri- (US) -t̬|ɚ **-ers** -əz (US) -ɚz **-ering** -ər.ɪŋ **-ered** -əd (US) -ɚd
re-entr|y ˌriːˈen.tr|i, ri- **-ies** -iz
Rees(e) riːs
re-establish ˌriː.ɪˈstæb.lɪʃ, -esˈtæb- **-es** -ɪz **-ing** -ɪŋ **-ed** -t **-ment** -mənt
reeve **(R)** riːv **-s** -z
Reeves riːvz
re-examination ˌriː.ɪgˌzæm.ɪˈneɪ.ʃən, -egˌ-, -əˈ- **-s** -z
re-examin|e ˌriː.ɪgˈzæm.ɪn, -egˈ- **-es** -z **-ing** -ɪŋ **-ed** -d
re-expor|t (*v.*) ˌriː.ɪkˈspɔː|t, -ekˈ- (US) -ˈspɔːr|t; -ˈek.spɔːr|t **-ts** -ts **-ting** -tɪŋ (US) -t̬ɪŋ **-ted** -tɪd (US) -t̬ɪd
ref **(R)** ref **-s** -s
refac|e ˌriːˈfeɪs **-es** -ɪz **-ing** -ɪŋ **-ed** -t
refashion ˌriːˈfæʃ.ən **-s** -z **-ing** -ɪŋ **-ed** -d
refection rɪˈfek.ʃən, rə-
refector|y rɪˈfek.tər|.i, rə-, ˈref.ɪk- (US) rɪˈfek-, rə- **-ies** -iz
refer rɪˈfɜːʳ, rə- (US) -ˈfɝː **-s** -z **-ring** -ɪŋ **-red** -d
referable rɪˈfɜː.rə.bl̩, rə-; ˈref.ər- (US) rɪˈfɝː.ə-, rə-; ˈref.ɚ-
referee ˌref.ərˈiː (US) -əˈriː **-s** -z **-ing** -ɪŋ **-d** -d
referenc|e ˈref.ər.ənts, ˈ-rənts **-es** -ɪz **ˈreference ˌbook**; **ˈreference ˌlibrary**
referend|um ˌref.ərˈen.d|əm (US) -əˈren- **-ums** -əmz **-a** -ə
referent ˈref.ər.ənt, ˈ-rənt **-s** -s
referential ˌref.ərˈen.tʃəl (US) -əˈrent.ʃəl **-ly** -i
referral rɪˈfɜː.rəl, rə- (US) -ˈfɝː.əl **-s** -z
refill (*n.*) ˈriː.fɪl **-s** -z
refill (*v.*) ˌriːˈfɪl **-s** -z **-ing** -ɪŋ **-ed** -d
refin|e rɪˈfaɪn, rə- **-es** -z **-ing** -ɪŋ **-ed** -d **-er/s** -əʳ/z (US) -ɚ/z **-ement/s** -mənt/s
refiner|y rɪˈfaɪ.nər|.i, rə- **-ies** -iz
refit (*n.*) ˈriː.fɪt, ˌ-ˈ-
re|fit (*v.*) ˌriː|ˈfɪt **-fits** -ˈfɪts **-fitting** -ˈfɪt.ɪŋ (US) -ˈfɪt̬.ɪŋ **-fitted** -ˈfɪt.ɪd (US) -ˈfɪt̬.ɪd
re|flate ˌriː|ˈfleɪt **-flates** -ˈfleɪts **-flating** -ˈfleɪ.tɪŋ (US) -ˈfleɪ.t̬ɪŋ **-flated** -ˈfleɪ.tɪd (US) -ˈfleɪ.t̬ɪd
reflation ˌriːˈfleɪ.ʃən
reflationary ˌriːˈfleɪ.ʃən.ər.i (US) -er-
reflect rɪˈflekt, rə- **-s** -s **-ing** -ɪŋ **-ed** -ɪd **-or/s** -əʳ/z (US) -ɚ/z
reflection rɪˈflek.ʃən, rə- **-s** -z
reflective rɪˈflek.tɪv, rə- **-ly** -li **-ness** -nəs, -nɪs
reflex ˈriː.fleks **-es** -ɪz
reflexed rɪˈflekst, ˌriː-; ˈriː.flekst
reflexive rɪˈflek.sɪv, rə- **-ly** -li **-ness** -nəs, -nɪs
reflexolog|y ˌriː.flekˈsɒl.ə.dʒ|i (US) -ˈsɑː.lə- **-ist/s** -ɪst/s
re|float ˌriː|ˈfləʊt (US) -ˈfloʊt **-floats** -ˈfləʊts (US) -ˈfloʊts **-floating** -ˈfləʊ.tɪŋ (US) -ˈfloʊ.t̬ɪŋ **-floated** -ˈfləʊ.tɪd (US) -ˈfloʊ.t̬ɪd
refluent ˈref.lu.ənt
reflux ˈriː.flʌks **-es** -ɪz
reforest ˌriːˈfɒr.ɪst (US) -ˈfɔːr.ɪst **-s** -s **-ing** -ɪŋ **-ed** -ɪd
reforestation ˌriː.fɒr.ɪˈsteɪ.ʃən, -əˈ- (US) -fɔːr.ɪˈ-
reform (*n. v.*) *make better, become better, etc.:* rɪˈfɔːm, rə- (US) -ˈfɔːrm **-s** -z **-ing** -ɪŋ **-ed** -d **-er/s** -əʳ/z (US) -ɚ/z **-able** -ə.bl̩ **reˈform ˌschool**
re-form (*v.*) *form again:* ˌriːˈfɔːm (US) -ˈfɔːrm **-s** -z **-ing** -ɪŋ **-ed** -d
reformation **(R)** ˌref.əˈmeɪ.ʃən, -ɔːˈ- (US) -ɚˈ- **-s** -z
reformative rɪˈfɔː.mə.tɪv, rə- (US) -ˈfɔːr.mə.t̬ɪv
reformator|y rɪˈfɔː.mə.tər|.i, rə- (US) -ˈfɔːr.mə.tɔːr- **-ies** -iz
reformist rɪˈfɔː.mɪst, rə- (US) -ˈfɔːr-
refract rɪˈfrækt, rə- **-s** -s **-ing** -ɪŋ **-ed** -ɪd **-or/s** -əʳ/z (US) -ɚ/z **-ive** -ɪv
refraction rɪˈfræk.ʃən, rə- **-s** -z
refractor|y rɪˈfræk.tər|.i, rə- **-ily** -əl.i, -ɪ.li **-iness** -ɪ.nəs, -ɪ.nɪs
refrain rɪˈfreɪn, rə- **-s** -z **-ing** -ɪŋ **-ed** -d
refresh rɪˈfreʃ, rə- **-es** -ɪz **-ing/ly** -ɪŋ/li **-ed** -t **-er/s** -əʳ/z (US) -ɚ/z **reˈfresher ˌcourse**
refreshment rɪˈfreʃ.mənt, rə- **-s** -s

refried *stress shift, see compound:* ˌriːˈfraɪd ˌ**refried** ˈ**beans**

refriger|ate rɪˈfrɪdʒ.ᵊr|.eɪt, rə- ⓤⓢ -ə.r|eɪt **-ates** -eɪts **-ating** -eɪ.tɪŋ ⓤⓢ -eɪ.t̬ɪŋ **-ated** -eɪ.tɪd ⓤⓢ -eɪ.t̬ɪd

refrigeration rɪˌfrɪdʒ.ᵊrˈeɪ.ʃᵊn, rə- ⓤⓢ -əˈreɪ-

refrigerator rɪˈfrɪdʒ.ᵊr.eɪ.təʳ, rə- ⓤⓢ -ə.reɪ.t̬ɚ **-s** -z

reft reft

re-fuel ˌriːˈfjuː.əl, -ˈfjʊəl ⓤⓢ -ˈfjuː.əl, -ˈfjuːl **-s** -z **-ling** -ɪŋ **-led** -d

refug|e ˈref.juːdʒ **-es** -ɪz

refugee ˌref.jʊˈdʒiː, -jəˈ- ⓤⓢ ˌref.jʊˈdʒiː, -jəˈ-; ˈref.jʊ.dʒi, -jə- **-s** -z

refulgen|ce rɪˈfʌl.dʒən|*t*s, rə- ⓤⓢ -ˈfʌl-, -ˈfʊl- **-t/ly** -t/li

refund (*n.*) ˈriː.fʌnd **-s** -z

refund (*v.*) ˌriːˈfʌnd, rɪ-, rə-; ˈriː.fʌnd ⓤⓢ ˌriːˈfʌnd, rɪ-, rə- **-s** -z **-ing** -ɪŋ **-ed** -ɪd

refurbish ˌriːˈfɜː.bɪʃ ⓤⓢ -ˈfɝː- **-es** -ɪz **-ing** -ɪŋ **-ed** -t **-ment/s** -mənt/s

refurnish ˌriːˈfɜː.nɪʃ ⓤⓢ -ˈfɝː- **-es** -ɪz **-ing** -ɪŋ **-ed** -t

refusal rɪˈfjuː.zᵊl, rə- **-s** -z

refuse (*n. adj.*) ˈref.juːs

refus|e (*v.*) rɪˈfjuːz, rə- **-es** -ɪz **-ing** -ɪŋ **-ed** -d **-able** -ə.bl̩

refusenik rɪˈfjuːz.nɪk, rə- **-s** -s

refutability ˌref.jʊ.təˈbɪl.ə.ti, -jə-, -ɪ.ti; rɪˌfjuː-, rə- ⓤⓢ rɪˌfjuː.t̬əˈbɪl.ə.t̬i; ˌref.jə.t̬əˈ-

refutab|le ˈref.jʊ.tə.b|l̩, -jə-; rɪˈfjuː-, rə- ⓤⓢ rɪˈfjuː.t̬ə-, rə-; ˈref.jə- **-ly** -li

refutation ˌref.jʊˈteɪ.ʃᵊn, -jəˈ- **-s** -z

re|fute rɪ|ˈfjuːt, rə- **-futes** -ˈfjuːts **-futing** -ˈfjuː.tɪŋ ⓤⓢ -ˈfjuː.t̬ɪŋ **-futed** -ˈfjuː.tɪd ⓤⓢ -ˈfjuː.t̬ɪd

Reg redʒ

-reg *car numberplate:* -ˌredʒ

Note: Used in the UK to refer to the year of registration of a car, which is indicated on the numberplate by a letter, e.g. **an F-reg**.

regain rɪˈgeɪn, ˌriː- **-s** -z **-ing** -ɪŋ **-ed** -d

regal ˈriː.gᵊl **-ly** -i

regal|e rɪˈgeɪl, rə- **-es** -z **-ing** -ɪŋ **-ed** -d

regalia rɪˈgeɪ.li.ə, rə- ⓤⓢ -ˈgeɪl.jə, -ˈgeɪ.li.ə

Regan ˈriː.gᵊn

regard rɪˈgɑːd, rə- ⓤⓢ -ˈgɑːrd **-s** -z **-ing** -ɪŋ **-ed** -ɪd **-ant** -ᵊnt

regardful rɪˈgɑːd.fᵊl, rə-, -fʊl ⓤⓢ -ˈgɑːrd- **-ly** -i **-ness** -nəs, -nɪs

regardless rɪˈgɑːd.ləs, rə-, -lɪs ⓤⓢ -ˈgɑːrd- **-ly** -li **-ness** -nəs, -nɪs

regatta rɪˈgæt.ə, rə- ⓤⓢ -ˈgɑː.t̬ə, -ˈgæt̬.ə **-s** -z

regenc|y (R) ˈriː.dʒᵊn*t*.s|i **-ies** -iz

regenerat|e (*adj.*) rɪˈdʒen.ᵊr.ət, rə-, -ɪt, -eɪt ⓤⓢ -ɪt **-ive** -ɪv

regener|ate (*v.*) rɪˈdʒen.ᵊr|.eɪt, rə-, ˌriː- ⓤⓢ -ə.r|eɪt **-ates** -eɪts **-ating** -eɪ.tɪŋ ⓤⓢ -eɪ.t̬ɪŋ **-ated** -eɪ.tɪd ⓤⓢ -eɪ.t̬ɪd

regeneration rɪˌdʒen.ᵊrˈeɪ.ʃᵊn, rə-, ˌriː.dʒen- ⓤⓢ -əˈreɪ- **-s** -z

Regensburg ˈreɪ.gᵊnz.bɜːg ⓤⓢ -bɝːg

regent (R) ˈriː.dʒᵊnt **-s** -s

regentship ˈriː.dʒᵊnt.ʃɪp **-s** -s

reggae ˈreg.eɪ

Reggie ˈredʒ.i

Reggio ˈredʒ.i.əʊ ⓤⓢ ˈ-oʊ

regicidal ˌredʒ.ɪˈsaɪ.dᵊl, -əˈ-

regicide ˈredʒ.ɪ.saɪd, ˈ-ə- **-s** -z

regime, régime reɪˈʒiːm, rɪ-, rə-, reʒˈiːm; ˈreɪ.ʒiːm ⓤⓢ rəˈʒiːm, rɪ-, reɪ- **-s** -z

regimen ˈredʒ.ɪ.mən, ˈ-ə-, -men ⓤⓢ ˈ-ə- **-s** -z

regiment (*n.*) ˈredʒ.ɪ.mənt, ˈ-ə- ⓤⓢ ˈ-ə- **-s** -s

regimen|t (*v.*) ˈredʒ.ɪ.men|t, ˈ-ə-, ˌ--ˈ- ⓤⓢ ˈredʒ.ə.men|t **-ts** -ts **-ting** -tɪŋ ⓤⓢ -t̬ɪŋ **-ted** -tɪd ⓤⓢ -t̬ɪd

regimental ˌredʒ.ɪˈmen.tᵊl, -əˈ- ⓤⓢ -əˈmen.t̬ᵊl **-s** -z *stress shift:* ˌregimental ˈcolours

regimentation ˌredʒ.ɪ.menˈteɪ.ʃᵊn, -ə-, -mənˈ- ⓤⓢ -ə.mənˈ-, -menˈ-

Regina rɪˈdʒaɪ.nə, rə- ⓤⓢ -ˈdʒaɪ-, -ˈdʒiː-

Note: In the US, /-ˈdʒiː-/ is especially suitable for the female name.

Reginald ˈredʒ.ɪ.nᵊld

region ˈriː.dʒᵊn **-s** -z

regional ˈriː.dʒᵊn.ᵊl **-ly** -i

regional|ism ˈriː.dʒᵊn.ᵊl|.ɪ.zᵊm **-ist/s** -ɪst/s

regionalistic ˌriː.dʒᵊn.ᵊlˈɪs.tɪk

Regis ˈriː.dʒɪs

regist|er ˈredʒ.ɪ.st|əʳ, ˈ-ə- ⓤⓢ -st|ɚ **-ers** -əz ⓤⓢ -ɚz **-ering** -ᵊr.ɪŋ **-ered** -əd ⓤⓢ -ɚd ˌ**registered** ˈ**mail**

registrant ˈredʒ.ɪ.strənt, ˈ-ə- **-s** -s

registrar ˌredʒ.ɪˈstrɑːʳ, -əˈ-, ˈ--- ⓤⓢ ˈredʒ.ɪ.strɑːr, ˌ--ˈ- **-s** -z

registrar|y ˈredʒ.ɪ.strᵊr|.i, ˈ-ə- ⓤⓢ -ɪ.strer- **-ies** -iz

registration ˌredʒ.ɪˈstreɪ.ʃᵊn, -əˈ- **-s** -z **regiˈstration** ˌ**number**

registr|y ˈredʒ.ɪ.str|i, ˈ-ə- **-ies** -iz ˈ**registry** ˌ**office**

Regius ˈriː.dʒi.əs, -dʒəs

regn|al ˈreg.n|ᵊl **-ant** -ənt

regress (*n.*) ˈriː.gres

regress (*v.*) rɪˈgres, ˌriː-, rə- **-es** -ɪz **-ing** -ɪŋ **-ed** -t

regression rɪˈgreʃ.ᵊn, ˌriː-, rə- **-s** -z

regressive rɪˈgres.ɪv, ˌriː-, rə- **-ly** -li **-ness** -nəs, -nɪs

re|gret rɪ|ˈgret, rə- **-grets** -ˈgrets **-gretting** -ˈgret.ɪŋ ⓤⓢ -ˈgret̬.ɪŋ **-gretted** -ˈgret.ɪd ⓤⓢ -ˈgret̬.ɪd

regretful rɪˈgret.fᵊl, rə-, -fʊl **-ly** -i

regrettab|le rɪˈgret.ə.b|l̩, rə- ⓤⓢ -ˈgre[t̬-] **-ly** -li

regroup ˌriːˈgruːp **-s** -s **-ing** -ɪŋ **-ed** -t

regular ˈreg.jə.ləʳ, -jʊ- ⓤⓢ -lɚ **-s** -z **-ly**

regularity ˌreg.jəˈlær.ə.ti, -jʊˈ-, -ɪ.ti ⓤⓢ -ˈler.ə.t̬i, -ˈlær-

regularization, -isa- ˌreg.jə.lᵊr.aɪˈzeɪ.ʃᵊn, -jʊ-, -ɪˈ- ⓤⓢ -[ɪ]

regulariz|e, -is|e ˈreg.jə.lᵊr.aɪz, -jʊ- ⓤⓢ -lə.raɪz **-es** -ɪz **-ing** -ɪŋ **-ed** -d

regu|late ˈreg.jə|.leɪt, -jʊ- **-lates** -leɪt[s] **-lating** -leɪ.tɪŋ ⓤⓢ -leɪ.t̬ɪŋ **-lated** -leɪ.tɪd ⓤⓢ -leɪ.t̬ɪd **-lator/s** -leɪ.təʳ/[z] ⓤⓢ -leɪ.t̬ɚ/z

regulation ˌreg.jəˈleɪ.ʃᵊn, -jʊˈ- **-s** -z

regulative ˈreg.jə.lə.tɪv, -jʊ-, -leɪ- ⓤⓢ -leɪ.t̬ɪv, -lə-

regulatory ˈreg.jə.lə.tᵊr.i, -jʊ-, ˌreg.jəˈleɪ-, -jəˈ- ⓤⓢ ˈreg.jə.lə.tɔːr-, -jʊ-

regul|us (R) ˈreg.jə.l|əs, -jʊ- **-uses** -ə.sɪz **-i** -aɪ

regurgi|tate rɪˈgɜː.dʒɪ|.teɪt, rə-, ˌriː-, -dʒə- ⓤⓢ -ˈgɝː.dʒə- **-tates** -teɪts **-tating** -teɪ.tɪŋ ⓤⓢ -teɪ.t̬ɪŋ **-tated** -teɪ.tɪd ⓤⓢ -teɪ.t̬ɪd

regurgitation rɪˌgɜː.dʒɪˈteɪ.ʃᵊn, rə-, ˌriː-, -dʒəˈ- ⓤⓢ -ˌgɝː.dʒəˈ-

rehab ˈriː.hæb **-s** -z **-bing** -ɪŋ **-bed** -d

rehabili|tate ˌriː.həˈbɪl.ɪ|.teɪt, -əˈ-, ˈ-[ə-] ⓤⓢ ˈ-ə- **-tates** -teɪts **-tating** -teɪ.tɪŋ ⓤⓢ -teɪ.t̬ɪŋ **-tated** -teɪ.tɪd ⓤⓢ -teɪ.t̬[ɪd]

rehabilitation ˌriː.həˌbɪl.ɪˈteɪ.ʃᵊn, -ə[ˈ-], -əˈ- ⓤⓢ -əˈ- **-s** -z

Rehan ˈriː.ən, ˈreɪ- ⓤⓢ ˈriː-

rehash (*n.*) ˈriː.hæʃ, ˌ-ˈ- **-es** -ɪz

rehash (*v.*) ˌriːˈhæʃ **-es** -ɪz **-ing** -ɪŋ **-ed**

rehear ˌriːˈhɪəʳ ⓤⓢ -ˈhɪr **-s** -z **-ing** -ɪŋ **reheard** ˌriːˈhɜːd ⓤⓢ -ˈhɝːd

rehearsal rɪˈhɜː.sᵊl, rə- ⓤⓢ -ˈhɝː- **-s** -z

rehears|e rɪˈhɜːs, rə- ⓤⓢ -ˈhɝːs **-es** -ɪz **-ing** -ɪŋ **-ed** -t

re|heat ˌriː|ˈhiːt **-heats** -ˈhiːts **-heatin[g]** -ˈhiː.tɪŋ ⓤⓢ -ˈhiː.t̬ɪŋ **-heated** -ˈhiː.[tɪd] ⓤⓢ -ˈhiː.t̬ɪd **-heater/s** -ˈhiː.təʳ/z ⓤⓢ -ˈhiː.t̬ɚ/z

Rehnquist ˈren.kwɪst, ˈreŋ-

rehoboam (R) ˌriː.əˈbəʊ.əm, -həˈ- ⓤⓢ -həˈboʊ- **-s** -z

re-hous|e ˌriːˈhaʊz **-es** -ɪz **-ing** -ɪŋ **-ed**

rehy|drate ˌriː.haɪ|ˈdreɪt ⓤⓢ -ˈhaɪ|.dr[eɪt] **-drates** -ˈdreɪts ⓤⓢ -dreɪts **-drating** -ˈdreɪ.tɪŋ ⓤⓢ -dreɪ.t̬ɪŋ **-drated** -ˈdreɪ.tɪd ⓤⓢ -dreɪ.t̬ɪd

rehydration ˌriː.haɪˈdreɪ.ʃᵊn

Reich raɪk *as if German:* raɪx

Reichstag ˈraɪk.stɑːg *as if German:* ˈraɪx-, -tɑːk ⓤⓢ ˈraɪk.stɑːg *as if German:* ˈraɪx-

Reid riːd
reification ˌreɪ.ɪ.fɪˈkeɪ.ʃᵊn, ˌriː-, ˌ-ə- (US) ˌ-ə-
rei|fy ˈreɪ.ɪ|.faɪ, ˈriː-, ˈ-ə- (US) ˈriː.ə- **-fies** -faɪz **-fying** -faɪ.ɪŋ **-fied** -faɪd
Reigate ˈraɪ.geɪt, -gɪt
reign (*n. v.*) reɪn **-s** -z **-ing** -ɪŋ **-ed** -d ˌ**reign of** ˈ**terror**
Reigny ˈreɪ.ni
Reill(e)y ˈraɪ.li
reimburs|e ˌriː.ɪmˈbɜːs, -əmˈ- (US) -ˈbɝːs **-es** -ɪz **-ing** -ɪŋ **-ed** -t **-ement/s** -mənt/s
re-im|port ˌriː.ɪm|ˈpɔːt (US) -ˈpɔːrt, -ˈ-- **-ports** -ˈpɔːts (US) -ˈpɔːrts **-porting** -ˈpɔː.tɪŋ (US) -ˈpɔːr.t̬ɪŋ **-ported** -ˈpɔː.tɪd (US) -ˈpɔːr.t̬ɪd
reimpos|e ˌriː.ɪmˈpəʊz (US) -ˈpoʊz **-es** -ɪz **-ing** -ɪŋ **-ed** -d
reimpression ˌriː.ɪmˈpreʃ.ᵊn **-s** -z
Reims riːmz
rein reɪn **-s** -z **-ing** -ɪŋ **-ed** -d
reincarnate (*adj.*) ˌriː.ɪnˈkɑː.nət, -ɪŋˈ-, -nɪt, -neɪt (US) -ɪnˈkɑːr.nɪt, -neɪt
reincarna|te (*v.*) ˌriː.ɪn.kɑːˈneɪ|t, -ɪŋ-, ˌriːˈɪn.kɑː.neɪ|t, -ˈɪŋ- (US) ˌriː.ɪnˈkɑːr.neɪ|t **-tes** -ts **-ting** -tɪŋ (US) -t̬ɪŋ **-ted** -tɪd (US) -t̬ɪd
reincarnation ˌriː.ɪn.kɑːˈneɪ.ʃᵊn, -ɪŋ- (US) -ɪn.kɑːrˈ- **-s** -z
reindeer ˈreɪn.dɪəʳ (US) -dɪr
reinforc|e ˌriː.ɪnˈfɔːs (US) -ˈfɔːrs **-es** -ɪz **-ing** -ɪŋ **-ed** -t **-ement/s** -mənt/s
Reinhard(t) ˈraɪn.hɑːt (US) -hɑːrt
reinstal|l ˌriː.ɪnˈstɔːl (US) -stɔːl, -stɑːl **-(l)s** -z **-(l)ing** -ɪŋ **-(l)ed** -d **-ment** -mənt
rein|state ˌriː.ɪn|ˈsteɪt **-states** -ˈsteɪts **-stating** -ˈsteɪ.tɪŋ (US) -ˈsteɪ.t̬ɪŋ **-stated** -ˈsteɪ.tɪd (US) -ˈsteɪ.t̬ɪd **-statement** -ˈsteɪt.mənt
reinsur|e ˌriː.ɪnˈʃʊəʳ, -ˈʃɔːʳ (US) -ˈʃʊr **-es** -z **-ing** -ɪŋ **-ed** -d **-ance/s** -ᵊnts/ɪz
reintroduc|e ˌriː.ɪn.trəˈdjuːs, -ˈdʒuːs (US) -ˈduːs, -ˈdjuːs **-es** -ɪz **-ing** -ɪŋ **-ed** -t
reintroduction ˌriː.ɪn.trəˈdʌk.ʃᵊn **-s** -z
rein|vent ˌriː.ɪn|ˈvent **-vents** -ˈvents **-venting** -ˈven.tɪŋ (US) -ˈven.t̬ɪŋ **-vented** -ˈven.tɪd (US) -ˈven.t̬ɪd
reinvention ˌriː.ɪnˈven.*t*ʃᵊn (US) -ˈven*t*.ʃᵊn
reinvest ˌriː.ɪnˈvest **-s** -s **-ing** -ɪŋ **-ed** -ɪd
reinvigor|ate ˌriː.ɪnˈvɪg.ᵊr|.eɪt (US) -ə.r|eɪt **-ates** -eɪts **-ating** -eɪ.tɪŋ (US) -eɪ.t̬ɪŋ **-ated** -eɪ.tɪd (US) -eɪ.t̬ɪd
reinvigoration ˌriː.ɪn.vɪ.gᵊrˈeɪ.ʃᵊn (US) -gəˈreɪ-
reissu|e ˌriːˈɪʃ.uː, -ˈɪs.juː (US) -ˈɪʃ.juː, -uː **-es** -z **-ing** -ɪŋ **-ed** -d
reiter|ate riˈɪt.ᵊr|.eɪt (US) -ˈɪt̬.ə.r|eɪt **-ates** -eɪts **-ating** -eɪ.tɪŋ (US) -eɪ.t̬ɪŋ **-ated** -eɪ.tɪd (US) -eɪ.t̬ɪd
reiteration riˌɪt.ᵊrˈeɪ.ʃᵊn (US) -ˌɪt̬.əˈreɪ- **-s** -z
reiterative riˈɪt.ᵊr.ə.tɪv, -eɪ- (US) -ˈɪt̬.ə.reɪ.t̬ɪv, ˈ-ɚ.ə- **-ly** -li **-ness** -nəs, -nɪs
Reith riːθ
reject (*n.*) ˈriː.dʒekt **-s** -s
reject (*v.*) rɪˈdʒekt, rə- **-s** -s **-ing** -ɪŋ **-ed** -ɪd **-or/s** -əʳ/z (US) -ɚ/z
rejection rɪˈdʒek.ʃᵊn, rə- **-s** -z
rejig ˌriːˈdʒɪg **-s** -z **-ging** -ɪŋ **-ged** -d
rejoic|e rɪˈdʒɔɪs, rə- **-es** -ɪz **-ing/ly** -ɪŋ/li **-ed** -t
rejoin *answer:* rɪˈdʒɔɪn, rə- **-s** -z **-ing** -ɪŋ **-ed** -d
rejoin *join again:* ˌriːˈdʒɔɪn, rɪ- **-s** -z **-ing** -ɪŋ **-ed** -d
rejoinder rɪˈdʒɔɪn.dəʳ, rə- (US) -dɚ **-s** -z
rejuven|ate rɪˈdʒuː.vᵊn|.eɪt, -vɪ.n|eɪt (US) -və- **-ates** -eɪts **-ating** -eɪ.tɪŋ (US) -eɪ.t̬ɪŋ **-ated** -eɪ.tɪd (US) -eɪ.t̬ɪd
rejuvenation rɪˌdʒuː.vᵊnˈeɪ.ʃᵊn, rə-, -vɪˈneɪ- (US) -vəˈ-
rejuvenescen|ce ˌriː.dʒuː.vᵊnˈes.ᵊn|*t*s, rɪˌdʒuː-, -vɪˈnes- (US) rɪˌdʒuː.vəˈ- **-t** -t
rekindl|e ˌriːˈkɪn.dl̩ **-es** -z **-ing** -ɪŋ, ˌriːˈkɪnd.lɪŋ **-ed** -d
re-label ˌriːˈleɪ.bᵊl **-s** -z **-ling** -ɪŋ, -ˈleɪ.blɪŋ **-led** -d
relaid (*past of* **relay** = *lay again*) riːˈleɪd, rɪ-, rə-
relapse (*n.*) rɪˈlæps, rə-; ˈriː.læps
relaps|e (*v.*) rɪˈlæps, rə- **-es** -ɪz **-ing** -ɪŋ **-ed** -t
re|late (R) rɪ|ˈleɪt, rə- **-lates** -ˈleɪts **-lating** -ˈleɪ.tɪŋ (US) -ˈleɪ.t̬ɪŋ **-lated** -ˈleɪ.tɪd (US) -ˈleɪ.t̬ɪd **-later/s** -ˈleɪ.təʳ/z (US) -ˈleɪ.t̬ɚ/z
relation rɪˈleɪ.ʃᵊn, rə- **-s** -z
relational rɪˈleɪ.ʃᵊn.ᵊl, rə-
relationship rɪˈleɪ.ʃᵊn.ʃɪp, rə- **-s** -s
relatival ˌrel.əˈtaɪ.vᵊl
relative ˈrel.ə.tɪv (US) -t̬ɪv **-s** -z **-ly** -li ˌ**relative** ˈ**clause**; ˌ**relative** ˈ**pronoun**
relativ|ism ˈrel.ə.tɪ.v|ɪ.zᵊm (US) -t̬ɪ- **-ist/s** -ɪst/s
relativistic ˌrel.ə.tɪˈvɪs.tɪk (US) -t̬ɪˈ-
relativity ˌrel.əˈtɪv.ə.ti, -ɪ.ti (US) -ə.t̬i
relaunch (*n.*) ˈriː.lɔːn*t*ʃ (US) -lɑːn*t*ʃ **-es** -ɪz
relaunch (*v.*) ˌriːˈlɔːn*t*ʃ (US) -ˈlɑːn*t*ʃ, -ˈlɔːn*t*ʃ **-es** -ɪz **-ing** -ɪŋ **-ed** -t
relax rɪˈlæks, rə- **-es** -ɪz **-ing** -ɪŋ **-ed** -t **-ant/s** -ᵊnt/s
relaxation ˌriː.lækˈseɪ.ʃᵊn **-s** -z
relay (*n.*) ˈriː.leɪ, rɪˈleɪ, rə- (US) ˈriː.leɪ **-s** -z ˈ**relay** ˌ**race**
relay (*v.*) *lay again:* ˌriːˈleɪ **-s** -z **-ing** -ɪŋ **relaid** ˌriːˈleɪd
relay (*v.*) *send, broadcast:* ˈriː.leɪ, rɪˈleɪ, rə-, riː- **-s** -z **-ing** -ɪŋ **-ed** -d
releas|e rɪˈliːs, rə- **-es** -ɪz **-ing** -ɪŋ **-ed** -t
rele|gate ˈrel.ɪ|.geɪt, ˈ-ə- (US) ˈ-ə- **-gates** -geɪts **-gating** -geɪ.tɪŋ (US) -geɪ.t̬ɪŋ **-gated** -geɪ.tɪd (US) -geɪ.t̬ɪd
relegation ˌrel.ɪˈgeɪ.ʃᵊn, -əˈ- (US) -əˈ-
re|lent rɪ|ˈlent, rə- **-lents** -ˈlents **-lenting** -ˈlen.tɪŋ (US) -ˈlen.t̬ɪŋ **-lented** -ˈlen.tɪd (US) -ˈlen.t̬ɪd
relentless rɪˈlent.ləs, rə-, -lɪs **-ly** -li **-ness** -nəs, -nɪs
Relenza rɪˈlen.zə
re|-let ˌriː|ˈlet **-lets** -ˈlets **-letting** -ˈlet.ɪŋ (US) -ˈlet̬.ɪŋ
relevan|ce ˈrel.ə.vən*t*|s, ˈ-ɪ- (US) ˈ-ə- **-cy** -si
relevant ˈrel.ə.vənt, ˈ-ɪ- (US) ˈ-ə- **-ly** -li
reliability rɪˌlaɪ.əˈbɪl.ə.ti, rə-, -ɪ.ti (US) -ə.t̬i
reliab|le rɪˈlaɪ.ə.b|l̩, rə- **-ly** -li **-leness** -l̩.nəs, -nɪs
relian|ce rɪˈlaɪ.ən|*t*s, rə- **-t** -t
reliant rɪˈlaɪ.ənt, rə-
relic ˈrel.ɪk **-s** -s
relict ˈrel.ɪkt **-s** -s
reliction rɪˈlɪk.ʃᵊn
relief rɪˈliːf, rə- **-s** -s **re**ˈ**lief** ˌ**map**
reliev|e rɪˈliːv, rə- **-es** -z **-ing** -ɪŋ **-ed** -d **-able** -ə.bl̩
relievo rɪˈliː.vəʊ (US) -voʊ
Religio Laici rɪˌlɪg.i.əʊˈlɑː.ɪ.siː, rə-, -kiː (US) rɪˌlɪdʒ.i.oʊˈleɪ.ə-
religion rɪˈlɪdʒ.ᵊn, rə- **-s** -z
religion|ism rɪˈlɪdʒ.ᵊn|.ɪ.zᵊm, rə- **-ist/s** -ɪst/s
religiosity rɪˌlɪdʒ.iˈɒs.ə.ti, rə-, -ɪ.ti (US) -ˈɑː.sə.t̬i
religious rɪˈlɪdʒ.əs, rə- **-ly** -li **-ness** -nəs, -nɪs
relin|e ˌriːˈlaɪn **-es** -z **-ing** -ɪŋ **-ed** -d
relinquish rɪˈlɪŋ.kwɪʃ, rə- **-es** -ɪz **-ing** -ɪŋ **-ed** -t **-ment** -mənt
reliquar|y ˈrel.ɪ.kwᵊr|.i (US) -ə.kwer- **-ies** -iz
relish ˈrel.ɪʃ **-es** -ɪz **-ing** -ɪŋ **-ed** -t
reliv|e ˌriːˈlɪv **-es** -z **-ing** -ɪŋ **-ed** -d
reload ˌriːˈləʊd (US) -ˈloʊd **-s** -z **-ing** -ɪŋ **-ed** -ɪd
relo|cate ˌriː.ləʊ|ˈkeɪt (US) -ˈloʊ|.keɪt **-cates** -ˈkeɪts (US) -keɪts **-cating** -ˈkeɪ.tɪŋ (US) -keɪ.t̬ɪŋ **-cated** -ˈkeɪ.tɪd (US) -keɪ.t̬ɪd
relocation ˌriː.ləʊˈkeɪ.ʃᵊn (US) -loʊˈ-
reluctance rɪˈlʌk.tᵊn*t*s, rə-
reluctant rɪˈlʌk.tᵊnt, rə- **-ly** -li
reluctivity ˌrel.ʌkˈtɪv.ə.ti, ˌriː.lʌkˈ-; rɪˌlʌkˈ-, rə-, -ɪ.ti (US) ˌrel.əkˈtɪv.ə.t̬i
re|ly rɪ|ˈlaɪ, rə- **-lies** -ˈlaɪz **-lying** -ˈlaɪ.ɪŋ **-lied** -ˈlaɪd
REM, rem ˌɑːʳ.iːˈem; rem (US) ˌɑːr.iːˈem; rem
remain rɪˈmeɪn, rə- **-s** -z **-ing** -ɪŋ **-ed** -d
remainder rɪˈmeɪn.dəʳ, rə- (US) -dɚ **-s** -z **-ing** -ɪŋ **-ed** -d

remak|e (*v.*) ˌriːˈmeɪk **-es** -s **-ing** -ɪŋ **remade** ˌriːˈmeɪd
re-make (*n.*) ˈriː.meɪk **-s** -s
remand rɪˈmɑːnd, rə- ⓤⓢ -ˈmænd **-s** -z **-ing** -ɪŋ **-ed** -ɪd **reˈmand ˌhome**
remanence ˈrem.ə.nənts
remark rɪˈmɑːk, rə- ⓤⓢ -ˈmɑːrk **-s** -s **-ing** -ɪŋ **-ed** -t
remarkab|le rɪˈmɑː.kə.bl̩, rə- ⓤⓢ -ˈmɑːr- **-ly** -li **-leness** -l̩.nəs, -nɪs
Remarque rɪˈmɑːk, rə- ⓤⓢ -ˈmɑːrk
remarriag|e ˌriːˈmær.ɪdʒ ⓤⓢ -ˈmer-, -ˈmær- **-es** -ɪz
remarr|y ˌriːˈmær|.i ⓤⓢ -ˈmer-, -ˈmær- **-ies** -iz **-ying** -i.ɪŋ **-ied** -id
rematch ˈriː.mætʃ **-es** -ɪz
Rembrandt ˈrem.brænt, -brənt ⓤⓢ -brænt, -brɑːnt **-s** -s
REME ˈriː.mi
remediable rɪˈmiː.di.ə.bl̩, rə-
remedial rɪˈmiː.di.əl, rə- **-ly** -i
remediation rɪˌmiː.diˈeɪ.ʃən, rə-
remed|y ˈrem.ə.d|i, ˈ-ɪ- **-ies** -iz **-ying** -i.ɪŋ **-ied** -id
rememb|er rɪˈmem.b|əʳ, rə- ⓤⓢ -b|ɚ **-ers** -əz ⓤⓢ -ɚz **-ering** -ər.ɪŋ **-ered** -əd ⓤⓢ -ɚd
remembranc|e rɪˈmem.brənts, rə- **-es** -ɪz **-er/s** -əʳ/z ⓤⓢ -ɚ/z **Reˈmembrance ˌDay**
re-militariz|e, -is|e ˌriːˈmɪl.ɪ.tər.aɪz, ˈ-ə- ⓤⓢ -t̬ə.raɪz **-es** -ɪz **-ing** -ɪŋ **-ed** -d
remind rɪˈmaɪnd, rə- **-s** -z **-ing** -ɪŋ **-ed** -ɪd **-er/s** -əʳ/z ⓤⓢ -ɚ/z
Remington ˈrem.ɪŋ.tən **-s** -z
reminisc|e ˌrem.ɪˈnɪs, -əˈ- ⓤⓢ -əˈ- **-es** -ɪz **-ing** -ɪŋ **-ed** -t
reminiscenc|e ˌrem.ɪˈnɪs.ənts, -əˈ- ⓤⓢ -əˈ- **-es** -ɪz
reminiscent ˌrem.ɪˈnɪs.ənt, -əˈ- ⓤⓢ -əˈ-
remiss rɪˈmɪs, rə- **-ly** -li **-ness** -nəs, -nɪs
remission rɪˈmɪʃ.ən, rə- **-s** -z
remit (*n.*) ˈriː.mɪt; rɪˈmɪt, rə-, riː- ⓤⓢ rɪˈmɪt, rə- **-s** -s
re|mit (*v.*) rɪ|ˈmɪt, rə- **-mits** -ˈmɪts **-mitting** -ˈmɪt.ɪŋ ⓤⓢ -ˈmɪt̬.ɪŋ **-mitted** -ˈmɪt.ɪd ⓤⓢ -ˈmɪt̬.ɪd **-mitter/s** -ˈmɪt.əʳ/z ⓤⓢ -ˈmɪt̬.ɚ/z
remittal rɪˈmɪt.əl, rə- ⓤⓢ -ˈmɪt̬- **-s** -z
remittanc|e rɪˈmɪt.ənts, rə- **-es** -ɪz
remittitur rɪˈmɪt.ɪ.tʊəʳ, rə-, -tɜːʳ ⓤⓢ rəˈmɪt̬.ə.t̬ɚ
remix (*n.*) ˈriː.mɪks **-es** -ɪz
remix (*v.*) ˌriːˈmɪks **-es** -ɪz **-ing** -ɪŋ **-ed** -t
remnant ˈrem.nənt **-s** -s
remodel ˌriːˈmɒd.əl ⓤⓢ -ˈmɑː.dəl **-s** -z **-(l)ing** -ɪŋ **-(l)ed** -d
remold (*v.*) ˌriːˈməʊld ⓤⓢ -ˈmoʊld **-s** -z **-ing** -ɪŋ **-ed** -ɪd
remold (*n.*) ˈriː.məʊld ⓤⓢ -moʊld **-s** -z
remonetiz|e, -is|e ˌriːˈmʌn.ɪ.taɪz, ˈ-ə- ⓤⓢ -ˈmɑː.nə-, -ˈmʌn.ə- **-es** -ɪz **-ing** -ɪŋ **-ed** -d
remonstranc|e rɪˈmɒnt.strənts, rə- ⓤⓢ -ˈmɑːnt- **-es** -ɪz
remonstrant rɪˈmɒnt.strənt, rə- ⓤⓢ -ˈmɑːnt- **-ly** -li
remon|strate ˈrem.ən|.streɪt; rɪˈmɒnt-, rə- ⓤⓢ rɪˈmɑːnt-, rə-; ˈrem.ənt- **-strates** -streɪts **-strating** -streɪ.tɪŋ ⓤⓢ -streɪ.t̬ɪŋ **-strated** -streɪ.tɪd ⓤⓢ -streɪ.t̬ɪd
remonstrative rɪˈmɒnt.strə.tɪv, rə- ⓤⓢ -ˈmɑːnt.strə.t̬ɪv **-ly** -li
remorse rɪˈmɔːs, rə- ⓤⓢ -ˈmɔːrs
remorseful rɪˈmɔːs.fəl, rə-, -fʊl ⓤⓢ -ˈmɔːrs- **-ly** -i
remorseless rɪˈmɔː.sləs, rə-, -lɪs ⓤⓢ -ˈmɔːrs- **-ly** -li **-ness** -nəs, -nɪs
remortgag|e ˌriːˈmɔː.gɪdʒ ⓤⓢ -ˈmɔːr- **-es** -ɪz **-ing** -ɪŋ **-ed** -d
remote rɪˈməʊt, rə- ⓤⓢ -ˈmoʊt **-ly** -li **-ness** -nəs, -nɪs **reˌmote conˈtrol**
remould (*v.*) ˌriːˈməʊld ⓤⓢ -ˈmoʊld **-s** -z **-ing** -ɪŋ **-ed** -ɪd
remould (*n.*) ˈriː.məʊld ⓤⓢ -moʊld **-s** -z
remount (*n.*) ˈriː.maʊnt, ˌ-ˈ- ⓤⓢ ˈriː.maʊnt **-s** -s
re|mount (*v.*) ˌriː|ˈmaʊnt **-mounts** -ˈmaʊnts **-mounting** -ˈmaʊn.tɪŋ ⓤⓢ -ˈmaʊn.t̬ɪŋ **-mounted** -ˈmaʊn.tɪd ⓤⓢ -ˈmaʊn.t̬ɪd
removability rɪˌmuː.vəˈbɪl.ə.ti, rə-, -ɪ.ti ⓤⓢ -ə.t̬i
removal rɪˈmuː.vəl, rə- **-s** -z **reˈmoval ˌvan**
remov|e rɪˈmuːv, rə- **-es** -z **-ing** -ɪŋ **-ed** -d **-er/s** -əʳ/z ⓤⓢ -ɚ/z **-able** -ə.bl̩
Remploy® ˈrem.plɔɪ
remuner|ate rɪˈmjuː.nər|.eɪt, rə- ⓤⓢ -nə.r|eɪt **-ates** -eɪts **-ating** -eɪ.tɪŋ ⓤⓢ -eɪ.t̬ɪŋ **-ated** -eɪ.tɪd ⓤⓢ -eɪ.t̬ɪd
remuneration rɪˌmjuː.nərˈeɪ.ʃən, rə- ⓤⓢ -nəˈreɪ- **-s** -z
remunerative rɪˈmjuː.nər.ə.tɪv, rə- ⓤⓢ -nə.reɪ.t̬ɪv, -nɚ.ə-
Remus ˈriː.məs
renaissance (R) rəˈneɪ.sənts, rɪ-, ˌren.eɪˈsɑ̃ːns, -ˈsɑːnts ⓤⓢ ˌren.əˈsɑːnts, -ˈzɑːnts, ˈ--- **Reˌnaissance ˈman**
renal ˈriː.nəl
renam|e ˌriːˈneɪm **-es** -z **-ing** -ɪŋ **-ed** -d
renascen|t rɪˈneɪ.sən|t, rə-, -ˈnæs.ən|t ⓤⓢ -ˈnæs.ən|t, -ˈneɪ.sən|t **-ce** -ts
Renault® ˈren.əʊ ⓤⓢ rəˈnoʊ, -ˈnɔːlt **-s** -z
rend rend **-s** -z **-ing** -ɪŋ **-ed** -ɪd **rent** rent
Rendell ˈren.dəl
rend|er ˈren.d|əʳ ⓤⓢ -d|ɚ **-ers** -əz ⓤⓢ -ɚz **-ering/s** -ər.ɪŋ/z **-ered** -əd ⓤⓢ -ɚd
rendezvous *singular:* ˈrɒn.dɪ.vuː, -deɪ- ⓤⓢ ˈrɑːn.deɪ-, -diː-, -dɪ- **-ing** -ɪŋ **-ed** -d *plural:* -z
rendition renˈdɪʃ.ən **-s** -z
Renee, Renée ˈren.eɪ; rəˈneɪ; ˈriː.ni ⓤⓢ rəˈneɪ
renegade ˈren.ɪ.geɪd, ˈ-ə- ⓤⓢ ˈ-ə- **-s** -z
renegoti|ate ˌriː.nɪˈgəʊ.ʃi|.eɪt, -nəˈ- ⓤⓢ -nəˈgoʊ- **-ates** -eɪts **-ating** -eɪ.tɪŋ ⓤⓢ -eɪ.t̬ɪŋ **-ated** -eɪ.tɪd ⓤⓢ -eɪ.t̬ɪd
renegotiation ˌriː.nɪˌgəʊ.ʃiˈeɪ.ʃən, -nəˌ- ⓤⓢ -nəˌgoʊ- **-s** -z
reneg(u)|e rɪˈniːg, rə-, -ˈneɪg, -ˈneg ⓤⓢ -ˈnɪg, -ˈneg, -ˈniːg **-es** -z **-ing** -ɪŋ **-ed** -d
renew rɪˈnjuː, rə- ⓤⓢ rɪˈnuː, -ˈnjuː **-s** -z **-ing** -ɪŋ **-ed** -d **-able/s** -ə.bl̩/z
renewal rɪˈnjuː.əl, rə-, -ˈnjʊəl ⓤⓢ -ˈnuː.əl, -ˈnjuː- **-s** -z
Renfrew ˈren.fruː **-shire** -ʃəʳ, -ˌʃɪəʳ ⓤⓢ -ʃɚ, -ˌʃɪr
renin ˈriː.nɪn ⓤⓢ ˈriː.nɪn, ˈren.ən
renminbi renˈmɪn.bi ⓤⓢ ˈren.mɪn-
Rennes ren
rennet ˈren.ɪt
Rennie ˈren.i
Rennies® ˈren.iz
rennin ˈren.ɪn
Reno ˈriː.nəʊ ⓤⓢ -noʊ
Renoir rənˈwɑːʳ; ˈren.wɑːʳ, ˌ-ˈ- ⓤⓢ rənˈwɑːr, ˈren.wɑːr
renounc|e rɪˈnaʊnts, rə- **-es** -ɪz **-ing** -ɪŋ **-ed** -t **-ement** -mənt
reno|vate ˈren.əʊ|.veɪt **-vates** -veɪts **-vating** -veɪ.tɪŋ ⓤⓢ -veɪ.t̬ɪŋ **-vated** -veɪ.tɪd ⓤⓢ -veɪ.t̬ɪd **-vator/s** -veɪ.təʳ/z ⓤⓢ -veɪ.t̬ɚ/z
renovation ˌren.əˈveɪ.ʃən **-s** -z
renown rɪˈnaʊn, rə- **-ed** -d
Renshaw ˈren.ʃɔː ⓤⓢ -ʃɑː, -ʃɔː
rent rent **-s** -s **-ing** -ɪŋ ⓤⓢ ˈren.t̬ɪŋ **-ed** -ɪd ⓤⓢ ˈren.t̬ɪd **-er/s** -əʳ/z ⓤⓢ ˈren.t̬ɚ/z
rent-a-crowd ˈrent.ə.kraʊd ⓤⓢ ˈrent̬-
rental ˈren.təl ⓤⓢ -t̬əl **-s** -z
rent-free ˌrentˈfriː *stress shift:* ˌrent-free ˈflat
rentier ˈrɑːn.ti.eɪ ⓤⓢ -ˈtjeɪ **-s** -z
Rentokil® ˈren.təʊ.kɪl ⓤⓢ -t̬ə-, -toʊ-
Renton ˈren.tən ⓤⓢ -tən
rent-roll ˈrent.rəʊl ⓤⓢ -roʊl **-s** -z
renunciation rɪˌnʌnt.siˈeɪ.ʃən, rə- **-s**
renvoi renˈvɔɪ
Renwick ˈren.ɪk, -wɪk
Note: For US names, /ˈren.wɪk/ is the likely pronunciation.
reoccupation riːˌɒk.jəˈpeɪ.ʃən, ri-, -jʊˈ- ⓤⓢ -ˌɑː.kjəˈ-, -kjʊˈ- **-s** -z
reoccup|y ˌriːˈɒk.jə.plaɪ, ri-, -jʊ- ⓤⓢ -ˈɑː.kjə-, -kjʊ- **-ies** -aɪz **-ying** -aɪ.ɪŋ **-ied** -aɪd
reoffend ˌriː.əˈfend **-s** -z **-ing** -ɪŋ **-ed** -**er/s** -əʳ/z ⓤⓢ -ɚ/z
reopen ˌriːˈəʊ.pən, ri-, -pəm ⓤⓢ -ˈoʊ. **-s** -z **-ing** -ɪŋ **-ed** -d

reorganization, -isa- ˌriːˌɔː.gᵊn.aɪˈzeɪ.ʃᵊn, ri-, -ɪˈ- (US) -ˌɔːr.gᵊn.ɪˈ-; ˌriː.ɔːr- **-s** -z

reorganiz|e, -is|e ˌriːˈɔː.gᵊn.aɪz, ri- (US) -ˈɔːr- **-es** -ɪz **-ing** -ɪŋ **-ed** -d

reori|ent ˌriːˈɔː.ri|.ənt, ri- (US) -ˈɔːr.i- **-ents** -ənts **-enting** -ən.tɪŋ (US) -ən.t̬ɪŋ **-ented** -ən.tɪd (US) -ən.t̬ɪd

reorien|tate ˌriːˈɔː.ri.ən|.teɪt, -ˈɒr.i-, -en- (US) ˌriːˈɔːr.i.en-, -ən- **-tates** -teɪts **-tating** -teɪ.tɪŋ (US) -teɪ.t̬ɪŋ **-tated** -teɪ.tɪd (US) -teɪ.t̬ɪd

reorientation riːˌɔː.ri.ənˈteɪ.ʃᵊn, -ˌɒr.i-, -enˈ- (US) -ˌɔːr.i.enˈ-, -ənˈ-

rep rep **-s** -s

repackag|e ˌriːˈpæk.ɪdʒ **-es** -ɪz **-ing** -ɪŋ **-ed** -d

repaid *(from* **repay**, *pay back)* rɪˈpeɪd, rə-, ˌriː- ˌriːˈpeɪd

repair rɪˈpeəʳ, rə- (US) -ˈper **-s** -z **-ing** -ɪŋ **-ed** -d **-er/s** -əʳ/z (US) -ɚ/z

repairable rɪˈpeə.rə.bl̩, rə- (US) -ˈper.ə-

reparability ˌrep.ᵊr.əˈbɪl.ə.ti, -ɪ.ti (US) -ə.t̬i

reparable ˈrep.ᵊr.ə.bl̩

reparation ˌrep.ᵊrˈeɪ.ʃᵊn (US) -əˈreɪ- **-s** -z

repartee ˌrep.ɑːˈtiː (US) -ɑːrˈ-, -ɚˈ-, -ˈteɪ

repass ˌriːˈpɑːs (US) -ˈpæs **-es** -ɪz **-ing** -ɪŋ **-ed** -t

repast rɪˈpɑːst, rə- (US) -ˈpæst **-s** -s

repatri|ate riːˈpæt.ri|.eɪt, rɪ- (US) -ˈpeɪ.tri- **-ates** -eɪts **-ating** -eɪ.tɪŋ (US) -eɪ.t̬ɪŋ **-ated** -eɪ.tɪd (US) -eɪ.t̬ɪd

repatriation ˌriː.pæt.riˈeɪ.ʃᵊn; rɪˌpæt- (US) rɪˌpeɪ.triˈ-

repay *pay back:* rɪˈpeɪ, rə-, ˌriː- **-s** -z **-ing** -ɪŋ **repaid** rɪˈpeɪd, rə-, ˌriː-

repay *pay again:* ˌriːˈpeɪ **-s** -z **-ing** -ɪŋ **repaid** ˌriːˈpeɪd

repayable rɪˈpeɪ.ə.bl̩, ˌriː-

repayment rɪˈpeɪ.mənt, ˌriː- **-s** -s

repeal rɪˈpiːl, rə- **-s** -z **-ing** -ɪŋ **-ed** -d

re|peat rɪ|ˈpiːt, rə- **-peats** -ˈpiːts **-peating** -ˈpiː.tɪŋ (US) -ˈpiː.t̬ɪŋ **-peated/ly** -ˈpiː.tɪd/li (US) -ˈpiː.t̬ɪd/li **-peater/s** -ˈpiː.təʳ/z (US) -ˈpiː.t̬ɚ/z

repeatability rɪˌpiː.təˈbɪl.ɪ.ti, rə-, -ə.ti (US) -t̬əˈbɪl.ə.t̬i

repêchage, repechage ˈrep.ə.ʃɑːʒ, ˈ-ɪ-, ˌ--ˈ- (US) ˌrep.əˈʃɑːʒ; rəˌpeʃˈ-

repel rɪˈpel, rə- **-s** -z **-ling** -ɪŋ **-led** -d

repellent, repellant rɪˈpel.ᵊnt, rə- **-s** -s

re|pent rɪ|ˈpent, rə- **-pents** -ˈpents **-penting** -ˈpen.tɪŋ (US) -ˈpen.t̬ɪŋ **-pented** -ˈpen.tɪd (US) -ˈpen.t̬ɪd

repentanc|e rɪˈpen.tənts, rə- (US) -tᵊnts **-es** -ɪz

repentant rɪˈpen.tənt, rə- (US) -tᵊnt **-ly** -li

repercussion ˌriː.pəˈkʌʃ.ᵊn (US) -pɚˈ-, ˌrep.ɚˈ- **-s** -z

repertoire ˈrep.ə.twɑːʳ (US) -ɚ.twɑːr, ˈ-ə- **-s** -z

repertor|y ˈrep.ə.tᵊr|.i (US) -ɚ.tɔːr-, ˈ-ə- **-ies** -iz

répétiteur rɪˌpet.ɪˈtɜːʳ, rə- (US) ˌreɪ.peɪˈtiː.tɚ **-s** -z

repetition ˌrep.ɪˈtɪʃ.ᵊn, -əˈ- (US) -əˈ- **-s** -z

repetitious ˌrep.ɪˈtɪʃ.əs, -əˈ- (US) -əˈ- **-ly** -li **-ness** -nəs, -nɪs

repetitive rɪˈpet.ə.tɪv, rə-, ˈ-ɪ- (US) -ˈpet̬.ə.t̬ɪv **-ly** -li **-ness** -nəs, -nɪs **reˌpetitive ˈstrain ˌinjury; reˌpetitive ˈmotion ˌinjury**

rephras|e ˌriːˈfreɪz **-es** -ɪz **-ing** -ɪŋ **-ed** -d

repin|e rɪˈpaɪn, rə- **-es** -z **-ing** -ɪŋ **-ed** -d

replac|e rɪˈpleɪs, rə-, ˌriː- **-es** -ɪz **-ing** -ɪŋ **-ed** -t

replaceable rɪˈpleɪ.sə.bl̩, rə-, ˌriː-

replacement rɪˈpleɪs.mənt, rə-, ˌriː- **-s** -s

re|plant ˌriː|ˈplɑːnt (US) -ˈplænt **-plants** -ˈplɑːnts (US) -ˈplænts **-planting** -ˈplɑːn.tɪŋ (US) -ˈplæn.t̬ɪŋ **-planted** -ˈplɑːn.tɪd (US) -ˈplæn.t̬ɪd

replay *(n.)* ˈriː.pleɪ **-s** -z

replay *(v.)* ˌriːˈpleɪ **-s** -z **-ing** -ɪŋ **-ed** -d

replenish rɪˈplen.ɪʃ, rə- **-es** -ɪz **-ing** -ɪŋ **-ed** -t **-ment** -mənt

replete rɪˈpliːt **-ness** -nəs, -nɪs

repletion rɪˈpliː.ʃᵊn

replevin rɪˈplev.ɪn, rə-

replevy rɪˈplev.i, rə-

replica ˈrep.lɪ.kə, -lə- (US) -lɪ- **-s** -z

replicable ˈrep.lɪ.kə.bl̩, -lə- (US) -lɪ-

repli|cate ˈrep.lɪ|.keɪt, -lə- (US) -lɪ- **-cates** -keɪts **-cating** -keɪ.tɪŋ (US) -keɪ.t̬ɪŋ **-cated** -keɪ.tɪd (US) -keɪ.t̬ɪd

replication ˌrep.lɪˈkeɪ.ʃᵊn, -ləˈ- (US) -ləˈ- **-s** -z

repl|y rɪˈpl|aɪ, rə- **-ies** -aɪz **-ying** -aɪ.ɪŋ **-ied** -aɪd

repo ˈriː.pəʊ (US) -poʊ **-s** -z

re|point ˌriː|ˈpɔɪnt **-points** -ˈpɔɪnts **-pointing** -ˈpɔɪn.tɪŋ (US) -ˈpɔɪn.t̬ɪŋ **-pointed** -ˈpɔɪn.tɪd (US) -ˈpɔɪn.t̬ɪd

repolish ˌriːˈpɒl.ɪʃ (US) -ˈpɑː.lɪʃ **-es** -ɪz **-ing** -ɪŋ **-ed** -t

repopu|late ˌriːˈpɒp.jə|.leɪt, rɪˈ-, -jʊ- (US) -ˈpɑː.pjə-, -pjʊ- **-lates** -leɪts **-lating** -leɪ.tɪŋ (US) -leɪ.t̬ɪŋ **-lated** -leɪ.tɪd (US) -leɪ.t̬ɪd

re|port rɪ|ˈpɔːt, rə- (US) -ˈpɔːrt **-ports** -ˈpɔːts (US) -ˈpɔːrts **-porting** -ˈpɔː.tɪŋ (US) -ˈpɔːr.t̬ɪŋ **-ported/ly** -ˈpɔː.tɪd/li (US) -ˈpɔːr.t̬ɪd/li **reˌported ˈspeech**

reportage ˌrep.ɔːˈtɑːʒ; rɪˈpɔː.tɪdʒ, rə- (US) rɪˈpɔːr.t̬ɪdʒ, rə-; ˌrep.ɚˈtɑːʒ

reporter rɪˈpɔː.təʳ, rə- (US) -ˈpɔːr.t̬ɚ **-s** -z

repos|e rɪˈpəʊz, rə- (US) -ˈpoʊz **-es** -ɪz **-ing** -ɪŋ **-ed** -d

reposeful rɪˈpəʊz.fᵊl, rə-, -fʊl (US) -ˈpoʊz- **-ly** -i

reposition ˌriː.pəˈzɪʃ.ᵊn **-s** -z **-ing** -ɪŋ **-ed** -d

repositor|y rɪˈpɒz.ɪ.tᵊr|.i, rə- (US) -ˈpɑː.zɪ.tɔːr- **-ies** -iz

repossess ˌriː.pəˈzes **-es** -ɪz **-ing** -ɪŋ **-ed** -t

repossession ˌriː.pəˈzeʃ.ᵊn **-s** -z

repoussé rəˈpuː.seɪ, rɪ- (US) rəˌpuːˈseɪ

reprehend ˌrep.rɪˈhend, -rəˈ- (US) -rɪˈ- **-s** -z **-ing** -ɪŋ **-ed** -ɪd

reprehensib|le ˌrep.rɪˈhent.sə.bl̩, -rəˈ-, -sɪ- (US) -sə- **-ly** -li

reprehension ˌrep.rɪˈhen.tʃᵊn, -rəˈ-

repre|sent ˌrep.rɪ|ˈzent, -rəˈ- (US) -rɪˈ- **-sents** -ˈzents **-senting** -ˈzen.tɪŋ (US) -ˈzen.t̬ɪŋ **-sented** -ˈzen.tɪd (US) -ˈzen.t̬ɪd

representation ˌrep.rɪ.zenˈteɪ.ʃᵊn, -rə-, -zᵊnˈ- (US) -rɪ.zenˈ- **-s** -z

representational ˌrep.rɪ.zenˈteɪ.ʃᵊn.ᵊl, -rə-, -zᵊnˈ- (US) -rɪ.zenˈ- **-ly** -i

representative ˌrep.rɪˈzen.tə.tɪv, -rəˈ- (US) -rɪˈzen.t̬ə.t̬ɪv **-s** -z **-ly** -li

repress rɪˈpres, rə- **-es** -ɪz **-ing** -ɪŋ **-ed** -t **-ible** -ə.bl̩, -ɪ.bl̩

repression rɪˈpreʃ.ᵊn, rə- **-s** -z

repressive rɪˈpres.ɪv, rə- **-ly** -li **-ness** -nəs, -nɪs

repriev|e rɪˈpriːv, rə- **-es** -z **-ing** -ɪŋ **-ed** -d

reprimand *(n.)* ˈrep.rɪ.mɑːnd, -rə- (US) -rə.mænd **-s** -z

reprimand *(v.)* ˈrep.rɪ.mɑːnd, -rə-, ˌ--ˈ- (US) ˈrep.rə.mænd, ˌ--ˈ- **-s** -z **-ing** -ɪŋ **-ed** -ɪd

reprint *(n.)* ˈriː.prɪnt, ˌ-ˈ- (US) ˈriː.prɪnt **-s** -s

re|print *(v.)* ˌriː|ˈprɪnt **-prints** -ˈprɪnts **-printing** -ˈprɪn.tɪŋ (US) -ˈprɪn.t̬ɪŋ **-printed** -ˈprɪn.tɪd (US) -ˈprɪn.t̬ɪd

reprisal rɪˈpraɪ.zᵊl, rə- **-s** -z

repris|e *(n. v.) in music:* rɪˈpriːz, rə- **-es** -ɪz **-ing** -ɪŋ **-ed** -d *legal term:* rɪˈpraɪz, rə-, -ˈpriːz (US) -ˈpraɪz **-es** -ɪz **-ing** -ɪŋ **-ed** -d

repro ˈriː.prəʊ (US) -proʊ **-s** -z

reproach rɪˈprəʊtʃ, rə- (US) -ˈproʊtʃ **-es** -ɪz **-ing** -ɪŋ **-ed** -t **-able** -ə.bl̩

reproachful rɪˈprəʊtʃ.fᵊl, rə-, -fʊl (US) -ˈproʊtʃ- **-ly** -i **-ness** -nəs, -nɪs

reprobate *(n. adj.)* ˈrep.rəʊ.beɪt, -bɪt (US) -rə.beɪt, -bɪt **-s** -s

repro|bate *(v.)* ˈrep.rəʊ|.beɪt (US) -rə- **-bates** -beɪts **-bating** -beɪ.tɪŋ (US) -beɪ.t̬ɪŋ **-bated** -beɪ.tɪd (US) -beɪ.t̬ɪd

reprobation ˌrep.rəʊˈbeɪ.ʃᵊn (US) -rəˈ-

reprocess ˌriːˈprəʊ.ses, -sɪs (US) -ˈprɑː.ses, -səs **-es** -ɪz **-ing** -ɪŋ **-ed** -t

reproduc|e ˌriː.prəˈdjuːs, -ˈdʒuːs (US) -ˈduːs, -ˈdjuːs **-es** -ɪz **-ing** -ɪŋ **-ed** -t **-er/s** -əʳ/z (US) -ɚ/z

reproduction ˌriː.prəˈdʌk.ʃᵊn **-s** -z
reproductive ˌriː.prəˈdʌk.tɪv **-ness** -nəs, -nɪs
reprogram ˌriːˈprəʊ.græm (US) -ˈproʊ- **-s** -z **-(m)ing** -ɪŋ **-(m)ed** -d
reprographic ˌriː.prəʊˈgræf.ɪk, ˌrep.rəʊˈ- (US) ˌriː.proʊˈ-, -prəˈ- **-s** -s
reprograph|y rɪˈprɒg.rə.f|i, riː- (US) -ˈprɑː.grə- **-er/s** -əʳ/z (US) -ɚ/z
reproof rɪˈpruːf, rə- **-s** -s
re-proof (*v.*) ˌriːˈpruːf **-s** -s **-ing** -ɪŋ **-ed** -t
reproval rɪˈpruː.vᵊl, rə- **-s** -z
reprov|e rɪˈpruːv, rə- **-es** -z **-ing/ly** -ɪŋ/li **-ed** -d **-er/s** -əʳ/z (US) -ɚ/z
reptile ˈrep.taɪl (US) -taɪl, -tᵊl **-s** -z
reptilian repˈtɪl.i.ən (US) -i.ən, ˈ-jən **-s** -z
Repton ˈrep.tən
republic (R) rɪˈpʌb.lɪk, rə- **-s** -s
republican (R) rɪˈpʌb.lɪ.kən, rə- **-s** -z **-ism** -ɪ.zᵊm
republication ˌriː.pʌb.lɪˈkeɪ.ʃᵊn, -ləˈ- (US) ˌriː.pʌb.lɪˈ- **-s** -z
republish ˌriːˈpʌb.lɪʃ **-es** -ɪz **-ing** -ɪŋ **-ed** -t
repudi|ate rɪˈpjuː.di|.eɪt, rə- **-ates** -eɪts **-ating** -eɪ.tɪŋ (US) -eɪ.t̬ɪŋ **-ated** -eɪ.tɪd (US) -eɪ.t̬ɪd **-ater/s** -eɪ.təʳ/z (US) -eɪ.t̬ɚ/z
repudiation rɪˌpjuː.diˈeɪ.ʃᵊn, rə-
repugnance rɪˈpʌg.nənts, rə-
repugnant rɪˈpʌg.nənt, rə- **-ly** -li
repuls|e rɪˈpʌls, rə- **-es** -ɪz **-ing** -ɪŋ **-ed** -t
repulsion rɪˈpʌl.ʃᵊn, rə-
repulsive rɪˈpʌl.sɪv, rə- **-ly** -li **-ness** -nəs, -nɪs
reputability ˌrep.jə.təˈbɪl.ə.ti, -jʊ-, -ɪ.ti (US) -t̬əˈbɪl.ə.t̬i
reputab|le ˈrep.jə.tə.b|ḷ, -jʊ- (US) -t̬ə- **-ly** -li
reputation ˌrep.jəˈteɪ.ʃᵊn, -jʊˈ- **-s** -z
re|pute rɪ|ˈpjuːt, rə- **-puted/ly** -ˈpjuː.tɪd/li (US) -ˈpjuː.t̬ɪd/li
request rɪˈkwest, rə- **-s** -s **-ing** -ɪŋ **-ed** -ɪd
requiem ˈrek.wi.əm, -em **-s** -z ˌ**requiem** ˈ**mass**
requiescat ˌrek.wiˈes.kæt (US) ˌreɪ.kwiˈ-, ˌrek.wiˈ-, -kɑːt
requir|e rɪˈkwaɪəʳ, rə- (US) -ˈkwaɪɚ **-es** -z **-ing** -ɪŋ **-ed** -d
requirement rɪˈkwaɪə.mənt, rə- (US) -ˈkwaɪɚ- **-s** -s
requisite ˈrek.wɪ.zɪt, -wə- **-s** -s **-ly** -li **-ness** -nəs, -nɪs
requisition ˌrek.wɪˈzɪʃ.ᵊn, -wəˈ- **-s** -z **-ing** -ɪŋ **-ed** -d
re|quite rɪ|ˈkwaɪt, rə- **-quites** -ˈkwaɪts **-quiting** -ˈkwaɪ.tɪŋ (US) -ˈkwaɪ.t̬ɪŋ **-quited** -ˈkwaɪ.tɪd (US) -ˈkwaɪ.t̬ɪd **-quital** -ˈkwaɪ.tᵊl (US) -ˈkwaɪ.t̬ᵊl
re-read *present tense:* ˌriːˈriːd **-s** -z **-ing** -ɪŋ *past tense:* ˌriːˈred
reredos ˈrɪə.dɒs (US) ˈrɪr.dɑːs **-es** -ɪz
releas|e (*v.*) ˌriː.rɪˈliːs **-es** -ɪz **-ing** -ɪŋ **-ed** -t
rereleas|e (*n.*) ˈriː.rɪ.liːs **-s** -es
rerou|te ˌriːˈruː|t (US) -ˈruː|t, -ˈraʊ|t **-tes** -ts **-ting** -tɪŋ (US) -t̬ɪŋ **-ted** -tɪd (US) -t̬ɪd
rerun (*v.*) ˌriːˈrʌn **-s** -z **-ning** -ɪŋ **reran** ˌriːˈræn
rerun (*n.*) ˈriː.rʌn **-s** -z
res reɪz, reɪs, riːz (US) reɪs, riːz
resale ˈriː.seɪl, ˌ-ˈ- (US) ˈriː.seɪl **-s** -z
reschedul|e ˌriːˈʃed.juːl, -ˈʃedʒ.uːl (US) -ˈskedʒ.uːl, -əl **-es** -z **-ing** -ɪŋ **-ed** -d
rescind rɪˈsɪnd, rə- **-s** -z **-ing** -ɪŋ **-ed** -ɪd
rescission rɪˈsɪʒ.ᵊn, rə-
rescript ˈriː.skrɪpt **-s** -s
rescu|e ˈres.kjuː **-es** -z **-ing** -ɪŋ **-ed** -d **-er/s** -əʳ/z (US) -ɚ/z
research (*n.*) rɪˈsɜːtʃ, rə-, ˈriː.sɜːtʃ (US) ˈriː.sɝːtʃ; rɪˈsɝːtʃ, rə- **-es** -ɪz
research (*v.*) rɪˈsɜːtʃ, rə- (US) -ˈsɝːtʃ; ˈriː.sɝːtʃ **-es** -ɪz **-ing** -ɪŋ **-ed** -t **-er/s** -əʳ/z (US) -ɚ/z
re|seat ˌriː|ˈsiːt **-seats** -ˈsiːts **-seating** -ˈsiː.tɪŋ (US) -ˈsiː.t̬ɪŋ **-seated** -ˈsiː.tɪd (US) -ˈsiː.t̬ɪd
resection ˌriːˈsek.ʃᵊn, rɪ- **-s** -z
reseda ˈres.ɪ.də, ˈrez-, ˈ-ə-; rɪˈsiː.də, rə- (US) rɪˈsiː.də, rə-, -ˈsed.ə **-s** -z
reselect ˌriː.sɪˈlekt, -səˈ- **-s** -s **-ing** -ɪŋ **-ed** -ɪd
reselection ˌriː.sɪˈlek.ʃᵊn, -səˈ-
resell ˌriːˈsel **-s** -z **-ing** -ɪŋ **resold** ˌriːˈsəʊld (US) -ˈsoʊld
resemblanc|e rɪˈzem.blənts, rə- **-es** -ɪz
resembl|e rɪˈzem.bḷ, rə- **-es** -z **-ing** -ɪŋ, -ˈzem.blɪŋ **-ed** -d
re|sent rɪ|ˈzent, rə- **-sents** -ˈzents **-senting** -ˈzen.tɪŋ (US) -ˈzen.t̬ɪŋ **-sented** -ˈzen.tɪd (US) -ˈzen.t̬ɪd
resentful rɪˈzent.fᵊl, rə-, -fʊl **-ly** -li
resentment rɪˈzent.mənt, rə-
reservation ˌrez.əˈveɪ.ʃᵊn (US) -ɚˈ- **-s** -z
reserv|e rɪˈzɜːv, rə- (US) -ˈzɝːv **-es** -z **-ing** -ɪŋ **-ed** -d
reservedly rɪˈzɜː.vɪd.li, rə- (US) -ˈzɝː-
reservist rɪˈzɜː.vɪst, rə- (US) -ˈzɝː- **-s** -s
reservoir ˈrez.əv.wɑːʳ (US) -ɚv.wɑːr, -wɔːr, ˈ-ɚ.vɔːr, ˈ-ə- **-s** -z
re|set ˌriː|ˈset **-sets** -ˈsets **-setting/s** -ˈset.ɪŋ/z (US) -ˈset̬.ɪŋ/z
resettle ˌriːˈset.ḷ **-s** -z **-ing** -ɪŋ **-ed** -d **-ment** -mənt
res gestae ˌreɪsˈges.taɪ, ˌreɪz-, ˌriːz-, -ˈdʒes-, -tiː
reshap|e ˌriːˈʃeɪp **-es** -s **-ing** -ɪŋ **-ed** -t
reship ˌriːˈʃɪp **-s** -s **-ping** -ɪŋ **-ped** -t **-ment/s** -mənt/s
reshuffle (*n.*) ˌriːˈʃʌf.ḷ, ˈ-ˌ-- (US) ˌriːˈʃʌf- **-s** -z
reshuffl|e (*v.*) ˌriːˈʃʌf.ḷ **-es** -z **-ing** -ɪŋ, -ˈʃʌf.lɪŋ **-ed** -d
resid|e rɪˈzaɪd, rə- **-es** -z **-ing** -ɪŋ **-ed** -ɪd
residenc|e ˈrez.ɪ.dᵊnts **-es** -ɪz
residenc|y ˈrez.ɪ.dᵊnt.s|i **-ies** -iz
resident ˈrez.ɪ.dᵊnt **-s** -s
residential ˌrez.ɪˈden.tʃᵊl
residual rɪˈzɪd.ju.əl, rə-, -ˈzɪdʒ.u- (US) -ˈzɪdʒ- **-ly** -i
residuary rɪˈzɪd.ju.əri, rə-, -ˈzɪdʒ.ʊə- (US) -ˈzɪdʒ.u.er-
residue ˈrez.ɪ.djuː, ˈ-ə-, -dʒuː (US) -ə.duː, -djuː **-s** -z
residu|um rɪˈzɪd.ju|.əm, rə-, -ˈzɪdʒ.u- (US) -ˈzɪdʒ- **-a** -ə
resign rɪˈzaɪn, rə- **-s** -z **-ing** -ɪŋ **-ed** -d **-edly** -ɪd.li
resignation ˌrez.ɪgˈneɪ.ʃᵊn, -əgˈ- (US) -ɪgˈ- **-s** -z
resilien|ce rɪˈzɪl.i.ənt|s, rə-, -ˈsɪl- (US) -ˈzɪl.jənt|s, ˈ-i.ənt|s **-cy** -si
resilient rɪˈzɪl.i.ənt, rə-, -ˈsɪl- (US) -ˈzɪl.jənt, ˈ-i.ənt **-ly** -li
resin ˈrez.ɪn **-s** -z **-ous** -əs
res ipsa loquitur ˌreɪs,ɪp.sɑːˈlɒk.wɪ.tʊəʳ, ˌreɪz-, ˌriːz-, -səˈ-, -təʳ (US) ˌreɪs,ɪp.səˈlɑː.wɪ.tʊr
resist rɪˈzɪst, rə- **-s** -s **-ing** -ɪŋ **-ed** -ɪd **-or/s** -əʳ/z (US) -ɚ/z
resistanc|e rɪˈzɪs.tᵊnts, rə- **-es** -ɪz
resistant rɪˈzɪs.tᵊnt, rə- **-ly** -li
resistivity ˌriː.zɪˈstɪv.ə.ti, ˌrez.ɪˈ-, -ɪ. (US) ˌriː.zɪˈstɪv.ə.t̬i; rɪˌzɪsˈtɪv-
resistless rɪˈzɪst.ləs, rə-, -lɪs
resistor rɪˈzɪs.təʳ, rə- (US) -tɚ **-s** -z
resit (*n.*) ˈriː.sɪt **-s** -s
re|sit (*v.*) ˌriː|ˈsɪt **-sits** -ˈsɪts **-sitting** -ˈsɪt.ɪŋ (US) -ˈsɪt̬.ɪŋ **resat** ˌriːˈsæt
res judicata ˌreɪs,dʒuː.dɪˈkɑː.tə, ˌreɪ… ˌriːz-, -dəˈ- (US) ˌreɪs-, ˌreɪz-, ˌriːz-, ˌriːs-
reskill ˌriːˈskɪl **-s** -z **-ing** -ɪŋ **-ed** -d
resnoid ˈrez.nɔɪd **-s** -z
resol|e ˌriːˈsəʊl (US) -ˈsoʊl **-es** -z **-ing** -ɪ… **-ed** -d
resoluble rɪˈzɒl.jə.bḷ, rə-, -jʊ-; ˈrez.ᵊ… (US) rɪˈzɑːl.jə-, rə-, -jʊ-; ˈrez.ᵊl-
resolute ˈrez.ᵊl.uːt, -juːt (US) -ə.luːt **-l**… -li **-ness** -nəs, -nɪs
resolution ˌrez.ᵊlˈuː.ʃᵊn, -ˈjuː- (US) -əˈluː- **-s** -z
resolvability rɪˌzɒl.vəˈbɪl.ə.ti, rə-, -… (US) -ˌzɑːl.vəˈbɪl.ə.t̬i
resolv|e rɪˈzɒlv, rə- (US) -ˈzɑːlv **-es** -z … -ɪŋ **-ed** -d **-able** -ə.bḷ
resonanc|e ˈrez.ᵊn.ənts **-es** -ɪz
resonant ˈrez.ᵊn.ənt **-ly** -li
reson|ate ˈrez.ᵊn|.eɪt **-ates** -eɪts **-ati…** -eɪ.tɪŋ (US) -eɪ.t̬ɪŋ **-ated** -eɪ.tɪd (US) -eɪ.t̬ɪd
resonator ˈrez.ᵊn.eɪ.təʳ (US) -t̬ɚ **-s** -z
resorb rɪˈzɔːb, rə-, -ˈsɔːb (US) -ˈsɔːrb, -ˈzɔːrb **-s** -z **-ing** -ɪŋ **-ed** -d

resorp|tion rɪˈsɔːp|.ʃən, rə-, -ˈzɔːp- (US) -ˈsɔːrp-, -ˈzɔːrp- **-tive** -tɪv

re|sort (*n. v.*) rɪ|ˈzɔːt, rə- (US) -ˈzɔːrt **-sorts** -ˈzɔːts (US) -ˈzɔːrts **-sorting** -ˈzɔː.tɪŋ (US) -ˈzɔːr.t̬ɪŋ **-sorted** -ˈzɔː.tɪd (US) -ˈzɔːr.t̬ɪd

re|-sort (*v.*) *sort again:* ˌriː|ˈsɔːt (US) -ˈsɔːrt **-sorts** -ˈsɔːts (US) -ˈsɔːrts **-sorting** -ˈsɔː.tɪŋ (US) -ˈsɔːr.t̬ɪŋ **-sorted** -ˈsɔː.tɪd (US) -ˈsɔːr.t̬ɪd

resound rɪˈzaʊnd, rə- **-s** -z **-ing** -ɪŋ **-ed** -ɪd

resourc|e rɪˈzɔːs, rə-, -ˈsɔːs; ˈriː.sɔːs (US) ˈriː.sɔːrs, -zɔːrs; rɪˈsɔːrs, rə-, -ˈzɔːrs **-es** -ɪz **-ing** -ɪŋ **-ed** -t

resourceful rɪˈzɔːs.fəl, rə-, -ˈsɔːs-, -fʊl (US) -ˈsɔːrs-, -ˈzɔːrs- **-ly** -i **-ness** -nəs, -nɪs

respect rɪˈspekt, rə- **-s** -s **-ing** -ɪŋ **-ed** -ɪd **-er/s** -əʳ/z (US) -ɚ/z

respectability rɪˌspek.təˈbɪl.ə.ti, rə-, -ɪ.ti (US) -ə.t̬i

respectab|le rɪˈspek.tə.b|l̩, rə- **-ly** -li **-leness** -l̩.nəs, -nɪs

respectful rɪˈspekt.fəl, rə-, -fʊl **-ly** -i **-ness** -nəs, -nɪs

respective rɪˈspek.tɪv, rə- **-ly** -li

Respighi resˈpiː.gi, rɪˈspiː-, rə-

respirable ˈres.pɪ.rə.bl̩, rɪˈspaɪə-, rə- (US) ˈres.pɚ.ə.bl̩; rɪˈspaɪ-, rə-

respiration ˌres.pərˈeɪ.ʃən, -pɪˈreɪ- (US) -pəˈreɪ- **-s** -z

respirator ˈres.pər.eɪ.təʳ, -pɪ.reɪ- (US) -pə.reɪ.t̬ɚ **-s** -z

respiratory rɪˈspɪr.ə.tər.i, -ˈspaɪə.rə-, rə-, resˈpaɪə-, ˈres.pɪ.rə-, -reɪ- (US) ˈres.pɚ.ə.tɔːr-; rɪˈspaɪ.rə-, rə-

respir|e rɪˈspaɪəʳ, rə- (US) -ˈspaɪɚ **-es** -z **-ing** -ɪŋ **-ed** -d

respi|te ˈres.paɪ|t, -pɪ|t (US) -pɪ|t **-tes** -ts **-ting** -tɪŋ (US) -t̬ɪŋ **-ted** -tɪd (US) -t̬ɪd

resplenden|ce rɪˈsplen.dən*t*|s, rə- **-cy** -si

resplendent rɪˈsplen.dənt, rə- **-ly** -li

respond rɪˈspɒnd, rə- (US) -ˈspɑːnd **-s** -z **-ing** -ɪŋ **-ed** -ɪd **-er/s** -əʳ/z (US) -ɚ/z

respondeat resˈpɒn.deɪ.æt, rɪs-, -di- (US) resˈpɑːn.di.ət

respondent rɪˈspɒn.dənt, rə- (US) -ˈspɑːn- **-s** -s

respons|e rɪˈspɒn*t*s, rə- (US) -ˈspɑːn*t*s **-es** -ɪz

responsibilit|y rɪˌspɒn*t*.səˈbɪl.ə.t|i, rə-, -sɪˈ-, -ɪ.t|i (US) -ˌspɑːn*t*.səˈbɪl.ə.t̬|i **-ies** -iz

responsib|le rɪˈspɒn*t*.sə.b|l̩, rə-, -sɪ- (US) -ˈspɑːn*t*.sə- **-ly** -li **-leness** -l̩.nəs, -nɪs

responsive rɪˈspɒn*t*.sɪv, rə- (US) -ˈspɑːn*t*- **-ly** -li **-ness** -nəs, -nɪs

respray (*n.*) ˈriː.spreɪ **-s** -z

respray (*v.*) ˌriːˈspreɪ **-s** -z **-ing** -ɪŋ **-ed** -d

rest rest **-s** -s **-ing** -ɪŋ **-ed** -ɪd ˈ**rest** ˌ**home**; ˈ**rest** ˌ**room**; ˈ**resting** ˌ**place**

re|start ˌriː|ˈstɑːt (US) -ˈstɑːrt **-starts** -ˈstɑːts (US) -ˈstɑːrts **-starting** -ˈstɑː.tɪŋ (US) -ˈstɑːr.t̬ɪŋ **-started** -ˈstɑː.tɪd (US) -ˈstɑːr.t̬ɪd

re|state ˌriː|ˈsteɪt **-states** -ˈsteɪts **-stating** -ˈsteɪ.tɪŋ (US) -ˈsteɪ.t̬ɪŋ **-stated** -ˈsteɪ.tɪd (US) -ˈsteɪ.t̬ɪd

re-statement ˌriːˈsteɪt.mənt **-s** -s

restaur|ant ˈres.tər|.ɔ̃ːŋ, -ɑ̃ːŋ, -ɑːŋ, -ɒnt, -ənt, ˈ-tr|ɔ̃ːŋ, -tr|ɑ̃ːŋ, -tr|ɑːŋ, -tr|ɒnt, -tr|ənt (US) -tə.r|ɑːnt, -tɚ|.ənt, ˈ-tr|ɑːnt, -tr|ənt **-ants** -ɔ̃ːŋz, -ɑ̃ːŋz, -ɑːŋz, -ɒŋz, -ɒnts, -ənts (US) -ɑːnts, -ənts ˈ**restaurant** ˌ**car**

restaurateur ˌres.tɒr.əˈtɜːʳ, -tər-, -tɔː.rəˈ- (US) -tɚ.əˈtɝː, -ˈtʊr **-s** -z

restful ˈrest.fəl, -fʊl **-ly** -i **-ness** -nəs, -nɪs

restitution ˌres.tɪˈtjuː.ʃən (US) -ˈtuː-, -ˈtjuː-

restive ˈres.tɪv **-ly** -li **-ness** -nəs, -nɪs

restless ˈrest.ləs, -lɪs **-ly** -li **-ness** -nəs, -nɪs

restock ˌriːˈstɒk (US) -ˈstɑːk **-s** -s **-ing** -ɪŋ **-ed** -t

restoration (R) ˌres.tərˈeɪ.ʃən (US) -təˈreɪ- **-s** -z

restorative rɪˈstɒr.ə.tɪv, rə-, resˈtɒr-, -ˈtɔː.rə- (US) rɪˈstɔːr.ə.t̬ɪv, rə- **-s** -z

restor|e rɪˈstɔːʳ, rə- (US) -ˈstɔːr **-es** -z **-ing** -ɪŋ **-ed** -d **-er/s** -əʳ/z (US) -ɚ/z **-able** -ə.bl̩

restrain rɪˈstreɪn, rə- **-s** -z **-ing** -ɪŋ **-ed** -d **-er/s** -əʳ/z (US) -ɚ/z

restraint rɪˈstreɪnt, rə- **-s** -s

restrict rɪˈstrɪkt, rə- **-s** -s **-ing** -ɪŋ **-ed** -ɪd

restriction rɪˈstrɪk.ʃən, rə- **-s** -z

restrictionism rɪˈstrɪk.ʃən.ɪ.zəm, rə-

restrictive rɪˈstrɪk.tɪv, rə- **-ly** -li **-ness** -nəs, -nɪs **re**ˌ**strictive** ˈ**practice**

restroom ˈrest.rʊm, -ruːm (US) -ruːm, -rʊm **-s** -z

restruct|ure ˌriːˈstrʌk.tʃ|əʳ (US) -tʃ|ɚ **-ures** -əz (US) -ɚz **-uring** -ər.ɪŋ **-ured** -əd (US) -ɚd

re|sult rɪ|ˈzʌlt, rə- **-sults** -ˈzʌlts **-sulting** -ˈzʌl.tɪŋ (US) -ˈzʌl.t̬ɪŋ **-sulted** -ˈzʌl.tɪd (US) -ˈzʌl.t̬ɪd **-sultant/s** -ˈzʌl.tənt/s

resultative rɪˈzʌl.tə.tɪv, rə- (US) -t̬ə.t̬ɪv

resum|e rɪˈzjuːm, rə-, -ˈzuːm (US) -ˈzuːm **-es** -z **-ing** -ɪŋ **-ed** -d

résumé, resumé ˈrez.juː.meɪ, ˈreɪ.zuː-, -zjʊ-, -zʊ-; rɪˈzjuː-, rə- (US) ˈrez.ʊ.meɪ, ˈ-ə-, ˌ--ˈ- **-s** -z

resumption rɪˈzʌm*p*.ʃən, rə- **-s** -z

resumptive rɪˈzʌm*p*.tɪv, rə-

resurfac|e ˌriːˈsɜː.fɪs, -fəs (US) -ˈsɝː- **-es** -ɪz **-ing** -ɪŋ **-ed** -t

resurgenc|e rɪˈsɜː.dʒən*t*s, rə- (US) -ˈsɝː- **-es** -ɪz

resurgent rɪˈsɜː.dʒənt, rə- (US) -ˈsɝː-

resurrect ˌrez.ərˈekt (US) -əˈrekt **-s** -s **-ing** -ɪŋ **-ed** -ɪd

resurrection (R) ˌrez.ərˈek.ʃən (US) -əˈrek- **-s** -z

resusci|tate rɪˈsʌs.ɪ|.teɪt, rə-, ˈ-ə- (US) ˈ-ə- **-tates** -teɪts **-tating** -teɪ.tɪŋ (US) -teɪ.t̬ɪŋ **-tated** -teɪ.tɪd (US) -teɪ.t̬ɪd **-tator/s** -teɪ.təʳ/z (US) -teɪ.t̬ɚ/z

resuscitation rɪˌsʌs.ɪˈteɪ.ʃən, rə-, -əˈ- (US) -əˈ- **-s** -z

retail (*n. adj.*) ˈriː.teɪl, ˌ-ˈ- (US) ˈriː.teɪl ˌ**retail** ˈ**price**

retail (*v.*) *sell:* ˈriː.teɪl, ˌ-ˈ- (US) ˈriː.teɪl; rɪˈteɪl **-s** -z **-ing** -ɪŋ **-ed** -d **-er/s** -əʳ/z (US) -ɚ/z

retail (*v.*) *tell:* rɪˈteɪl, rə-, ˌriː- **-s** -z **-ing** -ɪŋ **-ed** -d

retain rɪˈteɪn, rə- **-s** -z **-ing** -ɪŋ **-ed** -d **-er/s** -əʳ/z (US) -ɚ/z

retake (*n.*) ˈriː.teɪk **-s** -s

re|take (*v.*) ˌriːˈteɪk **-takes** -ˈteɪks **-taking** -ˈteɪ.kɪŋ **-took** -ˈtʊk **-taken** -ˈteɪ.kən

retali|ate rɪˈtæl.i|.eɪt, rə- **-ates** -eɪts **-ating** -eɪ.tɪŋ (US) -eɪ.t̬ɪŋ **-ated** -eɪ.tɪd (US) -eɪ.t̬ɪd

retaliation rɪˌtæl.iˈeɪ.ʃən, rə-

retaliatory rɪˈtæl.i.ə.tər.i, rə-, -eɪ-; rɪˌtæl.iˈeɪ-, rə- (US) rɪˈtæl.i.ə.tɔːr-, rə-, ˈ-jə-

retard (*v.*) rɪˈtɑːd, rə- (US) -ˈtɑːrd **-s** -z **-ing** -ɪŋ **-ed** -ɪd

retard (*n.*) ˈriː.tɑːd (US) -tɑːrd **-s** -z

retardant rɪˈtɑː.dənt, rə- (US) -ˈtɑːr- **-s** -s

retardation ˌriː.tɑːˈdeɪ.ʃən (US) -tɑːrˈ- **-s** -z

retch retʃ, riːtʃ (US) retʃ **-es** -ɪz **-ing** -ɪŋ **-ed** -t

retell ˌriːˈtel **-s** -z **-ing** -ɪŋ **retold** ˌriːˈtəʊld (US) -ˈtoʊld

retention rɪˈten.*t*ʃən, rə-

retentive rɪˈten.tɪv, rə- (US) -t̬ɪv **-ly** -li **-ness** -nəs, -nɪs

Retford ˈret.fəd (US) -fɚd

rethink (*v.*) ˌriːˈθɪŋk **-s** -s **-ing** -ɪŋ **rethought** ˌriːˈθɔːt (US) -ˈθɑːt, -ˈθɔːt

rethink (*n.*) ˈriː.θɪŋk **-s** -s

reticence ˈret.ɪ.sən*t*s, ˈ-ə- (US) ˈret̬.ə-

reticent ˈret.ɪ.sənt, ˈ-ə- (US) ˈret̬.ə- **-ly** -li

reticle ˈret.ɪ.kl̩ (US) ˈret̬.ɪ- **-s** -z

reticulate (*adj.*) rɪˈtɪk.jə.lət, rə-, retˈɪk-, -jʊ-, -lɪt, -leɪt (US) rɪˈtɪk.jə.lɪt, rə-, -jʊ-, -leɪt

reticu|late (*v.*) rɪˈtɪk.jə|.leɪt, rə-, retˈɪk-, -jʊ- (US) rɪˈtɪk-, rə- **-lates** -leɪts **-lating** -leɪ.tɪŋ (US) -leɪ.t̬ɪŋ **-lated** -leɪ.tɪd (US) -leɪ.t̬ɪd

reticulation rɪˌtɪk.jəˈleɪ.ʃən, rə-, retˌɪk-, -jʊˈ- (US) rɪˌtɪk-, rə- **-s** -z

reticule ˈret.ɪ.kjuːl, ˈ-ə- (US) ˈret̬.ə- **-s** -z

Retroflex

In a retroflex articulation the tip of the tongue is curled upward and backward.

Examples for English

The /r/ sound of some British and American accents is sometimes described as being retroflex, though in BBC pronunciation the degree of retroflexion is relatively small.

In US English and some accents of south-west England it is common for vowels preceding /r/ (e.g. /ɑː/ in *car*, or /ɜː/ in *bird*) to be affected by the consonant so that they have a retroflex quality for most of their duration. This 'r-colouring' is most common in back or central vowels where the forward part of the tongue is relatively free to change shape.

In other languages

Other languages have retroflex consonants with a more noticeable auditory quality, the best known examples being the great majority of the languages of the Indian sub-continent. The sound of retroflex consonants is fairly familiar to English listeners, since first-generation immigrants from India and Pakistan tend to carry the retroflex quality into their pronunciation of English consonants which are alveolar in BBC pronunciation.

retin|a ˈret.ɪ.nl|ə (US) -ᵊn|.ə **-as** -əz **-ae** -iː **-al** -əl

retinue ˈret.ɪ.njuː (US) -ᵊn.uː, -juː **-s** -z

retir|e rɪˈtaɪəʳ, rə- (US) -ˈtaɪɚ **-es** -z **-ing** -ɪŋ **-ed** -d **-ant/s** -ᵊnts

retiree rɪˌtaɪəˈriː, rə- (US) rɪˈtaɪ.riː, rə- **-s** -z

retirement rɪˈtaɪə.mənt, rə- (US) -ˈtaɪɚ- **reˈtirement ˌage; reˈtirement ˌhome**

retold *(from* **retell)** ˌriːˈtəʊld (US) -ˈtoʊld

re|tort rɪ|ˈtɔːt, rə- (US) -ˈtɔːrt **-torts** -ˈtɔːts (US) -ˈtɔːrts **-torting** -ˈtɔː.tɪŋ (US) -ˈtɔːr.t̬ɪŋ **-torted** -ˈtɔː.tɪd (US) -ˈtɔːr.t̬ɪd

retouch ˌriːˈtʌtʃ **-es** -ɪz **-ing** -ɪŋ **-ed** -t

retrac|e rɪˈtreɪs, ˌriː- **-es** -ɪz **-ing** -ɪŋ **-ed** -t

retract rɪˈtrækt, rə- **-s** -s **-ing** -ɪŋ **-ed** -ɪd **-or/s** -əʳ/z (US) -ɚ/z

retractable rɪˈtræk.tə.bl̩, rə-

retractation ˌriː.trækˈteɪ.ʃᵊn

retraction rɪˈtræk.ʃᵊn, rə- **-s** -z

retrain ˌriːˈtreɪn **-s** -z **-ing** -ɪŋ **-ed** -d

retransla|te ˌriː.trænˈsleɪ|t, -trɑːn'-, -trænzˈleɪ|t, -trɑːnz'-, -trᵊnˈsleɪ|t, -trᵊnzˈleɪ|t (US) ˌriːˈtræn.sleɪ|t, -ˈtrænz.leɪ|t, ˌ--ˈ- **-tes** -ts **-ting** -tɪŋ (US) -t̬ɪŋ **-ted** -tɪd (US) -t̬ɪd

retranslation ˌriː.trænˈsleɪ.ʃᵊn, -trɑːn'-, -trænzˈleɪ-, -trɑːnzˈ-, -trᵊnˈsleɪ-, -trᵊnzˈleɪ- (US) -trænˈsleɪ-, -trænzˈleɪ- **-s** -z

retread *(n.)* ˈriː.tred **-s** -z

retread *(v.)* ˌriːˈtred **-s** -z **-ing** -ɪŋ **retrod** ˌriːˈtrɒd (US) -ˈtrɑːd

re|treat rɪ|ˈtriːt, rə- **-treats** -ˈtriːts **-treating** -ˈtriː.tɪŋ (US) -ˈtriː.t̬ɪŋ **-treated** -ˈtriː.tɪd (US) -ˈtriː.t̬ɪd

retrench rɪˈtrentʃ, rə- (US) -ˈtrentʃ **-es** -ɪz **-ing** -ɪŋ **-ed** -t **-ment/s** -mənt/s

retrial ˌriːˈtraɪəl, ˈ-- (US) ˈriː.traɪəl, ˌ-ˈ- **-s** -z

retribution ˌret.rɪˈbjuː.ʃᵊn, -rəˈ- (US) -rəˈ-

retribu|tive rɪˈtrɪb.jə|.tɪv, rə-, -jʊ-, -t̬ɪv **-tory** -tᵊr.i (US) -tɔːr-

retrievab|le rɪˈtriː.və.b|l̩, rə- **-ly** -li **-leness** -l̩.nəs, -nɪs

retrieval rɪˈtriː.vᵊl, rə-

retriev|e rɪˈtriːv, rə- **-es** -z **-ing** -ɪŋ **-ed** -d **-er/s** -əʳ/z (US) -ɚ/z

retrim ˌriːˈtrɪm **-s** -z **-ming** -ɪŋ **-med** -d

retro- ret.rəʊ- (US) ret.roʊ-, -rə-

Note: Prefix. Normally takes primary or secondary stress on the first syllable, e.g. **retrograde** /ˈret.rəʊ.greɪd (US) -rə-/, **retroact** /ˌret.rəʊˈækt (US) -roʊˈ-/.

retro ˈret.rəʊ (US) -roʊ

retroact ˌret.rəʊˈækt (US) -roʊˈ- **-s** -s **-ing** -ɪŋ **-ed** -ɪd

retroaction ˌret.rəʊˈæk.ʃᵊn (US) -roʊˈ-

retroactive ˌret.rəʊˈæk.tɪv (US) -roʊˈ- **-ly** -li *stress shift:* ˌretroactive ˈlaws

retroced|e ˌret.rəʊˈsiːd (US) -roʊˈ-, -rəˈ- **-es** -z **-ing** -ɪŋ **-ed** -ɪd

retrocession ˌret.rəʊˈseʃ.ᵊn (US) -roʊˈ-, -rəˈ- **-s** -z

retroflex ˈret.rəʊ.fleks (US) -rə- **-ed** -t

retroflexion ˌret.rəʊˈflek.ʃᵊn (US) -rəˈ-

retrograde ˈret.rəʊ.greɪd (US) -rə-, -roʊ-

retrogress ˌret.rəʊˈgres (US) ˈret.rə.gres, -roʊ-, ˌ--ˈ- **-es** -ɪz **-ing** -ɪŋ **-ed** -t **-ive/ly** -ɪv/li

retrogression ˌret.rəʊˈgreʃ.ᵊn (US) -rəˈ-, -roʊˈ-

retro-rocket ˈret.rəʊˌrɒk.ɪt (US) -roʊˌrɑː.kɪt **-s** -s

retrospect ˈret.rəʊ.spekt (US) -rə- **-s** -s

retrospection ˌret.rəʊˈspek.ʃᵊn (US) -rəˈ- **-s** -z

retrospective ˌret.rəʊˈspek.tɪv (US) -rəˈ- **-s** -z **-ly** -li *stress shift:* ˌretrospective ˈview

retroussé rəˈtruː.seɪ, rɪ- (US) rəˌtruːˈseɪ, retˌruː-

retroversion ˌret.rəʊˈvɜː.ʃᵊn, -ʒᵊn (US) -roʊˈvɝː.ʒᵊn, -rəˈ-, -ʃᵊn **-s** -z

retrovert *(n.)* ˈret.rəʊ.vɜːt (US) -roʊ.vɝːt, -rə- **-s** -s

retro|vert *(v.)* ˌret.rəʊ|ˈvɜːt (US) -roʊ|ˈvɝːt, -rə- **-verts** -ˈvɜːts (US) -ˈvɝːts **-verting** -ˈvɜː.tɪŋ (US) -ˈvɝː.t̬ɪŋ **-verted** -ˈvɜː.tɪd (US) -ˈvɝː.t̬ɪd

retrovirus ˈret.rəʊ.vaɪə.rəs, ˌret.rəʊˈvaɪə- (US) ˈret.roʊˌvaɪ- **-es**

retr|y ˌriːˈtr|aɪ **-ies** -aɪz **-ying** -aɪ.ɪŋ **-ied** -aɪd

retsina retˈsiː.nə, ˈret.sɪ.nə

returf ˌriːˈtɜːf (US) -ˈtɝːf **-s** -s **-ing** -ɪŋ **-ed** -t

return rɪˈtɜːn, rə- (US) -ˈtɝːn **-s** -z **-ing** -ɪŋ **-ed** -d **-able** -ə.bl̩ **-er/s** -əʳ/z (US) -ɚ/z

returnee rɪˌtɜːˈniː, rə-, -ˈtɜː.niː (US) rɪˌtɝːˈniː, rə- **-s** -z

Reuben ˈruː.bən, -bɪn (US) -bən

reunification ˌriː.juː.nɪ.fɪˈkeɪ.ʃᵊn, riːˌjuː-, -nə- (US) riːˌjuː.nə- **-s** -z

reuni|fy ˌriːˈjuː.nɪ|.faɪ, -nə- (US) -nə- **-fies** -faɪ **-fying** -faɪ.ɪŋ **-fied** -faɪd

reunion ˌriːˈjuː.ni.ən (US) ˈ-njən **-s** -z

Réunion ˌriːˈjuː.ni.ən; *as if French:* ˌreɪ.uːˈnjɔ̃ːŋ (US) ˌriːˈjuːn.jən

reu|nite ˌriː.juː|ˈnaɪt **-nites** -ˈnaɪts **-niting** -ˈnaɪ.tɪŋ (US) -ˈnaɪ.t̬ɪŋ **-nited** -ˈnaɪ.tɪd (US) -ˈnaɪ.t̬ɪd

reusable ˌriːˈjuː.zə.bl̩

re-use *(n.)* ˌriːˈjuːs, ˈ-- (US) ˌriːˈjuːs

re-us|e *(v.)* ˌriːˈjuːz **-es** -ɪz **-ing** -ɪŋ **-ed**

Reuter ˈrɔɪ.təʳ (US) -t̬ɚ **-s** -z

Rev. *(abbrev. for* **Reverend)** ˈrev.ᵊr.ᵊnd, rev

rev *(n. v.)* rev **-s** -z **-ving** -ɪŋ **-ved** -d ˈ**rev** ˌ**counter**

revalu|e riːˈvæl.juː, ˌriː- **-es** -z **-ing** -ɪŋ **-ed** -d

revamp *(v.)* ˌriːˈvæmp **-s** -s **-ing** -ɪŋ **-ed** -t

revamp (*n.*) ˈriː.væmp **-s** -s
revanch|ist rɪˈvæntʃ|.ɪst **-ists** -ɪsts **-ism** -ɪ.zᵊm
Revd (*abbrev. for* **Reverend**) ˈrev.ᵊr.ᵊnd
reveal rɪˈviːl, rə- **-s** -z **-ing** -ɪŋ **-ed** -d **-er/s** -əʳ/z ⓤⓢ -ɚ/z **-able** -ə.bl̩
revealing rɪˈviː.lɪŋ **-ly** -li
reveille rɪˈvæl.i, rə-, -ˈvel- ⓤⓢ ˈrev.ᵊl.i **-s** -z
revel ˈrev.ᵊl **-s** -z **-(l)ing** -ɪŋ **-(l)ed** -d **-(l)er/s** -əʳ/z ⓤⓢ -ɚ/z
revelation (R) ˌrev.ᵊlˈeɪ.ʃᵊn **-s** -z
revelatory ˌrev.əˈleɪ.tᵊr.i ⓤⓢ ˈrev.ə.lə.tɔːr.i
Revell ˈrev.ᵊl
revelr|y ˈrev.ᵊl.r|i **-ies** -iz
Revelstoke ˈrev.ᵊl.stəʊk ⓤⓢ -stoʊk
revendication rɪˌven.dɪˈkeɪ.ʃᵊn, rə-, -dəˈ- ⓤⓢ -dəˈ- **-s** -z
reveng|e rɪˈvendʒ, rə- **-es** -ɪz **-ing** -ɪŋ **-ed** -d
revengeful rɪˈvendʒ.fᵊl, rə-, -fʊl **-ly** -i **-ness** -nəs, -nɪs
revenue ˈrev.ᵊn.juː, -ɪ.njuː ⓤⓢ ˈrev.ə.nuː, -njuː **-s** -z
reverber|ate rɪˈvɜː.bᵊr|.eɪt, rə- ⓤⓢ -ˈvɝː.bə.r|eɪt **-ates** -eɪts **-ating** -eɪ.tɪŋ ⓤⓢ -eɪ.t̬ɪŋ **-ated** -eɪ.tɪd ⓤⓢ -eɪ.t̬ɪd **-ator/s** -eɪ.təʳ/z ⓤⓢ -eɪ.t̬ɚ/z
reverberation rɪˌvɜː.bᵊrˈeɪ.ʃᵊn, rə- ⓤⓢ -ˌvɝː.bəˈreɪ- **-s** -z
reverberatory rɪˈvɜː.bᵊr.ə.tᵊr.i, rə-, -reɪ- ⓤⓢ -ˈvɝː.bɚ.ə.tɔːr-
rever|e (R) rɪˈvɪəʳ, rə- ⓤⓢ -ˈvɪr **-es** -z **-ing** -ɪŋ **-ed** -d
reverenc|e ˈrev.ᵊr.ᵊnts, ˈ-rᵊnts **-es** -ɪz **-ing** -ɪŋ **-ed** -t
reverend (R) ˈrev.ᵊr.ᵊnd, ˈ-rᵊnd **-s** -z
reverent ˈrev.ᵊr.ᵊnt, ˈ-rᵊnt **-ly** -li
reverential ˌrev.ᵊrˈen.tʃᵊl ⓤⓢ -əˈrent.ʃᵊl **-ly** -i
reverie ˈrev.ᵊr.i ⓤⓢ -ə.ri **-s** -z
revers *singular:* rɪˈvɪəʳ, rə-, -ˈveəʳ ⓤⓢ -ˈvɪr, -ˈver *plural:* -z
reversal rɪˈvɜː.sᵊl, rə- ⓤⓢ -ˈvɝː- **-s** -z
revers|e rɪˈvɜːs, rə- ⓤⓢ -ˈvɝːs **-es** -ɪz **-ing** -ɪŋ **-ed** -t
reversibility rɪˌvɜː.səˈbɪl.ə.ti, rə-, -sɪˈ-, -ɪ.ti ⓤⓢ -ˌvɝː.səˈbɪl.ə.t̬i
reversible rɪˈvɜː.sə.bl̩, rə-, -sɪ- ⓤⓢ -ˈvɝː.sə-
reversion rɪˈvɜː.ʃᵊn, rə- ⓤⓢ -ˈvɝː.ʒᵊn, -ʃᵊn **-s** -z
reversionary rɪˈvɜː.ʃᵊn.ᵊr.i, rə-, -ʒᵊn- ⓤⓢ -ˈvɝː.ʒᵊn.er-, -ʃᵊn-
re|vert rɪ|ˈvɜːt, rə- ⓤⓢ -ˈvɝːt **-verts** -ˈvɜːts ⓤⓢ -ˈvɝːts **-verting** -ˈvɜː.tɪŋ ⓤⓢ -ˈvɝː.t̬ɪŋ **-verted** -ˈvɜː.tɪd ⓤⓢ -ˈvɝː.t̬ɪd
reverter rɪˈvɜː.təʳ, rə- ⓤⓢ -ˈvɝː.t̬ɚ
re|vet rɪ|ˈvet, rə- **-vets** -ˈvets **-vetting** -ˈvet.ɪŋ ⓤⓢ -ˈvet̬.ɪŋ **-vetted** -ˈvet.ɪd ⓤⓢ -ˈvet̬.ɪd **-vetment/s** -ˈvet.mənt/s
review rɪˈvjuː, rə- **-s** -z **-ing** -ɪŋ **-ed** -d **-er/s** -əʳ/z ⓤⓢ -ɚ/z
revil|e rɪˈvaɪl, rə- **-es** -z **-ing** -ɪŋ **-ed** -d **-er/s** -əʳ/z ⓤⓢ -ɚ/z
revis|e rɪˈvaɪz, rə- **-es** -ɪz **-ing** -ɪŋ **-ed** -d **-er/s** -əʳ/z ⓤⓢ -ɚ/z **Reˌvised ˈVersion, Reˈvised ˌVersion**
revision rɪˈvɪʒ.ᵊn, rə- **-s** -z
revision|ism rɪˈvɪʒ.ᵊn|.ɪ.zᵊm, rə- **-ist/s** -ɪst/s
revis|it ˌriːˈvɪz|.ɪt **-its** -ɪts **-iting** -ɪ.tɪŋ ⓤⓢ -ɪ.t̬ɪŋ **-ited** -ɪ.tɪd ⓤⓢ -ɪ.t̬ɪd
revisualiz|e, -is|e ˌriːˈvɪz.ju.ᵊl.aɪz, -ˈvɪʒ-, -u- ⓤⓢ -ˈvɪʒ.u- **-es** -ɪz **-ing** -ɪŋ **-ed** -d
revitaliz|e, is|e ˌriːˈvaɪ.tᵊl.aɪz ⓤⓢ -t̬ᵊl- **-es** -ɪz **-ing** -ɪŋ **-ed** -d
revival rɪˈvaɪ.vᵊl, rə- **-s** -z
revival|ism rɪˈvaɪ.vᵊl|.ɪ.zᵊm, rə- **-ist/s** -ɪst/s
reviv|e rɪˈvaɪv, rə- **-es** -z **-ing** -ɪŋ **-ed** -d
revivi|fy ˌriːˈvɪv.ɪ|.faɪ, rɪ- **-fies** -faɪz **-fying** -faɪ.ɪŋ **-fied** -faɪd
reviviscence ˌrev.ɪˈvɪs.ᵊnts, ˌriː.vaɪˈ- ⓤⓢ ˌrev.əˈ-
Revlon® ˈrev.lɒn ⓤⓢ -lɑːn
revocability ˌrev.ə.kəˈbɪl.ə.ti, -ɪ.ti ⓤⓢ -ə.t̬i
revocable ˈrev.ə.kə.bl̩ *when applied to letters of credit:* rɪˈvəʊ.kə.bl̩, rə- ⓤⓢ -ˈvoʊ-
revocation ˌrev.əʊˈkeɪ.ʃᵊn ⓤⓢ -əˈ- **-s** -z
revok|e rɪˈvəʊk, rə- ⓤⓢ -ˈvoʊk **-es** -s **-ing** -ɪŋ **-ed** -t
re|volt rɪ|ˈvəʊlt, rə- ⓤⓢ -ˈvoʊlt **-volts** -ˈvəʊlts ⓤⓢ -ˈvoʊlts **-volting** -ˈvəʊl.tɪŋ ⓤⓢ -ˈvoʊl.t̬ɪŋ **-volted** -ˈvəʊl.tɪd ⓤⓢ -ˈvoʊl.t̬ɪd
revolution ˌrev.ᵊlˈuː.ʃᵊn, -ˈjuː- ⓤⓢ -əˈluː- **-s** -z
revolutionar|y ˌrev.ᵊlˈuː.ʃᵊn.ᵊr|.i, -ˈjuː- ⓤⓢ -əˈluː.ʃᵊn.er- **-ies** -iz
revolutionist ˌrev.ᵊlˈuː.ʃᵊn.ɪst, -ˈjuː- ⓤⓢ -əˈluː- **-s** -s
revolutioniz|e, -is|e ˌrev.ᵊlˈuː.ʃᵊn.aɪz, -ˈjuː- ⓤⓢ -əˈluː- **-es** -ɪz **-ing** -ɪŋ **-ed** -d
revolv|e rɪˈvɒlv, rə- ⓤⓢ -ˈvɑːlv **-es** -z **-ing** -ɪŋ **-ed** -d **reˌvolving ˈdoor; reˌvolving ˈcredit; reˌvolving ˈfund**
revolver rɪˈvɒl.vəʳ, rə- ⓤⓢ -ˈvɑːl.vɚ **-s** -z
revue rɪˈvjuː, rə- **-s** -z
revulsion rɪˈvʌl.ʃᵊn, rə- **-s** -z
reward rɪˈwɔːd, rə- ⓤⓢ -ˈwɔːrd **-s** -z **-ing** -ɪŋ **-ed** -ɪd
rewind ˌriːˈwaɪnd **-s** -z **-ing** -ɪŋ **rewound** ˌriːˈwaʊnd
rewir|e ˌriːˈwaɪəʳ ⓤⓢ -ˈwaɪɚ **-es** -z **-ing** -ɪŋ **-ed** -d
reword ˌriːˈwɜːd ⓤⓢ -ˈwɝːd **-s** -z **-ing** -ɪŋ **-ed** -ɪd
rework ˌriːˈwɜːk **-s** -s **-ing** -ɪŋ **-ed** -t
rewrite (*n.*) ˈriː.raɪt **-s** -s
re|write (*v.*) ˌriː|ˈraɪt **-writes** -ˈraɪts **-writing** -ˈraɪ.tɪŋ ⓤⓢ -ˈraɪ.t̬ɪŋ **-wrote** ˌriːˈrəʊt ⓤⓢ -ˈroʊt **-written** ˌriːˈrɪt.ᵊn
Rex reks
Reyes raɪz, reɪz
Reykjavik ˈreɪ.kjə.vɪk, ˈrek.jə-, -viːk ⓤⓢ ˈreɪ.kjə.viːk, -vɪk
reynard ˈren.ɑːd, ˈreɪ.nɑːd, -nəd ⓤⓢ ˈren.ɚd, ˈreɪ.nɚd, -nɑːrd **-s** -z
Reynard ˈren.əd, -ɑːd, ˈreɪ.nɑːd ⓤⓢ -nɑːrd, ˈreɪ.nɚd, ˈren.ɚd
Reynold ˈren.ᵊld **-s** -z
rezon|e ˌriːˈzəʊn ⓤⓢ -ˈzoʊn **-es** -z **-ing** -ɪŋ **-ed** -d
Rh (*abbrev. for* **rhesus**) ˈriː.səs
Rhadamanthus ˌræd.əˈmænt.θəs
Rhaeti|a ˈriː.ʃi|.ə, ˈ-ʃ|ə ⓤⓢ -ʃ|ə, ˈ-ʃi|.ə **-an** -ən
Rhaetic ˈriː.tɪk ⓤⓢ -t̬ɪk
Rhaeto-Roman|ce ˌriː.təʊ.rəʊˈmæn|ts ⓤⓢ -t̬oʊ.roʊˈ- **-ic** -ɪk
rhapsodic ræpˈsɒd.ɪk ⓤⓢ -ˈsɑː.dɪk **-al** -ᵊl **-ally** -ᵊl.i, -li
rhapsodiz|e, -is|e ˈræp.sə.daɪz **-es** -ɪz **-ing** -ɪŋ **-ed** -d
rhapsod|y ˈræp.sə.d|i **-ies** -iz
rhea (R) ˈriː.ə, rɪə ⓤⓢ ˈriː.ə **-s** -z
Rhea Silvia ˌriː.əˈsɪl.vi.ə, ˌrɪəˈ- ⓤⓢ ˌriː.əˈ-
Rheims riːmz
Rhenish ˈren.ɪʃ
rhenium ˈriː.ni.əm
rheostat ˈriː.əʊ.stæt ⓤⓢ -oʊ-, ˈ-ə- **-s** -s
rhesus ˈriː.səs **-es** -ɪz **ˈrhesus ˌfactor; ˌrhesus ˈmonkey, ˈrhesus ˌmonkey**
rhetoric ˈret.ᵊr.ɪk ⓤⓢ ˈret̬-
rhetoric|al rɪˈtɒr.ɪ.k|ᵊl, rə- ⓤⓢ -ˈtɔːr.ɪ- **-ally** -ᵊl.i, -li **rheˌtorical ˈquestion**
rhetorician ˌret.ᵊrˈɪʃ.ᵊn, -ɒrˈ- ⓤⓢ ˌret̬.əˈrɪʃ- **-s** -z
Rhett ret
rheum ruːm
rheumatic ruːˈmæt.ɪk ⓤⓢ -ˈmæt̬- **-s** -s **-ky** -i
rheumatism ˈruː.mə.tɪ.zᵊm
rheumatoid ˈruː.mə.tɔɪd **ˌrheumatoid arthˈritis**
rheumatolog|y ˌruː.məˈtɒl.ə.dʒ|i ⓤⓢ -ˈtɑː.lə- **-ist/s** -ɪst/s
rheumy ˈruː.mi
Rhiannon riˈæn.ən
Rhine raɪn **-land** -lænd, -lənd
Rhineland-Palatinate ˌraɪn.lænd.pəˈlæt.ɪ.nɪt, -lənd-, -nət, -neɪt ⓤⓢ -lænd.pəˈlæt.ᵊn.eɪt, -lənd-, -ɪt
rhinestone ˈraɪn.stəʊn ⓤⓢ -stoʊn **-s** -z
rhinitis ˌraɪˈnaɪ.tɪs ⓤⓢ -t̬ɪs

Rhotic

In rhotic varieties of English pronunciation the /r/ PHONEME is found in all phonological contexts.

Examples for English

In BBC pronunciation, /r/ is only found before vowels, and never before consonants or before a pause (see also LIAISON), e.g.:

red	/red/
around	/ə'raʊnd/
there is	/ðər ɪz/

In US English and other rhotic accents, on the other hand, /r/ may occur before consonants and before a pause, e.g.:

cart	/kɑːt/	(US)	/kɑːrt/
car	/kɑːʳ/	(US)	/kɑːr/

While the BBC accent is non-rhotic, many accents of the British Isles are rhotic, including most of the south and west of England, much of Wales and all of Scotland and Ireland. Most speakers of American English speak with a rhotic accent, but there are non-rhotic areas including the Boston area, lower-class New York and the Deep South.

Rhyme/Rime

In the phonological analysis of the syllable, this is a way of referring to the vowel in the middle of the syllable forming its 'peak' plus any sounds following the peak within the syllable (the CODA).

Examples for English

In the word *spoon* the rhyme (or rime) is /uːn/, in *tea* it is /iː/ and in *strengths* it is /eŋθs/ or /eŋkθs/.

Note

The spelling "rhyme" also refers to a pair of lines that end with the same sequence of sounds in verse. If we examine the sound sequences that must match each other, we find that these consist of the vowel and any final consonants of the last syllable: thus *moon* and *June* rhyme, and the initial consonants of these two words are not important (of course, we do find longer-running rhymes than this in verse, e.g. *ability* rhyming with *senility*).

rhino- raɪ.nəʊ-; raɪ'nɒ- (US) raɪ.noʊ-, -nə-; raɪ'nɑː-
Note: Prefix. Normally either takes primary or secondary stress on the first syllable, e.g. **rhinoplasty** /'raɪ.nəʊ.plæs.ti (US) -noʊ-/, or primary stress on the second syllable, e.g. **rhinoceros** /raɪ'nɒs.ᵊr.əs (US) -'nɑː.sɚ-/.
rhino 'raɪ.nəʊ (US) -noʊ **-s** -z
rhinoceri *(alternative plur. of* **rhinoceros***)* raɪ'nɒs.ᵊr.aɪ (US) -'nɑː.sə.raɪ
rhinoceros raɪ'nɒs.ᵊr.əs (US) -'nɑː.sɚ- **-es** -ɪz
rhinolog|y raɪ'nɒl.ə.dʒ|i (US) -'nɑː.lə- **-ist/s** -ɪst/s
rhinoplasty 'raɪ.nəʊ.plæs.ti (US) -noʊ-, -nə-
rhinoscope 'raɪ.nəʊ.skəʊp (US) -skoʊp **-s** -s
rhinoscopy raɪ'nɒs.kə.pi (US) -'nɑː.skə-
rhizome 'raɪ.zəʊm (US) -zoʊm **-s** -z
rho rəʊ (US) roʊ
Rhoads rəʊdz (US) roʊdz
Rhoda 'rəʊ.də (US) 'roʊ-
Rhode Island *state in US:* ˌrəʊd'aɪ.lənd (US) ˌroʊd- **-er/s** -əʳ/z (US) -ɚ/z *stress shift, see compound:* **ˌRhode Island 'Red**
Rhodes rəʊdz (US) roʊdz **ˌRhodes 'scholar**
Rhodesi|a rəʊ'diː.ʒ|ə, -ʃ|ə (US) roʊ-, '-ʒi|.ə **-an** -ən
Rhodian 'rəʊ.di.ən (US) 'roʊ- **-s** -z
rhodium 'rəʊ.di.əm (US) 'roʊ-
rhododendron ˌrəʊ.də'den.drən, -dɪ'- (US) ˌroʊ.də'- **-s** -z
rhomb rɒm (US) rɑːm*b* **-s** -z
rhomboid 'rɒm.bɔɪd (US) 'rɑːm- **-s** -z
rhomb|us 'rɒm.b|əs (US) 'rɑːm- **-uses** -ə.sɪz **-i** -aɪ
Rhona 'rəʊ.nə (US) 'roʊ-
Rhonda 'rɒn.də (US) 'rɑːn-
Rhondda 'rɒn.də, -ðə (US) 'rɑːn-
Rhone rəʊn (US) roʊn
Rhosllanerchrugog ˌrəʊs.*h*læn.ə'krɪg.ɒg, -θlæn- (US) ˌroʊs.*h*læn.ə'kriː.gɑːg
rhotacism 'rəʊ.tə.sɪ.zᵊm (US) 'roʊ.t̬ə-
rhotacization, -isa- ˌrəʊ.tə.saɪ'zeɪ.ʃᵊn, -tɪ- (US) ˌroʊ.t̬ə.sɪ'- **-s** -z
rhotaciz|e, -is|e 'rəʊ.tə.saɪz (US) 'roʊ.t̬ə- **-es** -ɪz **-ing** -ɪŋ **-ed** -d
rhotic 'rəʊ.tɪk (US) 'roʊ.t̬ɪk **-s** -s
rhoticity rəʊ'tɪs.ɪ.ti, -ə.ti (US) roʊ'tɪs.ə.t̬i
rhubarb 'ruː.bɑːb (US) -bɑːrb
Rhuddlan 'rɪð.lən, -læn
rhumb rʌm (US) rʌm*b* **-s** -z
Rhyl rɪl
rhym|e raɪm **-es** -z **-ing** -ɪŋ **-ed** -d **-er/s** -əʳ/z (US) -ɚ/z
rhymester 'raɪm.stəʳ (US) -stɚ **-s** -z
Rhymney 'rʌm.ni
Rhys *Welsh name:* riːs *family name of Baron Dynevor:* raɪs
Rhys-Jones ˌriːs'dʒəʊnz (US) -'dʒoʊnz
rhythm 'rɪð.ᵊm, 'rɪθ- (US) 'rɪð- **-s** -z **ˌrhythm and 'blues; 'rhythm ˌmethod**
rhythmic 'rɪð.mɪk, 'rɪθ- (US) 'rɪð- **-al** - **-ally** -ᵊl.i (US) -li
RI ˌɑːʳ'aɪ (US) ˌɑːr-
ria 'riː.ə, rɪə (US) 'riː.ə **-s** -z
rial ri'ɑːl; 'raɪ.əl, 'raɪ.əl; (US) 'riː.ɔːl, - **-s** -z
Note: The usual pronunciation for the Saudi Arabian currency is /ri'ɑːl (US) 'riː.ɔːl/.
rialto (R) ri'æl.təʊ (US) -toʊ **-s** -z
rib rɪb **-s** -z **-bing** -ɪŋ **-bed** -d **'rib ˌcag**
ribald 'rɪb.ᵊld, 'raɪ.bᵊld, -bɔːld (US) 'rɪb.ᵊld, 'raɪ.bɔːld **-s** -z **-ry** -ri
riband 'rɪb.ənd **-s** -z
Ribbentrop 'rɪb.ᵊn.trɒp (US) -trɑːp
Ribble 'rɪb.l̩
ribbon 'rɪb.ᵊn **-s** -z
Ribena® raɪ'biː.nə
riboflavin ˌraɪ.bəʊ'fleɪ.vɪn,

Rhythm

The way events in speech are distributed in time.

Examples for English

Obvious examples of vocal rhythms are chanting as part of games or physical activities. In conversational speech the rhythms are vastly more complicated, but it is clear that the timing of speech is not random. An extreme view (though a quite common one) is that English speech has a rhythm that allows us to divide it up into more or less equal intervals of time called 'feet', each of which begins with a stressed syllable: this is called the 'stress-timed rhythm hypothesis', e.g.:

London	'london
a return to London	a re | 'turn to | 'london
a day return to London	a | 'day re | 'turn to | 'london

Languages where the length of each syllable remains more or less the same as that of its neighbours whether or not it is stressed are called 'syllable-timed'.

Most evidence from the study of real speech suggests that such rhythms only exist in very careful, controlled speaking, but it appears from psychological research that listeners' brains tend to hear timing regularities even where there is little or no physical regularity.

'raɪ.bəʊ.fleɪ- (US) 'raɪ.bə.fleɪ.vɪn, ˌraɪ.bə'fleɪ-, -boʊ'-

ribosomal ˌraɪ.bəʊ'səʊ.məl (US) -bə'soʊ-

ribosome 'raɪ.bəʊ.səʊm (US) -bə.soʊm **-s** -z

Rica 'riː.kə

Ricardo rɪ'kɑː.dəʊ (US) -'kɑːr.doʊ

Ricci 'riː.tʃi

Riccio 'rɪtʃ.i.əʊ, 'rɪt.si- (US) 'rɪt.ʃi.oʊ; 'riːt.ʃoʊ

ric|e (R) raɪs **-es** -ɪz **-ing** -ɪŋ **-ed** -t **'rice ˌpaper; ˌrice 'pudding**

Rice Krispies® ˌraɪs'krɪs.piz

rich (R) rɪtʃ **-es** -ɪz **-er** -əʳ (US) -ɚ **-est** -ɪst, -əst **-ly** -li **-ness** -nəs, -nɪs

Richard 'rɪtʃ.əd (US) -ɚd **-s** -z

Richardson 'rɪtʃ.əd.sən (US) -ɚd-

Richelieu 'riː.ʃəl.jɜː, 'rɪʃ.əl-, -juː (US) 'rɪʃ.luː, 'riːʃ-, '-ə.luː

Riches 'rɪtʃ.ɪz

Richey, Richie 'rɪtʃ.i

Richler 'rɪtʃ.ləʳ (US) -lɚ

Richmond 'rɪtʃ.mənd

Richter 'rɪk.tə, 'rɪx- (US) 'rɪk.tɚ- **'Richter ˌscale**

Richthofen 'rɪk.təʊ.fən, 'rɪx- (US) -toʊ-

ick rɪk **-s** -s **-ing** -ɪŋ **-ed** -d

ickard 'rɪk.ɑːd (US) -ɑːrd **-s** -z

ickets 'rɪk.ɪts

ickett 'rɪk.ɪt

icketts 'rɪk.ɪts

ickettsi|a rɪ'ket.si|.ə **-ae** -iː **-as** -əz

icket|y 'rɪk.ə.t|i, -ɪ.t|i (US) -ə.ţ|i **-ier** -i.əʳ (US) -i.ɚ **-iest** -i.ɪst, -i.əst **-ily** -ɪ.li, -əl.i **-iness** -ɪ.nəs, -ɪ.nɪs

ickmansworth 'rɪk.mənz.wəθ, -wɜːθ (US) -wɚθ, -wɝːθ

ckshaw 'rɪk.ʃɔː (US) -ʃɑː, -ʃɔː **-s** -z

icky 'rɪk.i

ico 'riː.kəʊ (US) -koʊ

coch|et 'rɪk.ə.ʃ|eɪ, -ɒʃ|.eɪ, -et, ˌ--'- (US) 'rɪk.ə.ʃ|eɪ, ˌ--'- **-ets** -eɪz, -ets

(US) -eɪz **-eting** -eɪ.ɪŋ, -et.ɪŋ (US) -eɪ.ɪŋ **-eted** -eɪd, -et.ɪd (US) -eɪd

ricotta rɪ'kɒt.ə, rə- (US) -'kɑː.ţə

rictus 'rɪk.təs

rid rɪd **-s** -z **-ding** -ɪŋ

Ridd rɪd

riddance 'rɪd.ənts

Riddell 'rɪd.əl; rɪ'del

-ridden -ˌrɪd.ən

Ridding 'rɪd.ɪŋ

riddl|e 'rɪd.l̩ **-es** -z **-ing** -ɪŋ, 'rɪd.lɪŋ **-ed** -d

rid|e (R) raɪd **-es** -z **-ing** -ɪŋ **rode** rəʊd (US) roʊd **ridden** 'rɪd.ən

rid|er (R) 'raɪ.d|əʳ (US) -d|ɚ **-ers** -əz (US) -ɚz **-erless** -əl.əs, -ɪs, -es (US) -ɚ.ləs, -lɪs, -les

ridg|e (R) rɪdʒ **-es** -ɪz **-ed** -d

ridgepole 'rɪdʒ.pəʊl (US) -poʊl **-s** -z

Ridg(e)way 'rɪdʒ.weɪ

ridicul|e 'rɪd.ɪ.kjuːl, '-ə- **-es** -z **-ing** -ɪŋ **-ed** -d

ridiculous rɪ'dɪk.jə.ləs, rə-, -jʊ- **-ly** -li **-ness** -nəs, -nɪs

Riding 'raɪ.dɪŋ **-s** -z

Ridley 'rɪd.li

Ridout 'rɪd.aʊt, 'raɪ.daʊt

Ridpath 'rɪd.pɑːθ (US) -pæθ

riel 'riː.əl (US) ri'el

Rienzi ri'en.zi, -'ent.si (US) -'en.zi

Riesling 'riː.slɪŋ, 'riːz.lɪŋ (US) 'riːz-, 'riː.slɪŋ

Rievaulx 'riː.vəʊ, -vəʊz; 'rɪv.əz (US) 'riː.voʊ, -voʊz; 'rɪv.əz

Note: /'riː.vəʊ (US) -voʊ/ is the usual local pronunciation.

rife raɪf

riff rɪf **-s** -s

riffl|e 'rɪf.l̩ **-es** -z **-ing** -ɪŋ, 'rɪf.lɪŋ **-ed** -d

riff-raff 'rɪf.ræf

Rifkind 'rɪf.kɪnd

rifl|e 'raɪ.fl̩ **-es** -z **-ing** -ɪŋ, 'raɪ.flɪŋ **-ed** -d **'rifle ˌrange**

rift rɪft **-s** -s **-ing** -ɪŋ **-ed** -ɪd **ˌrift 'valley, 'rift ˌvalley**

rig rɪg **-s** -z **-ging** -ɪŋ **-ged** -d

Riga 'riː.gə

rigamarole 'rɪg.ə.mə.rəʊl (US) -roʊl **-s**

rigatoni ˌrɪg.ə'təʊ.ni (US) -'toʊ-

Rigby 'rɪg.bi

Rigel 'raɪ.gəl, -dʒəl (US) -dʒəl, -gəl

Rigg rɪg

rigger 'rɪg.əʳ (US) -ɚ **-s** -z

rigging (*n.*) 'rɪg.ɪŋ **-s** -z

right (R) raɪt **-s** -s **-ly** -li **-ness** -nəs, -nɪs **-ing** -ɪŋ (US) 'raɪ.ţɪŋ **-ed** -ɪd (US) 'raɪ.ţɪd **'right ˌangle; ˌright 'wing**

rightabout 'raɪt.əˌbaʊt (US) 'raɪţ-

right angle (*n.*) 'raɪtˌæŋ.gl̩ (US) 'raɪt- **-s** -z

right-angled (*adj.*) 'raɪtˌæŋ.gl̩d (US) 'raɪt-, ˌ-'--

righteous 'raɪ.tʃəs, -ti.əs (US) -tʃəs **-ly** -li **-ness** -nəs, -nɪs

rightful 'raɪt.fəl, -fʊl **-ly** -i **-ness** -nəs, -nɪs

right-hand ˌraɪt'hænd (US) ˌraɪt'hænd, '-- *stress shift, British only, see compound:* **ˌright-hand 'man**

right-handed ˌraɪt'hæn.dɪd *stress shift:* ˌright-handed 'player

right(h)o ˌraɪt'əʊ (US) -'oʊ

right|ism (R) 'raɪ.t|ɪ.zəm (US) -ţ|ɪ- **-ist/s** -ɪst/s

rightist 'raɪ.tɪst **-s** -s

right-minded ˌraɪt'maɪn.dɪd **-ly** -li **-ness** -nəs, -nɪs *stress shift:* ˌright-minded 'person

right-of-way ˌraɪt.əv'weɪ (US) ˌraɪt.əv'weɪ, '--ˌ- **rights-of-way** ˌraɪts- (US) ˌraɪts-, '--ˌ-

right-on ˌraɪt'ɒn (US) -'ɑːn *stress shift:* ˌright-on 'speaker

right-wing (*adj.*) ˌraɪt'wɪŋ **-er/s** -əʳ/s (US) -ɚ/z *stress shift:* ˌright-wing 'policies

righty-ho ˌraɪ.ti'həʊ (US) -t̬i'hoʊ
rigid 'rɪdʒ.ɪd **-ly** -li **-ness** -nəs, -nɪs
rigidity rɪ'dʒɪd.ə.ti, -ɪ.ti (US) -ə.t̬i
rigmarole 'rɪg.mᵊr.əʊl (US) -mə.roʊl **-s** -z
Rigoletto ˌrɪg.əʊ'let.əʊ (US) -ə'let.oʊ
rigor 'rɪg.əʳ (US) -ɚ
rigor mortis ˌrɪg.ə'mɔː.tɪs, ˌraɪ.gɔː'- (US) ˌrɪg.ɚ'mɔːr.t̬ɪs, ˌraɪ.gɔːr'-
rigorous 'rɪg.ᵊr.əs **-ly** -li **-ness** -nəs, -nɪs
rigour 'rɪg.əʳ (US) -ɚ **-s** -z
rig-out 'rɪg.aʊt
Rig-Veda ˌrɪg'veɪ.də (US) -'veɪ-, -'viː-
Rijeka ri'ek.ə (US) -'jek-, -'ek-
Rikki-Tiki-Tavi ˌrɪk.iˌtɪk.i'tɑː.vi, -'teɪ- (US) -'tɑː-, -'tæv.i
ril|e raɪl **-es** -z **-ing** -ɪŋ **-ed** -d
Riley 'raɪ.li
rilievo ˌrɪl.i'eɪ.vəʊ (US) -voʊ, -'jeɪ-
Rilke 'rɪl.kə
rill rɪl **-s** -z
rim rɪm **-s** -z **-ming** -ɪŋ **-med** -d **-less** -ləs, -lɪs
Rimbaud 'ræ̃m.bəʊ (US) ræm'boʊ
rime raɪm **-s** -z
Rimington 'rɪm.ɪŋ.tən
Rimini 'rɪm.ɪ.ni, '-ə- (US) '-ə-
Rimsky-Korsakov ˌrɪm*p*.ski'kɔː.sə.kɒf, -kɒv (US) -'kɔːr.sə.kɔːf
Rinaldo rɪ'næl.dəʊ (US) rɪ'nɑːl.doʊ, -næl-
rind raɪnd **-s** -z
Rind rɪnd
rinderpest 'rɪn.də.pest (US) -dɚ-
ring (*n. v.*) *encircle, put a ring on, etc.:* rɪŋ **-s** -z **-ing** -ɪŋ **-ed** -d **'ring ˌbinder, ˌring 'binder; 'ring ˌfinger; 'ring ˌroad; ˌrun 'rings round ˌsomeone**
ring (*n. v.*) *sound, etc.:* rɪŋ **-s** -z **-ing** -ɪŋ **rang** ræŋ **rung** rʌŋ **-er/s** -əʳ/z (US) -ɚ/z
ringgit 'rɪŋ.gɪt **-s** -s
ringleader 'rɪŋˌliː.dəʳ (US) -dɚ **-s** -z
ring|let 'rɪŋ|.lɪt, -lət (US) -lɪt **-lets** -lɪts, -ləts (US) -lɪts **-leted** -lɪ.tɪd, -lə.tɪd (US) -lɪ.t̬ɪd
ringmaster 'rɪŋˌmɑː.stəʳ (US) -ˌmæs.tɚ **-s** -z
Ringo 'rɪŋ.gəʊ (US) -goʊ
ringpull 'rɪŋ.pʊl **-s** -z
Ringshall 'rɪŋ.ʃᵊl
ringside 'rɪŋ.saɪd **ˌringside 'seat**
ring-tailed 'rɪŋ.teɪld
Ringwood 'rɪŋ.wʊd
ringworm 'rɪŋ.wɜːm (US) -wɝːm
rink rɪŋk **-s** -s
rinky-dink 'rɪŋ.ki.dɪŋk
rins|e rɪn*t*s **-es** -ɪz **-ing** -ɪŋ **-ed** -t
Rintoul 'rɪn.tuːl, -'-
Rio 'riː.əʊ (US) -oʊ
Rio de Janeiro ˌriː.əʊ.də.dʒə'nɪə.rəʊ, -deɪ-, -dɪ-, -ʒə'-, -'neə- (US) -oʊ.deɪ.ʒə'ner.oʊ, -diː-, -də-, -dʒə'-, -'nɪr-
Rio Grande ˌriː.əʊ'grænd, -'græn.di, -deɪ (US) -oʊ'grænd, -'græn.di, -'grɑːn.deɪ
rioja (R) ri'ɒk.ə, -'ɒx-, -'əʊ.kə (US) -'ɔː.hɑː, -'oʊ-
riot raɪət **-s** -s **-ing** -ɪŋ (US) 'raɪə.t̬ɪŋ **-ed** -ɪd (US) 'raɪə.t̬ɪd **-er/s** -əʳ/z (US) 'raɪə.t̬ɚ/z **'riot poˌlice; ˌread someone the 'riot act**
riotous 'raɪə.təs (US) -t̬əs **-ly** -li **-ness** -nəs, -nɪs
rip rɪp **-s** -s **-ping** -ɪŋ **-ped** -t
RIP ˌɑːʳ.aɪ'piː (US) ˌɑːr-
riparian raɪ'peə.ri.ən, rɪ- (US) rɪ'per.i-, raɪ-
ripcord 'rɪp.kɔːd (US) -kɔːrd **-s** -z
rip|e raɪp **-er** -əʳ (US) -ɚ **-est** -ɪst, -əst **-ely** -li **-eness** -nəs, -nɪs
ripen 'raɪ.pᵊn **-s** -z **-ing** -ɪŋ **-ed** -d
ripien|o ˌrɪp.i'eɪ.n|əʊ, rɪ'pjeɪ- (US) rɪ'pjeɪ.n|oʊ **-os** -əʊz (US) -oʊz **-i** -iː
Ripley 'rɪp.li
Ripman 'rɪp.mən
rip-off 'rɪp.ɒf (US) -ɑːf **-s** -s
Ripon 'rɪp.ən
ripost|e, ripost rɪ'pɒst, -'pəʊst (US) -'poʊst **-(e)s** -s **-ing** -ɪŋ **-ed** -ɪd
ripper 'rɪp.əʳ (US) -ɚ **-s** -z
ripping 'rɪp.ɪŋ **-ly** -li
rippl|e 'rɪp.l̩ **-es** -z **-ing** -ɪŋ, 'rɪp.lɪŋ **-ed** -d
Rippon 'rɪp.ᵊn
rip-roaring ˌrɪp'rɔː.rɪŋ (US) -'rɔːr.ɪŋ *stress shift:* ˌrip-roaring 'wave
ripsnort|ing ˌrɪp'snɔː.t|ɪŋ (US) -'snɔːr.t̬|ɪŋ **-er/s** -əʳ/z (US) -ɚ/z *stress shift:* ˌripsnorting 'finish
riptide 'rɪp.taɪd **-s** -z
Ripuarian ˌrɪp.ju'eə.ri.ən (US) -'er.i-
Rip van Winkle ˌrɪp.væn'wɪŋ.kl̩
Risborough, -boro' 'rɪz.bᵊr.ə (US) -bɚ.oʊ
Risca 'rɪs.kə
ris|e raɪz **-es** -ɪz **-ing** -ɪŋ **rose** rəʊz (US) roʊz **risen** 'rɪz.ᵊn
riser 'raɪ.zəʳ (US) -zɚ **-s** -z
Rishton 'rɪʃ.tᵊn
risibility ˌrɪz.ə'bɪl.ə.ti, ˌraɪ.zə'-, -zɪ'-, -ɪ.ti (US) ˌrɪz.ə'bɪl.ə.t̬i
risib|le 'rɪz.ə.b|l̩, 'raɪ.zə-, -zɪ- (US) 'rɪz.ə- **-ly** -li
rising 'raɪ.zɪŋ **-s** -z
risk rɪsk **-s** -s **-ing** -ɪŋ **-ed** -t
risk|y 'rɪs.k|i **-ier** -i.əʳ (US) -i.ɚ **-iest** -i.ɪst, -i.əst **-iness** -ɪ.nəs, -ɪ.nɪs
Risley 'rɪz.li
risotto rɪ'zɒt.əʊ, -'sɒt- (US) -'zɑː.t̬oʊ, -'sɑː- **-s** -z
risqué 'rɪs.keɪ, 'riː.skeɪ (US) rɪ'skeɪ
rissole 'rɪs.əʊl (US) -oʊl **-s** -z
Rita 'riː.tə (US) -t̬ə
Ritalin® 'rɪt.ᵊl.ɪn (US) 'rɪt̬-, 'rɪd.l̩n
ritardando ˌrɪt.ɑː'dæn.dəʊ (US) ˌriː.tɑːr'dɑːn.doʊ **-s** -z
Ritchie 'rɪtʃ.i
rite raɪt **-s** -s **ˌrite of 'passage**
ritornell|o ˌrɪt.ɔː'nel|.əʊ, -ᵊn'el- (US) -ɚ'nel|.oʊ, -ɔːr'- **-os** -əʊz (US) -oʊz **-i** -iː
Ritson 'rɪt.sᵊn
ritual 'rɪt.ju.əl, 'rɪtʃ.u- (US) 'rɪtʃ- **-s** -z **-ly**
ritual|ism 'rɪt.ju.ᵊl|.ɪ.zᵊm, 'rɪtʃ.u- (US) 'rɪtʃ- **-ist/s** -ɪst/s
ritualistic ˌrɪt.ju.ᵊl'ɪs.tɪk, ˌrɪtʃ.u- (US) ˌrɪtʃ- **-ally** -ᵊl.i, -li
ritualiz|e, -is|e 'rɪt.ju.ᵊl.aɪz, 'rɪtʃ.u- (US) 'rɪtʃ- **-es** -ɪz **-ing** -ɪŋ **-ed** -d
Ritz rɪts
ritz|y 'rɪt.s|i **-ier** -i.əʳ (US) -i.ɚ **-iest** -i.ɪst, -i.əst **-iness** -ɪ.nəs, -ɪ.nɪs
rival 'raɪ.vᵊl **-s** -z **-(l)ing** -ɪŋ **-(l)ed** -d
rivalr|y 'raɪ.vᵊl.r|i **-ies** -iz
riv|e raɪv **-es** -z **-ing** -ɪŋ **-ed** -d
riven 'rɪv.ᵊn
river (R) 'rɪv.əʳ (US) -ɚ **-s** -z **'river ˌbank, ˌriver 'bank; 'river ˌbed, ˌriver 'bed; ˌsell someone ˌdown the 'river**
Rivera rɪ'veə.rə (US) -'ver.ə
riverboat 'rɪv.ə.bəʊt (US) -ɚ.boʊt **-s** -s
Rivers 'rɪv.əz (US) -ɚz
riverside (R) 'rɪv.ə.saɪd (US) '-ɚ-
riv|et 'rɪv|.ɪt, -ət (US) -ɪt **-ets** -ɪts, -əts (US) -ɪts **-eting** -ɪ.tɪŋ, -ə.tɪŋ (US) -ɪ.t̬ɪŋ **-eted** -ɪ.tɪd, -ə.tɪd (US) -ɪ.t̬ɪd **-eter/s** -ɪ.təʳ/z, -ə.təʳ/z (US) -ɪ.t̬ɚ/z
Riviera ˌrɪv.i'eə.rə (US) -'er.ə
Rivington 'rɪv.ɪŋ.tən **-s** -z
rivulet 'rɪv.jə.lət, -jʊ-, -lɪt, -let (US) -lɪt **-s** -s
Rix rɪks
Riyadh 'riː.æd; -ɑːd, -'- (US) riː'jɑːd
riyal ri'ɑːl, -'æl; 'riː.ɑːl, -æl (US) riː'jɑːl, -'jɔːl, -'ɑːl, -'ɔːl **-s** -z
Rizla® 'rɪz.lə
Rizzio 'rɪt.si.əʊ (US) -oʊ
RN (*abbrev. for* **Royal Navy**) ˌɑːʳ'en; ˌrɔɪəl'neɪ.vi (US) ˌɑːr'en; ˌrɔɪəl'neɪ.
roach (R) rəʊtʃ (US) roʊtʃ **-es** -ɪz
road rəʊd (US) roʊd **-s** -z **'road ˌhog; 'road ˌrage; 'road ˌtax**
roadblock 'rəʊd.blɒk (US) 'roʊd.blɑːk **-s** -s
roadhou|se 'rəʊd.haʊ|s (US) 'roʊd- **-ses** -zɪz
roadie 'rəʊ.di (US) 'roʊ- **-s** -z
roadrunner 'rəʊdˌrʌn.əʳ (US) 'roʊdˌrʌn.ɚ **-s** -z
roadshow 'rəʊd.ʃəʊ (US) 'roʊd.ʃoʊ **-s** -z
roadside 'rəʊd.saɪd (US) 'roʊd-
roadstead 'rəʊd.sted (US) 'roʊd- **-s** -z
roadster 'rəʊd.stəʳ (US) 'roʊd.stɚ **-s** -

road-test ˈrəʊd.test ⓤⓢ ˈroʊd- -s -s -ing -ɪŋ -ed -ɪd
roadway ˈrəʊd.weɪ ⓤⓢ ˈroʊd- -s -z
roadworks ˈrəʊd.wɜːks ⓤⓢ ˈroʊd.wɝːks
roadworth|y ˈrəʊdˌwɜː.ð|i ⓤⓢ ˈroʊdˌwɝː- -iness -ɪ.nəs, -ɪ.nɪs
Roald rəʊəld ⓤⓢ roʊəld
roam rəʊm ⓤⓢ roʊm -s -z -ing -ɪŋ -ed -d
roan (R) rəʊn ⓤⓢ roʊn -s -z
Roanoke ˈrəʊə.nəʊk, ˈrəʊ-, ˌrəʊəˈnəʊk ⓤⓢ ˈroʊə.noʊk
roar rɔːʳ ⓤⓢ rɔːr -s -z -ing -ɪŋ -ed -d
roast rəʊst ⓤⓢ roʊst -s -s -ing -ɪŋ -ed -ɪd -er/s -əʳ/z ⓤⓢ -ɚ/z
rob (R) rɒb ⓤⓢ rɑːb -s -z -bing -ɪŋ -bed -d
Robards ˈrəʊ.bɑːdz ⓤⓢ ˈroʊ.bɑːrdz
Robb rɒb ⓤⓢ rɑːb
robber ˈrɒb.əʳ ⓤⓢ ˈrɑː.bɚ -s -z
robber|y ˈrɒb.ᵊr|.i ⓤⓢ ˈrɑː.bɚ|.i, ˈ-br|i -ies -iz
Robbins ˈrɒb.ɪnz ⓤⓢ ˈrɑː.bɪnz
rob|e rəʊb ⓤⓢ roʊb -es -z -ing -ɪŋ -ed -d
Robens ˈrəʊ.bɪnz ⓤⓢ ˈroʊ-
Roberson ˈrəʊ.bə.sᵊn, ˈrɒb.ə- ⓤⓢ ˈroʊ.bɚ-, ˈrɑː-
Note: In **Roberson's medium** the usual pronunciation is /ˈrɒb.ə- ⓤⓢ ˈrɑː.bɚ-/.
Robert ˈrɒb.ət ⓤⓢ ˈrɑː.bɚt -s -s
Roberta rəʊˈbɜː.tə, rɒbˈɜː- ⓤⓢ rəˈbɝː.t̬ə, roʊ-
Roberto rəʊˈbɜː.təʊ, rɒbˈɜː- ⓤⓢ rəˈbɝː.t̬oʊ, roʊ-, -toʊ
Robertson ˈrɒb.ət.sᵊn ⓤⓢ ˈrɑːb.ɚt-
Robeson ˈrəʊb.sᵊn ⓤⓢ ˈroʊb-
Robespierre ˈrəʊbz.pjeəʳ, -pɪəʳ, ˈrəʊb.spjeəʳ, -spɪəʳ ⓤⓢ ˌroʊbzˈpjer, -ˈpɪr, -piˈer
robin (R) ˈrɒb.ɪn ⓤⓢ ˈrɑː.bɪn -s -z ˌRobin ˈHood, ⓤⓢ ˈRobin ˌHood; ˌRobin Hood's ˈBay
Robina rɒbˈiː.nə, rəʊˈbiː- ⓤⓢ rəˈbiː-, roʊ-
Robins ˈrəʊ.bɪnz, ˈrɒb.ɪnz ⓤⓢ ˈrɑː.bɪnz, ˈroʊ-
Robinson ˈrɒb.ɪn.sᵊn ⓤⓢ ˈrɑː.bɪn- ˌRobinson ˈCrusoe
robot ˈrəʊ.bɒt ⓤⓢ ˈroʊ.bɑːt, -bət -s -s
Robotham ˈrəʊ.bɒθ.əm, -bɒt- ⓤⓢ ˈroʊ.bɑː.θəm, -bɑː.t̬əm
robotic rəʊˈbɒt.ɪk ⓤⓢ roʊˈbɑː.t̬ɪk -s -s
Rob Roy ˌrɒbˈrɔɪ ⓤⓢ ˌrɑːb-
Robsart ˈrɒb.sɑːt ⓤⓢ ˈrɑːb.sɑːrt
Robson ˈrɒb.sᵊn ⓤⓢ ˈrɑːb-
robust rəʊˈbʌst ⓤⓢ roʊ-, ˈ-- -ly -li -ness -nəs, -nɪs
Roby ˈrəʊ.bi ⓤⓢ ˈroʊ-
Robyn ˈrɒb.ɪn ⓤⓢ ˈrɑː.bɪn
Rocha ˈrɒʃ.ə ⓤⓢ ˈrɑː.ʃə
Rochdale ˈrɒtʃ.deɪl ⓤⓢ ˈrɑːtʃ-
Roche rəʊtʃ, rəʊʃ, rɒʃ ⓤⓢ roʊtʃ, roʊʃ, rɑːʃ
Rochester ˈrɒtʃ.ɪ.stəʳ, ˈ-ə- ⓤⓢ ˈrɑː.tʃə.stɚ, -tʃes.tɚ
rochet ˈrɒtʃ.ɪt ⓤⓢ ˈrɑː.tʃɪt -s -s
Rochford ˈrɒtʃ.fəd ⓤⓢ ˈrɑːtʃ.fɚd
rock (R) rɒk ⓤⓢ rɑːk -s -s -ing -ɪŋ -ed -t -er/s -əʳ/z ⓤⓢ -ɚ/z ˈrock ˌcake; ˈrock ˌclimbing; ˈrock ˌgarden; ˈrock ˌsalmon; ˈrock ˌsalt; ˈrocking ˌchair; ˈrocking ˌhorse
rockabilly ˈrɒk.əˌbɪl.i ⓤⓢ ˈrɑː.kəˌ-
rock-and-roll ˌrɒk.ᵊndˈrəʊl ⓤⓢ ˌrɑːk.ᵊndˈroʊl -er/s -əʳ/z ⓤⓢ -ɚ/z *stress shift:* ˌrock-and-roll ˈmusic
rock-bottom ˌrɒkˈbɒt.əm ⓤⓢ ˌrɑːkˈbɑː.t̬əm *stress shift:* ˌrock-bottom ˈlevel
rockbound ˈrɒk.baʊnd ⓤⓢ ˈrɑːk-
Rockefeller ˈrɒk.əˌfel.əʳ, -ɪˌ- ⓤⓢ ˈrɑː.kəˌfel.ɚ ˈRockefeller ˌCenter ⓤⓢ ˌRockefeller ˈCenter
rocker|y ˈrɒk.ᵊr|.i ⓤⓢ ˈrɑː.kɚ- -ies -iz
rock|et ˈrɒk|.ɪt ⓤⓢ ˈrɑː.k|ɪt -ets -ɪts -eting -ɪ.tɪŋ ⓤⓢ -ɪ.t̬ɪŋ -eted -ɪ.tɪd ⓤⓢ -ɪ.t̬ɪd ˈrocket ˌbase; ˈrocket ˌrange
rocketry ˈrɒk.ɪ.tri, ˈ-ə- ⓤⓢ ˈrɑː.kɪ-, -kə-
rockfall ˈrɒk.fɔːl ⓤⓢ ˈrɑːk-, -fɑːl -s -z
Rockhampton rɒkˈhæmp.tən ⓤⓢ rɑːk-
Rockies ˈrɒk.iz ⓤⓢ ˈrɑː.kiz
Rockingham ˈrɒk.ɪŋ.əm ⓤⓢ ˈrɑː.kɪŋ-
rockmelon ˈrɒkˌmel.ən ⓤⓢ ˈrɑːk- -s -z
Rockne ˈrɒk.ni ⓤⓢ ˈrɑːk-
rock 'n' roll ˌrɒk.ᵊndˈrəʊl ⓤⓢ ˌrɑːk.ᵊndˈroʊl -er/s -əʳ/z ⓤⓢ -ɚ/z *stress shift:* ˌrock 'n' roll ˈmusic
rockros|e ˈrɒk.rəʊz ⓤⓢ ˈrɑːk.roʊz -es -ɪz
Rockwell ˈrɒk.wel, -wəl ⓤⓢ ˈrɑː.kwel, -kwəl
rock|y (R) ˈrɒk|.i ⓤⓢ ˈrɑː.k|i -ier -i.əʳ ⓤⓢ -i.ɚ -iest -i.ɪst, -i.əst -iness -ɪ.nəs, -ɪ.nɪs ˌRocky ˈMountains
rococo rəʊˈkəʊ.kəʊ ⓤⓢ rəˈkoʊ.koʊ; ˌroʊ.kəˈkoʊ
rod (R) rɒd ⓤⓢ rɑːd -s -z make a ˌrod for one's ˌown ˈback; ˌrule someone with a ˌrod of ˈiron
Roddick ˈrɒd.ɪk ⓤⓢ ˈrɑː.dɪk
rode *(from* **ride***)* rəʊd ⓤⓢ roʊd
Roden ˈrəʊ.dᵊn ⓤⓢ ˈroʊ-
rodent ˈrəʊ.dᵊnt ⓤⓢ ˈroʊ- -s -s
rodeo rəʊˈdeɪ.əʊ; ˈrəʊ.di- ⓤⓢ ˈroʊ.di.oʊ; roʊˈdeɪ.oʊ -s -z
Roderic(k) ˈrɒd.ᵊr.ɪk ⓤⓢ ˈrɑː.dɚ-
Rodger ˈrɒdʒ.əʳ ⓤⓢ ˈrɑː.dʒɚ -s -z
Rodgers ˈrɒdʒ.əz ⓤⓢ ˈrɑː.dʒɚz
Rodin ˈrəʊ.dæ̃ŋ ⓤⓢ roʊˈdæ̃n
Roding ˈrəʊ.dɪŋ *locally sometimes:* ˈruː.dɪŋ, -ðɪŋ ⓤⓢ ˈroʊ.dɪŋ, ˈruː-, -ðɪŋ
Rodman ˈrɒd.mən, ˈrɒb- ⓤⓢ ˈrɑːd-
Rodmell ˈrɒd.mᵊl ⓤⓢ ˈrɑːd-
Rodney ˈrɒd.ni ⓤⓢ ˈrɑːd-
rodomontad|e ˌrɒd.ə.mɒnˈteɪd, ˌrəʊ.də-, -ˈtɑːd ⓤⓢ ˌrɑː.də.mənˈteɪd, ˌroʊ-, -ˈtɑːd -es -z -ing -ɪŋ -ed -ɪd
Rodriguez rɒdˈriː.gez ⓤⓢ rɑːˈdriː.ges, -geɪs, -geɪz, -gəz
Rodway ˈrɒd.weɪ ⓤⓢ ˈrɑːd-
roe (R) rəʊ ⓤⓢ roʊ -s -z
Roebling ˈrəʊ.blɪŋ ⓤⓢ ˈroʊ-
roebuck (R) ˈrəʊ.bʌk ⓤⓢ ˈroʊ- -s -s
Roedean ˈrəʊ.diːn ⓤⓢ ˈroʊ-
Roehampton rəʊˈhæmp.tən ⓤⓢ roʊ- *stress shift:* ˌRoehampton ˈCollege
roentgen (R) ˈrɒn.tjən, ˈrɜːn-, ˈrɒnt.gən, ˈrɜːn- ⓤⓢ ˈrent.gən, ˈrɝːnt-, ˈrʌnt-, ˈren.tʃən, ˈrɝːn-, ˈrʌn- -s -z
Roethke ˈret.kə ⓤⓢ ˈret-, ˈreθ-, -ki
rogation (R) rəʊˈgeɪ.ʃᵊn ⓤⓢ roʊ- -s -z
rogatory ˈrɒg.ə.tᵊr.i, -tri ⓤⓢ ˈrɑː.gə.tɔːr-
rog|er (R) ˈrɒdʒ|.əʳ ⓤⓢ ˈrɑː.dʒ|ɚ -ers -əz ⓤⓢ -ɚz -ering -ᵊr.ɪŋ -ered -əd ⓤⓢ -ɚz
Roget ˈrɒʒ.eɪ, ˈrəʊ.ʒeɪ ⓤⓢ ˌroʊˈʒeɪ, ˈ-- ˌRoget's Theˈsaurus
rogue rəʊg ⓤⓢ roʊg -s -z ˌrogue's ˈgallery
roguer|y ˈrəʊ.gᵊr|.i ⓤⓢ ˈroʊ- -ies -iz
roguish ˈrəʊ.gɪʃ ⓤⓢ ˈroʊ- -ly -li -ness -nəs, -nɪs
roil rɔɪl -s -z -ing -ɪŋ -ed -d
roist|er ˈrɔɪ.st|əʳ ⓤⓢ -st|ɚ -ers -əz ⓤⓢ -ɚz -ering -ᵊr.ɪŋ -ered -əd ⓤⓢ -ɚd -erer/s -ᵊr.əʳ/z ⓤⓢ -ɚ.ɚ/z
Rokeby ˈrəʊk.bi ⓤⓢ ˈroʊk-
Roker ˈrəʊ.kəʳ ⓤⓢ ˈroʊ.kɚ
Roland ˈrəʊ.lənd ⓤⓢ ˈroʊ-
role, rôle rəʊl ⓤⓢ roʊl -s -z ˈrole ˌmodel
roleplay ˈrəʊl.pleɪ ⓤⓢ ˈroʊl- -s -z -ing -ɪŋ -ed -d
Rolex® ˈrəʊ.leks ⓤⓢ ˈroʊ-
Rolf(e) rɒlf, rəʊf ⓤⓢ rɑːlf
roll rəʊl ⓤⓢ roʊl -s -z -ing -ɪŋ -ed -d ˈroll ˌbar; ˈroll ˌcall; ˈrolling ˌpin; ˈrolling ˌstock; ˌrolling ˈstone; ˌRolling ˈStones
Rollason ˈrɒl.ə.sᵊn ⓤⓢ ˈrɑː.lə-
roller ˈrəʊ.ləʳ ⓤⓢ ˈroʊ.lɚ -s -z ˈroller ˌblind; ˈroller ˌcoaster, ˌroller ˈcoaster
Rollerblade® ˈrəʊ.lə.bleɪd ⓤⓢ ˈroʊ.lɚ- -s -z
roller|-skate ˈrəʊ.lə|.skeɪt ⓤⓢ ˈroʊ.lɚ- -skates -skeɪts -skating -skeɪ.tɪŋ ⓤⓢ -skeɪ.t̬ɪŋ -skated -skeɪ.tɪd ⓤⓢ -skeɪ.t̬ɪd
Rolleston ˈrəʊl.stᵊn ⓤⓢ ˈroʊl-
rollicking ˈrɒl.ɪ.kɪŋ ⓤⓢ ˈrɑː.lɪ- -ly -li
Rollins ˈrɒl.ɪnz ⓤⓢ ˈrɑː.lɪnz
rollmop ˈrəʊl.mɒp ⓤⓢ ˈroʊl.mɑːp -s -s
rollneck ˈrəʊl.nek ⓤⓢ ˈroʊl- -s -s
Rollo ˈrɒl.əʊ ⓤⓢ ˈrɑː.loʊ
roll-on ˈrəʊl.ɒn ⓤⓢ ˈroʊl.ɑːn -s -z
roll-out ˈrəʊl.aʊt ⓤⓢ ˈroʊl- -s -s
rollover ˈrəʊˌləʊ.vəʳ, ˈroʊˌloʊ.vɚ -s -z

Rolls rəʊlz ⓤⓢ roʊlz
Rolls-Royc|e® ˌrəʊlz'rɔɪs ⓤⓢ ˌroʊlz- **-es** -ɪz *stress shift:* ˌRolls-Royce 'engine
roll-top 'rəʊl.tɒp ⓤⓢ 'roʊl.tɑːp **-s** -s
Rolo® 'rəʊ.ləʊ ⓤⓢ 'roʊ.loʊ
Rolodex® 'rəʊ.lə.deks ⓤⓢ 'roʊ-
Rolph rɒlf ⓤⓢ rɑːlf
roly-pol|y ˌrəʊ.li'pəʊ.l|i ⓤⓢ ˌroʊ.li'poʊ- **-ies** -iz *stress shift:* ˌroly-poly 'pudding
ROM rɒm ⓤⓢ rɑːm
Romagna rəʊ'mɑː.njə ⓤⓢ roʊ'-
Romaic rəʊ'meɪ.ɪk ⓤⓢ roʊ-
romaine rəʊ'meɪn ⓤⓢ rə-, roʊ- **roˌmaine 'lettuce, ˌromaine 'lettuce**
Roman 'rəʊ.mən ⓤⓢ 'roʊ- **-s** -z **ˌRoman 'candle; ˌRoman 'Catholic; ˌRoman Ca'tholicism; ˌRoman 'Empire; ˌRoman 'holiday; ˌRoman 'nose; ˌRoman 'numeral**
roman(s) à clef rəʊˌmɑ̃ːn.ɑː'kleɪ ⓤⓢ roʊ-
roman(s) à thèse rəʊˌmɑ̃ːn.ɑː'teɪz ⓤⓢ roʊ-
romanc|e (R) rəʊ'mænts; 'rəʊ.mænts ⓤⓢ roʊ'mænts, '-- **-es** -ɪz **-ing** -ɪŋ **-ed** -t **-er/s** -əʳ/z ⓤⓢ -ɚ/z
Romanes *surname:* rəʊ'mɑː.nɪz, -nɪs, -nes ⓤⓢ roʊ'mɑː.nɪz *gypsy language:* 'rɒm.ə.nes, -nɪs ⓤⓢ 'rɑː.mə-
Romanesque ˌrəʊ.mᵊn'esk ⓤⓢ ˌroʊ- *stress shift:* ˌRomanesque 'church
roman fleuve rəʊˌmɑ̃ːŋ'flɜːv ⓤⓢ roʊ-
Romani|a rʊ'meɪ.ni|.ə, rəʊ-, ruː- ⓤⓢ roʊ-, ruː-, '-nj|ə **-an/s** -ən/z
Romanic rəʊ'mæn.ɪk ⓤⓢ roʊ-
Roman|ism 'rəʊ.mᵊn|.ɪ.zᵊm ⓤⓢ 'roʊ- **-ist/s** -ɪst/s
romanization, -isa- ˌrəʊ.mᵊn.aɪ'zeɪ.ʃᵊn, -ɪ'- ⓤⓢ ˌroʊ.mᵊn.ɪ'- **-s** -z
romaniz|e, -is|e 'rəʊ.mᵊn.aɪz ⓤⓢ 'roʊ- **-es** -ɪz **-ing** -ɪŋ **-ed** -d
Romanov 'rəʊ.mᵊn.ɒf, -nɒv ⓤⓢ 'roʊ.mə.nɔːf; roʊ'mɑː-
Romans(c)h rəʊ'mænʃ, rʊ- ⓤⓢ roʊ'mɑːnʃ, -'mænʃ
romantic (R) rəʊ'mæn.tɪk ⓤⓢ roʊ'mæn.t̬ɪk **-ally** -ᵊl.i, -li
romantic|ism (R) rəʊ'mæn.tɪ.s|ɪ.zᵊm, -tə- ⓤⓢ roʊ'mæn.t̬ə- **-ist/s** -ɪst/s
romanticization, -isa- rəʊˌmæn.tɪ.saɪ'zeɪ.ʃᵊn, -tə-, -sɪ'- ⓤⓢ roʊˌmæn.t̬ə.sɪ'-
romanticiz|e, -is|e rəʊ'mæn.tɪ.saɪz, -tə- ⓤⓢ roʊ'mæn.t̬ə- **-es** -ɪz **-ing** -ɪŋ **-ed** -d
Roman|y 'rəʊ.mə.n|i, 'rɒm.ə- ⓤⓢ 'rɑː.mə-, 'roʊ- **-ies** -iz
romaunt rəʊ'mɔːnt ⓤⓢ roʊ'mɑːnt, -'mɔːnt **-s** -s
Rombauer 'rɒm.baʊəʳ ⓤⓢ 'rɑːm.baʊɚ
Rome rəʊm ⓤⓢ roʊm
Romeo 'rəʊ.mi.əʊ; rəʊ'meɪ- ⓤⓢ 'roʊ.mi.oʊ **-s** -z
Romero rəʊ'meə.rəʊ ⓤⓢ roʊ'mer.oʊ, rə-
Romford 'rɒm.fəd, 'rʌm- ⓤⓢ 'rɑːm.fɚd
romic (R) 'rəʊ.mɪk ⓤⓢ 'roʊ-
Romiley 'rɒm.ᵊl.i, -ɪ.li ⓤⓢ 'rɑː.mᵊl.i
Romilly 'rɒm.ᵊl.i, -ɪ.li ⓤⓢ 'rɑː.mᵊl.i
Romish 'rəʊ.mɪʃ ⓤⓢ 'roʊ-
Rommel 'rɒm.ᵊl ⓤⓢ 'rɑː.mᵊl
Romney 'rɒm.ni, 'rʌm- ⓤⓢ 'rɑːm-, 'rʌm- **-s** -z
Romola 'rɒm.ᵊl.ə ⓤⓢ 'rɑː.mᵊl-
romp rɒmp ⓤⓢ rɑːmp **-s** -s **-ing** -ɪŋ **-ed** -t
romper 'rɒm.pəʳ ⓤⓢ 'rɑːm.pɚ **-s** -z **'romper ˌsuit**
Romsey 'rʌm.zi, 'rɒm- ⓤⓢ 'rɑːm-
Romulus 'rɒm.jʊ.ləs, -jə- ⓤⓢ 'rɑː.mjə-, -mjʊ-
Ronald 'rɒn.ᵊld ⓤⓢ 'rɑː.nᵊld
Ronaldshay 'rɒn.ᵊld.ʃeɪ ⓤⓢ 'rɑː.nᵊld-
Ronaldsway 'rɒn.ᵊldz.weɪ ⓤⓢ 'rɑː.nᵊldz-
Ronan 'rəʊ.nən ⓤⓢ 'roʊ-
Ronay 'rəʊ.neɪ ⓤⓢ 'roʊ-
ron|deau 'rɒn|.dəʊ ⓤⓢ 'rɑːn|.doʊ **-deaus** -dəʊz, -dəʊ ⓤⓢ -doʊz **-deaux** -dəʊ ⓤⓢ -doʊ
rondel 'rɒn.dᵊl ⓤⓢ 'rɑːn-, -del **-s** -z
rondo 'rɒn.dəʊ ⓤⓢ 'rɑːn.doʊ **-s** -z
roneo (R®) 'rəʊ.ni.əʊ ⓤⓢ 'roʊ.ni.oʊ **-s** -z **-ing** -ɪŋ **-ed** -d
Ronnie 'rɒn.i ⓤⓢ 'rɑː.ni
Ronson 'rɒnt.sᵊn ⓤⓢ 'rɑːnt-
Ronstadt 'rɒn.stæt ⓤⓢ 'rɑːn-
röntgen, rontgen (R) 'rɒn.tjən, 'rɜːn-, 'rɒnt.gən, 'rɜːnt- ⓤⓢ 'rent.gən, 'rɜːnt-, 'rʌnt-, 'ren.tʃən, 'rɜːn-, 'rʌn- **-s** -z
röntgenogram 'rɒn.tʃən.ə.græm, 'rɜːn-, 'rɒnt.gən-, 'rɜːnt- ⓤⓢ 'rent.gə.nə-, 'rɜːnt-, 'rʌnt-, 'ren.tʃə-, 'rɜːn-, 'rʌn-, -dʒə- **-s** -z
Ronuk 'rɒn.ək ⓤⓢ 'rɑː.nək
roo ruː **-s** -z
rood ruːd **-s** -z **'rood ˌscreen**
roo|f (*n.*) ruː|f ⓤⓢ ruː|f, rʊ|f **-fs** -fs **-ves** -vz **'roof ˌgarden; 'roof ˌrack**
roof (*v.*) ruːf ⓤⓢ ruːf, rʊf **-s** -s **-ing** -ɪŋ **-ed** -t
roofer 'ruː.fəʳ ⓤⓢ -fɚ, 'rʊf.ɚ **-s** -z
rooftop 'ruːf.tɒp ⓤⓢ -tɑːp, 'rʊf- **-s** -s
rook rʊk **-s** -s **-ing** -ɪŋ **-ed** -t
Rooke rʊk **-s** -s
rooker|y 'rʊk.ᵊr|.i **-ies** -iz
rookie 'rʊk.i **-s** -z
room (R) ruːm, rʊm **-s** -z **-ing** **-ed** **-er/s** -əʳ/z ⓤⓢ -ɚ/z **'room ˌservice; 'rooming ˌhouse**
roomful 'ruːm.fʊl, 'rʊm- **-s** -z
roommate 'ruːm.meɪt, 'rʊm- **-s** -s
Rooms ruːmz
room|y 'ruː.m|i, 'rʊm|.i **-ier** -i.əʳ ⓤⓢ -i.ɚ **-iest** -i.ɪst, -i.əst **-ily** -ɪ.li, -ᵊl.i **-iness** -ɪ.nəs, -ɪ.nɪs
Rooney 'ruː.ni
Roosevelt 'rəʊ.zə.velt, 'ruː-, -sə-; 'ruːs.velt ⓤⓢ 'roʊ.zə.velt, 'ruː-, -vəlt; 'roʊz.velt
Note: /'rəʊ.zə.velt ⓤⓢ 'roʊ-/ is the pronunciation used in the families of the late presidents of the U.S.A..
roost (R) ruːst **-s** -s **-ing** -ɪŋ **-ed** -ɪd
rooster 'ruː.stəʳ ⓤⓢ -stɚ **-s** -z
root (R) ruːt **-s** -s **-ing** -ɪŋ ⓤⓢ 'ruː.t̬ɪŋ **-ed** -ɪd ⓤⓢ 'ruː.t̬ɪd **-less/ness** -ləs/nəs, -lɪs/nɪs **'root ˌbeer, ˌroot 'beer; 'root caˌnal; 'root ˌvegetable, ˌroot 'vegetable**
Rootham 'ruː.təm ⓤⓢ -t̬əm
rootstock 'ruːt.stɒk ⓤⓢ -stɑːk **-s** -s
rop|e rəʊp ⓤⓢ roʊp **-es** -s **-ing** -ɪŋ **-ed** -t **ˌrope 'ladder**
Roper 'rəʊ.pəʳ ⓤⓢ 'roʊ.pɚ
rop|ey, rop|y 'rəʊ.p|i ⓤⓢ 'roʊ- **-ier** -i.əʳ ⓤⓢ -i.ɚ **-iest** -i.ɪst, -i.əst **-iness** -ɪ.nə -ɪ.nɪs
Roquefort 'rɒk.fɔːʳ ⓤⓢ 'roʊk.fɚt
roquet 'rəʊ.ki, -keɪ ⓤⓢ roʊ'keɪ **-s** -z **-in** -ɪŋ **-ed** -d
Rorke rɔːk ⓤⓢ rɔːrk
Rorqual 'rɔː.kwᵊl, -kᵊl ⓤⓢ 'rɔːr.kwᵊl **-s**
Rorschach 'rɔː.ʃɑːk, -ʃæk ⓤⓢ 'rɔːr.ʃɑː
rort rɔːt ⓤⓢ rɔːrt **-s** -s **-ing** -ɪŋ, 'rɔːr.t̬ɪ **-ed** -ɪd ⓤⓢ 'rɔːr.t̬ɪd
Rory 'rɔː.ri ⓤⓢ 'rɔːr.i
Ros *(abbrev. for* **Rosalind***)* rɒz ⓤⓢ rɑː
Ros *surname:* rɒs ⓤⓢ rɑːs
Rosa 'rəʊ.zə ⓤⓢ 'roʊ-
rosaceous rəʊ'zeɪ.ʃəs ⓤⓢ roʊ-
Rosalba rəʊ'zæl.bə, rɒz'æl- ⓤⓢ roʊ'zɑːl-, -bɑː
Rosalie 'rəʊ.zᵊl.i, 'rɒz.ᵊl- ⓤⓢ 'roʊ.zə. 'rɑː-
Rosalind 'rɒz.ᵊl.ɪnd ⓤⓢ 'rɑː.zə.lɪnd
Rosaline 'rɒz.ᵊl.aɪn, -iːn ⓤⓢ 'rɑː.zə.lɪ -laɪn
Rosalynde 'rɒz.ᵊl.ɪnd ⓤⓢ 'rɑː.zə.lɪnd
Rosamond 'rɒz.ə.mənd ⓤⓢ 'rɑː.zə-, 'roʊ-
Rosario rəʊ'sɑː.ri.əʊ ⓤⓢ roʊ'zɑːr.i.o -sɑːr-
rosarium rəʊ'zeə.ri.əm ⓤⓢ roʊ'zer.i- **-s** -z
rosar|y 'rəʊ.zᵊr|.i ⓤⓢ 'roʊ- **-ies** -iz
Roscius 'rɒʃ.i.əs, 'rɒs-; 'rɒs.ki.əs ⓤⓢ 'rɑː.ʃi-, '-ʃəs
Roscoe 'rɒs.kəʊ ⓤⓢ 'rɑː.skoʊ
Roscommon rɒs'kɒm.ən ⓤⓢ rɑː'skɑː.mən
ros|e (R) rəʊz ⓤⓢ roʊz **-es** -ɪz **'rose ˌbush; 'rose ˌgarden; 'rose ˌwater; ˌrose 'window**

rose *(from* **rise)** rəʊz US roʊz
rosé ˈrəʊ.zeɪ, -ˈ- US roʊˈzeɪ
Roseanne rəʊˈzæn US roʊ-
roseate ˈrəʊ.zi.ət, -ɪt, -eɪt US ˈroʊ.zi.ɪt, -eɪt
Roseau rəʊˈzəʊ US roʊˈzoʊ
Rosebery ˈrəʊz.bᵊr.i US ˈroʊzˌber-
rosebud ˈrəʊz.bʌd US ˈroʊz- **-s** -z
rose-colo(u)red ˈrəʊzˌkʌl.əd US ˈroʊzˌkʌl.ɚd
rosehip ˈrəʊz.hɪp US ˈroʊz- **-s** -s
rosella rəʊˈzel.ə US roʊ-, rə- **-s** -z
rosemary (R) ˈrəʊz.mᵊr.i US ˈroʊz.mer-
Rosenberg ˈrəʊ.zᵊn.bɜːg, -zᵊm- US ˈroʊ.zᵊn.bɝːg
Rosencrantz ˈrəʊ.zᵊn.krænts, -zᵊŋ- US ˈroʊ-
Rosenkavalier ˌrəʊ.zᵊn.kæv.əˈlɪəʳ, -zᵊŋ-, ˈrəʊ.zᵊnˌkæv.ə.lɪə, ˌrəʊ- US ˈroʊ-
Rosenkranz US ˈrəʊ.zᵊn.krænts, -zᵊŋ- US ˈroʊ.zᵊn-
Rosenthal ˈrəʊ.zᵊn.tɑːl, -θɔːl US ˈroʊ.zᵊn.θɑːl, -θɔːl, -tɑːl, -tɔːl
roseola rəʊˈziː.ᵊl.ə; ˌrəʊ.ziˈəʊ.lə US roʊˈziː.ᵊl.ə; ˌroʊ.ziˈoʊ.lə
Rosetta rəʊˈzet.ə US roʊˈzet̬- **Roˌsetta ˈStone** US **Roˈsetta ˌStone**
rosette rəʊˈzet US roʊ- **-s** -s
rosewood ˈrəʊz.wʊd US ˈroʊz-
Rosh Hashana ˌrɒʃ.hæʃˈɑː.nə, -həˈʃɑː- US ˌroʊʃ.həˈʃɔː.nə, ˌrɑːʃ-, -ˈʃɑː-
Rosicrucian ˌrəʊ.zɪˈkruː.ʃᵊn, ˌrɒz.ɪˈ-, -ʃi.ən US ˌroʊ.zəˈkruː.ʃən, ˌrɑː- **-s** -z
Rosie ˈrəʊ.zi US ˈroʊ-
Rosier ˈrəʊ.zɪəʳ, -zi.əʳ US ˈroʊ.ʒɚ; roʊˈzɪr
rosin ˈrɒz.ɪn US ˈrɑː.zən
Rosina rəʊˈziː.nə US roʊ-
Roslin ˈrɒz.lɪn US ˈrɑːz-
Ross rɒs US rɑːs
Rossall ˈrɒs.ᵊl US ˈrɑː.sᵊl
Ross|e rɒs US rɑːs **-er** -əʳ US -ɚ
Rossellini ˌrɒs.əˈliː.ni US ˌrɑː.səˈ-
Rossetti rəˈzet.i, rɒzˈet-, rəˈset-, rɒsˈet- US roʊˈzet̬-, rə-, -ˈset̬-
Rossini rɒsˈiː.ni, rəˈsiː- US roʊˈsiː-, rɑː-
Rossiter ˈrɒs.ɪ.təʳ, ˈ-ə- US ˈrɑː.sə.t̬ɚ
Rosslare ˌrɒsˈleəʳ US rɑːˈsler *stress shift:* ˌRosslare ˈstreets
Rosslyn ˈrɒs.lɪn US ˈrɑː.slɪn
Ross-on-Wye ˌrɒs.ɒnˈwaɪ US ˌrɑːs.ɑːnˈ- *stress shift:* ˌRoss-on-Wye ˈstreets
rost|er ˈrɒs.t|əʳ US ˈrɑː.st|ɚ **-ers** -əz US -ɚz **-ering** -ᵊr.ɪŋ **-ered** -əd US -ɚd
Rostock ˈrɒs.tɒk US ˈrɑː.stɑːk
Rostov ˈrɒs.tɒv US ˈrɑː.stɑːf; rəˈstɔːf
Rostrevor rɒsˈtrev.əʳ US rɑːˈstrev.ɚ
Rostropovich ˌrɒs.trəˈpəʊ.vɪtʃ US ˌrɑː.strəˈpoʊ.viːtʃ, -strɑːˈpɔː-
rostr|um ˈrɒs.tr|əm US ˈrɑː.str|əm **-ums** -əmz **-a** -ə
ros|y (R) ˈrəʊ.z|i US ˈroʊ- **-ier** -i.əʳ US -i.ɚ **-iest** -i.ɪst, -i.əst **-ily** -ɪ.li, -ᵊl.i **-iness** -ɪ.nəs, -ɪ.nɪs
Rosyth rɒsˈaɪθ, rəˈsaɪθ US rɑːˈsaɪθ, rə-
rot rɒt US rɑːt **-s** -s **-ting** -ɪŋ US ˈrɑː.t̬ɪŋ **-ted** -ɪd US ˈrɑː.t̬ɪd
rota ˈrəʊ.tə US ˈroʊ.t̬ə **-s** -z
Rotarian rəʊˈteə.ri.ən US roʊˈter.i- **-s** -z
rotar|y ˈrəʊ.tᵊr|.i US ˈroʊ.t̬ɚ- **-ies** -iz **ˈRotary ˌClub**
rotatable rəʊˈteɪ.tə.bl̩ US ˈroʊ.teɪ.t̬ə-
rota|te rəʊˈteɪ|t US ˈroʊ.teɪ|t, -ˈ- **-tes** -ts **-ting** -tɪŋ US -t̬ɪŋ **-ted** -tɪd US -t̬ɪd **-tor/s** -təʳ/z US -t̬ɚ/z
rotation rəʊˈteɪ.ʃᵊn US roʊ- **-s** -z
rotatory ˈrəʊ.tə.tᵊr.i; rəʊˈteɪ- US ˈroʊ.tə.tɔːr-
ROTC ˌɑːʳ.əʊˌtiːˈsiː; ˌrɒtˈsiː US ˌɑːr.oʊ.tiːˈsiː; ˈrɑːt.si
rote rəʊt US roʊt
rotgut ˈrɒt.gʌt US ˈrɑːt-
Roth rɒθ, rəʊθ US rɑːθ
Rothamsted ˈrɒθ.ᵊm.sted US ˈrɑː.θəm-
Rothenstein ˈrəʊ.θᵊn.staɪn, -tᵊn-; ˈrɒθ.ᵊn- US ˈrɑː.θən-, ˈroʊ-
Rother ˈrɒð.əʳ US ˈrɑː.ðɚ
Rotherfield ˈrɒð.ə.fiːld US ˈrɑː.ðɚ-
Rotherham ˈrɒð.ᵊr.əm US ˈrɑː.ðɚ-
Rotherhithe ˈrɒð.ə.haɪð US ˈrɑː.ðɚ-
Rothermere ˈrɒð.ə.mɪəʳ US ˈrɑː.ðɚ.mɪr
Rotherston ˈrɒð.ə.stᵊn US ˈrɑː.ðɚ-
Rotherwick ˈrɒð.ᵊr.ɪk, -ə.wɪk US ˈrɑː.ðɚ.ɪk, -wɪk
Rothes ˈrɒθ.ɪs US ˈrɑː.θɪs
Rothesay ˈrɒθ.si, -seɪ US ˈrɑːθ-
Rothko ˈrɒθ.kəʊ US ˈrɑːθ.koʊ
Rothman ˈrɒθ.mən US ˈrɑːθ-
Rothschild ˈrɒθ.tʃaɪld, ˈrɒs-, ˈrɒθs- US ˈrɑːθ-, ˈrɔːθ-, ˈrɑːθs-, ˈrɔːθs-
Rothwell ˈrɒθ.wel, -wəl US ˈrɑːθ.wel, -wəl
roti ˈrəʊ.ti US roʊˈtiː **-s** -z
rotisserie rəʊˈtɪs.ᵊr.i, -ˈtiː.sᵊr- US roʊˈtɪs.ɚ- **-s** -z
rotogravure ˌrəʊ.təʊ.grəˈvjʊəʳ US ˌroʊ.t̬ə.grəˈvjʊr; ˈroʊ.t̬əˌgreɪ.vjɚ
rotor ˈrəʊ.təʳ US ˈroʊ.t̬ɚ **-s** -z
Rotorua ˌrəʊ.təˈruː.ə US ˌroʊ.t̬əˈ-
roto|vate ˈrəʊ.tə|.veɪt US ˈroʊ.t̬ə- **-vates** -veɪts **-vating** -veɪ.tɪŋ US -veɪ.t̬ɪŋ **-vated** -veɪ.tɪd US -veɪ.t̬ɪd
rotovator (R®) ˈrəʊ.tə.veɪ.təʳ US ˈroʊ.t̬ə.veɪ.t̬ɚ **-s** -z
rotten ˈrɒt.ᵊn US ˈrɑː.tᵊn **-est** -ɪst **-ly** -li **-ness** -nəs, -nɪs **ˌrotten ˈborough**
rottenstone ˈrɒt.ᵊn.stəʊn US ˈrɑː.tᵊn.stoʊn
rotter ˈrɒt.əʳ US ˈrɑː.t̬ɚ **-s** -z
Rotterdam ˈrɒt.ə.dæm, ˌ--ˈ- US ˈrɑː.t̬ɚ.dæm
Rottingdean ˈrɒt.ɪŋ.diːn, ˌ--ˈ- US ˈrɑː.t̬ɪŋ.diːn
rottweiler (R) ˈrɒt.waɪ.ləʳ, -vaɪ- US ˈrɑːt.waɪ.lɚ, ˈrɔːt.vaɪ- **-s** -z
rotund rəʊˈtʌnd; ˈrəʊ.tʌnd US roʊ- **-ity** -ə.ti, -ɪ.ti US -ə.t̬i **-ness** -nəs, -nɪs
rotunda (R) rəʊˈtʌn.də US roʊ- **-s** -z
rouble ˈruː.bl̩ **-s** -z
Rouch raʊtʃ
roué ˈruː.eɪ, -ˈ- US ruˈeɪ; ˈruː.eɪ **-s** -z
Rouen ˈruː.ɑ̃ːŋ, -ɑːŋ, -ˈ- US ruˈɑ̃ːŋ, -ˈɑːn
roug|e ruːʒ **-es** -ɪz **-ing** -ɪŋ **-ed** -d
rough rʌf **-s** -s **-er** -əʳ US -ɚ **-est** -ɪst, -əst **-ly** -li **-ness** -nəs, -nɪs **-ing** -ɪŋ **-ed** -t **ˌrough ˈdiamond; ˈrough ˌstuff; ˌrough ˈtrade; take the ˌrough with the ˈsmooth**
roughage ˈrʌf.ɪdʒ
rough-and-ready ˌrʌf.ᵊndˈred.i *stress shift:* ˌrough-and-ready ˈtreatment
rough-and-tumble ˌrʌf.ᵊndˈtʌm.bl̩ *stress shift:* ˌrough-and-tumble ˈgames
roughcast ˈrʌf.kɑːst US -kæst
roughen ˈrʌf.ᵊn **-s** -z **-ing** -ɪŋ, ˈrʌf.nɪŋ **-ed** -d
rough-hew ˌrʌfˈhjuː **-s** -z **-ing** -ɪŋ **-ed** -d **-n** -n *stress shift:* ˌrough-hewn ˈstone
roughhous|e ˈrʌf.haʊs **-es** -ɪz **-ing** -ɪŋ **-ed** -t
roughish ˈrʌf.ɪʃ
roughneck ˈrʌf.nek **-s** -s
roughrider ˈrʌfˌraɪ.dəʳ US -dɚ **-s** -z
roughshod ˈrʌf.ʃɒd US -ʃɑːd **ˌride ˈroughshod over**
rough-spoken ˌrʌfˈspəʊ.kᵊn US -ˈspoʊ- *stress shift:* ˌrough-spoken ˈperson
Rough Tor ˌraʊˈtɔːʳ US -ˈtɔːr
roulade ruːˈlɑːd **-s** -z
roulette ruːˈlet
Roulston ˈrəʊl.stᵊn US ˈroʊl-
Roumani|a ruˈmeɪ.ni|.ə, rʊ-, rəʊ- US ruː-, roʊ-, ˈ-nj|ə **-an/s** -ən/z
round (R) raʊnd **-s** -z **-er** -əʳ US -ɚ **-est** -ɪst, -əst **-ly** -li **-ness** -nəs, ˈraʊn.nəs, -nɪs **-ish** -ɪʃ **-ing** -ɪŋ **-ed** -ɪd **ˌround ˈrobin; ˌRound ˈTable** US **ˈRound ˌTable; ˌround ˈtrip**
roundabout ˈraʊnd.əˌbaʊt **-s** -s
roundel ˈraʊn.dᵊl **-s** -z
roundelay ˈraʊn.dɪ.leɪ, -dᵊl.eɪ US -də.leɪ **-s** -z
rounders ˈraʊn.dəz US -dɚz
roundhand ˈraʊnd.hænd
Roundhay ˈraʊn.deɪ, ˈraʊnd.heɪ
Roundhead ˈraʊnd.hed **-s** -z
roundhou|se ˈraʊnd.haʊ|s **-ses** -zɪz
round-shouldered ˌraʊndˈʃəʊl.dəd US -ˈʃoʊl.dɚd *stress shift:* ˌround-shouldered ˈperson

Rounding

A term used to describe lip configuration in speech sounds.

Examples for English

Practically any vowel or consonant may be produced with different amounts of lip-rounding. The lips are rounded by muscles that act rather like a draw-string round the neck of a bag, bringing the edges of the lips towards each other. Except in unusual cases, this results not only in the mouth opening adopting a round shape, but also in a protrusion or "pushing forward" of the lips. In theory, any vowel position (defined in terms of height and frontness/backness) may be produced rounded or unrounded, though we do not necessarily find all possible vowels in natural languages. BBC English has four rounded vowel monophthongs, while US English has three:

pot	/pɒt/	(US) /pɑːt/	(unrounded)
put	/pʊt/		
core	/kɔː/	(US) /kɔːr/	
coo	/kuː/		

Consonants, too, may have rounded lips (in [w], the basic consonantal articulation itself consists of lip-rounding): this lip-rounding in consonants is regarded as a 'secondary articulation', and it is usual to refer to it as 'labialisation'. In British English, it is common to find /ʃ/, /tʃ/ and /r/ with lip-rounding.

In other languages

Swedish is described as having a rounded vowel without lip protrusion.

rounds|man 'raʊndz|.mən **-men** -mən
round-table ˌraʊnd'teɪ.bl̩ (US) '-ˌ-- *stress shift:* ˌround-table 'conference
round-the-clock ˌraʊnd.ðə'klɒk (US) -'klɑːk *stress shift:* ˌround-the-clock 'vigil
round-up 'raʊnd.ʌp **-s** -s
roundworm 'raʊnd.wɜːm (US) -wɝːm **-s** -z
Rourke rɔːk (US) rɔːrk
Rous raʊs
rous|e raʊz **-es** -ɪz **-ing/ly** -ɪŋ/li **-ed** -d
Rouse raʊs, ruːs
Rousseau 'ruː.səʊ, -'- (US) ruː'soʊ
Roussillon ˌruː.si'jɔ̃ŋ, '---- (US) -'jõʊn
roustabout 'raʊst.əˌbaʊt **-s** -s
rout raʊt **-s** -s **-ing** -ɪŋ (US) 'raʊ.t̬ɪŋ **-ed** -ɪd (US) 'raʊ.t̬ɪd
rout|e ruːt (US) ruːt, raʊt **-es** -s **-(e)ing/s** -ɪŋ/z (US) 'ruː.t̬ɪŋ, 'raʊ- **-ed** -ɪd (US) 'ruː.t̬ɪd, 'raʊ- '**route** ˌ**march**
Routh raʊθ
routine ruː'tiːn **-s** -z
Routledge 'raʊt.lɪdʒ, -ledʒ, 'rʌt-
Routley 'raʊt.li
roux (R) ruː
rov|e rəʊv (US) roʊv **-es** -z **-ing** -ɪŋ **-ed** -d **-er/s** -əʳ/z (US) -ɚ/z
Rover® 'rəʊ.vəʳ (US) 'roʊ.vɚ **-s** -z
row *(n.v.) quarrel:* raʊ **-s** -z **-ing** -ɪŋ **-ed** -d
row *(n.v.) all other senses:* rəʊ (US) roʊ **-s** -z **-ing** -ɪŋ **-ed** -d '**row** ˌ**house**; '**rowing** ˌ**boat**
Rowallan rəʊ'æl.ən (US) roʊ-
rowan *tree:* rəʊən, raʊən; 'rəʊ.æn (US) roʊən, raʊən **-s** -z
Note: More commonly /raʊən/ in Scotland.
Rowan *name:* rəʊən, raʊən (US) roʊən, raʊən
rowanberr|y 'rəʊənˌberl.i, 'rəʊəm- (US) 'roʊən- **-ies** -iz
Rowant raʊənt
row-boat 'rəʊ.bəʊt (US) 'roʊ.boʊt **-s** -s
Rowbottom, Rowbotham 'rəʊˌbɒt.ᵊm (US) 'roʊˌbɑː.t̬əm
Rowden 'raʊ.dᵊn
rowd|y 'raʊ.dli **-ies** -iz **-ier** -i.əʳ (US) -i.ɚ **-iest** -i.ɪst, -i.əst **-ily** -ɪ.li, -ᵊl.i **-iness** -ɪ.nəs, -ɪ.nɪs **-yism** -i.ɪ.zᵊm
Rowe rəʊ (US) roʊ
rowel raʊəl **-s** -z
Rowell raʊəl
Rowena rəʊ'iː.nə (US) roʊ-, -'wiː-
Rowenta® rəʊ'en.tə (US) roʊ'en.t̬ə
rower 'rəʊ.əʳ (US) 'roʊ.ɚ **-s** -z
Rowland 'rəʊ.lənd (US) 'roʊ- **-s** -z
Rowlandson 'rəʊ.lənd.sən (US) 'roʊ-
Rowles rəʊlz (US) roʊlz
Rowley 'rəʊ.li, 'raʊ- (US) 'roʊ-, 'raʊ-
Rowling 'rəʊ.lɪŋ, 'raʊ- (US) 'roʊ-
Rowlinson 'rəʊ.lɪn.sᵊn (US) 'roʊ-
rowlock 'rɒl.ək, 'rəʊ.lɒk, 'rʌl.ək (US) 'rɑː.lək, 'rʌl.ək, 'roʊ.lɑːk **-s** -s
Rowney 'rəʊ.ni, 'raʊ- (US) 'roʊ-, 'raʊ-
Rowntree 'raʊn.triː ˌ**Rowntree** '**Mackintosh®**
Rowridge 'raʊ.rɪdʒ
Rowse raʊs
Rowton 'raʊ.tᵊn, 'rɔː-
Roxana rɒk'sɑː.nə, -'sæn.ə (US) rɑːk'sæn-
Roxanne rɒk'sæn (US) rɑːk-
Roxburgh(e) 'rɒks.bᵊr.ə (US) 'rɑːks- **-shire** -ʃəʳ, -ˌʃɪəʳ (US) -ʃɚ, -ˌʃɪr
Roxy 'rɒk.si (US) 'rɑːk-
Roy rɔɪ
royal 'rɔɪəl **-s** -ly -i ˌ**Royal** '**Air** ˌ**Force**; ˌ**royal** '**blue**; ˌ**royal** '**family**; ˌ**Royal** '**Highness**; ˌ**royal** '**jelly**; ˌ**Royal** '**Mail**; ˌ**Royal** '**Navy**
royal|ism 'rɔɪə.l|ɪ.zᵊm **-ist/s** -ɪst/s
royalt|y 'rɔɪəl.t|i (US) -t̬|i **-ies** -iz
Royce rɔɪs
Royle rɔɪl
Royston 'rɔɪ.stᵊn
Royton 'rɔɪ.tᵊn
RP ˌɑː'piː (US) ˌɑːr-
rpm (R) ˌɑː.piː'em (US) ˌɑːr-
RSA ˌɑːʳ.es'eɪ (US) ˌɑːr-
RSC ˌɑːʳ.es'siː (US) ˌɑːr-
RSPB ˌɑːʳ.esˌpiː'biː (US) ˌɑːr-
RSPCA ˌɑːʳ.esˌpiː.siː'eɪ (US) ˌɑːr-
RSVP ˌɑːʳ.es.viː'piː (US) ˌɑːr-
Rt. Hon. *(abbrev. for* **Right Honourable***)* ˌraɪt'ɒn.ᵊr.ə.bl̩ (US) -'ɑː.nɚ.ə- *stress shift:* ˌRt. Hon 'member
Ruabon ru'æb.ᵊn

Pronouncing the letters RRH

The consonant letter combination **rrh** behaves like the letter **r**, e.g.:

myrrh	/mɜːʳ/	(US) /mɜːr/
diarrh(o)ea	/ˌdaɪə'rɪə/	(US) /-'riː.ə/

Ruanda ru'æn.də (US) -'ɑːn-

rub rʌb **-s** -z **-bing** -ɪŋ **-bed** -d

Rubáiyát 'ruː.baɪ.jæt, -beɪ- (US) ˌruː.baɪ'jɑːt, -biː'-, '---

rubato ruː'bɑː.təʊ, rʊ- (US) ruː'bɑː.toʊ **-s** -z

rubb|er 'rʌb|.əʳ (US) -ɚ **-ers** -əz (US) -ɚz **-ery** -ᵊr.i ˌ**rubber 'band**; '**rubber ˌplant**

rubberiz|e, -is|e 'rʌb.ᵊr.aɪz (US) -ə.raɪz **-es** -ɪz **-ing** -ɪŋ **-ed** -d

rubberneck 'rʌb.ə.nek (US) '-ɚ- **-s** -s **-ing** -ɪŋ **-ed** -t **-er/s** -əʳ/z (US) -ɚ/z

rubber-stamp ˌrʌb.ə'stæmp (US) -ɚ'- **-s** -s **-ing** -ɪŋ **-ed** -t *stress shift:* ˌrubber-stamped 'document

rubbish 'rʌb.ɪʃ **-es** -ɪz **-ing** -ɪŋ **-ed** -t **-y** -i

rubble 'rʌb.l̩

Rubbra 'rʌb.rə

rubefacient ˌruː.bɪ'feɪ.ʃi.ənt, '-ʃᵊnt (US) -bə'feɪ.ʃᵊnt

Rube Goldberg ˌruːb'gəʊld.bɜːg (US) -'goʊld.bɝːg

rubella ruː'bel.ə, rʊ- (US) ruː-

Ruben 'ruː.bɪn, -bən (US) -bən

Rubenesque ˌruː.bɪ'nesk, -bᵊn'esk (US) -bə'nesk

Rubens 'ruː.bənz, -bɪnz (US) -bənz

rubeola ruː'biː.əʊ.lə, rʊ-; ˌruː.bi'əʊ.lə (US) ruː'bi.ᵊl.ə; ˌruː.bi'oʊ.lə

Rubicon 'ruː.bɪ.kᵊn, -kɒn (US) -kɑːn

rubicund 'ruː.bɪ.kənd, -kʌnd (US) -bə.kʌnd, -bɪ-, -kənd

rubidium ruː'bɪd.i.əm, rʊ- (US) ruː-

Rubik 'ruː.bɪk ˌ**Rubik's 'Cube**

Rubinstein 'ruː.bɪn.staɪn, -bən- (US) -bɪn-

ruble 'ruː.bl̩ **-s** -z

rubric 'ruː.brɪk **-s** -s

rub|y (R) 'ruː.b|i **-ies** -iz

RUC ˌɑː.juː'siː (US) ˌɑːr-

ruch|e ruːʃ **-es** -ɪz **-ing** -ɪŋ **-ed** -t

ruck rʌk **-s** -s **-ing** -ɪŋ **-ed** -t

rucksack 'rʌk.sæk, 'rʊk- **-s** -s

ruckus 'rʌk.əs

ruction 'rʌk.ʃᵊn **-s** -z

rudd (R) rʌd **-s** -z

rudd|er 'rʌd|.əʳ (US) -ɚ **-ers** -əz (US) -ɚz **-erless** -ᵊl.əs, -ɪs (US) -ɚ.ləs, -lɪs

Rudderham 'rʌd.ᵊr.əm

Ruddigore 'rʌd.ɪ.gɔːʳ (US) -gɔːr

ruddl|e 'rʌd.l̩ **-es** -z **-ing** -ɪŋ, 'rʌd.lɪŋ **-ed** -d

Ruddlington 'rʌd.lɪŋ.tən

Ruddock 'rʌd.ək

rudd|y 'rʌd|.i **-ier** -i.əʳ (US) -i.ɚ **-iest** -i.ɪst, -i.əst **-ily** -ɪ.li, -ᵊl.i **-iness** -ɪ.nəs, -ɪ.nɪs

rud|e ruːd **-er** -əʳ (US) -ɚ **-est** -ɪst, -əst **-ely** -li **-eness** -nəs, -nɪs

rudge rʌdʒ

Rudi 'ruː.di

rudiment 'ruː.dɪ.mənt, -də- (US) -də- **-s** -s

rudimentary ˌruː.dɪ'men.tᵊr.i, -də'-, '-tri (US) -də'- *stress shift:* ˌrudimentary 'knowledge

Rudolf, Rudolph 'ruː.dɒlf (US) -dɑːlf

Rudy 'ruː.di

Rudyard *first name:* 'rʌd.jəd, -jɑːd (US) -jɚd, -jɑːrd

Rudyard *in Staffordshire:* 'rʌdʒ.əd (US) -ɚd

rue ruː **-s** -z **-ing** -ɪŋ **-d** -d

rueful 'ruː.fᵊl, -fʊl **-ly** -i **-ness** -nəs, -nɪs

ruff rʌf **-s** -s **-ing** -ɪŋ **-ed** -t

ruffian 'rʌf.i.ən **-s** -z **-ly** -li **-ism** -ɪ.zᵊm

ruffl|e 'rʌf.l̩ **-es** -z **-ing** -ɪŋ, 'rʌf.lɪŋ **-ed** -d

rufiyaa 'ruː.fi.jɑː

rufous 'ruː.fəs

Rufus 'ruː.fəs

rug rʌg **-s** -z

Rugbeian rʌg'biː.ən **-s** -z

rugby (R) 'rʌg.bi ˌ**Rugby 'League**; ˌ**Rugby 'Union**

Rugeley 'ruːdʒ.li, 'ruːʒ-

rugged 'rʌg.ɪd **-ly** -li **-ness** -nəs, -nɪs

rugger 'rʌg.əʳ (US) -ɚ

rugrat (R) 'rʌg.ræt **-s** -s

Ruhr rʊəʳ (US) rʊr

ruin 'ruː.ɪn **-s** -z **-ing** -ɪŋ **-ed** -d

ruination ˌruː.ɪ'neɪ.ʃᵊn, rʊɪ'- (US) ˌruː.ə'-

ruinous 'ruː.ɪ.nəs (US) 'ruː.ə- **-ly** -li **-ness** -nəs, -nɪs

Ruislip 'raɪ.slɪp, 'raɪz.lɪp

Ruiz ru'iːθ (US) ru'iːθ; ruː'iːs

rul|e (R) ruːl **-es** -z **-ing** -ɪŋ **-ed** -d **-er/s** -əʳ/z (US) -ɚ/z

rulebook 'ruːl.bʊk **-s** -s

ruling 'ruː.lɪŋ **-s** -z ˌ**ruling 'class** (US) '**ruling ˌclass**

rum rʌm **-mer** -əʳ (US) -ɚ **-mest** -ɪst, -əst

Rumani|a rʊ'meɪ.ni|.ə, rəʊ-, ruː- (US) roʊ-, ruː-, '-nj|ə **-an/s** -ənz

rumba 'rʌm.bə **-s** -z

Rumbelow 'rʌm.bə.ləʊ, -bɪ- (US) -loʊ

rumbl|e 'rʌm.bl̩ **-es** -z **-ing/s** -ɪŋ/z, 'rʌm.blɪŋ/z **-ed** -d

Rumbold 'rʌm.bəʊld (US) -boʊld

rumbustious rʌm'bʌs.ti.əs, '-tʃəs (US) -tʃəs **-ness** -nəs, -nɪs

Rumelia ruː'miː.li.ə (US) -li.ə, -'miːl.jə

rumen 'ruː.men, -mɪn, -mən (US) -mən **-s** -z **rumina** 'ruː.mɪ.nə, -mə- (US) -mə-

Rumford 'rʌm.fəd (US) -fɚd

ruminant 'ruː.mɪ.nənt, -mə- (US) -mə- **-s** -s

rumi|nate 'ruː.mɪ|.neɪt, -mə- (US) -mə- **-nates** -neɪts **-nating** -neɪ.tɪŋ (US) -neɪ.t̬ɪŋ **-nated** -neɪ.tɪd (US) -neɪ.t̬ɪd

rumination ˌruː.mɪ'neɪ.ʃᵊn, -mə'- (US) -mə'- **-s** -z

ruminative 'ruː.mɪ.nə.tɪv, -mə-, -neɪ- (US) -məˌneɪ.t̬ɪv

rummag|e 'rʌm.ɪdʒ **-es** -ɪz **-ing** -ɪŋ **-ed** -d '**rummage ˌsale**

rumm|y 'rʌm|.i **-ier** -i.əʳ (US) -i.ɚ **-iest** -i.ɪst, -i.əst **-ily** -ɪ.li, -ᵊl.i **-iness** -ɪ.nəs, -ɪ.nɪs

rumo(u)r 'ruː.məʳ (US) -mɚ **-s** -z **-ed** -d

rumo(u)r-mong|er 'ruː.məˌmʌŋ.g|əʳ (US) -mɚˌmʌŋ.g|ɚ, -ˌmɑːŋ- **-ers** -əz (US) -ɚz **-ering** -ᵊr.ɪŋ

rump rʌmp **-s** -s ˌ**rump 'steak**

Rumpelstiltskin ˌrʌm.pᵊl'stɪlt.skɪn

rumpl|e 'rʌm.pl̩ **-es** -z **-ing** -ɪŋ, 'rʌm.plɪŋ **-ed** -d

Rumpole 'rʌm.pəʊl (US) -poʊl

rumpus 'rʌm.pəs **-es** -ɪz

rum-runner 'rʌmˌrʌn.əʳ (US) -ɚ **-s** -z

Rumsfeld 'rʌmz.felt (US) -feld

run rʌn **-s** -z **-ning** -ɪŋ **ran** ræn ˌ**running 'water**; ˌ**take a ˌrunning 'jump**; '**running ˌshoe**

runabout 'rʌn.əˌbaʊt **-s** -s

runagate 'rʌn.əˌgeɪt **-s** -s

runaround 'rʌn.ᵊrˌaʊnd

runaway 'rʌn.əˌweɪ **-s** -z

runcible 'rʌnt.sɪ.bl̩, -sə- (US) -sə-

Runcie 'rʌnt.si

Runciman 'rʌnt.sɪ.mən

Runcorn 'rʌŋ.kɔːn (US) -kɔːrn

run-down (*adj.*) ˌrʌn'daʊn *stress shift:* ˌrun-down 'area

rundown (*n.*) 'rʌn.daʊn **-s** -z

rune (R) ruːn **-s** -z

rung rʌŋ **-s** -z

rung (*from* **ring**) rʌŋ

Runham 'rʌn.əm

runic (R) 'ruː.nɪk

run-in 'rʌn.ɪn **-s** -z

runnel 'rʌn.ᵊl **-s** -z

runner 'rʌn.əʳ (US) -ɚ **-s** -z ˌ**runner 'bean**, '**runner ˌbean**

runner-up ˌrʌn.əʳ'ʌp (US) -ɚ'- **runners-up** ˌrʌn.əz'- (US) -ɚz'- *stress shift:* ˌrunner-up 'prizes

running-board 'rʌn.ɪŋ.bɔːd (US) -bɔːrd **-s** -z

runn|y 'rʌn|.i **-ier** -i.əʳ (US) -i.ɚ **-iest** -i.ɪst, -i.əst **-iness** -ɪ.nəs, -ɪ.nɪs

Runnymede 'rʌn.i.miːd

runoff 'rʌn.ɒf (US) -ɑːf **-s** -s

run-of-the-mill ˌrʌn.əv.ðə'mɪl *stress shift:* ˌrun-of-the-mill 'job

runt rʌnt **-s** -s **-y** -i (US) 'rʌn.t̬i

Runton 'rʌn.tən (US) -tᵊn

runway 'rʌn.weɪ **-s** -z

Runyon 'rʌn.jən

rupee ruː'piː (US) 'ruː.piː, -'- **-s** -z

Rupert 'ruː.pət (US) -pɚt

rupiah ruː'piː.ə **-s** -z

rupt|ure 'rʌp.tʃ|əʳ (US) -tʃ|ɚ **-ures** -əz (US) -ɚz **-uring** -ᵊr.ɪŋ **-ured** -əd (US) -ɚd

rural ˈrʊə.rəl ⓤⓢ ˈrʊr.əl **-ly** -i
ruridecanal ˌrʊə.rɪ.dɪˈkeɪ.nəl, -rə- ⓤⓢ ˌrʊr.ɪ.dəˈ-; -ˈdek.ə.næl
Ruritani|a ˌrʊə.rɪˈteɪ.ni|.ə, -rəˈ- ⓤⓢ ˌrʊr.ɪˈ- **-an** -ən
Rusbridger ˈrʌsˌbrɪdʒ.əʳ ⓤⓢ -ɚ
rus|e ruːz ⓤⓢ ruːz, ruːs **-es** -ɪz
rusé ˈruː.zeɪ ⓤⓢ ruːˈzeɪ
Rusedski rʊˈset.ski, -ˈsed-, -ˈzet-, -ˈzed-
rush (R) rʌʃ **-es** -ɪz **-ing** -ɪŋ **-ed** -t **-er/s** -əʳ/z ⓤⓢ -ɚ/z ˈ**rush** ˌ**hour**
Rushall ˈrʌʃ.əl
Rushden ˈrʌʃ.dən
Rushdie ˈrʊʃ.di, ˈrʌʃ-
Rushforth ˈrʌʃ.fɔːθ, -fəθ ⓤⓢ -fɔːrθ, -fɚθ
rushlight ˈrʌʃ.laɪt **-s** -s
Rushmere ˈrʌʃ.mɪəʳ ⓤⓢ -mɪr
Rushmore ˈrʌʃ.mɔːʳ ⓤⓢ -mɔːr
Rusholme ˈrʌʃ.əm, -həʊm ⓤⓢ -əm, -hoʊm
Rushton ˈrʌʃ.tən
Rushworth ˈrʌʃ.wəθ, -wɜːθ ⓤⓢ -wɚθ, -wɝːθ
rushy ˈrʌʃ.i
rusk (R) rʌsk **-s** -s
Ruskin ˈrʌs.kɪn
Rusper ˈrʌs.pəʳ ⓤⓢ -pɚ
Russell ˈrʌs.əl
russet ˈrʌs.ɪt **-s** -s
Russia ˈrʌʃ.ə
Russian ˈrʌʃ.ən **-s** -z ˌ**Russian rouˈlette**
russianism (R) ˈrʌʃ.ən.ɪ.zəm **-s** -z
russianiz|e, -is|e (R) ˈrʌʃ.ən.aɪz **-es** -ɪz **-ing** -ɪŋ **-ed** -d
Russo- ˌrʌs.əʊ- ⓤⓢ ˌrʌs.oʊ-, ˌ-ə-
Russo ˈrʌs.əʊ ⓤⓢ -oʊ

rust (R) rʌst **-s** -s **-ing** -ɪŋ **-ed** -ɪd
rustbelt ˈrʌst.belt
rustbucket ˈrʌstˌbʌk.ɪt **-s** -s
rustic ˈrʌs.tɪk **-s** -s **-ally** -əl.i, -li
rusti|cate ˈrʌs.tɪ|.keɪt ⓤⓢ -tə- **-cates** -keɪts **-cating** -keɪ.tɪŋ ⓤⓢ -keɪ.t̬ɪŋ **-cated** -keɪ.tɪd ⓤⓢ -keɪ.t̬ɪd
rustication ˌrʌs.tɪˈkeɪ.ʃən ⓤⓢ -təˈ-
rusticity rʌsˈtɪs.ə.ti, -ɪ.ti ⓤⓢ -ə.t̬i
rustl|e ˈrʌs.l̩ **-es** -z **-ing** -ɪŋ, ˈrʌs.lɪŋ **-ed** -d **-er/s** -əʳ/z ⓤⓢ -ɚ/z, ˈrʌs.ləʳ/z ⓤⓢ -lɚ/z
rustproof ˈrʌst.pruːf
Rustum ˈrʌs.təm
rust|y (R) ˈrʌs.t|i **-ier** -i.əʳ ⓤⓢ -i.ɚ **-iest** -i.ɪst, -i.əst **-iness** -ɪ.nəs, -ɪ.nɪs
Ruswarp ˈrʌs.əp, ˈrʌz- ⓤⓢ -ɚp
rut rʌt **-s** -s **-ting** -ɪŋ ⓤⓢ ˈrʌt̬.ɪŋ **-ted** -ɪd ⓤⓢ ˈrʌt̬.ɪd
rutabaga ˌruː.təˈbeɪ.gə, ˌrʊt.əˈ-, ˈruː.təˌbeɪ-, ˈrʊt.əˌ- ⓤⓢ ˌruː.t̬əˈbeɪ-, ˈruː.t̬əˌbeɪ- **-s** -z
Rutgers ˈrʌt.gəz ⓤⓢ -gɚz
Ruth, ruth ruːθ
Ruthenia ruːˈθiː.ni.ə ⓤⓢ -ni.ə, ˈ-njə
Ruthenian ruːˈθiː.ni.ən ⓤⓢ -ni.ən, ˈ-njən **-s** -z
ruthenium ruːˈθiː.ni.əm
Rutherford ˈrʌð.ə.fəd ⓤⓢ -ɚ.fɚd, ˈrʌθ-
rutherfordium ˌrʌð.əˈfɔː.di.əm ⓤⓢ -ɚˈfɔːr-
Rutherglen ˈrʌð.ə.glen ⓤⓢ ˈ-ɚ-
ruthful ˈruːθ.fəl, -fʊl **-ly** -li **-ness** -nəs, -nɪs
Ruthin ˈrɪθ.ɪn, ˈruː.θɪn
ruthless ˈruːθ.ləs, -lɪs **-ly** -li **-ness** -nəs, -nɪs

Ruthven *personal name:* ˈruːθ.vən, ˈrɪv.ən *Baron, place in Tayside region:* ˈrɪv.ən *place in Grampian region, loch in Highland region:* ˈrʌθ.vən
Ruthwell ˈrʌθ.wəl *locally:* ˈrɪð.əl
rutilant ˈruː.tɪ.lənt ⓤⓢ -təl.ənt
rutile ˈruː.taɪl ⓤⓢ -tiːl, -taɪl
rutin ˈruː.tɪn, -tən ⓤⓢ -tən
Rutland ˈrʌt.lənd
Rutledge ˈrʌt.lɪdʒ
Rutskoi ˌrʊtˈskɔɪ, ˌruːt-
Rutter ˈrʌt.əʳ ⓤⓢ ˈrʌt̬.ɚ
Rutterford ˈrʌt.ə.fəd ⓤⓢ ˈrʌt̬.ɚ.fɚd
rutt|y ˈrʌt|.i ⓤⓢ ˈrʌt̬- **-ier** -i.əʳ ⓤⓢ -i.ɚ **-iest** -i.ɪst, -i.əst **-iness** -ɪ.nəs, -ɪ.nɪs
Ruysdael ˈraɪz.dɑːl, ˈriːz-, -deɪl ⓤⓢ ˈraɪs.dɑːl, ˈraɪz-, ˈrɔɪs-
Ruyter ˈraɪ.təʳ ⓤⓢ ˈrɔɪ.t̬ɚ, ˈraɪ-
RV ˌɑːˈviː ⓤⓢ ˌɑːr-
Rwanda ruˈæn.də ⓤⓢ -ˈɑːn- **-n/s** -n/z
Ryan raɪən
Rydal ˈraɪ.dəl
Ryde raɪd
Ryder ˈraɪ.dəʳ ⓤⓢ -dɚ ˌ**Ryder** ˈ**Cup**
rye (R) raɪ ˈ**rye** ˌ**bread;** ˈ**rye** ˌ**grass**
Ryecroft ˈraɪ.krɒft ⓤⓢ -krɑːft
Ryle raɪl
Rylstone ˈrɪl.stən, -stəʊn ⓤⓢ -stən, -stoʊn
Ryman ˈraɪ.mən
Rymer ˈraɪ.məʳ ⓤⓢ -mɚ
ryot raɪət **-s** -s
Ryswick ˈrɪz.wɪk
Ryton ˈraɪ.tən
Ryukyu riˈuː.kjuː ⓤⓢ -ˈjuː-, -ˈuː-
Ryvita® raɪˈviː.tə ⓤⓢ -t̬ə

Pronouncing the letter S

See also SC, SCH, SH

The consonant letter **s** has five realisations: /s z ʃ ʒ/ and silent. The most obvious of these is /s/, e.g.

sack /sæk/
case /keɪs/

/z/ is a very common realisation of **s**, but it is not usually word-initial, e.g.:

rise /raɪz/
losing /ˈluː.zɪŋ/

It particularly occurs in the verb form of homographs, and in words ending **sm**.

close (v.) /kləʊz/ (US) /kloʊz/
use (v.) /juːz/
spasm /ˈspæz.əm/

In suffixes *-sion*, *-sure*, *-sia* and their derivatives, **s** is realised as /tʃ/ or /ʒ/, e.g.:

Asia /ˈeɪ.ʃə, -ʒə/ (US) /ˈeɪ.ʒə/
insure /ɪnˈʃʊəʳ/ (US) /ɪnˈʃʊr/
tension /ˈten.tʃᵊn/ (US) /ˈten*t*.ʃᵊn/
treasure /ˈtreʒ.əʳ/ (US) /-ɚ/
persuasion /pəˈsweɪ.ʒᵊn/ (US) /pɚ-/

In addition

s can be silent. This usually happens in word final position, where the word is a borrowing from French, e.g.:

debris /ˈdeɪ.briː/ (US) /dəˈbriː/

The grammatical inflections -(e)s, -'s

There are three possible ways of pronouncing the grammatical inflections *-(e)s* and *-'s*. Following /s z ʃ ʒ tʃ/ and /dʒ/ the inflection is realised as /ɪz/, e.g.:

horses /ˈhɔː.sɪz/ (US) /ˈhɔːr-/
rises /ˈraɪ.zɪz/

Following all other voiceless consonant sounds the inflection is realised as /s/, e.g.:

laughs /lɑːfs/ (US) /læfs/
shapes /ʃeɪps/

Following all other voiced consonant sounds and after vowel sounds, the inflection is realised as /z/, e.g.:

John's /dʒɒnz/ (US) /dʒɑːnz/
plays /pleɪz/

s (S) es **-'s** -ɪz
S (*abbrev. for* **south**) saʊθ
Saab® sɑːb
Saarbrücken ˌsɑːˈbrʊk.ᵊn *as if German:* ˌzɑː- (US) ˈsɑːrˌbrʊk- *as if German:* ˈzɑːr-
Saarland ˈsɑː.lænd *as if German:* ˈzɑː- (US) ˈsɑːr- *as if German:* ˈzɑːr-
Saatchi ˈsɑː.tʃi
Saba *in Arabia:* ˈsɑː.bə, ˈseɪ- (US) ˈseɪ.bə, ˈsɑː- *in West Indies:* ˈseɪ.bə, ˈsɑː- (US) ˈsɑː.bə
Sabaean səˈbiː.ən, sæbˈiː- (US) səˈbiː-
Sabah ˈsɑː.bɑː
Sabaoth sæbˈeɪ.ɒθ, səˈbeɪ-, ˈsæb.eɪ.ɒθ, -əθ (US) ˈsæb.eɪ.ɑːθ, -ə.ɔːθ; səˈbeɪ.ɔːθ
Sabatini ˌsæb.əˈtiː.ni
Sabbatarian ˌsæb.əˈteə.ri.ən (US) -ˈter.i- **-s** -z **-ism** -ɪ.zᵊm
Sabbath ˈsæb.əθ **-s** -s
sabbatical səˈbæt.ɪ.kᵊl (US) -ˈbæt̬-
Sabena® səˈbiː.nə, sæbˈiː-
sab|er ˈseɪ.b|əʳ (US) -b|ɚ **-ers** -əz (US) -ɚz **-ering** -ᵊr.ɪŋ **-ered** -əd (US) -ɚd
Sabin ˈseɪ.bɪn, ˈsæb.ɪn (US) ˈseɪ.bɪn
Sabine *Italian people:* ˈsæb.aɪn, ˈseɪ.baɪn (US) ˈseɪ.baɪn **-s** -z *surname:* ˈsæb.aɪn, ˈseɪ.baɪn, -bɪn (US) ˈseɪ- *river, lake, pass in US:* səˈbiːn, sæbˈiːn (US) səˈbiːn
sable ˈseɪ.bl̩ **-s** -z
sabot ˈsæb.əʊ, -ˈ- (US) sæbˈoʊ, ˈ-- **-s** -z
sabotag|e ˈsæb.ə.tɑːdʒ (US) -tɑːʒ, ˌ--ˈ- **-es** -ɪz **-ing** -ɪŋ **-ed** -d
saboteur ˌsæb.əˈtɜːʳ, ˈ--- (US) ˌsæb.əˈtɝː, -ˈtʊr **-s** -z
sabra (S) ˈsɑː.brə
sab|re ˈseɪ.b|əʳ (US) -b|ɚ **-res** -əz (US) -ɚz **-ring** -ᵊr.ɪŋ **-red** -əd (US) -ɚd **ˈsabre ˌrattling**
sabretach|e ˈsæb.ə.tæʃ (US) ˈseɪ.bɚ-, ˈsæb.ɚ- **-es** -ɪz
sabre-toothed ˌseɪ.bəˈtuːθt (US) ˈseɪ.bɚ.tuːθt *stress shift, British only, see compound:* **ˌsabre-toothed ˈtiger**
Sabrina səˈbriː.nə
sabulous ˈsæb.jə.ləs, -jʊ-
sac sæk **-s** -s
saccade sækˈɑːd, səˈkɑːd, -ˈkeɪd (US) sækˈɑːd, səˈkɑːd **-s** -z
Note: In British psychology, /sækˈeɪd, səˈkeɪd/ is the usual pronunciation.
saccharide ˈsæk.ᵊr.aɪd, -ɪd (US) -ə.raɪd **-s** -z
saccharin(e) (*n.*) ˈsæk.ᵊr.ɪn, -iːn (US) -ɪn, -ən
saccharine (*adj.*) ˈsæk.ᵊr.ɪn, -aɪn, -iːn (US) -ɚ.ɪn, -ə.raɪn
sacerdotal ˌsæs.əˈdəʊ.tᵊl (US) -ɚˈdoʊ.t̬ᵊl, ˌsæk- **-ly** -i
sachem ˈseɪ.tʃəm, -tʃem (US) -tʃəm **-s** -z
sachet ˈsæʃ.eɪ (US) -ˈ- **-s** -z
Sacheverell səˈʃev.ᵊr.ᵊl, sæʃˈev-
Sachs sæks
sack sæk **-s** -s **-ing/s** -ɪŋ/z **-ed** -t
sackbut ˈsæk.bʌt, -bət (US) -bʌt **-s** -s
sackcloth ˈsæk.klɒθ (US) -klɑːθ **ˌsackcloth and ˈashes**
sackful ˈsæk.fʊl **-s** -z **sacksful** ˈsæks.fʊl
sacking ˈsæk.ɪŋ
sackload ˈsæk.ləʊd (US) -loʊd
Sackville-West ˌsæk.vɪlˈwest
sacral ˈseɪ.krᵊl
sacrament (S) ˈsæk.rə.mənt **-s** -s
sacramental ˌsæk.rəˈmen.tᵊl (US) -t̬ᵊl **-ly** -i **-ism** -ɪ.zᵊm
Sacramento ˌsæk.rəˈmen.təʊ (US) -t̬oʊ
sacred ˈseɪ.krɪd **-ly** -li **-ness** -nəs, -nɪs **ˌsacred ˈcow**
sacrific|e ˈsæk.rɪ.faɪs, -rə- (US) -rə- **-es** -ɪz **-ing** -ɪŋ **-ed** -t
sacrificial ˌsæk.rɪˈfɪʃ.ᵊl, -rəˈ- (US) -rəˈ- **-ly** -i
sacrilege ˈsæk.rɪ.lɪdʒ, -rə- (US) -rə-
sacrilegious ˌsæk.rɪˈlɪdʒ.əs, -rəˈ- (US) -rəˈ- **-ly** -li **-ness** -nəs, -nɪs
sacristan ˈsæk.rɪ.stᵊn, -rə- (US) -rɪ- **-s** -z
Sacriston ˈsæk.rɪ.stᵊn, -rə- (US) -rɪ-
sacrist|y ˈsæk.rɪ.st|i, -rə- (US) -rɪ- **-ies** -iz
sacrosanct ˈsæk.rəʊ.sæŋ*k*t (US) -roʊ- **-ity** -ə.ti, -ɪ.ti (US) -ə.t̬i

sacr|um 'seɪ.kr|əm, 'sæk.r|əm **-a** -ə
sad sæd **-der** -əʳ (US) -ɚ **-dest** -ɪst, -əst **-ly** -li **-ness** -nəs, -nɪs
Sadat sə'dæt, sæd'æt (US) sə'dɑːt, sɑː-, -'dæt
Saddam sə'dæm, sæd'æm; 'sæd.əm (US) sɑː'dɑːm, sə-, sæd'æm, sə'dæm
sadden 'sæd.ᵊn **-s** -z **-ing** -ɪŋ **-ed** -d
saddhu 'sɑː.duː **-s** -z
saddl|e 'sæd.l̩ **-es** -z **-ing** -ɪŋ, 'sæd.lɪŋ **-ed** -d 'saddle ˌhorse; 'saddle ˌsore
saddleback 'sæd.l̩.bæk
saddlebag 'sæd.l̩.bæg **-s** -z
saddle|cloth 'sæd.l̩|.klɒθ (US) -klɑːθ **-cloths** -klɒθs, -klɒðz (US) -klɑːθs, -klɑːðz
saddler 'sæd.ləʳ, -l̩.əʳ (US) '-lɚ, -l̩.ɚ **-s** -z **-y** -i
Sadducee 'sæd.jʊ.siː, -jə- (US) 'sædʒ.ʊ-, 'sæd.jʊ- **-s** -z
Sade sɑːd (US) sɑːd, sæd
sadhu 'sɑː.duː **-s** -z
Sadie 'seɪ.di
sad|ism 'seɪ.dɪ.zᵊm (US) 'sæd|.ɪ-, 'seɪ.d|ɪ- **-ist/s** -ɪst/s
sadistic sə'dɪs.tɪk, sæd'ɪs- (US) sə'dɪs-, seɪ-, sæd'ɪs- **-ally** -ᵊl.i, -li
Sadleir 'sæd.ləʳ (US) -lɚ
Sadler 'sæd.ləʳ (US) -lɚ
sadomasoch|ism ˌseɪ.dəʊ'mæs.ə.k|ɪ.zᵊm, -'mæz- (US) ˌsæd.oʊ'-, ˌseɪ.doʊ'- **-ist/s** -ɪst/s
sadomasochistic ˌseɪ.dəʊˌmæs.ə'kɪs.tɪk, -ˌmæz- (US) ˌsæd.oʊˌ-, ˌseɪ.doʊˌ-
Sadova 'sɑː.dəʊ.ə, -və (US) -dɔː.vɑː, sɑː'dɔː-
sae, SAE ˌes.eɪ'iː
safari sə'fɑː.ri (US) -'fɑːr.i **-s** -z **sa'fari ˌpark; sa'fari ˌsuit**
saf|e seɪf **-es** -s **-er** -əʳ (US) -ɚ **-est** -ɪst, -əst **-ely** -li **-eness** -nəs, -nɪs **'safe ˌhouse,; ˌsafe 'house** (US) **'safe ˌhouse; ˌsafe 'sex**
safe-break|er 'seɪfˌbreɪ.k|əʳ (US) -k|ɚ **-s** -z **-ing** -ɪŋ
safe-conduct ˌseɪf'kɒn.dʌkt, -dəkt (US) -'kɑːn.dʌkt **-s** -s
safe-crack|er 'seɪfˌkræk|.əʳ (US) -ɚ **-s** -z **-ing** -ɪŋ
safe-deposit 'seɪf.dɪˌpɒz.ɪt, -dəˌ- (US) -dɪ'pɑː.zɪt **-s** -s **'safe-deˌposit ˌbox, ˌsafe-de'posit ˌbox** (US) **'safe-deˌposit ˌbox**
safeguard 'seɪf.gɑːd (US) -gɑːrd **-s** -z **-ing** -ɪŋ **-ed** -ɪd
safekeeping ˌseɪf'kiː.pɪŋ
safety 'seɪf.ti **'safety ˌbelt; 'safety ˌcurtain; 'safety ˌlamp; 'safety ˌmatch; 'safety ˌnet; 'safety ˌpin; 'safety ˌrazor; 'safety ˌvalve**
Safeway® 'seɪf.weɪ
Saffell sə'fel
safflower 'sæf.laʊəʳ (US) -laʊɚ **-s** -z
saffron (S) 'sæf.rən, -rɒn (US) -rən
Safin 'sɑː.fɪn
sag sæg **-s** -z **-ging** -ɪŋ **-ged** -d
saga 'sɑː.gə **-s** -z
sagacious sə'geɪ.ʃəs **-ly** -li **-ness** -nəs, -nɪs
sagacity sə'gæs.ə.ti, -ɪ.ti (US) -ə.t̬i
Sagan *English name:* 'seɪ.gən *French name:* sə'gɑ̃ːŋ, sæg'ɑ̃ːŋ (US) 'seɪ.gᵊn; sɑː'gɑ̃ːn
sag|e (S) seɪdʒ **-es** -ɪz **-ely** -li **-eness** -nəs, -nɪs
sagg|y 'sæg|.i **-ier** -i.əʳ (US) -i.ɚ **-iest** -i.ɪst, -i.əst **-iness** -i.nəs, -i.nɪs
sagitt|a (S) sə'dʒɪt|.ə, -'gɪt- (US) -'dʒɪt̬- **-ae** -iː, -aɪ
sagittal 'sædʒ.ɪ.tᵊl (US) -ə.t̬ᵊl **-ly** -i
Sagittarian ˌsædʒ.ɪ'teə.ri.ən, ˌsæg-, -ə'-, -'tɑː- (US) ˌsædʒ.ə'ter.i- **-s** -z
Sagittarius ˌsædʒ.ɪ'teə.ri.əs, ˌsæg-, -ə'-, -'tɑː- (US) ˌsædʒ.ə'ter.i-
sago 'seɪ.gəʊ (US) -goʊ
Sahara sə'hɑː.rə (US) -'her.ə, -'hær-, -'hɑːr-
Sahel sɑː'hel, sə- (US) sɑː-
sahib (S) sɑːb; 'sɑː.*h*ɪb (US) 'sɑː.*h*ɪb, -*h*iːb, -'- **-s** -z
said *(from* **say***)* sed
Said *(in* **Port Said***)* saɪd, seɪd, sɑː'iːd (US) sɑː'iːd
Saigon saɪ'gɒn (US) -'gɑːn, '--
Saigonese ˌsaɪ.gɒn'iːz, -gᵊn'- (US) -gɑː'niːz, -gə'- *stress shift:* ˌSaigonese 'exports
sail seɪl **-s** -z **-ing/s** -ɪŋ/z **-ed** -d **'sailing ˌboat; 'sailing ˌship**
sailboard 'seɪl.bɔːd (US) -bɔːrd **-s** -z **-ing** -ɪŋ **-er/s** -əʳ/z (US) -ɚ/z
sailboat 'seɪl.bəʊt (US) -boʊt **-s** -s
sailcloth 'seɪl.klɒθ (US) -klɑːθ
sailor 'seɪ.ləʳ (US) -lɚ **-s** -z **'sailor ˌsuit**
sailplane 'seɪl.pleɪn **-s** -z
sainfoin 'sæn.fɔɪn, 'seɪn- (US) 'seɪn-, 'sæn-
Sainsbury 'seɪnz.bᵊr.i (US) -bɚ-, -ber- **-'s** -z
saint (S) *strong form:* seɪnt **-s** -s **-ed** -ɪd **-hood** -hʊd *weak forms:* sᵊnt, sɪnt

Note: The weak forms are usual in British English for the names of saints (and places containing the word **Saint**), while the strong form is used when the word occurs on its own. For example, "This would try the patience of a saint" would have the strong form, while **St. John, St. Cecilia** (saints' names), **St. Alban's, St. Helen's** (placenames) have the weak forms. In American English, the strong form is usually used in all cases. When **Saint** occur in British family names (e.g. **St. Clair**) the pronunciation is variabl and individual names should be checked in their dictionary entries

Saint-Etienne ˌsæ̃*n*t.eɪ'tjen
Saint Laurent ˌsæ̃*n*.lɔː'rɑ̃ːŋ, -lə'- (US) -lɑː'rɑːnt, -lə'-
saintl|y 'seɪnt.l|i **-ier** -i.əʳ (US) -i.ɚ **-iest** -i.ɪst, -i.əst **-iness** -ɪ.nəs, -ɪ.nɪs
Saint-Saëns ˌsæ̃*n*'sɑ̃ːŋ, -'sɑ̃ː*n*s
Saintsbury 'seɪn*t*s.bᵊr.i
saith *(from* **say***)* seθ, seɪθ
sake *cause, purpose:* seɪk **-s** -s
sake *drink:* 'sɑː.ki, 'sæk.i (US) 'sɑː.ki
Sakhalin 'sæk.ə.liːn, 'sɑː.kə-, -lɪn *as if Russian:* ˌsæx.ə'liːn (US) 'sæk.ə.liːn
Sakharov 'sæk.ə.rɒf, -rɒv *as if Russian:* 'sæx- (US) 'sɑː.kə.rɔːf, 'sæk.ə-, -rɑːf
saki (S) 'sɑː.ki
salaam sə'lɑːm, sæl'ɑːm (US) sə'lɑːm **-s** -z **-ing** -ɪŋ **-ed** -d
salability ˌseɪ.lə'bɪl.ə.ti, -ɪ.ti (US) -ə.t̬i
salable 'seɪ.lə.bl̩
salacious sə'leɪ.ʃəs **-ly** -li **-ness** -nəs, -nɪs
salacity sə'læs.ə.ti, -ɪ.ti (US) -ə.t̬i
salad 'sæl.əd **-s** -z **'salad ˌbar; 'salad ˌcream, ˌsalad 'cream** (US) **'salad ˌcream; 'salad ˌdays; 'salad ˌdressin 'salad ˌonion**
Saladin 'sæl.ə.dɪn
Salamanca ˌsæl.ə'mæŋ.kə
salamander 'sæl.ə.mæn.dəʳ (US) -dɚ **-s** -z
salami sə'lɑː.mi **-s** -z
Salamis 'sæl.ə.mɪs
sal ammoniac ˌsæl.ə'məʊ.ni.æk (US) -'moʊ-
salariat sə'leə.ri.æt
salar|y 'sæl.ᵊr|.i **-ies** -iz **-ied** -id
Salcombe 'sɔːl.kəm, 'sɒl- (US) 'sɔːl-, 'sɑːl-
sale (S) seɪl **-s** -z **ˌsale or re'turn; ˌsale 'work; 'sales ˌtax**
saleability ˌseɪ.lə'bɪl.ə.ti, -ɪ.ti (US) -ə.
saleable 'seɪ.lə.bl̩
Salem 'seɪ.ləm, -lem (US) -ləm
Salerno sə'lɜː.nəʊ, -'leə- (US) -'lɝː.no sɑː'ler-
Salesbury 'seɪlz.bᵊr.i
salesclerk 'seɪlz.klɑːk (US) -klɝːk **-s** -s
salesgirl 'seɪlz.gɜːl (US) -gɝːl **-s** -z
sales|man 'seɪlz|.mən **-men** -mən, -men
salesmanship 'seɪlz.mən.ʃɪp
sales|person 'seɪlz|ˌpɜː.sᵊn (US) -ˌpɝː **-people** -ˌpiː.pl̩
salesroom 'seɪlz.rʊm, -ruːm (US) -ruː -rʊm **-s** -z
salestalk 'seɪlz.tɔːk (US) -tɑːk, -tɔːk

sales|woman ˈseɪlz|ˌwʊm.ən **-women** -ˌwɪm.ɪn
Salford ˈsɔːl.fəd, ˈsɒl- (US) ˈsɔːl.fɚd, ˈsɑːl-
Salfords ˈsæl.fədz (US) -fɚdz
Salian ˈseɪ.li.ən **-s** -z
Salic, **Salique** ˈsæl.ɪk, ˈseɪ.lɪk
salicylate səˈlɪs.ɪ.leɪt, sælˈɪs-, -ᵊl.eɪt (US) səˈlɪs.ə.leɪt; ˌsæl.əˈsɪl.eɪt, -ɪt **-s** -s
salicylic ˌsæl.ɪˈsɪl.ɪk, -əˈ- *stress shift, see compound:* (US) -əˈ- ˌ**salicylic** ˈ**acid**
salienc|e ˈseɪ.li.ənts **-y** -i
salient ˈseɪ.li.ənt (US) ˈseɪl.jənt, ˈseɪ.li.ənt **-s** -s **-ly** -li
Salieri ˌsæl.iˈeə.ri (US) -ˈer.i
saline *(adj.)* ˈseɪ.laɪn, ˈsæl.aɪn (US) ˈseɪ.liːn, -laɪn
saline *(n.)* ˈseɪ.laɪn, ˈsæl.aɪn (US) ˈseɪ.liːn, -laɪn; səˈliːn
Saline *in Fife:* ˈsæl.ɪn *in US:* səˈliːn
Salinger ˈsæl.ɪn.dʒəʳ, ˈseɪ.lɪn- (US) ˈsæl.ɪn.dʒɚ
salinity səˈlɪn.ə.ti, -ɪ.ti (US) -ə.t̬i
Salisbury ˈsɔːlz.bᵊr.i, ˈsɒlz- (US) ˈsɔːlz-, ˈsɑːlz-, -ber- ˌ**Salisbury** ˈ**Plain**
saliva səˈlaɪ.və
salivary ˈsæl.ɪ.vᵊr.i, ˈ-ə-; səˈlaɪ- (US) ˈsæl.ə.ver- **saˈlivary** ˌ**gland,** ˈ**salivary** ˌ**gland**
sali|vate ˈsæl.ɪ|.veɪt, ˈ-ə- (US) ˈ-ə- **-vates** -veɪts **-vating** -veɪ.tɪŋ (US) -veɪ.t̬ɪŋ **-vated** -veɪ.tɪd (US) -veɪ.t̬ɪd **-vation** ˌ--ˈveɪ.ʃᵊn
Salk sɔːlk ˈ**Salk** ˌ**vaccine**
sallet ˈsæl.ɪt, -ət (US) -ɪt **-s** -s
Sallis ˈsæl.ɪs
sallow ˈsæl.əʊ (US) -oʊ **-er -est -s** -z **-y** -i **-ness** -nəs, -nɪs
Sallust ˈsæl.əst
sall|y **(S)** ˈsæl|.i **-ies** -iz **-ying** -i.ɪŋ **-ied** -id ˌ**Sally** ˈ**Army**
Sally Lunn ˌsæl.iˈlʌn **-s** -z
salmagundi ˌsæl.məˈgʌn.di
Salman ˈsæl.mæn, -mən
salmi ˈsæl.mi **-s** -z
salmon ˈsæm.ən
Salmon *surname:* ˈsæm.ən, ˈsæl.mən, ˈsɑː- *river, etc. in Canada & US:* ˈsæm.ən *biblical name:* ˈsæl.mɒn, -mən (US) -mən
salmonberr|y ˈsæm.ən.bᵊr|.i, ˈ-əm- (US) -ˌber- **-ies** -iz
Salmond ˈsæm.ənd
salmonella ˌsæl.məˈnel.ə
Salome səˈləʊ.mi, -meɪ (US) -ˈloʊ-; ˈsæl.ə.meɪ
Salomon ˈsæl.ə.mən (US) ˈsɑːl-
salon ˈsæl.ɔ̃ːŋ, -lɒn (US) səˈlɑːn; ˈsæl.ɑːn **-s** -z
Salonika, **Salonica** səˈlɒn.ɪ.kə, ˌsæl.əˈniː- (US) səˈlɑː.nə-; ˌsæl.əˈnaɪ-, -ˈniː-
saloon səˈluːn **-s** -z **saˌloon** ˈ**bar; saˈloon** ˌ**car**
Salop ˈsæl.əp
Salopian səˈləʊ.pi.ən (US) -ˈloʊ- **-s** -z
Salpeter ˈsæl.piː.təʳ (US) -t̬ɚ
salpingitis ˌsæl.pɪnˈdʒaɪ.tɪs, -təs (US) -t̬ɪs
salsa ˈsæl.sə (US) ˈsɑːl-
salsify ˈsæl.sɪ.fi, -sə-, -faɪ (US) -sə-
salt, **SALT (S)** sɔːlt, sɒlt (US) sɔːlt, sɑːlt **-s** -s **-ing** -ɪŋ (US) ˈsɔːl.t̬ɪŋ **-ed** -ɪd (US) ˈsɔːl.t̬ɪd **-ness** -nəs, -nɪs ˈ**salt** ˌ**cellar;** ˌ**Salt** ˌ**Lake** ˈ**City;** ˈ**salt** ˌ**marsh;** ˈ**salt** ˌ**shaker; rub** ˌ**salt into someone's** ˈ**wounds;** ˌ**salt of the** ˈ**earth;** ˌ**take something with a** ˌ**pinch/grain of** ˈ**salt**
Saltaire sɔːlˈteəʳ, sɒl- (US) sɑːlˈter
saltant ˈsæl.tənt, ˈsɔːl-, ˈsɒl- (US) ˈsæl.tᵊnt
Saltash ˈsɔːl.tæʃ, ˈsɒl- (US) ˈsɑːl-
saltation sælˈteɪ.ʃᵊn **-s** -z
Saltburn ˈsɔːlt.bɜːn, ˈsɒlt- (US) ˈsɔːlt.bɝːn, ˈsɑːlt-
Saltcoats ˈsɔːlt.kəʊts, ˈsɒlt- (US) ˈsɔːlt.koʊts, ˈsɑːlt-
Saltdean ˈsɔːlt.diːn, ˈsɒlt- (US) ˈsɔːlt-, ˈsɑːlt-
Salter ˈsɔːl.təʳ, ˈsɒl- (US) ˈsɔːl.t̬ɚ, ˈsɑːl-
Salterton ˈsɔːl.tə.tᵊn, ˈsɒl- (US) ˈsɔːl.t̬ɚ.tən, ˈsɑːl-
Saltfleetby ˈsɔːltˌfliːt.bi, ˈsɒlt- *locally also:* ˈsɒl.ə.bi (US) ˈsɔːltˌfliːt.bi, ˈsɑːlt-
Salting ˈsɔːl.tɪŋ, ˈsɒl- (US) ˈsɔːl.t̬ɪŋ, ˈsɑːl-
saltire ˈsɔːl.taɪəʳ, ˈsɒl-, ˈsæl- (US) ˈsɔːl.tɪr, ˈsɑːl-, ˈsæl-, -taɪɚ **-s** -z
Saltmarsh ˈsɔːlt.mɑːʃ, ˈsɒlt- (US) ˈsɔːlt.mɑːrʃ, ˈsɑːlt-
Salto ˈsæl.təʊ (US) ˈsɑːl.toʊ
Saltoun ˈsɔːl.tᵊn, ˈsɒlt- (US) ˈsɔːl.tən, ˈsɑːl-
saltpan ˈsɔːlt.pæn, ˈsɒlt- (US) ˈsɔːlt-, ˈsɑːlt- **-s** -z
saltpetre, **saltpeter** ˌsɔːltˈpiː.təʳ, ˌsɒlt-, ˈ--- (US) ˈsɔːltˌpiː.t̬ɚ, ˈsɑːlt-
saltwater ˈsɔːltˌwɔː.təʳ, ˈsɒlt- (US) ˈsɔːltˌwɑː.t̬ɚ, ˈsɑːlt-, -ˌwɔː-
salt|y ˈsɔːl.t|i, ˈsɒl- (US) ˈsɔːl.t̬|i, ˈsɑːl- **-ier** -i.əʳ (US) -i.ɚ **-iest** -i.ɪst, -i.əst **-iness** -ɪ.nəs, -ɪ.nɪs
salubrious səˈluː.bri.əs, -ˈljuː- (US) -ˈluː- **-ly** -li **-ness** -nəs, -nɪs
salubrity səˈluː.brə.ti, -ˈljuː-, -brɪ- (US) -ˈluː.brə.t̬i
Salusbury ˈsɔːlz.bᵊr.i
Salut *(in* **Port Salut***)* səˈluː
salutar|y ˈsæl.jə.tᵊr|.i, -jʊ- (US) -ter- **-ily** -ᵊl.i, -ɪ.li **-iness** -ɪ.nəs, -ɪ.nɪs
salutation ˌsæl.jəˈteɪ.ʃᵊn, -jʊˈ- **-s** -z
salu|te səˈluː|t, -ˈljuː|t (US) -ˈluː|t **-tes** -ts **-ting** -tɪŋ (US) -t̬ɪŋ **-ted** -tɪd (US) -t̬ɪd
salvable ˈsæl.və.bl̩
Salvador ˈsæl.və.dɔːʳ, ˌ--ˈ- (US) ˈsæl.və.dɔːr **-an/s** -ən/z
Salvadorean, **Salvadorian** ˌsæl.vəˈdɔː.ri.ən (US) -ˈdɔːr.i- **-s** -z
salvag|e ˈsæl.vɪdʒ **-es** -ɪz **-ing** -ɪŋ **-ed** -d **-eable** -ə.bl̩ **-er/s** -əʳ/z (US) -ɚ/z
Salvarsan® ˈsæl.və.sən, -sæn (US) -vɚ-
salvation sælˈveɪ.ʃᵊn **-s** -z **Salˌvation** ˈ**Army**
salvation|ism sælˈveɪ.ʃᵊn|.ɪ.zᵊm **-ist/s** -ɪst/s
salv|e *anoint, soothe:* sælv, sɑːv (US) sæv, sɑːv **-es** -z **-ing** -ɪŋ **-ed** -d
salv|e *save ship, cargo:* sælv **-es** -z **-ing** -ɪŋ **-ed** -d
Salve *Catholic antiphon:* ˈsæl.veɪ **-s** -z
salver ˈsæl.vəʳ (US) -vɚ **-s** -z
salvia ˈsæl.vi.ə **-s** -z
salvo ˈsæl.vəʊ (US) -voʊ **-(e)s** -z **-ing** -ɪŋ **-ed** -d
sal volatile ˌsæl.vəʊˈlæt.ᵊl.i, -vɒlˈæt- (US) -voʊˈlæt̬.ᵊl-
Salyut səˈljuːt, sælˈjuːt (US) ˈsæl.juːt
Salzburg ˈsælts.bɜːg, ˈsɑːlts- (US) ˈsɔːlz.bɝːg, ˈsɑːlz-
Sam sæm ˌ**Sam** ˌ**Browne** ˈ**belt**
Samantha səˈmænt.θə
Samara səˈmɑː.rə (US) -ˈmɑːr.ə, -ˈmær-
Samaria səˈmeə.ri.ə (US) -ˈmer.i-, -ˈmær-
Samaritan səˈmær.ɪ.tᵊn (US) -ˈmer.ə-, -ˈmær- **-s** -z ˌ**good Saˈmaritan**
samarium səˈmeə.ri.əm (US) -ˈmer.i-, -ˈmær-
Samarkand ˌsæm.ɑːˈkænd, -əˈ-, ˈ--- (US) ˈsæm.ɚ.kænd, ˌ--ˈ-
samarskite səˈmɑː.skaɪt (US) -ˈmɑːr-; ˈsæm.ɚ-
samba ˈsæm.bə (US) ˈsɑːm-, ˈsæm- **-s** -z **-ing** -ɪŋ **-ed** -d
sambo **(S)** ˈsæm.bəʊ (US) -boʊ **-s** -z
same seɪm **-y** -i **-ness** -nəs, -nɪs
S. America *(abbrev. for* **South America***)* ˌsaʊθ.əˈmer.ɪ.kə
samite ˈseɪ.maɪt, ˈsæm.aɪt (US) ˈsæm.aɪt, ˈseɪ.maɪt
samizdat ˌsæm.ɪzˈdæt, ˈ--- (US) ˈsɑː.mɪz.dɑːt, ˌ--ˈ-
Sammy ˈsæm.i
Samnite ˈsæm.naɪt **-s** -s
Samo|a səˈməʊ|ə, sɑː- (US) səˈmoʊ|ə **-an/s** -ən/z
Samos ˈseɪ.mɒs, ˈsæm- (US) -mɑːs; ˈsæm.oʊs
samosa səˈməʊ.sə, sæmˈəʊ-, -zə (US) səˈmoʊ.sə **-s** -z
Samothrace ˈsæm.əʊ.θreɪs (US) ˈ-ə-, -oʊ-
samovar ˈsæm.ə.vɑːʳ, ˌ--ˈ- (US) ˈsæm.ə.vɑːr; ˌsɑː.məˈvɑːr **-s** -z
Samoyed *people:* ˌsæm.ɔɪˈed; -ˈ--, -ɪd (US) ˈsæm.ə.jed; səˈmɔɪ.ed **-s** -z *dog:* səˈmɔɪ.ed, -ɪd (US) ˈsæm.ə.jed; səˈmɔɪ.ed **-s** -z

sampan 'sæm.pæn **-s** -z
Samper 'sæm.pəʳ (US) -pɚ
samphire 'sæm*p*.faɪəʳ (US) -faɪɚ
sampl|e 'sɑːm.pl̩ (US) 'sæm- **-es** -z **-ing** -ɪŋ, 'sɑːm.plɪŋ (US) 'sæm- **-ed** -d
sampler 'sɑːm.pləʳ (US) 'sæm.plɚ **-s** -z
Sampras 'sæm.prəs, -præs
Sampson 'sæm*p*.sᵊn
Samson 'sæm*p*.sᵊn
Samsonite® 'sæm*p*.sᵊn.aɪt
Samsung® 'sæm.sʌŋ, -sʊŋ
Samuel 'sæm.jʊəl, -ju.əl (US) -ju.əl, -jʊl **-s** -z
samurai (S) 'sæm.ʊ.raɪ, -jʊ- (US) -ə.raɪ **-s** -z
San Antonio ˌsæn.æn'təʊ.ni.əʊ (US) -'toʊ.ni.oʊ
sanatari|um ˌsæn.ə'teə.ri|.əm (US) -'ter.i- **-ums** -əmz **-a** -ə
Sanatogen® sə'næt.ə.dʒᵊn, -dʒen (US) -'næt̬-
sanatori|um ˌsæn.ə'tɔː.ri|.əm (US) -'tɔːr.i- **-ums** -əmz **-a** -ə
Sancerre sæn'seəʳ, sɑ̃ː*n*- (US) sɑːn'ser
Sanchez 'sæn.tʃez
Sancho Panza ˌsæn.tʃəʊ'pæn.zə (US) ˌsɑːn.tʃoʊ'pɑːn-
San Cristóbal ˌsæn.krɪ'stəʊ.bæl, ˌsæŋ- (US) ˌsæn.krɪ'stoʊ.bəl, -bɑːl
sanctification ˌsæŋ*k*.tɪ.fɪ'keɪ.ʃᵊn, -tə-
sancti|fy 'sæŋ*k*.tɪ|.faɪ, -tə- **-fies** -faɪz **-fying** -faɪ.ɪŋ **-fied** -faɪd
sanctimonious ˌsæŋ*k*.tɪ'məʊ.ni.əs, -tə'- (US) -'moʊ- **-ly** -li **-ness** -nəs, -nɪs
sanction 'sæŋ*k*.ʃᵊn **-s** -z **-ing** -ɪŋ **-ed** -d
sanctity 'sæŋ*k*.tə.ti, -tɪ- (US) -tə.t̬i
sanctuar|y 'sæŋ*k*.tʃʊə.r|i, -tʃᵊ.r|i, -tjʊə.r|i, -tjᵊr|.i (US) -tʃu.er|.i **-ies** -ɪz
sanct|um 'sæŋ*k*.t|əm **-ums** -əmz **-a** -ə ˌ**inner** '**sanctum**
Sanctus 'sæŋ*k*.təs **-es** -ɪz
sand *on beach:* sænd **-s** -z **-ing** -ɪŋ **-ed** -ɪd **-er/s** -əʳ/z (US) -ɚ/z '**sand** ˌ**dollar**; '**sand** ˌ**trap**; ˌ**bury one's** ˌ**head in the** '**sand**, ˌ**bury one's** '**head in the** ˌ**sand** (US) ˌ**bury one's** ˌ**head in the** '**sand**
Sand *French novelist:* sɑ̃ː*n*d (US) sænd, sɑ̃ːnd
sandal 'sæn.dᵊl **-s** -z
sandalwood 'sæn.dᵊl.wʊd
Sanday 'sæn.deɪ, -di
Sandbach 'sæn*d*.bætʃ, 'sæm- (US) 'sæn*d*-
sandbag 'sæn*d*.bæg, 'sæm- (US) 'sæn*d*- **-s** -z **-ging** -ɪŋ **-ged** -d **-ger/s** -əʳ/z (US) -ɚ/z
sandbank 'sæn*d*.bæŋk, 'sæm- (US) 'sæn*d*- **-s** -s
sandbar 'sæn*d*.bɑːʳ, 'sæm- (US) 'sæn*d*.bɑːr **-s** -z
sandblast 'sæn*d*.blɑːst, 'sæm- (US) 'sæn*d*.blæst **-s** -s **-ing** -ɪŋ **-ed** -ɪd **-er/s** -əʳ/z (US) -ɚ/z
sandbox 'sænd.bɒks, 'sæm- (US) -bɑːks **-es** -ɪz
sandboy 'sæn*d*.bɔɪ, 'sæm- (US) 'sæn*d*- **-s** -z ˌ**happy as a** '**sandboy**
Sandburg 'sæn*d*.bɜːg (US) -bɝːg
sandcastle 'sæn*d*ˌkɑː.sl̩, 'sæŋ- (US) 'sæn*d*ˌkæs.l̩ **-s** -z
sanderling 'sæn.dᵊl.ɪŋ (US) -dɚ.lɪŋ **-s** -z
Sanders 'sɑːn.dəz (US) 'sæn.dɚz
Sanderson 'sɑːn.də.sᵊn (US) 'sæn.dɚ-
Sanderstead 'sɑːn.də.sted, -stɪd (US) 'sæn.dɚ-
sandfl|y 'sænd.fl|aɪ **-ies** -aɪz
Sandford 'sæn*d*.fəd, -fɔːd; 'sæn.əd (US) 'sæn*d*.fɚd, -fɔːrd
Sandgate 'sæn*d*.geɪt, 'sæŋ-, -gɪt (US) 'sæn*d*-
sandhi 'sæn.diː, 'sʌn-; 'sænd.hiː, 'sʌnd- (US) 'sæn.di, 'sɑːn-, 'sʌn-
sandhopper 'sændˌhɒp.əʳ (US) -ˌhɑː.pɚ **-s** -z
Sandhurst 'sænd.hɜːst (US) -hɝːst
San Diego ˌsæn.di'eɪ.gəʊ (US) -goʊ
Sandinista ˌsæn.də'nɪs.tə, -dɪ'- (US) -'niː.stə **-s** -z
Sanditon 'sæn.dɪ.tᵊn (US) -t̬ən
Sandling 'sænd.lɪŋ
sand|man 'sæn*d*|.mæn, 'sæm- (US) 'sæn*d*- **-men** -men
San Domingo ˌsæn.də'mɪŋ.gəʊ, -dəʊ'-, -dɒm'ɪŋ- (US) -də'mɪŋ.goʊ, -doʊ'-
Sandown 'sæn.daʊn
sandpail 'sæn*d*.peɪl, 'sæm- (US) 'sæn*d*- **-s** -z
sandpap|er 'sæn*d*ˌpeɪ.p|əʳ, 'sæm- (US) 'sæn*d*ˌpeɪ.p|ɚ **-ers** -əz (US) -ɚz **-ering** -ᵊr.ɪŋ **-ered** -əd (US) -ɚd
sandpiper 'sæn*d*ˌpaɪ.pəʳ, 'sæm- (US) 'sæn*d*ˌpaɪ.pɚ **-s** -z
sandpit 'sæn*d*.pɪt, 'sæm- (US) 'sæn*d*- **-s** -s
Sandra 'sæn.drə, 'sɑːn- (US) 'sæn-
Sandringham 'sæn.drɪŋ.əm
Sands sændz
sandstone 'sæn*d*.stəʊn (US) -stoʊn
sandstorm 'sæn*d*.stɔːm (US) -stɔːrm **-s** -z
sand|wich 'sæn|.wɪdʒ, 'sæm-, -wɪtʃ (US) 'sæn*d*|.wɪtʃ **-wiches** -wɪdʒ.ɪz, -wɪtʃ.ɪz (US) -wɪtʃ.ɪz **-wiching** -wɪdʒ.ɪŋ, -wɪtʃ.ɪŋ (US) -wɪtʃ.ɪŋ **-wiched** -wɪdʒd, -wɪtʃt (US) -wɪtʃt '**sandwich** ˌ**board**; '**sandwich** ˌ**course**
Note: Some British speakers use /-wɪtʃ/ in the uninflected form and /-wɪdʒ/ in the inflected forms of this word.
Sandwich *in Kent:* 'sæn*d*.wɪtʃ, 'sæm-, -wɪdʒ (US) 'sænd.wɪtʃ
sandwich|man 'sæn*d*.wɪdʒ|.mæn, 'sæm-, -wɪtʃ- (US) 'sæn*d*.wɪtʃ- **-men** -men
Sandwick 'sæn*d*.wɪk
sand|y (S) 'sæn.d|i **-ier** -i.əʳ (US) -i.ɚ **-iest** -i.ɪst, -i.əst **-iness** -ɪ.nəs, -ɪ.nɪs
Sandys sændz
san|e seɪn **-er** -əʳ (US) -ɚ **-est** -ɪst, -əst **-ely** -li **-eness** -nəs, -nɪs
San Fernando ˌsæn.fə'næn.dəʊ (US) -fɚ'næn.doʊ
Sanford 'sæn.fəd (US) -fɚd
sanforiz|e, -is|e 'sæn.fᵊr.aɪz (US) -fə.raɪz **-es** -ɪz **-ing** -ɪŋ **-ed** -d
San Francisco ˌsæn.frən'sɪs.kəʊ, -fræn'- (US) -koʊ
sang *(from* **sing***)* sæŋ
Sanger 'sæŋ.gəʳ, -əʳ (US) -ɚ
sang-froid ˌsɑ̃ː*ŋ*'frwɑː (US) ˌsɑ̃ː*ŋ*-, ˌsɑ̃ːn-
sangria 'sæŋ.gri.ə, sæŋ'griː- (US) sæn'griː-, sæŋ-
Sangster 'sæŋ*k*.stəʳ (US) -stɚ
sanguinar|y 'sæŋ.gwɪ.nᵊr|.i, -gwə- (US) -gwɪ.ner- **-ily** -ᵊl.i, -ɪ.li **-iness** -ɪ.nəs, -ɪ.nɪs
sanguine 'sæŋ.gwɪn **-ly** -li **-ness** -nəs, -nɪs
sanguineous sæŋ'gwɪn.i.əs
sanitari|um ˌsæn.ɪ'teə.ri|.əm, -ə'- (US) -'ter.i- **-ums** -əmz **-a** -ə
sanitar|y 'sæn.ɪ.tᵊr|.i, -tr|i (US) -ter|.i **-ily** -ᵊl.i, -ɪ.li **-iness** -ɪ.nəs, -ɪ.nɪs '**sanitary** ˌ**towel**; '**sanitary** ˌ**napkin**
sanitation ˌsæn.ɪ'teɪ.ʃᵊn, -ə'- **sani'tation** ˌ**worker**
sanitization, -isa- ˌsæn.ɪ.taɪ'zeɪ.ʃᵊn, ˌ-ə-, -tɪ'- (US) -tɪ'-
sanitiz|e, -is|e 'sæn.ɪ.taɪz, '-ə- **-es** -ɪz **-ing** -ɪŋ **-ed** -d
sanitori|um ˌsæn.ə'tɔː.ri|.əm, -ɪ'- (US) -'tɔːr.i- **-ums** -əmz **-a** -ə
sanity 'sæn.ə.ti, -ɪ.ti (US) -ə.t̬i
San José ˌsæn.həʊ'zeɪ, -əʊ'- (US) -hoʊ'-, -ə'-
San Juan ˌsæn'*h*wɑːn (US) -'hwɑːn, -'wɔːn
sank *(from* **sink***)* sæŋk
Sankey 'sæŋ.ki
San Marino ˌsæn.mə'riː.nəʊ, ˌsæm- (US) ˌsæn.mə'riː.noʊ
San Miguel ˌsæn.mɪ'gel, ˌsæm- (US) ˌsæn-
San Pedro Sula sænˌped.rəʊ'suː.lə, sæm- (US) sænˌpiː.droʊ'-, -ˌped.roʊ'-
San Remo ˌsæn'reɪ.məʊ, -'riː- (US) -'riː.moʊ, -'reɪ-
sans *English word:* sænz *in French phrases:* sɑ̃ː*ŋ* (US) sænz, sɑ̃ːn
San Salvador ˌsæn'sæl.və.dɔːʳ, -ˌsæl.və'dɔːʳ (US) -'sæl.və.dɔːr
sans-culotte ˌsænz.kjʊ'lɒt (US) -kuː'lɑːt, -kjuː'- **-s** -s
San Sebastian ˌsæn.sɪ'bæs.ti.ən, -sə'- (US) -sɪ'bæs.tʃən
Sanskrit 'sæn.skrɪt

sanskritic (S) sænˈskrɪt.ɪk US -ˈskrɪt̬-
sans serif ˌsænˈser.ɪf
Santa ˈsæn.tə US -t̬ə **-s** -z
Santa Ana ˌsæn.təˈæn.ə US -t̬əˈ-
Santa Claus ˌsæn.təˈklɔːz, ˈ--ˌ- US ˈsæn.t̬əˌklɑːz, -ˌklɔːz **-es** -ɪz
Santa Cruz ˌsæn.təˈkruːz US ˈsæn.t̬ə.kruːz, ˌ--ˈ-
Santa Fe ˌsæn.təˈfeɪ US ˈsæn.t̬ə.feɪ, ˌ--ˈ-
Santa Marta ˌsæn.təˈmɑː.tə US -t̬əˈmɑːr.t̬ə
Santander ˌsæn.tənˈdeəʳ, -tænˈ-; US ˌsɑːn.tɑːnˈder
Santayana ˌsæn.taɪˈɑː.nə US -t̬iˈæn-, -ˈɑː.nə
Santer ˈsæn.təʳ, sɑ̃ːˈteə US sɑːn.t̬ɚ
Santiago ˌsæn.tiˈɑː.gəʊ US -t̬iˈɑː.goʊ, ˌsɑːn-
Santley ˈsænt.li
Santo Domingo ˌsæn.təʊ.dəʊˈmɪŋ.gəʊ, -dɒmˈɪŋ- US -toʊ.dəˈmɪŋ.goʊ, ˌsɑːn-, -doʊˈ-
Sanyo® ˈsæn.jəʊ US -joʊ
Saône səʊn US soʊn
São Paulo saʊmˈpaʊ.ləʊ, saʊ- US sãʊˈpaʊ.lu, -loʊ
São Tomé ˌsaʊn.təˈmeɪ, ˌsaʊ- US ˌsãʊ.toʊˈ-, -təˈ-
sap sæp **-s** -s **-ping** -ɪŋ **-ped** -t
sapele (S) sæpˈɪl.i, səˈpɪl-, -ˈpiː.li US səˈpiː.li **saˌpele maˈhogany**
sapien|ce ˈseɪ.pi.ən|ts, ˈsæp.i- US ˈseɪ.pi- **-t/ly** -t/li
sapiens ˈsæp.i.enz, -seɪ.pi-
Sapir səˈpɪəʳ, sæpˈɪəʳ; ˈseɪ.pɪəʳ US sæpˈɪr, səˈpɪr
sapless ˈsæp.ləs, -lɪs **-ness** -nəs, -nɪs
sapling ˈsæp.lɪŋ **-s** -z
saponaceous ˌsæp.əʊˈneɪ.ʃəs US -əˈ- **-ness** -nəs, -nɪs
saponification səˌpɒn.ɪ.fɪˈkeɪ.ʃᵊn, sæpˌɒn-, ˌ-ə- US səˌpɑː.nə-
saponi|fy səˈpɒn.ɪ|.faɪ, sæpˈɒn-, ˈ-ə- US səˈpɑː.nə- **-fies** -faɪz **-fying** -faɪ.ɪŋ **-fied** -faɪd
sapper ˈsæp.əʳ US -ɚ **-s** -z
sapphic (S) ˈsæf.ɪk **-s** -s
Sapphira səˈfaɪə.rə, sæfˈaɪə- US səˈfaɪ-
sapphire ˈsæf.aɪəʳ US -aɪɚ **-s** -z
sapph|ism (S) ˈsæf|.ɪ.zᵊm **-ist/s** -ɪst/s
Sappho ˈsæf.əʊ US -oʊ
Sapporo səˈpɔː.rəʊ, sæpˈɔː-, -ˈpɒr.əʊ US səˈpɔːr.oʊ, sɑː-
sapp|y ˈsæp|.i **-iness** -ɪ.nəs, -ɪ.nɪs
saprogenic ˌsæp.rəʊˈdʒen.ɪk US -rəˈ-
saprophyte ˈsæp.rəʊ.faɪt US -rə- **-s** -s
sapwood ˈsæp.wʊd
Sara ˈsɑː.rə, ˈseə- US ˈser.ə, ˈsær-
saraband(e) ˈsær.ə.bænd, ˌ--ˈ- US ˈsær.ə.bænd, ˈser- **-s** -z
Saracen ˈsær.ə.sən, -sɪn, -sen US -sən, ˈser-, ˈsær- **-s** -z
Saracenic ˌsær.əˈsen.ɪk US ˌser-, ˌsær-
Saragossa ˌsær.əˈgɒs.ə US -ˈgɑː.sə, ˌser-, ˌsær-
Sarah ˈseə.rə US ˈser.ə, ˈsær-
Sarajevo ˌsær.əˈjeɪ.vəʊ US -voʊ, ˌser-, ˌsær-
Saran® səˈræn **Saˈran ˌwrap**
Sarandon ˈsær.ən.dən US səˈræn.dən
Sarasate ˌsær.əˈsɑː.teɪ US ˌsɑːr.ɑːˈsɑː.teɪ
Saratoga ˌsær.əˈtəʊ.gə US ˌser.əˈtoʊ-, ˌsær-
Sarawak səˈrɑː.wæk, -wək, -wə US -ˈrɑː.wɑːk
Sarawakian ˌsær.əˈwæk.i.ən US ˌser.əˈwɑː.ki-, ˌsær- **-s** -z
sarcasm ˈsɑː.kæz.ᵊm US ˈsɑːr- **-s** -z
sarcastic sɑːˈkæs.tɪk US sɑːr- **-ally** -ᵊl.i, -li
sarcenet ˈsɑːs.net, -nət, -nɪt US ˈsɑːr.snet
sarcoma sɑːˈkəʊ.mə US sɑːrˈkoʊ- **-s** -z **-ta** -tə **-tous** -təs
sarcopha|gus sɑːˈkɒf.ə|.gəs US sɑːrˈkɑː.fə- **-guses** -gə.sɪz **-gi** -gaɪ, -dʒaɪ
Sardanapalus ˌsɑː.dəˈnæp.ᵊl.əs; -nəˈpɑː.ləs US ˌsɑːr.dəˈnæp.ᵊl.əs; -nəˈpeɪ.ləs
sardine *fish:* sɑːˈdiːn US sɑːr- **-s** -z
sardine *stone:* ˈsɑː.daɪn US ˈsɑːr.dɪn, -daɪn
Sardini|a sɑːˈdɪn.i|.ə US sɑːr-, ˈ-j|ə **-an/s** -ən/z
Sardis ˈsɑː.dɪs US ˈsɑːr-
sardius ˈsɑː.di.əs US ˈsɑːr- **-es** -ɪz
sardonic sɑːˈdɒn.ɪk US sɑːrˈdɑː.nɪk **-ally** -ᵊl.i, -li
sardonyx ˈsɑː.dᵊn.ɪks; sɑːˈdɒn- US sɑːrˈdɑː.nɪks; ˈsɑːr.də- **-es** -ɪz
Sargant ˈsɑː.dʒᵊnt US ˈsɑːr-
sargasso (S) sɑːˈgæs.əʊ US sɑːrˈgæs.oʊ **-(e)s** -z **Sarˌgasso ˈSea**
sarge sɑːdʒ US sɑːrdʒ
Sargeant, Sargent ˈsɑː.dʒᵊnt US ˈsɑːr-
Sargeson ˈsɑː.dʒɪ.sᵊn US ˈsɑːr-
Sargon ˈsɑː.gɒn US ˈsɑːr.gɑːn
sari ˈsɑː.ri US ˈsɑːr.i **-s** -z
Sark sɑːk US sɑːrk
sark|y ˈsɑː.k|i US ˈsɑːr- **-ier** -i.əʳ US -i.ɚ **-iest** -i.ɪst, -i.əst
Sarmati|a sɑːˈmeɪ.ʃi|.ə, ˈ-ʃ|ə US sɑːrˈmeɪ.ʃ|ə, -ʃi|.ə **-an/s** -ən/z
sarnie ˈsɑː.ni US ˈsɑːr- **-s** -z
sarong səˈrɒŋ, sɑː-, særˈɒŋ US səˈrɔːŋ, -ˈrɑːŋ **-s** -z
Saro-Wiwa ˌsær.əʊˈwiː.wə, -wɑː US ˌsær.oʊˈwiː.wɑː, ˌsɑːr-
Saroyan səˈrɔɪ.ən
sarsaparilla ˌsɑː.spᵊrˈɪl.ə, -sə.pᵊrˈ- US ˌsɑːr.sə.pəˈrɪl-, ˌsɑːr.spəˈ- *popularly:* ˌsæs.pəˈ-
sarsenet ˈsɑːs.net, -nət, -nɪt US ˈsɑːr.snet
Sarton ˈsɑː.tᵊn US ˈsɑːr-
Sartor ˈsɑː.tɔːʳ, -təʳ US ˈsɑːr.tɔːr, -t̬ɚ
sartorial sɑːˈtɔː.ri.əl US sɑːrˈtɔːr.i-
Sartre ˈsɑː.trə US ˈsɑːr-; sɑːrt
Sarum ˈseə.rəm US ˈser.əm
SAS ˌes.eɪˈes
SASE ˌes.eɪ.esˈiː
sash sæʃ **-es** -ɪz **-ed** -t **ˌsash ˈwindow**
Sasha ˈsæʃ.ə US ˈsɑː.ʃə, ˈsæʃ.ə
sashay ˈsæʃ.eɪ, -ˈ- US sæʃˈeɪ **-s** -z **-ing** -ɪŋ **-ed** -d
sashimi sæʃˈiː.mi, səˈʃiː- US sɑːˈʃiː.mi
Saskatchewan səˈskætʃ.ɪ.wən, sæsˈkætʃ-, ˈ-ə-, -wɒn US sæsˈkætʃ.ə.wɑːn, -wən **-er/s** -əʳ/z US -ɚ/z
saskatoon (S) ˌsæs.kəˈtuːn
Saskia ˈsæs.ki.ə
sasquatch (S) ˈsæs.kwɒtʃ, -kwætʃ US -kwɑːtʃ, -kwætʃ **-es** -ɪz
sass sæs
sassafras ˈsæs.ə.fræs **-es** -ɪz
Sassenach ˈsæs.ə.næk, -næx, -nək, -nəx US -næk **-s** -s
Sassoon səˈsuːn, sæsˈuːn US sæsˈuːn, səˈsuːn
sass|y ˈsæs|.i **-ier** -i.əʳ US -i.ɚ **-iest** -i.ɪst, -i.əst
sat *(from* **sit***)* sæt
Sat. *(abbrev. for* **Saturday***)* ˈsæt.ə.deɪ, -di US ˈsæt̬.ɚ-
SAT sæt US es.eɪˈtiː **-s** -z
Satan ˈseɪ.tᵊn **-ism** -ɪ.zᵊm **-ist/s** -ɪst/s
satang sætˈæŋ US sɑːˈtæŋ **-s** -z
satanic səˈtæn.ɪk, seɪˈtæn- **-ally** -ᵊl.i US -li
satay, saté ˈsæt.eɪ, ˈsɑː.teɪ US sɑːˈteɪ **-s** -z **ˌsatay ˈsauce** US **ˈsatay ˌsauce**
satchel ˈsætʃ.ᵊl **-s** -z
Satchwell ˈsætʃ.wel
sateen sætˈiːn, səˈtiːn **-s** -z
satellite ˈsæt.ᵊl.aɪt, -ɪ.laɪt US ˈsæt̬.ᵊl.aɪt **-s** -s **ˈsatellite ˌdish; ˌsatellite ˈtelevision** US **ˈsatellite ˌtelevision**
sati ˈsɑː.tiː **-s** -z
satiable ˈseɪ.ʃi.ə.bl̩, ˈ-ʃə.bl̩ US -ʃə-, -ʃi.ə-
sati|ate (*v.*) ˈseɪ.ʃi|.eɪt **-ates** -eɪts **-ating** -eɪ.tɪŋ US -eɪ.t̬ɪŋ **-ated** -eɪ.tɪd US -eɪ.t̬ɪd
satiate (*adj.*) ˈseɪ.ʃi.ət, -ɪt, -eɪt US -ɪt
satiation ˌseɪ.ʃiˈeɪ.ʃᵊn
Satie ˈsæt.i, ˈsɑː.ti, -ˈ- US sɑːˈtiː
satiety səˈtaɪ.ə.ti, -ˈtaɪ.ɪ-; ˈseɪ.ʃə.ti, -ʃi.ə- US səˈtaɪ.ə.t̬i
satin ˈsæt.ɪn US -ᵊn **-s** -z **-y** -i

satinette, satinet ˌsæt.ɪˈnet ⓤⓢ -ənˈet
satinwood ˈsæt.ɪn.wʊd ⓤⓢ -ən-
satire ˈsæt.aɪəʳ ⓤⓢ -aɪɚ **-s** -z
satiric|al səˈtɪr.ɪ.k|əl, ˈ-ə- ⓤⓢ ˈ-ɪ- **-ally** -əl.i, -li
satirist ˈsæt.ər.ɪst, -ɪ.rɪst ⓤⓢ ˈsæt̬.ɚ.ɪst **-s** -s
satiriz|e, -is|e ˈsæt.ər.aɪz, -ɪ.raɪz ⓤⓢ ˈsæt̬.ə.raɪz **-es** -ɪz **-ing** -ɪŋ **-ed** -d
satisfaction ˌsæt.ɪsˈfæk.ʃən, -əsˈ- ⓤⓢ ˌsæt̬-
satisfactor|y ˌsæt.ɪsˈfæk.tər|.i, -əsˈ-, -tr|i ⓤⓢ ˌsæt̬- **-ily** -əl.i, -ɪ.li **-iness** -ɪ.nəs, -ɪ.nɪs
satis|fy ˈsæt.ɪs|.faɪ ⓤⓢ -əs-, ˈsæt̬- **-fies** -faɪz **-fying** -faɪ.ɪŋ **-fied** -faɪd
satrap ˈsæt.ræp, -rəp ⓤⓢ ˈseɪ.træp, ˈsæt.ræp **-s** -s **-y** -i **-ies** -iz
satsuma ˌsætˈsuː.mə; -sʊ- ⓤⓢ ˈsæt.sə.mɑː; sɑːtˈsuː.mə **-s** -z
satur|ate (*v.*) ˈsætʃ.ər|.eɪt, -ʊ.r|eɪt, -tjər|.eɪt, -tjʊ.r|eɪt ⓤⓢ ˈsætʃ.ə.r|eɪt **-ates** -eɪts **-ating** -eɪ.tɪŋ ⓤⓢ -eɪ.t̬ɪŋ **-ated** -eɪ.tɪd ⓤⓢ -eɪ.t̬ɪd ˌ**saturated** ˈ**fat**
saturate (*adj.*) ˈsætʃ.ər.eɪt, -ʊ.reɪt, ˈsæt.jər.eɪt, -jʊ.reɪt ⓤⓢ ˈsætʃ.ɚ.ɪt
saturation ˌsætʃ.ərˈeɪ.ʃən, -tʃʊˈreɪ-, -tjərˈeɪ-, -tjʊˈreɪ- ⓤⓢ ˌsætʃ.əˈreɪ- **satuˈration** ˌ**point**
Saturday ˈsæt.ə.deɪ, -di ⓤⓢ ˈsæt̬.ɚ- **-s** -z
Saturn ˈsæt.ən, -ɜːn ⓤⓢ ˈsæt̬.ɚn
saturnalia (S) ˌsæt.əˈneɪ.li.ə, -ɜːˈ- ⓤⓢ ˌsæt̬.ɚˈ-, -ˈneɪl.jə **-n** -n **-s** -z
saturnian (S) sætˈɜː.ni.ən, səˈtɜː- ⓤⓢ səˈtɝː-
saturnine ˈsæt.ə.naɪn ⓤⓢ ˈsæt̬.ɚ-
satyr ˈsæt.əʳ ⓤⓢ ˈseɪ.t̬ɚ, ˈsæt̬.ɚ **-s** -z
satyriasis ˌsæt.ərˈaɪə.sɪs ⓤⓢ ˌseɪ.t̬əˈraɪə.sɪs, ˌsæt̬-
satyric səˈtɪr.ɪk ⓤⓢ seɪ-, sə-
sauc|e sɔːs ⓤⓢ sɑːs, sɔːs **-es** -ɪz **-ing** -ɪŋ **-ed** -d ˈ**sauce** ˌ**boat**
saucepan ˈsɔːs.pən ⓤⓢ ˈsɑːs-, ˈsɔːs- **-s** -z
saucer ˈsɔː.səʳ ⓤⓢ ˈsɑː.sɚ, ˈsɔː- **-s** -z
Sauchiehall ˌsɔː.kɪˈhɔːl, ˌsɒk.ɪˈ-, ˈ--- ⓤⓢ ˌsɑː.kiˈ-, ˌsɔː-
sauc|y ˈsɔː.s|i ⓤⓢ ˈsɑː-, ˈsɔː- **-ier** -i.əʳ ⓤⓢ -i.ɚ **-iest** -i.ɪst, -i.əst **-ily** -ɪ.li, -əl.i **-iness** -ɪ.nəs, -ɪ.nɪs
Saudi ˈsaʊ.di, ˈsɔː- ⓤⓢ ˈsaʊ-, ˈsɔː-, ˈsɑː- **-s** -z ˌ**Saudi Aˈrabia**
sauerbraten ˈsaʊəˌbrɑː.tən ⓤⓢ ˈsaʊɚ-
sauerkraut ˈsaʊə.kraʊt ⓤⓢ ˈsaʊɚ-
Saul sɔːl ⓤⓢ sɔːl, sɑːl
Sault St. Marie ˌsuː.seɪnt.məˈriː
sauna ˈsɔː.nə, ˈsaʊ- ⓤⓢ ˈsaʊ-, ˈsɔː-, ˈsɑː- **-s** -z
Saunders ˈsɔːn.dəz, ˈsɑːn- ⓤⓢ ˈsɑːn.dɚz, ˈsɔːn-
Saunderson ˈsɔːn.də.sən, ˈsɑːn- ⓤⓢ ˈsɑːn.dɚ-, ˈsɔːn-
saunt|er ˈsɔːn.t|əʳ ⓤⓢ ˈsɑːn.t̬|ɚ, ˈsɔːn- **-ers** -əz ⓤⓢ -ɚz **-ering** -ər.ɪŋ **-ered** -əd ⓤⓢ -ɚd **-erer/s** -ə.rəʳ/z ⓤⓢ -ɚ.ɚ/z
saurian ˈsɔː.ri.ən ⓤⓢ ˈsɑːr.i-, ˈsɔːr- **-s** -z
sausag|e ˈsɒs.ɪdʒ ⓤⓢ ˈsɑː.sɪdʒ, ˈsɔː- **-es** -ɪz ˈ**sausage** ˌ**dog**; ˈ**sausage ma**ˌ**chine**; ˌ**sausage** ˈ**roll** ⓤⓢ ˈ**sausage** ˌ**roll**
Saussure səʊˈsjʊəʳ, -ˈsʊəʳ ⓤⓢ soʊˈsʊr
sauté ˈsəʊ.teɪ, ˈsɔː- ⓤⓢ sɔːˈteɪ, soʊ-, sɑː- **-s** -z **-ing** -ɪŋ **-(e)d** -d
Sauternes, Sauterne səʊˈtɜːn, -ˈteən ⓤⓢ soʊˈtɝːn, sɔː-, sɑː-
Sauvage ˈsæv.ɪdʒ; səʊˈvɑːʒ ⓤⓢ ˈsæv.ɪdʒ; soʊˈvɑːʒ
Sauvignon ˈsəʊ.viː.njɔ̃ːŋ, -vɪ-, -njɒn, ˌ--ˈ- ⓤⓢ ˌsoʊ.viːˈnjõʊn, ˈ--- ˌ**Sauvignon** ˈ**Blanc**
savag|e (S) ˈsæv.ɪdʒ **-es** -ɪz **-est** -ɪst, -əst **-ely** -li **-eness** -nəs, -nɪs **-ery** -ər.i, -ri **-ing** -ɪŋ **-ed** -d
savanna(h) (S) səˈvæn.ə **-s** -z
savant ˈsæv.ənt ⓤⓢ sævˈɑːnt; səˈvænt; ˈsæv.ənt **-s** -s
sav|e seɪv **-es** -z **-ing/s** -ɪŋ **-ed** -d **-er/s** -əʳ/z ⓤⓢ -ɚ/z **-(e)able** -ə.bl̩
saveloy ˈsæv.ə.lɔɪ, ˈ-ɪ-, ˌ--ˈ- ⓤⓢ ˈsæv.ə.lɔɪ **-s** -z
Savels ˈsæv.əlz
Savernake ˈsæv.ə.næk ⓤⓢ ˈ-ɚ-
Savery ˈsæv.ər.i
Savile ˈsæv.ɪl, -əl ˌ**Savile** ˈ**Row**
Savill(e) ˈsæv.ɪl, -əl
saving ˈseɪ.vɪŋ **-s** -z ˌ**saving** ˈ**grace**; ˈ**savings ac**ˌ**count**; ˈ**savings** ˌ**bank**; ˈ**savings** ˌ**bond**; ˈ**savings cer**ˌ**tificate**; ˈ**savings** ˌ**stamp**
savio(u)r (S) ˈseɪ.vjəʳ ⓤⓢ -vjɚ **-s** -z
Savlon® ˈsæv.lɒn ⓤⓢ -lɑːn
savoir faire ˌsæv.wɑːˈfeəʳ ⓤⓢ -wɑːrˈfer, -wɑːˈ-
savoir vivre ˌsæv.wɑːˈviː.vrə ⓤⓢ -wɑːrˈ-, -wɑːˈ-
Savonarola ˌsæv.ən.əˈrəʊ.lə ⓤⓢ -ˈroʊ-
sav|or ˈseɪ.v|əʳ ⓤⓢ -v|ɚ **-ors** -əz ⓤⓢ -ɚz **-oring** -ər.ɪŋ **-ored** -əd ⓤⓢ -ɚd **-orless** -ə.ləs, -lɪs ⓤⓢ -ɚ.ləs, -lɪs
savory (S) ˈseɪ.vər.i **-ies** -iz **-iness** -ɪ.nəs, -ɪ.nɪs
sav|our ˈseɪ.v|əʳ ⓤⓢ -v|ɚ **-ours** -əz ⓤⓢ -ɚz **-ouring** -ər.ɪŋ **-oured** -əd ⓤⓢ -ɚd **-ourless** -ə.ləs, -lɪs ⓤⓢ -ɚ.ləs, -lɪs
savour|y ˈseɪ.vər|.i **-ies** -iz **-iness** -ɪ.nəs, -ɪ.nɪs
savoy (S) səˈvɔɪ **-s** -z **sa**ˌ**voy** ˈ**cabbage**
Savoyard səˈvɔɪ.ɑːd; ˌsæv.ɔɪˈɑːd ⓤⓢ səˈvɔɪ.ɚd; ˌsæv.ɔɪˈɑːrd **-s** -z
savvy ˈsæv.i
saw sɔː ⓤⓢ sɑː, sɔː **-s** -z **-ing** -ɪŋ **-ed** -d **-n** -n
saw (*from* **see**) sɔː ⓤⓢ sɑː, sɔː
saw|bones *singular:* ˈsɔː|.bəʊnz ⓤⓢ ˈsɑː|.boʊnz, ˈsɔː- *plural:* ˈsɔː|.bəʊnz ⓤⓢ ˈsɑː|.boʊnz, ˈsɔː- **-boneses** -ˌbəʊn.zɪz ⓤⓢ -ˌboʊn-
Sawbridgeworth ˈsɔː.brɪdʒ.wɜːθ *old-fashioned:* ˈsæp.swəθ ⓤⓢ ˈsɑː.brɪdʒ.wɝːθ, ˈsɔː-
sawbuck ˈsɔː.bʌk ⓤⓢ ˈsɑː-, ˈsɔː- **-s** -s
sawd|er ˈsɔː.d|əʳ ⓤⓢ ˈsɑː.d|ɚ, ˈsɔː- **-ers** -əz ⓤⓢ -ɚz **-ering** -ər.ɪŋ **-ered** -əd ⓤⓢ -ɚd
sawdust ˈsɔː.dʌst ⓤⓢ ˈsɑː-, ˈsɔː-
sawfish ˈsɔː.fɪʃ ⓤⓢ ˈsɑː-, ˈsɔː-
sawfl|y ˈsɔː.fl|aɪ ⓤⓢ ˈsɑː-, ˈsɔː- **-ies** -aɪz
sawhors|e ˈsɔː.hɔːs ⓤⓢ ˈsɑː.hɔːrs, ˈsɔː- **-es** -ɪz
sawmill ˈsɔː.mɪl ⓤⓢ ˈsɑː-, ˈsɔː- **-s** -z
sawn (*from* **saw**) sɔːn ⓤⓢ sɑːn, sɔːn
Sawney ˈsɔː.ni ⓤⓢ ˈsɑː-, ˈsɔː- **-s** -z
sawn-off ˌsɔːnˈɒf ⓤⓢ ˌsɑːnˈɑːf, ˌsɔːn- *stress shift, see compound:* ˌ**sawn-off** ˈ**shotgun**
Sawoniuk səˈvɒn.i.ʊk ⓤⓢ -vɑːn-
Sawston ˈsɔːs.tən ⓤⓢ ˈsɑːz-, ˈsɔːz-
sawtooth ˈsɔː.tuːθ ⓤⓢ ˈsɑː-, ˈsɔː- **-ed** -t
Sawtry ˈsɔː.tri ⓤⓢ ˈsɑː-, ˈsɔː-
sawyer (S) ˈsɔː.jəʳ, ˈsɔɪ.əʳ ⓤⓢ ˈsɑː.jɚ, ˈsɔː-, ˈsɔɪ.ɚ **-s** -z
sax sæks **-es** -ɪz
Saxe-Coburg-Gotha ˌsæksˌkəʊ.bɜːgˈgəʊ.θə, -tə ⓤⓢ -ˌkoʊ.bɝːgˈgoʊ-
saxhorn ˈsæks.hɔːn ⓤⓢ -hɔːrn **-s** -z
saxifrag|e ˈsæk.sɪ.frɪdʒ, -sə-, -freɪdʒ ⓤⓢ -sə.frɪdʒ **-es** -ɪz
Saxmundham sæksˈmʌn.dəm
Saxon ˈsæk.sən **-s** -z
Saxone® ˈsæk.səʊn, -ˈ- ⓤⓢ -ˈsoʊn
saxony (S) ˈsæk.sən.i
saxophone ˈsæk.sə.fəʊn ⓤⓢ -foʊn **-s** -z
saxophonist sækˈsɒf.ən.ɪst ⓤⓢ ˈsæk.sə.foʊ.nɪst **-s** -s
say seɪ **says** sez **saying** ˈseɪ.ɪŋ **said** sed
Sayce seɪs
SAYE ˌes.eɪ.waɪˈiː
sayer (S) ˈseɪəʳ ⓤⓢ ˈseɪɚ **-s** -z
saying ˈseɪ.ɪŋ **-s** -z
Sayle seɪl
say-so ˈseɪ.səʊ ⓤⓢ -soʊ
SC (*abbrev. for* **South Carolina**) ˌsaʊθ.kær.əlˈaɪ.nə ⓤⓢ -ker.əˈlaɪ-, -kær-
scab skæb **-s** -z **-by** -i **-biness** -ɪ.nəs, -ɪ.nɪs **-bing** -ɪŋ **-bed** -d
scabbard ˈskæb.əd ⓤⓢ -ɚd **-s** -z
scabies ˈskeɪ.biːz, -biz
scabious ˈskeɪ.bi.əs **-es** -ɪz
scabrous ˈskeɪ.brəs ⓤⓢ ˈskæb.rəs, ˈskeɪ.brəs **-ly** -li **-ness** -nəs, -nɪs
Scacchi ˈskæk.i
scad skæd **-s** -z

Pronouncing the letters SC

The consonant digraph **sc** has two main pronunciations: /s/ and /sk/.

It is normally pronounced /s/ before the letters **e**, **i** or **y**, e.g.:

scene	/siːn/	
science	/saɪənts/	
scythe	/saɪð/	
coalesce	/ˌkəʊ.əˈles/	US /ˌkoʊ-/

However, the realisation /sk/ can occur before **e**, and /tʃ/ is possible before **i**, e.g.:

sceptic	/ˈskep.tɪk/	
conscious	/ˈkɒn.*t*ʃəs/	US /ˈkɑːn*t*.ʃəs/

In other cases, /sk/ is the usual pronunciation in word initial position, and /s/ in the combination **–scle**, e.g.:

scale	/skeɪl/	
Scotland	/ˈskɒt.lənd/	US /ˈskɑːt-/
muscle	/ˈmʌs.l̩/	

Scafell ˌskɔːˈfel *stress shift, see compound:* ˌ**Scafell** ˈ**Pike**
scaffold ˈskæf.əʊld, -əld US -əld, -oʊld **-s** -z
scaffolding ˈskæf.əl.dɪŋ **-s** -z
scag skæg
Scala ˈskɑː.lə
scalable ˈskeɪ.lə.bl̩
scalar ˈskeɪ.ləʳ, -lɑːʳ US -lɚ, -lɑːr
scalawag ˈskæl.ə.wæg, ˈ-ɪ- US ˈ-ə- **-s** -z
Scalby ˈskæl.bi
scald skɔːld US skɑːld, skɔːld **-s** -z **-ing** -ɪŋ **-ed** -ɪd
scal|e skeɪl **-es** -z **-ing** -ɪŋ **-ed** -d **-less** -ləs, -lɪs **-er/s** -əʳ/z US -ɚ/z
scalene ˈskeɪ.liːn; -ˈ-, skælˈiːn US ˈskeɪ.liːn, -ˈ-
scales (S) skeɪlz ˌ**tip the** ˈ**scales**
Scaliger ˈskæl.ɪ.dʒəʳ US -dʒɚ
scallion ˈskæl.i.ən, ˈ-jən US ˈ-jən **-s** -z
scallop ˈskæl.əp, ˈskɒl- US ˈskɑː.ləp, ˈskæl.əp **-s** -s **-ing** -ɪŋ **-ed** -t
scallywag ˈskæl.i.wæg **-s** -z
scalp skælp **-s** -s **-ing** -ɪŋ **-ed** -t **-er/s** -əʳ/z US -ɚ/z
scalpel ˈskæl.pəl **-s** -z
scal|y ˈskeɪ.l|i **-ier** -i.əʳ US -i.ɚ **-iest** -i.ɪst, -i.əst **-iness** -ɪ.nəs, -ɪ.nɪs
scam skæm **-s** -z
Scammell ˈskæm.əl
scamp skæmp **-s** -s **-ing** -ɪŋ **-ed** -t **-ish** -ɪʃ
scamp|er ˈskæm.p|əʳ US -p|ɚ **-ers** -əz US -ɚz **-ering** -ər.ɪŋ **-ered** -əd US -ɚd
scampi ˈskæm.pi
scan skæn **-s** -z **-ning** -ɪŋ **-ned** -d
scandal ˈskæn.dəl **-s** -z
scandalization, -isa- ˌskæn.dəl.aɪˈzeɪ.ʃən US -ɪˈ-
scandaliz|e, -is|e ˈskæn.dəl.aɪz US -də.laɪz **-es** -ɪz **-ing** -ɪŋ **-ed** -d
scandalmong|er ˈskæn.dəlˌmʌŋ.g|əʳ US -ˌmɑːŋ.g|ɚ, -ˌmʌŋ- **-ers** -əz US -ɚz **-ering** -ər.ɪŋ
scandalous ˈskæn.dəl.əs **-ly** -li **-ness** -nəs, -nɪs
scandent ˈskæn.dənt
Scandian ˈskæn.di.ən
Scandinavi|a ˌskæn.dɪˈneɪ.vi|.ə, -dəˈ- US -vi|.ə, ˈ-vj|ə **-an/s** -ən/z
scandium ˈskæn.di.əm
Scania® ˈskæn.i.ə, ˈ-jə
Scanlan, Scanlon ˈskæn.lən
Scannell ˈskæn.əl; skəˈnel
scanner ˈskæn.əʳ US -ɚ **-s** -z
scansion ˈskæn.ʃən **-s** -z
scant skænt **-ly** -li **-ness** -nəs, -nɪs
scant|y ˈskæn.t|i US -t̬|i **-ier** -i.əʳ US -i.ɚ **-iest** -i.ɪst, -i.əst **-ily** -ɪ.li, -əl.i **-iness** -ɪ.nəs, -ɪ.nɪs
Scapa Flow ˌskɑː.pəˈfləʊ, ˌskæp.əˈ- US -ˈfloʊ
scape skeɪp **-s** -s
-scape -skeɪp
Note: Suffix. Normally unstressed, e.g. **landscape** /ˈlænd.skeɪp/.
scapegoat ˈskeɪp.gəʊt US -goʊt **-s** -s **-ing** -ɪŋ **-ed** -ɪd
scapegrac|e ˈskeɪp.greɪs **-es** -ɪz
scapul|a ˈskæp.jə.l|ə, -jʊ- **-as** -əz **-ae** -iː **-ar/s** -əʳ
scar (S) skɑːʳ US skɑːr **-s** -z **-ring** -ɪŋ **-red** -d ˈ**scar** ˌ**tissue**
scarab ˈskær.əb US ˈsker-, ˈskær- **-s** -z
scarabae|us ˌskær.əˈbiː|.əs US ˌsker-, ˌskær- **-uses** -ə.sɪz **-i** -aɪ
scaramouch(e) (S) ˈskær.ə.muːʃ, -muːtʃ, -maʊtʃ, ˌ--ˈ- US ˈsker.ə.muːʃ, ˈskær-, -muːtʃ **-(e)s** -ɪz
Scarborough, Scarboro' ˈskɑː.bər.ə US ˈskɑːr.bɚ.oʊ, -ə
Scarbrough ˈskɑː.brə US ˈskɑːr-, -broʊ
scarc|e skeəs US skers **-er** -əʳ US -ɚ **-est** -ɪst, -əst **-ely** -li **-eness** -nəs, -nɪs
scarcity ˈskeə.sə.ti, -sɪ- US ˈsker.sə.t̬i
Scardino skɑːˈdiː.nəʊ US skɑːrˈdiː.noʊ
scar|e skeəʳ US sker **-es** -z **-ing** -ɪŋ **-ed** -d **-er/s** -əʳ/z US -ɚ/z ˈ**scare** ˌ**story**
scarecrow ˈskeə.krəʊ US ˈsker.kroʊ **-s** -z
scaredy-cat ˈskeə.di.kæt US ˈsker- **-s** -s
scaremong|er ˈskeəˌmʌŋ.g|əʳ US ˈskerˌmɑːŋ.g|ɚ, -ˌmʌŋ- **-ers** -əz US -ɚz **-ering** -ər.ɪŋ
scar|ey ˈskeə.r|i US ˈsker|.i **-ier** -i.əʳ US -i.ɚ **-iest** -i.ɪst, -i.əst **-ily** -ɪ.li **-iness** -ɪ.nəs, -ɪ.nɪs
scar|f (*n.*) skɑː|f US skɑːr|f **-ves** -vz **-fs** -fs
scarf (*v.*) skɑːf US skɑːrf **-s** -s **-ing** -ɪŋ **-ed** -t
Scarfe skɑːf US skɑːrf
Scargill ˈskɑː.gɪl US ˈskɑːr-
scarification ˌskær.ɪ.fɪˈkeɪ.ʃən, ˌskeə.rɪ-, -rə- US ˌsker.ə.fɪˈ-, ˌskær-
scari|fy ˈskær.ɪ|.faɪ, ˈskeə.rɪ-, -rə- US ˈsker.ə-, ˈskær- **-fies** -faɪz **-fying** -faɪ.ɪŋ **-fied** -faɪd
scarlatina ˌskɑː.ləˈtiː.nə, -lɪˈ- US ˌskɑːr.ləˈ-
Scarlatti skɑːˈlæt.i US skɑːrˈlɑː.t̬i
scarlet (S) ˈskɑː.lət, -lɪt US ˈskɑːr- ˌ**scarlet** ˈ**fever**; ˌ**scarlet** ˈ**pimpernel**; ˌ**scarlet** ˈ**woman**
Scarlett ˈskɑː.lət, -lɪt US ˈskɑːr-
Scarman ˈskɑː.mən US ˈskɑːr-
scarp skɑːp US skɑːrp **-s** -s **-ing** -ɪŋ **-ed** -t
scarper ˈskɑː.pəʳ US ˈskɑːr.pɚ **-s** -z **-ing** -ɪŋ **-ed** -d
scarves (*plur. of* **scarf**) skɑːvz US skɑːrvs
scar|y ˈskeə.r|i US ˈsker|.i **-ier** -i.əʳ US -i.ɚ **-iest** -i.ɪst, -i.əst **-ily** -ɪ.li, -əl.i **-iness** -ɪ.nəs, -ɪ.nɪs
Scase skeɪs
scat skæt **-s** -s **-ting** -ɪŋ US ˈskæt̬.ɪŋ **-ted** -ɪd US ˈskæt̬.ɪd
scath|e skeɪð **-es** -z **-ing** -ɪŋ/li **-ed** -d **-eless** -ləs, -lɪs
scathing ˈskeɪ.ðɪŋ **-ly** -li
scatological ˌskæt.əˈlɒdʒ.ɪ.kəl US ˌskæt̬.əˈlɑː.dʒɪ-
scatolog|y skætˈɒl.ə.dʒ|i US -ˈɑː.lə-, skəˈtɑː- **-ist/s** -ɪst/s
scatt|er ˈskæt|.əʳ US ˈskæt̬|.ɚ **-ers** -əz US -ɚz **-ering** -ər.ɪŋ **-ered** -əd US -ɚd
scatterbrain ˈskæt.ə.breɪn US ˈskæt̬.ɚ- **-s** -z **-ed** -d

Pronouncing the letters SCH

The consonant letter combination **sch** has several possible pronunciations, the most common being /sk/, e.g.:

school /skuːl/
scheme /skiːm/

Other possible realisations are /ʃ/ and /s/.

schedule /ˈʃed.juːl/ ⓤⓢ /ˈsked-/
schism /ˈskɪz.ᵊm, ˈsɪz-/

For words of German origin, the pronunciation is /ʃ/, e.g.:

schmalz /ʃmɔːlts/

In addition

When the three letters come together due to the addition of a prefix, the pronunciation is /s.tʃ/, e.g.:

mischance /ˈmɪs.tʃɑːnts/ ⓤⓢ /-tʃænts/

scatt|y ˈskæt|.i ⓤⓢ ˈskæt̬|.i **-ier** -i.əʳ ⓤⓢ -i.ɚ **-iest** -i.ɪst, -i.əst **-iness** -ɪ.nəs, -ɪ.nɪs
scaup skɔːp ⓤⓢ skɑːp, skɔːp **-s** -s
scaveng|e ˈskæv.ɪndʒ, -ᵊndʒ **-es** -ɪz **-ing** -ɪŋ **-ed** -d **-er/s** -əʳ/z ⓤⓢ -ɚ/z
Scawfell ˌskɔːˈfel ⓤⓢ ˌskɑː-, ˌskɔː- *stress shift, see compound:* ˌ**Scawfell** ˈ**Pike**
scena ˈʃeɪ.nə ⓤⓢ **-s** -z
scenario sɪˈnɑː.ri.əʊ, sə-, senˈɑː- ⓤⓢ səˈner.i.oʊ, -ˈnær-, -ˈnɑːr- **-s** -z
scenarist ˈsiː.nᵊr.ɪst ⓤⓢ səˈner-, -ˈnær-, -ˈnɑːr- **-s** -s
scene siːn **-s** -z
scenery ˈsiː.nᵊr.i
sceneshifter ˈsiːnˌʃɪf.təʳ ⓤⓢ -tɚ **-s** -z
scenic ˈsiː.nɪk, ˈsen.ɪk ⓤⓢ ˈsiː- **-ally** -ᵊl.i, -li ˌ**scenic** ˈ**railway**
scent sent **-s** -s **-ing** -ɪŋ ⓤⓢ ˈsen.t̬ɪŋ **-ed** -ɪd ⓤⓢ ˈsen.t̬ɪd
scepter ˈsep.təʳ ⓤⓢ -tɚ **-s** -z **-ed** -əd ˌ**scepter'd** ˈ**isle**
sceptic ˈskep.tɪk **-s** -s **-al** -ᵊl **-ally** -ᵊl.i, -li
scepticism ˈskep.tɪ.sɪ.zᵊm, -tə-
sceptre ˈsep.təʳ ⓤⓢ -tɚ **-s** -z **-d** -d
schadenfreude ˈʃɑː.dᵊnˌfrɔɪ.də
Schaefer ˈʃeɪ.fəʳ ⓤⓢ -fɚ
Schama ˈʃɑː.mə
schedul|e ˈʃed.juːl, ˈʃedʒ.uːl, -ᵊl; ˈsked.juːl, ˈskedʒ.uːl, -ᵊl ⓤⓢ ˈskedʒ.uːl, -u.əl, -ᵊl **-es** -z **-ing** -ɪŋ **-ed** -d
Scheherazade ʃɪˌher.əˈzɑː.də, ʃə-, -ˌhɪə.rəˈ-, -ˈzɑːd ⓤⓢ ʃəˌher.əˈzɑːd, -ˈzɑː.də
Scheldt skelt, ʃelt ⓤⓢ skelt
schema ˈskiː.mə **-s** -z **schemata** ˈskiː.mə.tə; skɪˈmɑː.tə ⓤⓢ skiːˈmɑː.t̬ə; ˈskiː.mə.t̬ə
schematic skiːˈmæt.ɪk, skɪ- ⓤⓢ skiːˈmæt̬-, skə- **-ally** -ᵊl.i, -li
schematiz|e, -is|e ˈskiː.mə.taɪz **-es** -ɪz **-ing** -ɪŋ **-ed** -d
schem|e skiːm **-es** -z **-ing/ly** -ɪŋ/li **-ed** -d **-er/s** -əʳ/z ⓤⓢ -ɚ/z
Schenectady skɪˈnek.tə.di, skə- ⓤⓢ skə-
scherzand|o skeətˈsæn.d|əʊ, skɜːt- ⓤⓢ skertˈsɑːn.d|oʊ, -ˈsæn- **-os** -əʊz ⓤⓢ -oʊz **-i** -i
scherz|o ˈskeət.s|əʊ, ˈskɜːt- ⓤⓢ ˈskert.s|oʊ **-os** -əʊz ⓤⓢ -oʊz **-i** -i
Schiaparelli ˌskæp.əˈrel.i, ˌskjæp-, ˌʃæp- ⓤⓢ ˌskæp-, ˌʃæp-, ˌskjɑː.pɑːˈ-
Schiedam skɪˈdæm, ˈskɪd.æm ⓤⓢ skɪˈdɑːm
Schiffer ˈʃɪf.əʳ ⓤⓢ -ɚ
Schiller ˈʃɪl.əʳ ⓤⓢ -ɚ
schilling (S) ˈʃɪl.ɪŋ **-s** -z
Schindler ˈʃɪnd.ləʳ ⓤⓢ -lɚ
schipperke (S) ˈʃɪp.ə.ki, ˈskɪ-; ˈʃɪp.ək ⓤⓢ ˈskɪp.ɚ.ki **schipperkes** ˈʃɪp.ə.kiz, ˈskɪ-; ˈʃɪp.əks ⓤⓢ ˈskɪp.ɚ.kiz
schism ˈskɪz.əm, ˈsɪz- ⓤⓢ ˈskɪz-, ˈsɪz- **-s** -z
schismatic skɪzˈmæt.ɪk, sɪz- ⓤⓢ skɪzˈmæt̬-, sɪz- **-al** -ᵊl **-ally** -ᵊl.i, -li
schist ʃɪst **-s** -s **-ose** -əʊs ⓤⓢ -oʊs
schizo ˈskɪt.səʊ ⓤⓢ -soʊ **-s** -z
schizoid ˈskɪt.sɔɪd
schizophrenia ˌskɪt.səʊˈfriː.ni.ə, ˌskɪd.zəʊˈ- ⓤⓢ ˌskɪt.səˈ-, -soʊˈ-, -ˈfren.i-
schizophrenic ˌskɪt.səʊˈfren.ɪk, ˌskɪd.zəʊˈ-, -ˈfriː.nɪk ⓤⓢ ˌskɪt.səˈ-, -soʊˈ- **-ally** -ᵊl.i, -li **-s** -s
Schlegel ˈʃleɪ.gᵊl
schlemiel ʃləˈmiːl **-s** -z
schlep(p) ʃlep **-s** -s **-ping** -ɪŋ **-ped** -t
Schlesinger ˈʃlez.ɪn.dʒəʳ, ˈʃles- ⓤⓢ ˈʃlees.ɪŋ.ɚ; ˈʃlez.ɪn.dʒɚ, ˈʃleɪ.zɪŋ-
Schleswig-Holstein ˌʃlez.vɪgˈhəʊl.staɪn, ˌʃles-, -wɪgˈ- ⓤⓢ -wɪgˈhoʊl-, ˌʃles.vɪgˈ-, -ˈhɔːl.ʃtaɪn
schlock ʃlɒk ⓤⓢ ʃlɑːk **-s** -s
schlockmeister ˈʃlɒkˌmaɪ.stəʳ ⓤⓢ ˈʃlɑːkˌmaɪ.stɚ **-s** -z
schmal(t)z ʃmɔːlts, ʃmɒlts, ʃmælts ⓤⓢ ʃmɑːlts, ʃmɔːlts **-y** -i **-ier** -i.əʳ ⓤⓢ -i.ɚ **-iest** -i.ɪst, -i.əst
Schmidt ʃmɪt
schmo ʃməʊ ⓤⓢ ʃmoʊ **-es** -z
schmooz|e ʃmuːz **-es** -ɪz **-ing** -ɪŋ **-ed** -d
schmuck ʃmʌk **-s** -s
Schnabel ʃnɑː.bᵊl
schnap(p)s ʃnæps ⓤⓢ ʃnɑːps, ʃnæps
schnauzer ˈʃnaʊt.səʳ ⓤⓢ ˈʃnaʊ.zɚ **-s** -z
Schneider ˈʃnaɪ.dəʳ ⓤⓢ -dɚ
schnitzel ˈʃnɪt.sᵊl **-s** -z
Schnitzler ˈʃnɪt.sləʳ ⓤⓢ -slɚ
schnorkel ˈʃnɔː.kᵊl ⓤⓢ ˈʃnɔːr- **-s** -z
schnozzle ˈʃnɒz.l̩ ⓤⓢ ˈʃnɑː.zl̩ **-s** -z
Schoen ʃəʊn, ʃɜːn ⓤⓢ ʃoʊn, ʃɜːrn
Schoenberg ˈʃɜːn.bɜːg, -beəg ⓤⓢ ˈʃɜːrn.bɚg, ˈʃoʊn-
Schofield ˈskəʊ.fiːld ⓤⓢ ˈskoʊ-
scholar ˈskɒl.əʳ ⓤⓢ ˈskɑː.lɚ **-s** -z **-ly** -li
scholarship ˈskɒl.ə.ʃɪp ⓤⓢ ˈskɑː.lɚ- **-s** -s
scholastic skəˈlæs.tɪk, skɒlˈæs- ⓤⓢ skəˈlæs- **-ally** -ᵊl.i, -li
scholasticism skəˈlæs.tɪ.sɪ.zᵊm, skɒlˈæs- ⓤⓢ skəˈlæs.tə-
Scholes skəʊlz ⓤⓢ skoʊlz
scholiast ˈskəʊ.li.æst ⓤⓢ ˈskoʊ-, -əst **-s** -s
scholi|um ˈskəʊ.li|.əm ⓤⓢ ˈskoʊ- **-a** -ə
Scholl ʃɒl, ʃəʊl, skɒl ⓤⓢ ʃoʊl
Schönberg ˈʃɜːn.bɜːg, -beəg ⓤⓢ ˈʃɜːrn.bɚg, ˈʃoʊn-
school skuːl **-s** -z **-ing** -ɪŋ **-ed** -d ˌ**school** ˈ**leaver**; ˌ**school** ˈ**tie**
schoolbag ˈskuːl.bæg **-s** -z
schoolbook ˈskuːl.bʊk **-s** -s
schoolboy ˈskuːl.bɔɪ **-s** -z **-ish** -ɪʃ
school|child ˈskuːl|.tʃaɪld **-children** -ˌtʃɪl.drᵊn
schooldays ˈskuːl.deɪz
schoolgirl ˈskuːl.gɜːl ⓤⓢ -gɝːl **-s** -z **-ish** -ɪʃ
schoolhou|se ˈskuːl.haʊ|s **-ses** -zɪz
schoolkid ˈskuːl.kɪd **-s** -z
schoolmarm ˈskuːl.mɑːm ⓤⓢ -mɑːrm **-s** -z **-ish** -ɪʃ
schoolmaster ˈskuːlˌmɑː.stəʳ ⓤⓢ -ˌmæs.tɚ **-s** -z
schoolmate ˈskuːl.meɪt **-s** -s
schoolmistress ˈskuːlˌmɪs.trɪs, -trəs **-es** -ɪz

Schwa

An unstressed central vowel.

Examples for English

One of the most noticeable features of English pronunciation is the phonetic difference between stressed and unstressed syllables. In most languages, any of the vowels of the language can occur in any syllable whether that syllable is stressed or not. In English, however, a syllable which bears no stress is more likely to have one of a small number of weak vowels. The most common weak vowel is one which never occurs in a stressed syllable, the schwa vowel (symbolised ə), which is generally described as being unrounded, central (i.e. between front and back) and mid (i.e. between close and open), e.g.:

appease	/ə'pi:z/		
syllable	/'sɪl.ə.bl̩/		
China	/'tʃaɪ.nə/		
mother	/'mʌð.əʳ/	(US)	/'mʌð.ɚ/

Statistically, schwa is reported to be the most frequently occurring vowel of English (over 10% of all vowels).

schoolroom 'sku:l.rʊm, -ru:m (US) -ru:m, -rʊm **-s** -z
schoolteacher 'sku:lˌti:.tʃəʳ (US) -tʃɚ **-s** -z
schooltime 'sku:l.taɪm
schoolwork 'sku:l.wɜ:k (US) -wɝ:k
schoolyard 'sku:l.jɑ:d (US) -jɑ:rd
schooner 'sku:.nəʳ (US) -nɚ **-s** -z
Schopenhauer 'ʃəʊ.pᵊn.haʊ.əʳ, 'ʃɒp.ᵊn- (US) 'ʃoʊ.pᵊn.haʊ.ɚ
schottisch|e ʃɒt'i:ʃ, ʃə'ti:ʃ (US) 'ʃɑ:.t̬ɪʃ **-es** -ɪz
Schreiner 'ʃraɪ.nəʳ (US) -nɚ
Schrödinger 'ʃrɜ:.dɪŋ.əʳ (US) 'ʃroʊ.dɪŋ.ɚ, 'ʃrɜ:r-
Schroeder 'ʃrɜ:.dəʳ (US) 'ʃroʊ.dɚ, 'ʃreɪ-
schtuck ʃtʊk
Schubert 'ʃu:.bət, -bɜ:t (US) -bɚt
Schultz ʃʊlts
Schumacher 'ʃu:ˌmæk.əʳ (US) -mɑ:k.ɚ, -mæk-
Schuman 'ʃu:.mən
Schumann 'ʃu:.mən, -mæn, -mɑ:n (US) -mɑ:n, -mən
schuss ʃʊs, ʃu:s **-es** -ɪz **-ing** -ɪŋ **-ed** -t
Schuster 'ʃʊs.tə, 'ʃu:.stəʳ (US) -stɚ
schwa ʃwɑ: **-s** -z
Schwabe ʃwɑ:b, 'ʃwɑ:.bə
Schwann ʃwɒn *as if German:* ʃvæn (US) ʃvɑ:n, ʃwɑ:n
Schwartz ʃwɔ:ts *as if German:* ʃvɑ:ts (US) ʃwɔ:rts
Schwarzenegger 'ʃwɔ:ts.ᵊn.eg.əʳ (US) 'ʃwɔ:rts.ᵊn.eg.ɚ
Schwarzkopf 'ʃvɑ:ts.kɒpf, 'ʃwɑ:ts-, 'ʃwɔ:ts- (US) 'ʃwɔ:rts.kɑ:pf
Schwarzwald 'ʃvɑ:ts.væld, 'ʃwɑ:ts-, -wæld (US) 'ʃvɑ:rts.vɑ:lt
Schweitzer 'ʃwaɪt.səʳ *as if German:* 'ʃvaɪt- (US) 'ʃwaɪt.sɚ *as if German:* 'ʃvaɪt-
Schweizer 'ʃwaɪt.səʳ *as if German:* 'ʃvaɪt- (US) 'ʃwaɪt.sɚ *as if German* 'ʃvaɪt-
Schweppes® ʃweps
Schwerin ʃveə'ri:n, ʃweə- (US) ʃver'i:n, ʃveɪ'ri:n
sciatic saɪ'æt.ɪk (US) -'æt̬-
sciatica saɪ'æt.ɪ.kə (US) -'æt̬-
scienc|e saɪənts **-es** -ɪz ˌ**science** '**fiction**; '**science** ˌ**park**
scientific ˌsaɪən'tɪf.ɪk **-ally** -ᵊl.i, -li
scientist 'saɪən.tɪst (US) -t̬ɪst **-s** -s
scientologist (S) ˌsaɪən'tɒl.ə.dʒɪst (US) -'tɑ:.lə- **-s** -s
Scientology® ˌsaɪən'tɒl.ə.dʒi (US) -'tɑ:.lə-
sci-fi 'saɪˌfaɪ
scilicet 'saɪ.lɪ.set, 'sɪl.ɪ- (US) 'sɪl.ɪ-
Scillonian sɪ'ləʊ.ni.ən (US) -'loʊ- **-s** -z
Scill|y 'sɪl|.i **-ies** -ɪz '**Scilly** ˌ**Isles**
scimitar 'sɪm.ɪ.təʳ, '-ə-, -tɑ:ʳ (US) -ə.t̬ɚ, -tɑ:r **-s** -z
scintilla sɪn'tɪl.ə
scintill|ate 'sɪn.tɪ.l|eɪt, -tᵊl|.eɪt (US) -t̬ᵊl|.eɪt **-ates** -eɪts **-ating** -eɪ.tɪŋ (US) -eɪ.t̬ɪŋ **-ated** -eɪ.tɪd (US) -eɪ.t̬ɪd
scintillation ˌsɪn.tɪ'leɪ.ʃᵊn, -tᵊl'eɪ- (US) -t̬ᵊl'eɪ- **-s** -z
sciol|ism 'saɪ.əʊ.l|ɪ.zᵊm (US) '-ə- **-ist/s** -ɪst/s
scion saɪən **-s** -z
Scipio 'skɪp.i.əʊ, 'sɪp- (US) 'sɪp.i.oʊ
scire facias ˌsaɪə.ri'feɪ.ʃi.æs, -əs (US) ˌsaɪ.ri'feɪ.ʃi.æs
scirocco ʃɪ'rɒk.əʊ, sɪ-, sə- (US) ʃɪ'rɑ:.koʊ, sə- **-s** -z
scission 'sɪʒ.ᵊn, 'sɪʃ- **-s** -z
sciss|or 'sɪz|.əʳ (US) -ɚ **-ors** -əz (US) -ɚz **-oring** -ᵊr.ɪŋ **-ored** -əd (US) -ɚd
scissors 'sɪz.əz (US) -ɚz
scissors-and-paste ˌsɪz.əz.ᵊnd'peɪst (US) -ɚz-
scler|a 'sklɪə.r|ə (US) 'sklɪr|.ə **-as** -əz **-ae** -i:
sclerос|is sklə'rəʊ.s|ɪs, sklɪ-, skler'əʊ-, sklɪə'rəʊ- (US) sklɪ'roʊ- **-es** -i:z
sclerotic sklə'rɒtɪk, sklɪ-, skler'ɒt-, sklɪə'rɒt- (US) sklɪ'rɑ:.t̬ɪk
scoff skɒf (US) skɑ:f **-s** -s **-ing/ly** -ɪŋ/li **-ed** -t **-er/s** -əʳ/z (US) -ɚ/z
scofflaw 'skɒf.lɔ: (US) 'skɑ:f.lɑ:, -lɔ: **-s** -z
Scofield 'skəʊ.fi:ld (US) 'skoʊ-
Scoggin 'skɒg.ɪn (US) 'skɑ:.gɪn **-s** -z
scold skəʊld (US) skoʊld **-s** -z **-ing/s** -ɪŋ/z **-ed** -ɪd
scoliosis ˌskɒl.i'əʊ.sɪs (US) ˌskoʊ.li'oʊ-, ˌskɑ:-
scollop 'skɒl.əp (US) 'skɑ:.ləp **-s** -s **-ing** -ɪŋ **-ed** -t
sconc|e skɒnts (US) skɑ:nts **-es** -ɪz **-ing** -ɪŋ **-ed** -t
scone skɒn, skəʊn (US) skoʊn, skɑ:n **-s** -z
Scone sku:n ˌ**Stone of** '**Scone**
scoop sku:p **-s** -s **-ing** -ɪŋ **-ed** -t
scoot sku:t **-s** -s **-ing** -ɪŋ (US) 'sku:.t̬ɪŋ **-ed** -ɪd (US) 'sku:.t̬ɪd
scooter 'sku:.təʳ (US) -t̬ɚ **-s** -z
scope skəʊp (US) skoʊp **-s** -s
-scope -skəʊp (US) -skoʊp
Note: Suffix. Normally unstressed, e.g. **microscope** /'maɪ.krə.skəʊp (US) -skoʊp/.
-scopic -'skɒp.ɪk (US) -'skɑ:.pɪk
Note: Suffix. Words containing **-scopic** normally carry primary stress on the penultimate syllable, e.g. **microscopic** /ˌmaɪ.krə'skɒp.ɪk (US) -'skɑ:.pɪk/.
scopolamine skə'pɒl.ə.mi:n, -mɪn; ˌskəʊ.pə'læm.ɪn (US) skə'pɑ:.lə.mi:n, skoʊ-, -mɪn
-scopy -skə.pi
Note: Suffix. Words containing **-scopy** normally carry primary stress on the antepenultimate syllable, e.g. **microscopy** /maɪ'krɒs.kə.pi (US) -'krɑ:.skə-/.
scorbutic skɔ:'bju:.tɪk (US) skɔ:r'bju:.t̬ɪk
scorch skɔ:tʃ (US) skɔ:rtʃ **-es** -ɪz **-ing/ly** -ɪŋ/li **-ed** -t **-er/s** -əʳ/z (US) -ɚ/z ˌ**scorched** '**earth**

scor|e skɔː^{r} US skɔːr **-es** -z **-ing** -ɪŋ **-ed** -d **-er/s** -ə^{r}/z US -ɚ/z **-less** -ləs, -lɪs
scoreboard 'skɔː.bɔːd US 'skɔːr.bɔːrd **-s** -z
scorecard 'skɔː.kɑːd US 'skɔːr.kɑːrd **-s** -z
scorekeeper 'skɔːˌkiː.pə^{r} US 'skɔːrˌkiː.pɚ **-s** -z
score-line 'skɔː.laɪn US 'skɔːr- **-s** -z
scoresheet 'skɔː.ʃiːt US 'skɔːr- **-s** -s
scoria 'skɔː.ri.ə, 'skɒr.i- US 'skɔːr.i-
scoriaceous ˌskɔː.ri'eɪ.ʃəs, ˌskɒr.i'- US ˌskɔːr.i'-
scorn skɔːn US skɔːrn **-s** -z **-ing** -ɪŋ **-ed** -d
scornful 'skɔːn.f^{ə}l, -fʊl US 'skɔːrn- **-ly** -i **-ness** -nəs, -nɪs
Scorpi|o 'skɔː.pi|.əʊ US 'skɔːr.pi|.oʊ **-os** -əʊz US -oʊz **-an/s** -ən/z
scorpion 'skɔː.pi.ən US 'skɔːr- **-s** -z
Scorsese skɔː'seɪ.zi, -zeɪ US skɔːr'seɪ.zi
scot (S) skɒt US skɑːt **-s** -s
scotch (S) skɒtʃ US skɑːtʃ **-es** -ɪz **-ing** -ɪŋ **-ed** -t **ˌScotch 'broth; ˌScotch 'egg; ˌScotch 'mist; ˌScotch 'pine; ˌScotch 'tape®**
Scotch|man 'skɒtʃ|.mən US 'skɑːtʃ- **-men** -mən
Scotch|woman 'skɒtʃ|ˌwʊm.ən US 'skɑːtʃ- **-women** -ˌwɪm.ɪn
scoter 'skəʊ.tə^{r} US 'skoʊ.t̬ɚ **-s** -z
scot-free ˌskɒt'friː US ˌskɑːt-
scotia (S) 'skəʊ.ʃə US 'skoʊ-
Scotland 'skɒt.lənd US 'skɑːt- **ˌScotland 'Yard**
Scots skɒts US skɑːts **ˌScots 'pine**
Scots|man 'skɒts|.mən US 'skɑːts- **-men** -mən
Scots|woman 'skɒts|ˌwʊm.ən US 'skɑːts- **-women** -ˌwɪm.ɪn
Scott skɒt US skɑːt
Scotticism 'skɒt.ɪ.sɪ.z^{ə}m US 'skɑː.t̬ɪ- **-s** -z
Scotticiz|e, -is|e 'skɒt.ɪ.saɪz US 'skɑː.t̬ɪ- **-es** -ɪz **-ing** -ɪŋ **-ed** -d
scottie (S) 'skɒt.i US 'skɑː.ti
Scottish 'skɒt.ɪʃ US 'skɑː.t̬ɪʃ **-ness** -nəs, -nɪs **ˌScottish 'terrier**
scoundrel 'skaʊn.drəl **-s** -z **-ly** -i
scour skaʊə^{r} US skaʊɚ **-s** -z **-ing** -ɪŋ **-ed** -d **-er/s** -ə^{r}/z US -ɚ/z **'scouring ˌpad**
scourg|e skɜːdʒ US skɝːdʒ **-es** -ɪz **-ing** -ɪŋ **-ed** -d
Scous|e skaʊs **-er/s** -ə^{r}/z US -ɚ/z
scout skaʊt **-s** -s **-ing** -ɪŋ US 'skaʊ.t̬ɪŋ **-ed** -ɪd US 'skaʊ.t̬ɪd **-er/s** -ə^{r}/z US 'skaʊ.t̬ɚ/z **ˌscout's 'hono(u)r**
scoutmaster 'skaʊtˌmɑː.stə^{r} US -ˌmæs.tɚ **-s** -z
scow skaʊ **-s** -z
scowl skaʊl **-s** -z **-ing/ly** -ɪŋ/li **-ed** -d

scrabbl|e (S®) 'skræb.l̩ **-es** -z **-ing** -ɪŋ, 'skræb.lɪŋ **-ed** -d
scrag skræg **-s** -z **-ging** -ɪŋ **-ged** -d
scrag-end ˌskræg'end **-s** -z
scraggly 'skræg.l̩.i **-ier** -i.ə^{r} US -i.ɚ **-iest** -i.ɪst **-iness** -ɪ.nəs, -ɪ.nɪs
scragg|y 'skræg|.i **-ier** -i.ə^{r} US -i.ɚ **-iest** -i.ɪst, -i.əst **-iness** -ɪ.nəs, -ɪ.nɪs
scram skræm **-s** -z **-ming** -ɪŋ **-med** -d
scrambl|e 'skræm.bl̩ **-es** -z **-ing** -ɪŋ, 'skræm.blɪŋ **-ed** -d **ˌscrambled 'eggs**
scramjet 'skræm.dʒet **-s** -s
scran skræn **-s** -z
scrap skræp **-s** -s **-ping** -ɪŋ **-ped** -t **-per/s** -ə^{r}/z US -ɚ/z **'scrap ˌheap; 'scrap ˌmerchant; ˌscrap 'metal** US **'scrap ˌmetal**
scrapbook 'skræp.bʊk **-s** -s
scrap|e skreɪp **-es** -s **-ing/s** -ɪŋ/z **-ed** -t **-er/s** -ə^{r}/z US -ɚ/z
scraperboard 'skreɪ.pə.bɔːd US -pɚ.bɔːrd **-s** -z
scrapie 'skreɪ.pi US 'skreɪ-, 'skræp.i
scrapple 'skræp.l̩
scrapp|y 'skræp|.i **-ier** -i.ə^{r} US -i.ɚ **-iest** -i.ɪst, -i.əst **-ily** -ɪ.li, -^{ə}l.i **-iness** -ɪ.nəs, -ɪ.nɪs
scrapyard 'skræp.jɑːd US -jɑːrd **-s** -z
scratch skrætʃ **-es** -ɪz **-ing** -ɪŋ **-ed** -t **-er/s** -ə^{r}/z US -ɚ/z **'scratch ˌpad; 'scratch ˌpaper**
scratchcard 'skrætʃ.kɑːd US -kɑːrd **-s** -z
scratchpad 'skrætʃ.pæd **-s** -z
scratch|y 'skrætʃ|.i **-ier** -i.ə^{r} US -i.ɚ **-iest** -i.ɪst, -i.əst **-ily** -ɪ.li, -^{ə}l.i **-iness** -ɪ.nəs, -ɪ.nɪs
scrawl skrɔːl US skrɑːl, skrɔːl **-s** -z **-ing** -ɪŋ **-ed** -d
scrawl|y 'skrɔː.l|i US 'skrɑː-, 'skrɔː- **-ier** -i.ə^{r} US -i.ɚ **-iest** -i.ɪst, -ɪ.əst **-iness** -ɪ.nəs, -ɪ.nɪs
scrawn|y 'skrɔː.n|i US 'skrɑː-, 'skrɔː- **-ier** -i.ə^{r} US -i.ɚ **-iest** -i.ɪst, -i.əst **-iness** -ɪ.nəs, -ɪ.nɪs
scray skreɪ **-s** -z
scream skriːm **-s** -z **-ing/ly** -ɪŋ **-ed** -d **-er/s** -ə^{r}/z US -ɚ/z
scree skriː **-s** -z
screech skriːtʃ **-es** -ɪz **-ing** -ɪŋ **-ed** -t **-er/s** -ə^{r}/z US -ɚ/z **'screech ˌowl**
screed skriːd **-s** -z
screen skriːn **-s** -z **-ing/s** -ɪŋ **-ed** -d **'screen ˌprinting; 'screen ˌtest**
screenplay 'skriːn.pleɪ, 'skriːm- US 'skriːn- **-s** -z
screensaver 'skriːnˌseɪ.və^{r} US -vɚ **-s** -z
screenwriter 'skriːnˌraɪ.tə^{r} US -t̬ɚ **-s** -z
screw skruː **-s** -z **-ing** -ɪŋ **-ed** -d **ˌscrew 'cap** US **'screw ˌcap; ˌscrew 'top** US **'screw ˌtop; ˌscrewed 'up**
screwball 'skruː.bɔːl US -bɔːl, -bɑːl **-s** -z

screwdriver 'skruːˌdraɪ.və^{r} US -vɚ **-s** -z
screw|y 'skruː|.i **-ier** -i.ə^{r} US -i.ɚ **-iest** -i.ɪst, -i.əst **-iness** -ɪ.nəs, -ɪ.nɪs
Scriabin 'skrɪə.bɪn, skri'æb.ɪn US skri'ɑː.bɪn
scribal 'skraɪ.b^{ə}l
scribbl|e 'skrɪb.l̩ **-es** -z **-ing** -ɪŋ, 'skrɪb.lɪŋ **-ed** -d **-er/s** -ə^{r}/z, 'skrɪb.lə^{r}/z US '-l̩.ɚ/z, '-lɚ/z
scribe skraɪb **-s** -z
Scriblerus skrɪ'blɪə.rəs US -'bler.əs, -'blɪr-
Scribner 'skrɪb.nə^{r} US -nɚ
scrim skrɪm
scrimmag|e 'skrɪm.ɪdʒ **-es** -ɪz **-ing** -ɪŋ **-ed** -d
scrimp skrɪmp **-s** -s **-ing** -ɪŋ **-ed** -t **-er/s** -ə^{r}/z US -ɚ/z
scrimshaw 'skrɪm.ʃɔː US -ʃɑː, -ʃɔː **-s** -z **-ing** -ɪŋ **-ed** -d
scrip skrɪp **-s** -s
script skrɪpt **-s** -s **-ing** -ɪŋ **-ed** -ɪd
scriptori|um skrɪp'tɔː.ri|.əm US -'tɔːr.i- **-ums** -əmz **-a** -ə
scriptural 'skrɪp.tʃ^{ə}r.^{ə}l, -tʃʊ.r^{ə}l US -tʃɚ.^{ə}l **-ly** -i
scripture (S) 'skrɪp.tʃə^{r} US -tʃɚ **-s** -z
scriptwriter 'skrɪptˌraɪ.tə^{r} US -t̬ɚ **-s** -z
Scriven 'skrɪv.^{ə}n
scrivener (S) 'skrɪv.^{ə}n.ə^{r}, '-nə^{r} US '-^{ə}n.ɚ, '-nɚ **-s** -z
scrofula 'skrɒf.jʊ.lə US 'skrɑː.fjə-
scrofulous 'skrɒf.jʊ.ləs US 'skrɑː.fjə- **-ly** -li **-ness** -nəs, -nɪs
scroll skrəʊl US skroʊl **-s** -z **-ing** -ɪŋ **-ed** -d
scrooge (S) skruːdʒ **-s** -ɪz
Scroope skruːp
Scrope skruːp, skrəʊp US skruːp, skroʊp
scrot|um 'skrəʊ.t|əm US 'skroʊ.t̬|əm **-ums** -əmz **-a** -ə **-al** -^{ə}l
scroung|e skraʊndʒ **-es** -ɪz **-ing** -ɪŋ **-ed** -d **-er/s** -ə^{r}/z US -ɚ/z
scrub skrʌb **-s** -z **-bing** -ɪŋ **-bed** -d **'scrubbing ˌbrush; 'scrub ˌbrush**
scrubber 'skrʌb.ə^{r} US -ɚ **-s** -z
scrubb|y 'skrʌb|.i **-ier** -i.ə^{r} US -i.ɚ **-iest** -i.ɪst, -i.əst **-iness** -ɪ.nəs, -ɪ.nɪs
scrubland 'skrʌb.lənd, -lænd US -lænd **-s** -z
scruff skrʌf **-s** -s
scruff|y 'skrʌf|.i **-ier** -i.ə^{r} US -i.ɚ **-iest** -i.ɪst, -i.əst **-iness** -ɪ.nəs, -ɪ.nɪs **-ily** -ɪ.li, -^{ə}l.i
scrum skrʌm **-s** -z
scrum-|half ˌskrʌm|'hɑːf US -'hæf **-halfs** -'hɑːfs US -'hæfs **-halves** -'hɑːvz US -'hævz
scrummag|e 'skrʌm.ɪdʒ **-es** -ɪz **-ing** -ɪŋ **-ed** -d **-er/s** -ə^{r}/z US -ɚ/z

scrummy ˈskrʌm.i **-ier** -i.əʳ ⓤⓢ -i.ɚ **-iest** -i.ɪst **-iness** -ɪ.nəs, -ɪ.nɪs
scrump skrʌmp **-s** -s **-ing** -ɪŋ **-ed** -t
scrumptious ˈskrʌmp.ʃəs, -tʃəs
scrumpy ˈskrʌm.pi
scrunch skrʌntʃ **-es** -ɪz **-ing** -ɪŋ **-ed** -t **-y** -i
scrupl|e ˈskruː.pl̩ **-es** -z **-ing** -ɪŋ, ˈskruː.plɪŋ **-ed** -d
scrupulosity ˌskruː.pjəˈlɒs.ə.ti, -pjʊˈ-, -ɪ.ti ⓤⓢ -ˈlɑː.sə.t̬i
scrupulous ˈskruː.pjə.ləs, -pjʊ- **-ly** -li **-ness** -nəs, -nɪs
scrutator skruːˈteɪ.təʳ ⓤⓢ -t̬ɚ **-s** -z
scrutineer ˌskruː.tɪˈnɪəʳ, -tᵊnˈɪəʳ ⓤⓢ -tᵊnˈɪr **-s** -z
scrutiniz|e, -is|e ˈskruː.tɪ.naɪz, -tᵊn.aɪz ⓤⓢ -tᵊn.aɪz **-es** -ɪz **-ing** -ɪŋ **-ed** -d
scrutin|y ˈskruː.tɪ.n|i, -tᵊn|.i ⓤⓢ -tᵊn|.i **-ies** -iz
Scruton ˈskruː.tᵊn
scr|y skr|aɪ **-ies** -aɪz **-ying** -aɪ.ɪŋ **-ied** -aɪd
Scrymgeour ˈskrɪm.dʒəʳ ⓤⓢ -dʒɚ
scuba ˈskuː.bə, ˈskjuː- ⓤⓢ ˈskuː- ˈ**scuba** ˌ**diving**
scud (S) skʌd **-s** -z **-ding** -ɪŋ **-ded** -ɪd
Scudamore ˈskjuː.də.mɔːʳ ⓤⓢ ˈskuː.də.mɔːr
scuff skʌf **-s** -s **-ing** -ɪŋ **-ed** -t
scuffl|e ˈskʌf.l̩ **-es** -z **-ing** -ɪŋ, ˈskʌf.lɪŋ **-ed** -d
scull skʌl **-s** -z **-ing** -ɪŋ **-ed** -d **-er/s** -əʳ/z ⓤⓢ -ɚ/z
sculler|y ˈskʌl.ᵊr|.i **-ies** -iz ˈ**scullery** ˌ**maid**
scullion (S) ˈskʌl.i.ən ⓤⓢ ˈ-jən **-s** -z
Scully ˈskʌl.i
sculpsit ˈskʌlp.sɪt
sculpt skʌlpt **-s** -s **-ing** -ɪŋ **-ed** -ɪd
sculptor ˈskʌlp.təʳ ⓤⓢ -tɚ **-s** -z
sculpt|ure ˈskʌlp.tʃ|əʳ ⓤⓢ -tʃ|ɚ **-ures** -əz ⓤⓢ -ɚz **-uring** -ᵊr.ɪŋ **-ured** -əd ⓤⓢ -ɚd **-ural** -ᵊr.ᵊl
scum skʌm **-s** -z **-ming** -ɪŋ **-med** -d **-my** -i
scumbag ˈskʌm.bæg **-s** -z
Scunthorpe ˈskʌn.θɔːp ⓤⓢ -θɔːrp
scupper ˈskʌp.əʳ ⓤⓢ -ɚ **-s** -z **-ing** -ɪŋ **-ed** -d
scurf skɜːf ⓤⓢ skɝːf **-y** -i **-iness** -ɪ.nəs, -ɪ.nɪs
scurrility skʌrˈɪl.ə.ti, skəˈrɪl-, -ɪ.ti ⓤⓢ skəˈrɪl.ə.t̬i
scurrilous ˈskʌr.ə.ləs, ˈ-ɪ- ⓤⓢ ˈskɝː- **-ly** -li **-ness** -nəs, -nɪs
scurr|y ˈskʌr|.i ⓤⓢ ˈskɝː- **-ies** -iz **-ying** -i.ɪŋ **-ied** -id
scurv|y ˈskɜː.v|i ⓤⓢ ˈskɝː- **-ier** -i.əʳ ⓤⓢ -i.ɚ **-iest** -i.ɪst, -i.əst **-ily** -ɪ.li, -ᵊl.i **-iness** -ɪ.nəs, -ɪ.nɪs
Scutari ˈskuː.tᵊr.i; skuːˈtɑː.ri, skʊ- ⓤⓢ ˈskuː.t̬ɚ.i, -tɑː-
scutcheon ˈskʌtʃ.ᵊn **-s** -z
scutt|er ˈskʌt|.əʳ ⓤⓢ ˈskʌt̬|.ɚ **-ers** -əz ⓤⓢ -ɚz **-ering** -ᵊr.ɪŋ **-ered** -əd ⓤⓢ -ɚd
scuttl|e ˈskʌt.l̩ ⓤⓢ ˈskʌt̬- **-es** -z **-ing** -ɪŋ, ˈskʌt.lɪŋ **-ed** -d
scuttlebutt ˈskʌt.l̩.bʌt **-s** -s
scut|um ˈskjuː.t|əm ⓤⓢ -t̬|əm **-ums** -əmz **-a** -ə
scuzz|y ˈskʌz|.i **-ier** -i.əʳ ⓤⓢ -i.ɚ **-iest** -i.ɪst, -i.əst **-iness** -ɪ.nəs, -ɪ.nɪs
Scylla ˈsɪl.ə
scyth|e saɪð **-es** -z **-ing** -ɪŋ **-ed** -d
Scythi|a ˈsɪð.i|.ə, ˈsɪθ- ⓤⓢ ˈsɪθ-, ˈsɪð- **-an/s** -ən/z
S.D. *(abbrev. for* **South Dakota***)* ˌsaʊθ.dəˈkəʊ.tə ⓤⓢ -ˈkoʊ.t̬ə
S.D.I. ˌes.diːˈaɪ
SDP ˌes.diːˈpiː
SE *(abbrev. for* **southeast***)* ˌesˈiː, ˌsaʊθˈiːst
sea siː **-s** -z ˌ**sea** ˈ**breeze** ⓤⓢ ˈ**sea** ˌ**breeze**; ˈ**sea** ˌ**captain**; ˈ**sea** ˌ**change**; ˈ**sea** ˌ**cow**; ˈ**sea** ˌ**elephant**; ˈ**sea** ˌ**fog**; ˌ**sea** ˈ**green**; ˈ**sea** ˌ**horse**; ˈ**sea** ˌ**legs**; ˈ**sea** ˌ**level**; ˈ**sea** ˌ**lion**; ˈ**sea** ˌ**power**; ˈ**sea** ˌ**serpent**; ˈ**sea** ˌ**slug**; ˈ**sea** ˌ**snail**; ˈ**sea** ˌ**urchin**; **between the** ˌ**devil and the** ˌ**deep** ˌ**blue** ˈ**sea**
seabed ˈsiː.bed, -ˈ-
seabird ˈsiː.bɜːd ⓤⓢ -bɝːd **-s** -z
seaboard ˈsiː.bɔːd ⓤⓢ -bɔːrd
seaborne ˈsiː.bɔːn ⓤⓢ -bɔːrn
Seabright ˈsiː.braɪt
seadog ˈsiː.dɒg ⓤⓢ -dɑːg, -dɔːg **-s** -z
seafar|er ˈsiːˌfeə.r|əʳ ⓤⓢ -ˌfer|.ɚ **-ers** -əz ⓤⓢ -ɚz **-ing** -ɪŋ
seafood ˈsiː.fuːd
Seaford ˈsiː.fəd, -fɔːd ⓤⓢ -fɚd, -fɔːrd
Seaforth ˈsiː.fɔːθ ⓤⓢ -fɔːrθ **-s** -s
seafront ˈsiː.frʌnt **-s** -s
Seager ˈsiː.gəʳ ⓤⓢ -gɚ
seagoing ˈsiːˌgəʊ.ɪŋ ⓤⓢ -ˌgoʊ-
Seagram® ˈsiː.grəm
seagull ˈsiː.gʌl **-s** -z
Seaham ˈsiː.əm
seakale ˈsiː.keɪl, ˌ-ˈ- ⓤⓢ ˈsiː.keɪl
seal siːl **-s** -z **-ing** -ɪŋ **-ed** -d ˈ**sealing** ˌ**wax**
sealant ˈsiː.lənt **-s** -s
sealer ˈsiː.ləʳ ⓤⓢ -lɚ **-s** -z
sealskin ˈsiːl.skɪn **-s** -z
Sealyham ˈsiː.li.əm **-s** -z
seam siːm **-s** -z **-ing** -ɪŋ **-ed** -d **-less/ly** -ləs/li, -lɪs/li
sea|man (S) ˈsiː|.mən **-men** -mən, -men **-manship** -mən.ʃɪp **-manlike** -mən.laɪk
Seamas ˈʃeɪ.məs
seamer ˈsiː.məʳ ⓤⓢ -mɚ **-s** -z
seamstress ˈsemp.strɪs, ˈsiːmp-, -strəs ⓤⓢ ˈsiːmp- **-es** -ɪz
Seamus ˈʃeɪ.məs
seamy ˈsiː.mi **-ier** -i.əʳ ⓤⓢ -i.ɚ **-iest** -i.ɪst, -i.əst **-iness** -ɪ.nəs, -ɪ.nɪs
Sean ʃɔːn ⓤⓢ ʃɑːn, ʃɔːn
seanc|e, séance ˈseɪ.ɑ̃ːnts ⓤⓢ ˈseɪ.ɑːnts **-es** -ɪz
sea-pink ˈsiː.pɪŋk
seaplane ˈsiː.pleɪn **-s** -z
seaport ˈsiː.pɔːt ⓤⓢ -pɔːrt **-s** -s
sear sɪəʳ ⓤⓢ sɪr **-s** -z **-ing/ly** -ɪŋ **-ed** -d
search sɜːtʃ ⓤⓢ sɝːtʃ **-es** -ɪz **-ing/ly** -ɪŋ/li **-ed** -t **-er/s** -əʳ/z ⓤⓢ -ɚ/z **-able** -ə.b|l̩ ˈ**search** ˌ**party**; ˈ**search** ˌ**warrant**
searchlight ˈsɜːtʃ.laɪt ⓤⓢ ˈsɝːtʃ- **-s** -s
Searle sɜːl ⓤⓢ sɝːl
Sears sɪəz ⓤⓢ sɪrz
Seascale ˈsiː.skeɪl
seascape ˈsiː.skeɪp **-s** -s
seashell ˈsiː.ʃel **-s** -z
seashore ˈsiː.ʃɔːʳ, ˌ-ˈ- ⓤⓢ ˈsiː.ʃɔːr **-s** -z
seasick ˈsiː.sɪk **-ness** -nəs, -nɪs
seaside ˈsiː.saɪd
season ˈsiː.zᵊn **-s** -z **-ing** -ɪŋ **-ed** -d ˌ**Season's** ˈ**Greetings**; ˈ**season** ˌ**ticket** ⓤⓢ ˌ**season** ˈ**ticket**
seasonab|le ˈsiː.zᵊn.ə.b|l̩, ˈsiːz.nə- **-ly** -li **-leness** -l̩.nəs, -nɪs
seasonal ˈsiː.zᵊn.ᵊl **-ly** -i
seasonality ˌsiː.zᵊnˈæl.ə.ti, -ɪ.ti ⓤⓢ -ə.t̬i
seasoning ˈsiː.zᵊn.ɪŋ **-s** -z
seat siːt **-s** -s **-ing** -ɪŋ ⓤⓢ ˈsiː.t̬ɪŋ **-ed** -ɪd ⓤⓢ ˈsiː.t̬ɪd **-er/s** -əʳ/z ⓤⓢ -ɚ/z ˈ**seat** ˌ**belt**
SEATO ˈsiː.təʊ ⓤⓢ -t̬oʊ
Seaton ˈsiː.tᵊn
Seaton Delavel ˌsiː.tᵊnˈdel.ə.vᵊl
Seattle siˈæt.l̩ ⓤⓢ -ˈæt̬-
seawall ˌsiːˈwɔːl, ˈ-- ⓤⓢ ˈsiː.wɔːl, -wɑːl **-s** -z
seaward ˈsiː.wəd ⓤⓢ -wɚd
seawater ˈsiːˌwɔː.təʳ ⓤⓢ -ˌwɑː.t̬ɚ, -ˌwɔː-
seaway ˈsiː.weɪ **-s** -z
seaweed ˈsiː.wiːd
seaworth|y ˈsiːˌwɜː.ð|i ⓤⓢ -ˌwɝː- **-iness** -ɪ.nəs, -ɪ.nɪs
sebaceous sɪˈbeɪ.ʃəs, sebˈeɪ- ⓤⓢ səˈbeɪ- **se**ˈ**baceous** ˌ**gland**
Sebastian sɪˈbæs.ti.ən, səˈbæs-, sebˈæs- ⓤⓢ səˈbæs.tʃən
Sebastopol sɪˈbæs.tə.pɒl, sə-, sebˈæs-, -pᵊl ⓤⓢ sɪˈbæs.tə.poʊl
seborrhea ˌseb.əˈriː.ə, -ˈrɪə ⓤⓢ -ˈriː.ə
sebum ˈsiː.bəm
sec sek **-s** -s
secant ˈsiː.kᵊnt, ˈsek.ᵊnt ⓤⓢ ˈsiː.kᵊnt, -kænt **-s** -s
secateurs ˌsek.əˈtɜːz; ˈ---, -təz ⓤⓢ ˈsek.ə.tɚz
seced|e sɪˈsiːd, siː-, sə- ⓤⓢ sɪ- **-es** -z **-ing** -ɪŋ **-ed** -ɪd **-er/s** -əʳ/z ⓤⓢ -ɚ/z
secession sɪˈseʃ.ᵊn, sə- **-s** -z **-ist/s** -ɪst/s

seclud|e sɪˈkluːd, sə- **-es** -z **-ing** -ɪŋ **-ed** -ɪd
seclusion sɪˈkluː.ʒᵊn, sə-
Secombe ˈsiː.kəm
second (*n. adj. v.*) *most senses:* ˈsek.ᵊnd **-s** -z **-ly** -li **-ing** -ɪŋ **-ed** -ɪd **-er/s** -əʳ/z (US) -ɚ/z ˌ**second ˈbest;** ˌ**Second ˈComing;** ˌ**second ˈcousin;** ˌ**second ˈfiddle;** ˌ**second ˈnature;** ˌ**second ˈperson;** *stress shift:* ˌsecond person ˈsingular; ˌ**second ˈreading;** ˌ**second ˈsight;** ˌ**second ˈthoughts;** ˌ**second ˈwind;** ˌ**Second** ˌ**World ˈWar**
second (*v.*) *to release for temporary service:* sɪˈkɒnd, sə- (US) -ˈkɑːnd **-s** -z **-ing** -ɪŋ **-ed** -ɪd **-ment/s**
secondar|y ˈsek.ᵊn.dᵊr|.i, -dr|i (US) -der|.i **-ies** -iz **-ily** -ᵊl.i, -ɪ.li ˌ**secondary ˈmodern;** ˈ**secondary** ˌ**school**
second-class ˌsek.ᵊndˈklɑːs (US) -ˈklæs ˌ**second-class ˈcitizen**
second-generation ˌsek.ᵊnˌdʒen.ᵊrˈeɪ.ʃᵊn (US) -əˈreɪ-
second-guess ˌsek.ᵊndˈges **-es** -ɪz **-ing** -ɪŋ **-ed** -t
secondhand ˌsek.ᵊndˈhænd *stress shift:* ˌsecondhand ˈbooks
Secondi *town in Ghana:* ˌsek.ənˈdiː *surname:* sɪˈkɒn.di, sə- (US) -ˈkɑːn-
secondment sɪˈkɒnd.mənt, sə- (US) -ˈkɑːnd-
secondo sekˈɒn.dəʊ, sɪˈkɒn- (US) sɪˈkɑːn.doʊ **-s** -z
second|-rate ˌsek.ᵊnd|ˈreɪt **-rater/s** -ˈreɪ.təʳ/z (US) -ˈreɪ.t̬ɚ/z
secrecy ˈsiː.krə.si, -krɪ-
secret ˈsiː.krət, -krɪt **-s** -s **-ly** -li ˌ**secret ˈagent;** ˌ**secret poˈlice;** ˌ**secret ˈservice**
secretarial ˌsek.rəˈteə.ri.əl, -rɪˈ- (US) -rəˈter.i-
secretariat ˌsek.rəˈteə.ri.ət, -rɪˈ-, -æt (US) -rəˈter.i.ət **-s** -s
secretar|y ˈsek.rə.tᵊr|.i, -rɪ-, -tr|i (US) -rə.ter|.i **-ies** -iz **-yship/s** -i.ʃɪp/s ˌ**Secretary of ˈState**
secretary-general, (S G) ˌsek.rə.tᵊr.iˈdʒen.ᵊr.ᵊl, -rɪ- (US) -rə.ter.iˈ- **-s** -z **secretaries-general** ˌsek.rə.tᵊr.izˈ-, -rɪ- (US) -rə.ter.izˈ-
se|crete sɪ|ˈkriːt, siː-, sə- (US) sɪ- **-cretes** -ˈkriːts **-creting** -ˈkriː.tɪŋ (US) -ˈkriː.t̬ɪŋ **-creted** -ˈkriː.tɪd (US) -ˈkriː.t̬ɪd
secretion sɪˈkriː.ʃᵊn, siː-, sə- (US) sɪ- **-s** -z
secretive *inclined to secrecy:* ˈsiː.krə.tɪv, -krɪ- (US) -krə.t̬ɪv **-ly** -li **-ness** -nəs, -nɪs
secretive *of secretion:* sɪˈkriː.tɪv, sə- (US) -t̬ɪv
sect sekt **-s** -s
sectarian sekˈteə.ri.ən (US) -ˈter.i- **-s** -z **-ism** -ɪ.zᵊm
sectar|y ˈsek.tᵊr|.i **-ies** -iz
section ˈsek.ʃᵊn **-s** -z **-ing** -ɪŋ **-ed** -d
sectional ˈsek.ʃᵊn.ᵊl **-ly** -i
sectional|ism ˈsek.ʃᵊn.ᵊl|.ɪ.zᵊm **-ist/s** -ɪst/s
sectionaliz|e, -is|e ˈsek.ʃᵊn.ᵊl.aɪz (US) -ə.laɪz **-es** -ɪz **-ing** -ɪŋ **-ed** -d
sector ˈsek.təʳ (US) -tɚ **-s** -z
secular ˈsek.jə.ləʳ, -jʊ- (US) -lɚ **-ly** -li
secular|ism ˈsek.jə.lᵊr|.ɪ.zᵊm, -jʊ- **-ist/s** -ɪst/s
secularity ˌsek.jəˈlær.ə.ti, -jʊˈ-, -ɪ.ti (US) -ˈler.ə.t̬i, -ˈlær-
secularization, -isa- ˌsek.jə.lᵊr.aɪˈzeɪ.ʃᵊn, -jʊ-, -ɪˈ- (US) -ɪˈ-
seculariz|e, -is|e ˈsek.jə.lᵊr.aɪz, -jʊ- (US) -lə.raɪz **-es** -ɪz **-ing** -ɪŋ **-ed** -d
secur|e sɪˈkjʊəʳ, sə-, -ˈkjɔːʳ (US) -ˈkjʊr **-er** -əʳ (US) -ɚ **-est** -ɪst, -əst **-ely** -li **-es** -z **-ing** -ɪŋ **-ed** -d **-able** -rə.bl̩
Securicor® sɪˈkjʊə.rɪ.kɔːʳ, sə-, -ˈkjɔː-, -rə- (US) -ˈkjʊr.ə.kɔːr
securit|y sɪˈkjʊə.rə.t|i, sə-, -ˈkjɔː-, -ɪ.t|i (US) -ˈkjʊr.ə.t̬|i **-ies** -iz **seˈcurity** ˌ**guard; Seˈcurity** ˌ**Council; seˈcurity** ˌ**risk**
sedan (S) sɪˈdæn, sə- **seˌdan ˈchair** (US) **seˈdan** ˌ**chair**
se|date (*v.*) sɪ|ˈdeɪt, sə- **-dates** -ˈdeɪts **-dating** -ˈdeɪ.tɪŋ (US) -ˈdeɪ.t̬ɪŋ **-dated** -ˈdeɪ.tɪd (US) -ˈdeɪ.t̬ɪd
sedate (*adj.*) sɪˈdeɪt, sə- **-ly** -li **-ness** -nəs, -nɪs
sedation sɪˈdeɪ.ʃᵊn, sə-
sedative ˈsed.ə.tɪv (US) -t̬ɪv **-s** -z
Sedbergh *public school:* ˈsed.bəʳ, -bɜːg (US) -bɜːg, -bɚ *name of town:* ˈsed.bəʳ (US) -bɚ
Sedding ˈsed.ɪŋ
Seddon ˈsed.ᵊn
sedentar|y ˈsed.ᵊn.tᵊr|.i, -tr|i (US) -ter|.i **-ily** -ᵊl.i, -ɪ.li **-iness** -ɪ.nəs, -ɪ.nɪs
sedg|e sedʒ **-es** -ɪz ˈ**sedge** ˌ**warbler,** ˌ**sedge ˈwarbler** (US) ˈ**sedge** ˌ**warbler**
Sedgefield ˈsedʒ.fiːld
Sedgemoor ˈsedʒ.mɔːʳ, -mʊəʳ (US) -mʊr, -mɔːr
Sedgley ˈsedʒ.li
Sedgwick ˈsedʒ.wɪk
sedilia sedˈiː.li.ə, sɪˈdiː-, sə-, -ˈdaɪ- (US) sɪˈdɪl.i.ə, ˈ-jə
sediment ˈsed.ɪ.mənt, ˈ-ə- (US) ˈ-ə- **-s** -s **-ation** ˌ--menˈteɪ.ʃᵊn
sedimentary ˌsed.ɪˈmen.tᵊr.i, -əˈ-, ˈ-tri
sedition sɪˈdɪʃ.ᵊn, sə- **-s** -z
seditious sɪˈdɪʃ.əs, sə- **-ly** -li **-ness** -nəs, -nɪs
Sedlescombe ˈsed.l̩z.kəm
Sedley ˈsed.li
seduc|e sɪˈdjuːs, sə-, -ˈdʒuːs (US) -ˈduːs, -ˈdjuːs **-es** -ɪz **-ing** -ɪŋ **-ed** -t **-er/s** -əʳ/z (US) -ɚ/z
seduction sɪˈdʌk.ʃᵊn, sə- **-s** -z
seductive sɪˈdʌk.tɪv, sə- **-ly** -li **-ness** -nəs, -nɪs
seductress sɪˈdʌk.trɪs, -trəs **-es** -ɪz
sedulous ˈsed.jʊ.ləs, -jə-, ˈsedʒ.ʊ-, ˈ-ə- (US) ˈsedʒ.ə-, ˈ-ʊ- **-ly** -li **-ness** -nəs, -nɪs
sedum ˈsiː.dəm **-s** -z
see (S) siː **-s** -z **-ing** -ɪŋ **saw** sɔː (US) sɑː, sɔː **seen** siːn
Seebeck ˈsiː.bek
seed siːd **-s** -z **-ing** -ɪŋ **-ed** -ɪd ˌ**go to ˈseed;** ˈ**seed po**ˌ**tato,** ˌ**seed poˈtato**
seedbed ˈsiːd.bed **-s** -z
seedcake ˈsiːd.keɪk **-s** -s
seedcas|e ˈsiːd.keɪs **-es** -ɪz
seedless ˈsiːd.ləs, -lɪs
seedling ˈsiːd.lɪŋ **-s** -z
seeds|man ˈsiːdz|.mən **-men** -mən, -men
seedtime ˈsiːd.taɪm **-s** -z
seed|y ˈsiː.d|i **-ier** -i.əʳ (US) -i.ɚ **-iest** -i.ɪst, -i.əst **-ily** -ɪ.li, -ᵊl.i **-iness** -ɪ.nəs, -ɪ.nɪs
Seeger ˈsiː.gəʳ (US) -gɚ
seek siːk **-s** -s **-ing** -ɪŋ **sought** sɔːt (US) sɑːt, sɔːt **seeker/s** ˈsiː.kəʳ/z (US) -kɚ/z
Seel(e)y ˈsiː.li
seem siːm **-s** -z **-ing/ly** -ɪŋ/li **-ed** -d
seeml|y ˈsiːm.l|i **-ier** -i.əʳ (US) -i.ɚ **-iest** -i.ɪst, -i.əst **-iness** -ɪ.nəs, -ɪ.nɪs
seen (*from* **see**) siːn
seep siːp **-s** -s **-ing** -ɪŋ **-ed** -t
seepage ˈsiː.pɪdʒ
seer *prophet:* ˈsiː.əʳ, sɪəʳ (US) sɪr, ˈsiː.ɚ **-s** -z
seer *Indian weight:* sɪəʳ (US) siːr, sɪr **-s** -z
seersucker ˈsɪəˌsʌk.əʳ (US) ˈsɪrˌsʌk.ɚ
seesaw ˈsiː.sɔː (US) -sɑː, -sɔː **-s** -z **-ing** -ɪŋ **-ed** -d
seeth|e siːð **-es** -z **-ing** -ɪŋ **-ed** -d
see-through ˈsiː.θruː
Sefton ˈsef.tᵊn (US) -tən
Sega® ˈseɪ.gə, ˈsiː-
Segal ˈsiː.gəl
segment (*n.*) ˈseg.mənt **-s** -s
segmen|t (*v.*) segˈmen|t, səg-, sɪg- (US) ˈseg.men|t, -ˈ- **-ts** -ts **-ting** -tɪŋ (US) -t̬ɪŋ **-ted** -tɪd (US) -t̬ɪd
segmental segˈmen.tᵊl, səg-, sɪg- (US) segˈmen.t̬ᵊl
segmentation ˌseg.menˈteɪ.ʃᵊn, -mənˈ-
segn|o ˈsen.j|əʊ, ˈseɪ.nj|əʊ (US) ˈseɪ.nj|oʊ **-i** -i
Segovia sɪˈgəʊ.vi.ə, sə-, segˈəʊ- (US) sɪˈgoʊ-, sə-
segregate (*n.*) ˈseg.rɪ.gət, -rə-, -geɪt, -gɪt (US) -rə.gɪt

segre|gate (*v.*) ˈseg.rɪ|.geɪt, -rə- (US) -rə- **-gates** -geɪts **-gating** -geɪ.tɪŋ (US) -geɪ.t̬ɪŋ **-gated** -geɪ.tɪd (US) -geɪ.t̬ɪd
segregation ˌseg.rɪˈgeɪ.ʃᵊn, -rəˈ- (US) -rəˈ-
segu|e ˈseg.weɪ, ˈseɪ.gweɪ, -gwi **-es** -z **-ing** -ɪŋ **-d** -d
seguidilla ˌseg.ɪˈdiː.jə, -li.ə (US) -əˈdiː.jə, ˌseɪ.gəˈ-, -ˈdiːl- **-s** -z
seich|e seɪʃ (US) seɪʃ, siːtʃ **-es** -ɪz
Seidlitz ˈsed.lɪts
seigneur senˈjɜːʳ, seɪˈnjɜːʳ; ˈseɪ.njəʳ (US) seɪˈnjɝː, senˈjɝː **-s** -z **-ial** -i.əl
seignior *lord:* ˈseɪ.njəʳ (US) ˈseɪ.njɚ; seɪˈnjɔːr **-s** -z
Seignior *surname:* ˈsiː.njəʳ (US) -njɚ
seignior|y ˈseɪ.njᵊr|.i (US) ˈseɪ- **-ies** -iz
Seiko® ˈseɪ.kəʊ (US) -koʊ
sein|e *net:* seɪn **-es** -z **-ing** -ɪŋ **-ed** -d
Seine *river in France:* seɪn, sen
Seinfeld ˈsaɪn.feld
Seir ˈsiː.əʳ (US) -ɚ
seis|e siːz **-es** -ɪz **-ing** -ɪŋ **-ed** -d
seisin ˈsiː.zɪn **-s** -z
seismic ˈsaɪz.mɪk (US) ˈsaɪz-, ˈsaɪs-
seismo- saɪz.məʊ-; saɪzˈmɒ- (US) saɪz.moʊ-, saɪs-, -mə-; saɪzˈmɑː-, saɪs-

Note: Prefix. Normally takes either primary or secondary stress on the first syllable, e.g. **seismograph** /ˈsaɪz.məʊ.grɑːf (US) -mə.græf/, **seismographic** /ˌsaɪz.məʊˈgræf.ɪk (US) -məˈ-/, or primary stress on the second syllable, e.g. **seismographer** /saɪzˈmɒg.rə.fəʳ (US) -ˈmɑː.grə.fɚ/.

seismograph ˈsaɪz.məʊ.grɑːf, -græf (US) -mə.græf, ˈsaɪs-, -moʊ- **-s** -s
seismograph|er saɪzˈmɒg.rə.f|əʳ (US) -ˈmɑː.grə.f|ɚ, saɪs- **-ers** -əz (US) -ɚz **-y** -i
seismographic ˌsaɪz.məʊˈgræf.ɪk (US) -məˈ-, saɪs-, -moʊˈ-
seismologic|al ˌsaɪz.məˈlɒdʒ.ɪ.k|ᵊl (US) -məˈlɑː.dʒɪ-, saɪs- **-ally** -ᵊl.i (US) -li
seismolog|y saɪzˈmɒl.ə.dʒ|i (US) -ˈmɑː.lə-, seɪs- **-ist/s** -ɪst/s
seismometer saɪzˈmɒm.ɪ.təʳ, ˈ-ə- (US) -ˈmɑː.mə.t̬ɚ, saɪs- **-s** -z
seizable ˈsiː.zə.bl̩
seiz|e siːz **-es** -ɪz **-ing** -ɪŋ **-ed** -d
seizin ˈsiː.zɪn **-s** -z
seizure ˈsiː.ʒəʳ (US) -ʒɚ **-s** -z
sejant ˈsiː.dʒənt
Sejanus sɪˈdʒeɪ.nəs, sə-, sedʒˈeɪ- (US) sɪˈdʒeɪ-
Sekhmet ˈsek.met
Sekondi-Takoradi ˌsek.ənˌdiː.tɑː.kəˈrɑː.di
selah ˈsiː.lə, -lɑː (US) ˈsiː.lə, ˈsel.ə, -ɑː **-s** -z
Selangor səˈlæŋ.əʳ, sɪ-, -ɔːʳ (US) selˈɑːŋ.gɔːr
Selassie səˈlæs.i (US) -ˈlæs-, -ˈlɑː.si
Selborne ˈsel.bɔːn, -bən (US) -bɔːrn, -bɚn
Selby ˈsel.bi
Selden ˈsel.dᵊn
seldom ˈsel.dəm
select sɪˈlekt, sə- (US) sə- **-ness** -nəs, -nɪs **-s** -s **-ing** -ɪŋ **-ed** -ɪd **seˌlect comˈmittee**
selection sɪˈlek.ʃᵊn, sə- (US) sə- **-s** -z
selective sɪˈlek.tɪv, sə- (US) sə- **-ly** -li **-ness** -nəs, -nɪs
selectivity ˌsɪl.ekˈtɪv.ə.ti, ˌsel-, ˌsiː.lekˈ-, -ɪ.ti; səˌlekˈ-, sɪ- (US) səˌlekˈtɪv.ə.t̬i, sɪ-; ˌsiː.lekˈ-
selector sɪˈlek.təʳ, sə- (US) səˈlek.tɚ **-s** -z
Selena sɪˈliː.nə, sə-
selenite *substance:* ˈsel.ɪ.naɪt, ˈ-ə- (US) ˈ-ə-
Selenite *inhabitant of moon:* sɪˈliː.naɪt, sə- (US) sɪˈliː-, sə-; ˈsel.ə- **-s** -s
selenium sɪˈliː.ni.əm, sə- (US) sə-
Seles ˈsel.ez, -əs
Seleuci|a sɪˈljuː.ʃi|.ə, sə-, -ˈluː-, -si- (US) səˈluː.ʃi-, ˈ-ʃ|ə **-an/s** -ən/z
Seleucid sɪˈljuː.sɪd, sə-, -ˈluː- (US) səˈluː- **-s** -z
Seleucus sɪˈljuː.kəs, sə-, -ˈluː- (US) səˈluː-
self- self-

Note: Many compounds beginning with **self-** have the stress pattern **ˌselfˈ-**; these are likely to undergo stress shift when a stressed syllable follows closely, especially in adjectives or adjectives derived from verbs.

sel|f sel|f **-ves** -vz
self-abuse ˌself.əˈbjuːs
self-addressed ˌself.əˈdrest
self-appointed ˌself.əˈpɔɪn.tɪd (US) -t̬ɪd
self-assurance ˌself.əˈʃʊə.rᵊnts (US) -ˈʃʊr.ᵊnts
self-assured ˌself.əˈʃʊəd (US) -ˈʃʊrd
self-catering ˌselfˈkeɪ.tᵊr.ɪŋ (US) -t̬ɚ-
self-centred, self-centered ˌselfˈsen.təd (US) -t̬ɚd **-ly** -li **-ness** -nəs, -nɪs
self-command ˌself.kəˈmɑːnd (US) -ˈmænd
self-confessed ˌself.kənˈfest
self-conscious ˌselfˈkɒn.tʃəs (US) -ˈkɑːnt.ʃəs **-ly** -li **-ness** -nəs, -nɪs
self-contained ˌself.kənˈteɪnd **-ly** -li **-ness** -nəs, -nɪs **-ment** -mənt
self-control ˌself.kənˈtrəʊl (US) -ˈtroʊl **-led** -d
self-critic|al ˌselfˈkrɪt.ɪ.k|ᵊl (US) -ˈkrɪt̬- **-ally** -ᵊl.i, -li
self-deception ˌself.dɪˈsep.ʃᵊn
self-defence, self-defense ˌself.dɪˈfents
self-denial ˌself.dɪˈnaɪ.əl
self-denying ˌself.dɪˈnaɪ.ɪŋ
self-destruct ˌself.dɪˈstrʌkt **-s** -s **-ing** -ɪŋ **-ed** -ɪd **-ive** -ɪv **-ion** -ʃᵊn
self-determination ˌself.dɪˌtɜː.mɪˈneɪ.ʃᵊn (US) -ˌtɝː-
self-discipline ˌselfˈdɪs.ɪ.plɪn, ˈ-ə- **-d** -d
self-drive ˌselfˈdraɪv
self-effac|ing ˌself.ɪˈfeɪ.s|ɪŋ **-ingly** -ɪŋ.li **-ement** -mənt
self-employed ˌself.ɪmˈplɔɪd, -emˈ-
self-esteem ˌself.ɪˈstiːm, -əˈ-
self-evident ˌselfˈev.ɪ.dᵊnt
self-explanatory ˌself.ɪkˈsplæn.ə.tᵊr.i, -ekˈ-, ˈ-ɪ- (US) -tɔːr-
self-fulfilling ˌself.fʊlˈfɪl.ɪŋ
self-governing ˌselfˈgʌv.ᵊn.ɪŋ (US) -ɚ.nɪŋ
self-government ˌselfˈgʌv.ᵊn.mənt, -ᵊm-, -və.mənt (US) -ɚn.mənt
self-heal ˌselfˈhiːl
self-help ˌselfˈhelp
self-image ˌselfˈɪm.ɪdʒ **-s** -ɪz
self-importan|ce ˌself.ɪmˈpɔː.tᵊn|ts (US) -ˈpɔːr- **-t/ly** -t/li
self-imposed ˌself.ɪmˈpəʊzd (US) -ˈpoʊzd
self-indulgen|ce ˌself.ɪnˈdʌl.dʒᵊn|ts **-t/ly** -t/li
self-inflicted ˌself.ɪnˈflɪk.tɪd
self-interest ˌselfˈɪn.trəst, -trɪst; -tᵊr.əst, -est, -ɪst (US) -ˈɪn.trɪst, -trəst, -trest; -t̬ɚ.ɪst, -əst, -est
selfish ˈsel.fɪʃ **-ly** -li **-ness** -nəs, -nɪs
selfless ˈsel.fləs, -flɪs **-ly** -li **-ness** -nəs, -nɪs
self-made ˌselfˈmeɪd
self-pity ˌselfˈpɪt.i (US) -ˈpɪt̬-
self-portrait ˌselfˈpɔː.trɪt, -trət, -treɪt (US) -ˈpɔːr.trɪt, -treɪt **-s** -s
self-possessed ˌself.pəˈzest
self-possession ˌself.pəˈzeʃ.ᵊn
self-preservation ˌselfˌprez.əˈveɪ.ʃᵊn (US) -ɚˈ-
self-proclaimed ˌself.prəʊˈkleɪmd (US) -proʊˈ-, -prəˈ-
self-raising ˌselfˈreɪ.zɪŋ **ˌself-raising ˈflour, selfˌ-raising ˈflour**
self-relian|ce ˌself.rɪˈlaɪ.ən|ts, -rəˈ- **-t** -t
self-respect ˌself.rɪˈspekt, -rəˈ-
self-respecting ˌself.rɪˈspek.tɪŋ, -rəˈ-
self-restraint ˌself.rɪˈstreɪnt, -rəˈ-
Selfridge ˈsel.frɪdʒ **-ˈs** -ɪz
Selfridges® ˈsel.frɪdʒ.ɪz
self-righteous ˌselfˈraɪ.tʃəs, -tjəs (US) -tʃəs **-ly** -li **-ness** -nəs, -nɪs
self-rising ˌselfˈraɪ.zɪŋ **ˌself-rising ˈflour, selfˌ-rising ˈflour**

self-rul|e ˌselfˈruːl **-ing** -ɪŋ
self-sacrific|e ˌselfˈsæk.rɪ.faɪs, -rə- **-ing/ly** -ɪŋ/li
selfsame ˈself.seɪm
self-satisfaction ˌselfˌsæt.ɪsˈfæk.ʃᵊn (US) -ˌsæt̬-
self-satisfied ˌselfˈsæt.ɪs.faɪd (US) -ˈsæt̬-
self-service ˌselfˈsɜː.vɪs (US) -ˈsɝː-
self-starter ˌselfˈstɑː.təʳ (US) -ˈstɑːr.t̬ɚ **-s** -z
self-styled ˌselfˈstaɪld
self-sufficien|cy ˌself.səˈfɪʃ.ᵊn|t.si **-t** -t
self-taught ˌselfˈtɔːt (US) -ˈtɑːt, -ˈtɔːt
self-will ˌselfˈwɪl **-ed** -d
self-winding ˌselfˈwaɪn.dɪŋ
Selhurst ˈsel.hɜːst (US) -hɝːst
Selina səˈliː.nə
Selkirk ˈsel.kɜːk (US) -kɝːk
sell (S) sel **-s** -z **-ing** -ɪŋ **sold** səʊld (US) soʊld **seller/s** ˈsel.əʳ/z (US) -ɚ/z
Sellafield ˈsel.ə.fiːld
Sellar ˈsel.əʳ (US) -ɚ
sell-by ˈsel.baɪ **ˈsell-by ˌdate**
Sellers ˈsel.əz (US) -ɚz
sellotap|e ˈsel.əʊ.teɪp (US) -oʊ- **-es** -s **-ing** -ɪŋ **-ed** -t
sellout ˈsel.aʊt **-s** -s
Selma ˈsel.mə
Selous səˈluː
Selsey ˈsel.si
Selston ˈsel.stᵊn
seltzer (S) ˈselt.səʳ (US) -sɚ **-s** -z
selva ˈsel.və **-s** -z
selvag|e, selvedg|e ˈsel.vɪdʒ **-es** -ɪz
selves *(plur. of* **self***)* selvz
Selwyn ˈsel.wɪn
Selznick ˈselz.nɪk
semantic sɪˈmæn.tɪk, sə-, semˈæn-, siːˈmæn- (US) səˈmæn.t̬ɪk, sɪ- **-s** -s **-ally** -ᵊl.i, -li
semanticism sɪˈmæn.tɪ.sɪ.zᵊm, sə-, semˈæn-, siːˈmæn- (US) səˈmæn.t̬ə-, sɪ-
semanticist sɪˈmæn.tɪ.sɪst, sə-, semˈæn-, siːˈmæn-, -tə- (US) səˈmæn.t̬ə-, sɪ- **-s** -s
semanticiz|e, -is|e sɪˈmæn.tɪ.saɪz, sə-, semˈæn-, siːˈmæn-, -tə- (US) səˈmæn.t̬ə-, sɪ- **-es** -ɪz **-ing** -ɪŋ **-ed** -d
semaphore ˈsem.ə.fɔːʳ (US) -fɔːr **-s** -z **-ing** -ɪŋ **-ed** -d
semaphoric ˌsem.əˈfɒr.ɪk (US) -ˈfɔːr- **-ally** -ᵊl.i, -li
semasiology sɪˌmeɪ.siˈɒl.ə.dʒi, sə-, semˌeɪ-, -ziˈ- (US) sɪˌmeɪ.siˈɑː.lə-
sematology ˌsem.əˈtɒl.ə.dʒi, ˌsiː.məˈ- (US) -ˈtɑː.lə-
semblanc|e ˈsem.blən*t*s **-es** -ɪz
seme siːm **-s** -z
Semele ˈsem.ɪ.li (US) ˈ-ə-
sememe ˈsiː.miːm (US) ˈsem.iːm **-s** -z
sememic sɪˈmiː.mɪk, sə- (US) sə-, sɪ- **-s** -s
semen ˈsiː.mən, -men (US) -mən
semester sɪˈmes.təʳ, sə- (US) səˈmes.tɚ **-s** -z
semi- sem.ɪ-, -i- (US) sem.ɪ-, -i-, -aɪ-, -ə-
Note: Many compounds beginning with **semi-** have the stress pattern ˈ**semi**ˌ-; these are likely to undergo stress shift when a stressed syllable follows closely, especially in adjectives and adjectives derived from verbs.
semi *house:* ˈsem.i **-s** -z
semiautomatic ˌsem.i.ɔː.təˈmæt.ɪk (US) -ɑː.t̬əˈmæt̬.ɪk, ˌ-aɪ-, -ɔː- **-s** -s
semiautonomous ˌsem.i.ɔːˈtɒn.ə.məs (US) -ɑːˈtɑː.nə-, ˌ-aɪ-, -ɔːˈ-
semibreve ˈsem.ɪ.briːv, -i- **-s** -z
semicircle ˈsem.ɪˌsɜː.kl̩, -iˌ- (US) -ˌsɝː-, -aɪˌ- **-s** -z
semicircular ˌsem.ɪˈsɜː.kjə.ləʳ, -iˈ-, -kjʊ- (US) -ˈsɝː.kjə.lɚ, -aiˈ-
semicolon ˌsem.ɪˈkəʊ.lən, ˈsem.ɪˌkəʊ-, -lɒn (US) ˈsem.ɪˌkoʊ.lən **-s** -z
semiconductivity ˌsem.ɪˌkɒn.dʌkˈtɪv.ə.ti, -iˌ-, -ɪ.ti (US) -ˌkɑːn.dʌkˈtɪv.ə.t̬i, -aɪˌ-
semiconduc|tor ˌsem.ɪ.kənˈdʌk|.təʳ, -i- (US) -tɚ, -aɪ- **-tors** -təz (US) -tɚz **-ting** -tɪŋ
semiconscious ˌsem.ɪˈkɒn.*t*ʃəs, -iˈ- (US) -ˈkɑːn-, -aɪˈ- **-ness** -nəs, -nɪs
semidesert ˌsem.ɪˈdez.ət, -iˈ- (US) -ɚt, -aɪˈ- **-s** -s
semidetached ˌsem.ɪ.dɪˈtætʃt, -i- (US) -ɪ-, -i-, ˌ-aɪ-
semifinal ˌsem.ɪˈfaɪ.nᵊl, -iˈ- (US) -ɪˈ-, -iˈ-, -aɪˈ- **-s** -z
semifinalist ˌsem.ɪˈfaɪ.nᵊl.ɪst, -iˈ- (US) -ɪˈ-, -iˈ-, -aɪˈ- **-s** -s
semiformal ˌsem.ɪˈfɔː.mᵊl, -iˈ- (US) -ˈfɔːr-, -aɪˈ-
Sémillon ˌseɪ.miːˈjɔ̃ː*ŋ* (US) -ˈjõʊ*n*, ˌsem.iːˈ-
seminal ˈsem.ɪ.nᵊl, ˈsiː.mɪ-, -mə- (US) ˈsem.ə- **-ly** -i
seminar ˈsem.ɪ.nɑːʳ, ˈ-ə- (US) -ə.nɑːr **-s** -z
seminarist ˈsem.ɪ.nᵊr.ɪst (US) ˌsem.ɪˈner- **-s** -s
seminar|y ˈsem.ɪ.nᵊr|.i (US) -ner- **-ies** -iz
seminiferous ˌsem.ɪˈnɪf.ᵊr.əs
Seminole ˈsem.ɪ.nəʊl (US) -noʊl **-s** -z
semiolog|y ˌsem.iˈɒl.ə.dʒ|i, ˌsiː.miˈ- (US) ˌsiː.miˈɑː.lə-, ˌsem.iˈ- **-ist/s** -ɪst/s
semiotic ˌsem.iˈɒt.ɪk, ˌsiː.miˈ- (US) ˌsiː.miˈɑː.t̬ɪk, ˌsem.iˈ- **-s** -s
Semipalatinsk ˌsem.i.pælˈæt.ɪnsk (US) -pəˈlɑː-
semiprecious ˌsem.ɪˈpreʃ.əs, -iˈ- (US) -ɪˈ-, -iˈ-, -aɪˈ-
semiprofessional ˌsem.ɪ.prəˈfeʃ.ᵊn.ᵊl, -i- (US) -ɪ.prəˈ-, -i-, ˌ-aɪ-, -proʊˈ-
semiquaver ˈsem.ɪˌkweɪ.vəʳ, -iˌ- (US) -ɪˌ-, -iˌ-, -vɚ **-s** -z
Semiramide ˌsem.ɪˈrɑː.mɪ.deɪ, -ˈræm.ɪ-, ˈ-ə-, -di
Semiramis semˈɪr.ə.mɪs, sɪˈmɪr- (US) sɪˈmɪr-
semiretired ˌsem.ɪ.rɪˈtaɪəd, -i- (US) -taɪrd, ˌ-aɪ-
semiretirement ˌsem.ɪ.rɪˈtaɪə.mənt, -i- (US) -ˈtaɪr-, ˌ-aɪ-
semiskilled ˌsem.ɪˈskɪld, -iˈ- (US) -ɪˈ-, -iˈ-, -aɪˈ-
semiskimmed ˌsem.ɪˈskɪmd, -iˈ- (US) -ɪˈ-, -iˈ-, -aɪˈ-
Semite ˈsiː.maɪt, ˈsem.aɪt (US) ˈsem.aɪt **-s** -s
Semitic sɪˈmɪt.ɪk, sə-, semˈɪt- (US) səˈmɪt̬-
Semitism ˈsem.ɪ.tɪ.zᵊm, ˈ-ə- (US) ˈ-ə-
semitone ˈsem.ɪ.təʊn, -i- (US) -toʊn, -aɪ- **-s** -z
semitrailer ˈsem.ɪˌtreɪ.ləʳ, -iˌ- (US) -lɚ, -aɪˌ- **-s** -z
semitropical ˌsem.ɪˈtrɒp.ɪ.kᵊl, -iˈ- (US) -ˈtrɑː.pɪ-, -aɪˈ-
semivowel ˈsem.ɪˌvaʊəl **-s** -z
semolina ˌsem.ᵊlˈiː.nə (US) -əˈliː-
semology semˈɒl.ə.dʒi, siːˈmɒl- (US) semˈɑː.lə-, siːˈmɑː-
Semon ˈsiː.mən
Sempill ˈsem.pᵊl
sempiternal ˌsem.pɪˈtɜː.nᵊl (US) -ˈtɝː- **-ly** -i
Semple ˈsem.pl̩
semplice ˈsem.plɪ.tʃeɪ
sempre ˈsem.preɪ
sempstress ˈsem*p*.strɪs, -strəs (US) -strɪs **-es** -ɪz
Semtex® ˈsem.teks
sen sen
senary ˈsiː.nᵊr.i
senate (S) ˈsen.ɪt, -ət (US) -ɪt **-s** -s
senator (S) ˈsen.ə.təʳ, ˈ-ɪ- (US) -ə.t̬ɚ **-s** -z
senatorial ˌsen.əˈtɔː.ri.əl (US) -ˈtɔːr.i- **-ly** -i
send send **-s** -z **-ing** -ɪŋ **sent** sent **sender/s** ˈsen.dəʳ/z (US) -dɚ/z
Sendai ˈsen.daɪ
Sendak ˈsen.dæk
send-off ˈsend.ɒf (US) -ɑːf **-s** -s
send-up ˈsend.ʌp **-s** -s
sene ˈseɪ.neɪ
Seneca ˈsen.ɪ.kə **-s** -z
Senegal ˌsen.ɪˈgɔːl (US) ˌsen.ɪˈgɔːl, -ˈgɑːl; ˈsen.ə.gᵊl
Senegalese ˌsen.ɪ.gəˈliːz, -gɔːˈ- (US) -gəˈ-
Senegambia ˌsen.ɪˈgæm.bi.ə
senescen|ce sɪˈnes.ᵊn|*t*s, sə-, senˈes- (US) səˈnes- **-t** -t

seneschal ˈsen.ɪ.ʃᵊl US ˈ-ə- -s -z

Senghenydd ˌseŋˈhen.ɪð

Senghor ˈseŋ.gɔːʳ *as if French:* ˈsæ̃ŋ- US sæ̃nˈgɔːr

senhor (S) senˈjɔːʳ US -ˈjɔːr, seɪˈnjɔːr -s -z -es -z *stress shift:* ˌSenhor Soˈares

senhora (S) senˈjɔː.rə US -ˈjɔːr.ə, seɪˈnjɔːr- -s -z

senhorita (S) ˌsen.jɔːˈriː.tə, -jəˈ- US ˌsen.jəˈriː.t̬ə, ˌseɪ.njəˈ-, -njɔːˈ- -s -z

senile ˈsiː.naɪl US ˈsiː-, ˈsen.aɪl

senility sɪˈnɪl.ə.ti, sə-, senˈɪl-, -ɪ.ti US səˈnɪl.ə.t̬i

senior (S) ˈsiː.ni.əʳ, ˈnjəʳ US -njɚ -s -z ˌsenior ˈcitizen

seniorit|y ˌsiː.niˈɒr.ə.t|i, -ɪ.t|i US siːˈnjɔːr.ə.t̬|i -ies -iz

seniti ˈsen.ɪ.ti US -ə.t̬i

Senlac ˈsen.læk

senna (S) ˈsen.ə

Sennacherib senˈæk.ə.rɪb, sɪˈnæk-, sə- US səˈnæk.ɚ.ɪb

sennet ˈsen.ɪt, -ət US -ɪt

sennight ˈsen.aɪt US -aɪt, -ɪt -s -s

señor, senor (S) senˈjɔːʳ US -ˈjɔːr, seɪˈnjɔːr -s -z *stress shift:* ˌSeñor ˈLopez

señora, senora (S) senˈjɔː.rə US -ˈjɔːr.ə, seɪˈnjɔːr- -s -z

señorita, senorita (S) ˌsen.jɔːˈriː.tə, -jəˈ- US ˌsen.jəˈriː.t̬ə, ˌseɪ.njəˈ-, -njɔːˈ- *stress shift:* ˌSeñorita ˈLopez

sensate ˈsen.seɪt US -seɪt, -sɪt -ly -li

sensation senˈseɪ.ʃᵊn, sᵊn- US sen- -s -z

sensational senˈseɪ.ʃᵊn.ᵊl, sᵊn-, -ˈseɪʃ.nᵊl US sen- -ly -i

sensational|ism senˈseɪ.ʃᵊn.ᵊl|.ɪ.zᵊm, sᵊn-, -ˈseɪʃ.nᵊl- US sen- -ist/s -ɪst/s

sensationaliz|e, -is|e ˌsenˈseɪ.ʃᵊn.ᵊl.aɪz -es -ɪz -ing -ɪŋ -ed -d

sens|e sen*t*s -es -ɪz -ing -ɪŋ -ed -d ˌsense of ˈhumo(u)r

senseless ˈsen*t*.sləs, -slɪs -ly -li -ness -nəs, -nɪs

sensibilit|y ˌsen*t*.sɪˈbɪl.ə.t|i, -səˈ-, -ɪ.t|i US -səˈbɪl.ə.t̬|i -ies -iz

sensib|le ˈsen*t*.sɪ.b|l̩, -sə- US -sə- -ly -li

sensitive ˈsen*t*.sɪ.tɪv, -sə- US -sə.t̬ɪv -s -z -ly -li -ness -nəs, -nɪs

sensitivit|y ˌsen*t*.sɪˈtɪv.ə.t|i, -səˈ-, -ɪ.t|i US -səˈtɪv.ə.t̬|i -ies -iz

sensitization, -isa- ˌsen*t*.sɪ.taɪˈzeɪ.ʃᵊn, -sə-, -tɪˈ- US -sə.tɪˈ-

sensitiz|e, -is|e ˈsen*t*.sɪ.taɪz, -sə- US -sə- -es -ɪz -ing -ɪŋ -ed -d

Sensodyne® ˈsen*t*.səʊ.daɪn US -soʊ-, -sə-

sensor ˈsen*t*.səʳ US -sɚ -s -z

sensorial sen*t*ˈsɔː.ri.əl US -ˈsɔːr.i- -ly -i

sensor|y ˈsen*t*.sᵊr|.i -ily -ᵊl.i, -ɪ.li

sensual ˈsen*t*.sjʊəl, -sju.əl, -ʃʊəl, -ʃu.əl US -ʃu.əl -ly -i -ness -nəs, -nɪs

sensual|ism ˈsen*t*.sjʊə.l|ɪ.zᵊm, -sju.ᵊl|.ɪ-, -ʃʊə.l|ɪ-, -ʃu.ᵊl|.ɪ- US -ʃu.ə.l|ɪ- -ist/s -ɪst/s

sensuality ˌsen*t*.sjuˈæl.ə.ti, -ʃuˈ-, -ɪ.ti US -ʃuˈæl.ə.t̬i

sensuous ˈsen*t*.sjʊəs, -sju.əs, -ʃʊəs, -ʃu.əs US -ʃu.əs -ly -li -ness -nəs, -nɪs

Sensurround® ˈsen*t*.sə.raʊnd

sent (*from* **send**) sent

sentenc|e ˈsen.tən*t*s US -t̬ən*t*s, -tᵊn*t*s -es -ɪz -ing -ɪŋ -ed -t

sentential senˈten.*t*ʃᵊl, sən- US senˈten*t*.ʃᵊl -ly -li

sententious senˈten.*t*ʃəs, sən- US senˈten*t*.ʃəs -ly -li -ness -nəs, -nɪs

sentience ˈsen.*t*ʃᵊn*t*s, -*t*ʃi.ən*t*s US ˈsen*t*.ʃᵊn*t*s, -ʃi.ən*t*s

sentient ˈsen.*t*ʃᵊnt, -*t*ʃi.ənt US ˈsen*t*.ʃᵊnt, -ʃi.ənt -ly -li

sentiment ˈsen.tɪ.mənt, -tə- US -t̬ə- -s -s

sentimental ˌsen.tɪˈmen.tᵊl, -təˈ- US -t̬əˈmen.t̬ᵊl -ly -i -ism -ɪ.zᵊm -ist/s -ɪst/s

sentimentality ˌsen.tɪ.menˈtæl.ə.ti, -tə-, -mən-, -ɪ.ti US -t̬ə.menˈtæl.ə.t̬i

sentimentalization, -isa- ˌsen.tɪ.men.tᵊl.aɪˈzeɪ.ʃᵊn, -ˌmen-, -tə-, -ɪˈ- US -t̬əˌmen.t̬ᵊl.ɪˈ-

sentimentaliz|e, -is|e ˌsen.tɪˈmen.tᵊl.aɪz, -təˈ- US -t̬əˈmen.t̬ə.laɪz -es -ɪz -ing -ɪŋ -ed -d

sentinel ˈsen.tɪ.nᵊl, -tə- US -t̬ɪ-, -tᵊn.ᵊl -s -z

sentr|y ˈsen.tr|i -ies -iz ˈsentry ˌbox

sentry-go ˈsen.tri.gəʊ US -goʊ

senza ˈsent.sə

Seoul səʊl US soʊl

sepal ˈsep.əl, ˈsiː.pəl US ˈsiː.pᵊl -s -z

separability ˌsep.ᵊr.əˈbɪl.ə.ti, -ɪ.ti US -ə.t̬i

separab|le ˈsep.ᵊr.ə.b|l̩ -ly -li -leness -l̩.nəs, -l̩.nɪs

separate (*adj.*) ˈsep.ᵊr.ət, -ɪt, ˈ-rət, -rɪt US -ɚ.ɪt, ˈ-rɪt -ly -li -ness -nəs, -nɪs

separ|ate (*v.*) ˈsep.ᵊr|.eɪt US -ə.r|eɪt -ates -eɪts -ating -eɪ.tɪŋ US -eɪ.t̬ɪŋ -ated -eɪ.tɪd US -eɪ.t̬ɪd -ator/s -eɪ.təʳ/z US -eɪ.t̬ɚ/z

separates ˈsep.ᵊr.əts, -ɪts, ˈ-rəts, ˈ-rɪts US -ɚ.ɪts, ˈ-rɪts

separation ˌsep.ᵊrˈeɪ.ʃᵊn US -əˈreɪ- -s -z

separat|ism ˈsep.ᵊr.ə.t|ɪ.zᵊm, ˈ-rə- -ist/s -ɪst/s

Sephardi səˈfɑː.di, sefˈɑː- US səˈfɑːr.di; -ˌfɑːrˈdi: **Sephardim** səˈfɑː.dɪm, sefˈɑː- US səˈfɑːr.dɪm; -ˌfɑːrˈdiːm

Sephardic səˈfɑː.dɪk, sefˈɑː- US səˈfɑːr-

sepia ˈsiː.pi.ə

sepoy ˈsiː.pɔɪ -s -z

seppuku sepˈuː.kuː

seps|is ˈsep.s|ɪs -es -iːz

Sept. (*abbrev. for* **September**) sepˈtem.bəʳ, səp-, sɪp- US sepˈtem.bɚ

September sepˈtem.bəʳ, səp-, sɪp- US sepˈtem.bɚ -s -z

Septembrist sepˈtem.brɪst, səp-, sɪp- US sep- -s -s

septennial sepˈten.i.əl

septet, septette sepˈtet -s -s

septic ˈsep.tɪk ˌseptic ˈtank, ˈseptic ˌtank US ˈseptic ˌtank

septic(a)emia ˌsep.tɪˈsiː.mi.ə US -təˈ-

septillion sepˈtɪl.jən -s -z

Septimus ˈsep.tɪ.məs

septuagenarian ˌsep.tjʊə.dʒɪˈneə.ri.ən, -tʃʊə-, -dʒəˈ- US -tu.ə.dʒəˈner.i-, -tju- -s -z

Septuagesima ˌsep.tjʊəˈdʒes.ɪ.mə, -tʃʊəˈ-, ˈ-ə- US -tu.əˈdʒes.ɪ-, -tju-, -ˈdʒeɪ.zɪ-

Septuagint ˈsep.tjʊə.dʒɪnt, -tʃʊə- US -tu.ə-, -tju-

sept|um ˈsep.t|əm -ums -əmz -a -ə

septuple ˈsep.tjʊ.pl, -tjuː- US sepˈtʌp.əl; ˈtuː.pəl

septuplet sepˈtjuː.plət, -plɪt, ˈsep.tjʊ.plət, -plɪt US -ˈtuː- -s -s

sepulcher ˈsep.ᵊl.kə US -kɚ -s -z

sepulchral sɪˈpʌl.krᵊl, sə-, sepˈʌl- US səˈpʌl- -ly -i

sepulchre ˈsep.ᵊl.kəʳ US -kɚ -s -z

sepulture ˈsep.ᵊl.tʃəʳ, -ˌtjʊəʳ US -tʃɚ

sequel ˈsiː.kwᵊl -s -z

sequel|a sɪˈkwiː.l|ə, sə- US sɪˈkwiː-, -ˈkwel|.ə -ae -iː

sequenc|e ˈsiː.kwən*t*s US -kwən*t*s, -kwen*t*s -es -ɪz -ing -ɪŋ -ed -t

sequential sɪˈkwen.*t*ʃᵊl US -ˈkwen*t*.ʃᵊl -ly -i

sequest|er sɪˈkwes.t|əʳ, sə- US sɪˈkwes.t|ɚ -ers -əz US -ɚz -ering -ᵊr.ɪŋ -ered -əd US -ɚd

seques|trate sɪˈkwes|.treɪt, sə-; ˈsiː.kwə.s|treɪt US sɪˈkwes|.treɪt; ˈsiː.kwə.s|treɪt, ˈsek.wə- -trates -treɪts -trating -treɪ.tɪŋ US -treɪ.t̬ɪŋ -trated -treɪ.tɪd US -treɪ.t̬ɪd

sequestration ˌsiː.kwesˈtreɪ.ʃᵊn, ˌsek.wesˈ-, -wəˈstreɪ-, -wɪˈ- US ˌsiː.kwəˈstreɪ-, ˌsek.wəˈ-; sɪˌkwesˈtreɪ- -s -z

sequin ˈsiː.kwɪn -s -z -(n)ed -d

sequoia sɪˈkwɔɪ.ə, sekˈwɔɪ.ə US sɪˈkwɔɪ.ə -s -z

seraglio serˈɑː.li.əʊ, sɪˈrɑː-, sə-, -ˈɑːl.jəʊ US sɪˈræl.joʊ, -ˈrɑːl- -s -z

serai serˈaɪ, səˈraɪ US sɪˈreɪ.i, sə- -s -z

seraph (S) 'ser.əf **-s** -s **-im** -ɪm
seraphic ser'æf.ɪk, sɪ'ræf-, sə- (US) sə'ræf- **-al** -ᵊl **-ally** -ᵊl.i, -li
Serapis 'ser.ə.pɪs, sə'reɪ-
Serb sɜːb (US) sɝːb **-s** -z
Serbi|a 'sɜː.bi|.ə (US) 'sɝː- **-an/s** -ən/z
Serbo-Croat ˌsɜː.bəʊ'krəʊ.æt (US) ˌsɝː.boʊ'kroʊ- **-s** -s
Serbo-Croatian ˌsɜː.bəʊ.krəʊ'eɪ.ʃᵊn (US) ˌsɝː.boʊ.kroʊ'- **-s** -z
sere sɪəʳ (US) sɪr **-s** -z
Serena sə'riː.nə, sɪ-, -'reɪ- (US) sə'riː-
serenad|e ˌser.ə'neɪd, -ɪ'- (US) -ə'- **-es** -z **-ing** -ɪŋ **-ed** -ɪd
serenata ˌser.ɪ'nɑː.tə, -ə'- (US) -ə'nɑː.t̬ə **-s** -z
serendipit|y ˌser.ᵊn'dɪp.ə.t|i, -en'-, -ɪ.t|i (US) -ən'dɪp.ə.t̬|i **-ous** -əs
seren|e sɪ'riːn, sə- (US) sə- **-est** -ɪst, -əst **-ely** -li
Serengeti ˌser.ᵊn'get.i, -ᵊŋ'-, -ɪn'-, -ɪŋ'- (US) -ᵊn'get̬-
serenity sɪ'ren.ɪ.ti, sə-, -ə.ti (US) sə'ren.ə.t̬i
serf sɜːf (US) sɝːf **-s** -s **-dom** -dəm
serg|e (S) sɜːdʒ (US) sɝːdʒ **-es** -ɪz
sergeant (S) 'sɑː.dʒᵊnt (US) 'sɑːr- **-s** -s **ˌsergeant 'major**
sergeant-at-arms, ˌsɑː.dʒᵊnt.ət'ɑːmz (US) ˌsɑːr.dʒᵊnt.ət'ɑːrmz **sergeants-at-arms** ˌsɑː.dʒᵊnts- (US) ˌsɑːr.dʒᵊnts-
Sergei 'seə.geɪ, 'sɜː-, -'- (US) 'ser.geɪ, 'sɝː-
serial 'sɪə.ri.əl (US) 'sɪr.i- **-s** -z **'serial ˌkiller; 'serial ˌnumber**
serialization, -isa- ˌsɪə.ri.ᵊl.aɪ'zeɪ.ʃᵊn, -ɪ'- (US) ˌsɪr.i.ᵊl.ɪ'- **-s** -z
serializ|e, -is|e 'sɪə.ri.ᵊl.aɪz (US) 'sɪr.i.ə.laɪz **-es** -ɪz **-ing** -ɪŋ **-ed** -d
seriatim ˌsɪə.ri'eɪ.tɪm, ˌser.i'-, -'ɑː- (US) ˌsɪr.i'eɪ.t̬ɪm
series 'sɪə.riːz, -rɪz (US) 'sɪr.iːz, 'siː.riːz
serif 'ser.ɪf **-s** -s
Serifos 'ser.ɪ.fɒs (US) sə'raɪ.fəs; 'ser.ɪ.fɑːs
serin 'ser.ɪn **-s** -z
seringa sɪ'rɪŋ.gə, sə- (US) sə- **-s** -z
Seringapatam səˌrɪŋ.gə.pə'tɑːm, sɪ-, -'tæm
seriocomic ˌsɪə.ri.əʊ'kɒm.ɪk (US) ˌsɪr.i.oʊ'kɑː.mɪk **-ally** -ᵊl.i, -li
serious 'sɪə.ri.əs (US) 'sɪr.i- **-ly** -li **-ness** -nəs, -nɪs
serjeant (S) 'sɑː.dʒᵊnt (US) 'sɑːr- **-s** -s **ˌserjeant-at-'arms**
Serjeantson 'sɑː.dʒᵊnt.sᵊn (US) 'sɑːr-
sermon 'sɜː.mən (US) 'sɝː- **-s** -z
sermonette ˌsɜː.mə'net (US) ˌsɝː- **-s** -s
sermoniz|e, -is|e 'sɜː.mə.naɪz (US) 'sɝː- **-es** -ɪz **-ing** -ɪŋ **-ed** -d
serolog|y sɪ'rɒl.ə.dʒ|i, sɪə- (US) sɪ'rɑː.lə- **-ist/s** -ɪst/s
seronegative ˌsɪə.rəʊ'neg.ə.tɪv (US) ˌsɪr.oʊ'neg.ə.t̬ɪv
seropositive ˌsɪə.rəʊ'pɒz.ɪ.tɪv, '-ə- (US) ˌsɪr.oʊ'pɑː.zə.t̬ɪv
Serota sə'rəʊ.tə, sɪ- (US) -'roʊ.t̬ə
serotonin ˌser.ə'təʊ.nɪn, ˌsɪə.rə'- (US) ˌser.ə'toʊ-, ˌsɪr-
serous 'sɪə.rəs (US) 'sɪr.əs
Serpell 'sɜː.pᵊl (US) 'sɝː-
Serpens 'sɜː.penz, -pᵊnz (US) 'sɝː-
serpent 'sɜː.pᵊnt (US) 'sɝː- **-s** -s
serpentine (S) 'sɜː.pᵊn.taɪn (US) 'sɝː-
SERPS, Serps sɜːps (US) sɝːps
serrate 'ser.ɪt, -eɪt, -ət (US) -eɪt, -ɪt
serrated sɪ'reɪ.tɪd, sə-, ser'eɪ- (US) 'ser.eɪ.t̬ɪd
serration sɪ'reɪ.ʃᵊn, sə-, ser'eɪ- (US) sə'reɪ-, ser'eɪ- **-s** -z
serried 'ser.id **ˌserried 'ranks**
ser|um 'sɪə.r|əm (US) 'sɪr|.əm **-ums** -əmz **-a** -ə
servant 'sɜː.vᵊnt (US) 'sɝː- **-s** -s
serv|e sɜːv (US) sɝːv **-es** -z **-ing** -ɪŋ **-ed** -d **-er/s** -əʳ/z (US) -ɚ/z
server|y 'sɜː.vᵊr|.i (US) 'sɝː- **-ies** -iz
servic|e (S) 'sɜː.vɪs (US) 'sɝː- **-es** -ɪz **-ing** -ɪŋ **-ed** -t **'service ˌcharge; 'service ˌstation**
serviceability ˌsɜː.vɪ.sə'bɪl.ə.ti, -ɪ.ti (US) ˌsɝː.vɪ.sə'bɪl.ə.t̬i
serviceab|le 'sɜː.vɪ.sə.b|l̩ (US) 'sɝː- **-ly** -li **-leness** -l̩.nəs, -l̩.nɪs
service|man 'sɜː.vɪs|.mən, -mæn (US) 'sɝː- **-men** -mən
service|woman 'sɜː.vɪs|ˌwʊm.ən (US) 'sɝː- **-women** -wɪm.ɪn
serviette ˌsɜː.vi'et, -s (US) ˌsɝː-
servile 'sɜː.vaɪl (US) 'sɝː.vᵊl, -vaɪl **-ly** -li
servility sɜː'vɪl.ə.ti, -ɪ.ti (US) sɝː'vɪl.ə.t̬i
serving 'sɜː.vɪŋ (US) 'sɝː- **-s** -z
serving-spoon 'sɜː.vɪŋ.spuːn (US) 'sɝː- **-s** -z
servitor 'sɜː.vɪ.təʳ (US) 'sɝː.və.t̬ɚ **-s** -z
servitude 'sɜː.vɪ.tjuːd, -tʃuːd (US) 'sɝː.və.tuːd, -tjuːd
servo 'sɜː.vəʊ (US) 'sɝː.voʊ **-s** -z
servomechanism 'sɜː.vəʊˌmek.ə.nɪ.zᵊm, ˌsɜː.vəʊ'mek- (US) ˌsɝː.voʊ'mek- **-s** -z
servomotor 'sɜː.vəʊˌməʊ.təʳ (US) 'sɝː.voʊˌmoʊ.t̬ɚ **-s** -z
sesame (S) 'ses.ə.mi **-s** -z **'sesame ˌseed**
Sesotho ses'uː.tuː, sɪ'suː-, sə-, -'səʊ.θəʊ (US) ses'uː.tuː, sɪ'suː-, sə-, -'soʊ.θoʊ
sesqui- 'ses.kwɪ-
sesquicentennial ˌses.kwɪ.sen'ten.i.əl, -sᵊn'- (US) -sen'-
sesquipedalian ˌses.kwɪ.pɪ'deɪ.li.ən, -pə'-, -ped'eɪ- (US) -pə'deɪ-, -'deɪl.jə
sessile 'ses.aɪl (US) -ɪl, -aɪl
session 'seʃ.ᵊn **-s** -z
sessional 'seʃ.ᵊn.ᵊl **-s** -z
sesterc|e 'ses.tɜːs, -təs (US) -tɝːs **-es** -ɪ
sesterti|um ses'tɜː.ti|.əm, -ʃi- (US) -'tɝː.ʃi-, '-ʃ|əm **-a** -ə
sestet ses'tet (US) ses'tet, '-- **-s** -s
set set **-s** -s **-ting** -ɪŋ (US) 'set̬.ɪŋ **ˌset 'book; ˌset 'piece;** (US) **'set ˌpiece; ˌse 'point** (US) **'set ˌpoint**
setaceous sɪ'teɪ.ʃəs, sə- (US) sɪ- **-ly** -li
setback 'set.bæk **-s** -s
Setchell 'setʃ.ᵊl
Setebos 'set.ɪ.bɒs (US) 'set̬.ə.bɑːs
Seth seθ
set-off 'set.ɒf (US) -ɑːf **-s** -s
seton (S) 'siː.tᵊn **-s** -z
setsquare 'set.skweəʳ (US) -skwer **-s** -z
sett set **-s** -s
settee set'iː **-s** -z
setter (S) 'set.əʳ (US) 'set̬.ɚ **-s** -z
setting 'set.ɪŋ (US) 'set̬.ɪŋ **-s** -z
settl|e (S) 'set.l̩ (US) 'set̬- **-es** -z **-ing** -ɪŋ, 'set.lɪŋ **-ed** -d
settlement 'set.l̩.mənt (US) 'set̬- **-s** -s
settler 'set.l̩.əʳ, '-ləʳ (US) 'set.lɚ, 'set̬.l̩.ɚ **-s** -z
set-to 'set.tuː
Setúbal sə'tuː.bəl, set'uː-
setup 'set.ʌp (US) 'set̬- **-s** -s
Seurat 'sɜː.rɑː, -'- (US) sɜː'rɑː
Seuss sjuːs (US) suːs
Sevastopol sə'væst.ə.pɒl (US) -poʊl
Seve 'sev.i
seven 'sev.ᵊn **-s** -z **-fold** -fəʊld (US) -foʊld **ˌseven 'seas**
sevenish 'sev.ᵊn.ɪʃ
Sevenoaks 'sev.ᵊn.əʊks (US) -oʊks
seven|pence 'sev.ᵊn|.pənts, -ᵊm- (US) -ᵊn- **-penny** -pən.i
Note: See note under **penny**.
seventeen ˌsev.ᵊn'tiːn **-s** -z **-th/s** -tθ/s
seventh 'sev.ᵊntθ **-s** -s **-ly** -li **ˌseventh 'heaven**
sevent|y 'sev.ᵊn.t|i (US) -t̬|i **-ies** -iz **-ieth/s** -i.əθ/s, -i.ɪθ/s
seventy-eight, 78 ˌsev.ᵊn.ti'eɪt (US) -t̬ **-s** -s
sev|er 'sev|.əʳ (US) -ɚ **-ers** -əz (US) -ɚz **-ering** -ᵊr.ɪŋ **-ered** -əd (US) -ɚd
several 'sev.ᵊr.ᵊl, '-rᵊl **-ly** -i
severalty 'sev.ᵊr.ᵊl.ti, '-rᵊl-
severance 'sev.ᵊr.ənts **'severance ˌp**
sever|e sɪ'vɪəʳ, sə- (US) sə'vɪr **-er** -əʳ (US) -ɚ **-est** -ɪst, -əst **-ely** -li **-eness** -nəs, -nɪs
severit|y sɪ'ver.ə.t|i, sə-, -ɪ.t|i (US) sə'ver.ə.t̬|i **-ies** -iz
Severn 'sev.ᵊn (US) -ɚn
Severus sɪ'vɪə.rəs, sə- (US) sə'vɪr.əs

Pronouncing the letters SH

The consonant digraph **sh** is most commonly pronounced /ʃ/, e.g.:

sheep /ʃiːp/

In addition

When the two letters come together due to the addition of a prefix, the pronunciation is /s.h/, or /s/ alone with a silent **h**, e.g.:

mishap /ˈmɪs.hæp/
dishonest /dɪsˈɒn.ɪst/ (US) /-ˈɑː.nɪst/

seviche sevˈiːʃ
Sevier ˈsev.i.əʳ (US) -ɚ; səˈvɪr
Seville səˈvɪl, sɪ-, sevˈɪl; ˈsev.ɪl, -əl *stress shift, see compound:* (US) səˈvɪl ˌ**Seville ˈorange**
Sèvres ˈseɪ.vrə, -vəʳ (US) -vrə
sew səʊ (US) soʊ **-s** -z **-ing** -ɪŋ **-ed** -d **-n** -n
sewage ˈsuː.ɪdʒ, ˈsjuː- (US) ˈsuː-
Sewanee səˈwɒn.i (US) -ˈwɑː.ni, -ˈwɔː-
Seward ˈsiː.wəd (US) ˈsuː.ɚd; ˈsiː.wɚd
Sewell ˈsjuː.əl, sjʊəl (US) ˈsuː.əl
sewer *one who sews:* ˈsəʊ.əʳ (US) ˈsoʊ.ɚ **-s** -z
sewer *drain:* sʊəʳ, sjʊəʳ (US) ˈsuː.ɚ **-s** -z
sewerage ˈsʊə.rɪdʒ, ˈsjʊə- (US) ˈsuː.ɚ.ɪdʒ
sewing ˈsəʊ.ɪŋ (US) ˈsoʊ- ˈ**sewing maˌchine**
sewn *(from* **sew***)* səʊn (US) soʊn
sex seks **-es** -ɪz **-ing** -ɪŋ **-ed** -t ˈ**sex apˌpeal**; ˈ**sex ˌchange**; ˈ**sex ˌkitten**; ˈ**sex ˌobject**
sexagenarian ˌsek.sə.dʒɪˈneə.ri.ən, -dʒəˈ- (US) -dʒɪˈner.i- **-s** -z
Sexagesi|ma ˌsek.səˈdʒes.ɪ|.mə (US) -ˈdʒes.ɪ|.mə, -ˈdʒeɪ.zɪ-
sexagesimal ˌsek.səˈdʒes.ɪ.məl, ˈ-ə-
sex|ism ˈsek.s|ɪ.zəm **-ist/s** -ɪst/s
sexless ˈsek.sləs, -slɪs **-ness** -nəs, -nɪs
sexolog|y sekˈsɒl.ə.dʒ|i (US) -ˈsɑː.lə- **-ist/s** -ɪst/s
sexploitation ˌsek.splɔɪˈteɪ.ʃən
sexpot ˈseks.pɒt (US) -pɑːt **-s** -s
sext sekst
sextant ˈsek.stənt **-s** -s
sextet, **sextette** sekˈstet **-s** -s
sextillion sekˈstɪl.jən, -i.ən (US) ˈ-jən **-s** -z
sexto ˈsek.stəʊ (US) -stoʊ **-s** -z
sexton **(S)** ˈsek.stən **-s** -z
sextuple ˈsek.stjʊ.pl̩, -stjə-; sekˈstjuː- (US) sekˈstuː-, -ˈstjuː-; ˈsek.stə.pl̩
sextuplet ˈsek.stjʊ.plet, -stjə-; -plət, -plɪt, sekˈstjuː- (US) sekˈstʌp.lɪt, -ˈstuː.plɪt, -ˈstjuː-; ˈsek.stə- **-s** -s
sexual ˈsek.ʃʊəl, -ʃu.əl, -sjʊəl, -sju.əl (US) -ʃu.əl **-ly** -i ˌ**sexual ˈintercourse**; ˌ**sexual reˈlations**; ˌ**sexual reproˈduction**
sexuality ˌsek.ʃuˈæl.ə.ti, -sjuˈ-, -ɪ.ti (US) -ʃuˈæl.ə.t̬i
sex|y ˈsek.s|i **-ier** -i.əʳ (US) -i.ɚ **-iest** -i.ɪst, -i.əst **-ily** -ɪ.li, -əl.i **-iness** -ɪ.nəs, -ɪ.nɪs
Sey seɪ
Seychelles seɪˈʃelz, ˈ-- (US) seɪˈʃelz, -ˈʃel
Seymour ˈsiː.mɔːʳ, ˈseɪ-, -məʳ (US) -mɔːr
Note: /ˈseɪ-/ chiefly in families of Scottish origin.
Sfax sfæks (US) sfɑːks
sferics ˈsfer.ɪks (US) ˈsfɪr-, ˈsfer-
sforzando sfɔːtˈsæn.dəʊ (US) sfɔːrtˈsɑːn.doʊ
sgian-dhu ˌskiː.ənˈduː, ˌskɪənˈ- (US) ˌskiː.ənˈ- **-s** -z
sgraffit|o sgræfˈiː.t|əʊ (US) skræfˈiː.t|oʊ, zgrɑːˈfiː- **-i** -i
Sgt. *(abbrev. for* **Sergeant***)* ˈsɑː.dʒənt (US) ˈsɑːr-
sh, **shh, ssh** ʃ
Note: Used to command silence.
Shabbat ʃəˈbæt
shabb|y ˈʃæb|.i **-ier** -i.əʳ (US) -i.ɚ **-iest** -i.ɪst, -i.əst **-ily** -ɪ.li, -əl.i **-iness** -ɪ.nəs, -ɪ.nɪs
Shabuoth ˈʃæb.u.ɒt (US) ˌʃɑː.vuːˈɑːt; ʃəˈvuː.oʊt, -oʊθ
shack ʃæk **-s** -s
shackl|e **(S)** ˈʃæk.l̩ **-es** -z **-ing** -ɪŋ, ˈʃæk.lɪŋ **-ed** -d
Shackleton ˈʃæk.l̩.tən
shad ʃæd **-s** -z
Shadbolt ˈʃæd.bəʊlt (US) -boʊlt
shaddock **(S)** ˈʃæd.ək
shad|e ʃeɪd **-es** -z **-ing** -ɪŋ **-ed** -ɪd
shadoof ʃædˈuːf, ʃəˈduːf (US) ʃɑː- **-s** -s
shadow ˈʃæd.əʊ (US) -oʊ **-s** -z **-ing** -ɪŋ **-ed** -d **-y** -i **-iness** -ɪ.nəs, -ɪ.nɪs
shadowbox ˈʃæd.əʊ.bɒks (US) -oʊ.bɑːks **-es** -ɪz **-ing** -ɪŋ **-ed** -t
shadowless ˈʃæd.əʊ.ləs, -lɪs (US) -oʊ-
Shadrach, **Shadrak** ˈʃæd.ræk
Note: Some Jews pronounce /-rɑːx/.
Shadwell ˈʃæd.wel, -wəl
shad|y ˈʃeɪ.d|i **-ier** -i.əʳ (US) -i.ɚ **-iest** -i.ɪst, -i.əst **-ily** -ɪ.li, -əl.i **-iness** -ɪ.nəs, -ɪ.nɪs
Shaffer ˈʃæf.əʳ (US) ˈʃeɪ.fɚ, ˈʃæf.ɚ
shaft ʃɑːft (US) ʃæft **-s** -s **-ing** -ɪŋ **-ed** -ɪd
Shaftesbury ˈʃɑːfts.bər.i (US) ˈʃæfts.ber-, ˈʃɑːfts-, -bɚ-
shag ʃæg **-s** -z **-ging** -ɪŋ **-ged** -d
shagg|y ˈʃæg|.i **-ier** -i.əʳ (US) -i.ɚ **-iest** -i.ɪst, -i.əst **-ily** -ɪ.li, -əl.i **-iness** -ɪ.nəs, -ɪ.nɪs ˌ**shaggy ˈdog ˌstory**
shagreen ʃægˈriːn, ʃəˈgriːn (US) ʃə-
shah **(S)** ʃɑː **-s** -z
Shairp ʃeəp, ʃɑːp (US) ʃerp, ʃɑːrp
shak|e ʃeɪk **-es** -s **-ing** -ɪŋ **shook** ʃʊk **shaken** ˈʃeɪ.kən
shakedown ˈʃeɪk.daʊn **-s** -z
shaken *(from* **shake***)* ˈʃeɪ.kən
shakeout ˈʃeɪk.aʊt **-s** -s
shaker **(S)** ˈʃeɪ.kəʳ (US) -kɚ **-s** -z **-ism** -ɪ.zəm
Shakespear(e) ˈʃeɪk.spɪəʳ (US) -spɪr
Shakespearean ˌʃeɪkˈspɪə.ri.ən (US) -ˈspɪr.i- **-s** -z
Shakespeareana ʃeɪkˌspɪə.riˈɑː.nə, ˌʃeɪk- (US) ˌʃeɪk.spɪr.i.æn.ə, -ˈɑː.nə
Shakespearian ʃeɪkˈspɪə.ri.ən (US) -ˈspɪr.i- **-s** -z
Shakespeariana ʃeɪkˌspɪə.riˈɑː.nə, ˌʃeɪk.spɪə- (US) ˌʃeɪk.spɪr.iˈæn.ə, -ˈɑː.nə
shake-up ˈʃeɪk.ʌp **-s** -s
shako ˈʃæk.əʊ, ˈʃeɪ.kəʊ, ˈʃɑː- (US) ˈʃæk.oʊ, ˈʃeɪ.koʊ, ˈʃɑː- **-(e)s** -z
shak|y ˈʃeɪ.k|i **-ier** -i.əʳ (US) -i.ɚ **-iest** -i.ɪst, -i.əst **-ily** -ɪ.li, -əl.i **-iness** -ɪ.nəs, -ɪ.nɪs
shale ʃeɪl
shall *strong form:* ʃæl *weak form:* ʃəl
Note: Weak form word. The strong form is used for strong insistence or prediction (e.g. "You **shall** go to the ball, Cinderella"), and in final position (e.g. "And so you **shall**"). The weak form is used elsewhere (e.g. "What shall we do today?" /ˌwɒt.ʃəl.wiˌduː.təˈdeɪ (US) ˌwɑːt-/). American English uses 'shall' much less frequently than British English.
shallop ˈʃæl.əp **-s** -s

shallot (S) ʃə'lɒt (US) -'lɑːt; 'ʃæl.ət **-s** -s
shallow (S) 'ʃæl.əʊ (US) -oʊ **-s** -z **-er** -əʳ (US) -ɚ **-est** -ɪst, -əst **-ly** -li **-ness** -nəs, -nɪs
shalom ʃæl'ɒm, ʃə'lɒm, -'ləʊm (US) ʃɑː'loʊm, ʃə-
shalt *(from* **shall***) strong form:* ʃælt *weak form:* ʃᵊlt
shal|y 'ʃeɪ.l|i **-iness** -ɪ.nəs, -ɪ.nɪs
sham ʃæm **-s** -z **-ming** -ɪŋ **-med** -d **-mer/s** -əʳ/z (US) -ɚ/z
shaman 'ʃeɪm.ən, 'ʃæ.mən, 'ʃɑː- (US) 'ʃɑː.mən, 'ʃeɪ-, 'ʃæm.ən **-s** -z **-ist/s** **-ism** -ɪ.zᵊm
shamateur ˌʃæm.ə'tɜːʳ (US) -'tɝː **-s** -z **-ism** -ɪ.zᵊm
shambl|e 'ʃæm.bl̩ **-es** -z **-ing** -ɪŋ, '-blɪŋ **-ed** -d
shambles *(n.)* 'ʃæm.bl̩z
shambolic ʃæm'bɒl.ɪk (US) -'bɑː.lɪk
sham|e ʃeɪm **-es** -z **-ing** -ɪŋ **-ed** -d
shamefaced ˌʃeɪm'feɪst (US) '-- *stress shift, British only:* ˌshamefaced 'person
shamefaced|ness ˌʃeɪm'feɪst|.nəs, -'feɪ.sɪd-, -nɪs (US) 'ʃeɪm.feɪst-; ˌʃeɪm'feɪ.sɪd- **-ly** -li
shameful 'ʃeɪm.fᵊl, -fʊl **-ly** -i **-ness** -nəs, -nɪs
shameless 'ʃeɪm.ləs, -lɪs **-ly** -li **-ness** -nəs, -nɪs ˌ**shameless 'hussy**
Shamir ʃæm'ɪəʳ, ʃə'mɪəʳ (US) ʃə'mɪr, ʃæm'ɪr
shamm|y 'ʃæm.i **-ies** -iz
shampoo ʃæm'puː **-(e)s** -z **-ing** -ɪŋ **-ed** -d
shamrock (S) 'ʃæm.rɒk (US) -rɑːk
Shan ʃɑːn (US) ʃɑːn, ʃæn
Shana 'ʃɑː.nə (US) 'ʃeɪ-, 'ʃɑː-
shand|y (S) 'ʃæn.d|i **-ies** -iz
Shane ʃɑːn, ʃɔːn, ʃeɪn (US) ʃeɪn
shanghai *(v.)* ˌʃæŋ'haɪ (US) 'ʃæŋ.haɪ, -'- **-s** -z **-ing** -ɪŋ **-ed** -d *stress shift, British only:* ˌShanghai 'trader
Shanghai ˌʃæŋ'haɪ (US) ˌʃæŋ-, ˌʃɑːŋ-, '--
Shangri-la ˌʃæŋ.gri'lɑː
shank ʃæŋk **-s** -s ˌ**shank's 'pony,** ˌ**shanks's 'pony**
Shankill 'ʃæŋ.kɪl
Shanklin 'ʃæŋ.klɪn
Shanks ʃæŋks
Shanna 'ʃæn.ə
Shannon 'ʃæn.ən
shan't ʃɑːnt (US) ʃænt
shantung *silk material:* ˌʃæn'tʌŋ
Shantung ˌʃæn'dʌŋ, -tʌŋ, -dʊŋ, -tʊŋ (US) ˌʃæn'-, ˌʃɑːn'-
shant|y 'ʃæn.t|i (US) -t̬|i **-ies** -iz
shantytown 'ʃæn.ti.taʊn (US) -t̬i- **-s** -z
shap|e ʃeɪp **-es** -s **-ing** -ɪŋ **-ed** -t
SHAPE ʃeɪp
shapeless 'ʃeɪp.ləs, -lɪs **-ly** -li **-ness** -nəs, -nɪs
shapel|y 'ʃeɪ.pl|i **-ier** -i.əʳ (US) -i.ɚ **-iest** -i.ɪst, -i.əst **-iness** -ɪ.nəs, -ɪ.nɪs
Shapiro ʃə'pɪə.rəʊ (US) -'pɪr.oʊ
shard ʃɑːd (US) ʃɑːrd **-s** -z
shar|e ʃeəʳ (US) ʃer **-es** -z **-ing** -ɪŋ **-ed** -d
sharecropp|er 'ʃeəˌkrɒp|.əʳ (US) 'ʃerˌkrɑː.p|ɚ **-ers** -əz (US) -ɚz **-ing** -ɪŋ
sharehold|er 'ʃeəˌhəʊl.d|əʳ (US) 'ʃerˌhoʊl.d|ɚ **-ers** -əz (US) -ɚz **-ing/s** -ɪŋ/z
share-out 'ʃeəʳ.aʊt (US) 'ʃer- **-s** -s
shareware 'ʃeə.weəʳ (US) 'ʃer.wer
sharia(h) ʃə'riː.ə
Sharif ʃə'riːf, ʃɑː-, ʃær'iːf
Sharjah 'ʃɑː.dʒɑː, -ʒɑː, -dʒə (US) 'ʃɑːr.dʒɑː
shark ʃɑːk (US) ʃɑːrk **-s** -s
sharkskin 'ʃɑːk.skɪn (US) 'ʃɑːrk-
Sharman 'ʃɑː.mən (US) 'ʃɑːr-
Sharon *female name & fruit:* 'ʃær.ən, 'ʃɑː.rən, 'ʃeə-, -rɒn (US) 'ʃer.ən, 'ʃær- *Israeli politician:* ʃə'rəʊn, -'rɒn (US) -'roʊn
sharp (S) ʃɑːp (US) ʃɑːrp **-s** -s **-er** -əʳ (US) -ɚ **-est** -ɪst, -əst **-ly** -li **-ness** -nəs, -nɪs ˌ**sharp 'end, 'sharp ˌend;** ˌ**sharp 'practice**
Sharpe ʃɑːp (US) ʃɑːrp
sharpen 'ʃɑː.pᵊn (US) 'ʃɑːr- **-s** -z **-ing** -ɪŋ, -ɪŋ **-ed** -d
sharpener 'ʃɑː.pᵊn.əʳ (US) 'ʃɑːr.pᵊn.ɚ **-s** -z
sharper 'ʃɑː.pəʳ (US) 'ʃɑːr.pɚ **-s** -z
Sharpeville 'ʃɑːp.vɪl (US) 'ʃɑːrp-
sharp-eyed ˌʃɑːp'aɪd (US) ˌʃɑːrp-
sharpish 'ʃɑː.pɪʃ (US) 'ʃɑːr-
Sharples 'ʃɑː.pl̩z (US) 'ʃɑːr-
sharp-set ˌʃɑːp'set (US) 'ʃɑːrp.set *stress shift, British only:* ˌsharp-set 'features
sharpshooter 'ʃɑːpˌʃuː.təʳ (US) 'ʃɑːrpˌʃuː.t̬ɚ **-s** -z
sharp-sighted ˌʃɑːp'saɪ.tɪd (US) 'ʃɑːrpˌsaɪ.t̬ɪd *stress shift, British only:* ˌsharp-sighted 'person
sharp-witted ˌʃɑːp'wɪt.ɪd (US) 'ʃɑːrpˌwɪt̬- *stress shift, British only:* ˌsharp-witted 'person
shashlik ʃɑːʃ'lɪk, ʃæʃ-, '-- (US) 'ʃɑːʃ- **-s** -s
Shasta 'ʃæs.tə
Shastri 'ʃæs.tri (US) 'ʃɑː.stri
shat *(from* **shit***)* ʃæt
Note: This past tense form is rarely used in American English.
Shatner 'ʃæt.nəʳ (US) -nɚ
Shatt-al-Arab ˌʃæt.æl'ær.əb (US) -əl'er-, -'ær-
shatt|er 'ʃæt|.əʳ (US) 'ʃæt̬|.ɚ **-ers** -əz (US) -ɚz **-ering** -ᵊr.ɪŋ **-ered** -əd (US) -ɚd
shatterproof 'ʃæt.ə.pruːf (US) 'ʃæt̬.ɚ-
Shaughnessy 'ʃɔː.nə.si (US) 'ʃɑː-, 'ʃɔː-
Shaula 'ʃəʊ.lə (US) 'ʃoʊ-, 'ʃɔː-
Shaun ʃɔːn (US) ʃɑːn, ʃɔːn
Shauna 'ʃɔː.nə (US) 'ʃɑː-, 'ʃɔː-
shav|e ʃeɪv **-es** -z **-ing** -ɪŋ **-ed** -d **'shaving ˌbrush; 'shaving ˌcream; 'shaving ˌfoam**
shaven 'ʃeɪ.vᵊn
shaver 'ʃeɪ.vəʳ (US) -vɚ **-s** -z
Shavian 'ʃeɪ.vi.ən
shaving 'ʃeɪ.vɪŋ **-s** -z
shaw (S) ʃɔː (US) ʃɑː, ʃɔː **-s** -z
shawl ʃɔːl (US) ʃɑːl, ʃɔːl **-s** -z
shawm ʃɔːm (US) ʃɑːm, ʃɔːm **-s** -z
Shawn ʃɔːn (US) ʃɑːn, ʃɔːn
Shawna 'ʃɔː.nə (US) 'ʃɑː-, 'ʃɔː-
Shawnee ʃɔː'niː (US) ʃɑː-, ʃɔː- **-s** -z
shay ʃeɪ **-s** -z
Shayler 'ʃeɪ.lə, -lɚ
she *normal form:* ʃiː *freq. weak form:* ʃi
Note: Weak form word. The strong form, /ʃiː/ is used mainly contrastively (e.g. "I wouldn't go, so SHE went") or emphatically (e.g. "What does SHE want?"). The weak form is /ʃi/ (e.g. "off she went", /ˌɒf.ʃi'went (US) ˌɑːf-/).
shea ʃɪə, 'ʃiː.ə, ʃiː (US) ʃiː, ʃeɪ **-s** -z
Shea ʃeɪ
shea|f ʃiː|f **-ves** -vz
Sheaffer 'ʃeɪ.fəʳ (US) -fɚ
shear ʃɪəʳ (US) ʃɪr **-s** -z **-ing** -ɪŋ **-ed** -d **shorn** ʃɔːn (US) ʃɔːrn
Sheard ʃeəd, ʃɪəd, ʃɜːd (US) ʃerd, ʃɪrd, ʃɝːd
shearer (S) 'ʃɪə.rəʳ (US) 'ʃɪr.ɚ **-s** -z
Shearman 'ʃɪə.mən, 'ʃɜː.mən (US) 'ʃɪr-, 'ʃɝː-
Shearn ʃɪən, ʃɜːn (US) ʃɪrn, ʃɝːn
shears (S) ʃɪəz (US) ʃɪrz
Shearson 'ʃɪə.sᵊn (US) 'ʃɪr-
shearwater 'ʃɪəˌwɔː.təʳ (US) 'ʃɪrˌwɑː.t̬ɚ, -ˌwɔː- **-s** -z
shea|th ʃiː|θ **-ths** -ðz, -θs
sheath|e ʃiːð **-es** -z **-ing** -ɪŋ **-ed** -d
sheaves *(plur. of* **sheaf***)* ʃiːvz
Sheba 'ʃiː.bə
shebang ʃɪ'bæŋ, ʃə-
she-bear 'ʃiː.beəʳ (US) -ber **-s** -z
shebeen ʃɪ'biːn, ʃə-, ʃeb'iːn (US) ʃɪ'biːn **-s** -z
she-cat 'ʃiː.kæt **-s** -s
Shechem 'ʃiː.kem, 'ʃek.em; *as if Jewish:* ʃə'xem (US) 'ʃiː.kəm, 'ʃek.əm
shed ʃed **-s** -z **-ding** -ɪŋ
she-devil 'ʃiːˌdev.ᵊl **-s** -z
Shee ʃiː
sheen (S) ʃiːn
Sheena 'ʃiː.nə
sheen|y 'ʃiː.n|i **-ies** -iz

sheep ʃiːp ˈsheep's ˌeyes; ˌseparate the ˌsheep from the ˈgoats
sheep-dip ˈʃiːp.dɪp
sheepdog ˈʃiːp.dɒg (US) -dɑːg, -dɔːg -s -z
sheepfold ˈʃiːp.fəʊld (US) -foʊld -s -z
sheepish ˈʃiː.pɪʃ -ly -li -ness -nəs, -nɪs
sheepshank ˈʃiːp.ʃæŋk -s -s
Sheepshanks ˈʃiːp.ʃæŋks
sheepshear|ing ˈʃiːpˌʃɪə.r|ɪŋ (US) -ˌʃɪr|.ɪŋ -er/s -əʳ/z (US) -ɚ/z
sheepskin ˈʃiːp.skɪn -s -z
sheer ʃɪəʳ (US) ʃɪr -s -z -ing -ɪŋ -ed -d
Sheerness ˌʃɪəˈnes (US) ˈʃɪr.nes
sheet ʃiːt -s -s -ing -ɪŋ (US) ˈʃiː.t̬ɪŋ ˈsheet ˌanchor; ˌsheet ˈlightning; (US) ˈsheet ˌlightning; ˌsheet ˈmetal; ˈsheet ˌmusic; ˌwhite as a ˈsheet
Sheffield ˈʃef.iːld *locally:* -ɪld (US) -iːld
Shefford ˈʃef.əd (US) -ɚd
she-goat ˈʃiː.gəʊt (US) -goʊt -s -s
sheik(h) ʃeɪk, ʃiːk, ʃek, ʃex (US) ʃiːk, ʃeɪk -s -s -dom/s -dəm/z
sheila (S) ˈʃiː.lə
shekel ˈʃek.əl -s -z
Shekinah ʃekˈaɪ.nə, ʃɪˈkaɪ- (US) ʃəˈkiː-, -ˈkaɪ-
Shelagh ˈʃiː.lə
Shelby ˈʃel.bi
Sheldon ˈʃel.dən
Sheldonian ʃelˈdəʊ.ni.ən (US) -ˈdoʊ-
sheldrake ˈʃel.dreɪk -s -s
Sheldrick ˈʃel.drɪk
shelduck ˈʃel.dʌk -s -s
shel|f ʃel|f -ves -vz
Shelfield ˈʃel.fiːld
shelf-life ˈʃelf.laɪf -lives -laɪvz
Shelford ˈʃel.fəd (US) -fɚd
shell (S) ʃel -s -z -ing -ɪŋ -ed -d ˈshell ˌshock; ˈshell ˌsuit
shellac ʃəˈlæk, ʃelˈæk; ˈʃel.æk (US) ʃəˈlæk -s -s -king -ɪŋ -ked -t
Shelley ˈʃel.i
shellfish ˈʃel.fɪʃ
Shelta ˈʃel.tə (US) -t̬ə
shelt|er ˈʃel.t|əʳ (US) -t̬|ɚ -ers -əz (US) -ɚz -ering -ər.ɪŋ -ered -əd (US) -ɚd
shelt|ie, shelt|y ˈʃel.t|i (US) -t̬|i -ies -iz
Shelton ˈʃel.tən (US) -tən
shelv|e ʃelv -es -z -ing -ɪŋ -ed -d
Shem ʃem
shemozzle ʃɪˈmɒz.l̩, ʃə- (US) -ˈmɑː.zl̩ -s -z
Shenandoah ˌʃen.ənˈdəʊə (US) -ˈdoʊə
shenanigan ʃɪˈnæn.ɪ.gən, ʃə- -s -z
Shennan ˈʃen.ən
Shenstone ˈʃen.stən
Shenyang ˌʃenˈjæŋ (US) ˌʃʌnˈjɑːŋ
Shepard ˈʃep.əd (US) -ɚd
shepherd (S) ˈʃep.əd (US) -ɚd -s -z -ing -ɪŋ -ed -ɪd ˌshepherd's ˈpie
shepherdess ˌʃep.əˈdes; ˈ---, -dɪs (US) ˈʃep.ɚ.dɪs -es -ɪz
Sheppard ˈʃep.əd (US) -ɚd
Shepperton ˈʃep.ə.tən (US) -ɚ.t̬ən
Sheppey ˈʃep.i
Shepreth ˈʃep.rəθ
Shepshed ˈʃep.ʃed
Shepton Mallet ˌʃep.tənˈmæl.ɪt
Sheraton ˈʃer.ə.tən (US) -t̬ən, -tən
sherbet, sherbert ˈʃɜː.bət (US) ˈʃɝː-, -bɚt
Note: Both pronunciations are possible for both variants in American English, even though only one is spelt with an **r**.
Sherborne ˈʃɜː.bən, -bɔːn (US) ˈʃɝː.bɔːrn, -bɚn
Sherbrooke ˈʃɜː.brʊk (US) ˈʃɝː-
sherd ʃɜːd (US) ʃɝːd -s -z
Shere ʃɪəʳ (US) ʃɪr
Shergar ˈʃɜː.gɑːʳ, ˈʃeə- (US) ˈʃɝː.gɑːr, ˈʃer-
Sheridan ˈʃer.ɪ.dən
sheriff (S) ˈʃer.ɪf -s -s
Sheringham ˈʃer.ɪŋ.əm
sherlock (S) ˈʃɜː.lɒk (US) ˈʃɝː.lɑːk
Sherman ˈʃɜː.mən (US) ˈʃɝː-
Sherpa ˈʃɜː.pə (US) ˈʃɝː- -s -z
Sherrin ˈʃer.ɪn
sherr|y (S) ˈʃer|.i -ies -iz
Sherwood ˈʃɜː.wʊd (US) ˈʃɝː- ˌSherwood ˈForest
she's *(from* **she is** *or* **she has**) *strong form:* ʃiːz *weak form:* ʃɪz
Note: The use of the strong form /ʃiːz/ and the weak form /ʃɪz/ is parallel to the two forms of **she**.
Shetland ˈʃet.lənd -s -z -er/s -əʳ/z (US) -ɚ/z ˈShetland ˌIslands; ˌShetland ˈpony
Shevardnadze ˌʃev.ədˈnɑːd.zeɪ, -zə (US) -ɚdˈnɑːtd.ziː
Shevington ˈʃev.ɪŋ.tən
shew ʃəʊ (US) ʃoʊ -s -z -ing -ɪŋ -ed -d -n -n
shewbread ˈʃəʊ.bred (US) ˈʃoʊ-
Shewell ʃʊəl, ˈʃuː.əl (US) ˈʃuː.əl
shewn *(from* **shew**) ʃəʊn (US) ʃoʊn
she-wol|f ˈʃiː.wʊl|f -ves -vz
shh, sh, ssh ʃ
Note: Used to command silence.
Shia(h) ˈʃiː.ə ˌShia ˈMuslim
shiatsu ʃiˈæt.su (US) -ˈɑːt-
shibboleth (S) ˈʃɪb.əl.eθ, -əθ, -ɪθ (US) -ə.leθ, -ləθ -s -s
shickered ˈʃɪk.əd (US) -ɚd
shield (S) ʃiːld -s -z -ing -ɪŋ -ed -ɪd
shieling ˈʃiː.lɪŋ -s -z
Shiels ʃiːlz
Shifnal ˈʃɪf.nəl
shift ʃɪft -s -s -ing -ɪŋ -ed -ɪd ˈshift ˌstick
shiftless ˈʃɪft.ləs, -lɪs -ly -li -ness -nəs, -nɪs
shiftwork ˈʃɪft.wɜːk (US) -wɝːk -er/s -əʳ/z (US) -ɚ/z
shift|y ˈʃɪf.t|i -ier -i.əʳ (US) -i.ɚ -iest -i.ɪst, -i.əst -ily -ɪ.li, -əl.i -iness -ɪ.nəs, -ɪ.nɪs
Shiism ˈʃiː.ɪ.zəm
Shiite ˈʃiː.aɪt -s -s
shikari ʃɪˈkɑː.ri, -ˈkær.i (US) -ˈkɑːr.i -s -z
Shikoku ʃɪˈkəʊ.kuː (US) -ˈkɑː-, ʃiː-, -ˈkɔː-
shiksa ˈʃɪk.sə -s -z
shikse ˈʃɪk.sə -s -z
Shildon ˈʃɪl.dən
Shillan ʃɪˈlæn
shillela(g)h (S) ʃɪˈleɪ.lə, -li (US) -li, -lə -s -z
Shilleto, Shillito ˈʃɪl.ɪ.təʊ (US) -toʊ
shilling ˈʃɪl.ɪŋ -s -z
shilly-shall|y ˈʃɪl.iˌʃæl|.i, ˌʃɪl.iˈʃæl- (US) ˈʃɪl.iˌʃæl- -ies -iz -ying -i.ɪŋ -ied -id
Shiloh ˈʃaɪ.ləʊ (US) -loʊ
Shilton ˈʃɪl.tən
shimm|er ˈʃɪm|.əʳ (US) -ɚ -ers -əz (US) -ɚz -ering -ər.ɪŋ -ered -əd (US) -ɚd
shimm|y ˈʃɪm|.i -ies -iz -ying -i.ɪŋ -ied -id
shin ʃɪn -s -z -ning -ɪŋ -ned -d
shinbone ˈʃɪn.bəʊn, ˈʃɪm- (US) ˈʃɪn.boʊn -s -z
shindig ˈʃɪn.dɪg -s -z
shind|y ˈʃɪn.d|i -ies -iz
shin|e ʃaɪn -es -z -ing -ɪŋ -ed -d shone ʃɒn (US) ʃoʊn, ʃɑːn
shiner ˈʃaɪ.nəʳ (US) -nɚ -s -z
shingle ˈʃɪŋ.gl̩ -s -z
shingly ˈʃɪŋ.gli, -gl̩.i
shinn|y ˈʃɪn|.i -ies -iz -ying -i.ɪŋ -ied -id
shinsplints ˈʃɪn.splɪnts
Shinto ˈʃɪn.təʊ (US) -toʊ -ism -ɪ.zəm -ist/s -ɪst/s
Shinwell ˈʃɪn.wəl, -wel
shin|y ˈʃaɪ.n|i -ier -i.əʳ (US) -i.ɚ -iest -i.ɪst, -i.əst -iness -ɪ.nəs, -ɪ.nɪs
ship ʃɪp -s -s -ping -ɪŋ -ped -t -per/s -əʳ/z (US) -ɚ/z
-ship -ʃɪp
Note: Suffix. Normally unstressed, e.g. **kinship** /ˈkɪn.ʃɪp/.
shipboard ˈʃɪp.bɔːd (US) -bɔːrd
shipbroker ˈʃɪpˌbrəʊ.kəʳ (US) -ˌbroʊ.kɚ -s -z
shipbuild|er ˈʃɪpˌbɪl.d|əʳ (US) -d|ɚ -ers -əz (US) -ɚz -ing -ɪŋ
Shiplake ˈʃɪp.leɪk
Shipley ˈʃɪp.li
shipload ˈʃɪp.ləʊd (US) -loʊd -s -z
Shipman ˈʃɪp.mən
shipmaster ˈʃɪpˌmɑː.stəʳ (US) -ˌmæs.tɚ -s -z
shipmate ˈʃɪp.meɪt -s -s
shipment ˈʃɪp.mənt -s -s
Shipp ʃɪp
shipping ˈʃɪp.ɪŋ ˈshipping ˌclerk
shipshape ˈʃɪp.ʃeɪp
Shipston ˈʃɪp.stən

Shipton 'ʃɪp.tən
shipway 'ʃɪp.weɪ **-s** -z
shipwreck 'ʃɪp.rek **-s** -s **-ing** -ɪŋ **-ed** -t
shipwright (S) 'ʃɪp.raɪt **-s** -s
shipyard 'ʃɪp.jɑːd (US) -jɑːrd **-s** -z
Shiraz ʃɪə'rɑːz, ʃɪ-, -'ræz (US) ʃiː-
shire ʃaɪə^r (US) ʃaɪɚ **-s** -z **'shire ˌhorse**
-shire -ʃə^r, -ˌʃɪə^r (US) -ʃɚ, -ˌʃɪr
Note: Suffix. Does not normally change the stress pattern of the stem to which it is added, e.g. **Lincoln** /'lɪŋ.kən/, **Lincolnshire** /'lɪŋ.kən.ʃə^r (US) -ʃɚ/. There is a free choice between the unstressed variant and that with secondary stress in all names ending **-shire**.
Shirebrook 'ʃaɪə.brʊk (US) 'ʃaɪɚ-
Shiremoor 'ʃaɪə.mɔː^r, -mʊə^r (US) 'ʃaɪɚ.mɔːr, -mʊr
shirk ʃɜːk (US) ʃɝːk **-s** -s **-ing** -ɪŋ **-ed** -t **-er/s** -ə^r/z (US) -ɚ/z
Shirley 'ʃɜː.li (US) 'ʃɝː-
shirr ʃɜː^r (US) ʃɝː **-s** -z **-ing** -ɪŋ **-ed** -d
shirt (S) ʃɜːt (US) ʃɝːt **-s** -s
shirtdress 'ʃɜːt.dres (US) 'ʃɝːt- **-es** -ɪz
shirt-front 'ʃɜːt.frʌnt (US) 'ʃɝːt- **-s** -s
shirting 'ʃɜː.tɪŋ (US) 'ʃɝː.t̬ɪŋ
shirt-sleev|es 'ʃɜːt.sliːv|z, -'- (US) 'ʃɝːt- **-ed** -d
shirt-tail 'ʃɜːt.teɪl (US) 'ʃɝːt- **-s** -z
shirtwaist 'ʃɜːt.weɪst (US) 'ʃɝːt- **-s** -s
shirtwaister 'ʃɜːtˌweɪ.stə^r, ˌ-'-- (US) 'ʃɝːtˌweɪ.stɚ **-s** -z
shirt|y 'ʃɜː.t|i (US) 'ʃɝː.t̬|i **-ier** -i.ə^r (US) -i.ɚ **-iest** -i.ɪst, -i.əst **-iness** -ɪ.nəs, -ɪ.nɪs
Shishak 'ʃaɪ.ʃæk, -ʃək *rarely:* 'ʃɪʃ.æk, -ək (US) 'ʃaɪ.ʃɑːk, -ʃæk
shish kebab 'ʃiːʃ.kɪˌbæb, -kə-, ˌ--'- (US) 'ʃɪʃ.kəˌbɑːb **-s** -z
shit ʃɪt **-s** -s **-ting** -ɪŋ (US) 'ʃɪt̬.ɪŋ **shat** ʃæt
Note: The past tense form **shat** is rarely used in American English, the normal past tense being **shit**.
shite ʃaɪt **-s** -s
shitfaced 'ʃɪt.feɪst
shithouse 'ʃɪt.haʊs
shitless 'ʃɪt.ləs, -lɪs
shitt|y 'ʃɪt|.i (US) 'ʃɪt̬|.i **-ier** -i.ə^r (US) -i.ɚ **-iest** -i.ɪst, -i.əst **-iness** -ɪ.nəs, -ɪ.nɪs
Shiva 'ʃiː.və, 'ʃɪv.ə (US) 'ʃiː.və
shiv|er 'ʃɪv|.ə^r (US) -ɚ **-ers** -əz (US) -ɚz **-ering/ly** -^{ə}r.ɪŋ/li **-ered** -əd (US) -ɚd
shiver|y 'ʃɪv.^{ə}r|.i **-iness** -ɪ.nəs, -ɪ.nɪs
shlemiel ʃlə'miːl **-s** -z
shlep ʃlep **-s** -s **-ping** -ɪŋ **-ped** -t
shlock ʃlɒk (US) ʃlɑːk **-s** -s
shlockmeister 'ʃlɒkˌmaɪ.stə^r (US) 'ʃlɑːkˌmaɪ.stɚ **-s** -z
Shloer® ʃlɜː^r (US) ʃlɝː
shmal(t)z ʃmɔːlts, ʃmɒlts, ʃmælts (US) ʃmɑːlts, ʃmɔːlts **-y** -i **-ier** -i.ə^r (US) -i.ɚ **-iest** -i.ɪst, -i.əst

shmooz|e ʃmuːz **-es** -ɪz **-ing** -ɪŋ **-ed** -d **-er/s** -ə^r/z (US) -ə/z
shmuck ʃmʌk **-s** -s
shoal ʃəʊl (US) ʃoʊl **-s** -z
shock ʃɒk (US) ʃɑːk **-s** -s **-ing** -ɪŋ **-ed** -t **-er/s** -ə^r/z (US) -ɚ/z **'shock abˌsorber; 'shock ˌtreatment; 'shock ˌwave**
shocking 'ʃɒk.ɪŋ (US) 'ʃɑː.kɪŋ **-ly** -li
shockproof 'ʃɒk.pruːf (US) 'ʃɑːk-
shodd|y 'ʃɒd|.i (US) 'ʃɑː.d|i **-ier** -i.ə^r (US) -i.ɚ **-iest** -i.ɪst, -i.əst **-ily** -ɪ.li, -^{ə}l.i **-iness** -ɪ.nəs, -ɪ.nɪs
shoe ʃuː **-s** -z **-ing** -ɪŋ **shod** ʃɒd (US) ʃɑːd **'shoe ˌleather**
shoeblack 'ʃuː.blæk **-s** -s
Shoeburyness ˌʃuː.b^{ə}r.i'nes
shoehorn 'ʃuː.hɔːn (US) -hɔːrn **-s** -z **-ing** -ɪŋ **-ed** -d
shoelac|e 'ʃuː.leɪs **-es** -ɪz
shoeless 'ʃuː.ləs, -lɪs
shoemaker (S) 'ʃuːˌmeɪ.kə^r (US) -kɚ **-s** -z
shoeshine 'ʃuː.ʃaɪn **-s** -z
shoestring 'ʃuː.strɪŋ
shoetree 'ʃuː.triː **-s** -z
shogun 'ʃəʊ.gʌn, -guːn, -gən (US) 'ʃoʊ.gʌn, -gʊn, -guːn **-s** -s
Sholokhov 'ʃɒl.ə.kɒf (US) 'ʃɔː.lə.kɔːf
Shona *female name:* 'ʃəʊ.nə (US) 'ʃoʊ- *African language & people:* 'ʃɒ.nə, 'ʃɔː-, 'ʃəʊ- (US) 'ʃoʊ-
shone *(from* **shine***)* ʃɒn (US) ʃoʊn
shonk|y 'ʃɒŋ.ki (US) 'ʃɑːŋ- **-ier** i.ə^r (US) i.ɚ **-iest** i.ɪst, i.əst
shoo ʃuː **-s** -z **-ing** -ɪŋ **-ed** -d
shoofl|y 'ʃuː.fl|aɪ **-ies** -aɪz
shoo-in 'ʃuː.ɪn **-s** -z
shook *(from* **shake***)* ʃʊk
shook-up ˌʃʊk'ʌp
shoot ʃuːt **-s** -s **-ing** -ɪŋ (US) 'ʃuː.t̬ɪŋ **shot** ʃɒt (US) ʃɑːt **ˌshoot the 'breeze**
shooter (S) 'ʃuː.tə^r (US) -t̬ɚ **-s** -z
shooting 'ʃuː.tɪŋ (US) -t̬ɪŋ **-s** -z **'shooting ˌgallery; ˌshooting 'star, 'shooting ˌstar;** (US) **ˌshooting 'star; 'shooting ˌstick**
shoot-out 'ʃuːt.aʊt **-s** -s
shop ʃɒp (US) ʃɑːp **-s** -s **-ping** -ɪŋ **-ped** -t **-per/s** -ə^r/z (US) -ɚ/z **'shop asˌsistant; ˌshop 'steward;** (US) **'shop ˌsteward; ˌshop 'window**
shopaholic ˌʃɒp.ə'hɒl.ɪk (US) ˌʃɑː.pə'hɑː.lɪk **-s** -s
shopfloor ˌʃɒp'flɔː^r (US) ˌʃɑːp'flɔːr
shopfront ˌʃɒp'frʌnt, '-- (US) 'ʃɑːp.frʌnt **-s** -s
shopgirl 'ʃɒp.gɜːl (US) 'ʃɑːp.gɝːl **-s** -z
shopkeeper 'ʃɒpˌkiː.pə^r (US) 'ʃɑːpˌkiː.pɚ **-s** -z
shoplift 'ʃɒp.lɪft (US) 'ʃɑːp- **-s** -s **-ing** -ɪŋ **-ed** -ɪd
shop-lifter 'ʃɒpˌlɪf.tə^r (US) 'ʃɑːpˌlɪf.tɚ **-s** -z

shopping 'ʃɒp.ɪŋ **'shopping ˌcentre/ˌcenter; 'shopping ˌlist; 'shopping ˌmall**
shop-soiled 'ʃɒp.sɔɪld (US) 'ʃɑːpˌsɔɪld
shoptalk 'ʃɒp.tɔːk (US) 'ʃɑːp.tɑːk, -tɔːk
shopwalker 'ʃɒpˌwɔː.kə^r (US) 'ʃɑːpˌwɔː.kɚ, -ˌwɑː- **-s** -z
shopworn 'ʃɒp.wɔːn (US) 'ʃɑːp.wɔːrn
shor|e ʃɔː^r (US) ʃɔːr **-es** -z **-ing** -ɪŋ **-ed** -d
Shoreditch 'ʃɔː.dɪtʃ (US) 'ʃɔːr-
Shoreham 'ʃɔː.rəm (US) 'ʃɔːr.əm
shoreline 'ʃɔː.laɪn (US) 'ʃɔːr-
shoreward 'ʃɔː.wəd (US) 'ʃɔːr.wɚd
shorn *(from* **shear***)* ʃɔːn (US) ʃɔːrn
Shorncliffe 'ʃɔːn.klɪf (US) 'ʃɔːrn-
short (S) ʃɔːt (US) ʃɔːrt **-s** -s **-er** -ə^r (US) 'ʃɔːr.t̬ɚ **-est** -ɪst, -əst (US) 'ʃɔːr.t̬ɪst, -t̬əst **-ly** -li **-ness** -nəs, -nɪs **-ing** -ɪŋ **-ed** -ɪd **ˌshort ˌback and 'sides; ˌshort 'shrift; ˌshort 'story; the ˌshort ˌend of the 'stick; the ˌlong and the 'short of it**
shortag|e 'ʃɔː.tɪdʒ (US) 'ʃɔːr.t̬ɪdʒ **-es** -ɪz
shortbread 'ʃɔːt.bred (US) 'ʃɔːrt- **-s** -z
shortcake 'ʃɔːt.keɪk (US) 'ʃɔːrt- **-s** -s
short-chang|e ˌʃɔːt'tʃeɪndʒ (US) ˌʃɔːrt- **-es** -ɪz **-ing** -ɪŋ **-ed** -d
short-cir|cuit ˌʃɔːt'sɜː|.kɪt (US) ˌʃɔːrt'sɝː- **-cuits** -kɪts **-cuiting** -kɪ.tɪŋ (US) -kɪ.t̬ɪŋ **-cuited** -kɪ.tɪd (US) -kɪ.t̬ɪd
shortcoming 'ʃɔːtˌkʌm.ɪŋ, ˌ-'-- (US) 'ʃɔːrtˌkʌm- **-s** -z
shortcrust 'ʃɔːt.krʌst (US) 'ʃɔːrt- **-s** -s **ˌshortcrust 'pastry**
shortcut 'ʃɔːt.kʌt (US) 'ʃɔːrt- **-s** -s
short-dated ˌʃɔːt'deɪ.tɪd (US) ˌʃɔːrt'deɪ.t̬ɪd
short-eared ˌʃɔːt'ɪəd (US) 'ʃɔːrt.ɪrd *stress shift, British only:* ˌshort-eared 'rabbit
shorten 'ʃɔː.t^{ə}n (US) 'ʃɔːr- **-s** -z **-ing** -ɪŋ, 'ʃɔːt.nɪŋ (US) 'ʃɔːr.t^{ə}n.ɪŋ, 'ʃɔːrt.nɪŋ **-ed** -d
shortening 'ʃɔːt.nɪŋ; 'ʃɔː.t^{ə}n.ɪŋ (US) 'ʃɔːrt.nɪŋ; 'ʃɔːr.t^{ə}n.ɪŋ
shortfall 'ʃɔːt.fɔːl (US) 'ʃɔːrt-, -fɑːl **-s** -z
shorthand 'ʃɔːt.hænd (US) 'ʃɔːrt- **ˌshorthand 'typist**
short-handed ˌʃɔːt'hæn.dɪd (US) ˌʃɔːrt- *stress shift:* ˌshort-handed 'vessel
short-haul 'ʃɔːt.hɔːl, ˌ-'- (US) 'ʃɔːrt.hɑːl, -hɔːl, ˌ-'-
shorthorn 'ʃɔːt.hɔːn (US) 'ʃɔːrt.hɔːrn **-s** -z
shortlist 'ʃɔːt.lɪst (US) 'ʃɔːrt- **-s** -s **-ing** -ɪŋ **-ed** -ɪd
short-lived ˌʃɔːt'lɪvd (US) 'ʃɔːrt.laɪvd, -lɪvd *stress shift, British only:* ˌshort-lived 'glory
short-order 'ʃɔːtˌɔː.də^r, ˌ-'-- (US) 'ʃɔːrtˌɔːr.dɚ

short-range ˌʃɔːt'reɪndʒ (US) ˌʃɔːrt- *stress shift:* ˌshort-range 'missile
shortsighted ˌʃɔːt'saɪ.tɪd (US) 'ʃɔːrtˌsaɪ.t̬ɪd **-ly** -li **-ness** -nəs, -nɪs *stress shift, British only:* ˌshort-sighted 'person
short-staffed ˌʃɔːt'stɑːft (US) ˌʃɔːrt'stæft *stress shift:* ˌshort-staffed 'bar
shortstop 'ʃɔːt.stɒp (US) 'ʃɔːrt.stɑːp **-s** -s
short-tempered ˌʃɔːt'tem.pəd (US) ˌʃɔːrt'tem.pɚd *stress shift:* ˌshort-tempered 'person
short-term ˌʃɔːt'tɜːm (US) 'ʃɔːrt.tɝːm **-ism** -ɪ.zᵊm *stress shift, British only:* ˌshort-term 'plans
shortwave 'ʃɔːt.weɪv (US) 'ʃɔːrt- **-s** -z
short-winded ˌʃɔːt'wɪn.dɪd (US) 'ʃɔːrtˌwɪn-, ˌ-'-- *stress shift, British only:* ˌshort-winded 'story
short|y 'ʃɔː.t|i (US) 'ʃɔːr.t̬|i **-ies** -iz
Shostakovich ˌʃɒs.tə'kəʊ.vɪtʃ (US) ˌʃɑː.stə'koʊ-
shot ʃɒt (US) ʃɑːt **-s** -s **'shot ˌput; 'shot ˌputter**
shotgun 'ʃɒt.gʌn (US) 'ʃɑːt- **-s** -z **ˌshotgun 'wedding**
Shotton 'ʃɒt.ᵊn (US) 'ʃɑː.tᵊn
Shotts ʃɒts (US) ʃɑːts
should *strong form:* ʃʊd *weak forms:* ʃəd, ʃd, ʃt
Note: Weak form word. The strong form is used for emphatic pronunciation (e.g. "He **should** have asked first"), or for contrast (e.g. "Don't tell me what I should or shouldn't do"). It is also used in final position (e.g. "We both should"). The most usual weak form is /ʃəd/, as in "When should it arrive?" /ˌwen.ʃəd.ɪt.ə'raɪv/, but in rapid speech we also find /ʃd/ before voiced sounds (e.g. "I should go now" /ˌaɪ.ʃd'gəʊ.naʊ (US) -'goʊ-/) and /ʃt/ before voiceless sounds (e.g. "You should try to finish" /ju.ʃtˌtraɪ.tə'fɪn.ɪʃ (US) -t̬ə'-/).
should|er 'ʃəʊl.d|əʳ (US) 'ʃoʊl.d|ɚ **-ers** -əz (US) -ɚz **-ering** -ᵊr.ɪŋ **-ered** -əd (US) -ɚd **'shoulder ˌbag; 'shoulder ˌblade; 'shoulder ˌpad; 'shoulder ˌstrap; a 'shoulder to ˌcry on, a ˌshoulder to 'cry on** (US) **a ˌshoulder to 'cry on**
shouldn't 'ʃʊd.ᵊnt
shout ʃaʊt **-s** -s **-ing** -ɪŋ (US) 'ʃaʊ.t̬ɪŋ **-ed** -ɪd (US) 'ʃaʊ.t̬ɪd
shov|e (*n. v.*) ʃʌv **-es** -z **-ing** -ɪŋ **-ed** -d
shove-halfpenny ˌʃʌv'heɪp.ni
shovel (S) 'ʃʌv.ᵊl **-s** -z **-(l)ing** -ɪŋ, 'ʃʌv.lɪŋ **-(l)ed** -d **-(l)er/s** -əʳ/z, 'ʃʌv.ləʳ/z (US) '-l̩.ɚ/z, '-lɚ/z **-ful/s** -fʊl/z
show ʃəʊ (US) ʃoʊ **-s** -z **-ing** -ɪŋ **-ed** -d **-n** -n **'show ˌbusiness; ˌshow 'trial, 'show ˌtrial**
showbiz 'ʃəʊ.bɪz (US) 'ʃoʊ-
showboat 'ʃəʊ.bəʊt (US) 'ʃoʊ.boʊt **-s** -s **-ing** -ɪŋ
showbread 'ʃəʊ.bred (US) 'ʃoʊ-
showcas|e 'ʃəʊ.keɪs (US) 'ʃoʊ- **-es** -ɪz **-ing** -ɪŋ **-ed** -t
showdown 'ʃəʊ.daʊn (US) 'ʃoʊ- **-s** -z
shower *fall of rain etc.:* ʃaʊəʳ (US) ʃaʊɚ **-s** -z **-ing** -ɪŋ **-ed** -d **-y** -i
shower *one who shows:* 'ʃəʊ.əʳ (US) 'ʃoʊ.ɚ **-s** -z
shower-ba|th 'ʃaʊə.bɑː|θ (US) 'ʃaʊɚ.bæ|θ **-ths** -ðz
showerhead 'ʃaʊə.hed (US) 'ʃaʊɚ- **-s** -z
showerproof 'ʃaʊə.pruːf (US) 'ʃaʊɚ-
showgirl 'ʃəʊ.gɜːl (US) 'ʃoʊ.gɝːl **-s** -z
showjump 'ʃəʊ.dʒʌmp (US) 'ʃoʊ- **-s** -s **-ing** -ɪŋ **-er/s** -əʳ/z (US) -ɚ/z
show|man 'ʃəʊ|.mən (US) 'ʃoʊ- **-men** -mən, -men
showmanship 'ʃəʊ.mən.ʃɪp (US) 'ʃoʊ-
shown (*from* **show**) ʃəʊn (US) ʃoʊn
show-off 'ʃəʊ.ɒf (US) 'ʃoʊ.ɑːf
showpiec|e 'ʃəʊ.piːs (US) 'ʃoʊ- **-es** -ɪz
showplac|e 'ʃəʊ.pleɪs (US) 'ʃoʊ- **-es** -ɪz
showroom 'ʃəʊ.rʊm, -ruːm (US) 'ʃoʊ.ruːm, -rʊm **-s** -z
showstopp|er 'ʃəʊˌstɒp|.əʳ (US) 'ʃoʊˌstɑː.p|ɚ **-ers** -əz (US) -ɚz **-ing** -ɪŋ
show|y 'ʃəʊ|.i (US) 'ʃoʊ- **-ier** -i.əʳ (US) -i.ɚ **-iest** -i.ɪst, -i.əst **-ily** -ɪ.li, -ᵊl.i **-iness** -ɪ.nəs, -ɪ.nɪs
shoyu 'ʃɔɪ.juː (US) 'ʃoʊ.juː
shrank (*from* **shrink**) ʃræŋk
shrapnel 'ʃræp.nᵊl
shred ʃred **-s** -z **-ding** -ɪŋ **-ded** -ɪd **-der/s** -əʳ/z (US) -ɚ/z
Shredded Wheat® ˌʃred.ɪd'*h*wiːt **-s** -s
shrew ʃruː **-s** -z
shrewd ʃruːd **-er** -əʳ (US) -ɚ **-est** -ɪst, -əst **-ly** -li **-ness** -nəs, -nɪs
shrewish 'ʃruː.ɪʃ **-ly** -li **-ness** -nəs, -nɪs
Shrewsbury *in the UK:* 'ʃrəʊz.bᵊr.i, 'ʃruːz-, '-bri (US) 'ʃruːzˌber.i, 'ʃroʊz-, -bɚ-
Note: /'ʃrəʊz-/ is the most widely used pronunciation, but /'ʃruːz-/ or /'ʃuːz-/ is more usually used by many local people.
Shrewsbury *in the US:* 'ʃruːz.bᵊr.i (US) -ˌber-, -bɚ-
shriek ʃriːk **-s** -s **-ing** -ɪŋ **-ed** -t
shrift ʃrɪft
shrike ʃraɪk **-s** -s
shrill ʃrɪl **-er** -əʳ (US) -ɚ **-est** -ɪst, -əst **-y** -i, -li **-ness** -nəs, -nɪs
shrimp ʃrɪmp **-s** -s **-ing** -ɪŋ **-er/s** -əʳ/z (US) -ɚ/z
Shrimpton 'ʃrɪmp.tən
shrine ʃraɪn **-s** -z
shriner (S) 'ʃraɪ.nəʳ (US) -nɚ **-s** -z
shrink ʃrɪŋk **-s** -s **-ing/ly** -ɪŋ/li **shrank** ʃræŋk **shrunk** ʃrʌŋk **shrunken** 'ʃrʌŋ.kən **ˌshrinking 'violet**
shrinkage 'ʃrɪŋ.kɪdʒ
shrink-wrap 'ʃrɪnk.ræp, -'- **-s** -s **-ping** -ɪŋ **-ped** -t
shriv|e (S) ʃraɪv **-es** -z **-ing** -ɪŋ **shrove** ʃrəʊv (US) ʃroʊv **shriven** 'ʃrɪv.ᵊn
shrivel 'ʃrɪv.ᵊl **-s** -z **-(l)ing** -ɪŋ, 'ʃrɪv.lɪŋ **-(l)ed** -d
shriven (*from* **shrive**) 'ʃrɪv.ᵊn
shroff ʃrɒf (US) ʃrɑːf **-s** -s **-ing** -ɪŋ **-ed** -t
Shropshire 'ʃrɒp.ʃəʳ, -ˌʃɪəʳ (US) 'ʃrɑːp.ʃɚ, -ˌʃɪr
shroud ʃraʊd **-s** -z **-ing** -ɪŋ **-ed** -ɪd **-less** -ləs, -lɪs
shrove (*from* **shrive**) ʃrəʊv (US) ʃroʊv
Shrove ʃrəʊv (US) ʃroʊv **ˌShrove 'Tuesday**
Shrovetide 'ʃrəʊv.taɪd (US) 'ʃroʊv-
shrub ʃrʌb **-s** -z
shrubber|y 'ʃrʌb.ᵊr|.i **-ies** -iz
shrubby 'ʃrʌb.i
shrug ʃrʌg **-s** -z **-ging** -ɪŋ **-ged** -d
shrunk (*from* **shrink**) ʃrʌŋk **-en** -ᵊn
shtick ʃtɪk
shuck ʃʌk **-s** -s **-ing** -ɪŋ **-ed** -d
Shuckburgh 'ʃʌk.bᵊr.ə (US) -bɝːg, -bɚ.ə
shudd|er 'ʃʌd|.əʳ (US) -ɚ **-ers** -əz (US) -ɚz **-ering** -ᵊr.ɪŋ **-ered** -əd (US) -ɚd
shuffl|e 'ʃʌf.l̩ **-es** -z **-ing** -ɪŋ, 'ʃʌf.lɪŋ **-ed** -d **-er/s** -əʳ/z, 'ʃʌf.ləʳ/z (US) '-l̩.ɚ/z, '-lɚ/z
shuffleboard 'ʃʌf.l̩.bɔːd (US) -bɔːrd **-s** -z
shufti 'ʃʊf.ti, 'ʃʌf- **-s** -z
Shulamite 'ʃuː.lə.maɪt
shun ʃʌn **-s** -z **-ning** -ɪŋ **-ned** -d
shunt ʃʌnt **-s** -s **-ing** -ɪŋ (US) 'ʃʌn.t̬ɪŋ **-ed** -ɪd (US) 'ʃʌn.t̬ɪd **-er/s** -əʳ/z (US) 'ʃʌn.t̬ɚ/z
shush ʃʊʃ, ʃʌʃ **-es** -ɪz **-ing** -ɪŋ **-ed** -t
shut ʃʌt **-s** -s **-ting** -ɪŋ (US) 'ʃʌt̬.ɪŋ
shutdown 'ʃʌt.daʊn **-s** -z
Shute ʃuːt
shut-eye 'ʃʌt.aɪ (US) 'ʃʌt̬-
shutout 'ʃʌt.aʊt **-s** -z
shutt|er 'ʃʌt|.əʳ (US) 'ʃʌt̬|.ɚ **-ers** -əz (US) -ɚz **-ering** -ᵊr.ɪŋ **-ered** -əd (US) -ɚd
shuttle 'ʃʌt.l̩ (US) 'ʃʌt̬- **-s** -z **-ling** -ɪŋ **-ed** -d **ˌshuttle di'plomacy**
shuttlecock 'ʃʌt.l̩.kɒk (US) 'ʃʌt̬.l̩.kɑːk **-s** -s
Shuttleworth 'ʃʌt.l̩.wəθ, -wɜːθ (US) 'ʃʌt̬.l̩.wɚθ, -wɝːθ
shwa ʃwɑː **-s** -z

sh|y ʃl|aɪ **-ies** -aɪz **-yer** -aɪ.əʳ US -aɪ.ɚ **-yest** -aɪ.ɪst, -aɪ.əst **-yly** -aɪ.li **-yness** -aɪ.nəs, -nɪs **-ying** -aɪ.ɪŋ **-ied** -aɪd
shylock (S) ˈʃaɪ.lɒk US -lɑːk
shyster ˈʃaɪ.stəʳ US -stɚ **-s** -z
si siː
Sialkot siˈæl.kɒt US -ˈɑːl.koʊt
Siam ˌsaɪˈæm, ˈ-- US saɪˈæm
Siamese ˌsaɪ.əˈmiːz US -ˈmiːz, -ˈmiːs *stress shift, see compounds:* **ˌSiamese ˈcat; ˌSiamese ˈtwins**
Sian, Siân ʃɑːn
Sibbald ˈsɪb.əld
Sibelius sɪˈbeɪ.li.əs US -li.əs, -ˈbeɪl.jəs
Siberi|a saɪˈbɪə.ri|.ə US -ˈbɪr.i- **-an/s** -ən/z
sibilan|ce ˈsɪb.ɪ.lᵊn|*t*s, -ᵊl.ᵊn|*t*s US -ᵊl.ᵊn|*t*s **-t/s** -t/s
sibilation ˌsɪb.ɪˈleɪ.ʃᵊn US -ᵊlˈeɪ-, -əˈleɪ **-s** -z
Sibley ˈsɪb.li
sibling ˈsɪb.lɪŋ **-s** -z **ˌsibling ˈrivalry**
sibyl (S) ˈsɪb.ᵊl, -ɪl US -ᵊl **-s** -z
sibylline ˈsɪb.ə.laɪn, ˈ-ɪ-; sɪˈbɪl.aɪn US ˈsɪb.ə.laɪn, -liːn, -lɪn
sic sɪk, siːk
Sichuan ˌsɪtʃˈwɑːn US ˈ-ˌ-
Sicilian sɪˈsɪl.jən, sə-, -i.ən **-s** -z
Sicil|y ˈsɪs.ɪ.l|i, -ᵊl|.i US -ᵊl|.i **-ies** -iz
sick sɪk **-er** -əʳ US -ɚ **-est** -ɪst, -əst **-ness** -nəs, -nɪs **ˈsick ˌbay; ˌsick ˈbuilding ˌsyndrome; ˈsick ˌleave; ˈsick ˌpay**
sickbed ˈsɪk.bed **-s** -z
sicken ˈsɪk.ᵊn **-s** -z **-ing/ly** -ɪŋ, ˈsɪk.nɪŋ **-ed** -d
Sickert ˈsɪk.ət US -ɚt
sickle ˈsɪk.l̩ **-s** -z **ˌsickle-cell aˈn(a)emia**
sickl|y ˈsɪk.l|i **-ier** -i.əʳ US -i.ɚ **-iest** -i.ɪst, -i.əst **-iness** -ɪ.nəs, -ɪ.nɪs
sickness ˈsɪk.nəs, -nɪs
sicko ˈsɪk.əʊ US -oʊ **-s** -z
sick-out ˈsɪk.aʊt **-s** -s
sickroom ˈsɪk.rʊm, -ruːm US -ruːm, -rʊm **-s** -z
sic transit gloria mundi ˌsɪkˌtræn.zɪtˌglɔː.ri.əˈmʊn.di, ˌsiːk-, -ˌtræn*t*.sɪt-, -ˌtrɑːn.zɪt-, -ˌtrɑːn*t*.sɪt- US ˌsɪkˌtræn.sɪtˌglɔːr.i.əˈmʌn.di
Sid sɪd
Sidcup ˈsɪd.kʌp, -kəp
Siddeley ˈsɪd.ᵊl.i
Siddharta sɪˈdɑː.tə US -ˈdɑːr.t̬ə
Siddons ˈsɪd.ᵊnz
sid|e saɪd **-es** -z **-ing** -ɪŋ **-ed** -ɪd **ˈside ˌarm; ˌside by ˈside; ˈside ˌdish; ˈside ˌdrum; ˈside efˌfect; ˈside ˌissue; ˈside ˌsalad; ˈside ˌstreet; ˌknow which ˌside one's ˌbread is ˈbuttered (on), ˌknow which ˌside one's ˈbread is ˌbuttered (on); ˌlaugh on the ˌother ˌside of one's ˈface; ˌlook on the ˈbright ˌside (of things)**
sidebar ˈsaɪd.bɑːʳ US -bɑːr **-s** -z
sideboard ˈsaɪd.bɔːd US -bɔːrd **-s** -z
Sidebotham ˈsaɪdˌbɒt.əm US -ˌbɑː.t̬əm
Sidebottom ˈsaɪdˌbɒt.əm, ˈsiːd-, ˌsɪd.ɪ.bəˈtəʊm US ˈsaɪdˌbɑː.t̬əm, ˈsiːd-; ˌsɪd.ɪ.bəˈtoʊm
sideburn ˈsaɪd.bɜːn US -bɝːn **-s** -z
sidecar ˈsaɪd.kɑːʳ US -kɑːr **-s** -z
sidedish ˈsaɪd.dɪʃ **-es** -ɪz
sidekick ˈsaɪd.kɪk **-s** -s
sidelight ˈsaɪd.laɪt **-s** -s
sidelin|e ˈsaɪd.laɪn **-es** -z **-ing** -ɪŋ **-ed** -d
sidelong ˈsaɪd.lɒŋ US -lɑːŋ, -lɔːŋ
sidereal saɪˈdɪə.ri.əl, sɪ- US saɪˈdɪr.i-
siderite ˈsaɪ.dᵊr.aɪt, ˈsɪd.ᵊr- US ˈsɪd.ə.raɪt
Sidery ˈsaɪ.dᵊr.i
sidesaddle ˈsaɪdˌsæd.l̩ **-s** -z
sideshow ˈsaɪd.ʃəʊ US -ʃoʊ **-s** -z
sideslip ˈsaɪd.slɪp **-s** -s **-ping** -ɪŋ **-ped** -t
sides|man ˈsaɪdz|.mən **-men** -mən, -men
sidespin ˈsaɪd.spɪn
sidesplitting ˈsaɪdˌsplɪt.ɪŋ US -ˌsplɪt̬-
sidestep ˈsaɪd.step **-s** -s **-ping** -ɪŋ **-ped** -t
sidestroke ˈsaɪd.strəʊk US -stroʊk **-s** -s
sideswip|e ˈsaɪd.swaɪp **-es** -s **-ing** -ɪŋ **-ed** -t
sidetrack ˈsaɪd.træk **-s** -s **-ing** -ɪŋ **-ed** -t
sidewalk ˈsaɪd.wɔːk US -wɑːk, -wɔːk **-s** -s
sideways ˈsaɪd.weɪz
sidewinder ˈsaɪdˌwaɪn.dəʳ US -dɚ **-s** -z
Sidgwick ˈsɪdʒ.wɪk
siding ˈsaɪ.dɪŋ **-s** -z
Sidlaw ˈsɪd.lɔː US -lɑː, -lɔː
sidl|e ˈsaɪ.dl̩ **-es** -z **-ing** -ɪŋ, ˈsaɪd.lɪŋ **-ed** -d
Sidmouth ˈsɪd.məθ
Sidney ˈsɪd.ni
Sidon ˈsaɪ.dᵊn, -dɒn US -dᵊn
Sidonian saɪˈdəʊ.ni.ən, sɪ- US saɪˈdoʊ.ni.ən **-s** -z
Sidonie sɪˈdəʊ.ni US -ˈdoʊ-
sieg|e siːdʒ **-es** -ɪz **ˈsiege menˌtality**
Siegfried ˈsiːg.friːd *as if German:* ˈziːg US ˈsɪg-, ˈsiːg-
Sieg Heil ˌsiːgˈhaɪl *as if German:* ˌziːk-
Sieglinde siːˈglɪn.də *as if German:* ziː- US siː-, ziː-, sɪ-
Siegmund ˈsiːg.mʊnd *as if German:* ˈziːg-, -mənd US ˈsɪg-, ˈsiːg-
Siemens ˈsiː.mənz *as if German:* ˈziː- **ˌSiemens-ˈNixdorf®**
Siena siˈen.ə
Sienese ˌsi.enˈiːz, -əˈniːz US -əˈniːz, -ˈniːs
sienna siˈen.ə
sierra (S) siˈer.ə, -ˈeə.rə; US siˈer.ə **-s** -z
Sierra Leone siˌer.ə.liˈəʊn, -ˌeə.rə-, -ˈəʊ.ni US siˌer.ə.liˈoʊn
Sierra Madre siˌer.əˈmɑː.dreɪ, -ˌeə.rəˈ-; US siˌer.əˈ-
Sierra Nevada siˌer.ə.nəˈvɑː.də, -ˈeə.rə-; US siˌer.ə.nəˈvæd.ə, -ˈvɑː.də
siesta siˈes.tə **-s** -z
siev|e sɪv **-es** -z **-ing** -ɪŋ **-ed** -d
sift sɪft **-s** -s **-ing** -ɪŋ **-ed** -ɪd **-er/s** -əʳ/z US -ɚ/z
sigh saɪ **-s** -z **-ing** -ɪŋ **-ed** -d
sight saɪt **-s** -s **-ing/s** -ɪŋ/s US ˈsaɪ.t̬ɪŋ/s **-ed** -ɪd US ˈsaɪ.t̬ɪd **-less/ness** -ləs, -lɪs **ˌsight unˈseen**
sightl|y ˈsaɪt.l|i **-iness** -ɪ.nəs, -ɪ.nɪs
sightread *present tense:* ˈsaɪt.riːd **-s** -z **-ing** -ɪŋ *past tense:* ˈsaɪt.red
sightreader ˈsaɪtˌriː.dəʳ US -dɚ **-s** -z
sightscreen ˈsaɪt.skriːn **-s** -z
sightsee ˈsaɪt.siː **-s** -z **-ing** -ɪŋ
sight-seeing ˈsaɪtˌsiː.ɪŋ
sightseer ˈsaɪtˌsiː.əʳ US -ɚ **-s** -z
Sigismond, Sigismund ˈsɪg.ɪs.mənd, ˈsɪdʒ-, -ɪz- US -ɪs-
sigma (S) ˈsɪg.mə **-s** -z
Sigmund ˈsɪg.mənd *as if German:* ˈzɪg-
sign saɪn **-s** -z **-ing/s** -ɪŋ/s **-ed** -d **-er/s** -əʳ/z US -ɚ/z **-age** -ɪdʒ **ˈsign ˌlanguage; ˌsign of the ˈtimes**
signal ˈsɪg.nᵊl **-s** -z **-(l)y** -i **-(l)ing** -ɪŋ **-(l)ed** -d **-(l)er/s** -əʳ/z US -ɚ/z **ˈsignal ˌbox**
signaliz|e, -is|e ˈsɪg.nᵊl.aɪz US -nə.laɪz **-es** -ɪz **-ing** -ɪŋ **-ed** -d
signal|man ˈsɪg.nᵊl|.mən, -mæn **-men** -mən, -men
signator|y ˈsɪg.nə.tᵊr|.i US -tɔːr- **-ies** -
signature ˈsɪg.nə.tʃəʳ, -nɪ- US -nə.tʃɚ **-s** -z **ˈsignature ˌtune**
signboard ˈsaɪn.bɔːd, ˈsaɪm- US ˈsaɪn.bɔːrd **-s** -z
signer ˈsaɪ.nəʳ US -nɚ **-s** -z
signet ˈsɪg.nɪt, -nət **-s** -s **ˈsignet ˌring**
significance sɪgˈnɪf.ɪ.kən*t*s, ˈ-ə- US ˈ-ə-
significant sɪgˈnɪf.ɪ.kənt, ˈ-ə- US ˈ-ə- **-ly** -li **sigˌnificant ˈother**
signification ˌsɪg.nɪ.fɪˈkeɪ.ʃᵊn, -nə- US -nə-
significative sɪgˈnɪf.ɪ.kə.tɪv, ˈ-ə-, -ke- US -keɪ.t̬ɪv **-ly** -li **-ness** -nəs, -nɪs
signi|fy ˈsɪg.nɪ|.faɪ, -nə- US -nə- **-fies** -faɪz **-fying** -faɪ.ɪŋ **-fied** -faɪd **-fier/s** -faɪ.əʳ/z US -faɪ.ɚ/z
signor (S) ˈsiː.njɔːʳ US siːˈnjɔːr **-s** -z
signora (S) siːˈnjɔː.r|ə US -ˈnɔːr|.ə **-az** -əz **-ez** -eɪz
signorina (S) ˌsiː.njɔːˈriː.nə, -njəˈ-
signpost ˈsaɪn.pəʊst, ˈsaɪm- US ˈsaɪn.poʊst **-s** -s **-ing** -ɪŋ **-ed** -ɪd
Sigourney sɪˈgɔː.ni, sə- US -ˈgɔːr-
Sigurd *English first name:* ˈsiː.gɜːd, ˈsɪg.ɜːd US ˈsɪg.ɚd *Scandinavian name:* ˈsɪg.ʊəd, -ɜːd US ˈsɪg.ɚd

Sikes saɪks
Sikh siːk **-s** -s **-ism** -ɪ.zᵊm
Sikkim 'sɪk.ɪm, sɪ'kɪm (US) 'sɪk.ɪm
Sikorsky sɪ'kɔː.ski (US) -'kɔːr-
silage 'saɪ.lɪdʒ
Silas 'saɪ.ləs, -læs (US) -ləs
Silchester 'sɪl.tʃɪ.stəʳ, -tʃə-, -tʃes.təʳ (US) -tʃes.tɚ
Sileby 'saɪl.bi
silenc|e 'saɪ.lənts **-es** -ɪz **-ing** -ɪŋ **-ed** -t
silencer 'saɪ.lənt.səʳ (US) -sɚ **-s** -z
silent 'saɪ.lənt **-ly** -li **-ness** -nəs, -nɪs **ˌsilent ma'jority; ˌsilent 'partner**
Silenus saɪ'liː.nəs, sɪ-, -'leɪ- (US) saɪ'liː-
Silesi|a saɪ'liː.zi|.ə, sɪ-, -ʒi|.ə, '-ʒ|ə, -si|.ə, -ʃi|.ə, '-ʃ|ə (US) saɪ'liː.ʃ|ə, sɪ-, -ʒ|ə **-an/s** -ən/z
silex 'saɪ.leks
silhouett|e ˌsɪl.u'et, '--- (US) ˌsɪl.u'et **-es** -s **-ing** -ɪŋ **-ed** -ɪd
silica 'sɪl.ɪ.kə **ˌsilica 'gel** (US) **'silica ˌgel**
silicate 'sɪl.ɪ.keɪt, '-ə-, -kət, -kɪt (US) -ɪ.keɪt, -kɪt
silicon 'sɪl.ɪ.kən, '-ə- (US) '-ɪ-, -kɑːn **ˌsilicon 'chip** (US) **'silicon ˌchip; ˌSilicon 'Valley**
silicone 'sɪl.ɪ.kəʊn, '-ə- (US) -ɪ.koʊn
silicosis ˌsɪl.ɪ'kəʊ.sɪs, -ə'- (US) -ɪ'koʊ-
silicotic ˌsɪl.ɪ'kɒt.ɪk, -ə'- (US) -ɪ'kɑː.t̬ɪk **-s** -s
silk (S) sɪlk **-s** -s **-en** -ᵊn
Silkin 'sɪl.kɪn
silk-screen 'sɪlk.skriːn **-s** -z **-ing** -ɪŋ **-ed** -d **ˌsilk-screen 'printing**
silkworm 'sɪlk.wɜːm (US) -wɝːm **-s** -z
silk|y 'sɪl.k|i **-ier** -i.əʳ (US) -i.ɚ **-iest** -i.ɪst, -i.əst **-iness** -ɪ.nəs, -ɪ.nɪs
sill (S) sɪl **-s** -z
sillabub 'sɪl.ə.bʌb, -bəb (US) -bʌb **-s** -z
sillery 'sɪl.ᵊr.i
Sillitoe 'sɪl.ɪ.təʊ (US) -toʊ
Silloth 'sɪl.əθ
sill|y 'sɪl|.i **-ies** -iz **-ier** -i.əʳ (US) -i.ɚ **-iest** -i.ɪst, -i.əst **-ily** -ɪ.li, -ᵊl.i **-iness** -ɪ.nəs, -ɪ.nɪs
silly-bill|y ˌsɪl.i'bɪl|.i **-ies** -iz
silo 'saɪ.ləʊ (US) -loʊ **-s** -z
Siloam saɪ'ləʊ.əm, sɪ-, -æm (US) sɪ'loʊ.əm, saɪ-
Silsden 'sɪlz.dən
silt sɪlt **-s** -s **-ing** -ɪŋ (US) 'sɪl.t̬ɪŋ **-ed** -ɪd (US) 'sɪl.t̬ɪd **-y** -i (US) 'sɪl.t̬i
Silurian saɪ'lʊə.ri.ən, sɪ-, -'ljʊə-, -'ljɔː- (US) sɪ'lʊr.i-, saɪ-
Silva 'sɪl.və
Silvan 'sɪl.vən
Silvanus sɪl'veɪ.nəs
silv|er (S) 'sɪl.v|əʳ (US) -v|ɚ **-ers** -əz (US) -ɚz **-ering** -ᵊr.ɪŋ **-ered** -əd (US) -ɚd **-ery** -ᵊr.i **-eriness** -ᵊr.ɪ.nəs, -nɪs **ˌsilver 'birch; ˌsilver 'foil** (US) **'silver ˌfoil; ˌsilver 'lining; ˌsilver 'nitrate; ˌsilver 'paper; ˌsilver 'plate;** (US) **'silver ˌplate; ˌsilver 'screen; ˌsilver 'spoon; ˌsilver 'wedding**
silverfish 'sɪl.və.fɪʃ (US) -vɚ- **-es** -ɪz
Silverman 'sɪl.və.mən (US) -vɚ-
Silvers 'sɪl.vəz (US) -vɚz
silverside 'sɪl.və.saɪd (US) -vɚ- **-s** -z
silversmith 'sɪl.və.smɪθ (US) -vɚ- **-s** -s
Silverstone 'sɪl.və.stəʊn, -stən (US) -vɚ.stoʊn, -stən
silver-tongued ˌsɪl.və'tʌŋd (US) -vɚ'- *stress shift:* ˌsilver-tongued 'devil
Silvertown 'sɪl.və.taʊn (US) -vɚ- **-s** -z
silverware 'sɪl.və.weəʳ (US) -vɚ.wer
Silvester sɪl'ves.təʳ (US) -tɚ
Silvia 'sɪl.vi.ə
Silvikrin® 'sɪl.vɪ.krɪn, -və-
Sim sɪm
Simca® 'sɪm.kə **-s** -z
Simcox 'sɪm.kɒks (US) -kɑːks
Simenon 'siː.mə.nɔ̃ːŋ, 'sɪm.ə-, -nɒn (US) 'siː.mə.noʊn, -nɔ̃ːn
Simeon 'sɪm.i.ən
simian 'sɪm.i.ən **-s** -z
similar 'sɪm.ɪ.ləʳ, '-ə- (US) -ə.lɚ **-ly** -li
similarit|y ˌsɪm.ɪ'lær.ə.t|i, -ə'-, -ɪ.t|i (US) -ə'ler.ə.t̬|i, -'lær- **-ies** -iz
simile 'sɪm.ɪ.li, -ᵊl.i (US) -ə.li **-s** -z
similitude sɪ'mɪl.ɪ.tjuːd, '-ə-, -tʃuːd (US) sə'mɪl.ə.tuːd, -tjuːd **-s** -z
Simla 'sɪm.lə
simm|er 'sɪm|.əʳ (US) -ɚ **-ers** -əz (US) -ɚz **-ering** -ᵊr.ɪŋ **-ered** -əd (US) -ɚd
Simmonds 'sɪm.əndz
Simmons 'sɪm.ənz
Simms sɪmz
simnel (S) 'sɪm.nᵊl **-s** -z **'simnel ˌcake**
Simon 'saɪ.mən
Simond 'saɪ.mənd, 'sɪm.ənd
Simonds 'sɪm.əndz
Simone sɪ'məʊn, sə- (US) -'moʊn
simoniacal ˌsaɪ.məʊ'naɪə.kᵊl (US) -mə'-, ˌsɪm.ə'-
Simons 'saɪ.mənz
simony 'saɪ.mə.ni, 'sɪm.ə-
simoom sɪ'muːm (US) sɪ-, saɪ- **-s** -z
simpatico sɪm'pæt.ɪ.kəʊ (US) -'pæt̬.ɪ.koʊ
simp|er 'sɪm.p|əʳ (US) -p|ɚ **-ers** -əz (US) -ɚz **-ering/ly** -ᵊr.ɪŋ **-ered** -əd (US) -ɚd
Simpkin 'sɪmp.kɪn **-s** -z **-son** -sən
simp|le 'sɪm.p|l **-ler** -ləʳ (US) -lɚ **-lest** -lɪst, -ləst **-ly** -li **-leness** -l̩.nəs, -nɪs
simplehearted ˌsɪm.pl̩'hɑː.tɪd (US) -'hɑːr.t̬ɪd *stress shift:* ˌsimplehearted 'person
simple-minded ˌsɪm.pl̩'maɪn.dɪd *stress shift:* ˌsimple-minded 'person
simpleton 'sɪm.pl̩.tᵊn (US) -tən **-s** -z
simplex 'sɪm.pleks **-es** -ɪz
simplicity sɪm'plɪs.ə.ti, -ɪ.ti (US) -ə.t̬i
simplification ˌsɪm.plɪ.fɪ'keɪ.ʃᵊn, -plə- (US) -plə- **-s** -z
simpli|fy 'sɪm.plɪ|.faɪ (US) -plə- **-fies** -faɪz **-fying** -faɪ.ɪŋ **-fied** -faɪd
simplistic sɪm'plɪs.tɪk **-ally** -ᵊl.i, -li
Simplon 'sæ̃m.plɔ̃ːŋ, 'sæm-, 'sɪm-, -plən (US) 'sɪm.plɑːn; 'sæ̃m.plɔ̃ːn
simply 'sɪm.pli
Simpson 'sɪmp.sən
Sims sɪmz
Simson 'sɪmp.sən
simulacr|um ˌsɪm.jə'leɪ.kr|əm, -jʊ'-, -'læk.r|əm (US) -'leɪ-, -'læk.r|əm **-ums** -əmz **-a** -ə
simu|late 'sɪm.jə|.leɪt, -jʊ- **-lates** -leɪts **-lating** -leɪ.tɪŋ (US) -leɪ.t̬ɪŋ **-lated** -leɪ.tɪd (US) -leɪ.t̬ɪd
simulation ˌsɪm.jə'leɪ.ʃᵊn, -jʊ'- **-s** -z
simulator 'sɪm.jə.leɪ.təʳ, -jʊ- (US) -t̬ɚ **-s** -z **'flight ˌsimulator**
simulcast 'sɪm.ᵊl.kɑːst (US) 'saɪ.mᵊl.kæst, 'sɪm.ᵊl- **-s** -s **-ing** -ɪŋ
simultaneity ˌsɪm.ᵊl.tə'neɪ.ə.ti, ˌsaɪ.mᵊl-, -'niː-, -ɪ.ti (US) ˌsaɪ.mᵊl.tə'niː.ə.t̬i, ˌsɪm.ᵊl-
simultaneous ˌsɪm.ᵊl'teɪ.ni.əs, ˌsaɪ.mᵊl'- (US) ˌsaɪ.mᵊl'teɪ.njəs, ˌsɪm.ᵊl'-, -ni.əs **-ly** -li **-ness** -nəs, -nɪs
sin *(n. v.) do wrong:* sɪn **-s** -z **-ning** -ɪŋ **-ned** -d **-ner/s** -əʳ/z (US) -ɚ/z **'sin ˌbin**
sin *in trigonometry:* saɪn
Sinai 'saɪ.naɪ, -ni.aɪ, -neɪ- (US) 'saɪ.naɪ
sinapism 'sɪn.ə.pɪ.zᵊm **-s** -z
Sinatra sɪ'nɑː.trə
Sinbad 'sɪn.bæd, 'sɪm- (US) 'sɪn-
since sɪnts
sincer|e sɪn'sɪəʳ, sᵊn- (US) sɪn'sɪr **-er** -əʳ (US) -ɚ **-est** -ɪst, -əst **-ely** -li **-eness** -nəs, -nɪs
sincerity sɪn'ser.ə.ti, sᵊn-, -ɪ.ti (US) sɪn'ser.ə.t̬i
Sinclair 'sɪŋ.kleəʳ, 'sɪn-, -kləʳ; sɪŋ'kleəʳ, sɪn- (US) sɪn'kler, '--
Sind sɪnd
Sindbad 'sɪnd.bæd
Sindh sɪnd
Sindhi 'sɪn.diː, -di
Sindlesham 'sɪn.dl̩.ʃəm
Sindy® 'sɪn.di **'Sindy ˌdoll**
sine saɪn **-s** -z
Sinead, Sinéad ʃɪ'neɪd, -'neəd (US) -'neɪd
sinecure 'saɪ.nɪ.kjʊəʳ, 'sɪn.ɪ-, -kjɔːʳ (US) 'saɪ.nə.kjʊr, 'sɪn.ə- **-s** -z
sine die ˌsaɪ.nɪ'daɪ.iː, -ɪ; ˌsɪn.ɪ'diː.eɪ (US) ˌsaɪ.ni'daɪ.i, ˌsɪn.eɪ'diː.eɪ
Sinel 'sɪn.ᵊl
sine qua non ˌsɪn.i.kwɑː'nəʊn, ˌsaɪ.ni.kweɪ'nɒn (US) ˌsɪn.eɪ.kwɑː'noʊn, ˌsaɪ.ni.kweɪ'nɑːn **-s** -z

sinew ˈsɪn.juː **-s** -z **-y** -i
sinfonia sɪnˈfəʊ.ni.ə; ˌsɪn.fəʊˈniː- US ˌsɪn.fəˈniː-; sɪnˈfoʊ.ni- **-s** -z
sinfonia concertante sɪnˌfəʊ.ni.əˌkɒn*t*.ʃəˈtæn.teɪ US ˌsɪn.fəˌniː.əˌkɑːn*t*.sɚˈtɑːn.teɪ, -ˌkɑːn.tʃɚˈ-; sɪnˌfoʊ.ni-
sinfonietta ˌsɪn.fəʊ.niˈet.ə, -fɒn.iˈ- US -fəˈnjet̬-, -foʊˈ- **-s** -z
sinful ˈsɪn.fᵊl, -fʊl **-ly** -i **-ness** -nəs, -nɪs
sing sɪŋ **-s** -z **-ing** -ɪŋ **sang** sæŋ **sung** sʌŋ **singer/s** ˈsɪŋ.əʳ/z US -ɚ/z
singable ˈsɪŋ.ə.bl̩
sing-along ˈsɪŋ.ə.lɒŋ US -lɑːŋ **-s** -z
Singapore ˌsɪŋ.əˈpɔːʳ, -gəˈ-, ˈ--- US ˈsɪŋ.ə.pɔːr, -gə-
Singaporean ˌsɪŋ.ə.pɔːˈriː.ən, -gə-; -ˈpɔː.ri- US ˌsɪŋ.ə.pɔːˈriː-, -gə-; -ˈpɔːr.i- **-s** -z
sing|e sɪndʒ **-es** -ɪz **-eing** -ɪŋ **-ed** -d
Singer ˈsɪŋ.əʳ, -gəʳ US -ɚ, -gɚ
Singh sɪŋ
Singhalese ˌsɪŋ.*h*əˈliːz, -gəˈ- US -gəˈliːz, -ˈliːs
sing|le (S) ˈsɪŋ.gl̩ **-les** -l̩z **-ling** -ɪŋ, -sɪŋ.glɪŋ **-led** -d **-ly** -li **-leness** -l̩.nəs, -nɪs ˌ**single ˈbed** US ˈ**single ˌbed**; ˌ**single ˈcurrency**; ˌ**single ˈfile**; ˌ**single ˈfigures**
single-breasted ˌsɪŋ.gl̩ˈbres.tɪd *stress shift:* ˌsingle-breasted ˈjacket
single-decker ˌsɪŋ.gl̩ˈdek.əʳ US -ɚ **-s** -z *stress shift:* ˌsingle-decker ˈbus
single-handed ˌsɪŋ.gl̩ˈhæn.dɪd **-ly** -li **-ness** -nəs, -nɪs *stress shift:* ˌsingle-handed ˈcrossing
single-hearted ˌsɪŋ.gl̩ˈhɑː.tɪd US ˈsɪŋ.gl̩ˌhɑːr.t̬ɪd **-ly** -li **-ness** -nəs, -nɪs *stress shift, British only:* ˌsingle-hearted ˈlove
single-minded ˌsɪŋ.gl̩ˈmaɪn.dɪd US ˈsɪŋ.gl̩ˌmaɪn- **-ly** -li **-ness** -nəs, -nɪs *stress shift, British only:* ˌsingle-minded ˈperson
singlestick ˈsɪŋ.gl̩.stɪk **-s** -s
singlet ˈsɪŋ.glɪt, -glət **-s** -s
singleton (S) ˈsɪŋ.gl̩.tən US -t̬ən, -tən **-s** -z
singly ˈsɪŋ.gli
singsong ˈsɪŋ.sɒŋ US -sɑːŋ, -sɔːŋ **-s** -z
singular ˈsɪŋ.gjə.ləʳ, -gjʊ- US -lɚ **-s** -z **-ly** -li
singularit|y ˌsɪŋ.gjəˈlær.ə.t|i, -gjʊˈ-, -ɪ.t|i US -ˈler.ə.t̬|i, -ˈlær- **-ies** -iz
Sinhalese ˌsɪŋ.*h*əˈliːz, ˌsɪn- US ˌsɪn.*h*əˈliːz, -ˈliːs
Sinim ˈsɪn.ɪm, ˈsaɪ.nɪm
sinister ˈsɪn.ɪ.stəʳ US -stɚ
sinistral ˈsɪn.ɪ.strᵊl **-ly** -i
Sinitic saɪˈnɪt.ɪk, sɪ- US -ˈnɪt̬-
sink sɪŋk **-s** -s **-ing** -ɪŋ **sank** sæŋk **sunk** sʌŋk **sunken** ˈsʌŋ.kᵊn
sinker ˈsɪŋ.kəʳ US -kɚ **-s** -z
sinless ˈsɪn.ləs, -lɪs **-ly** -li **-ness** -nəs, -nɪs
sinner ˈsɪn.əʳ US -ɚ **-s** -z
Sinn Fein ˌʃɪnˈfeɪn **-er/s** -əʳ/z US -ɚ/z
sinologue ˈsɪn.ə.lɒg, ˈsaɪ.nə-, -ləʊg US ˈsaɪ.nə.lɑːg, ˈsɪn.ə-, -lɔːg **-s** -z
sinolog|y saɪˈnɒl.ə.dʒ|i, sɪ- US -ˈnɑː.lə- **-ist/s** -ɪst/s
sinuosit|y ˌsɪn.juˈɒs.ə.t|i, -ɪ.t|i US -ˈɑː.sə.t̬|i **-ies** -iz
sinuous ˈsɪn.ju.əs **-ly** -li **-ness** -nəs, -nɪs
sinus ˈsaɪ.nəs **-es** -ɪz
sinusitis ˌsaɪ.nəˈsaɪ.tɪs US -t̬ɪs
sinusoid ˈsaɪ.nə.sɔɪd **-s** -z
Siobhan ʃɪˈvɔːn, ʃə- US -ˈvɑːn, -ˈvɔːn
Sion ˈsaɪ.ən, ˈzaɪ- US ˈsaɪ-
Sioux *singular:* suː, sjuː US suː *plural:* suːz, sjuːz, suː, sjuː US suːz, suː
sip sɪp **-s** -s **-ping** -ɪŋ **-ped** -t
siphon (*n. v.*) ˈsaɪ.fᵊn **-s** -z **-ing** -ɪŋ, ˈsaɪf.nɪŋ **-ed** -d
sir (S) *strong forms:* sɜːʳ US sɝː *weak forms:* səʳ US sɚ **-s** -z

Note: Weak form word. The strong form is used in various social situations. In school, it is often used by children to address a male teacher (e.g. "Sir, can I go now?"), and contrastively (e.g. "Dear Sir or Madam"). Similarly, in old-fashioned speech, the strong form would be used to begin addressing someone (e.g. "Sir, you are a scoundrel"). When it occurs utterance-finally in addressing someone, either form may be used, although the weak form is more common in military usage (e.g. "Ready to sail, sir"). In the title of a Knight (e.g. **Sir John Roberts**), the weak form is always used.

sirdar (S) ˈsɜː.dɑːʳ US sɚˈdɑːr; ˈsɝː.dɑːr **-s** -z
sir|e saɪəʳ US saɪɚ **-es** -z **-ing** -ɪŋ **-ed** -d
siren ˈsaɪə.rən, -rɪn US ˈsaɪ.rən **-s** -z
Sirion ˈsɪr.i.ən
Sirius ˈsɪr.i.əs
sirloin ˈsɜː.lɔɪn US ˈsɝː- **-s** -z
sirocco sɪˈrɒk.əʊ, sə- US səˈrɑː.koʊ, ʃə- **-s** -z
Siros ˈsɪə.rɒs US ˈsiː.rɑːs
sirrah ˈsɪr.ə
sirree, siree ˌsɜːˈriː, sə- US sə-
sis sɪs
sisal ˈsaɪ.sᵊl US ˈsaɪ-, ˈsɪs.ᵊl
Sisal *Mexican port:* sɪˈsɑːl US ˈsiː.səl, ˈsɪs.ɑːl
Sisera ˈsɪs.ᵊr.ə
siskin (S) ˈsɪs.kɪn **-s** -z
Sisley ˈsɪz.li
Sissinghurst ˈsɪs.ɪŋ.hɜːst US -hɝːst
Sisson ˈsɪs.ᵊn **-s** -z
siss|y ˈsɪs|.i **-ies** -iz
sist|er ˈsɪs.t|əʳ US -t|ɚ **-ers** -əz US -ɚz **-erly** -ᵊl.i US -ɚ.li
sisterhood ˈsɪs.tə.hʊd US -tɚ- **-s** -z
sister-in-law ˈsɪs.tᵊr.ɪn.lɔː US -tɚ.ɪn.lɑː, -lɔː **sisters-in-law** -t US -tɚz-
Sistine ˈsɪs.tiːn, -taɪn US -tiːn, -ˈ- ˌ**Sistine ˈChapel**
sistrum ˈsɪs.trəm **-s** -z
Sisulu sɪˈsuː.luː
Sisyphean, Sisyphian ˌsɪs.ɪˈfiː.ən, - US -əˈ-
Sisyphus ˈsɪs.ɪ.fəs, ˈ-ə- US ˈ-ə-
sit sɪt **-s** -s **-ting** -ɪŋ/z US ˈsɪt̬.ɪŋ/z **sat** sæt ˌ**Sitting ˈBull**; ˌ**sit on the ˈfenc**
Sita ˈsɪt.ə, ˈsiː.tə US ˈsiː.tɑː
sitar sɪˈtɑːʳ; ˈsɪt.ɑːʳ US sɪˈtɑːr
sitcom ˈsɪt.kɒm US -kɑːm **-s** -z
sit-down ˈsɪt.daʊn
sit|e saɪt **-es** -s **-ing** -ɪŋ **-ed** -ɪd
sit-in ˈsɪt.ɪn US ˈsɪt̬- **-s** -z
sitter ˈsɪt.əʳ US ˈsɪt̬.ɚ **-s** -z
sitting ˈsɪt.ɪŋ US ˈsɪt̬- **-s** -z ˌ**sitting ˈduck**; ˈ**sitting ˌroom**; ˌ**sitting ˈtarg** ˌ**sitting ˈtenant**
Sittingbourne ˈsɪt.ɪŋ.bɔːn US ˈsɪt̬.ɪŋ.bɔːrn
situate (*adj.*) ˈsɪt.ju.eɪt, ˈsɪtʃ.u-, -ɪt -ət US ˈsɪtʃ.u.ɪt, -eɪt
situ|ate (*v.*) ˈsɪt.ju|.eɪt, ˈsɪtʃ.u- US ˈsɪtʃ.u- **-ates** -eɪts **-ating** -eɪ.t US -eɪ.t̬ɪŋ **-ated** -eɪ.tɪd US -eɪ.t̬ɪd
situation ˌsɪt.juˈeɪ.ʃᵊn, ˌsɪtʃ.uˈ- US ˌsɪtʃ.uˈ- **-s** -z ˌ**situation ˈcome**
sit-up ˈsɪt.ʌp **-s** -s
Sitwell ˈsɪt.wəl, -wel
Siva ˈʃiː.və, ˈsiː-, ˈsɪv.ə, ˈʃɪv- US ˈʃiː ˈsiː-
Siward ˈsjuː.əd US -ɚd, ˈsuː-
six sɪks **-es** -ɪz **-fold** -fəʊld US -foʊld
sixer ˈsɪk.səʳ US -sɚ **-s** -z
sixish ˈsɪk.sɪʃ
six-pack ˈsɪks.pæk **-s** -s
six|pence ˈsɪks|.pən*t*s **-pences** -pən*t*.sɪz **-penny** -pᵊn.i

Note: See note under **penny**.

six-shooter ˈsɪksˌʃuː.təʳ, ˈsɪkʃ-, ˌ-ˈ- US ˈsɪksˌʃuː.t̬ɚ **-s** -z
sixte sɪkst
sixteen ˌsɪkˈstiːn **-s** -z **-th/s** -θ/s **-thl** -θ.li *stress shift, British only:* ˌsixteen ˈdays **sixˈteenth ˌnote**
sixteenmo, 16mo sɪkˈstiːn.məʊ US -moʊ **-s** -z
sixth sɪksθ US sɪkstθ **-s** -s **-ly** -li ˈ**sixt ˌform**; ˌ**sixth form ˈcollege**; ˌ**sixth ˈsense**
Sixtus ˈsɪk.stəs
sixt|y ˈsɪk.st|i **-ies** -iz **-ieth/s** -i.əθs, -i.ɪθ/s

sixty-nine, 69 ˌsɪk.stiˈnaɪn
sizar ˈsaɪ.zəʳ (US) -zɚ **-s** -z **-ship/s** -ʃɪp/s
siz|e saɪz **-es** -ɪz **-ing** -ɪŋ **-ed** -d
sizeab|le, sizab|le ˈsaɪ.zə.b|l̩ **-ly** -li **-leness** -l̩.nəs, -nɪs
Sizer ˈsaɪ.zəʳ (US) -zɚ
Sizewell ˈsaɪz.wəl, -wel
sizzl|e ˈsɪz.l̩ **-es** -z **-ing** -ɪŋ, ˈsɪz.lɪŋ **-ed** -d
sizzler ˈsɪz.ləʳ, -l̩.əʳ (US) ˈ-lɚ, -l̩.ɚ **-s** -z
sjambok ˈʃæm.bɒk, -bʌk (US) -bɑːk, -bʌk **-s** -s **-ing** -ɪŋ **-ed** -t
ska skɑː
Skagerrak ˈskæg.ə.ræk
Skara Brae ˌskær.əˈbreɪ
skat skæt
skat|e skeɪt **-es** -s **-ing** -ɪŋ (US) ˈskeɪ.t̬ɪŋ **-ed** -ɪd (US) ˈskeɪ.t̬ɪd **-er/s** -əʳ/z (US) ˈskeɪ.t̬ɚ/z
skateboard ˈskeɪt.bɔːd (US) -bɔːrd **-s** -z **-er/s** -əʳ/z (US) -ɚ/z **-ing** -ɪŋ
skating-rink ˈskeɪ.tɪŋ.rɪŋk **-s** -s
skean dhu ˌskiː.ənˈduː, ˌskiːnˈ- (US) ˌskiːn-, ˌʃkiːn- **-s** -z
Skeat skiːt
skedaddl|e skɪˈdæd.l̩ **-es** -z **-ing** -ɪŋ, -ˈdæd.lɪŋ **-ed** -d
Skeels skiːlz
Skeggs skegz
Skegness ˌskegˈnes *stress shift:* ˌSkegness ˈbeach
skein skeɪn **-s** -z
skeletal ˈskel.ɪ.tᵊl, ˈ-ə-; skɪˈliː-, skə- (US) ˈskel.ə.t̬ᵊl **-ly** -i
skeleton ˈskel.ɪ.tᵊn, ˈ-ə- (US) ˈ-ə- **-s** -z **ˈskeleton ˌkey; ˌskeleton in the ˈcupboard; ˌskeleton in the ˈcloset**
Skelmanthorpe ˈskel.mən.θɔːp (US) -θɔːrp
Skelmersdale ˈskel.məz.deɪl (US) -mɚz-
skelter ˈskel.təʳ (US) -t̬ɚ
Skelton ˈskel.tᵊn
skeptic ˈskep.tɪk **-s** -s **-al** -ᵊl **-ally** -ᵊl.i, -li
skepticism ˈskep.tɪ.sɪ.zᵊm, -tə- (US) -tə-
sketch sketʃ **-es** -ɪz **-ing** -ɪŋ **-ed** -t **-able** -ə.bl̩ **-er/s** -əʳ/z (US) -ɚ/z
sketchbook ˈsketʃ.bʊk **-s** -s
Sketchley ˈsketʃ.li
sketchpad ˈsketʃ.pæd **-s** -z
sketch|y ˈsketʃ|.i **-ier** -i.əʳ (US) -i.ɚ **-iest** -i.ɪst, -i.əst **-ily** -ɪ.li, -ᵊl.i **-iness** -ɪ.nəs, -ɪ.nɪs
skew skjuː **-s** -z **-ing** -ɪŋ **-ed** -d
skewbald ˈskjuː.bɔːld (US) -bɑːld, -bɔːld
skewer skjʊəʳ (US) ˈskjuː.ɚ, ˈskjuː.ɚ **-s** -z **-ing** -ɪŋ **-ed** -d
skew-whiff ˌskjuːˈhwɪf
Skey skiː
ski skiː **-s** -z **-ing** -ɪŋ **-ed** -d **ˈski ˌlift; ˈski ˌpants**
skibob ˈskiː.bɒb (US) -bɑːb **-s** -z **-bing** -ɪŋ **-bed** -d

skid skɪd **-s** -z **-ding** -ɪŋ **-ded** -ɪd **-dy** -i **ˌskid ˈrow**
Skiddaw ˈskɪd.ɔː *locally:* -ə (US) ˈskɪd.ɑː, -ɔː
Skidmore ˈskɪd.mɔːʳ (US) -mɔːr
skidpan ˈskɪd.pæn **-s** -z
skier ˈskiː.əʳ (US) -ɚ **-s** -z
skiff skɪf **-s** -s
skiffle ˈskɪf.l̩
ski-jump ˈskiː.dʒʌmp **-s** -s **-ing** -ɪŋ **-ed** -t **-er/s** -əʳ/z (US) -ɚ/z
skilful ˈskɪl.fᵊl, -fʊl **-ly** -i **-ness** -nəs, -nɪs
skill skɪl **-s** -z **-ed** -d
skillet ˈskɪl.ɪt **-s** -s
skilly ˈskɪl.i
skim skɪm **-s** -z **-ming** -ɪŋ **-med** -d **-mer/s** -əʳ/z (US) -ɚ/z
skimp skɪmp **-s** -s **-ing** -ɪŋ/li **-ed** -t
skimp|y ˈskɪm.p|i **-ier** -i.əʳ (US) -i.ɚ **-iest** -i.ɪst, -i.əst **-ily** -ɪ.li, -ᵊl.i **-iness** -ɪ.nəs, -ɪ.nɪs
skin skɪn **-s** -z **-ning** -ɪŋ **-ned** -d **-less** -ləs, -lɪs **by the ˌskin of one's ˈteeth**
skincare ˈskɪn.keəʳ, ˈskɪŋ- (US) -ker
skin-deep ˌskɪnˈdiːp (US) ˌskɪnˈdiːp, ˈ-- *stress shift, British only:* ˌskin-deep ˈwound
skin-div|ing ˈskɪnˌdaɪ.v|ɪŋ **-er/s** -əʳ/z (US) -ɚ/z
skinflint ˈskɪn.flɪnt **-s** -s
skinful ˈskɪn.fʊl **-s** -z
skinhead ˈskɪn.hed **-s** -z
skink skɪŋk **-s** -s
skinner (S) ˈskɪn.əʳ (US) -ɚ **-s** -z
skinn|y ˈskɪn|.i **-ier** -i.əʳ (US) -i.ɚ **-iest** -i.ɪst, -i.əst **-iness** -ɪ.nəs, -ɪ.nɪs
skinny-dip ˈskɪn.i.dɪp **-s** -s **-ping** -ɪŋ **-ped** -t
skint skɪnt
skintight ˈskɪn.taɪt
skip skɪp **-s** -s **-ping** -ɪŋ **-ped** -t
skipjack ˈskɪp.dʒæk **-s** -s
skipper ˈskɪp.əʳ (US) -ɚ **-s** -z **-ing** -ɪŋ **-ed** -d
skipping-rope ˈskɪp.ɪŋ.rəʊp (US) -roʊp **-s** -s
Skipton ˈskɪp.tən
skirl skɜːl (US) skɝːl **-s** -z
skirmish ˈskɜː.mɪʃ (US) ˈskɝː- **-es** -ɪz **-ing** -ɪŋ **-ed** -t **-er/s** -əʳ/z (US) -ɚ/z
skirt skɜːt (US) skɝːt **-s** -s **-ing** -ɪŋ/z (US) ˈskɝː.t̬ɪŋ/s **-ed** -ɪd (US) ˈskɝː.t̬ɪd
skirting ˈskɜː.tɪŋ (US) ˈskɝː.t̬ɪŋ **-s** -z
skirting-board ˈskɜː.tɪŋ.bɔːd (US) ˈskɝː.t̬ɪŋ.bɔːrd **-s** -z
skit skɪt **-s** -s
skitter ˈskɪt.əʳ (US) ˈskɪt̬.ɚ **-s** -z **-ing** -ɪŋ **-ed** -d
skittish ˈskɪt.ɪʃ (US) ˈskɪt̬- **-ly** -li **-ness** -nəs, -nɪs
skittle ˈskɪt.l̩ (US) ˈskɪt̬- **-s** -z
skiv|e skaɪv **-es** -z **-ing** -ɪŋ **-ed** -d **-er/s** -əʳ/z (US) -ɚ/z

skivv|y ˈskɪv|.i **-ies** -iz
Skoda® ˈskəʊ.də (US) ˈskoʊ-
Skol® skɒl, skəʊl (US) skoʊl, skɑːl
Skopje ˈskɔː.pjeɪ, ˈskɒp.jeɪ (US) ˈskɔː.pjeɪ, ˈskɑː-
Skrimshire ˈskrɪm.ʃəʳ, -ˌʃaɪəʳ (US) -ʃɚ, -ˌʃaɪɚ
Skrine skriːn
skua ˈskjuː.ə, skjʊə (US) ˈskjuː.ə **-s** -z
skulk skʌlk **-s** -s **-ing** -ɪŋ **-ed** -t
skull skʌl **-s** -z **ˌskull and ˈcrossbones**
skullcap ˈskʌl.kæp **-s** -s
skul(l)duggery skʌlˈdʌg.ᵊr.i
skunk skʌŋk **-s** -s
sk|y (S®) sk|aɪ **-ies** -aɪz **-ying** -aɪ.ɪŋ **-ied** -aɪd **-ier/s** -aɪ.əʳ/z (US) -aɪ.ɚ/z
sky-blue ˌskaɪˈbluː *stress shift:* ˌsky-blue ˈfabric
skycap (S) ˈskaɪ.kæp **-s** -s
skydiv|er ˈskaɪˌdaɪ.v|əʳ (US) -v|ɚ **-ers** -əz (US) -ɚz **-ing** -ɪŋ
Skye skaɪ
sky-high ˌskaɪˈhaɪ *stress shift:* ˌsky-high ˈprices
skyjack ˈskaɪ.dʒæk **-s** -s **-ing** -ɪŋ **-ed** -t **-er/s** -əʳ/z (US) -ɚ/z
skylark ˈskaɪ.lɑːk (US) -lɑːrk **-s** -s **-ing** -ɪŋ **-ed** -t **-er/s** -əʳ/z (US) -ɚ/z
skylight ˈskaɪ.laɪt **-s** -s
skyline ˈskaɪ.laɪn **-s** -z
skyrock|et ˈskaɪˌrɒk|.ɪt (US) -ˌrɑː.k|ɪt **-ets** -ɪts **-eting** -ɪ.tɪŋ (US) -ɪ.t̬ɪŋ **-eted** -ɪ.tɪd (US) -ɪ.t̬ɪd
skyscape ˈskaɪ.skeɪp **-s** -s
skyscraper ˈskaɪˌskreɪ.pəʳ (US) -pɚ **-s** -z
skyward ˈskaɪ.wəd (US) -wɚd **-s** -z
skywriting ˈskaɪˌraɪ.tɪŋ (US) -t̬ɪŋ
slab slæb **-s** -z **-bing** -ɪŋ **-bed** -d
slack slæk **-s** -s **-er** -əʳ (US) -ɚ **-est** -ɪst, -əst **-ly** -li **-ness** -nəs, -nɪs **-ing** -ɪŋ **-ed** -t **-er/s** -əʳ/z (US) -ɚ/z
slacken ˈslæk.ᵊn **-s** -z **-ing** -ɪŋ, ˈslæk.nɪŋ **-ed** -d
Slade sleɪd
slag slæg **-s** -z **-ging** -ɪŋ **-ged** -d **-gy** -i
slagheap ˈslæg.hiːp **-s** -s
slain *(from* **slay***)* sleɪn
slainte ˈslɑːn.tʃə, -tjə
Slaithwaite ˈslæθ.wət, -weɪt *locally also:* ˈslaʊ.ɪt
slak|e sleɪk **-es** -s **-ing** -ɪŋ **-ed** -t
slalom ˈslɑː.ləm **-s** -z
slam slæm **-s** -z **-ming** -ɪŋ **-med** -d
slam-bang ˌslæmˈbæŋ *stress shift:* ˌslam-bang ˈclatter
slam-dunk ˌslæmˈdʌŋk, ˈ-- **-s** -s **-ing** -ɪŋ **-ed** -t
slammer ˈslæm.əʳ (US) -ɚ **-s** -z
sland|er ˈslɑːn.d|əʳ (US) ˈslæn.d|ɚ **-ers** -əz (US) -ɚz **-ering** -ᵊr.ɪŋ **-ered** -əd (US) -ɚd **-erer/s** -ᵊr.əʳ/z (US) -ɚ.ɚ/z

slanderous 'slɑː n.dᵊr.əs, '-drəs (US) 'slæn.dɚ.əs, '-drəs **-ly** -li **-ness** -nəs, -nɪs

slang slæŋ **-s** -z **-ing** -ɪŋ **-ed** -d **-y** -i **-ier** -i.əʳ (US) -i.ɚ **-iest** -i.ɪst, -i.əst **-ily** -ɪ.li, -ᵊl.i **-iness** -ɪ.nəs, -ɪ.nɪs **'slanging ˌmatch**

slant slɑːnt (US) slænt **-s** -s **-ing/ly** -ɪŋ/li (US) 'slæn.t̬ɪŋ/li **-ed** -ɪd (US) 'slæn.t̬ɪd

slantways 'slɑːnt.weɪz (US) 'slænt-

slantwise 'slɑːnt.waɪz (US) 'slænt-

slap slæp **-s** -s **-ping** -ɪŋ **-ped** -t **ˌslap and 'tickle**

slap-bang ˌslæp'bæŋ *stress shift:* ˌslap-bang 'central

slapdash 'slæp.dæʃ, ˌ-'-

slaphappy ˌslæp'hæp.i (US) '-ˌ-- *stress shift, British only:* ˌslaphappy 'state

slapstick 'slæp.stɪk **-s** -s

slap-up ˌslæp'ʌp (US) '-- *stress shift, British only:* ˌslap-up 'meal

slash slæʃ **-es** -ɪz **-ing** -ɪŋ **-ed** -t **-er/s** -əʳ/z (US) -ɚ/z

slash-and-burn ˌslæʃ.ᵊn*d*'bɜːn, -ᵊm'- (US) -ᵊn*d*'bɝːn *stress shift:* ˌslash-and-burn 'farming

slat slæt **-s** -s **-ted** -ɪd

slat|e sleɪt **-es** -s **-ing** -ɪŋ (US) 'sleɪ.t̬ɪŋ **-ed** -ɪd (US) 'sleɪ.t̬ɪd **-er/s** -əʳ/z (US) 'sleɪ.t̬ɚ/z

Slater 'sleɪ.təʳ (US) -t̬ɚ

slath|er 'slæð|.əʳ (US) -ɚ **-ers** -əz (US) -ɚz **-ering** -ᵊr.ɪŋ **-ered** -əd (US) -ɚd

Slatkin 'slæt.kɪn

slattern 'slæt.ən, -ɜːn (US) 'slæt̬.ɚn **-s** -z **-ly** -li **-liness** -lɪ.nəs, -nɪs

Slattery 'slæt.ᵊr.i (US) 'slæt̬.ɚ-

slaty 'sleɪ.ti (US) -t̬i

slaught|er (S) (*n. v.*) 'slɔː.t|əʳ (US) 'slɑː.t̬|ɚ, 'slɔː- **-ers** -əz (US) -ɚz **-ering** -ᵊr.ɪŋ **-ered** -əd (US) -ɚd **-erer/s** -ᵊr.əʳ/z (US) -ɚ.ɚ/z **-erous/ly** -ᵊr.əs/li

slaughterhou|se 'slɔː.tə.haʊ|s (US) 'slɑː.t̬ɚ-, 'slɔː- **-ses** -zɪz

Slav slɑːv (US) slɑːv, slæv **-s** -z

slav|e sleɪv **-es** -z **-ing** -ɪŋ **-ed** -d **-er/s** -əʳ/z (US) -ɚ/z **'slave ˌdriver; ˌslave 'labour; 'slave ˌtrade**

slave-owner 'sleɪvˌəʊ.nəʳ (US) -ˌoʊ.nɚ **-s** -z

slaver *slave-trader:* 'sleɪ.vəʳ (US) -vɚ **-s** -z

slav|er (*n. v.*) *slobber:* 'slæv|.əʳ, 'sleɪ.v|əʳ (US) 'slæv|.ɚ **-ers** -əz (US) -ɚz **-ering** -ᵊr.ɪŋ **-ered** -əd (US) -ɚd

slavery 'sleɪ.vᵊr.i

slavey 'sleɪ.vi, 'slæv.i **-s** -z

Slavic 'slɑː.vɪk, 'slæv.ɪk

slavish 'sleɪ.vɪʃ **-ly** -li **-ness** -nəs, -nɪs

Slavonic slə'vɒn.ɪk, slæv'ɒn- (US) slə'vɑː.nɪk

slaw slɔː (US) slɑː, slɔː **-s** -z

slay sleɪ **-s** -z **-ing/s** -ɪŋ/z **-ed slew** sluː **slain** sleɪn **slayer/s** sleɪ.əʳ/z (US) -ɚ/z

Slazenger® 'slæz.ᵊn.dʒəʳ (US) -dʒɚ

Sleaford 'sliː.fəd (US) -fɚd

sleaze sliːz

sleazebag 'sliːz.bæg **-s** -z

sleazeball 'sliːz.bɔːl (US) -bɔːl, -bɑːl **-s** -z

sleaz|y 'sliː.z|i **-ier** -i.əʳ (US) -i.ɚ **-iest** -i.ɪst, -i.əst **-ily** -ɪ.li, -ᵊl.i **-iness** -ɪ.nəs, -ɪ.nɪs

sled sled **-s** -z **-ding** -ɪŋ **-ded** -ɪd

sledg|e sledʒ **-es** -ɪz **-ing** -ɪŋ **-ed** -d

sledgehammer 'sledʒˌhæm.əʳ (US) -ɚ **-s** -z **-ing** -ɪŋ **-ed** -d

sleek sliːk **-er** -əʳ (US) -ɚ **-est** -ɪst, -əst **-ly** -li **-ness** -nəs, -nɪs

sleep sliːp **-s** -s **-ing** -ɪŋ **slept** slept **'sleeping ˌbag; ˌSleeping 'Beauty; 'sleeping ˌcar; 'sleeping ˌdraught; 'sleeping ˌpill; 'sleeping ˌpartner; ˌsleeping po'liceman; 'sleeping ˌsickness**

sleeper 'sliː.pəʳ (US) -pɚ **-s** -z

sleepless 'sliː.pləs, -plɪs **-ly** -li **-ness** -nəs, -nɪs

sleepout 'sliːp.aʊt **-s** -s

sleepover 'sliːpˌəʊ.vəʳ (US) -ˌoʊ.vɚ **-s** -z

sleepwalk|er 'sliːpˌwɔː.k|əʳ (US) -ˌwɑː.k|ɚ, -ˌwɔː- **-ers** -əz (US) -ɚz **-ing** -ɪŋ

sleep|y 'sliː.p|i **-ier** -i.əʳ (US) -i.ɚ **-iest** -i.ɪst, -i.əst **-ily** -ɪ.li, -ᵊl.i **-iness** -ɪ.nəs, -ɪ.nɪs

sleepyhead 'sliː.pi.hed **-s** -z

sleet sliːt **-s** -s **-ing** -ɪŋ (US) 'sliː.t̬ɪŋ **-ed** -ɪd (US) 'sliː.t̬ɪd **-y** -i (US) 'sliː.t̬i **-iness** -ɪ.nəs, -ɪ.nɪs (US) 'sliː.t̬ɪ.nəs, -nɪs

sleeve sliːv **-s** -z **-d** -d **-less** -ləs, -lɪs

sleigh sleɪ **-s** -z **-ing** -ɪŋ **-ed** -d **'sleigh ˌbells**

sleight (S) slaɪt **ˌsleight of 'hand**

Sleights slaɪts

slender 'slen.dəʳ (US) -dɚ **-er** -əʳ (US) -ɚ **-est** -ɪst, -əst **-ly** -li **-ness** -nəs, -nɪs

slenderiz|e 'slen.dᵊr.aɪz (US) -də.raɪz **-es** -ɪz **-ing** -ɪŋ **-ed** -d

slept *(from* **sleep***)* slept

sleuth sluːθ, sljuːθ (US) sluːθ **-s** -s **-ing** -ɪŋ **-ed** -t

sleuthhound 'sluːθ.haʊnd, 'sljuːθ- (US) 'sluːθ- **-s** -z

slew sluː **-s** -z **-ing** -ɪŋ **-ed** -d

slic|e slaɪs **-es** -ɪz **-ing** -ɪŋ **-ed** -t **-er/s** -əʳ/z (US) -ɚ/z **ˌsliced 'bread**

slick slɪk **-er** -əʳ (US) -ɚ **-est** -ɪst, -əst **-s** -s **-z -ing** -ɪŋ **-ly** -li **-ed** -d **-ness** -nəs, -nɪs

slicker 'slɪk.əʳ (US) -ɚ **-s** -z

slid *(from* **slide***)* slɪd

slid|e slaɪd **-es** -z **-ing** -ɪŋ **slid** slɪd **'slide proˌjector; 'slide ˌrule; 'slide ˌvalve; ˌsliding 'door; ˌsliding 'scale**

slider 'slaɪ.dəʳ (US) -dɚ **-s** -z

slight slaɪt **-s** -s **-er** -əʳ (US) 'slaɪ.t̬ɚ **-est** -ɪst, -əst (US) 'slaɪ.t̬ɪst, -t̬əst **-ly** -li **-ness** -nəs, -nɪs **-ing/ly** -ɪŋ/li (US) 'slaɪ.t̬ɪŋ/li **-ed** -ɪd (US) 'slaɪ.t̬ɪd

Sligo 'slaɪ.gəʊ (US) -goʊ

slim (S) slɪm **-mer/s** -əʳ/z (US) -ɚ/z **-mest** -ɪst **-est** -əst **-ly** -li **-ness** -nəs, -nɪs **-s** -z **-ming** -ɪŋ **-med** -d **'Slim diˌsease**

Slimbridge 'slɪm.brɪdʒ

slim|e slaɪm **-es** -z **-ing** -ɪŋ **-ed** -d

slimline 'slɪm.laɪn

slim|y 'slaɪ.m|i **-ier** -i.əʳ (US) -i.ɚ **-iest** -i.ɪst, -i.əst **-ily** -ɪ.li, -ᵊl.i **-iness** -ɪ.nəs, -ɪ.nɪs

sling slɪŋ **-s** -z **-ing** -ɪŋ **slung** slʌŋ

slingback 'slɪŋ.bæk **-s** -s

slingshot 'slɪŋ.ʃɒt (US) -ʃɑːt **-s** -s

slink slɪŋk **-s** -s **-ing** -ɪŋ **slunk** slʌŋk

slink|y 'slɪŋ.k|i **-ier** -i.əʳ (US) -i.ɚ **-iest** -i.ɪst, -i.əst

slip slɪp **-s** -s **-ping** -ɪŋ **-ped** -t **ˌslipped 'disc; 'slip ˌroad; 'slip ˌstitch; ˌgive someone the 'slip**

slipcas|e 'slɪp.keɪs **-es** -ɪz

slipcover 'slɪpˌkʌv.əʳ (US) -ɚ **-s** -z

slipknot 'slɪp.nɒt (US) -nɑːt **-s** -s

slip-on 'slɪp.ɒn (US) -ɑːn **-s** -z

slipover 'slɪpˌəʊ.vəʳ (US) -ˌoʊ.vɚ **-s** -z

slippag|e 'slɪp.ɪdʒ **-es** -ɪz

slipper 'slɪp.əʳ (US) -ɚ **-s** -z **-ing** -ɪŋ **-ed** -d

slipper|y 'slɪp.ᵊr|.i **-ier** -i.əʳ (US) -i.ɚ **-iest** -i.ɪst, -i.əst **-ily** -ɪ.li, -ᵊl.i **-iness** -ɪ.nəs, -ɪ.nɪs **ˌslippery 'slope**

slipp|y 'slɪp|.i **-ier** -i.əʳ (US) -i.ɚ **-iest** -i.ɪst, -i.əst **-iness** -ɪ.nəs, -ɪ.nɪs

slipshod 'slɪp.ʃɒd (US) -ʃɑːd

slipstream 'slɪp.striːm **-s** -z **-ing** -ɪŋ **-ed** -d

slip-up 'slɪp.ʌp **-s** -s

slipway 'slɪp.weɪ **-s** -z

slit slɪt **-s** -s **-ting** -ɪŋ (US) 'slɪt̬.ɪŋ

slith|er 'slɪð|.əʳ (US) -ɚ **-ers** -əz (US) -ɚz **-ering** -ᵊr.ɪŋ **-ered** -əd (US) -ɚd **-ery** -ᵊr…

sliv|er 'slɪv|.əʳ (US) -ɚ **-ers** -əz (US) -ɚz **-ering** -ᵊr.ɪŋ **-ered** -əd (US) -ɚd

slivovitz 'slɪv.ə.vɪts, 'sliː.və- (US) 'slɪv.ə…

Sloan sləʊn (US) sloʊn

Sloan|e sləʊn (US) sloʊn **-es** -z **-ey** -i **-ier** -i.əʳ (US) -ɚ **-iest** -i.ɪst, -əst **ˌSloane 'Ranger; ˌSloane 'Square**

slob slɒb (US) slɑːb **-s** -z **-bing** -ɪŋ **-bed** -… **-bish** -ɪʃ

slobb|er 'slɒb|.əʳ (US) 'slɑː.b|ɚ **-ers** -əz (US) -ɚz **-ering** -ᵊr.ɪŋ **-ered** -əd (US) -ɚ… **-erer/s** -ə.rəʳ/z (US) -ɚ.ɚ/z

slobber|y 'slɒb.ᵊr|.i (US) 'slɑː.bɚ- **-ines…** -ɪ.nəs, -ɪ.nɪs

Slobodan 'slɒb.ə.dæn, slə'bɒd.ən (US) 'slɑː.bə-

Slocombe 'sləʊ.kəm (US) 'sloʊ-

Slocum 'sləʊ.kəm (US) 'sloʊ-

sloe sləʊ (US) sloʊ **-s** -z **ˌsloe 'gin**

slog slɒg (US) slɑːg, slɔːg **-s** -z **-ging** -ɪŋ **-ged** -d **-ger/s** -ər/z (US) -ɚ/z

slogan ˈsləʊ.gən (US) ˈsloʊ- **-s** -z

sloganeer ˌsləʊ.gəˈnɪər (US) ˌsloʊ.gəˈnɪr **-s** -z **-ing/s** -ɪŋ/z **-ed** -d

sloganiz|e, -is|e ˈsləʊ.gə.naɪz (US) ˈsloʊ- **-es** -ɪz **-ing** -ɪŋ **-ed** -d **-er/s** -ər/z (US) -ɚ/z

sloop sluːp **-s** -s

slop slɒp (US) slɑːp **-s** -s **-ping** -ɪŋ **-ped** -t

slop|e sləʊp (US) sloʊp **-es** -s **-ing** -ɪŋ/li **-ed** -t **-er/s** -ər/z (US) -ɚ/z

Sloper ˈsləʊ.pər (US) ˈsloʊ.pɚ

slopp|y ˈslɒp|.i (US) ˈslɑː.p|i **-ier** -i.ər (US) -i.ɚ **-iest** -i.ɪst, -i.əst **-ily** -ɪ.li, -əl.i **-iness** -ɪ.nəs, -ɪ.nɪs ˌ**sloppy** ˈ**joe**

slosh slɒʃ (US) slɑːʃ **-es** -ɪz **-ing** -ɪŋ **-ed** -t

slosh|y ˈslɒʃ|.i (US) ˈslɑː.ʃ|i **-ier** -i.ər (US) -i.ɚ **-iest** -i.ɪst, -i.əst **-iness** -ɪ.nəs, -ɪ.nɪs

slot slɒt (US) slɑːt **-s** -s **-ting** -ɪŋ (US) ˈslɑː.t̬ɪŋ **-ted** -ɪd (US) ˈslɑː.t̬ɪd

sloth sləʊθ (US) slɑːθ, slɔːθ, sloʊθ **-s** -s

slothful ˈsləʊθ.fəl, -fʊl (US) ˈslɑːθ-, ˈslɔːθ-, ˈsloʊθ- **-ly** -i **-ness** -nəs, -nɪs

slot-machine ˈslɒt.məˌʃiːn (US) ˈslɑːt- **-s** -z

slouch slaʊtʃ **-es** -ɪz **-ing/ly** -ɪŋ/li **-ed** -t

slough (*n.*) *bog:* slaʊ (US) sluː, slaʊ **-s** -z **-y** -i

slough (*v.*) *skin:* slʌf **-s** -s **-ing** -ɪŋ **-ed** -t

Slough slaʊ

Slovak ˈsləʊ.væk (US) ˈsloʊ.vɑːk, -væk **-s** -s

Slovaki|a sləʊˈvæk.i|.ə, -ˈvɑː.ki- (US) sloʊˈvɑː.ki-, -ˈvæk.i- **-an/s** -ən/z

sloven ˈslʌv.ən **-s** -z

Slovene sləʊˈviːn; ˈsləʊ.viːn (US) ˈsloʊ.viːn **-s** -z

Sloveni|a sləʊˈviː.ni|.ə, ˈ-nj|ə (US) sloʊ- **-an/s** -ən/z

slovenl|y ˈslʌv.ən.l|i **-iness** -ɪ.nəs, -ɪ.nɪs

slow sləʊ (US) sloʊ **-er** -ər (US) -ɚ **-est** -ɪst, -əst **-ly** -li **-ness** -nəs, -nɪs **-s** -z **-ing** -ɪŋ **-ed** -d ˌ**slow** ˈ**motion**

slowcoach ˈsləʊ.kəʊtʃ (US) ˈsloʊ.koʊtʃ **-es** -ɪz

slowdown ˈsləʊ.daʊn (US) ˈsloʊ- **-s** -z

slowpoke ˈsləʊ.pəʊk (US) ˈsloʊ.poʊk **-s** -s

slow-witted ˌsləʊˈwɪt.ɪd (US) ˌsloʊˈwɪt̬-

slowworm ˈsləʊ.wɜːm (US) ˈsloʊ.wɝːm **-s** -z

slub slʌb **-s** -z **-bing** -ɪŋ **-bed** -d

sludg|e slʌdʒ **-y** -i

slu|e sluː **-s** -z **-ing** -ɪŋ **-ed** -d

slug slʌg **-s** -z **-ging** -ɪŋ **-ged** -d

slugabed ˈslʌg.ə.bed **-s** -z

sluggard ˈslʌg.əd (US) -ɚd **-s** -z **-ly** -li

sluggish ˈslʌg.ɪʃ **-ly** -li **-ness** -nəs, -nɪs

sluic|e sluːs **-es** -ɪz **-ing** -ɪŋ **-ed** -t ˈ**sluice** ˌ**gate**

sluiceway ˈsluːs.weɪ **-s** -z

slum slʌm **-s** -z **-ming** -ɪŋ **-med** -d **-mer/s** -ər/z (US) -ɚ/z

slumb|er ˈslʌm.b|ər (US) -b|ɚ **-ers** -əz (US) -ɚz **-ering** -ər.ɪŋ **-ered** -əd (US) -ɚd **-erer/s** -ər.ər/z (US) -ɚ.ɚ/z ˈ**slumber** ˌ**party**

slumm|y ˈslʌm|.i **-ier** -i.ər (US) -i.ɚ **-iest** -i.ɪst, -i.əst **-iness** -ɪ.nəs, -ɪ.nɪs

slump slʌmp **-s** -s **-ing** -ɪŋ **-ed** -t

slung (*from* **sling**) slʌŋ

slunk (*from* **slink**) slʌŋk

slur slɜːr (US) slɝː **-s** -z **-ring** -ɪŋ **-red** -d

slurp slɜːp (US) slɝːp **-s** -s **-ing** -ɪŋ **-ed** -t

slurr|y ˈslʌr|.i (US) ˈslɝː- **-ies** -iz

slush slʌʃ **-y** -i **-ier** -i.ər (US) -i.ɚ **-iest** -i.ɪst, -i.əst **-iness** -ɪ.nəs, -ɪ.nɪs ˈ**slush** ˌ**fund**

slut slʌt **-s** -s **-ty** -i

sluttish ˈslʌt.ɪʃ (US) ˈslʌt̬- **-ly** -li **-ness** -nəs, -nɪs

Sluys slɔɪs

sly slaɪ **-er** -ər (US) -ɚ **-est** -ɪst, -əst **-ly** -li **-ness** -nəs, -nɪs

slyboots ˈslaɪ.buːts

SM ˌesˈem

smack smæk **-s** -s **-ing/s** -ɪŋ/z **-ed** -t **-er/s** -ər/z (US) -ɚ/z

smacker ˈsmæk.ər (US) -ɚ **-s** -z

smackeroo ˌsmæk.ərˈuː (US) -əˈruː **-s** -z

Smale smeɪl

small (S) smɔːl (US) smɔːl, smɑːl **-s** -z **-er** -ər (US) -ɚ **-est** -ɪst, -əst **-ness** -nəs, -nɪs **-ish** -ɪʃ ˈ**small** ˌ**ad,** ˌ**small** ˈ**ad;** ˌ**small** ˈ**arm;** ˌ**small** ˈ**beer;** ˌ**small** ˈ**change;** ˈ**small** ˌ**fry;** ˈ**small** ˌ**hours** (US) ˌ**small** ˈ**hours;** ˌ**small po**ˈ**tatoes;** ˌ**small** ˈ**print,;** ˈ**small** ˌ**print;** (US) ˌ**small** ˈ**print;** ˌ**small** ˈ**screen;** ˈ**small** ˌ**talk**

small-claims ˌsmɔːlˈkleɪmz (US) ˌsmɔːl-, ˌsmɑːl- ˌ**small-**ˈ**claims** ˌ**court,** ˌ**small-claims** ˈ**court**

Smalley ˈsmɔː.li (US) ˈsmɔː-, ˈsmɑː-

small-hold|er ˈsmɔːlˌhəʊl.d|ər (US) -ˌhoʊl.dɚ, ˈsmɑːl- **-ers** -əz (US) -ɚz **-ing/s** -ɪŋ/z

smallish ˈsmɔː.lɪʃ (US) ˈsmɔː-, ˈsmɑː-

small-minded ˌsmɔːlˈmaɪn.dɪd (US) ˌsmɔːl-, ˌsmɑːl- **-ly** -li **-ness** -nəs, -nɪs *stress shift:* ˌsmall-minded ˈperson

smallpox ˈsmɔːl.pɒks (US) -pɑːks, ˈsmɑːl-

small-scale ˌsmɔːlˈskeɪl (US) ˈ--, ˈsmɑːl- *stress shift, British only:* ˌsmall-scale ˈproject

small-tim|e ˌsmɔːlˈtaɪm (US) ˈ--, ˈsmɑːl- **-er/s** -ər/z (US) -ɚ/z

small-town ˈsmɔːl.taʊn (US) ˈsmɔːl-, ˈsmɑːl-

Smallwood ˈsmɔːl.wʊd (US) ˈsmɔːl-, ˈsmɑːl-

smalt smɔːlt, smɒlt (US) smɔːlt, smɑːlt

smarm smɑːm (US) smɑːrm **-s** -z **-ing** -ɪŋ **-ed** -d

smarm|y ˈsmɑː.m|i (US) ˈsmɑːr- **-ily** -ɪli, -əli **-iness** -ɪ.nəs, -ɪ.nɪs

smart (S) smɑːt (US) smɑːrt **-s** -s **-er** -ər (US) ˈsmɑːr.t̬ɚ **-est** -ɪst, -əst (US) ˈsmɑːr.t̬ɪst, -t̬əst **-ly** -li **-ness** -nəs, -nɪs **-ing** -ɪŋ (US) ˈsmɑːr.t̬ɪŋ **-ed** -ɪd (US) ˈsmɑːr.t̬ɪd ˈ**smart** ˌ**alec(k)** (US) ˌ**smart** ˈ**alec(k);** ˈ**smart** ˌ**card;** ˌ**smart** ˈ**money;** ˈ**smart** ˌ**set**

smartarse ˈsmɑːt.ɑːs (US) ˈsmɑːrt.ɑːrs

smartass ˈsmɑːt.ɑːs, -æs (US) ˈsmɑːrt.æs

smarten ˈsmɑː.tən (US) ˈsmɑːr- **-s** -z **-ing** -ɪŋ, ˈsmɑːt.nɪŋ (US) ˈsmɑːrt- **-ed** -d

Smarties® ˈsmɑː.tiz (US) ˈsmɑːr.t̬iz

smartish ˈsmɑː.tɪʃ (US) ˈsmɑːr.t̬ɪʃ

smarty-pants ˈsmɑː.ti.pænts (US) ˈsmɑːr.t̬i-

smash smæʃ **-es** -ɪz **-ing** -ɪŋ **-ed** -t **-er/s** -ər/z (US) -ɚ/z ˌ**smash** ˈ**hit**

smash-and-grab ˌsmæʃ.ənd̚ˈgræb, -əŋˈ- (US) -ənd̚- **-s** -z *stress shift:* ˌsmash-and-grab ˈraid

smattering ˈsmæt.ər.ɪŋ (US) ˈsmæt̬- **-s** -z

smear smɪər (US) smɪr **-s** -z **-ing** -ɪŋ **-ed** -d **-y** -i **-iness** -ɪ.nəs, -ɪ.nɪs ˈ**smear** **cam**ˌ**paign;** ˈ**smear** ˌ**test**

Smeaton ˈsmiː.tən

Smedley ˈsmed.li

Smeeth smiːð, smiːθ

smegma ˈsmeg.mə

smell smel **-s** -z **-ing** -ɪŋ **smelt** -t **smelled** -t, -d ˈ**smelling** ˌ**salts**

smell|y ˈsmel|.i **-ier** -i.ər (US) -i.ɚ **-iest** -i.ɪst, -i.əst **-iness** -ɪ.nəs, -ɪ.nɪs

smelt smelt **-s** -s **-ing** -ɪŋ (US) ˈsmel.t̬ɪŋ **-ed** -ɪd (US) ˈsmel.t̬ɪd **-er/s** -ər/z (US) -ɚ/z

Smetana ˈsmet.ən.ə

Smethwick ˈsmeð.ɪk

smew smjuː **-s** -z

smidgen, smidgin, smidgeon ˈsmɪdʒ.ən, -ɪn **-s** -z

Smieton ˈsmiː.tən

Smike smaɪk

smilax ˈsmaɪ.læks **-es** -ɪz

smil|e smaɪl **-es** -z **-ing/ly** -ɪŋ/li **-ed** -d

Smiles smaɪlz

smil|ey (S) ˈsmaɪ.l|i **-ier** -i.ər (US) -i.ɚ **-iest** -i.ɪst, -i.əst

Smillie ˈsmaɪ.li

smirch smɜːtʃ (US) smɝːtʃ **-es** -ɪz **-ing** -ɪŋ **-ed** -t

smirk smɜːk (US) smɝːk **-s** -s **-ing** -ɪŋ **-ed** -t **-er/s** -ər/z (US) -ɚ/z

Smirke smɜːk (US) smɝːk

Smirnoff® ˈsmɜː.nɒf (US) ˈsmɝː.nɔːf, ˈsmɪr-, -nɑːf

smit (*from* **smite**) smɪt

smit|e smaɪt **-es** -s **-ing** -ɪŋ (US) ˈsmaɪ.t̬ɪŋ **smote** sməʊt (US) smoʊt **smit** smɪt **smitten** ˈsmɪt.ən

smith (S) smɪθ -s -s
Smithells ˈsmɪð.ᵊlz
smithereens ˌsmɪð.ᵊrˈiːnz (US) -əˈriːnz
Smithers ˈsmɪð.əz (US) -ɚz
Smithfield ˈsmɪθ.fiːld
Smithson ˈsmɪθ.sᵊn
Smithsonian smɪθˈsəʊ.ni.ən (US) -ˈsoʊ-
smith|y ˈsmɪð|.i, ˈsmɪθ- (US) ˈsmɪθ-, ˈsmɪð- -ies -iz
smitten (*from* smite) ˈsmɪt.ᵊn
smock smɒk (US) smɑːk -s -s -ing -ɪŋ -ed -t
smog smɒg (US) smɑːg, smɔːg
smogg|y ˈsmɒg|.i (US) ˈsmɑː.g|i, ˈsmɔː- -ier -i.əʳ (US) -i.ɚ -iest -i.ɪst, -i.əst
smok|e sməʊk (US) smoʊk -es -s -ing -ɪŋ -ed -t -er/s -əʳ/z (US) -ɚ/z ˈsmoke aˌlarm; ˌsmoke and ˈmirrors; ˈsmoke ˌscreen; ˈsmoking comˌpartment; ˈsmoking ˌjacket; ˈsmoking ˌroom; ˌgo up in ˈsmoke; there's ˌno ˌsmoke without ˈfire
smokehou|se ˈsməʊk.haʊ|s (US) ˈsmoʊk- -ses -zɪz
smokeless ˈsməʊk.ləs, -lɪs (US) ˈsmoʊk-
smokestack ˈsməʊk.stæk (US) ˈsmoʊk- -s -s ˈsmokestack ˌindustry
Smokies ˈsməʊ.kiz (US) ˈsmoʊ-
smoko ˈsməʊ.kəʊ (US) ˈsmoʊ.koʊ -s -z
smok|y ˈsməʊ.k|i (US) ˈsmoʊ- -ier -i.əʳ (US) -i.ɚ -iest -i.ɪst, -i.əst -ily -ɪ.li, -ᵊl.i -iness -ɪ.nəs, -ɪ.nɪs
smold|er ˈsməʊl.d|əʳ (US) ˈsmoʊl.d|ɚ -ers -əz (US) -ɚz -ering -ᵊr.ɪŋ -ered -əd (US) -ɚd
Smollett ˈsmɒl.ɪt (US) ˈsmɑː.lɪt
smolt sməʊlt (US) smoʊlt
smooch smuːtʃ -es -ɪz -ing -ɪŋ -ed -t -y -i
smooth (*adj.*) smuːð -er -əʳ (US) -ɚ -est -ɪst, -əst -ly -li -ness -nəs, -nɪs
smoothbore ˈsmuːð.bɔːʳ (US) -bɔːr -s -z
smooth|(e) (*v.*) smuːð -(e)s -z -ing -ɪŋ -ed -d
smooth|ie, smooth|y ˈsmuː.ð|i -ies -iz
smorgasbord ˈsmɔː.gəs.bɔːd (US) ˈsmɔːr.gəs.bɔːrd -s -z
smote (*from* smite) sməʊt (US) smoʊt
smoth|er ˈsmʌð|.əʳ (US) -ɚ -ers -əz (US) -ɚz -ering -ᵊr.ɪŋ -ered -əd (US) -ɚd
smould|er ˈsməʊl.d|əʳ (US) ˈsmoʊl.d|ɚ -ers -əz (US) -ɚz -ering -ᵊr.ɪŋ -ered -əd (US) -ɚd
smudg|e smʌdʒ -es -ɪz -ing -ɪŋ -ed -d -y -i -ier -i.əʳ (US) -i.ɚ -iest -i.ɪst, -i.əst -ily -ɪ.li, -ᵊl.i -iness -ɪ.nəs, -ɪ.nɪs
smug smʌg -ly -li -ness -nəs, -nɪs -ger -əʳ (US) -gɚ -gest -ɪst, -gəst
smuggl|e ˈsmʌg|.l̩ -es -z -ing -ɪŋ, ˈsmʌg.lɪŋ -ed -d
smuggler ˈsmʌg.ləʳ, ˈ-l̩.əʳ (US) ˈ-lɚ, ˈ-l̩.ɚ -s -z
smut smʌt -s -s -ty -i (US) ˈsmʌt̬.i -tier -i.əʳ (US) ˈsmʌt̬.i.ɚ -tiest -i.ɪst, -i.əst (US) ˈsmʌt̬.i.ɪst, -i.əst -tily -ɪ.li, -ᵊl.i (US) ˈsmʌt̬.ɪ.li, -ᵊl.i -tiness -ɪ.nəs, -ɪ.nɪs (US) ˈsmʌt̬.ɪ.nəs, -ɪ.nɪs
Smylie ˈsmaɪ.li
Smyrna ˈsmɜː.nə (US) ˈsmɝː-
Smyth smɪθ, smaɪθ
Smythe smaɪð, smaɪθ
snack snæk -s -s -ing -ɪŋ -ed -d ˈsnack ˌbar
Snaefell ˌsneɪˈfel
snaffl|e ˈsnæf.l̩ -es -z -ing -ɪŋ, ˈsnæf.lɪŋ -ed -d
snafu snæfˈuː (US) snæfˈuː, ˈ-- -es -z -ing -ɪŋ -ed -d
snag snæg -s -z -ging -ɪŋ -ged -d
Snagge snæg
snail sneɪl -s -z -like -laɪk ˈsnail's ˌpace
snak|e sneɪk -es -s -ing -ɪŋ -ed -t ˈsnake ˌcharmer; ˌsnakes and ˈladders; ˌsnake in the ˈgrass (US) ˈsnake in the ˌgrass
snakebite ˈsneɪk.baɪt -s -s
snakeskin ˈsneɪk.skɪn
snak|y ˈsneɪ.k|i -iness -ɪ.nəs, -ɪ.nɪs
snap snæp -s -s -ping -ɪŋ -ped -t ˈsnap ˌfastener
snapdragon ˈsnæpˌdræg.ən -s -z
Snape sneɪp
snapper ˈsnæp.əʳ (US) -ɚ -s -z
snappish ˈsnæp.ɪʃ -ly -li -ness -nəs, -nɪs
Snapple® ˈsnæp.l̩
snapp|y ˈsnæp|.i -ier -i.əʳ (US) -i.ɚ -iest -i.ɪst, -i.əst -ily -ɪ.li, -ᵊl.i -iness -ɪ.nəs, -ɪ.nɪs
snapshot ˈsnæp|.ʃɒt (US) -ʃɑːt
snar|e sneəʳ (US) sner -es -z -ing -ɪŋ -ed -d ˈsnare ˌdrum
snark snɑːk (US) snɑːrk -s -s
snarl snɑːl (US) snɑːrl -s -z -ing -ɪŋ -ed -d
snarl-up ˈsnɑːl.ʌp (US) ˈsnɑːrl- -s -s
snatch snætʃ -es -ɪz -ing -ɪŋ -ed -t -er/s -əʳ/z (US) -ɚ/z
snatch|y ˈsnætʃ|.i -ier -i.əʳ (US) -i.ɚ -iest -i.ɪst, -i.əst -ily -ɪ.li, -ᵊl.i
snazz|y ˈsnæz|.i -ier -i.əʳ (US) -i.ɚ -iest -i.ɪst, -i.əst -ily -ɪ.li, -ᵊl.i -iness -ɪ.nəs, -ɪ.nɪs
sneak sniːk -s -s -ing/ly -ɪŋ/li -ed -t -y -i -ier -i.əʳ (US) -i.ɚ -iest -i.ɪst, -i.əst -ily -ɪ.li, -ᵊl.i -iness -ɪ.nəs, -ɪ.nɪs ˌsneak ˈpreview; ˈsneak ˌthief, ˌsneak ˈthief (US) ˈsneak ˌthief
sneaker ˈsniː.kəʳ (US) -kɚ -s -z
sneakers ˈsniː.kəz (US) -kɚz
sneaky ˈsniː.ki -ier -i.əʳ (US) -i.ɚ -iest -i.ɪst, -i.əst -iness -ɪ.nəs, -ɪ.nɪs
Snedden ˈsned.ᵊn
sneer snɪəʳ (US) snɪr -s -z -ing/ly -ɪŋ/li -ed -d
sneez|e sniːz -es -ɪz -ing -ɪŋ -ed -d
Snelgrove ˈsnel.grəʊv (US) -groʊv
snell (S) snel -s -z
Sneyd sniːd
snib snɪb -s -z
snick snɪk -s -s -ing -ɪŋ -ed -t
snick|er ˈsnɪk|.əʳ (US) -ɚ -ers -əz (US) -ɚz -ering -ᵊr.ɪŋ -ered -əd (US) -ɚd
Snickers® ˈsnɪk.əz (US) -ɚz
snickersnee ˌsnɪk.əˈsniː, ˈ--- (US) ˈsnɪk.ɚ.sniː -s -z
snide snaɪd -ly -li -ness -nəs, -nɪs
sniff snɪf -s -s -ing -ɪŋ -ed -t -y -i -ier -i.əʳ (US) -i.ɚ -iest -i.ɪst, -i.əst -ily -ɪ.li, -ᵊl.i -iness -ɪ.nəs, -ɪ.nɪs
sniffer ˈsnɪf.əʳ (US) -ɚ -s -z ˈsniffer ˌdog
sniffl|e ˈsnɪf.l̩ -es -z -ing -ɪŋ, ˈsnɪf.lɪŋ -ed -d
snifter ˈsnɪf.təʳ (US) -tɚ -s -z
snigg|er ˈsnɪg|.əʳ (US) -ɚ -ers -əz (US) -ɚz -ering -ᵊr.ɪŋ -ered -əd (US) -ɚd -erer/s -ə.rəʳ/z (US) -ɚ.ɚ/z
snip snɪp -s -s -ping -ɪŋ -ped -t -per/s -əʳ/z (US) -ɚ/z
snip|e snaɪp -es -s -ing -ɪŋ -ed -t -er/s -əʳ/z (US) -ɚ/z
snipp|et ˈsnɪp|.ɪt -ets -ɪts -ety -ɪ.ti (US) -ɪ.t̬i
snit snɪt -s -s
snitch snɪtʃ -es -ɪz -ing -ɪŋ -ed -t
snivel ˈsnɪv.ᵊl -s -z -(l)ing -ɪŋ, ˈsnɪv.lɪŋ -(l)ed -d -(l)er/s -əʳ/z, ˈsnɪv.ləʳ/z (US) ˈ-ᵊl.ɚ/z, ˈ-lɚ/z
snob snɒb (US) snɑːb -s -z -bism -ɪ.zᵊm
snobbery ˈsnɒb.ᵊr.i (US) ˈsnɑː.bɚ-
snobbish ˈsnɒb.ɪʃ (US) ˈsnɑː.bɪʃ -ly -li -ness -nəs, -nɪs
snobb|y ˈsnɒb|.i (US) ˈsnɑː.b|i -ier -i.əʳ (US) -i.ɚ -iest -i.ɪst, -i.əst
SNOBOL ˈsnəʊ.bɒl (US) ˈsnoʊ.bɔːl, -bɑːl
Snodgrass ˈsnɒd.grɑːs (US) ˈsnɑːd.græs
Snodland ˈsnɒd.lənd (US) ˈsnɑːd-
snoek snʊk, snuːk -s -s
snog snɒg (US) snɑːg, snɔːg -s -z -ging -ɪŋ -ged -d
snood snuːd, snʊd (US) snuːd -s -z -ed -ɪd
Snoody ˈsnuː.di
snook snuːk (US) snʊk, snuːk -s -s
snooker ˈsnuː.kəʳ (US) ˈsnʊk.ɚ -s -z -ing -ɪŋ -ed -d
snoop snuːp -s -s -ing -ɪŋ -ed -t -er/s -əʳ/z (US) -ɚ/z
Snoopy® ˈsnuː.pi
snoot|y ˈsnuː.t|i (US) -t̬|i -ily -ɪ.li, -ᵊl.i -iness -ɪ.nəs, -ɪ.nɪs -ier -i.əʳ (US) -i.ɚ -iest -i.ɪst, -i.əst
snooz|e snuːz -es -ɪz -ing -ɪŋ -ed -d -er/s -əʳ/z (US) -ɚ/z
snor|e snɔːʳ (US) snɔːr -es -z -ing -ɪŋ -ed -d -er/s -əʳ/z (US) -ɚ/z
snorkel ˈsnɔː.kᵊl (US) ˈsnɔːr- -s -z -(l)ing -ɪŋ -(l)ed -d -(l)er/s -əʳ/z (US) -ɚ/z

snort snɔːt ⓊⓈ snɔːrt **-s** -s **-ing** -ɪŋ ⓊⓈ ˈsnɔːr.t̬ɪŋ **-ed** -ɪd ⓊⓈ ˈsnɔːr.t̬ɪd
snorter ˈsnɔː.təʳ ⓊⓈ ˈsnɔːr.t̬ɚ **-s** -z
snort|y ˈsnɔː.t|i ⓊⓈ ˈsnɔːr.t̬|i **-ier** -i.əʳ ⓊⓈ -i.ɚ **-iest** -i.ɪst, -i.əst **-ily** -ɪ.li, -əl.i **-iness** -ɪ.nəs, -ɪ.nɪs
snot snɒt ⓊⓈ snɑːt **-ty** -i ⓊⓈ ˈsnɑː.t̬i
snout (S) snaʊt **-s** -s
snow (S) snəʊ ⓊⓈ snoʊ **-s** -z **-ing** -ɪŋ **-ed** -d **-er/s** **ˈsnow ˌblindness; ˈsnow ˌgoose; ˌSnow ˈWhite**
snowball ˈsnəʊ.bɔːl ⓊⓈ ˈsnoʊ.bɔːl, -bɑːl **-s** -z **-ing** -ɪŋ **-ed** -d
snowberr|y ˈsnəʊ.bər|.i, -br|i ⓊⓈ ˈsnoʊˌber|.i **-ies** -iz
snowblower ˈsnəʊˌbləʊ.əʳ ⓊⓈ ˈsnoʊˌbloʊ.ɚ **-s** -z
snowboard ˈsnəʊ.bɔːd ⓊⓈ ˈsnoʊ.bɔːrd **-s** -z **-ing** -ɪŋ **-ed** -ɪd **-er/s** -əʳ/z ⓊⓈ -ɚ/z
snowbound ˈsnəʊ.baʊnd ⓊⓈ ˈsnoʊ-
snowcap ˈsnəʊ.kæp ⓊⓈ ˈsnoʊ- **-s** -s **-ped** -t
Snowden, Snowdon ˈsnəʊ.dən ⓊⓈ ˈsnoʊ-
Snowdonia snəʊˈdəʊ.ni.ə ⓊⓈ snoʊˈdoʊ-
snowdrift ˈsnəʊ.drɪft ⓊⓈ ˈsnoʊ- **-s** -s
snowdrop ˈsnəʊ.drɒp ⓊⓈ ˈsnoʊ.drɑːp **-s** -s
snowfall ˈsnəʊ.fɔːl ⓊⓈ ˈsnoʊ-, -fɑːl **-s** -z
snowfield ˈsnəʊ.fiːld ⓊⓈ ˈsnoʊ- **-s** -z
snowflake ˈsnəʊ.fleɪk ⓊⓈ ˈsnoʊ- **-s** -s
snow|man ˈsnəʊ|.mæn ⓊⓈ ˈsnoʊ- **-men** -men
snowmobile ˈsnəʊ.məˌbiːl ⓊⓈ ˈsnoʊ.moʊˌ- **-s** -z
snowplough, snowplow ˈsnəʊ.plaʊ ⓊⓈ ˈsnoʊ- **-s** -z **-ing** -ɪŋ **-ed** -d
snowshoe ˈsnəʊ.ʃuː ⓊⓈ ˈsnoʊ- **-s** -z
snowstorm ˈsnəʊ.stɔːm ⓊⓈ ˈsnoʊ.stɔːrm **-s** -z
snowsuit ˈsnəʊ.suːt, -sjuːt ⓊⓈ ˈsnoʊ.suːt **-s** -s
snow-white ˌsnəʊˈhwaɪt ⓊⓈ ˌsnoʊ- *stress shift:* ˌsnow-white ˈhair
snow|y ˈsnəʊ|.i ⓊⓈ ˈsnoʊ- **-ier** -i.əʳ ⓊⓈ -i.ɚ **-iest** -i.ɪst, -i.əst **-ily** -ɪ.li, -əl.i **-iness** -ɪ.nəs, -ɪ.nɪs **ˌsnowy ˈowl**
SNP ˌes.enˈpiː, -emˈ- ⓊⓈ -enˈ-
snr (S) *(abbrev. for* **senior***)* ˈsiː.ni.əʳ, -njəʳ ⓊⓈ -njɚ
snub snʌb **-s** -z **-bing** -ɪŋ **-bed** -d
snub-nosed ˌsnʌbˈnəʊzd ⓊⓈ ˈsnʌb.noʊzd *stress shift, British only:* ˌsnub-nosed ˈbullet
snuck snʌk
snuff snʌf **-s** -s **-ing** -ɪŋ **-ed** -t **-er/s** -əʳ/z ⓊⓈ -ɚ/z **ˈsnuff ˌbox**
snuffl|e ˈsnʌf.l̩ **-es** -z **-ing** -ɪŋ, ˈsnʌf.lɪŋ **-ed** -d **-er/s** -əʳ/z, ˈsnʌf.ləʳ/z ⓊⓈ ˈ-l̩.ɚ/z, ˈ-lɚ/z **-y** -i
snug snʌg **-ger** -əʳ ⓊⓈ -ɚ **-gest** -ɪst, -əst **-ly** -li **-ness** -nəs, -nɪs
snugger|y ˈsnʌg.ər|.i **-ies** -iz
snuggl|e ˈsnʌg.l̩ **-es** -z **-ing** -ɪŋ, ˈsnʌg.lɪŋ **-ed** -d
Snyder ˈsnaɪ.dəʳ ⓊⓈ -dɚ
so *normal forms:* səʊ ⓊⓈ soʊ *occasional weak form:* sə **ˌso ˈlong, ˈso ˌlong**
Note: Weak form word. The weak form is used only rarely, and only in casual speech before adjectives and adverbs (e.g. "Not so bad" /ˌnɒt.səˈbæd ⓊⓈ ˌnɑːt-/, "Don't go so fast" /ˌdəʊnt.gəʊ.səˈfɑːst ⓊⓈ ˌdoʊnt.goʊ.səˈfæst/).
soak səʊk ⓊⓈ soʊk **-s** -s **-ing** -ɪŋ **-ed** -t
soakaway ˈsəʊk.əˌweɪ ⓊⓈ ˈsoʊk- **-s** -z
Soames səʊmz ⓊⓈ soʊmz
so-and-so ˈsəʊ.ənd.səʊ ⓊⓈ ˈsoʊ.ənd.soʊ **-(')s** -z
Soane səʊn ⓊⓈ soʊn **-s** -z
soap səʊp ⓊⓈ soʊp **-s** -s **-ing** -ɪŋ **-ed** -t **-y** -i **-ier** -i.əʳ ⓊⓈ -i.ɚ **-iest** -i.ɪst, -i.əst **-ily** -ɪ.li, -əl.i **-iness** -ɪ.nəs, -ɪ.nɪs
soapbox ˈsəʊp.bɒks ⓊⓈ ˈsoʊp.bɑːks **-es** -ɪz
soap opera ˈsəʊpˌɒp.ər.ə, ˌ-rə ⓊⓈ ˈsoʊpˌɑː.pɚ.ə, ˌ-prə **-s** -z
soapstone ˈsəʊp.stəʊn ⓊⓈ ˈsoʊp.stoʊn
soapsuds ˈsəʊp.sʌdz ⓊⓈ ˈsoʊp-
soar (S) sɔːʳ ⓊⓈ sɔːr **-s** -z **-ing** -ɪŋ **-ed** -d
soaraway ˈsɔː.rə.weɪ ⓊⓈ ˈsɔːr.ə-
Soares səʊˈɑː.rɪz ⓊⓈ soʊˈɑːr.ɪz
sob sɒb ⓊⓈ sɑːb **-s** -z **-bing** -ɪŋ **-bed** -d **ˈsob ˌstory**
SOB ˌes.əʊˈbiː ⓊⓈ -oʊˈ-
Sobel ˈsəʊ.bel ⓊⓈ ˈsoʊ-
sob|er ˈsəʊ.b|əʳ ⓊⓈ ˈsoʊ.b|ɚ **-erer** -ər.əʳ ⓊⓈ -ɚ.ɚ **-erest** -ər.ɪst, -ər.əst **-erly** -əl.i ⓊⓈ -ɚ.li **-erness** -ə.nəs, -ə.nɪs ⓊⓈ -ɚ.nəs, -ɚ.nɪs **-ers** -əz ⓊⓈ -ɚz **-ering/ly** -ər.ɪŋ/li **-ered** -əd ⓊⓈ -ɚd
Sobers ˈsəʊ.bəz ⓊⓈ ˈsoʊ.bɚz
sobersides ˈsəʊ.bə.saɪdz ⓊⓈ ˈsoʊ.bɚ-
sobriety səʊˈbraɪ.ɪ.ti, ˈ-ə- ⓊⓈ səˈbraɪ.ə.t̬i, soʊ-
sobriquet ˈsəʊ.brɪ.keɪ ⓊⓈ ˈsoʊ-, -ket, ˌ--ˈ- **-s** -z
so-called ˌsəʊˈkɔːld ⓊⓈ ˌsoʊˈkɑːld, -ˈkɔːld *stress shift:* ˌso-called ˈfriend
soc(c)age ˈsɒk.ɪdʒ ⓊⓈ ˈsɑː.kɪdʒ
soccer ˈsɒk.əʳ ⓊⓈ ˈsɑː.kɚ
sociability ˌsəʊ.ʃəˈbɪl.ə.ti, -ɪ.ti ⓊⓈ ˌsoʊ.ʃəˈbɪl.ə.t̬i
sociab|le ˈsəʊ.ʃə.b|l̩ ⓊⓈ ˈsoʊ- **-ly** -li **-leness** -l̩.nəs, -nɪs
social ˈsəʊ.ʃəl ⓊⓈ ˈsoʊ- **-s** -z **-ly** -i **ˌsocial ˈclimber** ⓊⓈ **ˈsocial ˌclimber; ˌsocial deˈmocracy; ˌsocial ˈdemocrat; ˈsocial ˌlife; ˌsocial ˈscience** ⓊⓈ **ˈsocial ˌscience; ˌsocial ˈsecretary; ˌsocial seˈcurity; ˌsocial ˈservice** ⓊⓈ **ˈsocial ˌservice; ˈsocial ˌwork**
social|ism ˈsəʊ.ʃəl|.ɪ.zəm ⓊⓈ ˈsoʊ- **-ist/s** -ɪst/s
socialistic ˌsəʊ.ʃəlˈɪs.tɪk ⓊⓈ ˌsoʊ.ʃəˈlɪs-
socialite ˈsəʊ.ʃəl.aɪt ⓊⓈ ˈsoʊ.ʃə.laɪt **-s** -s
socialization, -isa- ˌsəʊ.ʃəl.aɪˈzeɪ.ʃən ⓊⓈ ˌsoʊ.ʃəl.ɪˈ-
socializ|e, -is|e ˈsəʊ.ʃəl.aɪz ⓊⓈ ˈsoʊ.ʃə.laɪz **-es** -ɪz **-ing** -ɪŋ **-ed** -d
societal səˈsaɪ.ə.təl ⓊⓈ -t̬əl
societ|y (S) səˈsaɪ.ə.t|i ⓊⓈ -t̬|i **-ies** -iz
Socinian səʊˈsɪn.i.ən ⓊⓈ soʊ- **-s** -z
Socinus səʊˈsaɪ.nəs ⓊⓈ soʊ-
socio- səʊ.ʃi.əʊ-, -si-; ˌsəʊ.ʃiˈɒ-, -siˈ- ⓊⓈ soʊ.si.oʊ-, -ʃi-, -ə-; ˌsoʊ.siˈɑː-, -ʃiˈ-
Note: Prefix. Normally either takes primary or secondary stress on the first syllable, e.g. **sociopath** /ˈsəʊ.ʃi.əʊ.pæθ ⓊⓈ ˈsoʊ.si.ə-/, **sociopolitical** /ˌsəʊ.ʃi.əʊ.pəˈlɪt.ɪ.kəl ⓊⓈ ˌsoʊ.si.oʊ.pəˈlɪt̬-/, or secondary stress on the first syllable andprimary stress on the third syllable, e.g. **sociology** /ˌsəʊ.ʃiˈɒl.ə.dʒi ⓊⓈ ˌsoʊ.siˈɑː.lə-/.
sociobiolog|y ˌsəʊ.ʃi.əʊ.baɪˈɒl.ə.dʒ|i, -si- ⓊⓈ ˌsoʊ.si.oʊ.baɪˈɑː.lə-, -ʃi- **-ist/s** -ɪst/s
sociocultural ˌsəʊ.ʃi.əʊˈkʌl.tʃər.əl, -si- ⓊⓈ ˌsoʊ.si.oʊ-, -ʃi- **-ly** -i
socioeconomic ˌsəʊ.ʃi.əʊˌiː.kəˈnɒm.ɪk, -si-, -ˌek.əˈ- ⓊⓈ ˌsoʊ.si.oʊˌek.əˈnɑː.mɪk, -ʃi-, -ˌiː.kəˈ-
sociolinguist ˌsəʊ.ʃi.əʊˈlɪŋ.gwɪst, -si- ⓊⓈ ˌsoʊ.si.oʊˈ-, -ʃi- **-s** -s
sociolinguistic ˌsəʊ.ʃi.əʊ.lɪŋˈgwɪs.tɪk, -si- ⓊⓈ ˌsoʊ.si.oʊ-, -ʃi- **-s** -s
sociologic|al ˌsəʊ.ʃi.əˈlɒdʒ.ɪ.k|əl, -si- ⓊⓈ ˌsoʊ.si.əˈlɑː.dʒɪ-, -ʃi- **-ally** -əl.i, -li
sociologist ˌsəʊ.ʃiˈɒl.ə.dʒ|ɪst, -siˈ- ⓊⓈ ˌsoʊ.siˈɑː.lə-, -ʃiˈ- **-s** -s
sociolog|y ˌsəʊ.ʃiˈɒl.ə.dʒ|i, -siˈ- ⓊⓈ ˌsoʊ.siˈɑː.lə-, -ʃiˈ- **-ist/s** -ɪst/s
sociopath ˈsəʊ.ʃi.əʊ.pæθ, -si- ⓊⓈ ˈsoʊ.si.ə-, -ʃi- **-s** -s
sociopolitical ˌsəʊ.ʃi.əʊ.pəlˈɪt.ɪ.kəl, -si- ⓊⓈ ˌsoʊ.si.oʊ.pəˈlɪt̬-, -ʃi-
socioreligious ˌsəʊ.ʃi.əʊ.rɪˈlɪdʒ.əs, -si-, -rəˈ- ⓊⓈ ˌsoʊ.si.oʊ-, -ʃi-
sock sɒk ⓊⓈ sɑːk **-s** -s **-ing** -ɪŋ **-ed** -t
sockdolager, sockdologer sɒkˈdɒl.ə.dʒəʳ ⓊⓈ sɑːkˈdɑː.lə.dʒɚ **-s** -z
sock|et ˈsɒk|.ɪt ⓊⓈ ˈsɑː.k|ɪt **-ets** -ɪts **-eted** -ɪ.tɪd ⓊⓈ -ɪ.t̬ɪd
Socotra səʊˈkəʊ.trə, sɒkˈəʊ- ⓊⓈ soʊˈkoʊ-
Socrates ˈsɒk.rə.tiːz ⓊⓈ ˈsɑː.krə-

Soft palate

The rear part of the roof of the mouth.

Most of the roof of the mouth consists of 'hard palate', which has bone beneath the skin. Towards the back of the mouth, the layer of bone comes to an end but the layer of soft tissue continues for some distance, ending eventually in a loose appendage that can easily be seen by looking in a mirror. This dangling object is the 'uvula', and the layer of soft tissue attached to it is called the soft palate (it is also sometimes known as the 'velum'). In normal breathing the velum is allowed to hang down so that air may pass above it and escape through the nose, but for most speech sounds it is lifted up and pressed against the upper back wall of the throat so that no air can escape through the nose. This is necessary for a PLOSIVE, for example, so that air may be compressed within the vocal tract. However, for NASAL consonants (e.g., [m], [n]) the soft palate must be lowered since air should escape only through the nose in these sounds.

In nasalised vowels (such vowels are found in considerable numbers in French, for example) the soft palate is lowered and air escapes through the mouth and the nose together.

socratic (S) sɒk'ræt.ɪk, səʊ'kræt- (US) sə'kræt̬-, soʊ- **-ally** -ᵊl.i, -li

sod sɒd (US) sɑːd **-s** -z **-ding** -ɪŋ **-ded** -ɪd ˌ**sod's 'law, 'sod's ˌlaw**

soda 'səʊ.də (US) 'soʊ- **-s** -z **'soda ˌbiscuit; 'soda ˌbread; 'soda ˌcracker; 'soda ˌfountain; 'soda ˌpop; 'soda ˌsiphon; 'soda ˌwater**

sodalit|y səʊ'dæl.ə.t|i, -ɪ.t|i (US) soʊ'dæl.ə.t̬|i **-ies** -iz

sodden 'sɒd.ᵊn (US) 'sɑː.dᵊn **-ness** -nəs, -nɪs **-s** -z **-ing** -ɪŋ **-ed** -d

sodding 'sɒd.ɪŋ (US) 'sɑː.dɪŋ

sodium 'səʊ.di.əm (US) 'soʊ-

Sodom 'sɒd.əm (US) 'sɑː.dəm

sodomiz|e, -is|e 'sɒd.ə.maɪz (US) 'sɑː.də- **-es** -ɪz **-ing** -ɪŋ **-ed** -d

sodom|y 'sɒd.ə.m|i (US) 'sɑː.də- **-ite/s** -aɪt/s

Sodor 'səʊ.dəʳ (US) 'soʊ.dɚ

Soeharto sʊ'hɑː.təʊ (US) -'hɑːr.t̬oʊ

soever səʊ'ev.əʳ (US) soʊ'ev.ɚ

sofa 'səʊ.fə (US) 'soʊ- **-s** -z

sofabed 'səʊ.fə.bed (US) 'soʊ- **-s** -z

Sofala səʊ'fɑː.lə (US) soʊ-, sə-

soffit 'sɒf.ɪt (US) 'sɑː.fɪt **-s** -s

Sofia 'sɒf.i.ə, 'səʊ.fi- (US) 'soʊ.fi-; soʊ'fiː-

soft sɒft (US) sɑːft **-s** -s **-er** -əʳ (US) -ɚ **-est** -ɪst, -əst **-ly** -li **-ness** -nəs, -nɪs ˌ**soft 'copy; ˌsoft 'drink** (US) **'soft ˌdrink; ˌsoft 'fruit; ˌsoft 'furnishings; ˌsoft 'landing; ˌsoft 'option; ˌsoft 'sell; 'soft ˌspot, ˌsoft 'spot** (US) **'soft ˌspot; ˌsoft 'target; 'soft ˌtouch, ˌsoft 'touch**

softback 'sɒft.bæk (US) 'sɑːft- **-s** -s

softball 'sɒft.bɔːl (US) 'sɑːft-, -bɑːl

soft-boil ˌsɒft'bɔɪl (US) ˌsɑːft- **-s** -z **-ing** -ɪŋ **-ed** -d

soft-centred ˌsɒft'sen.təd (US) ˌsɑːft'sen.tɚd

soft-core 'sɒft.kɔːʳ (US) 'sɑːft.kɔːr

softcover ˌsɒft'kʌv.əʳ (US) 'sɑːft.kʌv.ɚ **-s** -z

soften 'sɒf.ᵊn (US) 'sɑː.fᵊn **-s** -z **-ing** -ɪŋ, 'sɒf.nɪŋ (US) 'sɑːf- **-ed** -d

softener 'sɒf.ᵊn.əʳ, '-nəʳ (US) 'sɑː.fᵊn.ɚ, 'sɑːf.nɚ **-s** -z

softhearted ˌsɒft'hɑː.tɪd (US) 'sɑːft.hɑːr.t̬ɪd **-ly** -li **-ness** -nəs, -nɪs *stress shift, British only:* ˌsofthearted 'person

soft|ie 'sɒf.t|i (US) 'sɑːf- **-ies** -iz

softish 'sɒf.tɪʃ (US) 'sɑːf-

softly-softly ˌsɒft.li'sɒft.li (US) ˌsɑːft.li'sɑːft-

soft-pedal ˌsɒf*t*'ped.ᵊl (US) ˌsɑːf*t*- **-s** -z **-(l)ing** -ɪŋ, -'ped.lɪŋ **-(l)ed** -d

soft-soap ˌsɒf*t*'səʊp (US) ˌsɑːf*t*'soʊp **-s** -s **-ing** -ɪŋ **-ed** -t

soft-spoken ˌsɒf*t*'spəʊ.kᵊn (US) ˌsɑːft'spoʊ- *stress shift:* ˌsoft-spoken 'person

software 'sɒf*t*.weəʳ (US) 'sɑːf*t*.wer

softwood 'sɒf*t*.wʊd (US) 'sɑːf*t*- **-s** -z

soft|y 'sɒf.t|i (US) 'sɑːf- **-ies** -iz

SOGAT 'səʊ.gæt (US) 'soʊ-

sogg|y 'sɒg|.i (US) 'sɑː.g|i **-ily** -ɪ.li, -ᵊl.i **-ier** -i.əʳ (US) -i.ɚ **-iest** -i.ɪst, -i.əst **-iness** -ɪ.nəs, -ɪ.nɪs

soh səʊ (US) soʊ **-s** -z

Soham 'səʊ.əm (US) 'soʊ-

Soho 'səʊ.həʊ; (US) 'soʊ.hoʊ

soi-disant ˌswɑː.diː'zɑ̃ː*ŋ*, ˌ-'-- (US) ˌswɑː.diː'zɑ̃ː*n*

soigné(e) 'swɑː.njeɪ, -'- (US) swɑː'njeɪ

soil sɔɪl **-s** -z **-ing** -ɪŋ **-ed** -d **'soil ˌpipe**

soirée, soiree 'swɑː.reɪ, 'swɒr.eɪ, -'- (US) swɑː'reɪ **-s** -z

soixante-neuf ˌswæs.ɑ̃ː*nt*'nɜːf, ˌswʌs- (US) ˌswɑː.sɑ̃ː*nt*'nɜːf

sojourn 'sɒdʒ.ɜːn, 'sʌdʒ-, -ən (US) 'soʊ.dʒɝːn, -'- **-s** -z **-ing** -ɪŋ **-ed** -d **-er/s** -əʳ/z (US) -ɚ/z

Sokoto 'səʊ.kə.təʊ, ˌ--'- (US) 'soʊ.koʊ.toʊ, ˌ--'-; sə'koʊ-

sol (S) sɒl (US) soʊl, sɑːl **-s** -z

sola 'səʊ.lə (US) 'soʊ-

solac|e 'sɒl.əs, -ɪs (US) 'sɑː.lɪs **-es** -ɪz **-ing** -ɪŋ **-ed** -t

solanum səʊ'leɪ.nəm, -'lɑː- (US) soʊ'leɪ-

solar 'səʊ.ləʳ (US) 'soʊ.lɚ ˌ**solar 'energy; ˌsolar 'panel; ˌsolar 'plexus; 'solar ˌsystem**

solari|um səʊ'leə.ri.əm (US) soʊ'ler.i-, sə- **-ums** -z **-a** -ə

solati|um səʊ'leɪ.ʃi|.əm (US) soʊ- **-ums** -əmz **-a** -ə

sold *(from* **sell***)* səʊld (US) soʊld

sold|er 'səʊl.d|əʳ, 'sɒl- (US) 'sɑː.d|ɚ **-ers** -əz (US) -ɚz **-ering** -ᵊr.ɪŋ **-ered** -əd (US) -ɚd **'soldering ˌiron**

soldi|er 'səʊl.dʒ|əʳ (US) 'soʊl.dʒ|ɚ **-ers** -əz (US) -ɚz **-ering** -ᵊr.ɪŋ **-ered** -əd (US) -ɚd ˌ**soldier of 'fortune**

soldierly 'səʊl.dʒᵊl.i (US) 'soʊl.dʒɚ.li

soldiery 'səʊl.dʒᵊr.i (US) 'soʊl-

sol|e (S) səʊl (US) soʊl **-es** -z **-ely** -li **-ing** -ɪŋ **-ed** -d

solecism 'sɒl.ɪ.sɪ.zᵊm, '-ə-, -es.ɪ- (US) 'sɑː.lə- **-s** -z

solemn 'sɒl.əm (US) 'sɑː.ləm **-ly** -li **-ness** -nəs, -nɪs

solemnif|y sə'lem.nɪ.f|aɪ, sɒl'em- (US) sə'lem- **-ies** -z **-ying** -ɪŋ **-ied** -d

solemnit|y sə'lem.nə.t|i, sɒl'em-, -nɪ- (US) sə'lem.nə.t̬|i **-ies** -z

solemnization, -isa- ˌsɒl.əm.naɪ'zeɪ.ʃᵊn, -nɪ'- (US) ˌsɑː.ləm.nɪ'- **-s** -z

solemniz|e, -is|e 'sɒl.əm.naɪz (US) 'sɑː.ləm- **-es** -ɪz **-ing** -ɪŋ **-ed** -d

solenoid 'səʊ.lə.nɔɪd, 'sɒl.ə-, '-ɪ- (US) 'soʊ.lə-, 'sɑː- **-s** -z

Solent 'səʊ.lənt (US) 'soʊ-

sol-fa (S) ˌsɒl'fɑː, '-- (US) ˌsoʊl-

solfegg|io sɒl'fedʒ|.i.əʊ (US) soʊl'fedʒ|.oʊ; sɑːl'fedʒ|.oʊ **-i** -iː

solferino (S) ˌsɒl.fᵊr'iː.nəʊ (US) ˌsoʊl.fə'riː.noʊ, ˌsɑːl-

solic|it sə'lɪs|.ɪt **-its** -ɪts **-iting** -ɪ.tɪŋ (US) -ɪ.t̬ɪŋ **-ited** -ɪ.tɪd (US) -ɪ.t̬ɪd

solicitation səˌlɪs.ɪˈteɪ.ʃᵊn -s -z

solicitor səˈlɪs.ɪ.təʳ, ˈ-ə- (US) -t̬ɚ -s -z **soˌlicitor ˈgeneral**

solicitous səˈlɪs.ɪ.təs (US) -t̬əs -ly -li -ness -nəs, -nɪs

solicitude səˈlɪs.ɪ.tjuːd, -tʃuːd (US) -tuːd, -tjuːd

solid ˈsɒl.ɪd (US) ˈsɑː.lɪd -s -z -est -ɪst, -əst -ly -li -ness -nəs, -nɪs

solidarity (S) ˌsɒl.ɪˈdær.ə.ti, -ɪ.ti (US) ˌsɑː.ləˈder.ə.t̬i, -ˈdær-

solidifiable səˈlɪd.ɪ.faɪ.ə.bl̩, sɒlˈɪd- (US) səˈlɪd-

solidification səˌlɪd.ɪ.fɪˈkeɪ.ʃᵊn, sɒlˌɪd- (US) səˌlɪd.ə-

solidi|fy səˈlɪd.ɪ.|faɪ, sɒlˈɪd- (US) səˈlɪd.ə- -fies -faɪz -fying -faɪ.ɪŋ -fied -faɪd

solidity səˈlɪd.ə.ti, sɒlˈɪd-, -ɪ.ti (US) səˈlɪd.ə.t̬i

solid-state ˌsɒl.ɪdˈsteɪt (US) ˌsɑː.lɪdˈ- *stress shift, see compound:* **ˌsolid-state ˈphysics**

solid|us ˈsɒl.ɪ.d|əs (US) ˈsɑː.lɪ- -i -aɪ, -iː

Solihull ˌsəʊ.lɪˈhʌl, ˌsɒl.ɪˈ- (US) ˌsoʊ.lɪˈ- *stress shift:* ˌSolihull ˈresidents

soliloquiz|e, -is|e səˈlɪl.ə.kwaɪz, sɒlˈɪl- (US) səˈlɪl- -es -ɪz -ing -ɪŋ -ed -d

soliloqu|y səˈlɪl.ə.kw|i, sɒlˈɪl- (US) səˈlɪl- -ies -iz

solipsism ˈsɒl.ɪp.sɪ.zᵊm, ˈsəʊ.lɪp- (US) ˈsɑː.lɪp-, ˈsoʊ- -s -z

solipsist ˈsɒl.ɪp.sɪst (US) ˈsɑː.lɪp- -s -s -ic -ɪk

solitaire ˌsɒl.ɪˈteəʳ, ˈ--- (US) ˈsɑː.lə.ter -s -z

solitar|y ˈsɒl.ɪ.tᵊr|.i, ˈ-ə-, -tr|i (US) ˈsɑː.lə.ter|.i -ies -iz -ily -ᵊl.i, -ɪ.li -iness -ɪ.nəs, -ɪ.nɪs **ˌsolitary conˈfinement**

solitude ˈsɒl.ɪ.tjuːd, ˈ-ə-, -tʃuːd (US) ˈsɑː.lə.tuːd, -tjuːd -s -z

Solloway ˈsɒl.ə.weɪ (US) ˈsɑː.lə-

solo ˈsəʊ.ləʊ (US) ˈsoʊ.loʊ -s -z

soloist ˈsəʊ.ləʊ.ɪst (US) ˈsoʊ.loʊ- -s -s

Solomon ˈsɒl.ə.mən (US) ˈsɑː.lə- **ˈSolomon ˌIslands**

Solon ˈsəʊ.lɒn, -lən (US) ˈsoʊ.lən, -lɑːn

so-long ˌsəʊˈlɒŋ; sə- (US) ˌsoʊˈlɑːŋ, sə-, -ˈlɔːŋ

solstic|e ˈsɒl.stɪs (US) ˈsɑːl- -es -ɪz

Solti ˈʃɒl.ti (US) ˈsoʊl.tiː

solubility ˌsɒl.jəˈbɪl.ə.ti, -jʊˈ-, -ɪ.ti (US) ˌsɑːl.jəˈbɪl.ə.t̬i, -jʊˈ-

soluble ˈsɒl.jə.bl̩, -jʊ- (US) ˈsɑːl-

solus ˈsəʊ.ləs (US) ˈsoʊ-

solution səˈluː.ʃᵊn, -ˈljuː- (US) -ˈluː- -s -z

solvability ˌsɒl.vəˈbɪl.ə.ti, -ɪ.ti (US) ˌsɑːl.vəˈbɪl.ə.t̬i

solv|e sɒlv (US) sɑːlv -es -z -ing -ɪŋ -ed -d -able -ə.bl̩

solvency ˈsɒl.vᵊnt.si (US) ˈsɑːl-

solvent ˈsɒl.vənt (US) ˈsɑːl- **ˈsolvent aˌbuse**

Solway ˈsɒl.weɪ (US) ˈsɑːl-

Solzhenitsyn ˌsɒl.ʒəˈnɪt.sɪn (US) ˌsoʊl.ʒəˈniːt-

som|a ˈsəʊ.m|ə (US) ˈsoʊ- -ata -ə.tə (US) -ə.t̬ə

Somali səˈmɑː.li (US) soʊ-, sə- -s -z

Somali|a səˈmɑː.li|.ə (US) soʊ-, sə- -an/s -ən/z

somatic səʊˈmæt.ɪk (US) soʊˈmæt̬-

somatostatin ˌsəʊ.mə.təˈstæt.ɪn (US) səˌmæt̬.əˈstæt.ᵊn; ˌsoʊ.mə.t̬əˈ-

somatotropin səʊˌmæt.əˈtrəʊ.pɪn; ˌsəʊ.mə.təˈ- (US) səˌmæt̬.əˈtroʊ.pən; ˌsoʊ.mə.t̬əˈ-

somb|er ˈsɒm.b|əʳ (US) ˈsɑːm.b|ɚ -erest -ᵊr.ɪst, -ᵊr.əst -erly -ə.li (US) -ɚ.li -erness -ə.nəs, -ə.nɪs (US) -ɚ.nəs, -ɚ.nɪs

sombr|e ˈsɒm.b|əʳ (US) ˈsɑːm.b|ɚ -est -ᵊr.ɪst, -ᵊr.əst -ely -ə.li -eli -ɚ.li -eness -ə.nəs, -ə.nɪs (US) -ɚ.nəs, -ɚ.nɪs

sombrero sɒmˈbreə.rəʊ (US) sɑːmˈbrer.oʊ, səm- -s -z

some *strong form:* sʌm *weak form:* sᵊm
Note: Weak form word. There are two grammatical functions for this word, one being the determiner, as in "some apples, some bananas", etc., where a weak form is used, the other being a quantifier, as in "some were tired and some were hungry", where the strong form is usual. In final position, the strong form is used (e.g. "I want some").

-some -səm
Note: Suffix. Does not normally change the stress pattern of the word to which it is added, e.g. **trouble** /ˈtrʌb.l̩/, **troublesome** /ˈtrʌb.l̩.səm/.

somebody ˈsʌm.bə.di, -ˌbɒd.i (US) -ˌbɑː.di, -ˌbʌd.i, -bə.di

someday ˈsʌm.deɪ

somehow ˈsʌm.haʊ

someone ˈsʌm.wʌn

someplace ˈsʌm.pleɪs

Somerfield® ˈsʌm.ə.fiːld (US) -ɚ-

Somers ˈsʌm.əz (US) -ɚz

somersault ˈsʌm.ə.sɔːlt, -sɒlt (US) -ɚ.sɑːlt, -sɔːlt -s -s -ing -ɪŋ -ed -ɪd

Somerset ˈsʌm.ə.set, -sɪt (US) ˈ-ɚ- -shire -ʃəʳ, -ˌʃɪəʳ (US) -ʃɚ, -ʃɪr

Somerton ˈsʌm.ə.tᵊn (US) -ɚ.t̬ən

Somervell ˈsʌm.ə.vɪl, -vel (US) ˈ-ɚ-

Somerville ˈsʌm.ə.vɪl (US) ˈ-ɚ-

something ˈsʌmp.θɪŋ

sometime ˈsʌm.taɪm

sometimes ˈsʌm.taɪmz

someway ˈsʌm.weɪ

somewhat ˈsʌm.*h*wɒt (US) -*h*wɑːt, -*h*wʌt, -*h*wət

somewhere ˈsʌm.*h*weəʳ (US) -*h*wer

Somme sɒm (US) sʌm

sommelier sɒmˈel.i.əʳ, sʌm-, -eɪ; ˈsʌm.ᵊl.jeɪ, ˈsɒm- (US) ˌsʌm.ᵊlˈjeɪ -s -z

somnambul|ism sɒmˈnæm.bjə.l|ɪ.zᵊm, -bjʊ- (US) sɑːmˈnæm- -ist/s -ɪst/s

somniferous sɒmˈnɪf.ᵊr.əs (US) sɑːm-

somnolen|ce ˈsɒm.nᵊl.ən|*t*s (US) ˈsɑːm- -t/ly -t/li

Sompting ˈsɒm*p*.tɪŋ, ˈsʌm*p*-

son (S) sʌn -s -z **ˌson of a ˈbitch**; **ˌson of a ˈgun**

sonagram ˈsəʊ.nə.græm, ˈsɒn.ə- (US) ˈsɑː.nə-, ˈsoʊ- -s -z

sonagraph (S®) ˈsəʊ.nə.grɑːf, ˈsɒn.ə-, -græf (US) ˈsɑː.nə.græf, ˈsoʊ- -s -s

sonant ˈsəʊ.nənt (US) ˈsoʊ- -s -s

sonar ˈsəʊ.nɑːʳ (US) ˈsoʊ.nɑːr

sonata səˈnɑː.tə (US) -t̬ə -s -z

sonatina ˌsɒn.əˈtiː.nə (US) ˌsɑː.nəˈ- -s -z

Sondheim ˈsɒnd.haɪm (US) ˈsɑːnd-

son et lumière ˌsɒn.eɪˈluː.mjeəʳ, ˌsɔːn-, -luːˈmjeəʳ (US) ˌsɑːn.eɪˈluː.mjer, ˌsɔːn-

song sɒŋ (US) sɑːŋ, sɔːŋ -s -z **ˌsong and ˈdance**; **ˈsong ˌthrush**

songbird ˈsɒŋ.bɜːd (US) ˈsɑːŋ.bɝːd, ˈsɔːŋ- -s -z

songbook ˈsɒŋ.bʊk (US) ˈsɑːŋ-, ˈsɔːŋ- -s -s

songfest ˈsɒŋ.fest (US) ˈsɑːŋ-, ˈsɔːŋ- -s -s

songster ˈsɒŋ*k*.stəʳ (US) ˈsɑːŋ*k*.stɚ, ˈsɔːŋ*k*- -s -z

songwrit|er ˈsɒŋˌraɪ.t|əʳ (US) ˈsɑːŋˌraɪ.t̬|ɚ, ˈsɔːŋ- -ers -əz (US) -ɚz -ing -ɪŋ

Sonia ˈsɒn.jə, ˈsəʊ.njə (US) ˈsɑː.njə, ˈsoʊ-

sonic ˈsɒn.ɪk (US) ˈsɑː.nɪk **ˌsonic ˈboom**

son-in-law ˈsʌn.ɪn.lɔː (US) -lɑː, -lɔː **sons-in-law** ˈsʌnz-

sonnet ˈsɒn.ɪt (US) ˈsɑː.nɪt -s -s

sonneteer ˌsɒn.ɪˈtɪəʳ, -əˈ- (US) ˌsɑː.nəˈtɪr -s -z

Sonning ˈsɒn.ɪŋ, ˈsʌn- (US) ˈsɑː.nɪŋ, ˈsʌn.ɪŋ

sonn|y ˈsʌn|.i -ies -iz

sonogram ˈsəʊ.nə.græm, ˈsɒn.ə- (US) ˈsɑː.nə-, ˈsoʊ- -s -z

sonograph ˈsəʊ.nə.grɑːf, ˈsɒn.ə-, -græf (US) ˈsɑː.nə.græf, ˈsoʊ- -s -s

sonometer səʊˈnɒm.ɪ.təʳ, ˈ-ə- (US) səˈnɑː.mə.t̬ɚ, soʊ- -s -z

Sonora səˈnɔː.rə (US) -ˈnɔːr.ə

sonorant ˈsɒn.ᵊr.ənt, ˈsəʊ.nᵊr- (US) ˈsɑː.nɚ-, ˈsoʊ-; səˈnɔːr-, soʊ- -s -s

sonorit|y səʊˈnɒr.ə.t|i, -ɪ.t|i (US) səˈnɔːr.ə.t̬|i, soʊ- -ies -iz

sonorous ˈsɒn.ᵊr.əs; səˈnɔː.rəs (US) səˈnɔːr.əs, soʊ-; ˈsɑː.nɚ-, ˈsoʊ- -ly -li

sonsie, sonsy 'sɒn*t*.si (US) 'sɑːn*t*-
Sontag 'sɒn.tæg (US) 'sɑːn-
Sony® 'səʊ.ni, 'sɒn.i (US) 'soʊ.ni
Sonya 'sɒn.jə, 'səʊ.njə (US) 'sɑː.njə, 'soʊ-
soon suːn **-er** -əʳ (US) -ɚ **-est** -ɪst, -əst ,**sooner or 'later**
soot sʊt (US) sʊt, suːt
sooth suːθ
sooth|e suːð **-es** -z **-ing/ly** -ɪŋ/li **-ed** -d
soothsayer 'suːθ,seɪ.əʳ (US) -ɚ **-s** -z
soot|y (S) 'sʊt|.i (US) 'sʊţ-, 'suː.ţ|i **-ier** -i.əʳ (US) -i.ɚ **-iest** -i.ɪst, -i.əst **-iness** -ɪ.nəs, -ɪ.nɪs
sop sɒp (US) sɑːp **-s** -s **-ping** -ɪŋ **-ped** -t
Sophia səʊ'fiː.ə, -'faɪ- (US) soʊ-
Sophie 'səʊ.fi (US) 'soʊ-
soph|ism 'sɒf|.ɪ.zᵊm (US) 'sɑː.f|ɪ- **-isms** -ɪ.zᵊmz **-ist/s** -ɪst/s
sophister 'sɒf.ɪ.stəʳ (US) 'sɑː.fɪ.stɚ **-s** -z
sophistic səʊ'fɪs.tɪk (US) sə- **-al** -ᵊl **-ally** -ᵊl.i, -li
sophisti|cate (*v.*) sə'fɪs.tɪ|.keɪt (US) -tə- **-cates** -keɪts **-cating** -keɪ.tɪŋ (US) -keɪ.ţɪŋ **-cated** -keɪ.tɪd (US) -keɪ.ţɪd
sophisticate (*n.*) sə'fɪs.tɪ.kət, -kɪt, -keɪt (US) -tə.kɪt **-s** -s
sophistication sə,fɪs.tɪ'keɪ.ʃᵊn (US) -tə'-
sophistr|y 'sɒf.ɪ.str|i (US) 'sɑː.fɪ- **-ies** -iz
Sophoclean ,sɒf.ə'kliː.ən (US) ,sɑː.fə'-
Sophocles 'sɒf.ə.kliːz (US) 'sɑː.fə-
sophomore 'sɒf.ə.mɔːʳ (US) 'sɑː.fə.mɔːr **-s** -z
sophomoric ,sɒf.ə'mɒr.ɪk (US) ,sɑː.fə'mɔːr-
Sophy 'səʊ.fi (US) 'soʊ-
soporific ,sɒp.ᵊr'ɪf.ɪk, ,səʊ.pᵊr'- (US) ,sɑː.pə'rɪf-, ,soʊ- **-ally** -ᵊl.i, -li
sopping 'sɒp.ɪŋ (US) 'sɑː.pɪŋ ,**sopping 'wet**
sopp|y 'sɒp|.i (US) 'sɑː.p|i **-ier** -i.əʳ (US) -i.ɚ **-iest** -i.ɪst, -i.əst **-iness** -ɪ.nəs, -ɪ.nɪs **-ily** -ɪ.li
sopranino ,sɒp.rə'niː.nəʊ (US) ,soʊ.prə'niː.noʊ **-s** -z
sopran|o sə'prɑː.n|əʊ (US) -'præn|.oʊ, -'prɑː.n|oʊ **-os** -əʊz (US) -oʊz **-i** -iː
Sopwith 'sɒp.wɪθ (US) 'sɑːp- **-s** -s
sorbet 'sɔː.beɪ (US) 'sɔːr.beɪ; sɔːr'bət **-s** -s
sorbic 'sɔː.bɪk (US) 'sɔːr- ,**sorbic 'acid**
sorbitol 'sɔː.bɪ.tɒl (US) 'sɔːr.bɪ.tɑːl, -tɔːl, -toʊl
Sorbonne sɔː'bɒn (US) sɔːr'bɑːn, -'bʌn
sorcer|y 'sɔː.sᵊr|.i (US) 'sɔːr- **-ies** -iz **-er/s** -əʳ/z (US) -ɚ/z **-ess/es** -ɪs/ɪz, -es/ɪz
Sorcha 'sɔː.ʃə
Sordello sɔː'del.əʊ (US) sɔːr'del.oʊ
sordid 'sɔː.dɪd (US) 'sɔːr- **-ly** -li **-ness** -nəs, -nɪs
sordin|o sɔː'diː.n|əʊ (US) sɔːr'diː.n|oʊ **-i** -iː
sor|e sɔːʳ (US) sɔːr **-es** -z **-er** -əʳ (US) -ɚ **-est** -ɪst, -əst **-ely** -li **-eness** -nəs, -nɪs
sorghum 'sɔː.gəm (US) 'sɔːr-
Soroptimist sə'rɒp.tɪ.mɪst, -tə- (US) -'rɑːp.tɪ- **-s** -s
sororit|y sə'rɒr.ə.t|i, sɒr'ɒr-, -ɪ.t|i (US) sə'rɔːr.ə.ţ|i **-ies** -iz
sorrel 'sɒr.ᵊl (US) 'sɔːr-
Sorrento sə'ren.təʊ (US) -toʊ
sorrow 'sɒr.əʊ (US) 'sɑːr.oʊ **-s** -z **-ing/ly** -ɪŋ/li **-ed** -d **-er/s** -əʳ/z (US) -ɚ/z
sorrow|ful 'sɒr.əʊ|.fᵊl, -fʊl (US) 'sɑːr.ə- **-fully** -fᵊl.i, -fli, -fʊl.i **-fulness** -fᵊl.nəs, -fʊl.nəs, -nɪs
sorr|y 'sɒr|.i (US) 'sɑːr- **-ier** -i.əʳ (US) -i.ɚ **-iest** -i.ɪst, -i.əst **-ily** -ᵊl.i, -ɪ.li **-iness** -ɪ.nəs, -ɪ.nɪs
sort sɔːt (US) sɔːrt **-s** -s **-ing** -ɪŋ (US) 'sɔːr.ţɪŋ **-ed** -ɪd (US) 'sɔːr.ţɪd **-er/s** -əʳ/z (US) 'sɔːr.ţɚ/z
sortie 'sɔː.ti (US) 'sɔːr.tiː, ,-'- **-s** -z
sortilege 'sɔː.tɪ.lɪdʒ (US) 'sɔːr.ţᵊl.ɪdʒ, -edʒ
SOS ,es.əʊ'es (US) -oʊ'-
so-so 'səʊ.səʊ, ,-'- (US) 'soʊ.soʊ, ,-'-
sostenuto ,sɒs.tə'nuː.təʊ, -tɪ'-, -'njuː- (US) ,sɑː.stə'nuː.ţoʊ, ,soʊ-
sot sɒt (US) sɑːt **-s** -s
Sotheby 'sʌð.ə.bi **-'s** -z
Sothern 'sʌð.ᵊn (US) -ɚn
Sotho 'suː.tuː, 'səʊ.təʊ (US) 'soʊ.toʊ **-s** -z
sottish 'sɒt.ɪʃ (US) 'sɑː.ţɪʃ **-ly** -li **-ness** -nəs, -nɪs
sotto voce ,sɒt.əʊ'vəʊ.tʃeɪ (US) ,sɑː.ţoʊ'voʊ-
sou suː **-s** -z
soubise suː'biːz
soubrette suː'bret, sʊ- (US) suː- **-s** -s
soubriquet 'suː.brɪ.keɪ, 'sʊ-, -brə- (US) 'suː.brə-, -ket **-s** -z
souchong ,suː'*t*ʃɒŋ, '-- (US) 'suː.tʃɑːŋ, -ʃɑːŋ
souffle 'suː.fl̩ **-s** -z
soufflé 'suː.fleɪ (US) suː'fleɪ, '-- **-s** -z **-ed** -d
sough saʊ, sʌf **-s** saʊz, sʌfs **-ing** 'saʊ.ɪŋ, 'sʌf.ɪŋ **-ed** saʊd, sʌft
sought (*from* **seek**) sɔːt (US) sɑːt, sɔːt
sought-after 'sɔːt,ɑːf.təʳ (US) 'sɑːt,æf.tɚ, 'sɔːt-
souk suːk **-s** -s
soul səʊl (US) soʊl **-s** -z '**soul** ,**food**; '**soul** ,**mate**
Soulbury 'səʊl.bᵊr.i (US) 'soʊl-, -ber.i
soul-destroying 'səʊl.dɪ,strɔɪ.ɪŋ (US) 'soʊl-
soulful 'səʊl.fᵊl, -fʊl (US) 'soʊl- **-ly** -i **-ness** -nəs, -nɪs
soulless 'səʊl.ləs, -lɪs (US) 'soʊl- **-ly** -li **-ness** -nəs, -nɪs
soulmate 'səʊl.meɪt (US) 'soʊl- **-s** -s
soul-searching 'səʊl,sɜː.tʃɪŋ (US) 'soʊl,sɝː-
sound saʊnd **-s** -z **-er** -əʳ (US) -ɚ **-est** -ɪst, -əst **-ly** -li **-ness** -nəs, -nɪs **-ing/s** -ɪŋ/z **-ed** -ɪd '**sound** ,**barrier**; '**sound** ,**bite**; '**sound** ,**box**; '**sound ef**,**fect**
soundbite 'saʊn*d*.baɪt, 'saʊm- (US) 'saʊn*d*- **-s** -s
soundboard 'saʊn*d*.bɔːd, 'saʊm- (US) 'saʊn*d*.bɔːrd **-s** -z
soundless 'saʊnd.ləs, -lɪs **-ly** -li
soundproof 'saʊn*d*.pruːf, 'saʊm- (US) 'saʊn*d*- **-s** -s **-ing** -ɪŋ **-ed** -t
soundtrack 'saʊn*d*.træk **-s** -s
soundwave 'saʊnd.weɪv **-s** -z
soup suːp **-s** -s **-y** -i **-ed** -t '**soup** ,**kitchen**; ,**souped 'up**
soupçon 'suːp.sɔ̃ː*ŋ*, -sɒŋ, -sɒn (US) suːp'sõʊn, suː-, -'sɑːn, '-- **-s** -z
soupspoon 'suːp.spuːn **-s** -z
sour saʊəʳ (US) saʊɚ **-er** -əʳ (US) -ɚ **-est** -ɪst, -əst **-ly** -li **-ness** -nəs, -nɪs **-s** -z **-ing** -ɪŋ **-ed** -d ,**sour 'cream**; ,**sour 'grapes**
sourc|e sɔːs (US) sɔːrs **-es** -ɪz **-ing** -ɪŋ **-ed** -t
sourdine sʊə'diːn (US) sʊr- **-s** -z
sourdough 'saʊə.dəʊ (US) 'saʊɚ.doʊ
sourpuss 'saʊə.pʊs (US) 'saʊɚ- **-es** -ɪz
Sousa 'suː.zə (US) -zə, -sə
sousaphone 'suː.zə.fəʊn (US) -zə.foʊn, -sə- **-s** -z
sous-chef 'suː.ʃef **-s** -s
sous|e saʊs **-es** -ɪz **-ing** -ɪŋ **-ed** -t
Sousse suːs
soutane suː'tɑːn (US) -'tæn, -'tɑːn **-s** -z
Souter 'suː.təʳ (US) -ţɚ
south (S) (*n. adj. adv.*) saʊθ ,**South 'Africa**; ,**South A'merica**; ,**South Caro'lina**; ,**South Da'kota**; ,**South 'Island** (US) '**South** ,**Island**; ,**South Ko'rea**; ,**south 'pole**; ,**South 'Seas**
Southall *place in London:* 'saʊ.θɔːl, -ðɔːl (US) -θɔːl, -θɑːl, -ðɔːl, -ðɑːl *surname:* 'sʌð.ɔːl, -ᵊl (US) -ɔːl, -ɑːl, -ᵊl
Southam 'saʊ.θəm
Southampton saʊ'θæm*p*.tən, saʊθ'hæm*p*-
southbound 'saʊθ.baʊnd
Southbourne 'saʊθ.bɔːn (US) -bɔːrn
Southdown 'saʊθ.daʊn
southeast (S) ,saʊθ'iːst *in nautical usage also:* ,saʊ- **-wards** -wədz (US) -wɚdz *stress shift:* ,southeast 'wind
south-easter ,saʊθ'iː.stəʳ (US) -stɚ *in nautical usage also:* ,saʊ- **-s** -z
southeasterl|y ,saʊθ'iː.stᵊl.i (US) -stɚ.li *in nautical usage also:* ,saʊ- **-ies** -iz
southeastern (S) ,saʊθ'iː.stən (US) -stɚn *in nautical usage also:* ,saʊ- **-er/s** -əʳ/z (US) -ɚ/z *stress shift:*

ˌsoutheastern ˈwind
southeastward ˌsaʊθˈiːst.wəd (US) -wɚd **-s** -z
Southend ˌsaʊθˈend *stress shift:* ˌSouthend ˈpier
southerl|y ˈsʌð.əl|.i (US) -ɚ.l|i **-ies** -iz
southern (S) ˈsʌð.ən (US) -ɚn **-most** -ən.məʊst, -əm.məʊst (US) -ɚn.moʊst ˌ**Southern** ˈ**Cross**
southerner (S) ˈsʌð.ən.əʳ (US) -ɚ.nɚ **-s** -z
southernwood ˈsʌð.ən.wʊd (US) -ɚn-
Southey ˈsaʊ.ði, ˈsʌð.i
Southgate ˈsaʊθ.geɪt, -gɪt
Southon ˈsaʊ.ðən
southpaw ˈsaʊθ.pɔː (US) -pɑː, -pɔː **-s** -z
Southport ˈsaʊθ.pɔːt (US) -pɔːrt
southron (S) ˈsʌð.rən **-s** -z
Southsea ˈsaʊθ.siː, -si
south-southeast ˌsaʊθ.saʊθˈiːst *in nautical usage also:* ˌsaʊ.saʊˈ-
south-southwest ˌsaʊθ.saʊθˈwest *in nautical usage also:* ˌsaʊ.saʊˈ-
southward ˈsaʊθ.wəd (US) -wɚd **-s** -z **-ly** -li
Southwark ˈsʌð.ək (US) -ɚk
Southwell *surname:* ˈsaʊθ.wəl, -wel; ˈsʌð.əl *town in Nottinghamshire:* ˈsaʊθ.wəl *locally:* ˈsʌð.əl
Note: Viscount Southwell is /sʌð.əl/
southwest (S) ˌsaʊθˈwest *in nautical usage also:* ˌsaʊ- **-wards** -wədz (US) -wɚdz *stress shift:* ˌsouthwest ˈwind
south-wester ˌsaʊθˈwes.təʳ (US) -tɚ *in nautical usage also:* ˌsaʊ- **-s** -z
south-westerl|y ˌsaʊθˈwes.təl|.i (US) -tɚ.l|i *in nautical usage also:* ˌsaʊ- **-ies** -iz
southwestern (S) ˌsaʊθˈwes.tən (US) -tɚn *in nautical usage also:* ˌsaʊ- **-er/s** -əʳ/z (US) -ɚ/z *stress shift:* ˌsouthwestern ˈwind
south-westward ˌsaʊθˈwest.wəd (US) -wɚd *in nautical usage also:* ˌsaʊ- **-s** -z
Southwick *in West Sussex:* ˈsaʊθ.wɪk *in Northamptonshire:* ˈsʌð.ɪk *in Hampshire:* ˈsʌð.ɪk, ˈsaʊθ.wɪk
Southwold ˈsaʊθ.wəʊld (US) -woʊld
Soutter ˈsuː.təʳ (US) -t̬ɚ
souvenir ˌsuː.vənˈɪəʳ, -vɪˈnɪəʳ, ˈ--- (US) ˌsuː.vəˈnɪr, ˈ--- **-s** -z
sou'wester ˌsaʊˈwes.təʳ (US) -tɚ **-s** -z
Souza ˈsuː.zə
sovereign ˈsɒv.ər.ɪn, ˈ-rɪn (US) ˈsɑːv.rən, -ɚ.ən **-s** -z **-ly** -li
sovereignty ˈsɒv.rən.ti, -rɪn- (US) ˈsɑːv.rən.t̬i, -ɚ.ən-
soviet (S) ˈsəʊ.vi.ət, ˈsɒv.i- (US) ˈsoʊ.vi.et, -ɪt; ˌ--ˈ- **-s** -s **-ism** -ɪ.zəm ˌ**Soviet** ˈ**Union**
sovran ˈsɒv.rən (US) ˈsɑːv- **-s** -z
sow *(n.) pig, metal, channel for metal:* saʊ **-s** -z
sow *(v.) plant seed:* səʊ (US) soʊ **-s** -z **-ing** -ɪŋ **-ed** -d **-n** -n **-er/s** -əʳ/z (US) -ɚ/z
Sowerby *in North Yorkshire:* ˈsaʊə.bi (US) ˈsaʊɚ- *in West Yorkshire, surname:* ˈsəʊə.bi, ˈsaʊə- (US) ˈsoʊɚ-, ˈsaʊɚ-
Soweto səˈwet.əʊ, -ˈweɪ.təʊ (US) -ˈwet̬.oʊ, -ˈweɪ.t̬oʊ
sox sɒks (US) sɑːks
soy sɔɪ ˌ**soy** ˈ**sauce** (US) ˈ**soy** ˌ**sauce**
soya ˈsɔɪ.ə ˈ**soya** ˌ**bean**
soybean ˈsɔɪ.biːn **-s** -z
Soyinka sɔɪˈɪŋ.kə
Soyuz sɔːˈjʊz, səˈjuːz (US) ˈsɑː.juːz, ˈsɔɪ.jʊz
sozzled ˈsɒz.l̩d (US) ˈsɑː.zl̩d
spa (S) spɑː **-s** -z
spac|e speɪs **-es** -ɪz **-ing** -ɪŋ **-ed** -t ˈ**space** ˌ**age**; ˈ**space** ˌ**bar**; ˈ**space** ˌ**shuttle**; ˈ**space** ˌ**station**; ˈ**space** ˌ**suit**; ˈ**space** ˌ**walk**
spacecraft ˈspeɪs.krɑːft (US) -kræft **-s** -s
spaced-out ˌspeɪstˈaʊt *stress shift:* ˌspaced-out ˈperson
spacelab ˈspeɪs.læb **-s** -z
space|man ˈspeɪs|.mæn, -mən **-men** -men, -mən
spaceship ˈspeɪs.ʃɪp, ˈspeɪʃ- (US) ˈspeɪs- **-s** -s
space-time ˌspeɪsˈtaɪm *stress shift:* ˌspace-time conˈtinuum
spacewalk ˈspeɪs.wɔːk (US) -wɔːk, -wɑːk **-s** -s **-ing** -ɪŋ **-ed** -t **-er/s** -əʳ/z (US) -ɚ/z
spac|ey ˈspeɪ.s|i **-ier** -i.əʳ (US) -i.ɚ **-iest** -i.ɪst, -i.əst **-iness** -ɪ.nəs, -ɪ.nɪs
spacious ˈspeɪ.ʃəs **-ly** -li **-ness** -nəs, -nɪs
spade speɪd **-s** -z **-ful/s** -fʊl/z ˌ**call a** ˌ**spade a** ˈ**spade**
spadework ˈspeɪd.wɜːk (US) -wɝːk
spaghetti spəˈget.i (US) -ˈget̬- **spa**ˌ**ghetti bolog**ˈ**nese**
spahi ˈspɑː.hiː, -iː (US) -hiː **-s** -z
Spain speɪn
spake *(archaic past tense of* **speak***)* speɪk
Spalding ˈspɔːl.dɪŋ, ˈspɒl- (US) ˈspɔːl-, ˈspɑːl-
spall spɔːl (US) spɔːl, spɑːl **-s** -z **-ing** -ɪŋ **-ed** -d
spam (S) spæm **-s** -z **-ming** -ɪŋ **-med** -d
span spæn **-s** -z **-ning** -ɪŋ **-ned** -d
Spandau ˈspæn.daʊ
spandex ˈspæn.deks
spandrel ˈspæn.drəl **-s** -z
spangl|e ˈspæŋ.gl̩ **-es** -z **-ing** -ɪŋ, ˈspæŋ.glɪŋ **-ed** -d
spangly ˈspæŋ.gli, -gl̩.i
Spaniard ˈspæn.jəd (US) -jɚd **-s** -z
spaniel ˈspæn.jəl **-s** -z
Spanish ˈspæn.ɪʃ ˌ**Spanish** ˈ**fly**; ˌ**Spanish** ˈ**omelette**; ˌ**Spanish** ˈ**onion**; ˌ**Spanish Sa**ˈ**hara**
spank spæŋk **-s** -s **-ing** -ɪŋ **-ed** -t **-er/s** -əʳ/z (US) -ɚ/z
spanking ˈspæŋ.kɪŋ **-s** -z
spanner ˈspæn.əʳ (US) -ɚ **-s** -z
spar spɑːʳ (US) spɑːr **-s** -z **-ring** -ɪŋ **-red** -d ˈ**sparring** ˌ**match**; ˈ**sparring** ˌ**partner**
spar|e speəʳ (US) sper **-ely** -li **-eness** -nəs, -nɪs **-es** -z **-ing** -ɪŋ/li **-ed** -d ˌ**spare** ˈ**part**; ˌ**spare** ˈ**rib**; ˌ**spare** ˈ**tyre**
sparing ˈspeə.rɪŋ (US) ˈsper.ɪŋ **-ly** -li
spark (S) spɑːk (US) spɑːrk **-s** -s **-ing** -ɪŋ **-ed** -t ˈ**spark** ˌ**plug**; ˈ**sparking** ˌ**plug**
Sparkes spɑːks (US) spɑːrks
sparkl|e ˈspɑː.kl̩ (US) ˈspɑːr- **-es** -z **-ing** -ɪŋ, ˈspɑː.klɪŋ (US) ˈspɑːr- **-ed** -d **-y** -i, ˈspɑː.kli (US) ˈspɑːr- ˌ**sparkling** ˈ**wine**
sparkler ˈspɑː.kləʳ (US) ˈspɑːr.klɚ **-s** -z
spark|y ˈspɑː.k|i (US) ˈspɑːr.k|i **-ier** -i.əʳ (US) -i.ɚ **-iest** -i.ɪst, -i.əst **-iness** -ɪ.nəs, -ɪ.nɪs **-ily** -ɪ.li
sparrow (S) ˈspær.əʊ (US) ˈsper.oʊ, ˈspær- **-s** -z
sparrowhawk ˈspær.əʊ.hɔːk (US) ˈsper.oʊ.hɑːk, ˈspær-, -hɔːk **-s** -s
spars|e spɑːs (US) spɑːrs **-er** -əʳ (US) -ɚ **-est** -ɪst, -əst **-ely** -li **-eness** -nəs, -nɪs **-ity** -ə.ti, -ɪ.ti (US) -ə.t̬i
Spar|ta ˈspɑː|.tə (US) ˈspɑːr|.t̬ə **-tan/s** -tən/z
Spartacus ˈspɑː.tə.kəs (US) ˈspɑːr.t̬ə-
spartan ˈspɑː.tən (US) ˈspɑːr-
spasm ˈspæz.əm **-s** -z
spasmodic spæzˈmɒd.ɪk (US) -ˈmɑː.dɪk **-ally** -əl.i, -li
spastic ˈspæs.tɪk **-s** -s
spasticity spæsˈtɪs.ə.ti, -ɪ.ti (US) -ə.t̬i
spat spæt **-s** -s **-ting** -ɪŋ **-ted** -ɪd
spatchcock ˈspætʃ.kɒk (US) -kɑːk **-s** -s **-ing** -ɪŋ **-ed** -t
spate speɪt **-s** -s
spatial ˈspeɪ.ʃəl **-ly** -i
spatt|er ˈspæt|.əʳ (US) ˈspæt̬|.ɚ **-ers** -əz (US) -ɚz **-ering** -ər.ɪŋ **-ered** -əd (US) -ɚd
spatul|a ˈspæt.jə.l|ə, -jʊ-, ˈspætʃ.ə-, ˈ-ʊ- (US) ˈspætʃ.ə- **-ae** -iː **-as** -əz
spatulate ˈspæt.jə.lət, -jʊ-, ˈspætʃ.ə-, ˈ-ʊ-, -lɪt, -leɪt (US) ˈspætʃ.ə.lɪt, -leɪt
spavin ˈspæv.ɪn **-ed** -d
spawn spɔːn (US) spɑːn, spɔːn **-s** -z **-ing** -ɪŋ **-ed** -d
spay speɪ **-s** -z **-ing** -ɪŋ **-ed** -d
Speaight speɪt
speak spiːk **-s** -s **-ing** -ɪŋ **spoke** spəʊk (US) spoʊk **spoken** ˈspəʊ.kən (US) ˈspoʊ- **speaker/s** ˈspiː.kəʳ/z (US) -kɚ/z
speakeas|y ˈspiːkˌiː.z|i **-ies** -iz
speakerphone ˈspiː.kə.fəʊn (US) -kɚ.foʊn **-s** -z

Spean spɪən, ˈspiː.ən US ˈspiː.ən
spear spɪəʳ US spɪr **-s** -z **-ing** -ɪŋ **-ed** -d
spearhead ˈspɪə.hed US ˈspɪr- **-s** -z **-ing** -ɪŋ **-ed** -ɪd
spear|man (S) ˈspɪə|.mən US ˈspɪr- **-men** -mən, -men
spearmint ˈspɪə.mɪnt US ˈspɪr-
spec spek
speci|al ˈspeʃ.ᵊl **-als** -ᵊlz **-ally** -ᵊl.i, -li **-alness** -ᵊl.nəs, -ᵊl.nɪs **ˈSpecial ˌBranch; ˌspecial deˈlivery; ˌspecial efˈfects**
special|ism ˈspeʃ.ᵊl.ɪ|.zᵊm, ˈ-lɪ- US ˈ-ᵊl.ɪ- **-s** -z
specialist ˈspeʃ.ᵊl.ɪst **-s** -s
specialit|y ˌspeʃ.iˈæl.ə.t|i, -ɪ.t|i US -ə.t̬|i **-ies** -iz
specialization, -isa- ˌspeʃ.ᵊl.aɪˈzeɪ.ʃᵊn, -ɪˈ- US -ɪˈ-
specializ|e, -is|e ˈspeʃ.ᵊl.aɪz US -ə.laɪz **-es** -ɪz **-ing** -ɪŋ **-ed** -d
specialt|y ˈspeʃ.ᵊl.t|i US -t̬|i **-ies** -iz
specie ˈspiː.ʃiː, -ʃi US -ʃiː, -siː
species ˈspiː.ʃiːz, -ʃɪz, -siːz, -sɪz US -ʃiːz, -siːz **-ism** -ɪ.zᵊm
specific spəˈsɪf.ɪk, spɪ- US spə- **-s** -s **-ally** -ᵊl.i, -li **speˌcific ˈgravity**
specification ˌspes.ɪ.fɪˈkeɪ.ʃᵊn, ˌ-ə- US ˌ-ə- **-s** -z
specificity ˌspes.ɪˈfɪs.ə.ti, -ɪ.ti US -əˈfɪs.ə.t̬i
speci|fy ˈspes.ɪ|.faɪ, ˈ-ə- US ˈ-ə- **-fies** -faɪz **-fying** -faɪ.ɪŋ **-fied** -faɪd **-fiable** -faɪ.ə.bl̩
specimen ˈspes.ə.mɪn, ˈ-ɪ-, -mən US -ə.mən **-s** -z
specious ˈspiː.ʃəs **-ly** -li **-ness** -nəs, -nɪs
speck spek **-s** -s **-ed** -t
speckle ˈspek.l̩ **-s** -z **-d** -d
speckless ˈspek.ləs, -lɪs
specs speks
spectacle ˈspek.tə.kl̩, -tɪ- **-s** -z **-d** -d
spectacular spekˈtæk.jə.ləʳ, -jʊ- US -lɚ **-ly** -li
spectat|e spekˈteɪt **-es** -s **-ing** -ɪŋ **-ed** -ɪd
spectator (S) spekˈteɪ.təʳ US -t̬ɚ **-s** -z **specˌtator ˈsport, specˈtator ˌsport**
specter ˈspek.təʳ US -tɚ **-s** -z
spectral ˈspek.trᵊl
spectre ˈspek.təʳ US -tɚ **-s** -z
spectrogram ˈspek.trəʊ.græm US -trə- **-s** -z
spectrograph ˈspek.trəʊ.grɑːf, -græf US -trə.græf **-s** -s
spectrographic ˌspek.trəʊˈgræf.ɪk US -trəˈ- *stress shift:* ˌspectrographic ˈsection
spectrography spekˈtrɒg.rə.fi US -ˈtrɑː.grə-
spectrometer spekˈtrɒm.ɪ.təʳ, ˈ-ə- US -ˈtrɑː.mə.t̬ɚ **-s** -z
spectroscope ˈspek.trə.skəʊp US -trə.skoʊp **-s** -s
spectroscopic ˌspek.trəˈskɒp.ɪk US -ˈskɑː.pɪk **-al** -ᵊl **-ally** -ᵊl.i, -li *stress shift:* ˌspectroscopic ˈpicture
spectroscop|ist spekˈtrɒs.kə.p|ɪst US -ˈtrɑː.skə- **-ists** -ɪsts **-y** -i
spectr|um ˈspek.tr|əm **-a** -ə **-ums** -əmz
specu|late ˈspek.jə|.leɪt, -jʊ- **-lates** -leɪts **-lating** -leɪ.tɪŋ US -leɪ.t̬ɪŋ **-lated** -leɪ.tɪd US -leɪ.t̬ɪd **-lator/s** -leɪ.təʳ/z US -leɪ.t̬ɚ/z
speculation ˌspek.jəˈleɪ.ʃᵊn, -jʊˈ- **-s** -z
speculative ˈspek.jə.lə.tɪv, -jʊ-, -leɪ- US -leɪ.t̬ɪv, -lə- **-ly** -li **-ness** -nəs, -nɪs
specul|um ˈspek.jə.l|əm, -jʊ- **-a** -ə **-ar** -əʳ US -ɚ
sped *(from* **speed)** sped
speech spiːtʃ **-es** -ɪz **ˈspeech ˌday; ˈspeech imˌpediment; ˌspeech ˈsynthesiser**
speechification ˌspiː.tʃɪ.fɪˈkeɪ.ʃᵊn, -tʃə- US -tʃə- **-s** -z
speechi|fy ˈspiː.tʃɪ|.faɪ, -tʃə- US -tʃə- **-fies** -faɪz **-fying** -faɪ.ɪŋ **-fied** -faɪd **-fier/s** -faɪ.əʳ/z US -faɪ.ɚ/z
speechless ˈspiːtʃ.ləs, -lɪs **-ly** -li **-ness** -nəs, -nɪs
speed (S) spiːd **-s** -z **-ing** -ɪŋ **-ed** -ɪd **sped** sped **ˈspeed ˌbump; ˈspeed ˌlimit; ˈspeed ˌtrap**
speedboat ˈspiːd.bəʊt US -boʊt **-s** -s
speed-cop ˈspiːd.kɒp US -kɑːp **-s** -s
speedo ˈspiː.dəʊ US -doʊ **-s** -z
speedometer spiːˈdɒm.ɪ.təʳ, spɪ-, -mə- US -ˈdɑː.mə.t̬ɚ **-s** -z
speed-read ˈspiːd.riːd **-s** -z **-ing** -ɪŋ *past tense:* ˈspiːd.red
speed|skate ˈspiːd|.skeɪt **-skating** -ˌskeɪ.tɪŋ US -t̬ɪŋ **-skater/s** -ˌskeɪ.təʳ/z US -t̬ɚ/z
speedway ˈspiːd.weɪ **-s** -z
speedwell (S) ˈspiːd.wel, -wᵊl **-s** -z
Speedwriting® ˈspiːdˌraɪ.tɪŋ US -t̬ɪŋ
speed|y ˈspiː.d|i **-ier** -i.əʳ US -i.ɚ **-iest** -i.ɪst, -i.əst **-ily** -ᵊl.i, -ɪ.li **-iness** -ɪ.nəs, -ɪ.nɪs
Speen spiːn
Speer speəʳ *as if German:* ʃpeəʳ US spɪr *as if German:* ʃper
Speight speɪt
Speirs spɪəz US spɪrz
speiss spaɪs
Speke spiːk
speleological ˌspiː.li.əˈlɒdʒ.ɪ.kᵊl, ˌspel.i- US -ˈlɑː.dʒɪ-
speleolog|y ˌspiː.liˈɒl.ə.dʒ|i, ˌspel.iˈ- US ˌspiː.liˈɑː.lə- **-ist/s** -ɪst/s
spell spel **-s** -z **-ing/s** -ɪŋ/z **-ed** -d, -t **spelt** -t **speller/s** ˈspel.əʳ/z US -ɚ/z **ˈspelling ˌbee**
spell|bind ˈspel|.baɪnd **-binds** -baɪndz **-binding** -baɪn.dɪŋ **-bound** -baʊnd **-binder/s** -ˌbaɪn.dəʳ/z US -ˌbaɪn.dɚ/z
spellbound ˈspel.baʊnd
spelt *(from* **spell)** spelt
spelt|er ˈspel.t|əʳ US -t̬|ɚ **-ers** -əz US -ɚz **-ering** -ᵊr.ɪŋ **-ered** -əd US -ɚd
spelunk|er spəˈlʌŋ.k|əʳ US -k|ɚ; ˈspiː.lʌŋ- **-er/s** -ᵊr.əʳ/z US -ɚ.ɚ/z **-ing** -ɪŋ
spenc|e (S) spen*t*s **-es** -ɪz
spencer (S) ˈspen*t*.səʳ US -sɚ **-s** -z
spend spend **-s** -z **-ing** -ɪŋ **spent** -t **spender/s** ˈspen.dəʳ/z US -dɚ/z
Spender ˈspen.dəʳ US -dɚ
spendthrift ˈspen*d*.θrɪft **-s** -s
Spengler ˈspeŋ.gləʳ US -glɚ
Spenlow ˈspen.ləʊ US -loʊ
Spennymoor ˈspen.i.mɔːʳ, -mʊəʳ US -mɔːr, -mʊr
Spens spenz
Spenser ˈspen*t*.səʳ US -sɚ
Spenserian spenˈsɪə.ri.ən US -ˈsɪr.i-
spent *(from* **spend)** spent
sperm spɜːm US spɝːm **-s** -z **ˈsperm ˌbank; ˈsperm ˌwhale**
spermaceti ˌspɜː.məˈset.i, -ˈsiː.ti US ˌspɝː.məˈsiː.ti, -ˈset.i
spermatozo|on ˌspɜː.mə.təʊˈzəʊ|.ɒn, -ən US ˌspɝː.mə.t̬əˈzoʊ|.ɑːn, -ən **-a** -ə
spermicidal ˌspɜː.mɪˈsaɪ.dᵊl US ˌspɝː.məˈ-
spermicide ˈspɜː.mɪ.saɪd US ˈspɝː.mə- **-s** -z
Sperrin ˈsper.ɪn
spew spjuː **-s** -z **-ing** -ɪŋ **-ed** -d
Spey speɪ
Spezia ˈspet.si.ə, ˈsped.zi- US ˈspet.si.ɑː
Spezzia ˈspet.si.ə
sphagnum ˈsfæg.nəm **ˌsphagnum ˈmoss**
sphene spiːn, sfiːn US sfiːn **-s** -z
sphere sfɪəʳ US sfɪr **-s** -z
spheric ˈsfer.ɪk US ˈsfɪr-, ˈsfer- **-s** -s **-al** -ᵊl **-ally** -ᵊl.i, -li
spheroid ˈsfɪə.rɔɪd US ˈsfɪr.ɔɪd, ˈsfer- **-s** -z
spheroidal sfɪəˈrɔɪ.dᵊl, sferˈɔɪ- US sfɪˈrɔɪ-, sferˈɔɪ-
spherometer sfɪəˈrɒm.ɪ.təʳ, sferˈɒm-, ˈ-ə- US sfɪˈrɑː.mə.tɚ, sferˈɑː- **-s** -z
sphincter ˈsfɪŋ*k*.təʳ US -tɚ **-s** -z
sphinx sfɪŋks **-es** -ɪz
sphragistics sfrəˈdʒɪs.tɪks
sphygmomanometer ˌsfɪg.məʊ.məˈnɒm.ɪ.təʳ, ˈ-ə- US -moʊ.məˈnɑː.mə.t̬ɚ **-s** -z
spic spɪk **-s** -s
spi|ca (S) ˈspaɪ|.kə **-cae** -siː **-cas** -kəz
spiccato spɪˈkɑː.təʊ US -t̬oʊ
spic|e (S) spaɪs **-es** -ɪz **-ing** -ɪŋ **-ed** -t

spiceberr|y ˈspaɪs.bᵊr|.i, -br|i (US) -ˌber|.i **-ies** -iz
Spicer ˈspaɪ.səʳ (US) -sɚ
spick spɪk ˌ**spick and** ˈ**span**
spicule ˈspɪk.juːl, ˈspaɪ.kjuːl (US) ˈspɪk.juːl **-s** -z
spic|y ˈspaɪ.s|i **-ier** -i.əʳ (US) -i.ɚ **-iest** -i.ɪst, -i.əst **-ily** -ɪ.li, -ᵊl.i **-iness** -ɪ.nəs, -ɪ.nɪs
spid|er ˈspaɪ.d|əʳ (US) -dɚ **-ers** -əz (US) -ɚz **-ery** -ᵊr.i ˈ**spider** ˌ**monkey**; ˈ**spider** ˌ**plant**
spidergram ˈspaɪ.də.græm (US) -dɚ- **-s** -z
spiderweb ˈspaɪ.də.web (US) -dɚ- **-s** -z
spiel ʃpiːl, spiːl (US) spiːl, ʃpiːl
Spielberg ˈspiːl.bɜːg (US) -bɝːg
spiffing ˈspɪf.ɪŋ **-ly** -li
spiff|y ˈspɪf|.i **-ier** -i.əʳ (US) -i.ɚ **-iest** -i.ɪst, -i.əst
spigot ˈspɪg.ət **-s** -s
spik spɪk **-s** -s
spik|e spaɪk **-es** -s **-ing** -ɪŋ **-ed** -t
spikenard ˈspaɪk.nɑːd, ˈspaɪ.kə- (US) ˈspaɪk.nɑːrd, -nɚd
Spikins ˈspaɪ.kɪnz
spik|y ˈspaɪ.k|i **-ier** -i.əʳ (US) -i.ɚ **-iest** -i.ɪst, -i.əst **-iness** -ɪ.nəs, -ɪ.nɪs
spill spɪl **-s** -z **-ing** -ɪŋ **-ed** -d **spilt** -t
spillag|e ˈspɪl.ɪdʒ **-es** -ɪz
spiller (S) ˈspɪl.əʳ (US) -ɚ **-s** -z
spillikin ˈspɪl.ɪ.kɪn **-s** -z
Spilling ˈspɪl.ɪŋ
spillover ˈspɪl.əʊ.vəʳ (US) -oʊ.vɚ **-s** -z
spilt *(from* **spill***)* spɪlt
spin spɪn **-s** -z **-ning** -ɪŋ **span** spæn **spun** spʌn **spinner/s** ˈspɪn.əʳ/z (US) -ɚ/z ˌ**spin** ˈ**bowling** (US) ˈ**spin** ˌ**bowling**; ˈ**spin** ˌ**doctor**; ˈ**spinning** ˌ**wheel**
spina bifida ˌspaɪ.nəˈbɪf.ɪ.də, -ˈbaɪ.fɪ- (US) -ˈbɪf.ɪ-
spinach ˈspɪn.ɪtʃ, -ɪdʒ (US) -ɪtʃ
spinal ˈspaɪ.nᵊl ˈ**spinal** ˌ**cord**, ˌ**spinal** ˈ**cord** (US) ˈ**spinal** ˌ**cord**
spindl|e ˈspɪn.dl̩ **-es** -z **-y** -i, ˈspɪnd.li
spindle-legged ˌspɪn.dl̩ˈlegd (US) ˈspɪn.dl̩.legd, -ˌleg.ɪd *stress shift, British only:* ˌspindle-legged ˈchair
spindrift ˈspɪn.drɪft
spin-dr|y ˌspɪnˈdr|aɪ, ˈ-- (US) ˈspɪn.dr|aɪ **-ies** -aɪz **-ying** -aɪ.ɪŋ **-ied** -aɪd **-ier/s** -aɪ.əʳ/z (US) -aɪ.ɚ/z
spine spaɪn **-s** -z **-d** -d
spine-chill|ing ˈspaɪnˌtʃɪl|.ɪŋ **-ingly** -ɪŋ.li **-er/s** -əʳ/z (US) -ɚ/z
spinel spɪˈnel (US) spɪˈnel; ˈspɪn.ᵊl
spineless ˈspaɪn.ləs, -lɪs **-ly** -li **-ness** -nəs, -nɪs
spinet spɪˈnet; ˈspɪn.et, -ɪt (US) ˈspɪn.ɪt **-s** -s
spinifex ˈspɪn.ɪ.feks, ˈ-ə-
Spink spɪŋk **-s** -s
spinnaker ˈspɪn.ə.kəʳ, ˈ-ɪ- (US) -ə.kɚ **-s** -z
spinney ˈspɪn.i **-s** -z
spinoff ˈspɪn.ɒf (US) -ɑːf **-s** -s
spinose ˈspaɪ.nəʊs, -ˈ- (US) ˈspaɪ.noʊs
spinous ˈspaɪ.nəs
Spinoza spɪˈnəʊ.zə (US) -ˈnoʊ-
spinster ˈspɪnt.stəʳ (US) -stɚ **-s** -z **-hood** -hʊd **-ish** -ɪʃ
spin|y ˈspaɪ.n|i **-iness** -ɪ.nəs, -ɪ.nɪs
Spion Kop ˌspaɪ.ənˈkɒp, -əŋˈ- (US) -ənˈkɑːp
spiraea spaɪˈriː.ə, -ˈrɪə (US) -ˈriː.ə **-s** -z
spiral ˈspaɪə.rᵊl (US) ˈspaɪ- **-s** -z **-ly** -i **-(l)ing** -ɪŋ **-(l)ed** -d ˌ**spiral** ˈ**staircase**
spirant ˈspaɪə.rᵊnt (US) ˈspaɪ- **-s** -s
spire spaɪəʳ (US) spaɪɚ **-s** -z **-d** -d
spirea spaɪˈrɪə, -ˈriː.ə (US) -ˈriː.ə **-s** -z
spiri|t ˈspɪr.ɪ|t, -ə|t **-ts** -ts **-ting** -tɪŋ (US) -t̬ɪŋ **-ted/ly** -tɪd/li (US) -t̬ɪd/li ˈ**spirit** ˌ**lamp**; ˈ**spirit** ˌ**level**
spiritism ˈspɪr.ɪ.tɪ.zᵊm (US) -t̬ɪ-
spiritless ˈspɪr.ɪt.ləs, -lɪs **-ly** -li **-ness** -nəs, -nɪs
spiritual ˈspɪr.ɪ.tʃu.əl, ˈ-ə-, -tju- (US) -tʃu- **-s** -z **-ly** -i
spiritual|ism ˈspɪr.ɪ.tʃu.ᵊl|.ɪ.zᵊm, ˈ-ə-, -tju- (US) -tʃu- **-ist/s** -ɪst/s
spiritualistic ˌspɪr.ɪ.tʃu.ᵊlˈɪs.tɪk, ˌ-ə-, -tju- (US) -tʃu-
spiritualit|y ˌspɪr.ɪ.tʃuˈæl.ə.t|i, ˌ-ə-, -tjuˈ-, -ɪ.t|i (US) -tʃuˈæl.ə.t̬|i **-ies** -iz
spirituous ˈspɪr.ɪ.tʃu.əs, -tju.əs (US) -tʃu-
spiritus ˈspɪr.ɪ.təs, ˈ-ə- (US) -t̬əs
spirogyra ˌspaɪə.rəʊˈdʒaɪə.rə (US) ˌspaɪ.roʊˈdʒaɪ-
spirt spɜːt (US) spɝːt **-s** -s **-ing** -ɪŋ (US) ˈspɝː.t̬ɪŋ **-ed** -ɪd (US) ˈspɝː.t̬ɪd
spit *(n. v.)* spɪt **-s** -s **-ting** -ɪŋ (US) ˈspɪt̬.ɪŋ **-ted** -ɪd (US) ˈspɪt̬.ɪd **spat** spæt ˌ**spitting** ˈ**image**; ˌ**spit and** ˈ**polish**
Spitalfields ˈspɪt.ᵊl.fiːldz (US) ˈspɪt̬-
spitball ˈspɪt.bɔːl (US) -bɔːl, -bɑːl **-s** -z
spit|e spaɪt **-es** -s **-ing** -ɪŋ (US) ˈspaɪ.t̬ɪŋ **-ed** -ɪd (US) ˈspaɪ.t̬ɪd
spiteful ˈspaɪt.fᵊl, -fʊl **-ly** -i **-ness** -nəs, -nɪs
spitfire (S) ˈspɪtˌfaɪəʳ (US) -ˌfaɪɚ **-s** -z
Spithead ˌspɪtˈhed *stress shift:* ˌSpithead ˈcoastline
Spitsbergen ˈspɪtsˌbɜː.gən, ˌ-ˈ-- (US) ˈspɪtsˌbɝː-
spittle ˈspɪt.l̩ (US) ˈspɪt̬-
spittoon spɪˈtuːn **-s** -z
Spitz spɪts
spiv spɪv **-s** -z **-vy** -i
splash splæʃ **-es** -ɪz **-ing** -ɪŋ **-ed** -t **-er/s** -əʳ/z (US) -ɚ/z ˈ**splash** ˌ**guard**
splashback ˈsplæʃ.bæk **-s** -s
splashboard ˈsplæʃ.bɔːd (US) -bɔːrd **-s** -z
splashdown ˈsplæʃ.daʊn **-s** -z
splash|y ˈsplæʃ|.i **-iness** -ɪ.nəs, -ɪ.nɪs
splat splæt **-s** -s **-ting** -ɪŋ **-ted** -ɪd
splatt|er ˈsplæt|.əʳ (US) ˈsplæt̬|.ɚ **-ers** -əz (US) -ɚz **-ering** -ᵊr.ɪŋ **-ered** -əd (US) -ɚd
splay spleɪ **-s** -z **-ing** -ɪŋ **-ed** -d
splayfooted ˌspleɪˈfʊt.ɪd (US) ˈspleɪˌfʊt̬- *stress shift, British only:* ˌsplayfooted ˈwalk
spleen spliːn **-s** -z **-ful** -fᵊl, -fʊl **-fully** -fᵊl.i, -fʊ.li
splendid ˈsplen.dɪd **-ly** -li **-ness** -nəs, -nɪs
splendiferous splenˈdɪf.ᵊr.əs **-ly** -li **-ness** -nəs, -nɪs
splendo(u)r ˈsplen.dəʳ (US) -dɚ **-s** -z
splenetic spləˈnet.ɪk, splɪ- (US) splɪˈnet̬- **-s** -s **-ally** -ᵊl.i, -li
splic|e splaɪs **-es** -ɪz **-ing** -ɪŋ **-ed** -t
spliff splɪf **-s** -s
splint splɪnt **-s** -s **-ing** -ɪŋ (US) ˈsplɪn.t̬ɪŋ **-ed** -ɪd (US) ˈsplɪn.t̬ɪd
splint|er ˈsplɪn.t|əʳ (US) -t̬|ɚ **-ers** -əz (US) -ɚz **-ering** -ᵊr.ɪŋ **-ered** -əd (US) -ɚd **-ery** -ᵊr.i ˈ**splinter** ˌ**group**
split (S) splɪt **-s** -s **-ting** -ɪŋ (US) ˈsplɪt̬.ɪŋ **-ter/s** -əʳ/z (US) ˈsplɪt̬.ɚ/z ˌ**split deˈcision**; ˌ**split** ˈ**ends**; ˌ**split** ˈ**hairs**; ˌ**split inˈfinitive**; ˌ**split** ˈ**pea**; ˌ**split persoˈnality**; ˌ**split** ˈ**screen** *stress shift:* ˌsplit screen ˈpicture; ˌ**split** ˈ**second**; *stress shift:* ˌsplit second ˈtiming
split-level ˌsplɪtˈlev.ᵊl *stress shift:* ˌsplit-level ˈflat
splodg|e splɒdʒ (US) splɑːdʒ **-es** -ɪz
splodg|y ˈsplɒdʒ|.i (US) ˈsplɑː.dʒ|i **-ier** -i.əʳ (US) -i.ɚ **-iest** -i.ɪst, -i.əst **-iness** -ɪ.nəs, -ɪ.nɪs
splosh splɒʃ (US) splɑːʃ **-es** -ɪz **-ing** -ɪŋ **-ed** -t
splotch splɒtʃ (US) splɑːtʃ **-es** -ɪz **-y** -i
splurg|e splɜːdʒ (US) splɝːdʒ **-es** -ɪz **-ing** -ɪŋ **-ed** -d
splutt|er ˈsplʌt|.əʳ (US) ˈsplʌt̬|.ɚ **-ers** -əz (US) -ɚz **-ering** -ᵊr.ɪŋ **-ered** -əd (US) -ɚd
Spock spɒk (US) spɑːk
Spode spəʊd (US) spoʊd
Spofforth ˈspɒf.əθ (US) ˈspɑː.fɚθ
Spohr spɔːʳ *as if German:* ʃpɔːʳ (US) spɔːr *as if German:* ʃpɔːr
spoil spɔɪl **-s** -z **-ing** -ɪŋ **-ed** -d, -t **-t** -t **-er/s** -əʳ/z (US) -ɚ/z **-age** -ɪdʒ
spoilsport ˈspɔɪl.spɔːt (US) -spɔːrt **-s** -s
spoke *of wheel:* spəʊk (US) spoʊk **-s** -s
spok|e *(from* **speak***)* spəʊk (US) spoʊk **-en** -ᵊn
spokes|man ˈspəʊks|.mən (US) ˈspoʊks- **-men** -mən
spokes|person ˈspəʊks|ˌpɜː.sᵊn (US) ˈspoʊks|ˌpɝː- **-persons** -ˌpɜː.sᵊnz (US) -ˌpɝː- **-people** -ˌpiː.pl̩

Spreading

A term used to describe lip positions in speech, produced by pulling the corners of the mouth away from each other, as in a smile.

Phonetics books tend to be rather inconsistent about this, sometimes implying that any sound that is not rounded has spread lips, but elsewhere treating lip-spreading as being different from NEUTRAL lip shape. Vowels with spreading are often referred to as 'unrounded'.

Examples for English

The English vowel /iː/ is thought of as having strong lip-spreading, while /ɪ/ has spreading to a lesser degree.

spokes|woman ˈspəʊksˌwʊm.ən (US) ˈspoʊks- **-women** -ˌwɪm.ɪn
spoliation ˌspəʊ.liˈeɪ.ʃᵊn (US) ˌspoʊ-
spoliator ˈspəʊ.li.eɪ.təʳ (US) ˈspoʊ.li.eɪ.t̬ɚ **-s** -z
spondee ˈspɒn.diː, -di (US) ˈspɑːn- **-s** -z
spondulicks spɒnˈduː.lɪks (US) spɑːnˈduː-
spondylitis ˌspɒn.dɪˈlaɪ.tɪs, -dəˈ- (US) ˌspɑːn.dəˈlaɪ.t̬ɪs
spong|e spʌndʒ **-es** -ɪz **-(e)ing** -ɪŋ **-ed** -d **-er/s** -əʳ/z (US) -ɚ/z **ˈsponge ˌbag; ˈsponge ˌcake; ˌsponge ˈfinger**
spongiform ˈspʌn.dʒɪ.fɔːm (US) -fɔːrm
spong|y ˈspʌn.dʒ|i **-ier** -i.əʳ (US) -i.ɚ **-iest** -i.ɪst, -i.əst **-iness** -ɪ.nəs, -ɪ.nɪs
sponson ˈspɒnt.sən (US) ˈspɑːnt- **-s** -z
spons|or ˈspɒnt.s|əʳ (US) ˈspɑːnt.s|ɚ **-ors** -əz (US) -ɚz **-oring** -ᵊr.ɪŋ **-ored** -əd (US) -ɚd **-orship** -ə.ʃɪp (US) -ɚ.ʃɪp
spontaneity ˌspɒn.təˈneɪ.ə.ti, -ˈniː.ə.ti, -ɪ.ti (US) ˌspɑːn.tᵊnˈeɪ.ə.t̬i, -ˈiː-
spontaneous spɒnˈteɪ.ni.əs, spən- (US) spɑːn- **-ly** -li **-ness** -nəs, -nɪs **sponˌtaneous comˈbustion**
spoof spuːf **-s** -s **-ing** -ɪŋ **-ed** -t
spook spuːk **-s** -s **-ing** -ɪŋ **-ed** -t **-ish** -ɪʃ
spook|y ˈspuː.k|i **-ier** -i.əʳ (US) -i.ɚ **-iest** -i.ɪst, -i.əst **-ily** -ɪ.li, -ᵊl.i **-iness** -ɪ.nəs, -ɪ.nɪs
spool spuːl **-s** -z **-ing** -ɪŋ **-ed** -d
spoon spuːn **-s** -z **-ing** -ɪŋ **-ed** -d
spoonbill ˈspuːn.bɪl, ˈspuːm- (US) ˈspuːn- **-s** -z **-ed** -d
Spooner ˈspuː.nəʳ (US) -nɚ
spoonerism ˈspuː.nᵊr.ɪ.zᵊm **-s** -z
spoon|-feed ˈspuːn|.fiːd **-feeds** -fiːdz **-feeding** -ˌfiː.dɪŋ **-fed** -fed
spoonful ˈspuːn.fʊl, -fᵊl **-s** -z **spoonsful** ˈspuːnz-
spoon|y ˈspuː.n|i **-ier** -i.əʳ (US) -i.ɚ **-iest** -i.ɪst, -i.əst **-ily** -ɪ.li, -ᵊl.i **-iness** -ɪ.nəs, -ɪ.nɪs
spoor spɔːʳ, spʊəʳ (US) spʊr **-s** -z **-ing** -ɪŋ **-ed** -d
Sporades ˈspɒr.ə.diːz (US) ˈspɔːr-
sporadic spəˈræd.ɪk, spɒrˈæd- (US) spəˈræd-, spɔː- **-ally** -ᵊl.i, -li
sporangi|um spəˈræn.dʒi|.əm (US) spə-, spoʊ- **-a** -ə
spore spɔːʳ (US) spɔːr **-s** -z
sporran ˈspɒr.ən (US) ˈspɔːr-, ˈspɑːr- **-s** -z
sport spɔːt (US) spɔːrt **-s** -s **-ing** -ɪŋ (US) ˈspɔːr.t̬ɪŋ **-ed** -ɪd (US) ˈspɔːr.t̬ɪd **ˈsports ˌcar; ˈsports ˌday; ˈsports ˌjacket**
sportive ˈspɔː.tɪv (US) ˈspɔːr.t̬ɪv **-ly** -li **-ness** -nəs, -nɪs
sportscast ˈspɔːts.kɑːst (US) ˈspɔːrts.kæst **-s** -s **-ing** -ɪŋ **-er/s** -əʳ/z (US) -ɚ/z
sports|man ˈspɔːts|.mən (US) ˈspɔːrts- **-men** -mən
sportsman|like ˈspɔːts.mən|.laɪk (US) ˈspɔːrts- **-ship** -ʃɪp
sports|person ˈspɔːts|ˌpɜː.sᵊn (US) ˈspɔːrts|ˌpɝː- **-persons** -ˌpɜː.sᵊnz (US) -ˌpɝː- **-people** -ˌpiː.pl̩
sportswear ˈspɔːts.weəʳ (US) ˈspɔːrts.wer
sports|woman ˈspɔːts|ˌwʊm.ən (US) ˈspɔːrts- **-women** -ˌwɪm.ɪn
sport|y ˈspɔː.t|i (US) ˈspɔːr.t̬|i **-ier** -i.əʳ (US) -i.ɚ **-iest** -i.ɪst, -i.əst **-ily** -ɪ.li, -ᵊl.i **-iness** -ɪ.nəs, -ɪ.nɪs
spot spɒt (US) spɑːt **-s** -s **-ting** -ɪŋ (US) ˈspɑː.t̬ɪŋ **-ted** -ɪd (US) ˈspɑː.t̬ɪd **ˌspotted ˈdick; ˌknock (the) ˈspots off**
spot-check ˌspɒtˈtʃek, ˈ-- (US) ˈspɑːt.tʃek **-s** -s **-ing** -ɪŋ **-ed** -t
spotless ˈspɒt.ləs, -lɪs (US) ˈspɑːt- **-ly** -li **-ness** -nəs, -nɪs
spotlight ˈspɒt.laɪt (US) ˈspɑːt- **-s** -s **-ing** -ɪŋ **-ed** -ɪd **spotlit** -lɪt
spot-on ˌspɒtˈɒn (US) spɑːtˈɑːn
Spottiswoode ˈspɒt.ɪs.wʊd, -ɪz-; ˈspɒt.swʊd (US) ˈspɑː.t̬ɪs-, ˈspɑːt.swʊd
spott|y ˈspɒt|.i (US) ˈspɑː.t̬|i **-ier** -i.əʳ (US) -i.ɚ **-iest** -i.ɪst, -i.əst **-iness** -ɪ.nəs, -ɪ.nɪs
spous|e spaʊs **-es** -ɪz
spout spaʊt **-s** -s **-ing** -ɪŋ (US) ˈspaʊ.t̬ɪŋ **-ed** -ɪd (US) ˈspaʊ.t̬ɪd **-er/s** -əʳ/z (US) ˈspaʊ.t̬ɚ/z
Spragge spræg
Sprague spreɪg
sprain spreɪn **-s** -z **-ing** -ɪŋ **-ed** -d
sprang *(from* **spring***)* spræŋ
Sprange spreɪndʒ
Sprangle ˈspræŋ.gl̩
sprat (S) spræt **-s** -s
Spratt spræt
sprawl sprɔːl (US) sprɑːl, sprɔːl **-s** -z **-ing** -ɪŋ **-ed** -d **-er/s** -əʳ/z (US) -ɚ/z
sprawl|y ˈsprɔː.l|i (US) ˈsprɑː-, ˈsprɔː- **-ier** -i.əʳ (US) -i.ɚ **-iest** -i.ɪst, -i.əst **-iness** -ɪ.nəs, -ɪ.nɪs
spray spreɪ **-s** -z **-ing** -ɪŋ **-ed** -d **-er/s** -əʳ/z (US) -ɚ/z **ˈspray ˌgun**
spraycan ˈspreɪ.kæn **-s** -z
spread spred **-s** -z **-ing** -ɪŋ **-er/s** -əʳ/z (US) -ɚ/z
spread-eagl|e ˌspredˈiː.gl̩ (US) ˈspredˌiː- **-es** -z **-ing** -ɪŋ, -ˈiː.glɪŋ (US) -ˌiː.glɪŋ **-ed** -d
spreadsheet ˈspred.ʃiːt **-s** -s
sprechgesang (S) ˈʃprek.gə.sæŋ *as if German:* ˈʃprex.gə.zæŋ (US) ˈʃprek.gə.sɑːŋ
spree spriː **-s** -z
sprig sprɪg **-s** -z
Sprigg sprɪg **-s** -z
sprightl|y ˈspraɪt.l|i **-ier** -i.əʳ (US) -i.ɚ **-iest** -i.ɪst, -i.əst **-iness** -ɪ.nəs, -ɪ.nɪs
spring (S) sprɪŋ **-s** -z **-ing** -ɪŋ **sprang** spræŋ **sprung** sprʌŋ **springer/s** ˈsprɪŋ.əʳ/z (US) -ɚ/z **ˌspring ˈbalance, ˈspring ˌbalance** (US) **ˈspring ˌbalance; ˌspring ˈchicken; ˌspring ˈfever; ˌspring ˈgreens; ˌspring ˈonion; ˌspring ˈroll** (US) **ˈspring ˌroll**
springboard ˈsprɪŋ.bɔːd (US) -bɔːrd **-s** -z
springbok (S) ˈsprɪŋ.bɒk (US) -bɑːk **-s** -s
spring-clean ˌsprɪŋˈkliːn **-s** -z **-ing** -ɪŋ **-ed** -d
spring|e sprɪndʒ **-es** -ɪz
Springell ˈsprɪŋ.ᵊl, -gᵊl
springer (S) ˈsprɪŋ.əʳ (US) -ɚ **ˌspringer ˈspaniel**
Springfield ˈsprɪŋ.fiːld
springlike ˈsprɪŋ.laɪk
Springsteen ˈsprɪŋ.stiːn
springtime ˈsprɪŋ.taɪm
spring|y ˈsprɪŋ|.i **-ier** -i.əʳ (US) -i.ɚ **-iest** -i.ɪst, -i.əst **-ily** -ɪ.li, -ᵊl.i **-iness** -ɪ.nəs, -ɪ.nɪs

sprinkl|e ˈsprɪŋ.kl̩ **-es** -z **-ing** -ɪŋ, ˈsprɪŋ.klɪŋ **-ed** -d **-er/s** -əʳ/z, ˈsprɪŋ.kləʳ/z (US) ˈ-kl̩.ɚ/z, ˈ-klɚ/z
sprinkling ˈsprɪŋ.klɪŋ, ˈ-kl̩.ɪŋ **-s** -z
sprint sprɪnt **-s** -s **-ing** -ɪŋ (US) ˈsprɪn.t̬ɪŋ **-ed** -ɪd (US) ˈsprɪn.t̬ɪd **-er/s** -əʳ/z (US) ˈsprɪn.t̬ɚ/z
sprit sprɪt **-s** -s
sprite spraɪt **-s** -s
spritsail ˈsprɪt.sᵊl, -seɪl (US) -seɪl, -sᵊl **-s** -z
spritz sprɪts **-es** -ɪz **-ing** -ɪŋ **-ed** -t
spritzer ˈsprɪt.səʳ (US) -sɚ **-s** -z
sprocket ˈsprɒk.ɪt (US) ˈsprɑː.kɪt **-s** -s
sprog sprɒg (US) sprɑːg, sprɔːg **-s** -z **-ging** -ɪŋ **-ged** -d
Sproule sprəʊl (US) sproʊl, spruːl
sprout spraʊt **-s** -s **-ing** -ɪŋ (US) ˈspraʊ.t̬ɪŋ **-ed** -ɪd (US) ˈspraʊ.t̬ɪd
spruc|e spruːs **-es** -ɪz **-er** -əʳ (US) -ɚ **-est** -ɪst, -əst **-ely** -li **-eness** -nəs, -nɪs **-ing** -ɪŋ **-ed** -t
sprue spruː **-s** -z
sprung *(from* **spring***)* sprʌŋ
spry (S) spraɪ **-er** -əʳ (US) -ɚ **-est** -ɪst, -əst **-ness** -nəs, -nɪs
spud spʌd **-s** -z
spu|e spjuː **-es** -z **-ing** -ɪŋ **-ed** -d
spum|e spjuːm **-es** -z **-ing** -ɪŋ **-ed** -d **-y** -i
spun *(from* **spin***)* spʌn
spunk spʌŋk **-y** -i **-ier** -i.əʳ (US) -i.ɚ **-iest** -i.ɪst, -i.əst **-iness** -ɪ.nəs, -ɪ.nɪs
spur spɜːʳ (US) spɝː **-s** -z **-ring** -ɪŋ **-red** -d **on the ˌspur of the ˈmoment**
spurg|e spɜːdʒ (US) spɝːdʒ **-es** -ɪz
Spurgeon ˈspɜː.dʒᵊn (US) ˈspɝː-
spurious ˈspjʊə.ri.əs, ˈspjɔː- (US) ˈspjʊr.i- **-ly** -li **-ness** -nəs, -nɪs
spurn (S) spɜːn (US) spɝːn **-s** -z **-ing** -ɪŋ **-ed** -d
Spurr spɜːʳ (US) spɝː
Spurrier ˈspʌr.i.əʳ (US) ˈspɝː.i.ɚ
spurt spɜːt (US) spɝːt **-s** -s **-ing** -ɪŋ (US) ˈspɝː.t̬ɪŋ **-ed** -ɪd (US) ˈspɝː.t̬ɪd
sputnik (S) ˈspʌt.nɪk, ˈspʊt-
sputt|er ˈspʌt|.əʳ (US) ˈspʌt̬|.ɚ **-ers** -əz (US) -ɚz **-ering** -ᵊr.ɪŋ **-ered** -əd (US) -ɚd **-erer/s** -ᵊr.əʳ/z (US) -ɚ.ɚ/z
sput|um ˈspjuː|.təm (US) -t̬əm **-a** -ə
sp|y sp|aɪ **-ies** -aɪz **-ying** -aɪ.ɪŋ **-ied** -aɪd
spyglass ˈspaɪ.glɑːs (US) -glæs **-es** -ɪz
spyhole ˈspaɪ.həʊl (US) -hoʊl **-s** -z
spymaster ˈspaɪˌmɑː.stəʳ (US) -ˌmæs.tɚ **-s** -z
sq *(abbrev. for* **square***)* skweəʳ (US) skwer
squab skwɒb (US) skwɑːb **-s** -z ˌ**squab ˈpie**
squabbl|e ˈskwɒb.l̩ (US) ˈskwɑː.bl̩ **-es** -z **-ing** -ɪŋ, ˈskwɒb.lɪŋ (US) ˈskwɑː.blɪŋ **-ed** -d **-er/s** -əʳ/z, ˈskwɒb.ləʳ/z (US) ˈskwɑː.bl̩.ɚ/z, ˈ-blɚ/z
squad skwɒd (US) skwɑːd **-s** -z ˈ**squad ˌcar**
squadd|y, squadd|ie ˈskwɒd|.i (US) ˈskwɑː.d|i **-ies** -iz
squadron ˈskwɒd.rᵊn (US) ˈskwɑː.drən **-s** -z
squalid ˈskwɒl.ɪd (US) ˈskwɑː.lɪd **-est** -ɪst, -əst **-ly** -li **-ness** -nəs, -nɪs
squall skwɔːl (US) skwɔːl, skwɑːl **-s** -z **-ing** -ɪŋ **-ed** -d **-y** -i
squalor ˈskwɒl.əʳ (US) ˈskwɑː.lɚ
squam|a ˈskweɪ.m|ə, ˈskwɑː- **-ae** -iː
squamate ˈskweɪ.meɪt, ˈskwɑː-
squam|ose ˈskweɪ.m|əʊs, ˈskwɑː- (US) -m|oʊs **-ous/ness** -əs/nəs, -nɪs
squand|er ˈskwɒn.d|əʳ (US) ˈskwɑːn.d|ɚ **-ers** -əz (US) -ɚz **-ering** -ᵊr.ɪŋ **-ered** -əd (US) -ɚd **-erer/s** -ᵊr.əʳ/z (US) -ɚ.ɚ/z
squar|e skweəʳ (US) skwer **-es** -z **-er** -əʳ (US) -ɚ **-est** -ɪst, -əst **-ely** -li **-eness** -nəs, -nɪs **-ing** -ɪŋ **-ed** -d ˈ**square ˌdance**; ˌ**square ˈdeal**; ˌ**square ˈfoot**; ˌ**square ˈleg**; ˌ**square ˈmeal**; ˌ**Square ˈMile**; ˌ**square ˈone**; ˌ**square ˈroot**
squarish ˈskweə.rɪʃ (US) ˈskwer.ɪʃ
squash skwɒʃ (US) skwɑːʃ **-es** -ɪz **-ing** -ɪŋ **-ed** -t
squash|y ˈskwɒʃ|.i (US) ˈskwɑː.ʃ|i **-ier** -i.əʳ (US) -i.ɚ **-iest** -i.ɪst, -i.əst **-iness** -ɪ.nəs, -ɪ.nɪs
squat skwɒt (US) skwɑːt **-ly** -li **-ness** -nəs, -nɪs **-s** -s **-ting** -ɪŋ (US) ˈskwɑː.t̬ɪŋ **-ted** -ɪd (US) ˈskwɑː.t̬ɪd **-ter/s** -əʳ/z (US) ˈskwɑː.t̬ɚ/z
squaw skwɔː (US) skwɑː, skwɔː **-s** -z
squawk skwɔːk (US) skwɑːk, skwɔːk **-s** -s **-ing** -ɪŋ **-ed** -t
squeak skwiːk **-s** -s **-ing** -ɪŋ **-ed** -t **-er/s** -əʳ/z (US) -ɚ/z
squeak|y ˈskwiː.k|i **-ier** -i.əʳ (US) -i.ɚ **-iest** -i.ɪst, -i.əst **-ily** -ɪ.li, -ᵊl.i **-iness** -ɪ.nəs, -ɪ.nɪs
squeaky-clean ˌskwiː.kiˈkliːn
squeal skwiːl **-s** -z **-ing** -ɪŋ **-ed** -d **-er/s** -əʳ/z (US) -ɚ/z
squeamish ˈskwiː.mɪʃ **-ly** -li **-ness** -nəs, -nɪs
squeegee ˈskwiː.dʒiː, ˌ-ˈ- (US) ˈskwiː.dʒiː **-s** -z **-ing** -ɪŋ **-d** -d
Squeers skwɪəz (US) skwɪrz
squeez|e skwiːz **-es** -ɪz **-ing** -ɪŋ **-ed** -d **-er/s** -əʳ/z (US) -ɚ/z **-able** -ə.bl̩ **-y** -i
squeeze-box ˈskwiːz.bɒks (US) -bɑːks **-es** -ɪz
squelch skweltʃ **-es** -ɪz **-ing** -ɪŋ **-ed** -t **-y** -i
squib skwɪb **-s** -z
squid skwɪd **-s** -z
squidg|y ˈskwɪdʒ|.i **-ier** -i.əʳ (US) -i.ɚ **-iest** -i.ɪst, -i.əst **-iness** -ɪ.nəs, -ɪ.nɪs
squiff|y ˈskwɪf|.i **-ed** -t **-ier** -i.əʳ (US) -i.ɚ **-iest** -i.ɪst, -i.əst **-iness** -ɪ.nəs, -ɪ.nɪs
squiggl|e ˈskwɪg|.l̩ **-es** -z **-ing** -ɪŋ, ˈskwɪg.lɪŋ **-ed** -d **-y** -i
squilgee ˈskwɪl.dʒiː, ˌ-ˈ- (US) ˈskwɪl.dʒiː **-s** -z **-ing** -ɪŋ **-d** -d
squill skwɪl **-s** -z
squinch skwɪntʃ **-es** -ɪz **-ing** -ɪŋ **-ed** -t
squint skwɪnt **-s** -s **-ing** -ɪŋ (US) ˈskwɪn.t̬ɪŋ **-ed** -ɪd (US) ˈskwɪn.t̬ɪd **-y** -i
squirarch|y ˈskwaɪə.rɑː.k|i (US) ˈskwaɪɚ.ɑːr- **-ies** -iz
squir|e (S) skwaɪəʳ (US) skwaɪɚ **-es** -z **-ing** -ɪŋ **-ed** -d
squirearch|y ˈskwaɪə.rɑː.k|i (US) ˈskwaɪɚ.ɑːr- **-ies** -iz
Squires skwaɪəz (US) skwaɪɚz
squirm skwɜːm (US) skwɝːm **-s** -z **-ing** -ɪŋ **-ed** -d **-y** -i
squirrel ˈskwɪr.ᵊl (US) ˈskwɝː- **-s** -z **-(l)ing** -ɪŋ **-(l)ed** -d
squirt skwɜːt (US) skwɝːt **-s** -s **-ing** -ɪŋ (US) ˈskwɝː.t̬ɪŋ **-ed** -ɪd (US) ˈskwɝː.t̬ɪd **-er/s** -əʳ/z (US) -ɚ/z
squish skwɪʃ **-es** -ɪz **-ing** -ɪŋ **-ed** -t **-y** -i
sr (S) *(abbrev. for* **senior***)* ˈsiː.ni.əʳ, -njəʳ (US) -njɚ
Srebrenica ˌsreb.rəˈniːt.sə, ˌʃreb-, -tʃə
Sri Lank|a ˌsriːˈlæŋ.kə, ˌsrɪ-, ˌʃriː- (US) -ˈlɑːŋ- **-an/s** -ən/z
Srinagar srɪˈnʌg.əʳ, sriː-, ʃrɪ-, ʃriː-, -ˈnɑː.gəʳ (US) ˌsriːˈnʌg.ɚ
SS *Nazi unit:* ˌesˈes *stress shift:* ˌ**SS ˈofficer**
SS *(abbrev. for* **steamship***)* ˌesˈes *stress shift:* ˌ**SS ˌGreat ˈBritian**
SSE *(abbrev. for* **south-southeast***)* ˌes.esˈiː, ˌsaʊθ.saʊθˈiːst *in nautical usage also:* ˌsaʊ.saʊ-
ssh, sh, shh ʃ
Note: Used to command silence
SSW *(abbrev. for* **south-southwest***)* ˌes.esˈdʌb.l̩.juː, -ju, ˌsaʊθ.saʊθˈwest (US) ˌesˌesˈdʌb.l̩.juː, -jə, ˌsaʊθ.saʊθˈwest *in nautical usage also:* ˌsaʊ.saʊ-
St. *(abbrev. for* **Street***)* striːt
St. *(abbrev. for* **Saint***)* sᵊnt, sɪnt, seɪnt (US) seɪnt
Note: See panel information at **Saint**.
st *(abbrev. for* **stone***)* stəʊn (US) stoʊn
stab stæb **-s** -z **-bing/s** -ɪŋ/z **-bed** -d
Stabat Mater ˌstɑː.bætˈmɑː.təʳ, -bətˈ- (US) -bɑːtˈmɑː.tɚ **-s** -z
St. Abb's sᵊntˈæbz, sɪnt- (US) seɪnt-
stability stəˈbɪl.ə.ti, -ɪ.ti (US) -ə.t̬i
stabilization, -isa- ˌsteɪ.bᵊl.aɪˈzeɪ.ʃᵊn, -bɪ.laɪ-, -lɪˈ- (US) -bᵊl.ɪˈ-
stabiliz|e, -is|e ˈsteɪ.bᵊl.aɪz, -bɪ.laɪz (US) -bə.laɪz **-es** -ɪz **-ing** -ɪŋ **-ed** -d **-er/s** -əʳ/z (US) -ɚ/z

stabl|e ˈsteɪ.bl̩ **-es** -z **-y** -i, ˈsteɪ.bli **-eness** -nəs, -nɪs **-ing** -ɪŋ, ˈsteɪ.blɪŋ **-ed** -d ˌ**stable** ˈ**door**; ˈ**stable** ˌ**lad**
stablemate ˈsteɪ.bl̩.meɪt **-s** -s
stabling ˈsteɪ.bl̩.ɪŋ, ˈ-blɪŋ
stablish ˈstæb.lɪʃ **-es** -ɪz **-ing** -ɪŋ **-ed** -t
staccato stəˈkɑː.təʊ (US) -t̬oʊ **-s** -z
Stacey, Stacie ˈsteɪ.si
stack stæk **-s** -s **-ing** -ɪŋ **-ed** -t
Stacpoole ˈstæk.puːl
Stacy ˈsteɪ.si
stadi|um ˈsteɪ.di|.əm **-ums** -əmz **-a** -ə
staff stɑːf (US) stæf **-s** -s **-ing** -ɪŋ **-ed** -t ˈ**staff** ˌ**nurse**; ˈ**staff** ˌ**sergeant**
Staffa ˈstæf.ə
staffer ˈstɑː.fə^{r} (US) ˈstæf.ɚ **-s** -z
Stafford ˈstæf.əd (US) -ɚd **-shire** -ʃə^{r}, -ˌʃɪə^{r} (US) -ʃɚ, -ˌʃɪr
staffroom ˈstɑːf.rʊm, -ruːm (US) ˈstæf.ruːm, -rʊm **-s** -z
Staffs. *(abbrev. for* **Staffordshire***)* stæfs
stag stæg **-s** -z ˈ**stag** ˌ**night**
stag|e steɪdʒ **-es** -ɪz **-ing** -ɪŋ **-ed** -d ˌ**stage** ˈ**door**; ˈ**stage** ˌ**fright**
stagecoach ˈsteɪdʒ.kəʊtʃ (US) -koʊtʃ **-es** -ɪz
stagecraft ˈsteɪdʒ.krɑːft (US) -kræft
stagehand ˈsteɪdʒ.hænd **-s** -z
stage-manag|e ˌsteɪdʒˈmæn.ɪdʒ, ˈ-ˌ-- (US) ˈsteɪdʒˌmæn- **-es** -ɪz **-ing** -ɪŋ **-ed** -d **-ment** -mənt
stage-manager ˌsteɪdʒˈmæn.ə.dʒə^{r}, ˈ-ɪ- (US) ˈsteɪdʒˌmæn.ə.dʒɚ
stager ˈsteɪ.dʒə^{r} (US) -dʒɚ **-s** -z
stage-struck ˈsteɪdʒ.strʌk
stag|ey ˈsteɪ.dʒ|i **-ier** -i.ə^{r} (US) -i.ɚ **-iest** -i.ɪst, -i.əst **-iness** -ɪ.nəs, -ɪ.nɪs
stagflation stægˈfleɪ.ʃ^{ə}n
stagg|er ˈstæg|.ə^{r} (US) -ɚ **-ers** -əz (US) -ɚz **-ering/ly** -^{ə}r.ɪŋ **-ered** -əd (US) -ɚd **-erer/s** -^{ə}r.ə^{r}/z (US) -ɚ.ɚ/z
staghound ˈstæg.haʊnd **-s** -z
staging ˈsteɪ.dʒɪŋ **-s** -z
Stagirite ˈstædʒ.ɪ.raɪt (US) ˈ-ə- **-s** -s
stagnancy ˈstæg.nənt.si
stagnant ˈstæg.nənt **-ly** -li
stagna|te stægˈneɪ|t, ˈ-- (US) ˈstæg.neɪ|t **-tes** -ts **-ting** -tɪŋ (US) -t̬ɪŋ **-ted** -tɪd (US) -t̬ɪd
stagnation stægˈneɪ.ʃ^{ə}n
St. Agnes s^{ə}ntˈæg.nɪs, sɪnt-, seɪnt- (US) seɪnt-
stag|y ˈsteɪ.dʒ|i **-ier** -i.ə^{r} (US) -i.ɚ **-iest** -i.ɪst, -i.əst **-ily** -ɪ.li, -^{ə}l.i **-iness** -ɪ.nəs, -ɪ.nɪs
staid steɪd **-ly** -li **-ness** -nəs, -nɪs
stain steɪn **-s** -z **-ing** -ɪŋ **-ed** -d **-er/s** -ə^{r}/z (US) -ɚ/z ˌ**stained** ˈ**glass**
Stainer *English name:* ˈsteɪ.nə^{r} (US) -nɚ *German name:* ˈstaɪ.nə^{r} *as if German:* ˈʃtaɪ- (US) -nɚ
Staines steɪnz
Stainforth ˈsteɪn.fəθ (US) -fɚθ
stainless ˈsteɪn.ləs, -lɪs **-ly** -li **-ness** -nəs, -nɪs ˌ**stainless** ˈ**steel**
stair steə^{r} (US) ster **-s** -z
staircas|e ˈsteə.keɪs (US) ˈster- **-es** -ɪz
stair-rod ˈsteə.rɒd (US) ˈster.rɑːd **-s** -z
stairway ˈsteə.weɪ (US) ˈster- **-s** -z
stairwell ˈsteə.wel (US) ˈster- **-s** -z
Staithes steɪðz
stak|e steɪk **-es** -s **-ing** -ɪŋ **-ed** -t
stakeholder ˈsteɪkˌhəʊl.də^{r} (US) -ˌhoʊl.dɚ **-s** -z
stakeout ˈsteɪk.aʊt **-s** -s
Stakhanov|ite stækˈæn.ə.v|aɪt (US) stəˈkɑː.nə- **-ites** -aɪts **-ism** -ɪ.z^{ə}m
Stakis ˈstæk.ɪs
stalactite ˈstæl.ək.taɪt (US) stəˈlæk-; ˈstæl.ək- **-s** -s
stalag ˈstæl.æg (US) ˈstɑː.lɑːg, ˈstæl.æg **-s** -z
stalagmite ˈstæl.əg.maɪt (US) stəˈlæg-; ˈstæl.əg- **-s** -s
St. Albans s^{ə}ntˈɔːl.bənz, sɪnt-, -ˈɒl- (US) seɪntˈɔːl-, -ˈɑːl-
Stalbridge ˈstɔːl.brɪdʒ (US) ˈstɔːl-
St. Aldate's s^{ə}ntˈɔːl.deɪts, sɪnt-, -ˈɒl-, -dɪts *old-fashioned:* -ˈəʊldz (US) seɪntˈɔːl.deɪts, -ˈɑːl-
stal|e steɪl **-er** -ə^{r} (US) -ɚ **-est** -ɪst, -əst **-ely** -li **-eness** -nəs, -nɪs
stale|mate ˈsteɪl|.meɪt **-mates** -meɪts **-mating** -meɪ.tɪŋ (US) -meɪ.t̬ɪŋ **-mated** -meɪ.tɪd (US) -meɪ.t̬ɪd
Stalin ˈstɑː.lɪn, ˈstæl.ɪn **-ism** -ɪ.z^{ə}m
Stalingrad ˈstɑː.lɪn.græd, ˈstæl.ɪn-, -grɑːd (US) ˈstɑː.lɪn.græd, ˈstæl.ɪn-
stalin|ism (S) ˈstɑː.lɪ.n|ɪ.z^{ə}m, ˈstæl.ɪ- (US) ˈstɑː.lɪ- **-ist/s** -ɪsts
stalk stɔːk (US) stɔːk, stɑːk **-s** -s **-ing** -ɪŋ **-ed** -t **-er/s** -ə^{r}/z (US) -ɚ/z
stalking-hors|e ˈstɔː.kɪŋ.hɔːs (US) -hɔːrs, ˈstɑː- **-es** -ɪz
Stalky ˈstɔː.ki (US) ˈstɔː-, ˈstɑː-
stall stɔːl (US) stɔːl, stɑːl **-s** -z **-ing** -ɪŋ **-ed** -d
stallage ˈstɔː.lɪdʒ
stallholder ˈstɔːlˌhəʊl.də^{r} (US) ˈstɔːlˌhoʊl.dɚ, ˈstɑːl- **-s** -z
stallion ˈstæl.jən, -i.ən (US) ˈ-jən **-s** -z
Stallone stəˈləʊn, stælˈəʊn (US) stəˈloʊn
stalwart ˈstɔːl.wət, ˈstɒl- (US) ˈstɔːl.wɚt, ˈstɑːl- **-s** -s **-ly** -li **-ness** -nəs, -nɪs
Stalybridge ˈsteɪ.lɪ.brɪdʒ
Stamboul stæmˈbuːl (US) stɑːm-
St. Ambrose s^{ə}ntˈæm.brəʊz, sɪnt-, -brəʊs (US) seɪntˈæm.broʊz, -broʊs
stamen ˈsteɪ.men, -mən **-s** -z
Stamford ˈstæmp.fəd (US) -fɚd
stamina ˈstæm.ɪ.nə, ˈ-ə- (US) ˈ-ə-
stamm|er ˈstæm|.ə^{r} (US) -ɚ **-ers** -əz (US) -ɚz **-ering** -^{ə}r.ɪŋ **-ered** -əd (US) -ɚd **-erer/s** -^{ə}r.ə^{r}/z (US) -ɚ.ɚ/z
stamp (S) stæmp **-s** -s **-ing** -ɪŋ **-ed** -t **-er/s** -ə^{r}/z (US) -ɚ/z ˈ**stamp** ˌ**album**; ˈ**stamp col**ˌ**lector**; ˈ**stamp** ˌ**duty**; ˈ**stamping** ˌ**ground**
stamped|e stæmˈpiːd **-es** -z **-ing** -ɪŋ **-ed** -ɪd
Stanbury ˈstæn.b^{ə}r.i, ˈstæm-, ˈ-bri (US) ˈstæn.ber.i, -bɚ-
stanc|e stænts, stɑːnts (US) stænts **-es** -ɪz
stanch stɑːntʃ (US) stɑːntʃ, stɔːntʃ, stæntʃ **-es** -ɪz **-ing** -ɪŋ **-ed** -t
stanchion ˈstɑːn.tʃ^{ə}n, ˈstæn- (US) ˈstæn- **-s** -z **-ing** -ɪŋ **-ed** -d
stand stænd **-s** -z **-ing** -ɪŋ **stood** stʊd
stand-alone ˈstænd.əˌləʊn, -^{ə}lˌəʊn (US) -əˌloʊn
standard ˈstæn.dəd (US) -dɚd **-s** -z ˌ**standard devi**ˈ**ation**; ˈ**standard** ˌ**lamp**; ˌ**standard of** ˈ**living**; ˈ**standard** ˌ**time**
standard-bearer ˈstæn.dədˌbeə.rə^{r} (US) -dɚdˌber.ɚ **-s** -z
standardization, -isa- ˌstæn.də.daɪˈzeɪ.ʃ^{ə}n, -dɪˈ- (US) -dɚ.dɪˈ-
standardiz|e, -is|e ˈstæn.də.daɪz (US) -dɚ- **-es** -ɪz **-ing** -ɪŋ **-ed** -d
standby ˈstænd.baɪ, ˈstæm- (US) ˈstænd- **-s** -z
stand-in ˈstænd.ɪn **-s** -z
standing ˈstæn.dɪŋ **-s** -z ˌ**standing** ˈ**joke**; ˌ**standing** ˈ**order**; ˈ**standing** ˌ**room**
standish (S) ˈstæn.dɪʃ **-es** -ɪz
standoff ˈstænd.ɒf (US) -ɑːf **-s** -s
standoffish ˌstændˈɒf.ɪʃ (US) -ˈɑː.fɪʃ **-ly** -li **-ness** -nəs, -nɪs
standout ˈstænd.aʊt **-s** -s
standpipe ˈstænd.paɪp, ˈstæm- (US) ˈstænd- **-s** -s
standpoint ˈstænd.pɔɪnt, ˈstæm- (US) ˈstænd- **-s** -s
St. Andrew s^{ə}ntˈæn.druː, sɪnt- (US) seɪnt- **-(')s** -z **St.** ˌ**Andrew's** ˈ**cross**
standstill ˈstænd.stɪl **-s** -z
stand-up ˈstænd.ʌp
Staneydale ˈsteɪ.ni.deɪl
Stanfield ˈstæn.fiːld
Stanford ˈstæn.fəd (US) -fɚd
Stanford-Binet ˌstæn.fədˈbiː.neɪ, ˌstæm-; -bɪˈneɪ (US) ˌstæn.fɚd.bɪˈneɪ
Stanford le Hope ˌstæn.fəd.lɪˈhəʊp (US) -fɚd.lɪˈhoʊp
stanhope (S) ˈstæn.əp, -həʊp (US) -hoʊp, -əp **-s** -s
staniel ˈstæn.jəl, -i.əl (US) ˈ-jəl **-s** -z
Stanis|las ˈstæn.ɪ.s|læs, ˈ-ə-, -s|ləs, -s|lɑːs (US) -s|lɑːs **-laus** -s|lɔːs

Stanislavski ˌstæn.ɪˈslæv.ski, -ˈslæf- (US) -əˈslɑːv-, -ˈslɑːf- **Staniˈslavski ˌmethod**
stank *(from* **stink***)* stæŋk
Stanley ˈstæn.li **ˈStanley ˌknife**
Stanmore ˈstæn.mɔː^{r}, ˈstæm- (US) ˈstæn.mɔːr
Stannard ˈstæn.əd (US) -ɚd
stannar|y ˈstæn.^{ə}r|.i **-ies** -iz
St. Anne s^{ə}ntˈæn, sɪnt- (US) seɪnt- **-'s** -z
stann|ic ˈstæn|.ɪk **-ous** -əs
Stansfield ˈstænz.fiːld, ˈstænts-
Stansted ˈstænt.sted, -stɪd, -stəd **ˌStansted ˈAirport**
Stansted Mountfitchet ˌstænt.sted.maʊntˈfɪtʃ.ɪt, -stɪd-, -stəd
St. Anthony s^{ə}ntˈæn.tə.ni, sɪnt- (US) seɪntˈæn.t^{ə}n.i, -θə.ni
Stanton ˈstæn.tən, ˈstɑːn- (US) ˈstæn.t^{ə}n
stanza ˈstæn.zə **-s** -z
stapes ˈsteɪ.piːz
staphylo|coccus ˌstæf.ɪ.ləʊ|ˈkɒk.əs, -^{ə}l.əʊ- (US) -ə.loʊ|ˈkɑː.kəs **-cocci** -ˈkɒk.saɪ, -aɪ, -iː (US) -ˈkɑːk.saɪ, -aɪ **-coccal** -ˈkɒk.^{ə}l (US) -ˈkɑː.k^{ə}l **-coccic** -ˈkɒk.ɪk (US) -ˈkɑː.kɪk
stapl|e (S) ˈsteɪ.pl̩ **-es** -z **-ing** -ɪŋ, ˈsteɪ.plɪŋ **-ed** -d
Stapleford ˈsteɪ.pl̩.fəd (US) -fɚd
stapler ˈsteɪ.plə^{r} (US) -plɚ **-s** -z
Stapleton ˈsteɪ.pl̩.tən (US) -t̬ən
Stapley ˈstæp.li, ˈsteɪ.pli
star stɑː^{r} (US) stɑːr **-s** -z **-ring** -ɪŋ **-red** -d **ˌStars and ˈBars**; **ˌstar ˈchamber**; **ˌStar of ˈDavid**; **ˈstar ˌsign**; **ˌStars and ˈStripes**; **ˈstar ˌwars**
starboard ˈstɑː.bəd, -bɔːd (US) ˈstɑːr.bɚd, -bɔːrd
Note: The nautical pronunciation is /ˈstɑː.bəd (US) -bɚd/.
Starbuck ˈstɑː.bʌk (US) ˈstɑːr- **-s** -s
starch stɑːtʃ (US) stɑːrtʃ **-es** -ɪz **-ing** -ɪŋ **-ed** -t **-y** -i **-ier** -i.ə^{r} (US) -i.ɚ **-iest** -i.ɪst, -i.əst **-iness** -ɪ.nəs, -ɪ.nɪs **-ily** -ɪ.li
starch-reduced ˌstɑːtʃ.rɪˈdjuːst, -rəˈ-, -ˈdʒuːst, ˈ--ˌ- (US) ˈstɑːrtʃ.rɪˌduːst, -ˌdjuːst
star-crossed ˈstɑː.krɒst (US) ˈstɑːr.krɑːst **ˌstar-crossed ˈlovers**
stardom ˈstɑː.dəm (US) ˈstɑːr-
stardust ˈstɑː.dʌst (US) ˈstɑːr-
star|e steə^{r} (US) ster **-es** -z **-ing/ly** -ɪŋ/li **-ed** -d **-er/s** -ə^{r}/z (US) -ɚ/z
starfish ˈstɑː.fɪʃ (US) ˈstɑːr- **-es** -ɪz
stargaz|e ˈstɑː.geɪz (US) ˈstɑːr- **-es** -ɪz **-ing** -ɪŋ **-er/s** -ə^{r}/z (US) -ɚ/z
stark (S) stɑːk (US) stɑːrk **-ly** -li **-ness** -nəs, -nɪs **ˌstark ˈnaked**; **ˌstark ˌraving ˈmad**
starkers ˈstɑː.kəz (US) ˈstɑːr.kɚz
Starks stɑːks (US) stɑːrks
star|less ˈstɑː|.ləs, -lɪs (US) ˈstɑːr-
starlet ˈstɑː.lət, -lɪt (US) ˈstɑːr- **-s** -s
starlight ˈstɑː.laɪt (US) ˈstɑːr-
starling (S) ˈstɑː.lɪŋ (US) ˈstɑːr- **-s** -z
starlit ˈstɑː.lɪt (US) ˈstɑːr-
Starr stɑː^{r} (US) stɑːr
starr|y ˈstɑː.r|i (US) ˈstɑːr|.i **-iness** -ɪ.nəs, -ɪ.nɪs
starry-eyed ˌstɑː.riˈaɪd (US) ˈstɑː.riˌaɪd *stress shift, British only:* ˌstarry-eyed ˈfan
star-spangled ˈstɑːˌspæŋ.gl̩d (US) ˈstɑːr- **ˌstar-ˌspangled ˈbanner**
starstruck ˈstɑː.strʌk (US) ˈstɑːr-
star-studded ˈstɑːˌstʌd.ɪd (US) ˈstɑːr-
start (S) stɑːt (US) stɑːrt **-s** -s **-ing** -ɪŋ (US) ˈstɑːr.t̬ɪŋ **-ed** -ɪd (US) ˈstɑːr.t̬ɪd **-er/s** -ə^{r}/z (US) ˈstɑːr.t̬ɚ/z **ˈstarting ˌblock**; **ˈstarting ˌpoint**
startl|e ˈstɑː.tl̩ (US) ˈstɑːr.t̬l̩ **-es** -z **-ing/ly** -ɪŋ, ˈstɑːt.lɪŋ (US) ˈstɑːrt- **-ed** -d **-er/s** -ə^{r}/z, ˈstɑːt.lə^{r}/z (US) ˈstɑːr.t̬l̩.ɚ/z, ˈstɑːrt.lɚ/z
Start-rite® ˈstɑːt.raɪt (US) ˈstɑːrt-
start-up ˈstɑːt.ʌp (US) ˈstɑːrt- **-s** -s
starvation stɑːˈveɪ.ʃ^{ə}n (US) stɑːr- **starˌvation ˈwages**
starv|e stɑːv (US) stɑːrv **-es** -z **-ing** -ɪŋ **-ed** -d
starveling ˈstɑːv.lɪŋ (US) ˈstɑːrv- **-s** -z
St. Asaph s^{ə}ntˈæs.əf, sɪnt- (US) seɪnt-
stash stæʃ **-es** -ɪz **-ing** -ɪŋ **-ed** -t
Stasi ˈstɑː.zi *as if German:* ˈʃtɑː-
stas|is ˈsteɪ.s|ɪs (US) ˈsteɪ-, ˈstæs|.ɪs **-es** -iːz
stat|e steɪt **-es** -s **-ing** -ɪŋ (US) ˈsteɪ.t̬ɪŋ **-ed/ly** -ɪd (US) ˈsteɪ.t̬ɪd **ˈState ˌDepartment**; **ˌstate of eˈmergency**; **ˈstate ˌschool**; **ˌstate ˈtrooper**
statecraft ˈsteɪt.krɑːft (US) -kræft
statehood ˈsteɪt.hʊd
stateless ˈsteɪt.ləs, -lɪs **-ness** -nəs, -nɪs
statel|y ˈsteɪt.l|i **-ier** -i.ə^{r} (US) -i.ɚ **-iest** -i.ɪst, -i.əst **-iness** -ɪ.nəs, -ɪ.nɪs **ˌstately ˈhome**
statement ˈsteɪt.mənt **-s** -s
Staten Island ˌstæt.^{ə}nˈaɪ.lənd
state-of-the-art ˌsteɪt.əv.ðiˈɑːt (US) -ˈɑːrt *stress shift:* ˌstate-of-the-art ˈgadget
state-owned ˌsteɪtˈəʊnd (US) -ˈoʊnd *stress shift:* ˌstate-owned ˈbusiness
stateroom ˈsteɪt.rʊm, -ruːm (US) -ruːm, -rʊm **-s** -z
States steɪts
stateside ˈsteɪt.saɪd
states|man ˈsteɪts|.mən **-men** -mən
statesman|like ˈsteɪts.mən|.laɪk **-ly** -li **-ship** -ʃɪp
states|woman ˈsteɪts|ˌwʊm.ən **-women** -ˌwɪm.ɪn
statewide ˈsteɪt.waɪd
Statham ˈsteɪ.θəm, -ðəm (US) -ðəm, -θəm, -t̬əm; ˈstæt̬.əm
St. Athan s^{ə}ntˈæθ.^{ə}n, sɪnt- (US) seɪnt-
static ˈstæt.ɪk (US) ˈstæt̬- **-s** -s **-al** -^{ə}l **-ally** -^{ə}l.i, -li
static|e ˈstæt.ɪs, -ɪ.s|i (US) ˈstæt̬.ə.s|i, ˈ-ɪs **-es** -ɪz, -iz
station ˈsteɪ.ʃ^{ə}n **-s** -z **-ing** -ɪŋ, ˈsteɪʃ.nɪŋ **-ed** -d **ˈstation ˌwagon**; **ˌstations of the ˈcross**
stationar|y ˈsteɪ.ʃ^{ə}n.^{ə}r|.i, ˈsteɪʃ.n^{ə}r- (US) ˈsteɪ.ʃə.ner- **-ily** -^{ə}l.i, -ɪ.li **-iness** -ɪ.nəs, -ɪ.nɪs
stationer ˈsteɪ.ʃ^{ə}n.ə^{r}, ˈsteɪʃ.nə^{r} (US) -ʃ^{ə}n.ɚ, ˈsteɪʃ.nɚ **-s** -z
stationery ˈsteɪ.ʃ^{ə}n.^{ə}r.i, ˈsteɪʃ.n^{ə}r- (US) ˈsteɪ.ʃə.ner-
stationmaster ˈsteɪ.ʃ^{ə}nˌmɑː.stə^{r} (US) -ˌmæs.tɚ **-s** -z
stat|ism ˈsteɪ.t|ɪ.z^{ə}m (US) -t̬|ɪ- **-ist/s** -ɪst/s
statistic stəˈtɪs.tɪk, stætˈɪs- (US) stəˈtɪs- **-s** -s **-al** -^{ə}l **-ally** -^{ə}l.i, -li
statistician ˌstæt.ɪˈstɪʃ.^{ə}n, -əˈ- (US) -ɪˈ- **-s** -z
Statius ˈsteɪ.ʃəs
stative ˈsteɪ.tɪv (US) -t̬ɪv
stator ˈsteɪ.tə^{r} (US) -t̬ɚ **-s** -z
statuary ˈstætʃ.u.^{ə}r.i, ˈstæt.ju- (US) ˈstætʃ.u.er-
statue ˈstætʃ.uː, ˈstæt.juː (US) ˈstætʃ.uː **-s** -z
statuesque ˌstæt.juˈesk, ˌstætʃ.uˈ- (US) ˌstætʃ.uˈ-
statuette ˌstæt.juˈet, ˌstætʃ.uˈ- (US) ˌstætʃ.uˈ- **-s** -s
stature ˈstætʃ.ə^{r}, ˈstæt.jə^{r} (US) ˈstætʃ.ɚ **-s** -z
status ˈsteɪ.təs (US) stæ.t̬əs **-es** -ɪz **ˈstatus ˌsymbol**
status quo ˌsteɪ.təsˈkwəʊ, ˌstæt.əsˈ- (US) ˌstæt̬.əsˈkwoʊ, ˌsteɪ.t̬əsˈ-
statute ˈstæt.juːt, ˈstætʃ.uːt (US) ˈstætʃ.uːt **-s** -s **ˈstatute ˌbook**
statutory ˈstæt.jə.t^{ə}r.i, -jʊ-, ˈstætʃ.ə-, ˈ-ʊ- (US) ˈstætʃ.ə.tɔːr-, ˈ-ʊ- **ˌstatutory ˈrape**
St. Augustine s^{ə}nt.ɔːˈgʌs.tɪn, sɪnt-, ˌsent-, ˌseɪnt-, -əˈ-; (US) seɪntˈɔː.gə.stiːn, -ˈɑː-
staunch stɔːntʃ (US) stɔːntʃ, stɑːntʃ **-er** -ə^{r} (US) -ɚ **-est** -ɪst, -əst **-ly** -li **-ness** -nəs, -nɪs **-es** -ɪz **-ing** -ɪŋ **-ed** -t
Staunton *English surname:* ˈstɔːn.tən (US) ˈstɑːn.t^{ə}n, ˈstɔːn- *towns in US:* ˈstæn.tən (US) -t^{ə}n
St. Austell s^{ə}ntˈɔː.st^{ə}l, sɪnt- *locally:* -ˈɔː.s^{ə}l (US) seɪntˈɑː.st^{ə}l, -ˈɔː-
Stavanger stəˈvæŋ.ə^{r}, stævˈæŋ- (US) stəˈvɑːŋ.ɚ, stɑː-
stav|e steɪv **-es** -z **-ing** -ɪŋ **-ed** -d **stove** stəʊv (US) stoʊv

Staveley ˈsteɪv.li
stay steɪ **-s** -z **-ing** -ɪŋ **-ed** -d **-er/s** -əʳ/z ⓤⓢ -ɚ/z
stay-at-home ˈsteɪ.ət.həʊm ⓤⓢ -hoʊm
staysail ˈsteɪ.seɪl *nautical pronunciation:* -sᵊl **-s** -z
St. Bartholomew sᵊn*t*.bɑːˈθɒl.ə.mjuː, sɪn*t*-, -bəˈ- ⓤⓢ ˌseɪnt.bɑːrˈθɑː.lə- **-ˈs** -z
St. Bees sᵊn*t*ˈbiːz, sɪn*t*- ⓤⓢ seɪnt-
St. Bernard sᵊn*t*ˈbɜː.nəd, sɪn*t*- ⓤⓢ ˌseɪnt.bɚˈnɑːrd **-s** -z
St. Blaize sᵊn*t*ˈbleɪz, sɪn*t*- ⓤⓢ seɪnt-
St. Blazey sᵊn*t*ˈbleɪ.zi, sɪn*t*- ⓤⓢ seɪnt-
St. Bride's sᵊn*t*ˈbraɪdz, sɪn*t*- ⓤⓢ seɪnt-
St. Bruno sᵊn*t*ˈbruː.nəʊ, sɪn*t*- ⓤⓢ seɪntˈbruː.noʊ
St. Catherine, St. Catharine sᵊn*t*ˈkæθ.ᵊr.ɪn, sɪn*t*-, sᵊŋˈ-, ˈ-rɪn ⓤⓢ seɪnt- **-ˈs** -z
St. Cecilia sᵊnt.sɪˈsɪl.i.ə, sɪnt-, -ˈsiː.li.ə, ˈ-ljə ⓤⓢ ˌseɪnt.sɪˈsiːl.jə
St. Christopher sᵊn*t*ˈkrɪs.tə.fəʳ, sɪn*t*-, sᵊŋ- ⓤⓢ seɪntˈkrɪs.tə.fɚ **-s** -z
St. Clair *surname:* ˈsɪŋ.kleəʳ, ˈsɪn- ⓤⓢ seɪntˈkler *place in US:* sᵊn*t*ˈkleəʳ, sɪn*t*-, sᵊŋ- ⓤⓢ seɪntˈkler
St. Columb sᵊn*t*ˈkɒl.əm, sɪn*t*- ⓤⓢ seɪntˈkɑː.ləm
STD ˌes.tiːˈdiː **STˈD ˌcode**
St. David sᵊn*t*ˈdeɪ.vɪd, sɪn*t*- ⓤⓢ seɪnt- **-ˈs** -z
stead (S) sted
steadfast ˈsted.fɑːst, -fəst ⓤⓢ -fæst, -fəst **-ly** -li **-ness** -nəs, -nɪs
steading ˈsted.ɪŋ **-s** -z
Steadman ˈsted.mən
stead|y ˈsted|.i **-ier** -i.əʳ ⓤⓢ -i.ɚ **-iest** -i.ɪst, -i.əst **-ily** -ɪ.li, -ᵊl.i **-iness** -ɪ.nəs, -ɪ.nɪs **-ies** -iz **-ying** -i.ɪŋ **-ied** -id **ˌsteady ˈstate; ˌsteady ˈstate ˌtheory**
steak steɪk **-s** -s **ˌsteak tarˈtare; ˌsteak and ˌkidney ˈpie**
steakhou|se ˈsteɪk.haʊ|s **-ses** -zɪz
steal stiːl **-s** -z **-ing** -ɪŋ **stole** stəʊl ⓤⓢ stoʊl **stolen** ˈstəʊ.lᵊn ⓤⓢ ˈstoʊ- **stealer/s** ˈstiː.ləʳ/z ⓤⓢ -lɚ/z
stealth stelθ
stealth|y ˈstel.θ|i **-ier** -i.əʳ ⓤⓢ -i.ɚ **-iest** -i.ɪst, -i.əst **-ily** -ɪ.li, -ᵊl.i **-iness** -ɪ.nəs, -ɪ.nɪs
steam stiːm **-s** -z **-ing** -ɪŋ **-ed** -d **-er/s** -əʳ/z ⓤⓢ -ɚ/z **ˈsteam ˌengine; ˈsteam ˌiron; ˈsteam ˌpower**
steamboat ˈstiːm.bəʊt ⓤⓢ -boʊt **-s** -s
steam-hammer ˈstiːmˌhæm.əʳ ⓤⓢ -ɚ **-s** -z
steamroll ˈstiːm.rəʊl ⓤⓢ -roʊl **-s** -z **-ing** -ɪŋ **-ed** -d
steamroll|er ˈstiːmˌrəʊ.l|əʳ ⓤⓢ -ˌroʊ.l|ɚ **-ers** -əz ⓤⓢ -ɚz **-ering** -ᵊr.ɪŋ **-ered** -əd ⓤⓢ -ɚd
steamship ˈstiːm.ʃɪp **-s** -s
steam|y ˈstiː.m|i **-ier** -i.əʳ ⓤⓢ -i.ɚ **-iest** -i.ɪst, -i.əst **-iness** -ɪ.nəs, -ɪ.nɪs
stearic stiˈær.ɪk ⓤⓢ stiˈær-; ˈstɪr-
stearin ˈstɪə.rɪn ⓤⓢ ˈstiː.ɚ.ɪn; ˈstɪr-
Stearn(e) stɜːn ⓤⓢ stɝːn **-s** -z
steatite ˈstɪə.taɪt ⓤⓢ ˈstiː.ə-
steatolysis stɪəˈtɒl.ə.sɪs, ˈ-ɪ- ⓤⓢ ˌstiː.əˈtɑː.lə-
steatopygia ˌstɪə.təʊˈpɪdʒ.i.ə, -ˈpaɪ.dʒi-, ˈ-dʒə ⓤⓢ ˌstiː.æt.əˈpaɪ.dʒi.ə, -ˈpɪdʒ.i-
steatopygous ˌstɪə.təʊˈpaɪ.gəs; stɪəˈtɒp.ɪ- ⓤⓢ ˌstiː.æt.əˈpaɪ-
Stedman ˈsted.mən
St. Edmunds sᵊntˈed.mən*d*z, sɪnt- ⓤⓢ seɪnt-
steed stiːd **-s** -z
steel (S) stiːl **-s** -z **-ing** -ɪŋ **-ed** -d **ˌsteel ˈwool**
Steele stiːl
steel-plated ˌstiːlˈpleɪ.tɪd ⓤⓢ ˈ-ˌ-- *stress shift, British only:* ˌsteel-plated ˈhull
steelworker ˈstiːlˌwɜː.kəʳ ⓤⓢ ˌwɝː.kɚ **-s** -z
steelworks ˈstiːl.wɜːks ⓤⓢ -wɝːks
steel|y ˈstiː.l|i **-ier** -i.əʳ ⓤⓢ -i.ɚ **-iest** -i.ɪst, -i.əst **-iness** -ɪ.nəs, -ɪ.nɪs
steelyard ˈstiːl.jɑːd, ˈstɪl.jəd ⓤⓢ ˈstiːl.jɑːrd, ˈstɪl.jɚd **-s** -z
steenbok ˈstiːn.bɒk, ˈsteɪn- ⓤⓢ -bɑːk **-s** -s
Steenson ˈstiːn*t*.sən
steep stiːp **-s** -s **-er** -əʳ ⓤⓢ -ɚ **-est** -ɪst, -əst **-ly** -li **-ness** -nəs, -nɪs **-ing** -ɪŋ **-ed** -t
steepen ˈstiː.pᵊn **-s** -z **-ing** -ɪŋ, ˈstiːp.nɪŋ **-ed** -d
steeple ˈstiː.pl̩ **-s** -z **-d** -d
steeplechas|e ˈstiː.pl̩.tʃeɪs **-es** -ɪz **-ing** -ɪŋ **-er/s** -əʳ/z ⓤⓢ -ɚ/z
steeplejack ˈstiː.pl̩.dʒæk **-s** -s
steer stɪəʳ ⓤⓢ stɪr **-s** -z **-ing** -ɪŋ **-ed** -d **-er/s** -əʳ/z ⓤⓢ -ɚ/z **ˈsteering ˌgear; ˈsteering comˌmittee; ˈsteering ˌwheel**
steerage ˈstɪə.rɪdʒ ⓤⓢ ˈstɪr.ɪdʒ
steers|man ˈstɪəz|.mən ⓤⓢ ˈstɪrz- **-men** -mən
steev|e stiːv **-es** -z **-ing** -ɪŋ **-ed** -d
Steevens ˈstiː.vᵊnz
Stefanie ˈstef.ᵊn.i
Steiger ˈstaɪ.gəʳ ⓤⓢ -gɚ
stein *beer mug:* staɪn *as if German:* ʃtaɪn **-s** -z
Stein *surname:* staɪn, stiːn *as if German:* ʃtaɪn
Steinbeck ˈstaɪn.bek, ˈstaɪm- ⓤⓢ ˈstaɪn-
steinbock ˈstaɪn.bɒk, ˈstaɪm- ⓤⓢ ˈstaɪn.bɑːk **-s** -s
Steinbrenner ˈstaɪnˌbren.əʳ, ˈstaɪm- ⓤⓢ ˈstaɪnˌbren.ɚ
Steinem ˈstaɪ.nəm
Steiner ˈstaɪ.nəʳ ⓤⓢ -nɚ
Steinway® ˈstaɪn.weɪ **-s** -z
stel|e *monument:* ˈstiː.l|i; stiːl ⓤⓢ ˈstiː.l|i **-ae** -iː **-es** ˈstiː.liz; stiːlz ⓤⓢ ˈstiː.liz *in architecture or botany:* ˈstiː.l|i; stiːl ⓤⓢ stiːl; ˈstiː.l|i **-ae** -iː **-es** ˈstiː.liz; stiːlz ⓤⓢ stiːlz; ˈstiː.liz
St. Elian sᵊntˈiː.li.ən, sɪnt- ⓤⓢ seɪnt-
St. Elias sᵊnt.ɪˈlaɪ.əs, sɪnt-, -æs ⓤⓢ ˌseɪnt.ɪˈlaɪ.əs
Stella ˈstel.ə **ˌStella ˈArtois®** *as if French:* **ˌStella Arˈtois**
stellar ˈstel.əʳ ⓤⓢ -ɚ
St. Elmo sᵊntˈel.məʊ, sɪnt- ⓤⓢ seɪntˈel.moʊ **-ˈs** -z **St. ˌElmo's ˈfire**
stem stem **-s** -z **-ming** -ɪŋ **-med** -d
stemple ˈstem.pl̩ **-s** -z
Sten sten **ˈSten ˌgun**
stench sten*t*ʃ ⓤⓢ stentʃ **-es** -ɪz
stencil ˈsten*t*.sᵊl, -ɪl ⓤⓢ -sᵊl **-s** -z **-(l)ing** -ɪŋ **-(l)ed** -d
Stendhal ˈstɑ̃ːn.dɑːl, -ˈ- ⓤⓢ ˈsten-, ˈstæn-
Stenhouse ˈsten.haʊs
Stenhousemuir ˌsten.haʊsˈmjʊəʳ, -əsˈ-, -ˈmjɔːʳ ⓤⓢ -ˈmjʊɚ
Stenness ˈsten.əs
steno ˈsten.əʊ ⓤⓢ -oʊ **-s** -z
stenograph ˈsten.əʊ.grɑːf, -græf ⓤⓢ -ə.græf **-s** -s
stenograph|er stəˈnɒg.rə.f|əʳ, stenˈɒg- ⓤⓢ stəˈnɑː.grə.f|ɚ **-ers** -əz ⓤⓢ -ɚz **-y** -i
stenotyp|e ˈsten.əʊ.taɪp ⓤⓢ ˈ-ə- **-ing** -ɪŋ **-ist/s** -ɪst/s
stentorian stenˈtɔː.ri.ən ⓤⓢ -ˈtɔːr.i-
step step **-s** -s **-ping** -ɪŋ **-ped** -t **-per/s** -əʳ/z ⓤⓢ -ɚ/z **ˌstep aeˈrobics; ˈstep ˌdance; ˌstep by ˈstep**
stepbrother ˈstepˌbrʌð.əʳ ⓤⓢ -ɚ **-s** -z
step|child ˈstep|.tʃaɪld **-children** -ˌtʃɪl.drᵊn
stepdad ˈstep.dæd **-s** -z
stepdaughter ˈstepˌdɔː.təʳ ⓤⓢ -ˌdɑː.t̬ɚ, -ˌdɔː- **-s** -z
stepfather ˈstepˌfɑː.ðəʳ ⓤⓢ -ðɚ **-s** -z
Stephanie ˈstef.ᵊn.i
Stephano ˈstef.ᵊn.əʊ ⓤⓢ -ə.noʊ
stephanotis ˌstef.əˈnəʊ.tɪs ⓤⓢ -ˈnoʊ.t̬ɪs
Stephen ˈstiː.vᵊn **-s** -z
Stephenson ˈstiː.vᵊn.sᵊn
stepladder ˈstepˌlæd.əʳ ⓤⓢ -ɚ **-s** -z
stepmother ˈstepˌmʌð.əʳ ⓤⓢ -ɚ **-s** -z
stepmum ˈstep.mʌm **-s** -z
Stepney ˈstep.ni
stepparent ˈstepˌpeə.rᵊnt ⓤⓢ -ˌper.ᵊnt, -ˌpær- **-s** -s
steppe step **-s** -s
Steppenwolf ˈstep.ᵊn.wʊlf
stepping-stone ˈstep.ɪŋ.stəʊn ⓤⓢ -stoʊn **-s** -z

stepsister ˈstepˌsɪs.təʳ (US) -tɚ **-s** -z
stepson ˈstep.sʌn **-s** -z
Steptoe ˈstep.təʊ (US) -toʊ
-ster -stəʳ (US) -stɚ
Note: Suffix. Does not normally change the stress pattern of the word to which it is added, e.g. **prank** /præŋk/, **prankster** /ˈpræŋk.stəʳ (US) -stɚ/.
stereo- ster.i.əʊ-, stɪə.ri-; ˌster.iˈɒ-, ˌstɪə.riˈ- (US) ster.i.oʊ-, stɪr-, -ə-; ˌster.iˈɑː-, ˌstɪr-
Note: Prefix. Normally either takes primary or secondary stress on the first syllable, e.g. **stereoscope** /ˈster.i.əʊ.skəʊp (US) -ə.skoʊp/, **stereophonic** /ˌster.i.əʊˈfɒn.ɪk (US) -əˈfɑː.nɪk/, or secondary stress on the first syllable and primary stress on the third syllable, e.g. **stereophony** /ˌster.iˈɒf.ən.i (US) -ˈɑː.fən-/.
stereo ˈster.i.əʊ, ˈstɪə.ri- (US) ˈster.i.oʊ, ˈstɪr- **-s** -z
stereophonic ˌster.i.əʊˈfɒn.ɪk, ˌstɪə.ri- (US) ˌster.i.əˈfɑː.nɪk, ˌstɪr-
stereophony ˌster.iˈɒf.ən.i, ˌstɪə.riˈ- (US) ˌster.iˈɑː.fən-, ˌstɪr-
stereopticon ˌster.iˈɒp.tɪ.kən, ˌstɪə.riˈ- (US) ˌster.iˈɑːp-, ˌstɪr-, -kɑːn **-s** -z
stereoscope ˈster.i.ə.skəʊp, ˈstɪə.ri- (US) ˈster.i.ə.skoʊp, ˈstɪr- **-s** -s
stereoscopic ˌster.i.əˈskɒp.ɪk, ˌstɪə.ri- (US) ˌster.i.əˈskɑː.pɪk, ˌstɪr- **-al** -əl **-ally** -əl.i, -li
stereoscopy ˌster.iˈɒs.kə.pi, ˌstɪə.riˈ- (US) ˌster.iˈɑː.skə-, ˌstɪr-
stereotyp|e ˈster.i.əʊ.taɪp, ˈstɪə.ri- (US) ˈster.i.ə-, ˈstɪr- **-es** -s **-ing** -ɪŋ **-ed** -t
stereotypic|al ˌster.i.əʊˈtɪp.ɪ.k|əl, ˌstɪə.ri- (US) ˌster.i.əˈ-, ˌstɪr- **-ally** -əl.i, -li
sterile ˈster.aɪl (US) -əl
sterility stəˈrɪl.ə.ti, sterˈɪl-, -ɪ.ti (US) stəˈrɪl.ə.t̬i
sterilization, -isa- ˌster.əl.aɪˈzeɪ.ʃən, -ɪ.laɪˈ-, -lɪˈ- (US) -əl.ɪˈ- **-s** -z
sterilize, -is|e ˈster.əl.aɪz, -ɪ.laɪz (US) -ə.laɪz **-es** -ɪz **-ing** -ɪŋ **-ed** -d **-er/s** -əʳ/z (US) -ɚ/z
sterling (S) ˈstɜː.lɪŋ (US) ˈstɝː-
stern (S) (*adj.*) stɜːn (US) stɝːn **-er** -əʳ (US) -ɚ **-est** -ɪst, -əst **-ly** -li **-ness** -nəs, -nɪs
Sterne stɜːn (US) stɝːn
stern|um ˈstɜː.n|əm (US) ˈstɝː- **-ums** -əmz **-a** -ə
steroid ˈster.ɔɪd, ˈstɪə.rɔɪd (US) ˈster-, ˈstɪr- **-s** -z
stertorous ˈstɜː.tər.əs (US) ˈstɝː.t̬ɚ- **-ly** -li **-ness** -nəs, -nɪs
stet stet **-s** -s **-ting** -ɪŋ (US) ˈstet̬.ɪŋ **-ted** -ɪd (US) ˈstet̬.ɪd
stethoscope ˈsteθ.ə.skəʊp (US) -skoʊp **-s** -s
stethoscopic ˌsteθ.əˈskɒp.ɪk (US) -ˈskɑː.pɪk **-al** -əl **-ally** -əl.i, -li
stethoscopy steθˈɒs.kə.pi (US) -ˈɑː.skə-
Stetson® ˈstet.sən
Steve stiːv
stevedore ˈstiː.və.dɔːʳ, -vɪ- (US) -və.dɔːr **-s** -z
Steven ˈstiː.vən **-s** -z
Stevenage ˈstiː.vən.ɪdʒ
Stevenson ˈstiː.vən.sən
Stevenston ˈstiː.vən.stən
Stevie ˈstiː.vi
stew stjuː (US) stuː, stjuː **-s** -z **-ing** -ɪŋ **-ed** -d
steward (S) ˈstjuː.əd, stjʊəd (US) ˈstuː.ɚd, ˈstjuː- **-s** -z **-ing** -ɪŋ **-ed** -ɪd
stewardess ˈstjuː.ə.dɪs, ˈstjʊə-, -dəs, -des; ˌstjuː.əˈdes (US) ˈstuː.ɚ.dɪs, ˈstjuː- **-es** -ɪz
stewardship ˈstjuː.əd.ʃɪp, ˈstjʊəd- (US) ˈstuː.ɚd-, ˈstjuː-
Stewart stjʊət, ˈstjuː.ət (US) ˈstuː.ɚt, ˈstjuː-, stʊrt
Stewarton ˈstjʊə.tən, ˈstjuː.ə- (US) ˈstuː.ɚ-, ˈstjuː-, stʊr.tən
Steyn staɪn
Steyne stiːn
Steyning ˈsten.ɪŋ
St. Fagans sənt̮ˈfæg.ənz, sɪnt- (US) seɪntˈfæg-, -ˈfeɪ.gənz
St. Francis sənt̮ˈfrɑːnt.sɪs, sɪnt- (US) seɪntˈfrænt-
stg. (*abbrev. for* **sterling**) ˈstɜː.lɪŋ (US) ˈstɝː-
St. Gall sənt̮ˈgæl, sɪnt-, -gɑːl, -gɔːl (US) seɪnt-
St. Gallen sənt̮ˈgæl.ən, sɪnt- (US) seɪntˈgɑː.lən
St. George sənt̮ˈdʒɔːdʒ, sɪnt- (US) seɪntˈdʒɔːrdʒ **-'s** -ɪz
St. Giles sənt̮ˈdʒaɪlz, sɪnt- (US) seɪnt- **-'s** -ɪz
St. Godric sənt̮ˈgɒd.rɪk, sɪnt- (US) seɪntˈgɑː.drɪk
St. Gotthard sənt̮ˈgɒt.əd, sɪnt-, -ɑːd (US) seɪntˈgɑː.t̬ɚd
St. Helen səntˈhel.ən, sɪnt-, -ɪn (US) seɪntˈhel.ən **-s** -z
St. Helena *Saint:* səntˈhel.ə.nə, sɪnt-, ˈ-ɪ- (US) ˌseɪnt.həˈliː-; seɪntˈhel.ə- *island:* ˌsent.hɪˈliː.nə, ˌsɪnt-, sənt-, -həˈ- (US) ˌseɪnt.həˈ-; seɪntˈhel.ə-
St. Helier səntˈhel.i.əʳ, sɪnt- (US) seɪntˈhel.jɚ **-s** -z
Stich stɪx *as if German:* ʃtiːx
stichomythia ˌstɪk.əʊˈmɪθ.i.ə (US) -əˈ-, -oʊˈ- **-s** -z
stick stɪk **-s** -s **-ing** -ɪŋ **stuck** stʌk ˈ**stick** ˌ**insect**; ˈ**sticking** ˌ**plaster**; ˈ**stick** ˌ**shift**; **get** (ˌ**hold of**) **the** ˌ**wrong** ˌ**end of the** ˈ**stick**
sticker ˈstɪk.əʳ (US) -ɚ **-s** -z
stick-in-the-mud ˈstɪk.ɪn.ðəˌmʌd **-s** -z
stickjaw ˈstɪk.dʒɔː (US) -dʒɑː, -dʒɔː **-s** -z
stickleback ˈstɪk.l̩.bæk **-s** -s
stickler ˈstɪk.ləʳ, -l̩.əʳ (US) ˈ-lɚ, -l̩.ɚ **-s** -z
stick-on ˈstɪk.ɒn (US) -ɑːn
stickpin ˈstɪk.pɪn
stick-up ˈstɪk.ʌp **-s** -s
stick|y ˈstɪk|.i **-ier** -i.əʳ (US) -i.ɚ **-iest** -i.ɪst, -i.əst **-ily** -ɪ.li, -əl.i **-iness** -ɪ.nəs, -ɪ.nɪs
stickybeak ˈstɪk.i.biːk **-s** -s
stiff stɪf **-er** -əʳ (US) -ɚ **-est** -ɪst, -əst **-ing** -ɪŋ **-ed** -t **-ly** -li **-ness** -nəs, -nɪs ˌ**stiff** ˌ**upper** ˈ**lip**
stiffen ˈstɪf.ən **-s** -z **-ing** -ɪŋ, ˈstɪf.nɪŋ **-ed** -d
Stiffkey ˈstɪf.ki *old-fashioned local pronunciation:* ˈstjuː.ki, ˈstuː-
stiff-necked ˌstɪfˈnekt (US) ˈstɪf.nekt *stress shift:* ˌstiff-necked ˈpride
stifl|e ˈstaɪ.fl̩ **-es** -z **-ing/ly** -ɪŋ/li, ˈstaɪ.flɪŋ/li **-ed** -d
Stiggins ˈstɪg.ɪnz
stigma ˈstɪg.mə **-s** -z **-tism** -tɪ.zəm
stigmata (*alternative plur. of* **stigmata**) stɪgˈmɑː.tə (US) -t̬ə, -ˈmæt̬.ə
stigmatic stɪgˈmæt.ɪk (US) -ˈmæt̬-
stigmatization, -isa- ˌstɪg.mə.taɪˈzeɪ.ʃən, -tɪˈ- (US) -t̬ɪˈ-
stigmatiz|e, -is|e ˈstɪg.mə.taɪz **-es** -ɪz **-ing** -ɪŋ **-ed** -d
stilbene ˈstɪl.biːn
stilbestrol stɪlˈbiː.strəl, -ˈbes.trəl (US) -ˈbes.trɔːl, -troʊl
stile staɪl **-s** -z
stiletto stɪˈlet.əʊ (US) -ˈlet̬.oʊ **-(e)s** -z
still (S) stɪl **-s** -z **-er** -əʳ (US) -ɚ/z **-est** -ɪst, -əst **-ness** -nəs, -nɪs **-ing** -ɪŋ **-ed** -d ˌ**still** ˈ**life** *stress shift:* ˌstill life ˈpainting
stillbirth ˈstɪl.bɜːθ (US) -bɝːθ **-s** -s
stillborn ˈstɪl.bɔːn (US) ˈstɪl.bɔːrn
Stillson ˈstɪl.sən ˈ**Stillson** ˌ**wrench®**
stilly ˈstɪl.i
stilt stɪlt **-s** -s
stilted ˈstɪl.tɪd (US) -t̬ɪd **-ly** -li **-ness** -nəs, -nɪs
Stilton ˈstɪl.tən **-s** -z
Stimpson ˈstɪmp.sən
Stimson ˈstɪmp.sən
stimulant ˈstɪm.jə.lənt, -jʊ- **-s** -s
stimu|late ˈstɪm.jə|.leɪt, -jʊ- **-lates** -leɪts **-lating** -leɪ.tɪŋ (US) -leɪ.t̬ɪŋ **-lated** -leɪ.tɪd (US) -leɪ.t̬ɪd **-lator/s** -leɪ.təʳ/z (US) -leɪ.t̬ɚ/z
stimulation ˌstɪm.jəˈleɪ.ʃən, -jʊˈ- **-s** -z

stimulative ˈstɪm.jə.lə.tɪv, -jʊ-, -leɪ- (US) -leɪ.t̬ɪv
stimul|us ˈstɪm.jə.l|əs, -jʊ- **-i** -aɪ, -iː
stim|y ˈstaɪ.m|i **-ies** -iz **-ying** -i.ɪŋ **-ied** -id
sting stɪŋ **-s** -z **-ing** -ɪŋ **stung** stʌŋ **stinger/s** ˈstɪŋ.əʳ/z (US) -ɚ/z ˈ**stinging** ˌ**nettle**
stingo ˈstɪŋ.gəʊ (US) -goʊ **-s** -z
stingray ˈstɪŋ.reɪ **-s** -z
sting|y ˈstɪn.dʒ|i **-ier** -i.əʳ (US) -i.ɚ **-iest** -i.ɪst, -i.əst **-ily** -ɪ.li, -ᵊl.i **-iness** -ɪ.nəs, -ɪ.nɪs
stink stɪŋk **-s** -s **-ing** -ɪŋ **stank** stæŋk **stunk** stʌŋk
stink-bomb ˈstɪŋk.bɒm (US) -bɑːm **-s** -z
stinker ˈstɪŋ.kəʳ (US) -kɚ **-s** -z
stinkpot ˈstɪŋk.pɒt (US) -pɑːt **-s** -s
stint stɪnt **-s** -s **-ing** -ɪŋ (US) ˈstɪn.t̬ɪŋ **-ed** -ɪd (US) ˈstɪn.t̬ɪd
stipend ˈstaɪ.pend, -pənd **-s** -z
stipendiar|y staɪˈpen.di.ᵊr|.i, stɪ- (US) staɪˈpen.di.er- **-ies** -iz
stippl|e ˈstɪp.l̩ **-es** -z **-ing** -ɪŋ, ˈstɪp.lɪŋ **-ed** -d **-er/s** -əʳ/z (US) -ɚ/z
stipu|late ˈstɪp.jə|.leɪt, -jʊ- **-lates** -leɪts **-lating** -leɪ.tɪŋ (US) -leɪ.t̬ɪŋ **-lated** -leɪ.tɪd (US) -leɪ.t̬ɪd
stipulation ˌstɪp.jəˈleɪ.ʃᵊn, -jʊˈ- **-s** -z
stipule ˈstɪp.juːl **-s** -z
stir stɜːʳ (US) stɝː **-s** -z **-ring/ly** -ɪŋ/li **-red** -d **-rer/s** -əʳ/z (US) -ɚ/z
stir|-fry ˈstɜː|ˌfraɪ (US) ˈstɝː- **-fries** -ˈfraɪz (US) -fraɪz **-frying** -ˈfraɪ.ɪŋ (US) -ˌfraɪ.ɪŋ **-fried** -ˈfraɪd (US) -fraɪd *stress shift, British only:* ˌstir-fried ˈvegetables
Stirling ˈstɜː.lɪŋ (US) ˈstɝː- **-shire** -ʃəʳ, -ˌʃɪəʳ (US) -ʃɚ, -ˌʃɪr
stirp|s stɜːp|s (US) stɝːp|s **-es** -iːz, -eɪz
stirrup ˈstɪr.əp (US) ˈstɝː-, ˈstɪr- **-s** -s ˈ**stirrup** ˌ**pump**
stitch stɪtʃ **-es** -ɪz **-ing** -ɪŋ **-ed** -t
St. Ivel sᵊntˈaɪ.vᵊl, sɪnt- (US) seɪnt-
St. Ives sᵊntˈaɪvz, sɪnt- (US) seɪnt-
St. James sᵊn*t*ˈdʒeɪmz, sɪn*t*- (US) seɪnt- **-'s** -ɪz
St. Joan sᵊn*t*ˈdʒəʊn, sɪn*t*- (US) seɪntˈdʒoʊn
St. John *Saint, place:* sᵊn*t*ˈdʒɒn, sɪn*t*- (US) seɪntˈdʒɑːn **-'s** -z *surname:* ˈsɪn.dʒᵊn (US) seɪntˈdʒɑːn **-'s** -z
St. Joseph sᵊn*t*ˈdʒəʊ.zɪf, sɪn*t*-, -zəf (US) seɪntˈdʒoʊ.zəf, -səf
St. Kilda sᵊn*t*ˈkɪl.də, sɪn*t*- (US) seɪnt-
St. Kitts sᵊn*t*ˈkɪts, sɪn*t*- (US) seɪnt-
St. Kitts-Nevis sᵊn*t*ˌkɪtsˈniː.vɪs, sɪnt- (US) seɪnt-
St. Laurent *Yves:* ˌsæ̃n.lɔːˈrɑ̃ːŋ, -ləˈ- (US) -lɔːˈrɑːn *place in Canada:* ˌsæn.lɔːˈrɒ̃ŋ, -ləˈ-, -ˈrɑːnt (US) ˌsæ̃.lɔːˈrɑːn, ˌsæn.lɔːˈrent
St. Lawrence sᵊn*t*ˈlɒr.ᵊn*t*s, sɪn*t*- (US) seɪntˈlɔːr- **St.** ˌ**Lawrence** ˈ**Seaway**
St. Leger *surname:* sᵊn*t*ˈledʒ.əʳ, sɪnt-; ˈsel.ɪn.dʒəʳ (US) seɪntˈledʒ.ɚ; ˈsel.ɪn.dʒɚ
Note: Most people bearing this name (including the Irish families) pronounce /sᵊn*t*ˈledʒ.əʳ (US) seɪnt-/. But there are members of the Doncaster family who pronounce /ˈsel.ɪn.dʒəʳ (US) -dʒɚ/.
St. Leger *race:* sᵊn*t*ˈledʒ.əʳ, sɪnt- (US) seɪntˈledʒ.ɚ
St. Leonards sᵊn*t*ˈlen.ədz, sɪnt- (US) seɪntˈlen.ɚdz *city in Quebec:* sænˈleɪ.əʊ.nɑːʳ, -oʊ.nɑːr
St. Levan sᵊn*t*ˈlev.ən, sɪnt- (US) seɪnt-
St. Louis *city in US:* sᵊn*t*ˈluː.ɪs, sɪnt- (US) seɪnt-, -i *sometimes locally:* sænt- *places in Canada:* sᵊn*t*ˈluː.i, sɪn*t*-, -ɪs (US) seɪnt-
St. Lucia sᵊn*t*ˈluː.ʃə, sɪnt-, -ʃi.ə, -si.ə (US) seɪntˈluː.ʃi.ə, -si-, ˈ-ʃə
St. Ludger sᵊn*t*ˈluː.dʒəʳ, sɪnt- (US) seɪntˈluː.dʒɚ
St. Luke sᵊn*t*ˈluːk, sɪnt- (US) seɪnt-
St. Malo sᵊn*t*ˈmɑː.ləʊ, sɪn*t*-, sæ̃n- *as if French:* ˌsæ̃n.mɑːˈləʊ (US) ˌsæn.mɑːˈloʊ
St. Margaret sᵊn*t*ˈmɑː.gᵊr.ɪt, sɪn*t*-, ˈ-grɪt (US) seɪntˈmɑːr.grət **-'s** -s
St. Mark sᵊn*t*ˈmɑːk, sɪn*t*- (US) seɪntˈmɑːrk **-'s** -s
St. Martin sᵊn*t*ˈmɑː.tɪn, sɪn*t*- (US) seɪntˈmɑːr.tᵊn **-'s** -z
St. Mary sᵊn*t*ˈmeə.ri, sɪn*t*- (US) seɪntˈmer.i **-'s** -z
St. Mary Axe sᵊn*t*ˌmeə.riˈæks, sɪn*t*- (US) seɪntˌmer.iˈ-
Note: The old form /ˌsɪm.ᵊr.iˈæks/ is used in Gilbert and Sullivan's opera 'The Sorcerer'.
St. Marylebone sᵊntˈmær.ᵊl.ə.bən, sɪn*t*-, -ɪ.lə- (US) seɪntˈmer.ᵊl.ə.boʊn
St. Mary-le-Bow sᵊn*t*ˌmeə.ri.ləˈbəʊ, sɪn*t*- (US) seɪntˌmer.i.ləˈboʊ
St. Matthew sᵊn*t*ˈmæθ.juː, sɪn*t*- (US) seɪnt-
St. Mawes sᵊn*t*ˈmɔːz, sɪn*t*- (US) seɪntˈmɑːz, -ˈmɔːz
St. Michael sᵊn*t*ˈmaɪ.kᵊl, sɪn*t*- (US) seɪnt- **-'s** -z
St. Moritz ˌsæn.mᵊrˈɪts, ˌsæm-; sᵊn*t*ˈmɒr.ɪts, sɪn*t*- (US) ˌsæn.məˈrɪts, ˌseɪnt-, -mɔːˈ-
St. Neots sᵊn*t*ˈniː.əts, sɪn*t*-, -niːts (US) seɪnt-
St. Nicholas sᵊn*t*ˈnɪk.ᵊl.əs, sɪn*t*-, ˈ-ləs (US) seɪnt-
stoat stəʊt (US) stoʊt **-s** -s
Stobart ˈstəʊ.bɑːt (US) ˈstoʊ.bɑːrt
stochastic stɒkˈæs.tɪk, stəˈkæs- (US) stoʊˈkæs-, stə-
stock stɒk (US) stɑːk **-s** -s **-ing** -ɪŋ **-ed** -t ˈ**stock** ˌ**car**; ˈ**stock** ˌ**cube**; ˈ**stock ex**ˌ**change**; ˈ**stock** ˌ**market**
stockad|e stɒkˈeɪd (US) stɑːˈkeɪd **-es** -z **-ing** -ɪŋ **-ed** -ɪd
stockbreed|er ˈstɒkˌbriː.d|əʳ (US) ˈstɑːkˌbriː.d|ɚ **-ers** -əz (US) -ɚz **-ing** -ɪŋ
Stockbridge ˈstɒk.brɪdʒ (US) ˈstɑːk-
stockbrok|er ˈstɒkˌbrəʊ.k|əʳ (US) ˈstɑːkˌbroʊ.k|ɚ **-ers** -əʳz (US) -ɚz **-ing** -ɪŋ ˈ**stockbroker** ˌ**belt**
stockfish ˈstɒk.fɪʃ (US) ˈstɑːk-
Stockhausen ˈstɒkˌhaʊ.zᵊn *as if German:* ˈʃtɒk- (US) ˈstɑːk-
stockholder ˈstɒkˌhəʊl.dəʳ (US) ˈstɑːkˌhoʊl.dɚ **-s** -z
Stockholm ˈstɒk.həʊm (US) ˈstɑːk.hoʊlm, -hoʊm
stockinet(te) ˌstɒk.ɪˈnet (US) ˌstɑː.kɪˈ-
stocking ˈstɒk.ɪŋ (US) ˈstɑː.kɪŋ **-s** -z **-ed** -d ˈ**stocking** ˌ**cap**; ˈ**stocking** ˌ**filler**; ˈ**stocking** ˌ**stitch**; **in one's** ˌ**stocking/ed** ˈ**feet**
stock-in-trade ˌstɒk.ɪnˈtreɪd (US) ˌstɑːk-
stockist ˈstɒk.ɪst (US) ˈstɑː.kɪst **-s** -s
stockjobb|er ˈstɒkˌdʒɒb|.əʳ (US) ˈstɑːkˌdʒɑː.b|ɚ **-ers** -əz (US) -ɚz **-ing** -ɪŋ
stock|man (S) ˈstɒk.mən (US) ˈstɑːk- **-men** -men, -mən
stockpil|e ˈstɒk.paɪl (US) ˈstɑːk- **-es** -z **-ing** -ɪŋ **-ed** -d
Stockport ˈstɒk.pɔːt (US) ˈstɑːk.pɔːrt
stockpot ˈstɒk.pɒt (US) ˈstɑːk.pɑːt **-s** -s
stockroom ˈstɒk.rʊm, -ruːm (US) ˈstɑːk.ruːm, -rʊm **-s** -z
Stocksbridge ˈstɒks.brɪdʒ (US) ˈstɑːks-
stock-still ˌstɒkˈstɪl (US) ˌstɑːk-
stocktaking ˈstɒkˌteɪ.kɪŋ (US) ˈstɑːk-
Stockton ˈstɒk.tən (US) ˈstɑːk-
Stockton-on-Tees ˌstɒk.tən.ɒnˈtiːz (US) ˌstɑːk.tən.ɑːnˈ-
Stockwell ˈstɒk.wel, -wəl (US) ˈstɑːk-
stock|y ˈstɒk|.i (US) ˈstɑː.k|i **-ier** -i.əʳ (US) -i.ɚ **-iest** -i.ɪst, -i.əst **-iness** -ɪ.nəs, -ɪ.nɪs **-ily** -ɪ.li
stockyard ˈstɒk.jɑːd (US) ˈstɑːk.jɑːrd **-s** -z
Stoddard ˈstɒd.əd, -ɑːd (US) ˈstɑː.dɚd
Stoddart ˈstɒd.ət, -ɑːt (US) ˈstɑː.dɚt
stodg|e stɒdʒ (US) stɑːdʒ **-es** -ɪz **-ing** -ɪŋ **-ed** -d **-y** -i **-ier** -i.əʳ (US) -i.ɚ **-iest** -i.ɪst, -i.əst **-iness** -ɪ.nəs, -ɪ.nɪs
stoep stuːp **-s** -s
Stogumber *in Somerset:* stəʊˈgʌm.bəʳ; ˈstɒg.əm- (US) stoʊˈgʌm.bɚ; ˈstɑː.gəm- *character in Shaw's 'Saint Joan':* ˈstɒg.əm.bəʳ (US) ˈstɑː.gəm.bɚ, ˈstɔː-

Stogursey stəʊ'gɜː.zi ⓤⓢ stoʊ'gɝː-
stoic (S) 'stəʊ.ɪk ⓤⓢ 'stoʊ- **-s** -s **-al** -ᵊl **-ally** -ᵊl.i, -li
stoicism (S) 'stəʊ.ɪ.sɪ.zᵊm, '-ə- ⓤⓢ 'stoʊ.ɪ-
stok|e (S) stəʊk ⓤⓢ stoʊk **-es** -s **-ing** -ɪŋ **-ed** -t **-er/s** -əʳ/z ⓤⓢ -ɚ/z
Stoke Courcy stəʊ'gɜː.zi ⓤⓢ stoʊ'gɝː-
Stoke d'Abernon ˌstəʊk'dæb.ᵊn.ən ⓤⓢ ˌstoʊk'dæb.ɚ.nən
stokehold 'stəʊk.həʊld ⓤⓢ 'stoʊk.hoʊld **-s** -z
stokehole 'stəʊk.həʊl ⓤⓢ 'stoʊk.hoʊl **-s** -z
Stoke Mandeville ˌstəʊk'mæn.də.vɪl, '-dɪ- ⓤⓢ ˌstoʊk-
Stoke on Trent ˌstəʊk.ɒn'trent ⓤⓢ ˌstoʊk.ɑːn'-
Stoke Poges ˌstəʊk'pəʊ.dʒɪz ⓤⓢ ˌstoʊk'poʊ-
stoker (S) 'stəʊ.kəʳ ⓤⓢ 'stoʊ.kɚ **-s** -z
STOL stɒl, 'es.tɒl ⓤⓢ stɑːl, 'es.tɑːl
St. Olaves, St. Olave's sᵊnt'ɒl.ɪvz, sɪnt-, -əvz ⓤⓢ seɪnt'ɑː.lɪvz, -ləvz
stole (S) stəʊl ⓤⓢ stoʊl **-s** -z
stol|e *(from* **steal***)* stəʊl ⓤⓢ stoʊl **-en** -ən
stolid 'stɒl.ɪd ⓤⓢ 'stɑː.lɪd **-est** -ɪst, -əst **-ly** -li
stolidity stɒl'ɪd.ə.ti, stə'lɪd-, -ɪ.ti ⓤⓢ stə'lɪd.ə.t̬i
Stoll stəʊl, stɒl ⓤⓢ stoʊl, stɑːl
stollen 'stɒl.ən *as if German:* 'ʃtɒl- ⓤⓢ 'stoʊ.lən *as if German:* 'ʃtoʊ- **-s** -z
stolon 'stəʊ.lɒn, -lən ⓤⓢ 'stoʊ.lɑːn, -lən **-s** -z
stoma 'stəʊ.mə ⓤⓢ 'stoʊ- **-s** -z **-ta** -tə
stomach 'stʌm.ək **-s** -s **-ing** -ɪŋ **-ed** -t 'stomach ˌpump
stomachache 'stʌm.ək.eɪk **-s** -s
stomacher 'stʌm.ə.kəʳ ⓤⓢ -kɚ **-s** -z
stomachic stəʊ'mæk.ɪk, stɒm'æk-; 'stʌm.ə.kɪk ⓤⓢ stə'mæk.ɪk
stomati|tis ˌstəʊ.mə'taɪ|.tɪs, ˌstɒm.ə'- ⓤⓢ ˌstoʊ.mə'taɪ|.t̬ɪs, ˌstɑː- **-tides** -tɪ.diːz **-tises** -tɪ.siːz, -tɪ.ziːz
stomatoscope stəʊ'mæt.ə.skəʊp, stɒm'æt- ⓤⓢ stoʊ'mæt̬.ə.skoʊp, stɑː- **-s** -s
stomp stɒmp ⓤⓢ stɑːmp **-s** -s **-ing** -ɪŋ **-ed** -t
ston|e (S) stəʊn ⓤⓢ stoʊn **-es** -z **-ing** -ɪŋ **-ed** -d **-y** -i **'Stone ˌAge; kill ˌtwo ˌbirds with ˌone 'stone; leave ˌno ˌstone un'turned; a 'stone's ˌthrow, a ˌstone's 'throw**
stone-blind ˌstəʊn'blaɪnd, ˌstəʊm- ⓤⓢ ˌstoʊn- **-ness** -nəs, -nɪs
stonechat 'stəʊn.tʃæt ⓤⓢ 'stoʊn- **-s** -s
stone-cold ˌstəʊn'kəʊld, ˌstəʊŋ- ⓤⓢ ˌstoʊn'koʊld *stress shift, see compound:* **ˌstone-cold 'sober**
stonecrop 'stəʊn.krɒp, 'stəʊŋ- ⓤⓢ 'stoʊn.krɑːp **-s** -s
stonecutter 'stəʊnˌkʌt.əʳ, 'stəʊŋ- ⓤⓢ 'stoʊnˌkʌt̬.ɚ **-s** -z
stone-dead ˌstəʊn'ded ⓤⓢ ˌstoʊn-
stone-deaf ˌstəʊn'def ⓤⓢ ˌstoʊn- **-ness** -nəs, -nɪs
stonefish 'stəʊn.fɪʃ ⓤⓢ 'stoʊn- **-es** -ɪz
stoneground ˌstəʊn'graʊnd, ˌstəʊŋ- ⓤⓢ ˌstoʊn-
Stonehaven 'stəʊnˌheɪ.vᵊn ⓤⓢ 'stoʊn-
Stonehenge ˌstəʊn'hendʒ ⓤⓢ 'stoʊn.hendʒ
Stonehouse 'stəʊn.haʊs ⓤⓢ 'stoʊn-
stonemason 'stəʊnˌmeɪ.sᵊn, 'stəʊm- ⓤⓢ 'stoʊn- **-s** -z
stonewall (S) ˌstəʊn'wɔːl ⓤⓢ 'stoʊn- **-s** -z **-ing** -ɪŋ **-ed** -d **-er/s** -əʳ/z ⓤⓢ -ɚ/z
stoneware 'stəʊn.weəʳ ⓤⓢ 'stoʊn.wer
stone-washed ˌstəʊn'wɒʃt ⓤⓢ ˌstoʊn'wɑːʃt *stress shift, British only:* ˌstonewashed 'jeans
stonework 'stəʊn.wɜːk ⓤⓢ 'stoʊn.wɝːk
Stoney 'stəʊ.ni ⓤⓢ 'stoʊ-
stonking 'stɒŋ.kɪŋ ⓤⓢ 'stɑːŋ- **-ly** -li
Stonor 'stəʊ.nəʳ, 'stɒn.əʳ ⓤⓢ 'stoʊ.nɚ, 'stɑː.nɚ
ston|y 'stəʊ.n|i ⓤⓢ 'stoʊ- **-ier** -i.əʳ ⓤⓢ -i.ɚ **-iest** -i.ɪst, -i.əst **-ily** -ɪ.li, -ᵊl.i **-iness** -ɪ.nəs, -ɪ.nɪs **ˌstony 'broke**
stony-hearted ˌstəʊ.ni'hɑː.tɪd ⓤⓢ 'stoʊ.niˌhɑːr.t̬ɪd **-ness** -nəs, -nɪs
Stony Stratford ˌstəʊ.ni'stræt.fəd ⓤⓢ ˌstoʊ.ni'stræt.fɚd
stood *(from* **stand***)* stʊd
stoog|e stuːdʒ **-es** -ɪz **-ing** -ɪŋ **-ed** -d
stook stuːk, stʊk **-s** -s
stool stuːl **-s** -z **'stool ˌpigeon; ˌfall beˌtween two 'stools**
stoop stuːp **-s** -s **-ing** -ɪŋ **-ed** -t **-er/s** -əʳ/z ⓤⓢ -ɚ/z
stop stɒp ⓤⓢ stɑːp **-s** -s **-ping** -ɪŋ **-ped** -t **-per/s** -əʳ/z ⓤⓢ -ɚ/z **'stop ˌvolley**
stopcock 'stɒp.kɒk ⓤⓢ 'stɑːp.kɑːk **-s** -s
Stopes stəʊps ⓤⓢ stoʊps
Stopford 'stɒp.fəd ⓤⓢ 'stɑːp.fɚd
stopgap 'stɒp.gæp ⓤⓢ 'stɑːp- **-s** -s
stop-go ˌstɒp'gəʊ ⓤⓢ ˌstɑːp'goʊ
stoplight 'stɒp.laɪt ⓤⓢ 'stɑːp- **-s** -s
stopover 'stɒpˌəʊ.vəʳ ⓤⓢ 'stɑːpˌoʊ.vɚ **-s** -z
stoppag|e 'stɒp.ɪdʒ ⓤⓢ 'stɑː.pɪdʒ **-es** -ɪz
Stoppard 'stɒp.ɑːd, -əd ⓤⓢ 'stɑː.pɚd
stopper 'stɒp.əʳ ⓤⓢ 'stɑː.pɚ **-s** -z **-ing** -ɪŋ **-ed** -d
stop-press ˌstɒp'pres ⓤⓢ ˌstɑːp-
stopwatch 'stɒp.wɒtʃ ⓤⓢ 'stɑːp.wɑːtʃ, -wɔːtʃ **-es** -ɪz
storage 'stɔː.rɪdʒ ⓤⓢ 'stɔːr.ɪdʒ **'storage ˌheater**
stor|e stɔːʳ ⓤⓢ stɔːr **-es** -z **-ing** -ɪŋ **-ed** -d **-able** -ə.bl̩ **'store ˌbrand; 'store deˌtective, ˌstore de'tective**
storefront 'stɔː.frʌnt ⓤⓢ 'stɔːr- **-s** -s
storehou|se 'stɔː.haʊ|s ⓤⓢ 'stɔːr- **-ses** -zɪz
storekeep|er 'stɔːˌkiː.p|əʳ ⓤⓢ 'stɔːrˌkiː.p|ɚ **-ers** -əz ⓤⓢ -ɚz **-ing** -ɪŋ
storeroom 'stɔː.rʊm, -ruːm ⓤⓢ 'stɔːr.ruːm, -rʊm **-s** -z
storey (S) 'stɔː.ri ⓤⓢ 'stɔːr.i **-s** -z **-ed** -d
storiated 'stɔː.ri.eɪ.tɪd ⓤⓢ 'stɔːr.i.eɪ.t̬ɪd
stork stɔːk ⓤⓢ stɔːrk **-s** -s
storm (S) stɔːm ⓤⓢ stɔːrm **-s** -z **-ing** -ɪŋ **-ed** -d **'storm ˌcloud; 'storm ˌlantern; 'storm ˌpetrel; 'storm ˌtrooper; 'storm ˌwindow; a ˌstorm in a 'teacup**
stormbound 'stɔːm.baʊnd ⓤⓢ 'stɔːrm-
Stormont 'stɔː.mɒnt, -mənt ⓤⓢ 'stɔːr.mɑːnt, -mənt
Stormonth 'stɔː.mən*t*θ, -mʌn*t*θ ⓤⓢ 'stɔːr-
stormproof 'stɔːm.pruːf ⓤⓢ 'stɔːrm-
storm|y 'stɔː.m|i ⓤⓢ 'stɔːr- **-ier** -i.əʳ ⓤⓢ -i.ɚ **-iest** -i.ɪst, -i.əst **-ily** -ɪ.li, -ᵊl.i **-iness** -ɪ.nəs, -ɪ.nɪs
Stornoway 'stɔː.nə.weɪ ⓤⓢ 'stɔːr-
Storr stɔːʳ ⓤⓢ stɔːr **-s** -z
Storrington 'stɒr.ɪŋ.tən ⓤⓢ 'stɔːr-
Stort stɔːt ⓤⓢ stɔːrt
Stortford 'stɔːt.fəd, 'stɔː- ⓤⓢ 'stɔːrt.fɚd, 'stɔːr-
Storthing 'stɔː.tɪŋ ⓤⓢ 'stɔːr.t̬ɪŋ
stor|y (S) 'stɔː.r|i ⓤⓢ 'stɔːr|.i **-ies** -iz **-ied** -id
storyboard 'stɔː.ri.bɔːd ⓤⓢ 'stɔːr.i.bɔːrd **-s** -z
storybook 'stɔː.ri.bʊk ⓤⓢ 'stɔːr.i- **-s** -s
storyline 'stɔː.ri.laɪn ⓤⓢ 'stɔːr.i- **-s** -z
storytell|er 'stɔː.riˌtel|.əʳ ⓤⓢ 'stɔːr.iˌtel|.ɚ **-ers** -əʳz ⓤⓢ -ɚz **-ing** -ɪŋ
St. Osyth sᵊnt'əʊ.zɪθ, sɪnt-, -sɪθ ⓤⓢ seɪnt'oʊ-
Stotfold 'stɒt.fəʊld ⓤⓢ 'stɑːt.foʊld
Stothard 'stɒð.əd ⓤⓢ 'stɑː.ðɚd
stotink|a stɒt'ɪŋ.k|ə ⓤⓢ stoʊ'tɪŋ- **-i** -iː
Stoughton *in West Sussex, Leicestershire and US:* 'stəʊ.tᵊn ⓤⓢ 'stoʊ- *in Somerset:* 'stɔː.tᵊn ⓤⓢ 'stɔː-, 'stɑː- *in Surrey:* 'staʊ.tᵊn *surname:* 'stɔː.tᵊn, 'staʊ-, 'stəʊ- ⓤⓢ 'stɔː-, 'stɑː-, 'staʊ-, 'stoʊ-
Note: /'stəʊ.tᵊn ⓤⓢ 'stoʊ-/ in **Hodder & Stoughton**, the publishers.
stoup stuːp **-s** -s
Stour *in Suffolk, Essex:* stʊəʳ ⓤⓢ stʊr *in Kent:* stʊəʳ, staʊəʳ ⓤⓢ stʊr, staʊɚ *in Hampshire:* staʊəʳ, stʊəʳ ⓤⓢ staʊɚ, stʊr *in Warwickshire, Hereford &*

Worcestershire and Oxfordshire: staʊəʳ, stauəʳ (US) stauɚ, stoʊɚ *in Dorset:* staʊəʳ (US) staʊɚ
Stourbridge *in West Midlands:* ˈstaʊə.brɪdʒ, ˈstəʊə- (US) ˈstaʊɚ-, ˈstoʊɚ- *Common in Cambridge:* ˈstaʊə.brɪdʒ (US) ˈstaʊɚ-
Stourhead ˈstɔː.hed, ˈstaʊə- (US) ˈstɔːr-, ˈstaʊɚ-
Stourmouth ˈstaʊə.maʊθ, ˈstʊə- (US) ˈstaʊɚ-, ˈstʊr-
Stourport ˈstaʊə.pɔːt, ˈstʊə- (US) ˈstaʊɚ.pɔːrt, ˈstʊr-
Stourton *surname:* ˈstɜː.tᵊn (US) ˈstɝː- *in Hereford & Worcestershire:* ˈstɔː.tᵊn (US) ˈstɔːr- *in Wiltshire:* ˈstɜː.tᵊn, ˈstɔː- (US) ˈstɝː-, ˈstɔːr-
stout (S) staʊt **-s** -s **-er** -əʳ (US) ˈstaʊ.t̬ɚ **-est** -ɪst, -əst (US) ˈstaʊ.t̬ɪst, -t̬əst **-ly** -li **-ness** -nəs, -nɪs
stout-hearted ˌstaʊtˈhɑː.tɪd (US) -ˈhɑːr.t̬ɪd **-ly** -li **-ness** -nəs, -nɪs
stoutish ˈstaʊ.tɪʃ (US) -t̬ɪʃ
stove stəʊv (US) stoʊv **-s** -z
stovepipe ˈstəʊv.paɪp (US) ˈstoʊv- **-s** -s
stovetop ˈstəʊv.tɒp (US) ˈstoʊv.tɑːp **-s** -s
stow (S) stəʊ (US) stoʊ **-s** -z **-ing** -ɪŋ **-ed** -d **-age** -ɪdʒ
stowaway ˈstəʊ.əˌweɪ (US) ˈstoʊ- **-s** -z
Stowe stəʊ (US) stoʊ
Stowers staʊəz (US) staʊɚz
Stowey ˈstəʊ.i (US) ˈstoʊ-
Stowmarket ˈstəʊˌmɑː.kɪt (US) ˈstoʊˌmɑːr-
Stow-on-the-Wold ˌstəʊ.ɒn.ðəˈwəʊld (US) ˌstoʊ.ɑːn.ðəˈwoʊld
St. Pancras sᵊnʈˈpæŋ.krəs, sɪnt-, sᵊm- (US) seɪnt-, -ˈpæn-
St. Patrick sᵊnʈˈpæt.rɪk, sɪnt-, sᵊm- (US) seɪnt- **St. ˈPatrick's ˌDay**
St. Paul sᵊnʈˈpɔːl, sɪnt-, sᵊm- (US) seɪntˈpɑːl, -ˈpɔːl **-'s** -z
St. Peter sᵊnʈˈpiː.təʳ, sɪnt-, sᵊm- (US) seɪntˈpiː.t̬ɚ **-'s** -z
St. Petersburg sᵊnʈˈpiː.təz.bɜːg, sɪnt-, sᵊm- (US) seɪntˈpiː.t̬ɚz.bɝːg
Strabane strəˈbæn
strabismus strəˈbɪz.məs, stræbˈɪz- (US) strəˈbɪz-
Strabo ˈstreɪ.bəʊ (US) -boʊ
Strabolgi strəˈbəʊ.gi (US) -ˈboʊ-
Strachan strɔːn; ˈstræk.ən (US) strɑːn, strɔːn; ˈstræk.ən
Strachey ˈstreɪ.tʃi (US) -ki, -tʃi
Strad stræd **-s** -z
Strada® ˈstrɑː.də **-s** -z
straddl|e ˈstræd.l̩ **-es** -z **-ing** -ɪŋ, ˈstræd.lɪŋ **-ed** -d
Stradivari ˌstræd.ɪˈvɑː.ri, -əˈ- (US) ˌstrɑː.diˈvɑːr.i **-s** -z
Stradivarius ˌstræd.ɪˈveə.ri.əs, -əˈ-, -ˈvɑː- (US) -əˈver.i- **-es** -ɪz
straf|e streɪf, strɑːf (US) streɪf **-es** -s **-ing/s** -ɪŋ/z **-ed** -t
Strafford ˈstræf.əd (US) -ɚd
straggl|e ˈstræg.l̩ **-es** -z **-ing** -ɪŋ, ˈstræg.lɪŋ **-ed** -d **-er/s** -əʳ/z, ˈstræg.ləʳ/z (US) ˈ-l̩.ɚ/z, ˈ-lɚ/z
straggl|y ˈstræg.l̩|.i, ˈ-l|i **-iness** -ɪ.nəs, -ɪ.nɪs
Strahan strɔːn, strɑːn
straight streɪt **-er** -əʳ (US) ˈstreɪ.t̬ɚ **-est** -ɪst, -əst (US) ˈstreɪ.t̬ɪst, -t̬əst **-ness** -nəs, -nɪs ˌ**straight ˈface;** ˌ**straight and ˈnarrow**
straightaway ˌstreɪt.əˈweɪ (US) ˌstreɪt̬-
straightedg|e ˈstreɪt.edʒ (US) ˈstreɪt̬- **-es** -ɪz
straighten ˈstreɪ.tᵊn **-s** -z **-ing** -ɪŋ, ˈstreɪt.nɪŋ **-ed** -d
straight-|faced ˌstreɪtˈfeɪst **-facedly** -ˈfeɪ.sɪd.li *stress shift:* ˌstraight-faced ˈspeaker
straightforward ˌstreɪtˈfɔː.wəd (US) -ˈfɔːr.wɚd **-ly** -li **-ness** -nəs, -nɪs
straightjacket ˈstreɪtˌdʒæk.ɪt **-s** -s **-ing** -ɪŋ **-ed** -ɪd
straightlaced ˌstreɪtˈleɪst (US) ˈ-- **-ly** -ˈleɪ.sɪd.li **-ness** -nəs, -nɪs *stress shift, British only:* ˌstraightlaced ˈteacher
straightway ˈstreɪt.weɪ
strain (S) streɪn **-s** -z **-ing** -ɪŋ **-ed** -d **-er/s** -əʳ/z (US) -ɚ/z
strait (S) streɪt **-s** -s **-ened** -ᵊnd
straitjacket ˈstreɪtˌdʒæk.ɪt **-s** -s **-ing** -ɪŋ **-ed** -ɪd
straitlaced ˌstreɪtˈleɪst (US) ˈ-- **-ly** -ˈleɪ.sɪd.li **-ness** -nəs, -nɪs *stress shift, British only:* ˌstraitlaced ˈteacher
Straker ˈstreɪ.kəʳ (US) -kɚ
strand (S) strænd **-s** -z **-ing** -ɪŋ **-ed** -ɪd
Strang stræŋ
strang|e (S) streɪndʒ **-er** -əʳ (US) -ɚ **-est** -ɪst, -əst **-ely** -li **-eness** -nəs, -nɪs
stranger ˈstreɪn.dʒəʳ (US) -dʒɚ **-s** -z
Strangeways ˈstreɪndʒ.weɪz
Strangford ˈstræŋ.fəd (US) -fɚd
strangl|e ˈstræŋ.gl̩ **-es** -z **-ing** -ɪŋ, ˈstræŋ.glɪŋ **-ed** -d **-er/s** -əʳ/z (US) -ɚ/z
stranglehold ˈstræŋ.gl̩.həʊld (US) -hoʊld **-s** -z
strangu|late ˈstræŋ.gjə|.leɪt, -gjʊ- **-lates** -leɪts **-lating** -leɪ.tɪŋ (US) -leɪ.t̬ɪŋ **-lated** -leɪ.tɪd (US) -leɪ.t̬ɪd
strangulation ˌstræŋ.gjəˈleɪ.ʃᵊn, -gjʊˈ- **-s** -z
Strangways ˈstræŋ.weɪz
Stranraer strænˈrɑːʳ, strən- (US) -ˈrɑːr
strap stræp **-s** -s **-ping** -ɪŋ **-ped** -t **-per/s** -əʳ/z (US) -ɚ/z **-py** -i
strap|hang ˈstræp|.hæŋ **-hangs** -hæŋz **-hanging** -ˌhæŋ.ɪŋ **-hung** -hʌŋ **-hanger/s** -ˌhæŋ.əʳ/z (US) -ɚ/z
strapless ˈstræp.ləs, -lɪs
Strasb(o)urg ˈstræz.bɜːg, -bʊəg, -bɔːg (US) ˈstrɑːs.bʊrg, ˈstrɑːz-; ˈstræs.bɝːg
strata *(plur. of* **stratum***)* ˈstrɑː.tə, ˈstreɪ- (US) ˈstreɪ.t̬ə, ˈstræt̬.ə
stratagem ˈstræt.ə.dʒəm, ˈ-ɪ-, -dʒɪm, -dʒem (US) ˈstræt̬.ə.dʒəm **-s** -z
strategic strəˈtiː.dʒɪk, strætˈiː- (US) strəˈtiː- **-al** -ᵊl **-ally** -ᵊl.i, -li **Straˌtegic DeˈfenceˌIˌnitiative**
strategist ˈstræt.ə.dʒɪst, ˈ-ɪ- (US) ˈstræt̬.ə- **-s** -s
strateg|y ˈstræt.ə.dʒ|i, ˈ-ɪ- (US) ˈstræt̬.ə- **-ies** -iz
Stratford ˈstræt.fəd (US) -fɚd
Stratford-atte-Bowe ˌstræt.fədˌæt.ɪˈbəʊ, -ˈbəʊ.i; -ˌæt.əˈbəʊ.ə (US) -fɚdˌæt̬.əˈboʊ
Stratford-upon-Avon ˌstræt.fəd.ə.pɒnˈeɪ.vᵊn (US) -fɚd.ə.pɑːnˈ-, -vɑːn
strath stræθ **-s** -s
Strathaven ˈstreɪ.vᵊn
Strathavon stræθˈɑːn
Strathclyde stræθˈklaɪd *stress shift:* ˌStrathclyde ˈcampus
Strathcona stræθˈkəʊ.nə (US) -ˈkoʊ-
Strathearn stræθˈɜːn (US) -ˈɝːn
Strathmore stræθˈmɔːʳ (US) -ˈmɔːr
strathspey (S) stræθˈspeɪ **-s** -z
stratification ˌstræt.ɪ.fɪˈkeɪ.ʃᵊn, ˌ-ə- (US) ˌstræt̬.ə-
strati|fy ˈstræt.ɪ|.faɪ, ˈ-ə- (US) ˈstræt̬.ə- **-fies** -faɪz **-fying** -faɪ.ɪŋ **-fied** -faɪd
stratocruiser ˈstræt.əˌkruː.zəʳ (US) ˈstræt̬.əˌkruː.zɚ **-s** -z
Straton ˈstræt.ᵊn
stratosphere ˈstræt.əʊˌsfɪəʳ (US) ˈstræt̬.ə.sfɪr **-s** -z
stratospheric ˌstræt.əʊˈsfer.ɪk (US) ˌstræt̬.əˈsfɪr-, -ˈsfer-
Stratton ˈstræt.ᵊn
strat|um ˈstrɑː.t|əm, ˈstreɪ- (US) ˈstreɪ.t̬|əm, ˈstræt̬|.əm **-a** -ə
stratus ˈstreɪ.təs, ˈstrɑː- (US) ˈstreɪ.t̬əs, ˈstræt̬.əs
Straus(s) straʊs *as if German:* ʃtraʊs
Stravinsky strəˈvɪnt.ski
straw (S) strɔː (US) strɑː, strɔː **-s** -z **-y** -i ˌ**straw ˈpoll** (US) ˈ**straw ˌpoll;** ˌ**straw ˈvote** (US) ˈ**straw ˌvote;** ˌ**clutch at ˈstraws; the ˌstraw that ˌbreaks the ˌcamel's ˈback**
strawberr|y ˈstrɔː.bᵊr|.i, -br|i (US) ˈstrɑːˌber|.i, ˈstrɔː- **-ies** -iz ˌ**strawberry ˈblonde; ˈstrawberry ˌmark**
strawboard ˈstrɔː.bɔːd (US) ˈstrɑː.bɔːrd, ˈstrɔː-

Stress

A property of syllables which makes them stand out as more noticeable than others.

Examples for English

Stress is a large topic, which cannot be covered in its entirety here. However, some examples follow.

The position of stress can change the meaning or word class of a word, and so forms part of the phonological composition of the word, e.g.:

import (n)	/ˈɪm.pɔːt/	(US) /-pɔːrt/
import (v)	/ɪmˈpɔːt/	(US) /-ˈpɔːrt/
record (n)	/ˈrek.ɔːd/	(US) /-ɚd/
record (v)	/rɪˈkɔːd/	(US) /-ˈkɔːrd/

It is necessary to consider what factors make a syllable count as stressed. It seems likely that stressed syllables are produced with greater effort than unstressed, and that this effort is manifested in the air pressure generated in the lungs for producing the syllable and also in the articulatory movements in the vocal tract. These effects of stress produce in turn various audible results: one is 'pitch prominence', in which the stressed syllable stands out from its context (for example, being higher if its unstressed neighbours are low in PITCH, or lower if those neighbours are high; often a pitch glide such as a fall or rise is used to give greater pitch prominence). Another effect of stress is that stressed syllables tend to be longer – this is very noticeable in English, less so in some other languages. Also, stressed syllables tend to be louder than unstressed, though experiments have shown that differences in loudness alone are not very noticeable to most listeners. It has been suggested by many writers that the term 'accent' should be used to refer to some of the manifestations of stress (particularly pitch prominence), but the word, though widely used, has never acquired a distinct meaning of its own.

One of the areas in which there is little agreement is that of 'levels' of stress. Some descriptions of languages manage with just two levels (stressed and unstressed), while others use more. In English, one can argue that if one takes the word *indicator* as an example, the first syllable is the most strongly stressed, the third syllable is the next most strongly stressed and the second and fourth syllables are weakly stressed, or unstressed. This gives us three levels: it is possible to argue for more, though this rarely seems to give any practical benefit.

Stress shift

A change in the position of the stress in a word when that word is combined with others in a phrase.

Examples for English

The RHYTHM of English prefers patterns in which two stressed syllables do not come together. In order to avoid this, stress in some polysyllabic words may move to an earlier syllable when combined with another in a phrase, e.g.:

Heathrow	/hiːθˈrəʊ/	(US) /-ˈroʊ/
Heathrow Airport	/ˌhiːθ.rəʊ ˈeə.pɔːt/	(US) /-roʊ ˈer.pɔːrt/
academic	/ˌæk.əˈdem.ɪk/	
academic dress	/ˌæk.ə.dem.ɪk ˈdres/	

In this dictionary, words which change their stress in this way are shown with an example demonstrating the stress shift.

stray (S) streɪ **-s** -z **-ing** -ɪŋ **-ed** -d

streak striːk **-s** -s **-ing** -ɪŋ **-ed** -t

streak|y ˈstriː.k|i **-ier** -i.əʳ (US) -i.ɚ **-iest** -i.ɪst, -i.əst **-iness** -ɪ.nəs, -ɪ.nɪs **ˌstreaky ˈbacon**

stream striːm **-s** -z **-ing** -ɪŋ **-ed** -d

streamer ˈstriː.məʳ (US) -mɚ **-s** -z

streamlet ˈstriːm.lət, -lɪt (US) -lɪt **-s** -s

streamlin|e ˈstriːm.laɪn **-es** -z **-ing** -ɪŋ **-ed** -d

stream-of-consciousness ˌstriːm.əvˈkɒn.*t*ʃəs.nəs, -nɪs (US) -ˈkɑːn*t*.ʃəs-

Streatham ˈstret.əm (US) ˈstreţ-

Streatley ˈstriːt.li

Streep striːp

street (S) striːt **-s** -s **ˈstreet ˌcred; ˌstreet crediˈbility** (US) **ˈstreet crediˌbility; ˌstreet ˈtheatre/ˈtheater** (US) **ˈstreet ˌtheatre/ˌtheater; ˈstreet ˌvalue**

streetcar ˈstriːt.kɑːʳ (US) -kɑːr **-s** -z

streetlight ˈstriːt.laɪt **-s** -s

streetwalk|er ˈstriːtˌwɔː.k|əʳ (US) -ˌwɑː.k|ɚ, -ˌwɔː- **-ers** -əz (US) -ɚz **-ing** -ɪŋ

streetwise ˈstriːt.waɪz

St. Regis sᵊntˈriː.dʒɪs, sɪnt- (US) seɪnt-

Streisand ˈstraɪ.zænd, -sənd, -sænd

strength streŋ*k*θ **-s** -s

strengthen ˈstreŋ*k*.θᵊn **-s** -z **-ing** -ɪŋ, ˈstreŋ*k*θ.nɪŋ **-ed** -d **-er/s** -əʳ/z, ˈstreŋ*k*θ.nəʳ/z (US) ˈstreŋ*k*.θᵊn.ɚ/z, ˈstreŋ*k*θ.nɚ/z

strenuous ˈstren.ju.əs **-ly** -li **-ness** -nəs, -nɪs

strep strep **ˌstrep ˈthroat**

strepto|coccus ˌstrep.təʊ|ˈkɒk.əs (US) -tə|ˈkɑː.kəs **-cocci** -ˈkɒk.saɪ, -aɪ, -iː (US) -ˈkɑːk.saɪ, -aɪ **-coccal** -ˈkɒk.ᵊl (US) -ˈkɑː.kᵊl **-coccic** -ˈkɒk.ɪk (US) -ˈkɑː.kɪk

streptomycin ˌstrep.təʊˈmaɪ.sɪn (US) -təˈ-

stress stres **-es** -ɪz **-ing** -ɪŋ **-ed** -t

stressful ˈstres.fʊl, -fᵊl **-ly** -i **-ness** -nəs, -nɪs

stressless ˈstres.ləs, -lɪs **-ness** -nəs, -nɪs

stretch stretʃ **-es** -ɪz **-ing** -ɪŋ **-ed** -t **ˌstretch(ed) ˈlimo**

stretcher ˈstretʃ.əʳ (US) -ɚ **-s** -z **-ing** -ɪŋ **-ed** -d

stretcher-bearer ˈstretʃ.əˌbeə.rəʳ (US) -ɚˌber.ɚ **-s** -z

stretchmark 'stretʃ.mɑːk (US) -mɑːrk **-s** -s
stretch|y 'stretʃ|.i **-ier** -i.əʳ (US) -i.ɚ **-iest** -i.ɪst, -i.əst
Stretford 'stret.fəd (US) -fɚd
Strevens 'strev.ᵊnz
strew struː **-s** -z **-ing** -ɪŋ **-ed** -d **-n** -n
strewth struːθ
stri|a 'straɪ|.ə **-ae** -iː
stri|ate (*v.*) 'stri|.eɪt **-ates** -eɪts **-ating** -eɪ.tɪŋ (US) -eɪ.t̬ɪŋ **-ated** -eɪ.tɪd (US) -eɪ.t̬ɪd **stri,ated 'muscle**
striation straɪ'eɪ.ʃᵊn **-s** -z
stricken *(from* **strike***)* 'strɪk.ᵊn
Strickland 'strɪk.lənd
strict strɪkt **-er** -əʳ (US) -ɚ **-est** -ɪst, -əst **-ly** -li **-ness** -nəs, -nɪs
stricture 'strɪk.tʃəʳ (US) -tʃɚ **-s** -z
strid|e straɪd **-es** -z **-ing** -ɪŋ **strode** strəʊd (US) stroʊd **stridden** 'strɪd.ᵊn
stridency 'straɪ.dᵊnt.si
strident 'straɪ.dᵊnt **-ly** -li
StrideRite® 'straɪd.raɪt
stridu|late 'strɪd.jə|.leɪt, -jʊ- (US) 'strɪdʒ.ə-, '-ʊ- **-lates** -leɪts **-lating** -leɪ.tɪŋ (US) -leɪ.t̬ɪŋ **-lated** -leɪ.tɪd (US) -leɪ.t̬ɪd **-lation/s** ,--'leɪ.ʃᵊn/z
strife straɪf
strigil 'strɪdʒ.ɪl **-s** -z
strik|e straɪk **-es** -s **-ing/ly** -ɪŋ/li **struck** strʌk **stricken** 'strɪk.ᵊn **striker/s** 'straɪ.kəʳ/z (US) -kɚ/z **'strike ,pay; ,strike while the ,iron's 'hot**
strikebound 'straɪk.baʊnd
strikebreak|er 'straɪk,breɪ.k|əʳ (US) -k|ɚ **-ers** -əz (US) -ɚz **-ing** -ɪŋ
strikeout 'straɪ.kaʊt **-s** -s
strike-pay 'straɪk.peɪ
strim strɪm **-s** -z **-ming** -ɪŋ **-med** -d
Strimmer® 'strɪm.əʳ (US) -ɚ
Strindberg 'strɪnd.bɜːg, 'strɪm- (US) 'strɪnd.bɝːg
string strɪŋ **-s** -z **-ing** -ɪŋ **-ed** -d **strung** strʌŋ **stringer/s** 'strɪŋ.əʳ/z (US) -ɚ/z **,string 'bean; ,string quar'tet**
stringency 'strɪn.dʒᵊnt.si
stringendo strɪn'dʒen.dəʊ (US) -doʊ
stringent 'strɪn.dʒᵊnt **-ly** -li
stringer (S) 'strɪŋ.əʳ (US) -ɚ
Stringfellow 'strɪŋ,fel.əʊ (US) -oʊ
string-pull|ing 'strɪŋ,pʊl|.ɪŋ **-er/s** -əʳ/z (US) -ɚ/z
string|y 'strɪŋ|.i **-ier** -i.əʳ (US) -i.ɚ **-iest** -i.ɪst, -i.əst **-iness** -ɪ.nəs, -ɪ.nɪs
strip strɪp **-s** -s **-ping** -ɪŋ **-ped** -t **-per/s** -əʳ/z (US) -ɚ/z **,strip car'toon; 'strip ,club; 'strip ,light; ,strip 'poker**
strip|e straɪp **-es** -s **-ing** -ɪŋ **-ed** -t **-(e)y** -i **-iness** -ɪ.nəs, -ɪ.nɪs
striplight 'strɪp.laɪt **-s** -s **-ing** -ɪŋ
stripling 'strɪp.lɪŋ **-s** -z
strippagram 'strɪp.ə.græm **-s** -z
strip-search ,strɪp'sɜːtʃ, '-- (US) 'strɪp.sɝːtʃ **-es** -ɪz **-ing** -ɪŋ **-ed** -t
stripteas|e 'strɪp.tiːz, ,-'- **-er/s** -əʳ/z (US) -ɚ/z
striv|e straɪv **-es** -z **-ing/s** -ɪŋ/z **-ed** -d **strove** strəʊv (US) stroʊv **striven** 'strɪv.ᵊn **striver/s** 'straɪ.vəʳ/z (US) -vɚ/z
strobe strəʊb (US) stroʊb **-s** -z **'strobe ,light**
stroboscope 'strəʊ.bə.skəʊp, 'strɒb.ə- (US) 'stroʊ.bə.skoʊp, 'strɑː- **-s** -s
stroboscopic ,strəʊ.bə'skɒp.ɪk, ,strɒb.ə'- (US) ,stroʊ.bə'skɑː.pɪk, ,strɑː-
stroboscopy strəʊ'bɒs.kə.pi, strɒb'ɒs- (US) strə'bɑː.skə-
strode *(from* **stride***)* strəʊd (US) stroʊd
stroganoff 'strɒg.ə.nɒf (US) 'strɔː.gə.nɔːf, 'stroʊ- **-s** -s
strok|e strəʊk (US) stroʊk **-es** -s **-ing** -ɪŋ **-ed** -t
strokeplay 'strəʊk.pleɪ (US) 'stroʊk-
stroll strəʊl (US) stroʊl **-s** -z **-ing** -ɪŋ **-ed** -d **-er/s** -əʳ/z (US) -ɚ/z
Stromberg 'strɒm.bɜːg (US) 'strɑːm.bɝːg
Stromboli 'strɒm.bᵊl.i, -bʊ.li, -bəʊ-; strɒm'bəʊ.li (US) 'strɑːm.bə-, -'boʊ.li
Stromness 'strɒm.nes, 'strʌm- (US) 'strɑːm-, 'strʌm-
St. Ronan sᵊnt'rəʊ.nən, sɪnt- (US) seɪnt'roʊ-
strong (S) strɒŋ (US) strɑːŋ, strɔːŋ **-er** -gəʳ (US) -gɚ **-est** -gɪst, -gəst **-ly** -li **-ish** -ɪʃ **,strong 'language; 'strong ,room; 'strong ,point**
strong-arm 'strɒŋ.ɑːm (US) 'strɑːŋ.ɑːrm, 'strɔːŋ- **-s** -z **-ing** -ɪŋ **-ed** -d
strongbox 'strɒŋ.bɒks (US) 'strɑːŋ.bɑːks, 'strɔːŋ- **-es** -ɪz
stronghold 'strɒŋ.həʊld (US) 'strɑːŋ.hoʊld, 'strɔːŋ- **-s** -z
strong|man 'strɒŋ|.mæn **-men** -men
strong-minded ,strɒŋ'maɪn.dɪd (US) 'strɑːŋ-, 'strɔːŋ- **-ly** -li **-ness** -nəs, -nɪs *stress shift:* ,strong-minded 'person
strong-willed ,strɒŋ'wɪld **-ness** -nəs, -nɪs *stress shift:* ,strong-willed 'child
stronti|a 'strɒn.ti|.ə, *-t*ʃi-, '-*t*ʃ|ə, -tj|ə (US) 'strɑːn*t*.ʃi.|ə, '-ʃ|ə **-an** -ən **-um** -əm
Strood struːd
strop strɒp (US) strɑːp **-s** -s **-ping** -ɪŋ **-ped** -t
strophe 'strəʊ.fi, 'strɒf.i (US) 'stroʊ.fi **-s** -z
strophic 'strɒf.ɪk, 'strəʊ.fɪk (US) 'strɑː.fɪk, 'stroʊ-
stropp|y 'strɒp|.i (US) 'strɑː.p|i **-ier** -i.əʳ (US) -i.ɚ **-iest** -i.ɪst, -i.əst **-iness** -ɪ.nəs, -ɪ.nɪs
Stroud straʊd
Note: *As a surname, the pronunciation* /struːd/ *is sometimes heard.*
strove *(from* **strive***)* strəʊv (US) stroʊv
strow strəʊ (US) stroʊ **-s** -z **-ing** -ɪŋ **-ed** -d **-n** -n
struck *(from* **strike***)* strʌk
structural 'strʌk.tʃᵊr.ᵊl **-ly** -i **,structural engi'neer**
structural|ism 'strʌk.tʃᵊr.ᵊl|.ɪ.zᵊm **-ist/s** -ɪst/s
structur|e 'strʌk.tʃəʳ (US) -tʃɚ **-es** -z **-ing** -ɪŋ **-ed** -d
strudel 'struː.dᵊl *as if German:* 'ʃtruː- **-s** -z
struggl|e 'strʌg.l̩ **-es** -z **-ing** -ɪŋ, 'strʌg.lɪŋ **-ed** -d **-er/s** -əʳ/z, 'strʌg.ləʳ/z (US) '-l̩.ɚ/z, '-lɚ/z
strum strʌm **-s** -z **-ming** -ɪŋ **-med** -d **-mer/s** -əʳ/z (US) -ɚ/z
strumpet 'strʌm.pɪt **-s** -s
strung *(from* **string***)* strʌŋ **,strung 'out**
strung-up ,strʌŋ'ʌp
strut strʌt **-s** -s **-ting** -ɪŋ (US) 'strʌt̬.ɪŋ **-ted** -ɪd (US) 'strʌt̬.ɪd
struth struːθ
Struthers 'strʌð.əz (US) -ɚz
Strutt strʌt
Struwwelpeter ,struː.əl'piː.təʳ, 'struː.əl,piː-; ,struːl'piː-, '-,-- (US) 'struː.əl,piː.t̬ɚ
strychnine 'strɪk.niːn, -nɪn (US) -naɪn, -nɪn, -niːn
St. Salvator's sᵊn*t*.sæl'veɪ.təz, sɪnt- (US) seɪnt'sæl.və.tɔːrz
St. Simon sᵊn*t*'saɪ.mən, sɪn*t*- (US) seɪnt-
St. Swithin sᵊn*t*'swɪð.ɪn, sɪn*t*- (US) seɪnt-
St. Thomas sᵊn*t*'tɒm.əs, sɪn*t*- (US) seɪnt'tɑː.məs **-'s** -ɪz
St. Trinian's sᵊnt'trɪn.i.ənz
St. Tropez ,sæ̃n.trəʊ'peɪ (US) ,sæ̃n.trɔː'peɪ, -troʊ'-
Stuart stjʊət, 'stjuː.ət (US) 'stuː.ɚt, 'stjuː-, stʊrt **-s** -s
stub stʌb **-s** -z **-bing** -ɪŋ **-bed** -d
Stubbings 'stʌb.ɪŋz
Stubbington 'stʌb.ɪŋ.tən
stubbl|e 'stʌb.l̩ **-y** -i, 'stʌb.li
stubborn 'stʌb.ən (US) -ɚn **-er** -əʳ (US) -ɚ **-est** -ɪst, -əst **-ly** -li **-ness** -nəs, -nɪs
Stubbs stʌbz
stubb|y 'stʌb|.i **-ier** -i.əʳ (US) -i.ɚ **-iest** -i.ɪst, -i.əst **-iness** -ɪ.nəs, -ɪ.nɪs **-ies** -iz
stucco 'stʌk.əʊ (US) -oʊ **-(e)s** -z **-ing** -ɪŋ **-ed** -d
stuck *(from* **stick***)* stʌk

stuck-up ˌstʌkˈʌp
Stucley ˈstjuː.kli (US) ˈstuː-, ˈstjuː-
stud stʌd **-s** -z **-ding** -ɪŋ **-ded** -ɪd ˌ**stud ˈpoker**
studding-sail ˈstʌd.ɪŋ.seɪl *nautical pronunciation:* ˈstʌnt.sᵊl **-s** -z
Studebaker ˈstjuː.dɪˌbeɪ.kəʳ (US) ˈstuː.dəˌbeɪ.kɚ, ˈstjuː-
student ˈstjuː.dᵊnt (US) ˈstuː-, ˈstjuː- **-s** -s ˌ**student ˈgrant**; ˌ**student ˈloan**; ˌ**student ˈteacher**; ˌ**student ˈunion**
studentship ˈstjuː.dᵊnt.ʃɪp (US) ˈstuː-, ˈstjuː- **-s** -s
studio ˈstjuː.di.əʊ (US) ˈstuː.di.oʊ, ˈstjuː- **-s** -z ˌ**studio ˈflat** (US) ˈ**studio** ˌ**flat**
studious ˈstjuː.di.əs (US) ˈstuː-, ˈstjuː- **-ly** -li **-ness** -nəs, -nɪs
Studley ˈstʌd.li
stud|y ˈstʌd|.i **-ies** -iz **-ying** -i.ɪŋ **-ied** -id
stuff stʌf **-s** -s **-ing** -ɪŋ **-ed** -t ˌ**stuffed ˈshirt**
stuffing ˈstʌf.ɪŋ **-s** -z
stuff|y ˈstʌf|.i **-ier** -i.əʳ (US) -i.ɚ **-iest** -i.ɪst, -i.əst **-iness** -ɪ.nəs, -ɪ.nɪs **-ily** -ɪ.li
stultification ˌstʌl.tɪ.fɪˈkeɪ.ʃᵊn, -tə- (US) -t̬ə-
stulti|fy ˈstʌl.tɪ|.faɪ, -tə- (US) -t̬ə- **-fies** -faɪz **-fying** -ˌfaɪ.ɪŋ **-fied** -faɪd
stum stʌm
stumbl|e ˈstʌm.bl̩ **-es** -z **-ing** -ɪŋ, ˈstʌm.blɪŋ **-ed** -d **-er/s** -əʳ/z, ˈstʌm.bləʳ/z (US) ˈ-bl̩.ɚ/z, ˈ-blɚ/z ˈ**stumbling** ˌ**block**
stumm ʃtʊm
stump stʌmp **-s** -s **-ing** -ɪŋ **-ed** -t **-y** -i **-ier** -i.əʳ (US) -i.ɚ **-iest** -i.ɪst, -i.st **-iness** -ɪ.nəs, -ɪ.nɪs
stun stʌn **-s** -z **-ning/ly** -ɪŋ/li **-ned** -d ˈ**stun** ˌ**gun**
stung *(from* **sting***)* stʌŋ
stunk *(from* **stink***)* stʌŋk
stunner ˈstʌn.əʳ (US) -ɚ **-s** -z
stunt stʌnt **-s** -s **-ing** -ɪŋ (US) ˈstʌn.t̬ɪŋ **-ed** -ɪd (US) ˈstʌn.t̬ɪd
stunt|man ˈstʌnt|.mæn **-men** -men
stunt|woman ˈstʌnt|ˌwʊm.ən **-women** -ˌwɪm.ɪn
stupa ˈstuː.pə **-s** -z
stupe stjuːp (US) stuːp, stjuːp **-s** -s
stupefaction ˌstjuː.pɪˈfæk.ʃᵊn (US) ˌstuː.pəˈ-, ˌstjuː-
stupe|fy ˈstjuː.pɪ|.faɪ (US) ˈstuː.pə-, ˈstjuː- **-fies** -faɪz **-fying/ly** -ˌfaɪ.ɪŋ **-fied** -faɪd
stupendous stjuːˈpen.dəs (US) stuː-, stjuː- **-ly** -li **-ness** -nəs, -nɪs
stupid ˈstjuː.pɪd (US) ˈstuː-, ˈstjuː- **-er** -əʳ (US) -ɚ **-est** -ɪst, -əst **-ly** -li **-ness** -nəs, -nɪs
stupidit|y stjuːˈpɪd.ə.t|i, -ɪ.t|i (US) stuːˈpɪd.ə.t̬|i, stjuː- **-ies** -iz
stupor ˈstjuː.pəʳ (US) ˈstuː.pɚ, ˈstjuː-
sturd|y ˈstɜː.d|i (US) ˈstɝː- **-ier** -i.əʳ (US) -i.ɚ **-iest** -i.ɪst, -i.əst **-ily** -ɪ.li, -ᵊl.i **-iness** -ɪ.nəs, -ɪ.nɪs
sturgeon **(S)** ˈstɜː.dʒᵊn (US) ˈstɝː- **-s** -z
Sturminster ˈstɜː.mɪnt.stəʳ (US) ˈstɝː.mɪnt.stɚ
Sturm und Drang ˌʃtʊəm.ʊntˈdræŋ, ˌstʊərm- (US) ˌʃtʊrm.ʊntˈdrɑːŋ
Sturtevant ˈstɜː.tɪ.vənt, -tə-, -vænt (US) ˈstɝː.t̬ə-
stutt|er ˈstʌt|.əʳ (US) ˈstʌt̬|.ɚ **-ers** -əz (US) -ɚz **-ering** -ᵊr.ɪŋ **-ered** -əd (US) -ɚd **-erer/s** -ᵊr.əʳ/z (US) -ɚ.ɚ/z
Stuttgart ˈʃtʊt.gɑːt, ˈstʊt- (US) ˈstʌt.gɑːrt, ˈstʊt-, ˈʃtʊt-
Stuyvesant ˈstaɪ.vɪ.sənt, -və- (US) -və-
St. Valentine sᵊntˈvæl.ᵊn.taɪn (US) seɪnt- **St. ˈValentine's** ˌ**Day**
St. Vincent sᵊntˈvɪnt.sᵊnt, sɪnt- (US) seɪnt-
St. Vitus sᵊntˈvaɪ.təs, sɪnt- (US) seɪntˈvaɪ.t̬əs **-'s** -ɪz **St.** ˌ**Vitus's ˈdance** (US) **St. ˈVitus's** ˌ**dance**
st|y st|aɪ **-ies** -aɪz
Styal staɪəl
stye staɪ **-s** -z
stygian **(S)** ˈstɪdʒ.i.ən (US) -i.ən, ˈ-ən
styl|e staɪl **-es** -z **-ing** -ɪŋ **-ed** -d
styleless ˈstaɪl.ləs, -lɪs **-ly** -li **-ness** -nəs, -nɪs
Styles staɪlz
stylet ˈstaɪ.lət, -lɪt (US) -lɪt **-s** -s
stylish ˈstaɪ.lɪʃ **-ly** -li **-ness** -nəs, -nɪs
stylist ˈstaɪ.lɪst **-s** -s
stylistic staɪˈlɪs.tɪk **-s** -s **-ally** -ᵊl.i, -li
stylite ˈstaɪ.laɪt **-s** -s
Stylites staɪˈlaɪ.tiːz (US) -t̬iːz
stylization, **-isa-** ˌstaɪ.laɪˈzeɪ.ʃᵊn, -lɪˈ- (US) -lɪˈ-
styliz|e, **-is|e** ˈstaɪ.laɪz **-es** -ɪz **-ing** -ɪŋ **-ed** -d
stylograph ˈstaɪ.ləʊ.grɑːf, -græf (US) -lə.græf **-s** -s
stylographic ˌstaɪ.ləʊˈgræf.ɪk (US) -ləˈ-
styl|us ˈstaɪ.l|əs **-uses** -ə.sɪz **-i** -aɪ
stym|ie ˈstaɪ.m|i **-ies** -iz **-ying** -i.ɪŋ **-ied** -id
styptic ˈstɪp.tɪk ˌ**styptic ˈpencil**
styrax ˈstaɪə.ræks (US) ˈstaɪ- **-es** -ɪz
Styrofoam® ˈstaɪə.rəʊ.fəʊm (US) -rə.foʊm
Styron ˈstaɪə.rən
Styx stɪks
suable ˈsuː.ə.bl̩, ˈsjuː- (US) ˈsuː-
Suak|im ˈsuː.ɑː.k|ɪm, ˈswɑː.k|ɪm (US) ˈswɑː- **-in** -ɪn
suasion ˈsweɪ.ʒᵊn
sua sponte ˌsuː.ɑːˈspɒn.teɪ (US) ˌswɑːˈspɑːn.teɪ
suav|e swɑːv **-er** -əʳ (US) -ɚ **-est** -ɪst, -əst **-ely** -li **-eness** -nəs, -nɪs
suavity ˈswɑː.və.ti, ˈsweɪ-, ˈswæv.ə-, -ɪ.ti (US) ˈswɑː.və.t̬i, ˈswæv.ə-
sub- sʌb-
sub sʌb **-s** -z **-bing** -ɪŋ **-bed** -d
subacid sʌbˈæs.ɪd, ˌsʌb-
subacute ˌsʌb.əˈkjuːt
subalpine sʌbˈæl.paɪn, ˌsʌb- (US) -paɪn, -pɪn
subaltern ˈsʌb.ᵊl.tən (US) səbˈɔːl.tɚn, -ˈɑːl- **-s** -z
subaqua sʌbˈæk.wə, ˌsʌb- (US) -ˈɑː.kwə, -ˈæk.wə
subarctic sʌbˈɑːk.tɪk, ˌsʌb- (US) -ˈɑːrk-
Subaru® ˌsuː.bᵊrˈuː, ˈ--- (US) ˈsuː.bə.ruː **-s** -z
subatomic ˌsʌb.əˈtɒm.ɪk (US) -ˈtɑː.mɪk ˌ**subatomic ˈparticles**
sub-bass ˌsʌbˈbeɪs (US) ˈ-- **-es** -ɪz
Subbuteo® səˈbjuː.ti.əʊ, sʌbˈjuː-, -ˈuː- (US) sʌbˈjuː.t̬i.oʊ
subclass ˈsʌb.klɑːs (US) -klæs **-es** -ɪz
subclassification sʌbˌklæs.ɪ.fɪˈkeɪ.ʃᵊn, ˌsʌb.klæs-, -ə- (US) ˌsʌb.klæs- **-s** -z
subclassi|fy sʌbˈklæs.ɪ|.faɪ, ˌsʌb-, ˈ-ə- (US) ˈ-ə- **-fies** -faɪz **-fying** -faɪ.ɪŋ **-fied** -faɪd
subclinical sʌbˈklɪn.ɪ.kᵊl, ˌsʌb-
subcommittee ˈsʌb.kəˌmɪt.i, ˌsʌb.kəˈmɪt.i (US) -ˌmɪt̬- **-s** -z
subcompact ˌsʌbˈkɒm.pækt (US) -ˈkɑːm- **-s** -s
subconscious sʌbˈkɒn.tʃəs, ˌsʌb- (US) -ˈkɑːnt.ʃəs **-ly** -li **-ness** -nəs, -nɪs
subcontinent sʌbˈkɒn.tɪ.nənt, ˌsʌb- (US) ˈsʌbˌkɑːn.tᵊn.ənt, ˌsʌbˈkɑːn-
subcontinental ˌsʌb.kɒn.tɪˈnen.tᵊl, -təˈ- (US) -kɑːn.t̬ᵊnˈen.t̬ᵊl **-ly** -i
subcontract *(v.)* ˌsʌb.kənˈtrækt (US) sʌbˈkɑːn.trækt **-s** -s **-ing** -ɪŋ **-ed** -ɪd **-or/s** -əʳ/z (US) -ɚ/z
subcontract *(n.)* ˈsʌbˌkɒn.trækt (US) -ˌkɑːn-, -ˈkɑːn- **-s** -s
subculture ˈsʌbˌkʌl.tʃəʳ (US) -tʃɚ **-s** -z
subcutaneous ˌsʌb.kjuːˈteɪ.ni.əs
subdean sʌbˈdiːn, ˌsʌb- **-s** -z
subdivid|e ˌsʌb.dɪˈvaɪd, -dəˈ-, ˈ--ˌ- **-es** -z **-ing** -ɪŋ **-ed** -ɪd
subdivision ˌsʌb.dɪˈvɪʒ.ᵊn, -dəˈ-, ˈsʌb.dɪˌvɪʒ-, -də,- (US) ˌsʌb.dɪˈvɪʒ.ᵊn, ˈsʌb.dɪˌvɪʒ- **-s** -z
subdominant sʌbˈdɒm.ɪ.nənt, ˌsʌb- (US) -ˈdɑː.mə- **-s** -s
subdu|e səbˈdjuː (US) -ˈduː, -ˈdjuː **-es** -z **-ing** -ɪŋ **-ed** -d **-er/s** -əʳ/z (US) -ɚ/z **-able** -ə.bl̩
subed|it sʌbˈed|.ɪt, ˌsʌb- **-its** -ɪts **-iting** -ɪ.tɪŋ (US) -ɪ.t̬ɪŋ **-ited** -ɪ.tɪd (US) -ɪ.t̬ɪd
subeditor sʌbˈed.ɪ.təʳ, ˈsʌbˌed- (US) sʌbˈed.ɪ.t̬ɚ **-s** -z **-ship/s** -ʃɪp/s
subentr|y ˈsʌbˌen.tr|i, ˌ-ˈ-- **-ies** -iz

subfamil|y 'sʌbˌfæm.ᵊl|.i, -ɪ.l|i US -ᵊl|.i **-ies** -iz

subfusc 'sʌb.fʌsk, -'-

subgroup 'sʌb.gruːp **-s** -s

subhead sʌb'hed, ˌsʌb- US 'sʌb.hed **-s** -z

subheading 'sʌbˌhed.ɪŋ, -'-- US 'sʌbˌhed- **-s** -z

subhuman sʌb'hjuː.mən, ˌsʌb- **-s** -z

subito 'suː.bɪ.təʊ, 'sʊb.ɪ- US -t̬oʊ

subjacency sʌb'dʒeɪ.sᵊnt.si, səb- US sʌb-

subjacent sʌb'dʒeɪ.sᵊnt, səb- US sʌb-

subject (*n. adj.*) 'sʌb.dʒɪkt, -dʒekt **-s** -s **'subject ˌmatter**

subject (*v.*) səb'dʒekt, sʌb-; 'sʌb.dʒekt, -dʒɪkt US səb'dʒekt **-s** -s **-ing** -ɪŋ **-ed** -ɪd

subjection səb'dʒek.ʃᵊn

subjective səb'dʒek.tɪv, sʌb- US səb- **-ly** -li **-ness** -nəs, -nɪs

subjectivism səb'dʒek.tɪ.vɪ.zᵊm, sʌb- US səb-

subjectivity ˌsʌb.dʒek'tɪv.ə.ti, -dʒɪk-, -ɪ.ti US -ə.t̬i

subjoin sʌb'dʒɔɪn, ˌsʌb- US səb- **-s** -z **-ing** -ɪŋ **-ed** -d

sub judice ˌsʌb'dʒuː.dɪ.si, ˌsʊb-, -də-, -seɪ; US ˌsʌb'dʒuː.də.si

subju|gate 'sʌb.dʒə|.geɪt, -dʒʊ- **-gates** -geɪts **-gating** -geɪ.tɪŋ US -geɪ.t̬ɪŋ **-gated** -geɪ.tɪd US -geɪ.t̬ɪd **-gator/s** -geɪ.təʳ/z US -geɪ.t̬ɚ/s

subjugation ˌsʌb.dʒə'geɪ.ʃᵊn, -dʒʊ'-

subjunct 'sʌb.dʒʌŋ*k*t **-s** -s

subjunctive səb'dʒʌŋ*k*.tɪv **-s** -z

subleas|e (*n.*) 'sʌb.liːs **-s** -ɪz

subleas|e (*v.*) sʌb'liːs, ˌsʌb- **-es** -ɪz **-ing** -ɪŋ **-ed** -t

sublessee ˌsʌb.les'iː **-s** -z

sublessor ˌsʌb.les'ɔːʳ US -'ɔːr; sʌb'les.ɔːr **-s** -z

suble|t sʌb'le|t, ˌsʌb- US sʌb'le|t, ˌsʌb-, '-- **-ts** -ts **-tting** -tɪŋ US -t̬ɪŋ

sublieutenanc|y ˌsʌb.lef'ten.ən*t*.s|i, -ləf- US -luː- **-ies** -iz

sublieutenant ˌsʌb.lef'ten.ənt, -ləf'- US -luː'- **-s** -s

sublimate (*n.*) 'sʌb.lɪ.mət, -lə-, -mɪt, -meɪt US -meɪt, -mɪt **-s** -s

subli|mate (*v.*) 'sʌb.lɪ|.meɪt, -lə- **-mates** -meɪts **-mating** -meɪ.tɪŋ US -meɪ.t̬ɪŋ **-mated** -meɪ.tɪd US -meɪ.t̬ɪd

sublimation ˌsʌb.lɪ'meɪ.ʃᵊn, -lə'-

sublim|e sə'blaɪm **-ely** -li **-eness** -nəs, -nɪs **-es** -z **-ing** -ɪŋ **-ed** -d

subliminal sʌb'lɪm.ɪ.nᵊl, sə'blɪm-, -ᵊn.ᵊl US sʌb'lɪm.ᵊn- **-ly** -i

sublimity sə'blɪm.ə.ti, -ɪ.ti US -ə.t̬i

submachine gun ˌsʌb.mə'ʃiːnˌgʌn, -'ʃiːŋˌ- US -'ʃiːnˌ- **-s** -z

submarin|e ˌsʌb.mᵊr'iːn, '--- US 'sʌb.mə.riːn, ˌ--'- **-es** -z **-ing** -ɪŋ **-ed** -d

submariner sʌb'mær.ɪ.nəʳ, ˌsʌb-, -ᵊn.əʳ US ˌsʌb.mə'riː.nɚ, 'sʌb.məˌriː-; sʌb'mer.ᵊn.ɚ, -'mær- **-s** -z

submerg|e səb'mɜːdʒ, sʌb- US -'mɝːdʒ **-es** -ɪz **-ing** -ɪŋ **-ed** -d **-ence** -ᵊn*t*s

submers|e səb'mɜːs, sʌb'- US səb'mɝːs **-es** -ɪz **-ing** -ɪŋ **-ed** -t

submersible səb'mɜː.sə.bl̩, sʌb-, -sɪ- US -'mɝː.sə- **-s** -z

submersion səb'mɜː.ʃᵊn, sʌb- US -'mɝː.ʒᵊn, -ʃᵊn **-s** -z

submission səb'mɪʃ.ᵊn **-s** -z

submissive səb'mɪs.ɪv **-ly** -li **-ness** -nəs, -nɪs

sub|mit səb|'mɪt **-mits** -'mɪts **-mitting** -'mɪt.ɪŋ US -'mɪt̬.ɪŋ **-mitted** -'mɪt.ɪd US -'mɪt̬.ɪd

submultiple sʌb'mʌl.tɪ.pl̩, ˌsʌb- US -t̬ə- **-s** -z

subnormal sʌb'nɔː.mᵊl, ˌsʌb- US -'nɔːr- **-ly** -i

subnormality ˌsʌb.nɔː'mæl.ə.ti, -ɪ.ti US -nɔːr.mæl.ə.t̬i

subnuclear sʌb'njuː.kli.əʳ, ˌsʌb- US -'nuː.kli.ɚ, -'njuː-

suboctave 'sʌbˌɒk.tɪv US -ˌɑːk- **-s** -z

suborbital sʌb'ɔː.bɪ.tᵊl, ˌsʌb- US -'ɔːr.bə.t̬ᵊl

subordinate (*n. adj.*) sə'bɔː.dᵊn.ət, -dɪ.nət, -'bɔːd.nət, -nɪt US -'bɔːr.dᵊn.ɪt **-s** -s **-ly** -li

subordin|ate (*v.*) sə'bɔː.dɪ.n|eɪt US -'bɔːr.dᵊn|.eɪt **-ates** -eɪts **-ating** -eɪ.tɪŋ US -eɪ.t̬ɪŋ **-ated** -eɪ.tɪd US -eɪ.t̬ɪd

subordination səˌbɔː.dɪ'neɪ.ʃᵊn US -ˌbɔːr.dᵊn'eɪ-

subordinative sə'bɔː.dɪ.nə.tɪv, -dᵊn.ə- US -'bɔːr.dᵊn.eɪ.t̬ɪv, -dɪ.nə-

suborn sə'bɔːn, sʌb'ɔːn US sə'bɔːrn **-s** -z **-ing** -ɪŋ **-ed** -d **-er/s** -əʳ/z US -ɚ/z

subornation ˌsʌb.ɔː'neɪ.ʃᵊn US -ɔːr'-

Subotica sə'bɒt.ɪ.tʃə, sʊ- US 'suː.bɔː.tiːt.sə, -bə-

subplot 'sʌb.plɒt US -plɑːt **-s** -s

subpoena səb'piː.nə, sʌb-, sə- US sə- **-s** -z **-ing** -ɪŋ **-ed** -d

subpostmaster ˌsʌb'pəʊs*t*ˌmɑː.stəʳ US -'poʊs*t*ˌmæs.tɚ **-s** -z

subpostmistress ˌsʌb'pəʊs*t*ˌmɪs.trəs, -trɪs US -'poʊs*t*- **-es** -ɪz

subpostoffice ˌsʌb'pəʊstˌɒf.ɪs US -'poʊstˌɑː.fɪs **-s** -ɪz

subprefect sʌb'priː.fekt, ˌsʌb- **-s** -s

subprogram ˌsʌb'prəʊ.græm US 'sʌbˌproʊ-, -grəm **-s** -z

subrogation ˌsʌb.rəʊ'geɪ.ʃᵊn US -roʊ'-, -rə'-

subrogee ˌsʌb.rəʊ'giː US -roʊ'-, -rə'- **-s** -z

subrogor ˌsʌb.rəʊ'gɔːʳ US 'sʌb.rə.gɔːr **-s** -z

sub rosa ˌsʌb'rəʊ.zə, -zɑː US -'roʊ.zə

subroutine 'sʌb.ruːˌtiːn **-s** -z

subscrib|e səb'skraɪb **-es** -z **-ing** -ɪŋ **-ed** -d **-er/s** -əʳ/z US -ɚ/z

subscript 'sʌb.skrɪpt

subscription səb'skrɪp.ʃᵊn **-s** -z

subsection 'sʌbˌsek.ʃᵊn **-s** -z

subsequent 'sʌb.sɪ.kwənt, -sə- US -sɪ- **-ly** -li

subserv|e səb'sɜːv, sʌb- US səb'sɝːv **-es** -z **-ing** -ɪŋ **-ed** -d

subservien|ce səb'sɜː.vi.ən*t*|s, sʌb- US səb'sɝː- **-cy** -si

subservient səb'sɜː.vi.ənt, sʌb- US səb'sɝː- **-ly** -li

subset 'sʌb.set **-s** -s

subsid|e səb'saɪd **-es** -z **-ing** -ɪŋ **-ed** -ɪd

subsidence səb'saɪ.dᵊn*t*s; 'sʌb.sɪ.dᵊn*t*s, -sə- **-s** -ɪz

subsidiarity səbˌsɪd.i'ær.ə.ti, -ɪ.ti US -'er.ə.t̬i, -'ær-

subsidiar|y səb'sɪd.i.ᵊr|.i US -er-, -ɚ- **-ies** -iz **-ily** -ᵊl.i, -ɪ.li

subsidization ˌsʌb.sɪ.daɪ'zeɪ.ʃᵊn, -sə- US -dɪ'- **-s** -z

subsidiz|e, -is|e 'sʌb.sɪ.daɪz, -sə- US -sə- **-es** -ɪz **-ing** -ɪŋ **-ed** -d

subsid|y 'sʌb.sɪ.d|i, -sə- US -sə- **-ies** -iz

sub silentio ˌsʌb.sɪ'len.ti.əʊ US ˌsʌb.sɪ'len.ti.oʊ, -'len*t*.ʃi-

subsist səb'sɪst **-s** -s **-ing** -ɪŋ **-ed** -ɪd

subsistence səb'sɪs.tᵊn*t*s **sub'sistence ˌlevel**

subsoil 'sʌb.sɔɪl **-s** -z

subsonic sʌb'sɒn.ɪk, ˌsʌb- US -'sɑː.nɪk

subspecies 'sʌbˌspiː.ʃiːz, -ʃɪz, -siːz, -sɪz US -ʃiːz, -siːz

substanc|e 'sʌb.stᵊn*t*s **-es** -ɪz **-less** -ləs, -lɪs

substandard sʌb'stæn.dəd, ˌsʌb- US -dɚd

substantial səb'stæn.*t*ʃᵊl, -'stɑːn- US -'stæn*t*.ʃᵊl **-ly** -i **-ness** -nəs, -nɪs

substantiality səbˌstæn.*t*ʃi'æl.ə.ti, -ˌstɑːn-, -ɪ.ti US -ˌstæn*t*.ʃi'æl.ə.t̬i

substanti|ate səb'stæn.*t*ʃi|.eɪt, -'stɑːn-, -'stæn*t*.si-, -'stɑːn*t*- US -'stæn*t*.ʃi- **-ates** -eɪts **-ating** -eɪ.tɪŋ US -eɪ.t̬ɪŋ **-ated** -eɪ.tɪd US -eɪ.t̬ɪd

substantiation səbˌstæn.*t*ʃi'eɪ.ʃᵊn, -ˌstɑːn-, -ˌstæn*t*.si'-, -ˌstɑːn*t*- US -ˌstæn*t*.ʃi'-

substantival ˌsʌb.stᵊn'taɪ.vᵊl

substantive (*n.*) 'sʌb.stᵊn.tɪv US -t̬ɪv **-s** -z

substantive (*adj.*) 'sʌb.stᵊn.tɪv; səb'stæn- US -t̬ɪv **-s** -z **-ly** -li **-ness** -nəs, -nɪs

Note: In British English, generally /səb'stæn.tɪv/ when applied to rank, pay, etc.

substation 'sʌbˌsteɪ.ʃᵊn **-s** -z

substitutable 'sʌb.stɪ.tjuː.tə.bl̩, ˌsʌb.stɪ'tjuː- ⓊⓈ 'sʌb.stə.tuː.t̬ə-, -tjuː-

substitu|te 'sʌb.stɪ.tjuː|t ⓊⓈ -stə.tuː|t, -tjuː|t **-tes** -ts **-ting** -tɪŋ ⓊⓈ -t̬ɪŋ **-ted** -tɪd ⓊⓈ -t̬ɪd

substitution ˌsʌb.stɪ'tjuː.ʃᵊn ⓊⓈ -stə'tuː-, -'tjuː- **-s** -z

substitutional ˌsʌb.stɪ'tjuː.ʃᵊn.ᵊl, -'tjuːʃ.nᵊl ⓊⓈ -stə'tuː.ʃᵊn.ᵊl, -'tjuː- **-ly** -i

substitutive 'sʌb.stɪ.tjuː.tɪv ⓊⓈ -stə.tuː.t̬ɪv, -tjuː-

substrate 'sʌb.streɪt **-s** -s

substratosphere sʌb'stræt.əʊˌsfɪəʳ, -'strɑː.təʊ- ⓊⓈ -'stræt̬.ə.sfɪr **-s** -z

substrat|um sʌb'strɑː.t|əm, -'streɪ-, '-ˌ-- ⓊⓈ 'sʌbˌstreɪ.t̬|əm, -ˌstræt̬|.əm **-a** -ə

substructure 'sʌbˌstrʌk.tʃəʳ ⓊⓈ -tʃɚ **-s** -z

subsum|e səb'sjuːm ⓊⓈ -'suːm **-es** -z **-ing** -ɪŋ **-ed** -d

subsystem 'sʌbˌsɪs.təm, -tɪm ⓊⓈ -təm **-s** -z

subtangent sʌb'tæn.dʒᵊnt, ˌsʌb- **-s** -s

subtenancy sʌb'ten.ənt.si, ˌsʌb-, 'sʌbˌten- ⓊⓈ sʌb'ten-, ˌsʌb-

subtenant sʌb'ten.ᵊnt, ˌsʌb-, '-ˌ-- ⓊⓈ 'sʌbˌten- **-s** -s

subtend səb'tend, sʌb- **-s** -z **-ing** -ɪŋ **-ed** -ɪd

subterfug|e 'sʌb.tə.fjuːdʒ ⓊⓈ -tɚ- **-es** -ɪz

subterrane|an ˌsʌb.tᵊr'eɪ.ni|.ən ⓊⓈ -tə'reɪ- **-ous** -əs

subtext 'sʌb.tekst **-s** -s

subtil(e) 'sʌt.ᵊl ⓊⓈ 'sʌt̬.ᵊl; 'sʌb.tɪl

subtility sʌb'tɪl.ə.ti, -ɪ.ti ⓊⓈ -ə.t̬i

subtiliz|e, -is|e 'sʌt.ᵊl.aɪz, -ɪ.laɪz ⓊⓈ 'sʌt̬.ᵊl.aɪz, 'sʌb.tɪ.laɪz **-es** -ɪz **-ing** -ɪŋ **-ed** -d

subtilty 'sʌt.ᵊl.ti, -ɪl- ⓊⓈ 'sʌt̬.ᵊl.t̬i, 'sʌb.tɪl-

subtitl|e 'sʌbˌtaɪ.tl̩, -'-- ⓊⓈ 'sʌbˌtaɪ.t̬l̩ **-es** -z **-ing** -ɪŋ **-ed** -d

subtl|e 'sʌt.l̩ ⓊⓈ 'sʌt̬- **-er** -əʳ, 'sʌt.ləʳ ⓊⓈ 'sʌt̬.l̩.ɚ, 'sʌt.lɚ **-est** -ɪst, -əst, 'sʌt.lɪst, -ləst ⓊⓈ 'sʌt̬.l̩.ɪst, -əst, 'sʌt.lɪst, -ləst **-y** -i **-eness** -nəs, -nɪs

subtlet|y 'sʌt.l̩.t|i ⓊⓈ 'sʌt̬.l̩.t̬|i **-ies** -iz

subtopia sʌb'təʊ.pi.ə ⓊⓈ -'toʊ-

subtotal 'sʌbˌtəʊ.tᵊl, -'--, ˌ-'-- ⓊⓈ 'sʌbˌtoʊ.t̬ᵊl **-s** -s **-(l)ing** -ɪŋ **-(l)ed** -d

subtract səb'trækt **-s** -s **-ing** -ɪŋ **-ed** -ɪd

subtraction səb'træk.ʃᵊn **-s** -z

subtrahend 'sʌb.trə.hend **-s** -z

subtropic sʌb'trɒp.ɪk ⓊⓈ -'trɑː.pɪk **-s** -s

subtropical sʌb'trɒp.ɪ.kᵊl, ˌsʌb- ⓊⓈ -'trɑː.pɪ-

suburb 'sʌb.ɜːb ⓊⓈ -ɝːb **-s** -z

suburban sə'bɜː.bᵊn ⓊⓈ -'bɝː-

suburbanite sə'bɜː.bᵊn.aɪt ⓊⓈ -'bɝː- **-s** -s

suburbanization, -isa- səˌbɜː.bᵊn.aɪ'zeɪ.ʃᵊn ⓊⓈ -ˌbɝː-, -ɪ'-

suburbaniz|e, -is|e sə'bɜː.bᵊn.aɪz ⓊⓈ -'bɝː- **-es** -ɪz **-ing** -ɪŋ **-ed** -d

suburbia sə'bɜː.bi.ə ⓊⓈ -'bɝː-

subvariet|y 'sʌb.vᵊrˌaɪ.ə.t|i ⓊⓈ -vəˌraɪ.ə.t̬|i **-ies** -iz

subvention səb'ven.tʃᵊn, sʌb- ⓊⓈ -'vent.ʃᵊn **-s** -z

subversion səb'vɜː.ʃᵊn, sʌb-, -ʒᵊn ⓊⓈ -'vɝː.ʒᵊn, -ʃᵊn

subversive səb'vɜː.sɪv, sʌb- ⓊⓈ -'vɝː- **-ly** -li **-ness** -nəs, -nɪs

sub|vert sʌb|'vɜːt, səb- ⓊⓈ -'vɝːt **-verts** -'vɜːts ⓊⓈ -'vɝːts **-verting** -'vɜː.tɪŋ ⓊⓈ -'vɝː.t̬ɪŋ **-verted** -'vɜː.tɪd ⓊⓈ -'vɝː.t̬ɪd

subway 'sʌb.weɪ **-s** -z

subzero sʌb'zɪə.rəʊ, ˌsʌb- ⓊⓈ -'zɪr.oʊ, -'ziː.roʊ

succeed sək'siːd **-s** -z **-ing** -ɪŋ **-ed** -ɪd

succès de scandale sjuːkˌseɪ.dəˌskɑ̃ːn'dɑːl *as if French:* sʊk-

success sək'ses **-es** -ɪz **suc'cess ˌstory**

successful sək'ses.fᵊl, -fʊl **-ly** -li **-ness** -nəs, -nɪs

succession sək'seʃ.ᵊn **-s** -z

successive sək'ses.ɪv **-ly** -li

successor sək'ses.əʳ ⓊⓈ -ɚ **-s** -z

succinct sək'sɪŋkt, sʌk- **-ly** -li **-ness** -nəs, -nɪs

succ|or 'sʌk|.əʳ ⓊⓈ -ɚ **-ors** -əz ⓊⓈ -ɚz **-oring** -ᵊr.ɪŋ **-ored** -əd ⓊⓈ -ɚd

succory 'sʌk.ᵊr.i

succotash 'sʌk.ə.tæʃ

Succoth 'sʌk.əs, 'sʊk-; sʊ'kɒt ⓊⓈ 'sʊk.əs; 'suː.kɔːt

succ|our 'sʌk|.əʳ ⓊⓈ -ɚ **-ours** -əz ⓊⓈ -ɚz **-ouring** -ᵊr.ɪŋ **-oured** -əd ⓊⓈ -ɚd

succub|a 'sʌk.jə.b|ə, -jʊ- **-ae** -iː

succub|us 'sʌk.jə.b|əs, -jʊ- **-i** -aɪ

succulence 'sʌk.jə.lənts, -jʊ-

succulent 'sʌk.jə.lənt, -jʊ- **-ly** -li

succumb sə'kʌm **-s** -z **-ing** -ɪŋ **-ed** -d

such *usual form:* sʌtʃ *occasional weak form:* sətʃ

such-and-such 'sʌtʃ.ᵊn.sʌtʃ

Suchard® 'suː.ʃɑːd, -ʃɑː ⓊⓈ -ʃɑːrd

suchlike 'sʌtʃ.laɪk

suck sʌk **-s** -s **-ing** -ɪŋ **-ed** -t **'sucking ˌpig**

sucker 'sʌk.əʳ ⓊⓈ -ɚ **-s** -z

suckl|e 'sʌk.l̩ **-es** -z **-ing** -ɪŋ, 'sʌk.lɪŋ **-ed** -d

suckling (S) 'sʌk.lɪŋ, '-l̩.ɪŋ **-s** -z

sucre *currency:* 'suː.kreɪ **-s** -z

Sucre *in Bolivia:* 'suː.kreɪ

sucrose 'suː.krəʊs, 'sjuː-, -krəʊz ⓊⓈ 'suː.kroʊs

suction 'sʌk.ʃᵊn **'suction ˌpad; 'suction ˌpump**

Sudan suː'dɑːn, sʊ-, -'dæn ⓊⓈ suː'dæn

Sudanese ˌsuː.dᵊn'iːz

Sudanic suː'dæn.ɪk, sʊ- ⓊⓈ suː-

sudarium sjuː'deə.ri.əm, suː- ⓊⓈ suː'der.i- **-s** -z

sudatory 'sjuː.də.tᵊr.i, 'suː- ⓊⓈ 'suː.də.tɔːr-

Sudbury 'sʌd.bᵊr.i, 'sʌb- ⓊⓈ 'sʌd.ber-, -bɚ-

sudd sʌd

sudden 'sʌd.ᵊn **-est** -ɪst, -əst **-ly** -li **-ness** -nəs, -nɪs **ˌsudden 'death**

Sudetenland sʊ'deɪ.tᵊn.lænd ⓊⓈ suː-

sudorific ˌsjuː.dᵊr'ɪf.ɪk, ˌsuː-, -dɒr'- ⓊⓈ ˌsuː.də'rɪf- **-s** -s

suds sʌdz

suds|y 'sʌd.z|i **-ier** -i.əʳ ⓊⓈ -i.ɚ **-iest** -i.ɪst, -i.əst **-iness** -ɪ.nəs, -ɪ.nɪs

su|e (S) suː, sjuː ⓊⓈ suː **-es** -z **-ing** -ɪŋ **-ed** -d

suede sweɪd

su|et 'suː|.ɪt, 'sjuː- ⓊⓈ 'suː- **-ety** -ɪ.ti ⓊⓈ -ɪ.t̬i **ˌsuet 'pudding**

Suetonius swɪ'təʊ.ni.əs, swiː-, ˌsjuː.ɪ'-, ˌsuː-, -iː'- ⓊⓈ swiː'toʊ-, swɪ-

Suez 'suː.ɪz, 'sjuː- ⓊⓈ suː'ez, '-- **ˌSuez Ca'nal**

suff|er 'sʌf|.əʳ ⓊⓈ -ɚ **-ers** -əz ⓊⓈ -ɚz **-ering/s** -ᵊr.ɪŋ/z **-ered** -əd ⓊⓈ -ɚd **-erer/s** -ᵊr.əʳ/z ⓊⓈ -ɚ.ɚ/z **-erable** -ᵊr.ə.bl̩ **-erance** -ᵊr.ᵊnts

suffic|e sə'faɪs **-es** -ɪz **-ing** -ɪŋ **-ed** -t

sufficiency sə'fɪʃ.ᵊnt.si

sufficient sə'fɪʃ.ᵊnt **-ly** -li

suffix (*v.*) 'sʌf.ɪks; sə'fɪks, sʌf'ɪks ⓊⓈ 'sʌf.ɪks; sə'fɪks **-es** -ɪz **-ing** -ɪŋ **-ed** -t

suffix (*n.*) 'sʌf.ɪks **-es** -ɪz

suffo|cate 'sʌf.ə|.keɪt **-cates** -keɪts **-cating/ly** -keɪ.tɪŋ/li ⓊⓈ -keɪ.t̬ɪŋ/li **-cated** -keɪ.tɪd ⓊⓈ -keɪ.t̬ɪd

suffocation ˌsʌf.ə'keɪ.ʃᵊn

Suffolk 'sʌf.ək

suffragan 'sʌf.rə.gən **-s** -z

suffrag|e 'sʌf.rɪdʒ **-es** -ɪz

suffragette ˌsʌf.rə'dʒet **-s** -s

suffragist 'sʌf.rə.dʒɪst **-s** -s

suffus|e sə'fjuːz, sʌf'juːz ⓊⓈ sə'fjuːz **-es** -ɪz **-ing** -ɪŋ **-ed** -d

suffusion sə'fjuː.ʒᵊn, sʌf'juː- ⓊⓈ sə'fjuː- **-s** -z

Suf|i 'suː.f|i **-is** -iz **-ism** -ɪ.zᵊm **-ic** -ɪk

sug|ar 'ʃʊg|.əʳ ⓊⓈ -ɚ **-ars** -əz ⓊⓈ -ɚz **-aring** -ᵊr.ɪŋ **-ared** -əd ⓊⓈ -ɚd **'sugar ˌbeet; 'sugar ˌdaddy**

Suffixes

A suffix is an element placed at the end of a word to modify or alter its meaning. Unlike PREFIXES, it is possible for a suffix to alter the original pronunciation of the word stem on to which they are affixed. This depends on whether the suffix is stress-neutral, pre-stressed or stress-attracting.

Examples

Some suffixes do not change the pronunciation of the word stem. These are known as 'stress-neutral' suffixes. Some words containing stress-neutral suffixes follow:

eleventh	/ɪˈlev.ənᵗθ/	
dramatise	/ˈdræm.ə.taɪz/	(US) /ˈdrɑː.mə-/
fatherhood	/ˈfɑː.ðə.hʊd/	(US) /-ðɚ-/
happily	/ˈhæp.ɪ.li/	

A suffix which attracts stress is known as 'stress-attracting'. Some words containing stress-attracting suffixes follow:

engineer	/ˌen.dʒɪˈnɪəʳ/	(US) /-ˈnɪr/
Japanese	/ˌdʒæp.əˈniːz/	
nineteen	/ˌnaɪnˈtiːn/	

A 'pre-stressed' suffix is one in which the affixation of the suffix causes stress to be assigned to a syllable before it. There are a number of different types of pre-stressed suffixes. Here is an example where the stress falls on the syllable immediately before the suffix:

despotic	/dɪˈspɒt.ɪk/	(US) /desˈpɑː.t̬ɪk/

In other words, the stress falls two syllables ahead of the suffix:

insecticide	/ɪnˈsek.tɪ.saɪd/

There are also 'mixed' pre-stressed suffixes where the stress may fall either one or two syllables before the suffix.

The suffix *–ation* is actually a combination of the stress-neutral *–ate* and the pre-stressed suffix *–ion*. In words containing *–ation*, the strongest stress is always on the penultimate syllable, e.g.:

condemnation	/ˌkɒn.demˈneɪ.ʃən/ (US) /ˌkɑːn-/

sugarcane ˈʃʊg.ə.keɪn (US) ˈ-ɚ- **-s** -z
sugarloa|f ˈʃʊg.ə.ləʊ|f (US) -ɚ.loʊ|f **-ves** -vz ˌ**Sugarloaf 'Mountain**
sugarplum ˈʃʊg.ə.plʌm (US) ˈ-ɚ- **-s** -z
sugar|y ˈʃʊg.ᵊr|.i **-iest** -i.ɪst, -i.əst **-iness** -ɪ.nəs, -ɪ.nɪs
suggest səˈdʒest (US) səg- **-s** -s **-ing** -ɪŋ **-ed** -ɪd
suggestibility səˌdʒes.təˈbɪl.ə.ti, -tɪˈ-, -ɪ.ti (US) səgˌdʒes.təˈbɪl.ə.t̬i
suggestible səˈdʒes.tə.bl̩, -tɪ- (US) səgˈdʒes.tə-
suggestion səˈdʒes.tʃən, -ˈdʒeʃ- (US) səgˈdʒes- **-s** -z
suggestive səˈdʒes.tɪv (US) səgˈdʒes- **-ly** -li **-ness** -nəs, -nɪs
Suharto sʊˈhɑː.təʊ (US) -ˈhɑːr.t̬oʊ
suicidal ˌsuː.ɪˈsaɪ.dᵊl, ˌsjuː- (US) ˌsuː.əˈ- **-ly** -i
suicide ˈsuː.ɪ.saɪd, ˈsjuː- (US) ˈsuː.ə- **-s** -z
sui generis ˌsjuː.iːˈdʒen.ᵊr.ɪs, ˌsuː-, -aɪˈ-, -ˈgen- (US) ˌsuː.iːˈdʒen-, -aɪˈ-
sui juris ˌsjuː.iːˈdʒʊə.rɪs, ˌsuː-, -aɪˈ-, -ˈdʒɔː- (US) ˌsuː.iːˈdʒʊr.ɪs, -aɪˈ-
suit suːt, sjuːt (US) suːt **-s** -s **-ing/s** -ɪŋ/z (US) ˈsuː.t̬ɪŋ/z **-ed** -ɪd (US) ˈsuː.t̬ɪd
suitability ˌsuː.təˈbɪl.ə.ti, ˌsjuː-, -ɪ.ti (US) ˌsuː.t̬əˈbɪl.ə.t̬i
suitab|le ˈsuː.tə.bl|̩, ˈsjuː- (US) ˈsuː.t̬ə- **-ly** -li **-leness** -l̩.nɪs, -nəs
suitcas|e ˈsuːt.keɪs, ˈsjuːt- (US) ˈsuːt- **-es** -ɪz
suite swiːt **-s** -s
suitor ˈsuː.təʳ, ˈsjuː- (US) ˈsuː.t̬ɚ **-s** -z
sukiyaki ˌsuː.kiˈjæk.i (US) -ˈjɑː.ki, ˌsʊk.iˈ-
Sukkot(h) ˈsʊk.ɒt
Sukkur ˈsʊk.ʊə (US) ˈsʊk.ʊr, -ɚ
Sulawesi ˌsuː.ləˈweɪ.si, -læˈ- (US) -lɑːˈ-
sulcal ˈsʌl.kᵊl
sulcalization, -isa- ˌsʌl.kᵊl.aɪˈzeɪ.ʃᵊn, -lɪˈ- (US) -lɪˈ-
sulcaliz|e, -is|e ˈsʌl.kᵊl.aɪz **-es** -ɪz **-ing** -ɪŋ **-ed** -d
sulcate ˈsʌl.keɪt, -kɪt, -kət (US) -keɪt
Suleiman ˌsʊl.eɪˈmɑːn, ˌsuː.leɪˈ-, -lɪˈ-, ˈ--- (US) ˈsuː.leɪ.mɑːn, -lə-
sulfanilamide ˌsʌl.fəˈnɪl.ə.maɪd (US) -maɪd, -mɪd
sulfate ˈsʌl.feɪt, -fɪt, -fət (US) -feɪt **-s** -s
sulf|ide ˈsʌl.f|aɪd **-ides** -aɪdz **-ite/s** -aɪt/s
sulfonamide sʌlˈfɒn.ə.maɪd (US) -ˈfɑː.nə-, -mɪd **-s** -z
sulfur ˈsʌl.fəʳ (US) -fɚ
sulfureous sʌlˈfjʊə.ri.əs, -ˈfjɔː- (US) -ˈfjʊr.i-
sulfuretted ˈsʌl.fjʊ.ret.ɪd, -fjʊə-, -fə- (US) -fjə.ret̬-, -fə-, -fjʊ-
sulfuric sʌlˈfjʊə.rɪk, -ˈfjɔː- (US) -ˈfjʊr.ɪk **sulˌfuric 'acid**
sulfurous ˈsʌl.fᵊr.əs, -fjʊ.rəs (US) -fɚ-; sʌlˈfjʊr.əs
sulfury ˈsʌl.fᵊr.i
Suliman ˌsʊl.ɪˈmɑːn, ˈ--- (US) ˈsuː.leɪ.mɑːn, -lə-
sulk sʌlk **-s** -s **-ing** -ɪŋ **-ed** -t **-y** -i **-ier** -i.əʳ (US) -i.ɚ **-iest** -i.ɪst, -i.əst **-ily** -ɪ.li, -ᵊl.i **-iness** -ɪ.nəs, -ɪ.nɪs
Sulla ˈsʌl.ə, ˈsʊl- (US) ˈsʌl-
sullen ˈsʌl.ən **-est** -ɪst, -əst **-ly** -li **-ness** -nəs, -nɪs
Sullivan ˈsʌl.ɪ.vᵊn
Sullom Voe ˌsuː.ləmˈvəʊ, ˌsʌl.əmˈ- (US) -ˈvoʊ
sull|y (S) ˈsʌl|.i **-ies** -iz **-ying** -i.ɪŋ **-ied** -id
sulphanilamide ˌsʌl.fəˈnɪl.ə.maɪd (US) -maɪd, -mɪd
sulphate ˈsʌl.feɪt, -fɪt, -fət (US) -feɪt **-s** -s
sulph|ide ˈsʌl.f|aɪd **-ides** -aɪdz **-ite/s** -aɪt/s
sulphonamide sʌlˈfɒn.ə.maɪd (US) -ˈfɑː.nə-, -mɪd **-s** -z
sulphur ˈsʌl.fəʳ (US) -fɚ
sulphureous sʌlˈfjʊə.ri.əs, -ˈfjɔː- (US) -ˈfjʊr.i-
sulphuretted ˈsʌl.fjʊ.ret.ɪd, -fjʊə-, -fə- (US) -fjə.ret̬-, -fə-, -fjʊ-
sulphuric sʌlˈfjʊə.rɪk, -ˈfjɔː- (US) -ˈfjʊr.ɪk **sulˌphuric 'acid**
sulphurous ˈsʌl.fᵊr.əs, -fjʊ.rəs (US) -fɚ.əs; sʌlˈfjʊr.əs
sulphury ˈsʌl.fᵊr.i
sultan (S) ˈsʌl.tᵊn **-s** -z
sultana *kind of raisin:* sᵊlˈtɑː.nə, sʌl- (US) sʌlˈtæn.ə, -ˈtɑː.nə **-s** -z
sultana (S) *sultan's wife, mother, etc.:* sʌlˈtɑː.nə, sʊl- (US) sʌlˈtæn.ə, -ˈtɑː.nə **-s** -z
sultanate ˈsʌl.tə.nət, -neɪt, -nɪt (US) -tᵊn.ɪt, -eɪt **-s** -s
sultr|y ˈsʌl.tr|i **-ier** -i.əʳ (US) -i.ɚ **-iest** -i.ɪst, -i.əst **-ily** -ᵊl.i, -ɪ.li **-iness** -ɪ.nəs, -ɪ.nɪs

Sulu 'suː.luː
sum sʌm **-s** -z **-ming** -ɪŋ **-med** -d ˌ**sum** ˈ**total**
sumac(h) 'ʃuː.mæk, 'suː-, 'sjuː- (US) 'suː.mæk, 'ʃʊm.æk **-s** -s
Sumatr|a sʊ'mɑː.tr|ə, sjʊ- (US) suː- **-an/s** -ən/z
Sumburgh 'sʌm.bᵊr.ə
Sumerian sʊ'mɪə.ri.ən, suː-, sjʊ-, sjuː-, -'meə- (US) suː'mɪr.i-, -'mer-
summa cum laude ˌsʊm.ɑː.kʊm'laʊ.deɪ (US) -əˌ-, -di; ˌsʌm.əˌkʌm'lɔː.di
summariz|e, is|e 'sʌm.ᵊr.aɪz (US) -ə.raɪz **-es** -ɪz **-ing** -ɪŋ **-ed** -d
summar|y 'sʌm.ᵊr|.i **-ies** -iz **-ily** -ᵊl.i, -ɪ.li **-iness** -ɪ.nəs, -ɪ.nɪs
summat 'sʌm.ət
summation sʌm'eɪ.ʃᵊn, sə'meɪ- (US) sə'meɪ- **-s** -z
summer (S) 'sʌm.əʳ (US) -ɚ **-s** -z **-ing** -ɪŋ **-ed** -d **-like** -laɪk ˌ**summer** ˈ**pudding**; ˈ**summer** ˌ**school**; ˈ**Summer** ˌ**Time**
Summerfield 'sʌm.ə.fiːld (US) '-ɚ- **-s** -z
summerhou|se 'sʌm.ə.haʊ|s (US) '-ɚ- **-ses** -zɪz
Summers 'sʌm.əz (US) -ɚz
summertime 'sʌm.ə.taɪm (US) '-ɚ-
Summerville 'sʌm.ə.vɪl (US) '-ɚ-
summery 'sʌm.ᵊr.i
summing-up ˌsʌm.ɪŋ'ʌp **summings-up** ˌsʌm.ɪŋz'-
summit 'sʌm.ɪt **-s** -s
summiteer ˌsʌm.ɪ'tɪəʳ (US) -tɪɚ **-s** -z
summon 'sʌm.ən **-s** -z **-ing** -ɪŋ **-ed** -d **-er/s** -əʳ/z (US) -ɚ/z
summons 'sʌm.ənz **-es** -ɪz **-ing** -ɪŋ **-ed** -d
Sumner 'sʌm.nəʳ (US) -nɚ
sumo 'suː.məʊ (US) -moʊ ˈ**sumo** ˌ**wrestler**, ˌ**sumo** ˈ**wrestler**; ˌ**sumo** ˈ**wrestling**, ˈ**sumo** ˌ**wrestling**
sump sʌmp **-s** -s
sumpter (S) 'sʌmp.təʳ (US) -tɚ **-s** -z
sumptuary 'sʌmp.tjʊə.ri, -tjʊ-, -tʃʊə-, -tʃʊ- (US) -tʃu.er.i
sumptuous 'sʌmp.tʃu.əs, -tju- (US) -tʃu- **-ly** -li **-ness** -nəs, -nɪs
sun (S) sʌn **-s** -z **-ning** -ɪŋ **-ned** -d ˌ**Sun** ˈ**City**; ˈ**sun** ˌ**deck**; ˈ**sun** ˌ**hat**; ˈ**sun** ˌ**lounge**
Sun. *(abbrev. for* **Sunday***)* 'sʌn.deɪ, -di
sunbaked 'sʌn.beɪkt, 'sʌm- (US) 'sʌn-
sunba|th 'sʌn.bɑː|θ, 'sʌm- (US) 'sʌn.bæ|θ **-ths** -ðz
sunbath|e 'sʌn.beɪð, 'sʌm- (US) 'sʌn- **-es** -z **-ing** -ɪŋ **-ed** -d **-er/s** -əʳ/z (US) -ɚ/z
sunbeam (S) 'sʌn.biːm, 'sʌm- (US) 'sʌn- **-s** -z
sunbed 'sʌn.bed, 'sʌm- (US) 'sʌn- **-s** -z
sun-belt 'sʌn.belt, 'sʌm- **-s** -s
sunblind 'sʌn.blaɪnd, 'sʌm- (US) 'sʌn- **-s** -z
sunblock 'sʌn.blɒk, 'sʌm- (US) 'sʌn.blɑːk **-s** -s
sun-bonnet 'sʌnˌbɒn.ɪt, 'sʌm- (US) 'sʌnˌbɑː.nɪt **-s** -s
sunburn 'sʌn.bɜːn, 'sʌm- (US) 'sʌn.bɝːn **-s** -z **-ed** -d **-t** -t
sunburst 'sʌn.bɜːst, 'sʌm- (US) 'sʌn.bɝːst **-s** -s
Sunbury 'sʌn.bᵊr.i, 'sʌm- (US) 'sʌn-, -beri
Sunda 'sʌn.də
sundae 'sʌn.deɪ (US) -di, -deɪ **-s** -z
Sundanese ˌsʌn.də'niːz
Sunday 'sʌn.deɪ, -di **-s** -z ˌ**Sunday** ˈ**best**; ˈ**Sunday** ˌ**school**; **in a** ˌ**month of** ˈ**Sundays**
sund|er 'sʌn.d|əʳ (US) -d|ɚ **-ers** -əz (US) -ɚz **-ering** -ᵊr.ɪŋ **-ered** -əd (US) -ɚd
Sunderland 'sʌn.dᵊl.ənd (US) -dɚ.lənd
sundial 'sʌn.daɪl **-s** -z
sundown 'sʌn.daʊn
sundowner 'sʌnˌdaʊ.nəʳ (US) -nɚ **-s** -z
sundrenched 'sʌn.drentʃt
sundress 'sʌn.dres **-es** -ɪz
sun-dried 'sʌn.draɪd
sundr|y 'sʌn.dr|i **-ies** -iz
sunfish 'sʌn.fɪʃ
sunflower 'sʌn.flaʊəʳ (US) -flaʊɚ **-s** -z ˈ**sunflower** ˌ**seed**
sung *(from* **sing***)* sʌŋ
Sung sʊŋ, sʌŋ (US) sʊŋ
sunglasses 'sʌnˌglɑː.sɪz, 'sʌŋ- (US) 'sʌnˌglæs.ɪs
sunk *(from* **sink***)* sʌŋk
sunken *(from* **sink***)* 'sʌŋ.kən
sunkissed 'sʌn.kɪst, 'sʌŋ-
sunlamp 'sʌn.læmp **-s** -s
sunless 'sʌn.ləs, -lɪs
sun|light 'sʌn|.laɪt **-lit** -lɪt
sunlounger 'sʌnˌlaʊn.dʒəʳ (US) -dʒɚ **-s** -z
Sunn|i 'sʊn|.i, 'sʌn- (US) 'sʊn- **-ite/s** -aɪt/s **-ism** -ɪ.zᵊm ˌ**Sunni** ˈ**Muslim**
Sunningdale 'sʌn.ɪŋ.deɪl
sunn|y 'sʌn|.i **-ier** -i.əʳ (US) -i.ɚ **-iest** -i.ɪst, -i.əst **-iness** -ɪ.nəs, -ɪ.nɪs ˌ**sunny-side** ˈ**up**
Sunnyside 'sʌn.i.saɪd
sunproof 'sʌn.pruːf, 'sʌm- (US) 'sʌn-
sunray 'sʌn.reɪ **-s** -z
sunris|e 'sʌn.raɪz **-es** -ɪz
sunroo|f 'sʌn.ruː|f (US) -ruː|f, -rʊ|f **-fs** -fs **-ves** -vz
sunscreen 'sʌn.skriːn **-s** -z **-ing** -ɪŋ
sunset 'sʌn.set **-s** -s
sunshade 'sʌn.ʃeɪd **-s** -z
sunshin|e 'sʌn.ʃaɪn **-y** -i
sunspot 'sʌn.spɒt (US) -spɑːt **-s** -s
sunstroke 'sʌn.strəʊk (US) -stroʊk **-s** -s
suntan 'sʌn.tæn **-s** -z **-ned** -d
suntrap 'sʌn.træp **-s** -s
sunup 'sʌn.ʌp **-s** -s
sun-worship 'sʌnˌwɜː.ʃɪp (US) -ˌwɝː- **-per/s** -əʳ/z (US) -ɚ/z
suo nomine ˌsuː.əʊ'nəʊ.mɪ.neɪ, ˌsjuː-, -'nɒm.ɪ- (US) ˌsuː.oʊ'noʊ.mɪ-, -'nɑː-
sup sʌp **-s** -s **-ping** -ɪŋ **-ped** -t
super- 'suː.pəʳ-, 'sjuː- (US) 'suː.pɚ-
super 'suː.pəʳ, 'sjuː- (US) 'suː.pɚ **-s** -z
superab|le 'suː.pᵊr.ə.b|l̩, 'sjuː- (US) 'suː- **-ly** -li **-leness** -l̩.nəs, -nɪs
superabundan|ce ˌsuː.pᵊr.ə'bʌn.dən|*t*s, ˌsjuː- (US) ˌsuː- **-t/ly** -t/li
superannu|ate ˌsuː.pᵊr'æn.ju|.eɪt, ˌsjuː- (US) ˌsuː- **-ates** -eɪts **-ating** -eɪ.tɪŋ (US) -eɪ.t̬ɪŋ **-ated** -eɪ.tɪd (US) -eɪ.t̬ɪd
superannuation ˌsuː.pᵊrˌæn.ju'eɪ.ʃᵊn, ˌsjuː- (US) ˌsuː- **-s** -z
superb suː'pɜːb, sjuː-, sʊ-, sjʊ- (US) sə'pɝːb, sʊ-, suː- **-ly** -li **-ness** -nəs, -nɪs
Superbowl 'suː.pə.bəʊl, 'sjuː- (US) 'suː.pɚ.boʊl
superbug 'suː.pə.bʌg, 'sjuː- (US) 'suː.pɚ- **-s** -z
supercargo 'suː.pəˌkɑː.gəʊ, 'sjuː- (US) 'suː.pɚˌkɑːr.goʊ **-es** -z
supercharg|e 'suː.pə.tʃɑːdʒ, 'sjuː- (US) 'suː.pɚ.tʃɑːrdʒ **-es** -ɪz **-ing** -ɪŋ **-ed** -d
supercharger 'suː.pəˌtʃɑː.dʒəʳ, 'sjuː- (US) 'suː.pɚˌtʃɑːr.dʒɚ **-s** -z
superchip 'suː.pə.tʃɪp, 'sjuː- (US) 'suː.pɚ- **-s** -s
supercilious ˌsuː.pə'sɪl.i.əs, ˌsjuː- (US) ˌsuː.pɚ'- **-ly** -li **-ness** -nəs, -nɪs
supercomputer 'suː.pə.kəmˌpjuː.təʳ, 'sjuː- (US) 'suː.pɚ.kəmˌpjuː.t̬ɚ **-s** -z
superconductivity ˌsuː.pəˌkɒn.dʌk'tɪv.ə.ti, ˌsjuː-, -dək'-, -ɪ.ti (US) ˌsuː.pɚˌkɑːn.dʌk'tɪv.ə.t̬i
superconduct|or 'suː.pə.kənˌdʌk.t|əʳ, 'sjuː- (US) 'suː.pɚ.kənˌdʌk.t|ɚ **-ors** -əz (US) -ɚz **-ing** -ɪŋ
supercool ˌsuː.pə'kuːl, ˌsjuː- (US) ˌsuː.pɚ'- **-s** -z **-ing** -ɪŋ **-ed** -d
Superdrug® 'suː.pə.drʌg, 'sjuː- (US) 'suː.pɚ-
super-duper ˌsuː.pə'duː.pəʳ, ˌsjuː- (US) ˌsuː.pɚ'duː.pɚ
superego ˌsuː.pᵊr'iː.gəʊ, ˌsjuː-, -'eg.əʊ (US) ˌsuː.pɚ'iː.goʊ **-s** -z
supererogation ˌsuː.pᵊrˌer.əʊ'geɪ.ʃᵊn, ˌsjuː- (US) ˌsuː.pɚˌer.ə'-
supererogatory ˌsuː.pᵊr.er'ɒg.ə.tᵊr.i, ˌsjuː-, -ɪ'rɒg- (US) ˌsuː.pɚ.ɪ'rɑː.gə.tɔːr-
superfici|al ˌsuː.pə'fɪʃ|.ᵊl, ˌsjuː- (US) ˌsuː.pɚ'- **-ally** -ᵊl.i **-alness** -ᵊl.nəs, -nɪs

superficialit|y ˌsuː.pəˌfɪʃ.iˈæl.ə.t|i, ˌsjuː-, -ɪ.t|i (US) ˌsuː.pɚˌfɪʃ.iˈæl.ə.ţ|i **-ies** -iz
superficies ˌsuː.pəˈfɪʃ.iːz, ˌsjuː-, -i.iːz (US) ˌsuː.pɚˈfɪʃ.i.iːz, ˈ-iːz
superfine ˌsuː.pəˈfaɪn, ˌsjuː-, ˈ--- (US) ˈsuː.pɚ.faɪn, ˌ--ˈ-
superfix ˈsuː.pə.fɪks, ˈsjuː- (US) ˈsuː.pɚ-
superfluit|y ˌsuː.pəˈfluː.ə.t|i, ˌsjuː-, -ɪ.t|i (US) ˌsuː.pɚˈfluː.ə.ţ|i **-ies** -iz
superfluous suːˈpɜː.flu.əs, sjuː-, sʊ-, sjʊ- (US) -ˈpɝː- **-ly** -li **-ness** -nəs, -nɪs
superglottal ˌsuː.pəˈglɒt.əl, ˌsjuː- (US) ˌsuː.pɚˈglɑː.ţəl
Superglue® ˈsuː.pə.gluː, ˈsjuː- (US) ˈsuː.pɚ-
supergrass ˈsuː.pə.grɑːs, ˈsjuː- (US) ˈsuː.pɚ.græs **-es** -ɪz
supergravity ˌsuː.pəˈgræv.ə.ti, ˌsjuː-, -ɪ.ti (US) ˌsuː.pɚˈgræv.ə.ţi
supergun ˈsuː.pə.gʌn, ˈsjuː- (US) ˈsuː.pɚ- **-s** -z
superhead ˈsuː.pə.hed, ˈsjuː-, ˈsuː.pɚ- **-s** -z
superheat (*v.*) ˌsuː.pəˈhiːt, ˌsjuː- (US) ˌsuː.pɚˈ- **-s** -s **-ing** -ɪŋ **-ed** -ɪd
superheat (*n.*) ˈsuː.pə.hiːt, ˈsjuː- (US) ˈsuː.pɚ-
superhero ˈsuː.pəˌhɪə.rəʊ, ˈsjuː-, ˌsuː.pəˈhɪə.rəʊ (US) ˈsuː.pɚ- **-es** -z
superheterodyne ˌsuː.pəˈhet.ər.əʊ.daɪn, ˌsjuː- (US) ˌsuː.pɚˈheţ.ə.roʊ.daɪn **-s** -z
superhighway ˌsuː.pəˈhaɪ.weɪ, ˌsjuː-, ˈsuː.pəˌhaɪ.weɪ (US) ˈsuː.pɚ- **-s** -z **ˌinformation ˈsuperˌhighway, ˌinformation ˌsuperˈhighway**
superhuman ˌsuː.pəˈhjuː.mən, ˌsjuː- (US) ˌsuː.pɚˈ- **-ly** -li **-ness** -nəs, -nɪs
superimpos|e ˌsuː.pər.ɪmˈpəʊz, ˌsjuː- (US) ˌsuː.pɚ.ɪmˈpoʊz **-es** -ɪz **-ing** -ɪŋ **-ed** -d
superintend ˌsuː.pər.ɪnˈtend, ˌsjuː- (US) ˌsuː.pɚ- **-s** -z **-ing** -ɪŋ **-ed** -ɪd **-ence** -ənts
superintendenc|y ˌsuː.pər.ɪnˈten.dənt.s|i, ˌsjuː- (US) ˌsuː.pɚ- **-ies** -iz
superintendent ˌsuː.pər.ɪnˈten.dənt, ˌsjuː- (US) ˌsuː.pɚ- **-s** -s
superior (S) suːˈpɪə.ri.əʳ, sjuː-, sʊ-, sjʊ-, sə- (US) səˈpɪr.i.ɚ, sʊ- **-s** -z
superiorit|y suːˌpɪə.riˈɒr.ə.t|i, sjuː-, sʊ-, sjʊ-, sə-, -ɪ.t|i (US) səˌpɪr.iˈɔːr.ə.ţ|i, sʊ- **-ies** -iz
superlative suːˈpɜː.lə.tɪv, sjuː-, sʊ-, sjʊ- (US) səˈpɝː.lə.ţɪv, sʊ-, suː- **-s** -z **-ly** -li **-ness** -nəs, -nɪs
Superleague ˈsuː.pə.liːg, ˈsjuː- (US) ˈsuː.pɚ- **-s** -z
super|man (S) ˈsuː.pə|.mæn, ˈsjuː- (US) ˈsuː.pɚ- **-men** -men
supermarket ˈsuː.pəˌmɑː.kɪt, ˈsjuː- (US) ˈsuː.pɚˌmɑːr- **-s** -s
supermodel ˈsuː.pəˌmɒd.əl, ˈsjuː- (US) ˈsuː.pɚˌmɑː.dəl **-s** -z
supernal suːˈpɜː.nəl, sjuː-, sʊ-, sjʊ- (US) səˈpɝː-, sʊ-, suː-
supernatural ˌsuː.pəˈnætʃ.ər.əl, ˌsjuː-, ˌsjʊ.pəˈ-, ˌsʊ-, -ʊ.rəl (US) ˌsuː.pɚˈnæt.ʃɚ.əl **-ly** -i **-ness** -nəs, -nɪs
supernormal ˌsuː.pəˈnɔː.məl, ˌsjuː- (US) ˌsuː.pɚˈnɔːr-
supernov|a ˌsuː.pəˈnəʊ.v|ə, ˌsjuː- (US) ˌsuː.pɚˈnoʊ- **-ae** -iː **-as** -əz
supernumerar|y ˌsuː.pəˈnjuː.mər.ər|.i, ˌsjuː- (US) ˌsuː.pɚˈnuː.mə.rer|.i, -ˈnjuː- **-ies** -iz
superoctave ˈsuː.pərˌɒk.tɪv, ˈsjuː- (US) ˈsuː.pɚˌɑːk- **-s** -z
superordinate ˌsuː.pərˈɔː.dən.ət, ˌsjuː-, -dɪ.nət, -nɪt, -neɪt (US) ˌsuː.pɚˈɔːr.dən.ɪt **-s** -s
superpos|e ˌsuː.pəˈpəʊz, ˌsjuː- (US) ˌsuː.pɚˈpoʊz **-es** -ɪz **-ing** -ɪŋ **-ed** -d
superposition ˌsuː.pə.pəˈzɪʃ.ən, ˌsjuː- (US) ˌsuː.pɚ- **-s** -z
superpower ˈsuː.pəˌpaʊəʳ, ˈsjuː- (US) ˈsuː.pɚˌpaʊɚ **-s** -z
superpriorit|y ˌsuː.pə.praɪˈɒr.ə.t|i, ˌsjuː-, -ɪ.t|i (US) ˌsuː.pɚ.praɪˈɔːr.ə.ţ|i **-ies** -iz
supersaver ˈsuː.pəˌseɪ.vəʳ, ˈsjuː- (US) ˈsuː.pɚˌseɪ.vɚ **-s** -z
superscrib|e ˌsuː.pəˈskraɪb, ˌsjuː-, ˈ--- (US) ˈsuː.pɚ.skraɪb **-es** -z **-ing** -ɪŋ **-ed** -d
superscript ˈsuː.pə.skrɪpt, ˈsjuː- (US) ˈsuː.pɚ-
superscription ˌsuː.pəˈskrɪp.ʃən, ˌsjuː- (US) ˌsuː.pɚˈ- **-s** -z
supersed|e ˌsuː.pəˈsiːd, ˌsjuː- (US) ˌsuː.pɚˈ- **-es** -z **-ing** -ɪŋ **-ed** -ɪd
supersession ˌsuː.pəˈseʃ.ən, ˌsjuː- (US) ˌsuː.pɚˈ-
supersonic ˌsuː.pəˈsɒn.ɪk, ˌsjuː- (US) ˌsuː.pɚˈsɑː.nɪk **-s** -z **-ally** -əl.i, -li
superstar ˈsuː.pə.stɑːʳ, ˈsjuː- (US) ˈsuː.pɚ.stɑːr **-s** -z **-dom** -dəm
superstate ˈsuː.pə.steɪt, ˈsjuː- (US) ˈsuː.pɚ- **-s** -s
superstition ˌsuː.pəˈstɪʃ.ən, ˌsjuː- (US) ˌsuː.pɚˈ- **-s** -z
superstitious ˌsuː.pəˈstɪʃ.əs, ˌsjuː- (US) ˌsuː.pɚˈ- **-ly** -li **-ness** -nəs, -nɪs
superstore ˈsuː.pə.stɔːʳ, ˈsjuː- (US) ˈsuː.pɚ.stɔːr **-s** -z
superstring ˈsuː.pə.strɪŋ, ˈsjuː- (US) ˈsuː.pɚ- **-s** -z
superstructure ˈsuː.pəˌstrʌk.tʃəʳ, ˈsjuː- (US) ˈsuː.pɚˌstrʌk.tʃɚ **-s** -z
supertanker ˈsuː.pəˌtæŋ.kəʳ, ˈsjuː- (US) ˈsuː.pɚˌtæŋ.kɚ **-s** -z
supertax ˈsuː.pə.tæks, ˈsjuː-, ˌ--ˈ- (US) ˈsuː.pɚ.tæks **-es** -ɪz
supertitle ˈsuː.pəˌtaɪ.tl̩, ˈsjuː- (US) ˈsuː.pɚ- **-s** -z
supertonic ˌsuː.pəˈtɒn.ɪk, ˌsjuː- (US) ˌsuː.pɚˈtɑː.nɪk **-s** -s
superven|e ˌsuː.pəˈviːn, ˌsjuː- (US) ˌsuː.pɚˈ- **-es** -z **-ing** -ɪŋ **-ed** -d
supervis|e ˈsuː.pə.vaɪz, ˈsjuː- (US) ˈsuː.pɚ- **-es** -ɪz **-ing** -ɪŋ **-ed** -d
supervision ˌsuː.pəˈvɪʒ.ən, ˌsjuː- (US) ˌsuː.pɚˈ- **-s** -z
supervisor ˈsuː.pə.vaɪ.zəʳ, ˈsjuː- (US) ˈsuː.pɚ.vaɪ.zɚ **-s** -z
supervisory ˌsuː.pəˈvaɪ.zər.i, ˌsjuː-, ˈsuː.pə.vaɪ-, ˈsjuː- (US) ˌsuː.pɚˈvaɪ.zɚ-
super|woman ˈsuː.pə|ˌwʊm.ən, ˈsjuː- (US) ˈsuː.pɚˌ- **-women** -ˌwɪm.ɪn
supine (*n.*) ˈsuː.paɪn, ˈsjuː- (US) ˈsuː- **-s** -z
supine (*adj.*) ˈsuː.paɪn, ˈsjuː-, -ˈ- (US) suːˈpaɪn, ˈ-- **-ly** -li **-ness** -nəs, -nɪs
supper ˈsʌp.əʳ (US) -ɚ **-s** -z **-less** -ləs, -lɪs
sup|plant sə|ˈplɑːnt (US) -ˈplænt **-plants** -ˈplɑːnts (US) -ˈplænts **-planting** -ˈplɑːn.tɪŋ (US) -ˈplæn.ţɪŋ **-planted** -ˈplɑːn.tɪd (US) -ˈplæn.ţɪd **-planter/s** -ˈplɑːn.təʳ/z (US) -ˈplæn.ţɚ/z
supp|le ˈsʌp|.l̩ **-leness** -l̩.nəs, -nɪs **-ly** -li, -l̩.i
supplement (*n.*) ˈsʌp.lɪ.mənt, -lə- (US) -lə- **-s** -s
supple|ment (*v.*) ˈsʌp.lɪ|.ment, -lə-, ˌ--ˈ- (US) ˈsʌp.lə- **-ments** -ments **-menting** -men.tɪŋ (US) -men.ţɪŋ **-mented** -men.tɪd (US) -men.ţɪd
supplemental ˌsʌp.lɪˈmen.təl, -ləˈ- (US) -ləˈmen.ţəl
supplementary ˌsʌp.lɪˈmen.tər.i, -ləˈ-, ˈ-tri (US) -ləˈmen.ţɚ.i *stress shift, see compound:* **ˌsupplementary ˈbenefit**
supplementation ˌsʌp.lɪ.menˈteɪ.ʃən, -lə- (US) -lə-
suppliant ˈsʌp.li.ənt **-s** -s **-ly** -li
supplicant ˈsʌp.lɪ.kənt, -lə- (US) -lə- **-s** -s
suppli|cate ˈsʌp.lɪ|.keɪt, -lə- (US) -lə- **-cates** -keɪts **-cating/ly** -keɪ.tɪŋ/li (US) -keɪ.ţɪŋ/li **-cated** -keɪ.tɪd (US) -keɪ.ţɪd
supplication ˌsʌp.lɪˈkeɪ.ʃən, -ləˈ- (US) -ləˈ- **-s** -z
supplicatory ˈsʌp.lɪ.kə.tər.i, -lə-, -keɪ- (US) -lə.kə.tɔːr-
supplier səˈplaɪ.əʳ (US) -ɚ **-s** -z
suppl|y səˈpl|aɪ **-ies** -aɪz **-ying** -aɪ.ɪŋ **-ied** -aɪd **supˌply and deˈmand; supˈply ˌteacher**
supply-sid|e səˈplaɪ.saɪd **-er/s** -əʳ/z (US) -ɚ/z

sup|port sə|ˈpɔːt ⓤⓢ -ˈpɔːrt **-ports** -ˈpɔːts ⓤⓢ -ˈpɔːrts **-porting** -ˈpɔː.tɪŋ ⓤⓢ -ˈpɔːr.t̬ɪŋ **-ported** -ˈpɔː.tɪd ⓤⓢ -ˈpɔːr.t̬ɪd **-porter/s** -ˈpɔː.təʳ/z ⓤⓢ -ˈpɔːr.t̬ɚ/z
supportab|le səˈpɔː.tə.b|l̩ ⓤⓢ -ˈpɔːr.t̬ə- **-ly** -li
supportive səˈpɔː.tɪv ⓤⓢ -ˈpɔːr.t̬ɪv
suppos|e səˈpəʊz ⓤⓢ -ˈpoʊz **-es** -ɪz **-ing** -ɪŋ **-ed** -d
supposedly səˈpəʊ.zɪd.li ⓤⓢ -ˈpoʊ-
supposition ˌsʌp.əˈzɪʃ.ᵊn **-s** -z
suppositional ˌsʌp.əˈzɪʃ.ᵊn.ᵊl, ˈ-nᵊl **-li** -i
supposititious səˌpɒz.ɪˈtɪʃ.əs, -əˈ- ⓤⓢ -ˌpɑː.zəˈ- **-ly** -li **-ness** -nəs, -nɪs
suppositor|y səˈpɒz.ɪ.tᵊr|.i, ˈ-ə-, -tr|i ⓤⓢ -ˈpɑː.zə.tɔːr|.i **-ies** -iz
suppress səˈpres **-es** -ɪz **-ing** -ɪŋ **-ed** -t **-or/s** -əʳ/z ⓤⓢ -ɚ/z **-ible** -ə.bl̩, -ɪ.bl̩
suppressant səˈpres.ᵊnt **-s** -s
suppression səˈpreʃ.ᵊn **-s** -z
suppu|rate ˈsʌp.jə|.reɪt, -jʊ- **-rates** -reɪts **-rating** -reɪ.tɪŋ ⓤⓢ -reɪ.t̬ɪŋ **-rated** -reɪ.tɪd ⓤⓢ -reɪ.t̬ɪd
suppuration ˌsʌp.jəʳˈreɪ.ʃᵊn, -jʊˈreɪ- ⓤⓢ -jəˈreɪ-, -jʊˈ- **-s** -z
supra- ˈsuː.prə, ˈsjuː- ⓤⓢ ˈsuː.prə-
supradental ˌsuː.prəˈden.tᵊl, ˌsjuː- ⓤⓢ ˌsuː.prəˈden.t̬ᵊl
suprafix ˈsuː.prə.fɪks, ˈsjuː- ⓤⓢ ˈsuː-
supranational ˌsuː.prəˈnæʃ.ᵊn.ᵊl, ˌsjuː-, ˈ-nᵊl ⓤⓢ ˌsuː- **-ly** -li
suprarenal ˌsuː.prəˈriː.nᵊl, ˌsjuː-, ˈsuː.prəˌriː-, ˈsjuː- ⓤⓢ ˌsuː.prəˈriː
suprasegmental ˌsuː.prə.segˈmen.tᵊl, ˌsjuː- ⓤⓢ ˌsuː.prə.segˈmen.t̬ᵊl
supremacist suːˈprem.ə.sɪst, sjuː-, sʊ-, sjʊ- ⓤⓢ səˈ-, sʊ-, suː- **-s** -s
supremac|y suːˈprem.ə.s|i, sjuː-, sʊ-, sjʊ- ⓤⓢ sə-, sʊ-, suː- **-ies** -iz
supreme suːˈpriːm, sjuː-, sʊ-, sjʊ- ⓤⓢ sə-, sʊ-, suː- **-ly** -li **-ness** -nəs, -nɪs **Suˌpreme ˈCourt**; **Suˌpreme ˈSoviet**
supremo suːˈpriː.məʊ, sjuː-, sʊ-, sjʊ- ⓤⓢ suːˈpriː.moʊ, sʊ-, sə- **-s** -z
supt (S) *(abbrev. for* **superintendent***)* ˌsuː.pᵊr.ɪnˈten.dənt, ˌsjuː- ⓤⓢ ˌsuː.pɚ-
sura ˈsʊə.rə ⓤⓢ ˈsʊr.ə **-s** -z
surah ˈsjʊə.rə ⓤⓢ ˈsʊr.ə
surat sʊˈræt, sjuː- ⓤⓢ ˈsʊr.æt
Surat ˈsʊə.rət, ˈsuː-; sʊˈrɑːt, -ˈræt ⓤⓢ ˈsʊr.ət; səˈræt
Surbiton ˈsɜː.bɪ.tᵊn ⓤⓢ ˈsɝː.bɪ.t̬ən
surceas|e *(v.)* sɜːˈsiːs ⓤⓢ sɝː- **-es** -ɪz **-ing** -ɪŋ **-ed** -t
surceas|e *(n.)* sɜːˈsiːs ⓤⓢ sɝː-, ˈ-- **-es** -ɪz
surcharg|e *(n.)* ˈsɜː.tʃɑːdʒ, ˌ-ˈ- ⓤⓢ ˈsɝː.tʃɑːrdʒ **-es** -ɪz
surcharg|e *(v.)* ˈsɜː.tʃɑːdʒ, ˌ-ˈ- ⓤⓢ ˈsɝː.tʃɑːrdʒ, -ˈ- **-es** -ɪz **-ing** -ɪŋ **-ed** -d
surcingle ˈsɜː.sɪŋ.gl̩ ⓤⓢ ˈsɝː- **-s** -z
surcoat ˈsɜː.kəʊt ⓤⓢ ˈsɝː.koʊt **-s** -s
surd sɜːd ⓤⓢ sɝːd **-s** -z **-ity** -ə.ti, -ɪ.ti ⓤⓢ -ə.t̬i
sur|e ʃɔːʳ, ʃʊəʳ ⓤⓢ ʃʊr **-er** -əʳ ⓤⓢ -ɚ **-est** -ɪst, -əst **-ness** -nəs, -nɪs
surefire ˈʃɔːˌfaɪəʳ, ˈʃʊə- ⓤⓢ ˈʃʊrˌfaɪɚ
surefooted ˌʃɔːˈfʊt.ɪd, ˌʃʊə- ⓤⓢ ˈʃʊrˌfʊt̬.ɪd **-ly** -li **-ness** -nəs, -nɪs
surely ˈʃɔː.li, ˈʃʊə- ⓤⓢ ˈʃʊr-
suret|y ˈʃɔː.rə.t|i, ˈʃʊə- ⓤⓢ ˈʃʊr.ə.t̬|i, ˈ-t̬|i **-ies** -iz **-yship/s** -i.ʃɪp/s
surf sɜːf ⓤⓢ sɝːf **-s** -s **-ing** -ɪŋ **-ed** -t
surfac|e ˈsɜː.fɪs, -fəs ⓤⓢ ˈsɝː- **-es** -ɪz **-ing** -ɪŋ **-ed** -t ˈ**surface** ˌ**mail**; ˈ**surface** ˌ**structure**; ˌ**surface** ˈ**tension** ⓤⓢ ˈ**surface** ˌ**tension**
surface-to-air ˌsɜː.fɪs.tuˈeəʳ ⓤⓢ ˌsɝː.fɪs.tuˈer ˌ**surface-to-air** ˈ**missile**
surface-to-surface ˌsɜː.fɪs.təˈsɜː.fɪs ⓤⓢ ˌsɝː.fɪs.təˈsɝːr- *stress shift:* ˌsurface-to-surface ˈmissile
surfactant sɜːˈfæk.tənt ⓤⓢ sɝː- **-s** -s
surfboard ˈsɜːf.bɔːd ⓤⓢ ˈsɝːf.bɔːrd **-s** -z **-er/s** -əʳ/z ⓤⓢ -ɚ/z
surfboat ˈsɜːf.bəʊt ⓤⓢ ˈsɝːf.boʊt **-s** -s
surfei|t ˈsɜː.fɪ|t, -ə|t ⓤⓢ ˈsɝː.fɪ|t **-ts** -ts **-ting** -tɪŋ ⓤⓢ -t̬ɪŋ **-ted** -tɪd ⓤⓢ -t̬ɪd
surfer ˈsɜː.fəʳ ⓤⓢ ˈsɝː.fɚ **-s** -z
surfing ˈsɜː.fɪŋ ⓤⓢ ˈsɝː-
surg|e sɜːdʒ ⓤⓢ sɝːdʒ **-es** -ɪz **-ing** -ɪŋ **-ed** -d
surgeon ˈsɜː.dʒᵊn ⓤⓢ ˈsɝː- **-s** -z
surger|y ˈsɜː.dʒᵊr|.i ⓤⓢ ˈsɝː- **-ies** -iz
surgic|al ˈsɜː.dʒɪ.k|ᵊl ⓤⓢ ˈsɝː- **-ally** -ᵊl.i, -li ˌ**surgical** ˈ**spirit**
Suriname, Surinam ˌsʊə.rɪˈnæm, ˌsjʊə-, ˈ--- ⓤⓢ ˌsʊr.ɪˈnɑːm; ˈsʊr.ɪ.næm
Surinamese ˌsʊə.rɪ.næmˈiːz, ˌsjʊə-
surl|y ˈsɜː.l|i ⓤⓢ ˈsɝː- **-ier** -i.əʳ ⓤⓢ -i.ɚ **-iest** -i.ɪst, -i.əst **-ily** -ɪ.li, -ᵊl.i **-iness** -ɪ.nəs, -ɪ.nɪs
surmis|e *(n.)* ˈsɜː.maɪz; ˌ-ˈ-, sə- ⓤⓢ sɚˈmaɪz; ˈsɜːr.maɪz **-es** -ɪz
surmis|e *(v.)* sɜːˈmaɪz, sə-; ˈsɜː.maɪz ⓤⓢ sɚˈmaɪz **-es** -ɪz **-ing** -ɪŋ **-ed** -d
sur|mount sə|ˈmaʊnt, sɜː- ⓤⓢ sɚ- **-mounts** -ˈmaʊnts **-mounting** -ˈmaʊn.tɪŋ ⓤⓢ -ˈmaʊn.t̬ɪŋ **-mounted** -ˈmaʊn.tɪd ⓤⓢ -ˈmaʊn.t̬ɪd **-mountable** -ˈmaʊn.tə.bl̩ ⓤⓢ -ˈmaʊn.t̬ə.bl̩
surnam|e ˈsɜː.neɪm ⓤⓢ ˈsɝː- **-es** -z **-ing** -ɪŋ **-ed** -d
surpass səˈpɑːs, sɜː- ⓤⓢ sɚˈpæs **-es** -ɪz **-ing/ly** -ɪŋ/li **-ed** -t **-able** -ə.bl̩
surplic|e ˈsɜː.plɪs, -pləs ⓤⓢ ˈsɝː- **-es** -ɪz **-ed** -t
surplus ˈsɜː.pləs ⓤⓢ ˈsɝː-, -plʌs **-es** -ɪz **-age** -ɪdʒ
surpris|e səˈpraɪz ⓤⓢ sɚ- **-es** -ɪz **-ing/ly** -ɪŋ/li **-ed/ly** -ɪd/li, -d/li
surreal səˈrɪəl ⓤⓢ səˈriː.əl, -ˈriːl
surreal|ism səˈrɪə.lɪ|.zᵊm ⓤⓢ -ˈriː.ə-, -ˈriː.lɪ- **-ist/s** -ɪst/s
surrealistic səˌrɪəˈlɪs.tɪk ⓤⓢ -ˌriː.əˈ-, -ˌriːˈ-
surrend|er sᵊrˈen.d|əʳ ⓤⓢ səˈren.d|ɚ **-ers** -əz ⓤⓢ -ɚz **-ering** -ᵊr.ɪŋ **-ered** -əd ⓤⓢ -ɚd
surreptitious ˌsʌr.əpˈtɪʃ.əs, -ɪpˈ-, -epˈ- ⓤⓢ ˌsɝː.əpˈ- **-ly** -li **-ness** -nəs, -nɪs
Surrey, surrey ˈsʌr.i ⓤⓢ ˈsɝː-
surrogac|y ˈsʌr.ə.gə.s|i **-ies** -iz
surrogate ˈsʌr.ə.gɪt, -gət, -geɪt ⓤⓢ ˈsɝː.ə.gɪt, -geɪt **-s** -s ˌ**surrogate** ˈ**mother**
surround səˈraʊnd **-s** -z **-ing/s** -ɪŋ/z **-ed** -ɪd **surˌround** ˈ**sound**
sursum corda ˌsɜː.səmˈkɔː.də, -sʊmˈ- ⓤⓢ ˌsɝː.səmˈkɔːr-, -sʊmˈ-
surtax ˈsɜː.tæks ⓤⓢ ˈsɝː- **-es** -ɪz
Surtees ˈsɜː.tiːz ⓤⓢ ˈsɝː-
surtitl|e ˈsɜːˌtaɪ.tl̩ ⓤⓢ ˈsɝːˌtaɪ.t̬l̩ **-es** -z **-ing** -ɪŋ, -ˌtaɪt.lɪŋ **-ed** -d
Surtsey ˈsɜːt.si, -seɪ ⓤⓢ ˈsɝːt-
surveil səˈveɪ **-s** -z **-ing** -ɪŋ **-led** -d **-lant/s** -ənt/s
surveillance sɜːˈveɪ.lənts, sə- ⓤⓢ sɚ-, -ˈveɪl.jənts
survey *(n.)* ˈsɜː.veɪ; ˌ-ˈ-, sə- ⓤⓢ ˈsɝː.veɪ **-s** -z
survey *(v.)* səˈveɪ, sɜː-; ˈsɜː.veɪ ⓤⓢ sɚˈveɪ; ˈsɝː.veɪ **-s** -z **-ing** -ɪŋ **-ed** -d
surveyor səˈveɪ.əʳ ⓤⓢ sɚˈveɪ.ɚ **-s** -z
survival səˈvaɪ.vᵊl ⓤⓢ sɚ- **-s** -z **surˌvival of the** ˈ**fittest**
survivalist səˈvaɪ.vᵊl.ɪst ⓤⓢ sɚ- **-s** -s
surviv|e səˈvaɪv ⓤⓢ sɚ- **-es** -z **-ing** -ɪŋ **-ed** -d **-able** -ə.bl̩
survivor səˈvaɪ.vəʳ ⓤⓢ sɚˈvaɪ.vɚ **-s** -z
Susan ˈsuː.zᵊn
Susanna(h) suːˈzæn.ə, sʊ-
susceptibilit|y səˌsep.təˈbɪl.ə.t|i, -tɪˈ-, -ɪ.t|i ⓤⓢ -təˈbɪl.ə.t̬|i **-ies** -iz
susceptib|le səˈsep.tə.b|l̩, -tɪ- ⓤⓢ -tə- **-ly** -li
susceptive səˈsep.tɪv
sushi ˈsuː.ʃi
Susie ˈsuː.zi
suspect *(n. adj.)* ˈsʌs.pekt **-s** -s
suspect *(v.)* səˈspekt **-s** -s **-ing** -ɪŋ **-ed** -ɪd
suspend səˈspend **-s** -z **-ing** -ɪŋ **-ed** -ɪd
suspender səˈspen.dəʳ ⓤⓢ -dɚ **-s** -z **suˈspender** ˌ**belt**
suspens|e səˈspen*t*s **-ible** -ə.bl̩, -ɪ.bl̩
suspensibility səˌspen*t*.sɪˈbɪl.ə.ti, -səˈ-, -ɪ.ti ⓤⓢ -səˈbɪl.ə.t̬i
suspension səˈspen.*t*ʃᵊn ⓤⓢ -ˈspen*t*.ʃᵊn **-s** -z **suˈspension** ˌ**bridge**
suspens|ive səˈspen*t*.s|ɪv **-ory** -ᵊr.i

suspicion sə'spɪʃ.ᵊn **-s** -z

suspicious sə'spɪʃ.əs **-ly** -li **-ness** -nəs, -nɪs

suss sʌs **-es** -ɪz **-ing** -ɪŋ **-ed** -t

Sussex 'sʌs.ɪks

Susskind 'sʊs.kɪnd (US) 'sʌs-

sustain sə'steɪn **-s** -z **-ing** -ɪŋ **-ed** -d **-er/s** -əʳ/z (US) -ɚ/z **-able** -ə.bl̩

sustainability sə,steɪ.nə'bɪl.ə.ti, -ɪ.ti (US) -ə.t̬i

sustenance 'sʌs.tɪ.nənts, -tᵊn.ənts (US) -tᵊn.ənts

sustentation ,sʌs.ten'teɪ.ʃᵊn, -tən'-

susurr|ate 'suː.sᵊr|.eɪt, 'sjuː- (US) suː'sɝː|.eɪt, sʊ-, sə- **-ates** -eɪts **-ating** -eɪ.tɪŋ (US) -eɪ.t̬ɪŋ **-ated** -eɪ.tɪd (US) -eɪ.t̬ɪd

susurration ,suː.sᵊr'eɪ.ʃᵊn, ,sjuː- (US) ,suː.sə'reɪ- **-s** -z

Sutcliffe 'sʌt.klɪf

Sutherland 'sʌð.ᵊl.ənd (US) -ɚ.lənd

Sutlej 'sʌt.lɪdʒ, -ledʒ (US) -ledʒ

sutler 'sʌt.ləʳ (US) -lɚ **-s** -z

Sutro 'suː.trəʊ (US) -troʊ

suttee 'sʌt.iː, -'- (US) sə'tiː; 'sʌt.iː **-s** -z

Sutton 'sʌt.ᵊn

Sutton Coldfield ,sʌt.ᵊn'kəʊld.fiːld (US) -'koʊld-

Sutton Hoo ,sʌt.ᵊn'huː

sutur|e 'suː.tʃəʳ, 'sjuː-, -tjəʳ (US) 'suː.tʃɚ **-es** -z **-ing** -ɪŋ **-ed** -d

Suva 'suː.və

Suzanne suː'zæn, sʊ-

suzerain 'suː.zᵊr.eɪn, 'sjuː- (US) 'suː.zɚ.ɪn, -zə.raɪn **-s** -z

suzeraint|y 'suː.zᵊr.eɪn.t|i, 'sjuː-, -ᵊn- (US) 'suː.zɚ.ɪn-, -zə.raɪn- **-ies** -iz

Suzuki® sə'zuː.ki, sʊ- **-s** -z

Suzy 'suː.zi

svarabhakti ,svʌr.ə'bʌk.ti, ,svɑː.rə'-, -'bæk-, -tiː (US) ,svɑːr.ɑː'bɑːk-

svelt|e svelt, sfelt **-ely** -li **-eness** -nəs, -nɪs

Svengali sveŋ'gɑː.li, sfeŋ- (US) sven-, sfen- **-s** -z

Sverdlovsk sveəd'lɒvsk, -'lɒfsk; '--, -ləvsk, -ləfsk (US) sverd'lɔːfsk

SW *(abbrev. for* **southwest***)* ,es'dʌb.l̩.juː, saʊθ'west

swab swɒb (US) swɑːb **-s** -z **-bing** -ɪŋ **-bed** -d **-ber/s** -əʳ/z (US) -ɚ/z

Swabi|a 'sweɪ.bi|.ə **-an/s** -ən/z

swaddl|e 'swɒd.l̩ (US) 'swɑː.dl̩ **-es** -z **-ing** -ɪŋ, 'swɒd.lɪŋ (US) 'swɑːd- **-ed** -d **'swaddling ,clothes**

Swadlincoat 'swɒd.lɪn.kəʊt, -lɪŋ- (US) 'swɑːd.lɪn.koʊt

Swadling 'swɒd.lɪŋ (US) 'swɑːd-

Swaffer 'swɒf.əʳ (US) 'swɑː.fɚ

Swaffham 'swɒf.əm (US) 'swɑː.fəm

swag swæg

swag|e sweɪdʒ **-es** -ɪz **-ing** -ɪŋ **-ed** -d

Swaggart 'swæg.ət (US) -ɚt

swagg|er 'swæg|.əʳ (US) -ɚ **-ers** -əz (US) -ɚz **-ering/ly** -ᵊr.ɪŋ/li **-ered** -əd (US) -ɚd **-erer/s** -ᵊr.əʳ/z (US) -ɚ.ɚ/z **'swagger ,stick**

swag|man 'swæg|.mæn, -mən **-men** -men, -mən

Swahili swɑː'hiː.li, swə- (US) swɑː- **-s** -z

swain (S) sweɪn **-s** -z

swale (S) sweɪl

Swaledale 'sweɪl.deɪl

SWALK swɔːlk (US) swɑːk, swɔːk

swallow 'swɒl.əʊ (US) 'swɑː.loʊ **-s** -z **-ing** -ɪŋ **-ed** -d

swallowtail 'swɒl.əʊ.teɪl (US) 'swɑː.loʊ- **-s** -z **-ed** -d

swam *(from* **swim***)* swæm

swami 'swɑː.mi **-(e)s** -z

swamp swɒmp (US) swɑːmp, swɔːmp **-s** -s **-ing** -ɪŋ **-ed** -t **-y** -i **-ier** -i.əʳ (US) -i.ɚ **-iest** -i.ɪst, -i.əst **-iness** -ɪ.nəs, -ɪ.nɪs

swampland 'swɒmp.lænd (US) 'swɑːmp- **-s** -z

swan (S) swɒn (US) swɑːn **-s** -z **-ning** -ɪŋ **-ned** -d **'swan ,song**

Swanage 'swɒn.ɪdʒ (US) 'swɑː.nɪdʒ

Swanee 'swɒn.i (US) 'swɑː.ni

swank swæŋk **-y** -i **-ier** -i.əʳ (US) -i.ɚ **-iest** -i.ɪst, -i.əst **-ily** -ɪ.li, -ᵊl.i **-iness** -ɪ.nəs, -ɪ.nɪs

Swanley 'swɒn.li (US) 'swɑːn-

Swann swɒn (US) swɑːn

swanner|y 'swɒn.ᵊr|.i (US) 'swɑː.nɚ- **-ies** -iz

Swanscombe 'swɒnz.kəm (US) 'swɑːnz-

swansdown 'swɒnz.daʊn (US) 'swɑːnz-

Swansea *in Wales:* 'swɒn.zi (US) 'swɑːn- *in Tasmania:* 'swɒnt.si, -siː (US) 'swɑːnt-

Swanson 'swɒnt.sən (US) 'swɑːnt-

swan-upp|ing 'swɒn,ʌp|.ɪŋ (US) 'swɑːn- **-er/s** -əʳ/z (US) -ɚ/z

Swanwick 'swɒn.ɪk (US) 'swɑː.nɪk

swap swɒp (US) swɑːp **-s** -s **-ping** -ɪŋ **-ped** -t **'swap ,shop**

Swapo, SWAPO 'swɑː.pəʊ, 'swɒp.əʊ (US) 'swɑː.poʊ

sward swɔːd (US) swɔːrd **-s** -z

swarf swɔːf (US) swɔːrf

Swarfega® swɔː'fiː.gə (US) swɔːr-

swarm swɔːm (US) swɔːrm **-s** -z **-ing** -ɪŋ **-ed** -d

swart swɔːt (US) swɔːrt

swarth|y 'swɔː.ð|i (US) 'swɔːr-, -θ|i **-ier** -i.əʳ (US) -i.ɚ **-iest** -i.ɪst, -i.əst **-ily** -ɪ.li, -ᵊl.i **-iness** -ɪ.nəs, -ɪ.nɪs

swash swɒʃ (US) swɑːʃ **-es** -ɪz **-ing** -ɪŋ **-ed** -t

swashbuckl|er 'swɒʃ,bʌk.l̩|.əʳ, ,-l|əʳ (US) 'swɑːʃ,bʌk.l̩|.ɚ, ,-l|ɚ **-ers** -əz (US) -ɚz **-ing** -ɪŋ

swastika 'swɒs.tɪ.kə (US) 'swɑː.stɪ- **-s** -z

swat swɒt (US) swɑːt **-s** -s **-ting** -ɪŋ (US) 'swɑː.t̬ɪŋ **-ted** -ɪd (US) 'swɑː.t̬ɪd **-ter/s** -əʳ/z (US) 'swɑː.t̬ɚ/s

swatch (S®) swɒtʃ (US) swɑːtʃ **-es** -ɪz

swa|th swɒ|θ, swɔː|θ (US) swɑː|θ, swɔː|θ **-ths** -θs, -ðz

swath|e sweɪð **-es** -z **-ing** -ɪŋ **-ed** -d

sway sweɪ **-s** -z **-ing** -ɪŋ **-ed** -d

Swazi 'swɑː.zi **-s** -z

Swaziland 'swɑː.zi.lænd

swear sweəʳ (US) swer **-s** -z **-ing** -ɪŋ **swore** swɔːʳ (US) swɔːr **sworn** swɔːn (US) swɔːrn

swearword 'sweə.wɜːd (US) 'swer.wɝːd **-s** -z

sweat swet **-s** -s **-ing** -ɪŋ (US) 'swet̬.ɪŋ **-ed** -ɪd (US) 'swet̬.ɪd

sweatband 'swet.bænd **-s** -z

sweater 'swet.əʳ (US) 'swet̬.ɚ **-s** -z

sweatpants 'swet.pænts

sweatshirt 'swet.ʃɜːt (US) -ʃɝːt **-s** -s

sweatshop 'swet.ʃɒp (US) -ʃɑːp **-s** -s

sweat|y 'swet|.i (US) 'swet̬- **-ier** -i.əʳ (US) -i.ɚ **-iest** -i.ɪst, -i.əst **-iness** -ɪ.nəs, -ɪ.nɪs

swede (S) swiːd **-s** -z

Sweden 'swiː.dᵊn

Swedenborg 'swiː.dᵊn.bɔːg, -dᵊm- (US) -dᵊn.bɔːrg

Swedenborgian ,swiː.dᵊn'bɔː.dʒən, -dᵊm'-, -dʒi.ən, -gən, -gi.ən (US) -dᵊn'bɔːr.dʒi.ən, -gi- **-s** -z

Swedish 'swiː.dɪʃ **,Swedish 'massage** (US) **,Swedish mas'sage**

Sweeney 'swiː.ni

sweep swiːp **-s** -s **-ing/s** -ɪŋ **swept** swept **sweeper/s** 'swiː.pəʳ/z (US) -pɚ/z

sweepstake 'swiːp.steɪk **-s** -s

sweet (S) swiːt **-s** -s **-er** -əʳ (US) 'swiː.t̬ɚ **-est** -ɪst, -əst (US) 'swiː.t̬ɪst, -t̬əst **-ly** -li **-ness** -nəs, -nɪs **,sweet 'nothings; ,sweet 'pea; ,sweet po'tato** (US) **'sweet po,tato; ,sweet 'tooth** (US) **'sweet ,tooth; ,sweet 'William; ,sweetness and 'light**

sweet-and-sour ,swiːt.ᵊn'saʊəʳ (US) -'saʊɚ

sweetbread 'swiːt.bred **-s** -z

sweetbrier 'swiːt.braɪəʳ (US) -braɪɚ **-s** -z

sweetcorn 'swiːt.kɔːn (US) -kɔːrn

sweeten 'swiː.tᵊn **-s** -z **-ing** -ɪŋ, 'swiːt.nɪŋ **-ed** -d **-er/s** -əʳ/z, 'swiːt.nəʳ/z (US) 'swiː.tᵊn.ɚ/z, 'swiːt.nɚ/z

Sweetex® 'swiː.teks

sweetheart 'swiːt.hɑːt (US) -hɑːrt **-s** -s

sweetie 'swiː.ti (US) -t̬i **-s** -z

sweeting (S) 'swiː.tɪŋ (US) -t̬ɪŋ **-s** -z

sweetish 'swiː.tɪʃ (US) -t̬ɪʃ

sweetmeal 'swiːt.miːl

sweetmeat 'swiːt.miːt **-s** -s

sweet-talk 'swiːt.tɔːk ⓊⓈ -tɑːk, -tɔːk **-s** -s **-ing** -ɪŋ **-ed** -t
sweet|y 'swiː.t|i ⓊⓈ -ţ|i **-ies** -iz
swell swel **-s** -z **-ing/s** -ɪŋ/z **-ed** -d **swollen** 'swəʊ.lən ⓊⓈ 'swoʊ- ˌ**swelled** '**head**
swelt|er 'swel.t|əʳ ⓊⓈ -ţ|ɚ **-ers** -əz ⓊⓈ -ɚz **-ering/ly** -ᵊr.ɪŋ/li **-ered** -əd ⓊⓈ -ɚd
swept *(from* **sweep***)* swept
swerv|e swɜːv ⓊⓈ swɝːv **-es** -z **-ing** -ɪŋ **-ed** -d
Swettenham 'swet.ᵊn.əm
swift (S) swɪft **-s** -s **-er** -əʳ ⓊⓈ -ɚ **-est** -ɪst, -əst **-ly** -li **-ness** -nəs, -nɪs
Swiftsure 'swɪft.ʃɔːʳ, -ʃʊəʳ ⓊⓈ -ʃʊr
swig swɪg **-s** -z **-ging** -ɪŋ **-ged** -d
swill swɪl **-s** -z **-ing** -ɪŋ **-ed** -d **-er/s** -əʳ/z ⓊⓈ -ɚ/z
swim swɪm **-s** -z **-ming/ly** -ɪŋ/li **swam** swæm **swum** swʌm **swimmer/s** 'swɪm.əʳ/z ⓊⓈ -ɚ/z '**swimming** ˌ**bath(s)**; '**swimming** ˌ**costume**; '**swimming** ˌ**pool**
swimsuit 'swɪm.suːt, -sjuːt ⓊⓈ -suːt **-s** -s
swimwear 'swɪm.weəʳ ⓊⓈ -wer
Swinbourne 'swɪn.bɔːn, 'swɪm- ⓊⓈ 'swɪn.bɔːrn
Swinburne 'swɪn.bɜːn, 'swɪm-, -bən ⓊⓈ 'swɪn.bɝːn, -bɚn
swindl|e 'swɪn.dl̩ **-es** -z **-ing** -ɪŋ, 'swɪnd.lɪŋ **-ed** -d **-er/s** -əʳ/z, 'swɪnd.ləʳ/z ⓊⓈ 'swɪn.dl̩.ɚ/z, 'swɪnd.lɚ/z
Swindon 'swɪn.dən
swine swaɪn **-s** -z
swineherd 'swaɪn.hɜːd ⓊⓈ -hɝːd **-s** -z
swing swɪŋ **-s** -z **-ing** -ɪŋ **swung** swʌŋ **swinger/s** 'swɪŋ.əʳ/z ⓊⓈ -ɚ/z ˌ**swing** '**door**; ˌ**swings and** '**roundabouts**
swingbridge swɪŋ'brɪdʒ **-s** -ɪz
swingeing 'swɪn.dʒɪŋ
swingl|e 'swɪŋ.gl̩ **-es** -z **-ing** -ɪŋ, 'swɪŋ.glɪŋ **-ed** -d
swingometer swɪŋ'ɒm.ɪ.təʳ, -ə.təʳ ⓊⓈ 'ɑː.mə.ţɚ **-s** -z
swing-wing ˌswɪŋ'wɪŋ ⓊⓈ '-- *stress shift:* ˌswing-wing 'plane
swinish 'swaɪ.nɪʃ **-ly** -li **-ness** -nəs, -nɪs
Swinton 'swɪn.tən ⓊⓈ -tᵊn
swip|e swaɪp **-es** -s **-ing** -ɪŋ **-ed** -t **-er/s** -əʳ/z ⓊⓈ -ɚ/z
swirl swɜːl ⓊⓈ swɝːl **-s** -z **-ing** -ɪŋ **-ed** -d **-y** -i
swish swɪʃ **-es** -ɪz **-ing** -ɪŋ **-ed** -t
swish|y 'swɪʃ|.i **-ier** -i.əʳ ⓊⓈ -i.ɚ **-iest** -i.ɪst, -i.əst
Swiss swɪs ˌ**Swiss** '**cheese**; ˌ**Swiss** '**cheese** ˌ**plant**; ˌ**Swiss** '**roll**
Swissair® swɪs'eəʳ ⓊⓈ -er
switch (S®) swɪtʃ **-es** -ɪz **-ing** -ɪŋ **-ed** -t
switchback 'swɪtʃ.bæk **-s** -s
switchblade 'swɪtʃ.bleɪd **-s** -z
switchboard 'swɪtʃ.bɔːd ⓊⓈ -bɔːrd **-s** -z
switchgear 'swɪtʃ.gɪəʳ ⓊⓈ -gɪr
Swithin 'swɪð.ɪn, 'swɪθ-
Switzerland 'swɪt.sᵊl.ənd ⓊⓈ -sɚ.lənd
swivel 'swɪv.ᵊl **-s** -z **-(l)ing** -ɪŋ, 'swɪv.lɪŋ **-(l)ed** -d ˌ**swivel** '**chair**
swiz(z) swɪz **-es** -ɪz
swizzl|e 'swɪz.l̩ **-es** -z **-ing** -ɪŋ, 'swɪz.lɪŋ **-ed** -d **-er/s** -əʳ/z, 'swɪz.ləʳ/z ⓊⓈ '-l̩.ɚ/z, '-lɚ/z '**swizzle** ˌ**stick**
swollen *(from* **swell***)* 'swəʊ.lən ⓊⓈ 'swoʊ- ˌ**swollen** '**head**
swoon swuːn **-s** -z **-ing** -ɪŋ **-ed** -d
swoop swuːp **-s** -s **-ing** -ɪŋ **-ed** -t
swoosh swuːʃ, swʊʃ **-es** -ɪz **-ing** -ɪŋ **-ed** -t
swop swɒp ⓊⓈ swɑːp **-s** -s **-ping** -ɪŋ **-ped** -t
sword sɔːd ⓊⓈ sɔːrd **-s** -z '**sword** ˌ**dance**
Sworder 'sɔː.dəʳ ⓊⓈ 'sɔːr.dɚ
swordfish 'sɔːd.fɪʃ ⓊⓈ 'sɔːrd-
swordplay 'sɔːd.pleɪ ⓊⓈ 'sɔːrd-
swords|man 'sɔːdz|.mən ⓊⓈ 'sɔːrdz- **-men** -mən **-manship** -mən.ʃɪp
swordstick 'sɔːd.stɪk ⓊⓈ 'sɔːrd- **-s** -s
sword-swallower 'sɔːdˌswɒl.əʊ.əʳ ⓊⓈ 'sɔːrdˌswɑː.loʊ.ɚ **-s** -z
swore *(from* **swear***)* swɔːʳ ⓊⓈ swɔːr
sworn *(from* **swear***)* swɔːn ⓊⓈ swɔːrn
swot swɒt ⓊⓈ swɑːt **-s** -s **-ting** -ɪŋ ⓊⓈ 'swɑː.ţɪŋ **-ted** -ɪd ⓊⓈ 'swɑː.ţɪd **-ter/s** -əʳ/z ⓊⓈ 'swɑː.ţɚ/z
swum *(from* **swim***)* swʌm
swung *(from* **swing***)* swʌŋ
Sybaris 'sɪb.ᵊr.ɪs; sɪ'bɑːr- ⓊⓈ 'sɪb.ɚ.ɪs
sybarite 'sɪb.ᵊr.aɪt ⓊⓈ -ə.raɪt **-s** -s
sybaritic ˌsɪb.ᵊr'ɪt.ɪk ⓊⓈ -ə'rɪţ- **-ally** -ᵊl.i, -li
Sybil 'sɪb.ɪl, -ᵊl ⓊⓈ -ᵊl
Note: As a feminine name, /'sɪb.ᵊl/ is more common in British English; the /-ɪl/ ending is more usual for the soothsayer.
sycamore (S) 'sɪk.ə.mɔːʳ ⓊⓈ -mɔːr **-s** -z
syc|e saɪs **-es** -ɪz
sycophancy 'sɪk.ə.fᵊn*t*.si, 'saɪ.kə-, -'fæn*t*- ⓊⓈ -fᵊn*t*-
sycophant 'sɪk.ə.fænt, 'saɪ.kə-, -fənt ⓊⓈ -fᵊnt **-s** -s
sycophantic ˌsɪk.əʊ'fæn.tɪk, ˌsaɪ.kə'- ⓊⓈ -ţɪk
Sydenham 'sɪd.ᵊn.əm, '-nəm
Sydney 'sɪd.ni
Sydneysider 'sɪd.niˌsaɪ.dəʳ ⓊⓈ -dɚ
syenite 'saɪ.ə.naɪt, '-ɪ- ⓊⓈ '-ə-
Sykes saɪks
syllabar|y 'sɪl.ə.bᵊr|.i ⓊⓈ -ber- **-ies** -iz
syllabic sɪ'læb.ɪk, sə- ⓊⓈ sɪ- **-ally** -ᵊl.i, -li
syllabi|cate sɪ'læb.ɪ|.keɪt, sə-, '-ə- ⓊⓈ sɪ'læb.ə- **-cates** -keɪts **-cating** -keɪ.tɪŋ ⓊⓈ -keɪ.ţɪŋ **-cated** -keɪ.tɪd ⓊⓈ -keɪ.ţɪd
syllabication sɪˌlæb.ɪ'keɪ.ʃᵊn, sə-, -ə'- ⓊⓈ sɪˌlæb.ə'-
syllabicity ˌsɪl.ə'bɪs.ə.ti, -ɪ.ti ⓊⓈ -ə.ţi
syllabification sɪˌlæb.ɪ.fɪ'keɪ.ʃᵊn, sə-, ˌ-ə- ⓊⓈ sɪˌlæb.ə-
syllabi|fy sɪ'læb.ɪ|.faɪ, sə-, '-ə- ⓊⓈ sɪ'læb.ə- **-fies** -faɪz **-fying** -faɪ.ɪŋ **-fied** -faɪd
syllabism 'sɪl.ə.bɪ.zᵊm
syllable 'sɪl.ə.bl̩ **-s** -z
syllabub 'sɪl.ə.bʌb
syllab|us 'sɪl.ə.b|əs **-uses** -əs.ɪz **-i** -aɪ
syllep|sis sɪ'lep|.sɪs, sə- ⓊⓈ sɪ- **-tic** -tɪk
syllogism 'sɪl.ə.dʒɪ.zᵊm **-s** -z
syllogistic ˌsɪl.ə'dʒɪs.tɪk **-ally** -ᵊl.i, -li
syllogiz|e, -is|e 'sɪl.ə.dʒaɪz **-es** -ɪz **-ing** -ɪŋ **-ed** -d
sylph sɪlf **-s** -s
sylphlike 'sɪlf.laɪk
sylvan 'sɪl.vən
Sylvester sɪl'ves.təʳ ⓊⓈ -tɚ
Sylvia 'sɪl.vi.ə
symbiont 'sɪm.baɪ.ɒnt, -bi- ⓊⓈ -bi-, -baɪ-, -ɑːnt **-s** -s
symbiosis ˌsɪm.baɪ'əʊ.sɪs, -bi'- ⓊⓈ -bi-, -baɪ-, -'oʊ-
symbiotic ˌsɪm.baɪ'ɒt.ɪk, -bi'- ⓊⓈ -bi-, -baɪ-, -'ɑː.ţɪk
symbol 'sɪm.bᵊl **-s** -z
symbolic sɪm'bɒl.ɪk ⓊⓈ -'bɑː.lɪk **-al** -ᵊl **-ally** -ᵊl.i, -li
symbolism 'sɪm.bᵊl.ɪ.zᵊm
symbolist 'sɪm.bᵊl.ɪst **-s** -s
symbolization, -isa- ˌsɪm.bᵊl.aɪ'zeɪ.ʃᵊn, -ɪ'- ⓊⓈ -ɪ'-
symboliz|e, -is|e 'sɪm.bᵊl.aɪz ⓊⓈ -bə.laɪz **-es** -ɪz **-ing** -ɪŋ **-ed** -d
Syme saɪm
Symington 'saɪ.mɪŋ.tən, 'sɪm.ɪŋ-
symmetric sɪ'met.rɪk, sə- ⓊⓈ sɪ- **-al** -ᵊl **-ally** -ᵊl.i, -li **-alness** -ᵊl.nəs, -nɪs
symmetry 'sɪm.ə.tri, '-ɪ- ⓊⓈ '-ə-
Symond 'saɪ.mənd
Symonds 'saɪ.mən*d*z, 'sɪm.ən*d*z
Symonds Yat ˌsɪm.ən*d*z'jæt
Symons 'saɪ.mənz, 'sɪm.ənz
sympathetic ˌsɪm.pə'θet.ɪk ⓊⓈ -'θeţ- **-al** -ᵊl **-ally** -ᵊl.i, -li
sympathiz|e, is|e 'sɪm.pə.θaɪz **-es** -ɪz **-ing** -ɪŋ **-ed** -d **-er/s** -əʳ/z ⓊⓈ -ɚ/z
sympath|y 'sɪm.pə.θ|i **-ies** -iz
symphonic sɪm'fɒn.ɪk ⓊⓈ -'fɑː.nɪk
symphon|y 'sɪm*p*.fə.n|i **-ies** -iz '**symphony** ˌ**orchestra** ⓊⓈ ˌ**symphony** '**orchestra**
symposi|um sɪm'pəʊ.zi|.əm ⓊⓈ -'poʊ- **-ums** -əmz **-a** -ə
symptom 'sɪm*p*.təm **-s** -z
symptomatic ˌsɪm*p*.tə'mæt.ɪk ⓊⓈ -'mæţ- **-ally** -ᵊl.i, -li

Syllabic consonant

A consonant which can stand alone as a syllable.

Examples for English

The great majority of syllables in all languages have a vowel at their centre, and may have one or more consonants preceding and following the vowel (though languages differ greatly in the possible occurrences of consonants in syllables). However, in a few cases we find syllables which contain nothing that could conventionally be classed as a vowel. In English, syllabic consonants appear to arise as a consequence of a weak vowel becoming lost, and some appear to have become obligatory in present-day speech, e.g.:

bottle /ˈbɒt.l̩/ (US) /ˈbɑː.t̬l̩/

In many other cases in English it appears to be possible either to pronounce /m n ŋ l r/ as syllabic consonants or to pronounce them with a preceding vowel, e.g.:

button /ˈbʌt.n̩/
orderly /ˈɔː.dl̩.i, -də.li/ (US) /ˈɔːr.dɚ.li/
history /ˈhɪs.tr̩.i, -tə.ri/ (US) /-tr̩.i, -tɚ-/

In this dictionary, the use of a superscript schwa (ᵊ) indicates the possibility of a syllabic consonant.

The matter is more confusing because of the fact that speakers do not agree in their intuitions about whether a consonant (particularly /l/) is syllabic or not: while most would agree that, for example, *cuddle* and *cycle* are disyllabic (i.e. contain two syllables), *cuddly* and *cycling* are disyllabic for some people (and therefore do not contain a syllabic consonant) while for others they are trisyllabic.

In other languages

For syllables not to contain a vowel is a normal state of affairs in some languages (consider the first syllables of the Czech names *Brno* and *Vltava*). In Japanese some consonants appear to be able to stand as syllables by themselves, according to the intuitions of native speakers who are asked to divide speech up into rhythmical beats.

Syllable

A fundamentally important unit - the most basic unit in speech. Here we are concerned with the phonological notion of the syllable.

Examples for English

Phonologists are interested in the structure of the syllable, since there appear to be interesting observations to be made about which phonemes may occur at the beginning, in the middle and at the end of syllables. In English, it is possible to have from zero to up to three consonants in the ONSET of a syllable, and from zero to up to four in the CODA.

The study of sequences of phonemes is called 'phonotactics', and it seems that the phonotactic possibilities of a language are determined by syllabic structure. This means that any sequence of sounds that a native speaker produces can be broken down into syllables without any segments being left over. For example, in *Their strengths triumphed frequently*, we find the rather daunting sequences of consonant phonemes /ŋθstr/ and /mftfr/, but using what we know of English phonotactics we can split these clusters into one part that belongs to the end of one syllable and another part that belongs to the beginning of another. Thus the first one can only be divided /ŋθ | str/ or /ŋθs | tr/ and the second can only be /mft | fr/.

Phonological treatments of syllable structure usually call the first part of a syllable the ONSET, the middle part the 'peak' and the end part the CODA. The combination of peak and coda is called the RHYME. Syllable breaks, however, may be problematic when approximants occur at syllable boundaries.

synaesthesia ˌsɪn.ɪsˈθiː.zi.ə, -iːsˈ-, -əsˈ-, -ʒə, -ʒi.ə (US) -ɪsˈθiː.ʒə, -ʒi.ə, -zi-
synagogue ˈsɪn.ə.gɒg (US) -gɑːg, -gɔːg **-s** -z
synaloepha ˌsɪn.ᵊlˈiː.fə (US) -əˈliː-
synapse ˈsaɪ.næps, ˈsɪn.æps; sɪˈnæps (US) ˈsɪn.æps; sɪˈnæps
synap|sis sɪˈnæp|.sɪs **-ses** -siːz **-tic/ally** -tɪk/.ᵊl.i, -tɪk/.li
sync(h) sɪŋk **-s** -s **-ing** -ɪŋ **-ed** -t
synchromesh ˈsɪŋ.krəʊ.meʃ, ˈsɪn-, ˌ--ˈ- (US) ˈsɪŋ.krə-, ˈsɪn-, -kroʊ- **-es** -ɪz
synchronic sɪŋˈkrɒn.ɪk, sɪn- (US) sɪnˈkrɑː.nɪk, sɪŋ-
synchronicity ˌsɪŋ.krəˈnɪs.ə.ti, ˌsɪn-, -krɒnˈɪs-, -ɪ.ti (US) -krəˈnɪs.ə.t̬i
synchronism ˈsɪŋ.krə.nɪ.zᵊm, ˈsɪn-
synchronistic ˌsɪŋ.krəˈnɪs.tɪk, ˌsɪn-
synchronization, -isa- ˌsɪŋ.krə.naɪˈzeɪ.ʃᵊn, ˌsɪn-, -nɪˈ- (US) -nɪˈ- **-s** -z
synchroniz|e, -is|e ˈsɪŋ.krə.naɪz, ˈsɪn- **-es** -ɪz **-ing** -ɪŋ **-ed** -d ˌ**synchronized** ˈ**swimming**
synchronous ˈsɪŋ.krə.nəs, ˈsɪn- **-ly** -li **-ness** -nəs, -nɪs
synchrony ˈsɪŋ.krə.ni, ˈsɪn-
synchrotron ˈsɪŋ.krəʊ.trɒn, ˈsɪn- (US) -krə.trɑːn **-s** -z
synco|pate ˈsɪŋ.kə|.peɪt (US) ˈsɪŋ-, ˈsɪn- **-pates** -peɪts **-pating** -peɪ.tɪŋ (US) -peɪ.t̬ɪŋ **-pated** -peɪ.tɪd (US) -peɪ.t̬ɪd
syncopation ˌsɪn.kəˈpeɪ.ʃᵊn, ˌsɪŋ- (US) ˌsɪŋ-, ˌsɪn- **-s** -z
syncope ˈsɪŋ.kə.pi, ˈsɪn-

syncretic sɪŋˈkriː.tɪk, sɪn-, -ˈkret.ɪk (US) -ˈkreţ.ɪk
syncretism ˈsɪŋ.krɪ.tɪ.zᵊm, ˈsɪn- (US) -krə-
syndesis sɪnˈdiː.sɪs (US) ˈsɪn.də-; sɪnˈdiː-
syndetic sɪnˈdet.ɪk (US) -ˈdeţ-
syndic ˈsɪn.dɪk **-s** -s
syndical|ism ˈsɪn.dɪ.kᵊl|.ɪ.zᵊm **-ist/s** -ɪst/s
syndicate (*n.*) ˈsɪn.dɪ.kət, -kɪt (US) -də.kɪt **-s** -s
syndi|cate (*v.*) ˈsɪn.dɪ|.keɪt (US) -də- **-cates** -keɪts **-cating** -keɪ.tɪŋ (US) -keɪ.ţɪŋ **-cated** -keɪ.tɪd (US) -keɪ.ţɪd
syndication ˌsɪn.dɪˈkeɪ.ʃᵊn (US) -dəˈ-
syndrome ˈsɪn.drəʊm (US) -droʊm **-s** -z
syne saɪn
synecdoche sɪˈnek.də.ki
synereslis sɪˈnɪə.rə.s|ɪs, -rɪ- (US) -ˈner.ə- **-es** -iːz
synergism ˈsɪn.ə.dʒɪ.zᵊm (US) ˈ-ɚ-
synerg|y ˈsɪn.ə.dʒ|i (US) ˈ-ɚ- **-ies** -iz
synesthesia ˌsɪn.ɪsˈθiː.zi.ə, -iːsˈ-, -əsˈ-, -ʒə, -ʒi.ə (US) -ɪsˈθiː.ʒə, -ʒi.ə, -zi-
Synge sɪŋ
synod ˈsɪn.əd, -ɒd (US) -əd **-s** -z **-al** -ᵊl
synodic sɪˈnɒd.ɪk (US) -ˈnɑː.dɪk **-al** -ᵊl **-ally** -ᵊl.i, -li
synonym ˈsɪn.ə.nɪm **-s** -z
synonymous sɪˈnɒn.ɪ.məs, ˈ-ə- (US) -ˈnɑː.nə- **-ly** -li
synonymy sɪˈnɒn.ɪ.mi, ˈ-ə- (US) -ˈnɑː.nə-
synops|is sɪˈnɒp.s|ɪs (US) -ˈnɑːp- **-es** -iːz
synoptic sɪˈnɒp.tɪk (US) -ˈnɑːp- **-s** -s **-al** -ᵊl **-ally** -ᵊl.i, -li
synovi|a saɪˈnəʊ.vi|.ə, sɪ- (US) sɪˈnoʊ- **-al** -ᵊl
synovitis ˌsaɪ.nəʊˈvaɪ.tɪs, ˌsɪn.əʊˈ- (US) ˌsaɪ.nəˈvaɪ.ţɪs, ˌsɪn.əˈ-
syntactic sɪnˈtæk.tɪk **-al** -ᵊl **-ally** -ᵊl.i, -li
syntagm ˈsɪn.tæm **-s** -z
syntagmatic ˌsɪn.tægˈmæt.ɪk (US) -ˈmæţ-
syntax ˈsɪn.tæks **-es** -ɪz
synthes|is ˈsɪnt.θə.s|ɪs, -θɪ- (US) -θə- **-es** -iːz
synthesiz|e, -is|e ˈsɪnt.θə.saɪz, -θɪ- (US) -θə- **-es** -ɪz **-ing** -ɪŋ **-ed** -d **-er/s** -əʳ/z (US) -ɚ/z
synthespian sɪnˈθes.pi.ən **-s** -z
synthetic sɪnˈθet.ɪk (US) -ˈθeţ- **-s** -s **-ally** -ᵊl.i, -li
syphilis ˈsɪf.ɪ.lɪs, -ᵊl.ɪs (US) -ᵊl.ɪs
syphilitic ˌsɪf.ɪˈlɪt.ɪk, -ᵊlˈɪt- (US) -əˈlɪţ-
syphon ˈsaɪ.fᵊn **-s** -z **-ing** -ɪŋ **-ed** -d
Syracusan ˌsaɪə.rəˈkjuː.zᵊn, ˌsɪr.əˈ- (US) ˌsɪr.əˈ-
Syracuse *in classical history:* ˈsaɪə.rə.kjuːz (US) ˈsɪr.ə- *modern town in Sicily:* ˈsaɪə.rə.kjuːz, ˈsɪr.ə- (US) ˈsɪr.ə- *town in US:* ˈsɪr.ə.kjuːs, -kjuːz
Syri|a ˈsɪr.i|.ə **-an/s** -ən/z
Syriac ˈsɪr.i.æk
syringa sɪˈrɪŋ.gə **-s** -z
syring|e sɪˈrɪndʒ, sə-; ˈsɪr.ɪndʒ (US) səˈrɪndʒ; ˈsɪr.ɪndʒ **-es** -ɪz **-ing** -ɪŋ **-ed** -d
syrinx ˈsɪr.ɪŋks **-es** -ɪz
syrophoenician ˌsaɪə.rəʊ.fɪˈnɪʃ.ᵊn, -fiːˈ-, -ʃi.ən, -si.ən (US) ˌsaɪ.roʊ.fiːˈnɪʃ.ᵊn, -fɪˈ-
syr|tis (S) ˈsɜː|.tɪs (US) ˈsɝː|.ţɪs **-tes** -tiːz
syrup ˈsɪr.əp (US) ˈsɪr-, ˈsɝː- **-s** -s **-y** -i
systaltic sɪˈstæl.tɪk (US) -ˈstɑːl.ţɪk, -ˈstæl-
system ˈsɪs.təm, -tɪm (US) -təm **-s** -z ˌ**systems** ˈ**analyst**
systematic ˌsɪs.təˈmæt.ɪk, -tɪˈ- (US) -təˈmæţ- **-ally** -ᵊl.i, -li
systematization, -isa- ˌsɪs.tə.mə.taɪˈzeɪ.ʃᵊn, -tɪ-, -tɪˈ- (US) -tə.mə.ţɪˈ-
systematiz|e, -is|e ˈsɪs.tə.mə.taɪz, -tɪ- (US) -tə- **-es** -ɪz **-ing** -ɪŋ **-ed** -d **-er/s** -əʳ/z (US) -ɚ/z
systemic sɪˈstem.ɪk, -ˈstiː.mɪk (US) -ˈstem.ɪk
systemiz|e ˈsɪs.tə.maɪz, -tɪ- (US) -tə- **-es** -ɪz **-ing** -ɪŋ **-ed** -d
systole ˈsɪs.tᵊl.i
systolic sɪˈstɒl.ɪk (US) -ˈɑː.lɪk
syzyg|y ˈsɪz.ɪ.dʒ|i, ˈ-ə- (US) ˈ-ə- **-ies** -iz
Szczecin ˈʃtʃet.ʃiːn
Szeged ˈseg.ed

Pronouncing the letter T

See also TH, TZ

The consonant letter **t** has several possible realisations. In word initial and final position, it is most often realised as /t/, e.g.:

tap /tæp/
get /get/

However, in consonant clusters /t/ may be elided, and it is silent in some words borrowed from French, e.g.:

castle /ˈkɑː.sl̩/ (US) /ˈkæs.l̩/
depot /ˈdep.əʊ/ (US) /ˈdiː.poʊ/

In US English, **t** is often pronounced as a voiced consonant in certain environments. The **t** must be at the end of a stressed syllable, preceded either by one of /n/, /l/, or /r/ or a vowel, and followed by an unstressed syllable, either beginning with a vowel or containing a syllabic consonant other than /n/. Such a pronunciation is shown in EPD as /t̬/.

When appearing between two vowels, **t** is most likely to be pronounced as a tap or flap, e.g.:

butter /ˈbʌt.əʳ/ (US) ˈbʌt̬.ɚ/

Before a syllabic consonant, and following /n/ or /l/, **t** is pronounced as a brief voiced plosive rather than a tap or flap, e.g.:

little /ˈlɪt.l̩/ (US) /ˈlɪt̬-/
canter /ˈkæn.təʳ/ (US) /-t̬ɚ/

In careful speech, these words may be pronounced with a voiceless /t/, as in British English.

Another common pronunciation for **t** is /ʃ/ where it is followed by a suffix which begins with the letter **i**, e.g.:

negotiate /nɪˈgəʊ.ʃi.eɪt/ (US) /-ˈgoʊ-/
affection /əˈfek.ʃᵊn/

In addition

t can be pronounced as a GLOTTAL STOP either word finally or between two vowels.

t is also sometimes realised as /tʃ/, e.g.:

adventure /ədˈven.tʃəʳ/ (US) /-tʃɚ/
picture /ˈpɪk.tʃəʳ/ (US) /-tʃɚ/

Due to coalescence between /t/ and /j/ in British English and omission of /j/ in US English, syllables beginning with **tu** do not always sound the same, e.g.:

Tuesday /ˈtʃuːz.deɪ/ (US) /ˈtuːz-/

t (T) tiː **-'s** -z
ta *Tonic Sol-fa name for diminished seventh from the tonic:* tɔː (US) tɑː **-s** -z
ta *syllable used in Tonic Sol-fa for counting time:* tɑː
ta *thank you:* tɑː
Note: This form is used in casual British English.
Taal tɑːl
tab tæb **-s** -z **-bing** -ɪŋ **-bed** -d
tabard 'tæb.ɑːd, -əd (US) -ɚd **-s** -z
Tabasco® tə'bæs.kəʊ (US) -koʊ
Tabatha 'tæb.ə.θə
tabbouleh tə'buː.lə, -li
tabb|y 'tæb|.i **-ies** -iz
tabernacle 'tæb.əˌnæk.l̩ (US) -ɚˌ- **-s** -z
Taberner tə'bɜː.nəʳ; 'tæb.ᵊn.əʳ (US) tə'bɝː.nɚ; 'tæb.ɚ.nɚ
tabes 'teɪ.biːz
Tabitha 'tæb.ɪ.θə, '-ə-
tabla 'tæb.lə (US) 'tɑː.blə, -blɑː **-s** -z
tablature 'tæb.lə.tʃəʳ, -lɪ-, -tjʊəʳ (US) -lə.tʃɚ **-s** -z
tabl|e (T) 'teɪ.bl̩ **-es** -z **-ing** -ɪŋ, 'teɪ.blɪŋ **-ed** -d **'table ˌlinen; 'table ˌmanners; 'table ˌtennis, ˌtable 'tennis; 'table ˌwine; ˌdrink someone ˌunder the 'table; ˌturn the 'tables on ˌsomeone**
tableau 'tæb.ləʊ (US) -loʊ, -'- **-s** -z
tableaux *(alternative plur. of* **tableau***)* 'tæb.ləʊ, -ləʊz (US) -loʊ, -loʊz, -'-
table|cloth 'teɪ.bl̩|.klɒθ (US) -klɑːθ **-cloths** -klɒθs, -klɒðz (US) -klɑːθs, -klɑːðz
table d'hôte ˌtɑː.bl̩'dəʊt, -blə'- (US) -bl̩'doʊt, ˌtæb.l̩'-
table-hop 'teɪ.bl̩.hɒp (US) -hɑːp **-s** -s **-ping** -ɪŋ **-ped** -t **-per/s** -əʳ/z (US) -ɚ/z
tableland 'teɪ.bl̩.lænd **-s** -z
tablemat 'teɪ.bl̩.mæt **-s** -s
tablespoon 'teɪ.bl̩.spuːn **-s** -z
tablespoonful 'teɪ.bl̩ˌspuːn.fʊl **-s** -z
tablespoonsful *(alternative plur. of* **tablespoonful***)* 'teɪ.bl̩ˌspuːnz.fʊl
tablet 'tæb.lət, -lɪt (US) -lɪt **-s** -s **ˌtablets of 'stone**
table-turning 'teɪ.bl̩ˌtɜː.nɪŋ (US) -ˌtɝː-
tableware 'teɪ.bl̩.weəʳ (US) -wer
tabloid 'tæb.lɔɪd **-s** -z
taboo tə'buː, tæb'uː **-s** -z **-ing** -ɪŋ **-ed** -d
tabor 'teɪ.bəʳ, -bɔːʳ (US) -bɚ **-s** -z
Tabor 'teɪ.bɔːʳ, -bəʳ (US) -bɚ
tabo(u)ret 'tæb.ᵊr.ɪt, -et (US) ˌtæb.ə'ret, '--- **-s** -s
Tabriz tæb'riːz (US) tɑː'briːz, tə-
tabular 'tæb.jə.ləʳ, -jʊ- (US) -lɚ
tabula rasa ˌtæb.jə.lə'rɑː.sə, -jʊ-, -zə
tabulae rasae ˌtæb.jə.liː'rɑː.siː, -jʊ-, -ziː
tabu|late 'tæb.jə|.leɪt, -jʊ- **-lates** -leɪts **-lating** -leɪ.tɪŋ (US) -leɪ.t̬ɪŋ **-lated** -leɪ.tɪd (US) -leɪ.t̬ɪd **-lator/s** -leɪ.təʳ/z (US) -leɪ.t̬ɚ/z
tabulation ˌtæb.jə'leɪ.ʃᵊn, -jʊ'- **-s** -z
tacet 'teɪ.set, 'tæs.et, -ɪt (US) 'teɪ.set, 'tæs.et; 'tɑː.ket
tach|e tɑːʃ, tæʃ (US) tætʃ **-es** -ɪz
tach|ism (T) 'tæʃ|.ɪ.zᵊm **-ist/s** -ɪst/s **-iste/s** -'iːst/s
tachograph 'tæk.əʊ.grɑːf, -græf (US) -ə.græf **-s** -s
tachometer tæk'ɒm.ɪ.təʳ, '-ə- (US) tæk'ɑː.mə.t̬ɚ, tə'kɑː- **-s** -z
tachycardia ˌtæk.ɪ'kɑː.di.ə (US) -'kɑːr-
tachygraph 'tæk.ɪ.grɑːf, -græf (US) -græf **-s** -s
tachygraph|y tæk'ɪ.grə.f|i, tə'kɪg- **-er/s** -əʳ/z (US) -ɚ/z
tacit 'tæs.ɪt **-ly** -li **-ness** -nəs, -nɪs
taciturn 'tæs.ɪ.tɜːn (US) -ə.tɝːn **-ly** -li
taciturnity ˌtæs.ɪ'tɜː.nə.ti, -nɪ- (US) -ə'tɝː.nə.t̬i
Tacitus 'tæs.ɪ.təs (US) -t̬əs
tack tæk **-s** -s **-ing** -ɪŋ **-ed** -t
tackl|e 'tæk.l̩ *nautical often:* 'teɪ.kl̩ **-es** -z **-ing** -ɪŋ, 'tæk.lɪŋ, 'teɪ.klɪŋ **-ed** -d

-er/s -əʳ/z, ˈtæk.ləʳ/z, ˈteɪ.kləʳ/z (US) ˈtæk.l̩.ɚ/z, ˈteɪ.kl̩.ɚ/z, ˈtæk.lɚ/z, ˈteɪ.klɚ/z
tack|y ˈtæk|.i **-ier** -i.əʳ (US) -i.ɚ **-iest** -i.ɪst, -i.əst **-ily** -ɪ.li, -əl.i **-iness** -ɪ.nəs, -ɪ.nɪs
taco ˈtæk.əʊ, ˈtɑː.kəʊ (US) ˈtɑː.koʊ **-s** -z
Tacoma təˈkəʊ.mə (US) -ˈkoʊ-
tact tækt
tactful ˈtækt.fəl, -fʊl **-ly** -i **-ness** -nəs, -nɪs
tactic ˈtæk.tɪk **-s** -s **-al** -əl **-ally** -əl.i, -li
tactician tækˈtɪʃ.ən **-s** -z
tactile ˈtæk.taɪl (US) -təl
tactless ˈtækt.ləs, -lɪs **-ly** -li **-ness** -nəs, -nɪs
tactual ˈtæk.tju.əl, -tʃu- (US) -tʃu- **-ly** -i
tad tæd **-s** -z
Tadcaster ˈtædˌkæs.təʳ, -kə.stəʳ (US) -ˌkæs.tɚ
Tadema ˈtæd.ɪ.mə, ˈ-ə-
Tadley ˈtæd.li
tadpole ˈtæd.pəʊl (US) -poʊl **-s** -z
Tadworth ˈtæd.wəθ, -wɜːθ (US) -wɚθ, -wɝːθ
Tadzhik ˈtɑː.dʒiːk, -ˈ- (US) ˌtɑːˈdʒɪk, -ˈdʒiːk
Tadzhikistan tɑːˌdʒɪk.ɪˈstɑːn, -ˌdʒiː.kɪˈ- (US) -ˈdʒɪk.ɪ.stæn, -ˈdʒiː.kɪ-, -stɑːn
Taegu ˌteɪˈguː (US) ˈtaɪ.guː, -ˈ-
Tae Kwon Do ˌtaɪˈkwɒn.dəʊ, ˌteɪ-, ˌ--ˈ- (US) ˌtaɪ.kwɑːnˈdoʊ, ˌ-ˈ--
tael teɪl **-s** -z
ta'en *(dialectal for* **taken***)* teɪn
Taff tæf
Taff-Ely ˌtæfˈiː.li
taffeta ˈtæf.ɪ.tə, ˈ-ə- (US) -ɪ.t̬ə
taffrail ˈtæf.reɪl, -rɪl, -rəl (US) -reɪl **-s** -z
Taff|y *Brit slang for Welsh:* ˈtæf|.i **-ies** -iz
taffy *US for toffee:* ˈtæf.i
Taft *surname* tæft, tɑːft (US) tæft *town in Iran:* tɑːft
tag tæg **-s** -z **-ging** -ɪŋ **-ged** -d **ˈtag ˌquestion**
Tagalog təˈgɑː.lɒg, -ləg (US) -lɑːg, -lɔːg
tagetes tædʒˈiː.tiːz
Taggart ˈtæg.ət (US) -ɚt
tagliatelle ˌtæl.jəˈtel.i (US) ˌtɑːl.jəˈ-
tagmeme ˈtæg.miːm **-s** -z
tagmemic tægˈmiː.mɪk **-s** -s
Tagore təˈgɔːʳ (US) -ˈgɔːr
Tagus ˈteɪ.gəs
tahini tɑːˈhiː.ni, tə- (US) tə-, tɑː-
Tahi|ti tɑːˈhiː|.ti, tə- (US) təˈhiː|.t̬i **-tian/s** -ʃən/z (US) -ʃən/z, -t̬i.ənz
Tahoe ˈtɑː.həʊ (US) -hoʊ
t'ai chi, **tai chi** ˌtaɪˈtʃiː, -ˈdʒiː (US) -ˈdʒiː, -ˈtʃiː
Taichung, **T'ai-chung** ˌtaɪˈtʃʊŋ
Taig taɪk, taɪx **-s** -s

taiga ˈtaɪ.gə, -gɑː (US) -gə
tail teɪl **-s** -z **-ing** -ɪŋ **-ed** -d **-less** -ləs, -lɪs **ˌtail ˈend; ˈtail ˌpipe; make ˌhead or ˈtail of; with one's ˌtail between one's ˈlegs**
tailback ˈteɪl.bæk **-s** -s
tailboard ˈteɪl.bɔːd (US) -bɔːrd **-s** -z
tailbone ˈteɪl.bəʊn (US) -boʊn **-s** -z
tailcoat ˌteɪlˈkəʊt, ˈ-- (US) ˈteɪl.koʊt **-s** -s
tail|gate ˈteɪl|.geɪt **-gates** -geɪts **-gating** -geɪ.tɪŋ (US) -geɪ.t̬ɪŋ **-gated** -geɪ.tɪd (US) -geɪ.t̬ɪd **-gater/s** -ˌgeɪ.təʳ/z (US) -ˌgeɪ.t̬ɚ/z
taille taɪ (US) teɪl
tail|or ˈteɪ.l|əʳ (US) -l|ɚ **-ors** -əz (US) -ɚz **-oring** -ər.ɪŋ **-ored** -əd (US) -ɚd
tailor-made ˌteɪ.ləˈmeɪd (US) -lɚˈ- **-s** -z *stress shift:* ˌtailor-made ˈsuit
tailpiec|e ˈteɪl.piːs **-es** -ɪz
tailpipe ˈteɪl.paɪp **-s** -s
tail-rhyme ˈteɪl.raɪm
tailspin ˈteɪl.spɪn **-s** -z
tailwind ˈteɪl.wɪnd **-s** -z
Taine teɪn
taint teɪnt **-s** -s **-ing** -ɪŋ (US) ˈteɪn.t̬ɪŋ **-ed** -ɪd (US) ˈteɪn.t̬ɪd **-less** -ləs, -lɪs
taipan ˈtaɪ.pæn (US) ˈ--, -ˈ- **-s** -z
Taipei ˌtaɪˈpeɪ
Taiping ˌtaɪˈpɪŋ
Tait teɪt
Taiwan ˌtaɪˈwɑːn, -ˈwæn (US) -ˈwɑːn
Taiwanese ˌtaɪ.wəˈniːz, -wɑːˈ- (US) -wəˈniːz, -ˈniːs
Ta'izz teɪˈiːz, tæ- (US) tæˈɪz
Tajik tɑːˈdʒiːk; ˈtɑː.dʒɪk **-s** -s
Tajikistan tɑːˈdʒiː.kɪˌstɑːn, -ˌstæn
Taj Mahal ˌtɑːdʒ.məˈhɑːl
taka ˈtɑː.kɑː
tak|e teɪk **-es** -s **-ing** -ɪŋ **took** tʊk **taken** ˈteɪ.kən **taker/s** ˈteɪ.kəʳ/z (US) -kɚ/z **ˌtake a ˈwalk; ˌtake a ˈhike**
takeaway ˈteɪk.ə.weɪ **-s** -z
take-home pay ˈteɪk.həʊmˌpeɪ, ˌ--ˈ- (US) ˈteɪk.hoʊmˌpeɪ
take-it-or-leave-it ˌteɪk.ɪt.ɔːˈliːv.ɪt, -əˈ- (US) -ɔːrˈ-, -ɚˈ-
take-off ˈteɪk.ɒf (US) -ɑːf **-s** -s
takeout ˈteɪk.aʊt **-s** -s
takeover ˈteɪkˌəʊ.vəʳ (US) -ˌoʊ.vɚ **-s** -z **ˈtakeover ˌbid**
take-up ˈteɪk.ʌp **-s** -s
taking ˈteɪ.kɪŋ **-s** -z **-ly** -li **-ness** -nəs, -nɪs
tala ˈtɑː.lɑː
Talbot ˈtɔːl.bət, ˈtɒl- (US) ˈtɔːl-, ˈtæl-
Note: Both pronunciations are current for **Port Talbot** in Wales.
talc tælk **-s** -s
Talcahuano ˌtæl.kəˈwɑː.nəʊ (US) ˌtɑːl.kɑːˈwɑː.noʊ, ˌtæl.kəˈ-
talcum powder ˈtæl.kəmˌpaʊ.dəʳ (US) -dɚ **-s** -z

tale teɪl **-s** -z
talebearer ˈteɪlˌbeə.rəʳ (US) -ˌber.ɚ **-s** -z
tal|ent ˈtæl|.ənt **-ents** -ənts **-ented** -ən.tɪd (US) -ən.t̬ɪd **-entless** -ənt.ləs, -lɪs **ˈtalent ˌcontest; ˈtalent ˌscout**
talent|-spot ˈtæl.ənt|.spɒt (US) -spɑːt **-spots** -spɒts (US) -spɑːts **-spotting** -ˌspɒt.ɪŋ (US) -ˌspɑː.t̬ɪŋ **-spotted** -ˌspɒt.ɪd (US) -ˌspɑː.t̬ɪd **-spotter/s** -ˌspɒt.əʳ/z (US) -ˌspɑː.t̬ɚ/z
tales *law:* ˈteɪ.liːz (US) ˈteɪ.liːz; teɪlz
tales|man ˈteɪ.liːz|.mən, ˈteɪlz-, -mæn (US) ˈteɪlz-, ˈteɪl.iːz- **-men** -mən, -men
taletell|er ˈteɪlˌtel|.əʳ (US) -ɚ **-er/s** -əʳ/z (US) -ɚ/z **-ing** -ɪŋ
Talfourd ˈtæl.fəd (US) -fɚd
Taliban ˈtæl.ɪ.bæn, ˈtɑː.lɪ-, -lə-, -bɑːn, ˌ--ˈ- (US) ˈtæl.ə.bæn, -bɑːn, ˈtɑː.l-, -ɪ-
Taliesin ˌtæl.iˈes.ɪn, ˌ-ˈjes- (US) -iˈes.ɪn
talisman ˈtæl.ɪz.mən, -ɪs- **-s** -z
talismanic ˌtæl.ɪzˈmæn.ɪk, -ɪsˈ- **-ally** -əl.i, -li
talk tɔːk (US) tɔːk, tɑːk **-s** -s **-ing** -ɪŋ **-ed** -t **-er/s** -əʳ/z (US) -ɚ/z **ˌtalking ˈhead; ˈtalking ˌpoint; ˈtalk ˌshow; (to) ˌtalk ˈshop**
talkathon ˈtɔː.kə.θɒn (US) -θɑːn, ˈtɑː- **-s** -z
talkative ˈtɔː.kə.tɪv (US) -t̬ɪv, ˈtɑː- **-ly** -li **-ness** -nəs, -nɪs
talkback ˈtɔːk.bæk (US) ˈtɔːk-, ˈtɑːk- **-s** -s
talkie ˈtɔː.ki (US) ˈtɔː-, ˈtɑː- **-s** -z
talking-to ˈtɔː.kɪŋ.tuː (US) ˈtɔː-, ˈtɑː- **-s** -z
tall tɔːl **-er** -əʳ (US) -ɚ **-est** -ɪst, -əst **-ness** -nəs, -nɪs **ˌtall ˈstory**
tallage ˈtæl.ɪdʒ
Tallahassee ˌtæl.əˈhæs.i
tallboy ˈtɔːl.bɔɪ **-s** -z
Talleyrand ˈtæl.i.rænd
Tallin(n) ˈtæl.ɪn, -ˈ-, -ˈiːn (US) ˈtɑː.lɪn, ˈtæl.ɪn
Tallis ˈtæl.ɪs
tallish ˈtɔː.lɪʃ
tallow ˈtæl.əʊ (US) -oʊ **-y** -i
Tallulah təˈluː.lə
tall|y ˈtæl|.i **-ies** -iz **-ying** -i.ɪŋ **-ied** -id
tally-ho ˌtæl.iˈhəʊ (US) -ˈhoʊ **-s** -z
tally|man ˈtæl.i|.mən **-men** -mən, -men
Talman ˈtɔːl.mən
Talmud ˈtæl.mʊd, -məd, -mʌd (US) ˈtɑːl.mʊd, ˈtæl-, -məd
talmudic (T) tælˈmʊd.ɪk, -ˈmʌd-, -ˈmjuː.dɪk (US) tɑːlˈmʊd.ɪk, tæl- **-al** -əl
talmud|ism (T) ˈtæl.mʊd|.ɪ.zəm, -məd-, -mʌd- **-ist/s** -ɪst/s
talon ˈtæl.ən **-s** -z
Tal-y-llyn ˌtæl.iˈhlɪn, -əˈ-, -ˈθlɪn
tamable ˈteɪ.mə.bl̩
tamagotchi ˌtæm.əˈgɒtʃ.i (US) ˌtɑː.məˈgɑː.tʃ.i, ˈtæm- **-s** -z

tamale *Mexican dish:* tə'mɑː.li, -leɪ
Tamale *in Ghana:* tə'mɑː.leɪ
Tamaqua tə'mɑː.kwə
Tamar *river in W. of England:* 'teɪ.məʳ, -mɑːʳ (US) -mɚ, -mɑːr
Tamar *biblical name:* 'teɪ.mɑːʳ, -məʳ (US) -mɑːr, -mɚ
Tamara tə'mɑː.rə, -'mær.ə; 'tæm.ᵊr.ə (US) tə'mɑːr.ə, -'mær-, -'mer-
tamarillo ˌtæm.ᵊr'ɪl.əʊ (US) -ə'rɪl.oʊ **-s** -z
tamarin 'tæm.ᵊr.ɪn (US) -ɚ.ɪn, -ə.ræn **-s** -z
tamarind 'tæm.ᵊr.ɪnd **-s** -z
tamarisk 'tæm.ᵊr.ɪsk **-s** -s
tambala tæm'bɑː.lə (US) tɑːm'bɑː.lɑː **-s** -z
tamber 'tæm.bəʳ (US) -bɚ **-s** -z
Tambo 'tæm.bəʊ (US) -boʊ
tambour 'tæm.bʊəʳ, -bɔːʳ, -bəʳ (US) -bʊr **-s** -z
tamboura tæm'bʊə.rə, -'bɔː- (US) tɑːm'bʊr.ə **-s** -z
tambourine ˌtæm.bᵊr'iːn (US) -bə'riːn **-s** -z
Tamburlaine 'tæm.bə.leɪn (US) -bɚ-
tam|e teɪm **-er/s** -əʳ/z (US) -ɚ/z **-est** -ɪst, -əst **-ely** -li **-eness** -nəs, -nɪs **-es** -z **-ing** -ɪŋ **-ed** -d
tameable 'teɪ.mə.bl̩
Tamerlane 'tæm.ə.leɪn (US) '-ɚ-
Tameside 'teɪm.saɪd
Tamil 'tæm.ɪl, -ᵊl (US) -ᵊl, 'tɑː.mᵊl, 'tʊm.ᵊl **-s** -z
Tamil Nadu ˌtæm.ɪl'nɑː.duː, -ᵊl- (US) -ᵊl'nɑː.duː, ˌtɑː.mᵊl'-, ˌtʊm.ᵊl'-, -nɑː'duː
Tammany 'tæm.ᵊn.i
Tammerfors 'tæm.ə.fɔːz (US) -ɚ.fɔːrz
Tammuz 'tæm.uːz, -ʊz (US) 'tɑː.mʊz
Tammy 'tæm.i
Tamora 'tæm.ᵊr.ə
tam-o'-shanter ˌtæm.ə'ʃæn.təʳ (US) 'tæm.əˌʃæn.t̬ɚ **-s** -z
tamoxifen tə'mɒk.sɪ.fen, tæm'ɒk-, -sə- (US) tə'mɑːk-, tæm'ɑːk-
tamp tæmp **-s** -s **-ing** -ɪŋ **-ed** -t **-er/s** -əʳ/z (US) -ɚ/z
Tampa 'tæm.pə
Tampax® 'tæm.pæks
tamp|er 'tæm.p|əʳ (US) -p|ɚ **-ers** -əz (US) -ɚz **-ering** -ᵊr.ɪŋ **-ered** -əd (US) -ɚd **-erer/s** -ə.rəʳ/z (US) -ɚ.ɚ/z
Tampere 'tæm.pᵊr.eɪ (US) 'tɑːm.pə.reɪ
tamper-evident ˌtæm.pᵊr'ev.ɪ.dᵊnt (US) -pɚ'-
tamper-proof 'tæm.pə.pruːf (US) -pɚ-
Tampico tæm'piː.kəʊ (US) -koʊ, tɑːm-
tampon 'tæm.pɒn (US) -pɑːn **-s** -z
Tamsin 'tæm.zɪn, -sɪn
Tamworth 'tæm.wəθ, -wɜːθ (US) -wɚθ, -wɝːθ

tan tæn **-s** -z **-ning** -ɪŋ **-ned** -d **-ner/s** -əʳ/z (US) -ɚ/z
Tancred 'tæŋ.kred, -krɪd (US) -krɪd
tandem 'tæn.dəm, -dem (US) -dəm **-s** -z
tandoori tæn'dʊə.ri, -'dɔː- (US) tɑːn'dʊr.i
Tandy 'tæn.di
Tanfield 'tæn.fiːld
tang tæŋ **-s** -z **-y** -i
Tang tæŋ (US) tɑːŋ
Tanga 'tæŋ.gə
Tanganyika ˌtæŋ.gə'njiː.kə, -gæn'jiː- (US) -gə'njiː-
tangenc|y 'tæn.dʒənt.s|i **-ies** -iz
tangent 'tæn.dʒᵊnt **-s** -s
tangential tæn'dʒen.*t*ʃᵊl (US) -'dʒent.ʃᵊl **-ly** -i **-ness** -nəs, -nɪs
tangerine ˌtæn.dʒᵊr'iːn, '--- (US) ˌtæn.dʒə'riːn, '--- **-s** -z
tangibility ˌtæn.dʒə'bɪl.ə.ti, -dʒɪ'-, -ɪ.ti (US) -dʒə'bɪl.ə.t̬i
tangib|le 'tæn.dʒə.b|l̩, -dʒɪ- (US) -dʒə- **-ly** -li **-leness** -l̩.nəs, -nɪs
Tangier tæn'dʒɪəʳ, '-- (US) tæn'dʒɪr **-s** -z
tangl|e 'tæŋ.gl̩ **-es** -z **-ing** -ɪŋ, 'tæŋ.glɪŋ **-ed** -d
Tanglewood 'tæŋ.gl̩.wʊd
tangly 'tæŋ.gli, '-gl̩.i
tango 'tæŋ.gəʊ (US) -goʊ **-s** -z **-ing** -ɪŋ **-ed** -d
tang|y 'tæŋ|.i **-ier** -i.əʳ (US) -i.ɚ **-iest** -i.ɪst, -i.əst **-iness** -ɪ.nəs, -ɪ.nɪs
Tangye 'tæŋ.gi
tanh θæn, tæn*t*ʃ
tank tæŋk **-s** -s **-age** -ɪdʒ **-er/s** -əʳ/z (US) -ɚ/z **'tank ˌtop; ˌtanked 'up**
tankard 'tæŋ.kəd (US) -kɚd **-s** -z
tankful 'tæŋk.fʊl **-s** -z
tanner (T) 'tæn.əʳ (US) -ɚ **-s** -z
tanner|y 'tæn.ᵊr|.i **-ies** -iz
Tannhäuser 'tænˌhɔɪ.zəʳ (US) 'tɑːnˌhɔɪ.zɚ, 'tæn-
tann|ic 'tæn|.ɪk **-in** -ɪn **ˌtannic 'acid**
tannin 'tæn.ɪn **-s** -z
Tannoy® 'tæn.ɔɪ
Tanqueray 'tæŋ.kᵊr.i, -eɪ (US) -kə.reɪ, -kɚ.i
tansy (T) 'tæn.zi
tantalization, -isa- ˌtæn.tᵊl.aɪ'zeɪ.ʃᵊn, -ɪ'- (US) -t̬ᵊl.ɪ'- **-s** -z
tantaliz|e, -is|e 'tæn.tᵊl.aɪz (US) -t̬ə.laɪz **-es** -ɪz **-ing/ly** -ɪŋ/li **-ed** -d **-er/s** -əʳ/z (US) -ɚ/z
tantalum 'tæn.tᵊl.əm (US) -t̬ᵊl- **-s** -z
tantalus (T) 'tæn.tᵊl.əs (US) -t̬ᵊl- **-es** -ɪz
tantamount 'tæn.tə.maʊnt (US) -t̬ə-
tantiv|y tæn'tɪv|.i **-ies** -iz
tanto 'tæn.təʊ (US) -toʊ
tantr|a (T) 'tæn.tr|ə, 'tʌn- (US) 'tʌn-, 'tɑːn-, 'tæn- **-ic** -ɪk
tantrum 'tæn.trəm **-s** -z
Tanya 'tæn.jə, 'tɑː.njə (US) 'tɑː.njə, 'tæn.jə

Tanzani|a ˌtæn.zə'niː|.ə; tæn'zeɪ.ni- (US) ˌtæn.zə'niː- **-an/s** -ən/z
Tao taʊ (US) daʊ, taʊ
Taoiseach 'tiː.ʃək, -ʃəx (US) -ʃək
Tao|ism 'taʊ|.ɪ.zᵊm, 'teɪ.əʊ- (US) 'daʊ|.ɪ-, 'taʊ- **-ist/s** -ɪst/s
tap tæp **-s** -s **-ping** -ɪŋ **-ped** -t **-per/s** -əʳ/z (US) -ɚ/z
tapas 'tæp.æs, -əs **'tapas ˌbar**
tap-danc|e 'tæpˌdɑːn*t*s (US) -ˌdæn*t*s **-es** -ɪz **-ing** -ɪŋ **-ed** -t **-er/s** -əʳ/z (US) -ɚ/z
tap|e (T) teɪp **-es** -s **-ing** -ɪŋ **-ed** -t **'tape ˌdeck; 'tape ˌmeasure; 'tape reˌcorder**
tap|er 'teɪ.p|əʳ (US) -p|ɚ **-ers** -əz (US) -ɚz **-ering** -ᵊr.ɪŋ **-ered** -əd (US) -ɚd
tapestr|y 'tæp.ɪ.str|i, '-ə- (US) '-ə- **-ies** -iz
tapeworm 'teɪp.wɜːm (US) -wɝːm **-s** -z
tapioca ˌtæp.i'əʊ.kə (US) -'oʊ-
tapir 'teɪ.pəʳ, -pɪəʳ (US) -pɚ **-s** -z
tapis 'tæp.iː, -pi (US) -i, -ɪs; tæp'iː
Tapling 'tæp.lɪŋ
Tappertit 'tæp.ə.tɪt (US) '-ɚ-
tappet 'tæp.ɪt **-s** -s
taproom 'tæp.rʊm, -ruːm (US) -ruːm, -rʊm **-s** -z
tap-root 'tæp.ruːt **-s** -s
tapster 'tæp.stəʳ (US) -stɚ **-s** -z
tar tɑːʳ (US) tɑːr **-s** -z **-ring** -ɪŋ **-red** -d
Tara *literary location, place in Ireland:* 'tɑː.rə (US) 'ter.ə, 'tær- *female name:* 'tɑː.rə (US) 'tɑːr.ə
taradiddle 'tær.əˌdɪd.l̩ (US) 'ter-, 'tær- **-s** -z
taramasalata, taramosalata ˌtær.ə.mə.sə'lɑː.tə (US) ˌtɑːr.ɑː.mɑː.sɑː'lɑː.tɑː
Taransay 'tær.ən.seɪ
tarantella ˌtær.ᵊn'tel.ə (US) ˌter-, ˌtær- **-s** -z
Tarantino ˌtær.ᵊn'tiː.nəʊ (US) ˌter.ᵊn'tiː.noʊ, ˌtær-
Taranto tə'ræn.təʊ; (US) -toʊ; 'tɑːr.ɑːn-
tarantula tə'ræn.tjə.lə, -tjʊ-, -tʃə- (US) -tʃə-, -tʃʊ-, -tjʊ-, -t̬ə- **-s** -z
Tarawa tə'rɑː.wə (US) tə'rɑː-; 'tɑːr.ə-
taraxacum tə'ræk.sə.kəm
Tarbuck 'tɑː.bʌk (US) 'tɑːr-
Tardis 'tɑː.dɪs (US) 'tɑːr- **-es** -ɪz
tard|y 'tɑː.d|i (US) 'tɑːr- **-ier** -i.əʳ (US) -i.ɚ **-iest** -i.ɪst, -i.əst **-ily** -ɪ.li, -ᵊl.i **-iness** -ɪ.nəs, -ɪ.nɪs
tare teəʳ (US) ter **-s** -z
tar|get 'tɑː|.gɪt (US) 'tɑːr- **-gets** -gɪts **-geting** -gɪ.tɪŋ (US) -gɪ.t̬ɪŋ **-geted** -gɪ.tɪd (US) -gɪ.t̬ɪd **'target ˌpractice**
tariff 'tær.ɪf (US) 'ter-, 'tær- **-s** -s
Tariq 'tær.ɪk, 'tɑː.rɪk (US) 'tɑːr.ɪk
Tarka 'tɑː.kə (US) 'tɑːr-
Tarkington 'tɑː.kɪŋ.tən (US) 'tɑːr-
Tarleton 'tɑːl.tən, 'tɑː.lə- (US) 'tɑːrl.tən, 'tɑːr.lə-

Tap

A sound which resembles [t] or [d], being made by a complete closure between the tongue and the alveolar region, but which is very brief and is produced by a sharp upward throw of the tongue blade. As soon as contact is made, the effects of gravity and air pressure cause the tongue to fall again.

Examples for English

The tap sound (for which the phonetic symbol is [ɾ]) is noticeable in Scottish accents as the realisation of /r/, and in US English it is often heard as a (voiced) realisation of /t/ when it occurs after a stressed vowel and before an unstressed one, e.g.:

getting better ⓤⓢ /ˈget̬.ɪŋ ˈbet̬.ɚ/ [g̊eɾɪŋb̥eɾɚ]

In British English it used to be quite common to hear a tap for /r/ in careful or emphatic speech (e.g. *very* [ve̥ɾɪ]), though this is less often heard now. It is increasingly common to hear the American-style tapped /t/ in England.

Several varieties of tap are possible: they may be voiced or voiceless. For instance, Scottish pre-pausal /r/ is often realised as a voiceless tap, as in *here* [hiɾ̥]. Taps may also be produced with the SOFT PALATE lowered, resulting in a nasalised tap which is sometimes heard in the US English pronunciation of words like *mental* [meɾ̃əɫ]. A closely related sound is the FLAP, and the TRILL also has some similar characteristics.

tarmac (T®) ˈtɑː.mæk ⓤⓢ ˈtɑːr- **-s** -s **-king** -ɪŋ **-ked** -t

tarmacadam ˌtɑː.məˈkæd.əm ⓤⓢ ˌtɑːr-

tarn tɑːn ⓤⓢ tɑːrn **-s** -z

tarnation tɑːˈneɪ.ʃᵊn ⓤⓢ tɑːr-

tarnish ˈtɑː.nɪʃ ⓤⓢ ˈtɑːr- **-es** -ɪz **-ing** -ɪŋ **-ed** -t

tarot ˈtær.əʊ ⓤⓢ -oʊ, -ət, ˈter-; təˈroʊ **-s** -z ˈ**tarot** ˌ**card** ⓤⓢ **taˈrot** ˌ**card**

tarp tɑːp ⓤⓢ tɑːrp **-s** -s

tarpaulin tɑːˈpɔː.lɪn ⓤⓢ tɑːrˈpɑː-, -ˈpɔː-; ˈtɑːr.pə- **-s** -z

Tarpeian tɑːˈpiː.ən ⓤⓢ tɑːr-

tarpon ˈtɑː.pɒn ⓤⓢ ˈtɑːr.pən, -pɑːn **-s** -z

Tarquin ˈtɑː.kwɪn ⓤⓢ ˈtɑːr- **-s** -z

Tarquini|us tɑːˈkwɪn.i|.əs ⓤⓢ tɑːr- **-i** -aɪ, -iː

tarradiddle ˈtær.əˌdɪd.l̩ ⓤⓢ ˈter-, ˈtær- **-s** -z

tarragon ˈtær.ə.gən ⓤⓢ ˈter.ə.gɑːn, ˈtær-

Tarragona ˌtær.əˈgəʊ.nə ⓤⓢ ˌter.əˈgoʊ-, ˌtær-, ˌtɑːr.ɑːˈ-

tarrah təˈrɑː; trɑː

Tarrant ˈtær.ᵊnt ⓤⓢ ˈter-, ˈtær-

Tarring ˈtær.ɪŋ ⓤⓢ ˈter-, ˈtær-

tarrock ˈtær.ək ⓤⓢ ˈter-, ˈtær- **-s** -s

tarry (*adj.*) *tarred, like tar:* ˈtɑː.ri ⓤⓢ ˈtɑːr.i

tarr|y (*v.*) *wait:* ˈtær|.i ⓤⓢ ˈter-, ˈtær- **-ies** -iz **-ying** -i.ɪŋ **-ied** -id **-ier/s** -i.əʳ/z ⓤⓢ -i.ɚ/z

Tarshish ˈtɑː.ʃɪʃ ⓤⓢ ˈtɑːr-

tars|us (T) ˈtɑː.s|əs ⓤⓢ ˈtɑːr- **-i** -aɪ

tart tɑːt ⓤⓢ tɑːrt **-s** -s **-ly** -li **-ness** -nəs, -nɪs

tartan ˈtɑː.tᵊn ⓤⓢ ˈtɑːr- **-s** -z

tartar, tartare (T) ˈtɑː.təʳ ⓤⓢ ˈtɑːr.t̬ɚ **-s** -z ˌ**tartar** ˈ**sauce** ⓤⓢ ˈ**tartar** ˌ**sauce**

tartaric tɑːˈtær.ɪk ⓤⓢ tɑːr-, -ˈter-, -ˈtɑːr- **tar**ˌ**taric** ˈ**acid**

Tartar|us ˈtɑː.tᵊr|.əs ⓤⓢ ˈtɑːr.t̬ɚ- **-y** -i

tartlet ˈtɑːt.lət, -lɪt ⓤⓢ ˈtɑːrt.lət, -lɪt **-s** -s

tartrazine ˈtɑː.trə.ziːn, -zɪn ⓤⓢ ˈtɑːr-

Tartu ˈtɑː.tu ⓤⓢ ˈtɑːr-

Tartuffe tɑːˈtʊf, -ˈtuːf ⓤⓢ tɑːr-

tart|y ˈtɑː.t|i ⓤⓢ ˈtɑːr.t̬|i **-ier** -i.əʳ ⓤⓢ -i.ɚ **-iest** -i.ɪst, -i.əst **-ily** -ɪ.li, -ᵊl.i **-iness** -ɪ.nəs, -ɪ.nɪs

Tarzan ˈtɑː.zᵊn, -zæn ⓤⓢ ˈtɑːr-

Tasha ˈtæʃ.ə

Tashkent tæʃˈkent ⓤⓢ tæʃ-, tɑːʃ-

Tashtego tæʃˈtiː.gəʊ ⓤⓢ -goʊ

task tɑːsk ⓤⓢ tæsk **-s** -s **-ing** -ɪŋ **-ed** -t ˈ**task** ˌ**force**

Tasker ˈtæs.kəʳ ⓤⓢ -kɚ

taskmaster ˈtɑːskˌmɑː.stəʳ ⓤⓢ ˈtæskˌmæs.tɚ **-s** -z

taskmistress ˈtɑːskˌmɪs.trəs, -trɪs ⓤⓢ ˈtæskˌmɪs.trɪs **-es** -ɪz

Tasman ˈtæz.mən

Tasmani|a tæzˈmeɪ.ni|.ə, -nj|ə **-an/s** -ən/z

Tass, TASS tæs

tassel ˈtæs.ᵊl **-s** -z **-led** -d

tassie (T) ˈtæs.i

Tasso ˈtæs.əʊ ⓤⓢ -oʊ

tast|e teɪst **-es** -s **-ing** -ɪŋ **-ed** -ɪd **-er/s** -əʳ/z ⓤⓢ -ɚ/z **give someone a** ˌ**taste of their** ˌ**own** ˈ**medicine**

tastebud ˈteɪst.bʌd **-s** -z

tasteful ˈteɪst.fᵊl, -fʊl **-ly** -i **-ness** -nəs, -nɪs

tasteless ˈteɪst.ləs, -lɪs **-ly** -li **-ness** -nəs, -nɪs

tast|y ˈteɪ.st|i **-ier** -i.əʳ ⓤⓢ -i.ɚ **-iest** -i.ɪst, -i.əst **-ily** -ɪ.li, -ᵊl.i **-iness** -ɪ.nəs, -ɪ.nɪs

tat tæt **-s** -s **-ting** -ɪŋ ⓤⓢ ˈtæt̬.ɪŋ **-ted** -ɪd ⓤⓢ ˈtæt̬.ɪd

ta-ta təˈtɑː, tætˈɑː ⓤⓢ tɑːˈtɑː

tatami təˈtɑː.mi, tɑː-, tætˈɑː- ⓤⓢ təˈtɑː- **-s** -z

Tatar ˈtɑː.təʳ ⓤⓢ -t̬ɚ **-s** -z

Tatchell ˈtætʃ.ᵊl

Tate teɪt ˌ**Tate** ˈ**Gallery**

Tatham ˈteɪ.θᵊm, -ðəm; ˈtæt.əm

Tati ˈtæt.i, -ˈ- ⓤⓢ tɑːˈtiː

Tatiana ˌtæt.iˈɑː.nə ⓤⓢ ˌ-ˈjɑː.nə

tatler (T®) ˈtæt.ləʳ ⓤⓢ -lɚ **-s** -z

Tatra ˈtɑː.trə, ˈtæt.rə ⓤⓢ ˈtɑː.trə

tatter ˈtæt.əʳ ⓤⓢ ˈtæt̬.ɚ **-s** -z **-ed** -d

tatterdemalion ˌtæt.ə.dəˈmeɪ.li.ən, -dɪˈ-, -ˈmæl.i- ⓤⓢ ˌtæt̬.ɚ-

tattersall (T) ˈtæt.ə.sɔːl, -sᵊl ⓤⓢ ˈtæt̬.ɚ.sɔːl, -sɑːl **-s** -z

tattl|e ˈtæt.l̩ ⓤⓢ ˈtæt̬- **-es** -z **-ing** -ɪŋ, ˈtæt.lɪŋ **-ed** -d **-er/s** -əʳ/z, ˈtæt.ləʳ/z ⓤⓢ ˈ-l̩.ɚ/z, ˈ-lɚ/z

tattletale ˈtæt.l̩.teɪl ⓤⓢ ˈtæt̬- **-s** -z

Tatton ˈtæt.ᵊn

tattoo tætˈuː, təˈtuː ⓤⓢ tætˈuː **-s** -z **-ing** -ɪŋ **-ed** -d **-er/s** -əʳ/z ⓤⓢ -ɚ/z

tattooist tætˈuː.ɪst, təˈtuː- ⓤⓢ tætˈuː- **-s** -s

tatt|y ˈtæt|.i ⓤⓢ ˈtæt̬- **-ier** -i.əʳ ⓤⓢ -i.ɚ **-iest** -i.ɪst, -i.əst **-ily** -ɪ.li, -ᵊl.i **-iness** -ɪ.nəs, -ɪ.nɪs

Tatum ˈteɪ.təm ⓤⓢ -t̬əm

tau taʊ, tɔː ⓤⓢ taʊ, tɔː, tɑː

Tauchnitz ˈtaʊk.nɪts *as if German:* ˈtaʊx-

taught (*from* **teach**) tɔːt ⓤⓢ tɑːt, tɔːt

taun|t tɔːn|t ⓤⓢ tɑːn|t, tɔːn|t **-ts** -ts **-ting/ly** -tɪŋ/li ⓤⓢ -t̬ɪŋ/li **-ted** -tɪd ⓤⓢ -t̬ɪd **-ter/s** -təʳ/z ⓤⓢ -t̬ɚ/z

Taunton ˈtɔːn.tən *locally:* ˈtɑːn- ⓤⓢ ˈtɑːn.tᵊn, ˈtɔːn-

taupe təʊp ⓤⓢ toʊp

Taupo ˈtaʊ.pəʊ ⓤⓢ ˈtoʊ.poʊ

Taurean ˈtɔː.ri.ən; tɔːˈriː- ⓤⓢ ˈtɔːr.i- **-s** -z

Taurus 'tɔː.rəs ⓤⓢ 'tɔːr.əs
taut tɔːt ⓤⓢ tɑːt, tɔːt **-er** -əʳ ⓤⓢ -ɚ **-est** -ɪst, -əst **-ly** -li **-ness** -nəs, -nɪs
tauten 'tɔː.tᵊn ⓤⓢ 'tɑː- **-s** -z **-ing** -ɪŋ **-ed** -d
tautologic ˌtɔː.tə'lɒdʒ.ɪk ⓤⓢ ˌtɑː.t̬ə'lɑː.dʒɪ-, ˌtɔː- **-al** -ᵊl **-ally** -ᵊl.i, -li
tautologic|al ˌtɔː.tə'lɒdʒ.ɪk|.ᵊl ⓤⓢ ˌtɑː.t̬ə'lɑː.dʒɪk-, ˌtɔː- **-ally** -ᵊl.i, -li
tautologism tɔː'tɒl.ə.dʒɪ.zᵊm ⓤⓢ tɑː'tɑː.lə-, tɔː'- **-s** -z
tautologiz|e, -is|e tɔː'tɒl.ə.dʒaɪz ⓤⓢ tɑː'tɑː.lə-, tɔː- **-es** -ɪz **-ing** -ɪŋ **-ed** -d
tautologous tɔː'tɒl.ə.gəs ⓤⓢ tɑː'tɑː.lə-, tɔː-
tautolog|y tɔː'tɒl.ə.dʒ|i ⓤⓢ tɑː'tɑː.lə-, tɔː- **-ies** -iz
Tavener 'tæv.ᵊn.əʳ, -nəʳ ⓤⓢ -ᵊn.ɚ, -nɚ
Taverham 'teɪ.vᵊr.əm
tavern 'tæv.ᵊn ⓤⓢ -ɚn **-s** -z **-er/s** -əʳ/z ⓤⓢ -ɚ/z
taverna tə'vɜː.nə, ˌtæv'ɜː- ⓤⓢ tɑː'vɝː-, tə- **-s** -z
Tavistock 'tæv.ɪ.stɒk, '-ə- ⓤⓢ -ə.stɑːk
taw tɔː ⓤⓢ tɑː, tɔː **-s** -z **-ing** -ɪŋ **-ed** -d
tawdr|y 'tɔː.dr|i ⓤⓢ 'tɑː-, 'tɔː- **-ier** -i.əʳ ⓤⓢ -i.ɚ **-iest** -i.ɪst, -i.əst **-ily** -ᵊl.i, -ɪ.li **-iness** -ɪ.nəs, -ɪ.nɪs
Tawe 'taʊ.i, -eɪ
Tawell tɔːl; 'tɔː.əl ⓤⓢ tɑːl, tɔːl, 'tɑː.əl, 'tɔː-
tawn|y 'tɔː.n|i ⓤⓢ 'tɑː-, 'tɔː- **-ier** -i.əʳ ⓤⓢ -i.ɚ **-iest** -i.ɪst, -i.əst **-iness** -ɪ.nəs, -ɪ.nɪs **ˌtawny 'owl, 'tawny ˌowl**
tax tæks **-es** -ɪz **-ing/ly** -ɪŋ/li **-ed** -t **-er/s** -əʳ/z ⓤⓢ -ɚ/z **'tax eˌvasion; 'tax ˌexile; 'tax ˌhaven; 'tax inˌspector; 'tax ˌoffice; 'tax reˌturn; 'tax ˌyear**
taxability ˌtæk.sə'bɪl.ə.ti, -ɪ.ti ⓤⓢ -ə.t̬i
taxable 'tæk.sə.bl̩ **-ness** -nəs, -nɪs
taxation tæk'seɪ.ʃᵊn **-s** -z
tax-deductible ˌtæks.dɪ'dʌk.tə.bl̩, -də'- *stress shift:* ˌtax-deductible 'earnings
tax-deferred ˌtæks.dɪ'fɜːd ⓤⓢ -'fɝːd *stress shift:* ˌtax-deferred 'earnings
taxeme 'tæk.siːm
taxemic tæk'siː.mɪk
tax-exempt ˌtæks.ɪg'zempt, -eg'-; -ɪk'sempt, -ek'- ⓤⓢ -ɪg'zempt, -eg'- *stress shift:* ˌtax-exempt 'earnings
tax-free ˌtæks'friː *stress shift:* ˌtax-free 'bonus
tax|i (*v.*) 'tæk.s|i **-i(e)s** -iz **-ying** -i.ɪŋ **-iing** -i.ɪŋ **-ied** -id **'taxi ˌrank; 'taxi ˌstand**
taxicab 'tæk.si.kæb **-s** -z
taxidermic ˌtæk.sɪ'dɜː.mɪk ⓤⓢ -'dɝː-
taxidermist 'tæk.sɪ.dɜː.mɪst, ˌtæk.sɪ'dɜː-; tæk'sɪd.ə- ⓤⓢ 'tæk.sɪ.dɝː- **-s** -s
taxidermy 'tæk.sɪ.dɜː.mi ⓤⓢ -dɝː-
taximeter 'tæk.siˌmiː.təʳ ⓤⓢ -t̬ɚ **-s** -z
tax|is (T) 'tæk.s|ɪs **-es** -iːz
taxiway 'tæk.si.weɪ **-s** -z
taxman 'tæks.mæn **-men** -men
taxonomic ˌtæk.sə'nɒm.ɪk ⓤⓢ -'nɑː.mɪk **-ally** -ᵊl.i, -li
taxonom|y tæk'sɒn.ə.m|i ⓤⓢ -'sɑː.nə- **-ist/s** -ɪst/s
taxpayer 'tæksˌpeɪ.əʳ ⓤⓢ -ɚ **-s** -z
tay *syllable used in Tonic Sol-fa in counting time:* teɪ, te
Note: In the sequence 'tay fe' this may be pronounced /te/.
Tay teɪ
tayberr|y 'teɪ.bᵊr|.i, '-br|i, -ˌber|.i ⓤⓢ -ˌber|.i **-ies** -iz
Taylor 'teɪ.ləʳ ⓤⓢ -lɚ
Taylorian teɪ'lɔː.ri.ən ⓤⓢ -'lɔːr.i-
Taymouth 'teɪ.maʊθ, -məθ
Tay-Sachs ˌteɪ'sæks ⓤⓢ ˌ-'-, '-- **ˌTay-'Sachs diˌsease**
Tayside 'teɪ.saɪd
TB ˌtiː'biː
T-bar 'tiː.bɑːʳ ⓤⓢ -bɑːr **-s** -z
Tbilisi tə.bɪ'liː.si; tə'bɪl.ɪ- ⓤⓢ təˌbɪl.i'siː; ˌtʌb.ɪ'liː.si; tə'bɪl.i-
T-bone 'tiː.bəʊn ⓤⓢ -boʊn **-s** -z **ˌT-bone 'steak**
tbs., tbsp. *(abbrev. for* **tablespoon, tablespoonful***)* 'teɪ.bl̩.spuːn, 'teɪ.bl̩ˌspuːn.fʊl
Tchad tʃæd
Tchaikovsky tʃaɪ'kɒf.ski, -'kɒv- ⓤⓢ -'kɔːf-, -'kɑːv-
Tcherkasy tʃɜː'kæs.i ⓤⓢ tʃɝː-
TCP® ˌtiː.siː'piː
te *Tonic Sol-fa name for leading note:* tiː **-s** -z
tea tiː **-s** -z **'tea ˌbag; 'tea ˌbreak; 'tea ˌchest; 'tea ˌcosy; 'tea ˌdance; 'tea ˌlady; 'tea ˌleaf; 'tea ˌparty; 'tea ˌset; 'tea ˌshop; 'tea ˌtowel; 'tea ˌtray; 'tea ˌtrolley; 'tea ˌwagon; not for ˌall the ˌtea in 'China**
teabread 'tiː.bred
tea-cadd|y 'tiːˌkæd|.i **-ies** -iz
teacake 'tiː.keɪk **-s** -s
teach tiːtʃ **-es** -ɪz **-ing/s** -ɪŋ/z **taught** tɔːt ⓤⓢ tɑːt, tɔːt **'teaching ˌpractice**
teachability ˌtiː.tʃə'bɪl.ə.ti, -ɪ.ti ⓤⓢ -ə.t̬i
teachable 'tiː.tʃə.bl̩ **-ness** -nəs, -nɪs
teacher 'tiː.tʃəʳ ⓤⓢ -tʃɚ **-s** -z **ˌteacher(s') 'training ˌcollege**
teach-in 'tiːtʃ.ɪn **-s** -z
tea|cloth 'tiː|.klɒθ ⓤⓢ -klɑːθ **-cloths** -klɒθs, -klɒðz ⓤⓢ -klɑːθs, -klɑːðz
teacup 'tiː.kʌp **-s** -s **-ful/s** -fʊl/z
Teague tiːg **-s** -z
teahou|se 'tiː.haʊ|s **-ses** -zɪz
teak tiːk
teakettle 'tiːˌket.l̩ ⓤⓢ -ˌket̬- **-s** -z
teal tiːl **-s** -z
team tiːm **-s** -z **-ing** -ɪŋ **-ed** -d **ˌteam 'spirit, 'team ˌspirit**
teammate 'tiːm.meɪt **-s** -s
teamster (T) 'tiːmp.stəʳ ⓤⓢ -stɚ **-s** -z **ˌTeamsters' 'Union** ⓤⓢ **'Teamsters' ˌUnion**
teamwork 'tiːm.wɜːk ⓤⓢ -wɝːk
teapot 'tiː.pɒt ⓤⓢ -pɑːt **-s** -s
teapoy 'tiː.pɔɪ **-s** -z
tear (*n.*) *fluid from the eye:* tɪəʳ ⓤⓢ tɪr **-s** -z **'tear ˌgas**
tear (*n. v.*) *pull apart, rush, a rent etc.:* teəʳ ⓤⓢ ter **-s** -z **-ing** -ɪŋ **tore** tɔːʳ ⓤⓢ tɔːr **torn** tɔːn ⓤⓢ tɔːrn
tearaway 'teə.rə.weɪ ⓤⓢ 'ter.ə- **-s** -z
teardrop 'tɪə.drɒp ⓤⓢ 'tɪr.drɑːp **-s** -s
tearful 'tɪə.fᵊl, -fʊl ⓤⓢ 'tɪr- **-ly** -i **-ness** -nəs, -nɪs
teargas 'tɪə.gæs ⓤⓢ 'tɪr- **-es** -ɪz **-sing** -ɪŋ **-sed** -t
tearjerker 'tɪəˌdʒɜː.kəʳ ⓤⓢ 'tɪrˌdʒɝː.kɚ **-s** -z
tearless 'tɪə.ləs, -lɪs ⓤⓢ 'tɪr- **-ly** -li **-ness** -nəs, -nɪs
tearoom 'tiː.rʊm, -ruːm ⓤⓢ -ruːm, -rʊm **-s** -z
tearstained 'tɪə.steɪnd ⓤⓢ 'tɪr-
tear|y 'tɪə.r|i ⓤⓢ 'tɪr|.i **-ily** -ɪ.li
teas|e tiːz **-es** -ɪz **-ing/ly** -ɪŋ/li **-ed** -d **-er/s** -əʳ/z ⓤⓢ -ɚ/z
teasel 'tiː.zᵊl **-s** -z **-(l)ing** -ɪŋ, 'tiːz.lɪŋ **-(l)ed** -d
Teasmade® 'tiːz.meɪd
teaspoon 'tiː.spuːn **-s** -z
teaspoonful 'tiː.spuːn.fʊl **-s** -z
teaspoonsful *(alternative plur. of* **teaspoonful***)* 'tiː.spuːnz.fʊl
tea-strainer 'tiːˌstreɪ.nəʳ ⓤⓢ -nɚ **-s** -z
teat tiːt **-s** -s
tea-table 'tiːˌteɪ.bl̩ **-s** -z
teatime 'tiː.taɪm
tea-tree 'tiː.triː **-s** -z **'tea-tree ˌoil**
tea-urn 'tiː.ɜːn ⓤⓢ -ɝːn **-s** -z
teazel 'tiː.zᵊl **-s** -z
teazle (T) 'tiː.zᵊl **-s** -z
Tebay 'tiː.beɪ *locally:* -bi
Tebbitt 'teb.ɪt
tec tek **-s** -s
tech tek **-s** -s
techie 'tek.i **-s** -z
technetium tek'niː.ʃi.əm, -si-, '-ʃəm ⓤⓢ -ʃi.əm, '-ʃəm
technic|al 'tek.nɪ.k|ᵊl **-ally** -ᵊl.i, -li **-alness** -l̩.nəs, -nɪs **'technical ˌcolleg**
technicalit|y ˌtek.nɪ'kæl.ə.t|i, -nə'-, -ɪ.t|i ⓤⓢ -nə'kæl.ə.t̬|i **-ies** -iz
technician tek'nɪʃ.ᵊn **-s** -z
Technicolor® 'tek.nɪˌkʌl.əʳ ⓤⓢ -ɚ

technicolo(u)r ˈtek.nɪˌkʌl.əʳ (US) -ɚ **-ed** -d
technics (T®) ˈtek.nɪks
technique tekˈniːk **-s** -s
techno- tek.nəʊ-; tekˈnɒ- (US) ˈtek.noʊ-, -nə-; tekˈnɑː-
Note: Prefix. This may carry primary or secondary stress on the first syllable, e.g. **technophobe** /ˈtek.nə.fəʊb (US) -foʊb/, **technophobia** /ˌtek.nəˈfəʊ.bi.ə (US) -ˈfoʊ-/, or on the second syllable, e.g. **technology** /tekˈnɒl.ə.dʒi (US) tekˈnɑː-/.
technocrat ˈtek.nəʊ.kræt (US) -nə- **-s** -s
technocratic ˌtek.nəʊˈkræt.ɪk (US) -nəˈkræt̬-
technologic|al ˌtek.nəˈlɒdʒ.ɪ.k|əl (US) -ˈlɑː.dʒɪ- **-ly** -əl.i, -li
technolog|y tekˈnɒl.ə.dʒ|i (US) -ˈnɑː.lə- **-ist/s** -ɪst/s **-ies**
technophobe ˈtek.nəʊ.fəʊb (US) -nə.foʊb **-s** -z
technophob|ia ˌtek.nəʊˈfəʊ.b|i.ə (US) -nəˈfoʊ- **-ic** -ɪk
tech|y ˈtetʃ|.i **-ier** -i.əʳ (US) -i.ɚ **-iest** -i.ɪst, -i.əst **-ily** -ɪ.li, -əl.i **-iness** -ɪ.nəs, -ɪ.nɪs
Teck tek
tectonic tekˈtɒn.ɪk (US) -ˈtɑː.nɪk **-s** -s **tecˌtonic ˈplates**
ted (T) ted **-s** -z **-ding** -ɪŋ **-ded** -ɪd **-der/s** -əʳ/z (US) -ɚ/z
Teddington ˈted.ɪŋ.tən
tedd|y (T) ˈted|.i **-ies** -iz **ˈteddy ˌbear; ˌTeddy Bear's ˈPicnic; ˈteddy ˌboy**
Te Deum ˌteɪˈdeɪ.ʊm, ˌtiːˈdiː.əm; **-s** -z
tedious ˈtiː.di.əs (US) -di.əs, -dʒəs **-ly** -li **-ness** -nəs, -nɪs
tedium ˈtiː.di.əm
tee tiː **-s** -z **-ing** -ɪŋ **-d** -d
tee-hee ˌtiːˈhiː **-s** -z
teem tiːm **-s** -z **-ing** -ɪŋ **-ed** -d
teen tiːn **-s** -z
teenage ˈtiːn.eɪdʒ **-d** -d
teenager ˈtiːnˌeɪ.dʒəʳ (US) -dʒɚ **-s** -z
teens|y ˈtiːn.z|i **-ier** -i.əʳ (US) -i.ɚ **-iest** -i.ɪst, -i.əst
teensy-weensy ˌtiːn.ziˈwiːn.zi, ˌtiːnt.siˈwiːnt.si *stress shift:* ˌteensy-weensy ˈhouse
teen|y ˈtiː.n|i **-iest** -i.ɪst, -i.əst
teenybopper ˈtiː.niˌbɒp.əʳ (US) -ˌbɑː.pɚ **-s** -z
teeny-weeny ˌtiː.niˈwiː.ni *stress shift:* ˌteeny-weeny ˈhouse
teepee ˈtiː.piː **-s** -z
Tees tiːz
Teesdale ˈtiːz.deɪl
teeshirt ˈtiː.ʃɜːt (US) -ʃɝːt **-s** -s
tee-square ˈtiː.skweəʳ, ˌ-ˈ- (US) ˈtiː.skwer **-s** -z
Teesside ˈtiː.saɪd, ˈtiːz-
teet|er ˈtiː.t|əʳ (US) -t̬|ɚ **-ers** -əz (US) -ɚz **-ering** -ər.ɪŋ **-ered** -əd (US) -ɚd
teeter-tott|er ˌtiː.təˈtɒt|.əʳ (US) -t̬ɚˈtɑː.t̬|ɚ **-ers** -əz (US) -ɚz **-ering** -ər.ɪŋ **-ered** -əd (US) -ɚd
teeth *(plur. of* **tooth***)* tiːθ **ˌgrit one's ˈteeth; ˌset someone's ˈteeth on ˌedge**
teeth|e tiːð **-es** -z **-ing** -ɪŋ **-ed** -d **ˈteething ˌring; ˈteething ˌtroubles**
teetotal ˌtiːˈtəʊ.təl (US) -ˈtoʊ.t̬əl, ˈ-ˌ--
-ism -ɪ.zəm
teetotal(l)er ˌtiːˈtəʊ.təl.əʳ, -ˈtəʊt.ləʳ (US) -ˈtoʊ.t̬əl.ɚ, -ˈtoʊt.lɚ, ˈtiːˌtoʊ.t̬əl.ɚ, -ˌtoʊt.lɚ **-s** -z
teetotum ˌtiːˈtəʊ.təm, ˈ---; ˌtiː.təʊˈtʌm (US) ˌtiːˈtoʊt̬.əm **-s** -z
TEFL ˈtef.l̩
Teflon® ˈtef.lɒn (US) -lɑːn
Tegucigalpa teɡˌuː.sɪˈɡæl.pə (US) -səˈɡæl.pɑː, -ˈɡɑːl-
tegument ˈteɡ.jʊ.mənt, -jə- **-s** -s
Tehran, **Teheran** teəˈrɑːn, -ˈræn; ˌte.həˈrɑːn, ˌteɪ.əˈr-, -ˈæn (US) terˈɑːn, təˈrɑːn, teə-, -ˈræn
Tehuantepec təˈwɑːn.tə.pek (US) -t̬ə-
Teifi ˈtaɪ.vi
Teign tɪn, tiːn
Teignbridge ˈtɪn.brɪdʒ, ˈtiːn-, ˈtɪm-, ˈtiːm- (US) ˈtɪn-, ˈtiːn-
Teignmouth ˈtɪn.məθ, ˈtiːn-, ˈtɪm-, ˈtiːm- *locally also:* ˈtɪŋ- (US) ˈtɪn-, ˈtiːn-
Teignton ˈteɪn.tən (US) -tən
Teiresias taɪəˈriː.si.əs (US) taɪ-
Te Kanawa teɪˈkɑː.nə.wə, tɪ-
tel. *(abbrev. for* **telephone***)* ˈtel.ɪ.fəʊn (US) -ə.foʊn
telaesthesia ˌtel.əsˈθiː.zi.ə, -ɪsˈ-, -iːsˈ-, -ʒi-, ˈ-ʒə (US) ˌtel.əsˈθiː.ʒə
telaesthetic ˌtel.əsˈθet.ɪk, -ɪsˈ-, -iːsˈ- (US) -ˈθet̬- **-s** -s **-ally** -əl.i, -li
telamon (T) ˈtel.ə.mən, -mɒn (US) -mən, -mɑːn **-s** -z
TelAutograph® telˈɔː.tə.ɡrɑːf, -ɡræf (US) -ˈɑː.t̬ə.ɡræf, -ˈɔː-
Tel Aviv ˌtel.əˈviːv, -ævˈiːv, -ˈɪv (US) -əˈviːv, -ɑːˈ-
tele- tel.ɪ-; tɪˈle-, tə- (US) ˈtel.ə-; tɪˈle-, tə-, tel.ɪ-
Note: Prefix. This may carry primary or secondary stress on the first syllable, e.g. **telephone** /ˈtel.ɪ.fəʊn (US) ˈtel.ə.foʊn/, **telegraphic** /ˌtel.ɪˈɡræf.ɪk (US) -əˈ-/, or on the second syllable, e.g. **telephony** /təˈlef.ə.ni/.
tele ˈtel.i **-s** -z
telebanking ˈtel.ɪˌbæŋ.kɪŋ
telecamera ˈtel.ɪˌkæm.ər.ə, ˌ-rə **-s** -z
telecast ˈtel.ɪ.kɑːst (US) -kæst **-s** -s **-ing** -ɪŋ **-ed** -ɪd **-er/s** -əʳ/z (US) -ɚ/z
tele-cine ˌtel.ɪˈsɪn.i
telecom ˈtel.ɪ.kɒm (US) -kɑːm **-s** -z
telecommunications ˌtel.ɪ.kəˌmjuː.nɪˈkeɪ.ʃənz, -nəˈ-
telecom|mute ˌtel.ɪ.kə|ˈmjuːt (US) ˈ----
-mutes -ˈmjuːts **-muting** -ˈmjuː.tɪŋ (US) -mjuː.t̬ɪŋ **-muted** -ˈmjuː.tɪd (US) -mjuː.t̬ɪd **-muter/s** -ˈmjuː.təʳ/z (US) -mjuː.t̬ɚ/z
teleconferenc|e ˌtel.ɪˈkɒn.fər.ənts (US) ˈtel.ɪˌkɑːn- **-es** -ɪz
telecottag|e ˈtel.ɪˌkɒt.ɪdʒ (US) -ˌkɑː.t̬ɪdʒ **-ing** -ɪŋ
telefilm ˈtel.ɪ.fɪlm (US) ˈ-ə- **-s** -z
telegenic ˌtel.ɪˈdʒen.ɪk (US) -əˈ-
telegram ˈtel.ɪ.ɡræm **-s** -z **-ming** -ɪŋ **-med** -d
telegramese ˌtel.ɪ.ɡræmˈiːz
telegraph ˈtel.ɪ.ɡrɑːf, -ɡræf (US) -ɡræf **-s** -s **-ing** -ɪŋ **-ed** -t **ˈtelegraph ˌpole; ˈtelegraph ˌwire**
telegrapher tɪˈleɡ.rə.fəʳ, telˈeɡ-, təˈleɡ- (US) təˈleɡ.rə.fɚ **-s** -z
telegraphese ˌtel.ɪ.ɡrɑːˈfiːz, -ɡræfˈiːz, -ɡrəˈfiːz (US) -ɡræfˈiːz, -ɡrəˈfiːz
telegraphic ˌtel.ɪˈɡræf.ɪk (US) -əˈ- **-ally** -əl.i, -li
telegraph|y tɪˈleɡ.rə.f|i, telˈeɡ-, təˈleɡ- (US) təˈleɡ- **-ist/s** -ɪst/s
teleki|nesis ˌtel.ɪ.kɪ|ˈniː.sɪs, ˌ-ə-, -kaɪˈ- (US) -kɪˈ- **-netic** -ˈnet.ɪk (US) -ˈnet̬-
Telemachus tɪˈlem.ə.kəs, telˈem-, təˈlem- (US) təˈlem-
Telemann ˈteɪ.lə.mæn (US) -mɑːn
telemark ˈtel.ɪ.mɑːk, ˈ-ə- (US) -ə.mɑːrk **-s** -s **-ing** -ɪŋ **-ed** -t
telemarketing ˌtel.ɪˈmɑː.kɪ.tɪŋ, -kə-, ˈtel.ɪˌmɑː- (US) ˈtel.əˌmɑːr.kə.t̬ɪŋ
Telemessag|e® ˈtel.ɪˌmes.ɪdʒ **-es** -ɪz
telemet|er təˈlem.ɪ.t|əʳ, ˈ-ə-; ˈtel.ɪˌmiː- (US) ˈtel.əˌmiː.t̬|ɚ; təˈlem.ə- **-ers** -əz (US) -ɚz **-ering** -ər.ɪŋ **-ered** -əd (US) -ɚd
telemetric ˌtel.ɪˈmet.rɪk (US) -əˈ- **-ally** -əl.i, -li
telemetry tɪˈlem.ɪ.tri, tə-, ˈ-ə- (US) təˈlem.ə-
teleological ˌtel.i.əˈlɒdʒ.ɪ.kəl, ˌtiː.li- (US) ˌtiː.li.əˈlɑː.dʒɪ-, ˌtel.i-
teleolog|y ˌtel.iˈɒl.ə.dʒ|i, ˌtiː.liˈ- (US) ˌtiː.liˈɑː.lə-, ˌtel.iˈ- **-ist/s** -ɪst/s
telepathic ˌtel.ɪˈpæθ.ɪk (US) -əˈ- **-ally** -əl.i, -li
telepathiz|e, **-is|e** tɪˈlep.ə.θaɪz, telˈep-, təˈlep- (US) təˈlep- **-es** -ɪz **-ing** -ɪŋ **-ed** -d
telepath|y tɪˈlep.ə.θ|i, telˈep-, təˈlep- (US) təˈlep- **-ist/s** -ɪst/s
telephon|e ˈtel.ɪ.fəʊn (US) -ə.foʊn **-es** -z **-ing** -ɪŋ **-ed** -d **-er/s** -əʳ/z (US) -ɚ/z **ˈtelephone ˌbooth; ˈtelephone ˌbook; ˈtelephone ˌbox; ˈtelephone ˌcall; ˈtelephone diˌrectory; ˈtelephone ˌnumber; ˈtelephone ˌpole**

telephonic ˌtel.ɪˈfɒn.ɪk, -əˈ- (US) -əˈfɑː.nɪk **-ally** -^{ə}l.i, -li
telephonist tɪˈlef.^{ə}n.ɪst, telˈef-, təˈlef- (US) təˈlef- **-s** -s
telephony tɪˈlef.^{ə}n.i, telˈef-, təˈlef- (US) təˈlef-
telephoto ˌtel.ɪˈfəʊ.təʊ (US) ˈtel.ə.foʊ.t̬oʊ **-s** -z *stress shift, see compound:* ˌ**telephoto** ˈ**lens**
telephotography ˌtel.ɪ.fəˈtɒg.rə.fi (US) -ə.fəˈtɑː.grə-
teleprinter ˈtel.ɪˌprɪn.tə^{r} (US) -əˌprɪn.t̬ɚ **-s** -z
TelePrompTer® ˈtel.ɪˌprɒmp.tə^{r} (US) -əˌprɑːmp.tɚ **-s** -z
telerecord *(n.)* ˈtel.ɪˌrek.ɔːd (US) -ɚd **-s** -z
telerecord *(v.)* ˈtel.ɪ.rɪˌkɔːd, -rəˌ-, ˌtel.ɪ.rɪˈkɔːd, -rəˈ- (US) ˈtel.ɪ.rɪˌkɔːrd, -rə-, ˌtel.ɪ.rɪˈkɔːrd, -rəˈ- **-s** -z **-ing/s** -ɪŋ/z **-ed** -ɪd
telesales ˈtel.ɪ.seɪlz
telescop|e ˈtel.ɪ.skəʊp (US) -ə.skoʊp **-es** -s **-ing** -ɪŋ **-ed** -t
telescopic ˌtel.ɪˈskɒp.ɪk (US) -əˈskɑː.pɪk **-ally** -^{ə}l.i, -li
telescreen ˈtel.ɪ.skriːn **-s** -z
teleshopping ˈtel.ɪˌʃɒp.ɪŋ, ˌtel.ɪˈʃɒp- (US) ˈtel.əˌʃɑː.pɪŋ
telesthesia ˌtel.əsˈθiː.zi.ə, -ɪsˈ-, -iːsˈ-, -ʒi-, ˈ-ʒə- (US) ˌtel.əsˈθiː.ʒə
telesthetic ˌtel.əsˈθet.ɪk, -ɪsˈ-, -iːsˈ- (US) -ˈθet̬- **-s** -s **-ally** -^{ə}l.i, -li
Teletex® ˈtel.ɪ.teks
teletext ˈtel.ɪ.tekst (US) ˈ-ə- **-s** -s
telethon ˈtel.ɪ.θɒn (US) -ə.θɑːn **-s** -z
Teletype® ˈtel.ɪ.taɪp (US) ˈ-ə- **-s** -s
Teletypesetter® ˌtel.ɪˈtaɪpˌset.ə^{r} (US) -əˈtaɪpˌset̬.ɚ **-s** -z
televangel|ism ˌtel.ɪˈvæn.dʒə.l|ɪ.z^{ə}m, -dʒɪ- **-ist/s** -ɪst/s
teleview ˈtel.ɪ.vjuː (US) ˈ-ə- **-s** -z **-ing** -ɪŋ **-ed** -d **-er/s** -ə^{r}/z (US) -ɚ/z
televis|e ˈtel.ɪ.vaɪz (US) ˈ-ə- **-es** -ɪz **-ing** -ɪŋ **-ed** -d
television ˈtel.ɪ.vɪʒ.^{ə}n, ˌtel.ɪˈvɪʒ- (US) ˈtel.ə.vɪʒ- **-s** -z ˈ**television** ˌ**set**, **tele**ˈ**vision** ˌ**set**
televisor ˈtel.ɪ.vaɪ.zə^{r} (US) -ə.vaɪ.zɚ **-s** -z
televisual ˌtel.ɪˈvɪʒ.u.əl, -ˈvɪz.ju- (US) -əˈvɪʒ.u- **-ly** -i
telework|ing ˈtel.ɪˌwɜː.k|ɪŋ (US) -ˌwɝː- **-er/s** -ə^{r}/z (US) -ɚ/z
telex ˈtel.eks **-es** -ɪz **-ing** -ɪŋ **-ed** -t
Telfer ˈtel.fə^{r} (US) -fɚ
Telford ˈtel.fəd (US) -fɚd
telic ˈtel.ɪk (US) ˈtiː.lɪk, ˈtel.ɪk
tell (T) tel **-s** -z **-ing/ly** -ɪŋ/li **told** təʊld (US) toʊld
teller (T) ˈtel.ə^{r} (US) -ɚ **-s** -z
telling-off ˌtel.ɪŋˈɒf (US) -ˈɑːf **tellings-off** ˌtel.ɪŋzˈɒf (US) -ˈɑːf
telltale ˈtel.teɪl **-s** -z
tellurian telˈʊə.ri.ən, təˈlʊə-, tɪ-, -ˈljʊə- (US) telˈʊr.i-, təˈlʊr- **-s** -z
telluric telˈʊə.rɪk, təˈlʊə-, tɪ-, -ˈljʊə- (US) telˈʊr.ɪk, təˈlʊr-
tellurium telˈʊə.ri.əm, təˈlʊə-, tɪ-, -ˈljʊə- (US) telˈʊr.i-, təˈlʊr-
tell|y ˈtel|.i **-ies** -iz
Telstar® ˈtel.stɑː^{r} (US) -stɑːr
Telugu ˈtel.ə.guː, ˈ-ʊ- (US) ˈ-ə-
temerity tɪˈmer.ə.ti, tə-, temˈer-, -ɪ.ti (US) təˈmer.ə.t̬i
temp temp **-s** -s **-ing** -ɪŋ **-ed** -t
Tempe ˈtem.pi
tempeh ˈtem.peɪ **-s** -z
temp|er ˈtem.p|ə^{r} (US) -p|ɚ **-ers** -əz (US) -ɚz **-ering** -^{ə}r.ɪŋ **-ered** -əd (US) -ɚd **-erer/s** -^{ə}r.ə^{r}/z (US) -ɚ.ɚ/z
tempera ˈtem.p^{ə}r.ə
temperable ˈtem.p^{ə}r.ə.bl̩, -prə.bl̩
temperament ˈtem.p^{ə}r.ə.mənt, -prə.mənt **-s** -s
temperamental ˌtem.p^{ə}r.əˈmen.t^{ə}l, -prəˈ- (US) -t̬^{ə}l **-ly** -i
temperance ˈtem.p^{ə}r.^{ə}n*t*s, ˈ-prən*t*s
temperate ˈtem.p^{ə}r.ət, ˈ-prət, -prɪt **-ly** -li **-ness** -nəs, -nɪs
temperature ˈtem.prə.tʃə^{r}, -prɪ-, -p^{ə}r.ə-, -ɪ- (US) -pɚ.ə.tʃɚ, ˈ-prə-, -pɚ-, -pə- **-s** -z
-tempered -ˈtem.pəd (US) -pɚd **-ly** -li
Temperley ˈtem.p^{ə}l.i (US) -pɚ.li
tempest ˈtem.pɪst, -pəst **-s** -s
tempestuous temˈpes.tju.əs, -tʃu- (US) -tʃu-, -tʃə.wəs **-ly** -li **-ness** -nəs, -nɪs
Templar ˈtem.plə^{r}, -plɑː^{r} (US) -plɚ **-s** -z
template ˈtem.pleɪt, -plɪt (US) -plɪt **-s** -s
temple (T) ˈtem.pl̩ **-s** -z
templet ˈtem.plɪt, -plət (US) -plɪt **-s** -s
Templeton ˈtem.pl̩.tən
temp|o ˈtem.p|əʊ (US) -p|oʊ **-os** -əʊz (US) -oʊz **-i** -iː
temporal ˈtem.p^{ə}r.^{ə}l **-ly** -i
temporality ˌtem.p^{ə}rˈæl.ə.ti, -ɪ.ti (US) -pəˈræl.ə.t̬i
temporar|y ˈtem.p^{ə}r.^{ə}r|.i, -pr^{ə}r- (US) -pə.rer|.i **-ies** -iz **-ily** -^{ə}l.i, -ɪ.li **-iness** -ɪ.nəs, -ɪ.nɪs
temporization, -isa- ˌtem.p^{ə}r.aɪˈzeɪ.ʃ^{ə}n, -ɪˈ- (US) -ɪˈ-
temporiz|e, -is|e ˈtem.p^{ə}r.aɪz (US) -pə.raɪz **-es** -ɪz **-ing/ly** -ɪŋ/li **-ed** -d **-er/s** -ə^{r}/z (US) -ɚ/z
tempt tempt **-s** -s **-ing** -ɪŋ **-ed** -ɪd **-er/s** -ə^{r}/z (US) -ɚ/z
temptation tempˈteɪ.ʃ^{ə}n **-s** -z
tempting ˈtemp.tɪŋ **-ly** -li **-ness** -nəs, -nɪs
temptress ˈtemp.trəs, -trɪs (US) -trɪs **-es** -ɪz
tempura ˈtem.p^{ə}r.ə; temˈpʊə.rə (US) ˈtem.pʊ.rɑː; temˈpʊr.ə
tempus fugit ˌtem.pəsˈfjuː.dʒɪt, -pʊsˈ-, -gɪt (US) -pəsˈfjuː.dʒɪt
ten ten **-s** -z ˌ**Ten Com**ˈ**mandments**
tenability ˌten.əˈbɪl.ə.ti, -ɪ.ti (US) -ə.t̬i
tenable ˈten.ə.bl̩ **-ness** -nəs, -nɪs
tenacious tɪˈneɪ.ʃəs, tə-, tenˈeɪ- (US) təˈneɪ- **-ly** -li **-ness** -nəs, -nɪs
tenacity tɪˈnæs.ə.ti, tə-, tenˈæs-, -ɪ.ti (US) təˈnæs.ə.t̬i
tenanc|y ˈten.ən*t*.s|i **-ies** -iz
tenant ˈten.ənt **-s** -s **-ing** -ɪŋ **-ed** -ɪd
tenantry ˈten.ən.tri
Tenbury ˈten.b^{ə}r.i, ˈtem- (US) ˈten.ber-, -bɚ-
Tenby ˈten.bi, ˈtem- (US) ˈten-
tench ten*t*ʃ
tend tend **-s** -z **-ing** -ɪŋ **-ed** -ɪd
tendencious tenˈden.*t*ʃəs (US) -ˈden*t*.ʃəs **-ly** -li **-ness** -nəs, -nɪs
tendenc|y ˈten.dən*t*.s|i **-ies** -iz
tendentious tenˈden.*t*ʃəs (US) -ˈden*t*.ʃəs **-ly** -li **-ness** -nəs, -nɪs
tend|er ˈten.d|ə^{r} (US) -d|ɚ **-ers** -əz (US) -ɚz **-erer** -^{ə}r.ə^{r} (US) -ɚ.ɚ **-erest** -^{ə}r.ɪst, -əst **-erly** -^{ə}l.i (US) -ɚ.li **-erness** -ə.nəs, -nɪs (US) -ɚ.nəs, -nɪs **-ering** -^{ə}r.ɪŋ **-ered** -əd (US) -ɚd
tender|foot ˈten.də|.fʊt (US) -dɚ- **-foots** -s **-feet** -fiːt
tender-hearted ˌten.dəˈhɑː.tɪd, ˈten.dəˌhɑː- (US) ˈten.dɚˌhɑːr.t̬ɪd, ˌten.dɚˈhɑːr- **-ly** -li **-ness** -nəs, -nɪs *stress shift, British only:* ˌtender-hearted ˈperson
tenderization, -isa- ˌten.d^{ə}r.aɪˈzeɪ.ʃ^{ə}n -ɪˈ- (US) -ɪˈ-
tenderiz|e, -is|e ˈten.d^{ə}r.aɪz (US) -də.raɪz **-es** -ɪz **-ing** -ɪŋ **-ed** -d **-er/s** -ə^{r}/z (US) -ɚ/z
tenderloin ˈten.d^{ə}l.ɔɪn (US) -dɚ.lɔɪn **-s** -z
tendinitis ˌten.dɪˈnaɪ.tɪs, -dəˈ-
tendon ˈten.dən **-s** -z
tendonitis ˌten.dəˈnaɪ.tɪs (US) -t̬ɪs
tendril ˈten.dr^{ə}l, -drɪl (US) -dr^{ə}l **-s** -z
Tenebrae ˈten.ɪ.briː, ˈ-ə-, -breɪ, -braɪ (US) -ə.breɪ, -briː
tenebrous ˈten.ɪ.brəs, ˈ-ə- (US) ˈ-ə-
tenement ˈten.ə.mənt, ˈ-ɪ- (US) ˈ-ə- **-s** -s
Tenerif(f)e ˌten.^{ə}rˈiːf (US) -əˈriːf
tenet ˈten.ɪt **-s** -s
tenfold ˈten.fəʊld (US) -foʊld
ten-gallon hat ˌtenˌgæl.ənˈhæt, ˌteŋ- (US) ˌten- **-s** -s
Tengu ˈteŋ.gu **-s** -z
Teniers ˈten.i.əz, ˈ-jəz (US) -i.ɚz, ˈ-jɚz; təˈnɪrz
Tenison ˈten.ɪ.s^{ə}n
Tenko ˈteŋ.kəʊ (US) -koʊ

Tense
See LAX.

Tenn. *(abbrev. for* Tennessee*)* ˌten.əˈsiː, -ɪˈ- (US) ˌten.ɪˈsiː *regionally:* ˈten.ɪ.si, -ə-
Tennant ˈten.ənt
tenner ˈten.əʳ (US) -ɚ **-s** -z
Tennessee ˌten.əˈsiː, -ɪˈ- (US) ˌten.ɪˈsiː *regionally:* ˈten.ɪ.si, -ə-
Tenniel ˈten.i.əl, ˈ-jəl
tennis ˈten.ɪs ˈ**tennis** ˌ**ball**; ˈ**tennis** ˌ**court**; ˌ**tennis** ˈ**elbow**; ˈ**tennis** ˌ**racket**
Tennyson ˈten.ɪ.sᵊn
tenon ˈten.ən **-s** -z
tenor ˈten.əʳ (US) -ɚ **-s** -z
tenour ˈten.əʳ (US) -ɚ
ten|pence ˈten|.pənts, ˈtem- (US) ˈten- **-penny** -pᵊn.i
tenpin ˈten.pɪn, ˈtem- (US) ˈten- **-s** -z ˌ**tenpin** ˈ**bowling**
tenpins ˈten.pɪnz, ˈtem- (US) ˈten-
tens|e tents **-es** -ɪz **-er** -əʳ (US) -ɚ **-est** -ɪst, -əst **-ing** -ɪŋ **-ed** -t **-ely** -li **-eness** -nəs, -nɪs
tensile ˈtent.saɪl (US) -sɪl, -saɪl
tension ˈten.tʃᵊn (US) ˈtent.ʃᵊn **-s** -z
tensity ˈtent.sə.ti, -sɪ- (US) -sə.ţi
tensor ˈtent.səʳ (US) -sɚ **-s** -z
tent tent **-s** -s **-ing** -ɪŋ (US) ˈten.ţɪŋ **-ed** -ɪd (US) ˈten.ţɪd
tentacle ˈten.tə.kl̩, -tɪ- (US) -ţə- **-s** -z
tentacular tenˈtæk.jə.ləʳ, -jʊ- (US) -lɚ
tentative ˈten.tə.tɪv (US) -ţə.ţɪv **-s** -z **-ly** -li
tenter ˈten.təʳ (US) -ţɚ **-s** -z
Tenterden ˈten.tə.dᵊn (US) -ţɚ-
tenterhook ˈten.tə.hʊk (US) -ţɚ- **-s** -s
tenth tentθ **-s** -s **-ly** -li
tentpegging ˈtentˌpeg.ɪŋ
Tentsmuir tentsˈmjʊəʳ (US) -ˈmjʊr
tenu|is ˈten.ju|.ɪs **-es** -iːz, -eɪz
tenuity tenˈjuː.ə.ti, təˈnjuː-, tɪ-, -ɪ.ti (US) təˈnuː.ə.ţi, -ˈnjuː-
tenuous ˈten.ju.əs **-ly** -li **-ness** -nəs, -nɪs
tenur|e ˈten.jəʳ, -jʊəʳ (US) -jɚ, -jʊr **-es** -z **-ed** -d
tepal ˈtiː.pᵊl, ˈtep.ᵊl
tepee ˈtiː.piː **-s** -z
tepid ˈtep.ɪd **-est** -ɪst, -əst **-ly** -li **-ness** -nəs, -nɪs
tepidity tepˈɪd.ə.ti, -ɪ.ti (US) təˈpɪd.ə.ţi
tequila təˈkiː.lə, tɪ- (US) tə- **-s** -z **te**ˌ**quila** ˈ**sunrise**
ter *three times:* tɜːʳ (US) tɝː, ter
Ter *river in Essex:* tɑːʳ (US) tɑːr
teraph ˈter.əf **-im** -ɪm
terbium ˈtɜː.bi.əm (US) ˈtɝː-
tercel *hawk:* ˈtɜː.sᵊl (US) ˈtɝː- **-s** -z
Tercel *car:* ˈtɜː.sel (US) tɚˈsel
tercentenar|y ˌtɜː.senˈtiː.nᵊr|.i, -ˈten.ᵊr-; tɜːˈsen.tɪ.nᵊr- (US) tɚˈsen.tᵊn.er-; ˌtɝː.senˈten.ɚ- **-ies** -iz
tercentennial ˌtɜː.senˈten.i.əl (US) ˌtɝː-
tercet ˈtɜː.sɪt, -set (US) ˈtɝː.sɪt; tɚˈset **-s** -s
terebene ˈter.ə.biːn, ˈ-ɪ- (US) ˈ-ə-
terebinth ˈter.ə.bɪntθ, ˈ-ɪ- (US) ˈ-ə- **-s** -s
Terence ˈter.ᵊnts
Teresa təˈriː.zə, tɪ-, -ˈreɪ-, terˈiː- (US) təˈriː.sə, -zə, -ˈreɪ-
tergiver|sate ˈtɜː.dʒɪ.vɜː|.seɪt, -və- (US) ˈtɝː.dʒɪ.vɚ- **-sates** -seɪts **-sating** -seɪ.tɪŋ (US) -seɪ.ţɪŋ **-sated** -seɪ.tɪd (US) -seɪ.ţɪd
tergiversation ˌtɜː.dʒɪ.vɜːˈseɪ.ʃᵊn, -vəˈ- (US) ˌtɝː.dʒɪ.vɚ-
teriyaki ˌter.iˈæk.i (US) -ˈjɑː.ki
Terling ˈtɑː.lɪŋ, ˈtɜː- (US) ˈtɑːr-, ˈtɝː-
term tɜːm (US) tɝːm **-s** -z **-ing** -ɪŋ **-ed** -d **-ly** -li
termagant **(T)** ˈtɜː.mə.gənt (US) ˈtɝː- **-s** -s **-ly** -li
terminab|le ˈtɜː.mɪ.nə.b|l̩, -mə- (US) ˈtɝː- **-ly** -li **-leness** -l̩.nəs, -nɪs
terminal ˈtɜː.mɪ.nᵊl, -mə- (US) ˈtɝː- **-s** -z **-ly** -i
termi|nate ˈtɜː.mɪ|.neɪt, -mə- (US) ˈtɝː- **-nates** -neɪts **-nating** -neɪ.tɪŋ (US) -neɪ.ţɪŋ **-nated** -neɪ.tɪd (US) -neɪ.ţɪd **-nator/s** -neɪ.təʳ/z (US) -neɪ.ţɚ/z
termination ˌtɜː.mɪˈneɪ.ʃᵊn, -məˈ- (US) ˌtɝː- **-s** -z
terminative ˈtɜː.mɪ.nə.tɪv, -mə-, -neɪ- (US) ˈtɝː.mɪ.neɪ.ţɪv, -mə- **-ly** -li
terminer ˈtɜː.mɪ.nəʳ, -mə- (US) ˈtɝː.mɪ.nɚ, -mə-
terminologic|al ˌtɜː.mɪ.nəˈlɒdʒ.ɪ.k|ᵊl, -mə- (US) ˌtɝː.mɪ.nəˈlɑː.dʒɪ-, -mə- **-ally** -ᵊl.i, -li
terminolog|y ˌtɜː.mɪˈnɒl.ə.dʒ|i, -məˈ- (US) ˌtɝː.mɪˈnɑː.lə-, -məˈ- **-ies** -iz
termin|us ˈtɜː.mɪ.n|əs, -mə- (US) ˈtɝː- **-i** -aɪ **-uses** -ə.sɪz
termite ˈtɜː.maɪt (US) ˈtɝː- **-s** -s
termtime ˈtɜːm.taɪm (US) ˈtɝːm-
tern tɜːn (US) tɝːn **-s** -z
ternary ˈtɜː.nᵊr.i (US) ˈtɝː-
Ternate tɜːˈnɑː.ti (US) tɝːˈnɑː.teɪ
Terpsichore tɜːpˈsɪk.ᵊr.i (US) tɚp-
terpsichorean ˌtɜːp.sɪ.kᵊrˈiː.ən, -kɒrˈ- (US) ˌtɝːp.sɪ.kəˈriː-; ˌtɝːp.sɪˈkɔːr.i-
terra ˈter.ə
terrac|e ˈter.ɪs, -əs **-es** -ɪz **-ing** -ɪŋ **-ed** -t
terracotta ˌter.əˈkɒt.ə (US) -ˈkɑː.ţə
terra firma ˌter.əˈfɜː.mə (US) -ˈfɝː-
terrain təˈreɪn, tɪ-, terˈeɪn; ˈter.eɪn (US) terˈeɪn, təˈreɪn; ˈter.eɪn **-s** -z
terra incognita ˌter.ə.ɪŋˈkɒg.nɪ.tə, -ɪnˈ-; -kɒgˈniː.tə- (US) -ɪnˈkɑːg.niː.ţə, -nɪ- **terrae incognitae** ˌter.i.ɪŋˈkɒg.nɪ.ti, -ɪnˈ-; -kɒgˈniː.ti (US) -ɪnˈkɑːg.niː.ţi, -nɪ-
Terramycin® ˌter.əˈmaɪ.sɪn
Terrance ˈter.ᵊnts
terrapin ˈter.ə.pɪn **-s** -z
terrari|um təˈreə.ri|.əm, terˈeə-, tɪˈreə- (US) təˈrer.i- **-ums** -əmz **-a** -ə
terrazzo terˈæt.səʊ, təˈræt-, tɪ- (US) təˈrɑːt.soʊ, terˈɑːt-; təˈræz.oʊ **-s** -z
Terrell ˈter.ᵊl
Terrence ˈter.ᵊnts
terrestrial təˈres.tri.əl, terˈes-, tɪˈres- (US) təˈres- **-s** -z **-ly** -i **-ness** -nəs, -nɪs
terret ˈter.ɪt **-s** -s
Terri ˈter.i
terrib|le ˈter.ə.b|l̩, ˈ-ɪ- (US) ˈ-ə- **-ly** -li **-leness** -l̩.nəs, -nɪs
terricolous təˈrɪk.ᵊl.əs, terˈɪk-, tɪˈrɪk- (US) terˈɪk-, təˈrɪk-
terrier ˈter.i.əʳ (US) -ɚ **-s** -z
terrific təˈrɪf.ɪk, tɪ- (US) tə- **-ally** -ᵊl.i, -li
terri|fy ˈter.ə|.faɪ, ˈ-ɪ- (US) ˈ-ə- **-fies** -faɪz **-fying/ly** -faɪ.ɪŋ/li **-fied** -faɪd
terrine terˈiːn, təˈriːn; ˈter.iːn (US) terˈiːn **-s** -z
territorial ˌter.ɪˈtɔː.ri.əl, -əˈ- (US) -əˈtɔːr.i- **-s** -z **-ly** -i *stress shift, see compounds:* ˌ**Territorial** ˈ**Army**, **Terri**ˌ**torial** ˈ**Army**; **terri**ˌ**torial** ˈ**waters**
territorializ|e, -is|e ˌter.ɪˈtɔː.ri.ᵊl.aɪz, -əˈ- (US) -əˈtɔːr.i- **-es** -ɪz **-ing** -ɪŋ **-ed** -d
territor|y ˈter.ɪ.tᵊr|.i, ˈ-ə-, -tr|i (US) -ə.tɔːr|.i **-ies** -iz
terror ˈter.əʳ (US) -ɚ **-s** -z
terror|ism ˈter.ᵊr|.ɪ.zᵊm **-ist/s** -ɪst/s
terrorization, -isa-, ˌter.ᵊr.aɪˈzeɪ.ʃᵊn, -ɪˈ- (US) -ɪˈ-
terroriz|e, -is|e ˈter.ᵊr.aɪz (US) -ə.raɪz **-es** -ɪz **-ing** -ɪŋ **-ed** -d **-er/s** -əʳ/z (US) -ɚ/z
terror-stricken ˈter.əˌstrɪk.ᵊn (US) -ɚˌ-
terror-struck ˈter.ə.strʌk (US) ˈ-ɚ-
terr|y **(T)** ˈter|.i **-ies** -iz ˌ**terry** ˈ**nappy**; ˌ**terry** ˈ**towelling**
ters|e tɜːs (US) tɝːs **-er** -əʳ (US) -ɚ **-est** -ɪst, -əst **-ely** -li **-eness** -nəs, -nɪs
tertian ˈtɜː.ʃᵊn, -ʃi.ən (US) ˈtɝː.ʃᵊn
tertiary ˈtɜː.ʃᵊr.i, -ʃi.ᵊr- (US) ˈtɝː.ʃi.er-, -ʃɚ.i ˌ**tertiary edu**ˈ**cation**
tertium quid ˌtɜː.ti.əmˈkwɪd, ˌ-ʃəmˈ-, -ʃi.əmˈ- (US) ˌtɝː.ʃi.əmˈ-; ˌter.ti.ʊmˈ-
Tertius ˈtɜː.ʃəs, -ʃi.əs, -ti-
Tertullian tɜːˈtʌl.i.ən, ˈ-jən (US) tɚ-
terylene **(T®)** ˈter.ə.liːn, ˈ-ɪ- (US) ˈ-ɪ-
terza rima ˌteət.səˈriː.mə, ˌtɜːt- (US) ˌtert-
Tesco® ˈtes.kəʊ (US) -koʊ **-'s** -z
TESL ˈtes.l̩
tesla **(T)** ˈtes.lə
TESOL ˈtiː.sɒl (US) -sɑːl; ˈtes.ᵊl
Tess tes

Tessa, TESSA 'tes.ə

tesse(l)l|ate 'tes.ᵊl|.eɪt, -ɪ.l|eɪt (US) -ə.l|eɪt **-ates** -eɪts **-ating** -eɪ.tɪŋ (US) -eɪ.t̬ɪŋ **-ated** -eɪ.tɪd (US) -eɪ.t̬ɪd

tessellation ˌtes.ᵊl'eɪ.ʃᵊn, -ɪ'leɪ- (US) -ə'leɪ- **-s** -z

tessitura ˌtes.ɪ'tʊə.rə, -ə'-, -'tjʊə-, -'tɔː-, -'tjɔː- (US) -ɪ'tʊr.ə

test (T) test **-s** -s **-ing** -ɪŋ **-ed** -ɪd **-able** -ə.bl̩ **-er/s** -əʳ/z (US) -ɚ/z 'test ˌcard; 'test ˌcase; 'test ˌmatch

testace|an tes'teɪ.ʃ|ᵊn, -ʃi|.ən (US) '-ʃ|ən **-ous** -əs

testacy 'tes.tə.si

testament (T) 'tes.tə.mənt **-s** -s

testament|ary ˌtes.tə'men.t|ᵊr.i (US) -t̬ɚ- **-al** -ᵊl

testate 'tes.teɪt, -tɪt (US) -teɪt **-s** -s

testator tes'teɪ.təʳ (US) 'tes.teɪ.t̬ɚ, -'-- **-s** -z

testatri|x tes'teɪ.trɪ|ks **-ces** -siːz

test-bed 'test.bed **-s** -z

test-|drive 'test|.draɪv **-drives** -draɪvz **-driving** -ˌdraɪ.vɪŋ **-drove** -drəʊv (US) -droʊv **-driven** -ˌdrɪv.ᵊn

testes *(plur. of* **testis***)* 'tes.tiːz

testicle 'tes.tɪ.kl̩, -tə- **-s** -z

testicular tes'tɪk.jə.ləʳ, -jʊ- (US) -lɚ

testification ˌtes.tɪ.fɪ'keɪ.ʃᵊn, -tə- **-s** -z

testi|fy 'tes.tɪ|.faɪ, -tə- **-fies** -faɪz **-fying** -faɪ.ɪŋ **-fied** -faɪd **-fier/s** -faɪ.əʳ/z (US) -faɪ.ɚ/z

testimonial ˌtes.tɪ'məʊ.ni.əl, -tə'- (US) -'moʊ- **-s** -z

testimonializ|e, -is|e ˌtes.tɪ'məʊ.ni.ᵊl.aɪz, -tə'- (US) -'moʊ.ni.ə.laɪz **-es** -ɪz **-ing** -ɪŋ **-ed** -d

testimon|y 'tes.tɪ.mə.n|i, -tə- (US) -moʊ.n|i **-ies** -iz

test|is 'tes.t|ɪs **-es** -iːz

Teston 'tiː.sᵊn

testosterone tes'tɒs.tᵊr.əʊn (US) -'tɑː.stə.roʊn

test-tube 'test.tjuːb, -tʃuːb (US) -tuːb, -tjuːb **-s** -z ˌtest-tube 'baby (US) 'test-tube ˌbaby

testud|o tes'tjuː.d|əʊ, -'tuː- (US) -'tuː.d|oʊ, -'tjuː- **-os** -əʊz (US) -oʊz **-ines** -dɪ.niːz, -neɪz (US) -dɪ.niːz

test|y 'tes.t|i **-ier** -i.əʳ (US) -i.ɚ **-iest** -i.ɪst, -i.əst **-ily** -ɪ.li, -ᵊl.i **-iness** -ɪ.nəs, -ɪ.nɪs

tetanus 'tet.ᵊn.əs

Tetbury 'tet.bᵊr.i (US) -ber-, -bɚ-

tetch|y 'tetʃ|.i **-ier** -i.əʳ (US) -i.ɚ **-iest** -i.ɪst, -i.əst **-ily** -ɪ.li, -ᵊl.i **-iness** -ɪ.nəs, -ɪ.nɪs

tête-à-tête ˌteɪt.ɑː'teɪt, ˌtet.ə'tet (US) ˌteɪt.ə'teɪt, ˌtet.ə'tet **-s** -s

teth|er 'teð|.əʳ (US) -ɚ **-ers** -əz (US) -ɚz **-ering** -ᵊr.ɪŋ **-ered** -əd (US) -ɚd

Tetley 'tet.li

Tétouan tet'wɑːn (US) tet'wɑːn; 'teɪ.twɑːn

Tetovo tet'əʊ.vəʊ (US) -'oʊ.voʊ

tetrachord 'tet.rə.kɔːd (US) -kɔːrd **-s** -z

tetrad 'tet.ræd, -rəd (US) -ræd **-s** -z

tetragon 'tet.rə.gən (US) -gɑːn **-s** -z

tetrahedr|on ˌtet.rə'hiː.dr|ᵊn, -'hed.r|ᵊn (US) -'hiː- **-ons** -ᵊnz **-a** -ə **-al** -ᵊl

tetralog|y tet'ræl.ə.dʒ|i, tə'træl- (US) tet'rɑː.lə- **-ies** -iz

tetrameter tet'ræm.ɪ.təʳ, '-ə- (US) -ə.t̬ɚ **-s** -z

tetrarch 'tet.rɑːk (US) -rɑːrk **-s** -s **-y** -i **-ies** -iz

tetrasyllabic ˌtet.rə.sɪ'læb.ɪk, -sə'- (US) -sɪ'-

tetrasyllable 'tet.rəˌsɪl.ə.bl̩, ˌtet.rə'sɪl- **-s** -z

tetrathlon tet'ræθ.lɒn, tɪ'træθ-, tə-, -lən (US) tet'ræθ.lɑːn

Tettenhall 'tet.ᵊn.hɔːl

tetter 'tet.əʳ (US) 'tet̬.ɚ

Teucer 'tjuː.səʳ (US) 'tuː.sɚ, 'tjuː-

Teuton 'tjuː.tᵊn (US) 'tuː-, 'tjuː- **-s** -z

Teutonic tjuː'tɒn.ɪk (US) tuː'tɑː.nɪk, tjuː-

teutonization, -isa- ˌtjuː.tᵊn.aɪ'zeɪ.ʃᵊn, -ɪ'- (US) ˌtuː.tᵊn.ɪ'-, ˌtjuː-

teutoniz|e, -is|e 'tjuː.tᵊn.aɪz (US) 'tuː-, 'tjuː- **-es** -ɪz **-ing** -ɪŋ **-ed** -d

Teviot *river:* 'tiː.vi.ət *Lord:* 'tev.i.ət

Teviotdale 'tiː.vi.ət.deɪl

Tewfik 'tjuː.fɪk (US) 'tuː-, 'tjuː-

Tewkesbury 'tjuːks.bᵊr.i (US) 'tuːks.ber-, 'tjuːks-, -bɚ-

Tex. *(abbrev. for* **Texas***)* 'tek.səs

Texaco® 'tek.sə.kəʊ (US) -sɪ.koʊ, -sə-

Texan 'tek.sᵊn **-s** -z

Texas 'tek.səs

Texel 'tek.sᵊl

Tex-Mex ˌteks'meks *stress shift:* ˌTex-Mex 'food

text tekst **-s** -s **-ing** -ɪŋ **-ed** -ɪd

textbook 'tekst.bʊk **-s** -s

textile 'tek.staɪl (US) -staɪl, -stɪl **-s** -z

textual 'teks.tju.əl (US) -tʃu- **-ly** -i

textural 'teks.tʃᵊr.ᵊl

textur|e 'teks.tʃəʳ (US) -tʃɚ **-es** -z **-ing** -ɪŋ **-ed** -d

Tey teɪ

Teynham 'ten.əm, 'teɪ.nəm

Note: The former is appropriate for Baron Teynham.

-th -θ

Note: Suffix. Not a syllable in itself, and does not affect the word stress, e.g. **tenth** /tenθ/.

Thacker 'θæk.əʳ (US) -ɚ

Thackeray 'θæk.ᵊr.i, '-ri

Thackley 'θæk.li

Thaddeus 'θæd.i.əs; θæd'iː-

Thai taɪ **-s** -z

Thailand 'taɪ.lænd, -lənd

Thake θeɪk

thalam|us 'θæl.ə.m|əs **-i** -aɪ, -iː

thalassotherapy θəˌlæs.əʊ'θer.ə.pi, θælˌæs- (US) -ə'-

Thalben 'θæl.bən, 'θɔːl-

thaler 'tɑː.ləʳ (US) -lɚ **-s** -z

Thales 'θeɪ.liːz

Thali|a *of the three Graces:* θə'laɪ|.ə **-an** -ən *Greek Muse:* 'θæl.i.ə, '-jə (US) 'θeɪ.li.ə, 'θeɪl.jə

thalidomide θə'lɪd.ə.maɪd, θæl'ɪd- (US) θə'lɪd-

thallium 'θæl.i.əm

Thame teɪm

Thames *in England, Canada, New Zealand:* temz *in Connecticut:* θeɪmz, teɪmz, temz

Thamesmead 'temz.miːd

than *strong form:* ðæn *weak forms:* ðᵊn, ðən, ðn̩

Note: Weak form word. The strong form /ðæn/ is rarely used; it is sometimes found in emphatic utterances such as 'The Queen, than whom no-one is richer...', but it normally has the weak pronunciation /ðən/, e.g. 'faster than sound', /ˌfɑː.stə.ðən'saʊnd (US) -stɚ-/, or in rapid speech /ðn̩/, e.g. 'better than ever', /ˌbet.ə.ðn̩'ev.ə (US) ˌbet̬.ɚ.ðn̩'ev.ɚ/.

Thanatos 'θæn.ə.tɒs (US) -tɑːs

thane (T) θeɪn **-s** -z

Thanet 'θæn.ɪt

thank θæŋk **-s** -s **-ing** -ɪŋ **-ed** -t **-er/s** -əʳ/z (US) -ɚ/z

thankful 'θæŋk.fᵊl, -fʊl **-ly** -i **-ness** -nəs -nɪs

thankless 'θæŋ.kləs, -klɪs **-ly** -li **-ness** -nəs, -nɪs

thanksgiving (T) ˌθæŋks'gɪv.ɪŋ (US) ˌ-'--, '-ˌ-- **-s** -z **Thanks'giving ˌDay** (US) **Thanks'giving ˌDay** (US) **'Thanksgiving ˌDay**

thankworth|y 'θæŋkˌwɜː.ð|i (US) -ˌwɝː- **-iness** -ɪ.nəs, -ɪ.nɪs

thank-you 'θæŋk.ju **-s** -z **'thank-you ˌletter**

Note: Although the most common abbreviation for 'thank you' is 'thanks', the pronunciation /kjuː/ is also heard in British English, usually with high pitch, in casual speech.

Thant θænt

that *(adj., demonstr. pron., adv.)* ðæt

Note: Weak form word. When used demonstratively it is always

Pronouncing the letters TH

The consonant digraph **th** is most commonly pronounced /θ/ or /ð/. In initial position, /ð/ occurs mostly in function or grammar words like determiners and conjunctions, e.g.:

the	/ðə/	
that	/ðæt, ðət/	

In content words like nouns and main verbs, /θ/ most usually appears in initial position, e.g.:

theme	/θiːm/	
think	/θɪŋk/	

At the ends of words, it is more difficult to predict which realisation will occur. However, /ð/ is more common here than /θ/, and is highly likely in verbs. For example, before **e** or the grammatical inflection *-ing*, the pronunciation is usually /ð/, e.g.:

loathe	/ləʊð/	(US) /loʊð/
loath	/ləʊθ, ləʊð/	
bathe	/beɪð/	
bath	/bɑːθ/	(US) /bæθ/

Note that the verb *bathe* and *bath* when used as a verb both have the same spelling for the present participle, *bathing*, but different pronunciations.

In addition

In some names and a few other words, **th** is pronounced as /t/, e.g.:

Thames	/temz/	
thyme	/taɪm/	

The suffix *-th* when applied to numbers is always pronounced /θ/, e.g.:

eighth	/eɪtθ/	
sixteenth	/sɪkˈstiːnθ/	

When the two letters come together due to the addition of a prefix, the pronunciation is /t.h/, e.g.:

lighthouse	/ˈlaɪt.haʊs/	
sweetheart	/ˈswiːt.hɑːt/	(US) /-hɑːrt/

Occasionally, **th** may be silent, e.g.:

asthma	/ˈæsθ.mə, ˈæs-/	(US) /ˈæz-/

pronounced with its strong form /ðæt/, e.g. 'that's final', 'I like **that** one'.

that (*relative pron.*) *strong form:* ðæt *weak form:* ðət *weak form:* ðt

Note: The strong form is seldom used, except in very deliberate speech or when the word is said in isolation.

that (*conj.*) *strong form:* ðæt *weak form:* ðət

Note: The strong form is rarely used.

thataway ˈðæt.ə,weɪ (US) ˈðæt̬-

thatch θætʃ **-es** -ɪz **-ing** -ɪŋ **-ed** -t **-er/s** -əʳ/z (US) -ɚ/z

Thatcham ˈθætʃ.əm

Thatch|er ˈθætʃ|.əʳ (US) -ɚ **-erism** -ᵊr.ɪ.zᵊm **-erite/s** -ᵊr.aɪt/s (US) -ə.raɪt/s

thaumaturg|e ˈθɔː.mə.tɜːdʒ (US) -tɝːdʒ, ˈθɑː- **-es** -ɪz

thaumaturgic ˌθɔː.məˈtɜː.dʒɪk (US) -ˈtɝː-, ˌθɑː-

thaumaturg|y ˈθɔː.mə.tɜː.dʒ|i (US) -tɝː-, ˈθɑː- **-ist/s** -ɪst/s

thaw (T) θɔː (US) θɑː, θɔː **-s** -z **-ing** -ɪŋ **-ed** -d

the *strong form:* ðiː *weak form before vowels:* ði; *weak form before consonants:* ðə

Note: Weak form word. The strong form /ðiː/ is used for emphasis, e.g. 'This is **the** place to eat' or contrast, e.g. 'It's not **a** solution, but **the** solution'. Weak forms are /ðə/ before consonants, e.g 'the cat' /ðəˈkæt/ and /ði/ before vowels, e.g. 'the apple' /ðiˈæp.l̩/.

Thea θɪə, ˈθiː.ə (US) ˈθiː.ə

Theakston ˈθiːk.stən **-'s** -z

theatre, **theater** ˈθɪə.təʳ, ˈθiː.ə-; θiˈet.əʳ (US) ˈθiː.ə.t̬ɚ **-s** -z

theatregoer, **theatergoer** ˈθɪə.tə,gəʊ.əʳ, ˈθiː.ə-; θiˈet.ə,- (US) ˈθiː.ə.t̬ɚ,goʊ.ɚ **-s** -z

theatreland, **theaterland** ˈθɪə.tə.lænd, ˈθiː.ə-; θiˈet.ə- (US) ˈθiː.ə.t̬ɚ-

theatric|al θiˈæt.rɪ.k|ᵊl **-als** -ᵊlz **-ally** -ᵊl.i, -li **-alness** -ᵊl.nəs, -nɪs **-alism** -ᵊl.ɪ.zᵊm

theatricality θi,æt.rɪˈkæl.ə.ti, -ɪ.ti (US) -ə.t̬i

theatrics θiˈæt.rɪks

Thebaid ˈθiː.beɪ.ɪd, -bi-

Theban ˈθiː.bən **-s** -z

thebe ˈtiː.beɪ

Thebes θiːbz

thee *normal form:* ðiː *occasional weak form:* ði

theft θeft **-s** -s

thegn θeɪn **-s** -z

their *normal form:* ðeəʳ (US) ðer *occasional weak form when a vowel follows:* ðᵊr (US) ðɚ

Note: The weak form is found in commonly-used phrases such as 'on their own' /ˌɒn.ðᵊrˈəʊn (US) ˌɑːn.ðɚˈoʊn/.

theirs ðeəz (US) ðerz

the|ism ˈθiː|.ɪ.zᵊm **-ist/s** -ɪst/s

theistic θiːˈɪs.tɪk **-al** -ᵊl

Thelma ˈθel.mə

Thelwall ˈθel.wɔːl

Thelwell ˈθel.wəl, -wel

them *strong form:* ðem *weak forms:* ðəm, ðm *occasional weak forms:* əm, ᵊm

Note: Weak form word. The strong form /ðem/ is used for contrast, e.g. 'them and us' or for emphasis, e.g. 'look at **them**'. The weak form is usually /ðəm/, e.g. 'leave them alone' /ˌliːv.ðəm.əˈləʊn (US) -ˈloʊn/, or in rapid, casual speech /ðm/, e.g. 'run them out', /ˌrʌn.ðmˈaʊt/.

thematic θɪˈmæt.ɪk, θiː- (US) θiːˈmæt̬- **-ally** -ᵊl.i, -li

them|e θiːm **-es** -z **-ing** -ɪŋ **-ed** -d ˈ**theme** ˌ**park**

Themistocles θɪˈmɪs.tə.kliːz, θemˈɪs-, θəˈmɪs- (US) θəˈmɪs-

themselves ðəmˈselvz (US) ðəm-, ðem-

then ðen

thence ðents

thenceforth ˌðentsˈfɔːθ (US) -ˈfɔːrθ

thenceforward ˌðentsˈfɔː.wəd (US) -ˈfɔːr.wɚd

theo- θiː.əʊ-, θɪə-; θiˈɒ- US θi.oʊ-, -ə-, θiˈɑː-
Note: Prefix. Normally stressed on the second syllable, e.g. **theology** /θiˈɒl.ə.dʒi US θiˈɑː-/, but may also carry secondary stress on the first syllable with primary stress on the third syllable, e.g. **theological** /ˌθiː.əˈlɒdʒ.ɪ.kl̩ US -ˈlɑː.dʒ-/. This prefix is not present in 'theory' and related words.
Theo ˈθiː.əʊ US -oʊ
Theobald ˈθiː.ə.bɔːld, ˈθɪə- *formerly:* ˈθɪb.ᵊld, ˈtɪb- US ˈθiː.ə.bɔːld, -bɑːld; ˈtɪb.ᵊld
Theobalds *in Hertfordshire:* ˈθiː.ə.bɔːldz, ˈθɪə- US ˈθiː.ə-, -bɑːldz *road in London:* ˈθiː.ə.bɔːldz, ˈθɪə- *formerly:* ˈtɪb.ᵊldz US ˈθiː.ə.bɔːldz, -bɑːldz; ˈtɪb.ᵊldz
theocrac|y θiˈɒk.rə.s|i US -ˈɑː.krə- **-ies** -iz
theocratic ˌθiː.əʊˈkræt.ɪk, ˌθɪəˈ- US ˌθiː.əˈkræt̬- **-al** -ᵊl
Theocritus θiˈɒk.rɪ.təs US -ˈɑː.krə.t̬əs
theodicy θiˈɒd.ɪ.si, ˈ-ə- US -ˈɑː.də-
theodolite θiˈɒd.ᵊl.aɪt US -ˈɑː.də.laɪt **-s** -s
Theodora ˌθiː.əˈdɔː.rə, ˌθɪəˈ- US ˌθiː.əˈdɔːr.ə
Theodore ˈθiː.ə.dɔːʳ, ˈθɪə- US ˈθiː.ə.dɔːr
Theodoric θiˈɒd.ᵊr.ɪk US -ˈɑː.dɚ-
Theodosi|a ˌθiː.əˈdəʊ.si|.ə, ˌθɪəˈ- US ˌθiː.oʊˈdoʊ.ʃi|.ə, -əˈ-, ˈ-ʃ|ə **-us** -əs
theologian ˌθiː.əˈləʊ.dʒᵊn, ˌθɪəˈ-, -dʒi.ən US ˌθiː.əˈloʊ.dʒᵊn, -dʒi.ən **-s** -z
theologic ˌθiː.əˈlɒdʒ.ɪk, ˌθɪəˈ- US ˌθiː.əˈlɑː.dʒɪk **-al** -ᵊl **-ally** -ᵊl.i, -li
theologi|cal ˌθiː.əˈlɒdʒ.ɪ|.kᵊl, ˌθɪəˈ- US ˌθiː.əˈlɑː.dʒɪ- **-cally** -kᵊl.i, -kli
theologiz|e, -is|e θiˈɒl.ə.dʒaɪz US -ˈɑː.lə- **-es** -ɪz **-ing** -ɪŋ **-ed** -d
theolog|y θiˈɒl.ə.dʒ|i US -ˈɑː.lə- **-ist/s** -ɪst/s
Theophilus θiˈɒf.ɪ.ləs, -ᵊl.əs US -ˈɑː.fᵊl-
Theophrastus ˌθiː.əʊˈfræs.təs, ˌθɪəˈ- US ˌθiː.oʊˈ-, -əˈ-
theorbo θiˈɔː.bəʊ US -ˈɔːr.boʊ **-s** -z
theorem ˈθɪə.rəm, -rem, -rɪm US ˈθiː.ɚ.əm, ˈθɪr.əm, -em **-s** -z
theoretic θɪəˈret.ɪk, ˌθiː.əˈ- US ˌθiː.əˈret̬- **-al** -ᵊl **-ally** -ᵊl.i, -li
theoreti|cal θɪəˈret.ɪ|.kᵊl, ˌθiː.əˈ- US ˌθiː.əˈret̬- **-cally** -kᵊl.i, -kli
theoretician ˌθɪə.rəˈtɪʃ.ᵊn, ˌθiː.ə-, -rɪˈ-, -retˈɪʃ- US ˌθiː.ə.rəˈtɪʃ-, ˌθɪr.əˈ- **-s** -z
theorist ˈθɪə.rɪst, ˈθiː.ə- US ˈθiː.ɚ.ɪst, ˈθɪr.ɪst **-s** -s
theoriz|e, -is|e ˈθɪə.raɪz, ˈθiː.ə- US ˈθiː.ə-, ˈθɪr.aɪz **-es** -ɪz **-ing** -ɪŋ **-ed** -d **-er/s** -əʳ/z US -ɚ/z
theor|y ˈθɪə.r|i, ˈθiː.ə- US ˈθiː.ə-, ˈθɪr|.i **-ies** -iz
theosophic ˌθiː.əˈsɒf.ɪk, ˌθɪəˈ- US ˌθiː.əˈsɑː.fɪk **-al** -ᵊl **-ally** -ᵊl.i, -li
theosophiz|e, -is|e θiˈɒs.ə.faɪz US -ˈɑː.sə- **-es** -ɪz **-ing** -ɪŋ **-ed** -d
theosoph|y θiˈɒs.ə.f|i US -ˈɑː.sə- **-ist/s** -ɪst/s **-ism** -ɪ.zᵊm
Thera ˈθɪə.rə US ˈθɪr.ə
therapeutic ˌθer.əˈpjuː.tɪk US -t̬ɪk **-s** -s **-ally** -ᵊl.i, -li
therapeutist ˌθer.əˈpjuː.tɪst US -t̬ɪst **-s** -s
therap|y ˈθer.ə.p|i **-ies** -iz **-ist/s** -ɪst/s
Theravada ˌθer.əˈvɑː.də
there *strong form:* ðeəʳ US ðer *weak form:* ðəʳ US ðɚ *alternative weak form before vowels:* ðᵊr US ðɚ
Note: Weak form word. The weak forms occur only when 'there' is used existentially as in 'there is', 'there are', 'there was', 'there won't be', etc. The strong form /ðeəʳ US ðer/ is also used in such expressions, and is the normal pronunciation for 'there' as a place adverbial, e.g. 'there it is'.
thereabout ˈðeə.rə.baʊt, ˌ--ˈ- US ˈðer.ə.baʊt, ˌ--ˈ- **-s** -s
Note: The form /ˌðeəʳ.əˈbaʊts US ˌðer-/ is always used in the expression 'there or thereabouts'.
thereafter ˌðeəˈrɑːf.təʳ US ˌðerˈæf.tɚ
thereat ˌðeəˈræt US ˌðer-
thereby ˌðeəˈbaɪ US ˌðer-
there'd ðeəd US ðerd
therefor ˌðeəˈfɔːʳ US ˌðerˈfɔːr
therefore ˈðeə.fɔːʳ US ˈðer.fɔːr
therefrom ˌðeəˈfrɒm US ˌðerˈfrʌm, -ˈfrɑːm
therein ˌðeəˈrɪn US ˌðerˈɪn
thereinafter ˌðeə.rɪnˈɑːf.təʳ US ˌðer.ɪnˈæf.tɚ
thereinto ˌðeəˈrɪn.tuː US ˌðerˈɪn-
there'll ðeəl *weak form:* ðəl, ðl̩ US ðerl
Note: See note for 'there'.
thereof ˌðeəˈrɒv US ˌðerˈɑːv, -ˈʌv
thereon ˌðeəˈrɒn US ˌðerˈɑːn
there's *(=* **there is, there has***) strong form:* ðeəz US ðerz *weak form:* ðəz US ðɚz
Note: See note for 'there'.
Theresa tɪˈriː.zə, tə- US təˈriː.sə, -zə
thereto ˌðeəˈtuː US ˌðer-
theretofore ˌðeə.tuːˈfɔːʳ US ˌðer.t̬əˈfɔːr, ˈ---
thereunder ˌðeəˈrʌn.dəʳ US ˌðerˈʌn.dɚ
thereunto ˌðeəˈrʌn.tuː, ˌ--ˈ- US ˌðerˈʌn.tuː, ˌ--ˈ-
thereupon ˌðeə.rəˈpɒn, ˈ--- US ˌðer.əˈpɑːn, ˈ---
there've *strong forms:* ˈðeəʳ.əv US ˈðer- *weak forms:* ðəʳ.əv, ðəv US ðɚ.əv
therewith ˌðeəˈwɪð, -ˈwɪθ US ˌðer-
therewithal ˌðeə.wɪðˈɔːl, -wɪθˈ- *when used as a noun:* ˈ--- US ˌðer-, ˈ---
therm θɜːm US θɝːm **-s** -z
thermal ˈθɜː.mᵊl US ˈθɝː- **-ly** -i
thermic ˈθɜː.mɪk US ˈθɝː- **-ally** -ᵊl.i, -li
Thermidor ˈθɜː.mɪ.dɔːʳ US ˈθɝː.mə.dɔːr
thermion ˈθɜː.mi.ən US ˈθɝː- **-s** -z
thermionic ˌθɜː.miˈɒn.ɪk US ˌθɝː.miˈɑː.nɪk **-s** -s
thermistor θɜːˈmɪs.təʳ US ˈθɝː.mɪ.stɚ, θɚˈmɪs.tɚ **-s** -z
Thermit® ˈθɜː.mɪt US ˈθɝː-
thermite ˈθɜː.maɪt US ˈθɝː-
thermo- θɜː.məʊ-; θəˈmɒ- US θɝː.moʊ-, -mə-, θɚˈmɑː-
Note: Prefix. There may be primary or secondary stress on the first syllable, e.g. **thermocouple** /ˈθɜː.məˌkʌp.l̩ US ˈθɜːr.mə-/, **thermometric** /ˌθɜː.məʊˈmet.rɪk US ˌθɜːr.moʊˈ-/, or on the second syllable, e.g. **thermometer** /θəˈmɒm.ɪ.tə US θɚˈmɑː.mə.t̬ɚ/.
thermocouple ˈθɜː.məʊˌkʌp.l̩ US ˈθɝː.moʊ-, -mə- **-s** -z
thermodynamic ˌθɜː.məʊ.daɪˈnæm.ɪk, -dɪˈ- US ˌθɝː.moʊ.daɪˈ-, -mə- **-s** -s **-ally** -ᵊl.i, -li
thermoelectric ˌθɜː.məʊ.ɪˈlek.trɪk, -əˈ- US ˌθɝː.moʊ- **-ally** -ᵊl.i, -li
thermoelectricity ˌθɜː.məʊ.ɪˌlekˈtrɪs.ə.ti, -əˌ-, -ˌiː.lekˈ-, -ˈtrɪz-, -ɪ.ti US ˌθɝː.moʊˌiː.lekˈtrɪs.ə.t̬i
thermograph ˈθɜː.məʊ.grɑːf, -græf US ˈθɝː.moʊ.græf, -mə- **-s** -s
thermometer θəˈmɒm.ɪ.təʳ, ˈ-ə- US θɚˈmɑː.mə.t̬ɚ **-s** -z
thermometric ˌθɜː.məʊˈmet.rɪk US ˌθɝː.moʊˈ-, -məˈ- **-al** -ᵊl **-ally** -ᵊl.i, -li
thermonuclear ˌθɜː.məʊˈnjuː.kli.əʳ US ˌθɝː.moʊˈnuː.kli.ɚ, -məˈ-, -ˈnjuː-
thermopile ˈθɜː.məʊ.paɪl US ˈθɝː.moʊ-, -mə- **-s** -z
thermoplastic ˌθɜː.məʊˈplæs.tɪk, -ˈplɑː.stɪk US ˌθɝː.moʊˈplæs.tɪk, -məˈ- **-s** -s
Thermopylae θɜːˈmɒp.ɪ.liː, θə-, -ᵊl.iː, -i, -aɪ US θɚˈmɑː.pə.liː
Thermos® ˈθɜː.mɒs, -məs US ˈθɝː.məs **-es** -ɪz ˈ**Thermos** ˌ**flask**
thermosetting ˈθɜː.məʊˌset.ɪŋ US ˈθɝː.moʊˌset̬-, -məˌ-
thermostat ˈθɜː.mə.stæt US ˈθɝː.mə- **-s** -s **-(t)ing** -ɪŋ **-(t)ed** -ɪd
thermostatic ˌθɜː.məˈstæt.ɪk US ˌθɝː.məˈstæt̬-

Theroux θəˈruː
Thersites θɜːˈsaɪ.tiːz, θə- (US) θɚˈsaɪ-
thesaur|us θɪˈsɔː.r|əs, θiː-, θə- (US) θɪˈsɔːr|.əs **-i** -aɪ **-uses** -ə.sɪz
these *(plur. of* **this**) ðiːz
Theseus *in Greek legend:* ˈθiː.sjuːs, -sjəs, -si.əs (US) -si.əs, -sjuːs *Shakespearian character, and as name of ship:* ˈθiː.sjəs, -si.əs
Thesiger ˈθes.ɪ.dʒəʳ (US) -dʒɚ
thes|is *dissertation:* ˈθiː.s|ɪs **-es** -iːz
thesis *metrical term:* ˈθes.ɪs, ˈθiː.sɪs (US) ˈθiː.sɪs
thespian (T) ˈθes.pi.ən **-s** -z
Thespis ˈθes.pɪs
Thessalonian ˌθes.əˈləʊ.ni.ən (US) -əˈloʊ- **-s** -z
Thessalonika ˌθes.əlˈɒn.ɪ.kə (US) -əˈlɑː.nɪ-
Thessaly ˈθes.əl.i
theta ˈθiː.tə (US) ˈθeɪ.t̬ə, ˈθiː- **-s** -z
Thetford ˈθet.fəd (US) -fɚd
Thetis *Greek:* ˈθet.ɪs (US) ˈθet̬- *otherwise:* ˈθiː.tɪs (US) -t̬ɪs
thews θjuːz
they ðeɪ
they'd ðeɪd
Theydon Bois ˌθeɪ.dənˈbɔɪz
they'd've ˈðeɪ.dəv
they'll ðeɪl
they're ðeəʳ (US) ðer
they've ðeɪv
thiamin(e) ˈθaɪə.miːn, -mɪn (US) -mɪn, -miːn
thick θɪk **-er** -əʳ (US) -ɚ **-est** -ɪst, -əst **-ly** -li **-ness/es** -nəs/ɪz, -nɪs/ɪz **as ˌthick as ˈthieves; as ˌthick as ˌtwo ˌshort ˈplanks; ˌgive someone a ˌthick ˈear; through ˌthick and ˈthin**
thicken ˈθɪk.ən **-s** -z **-ing** -ɪŋ, ˈθɪk.nɪŋ **-ed** -d **-er/s** -əʳ/z (US) -ɚ/z
thicket ˈθɪk.ɪt **-s** -s
thickhead ˈθɪk.hed **-s** -z
thickheaded ˌθɪkˈhed.ɪd (US) ˈ-ˌ--, ˌ-ˈ-- **-ness** -nəs, -nɪs *stress shift, British only:* ˌthickheaded ˈfool
thickish ˈθɪk.ɪʃ
thicko ˈθɪk.əʊ (US) -oʊ **-s** -z
thickset ˌθɪkˈset (US) ˈ--, ˌ-ˈ- *stress shift, British only:* ˌthickset ˈman
thick-skinned ˌθɪkˈskɪnd (US) ˈ--, ˌ-ˈ- *stress shift, British only:* ˌthick-skinned ˈman
thick-skulled ˌθɪkˈskʌld (US) ˈ--, ˌ-ˈ- *stress shift, British only:* ˌthick-skulled ˈidiot
thick-witted ˌθɪkˈwɪt.ɪd (US) ˈθɪkˌwɪt̬.ɪd, ˌ-ˈ-- *stress shift, British only:* ˌthick-witted ˈfool
thie|f θiː|f **-ves** -vz
Thiès tjez (US) tjes
thiev|e θiːv **-es** -z **-ing** -ɪŋ **-ed** -d **-ery** -ər.i
thievish ˈθiː.vɪʃ **-ly** -li **-ness** -nəs, -nɪs
thigh θaɪ **-s** -z
thighbone ˈθaɪ.bəʊn (US) -boʊn **-s** -z
thill θɪl **-s** -z
thimble ˈθɪm.bl̩ **-s** -z **-ful/s** -fʊl/z
thimblerig ˈθɪm.bl̩.rɪg **-s** -z **-ging** -ɪŋ **-ged** -d
Thimbu ˈθɪm.buː
Thimphu ˈθɪmp.fuː
thin θɪn **-ner** -əʳ (US) -ɚ **-nest** -ɪst, -əst **-ly** -li **-ness** -nəs, -nɪs **-s** -z **-ning** -ɪŋ **-ned** -d **into ˌthin ˈair**
thine ðaɪn
thing θɪŋ **-s** -z
thingamabob ˈθɪŋ.ə.məˌbɒb (US) -ˌbɑːb **-s** -z
thingamajig ˈθɪŋ.ə.məˌdʒɪg **-s** -z
thingam|y ˈθɪŋ.ə.m|i **-ies** -iz
thingie ˈθɪŋ.i **-s** -z
thingumabob ˈθɪŋ.ə.məˌbɒb (US) -ˌbɑːb **-s** -z
thingumajig ˈθɪŋ.ə.məˌdʒɪg **-s** -z
thingumm|y ˈθɪŋ.ə.m|i **-ies** -iz
thing|y ˈθɪŋ|.i **-ies** -z
think θɪŋk **-s** -s **-ing/ly** -ɪŋ/li **thought** θɔːt (US) θɑːt, θɔːt **thinker/s** ˈθɪŋ.kəʳ/z (US) -kɚ/z **ˈthink ˌtank**
thinkable ˈθɪŋ.kə.bl̩
thinktank ˈθɪŋkˌtæŋk **-s** -s
Thinn θɪn
thinnish ˈθɪn.ɪʃ
thin-skinned ˌθɪnˈskɪnd (US) ˈ-- *stress shift, British only:* ˌthin-skinned ˈperson
third θɜːd (US) θɝːd **-s** -z **-ly** -li **ˌthird ˈclass; ˌthird diˈmension; ˌthird ˈparty; ˌthird ˈperson; ˌThird ˈWorld; ˌgive someone the ˌthird deˈgree**
third-degree ˌθɜːd.dɪˈgriː, -dəˈ- (US) ˌθɝːd- *stress shift, see compound:* **ˌthird-degree ˈburn**
thirdhand ˌθɜːdˈhænd (US) ˌθɝːd- *stress shift:* ˌthirdhand ˈgossip
third-ra|te ˌθɜːdˈreɪ|t (US) ˌθɝːd- **-ter/s** -təʳ/z (US) -t̬ɚ/z *stress shift:* ˌthird-rate ˈdrama
Thirsk θɜːsk (US) θɝːsk
thirst θɜːst (US) θɝːst **-s** -s **-ing** -ɪŋ **-ed** -ɪd
thirst|y ˈθɜː.st|i (US) ˈθɝː- **-ier** -i.əʳ (US) -i.ɚ **-iest** -i.ɪst, -i.əst **-ily** -ɪ.li, -əl.i **-iness** -ɪ.nəs, -ɪ.nɪs
thirteen θɜːˈtiːn (US) θɝː- **-s** -z *stress shift:* ˌthirteen ˈpounds
thirteenth θɜːˈtiːntθ (US) θɝː- **-s** -s *stress shift:* ˌthirteenth ˈplace
thirtieth ˈθɜː.ti.əθ (US) ˈθɝː.t̬i- **-s** -s
thirt|y ˈθɜː.t|i (US) ˈθɝː.t̬|i **-ies** -iz **ˈthirty ˌsomething; ˌThirty ˌYears' ˈWar**
thirtyfold ˈθɜː.ti.fəʊld (US) ˈθɝː.t̬i.foʊld
this ðɪs *occasional weak form:* ðəs **ˌthis ˌthat, and the ˈother**
Note: Some speakers use a weak form /ðəs/ in 'this morning, afternoon, evening'.
Thisbe ˈθɪz.bi
Thiselton ˈθɪs.l̩.tən
thistle ˈθɪs.l̩ **-s** -z
thistledown ˈθɪs.l̩.daʊn
thistly ˈθɪs.l̩.i, ˈ-li
thither ˈðɪð.əʳ (US) ˈθɪð.ɚ, ˈðɪð- **-ward/s** -wəd/z (US) -wɚd/z
tho' ðəʊ (US) ðoʊ
Thoday ˈθəʊ.deɪ (US) ˈθoʊ-
thole θəʊl (US) θoʊl **-s** -z
Thom tɒm (US) tɑːm
Thomas ˈtɒm.əs (US) ˈtɑː.məs
Thomasin ˈtɒm.ə.sɪn (US) ˈtɑː.mə-
Thomond ˈθəʊ.mənd (US) ˈθoʊ-
Thompson ˈtɒmp.sən (US) ˈtɑːmp-
Thompstone ˈtɒmp.stəʊn (US) ˈtɑːmp.stoʊn
Thomson ˈtɒmp.sən (US) ˈtɑːmp-
-thon -θɒn, -θən (US) -θɑːn
Note: Suffix. Normally unstressed, e.g. /ˈmær.ə.θən (US) ˈmer.ə.θɑːn/.
thong θɒŋ (US) θɑːŋ, θɔːŋ **-s** -z
Thor θɔːʳ (US) θɔːr
Thora ˈθɔː.rə (US) ˈθɔːr.ə
thoraces *(alternative plur. of* **thorax**) ˈθɔː.rə.siːz
thoracic θɔːˈræs.ɪk, θɒrˈæs-, θəˈræs- (US) θɔːˈræs-, θə-
thorax ˈθɔː.ræks (US) ˈθɔːr.æks **-es** -ɪz
Thorburn ˈθɔː.bɜːn (US) ˈθɔːr.bɝn
Thoreau θɔːˈrəʊ, θə-; ˈθɔː.rəʊ (US) θəˈroʊ, θɔː-; ˈθɔːr.oʊ
thorium ˈθɔː.ri.əm (US) ˈθɔːr.i-
thorn (T) θɔːn (US) θɔːrn **-s** -z **a ˌthorn in one's ˈflesh/side**
Thornaby ˈθɔː.nə.bi (US) ˈθɔːr-
Thornbury ˈθɔːn.bər.i, ˈθɔːm- (US) ˈθɔːrn.ber-, -bɚ-
thornbush ˈθɔːn.bʊʃ, ˈθɔːm- (US) ˈθɔːrn- **-es** -ɪz
Thorndike ˈθɔːn.daɪk (US) ˈθɔːrn-
Thorne θɔːn (US) θɔːrn
Thorneycroft ˈθɔː.nɪ.krɒft (US) ˈθɔːr.nɪ.krɑːft
Thornhill ˈθɔːn.hɪl (US) ˈθɔːrn-
thornless ˈθɔːn.ləs, -lɪs (US) ˈθɔːrn-
Thornton ˈθɔːn.tən (US) ˈθɔːrn.tən
thorn|y ˈθɔː.n|i (US) ˈθɔːr- **-ier** -i.əʳ (US) -i.ɚ **-iest** -i.ɪst, -i.əst **-ily** -ɪ.li, -əl.i **-iness** -ɪ.nəs, -ɪ.nɪs
Thorold ˈθɒr.əld, ˈθʌr- (US) ˈθɔːr-, ˈθɝː-
thorough ˈθʌr.ə (US) ˈθɝː.oʊ, -ə **-ly** -li **-ness** -nəs, -nɪs
thoroughbass ˈθʌr.ə.beɪs (US) ˈθɝː.oʊ-, ˈ-ə-
thoroughbred ˈθʌr.ə.bred (US) ˈθɝː.oʊ-, ˈ-ə- **-s** -z

thoroughfare ˈθʌr.ə.feəʳ ⓤⓢ ˈθɝː.oʊ.fer, ˈ-ə- **-s** -z

thoroughgoing ˌθʌr.əˈɡəʊ.ɪŋ ⓤⓢ ˌθɝː.oʊˈɡoʊ-, -əˈ-

thorough-paced ˌθʌr.əˈpeɪst ⓤⓢ ˈθɝː.oʊ.peɪst, ˈ-ə-

Thorowgood ˈθʌr.ə.ɡʊd ⓤⓢ ˈθɝː.oʊ-

Thorpe θɔːp ⓤⓢ θɔːrp

Thorrowgood ˈθʌr.ə.ɡʊd ⓤⓢ ˈθɝː-

those *(plur. of* **that***)* ðəʊz ⓤⓢ ðoʊz

Thoth θəʊθ, təʊt, θɒθ ⓤⓢ θoʊθ, toʊt

thou *you:* ðaʊ

thou *(abbrev. for* **thousand***)* θaʊ

though ðəʊ ⓤⓢ ðoʊ

thought *(from* **think***)* θɔːt ⓤⓢ θɑːt, θɔːt **-s** -s

thoughtful ˈθɔːt.fᵊl, -fʊl ⓤⓢ ˈθɑːt-, ˈθɔːt- **-ly** -i **-ness** -nəs, -nɪs

thoughtless ˈθɔːt.ləs, -lɪs ⓤⓢ ˈθɑːt-, ˈθɔːt- **-ly** -li **-ness** -nəs, -nɪs

thought-out ˌθɔːtˈaʊt ⓤⓢ ˌθɑːt̬-, ˌθɔːt̬-

thought-provoking ˈθɔːt.prəˌvəʊ.kɪŋ ⓤⓢ ˈθɑːt.prəˌvoʊ-, ˈθɔːt-

Thouless ˈθaʊ.les, -lɪs

thous|and ˈθaʊ.z|ᵊnd **-ands** -ᵊn*d*z ˌ**Thousand** ˌ**Island** ˈ**dressing**

thousandfold ˈθaʊ.zᵊn*d*.fəʊld ⓤⓢ -foʊld

thousandth ˈθaʊ.zᵊn*d*θ **-s** -s

Thrace θreɪs

Thracian ˈθreɪ.ʃᵊn, -ʃi.ən ⓤⓢ ˈ-ʃᵊn **-s** -z

thrall θrɔːl ⓤⓢ θrɔːl, θrɑːl **-s** -z **-ing** -ɪŋ **-ed** -d

thral(l)dom ˈθrɔːl.dəm ⓤⓢ ˈθrɔːl-, ˈθrɑːl-

thrash θræʃ **-es** -ɪz **-ing** -ɪŋ **-ed** -t **-er/s** -əʳ/z ⓤⓢ -ɚ/z

thread θred **-s** -z **-ing** -ɪŋ **-ed** -ɪd

threadbare ˈθred.beəʳ ⓤⓢ -ber

Threadneedle ˌθredˈniː.dl̩, ˈ-ˌ--

thread|y ˈθred|.i **-iness** -ɪ.nəs, -ɪ.nɪs

threat θret **-s** -s

threaten ˈθret.ᵊn **-s** -z **-ing/ly** -ɪŋ/li, ˈθret.nɪŋ/li **-ed** -d

three θriː **-s** -z

three-cornered ˌθriːˈkɔː.nəd ⓤⓢ -ˈkɔːr- *stress shift:* ˌthree-cornered ˈhat

three-D, 3-D ˌθriːˈdiː *stress shift:* ˌthree-D ˈglasses

three-day ˌθriːˈdeɪ ˌ**three-day eˈvent**; ˌ**three-day ˈweek**

three-decker ˌθriːˈdek.əʳ ⓤⓢ ˈθriːˌdek.ɚ **-s** -z

three-dimensional ˌθriː.dɪˈmen.*t*ʃᵊn.ᵊl, -daɪˈ-, -ˈmen*t*ʃ.nᵊl ⓤⓢ -dəˈment.ʃᵊn.ᵊl

threefold ˈθriː.fəʊld ⓤⓢ -foʊld

threeish ˈθriː.ɪʃ

three-legged ˌθriːˈleɡd, -ˈleɡ.ɪd ⓤⓢ ˈθriː.leɡd, -ˌleɡ.ɪd *stress shift:* ˌthree-legged ˈstool ˌthree-ˈlegged ˌrace

three-line ˌθriːˈlaɪn *stress shift, see compound:* ˌ**three-line ˈwhip**

three|pence ˈθre|p.ᵊn*t*s, ˈθrɪ|p-, ˈθrʌ|p-, ˈθrʊ|p- **-pences** -pᵊn*t*.sɪz **-penny** -pᵊn.i, -p.ni

Note: See note for **penny**.

three-piece ˌθriːˈpiːs *stress shift, see compound:* ˌ**three-piece ˈsuite**

three-ply ˈθriː.plaɪ, ˌ-ˈ-

three-point ˌθriːˈpɔɪnt *stress shift, see compound:* ˌ**three-point ˈturn**

three-quarter ˌθriːˈkwɔː.təʳ ⓤⓢ -ˈkwɔːr.t̬ɚ **-s** -z *stress shift:* ˌthree-quarter ˈlength

three-ring ˌθriːˈrɪŋ *stress shift, see compound:* ˌ**three-ring ˈcircus**

three Rs θriːˈɑːz ⓤⓢ -ˈɑːrz

threescore ˌθriːˈskɔːʳ ⓤⓢ ˈθriː.skɔːr *stress shift:* ˌthreescore ˈyears ˌ**threescore** ˌ**years and ˈten**

threesome ˈθriː.səm **-s** -z

three-star ˌθriːˈstɑːʳ ⓤⓢ -ˈstɑːr *stress shift:* ˌthree-star hoˈtel

threnod|y ˈθren.ə.d|i, ˈθriː.nə- ⓤⓢ ˈθren.ə- **-ies** -iz

thresh θreʃ **-es** -ɪz **-ing** -ɪŋ **-ed** -t **-er/s** -əʳ/z ⓤⓢ -ɚ/z ˈ**threshing maˌchine**

thresher (T®) ˈθreʃ.əʳ ⓤⓢ -ɚ **-s** -z

threshold ˈθreʃ.*h*əʊld ⓤⓢ -*h*oʊld **-s** -z

threw *(from* **throw***)* θruː

thrice θraɪs

thrift θrɪft ˈ**thrift** ˌ**shop**

thriftless ˈθrɪft.ləs, -lɪs **-ly** -li **-ness** -nəs, -nɪs

thrift|y ˈθrɪf.t|i **-ier** -i.əʳ ⓤⓢ -i.ɚ **-iest** -i.ɪst, -i.əst **-ily** -ɪ.li, -ᵊl.i **-iness** -ɪ.nəs, -ɪ.nɪs

thrill θrɪl **-s** -z **-ing/ly** -ɪŋ/li **-ed** -d **-er/s** -əʳ/z ⓤⓢ -ɚ/z

Thring θrɪŋ

thrip θrɪp **-s** -s

thriv|e θraɪv **-es** -z **-ing** -ɪŋ **-ed** -d **throve** θrəʊv ⓤⓢ θroʊv **thriven** ˈθrɪv.ᵊn

thro' θruː

throat θrəʊt ⓤⓢ θroʊt **-s** -s **-ed** -ɪd ⓤⓢ ˈθroʊ.t̬ɪd

throat|y ˈθrəʊ.t|i ⓤⓢ ˈθroʊ.t̬|i **-ier** -i.əʳ ⓤⓢ -i.ɚ **-iest** -i.ɪst, -i.əst **-ily** -ɪ.li, -ᵊl.i **-iness** -ɪ.nəs, -ɪ.nɪs

throb θrɒb ⓤⓢ θrɑːb **-s** -z **-bing/ly** -ɪŋ/li **-bed** -d

throes θrəʊz ⓤⓢ θroʊz

Throgmorton θrɒɡˈmɔː.tᵊn, ˈ--- ⓤⓢ θrɑːɡˈmɔːr-, θrɔːɡ-, ˈ---

thrombin ˈθrɒm.bɪn ⓤⓢ ˈθrɑːm-

thrombos|is θrɒmˈbəʊ.s|ɪs ⓤⓢ θrɑːmˈboʊ- **-es** -iːz

thromb|us ˈθrɒm.b|əs ⓤⓢ ˈθrɑːm- **-i** -aɪ

thron|e θrəʊn ⓤⓢ θroʊn **-es** -z **-ing** -ɪŋ **-ed** -d

throng θrɒŋ ⓤⓢ θrɑːŋ, θrɔːŋ **-s** -z **-ing** -ɪŋ **-ed** -d

throstle ˈθrɒs.l̩ ⓤⓢ ˈθrɑː.sl̩ **-s** -z

throttl|e ˈθrɒt.l̩ ⓤⓢ ˈθrɑː.t̬l̩ **-es** -z **-ing** -ɪŋ, ˈθrɒt.lɪŋ ⓤⓢ ˈθrɑːt- **-ed** -d

through θruː ˌ**through and ˈthrough**

Througham ˈθrʌf.əm

throughout θruˈaʊt

throughput ˈθruː.pʊt **-s** -s

throughway ˈθruː.weɪ **-s** -z

throve *(from* **thrive***)* θrəʊv ⓤⓢ θroʊv

throw θrəʊ ⓤⓢ θroʊ **-s** -z **-ing** -ɪŋ **threw** θruː **thrown** θrəʊn ⓤⓢ θroʊn **thrower/s** ˈθrəʊ.əʳ/z ⓤⓢ ˈθroʊ.ɚ/z

throwaway ˈθrəʊ.ə.weɪ ⓤⓢ ˈθroʊ-

throwback ˈθrəʊ.bæk ⓤⓢ ˈθroʊ- **-s** -s

thru θruː

thrum θrʌm **-s** -z **-ming** -ɪŋ **-med** -d

thrush θrʌʃ **-es** -ɪz

thrust θrʌst **-s** -s **-ing** -ɪŋ

thruway ˈθruː.weɪ **-s** -z

Thucydides θjuːˈsɪd.ɪ.diːz, θjʊ-, ˈ-ə- ⓤⓢ θuːˈsɪd.ə-

thud θʌd **-s** -z **-ding** -ɪŋ **-ded** -ɪd

thug θʌɡ **-s** -z

thuggery ˈθʌɡ.ᵊr.i

thuggish ˈθʌɡ.ɪʃ **-ly** -li **-ness** -nəs, -nɪs

thuja ˈθuː.jə ⓤⓢ ˈθuː-, ˈθjuː- **-s** -z

Thule *Northernmost region of the world:* ˈθjuː.liː, ˈθuː-, -li; θuːl ⓤⓢ ˈθuː.li, ˈθjuː-, ˈtuː-, ˈtjuː- *Eskimo settlement:* ˈtuː.li ⓤⓢ ˈθuː-, ˈθjuː-

thulium ˈθjuː.li.əm ⓤⓢ ˈθuː-, ˈθjuː-

thumb θʌm **-s** -z **-ing** -ɪŋ **-ed** -d ˌ**thumb** ˈ**index**

thumbnail ˈθʌm.neɪl **-s** -z ˌ**thumbnail** ˈ**sketch**

thumbprint ˈθʌm.prɪnt **-s** -s

thumbscrew ˈθʌm.skruː **-s** -z

thumbs-down ˌθʌmzˈdaʊn

thumbstall ˈθʌm.stɔːl ⓤⓢ -stɔːl, -stɑːl **-s** -z

thumbs-up ˌθʌmzˈʌp

thumbtack ˈθʌm.tæk **-s** -s

Thummim ˈθʌm.ɪm *in Jewish usage also:* ˈθʊm-, ˈtʊm-

thump θʌmp **-s** -s **-ing** -ɪŋ **-ed** -t **-er/s** -əʳ/z ⓤⓢ -ɚ/z

Thun tuːn

thund|er ˈθʌn.d|əʳ ⓤⓢ -d|ɚ **-ers** -əz ⓤⓢ -ɚz **-ering/ly** -ᵊr.ɪŋ/li **-ered** -əd ⓤⓢ -ɚd **-erer/s** -ᵊr.əʳ/z ⓤⓢ -ɚ.ɚ/z

Thunderball ˈθʌn.də.bɔːl ⓤⓢ -dɚ-, -bɑːl

thunderbird (T) ˈθʌn.də.bɜːd ⓤⓢ -dɚ.bɝːd **-s** -z

thunderbolt ˈθʌn.də.bəʊlt ⓤⓢ -dɚ.boʊlt **-s** -s

thunderclap ˈθʌn.də.klæp ⓤⓢ -dɚ- **-s** -s

thundercloud ˈθʌn.də.klaʊd ⓤⓢ -dɚ- **-s** -z

thunderfl|y ˈθʌn.də.fl|aɪ ⓤⓢ -dɚ- **-ies** -aɪz

thunderhead ˈθʌn.də.hed ⓤⓢ -dɚ- **-s** -z

thunderous ˈθʌn.dᵊr.əs **-ly** -li

thunderstorm 'θʌn.də.stɔːm (US) -dɚ.stɔːrm -s -z
thunderstruck 'θʌn.də.strʌk (US) -dɚ-
thunder|y 'θʌn.dᵊr|.i -iness -ɪ.nəs, -ɪ.nɪs
Thur. *(abbrev. for* **Thursday***)* 'θɜːz.deɪ, -di (US) 'θɝːz-
Note: This abbreviation may also be pronounced /θɜːʳ/ in British English.
Thurber 'θɜː.bəʳ (US) 'θɝː.bɚ
Thurcroft 'θɜː.krɒft (US) 'θɝː.krɑːft
thurible 'θjʊə.rɪ.bl̩, 'θjɔː-, -rə- (US) 'θɝː.ə-, 'θʊr-, 'θjʊr- -s -z
Thuringi|a θjʊə'rɪn.dʒi|.ə, tʊə-, -'rɪŋ.gi|.ə (US) θʊ'rɪn.dʒi|.ə, θjʊ-, '-dʒ|ə -an/s -ən/z
Thurloe, **Thurlow** 'θɜː.ləʊ (US) 'θɝː.loʊ
Thurman 'θɜː.mən (US) θɝː-
Thurnscoe 'θɜːnz.kəʊ (US) 'θɝːnz.koʊ
Thuron tʊə'rɒn, tə- (US) -'rɑːn
Thurs. *(abbrev. for* **Thursday***)* 'θɜːz.deɪ, -di (US) 'θɝːz-
Note: This abbreviation may also be pronounced /θɜːz/in British English.
Thursday 'θɜːz.deɪ, -di (US) 'θɝːz- -s -z
Thurso 'θɜː.səʊ, -zəʊ (US) 'θɝː.soʊ, -zoʊ
Thurston 'θɜː.stᵊn (US) 'θɝː-
thus ðʌs
thwack θwæk -s -s -ing -ɪŋ -ed -t
Thwackum 'θwæk.əm
thwaite (T) θweɪt -s -s
thwart *of a boat:* θwɔːt (US) θwɔːrt *in nautical usage also:* θɔːt (US) θɔːrt -s -s
thwart (*v.*) θwɔːt (US) θwɔːrt -s -s -ing -ɪŋ (US) 'θwɔːr.t̬ɪŋ -ed -ɪd (US) 'θwɔːr.t̬ɪd
thy ðaɪ
thyme taɪm -s -z
thymine 'θaɪ.miːn (US) -miːn, -mɪn
thymol 'θaɪ.mɒl (US) -mɔːl, -moʊl
thymus 'θaɪ.məs -es -ɪz
Thynne θɪn
thyroid 'θaɪ.rɔɪd -s -z 'thyroid ˌgland
thyroxin θaɪ'rɒk.siːn, -sɪn (US) -'rɑːk-
Thyrsis 'θɜː.sɪs (US) 'θɝː-
thyself ðaɪ'self
Tia Maria® ˌtiː.ə.mə'riː.ə
Tiananmen Square ti,æn.ən.mɪn'skweəʳ, -men'- (US) ˌtjɑː.nɑːn.mɪn'skwer; ti,æn.ən-
Tianjin ˌtjen'dʒɪn
tiara ti'ɑː.rə (US) -'er.ə, -'ær-, -'ɑːr- -s -z -ed -d
Tibbitts 'tɪb.ɪts
Tibbs tɪbz
Tiber 'taɪ.bəʳ (US) -bɚ
Tiberias taɪ'bɪə.ri.æs, -əs (US) -'bɪr.i.əs
Tiberius taɪ'bɪə.ri.əs (US) -'bɪr.i-
Tibet tɪ'bet
Tibetan tɪ'bet.ᵊn -s -s

tibi|a 'tɪb.i|.ə, 'taɪ.bi- (US) 'tɪb.i- -ae -iː -as -əz
Tibullus tɪ'bʌl.əs, -'bʊl-
tic tɪk -s -s
tic douloureux ˌtɪk.duː.lᵊr'ɜː (US) -lʊ'ruː
tic|e taɪs -es -ɪz -ing -ɪŋ -ed -t
Ticehurst 'taɪs.hɜːst (US) -hɝːst
Tichborne 'tɪtʃ.bɔːn, -bən (US) -bɔːrn, -bɚn
Ticino tɪ'tʃiː.nəʊ (US) -noʊ
tick tɪk -s -s -ing -ɪŋ -ed -t -er/s -əʳ/z (US) -ɚ/z ˌticking 'off
tickertape 'tɪk.ə.teɪp (US) '-ɚ- ˌtickertape re'ception; 'tickertape ˌparade
tick|et 'tɪk|.ɪt -ets -ɪts -eting -ɪ.tɪŋ (US) -ɪ.t̬ɪŋ -eted -ɪ.tɪd (US) -ɪ.t̬ɪd 'ticket ˌoffice
tickety-boo ˌtɪk.ɪ.ti'buː, ˌ-ə- (US) -ə.t̬i'-
ticking 'tɪk.ɪŋ -s -z
ticking-off ˌtɪk.ɪŋ'ɒf (US) -'ɑːf
tickings-off ˌtɪk.ɪŋz'ɒf (US) -'ɑːf
tickl|e 'tɪk.l̩ -es -z -ing -ɪŋ, 'tɪk.lɪŋ -ed -d -er/s -əʳ/z, 'tɪk.ləʳ/z (US) '-l̩.ɚ/z, '-lɚ/z
Tickler 'tɪk.ləʳ (US) -lɚ
ticklish 'tɪk.lɪʃ, '-l̩.ɪʃ -ly -li -ness -nəs, -nɪs
tickl|y 'tɪk.l̩|.i, '-l|i -ier -i.əʳ (US) -i.ɚ -iest -i.ɪst, -i.əst -iness -ɪ.nəs, -ɪ.nɪs
ticktacktoe ˌtɪkˌtæk'təʊ (US) -'toʊ
ticktock 'tɪk.tɒk (US) -tɑːk -s -s
tic-tac-toe ˌtɪkˌtæk'təʊ (US) -'toʊ
tidal 'taɪ.dᵊl 'tidal ˌwave, ˌtidal 'wave
tidbit 'tɪd.bɪt -s -s
tiddledywink 'tɪd.l̩.di.wɪŋk -s -s
tiddler 'tɪd.l̩.əʳ, '-ləʳ (US) '-lɚ, '-l̩.ɚ -s -z
Tiddles 'tɪd.l̩z
tiddl|y 'tɪd.l|i, '-l̩|.i -ier -i.əʳ (US) -i.ɚ -iest -i.ɪst, -i.əst -iness -ɪ.nəs, -ɪ.nɪs
tiddlywink 'tɪd.l̩.i.wɪŋk, '-li- (US) '-li-, '-l̩.i- -s -s
tid|e taɪd -es -z -ing -ɪŋ -ed -ɪd
tideland 'taɪd.lænd -s -z
tidemark 'taɪd.mɑːk (US) -mɑːrk -s -s
tidewater 'taɪdˌwɔː.təʳ (US) -ˌwɑː.t̬ɚ, -ˌwɔː-
tideway 'taɪd.weɪ
tidings 'taɪ.dɪŋz
Tidworth 'tɪd.wəθ, -wɜːθ (US) -wɚθ, -wɝːθ
tid|y 'taɪ.d|i -ies -iz -ier -i.əʳ (US) -i.ɚ -iest -i.ɪst, -i.əst -ily -ɪ.li, -ᵊl.i -iness -ɪ.nəs, -ɪ.nɪs -ying -i.ɪŋ -ied -id
tie taɪ -s -z tying 'taɪ.ɪŋ tieing 'taɪ.ɪŋ tied taɪd ˌtied 'house
tie-break 'taɪ.breɪk -s -s -er/s -əʳ/z (US) -ɚ/z
tie-dy|e 'taɪ.daɪ -es -z -ing -ɪŋ -ed -d
tie-in 'taɪ.ɪn -s -z
Tientsin ˌtjent'sɪn
tiepin 'taɪ.pɪn -s -z

Tiepolo ti'ep.ᵊl.əʊ (US) -ə.loʊ
tier *one who ties:* 'taɪ.əʳ (US) -ɚ -s -z
tier *set of seats in theatre, etc.:* tɪəʳ (US) tɪr -s -z -ed -d
tierc|e *in music, fencing, cash:* tɪəs (US) tɪrs -es -ɪz
tierc|e *in cards:* tɜːs, tɪəs (US) tɪrs -es -ɪz
tiercel 'tɜː.sᵊl, 'tɪə- (US) 'tɪr- -s -z
Tierra del Fuego ti,er.ə.del'fweɪ.gəʊ, ˌtjer.ə-, -fu'eɪ- (US) ti,er.ə.del'fweɪ.goʊ
tiff tɪf -s -s -ing -ɪŋ -ed -t
tiffany (T) 'tɪf.ᵊn.i
tiffin (T) 'tɪf.ɪn -s -z
Tiflis 'tɪf.lɪs
tig tɪg -s -z
tig|e tiːʒ -es -ɪz
tiger 'taɪ.gəʳ (US) -gɚ -s -z 'tiger ˌlily; 'tiger ˌmoth
tigerish 'taɪ.gᵊr.ɪʃ -ly -li -ness -nəs, -nɪ
Tigger 'tɪg.əʳ (US) -ɚ
Tiggy-Winkle 'tɪg.iˌwɪŋ.kl̩
Tighe taɪ
tight taɪt -er -əʳ (US) 'taɪ.t̬ɚ -est -ɪst, -əst (US) 'taɪ.t̬ɪst, -t̬əst -ly -li -ness -nəs, -nɪs
tighten 'taɪ.tᵊn -s -z -ing -ɪŋ, 'taɪt.nɪŋ -ed -d -er/s -əʳ/z, 'taɪt.nəʳ/z (US) 'taɪ.tᵊn.ɚ/z, 'taɪt.nɚ/z
tightfisted ˌtaɪt'fɪs.tɪd (US) '-ˌ--, ˌ-'-- -ly -li -ness -nəs, -nɪs *stress shift, British only:* ˌtightfisted 'miser
tightknit ˌtaɪt'nɪt (US) '--, ˌ-'- *stress shift, British only:* ˌtightknit 'group
tight-lipped ˌtaɪt'lɪpt (US) '--, ˌ-'- *stress shift, British only:* ˌtight-lipped 'speaker
tightrope 'taɪt.rəʊp (US) -roʊp 'tightrope ˌwalker
tights taɪts
tightwad 'taɪt.wɒd (US) 'wɑːd -s -z
Tiglath-pileser ˌtɪg.læθ.paɪ'liː.zəʳ, -pɪ'-, -pə'- (US) -zɚ
tigon 'taɪ.gən -s -z
Tigré 'tiː.greɪ
tigress 'taɪ.gres, -grɪs (US) -grɪs -es -ɪz
Tigris 'taɪ.grɪs
Tijuana tɪ'*h*wɑː.nə, ˌtiː.ə'- (US) ˌtiː.ə'wɑː-, tiː'*h*wɑː-
tike taɪk -s -s
tikka 'tɪk.ə, 'tiː.kə
tilbur|y (T) 'tɪl.bᵊr|.i (US) -ber-, -bɚ- -ies -iz
tilde 'tɪl.də, -di, -deɪ; tɪld (US) 'tɪl.də -s -z
til|e taɪl -es -z -ing -ɪŋ -ed -d -er/s -əʳ/z (US) -ɚ/z
Tilehurst 'taɪl.hɜːst (US) -hɝːst
till (T) tɪl -s -z -ing -ɪŋ -ed -d -er/s -əʳ/z (US) -ɚ/z -able -ə.bl̩ -age -ɪdʒ
tiller 'tɪl.əʳ (US) -ɚ -s -z
Tilley 'tɪl.i
Tillicoultry ˌtɪl.ɪ'kuː.tri, -ə'-

Tilling 'tɪl.ɪŋ **-s** -z
Tillotson 'tɪl.ət.sᵊn
Tilly 'tɪl.i
tilt tɪlt **-s** -s **-ing** -ɪŋ US 'tɪl.t̬ɪŋ **-ed** -ɪd US 'tɪl.t̬ɪd **-er/s** -əʳ/z US 'tɪl.t̬ɚ/z
tilth tɪlθ
tilt-yard 'tɪlt.jɑːd US -jɑːrd **-s** -z
Tim tɪm
Timaeus taɪ'miː.əs, tɪ- US taɪ'-
timbal 'tɪm.bᵊl **-s** -z
timbale tæm'bɑːl; tɪm'-, 'tɪm.bᵊl, tɪm'bɑːl US 'tɪm.bᵊl; tɪm'bɑːl, tæm- **-s** -z
timb|er 'tɪm.b|əʳ US -b|ɚ **-ers** -əz US -ɚz **-ering** -ᵊr.ɪŋ **-ered** -əd US -ɚd
Timberlake 'tɪm.bə.leɪk US -bɚ-
timberland (T®) 'tɪm.bə.lænd US -bɚ- **-s** -z
timberline 'tɪm.bə.laɪn US -bɚ-
timbre 'tæ̃m.brə, 'tæm-, -bəʳ; 'tɪm.bəʳ US 'tæm.bɚ, 'tɪm- **-s** -z
timbrel 'tɪm.brᵊl **-s** -z
Timbuktu, Timbuctoo ˌtɪm.bʌk'tuː, -bək'- US -bʌk'-
tim|e taɪm **-es** -z **-ing** -ɪŋ **-ed** -d **-er/s** -əʳ/z US -ɚ/z **ˌtime and a 'half; ˌtime and 'motion; ˌtime after 'time; since ˌtime imme'morial; 'time ˌbomb; 'time ˌcapsule; ˌtime 'off; 'time ˌswitch; 'time ˌwarp; 'time ˌzone; ˌfall on ˌhard 'times**
time-consuming 'taɪm.kənˌsjuː.mɪŋ, -ˌsuː- US -ˌsuː-
time-hono(u)red 'taɪmˌɒn.əd, ˌ-'-- US 'taɪmˌɑː.nɚd
timekeep|er 'taɪmˌkiː.p|əʳ US -p|ɚ **-ers** -əz US -ɚz **-ing** -ɪŋ
time-lapse 'taɪm.læps **-s** -ɪz **ˌtime-lapse pho'tography**
timeless 'taɪm.ləs, -lɪs **-ly** -li **-ness** -nəs, -nɪs
time-lock 'taɪm.lɒk US -lɑːk **-s** -s
timel|y 'taɪm.l|i **-ier** -i.əʳ US -i.ɚ **-iest** -i.ɪst, -i.əst **-iness** -ɪ.nəs, -ɪ.nɪs
timeous 'taɪ.məs
time-out ˌtaɪm'aʊt, '-- **time-outs** ˌtaɪm'aʊts, '-- **times-out** ˌtaɪmz'aʊt, '--
timepiec|e 'taɪm.piːs **-es** -ɪz
time-saving 'taɪmˌseɪ.vɪŋ
timescale 'taɪm.skeɪl
timeserv|er 'taɪmˌsɜː.v|əʳ US -ˌsɝː.v|ɚ **-ers** -əz US -ɚz **-ing** -ɪŋ
timeshar|e 'taɪm.ʃeəʳ US -ʃer **-es** -z **-er/s** -əʳ/z US -ɚ/z **-ing** -ɪŋ
timesheet 'taɪm.ʃiːt **-s** -s
time-switch 'taɪm.swɪtʃ **-es** -ɪz
timetabl|e 'taɪmˌteɪ.bl̩ **-es** -z **-ing** -ɪŋ, -ˌteɪ.blɪŋ **-ed** -d
timework 'taɪm.wɜːk US -wɝːk **-er/s** -əʳ/z US -ɚ/z
timeworn 'taɪm.wɔːn US -wɔːrn
Timex® 'taɪ.meks
timid 'tɪm.ɪd **-est** -ɪst, -əst **-ly** -li **-ness** -nəs, -nɪs
timidity tɪ'mɪd.ə.ti, -ɪ.ti US -ə.t̬i
Timisoara ˌtɪm.ɪ'ʃwɑː.rə US ˌtiː.miː'ʃwɑːr.ə
Timmins 'tɪm.ɪnz
Timms tɪmz
Timon 'taɪ.mən, -mɒn US -mən
Timor 'tiː.mɔːʳ, 'taɪ- US -mɔːr; tiː'mɔːr
timorous 'tɪm.ᵊr.əs **-ly** -li **-ness** -nəs, -nɪs
Timotheus tɪ'məʊ.θi.əs US -'moʊ-, taɪ-, -'mɑː-
Timothy 'tɪm.ə.θi
timpan|i, timpan|y 'tɪm.pə.n|i **-ist/s** -ɪst/s
Timpson 'tɪmp.sᵊn
tin tɪn **-s** -z **-ning** -ɪŋ **-ned** -d **ˌtin 'can; ˌtin 'god; 'tin ˌopener; ˌtin ˌpan 'alley**
Tina 'tiː.nə
tinctorial tɪŋk'tɔː.ri.əl US -'tɔːr.i-
tinct|ure 'tɪŋk.tʃ|əʳ US -tʃ|ɚ **-ures** -əz US -ɚz **-uring** -ᵊr.ɪŋ **-ured** -əd US -ɚd
Tindal(l), Tindale 'tɪn.dᵊl
tinder 'tɪn.dəʳ US -dɚ
tinderbox 'tɪn.də.bɒks US -dɚ.bɑːks **-es** -ɪz
tine taɪn **-s** -z
tinfoil 'tɪn.fɔɪl, ˌ-'- US 'tɪn.fɔɪl
ting tɪŋ
ting|e tɪndʒ **-es** -ɪz **-(e)ing** -ɪŋ **-ed** -d
Tingey 'tɪŋ.gi
tingl|e 'tɪŋ.gl̩ **-es** -z **-ing** -ɪŋ, 'tɪŋ.glɪŋ **-ed** -d
tingly 'tɪŋ.gli, '-gl̩.i
tink|er 'tɪŋ.k|əʳ US -k|ɚ **-ers** -əz US -ɚz **-ering** -ᵊr.ɪŋ **-ered** -əd US -ɚd **ˌtinker's 'cuss; ˌtinker's 'damn**
Tinkerbell 'tɪŋ.kə.bel US -kɚ-
Tinkertoy® 'tɪŋ.kə.tɔɪ US -kɚ-
tinkl|e 'tɪŋ.kl̩ **-es** -z **-ing/s** -ɪŋ/z, 'tɪŋ.klɪŋ/z **-ed** -d
Tinnevelly tɪ'nev.ᵊl.i; ˌtɪn.ɪ'vel.i
tinnitus 'tɪn.ɪ.təs, '-ə- US tɪ'naɪ.t̬əs; 'tɪn.ɪ-
tinn|y 'tɪn|.i **-ies** -iz **-ier** -i.əʳ US -i.ɚ **-iest** -i.ɪst, -i.əst **-ily** -ɪ.li, -ᵊl.i **-iness** -ɪ.nəs, -ɪ.nɪs
Tinos 'tiː.nɒs US -nɑːs
tinplate 'tɪn.pleɪt, 'tɪm-, ˌ-'- US 'tɪn.pleɪt **-d** -ɪd
tin-pot 'tɪn.pɒt, 'tɪm- US 'tɪn.pɑːt **ˌtin-pot dic'tator**
tinsel 'tɪnt.sᵊl **-ly** -i **'tinsel ˌtown**
Tinseltown 'tɪnt.sᵊl.taʊn
tint tɪnt **-s** -s **-ing** -ɪŋ US 'tɪn.t̬ɪŋ **-ed** -ɪd US 'tɪn.t̬ɪd **-er/s** -əʳ/z US 'tɪn.t̬ɚ/z
Tintagel tɪn'tædʒ.ᵊl
Tintern 'tɪn.tən, -tɜːn US -tɚn, -tɝːn
Tintin 'tɪn.tɪn
tintinnabulation ˌtɪn.tɪˌnæb.jə'leɪ.ʃᵊn, -jʊ'- **-s** -z
tintinnabul|um ˌtɪn.tɪ'næb.jə.l|əm, -jʊ- **-a** -ə **-ar** -əʳ US -ɚ **-ary** -ᵊr.i **-ous** -əs
Tintoretto ˌtɪn.tᵊr'et.əʊ, -tɒr'- US -tə'ret̬.oʊ **-s** -z
tin|y 'taɪ.n|i **-ier** -i.əʳ US -i.ɚ **-iest** -i.ɪst, -i.əst **-iness** -ɪ.nəs, -ɪ.nɪs
-tion -ʃᵊn
Note: Suffix. Words containing **-tion** are normally stressed on the penultimate syllable, e.g. **fruition** /fru'ɪʃ.ᵊn/.
Tio Pepe® ˌtiː.əʊ'pep.eɪ, -i US -oʊ'-
-tious -ʃəs
Note: Suffix. Words containing **-tious** are normally stressed on the penultimate syllable, e.g. **propitious** /prə'pɪʃ.əs/.
tip tɪp **-s** -s **-ping** -ɪŋ **-ped** -t **-per/s** -əʳ/z US -ɚ/z
tipcat 'tɪp.kæt
tipi 'tiː.piː **-s** -z
Tipo® 'tiː.pəʊ US -poʊ
tip-off 'tɪp.ɒf US -ɑːf **-s** -s
Tippell 'tɪp.ᵊl
Tipperary ˌtɪp.ᵊr'eə.ri US -ə'rer.i
tippet 'tɪp.ɪt **-s** -s
Tippett 'tɪp.ɪt
Tipp-Ex® 'tɪp.eks
Tippex 'tɪp.eks **-es** -ɪz **-ing** -ɪŋ **-ed** -t
tippl|e 'tɪp.l̩ **-es** -z **-ing** -ɪŋ, 'tɪp.lɪŋ **-ed** -d **-er/s** -əʳ/z, 'tɪp.ləʳ/z US '-l̩.ɚ/z, '-lɚ/z
tip|staff 'tɪp|.stɑːf US -stæf **-staves** -steɪvz
tipster 'tɪp.stəʳ US -stɚ **-s** -z
tips|y 'tɪp.s|i **-ier** -i.əʳ US -i.ɚ **-iest** -i.ɪst, -i.əst **-ily** -ɪ.li, -ᵊl.i **-iness** -ɪ.nəs, -ɪ.nɪs
tipto|e 'tɪp.təʊ US -toʊ **-es** -z **-(e)ing** -ɪŋ **-ed** -d
Tipton 'tɪp.tᵊn
tiptop ˌtɪp'tɒp US 'tɪp.tɑːp *stress shift:* ˌtiptop 'shape
Tiptree 'tɪp.triː
tirade taɪ'reɪd, tɪ-, -'rɑːd US 'taɪ.reɪd, -'- **-s** -z
tiramisu ˌtɪr.ə.mɪ'suː US -'miː.suː
Tirana, Tiranë tɪ'rɑː.nə US tɪ-, tiː-
tirass|e tɪ'ræs **-es** -ɪz
tir|e taɪəʳ US taɪɚ **-es** -z **-ing** -ɪŋ **-ed** -d
tired taɪəd US taɪɚd **-ly** -li **-ness** -nəs, -nɪs
Tiree taɪ'riː
tireless 'taɪə.ləs, -lɪs US 'taɪɚ- **-ly** -li **-ness** -nəs, -nɪs
Tiresias taɪə'riː.si.æs, -'res.i-, -əs, '-sjəs US taɪ'riː.si.əs
tiresome 'taɪə.səm US 'taɪɚ- **-ly** -li **-ness** -nəs, -nɪs
Tirney 'tɜː.ni US 'tɝː-
tiro 'taɪə.rəʊ US 'taɪ.roʊ **-s** -z

Tirol tɪˈrəʊl; ˈtɪr.əʊl US tɪˈroʊl, -ˈrɑːl; ˈtɪr.oʊl, ˈtaɪ.roʊl, -rɑːl
Tirolean ˌtɪr.əʊˈliː.ən US tɪˈroʊ.li-, taɪ-; ˌtɪr.əˈliː-
Tirolese ˌtɪr.əʊˈliːz US -əˈliːz, -ˈliːs
Tiruchchirappalli ˌtɪr.əˌtʃɪr.əˈpʌl.i; tɪˌruː.tʃɪˈrɑː.pᵊl- US ˌtɪr.ə.tʃɪˈrɑː.pᵊl-; -ˌtʃɪr.əˈpuː.li, -ˈpʌl.i
'tis tɪz
tisane tɪˈzæn, tiː-, -ˈsæn US tɪˈzæn **-s** -z
Tishbite ˈtɪʃ.baɪt **-s** -s
Tissaphernes ˌtɪs.əˈfɜː.niːz US -ˈfɝː-
Tissot ˈtiː.səʊ US tiːˈsoʊ
tissue ˈtɪʃ.uː, ˈtɪs.juː US ˈtɪʃ.uː **-s** -z **ˈtissue ˌpaper**
tit tɪt **-s** -s **ˌtit for ˈtat**
titan (T) ˈtaɪ.tᵊn **-s** -z
Titania tɪˈtɑː.njə, taɪ-, -ˈteɪ-, -ni.ə US tɪˈteɪ.ni.ə, taɪ-, -ˈtɑː-
titanic (T) taɪˈtæn.ɪk, tɪ- **-ally** -ᵊl.i, -li
titanium tɪˈteɪ.ni.əm, taɪ- US taɪ-, tɪ-
titbit ˈtɪt.bɪt **-s** -s
titch tɪtʃ
Titchmarsh ˈtɪtʃ.mɑːʃ US -mɑːrʃ
titch|y ˈtɪtʃ|.i **-ier** -i.əʳ US -i.ɚ **-iest** -i.ɪst, -i.əst
tith|e taɪð **-es** -z **-ing** -ɪŋ **-ed** -d
tithing ˈtaɪ.ðɪŋ **-s** -z
Tithonus tɪˈθəʊ.nəs, taɪ- US -ˈθoʊ-
Titian ˈtɪʃ.ᵊn, -i.ən US -ᵊn **-s** -z
Titicaca ˌtɪt.ɪˈkɑː.kɑː, -kə US ˌtɪt.ɪ-, ˌtiː.tɪˈ-
titill|ate ˈtɪt.ɪ.l|eɪt, -ᵊl|.eɪt US -ᵊl|.eɪt **-ates** -eɪts **-ating** -eɪ.tɪŋ US -eɪ.t̬ɪŋ **-ated** -eɪ.tɪd US -eɪ.t̬ɪd
titillation ˌtɪt.ɪˈleɪ.ʃᵊn, -ᵊlˈeɪ- US -ᵊlˈeɪ- **-s** -z
titi|vate ˈtɪt.ɪ|.veɪt, ˈ-ə- US ˈtɪt̬.ə- **-vates** -veɪts **-vating** -veɪ.tɪŋ US -veɪ.t̬ɪŋ **-vated** -veɪ.tɪd US -veɪ.t̬ɪd
titivation ˌtɪt.ɪˈveɪ.ʃᵊn, -əˈ- US ˌtɪt̬.əˈ- **-s** -z
title ˈtaɪ.tl̩ US -t̬l̩ **-s** -z **-ing** -ɪŋ **-d** -d **-less** -ləs, -lɪs **ˈtitle ˌdeed**
titleholder ˈtaɪ.tl̩ˌhəʊl.dəʳ US -ˌhoʊl.dɚ **-s** -z
titling ˈtaɪt.lɪŋ, ˈtaɪ.tl̩.ɪŋ US ˈtaɪt.lɪŋ, ˈtaɪ.t̬l̩.ɪŋ **-s** -z
Titmarsh ˈtɪt.mɑːʃ US -mɑːrʃ
tit|mouse ˈtɪt|.maʊs **-mice** -maɪs
Tito ˈtiː.təʊ US -t̬oʊ, -toʊ
Titograd ˈtiː.təʊ.græd US -t̬oʊ-, -grɑːd
titration taɪˈtreɪ.ʃᵊn, tɪ- US taɪ-
titt|er ˈtɪt|.əʳ US ˈtɪt̬|.ɚ **-ers** -əz US -ɚz **-ering** -ᵊr.ɪŋ **-ered** -əd US -ɚd **-erer/s** -ᵊr.əʳ/z US -ɚ.ɚ/z
tittle ˈtɪt.l̩ US ˈtɪt̬- **-s** -z
tittle-tattle ˈtɪt.l̩ˌtæt.l̩ US ˈtɪt̬.l̩ˌtæt̬-
titular ˈtɪt.jə.ləʳ, -jʊ- US ˈtɪtʃ.ə.lɚ, ˈ-ʊ-, ˈtɪt.jə-, -jʊ- **-s** -z **-ly** -li
titular|y ˈtɪt.jə.lᵊr|.i, -jʊ- US ˈtɪtʃ.ə.ler-, ˈ-ʊ-, ˈtɪt.jə-, -jʊ- **-ies** -iz
Titus ˈtaɪ.təs US -t̬əs
Tiverton ˈtɪv.ə.tᵊn US -ɚ.t̬ən
Tivoli ˈtɪv.ᵊl.i
Tivy ˈtaɪ.vi
Tizard ˈtɪz.əd US -ɚd
Tizer® ˈtaɪ.zəʳ US -zɚ
tizz tɪz **-es** -ɪz
tizz|y ˈtɪz|.i **-ies** -iz
T-junction ˈtiːˌdʒʌŋk.ʃᵊn **-s** -z
Tlaxcala tləˈskɑː.lə, tlæsˈkɑː- US tlɑːˈskɑː.lə
Tlemcen tlemˈsen
TM ˌtiːˈem
tmesis ˈtmiː.sɪs, ˈmiː-; təˈmiː- US təˈmiː-, ˈmiː-
TN *(abbrev. for* **Tennessee***)* ten.əˈsiː, -ɪˈ- US ˈten.ə.siː *regionally:* ˈten.ɪ.si, -ə-
TNT ˌtiː.enˈtiː
to *(adv.)* tuː
Note: This form of **to** is found in expressions such as ‘to and fro’.
to *(prep.) strong form:* tuː *weak forms:* tʊ, tu, tə US tə, t̬ə, tu
Note: Weak form word. The strong form /tuː/ is used contrastively, e.g. ‘the letter was **to** him, not **from** him’, and sometimes in final position, e.g. ‘I don’t want to’, though the /ʊ/ vowel is more often used in this context. The weak form /tə/ is used before consonants, e.g. ‘to cut’ /təˈkʌt/, while the pronunciation /tu/ is used before vowels in British English, e.g. ‘to eat’ /tuˈiːt/. In American English, the schwa form is usual before both vowels and consonants, so the latter is /təˈiːt/.
toad təʊd US toʊd **-s** -z
toadflax ˈtəʊd.flæks US ˈtoʊd-
toad-in-the-hole ˌtəʊd.ɪn.ðəˈhəʊl US ˌtoʊd.ɪn.ðəˈhoʊl
toadstool ˈtəʊd.stuːl US ˈtoʊd- **-s** -z
toad|y ˈtəʊ.d|i US ˈtoʊ- **-ies** -iz **-ying** -i.ɪŋ **-ied** -id
Toal təʊl US toʊl
to-and-fro ˌtuː.əndˈfrəʊ US -ˈfroʊ
toast təʊst US toʊst **-s** -s **-ing** -ɪŋ **-ed** -ɪd **-er/s** -əʳ/z US -ɚ/z **-y** **ˈtoasting ˌfork; ˈtoast ˌrack**
toastmaster ˈtəʊs*t*ˌmɑː.stəʳ US ˈtoʊs*t*ˌmæs.tɚ **-s** -z
tobacco təˈbæk.əʊ US -oʊ **-s** -z
tobacconist təˈbæk.ᵊn.ɪst **-s** -s
Tobagan təʊˈbeɪ.gən US tə- **-s** -z
Tobago təʊˈbeɪ.gəʊ US toʊˈbeɪ.goʊ, tə-
Tobagonian ˌtəʊ.bəˈgəʊ.ni.ən US ˌtoʊ.bəˈgoʊ- **-s** -z
to-be təˈbiː
Tobermory ˌtəʊ.bəˈmɔː.ri US ˌtoʊ.bɚˈmɔːr.i
Tobias təʊˈbaɪ.əs US toʊ-, tə-
Tobin ˈtəʊ.bɪn US ˈtoʊ-
Tobit ˈtəʊ.bɪt US ˈtoʊ-
Toblerone® ˈtəʊ.blə.rəʊn US ˈtoʊ.blə.roʊn
toboggan təˈbɒg.ᵊn US -ˈbɑː.gᵊn **-s** -z **-ing** -ɪŋ **-ed** -d **-er/s** -əʳ/z US -ɚ/z
Tobruk təˈbrʊk US tə-, toʊ-
tob|y (T) ˈtəʊ.b|i US ˈtoʊ- **-ies** -iz **ˈtoby ˌjug**
toccata təˈkɑː.tə, tɒkˈɑː- US təˈkɑː.t̬ə **-s** -z
Toc H ˌtɒkˈeɪtʃ US ˌtɑːk-
Tocharian tɒkˈeə.ri.ən, təʊˈkeə-, -ˈkɑː- US toʊˈker.i-, -ˈkær-, -ˈkɑːr-
Tocqueville ˈtɒk.vɪl, ˈtəʊk- US ˈtoʊk-, ˈtɑːk-
tocsin ˈtɒk.sɪn US ˈtɑːk- **-s** -z
tod (T) tɒd US tɑːd **-s** -z
today təˈdeɪ, tʊ- US tə-, tʊ-, tu-
Todd tɒd US tɑːd
toddl|e ˈtɒd.l̩ US ˈtɑː.dl̩ **-es** -z **-ing** -ɪŋ, ˈtɒd.lɪŋ US ˈtɑːd- **-ed** -d **-er/s** -əʳ/z, ˈtɒd.ləʳ/z US ˈtɑːd.l̩.ɚ/z, ˈ-lɚ/z
todd|y ˈtɒd|.i US ˈtɑː.d|i **-ies** -iz
Todhunter ˈtɒdˌhʌn.təʳ, -*h*ən.təʳ US ˈtɑːdˌhʌn.t̬ɚ, -*h*ən.t̬ɚ
Todmorden ˈtɒd.mə.dən, -ˌmɔː.dᵊn US ˈtɑːd.mɚ.dən, -ˌmɔːr.dᵊn
to-do təˈduː, tʊ- **-s** -z
toe təʊ US toʊ **-s** -z **-ing** -ɪŋ **-d** -d **ˈtoe ˌcap; ˌtoe the ˈline; ˌtread on someone's ˈtoes**
toea ˈtəʊ.ɑː US ˈtoʊ-
TOEFL ˈtəʊ.fl̩ US ˈtoʊ-
toehold ˈtəʊ.həʊld US ˈtoʊ.hoʊld **-s** -z
toenail ˈtəʊ.neɪl US ˈtoʊ- **-s** -z
toerag ˈtəʊ.ræg US ˈtoʊ- **-s** -z
toff tɒf US tɑːf **-s** -s
toffee ˈtɒf.i US ˈtɑː.fi **-s** -z **ˈtoffee ˌapple, ˌtoffee ˈapple**
toffee-nosed ˈtɒf.i.nəʊzd US ˈtɑː.fi.noʊzd
toff|y ˈtɒf|.i US ˈtɑː.f|i **-ies** -iz
Tofts tɒfts US tɑːfts
tofu ˈtəʊ.fuː US ˈtoʊ-
tog tɒg US tɑːg, tɔːg **-s** -z **-ging** -ɪŋ **-ged** -d
toga ˈtəʊ.gə US ˈtoʊ- **-s** -z **-ed** -d
together təˈgeð.əʳ US -ɚ **-ness** -nəs, -nɪs
toggery ˈtɒg.ᵊr.i US ˈtɑː.gɚ-, ˈtɔː-
toggl|e ˈtɒg.l̩ US ˈtɑː.gl̩, ˈtɔː- **-es** -z **-ing** -ɪŋ **-ed** -d
Togo ˈtəʊ.gəʊ US ˈtoʊ.goʊ **-land** -lænd
Togolese ˌtəʊ.gəʊˈliːz US ˌtoʊ.goʊˈ-, -ˈliːs *stress shift:* ˌTogolese ˈpeople
Toibin təʊˈbiːn US ˈtɔɪ.bɪn
toil tɔɪl **-s** -z **-ing** -ɪŋ **-ed** -d **-er/s** -əʳ/z US -ɚ/z

Tone

An identifiable movement or level of PITCH that is used in a linguistically contrastive way.

Examples for English

In English, tone forms the central part of INTONATION, and the difference between, for example, a rising and a falling tone on a particular word may cause a different interpretation of the sentence in which it occurs, e.g.:

▶ it was ˋ cold
(meaning 'it was cold')

▶ it was ˊ cold
(meaning 'was it cold?')

There are often recognised as being at least five tones in English: a fall, a rise, a fall-rise, a rise-fall and a level tone.

Meanings are frequently ascribed to each tone; the scope of this panel does not allow us to discuss this further.

In intonation, tone may be spread over many syllables. E.g., in:

▶ his ˇ car could have broken down
(in which the pitch movement falls on *car* and rises on *down*)

In other languages

In some languages (known as 'tone languages') the linguistic function of tone is to change the meaning of a word: in Mandarin Chinese, for example, [ma] said on a high pitch means *mother* while [ma] said on a low rising tone means *hemp*. It is usual to identify tones as being a property of individual syllables.

toile twɑːl, twɔːl US twɑːl **-s** -z
toilet 'tɔɪ.lət **-s** -s **'toilet ˌbag; 'toilet ˌpaper; 'toilet ˌroll; 'toilet ˌtraining; 'toilet ˌwater**
toiletr|y 'tɔɪ.lɪ.tr|i, -lə- **-ies** -iz
toilette twɑː'let **-s** -s
toilsome 'tɔɪl.səm **-ly** -li **-ness** -nəs, -nɪs
toilworn 'tɔɪl.wɔːn US -wɔːrn
to-ing and fro-ing ˌtuː.ɪŋ.ənd'frəʊ.ɪŋ US -'froʊ- **to-ings and fro-ings** ˌtuː.ɪŋz.ənd'frəʊ.ɪŋz US -'froʊ-
tokay (T) təʊ'keɪ, -'kaɪ, '--; tɒk'aɪ, -'eɪ US toʊ'keɪ
Tokelau 'təʊ.kə.laʊ, 'tɒk.ə- US 'toʊ.kə-
token 'təʊ.kən US 'toʊ- **-s** -z **-ism** -ɪ.zəm
Tokharian tɒk'eə.ri.ən, təʊ'keə-, -'kɑː- US toʊ'ker.i-, -'kær-
Toklas 'tɒk.ləs, 'təʊk-, -læs US 'toʊk.ləs
Tokley 'təʊ.kli US 'toʊ-
Tokyo 'təʊ.ki.əʊ US 'toʊ.ki.oʊ
Toland 'təʊ.lənd US 'toʊ-
told *(from* **tell***)* təʊld US toʊld
toledo *blade:* tə'liː.dəʊ, tɒl'iː- US tə'liː.doʊ **-s** -z
Toledo *in Spain:* tɒl'eɪ.dəʊ, tə'leɪ-, -'liː- US tə'liː.doʊ, -'leɪ- *in US:* tə'liː.dəʊ US -doʊ
tolerability ˌtɒl.ər.ə'bɪl.ə.ti, -ɪ.ti US ˌtɑː.lɚ.ə'bɪl.ə.t̬i
tolerab|le 'tɒl.ər.ə.b|l̩ US 'tɑː.lɚ- **-ly** -li **-leness** -l̩.nəs, -nɪs
tolerance 'tɒl.ər.ənts US 'tɑː.lɚ-
tolerant 'tɒl.ər.ənt US 'tɑː.lɚ- **-ly** -li
toler|ate 'tɒl.ər|.eɪt US 'tɑː.lə.r|eɪt **-ates** -eɪts **-ating** -eɪ.tɪŋ US -eɪ.t̬ɪŋ **-ated** -eɪ.tɪd US -eɪ.t̬ɪd
toleration ˌtɒl.ər'eɪ.ʃən US ˌtɑː.lə'reɪ-
Tolkien 'tɒl.kiːn, -'- US 'toʊl.kiːn, 'tɑːl-
toll təʊl US toʊl **-s** -z **-ing** -ɪŋ **-ed** -d **-er/s** -ər/z US -ɚ/z **'toll ˌbridge; 'toll ˌcall**
toll|booth 'tɒl|.buːθ, 'təʊl-, -buːð US 'toʊl- **-booths** -buːθs, -buːðz
Tollemache 'tɒl.mæʃ, -mɑːʃ US 'tɑːl-
Tollesbury 'təʊlz.bər.i US 'toʊlz.ber-, -bɚ-
Tolleshunt 'təʊlz.hʌnt US 'toʊlz-
Tolley 'tɒl.i US 'tɑː.li
toll-free ˌtəʊl'friː, ˌtoʊl- *stress shift:* ˌtoll-free 'call
tollgate 'təʊl.geɪt US 'toʊl- **-s** -s
tollhou|se 'təʊl.haʊ|s US 'toʊl- **-ses** -zɪz
Tolpuddle 'tɒlˌpʌd.l̩ *locally also:* -ˌpɪd- US 'tɑːl-
Tolstoy 'tɒl.stɔɪ US 'tɑːl-, 'toʊl-
Toltec 'tɒl.tek US 'tɑːl-, 'toʊl- **-s** -s
tolu (T) tɒl'uː, təʊ'luː, -'ljuː US toʊ'luː
toluene 'tɒl.ju.iːn US 'tɑːl-
Tolworth 'tɒl.wəθ, -wɜːθ US 'tɑːl.wɚθ, -wɝːθ
tom (T) tɒm US tɑːm **-s** -z **ˌTom 'Collins; ˌTom, ˌDick and 'Harry; ˌTom and 'Jerry; ˌTom 'Thumb**
tomahawk 'tɒm.ə.hɔːk US 'tɑː.mə.hɑːk, -hɔːk **-s** -s **-ing** -ɪŋ **-ed** -t
Tomalin 'tɒm.əl.ɪn US 'tɑː.məl-
toman təʊ'mɑːn US toʊ-, tə- **-s** -z
tomato tə'mɑː.təʊ US -'meɪ.t̬oʊ **-es** -z
tomb tuːm **-s** -z
tombola tɒm'bəʊ.lə US tɑːm'boʊ-, 'tɑːm.bəl.ə **-s** -z
tomboy 'tɒm.bɔɪ US 'tɑːm- **-s** -z
tombstone (T) 'tuːm.stəʊn US -stoʊn **-s** -z
tomcat 'tɒm.kæt US 'tɑːm- **-s** -s
tome təʊm US toʊm **-s** -z
Tomelty 'tʌm.əl.ti US -t̬i
tomfool ˌtɒm'fuːl US ˌtɑːm- **-s** -z **-ery** -ər.i US -ɚ.i
Tomintoul ˌtɒm.ɪn'taʊl, -ən'- US ˌtɑːm-
Tomkins 'tɒmp.kɪnz US 'tɑːmp-
Tomlinson 'tɒm.lɪn.sən US 'tɑːm-
tomm|y, tomm|ie (T) 'tɒm|.i US 'tɑː.m|i **-ies** -iz **'tommy ˌgun**
tommy-gun 'tɒm.i.gʌn US 'tɑː.mi- **-s** -z
tommyrot 'tɒm.i.rɒt, ˌ--'- US 'tɑː.mi.rɑːt
tomogram 'təʊ.mə.græm, 'tɒm.ə- US 'toʊ.mə- **-s** -z
tomography tə'mɒg.rə.fi US toʊ'mɑː.grə-, tə'-
tomorrow tə'mɒr.əʊ, tʊ- US -'mɑːr.oʊ **-s** -z **toˌmorrow after'noon; toˌmorrow 'evening; toˌmorrow 'morning; toˌmorrow 'night**
Tompion 'tɒm.pi.ən US 'tɑːm-
Tompkins 'tɒmp.kɪnz US 'tɑːmp-
Tomsk tɒmpsk US tɑːmpsk
tomtit 'tɒm.tɪt, ˌ-'- US ˌtɑːm'tɪt, '-- **-s** -s
tom-tom 'tɒm.tɒm US 'tɑːm.tɑːm **-s** -z
ton *weight:* tʌn **-s** -z
ton *fashion:* tɔ̃ːŋ US tõʊn
tonal 'təʊ.nəl US 'toʊ-
tonalit|y təʊ'næl.ə.t|i, -ɪ.t|i US toʊ'næl.ə.t̬|i, tə- **-ies** -iz
Tonbridge 'tʌn.brɪdʒ, 'tʌm- US 'tʌn-
ton|e təʊn US toʊn **-es** -z **-ing** -ɪŋ **-ed** -d
tone-deaf ˌtəʊn'def US 'toʊn-, ˌ-'- **-ness** -nəs, -nɪs *stress shift, British only:* ˌtone-deaf 'person
toneless 'təʊn.ləs, -lɪs US 'toʊn- **-ly** -li **-ness** -nəs, -nɪs
tonematic ˌtəʊ.nɪ'mæt.ɪk US ˌtoʊ.nɪ'mæt̬.ɪk **-s** -s
toneme 'təʊ.niːm US 'toʊ- **-s** -z
tonemic təʊ'niː.mɪk US toʊ-, tə- **-s** -s
toner (T) 'təʊ.nər US 'toʊ.nɚ **-s** -z

Tone unit

A unit of speech consisting of one or more syllables or feet.

Examples for English

A tone unit must contain a tonic syllable, that is, a syllable on which a pitch movement begins. Only one tonic syllable is allowed in an English tone unit. The tone unit may also contain a 'head' (from the first stressed syllable up to the tonic syllable), a 'pre-head' (any unstressed syllables preceding the head) and a 'tail' (all syllables after the tonic syllable). The tonic syllable is underlined in each of the examples which follow:

- ˋyes
  tonic
- ˈJoe said ˋyes
  head + tonic
- and then ˈJoe said ˋyes
  pre-head + head + tonic
- and then ˈJoe said ˋyes to me
  pre-head + head + tonic + tail

As each of the non-tonic elements is optional, it is possible to have any combination together with the tonic syllable, e.g.:

- was it ˇyou
  pre-head + tonic
- it was ˇyesterday
  pre-head + tonic + tail
- ˇnow I understand
  tonic + tail

In the study of INTONATION it is usual to divide speech into larger units than syllables. If one studies only short sentences said in isolation it may be sufficient to make no subdivision of the utterance, but in longer utterances there must be some points at which the analyst marks a break between the end of one pattern and the beginning of the next. These breaks divide speech into 'tone-units', and are called 'tone-unit boundaries', e.g.:

| the ˇlast time I saw her | was ˋyesterday |

If the study of intonation is part of phonology, these boundaries should be identifiable with reference to their effect on pronunciation rather than to grammatical information about word and clause boundaries; statistically, however, we find that in most cases tone-unit boundaries do fall at obvious syntactic boundaries, and it would be rather odd to divide two tone-units in the middle of a phrase. The most obvious factor to look for in trying to establish boundaries is the presence of a pause, and in slow careful speech (e.g. in lectures, sermons and political speeches) this may be done quite regularly. However, it seems that we detect tone-unit boundaries even when the speaker does not make a pause, if there is an identifiable break or discontinuity in the rhythm or in the intonation pattern.

There is evidence that we use a larger number of shorter tone-units in informal conversational speech, and fewer, longer tone units in formal styles.

tonetic təʊˈnet.ɪk (US) toʊˈnet̬-, tə- **-s** -s

ton|ey ˈtəʊ.n|i (US) ˈtoʊ- **-ier** -i.əʳ (US) -i.ɚ **-iest** -i.ɪst, -i.əst

tonga *cart, medicinal bark:* ˈtɒŋ.gə (US) ˈtɑːŋ-, ˈtɔːŋ- **-s** -z

Tong|a *Pacific islands:* ˈtɒŋ|.ə, -g|ə (US) ˈtɑːŋ-, ˈtɔːŋ- **-an/s** -ᵊn/z

Tong|a *East Africa:* ˈtɒŋ.g|ə (US) ˈtɑːŋ-, ˈtɔːŋ- **-as** -əz **-an** -ən

Tongking ˌtɒŋˈkɪŋ (US) ˌtɑːŋ-, ˌtɔːŋ-

tongs tɒŋz (US) tɑːŋz, tɔːŋz

tongu|e tʌŋ **-es** -z **-ing** -ɪŋ **-ed** -d **-eless** -ləs, -lɪs **ˌtongue and ˈgroove; ˈtongue ˌtwister; ˌbite one's ˈtongue;**

tongue-in-cheek ˌtʌŋ.ɪnˈtʃiːk *stress shift:* ˌtongue-in-cheek ˈarticle

tongue-lashing ˈtʌŋˌlæʃ.ɪŋ **-s** -z

tongue-tied ˈtʌŋ.taɪd

Toni ˈtəʊ.ni (US) ˈtoʊ-

tonic ˈtɒn.ɪk (US) ˈtɑː.nɪk **-s** -s **-ally** -ᵊl.i, -li

tonicity təʊˈnɪs.ə.ti, -ɪ.ti (US) toʊˈnɪs.ə.t̬i, tə-

tonic-solfa, ˌtɒn.ɪk.sɒlˈfɑː (US) ˌtɑː.nɪk.soʊlˈfɑː, -sɑːlˈ-

tonight təˈnaɪt

tonka bean ˈtɒŋ.kə.biːn (US) ˈtɑːŋ-, ˈtɔːŋ- **-s** -z

Tonks tɒŋks (US) tɑːŋks, tɔːŋks

tonnag|e ˈtʌn.ɪdʒ **-es** -ɪz

tonne tʌn **-s** -z

tonsil ˈtɒn*t*.sᵊl, -sɪl (US) ˈtɑːn*t*.sᵊl **-s** -z

tonsillectom|y ˌtɒn*t*.sᵊlˈek.tə.m|i, -sɪˈlek- (US) ˌtɑːn*t*.səˈlek- **-ies** -iz

tonsil(l)itis ˌtɒn*t*.sᵊlˈaɪ.tɪs, -sɪˈlaɪ- (US) ˌtɑːn*t*.səˈlaɪ.t̬ɪs

tonsorial tɒnˈsɔː.ri.əl (US) tɑːnˈsɔːr.i-

tonsure ˈtɒn.*t*ʃəʳ, ˈtɒn*t*.ʃʊəʳ, -ˌsjʊəʳ (US) ˈtɑːn*t*.ʃɚ **-s** -z **-d** -d

tontine ˈtɒn.tiːn, -taɪn; tɒnˈtiːn (US) ˈtɑːn.tiːn, -ˈ-

Tonto ˈtɒn.təʊ (US) ˈtɑːn.t̬oʊ

ton-up ˌtʌnˈʌp *stress shift:* ˌton-up ˈbike

ton|y (T) ˈtəʊ.n|i (US) ˈtoʊ- **-ier** -i.əʳ (US) -i.ɚ **-iest** -i.ɪst, -i.əst **ˈTony AˌWard**

Tonya ˈtɒn.jə (US) ˈtɑːn-

Tonypandy ˌtɒn.iˈpæn.di (US) ˌtɑː.niˈ-

Tonyrefail ˌtɒn.iˈrev.aɪl (US) ˌtɑː.niˈ-

too tuː

toodle-oo ˌtuː.dl̩ˈuː

toodle-pip ˌtuː.dl̩ˈpɪp

took *(from* **take***)* tʊk

Tooke tʊk

tool tuːl **-s** z **-ing** ɪŋ **-ed** -d

toolbox ˈtuːl.bɒks (US) -bɑːks **-es** -ɪz

Toole tuːl

Tooley ˈtuː.li

toolmaker ˈtuːlˌmeɪ.kəʳ (US) -kɚ **-s** -z

toonie ˈtuː.ni **-s** -z

toot tuːt **-s** -s **-ing** -ɪŋ (US) ˈtuː.t̬ɪŋ **-ed** -ɪd (US) ˈtuː.t̬ɪd **-er/s** -əʳ/z (US) ˈtuː.t̬ɚ/z

tooth tuːθ **-s** -s **-ing** -ɪŋ **-ed** -t **teeth** tiːθ **ˈtooth ˌfairy; ˈtooth ˌpowder; ˌtooth and ˈnail; ˌlong in the ˈtooth**

toothache ˈtuːθ.eɪk

toothbrush ˈtuːθ.brʌʃ **-es** -ɪz **-ing** -ɪŋ

toothless ˈtuːθ.ləs, -lɪs **-ly** -li **-ness** -nəs, -nɪs

toothpaste ˈtuːθ.peɪst **-s** -s

toothpick ˈtuːθ.pɪk **-s** -s

toothsome ˈtuːθ.səm **-ly** -li **-ness** -nəs, -nɪs

tooth|y ˈtuː.θ|i **-ier** -i.əʳ (US) -i.ɚ **-iest** -i.ɪst, -i.əst **-ily** -ɪ.li, -ᵊl.i **-iness** -ɪ.nəs, -ɪ.nɪs

Tooting ˈtuː.tɪŋ (US) -t̬ɪŋ

tootl|e ˈtuː.tl̩ (US) -t̬l̩ **-es** -z **-ing** -ɪŋ, ˈtuːt.lɪŋ **-ed** -d

toots|y, toots|ie 'tʊt.s|i, 'tuːt- (US) 'tʊt- **-ies** -iz

Toowoomba tə'wʊm.bə, tʊ-

top tɒp (US) tɑːp **-s** -s **-ping** -ɪŋ **-ped** -t **ˌtop 'brass; ˌtop 'dog; ˌtop 'drawer; ˌtop 'gear; ˌtop 'hat** (US) **'top ˌhat; ˌtop 'secret; at the ˌtop of one's 'voice; ˌoff the ˌtop of one's 'head; on ˌtop of the 'world**

topaz 'təʊ.pæz (US) 'toʊ- **-es** -ɪz

top-class ˌtɒp'klɑːs (US) ˌtɑːp'klæs *stress shift:* ˌtop-class 'model

topcoat 'tɒp.kəʊt (US) 'tɑːp.koʊt **-s** -s

top-down ˌtɒp'daʊn (US) ˌtɑːp- *stress shift:* ˌtop-down 'processing

top-dress ˌtɒp'dres, '-- (US) 'tɑːp.dres **-es** -ɪz **-ing** -ɪŋ **-ed** -t

top|e təʊp (US) toʊp **-es** -s **-ing** -ɪŋ **-ed** -t **-er/s** -əʳ/z (US) -ɚ/z

topee 'təʊ.piː, -pi; toʊ'piː (US) toʊ'piː, '-- **-s** -z

Topeka təʊ'piː.kə (US) tə-

top-flight ˌtɒp'flaɪt (US) 'tɑːp.flaɪt, ˌ-'- *stress shift:* ˌtop-flight 'surgeon

topgallant ˌtɒp'gæl.ᵊnt (US) ˌtɑːp- *nautical pronunciation:* tə'gæl-

Topham 'tɒp.əm (US) 'tɑː.pəm

top-heav|y ˌtɒp'hev|.i (US) 'tɑːpˌhev- **-iness** -ɪ.nəs, -ɪ.nɪs *stress shift:* ˌtop-heavy 'cargo

Tophet(h) 'təʊ.fet (US) 'toʊ-

top-hole ˌtɒp'həʊl (US) ˌtɑːp'hoʊl

topi 'təʊ.piː, -pi; toʊ'piː (US) toʊ'piː, '-- **-s** -z

topiary 'təʊ.pjᵊr.i, -pi.ᵊr- (US) 'toʊ.pi.er-

topic 'tɒp.ɪk (US) 'tɑː.pɪk **-s** -s **-al** -ᵊl **-ally** -ᵊl.i, -li

topicalit|y ˌtɒp.ɪ'kæl.ə.t|i, -ɪ.t|i (US) ˌtɑː.pɪ'kæl.ə.t̬|i **-ies** -iz

topknot 'tɒp.nɒt (US) 'tɑːp.nɑːt **-s** -s

Toplady 'tɒpˌleɪ.di (US) 'tɑːp-

topless 'tɒp.ləs, -lɪs (US) 'tɑːp- **-ness** -nəs, -nɪs

top-level ˌtɒp'lev.ᵊl (US) 'tɑːpˌlev- *stress shift, British only:* ˌtop-level 'leak

topmast 'tɒp.mɑːst (US) 'tɑːp.mæst *nautical pronunciation:* -məst **-s** -s

topmost 'tɒp.məʊst (US) 'tɑːp-

top-notch ˌtɒp'nɒtʃ (US) ˌtɑːp'nɑːtʃ, ˌ-'- *stress shift:* ˌtop-notch 'person

topographic ˌtɒp.əʊ'græf.ɪk (US) ˌtɑː.pə'- **-al** -ᵊl **-ally** -ᵊl.i, -li

topograph|y tɒp'ɒg.rə.f|i, tə'pɒg- (US) tə'pɑː.grə- **-er/s** -əʳ/z (US) -ɚ/z

topologic|al ˌtɒp.ᵊl'ɒdʒ.ɪ.k|ᵊl (US) ˌtɑː.pə'lɑː.dʒɪ- **-ally** -ᵊl.i, -li

topolog|y tɒp'ɒl.ə.dʒ|i, tə'pɒl- (US) tə'pɑː.lə- **-ies** -iz **-ist/s** -ɪst/s

toponymy tɒp'ɒn.ɪ.mi, tə'pɒn-, '-ə- (US) tə'pɑː.nə-, toʊ-

top|os 'tɒp|.ɒs (US) 'toʊ.ploʊs, -ɑːs **-oi** -ɔɪ

topper 'tɒp.əʳ (US) 'tɑː.pɚ **-s** -z

topping (T) 'tɒp.ɪŋ (US) 'tɑː.pɪŋ **-s** -z **-ly** -li

toppl|e 'tɒp.l̩ (US) 'tɑː.pl̩ **-es** -z **-ing** -ɪŋ, 'tɒp.lɪŋ (US) 'tɑː.plɪŋ **-ed** -d

top-ranking ˌtɒp'ræŋ.kɪŋ (US) ˌtɑːp- *stress shift:* ˌtop-ranking 'amateur

topsail 'tɒp.seɪl (US) 'tɑːp- *nautical pronunciation:* -sᵊl **-s** -z

Topsham 'tɒp.səm (US) 'tɑːp-

topside 'tɒp.saɪd (US) 'tɑːp-

topsoil 'tɒp.sɔɪl (US) 'tɑːp- **-s** -z

topspin 'tɒp.spɪn (US) 'tɑːp-

topsy-turv|y ˌtɒp.si'tɜː.v|i (US) ˌtɑːp.si'tɝː- **-ily** -ɪ.li, -ᵊl.i **-yness** -ɪ.nəs, -nɪs **-iness** -ɪ.nəs, -nɪs **-ydom** -ɪ.dəm

top-up 'tɒp.ʌp, ˌ-'- (US) 'tɑːp.ʌp, ˌ-'- **-s** -s

toque təʊk (US) toʊk **-s** -s

tor tɔːʳ (US) tɔːr **-s** -z

Torah 'tɔː.rə *with some Jews:* 'təʊ.rɑː, ˌ-'-, ˌtɔː- (US) 'tɔːr.ə; tɔː'rɑː; 'toʊ.rə

Torbay ˌtɔː'beɪ (US) ˌtɔːr- *stress shift:* ˌTorbay 'guesthouse

torch tɔːtʃ (US) tɔːrtʃ **-es** -ɪz **-ing** -ɪŋ **-ed** -t **'torch ˌsong**

torchlight 'tɔːtʃ.laɪt (US) 'tɔːrtʃ-

torchon 'tɔː.ʃᵊn, -ʃɒn (US) 'tɔːr.ʃɑːn

tore *(from* **tear***)* tɔːʳ (US) tɔːr

toreador 'tɒr.i.ə.dɔːʳ (US) 'tɔːr.i.ə.dɔːr **-s** -z

Torfaen ˌtɔː'veɪn (US) ˌtɔːr-

torment *(n.)* 'tɔː.ment (US) 'tɔːr- **-s** -s

tormen|t *(v.)* tɔː'men|t (US) tɔːr-, '-- **-ts** -ts **-ting/ly** -tɪŋ/li (US) -t̬ɪŋ/li **-ted** -tɪd (US) -t̬ɪd

tormentor, tormenter tɔː'men.təʳ (US) tɔːr'men.t̬ɚ, '--- **-s** -z

torn *(from* **tear***)* tɔːn (US) tɔːrn

tornado tɔː'neɪ.dəʊ (US) tɔːr'neɪ.doʊ **-(e)s** -z

Toronto tə'rɒn.təʊ (US) -'rɑːn.t̬oʊ

torpedo tɔː'piː.dəʊ (US) tɔːr'piː.doʊ **-es** -z **-ing** -ɪŋ **-ed** -d

Torpenhow 'tɔː.pən.haʊ, trɪ'pen.ə *locally:* trə- (US) 'tɔːr.pen.haʊ

torpid 'tɔː.pɪd (US) 'tɔːr- **-s** -z **-ly** -li **-ness** -nəs, -nɪs

torpidity tɔː'pɪd.ə.ti, -ɪ.ti (US) tɔːr'pɪd.ə.t̬i

Torpoint ˌtɔː'pɔɪnt (US) ˌtɔːr-

torpor 'tɔː.pəʳ (US) 'tɔːr.pɚ

Torquay ˌtɔː'kiː (US) ˌtɔːr- *stress shift:* ˌTorquay 'guesthouse

torque tɔːk (US) tɔːrk **-s** -s

Torquemada ˌtɔː.kɪ'mɑː.də, -kem'ɑː-, -kwɪ'mɑː-, -kwem'ɑː- (US) ˌtɔːr.kə'mɑː-, -kwə'-

torr tɔːʳ (US) tɔːr

Torrance 'tɒr.ᵊn*t*s (US) 'tɔːr-

torrefaction ˌtɒr.ɪ'fæk.ʃᵊn, -ə'- (US) ˌtɔːr.ə'-

torre|fy 'tɒr.ɪ|.faɪ, '-ə- (US) 'tɔːr.ə- **-fies** -faɪz **-fying** -faɪ.ɪŋ **-fied** -faɪd

Torremolinos ˌtɒr.ɪ.mə'liː.nɒs, ˌ-ə- (US) ˌtɔːr.ə.mə'liː.nɑːs, -əs

Torrens 'tɒr.ᵊnz (US) 'tɔːr-

torrent 'tɒr.ᵊnt (US) 'tɔːr- **-s** -s

torrential tə'ren.*t*ʃᵊl, tɒr'en- (US) tɔː'rent.ʃᵊl, tə- **-ly** -i

torrentiality təˌren.*t*ʃi'æl.ə.ti, tɒrˌen-, -ɪ.ti (US) tɔːˌrent.ʃi'æl.ə.t̬i, tə-

Torres 'tɒr.ɪs, 'tɔː.rɪs, -rɪz (US) 'tɔːr.ɪz, -ɪs

Torricelli ˌtɒr.ɪ'tʃel.i (US) ˌtɔːr.ə'- **-an** -ən

torrid 'tɒr.ɪd (US) 'tɔːr.ɪd **-ly** -li **-ness** -nəs, -nɪs

Torridge 'tɒr.ɪdʒ (US) 'tɔːr-

Torrington 'tɒr.ɪŋ.tən (US) 'tɔːr-

torsion 'tɔː.ʃᵊn (US) 'tɔːr-

torso 'tɔː.səʊ (US) 'tɔːr.soʊ **-s** -z

tort tɔːt (US) tɔːrt **-s** -s

torte 'tɔː.tə; tɔːt (US) tɔːrt; 'tɔːr.tə **-s** -z

Tortelier tɔː'tel.i.eɪ (US) tɔːr-

tortellini ˌtɔː.tᵊl'iː.ni (US) ˌtɔːr.t̬ə'liː-

tortelloni ˌtɔː.tᵊl'əʊ.ni (US) ˌtɔːr.t̬ə'loʊ-

tortfeasor ˌtɔːt'fiː.zəʳ (US) ˌtɔːrt'fiː.zɚ **-s** -z

tortilla tɔː'tiː.ə, -jə; -'tɪl.ə (US) tɔːr'tiː.jə **torˈtilla ˌchip**

tortious 'tɔː.ʃəs (US) 'tɔːr- **-ly** -li

tortois|e 'tɔː.təs (US) 'tɔːr.t̬əs **-es** -ɪz

tortoiseshell 'tɔː.təʃ.ʃel, -tə.ʃel (US) 'tɔːr.t̬əs.ʃel

tortuosity ˌtɔː.tʃu'ɒs.ə.ti, -tju'-, -ɪ.ti (US) ˌtɔːr.tʃu'ɑː.sə.t̬i

tortuous 'tɔː.tʃu.əs, -tju- (US) 'tɔːr.tʃu- **-ly** -li **-ness** -nəs, -nɪs

tort|ure 'tɔː.tʃ|əʳ (US) 'tɔːr.tʃ|ɚ **-ures** -əz (US) -ɚz **-uring/ly** -ᵊr.ɪŋ/li **-ured** -əd (US) -ɚd **-urer/s** -ᵊr.əʳ/z (US) -ɚ.ɚ/z **'torture ˌchamber**

torturous 'tɔː.tʃᵊr.əs (US) 'tɔːr- **-ly** -li **-ness** -nəs, -nɪs

tor|us 'tɔː.r|əs (US) 'tɔːr|.əs **-i** -aɪ

Torvill 'tɔː.vɪl (US) 'tɔːr-

tor|y (T) 'tɔː.r|i (US) 'tɔːr|.i **-ies** -iz **-yism** -i.ɪ.zᵊm **'Tory ˌparty**

Tosca 'tɒs.kə (US) 'tɑː.skə

Toscanini ˌtɒs.kə'niː.ni (US) ˌtɑː.skə'-

tosh tɒʃ (US) tɑːʃ

Toshiba® tə'ʃiː.bə, tɒʃ'iː- (US) toʊ'ʃiː.bə, tə-

toss tɒs (US) tɑːs **-es** -ɪz **-ing** -ɪŋ **-ed** -t **-er/s** -əʳ/z (US) -ɚ/z **ˌargue the 'toss**

tosspot 'tɒs.pɒt (US) 'tɑːs.pɑːt **-s** -s

toss-up 'tɒs.ʌp (US) 'tɑːs- **-s** -s

tostad|a tɒs'tɑː.d|ə (US) toʊ'stɑː- **-as** -əz **-o** -əʊ (US) -oʊ **-os** -əʊz (US) -oʊz

tot tɒt (US) tɑːt **-s** -s **-ting** -ɪŋ (US) 'tɑː.t̬ɪŋ **-ted** -ɪd (US) 'tɑː.t̬ɪd

total (T) 'təʊ.tᵊl (US) 'toʊ.t̬ᵊl **-s** -z **-ly** -i

-(l)ing -ɪŋ, -ɪŋ -(l)ed -d ˌtotal ˈrecall, ˌtotal reˈcall
totalitarian təʊˌtæl.ɪˈteə.ri.ən, -əˈ-; ˌtəʊ.tæl- (US) toʊˌtæl.əˈter.i-, ˌtoʊ.tæl- **-ism** -ɪ.zᵊm
totalit|y təʊˈtæl.ə.t|i, -ɪ.t|i (US) toʊˈtæl.ə.t̬|i **-ies** -iz
totalizator, **-isa-** ˈtəʊ.tᵊl.aɪ.zeɪ.təʳ, -ɪ- (US) ˈtoʊ.t̬ᵊl.ɪ.zeɪ.t̬ɚ **-s** -z
totaliz|e, **-is|e** ˈtəʊ.tᵊl.aɪz (US) ˈtoʊ.t̬ə.laɪz **-es** -ɪz **-ing** -ɪŋ **-ed** -d **-er/s** -əʳ/z (US) -ɚ/z
tot|e təʊt (US) toʊt **-es** -s **-ing** -ɪŋ **-ed** -ɪd ˈ**tote** ˌ**bag**
totem ˈtəʊ.təm (US) ˈtoʊ.t̬əm **-s** -z **-ism** -ɪ.zᵊm ˈ**totem** ˌ**pole**
totemic təʊˈtem.ɪk (US) toʊ- **-ally** -ᵊl.i, -li
t'other, **tother** ˈtʌð.əʳ (US) -ɚ
Tothill ˈtɒt.*h*ɪl (US) ˈtɑː.tɪl, ˈtɑːt.hɪl
Totnes ˈtɒt.nɪs, -nəs (US) ˈtɑːt-
Totten ˈtɒt.ᵊn (US) ˈtɑː.tᵊn
Tottenham ˈtɒt.ᵊn.əm, ˈ-nəm (US) ˈtɑː.tᵊn.əm ˌ**Tottenham Court** ˈ**Road**; ˌ**Tottenham** ˈ**Hotspur**
tott|er ˈtɒt|.əʳ (US) ˈtɑː.t̬|ɚ **-ers** -əz (US) -ɚz **-ering/ly** -ᵊr.ɪŋ/li **-ered** -əd (US) -ɚd **-erer/s** -ᵊr.əʳ/z (US) -ɚ.ɚ/z **-ery** -ᵊr.i
Totteridge ˈtɒt.ᵊr.ɪdʒ (US) ˈtɑː.t̬ɚ-
Tottington ˈtɒt.ɪŋ.tən (US) ˈtɑː.t̬ɪŋ-
Totton ˈtɒt.ᵊn (US) ˈtɑː.tᵊn
totty ˈtɒt.i (US) ˈtɑː.t̬i
toucan ˈtuː.kæn, -kən (US) -kæn, -kɑːn, -kən; tuːˈkæn, -ˈkɑːn **-s** -z
touch tʌtʃ **-es** -ɪz **-ing** -ɪŋ **-ed** -t ˌ**touch and** ˈ**go**
touchable ˈtʌtʃ.ə.bl̩
touchdown ˈtʌtʃ.daʊn **-s** -z
touché ˈtuː.ʃeɪ, -ˈ- (US) tuːˈʃeɪ
touching ˈtʌtʃ.ɪŋ **-ly** -li **-ness** -nəs, -nɪs
touchline ˈtʌtʃ.laɪn **-s** -z
touchpaper ˈtʌtʃˌpeɪ.pəʳ (US) -pɚ
touchstone (T) ˈtʌtʃ.stəʊn (US) -stoʊn **-s** -z
touch-tone ˈtʌtʃ.təʊn (US) -toʊn
touch-typ|e ˈtʌtʃ.taɪp **-es** -s **-ing** -ɪŋ **-ed** -t **-ist/s** -ɪst/s
touchwood ˈtʌtʃ.wʊd
touch|y ˈtʌtʃ|.i **-ier** -i.əʳ (US) -i.ɚ **-iest** -i.ɪst, -i.əst **-ily** -ɪ.li, -ᵊl.i **-iness** -ɪ.nəs, -ɪ.nɪs
tough tʌf **-s** -s **-er** -əʳ (US) -ɚ **-est** -ɪst, -əst **-ly** -li **-ness** -nəs, -nɪs
toughen ˈtʌf.ᵊn **-s** -z **-ing** -ɪŋ, ˈtʌf.nɪŋ **-ed** -d
tough|ie, **tough|y** ˈtʌf|.i **-ies** -z
Toulon tuːˈlɔ̃ːŋ (US) -ˈlõʊn, -ˈlɑːn
Toulouse tuːˈluːz
Toulouse-Lautrec ˌtuː.luːz.ləʊˈtrek, tuːˌluːz- (US) tuːˌluːz.loʊˈ-, -ˌluːs-, -ləˈ-
toupée, **toupee** ˈtuː.peɪ, -ˈ- (US) tuːˈpeɪ **-s** -z
tour tʊəʳ, tɔːʳ (US) tʊr **-s** -z **-ing** -ɪŋ **-ed** -d **-er/s** -əʳ/z (US) -ɚ/z ˈ**tour** ˌ**operator**
Touraine tʊˈreɪn (US) -ˈreɪn, -ˈren
tourbillion tʊəˈbɪl.i.ən, ˈ-jən (US) tʊrˈbɪl.jən **-s** -z
tour de force ˌtʊə.dəˈfɔːs, ˌtɔː- (US) ˌtʊr.dəˈfɔːrs **tours de force** ˌtʊəz-, ˌtɔːz- (US) ˌtʊrz-
Tour de France ˌtʊə.dəˈfrɑːn*t*s, ˌtɔː- (US) ˌtʊr-
Tourette syndrome tʊəˈretˌsɪn.drəʊm, tɔː- (US) tʊˈretˌsɪn.droʊm
tourism ˈtʊə.rɪ.zᵊm, ˈtɔː- (US) ˈtʊr.ɪ-
tourist ˈtʊə.rɪst, ˈtɔː- (US) ˈtʊr.ɪst **-s** -s ˈ**tourist at**ˌ**traction**; ˈ**tourist** ˌ**class**; ˌ**tourist infor**ˈ**mation office**
touristic tʊəˈrɪs.tɪk, tɔː- (US) tʊˈrɪs- **-ally** -ᵊl.i, -li
touristy ˈtʊə.rɪ.sti, ˈtɔː- (US) ˈtʊr.ɪ-
tourmaline ˈtʊə.mə.liːn, ˈtɜː-, ˈtɔː-, -lɪn (US) ˈtʊr.mə.lɪn, -liːn
Tournai ˈtʊə.neɪ, -ˈ- (US) tʊrˈneɪ
tournament ˈtʊə.nə.mənt, ˈtɔː-, ˈtɜː- (US) ˈtɝː-, ˈtʊr- **-s** -s
tournedos (*sing.*) ˈtʊə.nə.dəʊ, ˈtɔː-, ˈtɜː- (US) ˈtʊr.nə.doʊ, ˌ--ˈ- (*plur.*) -z
Tourneur ˈtɜː.nəʳ (US) ˈtɝː.nɚ
tourney ˈtʊə.ni, ˈtɔː- (US) ˈtɝː-, ˈtʊr- **-s** -z
tourniquet ˈtʊə.nɪ.keɪ, ˈtɔː-, ˈtɜː- (US) ˈtɝː.nɪ.kɪt, ˈtʊr-, -ket **-s** -z
tournure ˈtʊə.njʊəʳ, ˈtɔː-, -ˈ- (US) ˈtɝː.njʊr **-s** -z
Tours *French town:* tʊəʳ (US) tʊr *English musical composer:* tʊəz, tɔːz (US) tʊrz
tousl|e ˈtaʊ.zl̩ **-es** -z **-ing** -ɪŋ, ˈtaʊz.lɪŋ **-ed** -d
tout taʊt **-s** -s **-ing** -ɪŋ (US) ˈtaʊ.t̬ɪŋ **-ed** -ɪd (US) ˈtaʊ.t̬ɪd
Tout *in* **Belle Tout** *in East Sussex:* tuːt *surname:* taʊt
tout court ˌtuːˈkʊəʳ, -ˈkɔːʳ (US) -ˈkʊr
tout de suite ˌtuːtˈswiːt
Tovey ˈtəʊ.vi, ˈtʌv.i (US) ˈtoʊ.vi, ˈtʌv.i
tow (T) təʊ (US) toʊ **-s** -z **-ing** -ɪŋ **-ed** -d
towage ˈtəʊ.ɪdʒ (US) ˈtoʊ-
toward (*adj.*) ˈtəʊ.əd; tɔːd (US) tɔːrd; ˈtoʊ.ɚd **-ly** -li **-ness** -nəs, -nɪs
toward (*prep.*) təˈwɔːd, tʊ-; twɔːd, tɔːd (US) tɔːrd, twɔːrd; ˈtoʊ.ɚd; təˈwɔːrd **-s** -z
towaway ˈtəʊ.ə.weɪ (US) ˈtoʊ- **-s** -z
towbar ˈtəʊ.bɑːʳ (US) ˈtoʊ.bɑːr **-s** -z
Towcester ˈtəʊ.stəʳ (US) ˈtoʊ.stɚ
towel taʊəl **-s** -z **-(l)ing** -ɪŋ **-(l)ed** -d ˌ**throw in the** ˈ**towel**
towelette ˌtaʊəˈlet (US) ˌtaʊə- **-s** -s
tower (T) taʊəʳ (US) taʊɚ **-s** -z **-ing/ly** -ɪŋ/li **-ed** -d ˈ**tower** ˌ**block**; ˌ**Tower** ˈ**Hamlets**; ˌ**Tower of** ˈ**London**; ˌ**tower of** ˈ**strength**
towhead ˈtəʊ.hed (US) ˈtoʊ- **-s** -z **-ed** -ɪd
Towle təʊl (US) toʊl
Towler ˈtaʊ.ləʳ (US) -lɚ
town taʊn **-s** -z ˌ**town** ˈ**centre**; ˌ**town** ˈ**crier**; ˌ**town** ˈ**hall**; ˈ**town** ˌ**house**; ˌ**town** ˈ**planning**; ˌ**paint the** ˌ**town** ˈ**red**
Towne taʊn **-s** -z
townee taʊˈniː, ˈ-- **-s** -z
townie ˈtaʊ.ni **-s** -z
townscape ˈtaʊn.skeɪp **-s** -s
Townsend ˈtaʊn.zend
townsfolk ˈtaʊnz.fəʊk (US) -foʊk
Townshend ˈtaʊn.zend
township ˈtaʊn.ʃɪp **-s** -s
towns|man ˈtaʊnz|.mən **-men** -mən, -men
townspeople ˈtaʊnzˌpiː.pl̩
Townsville ˈtaʊnz.vɪl
towns|woman ˈtaʊnz|ˌwʊm.ən **-women** -ˌwɪm.ɪn
town|y ˈtaʊ.n|i **-ies** -iz
towpa|th ˈtəʊ.pɑː|θ (US) ˈtoʊ.pæ|θ **-ths** -ðz (US) -θs, -ðz
towrope ˈtəʊ.rəʊp (US) ˈtoʊ.roʊp **-s** -z
Towton ˈtaʊ.tᵊn
Towy ˈtaʊ.i
Towyn ˈtaʊ.ɪn
tox(a)emia tɒkˈsiː.mi.ə (US) tɑːk-
toxic ˈtɒk.sɪk (US) ˈtɑːk- **-al** -ᵊl **-ally** -ᵊl.i, -li ˌ**toxic** ˈ**shock** ˌ**syndrome**; ˌ**toxic** ˈ**waste**
toxicity tɒkˈsɪs.ə.ti, -ɪ.ti (US) tɑːkˈsɪs.ə.t̬i
toxicological ˌtɒk.sɪ.kᵊlˈɒdʒ.ɪ.kᵊl (US) ˌtɑːk.sɪ.kəˈlɑː.dʒɪ-
toxicolog|y ˌtɒk.sɪˈkɒl.ə.dʒ|i (US) ˌtɑːk.sɪˈkɑː.lə- **-ist/s** -ɪst/s
toxin ˈtɒk.sɪn (US) ˈtɑːk- **-s** -z
toxophilite tɒkˈsɒf.ɪ.laɪt, -ᵊl.aɪt (US) tɑːkˈsɑː.fə.laɪt **-s** -s
toxoplasmosis ˌtɒk.səʊ.plæzˈməʊ.sɪs (US) ˌtɑːk.soʊ.plæzˈmoʊ-
Toxteth ˈtɒk.steθ, -stəθ (US) ˈtɑːk-
toy tɔɪ **-s** -z **-ing** -ɪŋ **-ed** -d
Toya(h) ˈtɔɪ.ə
toyboy ˈtɔɪ.bɔɪ **-s** -z
Toye tɔɪ
Toynbee ˈtɔɪn.biː, ˈtɔɪm- (US) ˈtɔɪn-
Toyota® tɔɪˈəʊ.tə, tɔːˈjəʊ- (US) tɔɪˈjoʊ.t̬ə, -ˈoʊ-
toyshop ˈtɔɪ.ʃɒp (US) -ʃɑːp **-s** -s
Tozer ˈtəʊ.zəʳ (US) ˈtoʊ.zɚ
trac|e treɪs **-es** -ɪz **-ing** -ɪŋ **-ed** -t **-er/s** -əʳ/z (US) -ɚ/z ˈ**trace** ˌ**element**; ˈ**tracing** ˌ**paper**
traceab|le ˈtreɪ.sə.b|l̩ **-ly** -li **-leness** -l̩.nəs, -nɪs
tracer|y ˈtreɪ.sᵊr|.i **-ies** -iz
Tracey ˈtreɪ.si
trache|a trəˈkiː|.ə; ˈtreɪ.ki- (US) ˈtreɪ.ki- **-as** -əz **-ae** -iː

tracheal trəˈkiː.əl; ˈtreɪ.ki- US ˈtreɪ.ki-

tracheotomy ˌtræk.iˈɒt.ə.mi US ˌtreɪ.kiˈɑː.t̬ə-

trachoma trəˈkəʊ.mə, trækˈəʊ- US trəˈkoʊ-

Traci ˈtreɪ.si

tracing ˈtreɪ.sɪŋ **-s** -z

track træk **-s** -s **-ing** -ɪŋ **-ed** -t **-er/s** -əʳ/z US -ɚ/z ˌ**track and ˈfield; ˈtrack eˌvent; ˈtrack ˌrecord, ˌtrack ˈrecord** US ˈ**track ˌrecord; keep ˈtrack of ˌsomeone/something; ˌoff the ˌbeaten ˈtrack**

trackless ˈtræk.ləs, -lɪs

trackpad ˈtræk.pæd **-s** -z

tracksuit ˈtræk.suːt, -sjuːt US -suːt **-s** -s **-ed** -ɪd

tract trækt **-s** -s

tractability ˌtræk.təˈbɪl.ə.ti, -ɪ.ti US -ə.t̬i

tractab|le ˈtræk.tə.b|l̩ **-ly** -li **-leness** -l̩.nəs, -nɪs

Tractarian trækˈteə.ri.ən US -ˈter.i- **-s** -z **-ism** -ɪ.zᵊm

tractate ˈtræk.teɪt **-s** -s

tractile ˈtræk.taɪl US -tɪl, -taɪl

traction ˈtræk.ʃᵊn ˈ**traction ˌengine**

tractor ˈtræk.təʳ US -tɚ **-s** -z

Tracy ˈtreɪ.si

trad træd ˌ**trad ˈjazz**

trad|e treɪd **-es** -z **-ing** -ɪŋ **-ed** -ɪd **-er/s** -əʳ/z US -ɚ/z ˈ**trade ˌbook; ˌTrades Desˈcription ˌAct; ˈtrading eˌstate; ˈtrade ˌfair; ˈtrade ˌgap; ˈtrade ˌname; ˈtrading ˌpost; ˈtrade ˌprice; ˈtrade ˌroute; ˌtrade ˈsecret; ˌtrade(s) ˈunion** US ˈ**trade(s) ˌunion; ˈtrade ˌwind**

trade-in ˈtreɪd.ɪn **-s** -z

trademark ˈtreɪd.mɑːk US -mɑːrk **-s** -s **-ing** -ɪŋ **-ed** -t

trade-off ˈtreɪd.ɒf US -ɑːf **-s** -s

Tradescant trəˈdes.kənt

tradescantia ˌtræd.ɪˈskæn.ti.ə, ˌtreɪ.dɪˈ-, -desˈkæn-, -dəˈskæn- US ˌtræd.esˈkænt.ʃi.ə, ˈ-ʃə **-s** -z

tradesfolk ˈtreɪdz.fəʊk US -foʊk

trades|man ˈtreɪdz|.mən **-men** -mən

tradespeople ˈtreɪdzˌpiː.pl̩

tradition trəˈdɪʃ.ᵊn **-s** -z

traditional trəˈdɪʃ.ᵊn.ᵊl, -ˈdɪʃ.nᵊl **-ly** -i

traditional|ism trəˈdɪʃ.ᵊn.ᵊl|.ɪ.zᵊm, ˈ-nᵊl- **-ist/s** -ɪst/s

traduc|e trəˈdjuːs, -ˈdʒuːs US -ˈduːs, -ˈdjuːs **-es** -ɪz **-ing** -ɪŋ **-ed** -t **-er/s** -əʳ/z US -ɚ/z **-ement** -mənt

Trafalgar *in Spain:* trəˈfæl.gəʳ *archaic and poetical:* ˌtræf.ᵊlˈgɑːʳ US trəˈfæl.gɚ

Trafalgar *Square:* trəˈfæl.gəʳ US -gɚ *Viscount:* trəˈfæl.gəʳ US -gɚ *House near Salisbury:* ˌtræf.ᵊlˈgɑːʳ; trəˈfæl.gəʳ US ˌtræf.ᵊlˈgɑːr; trəˈfæl.gɚ

traffic ˈtræf.ɪk **-s** -s **-king** -ɪŋ **-ked** -t **-ker/s** -əʳ/z US -ɚ/z ˈ**traffic ˌcalming; ˈtraffic ˌcircle; ˈtraffic ˌjam; ˈtraffic ˌlight; ˈtraffic ˌwarden**

trafficator ˈtræf.ɪ.keɪ.təʳ US -t̬ɚ **-s** -z

Trafford ˈtræf.əd US -ɚd

tragacanth ˈtræg.ə.kænʔθ, ˈtrædʒ-, -sænʔθ US -kænʔθ

tragedian trəˈdʒiː.di.ən **-s** -z

traged|y ˈtrædʒ.ə.d|i, ˈ-ɪ- US ˈ-ə- **-ies** -iz

Trager ˈtreɪ.gəʳ US -gɚ

tragic ˈtrædʒ.ɪk **-al** -ᵊl **-ally** -ᵊl.i, -li

tragicomed|y ˌtrædʒ.ɪˈkɒm.ə.d|i, ˈ-ɪ- US -ˈkɑː.mə- **-ies** -iz

tragicomic ˌtrædʒ.ɪˈkɒm.ɪk US -ˈkɑː.mɪk **-al** -ᵊl **-ally** -ᵊl.i, -li

tra|gus ˈtreɪ|.gəs **-gi** -gaɪ, -dʒaɪ US -dʒaɪ

Traherne trəˈhɜːn US -ˈhɝːn

trail treɪl **-s** -z **-ing** -ɪŋ **-ed** -d **-er/s** -əʳ/z US -ɚ/z

trailblaz|er ˈtreɪlˌbleɪ.z|əʳ US -z|ɚ **-ers** -əz US -ɚz **-ing** -ɪŋ

train treɪn **-s** -z **-ing/s** -ɪŋ/z **-ed** -d **-er/s** -əʳ/z US -ɚ/z ˈ**training ˌcollege; ˈtraining ˌcourse; ˈtrain ˌset; ˈtraining ˌshoe; ˈtrain ˌspotter**

trainbearer ˈtreɪnˌbeə.rəʳ, ˈtreɪm- US ˈtreɪnˌber.ɚ **-s** -z

trainee ˌtreɪˈniː **-s** -z **-ship/s** -ʃɪp/s

Trainor ˈtreɪ.nəʳ US -nɚ

traips|e treɪps **-es** -ɪz **-ing** -ɪŋ **-ed** -t

trait treɪt, treɪ US treɪt **traits** treɪz, treɪts US treɪts

traitor ˈtreɪ.təʳ US -t̬ɚ **-s** -z

traitoress ˈtreɪ.tᵊr.ɪs, -əs US -t̬ɚ- **-es** -ɪz

traitorous ˈtreɪ.tᵊr.əs US -t̬ɚ- **-ly** -li **-ness** -nəs, -nɪs

traitress ˈtreɪ.trəs, -trɪs US -trɪs **-es** -ɪz

Trajan ˈtreɪ.dʒᵊn

trajector|y trəˈdʒek.tᵊr|.i, ˈ-tr|i US -tɚ|.i **-ies** -iz

Tralee trəˈliː

tram træm **-s** -z

tramcar ˈtræm.kɑːʳ US -kɑːr **-s** -z

tramline ˈtræm.laɪn **-s** -z

trammel ˈtræm.ᵊl **-s** -z **-(l)ing** -ɪŋ **-(l)ed** -d

tramontane trəˈmɒn.teɪn US trəˈmɑːn-; træmˈɑːn-; ˌtræm.ɑːnˈteɪn

tramp træmp **-s** -s **-ing** -ɪŋ **-ed** -t **-er/s** -əʳ/z US -ɚ/z

trampl|e ˈtræm.pl̩ **-es** -z **-ing** -ɪŋ, ˈtræm.plɪŋ **-ed** -d **-er/s** -əʳ/z, ˈtræm.pləʳ/z US ˈ-pl̩.ɚ/z, ˈ-plɚ/z

trampolin|e ˈtræm.pᵊl.iːn, -ɪn; ˌtræm.pᵊlˈiːn US ˈtræm.pə.liːn, -pᵊl.ɪn; ˌtræm.pəˈliːn **-es** -z **-ing** -ɪŋ **-ist/s** -ɪst/s

tramway ˈtræm.weɪ **-s** -z

tranc|e trɑːnʔs US trænʔs **-es** -ɪz

tranch|e trɑːnʔʃ, trɔːnʔʃ, trænʔʃ US trɑːnʔʃ **-es** -ɪz

Tranent trəˈnent

Tranmere træn.mɪəʳ US -mɪə

trann|y, trann|ie ˈtræn|.i **-ies** -iz

tranquil ˈtræŋ.kwɪl US ˈtræŋ-, ˈtræn- **-ly** -i **-ness** -nəs, -nɪs

tranquil(l)ity træŋˈkwɪl.ə.ti, -ɪ.ti US -ə.t̬i, træn-

tranquil(l)ization, -isa- ˌtræŋ.kwɪ.laɪˈzeɪ.ʃᵊn, -kwə-, -lɪˈ- US -kwə.lɪˈ-, ˌtræn-

tranquil(l)iz|e, -is|e ˈtræŋ.kwɪ.laɪz, -kwə- US ˈtræŋ-, ˈtræn- **-es** -ɪz **-ing/ly** -ɪŋ/li **-ed** -d **-er/s** -əʳ/z US -ɚ/z

trans- trænʔs-, trɑːnʔs-, trænz-, trɑːnz- US trænʔs-, trænz-

Note: Prefix. May carry primary or secondary stress, or be unstressed; see individual entries.

transact trænˈzækt, trɑːn-, -ˈsækt US træn- **-s** -s **-ing** -ɪŋ **-ed** -ɪd **-or/s** -əʳ/z US -ɚ/z

transaction trænˈzæk.ʃᵊn, trɑːn-, -ˈsæk- US træn- **-s** -z

transalpine trænˈzæl.paɪn, trɑːn- US træn-

transatlantic ˌtræn.zətˈlæn.tɪk, ˌtrɑːn- US ˌtrænʔ.sætˈ-, ˌtræn.zætˈ- *stress shift:* ˌtransatlantic ˈyacht

transcend trænˈsend, trɑːn- US træn- **-s** -z **-ing** -ɪŋ **-ed** -ɪd

transcenden|ce trænˈsen.dənʔ|s, trɑːn- US træn- **-cy** -si

transcendent trænˈsen.dənt, trɑːn- US træn- **-ly** -li

transcendental ˌtrænʔ.senˈden.tᵊl, ˌtrɑːnʔ-, -sᵊnˈ- US ˌtrænʔ.senˈden.t̬ᵊl **-ly** -i ˌ**transcendental mediˈtation**

transcendental|ism ˌtrænʔ.senˈden.tᵊl|.ɪ.zᵊm, ˌtrɑːnʔ-, -sᵊnˈ- US ˌtrænʔ.senˈden.t̬ᵊl- **-ist/s** -ɪst/s

transcontinental ˌtrænsˌkɒn.tɪˈnen.tᵊl, ˌtrɑːns-, -təˈ- US ˌtrænʔsˌkɑːn.tᵊnˈen-, ˌtrænz-

transcrib|e trænˈskraɪb, trɑːn- US træn- **-es** -z **-ing** -ɪŋ **-ed** -d **-er/s** -əʳ/z US -ɚ/z

transcript ˈtrænʔ.skrɪpt, ˈtrɑːnʔ- US ˈtrænʔ- **-s** -s

transcription trænˈskrɪp.ʃᵊn, trɑːn- US træn- **-s** -z

transducer trænzˈdjuː.səʳ, trɑːnz-, trænʔs-, trɑːnʔs- US trænʔsˈduː.sɚ, trænz-, -ˈdjuː- **-s** -z

transept ˈtrænʔ.sept, ˈtrɑːnʔ- US ˈtrænʔ- **-s** -s

transexual trænˈsek.ʃʊəl, trɑːn-, -ʃu.əl, -sjʊəl, -sju.əl US trænˈsek.ʃu.əl **-s** -z **-ism** -ɪ.zᵊm

transexuality træn̩ˌsek.ʃuˈæl.ɪ.ti, -sju-, -ə.ti ⓤⓢ -ʃuˈæl.ə.t̬i

transfer (*n.*) ˈtrænts.fɜːʳ, ˈtrɑːnts- ⓤⓢ ˈtrænts.fɝː -s -z

transfer (*v.*) træntsˈfɜːʳ, trɑːnts- ⓤⓢ træntsˈfɝː, ˈ-- -s -z -ring -ɪŋ -red -d -rer/s -əʳ/z ⓤⓢ -ɚ/z

transferability ˌtrænts.fᵊr.əˈbɪl.ə.ti, ˌtrɑːnts-, -ɪ.ti; træntsˌfɜː.rəˈ-, trɑːnts- ⓤⓢ træntsˌfɝː.əˈbɪl.ə.t̬i

transferable træntsˈfɜː.rə.bl̩, trɑːnts-; ˈtrænts.fᵊr.ə-, ˈtrɑːnts- ⓤⓢ træntsˈfɝː.ə-

transferee ˌtrænts.fɜːˈriː, ˌtrɑːnts-, -fəˈ- ⓤⓢ ˌtrænts.fəˈriː -s -z

transferenc|e træntsˈfɜː.rᵊnts, trɑːnts-; ˈtrænts.fᵊr.ᵊnts, ˈtrɑːnts- ⓤⓢ træntsˈfɝː-; ˈtrænts.fɚ- -es -ɪz

transfiguration (T) ˌtrænts.fɪ.gᵊrˈeɪ.ʃᵊn, ˌtrɑːnts-, -fɪg.jᵊrˈeɪ-; træntsˌfɪg.ᵊrˈ-, trɑːnts-, -jᵊrˈ- ⓤⓢ ˌtrænts.fɪg.jəˈreɪ-, træntsˌfɪg-, -jʊˈ- -s -z

transfig|ure træntsˈfɪg|.əʳ, trɑːnts- ⓤⓢ træntsˈfɪg.j|ɚ -ures -əz ⓤⓢ -ɚz -uring -ᵊr.ɪŋ -ured -əd ⓤⓢ -ɚd -urement/s -ə.mənt/s ⓤⓢ -ɚ.mənt/s

transfinite træntsˈfaɪ.naɪt, trɑːnts- ⓤⓢ trænts-

transfix træntsˈfɪks, trɑːnts- ⓤⓢ trænts- -es -ɪz -ing -ɪŋ -ed -t

transfixion træntsˈfɪk.ʃᵊn, trɑːnts- ⓤⓢ trænts- -s -z

transform træntsˈfɔːm, trɑːnts- ⓤⓢ træntsˈfɔːrm -s -z -ing -ɪŋ -ed -d -er/s -əʳ/z ⓤⓢ -ɚ/z -able -ə.bl̩

transformation ˌtrænts.fəˈmeɪ.ʃᵊn, ˌtrɑːnts-, -fɔːˈ- ⓤⓢ ˌtrænts.fɚˈ-, -fɔːrˈ- -s -z

transformational ˌtrænts.fəˈmeɪ.ʃᵊn.ᵊl, ˌtrɑːnts-, -ˈmeɪʃ.nᵊl ⓤⓢ ˌtrænts.fɚˈ-, -fɔːrˈ- *stress shift, see compound:* ˌ**transformational** ˈ**grammar**

transfusable træntsˈfjuː.zə.bl̩, trɑːnts- ⓤⓢ trænts-

transfus|e træntsˈfjuːz, trɑːnts- ⓤⓢ trænts- -es -ɪz -ing -ɪŋ -ed -d -er/s -əʳ/z ⓤⓢ -ɚ/z

transfusible træntsˈfjuː.zə.bl̩, trɑːnts-, -zɪ- ⓤⓢ trænts-

transfusion træntsˈfjuː.ʒᵊn, trɑːnts- ⓤⓢ trænts- -s -z

transgenic trænzˈdʒen.ɪk, trɑːnz- ⓤⓢ trænz-

transgress trænzˈgres, trɑːnz-, trænts-, trɑːnts- ⓤⓢ trænts-, trænz- -es -ɪz -ing -ɪŋ -ed -t -or/s -əʳ/z ⓤⓢ -ɚ/z

transgression trænzˈgreʃ.ᵊn, trɑːnz-, trænts-, trɑːnts- ⓤⓢ trænts-, trænz- -s -z

tranship træntsˈʃɪp, trɑːnts-, trænz-, trɑːnz-, træn-, trɑːn- ⓤⓢ træn- -s -s -ping -ɪŋ -ped -t -ment/s -mənt/s

transhuman|ce træntsˈhjuː.mən|ts, trɑːnts- ⓤⓢ trænts-, trænz- -t -t

transien|ce ˈtræn.zi.ənt|s, ˈtrɑːn-; ˈtrænt.si-, ˈtrɑːnt- ⓤⓢ ˈtrænt.ʃᵊnt|s, -si.ənt|s; ˈtræn.ʒᵊnt|s, -zi.ənt|s -cy -si

transient ˈtræn.zi.ənt, ˈtrɑːn-; ˈtrænt.si.ənt, ˈtrɑːnt- ⓤⓢ ˈtrænt.ʃᵊnt, -si.ənt; ˈtræn.ʒᵊnt, -zi.ənt -ly -li -ness -nəs, -nɪs

transilient trænˈsɪl.i.ənt, trɑːn-, -ˈzɪl-, ˈ-jənt ⓤⓢ træn-

transistor trænˈzɪs.təʳ, trɑːn-, -ˈsɪs- ⓤⓢ trænˈzɪs.tɚ, -ˈsɪs- -s -z **tranˌsistor** ˈ**radio**, ˌ**transistor** ˈ**radio**

transistoriz|e, -is|e trænˈzɪs.tᵊr.aɪz, trɑːn-, -ˈsɪs- ⓤⓢ trænˈzɪs.tə.raɪz, -ˈsɪs- -es -ɪz -ing -ɪŋ -ed -d

transit ˈtrænt.sɪt, ˈtrɑːnt-; ˈtræn.zɪt, ˈtrɑːn- ⓤⓢ ˈtrænt.sɪt; ˈtræn.zɪt -s -s ˈ**transit** ˌ**lounge**

transition trænˈzɪʃ.ᵊn, trɑːn-, trən-, -ˈsɪʒ- ⓤⓢ trænˈzɪʃ-, -ˈsɪʃ-, -ˈsɪʒ- -s -z

transitional trænˈzɪʃ.ᵊn.əl, trɑːn-, trən-, -ˈsɪʒ-, ˈ-nᵊl ⓤⓢ trænˈzɪʃ-, -ˈsɪʃ-, -ˈsɪʒ- -li -i

transitive ˈtrænt.sə.tɪv, ˈtrɑːnt-, -sɪ-; ˈtræn.zə-, ˈtrɑːn-, -zɪ- ⓤⓢ ˈtrænt.sə.t̬ɪv; ˈtræn.zə- -ly -li -ness -nəs, -nɪs

transitivity ˌtrænt.səˈtɪv.ɪ.ti, ˌtrɑːnt-, -sɪˈ-; ˌtræn.zəˈ-, ˌtrɑːn-, -zɪˈ- ⓤⓢ ˌtrænt.səˈtɪv.ə.t̬i; ˌtræn.zəˈ-

transitor|y ˈtrænt.sɪ.tᵊr|.i, ˈtrɑːnt-, -sə-; ˈtræn.zɪ-, ˈtrɑːn-, -zə- ⓤⓢ ˈtrænt.sə.tɔːr-; ˈtræn.zə- -ily -ᵊl.i, -ɪ.li -iness -ɪ.nəs, -ɪ.nɪs

Transkei ˌtræntˈskaɪ, ˌtrɑːnt-; ˌtrænzˈkaɪ, ˌtrɑːnz- ⓤⓢ trænˈskeɪ, -ˈskaɪ

transla|te trænzˈleɪ|t, trɑːnz-; træntˈsleɪ|t, trɑːnt- ⓤⓢ trænˈsleɪ|t, ˈ--; trænzˈleɪ|t, ˈ-- -tes -ts -ting -tɪŋ ⓤⓢ -t̬ɪŋ -ted -tɪd ⓤⓢ -t̬ɪd -tor/s -təʳ/z ⓤⓢ -t̬ɚ/z -table -tə.bl̩ ⓤⓢ -t̬ə.bl̩

translation trænzˈleɪ.ʃᵊn, trɑːnz-; træntˈsleɪ-, trɑːnt- ⓤⓢ trænˈsleɪ-; trænzˈleɪ- -s -z

translative trænzˈleɪ.tɪv, trɑːnz-; træntˈsleɪ-, trɑːnt- ⓤⓢ trænˈsleɪ.t̬ɪv; trænzˈleɪ-

translatory trænzˈleɪ.tᵊr.i, trɑːnz-; træntˈsleɪ-, trɑːnt- ⓤⓢ trænˈsleɪ.t̬ɚ-; trænzˈleɪ-

transliter|ate trænzˈlɪt.ᵊr|.eɪt, trɑːnz-; træntˈslɪt-, trɑːnt- ⓤⓢ trænˈslɪt̬.ə.r|eɪt; trænzˈlɪt̬- -ates -eɪts -ating -eɪ.tɪŋ ⓤⓢ -eɪ.t̬ɪŋ -ated -eɪ.tɪd ⓤⓢ -eɪ.t̬ɪd -ator/s -eɪ.təʳ/z ⓤⓢ -eɪ.t̬ɚ/z

transliteration ˌtrænz.lɪ.tᵊrˈeɪ.ʃᵊn, ˌtrɑːnz-; trænzˌlɪt.ᵊrˈ-, trɑːnz-; ˌtrænt.slɪ.tᵊr-, ˌtrɑːnt-; trænˌslɪt.ᵊrˈ-, trɑːn- ⓤⓢ trænˌslɪt̬.əˈreɪ-; trænzˌlɪt̬- -s -z

translocation ˌtrænz.ləʊˈkeɪ.ʃᵊn, ˌtrɑːnz- ⓤⓢ ˌtrænz.loʊ-

translucenc|e trænzˈluː.sᵊnts, trɑːnz-, -ˈljuː-; trænˈsluː-, trɑːn-; trænsˈljuː-, trɑːns- ⓤⓢ trænˈsluː-; trænzˈluː- -y -i

translucent trænzˈluː.sᵊnt, trɑːnz-, -ˈljuː-; trænˈsluː-, trɑːn-; trænsˈljuː-, trɑːns- ⓤⓢ trænˈsluː-; trænzˈluː- -ly -li

transmigra|te ˌtrænz.maɪˈgreɪ|t, ˌtrɑːnz-; ˌtrænt.smaɪˈ-, ˌtrɑːnt- ⓤⓢ ˌtræntˈsmaɪ.greɪ|t; ˌtrænzˈmaɪ- -tes -ts -ting -tɪŋ ⓤⓢ -t̬ɪŋ -ted -tɪd ⓤⓢ -t̬ɪd -tor/s -təʳ/z ⓤⓢ -t̬ɚ/z

transmigration ˌtrænz.maɪˈgreɪ.ʃᵊn, ˌtrɑːnz-; ˌtrænt.smaɪˈ-, ˌtrɑːnt- ⓤⓢ ˌtrænt.smaɪˈ-; ˌtrænz.maɪˈ- -s -z

transmigratory trænzˈmaɪ.grə.tᵊr.i, trɑːnz-; trænˈsmaɪ-, trɑːn- ⓤⓢ trænˈsmaɪ.grə.tɔːr-; trænzˈmaɪ-

transmissibility trænzˌmɪs.əˈbɪl.ə.ti, trɑːnz-, -ɪˈ-, -ɪ.ti; trænˌsmɪs-, trɑːn-; ˌtrænz.mɪ.səˈ-, ˌtrɑːnz-, -sɪˈ-; ˌtrænt.smɪ-, ˌtrɑːnt- ⓤⓢ ˌtrænt.smɪs.əˈbɪl.ə.t̬i; ˌtrænz.mɪs-

transmissible trænzˈmɪs.ə.bl̩, trɑːnz-, ˈ-ɪ-; trænˈsmɪs-, trɑːn- ⓤⓢ trænˈsmɪs-; trænzˈmɪs-

transmission trænzˈmɪʃ.ᵊn, trɑːnz-; trænˈsmɪʃ-, trɑːn- ⓤⓢ trænˈsmɪʃ-; trænzˈmɪʃ- -s -z

transmi|t trænzˈmɪ|t, trɑːnz-; trænˈsmɪ|t, trɑːn- ⓤⓢ trænˈsmɪ|t; trænzˈmɪ|t -ts -ts -tting -tɪŋ ⓤⓢ -t̬ɪŋ -tted -tɪd ⓤⓢ -t̬ɪd -tter/s -təʳ/z ⓤⓢ -t̬ɚ/z

transmittal trænzˈmɪt.ᵊl, trɑːnz-; trænˈsmɪt-, trɑːn- ⓤⓢ trænˈsmɪt̬-; trænzˈmɪt̬- -s -z

transmittanc|e trænzˈmɪt.ᵊnts, trɑːnz-; trænˈsmɪt-, trɑːn- ⓤⓢ trænˈsmɪt̬-; trænzˈmɪt̬- -es -ɪz

transmogrification ˌtrænz.mɒg.rɪ.fɪˈkeɪ.ʃᵊn, ˌtrɑːnz-, trænzˌmɒg-, trɑːnz-, -rə-; ˌtrænt.smɒg-, ˌtrɑːnt-, trænˌsmɒg-, trɑːn- ⓤⓢ trænˌsmɑː.grə-; trænzˌmɑːg-

transmogri|fy trænzˈmɒg.rɪ|.faɪ, trɑːnz-, -rə-; trænˈsmɒg-, trɑːn- ⓤⓢ trænˈsmɑː.grə-; trænzˈmɑː- -fies -faɪz -fying -faɪ.ɪŋ -fied -faɪd

transmutability trænz,mjuː.tə'bɪl.ə.ti, trɑːnz-, træn*t*s-, trɑːn*t*s-, ˌtrænz.mjuː-, ˌtrɑːnz-, ˌtræn*t*s-, ˌtrɑːn*t*s-, -ɪ.ti (US) ˌtræn*t*s.mjuː.t̬ə'bɪl.ə.t̬i, ˌtrænz-

transmutation ˌtrænz.mjuː'teɪ.ʃən, ˌtrɑːnz-, ˌtræn*t*s-, ˌtrɑːn*t*s-, -mjʊ'- (US) ˌtræn*t*s-, ˌtrænz- **-s** -z

trans|mute trænz|'mjuːt, trɑːnz-, træn*t*s-, trɑːn*t*s- (US) træn*t*s-, trænz- **-mutes** -'mjuːts **-muting** -'mjuː.tɪŋ (US) -'mjuː.t̬ɪŋ **-muted** -'mjuː.tɪd (US) -'mjuː.t̬ɪd **-muter/s** -'mjuː.təʳ/z (US) -'mjuː.t̬ɚ/z **-mutable** -'mjuː.tə.bl̩ (US) -'mjuː.t̬ə.bl̩

transnational trænz'næʃ.ən.əl, trɑːnz-, '-nəl; træn'snæʃ-, trɑːn- (US) træn'snæʃ-; trænz'næʃ-

transoceanic ˌtræn.zəʊ.ʃi'æn.ɪk, -si'-; ˌtræn*t*.səʊ- (US) ˌtræn*t*.soʊ.ʃi'-; ˌtræn.zoʊ-

transom 'træn*t*.səm **-s** -z

transpacific ˌtræn*t*.spə'sɪf.ɪk, ˌtrɑːn*t*s-; ˌtrænz.pə'-, ˌtrɑːnz- (US) ˌtræn*t*.spə-, ˌtrænz-

transparenc|y træn'spær.ən*t*.s|i, trɑːn-, trən-, -'speə.rən*t*-; trænz'pær.ən*t*-, trɑːnz-, trənz-, -'peə.rən*t*- (US) træn'sper.ən*t*-, -'spær- **-ies** -iz

transparen|t træn*t*'spær.ən|t, trɑːn*t*-, trən*t*-, -speə.rən|t; trænz'pær.ən|t, trɑːnz-, trənz-, -'peə.rən|t (US) træn'sper.ən|t, -'spær- **-tly** -t.li **-tness** -t.nəs, -t.nɪs **-ce** -*t*s

transpiration ˌtræn*t*.spɪ'reɪ.ʃən, ˌtrɑːn*t*-, -spə'- (US) ˌtræn*t*-

transpir|e træn'spaɪəʳ, trɑːn- (US) træn'spaɪɚ **-es** -z **-ing** -ɪŋ **-ed** -d

transplan|t (*v.*) træn'splɑːn|t, trɑːn- (US) træn'splæn|t; 'træn*t*.splæn|t **-ts** -ts **-ting** -tɪŋ (US) -t̬ɪŋ **-ted** -tɪd (US) -t̬ɪd **-table** -tə.bl̩ (US) -t̬ə.bl̩

transplant (*n.*) 'træn*t*.splɑːnt, 'trɑːn- (US) 'træn*t*.splænt **-s** -s

transplantation ˌtræn*t*.splɑːn'teɪ.ʃən, ˌtrɑːn*t*- (US) ˌtræn*t*.splæn'- **-s** -z

transponder træn'spɒn.dəʳ, trɑːn- (US) træn'spɑːn.dɚ **-s** -z

transpontine træn*t*'spɒn.taɪn, trɑːn*t*-; trænz'pɒn-, trɑːnz- (US) træn'spɑːn.taɪn, -tɪn, -tiːn

transport (*n.*) 'træn*t*.spɔːt, 'trɑːn*t*- (US) 'træn*t*.spɔːrt **-s** -s **'transport ˌcafe**

transpor|t (*v.*) træn'spɔː|t, trɑːn- (US) træn'spɔːr|t, '-- **-ts** -ts **-ting** -tɪŋ (US) -t̬ɪŋ **-ted** -tɪd (US) -t̬ɪd **-table** -tə.bl̩ (US) -t̬ə.bl̩

transportability ˌtræn*t*.spɔː.tə'bɪl.ə.ti, ˌtrɑːn*t*-, trænˌspɔː-, trɑːn-, -ɪ.ti (US) trænˌspɔːr.t̬ə'bɪl.ə.t̬i

transportation ˌtræn*t*.spɔː'teɪ.ʃən, ˌtrɑːn*t*-, -spə'- (US) ˌtræn*t*.spɚ'- **-s** -z

transporter træn'spɔː.təʳ, trɑːn- (US) træn'spɔːr.t̬ɚ **-s** -z

transpos|e træn'spəʊz, trɑːn- (US) træn'spoʊz **-es** -ɪz **-ing** -ɪŋ **-ed** -d **-er/s** -əʳ/z (US) -ɚ/z **-able** -ə.bl̩ **-al/s** -əl/z

transposition ˌtræn*t*.spə'zɪʃ.ən, ˌtrɑːn*t*- (US) ˌtræn*t*- **-s** -z

transputer træn'spjuː.təʳ, trɑːn-; trænz'pjuː-, trɑːnz- (US) træn'spjuː.t̬ɚ **-s** -z

transsexual træn'sek.ʃʊəl, trɑːn-, træn*t*s-, trɑːn*t*s-, -ʃu.əl, -sjʊəl, -sju.əl (US) træn'sek.ʃu.əl, træn*t*s- **-s** -z **-ism** -ɪ.zəm

transsexuality trænˌsek.ʃu'æl.ɪ.ti, -sju-, -ə.ti (US) -ʃu'æl.ə.t̬i

transship træn*t*s'ʃɪp, trɑːn*t*s-, trænz-, trɑːnz-, træn-, trɑːn- (US) træns'ʃɪp **-s** -s **-ping** -ɪŋ **-ped** -t **-ment/s** -mənt/s

Trans-Siberian ˌtræn*t*s.saɪ'bɪə.ri.ən, ˌtrɑːn*t*s-, ˌtrænz-, ˌtrɑːnz- (US) ˌtræn*t*s.saɪ'bɪr.i-, ˌtrænz-

transubstanti|ate ˌtræn*t*.səb'stæn.*t*ʃi|.eɪt, ˌtrɑːn*t*-, -'stɑːn-; -'stæn*t*.si-, -'stɑːn*t*- (US) ˌtræn*t*.səb'stæn*t*.ʃi- **-ates** -eɪts **-ating** -eɪ.tɪŋ (US) -eɪ.t̬ɪŋ **-ated** -eɪ.tɪd (US) -eɪ.t̬ɪd

transubstantiation ˌtræn*t*.səbˌstæn.*t*ʃi'eɪ.ʃən, ˌtrɑːn*t*-, -ˌstɑːn-; -ˌstæn*t*s.i-, -ˌstɑːn*t*- (US) ˌtræn*t*.səbˌstæn*t*.ʃi'- **-s** -z

Transvaal 'trænz.vɑːl, 'trɑːnz-, 'træn*t*s-, 'trɑːn*t*s-, ˌ-'- (US) ˌtræn*t*s'vɑːl, ˌtrænz-

Transvaaler 'trænzˌvɑː.ləʳ, 'trɑːnz-, 'træn*t*s-, 'trɑːn*t*s-, ˌ-'-- (US) ˌtræn*t*s'vɑː.lɚ, ˌtrænz- **-s** -z

transversal trænz'vɜː.səl, trɑːnz-, træn*t*s-, trɑːn*t*s- (US) træn*t*s'vɝː-, trænz- **-s** -z

transverse trænz'vɜːs, trɑːnz-, træn*t*s-, trɑːn*t*s- (US) træn*t*s'vɝːs, trænz- **-ly** -li *stress shift:* ˌtransverse 'engine

transverse (*n.*) 'trænz.vɜːs, 'trɑːnz-, 'træn*t*s-, 'trɑːn*t*s-, ˌ-'- (US) 'træn*t*s-, 'trænz-

transvestism trænz'ves.tɪ.zəm, trɑːnz-, træn*t*s-, trɑːn*t*s- (US) træn*t*s-, trænz-

transvestite trænz'ves.taɪt, trɑːnz-, træn*t*s-, trɑːn*t*s- (US) træn*t*s-, trænz- **-s** -s

Transylvani|a ˌtræn*t*.sɪl'veɪ.ni|.ə, ˌtrɑːn*t*-, -səl'-, '-nj|ə (US) ˌtræn*t*- **-an/s** -ən

tranter (T) 'træn.təʳ (US) -t̬ɚ **-s** -z

trap træp **-s** -s **-ping/s** -ɪŋ/z **-ped** -t **-per/s** -əʳ/z (US) -ɚ/z

trapdoor ˌtræp'dɔːʳ (US) 'træp.dɔːr, ˌ-'- **-s** -z *stress shift, British only:* ˌtrapdoor 'spider

trapes treɪps **-es** -ɪz **-ing** -ɪŋ **-ed** -t

trapez|e trə'piːz (US) træp'iːz, trə'piːz **-es** -ɪz

trapezi|um trə'piː.zi|.əm **-ums** -əmz **-a** -ə

trapezoid 'træp.ɪ.zɔɪd **-s** -z

Trapp træp

trappings 'træp.ɪŋz

Trappist 'træp.ɪst **-s** -s

trapshoot|ing 'træpˌʃuː.t|ɪŋ **-er/s** -əʳ/z (US) -ɚ/z

Traquair trə'kweəʳ (US) -'kwer

trash træʃ **-es** -ɪz **-ing** -ɪŋ **-ed** -t

trashcan 'træʃ.kæn **-s** -z

trash|man 'træʃ|.mæn, -mən **-men** -men, -mən

trash|y 'træʃ|.i **-ier** -i.əʳ (US) -i.ɚ **-iest** -i.ɪst, -i.əst **-iness** -ɪ.nəs, -ɪ.nɪs

Trasimene 'træz.ɪ.miːn, '-ə- (US) 'trɑː.zɪ.miːn, -zə-

trattoria ˌtræt.ər'iː.ə (US) ˌtrɑː.t̬ə'riː.ə, -tɔː'-; trɑː'tɔːr.i- **-s** -z

traum|a 'trɔː.m|ə, 'traʊ- (US) 'trɑː-, 'trɔː-, 'traʊ- **-as** -əz **-ata** -ə.tə (US) -ə.t̬ə

traumatic trɔː'mæt.ɪk, traʊ- (US) trɑː'mæt̬-, trɔː-, traʊ- **-ally** -əl.i, -li

traumatism 'trɔː.mə.tɪ.zəm (US) 'trɑː-, 'trɔː- **-s** -z

traumatization, -isa- ˌtrɔː.mə.taɪ'zeɪ.ʃən, ˌtraʊ-, -tɪ'- (US) ˌtrɑː.mə.t̬ɪ'-, ˌtrɔː-, ˌtraʊ-

traumatiz|e, -is|e 'trɔː.mə.taɪz, 'traʊ- (US) 'trɑː-, 'trɔː-, 'traʊ- **-es** -ɪz **-ing** -ɪŋ **-ed** -d

travail 'træv.eɪl; trə'veɪl (US) trə'veɪl; 'træv.eɪl **-s** -z **-ing** -ɪŋ **-ed** -d

Travancore ˌtræv.əŋ'kɔːʳ (US) -'kɔːr

travel 'træv.əl **-s** -z **-(l)ing** -ɪŋ, 'træv.lɪŋ **-(l)ed** -d **'travel ˌagency; 'travel ˌagent; 'travelling exˌpenses; ˌtravelling 'salesman; 'travel ˌsickness**

travelator 'træv.əl.eɪ.təʳ (US) -ə.leɪ.t̬ɚ **-s** -z

Travelcard 'træv.əl.kɑːd (US) -kɑːrd

travel(l)er 'træv.əl.əʳ, '-ləʳ (US) '-əl.ɚ, '-lɚ **-s** -z **'travel(l)er's ˌcheque**

travelogue, travelog 'træv.əl.ɒg (US) -ə.lɑːg, -lɔːg **-s** -z

Travers 'træv.əz (US) -ɚz

travers|e (*n. adj.*) 'træv.əs, -ɜːs; trə'vɜːs, træv'ɜːs (US) 'træv.ɚs, -ɝːs; trə'vɝːs, træv'ɝːs **-es** -ɪz

travers|e (*v.*) trə'vɜːs, træv'ɜːs; 'træv.ɜːs (US) trə'vɝːs, træv'ɝːs; 'træv.ɚs **-es** -ɪz **-ing** -ɪŋ **-ed** -t

travest|y 'træv.ə.st|i, '-ɪ- (US) '-ɪ- **-ies** -iz **-ying** -i.ɪŋ **-ied** -id ˌ**travesty of 'justice**

Traviata ˌtræv.iˈɑː.tə ⓤⓢ ˌtrɑː.viˈɑː.t̬ə
Travis ˈtræv.ɪs
travolator ˈtræv.ᵊl.eɪ.təʳ ⓤⓢ -t̬ɚ **-s** -z
Travolta trəˈvəʊl.tə, -ˈvɒl- ⓤⓢ -ˈvoʊl.t̬ə
trawl trɔːl ⓤⓢ trɑːl, trɔːl **-s** -z **-ing** -ɪŋ **-ed** -d
trawler ˈtrɔː.ləʳ ⓤⓢ ˈtrɑː.lɚ, ˈtrɔː- **-s** -z
trawler|man ˈtrɔː.lə|.mən ⓤⓢ ˈtrɑː.lɚ-, ˈtrɔː- **-men** -mən
tray treɪ **-s** -z
Traynor ˈtreɪ.nəʳ ⓤⓢ -nɚ
treacherous ˈtretʃ.ᵊr.əs **-ly** -li **-ness** -nəs, -nɪs
treacher|y ˈtretʃ.ᵊr|.i **-ies** -iz
treacle ˈtriː.kl̩ **-s** -z ˌ**treacle** ˈ**tart**
treacl|y ˈtriː.kl̩|.i, ˈ-kl|i **-iness** -ɪ.nəs, -ɪ.nɪs
tread tred **-s** -z **-ing** -ɪŋ **trod** trɒd ⓤⓢ trɑːd **trodden** ˈtrɒd.ᵊn ⓤⓢ ˈtrɑː.dᵊn **treader/s** ˈtred.əʳ/z ⓤⓢ -ɚ/z ˌ**tread on someone's** ˈ**toes**
treadle ˈtred.l̩ **-s** -z
treadmill ˈtred.mɪl **-s** -z
Treadwell ˈtred.wel
treason ˈtriː.zᵊn **-s** -z
treasonab|le ˈtriː.zᵊn.ə.b|l̩, ˈtriːz.nə- **-ly** -li **-leness** -l̩.nəs, -nɪs
treasonous ˈtriː.zᵊn.əs, ˈtriːz.nəs
treas|ure ˈtreʒ|.əʳ ⓤⓢ -ɚ **-ures** -əz ⓤⓢ -ɚz **-uring** -ᵊr.ɪŋ **-ured** -əd ⓤⓢ -ɚd ˈ**treasure** ˌ**hunt**; ˈ**treasure** ˌ**trove**
treasure-hou|se ˈtreʒ.ə.haʊ|s ⓤⓢ ˈ-ɚ- **-ses** -zɪz
treasurer ˈtreʒ.ᵊr.əʳ ⓤⓢ -ɚ **-s** -z
treasurership ˈtreʒ.ᵊr.ə.ʃɪp ⓤⓢ -ɚ- **-s** -s
treasure-trove ˈtreʒ.ə.trəʊv ⓤⓢ ˈ-ɚ.troʊv
treasur|y (T) ˈtreʒ.ᵊr|.i **-ies** -iz
treat triːt **-s** -s **-ing** -ɪŋ ⓤⓢ ˈtriː.t̬ɪŋ **-ed** -ɪd ⓤⓢ ˈtriː.t̬ɪd
treatable ˈtriː.tə.bl̩ ⓤⓢ -t̬ə-
treatis|e ˈtriː.tɪz, -tɪs ⓤⓢ -t̬ɪs **-es** -ɪz
treatment ˈtriːt.mənt **-s** -s
treat|y ˈtriː.t|i ⓤⓢ -t̬|i **-ies** -iz
Trebizond ˈtreb.ɪ.zɒnd ⓤⓢ -zɑːnd
trebl|e ˈtreb.l̩ **-es** -z **-y** -i, ˈtreb.li **-ing** -ɪŋ, ˈtreb.lɪŋ **-ed** -d
Treblinka trəˈblɪŋ.kə, trebˈlɪŋ- ⓤⓢ trəˈblɪŋ-; trebˈliːŋ-
Trebor ˈtriː.bɔːʳ ⓤⓢ -bɔːr
Tredegar trɪˈdiː.gəʳ, trə- ⓤⓢ -gɚ
tree (T) triː **-s** -z **-ing** -ɪŋ **-d** -d ˈ**tree** ˌ**frog**; ˌ**Tree of** ˈ**Knowledge**; ˈ**tree** ˌ**surgeon**; ˌ**bark up the** ˌ**wrong** ˈ**tree**
treecreeper ˈtriːˌkriː.pəʳ ⓤⓢ -pɚ **-s** -z
treeless ˈtriː.ləs, -lɪs
treeline ˈtriː.laɪn
tree-lined ˈtriː.laɪnd
treetop ˈtriː.tɒp ⓤⓢ -tɑːp **-s** -z
trefoil ˈtref.ɔɪl, ˈtriː.fɔɪl, ˈtrɪf.ɔɪl ⓤⓢ ˈtriː.fɔɪl, ˈtref.ɔɪl **-s** -z
Trefor ˈtrev.əʳ ⓤⓢ -ɚ

Trefusis trɪˈfjuː.sɪs, trə-
Tregear trɪˈgɪəʳ, trə- ⓤⓢ -ˈgɪr
Treharne trɪˈhɑːn, trə-, -ˈhɜːn ⓤⓢ -ˈhɑːrn, -ˈhɝːn
Treharris trɪˈhær.ɪs, trə- ⓤⓢ -ˈher-, -ˈhær-
Treherne trɪˈhɜːn, trə- ⓤⓢ -ˈhɝːn
trek trek **-s** -s **-king** -ɪŋ **-ked** -t **-ker/s** -əʳ/z ⓤⓢ -ɚ/z
Trekkie ˈtrek.i **-s** -z
Trelawn(e)y trɪˈlɔː.ni, trə- ⓤⓢ -ˈlɑː-, -ˈlɔː-
Treleaven trɪˈlev.ᵊn, trə-
trellis ˈtrel.ɪs **-es** -ɪz **-ed** -t
trelliswork ˈtrel.ɪs.wɜːk ⓤⓢ -wɝːk
Tremadoc trɪˈmæd.ək, trə-
Tremain, Tremayne trɪˈmeɪn, trə-
trembl|e ˈtrem.bl̩ **-es** -z **-ing/ly** -ɪŋ/li, ˈtrem.blɪŋ/li **-ed** -d **-er/s** -əʳ/z, ˈtrem.bləʳ/z ⓤⓢ ˈ-l̩.ɚ/z, ˈ-lɚ/z
trembl|y ˈtrem.bl|i, ˈ-bl̩|.i **-ier** -i.əʳ ⓤⓢ -i.ɚ **-iest** -i.ɪst, -i.əst **-iness** -ɪ.nəs, -ɪ.nɪs
tremendous trɪˈmen.dəs, trə- **-ly** -li **-ness** -nəs, -nɪs
tremolo ˈtrem.ᵊl.əʊ ⓤⓢ -ə.loʊ **-s** -z
tremor ˈtrem.əʳ ⓤⓢ -ɚ **-s** -z
tremulant ˈtrem.jə.lənt, -jʊ- **-s** -s
tremulous ˈtrem.jə.ləs, -jʊ- **-ly** -li **-ness** -nəs, -nɪs
trench (T) tren*t*ʃ **-es** -ɪz **-ing** -ɪŋ **-ed** -t **-er/s** -əʳ/z ⓤⓢ -ɚ/z ˈ**trench** ˌ**coat**; ˌ**trench** ˈ**foot**; ˌ**trench** ˈ**warfare**
trenchancy ˈtren.*t*ʃən*t*.si
trenchant ˈtren.*t*ʃənt **-ly** -li
Trenchard ˈtren.*t*ʃɑːd, -*t*ʃəd ⓤⓢ -*t*ʃɑːrd, -*t*ʃɚd
trencher|man ˈtren.*t*ʃə|.mən ⓤⓢ -*t*ʃɚ- **-men** -mən
trend trend **-s** -z **-ing** -ɪŋ **-ed** -ɪd
trendsett|er ˈtrendˌset|.əʳ ⓤⓢ -ˌset̬|.ɚ **-s** -əʳ/z ⓤⓢ -ɚ/z **-ing** -ɪŋ
trend|y ˈtren.d|i **-ies** -iz **-ier** -i.əʳ ⓤⓢ -i.ɚ **-iest** -i.ɪst, -i.əst **-ily** -ɪ.li **-iness** -ɪ.nəs, -ɪ.nɪs
Trent trent
Trentham ˈtren.təm
Trenton ˈtren.tən ⓤⓢ -tᵊn
trepan trɪˈpæn, trə- **-s** -z **-ning** -ɪŋ **-ned** -d
trepang trɪˈpæŋ, trə- **-s** -z
trephin|e trɪˈfiːn, trefˈiːn, trəˈfiːn, -ˈfaɪn ⓤⓢ trɪˈfaɪn, triː-, -ˈfiːn **-es** -z **-ing** -ɪŋ **-ed** -d
trepidation ˌtrep.ɪˈdeɪ.ʃᵊn, -əˈ-
Tresilian trɪˈsɪl.i.ən, trə-, ˈ-jən
trespass (*v.*) ˈtres.pəs ⓤⓢ -pæs, -pəs **-es** -ɪz **-ing** -ɪŋ **-ed** -t **-er/s** -əʳ/z ⓤⓢ -ɚ/z
trespass (*n.*) ˈtres.pəs **-es** -ɪz
tress tres **-es** -ɪz **-ed** -t
trestle ˈtres.l̩ **-s** -z ˌ**trestle** ˈ**table**, ˈ**trestle** ˌ**table**

Trethowan trɪˈθəʊən, trə-, -ˈθaʊən, -ˈθɔː.ən ⓤⓢ -ˈθoʊən, -ˈθaʊən, -ˈθɑː.ən, -ˈθɔː-
Trevelyan *in Cornwall:* trɪˈvɪl.jən, trə- ⓤⓢ trɪˈvel-, -ˈvɪl- *in Northumbria:* trɪˈvel.jən, trə-
Treves triːvz
Trevethick trɪˈveθ.ɪk, trə-
Trevisa trɪˈviː.sə, trə-
Treviso trɪˈviː.səʊ, -zəʊ ⓤⓢ -soʊ
Trevithick ˈtrev.ɪ.θɪk ⓤⓢ -ə-
Trevor ˈtrev.əʳ ⓤⓢ -ɚ
Trevor-Roper ˌtrev.əˈrəʊ.pəʳ ⓤⓢ -ɚˈroʊ.pɚ
Trewin trɪˈwɪn, trə-
trews truːz
trey treɪ **-s** -z
tri- traɪ-, trɪ-, triː-
Note: Prefix. See individual entries for pronunciation and stressing.
triable ˈtraɪ.ə.bl̩ **-ness** -nəs, -nɪs
triad (T) ˈtraɪ.æd, -əd **-s** -z
triage ˈtriː.ɑːʒ; ˈtraɪ.ɪdʒ ⓤⓢ ˈtriː.ɑːʒ
trial traɪəl **-s** -z **-(l)ing** -ɪŋ **-(l)ed** -d ˌ**trial and** ˈ**error**; ˌ**trials and tribu**ˈ**lations**; ˌ**trial** ˈ**run**
trialogue ˈtraɪ.ə.lɒg ⓤⓢ -lɑːg, -lɔːg **-s** -z
triangle ˈtraɪ.æŋ.gl̩ **-s** -z **-d** -d
triangular traɪˈæŋ.gjə.ləʳ, -gjʊ- ⓤⓢ -lɚ **-ly** -li
triangularity traɪˌæŋ.gjəˈlær.ə.ti, ˌtraɪ.æŋ-, -jʊˈ-, -ɪ.ti ⓤⓢ traɪˌæŋ.gjəˈler.ə.t̬i, -gjʊˈ-, -ˈlær-
triangu|late traɪˈæŋ.gjə|.leɪt, -gjʊ- **-lates** -leɪts **-lating** -leɪ.tɪŋ ⓤⓢ -leɪ.t̬ɪŋ **-lated** -leɪ.tɪd ⓤⓢ -leɪ.t̬ɪd
triangulation traɪˌæŋ.gjəˈleɪ.ʃᵊn, ˌtraɪ.æŋ-, -gjʊˈ- ⓤⓢ traɪˌæŋ-
Triangulum traɪˈæŋ.gjə.ləm, -gjʊ-
Triassic traɪˈæs.ɪk
triathlete traɪˈæθ.liːt **-s** -s
triathlon traɪˈæθ.lɒn, -lən ⓤⓢ -lɑːn, -lən **-s** -z
triatomic ˌtraɪ.əˈtɒm.ɪk ⓤⓢ -ˈtɑː.mɪk
tribadism ˈtrɪb.ə.dɪ.zᵊm, ˈtraɪ.bə-
tribal ˈtraɪ.bᵊl **-ly** -i **-ism** -ɪ.zᵊm
tribalistic ˌtraɪ.bᵊlˈɪs.tɪk ⓤⓢ -bəˈlɪs-
tribasic traɪˈbeɪ.sɪk
tribe traɪb **-s** -z
tribes|man ˈtraɪbz|.mən **-men** -mən, -men **-woman** -ˌwʊm.ən **-women** -ˌwɪm.ɪn
tribespeople ˈtraɪbzˌpiː.pl̩
tribrach ˈtraɪ.bræk, ˈtrɪb.ræk **-s** -s
tribrachic traɪˈbræk.ɪk, trɪ-
tribulation ˌtrɪb.jəˈleɪ.ʃᵊn, -jʊˈ- **-s** -z
tribunal traɪˈbjuː.nᵊl, trɪ- **-s** -z
tribunate ˈtrɪb.jə.neɪt, -jʊ-, -nɪt, -nət ⓤⓢ -nɪt, -neɪt **-s** -s
tribune (T) ˈtrɪb.juːn **-s** -z
tributar|y ˈtrɪb.jə.tᵊr|.i, -jʊ-, -tr|i ⓤⓢ -ter|.i **-ies** -iz

Trill

A speech sound produced by the rapid vibration of one of the vocal organs.

Examples

The parts of the body that are used in speaking (the 'vocal apparatus') include some 'wobbly bits' that can be made to vibrate. When this type of vibration is made as a speech sound, it is called a trill. The possibilities include a **BILABIAL** trill, where the lips vibrate (used as a mild insult, this is sometimes called "blowing a raspberry", or, in the US, a 'Bronx Cheer'), a tongue-tip trill which is produced in many languages for a sound represented alphabetically as r, and a uvular trill, which is a rather dramatic way of pronouncing a "uvular r" as found in French, German and many other European languages, most commonly used in acting and singing.

In British English, the trill most likely to occur is the **ALVEOLAR** trill, which is (perhaps confusingly) represented by the symbol [r], and is an allophone of the English phoneme /r/. However, it most frequently occurs in restricted contexts, such as singing.

tribute 'trɪb.juːt **-s** -s
trice traɪs
Tricel® 'traɪ.sel
triceps 'traɪ.seps **-es** -ɪz
trichin|a trɪ'kaɪ.n|ə, trə- **-ae** -iː **-as** -əz
Trichinopoly ˌtrɪtʃ.ɪ'nɒp.ᵊl.i, -ə'- (US) -'nɑː.pᵊl-
trichinosis ˌtrɪk.ɪ'nəʊ.sɪs, -ə'- (US) -ɪ'noʊ-
trichloride traɪ'klɔː.raɪd (US) -'klɔːr.aɪd **-s** -z
trichologly trɪ'kɒl.ə.dʒ|i, trə- (US) -'kɑː.lə- **-ist/s** -ɪst/s
trichord 'traɪ.kɔːd (US) -kɔːrd **-s** -z
trichosis trɪ'kəʊ.sɪs, trə- (US) -'koʊ-
trichotomy trɪ'kɒt.ə.mi, trə- (US) -'kɑː.t̬ə-
Tricia 'trɪʃ.ə
Tricity® 'trɪs.ə.ti, -ɪ.ti (US) -ə.t̬i
trick trɪk **-s** -s **-ing** -ɪŋ **-ed** -t **-er/s** -əʳ/z (US) -ɚ/z ˌ**trick 'cyclist**; ˌ**trick or 'treat**
tricker|y 'trɪk.ᵊr|.i **-ies** -iz
trickl|e 'trɪk.l̩ **-es** -z **-ing** -ɪŋ, 'trɪk.lɪŋ **-ed** -d '**trickle** ˌ**charger**
trickledown 'trɪk.l̩.daʊn
trickly 'trɪk.l̩.i, '-li
trickster 'trɪk.stəʳ (US) -stɚ **-s** -z
tricks|y 'trɪk.s|i **-ier** -i.əʳ (US) -i.ɚ **-iest** -i.ɪst, -i.əst **-iness** -ɪ.nəs, -ɪ.nɪs
trick|y 'trɪk|.i **-ier** -i.əʳ (US) -i.ɚ **-iest** -i.ɪst, -i.əst **-ily** -ɪ.li, -ᵊl.i **-iness** -ɪ.nəs, -ɪ.nɪs
tricolo(u)r 'trɪk.ᵊl.əʳ; 'traɪˌkʌl.əʳ (US) 'traɪˌkʌl.ɚ **-s** -z
tricorn(e) 'traɪ.kɔːn (US) -kɔːrn
tricot 'triː.kəʊ, 'trɪk.əʊ (US) 'triː.koʊ **-s** -z
tricycl|e 'traɪ.sɪ.kl̩, -sə- **-es** -z **-ing** -ɪŋ, -klɪŋ **-ed** -d
trident (T) 'traɪ.dᵊnt **-s** -s
Tridentine traɪ'den.taɪn, trɪ-, trə-, -tiːn (US) traɪ'den.taɪn, -tiːn, -tɪn
tried *(from* **try***)* traɪd
triennial traɪ'en.i.əl, '-jəl **-ly** -i
trier 'traɪ.əʳ (US) -ɚ **-s** -z
Trier trɪəʳ (US) trɪr
trierarch 'traɪ.ᵊr.ɑːk (US) -ə.rɑːrk **-s** -s **-y** -i **-ies** -iz
tries *(from* **try***)* traɪz
Trieste tri'est; -'es.teɪ
triffid (T) 'trɪf.ɪd **-s** -z
trifid 'traɪ.fɪd
trifl|e 'traɪ.fl̩ **-es** -z **-ing/ly** -ɪŋ/li, 'traɪ.flɪŋ/li **-ed** -d **-er/s** -əʳ/z, 'traɪ.fləʳ/z (US) '-fl̩.ɚ/z, '-flɚ/z
trifolium traɪ'fəʊ.li.əm (US) -'foʊ- **-s** -z
trifori|um traɪ'fɔː.ri|.əm (US) -'fɔːr.i- **-a** -ə
trig trɪg **-s** -z **-ging** -ɪŋ **-ged** -d
Trigg trɪg
trigg|er 'trɪg|.əʳ (US) -ɚ **-ers** -əz (US) -ɚz **-ering** -ᵊr.ɪŋ **-ered** -əd (US) -ɚd
trigger-happy 'trɪg.əˌhæp.i (US) -ɚˌ-
triglyph 'traɪ.glɪf, 'trɪg.lɪf (US) 'traɪ.glɪf **-s** -s
trigon 'traɪ.gən, -gɒn (US) -gɑːn **-s** -z
trigonometric ˌtrɪg.ə.nəʊ'met.rɪk (US) -nə'- **-al** -ᵊl **-ally** -ᵊl.i, -li
trigonometr|y ˌtrɪg.ə'nɒm.ɪ.tr|i, '-ə- (US) -'nɑː.mə- **-ies** -iz
trigraph 'traɪ.grɑːf, -græf (US) -græf **-s** -s
trihedral traɪ'hiː.drəl
trike traɪk **-s** -s
trilateral traɪ'læt.ᵊr.ᵊl, '-rᵊl (US) -'læt̬.ɚ.ᵊl, -'læt.rᵊl **-ly** -i **-ness** -nəs, -nɪs
trilb|y (T) 'trɪl.b|i **-ies** -iz
trilingual traɪ'lɪŋ.gwᵊl **-ly** -i
triliteral traɪ'lɪt.ᵊr.ᵊl, '-rᵊl (US) -'lɪt̬.ɚ.ᵊl, -'lɪt.rᵊl
trill trɪl **-s** -z **-ing** -ɪŋ **-ed** -d
Trilling 'trɪl.ɪŋ
trillion 'trɪl.jən, -i.ən (US) '-jən **-s** -z **-th/s** -*t*.θ/s
trilobite 'traɪ.ləʊ.baɪt (US) -loʊ-, -lə- **-s** -s
trilog|y 'trɪl.ə.dʒ|i **-ies** -iz
trim (T) trɪm **-mer/s** -əʳ/z (US) -ɚ/z **-mest** -ɪst, -əst **-ly** -li **-ness** -nəs, -nɪs **-s** -z **-ming/s** -ɪŋ/z **-med** -d
trimaran 'traɪ.mᵊr.æn, ˌ--'- (US) 'traɪ.mə.ræn **-s** -z
Trimble 'trɪm.bl̩
trimester trɪ'mes.təʳ, traɪ- (US) traɪ'mes.tɚ, '--- **-s** -z
trimestral trɪ'mes.trᵊl, traɪ- (US) traɪ-, '---
trimestrial trɪ'mes.tri.əl, traɪ- (US) traɪ-
trimeter 'trɪm.ɪ.təʳ, '-ə- (US) -ə.t̬ɚ **-s** -z
Trincomalee ˌtrɪŋ.kəʊ.mᵊl'iː (US) -koʊ.mə'liː
Trinculo 'trɪŋ.kjə.ləʊ, -kjʊ- (US) -loʊ
Trinder 'trɪn.dəʳ (US) -dɚ
trine (T) traɪn **-s** -z
Tring trɪŋ
Trinidad 'trɪn.ɪ.dæd, '-ə-, ˌ--'- (US) 'trɪn.ɪ.dæd ˌ**Trinidad and To'bago**
Trinidadian ˌtrɪn.ɪ'dæd.i.ən, -ə'-, -'deɪ.di- (US) -ɪ'dæd.i- **-s** -z
Trinitarian ˌtrɪn.ɪ'teə.ri.ən, -ə'- (US) -ɪ'ter.i- **-s** -z **-ism** -ɪ.zᵊm
trinitroglycerin(e) ˌtraɪ.naɪ.trəʊ'glɪs.ᵊr.ɪn, traɪˌnaɪ-, -iːn (US) traɪˌnaɪ.troʊ'glɪs.ɚ.ɪn
trinitrotoluene ˌtraɪ.naɪ.trəʊ'tɒl.ju.iːn, traɪˌnaɪ- (US) traɪˌnaɪ.troʊ'tɑːl-
trinit|y (T) 'trɪn.ə.t|i, -ɪ.t|i (US) -ə.t̬|i **-ies** -iz
trinket 'trɪŋ.kɪt, -kət **-s** -s
trinomial traɪ'nəʊ.mi.əl (US) -'noʊ- **-s** -z
trio 'triː.əʊ (US) -oʊ **-s** -z
triode 'traɪ.əʊd (US) -oʊd **-s** -z
triolet 'triː.əʊ.let, 'traɪ-, 'trɪə.let, -lɪt, -lət (US) 'triː.ə-, 'traɪ- **-s** -s
trioxide traɪ'ɒk.saɪd (US) -'ɑːk- **-s** -z
trip trɪp **-s** -s **-ping/ly** -ɪŋ/li **-ped** -t **-per/s** -əʳ/z (US) -ɚ/z '**trip** ˌ**wire**
tripartite ˌtraɪ'pɑː.taɪt (US) -'pɑːr- **-ly** -li *stress shift:* ˌtripartite 'talks
tripe traɪp

Triphthong

A vowel glide with three distinguishable vowel qualities.

Examples for English

In British English there are said to be five triphthongs, formed by adding /ə/ to the diphthongs /eɪ aɪ ɔɪ aʊ əʊ/. US English treats most of these sequences differently, e.g.:

layer	/leɪəʳ/	(US) /ˈleɪ.ɚ/
liar	/laɪəʳ/	(US) /ˈlaɪ.ɚ/
loyal	/lɔɪəl/	(US) /ˈlɔɪ.əl/
power	/paʊəʳ/	(US) /paʊɚ/
mower	/məʊəʳ/	(US) /ˈmoʊ.ɚ/

There are many other examples of sequences of three vowel qualities, e.g. *play-off* /pleɪɒf/, *reopen* /riəʊpən/, so the five listed above must have some special characteristic. One possibility is that speakers feel them to be one syllable; this may be the case, but there does not seem to be any clear way of proving this. This is a matter which depends to some extent on the accent: many BBC speakers pronounce these sequences almost as pure vowels (prolongations of the first element of the triphthong), so that the word *Ireland*, for example, sounds like /ˈɑː.lənd/. In Lancashire and Yorkshire accents, on the other hand, the middle vowel (/ɪ/ or /ʊ/) is pronounced with such a close vowel quality that it would seem more appropriate to transcribe the triphthongs with /j/ or /w/ in the middle (e.g. *fire* /ˈfaj.ər/), emphasising the disyllabic aspect of their pronunciation.

triphibi|ous traɪˈfɪb.i|.əs **-an/s** -ən/z
triphthong ˈtrɪf.θɒŋ, ˈtrɪp- (US) -θɑːŋ, -θɔːŋ **-s** -z
triphthongal trɪfˈθɒŋ.gᵊl, trɪp- (US) -ˈθɑːŋ-, -ˈθɔːŋ- **-ly** -i
triplane ˈtraɪ.pleɪn **-s** -z
tripl|e ˈtrɪp.l̩ **-y** -i **-es** -z **-ing** -ɪŋ, ˈtrɪp.lɪŋ **-ed** -d **ˈtriple ˌjump, ˌtriple ˈjump**
triplet ˈtrɪp.lət, -lɪt **-s** -s
triplex **(T®)** ˈtrɪp.leks **-es** -ɪz
triplicate *(adj.)* ˈtrɪp.lɪ.kət, -lə-, -kɪt (US) -kɪt
tripli|cate *(v.)* ˈtrɪp.lɪ|.keɪt, -lə- **-cates** -keɪts **-cating** -keɪ.tɪŋ (US) -keɪ.t̬ɪŋ **-cated** -keɪ.tɪd (US) -keɪ.t̬ɪd
triploid ˈtrɪp.lɔɪd **-s** -z **-y** -i
tripod ˈtraɪ.pɒd (US) -pɑːd **-s** -z
Tripoli, **tripoli** ˈtrɪp.ᵊl.i
Tripolitania ˌtrɪp.ᵊl.ɪˈteɪ.ni.ə, -ɒl-; trɪˌpɒl- (US) ˌtrɪp.ᵊl.əˈ-; trɪˌpɑː.ləˈ-
tripos ˈtraɪ.pɒs (US) -pɑːs **-es** -ɪz
Tripp trɪp
triptych ˈtrɪp.tɪk **-s** -s
tripwire ˈtrɪp.waɪəʳ (US) -waɪɚ **-s** -z
trireme ˈtraɪ.riːm **-s** -z
trisect traɪˈsekt **-s** -s **-ing** -ɪŋ **-ed** -ɪd **-or/s** -əʳ/z (US) -ɚ/z
trisection traɪˈsek.ʃᵊn **-s** -z
Trisha ˈtrɪʃ.ə
Tristan ˈtrɪs.tən, -tæn (US) -tən, -tæn, -tɑːn
Tristan da Cunha ˌtrɪs.tən.dəˈkuː.nə, -njə
Tristram ˈtrɪs.trəm, -træm (US) -trəm
trisyllabic ˌtraɪ.sɪˈlæb.ɪk, -səˈ- (US) -sɪˈ- **-al** -ᵊl **-ally** -ᵊl.i, -li
trisyllable traɪˈsɪl.ə.bl̩ **-s** -z
trit|e traɪt **-er** -əʳ (US) ˈtraɪ.t̬ɚ **-est** -ɪst, -əst (US) ˈtraɪ.t̬ɪst, -t̬əst **-ely** -li **-eness** -nəs, -nɪs

tritium ˈtrɪt.i.əm, ˈ-jəm (US) ˈtrɪt̬.i.əm, ˈtrɪʃ-
triton **(T)** *sea god, mollusc:* ˈtraɪ.tɒn, -tᵊn (US) -tᵊn *physics:* ˈtraɪ.tɒn, -tᵊn (US) -tɑːn **-s** -z
tritone ˈtraɪ.təʊn (US) -toʊn **-s** -z
triumph **(T®)** ˈtraɪ.əmpf, -ʌmpf **-s** -s **-ing** -ɪŋ **-ed** -t
triumphal traɪˈʌmp.fᵊl **-ism** -ɪ.zᵊm **-ist/s** -ɪsts
triumphant traɪˈʌmp.fənt **-ly** -li
triumv|ir traɪˈʌm.v|əʳ, tri-, -ˈʊm-, -v|ɪəʳ, -v|ɜːʳ; ˈtraɪ.ʌm-, -əm- (US) traɪˈʌm.v|ɪr, -v|ɚ **-irs** -əz, -ɪəz, -ɜːz (US) -ɪrz, -ɚz **-iri** -ɪˌriː, -ᵊr.iː, -aɪ (US) -ɪˌraɪ
triumvirate traɪˈʌm.vɪ.rət, tri-, -vᵊr.ət, -ɪt (US) traɪˈʌm.vɪ.rɪt, -vɚ.ɪt **-s** -s
triumviri traɪˈʌm.vɪˌriː, tri-, -vᵊr.iː, -aɪ, ˈtraɪ.ʌm-, -əm- (US) traɪˈʌm.vɪˌraɪ, -və-
triune **(T)** ˈtraɪ.uːn (US) -juːn
trivalent traɪˈveɪ.lᵊnt; ˈtrɪv.ᵊl.ᵊnt (US) traɪˈveɪ.lᵊnt, ˌtraɪ-, ˈ---
trivet ˈtrɪv.ɪt **-s** -s
trivia ˈtrɪv.i.ə
trivial ˈtrɪv.i.əl **-ly** -i **-ness** -nəs, -nɪs **ˌTrivial Purˈsuit®**
trivialit|y ˌtrɪv.iˈæl.ə.t|i, -ɪ.t|i (US) -ə.t̬|i **-ies** -iz
trivializ|e, **-is|e** ˈtrɪv.i.ᵊl.aɪz, ˈ-jᵊl- (US) -i.ᵊl- **-es** -ɪz **-ing** -ɪŋ **-ed** -d
trivi|um ˈtrɪv.i|.əm **-a** -ə
Trixie ˈtrɪk.si
trizonal traɪˈzəʊ.nᵊl (US) -ˈzoʊ-
Trizone ˈtraɪ.zəʊn (US) -zoʊn
Troad ˈtrəʊ.æd (US) ˈtroʊ-
Troas ˈtrəʊ.æs (US) ˈtroʊ-
Trocadero ˌtrɒk.əˈdɪə.rəʊ (US) ˌtrɑː.kəˈder.oʊ, ˌtroʊ-

trochaic trəʊˈkeɪ.ɪk, trɒkˈeɪ- (US) troʊˈkeɪ-
troch|e trəʊʃ (US) ˈtroʊ.ki **-es** -ɪz
trochee ˈtrəʊ.kiː, -ki (US) ˈtroʊ- **-s** -z
trod *(from* **tread***)* trɒd (US) trɑːd **-den** -ᵊn
Troed-y-rhiw ˌtrɔɪd.ə.riˈuː
trog trɒg (US) trɑːg, trɔːg **-s** -z **-ging** -ɪŋ **-ged** -d
troglodyte ˈtrɒg.ləʊ.daɪt (US) ˈtrɑː.glə- **-s** -s
troika ˈtrɔɪ.kə **-s** -z
troilism ˈtrɔɪ.lɪ.zᵊm
Troilus ˈtrɔɪ.ləs, ˈtrəʊ.ɪ.ləs (US) ˈtrɔɪ.ləs, ˈtroʊ.ə-
Trojan ˈtrəʊ.dʒᵊn (US) ˈtroʊ- **-s** -z **ˌTrojan ˈhorse; ˌTrojan ˈWar**
troll trəʊl, trɒl (US) troʊl **-s** -z **-ing** -ɪŋ **-ed** -d
trolley ˈtrɒl.i (US) ˈtrɑː.li **-s** -z
trolleybus ˈtrɒl.i.bʌs (US) ˈtrɑː.li- **-es** -ɪz
trollop ˈtrɒl.əp (US) ˈtrɑː.ləp **-s** -s
Trollope ˈtrɒl.əp (US) ˈtrɑː.ləp
Tromans ˈtrəʊ.mənz (US) ˈtroʊ-
trombone trɒmˈbəʊn (US) trɑːmˈboʊn, trəm-; ˈtrɑːm.boʊn **-s** -z
trombonist trɒmˈbəʊ.nɪst (US) trɑːmˈboʊ-, ˈ--- **-s** -s
tromp trɒmp (US) trɑːmp, trɔːmp **-s** -s **-ing** -ɪŋ **-ed** -d
trompe l'oeil ˌtrɒmpˈlɔɪ *as if French:* ˌtrɔ̃ːmpˈlɜː.i (US) ˌtrɔːmpˈlɔɪ **-s** -z
Trondheim ˈtrɒnd.haɪm (US) ˈtrɑːn.heɪm
Troon truːn
troop truːp **-s** -s **-ing** -ɪŋ **-ed** -t **-er/s** -əʳ/z (US) -ɚ/z **ˈtroop ˌcarrier**
trope trəʊp (US) troʊp **-s** -s
trophic ˈtrɒf.ɪk (US) ˈtrɑː.fɪk
troph|y ˈtrəʊ.f|i (US) ˈtroʊ- **-ies** -iz
tropic ˈtrɒp.ɪk (US) ˈtrɑː.pɪk **-s** -s **-al** -ᵊl **-ally** -ᵊl.i, -li **ˌtropic of ˈCancer; ˌtropic of ˈCapricorn**

tropism ˈtrəʊ.pɪ.zᵊm (US) ˈtroʊ- **-s** -z
tropistic trəʊˈpɪs.tɪk (US) troʊ-
troppo ˈtrɒp.əʊ (US) ˈtrɑː.poʊ
Trossachs ˈtrɒs.əks, -æks, -əxs (US) ˈtrɑː.səks, -sæks
trot (T) trɒt (US) trɑːt **-s** -s **-ting** -ɪŋ (US) ˈtrɑː.t̬ɪŋ **-ted** -ɪd (US) ˈtrɑː.t̬ɪd
troth trəʊθ, trɒθ (US) trɑːθ, trɔːθ, troʊθ
Trotsky ˈtrɒt.ski (US) ˈtrɑːt- **-ist/s** -ɪst/s **-ite/s** -aɪt/s **-ism** -ɪ.zᵊm
Trotskyite ˈtrɒt.ski.aɪt (US) ˈtrɑːt- **-s** -s
Trott trɒt (US) trɑːt
trotter (T) ˈtrɒt.əʳ (US) ˈtrɑː.t̬ɚ **-s** -z
Trottiscliffe ˈtrɒz.li, ˈtrɒs- (US) ˈtrɑːz-, ˈtrɑːs-
troubadour ˈtruː.bə.dɔːʳ, -dʊəʳ (US) -dɔːr **-s** -z
troubl|e ˈtrʌb.l̩ **-es** -z **-ing/ly** -ɪŋ/li, ˈtrʌb.lɪŋ/li **-ed** -d **-er/s** -əʳ/z, ˈtrʌb.ləʳ/z (US) ˈ-l̩.ɚ/z, ˈ-lɚ/z ˌ**trouble and ˈstrife**; ˈ**trouble** ˌ**spot**
trouble-free ˌtrʌb.l̩ˈfriː *stress shift:* ˌtrouble-free ˈjourney
troublemaker ˈtrʌb.l̩ˌmeɪ.kəʳ (US) -kɚ **-s** -z
troubleshoot|er ˈtrʌb.l̩ˌʃuː.t|əʳ (US) -t̬|ɚ **-ers** -əz (US) -ɚz **-ing** -ɪŋ
troublesome ˈtrʌb.l̩.səm **-ly** -li **-ness** -nəs, -nɪs
troublous ˈtrʌb.ləs **-ly** -li **-ness** -nəs, -nɪs
Troubridge ˈtruː.brɪdʒ
trough trɒf (US) trɑːf, trɔːf **-s** -s
Note: Some bakers pronounce /traʊ/.
Troughton ˈtraʊ.tᵊn, ˈtrɔː-
trounc|e traʊn*t*s **-es** -ɪz **-ing/s** -ɪŋ/z **-ed** -t
Troup truːp
troup|e truːp **-es** -s **-er/s** -əʳ/z (US) -ɚ/z
trouper ˈtruː.pəʳ (US) -pɚ **-s** -z
trouser ˈtraʊ.zəʳ (US) -zɚ ˈ**trouser** ˌ**press**; ˈ**trouser** ˌ**suit**
trousers ˈtraʊ.zəz (US) -zɚz
trousseau ˈtruː.səʊ, -ˈ- (US) ˈtruː.soʊ, -ˈ- **-s** -z **-x** -z
trout traʊt **-s** -s
trove trəʊv (US) troʊv
trover ˈtrəʊ.vəʳ (US) ˈtroʊ.vɚ
trow trəʊ, traʊ (US) troʊ
Trowbridge ˈtrəʊ.brɪdʒ (US) ˈtroʊ-
trowel traʊəl **-s** -z **-(l)ing** -ɪŋ **-(l)ed** -d
Trowell trəʊəl, traʊəl (US) troʊəl, traʊəl
troy (T) trɔɪ
truancy ˈtruː.ən*t*.si
truant ˈtruː.ənt **-s** -s **-ing** -ɪŋ **-ed** -ɪd
Trübner ˈtruːb.nəʳ (US) -nɚ
truc|e truːs **-es** -ɪz
trucial (T) ˈtruː.ʃᵊl (US) ˈ-ʃᵊl
truck trʌk **-s** -s **-ing** -ɪŋ **-ed** -t **-age** -ɪdʒ **-er/s** -əʳ/z (US) -ɚ/z ˈ**truck** ˌ**stop**
truckl|e ˈtrʌk.l̩ **-es** -z **-ing** -ɪŋ, ˈtrʌk.lɪŋ **-ed** -d ˈ**truckle** ˌ**bed**
truckload ˈtrʌk.ləʊd (US) -loʊd **-s** -z
truculen|ce ˈtrʌk.jə.lᵊn*t*|s, -jʊ- **-cy** -si
truculent ˈtrʌk.jə.lᵊnt, -jʊ- **-ly** -li
Trudeau ˈtruː.dəʊ (US) truːˈdoʊ, ˈ--
trudg|e trʌdʒ **-es** -ɪz **-ing** -ɪŋ **-ed** -d **-er/s** -əʳ/z (US) -ɚ/z
trudgen (T) ˈtrʌdʒ.ᵊn
Trudgill ˈtrʌd.gɪl
Trudy, Trudi ˈtruː.di
tru|e (T) truː **-er** -əʳ (US) -ɚ **-est** -ɪst, -əst **-ly** -li **-eness** -nəs, -nɪs
true-blue ˌtruːˈbluː **-s** -z *stress shift:* ˌtrue-blue ˈTory
trueborn ˈtruː.bɔːn (US) -bɔːrn
Truefitt ˈtruː.fɪt
truehearted ˌtruːˈhɑː.tɪd (US) ˈtruːˌhɑːr.t̬ɪd **-ness** -nəs, -nɪs *stress shift, British only:* ˌtruehearted ˈperson
true-life ˌtruːˈlaɪf *stress shift:* ˌtrue-life ˈstory
truelove ˈtruː.lʌv
Trueman ˈtruː.mən
Truffaut ˈtruː.fəʊ, ˈtrʊf.əʊ (US) truːˈfoʊ
truffle ˈtrʌf.l̩ **-s** -z **-d** -d
trug trʌg **-s** -z
truism ˈtruː.ɪ.zᵊm **-s** -z
Trujillo trʊˈhiː.jəʊ (US) truːˈhiː.joʊ
Truk trʌk, trʊk
truly ˈtruː.li
Truman ˈtruː.mən
Trumbull ˈtrʌm.bʊl (US) -bʊl, -bᵊl
trump (T) trʌmp **-s** -s **-ing** -ɪŋ **-ed** -t ˈ**trump** ˌ**card**, ˌ**trump** ˈ**card**
trumped-up ˌtrʌmptˈʌp *stress shift:* ˌtrumped-up ˈcharges
Trumper ˈtrʌm.pəʳ (US) -pɚ
trumpery ˈtrʌm.pᵊr.i
trum|pet ˈtrʌm|.pɪt (US) -pət **-pets** -pɪts (US) -pəts **-peting/s** -pɪ.tɪŋ/z (US) -pə.t̬ɪŋ/z **-peted** -pɪ.tɪd (US) -pə.t̬ɪd **-peter/s** -pɪ.təʳ/z (US) -pə.t̬ɚ/z ˌ**blow one's** ˌ**own** ˈ**trumpet**
trunca|te trʌŋˈkeɪ|t, ˈ-- (US) ˈtrʌŋ.keɪ|t, ˈtrʌn- **-tes** -ts **-ting** -tɪŋ (US) -t̬ɪŋ **-ted** -tɪd (US) -t̬ɪd
truncation trʌŋˈkeɪ.ʃᵊn (US) trʌŋ-, trʌn- **-s** -z
truncheon ˈtrʌn.*t*ʃᵊn (US) ˈtrʌn*t*.ʃᵊn **-s** -z **-ing** -ɪŋ **-ed** -d
trundl|e ˈtrʌn.dl̩ **-es** -z **-ing** -ɪŋ, ˈtrʌnd.lɪŋ **-ed** -d **-er/s** -əʳ/z (US) -ɚ/z
trunk trʌŋk **-s** -s **-ful/s** -fʊl/z ˈ**trunk** ˌ**call**; ˈ**trunk** ˌ**road**
trunnion ˈtrʌn.i.ən, ˈ-jən (US) ˈ-jən **-s** -z **-ed** -d
Truro ˈtrʊə.rəʊ (US) ˈtrʊr.oʊ
Truscott ˈtrʌs.kət (US) -kət, -kɑːt
Truslove ˈtrʌs.lʌv
truss trʌs **-es** -ɪz **-ing** -ɪŋ **-ed** -t
trust trʌst **-s** -s **-ing/ly** -ɪŋ/li **-ed** -ɪd ˈ**trust** ˌ**fund**
trustee trʌsˈtiː **-s** -z
trusteeship trʌsˈtiː.ʃɪp **-s** -s
trustful ˈtrʌst.fᵊl, -fʊl **-ly** -i **-ness** -nəs, -nɪs
Trusthouse Forte® ˌtrʌst.haʊsˈfɔː.teɪ (US) -ˈfɔːr-
trustworth|y ˈtrʌstˌwɜː.ðli (US) -ˌwɝː- **-iness** -ɪ.nəs, -ɪ.nɪs
trust|y ˈtrʌs.t|i **-ier** -i.əʳ (US) -i.ɚ **-iest** -i.ɪst, -i.əst **-ily** -ɪ.li, -ᵊl.i **-iness** -ɪ.nəs, -ɪ.nɪs
tru|th truː|θ **-ths** -ðz, -θs ˈ**truth** ˌ**drug**
truthful ˈtruːθ.fᵊl, -fʊl **-ly** -i **-ness** -nəs, -nɪs
tr|y tr|aɪ **-ies** -aɪz **-ying/ly** -aɪ.ɪŋ/li **-ied** -aɪd **-ier/s** -aɪ.əʳ/z (US) -aɪ.ɚ/z
Tryon traɪən
try-on ˈtraɪ.ɒn (US) -ɑːn **-s** -z
tryout ˈtraɪ.aʊt **-s** -s
trypanosome ˈtrɪp.ə.nəʊ.səʊm; trɪˈpæn.ə- (US) trɪˈpæn.ə.soʊm; ˈtrɪp.ə.noʊ- **-s** -z
trypanosomiasis ˌtrɪp.ə.nəʊ.səʊˈmaɪ.ə.sɪs; trɪˌpæn.əʊ- (US) trɪˌpæn.ə.soʊˈ-; ˌtrɪp.ə.noʊ-;
trypsin ˈtrɪp.sɪn
trypsinogen trɪpˈsɪn.ə.dʒᵊn (US) ˈ-oʊ-
tryst trɪst **-s** -s **-ing** -ɪŋ **-ed** -ɪd
Trystan ˈtrɪs.tæn, -tən
tsar (T) zɑːʳ, tsɑːʳ (US) zɑːr, tsɑːr **-s** -z
tsarevitch, tsarevich (T) ˈzɑː.rə.vɪtʃ, ˈtsɑː-, -rɪ- (US) ˈzɑːr.ə-, ˈtsɑːr- **-es** -ɪz
tsarina (T) zɑːˈriː.nə, tsɑː- **-s** -z
tsarism ˈzɑː.rɪ.zᵊm, ˈtsɑː- (US) ˈzɑːr.ɪ-, ˈtsɑːr-
tsarist ˈzɑː.rɪst, ˈtsɑː- (US) ˈzɑːr.ɪst, ˈtsɑːr- **-s** -s
TSB® ˌtiː.esˈbiː
tsetse ˈtet.si, ˈtset- (US) ˈtset-, ˈtsiːt-, ˈtet-, ˈtiːt- **-s** -z ˈ**tsetse** ˌ**fly**
T-shirt ˈtiː.ʃɜːt (US) -ʃɝːt **-s** -s
tsk *(interj.)* tɪsk
Note: This spelling represents the tongue click used (usually repeated) to indicate disapproval; it may be described as a voiceless affricated alveolar click, symbolized as [!Ús]. The transcription given above is only used in mock disapproval. See also **tut**.
tsp *(abbrev. for* **teaspoon, teaspoonful***)* ˈtiː.spuːn, ˈtiː.spuːn.fʊl
T-square ˈtiː.skweəʳ (US) -skwer **-s** -z
tsunam|i tsʊˈnɑː.m|i, sʊ-, -ˈnæm|.i (US) tsuːˈnɑː.m|i **-is** -iz **-ic** -ɪk
Tswana ˈtswɑː.nə, ˈswɑː- **-s** -z
TT ˌtiːˈtiː ˌ**T'T** ˌ**races**
Tuamotu ˌtuː.əˈməʊ.tuː (US) -ˈmoʊ-

Tuareg ˈtwɑː.reg ⓤⓢ ˈtwɑːr.eg **-s** -z
tub tʌb **-s** -z **-bing** -ɪŋ **-bed** -d
tuba ˈtjuː.bə, ˈtʃuː- ⓤⓢ ˈtuː-, ˈtjuː- **-s** -z
tubb|y ˈtʌb|.i **-ier** -i.əʳ ⓤⓢ -i.ɚ **-iest** -i.ɪst, -i.əst **-iness** -ɪ.nəs, -ɪ.nɪs
tube tjuːb, tʃuːb ⓤⓢ tuːb, tjuːb **-s** -z
tubeless ˈtjuː.bləs, ˈtʃuː-, -blɪs ⓤⓢ ˈtuː-, ˈtjuː-
tuber ˈtjuː.bəʳ ⓤⓢ ˈtuː.bɚ, ˈtjuː- **-s** -z
tubercle ˈtjuː.bə.kl̩, -bɜː- ⓤⓢ ˈtuː.bɚ-, ˈtjuː- **-s** -z
tubercular tjuːˈbɜː.kjə.ləʳ, tjʊ-, -kjʊ- ⓤⓢ tuːˈbɝː.kjə.lɚ, tjuː-, tə-, -kjʊ-
tuberculin tjuːˈbɜː.kjə.lɪn, tjʊ-, -kjʊ- ⓤⓢ tuːˈbɝː-, tjuː-, tə-
tuberculization, -isa- tjuːˌbɜː.kjə.laɪˈzeɪ.ʃᵊn, tjʊ-, -kjʊ-, -lɪˈ- ⓤⓢ tuːˌbɝː.kjə.lɪˈ-, tjuː-, tə-, -kjʊ-
tuberculiz|e, -is|e tjuːˈbɜː.kjə.laɪz, tjʊ-, -kjʊ- ⓤⓢ tuːˈbɝː-, tjuː-, tə- **-es** -ɪz **-ing** -ɪŋ **-ed** -d
tuberculoid tjuːˈbɜː.kjə.lɔɪd, tjʊ-, -kjʊ- ⓤⓢ tuːˈbɝː-, tjuː-, tə-
tuberculosis tjuːˌbɜː.kjəˈləʊ.sɪs, tjʊ-, -kjʊ- ⓤⓢ tuːˌbɝː.kjəˈloʊ-, tjuː-, tə-, -kjʊ-
tuberculous tjuːˈbɜː.kjə.ləs, tjʊ-, -kjʊ- ⓤⓢ tuːˈbɝː-, tjuː-, tə-
tuberose *(n.)* ˈtjuː.bᵊr.əʊz ⓤⓢ ˈtuː.broʊz, ˈtjuː-, -bə.roʊz
tuberose *(adj.)* ˈtjuː.bᵊr.əʊs ⓤⓢ ˈtuː.bə.roʊs, ˈtjuː-
tuberous ˈtjuː.bᵊr.əs ⓤⓢ ˈtuː-, ˈtjuː-
tubful ˈtʌb.fʊl **-s** -z
tubiform ˈtjuː.bɪ.fɔːm, ˈtʃuː- ⓤⓢ ˈtuː.bɪ.fɔːrm, ˈtjuː-
tubing ˈtjuː.bɪŋ, ˈtʃuː- ⓤⓢ ˈtuː-, ˈtjuː- **-s** -z
Tübingen ˈtuː.bɪŋ.ən, ˈtjuː-
tub-thump|ing ˈtʌbˌθʌm.p|ɪŋ **-er/s** -əʳ/z ⓤⓢ -ɚ/z
Tubuai ˌtuː.buˈaɪ
tubular ˈtjuː.bjə.ləʳ, ˈtʃuː-, -bjʊ- ⓤⓢ ˈtuː.bjə.lɚ, ˈtjuː-, -bjʊ-
tubule ˈtjuː.bjuːl, ˈtʃuː- ⓤⓢ ˈtuː-, ˈtjuː- **-s** -z
TUC ˌtiː.juːˈsiː
tuck (T) tʌk **-s** -s **-ing** -ɪŋ **-ed** -t
tucker (T) ˈtʌk.əʳ ⓤⓢ -ɚ **-s** -z
tuck-shop ˈtʌk.ʃɒp ⓤⓢ -ʃɑːp **-s** -s
Tucson ˈtuː.sɒn ⓤⓢ ˈtuː.sɑːn
Tudjman ˈtʊdʒ.mən, ˈtʊdz-, ˈtʌdʒ-
Tudor ˈtjuː.dəʳ, ˈtʃuː- ⓤⓢ ˈtuː.dɚ, ˈtjuː- **-s** -z
Tue. *(abbrev. for* **Tuesday***)* ˈtjuːz.deɪ, ˈtʃuːz-, -di ⓤⓢ ˈtuːz-, ˈtjuːz-
Note: This abbreviation may also be pronounced /tjuː/ in British English.
Tues. *(abbrev. for* **Tuesday***)* ˈtjuːz.deɪ, ˈtʃuːz-, -di ⓤⓢ ˈtuːz-, ˈtjuːz-
Note: This abbreviation may also be pronounced /tjuːz/ in British English.
Tuesday ˈtjuːz.deɪ, ˈtʃuːz-, -di ⓤⓢ ˈtuːz-, ˈtjuːz- **-s** -z
tufa ˈtjuː.fə ⓤⓢ ˈtuː-, ˈtjuː-
tuffet ˈtʌf.ɪt, -ət **-s** -s
Tufnell ˈtʌf.nᵊl ˌ**Tufnell** ˈ**Park**
tuft tʌft **-s** -s **-ing** -ɪŋ **-ed** -ɪd
tuft|y ˈtʌf.t|i **-ier** -i.əʳ ⓤⓢ -i.ɚ **-iest** -i.ɪst, -i.əst **-iness** -ɪ.nəs, -ɪ.nɪs
tug tʌg **-s** -z **-ging** -ɪŋ **-ged** -d **-ger/s** -əʳ/z ⓤⓢ -ɚ/z
tugboat ˈtʌg.bəʊt ⓤⓢ -boʊt **-s** -s
tug-of-love ˌtʌg.əvˈlʌv
tug-of-war ˌtʌg.əvˈwɔːʳ ⓤⓢ -ˈwɔːr **-s** -z **tugs-of-war** ˌtʌgz.əvˈwɔːʳ ⓤⓢ -ˈwɔːr
tugrik ˈtuː.griːk **-s** -s
Tuileries ˈtwiː.lᵊr.iː, -i ⓤⓢ -iː, -i, -iz
tuition tjuˈɪʃ.ᵊn ⓤⓢ tu-, tju- **-s** -z **-al** -ᵊl
Tuke tjuːk ⓤⓢ tuːk, tjuːk
tulip ˈtjuː.lɪp, ˈtʃuː- ⓤⓢ ˈtuː-, ˈtjuː- **-s** -s
Tull tʌl
tulle tjuːl ⓤⓢ tuːl **-s** -z
Tulloch ˈtʌl.ək, -əx ⓤⓢ -ək
Tully ˈtʌl.i
Tulsa ˈtʌl.sə
Tulse tʌls
tum tʌm **-s** -z
tumbl|e ˈtʌm.bl̩ **-es** -z **-ing** -ɪŋ, -blɪŋ **-ed** -d **-er/s** -əʳ/z ⓤⓢ -ɚ/z
tumbledown (T) ˈtʌm.bl̩.daʊn
tumble-drier, tumble-dryer ˌtʌm.bl̩ˈdraɪ.əʳ, ˈtʌm.bl̩ˌdraɪ- ⓤⓢ -ɚ **-s** -z
tumble-dr|y ˌtʌm.bl̩ˈdr|aɪ, ˈ--- **-ies** -aɪz **-ying** -aɪ.ɪŋ **-ied** -aɪd
tumbler ˈtʌm.bləʳ, ˈ-bl̩.əʳ ⓤⓢ ˈ-blɚ, ˈ-bl̩.ɚ **-s** -z **-ful/s** -fʊl/z
tumbleweed ˈtʌm.bl̩.wiːd
tumbrel ˈtʌm.brᵊl **-s** -z
tumbril ˈtʌm.brɪl, -brᵊl **-s** -z
tumefaction ˌtjuː.mɪˈfæk.ʃᵊn, -məˈ- ⓤⓢ ˌtuː.məˈ-, ˌtjuː-
tume|fy ˈtjuː.mɪ|.faɪ, -mə- ⓤⓢ ˈtuː.mə-, ˈtjuː- **-fies** -faɪz **-fying** -faɪ.ɪŋ **-fied** -faɪd
tumescen|t tjuːˈmes.ᵊn|t, tjʊ- ⓤⓢ tuː-, tjuː- **-ce** -*t*s
tumid ˈtjuː.mɪd ⓤⓢ ˈtuː-, ˈtjuː- **-ly** -li
tumidity tjuːˈmɪd.ə.ti, tjʊ-, -ɪ.ti ⓤⓢ tuːˈmɪd.ə.t̬i, tjuː-
Tummel ˈtʌm.ᵊl
tumm|y ˈtʌm|.i **-ies** -iz ˈ**tummy** ˌ**ache**; ˈ**tummy** ˌ**button**
tumo(u)r ˈtjuː.məʳ, ˈtʃuː- ⓤⓢ ˈtuː.mɚ, ˈtjuː- **-s** -z
tumo(u)rous ˈtjuː.mᵊr.əs, ˈtʃuː- ⓤⓢ ˈtuː-, ˈtjuː-
tumult ˈtjuː.mʌlt, -məlt ⓤⓢ ˈtuː-, ˈtjuː- **-s** -s
tumultuous tjuːˈmʌl.tju.əs, tjʊ- ⓤⓢ tuːˈmʌl.tʃuː.əs, tjuː-, tə-, -tʃə.wəs **-ly** -li **-ness** -nəs, -nɪs
tumul|us ˈtjuː.mjə.l|əs, -mju- ⓤⓢ ˈtuː-, ˈtjuː- **-i** -aɪ
tun tʌn **-s** -z
tuna ˈtjuː.nə, ˈtuː- ⓤⓢ ˈtuː-, ˈtjuː- **-s** -z ˈ**tuna** ˌ**fish**
Tunbridge ˈtʌn.brɪdʒ, ˈtʌm- ⓤⓢ ˈtʌn- ˌ**Tunbridge** ˈ**Wells**
tundra ˈtʌn.drə **-s** -z
tun|e tjuːn, tʃuːn ⓤⓢ tuːn, tjuːn **-es** -z **-ing** -ɪŋ **-ed** -d **-er/s** -əʳ/z ⓤⓢ -ɚ/z ˈ**tuning** ˌ**fork**; ˈ**tuning** ˌ**peg**; ˌ**change one's** ˈ**tune**
tuneful ˈtjuːn.fᵊl, ˈtʃuːn-, -fʊl ⓤⓢ ˈtuːn-, ˈtjuːn- **-ly** -i **-ness** -nəs, -nɪs
tuneless ˈtjuːn.ləs, ˈtʃuːn-, -lɪs ⓤⓢ ˈtuːn-, ˈtjuːn- **-ly** -li **-ness** -nəs, -nɪs
tunesmith ˈtjuːn.smɪθ, ˈtʃuːn- ⓤⓢ ˈtuːn-, ˈtjuːn- **-s** -s
tungsten ˈtʌŋ*k*.stən
tunic ˈtjuː.nɪk, ˈtʃuː- ⓤⓢ ˈtuː-, ˈtjuː- **-s** -s
tunicle ˈtjuː.nɪ.kl̩ ⓤⓢ ˈtuː-, ˈtjuː- **-s** -z
Tunis ˈtjuː.nɪs ⓤⓢ ˈtuː-, ˈtjuː-
Tunisi|a tjuːˈnɪz.i|.ə, tjʊ-, -ˈnɪs- ⓤⓢ tuːˈniː.ʒ|ə, tjuː-, -ˈnɪʒ|.ə, -ˈnɪʃ|.ə **-an/s** -ən/z
Tunnard ˈtʌn.əd ⓤⓢ -ɚd
tunnel ˈtʌn.ᵊl **-s** -z **-(l)ing** -ɪŋ **-(l)ed** -d **-(l)er/s** -əʳ/z ⓤⓢ -ɚ/z ˌ**tunnel** ˈ**vision**; ˌ**light at the** ˌ**end of the** ˈ**tunnel**
Tunnicliff(e) ˈtʌn.ɪ.klɪf
tunn|y ˈtʌn|.i **-ies** -iz
Tunstall ˈtʌn*t*.stᵊl, -stɔːl
Tuoh(e)y ˈtuː.i, -hi
Tupman ˈtʌp.mən
tuppenc|e ˈtʌp.ᵊn*t*s, -ᵊm*p*s **-es** -ɪz
tuppenny ˈtʌp.ᵊn.i, ˈ-ni
tuppeny ˈtʌp.ᵊn.i, ˈ-ni
Tupperware® ˈtʌp.ə.weəʳ ⓤⓢ -ɚ.wer
tuque tjuːk ⓤⓢ tuːk, tjuːk **-s** -s
tu quoque ˌtuːˈkwəʊ.kwi, -ˈkwɒk.weɪ ⓤⓢ ˌtuːˈkwoʊ.kwi, ˌtjuː-, -kweɪ **-s** -z
Turandot ˈtʊə.rən.dɒt, ˈtjʊə-, -dəʊ ⓤⓢ ˈtʊr.ən.dɑːt, -doʊ
Turani|a tjʊəˈreɪ.ni|.ə ⓤⓢ tʊˈreɪ-, tjʊ-, -ˈrɑː- **-an/s** -ən/z
turban ˈtɜː.bən ⓤⓢ ˈtɝː- **-s** -z **-(n)ed** -d
turbid ˈtɜː.bɪd ⓤⓢ ˈtɝː- **-ly** -li **-ness** -nəs, -nɪs
turbidity tɜːˈbɪd.ə.ti, -ɪ.ti ⓤⓢ tɝːˈbɪd.ə.t̬i
turbine ˈtɜː.baɪn, -bɪn ⓤⓢ ˈtɝː.bɪn, -baɪn **-s** -z
turbo ˈtɜː.bəʊ ⓤⓢ ˈtɝː.boʊ **-s** -z
turbocharg|e ˈtɜː.bəʊ.tʃɑːdʒ ⓤⓢ ˈtɝː.boʊ.tʃɑːrdʒ **-es** -ɪz **-ing** -ɪŋ **-ed** -d **-er/s** -əʳ/z ⓤⓢ -ɚ/z
turbofan ˈtɜː.bəʊ.fæn ⓤⓢ ˈtɝː.boʊ- **-s** -z

turbo-jet 'tɜː.bəʊ.dʒet, ˌ--'- (US) 'tɝː.boʊ.dʒet **-s** -s

turbo-prop 'tɜː.bəʊ.prɒp, ˌ--'- (US) 'tɝː.boʊ.prɑːp **-s** -s

turbot 'tɜː.bət (US) 'tɝː- **-s** -s

turbulence 'tɜː.bjə.lənts, -jʊ- (US) 'tɝː-

turbulent 'tɜː.bjə.lənt, -bjʊ- (US) 'tɝː- **-ly** -li

Turco- 'tɜː.kəʊ- (US) 'tɝː.koʊ-, -kə-

Turcoman 'tɜː.kəʊ.mən, -mæn, -mɑːn (US) 'tɝː.koʊ.mən, -kə- **-s** -z

turd tɜːd (US) tɝːd **-s** -z

tureen tjʊ'riːn, tjə-, tə-, tʊ- (US) tʊ-, tjʊ- **-s** -z

tur|f tɜː|f (US) tɝː|f **-fs** -fs **-ves** -vz **-ing** -ɪŋ **-ed** -t **'turf acˌcountant**

turf (*v.*) tɜːf (US) tɝːf **-s** -s **-ing** -ɪŋ **-ed** -t

Turgenev tɜː'geɪ.njev, tʊə-, -'gen.jev, -jef, -jɪf, -ev, -əv (US) tʊr'geɪ.nəf, tɝː-, -gen-, -njef, -njev

turgescen|ce tɜː'dʒes.ᵊn|ts **-t** -t

turgid 'tɜː.dʒɪd (US) 'tɝː- **-ly** -li **-ness** -nəs, -nɪs

turgidity tɜː'dʒɪd.ə.ti, -ɪ.ti (US) tɝː'dʒɪd.ə.t̬i

turgor 'tɜː.gəʳ (US) 'tɝː.gɚ

Turin tjʊə'rɪn (US) tʊ-, tjʊ- *stress shift, see compound:* **ˌTurin 'Shroud**

Turing 'tjʊə.rɪŋ (US) 'tʊr.ɪŋ, 'tjʊr-

Turk tɜːk (US) tɝːk **-s** -s

Turkestan ˌtɜː.kɪ'stɑːn, -kə'-, -stæn (US) 'tɝː.kɪ.stæn, -stɑːn

turkey (T) 'tɜː.ki (US) 'tɝː- **-s** -z

turkey-cock 'tɜː.ki.kɒk (US) 'tɝː.ki.kɑːk **-s** -s

Turki 'tɜː.kiː, -ki (US) 'tɝː-

Turkic 'tɜː.kɪk (US) 'tɝː-

Turkington 'tɜː.kɪŋ.tən (US) 'tɝː-

Turkish 'tɜː.kɪʃ (US) 'tɝː- **ˌTurkish 'bath; ˌTurkish de'light**

Turkmenia tɜːk'miː.ni.ə (US) tɝːk-

Turkmenistan tɜːkˌmen.ɪ'stɑːn, -'stæn (US) tɝːk'men.ɪ.stæn, -stɑːn

Turko- 'tɜː.kəʊ- (US) 'tɝː.koʊ-, -kə-

Turkoman 'tɜːk.əʊ.mən, -mæn, -mɑːn (US) 'tɝː.koʊ.mən, -kə- **-s** -z

Turku 'tʊə.kuː, 'tɜː- (US) 'tʊr-

Turley 'tɜː.li (US) 'tɝː-

turmeric 'tɜː.mᵊr.ɪk (US) 'tɝː-

turmoil 'tɜː.mɔɪl (US) 'tɝː-

turn tɜːn (US) tɝːn **-s** -z **-ing** -ɪŋ **-ed** -d **-er/s** -əʳ/z (US) -ɚ/z **'turning ˌpoint; ˌturn of 'phrase**

turnabout 'tɜːn.əˌbaʊt (US) 'tɝːn- **-s** -s

Turnage 'tɜː.nɪdʒ (US) tɝː-

turnaround 'tɜːn.ᵊr'aʊnd (US) 'tɝːn.ɚ- **-s** -z

Turnbull 'tɜːn.bʊl, 'tɜːm- (US) 'tɝːn-, -bᵊl

turncoat 'tɜːn.kəʊt, 'tɜːŋ- (US) 'tɝːn.koʊt **-s** -s

turned-on ˌtɜːnd'ɒn (US) ˌtɝːnd'ɑːn

turner (T) 'tɜː.nəʳ (US) 'tɝː.nɚ **-s** -z

turnery 'tɜː.nᵊr.i (US) 'tɝː-

Turnham 'tɜː.nəm (US) 'tɝː-

Turnhouse 'tɜːn.haʊs (US) 'tɝːn-

turning 'tɜː.nɪŋ (US) 'tɝː- **-s** -z

turning-point 'tɜː.nɪŋ.pɔɪnt (US) 'tɝː- **-s** -s

turnip 'tɜː.nɪp (US) 'tɝː- **-s** -s

turnkey 'tɜːn.kiː, 'tɜːŋ- (US) 'tɝːn- **-s** -z

turn-off 'tɜːn.ɒf (US) 'tɝːn.ɑːf **-s** -s

turn-on 'tɜːn.ɒn (US) 'tɝːn.ɑːn **-s** -z

turnout 'tɜːn.aʊt (US) 'tɝːn- **-s** -s

turnover 'tɜːnˌəʊ.vəʳ (US) 'tɝːnˌoʊ.vɚ **-s** -z

turnpike 'tɜːn.paɪk, 'tɜːm- (US) 'tɝːn- **-s** -s

turnround 'tɜːn.raʊnd (US) 'tɝːn- **-s** -z

turnstile 'tɜːn.staɪl (US) 'tɝːn- **-s** (US) -z

turnstone 'tɜːn.stəʊn (US) 'tɝːn.stoʊn **-s** -z

turntable 'tɜːnˌteɪ.bl̩ (US) 'tɝːn- **-s** -z

turn-up 'tɜːn.ʌp (US) 'tɝːn- **-s** -s

turpentine 'tɜː.pᵊn.taɪn, -pᵊm- (US) 'tɝː.pᵊn-

Turpin 'tɜː.pɪn (US) 'tɝː-

turpitude 'tɜː.pɪ.tjuːd, -tʃuːd (US) 'tɝː.pɪ.tuːd, -tjuːd

turps tɜːps (US) tɝːps

turquois|e 'tɜː.kwɑːz, -kwɔɪz (US) 'tɝː.kwɔɪz, -kɔɪz **-es** -ɪz

turre|t 'tʌr.ɪ|t, -ə|t (US) 'tɝː.ɪ|t **-ts** -ts **-ted** -tɪd (US) -t̬ɪd

turtle 'tɜː.tl̩ (US) 'tɝː.t̬l̩ **-s** -z

turtledove 'tɜː.tl̩.dʌv (US) 'tɝː.t̬l̩- **-s** -z

turtleneck 'tɜː.tl̩.nek (US) 'tɝː.t̬l̩- **-s** -s

Turton 'tɜː.tᵊn (US) 'tɝː-

turves (*plur. of* **turf**) tɜːvz (US) tɝːvz

Tuscan 'tʌs.kən **-s** -z

Tuscany 'tʌs.kə.ni

tush (*interj.*) tʌʃ

tush *tooth:* tʌʃ **-es** -ɪz

tush *buttocks:* tʊʃ **-es** -ɪz

tusk tʌsk **-s** -s **-ed** -t

tusker 'tʌs.kəʳ (US) -kɚ **-s** -z

tussah 'tʌs.ə

Tussaud *surname:* 'tuː.səʊ (US) tuː'soʊ

Tussaud's *exhibition:* tʊ'sɔːdz, tjʊ-, tə-, -'səʊdz, -'səʊz (US) tʊ'soʊz, tə-, -'sɑːd, -'sɔːd; 'tuː.soʊz

Tusser 'tʌs.əʳ (US) -ɚ

tussl|e 'tʌs.l̩ **-es** -z **-ing** -ɪŋ, 'tʌs.lɪŋ **-ed** -d **-er/s** -əʳ/z (US) -ɚ/z

tussock 'tʌs.ək **-s** -s **-y** -i

tussore 'tʌs.əʳ, -ɔːʳ (US) -ɚ

tut tʌt **-s** -s **-ting** -ɪŋ (US) 'tʌt̬.ɪŋ **-ted** -ɪd (US) 'tʌt̬.ɪd

tut (*interj.*) tʌt

Note: This spelling represents the tongue click used (usually repeated - see **tut-tut**) to indicate disapproval; it may be described as a voiceless affricated alveolar click, symbolised as [ǃˢ].

Tutankhamen, Tutankhamon ˌtuː.tᵊn'kɑː.mən, -təŋ-, -tæŋ-, -tɑːŋ-, -kɑː'muːn

Tutbury 'tʌt.bᵊr.i (US) -ber-, -bɚ-

tutee ˌtjuː'tiː, ˌtʃuː- (US) ˌtuː-, ˌtjuː- **-s** -z

tutelage 'tjuː.tɪ.lɪdʒ, -tᵊl.ɪdʒ (US) 'tuː.t̬ᵊl.ɪdʒ, 'tjuː-

tutelar 'tjuː.tᵊl.əʳ (US) 'tuː.t̬ᵊl.ɚ, 'tjuː-

tutelary 'tjuː.tᵊl.ᵊr.i (US) 'tuː.t̬ᵊl.er.i, 'tjuː-

Tutin 'tjuː.tɪn (US) 'tuː-, 'tjuː-

tut|or 'tjuː.t|əʳ, 'tʃuː- (US) 'tuː.t̬|ɚ, 'tjuː- **-ors** -əz (US) -ɚz **-oring** -ᵊr.ɪŋ **-ored** -əd (US) -ɚd **-orage** -ᵊr.ɪdʒ

tutorial tjuː'tɔː.ri.əl, tjʊ-, tʃuː-, tʃʊ- (US) tuː'tɔːr.i-, tjuː- **-s** -z **-ly** -i

tutorship 'tjuː.tə.ʃɪp, 'tʃuː- (US) 'tuː.t̬ɚ-, 'tjuː- **-s** -s

Tutsi 'tʊt.si **-s** -z

tutti 'tʊt.i, 'tuː.ti, -tiː (US) 'tuː.t̬i **-s** -z

tutti-frutti ˌtuː.ti'fruː.ti, ˌtʊt.i'-, -'frʊt.i (US) ˌtuː.t̬i'fruː.t̬i **-s** -z

Tuttle 'tʌt.l̩ (US) 'tʌt̬-

tut|-tut ˌtʌt|'tʌt **-tuts** -'tʌts **-tutting** -'tʌt.ɪŋ (US) -'tʌt̬.ɪŋ **-tutted** -'tʌt.ɪd (US) -'tʌt̬.ɪd

tutu (T) 'tuː.tuː **-s** -z

Tuvalu tuː'vɑː.luː; 'tuː.və- (US) ˌtuː.və'luː; tuː'vɑː.luː

tu-whit tu-whoo tʊˌ*h*wɪt.tʊ'*h*wuː, tə-, -tə'-

tux tʌks **-es** -ɪz

tuxedo (T) tʌk'siː.dəʊ (US) -doʊ **-(e)s** -z

Tuxford 'tʌks.fəd (US) -fɚd

Tuzla 'tʊz.lə, 'tuːz- (US) 'tuːz.lɑː

TV ˌtiː'viː **-s** -z **ˌTV 'dinner; ˌT'V ˌprogram(me)**

Twaddell 'twɒd.ᵊl; twɒd'el (US) twɑː'del; 'twɑː.dᵊl

twaddl|e 'twɒd.l̩ (US) 'twɑː.dl̩ **-es** -z **-ing** -ɪŋ, 'twɒd.lɪŋ (US) 'twɑːd- **-ed** -d **-er/s** -əʳ/z, 'twɒd.ləʳ/z (US) 'twɑː.dl̩.ɚ/z, 'twɑːd.lɚ/z **-y** -i, 'twɒd.li (US) 'twɑː.dl̩.i, 'twɑːd.li

twain (T) tweɪn

twang twæŋ **-s** -z **-ing** -ɪŋ **-ed** -d **-y** -i

Twank(e)y 'twæŋ.ki

'twas *strong form:* twɒz (US) twɑːz *weak form:* twəz

twat twæt, twɒt (US) twɑːt **-s** -s

tweak twiːk **-s** -s **-ing** -ɪŋ **-ed** -t

twee twiː

tweed (T) twiːd **-s** -z

Tweeddale 'twiːd.deɪl

Tweedie 'twiː.di

tweedl|e 'twiː.dl̩ **-es** -z **-ing** -ɪŋ, 'twiːd.lɪŋ **-ed** -d

Tweedledee ˌtwiː.dl̩'diː

Tweedledum ˌtwiː.dl̩'dʌm

Tweedmouth 'twiːd.məθ, -maʊθ

Tweedsmuir 'twiːdz.mjʊəʳ, -mjɔːʳ (US) -mjʊr, -mjʊɚ

tweed|y 'twiː.d|i **-ier** -i.əʳ (US) -i.ɚ **-iest** -i.ɪst, -i.əst **-iness** -ɪ.nəs, -ɪ.nɪs
'tween twiːn
tween|y 'twiː.n|i **-ies** -iz
tweet twiːt **-s** -s **-ing** -ɪŋ (US) 'twiː.t̬ɪŋ **-ed** -ɪd (US) 'twiː.t̬ɪd **-er/s** -əʳ/z (US) 'twiː.t̬ɚ/z
tweezers 'twiː.zəz (US) -zɚz
twelfth twelfθ **-s** -s **-ly** -li **ˌTwelfth 'Night** (US) **'Twelfth ˌNight**
twelve twelv **-s** -z
twelvemonth 'twelv.mʌntθ **-s** -s
twelvish 'twel.vɪʃ
twentieth 'twen.ti.ɪθ, -əθ (US) -t̬i- **-s** -s
twent|y 'twen.t|i (US) -t̬|i **-ies** -iz **ˌtwenty-ˌtwenty 'vision**
twenty-first ˌtwen.ti'fɜːst (US) -t̬i'fɝːst *stress shift:* ˌtwenty-first 'birthday
twentyfold 'twen.ti.fəʊld (US) -t̬i.foʊld
Twentyman 'twen.ti.mən (US) -t̬i-
twenty-one ˌtwen.ti'wʌn (US) -t̬i'- *stress shift:* ˌtwenty-one 'years
'twere *strong form:* twɜːʳ (US) twɝː; *weak form:* twəʳ (US) twɚ
twerp twɜːp (US) twɝːp **-s** -s
Twi twiː
twice twaɪs
twice-told twaɪs'təʊld (US) -'toʊld *stress shift:* ˌtwice-told 'tale
Twickenham 'twɪk.ən.əm, '-nəm
twiddl|e 'twɪd.l̩ **-es** -z **-ing** -ɪŋ, 'twɪd.lɪŋ **-ed** -d **ˌtwiddle your 'thumbs**
twiddl|y 'twɪd.l|i, -l̩|.i **-ier** -i.əʳ (US) -i.ɚ **-iest** -i.ɪst iest -i.əst
twig twɪg **-s** -z **-ging** -ɪŋ **-ged** -d
Twigg twɪg
twiggy (T) 'twɪg.i
twilight 'twaɪ.laɪt **-s** -s **'twilight ˌzone**
twilit 'twaɪ.lɪt
twill twɪl **-s** -z **-ing** -ɪŋ **-ed** -d **-y** -i
'twill *normal form:* twɪl *occasional weak form:* twəl
twin twɪn **-s** -z **-ning** -ɪŋ **-ned** -d **ˌtwin 'bed; 'twin ˌset**
twin|e twaɪn **-es** -z **-ing/ly** -ɪŋ/li **-ed** -d **-er/s** -əʳ/z (US) -ɚ/z
twing|e twɪndʒ **-es** -ɪz **-(e)ing** -ɪŋ **-ed** -d
Twingo 'twɪn.gəʊ, 'twɪŋ- (US) -goʊ
Twining 'twaɪ.nɪŋ
Twinkie® 'twɪŋ.ki **-s** -z
twinkl|e 'twɪŋ.kl̩ **-es** -z **-ing** -ɪŋ, 'twɪŋ.klɪŋ **-ed** -d **-er/s** -əʳ/z, 'twɪŋ.kləʳ/z (US) '-kl.ɚ/z, '-klɚ/z
Twinn twɪn
twinset 'twɪn.set **-s** -s
twin-track ˌtwɪn'træk *stress shift:* ˌtwin-track 'railway
twin-tub 'twɪn.tʌb **-s** -z
twirl twɜːl (US) twɝːl **-s** -z **-ing** -ɪŋ **-ed** -d **-y** -i
twirp twɜːp (US) twɝːp **-s** -s
twist (T) twɪst **-s** -s **-ing** -ɪŋ **-ed** -ɪd **-er/s** -əʳ/z (US) -ɚ/z
Twistington 'twɪs.tɪŋ.tən
twist|y 'twɪs.t|i **-ier** -i.əʳ (US) -i.ɚ **-iest** -i.ɪst, -i.əst **-iness** -ɪ.nəs, -ɪ.nɪs
twit twɪt **-s** -s **-ting/ly** -ɪŋ/li (US) 'twɪt̬.ɪŋ/li **-ted** -ɪd (US) 'twɪt̬.ɪd
twitch twɪtʃ **-es** -ɪz **-ing/s** -ɪŋ/z **-ed** -t **-er/s** -əʳ/z (US) -ɚ/z
twitch|y 'twɪtʃ|.i **-ier** -i.əʳ (US) -i.ɚ **-iest** -i.ɪst, -i.əst
twite twaɪt **-s** -s
twitt|er 'twɪt|.əʳ (US) 'twɪt̬|.ɚ **-ers** -əz (US) -ɚz **-ering** -ər.ɪŋ (US) -ɚ.ɪŋ **-ered** -əd (US) -ɚd **-ery** -ər.i (US) -ɚ.i
'twixt twɪkst
two tuː **-s** -z **put ˌtwo and ˌtwo to'gether**
two-bit tuː'bɪt (US) '-- *stress shift, British only:* ˌtwo-bit 'liar
two-by-four ˌtuː.baɪ'fɔːʳ, -bə'-, -bɪ'- (US) 'tuː.baɪ.fɔːr, -bə-
two-dimensional ˌtuː.dɪ'men.*t*ʃən.əl, -daɪ'-, -'men*t*ʃ.nəl (US) -də'-, -dɪ'-, -daɪ'-
two-edged ˌtuː'edʒd *stress shift:* ˌtwo-edged 'sword
two-|faced ˌtuː|'feɪst (US) '-- **-facedly** -'feɪ.sɪd.li; -'feɪst.li (US) -feɪ.sɪd.li, -feɪst.li **-facedness** -'feɪ.sɪd.nəs, -nɪs; -'feɪst.nəs, -nɪs (US) -feɪ.sɪd.nəs, -nɪs; -feɪst.nəs, -nɪs *stress shift, British only:* ˌtwo-faced 'liar
twofold 'tuː.fəʊld (US) -foʊld
two-ish 'tuː.ɪʃ
two-legged ˌtuː'legd; -'leg.ɪd (US) 'tuː.legd; -ˌleg.ɪd *stress shift, British only:* ˌtwo-legged 'creature
twopenc|e 'tʌp.ən*t*s, -əm*p*s **-es** -ɪz
Note: The British English pronunciation of **twopenny, twopence,** etc., date from the period before the introduction of decimal coinage in 1971. They remain in use to suggest a very small value (e.g. a twopenny-halfpenny bus ride).
twopenny 'tʌp.ən.i, '-ni
twopenny-halfpenny ˌtʌp.ni'heɪp.ni, ˌtʌp.ən.i'heɪ.pən.i
twopennyworth ˌtuː'pen.i.wɜːθ, '-əθ; 'tʌp.ən.i.wɜːθ, '-ni-, -wəθ (US) -wɝːθ, -wɚθ **-s** -s
two-piece 'tuː.piːs
two-ply 'tuː.plaɪ
two-seater ˌtuː'siː.təʳ (US) -t̬ɚ, '-ˌ-- **-s** -z *stress shift:* ˌtwo-seater 'sportscar
twosome 'tuː.səm **-s** -z
two-step 'tuː.step **-s** -s
two-stroke 'tuː.strəʊk (US) -stroʊk
two-time ˌtuː'taɪm, '-- (US) '-- **-s** -z **-ing** -ɪŋ **-ed** -d **-er/s** -əʳ/z (US) -ɚ/z
two-tone ˌtuː'təʊn, '-- (US) 'tuː.toʊn **-d** -d
two-way ˌtuː'weɪ (US) '-- *stress shift, British only:* ˌtwo-way 'mirror
Twyford 'twaɪ.fəd (US) -fɚd
TX *(abbrev. for* **Texas***)* 'tek.səs
Tybalt 'tɪb.əlt
Tyburn 'taɪ.bɜːn (US) -bɝːn
Tycho 'taɪ.kəʊ (US) -koʊ
tycoon taɪ'kuːn **-s** -z
Tydeus 'taɪ.djuːs, -djəs, -di.əs (US) 'taɪ.di.əs, '-djəs
Tydfil 'tɪd.vɪl
tyger 'taɪ.gəʳ (US) -gɚ
tying *(from* **tie***)* 'taɪ.ɪŋ
tyke taɪk **-s** -s
Tyldesley 'tɪldz.li
Tyler 'taɪ.ləʳ (US) -lɚ
tympan|i 'tɪm.pə.n|i **-ist/s** -ɪst/s
tympanic tɪm'pæn.ɪk
tympan|um 'tɪm.pən|.əm **-ums** -əmz **-a** -ə
tympan|y 'tɪm.pən|.i **-ies** -iz
Tynan 'taɪ.nən
Tyndale, Tyndall 'tɪn.dəl
Tyndrum 'taɪn.drʌm
Tyne taɪn **ˌTyne and 'Wear**
Tynemouth 'taɪn.məθ, 'taɪm-, -maʊθ; 'tɪn.məθ, 'tɪm- (US) 'taɪn-
Tynesid|e 'taɪn.saɪd **-er/s** -əʳ/z (US) -ɚ/z
Tynwald 'tɪn.wəld
typ|e taɪp **-es** -s **-ing** -ɪŋ **-ed** -t **'typing ˌpool**
typecast 'taɪp.kɑːst (US) -kæst **-s** -s **-ing** -ɪŋ
Typee ˌtaɪ'piː
typefac|e 'taɪp.feɪs **-es** -ɪz
typefounder 'taɪpˌfaʊn.dəʳ (US) -dɚ **-s** -z
typefoundr|y 'taɪpˌfaʊn.dr|i **-ies** -iz
typescript 'taɪp.skrɪpt **-s** -s
type|set 'taɪp|.set **-sets** -sets **-setting** -ˌset.ɪŋ (US) -ˌset̬.ɪŋ **-setter/s** -ˌset.əʳ/z (US) -ˌset̬.ɚ/z
typesetter 'taɪpˌset.əʳ (US) -ˌset̬.ɚ **-s** -z
type|write 'taɪp|.raɪt **-writes** -raɪts **-writing** -ˌraɪ.tɪŋ (US) -ˌraɪ.t̬ɪŋ **-wrote** -rəʊt (US) -roʊt **-written** -ˌrɪt.ən
typewriter 'taɪpˌraɪ.təʳ (US) -t̬ɚ **-s** -z
typhoid 'taɪ.fɔɪd
typhonic taɪ'fɒn.ɪk (US) -'fɑː.nɪk
Typhoo® taɪ'fuː
typhoon taɪ'fuːn **-s** -z
typh|us 'taɪ.f|əs **-ous** -əs
typic|al 'tɪp.ɪ.k|əl **-ally** -əl.i, -li **-alness** -əl.nəs, -nɪs
typicality ˌtɪp.ɪ'kæl.ə.ti, -ɪ.ti (US) -ə.t̬i
typi|fy 'tɪp.ɪ|.faɪ **-fies** -faɪz **-fying** -faɪ.ɪŋ **-fied** -faɪd
typist 'taɪ.pɪst **-s** -s
typo 'taɪ.pəʊ (US) -poʊ **-s** -z
typographic ˌtaɪ.pəʊ'græf.ɪk (US) -pə'-, -poʊ'- **-al** -əl **-ally** -əl.i, -li
typograph|y taɪ'pɒg.rə.f|i (US) -'pɑː.grə- **-er/s** -əʳ/z (US) -ɚ/z

Pronouncing the letters TZ

The consonant digraph **tz** is most commonly pronounced /ts/, e.g.:

chintz /tʃɪnts/
quartz /kwɔːts/ (US) /kwɔːrts/

However, the /t/ is sometimes optional in British English, e.g.:

waltz /wɒlts, wɔːlts/ (US) /wɑːlts, wɔːlts/

typolog|y taɪˈpɒl.ə.dʒ|i (US) -ˈpɑː.lə- **-ies** -iz
tyrannic|al tɪˈræn.ɪ.k|ᵊl, tə-, taɪ- (US) tə-, tɪ-, taɪ- **-ally** -ᵊl.i, -li **-alness** -ᵊl.nəs, -nɪs
tyrannicide tɪˈræn.ɪ.saɪd, tə-, taɪ- (US) tə-, tɪ-, taɪ- **-s** -z
tyranniz|e, -is|e ˈtɪr.ᵊn.aɪz **-es** -ɪz **-ing** -ɪŋ **-ed** -d
tyrannosaur tɪˈræn.ə.sɔːʳ, tə-, taɪ- (US) təˈræn.ə.sɔːr, tɪ-, taɪ- **-s** -z
tyrannosaurus tɪˌræn.əˈsɔː.rəs, tə-, taɪ- (US) təˌræn.əˈsɔːr.əs, tɪ-, taɪ- **-es** -ɪz **tyˌrannoˌsaurus ˈrex**
tyrannous ˈtɪr.ᵊn.əs **-ly** -li
tyrann|y ˈtɪr.ᵊn|.i **-ies** -iz
tyrant ˈtaɪə.rənt (US) ˈtaɪ- **-s** -s
tyre (T) taɪəʳ (US) taɪɚ **-s** -z
Tyrian ˈtɪr.i.ən **-s** -z
tyro ˈtaɪə.rəʊ (US) ˈtaɪ.roʊ **-s** -z
Tyrol tɪˈrəʊl, tə-; ˈtɪr.ᵊl (US) tɪˈroʊl, taɪ-; ˈtɪr.oʊl, -ɑːl
Tyrolean ˌtɪr.əʊˈliː.ən; tɪˈrəʊ.li-, tə- (US) tɪˈroʊ.li-, taɪ-; ˌtɪr.əˈliː-
Tyrolese ˌtɪr.əʊˈliːz (US) -əˈliːz, -ˈliːs
Tyrolienne tɪˌrəʊ.liˈen, tə-; ˌtɪr.əʊ- (US) tɪˈroʊ.li.ən; ˌtɪr.əˈliː-, ˌtaɪ.rəˈ- **-s** -z
Tyrone *in Ireland:* tɪˈrəʊn, tə- (US) -ˈroʊn
Tyrone *person's name:* ˈtaɪə.rəʊn; taɪˈrəʊn, tɪ-, tə- (US) ˈtaɪ.roʊn, ˌ-ˈ-
Tyrrell ˈtɪr.ᵊl
Tyrrhenian tɪˈriː.ni.ən, tə- (US) tɪ-
Tyrtaeus tɜːˈtiː.əs (US) tɝː-
Tyrwhitt ˈtɪr.ɪt
Tyser ˈtaɪ.zəʳ (US) -zɚ
Tyson ˈtaɪ.sᵊn
Tytler ˈtaɪt.ləʳ (US) -lɚ
Tyzack ˈtaɪ.zæk, ˈtɪz.æk, -ək
tzar (T) zɑːʳ, tsɑːʳ (US) zɑːr, tsɑːr **-s** -z
tzarina (T) zɑːˈriː.nə, tsɑː- **-s** -z
tzar|ism ˈzɑː.r|ɪ.zᵊm, ˈtsɑː- (US) ˈzɑːr.ɪ-, ˈtsɑːr- **-ist/s** -ɪst/s
tzetze ˈtet.si, ˈtset- (US) ˈtset-, ˈtsiːt-, ˈtet-, ˈtiːt- **-s** -z **ˈtzetze ˌfly**

Pronouncing the letter U

See also UE, UI, UOU, UY

The vowel letter **u** has several strong pronunciations linked to spelling. 'Short' pronunciations include /ʌ/ and /ʊ/, and 'long' pronunciations include /uː/ and /juː/. In 'short' pronunciations pronounced /ʌ/, the **u** is generally followed by a consonant letter which ends the word, or a double consonant before another vowel. Words containing /ʊ/ which end with a consonant sound often have two consonant letters finally, a notable exception being *put* /pʊt/, e.g.:

tub	/tʌb/	
tubby	/ˈtʌb.i/	
bull	/bʊl/	
bully	/ˈbʊl.i/	

The 'long' pronunciations usually mean the **u** is followed by a single consonant letter and then a vowel, e.g.:

tube	/tjuːb/	(US) /tuːb/
tubing	/ˈtjuː.bɪŋ/	(US) /ˈtuː-/
supervise	/ˈsuː.pə.vaɪz/	(US) /-pɚ-/

In word initial position, the 'long' pronunciation is almost always pronounced /juː/, e.g.:

unique	/juːˈniːk/	
useful	/ˈjuːs.fəl/	

However, there are exceptions to these guidelines, e.g.:

study	/ˈstʌd.i/	
sugar	/ˈʃʊg.əʳ/	(US) /-ɚ/
truth	/truːθ/	

When **u** is followed by **r**, the strong pronunciation is one of several possibilities: /jʊə, jɔː (US) jʊr/, /ʊə, ɔː (US) ʊr/, /ɜː (US) ɝː/, or /ʌ (US) ɝː/, e.g.:

cure	/kjʊəʳ, kjɔːʳ/	(US) /kjʊr/
plural	/ˈplʊə.rəl, ˈplɔː-/	(US) /ˈplʊr.əl/
burn	/bɜːn/	(US) /bɝːn/
hurry	/ˈhʌr.i/	(US) /ˈhɝː.i/

In weak syllables

The vowel letter **u** is realised as one of /jə/, /jʊ/, /ə/ or /ʊ/ in weak syllables, e.g.:

failure	/ˈfeɪ.ljəʳ/	(US) /ˈfeɪl.jɚ/
accurate	/ˈæk.jə.rət, -jʊ-/	(US) /-jɚ.ət, -jʊ.rət/
status	/ˈsteɪ.təs/	(US) /ˈstæt̬əs/
July	/dʒʊˈlaɪ/	

It may also result in a syllabic consonant, e.g.:

hopeful	/ˈhəʊp.fəl, -fʊl/	(US) /ˈhoʊp-/

u (U) juː **-'s** -z
UAE ˌjuː.eɪˈiː
UB40 ˌjuː.biːˈfɔː.ti (US) -ˈfɔːr.t̬i **-s** -z
Ubbelohde ˈʌb.əl.əʊd (US) -oʊd
U-bend ˈjuː.bend **-s** -z
Übermensch ˈuː.bə.mentʃ (US) -bɚ- **-en** -ən
ubiquitarian (U) juːˌbɪk.wɪˈteə.ri.ən, ˌjuː.bɪ.kwɪˈ- (US) juːˌbɪk.wəˈter.i- **-s** -z
ubiquitous juːˈbɪk.wɪ.təs (US) -wə.t̬əs **-ly** -li **-ness** -nəs, -nɪs
ubiquity juːˈbɪk.wə.ti, -wɪ- (US) -wə.t̬i
U-boat ˈjuː.bəʊt (US) -boʊt **-s** -s
Ubu Roi ˌuː.buːˈrwɑː
UCAS, Ucas ˈjuː.kæs
UCATT ˈʌk.ət, ˈjuː.kæt
UCCA ˈʌk.ə
Uccello uːˈtʃel.əʊ (US) -oʊ
Uckfield ˈʌk.fiːld
UDA ˌjuː.diːˈeɪ
Udall ˈjuː.dəl (US) -dɔːl, -dɑːl, -dəl
udder ˈʌd.əʳ (US) -ɚ **-s** -z
Uddin ˈʌd.ɪn
Uddingston ˈʌd.ɪŋ.stən
UDI ˌjuː.diːˈaɪ
Udolpho uːˈdɒl.fəʊ, juː- (US) -ˈdɑːl.foʊ
udometer juːˈdɒm.ɪ.təʳ, ˈ-ə- (US) -ˈdɑː.mə.t̬ɚ **-s** -z
UDR ˌjuː.diːˈɑːʳ (US) -ˈɑːr
UEFA, Uefa juːˈeɪ.fə, -ˈiː-
Uffizi juːˈfɪt.si, uː-, -ˈfiːt-
UFO ˌjuː.efˈəʊ (US) -ˈoʊ **-(')s** -z
ufolog|y juːˈfɒl.ə.dʒ|i (US) -ˈfɑː.lə- **-ist/s** -ɪst/s
Ugand|a juːˈgæn.d|ə, jʊ- (US) juː-, uː- **-an/s** -ən/z
Ugaritic ˌuː.gəˈrɪt.ɪk, ˌjuː- (US) -gəˈrɪt̬-
ugh ʊːx, ʊh, ʌx, ʊɸ, ʊh, ɜːh, ʌg
Note: Used to indicate disgust.
ugli ˈʌg.li **-s** -z ˈ**ugli** ˌ**fruit**
uglification ˌʌg.lɪ.fɪˈkeɪ.ʃən, -lə-
ugli|fy ˈʌg.lɪ|.faɪ **-fies** -faɪz **-fying** -faɪ.ɪŋ **-fied** -faɪd
ugl|y ˈʌg.l|i **-ier** -i.əʳ (US) -i.ɚ **-iest** -i.ɪst, -i.əst **-iness** -ɪ.nəs, -ɪ.nɪs ˌ**ugly** ˈ**duckling**
Ugrian ˈuː.gri.ən, ˈjuː- **-s** -z
Ugric ˈuː.grɪk, ˈjuː-
UHF ˌjuː.eɪtʃˈef
uh-huh ʌˈhʌ, ˈʌ.hʌ
uhlan ˈuː.lɑːn, ˈjuː-, -lən; uːˈlɑːn, juː- **-s** -z
Uhland ˈuː.lənd, -lænd, -lɑːnd (US) -lɑːnt, -lɑːnd
UHT ˌjuː.eɪtʃˈtiː *stress shift, see compound:* ˌ**UHT** ˈ**milk**
Uhu® ˈjuː.huː, ˈuː-
uh-uh ˈʌʔˌʌʔ (US) ˈʌ̃ʔˌʌ̃
Note: Used to indicate alarm or anxiety.
uhuru (U) uːˈhuː.ruː, -ˈhʊə-
Uig ˈuː.ɪg, ˈjuː-
Uist ˈjuː.ɪst
uitlander (U) ˈeɪtˌlæn.dəʳ, ˈɔɪt- (US) ˈɔɪtˌlæn.dɚ, ˈeɪt-, ˈaɪt- **-s** -z
UK ˌjuːˈkeɪ *stress shift:* ˌUK ˈcitizen
ukas|e juːˈkeɪz, -ˈkeɪs (US) juːˈkeɪz, -ˈkeɪs, ˈ-- **-es** -ɪz
uke juːk **-s** -s
ukelele ˌjuː.kəlˈeɪ.li (US) -kəˈleɪ- **-s** -z
Ukraine juːˈkreɪn (US) -ˈkreɪn, ˈjuː.kreɪn
ukulele ˌjuː.kəlˈeɪ.li (US) -kəˈleɪ- **-s** -z
ulan ˈuː.lɑːn, ˈjuː-, -lən; uːˈlɑːn, juː- **-s** -z
Ulan Bator uːˌlɑːnˈbɑː.tɔːʳ (US) ˌuː.lɑːnˈbɑː.tɔːr
Ulan-Ude uːˌlɑːn.uːˈdeɪ (US) uːˌlɑːn.uːˈdeɪ, uːˈlɑːn.uːˌdeɪ
ulcer ˈʌl.səʳ (US) -sɚ **-s** -z
ulcer|ate ˈʌl.sər|.eɪt (US) -sə.r|eɪt **-ates** -eɪts **-ating** -eɪ.tɪŋ (US) -eɪ.t̬ɪŋ **-ated** -eɪ.tɪd (US) -eɪ.t̬ɪd
ulceration ˌʌl.sərˈeɪ.ʃən (US) -səˈreɪ- **-s** -z
ulcerative ˈʌl.sər.ə.tɪv, -eɪ- (US) -sə.reɪ.t̬ɪv, -sɚ.ə-
ulcerous ˈʌl.sər.əs
ulema ˈuː.lɪ.mə, -lə-, -mɑː; ˌuː.lɪˈmɑː, -ləˈ- (US) ˌuː.ləˈmɑː, ˈ--- **-s** -z
Ulfilas ˈʊl.fɪ.læs, -fə-, -ləs (US) ˈʌl.fɪ.ləs
Ulgham ˈʌf.əm
ullage ˈʌl.ɪdʒ

Pronouncing the letters UE

The vowel digraph **ue** is most commonly pronounced as /juː/ or /uː/. The /j/ sound is not always present in US English where it is found in British English. In general, the /j/ is dropped in US English where it appears in British English following an alveolar consonant such as /t/, /d/ or /n/, e.g.:

cue	/kjuː/	
due	/djuː/	(US) /duː/

Another possible pronunciation is /juː.ə/ or /jʊə/, e.g.:

dual	/ˈdjuː.əl, djʊəl/	(US) /ˈduː.ᵊl/

In addition

Other sounds are associated with the digraph **ue**, e.g.:

/weɪ/	suede	/sweɪd/
/e/	guess	/ges/
/uː.ɪ/	suet, bluest	/ˈsuː.ɪt/, /ˈbluː.ɪst/
silent	league	/liːg/

Pronouncing the letters UI

There are several pronunciation possibilities for the vowel digraph **ui**. The most common is likely to be /uː/, e.g.:

fruit	/fruːt/

A similar pronunciation is /juː/ in British English, realised as /uː/ in US English, e.g.:

nuisance	/ˈnjuː.sᵊnts/	(US) /ˈnuː-/
suit	/sjuːt, suːt/	(US) /suːt/

In addition

Other sounds are associated with the digraph **ui**, e.g.:

/wiː/	suite	/swiːt/
/wɪ/	linguist	/ˈlɪŋ.gwɪst/
/ɪ/	build	/bɪld/
/aɪ/	guide	/gaɪd/
/u.ɪ/	fruition	/fruˈɪʃ.ᵊn/
/uː.ɪ/	ruin	/ˈruː.ɪn/

It should also be noted that **ui** may follow **q**, producing the sound /kwɪ/ or /kwaɪ/.

Ullah ˈʌl.ə
Ullapool ˈʌl.ə.puːl
Ullman(n) ˈʊl.mən, ˈʌl- (US) ˈʌl-, ˈʊl-
Ullswater ˈʌlzˌwɔː.təʳ (US) -ˌwɑː.t̬ɚ, -ˌwɔː-
Ulm ʊlm
uln|a ˈʌl.n|ə **-as** -əz **-ae** -iː **-ar** -əʳ (US) -ɚ
Ulrica ˈʊl.rɪkə, ˈʌl-
Ulrich ˈʊl.rɪk *as if German:* -rɪx (US) ˈʌl-, ˈʊl-
Ulrika ʊlˈriː.kə
Ulster, ulster ˈʌl.stəʳ (US) -stɚ **-s** -z
Ulster|man ˈʌl.stə|.mən (US) -stɚ- **-men** -mən
Ulster|woman ˈʌl.stə|ˌwʊm.ən (US) -stɚ- **-women** -ˌwɪm.ɪn
ulterior ʌlˈtɪə.ri.əʳ (US) -ˈtɪr.i.ɚ **-ly** -li **ulˌterior ˈmotive**
ultima ˈʌl.tɪ.mə, -tə- (US) -t̬ɪ- **ˌultima ˈThule**
ultimate ˈʌl.tɪ.mət, -tə-, -mət (US) -t̬ə.mɪt **-ly** -li
ultimat|um ˌʌl.tɪˈmeɪ.t|əm (US) -t̬əˈmeɪ.t̬|əm **-ums** -əmz **-a** -ə
ultimo ˈʌl.tɪ.məʊ, -tə- (US) -t̬ɪ.moʊ
ultra- ʌl.trə-
Note: Prefix. Normally takes primary or secondary stress on the first syllable, e.g. **ultrasound** /ˈʌl.trə.saʊnd/, **ultrasonic** /ˌʌl.trəˈsɒn.ɪk (US) -ˈsɑː.nɪk/.
ultra ˈʌl.trə **-s** -z
ultra-high frequenc|y ˌʌl.trəˌhaɪˈfriː.kwənt.s|i **-ies** -iz
ultramarine ˌʌl.trə.məˈriːn *stress shift:* ˌultramarine ˈblue
ultramodern ˌʌl.trəˈmɒd.ən (US) -ˈmɑː.dɚn **-ist/s** -ɪst/s *stress shift:* ˌultramodern ˈstyling
ultramontane ˌʌl.trəˈmɒn.teɪn, -mɒnˈteɪn (US) -ˈmɑːn.teɪn, -mɑːnˈteɪn
ultramontanism (U) ˌʌl.trəˈmɒn.tə.nɪ.zᵊm, -tɪ-, -teɪ- (US) -ˈmɑːn.tə-
ultrasonic ˌʌl.trəˈsɒn.ɪk (US) -ˈsɑː.nɪk **-s** -s **-ally** -ᵊl.i, -li *stress shift:* ˌultrasonic ˈscanner
ultrasound ˈʌl.trə.saʊnd
ultraviolet ˌʌl.trəˈvaɪə.lət, -lɪt (US) -lɪt *stress shift, see compound:* **ˌultraviolet ˈlight**
ultra vires ˌʌl.trəˈvaɪə.riːz, ˌʊl.trɑːˈviə.reɪz (US) ˌʌl.trəˈvaɪ.riːz
ululant ˈjuː.ljə.lənt, ˈʌl.jə-, -jʊ- (US) ˈjuːl.juː.lənt, ˈʌl-, -jə-
ulu|late ˈjuː.ljə|.leɪt, ˈʌl.jə-, -jʊ- (US) ˈjuːl.juː-, ˈʌl-, -jə- **-lates** -leɪts **-lating** -leɪ.tɪŋ (US) -leɪ.t̬ɪŋ **-lated** -leɪ.tɪd (US) -leɪ.t̬ɪd
ululation ˌjuː.ljəˈleɪ.ʃᵊn, ˌʌl.jəˈ-, -jʊˈ- (US) ˌjuːl.juːˈ-, ˌʌl-, -jəˈ- **-s** -z
Uluru uːˈluː.ruː; ˌʊl.əˈruː
Ulverston ˈʌl.və.stən (US) -vɚ-
Ulyanovsk ʊlˈjɑː.nɒfsk (US) uːlˈjɑː.nɔːfsk
Ulysses ˈjuː.lɪ.siːz; juːˈlɪs.iːz (US) juːˈlɪs-
umbel ˈʌm.bəl, -bel **-s** -z
umbellifer ʌmˈbel.ɪ.fəʳ (US) -fɚ
umbelliferae ˌʌm.bᵊlˈɪf.ᵊr.iː, -belˈ- (US) -bəˈlɪf.ə.riː
umbelliferous ˌʌm.bᵊlˈɪf.ᵊr.əs, -belˈ- (US) -bəˈlɪf-
umber ˈʌm.bəʳ (US) -bɚ **-s** -z
Umberto ʊmˈbeə.təʊ, -ˈbɜː- (US) -ˈber.toʊ
umbilical ʌmˈbɪl.ɪ.kl̩, ˈ-ə-, ˌʌm.bɪˈlaɪ-, -bəˈ- (US) ʌmˈbɪl.ɪ-, ˈ-ə- **umˌbilical ˈcord, ˌumbiˌlical ˈcord** (US) **umˈbilical ˌcord**
umbilic|us ʌmˈbɪl.ɪ.k|əs, ˈ-ə-; ˌʌm.bɪˈlaɪ-, -bəˈ- **-uses** -ə.sɪz **-i** -aɪ
umbles ˈʌm.bl̩z

um|bo 'ʌm|.bəʊ (US) -boʊ **-bos** -bəʊz (US) -boʊz **-bones** -'bəʊ.neɪz (US) -'boʊ-
umbr|a 'ʌm.br|ə **-as** -əz **-ae** -iː **-al** -ᵊl
umbrage 'ʌm.brɪdʒ
umbrageous ʌm'breɪ.dʒəs **-ly** -li **-ness** -nəs, -nɪs
umbrated 'ʌm.breɪ.tɪd (US) -t̬ɪd
umbration ʌm'breɪ.ʃᵊn **-s** -z
umbrella ʌm'brel.ə **-s** -z
Umbri|a 'ʌm.bri|.ə **-an/s** -ən/z
Umbro® 'ʌm.brəʊ (US) -broʊ
Umfreville 'ʌm.frə.vɪl
umiak 'uː.mi.æk, -mjæk **-s** -s
umlaut 'ʊm.laʊt **-s** -s
umpirag|e 'ʌm.paɪ.ᵊr.ɪdʒ **-es** -ɪz
umpir|e 'ʌm.paɪəʳ (US) -paɪɚ **-es** -z **-ing** -ɪŋ **-ed** -d
umpteen ʌm*p*'tiːn **-th** -θ *stress shift:* ˌumpteen 'times
un- ʌn-
Note: Prefix. It may be unstressed, usually when a stressed syllable follows it and it is a frequently-used word, e.g. **unable** /ʌn'eɪ.bl̩/. Otherwise it will have secondary stress, e.g. **unadvisable** /ˌʌn.əd'vaɪ.zə.bl̩/. This syllable frequently becomes the main stress in the word through stress-shift, e.g. **unattended** /ˌʌn.ə'ten.dɪd/, **unattended parking** /ˌʌn.ə.ten.dɪd'pɑː.kɪŋ (US) -'pɑːr-/. There are so many such cases that individual examples are not given for each word.
'un ən **-s** -z
Note: Old-fashioned colloquial form for 'one', as in 'little 'un'.
UN ˌjuː'en
Una 'juː.nə, 'uː-
unabash|ed ˌʌn.ə'bæʃ|t **-edly** -ɪd.li
unabated ˌʌn.ə'beɪ.tɪd (US) -t̬ɪd **-ly** -li
unable ʌn'eɪ.bl̩, ˌʌn-
Unabomber 'juː.nəˌbɒm.əʳ (US) -ˌbɑː.mɚ
unabridged ˌʌn.ə'brɪdʒd
unaccented ˌʌn.ək'sen.tɪd, -æk'- (US) ʌn'æk.sen.t̬ɪd
unacceptability ˌʌn.ək.sep.tə'bɪl.ə.ti, -ɪ.ti (US) -ə.t̬i
unaccepta|ble ˌʌn.ək'sep.tə|.bl̩, -æk'- **-bly** -bli
unaccompanied ˌʌn.ə'kʌm.pə.nid, -'kʌmp.nid
unaccountability ˌʌn.əˌkaʊn.tə'bɪl.ɪ.ti, -ə.ti (US) -t̬ə'bɪl.ə.t̬i
unaccountab|le ˌʌn.ə'kaʊn.tə.b|l̩ (US) -t̬ə- **-ly** -li **-leness** -l̩.nəs, -nɪs
unaccounted ˌʌn.ə'kaʊn.tɪd (US) -t̬ɪd **ˌunac'counted ˌfor**
unaccustomed ˌʌn.ə'kʌs.təmd **-ly** -li
unacknowledged ˌʌn.ək'nɒl.ɪdʒd (US) -'nɑː.lɪdʒd
unacquainted ˌʌn.ə'kweɪn.tɪd (US) -t̬ɪd
unadaptable ˌʌn.ə'dæp.tə.bl̩
unaddressed ˌʌn.ə'drest
unadopted ˌʌn.ə'dɒp.tɪd (US) -'dɑːp-
unadorned ˌʌn.ə'dɔːnd (US) -'dɔːrnd
unadulterated ˌʌn.ə'dʌl.tᵊr.eɪ.tɪd (US) -t̬ə.reɪ.t̬ɪd
unadvised ˌʌn.əd'vaɪzd
unadvisedly ˌʌn.əd'vaɪ.zɪd.li
unaffected ˌʌn.ə'fek.tɪd **-ly** -li **-ness** -nəs, -nɪs
unaffectionate ˌʌn.ə'fek.ʃᵊn.ət **-ly** -li
unafraid ˌʌn.ə'freɪd
unaided ʌn'eɪ.dɪd, ˌʌn-
unalienab|le ʌn'eɪ.li.ə.nə.b|l̩, ˌʌn-, '-ljə- (US) -li.ə-, -'eɪl.jə- **-ly** -li
unaligned ˌʌn.ə'laɪnd
unalloyed ˌʌn.ə'lɔɪd
unalterability ʌnˌɔːl.tᵊr.ə'bɪl.ɪ.ti, ˌʌn-, -ə.ti (US) -ˌɑːl.t̬ɚ.ə'bɪl.ə.t̬i, -ˌɔːl-
unalterab|le ʌn'ɔːl.tᵊr.ə.b|l̩, ˌʌn- (US) -'ɔːl.t̬ɚ-, -'ɑːl- **-ly** -li **-leness** -l̩.nəs (US) -nɪs
unaltered ʌn'ɔːl.təd, ˌʌn- (US) -t̬ɚd, -'ɑːl-
unambiguous ˌʌn.æm'bɪg.ju.əs **-ly** -li **-ness** -nəs, -nɪs
unambivalent ˌʌn.æm'bɪv.ᵊl.ənt **-ly** -li
un-American ˌʌn.ə'mer.ɪ.kən
unanalysab|le ʌnˌæn.ᵊl'aɪ.zə.b|l̩, ˌʌn-, -'æn.ᵊl.aɪ- (US) -ˌæn.ə'laɪ-, -'æn.ə.laɪ- **-ly** -li **-leness** -l̩.nəs, -nɪs
unanimity ˌjuː.nə'nɪm.ə.ti, -næn'ɪm-, -ɪ.ti (US) -nə'nɪm.ə.t̬i
unanimous juː'næn.ɪ.məs, '-ə- (US) '-ə- **-ly** -li **-ness** -nəs, -nɪs, -nəs
unannounced ˌʌn.ə'naʊn*t*st
unanswerability ʌnˌɑːn*t*.sᵊr.ə'bɪl.ɪ.ti, ˌʌn-, -ə.ti (US) -ˌæn*t*.sɚ.ə'bɪl.ə.t̬i
unanswerab|le ʌn'ɑːn*t*.sᵊr.ə.b|l̩, ˌʌn- (US) -'æn*t*- **-ly** -li
unanswered ʌn'ɑːn*t*.səd, ˌʌn- (US) -'æn*t*.sɚd
unappealing ˌʌn.ə'piː.lɪŋ **-ly** -li
unappeasable ˌʌn.ə'piː.zə.bl̩
unappeased ˌʌn.ə'piːzd
unappetizing, -ising ʌn'æp.ɪ.taɪ.zɪŋ, ˌʌn-, '-ə- (US) '-ə- **-ly** -li
unapplied ˌʌn.ə'plaɪd
unappreciated ˌʌn.ə'priː.ʃi.eɪ.tɪd (US) -t̬ɪd
unappreciative ˌʌn.ə'priː.ʃi.ə.tɪv (US) -t̬ɪv **-ly** -li
unapproachability ˌʌn.əˌprəʊ.tʃə'bɪl.ɪ.ti, -ə.ti (US) -ˌproʊ.tʃə'bɪl.ə.t̬i
unapproachab|le ˌʌn.ə'prəʊ.tʃə.b|l̩ (US) -'proʊ- **-ly** -bli **-leness** -bl̩.nəs, -nɪs
unappropriate ˌʌn.ə'prəʊ.pri.ət (US) -'proʊ- **-ly** -li **-ness** -nəs, -nɪs
unappropriated ˌʌn.ə'prəʊ.pri.eɪ.tɪ (US) -'proʊ.pri.eɪ.t̬ɪd
unapproved ˌʌn.ə'pruːvd
unapt ʌn'æpt **-ly** -li **-ness** -nəs, -nɪs
unarguab|le ʌn'ɑː.gju.ə.b|l̩ (US) -'ɑːr- **-ly** -li **-leness** -l̩.nəs, -nɪs
unarm ʌn'ɑːm, ˌʌn- (US) -'ɑːrm **-s** -z **-ing** -ɪŋ **-ed** -d **ˌunarmed 'combat**
unarticulated ˌʌn.ɑː'tɪk.jə.leɪ.tɪd, -j (US) -ɑːr'tɪk.jə.leɪ.t̬ɪd
unary 'juː.nᵊr.i
unasha|med ˌʌn.ə'ʃeɪ|md **-medly** -mɪd.li **-medness** -mɪd.nəs, -nɪs
unasked ʌn'ɑːskt, ˌʌn- (US) -'æskt
unaspirated ʌn'æs.pᵊr.eɪ.tɪd, ˌʌn- (US) -pə.reɪ.t̬ɪd
unassailability ˌʌn.əˌseɪ.lə'bɪl.ɪ.ti, -ə.ti (US) -ə.t̬i
unassailab|le ˌʌn.ə'seɪ.lə.b|l̩ **-ly** -li **-leness** -l̩.nəs, -nɪs
unassertive ˌʌn.ə'sɜː.tɪv (US) -'sɝː.t̬ɪv **-ly** -li **-ness** -nəs, -nɪs
unassigned ˌʌn.ə'saɪnd
unassimilated ˌʌn.ə'sɪm.ᵊl.eɪ.tɪd, -ɪ.leɪ- (US) -t̬ɪd
unassisted ˌʌn.ə'sɪs.tɪd
unassuageable ˌʌn.ə'sweɪ.dʒə.bl̩
unassuming ˌʌn.ə'sjuː.mɪŋ (US), -'suː- (US) -'suː- **-ly** -li **-ness** -nəs, -nɪs
unattached ˌʌn.ə'tætʃt
unattainab|le ˌʌn.ə'teɪ.nə.b|l̩ **-ly** -li **-ness** -nəs, -nɪs
unattended ˌʌn.ə'ten.dɪd
unattested ˌʌn.ə'tes.tɪd
unattractive ˌʌn.ə'træk.tɪv **-ly** -li **-ness** -nəs, -nɪs
unauthenticated ˌʌn.ɔː'θen.tɪ.keɪ.tɪd (US) -ɑː'θen.t̬ɪ.keɪ.t̬ɪd, -ɔː'-
unauthorized, -ised ʌn'ɔː.θᵊr.aɪzd, ˌʌn- (US) -'ɑː.θə.raɪzd, -'ɔː-
unavailability ˌʌn.əˌveɪ.lə'bɪl.ɪ.ti, -ə.t (US) -ə.t̬i
unavailable ˌʌn.ə'veɪ.lə.bl̩
unavailing ˌʌn.ə'veɪ.lɪŋ **-ly** -li **-ness** -nəs, -nɪs
unavenged ˌʌn.ə'ven*d*ʒd
unavoidab|le ˌʌn.ə'vɔɪ.də.b|l̩ **-ly** -li
unaware ˌʌn.ə'weəʳ (US) -'wer **-s** -z **-ly** -li **-ness** -nəs, -nɪs
unbalanc|e ʌn'bæl.ən*t*s, ˌʌn-, ʌm-, ˌʌm- (US) ʌn-, ˌʌn- **-es** -ɪz **-ing** -ɪŋ **-ed** -t
unbaptized ˌʌn.bæp'taɪzd, ˌʌm- (US) ʌn'bæp.taɪzd
unbar ʌn'bɑːʳ, ˌʌn-, ʌm-, ˌʌm- (US) ʌn'bɑːr, ˌʌn- **-s** -z **-ring** -ɪŋ **-red** -d
unbearab|le ʌn'beə.rə.b|l̩, ˌʌn-, ʌm-, ˌʌm- (US) ʌn'ber.ə-, -nəs, ˌʌn- **-ly** -li **-leness** -l̩.nəs, -nɪs
unbeatab|le ʌn'biː.tə.b|l̩, ˌʌn-, ʌm-, ˌʌm- (US) ʌn'biː.t̬ə-, ˌʌn- **-ly** -li
unbeaten ʌn'biː.tᵊn, ˌʌn-, ʌm-, ˌʌm- (US) ʌn-, ˌʌn-

unbecoming ˌʌn.bɪˈkʌm.ɪŋ, ˌʌm-, -bəˈ- US ˌʌn- **-ly** -li **-ness** -nəs, -nɪs
unbegotten ˌʌn.bɪˈɡɒt.ᵊn, ˌʌm-, -bəˈ- US ˌʌn.bɪˈɡɑː.tᵊn, -bəˈ-
unbeknown ˌʌn.bɪˈnəʊn, ˌʌm-, -bəˈ- US ˌʌn.bɪˈnoʊn, -bəˈ- **-st** -*t*st
unbelief ˌʌn.bɪˈliːf, ˌʌm-, -bəˈ- US ˌʌn-
unbelievab|le ˌʌn.bɪˈliː.və.bl̩, ˌʌm-, -bəˈ- US ˌʌn- **-ly** -li
unbeliever ˌʌn.bɪˈliː.vəʳ, ˌʌm-, -bəˈ- US ˌʌn.bɪˈliː.vɚ, -bəˈ- **-s** -z
unbelieving ˌʌn.bɪˈliː.vɪŋ, ˌʌm-, -bəˈ- US ˌʌn- **-ly** -li
un|bend ʌnˈbend, ˌʌn-, ʌm-, ˌʌm- US ʌn-, ˌʌn- **-bends** -ˈbendz **-bending** -ˈben.dɪŋ **-bended** -ˈben.dɪd **-bent** -ˈbent
unbeneficed ʌnˈben.ɪ.fɪst, ˌʌn-, ʌm-, ˌʌm- US ʌn-, ˌʌn-
unbias(s)ed ʌnˈbaɪəst, ˌʌn-, ʌm-, ˌʌm- US ʌn-, ˌʌn- **-ness** -nəs, -nɪs
unbidden ʌnˈbɪd.ᵊn, ˌʌn-, ʌm-, ˌʌm- US ʌn-, ˌʌn-
un|bind ʌn|ˈbaɪnd, ˌʌn-, ʌm-, ˌʌm- US ʌn-, ˌʌn- **-binds** -ˈbaɪndz **-binding** -ˈbaɪn.dɪŋ **-bound** -ˈbaʊnd
unbleached ʌnˈbliːtʃt, ˌʌn-, ʌm-, ˌʌm- US ʌn-, ˌʌn-
unblemished ʌnˈblem.ɪʃt, ˌʌn-, ʌm-, ˌʌm- US ʌn-, ˌʌn-
unblinking ʌnˈblɪŋ.kɪŋ, ʌm- US ʌn- **-ly** -li **-ness** -nəs, -nɪs
unblock ʌnˈblɒk, ʌm- US ʌnˈblɑːk **-s** -s **-ing** -ɪŋ **-ed** -t **-er/s** -əʳ/z US -ɚ/z
unblushing ʌnˈblʌʃ.ɪŋ, ˌʌn-, ʌm-, ˌʌm- US ʌn-, ˌʌn- **-ly** -li
un|bolt ʌn|ˈbəʊlt, ˌʌn-, ʌm-, ˌʌm- US ʌn|ˈboʊlt, ˌʌn- **-bolts** -ˈbəʊlts US -ˈboʊlts **-bolting** -ˈbəʊl.tɪŋ US -ˈboʊl.t̬ɪŋ **-bolted** -ˈbəʊl.tɪd US -ˈboʊl.t̬ɪd
unborn ʌnˈbɔːn, ˈʌn-, ʌm-, ˌʌm- US ʌnˈbɔːrn, ˌʌn- ˌ**unborn ˈchild**
unbosom ʌnˈbʊz.əm, ˌʌn-, ʌm-, ˌʌm- US ʌn-, ˌʌn- **-s** -z **-ing** -ɪŋ **-ed** -d
unbound ʌnˈbaʊnd, ˌʌn-, ʌm-, ˌʌm- US ʌn-, ˌʌn-
unbounded ʌnˈbaʊn.dɪd, ˌʌn-, ʌm-, ˌʌm- US ʌn-, ˌʌn- **-ness** -nəs, -nɪs
unbowed ʌnˈbaʊd, ˌʌn-, ʌm-, ˌʌm- US ʌn-, ˌʌn-
unbridled ʌnˈbraɪ.dl̩d, ˌʌn-, ʌm-, ˌʌm- US ʌn-, ˌʌn-
unbroken ʌnˈbrəʊ.kᵊn, ˌʌn-, ʌm-, ˌʌm- US ʌnˈbroʊ-, ˌʌn-
unbuckl|e ʌnˈbʌk.l̩, ˌʌn-, ʌm-, ˌʌm- US ʌn-, ˌʌn- **-es** -z **-ing** -ɪŋ, -ˈbʌk.lɪŋ **-ed** -d
unbuilt ʌnˈbɪlt, ʌm- US ʌn-
unburden ʌnˈbɜː.dᵊn, ˌʌn-, ʌm-, ˌʌm- US ʌnˈbɝː-, ˌʌn- **-s** -z **-ing** -ɪŋ **-ed** -d
unburied ʌnˈber.id, ˌʌn-, ʌm-, ˌʌm- US ʌn-, ˌʌn-
unbusiness-like ʌnˈbɪz.nɪs.laɪk, -nəs-, ˌʌn-, ʌm-, ˌʌm- US ʌn-, ˌʌn-
unbutton ʌnˈbʌt.ᵊn, ˌʌn-, ʌm-, ˌʌm- US ʌn-, ˌʌn- **-s** -z **-ing** -ɪŋ, -ˈbʌt.nɪŋ **-ed** -d
uncalculat|ed ʌnˈkæl.kjə.leɪ.t|ɪd, ʌŋ-, -kjʊ- US ʌn- **-ing** -ɪŋ
uncalled-for ʌnˈkɔːld.fɔːʳ, ˌʌn-, ʌŋ-, ˌʌŋ- US ʌnˈkɔːld.fɔːr, ˌʌn-, -ˈkɑːld-
uncann|y ʌnˈkæn|.i, ˌʌn-, ʌŋ-, ˌʌŋ- US ʌn-, ˌʌn- **-ier** -i.əʳ US -i.ɚ **-iest** -i.ɪst, -i.əst **-ily** -ɪ.li, -ᵊl.i **-iness** -ɪ.nəs, -ɪ.nɪs
uncanonical ˌʌn.kəˈnɒn.ɪ.kᵊl, ˌʌŋ- US ˌʌn.kəˈnɑː.nɪ-
uncap ʌnˈkæp, ˌʌn-, ʌŋ-, ˌʌŋ- US ʌn-, ˌʌn- **-s** -s **-ping** -ɪŋ **-ped** -t
uncared-for ʌnˈkeəd.fɔːʳ, ˌʌn-, ʌŋ-, ˌʌŋ- US ʌnˈkerd.fɔːr, ˌʌn-
uncaring ʌnˈkeə.rɪŋ, ʌŋ- US ʌn- **-ly** -li **-ness** -nəs, -nɪs
Uncas ˈʌŋ.kəs
uncatalog(u)ed ʌnˈkæt.ᵊl.ɒɡd, ˌʌn-, ʌŋ-, ˌʌŋ- US ʌnˈkæt̬.ᵊl.ɑːɡd, ˌʌn-, -ɔːɡd
unceasing ʌnˈsiː.sɪŋ, ˌʌn- **-ly** -li **-ness** -nəs, -nɪs
uncensored ʌnˈsen*t*.səd, ˌʌn- US -sɚd
unceremonious ʌnˌser.ɪˈməʊ.ni.əs, ˌʌn-, -əˈ- US -ˈmoʊ- **-ly** -li **-ness** -nəs, -nɪs
uncertain ʌnˈsɜː.tᵊn, ˌʌn- US -ˈsɝː- **-ly** -li
uncertaint|y ʌnˈsɜː.tᵊn.t|i, ˌʌn- US -ˈsɝː.tᵊn.t̬|i **-ies** -iz
unchain ʌnˈtʃeɪn, ˌʌn- **-s** -z **-ing** -ɪŋ **-ed** -d
unchallenged ʌnˈtʃæl.ɪndʒd, ˌʌn-, -əndʒd
unchangeability ʌnˌtʃeɪn.dʒəˈbɪl.ɪ.ti, ˌʌn-, -ə.ti US -ə.t̬i
unchangeab|le ʌnˈtʃeɪn.dʒə.bl̩, ˌʌn- **-ly** -li **-leness** -l̩.nəs, -nɪs
unchanged ʌnˈtʃeɪndʒd, ˌʌn-
unchanging ʌnˈtʃeɪn.dʒɪŋ, ˌʌn-
uncharacteristic ˌʌn.kær.ək.tᵊrˈɪs.tɪk, ʌnˈkær-, ˌʌŋ- US ʌnˌker.ɪk.təˈrɪs.tɪk, -ˌkær- **-ally** -ᵊl.i, -li
uncharged ʌnˈtʃɑːdʒd, ˌʌn- US -ˈtʃɑːrdʒd
uncharitab|le ʌnˈtʃær.ɪ.tə.bl̩, ˌʌn-, ˈ-ə- US -ˈtʃer.ə.t̬ə-, -ˈtʃær- **-ly** -li **-leness** -l̩.nəs, -nɪs
uncharted ʌnˈtʃɑː.tɪd, ˌʌn- US -ˈtʃɑːr.t̬ɪd **unˌcharted ˈwaters, ˌuncharted ˈwaters**
unchartered ʌnˈtʃɑː.təd, ˌʌn- US -ˈtʃɑːr.t̬ɚd
unchaste ʌnˈtʃeɪst US ˌʌn- **-ly** -li
unchastened ʌnˈtʃeɪ.sᵊnd, ˌʌn-
unchecked ʌnˈtʃekt, ˌʌn-
unchivalrous ʌnˈʃɪv.ᵊl.rəs **-ly** -li **-ness** -nəs, -nɪs
unchristian ʌnˈkrɪs.tʃən, ˌʌn-, ʌŋ-, ˌʌŋ-, -ˈkrɪʃ-, -ti.ən US ʌnˈkrɪs-, ˌʌn-
uncial ˈʌn*t*.si.əl US -ʃi-, ˈ-ʃᵊl **-s** -z
unciform ˈʌn*t*.sɪ.fɔːm US -fɔːrm
uncinate ˈʌn.sɪ.nɪt, -neɪt, -nət
uncircumcised ʌnˈsɜː.kəm.saɪzd, ˌʌn- US -ˈsɝː-
uncircumcision ʌnˌsɜː.kəmˈsɪʒ.ᵊn, ˌʌn- US -ˌsɝː-
uncivil ʌnˈsɪv.ᵊl, -ɪl, ˌʌn- **-ly** -i
uncivilized, -ised ʌnˈsɪv.ᵊl.aɪzd, ˌʌn-, -ɪ.laɪzd
unclaimed ʌnˈkleɪmd, ˌʌn-, ʌŋ-, ˌʌŋ- US ʌn-, ˌʌn-
unclamp ʌnˈklæmp, ʌŋ- US ʌn- **-s** -s **-ing** -ɪŋ **-ed** -t
unclasp ʌnˈklɑːsp, ˌʌn-, ʌŋ-, ˌʌŋ- US ʌnˈklæsp, ˌʌn- **-s** -s **-ing** -ɪŋ **-ed** -t
unclassified ʌnˈklæs.ɪ.faɪd, ˌʌn-, ʌŋ-, ˌʌŋ- US ʌn-, ˌʌn-
uncle ˈʌŋ.kl̩ **-s** -z ˌ**Uncle ˈSam**; ˌ**Uncle ˈTom**
unclean ʌnˈkliːn, ˌʌn-, ʌŋ-, ˌʌŋ- US ʌn-, ˌʌn- **-ly** -li **-ness** -nəs, -nɪs
uncleanl|y ʌnˈklen.l|i, ˌʌn-, ʌŋ-, ˌʌŋ- US ʌn-, ˌʌn- **-iness** -ɪ.nəs, -ɪ.nɪs
unclear ʌnˈklɪəʳ, ˌʌn-, ʌŋ-, ˌʌŋ- US ʌnˈklɪr, ˌʌn-
unclench ʌnˈklen*t*ʃ, ˌʌn-, ʌŋ-, ˌʌŋ- US ʌnˈklentʃ, ˌʌn- **-es** -ɪz **-ing** -ɪŋ **-ed** -t
unclog ʌnˈklɒɡ, ʌŋ- US ʌnˈklɑːɡ, -ˈklɔːɡ **-s** -z **-ging** -ɪŋ **-ged** -d
unclos|e ʌnˈkləʊz, ˌʌn-, ʌŋ-, ˌʌŋ- US ʌnˈkloʊz, ˌʌn- **-es** -ɪz **-ing** -ɪŋ **-ed** -d
unclothed ʌnˈkləʊðd, ˌʌn-, ʌŋ-, ˌʌŋ- US ʌnˈkloʊðd, ˌʌn-
unclouded ʌnˈklaʊ.dɪd, ˌʌn-, ʌŋ-, ˌʌŋ- US ʌn-, ˌʌn-
uncluttered ʌnˈklʌt.əd, ˌʌn-, ʌŋ-, ˌʌŋ- US ʌnˈklʌt̬.ɚd, ˌʌn-
uncoil ʌnˈkɔɪl, ˌʌn-, ʌŋ-, ˌʌŋ- US ʌn-, ˌʌn- **-s** -z **-ing** -ɪŋ **-ed** -d
uncollected ˌʌn.kəˈlek.tɪd, ˌʌŋ- US ˌʌn-
uncolo(u)red ʌnˈkʌl.əd, ˌʌn-, ʌŋ-, ˌʌŋ- US ʌnˈkʌl.ɚd, ˌʌn-
uncomfortab|le ʌnˈkʌm*p*f.tə.bl̩, ˌʌn-, ʌŋ-, ˌʌŋ-, -ˈkʌm*p*.fə.tə- US ʌnˈkʌm*p*.fɚ.t̬ə-, ˌʌn-, -ˈkʌm*p*f.tə- **-ly** -li **-leness** -l̩.nəs, -nɪs
uncommercial ˌʌn.kəˈmɜː.ʃᵊl, ˌʌŋ- US ˌʌn.kəˈmɝː-
uncommercialized, -ised ˌʌn.kəˈmɜː.ʃᵊl.aɪzd, ˌʌŋ- US ˌʌn.kəˈmɝː-
uncommitted ˌʌn.kəˈmɪt.ɪd, ˌʌŋ- US ˌʌn.kəˈmɪt̬-

uncommon ʌn'kɒm.ən, ˌʌn-, ʌŋ-, ˌʌŋ- US ʌn'kɑː.mən, ˌʌn- **-ly** -li **-ness** -nəs, -nɪs

uncommunicable ˌʌn.kə'mjuː.nɪ.kə.bl̩, ˌʌŋ-, -nə- US ˌʌn-

uncommunicated ˌʌn.kə'mjuː.nɪ.keɪ.tɪd, ˌʌŋ-, -nə- US ˌʌn.kə'mjuː.nɪ.keɪ.t̬ɪd, -nə-

uncommunicative ˌʌn.kə'mjuː.nɪ.kə.tɪv, ˌʌŋ-, -nə-, -keɪ- US ˌʌn.kə'mjuː.nɪ.kə.t̬ɪv, -nə-, -keɪ- **-ness** -nəs, -nɪs

uncompetitive ˌʌn.kəm'pet.ɪ.tɪv, ˌʌŋ-, '-ə- US ˌʌn.kəm'pet̬.ə.t̬ɪv **-ly** -li **-ness** -nəs, -nɪs

uncomplaining ˌʌn.kəm'pleɪ.nɪŋ, ˌʌŋ- US ˌʌn- **-ly** -li

uncompleted ˌʌn.kəm'pliː.tɪd, ˌʌŋ- US ˌʌn.kəm'pliː.t̬ɪd

uncomplicated ˌʌn'kɒm.plɪ.keɪ.tɪd, ˌʌŋ- US ʌn'kɑːm.plɪ.keɪ.t̬ɪd

uncomplimentary ʌnˌkɒm.plɪ'men.tᵊr.i, ˌʌn-, ʌŋ-, ˌʌŋ-, -plə'- US ʌnˌkɑːm.plə'men.t̬ɚ-, ˌʌn-

uncompounded ˌʌn.kəm'paʊn.dɪd, ˌʌŋ- US ˌʌn-

uncomprehending ˌʌn.kɒm.prɪ'hen.dɪŋ, ˌʌŋ- US ˌʌn.kɑːm- **-ly** -li

uncompromising ʌn'kɒm.prə.maɪ.zɪŋ, ˌʌn-, ʌŋ-, ˌʌŋ- US ʌn'kɑːm-, ˌʌn- **-ly** -li **-ness** -nəs, -nɪs

unconcealed ˌʌn.kən'siːld, ˌʌŋ- US ˌʌn-

unconcern ˌʌn.kən'sɜːn, ˌʌŋ- US ˌʌn.kən'sɝːn **-ed** -d **-edly** -d.li, -ɪd.li **-edness** -d.nəs, -nɪs, -ɪd.nəs, -nɪs

unconditional ˌʌn.kən'dɪʃ.ᵊn.ᵊl, ˌʌŋ-, '-nᵊl US ˌʌn- **-ly** -i **ˌunconditional 'offer**

unconditioned ˌʌn.kən'dɪʃ.ᵊnd, ˌʌŋ- US ˌʌn-

unconfined ˌʌn.kən'faɪnd, ˌʌŋ- US ˌʌn-

unconfirmed ˌʌn.kən'fɜːmd, ˌʌŋ- US ˌʌn.kən'fɝːmd

unconformit|y ˌʌn.kən'fɔː.mə.t|i, ˌʌŋ-, -mɪ.t|i US ˌʌn.kən'fɔːr.mə.t̬|i **-ies** -iz

uncongenial ˌʌn.kən'dʒiː.ni.əl, ˌʌŋ- US ˌʌn-, -jəl

uncongeniality ˌʌn.kənˌdʒiː.ni'æl.ɪ.ti, ˌʌŋ-, -ə.ti US ˌʌn.kənˌdʒiː.ni'æl.ə.t̬i

unconnected ˌʌn.kə'nek.tɪd, ˌʌŋ- US ˌʌn- **-ness** -nəs, -nɪs

unconquerab|le ʌn'kɒŋ.kᵊr.ə.b|l̩, ˌʌn-, ʌŋ-, ˌʌŋ- US ʌn'kɑːŋ-, ˌʌn- **-ly** -li

unconquered ʌn'kɒŋ.kəd, ˌʌn-, ʌŋ-, ˌʌŋ- US ʌn'kɑːŋ.kɚd, ˌʌn-

unconscionab|le ʌn'kɒn.tʃᵊn.ə.b|l̩, ˌʌn-, ʌŋ-, ˌʌŋ- US ʌn'kɑːn-, ˌʌn- **-ly** -li **-leness** -l̩.nəs, -nɪs

unconscious ʌn'kɒn.tʃəs, ˌʌn-, ʌŋ-, ˌʌŋ- US ʌn'kɑːn-, ˌʌn- **-ly** -li **-ness** -nəs, -nɪs

unconsecrated ʌn'kɒnt.sɪ.kreɪ.tɪd, ˌʌn-, ʌŋ-, ˌʌŋ-, -sə- US ʌn'kɑːnt.sə-, ˌʌn-

unconsidered ˌʌn.kən'sɪd.əd, ˌʌŋ- US ˌʌn.kən'sɪd.ɚd

unconstitutional ʌnˌkɒnt.stɪ'tjuː.ʃᵊn.ᵊl, ˌʌn-, ʌŋ-, ˌʌŋ-, -stə'-, -'tʃuː-, -'tjuːʃ.nᵊl, -'tʃuːʃ- US ʌnˌkɑːnt.stə'tuː-, ˌʌn-, -'tjuː- **-ly** -i

unconstrain|ed ˌʌn.kən'streɪn|d, ˌʌŋ- US ˌʌn- **-edly** -d.li, -ɪd.li

uncontaminated ˌʌn.kən'tæm.ɪ.neɪ.tɪd, ˌʌŋ-, '-ə- US ˌʌn.kən'tæm.ɪ.neɪ.t̬ɪd, '-ə-

uncontestable ˌʌn.kən'tes.tə.bl̩, ˌʌŋ- US ˌʌn-

uncontested ˌʌn.kən'tes.tɪd, ˌʌŋ- US ˌʌn-

uncontradicted ʌnˌkɒn.trə'dɪk.tɪd, ˌʌn-, ʌŋ-, ˌʌŋ- US ʌnˌkɑːn-, ˌʌn-

uncontrollab|le ˌʌn.kən'trəʊ.lə.b|l̩, ˌʌŋ- US ˌʌn.kən'troʊ- **-ly** -li **-leness** -l̩.nəs, -nɪs

uncontrolled ˌʌn.kən'trəʊld, ˌʌŋ- US ˌʌn.kən'troʊld

unconvention|al ˌʌn.kən'ven.tʃᵊn|.ᵊl, ˌʌŋ-, -'ventʃ.n|ᵊl US ˌʌn.kən'vent.ʃᵊn|.ᵊl, -'ventʃ.n|ᵊl **-ally** -ᵊl.i

unconventionalit|y ˌʌn.kənˌven.tʃᵊn'æl.ə.t|i, ˌʌŋ-, -ɪ.t|i US ˌʌn.kənˌven.tʃᵊn'æl.ə.t̬|i **-ies** -iz

unconverted ˌʌn.kən'vɜː.tɪd, ˌʌŋ- US ˌʌn.kən'vɝː.t̬ɪd

unconvertible ˌʌn.kən'vɜː.tə.bl̩, ˌʌŋ-, -tɪ- US ˌʌn.kən'vɝː.t̬ə-

unconvinced ˌʌn.kən'vɪntst, ˌʌŋ- US ˌʌn-

unconvincing ˌʌn.kən'vɪnt.sɪŋ, ˌʌŋ- US ˌʌn- **-ly** -li

uncooked ʌn'kʊkt, ˌʌn-, ʌŋ-, ˌʌŋ- US ʌn-, ˌʌn-

uncool ʌn'kuːl, ˌʌn-, ʌŋ- US ʌn-, ˌʌn- **-ly** -li **-ness** -nəs, -nɪs

uncooperative ˌʌn.kəʊ'ɒp.ᵊr.ə.tɪv, ˌʌŋ-, '-rə- US ˌʌn.koʊ'ɑː.pɚ.ə.t̬ɪv, '-prə- **-ly** -li **-ness** -nəs, -nɪs

uncoordinated ˌʌn.kəʊ'ɔː.dɪ.neɪ.tɪd, ˌʌŋ- US ˌʌn.koʊ'ɔːr.dᵊn.eɪ.t̬ɪd

uncork ʌn'kɔːk, ˌʌn-, ʌŋ-, ˌʌŋ- US ʌn'kɔːrk, ˌʌn- **-s** -s **-ing** -ɪŋ **-ed** -t

uncorrected ˌʌn.kᵊr'ek.tɪd, ˌʌŋ- US ˌʌn.kə'rek-

uncorroborated ˌʌn.kᵊr'ɒb.ᵊr.eɪ.tɪd, ˌʌŋ- US ˌʌn.kə'rɑː.bə.reɪ.t̬ɪd

uncorrupt ˌʌn.kᵊr'ʌpt, ˌʌŋ- US ˌʌn.kə'rʌpt **-ness** -nəs, -nɪs

uncorrupted ˌʌn.kᵊr'ʌp.tɪd, ˌʌŋ- US ˌʌn.kə'rʌp-

uncountable ʌn'kaʊn.tə.bl̩, ˌʌn-, ʌŋ-, ˌʌŋ- US ʌn'kaʊn.t̬ə-, ˌʌn- **unˌcountable 'noun**

uncounted ʌn'kaʊn.tɪd, ˌʌn-, ʌŋ-, ˌʌŋ US ʌn'kaʊn.t̬ɪd, ˌʌn-

uncoupl|e ʌn'kʌp.l̩, ˌʌn-, ʌŋ-, ˌʌŋ- US ʌn-, ˌʌn- **-es** -z **-ing** -ɪŋ, -'kʌp.lɪŋ **-ed** -d

uncouth ʌn'kuːθ, ˌʌn-, ʌŋ-, ˌʌŋ- US ʌn-, ˌʌn- **-ly** -li **-ness** -nəs, -nɪs

uncov|er ʌn'kʌv|.əʳ, ˌʌn-, ʌŋ-, ˌʌŋ- US ʌn'kʌv|.ɚ, ˌʌn- **-ers** -əz US -ɚz **-ering** -ᵊr.ɪŋ **-ered** -əd US -ɚd

uncritic|al ʌn'krɪt.ɪ.k|ᵊl, ˌʌn-, ʌŋ-, ˌʌŋ- US ʌn'krɪt̬.ɪ-, ˌʌn- **-ally** -ᵊl.i, -li

uncrossed ʌn'krɒst, ˌʌn-, ʌŋ-, ˌʌŋ- US ʌn'krɑːst, ˌʌn-

uncrowned ʌn'kraʊnd, ˌʌn-, ʌŋ-, ˌʌŋ- US ʌn-, ˌʌn- *stress shift, see compounds:* **ˌuncrowned 'king; ˌuncrowned 'queen**

uncrushable ʌn'krʌʃ.ə.bl̩, ˌʌn-, ʌŋ-, ˌʌŋ- US ʌn-, ˌʌn-

unction 'ʌŋk.ʃᵊn **-s** -z

unctuosity ˌʌŋk.tju'ɒs.ə.ti, -tʃu'-, -ɪ.t US -tʃu'ɑː.sə.t̬i

unctuous 'ʌŋk.tju.əs, -tʃu- US -tʃu-, '-tʃəs **-ly** -li **-ness** -nəs, -nɪs

uncultivated ʌn'kʌl.tɪ.veɪ.tɪd, ˌʌn-, ʌŋ-, ˌʌŋ-, -tə- US ʌn'kʌl.t̬ə.veɪ.t̬ɪd, ˌʌn-

uncultured ʌn'kʌl.tʃəd, ˌʌn-, ʌŋ-, ˌʌŋ- US ʌn'kʌl.tʃɚd, ˌʌn-

uncurbed ʌn'kɜːbd, ˌʌn-, ʌŋ-, ˌʌŋ- US ʌn'kɝːbd, ˌʌn-

uncurl ʌn'kɜːl, ˌʌn-, ʌŋ-, ˌʌŋ- US ʌn'kɝːl, ˌʌn- **-s** -z **-ing** -ɪŋ **-ed** -d

uncut ʌn'kʌt, ˌʌn-, ʌŋ-, ˌʌŋ- US ʌn-, ˌʌn-

undamaged ʌn'dæm.ɪdʒd, ˌʌn-

undated *wavy:* 'ʌn.deɪ.tɪd US -t̬ɪd

undated *not dated:* ʌn'deɪ.tɪd, ˌʌn- US -t̬ɪd

undaunted ʌn'dɔːn.tɪd, ˌʌn- US -'dɑːn.t̬ɪd, -'dɔːn- **-ly** -li **-ness** -nəs, -nɪs

undebated ˌʌn.dɪ'beɪ.tɪd, -də'- US -t̬ɪd

undeceiv|e ˌʌn.dɪ'siːv, -də'- **-es** -z **-ing** -ɪŋ **-ed** -d

undecided ˌʌn.dɪ'saɪ.dɪd, -də'- **-ly** -li **-ness** -nəs, -nɪs

undecipherab|le ˌʌn.dɪ'saɪ.fᵊr.ə.b|l̩, -də'- **-ly** -li

undecisive ˌʌn.dɪ'saɪ.sɪv, -də'-, -zɪv US -sɪv **-ly** -li **-ness** -nəs, -nɪs

undeclared ˌʌn.dɪ'kleəd, -də'- US -'klerd

undefeated ˌʌn.dɪ'fiː.tɪd, -də'- US -dɪ'fiː.t̬ɪd

undefended ˌʌn.dɪ'fen.dɪd, -də'-

undefiled ˌʌn.dɪˈfaɪld, -dəˈ-

undefinab|le ˌʌn.dɪˈfaɪ.nə.b|l̩, -dəˈ- **-ly** -li

undefined ˌʌn.dɪˈfaɪnd, -dəˈ-

unde|lete ˌʌn.dɪ|ˈliːt, -dəˈ- US -dɪˈ- **-letes** -ˈliːts **-leting** -ˈliː.tɪŋ US -ˈliː.t̬ɪŋ **-leted** -ˈliː.tɪd US -ˈliː.t̬ɪd

undelivered ˌʌn.dɪˈlɪv.əd, -dəˈ- US -ɚd

undemanding ˌʌn.dɪˈmɑːn.dɪŋ, -dəˈ- US -dɪˈmæn-

undemocratic ʌn.dem.əˈkræt.ɪk, ˌʌn- **-ally** -ᵊl.i, -li

undemonstrative ˌʌn.dɪˈmɒn*t*.strə.tɪv, -dəˈ- US -ˈmɑːn*t*.strə.t̬ɪv **-ly** -li **-ness** -nəs, -nɪs

undeniab|le ˌʌn.dɪˈnaɪ.ə.b|l̩, -dəˈ- **-ly** -li

undenominational ˌʌn.dɪˌnɒm.ɪˈneɪ.ʃᵊn.ᵊl, -dəˌ-, -əˈ-, -ˈneɪʃ.nᵊl US -ˌnɑː.mɪˈ-, -məˈ- **-ism** -ɪ.zᵊm

under- ʌn.dəʳ- US ʌn.dɚ-

Note: Prefix. May receive primary stress, e.g. **undercarriage** /ˈʌn.dəˌkær.ɪdʒ US ˈʌn.dɚ-/, or secondary stress, e.g. **understand** /ˌʌn.dəˈstænd US -dɚˈ-/. Such secondary-stressed syllables may come to carry the strongest stress in the word through stress-shift, e.g. **understand** /ˌʌn.dəˈstænd US ˌʌn.dɚ-/, **understand problems** /ˌʌn.də.stændˈprɒb.ləmz US ˌʌn.dɚ.stændˈprɑː.bləmz/. Although /r/ is normally assigned to a following strong syllable in American English, when /ɚ/ is perceived to be morphemically linked to the preceding unit /r/ is retained as /ɚ/.

under ˈʌn.dəʳ US -dɚ **-s** -z ˌ**under** ˈ**way**

underachiev|e ˌʌn.dəʳ.əˈtʃiːv US -dɚ- **-es** -z **-ing** -ɪŋ **-ed** -d **-er/s** -əʳ/z US -ɚ/z **-ment/s** -mənt/s

underact ˌʌn.dəʳˈækt US -dɚˈ- **-s** -s **-ing** -ɪŋ **-ed** -ɪd

under-age ˌʌn.dəʳˈeɪdʒ US -dɚˈ- *stress shift:* ˌunder-age ˈdrinking

underarm ˈʌn.dəʳ.ɑːm US -dɚ.ɑːrm

underbell|y ˈʌn.dəˌbel|.i US -dɚˌ- **-ies** -iz

underbid ˌʌn.dəˈbɪd US -dɚˈ- **-s** -z **-ding** -ɪŋ **-der/s** -əʳ/z US -ɚ/z

underbred ˌʌn.dəˈbred US -dɚˈ- *stress shift:* ˌunderbred ˈstock

underbrush ˈʌn.də.brʌʃ US -dɚ-

underbudgeted ˌʌn.dəˈbʌdʒ.ɪ.tɪd, ˈ-ə- US -dɚˈbʌdʒ.ɪ.t̬ɪd

under|buy ˌʌn.də|ˈbaɪ US -dɚˈ- **-buys** -ˈbaɪz **-buying** -ˈbaɪ.ɪŋ **-bought** -ˈbɔːt US -ˈbɑːt, -ˈbɔːt

undercapitaliz|e, -is|e ˌʌn.dəˈkæp.ɪ.tᵊl.aɪz US -dɚˈ- **-es** -ɪz **-ing** -ɪŋ **-ed** -d

undercard ˈʌn.də.kɑːd US -dɚ.kɑːrd **-s** -z

undercarriag|e ˈʌn.dəˌkær.ɪdʒ US -dɚˌker-, -ˌkær- **-es** -ɪz

undercharg|e (*n.*) ˈʌn.dəˌtʃɑːdʒ, ˌ--ˈ- US ˈʌn.dɚ.tʃɑːrdʒ **-es** -ɪz

undercharg|e (*v.*) ˌʌn.dəˈtʃɑːdʒ US -dɚˈtʃɑːrdʒ **-es** -ɪz **-ing** -ɪŋ **-ed** -d

underclass ˈʌn.də.klɑːs US -dɚ.klæs **-es** -ɪz

under-clerk ˈʌn.də.klɑːk US -dɚ.klɝːk **-s** -s

underclothes ˈʌn.də.kləʊðz US -dɚ.kloʊðz, -kloʊz

underclothing ˈʌn.dəˌkləʊ.ðɪŋ US -dɚˌkloʊ-

undercoat ˈʌn.də.kəʊt US -dɚ.koʊt **-s** -s **-ing** -ɪŋ

undercook ˌʌn.dəˈkʊk US -dɚˈ- **-s** -s **-ing** -ɪŋ **-ed** -t

undercover ˌʌn.dəˈkʌv.əʳ US -dɚˈkʌv.ɚ *stress shift:* ˌundercover ˈagent

undercroft ˈʌn.də.krɒft US -dɚ.krɑːft **-s** -s

undercurrent ˈʌn.dəˌkʌr.ᵊnt US -dɚˌkɝː- **-s** -s

undercut (*n.*) ˈʌn.də.kʌt US -dɚ- **-s** -s

under|cut (*adj. v.*) ˌʌn.də|ˈkʌt US -dɚˈ- **-cuts** -ˈkʌts **-cutting** -ˈkʌt.ɪŋ US -ˈkʌt̬.ɪŋ

underdevelop|ed ˌʌn.də.dɪˈvel.əp|t, -dəˈ- US -dɚ- **-ment** -mənt *stress shift:* ˌunderdeveloped ˈbrain

under|do ˌʌn.də|ˈduː US -dɚˈ- **-does** -ˈdʌz **-doing** -ˈduː.ɪŋ **-did** -ˈdɪd **-done** -ˈdʌn

underdog ˈʌn.də.dɒg US -dɚ.dɑːg, -dɔːg **-s** -z

underdone ˌʌn.dəˈdʌn US -dɚˈ- *stress shift:* ˌunderdone ˈbeef

underdress ˌʌn.dəˈdres US -dɚˈ- **-es** -ɪz **-ing** -ɪŋ **-ed** -t

undereducated ˌʌn.dᵊrˈedʒ.ʊ.keɪ.tɪd, -ˈed.jʊ- US -dɚˈedʒ.ʊ.keɪ.t̬ɪd, ˈ-ə-

undereducation ˌʌn.dᵊr.edʒ.ʊˈkeɪ.ʃᵊn, -ed.jʊ- US -dɚ.edʒ.ʊ-, -əˈ-

underemployed ˌʌn.dᵊr.ɪmˈplɔɪd, -emˈ- US -dɚ- *stress shift:* ˌunderemployed ˈworkforce

underemployment ˌʌn.dᵊr.ɪmˈplɔɪ.mənt US -dɚ-

underestimate (*n.*) ˌʌn.dᵊrˈes.tɪ.mət, -tə-, -mɪt, -meɪt US -dɚˈes.tə.mɪt, -mət **-s** -s

underesti|mate (*v.*) ˌʌn.dᵊrˈes.tɪ|.meɪt, -tə- US -dɚˈes.tə- **-mates** -meɪts **-mating** -meɪ.tɪŋ US -meɪ.t̬ɪŋ **-mated** -meɪ.tɪd US -meɪ.t̬ɪd

underestimation ˌʌn.dᵊrˌes.tɪˈmeɪ.ʃᵊn, -təˈ- US -dɚˌes.təˈ- **-s** -z

under-expos|e ˌʌn.dᵊr.ɪkˈspəʊz, -ekˈ- US -dɚ.ɪkˈspoʊz, -ekˈ- **-es** -ɪz **-ing** -ɪŋ **-ed** -d

underexposure ˌʌn.dᵊr.ɪkˈspəʊ.ʒəʳ, -ekˈ- US -dɚ.ɪkˈspoʊ.ʒɚ, -ekˈ- **-s** -z

under-eye ˈʌn.dᵊr.aɪ

under|feed ˌʌn.də|ˈfiːd US -dɚˈ- **-feeds** -ˈfiːdz **-feeding** -ˈfiː.dɪŋ **-fed** -ˈfed *stress shift:* ˌunderfed ˈchickens

underfelt ˈʌn.də.felt US -dɚ- **-s** -s

underfinanced ˌʌn.dəˈfaɪ.næn*t*st US -dɚˈ-

underfloor ˌʌn.dəˈflɔːʳ US -dɚˈflɔːr *stress shift:* ˌunderfloor ˈheating

underfoot ˌʌn.dəˈfʊt US -dɚˈ-

underfund ˌʌn.dəˈfʌnd US -dɚˈ- **-s** -z **-ing** -ɪŋ **-ed** -ɪd

undergarment ˈʌn.dəˌgɑː.mənt US -dɚˌgɑːr- **-s** -s

under|go ˌʌn.də|ˈgəʊ US -dɚ|ˈgoʊ **-goes** -ˈgəʊz US -ˈgoʊz **-going** -ˈgəʊ.ɪŋ US -ˈgoʊ.ɪŋ **-went** -ˈwent **-gone** -ˈgɒn US -ˈgɑːn *stress shift:* ˌundergo ˈtreatment

undergrad ˈʌn.də.græd US -dɚ- **-s** -z

undergraduate ˌʌn.dəˈgrædʒ.u.ət, -ˈgræd.ju-, -ɪt US -dɚˈgrædʒ.u.ət, -ə.wət **-s** -s *stress shift:* ˌundergraduate ˈhumour

underground (U) (*n. adj.*) ˈʌn.də.graʊnd US -dɚ- **-er/s** -əʳ/z US -ɚ/z

underground (*adv.*) ˌʌn.dəˈgraʊnd US -dɚˈ-

undergrown ˌʌn.dəˈgrəʊn US -dɚˈgroʊn *stress shift:* ˌundergrown ˈtrees

undergrowth ˈʌn.də.grəʊθ US -dɚ.groʊθ

underhand ˌʌn.dəˈhænd US -dɚˈ- **-ed/ly** -ɪd/li **-edness** -ɪd.nəs, -nɪs *stress shift:* ˌunderhand ˈtrick

Underhill ˈʌn.də.hɪl US -dɚ-

underhung ˌʌn.dəˈhʌŋ US -dɚˈ- *stress shift:* ˌunderhung ˈaxle

underinsured ˌʌn.dᵊr.ɪnˈʃʊəd, -ˈʃɔːd US -dɚ.ɪnˈʃʊrd

underlay (*n.*) ˈʌn.dᵊl.eɪ US -dɚ.leɪ **-s** -z

under|lay (*v.*) ˌʌn.də|ˈleɪ US -dɚˈ- **-lays** -ˈleɪz **-laying** -ˈleɪ.ɪŋ **-laid** -ˈleɪd

under|let ˌʌn.də|ˈlet US -dɚˈ- **-lets** -ˈlets **-letting** -ˈlet.ɪŋ US -ˈlet̬.ɪŋ

under|lie ˌʌn.də|ˈlaɪ US -dɚˈ- **-lies** -ˈlaɪz **-lying** -ˈlaɪ.ɪŋ **-lay** -ˈleɪ **-lain** -ˈleɪn

underline (*n.*) ˈʌn.dᵊl.aɪn US ˈʌn.dɚ.laɪn **-s** -z

underlin|e (*v.*) ˌʌn.dəˈlaɪn US -dɚˈ-, ˈ--- **-es** -z **-ing** -ɪŋ **-ed** -d

underling ˈʌn.dᵊl.ɪŋ US -dɚ.lɪŋ **-s** -z

underlip ˈʌn.dᵊl.ɪp US -dɚ.lɪp **-s** -s

underlying ˌʌn.dəˈlaɪ.ɪŋ US -dɚˈ-, ˈʌn.dɚˌlaɪ.ɪŋ *stress shift, British only:* ˌunderlying ˈcause

underman ˌʌn.dəˈmæn US -dɚˈ- **-s** -z **-ning** -ɪŋ **-ned** -d *stress shift:* ˌundermanned ˈindustry

undermentioned ˌʌn.dəˈmen.tʃᵊnd US -dɚˈ- *stress shift:* ˌundermentioned ˈclause

undermin|e ˌʌn.dəˈmaɪn US -dɚˈ-, ˈ--- **-es** -z **-ing** -ɪŋ **-ed** -d **-er/s** -əʳ/z US -ɚ/z *stress shift, British only:* ˌundermine ˈconfidence

undermost ˈʌn.də.məʊst US -dɚ.moʊst

underneath ˌʌn.dəˈniːθ US -dɚˈ- *stress shift:* ˌunderneath ˈeverything

undernourish ˌʌn.dəˈnʌr.ɪʃ US -dɚˈnɝː- **-es** -ɪz **-ing** -ɪŋ **-ed** -t **-ment** -mənt

underpants ˈʌn.də.pænts US -dɚ-

underpass ˈʌn.də.pɑːs US -dɚ.pæs **-es** -ɪz

under|pay ˌʌn.də|ˈpeɪ US -dɚˈ- **-pays** -ˈpeɪz **-paying** -ˈpeɪ.ɪŋ **-paid** -ˈpeɪd *stress shift:* ˌunderpaid ˈstaff

underpayment ˌʌn.dəˈpeɪ.mənt US -dɚˈ- **-s** -s

underperform ˌʌn.də.pəˈfɔːm US -dɚ.pɚˈfɔːrm **-s** -z **-ing** -ɪŋ **-ed** -d **-er/s** -əʳ/z US -ɚ/z *stress shift:* ˌunderperforming ˈworker

underpin ˌʌn.dəˈpɪn US -dɚˈ-, ˈ--- **-s** -z **-ning** -ɪŋ **-ned** -d

underpinning ˈʌn.dəˌpɪn.ɪŋ US -dɚˌ- **-s** -z

underplay ˌʌn.dəˈpleɪ US -dɚˈ-, ˈ--- **-s** -z **-ing** -ɪŋ **-ed** -d

underpopulated ˌʌn.dəˈpɒp.jə.leɪ.tɪd, -pjʊ- US -dɚˈpɑː.pjə-, -pjʊ-

underpri|ce ˌʌn.dəˈpraɪ|s US -dɚˈ- **-ces** -sɪz **-ced** -st **-cing** -sɪŋ

underprivileged ˌʌn.dəˈprɪv.ᵊl.ɪdʒd, -vɪ.lɪdʒd US -dɚˈprɪv.ᵊl.ɪdʒd, ˈ-lɪdʒd

underproduc|e ˌʌn.də.prəˈdjuːs, -ˈdʒuːs US -dɚ.prəˈduːs, -ˈdjuːs **-es** -ɪz **-ing** -ɪŋ **-ed** -t

underproduction ˌʌn.də.prəˈdʌk.ʃᵊn US -dɚ-

underprop ˌʌn.dəˈprɒp US -dɚˈprɑːp **-s** -s **-ping** -ɪŋ **-ped** -t

under|rate ˌʌn.də|ˈreɪt US -dɚˈ- **-rates** -ˈreɪts **-rating** -ˈreɪ.tɪŋ US -ˈreɪ.t̬ɪŋ **-rated** -ˈreɪ.tɪd US -ˈreɪ.t̬ɪd

underrepresentation ˌʌn.dəˌrep.rɪ.zenˈteɪ.ʃᵊn US -dɚˌrep- **-s** -z

underrepresented ˌʌn.dəˌrep.rɪˈzen.tɪd, -rəˈ- US -dɚˌrep.rɪˈzen.t̬ɪd

underripe ˌʌn.dəˈraɪp US -dɚˈ- *stress shift:* ˌunderripe ˈfruit

under|run ˌʌn.də|ˈrʌn US -dɚˈ- **-runs** -ˈrʌnz **-running** -ˈrʌn.ɪŋ **-ran** -ˈræn

underscor|e (*v.*) ˌʌn.dəˈskɔːʳ US -dɚˈskɔːr, ˈ--- **-es** -z **-ing** -ɪŋ **-ed** -d

underscore (*n.*) ˈʌn.də.skɔːʳ US -dɚ.skɔːr **-s** -z

undersea ˌʌn.dəˈsiː US -dɚˈ- **-s** -z *stress shift:* ˌundersea ˈcable

underseal ˈʌn.də.siːl US -dɚ- **-s** -z **-ing** -ɪŋ **-ed** -d

undersecretar|y ˌʌn.dəˈsek.rə.tᵊr|.i, -rɪ-, -tr|i US -dɚˈsek.rə.ter- **-ies** -iz **-yship/s** -i.ʃɪp/s

under|sell ˌʌn.də|ˈsel US -dɚˈ- **-sells** -ˈselz **-selling** -ˈsel.ɪŋ **-sold** -ˈsəʊld US -ˈsoʊld

undersexed ˌʌn.dəˈsekst US -dɚˈ-

Undershaft ˈʌn.də.ʃɑːft US -dɚ.ʃæft

undersheriff ˈʌn.dəˌʃer.ɪf US -dɚˌ- **-s** -s

undershirt ˈʌn.də.ʃɜːt US -dɚ.ʃɝːt **-s** -s

under|shoot (*v.*) ˌʌn.də|ˈʃuːt US -dɚˈ- **-shoots** -ˈʃuːts **-shooting** -ˈʃuː.tɪŋ US -ˈʃuː.t̬ɪŋ **-shot** -ˈʃɒt US -ˈʃɑːt

undershoot (*n.*) ˈʌn.də.ʃuːt, ˌ--ˈ- US ˈʌn.dɚ.ʃuːt, ˌ--ˈ- **-s** -s

undershorts ˈʌn.də.ʃɔːts US -dɚˈʃɔːrts

undershot (*adj.*) ˌʌn.dəˈʃɒt US -ˈʃɑːt *stress shift:* ˌundershot ˈwheel

undershot (*from* **undershoot**) ˌʌn.dəˈʃɒt US -dɚˈʃɑːt

underside ˈʌn.də.saɪd US -dɚ- **-s** -z

undersigned ˈʌn.də.saɪnd, ˌ--ˈ- US ˈʌn.dɚ.saɪnd

undersized ˌʌn.dəˈsaɪzd US ˈʌn.dɚ.saɪzd *stress shift, British only:* ˌundersized ˈbelt

underskirt ˈʌn.də.skɜːt US -dɚ.skɝːt **-s** -s

underspend ˌʌn.dəˈspend US -dɚˈ- **-s** -z **-ing** -ɪŋ **underspent** ˌʌn.dəˈspent US -dɚˈ-

understaffed ˌʌn.dəˈstɑːft US -dɚˈstæft *stress shift:* ˌunderstaffed ˈschool

under|stand ˌʌn.də|ˈstænd US -dɚˈ- **-stands** -ˈstændz **-standing** -ˈstæn.dɪŋ **-stood** -ˈstʊd

understandab|le ˌʌn.dəˈstæn.də.b|l̩ US -dɚˈ- **-ly** -li

under|state ˌʌn.də|ˈsteɪt US -dɚˈ- **-states** -ˈsteɪts **-stating** -ˈsteɪ.tɪŋ US -ˈsteɪ.t̬ɪŋ **-stated** -ˈsteɪ.tɪd US -ˈsteɪ.t̬ɪd

understatement ˌʌn.dəˈsteɪt.mənt, ˈʌn.dəˌsteɪt- US ˌʌn.dɚˈsteɪt-, ˈʌn.dɚˌsteɪt- **-s** -s

understocked ˌʌn.dəˈstɒkt US -dɚˈstɑːkt *stress shift:* ˌunderstocked ˈshelves

understood (*from* **understand**) ˌʌn.dəˈstʊd US -dɚˈ- *stress shift:* ˌunderstood ˈplan

understrapper ˈʌn.dəˌstræp.əʳ US -dɚˌstræp.ɚ **-s** -z

understud|y ˈʌn.dəˌstʌd|.i US -dɚˌ- **-ies** -iz **-ying** -i.ɪŋ **-ied** -id

undersubscrib|e ˌʌn.də.səbˈskraɪb US -dɚ- **-es** -z **-ing** -ɪŋ **-ed** -d

under|take *agree or promise to do something:* ˌʌn.də|ˈteɪk US -dɚˈ- **-takes** -ˈteɪks **-taking** -ˈteɪ.kɪŋ **-took** -ˈtʊk **-taken** -ˈteɪ.kᵊn, -kᵊŋ US -kᵊn

undertaker *person who agrees to do something:* ˌʌn.dəˈteɪ.kəʳ US -dɚˈteɪ.kɚ **-s** -z *person who arranges funerals:* ˈʌn.dəˌteɪ.kəʳ US -dɚˌteɪ.kɚ **-s** -z

undertaking *enterprise, promise:* ˌʌn.dəˈteɪ.kɪŋ, ˈʌn.dəˌteɪ- US ˌʌn.dɚˈteɪ-, ˈʌn.dɚˌteɪ- **-s** -z *arranging funerals:* ˈʌn.dəˌteɪ.kɪŋ US -dɚˌ-

under-the-counter ˌʌn.də.ðəˈkaʊn.tə US -dɚ.ðəˈkaʊn.t̬ɚ *stress shift:* ˌunder-the-counter ˈdeal

underthings ˈʌn.də.θɪŋz US -dɚ-

undertint ˈʌn.də.tɪnt US -dɚ- **-s** -s

undertone ˈʌn.də.təʊn US -dɚ.toʊn **-s** -z

undertook (*from* **undertake**) ˌʌn.dəˈtʊk US -dɚˈ-

undertow ˈʌn.də.təʊ US -dɚ.toʊ **-s** -z

underused ˌʌn.dəˈjuːzd US -dɚˈ- *stress shift:* ˌunderused ˈpath

underutiliz|e, -is|e ˌʌn.dəˈjuː.tɪ.laɪz, -tᵊl.aɪz US -dɚˈjuː.t̬ᵊl.aɪz **-es** -ɪz **-ing** -ɪŋ **-ed** -d

undervaluation ˌʌn.dəˌvæl.juˈeɪ.ʃᵊn US -dɚˌ- **-s** -z

underval|ue ˌʌn.dəˈvæl|.juː US -dɚˈ- **-ues** -juːz **-uing** -juː.ɪŋ **-ued** -juːd *stress shift:* ˌundervalued ˈshares

underwater ˌʌn.dəˈwɔː.təʳ US -dɚˈwɑː.t̬ɚ, -ˈwɔː- *stress shift:* ˌunderwater ˈcamera

underway ˌʌn.dəˈweɪ US -dɚˈ-

underwear ˈʌn.də.weəʳ US -dɚ.wer

underweight ˌʌn.dəˈweɪt US -dɚˈ-, ˈ--- *stress shift:* ˌunderweight ˈbaggage

underwent (*from* **undergo**) ˌʌn.dəˈwent US -dɚˈ- *stress shift:* ˌunderwent ˈsurgery

underwhelm ˌʌn.dəˈhwelm US -dɚˈ- **-s** -z **-ing** -ɪŋ **-ed** -d

underwing ˈʌn.də.wɪŋ US -dɚ- **-s** -z

underwired ˌʌn.dəˈwaɪəd US -dɚˈwaɪɚd, ˈ--- *stress shift:* ˌunderwired ˈbra

underwood (U) ˈʌn.də.wʊd **underwood** US -dɚ- **-s** -z

nderworld (U) ˈʌn.də.wɜːld
underworld ⓤⓢ -dɚ.wɝːld
nderwri|te ˌʌn.dᵊrˈraɪ|t, ˈ---
ⓤⓢ ˈʌn.dɚ.raɪ|t **-tes** -ts **-ting** -tɪŋ
ⓤⓢ -t̬ɪŋ **underwrote** ˌʌn.dᵊrˈəʊt, ˈ---
ⓤⓢ ˈʌn.dɚ.roʊt **underwritten**
ˌʌn.dᵊrˈɪt.ᵊn, ˈʌn.dᵊr,ɪt-
ⓤⓢ ˈʌn.dɚ,rɪt.ᵊn
nderwriter ˈʌn.dᵊr,aɪ.təʳ
ⓤⓢ -dɚ,raɪ.t̬ɚ **-s** -z
ndescended ˌʌn.dɪˈsen.dɪd
ndescribab|le ˌʌn.dɪˈskraɪ.bə.b|l̩,
-dəˈ- **-ly** -li
ndeserv|ed ˌʌn.dɪˈzɜː.v|d, -dəˈ-
ⓤⓢ -ˈzɝː.v|d **-edly** -ɪd.li **-edness**
-ɪd.nəs, -nɪs
ndeserving ˌʌn.dɪˈzɜː.vɪŋ, -dəˈ-
ⓤⓢ -ˈzɝː- **-ly** -li
ndesigning ˌʌn.dɪˈzaɪ.nɪŋ
ndesirability ˌʌn.dɪ,zaɪə.rəˈbɪl.ə.ti,
-də,-, -ɪ.ti ⓤⓢ -,zaɪ.rəˈbɪl.ə.t̬i
ndesirab|le ˌʌn.dɪˈzaɪə.rə.b|l̩, -dəˈ-
ⓤⓢ -ˈzaɪ- **-ly** -li **-leness** -l̩.nəs, -nɪs
ndetected ˌʌn.dɪˈtek.tɪd, -dəˈ-
ndeterminable ˌʌn.dɪˈtɜː.mɪ.nə.bl̩,
-dəˈ-, -mə- ⓤⓢ -ˈtɝː-
ndeterminate ˌʌn.dɪˈtɜː.mɪ.nət,
-dəˈ-, -mə-, -nɪt ⓤⓢ -ˈtɝː- **-ly** -li
-ness -nəs, -nɪs
undetermination
ˌʌn.dɪ,tɜː.mɪˈneɪ.ʃᵊn, -də-, -məˈ-
ⓤⓢ -,tɝː-
undetermined ˌʌn.dɪˈtɜː.mɪnd, -dəˈ-
ⓤⓢ -ˈtɝː-
undeterred ˌʌn.dɪˈtɜːd, -dəˈ- ⓤⓢ -ˈtɝːd
undeveloped ˌʌn.dɪˈvel.əpt, -dəˈ-
undeviating ʌnˈdiː.vi.eɪ.tɪŋ, ˌʌn-
ⓤⓢ -t̬ɪŋ **-ly** -li
undid *(from* **undo***)* ʌnˈdɪd, ˌʌn-
undies ˈʌn.diz
undigested ˌʌn.daɪˈdʒes.tɪd, -dɪˈ-, -dəˈ-
undignified ʌnˈdɪg.nɪ.faɪd, ˌʌn-, -nə-
undiluted ˌʌn.daɪˈluː.tɪd, -dɪˈ-, -ˈljuː-
ⓤⓢ -ˈluː.t̬ɪd
undiminished ˌʌn.dɪˈmɪn.ɪʃt, -dəˈ-
undimmed ʌnˈdɪmd, ˌʌn-
undine (U) ˈʌn.diːn; ʌnˈdiːn, ʊn-
ⓤⓢ ʌnˈdiːn; ˈʌn.diːn, -daɪn **-s** -z
undiplomatic ˌʌn.dɪp.ləˈmæt.ɪk
ⓤⓢ -ˈmæt̬- **-ally** -ᵊl.i, -li
undiscerning ˌʌn.dɪˈsɜː.nɪŋ, -dəˈ-,
-ˈzɜː- ⓤⓢ -ˈsɝː-, -ˈzɝː-
undischarged ˌʌn.dɪsˈtʃɑːdʒd
ⓤⓢ -ˈtʃɑːrdʒd
undisciplined ʌnˈdɪs.ɪ.plɪnd, ˌʌn-, ˈ-ə-
undisclosed ˌʌn.dɪsˈkləʊzd ⓤⓢ -ˈkloʊzd
undiscouraged ˌʌn.dɪˈskʌr.ɪdʒd
ⓤⓢ -ˈskɝː-
undiscovered ˌʌn.dɪˈskʌv.əd ⓤⓢ -ɚd
undiscussed ˌʌn.dɪˈskʌst
undisguised ˌʌn.dɪsˈgaɪzd, -dɪzˈ-
undismayed ˌʌn.dɪˈsmeɪd, -dəˈ-
undisputed ˌʌn.dɪˈspjuː.tɪd, -dəˈ-
ⓤⓢ -t̬ɪd
undissolved ˌʌn.dɪˈzɒlvd, -ˈsɒlvd
ⓤⓢ -ˈzɑːlvd
undistinguishab|le
ˌʌn.dɪˈstɪŋ.gwɪ.ʃə.b|l̩, -dəˈ- **-ly** -li
-leness -l̩.nəs, -nɪs
undistinguished ˌʌn.dɪˈstɪŋ.gwɪʃt, -dəˈ-
undistracted ˌʌn.dɪˈstræk.tɪd, -dəˈ-
undisturbed ˌʌn.dɪˈstɜːbd, -dəˈ-
ⓤⓢ -ˈstɝːbd
undivided ˌʌn.dɪˈvaɪ.dɪd, -dəˈ- **-ly** -li
-ness -nəs, -nɪs
un|do ʌn|ˈduː, ˌʌn- **-does** -ˈdʌz **-doing**
-ˈduː.ɪŋ **-did** -ˈdɪd **-done** -ˈdʌn
-doer/s -ˈduː.əʳ/z ⓤⓢ -ˈduː.ɚ/z
undock ʌnˈdɒk, ˌʌn- ⓤⓢ -ˈdɑːk **-s** -s
-ing -ɪŋ **-ed** -t
undomesticated ˌʌn.dəˈmes.tɪ.keɪ.tɪd
ⓤⓢ -t̬ɪd
undone *(from* **undo***)* ʌnˈdʌn, ˌʌn-
undoubted ʌnˈdaʊ.tɪd, ˌʌn- ⓤⓢ -t̬ɪd
-ly -li
undreamed, undreamt ʌnˈdriːmd,
ˌʌnˈdrem*p*t **unˈdreamed ˌof**
undress ʌnˈdres, ˌʌn- **-es** -ɪz **-ing** -ɪŋ
-ed -t
undrinkable ʌnˈdrɪŋ.kə.bl̩, ˌʌn-
undrunk ʌnˈdrʌŋk
undue ʌnˈdjuː, ˌʌn- ⓤⓢ -ˈduː, -ˈdjuː
undulant ˈʌn.djᵊl.ənt, -djʊ.lənt,
-dʒᵊl.ənt, -dʒʊ.lənt ⓤⓢ -dʒᵊl.ənt,
-djᵊl-
undu|late ˈʌn.djə|l.leɪt, -djʊ-, -dʒə-,
-dʒʊ- ⓤⓢ -dʒə-, -djə- **-lates** -leɪts
-lating/ly -leɪ.tɪŋ/li ⓤⓢ -leɪ.t̬ɪŋ/li
-lated -leɪ.tɪd ⓤⓢ -leɪ.t̬ɪd
undulation ˌʌn.djəˈleɪ.ʃᵊn, -djʊˈ-,
-dʒəˈ-, -dʒʊˈ- ⓤⓢ -dʒəˈ-, -djəˈ-, -dəˈ-
-s -z
undulatory ˈʌn.djᵊl.ə.tᵊr.i, -djʊ.lə-,
-dʒᵊl.ə-, -dʒʊ.lə-, -tri;
ˌʌn.djəˈleɪ.tᵊr-, -djʊˈ-
ⓤⓢ ˈʌn.dʒᵊl.ə.tɔːr.i, -djᵊl-, -dᵊl-
unduly ʌnˈdjuː.li, ˌʌn-, -ˈdʒuː-
ⓤⓢ -ˈduː-, -ˈdjuː-
undutiful ʌnˈdjuː.tɪ.fᵊl, ˌʌn-, -ˈdʒuː-,
-fʊl ⓤⓢ -ˈduː.t̬ɪ-, -ˈdjuː- **-ly** -i **-ness**
-nəs, -nɪs
undying ʌnˈdaɪ.ɪŋ, ˌʌn- **-ly** -li
unearned ʌnˈɜːnd, ˌʌn- ⓤⓢ -ˈɝːnd
unearth ʌnˈɜːθ, ˌʌn- ⓤⓢ -ˈɝːθ **-s** -s **-ing**
-ɪŋ **-ed** -t
unearthl|y ʌnˈɜːθ.l|i, ˌʌn- ⓤⓢ -ˈɝːθ-
-iness -ɪ.nəs, -ɪ.nɪs
unease ʌnˈiːz, ˌʌn-
uneas|y ʌnˈiː.z|i, ˌʌn- **-ier** -i.əʳ ⓤⓢ -i.ɚ
-iest -i.ɪst, -i.əst **-ily** -ɪ.li, -ᵊl.i **-iness**
-ɪ.nəs, -ɪ.nɪs
uneatable ʌnˈiː.tə.bl̩, ˌʌn- ⓤⓢ -t̬ə- **-ness**
-nəs, -nɪs
uneaten ʌnˈiː.tᵊn, ˌʌn-
uneconomic ʌn,iː.kəˈnɒm.ɪk, ˌʌn-,
-,ek.əˈ- ⓤⓢ -,ek.əˈnɑː.mɪk, -,iː.kəˈ-
-al -ᵊl **-ally** -ᵊl.i, -li
unedifying ʌnˈed.ɪ.faɪ.ɪŋ, ˌʌn-
unedited ʌnˈed.ɪ.tɪd ⓤⓢ -t̬ɪd
uneducated ʌnˈedʒ.ʊ.keɪ.tɪd, ˌʌn-,
ˈ-ə-, -ˈed.jʊ-, -jə- ⓤⓢ -ˈedʒ.ʊ.keɪ.t̬ɪd,
ˈ-ə-
unelected ˌʌn.ɪˈlek.tɪd
unembarrassed ˌʌn.ɪmˈbær.əst, -emˈ-
ⓤⓢ -emˈber-, -ɪmˈ-, -ˈbær-
unemotional ˌʌn.ɪˈməʊ.ʃᵊn.ᵊl
ⓤⓢ -ˈmoʊ- **-ly** -i
unemphatic ˌʌn.ɪmˈfæt.ɪk, -emˈ-
ⓤⓢ -ˈfæt̬- **-ally** -ᵊl.i, -li
unemployability ˌʌn.ɪm,plɔɪ.əˈbɪl.ɪ.ti,
-em,-, -ə.ti ⓤⓢ -ə.t̬i
unemployable ˌʌn.ɪmˈplɔɪ.ə.bl̩, -emˈ-
unemployed ˌʌn.ɪmˈplɔɪd, -emˈ-
unemployment ˌʌn.ɪm̩ˈplɔɪ.mənt,
-emˈ- **unemˈployment ˌbenefit,**
ˌunemployment ˈbenefit
ⓤⓢ **unemˈployment ˌbenefit**
unenclosed ˌʌn.ɪnˈkləʊzd, -ɪŋˈ-, -enˈ-,
-eŋˈ- ⓤⓢ -ɪnˈkloʊzd, -enˈ-
unencumbered ˌʌn.ɪŋˈkʌm.bəd, -ɪnˈ-,
-eŋˈ-, -enˈ- ⓤⓢ -ɪnˈkʌm.bɚd, -enˈ-
unending ʌnˈen.dɪŋ, ˌʌn- **-ly** -li
unendowed ˌʌn.ɪnˈdaʊd, -enˈ-
unendurab|le ˌʌn.ɪnˈdjʊə.rə.b|l̩, -enˈ-,
-ˈdjɔː- ⓤⓢ -ˈdʊr.ə-, -ˈdjʊr-, -ˈdɝː-
-ly -li **-leness** -l̩.nəs, -nɪs
unenforceable ˌʌn.ɪnˈfɔː.sə.bl̩
ⓤⓢ -ˈfɔːr-
unengaged ˌʌn.ɪŋˈgeɪdʒd, -ɪnˈ-, -eŋˈ-,
-enˈ- ⓤⓢ -ɪnˈ-, -enˈ-
un-English ˌʌnˈɪŋ.glɪʃ **-ness** -nəs, -nɪs
unenlightened ˌʌn.ɪnˈlaɪ.tᵊnd, -enˈ-
unenterprising ʌnˈen.tə.praɪ.zɪŋ, ˌʌn-
ⓤⓢ -t̬ɚ- **-ly** -li
unenthusiastic ˌʌn.ɪn,θjuː.ziˈæs.tɪk,
-en,- ⓤⓢ -,θuː-, -,θjuː- **-ally** -ᵊl.i, -li
unenviab|le ʌnˈen.vi.ə.b|l̩, ˌʌn- **-ly** -li
unequal ʌnˈiː.kwᵊl, ˌʌn- **-s** -z **-ly** -i
-ness -nəs, -nɪs **-(l)ed** -d
unequitab|le ʌnˈek.wɪ.tə.b|l̩, ˌʌn-,
-wə- ⓤⓢ -t̬ə- **-ly** -li
unequivoc|al ˌʌn.ɪˈkwɪv.ə.k|ᵊl **-ally**
-ᵊl.i, -li **-alness** -ᵊl.nəs, -nɪs
unerring ʌnˈɜː.rɪŋ, ˌʌn- ⓤⓢ -ˈɝː.ɪŋ, -ˈer-
-ly -li **-ness** -nəs, -nɪs
unescapable ˌʌn.ɪˈskeɪ.pə.bl̩
UNESCO, Unesco juːˈnes.kəʊ ⓤⓢ -koʊ
unessential ˌʌn.ɪˈsen.*t*ʃᵊl
unethic|al ʌnˈeθ.ɪ.k|ᵊl **-ly** -ᵊl.i, -li **-ness**
-nəs, -nɪs
uneven ʌnˈiː.vᵊn, ˌʌn- **-ly** -li **-ness** -nəs,
-nɪs
uneventful ˌʌn.ɪˈvent.fᵊl, -fʊl **-ly** -i
-ness -nəs, -nɪs
unexampled ˌʌn.ɪgˈzɑːm.pl̩d, -egˈ-,
-ɪkˈsɑːm-, -ekˈ- ⓤⓢ -ɪgˈzæm-, -egˈ-

unexceptionab|le ˌʌn.ɪkˈsep.ʃən.ə.b|l̩, -ekˈ-, -ˈsepʃ.nə- -ly -li -leness -l̩.nəs (US) -nɪs

unexceptional ˌʌn.ɪkˈsep.ʃən.əl, -ekˈ-, -ˈsepʃ.nəl -ly -i

unexhausted ˌʌn.ɪɡˈzɔː.stɪd, -eɡˈ-, -ɪkˈsɔː-, -ekˈ- (US) -ɪɡˈzɑː-, -eɡˈ-, -ˈzɔː-

unexpected ˌʌn.ɪkˈspek.tɪd, -ekˈ- -ly -li -ness -nəs, -nɪs

unexpired ˌʌn.ɪkˈspaɪəd, -ekˈ- (US) -ˈspaɪɚd

unexplained ˌʌn.ɪkˈspleɪnd, -ekˈ-

unexplored ˌʌn.ɪkˈsplɔːd, -ekˈ- (US) -ˈsplɔːrd

unexposed ˌʌn.ɪkˈspəʊzd, -ekˈ- (US) -ˈspoʊzd

unexpressib|le ˌʌn.ɪkˈspres.ə.b|l̩, -ekˈ-, ˈ-ɪ- -ly -li

unexpressive ˌʌn.ɪkˈspres.ɪv, -ekˈ-

unexpurgated ʌnˈek.spə.ɡeɪ.tɪd, ˌʌn-, -spɜː- (US) -spɚ.ɡeɪ.t̬ɪd

unfading ʌnˈfeɪ.dɪŋ, ˌʌn- -ly -li

unfailing ʌnˈfeɪ.lɪŋ, ˌʌn- -ly -li -ness -nəs, -nɪs

unfair ʌnˈfeəʳ, ˌʌn- (US) -ˈfer -ly -li -ness -nəs, -nɪs ˌunfair disˈmissal

unfaithful ʌnˈfeɪθ.fəl, ˌʌn-, -fʊl -ly -i -ness -nəs, -nɪs

unfaltering ʌnˈfɔːl.tər.ɪŋ, ˌʌn-, -ˈfɒl- (US) -ˈfɑːl.t̬ɚ-, -ˈfɔːl- -ly -li

unfamiliar ˌʌn.fəˈmɪl.jəʳ, ˈ-i.əʳ (US) ˈ-jɚ -ly -li

unfamiliarity ˌʌn.fəˌmɪl.iˈær.ə.ti, -ɪ.ti (US) -ˈer.ə.t̬i, -ˈær-

unfashionab|le ʌnˈfæʃ.ən.ə.b|l̩, ˌʌn-, ˈ-nə- -ly -li

unfasten ʌnˈfɑː.sən, ˌʌn- (US) -ˈfæs- -s -z -ing -ɪŋ, -ˈfɑːs.nɪŋ (US) -ˈfæs.nɪŋ -ed -d

unfathomab|le ʌnˈfæð.ə.mə.b|l̩, ˌʌn- -ly -li -leness -l̩.nəs, -nɪs

unfathomed ʌnˈfæð.əmd, ˌʌn-

unfavo(u)rab|le ʌnˈfeɪ.vər.ə.b|l̩, ˌʌn-, -ˈfeɪv.rə- -ly -li -leness -l̩.nəs, -nɪs

unfavo(u)rite ʌnˈfeɪ.vər.ɪt, ˌʌn-, -ˈfeɪv.rɪt

unfazed ʌnˈfeɪzd

unfed ʌnˈfed, ˌʌn-

unfeeling ʌnˈfiː.lɪŋ, ˌʌn- -ly -li -ness -nəs, -nɪs

unfeigned ʌnˈfeɪnd, ˌʌn-

unfeigned|ly ʌnˈfeɪ.nɪd|.li, ˌʌn- -ness -nəs, -nɪs

unfelt ʌnˈfelt, ˌʌn-

unfermented ˌʌn.fəˈmen.tɪd, -fɜːˈ- (US) -fɚˈmen.t̬ɪd

unfertilized, -ised ʌnˈfɜː.təl.aɪzd, ˌʌn-, -tɪ.laɪzd (US) -ˈfɝː.t̬əl.aɪzd

unfett|er ʌnˈfet|.əʳ, ˌʌn- (US) -ˈfet̬|.ɚ -ers -əz (US) -ɚz -ering -ər.ɪŋ -ed -əd (US) -ɚd

unfettered ʌnˈfet.əd (US) -ˈfet̬.ɚd

unfilial ʌnˈfɪl.i.əl, ˌʌn- -ly -i

unfinished ʌnˈfɪn.ɪʃt, ˌʌn- ˌunfinished ˈbusiness, unˌfinished ˈbusiness

unfit (*adj.*) ʌnˈfɪt -ly -li -ness -nəs, -nɪs

un|fit (*v.*) ʌn|ˈfɪt, ˌʌn- -fits -ˈfɪts -fitting/ly -ˈfɪt.ɪŋ/li (US) -ˈfɪt̬.ɪŋ/li -fitted -ˈfɪt.ɪd (US) -ˈfɪt̬.ɪd

unfix ʌnˈfɪks, ˌʌn- -es -ɪz -ing -ɪŋ -ed -t

unflagging ʌnˈflæɡ.ɪŋ, ˌʌn- -ly -li

unflappab|le ʌnˈflæp.ə.b|l̩, ˌʌn- -ly -li

unflattering ʌnˈflæt.ər.ɪŋ, ˌʌn- (US) -ˈflæt̬- -ly -li

unfledged ʌnˈfledʒd, ˌʌn-

unflinching ʌnˈflɪn.tʃɪŋ, ˌʌn- -ly -li -ness -nəs, -nɪs

unfold ʌnˈfəʊld, ˌʌn- (US) -ˈfoʊld -s -z -ing -ɪŋ -ed -ɪd

unforeseeable ˌʌn.fɔːˈsiː.ə.bl̩, -fəˈ- (US) -fɔːrˈ-, -fɚˈ-

unforeseen ˌʌn.fɔːˈsiːn, -fəˈ- (US) -fɔːrˈ-, -fɚˈ- ˌunforeseen ˈcircumstances

unforgettab|le ˌʌn.fəˈɡet.ə.b|l̩ (US) -fɚˈɡet̬- -ly -li

unforgivable ˌʌn.fəˈɡɪv.ə.bl̩ (US) -fɚˈ-

unforgiven ˌʌn.fəˈɡɪv.ən (US) -fɚˈ-

unforgiving ˌʌn.fəˈɡɪv.ɪŋ (US) -fɚˈ- -ly -li -ness -nəs, -nɪs

unforgotten ˌʌn.fəˈɡɒt.ən (US) -fɚˈɡɑː.tən

unformatted ʌnˈfɔː.mæt.ɪd (US) -ˈfɔːr.mæt̬-

unformed ʌnˈfɔːmd, ˌʌn- (US) -ˈfɔːrmd

unforthcoming ˌʌn.fɔːθˈkʌm.ɪŋ (US) -fɔːrθ-

unfortified ʌnˈfɔː.tɪ.faɪd, ˌʌn- (US) -ˈfɔːr.t̬ɪ-

unfortunate ʌnˈfɔː.tʃən.ət, ˌʌn-, -ɪt (US) -ˈfɔːr- -ly -li -ness -nəs, -nɪs

unfounded ʌnˈfaʊn.dɪd, ˌʌn-

unframed ʌnˈfreɪmd, ˌʌn-

un|freeze ʌn|ˈfriːz (US) ˌʌn- -freezes -ˈfriː.zɪz -froze -ˈfrəʊz (US) -ˈfroʊz -frozen -ˈfrəʊ.zən (US) -ˈfroʊ.zən

unfrequented ˌʌn.frɪˈkwen.tɪd (US) ʌnˈfriː.kwen.t̬ɪd, ˌʌn-

unfriend|ly ʌnˈfrend|.li, ˌʌn- -liness -lɪ.nəs, -lɪ.nɪs

unfrock ʌnˈfrɒk, ˌʌn- (US) -ˈfrɑːk -s -s -ing -ɪŋ -ed -t

unfruitful ʌnˈfruːt.fəl, ˌʌn-, -fʊl -ly -i -ness -nəs, -nɪs

unfulfilled ˌʌn.fʊlˈfɪld

unfunny ʌnˈfʌn.i, ˌʌn-

unfurl ʌnˈfɜːl, ˌʌn- (US) -ˈfɝːl -s -z -ing -ɪŋ -ed -d

unfurnished ʌnˈfɜː.nɪʃt, ˌʌn- (US) -ˈfɝː-

ungainl|y ʌnˈɡeɪn.l|i, ˌʌn-, ʌŋ-, ˌʌŋ- (US) ʌn-, ˌʌn- -iest -i.ɪst, -i.əst -iness -ɪ.nəs, -ɪ.nɪs

ungallant ʌnˈɡæl.ənt, ˌʌn.ɡəˈlænt, ʌŋ-, ˌʌŋ- (US) ʌnˈɡæl.ənt, ˌʌn.ɡəˈlænt, -ˈlɑːnt -ly -li

ungenerous ʌnˈdʒen.ər.əs, ˌʌn- -ly -li

ungentlemanl|y ʌnˈdʒent.l̩.mən.l|i, ˌʌn- -iness -ɪ.nəs, -ɪ.nɪs

un-get-at-able ˌʌn.ɡetˈæt.ə.bl̩, ˌʌŋ- (US) ˌʌn.ɡet̬ˈæt̬-

ungird ʌnˈɡɜːd, ˌʌn-, ʌŋ-, ˌʌŋ- (US) ʌnˈɡɝːd, ˌʌn- -s -z -ing -ɪŋ -ed -ɪ

unglazed ʌnˈɡleɪzd, ˌʌn-, ʌŋ-, ˌʌŋ- (US) ʌn-, ˌʌn-

ungloved ʌnˈɡlʌvd, ˌʌn-, ʌŋ-, ˌʌŋ- (US) ʌn-, ˌʌn-

unglu|e ʌnˈɡluː, ˌʌn-, ʌŋ-, ˌʌŋ- (US) ʌn-, ˌʌn- -es -z -ing -ɪŋ -ed -d

ungodl|y ʌnˈɡɒd.l|i, ˌʌn-, ʌŋ-, ˌʌŋ- (US) ʌnˈɡɑːd.l|i, ˌʌn- -ier -i.əʳ (US) -i.ɚ -iest -i.ɪst, -i.əst -iness -ɪ.nəs, -ɪ.nɪs

Ungoed ˈʌŋ.ɡɔɪd

ungotten ʌnˈɡɒt.ən, ˌʌn-, ʌŋ-, ˌʌŋ- (US) ʌnˈɡɑː.tən, ˌʌn-

ungovernab|le ʌnˈɡʌv.ən.ə.b|l̩, ˌʌn-, ʌŋ-, ˌʌŋ-, ˈ-nə- (US) ʌnˈɡʌv.ɚ.nə-, ˌʌ -ly -li -leness -l̩.nəs (US) -nɪs

ungoverned ʌnˈɡʌv.ənd, ˌʌn-, ʌŋ-, ˌʌ (US) ʌnˈɡʌv.ɚnd, ˌʌn-

ungraceful ʌnˈɡreɪs.fəl, ˌʌn-, ʌŋ-, ˌʌŋ -fʊl (US) ʌn-, ˌʌn- -ly -i -ness -nəs, -nɪ

ungracious ʌnˈɡreɪ.ʃəs, ˌʌn-, ʌŋ-, ˌʌŋ (US) ʌn-, ˌʌn- -ly -li -ness -nəs, -nɪs

ungrammatic|al ˌʌn.ɡrəˈmæt.ɪ.k|əl, ˌʌŋ- (US) ˌʌn.ɡrəˈmæt̬- -ally -əl.i, -li

ungrateful ʌnˈɡreɪt.fəl, ˌʌn-, ʌŋ-, ˌʌŋ- -fʊl (US) ʌn-, ˌʌn- -ly -li -ness -nəs, -nɪ

ungrounded ʌnˈɡraʊn.dɪd, ˌʌn-, ʌŋ-, ˌʌŋ- (US) ʌn-, ˌʌn-

ungrudging ʌnˈɡrʌdʒ.ɪŋ, ˌʌn-, ʌŋ-, ˌʌŋ- (US) ʌn-, ˌʌn- -ly -li

unguarded ʌnˈɡɑː.dɪd, ˌʌn-, ʌŋ-, ˌʌŋ- (US) ʌnˈɡɑːr-, ˌʌn- -ly -li -ness -nəs, -nɪs

unguent ˈʌŋ.ɡwənt, -ɡju.ənt (US) -ɡwənt -s -s

unguided ʌnˈɡaɪ.dɪd, ˌʌn-, ʌŋ-, ˌʌŋ- (US) ʌn-, ˌʌn-

ungul|a ˈʌŋ.ɡjə.l|ə, -ɡjʊ- -ae -iː

ungulate ˈʌŋ.ɡjə.leɪt, -ɡjʊ-, -lət, -lɪt (US) -lɪt, -leɪt -s -s

unhallowed ʌnˈhæl.əʊd, ˌʌn- (US) -oʊd

unhampered ʌnˈhæm.pəd, ˌʌn- (US) -pɚd

unhand ʌnˈhænd, ˌʌn- -s -z -ing -ɪŋ -ed -ɪd

unhandy ʌnˈhæn.di, ˌʌn-

unhapp|y ʌnˈhæp|.i, ˌʌn- -ier -i.əʳ (US) -i.ɚ -iest -i.ɪst, -i.əst -ily -ɪ.li, -əl.i -iness -ɪ.nɪs, -ɪ.nəs

unharmed ʌnˈhɑːmd, ˌʌn- (US) -ˈhɑːrmd

unharness ʌnˈhɑː.nɪs, ˌʌn- (US) -ˈhɑːr- -es -ɪz -ing -ɪŋ -ed -t

unhatched ʌnˈhætʃt, ˌʌn-

unhealth|y ʌnˈhel.θ|i, ˌʌn- -ier -i.əʳ (US) -i.ɚ -iest -i.ɪst, -i.əst -ily -ɪ.li, -əl.i -iness -ɪ.nəs, -ɪ.nɪs

unheard ʌn'hɜːd, ˌʌn- ⓤⓢ -'hɝːd
unheard-of ʌn'hɜːdˌɒv ⓤⓢ -'hɝːdˌɑːv, -əv
unheeded ʌn'hiː.dɪd, ˌʌn-
unheeding ʌn'hiː.dɪŋ **-ly** -li
unhelpful ʌn'help.fʊl, -fəl **-ly** -i **-ness** -nəs, -nɪs
unheralded ʌn'her.əl.dɪd
unhesitating ʌn'hez.ɪ.teɪ.tɪŋ, ˌʌn-, '-ə- ⓤⓢ -t̬ɪŋ **-ly** -li
unhing|e ʌn'hɪndʒ, ˌʌn- **-es** -ɪz **-ing** -ɪŋ **-ed** -d
unhistoric ˌʌn.hɪ'stɒr.ɪk, -ɪ'- ⓤⓢ -hɪ'stɔːr- **-al** -əl
unhitch ʌn'hɪtʃ, ˌʌn- **-es** -ɪz **-ing** -ɪŋ **-ed** -t
unhol|y ʌn'həʊ.l|i, ˌʌn- ⓤⓢ -'hoʊ- **-iness** -ɪ.nəs, -ɪ.nɪs **unˌholy al'liance**
unhook ʌn'hʊk, ˌʌn- **-s** -s **-ing** -ɪŋ **-ed** -t
unhoped-for ʌn'həʊptˌfɔːr ⓤⓢ -'hoʊptˌfɔːr
unhors|e ʌn'hɔːs, ˌʌn- ⓤⓢ -'hɔːrs **-es** -ɪz **-ing** -ɪŋ **-ed** -t
unhous|e ʌn'haʊz, ˌʌn- **-es** -ɪz **-ing** -ɪŋ **-ed** -d
unhuman ʌn'hjuː.mən, ˌʌn-
unhung ʌn'hʌŋ, ˌʌn-
unhurried ʌn'hʌr.ɪd, ˌʌn- ⓤⓢ -'hɝː- **-ly** -li **-ness** -nəs, -nɪs
unhurt ʌn'hɜːt, ˌʌn- ⓤⓢ -'hɝːt
uni- juː.nɪ-, -ni-
Note: Prefix. Normally takes primary or secondary stress on the first syllable, e.g. **unify** /'juː.nɪ.faɪ ⓤⓢ -nə-/, **unification** /ˌjuː.nɪ.fɪ'keɪ.ʃən ⓤⓢ -nə-/.
uni 'juː.ni **-s** -z
Uniate 'juː.ni.ət, -ɪt, -eɪt ⓤⓢ -ɪt, -eɪt **-s** -s
unicameral ˌjuː.nɪ'kæm.ər.əl
UNICEF, Unicef 'juː.nɪ.sef
unicellular ˌjuː.nɪ'sel.jə.lər, -jʊ- ⓤⓢ -jə.lɚ
unicorn 'juː.nɪ.kɔːn ⓤⓢ -kɔːrn **-s** -z
unicycl|e 'juː.nɪˌsaɪ.kl̩ ⓤⓢ -nə- **-es** -z **-ist/s** -ɪst/s
unidentified ˌʌn.aɪ'den.tɪ.faɪd ⓤⓢ -t̬ə- **ˌunidentified ˌflying 'object**
unidimensional ˌjuː.nɪ.daɪ'men.*t*ʃən.əl, -dɪ'-, -də'- ⓤⓢ -nə.də'men*t*.ʃə-, -dɪ'-, -daɪ-
unidiomatic ʌnˌɪd.i.əʊ'mæt.ɪk, ˌʌn- ⓤⓢ -ə'mæt̬- **-ally** -əl.i, -li
unifiable 'juː.nɪ.faɪ.ə.bl̩ ⓤⓢ -nə-
unification ˌjuː.nɪ.fɪ'keɪ.ʃən, -nə- ⓤⓢ -nə- **-s** -z
uniform 'juː.nɪ.fɔːm, -nə- ⓤⓢ -nə.fɔːrm **-s** -z **-ed** -d **-ly** -li **-ness** -nəs, -nɪs
uniformity ˌjuː.nɪ'fɔː.mə.ti, -nə'-, -mɪ- ⓤⓢ -nə'fɔːr.mə.t̬i
uni|fy 'juː.nɪ|.faɪ, -nə- ⓤⓢ -nə- **-fies** -faɪz **-fying** -faɪ.ɪŋ **-fied** -faɪd **-fier/s** -faɪ.ər/z ⓤⓢ -faɪ.ɚ/z
Unigate® 'juː.nɪ.geɪt, -nə- ⓤⓢ -nə-
unilateral ˌjuː.nɪ'læt.ər.əl ⓤⓢ -nə'læt̬- **-ly** -i **-ism** -ɪ.zəm **-ist/s** -ɪst/s
Unilever® 'juː.nɪ.liː.vər ⓤⓢ -nə.liː.vɚ
unimaginab|le ˌʌn.ɪ'mædʒ.ɪ.nə.bl̩, -ən.ə- **-ly** -li **-leness** -l̩.nəs, -nɪs
unimaginative ˌʌn.ɪ'mædʒ.ɪ.nə.tɪv, -ən.ə- ⓤⓢ -t̬ɪv **-ly** -li **-ness** -nəs, -nɪs
unimagined ˌʌn.ɪ'mædʒ.ɪnd, -ənd
unimpaired ˌʌn.ɪm'peəd ⓤⓢ -'perd
unimpassioned ʌn.ɪm'pæʃ.ənd
unimpeachab|le ˌʌn.ɪm'piː.tʃə.bl̩ **-ly** -li **-leness** -l̩.nəs, -nɪs
unimpeded ˌʌn.ɪm'piː.dɪd
unimportance ˌʌn.ɪm'pɔː.tənts ⓤⓢ -'pɔːr-
unimportant ˌʌn.ɪm'pɔː.tənt ⓤⓢ -'pɔːr- **-ly** -li
unimpressed ˌʌn.ɪm'prest
unimpressive ˌʌn.ɪm'pres.ɪv **-ly** -li
unimproved ʌn.ɪm'pruːvd
uninflated ˌʌn.ɪn'fleɪ.tɪd ⓤⓢ -t̬ɪd
uninflected ˌʌn.ɪn'flek.tɪd
uninfluenced ʌn'ɪn.flu.əntst, ˌʌn-, -fluən*t*st ⓤⓢ -flu.ən*t*st
uninformative ˌʌn.ɪn'fɔː.mə.tɪv ⓤⓢ -'fɔːr.mə.t̬ɪv **-ly** -li
uninformed ˌʌn.ɪn'fɔːmd ⓤⓢ -'fɔːrmd
uninhabitable ˌʌn.ɪn'hæb.ɪ.tə.bl̩, '-ə- ⓤⓢ -t̬ə- **-ness** -nəs, -nɪs
uninhabited ˌʌn.ɪn'hæb.ɪ.tɪd, '-ə- ⓤⓢ -t̬ɪd
uninhibited ˌʌn.ɪn'hɪb.ɪ.tɪd, '-ə- ⓤⓢ -t̬ɪd **-ly** -li **-ness** -nəs, -nɪs
uninitiated ˌʌn.ɪ'nɪʃ.i.eɪ.tɪd ⓤⓢ -t̬ɪd
uninjured ʌn'ɪn.dʒəd, ˌʌn- ⓤⓢ -dʒɚd
uninspired ˌʌn.ɪn'spaɪəd ⓤⓢ -'spaɪɚd
uninspiring ˌʌn.ɪn'spaɪə.rɪŋ ⓤⓢ -'spaɪ- **-ly** -li
uninstall ˌʌn.ɪn'stɔːl ⓤⓢ -'stɔːl, -'stɑːl **-s** -z **-ing** -ɪŋ **-ed** -d
uninstructed ˌʌn.ɪn'strʌk.tɪd
uninsured ˌʌn.ɪn'ʃʊəd, -'ʃɔːd ⓤⓢ -'ʃʊrd
unintelligent ˌʌn.ɪn'tel.ɪ.dʒənt, '-ə- **-ly** -li
unintelligibility ˌʌn.ɪnˌtel.ɪ.dʒə'bɪl.ə.ti, ˌ-ə-, -dʒɪ'-, -ɪ.ti ⓤⓢ -ə.t̬i
unintelligib|le ˌʌn.ɪn'tel.ɪ.dʒə.bl̩, '-ə-, -dʒɪ- **-ly** -li
unintentional ˌʌn.ɪn'ten.*t*ʃən.əl, -'ten*t*ʃ.nəl **-ly** -i
uninterest|ed ʌn'ɪn.trə.st|ɪd, ˌʌn-, -trɪ-, -tres.t|ɪd, -tər.ə.st|ɪd, -ɪ-, -es.t|ɪd ⓤⓢ -trɪ.st|ɪd, -trə-, -tres.t|ɪd, -tɚ.es-, -ə.st|ɪd **-ing** -ɪŋ
uninterrupted ʌnˌɪn.tər'ʌp.tɪd, ˌʌn- ⓤⓢ -tə'rʌp- **-ly** -li
uninvited ˌʌn.ɪn'vaɪ.tɪd ⓤⓢ -t̬ɪd
uninviting ʌn.ɪn'vaɪ.tɪŋ ⓤⓢ -t̬ɪŋ **-ly** -li **-ness** -nəs, -nɪs
union (U) 'juː.njən, -ni.ən ⓤⓢ '-njən **-s** -z **ˌUnion 'Jack**
union|ism (U) 'juː.njə.n|ɪ.zəm, -ni.ə- ⓤⓢ -njə- **-ist/s** -ɪst/s
unionization, -isa- ˌjuː.njə.naɪ'zeɪ.ʃən, -ni.ə-, -ɪ'- ⓤⓢ -njə.nɪ'-
unioniz|e, -is|e 'juː.njə.naɪz, -ni.ə- ⓤⓢ -'njə- **-es** -ɪz **-ing** -ɪŋ **-ed** -d
unipartite ˌjuː.nɪ'pɑː.taɪt ⓤⓢ -'pɑːr-
unique juː'niːk **-ly** -li **-ness** -nəs, -nɪs
Uniroyal® 'juː.nɪ.rɔɪəl
unisex 'juː.nɪ.seks ⓤⓢ -nə-
unisexual ˌjuː.nɪ'sek.ʃʊəl, -sjʊəl ⓤⓢ -nə'sek.ʃu.əl
unison 'juː.nɪ.sən, -nə-, -zən ⓤⓢ -nə- **-s** -z
unissued ʌn'ɪʃ.uːd, ˌʌn-, -'ɪs.juːd ⓤⓢ -'ɪʃ.uːd
unit 'juː.nɪt **-s** -s **ˌunit 'trust**
UNITA, Unita juː'niː.tə ⓤⓢ -t̬ə
unitable juː'naɪ.tə.bl̩ ⓤⓢ -t̬ə-
unitarian (U) ˌjuː.nɪ'teə.ri.ən ⓤⓢ -'ter.i- **-s** -z **-ism** -ɪ.zəm
unitary 'juː.nɪ.tər.i, -tri ⓤⓢ -ter.i
u|nite juː|'naɪt, jʊ- **-nites** -'naɪts **-niting** -'naɪ.tɪŋ ⓤⓢ -'naɪ.t̬ɪŋ **-nited/ly** -'naɪ.tɪd/li ⓤⓢ -'naɪ.t̬ɪd/li **-niter/s** -'naɪ.tər/z ⓤⓢ -'naɪ.t̬ɚ/z
United Arab Emirates juːˌnaɪ.tɪdˌær.əb'em.ɪ.rəts, jʊ-, -ər.əts, -ɪts, -eɪts ⓤⓢ -t̬ɪdˌer.əb'em.ɚ.əts, -ˌær-; -ɪ'mɪr-
United Kingdom juːˌnaɪ.tɪd'kɪŋ.dəm, jʊ- ⓤⓢ -t̬ɪd'-
United Nations juːˌnaɪ.tɪd'neɪ.ʃənz, jʊ- ⓤⓢ -t̬ɪd'-
United Reformed Church juːˌnaɪ.tɪd.rɪ'fɔːmdˌtʃɜːtʃ, jʊ- ⓤⓢ -t̬ɪd.rɪ'fɔːrmdˌtʃɝːtʃ
United States juːˌnaɪ.tɪd'steɪts, jʊ- ⓤⓢ -t̬ɪd'- **UˌnitedˌStates of A'merica**
unit|y (U) 'juː.nə.t|i, -nɪ- ⓤⓢ -nə.t̬|i **-ies** -iz
univalen|t ˌjuː.nɪ'veɪ.lən|t ⓤⓢ -nə'-; juː'nɪv.əl.ən|t **-ce** -*t*s
univalve 'juː.nɪ.vælv ⓤⓢ -nə- **-s** -z
universal ˌjuː.nɪ'vɜː.səl, -nə'- ⓤⓢ -nə'vɝː- **-s** -z **-ly** -i **-ness** -nəs, -nɪs **-ism** -ɪ.zəm **-ist/s** -ɪst/s *stress shift:* ˌuniversal 'joint
universality ˌjuː.nɪ.vɜː'sæl.ə.ti, -nə-, -ɪ.ti ⓤⓢ -nə.vɝː'sæl.ə.t̬i
universaliz|e, -is|e ˌjuː.nɪ'vɜː.səl.aɪz, -nə'- ⓤⓢ -nə'vɝː.sə.laɪz **-es** -ɪz **-ing** -ɪŋ **-ed** -d
univers|e 'juː.nɪ.vɜːs, -nə- ⓤⓢ -nə.vɝːs **-es** -ɪz
universit|y ˌjuː.nɪ'vɜː.sə.t|i, -nə'-, -sɪ- ⓤⓢ -nə'vɝː.sə.t̬|i **-ies** -iz *stress shift:* ˌuniversity 'grant
univocal ˌjuː.nɪ'vəʊ.kəl ⓤⓢ -'nɪv.ə- **-s** -z

Unix®, UNIX ˈjuː.nɪks
unjust ʌnˈdʒʌst, ˌʌn- **-ly** -li **-ness** -nəs, -nɪs
unjustifiab|le ʌnˌdʒʌs.tɪˈfaɪ.ə.b|l̩, ˌʌn.dʒʌs-, ˌʌnˌdʒʌs-, -təˈ- ⓊⓈ ʌnˌdʒʌs.tɪˈfaɪ.ə.b|l̩, ˌʌn-, -təˈ-, -ˈdʒʌs.tɪ.faɪ-, -tə- **-ly** -li **-leness** -l̩.nəs, -nɪs
unjustified ʌnˈdʒʌs.tɪ.faɪd, ˌʌn-, -tə- **-ly** -li
unkempt ʌnˈkempt, ˌʌn-, ʌŋ-, ˌʌŋ- ⓊⓈ ʌn-, ˌʌn-
unkept ʌnˈkept, ˌʌn-, ʌŋ-, ˌʌŋ- ⓊⓈ ʌn-, ˌʌn-
unkin|d ʌnˈkaɪn|d, ˌʌn-, ʌŋ-, ˌʌŋ- ⓊⓈ ʌn-, ˌʌn- **-der** -dəʳ ⓊⓈ -dɚ **-dest** -dɪst, -dəst **-dly** -d.li **-dness** -*d*.nɪs, -nəs
un|knot ʌn|ˈnɒt, ˌʌn- ⓊⓈ -ˈnɑːt **-knots** -ˈnɒts ⓊⓈ -ˈnɑːts **-knotting** -ˈnɒt.ɪŋ ⓊⓈ -ˈnɑː.t̬ɪŋ **-knotted** -ˈnɒt.ɪd ⓊⓈ -ˈnɑː.t̬ɪd
unknowable ʌnˈnəʊ.ə.bl̩, ˌʌn- ⓊⓈ -ˈnoʊ-
unknowing ʌnˈnəʊ.ɪŋ, ˌʌn- ⓊⓈ -ˈnoʊ- **-ly** -li **-ness** -nəs, -nɪs
unknown ʌnˈnəʊn, ˌʌn- ⓊⓈ -ˈnoʊn **-s** -z ˌ**Unknown** ˈ**Soldier**; ˌ**unknown** ˈ**quantity**
unlac|e ʌnˈleɪs, ˌʌn- **-es** -ɪz **-ing** -ɪŋ **-ed** -t
unlad|e ʌnˈleɪd ⓊⓈ ˌʌn- **-es** -z **-ing** -ɪŋ **-ed** -ɪd **-en** -ᵊn
unladylike ʌnˈleɪ.di.laɪk, ˌʌn-
unlamented ˌʌn.ləˈmen.tɪd ⓊⓈ -t̬ɪd
unlash ʌnˈlæʃ ⓊⓈ ˌʌn- **-es** -ɪz **-ing** -ɪŋ **-ed** -t
unlatch ʌnˈlætʃ ⓊⓈ ˌʌn- **-es** -ɪz **-ing** -ɪŋ **-ed** -t
unlawful ʌnˈlɔː.fᵊl, ˌʌn-, -fʊl ⓊⓈ -ˈlɑː-, -ˈlɔː- **-ly** -i **-ness** -nəs, -nɪs
unleaded ʌnˈled.ɪd, ˌʌn- ˌ**unleaded** ˈ**petrol, un**ˌ**leaded** ˈ**petrol**
unlearn ʌnˈlɜːn, ˌʌn- ⓊⓈ -ˈlɝːn **-s** -z **-ing** -ɪŋ **-ed** -t, -d **-t** -t
unlearned ʌnˈlɜː.nɪd, ˌʌn- ⓊⓈ -ˈlɝː- **-ly** -li **-ness** -nəs, -nɪs
unleash ʌnˈliːʃ, ˌʌn- **-es** -ɪz **-ing** -ɪŋ **-ed** -t
unleavened ʌnˈlev.ᵊnd, ˌʌn- ˌ**unleavened** ˈ**bread, un**ˌ**leavened** ˈ**bread**
unled ʌnˈled, ˌʌn-
unless ənˈles, ʌn-
unlettered ʌnˈlet.əd, ˌʌn- ⓊⓈ -ˈlet̬.ɚd
unliberated ʌnˈlɪb.ᵊr.eɪ.tɪd, ˌʌn- ⓊⓈ -ə.reɪ.t̬ɪd
unlicensed ʌnˈlaɪ.sᵊntst, ˌʌn-
unlike ʌnˈlaɪk, ˌʌn-
unlikel|y ʌnˈlaɪ.kl|i, ˌʌn- **-ier** -i.əʳ ⓊⓈ -i.ɚ **-iest** -i.ɪst, -i.əst **-ihood** -ɪ.hʊd **-iness** -ɪ.nəs, -ɪ.nɪs
unlikeness ʌnˈlaɪk.nəs, ˌʌn-, -nɪs
unlimb|er ʌnˈlɪm.b|əʳ, ˌʌn- ⓊⓈ -b|ɚ **-ers** -əz ⓊⓈ -ɚz **-ering** -ᵊr.ɪŋ **-ered** -əd ⓊⓈ -ɚd
unlimited ʌnˈlɪm.ɪ.tɪd, ˌʌn- ⓊⓈ -t̬ɪd
unlink ʌnˈlɪŋk ⓊⓈ ˌʌn- **-s** -s **-ing** -ɪŋ **-ed** -t
unliquidated ʌnˈlɪk.wɪ.deɪ.tɪd, ˌʌn-, -wə- ⓊⓈ -wə.deɪ.t̬ɪd
unlisted ʌnˈlɪs.tɪd
unlit ʌnˈlɪt, ˌʌn-
unload ʌnˈləʊd, ˌʌn- ⓊⓈ -ˈloʊd **-s** -z **-ing** -ɪŋ **-ed** -ɪd **-er/s** -əʳ/z ⓊⓈ -ɚ/z
unlock ʌnˈlɒk, ˌʌn- ⓊⓈ -ˈlɑːk **-s** -s **-ing** -ɪŋ **-ed** -t
unlooked-for ʌnˈlʊkt.fɔːʳ, ˌʌn- ⓊⓈ -ˌfɔːr
unloos|e ʌnˈluːs, ˌʌn- **-es** -ɪz **-ing** -ɪŋ **-ed** -t
unloosen ʌnˈluː.sᵊn, ˌʌn- **-s** -z **-ing** -ɪŋ, -ˈluːs.nɪŋ **-ed** -d
unlovel|y ʌnˈlʌv.l|i, ˌʌn- **-iness** -ɪ.nəs, -ɪ.nɪs
unloving ʌnˈlʌv.ɪŋ, ˌʌn-
unluck|y ʌnˈlʌk|.i, ˌʌn- **-ier** -i.əʳ ⓊⓈ -i.ɚ **-iest** -i.ɪst, -i.əst **-ily** -ɪ.li, -ᵊl.i **-iness** -ɪ.nəs, -ɪ.nɪs
unmade ʌnˈmeɪd, ˌʌn-
un|make ʌn|ˈmeɪk, ˌʌn- **-makes** -ˈmeɪks **-making** -ˈmeɪ.kɪŋ **-made** -ˈmeɪd
unman ʌnˈmæn, ˌʌn- **-s** -z **-ning** -ɪŋ **-ned** -d
unmanageab|le ʌnˈmæn.ɪ.dʒə.b|l̩, ˌʌn-, ˈ-ə- **-ly** -li **-leness** -l̩.nəs, -nɪs
unmanl|y ʌnˈmæn.l|i, ˌʌn- **-iness** -ɪ.nəs, -ɪ.nɪs
unmannered ʌnˈmæn.əd ⓊⓈ -ɚd **-ly** -li
unmannerl|y ʌnˈmæn.ᵊl|.i, ˌʌn- ⓊⓈ -ɚ.l|i **-iness** -ɪ.nəs, -ɪ.nɪs
unmarked ʌnˈmɑːkt, ˌʌn- ⓊⓈ -ˈmɑːrkt
unmarriageable ʌnˈmær.ɪ.dʒə.bl̩, ˌʌn- ⓊⓈ -ˈmer-, -ˈmær-
unmarried ʌnˈmær.ɪd, ˌʌn- ⓊⓈ -ˈmer-, -ˈmær-
unmask ʌnˈmɑːsk, ˌʌn- ⓊⓈ -ˈmæsk **-s** -s **-ing** -ɪŋ **-ed** -t
unmatched ʌnˈmætʃt, ˌʌn-
unmeaning ʌnˈmiː.nɪŋ, ˌʌn-
unmeaning|ly ʌnˈmiː.nɪŋ|.li, ˌʌn- **-ness** -nəs, -nɪs
unmeasurable ʌnˈmeʒ.ᵊr.ə.bl̩, ˌʌn-
unmeasured ʌnˈmeʒ.əd, ˌʌn- ⓊⓈ -ɚd
unmentionable ʌnˈmen.*t*ʃᵊn.ə.bl̩, ˌʌn-, -ˈmen*t*ʃ.nə- ⓊⓈ -ˈmen*t*.ʃᵊn.ə-, -ˈmen*t*ʃ.nə- **-s** -z **-ness** -nəs, -nɪs
unmentioned ʌnˈmen.*t*ʃᵊnd, ˌʌn- ⓊⓈ -ˈmen*t*.ʃᵊnd
unmerciful ʌnˈmɜː.sɪ.fᵊl, ˌʌn-, -sə-, -fʊl ⓊⓈ -ˈmɝː- **-ly** -i **-ness** -nəs, -nɪs
unmerited ʌnˈmer.ɪ.tɪd, ˌʌn- ⓊⓈ -t̬ɪd
unmethodic|al ˌʌn.məˈθɒd.ɪ.k|ᵊl, -mɪˈ-, -meθˈɒd- ⓊⓈ -məˈθɑː.dɪ- **-ally** -ᵊl.i, -li
unmetred, unmetered ʌnˈmiː.təd ⓊⓈ -t̬ɚd
unmindful ʌnˈmaɪn*d*.fᵊl, ˌʌn-, -fʊl **-ly** **-ness** -nəs, -nɪs
unmissable ʌnˈmɪs.ə.bl̩
unmistakab|le ˌʌn.mɪˈsteɪ.kə.b|l̩ **-ly** **-leness** -l̩.nəs, -nɪs
unmitigated ʌnˈmɪt.ɪ.geɪ.tɪd, ˌʌn-, ˈ- ⓊⓈ -ˈmɪt̬.ə.geɪ.t̬ɪd
unmixed ʌnˈmɪkst, ˌʌn-
unmodifiable ʌnˈmɒd.ɪ.faɪ.ə.bl̩, ˌʌn- ⓊⓈ -ˈmɑː.dɪ-
unmodified ʌnˈmɒd.ɪ.faɪd, ˌʌn- ⓊⓈ -ˈmɑː.dɪ-
unmolested ˌʌn.məʊˈles.tɪd ⓊⓈ -məˈ-
unmounted ʌnˈmaʊn.tɪd, ˌʌn- ⓊⓈ -t̬ɪd
unmourned ʌnˈmɔːnd, ˌʌn- ⓊⓈ -ˈmɔːrnd
unmov(e)able ʌnˈmuː.və.bl̩, ˌʌn-
unmoved ʌnˈmuːvd, ˌʌn-
unmuffl|e ʌnˈmʌf.l̩, ˌʌn- **-es** -z **-ing** -ɪŋ, -ˈmʌf.lɪŋ **-ed** -d
unmusic|al ʌnˈmjuː.zɪ.k|ᵊl, ˌʌn- **-ally** -ᵊl.i, -li
unmuzzl|e ʌnˈmʌz.l̩, ˌʌn- **-es** -z **-ing** -ˈmʌz.lɪŋ **-ed** -d
unnamed ʌnˈneɪmd, ˌʌn-
unnatural ʌnˈnætʃ.ᵊr.ᵊl, ˌʌn-, -ʊ.rᵊl ⓊⓈ -ɚ.əl, ˈ-rᵊl **-ly** -i **-ness** -nəs, -nɪs
unnavigable ʌnˈnæv.ɪ.gə.bl̩, ˌʌn-
unnecessarily ʌnˈnes.ə.sᵊr.ᵊl.i, ˌʌn-, ˈ-ɪ-, -ɪ.li; -ˌnes.əˈser-, -ɪˈ- ⓊⓈ -ˌnes.əˈser-; -ˈnes.ə.ser-
unnecessary ʌnˈnes.ə.sᵊr.i, ˌʌn-, ˈ-ɪ-, -ser- ⓊⓈ -ser-
unneighbo(u)rl|y ʌnˈneɪ.bᵊl|.i, ˌʌn- ⓊⓈ -bɚ.l|i **-iness** -ɪ.nəs, -ɪ.nɪs
unnerv|e ʌnˈnɜːv, ˌʌn- ⓊⓈ -ˈnɝːv **-es** -z **-ing/ly** -ɪŋ/li **-ed** -d
unnoticeab|le ʌnˈnəʊ.tɪ.sə.b|l̩, ˌʌn-, -tə- ⓊⓈ -ˈnoʊ.t̬ə- **-ly** -li
unnoticed ʌnˈnəʊ.tɪst, ˌʌn- ⓊⓈ -ˈnoʊ.t̬ɪst
unnumbered ʌnˈnʌm.bəd, ˌʌn- ⓊⓈ -bɚd
UNO ˈjuː.nəʊ ⓊⓈ -noʊ
uno (U) ˈuː.nəʊ, ˈjuː- ⓊⓈ -noʊ ˌ**Fiat** ˈ**Uno**
unobjectionab|le ˌʌn.əbˈdʒek.ʃᵊn.ə.b|l̩, -ˈdʒekʃ.nə- **-ly** -li
unobliging ˌʌn.əˈblaɪ.dʒɪŋ **-ly** -li
unobliterated ˌʌn.əˈblɪt.ᵊr.eɪ.tɪd ⓊⓈ -ˈblɪt̬.ə.reɪ.t̬ɪd
unobservant ˌʌn.əbˈzɜː.vᵊnt ⓊⓈ -ˈzɝː- **-ly** -li
unobserv|ed ˌʌn.əbˈzɜːv|d ⓊⓈ -ˈzɝːv|d **-edly** -ɪd.li
unobstructed ˌʌn.əbˈstrʌk.tɪd
unobtainable ˌʌn.əbˈteɪ.nə.bl̩
unobtrusive ˌʌn.əbˈtruː.sɪv ⓊⓈ -əbˈ- **-ly** -li **-ness** -nəs, -nɪs
unoccupied ʌnˈɒk.jə.paɪd, ˌʌn-, -jʊ- ⓊⓈ -ˈɑː.kjə-

noffending ˌʌn.əˈfen.dɪŋ

noffensive ˌʌn.əˈfen*t*.sɪv

nofficial ˌʌn.əˈfɪʃ.ᵊl **-ly** -li

nopened ʌnˈəʊ.pᵊnd, ʌn- ⓤⓢ -ˈoʊ-

nopposed ˌʌn.əˈpəʊzd ⓤⓢ -ˈpoʊzd

nordained ˌʌn.ɔːˈdeɪnd ⓤⓢ -ɔːrˈ-

nordered ʌnˈɔː.dəd, ˌʌn- ⓤⓢ -ˈɔːr.dɚd

norganized, -ise- ʌnˈɔː.gᵊn.aɪzd, ˌʌn- ⓤⓢ -ˈɔːr-

northodox ʌnˈɔː.θə.dɒks, ˌʌn- ⓤⓢ -ˈɔːr.θə.dɑːks **-ly** -li

northodoxy ʌnˈɔː.θə.dɒk.si, ˌʌn- ⓤⓢ -ˈɔːr.θə.dɑːk-

nostentatious ʌnˌɒs.tenˈteɪ.ʃəs, ˌʌn-, -tənˈ- ⓤⓢ -ˌɑː.stənˈ- **-ly** -li **-ness** -nəs, -nɪs

nowned ʌnˈəʊnd, ˌʌn- ⓤⓢ -ˈoʊnd

npack ʌnˈpæk, ˌʌn-, ʌm-, ˌʌm- ⓤⓢ ʌn-, ˌʌn- **-s** -s **-ing** -ɪŋ **-ed** -t **-er/s** -əʳ/z ⓤⓢ -ɚ/z

npaid ʌnˈpeɪd, ˌʌn-, ʌm-, ˌʌm- ⓤⓢ ʌn-, ˌʌn-

npaired ʌnˈpeəd, ˌʌn-, ʌm-, ˌʌm- ⓤⓢ ʌnˈperd, ˌʌn-

npalatability ʌnˌpæl.ə.təˈbɪl.ɪ.ti, ˌʌn-, ʌm-, ˌʌm-, ˌ-ɪ-, -ə.ti ⓤⓢ ʌnˌpæl.ə.t̬əˈbɪl.ə.t̬i, ˌʌn-

npalatab|le ʌnˈpæl.ə.tə.b|l̩, ˌʌn-, ʌm-, ˌʌm-, ˈ-ɪ- ⓤⓢ ʌnˈpæl.ə.t̬ə-, ˌʌn- **-leness** -l̩.nəs, -nɪs

nparalleled ʌnˈpær.ᵊl.eld, ˌʌn-, ʌm-, ˌʌm- ⓤⓢ ʌnˈper-, ˌʌn-, -ˈpær-

npardonab|le ʌnˈpɑː.dᵊn.ə.b|l̩, ˌʌn-, ʌm-, ˌʌm-, -ˈpɑːd.nə- ⓤⓢ ʌnˈpɑːr.dᵊn.ə-, ˌʌn-, -ˈpɑːrd.nə- **-leness** -l̩.nəs, -nɪs

npardonab|ly ʌnˈpɑː.dᵊn.ə.b|li, ˌʌn-, ʌm-, ˌʌm-, -ˈpɑːd.nə- ⓤⓢ ʌnˈpɑːr.dᵊn.ə-, ˌʌn-, -ˈpɑːrd.nə-

nparliamentary ʌnˌpɑː.ləˈmen.tᵊr.i, ˌʌn-, ʌm-, ˌʌm-, -lɪˈ-, -li.əˈ- ⓤⓢ ʌnˌpɑːr.ləˈmen.t̬ɚ-, ˌʌn-, ˈ-tri

npasteurized, -ised ʌnˈpæs.tʃᵊr.aɪzd, ˌʌn-, ʌm-, ˌʌm-, -ˈpɑːs-, -tjᵊr-, -tᵊr- ⓤⓢ ʌnˈpæs.tʃə.raɪzd, ˌʌn-, -tə-

npatriotic ʌnˌpæt.riˈɒt.ɪk, ˌʌn-, ʌm-, ˌʌm-, -ˌpeɪ.triˈ- ⓤⓢ ʌnˌpeɪ.triˈɑː.t̬ɪk, ˌʌn- **-ally** -ᵊl.i, -li

npaved ʌnˈpeɪvd, ˌʌn-, ʌm-, ˌʌm- ⓤⓢ ʌn-, ˌʌn-

npeeled ʌnˈpiːld, ˌʌn-, ʌm-, ˌʌm- ⓤⓢ ʌn-, ˌʌn-

nperceiv|able ˌʌn.pəˈsiː.v|ə.bl̩, ˌʌm- ⓤⓢ ˌʌn.pɚˈ- **-ed** -d

nperforated ʌnˈpɜː.fᵊr.eɪ.tɪd, ˌʌn-, ʌm-, ˌʌm- ⓤⓢ ʌnˈpɝː.fə.reɪ.t̬ɪd, ˌʌn-

nperformed ˌʌn.pəˈfɔːmd, ˌʌm- ⓤⓢ ˌʌn.pɚˈfɔːrmd

npersuadable ˌʌn.pəˈsweɪ.də.bl̩, ˌʌm- ⓤⓢ ˌʌn.pɚˈ-

unpersuaded ˌʌn.pəˈsweɪ.dɪd, ˌʌm- ⓤⓢ ˌʌn.pɚˈ-

unpersuasive ˌʌn.pəˈsweɪ.sɪv, ˌʌm-, -zɪv ⓤⓢ ˌʌn.pɚˈ-

unperturbable ˌʌn.pəˈtɜː.bə.bl̩, ˌʌm- ⓤⓢ ˌʌn.pɚˈtɝː-

unperturbed ˌʌn.pəˈtɜːbd, ˌʌm- ⓤⓢ ˌʌn.pɚˈtɝːbd

unphilosophic|al ʌnˌfɪl.əˈsɒf.ɪ.k|ᵊl ⓤⓢ -ˈsɑː.fɪ- **-ally** -ᵊl.i, -li **-alness** -ᵊl.nəs, -nɪs

unpick ʌnˈpɪk, ˌʌn-, ʌm-, ˌʌm- ⓤⓢ ʌn-, ˌʌn- **-s** -s **-ing** -ɪŋ **-ed** -t

unpiloted ʌnˈpaɪ.lə.tɪd, ˌʌn-, ʌm-, ˌʌm- ⓤⓢ ʌnˈpaɪ.lə.t̬ɪd, ˌʌn-

unpin ʌnˈpɪn, ˌʌn-, ʌm-, ˌʌm- ⓤⓢ ʌn-, ˌʌn- **-s** -z **-ning** -ɪŋ **-ned** -d

unpitying ʌnˈpɪt.i.ɪŋ, ˌʌn-, ʌm-, ˌʌm- ⓤⓢ ʌnˈpɪt̬.i-, ˌʌn- **-ly** -li

unplaced ʌnˈpleɪst, ˌʌn-, ʌm-, ˌʌm- ⓤⓢ ʌn-, ˌʌn-

unplanned ʌnˈplænd, ˌʌn-, ʌm-, ˌʌm- ⓤⓢ ʌn-, ˌʌn-

unplayable ʌnˈpleɪ.ə.bl̩, ˌʌn-, ʌm-, ˌʌm- ⓤⓢ ʌn-, ˌʌn-

unpleasant ʌnˈplez.ᵊnt, ˌʌn-, ʌm-, ˌʌm- ⓤⓢ ʌn-, ˌʌn- **-ly** -li **-ness** -nəs, -nɪs

unpleasing ʌnˈpliː.zɪŋ, ˌʌn-, ʌm-, ˌʌm- ⓤⓢ ʌn-, ˌʌn- **-ly** -li **-ness** -nəs, -nɪs

unplug ʌnˈplʌg, ˌʌn-, ʌm-, ˌʌm- ⓤⓢ ʌn-, ˌʌn- **-s** -z **-ging** -ɪŋ **-ged** -d

unplumbed ʌnˈplʌmd, ˌʌn-, ʌm-, ˌʌm- ⓤⓢ ʌn-, ˌʌm-

unpoetic|al ˌʌn.pəʊˈet.ɪ.k|ᵊl, ˌʌm- ⓤⓢ ˌʌn.poʊˈet̬- **-ally** -ᵊl.i, -li **-alness** -ᵊl.nəs, -nɪs

unpolished ʌnˈpɒl.ɪʃt, ˌʌn-, ʌm-, ˌʌm- ⓤⓢ ʌnˈpɑː.lɪʃt, ˌʌn-

unpolitical ˌʌn.pəˈlɪt.ɪ.kᵊl, ˌʌm- ⓤⓢ ˌʌn.pəˈlɪt̬-

unpolluted ˌʌn.pəˈluː.tɪd, ˌʌm-, -ˈljuː- ⓤⓢ ˌʌn.pəˈluː.t̬ɪd

unpopular ʌnˈpɒp.jə.ləʳ, ˌʌn-, ʌm-, ˌʌm-, -jʊ- ⓤⓢ ʌnˈpɑː.pjə.lɚ, ˌʌn-

unpopularity ʌnˌpɒp.jəˈlær.ə.ti, ˌʌn-, ʌm-, ˌʌm-, -jʊˈ-, -ɪ.ti ⓤⓢ ʌnˌpɑː.pjəˈler.ə.t̬i, ˌʌn-, -pjʊˈ-, -ˈlær-

unpractic|al ʌnˈpræk.tɪ.k|ᵊl, ˌʌn-, ʌm-, ˌʌm- ⓤⓢ ʌn-, ˌʌn- **-ally** -ᵊl.i, -li

unpracticality ʌnˌpræk.tɪˈkæl.ə.ti, ˌʌn-, ʌm-, ˌʌm-, -təˈ-, -ɪ.ti ⓤⓢ ʌnˌpræk.təˈkæl.ə.t̬i, ˌʌn-

unpractised, -iced ʌnˈpræk.tɪst, ˌʌn-, ʌm-, ˌʌm- ⓤⓢ ʌn-, ˌʌn-

unprecedented ʌnˈpres.ɪ.dᵊn.tɪd, ˌʌn-, ʌm-, ˌʌm-, -ˈpriː.sɪ-, -den- ⓤⓢ ʌnˈpres.ə.den.t̬ɪd, ˌʌn-

unpredictability ˌʌn.prɪˌdɪk.təˈbɪl.ɪ.ti, ˌʌm-, -prə-, -ɪ.ti ⓤⓢ ˌʌn.prɪˌdɪk.təˈbɪl.ə.t̬i, -ˌpriː-

unpredictab|le ˌʌn.prɪˈdɪk.tə.b|l̩, ˌʌm-, -prəˈ- ⓤⓢ ˌʌn.prɪˈ-, -priːˈ- **-ly** -li

unprejudiced ʌnˈpredʒ.ə.dɪst, ˌʌn-, ʌm-, ˌʌm-, ˈ-ʊ- ⓤⓢ ʌnˈpredʒ.ə-, ˌʌn-

unpremeditated ˌʌn.priːˈmed.ɪ.teɪ.tɪd, ˌʌm-, -prɪˈ-, ˈ-ə- ⓤⓢ ˌʌn.priːˈmed.ɪ.teɪ.t̬ɪd

unpre|pared ˌʌn.prɪ|ˈpeəd, ˌʌm-, -prəˈ- ⓤⓢ ˌʌn.prɪ|ˈperd, -priːˈ- **-paredly** -ˈpeə.rɪd.li, -ˈpeəd.li ⓤⓢ -ˈper.ɪd.li, -ˈperd.li **-paredness** -ˈpeə.rɪd.nəs, -ˈpeəd.nəs, -nɪs ⓤⓢ -ˈper.ɪd.nəs, -ˈperd.nəs, -nɪs

unprepossessing ʌnˌpriː.pəˈzes.ɪŋ, ˌʌn-, ʌm-, ˌʌm- ⓤⓢ ʌn-, ˌʌn- **-ly** -li

unpresentable ˌʌn.prɪˈzen.tə.bl̩, ˌʌm-, -prəˈ- ⓤⓢ ˌʌn.prɪˈzen.t̬ə-, -priːˈ-

unpresuming ˌʌn.prɪˈzjuː.mɪŋ, ˌʌm-, -prəˈ-, -ˈzuː- ⓤⓢ ˌʌn.prɪˈzuː-, -priːˈ-, -ˈzjuː-

unpretending ˌʌn.prɪˈten.dɪŋ, ˌʌm-, -prəˈ- ⓤⓢ ˌʌn.prɪˈten.dɪŋ, -priːˈ- **-ly** -li

unpretentious ˌʌn.prɪˈten.*t*ʃəs, ˌʌm-, -prəˈ- ⓤⓢ ˌʌn.prɪˈ-, -priːˈ- **-ly** -li **-ness** -nəs, -nɪs

unpreventable ˌʌn.prɪˈven.tə.bl̩, ˌʌm-, -prəˈ- ⓤⓢ ˌʌn.prɪˈven.t̬ə-, -priːˈ-

unpriced ʌnˈpraɪst, ˌʌn-, ʌm-, ˌʌm- ⓤⓢ ʌn-, ˌʌn-

unprincipled ʌnˈprɪn*t*.sə.pl̩d, ˌʌn-, ʌm-, ˌʌm-, -sɪ- ⓤⓢ ʌn-, ˌʌn-

unprintable ʌnˈprɪn.tə.bl̩, ˌʌn-, ʌm-, ˌʌm- ⓤⓢ ʌnˈprɪn.t̬ə-, ˌʌn-

unprinted ʌnˈprɪn.tɪd, ˌʌn-, ʌm-, ˌʌm- ⓤⓢ ʌnˈprɪn.t̬ɪd, ˌʌn-

unproclaimed ˌʌn.prəʊˈkleɪmd, ˌʌm- ⓤⓢ ˌʌn.proʊˈ-, -prəˈ-

unprocurable ˌʌn.prəˈkjʊə.rə.bl̩, ˌʌm-, -ˈkjɔː- ⓤⓢ ˌʌn.prəˈkjʊr.ə-, -proʊˈ-

unproductive ˌʌn.prəˈdʌk.tɪv, ˌʌm- ⓤⓢ ˌʌn- **-ly** -li **-ness** -nəs, -nɪs

unprofessional ˌʌn.prəˈfeʃ.ᵊn.ᵊl, ˌʌm-, -ˈfeʃ.nᵊl ⓤⓢ ˌʌn- **-ly** -i **-ness** -nəs, -nɪs

unprofitab|le ʌnˈprɒf.ɪ.tə.b|l̩, ˌʌn-, ʌm-, ˌʌm-, ˈ-ə- ⓤⓢ ʌnˈprɑː.fɪ.t̬ə-, ˌʌn- **-ly** -li **-leness** -l̩.nəs, -nɪs

Unprofor ˈʌn.prə.fɔːʳ, ˈʌm- ⓤⓢ ˈʌn.prə.fɔːr

unprohibited ˌʌn.prəʊˈhɪb.ɪ.tɪd, ˌʌm-, ˈ-ə- ⓤⓢ ˌʌn.proʊˈhɪb.ə.t̬ɪd, -prəˈ-

unpromising ʌnˈprɒm.ɪ.sɪŋ, ˌʌn-, ʌm-, ˌʌm-, ˈ-ə- ⓤⓢ ʌnˈprɑː.mə-, ˌʌn- **-ly** -li

unprompted ʌnˈprɒm*p*.tɪd, ˌʌn-, ʌm-, ˌʌm- ⓤⓢ ʌnˈprɑːm*p*-, ˌʌn-

unpronounceable ˌʌn.prəˈnaʊn*t*.sə.bl̩, ˌʌm- ⓤⓢ ˌʌn-

unprop ʌnˈprɒp, ˌʌn-, ʌm-, ˌʌn- ⓤⓢ ʌnˈprɑːp, ˌʌn- **-s** -s **-ping** -ɪŋ **-ped** -t

unpropitious ˌʌn.prəˈpɪʃ.əs, ˌʌm- (US) ˌʌn.prəˈ-, -proʊˈ- **-ly** -li **-ness** -nəs, -nɪs
unprotected ˌʌn.prəˈtek.tɪd, ˌʌm- (US) ˌʌn-
unproved ʌnˈpruːvd, ˌʌn-, ʌm-, ˌʌm- (US) ʌn-, ˌʌn-
unproven ʌnˈpruː.vᵊn, ˌʌn-, ʌm-, ˌʌm-, -ˈprəʊ- (US) ʌnˈpruː-, ˌʌn-
unprovided ˌʌn.prəˈvaɪ.dɪd, ˌʌm- (US) ˌʌn-
unprovok|ed ˌʌn.prəˈvəʊk|t, ˌʌm- (US) ˌʌn.prəˈvoʊk|t **-edly** -ɪd.li, -t.li
unpublished ʌnˈpʌb.lɪʃt, ˌʌn-, ʌm-, ˌʌm- (US) ʌn-, ˌʌn-
unpunctual ʌnˈpʌŋk.tʃu.əl, ˌʌn-, ʌm-, ˌʌm-, -tʃʊəl, -tju.əl, -tjʊəl (US) ʌnˈpʌŋk.tʃu.əl, ˌʌn- **-ly** -i
unpunctuality ʌnˌpʌŋk.tʃuˈæl.ə.ti, ˌʌn-, ʌm-, ˌʌm-, -tjuˈ-, -ɪ.ti (US) ʌnˌpʌŋk.tʃuˈæl.ə.t̬i, ˌʌn-
unpunished ʌnˈpʌn.ɪʃt, ˌʌn-, ʌm-, ˌʌm- (US) ʌn-, ˌʌn-
unputdownable ˌʌn.pʊtˈdaʊ.nə.bl̩, ˌʌm- (US) ˌʌn-
unqualified ʌnˈkwɒl.ɪ.faɪd, ˌʌn-, ʌŋ-, ˌʌŋ-, ˈ-ə- (US) ʌnˈkwɑː.lə-, ˌʌn-
unquenchable ʌnˈkwen.tʃə.bl̩, ˌʌn-, ʌŋ-, ˌʌŋ- (US) ʌn-, ˌʌn-
unquestionab|le ʌnˈkwes.tʃə.nə.b|l̩, ˌʌn-, ʌŋ-, ˌʌŋ-, -ˈkweʃ- (US) ʌnˈkwes.tʃə-, ˌʌn-, -tjə- **-ly** -li **-leness** -l̩.nəs, -nɪs
unquestioned ʌnˈkwes.tʃənd, ˌʌn-, ʌŋ-, ˌʌŋ-, -ˈkweʃ- (US) ʌnˈkwes.tʃənd, ˌʌn-, -tjənd
unquestioning ʌnˈkwes.tʃə.nɪŋ, ˌʌn-, ʌŋ-, ˌʌŋ-, -ˈkweʃ- (US) ʌnˈkwes.tʃə-, ˌʌn-, -tjə- **-ly** -li
unquiet ʌnˈkwaɪət, ʌŋ- **-ly** -li **-ness** -nəs, -nɪs
unquote ʌnˈkwəʊt, ˌʌn-, ʌŋ-, ˌʌŋ- (US) ʌnˈkwoʊt, ˌʌn-
unravel ʌnˈræv.ᵊl, ˌʌn- **-s** -z **-(l)ing** -ɪŋ, -ˈræv.lɪŋ **-(l)ed** -d **-(l)er/s** -əʳ/z, -ɚ/z (US) -ˈræv.ləʳ/z, -lɚ/z
unread ʌnˈred, ˌʌn-
unreadable ʌnˈriː.də.bl̩, ˌʌn- **-ness** -nəs, -nɪs
unread|y ʌnˈred|.i, ˌʌn- **-ily** -ɪ.li, -ᵊl.i **-iness** -ɪ.nəs, -ɪ.nɪs
unreal ʌnˈrɪəl, ˌʌn- (US) -ˈriːl, -ˈriː.əl
unrealistic ˌʌn.rɪəˈlɪs.tɪk (US) -ri.əˈ- **-ally** -ᵊl.i, -li
unrealit|y ˌʌn.riˈæl.ə.t|i, -ɪ.t|i (US) -ə.t̬|i **-ies** -iz
unreason ʌnˈriː.zᵊn, ˌʌn-
unreasonab|le ʌnˈriː.zᵊn.ə.b|l̩, ˌʌn-, -ˈriːz.nə- **-ly** -li **-leness** -l̩.nəs, -nɪs
unreasoning ʌnˈriː.zᵊn.ɪŋ, ˌʌn-, -ˈriːz.nɪŋ
unreceived ˌʌn.rɪˈsiːvd, -rəˈ- (US) -rɪˈ-
unreciprocated ˌʌn.rɪˈsɪp.rə.keɪ.tɪd, -rəˈ- (US) -rɪˈsɪp.rə.keɪ.t̬ɪd
unreckoned ʌnˈrek.ᵊnd, ˌʌn-
unreclaimed ˌʌn.rɪˈkleɪmd
unrecognizable, -isa- ʌnˈrek.əg.naɪ.zə.bl̩, ˌʌn-, ˌʌn.rek.əgˈnaɪ- (US) ˌʌn.rek.əgˈnaɪ-, ʌnˈrek.əg.naɪ-, ˌʌn-
unrecognized, -ised ʌnˈrek.əg.naɪzd, ˌʌn-
unreconcilable ʌnˈrek.ᵊn.saɪ.lə.bl̩, ˌʌn-, ˌʌn.rek.ᵊnˈsaɪ-
unreconciled ʌnˈrek.ᵊn.saɪld, ˌʌn-
unreconstructed ˌʌn.riː.kənˈstrʌk.tɪd
unrecorded ˌʌn.rɪˈkɔː.dɪd, -rəˈ- (US) -rɪˈkɔːr-
unrecounted ˌʌn.rɪˈkaʊn.tɪd, -rəˈ- (US) -rɪˈkaʊn.t̬ɪd
unredeemable ˌʌn.rɪˈdiː.mə.bl̩, -rəˈ- (US) -rɪˈ-
unredeemed ˌʌn.rɪˈdiːmd, -rəˈ- (US) -rɪˈ-
unrefined ˌʌn.rɪˈfaɪnd, -rəˈ- (US) -rɪˈ-
unreflecting ˌʌn.rɪˈflek.tɪŋ, -rəˈ- (US) -rɪˈ-
unreformed ˌʌn.rɪˈfɔːmd, -rəˈ- (US) -rɪˈfɔːrmd
unrefuted ˌʌn.rɪˈfjuː.tɪd, -rəˈ- (US) -rɪˈfjuː.t̬ɪd
unregenerate ˌʌn.rɪˈdʒen.ᵊr.ət, -rəˈ-, -ɪt (US) -rəˈdʒen.ɚ.ɪt
unregistered ʌnˈredʒ.ɪ.stəd, ˌʌn- (US) -stɚd
unregulated ʌnˈreg.jə.leɪ.tɪd, -jʊ- (US) -t̬ɪd
unrehearsed ˌʌn.rɪˈhɜːst, -rəˈ- (US) -rɪˈhɝːst
unrelated ˌʌn.rɪˈleɪ.tɪd, -rəˈ- (US) -rɪˈleɪ.t̬ɪd
unrelaxed ˌʌn.rɪˈlækst, -rəˈ- (US) -rɪˈ-
unrelenting ˌʌn.rɪˈlen.tɪŋ, -rəˈ- (US) -rɪˈlen.t̬ɪŋ **-ly** -li **-ness** -nəs, -nɪs
unreliability ˌʌn.rɪ.laɪ.əˈbɪl.ɪ.ti, -rə-, -ə.ti (US) -rɪ.laɪ.əˈbɪl.ə.t̬i
unreliab|le ˌʌn.rɪˈlaɪ.ə.b|l̩, -rəˈ- (US) -rɪˈ- **-ly** -li **-leness** -l̩.nəs, -nɪs
unreliev|ed ˌʌn.rɪˈliːv|d, -rəˈ- (US) -rɪˈ- **-edly** -ɪd.li
unremarkable ˌʌn.rɪˈmɑː.kə.bl̩, -rəˈ- (US) -ˈmɑːr-
unremembered ˌʌn.rɪˈmem.bəd, -rəˈ- (US) -rɪˈmem.bɚd
unremitting ˌʌn.rɪˈmɪt.ɪŋ, -rəˈ- (US) -rɪˈmɪt̬- **-ly** -li **-ness** -nəs, -nɪs
unremonstrative ˌʌn.rɪˈmɒnt.strə.tɪv, -rəˈ- (US) -rɪˈmɑːnt.strə.t̬ɪv
unremovable ˌʌn.rɪˈmuː.və.bl̩, -rəˈ- (US) -rɪˈ-
unremunerative ˌʌn.rɪˈmjuː.nᵊr.ə.tɪv, -rəˈ- (US) -rɪˈmjuː.nɚ.ə.t̬ɪv, -nə.reɪ-
unrepaired ˌʌn.rɪˈpeəd (US) -ˈperd
unrepeatable ˌʌn.rɪˈpiː.tə.bl̩, -rəˈ- (US) -rɪˈpiː.t̬ə-
unrepentant ˌʌn.rɪˈpen.tənt, -rəˈ- (US) -rɪˈpen.tᵊnt
unreplaceable ˌʌn.rɪˈpleɪs.ə.bl̩
unreported ˌʌn.rɪˈpɔː.tɪd, -rəˈ- (US) -rɪˈpɔːr.t̬ɪd
unrepresentative ˌʌn.rep.rɪˈzen.tə.tɪv (US) -t̬ə.t̬ɪv
unrepresented ˌʌn.rep.rɪˈzen.tɪd (US) -t̬ɪd
unrequested ˌʌn.rɪˈkwes.tɪd, -rəˈ- (US) -rɪˈ-
unrequited ˌʌn.rɪˈkwaɪ.tɪd, -rəˈ- (US) -rɪˈkwaɪ.t̬ɪd ˌ**unrequited** ˈ**love**
unreserv|ed ˌʌn.rɪˈzɜːv|d, -rəˈ- (US) -rɪˈzɝːv|d **-edly** -ɪd.li **-edness** -ɪd.nəs, -nɪs
unresisting ˌʌn.rɪˈzɪs.tɪŋ, -rəˈ- (US) -rɪ **-ly** -li
unresolved ˌʌn.rɪˈzɒlvd, -rəˈ- (US) -rɪˈzɑːlvd
unresponsive ˌʌn.rɪˈspɒnt.sɪv, -rəˈ- (US) -rɪˈspɑːnt- **-ly** -li **-ness** -nəs, -nɪs
unrest ʌnˈrest, ˌʌn- (US) ʌnˈrest, ˌʌn-,
unrestful ʌnˈrest.fᵊl, ˌʌn-, -fʊl **-ly** -i **-ness** -nəs, -nɪs
unresting ʌnˈres.tɪŋ, ˌʌn-
unrestored ˌʌn.rɪˈstɔːd, -rəˈ- (US) -rɪˈstɔːrd
unrestrain|ed ˌʌn.rɪˈstreɪn|d, -rəˈ- (US) -rɪˈ- **-edly** -ɪd.li
unrestraint ˌʌn.rɪˈstreɪnt
unrestricted ˌʌn.rɪˈstrɪk.tɪd, -rəˈ- (US) -rɪˈ-
unretentive ˌʌn.rɪˈten.tɪv, -rəˈ- (US) -rɪˈten.t̬ɪv
unreveal|ed ˌʌn.rɪˈviːl|d, -rəˈ- (US) -rɪˈ- **-ing** -ɪŋ
unrevoked ˌʌn.rɪˈvəʊkt, -rəˈ- (US) -rɪˈvoʊkt
unrewarded ˌʌn.rɪˈwɔː.dɪd, -rəˈ- (US) -rɪˈwɔːr-
unriddl|e ʌnˈrɪd.l̩ **-es** -z **-ing** -ɪŋ **-ed** -d
unrighteous ʌnˈraɪ.tʃəs, -ti.əs (US) -tʃ **-ly** -li **-ness** -nəs, -nɪs
unrightful ʌnˈraɪt.fᵊl, ˌʌn-, -fʊl **-ly** -i **-ness** -nəs, -nɪs
unripe ʌnˈraɪp, ˌʌn- **-ness** -nəs, -nɪs
unrivalled ʌnˈraɪ.vᵊld, ˌʌn-
unrob|e ʌnˈrəʊb, ˌʌn- (US) -ˈroʊb **-es** -z **-ing** -ɪŋ **-ed** -d
unroll ʌnˈrəʊl, ˌʌn- (US) -ˈroʊl **-s** -z **-ing** -ɪŋ **-ed** -d
unromantic ˌʌn.rəʊˈmæn.tɪk (US) -roʊˈmæn.t̬ɪk, -rəˈ- **-ally** -ᵊl.i, -li
unrounded ʌnˈraʊn.dɪd, ˌʌn-
unruffled ʌnˈrʌf.l̩d, ˌʌn-
unrul|y ʌnˈruː.l|i, ˌʌn- **-ier** -i.əʳ (US) -i.ɚ **-iest** -i.ɪst, -i.əst **-iness** -ɪ.nəs, -ɪ.nɪs
unsaddl|e ʌnˈsæd.l̩, ˌʌn- **-es** -z **-ing** -ɪŋ, -ˈsæd.lɪŋ **-ed** -d
unsafe ʌnˈseɪf, ˌʌn- **-ly** -li **-ness** -nəs, -n
unsaid ʌnˈsed, ˌʌn-

sal(e)able ʌn'seɪ.lə.bl̩, ˌʌn-
salted ʌn'sɔːl.tɪd, ˌʌn-, -'sɒl- (US) -'sɔːl.t̬ɪd, -sɑː-
sanctified ʌn'sæŋk.tɪ.faɪd, ˌʌn-
sanitary ʌn'sæn.ɪ.tᵊr.i, ˌʌn-, '-ə-, -tri (US) -'sæn.ə.ter.i
satisfactor|y ʌnˌsæt.ɪs'fæk.tᵊr|.i, ˌʌn.sæt-, ˌʌnˌsæt- (US) ʌnˌsæt̬-, ˌʌn- **-ily** -ᵊl.i, -ɪ.li **-iness** -ɪ.nəs, -ɪ.nɪs
satisf|ied ʌn'sæt.ɪs.f|aɪd, ˌʌn- (US) -'sæt̬- **-ying** -aɪ.ɪŋ
saturated ʌn'sætʃ.ᵊr.eɪ.tɪd, ˌʌn-, -tʃʊ.reɪ-, -tjᵊr.eɪ, -tjʊ.reɪ- (US) -'sætʃ.ə.reɪ.t̬ɪd **unˌsaturated 'fat**
savo(u)r|y ʌn'seɪ.vᵊr|.i, ˌʌn- **-iness** -ɪ.nəs, -ɪ.nɪs
|say ʌn|'seɪ, ˌʌn- **-says** -'sez **-saying** -'seɪ.ɪŋ **-said** -'sed **-sayable** -'seɪ.ə.bl̩
scathed ʌn'skeɪðd, ˌʌn-
scented ʌn'sen.tɪd, ˌʌn- (US) -t̬ɪd
scheduled ʌn'ʃed.juːld, ˌʌn-, -'ʃedʒ.uːld, -'sked.juːld, -'skedʒ.uːld, -ᵊld (US) -'skedʒ.ʊld, -uːld, -u.əld
scholarly ʌn'skɒl.ə.li, ˌʌn- (US) -'skɑː.lɚ-
schooled ʌn'skuːld, ˌʌn-
scientific ˌʌn.saɪən'tɪf.ɪk **-ally** -ᵊl.i, -li
scom 'ʌn.skɒm (US) -skɑːm
scrambl|e ʌn'skræm.bl̩, ˌʌn- **-es** -z **-ing** -ɪŋ, -'skræm.blɪŋ **-ed** -d
screw ʌn'skruː, ˌʌn- **-s** -z **-ing** -ɪŋ **-ed** -d
scripted ʌn'skrɪp.tɪd, ˌʌn-
scriptural ʌn'skrɪp.tʃᵊr.ᵊl, ˌʌn-, -tʃʊ.rᵊl (US) -tʃɚ.ᵊl **-ly** -i
scrupulous ʌn'skruː.pjə.ləs, ˌʌn-, -pjʊ- (US) -pjə- **-ly** -li **-ness** -nəs, -nɪs
seal ʌn'siːl, ˌʌn- **-s** -z **-ing** -ɪŋ **-ed** -d
seasonab|le ʌn'siː.zᵊn.ə.bl|̩, ˌʌn-, -'siːz.nə- **-ly** -li **-leness** -l̩.nəs, -nɪs
seasoned ʌn'siː.zᵊnd, ˌʌn-
|seat ʌn|'siːt, ˌʌn- **-seats** -'siːts **-seating** -'siː.tɪŋ (US) -'siː.t̬ɪŋ **-seated** -'siː.tɪd (US) -'siː.t̬ɪd
seaworth|y ʌn'siːˌwɜː.ð|i, ˌʌn- (US) -ˌwɝː- **-iness** -ɪ.nəs, -ɪ.nɪs
sectarian ˌʌn.sek'teə.ri.ən (US) -'ter.i-
secured ˌʌn.sɪ'kjʊəd, -sə'-, -'kjɔːd (US) -'kjʊrd
seeded ʌn'siː.dɪd, ˌʌn-
seeing ʌn'siː.ɪŋ, ˌʌn- **-ly** -li
seeml|y ʌn'siːm.l|i (US), ˌʌn- **-iness** -ɪ.nəs, -ɪ.nɪs
seen ʌn'siːn, ˌʌn-
selfconscious ˌʌn.self'kɒn.tʃəs (US) -'kɑːn- **-ly** -li **-ness** -nəs, -nɪs
selfish ʌn'sel.fɪʃ, ˌʌn- **-ly** -li **-ness** -nəs, -nɪs
sensational ˌʌn.sen'seɪ.ʃᵊn.ᵊl, -sᵊn'-, -'seɪʃ.nᵊl

unsensitive ʌn'sent.sə.tɪv, ˌʌn-, -sɪ- (US) -sə.t̬ɪv **-ly** -li **-ness** -nəs, -nɪs
unsentimental ˌʌn.sen.tɪ'men.tᵊl (US) -t̬ᵊl **-ly** -i
unserviceable ʌn'sɜː.vɪ.sə.bl̩, ˌʌn- (US) -'sɝː-
unsettl|e ʌn'set.l̩, ˌʌn- (US) -'set̬- **-es** -z **-ing/ly** -ɪŋ/li, -'set.lɪŋ/li **-ness** -nəs, -nɪs
unsettled ʌn'set.l̩d (US) -'set̬-
unsevered ʌn'sev.əd, ˌʌn- (US) -ɚd
unshackl|e ʌn'ʃæk.l̩, ˌʌn- **-es** -z **-ing** -ɪŋ, -'ʃæk.lɪŋ **-ed** -d
unshak(e)able ʌn'ʃeɪ.kə.bl̩, ˌʌn-
unshaken ʌn'ʃeɪ.kᵊn, ˌʌn-
unshapely ʌn'ʃeɪ.pli, ˌʌn-
unshaven ʌn'ʃeɪ.vᵊn, ˌʌn-
unsheath|e ʌn'ʃiːð, ˌʌn- **-es** -z **-ing** -ɪŋ **-ed** -d
unship ʌn'ʃɪp, ˌʌn- **-s** -s **-ping** -ɪŋ **-ped** -t
unshockability ˌʌn.ʃɒk.ə'bɪl.ɪ.ti, -ˌʃɒk-, -ə.ti (US) -ʃɑː.kə'bɪl.ə.t̬i, -ˌʃɑː-
unshockable ʌn'ʃɒk.ə.bl̩, ˌʌn- (US) -'ʃɑː.kə-
unshod ʌn'ʃɒd, ˌʌn- (US) -'ʃɑːd
unshorn ʌn'ʃɔːn, ˌʌn- (US) -'ʃɔːrn
unshrinkable ʌn'ʃrɪŋ.kə.bl̩, ˌʌn-
unshrinking ʌn'ʃrɪŋ.kɪŋ, ˌʌn- **-ly** -li
unsighted ʌn'saɪ.tɪd, ˌʌn- (US) -t̬ɪd
unsightl|y ʌn'saɪt.l|i, ˌʌn- **-ier** -i.əʳ (US) -i.ɚ **-iest** -i.ɪst, -i.əst **-iness** -ɪ.nəs, -ɪ.nɪs
unsigned ʌn'saɪnd, ˌʌn-
unskilful ʌn'skɪl.fᵊl, ˌʌn-, -fʊl **-ly** -i
unskilled ʌn'skɪld, ˌʌn- **ˌunskilled 'worker**
unslaked ʌn'sleɪkt, ˌʌn-
unsliced ʌn'slaɪst
unsociability ˌʌn.səʊ.ʃə'bɪl.ɪ.ti, -ˌsəʊ-, -ə.ti (US) -soʊ.ʃə'bɪl.ə.t̬i, -ˌsoʊ-
unsociab|le ʌn'səʊ.ʃə.bl|̩, ˌʌn- (US) -'soʊ- **-ly** -li **-leness** -l̩.nəs, -nɪs
unsocial ʌn'səʊ.ʃᵊl, ˌʌn- (US) -'soʊ- **-ly** -i **ˌunsocial 'hours, unˌsocial 'hours**
unsold ʌn'səʊld, ˌʌn- (US) -'soʊld
unsold|er ʌn'səʊl.d|əʳ, ˌʌn-, -'sɒl- (US) -'sɑː.d|ɚ **-ers** -əz (US) -ɚz **-ering** -ᵊr.ɪŋ **-ered** -əd (US) -ɚd
unsolicited ˌʌn.sə'lɪs.ɪ.tɪd (US) -t̬ɪd
unsolved ʌn'sɒlvd, ˌʌn- (US) -'sɑːlvd, -'sɔːlvd
unsophisticated ˌʌn.sə'fɪs.tɪ.keɪ.tɪd, -tə- (US) -tə.keɪ.t̬ɪd **-ly** -li **-ness** -nəs, -nɪs
unsophistication ˌʌn.səˌfɪs.tɪ'keɪ.ʃᵊn, -tə'-
unsorted ʌn'sɔː.tɪd, ˌʌn- (US) -'sɔːr.t̬ɪd
unsought ʌn'sɔːt, ˌʌn- (US) -'sɑːt, -'sɔːt
unsound ʌn'saʊnd, ˌʌn- **-ly** -li **-ness** -nəs, -nɪs
unsparing ʌn'speə.rɪŋ, ˌʌn- (US) -'sper.ɪŋ **-ly** -li **-ness** -nəs, -nɪs

unspeakab|le ʌn'spiː.kə.bl|̩, ˌʌn- **-ly** -li
unspecified ʌn'spes.ɪ.faɪd, ˌʌn-, -'ə-
unspent ʌn'spent, ˌʌn-
unspoiled ʌn'spɔɪlt, ˌʌn-, -'spɔɪld (US) -'spɔɪld
unspoilt ʌn'spɔɪlt, ˌʌn-
unspoken ʌn'spəʊ.kᵊn, ˌʌn- (US) -'spoʊ-
unsporting ʌn'spɔː.tɪŋ, ˌʌn- (US) -'spɔːr.t̬ɪŋ **-ly** -li **-ness** -nəs, -nɪs
unsportsmanlike ʌn'spɔːts.mən.laɪk, ˌʌn- (US) -'spɔːrts-
unspotted ʌn'spɒt.ɪd, ˌʌn- (US) -'spɑː.t̬ɪd
Unst ʌntst
unstable ʌn'steɪ.bl̩, ˌʌn- **-ness** -nəs, -nɪs
unstack ʌn'stæk, ˌʌn- **-s** -s **-ing** -ɪŋ **-ed** -t
unstamped ʌn'stæmpt, ˌʌn-
unstarched ʌn'stɑːtʃt, ˌʌn- (US) -'stɑːrtʃt
unstated ʌn'steɪ.tɪd (US) -t̬ɪd
unstatesmanlike ʌn'steɪts.mən.laɪk, ˌʌn-
unsteadfast ʌn'sted.fɑːst, ˌʌn-, -fəst (US) -fæst, -fəst **-ly** -li **-ness** -nəs, -nɪs
unstead|y ʌn'sted|.i, ˌʌn- **-ier** -i.əʳ (US) -i.ɚ **-iest** -i.ɪst, -i.əst **-ily** -ɪ.li, -ᵊl.i **-iness** -ɪ.nəs, -ɪ.nɪs
unstick ʌn'stɪk, ˌʌn- **-s** -s **-ing** -ɪŋ **unstuck** ʌn'stʌk, ˌʌn-
unstinted ʌn'stɪn.tɪd, ˌʌn- (US) -t̬ɪd
unstinting ʌn'stɪn.tɪŋ, ˌʌn- (US) -t̬ɪŋ **-ly** -li
unstitch ʌn'stɪtʃ, ˌʌn- **-es** -ɪz **-ing** -ɪŋ **-ed** -t
unstop ʌn'stɒp, ˌʌn- (US) -'stɑːp **-s** -s **-ping** -ɪŋ **-ped** -t
unstoppab|le ʌn'stɒp.ə.bl|̩, ˌʌn- (US) -'stɑː.pə- **-ly** -li
unstrap ʌn'stræp, ˌʌn- **-s** -s **-ping** -ɪŋ **-ped** -t
unstressed ʌn'strest, ˌʌn-
unstructured ʌn'strʌk.tʃəd (US) -tʃɚd
unstrung ʌn'strʌŋ, ˌʌn-
unstuck *(from* **unstick)** ʌn'stʌk, ˌʌn- **ˌcome un'stuck**
unstudied ʌn'stʌd.ɪd, ˌʌn-
unstylish ʌn'staɪ.lɪʃ, ˌʌn- **-ly** -li
unsubmissive ˌʌn.səb'mɪs.ɪv **-ly** -li **-ness** -nəs, -nɪs
unsubstantial ˌʌn.səb'stæn.tʃᵊl, -'stɑːn- (US) -'stænt.ʃᵊl **-ly** -i
unsubstantiality ˌʌn.səbˌstæn.tʃi'æl.ə.ti, -ˌstɑːn-, -ɪ.ti (US) -ˌstænt.ʃi'æl.ə.t̬i
unsubstantiated ˌʌn.səb'stæn.tʃi.eɪ.tɪd, -'stɑːn- (US) -'stænt.ʃi.eɪ.t̬ɪd
unsuccess ˌʌn.sək'ses, '--- (US) ˌʌn.sək'ses
unsuccessful ˌʌn.sək'ses.fᵊl, -fʊl **-ly** -i **-ness** -nəs, -nɪs

unsuitability ˌʌn.suː.təˈbɪl.ə.ti, -sjuː-, ʌnˌsuː-, -ˌsjuː-, -ɪ.ti (US) ˌʌn.suː.t̬əˈbɪl.ə.t̬i, ʌnˌsuː-
unsuitab|le ʌnˈsuː.tə.b|l̩, ˌʌn-, -ˈsjuː- (US) -ˈsuː.t̬ə- **-ly** -li **-leness** -l̩.nəs, -nɪs
unsuited ʌnˈsuː.tɪd, ˌʌn-, -ˈsjuː- (US) -ˈsuː.t̬ɪd
unsullied ʌnˈsʌl.ɪd, ˌʌn-
unsung ʌnˈsʌŋ, ˌʌn-
unsupportab|le ˌʌn.səˈpɔː.tə.b|l̩ (US) -ˈpɔːr.t̬ə- **-ly** -li **-leness** -l̩.nəs, -nɪs
unsupported ˌʌn.səˈpɔː.tɪd (US) -ˈpɔːr.t̬ɪd
unsure ʌnˈʃɔːʳ, ˌʌn-, -ʃʊəʳ (US) -ˈʃʊr
unsurmountab|le ˌʌn.səˈmaʊn.tə.b|l̩ (US) -sɚˈmaʊn.t̬ə- **-ly** -li
unsurpassable ˌʌn.səˈpɑː.sə.bl̩ (US) -sɚˈpæs.ə-
unsurpassed ˌʌn.səˈpɑːst (US) -sɚˈpæst
unsurprising ʌn.səˈpraɪ.zɪŋ (US) -sɚ- **-ly** -li
unsusceptibility ˌʌn.səˌsep.təˈbɪl.ə.ti, -tɪˈ-, -ɪ.ti (US) -ə.t̬i
unsusceptible ˌʌn.səˈsep.tə.bl̩, -tɪ-
unsuspected ˌʌn.səˈspek.tɪd
unsuspecting ˌʌn.səˈspek.tɪŋ **-ly** -li **-ness** -nəs, -nɪs
unsuspicious ˌʌn.səˈspɪʃ.əs **-ly** -li **-ness** -nəs, -nɪs
unsustainable ˌʌn.səˈsteɪ.nə.bl̩
unsweetened ʌnˈswiː.tᵊnd, ˌʌn-
unswerving ʌnˈswɜː.vɪŋ, ˌʌn- (US) -ˈswɝː- **-ly** -li
Unsworth ˈʌnz.wəθ, -wɜːθ (US) -wɚθ, -wɝːθ
unsymmetric ˌʌn.sɪˈmet.rɪk, -səˈ- **-al** -ᵊl **-ally** -ᵊl.i, -li
unsymmetry ʌnˈsɪm.ɪ.tri, ˌʌn-, ˈ-ə-
unsympathetic ˌʌn.sɪm.pəˈθet.ɪk, -ˌsɪm- (US) -ˈθet̬- **-ally** -ᵊl.i, -li
unsystematic ˌʌn.sɪ.stəˈmæt.ɪk, -ˌsɪs.təˈ-, -tɪˈ- (US) -stəˈmæt̬- **-al** -ᵊl **-ally** -ᵊl.i, -li
untainted ʌnˈteɪn.tɪd, ˌʌn- (US) -t̬ɪd
untamable, untameable ʌnˈteɪ.mə.bl̩, ˌʌn-
untangl|e ʌnˈtæŋ.gl̩, ˌʌn- **-es** -z **-ing** -ɪŋ, -ˈtæŋ.glɪŋ **-ed** -d
untapped ʌnˈtæpt, ˌʌn-
untarnished ʌnˈtɑː.nɪʃt, ˌʌn- (US) -ˈtɑːr-
untaught ʌnˈtɔːt, ˌʌn- (US) -ˈtɑːt, -ˈtɔːt
untaxed ʌnˈtækst, ˌʌn-
unteachable ʌnˈtiː.tʃə.bl̩, ˌʌn-
untempered ʌnˈtem.pəd, ˌʌn- (US) -pɚd
untenability ˌʌn.ten.əˈbɪl.ɪ.ti, -ˌten-, -ə.ti (US) -ə.t̬i
untenable ʌnˈten.ə.bl̩, ˌʌn-
untenanted ʌnˈten.ən.tɪd, ˌʌn- (US) -t̬ɪd
unthankful ʌnˈθæŋk.fᵊl, ˌʌn-, -fʊl **-ly** -i **-ness** -nəs, -nɪs
unthinka|ble ʌnˈθɪŋ.kə|.bl̩, ˌʌn- **-bly** -bli
unthinking ʌnˈθɪŋ.kɪŋ, ˌʌn- **-ly** -li
unthought ʌnˈθɔːt (US) -ˈθɑːt, -ˈθɔːt
unˈthought of
unthoughtful ʌnˈθɔːt.fᵊl, ˌʌn-, -fʊl (US) -ˈθɑːt-, -ˈθɔːt- **-ly** -i **-ness** -nəs, -nɪs
unthread ʌnˈθred, ˌʌn- **-s** -z **-ing** -ɪŋ **-ed** -ɪd
untid|y ʌnˈtaɪ.d|i, ˌʌn- **-ier** -i.əʳ (US) -i.ɚ **-iest** -i.ɪst, -i.əst **-ily** -ɪ.li, -ᵊl.i **-iness** -ɪ.nəs, -ɪ.nɪs **-ies** -iz **-ying** -i.ɪŋ **-ied** -id
un|tie ʌn|ˈtaɪ, ˌʌn- **-ties** -ˈtaɪz **-tying** -ˈtaɪ.ɪŋ **-tied** -ˈtaɪd
until ᵊnˈtɪl, ʌnˈtɪl
Note: There is an occasional weak form /ˈʌn.tɪl, -tᵊl/ in stress-shift environments (e.g. ˈuntil ˌdeath), but this is rare.
untimel|y ʌnˈtaɪm.l|i, ˌʌn- **-iness** -ɪ.nəs, -ɪ.nɪs
untinged ʌnˈtɪndʒd, ˌʌn-
untiring ʌnˈtaɪə.rɪŋ, ˌʌn- (US) -ˈtaɪ- **-ly** -li **-ness** -nəs, -nɪs
untitled ʌnˈtaɪ.tl̩d, ˌʌn- (US) -t̬l̩d
unto ˈʌn.tuː, -tu, -tə (US) -tuː, -t̬ə, -tu
untold ʌnˈtəʊld, ˌʌn- (US) -ˈtoʊld
untouchability ʌnˌtʌtʃ.əˈbɪl.ə.ti, ˌʌn-, -ɪ.ti (US) -ə.t̬i
untouchable ʌnˈtʌtʃ.ə.bl̩, ˌʌn- **-s** -z
untouched ʌnˈtʌtʃt, ˌʌn-
untoward ˌʌn.təˈwɔːd, -tʊˈ-; -ˈtəʊəd (US) -ˈtɔːrd, -təˈwɔːrd **-ly** -li **-ness** -nəs, -nɪs
untraceable ʌnˈtreɪ.sə.bl̩, ˌʌn-
untrained ʌnˈtreɪnd, ˌʌn-
untrammel(l)ed ʌnˈtræm.ᵊld, ˌʌn-
untransferable ˌʌn.træntsˈfɜː.rə.bl̩, -trɑːntsˈ-, ʌnˈtrænts.fɜː-, -ˈtrɑːnts- (US) ˌʌn.træntsˈfɝː.ə-, ʌnˈtrænts.fɚ-
untranslat|able ˌʌn.træntˈsleɪ.t|ə.bl̩, -trɑːntˈ-, -trᵊnˈ-; -trænzˈleɪ-, -trɑːnzˈ-, -trᵊnzˈ- (US) -trænˈsleɪ.t̬|ə-, -trænzˈleɪ- **-ed** -ɪd
untried ʌnˈtraɪd, ˌʌn-
untrimmed ʌnˈtrɪmd, ˌʌn-
untrodden ʌnˈtrɒd.ᵊn, ˌʌn- (US) -ˈtrɑː.dᵊn
untroubled ʌnˈtrʌb.l̩d, ˌʌn-
untrue ʌnˈtruː, ˌʌn- **-ness** -nəs, -nɪs
untruly ʌnˈtruː.li, ˌʌn-
untrustworth|y ʌnˈtrʌstˌwɜː.ð|i, ˌʌn- (US) -ˌwɝː- **-ily** -ɪ.li, -ᵊl.i **-iness** -ɪ.nəs, -ɪ.nɪs
untru|th ʌnˈtruː|θ, ˌʌn- **-ths** -ðz, -θs
untruthful ʌnˈtruːθ.fᵊl, ˌʌn-, -fʊl **-ly** -i **-ness** -nəs, -nɪs
untuck ʌnˈtʌk, ˌʌn- **-s** -s **-ing** -ɪŋ **-ed** -t
unturned ʌnˈtɜːnd, ˌʌn- (US) -ˈtɝːnd
ˌleave no ˌstone unˈturned, leave ˌno ˌstone unˈturned
untutored ʌnˈtjuː.təd, ˌʌn- (US) -ˈtuː.t̬ɚd, -ˈtjuː-
untwist ʌnˈtwɪst, ˌʌn- **-s** -s **-ing** -ɪŋ **-ed** -ɪd
untypic|al ʌnˈtɪp.ɪ.k|ᵊl **-ly** -ᵊl.i, -li
unused *not made use of:* ʌnˈjuːzd, ˌʌ…
unused *not accustomed:* ʌnˈjuːst, ˌʌ…
unusual ʌnˈjuː.ʒᵊl, ˌʌn-, -ʒu.əl (US) -ʒu-ˈjuːʒ.wəl **-ly** -i **-ness** -nəs, -nɪs
unutterab|le ʌnˈʌt.ᵊr.ə.b|l̩, ˌʌn- (US) -ˈʌt̬- **-ly** -li **-leness** -l̩.nəs, -nɪs
unvariable ʌnˈveə.ri.ə.bl̩, ˌʌn- (US) -ˈver.i-
unvaried ʌnˈveə.rid, ˌʌn- (US) -ˈver.id, -ˈvær-
unvarnished ʌnˈvɑː.nɪʃt, ˌʌn- (US) -ˈvɑːr-
unvarying ʌnˈveə.ri.ɪŋ, ˌʌn- (US) -ˈver…, -ˈvær.i-
unveil ʌnˈveɪl, ˌʌn- **-s** -z **-ing** -ɪŋ **-ed** -…
unventilated ʌnˈven.tɪ.leɪ.tɪd, ˌʌn-, -tə- (US) -t̬ə.leɪ.t̬ɪd
unversed ʌnˈvɜːst, ˌʌn- (US) -ˈvɝːst
unvoiced ʌnˈvɔɪst, ˌʌn-
unwaged ʌnˈweɪdʒd, ˌʌn-
unwanted ʌnˈwɒn.tɪd, ˌʌn- (US) -ˈwɑːn.t̬ɪd
unwarlike ʌnˈwɔː.laɪk, ˌʌn- (US) -ˈwɔː…
unwarmed ʌnˈwɔːmd, ˌʌn- (US) -ˈwɔːrmd
unwarned ʌnˈwɔːnd, ˌʌn- (US) -ˈwɔːrn…
unwarrantab|le ʌnˈwɒr.ᵊn.tə.b|l̩, ˌʌ… (US) -ˈwɔːr.ᵊn.t̬ə-, -ˈwɑːr- **-ly** -li **-leness** -l̩.nəs, -nɪs
unwarranted ʌnˈwɒr.ᵊn.tɪd, ˌʌn- (US) -ˈwɔːr.ᵊn.t̬ɪd, -ˈwɑːr-
unwar|y ʌnˈweə.r|i, ˌʌn- (US) -ˈwer|.i **-ily** -ɪ.li, -ᵊl.i **-iness** -ɪ.nəs, -ɪ.nɪs
unwashed ʌnˈwɒʃt, ˌʌn- (US) -ˈwɑːʃt, -ˈwɔːʃt
unwavering ʌnˈweɪ.vᵊr.ɪŋ, ˌʌn- **-ly** -l…
unwearable ʌnˈweə.rə.bl̩, ˌʌn- (US) -ˈwer.ə-
unwearied ʌnˈwɪə.rid, ˌʌn- (US) -ˈwɪr.i…
unwearying ʌnˈwɪə.ri.ɪŋ, ˌʌn- (US) -ˈwɪr.i-
unwed ʌnˈwed, ˌʌn-
unwelcome ʌnˈwel.kəm, ˌʌn-
unwell ʌnˈwel, ˌʌn-
unwholesome ʌnˈhəʊl.səm, ˌʌn- (US) -ˈhoʊl- **-ly** -li **-ness** -nəs, -nɪs
unwield|y ʌnˈwiːl.d|i, ˌʌn- **-ier** -i.əʳ (US) -i.ɚ **-iest** -i.ɪst, -i.əst **-ily** -ɪ.li, -ᵊ… **-iness** -ɪ.nəs, -ɪ.nɪs
unwilling ʌnˈwɪl.ɪŋ, ˌʌn- **-ly** -li **-ness** -nəs, -nɪs
Unwin ˈʌn.wɪn
unwind ʌnˈwaɪnd, ˌʌn- **-s** -z **-ing** -ɪŋ
unwound ʌnˈwaʊnd, ˌʌn-
unwise ʌnˈwaɪz, ˌʌn- **-ly** -li
unwish ʌnˈwɪʃ **-es** -ɪz **-ing** -ɪŋ **-ed** -t
unˈwished ˌfor
unwitting ʌnˈwɪt.ɪŋ, ˌʌn- (US) -ˈwɪt̬- **-ly** -li

nwomanl|y ʌn'wʊm.ən.l|i, ˌʌn- **-iness** -ɪ.nəs, -ɪ.nɪs

nwonted ʌn'wəʊn.tɪd, ˌʌn- US -'wɔːn.t̬ɪd, -'woʊn-, -'wɑːn-, -'wʌn- **-ly** -li **-ness** -nəs, -nɪs

nworkable ʌn'wɜː.kə.bl̩, ˌʌn- US -'wɝː-

nworkmanlike ʌn'wɜːk.mən.laɪk, ˌʌn- US -'wɝːk-

nworldl|y ʌn'wɜːld.l|i, ˌʌn- US -'wɝːld- **-iness** -ɪ.nəs, -ɪ.nɪs

nworn ʌn'wɔːn, ˌʌn- US -'wɔːrn

nworth|y ʌn'wɜː.ð|i, ˌʌn- US -'wɝː- **-ily** -ɪ.li, -ᵊl.i **-iness** -ɪ.nəs, -ɪ.nɪs

nwound *(from* **unwind***)* ʌn'waʊnd, ˌʌn-

nwounded ʌn'wuːn.dɪd, ˌʌn-

nwrap ʌn'ræp, ˌʌn- **-s** -s **-ping** -ɪŋ **-ped** -t

nwritten ʌn'rɪt.ᵊn, ˌʌn- **ˌunwritten ˌconsti'tution; ˌunwritten 'law; ˌunwritten 'rule**

nwrought ʌn'rɔːt, ˌʌn- US -'rɑːt, -'rɔːt

nyielding ʌn'jiːl.dɪŋ, ˌʌn- **-ly** -li **-ness** -nəs, -nɪs

nyok|e ʌn'jəʊk, ˌʌn- US -'joʊk **-es** -s **-ing** -ɪŋ **-ed** -t

nzip ʌn'zɪp, ˌʌn- **-s** -s **-ping** -ɪŋ **-ped** -t

p- ʌp-

Note: Prefix. It is normally unstressed or receives secondary stress. It may carry the strongest stress in stress shift cases.

p ʌp **-s** -s **-ping** -ɪŋ **-ped** -t

p-and-coming ˌʌp.ᵊŋ'kʌm.ɪŋ, -ᵊnd̚- US -ᵊnd̚- *stress shift:* ˌup-and-coming 'leader

p-and-down ˌʌp.ᵊnd̚'daʊn *stress shift:* ˌup-and-down 'motion

p-and-up ˌʌp.ᵊnd̚'ʌp

panishad ʊ'pʌn.ɪ.ʃəd, jʊ-, -'pæn-, -ʃæd US uː'pæn.ɪ.ʃæd, juː-, -'pɑː.nɪ-, -ʃɑːd **-s** -z

pas 'juː.pəs **-es** -ɪz

pbeat *(adj.)* ʌp'biːt US '-- *stress shift, British only:* ˌupbeat 'ending

pbeat *(n.)* 'ʌp.biːt **-s** -s

pbraid ʌp'breɪd, ˌʌp- **-s** -z **-ing** -ɪŋ **-ed** -ɪd

pbringing 'ʌpˌbrɪŋ.ɪŋ

pcast 'ʌp.kɑːst US -kæst **-s** -s

pchuck 'ʌp.tʃʌk **-s** -s **-ing** -ɪŋ **-ed** -t

upcoming 'ʌpˌkʌm.ɪŋ, -'-- US 'ʌpˌkʌm-

Upcott 'ʌp.kət, -kɒt US -kət, -kɑːt

up-countr|y *(n. adj.)* ˌʌp'kʌn.tr|i US '--- **-ies** -iz *stress shift, British only:* ˌup-country 'farm

up-country *(adv.)* ʌp'kʌn.tri

update *(n.)* 'ʌp.deɪt **-s** -s

up|date *(v.)* ʌp|'deɪt, ˌʌp- **-dates** -'deɪts **-dating** -'deɪ.tɪŋ US -'deɪ.t̬ɪŋ **-dated** -'deɪ.tɪd US -'deɪ.t̬ɪd

Updike 'ʌp.daɪk

upend ʌp'end, ˌʌp- **-s** -z **-ing** -ɪŋ **-ed** -ɪd

up-front ʌp'frʌnt, ˌʌp- *stress shift:* ˌup-front 'payment

upgrad|e *(v.)* ʌp'greɪd, ˌʌp- **-es** -z **-ing** -ɪŋ **-ed** -ɪd

upgrade *(n.)* 'ʌp.greɪd **-s** -z

Upham 'ʌp.əm

upheaval ʌp'hiː.vᵊl **-s** -z

upheav|e ʌp'hiːv **-es** -z **-ing** -ɪŋ **-ed** -d

upheld *(from* **uphold***)* ʌp'held

uphill ʌp'hɪl, ˌʌp- *stress shift:* ˌuphill 'struggle

up|hold ʌp|'həʊld US -'hoʊld **-holds** -'həʊldz US -'hoʊldz **-holding** -'həʊl.dɪŋ US -'hoʊl.dɪŋ **-held** -'held **-holder/s** -'həʊl.dəʳ/z US -'hoʊl.dɚ/z

upholst|er ʌp'həʊl.st|əʳ, əp- US ʌp'hoʊl.st|ɚ **-ers** -əz US -ɚz **-ering** -ᵊr.ɪŋ **-ered** -əd US -ɚd **-erer/s** -ᵊr.əʳ/z US -ɚ.ɚ/z **-ery** -ᵊr.i

Upjohn 'ʌp.dʒɒn US -dʒɑːn

upkeep 'ʌp.kiːp

upland 'ʌp.lənd US -lənd, -lænd **-s** -z **-er/s** -əʳ/z US -ɚ/z

uplift *(n.)* 'ʌp.lɪft

uplift *(v.)* ʌp'lɪft, ˌʌp- **-s** -s **-ing** -ɪŋ **-ed** -ɪd

uplifting ʌp'lɪf.tɪŋ, ˌʌp- *stress shift:* ˌuplifting 'day

uplighter 'ʌpˌlaɪ.təʳ US -t̬ɚ **-s** -z

upload ʌp'ləʊd, 'ʌp.ləʊd US -loʊd **-s** -z **-ing** -ɪŋ **-ed** -ɪd

up-market ˌʌp'mɑː.kɪt US 'ʌpˌmɑːr- *stress shift, British only:* ˌup-market 'shop

Upminster 'ʌpˌmɪnt.stəʳ US -stɚ

upmost 'ʌp.məʊst US -moʊst

upon *strong form:* ə'pɒn US -'pɑːn *occasional weak form:* ə.pən

upper 'ʌp.əʳ US -ɚ **-s** -z **ˌupper 'class; ˌupper 'crust; ˌUpper 'House; ˌstiff upper 'lip; have the ˌupper 'hand**

upper-case ˌʌp.ə'keɪs US -ɚ'- *stress shift, see compound:* **ˌupper-case 'letters**

uppercut 'ʌp.ə.kʌt US '-ɚ- **-s** -s

Uppermill 'ʌp.ə.mɪl US '-ɚ-

uppermost 'ʌp.ə.məʊst US -ɚ.moʊst

Uppingham 'ʌp.ɪŋ.əm

uppish 'ʌp.ɪʃ **-ly** -li **-ness** -nəs, -nɪs

uppity 'ʌp.ɪ.ti US -t̬i **-ness** -nəs, -nɪs

Uppsala ʊp'sɑː.lə, ʌp-, '---; 'ʌp.sᵊl.ə, 'ʊp-, -sɑː.lɑː US ʌp'sɑː.lɑː, ʊp-; 'ʌp.sᵊl.ə

uprais|e ʌp'reɪz, ˌʌp- **-es** -ɪz **-ing** -ɪŋ **-ed** -d

uprear ʌp'rɪəʳ, ˌʌp- US -'rɪr **-s** -z **-ing** -ɪŋ **-ed** -d

Uprichard juː'prɪtʃ.ɑːd, -əd; ʌp'rɪtʃ.əd US juː'prɪtʃ.ɑːrd, -ɚd; ʌp'rɪtʃ.ɚd

upright 'ʌp.raɪt **-s** -s **-ly** -li **-ness** -nəs, -nɪs

uprising 'ʌpˌraɪ.zɪŋ, -'--, ˌ-'-- US 'ʌpˌraɪ- **-s** -z

upriver ˌʌp'rɪv.əʳ US -ɚ

uproar 'ʌp.rɔːʳ US -rɔːr **-s** -z

uproarious ʌp'rɔː.ri.əs US -'rɔːr.i- **-ly** -li **-ness** -nəs, -nɪs

up|root ʌp|'ruːt, ˌʌp- **-roots** -'ruːts **-rooting** -'ruː.tɪŋ US -'ruː.t̬ɪŋ **-rooted** -'ruː.tɪd US -'ruː.t̬ɪd **-rooter/s** -'ruː.təʳ/z US -'ruː.t̬ɚ/z

upsadaisy ˌʌps.ə'deɪ.zi, ˌʊps-

Upsala ʊp'sɑː.lə, ʌp-, '---; 'ʌp.sᵊl.ə, 'ʊp-, -sɑː.lɑː US ʌp'sɑː.lɑː, ʊp-; 'ʌp.sᵊl.ə

upscale ˌʌp'skeɪl

upset *(n.)* 'ʌp.set **-s** -s

upset *(adj.)* ʌp'set, ˌʌp- *stress shift, see compound:* **ˌupset 'stomach**

up|set *(v.)* ʌp|'set, ˌʌp- **-sets** -'sets **-setting** -'set.ɪŋ US -'set̬.ɪŋ

upshot 'ʌp.ʃɒt US -ʃɑːt

upside 'ʌp.saɪd **-s** -z **ˌupside 'down**

upsilon juːp'saɪ.lən, ʊp-, ʌp-, -lɒn; 'juːp.sɪl.ən, 'ʌp-, -ɒn US 'ʌp.sə.lɑːn, 'uːp- **-s** -z

upstag|e *(v.)* ʌp'steɪdʒ, ˌʌp- **-es** -ɪz **-ing** -ɪŋ **-ed** -d *stress shift, British only:* ˌupstage 'speech

upstage *(adj.)* ʌp'steɪdʒ, ˌʌp- US 'ʌp.steɪdʒ

upstairs ʌp'steəz, ˌʌp- US -'sterz *stress shift:* ˌupstairs 'window

upstanding ʌp'stæn.dɪŋ, ˌʌp- **-ness** -nəs, -nɪs *stress shift:* ˌupstanding 'soldier

upstart 'ʌp.stɑːt US -stɑːrt **-s** -s

upstate ˌʌp'steɪt US 'ʌp-, -'- *stress shift, British only:* ˌupstate 'town

upstream ʌp'striːm, ˌʌp- *stress shift:* ˌupstream 'journey

upstretched ʌp'stretʃt, ˌʌp- *stress shift:* ˌupstretched 'hands

Pronouncing the letters UOU

The vowel letter combination **uou** has only one possible pronunciation: /ju.ə/, e.g.:

ambiguous /æm'bɪg.ju.əs/

upstroke ˈʌp.strəʊk US -stroʊk **-s** -s
upsurg|e ˈʌp.sɜːdʒ US -sɝːdʒ **-es** -ɪz
upswept ʌpˈswept, ˌʌp- *stress shift:* ˌupswept ˈwings
upswing (*n.*) ˈʌp.swɪŋ **-s** -z
upswing (*v.*) ʌpˈswɪŋ, ˌʌp- **-s** -z **-ing** -ɪŋ **upswung** ʌpˈswʌŋ, ˌʌp-
uptake ˈʌp.teɪk **-s** -s
up-tempo ˌʌpˈtem.pəʊ US -poʊ
upthrust ˈʌp.θrʌst **-s** -s
uptight ʌpˈtaɪt, ˌʌp- **-ness** -nəs, -nɪs *stress shift:* ˌuptight ˈperson
up|tilt ʌpˈ|tɪlt, ˌʌp- **-tilts** -ˈtɪlts **-tilting** -ˈtɪl.tɪŋ US -ˈtɪl.t̬ɪŋ **-tilted** -ˈtɪl.tɪd US -ˈtɪl.t̬ɪd
up-to-date ˌʌp.təˈdeɪt **-ness** -nəs, -nɪs *stress shift:* ˌup-to-date ˈmethod
Upton ˈʌp.tən
up-to-the-minute ˌʌp.tə.ðəˈmɪn.ɪt, -tʊ- *stress shift:* ˌup-to-the-minute ˈstyling
uptown ʌpˈtaʊn, ˌʌp- US ˈʌp.taʊn, ˌ-ˈ- *stress shift, British only:* ˌuptown ˈhouse
upturn (*v.*) ʌpˈtɜːn US -ˈtɝːn **-s** -z **-ing** -ɪŋ **-ed** -d
upturn (*n.*) ˈʌp.tɜːn US -tɝːn **-s** -z
upturned ʌpˈtɜːnd, ˌʌp- US -ˈtɝːnd *stress shift:* ˌupturned ˈboat
upward ˈʌp.wəd US -wɚd **-ly** -li **-s** -z **ˌupwardly ˈmobile**
upwind ʌpˈwɪnd
Ur ɜːʳ, ʊəʳ US ɝː, ʊr
uraemia jʊəˈriː.mi.ə, jə-, jɔː- US juːˈriː-, jʊ-
Ural ˈjʊə.rᵊl, ˈjɔː- US ˈjʊr.ᵊl **-s** -z **ˌUral ˈMountains**
uralite ˈjʊə.rᵊl.aɪt, ˈjɔː- US ˈjʊr.ə.laɪt
Urani|a jʊəˈreɪ.ni|.ə, jə-, jɔː- US jʊ- **-an** -ən
uranium jʊəˈreɪ.ni.əm, jə-, jɔː- US jʊ-, jə-
Uranus ˈjʊə.rᵊn.əs, ˈjɔː-; jʊəˈreɪ.nəs, jə- US ˈjʊr.ᵊn.əs; juːˈreɪ.nəs
urate ˈjʊə.reɪt, ˈjɔː-, -rɪt US ˈjʊr.eɪt **-s** -s
urban (U) ˈɜː.bᵊn **urban** US ˈɝː- **-ite/s** -aɪt/s **ˌurban gueˈrrilla**
Urbana ɜːˈbæn.ə, -ˈbɑː.nə US ɝːˈbæn.ə
urbane ɜːˈbeɪn US ɝː- **-ly** -li **-ness** -nəs, -nɪs
urban|ism ˈɜː.bᵊn|.ɪ.zᵊm US ˈɝː- **-ist/s** -ɪst/s
urbanistic ˌɜː.bᵊnˈɪs.tɪk US ˌɝː- **-ally** -ᵊl.i, -li
urbanity ɜːˈbæn.ə.ti, -ɪ.ti US ɝːˈbæn.ə.t̬i
urbanization, -isa- ˌɜː.bᵊn.aɪˈzeɪ.ʃᵊn, -ɪˈ- US ˌɝː.bᵊn.ɪˈ-
urbaniz|e, -is|e ˈɜː.bᵊn.aɪz US ˈɝː- **-es** -ɪz **-ing** -ɪŋ **-ed** -d
Urbervilles ˈɜː.bə.vɪlz US ˈɝː-
urchin ˈɜː.tʃɪn US ˈɝː- **-s** -z
Urdu ˈʊə.duː, ˈɜː-, ˌ-ˈ- US ˈʊr.duː, ˈɝː-
Ure jʊəʳ US jʊr
-ure -əʳ US -ɚ

Note: Suffix. In words containing **-ure** where the stem is free, **-ure** does not normally affect the stress pattern of the word, e.g. **proceed** /prəʊˈsiːd US prə-/, **procedure** /prəʊˈsiː.dʒəʳ US prəˈsiː.dʒɚ/. Where the stem is bound, the word is normally stressed on the penultimate or antepenultimate syllable, e.g. **furniture** /ˈfɜː.nɪ.tʃəʳ US ˈfɝːr.nɪ.tʃɚ/. Exceptions exist; see individual entries.

ure|a jʊəˈriː|.ə; ˈjʊə.ri-, ˈjɔː- US jʊˈriː-; ˈjʊr.i- **-al** -ᵊl
ureter jʊəˈriː.təʳ; ˈjʊə.rɪ-, -rə- US jʊˈriː.t̬ɚ **-s** -z
ureth|ra jʊəˈriː.θ|rə US jʊ- **-rae** -riː **-ras** -rəz
urethritis ˌjʊə.rəˈθraɪ.tɪs, ˌjɔː-, -rɪˈ- US ˌjʊr.əˈθraɪ.t̬ɪs
uretic jʊəˈret.ɪk, jə- US jʊˈret̬.ɪk **-s** -s
urg|e ɜːdʒ US ɝːdʒ **-es** -ɪz **-ing** -ɪŋ **-ed** -d **-er/s** -əʳ/z US -ɚ/z
urgency ˈɜː.dʒᵊnt.si US ˈɝː-
urgent ˈɜː.dʒᵊnt US ˈɝː- **-ly** -li
Uriah jʊəˈraɪə, jə- US jʊ-
uric ˈjʊə.rɪk, ˈjɔː- US ˈjʊr.ɪk
Uriel ˈjʊə.ri.əl, ˈjɔː- US ˈjʊr.i-
Urim ˈjʊə.rɪm, ˈjɔː-, ˈʊə- US ˈjʊr.ɪm
urinal jʊəˈraɪ.nᵊl, jə-; ˈjʊə.rɪ.nᵊl, ˈjɔː-, -rᵊn.ᵊl; US ˈjʊr.ᵊn.ᵊl **-s** -z
urinary ˈjʊə.rɪ.nᵊr.i, ˈjɔː-, -rᵊn.ᵊr- US ˈjʊr.ə.ner.i
urin|ate ˈjʊə.rɪ.n|eɪt, ˈjɔː-, -rᵊn|.eɪt US ˈjʊr.ə.n|eɪt **-ates** -eɪts **-ating** -eɪ.tɪŋ US -eɪ.t̬ɪŋ **-ated** -eɪ.tɪd US -eɪ.t̬ɪd
urination ˌjʊə.rɪˈneɪ.ʃᵊn, ˌjɔː-, -rᵊnˈeɪ- US ˌjʊr.əˈneɪ-
urine ˈjʊə.rɪn, ˈjɔː- US ˈjʊr.ɪn **-s** -z
uriniferous ˌjʊə.rɪˈnɪf.ᵊr.əs, ˌjɔː-, -rᵊnˈɪf- US ˌjʊr.əˈnɪf-
urinogenital ˌjʊə.rɪ.nəʊˈdʒen.ɪ.tᵊl, ˌjɔː-, ˈ-ə- US ˌjʊr.ə.noʊˈdʒen.ə.t̬ᵊl
Urmia ˈɜː.mi.ə, ˈʊə- US ˈʊr-
Urmston ˈɜːm.stᵊn US ˈɝːm-
urn ɜːn US ɝːn **-s** -z
uro- ˌjʊə.rəʊ-, ˌjɔː- US ˌjʊr.oʊ-, ˌ-ə-
urolog|y jʊəˈrɒl.ə.dʒ|i US jʊrˈɑː- **-ist/s** -ɪst/s
Urquhart ˈɜː.kət US ˈɝː.kɚt, -kɑːrt
Ursa ˈɜː.sə US ˈɝː- **ˌUrsa ˈMajor; ˌUrsa ˈMinor**
ursine ˈɜː.saɪn US ˈɝː-, -sɪn
Ursula ˈɜː.sjə.lə, -sjʊ-, -ʃə-, -ʃʊ- US ˈɝː.sə.lə
Ursuline ˈɜː.sjə.laɪn, -sjʊ-, -ʃə-, -ʃʊ-, -lɪn US ˈɝː.sə.lɪn, -laɪn **-s** -z
urticaria ˌɜː.tɪˈkeə.ri.ə US ˌɝː.t̬ɪˈker.i-
Uruguay ˈjʊə.rə.gwaɪ, ˈʊr.ə-, ˈ-ʊ-, -gweɪ US ˈjʊr.ə.gweɪ, ˈʊr-, ˈuː.ruː-, -gwaɪ
Uruguayan ˌjʊə.rəˈgwaɪ.ən, ˌʊr.əˈ-, -ʊˈ-, -ˈgweɪ- US ˌjʊr.əˈgweɪ-, ˌʊr-, ˌuː.ruː-, -ˈgwaɪ- **-s** -z
urus ˈjʊə.rəs, ˈjɔː- US ˈjʊr.əs
us *strong form:* ʌs *weak forms:* əs, s

Note: Weak form word. The strong form is used mainly for contrast, e.g. 'a them and us attitude', or for emphasis, e.g. 'This land belongs to **us**'. The weak form is used when unstressed, and can occur in final position, e.g. 'They joined us' /ðeɪˈdʒɔɪnd.əs/.

US ˌjuːˈes
USA ˌjuː.es.ˈeɪ
usability ˌjuː.zəˈbɪl.ə.ti, -ɪ.ti US -ə.t̬i
usable ˈjuː.zə.bl̩
USAF ˌjuː.es.eɪˈef
usag|e ˈjuː.sɪdʒ, -zɪdʒ **-es** -ɪz
usanc|e ˈjuː.zᵊnts **-es** -ɪz
USDAW ˈʌs.dɔː, ˈʌz- US -dɑː, -dɔː
use (*n.*) juːs **uses** ˈjuː.sɪz
us|e (*v.*) *make use of:* juːz **-es** -ɪz **-ing** -ɪŋ **-ed** -d **-er/s** -əʳ/z US -ɚ/z
useab|le ˈjuː.zə.b|l̩ **-ly** -li **-leness** -l̩.nəs, -nɪs
used *(from* **use** *v.)* juːzd
used (*adj.*) *accustomed:* juːst, juːzd
used (*v.*) *was or were accustomed; when followed by* **to**: juːst *when not followed by* **to**: juːst, juːzd
usedn't *when followed by* **to**: ˈjuː.sᵊnt *when not followed by* **to**: ˈjuː.sᵊnt

Note: This form is rare in present-day English, especially in American English.

useful ˈjuːs.fᵊl, -fʊl **-ly** -i **-ness** -nəs, -nɪs
useless ˈjuː.sləs, -slɪs **-ly** -li **-ness** -nəs, -nɪs
usen't *when followed by* **to**: ˈjuː.sᵊnt *when not followed by* **to**: ˈjuː.sᵊnt

Note: See note for 'usedn't'.

user-friendl|y ˌjuː.zəˈfrend.l|i US -zɚˈ- **-iness** -ɪ.nəs, -ɪ.nɪs *stress shift:* ˌuser-friendly ˈproduct
uses *(plur. of* **use** *n.)* ˈjuː.sɪz
uses *(from* **use** *v.)* ˈjuː.zɪz
Ushant ˈʌʃ.ᵊnt
Ushaw ˈʌʃ.ə, -ɔː US -ə, -ɑː, -ɔː
ush|er (U) ˈʌʃ|.əʳ US -ɚ **-ers** -əz US -ɚz **-ering** -ᵊr.ɪŋ **-ered** -əd US -ɚd
usherette ˌʌʃ.ᵊrˈet **-s** -s
Usk ʌsk
USN ˌjuː.esˈen
usquebaugh ˈʌs.kwɪ.bɔː, -kwə- US -bɑː, -bɔː **-s** -z
Ussher ˈʌʃ.əʳ US -ɚ
USSR ˌjuː.es.esˈɑːʳ US -ˈɑːr

Uvular

A consonant sound made between the back of the tongue and a lump of soft tissue (uvula) which is in the back of the mouth, dangling from the end of the soft palate.

Examples for English

English does not have any examples of uvular sounds as phonemes, but sounds with this place of articulation are widely found in other languages.

In other languages

The voiceless uvular PLOSIVE [q] is found as the phoneme /q/ in many dialects of Arabic. Uvular FRICATIVES [χ ʁ] are found quite commonly: German, Hebrew, Dutch and Spanish, for example, have voiceless ones, and French, Arabic and Danish have voiced ones. The uvular NASAL [ɴ] is found in some Inuit languages. The uvula itself is active only when it vibrates in a uvular TRILL, [ʀ].

Pronouncing the letters UY

The vowel digraph **uy** has two possible pronunciations: /aɪ/ and, at the end of words where it is usually preceded by the letter **q**, /wi/, e.g.:

buy /baɪ/
soliloquy /səˈlɪl.ə.kwi/

An exceptional case is the word Gruyère, borrowed from French.

Gruyère /ˈgruː.jeə^{r}; gruˈjeə^{r}/ (US) /gruˈjer/

Ustinov ˈjuː.stɪ.nɒf, ˈuː-, -stə-, -nɒv (US) -nɑːf, -nɔːf, -nɑːv
usu. *(abbrev. for* **usual/ly***)* ˈjuː.ʒ^{ə}l/i, -ʒu.əl- (US) -ʒu.əl-, ˈjuːʒ.wəl-
usual ˈjuː.ʒ^{ə}l, -ʒu.əl (US) -ʒu.əl, ˈjuːʒ.wəl **-ly** -i **-ness** -nəs, -nɪs
usufruct ˈjuː.sjʊ.frʌkt, -zjʊ- (US) -zʊ-, -sʊ-, -zə-, -sə- **-s** -s
usurer ˈjuː.ʒ^{ə}r.ə^{r} (US) -ɚ **-s** -z
usurious juːˈzjʊə.ri.əs, -ˈʒʊə-, -ˈzjɔː- (US) juːˈʒʊr.i- **-ly** -li **-ness** -nəs, -nɪs
usurp juːˈzɜːp, -ˈsɜːp (US) -ˈsɝːp, -ˈzɝːp **-s** -s **-ing** -ɪŋ **-ed** -t **-er/s** -ə^{r}/z (US) -ɚ/z
usurpation ˌjuː.zɜːˈpeɪ.ʃ^{ə}n, -sɜːˈ- (US) -sɚˈ-, -zɚˈ- **-s** -z
usury ˈjuː.ʒ^{ə}r.i (US) -ʒɚ.i
Ut. *(abbrev. for* **Utah***)* ˈjuː.tɑː (US) -tɔː, -tɑː
Utah ˈjuː.tɑː (US) -tɔː, -tɑː
Ute juːt **-s** -s
utensil juːˈten*t*.s^{ə}l, -sɪl (US) -s^{ə}l **-s** -z
uteri *(alternative plur. of* **uterus***)* ˈjuː.t^{ə}r.aɪ (US) -t̬ə.raɪ
uterine ˈjuː.t^{ə}r.aɪn (US) -t̬ɚ.ɪn, -t̬ə.raɪn
uterus ˈjuː.t^{ə}r.əs (US) -t̬ɚ- **-es** -ɪz
Uther ˈjuː.θə^{r} (US) -θɚ
Utica ˈjuː.tɪ.kə (US) -t̬ɪ-
utilitarian ˌjuː.tɪ.lɪˈteə.ri.ən, -ləˈ-; juːˌtɪl.ɪˈ-, -əˈ- (US) juːˌtɪl.əˈter.i- **-s** -z **-ism** -ɪ.z^{ə}m
utilit|y juːˈtɪl.ə.t|i, -ɪ.t|i (US) -ə.t̬|i **-ies** -iz **uˈtility ˌroom**
utilization, -isa- ˌjuː.t^{ə}l.aɪˈzeɪ.ʃ^{ə}n, -tɪ.laɪˈ-, -lɪˈ- (US) -t̬^{ə}l.ɪˈ-
utiliz|e, -is|e ˈjuː.tɪ.laɪz, -t^{ə}l.aɪz (US) -t̬^{ə}l.aɪz **-es** -ɪz **-ing** -ɪŋ **-ed** -d **-er/s** -ə^{r}/z (US) -ɚ/z **-able** -ə.bl̩
utmost ˈʌt.məʊst, -məst (US) -moʊst
utopi|a (U) juːˈtəʊ.pi|.ə (US) -ˈtoʊ- **-an/s** -ən/z
utopianism (U) juːˈtəʊ.pi.ə.nɪ.z^{ə}m (US) -ˈtoʊ-
Utrecht ˈjuː.trekt, -trext, -ˈ- (US) ˈjuː.trekt
utricle ˈjuː.trɪ.kl̩ **-s** -z
Utrillo juːˈtrɪl.əʊ, uː- (US) -oʊ
Utsira uːtˈsɪə.rə (US) -ˈsɪr.ə
Uttar Pradesh ˌʊt.ə.prəˈdeʃ, -ˈdeɪʃ (US) ˌuː.t̬ɚ-
utt|er ˈʌt|.ə^{r} (US) ˈʌt̬|.ɚ **-erly** -^{ə}l.i (US) -ɚ.li **-erness** -ə.nəs, -nɪs (US) -ɚ- **-ers** -əz (US) -ɚz **-ering** -^{ə}r.ɪŋ **-ered** -əd (US) -ɚd **-erer/s** -^{ə}r.ə^{r}/z (US) -ɚ.ɚ/z **-erable** -^{ə}r.ə.bl̩
utteranc|e ˈʌt.^{ə}r.^{ə}n*t*s (US) ˈʌt̬- **-es** -ɪz
uttermost ˈʌt.ə.məʊst (US) ˈʌt̬.ɚ.moʊst
Uttley ˈʌt.li
Uttoxeter juːˈtɒk.sɪ.tə^{r}, ʌtˈɒk-, ˈʌk.sɪ- (US) juːˈtɑːk.sɪ.t̬ɚ, ʌt̬ˈɑːk-, ˈʌk.sɪ-
Note: The common pronunciation is /juːˈtɒk.sɪ.tə^{r} (US) -ˈtɑːk.sɪ.t̬ɚ/ or /ʌtˈɒk.sɪ.tə^{r} (US) -ˈɑːk.sɪ.t̬ɚ/. The former is more frequent, and is the pronunciation of most outsiders.
U-turn ˈjuː.tɜːn, ˌjuːˈtɜːn (US) ˈjuː.tɝːn, ˌ-ˈ- **-s** -z
UV ˌjuːˈviː *stress shift, see compound:* **ˌUV ˈlight**
uvul|a ˈjuː.vjə.l|ə, -vjʊ- **-as** -z **-ae** -i
uvular ˈjuː.vjə.lə^{r}, -vjʊ- (US) -lɚ
Uxbridge ˈʌks.brɪdʒ
uxorial ʌkˈsɔː.ri.əl (US) -ˈsɔːr.i-; ʌgˈzɔːr-
uxorious ʌkˈsɔː.ri.əs (US) -ˈsɔːr.i-; ʌgˈzɔːr- **-ly** -li **-ness** -nəs, -nɪs
Uzbek ˈʊz.bek, ˈʌz- **-s** -s
Uzbekistan ʊzˌbek.ɪˈstɑːn, ʌz- (US) -ˈstæn, -ˈstɑːn **-i/s** -i/z
Uzi® ˈuː.zi

Pronouncing the letter V

The consonant letter **v** is always realised as /v/ in English words, e.g.:

van /væn/
love /lʌv/

However, in words borrowed from German and Slavic languages, the pronunciation may be /f/, e.g.:

Volkswagen /ˈfɒlksˌvɑː.gən, ˈvɒlks-/ (US) /ˈfoʊlks-, ˈvoʊlks-/
Gorbachev /ˈgɔː.bə.tʃɒf/ (US) /ˈgɔːr.bə.tʃɑːf/

v (V) viː **-'s** -z **ˈv ˌsign**
v. *versus:* viː, ˈvɜː.səs (US) viː, ˈvɝː- *vide:* viː, siː, ˈviː.deɪ, ˈvaɪ.di (US) ˈviː.deɪ
Va. *(abbrev. for* **Virginia***)* vəˈdʒɪn.jə, vɜː-, -i.ə; ˌviːˈeɪ (US) vɚˈdʒɪn.jə; ˌviːˈeɪ
Vaal vɑːl
vac væk **-s** -s
vacanc|y ˈveɪ.kᵊnt.s|i **-ies** -iz
vacant ˈveɪ.kᵊnt **-ly** -li ˌ**vacant ˈlot**
vaca|te vəˈkeɪ|t, veɪ- (US) ˈveɪ.keɪ|t, -ˈ- **-tes** -ts **-ting** -tɪŋ (US) -t̬ɪŋ **-ted** -tɪd (US) -t̬ɪd
vacation vəˈkeɪ.ʃᵊn (US) veɪ-, və- **-s** -z **-ing** -ɪŋ **-ed** -d **-er/s** -əʳ/z (US) -ɚ/z **-ist/s** -ɪst/s
vaccin|ate ˈvæk.sɪ.n|eɪt, -sᵊn|.eɪt (US) -sə.n|eɪt **-ates** -eɪts **-ating** -eɪ.tɪŋ (US) -eɪ.t̬ɪŋ **-ated** -eɪ.tɪd (US) -eɪ.t̬ɪd **-ator/s** -eɪ.təʳ/z (US) -eɪ.t̬ɚ/z
vaccination ˌvæk.sɪˈneɪ.ʃᵊn, -sᵊnˈeɪ- (US) -səˈneɪ- **-s** -z
vaccine ˈvæk.siːn, -sɪn (US) vækˈsiːn, ˈ-- **-s** -z
Vachel(l) ˈveɪ.tʃᵊl
Vacher ˈvæʃ.əʳ, ˈveɪ.tʃəʳ (US) ˈvæʃ.ɚ, ˈveɪ.tʃɚ
vacill|ate ˈvæs.ᵊl|.eɪt, -sɪ.l|eɪt (US) -ə.l|eɪt **-ates** -eɪts **-ating/ly** -eɪ.tɪŋ/li (US) -eɪ.t̬ɪŋ/li **-ated** -eɪ.tɪd (US) -eɪ.t̬ɪd **-ator/s** -eɪ.təʳ/z (US) -eɪ.t̬ɚ/z
vacillation ˌvæs.ᵊlˈeɪ.ʃᵊn, -ɪˈleɪ- (US) -əˈleɪ- **-s** -z
Václav ˈvæt.slæv (US) ˈvɑːt.slɑːf
vacuity vækˈjuː.ə.ti, vəˈkjuː-, -ɪ.ti (US) -ə.t̬i
vacuolar ˌvæk.juˈəʊ.ləʳ (US) ˈvæk.ju.wə.lɚ; ˌvæk.juˈoʊ-, -lɑːr
vacuole ˈvæk.ju.əʊl (US) -oʊl **-s** -z
vacuous ˈvæk.ju.əs **-ly** -li **-ness** -nəs, -nɪs
vacuum ˈvæk.juːm, -jʊm, -jʊəm (US) -juːm, -ju.əm, -jʊm, -jəm **-s** -z **-ing** -ɪŋ **-ed** -d ˈ**vacuum ˌcleaner**; ˈ**vacuum ˌflask**; ˈ**vacuum ˌpump**
vacuum-packed ˌvæk.juːmˈpækt, -jʊmˈ-, -jʊəmˈ- (US) -ju.əmˈ-, -juːmˈ-, -jʊmˈ-, -jəmˈ-, ˈ---
vade-mecum ˌvɑː.deɪˈmeɪ.kəm, -kʊm; ˌveɪ.diˈmiː.kəm, -kʌm (US) ˌveɪ.diˈmiː.kəm, ˌvɑː-, -ˈmeɪ- **-s** -z
Vaduz vɑːˈduːts
vagabond ˈvæg.ə.bɒnd, -bənd (US) -bɑːnd **-s** -z **-ish** -ɪʃ **-ism** -ɪ.zᵊm
vagabondage ˈvæg.əˌbɒn.dɪdʒ (US) -ˌbɑːn-
vagar|y ˈveɪ.gᵊr|.i; vəˈgeə.r|i (US) ˈveɪ.gɚ.|i; vəˈger|.i **-ies** -iz
vagina vəˈdʒaɪ.nə **-s** -z
vaginal vəˈdʒaɪ.nᵊl; ˈvædʒ.ɪ-, -ᵊn.ᵊl (US) ˈvædʒ.ᵊn.ᵊl **-ly** -i
vaginismus ˌvædʒ.ɪˈnɪz.məs, -əˈ-, -ˈnɪs- (US) -əˈnɪz-
vagrancy ˈveɪ.grᵊnt.si
vagrant ˈveɪ.grᵊnt **-s** -s
vagu|e veɪg **-er** -əʳ (US) -ɚ **-est** -ɪst, -əst **-ely** -li **-eness** -nəs, -nɪs
vail (V) veɪl **-s** -z **-ing** -ɪŋ **-ed** -d
Vaile veɪl
vain veɪn **-er** -əʳ (US) -ɚ **-est** -ɪst, -əst **-ly** -li **-ness** -nəs, -nɪs
vainglorious ˌveɪnˈglɔː.ri.əs, ˌveɪŋˈ- (US) ˌveɪnˈglɔːr.i- **-ly** -li **-ness** -nəs, -nɪs
vainglory ˌveɪnˈglɔː.ri, ˌveɪŋ- (US) ˈveɪnˌglɔːr.i, ˌ-ˈ--
Vaishnav|a ˈveʃ.nə.v|ɑː **-ism** -ɪ.zᵊm
Val væl
Valais ˈvæl.eɪ
valanc|e ˈvæl.ənts (US) ˈvæl-, ˈveɪ.lᵊnts **-es** -ɪz **-ed** -t
Valdez vælˈdiːz
vale (V) *valley:* veɪl **-s** -z
vale *latin word meaning "goodbye":* ˈvɑː.leɪ, ˈveɪ.li, ˈvæl.eɪ (US) ˈveɪ.li, ˈvɑː.leɪ
valediction ˌvæl.ɪˈdɪk.ʃᵊn, -əˈ- (US) ˌvæl.əˈdɪk.ʃᵊn **-s** -z
valedictorian ˌvæl.ɪ.dɪkˈtɔː.ri.ən, ˌ-ə- (US) ˌvæl.ə.dɪkˈtɔːr.i- **-s** -z
valedictor|y ˌvæl.ɪˈdɪk.tᵊr|.i, -əˈ- (US) ˌvæl.əˈdɪk.tɚ- **-ies** -iz
valence ˈveɪ.lᵊnts
Valencia vəˈlent.si.ə
Valenciennes ˌvæl.ən.siˈen, -ɑ̃ːn-, -ɑːnt-, -ˈsjen (US) -siˈenz, -ˈsjenz; vəˌlent.siˈenz, -ˌlɑːnt-
valenc|y ˈveɪ.lənt.s|i **-ies** -iz
valentine (V) *person or card:* ˈvæl.ən.taɪn **-s** -z ˈ**Valentine's ˌcard**; ˈ**Valentine's ˌDay**
Valentine *first name/surname:* ˈvæl.ən.taɪn, -tɪn (US) -taɪn
Valentinian ˌvæl.ənˈtɪn.i.ən
Valentino ˌvæl.ənˈtiː.nəʊ (US) -noʊ
valerian (V) vəˈlɪə.ri.ən, -ˈleə- (US) -ˈlɪr.i- **-s** -z
Valerie, Valery ˈvæl.ᵊr.i
Valerius vəˈlɪə.ri.əs, -ˈleə- (US) -ˈlɪr.i-
Valéry ˈvæl.eə.riː, ˌvæl.eəˈriː (US) ˌvæl.əˈriː, ˌvɑː.leɪˈiː
valet ˈvæl.eɪ, -ɪt, -ət, -i (US) ˈvæl.ɪt; vəˈleɪ, vælˈeɪ; ˈvæl.eɪ **valets** ˈvæl.eɪz, -ɪts, -əts, -iz (US) ˈvæl.ɪts; vəˈleɪz, vælˈeɪz; ˈvæl.eɪz **valeting** ˈvæl.eɪ.ɪŋ, -ɪ.tɪŋ, -ə.tɪŋ, -i.ɪŋ (US) ˈvæl.ɪ.t̬ɪŋ; vəˈleɪ.ɪŋ, vælˈeɪ.ɪŋ; ˈvæl.eɪ.ɪŋ **valeted** ˈvæl.eɪd, -ɪ.tɪd, -ə.tɪd, ˈ-id (US) ˈvæl.ɪ.t̬ɪd; vəˈleɪd, vælˈeɪd; ˈvæl.eɪd ˈ**valet ˌparking**
valetudinarian ˌvæl.ɪ.tjuː.dɪˈneə.ri.ən, ˌ-ə-, -tʃuː- (US) -əˌtuː.dəˈner.i-, -ˌtjuː- **-s** -z **-ism** -ɪ.zᵊm
Valhalla vælˈhæl.ə (US) vælˈhæl-, vɑːlˈhɑː.lə
valiant ˈvæl.i.ənt, ˈ-jənt (US) ˈ-jənt **-ly** -li **-ness** -nəs, -nɪs
valid ˈvæl.ɪd **-ly** -li **-ness** -nəs, -nɪs
vali|date ˈvæl.ɪ|.deɪt, ˈ-ə- (US) ˈ-ə- **-dates** -deɪts **-dating** -deɪ.tɪŋ (US) -deɪ.t̬ɪŋ **-dated** -deɪ.tɪd (US) -deɪ.t̬ɪd
validation ˌvæl.ɪˈdeɪ.ʃᵊn, -əˈ- (US) -əˈ- **-s** -z
validit|y vəˈlɪd.ə.t|i, vælˈɪd-, -ɪ.t|i (US) vəˈlɪd.ə.t̬|i **-ies** -iz
valis|e vəˈliːz, vælˈiːz, -ˈiːs (US) vəˈliːs, -ˈliːz **-es** -ɪz
Valium® ˈvæl.i.əm (US) ˈ-i.əm, ˈ-jəm **-s** -z
Valkyrie vælˈkɪə.ri, ˈvæl.kᵊr.i, -kɪ.ri (US) vælˈkɪr.i, ˈvæl.kɚ.i, -kɪ.ri **-s** -z
Valladolid ˌvæl.ə.dəʊˈlɪd, -dɒlˈɪd *as if Spanish:* ˌvaɪ.ɑː.dɒlˈiːd (US) -doʊˈlɪd
Vallance ˈvæl.ənts
Valletta vəˈlet.ə (US) vɑːˈlet.ɑː
valley ˈvæl.i **-s** -z
Vallone vəˈləʊn (US) -ˈloʊn

Valois 'væl.wɑː ⓤⓢ vɑːl'wɑː; 'væl.wɑː
valor 'væl.əʳ ⓤⓢ -ɚ
valorization, -isa- ˌvæl.ᵊr.aɪ'zeɪ.ʃᵊn, -ɪ'- ⓤⓢ -ɪ'- **-s** -z
valoriz|e, -is|e 'væl.ᵊr.aɪz ⓤⓢ -ə.raɪz **-es** -ɪz **-ing** -ɪŋ **-ed** -d
valorous 'væl.ᵊr.əs **-ly** -li **-ness** -nəs, -nɪs
valour 'væl.əʳ ⓤⓢ -ɚ
Valparaiso ˌvæl.pᵊr'aɪ.zəʊ, -'eɪ- ⓤⓢ -pə'raɪ.zoʊ, -'reɪ-
Valpolicella ˌvæl.pɒl.ɪ'tʃel.ə ⓤⓢ ˌvɑːl.poʊ.lɪ-
vals|e vɑːls, væls, vɔːls ⓤⓢ vɑːls, vʌls **-es** -ɪz
valuab|le 'væl.ju.ə.bl̩, -jə.bl̩, -jʊ- **-les** -l̩z **-ly** -li **-leness** -l̩.nəs, -nɪs
valuat|e 'væl.ju.eɪt **-es** -s **-ing** -ɪŋ **-ed** -ɪd
valuation ˌvæl.ju'eɪ.ʃᵊn **-s** -z
valu|e 'væl.juː **-es** -z **-ing** -ɪŋ **-ed** -d **-er/s** -əʳ/z ⓤⓢ -ɚ/z **'value ˌjudgment; ˌfamily 'values**
value-added ˌvæl.juː'æd.ɪd **ˌvalue-ˌadded 'tax, ˌvalue-'added ˌtax**
valueless 'væl.juː.ləs, -jʊ-, -lɪs
valve vælv **-s** -z
valvular 'væl.vjə.ləʳ, -vjʊ- ⓤⓢ -vjə.lɚ
valvule 'væl.vjuːl **-s** -z
vamoos|e və'muːs, væm'uːs ⓤⓢ væm'uːs, və'muːs **-es** -ɪz **-ing** -ɪŋ **-ed** -t
vamp væmp **-s** -s **-ing** -ɪŋ **-ed** -t
vampire 'væm.paɪəʳ ⓤⓢ -paɪɚ **-s** -z **'vampire ˌbat**
vampirism 'væm.paɪə.rɪ.zᵊm ⓤⓢ -paɪ-, -pɪ-
vampish 'væm.pɪʃ **-ly** -li **-ness** -nəs, -nɪs
van (V) væn **-s** -z
vanadium və'neɪ.di.əm
Van Allen væn'æl.ən **Van ˌAllen 'belt** ⓤⓢ **Van 'Allen ˌbelt**
Vanbrugh 'væn.brə, 'væm- ⓤⓢ 'væn.bruː
Note: **Sir John Vanbrugh**, the seventeenth-century dramatist and architect, is also sometimes referred to as /'væn.bruː/ in British English.
Vance vænts, vɑːnts ⓤⓢ vænts
Vancouver væn'kuː.vəʳ, væŋ- ⓤⓢ væn'kuː.vɚ
V and A, V & A *(abbrev. for* **Victoria and Albert Museum***)* ˌviː.ənd'eɪ
vandal (V) 'væn.dᵊl **-s** -z
vandalism 'væn.dᵊl.ɪ.zᵊm
vandaliz|e, -is|e 'væn.dᵊl.aɪz **-es** -ɪz **-ing** -ɪŋ **-ed** -d
Van de Graaff generator ˌvæn.də.grɑːf'dʒen.ᵊ.reɪ.təʳ ⓤⓢ -t̬ɚ, -ˌgræf'- **-s** -z
Vanderbilt 'væn.də.bɪlt ⓤⓢ -dɚ-
Vanderbyl 'væn.də.bɪl ⓤⓢ -dɚ-
Vandermeer ˌvæn.də'mɪəʳ ⓤⓢ -dɚ'mɪr
van der Post ˌvæn.də'pɒst ⓤⓢ -dɚ'pɑːst
Van Diemen væn'diː.mən
Vandyke, Van Dyck væn'daɪk *stress shift, see compounds:* **ˌVandyke 'brown; ˌVandyke 'collar**
vane (V) veɪn **-s** -z **-d** -d
Vanessa və'nes.ə
Van Eyck væn'aɪk **-s** -s
Vange vændʒ
Van Gogh væn'gɒf, væŋ-, -'gɒk, -'gɒx ⓤⓢ væn'goʊ, -'gɔːx
vanguard 'væn.gɑːd, 'væŋ- ⓤⓢ 'væn.gɑːrd **-s** -z
Van Helsing væn'hel.sɪŋ ⓤⓢ væn-, vɑːn-
vanilla və'nɪl.ə **vaˌnilla ˌpod**
vanish 'væn.ɪʃ **-es** -ɪz **-ing** -ɪŋ **-ed** -t **'vanishing ˌcream; 'vanishing ˌpoint**
Vanitory® 'væn.ɪ.tᵊr.i **'Vanitory ˌunit**
vanit|y 'væn.ə.t|i, -ɪ.t|i ⓤⓢ -ə.t̬|i **-ies** -iz **'vanity ˌcase; ˌVanity 'Fair; 'vanity ˌplates; 'vanity ˌtable**
vanquish 'væŋ.kwɪʃ ⓤⓢ 'væŋ-, 'væn- **-es** -ɪz **-ing** -ɪŋ **-ed** -t **-er/s** -əʳ/z ⓤⓢ -ɚ/z **-able** -ə.bl̩
Vansittart væn'sɪt.ət, -ɑːt ⓤⓢ -'sɪt̬.ɚt
van Straubenzee ˌvæn.strɔː'ben.zi ⓤⓢ -strɑː'-, -strɔː'-
vantag|e 'vɑːn.tɪdʒ ⓤⓢ 'væn.t̬ɪdʒ **-es** -ɪz **'vantage ˌpoint**
Vanuatu ˌvæn.u'ɑː.tuː, -'æt.uː ⓤⓢ væn'wɑː.tuː
Vanunu və'nuː.nuː
Van Vechten væn'vek.tən
Vanya 'vɑː.njə, 'væn.jə ⓤⓢ 'vɑː.njə
vapid 'væp.ɪd **-ly** -li **-ness** -nəs, -nɪs
vapidity væp'ɪd.ə.ti, və'pɪd-, -ɪ.ti ⓤⓢ væp'ɪd.ə.t̬i
vap|or 'veɪ.p|əʳ ⓤⓢ -p|ɚ **-ors** -əz ⓤⓢ -ɚz **-ory** -ᵊr.i **'vapor ˌtrail**
vaporett|o ˌvæp.ᵊr'et|.əʊ ⓤⓢ -pə'ret̬|.oʊ **-os** -əʊz ⓤⓢ -oʊz **-i** -i
vaporization, -isa- ˌveɪ.pᵊr.aɪ'zeɪ.ʃᵊn, -ɪ'- ⓤⓢ -ɪ'- **-s** -z
vaporiz|e, -is|e 'veɪ.pᵊr.aɪz ⓤⓢ -pə.raɪz **-es** -ɪz **-ing** -ɪŋ **-ed** -d **-er/s** -əʳ/z ⓤⓢ -ɚ/z
vaporosity ˌveɪ.pᵊr'ɒs.ə.ti, -ɪ.ti ⓤⓢ -pə'rɑː.sə.t̬i
vaporous 'veɪ.pᵊr.əs **-ly** -li **-ness** -nəs, -nɪs
vap|our 'veɪ.p|əʳ ⓤⓢ -p|ɚ **-ours** -əz ⓤⓢ -ɚz **-oury** -ᵊr.i **'vapour ˌtrail**
Varah 'vɑː.rə ⓤⓢ 'vɑːr.ə
Varden 'vɑː.dᵊn ⓤⓢ 'vɑːr-
varec 'vær.ek, -ɪk ⓤⓢ 'ver-, 'vær-
variability ˌveə.ri.ə'bɪl.ə.ti, -ɪ.ti ⓤⓢ ˌver.i.ə'bɪl.ə.t̬i, ˌvær-
variab|le 'veə.ri.ə.bl̩ ⓤⓢ 'ver.i-, 'vær- **-les** -l̩z **-ly** -li **-leness** -l̩.nəs, -nɪs
variance 'veə.ri.ənts ⓤⓢ 'ver.i-, 'vær-
variant 'veə.ri.ənt ⓤⓢ 'ver.i-, 'vær- **-s** -s
variate 'veə.ri.ət, -ɪt ⓤⓢ 'ver.i.ɪt, 'vær- **-s** -s
variation ˌveə.ri'eɪ.ʃᵊn ⓤⓢ ˌver.i'-, ˌvær- **-s** -z
varicella ˌvær.ɪ'sel.ə ⓤⓢ ˌver-, ˌvær-, -ə-
varices *(plur. of* **varix***)* 'vær.ɪ.siːz, 'veə.rɪ- ⓤⓢ 'ver.ə.siːz, 'vær-
varicose 'vær.ɪ.kəʊs ⓤⓢ 'ver.ə.koʊs, 'vær- **ˌvaricose 'veins**
varicosity ˌvær.ɪ'kɒs.ə.ti, -ɪ.ti ⓤⓢ ˌver.ɪ'kɑː.sə.t̬i, ˌvær-
varied 'veə.rɪd ⓤⓢ 'ver.ɪd, 'vær- **-ly** -li
varie|gate 'veə.rɪ|.geɪt, -ri.ə- ⓤⓢ 'ver.i.ə-, 'vær- **-gates** -geɪts **-gating** -geɪ.tɪŋ ⓤⓢ -geɪ.t̬ɪŋ **-gated** -geɪ.tɪd ⓤⓢ -geɪ.t̬ɪd **-gator/s** -geɪ.təʳ/z ⓤⓢ -geɪ.t̬ɚ/z
variegation ˌveə.rɪ'geɪ.ʃᵊn, -ri.ə'- ⓤⓢ ˌver.i.ə'-, ˌvær- **-s** -z
varietal və'raɪə.tᵊl ⓤⓢ -t̬ᵊl
variet|y və'raɪə.t|i ⓤⓢ -t̬|i **-ies** -iz **va'riety ˌshow; va'riety ˌstore**
variform 'veə.rɪ.fɔːm ⓤⓢ 'ver.ə.fɔːrm, 'vær-
Varig® 'vær.ɪg ⓤⓢ 'ver-, 'vær-
variola və'raɪ.ə.lə
variole 'veə.ri.əʊl ⓤⓢ 'ver.i.oʊl, 'vær- **-s** -z
variorum ˌveə.ri'ɔː.rəm, ˌvær- ⓤⓢ ˌver.i'ɔːr.əm, ˌvær-
various 'veə.ri.əs ⓤⓢ 'ver.i-, 'vær- **-ly** -li **-ness** -nəs, -nɪs
variphone 'veə.rɪ.fəʊn ⓤⓢ 'ver.ɪ.foʊn, 'vær- **-s** -z
varix 'veə.rɪks ⓤⓢ 'ver.ɪks, 'vær- **varices** 'vær.ɪ.siːz, 'veə.rɪ- ⓤⓢ 'vær.ə-, 'ver-
varlet 'vɑː.lət, -lɪt ⓤⓢ 'vɑːr- **-s** -s
Varley 'vɑː.li ⓤⓢ 'vɑːr-
varmint 'vɑː.mɪnt ⓤⓢ 'vɑːr- **-s** -s
Varna 'vɑː.nə ⓤⓢ 'vɑːr-
Varney 'vɑː.ni ⓤⓢ 'vɑːr-
varnish 'vɑː.nɪʃ ⓤⓢ 'vɑːr- **-es** -ɪz **-ing** -ɪŋ **-ed** -t **-er/s** -əʳ/z ⓤⓢ -ɚ/z
Varro 'vær.əʊ ⓤⓢ -oʊ, 'ver-
varsit|y 'vɑː.sə.t|i, -ɪ.t|i ⓤⓢ 'vɑːr.sə.t̬|i **-ies** -iz
Varuna vær'uː.nə ⓤⓢ vʌr-, vɑː'ruː-
var|y 'veə.r|i ⓤⓢ 'ver|.i, 'vær- **-ies** -iz **-ying/ly** -i.ɪŋ/li **-ied** -id
Vasari və'sɑː.ri ⓤⓢ vɑː'sɑːr.i
Vasco da Gama ˌvæs.kəʊ.də'gɑː.mə, -dɑː'- ⓤⓢ ˌvɑː.skoʊ-, -'gæm.ə
vascular 'væs.kjə.ləʳ, -kjʊ- ⓤⓢ -kjə.lɚ
vascularity ˌvæs.kjə'lær.ə.ti, -kjʊ'-, -ɪ.ti ⓤⓢ -kjə'ler.ə.t̬i, -'lær-
vascul|um 'væs.kjə.l|əm, -kjʊ- ⓤⓢ -kjə- **-a** -ə

vas deferens ˌvæsˈdef.ə.renz, ˌvæz- ⓤⓢ ˌvæsˈdef.ə.renz
vas|e vɑːz ⓤⓢ veɪs, veɪz, vɑːz **-es** -ɪz
vasectom|y vəˈsek.tə.m|i, væsˈek- **-ies** -ɪz
Vaseline® ˈvæs.əl.iːn, -ɪ.liːn, ˌ--ˈ- ⓤⓢ ˈvæs.ə.liːn, ˌ--ˈ-
Vashti ˈvæʃ.ti ⓤⓢ ˈvɑːʃ.ti, -taɪ
vasoconstriction ˌveɪ.zəʊ.kənˈstrɪk.ʃən, ˌvæs.əʊ- ⓤⓢ ˌvæs.oʊ-, ˌveɪ.zoʊ-
vasoconstrictor ˌveɪ.zəʊ.kənˈstrɪk.təʳ, ˌvæs.əʊ- ⓤⓢ ˌvæs.oʊ-, ˌveɪ.zoʊ- **-s** -z
vasodilation ˌveɪ.zəʊ.daɪˈleɪ.ʃən, ˌvæs.əʊ- ⓤⓢ ˌvæs.oʊ-, ˌveɪ.zoʊ-
vasodilator ˌveɪ.zəʊ.daɪˈleɪ.təʳ, ˌvæs.əʊ- ⓤⓢ ˌvæs.oʊˈdaɪ.leɪ.t̬ɚ, ˌveɪ.zoʊ-, -dəˈ-; -daɪˈleɪ- **-s** -z
vasomotor ˌveɪ.zəʊˈməʊ.təʳ, ˌvæs.əʊ- ⓤⓢ ˌvæs.oʊˈmoʊ.t̬ɚ, ˌveɪ.zoʊˈ-
vassal ˈvæs.əl **-s** -z
vassalage ˈvæs.əl.ɪdʒ
vast vɑːst ⓤⓢ væst **-er** -əʳ ⓤⓢ -ɚ **-est** -ɪst, -əst **-ly** -li **-ness/es** -nəs/ɪz, -nɪs/ɪz
Västerås ˌves.təˈrɔːs
vat væt **-s** -s **-ting** -ɪŋ ⓤⓢ ˈvæt̬.ɪŋ **-ted** -ɪd ⓤⓢ ˈvæt̬.ɪd
VAT ˌviː.eɪˈtiː, væt **-able** ˈvæt.ə.bl̩
Vathek ˈvæθ.ek, ˈvɑː.θek
vatic ˈvæt.ɪk ⓤⓢ ˈvæt̬-
Vatican ˈvæt.ɪ.kən ⓤⓢ ˈvæt̬- ˌ**Vatican** ˈ**City**
vatici|nate vəˈtɪs.ɪ|.neɪt, vætˈɪs- ⓤⓢ ˈ-ə- **-nates** -neɪts **-nating** -neɪ.tɪŋ ⓤⓢ -neɪ.t̬ɪŋ **-nated** -neɪ.tɪd ⓤⓢ -neɪ.t̬ɪd
vaticination ˌvæt.ɪ.sɪˈneɪ.ʃən, ˌ-ə-; vəˌtɪs.ɪˈ-, vætˌɪs- ⓤⓢ ˌvæt̬.ə.səˈ-; vəˌtɪs-, vætˌɪs- **-s** -z
vatu ˈvɑː.tuː **-s** -z
Vaucluse vəʊˈkluːz ⓤⓢ voʊ-
Vaud vəʊ ⓤⓢ voʊ
vaudeville ˈvɔː.də.vɪl, ˈvəʊ-; ˈvɔːd.vɪl, -vəl ⓤⓢ ˈvɑːd.vɪl, ˈvɔːd-, ˈvoʊd-, ˈvɑː.də-, ˈvɔː-, ˈvoʊ- **-s** -z
vaudevillian ˌvɔː.dəˈvɪl.i.ən, ˌvəʊ-, ˌvɔːdˈvɪl- ⓤⓢ ˌvɑːdˈvɪl-, ˌvɔːd-, ˌvoʊd-, ˌvɑː.dəˈ-, ˌvɔː-, ˌvoʊ- **-s** -z
Vaudin ˈvəʊ.dɪn ⓤⓢ ˈvoʊ-
Vaudois *(sing.)* ˈvəʊ.dwɑː, -ˈ-, -dwɔː ⓤⓢ voʊˈdwɑː *(plur.)* -z
Vaughan vɔːn ⓤⓢ vɑːn, vɔːn
Vaughan Williams ˌvɔːnˈwɪl.jəmz, -i.əmz ⓤⓢ ˌvɑːnˈ-, ˌvɔːnˈ-
Vaughn vɔːn ⓤⓢ vɑːn, vɔːn
vault vɔːlt, vɒlt ⓤⓢ vɑːlt, vɔːlt **-s** -s **-ing/s** -ɪŋ/z ⓤⓢ ˈvɑːl.t̬ɪŋz, ˈvɔːl- **-ed** -ɪd ⓤⓢ ˈvɑːl.t̬ɪd, ˈvɔːl- **-er/s** -əʳ/z ⓤⓢ ˈvɑːl.t̬ɚ/z, -ˈvɔːl- ˈ**vaulting** ˌ**horse**
vaunt vɔːnt ⓤⓢ vɑːnt, vɔːnt **-s** -s **-ing/ly** -ɪŋ/li ⓤⓢ ˈvɑːn.t̬ɪŋ/li, ˈvɔːn- **-ed** -ɪd ⓤⓢ ˈvɑːn.t̬ɪd, ˈvɔːn- **-er/s** -əʳ/z ⓤⓢ ˈvɑːn.t̬ɚ/z, ˈvɔːn-
Vaux *English surname:* vɔːz, vɒks, vɔːks, vəʊks ⓤⓢ vɔːks, vɑːks *in* **de Vaux**: *vəʊ* ⓤⓢ *voʊ*
Vauxhall® ˈvɒk.sɔːl, ˈvɒks.hɔːl, -ˈ- ⓤⓢ ˈvɑːks.hɔːl, ˈvɔːks-
vavaso(u)r (V) ˈvæv.ə.sʊəʳ, -sɔːʳ ⓤⓢ -sɔːr **-s** -z
VAX® væks
Vaz væz
VC ˌviːˈsiː **-s** -z
VCR ˌviː.siːˈɑːʳ ⓤⓢ -ˈɑːr **-s** -z
VD ˌviːˈdiː
VDT ˌviː.diːˈtiː **-s** -z
VDU, vdu ˌviː.diːˈjuː **-s** -z
-'ve *(=* **have***)* -v, -əv
veal viːl **-y** -i
Veblen ˈveb.lən
vector *(n.)* ˈvek.təʳ, -tɔːʳ ⓤⓢ -tɚ **-s** -z
vect|or *(v.)* ˈvek.t|əʳ ⓤⓢ -t|ɚ **-ors** -əz ⓤⓢ -ɚz **-oring** -ər.ɪŋ **-ored** -əd ⓤⓢ -ɚd
vectorial vekˈtɔː.ri.əl ⓤⓢ -ˈtɔːr.i-
Veda ˈveɪ.də, ˈviː- **-s** -z
Vedanta vedˈɑːn.tə, vɪˈdɑːn-, və-, -ˈdæn- ⓤⓢ vɪˈdɑːn-, -ˈdæn-
V-E Day ˌviːˈiː.deɪ
vedette vɪˈdet, və-, vedˈet ⓤⓢ və- **-s** -s
Vedic ˈveɪ.dɪk, ˈviː-
veep (V) viːp
veer vɪəʳ ⓤⓢ vɪr **-s** -z **-ing/ly** -ɪŋ/li **-ed** -d
veg vedʒ ˌ**meat and two** ˈ**veg**
Vega *star:* ˈviː.gə ⓤⓢ ˈviː-, ˈveɪ- *Spanish dramatist:* ˈveɪ.gə
vegan ˈviː.gən **-s** -z **-ism** -ɪ.zəm
Vegas ˈveɪ.gəs
vegeburger ˈvedʒ.iˌbɜː.gəʳ ⓤⓢ -ˌbɝː.gɚ **-s** -z
Vegemite® ˈvedʒ.i.maɪt, ˈ-ə-
vegetable ˈvedʒ.tə.bl̩, ˈ-ə.tə-, ˈ-ɪ- ⓤⓢ ˈvedʒ.tə-, -ə.t̬ə- **-s** -z
vegetal ˈvedʒ.ɪ.təl, ˈ-ə- ⓤⓢ ˈ-ə-
vegetarian ˌvedʒ.ɪˈteə.ri.ən, -əˈ- ⓤⓢ -əˈter.i- **-s** -z **-ism** -ɪ.zəm
vege|tate ˈvedʒ.ɪ|.teɪt, ˈ-ə- ⓤⓢ ˈ-ə- **-tates** -teɪts **-tating** -teɪ.tɪŋ ⓤⓢ -teɪ.t̬ɪŋ **-tated** -teɪ.tɪd ⓤⓢ -teɪ.t̬ɪd
vegetation ˌvedʒ.ɪˈteɪ.ʃən, -əˈ- ⓤⓢ -əˈ- **-s** -z
vegetative ˈvedʒ.ɪ.tə.tɪv, ˈ-ə-, -teɪ- ⓤⓢ -ə.teɪ.t̬ɪv **-ly** -li
veggie ˈvedʒ.i **-s** -z
veggieburger ˈvedʒ.iˌbɜː.gəʳ ⓤⓢ ˌbɝː.gɚ **-s** -z
vegg|y ˈvedʒ|.i **-ies** -iz
vehemence ˈviː.ə.mənts, ˈ-ɪ-, -hɪ-, -hə-, ˈvɪə.mənts ⓤⓢ ˈviː.ə-, -hə-
vehement ˈviː.ə.mənt, ˈ-ɪ-, -hɪ-, -hə-, ˈvɪə.mənt ⓤⓢ ˈviː.ə-, -hə- **-ly** -li
vehicle ˈvɪə.kl̩, ˈviː.ɪ- ⓤⓢ ˈviː.ə-, -hɪ- **-s** -z
vehicular viˈɪk.jə.ləʳ, vɪˈhɪk-, və-, -jʊ- ⓤⓢ viːˈhɪk.jə.lɚ, -jʊ-
veil veɪl **-s** -z **-ing/s** -ɪŋ/z **-ed** -d
Veil viːl ⓤⓢ veɪ, viːl
vein veɪn **-s** -z **-ed** -d **-less** -ləs, -lɪs
vein|y ˈveɪ.n|i **-ier** -i.əʳ ⓤⓢ -i.ɚ **-iest** -i.ɪst, -i.əst
Veitch viːtʃ
velar ˈviː.ləʳ ⓤⓢ -lɚ **-s** -z
velaric viːˈlær.ɪk, vɪ- ⓤⓢ -ˈler-, -ˈlær-
velarization, -isa- ˌviː.lər.aɪˈzeɪ.ʃən, -ɪˈ- ⓤⓢ -ɪˈ- **-s** -z
velariz|e, -is|e ˈviː.lər.aɪz ⓤⓢ -lə.raɪz **-es** -ɪz **-ing** -ɪŋ **-ed** -d
Velasquez, Velazquez vɪˈlæs.kwɪz, velˈæs-, -kɪz, -kez, -kwɪθ ⓤⓢ vəˈlɑː.skes, -ˈlæs.kes, -kwez
Velcro® ˈvel.krəʊ ⓤⓢ -kroʊ

Velar

Velar consonant sounds are produced between the tongue and the SOFT PALATE, or 'velum'.

Examples for English

Velar sounds occurring as English phonemes are /k g/ and /ŋ/. The first two are PLOSIVES, and the last, a NASAL. Although /k g/ can occur syllable-initially and finally, /ŋ/ is restricted to syllable-final position only in English, e.g.:

cap	/kæp/
gap	/gæp/
sack	/sæk/
sag	/sæg/
sang	/sæŋ/

/k/ and /g/ are one of the pairs of consonants said to be distinguished from each other by being FORTIS or LENIS rather than voiced or voiceless.

Velarisation

A type of secondary articulation in which a constriction in the vocal tract is added to the primary constriction which gives a consonant its place of articulation.

Examples for English

In the case of English DARK L, the /l/ phoneme is articulated with its usual primary constriction in the alveolar region, while the back of the tongue is raised as for an [u] vowel creating a secondary constriction (see DARK L).

In other languages

Arabic has a number of consonant phonemes that are velarized, and are known as 'emphatic' consonants.

veldt, veld (V) velt ⓤⓢ velt, felt **-s** -z
velic 'viː.lɪk
velleity vel'iː.ə.ti, və'liː-, -ɪ.ti ⓤⓢ və'liː-
vellum 'vel.əm **-s** -z
veloce vɪ'ləʊ.tʃeɪ, vel'əʊ-, və'ləʊ- ⓤⓢ veɪ'loʊ.tʃeɪ
velocipede vɪ'lɒs.ɪ.piːd, və-, '-ə- ⓤⓢ və'lɑː.sə- **-s** -z
velocit|y vɪ'lɒs.ə.t|i, və-, -ɪ.t|i ⓤⓢ və'lɑː.sə.t̬|i **-ies** -iz
velodrome 'vel.ə.drəʊm, 'viː.ləʊ- ⓤⓢ 'vel.ə.droʊm **-s** -z
velour və'lʊəʳ ⓤⓢ -'lʊr **-s** -z
velouté və'luː.teɪ **-s** -z
vel|um 'viː.l|əm **-a** -ə
velvet 'vel.vɪt, -vət **-s** -s
velveteen ˌvel.vɪ'tiːn, -və'-, '--- **-s** -z
velvet|y 'vel.vɪ.t|i, -və- ⓤⓢ -və.t̬|i **-iness** -ɪ.nəs, -nɪs
Venables 'ven.ə.bl̩z
vena cava ˌviː.nə'keɪ.və, -'kɑː- ⓤⓢ -'keɪ- **venae cavae** -niː'keɪ.viː, -'kɑː- ⓤⓢ -'keɪ-
venal 'viː.nᵊl **-ly** ⓤⓢ -i
venality viː'næl.ə.ti, vɪ-, -ɪ.ti ⓤⓢ vɪ'næl.ə.t̬i
venation viː'neɪ.ʃᵊn
vend vend **-s** -z **-ing** -ɪŋ **-ed** -ɪd **-er/s** -əʳ/z ⓤⓢ -ɚ/z **'vending maˌchine**
Venda 'ven.də
vendee ven'diː **-s** -z
vendetta ven'det.ə ⓤⓢ -'det̬- **-s** -z
vendor 'ven.dɔːʳ, -dəʳ ⓤⓢ -dɚ, -dɔːr **-s** -z
veneer və'nɪəʳ, vɪ- ⓤⓢ -'nɪr **-s** -z **-ing** -ɪŋ **-ed** -d
venerab|le 'ven.ᵊr.ə.b|l̩ **-ly** -li **-leness** -l̩.nəs, -nɪs
vener|ate 'ven.ᵊr|.eɪt ⓤⓢ -ə.r|eɪt **-ates** -eɪts **-ating** -eɪ.tɪŋ ⓤⓢ -eɪ.t̬ɪŋ **-ated** -eɪ.tɪd ⓤⓢ -eɪ.t̬ɪd **-ator/s** -eɪ.təʳ/z ⓤⓢ -eɪ.t̬ɚ/z
veneration ˌven.ᵊr'eɪ.ʃᵊn ⓤⓢ -ə'reɪ-
venereal və'nɪə.ri.əl, vɪ- ⓤⓢ və'nɪr.i- **ve'nereal diˌsease**
venery 'ven.ᵊr.i
Venetia və'niː.ʃi.ə, vɪ-, '-ʃə
Venetian, venetian və'niː.ʃᵊn, vɪ- ⓤⓢ '-ʃᵊn **-s** -z **veˌnetian 'blind**
Venezuel|a ˌven.ɪ'zweɪ.l|ə, -ez'weɪ-, -ə'zweɪ- ⓤⓢ -ə'zweɪ-, -'zwiː- **-an/s** -ən/z
veng|e vendʒ **-es** -ɪz **-ing** -ɪŋ **-ed** -d
vengeance 'ven.dʒᵊnts
vengeful 'vendʒ.fᵊl, -fʊl **-ly** -i **-ness** -nəs ⓤⓢ -nɪs
Vengerov 'veŋ.gə.rɒf ⓤⓢ -gɚ.ɑːf
veni, vidi, vici ˌveɪ.niː,viː.diː'viː.kiː, ˌweɪ.niː,wiː.diː'wiː.kiː
venial 'viː.ni.əl, '-njəl **-ly** -i **-ness** -nəs, -nɪs ˌ**venial 'sin**
veniality ˌviː.ni'æl.ə.ti, -ɪ.ti ⓤⓢ -ə.t̬i
Venice 'ven.ɪs
venire və'nɪə.riː ⓤⓢ -'naɪ-, -'nɪr.iː
venison 'ven.ɪ.sᵊn, '-ə-, -zᵊn
Venite vɪ'naɪ.ti, ven'aɪ-, -'niː- ⓤⓢ və'niː- **-s** -z
Venn ven **'Venn ˌdiagram, ˌVenn 'diagram**
Venner 'ven.əʳ ⓤⓢ -ɚ
venom 'ven.əm **-s** -z **-ed** -d
venomous 'ven.ə.məs **-ly** -li **-ness** -nəs, -nɪs
venous 'viː.nəs **-ly** -li
vent vent **-s** -s **-ing** -ɪŋ ⓤⓢ 'ven.t̬ɪŋ **-ed** -ɪd ⓤⓢ 'ven.t̬ɪd
Vent-Axia® ˌvent'æk.si.ə
ventil|ate 'ven.tɪ.l|eɪt, -tᵊl|.eɪt ⓤⓢ -t̬ə.l|eɪt **-ates** -eɪts **-ating** -eɪ.tɪŋ ⓤⓢ -eɪ.t̬ɪŋ **-ated** -eɪ.tɪd ⓤⓢ -eɪ.t̬ɪd
ventilation ˌven.tɪ'leɪ.ʃᵊn, -tᵊl'eɪ- ⓤⓢ -t̬ə'leɪ-
ventilator 'ven.tɪ.leɪ.təʳ, -tᵊl.eɪ- ⓤⓢ -t̬ə.leɪ.t̬ɚ **-s** -z
Ventnor 'vent.nəʳ ⓤⓢ -nɚ
Ventolin® 'ven.təʊ.lɪn, -tᵊl.ɪn ⓤⓢ -t̬ᵊl.ɪn, -toʊ.lɪn
ventral 'ven.trᵊl **-ly** -i
ventricle 'ven.trɪ.kl̩ **-s** -z
ventricular ven'trɪk.jə.ləʳ, -jʊ- ⓤⓢ -jə.lɚ
ventriloquial ˌven.trɪ'ləʊ.kwi.əl, -trə'- ⓤⓢ -trə'loʊ- **-ly** -i
ventriloquism ven'trɪl.ə.kwɪ.zᵊm
ventriloquist ven'trɪl.ə.kwɪst **-s** -s
ventriloquiz|e, -is|e ven'trɪl.ə.kwaɪz **-es** -ɪz **-ing** -ɪŋ **-ed** -d
ventriloquy ven'trɪl.ə.kwi
vent|ure 'ven.tʃ|əʳ ⓤⓢ -tʃ|ɚ **-ures** -əz ⓤⓢ -ɚz **-uring** -ᵊr.ɪŋ **-ured** -əd ⓤⓢ -ɚd **-urer/s** -ᵊr.əʳ/z ⓤⓢ -ɚ.ɚ/z ˌ**venture 'capital** ⓤⓢ **'venture ˌcapital; 'Venture ˌScout**
venturesome 'ven.tʃə.səm ⓤⓢ -tʃɚ- **-ly** -li **-ness** -nəs, -nɪs
venturi ven'tjʊə.ri, -'tʃʊə- ⓤⓢ -'tʊr.i **-s** -z
venturous 'ven.tʃᵊr.əs **-ly** -li **-ness** -nəs, -nɪs
venue 'ven.juː **-s** -z
venul|ar 'ven.jʊ.l|əʳ, -jə- ⓤⓢ -juː.l|ɚ, 'viː.njuː-, -njə- **-ose** -əʊs ⓤⓢ -oʊs
venule 'ven.juːl ⓤⓢ 'ven.juːl, 'viː.njuːl **-s** -z
Venus 'viː.nəs **-es** -ɪz ˌ**Venus' 'flytrap**
Venusian vɪ'njuː.si.ən, və-, -zi.ən ⓤⓢ vɪ'nuː.ʃᵊn, -ʒᵊn, -zi.ən **-s** -z
Vera 'vɪə.rə ⓤⓢ 'vɪr.ə
veracious və'reɪ.ʃəs, vɪ-, ver'eɪ- ⓤⓢ və'reɪ- **-ly** -li **-ness** -nəs, -nɪs
veracity və'ræs.ə.ti, vɪ-, ver'æs-, -ɪ.ti ⓤⓢ və'ræs.ə.t̬i
Veracruz ˌvɪə.rə'kruːz, ˌver.ə'-, ˌveə.rə'- ⓤⓢ ˌver.ə'-
veranda(h) və'ræn.də **-s** -z
verb vɜːb ⓤⓢ vɝːb **-s** -z
verbal 'vɜː.bᵊl ⓤⓢ 'vɝː- **-ly** -i
verbal|ism 'vɜː.bᵊl|.ɪ.zᵊm ⓤⓢ 'vɝː- **-ist/s** -ɪst/s
verbalization ˌvɜː.bᵊl.aɪ'zeɪ.ʃᵊn, -ɪ'- ⓤⓢ ˌvɝː.bᵊl.ɪ'-
verbaliz|e, -is|e 'vɜː.bᵊl.aɪz ⓤⓢ 'vɝː.bə.laɪz **-es** -ɪz **-ing** -ɪŋ **-ed** -d
verbatim vɜː'beɪ.tɪm, və- ⓤⓢ vɚ'beɪ.t̬ɪm, -t̬əm
verbena vɜː'biː.nə, və- ⓤⓢ vɚ- **-s** -z
verbiage 'vɜː.bi.ɪdʒ ⓤⓢ 'vɝː-
Verbier 'veə.bi.eɪ ⓤⓢ 'ver-
verbose vɜː'bəʊs, və- ⓤⓢ vɚ'boʊs **-ly** -li **-ness** -nəs, -nɪs
verbosity vɜː'bɒs.ə.ti, və-, -ɪ.ti ⓤⓢ vɚ'bɑː.sə.t̬i
verboten vɜː'bəʊ.tᵊn *as if German:* fə'- ⓤⓢ vɚ'boʊ-

Vercingetorix ˌvɜː.sɪnˈdʒet.ə.rɪks, -sᵊnˈ-, -ˈget- (US) ˌvɝː.sɪnˈdʒet̬.ɚ.ɪks, -ˈget̬-

verdancy ˈvɜː.dᵊnt.si (US) ˈvɝː-

verdant ˈvɜː.dᵊnt (US) ˈvɝː- **-ly** -li

Verde vɜːd (US) vɝːd

Verdi ˈveə.diː, -di (US) ˈver- **-an** -ən

verdict ˈvɜː.dɪkt (US) ˈvɝː- **-s** -s

verdigris ˈvɜː.dɪ.griːs, -griː (US) ˈvɝː.dɪ.griːs, -grɪs, -griː

Verdun vɜːˈdʌn, ˈ-- (US) verˈdʌn, ˌvɝː-

verdure ˈvɜː.djəʳ, -dʒəʳ, -djʊəʳ (US) ˈvɝː.dʒɚ

Vere vɪəʳ (US) vɪr

verg|e vɜːdʒ (US) vɝːdʒ **-es** -ɪz **-ing** -ɪŋ **-ed** -d

verger ˈvɜː.dʒəʳ (US) ˈvɝː.dʒɚ **-s** -z

Vergil ˈvɜː.dʒɪl (US) ˈvɝː- **-s** -z

Vergilian vɜːˈdʒɪl.i.ən, və- (US) vɝː-, ˈ-jən

verifiable ˈver.ɪ.faɪ.ə.bl̩, ˈ-ə-, ˌver.ɪˈfaɪ-, -əˈ- (US) ˈver.ə.faɪ-

verification ˌver.ɪ.fɪˈkeɪ.ʃᵊn, ˌ-ə- (US) ˌ-ə- **-s** -z

veri|fy ˈver.ɪ|.faɪ, ˈ-ə- (US) ˈ-ə- **-fies** -faɪz **-fying** -faɪ.ɪŋ **-fied** -faɪd **-fier/s** -faɪ.əʳ/z (US) -faɪ.ɚ/z

verily ˈver.ᵊl.i, -ɪ.li

verisimilitude ˌver.ɪ.sɪˈmɪl.ɪ.tjuːd, ˌ-ə-, -səˈ- (US) -ə.səˈmɪl.ə.tuːd, -tjuːd

verismo vəˈrɪz.moʊ

veritab|le ˈver.ɪ.tə.b|l̩ (US) -ə.t̬ə- **-ly** -li

verit|y (V) ˈver.ə.t|i -ɪ.t|i (US) -ə.t̬|i **-ies** -iz

verjuice ˈvɜː.dʒuːs (US) ˈvɝː-

Verlaine veəˈlen, vɜː- (US) vɚˈleɪn, -ˈlen

Vermeer vəˈmɪəʳ, vɜː-, -ˈmeəʳ (US) vɚˈmɪr **-s** -z

vermeil ˈvɜː.meɪl, -mɪl (US) ˈvɝː.mɪl; vɚˈmeɪl

vermicelli ˌvɜː.mɪˈtʃel.i, -ˈsel- (US) ˌvɝː.məˈtʃel-, -ˈsel-

vermicide ˈvɜː.mɪ.saɪd (US) ˈvɝː.mə- **-s** -z

vermicular vɜːˈmɪk.jə.ləʳ, -jʊ- (US) vɚˈmɪk.jə.lɚ

vermiform ˈvɜː.mɪ.fɔːm (US) ˈvɝː.mə.fɔːrm ˌ**vermiform apˈpendix**

vermil(l)ion vəˈmɪl.jən, vɜː-, -i.ən (US) vɚˈmɪl.jən **-s** -z

vermin ˈvɜː.mɪn (US) ˈvɝː- **-ous** -əs

Vermont vəˈmɒnt, vɜː- (US) vɚˈmɑːnt

vermouth ˈvɜː.məθ, -muːθ; vɜːˈmuːθ, və- (US) vɚˈmuːθ **-s** -s

vernacular vəˈnæk.jə.ləʳ, vɜː-, -jʊ- (US) vɚˈnæk.jə.lɚ **-s** -z **-ly** -li

vernal ˈvɜː.nᵊl (US) ˈvɝː- **-ly** -i ˌ**vernal ˈequinox**

Verne vɜːn, veən (US) vɝːn

Verner *English surname:* ˈvɜː.nəʳ (US) ˈvɝː.nɚ *Danish grammarian:* ˈvɜː.nəʳ, ˈveə- (US) ˈvɝː.nɚ, ˈver-

Verney ˈvɜː.ni (US) ˈvɝː-

vernier ˈvɜː.ni.əʳ (US) ˈvɝː.ni.ɚ **-s** -z

Vernon ˈvɜː.nən (US) ˈvɝː-

Verona vəˈrəʊ.nə, vɪ-, verˈəʊ- (US) vəˈroʊ-

Veronal® ˈver.ə.nᵊl

Veronese *artist:* ˌver.əʊˈneɪ.zeɪ (US) -əˈneɪ.si, -zi

Veronese *(person) from Verona:* ˌver.əˈniːz, -əʊˈ- (US) -əˈniːz

veronica (V) vəˈrɒn.ɪ.kə, vɪ- verˈɒn- (US) vəˈrɑː.nɪ- **-s** -z

Verrazano ˌver.əˈzɑː.nəʊ (US) -noʊ *stress shift, see compound:* ˌ**Verrazano ˈNarrows**

verru|ca vəˈruː|.kə, vɪ-, verˈuː- (US) vəˈruː- **-cas** -kəz **-cae** -kiː, -kaɪ

verrucose vəˈruː.kəʊs, vɪ-, verˈuː- (US) ˈver.uː.koʊs, -jə-

Versace vəˈsɑː.tʃi, vɜː- (US) vɚ-

Versailles *in France:* veəˈsaɪ, vɜː- (US) vɝːˈsaɪ-, ver- *in US:* vɜːˈseɪlz (US) vɝː-

versant ˈvɜː.sᵊnt (US) ˈvɝː- **-s** -s

versatile ˈvɜː.sə.taɪl (US) ˈvɝː.sə.t̬ᵊl **-ly** -li **-ness** -nəs, -nɪs

versatility ˌvɜː.səˈtɪl.ə.ti, -ɪ.ti (US) ˌvɝː.səˈtɪl.ə.t̬i

vers de société ˌveə.dəˌsɒs.jeɪˈteɪ (US) ˌver.dɪ.soʊˈsiː.eɪ.teɪ; -dəˌsɑː.sjeɪˈteɪ

vers|e vɜːs (US) vɝːs **-es** -ɪz **-ed** -t

versicle ˈvɜː.sɪ.kl̩ (US) ˈvɝː- **-s** -z

versification ˌvɜː.sɪ.fɪˈkeɪ.ʃᵊn, -sə- (US) ˌvɝː.sə-

versificator ˈvɜː.sɪ.fɪ.keɪ.təʳ, -sə- (US) ˈvɝː.sə.fɪ.keɪ.t̬ɚ **-s** -z

versi|fy ˈvɜː.sɪ|.faɪ, -sə- (US) ˈvɝː.sə- **-fies** -faɪz **-fying** -faɪ.ɪŋ **-fied** -faɪd **-fier/s** -faɪ.əʳ/z (US) -faɪ.ɚ/z

version ˈvɜː.ʃᵊn, -ʒᵊn (US) ˈvɝː.ʒᵊn, -ʃᵊn **-s** -z

verso ˈvɜː.səʊ (US) ˈvɝː.soʊ **-s** -z

versus ˈvɜː.səs (US) ˈvɝː-

vert (V) vɜːt (US) vɝːt **-s** -s

vertebr|a ˈvɜː.tɪ.br|ə, -tə- (US) ˈvɝː.t̬ə- **-ae** -iː, -aɪ, -eɪ **-as** -əz

vertebral ˈvɜː.tɪ.brᵊl, -tə- (US) ˈvɝː.t̬ə- **-ly** -i ˌ**vertebral ˈcolumn**

vertebrata ˌvɜː.tɪˈbrɑː.tə, -təˈ-, -ˈbreɪ- (US) -ˈbreɪ.t̬ə, -ˈbrɑː-

vertebrate ˈvɜː.tɪ.breɪt, -tə-, -brət, -brɪt (US) ˈvɝː.tə.brɪt, -breɪt **-s** -s

ver|tex ˈvɜː|.teks (US) ˈvɝː- **-tices** -tɪ.siːz (US) -t̬ɪ- **-texes** -tek.sɪz

vertic|al ˈvɜː.tɪ.k|ᵊl, -tə- (US) ˈvɝː.t̬ə- **-ally** -ᵊl.i, -li **-alness** -ᵊl.nəs, -nɪs

vertiginous vɜːˈtɪdʒ.ɪ.nəs, ˈ-ə- (US) vɚˈtɪdʒ.ə- **-ly** -li

vertigo ˈvɜː.tɪ.gəʊ, -tə- (US) ˈvɝː.t̬ə.goʊ

Verulam ˈver.ʊ.ləm (US) -juː-

Verulamium ˌver.ʊˈleɪ.mi.əm (US) -juːˈ-

vervain ˈvɜː.veɪn (US) ˈvɝː-

verve vɜːv (US) vɝːv

Verwoerd fəˈvʊət, feə-, -ˈvɔːt (US) fɚ-ˈvɔːrt, -ˈvʊrt

Verwood ˈvɜː.wʊd (US) ˈvɝː-

very *(adj. adv.)* ˈver.i

Very *surname:* ˈvɪə.ri, ˈver.i (US) ˈvɪr.i, ˈver-

Vesalius vesˈeɪ.li.əs

Vesey ˈviː.zi

vesi|ca ˈves.ɪ|.kə; vɪˈsaɪ|.kə, və- (US) vɪˈsaɪ-, -ˈsiː- **-cae** -kiː

vesicle ˈves.ɪ.kl̩ **-s** -z

vesicular vɪˈsɪk.jə.ləʳ, vəˈ- (US) -lɚ

vesiculate vɪˈsɪk.jə.leɪt, vəˈ-

Vespa® ˈves.pə

Vespasian vesˈpeɪ.zi.ən, -ʒi-, ˈ-ʒᵊn (US) ˈ-ʒᵊn, -ʒi.ən

vesper (V) ˈves.pəʳ (US) -pɚ **-s** -z

vespertine ˈves.pə.taɪn (US) -pɚ.tɪn, -taɪn

Vespucci vesˈpuː.tʃi

vessel ˈves.ᵊl **-s** -z

vest vest **-s** -s **-ing** -ɪŋ **-ed** -ɪd ˌ**vested ˈinterest**

vesta (V) ˈves.tə **-s** -z

vestal ˈves.tᵊl **-s** -z ˌ**vestal ˈvirgin**

vestiar|y ˈvest.jə.r|i **-ies** -iz

vestibular vesˈtɪb.jə.ləʳ, -jʊ- (US) -jə.lɚ

vestibule ˈves.tɪ.bjuːl (US) -tə- **-s** -z **-d** -d

vestig|e ˈves.tɪdʒ **-es** -ɪz

vestigial vesˈtɪdʒ.i.əl, ˈ-əl **-ly** -i

vestiture ˈves.tɪ.tʃəʳ (US) -tʃɚ

vestment ˈvest.mənt **-s** -s

vest-pocket ˌvestˈpɒk.ɪt (US) -ˈpɑː.kɪt, ˈ-ˌ--

Vestris ˈves.trɪs

vestr|y ˈves.tr|i **-ies** -iz

vesture ˈves.tʃəʳ, -tjəʳ (US) -tʃɚ **-s** -z

vesuvian (V) vɪˈsuː.vi.ən və-, -ˈsjuː- (US) vəˈsuː- **-s** -z **-ite** -aɪt

Vesuvius vɪˈsuː.vi.əs, və-, -ˈsjuː- (US) vəˈsuː-

vet vet **-s** -s **-ting** -ɪŋ (US) ˈvet̬.ɪŋ **-ted** -ɪd (US) ˈvet̬.ɪd

vetch vetʃ **-es** -ɪz

veteran ˈvet.ᵊr.ᵊn, -rən (US) ˈvet̬.ɚ.ᵊn; ˈvet.rən **-s** -z ˈ**Veterans ˌDay**

veterinarian ˌvet.ᵊr.ɪˈneə.ri.ən, ˌ-rəˈ- (US) -ˈner.i- **-s** -z

veterinar|y ˈvet.ᵊr.ɪ.nᵊr|.i, ˈ-rə.nᵊr- (US) -ner- **-ies** -iz ˈ**veterinary ˌsurgeon**

veto ˈviː.təʊ (US) -t̬oʊ **-es** -z **-ing** -ɪŋ **-ed** -d **-er/s** -əʳ/z (US) -ɚ/z

Vevey ˈvev.eɪ, -i (US) vəˈveɪ

vex veks **-es** -ɪz **-ing** -ɪŋ **-ed** -t ˌ**vexed ˈquestion**

vexation vekˈseɪ.ʃᵊn **-s** -z

vexatious vekˈseɪ.ʃəs **-ly** -li **-ness** -nəs -nɪs

vgc ˌviː.dʒiːˈsiː

VHF ˌviː.eɪtʃˈef
via vaɪə ⓤⓢ vaɪə, ˈviː.ə
viability ˌvaɪ.əˈbɪl.ə.ti, -ɪ.ti ⓤⓢ -ə.t̬i
viab|le ˈvaɪ.ə.b|l̩ **-ly** -li
via dolorosa, (V D) ˌviː.əˌdɒl.əˈrəʊ.sə ⓤⓢ -ˌdɑː.ləˈroʊ-, -ˌdoʊ-
viaduct ˈvaɪə.dʌkt **-s** -s
Viagra vaɪˈæg.rə, vi-
vial vaɪəl ⓤⓢ ˈvaɪ.əl; vaɪl **-s** -z
Vialli viˈɑː.li
viand ˈvaɪ.ənd **-s** -z
viatic|um vaɪˈæt.ɪ.k|əm, vi- ⓤⓢ vaɪˈæt̬- **-ums** -əmz **-a** -ə
vibe vaɪb **-s** -z
vibrancy ˈvaɪ.brənt.si
vibrant ˈvaɪ.brənt **-ly** -li
vibraphone ˈvaɪ.brə.fəʊn ⓤⓢ -foʊn **-s** -z
vibra|te vaɪˈbreɪ|t ⓤⓢ ˈ-- **-tes** -ts **-ting** -tɪŋ ⓤⓢ -t̬ɪŋ **-ted** -tɪd ⓤⓢ -t̬ɪd
vibration vaɪˈbreɪ.ʃᵊn **-s** -z
vibrational vaɪˈbreɪ.ʃᵊn.ᵊl, -ˈbreɪʃ.nᵊl
vibrative vaɪˈbreɪ.tɪv ⓤⓢ ˈvaɪ.brə.t̬ɪv
vibrato vɪˈbrɑː.təʊ ⓤⓢ -t̬oʊ **-s** -z
vibrator vaɪˈbreɪ.təʳ ⓤⓢ ˈvaɪ.breɪ.t̬ɚ **-s** -z
vibratory ˈvaɪ.brə.tᵊr.i; vaɪˈbreɪ- ⓤⓢ ˈvaɪ.brə.tɔːr-
viburnum vaɪˈbɜː.nəm ⓤⓢ -ˈbɝː- **-s** -z
vic (V) vɪk **-s** -s
vicar ˈvɪk.əʳ ⓤⓢ -ɚ **-s** -z
vicarag|e ˈvɪk.ᵊr.ɪdʒ **-es** -ɪz
vicarial vɪˈkeə.ri.əl, vaɪ-, və- ⓤⓢ -ˈker.i-, -ˈkær-
vicarious vɪˈkeə.ri.əs, vaɪ-, və- ⓤⓢ -ˈker.i-, -ˈkær- **-ly** -li **-ness** -nəs, -nɪs
vice- ˌvaɪs-
Note: Prefix. This usually receives secondary stress. It may carry the strongest stress in the word in stress shift cases.
vic|e (*n.*) vaɪs **-es** -ɪz **ˈvice ˌsquad**
vice (*prep.*) ˈvaɪ.si, -sə ⓤⓢ -sə, -si
vice-admiral ˌvaɪsˈæd.mᵊr.ᵊl, -mɪ.rᵊl **-s** -z *stress shift:* ˌvice-admiral's ˈflag
vice-chair|man ˌvaɪsˈtʃeəl.mən ⓤⓢ -ˈtʃer- **-men** -mən *stress shift:* ˌvice-chairman's ˈprivilege
vice-chancellor ˌvaɪsˈtʃɑːnt.sᵊl.əʳ ⓤⓢ -ˈtʃænt- **-s** -z *stress shift:* ˌvice-chancellor's ˈsecretary
vice-consul ˌvaɪsˈkɒnt.sᵊl ⓤⓢ -ˈkɑːnt- **-s** -z *stress shift:* ˌvice-consul's ˈpost
vice-consulate ˌvaɪsˈkɒnt.sjə.lət, -sjʊ-, -lɪt ⓤⓢ -ˈkɑːnt.sə.lət **-s** -s
vicegerent ˌvaɪsˈdʒer.ᵊnt, -ˈdʒɪə.rᵊnt ⓤⓢ -ˈdʒɪr.ᵊnt **-s** -s
vice-presidenc|y ˌvaɪsˈprez.ɪ.dᵊnt.s|i **-ies** -iz
vice-president ˌvaɪsˈprez.ɪ.dᵊnt **-s** -s *stress shift:* ˌvice-president's ˈvote
vice-presidential ˌvaɪs.prez.ɪˈdent.ʃᵊl
vice-principal ˌvaɪsˈprɪnt.sə.pᵊl, -sɪ.pᵊl **-s** -z *stress shift:* ˌvice-principal's ˈoffice
viceregal ˌvaɪsˈriː.gᵊl *stress shift:* ˌviceregal ˈprivilege
vicereine ˌvaɪsˈreɪn, ˈ-- ⓤⓢ ˈvaɪs.reɪn **-s** -z
viceroy ˈvaɪs.rɔɪ **-s** -z
viceroyalt|y ˌvaɪsˈrɔɪ.əl.t|i ⓤⓢ -t̬|i **-ies** -iz
viceroyship ˈvaɪs.rɔɪ.ʃɪp **-s** -s
vice versa ˌvaɪ.siˈvɜː.sə, -səˈ-, ˌvaɪsˈ- ⓤⓢ ˌvaɪ.səˈvɝː-, ˌvaɪsˈ-
Vichy ˈviː.ʃiː, -ʃi, ˈvɪʃ.iː, -i
vichyssoise ˌviː.ʃiˈswɑːz, ˌvɪʃ.iˈ-
vicinage ˈvɪs.ɪ.nɪdʒ, ˈ-ə- ⓤⓢ ˈ-ə-
vicinity vɪˈsɪn.ə.ti, və-, vaɪ-, -ɪ.ti ⓤⓢ vəˈsɪn.ə.t̬i
vicious ˈvɪʃ.əs **-ly** -li **-ness** -nəs, -nɪs **ˌvicious ˈcircle**
vicissitude vɪˈsɪs.ɪ.tjuːd, və-, vaɪs-, ˈ-ə- ⓤⓢ vɪˈsɪs.ə.tuːd, -tjuːd **-s** -z
Vick® vɪk
Vickers ˈvɪk.əz ⓤⓢ -ɚz
Vickery ˈvɪk.ᵊr.i
Vicki, Vicky ˈvɪk.i
victim ˈvɪk.tɪm, -təm **-s** -z **-less** -ləs, -lɪs
victimization, -isa- ˌvɪk.tɪ.maɪˈzeɪ.ʃᵊn, -tə-, -mɪˈ- ⓤⓢ -tə.mɪˈ-
victimiz|e, -is|e ˈvɪk.tɪ.maɪz, -tə- ⓤⓢ -tə- **-es** -ɪz **-ing** -ɪŋ **-ed** -d **-er/s** -əʳ/z ⓤⓢ -ɚ/z
victor (V) ˈvɪk.təʳ ⓤⓢ -tɚ **-s** -z
Victoria, victoria vɪkˈtɔː.ri.ə ⓤⓢ -ˈtɔːr.i- **-s** -z **Vicˌtoria ˈCross; Vicˈtoria ˌDay; Vicˌtoria ˈFalls; Vicˌtoria ˈsandwich**
Victorian, victorian vɪkˈtɔː.ri.ən ⓤⓢ -ˈtɔːr.i- **-s** -z **Vicˌtorian ˈvalues**
Victoriana ˌvɪk.tɔː.riˈɑː.nə, vɪkˌtɔː- ⓤⓢ vɪkˌtɔːr.iˈæn.ə
victorious vɪkˈtɔː.ri.əs ⓤⓢ -ˈtɔːr.i- **-ly** -li **-ness** -nəs, -nɪs
victor ludorum ˌvɪk.təˌluːˈdɔː.rəm ⓤⓢ -tɚ.luːˈdɔːr.əm **victores ludorum** vɪkˌtɔː.reɪs,- ⓤⓢ -ˌtɔːr.eɪs-
victor|y ˈvɪk.tᵊr|.i, ˈ-tr|i **-ies** -iz
Victory-V® ˌvɪk.tᵊr.iˈviː
victual ˈvɪt.ᵊl ⓤⓢ ˈvɪt̬- **-s** -z **-(l)ing** -ɪŋ **-(l)ed** -d **-(l)er/s** -əʳ/z ⓤⓢ -ɚ/z
vicuña, vicuna vɪˈkjuː.nə, vaɪ-, və-, -ˈkuː-, -ˈkuː.njə ⓤⓢ vaɪˈkjuː.nə, vɪ-, -ˈkuː-, -ˈkuː.njə
Vidal vɪˈdɑːl, və-, -ˈdæl; ˈvaɪ.dᵊl ⓤⓢ vɪˈdæl, -ˈdɑːl
Note: The author Gore Vidal is normally /vɪˈdɑːl/; Vidal Sassoon is normally /vɪˈdæl/.
vide ˈvaɪ.diː, -di; ˈvɪd.eɪ ⓤⓢ ˈvaɪ.diː, -di; ˈviː.deɪ, ˈwiː-
videlicet vɪˈdiː.lɪ.set, vaɪ-, və-; -ˈdeɪ.lɪ.ket ⓤⓢ vɪˈdel.ə.sɪt, wɪ-
video ˈvɪd.i.əʊ ⓤⓢ -oʊ **-s** -z **-ing** -ɪŋ **-ed** -d **ˈvideo arˌcade; ˈvideo ˌcamera; ˈvideo ˌgame; ˌvideo ˈnasty; ˈvideo recˌorder**
videocassette ˌvɪd.i.əʊ.kəˈset, -kæsˈet ⓤⓢ -oʊ.kəˈset **-s** -s **ˌvideo-casˈsette recˌorder**
videoconferenc|e ˌvɪd.i.əʊˈkɒn.fᵊr.ᵊnts ⓤⓢ ˈvɪd.i.oʊˌkɑːn.fɚ-, -frəns **-es** -ɪz **-ing** -ɪŋ
videodisc ˈvɪd.i.əʊ.dɪsk ⓤⓢ -oʊ- **-s** -s
videofit ˈvɪd.i.əʊ.fɪt ⓤⓢ -oʊ **-s** -s
video-link ˈvɪd.i.əʊ.lɪŋk ⓤⓢ -oʊ- **-s** -s **-ing** -ɪŋ **-ed** -t
Videophone® ˈvɪd.i.əʊ.fəʊn ⓤⓢ -oʊ.foʊn
videorecorder ˈvɪd.i.əʊ.rɪˌkɔː.dəʳ ⓤⓢ -oʊ.rɪˌkɔːr.dɚ **-s** -z
videorecording ˈvɪd.i.əʊ.rɪˌkɔː.dɪŋ, -rəˌ- ⓤⓢ -oʊ.rɪˌkɔːr-, -rəˌ- **-s** -z
videotap|e ˈvɪd.i.əʊ.teɪp ⓤⓢ -oʊ- **-es** -s **-ing** -ɪŋ **-ed** -t
videotext ˈvɪd.i.əʊ.tekst ⓤⓢ -oʊ- **-s** -s
vie vaɪ **vies** vaɪz **vying** ˈvaɪ.ɪŋ **vied** vaɪd
Vienna viˈen.ə
Viennese ˌvɪəˈniːz ⓤⓢ ˌviː.əˈ-
Vientiane ˌvjenˈtjɑːn
Vietcong, Viet Cong ˌvjetˈkɒŋ ⓤⓢ ˌviː.etˈkɑːŋ, -ˈkɔːŋ; viˌetˈ-; ˌvjetˈ- *stress shift:* ˌVietcong ˈfighters
Vietminh ˌvjetˈmɪn ⓤⓢ ˌviː.etˈ-; viˌetˈ-; ˌvjetˈ-
Vietnam, Viet Nam ˌvjetˈnæm, -ˈnɑːm ⓤⓢ ˌviː.etˈnɑːm, -ətˈ-, -ˈnæm; vɪˌetˈ-; ˌvjetˈ- *stress shift:* ˌVietnam ˈwar
Vietnamese ˌvjet.nəˈmiːz ⓤⓢ viˌet-; ˌvjet-, ˌviː.ət- *stress shift:* ˌVietnamese ˈpeople
view vjuː **-s** -z **-ing** -ɪŋ **-ed** -d **-er/s** -əʳ/z ⓤⓢ -ɚ/z **-able** -ə.bl̩ **-less** -ləs, -lɪs
viewfinder ˈvjuːˌfaɪn.dəʳ ⓤⓢ -dɚ **-s** -z
Viewpark ˈvjuː.pɑːk ⓤⓢ -pɑːrk
viewpoint ˈvjuː.pɔɪnt **-s** -s
Vigar ˈvaɪ.gəʳ ⓤⓢ -gɚ
Vigers ˈvaɪ.gəz ⓤⓢ -gɚz
vigil ˈvɪdʒ.ɪl, -ᵊl ⓤⓢ -ᵊl **-s** -z
vigilance ˈvɪdʒ.ɪ.ləns, -ᵊl.ənts
vigilant ˈvɪdʒ.ɪ.lənt, -ᵊl.ənt **-ly** -li
vigilant|e ˌvɪdʒ.ɪˈlæn.t|i, -əˈ- ⓤⓢ -t̬|i **-es** -iz **-ism** -ɪ.zᵊm
vig|nette vɪˈnjet, -ˈnet ⓤⓢ -ˈnjet **-nettes** -ˈnjets, -ˈnets ⓤⓢ -ˈnjets **-netting** -ˈnjet.ɪŋ, -ˈnet- ⓤⓢ -ˈnjet̬.ɪŋ **-netted** -ˈnjet.ɪd, -ˈnet- ⓤⓢ -ˈnjet̬.ɪd **-nettist/s** -ˈnjet.ɪst/s ⓤⓢ -ˈnjet̬.ɪst/s
Vignoles ˈviː.njəʊlz, ˈvɪn.jəʊlz, -jəʊl, -jɒlz; vɪˈnjɒlz, -ˈnjəʊlz ⓤⓢ viːˈnjoʊl, -ˈnjoʊlz, ˈ--
Vigo ˈviː.gəʊ, ˈvaɪ- ⓤⓢ ˈviː.goʊ
vigor ˈvɪg.əʳ ⓤⓢ -ɚ

vigorous ˈvɪg.ər.əs **-ly** -li **-ness** -nəs, -nɪs
vigour ˈvɪg.əʳ ⓤⓢ -ɚ
viking (V) ˈvaɪ.kɪŋ **-s** -z
Vila ˈviː.lə
vil|e vaɪl **-er** -əʳ ⓤⓢ -ɚ **-est** -ɪst, -əst **-ely** -li **-eness** -nəs, -nɪs
vilification ˌvɪl.ɪ.fɪˈkeɪ.ʃən, ˌ-ə- ⓤⓢ ˌ-ə-
vili|fy ˈvɪl.ɪ|.faɪ, ˈ-ə- ⓤⓢ ˈ-ə- **-fies** -faɪz **-fying** -faɪ.ɪŋ **-fied** -faɪd **-fier/s** -faɪ.əʳ/z ⓤⓢ -faɪ.ɚ/z
villa (V) *house:* ˈvɪl.ə **-s** -z
Villa *foreign name:* ˈviː.ə
villag|e ˈvɪl.ɪdʒ **-es** -ɪz
villager ˈvɪl.ɪ.dʒəʳ, ˈ-ə- ⓤⓢ -ə.dʒɚ **-s** -z
villain ˈvɪl.ən *in historical sense also:* -ɪn, -eɪn ⓤⓢ -ən **-s** -z
villainage ˈvɪl.ɪ.nɪdʒ, ˈ-ə- ⓤⓢ ˈ-ə-
villainess ˌvɪl.əˈnes **-es** -ɪz
villainous ˈvɪl.ə.nəs **-ly** -li **-ness** -nəs, -nɪs
villain|y ˈvɪl.ə.n|i **-ies** -iz
Villa-Lobos ˌviː.əˈləʊ.bɒs, ˌviː.lə- ⓤⓢ ˌviː.ləˈloʊ.bəs, -boʊs
villanelle ˌvɪl.əˈnel **-s** -z
-ville -vɪl, -viːl ⓤⓢ -vɪl, -vəl
villein ˈvɪl.ɪn, -eɪn ⓤⓢ -ən **-s** -z **-age** -ɪdʒ
villenage ˈvɪl.ə.nɪdʒ, -ɪ-
Villeneuve ˈviːl.nɜːv ⓤⓢ vɪl.əˈnɜːv
Villette vɪˈlet
Villiers ˈvɪl.əz, -jəz, -i.əz ⓤⓢ ˈ-ɚz, -jɚz
Villon ˈvɪl.ən *as if French:* viːˈjɔ̃ːŋ ⓤⓢ viːˈjoʊn
vill|us ˈvɪl|.əs **-i** -aɪ
Vilna ˈvɪl.nə
Vilnius ˈvɪl.ni.əs ⓤⓢ -ʊs, -əs
vim® (V) vɪm
Vimto® ˈvɪmp.təʊ ⓤⓢ -toʊ
Viña del Mar ˌviː.njə.delˈmɑːʳ ⓤⓢ -ˈmɑːr
vinaigrette ˌvɪn.ɪˈgret, -eɪˈ- ⓤⓢ -əˈ- **-s** -s
Vince vɪnts
Vincennes *in France:* væ̃nˈsen, væn- ⓤⓢ væn- *in Indiana:* vɪnˈsenz
Vincent ˈvɪnt.sənt
Vinci ˈvɪn.tʃiː, -tʃi
vincul|um ˈvɪŋ.kjə.l|əm, -kjʊ- ⓤⓢ -kjə- **-a** -ə **-ums** -əmz
vindaloo ˌvɪn.dəlˈuː ⓤⓢ -dəˈluː **-s** -z
vin(s) de pays ˌvæ̃n.də.peɪˈiː, ˌvæn-
vindicability ˌvɪn.dɪ.kəˈbɪl.ə.ti, -ɪ.ti ⓤⓢ -ə.t̬i
vindicable ˈvɪn.dɪ.kə.bl̩
vindi|cate ˈvɪn.dɪ|.keɪt ⓤⓢ -də- **-cates** -keɪts **-cating** -keɪ.tɪŋ ⓤⓢ -keɪ.t̬ɪŋ **-cated** -keɪ.tɪd ⓤⓢ -keɪ.t̬ɪd **-cator/s** -keɪ.təʳ/z ⓤⓢ -keɪ.t̬ɚ/z
vindication ˌvɪn.dɪˈkeɪ.ʃən ⓤⓢ -dəˈ-
vindicative ˈvɪn.dɪ.kə.tɪv, -keɪ-; vɪnˈdɪk.ə- ⓤⓢ vɪnˈdɪk.ə.t̬ɪv; ˈvɪn.dɪ.keɪ-
vindictive vɪnˈdɪk.tɪv **-ly** -li **-ness** -nəs, -nɪs

vine vaɪn **-s** -z
vineg|ar ˈvɪn.ɪ.g|əʳ, ˈ-ə- ⓤⓢ -ə.g|ɚ **-ars** -əz ⓤⓢ -ɚz **-ary** -ər.i
viner|y ˈvaɪ.nər|.i **-ies** -iz
Viney ˈvaɪ.ni
vineyard ˈvɪn.jəd, -jɑːd ⓤⓢ -jɚd **-s** -z
vingt-et-un ˌvæ̃n.teɪˈɜ̃ːŋ, ˌvæn-, -ˈɜːn ⓤⓢ ˌvæn.teɪˈɜːn
viniculture ˈvɪn.ɪˌkʌl.tʃəʳ, ˌvɪn.ɪˈkʌl- ⓤⓢ ˈvɪn.ɪˌkʌl.tʃɚ
viniculturist ˌvɪn.ɪˈkʌl.tʃər.ɪst, ˈvɪn.ɪˌkʌl- ⓤⓢ ˌvɪn.ɪˈkʌl- **-s** -s
vino ˈviː.nəʊ ⓤⓢ -noʊ
vin(s) ordinaire(s) ˌvæ̃nˌɔː.dɪˈneəʳ, ˌvæn- ⓤⓢ ˌvæ̃nˌɔːr.dənˈer
vinous ˈvaɪ.nəs
vin(s) væ̃ŋ, væn
vintag|e ˈvɪn.tɪdʒ ⓤⓢ -t̬ɪdʒ **-es** -ɪz **ˌvintage ˈyear**
Vinter ˈvɪn.təʳ ⓤⓢ -t̬ɚ
vintner ˈvɪnt.nəʳ ⓤⓢ -nɚ **-s** -z
viny ˈvaɪ.ni
vinyl ˈvaɪ.nəl, -nɪl ⓤⓢ -nəl
viol vaɪəl, vaɪl, vɪəl ⓤⓢ vaɪəl **-s** -z
viola *flower:* ˈvaɪə.lə, ˈvaɪ.əʊ-, ˈviː.ə-, -əʊ-; vaɪˈəʊ-, viˈ- ⓤⓢ ˈviː.ə.lə; vaɪˈoʊ- **-s** -z
viola *musical instrument:* viˈəʊ.lə ⓤⓢ viˈoʊ- **-s** -z
Viola *female name:* ˈvaɪə.lə, ˈvaɪ.əʊ-, ˈviː.ə.lə; viˈəʊ-, vaɪ- ⓤⓢ vaɪˈoʊ.lə, vi-; viː.ə-
violable ˈvaɪə.lə.bl̩
viola da gamba viˌəʊ.lə.dəˈgæm.bə ⓤⓢ -ˌoʊ.lə.dəˈgɑːm- **-s** -z **viole da gamba** viˌəʊ.leɪ- ⓤⓢ -ˌoʊ-
viola d'amore viˌəʊ.lə.dæmˈɔː.reɪ ⓤⓢ -ˌoʊ.lə.dɑːˈmɔːr.eɪ, -ˌoʊ- **viole d'amore** viˌəʊ.leɪ-
vio|late (*v.*) ˈvaɪə|.leɪt, ˈvaɪ.əʊ- ⓤⓢ ˈvaɪə- **-lates** -leɪts **-lating** -leɪ.tɪŋ ⓤⓢ -leɪ.t̬ɪŋ **-lated** -leɪ.tɪd ⓤⓢ -leɪ.t̬ɪd **-lator/s** -leɪ.təʳ/z ⓤⓢ -leɪ.t̬ɚ/z
violate (*adj.*) ˈvaɪə.lɪt, ˈvaɪ.əʊ- ⓤⓢ ˈvaɪə-
violation ˌvaɪəˈleɪ.ʃən, ˌvaɪ.əʊˈ- ⓤⓢ ˌvaɪəˈ- **-s** -z
violence ˈvaɪə.lənts
violent ˈvaɪə.lənt **-ly** -li
violet (V) ˈvaɪə.lət, -lɪt ⓤⓢ -lɪt **-s** -s
violin ˌvaɪəˈlɪn **-s** -z
violinist vaɪəˈlɪn.ɪst, ˌvaɪə- **-s** -s
violist *viola player:* viˈəʊ.lɪst ⓤⓢ -ˈoʊ- **-s** -s *viol player:* ˈvaɪə.lɪst **-s** -s
violoncellist ˌvaɪə.lənˈtʃel.ɪst, ˌvɪə.lənˈ-, -lɪnˈ- ⓤⓢ ˌviː.ə.lɑːnˈ-, ˌvaɪə.lɑːnˈ- **-s** -s
violoncello ˌvaɪə.lənˈtʃel.əʊ, ˌvɪə.lənˈ-, -lɪnˈ- ⓤⓢ ˌviː.ə.lɑːnˈtʃel.oʊ, ˌvaɪə.lɑːnˈ- **-s** -z

violone ˈvaɪə.ləʊn, ˈvɪə-, ˌvɪəˈləʊ.neɪ ⓤⓢ ˌviː.əˈloʊ- **-s** -z
VIP ˌviː.aɪˈpiː **-s** -z
vip|er ˈvaɪ.p|əʳ ⓤⓢ -p|ɚ **-ers** -əz ⓤⓢ -ɚz **-erish** -ər.ɪʃ **-erous** -ər.əs
virago (V) vɪˈrɑː.gəʊ, -ˈreɪ- ⓤⓢ vəˈrɑː.goʊ, -ˈreɪ-; ˈvɪr.ə- **-(e)s** -z
viral ˈvaɪə.rəl ⓤⓢ ˈvaɪ-
vires ˈvaɪə.riːz ⓤⓢ ˈvaɪ-
Virgil ˈvɜː.dʒɪl ⓤⓢ ˈvɝː.dʒəl **-s** -z
Virgilian vɜːˈdʒɪl.i.ən, və- ⓤⓢ vɝː-, ˈ-jən
virgin (V®) ˈvɜː.dʒɪn ⓤⓢ ˈvɝː- **-s** -z **ˌvirgin ˈbirth; ˈVirgin ˌIslands** ⓤⓢ **ˌVirgin ˈIslands; ˌVirgin ˈMary**
virginal ˈvɜː.dʒɪ.nəl, -dʒən.əl ⓤⓢ ˈvɝː- **-s** -z **-ly** -li
Virgini|a, virgini|a vəˈdʒɪn.j|ə, vɜː-, -i|.ə ⓤⓢ vɚ- **-as** -əz **-an/s** -ən/z **virˌginia ˈcreeper**
virginity vəˈdʒɪn.ə.ti, vɜː-, -ɪ.ti ⓤⓢ vɚˈdʒɪn.ə.t̬i
Virgo *constellation:* ˈvɜː.gəʊ, ˈvɪə- ⓤⓢ ˈvɝː.goʊ **-s** -z
Virgoan vɜːˈgəʊ.ən ⓤⓢ vɝːˈgoʊ- **-s** -z
virgule ˈvɜː.gjuːl ⓤⓢ ˈvɝː- **-s** -z
viridescen|t ˌvɪr.ɪˈdes.ən|t ⓤⓢ -əˈ- **-ce** -ts
viridian vɪˈrɪd.i.ən, və- ⓤⓢ və-
virile ˈvɪr.aɪl ⓤⓢ -əl, -aɪl
virility vɪˈrɪl.ə.ti, və-, -ɪ.ti ⓤⓢ vəˈrɪl.ə.t̬i
virolog|y vaɪəˈrɒl.ə.dʒ|i ⓤⓢ vaɪˈrɑː.lə- **-ist/s** -ɪst/s
virtu vɜːˈtuː ⓤⓢ vɚ-; ˈvɜː.tuː
virtual ˈvɜː.tʃu.əl, -tju-, ˈ-tʃʊəl, -tjʊəl ⓤⓢ ˈvɝː.tʃu- **-ly** -i **ˌvirtual reˈality**
virtue ˈvɜː.tjuː, -tʃuː ⓤⓢ ˈvɝː.tʃuː **-s** -z
virtuosity ˌvɜː.tjuˈɒs.ə.ti, -tʃuˈ-, -ɪ.ti ⓤⓢ ˌvɝː.tʃuˈɑː.sə.t̬i
virtuos|o ˌvɜː.tjuˈəʊ.s|əʊ, -tʃuˈ-, -z|əʊ ⓤⓢ ˌvɝː.tʃuˈoʊ.s|oʊ **-os** -əʊz ⓤⓢ -oʊz **-i** -i
virtuous ˈvɜː.tʃu.əs, -tju- ⓤⓢ ˈvɝː.tʃu- **-ly** -li **-ness** -nəs, -nɪs
virulence ˈvɪr.ʊ.lənts, ˈ-ə-, -jʊ-, -jə- ⓤⓢ -jə-, ˈ-ə-, -jʊ-
virulent ˈvɪr.ʊ.lənt, ˈ-ə-, -jʊ-, -jə- ⓤⓢ -jə-, ˈ-ə-, -jʊ- **-ly** -li
virus ˈvaɪə.rəs ⓤⓢ ˈvaɪ- **-es** -ɪz
vis vɪs
visa (V®) ˈviː.zə ⓤⓢ -zə, -sə **-s** -z **-ing** -ɪŋ **-ed** -d
visag|e ˈvɪz.ɪdʒ **-es** -ɪz
visagiste ˌvɪz.ɑːˈʒiːst **-s** -s
vis-à-vis ˌviːz.ɑːˈviː, ˌvɪz-, -əˈ-, -æˈ- ⓤⓢ ˌviːz.əˈviː
viscera ˈvɪs.ər|.ə
visceral ˈvɪs.ər.əl **-ly** -i
viscid ˈvɪs.ɪd
viscidity vɪˈsɪd.ə.ti, -ɪ.ti ⓤⓢ -ə.t̬i
Visconti vɪˈskɒn.ti ⓤⓢ -ˈskɑːn-

viscose 'vɪs.kəʊs, -kəʊz ⓤⓢ -koʊs, -koʊz
viscosity vɪ'skɒs.ə.ti, -ɪ.ti ⓤⓢ -'skɑː.sə.t̬i
vis|count 'vaɪ.kaʊnt **-counts** -kaʊnts **-county** -kaʊn.ti ⓤⓢ -kaʊn.t̬i **-counties** -kaʊn.tiz ⓤⓢ -kaʊn.t̬iz
viscountc|y 'vaɪ.kaʊnt.s|i **-ies** -iz
viscountess ˌvaɪ.kaʊn'tes; 'vaɪ.kaʊn.tɪs, -təs ⓤⓢ 'vaɪ.kaʊn.t̬ɪs **-es** -ɪz
viscous 'vɪs.kəs **-ness** -nəs, -nɪs
visé 'viː.zeɪ ⓤⓢ 'viː.zeɪ, -'- **-s** -z **-ing** -ɪŋ **-d** -d
vis|e vaɪs **-es** -ɪz **-ing** -ɪŋ **-ed** -t
Vishnu 'vɪʃ.nuː
visibility ˌvɪz.ə'bɪl.ə.ti, -ɪ'-, -ɪ.ti ⓤⓢ -ə'bɪl.ə.t̬i
visib|le 'vɪz.ə.b|l̩, '-ɪ- ⓤⓢ '-ə- **-ly** -li **-leness** -l̩.nəs, -nɪs
Visigoth 'vɪz.ɪ.gɒθ, 'vɪs- ⓤⓢ -ə.gɑːθ **-s** -s
Visigothic ˌvɪz.ɪ'gɒθ.ɪk, ˌvɪs- ⓤⓢ -ə'gɑː.θɪk
vision 'vɪʒ.ən **-s** -z
visional 'vɪʒ.ən.əl, '-nəl ⓤⓢ 'vɪʒ.ən.əl **-ly** -i
visionar|y 'vɪʒ.ən.ər|.i, -ən.r|i ⓤⓢ -ən.er|.i **-ies** -iz
vis|it 'vɪz|.ɪt **-its** -ɪts **-iting** -ɪ.tɪŋ ⓤⓢ -ɪ.t̬ɪŋ **-ited** -ɪ.tɪd ⓤⓢ -ɪ.t̬ɪd **'visiting ˌcard; ˌvisiting pro'fessor**
visitant 'vɪz.ɪ.tənt ⓤⓢ -t̬ənt **-s** -s
visitation ˌvɪz.ɪ'teɪ.ʃən ⓤⓢ -ə'- **-s** -z
visitor 'vɪz.ɪ.təʳ ⓤⓢ -t̬ɚ **-s** -z **'visitors' ˌbook**
vis major ˌvɪs'meɪ.dʒəʳ ⓤⓢ -dʒɚ
visor 'vaɪ.zəʳ ⓤⓢ -zɚ **-s** -z
vista 'vɪs.tə **-s** -z
Vistula 'vɪs.tjʊ.lə ⓤⓢ -tʃuː-
visual 'vɪʒ.u.əl, 'vɪz.ju- ⓤⓢ 'vɪʒ.u- **-s** -z **-ly** -i **ˌvisual 'aid; ˌvisual di'splay ˌunit**
visualization, -isa- ˌvɪʒ.u.əl.aɪ'zeɪ.ʃən, ˌvɪz.ju-, -ɪ'- ⓤⓢ ˌvɪʒ.u.əl.ɪ'-
visualiz|e, -is|e 'vɪʒ.u.əl.aɪz, 'vɪz.ju- ⓤⓢ 'vɪʒ.u.ə.laɪz **-es** -ɪz **-ing** -ɪŋ **-ed** -d **-er/s** -əʳ/z ⓤⓢ -ɚ/z
vita *glass:* 'vaɪ.tə ⓤⓢ -t̬ə *aqua:* 'viː.tə ⓤⓢ -t̬ə
Vita 'viː.tə ⓤⓢ -t̬ə
vitae *curriculum:* 'viː.taɪ, 'vaɪ.tiː ⓤⓢ 'vaɪ.t̬iː, 'viː-, -taɪ
vital 'vaɪ.təl ⓤⓢ -t̬əl **-ly** -i **ˌvital 'signs** ⓤⓢ **'vital ˌsigns; ˌvital sta'tistics**
Vitalite® 'vaɪ.tə.laɪt
vitality vaɪ'tæl.ə.ti, -ɪ.ti ⓤⓢ -ə.t̬i
vitalization, -isa- ˌvaɪ.təl.aɪ'zeɪ.ʃən ⓤⓢ -təl.ɪ'-
vitaliz|e, -is|e 'vaɪ.təl.aɪz ⓤⓢ -t̬ə.laɪz **-es** -ɪz **-ing** -ɪŋ **-ed** -d
vitals 'vaɪ.təlz ⓤⓢ -t̬əlz
vitamin 'vɪt.ə.mɪn, 'vaɪ- ⓤⓢ 'vaɪ.t̬ə- **-s** -z **ˌvitamin 'C**
VitBe® 'vɪt.biː
vitellus vɪ'tel.əs ⓤⓢ vɪ-, vaɪ-
Vitez 'viː.tez
viti|ate 'vɪʃ.i|.eɪt **-ates** -eɪts **-ating** -eɪ.tɪŋ ⓤⓢ -eɪ.t̬ɪŋ **-ated** -eɪ.tɪd ⓤⓢ -eɪ.t̬ɪd **-ator/s** -eɪ.təʳ/z ⓤⓢ -eɪ.t̬ɚ/z
vitiation ˌvɪʃ.i'eɪ.ʃən
viticulture 'vɪt.ɪˌkʌl.tʃəʳ, 'vaɪ- ⓤⓢ -t̬əˌkʌl.tʃɚ
vitiligo ˌvɪt.ɪ'laɪ.gəʊ ⓤⓢ ˌvɪt̬.ɪ'laɪ.goʊ
vitreous 'vɪt.ri.əs **-ness** -nəs, -nɪs
vitrescen|t vɪ'tres.ən|t **-ce** -*t*s
vitric 'vɪt.rɪk
vitrifaction ˌvɪt.rɪ'fæk.ʃən ⓤⓢ -rə'-
vitrification ˌvɪt.rɪ.fɪ'keɪ.ʃən, -rə- ⓤⓢ -rə-
vitri|fy 'vɪt.rɪ|.faɪ ⓤⓢ -trə- **-fies** -faɪz **-fying** -faɪ.ɪŋ **-fied** -faɪd **-fiable** -faɪ.ə.bl̩
vitriol 'vɪt.ri.əl, -ɒl ⓤⓢ -əl, -ɔːl
vitriolic ˌvɪt.ri'ɒl.ɪk ⓤⓢ -'ɑː.lɪk **-ally** -əl.i, -li
vitro 'viː.trəʊ ⓤⓢ -troʊ
Vitruvius vɪ'truː.vi.əs
vittles 'vɪt.l̩z ⓤⓢ 'vɪt̬-
Vittoria vɪ'tɔː.ri.ə ⓤⓢ -'tɔːr.i-
vituper|ate vɪ'tjuː.pər|.eɪt, vaɪ- ⓤⓢ vaɪ'tuː.pə.r|eɪt, vɪ-, -'tjuː- **-ates** -eɪts **-ating** -eɪ.tɪŋ ⓤⓢ -eɪ.t̬ɪŋ **-ated** -eɪ.tɪd ⓤⓢ -eɪ.t̬ɪd **-ator/s** -eɪ.təʳ/z ⓤⓢ -eɪ.t̬ɚ/z
vituperation vɪˌtjuː.pər'eɪ.ʃən, vaɪ- ⓤⓢ vaɪˌtuː.pə'reɪ-, vɪ-, -ˌtjuː- **-s** -z
vituperative vɪ'tjuː.pər.ə.tɪv, vaɪ-, -eɪ- ⓤⓢ vaɪ'tuː.pɚ.ə.t̬ɪv, vɪ-, -'tjuː-, -pə.reɪ- **-ly** -li
vituperatory vɪ'tjuː.pər.ə.tər.i, vaɪ- ⓤⓢ vaɪ'tuː.pɚ.ə.tɔːr-, -tjuː-, -prə.tɔːr-
Vitus 'vaɪ.təs ⓤⓢ -t̬əs
viva *long live:* 'viː.və
viva *examination:* 'vaɪ.və ⓤⓢ 'vaɪ.və, 'viː- **-s** -z **ˌviva 'voce**
Viva® 'viː.və
vivace vɪ'vɑː.tʃeɪ ⓤⓢ -tʃeɪ **-s** -z
vivacious vɪ'veɪ.ʃəs, vaɪ- **-ly** -li **-ness** -nəs, -nɪs
vivacity vɪ'væs.ə.ti, vaɪ-, -ɪ.ti ⓤⓢ -ə.t̬i
Vivaldi vɪ'væl.di ⓤⓢ -'vɑːl-
vivari|um vaɪ'veə.ri|.əm, vɪ- ⓤⓢ vaɪ'ver.i- **-ums** -əmz **-a** -ə
vivat 'vaɪ.væt, 'viː-
vive viːv
Vivendi® vɪ'ven.di
Vivian 'vɪv.i.ən
vivid 'vɪv.ɪd **-ly** -li **-ness** -nəs, -nɪs
Vivien 'vɪv.i.ən
Vivienne 'vɪv.i.ən, ˌvɪv.i'en
vivification ˌvɪv.ɪ.fɪ'keɪ.ʃən ⓤⓢ ˌ-ə-
vivi|fy 'vɪv.ɪ|.faɪ ⓤⓢ '-ə- **-fies** -faɪz **-fying** -faɪ.ɪŋ **-fied** -faɪd
viviparity ˌvɪv.ɪ'pær.ə.ti, -ɪ.ti ⓤⓢ -ə'per.ə.t̬i, -'pær-
viviparous vɪ'vɪp.ər.əs, vaɪ- ⓤⓢ vaɪ- **-ly** -li **-ness** -nəs, -nɪs
vivisect ˌvɪv.ɪ'sekt, '--- ⓤⓢ 'vɪv.ə.sekt **-s** -s **-ing** -ɪŋ **-ed** -ɪd **-or/s** -əʳ/z ⓤⓢ -ɚ/z
vivisection ˌvɪv.ɪ'sek.ʃən ⓤⓢ -ə'-, 'vɪv.ə.sek-
vivisectionist ˌvɪv.ɪ'sek.ʃən.ɪst ⓤⓢ -ə'- **-s** -s
vixen 'vɪk.sən **-s** -z
vixenish 'vɪk.sən.ɪʃ
Viyella® vaɪ'el.ə
viz. vɪz; vɪ'diː.lɪ.set, vaɪ-; vɪ'deɪ.lɪ.ket ⓤⓢ vɪz; vɪ'del.ɪ.set, wɪ-
Note: Many people in reading aloud substitute **namely** (/'neɪm.li/) for this word.
Vizetelly ˌvɪz.ɪ'tel.i
vizier vɪ'zɪəʳ, 'vɪz.ɪəʳ; ⓤⓢ vɪ'zɪr; 'vɪz.jɚ **-s** -z
vizor 'vaɪ.zəʳ ⓤⓢ -zɚ **-s** -z
VJ-Day ˌviː'dʒeɪ.deɪ
Vladimir 'vlæd.ɪ.mɪəʳ, -məʳ, vlæd'iː.mɪəʳ ⓤⓢ -ə.mɪr
Vladivostok ˌvlæd.ɪ'vɒs.tɒk ⓤⓢ -'vɑː.stɑːk
V-neck ˌviː'nek ⓤⓢ '-- **-s** -s **-ed** -t
vocab 'vəʊ.kæb ⓤⓢ 'voʊ-
vocable 'vəʊ.kə.bl̩ ⓤⓢ 'voʊ- **-s** -z
vocabular|y vəʊ'kæb.jə.lər|.i, -jʊ- ⓤⓢ voʊ'kæb.jə.ler-, -jʊ- **-ies** -iz
vocal 'vəʊ.kəl ⓤⓢ 'voʊ- **-s** -z **-ly** -i **ˌvocal 'cords** ⓤⓢ **'vocal ˌcords**
vocalic vəʊ'kæl.ɪk ⓤⓢ voʊ-
vocalism 'vəʊ.kəl.ɪ.zəm ⓤⓢ 'voʊ-
vocalist 'vəʊ.kəl.ɪst ⓤⓢ 'voʊ- **-s** -s
vocality vəʊ'kæl.ə.ti, -ɪ.ti ⓤⓢ voʊ'kæl.ə.t̬i
vocalization, -isa- ˌvəʊ.kəl.aɪ'zeɪ.ʃən, -ɪ'- ⓤⓢ ˌvoʊ.kəl.ɪ'- **-s** -z
vocaliz|e, -is|e 'vəʊ.kəl.aɪz ⓤⓢ 'voʊ.kə.laɪz **-es** -ɪz **-ing** -ɪŋ **-ed** -d **-er/s** -əʳ/z ⓤⓢ -ɚ/z
vocation vəʊ'keɪ.ʃən ⓤⓢ voʊ- **-s** -z
vocational vəʊ'keɪ.ʃən.əl, -'keɪʃ.nəl ⓤⓢ voʊ- **-ly** -i
vocational|ism vəʊ'keɪ.ʃən.əl|.ɪ.zəm, -'keɪʃ.nəl- ⓤⓢ voʊ- **-ist/s** -ɪst/s
vocative 'vɒk.ə.tɪv ⓤⓢ 'vɑː.kə.t̬ɪv **-s** -z
voce *(in* **viva voce***)* 'vəʊ.si, -tʃi, -tʃeɪ ⓤⓢ 'voʊ.siː *(in* **sotto voce***)* 'vəʊ.tʃi ⓤⓢ 'voʊ.tʃi, -tʃeɪ
vocifer|ate vəʊ'sɪf.ər|.eɪt ⓤⓢ voʊ'sɪf.ə.r|eɪt **-ates** -eɪts **-ating** -eɪ.tɪŋ ⓤⓢ -eɪ.t̬ɪŋ **-ated** -eɪ.tɪd ⓤⓢ -eɪ.t̬ɪd **-ator/s** -eɪ.təʳ/z ⓤⓢ -eɪ.t̬ɚ/z
vociferation vəʊˌsɪf.ə'reɪ.ʃən ⓤⓢ voʊ- **-s** -z
vociferous vəʊ'sɪf.ər.əs ⓤⓢ voʊ- **-ly** -li **-ness** -nəs, -nɪs
vocoid 'vəʊ.kɔɪd ⓤⓢ 'voʊ- **-s** -z

Vocal folds

An essential part of the larynx, performing a number of important linguistic functions. The term 'vocal cords' is also used.

The vocal folds may be firmly closed to produce what is sometimes called a GLOTTAL STOP, and while they are closed the larynx may be moved up or down move air out of or into the vocal tract; this is done in the production of 'ejective' and 'implosive' consonants. When brought into light contact with each other the vocal folds tend to vibrate if air is forced through them, producing VOICING, also called 'phonation'. This vibration can be made to vary in many ways, resulting in differences in such things as PITCH, loudness and voice quality. If a narrow opening is made between the vocal folds, friction noise can result and this is found in whispering and in the glottal fricative [h]. A more widely open glottis is found in most voiceless consonants.

Voice onset time

A measure of the timing of the start of voicing.

All languages distinguish between voiced and voiceless consonants, and PLOSIVES are the most common consonants to be distinguished in this way. However, this is not a simple matter of a plosive being either completely voiced or completely voiceless: the timing of the voicing in relation to the consonant articulation is very important. In one particular case this is so noticeable that it has for a long time been given its own name: ASPIRATION, in which the beginning of full voicing does not happen until some time after the release of the plosive (usually voiceless). This delay, or 'lag', has been the subject of much experimental investigation which has led to the development of a scientific measure of voice timing called voice onset time or V.O.T.. The onset of voicing in a plosive may lag behind the plosive release, or it may precede ('lead') it, resulting in a fully or partially voiced plosive. Both can be represented on the V.O.T. scale, one case having positive values and the other negative values.

Voicing

A term used to refer to the vibration of the VOCAL FOLDS. A sound made with this vibration is called *voiced*, and one without vibration is called *voiceless*. Most vowels in most languages are voiced, though voiceless vowels are found in some languages. Among consonants, it is very common to find pairs that are distinguished from each other by the presence or absence of voicing, but in English we find that consonants such as /b d g v ð z ʒ/, though frequently described as voiced (in contrast with the corresponding voiceless consonants /p t k f θ s ʃ/) often have little or no voicing. See FORTIS, LENIS, ONSET TIME. Whispering is speech that is entirely voiceless.

In other languages

Many pairs of consonants distinguished by the voiced-voiceless contrast are found in different languages. Welsh has voiced and voiceless LATERAL consonants, while Burmese has voiced and voiceless NASAL consonants.

Vodafone®, **Vodaphone** ˈvəʊ.də.fəʊn (US) ˈvoʊ.də.foʊn
vodka ˈvɒd.kə (US) ˈvɑːd- **-s** -z
Vogt *English surname:* vəʊkt (US) voʊkt
vogue **(V®)** vəʊg (US) voʊg
voic|e vɔɪs **-es** -ɪz **-ing** -ɪŋ **-ed** -t **ˌVoice of Aˈmerica; ˈvoice ˌbox**
voiceless ˈvɔɪ.sləs, -slɪs **-ly** -li **-ness** -nəs, -nɪs
voicemail ˈvɔɪs.meɪl
voice-over ˈvɔɪsˌəʊ.vəʳ (US) -ˌoʊ.vɚ **-s** -z
voiceprint ˈvɔɪs.prɪnt **-s** -s
void vɔɪd **-s** -z **-ing** -ɪŋ **-ed** -ɪd **-able** -ə.bl̩ **-ance** -ᵊnts **-ness** -nəs, -nɪs
voilà vwælˈɑː, vwɒl-, vwɑːˈlɑː (US) vwɑːˈlɑː
voile vɔɪl
voir dire ˌvwɑːˈdɪəʳ (US) ˌvwɑːrˈdɪr
vol vɒl (US) vɑːl
volant ˈvəʊ.lənt (US) ˈvoʊ-
Volapük ˈvɒl.ə.puːk, ˈvəʊl-, -pʊk, ˌ--ˈ- (US) ˈvoʊ.lɑː-, ˈvɑː-
volatile *(adj.)* ˈvɒl.ə.taɪl (US) ˈvɑː.lə.t̬ᵊl **-ness** -nəs, -nɪs
volatile *(in* **sal volatile***)* vəʊˈlæt.ə.li, vɒlˈæt- (US) voʊˈlæt.li
volatility ˌvɒl.əˈtɪl.ə.ti, -ɪ.ti (US) ˌvɑː.ləˈtɪl.ə.t̬i
volatilization, **-isa-** vɒlˌæt.ɪ.laɪˈzeɪ.ʃᵊn, vəʊˌlæt-, -ᵊl.aɪˈ-, -ɪˈ-; ˌvɒl.ə.tɪ.laɪˈ-, -tᵊl.aɪˈ-, -ɪˈ- (US) ˌvɑː.lə.tᵊl.ɪˈ-
volatiliz|e, **-is|e** vɒlˈæt.ɪ.laɪz, vəʊˈlæt- -ᵊl.aɪz; ˈvɒl.ə.tɪ.laɪz, -tᵊl.aɪz (US) ˈvɑː.lə.tə.laɪz **-es** -ɪz **-ing** -ɪŋ **-ed** -d
vol-au-vent ˈvɒl.əʊ.vɑ̃ːŋ, ˌ--ˈ- (US) ˌvɔː.loʊˈvɑ̃ːn, ˌvoʊ- **-s** -z
volcanic vɒlˈkæn.ɪk (US) vɑːl- **-ally** -ᵊl.i, -li
volcanicity ˌvɒl.kəˈnɪs.ə.ti, -ɪ.ti (US) ˌvɑːl.kəˈnɪs.ə.t̬i
volcanism ˈvɒl.kə.nɪ.zᵊm (US) ˈvɑːl-
volcano vɒlˈkeɪ.nəʊ (US) vɑːlˈkeɪ.noʊ **-(e)s** -z
volcanology ˌvɒl.kəˈnɒl.ə.dʒi (US) ˌvɑːl.kəˈnɑː.lə-
vole vəʊl (US) voʊl **-s** -z

volenti non fit injuria vɒlˌen.tiːˌnəʊn.fɪt.ɪn'dʒʊə.ri.ə, -'jɔː- (US) voʊˌlen.ti.nɑːnˌfɪt.ɪn'dʒʊr.i.ə
volet 'vɒl.eɪ (US) 'voʊ.leɪ, -'- **-s** -z
Volga 'vɒl.gə (US) 'vɑːl-, 'voʊl-
Volgograd 'vɒl.gəʊ.græd (US) 'vɑːl.gə-, 'voʊl-
volition vəʊ'lɪʃ.ᵊn (US) voʊ-, və- **-al** -ᵊl
volitive 'vɒl.ɪ.tɪv, '-ə- (US) 'vɑː.lə.t̬ɪv
volks|lied 'fɒlks|.liːd, 'vɒlks- *as if German:* -liːt (US) 'fɔːlks|.liːt **-lieder** -ˌliː.dəʳ (US) -ˌliː.dɚ
volkstaat 'fɒlk.ʃtɑːt (US) 'fɔːlk- **-s** -s
Volkswagen® 'fɒlksˌvɑː.gən, 'vɒlks- (US) 'fɔːlks-, 'vɔːlks-, 'voʊks-, -ˌwɑː-, -ˌwæg.ᵊn **-s** -z
volley 'vɒl.i (US) 'vɑː.li **-s** -z **-ing** -ɪŋ **-ed** -d **-er/s** -əʳ/z (US) -ɚ/z
volleyball 'vɒl.i.bɔːl (US) 'vɑː.li-
Volos 'vɒl.ɒs (US) 'vɔː.lɑːs
volplan|e 'vɒl.pleɪn (US) 'vɑːl- **-es** -z **-ing** -ɪŋ **-ed** -d
Volpone vɒl'pəʊ.neɪ, -ni (US) vɑːl'poʊ-
Volsci 'vɒl.skiː, -saɪ (US) 'vɑːl.saɪ, -skiː
Volscian 'vɒl.ski.ən, -ʃi-, -si- (US) 'vɑːl.ʃᵊn, -ski.ən
Volstead 'vɒl.sted (US) 'vɑːl-
Volsung 'vɒl.sʊŋ (US) 'vɑːl-
volt *electric unit:* vəʊlt, vɒlt (US) voʊlt **-s** -s
volt *movement of horse, movement in fencing:* vɒlt (US) voʊlt, vɑːlt, vɔːlt **-s** -s
Volta (V) *physicist:* 'vɒl.tə, 'vəʊl- (US) 'voʊl.t̬ə
Volta *lake and river:* 'vɒl.tə (US) 'vɑːl.t̬ə, 'vɔːl-, 'voʊl-
volta *dance:* 'vɒl.tə (US) 'vɑːl- **-s** -z
voltag|e 'vəʊl.tɪdʒ, 'vɒl- (US) 'voʊl.t̬ɪdʒ **-es** -ɪz
voltaic vɒl'teɪ.ɪk (US) vɑːl-, voʊl-
Voltaire vɒl'teəʳ, '-- (US) voʊl'ter, vɑːl-
voltameter vɒl'tæm.ɪ.təʳ, vəʊl-, '-ə- (US) voʊl'tæm.ə.t̬ɚ, vɑːl- **-s** -z
volte 'vɒl.teɪ, -ti (US) vɑːlt, voʊlt **-s** -z
volte-fac|e ˌvɒlt'fæs (US) ˌvɑːlt'fɑːs **-es** -ɪz
voltmeter 'vəʊltˌmiː.təʳ, 'vɒlt- (US) 'voʊltˌmiː.t̬ɚ **-s** -z
volubility ˌvɒl.jə'bɪl.ə.ti, -jʊ'-, -ɪ.ti (US) ˌvɑːl.jə'bɪl.ə.t̬i, -jʊ'-
volub|le 'vɒl.jə.bl̩, -jʊ- (US) 'vɑːl- **-ly** -li **-leness** -l̩.nəs, -nɪs
volume 'vɒl.juːm, -jʊm, -jəm (US) 'vɑːl.juːm, -jəm **-s** -z
volumeter vɒl'juː.mɪ.təʳ, və'ljuː-, -'luː-, -mə- (US) 'vɑːl.jʊˌmiː.t̬ɚ **-s** -z
volumetric ˌvɒl.jə'met.rɪk, -jʊ'- (US) ˌvɑːl- **-al** -ᵊl **-ally** -ᵊl.i, -li
voluminous və'luː.mɪ.nəs, vɒl'uː-, -'juː-, -mə- (US) və'luː.mə- **-ly** -li **-ness** -nəs, -nɪs
voluntar|y 'vɒl.ən.tᵊr|.i, -tr|i (US) 'vɑː.lᵊn.ter|.i **-ies** -iz **-ily** -ᵊl.i, -ɪ.li, ˌvɒl.ən'teə.rᵊl.i, -'tær-, -ɪ.li **-iness** -ɪ.nəs, -ɪ.nɪs
volunteer ˌvɒl.ən'tɪəʳ (US) ˌvɑː.lən'tɪr **-s** -z **-ing** -ɪŋ **-ed** -d
voluptuar|y və'lʌp.tʃʊə.r|i, -tʃʊə- (US) -tʃu.er|.i **-ies** -iz
voluptuous və'lʌp.tʃu.əs, -tju.əs (US) -tʃu- **-ly** -li **-ness** -nəs, -nɪs
volu|te vəʊ'luː|t, vɒl'uː|t, -'juː|t (US) və'luː|t **-tes** -ts **-ted** -tɪd (US) -t̬ɪd
volution vəʊ'luː.ʃᵊn, vɒl'uː-, -'juː- (US) və'luː- **-s** -z
Volvo® 'vɒl.vəʊ (US) 'vɑːl.voʊ **-s** -z
vom|it 'vɒm|.ɪt (US) 'vɑː.m|ɪt **-its** -ɪts **-iting** -ɪ.tɪŋ (US) -ɪ.t̬ɪŋ **-ited** -ɪ.tɪd (US) -ɪ.t̬ɪd
vomitor|y 'vɒm.ɪ.tᵊr|.i, -tr|i (US) 'vɑː.mə.tɔːr|.i **-ies** -iz
von (V) vɒn, fɒn (US) vɑːn, fɑːn
Vonnegut 'vɒn.ɪ.gət (US) 'vɑː.nə-
voodoo 'vuː.duː **-s** -z **-ing** -ɪŋ **-ed** -d **-ist/s** -ɪst/s **-ism** -ɪ.zᵊm
Vooght vuːt
voracious və'reɪ.ʃəs, vɔː-, vɒr'eɪ- (US) vɔː'reɪ-, və- **-ly** -li **-ness** -nəs, -nɪs
voracity və'ræs.ə.ti, vɔː-, vɒr'æs-, -ɪ.ti (US) vɔː'ræs.ə.t̬i, və-
Vorderman 'vɔː.də.mən (US) 'vɔːr.dɚ-
Vorster 'fɔː.stəʳ (US) 'fɔːr.stɚ
vort|ex 'vɔː.t|eks (US) 'vɔːr- **-ices** -ɪ.siːz **-exes** -ek.sɪz
vortic|al 'vɔː.tɪ.k|ᵊl (US) 'vɔːr.t̬ɪ- **-ally** -ᵊl.i, -li
vortices *(plur. of* **vortex***)* 'vɔː.tɪ.siːz (US) 'vɔːr.t̬ɪ-
vortic|ism (V) 'vɔː.tɪ.s|ɪ.zᵊm (US) 'vɔːr.t̬ɪ- **-ist/s** -ɪst/s
Vortigern 'vɔː.tɪ.gɜːn, -gən (US) 'vɔːr.t̬ɪ.gɝːn
Vosges vəʊʒ (US) voʊʒ
Voss vɒs (US) vɑːs
votaress 'vəʊ.tᵊr.es, -ɪs (US) 'voʊ.t̬ɚ.əs, '-trəs **-es** -ɪz
votar|y 'vəʊ.tᵊr|.i (US) 'voʊ.t̬ɚ- **-ies** -iz **-ist/s** -ɪst/s
vot|e vəʊt (US) voʊt **-es** -s **-ing** -ɪŋ (US) 'voʊ.t̬ɪŋ **-ed** -ɪd (US) 'voʊ.t̬ɪd **-er/s** -əʳ/z (US) 'voʊ.t̬ɚ/z **ˌvote of (ˌno) 'confidence; ˌvote of 'thanks; ˌvote with one's 'feet**
voteless 'vəʊt.ləs, -lɪs (US) 'voʊt-
votive 'vəʊ.tɪv (US) 'voʊ.t̬ɪv **-ly** -li **-ness** -nəs, -nɪs
vouch vaʊtʃ **-es** -ɪz **-ing** -ɪŋ **-ed** -t
voucher 'vaʊ.tʃəʳ (US) -tʃɚ **-s** -z **'voucher ˌsystem**
vouchsaf|e ˌvaʊtʃ'seɪf, '-- **-es** -s **-ing** -ɪŋ **-ed** -t
Vouvray 'vuː.vreɪ (US) -'-
vow vaʊ **-s** -z **-ing** -ɪŋ **-ed** -d
vowel vaʊəl **-s** -z **-(l)ing** -ɪŋ **-(l)ed** -d
Vowles vəʊlz, vaʊlz (US) voʊlz, vaʊlz
vox (V) vɒks (US) vɑːks
vox humana ˌvɒks.hjuː'mɑː.nə (US) ˌvɑːks-, -'meɪ- **-s** -z
vox pop ˌvɒks'pɒp (US) ˌvɑːks'pɑːp
vox populi ˌvɒks'pɒp.jʊ.liː, -jə- (US) ˌvɑːks'pɑː.pjuː.laɪ, -liː
voyag|e 'vɔɪ.ɪdʒ **-es** -ɪz **-ing** -ɪŋ **-ed** -d
voyager 'vɔɪ.ɪ.dʒəʳ, 'vɔɪ.ə- (US) 'vɔɪ.ɪ.dʒɚ **-s** -z
voyeur vwɑː'jɜːʳ, vɔɪ'ɜːʳ (US) vɔɪ'jɝː, vwɑː- **-s** -z
voyeurism vwɑː'jɜː.rɪ.zᵊm, vɔɪ'ɜː-, 'vwɑː.jɜː-, 'vɔɪ.ɜː- (US) vɔɪ'jɝː.ɪ-, vwɑː-; 'vɔɪ.jɚ.ɪ-
voyeuristic ˌvɔɪ.ə'rɪ.stɪk, ˌvwɑː.jɜː'- (US) ˌvɔɪ.jə'-, ˌvwɑː- **-ally** -ᵊl.i, li
VP ˌviː'piː **-s** -z
vroom vruːm, vrʊm
vs. 'vɜː.səs (US) 'vɝː-
VSO ˌviː.es'əʊ (US) -'oʊ
V/STOL 'viːˌstɒl (US) -ˌstɑːl
Vt. *(abbrev. for* **Vermont***)* və'mɒnt, vɜː- (US) vɚ'mɑːnt
VTOL 'viː.tɒl (US) -tɑːl
Vuillard 'vuː.jɑː, -'-
Vuitton® 'vjuː.ɪ.tɔ̃ːŋ, 'vwiː.tɒn (US) vwiː'tɔ̃ːn
Vukovar 'vʊk.ə.vəʳ, -vɑːʳ (US) -vɚ
Vulcan 'vʌl.kən **-s** -z
vulcanite 'vʌl.kə.naɪt
vulcanization, -isa- ˌvʌl.kə.naɪ'zeɪ.ʃᵊn, -nɪ'- (US) -nɪ'-
vulcaniz|e, -is|e 'vʌl.kə.naɪz **-es** -ɪz **-ing** -ɪŋ **-ed** -d
vulgar (V) 'vʌl.gəʳ (US) -gɚ **-ly** -li **ˌVulgar 'Latin**
vulgarian vʌl'geə.ri.ən (US) -'ger.i- **-s** -z
vulgarism 'vʌl.gᵊr.ɪ.zᵊm **-s** -z
vulgarit|y vʌl'gær.ə.t|i, -ɪ.t|i (US) -'ger.ə.t̬|i, -'gær- **-ies** -iz
vulgarization, -isa- ˌvʌl.gᵊr.aɪ'zeɪ.ʃᵊn, -ɪ'- (US) -ɪ'-
vulgariz|e, -is|e 'vʌl.gᵊr.aɪz (US) -gə.raɪz **-es** -ɪz **-ing** -ɪŋ **-ed** -d **-er/s** -əʳ/z (US) -ɚ/z
vulgate (V) 'vʌl.geɪt, -gɪt, -gət (US) -geɪt, -gɪt
Vulliamy 'vʌl.jə.mi
vulnerability ˌvʌl.nᵊr.ə'bɪl.ə.ti, ˌvʌn.ᵊr-, ˌvʌn.rə'-, -ɪ.ti (US) ˌvʌl.nɚ.ə'bɪl.ə.t̬i
vulnerab|le 'vʌl.nᵊr.ə.bl̩, 'vʌn.ᵊr-, 'vʌn.rə.bl̩ (US) 'vʌl.nɚ.ə- **-ly** -li **-leness** -l̩.nəs, -nɪs
Vulpecula vʌl'pek.jə.lə, -jʊ-
vulpine 'vʌl.paɪn (US) -paɪn, -pɪn
vulture 'vʌl.tʃəʳ (US) -tʃɚ **-s** -z

Vowel

Definition

The class of sound which makes the least obstruction to the flow of air. They are almost always found at the centre of a syllable, and it is rare to find any sound other than a vowel which is able to stand alone as a whole syllable.

Examples for English

Here we examine the vowel monophthongs of English. In phonetic terms, each vowel has a number of properties that distinguish it from other vowels. These include the shape of the lips, which may be rounded (as for an [u] vowel), NEUTRAL (as for [ə]) or spread (as in a smile, or an [i] vowel – photographers traditionally ask their subjects to say *cheese* /tʃiːz/ so that they will seem to be smiling):

Unrounded	Rounded	(US) Unrounded	Rounded
iː	uː	iː	uː
ɪ	ʊ	ɪ	ʊ
e	ɔː	e	ɔː
æ	ɒ	æ	
ʌ		ʌ	
ɑː		ɑː	
ɜː		ɝː	
ə		ə ɚ	

Secondly, the front, the middle or the back of the tongue may be raised, giving different vowel qualities: the BBC English /æ/ vowel (*cat*) is a front vowel, while the /ɑː/ of *cart* is a back vowel:

Front	Central	Back	(US) Front	Central	Back
iː	ʌ	uː	iː	ʌ	uː
ɪ	ɜː	ʊ	ɪ	ɝː	ʊ
e	ə	ɔː	e	ə ɚ	ɔː
æ		ɒ	æ		ɑː
		ɑː			

The tongue (and the lower jaw) may be raised close to the roof of the mouth, or the tongue may be left low in the mouth with the jaw comparatively open. In British phonetics we talk about 'close' and 'open' vowels, whereas American phoneticians more often talk about 'high' and 'low' vowels. The meaning is clear in either case, e.g.:

Close	Mid	Open	(US) High	Mid	Low
iː	e	ʌ	iː	e	ʌ
ɪ	ɜː	ɒ	ɪ	ɝː	ɑː
uː	ə	ɑː	uː	ə ɚ	æ
ʊ	ɔː	æ	ʊ	ɔː	

Vowels also differ in other ways: they may be 'nasalised' (see NASALISATION) by being pronounced with the soft palate lowered as for [m n] or [ŋ]. Vowels may be voiced, as the great majority are, or voiceless: in English the first vowel in *perhaps* or *potato* is often voiceless. It is claimed that in some languages (including English) there is a distinction to be made between TENSE and LAX vowels, the former being made with greater force than the latter.

In other languages

Nasalisation is phonemically contrastive in French, where we find 'minimal pairs' such as *très* /trɛ/ (*very*) and *train* /trɛ̃/ (*train*), where the [˜] diacritic indicates nasality. Concerning voiceless vowels: in Portuguese, for example, unstressed vowels in the last syllable of a word are often voiceless. Less usual is the case of stressed voiceless vowels, but these are found in French: close vowels, particularly /i/ but also the close front rounded /y/, become voiceless for some speakers when they are word-final before a pause (for example *oui* [wi̥], *midi* [midi̥], and also *entendu* [ɑ̃tɑ̃dẙ]).

Vowel Reduction

The process by which an unstressed vowel may change to become like the mid central vowel 'schwa' /ə/. In the words 'photograph', 'photographic' and 'photography', the vowels in the first three syllables alternate between full vowels and /ə/ according to the position of stress, e.g.:

photograph /ˈfəʊ.tə.grɑːf/ (US) /ˈfoʊ.t̬ə.græf/
photographic /ˌfəʊ.təˈgræf.ɪk/ (US) /ˈfoʊ.t̬əˈ-/
photography /fəˈtɒg.rəfi/ (US) /-ˈtɑː.grə/

Although the word 'man' is pronounced /mæn/, the reduced form can be seen in 'postman' /ˈpəʊs*t*.mən (US) ˈpoʊs*t*-/, 'chairman' /ˈtʃeə.mən (US) tʃer-/, etc.

Another example of vowel reduction is found in the alternation between /e/ and /ɪ/ in, for example, the first syllables of 'exhibition' /ˌek.sɪˈbɪʃ.ən/ and /ɪgˈzɪb.ɪt/.

vulturine ˈvʌl.tʃᵊr.aɪn, -tʃʊ.raɪn, -tjᵊr.aɪn, -tjʊ.raɪn (US) -tʃə.raɪn, -rɪn

vulturous ˈvʌl.tʃᵊr.əs, -tʃʊ.rəs, -tjᵊr.əs, -tjʊ.rəs (US) -tʃɚ.əs

vulv|a ˈvʌl.v|ə **-as** -əz **-ae** -iː

VW ˌviːˈdʌb.l̩.ju, -juː (US) -juː, -jə **-s** -z

Vye vaɪ

vying (*from* **vie**) ˈvaɪ.ɪŋ

Pronouncing the letter W

See also WH

The consonant letter **w** is most often realised as /w/, e.g.:

wet /wet/
swing /swɪŋ/

In addition

w can be silent. There are four conditions under which this can occur. In the spelling combination **wr**, **w** is not pronounced and the realisation is /r/. In some instances of **tw** when at the beginning of a word, the pronunciation is /t/. Some word-medial **sw** spellings are pronounced /s/. Finally, in (mostly) British place names ending *–wich*, **w** is not normally pronounced, although exceptions do exist. E.g.:

write /raɪt/
two /tuː/
answer /ˈɑːnt.səʳ/ (US) /ˈæn .sɚ/
Greenwich /ˈgren.ɪdʒ/

The examples given above are for **w** in word or syllable-initial position. The letter **w** can also appear at the end of a word or syllable. These instances of **w** are covered at the panels for **aw** and **ow**.

In words borrowed from German, **w** may be pronounced /v/. Words borrowed from Slavic may have /v/ or /f/. E.g.:

Wagner /ˈwɑːg.nəʳ/ (US) /-nɚ/
Krakow /ˈkræk.ɒv, -ɒf/ (US) /ˈkrɑː.kʊf/

w (W) ˈdʌb.l̩.juː, -ju (US) -juː, -jə **-'s** -z
W *(abbrev. for* **west)** west
Waaf, WAAF wæf **-s** -s
Wabash ˈwɔː.bæʃ (US) ˈwɔː-, ˈwɑː-
Wace weɪs
wacko ˈwæk.əʊ (US) -oʊ **-s** -z
wack|y ˈwæk|.i **-ier** -i.əʳ (US) -i.ɚ **-iest** -i.ɪst, -i.əst **-ily** -ɪ.li, -ᵊl.i **-iness** -ɪ.nəs, -ɪ.nɪs
Waco ˈweɪ.kəʊ (US) -koʊ
wad wɒd (US) wɑːd **-s** -z **-ding** -ɪŋ **-ded** -ɪd
Waddell wɒdˈel, ˈwɒd.ᵊl (US) wɑːˈdel, ˈwɑː.dᵊl
wadding ˈwɒd.ɪŋ (US) ˈwɑː.dɪŋ
Waddington ˈwɒd.ɪŋ.tən (US) ˈwɑː.dɪŋ-
waddl|e ˈwɒd.l̩ (US) ˈwɑː.dl̩ **-es** -z **-ing** -ɪŋ, ˈwɒd.lɪŋ (US) ˈwɑːd- **-ed** -d **-er/s** -əʳ/z, ˈwɒd.ləʳ/z (US) ˈwɑː.dl̩.ɚ/z, ˈwɑːd.lɚ/z
wadd|y (W) ˈwɒd|.i (US) ˈwɑː.d|i **-ies** -iz
wad|e (W) weɪd **-es** -z **-ing** -ɪŋ **-ed** -ɪd
Wadebridge ˈweɪd.brɪdʒ
Wade-Giles ˌweɪdˈdʒaɪlz
wader ˈweɪ.dəʳ (US) -dɚ **-s** -z
Wadey ˈweɪ.di
wadg|e wɒdʒ (US) wɑːdʒ **-es** -ɪz
Wadham ˈwɒd.əm (US) ˈwɑː.dəm
Wadhurst ˈwɒd.hɜːst (US) ˈwɑːd.hɝːst
wadi ˈwɒd.i, ˈwæd-, ˈwɑː.di (US) ˈwɑː.di **-s** -z
Wadi Halfa ˌwɒd.iˈhæl.fə, ˌwæd-, ˌwɑː.diˈ- (US) ˌwɑː.diˈhɑːl.fə
Wadman ˈwɒd.mən (US) ˈwɑːd-
Wad Medani ˌwɑːd.məˈdɑː.ni
Wadsworth ˈwɒdz.wəθ, -wɜːθ (US) ˈwɑːdz.wɚθ, -wɝːθ
WAF, Waf wæf **-s** -s
Wafd wɒft, wæft, wɑːft (US) wɑːft
waf|er ˈweɪ.f|əʳ (US) -f|ɚ **-ers** -əz (US) -ɚz **-ery** -ᵊr.i
wafer-thin ˌweɪ.fəˈθɪn (US) -fɚˈ- *stress shift:* ˌwafer-thin ˈmints
waffl|e ˈwɒf.l̩ (US) ˈwɑː.fl̩ **-es** -z **-ing** -ɪŋ, ˈwɒf.lɪŋ (US) ˈwɑːf- **-ed** -d **-er/s** -əʳ/z, ˈwɒf.ləʳ/z (US) ˈwɑː.fl̩.ɚ/z, ˈwɑːf.lɚ/z **-y** -i, ˈwɒf.li (US) ˈwɑː.fl̩.i, ˈwɑːf.li
waffle-iron ˈwɒf.l̩ˌaɪən (US) ˈwɑː.fl̩ˌaɪɚn **-s** -z
waft wɒft, wɑːft (US) wɑːft, wæft **-s** -s **-ing** -ɪŋ **-ed** -ɪd
wag wæg **-s** -z **-ging** -ɪŋ **-ged** -d
wag|e weɪdʒ **-es** -ɪz **-ing** -ɪŋ **-ed** -d ˈ**wage** ˌ**packet**
wage-earner ˈweɪdʒˌɜː.nəʳ (US) -ˌɝː.nɚ **-s** -z
wag|er ˈweɪ.dʒ|əʳ (US) -dʒ|ɚ **-ers** -əz (US) -ɚz **-ering** -ᵊr.ɪŋ **-ered** -əd (US) -ɚd **-erer/s** -ᵊr.əʳ/z (US) -ɚ.ɚ/z
wageworker ˈweɪdʒˌwɜː.kəʳ (US) -ˌwɝː.kɚ **-s** -z
waggish ˈwæg.ɪʃ **-ly** -li **-ness** -nəs, -nɪs
waggl|e ˈwæg.l̩ **-es** -z **-ing** -ɪŋ, ˈwæg.lɪŋ **-ed** -d
waggon ˈwæg.ən **-s** -z
waggoner ˈwæg.ᵊn.əʳ (US) -ɚ **-s** -z
waggonette ˌwæg.əˈnet **-s** -s
Waghorn ˈwæg.hɔːn (US) -hɔːrn
Wagnall ˈwæg.nᵊl
Wagner *English name:* ˈwæg.nəʳ (US) -nɚ *German composer:* ˈvɑːg.nəʳ (US) -nɚ
Wagnerian vɑːgˈnɪə.ri.ən (US) -ˈnɪr.i-, -ˈner- **-s** -z
wagon ˈwæg.ən **-s** -z
wagoner ˈwæg.ə.nəʳ (US) -nɚ **-s** -z
wagonette ˌwæg.əˈnet **-s** -s
wagon-lit ˌvæg.ɔ̃ːnˈliː, ˌvɑːg-, -gɒnˈ-, ˈ--- (US) ˌvɑː.gɔ̃ːnˈliː **-s** -z
Wagstaff ˈwæg.stɑːf (US) -stæf
wagtail ˈwæg.teɪl **-s** -z
Wah(h)abi wəˈhɑː.bi, wɑː- **-s** -z
Wahlberg ˈwɑːl.bɜːg (US) -bɝːg
waif weɪf **-s** -s
Waikiki ˌwaɪ.kiˈkiː, ˈ---
wail weɪl **-s** -z **-ing/ly** -ɪŋ/li **-ed** -d
wain (W) weɪn **-s** -z
Wain(e) weɪn
Wainfleet ˈweɪn.fliːt
wainsco|t ˈweɪn.skə|t, ˈwen-, -skɒ|t (US) ˈweɪn.skə|t, -skɑː|t, -skoʊ|t **-ts** -ts **-t(t)ing** -tɪŋ (US) -t̬ɪŋ **-t(t)ed** -tɪd (US) -t̬ɪd
Wainwright ˈweɪn.raɪt
waist weɪst **-s** -s **-ed** -ɪd
waistband ˈweɪst.bænd **-s** -z
waistcoat ˈweɪst.kəʊt *old-fashioned:* ˈwes.kət, -kɪt (US) ˈwes.kət, ˈweɪst.koʊt **-s** -s
waist-deep ˌweɪstˈdiːp *stress shift:* ˌwaist-deep ˈwater
waist-high ˌweɪstˈhaɪ *stress shift:* ˌwaist-high ˈwater
waistline ˈweɪst.laɪn **-s** -z
wait weɪt **-s** -s **-ing** -ɪŋ (US) ˈweɪ.t̬ɪŋ **-ed** -ɪd (US) ˈweɪ.t̬ɪd ˈ**waiting** ˌ**list**
Waite weɪt
waiter ˈweɪ.təʳ (US) -t̬ɚ **-s** -z
waiting-room ˈweɪ.tɪŋ.rʊm, -ruːm (US) -t̬ɪŋ.ruːm, -rʊm **-s** -z
wait|person ˈweɪt|ˌpɜː.sᵊn (US) -ˌpɝː- **-people** -ˌpiː.pl̩
waitress ˈweɪ.trəs, -trɪs (US) -trɪs **-es** -ɪz
Waitrose® ˈweɪ.trəʊz (US) -troʊz
waiv|e weɪv **-es** -z **-ing** -ɪŋ **-ed** -d
waiver ˈweɪ.vəʳ (US) -vɚ **-s** -z
Wajda ˈvaɪ.də
wak|e weɪk **-es** -s **-ing** -ɪŋ **-ed** -t **woke** wəʊk (US) woʊk **woken** ˈwəʊ.kᵊn (US) ˈwoʊ-
Wakefield ˈweɪk.fiːld
wakeful ˈweɪk.fᵊl, -fʊl **-ly** -i **-ness** -nəs, -nɪs

Wakeham ˈweɪ.kəm
Wakehurst ˈweɪk.hɜːst (US) -hɝːst
Wakeling ˈweɪ.klɪŋ
Wakeman ˈweɪk.mən
waken ˈweɪ.kᵊn **-s** -z **-ing** -ɪŋ, ˈweɪk.nɪŋ **-ed** -d
wakey wakey ˌweɪ.kiˈweɪ.ki
Wakley ˈweɪ.kli
Wakonda wəˈkɒn.də (US) wɑːˈkɑːn-
Wal wɒl, wɔːl (US) wɑːl
Walachi|a wɒlˈeɪ.ki|.ə, wəˈleɪ- (US) wɑːˈleɪ-, wə- **-an/s** -ən/z
Walberswick ˈwɔːl.bəz.wɪk, ˈwɒl- (US) ˈwɔːl.bɚz-, ˈwɑːl-
Walbrook ˈwɔːl.brʊk, ˈwɒl- (US) ˈwɔːl-, ˈwɑːl-
Walcott ˈwɔːl.kət, ˈwɒl-, -kɒt (US) ˈwɔːl.kət, ˈwɑːl-, -kɑːt
Waldeck ˈwɔːl.dek, ˈwɒl- (US) ˈwɔːl-, ˈvɑːl-
Waldegrave ˈwɔːl.greɪv, ˈwɒl-, -də.greɪv (US) ˈwɔːl-, ˈwɑːl-
Note: Earl Waldegrave is /ˈwɔːl.greɪv, ˈwɒl- (US) ˈwɔːl-, ˈwɑːl-/; the politician William Waldegrave is /ˈwɔːl.də.greɪv, ˈwɒl- (US) ˈwɔːl-, ˈwɑːl-/.
Waldemar ˈvæl.də.mɑːʳ, ˈvɑːl-, ˈwɔːl-, -dɪ- (US) ˈvɑːl.də.mɑːr
Walden ˈwɔːl.dᵊn, ˈwɒl- (US) ˈwɔːl-, ˈwɑːl-
Waldheim ˈvɑːld.haɪm *as if German:* ˈvælt- (US) ˈwɑːld- *as if German:* ˈvɑːlt-
Waldhere ˈwɑːldˌheə.rə (US) ˈwɔːldˌher.ə, ˈwɑːld-
Waldo ˈwɔːl.dəʊ, ˈwɒl- (US) ˈwɔːl.doʊ, ˈwɑːl-
Waldock ˈwɔːl.dɒk, ˈwɒl- (US) ˈwɔːl.dɑːk, ˈwɑːl-
Waldorf ˈwɔːl.dɔːf, ˈwɒl- (US) ˈwɔːl.dɔːrf, ˈwɑːl- **ˌWaldorf ˈsalad**
Waldron ˈwɔːl.drən, ˈwɒl- (US) ˈwɔːl-, ˈwɑːl-
Waldstein *American name:* ˈwɔːld.staɪn, ˈwɒld- (US) ˈwɔːld-, ˈwɑːld- *German name, Beethoven sonata:* ˈvæld.staɪn, ˈvɑːld-, ˈvɔːld-, ˈvɒld-, ˈwɔːld-, ˈwɒld-, -ʃtaɪn (US) ˈvɑːlt.ʃtaɪn, ˈvɑːld-
wale weɪl **-s** -z
waler (W) ˈweɪ.ləʳ (US) -lɚ **-s** -z
Waleran *Baron:* ˈwɔːl.rən, ˈwɒl- (US) ˈwɔːl-, ˈwɑːl- *buildings in Borough High Street, London:* ˈwɒl.ᵊr.ən (US) ˈwɑː.lɚ-, ˈwɔː-
Wales weɪlz
Walesa vɑːˈwent.sə, væˈ- (US) wɑːˈlent.sə; vɑːˈwent.sɑː
Waley ˈweɪ.li
Walfish ˈwɔːl.fɪʃ, ˈwɒl- (US) ˈwɔːl-, ˈwɑːl-
Walford ˈwɔːl.fəd, ˈwɒl- (US) ˈwɔːl.fɚd, ˈwɑːl-
Walhalla vælˈhæl.ə (US) wɑːlˈhɑː.lə; wælˈhæl.ə, væl-
Walham ˈwɒl.əm (US) ˈwɑː.ləm
walk wɔːk (US) wɑːk, wɔːk **-s** -s **-ing** -ɪŋ **-ed** -t **-er/s** -əʳ/z (US) -ɚ/z **ˈwalking ˌstick**
walkabout ˈwɔː.kəˌbaʊt (US) ˈwɑː-, ˈwɔː- **-s** -s
walkaway ˈwɔː.kə.weɪ (US) ˈwɑː-, ˈwɔː-
Walkden ˈwɔːk.dən (US) ˈwɑːk-, ˈwɔːk-
Walker ˈwɔː.kəʳ (US) ˈwɑː.kɚ, ˈwɔː-
Walkern ˈwɔːl.kən, -kɜːn (US) ˈwɔːl.kɚn, ˈwɑːl-, -kɝːn
walkies ˈwɔː.kiz (US) ˈwɑː-, ˈwɔː-
walkie-talkie ˌwɔː.kiˈtɔː.ki (US) ˌwɑː.kiˈtɑː-, ˌwɔː-, -ˈtɔː- **-s** -z
walk-in ˈwɔːk.ɪn (US) ˈwɑːk-, ˈwɔːk-
Walkman® ˈwɔːk.mən (US) ˈwɑːk-, ˈwɔːk- **-s** -z
walk-on ˈwɔːk.ɒn (US) ˈwɑːk.ɑːn, ˈwɔːk- **-s** -z
walkout ˈwɔːk.aʊt (US) ˈwɑːk-, ˈwɔːk- **-s** -s
walkover ˈwɔːkˌəʊ.vəʳ (US) ˈwɑːkˌoʊ.vɚ, ˈwɔːk- **-s** -z
walkway ˈwɔːk.weɪ (US) ˈwɑːk-, ˈwɔːk- **-s** -z
Walkyrie vælˈkɪə.ri; ˈvæl.kᵊr.i, -kɪ.ri (US) wɑːlˈkɪr.i; ˈwɑːl.kɚ-, ˈvɑːl- **-s** -z
walky-talk|y ˌwɔː.kiˈtɔː.k|i (US) ˌwɑː.kiˈtɑː-, ˌwɔː-, -ˈtɔː- **-ies** -iz
wall (W) wɔːl (US) wɔːl, wɑːl **-s** -z **-ing** -ɪŋ **-ed** -d **ˈWall ˌStreet; ˌWall Street ˈJournal; ˌbang one's ˌhead against a ˌbrick ˈwall**
wallab|y (W) ˈwɒl.ə.b|i (US) ˈwɑː.lə- **-ies** -iz
Wallace ˈwɒl.ɪs, -əs (US) ˈwɑː.lɪs, -ləs
Wallach ˈwɒl.ək (US) ˈwɑː.lək **-s** -s
Wallachi|a wɒlˈeɪ.ki|.ə, wəˈleɪ- (US) wɑːˈleɪ- **-an/s** -an/z
walla(h) ˈwɒl.ə (US) ˈwɑː.lɑː **-s** -z
Wallasey ˈwɒl.ə.si (US) ˈwɑː.lə-
wallboard ˈwɔːl.bɔːd (US) ˈwɔːl.bɔːrd, ˈwɑːl-
wallchart ˈwɔːl.tʃɑːt (US) -tʃɑːrt, ˈwɑːl- **-s** -s
Waller ˈwɒl.əʳ (US) ˈwɑː.lɚ
wallet ˈwɒl.ɪt (US) ˈwɑː.lɪt **-s** -s
wall-eye ˈwɔːl.aɪ (US) ˈwɔːl-, ˈwɑːl- **-s** -z **-d** -d
wallflower ˈwɔːl.flaʊəʳ (US) -flaʊɚ, ˈwɑːl- **-s** -z
Wallingford ˈwɒl.ɪŋ.fəd (US) ˈwɑː.lɪŋ.fɚd
Wallington ˈwɒl.ɪŋ.tən (US) ˈwɑː.lɪŋ-
Wallis ˈwɒl.ɪs (US) ˈwɑː.lɪs
Wallonia wəˈləʊ.ni.ə (US) wɑːˈloʊ-
Walloon wɒlˈuːn, wəˈluːn (US) wɑːˈluːn **-s** -z
wallop ˈwɒl.əp (US) ˈwɑː.ləp **-s** -s **-ing/s** -ɪŋ/z **-ed** -t
wallow ˈwɒl.əʊ (US) ˈwɑː.loʊ **-s** -z **-ing** -ɪŋ **-ed** -d **-er/s** -əʳ/z (US) -ɚ/z
wallpap|er ˈwɔːlˌpeɪ.p|əʳ (US) -p|ɚ, ˈwɑːl- **-ers** -əz (US) -ɚz **-ering** -ᵊr.ɪŋ **-ered** -əd (US) -ɚd
Wallsend ˈwɔːl.zend (US) ˈwɔːl-, ˈwɑːl-
wall-to-wall ˌwɔːl.təˈwɔːl, -tuˈ- (US) -t̬əˈ-, ˌwɑːl-, -ˈwɑːl
Wallwork ˈwɔːl.wɜːk, ˈwɒl- (US) ˈwɔːl.wɝːk, ˈwɑːl-
wall|y (W) ˈwɒl|.i (US) ˈwɑː.l|i **-ies** -iz
Wal-Mart® ˈwɒl.mɑːt (US) ˈwɔːl.mɑːrt, ˈwɑːl-
Walmer ˈwɔːl.məʳ, ˈwɒl- (US) ˈwɔːl.mɚ, ˈwɑːl-
Walm(e)sley ˈwɔːmz.li (US) ˈwɑːmz-, ˈwɔːmz-
Walmisley ˈwɔːmz.li (US) ˈwɑːmz-, ˈwɔːmz-
Walney ˈwɔːl.ni, ˈwɒl- (US) ˈwɔːl-, ˈwɑːl-
walnut ˈwɔːl.nʌt, -nət (US) ˈwɔːl-, ˈwɑːl- **-s** -s
Walpole ˈwɔːl.pəʊl, ˈwɒl- (US) ˈwɔːl.poʊl, ˈwɑːl-
Walpurgis vælˈpʊə.gɪs, vɑːl-, -ˈpɜː- (US) vɑːlˈpʊr.gɪs
walrus ˈwɔːl.rəs, ˈwɒl-, -rʌs (US) ˈwɔːl.rəs, ˈwɑːl- **-es** -ɪz
Walsall ˈwɔːl.sɔːl, ˈwɒl-, -sᵊl (US) ˈwɔːl.sɔːl, ˈwɑːl-, -sɑːl
Walsh wɒlʃ, wɔːlʃ (US) wɔːlʃ, wɑːlʃ
Walsham ˈwɔːl.ʃəm *locally:* -səm (US) ˈwɔːl-, ˈwɑːl-
Walsingham *surname:* ˈwɔːl.sɪŋ.əm, ˈwɒl- (US) ˈwɔːl-, ˈwɑːl- *place:* ˈwɔːl.zɪŋ.əm, ˈwɒl-, -sɪŋ- (US) ˈwɔːl-, ˈwɑːl-
Walt wɒlt, wɔːlt (US) wɔːlt, wɑːlt
Walter *English name:* ˈwɒl.təʳ, ˈwɔːl- (US) ˈwɔːl.t̬ɚ, ˈwɑːl- *German name:* ˈvɑːl.təʳ (US) -t̬ɚ
Walter Mitty ˌwɒl.təˈmɪt.i, ˌwɔːl- (US) ˌwɔːl.t̬ɚˈmɪt̬-, ˌwɑːl-
Walters ˈwɒl.təz, ˈwɔːl- (US) ˈwɔːl.t̬ɚz, ˈwɑːl-
Waltham ***Great** and **Little**, in Essex:* ˈwɔːl.təm, ˈwɒl- (US) ˈwɔːl-, ˈwɑːl-
Note: Some new residents pronounce /-θəm/. *other places:* ˈwɔːl.θəm, ˈwɒl- (US) ˈwɔːl-, ˈwɑːl- **ˌWaltham ˈForest**
Walthamstow ˈwɒl.θəm.stəʊ, ˈwɔːl- (US) ˈwɔːl.θəm.stoʊ, ˈwɑːl-
Walther ˈvɑːl.təʳ (US) -t̬ɚ
Walton ˈwɒl.tᵊn, ˈwɔːl- (US) ˈwɔːl-, ˈwɑːl-
Walton-on-the-Naze ˌwɒl.tᵊnˌɒn.ðəˈneɪz, ˌwɔːl- (US) ˌwɔːl.tᵊnˌɑːn-, ˌwɑːl-
waltz wɒls, wɔːls, wɒlts, wɔːlts (US) wɔːlts, wɑːlts **-es** -ɪz **-ing** -ɪŋ **-ed** -t **-er/s** -əʳ/z (US) -ɚ/z

Walworth ˈwɒl.wəθ, ˈwɔːl-, -wɜːθ (US) ˈwɔːl.wɝːθ, ˈwɑːl-, -wɚθ
wampum ˈwɒm.pəm (US) ˈwɑːm-, ˈwɔːm- **-s** -z
WAN wæn
wan wɒn (US) wɑːn **-ner** -əʳ (US) -ɚ **-nest** -ɪst, -əst **-ly** -li **-ness** -nəs, -nɪs
Wanamaker ˈwɒn.ə.meɪ.kəʳ (US) ˈwɑː.nə.meɪ.kɚ
wand (W) wɒnd (US) wɑːnd **-s** -z
Wanda ˈwɒn.də (US) ˈwɑːn-
wand|er ˈwɒn.d|əʳ (US) ˈwɑːn.d|ɚ **-ers** -əz (US) -ɚz **-ering/s** -ər.ɪŋ/z **-ered** -əd (US) -ɚd **-erer/s** -ər.əʳ/z (US) -ɚ.ɚ/z
wanderlust ˈwɒn.də.lʌst, ˈvɑːn.də.lʊst (US) ˈwɑːn.dɚ.lʌst
Wandle ˈwɒn.dl̩ (US) ˈwɑːn-
Wandsworth ˈwɒn*dz*.wəθ (US) ˈwɑːn*dz*.wɚθ
wan|e weɪn **-es** -z **-ing** -ɪŋ **-ed** -d
Wang® wæŋ
Wanganui *in New Zealand:* ˌwɒŋ.əˈnuː.i, ˌwɒn.gə- (US) ˌwɔːŋ.gə-, ˌwɑːn-
Note: The first is the form always used by those of Polynesian descent.
wangl|e ˈwæŋ.gl̩ **-es** -z **-ing** -ɪŋ (US) ˈwæŋ.glɪŋ **-ed** -d
wank wæŋk **-s** -s **-ing** -ɪŋ **-ed** -t
wanker ˈwæŋ.kəʳ (US) -kɚ **-s** -z
Wann wɒn (US) wɑːn
wanna ˈwɒn.ə (US) ˈwɑː.nə
wannabe(e) ˈwɒn.ə.bi, -biː (US) ˈwɑː.nə- **-s** -z
Wansbeck ˈwɒnz.bek (US) ˈwɑːnz-
Wanstall ˈwɒn.stɔːl (US) ˈwɑːn.stɑːl, -stɔːl
Wanstead ˈwɒn*t*.sted, -stɪd (US) ˈwɑːn*t*-
wan|t wɒn|t (US) wɑːn|t, wɔːn|t, wʌn|t **-ts** -ts **-ting** -tɪŋ (US) -t̬ɪŋ **-ted** -tɪd (US) -t̬ɪd
Wantage ˈwɒn.tɪdʒ (US) ˈwɑːn.t̬ɪdʒ
wanton ˈwɒn.tən (US) ˈwɑːn.tən **-ly** -li **-ness** -nəs, -nɪs
WAP, Wap wæp, wɒp (US) wɑːp, wæp
wapentake ˈwæp.ən.teɪk, ˈwɒp- (US) ˈwɑː.pən-, ˈwæp.ən- **-s** -s
wapiti ˈwɒp.ɪ.ti (US) ˈwɑː.pə.t̬i **-s** -z
Wapping ˈwɒp.ɪŋ (US) ˈwɑː.pɪŋ
Wappinger ˈwɒp.ɪn.dʒəʳ (US) ˈwɑː.pɪn.dʒɚ
war wɔːʳ (US) wɔːr **-s** -z **-ring** -ɪŋ **-red** -d **ˈwar ˌcrime; ˈwar ˌdance; ˈwar ˌgame; ˈwar meˌmorial; ˌwar of ˈnerves; ˈwar ˌpaint; ˈwar ˌwidow**
Warbeck ˈwɔː.bek (US) ˈwɔːr-
warbl|e ˈwɔː.bl̩ (US) ˈwɔːr- **-es** -z **-ing** -ɪŋ, ˈ-blɪŋ (US) ˈwɔːr.bl̩.ɪŋ, ˈ-blɪŋ **-ed** -d
warbler ˈwɔː.bləʳ, -bl̩.əʳ (US) ˈwɔːr.blɚ, -bl̩.ɚ **-s** -z
Warburg ˈwɔː.bɜːg (US) ˈwɔːr.bɝːg
Warburton ˈwɔː.bə.tən, -bɜː- (US) ˈwɔːr.bɚ-, -bɝː-
war-cr|y ˈwɔː.kr|aɪ (US) ˈwɔːr- **-ies** -aɪz
ward (W) wɔːd (US) wɔːrd **-s** -z **-ing** -ɪŋ **-ed** -ɪd
-ward -wəd (US) -wɚd
Note: Suffix. Normally unstressed, e.g. **homeward** /ˈhəʊm.wəd (US) ˈhoʊm.wɚd/.
warden (W) ˈwɔː.dən (US) ˈwɔːr- **-s** -z
warder (W) ˈwɔː.dəʳ (US) ˈwɔːr.dɚ **-s** -z
Wardlaw ˈwɔːd.lɔː (US) ˈwɔːrd.lɑː, -lɔː
Wardle ˈwɔː.dl̩ (US) ˈwɔːr-
Wardour ˈwɔː.dəʳ (US) ˈwɔːr.dɚ
wardress *fem. warder:* ˈwɔː.drɪs, -drəs (US) ˈwɔːr.drɪs **-es** -ɪz
war-dress *war costume:* ˈwɔː.dres (US) ˈwɔːr- **-es** -ɪz
wardrobe ˈwɔː.drəʊb (US) ˈwɔːr.droʊb **-s** -z
wardroom ˈwɔːd.rʊm, -ruːm (US) ˈwɔːrd.ruːm, -rʊm **-s** -z
-wards -wədz (US) -wɚdz
Note: See note for **-ward**.
wardship ˈwɔːd.ʃɪp (US) ˈwɔːrd- **-s** -s
ware (W) weəʳ (US) wer **-s** -z
-ware -weəʳ (US) -wer
Note: Suffix. Normally unstressed, e.g. **tableware** /ˈteɪ.bl̩.weəʳ (US) -wer/.
Wareham ˈweə.rəm (US) ˈwer.əm
warehou|se (*n.*) ˈweə.haʊ|s (US) ˈwer- **-ses** -zɪz
warehou|se (*v.*) ˈweə.haʊ|z, -haʊ|s (US) ˈwer- **-ses** -zɪz, -sɪz **-sing** -zɪŋ, -sɪŋ **-sed** -zd, -st
warehouse|man ˈweə.haʊs|.mən (US) ˈwer- **-men** -mən
warfare ˈwɔː.feəʳ (US) ˈwɔːr.fer
warfarin ˈwɔː.fər.ɪn (US) ˈwɔːr-
Wargrave ˈwɔː.greɪv (US) ˈwɔːr-
Warham ˈwɔː.rəm (US) ˈwɔːr.əm
warhead ˈwɔː.hed (US) ˈwɔːr- **-s** -z
Warhol ˈwɔː.həʊl (US) ˈwɔːr.hɔːl, -hoʊl
warhors|e ˈwɔː.hɔːs (US) ˈwɔːr.hɔːrs **-es** -ɪz
Waring ˈweə.rɪŋ (US) ˈwer.ɪŋ
warlike ˈwɔː.laɪk (US) ˈwɔːr-
Warlingham ˈwɔː.lɪŋ.əm (US) ˈwɔːr-
warlock (W) ˈwɔː.lɒk (US) ˈwɔːr- **-s** -s
warlord ˈwɔː.lɔːd (US) ˈwɔːr.lɔːrd **-s** -z
warm wɔːm (US) wɔːrm **-er** -əʳ (US) -ɚ **-est** -ɪst, -əst **-ly** -li **-ness** -nəs, -nɪs **-s** -z **-ing** -ɪŋ **-ed** -d
warm-blooded ˌwɔːmˈblʌd.ɪd (US) ˌwɔːrm- **-ness** -nəs, -nɪs *stress shift:* ˌwarm-blooded ˈanimal
warmer ˈwɔː.məʳ (US) ˈwɔːr.mɚ **-s** -z
warm-hearted ˌwɔːmˈhɑː.tɪd (US) ˌwɔːrmˈhɑːr.t̬ɪd **-ly** -li **-ness** -nəs, -nɪs *stress shift:* ˌwarm-hearted ˈperson
warming-pan ˈwɔː.mɪŋ.pæn (US) ˈwɔːr- **-s** -z
Warmington ˈwɔː.mɪŋ.tən (US) ˈwɔːr-
Warminster ˈwɔː.mɪn*t*.stəʳ (US) ˈwɔːr.mɪn*t*.stɚ
warmong|er ˈwɔːˌmʌŋ.g|əʳ (US) ˈwɑːrˌmʌŋ.g|ɚ, ˈwɔːr-, -ˌmɑːŋ- **-ers** -əz (US) -ɚz **-ering** -ər.ɪŋ
warmth wɔːm*p*θ (US) wɔːrm*p*θ
warn wɔːn (US) wɔːrn **-s** -z **-ing/ly** -ɪŋ/li **-ed** -d
Warne wɔːn (US) wɔːrn
Warner ˈwɔː.nəʳ (US) ˈwɔːr.nɚ
warning ˈwɔː.nɪŋ (US) ˈwɔːr- **-s** -z
Warnock ˈwɔː.nɒk (US) ˈwɔːr.nɑːk
warp wɔːp (US) wɔːrp **-s** -s **-ing** -ɪŋ **-ed** -t
warpath ˈwɔː.pɑːθ (US) ˈwɔːr.pæθ
warr|ant ˈwɒr|.ənt (US) ˈwɔːr-, ˈwɑːr- **-ants** -ənts **-anting** -ən.tɪŋ (US) -ən.t̬ɪŋ **-anted** -ən.tɪd (US) -ən.t̬ɪd **-anter/s** -ən.təʳ/z (US) -ən.t̬ɚ/z **ˈwarrant ˌofficer**
warrantab|le ˈwɒr.ən.tə.bl̩ (US) ˈwɔːr.ən.t̬ə-, ˈwɑːr- **-ly** -li **-leness** -l̩.nəs, -nɪs
warrantee ˌwɒr.ənˈtiː (US) ˌwɔːr-, ˌwɑːr- **-s** -z
warrantor ˈwɒr.ən.tɔːʳ, -təʳ, ˌwɒr.ənˈtɔːʳ (US) ˈwɔːr.ən.tɔːr, ˈwɑːr-, -t̬ɚ **-s** -z
warrant|y ˈwɒr.ən.t|i (US) ˈwɔːr.ən.t̬|i, ˈwɑːr- **-ies** -iz
Warre wɔːʳ (US) wɔːr
warren (W) ˈwɒr.ən, -ɪn (US) ˈwɔːr.ən, ˈwɑːr- **-s** -z
Warrender ˈwɒr.ən.dəʳ, -ɪn- (US) ˈwɔːr.ən.dɚ, ˈwɑːr-, -ɪn-
Warrenpoint ˈwɒr.ən.pɔɪnt, -əm- (US) ˈwɔːr.ən-, ˈwɑːr-
Warrington ˈwɒr.ɪŋ.tən (US) ˈwɔːr-, ˈwɑːr-
warrior (W) ˈwɒr.i.əʳ (US) ˈwɔːr.jɚ, ˈwɑːr-, -i.ɚ **-s** -z
Warrnambool ˈwɔː.nəm.buːl (US) ˈwɔːr-
Warsaw ˈwɔː.sɔː (US) ˈwɔːr.sɑː, -sɔː **ˌWarsaw ˈPact**
warship ˈwɔː.ʃɪp (US) ˈwɔːr- **-s** -s
Warsop ˈwɔː.səp (US) ˈwɔːr-
Warspite ˈwɔː.spaɪt (US) ˈwɔːr-
wart wɔːt (US) wɔːrt **-s** -s **-y** -i (US) ˈwɔːr.t̬i
warthog ˈwɔːt.hɒg (US) ˈwɔːrt.hɑːg, -hɔːg **-s** -z
wartime ˈwɔː.taɪm (US) ˈwɔːr-
Warton ˈwɔː.tən (US) ˈwɔːr-
war-weary ˈwɔːˌwɪə.ri (US) ˈwɔːrˌwɪr.i
Warwick *in Britain:* ˈwɒr.ɪk (US) ˈwɔːr.ɪk, ˈwɑːr- **-shire** -ʃəʳ, -ˌʃɪəʳ (US) -ʃɚ, -ˌʃɪr *in US:* ˈwɔː.wɪk (US) ˈwɔːr-
war-worn ˈwɔː.wɔːn (US) ˈwɔːr.wɔːrn
war|y ˈweə.r|i (US) ˈwer|.i **-ier** -i.əʳ (US) -i.ɚ **-iest** -i.ɪst, -i.əst **-ily** -əl.i, -ɪ.li **-iness** -ɪ.nəs, -ɪ.nɪs

was *(from* **be***) strong forms:* wɒz
(US) wɑːz, wʌz *weak forms:* wəz, wz
Note: Weak form word. The strong forms are used in contrastive contexts (e.g. 'I don't know whether it **was** or it **wasn't**), and for emphasis (e.g. 'I **was** right!'). The strong form is also usual in final position (e.g. 'That's where it was'). The weak forms are used elsewhere; the form /wz/ is found only in rapid, casual speech.
Wasbrough ˈwɒz.brə (US) ˈwɑːz-
wash (W) wɒʃ (US) wɑːʃ, wɔːʃ **-es** -ɪz **-ing** -ɪŋ **-ed** -t **-able** -ə.bl̩ ˌ**wash and** ˈ**wear**
Wash. *(abbrev. for* **Washington***)* ˈwɒʃ.ɪŋ.tən (US) ˈwɑː.ʃɪŋ-, ˈwɔː-
washbasin ˈwɒʃˌbeɪ.sᵊn (US) ˈwɑːʃ-, ˈwɔːʃ- **-s** -z
washboard ˈwɒʃ.bɔːd (US) ˈwɑːʃ.bɔːrd, ˈwɔːʃ- **-s** -z
washbowl ˈwɒʃ.bəʊl (US) ˈwɑːʃ.boʊl, ˈwɔːʃ- **-s** -z
wash|cloth ˈwɒʃ|.klɒθ (US) ˈwɑːʃ|.klɑːθ, ˈwɔːʃ- **-cloths** -klɒθs, -klɒðz (US) -klɑːθs, -klɑːðz
washday ˈwɒʃ.deɪ (US) ˈwɑːʃ-, ˈwɔːʃ- **-s** -z
washed-out ˌwɒʃtˈaʊt (US) ˌwɑːʃt-, ˌwɔːʃt- *stress shift:* ˌwashed-out ˈcolour
washed-up ˌwɒʃtˈʌp (US) ˌwɑːʃt-, ˌwɔːʃt- *stress shift:* ˌwashed-up ˈwriter
washer ˈwɒʃ.əʳ (US) ˈwɑː.ʃɚ, ˈwɔː- **-s** -z
washer-dryer ˌwɒʃ.əˈdraɪ.əʳ (US) ˌwɑː.ʃɚˈdraɪ.ɚ, ˌwɔː- **-s** -z
washer-up ˌwɒʃ.əʳˈʌp (US) ˌwɑː.ʃɚ-, ˌwɔː- **washers-up** ˌwɒʃ.əzˈ- (US) ˌwɑː.ʃɚzˈ-, ˌwɔː-
washer|woman ˈwɒʃ.ə|ˌwʊm.ən (US) ˈwɑː.ʃɚ-, ˈwɔː- **-women** -ˌwɪm.ɪn
wash-hou|se ˈwɒʃ.haʊ|s (US) ˈwɑːʃ-, ˈwɔːʃ- **-ses** -zɪz
washing ˈwɒʃ.ɪŋ (US) ˈwɑː.ʃɪŋ, ˈwɔː- ˈwashing maˌchine; ˈwashing ˌpowder
Washingborough ˈwɒʃ.ɪŋˌbʌr.ə (US) ˈwɑː.ʃɪŋ.bɚ.oʊ, ˈwɔː-
Washington ˈwɒʃ.ɪŋ.tən (US) ˈwɑː.ʃɪŋ-, ˈwɔː- ˌWashington ˌDˈC; ˌWashington ˈState
Washingtonian ˌwɒʃ.ɪŋˈtəʊ.ni.ən (US) ˌwɑː.ʃɪŋˈtoʊ-, ˌwɔː- **-s** -z
washing-up ˌwɒʃ.ɪŋˈʌp (US) ˌwɑː.ʃɪŋˈ-, ˌwɔː-
washout ˈwɒʃ.aʊt (US) ˈwɑːʃ-, ˈwɔːʃ- **-s** -s
washrag ˈwɒʃ.ræg (US) ˈwɑːʃ-, ˈwɔːʃ- **-s** -z
washroom ˈwɒʃ.rʊm, -ruːm (US) ˈwɑːʃ.ruːm, ˈwɔːʃ-, -rʊm **-s** -z
washstand ˈwɒʃ.stænd (US) ˈwɑːʃ-, ˈwɔːʃ- **-s** -z
wash-tub ˈwɒʃ.tʌb (US) ˈwɑːʃ-, ˈwɔːʃ- **-s** -z
wash|y ˈwɒʃ|.i (US) ˈwɑː.ʃ|i, ˈwɔː- **-ier** -i.əʳ (US) -i.ɚ **-iest** -i.ɪst, -i.əst **-iness** -ɪ.nəs, -ɪ.nɪs
wasn't ˈwɒz.ᵊnt (US) ˈwɑː.zᵊnt, ˈwʌz-
wasp, WASP (W) wɒsp (US) wɑːsp **-s** -s
waspish ˈwɒs.pɪʃ (US) ˈwɑː.spɪʃ **-ly** -li **-ness** -nəs, -nɪs
wassail ˈwɒs.eɪl, ˈwæs-, -ᵊl (US) ˈwɑː.sᵊl, ˈwæs.ᵊl, -eɪl; wɑːˈseɪl **-s** -z
wassailing ˈwɒs.ᵊl.ɪŋ, ˈwæs-, -eɪ.lɪŋ (US) ˈwɑː.sᵊl.ɪŋ, ˈwæs.ᵊl-, -eɪ.lɪŋ; wɑːˈseɪ.lɪŋ
Wassell ˈwæs.ᵊl
Wasson ˈwɒs.ᵊn (US) ˈwɑː.sᵊn
wast *(from* **be***) strong forms:* wɒst (US) wɑːst *weak form:* wəst
Wast wɒst (US) wɑːst
wast|e weɪst **-es** -s **-ing** -ɪŋ **-ed** -ɪd **-er/s** -əʳ/z (US) -ɚ/z **-age** -ɪdʒ ˈwaste ˌproduct, ˌwaste ˈproduct
wastebasket ˈweɪst*t*ˌbɑː.skɪt (US) -ˌbæs.kət **-s** -s
wasteful ˈweɪst*t*.fᵊl, -fʊl **-ly** -i **-ness** -nəs, -nɪs
wasteland ˈweɪst*t*.lænd **-s** -z
wastepaper ˌweɪst*t*ˈpeɪ.pəʳ, ˈ-ˌ-- (US) ˈweɪst*t*ˌpeɪ.pɚ wasteˈpaper ˌbasket, ˈwastepaper ˌbasket; wasteˈpaper ˌbin
wastepipe ˈweɪst*t*.paɪp **-s** -s
wastrel ˈweɪ.strᵊl **-s** -z
Wastwater ˈwɒstˌwɔː.təʳ (US) ˈwɑːstˌwɑː.t̬ɚ, -ˌwɔː-
Wat wɒt (US) wɑːt
watch wɒtʃ (US) wɑːtʃ, wɔːtʃ **-es** -ɪz **-ing** -ɪŋ **-ed** -t **-er/s** -əʳ/z (US) -ɚ/z
watchable ˈwɒtʃ.ə.bl̩ (US) ˈwɑː.tʃə-, ˈwɔː-
watchamacallit ˈwɒtʃ.ə.məˌkɔːl.ɪt (US) ˈwɑː.tʃə-, ˈwɔː-, -ˌkɑːl- **-s** -s
watch-cas|e ˈwɒtʃ.keɪs (US) ˈwɑːtʃ-, ˈwɔːtʃ- **-es** -ɪz
watchdog ˈwɒtʃ.dɒg (US) ˈwɑːtʃ.dɑːg, ˈwɔːtʃ-, -dɔːg **-s** -z
Watchet ˈwɒtʃ.ɪt (US) ˈwɑː.tʃɪt, ˈwɔː-
watchful ˈwɒtʃ.fᵊl, -fʊl (US) ˈwɑːtʃ-, ˈwɔːtʃ- **-ly** -i **-ness** -nəs, -nɪs
watchmak|er ˈwɒtʃˌmeɪ.k|əʳ (US) ˈwɑːtʃˌmeɪ.k|ɚ, ˈwɔːtʃ- **-ers** -əz (US) -ɚz **-ing** -ɪŋ
watch|man ˈwɒtʃ|.mən (US) ˈwɑːtʃ-, ˈwɔːtʃ- **-men** -mən, -men
watchstrap ˈwɒtʃ.stræp (US) ˈwɑːtʃ-, ˈwɔːtʃ- **-s** -s
watchtower (W) ˈwɒtʃ.taʊəʳ (US) ˈwɑːtʃ.taʊɚ, ˈwɔːtʃ- **-s** -z
watchword ˈwɒtʃ.wɜːd (US) ˈwɑːtʃ.wɝːd, ˈwɔːtʃ- **-s** -z
wat|er ˈwɔː.t|əʳ (US) ˈwɑː.t̬|ɚ, ˈwɔː- **-ers** -əz (US) -ɚz **-ering** -ᵊr.ɪŋ **-ered** -əd (US) -ɚd ˈwater ˌbed; ˈwater ˌbeetle ˈwater ˌbottle; ˈwater ˌbuffalo,; ˌwater ˈbuffalo (US) ˈwater ˌbuffalo; ˈwater ˌcannon; ˌwater ˈchestnut (US) ˈwater ˌchestnut; ˈwater ˌcloset ˈwater ˌice; ˈwater ˌmain; ˈwater ˌmeadow; ˈwater ˌmill; ˈwater supˌply; ˈwater ˌtable; ˈwater ˌtow ˌkeep one's ˌhead above ˈwater; ˌpour cold ˈwater on; like ˌwater of ˌduck's ˈback; (US) like ˌwater off a ˈduck's ˌback; ˌwater ˌunder the ˈbridge
water-borne ˈwɔː.tə.bɔːn (US) ˈwɑː.t̬ɚ.bɔːrn, ˈwɔː-
waterbuck ˈwɔː.tə.bʌk (US) ˈwɑː.t̬ɚ-, ˈwɔː-
Waterbur|y ˈwɔː.tə.bᵊr|.i (US) ˈwɑː.t̬ɚˌber-, ˈwɔː-, -bɚ- **-ies** -i
water-chute ˈwɔː.tə.ʃuːt (US) ˈwɑː.t̬ɚ ˈwɔː- **-s** -s
watercolo(u)r ˈwɔː.təˌkʌl.əʳ (US) ˈwɑː.t̬ɚˌkʌl.ɚ, ˈwɔː- **-s** -z
watercolo(u)rist ˈwɔː.təˌkʌl.ᵊr.ɪst (US) ˈwɑː.t̬ɚ-, ˈwɔː- **-s** -s
water-cooled ˌwɔː.təˈkuːld (US) ˈwɑː.t̬ɚ.kuːld, ˈwɔː- *stress shif British only:* ˌwater-cooled ˈengine
watercours|e ˈwɔː.tə.kɔːs (US) ˈwɑː.t̬ɚ.kɔːrs, ˈwɔː- **-es** -ɪz
watercress ˈwɔː.tə.kres (US) ˈwɑː.t̬ɚ-, ˈwɔː-
water-divin|ing ˈwɔː.tə.dɪˌvaɪ.n|ɪŋ, -dəˌ- (US) ˈwɑː.t̬ɚ-, ˈwɔː- **-er/s** -əʳ/z (US) -ɚ/z
watered-down ˌwɔː.tədˈdaʊn (US) ˌwɑː.t̬ɚdˈ-, ˌwɔː- *stress shift:* ˌwatered-down ˈrum
waterfall ˈwɔː.tə.fɔːl (US) ˈwɑː.t̬ɚ.fɔː ˈwɔː-, -fɑːl **-s** -z
water-finder ˈwɔː.təˌfaɪn.dəʳ (US) ˈwɑː.t̬ɚˌfaɪn.dɚ, ˈwɔː- **-s** -z
Waterford ˈwɔː.tə.fəd (US) ˈwɑː.t̬ɚ.fɚd, ˈwɔː-
waterfowl ˈwɔː.tə.faʊl (US) ˈwɑː.t̬ɚ-, ˈwɔː- **-s** -z **-er/s** -əʳ/z (US) -ɚ/z
waterfront ˈwɔː.tə.frʌnt (US) ˈwɑː.t̬ɚ ˈwɔː- **-s** -s
Watergate ˈwɔː.tə.geɪt (US) ˈwɑː.t̬ɚ-, ˈwɔː-
waterhole ˈwɔː.tə.həʊl (US) ˈwɑː.t̬ɚ.hoʊl, ˈwɔː- **-s** -z
Waterhouse ˈwɔː.tə.haʊs (US) ˈwɑː.t̬ɚ ˈwɔː-
wateriness ˈwɔː.tᵊr.ɪ.nəs, -nəs (US) ˈwɑː.t̬ɚ-, ˈwɔː-
watering-can ˈwɔː.tᵊr.ɪŋ.kæn (US) ˈwɑː.t̬ɚ-, ˈwɔː- **-s** -z
watering-hole ˈwɔː.tᵊr.ɪŋ.həʊl (US) ˈwɑː.t̬ɚ.ɪŋ.hoʊl, ˈwɔː- **-s** -z

atering-plac|e ˈwɔː.tᵊr.ɪŋ.pleɪs US ˈwɑː.t̬ɚ-, ˈwɔː- **-es** -ɪz
aterless ˈwɔː.tᵊl.əs, -lɪs US ˈwɑː.t̬ɚ.ləs, ˈwɔː-
ater-level ˈwɔː.təˌlev.ᵊl US ˈwɑː.t̬ɚ-, ˈwɔː- **-s** -z
ater-lil|y ˈwɔː.təˌlɪl|.i US ˈwɑː.t̬ɚ-, ˈwɔː- **-ies** -iz
ater-line ˈwɔː.tə.laɪn US ˈwɑː.t̬ɚ-, ˈwɔː- **-s** -z
aterlog ˈwɔː.tə.lɒg US ˈwɑː.t̬ɚ.lɑːg, ˈwɔː-, -lɔːg **-s** -z **-ging** -ɪŋ **-ged** -d
aterlogged ˈwɔː.tə.lɒgd US ˈwɑː.t̬ɚ.lɑːgd, ˈwɔː-, -lɔːgd
aterloo **(W)** ˌwɔː.təˈluː US ˈwɑː.t̬ɚ-, ˈwɔː-, ˌ--ˈ- **-s** -z *stress shift, British only:* ˌWaterloo ˈBridge
/aterlooville ˌwɔː.təˈluː.vɪl, ˌwɔː.tᵊl.uːˈvɪl US ˌwɑː.t̬ɚ.luːˈ-, ˌwɔː-, ˈwɑː.t̬ɚ.luː.vɪl
/ater|man **(W)** ˈwɔː.tə|.mən US ˈwɔː- US ˈwɑː.t̬ɚ- **-men** -mən, -men
/atermark ˈwɔː.tə.mɑːk US ˈwɑː.t̬ɚ.mɑːrk, ˈwɔː- **-s** -s **-ing** -ɪŋ **-ed** -t
/atermelon ˈwɔː.təˌmel.ən US ˈwɑː.t̬ɚ-, ˈwɔː- **-s** -z
/atermill ˈwɔː.tə.mɪl US ˈwɑː.tɚ-, ˈwɔː- **-s** -z
/ater-nymph ˈwɔː.tə.nɪmpf US ˈwɑː.t̬ɚ-, ˈwɔː- **-s** -s
/aterpolo ˈwɔː.təˌpəʊ.ləʊ US ˈwɑː.t̬ɚˌpoʊ.loʊ, ˈwɔː-
/aterproof ˈwɔː.tə.pruːf US ˈwɑː.t̬ɚ-, ˈwɔː- **-s** -s **-ing** -ɪŋ **-ed** -t
/ater-resistant ˈwɔː.tə.rɪˌzɪs.tənt, -rə- US ˈwɑː.t̬ɚ-, ˈwɔː-
Vaters ˈwɔː.təz US ˈwɑː.t̬ɚz, ˈwɔː-
/atershed ˈwɔː.tə.ʃed US ˈwɑː.t̬ɚ-, ˈwɔː- **-s** -z
Vatership ˈwɔː.tə.ʃɪp US ˈwɑː.tɚ-, ˈwɔː-
/atersid|e ˈwɔː.tə.saɪd US ˈwɑː.t̬ɚ-, ˈwɔː- **-er/s** -əʳ/z US -ɚ/z
/ater-ski ˈwɔː.tə.skiː US ˈwɑː.t̬ɚ-, ˈwɔː- **-s** -z **-ing** -ɪŋ **-ed** -d **-er/s** -əʳ/z US -ɚ/z
/atersport ˈwɔː.tə.spɔːt US ˈwɑː.t̬ɚ.spɔːrt, ˈwɔː- **-s** -s
/aterspout ˈwɔː.tə.spaʊt US ˈwɑː.t̬ɚ-, ˈwɔː- **-s** -s
Vaterstone ˈwɔː.tə.stəʊn US ˈwɑː.t̬ɚ.stoʊn, ˈwɔː-, -stən **'s** -z
/atertight ˈwɔː.tə.taɪt US ˈwɑː.t̬ɚ-, ˈwɔː-
/aterway ˈwɔː.tə.weɪ US ˈwɑː.t̬ɚ-, ˈwɔː- **-s** -z
/aterwheel ˈwɔː.tə.*h*wiːl US ˈwɑː.t̬ɚ-, ˈwɔː- **-s** -z
/aterwings ˈwɔː.tə.wɪŋz US ˈwɑː.tɚ-, ˈwɔː-

waterworks ˈwɔː.tə.wɜːks US ˈwɑː.t̬ɚ.wɝːks, ˈwɔː-
water|y ˈwɔː.tᵊr|.i, -tr|i US ˈwɑː.t̬ɚ|.i, ˈwɔː- **-iness** -ɪ.nəs, -ɪ.nɪs
Watford ˈwɒt.fəd US ˈwɑːt.fɚd
Wath upon Dearne ˌwɒθ.əˌpɒnˈdɜːn, ˌwæθ- US ˌwɑːθ.əˌpɑːnˈdɝːn, ˌwæθ-
Watkin ˈwɒt.kɪn US ˈwɑːt- **-s** -z
Watling ˈwɒt.lɪŋ US ˈwɑːt-
Watson ˈwɒt.sᵊn US ˈwɑːt-
watt **(W)** wɒt US wɑːt **-s** -s
wattag|e ˈwɒt.ɪdʒ US ˈwɑː.t̬ɪdʒ **-es** -ɪz
Watteau ˈwɒt.əʊ US wɑːˈtoʊ
Watters ˈwɔː.təz, ˈwɒt.əz US ˈwɑː.t̬ɚz, ˈwɔː-
Watterson ˈwɔː.tə.sᵊn, ˈwɒt.ə- US ˈwɑː.t̬ɚ-, ˈwɔː-
wattle ˈwɒt.l̩ US ˈwɑː.t̬l̩ **-s** -z **-d** -d
wattmeter ˈwɒtˌmiː.təʳ US ˈwɑːtˌmiː.t̬ɚ **-s** -z
Watton ˈwɒt.ᵊn US ˈwɑː.tᵊn
Wauchope ˈwɔː.kəp, ˈwɒx.əp US ˈwɑː.kəp, ˈwɔː-
Waugh wɔː, wɒx, wɒf, wɑːf US wɑː, wɔː
Note: /wɔː US wɑː, wɔː/ are the appropriate pronunciations for authors Auberon and Evelyn Waugh.
wav|e weɪv **-es** -z **-ing** -ɪŋ **-ed** -d **-eless** -ləs, -lɪs
waveband ˈweɪv.bænd **-s** -z
waveform ˈweɪv.fɔːm US -fɔːrm **-s** -z
wavelength ˈweɪv.leŋ*k*θ **-s** -s
wavelet ˈweɪv.lət, -lɪt **-s** -s
Wavell ˈweɪ.vᵊl
Waveney ˈweɪv.ni
wav|er ˈweɪ.v|əʳ US -v|ɚ **-ers** -əz US -ɚz **-ering/ly** -ᵊr.ɪŋ/li **-ered** -əd US -ɚd **-erer/s** -ᵊr.əʳ/z US -ɚ.ɚ/z
Waverley ˈweɪ.vᵊl.i US -vɚ.li
wav|y ˈweɪ.v|i **-ier** -i.əʳ US -i.ɚ **-iest** -i.ɪst, -i.əst **-ily** -ɪ.li, -ᵊl.i **-iness** -ɪ.nəs, -ɪ.nɪs
wax wæks **-es** -ɪz **-ing** -ɪŋ **-ed** -t **-en** -ᵊn
waxhead ˈwæks.hed **-s** -z
waxwing ˈwæks.wɪŋ **-s** -z
waxwork ˈwæks.wɜːk US -wɝːk **-s** -s
wax|y ˈwæk.s|i **-ier** -i.əʳ US -i.ɚ **-iest** -i.ɪst, -i.əst **-iness** -ɪ.nəs, -ɪ.nɪs
way **(W)** weɪ **-s** -z ˌ**right of ˈway** US ˈ**right of ˌway**; ˌ**ways and ˈmeans**
waybill ˈweɪ.bɪl **-s** -z
wayfar|er ˈweɪˌfeə.r|əʳ US -ˌfer|.ɚ **-ers** -əz US -ɚz **-ing** -ɪŋ
Wayland ˈweɪ.lənd
way|lay ˌweɪ|ˈleɪ US ˈweɪ|.leɪ, -ˈ- **-lays** -ˈleɪz US -leɪz, -ˈleɪz **-laying** -ˈleɪ.ɪŋ US -ˌleɪ.ɪŋ, -ˈleɪ.ɪŋ **-laid** -ˈleɪd US -leɪd, -ˈleɪd **-layer/s** -ˈleɪ.əʳ/z US -ˌleɪ.ɚ/z, -ˈleɪ.ɚ/z
Wayman ˈweɪ.mən

Wayne weɪn
Waynflete ˈweɪn.fliːt
way-out *unusual and daring:* ˌweɪˈaʊt *stress shift:* ˌway-out ˈclothes
way out *exit:* ˌweɪˈaʊt
-ways -weɪz, -wɪz
Note: Suffix. Normally unstressed, e.g. **lengthways** /ˈleŋ*k*θ.weɪz/.
wayside ˈweɪ.saɪd ˌ**fall by the ˈwayside**
wayward ˈweɪ.wəd US -wɚd **-ly** -li **-ness** -nəs, -nɪs
wazoo wæzˈuː, wəˈzuː US wɑːˈzuː **-s** -z
wazzock ˈwæz.ək **-s** -s
WC ˌdʌb.l̩.juːˈsiː, -jʊ- US -juːˈ-, -jəˈ- **-s** -z
we *strong form:* wiː *weak form:* wi
Note: Weak form word. The strong form is used contrastively (e.g. 'We, not they, will win it') or for emphasis (e.g. '**We** are the winners'). It is also used in final position (e.g. 'So are we'). The weak form is used elsewhere.
weak wiːk **-er** -əʳ US -ɚ **-est** -ɪst, -əst **-ly** -li ˌ**weak at the ˈknees**
weaken ˈwiː.kᵊn **-s** -z **-ing** -ɪŋ, ˈwiːk.nɪŋ **-ed** -d
weak-kneed ˌwiːkˈniːd US ˈwiːk.niːd *stress shift, British only:* ˌweak-kneed ˈcoward
weakling ˈwiː.klɪŋ **-s** -z
weak-minded ˌwiːkˈmaɪn.dɪd **-ness** -nəs, -nɪs *stress shift:* ˌweak-minded ˈperson
weakness ˈwiːk.nəs, -nɪs **-es** -ɪz
weal wiːl **-s** -z
weald **(W)** wiːld **-s** -z
wealden **(W)** ˈwiːl.dᵊn
Wealdstone ˈwiːld.stəʊn US -stoʊn
wealth welθ
wealth|y ˈwel.θ|i **-ier** -i.əʳ US -i.ɚ **-iest** -i.ɪst, -i.əst **-ily** -ɪ.li, -ᵊl.i **-iness** -ɪ.nəs, -ɪ.nɪs
wean *child or baby:* weɪn **-s** -z
wean *withdraw mother's milk:* wiːn **-s** -z **-ing** -ɪŋ **-ed** -d
weaner ˈwiː.nəʳ US -nɚ **-s** -z
weanling ˈwiːn.lɪŋ **-s** -z
weapon ˈwep.ən **-s** -z **-less** -ləs, -lɪs **-ry** -ri
wear (*v.*) weəʳ US wer **-s** -z **-ing** -ɪŋ **wore** wɔːʳ US wɔːr **worn** wɔːn US wɔːrn **wearer/s** ˈweə.rəʳ/z US ˈwer.ɚ/z ˌ**wear and ˈtear**
Wear *river:* wɪəʳ US wɪr
wearability ˌweə.rəˈbɪl.ə.ti, -ɪ.ti US ˌwer.əˈbɪl.ə.t̬i
wearable ˈweə.rə.bl̩ US ˈwer.ə-
Wearing ˈweə.rɪŋ US ˈwer.ɪŋ
wearisome ˈwɪə.rɪ.sᵊm US ˈwɪr.ɪ- **-ly** -li **-ness** -nəs, -nɪs
Wearmouth ˈwɪə.məθ, -maʊθ US ˈwɪr-

Weak form

A variant form of a word, used when it is unstressed.

Examples for English

A very important aspect of the dynamics of English pronunciation is that many very common words have not only a 'strong' or 'full' pronunciation (which is used when the word is said in isolation), but also one or more weak forms which are used when the word occurs in certain contexts. Words which have weak forms are, for the most part, function words such as conjunctions (e.g. and, but), articles (e.g. a, the), pronouns (e.g. she, he her), prepositions (e.g. for, to) and some auxiliary and modal verbs (e.g. do, must). Generally the strong form of such words is used when the word is being quoted (e.g. the word *and* is given its strong form in the sentence 'We use the word and to join clauses'), when it is being contrasted (e.g. *for* in 'There are arguments for and against') and when it is at the end of a sentence (e.g. *from* in 'Where did you get it from?'). Often the pronunciation of a weak-form word is so different from its strong form that if it were heard in isolation it would be impossible to recognise it: for example, *and* can become /n̩/ in *us and them, fish and chips*, and *of* can become /f/ or /v/ in *of course*. The reason for this is that to someone who knows the language well these words are usually highly predictable in their normal context.

Wearn wɜːn (US) wɝːn
wear|y 'wɪə.r|i (US) 'wɪr|.i **-ier** -i.əʳ (US) -i.ɚ **-iest** -i.ɪst, -i.əst **-ily** -əl.i, -ɪ.li **-iness** -ɪ.nəs, -ɪ.nɪs **-ies** -iz **-ying** -i.ɪŋ **-ied** -id
weasel 'wiː.zəl **-s** -z
weaselly 'wiː.zəl.i, 'wiːz.li
weath|er 'weð|.əʳ (US) -ɚ **-ers** -əz (US) -ɚz **-ering** -ər.ɪŋ **-ered** -əd (US) -ɚd **'weather ˌforecast; make ˌheavy 'weather of ˌsomething**
weather-beaten 'weð.əˌbiː.tən (US) -ɚˌ-
weatherboard 'weð.ə.bɔːd (US) -ɚ.bɔːrd **-s** -z **-ing** -ɪŋ
weather-bound 'weð.ə.baʊnd (US) '-ɚ-
weathercock 'weð.ə.kɒk (US) -ɚ.kɑːk **-s** -s
weather-eye 'weð.əʳ.aɪ, ˌ--'- (US) 'weð.ɚ.aɪ **-s** -z **ˌkeep a 'weather-eye open for something**
weather-glass 'weð.ə.glɑːs (US) -ɚ.glæs **-es** -ɪz
Weatherhead 'weð.ə.hed (US) '-ɚ-
weatherly **(W)** 'weð.əl.i (US) -ɚ.li
weather|man 'weð.ə|.mæn (US) '-ɚ- **-men** -men
weatherproof 'weð.ə.pruːf (US) '-ɚ-
weathership 'weð.ə.ʃɪp (US) '-ɚ- **-s** -s
weathervane 'weð.ə.veɪn (US) '-ɚ- **-s** -z
weather-wise 'weð.ə.waɪz (US) '-ɚ-
weather-worn 'weð.ə.wɔːn (US) -ɚ.wɔːrn
Weatly 'wiːt.li
weav|e wiːv **-es** -z **-ing** -ɪŋ **-ed** -d **wove** wəʊv (US) woʊv **woven** 'wəʊ.vən (US) 'woʊ-
weaver **(W)** 'wiː.vəʳ (US) -vɚ **-s** -z
Weaverham 'wiː.və.hæm, -vər.əm (US) -vɚ.hæm, -əm
web web **-s** -z
web-based 'web.beɪst
Webb(e) web
webbed webd **ˌwebbed 'feet**
Webber 'web.əʳ (US) -ɚ
webb|ing 'webl.ɪŋ **-y** -i
webcam 'web.kæm **-s** -z
webcast 'web.kɑːst (US) -kæst **-s** -s **-ing** -ɪŋ
Weber *English name:* 'web.əʳ, 'weɪ.bəʳ, 'wiː- (US) 'web.ɚ, 'weɪ.bɚ, 'wiː- *German composer:* 'veɪ.bəʳ (US) -bɚ
Webern 'veɪ.bɜːn (US) -bɚn
webfooted ˌweb'fʊt.ɪd, 'webˌfʊt̬.ɪd *stress shift, British only:* ˌwebfooted 'bird
webmaster 'webˌmɑː.stəʳ (US) -ˌmæs.tɚ **-s** -z
webpag|e 'web.peɪdʒ **-es** -ɪz
website 'web.saɪt **-s** -s
Webster 'web.stəʳ (US) -stɚ **-s** -z
we'd *(=* **we had, we would***) strong form:* wiːd *weak form:* wid
Note: Weak form word. The weak form is used when the word is unstressed (e.g. 'We'd be silly to do it' /wid.bi'sɪl.i.təˌduː.ɪt/).
wed wed **-s** -z **-ding** -ɪŋ **-ded** -ɪd
Wed. *(abbrev. for* **Wednesday***)* 'wenz.deɪ, 'wed.ənz-, -di (US) 'wenz.deɪ, -di
Note: This abbreviation may also be pronounced /wed/ in British English.
Weddell *surname:* wə'del, 'wed.əl *Sea:* 'wed.əl
Wedderburn 'wed.ə.bɜːn (US) -ɚ.bɝːn
wedding 'wed.ɪŋ **-s** -z **'wedding ˌbreakfast; 'wedding ˌcake; 'wedding ˌday; 'wedding ˌdress; 'wedding ˌmarch; 'wedding ˌring**
Wedekind 'veɪ.də.kɪnd, -kɪnt (US) -kɪnt, -kɪnd
wedg|e wedʒ **-es** -ɪz **-ing** -ɪŋ **-ed** -d **-ewise** -waɪz
wedge-shaped 'wedʒ.ʃeɪpt
Wedg(e)wood 'wedʒ.wʊd
wedlock 'wed.lɒk (US) -lɑːk
Wednesbury 'wenz.bər.i *locally also:* 'wedʒ- (US) 'wenz.bɚ-
Wednesday 'wenz.deɪ, 'wed.nz-, -di (US) 'wenz.deɪ, -di **-s** -z
Wednesfield 'wenz.fiːld *locally also:* 'wedʒ- (US) 'wenz-
Weds. *(abbrev. for* **Wednesday***)* 'wenz.deɪ, 'wed.nz-, -di (US) 'wenz.deɪ, -di
Note: This abbreviation may also be pronounced /wedz/ in British English.
wee wiː
weed wiːd **-s** -z **-ing** -ɪŋ **-ed** -ɪd
weedkiller 'wiːdˌkɪl.əʳ (US) -ɚ **-s** -z
Weedon 'wiː.dən
weed|y 'wiː.d|i **-ier** -i.əʳ (US) -i.ɚ **-iest** -i.ɪst, -i.əst **-iness** -ɪ.nəs, -ɪ.nɪs
week wiːk **-s** -s
weekday 'wiːk.deɪ **-s** -z
weekend ˌwiːk'end, '-- (US) 'wiːk.end **-s** -z *stress shift, British only:* ˌweekend 'traffic
weekender ˌwiːk'en.dəʳ (US) 'wiːk.ˌen.dɚ **-s** -z
Weekes wiːks
Weekl(e)y 'wiː.kli
weekl|y *(n. adv.)* 'wiː.kl|i **-ies** -iz
weeknight 'wiːk.naɪt **-s** -s
Weeks wiːks
Weelkes wiːlks
ween wiːn **-s** -z **-ing** -ɪŋ **-ed** -d
ween|y 'wiː.n|i **-ies** -iz **-ier** -i.əʳ (US) -i.ɚ **-iest** -i.ɪst, -i.əst
weenybopper 'wiː.niˌbɒp.əʳ (US) -ˌbɑː.pɚ **-s** -z
weep wiːp **-s** -s **-ing** -ɪŋ **wept** wept
weeper 'wiː.pəʳ (US) -pɚ **-s** -z
weepie 'wiː.pi **-s** -z
weep|y 'wiː.p|i **-ier** -i.əʳ (US) -i.ɚ **-iest** -i.ɪst, -i.əst **-ily** -ɪ.li, -əl.i **-iness** -ɪ.nəs, -ɪ.nɪs

Weetabix® ˈwiː.tə.bɪks
weever ˈwiː.vəʳ (US) -vɚ **-s** -z
weevil ˈwiː.vəl, -vɪl (US) -vəl **-s** -z
wee-wee ˈwiː.wiː **-s** -z **-ing** -ɪŋ **-d** -d
weft weft
Weidenfeld ˈvaɪ.dən.felt, ˈwaɪ-
Weigall ˈwaɪ.gɔːl
weigela waɪˈdʒiː.lə, -ˈgiː- (US) waɪˈgiː-, -ˈjiː-; ˈwaɪ.gə- **-s** -z
weigelia waɪˈdʒiː.li.ə, -ˈgiː- (US) waɪˈgiː- **-s** -z
weigh weɪ **-s** -z **-ing** -ɪŋ **-ed** -d **-able** -ə.bl̩
weighbridg|e ˈweɪ.brɪdʒ **-es** -ɪz
weight weɪt **-s** -s **-ing** -ɪŋ (US) ˈweɪ.t̬ɪŋ **-ed** -ɪd (US) ˈweɪ.t̬ɪd **ˈweight ˌtraining**
weightless ˈweɪt.ləs, -lɪs **-ly** -li **-ness** -nəs, -nɪs
weightlift|ing ˈweɪtˌlɪf.t|ɪŋ **-er/s** -əʳ/z (US) -ɚ/z
Weighton *in* ***Market Weighton****, Humberside* ˈwiː.tən
WeightWatchers® ˈweɪtˌwɒtʃ.əz (US) -ˌwɑː.tʃɚz
weightwatch|ing ˈweɪtˌwɒtʃ|.ɪŋ (US) -ˌwɑː.tʃ|ɪŋ **-er/s** -əʳ/z (US) -ɚ/z
weight|y ˈweɪ.t|i (US) -t̬|i **-ier** -i.əʳ (US) -i.ɚ **-iest** -i.ɪst, -i.əst **-ily** -ɪ.li, -əl.i **-iness** -ɪ.nəs, -ɪ.nɪs
Weill *English surname:* wiːl, vaɪl *German composer:* vaɪl
Weimar ˈvaɪ.mɑːʳ (US) -mɑːr
Weinberger ˈwaɪnˌbɜː.gəʳ, ˈwaɪm- (US) ˈwaɪnˌbɝː.gɚ
weir (W) wɪəʳ **weir** (US) wɪr **-s** -z
weird wɪəd (US) wɪrd **-er** -əʳ (US) -ɚ **-est** -ɪst, -əst **-ly** -li **-ness** -nəs, -nɪs
weirdo ˈwɪə.dəʊ (US) ˈwɪr.doʊ **-s** -z
Weiss vaɪs
Weisshorn ˈvaɪs.hɔːn (US) -hɔːrn
Weissmuller ˈvaɪsˌmʊl.əʳ, ˈwaɪs- (US) ˈwaɪsˌmʌl.ɚ
Weland ˈweɪ.lənd, ˈwiː-
Welbeck ˈwel.bek
Welby ˈwel.bi
welch (W) (*v. adj.*) wel*t*ʃ **-es** -ɪz **-ing** -ɪŋ **-ed** -t **-er/s** -əʳ/z (US) -ɚ/z
Welcombe ˈwel.kəm
welcom|e ˈwel.kəm **-es** -z **-ing** -ɪŋ **-ed** -d
weld weld **-s** -z **-ing** -ɪŋ **-ed** -ɪd **-er/s** -əʳ/z (US) -ɚ/z
Weldon ˈwel.dən
welfare ˈwel.feəʳ (US) -fer **ˌwelfare ˈstate** (US) **ˈwelfare ˌstate**
Welford ˈwel.fəd (US) -fɚd
welkin ˈwel.kɪn
we'll *(=* **we will, we shall***) strong form:* wiːl *weak form:* wil
Note: Weak form word. The weak form is used when the word is unstressed (e.g. 'We'll write today' /wilˌraɪt.təˈdeɪ/).
well wel **-s** -z **-ing** -ɪŋ **-ed** -d **-ness** -nəs, -nɪs
well-advised ˌwel.ədˈvaɪzd *stress shift:* ˌwell-advised ˈaction
Welland ˈwel.ənd
well-appointed ˌwel.əˈpɔɪn.tɪd (US) -t̬ɪd *stress shift:* ˌwell-appointed ˈoffice
well-balanced ˌwelˈbæl.ən*t*st *stress shift:* ˌwell-balanced ˈdiet
well-behaved ˌwel.bɪˈheɪvd, -bəˈ- *stress shift:* ˌwell-behaved ˈdog
well-being ˈwelˌbiː.ɪŋ, ˌ-ˈ--
well-born ˌwelˈbɔːn (US) -ˈbɔːrn *stress shift:* ˌwell-born ˈlady
well-bred ˌwelˈbred *stress shift:* ˌwell-bred ˈchild
well-built ˌwelˈbɪlt *stress shift:* ˌwell-built ˈperson
Wellby ˈwel.bi
well-chosen ˌwelˈtʃəʊ.zən (US) -ˈtʃoʊ- *stress shift:* ˌwell-chosen ˈwords
Wellcome ˈwel.kəm
well-conducted ˌwel.kənˈdʌk.tɪd *stress shift:* ˌwell-conducted ˈscheme
well-connected ˌwel.kəˈnek.tɪd *stress shift:* ˌwell-connected ˈperson
well-cooked ˌwelˈkʊkt *stress shift:* ˌwell-cooked ˈfood
well-disposed ˌwel.dɪˈspəʊzd (US) -ˈspoʊzd *stress shift:* ˌwell-disposed ˈmanner
well-do|er ˈwelˌduː|.əʳ, ˌ-ˈ-- (US) ˈwelˌduː|.ɚ **-ers** -əz (US) -ɚz **-ing** -ɪŋ
Welldon ˈwel.dən
well-done ˌwelˈdʌn *stress shift:* ˌwell-done ˈfood
well-earned ˌwelˈɜːnd (US) -ˈɝːnd *stress shift:* ˌwell-earned ˈrest
Weller ˈwel.əʳ (US) -ɚ
Welles welz
Wellesley ˈwelz.li
well-fed ˌwelˈfed *stress shift:* ˌwell-fed ˈcat
well-formed ˌwelˈfɔːmd (US) -ˈfɔːrmd *stress shift:* ˌwell-formed ˈsentence
well-found ˌwelˈfaʊnd *stress shift:* ˌwell-found ˈship
well-groomed ˌwelˈgruːmd *stress shift:* ˌwell-groomed ˈman
well-grounded ˌwelˈgraʊn.dɪd *stress shift:* ˌwell-grounded ˈargument
well-heeled ˌwelˈhiːld *stress shift:* ˌwell-heeled ˈowner
wellie ˈwel.i **-s** -z
well-informed ˌwel.ɪnˈfɔːmd (US) -ˈfɔːrmd *stress shift:* ˌwell-informed ˈjournalist
Welling ˈwel.ɪŋ
Wellingborough ˈwel.ɪŋ.bər.ə (US) -bɚ.oʊ
wellington (W) ˈwel.ɪŋ.tən **-s** -z **ˌwellington ˈboot** (US) **ˈwellington ˌboot**
wellingtonia ˌwel.ɪŋˈtəʊ.ni.ə (US) -ˈtoʊ- **-s** -z
well-intentioned ˌwel.ɪnˈten.*t*ʃənd *stress shift:* ˌwell-intentioned ˈaction
well-judged ˌwelˈdʒʌdʒd *stress shift:* ˌwell-judged ˈshot
well-known ˌwelˈnəʊn (US) -ˈnoʊn *stress shift:* ˌwell-known ˈwriter
well-made ˌwelˈmeɪd *stress shift:* ˌwell-made ˈproduct
well-meaning ˌwelˈmiː.nɪŋ *stress shift:* ˌwell-meaning ˈaction
well-meant ˌwelˈment *stress shift:* ˌwell-meant ˈgesture
well-nigh ˌwelˈnaɪ *stress shift:* ˌwell-nigh imˈpossible
well-off ˌwelˈɒf (US) -ˈɑːf *stress shift:* ˌwell-off ˈperson
well-ordered ˌwelˈɔː.dəd (US) -ˈɔːr.dɚd *stress shift:* ˌwell-ordered ˈhousehold
well-proportioned ˌwel.prəˈpɔː.ʃənd (US) -ˈpɔːr- *stress shift:* ˌwell-proportioned ˈroom
well-read ˌwelˈred *stress shift:* ˌwell-read ˈperson
well-rounded ˌwelˈraʊn.dɪd *stress shift:* ˌwell-rounded ˈcharacter
Wells welz
well-spoken ˌwelˈspəʊ.kən (US) -ˈspoʊ- *stress shift:* ˌwell-spoken ˈperson
wellspring ˈwel.sprɪŋ **-s** -z
well-thumbed ˌwelˈθʌmd *stress shift:* ˌwell-thumbed ˈbook
well-timed ˌwelˈtaɪmd *stress shift:* ˌwell-timed ˈaction
well-to-do ˌwel.təˈduː *stress shift:* ˌwell-to-do ˈperson
well-versed ˌwelˈvɜːst (US) -ˈvɝːst *stress shift:* ˌwell-versed ˈteacher
well-wisher ˈwelˌwɪʃ.əʳ, ˌ-ˈ-- (US) ˈwelˌwɪʃ.ɚ **-s** -z
well-worn ˌwelˈwɔːn (US) -ˈwɔːrn *stress shift:* ˌwell-worn ˈphrase
well|y ˈwel|.i **-ies** -iz
Welsch wel*t*ʃ
welsh (W) welʃ **-es** -ɪz **-ing** -ɪŋ **-ed** -t **-er/s** -əʳ/z (US) -ɚ/z **ˌWelsh ˈdresser; ˌWelsh ˈNationalists; ˌWelsh ˈrarebit**
Welsh|man ˈwelʃ|.mən **-men** -mən
Welshpool ˈwelʃ.puːl, ˌ-ˈ-
Welsh|woman ˈwelʃ|ˌwʊm.ən **-women** -ˌwɪm.ɪn
welt welt **-s** -s **-ing** -ɪŋ (US) ˈwel.t̬ɪŋ **-ed** -ɪd (US) ˈwel.t̬ɪd
weltanschauung (W) ˈvelt.ænˌʃaʊ.ʊŋ (US) -ɑːnˌ-
welt|er ˈwel.t|əʳ (US) -t̬|ɚ **-ers** -əz (US) -ɚz **-ering** -ər.ɪŋ **-ered** -əd (US) -ɚd
welterweight ˈwel.tə.weɪt (US) -t̬ɚ- **-s** -s

weltschmerz (W) ˈvelt.ʃmeəts (US) -ʃmerts

Welty ˈwel.ti (US) -t̬i

Welwyn ˈwel.ɪn ˌ**Welwyn** ˌ**Garden** ˈ**City**

Wembley ˈwem.bli

Wemyss wiːmz

wen wen **-s** -z

Wenceslas ˈwen.sɪ.sləs, -sə-, -slæs (US) -sɪ.slɑːs, -slɔːs

wench wentʃ **-es** -ɪz

wend wend **-s** -z **-ing** -ɪŋ **-ed** -ɪd

Wend wend, vend **-s** -z **-ic** -ɪk **-ish** -ɪʃ

Wendell ˈwen.dᵊl

Wenders ˈwen.dəz (US) ˈven.dɚz

Wendover ˈwen.dəʊ.vəʳ (US) -doʊ.vɚ

Wendy ˈwen.di ˈ**Wendy** ˌ**house**

Wengen ˈveŋ.ən

Wenger ˈveŋ.gəʳ (US) -gɚ

Wengern Alp ˌveŋ.ənˈælp (US) -ɚnˈ-

Wenham ˈwen.əm

Wenlock ˈwen.lɒk (US) -lɑːk ˌ**Wenlock** ˈ**Edge**

Wensleydale ˈwenz.lɪ.deɪl

went (*from* **go**) went

Wentworth ˈwent.wəθ, -wɜːθ (US) -wɚθ, -wɝːθ

wept (*from* **weep**) wept

we're (= **we are**) wɪəʳ (US) wɪr

were (*from* **be**) *strong forms:* wɜːʳ (US) wɝː *weak forms:* wəʳ (US) wɚ

Note: Weak form word. The strong form is used for emphasis (e.g. 'You **were** a long time') and for contrast (e.g. 'what they were and what they might have been'). The strong form is also usual in final position (e.g. 'We didn't know where we were'). The weak form is used elsewhere.

weren't wɜːnt (US) wɝːnt

werewol|f ˈweə.wʊl|f, ˈwɪə-, ˈwɜː- (US) ˈwer-, ˈwɪr-, ˈwɝː- **-ves** -vz

Werner ˈwɜː.nəʳ *as if German:* ˈveə- (US) ˈwɝː.nɚ *as if German:* ˈvɝː-

wert (*from* **be**) *strong forms:* wɜːt (US) wɝːt *weak forms:* wət (US) wɚt

Note: Archaic form; see information at **were**.

Weser *German river:* ˈveɪ.zəʳ (US) -zɚ

Note: /ˈwiː.zəʳ (US) -zɚ/ is necessary for rhyme in Browning's 'Pied Piper', but this pronunciation is exceptional.

Wesker ˈwes.kəʳ (US) -kɚ

Wesley ˈwez.li, ˈwes- (US) ˈwes-, ˈwez-

Note: Most people bearing the name **Wesley** pronounce /ˈwes.li/, but in Britain the pronunciation is commonly /ˈwez.li/.

Wesleyan ˈwez.li.ən, ˈwes- (US) ˈwes-, ˈwez- **-s** -z **-ism** -ɪ.zᵊm

Note: /ˈwes-/ appears to be the more usual pronunciation among Wesleyans; with those who are not Wesleyans /ˈwez-/ is probably the commoner form in British English. There exists also an old-fashioned pronunciation /wesˈliː.ən/.

Wessex ˈwes.ɪks

west (W) west ˌ**West** ˈ**Bank** *stress shift:* ˌWest Bank ˈsettlement; ˌ**West** ˈ**Coast**; *stress shift:* ˌWest Coast ˈsinger; ˈ**West** ˌ**Country**; ˌ**West** ˈ**End**; *stress shift:* ˌWest End ˈplay; ˌ**West** ˈ**Indian**; ˌ**West** ˈ**Indies**; ˌ**West** ˈ**Point**; (US) ˈ**West** ˌ**Point**; ˌ**West** ˌ**Side** ˈ**Story** (US) ˈ**West Side** ˌ**Story**; ˌ**West Vir**ˈ**ginia**

westbound ˈwes*t*.baʊnd

Westbourne ˈwes*t*.bɔːn, -bən (US) -bɔːrn, -bɚn

West Bridgford ˌwes*t*ˈbrɪdʒ.fəd (US) -fɚd

Westbrook ˈwes*t*.brʊk

Westbury ˈwes*t*.bᵊr.i

Westchester ˈwes*t*ˌtʃes.təʳ (US) -tɚ

Westcott ˈwes*t*.kət

Westergate ˈwes.tə.geɪt (US) -tɚ-

Westerham ˈwes.tᵊr.əm

westering ˈwes.tᵊr.ɪŋ

westerl|y ˈwes.tᵊl|.i (US) -tɚ.l|i **-ies** -iz

western (W) ˈwes.tən (US) -tɚn **-s** -z **-er/s** -əʳ/z (US) -ɚ/z **-most** -məʊst (US) -moʊst ˌ**Western Aus**ˈ**tralia**; ˈ**Western** ˌ**Isles**,; ˌ**Western** ˈ**Isles**

westernization, **-isa-** ˌwes.tᵊn.aɪˈzeɪ.ʃᵊn, -ɪˈ- (US) -tɚ.nɪˈ-

westerniz|e, **-is|e** ˈwes.tən.aɪz (US) -tɚ.naɪz **-es** -ɪz **-ing** -ɪŋ **-ed** -d

Westfield ˈwest.fiːld

Westgate ˈwes*t*.geɪt, -gɪt

Westhill ˈwest.hɪl

Westhoughton ˌwestˈhɔː.tᵊn (US) -ˈhɑː-, -ˈhɔː-

Westinghouse ˈwes.tɪŋ.haʊs

Westlake ˈwes*t*.leɪk

Westland® ˈwes*t*.lənd

Westlife ˈwes*t*.laɪf

Westly ˈwes*t*.li

Westmeath ˌwes*t*ˈmiːð

West Mersea ˌwes*t*ˈmɜː.zi (US) -ˈmɝː-

Westminster wes*t*ˈmɪn*t*.stəʳ, ˈ--- (US) wes*t*ˈmɪn*t*.stɚ, ˈ--- ˌ**Westminster** ˈ**Abbey**

Westmor(e)land ˈwes*t*.mᵊl.ənd (US) -mɔːr.lənd

west-northwest ˌwest.nɔːθˈwest (US) -nɔːrθˈ- *nautical pronunciation:* -nɔːˈ- (US) -nɔːrˈ-

Weston ˈwes.tən

Weston-super-Mare ˌwes.tənˌsuː.pəˈmeəʳ, -ˌsjuː-; -ˈsuː.pə.meəʳ, -ˈsjuː- (US) -ˌsuː.pɚˈmer, -ˈsuː.pɚ.mer

Westphali|a ˌwes*t*ˈfeɪ.li|.ə, ˈ-lj|ə (US) ˈ-li|.ə, -ˈfeɪl.j|ə **-an/s** -ən/z

Westray ˈwes.treɪ

Westside ˈwes*t*.saɪd

west-southwest ˌwest.saʊθˈwest *nautical pronunciation:* -saʊˈ-

westward ˈwes*t*.wəd (US) -wɚd **-s** -z **-ly** -li

Westward Ho! ˌwes*t*.wədˈhəʊ (US) -wɚdˈhoʊ

Westwood ˈwes*t*.wʊd

wet wet **-ter** -əʳ (US) ˈwet̬.ɚ **-test** -ɪst, -əst (US) ˈwet̬.ɪst, -əst **-s** -s **-ting** -ɪŋ (US) ˈwet̬.ɪŋ **-ted** -ɪd (US) ˈwet̬.ɪd **-ly** -li **-ness** -nəs, -nɪs ˌ**wet** ˈ**blanket**; ˈ**wet** ˌ**suit**; (**still**) ˌ**wet behind the** ˈ**ears**

wetback ˈwet.bæk **-s** -s

wether ˈweð.əʳ (US) -ɚ **-s** -z

Wetherby ˈweð.ə.bi (US) ˈ-ɚ-

wetland ˈwet.lənd (US) -lænd **-s** -z

wet-look ˈwet.lʊk

wet-nurs|e ˈwet.nɜːs (US) -nɝːs **-es** -ɪz

we've (= **we have**) *strong form:* wiːv *weak form:* wiv

Note: Weak form word. The weak form is usually found when the word is unstressed, but the strong form may also be used in this situation.

Wexford ˈweks.fəd (US) -fɚd

Wey weɪ

Weybridge ˈweɪ.brɪdʒ

Weyman ˈweɪ.mən

Weymouth ˈweɪ.məθ

whack *h*wæk **-s** -s **-ing/s** -ɪŋ/z **-ed** -t **-er/s** -əʳ/z (US) -ɚ/z

whacko ˈ*h*wæk.əʊ (US) -oʊ

whack|y ˈ*h*wæk|.i **-ier** -i.əʳ (US) -i.ɚ **-iest** -i.ɪst, -i.əst **-ily** -ɪ.li, -ᵊl.i

whal|e (W) *h*weɪl **-es** -z **-ing** -ɪŋ **-er/s** -əʳ/z (US) -ɚ/z ˌ**have a** ˈ**whale of a** ˌ**time**

whalebone ˈ*h*weɪl.bəʊn (US) -boʊn

whale-oil ˈ*h*weɪl.ɔɪl

Whaley ˈ*h*weɪ.li

Whalley *surname:* ˈ*h*weɪ.li, ˈ*h*wɔː-, ˈ*h*wɒl.i (US) ˈ*h*weɪ.li, ˈ*h*wɑː.li *abbey near Blackburn:* ˈ*h*wɔː.li (US) ˈ*h*wɑː-

wham *h*wæm **-s** -z **-ming** -ɪŋ **-med** -d

whammo ˈ*h*wæm.əʊ (US) -oʊ

whamm|y ˈ*h*wæm|.i **-ies** -iz

whamo ˈ*h*wæm.əʊ (US) -oʊ

whang *h*wæŋ **-s** -z **-ing** -ɪŋ **-ed** -d

whangee ˌ*h*wæŋˈgiː, -ˈiː (US) -ˈiː

whar|f *h*wɔː|f (US) *h*wɔːr|f **-ves** -vz **-fs** -fs

wharfage ˈ*h*wɔː.fɪdʒ (US) ˈ*h*wɔːr-

Wharfedale ˈ*h*wɔːf.deɪl (US) ˈ*h*wɔːrf-

wharfinger ˈ*h*wɔː.fɪn.dʒəʳ (US) ˈ*h*wɔːr.fɪn.dʒɚ **-s** -z

Wharton ˈ*h*wɔː.tᵊn (US) ˈ*h*wɔːr-

what *h*wɒt (US) *h*wʌt, *h*wɑːt

whatchamacallit ˈ*h*wɒtʃ.ə.məˌkɔː.lɪt (US) ˈ*h*wʌtʃ-

what-d'you-call-it ˈ*h*wɒt.djʊˌkɔː.lɪt, -djəˌ-, -dʒʊˌ-, -dʒəˌ- (US) ˈ*h*wʌt̬.i.jəˌkɔː-, ˈ*h*wʌtʃ.əˌ-, -ˌkɑː-

Pronouncing the letters WH

The consonant digraph **wh** is found in word or morpheme initial position in English, and usually pronounced as /w/ in British English and /hw/ in US English. The realisation /hw/ also occurs amongst some speakers of British English. In this dictionary, the transcription /*h*w/ is used to cover both variants, e.g.:

when /*h*wen/
where /*h*weəʳ/ ⓤⓢ /*h*wer/

Another realisation of the consonant digraph **wh** is /h/, e.g.:

who /huː/
wholesome /ˈhəʊl.sᵊm/ ⓤⓢ /ˈhoʊl-/

what-d'you-ma-call-it ˈ*h*wɒt.djʊ.mə,kɔː.lɪt, -djə-, -dʒʊ-, -dʒə- ⓤⓢ ˈ*h*wʌt̬.i.jə.mə,kɔː-, -*h*wʌtʃ.ə-, -kɑː-
whate'er *h*wɒtˈeəʳ ⓤⓢ *h*wʌtˈer, *h*wɑːt-
Whateley ˈ*h*weɪt.li
whatever *h*wɒtˈev.əʳ ⓤⓢ *h*wʌtˈev.ɚ, *h*wɑːt-
Whatley ˈ*h*wɒt.li ⓤⓢ ˈ*h*wɑːt-
Whatman ˈ*h*wɒt.mən ⓤⓢ ˈ*h*wɑːt-
Whatmough ˈ*h*wɒt.məʊ ⓤⓢ ˈ*h*wɑːt.moʊ
whatnot ˈ*h*wɒt.nɒt ⓤⓢ ˈ*h*wʌt.nɑːt, ˈ*h*wɑːt- **-s** -s
what's-her-name ˈ*h*wɒt.sᵊn.eɪm ⓤⓢ ˈ*h*wʌt.sɚ.neɪm, ˈ*h*wɑːt-
what's-his-name ˈ*h*wɒt.sɪz.neɪm ⓤⓢ ˈ*h*wʌt-, ˈ*h*wɑːt-
whatsit ˈ*h*wɒt.sɪt ⓤⓢ ˈ*h*wʌt- **-s** -s
whatsoe'er ,*h*wɒt.səʊˈeəʳ ⓤⓢ ,*h*wʌt.soʊˈer, ,*h*wɑːt-
whatsoever ,*h*wɒt.səʊˈev.əʳ ⓤⓢ ,*h*wʌt.soʊˈev.ɚ, ,*h*wɑːt-
wheal *h*wiːl **-s** -z
wheat *h*wiːt **-en** -ᵊn
wheatgerm ˈ*h*wiːt.dʒɜːm ⓤⓢ -dʒɝːm
Wheathampstead ˈ*h*wiː.təm*p*.sted, ˈ*h*wet.əm*p*-
Wheatley ˈ*h*wiːt.li
wheatmeal ˈ*h*wiːt.miːl
Wheaton ˈ*h*wiː.tᵊn
Wheatstone ˈ*h*wiːt.stᵊn, -stəʊn ⓤⓢ -stoʊn, -stᵊn
wheedl|e ˈ*h*wiː.dl̩ **-es** -z **-ing** -ɪŋ, ˈ*h*wiːd.lɪŋ **-ed** -d **-er/s** -əʳ/z, ˈ*h*wiːd.ləʳ/z ⓤⓢ ˈ*h*wiː.dl̩.əʳ/z, ˈ*h*wiːd.lɚ/z
wheel *h*wiːl **-s** -z **-ing** -ɪŋ **-ed** -d ˈ**wheel** ,**clamp**
wheelbarrow ˈ*h*wiːl,bær.əʊ ⓤⓢ -,ber.oʊ, -,bær- **-s** -z
wheelbas|e ˈ*h*wiːl.beɪs **-es** -ɪz
wheelchair ˈ*h*wiːl.tʃeəʳ ⓤⓢ -tʃer **-s** -z
wheeler (W) ˈ*h*wiː.ləʳ ⓤⓢ -lɚ **-s** -z
wheeler-dealer ,*h*wiː.ləˈdiː.ləʳ ⓤⓢ -lɚˈdiː.lɚ **-s** -z
wheelhou|se ˈ*h*wiːl.haʊ|s **-ses** -zɪz
wheelie ˈ*h*wiː.li **-s** -z ˈ**wheelie** ,**bin**
Wheelock ˈ*h*wiː.lək
wheelwright, wheelright (W) ˈ*h*wiːl.raɪt **-s** -s
Wheen ˈ*h*wiːn
wheez|e *h*wiːz **-es** -ɪz **-ing** -ɪŋ **-ed** -d **-y** -i **-ier** -i.əʳ ⓤⓢ -i.ɚ **-iest** -i.ɪst, -i.əst **-iness** -ɪ.nəs, -ɪ.nɪs
Whelan ˈ*h*wiː.lən
whelk welk ⓤⓢ *h*welk **-s** -s
whelm *h*welm **-s** -z **-ing** -ɪŋ **-ed** -d
whelp *h*welp **-s** -s **-ing** -ɪŋ **-ed** -t
when *h*wen
whence *h*wen*t*s
whene'er *h*wenˈeəʳ ⓤⓢ -ˈer
whenever *h*wenˈev.əʳ, *h*wənˈ- ⓤⓢ -ɚ
whensoever ,*h*wen.səʊˈev.əʳ ⓤⓢ -soʊˈev.ɚ
where *h*weəʳ ⓤⓢ *h*wer
whereabout ,*h*weə.rəˈbaʊt ⓤⓢ ˈ*h*wer.ə,-
whereabouts (*n.*) ˈ*h*weə.rə.baʊts ⓤⓢ ˈ*h*wer.ə-
whereabouts *interrogation:* ,*h*weə.rəˈbaʊts ⓤⓢ ,*h*wer.əˈ-
whereas *h*weəˈræz, *h*wər- ⓤⓢ *h*werˈæz, *h*wɚ-
whereat *h*weəˈræt, *h*wər- ⓤⓢ *h*werˈæt, *h*wɚ-
whereby *h*weəˈbaɪ ⓤⓢ *h*wer-
where'er *h*weəˈreəʳ, *h*wə- ⓤⓢ *h*werˈer, *h*wɚ-
wherefore ˈ*h*weə.fɔːʳ ⓤⓢ ˈ*h*wer.fɔːr **-s** -z
wherein *h*weəˈrɪn ⓤⓢ *h*werˈɪn
whereof *h*weəˈrɒv ⓤⓢ *h*werˈɑːv
whereon *h*weəˈrɒn ⓤⓢ *h*werˈɑːn
wheresoe'er ,*h*weə.səʊˈeəʳ ⓤⓢ ,*h*wer.soʊˈer
wheresoever ,*h*weə.səʊˈev.əʳ ⓤⓢ ,*h*wer.soʊˈev.ɚ
whereto *h*weəˈtuː ⓤⓢ *h*wer-
whereunder *h*weəˈrʌn.dəʳ ⓤⓢ *h*werˈʌn.dɚ
whereunto ,*h*weə.rʌnˈtuː ⓤⓢ ,*h*wer.ʌnˈ-
whereupon ,*h*weə.rəˈpɒn, ˈ--,- ⓤⓢ ˈ*h*wer.ə,pɑːn
wherever *h*weəˈrev.əʳ, *h*wər- ⓤⓢ *h*werˈev.ɚ, *h*wɚ-
wherewith *h*weəˈwɪθ, -ˈwɪð ⓤⓢ *h*wer-
wherewithal (*n.*) ˈ*h*weə.wɪ.ðɔːl ⓤⓢ ˈ*h*wer-, -θɔːl, -ðɑːl, -θɑːl
wherewithal (*adv.*) ,*h*weə.wɪˈðɔːl, ˈ--- ⓤⓢ ˈ*h*wer.wɪ.ðɔːl, -θɔːl, -ðɑːl, -θɑːl
Whernside ˈ*h*wɜːn.saɪd ⓤⓢ ˈ*h*wɝːn-
wherr|y ˈ*h*wer|.i **-ies** -iz
whet *h*wet **-s** -s **-ting** -ɪŋ ⓤⓢ ˈ*h*wet̬.ɪŋ **-ted** -ɪd ⓤⓢ ˈ*h*wet̬.ɪd
whether ˈ*h*weð.əʳ ⓤⓢ -ɚ
whetstone (W) ˈ*h*wet.stəʊn ⓤⓢ -stoʊn **-s** -z
whew ,ɣ,u, fjuː
Note: This is an attempt at a symbolic representation of an interjection used to indicate that the speaker is either surprised, or suffering from the heat. The sound is related to a whistle (falling or rising-falling pitch), but in speech is more usually a whispered sound. The pronunciation /fjuː/ is an alternative based on the spelling.
Whewell ˈhjuː.əl, -el, -ɪl; hjʊəl ⓤⓢ ˈhjuː.əl
whey *h*weɪ
which *h*wɪtʃ
whichever *h*wɪˈtʃev.əʳ ⓤⓢ -ɚ
whick|er (W) ˈ*h*wɪk|.əʳ ⓤⓢ -ɚ **-ers** -əz ⓤⓢ -ɚz **-ering** -ᵊr.ɪŋ **-ered** -əd ⓤⓢ -ɚd
Whickham ˈ*h*wɪk.əm
whiff *h*wɪf **-s** -s **-ing** -ɪŋ **-ed** -t
Whiffen ˈ*h*wɪf.ɪn, -ən
Whig *h*wɪg **-s** -z
Whigg|ery ˈ*h*wɪg|.ᵊr.i **-ism** -ɪ.zᵊm
Whiggish ˈ*h*wɪg.ɪʃ
Whigham ˈ*h*wɪg.əm
whil|e ˈ*h*waɪl **-es** -z **-ing** -ɪŋ **-ed** -d
whilst *h*waɪlst
whim *h*wɪm **-s** -z
whimbrel ˈ*h*wɪm.brᵊl **-s** -z
whimp|er ˈ*h*wɪm.p|əʳ ⓤⓢ -p|ɚ **-ers** -əz ⓤⓢ -ɚz **-ering/ly** -ᵊr.ɪŋ/li **-ered** -əd ⓤⓢ -ɚd
whimsic|al ˈ*h*wɪm.zɪ.k|ᵊl, -sɪ- ⓤⓢ -zɪ- **-ally** -ᵊl.i, -li **-alness** -ᵊl.nəs, -nɪs
whimsicality ,*h*wɪm.zɪˈkæl.ə.ti, -sɪˈ-, -ɪ.ti ⓤⓢ -zɪˈkæl.ə.t̬i
whims|y ˈ*h*wɪm.z|i **-ies** -iz
whin *h*wɪn **-s** -z
whinchat ˈ*h*wɪn.tʃæt **-s** -s
whin|e *h*waɪn **-es** -z **-ing/ly** -ɪŋ/li **-ed** -d **-er/s** -əʳ/z ⓤⓢ -ɚ/z

whing|e hwɪndʒ -es -ɪz -(e)ing -ɪŋ -ed -d -er/s -ə^r/z (US) -ɚ/z
whinn|y 'hwɪn|.i -ies -iz -ying -i.ɪŋ -ied -id
whin|y 'hwaɪ.n|i -ier -i.ə^r (US) -i.ɚ -iest -i.ɪst, -i.əst -iness -ɪ.nəs, -ɪ.nɪs
whip hwɪp -s -s -ping/s -ɪŋ/z -ped -t have the ˌwhip 'hand
whipcord 'hwɪp.kɔːd (US) -kɔːrd
whiplash 'hwɪp.læʃ
whipp|er-in ˌhwɪp|.ə^r'ɪn (US) -ɚ'- -ers-in -əz'ɪn (US) -ɚz'-
whippersnapper 'hwɪp.əˌsnæp.ə^r (US) -ɚˌsnæp.ɚ -s -z
whippet 'hwɪp.ɪt -s -s
whipping-boy 'hwɪp.ɪŋ.bɔɪ -s -z
Whippingham 'hwɪp.ɪŋ.əm
Whipple 'hwɪp.l̩
whippoorwill 'hwɪp.ə.wɪl, -ʊə-, -pʊə-, -pɔː- (US) '-ɚ- -s -z
whip-round 'hwɪp.raʊnd -s -z
whipsaw 'hwɪp.sɔː (US) -sɑː, -sɔː -s -z
Whipsnade 'hwɪp.sneɪd
whir hwɜː^r (US) hwɝː -s -z -ring/s -ɪŋ/z -red -d
whirl hwɜːl (US) hwɝːl -s -z -ing -ɪŋ -ed -d
whirligig 'hwɜː.lɪ.gɪg (US) 'hwɝː- -s -z
whirlpool 'hwɜːl.puːl (US) 'hwɝːl- -s -z
whirlwind 'hwɜːl.wɪnd (US) 'hwɝːl- -s -z
whirlybird 'hwɜː.lɪ.bɜːd (US) 'hwɝː.lɪ.bɝːd -s -z
whirr hwɜː^r (US) hwɝː -s -z -ing/s -ɪŋ/z -ed -d
whisk hwɪsk -s -s -ing -ɪŋ -ed -t
Whiskas® 'hwɪs.kəz
whisker 'hwɪs.kə^r (US) -kɚ -s -z -ed -d
whiskey 'hwɪs.ki -s -z
whisk|y 'hwɪs.k|i -ies -iz
whisp|er 'hwɪs.p|ə^r (US) -p|ɚ -ers -əz (US) -ɚz -ering/s -^{ə}r.ɪŋ/z -ered -əd (US) -ɚd -erer/s -^{ə}r.ə^r/z (US) -ɚ.ɚ/z
whist hwɪst 'whist ˌdrive
whistl|e 'hwɪs.l̩ -es -z -ing -ɪŋ, 'hwɪs.lɪŋ -ed -d ˌblow the 'whistle ˌon
whistle-blower 'hwɪs.l̩ˌbləʊ.ə^r (US) -ˌbloʊ.ɚ -s -z
whistler (W) 'hwɪs.lə^r, -l̩.ə^r (US) '-lɚ, -l̩.ɚ -s -z
whistle-stop 'hwɪs.l̩.stɒp (US) -stɑːp -s -s -ping -ɪŋ -ped -t ˌwhistle-stop 'tour
whit (W) hwɪt
Whitaker 'hwɪt.ə.kə^r, '-ɪ- (US) hwɪt̬.ə.kɚ
Whitbread 'hwɪt.bred
Whitburn 'hwɪt.bɜːn (US) -bɝːn
Whitby 'hwɪt.bi
Whitchurch 'hwɪt.tʃɜːtʃ (US) -tʃɝːtʃ
Whitcombe 'hwɪt.kəm
Whitcut 'hwɪt.kʌt
whit|e (W) hwaɪt -es -s -er -ə^r (US) 'hwaɪ.t̬ɚ -est -ɪst, -əst (US) 'hwaɪ.t̬ɪst, -t̬əst -ely -li -eness -nəs, -nɪs -ing -ɪŋ (US) 'hwaɪ.t̬ɪŋ -ed -ɪd (US) 'hwaɪ.t̬ɪd ˌwhite 'elephant; ˌwhite 'flag; 'white ˌgoods; 'White ˌHouse; ˌwhite 'knight; ˌwhite 'lie; 'white ˌman; ˌwhite 'paper (US) 'white ˌpaper; ˌwhite 'sauce; (US) 'white ˌsauce; ˌwhite 'trash; ˌwhite 'wedding; ˌwhite as a 'sheet
whitebait 'hwaɪt.beɪt
whitebeard 'hwaɪt.bɪəd (US) -bɪrd -s -z -ed -ɪd
whiteboard 'hwaɪt.bɔːd (US) -bɔːrd -s -z
whitecap 'hwaɪt.kæp -s -s
Whitechapel 'hwaɪtˌtʃæp.^{ə}l
white-collar ˌhwaɪt'kɒl.ə^r (US) -'kɑː.lɚ *stress shift:* ˌwhite-collar 'worker
Whitefield 'hwaɪt.fiːld, 'hwɪt-
whitefl|y 'hwaɪt.fl|aɪ -ies -aɪz
Whitefriars 'hwaɪt.fraɪəz, ˌ-'- (US) 'hwaɪt.fraɪɚz, ˌ-'-
Whitehall 'hwaɪt.hɔːl, ˌ-'- (US) 'hwaɪt.hɔːl, -hɑːl
Whitehaven 'hwaɪtˌheɪ.v^{ə}n
whitehead (W) 'hwaɪt.hed -s -z
Whitehorn 'hwaɪt.hɔːn (US) -hɔːrn
Whitehorse 'hwaɪt.hɔːs (US) -hɔːrs
white-hot ˌhwaɪt'hɒt (US) -'hɑːt *stress shift:* ˌwhite-hot 'metal
Whitehouse 'hwaɪt.haʊs
Whitelaw 'hwaɪt.lɔː (US) -lɑː, -lɔː
Whiteley 'hwaɪt.li
white-livered 'hwaɪtˌlɪv.əd, ˌ-'-- (US) -ɚd
whiten 'hwaɪ.t^{ə}n -s -z -ing -ɪŋ, 'hwaɪt.nɪŋ -ed -d
whitener 'hwaɪt.nə^r, 'hwaɪ.t^{ə}n.ə^r (US) 'hwaɪt.nɚ, 'hwaɪ.t^{ə}n.ɚ -s -z
whiteout 'hwaɪt.aʊt -s -s
Whiteread 'hwaɪt.riːd
Whiteside 'hwaɪt.saɪd
whitethorn 'hwaɪt.θɔːn (US) -θɔːrn -s -z
whitethroat 'hwaɪt.θrəʊt (US) -θroʊt -s -s
whitewash 'hwaɪt.wɒʃ (US) -wɑːʃ -es -ɪz -ing -ɪŋ -ed -t -er/s -ə^r/z (US) -ɚ/z
whitewater (W) 'hwaɪt.wɔː.tə^r (US) -wɑː.t̬ɚ, -wɔː- ˌwhitewater 'rafting
whitewood 'hwaɪt.wʊd
whitey 'hwaɪ.ti (US) -t̬i
Whitfield 'hwɪt.fiːld
Whitgift 'hwɪt.gɪft
whither 'hwɪð.ə^r (US) -ɚ
whithersoever ˌhwɪð.ə.səʊ'ev.ə^r (US) -ɚ.soʊ'ev.ɚ
whiting (W) 'hwaɪ.tɪŋ (US) -t̬ɪŋ -s -z
whitish 'hwaɪ.tɪʃ (US) -t̬ɪʃ
Whitlam 'hwɪt.ləm
Whitley 'hwɪt.li
whitlow 'hwɪt.ləʊ (US) -loʊ -s -z
Whitman 'hwɪt.mən
Whitmarsh 'hwɪt.mɑːʃ (US) -mɑːrʃ
Whitmore 'hwɪt.mɔː^r (US) -mɔːr
Whitney 'hwɪt.ni
Whitstable 'hwɪt.stə.bl̩
Whitstone 'hwɪt.stəʊn, -st^{ə}n (US) -stoʊn, -st^{ə}n
Whitsun 'hwɪt.s^{ə}n
Whitsunday ˌhwɪt'sʌn.deɪ, -di; -s^{ə}n'deɪ -s -z
Whitsuntide 'hwɪt.s^{ə}n.taɪd -s -z
Whittaker 'hwɪt.ə.kə^r, '-ɪ- (US) 'hwɪt̬.ə.kɚ
Whittall 'hwɪt.^{ə}l, -ɔːl (US) 'hwɪt̬-
Whittier 'hwɪt.i.ə^r (US) 'hwɪt̬.i.ɚ
Whittingeham(e) 'hwɪt.ɪn.dʒəm (US) 'hwɪt̬-
Whittington 'hwɪt.ɪŋ.tən (US) 'hwɪt̬-
whittl|e (W) 'hwɪt.l̩ (US) 'hwɪt̬- -es -z -ing -ɪŋ, 'hwɪt.lɪŋ -ed -d
Whittlesey 'hwɪt.l̩.si (US) 'hwɪt̬-
Whitworth 'hwɪt.wəθ, -wɜːθ (US) -wɚθ, -wɝːθ
whit|y 'hwaɪ.t|i (US) -t̬|i -iness -ɪ.nəs, -ɪ.nɪs
whiz, whiz|z hwɪz -zes -ɪz -zing -ɪŋ -zed -d ˌgee 'whiz(z); 'whiz(z) ˌkid
whiz(z)-bang 'hwɪz.bæŋ -s -z
who *strong form:* huː *weak form:* hu ˌWho's 'Who
Note: Weak form word. The weak form is only found in unstressed syllables, and the /h/ is frequently not pronounced. The strong form is also found in unstressed syllables.
WHO ˌdʌb.l̩.juːˌeɪtʃ'əʊ (US) ˌdʌb.l̩.juːˌeɪtʃ'oʊ, -jəˌ-
whoa hwəʊ (US) hwoʊ
who'd huːd
whodun(n)it ˌhuː'dʌn.ɪt -s -s
whoe'er huː'eə^r, hu- (US) -'er
whoever huː'ev.ə^r, hu- (US) -ɚ
whole həʊl (US) hoʊl -ness -nəs, -nɪs go the ˌwhole 'hog
wholefood 'həʊl.fuːd (US) 'hoʊl- -s -z
wholegrain 'həʊl.greɪn (US) 'hoʊl-
whole-hearted ˌhəʊl'hɑː.tɪd (US) ˌhoʊl'hɑːr.t̬ɪd -ly -li -ness -nəs, -nɪs *stress shift:* ˌwhole-hearted 'effort
wholemeal 'həʊl.miːl (US) 'hoʊl-
wholesale 'həʊl.seɪl (US) 'hoʊl-
wholesaler 'həʊlˌseɪ.lə^r (US) 'hoʊlˌseɪ.lɚ -s -z
wholesom|e 'həʊl.s^{ə}m (US) 'hoʊl- -est -ɪst, -əst -ely -li -eness -nəs, -nɪs
wholewheat 'həʊl.hwiːt (US) ˌhoʊl'hwiːt
wholism 'həʊ.lɪ.z^{ə}m (US) 'hoʊ-
wholistic həʊ'lɪs.tɪk (US) hoʊ-
who'll huːl
wholly 'həʊl.li, 'həʊ- (US) 'hoʊl.li, 'hoʊ-
whom huːm

whomever ˌhuːˈmev.əʳ, hʊˈ-
whomsoever ˌhuːm.səʊˈev.əʳ, ˌhʊm- (US) -soʊˈev.ɚ
whoop *h*wuːp, huːp **-s** -s **-ing** -ɪŋ **-ed** -t
whoopee (*n.*) ˈ*h*wʊp.i (US) ˈ*h*wuː.pi ˈ**whoopee** ˌ**cushion** (*interj.*) *h*wʊˈpiː
Whoopi ˈ*h*wʊp.i (US) ˈ*h*wʊp.i, ˈ*h*wuː.pi
whooping-cough ˈhuː.pɪŋ.kɒf (US) -kɑːf, ˈhʊp.ɪŋ-, ˈwuː.pɪŋ-, ˈwʊp.ɪŋ-
whoops *h*wʊps (US) *h*wʊps, *h*wuːps
whoops-a-daisy ˈ*h*wʊps.əˌdeɪ.zi (US) ˈ*h*wʊps-, ˈ*h*wuːps-
whoosh *h*wʊʃ (US) *h*wʊʃ, *h*wuːʃ **-es** -ɪz **-ing** -ɪŋ **-ed** -t
whop *h*wɒp (US) *h*wɑːp **-s** -s **-ping/s** -ɪŋ/z **-ped** -t
whopper ˈ*h*wɒp.əʳ (US) ˈ*h*wɑː.pɚ **-s** -z
whopping ˈ*h*wɒp.ɪŋ (US) ˈ*h*wɑː.pɪŋ
whor|e hɔːʳ (US) hɔːr **-es** -z **-ing** -ɪŋ **-ed** -d
whoredom ˈhɔː.dəm (US) ˈhɔːr-
whorehou|se ˈhɔː.haʊ|s (US) ˈhɔːr- **-ses** -zɪz
whoreson ˈhɔː.sᵊn (US) ˈhɔːr- **-s** -z
Whorf *h*wɔːf (US) *h*wɔːrf
whorish ˈhɔː.rɪʃ (US) ˈhɔːr.ɪʃ
whorl *h*wɜːl (US) *h*wɝːl, *h*wɔːrl **-s** -z **-ed** -d
whortle ˈ*h*wɜː.tl̩ (US) ˈ*h*wɝː.ţl̩ **-s** -z
whortleberr|y ˈ*h*wɜː.tl̩ˌber|.i, -bᵊr- (US) ˈ*h*wɝː.ţl̩ˌber- **-ies** -iz
who's huːz
whose huːz
whoso ˈhuː.səʊ (US) -soʊ
whosoever ˌhuː.səʊˈev.əʳ (US) -soʊˈev.ɚ
who've huːv
why *h*waɪ **-s** -z
Whybrow ˈ*h*waɪ.braʊ
Whyle ˈ*h*waɪ.li
why'll *h*waɪl
Whymper ˈ*h*wɪm.pəʳ (US) -pɚ
why're ˈ*h*waɪ.əʳ (US) -ɚ
why's *h*waɪz
Whyte *h*waɪt
Whytt *h*waɪt
why've *h*waɪv, ˈ*h*waɪ.əv
WI ˌdʌb.l̩.juːˈaɪ
Wichita ˈwɪtʃ.ɪ.tɔː, ˈ-ə- (US) -ə.tɔː, -tɑː
wick (W) wɪk **-s** -s
wicked ˈwɪk.ɪd **-est** -ɪst, -əst **-ly** -li **-ness/es** -nəs/ɪz, -nɪs/ɪz
Wicken ˈwɪk.ᵊn
Wickens ˈwɪk.ɪnz
wicker (W) ˈwɪk.əʳ (US) -ɚ
wickerwork ˈwɪk.ə.wɜːk (US) -ɚ.wɝːk
wicket ˈwɪk.ɪt **-s** -s ˈ**wicket** ˌ**gate**
wicket-keeper ˈwɪk.ɪtˌkiː.pəʳ (US) -pɚ **-s** -z
Wickford ˈwɪk.fəd (US) -fɚd
Wickham ˈwɪk.əm
Wickliffe ˈwɪk.lɪf
Wicklow ˈwɪk.ləʊ (US) -loʊ
Widdecombe, Widdicombe ˈwɪd.ɪ.kəm
Widdowson ˈwɪd.əʊ.sᵊn (US) -oʊ-, ˈ-ə-
wid|e waɪd **-es** -z **-er** -əʳ (US) -ɚ **-est** -ɪst, -əst **-ely** -li **-eness** -nəs, -nɪs ˈ**wide** ˌ**boy**
wide-angle ˌwaɪdˈæŋ.gl̩ *stress shift:* ˌwide-angle ˈlens
wide-awake (*adj.*) ˌwaɪd.əˈweɪk
Widecombe ˈwɪd.ɪ.kəm
wide-eyed ˌwaɪdˈaɪd (US) ˈ-- *stress shift, British only:* ˌwide-eyed ˈstare
Widemouth ˈwɪd.maθ
widen ˈwaɪ.dᵊn **-s** -z **-ing** -ɪŋ, ˈwaɪd.nɪŋ **-ed** -d
Wideopen ˈwaɪdˌəʊ.pᵊn (US) -ˌoʊ-
widescreen ˈwaɪd.skriːn
widespread ˈwaɪd.spred
widgeon ˈwɪdʒ.ən, -ɪn **-s** -z
widget ˈwɪdʒ.ɪt **-s** -s
widish ˈwaɪ.dɪʃ
Widmerpool ˈwɪd.mə.puːl (US) -mɚ-
Widnes ˈwɪd.nəs, -nɪs
widow ˈwɪd.əʊ (US) -oʊ **-s** -z **-ed** -d
widower ˈwɪd.əʊ.əʳ (US) -oʊ.ɚ **-s** -z
widowhood ˈwɪd.əʊ.hʊd (US) -oʊ-
Widsith ˈwɪd.sɪθ
width wɪtθ, wɪdθ **-s** -s
wield wiːld **-s** -z **-ing** -ɪŋ **-ed** -ɪd
Wiener schnitzel ˌviː.nəˈʃnɪt.sᵊl (US) ˈviː.nɚˌʃnɪt- **-s** -z
Wiesbaden ˈviːsˌbɑː.dᵊn, ˈviːz-, ˌ-ˈ-- (US) ˈviːsˌbɑː-
Wiesenthal ˈwiː.zᵊn.tɑːl, ˈviː- (US) ˈwiː.zᵊn.tɑːl, ˈviː-, -θɔːl
wi|fe waɪ|f **-ves** -vz
wife|hood ˈwaɪf|.hʊd **-less** -ləs, -lɪs
wifelike ˈwaɪf.laɪk
wifely ˈwaɪ.fli
wife-swapping ˈwaɪfˌswɒp.ɪŋ (US) -ˌswɑː.pɪŋ
Wiffen ˈwɪf.ɪn
Wiffle ball® ˈwɪf.l̩ˌbɔːl (US) -ˌbɑːl, -ˌbɔːl
wig wɪg **-s** -z **-ging** -ɪŋ **-ged** -d
Wigan ˈwɪg.ən
wigeon ˈwɪdʒ.ən, -ɪn **-s** -z
Wiggin ˈwɪg.ɪn **-s** -z
wigging ˈwɪg.ɪŋ **-s** -z
wiggl|e ˈwɪg.l̩ **-es** -z **-ing** -ɪŋ, ˈwɪg.lɪŋ **-ed** -d
Wigglesworth ˈwɪg.l̩z.wəθ, -wɜːθ (US) -wɚθ, -wɝːθ
wiggly ˈwɪg.l̩.i, ˈwɪg.li
wight (W) waɪt **-s** -s
Wigley ˈwɪg.li
Wigmore ˈwɪg.mɔːʳ (US) -mɔːr
Wigram ˈwɪg.rəm
Wigston ˈwɪg.stən
Wigton ˈwɪg.tən
Wigtown ˈwɪg.taʊn, -tən
Wigtownshire ˈwɪg.tən.ʃəʳ, -ˌʃɪəʳ (US) -ʃɚ, -ˌʃɪr
wigwam ˈwɪg.wæm (US) -wɑːm **-s** -z
Wilberforce ˈwɪl.bə.fɔːs (US) -bɚ.fɔːrs
Wilbraham *surname:* ˈwɪl.brə.hæm, ˈ-brəm, ˈ-bri.əm (US) ˈ-brə.hæm, ˈ-brəm ***Great and Little** in Cambridgeshire:* ˈwɪl.brəm, -brə.hæm
Wilbur ˈwɪl.bəʳ (US) -bɚ
Wilbye ˈwɪl.bi
wilco ˈwɪl.kəʊ (US) -koʊ
Wilcox ˈwɪl.kɒks (US) -kɑːks
wild (W) waɪld **-s** -z **-er** -əʳ (US) -ɚ **-est** -ɪst, -əst **-ly** -li **-ness** -nəs, -nɪs ˈ**wild** ˌ**card**; ˈ**wild** ˌ**child**; ˌ**Wild** ˈ**West**; ˌ**sow one's** ˌ**wild** ˈ**oats**
wild|cat ˈwaɪld|.kæt **-cats** -kæts **-catting** -ˌkæt.ɪŋ (US) -ˌkæţ.ɪŋ **-catted** -ˌkæt.ɪd (US) -ˌkæţ.ɪd **-catter/s** -ˌkæt.əʳ/z (US) -ˌkæţ.ɚ/z ˌ**wildcat** ˈ**strike**
Wilde waɪld
wildebeest ˈwɪl.dɪ.biːst, ˈvɪl-, -də- (US) -də- **-s** -s
Wilder ˈwaɪl.dəʳ (US) -dɚ
wilderness ˈwɪl.də.nəs, -nɪs (US) -dɚ- **-es** -ɪz
Wilderspin ˈwɪl.də.spɪn (US) -dɚ-
Wildfell ˈwaɪld.fel
wildfire ˈwaɪld.faɪəʳ (US) -faɪɚ
wildfowl ˈwaɪld.faʊl **-ing** -ɪŋ **-er/s** -əʳ/z (US) -ɚ/z
wild-goose chase ˌwaɪldˈguːs.tʃeɪs
wilding (W) ˈwaɪl.dɪŋ **-s** -z
wildlife ˈwaɪld.laɪf ˈ**wildlife** ˌ**park**
wil|e (W) waɪl **-es** -z **-ing** -ɪŋ **-ed** -d
Wiley ˈwaɪ.li
Wilfred, Wilfrid ˈwɪl.frɪd, -frəd (US) ˈwɪl-
wilful ˈwɪl.fᵊl, -fʊl **-ly** -i **-ness** -nəs, -nɪs
Wilhelmina ˌwɪl.helˈmiː.nə, -əˈ-
Wilkerson ˈwɪl.kə.sᵊn (US) -kɚ-
Wilkes wɪlks
Wilkie ˈwɪl.ki
Wilkin ˈwɪl.kɪn
Wilkins ˈwɪl.kɪnz
Wilkinson ˈwɪl.kɪn.sᵊn
Wilks wɪlks
will (W) (*n.*) wɪl **-s** -z
will (*transitive v.*) wɪl **-s** -z **-ing** -ɪŋ **-ed** -d
will (*auxil. v.*) *strong form:* wɪl *weak forms:* wᵊl, ᵊl
Note: Weak form word. The strong form is used for emphasis (e.g. 'I **will** do it') and contrast (e.g. 'I don't know if I will or not'). It is also the usual form of 'will' in final position (e.g. 'I think they both will'). Elsewhere the weak form (often speltin contracted form as **'ll**) is used.
Willard ˈwɪl.ɑːd, -əd (US) -ɚd
Willcocks, -cox ˈwɪl.kɒks (US) -kɑːks

Willenhall 'wɪl.ən.hɔːl
Willes wɪlz
Willesden 'wɪlz.dᵊn
Willett 'wɪl.ɪt **-s** -s
willful 'wɪl.fᵊl, -fʊl **-ly** -i **-ness** -nəs, -nɪs
William 'wɪl.jəm, -i.əm ⓤⓢ '-jəm **-s** -z **-son** -sᵊn
willie (W) 'wɪl.i **-s** -z
willing (W) 'wɪl.ɪŋ **-ly** -li **-ness** -nəs, -nɪs
Willingdon 'wɪl.ɪŋ.dən
Willington 'wɪl.ɪŋ.tən
Willis 'wɪl.ɪs
Willmott 'wɪl.mɒt, -mət ⓤⓢ -mɑːt, -mət
will-o'-the-wisp ˌwɪl.ə.ðə'wɪsp, 'wɪl.ə.ðə.wɪsp ⓤⓢ ˌwɪl.ə.ðə'wɪsp **-s** -s
Willoughby 'wɪl.ə.bi
willow 'wɪl.əʊ ⓤⓢ -oʊ **-s** -z **-ing** -ɪŋ **-ed** -d
willowherb 'wɪl.əʊ.hɜːb ⓤⓢ -oʊ.hɝːb
willow-pattern 'wɪl.əʊˌpæt.ᵊn ⓤⓢ -oʊˌpæt̬.ɚn
willowy 'wɪl.əʊ.i ⓤⓢ -oʊ-
willpower 'wɪl.paʊəʳ ⓤⓢ -paʊɚ **-s** -z
Wills wɪlz
Willson 'wɪl.sᵊn
Willsteed 'wɪl.stiːd
will|y (W) 'wɪl|.i **-ies** -iz
willy-nilly ˌwɪl.i'nɪl.i
Wilma 'wɪl.mə
Wilmcote 'wɪlm.kəʊt ⓤⓢ -koʊt, -kət
Wilmington 'wɪl.mɪŋ.tən
Wilmot(t) 'wɪl.mɒt, -mət ⓤⓢ -mɑːt, -mət
Wilmslow 'wɪlmz.ləʊ *locally:* 'wɪmz.ləʊ ⓤⓢ 'wɪlmz.loʊ
Wilna 'vɪl.nə
Wilno 'wɪl.nəʊ ⓤⓢ -noʊ
Wilsden 'wɪlz.dᵊn
Wilshire 'wɪl.ʃəʳ, -ˌʃɪəʳ ⓤⓢ -ʃɚ, -ˌʃɪr
Wilson 'wɪl.sᵊn
wilt *(from* **will,** *auxil. v.) normal form:* wɪlt *occasional weak form:* ᵊlt
Note: This archaic form is rarely used.
wilt wɪlt **-s** -s **-ing** -ɪŋ ⓤⓢ 'wɪl.t̬ɪŋ **-ed** -ɪd ⓤⓢ 'wɪl.t̬ɪd
Wilton 'wɪl.tən ⓤⓢ -tən, -tᵊn **-s** -z
Wilts. *(abbrev. for* **Wiltshire***)* wɪlts
Wiltshire 'wɪlt.ʃəʳ, -ˌʃɪəʳ ⓤⓢ -ʃɚ, -ˌʃɪr
wil|y 'waɪ.l|i **-ier** -i.əʳ ⓤⓢ -i.ɚ **-iest** -i.ɪst, -i.əst **-iness** -ɪ.nəs, -ɪ.nɪs
wimble 'wɪm.bl̩ **-s** -z
Wimbledon 'wɪm.bl̩.dᵊn ˌ**Wimbledon 'Common**
Wimborne 'wɪm.bɔːn ⓤⓢ -bɔːrn
Wimms wɪmz
wimp wɪmp **-s** -s **-y** -i
WIMP wɪmp
Wimpey 'wɪm.pi
wimpish 'wɪm.pɪʃ **-ly** -li **-ness** -nəs, -nɪs
wimple 'wɪm.pl̩ **-s** -z
Wimpole 'wɪm.pəʊl ⓤⓢ -poʊl
Wimpy® 'wɪm.pi **-bar/s** -bɑːʳ/z ⓤⓢ -bɑːr/z
Wimsey 'wɪm.zi
win wɪn **-s** -z **-ning** -ɪŋ **won** wʌn **winner/s** 'wɪn.əʳ/z ⓤⓢ -ɚ/z
Winalot® 'wɪn.ə.lɒt ⓤⓢ -lɑːt
Wincanton wɪŋ'kæn.tən, wɪn- ⓤⓢ wɪn'kæn.tᵊn
winc|e wɪnts **-es** -ɪz **-ing** -ɪŋ **-ed** -t
wincey 'wɪnt.si
winceyette ˌwɪnt.si'et
winch wɪntʃ **-es** -ɪz **-ing** -ɪŋ **-ed** -t
Winchelsea 'wɪn.tʃᵊl.si
Winchester 'wɪn.tʃɪ.stəʳ, -tʃə- ⓤⓢ -tʃes.tɚ, -tʃə.stɚ
Winchfield 'wɪntʃ.fiːld
Winchilsea 'wɪn.tʃᵊl.si
Winchmore 'wɪntʃ.mɔːʳ ⓤⓢ -mɔːr
wind *(n.) air blowing:* wɪnd **-s** -z **'wind ˌtunnel; take the ˌwind out of someone's 'sails**
wind *(v.) go round, roll round:* waɪnd **-s** -z **-ing** -ɪŋ **wound** waʊnd **-er/s** -əʳ/z ⓤⓢ -ɚ/z
wind *(v.) blow horn:* waɪnd ⓤⓢ waɪnd, wɪnd **-s** -z **-ing** -ɪŋ **-ed** -ɪd
wind *(v.) detect by scent, make unable to breathe:* wɪnd **-s** -z **-ing** -ɪŋ **-ed** -ɪd
windage 'wɪn.dɪdʒ
windbag 'wɪnd.bæg **-s** -z
windblown 'wɪnd.bləʊn ⓤⓢ -bloʊn
windbreak 'wɪnd.breɪk **-s** -s **-er/s** -əʳ/z ⓤⓢ -ɚ/z
windburn 'wɪnd.bɜːn ⓤⓢ -bɝːn **-ed** -t, -d **-t** -t
windcheater 'wɪndˌtʃiː.təʳ ⓤⓢ -t̬ɚ **-s** -z
wind-chest 'wɪnd.tʃest **-s** -s
windchill 'wɪnd.tʃɪl
wind-cone 'wɪnd.kəʊn ⓤⓢ -koʊn **-s** -z
Windermere 'wɪn.də.mɪəʳ ⓤⓢ -dɚ.mɪr
windfall 'wɪnd.fɔːl ⓤⓢ -fɔːl, -fɑːl **-s** -z
Windham 'wɪn.dəm
Windhoek 'wɪnd.hʊk, 'wɪnt-, 'vɪnt- ⓤⓢ 'vɪnt-
windhover 'wɪndˌhɒv.əʳ ⓤⓢ -ˌhʌv.ɚ, -ˌhɑː.vɚ **-s** -z
winding *in furnaces:* 'wɪn.dɪŋ
winding *(n. adj.)* 'waɪn.dɪŋ **-s** -z **-ly** -li
winding-sheet 'waɪn.dɪŋ.ʃiːt **-s** -s
winding-up ˌwaɪn.dɪŋ'ʌp
wind-instrument 'wɪndˌɪn.strə.mənt, -strʊ- **-s** -s
windjammer 'wɪndˌdʒæm.əʳ ⓤⓢ -ɚ **-s** -z
windlass 'wɪnd.ləs **-es** -ɪz
Windley 'wɪnd.li
windmill 'wɪnd.mɪl **-s** -z
Windolene® 'wɪn.dəʊ.liːn ⓤⓢ -doʊ-, -də-
window 'wɪn.dəʊ ⓤⓢ -doʊ **-s** -z **'window ˌbox; 'window ˌcleaner; 'window ˌdressing; 'window ˌseat**
windowpane 'wɪn.dəʊ.peɪn ⓤⓢ -do **-s** -z
window-shop 'wɪn.dəʊ.ʃɒp ⓤⓢ -doʊ.ʃɑːp **-s** -s **-ing** -ɪŋ **-ed** -t
windowsill 'wɪn.dəʊ.sɪl ⓤⓢ -doʊ- **-s**
windpipe 'wɪnd.paɪp **-s** -s
windproof 'wɪnd.pruːf
windrow 'wɪn.drəʊ ⓤⓢ -droʊ **-s** -z
Windrush 'wɪn.drʌʃ
Windscale 'wɪnd.skeɪl
windscreen 'wɪnd.skriːn **-s** -z **'windscreen ˌwiper**
windshield 'wɪnd.ʃiːld **-s** -z **'windsh ˌwiper**
windsock 'wɪnd.sɒk ⓤⓢ -sɑːk **-s** -s
Windsor 'wɪnd.zəʳ ⓤⓢ -zɚ ˌ**Windsor 'Castle; ˌDuke of 'Windsor; ˌDuche of 'Windsor**
windstorm 'wɪnd.stɔːm ⓤⓢ -stɔːrm **-s** -z
windsurf 'wɪnd.sɜːf ⓤⓢ -sɝːf **-s** -s **-i** -ɪŋ **-ed** -t **-er/s** -əʳ/z ⓤⓢ -ɚ/z
windswept 'wɪnd.swept
wind-up 'waɪnd.ʌp **-s** -s
Windus 'wɪn.dəs
windward (W) 'wɪnd.wəd ⓤⓢ -wɚd
wind|y 'wɪn.d|i **-ier** -i.əʳ ⓤⓢ -i.ɚ **-iest** -i.ɪst, -i.əst **-ily** -ɪ.li, -ᵊl.i **-iness** -ɪ.nəs, -ɪ.nɪs ˌ**Windy 'City**
win|e waɪn **-es** -z **-ing** -ɪŋ **-ed** -d **'wine ˌbar; 'wine ˌbottle; 'wine ˌcellar; ˌwine 'vinegar**
winebibber 'waɪnˌbɪb.əʳ ⓤⓢ -ɚ **-s** -z
wineglass 'waɪn.glɑːs ⓤⓢ -glæs **-es** -
winemaker 'waɪnˌmeɪ.kəʳ, 'waɪm- ⓤⓢ 'waɪnˌmeɪ.kɚ **-s** -z
winer|y 'waɪ.nᵊr|.i **-ies** -iz
winey 'waɪ.ni
Winfrey 'wɪn.fri
wing (W) wɪŋ **-s** -z **-ing** -ɪŋ **-ed** -d **'wir ˌnut; ˌclip someone's 'wings**
Wingate 'wɪn.geɪt, 'wɪŋ-, -gɪt ⓤⓢ 'w
wing-commander ˌwɪŋ.kə'mɑːn.dəʳ ⓤⓢ 'wɪŋ.kəˌmæn.dɚ **-s** -z *stress sh British only:* ˌwing-commander 'Smith
winged wɪŋd
-winger -'wɪŋ.əʳ ⓤⓢ -ɚ **-s** -z
Note: Suffix. Normally carries primary stress as shown, e.g. **left winger** /ˌleft'wɪŋ.əʳ ⓤⓢ -ɚ/.
winger 'wɪŋ.əʳ ⓤⓢ -ɚ **-s** -z
Wingerworth 'wɪŋ.ə.wəθ, -wɜːθ ⓤⓢ -ɚ.wɚθ, -wɝːθ
Wingfield 'wɪŋ.fiːld
wingspan 'wɪŋ.spæn
Winifred 'wɪn.ɪ.frɪd ⓤⓢ '-ə-
wink (W) wɪŋk **-s** -s **-ing** -ɪŋ **-ed** -t **-er/** -əʳ/z ⓤⓢ -ɚ/z
Winkfield 'wɪŋk.fiːld
Winkie 'wɪŋ.ki
winkle (W) 'wɪŋ.kl̩ **-s** -z

nkle-picker 'wɪŋ.kl̩ˌpɪk.əʳ (US) -ɚ **-s** -z
nnable 'wɪn.ə.bl̩
nner 'wɪn.əʳ (US) -ɚ **-s** -z
nnie 'wɪn.i
nnie-the-Pooh ˌwɪn.i.ðə'puː
nning (W) 'wɪn.ɪŋ **-s** -z **-ly** -li
nning-post 'wɪn.ɪŋ.pəʊst (US) -poʊst **-s** -s
innipeg 'wɪn.ɪ.peg
nnow 'wɪn.əʊ (US) -oʊ **-s** -z **-ing** -ɪŋ **-ed** -d **-er/s** -əʳ/z (US) -ɚ/z
no 'waɪ.nəʊ (US) -noʊ **-s** -z
inona wɪ'nəʊ.nə (US) -'noʊ-
insford 'wɪnz.fəd, 'wɪns- (US) -fɚd
inslet 'wɪn*d*z.lɪt, -lət
inslow 'wɪnz.ləʊ (US) -loʊ
insome 'wɪn.səm **-ly** -li **-ness** -nəs, -nɪs
instanley *in Greater Manchester:* 'wɪn*t*.stᵊn.li; wɪn'stæn- *surname:* wɪn'stæn.li; 'wɪn*t*.stᵊn-
inston 'wɪn*t*.stᵊn
instone 'wɪn*t*.stəʊn, -stᵊn (US) -stoʊn, -stən
int|er (W) 'wɪn.t|əʳ (US) -t̬|ɚ **-ers** -əz (US) -ɚz **-ering** -ᵊr.ɪŋ **-ered** -əd (US) -ɚd ˌ**winter 'sports;** ˌ**Winter O'lympics**
interbottom 'wɪn.təˌbɒt.əm (US) -t̬ɚˌbɑː.t̬əm
interbourne 'wɪn.tə.bɔːn (US) -t̬ɚ.bɔːrn
inters 'wɪn.təz (US) -t̬ɚz
interson 'wɪn.tə.sᵊn (US) -t̬ɚ-
interthur 'vɪn.tə.tʊəʳ (US) -t̬ɚ.tʊr
intertime 'wɪn.tə.taɪm (US) -t̬ɚ-
interton 'wɪn.tə.tᵊn (US) -t̬ɚ.tən
inthrop 'wɪn.θrɒp, 'wɪn*t*.θrəp (US) 'wɪn*t*.θrəp
inton 'wɪn.tən (US) -tᵊn
intour 'wɪn.təʳ (US) -t̬ɚ
intr|y 'wɪn.tr|i **-iness** -ɪ.nəs (US) -ɪ.nɪs
inwick 'wɪn.ɪk
inwood 'wɪn.wʊd
iny 'waɪ.ni
ip|e waɪp **-es** -s **-ing** -ɪŋ **-ed** -t **-er/s** -əʳ/z (US) -ɚ/z ˌ**wiped 'out**
ipeout 'waɪp.aʊt **-s** -s
ir|e waɪəʳ (US) waɪɚ **-es** -z **-ing** -ɪŋ **-ed** -d
ire-cutter 'waɪəˌkʌt.əʳ (US) 'waɪɚˌkʌt̬.ɚ **-s** -z
ire|draw 'waɪə|.drɔː (US) 'waɪɚ|.drɑː, -drɔː **-draws** -drɔːz (US) -drɑːz, -drɔːz **-drawing** -ˌdrɔː.ɪŋ (US) -ˌdrɑː.ɪŋ, -ˌdrɔː- **-drew** -druː **-drawn** -drɔːn (US) -drɑːn, -drɔːn **-drawer/s** -ˌdrɔː.əʳ/z (US) -ˌdrɑː.ɚ/z, -ˌdrɔː-
ire-haired 'waɪə.heəd (US) 'waɪɚ.herd
ireless 'waɪə.ləs, -lɪs (US) 'waɪɚ- **-es** -ɪz
iretap 'waɪə.tæp (US) 'waɪɚ- **-s** -s **-ping** -ɪŋ **-ped** -t

wireworm 'waɪə.wɜːm (US) 'waɪɚ.wɝːm **-s** -z
wiring 'waɪə.rɪŋ (US) 'waɪɚ.ɪŋ
Wirksworth 'wɜːk.swəθ, -swɜːθ (US) 'wɝːk.swɚθ, -swɝːθ
Wirral 'wɪr.ᵊl
wir|y 'waɪə.r|i (US) 'waɪɚ|.i **-ier** -i.əʳ (US) -i.ɚ **-iest** -i.ɪst, -i.əst **-iness** -ɪ.nəs, -ɪ.nɪs
Wis. *(abbrev. for* **Wisconsin***)* wɪ'skɒn*t*.sɪn (US) -'skɑːn*t*.sən
Wisbech 'wɪz.biːtʃ *locally:* -bɪtʃ
Wisbey 'wɪz.bi
Wisconsin wɪ'skɒn*t*.sɪn (US) -'skɑːn*t*.sən
Wisden 'wɪz.dən
wisdom 'wɪz.dəm '**wisdom** ˌ**tooth**
wis|e (W) waɪz **-er** -əʳ (US) -ɚ **-est** -ɪst, -əst **-ely** -li **-eness** -nəs, -nɪs '**wise** ˌ**guy;** ˌ**three** ˌ**wise 'men**
wiseacre 'waɪzˌeɪ.kəʳ (US) -kɚ **-s** -z
wisecrack 'waɪz.kræk **-s** -s
Wiseman 'waɪz.mən
wish wɪʃ **-es** -ɪz **-ing** -ɪŋ **-ed** -t **-er/s** -əʳ/z (US) -ɚ/z
Wishart 'wɪʃ.ət (US) -ɚt
Wishaw 'wɪʃ.ɔː (US) -ɑː, -ɔː
wishbone 'wɪʃ.bəʊn (US) -boʊn **-s** -z
wishful 'wɪʃ.fᵊl, -fʊl **-ly** -i **-ness** -nəs, -nɪs ˌ**wishful 'thinking**
wishing-well 'wɪʃ.ɪŋ.wel **-s** -z
wish-wash 'wɪʃ.wɒʃ (US) -wɑːʃ, -wɔːʃ
wishy-washy 'wɪʃ.iˌwɒʃ.i, ˌwɪʃ.i'wɒʃ- (US) 'wɪʃ.iˌwɑː.ʃi, -ˌwɔː-
wisp wɪsp **-s** -s
wisp|y 'wɪs.p|i **-ier** -i.əʳ (US) -i.ɚ **-iest** -i.ɪst, -i.əst **-ily** -ɪ.li, -ᵊl.i **-iness** -ɪ.nəs, -ɪ.nɪs
wist wɪst
Wistar 'wɪs.təʳ (US) -tɚ
wistaria wɪ'steə.ri.ə, -'stɪə- (US) -'ster.i-, -'stɪr- **-s** -z
Wister 'wɪs.təʳ (US) -tɚ
wisteria wɪ'stɪə.ri.ə, -'steə- (US) -'stɪr.i-, -'ster- **-s** -z
wistful 'wɪs*t*.fᵊl, -fʊl **-ly** -i **-ness** -nəs, -nɪs
wit wɪt **-s** -s
witch wɪtʃ **-es** -ɪz **-ing/ly** -ɪŋ/li **-ed** -t
witchcraft 'wɪtʃ.krɑːft (US) -kræft
witchdoctor 'wɪtʃˌdɒk.təʳ (US) -ˌdɑːk.tɚ **-s** -z
witcher|y 'wɪtʃ.ᵊr|.i **-ies** -iz
witch-hazel 'wɪtʃˌheɪ.zᵊl, ˌ-'-- (US) 'wɪtʃˌheɪ- **-s** -z
witch-hunt 'wɪtʃ.hʌnt **-s** -s **-er/s** -əʳ/z (US) -ɚ/z
witching 'wɪtʃ.ɪŋ '**witching** ˌ**hour**
witenagemot(e) ˌwɪt.ɪ.nə.gɪ'məʊt, -ᵊn.ə-, -gə'- (US) ˌwɪt.ᵊn.ə.gə'moʊt
with wɪð, wɪθ
Note: The pronunciation /wɪθ/ is most frequently found when followed by a voiceless consonant (e.g. 'with care' /wɪθ'keə (US) -'ker/).
withal wɪ'ðɔːl (US) wɪ'ðɔːl, -'ðɑːl
Witham 'wɪð.əm *town in Essex:* 'wɪt.əm (US) 'wɪt̬-
withdraw wɪð'drɔː, wɪθ- (US) -'drɑː, -'drɔː **-s** -z **-ing** -ɪŋ **withdrew** wɪð'druː, wɪθ- **withdrawn** wɪð'drɔːn, wɪθ- (US) -'drɑːn, -'drɔːn
withdrawal wɪð'drɔː.ᵊl, wɪθ- (US) -'drɑː-, -'drɔː- **-s** -z **with'drawal** ˌ**method; with'drawal** ˌ**symptoms**
withe wɪθ, wɪð, waɪð **-s** -s, -z
with|er (W) 'wɪð|.əʳ (US) -ɚ **-ers** -əz (US) -ɚz **-ering/ly** -ᵊr.ɪŋ/li **-ered** -əd (US) -ɚd
Withernsea 'wɪð.ən.siː (US) -ɚn-
withers (W) *(n.)* 'wɪð.əz (US) -ɚz
Witherspoon 'wɪð.ə.spuːn (US) '-ɚ-
with|hold wɪθ|'həʊld, wɪð- (US) -'hoʊld **-holds** -'həʊldz (US) -'hoʊldz **-holding** -'həʊl.dɪŋ (US) -'hoʊl.dɪŋ **-held** -'held **-holden** -'həʊl.dᵊn (US) -'hoʊl.dᵊn **-holder/s** -'həʊl.dəʳ/z (US) -'hoʊl.dɚ/z
within wɪ'ðɪn; 'wɪð.ɪn (US) wɪ'ðɪn, -'θɪn
with-it 'wɪð.ɪt (US) 'wɪð-, 'wɪθ-
withless 'wɪt.ləs, -lɪs **-ly** -li **-ness** -nəs, -nɪs
without wɪ'ðaʊt; 'wɪð.aʊt (US) wɪ'ðaʊt, -'θaʊt
withstand wɪð'stænd, wɪθ- (US) wɪθ-, wɪð- **-s** -z **-ing** -ɪŋ **withstood** wɪð'stʊd, wɪθ- (US) wɪθ-, wɪð-
with|y 'wɪð|.i (US) 'wɪð-, 'wɪθ- **-ies** -iz
witless 'wɪt.ləs, -lɪs **-ly** -li **-ness** -nəs, -nɪs
Witley 'wɪt.li
witness *(n. v.)* 'wɪt.nəs, -nɪs **-es** -ɪz **-ing** -ɪŋ **-ed** -t '**witness** ˌ**box**
witney (W) 'wɪt.ni
-witted -'wɪt.ɪd, -ˌwɪt.ɪd (US) -ˌwɪt̬.ɪd
Note: Suffix. May take either primary or secondary stress in British English, unless it is used attributively, in which case it always takes secondary stress, e.g. **quick-witted** /ˌkwɪk'wɪt.ɪd/, 'quick-witted ˌfox. Normally takes only secondary stress in American English.
Wittenberg 'vɪt.ᵊn.bɜːg, -beəg *old-fashioned:* 'wɪt.ᵊn.bɜːg (US) 'wɪt.ᵊn.bɝːg, 'vɪt-
witter 'wɪt.əʳ (US) 'wɪt̬- **-s** -z **-ing** -ɪŋ **-ed** -d **-er/s** -əʳ/z (US) -ɚ/z
Wittgenstein 'vɪt.gən.ʃtaɪn, -staɪn
witticism 'wɪt.ɪ.sɪ.zᵊm (US) 'wɪt̬.ə- **-s** -z
wittingly 'wɪt.ɪŋ.li (US) 'wɪt̬-
witt|y 'wɪt|.i (US) 'wɪt̬- **-ier** -i.əʳ (US) -i.ɚ **-iest** -i.ɪst, -i.əst **-ily** -ɪ.li, -ᵊl.i **-iness** -ɪ.nəs, -ɪ.nɪs

Witwatersrand wɪtˈwɔː.təz.rænd, -rɑːnd, -rɑːnt; ˈwɪtˌwɔː-, ˈvɪtˌvɑː.təz.rɒnt ⓤⓢ wɪtˈwɔː.t̬ɚz.rænd, -ˈwɑː-
Wiveliscombe ˈwɪv.əl.ɪ.skəm, ˌwɪv.əˈlɪs.kəm *locally also:* ˈwɪl.skəm
Wivelsfield ˈwɪv.əlz.fiːld
Wivenhoe ˈwɪv.ən.həʊ ⓤⓢ -hoʊ
wivern ˈwaɪ.vən, -vɜːn ⓤⓢ -vɚn, -vɝːn **-s** -z
wives *(plur. of* **wife***)* waɪvz
wizard ˈwɪz.əd ⓤⓢ -ɚd **-s** -z **-ry** -ri
wizen ˈwɪz.ən **-ed** -d
wk *(abbrev. for* **week***)* wiːk
WNW *(abbrev. for* **west-northwest***)* ˌwest.nɔːθˈwest ⓤⓢ -nɔːrθˈ- *nautical pronunciation:* -nɔːˈ- ⓤⓢ -nɔːrˈ-
wo wəʊ ⓤⓢ woʊ
woad wəʊd ⓤⓢ woʊd
wobbl|e ˈwɒb.l̩ ⓤⓢ ˈwɑː.bl̩ **-es** -z **-ing** -ɪŋ, ˈwɒb.lɪŋ ⓤⓢ ˈwɑː.blɪŋ **-ed** -d **-er/s** -əʳ/z ⓤⓢ ˈwɒb.ləʳ/z, ˈwɑː.bl̩.əʳ/z ⓤⓢ ˈwɑː.blɚ/z
wobbl|y ˈwɒb.l̩|.i, ˈ-l|i ⓤⓢ ˈwɑː.bl̩|.i, ˈ-bl|i **-iness** -ɪ.nəs, -ɪ.nɪs
Wobegon ˈwəʊ.bɪ.gɒn ⓤⓢ ˈwoʊ.bɪ.gɑːn
Woburn *Abbey:* ˈwuː.bɜːn, -bən ⓤⓢ -bɝːn, -bɚn *street and square in London:* ˈwəʊ.bən, -bɜːn ⓤⓢ ˈwoʊ.bɚn, -bɝːn *village:* ˈwəʊ.bən, ˈwuː- ⓤⓢ ˈwoʊ.bɚn, ˈwuː-
Wodehouse ˈwʊd.haʊs
Woden ˈwəʊ.dən ⓤⓢ ˈwoʊ-
wodge wɒdʒ ⓤⓢ wɑːdʒ **-s** -ɪz
woe wəʊ ⓤⓢ woʊ **-s** -z
woebegone ˈwəʊ.bɪ.gɒn ⓤⓢ ˈwoʊ.bɪ.gɑːn
woeful ˈwəʊ.fəl, -fʊl ⓤⓢ ˈwoʊ- **-ly** -i **-ness** -nəs, -nɪs
Woffington ˈwɒf.ɪŋ.tən ⓤⓢ ˈwɑː.fɪŋ-
wog wɒg ⓤⓢ wɑːg, wɔːg **-s** -z
Wogan ˈwəʊ.gən ⓤⓢ ˈwoʊ-
wok wɒk ⓤⓢ wɑːk **-s** -s
woke *(from* **wake***)* wəʊk ⓤⓢ woʊk
woken *(from* **wake***)* ˈwəʊ.kən ⓤⓢ ˈwoʊ-
Woking ˈwəʊ.kɪŋ ⓤⓢ ˈwoʊ-
Wokingham ˈwəʊ.kɪŋ.əm ⓤⓢ ˈwoʊ-
Wolborough ˈwɒl.bər.ə ⓤⓢ ˈwɑːl.bɚ.oʊ
Wolcot(t) ˈwʊl.kət ⓤⓢ ˈwʊl-, ˈwɔːl-
wold wəʊld ⓤⓢ woʊld **-s** -z
Woldingham ˈwəʊl.dɪŋ.əm ⓤⓢ ˈwoʊl-
Woledge ˈwʊl.ɪdʒ
wol|f (W) *(n.)* wʊl|f **-ves** -vz **a ˌwolf in ˌsheep's ˈclothing; keep the ˌwolf from, the ˈdoor, keep the ˈwolf from the ˌdoor**
wolf *(v.)* wʊlf **-s** -s **-ing** -ɪŋ **-ed** -t
wolf-cub ˈwʊlf.kʌb **-s** -z
Wolfe wʊlf
Wolfenden ˈwʊl.fən.dən
Wolff wʊlf, vɒlf ⓤⓢ wʊlf, vɔːlf
Wolfgang ˈwʊlf.gæŋ
wolfhound ˈwʊlf.haʊnd **-s** -z
wolfish ˈwʊl.fɪʃ **-ly** -li **-ness** -nəs, -nɪs
wolfram (W) ˈwʊl.frəm **-ite** -aɪt
Wolfson ˈwʊlf.sən
wolf-whistl|e ˈwʊlfˌhwɪs.l̩ **-es** -z **-ing** -ɪŋ, -ˌhwɪs.lɪŋ **-ed** -d
Wollard ˈwʊl.ɑːd ⓤⓢ -ɑːrd, -ɚd
Wollaston ˈwʊl.ə.stən
Wollaton ˈwʊl.ə.tən ⓤⓢ -tən
Wollongong ˈwʊl.ən.gɒŋ, -əŋ- ⓤⓢ -ən.gɑːŋ
Wollstonecraft ˈwʊl.stən.krɑːft ⓤⓢ -kræft, -krɑːft
Wolmer ˈwʊl.məʳ ⓤⓢ -mɚ
Wolseley® ˈwʊlz.li
Wolsey ˈwʊl.zi
Wolsingham ˈwɒl.sɪŋ.əm ⓤⓢ ˈwɑːl-
Wolstenholme ˈwʊl.stən.həʊm ⓤⓢ -hoʊm
Wolverhampton ˈwʊl.vəˌhæmp.tən, ˌwʊl.vəˈhæmp- ⓤⓢ ˈwʊl.vɚˌhæmp-
wolverine ˈwʊl.vər.iːn ⓤⓢ ˌwʊl.vəˈriːn, ˈ--- **-s** -z
Wolverton ˈwʊl.və.tən ⓤⓢ -vɚ-
wolves *(plur. of* **wolf***)* wʊlvz
Womad ˈwəʊ.mæd ⓤⓢ ˈwoʊ-
woman ˈwʊm.ən **women** ˈwɪm.ɪn **ˌwoman of the ˈworld**
woman-hat|er ˈwʊm.ənˌheɪ.t|əʳ ⓤⓢ -t̬|ɚ **-ers** -əz ⓤⓢ -ɚz **-ing** -ɪŋ
womanhood ˈwʊm.ən.hʊd
womanish ˈwʊm.ə.nɪʃ **-ly** -li **-ness** -nəs, -nɪs
womanist ˈwʊm.ə.nɪst **-s** -s
womaniz|e, -is|e ˈwʊm.ə.naɪz **-es** -ɪz **-ing** -ɪŋ **-ed** -d **-er/s** -əʳ/z ⓤⓢ -ɚ/z
womankind ˌwʊm.ənˈkaɪnd, -əŋˈ-, ˈ--- ⓤⓢ ˈwʊm.ən.kaɪnd
womanlike ˈwʊm.ən.laɪk
womanl|y ˈwʊm.ən.l|i **-iness** -ɪ.nəs, -ɪ.nɪs
womb wuːm **-s** -z
wombat ˈwɒm.bæt ⓤⓢ ˈwɑːm- **-s** -s
Womble ˈwɒm.bl̩, ˈwʌm- ⓤⓢ ˈwɑː.m-
Wombourne ˈwɒm.bɔːn ⓤⓢ ˈwɑːm.bɔːrn
Wombwell *place in South Yorkshire:* ˈwʊm.wel, -wəl *surname:* ˈwʊm.wəl, ˈwʌm-, ˈwɒm- ⓤⓢ ˈwʊm-, ˈwʌm-, ˈwɑːm-
women *(plur. of* **woman***)* ˈwɪm.ɪn **ˌWomen's ˈInstitute; ˌwomen's ˈlib; ˈwomen's ˌmovement; ˈwomen's ˌroom**
womenfolk ˈwɪm.ɪn.fəʊk ⓤⓢ -foʊk
womenkind ˌwɪm.ɪnˈkaɪnd, -ɪŋˈ-, ˈ--- ⓤⓢ ˈwɪm.ɪn.kaɪnd
womenswear ˈwɪm.ɪnz.weəʳ ⓤⓢ -wer
won *(from* **win***)* wʌn
won *Korean money:* wɒn ⓤⓢ wɑːn
wond|er (W) ˈwʌn.d|əʳ ⓤⓢ -d|ɚ **-ers** -əz ⓤⓢ -ɚz **-ering/ly** -ər.ɪŋ/li **-ered** -əd ⓤⓢ -ɚd **-erer/s** -ər.əʳ/z ⓤⓢ -ɚ.ɚ/z
wonder|ful ˈwʌn.də|.fəl, -fʊl ⓤⓢ -dɚ- **-fully** -fəl.i, -fʊl-, -fli **-fulness** -fəl.-, -fʊl-, -nɪs
wonderland (W) ˈwʌn.dəl.ænd ⓤⓢ -dɚ.lænd **ˌAlice in ˈWonderlan[d]**
wonderment ˈwʌn.də.mənt ⓤⓢ -dɚ-
wondrous ˈwʌn.drəs **-ly** -li **-ness** -nə[s], -nɪs
wonk ˈwɒŋk ⓤⓢ ˈwɑːŋk **-s** -s
wonk|y ˈwɒŋ.k|i ⓤⓢ ˈwɑːŋ-, ˈwɔːŋ- **-ier** -i.əʳ ⓤⓢ -i.ɚ **-iest** -i.ɪst, -i.əst **-ily** -əl.i **-iness** -ɪ.nəs, -ɪ.nɪs
Wonsan ˌwɒnˈsæn ⓤⓢ ˌwɑːnˈsɑːn, ˌw[ɔːn-]
won|t *(n. adj.)* wəʊn|t ⓤⓢ wɔːn|t, wɑːn|t, woʊn|t, wʌn|t **-ted** -tɪd ⓤⓢ -t̬ɪd
won't wəʊnt ⓤⓢ woʊnt
wonton ˌwɒnˈtɒn ⓤⓢ ˈwɑːn.tɑːn
woo wuː **-s** -z **-ing** -ɪŋ **-ed** -d **-er/s** -əʳ/z ⓤⓢ -ɚ/z
wood (W) wʊd **-s** -z **-ed** -ɪd **not see th[e] ˌwood for the ˈtrees**
Woodall ˈwʊd.ɔːl ⓤⓢ -ɔːl, -ɑːl
Woodard ˈwʊd.ɑːd ⓤⓢ -ɚd
woodbine (W) ˈwʊd.baɪn **-s** -z
woodblock ˈwʊd.blɒk ⓤⓢ -blɑːk **-s** -s
Woodbridge ˈwʊd.brɪdʒ
Woodbury ˈwʊd.bər.i ⓤⓢ -ber-, -bɚ-
wood-carv|er ˈwʊdˌkɑː.v|əʳ ⓤⓢ -ˌkɑːr.v|ɚ **-ers** -əz ⓤⓢ -ɚz **-ing/s** -ɪŋ/z
woodchuck ˈwʊd.tʃʌk **-s** -s
woodcock (W) ˈwʊd.kɒk ⓤⓢ -kɑːk **-s**
woodcut ˈwʊd.kʌt **-s** -s
woodcutter ˈwʊdˌkʌt.əʳ ⓤⓢ -ˌkʌt̬.ɚ **-s** -z
wooden ˈwʊd.ən **-ly** -li **-ness** -nəs, -n[ɪs]
wooden-headed ˌwʊd.ənˈhed.ɪd *str[ess] shift:* ˌwooden-headed ˈperson
Woodfield ˈwʊd.fiːld
Woodford(e) ˈwʊd.fəd ⓤⓢ -fɚd
Woodgate ˈwʊd.geɪt, ˈwʊg- ⓤⓢ ˈwʊ[d-]
Woodhead ˈwʊd.hed
Woodhouse ˈwʊd.haʊs
woodland ˈwʊd.lənd **-s** -z
Woodley ˈwʊd.li
wood-|louse ˈwʊd|.laʊs **-lice** -laɪs
wood|man (W) ˈwʊd|.mən **-men** -mə[n]
wood-nymph ˈwʊd.nɪmpf **-s** -s
woodpecker ˈwʊdˌpek.əʳ ⓤⓢ -ɚ **-s** -z
wood-pigeon ˈwʊdˌpɪdʒ.ən, -ɪn **-s** -z
Woodroffe ˈwʊd.rɒf, -rʌf ⓤⓢ -rɑːf, -r[ʌf]
Woodrow ˈwʊd.rəʊ ⓤⓢ -roʊ
woodruff (W) ˈwʊd.rʌf **-s** -s
Woods wʊdz
woodshed ˈwʊd.ʃed **-s** -z **-ing** -ɪŋ **-ed** -ɪd
Woodside ˌwʊdˈsaɪd, ˈ-- ⓤⓢ ˈwʊd.saɪ[d]
woodsman ˈwʊdz.mən

odstock 'wʊd.stɒk US -stɑːk
odward 'wʊd.wəd US -wɚd
odwind 'wʊd.wɪnd **-s** -z
odwork 'wʊd.wɜːk US -wɝːk **-ing** -ɪŋ
odworm 'wʊd.wɜːm US -wɝːm
od|y (W) 'wʊd|.i **-ier** -i.əʳ US -i.ɚ **-iest** -i.ɪst, -i.əst **-iness** -ɪ.nəs, -ɪ.nɪs
of *weaving:* wuːf US wuːf, wʊf **-s** -s
of *dog's bark:* wʊf **-s** -s
of *surname:* wʊf
ofer 'wʊf.əʳ US -ɚ **-s** -z
ofter 'wʊf.təʳ US -tɚ **-s** -z
okey 'wʊk.i
ol wʊl **-s** -z
olacombe 'wʊl.ə.kəm
oldridge 'wʊl.drɪdʒ
olen 'wʊl.ən **-s** -z
oler 'wʊl.əʳ US -ɚ
olf wʊlf
olfardisworthy *near Bideford, Devon:* 'wʊl.zᵊr.i, 'wʊl.fɑː.dɪˌswɜː.ði US 'wʊl.zɚ.i, 'wʊl.fɑːr.dɪ.swɝː.ði *near Crediton, Devon:* 'wʊl.fɑː.dɪˌswɜː.ði US -fɑːr.dɪˌswɝː-
olford 'wʊl.fəd US -fɚd
ol-gathering 'wʊlˌgæð.ᵊr.ɪŋ
ollard 'wʊl.ɑːd US -ɚd
ollen 'wʊl.ən **-s** -z
olley 'wʊl.i
oll|y 'wʊl|.i **-ies** -iz **-ier** -i.əʳ US -i.ɚ **-iest** -i.ɪst, -i.əst **-iness** -ɪ.nəs, -ɪ.nɪs
olly-headed ˌwʊl.i'hed.ɪd US 'wʊl.iˌhed- *stress shift, British only:* ˌwoolly-headed 'person
olner 'wʊl.nəʳ US -nɚ
olnough 'wʊl.nəʊ US -noʊ
olpack 'wʊl.pæk **-s** -s
olsack 'wʊl.sæk **-s** -s
olsey 'wʊl.zi
olwich 'wʊl.ɪdʒ, -ɪtʃ
olworth 'wʊl.wəθ, -wɜːθ US -wɚθ, -wɝːθ **-'s** -s
ol|y 'wʊl|.i **-ier** -i.əʳ US -i.ɚ **-iest** -i.ɪst, -i.əst **-iness** -ɪ.nəs, -ɪ.nɪs
omera 'wʊm.ᵊr.ə, 'wuː.mᵊr-
orstead 'wʊs.tɪd, -təd US 'wʊs-, 'wɜː-
osley 'wuːz.li
osnam 'wuːz.nəm
ooster 'wʊs.təʳ US -tɚ
oot(t)on 'wʊt.ᵊn
ooz|y 'wuː.z|i **-ier** -i.əʳ US -i.ɚ **-iest** -i.ɪst, -i.əst **-ily** -ɪ.li, -ᵊl.i **-iness** -ɪ.nəs, -ɪ.nɪs
op wɒp US wɑːp **-s** -s
orboys 'wɔː.bɔɪz US 'wɔːr-
orcester 'wʊs.təʳ US -tɚ **-shire** -ʃəʳ, -ˌʃɪəʳ US -ʃɚ, -ˌʃɪr ˌ**Worcester 'sauce**
orcs. *(abbrev. for* **Worcestershire***)* 'wʊs.tə.ʃəʳ, -ˌʃɪəʳ US -tɚ.ʃɚ, -ˌʃɪr

word wɜːd US wɝːd **-s** -z **-ing/s** -ɪŋ/z **-ed** -ɪd **-less** -ləs, -lɪs **'word ˌorder; 'word ˌprocessor, ˌword 'processor; ˌeat one's 'words; get a ˌword in 'edgewise; put ˌwords in(to) someone's 'mouth** US **put 'words in(to) someone's ˌmouth**
wordbook 'wɜːd.bʊk US 'wɝːd- **-s** -s
Worde wɔːd US wɔːrd
word-formation 'wɜːd.fɔːˌmeɪ.ʃᵊn US 'wɝːd.fɔːrˌ-
word-for-word ˌwɜːd.fə'wɜːd US ˌwɝːd.fɚ'wɜːrd
wordless 'wɜːd.ləs, -lɪs US 'wɝːd- **-ly** -li **-ness** -nəs, -nɪs
word-of-mouth ˌwɜːd.əv'maʊθ US ˌwɝːd-
word-perfect ˌwɜːd'pɜː.fɪkt, -fekt US ˌwɝːd'pɜːr.fɪkt
wordplay 'wɜːd.pleɪ US 'wɝːd- **-s** -z
word processing 'wɜːdˌprəʊ.ses.ɪŋ, ˌ-'--- US 'wɝːdˌprɑː-, -ˌproʊ-
wordsmith 'wɜːd.smɪθ US 'wɝːd- **-s** -s
Wordsworth 'wɜːdz.wəθ, -wɜːθ US 'wɝːdz.wɚθ, -wɝːθ
Wordsworthian ˌwɜːdz'wɜː.θi.ən US ˌwɝːdz'wɜːr-
word|y 'wɜː.d|i US 'wɝː- **-ier** -i.əʳ US -i.ɚ **-iest** -i.ɪst, -i.əst **-ily** -ɪ.li, -ᵊl.i **-iness** -ɪ.nəs, -ɪ.nɪs
wore *(from* **wear***)* wɔːʳ US wɔːr
work wɜːk US wɝːk **-s** -s **-ing/s** -ɪŋ/z **-ed** -t **-er/s** -əʳ/z US -ɚ/z **ˌworking 'day** US **'working ˌday; ˌworking 'knowledge** US **'working ˌknowledge; ˌwork of 'art; ˌworking 'order** US **'working ˌorder**
workable 'wɜː.kə.bl̩ US 'wɝː- **-ness** -nəs, -nɪs
workaday 'wɜː.kə.deɪ US 'wɝː-
workaholic ˌwɜː.kə'hɒl.ɪk US ˌwɝː.kə'hɑː.lɪk **-s** -s
workaholism 'wɜː.kə.hɒl.ɪ.zᵊm US 'wɝː.kə.hɑː.lɪ-
workbag 'wɜːk.bæg US 'wɝːk- **-s** -z
workbasket 'wɜːkˌbɑː.skɪt US 'wɝːkˌbæs.kɪt **-s** -s
workbench 'wɜːk.bentʃ US 'wɝːk- **-es** -ɪz
workbook 'wɜːk.bʊk US 'wɝːk- **-s** -s
workbox 'wɜːk.bɒks US 'wɝːk.bɑːks **-es** -ɪz
workday 'wɜːk.deɪ US 'wɝːk- **-s** -z
worker 'wɜː.kəʳ US 'wɝː.kɚ **-s** -z
workfare 'wɜːk.feəʳ US 'wɝːk.fer
workforc|e 'wɜːk.fɔːs US 'wɝːk.fɔːrs **-es** -ɪz
workhors|e 'wɜːk.hɔːs US 'wɝːk.hɔːrs **-es** -ɪz
workhou|se 'wɜːk.haʊ|s US 'wɝːk- **-ses** -zɪz
working-class *(adj.)* ˌwɜː.kɪŋ'klɑːs US 'wɝː.kɪŋˌklæs *stress shift, British only:* ˌworking-class 'origins
working class *(n.)* ˌwɜː.kɪŋ'klɑːs US 'wɝː.kɪŋˌklæs **-es** -ɪz
Workington 'wɜː.kɪŋ.tən US 'wɝː-
workload 'wɜːk.ləʊd US 'wɝːk.loʊd **-s** -z
work|man (W) 'wɜːk|.mən US 'wɝːk- **-men** -mən
workman|like 'wɜːk.mən|.laɪk US 'wɝːk- **-ly** -li
workmanship 'wɜːk.mən.ʃɪp US 'wɝːk-
workmate 'wɜːk.meɪt US 'wɝːk- **-s** -s
workout 'wɜːk.aʊt US 'wɝːk- **-s** -s
workpeople 'wɜːkˌpiː.pl̩ US 'wɝːk-
workplac|e 'wɜːk.pleɪs US 'wɝːk- **-es** -ɪz
workroom 'wɜːk.rʊm, -ruːm US 'wɝːk.ruːm, -rʊm **-s** -z
workshop 'wɜːk.ʃɒp US 'wɝːk.ʃɑːp **-s** -s
work-shy 'wɜːk.ʃaɪ US 'wɝːk-
Worksop 'wɜːk.sɒp, -səp US 'wɝːk.sɑːp, -səp
workstation 'wɜːkˌsteɪ.ʃᵊn US 'wɝːk- **-s** -s
worktable 'wɜːkˌteɪ.bl̩ US 'wɝːk- **-s** -z
worktop 'wɜːk.tɒp US 'wɝːk.tɑːp **-s** -s
work-to-rule ˌwɜːk.tə'ruːl US ˌwɝːk- **-s** -z
world wɜːld US wɝːld **-s** -z **ˌWorld 'Cup; ˌWorld 'Series; ˌWorld 'Service; ˌworld 'war; ˌWorld ˌWar 'I; ˌWorld ˌWar 'II; ˌWorld Wide 'Web; ˌout of this 'world**
world-class ˌwɜːld'klɑːs US 'wɝːld.klæs, ˌ-'- *stress shift, British only:* ˌworld-class 'sportsman
world-famous ˌwɜːld'feɪ.məs US 'wɝːldˌfeɪ-, ˌ-'-- *stress shift, British only:* ˌworld-famous 'actor
worldling 'wɜːld.lɪŋ US 'wɝːld- **-s** -z
worldl|y 'wɜːld.l|i US 'wɝːld- **-ier** -i.əʳ US -i.ɚ **-iest** -i.ɪst, -i.əst **-iness** -ɪ.nəs, -ɪ.nɪs
worldly-wise ˌwɜːld.li'waɪz US 'wɝːld.liˌwaɪz, ˌ--'- *stress shift, British only:* ˌworldly-wise 'person
worldview 'wɜːld.vjuː, ˌ-'- US 'wɝːld- **-s** -z
world-wear|y ˌwɜːld'wɪə.r|i, '-ˌ-- US 'wɝːldˌwɪr|.i **-ier** -i.əʳ US -i.ɚ **-iest** -i.ɪst, -i.əst **-ily** -ɪ.li, -ᵊl.i **-iness** -ɪ.nəs, -ɪ.nɪs *stress shift, British only:* ˌworld-weary 'attitude
worldwide ˌwɜːld'waɪd US 'wɝːld.waɪd, ˌ-'- *stress shift, British only:* ˌworldwide 'coverage
worm wɜːm US wɝːm **-s** -z **-ing** -ɪŋ **-ed** -d

WORM wɜːm US wɝːm

wormcast ˈwɜːm.kɑːst US ˈwɝːm.kæst -s -s

worm-eaten ˈwɜːmˌiː.tᵊn US ˈwɝːm-

wormhole ˈwɜːm.həʊl US ˈwɝːm.hoʊl -s -z

Worms vɔːmz, wɜːmz US wɝːmz, vɔːrmz

wormwood (W) ˈwɜːm.wʊd US ˈwɝːm- ˌWormwood ˈScrubs

worm|y ˈwɜː.m|i US ˈwɝː- -iness -ɪ.nəs, -ɪ.nɪs

worn *(from* wear*)* wɔːn US wɔːrn

worn-out ˌwɔːnˈaʊt US ˌwɔːrn- *stress shift:* ˌworn-out ˈshoes

Worple ˈwɔː.pl̩ US ˈwɔːr-

Worplesdon ˈwɔː.pl̩z.dən US ˈwɔːr-

Worrall ˈwʌr.ᵊl, ˈwɒr- US ˈwɔːr-, ˈwɝː-

worrisome ˈwʌr.ɪ.səm US ˈwɝː.i- -ly -li

worr|y ˈwʌr|.i US ˈwɝː- -ies -iz -ying/ly -i.ɪŋ/li -ied -id -ier/s -i.əʳ/z US -i.ɚ/z ˈworry ˌbeads

worrywart ˈwʌr.i.wɔːt US ˈwɝː.i.wɔːrt -s -s

Worsborough ˈwɜːz.bᵊr.ə US ˈwɝːz.bɚ.oʊ, -ə

worse wɜːs US wɝːs

worsen ˈwɜː.sᵊn US ˈwɝː- -s -z -ing -ɪŋ, ˈwɜːs.nɪŋ US ˈwɝːs- -ed -d

worse-off ˌwɜːsˈɒf US ˌwɝːsˈɑːf *stress shift:* ˌworse-off ˈcircumstances

Worsfold ˈwɜːs.fəʊld, ˈwɔːz- US ˈwɝːs.foʊld, ˈwɔːrz-

worship (W) ˈwɜː.ʃɪp US ˈwɝː- -s -s -(p)ing -ɪŋ -(p)ed -t -(p)er/s -əʳ/z US -ɚ/z

worshipful ˈwɜː.ʃɪp.fᵊl, -fʊl US ˈwɝː- -ly -i -ness -nəs, -nɪs

Worsley *surname:* ˈwɜː.sli, ˈwɜːz.li US ˈwɝː.sli, ˈwɝːz.li *place near Manchester:* ˈwɜː.sli US ˈwɝː-

worst wɜːst US wɝːst -s -s -ing -ɪŋ -ed -ɪd

worst-case ˌwɜːs*t*ˈkeɪs US ˌwɝːs*t*- *stress shift:* ˌworst-case sceˈnario

Worstead ˈwʊs.tɪd, -təd US ˈwʊs-, ˈwɝː.stɪd, -stəd

worsted *yarn, cloth:* ˈwʊs.tɪd, -təd US ˈwʊs-, ˈwɝː.stɪd, -stəd

worsted *(from* worst*)* ˈwɜː.stɪd US ˈwɝː-

Worsthorne ˈwɜːs.θɔːn US ˈwɝːs.θɔːrn

Worswick ˈwɜː.sɪk US ˈwɝː-

wort wɜːt US wɝːt, wɔːrt -s -s

worth (W) wɜːθ US wɝːθ

Worthing ˈwɜː.ðɪŋ US ˈwɝː- -ton -tən

worthless ˈwɜːθ.ləs, -lɪs US ˈwɝːθ- -ly -li -ness -nəs, -nɪs

worthwhile ˌwɜːθˈ*h*waɪl US ˌwɝːθ- *stress shift:* ˌworthwhile ˈprogress

worth|y ˈwɜː.ð|i US ˈwɝː- -ies -iz -ier -i.əʳ US -i.ɚ -iest -i.ɪst, -i.əst -ily -ɪ.li US -ᵊl.i -iness -ɪ.nəs, -ɪ.nɪs

Wortley ˈwɜːt.li US ˈwɝːt-

wot wɒt US wɑːt

Wotan ˈwəʊ.tæn, ˈvəʊ- US ˈvoʊ.tɑːn

wotcha ˈwɒtʃ.ə US ˈwɑː.tʃə

wotcher ˈwɒt.ʃəʳ US ˈwɑː.tʃɚ

Wotherspoon ˈwɒð.ə.spuːn US ˈwɑː.ðɚ-

Wotton ˈwɒt.ᵊn, ˈwʊt- US ˈwɑː.tᵊn, ˈwʊt.ᵊn

Note: The place in Buckinghamshire is pronounced /ˈwʊt.ᵊn/.

would *(from* will*) strong form:* wʊd *weak forms:* wəd, əd, d

Note: Weak form word. The strong form is used contrastively (e.g. 'I don't know if he would or he wouldn't') and emphatically (e.g. 'I certainly **would**'). The strong form is always used in final position, even when unstressed (e.g. 'I **knew** she would'). The weak forms are used elsewhere. The forms /əd/ and /d/ are usually represented in spelling as 'd (e.g 'John'd do it' /ˈdʒɒn.əd̩duː.ɪt US ˈdʒɑːn- /; 'I'd do it' /ˈaɪdˌduː.ɪt/).

would-be ˈwʊd.bi

wouldn't ˈwʊd.ᵊnt

wouldst wʊdst

wound *(n. v.)* wuːnd -s -z -ing -ɪŋ -ed -ɪd

wound *(from* wind, *v.)* waʊnd

wov|e *(from* weave*)* wəʊv US woʊv -en -ᵊn

wow waʊ -s -z -ing -ɪŋ -ed -d

wowser ˈwaʊ.zəʳ US -zɚ -s -z

Wozzeck ˈvɒt.sek US ˈvɑːt.sek

WP ˌdʌb.l̩.juːˈpiː

WPC ˌdʌb.l̩.juːˌpiːˈsiː, -jʊˌ- US -juːˌ-, -jəˌ- -s -z *stress shift:* ˌWPC ˈSmith

WRAC ræk, ˌdʌb.l̩.juːˌɑːʳˌeɪˈsiː, -jʊ- US ræk, -juːˌɑːr-, -jəˌ-

wrack ræk -s -s -ing -ɪŋ -ed -t

WRAF ræf; ˌdʌb.l̩.juːˌɑːʳ.eɪˈef US ræf; ˌdʌb.l̩.juːˌɑːr.eɪˈef

Wragg ræg

wraith reɪθ -s -s

wrangl|e ˈræŋ.gl̩ -es -z -ing -ɪŋ, ˈ-glɪŋ -ed -d -er/s -əʳ/z, ˈ-gləʳ/z US ˈ-gl̩.ɚ/z, ˈ-glɚ/z

wrangler (W®) ˈræŋ.gləʳ US -glɚ -s -z

wrap ræp -s -s -ping/s -ɪŋ/z -ped -t

wraparound ˈræp.ə.raʊnd -s -z

wrapper ˈræp.əʳ US -ɚ -s -z

wrapround ˈræp.raʊnd

wrass|e ræs -es -ɪz

wrath rɒθ, rɔːθ US ræθ, rɑːθ

Wrath *Cape:* rɔːθ, rɑːθ, ræθ US ræθ, rɑːθ

wrathful ˈrɒθ.fᵊl, ˈrɔːθ-, -fʊl US ˈræθ-, ˈrɑːθ- -ly -i -ness -nəs, -nɪs

Wratislaw ˈræt.ɪ.slɔː US ˈræt̬.ɪ.slɑː, -slɔː

Wraxall ˈræk.sɔːl

Wray reɪ

wreak riːk -s -s -ing -ɪŋ -ed -t

wrea|th riː|θ -ths -ðz, -θs

wreath|e riːð -es -z -ing -ɪŋ -ed -d

Wreay reɪ *locally:* rɪə

wreck rek -s -s -ing -ɪŋ -ed -t -er/s -əʳ/z US -ɚ/z

wreckag|e ˈrek.ɪdʒ -es -ɪz

Wrekin ˈriː.kɪn

wren (W) ren -s -z

wrench ren*t*ʃ -es -ɪz -ing -ɪŋ -ed -t

Wrenn ren

wrest rest -s -s -ing -ɪŋ -ed -ɪd

wrestl|e ˈres.l̩ -es -z -ing -ɪŋ, ˈres.lɪŋ - -d -er/s -əʳ/z, ˈres.ləʳ/z US ˈres.l̩.ɚ/z ˈres.lɚ/z

wretch retʃ -es -ɪz

wretched ˈretʃ.ɪd -ly -li -ness -nəs, -n

Wrexham ˈrek.səm

wriggl|e ˈrɪg.l̩ -es -z -ing -ɪŋ, ˈrɪg.lɪŋ - -d -er/s -əʳ/z, ˈrɪg.ləʳ/z US ˈrɪg.l̩.ɚ/z ˈrɪg.lɚ/z

wright (W) raɪt -s -s

Wrigley ˈrɪg.li

wring rɪŋ -s -z -ing -ɪŋ -er/s -əʳ/z US -ɚ wrung rʌŋ

wringing-wet ˌrɪŋ.ɪŋˈwet *stress shift:* ˌwringing-wet ˈcloth

wrinkl|e ˈrɪŋ.kl̩ -es -z -ing -ɪŋ, ˈrɪŋ.klɪ -ed -d

wrinkl|y ˈrɪŋ.kl|i -ies -iz

Wriothesley ˈraɪəθ.sli

wrist rɪst -s -s

wristband ˈrɪs*t*.bænd -s -z

wristlet ˈrɪs*t*.lɪt, -lət -s -s

wristwatch ˈrɪs*t*.wɒtʃ US -wɑːtʃ -es -ɪz

wristy ˈrɪs.ti

writ rɪt -s -s

writ *(=* written*)* rɪt

writ|e raɪt -es -s -ing/s -ɪŋ/z US ˈraɪ.t̬ɪŋ/z wrote rəʊt US roʊt written ˈrɪt.ᵊn writer/s ˈraɪ.təʳ/z US ˈraɪ.t̬ɚ/z ˌwriter's ˈcramp

writh|e raɪð -es -z -ing -ɪŋ -ed -d

writing ˈraɪ.tɪŋ US -t̬ɪŋ -s -z see the ˌwriting on the ˈwall

writing-cas|e ˈraɪ.tɪŋ.keɪs US -t̬ɪŋ- -es -ɪz

writing-paper ˈraɪ.tɪŋˌpeɪ.pəʳ US -t̬ɪŋˌpeɪ.pɚ

written-off ˌrɪt.ᵊnˈɒf US -ˈɑːf

Writtle ˈrɪt.l̩ US ˈrɪt̬-

WRNS *(abbrev. for* Women's Royal Navy Service*)* renz; ˌdʌb.l̩.juːˌɑːʳ.enˈes US renz; ˌdʌb.l̩.juːˌɑːr.enˈes

Wroclaw ˈvrɒt.slɑːf, -slæf, -swɑːf US ˈvrɑːt.slɑːf

wrong (W) rɒŋ US rɑːŋ, rɔːŋ **-s** -z **-ly** -li **-ness** -nəs, -nɪs **-ing** -ɪŋ **-ed** -d
wrong-doer ˈrɒŋˌduː.əʳ, ˌ-ˈ-- US ˈrɑːŋˌduː.ɚ, ˈrɔːŋ- **-s** -z
wrong-doing ˈrɒŋˌduː.ɪŋ, ˌ-ˈ-- US ˈrɑːŋˌduː-, ˈrɔːŋ-
wrong|-foot ˌrɒŋˈfʊt US ˌrɑːŋ-, ˌrɔːŋ- **-foots** -ˈfʊts **-footing** -ˈfʊt.ɪŋ US -ˈfʊt̬.ɪŋ **-footed** -ˈfʊt.ɪd US -ˈfʊt̬.ɪd
wrongful ˈrɒŋ.fᵊl, -fʊl US ˈrɑːŋ-, ˈrɔːŋ- **-ly** -i **-ness** -nəs, -nɪs
wrongheaded ˌrɒŋˈhed.ɪd US ˌrɑːŋ-, ˌrɔːŋ-, ˈ-ˌ-- **-ly** -li **-ness** -nəs, -nɪs
wrote *(from* **write***)* rəʊt US roʊt
wroth rəʊθ, rɔːθ, rɒθ US rɔːθ, rɑːθ
Wrotham ˈruː.təm US -t̬əm
Wrottesley ˈrɒt.sli US ˈrɑːt-
wrought rɔːt US rɑːt, rɔːt
wrought-iron ˌrɔːtˈaɪən US ˌrɑːtˈaɪɚn, ˌrɔːt- *stress shift:* ˌwrought-iron ˈgate
Wroughton ˈrɔː.tᵊn US ˈrɑː-, ˈrɔː-
Wroxham ˈrɒk.səm US ˈrɑːk-
wrung *(from* **wring***)* rʌŋ
W.R.V.S. ˌdʌb.l̩.juːˌɑːˌviːˈes, -jʊˌ- US -juːˌɑːrˌ-, -jəˌ-
wry raɪ **wrier, wryer** ˈraɪ.əʳ US -ɚ **wriest, wryest** ˈraɪ.ɪst, -əst **wryly** ˈraɪ.li **wryness** ˈraɪ.nəs, -nɪs
wryneck ˈraɪ.nek **-s** -s
Wrythe raɪð
WSW *(abbrev. for* **west southwest***)* ˌwest.saʊθˈwest *nautical pronunciation:* -saʊˈ-
wt *(abbrev. for* **weight***)* weɪt
Wuhan ˌwuːˈhæn US -ˈhɑːn
Wulf wʊlf
Wulfila ˈwʊl.fɪ.lə
Wulfstan ˈwʊlf.stən US -stæn, -stɑːn
wunder|kind ˈwʊn.dəl.kɪnd, ˈvʊn- US -dɚl.kɪnt, ˈwʌn- **-kinder** -ˌkɪn.dəʳ US -ˌkɪn.dɚ
Wurlitzer ˈwɜː.lɪt.səʳ, -lət- US ˈwɝː.lət.sɚ **-s** -z
Württemberg ˈvɜː.təm.beəg; ˈwɜː.təm.bɜːg US ˈwɝː.t̬əm.bɜːrg; ˈvɝː.təm.berk
Würzburg ˈvɜːts.bʊəg; ˈwɜːts.bɜːg US ˈwɝːts.bɜːrg; ˈvɝːts.burk
wuss wʊs
Wuthering ˈwʌð.ᵊr.ɪŋ ˌ**Wuthering ˈHeights**
W.Va. *(abbrev. for* **West Virginia***)* ˌwest.vəˈdʒɪn.jə, -vɜːˈ-, -i.ə US -vɚˈ-
WVS ˌdʌb.l̩.juːˌviːˈes, -jʊˌ- US -juːˌ-, -jəˌ-
Wyandotte ˈwaɪən.dɒt US -dɑːt **-s** -s
Wyat(t) waɪət
Wych waɪtʃ, wɪtʃ
Wycherley ˈwɪtʃ.ᵊl.i US -ɚ.li
wych-hazel ˈwɪtʃˌheɪ.zᵊl, ˌ-ˈ-- US ˈwɪtʃˌheɪ- **-s** -z
Wycliffe, Wyclif ˈwɪk.lɪf
Wycliffite ˈwɪk.lɪ.faɪt **-s** -s
Wycombe ˈwɪk.əm
Wye waɪ
Wygram ˈwaɪ.grəm
Wykeham ˈwɪk.əm **-ist/s** -ɪst/s
Wyld(e) waɪld
Wyl(l)ie ˈwaɪ.li
Wyman ˈwaɪ.mən
Wymondham *in Norfolk:* ˈwɪm.ən.dəm *locally:* ˈwɪn.dəm *in Leicestershire:* ˈwaɪ.mən.dəm
Wyndham ˈwɪn.dəm
Wynn(e) wɪn
Wynyard ˈwɪn.jəd, -jɑːd US -jɚd, -jɑːrd
Wyo. *(abbrev. for* **Wyoming***)* waɪˈəʊ.mɪŋ US -ˈoʊ-
Wyoming waɪˈəʊ.mɪŋ US -ˈoʊ-
WYSIWYG ˈwɪz.i.wɪg
Wyss waɪs
Wystan ˈwɪs.tən
Wytch Farm ˌwɪtʃˈfɑːm US -ˈfɑːrm
Wytham ˈwaɪ.təm US -t̬əm
Wythenshawe ˈwɪð.ᵊn.ʃɔː US -ʃɑː, -ʃɔː
wyvern (W) ˈwaɪ.vən, -vɜːn US -vɚn, -vɜːrn **-s** -z

Pronouncing the letter X

See also XC

The consonant letter **x**, which rarely occurs at the beginning of a word, has three main pronuncations: /ks gz/ and /kʃ/, e.g.:

box	/bɒks/	(US) /bɑːks/
examine	/ɪgˈzæm.ɪn, ɪkˈsæm-/	(US) /ɪgˈzæm-/
noxious	/ˈnɒk.ʃəs/	(US) /ˈnɑːk-/

When **x** does appear at the beginning of a word, it is almost always pronounced /z/, e.g.:

/z/	xylophone	/ˈzaɪ.lə.fəʊn/	(US) /-foʊn/

Another pronunciation associated with **x is** /eks/, e.g.:

/eks/	X-ray	/ˈeks.reɪ/	(US) /ˈek.sreɪ/

Pronouncing the letters XC

The consonant digraph **xc** has two pronunciations: /ks/ and /ksk/.

Before the vowel letters **i** or **e**, it is pronounced as /ks/, e.g.:

exceed /ɪkˈsiːd/

In other situations, **xc** is pronounced as /ksk/, e.g.:

exclaim /ɪksˈkleɪm/

x (**X**) eks **-'s** -ɪz

Xanadu ˈzæn.ə.duː, ˌ--ˈ- (US) ˈzæn.ə.duː, -djuː, ˌ--ˈ-

Xanthe ˈzænt.θi

Xanthipp|e zæntˈθɪp|.i, zænˈtɪp- (US) zænˈtɪp- **-us** -əs

Xanthus ˈzænt.θəs

Xantia® ˈzæn.ti.ə (US) zænˈtiː-

Xavier ˈzæv.i.əʳ, -eɪ, ˈzeɪ.vi.əʳ, ˈ-vjəʳ (US) ˈzeɪ.vjɚ, ˈzæv.jɚ, -i.ɚ

X-certificate ˌeks.səˈtɪf.ɪ.kət, -sɜːˈ-, ˈ-ə-, -kɪt (US) -sɚˈ- **-s** -s

xebec ˈziː.bek **-s** -s

Xenia ˈzen.i.ə, ˈksen-, ˈziː.ni-, ˈksiː-, ˈ-njə (US) ˈziː.njə, ˈ-ni.ə

xeno- zen.əʊ-, ziː.nəʊ-; zɪˈnɒ- (US) zen.oʊ-, ziː.noʊ-, -nə-; zɪˈnɑː-

Note: Prefix. Normally either takes primary or secondary stress on the first syllable, e.g. **xenophobe** /ˈzen.əʊ.fəʊb (US) -ə.foʊb/, **xenophobia** /ˌzen.əʊˈfəʊ.bi.ə (US) -əˈfoʊ-/, or primary stress on the second syllable, e.g. **xenogamy** /zɪˈnɒg.ə.mi (US) -ˈnɑː.gə-/.

xenogamy zɪˈnɒg.ə.mi (US) -ˈnɑː.gə-

xenon ˈziː.nɒn (US) -nɑːn, ˈzen.ɑːn

xenophobe ˈzen.əʊ.fəʊb (US) -ə.foʊb, ˈziː.nə-, -noʊ- **-s** -z

xenophobia ˌzen.əʊˈfəʊ.bi.ə (US) -əˈfoʊ-, ˌziː.nəˈ-, -noʊˈ-

xenophobic ˌzen.əʊˈfəʊ.bɪk (US) -əˈfoʊ-, ˌziː.nə-, -noʊ- *stress shift:* ˌxenophobic ˈsentiment

Xenophon ˈzen.ə.fᵊn (US) -fən, -fɑːn

xerography zɪəˈrɒg.rə.fi, zerˈɒg- (US) zɪˈrɑː.grə-

xerox® (**X**) (*n. v.*) ˈzɪə.rɒks (US) ˈzɪr.ɑːks, ˈziː.rɑːks **-es** -ɪz **-ing** -ɪŋ **-ed** -t

Xerxes ˈzɜːk.siːz (US) ˈzɝːk-

Xhosa ˈkɔː.sə, ˈkəʊ-, -zə (US) ˈkoʊ.sɑː, -zɑː

xi saɪ, ksaɪ (US) zaɪ, saɪ **-'s** -z

Xiaoping ˌʃaʊˈpɪŋ

Xinhua ˌʃɪnˈhwɑː *stress shift:* ˌXinhua ˈNews Agency

Xmas ˈkrɪst.məs, ˈeks.məs (US) ˈkrɪs-

X-rated ˈeksˌreɪ.tɪd (US) -t̬ɪd

X-ray ˈeks.reɪ, ˌ-ˈ- (US) ˈek.sreɪ **-s** -z **-ing** -ɪŋ **-ed** -d

xu suː

xylem ˈzaɪ.ləm, -lem (US) ˈzaɪ-

xylene ˈzaɪ.liːn

xylograph ˈzaɪ.ləʊ.grɑːf, -græf (US) -loʊ.græf, -lə- **-s** -s

xylograph|y zaɪˈlɒg.rə.f|i (US) -ˈlɑː.grə- **-er/s** -əʳ/z (US) -ɚ/z

xylonite ˈzaɪ.lə.naɪt

xylophone ˈzaɪ.lə.fəʊn (US) -foʊn **-s** -z

xylose ˈzaɪ.ləʊs, -ləʊz (US) -loʊs

xyster ˈzɪs.t əʳ (US) -tɚ

Pronouncing the letter Y

The consonant letter **y** is special in that it can act as both vowel and consonant. At the beginning of a word, it most often behaves as a consonant and, when doing so, is pronounced as /j/, e.g.:

yes	/jes/
youth	/juːθ/

When acting as a vowel, the letter **y** has two main strong pronunciations: a 'short' pronunciation /ɪ/ and a 'long' pronunciation /aɪ/. There are no definite rules for when either of these pronunciations will occur, e.g.:

myth	/mɪθ/
cycle	/ˈsaɪ.kl̩/

At the end of a word, in adjectives and adverbs ending with a letter **y**, a short /i/ is usually used. However, for other types of word, either /i/ or /aɪ/ may occur, e.g.:

happy	/ˈhæp.i/
happily	/ˈhæp.ɪ.li/
study	/ˈstʌd.i/
apply	/əˈplaɪ/

When **y** is followed by **r**, the strong pronunciation is one of four possibilities: /aɪə (US) aɪɚ/, /aɪə.r (US) aɪ.r/ or /ɪ/ when followed by a single consonant and then a vowel, otherwise /ɜː, (US) ɝː/, e.g.:

tyre	/taɪəʳ/	(US) /taɪɚ/
gyrate (v.)	/dʒaɪəˈreɪt/	(US) /ˈdʒaɪ.reɪt/
lyric	/ˈlɪr.ɪk/	
myrrh	/mɜːʳ/	(US) /mɝː/

In addition

When acting as a vowel, **y** can also be realised as /iː/ or /ɪ/ in a small number of words, usually proper nouns, e.g.:

Yves	/iːv/

In weak syllables

When acting as a vowel, the letter **y** is realised with the vowels /ɪ/ and, occasionally, /ə/ and /i/ in word-medial weak syllables, e.g.:

oxygen	/ˈɒk.sɪ.dʒən, -sə-/	(US) /ˈɑːk.sɪ-/
anybody	/ˈen.iˌbɒd.i/	(US) /-ˌbɑː.di/

y (Y) waɪ **-'s** -z
yacht jɒt (US) jɑːt **-s** -s **-ing** -ɪŋ (US) ˈjɑː.t̬ɪŋ **-ed** -ɪd (US) ˈjɑː.t̬ɪd
yachts|man ˈjɒts|.mən (US) ˈjɑːts- **-men** -mən **-woman** -ˌwʊm.ən **-women** -ˌwɪm.ɪn
yack jæk **-s** -s **-ing** -ɪŋ **-ed** -t
yah jɑː
yahoo (Y) (*interj.*) jəˈhuː, jɑː- **-s** -z (*n.*) ˈjɑː.huː (US) ˈjɑː-, ˈjeɪ-
Yahveh ˈjɑː.veɪ, -və, jɑːˈveɪ (US) ˈjɑː.veɪ
Yahweh ˈjɑː.weɪ
yak jæk **-s** -s
yakka ˈjæk.ə
Yakutsk jækˈʊtsk, jɑːˈkʊtsk, jə- (US) jɑː-
yakuza ˈjæk.ʊ.zɑː (US) ˈjɑː.kʊ- **-s** -z
Yalding *surname:* ˈjæl.dɪŋ *place name:* ˈjɔːl.dɪŋ (US) ˈjɑːl-, ˈjɔːl-
Yale jeɪl
y'all jɔːl
Yalta ˈjæl.tə, ˈjɔːl-, ˈjɒl- (US) ˈjɑːl.t̬ə, ˈjɔːl-, -tə
yam jæm **-s** -z
Yamaha ˈjæm.ə.hɑː, -hə (US) ˈjɑː.mə-
Yamamoto ˌjæm.əˈməʊ.təʊ (US) ˌjɑː.məˈmoʊ.t̬oʊ, -toʊ
yamm|er ˈjæm|.əʳ (US) -ɚ **-ers** -əz (US) -ɚz **-ering** -ᵊr.ɪŋ **-ed** -əd (US) -ɚd
yang jæŋ (US) jæŋ, jɑːŋ
Yangtze, Yangtse, Yangzi ˈjæŋ*k*t.si (US) ˈjæŋ*k*t-, ˈjɑːŋ*k*t-
yank (Y) jæŋk **-s** -s **-ing** -ɪŋ **-ed** -t
Yankee ˈjæŋ.ki **-s** -z
Yaoundé jɑːˈʊn.deɪ, -ˈuːn- (US) ˌjɑː.ʊnˈdeɪ
yap jæp **-s** -s **-ping** -ɪŋ **-ped** -t
Yap jæp (US) jɑːp, jæp
yard jɑːd (US) jɑːrd **-s** -z **ˈyard ˌsale**
yardage ˈjɑː.dɪdʒ (US) ˈjɑːr- **-s** -ɪz
yardarm ˈjɑːd.ɑːm (US) ˈjɑːrd.ɑːrm **-s** -z
yardbird ˈjɑːd.bɜːd (US) ˈjɑːrd.bɝːd **-s** -z
Yardie ˈjɑː.di (US) ˈjɑːr- **-s** -z
Yardley ˈjɑːd.li (US) ˈjɑːrd-
yardstick ˈjɑːd.stɪk (US) ˈjɑːrd- **-s** -s
Yare *in Norfolk:* jeəʳ (US) jer *in the Isle of Wight:* jɑːʳ (US) jɑːr
Yarm jɑːm (US) jɑːrm
yarmelke ˈjʌm.ʊl.kə, ˈjɑː.mʊl-, -mᵊl- (US) ˈjɑːr.məl-, ˈjɑː- **-s** -z
Yarmouth ˈjɑː.məθ (US) ˈjɑːr-
yarmulke, yarmulka ˈjʌm.ʊl.kə, ˈjɑː.mʊl-, -mᵊl- (US) ˈjɑːr.məl-, ˈjɑː- **-s** -z
yarn jɑːn (US) jɑːrn **-s** -z **-ing** -ɪŋ **-ed** -d
Yaroslavl ˌjær.əʊˈslɑː.vᵊl (US) ˌjɑːr.oʊˈslɑː.vᵊl, -əˈ-
yarrow (Y) ˈjær.əʊ (US) ˈjer.oʊ, ˈjær-
yashmak ˈjæʃ.mæk (US) ˈjɑːʃ.mɑːk, ˈjæʃ.mæk **-s** -s
Yasmin ˈjæz.mɪn
Yasser ˈjæs.əʳ (US) -ɚ, ˈjɑː.sɚ
yataghan ˈjæt.ə.gən (US) -gæn, -gən **-s** -z
Yate jeɪt **-s** -s
Yately ˈjeɪt.li
Yatman ˈjæt.mən
Yatton ˈjæt.ᵊn
yaw jɔː (US) jɑː, jɔː **-s** -z **-ing** -ɪŋ **-ed** -d
Yaweh ˈjɑː.weɪ
yawl jɔːl (US) jɑːl, jɔːl **-s** -z
yawn jɔːn (US) jɑːn, jɔːn **-s** -z **-ing/ly** -ɪŋ/li **-ed** -d
yaws jɔːz (US) jɑːz, jɔːz
Yaxley ˈjæk.sli
yclept ɪˈklept (US) i-
yd *(abbrev. for* **yard***) singular:* jɑːd (US) jɑːrd *plural:* jɑːdz (US) jɑːrdz
ye *you. Normal form:* jiː *occasional weak form:* ji
Note: The weak form is rarely used, and only in imitation of archaic or dialect sayings such as 'Sit ye down' /ˌsɪt.jiˈdaʊn/.
ye *the:* jiː
Note: As a pronunciation of the definite article, this is rarely used except in joking. It is a mistake resulting from reading the Old English letter "thorn" (which represented 'th' sounds) as a 'y', which it resembles.
yea jeɪ
Yeading ˈjed.ɪŋ
Yeadon ˈjiː.dᵊn
yeah jeə (US) jeə, jæə
Note: Aside from the examples given for American English, there are many possibilities here, another being /jɑː/.
Yeames jiːmz

yean jiːn **-s** -z **-ing** -ɪŋ **-ed** -d
year jɪə^r, jɜː^r (US) jɪr **-s** -z **-ly** -li **ˌyear in (and) ˌyear ˈout**
yearbook ˈjɪə.bʊk, ˈjɜː- (US) ˈjɪr- **-s** -s
yearling ˈjɪə.lɪŋ, ˈjɜː- (US) ˈjɪr- **-s** -z
yearlong ˌjɪəˈlɒŋ, ˌjɜː- (US) ˈjɪr.lɑːŋ, -lɔːŋ, ˌ-ˈ- *stress shift, British only:* ˌyearlong ˈtruce
yearn jɜːn (US) jɝːn **-s** -z **-ing/s** -ɪŋ/z **-ed** -d
yeast jiːst **-y** -i **-iness** -ɪ.nəs, -ɪ.nɪs
Yeates jeɪts
Yeatman ˈjiːt.mən, ˈjeɪt-, ˈjet-
Yeats jeɪts
Yeddo ˈjed.əʊ (US) -oʊ
Yehudi jeˈhuː.di, jɪ-, jə-
yell (Y) jel **-s** -z **-ing** -ɪŋ **-ed** -d
Yelland ˈjel.ənd
yellow ˈjel.əʊ (US) -oʊ **-s** -z **-ing** -ɪŋ **-ed** -d **-y** -i **ˌyellow ˈfever; ˌyellow ˈline; ˌYellow ˈPages** (US) **ˈYellow ˌPages; ˌyellow ˈperil; ˌyellow ˌbrick ˈroad**
yellowhammer ˈjel.əʊˌhæm.ə^r (US) -oʊˌhæm.ɚ **-s** -z
yellowish ˈjel.əʊ.ɪʃ (US) -oʊ- **-ness** -nəs, -nɪs
yellowjacket ˈjel.əʊˌdʒæk.ɪt (US) -oʊ- **-s** -s
Yellowknife ˈjel.əʊ.naɪf (US) -oʊ-
yellowness ˈjel.əʊ.nəs, -nɪs (US) -oʊ-
Yellowstone ˈjel.əʊ.stəʊn, -stən (US) -oʊ.stoʊn
yelp jelp **-s** -s **-ing** -ɪŋ **-ed** -t
Yeltsin ˈjelt.sɪn
Yemen ˈjem.ən, -en (US) -ən, ˈjeɪ.mən **-i** -i **-is** -iz
Yemenite ˈjem.ən.aɪt (US) ˈjem-, ˈjeɪ.mən- **-s** -s
yen jen **-s** -z
Yentob ˈjen.tɒb (US) -tɑːb
Yeo jəʊ (US) joʊ
Yeoburgh ˈjɑː.b^{ə}r.ə
yeo|man ˈjəʊ|.mən (US) ˈjoʊ- **-men** -mən **-manly** -mən.li
yeomanry ˈjəʊ.mən.ri (US) ˈjoʊ-
Yeomans ˈjəʊ.mənz (US) ˈjoʊ-
Yeovil ˈjəʊ.vɪl (US) ˈjoʊ-
yep jep
yer jeə, jɜː (US) je
Note: This is a written or spoken informal form of **yes** in British English. The **r** in the spelling is not pronounced in American English forms and is not linking in British English.
Yerby ˈjɜː.bi (US) ˈjɝː-
Yerevan ˌjer.əˈvɑːn
Yerkes ˈjɜː.kiːz (US) ˈjɝː-
yes jes
yes|-man ˈjes|.mæn **-men** -men
yesterday ˈjes.tə.deɪ, ˌ--ˈ-, -di (US) -tɚ-
yesteryear ˈjes.tə.jɪə^r, ˌ--ˈ- (US) -tɚ.jɪr

yet jet
Yetholm ˈjet.əm (US) ˈjet̬-
yeti ˈjet.i (US) ˈjet̬- **-s** -z
Yevtushenko ˌjev.tʊˈʃeŋ.kəʊ, -tuːˈ- (US) -koʊ
yew juː **-s** -z
Y-Front® ˈwaɪ.frʌnt **-s** -s
Yg(g)drasil ˈɪg.drə.sɪl, ɪgˈdræs.^{ə}l (US) ˈɪg.drə.sɪl
yid jɪd
Yiddish ˈjɪd.ɪʃ
yield jiːld **-s** -z **-ing/ly** -ɪŋ/li **-ed** -ɪd
yin jɪn
yippee jɪˈpiː (US) ˈjɪp.iː
Yitzhak ˈjɪt.sɑːk, -sæk
ylang-ylang ˌiː.læŋ.iːˈlæŋ (US) -lɑːŋˈiː.lɑːŋ
YMCA ˌwaɪ.em.siːˈeɪ
Ynys Mon ˌʌn.ɪsˈmɔːn
yo jəʊ (US) joʊ
yob jɒb (US) jɑːb **-s** -z
yobbish ˈjɒb.ɪʃ (US) ˈjɑː.bɪʃ **-ly** -li **-ness** -nəs, -nɪs
yobbo ˈjɒb.əʊ (US) ˈjɑː.boʊ **-s** -z
yod jɒd (US) jɑːd **-s** -z
yodel ˈjəʊ.d^{ə}l (US) ˈjoʊ- **-s** -z **-(l)ing** -ɪŋ, ˈjəʊd.lɪŋ (US) ˈjoʊd- **-(l)ed** -d **-ler/s** -ə^r/z (US) -ɚ/z
yog|a ˈjəʊ.g|ə (US) ˈjoʊ- **-ic** -ɪk
yogh(o)urt ˈjɒg.ət, ˈjəʊ.gət, -gɜːt (US) ˈjoʊ.gɚt **-s** -s
yog|i ˈjəʊ.g|i (US) ˈjoʊ- **-is** -iz **-ism** -ɪ.z^{ə}m **ˌYogi ˈBear, ˈYogi ˌBear**
yogic ˈjəʊ.gɪk (US) ˈjoʊ-
yogurt ˈjɒg.ət, ˈjəʊ.gət, -gɜːt (US) ˈjoʊ.gɚt **-s** -s
Yohji ˈjəʊ.dʒi, ˈjɒdʒ.i (US) ˈjoʊ.dʒi
yoicks jɔɪks
yok|e jəʊk (US) joʊk **-es** -s **-ing** -ɪŋ **-ed** -t
yokel ˈjəʊ.k^{ə}l (US) ˈjoʊ- **-s** -z
Yokohama ˌjəʊ.kəʊˈhɑː.mə (US) ˌjoʊ.kə-
Yolanda, Yolande jəʊˈlæn.də (US) joʊˈlɑːn-, -ˈlæn-
yolk jəʊk (US) joʊk **-s** -s **-y** -i
Yom Kippur ˌjɒm.kɪˈpʊə^r; -ˈkɪp.ə^r (US) ˌjɑːmˈkɪp.ɚ, ˌjɔːm-; -kɪˈpʊr
yomp jɒmp (US) jɑːmp **-s** -s **-ing** -ɪŋ **-ed** -t **-er/s** -ə^r/z (US) -ɚ/z
yon jɒn (US) jɑːn
yond jɒnd (US) jɑːnd
yonder ˈjɒn.də^r (US) ˈjɑːn.dɚ
Yonge jʌŋ
Yonkers ˈjɒŋ.kəz (US) ˈjɑːŋ.kɚz, ˈjɔːŋ-
yonks jɒŋks (US) jɑːŋks, jɔːŋks
yoof juːf
Yorba Linda ˌjɔː.bəˈlɪn.də (US) ˌjɔːr-
yore jɔː^r (US) jɔːr
Yorick ˈjɒr.ɪk (US) ˈjɔːr-
York jɔːk (US) jɔːrk
Yorke jɔːk (US) jɔːrk

yorker ˈjɔː.kə^r (US) ˈjɔːr.kɚ **-s** -z
Yorkist ˈjɔː.kɪst (US) ˈjɔːr- **-s** -s
Yorks. *(abbrev. for* **Yorkshire***)* jɔːks (US) jɔːrks
Yorkshire ˈjɔːk.ʃə^r, -ˌʃɪə^r (US) ˈjɔːrk.ʃɚ, -ˌʃɪr **ˌYorkshire ˈpudding; ˌYorkshire ˈterrier**
Yorkshire|man ˈjɔːk.ʃə.|mən (US) ˈjɔːrk.ʃɚ- **-men** -mən, -men **-woman** -ˌwʊm.ən **-women** -ˌwɪm.
Yorktown ˈjɔːk.taʊn (US) ˈjɔːrk-
Yoruba ˈjɒr.ʊ.bə, ˈjəʊ.rʊ- (US) ˈjɔːr.ə.bə, ˈjoʊ.rə-, -ruː-, -bɑː
Yosemite jəʊˈsem.ɪ.ti (US) joʊˈsem.ə. **Yoˌsemite ˌNational ˈPark; Yoˌsemi ˈSam**
Yossarian jɒsˈeə.ri.ən (US) joʊˈser.i-, -ˈsɑːr-
Yost jəʊst (US) joʊst **-s** -s
you *strong form:* juː *weak forms:* ju, j
Note: Weak form word. The strong form is used contrastively (e.g. 'W it be you, or me?') or emphatically (e.g. 'It was **you** that broke it'). Elsewhere the weak forms are use in British English, /ju/ is the form found before vowels and in final position (e.g. 'You ought' /juˈɔːt (US) -ɑːt/; 'Thank you' /ˈθæŋk.ju/), while /jə/ is only used before consonants (e.g. 'if you can' /ɪf.jəˈkæn/); in American English /jə/ predominates in both environments. The strong form is also found in unstressed syllables Sometimes when 'you' is weakly stressed and is preceded by a word normally ending in /d/, the two words are joined closely together if they formed a single word with the affricate sound /dʒ/ linking th two parts. Thus 'did you' is often pronounced /ˈdɪdʒ.u/, and 'behind you' /bɪˈhaɪn.dʒu/. Similarly whe the preceding word normally ends in /t/ (e.g. 'hurt you') it is sometim pronounced /ˈhɜː.tʃu (US) ˈhɝː-/ an 'don't you know' as /ˌdəʊn.tʃəˈnəʊ (US) ˌdoʊn.tʃəˈnoʊ/.
you-all juˈɔːl (US) juˈɔːl, jɔːl, jɑːl
Youens ˈjuː.ɪnz
Youghal *near Cork:* jɔːl *on Lake Derg* ˈjɒk.^{ə}l, ˈjɒx- (US) ˈjɑː.k^{ə}l
Youmans ˈjuː.mənz
young (Y) jʌŋ **-er** -gə^r (US) -gɚ **-est** -gɪs -gəst
Younger ˈjʌŋ.ə^r, -gə^r (US) -gɚ, -ɚ
Younghusband ˈjʌŋˌhʌz.bənd
youngish ˈjʌŋ.ɪʃ, -gɪʃ
Youngman ˈjʌŋ.mən
youngster ˈjʌŋ*k*.stə^r (US) -stɚ **-s** -z
younker ˈjʌŋ.kə^r (US) -kɚ **-s** -z

our *normal forms:* jɔːʳ, jʊəʳ ⓤⓢ jʊr, jɔːr *occasional weak forms:* jəʳ ⓤⓢ jɚ
Note: Weak form word. The strong form /jʊə ⓤⓢ jʊr/ or /jɔː ⓤⓢ jɔːr/ is usually used for emphasis (e.g. 'It's **your** fault') or contrast (e.g. 'with **your** looks and **my** brains'). This pronunciation is quite common also in weakly stressed positions in careful speech. In British English, the weak form is /jə/ before consonants (e.g. 'take your time' /ˌteɪk.jə'taɪm/) and /jər/ before vowels (e.g. 'on your own' /ɒn.jər'əʊn/); in American English, /jɚ/ is used in both cases.
ou're *(=* **you are***) strong forms:* jɔːʳ, jʊəʳ ⓤⓢ jʊr, jɔːr *occasional weak forms:* jəʳ ⓤⓢ jɚ
Note: The use of strong and weak forms follows that of **your**.
ours jɔːz, jʊəz ⓤⓢ jʊrz, jɔːrz
oursel|f jɔː'sel|f, jʊə-, jə- ⓤⓢ jʊr-, jɔːr-, jɚ- **-ves** -vz
ou|th juː|θ **-ths** -ðz **'youth ˌclub; 'youth ˌhostel; ˌyouth 'training ˌscheme**
youthful 'juːθ.fᵊl, -fʊl **-ly** -i **-ness** -nəs, -nɪs
you've *(=* **you have***) normal form:* juːv *occasional weak forms:* jʊv, jəv
yowl jaʊl **-s** -z **-ing** -ɪŋ **-ed** -d
yo-yo 'jəʊ.jəʊ ⓤⓢ 'joʊ.joʊ **-s** -z **-ing** -ɪŋ **-ed** -d
Ypres *in Belgium:* 'iː.prə, 'iː.pəz *sometimes facetiously:* 'aɪ.pəz, 'waɪ.pəz ⓤⓢ 'iː.prə
Ypres *tower at Rye:* 'iː.prə, 'iː.preɪ, 'waɪ.pəz ⓤⓢ 'iː.prə
Note: The 'Ypres Castle', a public house near by, is called locally the /'waɪ.pəz/.
Yser 'iː.zəʳ ⓤⓢ -zɚ, -zer
Ysolde ɪ'zɒl.də ⓤⓢ -'zoʊl-
Ystradgynlais ˌʌs.træd'gʌn.laɪs, -trəd'-
Ystwyth 'ʌs.twɪθ
Ythan 'aɪ.θən
YTS ˌwaɪ.tiː'es
ytterbium ɪ'tɜː.bi.əm ⓤⓢ -'tɝː-
yttrium 'ɪt.ri.əm
Yucatan ˌjuː.kə'tɑːn, ˌjʊk.ə'-, -'tæn ⓤⓢ ˌjuː.kə'tæn, -'tɑːn
yucca 'jʌk.ə **-s** -z
yuck jʌk **-y** -i **-ier** -i.əʳ ⓤⓢ -i.ɚ **-iest** -i.ɪst, -i.əst
Yugoslav 'juː.gəʊ.slɑːv, ˌ--'- ⓤⓢ 'juː.goʊ.slɑːv, -gə- **-s** -z
Yugoslavi|a ˌjuː.gəʊ'slɑː.vi|.ə ⓤⓢ -goʊ'- **-an** -ən
Yuill 'juː.ɪl
yuk jʌk **-ky** -i
Yukon 'juː.kɒn ⓤⓢ -kɑːn
yule (Y) juːl **'yule ˌlog**
yuletide (Y) 'juːl.taɪd
yumm|y 'jʌm|.i **-ier** -i.əʳ ⓤⓢ -i.ɚ **-iest** -i.ɪst, -i.əst
Yum-Yum ˌjʌm'jʌm
Yunnan jʊ'næn
yuppie 'jʌp.i **-s** -z
yuppif|y 'jʌp.ɪ.f|aɪ **-ies** -aɪz **-ying** -aɪ.ɪŋ **-ied** -aɪd
yupp|y, yupp|ie 'jʌp|.i **-ies** -iz
yurt jɜːt, jʊət ⓤⓢ jʊrt, jɝːt **-s** -s
Yussuf 'jʊs.ʊf, -əf
Yves iːv
Yvette ɪ'vet, iː'- ⓤⓢ iː-
Yvonne ɪ'vɒn, iː'- ⓤⓢ iː'vɑːn
Ywain ɪ'weɪn, iː'-
YWCA ˌwaɪˌdʌb.l̩.juː.siː'eɪ, -ju- ⓤⓢ -juː-, -jə-

Pronouncing the letter Z

The consonant letter **z** is most often realised as /z/, e.g.:

zest /zest/
gaze /geɪz/

It can also be pronounced /ʒ/ in words where it is followed by the letter **u**, e.g.:

seizure /ˈsiː.ʒəʳ/ (US) /-ʒɚ/

In addition

In the word rendezvous, **z** is silent, e.g.:

rendezvous /ˈrɒn.dɪ.vuː/ (US) /ˈrɑːn.deɪ-/

This is an exceptional case; the word is a borrowing from French.

z (Z) zed (US) ziː **-'s** -z
zabaglione ˌzæb.ᵊlˈjəʊ.ni, -neɪ, -ælˈ- (US) ˌzɑː.bᵊlˈjoʊ-, -bɑːlˈ-, -neɪ
Zacchaeus zækˈiː.əs, zəˈkiː-
Zachariah ˌzæk.ᵊrˈaɪ.ə (US) -əˈraɪ-
Zacharias ˌzæk.ᵊrˈaɪ.əs, -æs (US) -əˈraɪ-
Zachary ˈzæk.ᵊr.i
Zadar ˈzæd.ɑːʳ (US) ˈzɑː.dɑːr
Zadok ˈzeɪ.dɒk (US) -dɑːk
Zagreb ˈzɑː.greb, ˈzæg.reb; zɑːˈgreb (US) ˈzɑː.greb
zaire zaɪˈɪəʳ, zɑː- (US) -ˈɪr
Zaïr|e, Zair|e zaɪˈɪəʳ, zɑː- (US) -ˈɪr **-ean** -i.ən
Zambezi, Zambesi zæmˈbiː.zi
Zambi|a ˈzæm.bi|.ə **-an** -ən
Zamboni® zæmˈbəʊ.ni (US) -ˈboʊ-
Zamenhof ˈzɑː.mᵊn.hɒf (US) -hɑːf
Zangwill ˈzæŋ.gwɪl (US) -gwɪl, -wɪl
Zanu ˈzæn.uː, ˈzɑː.nuː
zan|y ˈzeɪ.n|i **-ies** -iz **-ier** -i.əʳ (US) -i.ɚ **-iest** -i.ɪst, -i.əst
Zanzibar ˈzæn.zɪ.bɑːʳ, ˌ--ˈ- (US) -zə.bɑːr
zap zæp **-s** -s **-ping** -ɪŋ **-ped** -t **-per/s** -əʳ/z (US) -ɚ/z
Zapata zəˈpɑː.tə, zæpˈɑː- (US) -t̬ə
Zapatista ˌzæp.əˈtɪs.tə **-s** -z
Zaporozhye ˌzæp.əˈrəʊ.ʒeɪ, -ɔːˈ- (US) ˌzɑː.pəˈroʊ.ʒə
Zapotek ˈzæp.ə.tek, ˈzɑː.pə-, ˌ--ˈ- (US) ˈzɑː.pə.tek, ˈsɑː- **-s** -s
Zappa ˈzæp.ə
zapp|y ˈzæp|.i **-ier** -i.əʳ (US) -i.ɚ **-iest** -i.ɪst, -əst
Zaragoza ˌsær.əˈgɒs.ə *as if Spanish:* ˌθær.əˈgɒθ.ə (US) ˌzær.əˈgoʊ.zə, ˌzer-
Zarathustra ˌzær.əˈθuː.strə, ˌzɑː.rəˈ- (US) ˌzer.əˈ-, ˌzær-
zareba zəˈriː.bə **-s** -z
Zaria ˈzɑː.ri.ə (US) ˈzɑːr.i-
Zarqa ˈzɑː.kə (US) ˈzɑːr-
Zatopek ˈzæt.ə.pek (US) ˈzæt̬-
zeal ziːl
Zealand ˈziː.lənd **-er/s** -əʳ/z (US) -ɚ/z
zealot ˈzel.ət **-s** -s **-ry** -ri
zealous ˈzel.əs **-ly** -li **-ness** -nəs, -nɪs
Zebedee ˈzeb.ɪ.diː, ˈ-ə- (US) ˈ-ə-
zebra ˈzeb.rə, ˈziː.brə (US) ˈziː.brə **-s** -z ˌ**zebra** ˈ**crossing**
zebu ˈziː.buː, -bjuː (US) -bjuː, -buː **-s** -z
Zebulon, Zebulun ˈzeb.jʊ.lən; zebˈjuː-, zəˈbjuː- (US) ˈzeb.jʊ-, -lɑːn
Zechariah ˌzek.əˈraɪ.ə
zed zed **-s** -z
Zedekiah ˌzed.ɪˈkaɪ.ə, -əˈ- (US) -əˈ-
Zeebrugge ziːˈbrʊg.ə, zeɪ-, ˈ--- (US) ˈziː.brʊg-
Zeeland ˈziː.lənd, ˈzeɪ- (US) ˈziː-
Zeffirelli ˌzef.əˈrel.i, -ɪˈ-
Zeiss zaɪs *as German:* tsaɪs **-es** -ɪz
zeitgeist ˈtsaɪt.gaɪst, ˈzaɪt-
Zelazny zelˈæz.ni (US) zəˈlɑːz.ni
Zelda ˈzel.də
Zeller ˈzel.əʳ (US) -ɚ
Zellweger ˈzelˌweg.əʳ (US) -ɚ
Zelotes ziːˈləʊ.tiːz, zɪ-, zə- (US) -ˈloʊ-
zemindar ˈzem.ɪn.dɑːʳ (US) -dɑːr; zəˈmiːn- **-s** -z
zemstvo ˈzemst.vəʊ (US) -voʊ **-s** -z
Zen zen
Zena ˈziː.nə
zenana zenˈɑː.nə, zɪˈnɑː- (US) zenˈɑː- **-s** -z
Zenawi zenˈɑː.wi
Zend zend
Zenda ˈzen.də
Zeneca® ˈzen.ɪ.kə, -ə-
zenica ˈzen.ɪ.kə, ˈzen.ɪt.sə
zenith ˈzen.ɪθ (US) ˈziː.nɪθ **-s** -s
Zeno ˈziː.nəʊ (US) -noʊ
Zenobia zɪˈnəʊ.bi.ə, zenˈəʊ- (US) zəˈnoʊ-
Zenocrate ˈzen.əʊ.kræt (US) -oʊ-
Zepa ˈʒep.ə
Zephaniah ˌzef.əˈnaɪ.ə
zephyr (Z) ˈzef.əʳ (US) -ɚ **-s** -z
Zephyrus ˈzef.ᵊr.əs
zeppelin (Z) ˈzep.ᵊl.ɪn (US) ˈ-lɪn, ˈzep.ə.lɪn **-s** -z
Zermatt ˈzɜː.mæt (US) ˈzɝː.mɑːt, -ˈ-
zero ˈzɪə.rəʊ (US) ˈzɪr.oʊ, ˈziː.roʊ **-(e)s** -z ˈ**zero** ˌ**hour**
Zerubbabel zɪˈrʌb.ə.bᵊl, zə-; *in Jewish usage also:* zɪˈruːˌbɑː-, zə- (US) zəˈrʌb.ə-
zest zest **-ful/ly** -fᵊl/i, fʊl/i
zest|y ˈzes.t|i **-ier** -i.əʳ (US) -i.ɚ **-iest** -i.ɪst, -i.əst
zeta ˈziː.tə (US) ˈzeɪ.t̬ə, ˈziː- **-s** -z
Zetland ˈzet.lənd
zeugma ˈzjuːg.mə, ˈzuːg- (US) ˈzuːg- **-s** -z
Zeus zjuːs (US) zuːs
Zhirinovsky ˌʒɪr.ɪˈnɒf.ski (US) -ˈnɑːf-
Zhivago ʒɪˈvɑː.gəʊ, ʒə- (US) -goʊ
Zhou ʒuː (US) dʒoʊ
ziggurat ˈzɪg.ə.ræt, ˈ-ʊ- **-s** -s
zigzag ˈzɪg.zæg **-s** -z **-ging** -ɪŋ **-ged** -d
zilch zɪltʃ
zillion ˈzɪl.jən, -i.ən (US) ˈ-jən **-s** -z
Zimbabwe zɪmˈbɑːb.weɪ, -ˈbæb-, -wi (US) -ˈbɑːb-
Zimbabwean zɪmˈbɑːb.wi.ən, -ˈbæb-, -weɪ- (US) -ˈbɑːb- **-s** -z
Zimmer® ˈzɪm.əʳ (US) -ɚ ˈ**Zimmer** ˌ**fram**
Zimmerman ˈzɪm.ə.mən (US) ˈ-ɚ-
zinc zɪŋk **-s** -s **-king** -ɪŋ **-ked** -t **-ky** -i
zinco ˈzɪŋ.kəʊ (US) -koʊ **-s** -z
zincograph ˈzɪŋ.kəʊ.grɑːf, -græf (US) -koʊ.græf, -kə- **-s** -s
zinfandel (Z) ˈzɪn.fən.del, ˌ--ˈ- (US) ˈzɪn.fən.del
zing zɪŋ **-s** -z **-ing** -ɪŋ **-ed** -d **-y** -i
zingar|o (Z) ˈzɪŋ.gᵊr|.əʊ (US) -gə.r|oʊ **-i** -iː
zinnia ˈzɪn.i.ə **-s** -z
Zion ˈzaɪ.ən **-ism** -ɪ.zᵊm **-ist/s** -ɪst/s
zip zɪp **-s** -s **-ping** -ɪŋ **-ped** -t ˈ**zip** ˌ**code** ˌ**zip** ˈ**fastener**
zipper ˈzɪp.əʳ (US) -ɚ **-s** -z
Zipporah zɪˈpɔː.rə, ˈzɪp.ᵊr.ə (US) ˈzɪp.ɚ.ə
zipp|y ˈzɪp|.i **-ier** -i.əʳ (US) -i.ɚ **-iest** -i.ɪs -i.əst
zircon ˈzɜː.kɒn (US) ˈzɝː.kɑːn
zirconia zɜːˈkəʊ.ni.ə, zə- (US) zɚˈkoʊ-
zirconium zɜːˈkəʊ.ni.əm, zə- (US) zɚˈkoʊ-
zit zɪt **-s** -s
zither ˈzɪð.əʳ, ˈzɪθ- (US) ˈzɪθ.ɚ, ˈzɪð- **-s**
zloty ˈzlɒt.i *as if Polish:* ˈzwɒt- (US) ˈzlɔː.t̬i, ˈzlɑː- **-s** -z
Zoar ˈzəʊ.ɑːʳ, zəʊəʳ (US) ˈzoʊ.ɑːr, zoʊɚ

odiac 'zəʊ.di.æk (US) 'zoʊ-
odiacal zəʊ'daɪ.ə.kᵊl (US) zoʊ-
oe, **Zoë** 'zəʊ.i (US) 'zoʊ-
og zɒg (US) zɔːg, zɑːg
zoic -'zəʊ.ɪk (US) -'zoʊ.ɪk
ola 'zəʊ.lə (US) 'zoʊ-; zoʊ'lɑː
ollverein 'tsɒl.fᵊr.aɪn, 'zɒl.vᵊr- (US) 'tsɔːl.fə.raɪn **-s** -z
ombie 'zɒm.bi (US) 'zɑːm- **-s** -z
onal 'zəʊ.nᵊl (US) 'zoʊ- **-ly** -i
on|e zəʊn (US) zoʊn **-es** -z **-ing** -ɪŋ **-ed** -d **-eless** -ləs, -lɪs
onked zɒŋkt (US) zɑːŋkt, zɔːŋkt
oo- zuː.əʊ-, zəʊ.əʊ-; zu'ɒ,- zəʊ'ɒ- (US) zoʊ.oʊ-, zuː.oʊ-, -ə-; zoʊ'ɑː-, zu'ɑː-
Note: Prefix. Normally either takes primary or secondary stress on the first syllable, e.g. **zoophyte** /'zuː.ə.faɪt (US) 'zoʊ-/, **zoomorphic** /ˌzuː.ə'mɔː.fɪk (US) ˌzoʊ.ə'mɔːr-/, or primary stress on the second syllable, e.g. **zoology** /zu'ɒl.ə.dʒi (US) zoʊ'ɑː.lə-/.
oo zuː **-s** -z
oochemi|stry ˌzuː.əʊ'kem.ɪ|.stri (US) ˌzoʊ.ə'- **-cal** -kᵊl
ograph|er zuː'ɒg.rə.f|əʳ (US) zoʊ'ɑː.grə.f|ɚ **-ers** -əz (US) -ɚz **-y** -i
ooks zuːks (US) zuːks, zʊks
oolite 'zuː.əʊ.laɪt (US) 'zoʊ.oʊ.laɪt, '-ə- **-s** -s
zoologic|al ˌzuː.əʊ'lɒdʒ.ɪ.k|ᵊl, ˌzəʊ.ə'- (US) ˌzoʊ.ə'lɑː.dʒɪ- **-ally** -ᵊl.i, -li **zooˌlogical 'gardens**
zoologist zu'ɒl.ə.dʒ|ɪst, zəʊ- (US) zoʊ'ɑːlə-, zu- **-s** -s
zoolog|y zu'ɒl.ə.dʒ|i, zəʊ- (US) zoʊ'ɑː.lə-, zu- **-ist/s** -ɪst/s
zoom zuːm **-s** -z **-ing** -ɪŋ **-ed** -d **'zoom ˌlens**
zoomorphic ˌzuː.ə'mɔː.fɪk (US) ˌzoʊ.ə'mɔːr-
-zo|on -'zəʊ|.ɒn (US) -'zoʊ|.ɑːn, -ən **-a** -ə
Note: Suffix. Normally carries primary stress as shown, e.g. **protozoon** /ˌprəʊ.təʊ'zəʊ.ɒn (US) ˌproʊ.t̬oʊ'zoʊ.ɑːn/.
zoophyte 'zuː.ə.faɪt (US) 'zoʊ.ə- **-s** -s
zooplankton ˌzuː.əʊ'plæŋk.tən, -tɒn (US) ˌzoʊ.ə'plæŋk.tən **-s** -z
zoot zuːt **-s** -s **'zoot ˌsuit**
zoril 'zɒr.ɪl (US) 'zɔːr- **-s** -z
Zoroaster ˌzɒr.əʊ'æs.təʳ, 'zɒr.əʊ.æs- (US) 'zɔːr.oʊ.æs.tɚ
Zoroastrian ˌzɒr.əʊ'æs.tri.ən (US) ˌzɔːr.oʊ'- **-s** -z **-ism** -ɪ.zᵊm
Zorro 'zɒr.əʊ (US) 'zɔːr.oʊ
zouave (Z) zu'ɑːv; zwɑːv; 'zuː.ɑːv (US) zu'ɑːv, zwɑːv **-s** -z
Zouch(e) zuːʃ
zounds zuːndz, zaʊndz (US) zaʊndz
Zsa Zsa 'ʒɑː.ʒɑː
zucchini zʊ'kiː.ni (US) zuː- **-s** -z
Zugspitze 'zʊg.ʃpɪt.sə *as if German:* 'tsuːk-
Zuider Zee ˌzaɪ.də'ziː, -'zeɪ (US) -dɚ'ziː
Zuleika zuː'leɪ.kə, zʊ-, -'laɪ-
Zulu 'zuː.luː **-s** -z
Zululand 'zuː.luː.lænd
Zuñi, Zuni 'zʊn.ji (US) 'zuː.ni, -nji
zuppa inglese ˌzʊp.ɑː.ɪŋ'gleɪ.zeɪ, -zi (US) ˌzuː.pə.ɪn'gleɪ.zeɪ, ˌtsuː-, -ɪŋ'-
Zürich 'zjʊə.rɪk, 'zʊə- *as if German:* 'tsjʊə- (US) 'zʊr.ɪk
Zutphen 'zʌt.fən
Zwelithini ˌzwel.ɪ'θiː.ni
zwieback 'zwiː.bæk, -bɑːk (US) 'zwaɪ.bæk, 'zwiː-, 'swiː-, 'swaɪ-, -bɑːk **-s** -s
zygoma zaɪ'gəʊ.mə, zɪ- (US) -'goʊ- **-ta** -tə (US) -t̬ə
zygote 'zaɪ.gəʊt, 'zɪg.əʊt (US) 'zaɪ.goʊt, 'zɪg.oʊt **-s** -s
zymosis zaɪ'məʊ.sɪs, zɪ- (US) -'moʊ-
zymotic zaɪ'mɒt.ɪk, zɪ- (US) -'mɑː.t̬ɪk
Zyuganov ʒʊ'gɑː.nɒf
zzz zː
Note: This is rarely pronounced, but is used in comic strips to represent sleeping, or, more specifically, snoring. The suggested pronunciation derives from the spelling.